CONGRESSIONAL QUARTERLY

Almanac®

103rd CONGRESS
1st SESSION . . . 1993

VOLUME XLIX

Congressional Quarterly Inc.

1414 22nd Street N.W.
Washington, D.C. 20037

Congressional Quarterly Inc.

Congressional Quarterly Inc. is a publishing and information services company and a recognized leader in political journalism. For almost half a century, CQ has served clients in the fields of news, education, business and government with timely, complete, unbiased and accurate information on Congress, politics and national issues.

At the heart of CQ is its acclaimed publication, the Weekly Report, a weekly magazine offering news and analyses on Congress and legislation. The CQ Researcher (formerly Editorial Research Reports), with its focus on current issues, provides weekly balanced summaries on topics of widespread interest.

Congressional Quarterly Inc. publishes the Congressional Monitor, a daily report on Congress and current and future activities of congressional committees, and several newsletters, including Congressional Insight, a weekly analysis of congressional action.

Congressional Quarterly Inc. also publishes a variety of books, including political science textbooks, under the CQ Press imprint and public affairs paperbacks to keep journalists, scholars and the public abreast of developing issues and events. CQ Books publishes highly regarded information directories and reference books on the federal government, national elections and politics, including the Guide to the Presidency, the Guide to Congress, the Guide to the U.S. Supreme Court, the Guide to U.S. Elections, Politics in America, the Federal Regulatory Directory and Washington Information Directory. The CQ Almanac®, a compendium of legislation for one session of Congress, is published each year. Congress and the Nation, a record of government for a presidential term, is published every four years.

Washington Alert, Congressional Quarterly's online congressional and regulatory tracking service, provides immediate access to both proprietary and public databases of legislative action, votes, schedules, profiles and analyses.

Library of Congress Catalog Number 47-41081
ISBN: 1-56802-020-1 ISSN: 0095-6007

What You Will Find in This Book

This is the 49th edition of the Congressional Quarterly Almanac, an annual book that chronicles the course of major legislation and national politics.

Drawing on reporting and writing done throughout the year by the staffs of the Congressional Quarterly Weekly Report and the Congressional Monitor, the Almanac organizes, distills and cross-indexes for permanent reference the full year in Congress and in national politics. The current volume covers the first session of the 103rd Congress.

The following are the major elements of the volume:

● **103rd Congress.** The first chapter gives an overview of the year in Congress. It includes statistical information on the session and stories on legislation governing Congress as a whole, such as campaign finance and lobbying disclosure. This year the section includes a series of stories on lawmakers' ethics problems, including those of Sen. Bob Packwood, R-Ore.; Rep. Dan Rostenkowski, D-Ill.; and other members.

● **Legislative Chapters.** The next nine chapters cover legislative action during the session on economics and finance, government and commerce, social policy, defense, and foreign policy.

● **Appropriations.** Chapter 11 contains separate stories detailing the substance and legislative history of each of the 13 regular fiscal 1994 appropriations bills, including charts and provisions. It also includes stories on the three supplemental appropriations bills enacted during the year.

● **Political report.** Appendix A covers special House and Senate elections and gubernatorial elections in 1993, along with other political information.

● **Appendixes.** The volume also includes appendixes on the following topics:

▶ **Congress and Its Members**. Membership lists for all committees and subcommittees, characteristics of Congress, and a description of the legislative process.

▶ **Glossary.** A 10-page glossary of terms used in Congress.

▶ **Vote Studies.** Studies of presidential support, party unity, conservative coalition, and freshmen patterns, as well as the key votes of 1993.

▶ **Texts.** Key presidential and other texts.

▶ **Public Laws.** A complete listing of public laws enacted during the session in the order they were signed by the president.

▶ **Roll Call Votes.** A complete set of roll call vote charts for the House and Senate during the session.

"By providing a link between the local newspaper and Capitol Hill we hope Congressional Quarterly can help to make public opinion the only effective pressure group in the country. Since many citizens other than editors are also interested in Congress, we hope that they too will find Congressional Quarterly an aid to a better understanding of their government.

"Congressional Quarterly presents the facts in as complete, concise and unbiased form as we know how. The editorial comment on the acts and votes of Congress, we leave to our subscribers."

Foreword, Congressional Quarterly, Vol. I, 1945
Henrietta Poynter, 1901-1968
Nelson Poynter, 1903-1978

Errata: 1992 CQ Almanac

p. 128, CFTC Reauthorization, col. 1, first paragraph under 1991 Action: Both chambers passed HR 707 in 1991; the Senate substituted the text of its own bill, S 207, before passing HR 707.

p. 131, Defense Production Act, col. 2, fourth paragraph: The House adopted the conference report on S 347 on Oct. 6 in the session that began Oct. 5.

p. 144, Urban Aid Tax Bill Highlights, col. 2, third paragraph under Extenders: The Senate provision dropped by conferees would have allowed self-employed individuals to deduct 100 percent of the cost of health insurance.

p. 195, Transportation Corrections, col. 1, second paragraph under House Action: The House committee report on HR 5753 was H Rept 102-833.

p. 205, Aviation Worker Fines and Appeals, col. 2, second paragraph: President George Bush signed HR 5481 (PL 102-345) into law Aug. 26.

p. 209, Product Safety, col. 2, fourth paragraph: The fiscal 1993 spending bill for the VA, HUD and independent agencies was HR 5679.

p. 217, New Farmer Loans, col. 1, fifth full paragraph: The House passed HR 6129 on Oct. 4.

p. 226, Government Ethics, col. 1, first paragraph: President Bush signed S 1145 (PL 102-506) on Oct. 24.

p. 306, Joint Ventures, col. 2, fifth full paragraph: The paragraph describes the Senate-passed bill; the House did not act on S 479.

p. 339, Urban Aid, col. 1, second paragraph: HR 5132 became PL 102-302.

p. 357, Family Leave, col. 1, second paragraph under Senate Overrides Veto: The House voted 239-139 to postpone the veto-override vote on S 5.

p. 379, Loan Guarantees, col. 2, fourth paragraph under Legislative Action: The House agreed to a compromise version of HR 939 on Oct. 6 in the session that began Oct. 5.

p. 380, Veterans Health Care, col. 2, first paragraph under Final Action: The House accepted the Senate amendments to HR 5193 with further amendments Oct. 6 in the session that began Oct. 5.

p. 382, Radiation Compensation, col. 1, sixth paragraph: The Senate passed S 775 by voice vote Nov. 20, 1991.

p. 435 Rehabilitation Act, col. 1, eighth paragraph: The House passed HR 5482 by voice vote Aug. 10.

p. 455, School Improvement, col. 2, third paragraph under Background: Education Secretary Lauro F. Cavazos was asked to leave and resigned on Dec. 12, 1990.

p. 466, Older Americans Act, col. 1, sixth paragraph; boxscore: The Senate on Sept. 15 approved HR 2967 by voice vote after substituting the text of its own bill, S 3008.

p. 468, Older Americans Act, col. 1, first paragraph under Senate Action: The Senate on Sept. 15 approved HR 2967 by voice vote after substituting the text of its own bill, S 3008.

p. 579, Urban Aid Supplemental, boxscore: The House passed HR 5132 on May 14.

p. 22-H, House Vote 87: The resolution was H Res 433.

SUMMARY TABLE OF CONTENTS

APPENDIXES

INDEXES

TABLE OF CONTENTS

Chapter 1 — 103rd Congress

Chapter 2 — Economics & Finance

Chapter 3 — Government/Commerce

Chapter 4 — Sciency & Technology/Communications

Chapter 5 — Environment/Energy

Chapter 6 — Law & Judiciary

Chapter 7 — Health/Human Services

Chapter 8 — Labor/Education/Veterans/Housing

Chapter 9 — Defense

Chapter 10 — Foreign Policy

Chapter 11 — Appropriations

Appendixes

Political Report

Congress and Its Members

Vote Studies

Vote Studies (cont'd)

Text

Public Laws

Roll Call Votes

Indexes

committee meetings and routine floor action. Republicans argued that the new rule would discourage floor participation and permit chairmen to abuse the system.

● **Rolling quorums.** Committee chairmen were allowed to declare the quorum needed to draft legislation once a majority of members had been in attendance for some part of the session. Previously, a bill could be ruled out of order on the House floor if the quorum was not present at the same time.

● **Conferees.** The Speaker was given power to remove any House conferee from a House-Senate conference or to add members. Democrats said the power would prevent deadlock. Republicans said it would give the Speaker too much power.

● **Privileged motions.** The Speaker was given power to delay for two legislative days debate on privileged motions dealing with the rights of the House collectively and the integrity of its proceedings. Previously, these motions took precedence over other floor action. An exception was provided for the majority and minority leaders, whose motions would receive immediate attention. Privileged motions regarding an individual member's rights were not affected.

House Republicans argued that by threatening to bring up privileged motions on the House bank, they had persuaded the Democrats to release key information.

● **Teller votes.** Once a principal method of voting, "teller votes" — in which members filed past stations where the number for and against a question was counted — were abolished on the grounds that they wasted time.

● **Authorizing language on appropriations bills.** The chairmen of the authorizing committees, who frequently complained about the Senate's adding legislation to appropriations bills that the House could not, were given an opportunity to offer a preferential motion to insist on disagreement with the Senate in consideration of a conference report.

Before the rules package was sent to the House, Democrats reversed course and backed away from a previously approved proposal to limit special orders, time reserved at the end of the day for members to speak on any subject for three hours total or until 9 p.m., whichever came first. Democrats maintained that this would save money and was not intended to stifle the GOP. But they backed off when Republicans cried foul.

More Committee Changes

Democrats in the House had filled committee chairmanships and most committee seats in their December 1992 organizational meetings. But Clinton opened important posts in both chambers with his Cabinet choices. Defense Secretary Les Aspin, D-Wis., had headed House Armed Services; Office of Management and Budget Director Leon E. Panetta, D-Calif., had chaired House Budget; Treasury Secretary Lloyd Bentsen, D-Texas, had headed

Public Laws

A total of 210 bills cleared Congress in 1993 and became public laws. Following is a list of the number of public laws enacted since 1972:

Year	Public Laws
1993	210
1992	347
1991	243
1990	410
1989	240
1988	471
1987	242
1986	424
1985	240
1984	408
1983	215
1982	328
1981	145
1980	426
1979	187
1978	410
1977	223
1976	383
1975	205
1974	402
1973	247
1972	383

Senate Finance.

House Democrats picked Martin Olav Sabo, D-Minn., to head the House Budget Committee for two years, replacing the voluble and passionate Panetta with a laconic, behind-the-scenes legislator.

In a Jan. 6 election that gave them a clear choice between a liberal and a right-leaning centrist, Democrats chose Sabo over centrist John M. Spratt Jr., D-S.C., by 149-112 in a closed-door vote. Despite the stark philosophical differences between the two, however, observers said Sabo's win was more the result of the well-liked congressman's networking and pre-emptive campaigning than a measure of House Democrats' political temperature.

Ronald V. Dellums, D-Calif., faced no opposition for the nomination to head Armed Services. Despite his left-wing principles, Dellums' political savvy and procedural fair play smoothed over any skepticism about the ability of the 22-year House veteran to handle the job. Dellums was officially named on Jan. 27 after a 198-10 vote of the Democratic Caucus.

Speaker Foley created another vacancy when he informed Dave McCurdy, D-Okla., who had been at odds with the Speaker, that he would not be reappointed chairman of the Intelligence Committee. McCurdy, who announced the decision to reporters Jan. 8, said he thought the change indicated Foley's "desire to place his own team on the committee."

He said Foley, in a private meeting between the two the previous day, did not mention 1992 reports that McCurdy was considering challenging Foley for the speakership. Instead, McCurdy said he was told he was being replaced mainly because he had been a committee member for nine years, far longer than the usual six-year term. But McCurdy had been known to rub the leadership and other colleagues the wrong way with his aggressiveness and ambition. He had floated his name as a possible replacement to Foley during the 1992 House bank scandal.

On Jan. 11, Foley named Dan Glickman, D-Kan., as Intelligence chairman.

Sen. Daniel Patrick Moynihan, D-N.Y., had no opposition in taking over for Bentsen as Finance Committee chairman.

Congress approved legislation — S J Res 1 — designed to allow Bentsen to become Treasury secretary. The Senate passed it Jan. 5, and the House cleared it Jan. 6. It reduced the Treasury secretary's pay from $148,400 to $99,500 — the level in effect four years before. That was necessary because the Constitution prohibited a member from taking an office for which the pay was increased during the same term the appointment was made. Bentsen's six-year term began in 1989, the year in which Cabinet pay was increased.

Reorganizing Subcommittees

Many House committees had to reorganize their subcommittee structure, which under the new rules required

Inhofe Breaks With House Tradition ...

Republicans blew a rare hole in Democrats' ironclad rule of the House in early autumn: They forced through a resolution making public the signatures on petitions to bring measures that had been bottled up in committee to the floor.

With the help of The Wall Street Journal's editorial page, independent presidential candidate Ross Perot and talk show hosts across the country, Republicans persuaded the House to overturn a 61-year-old precedent under which signatures on so-called discharge petitions were kept secret until a majority (218 members) had signed them.

Democratic leaders backed down after several weeks of fighting a losing battle against the effort. The House on Sept. 28 voted 384-40 to approve Oklahoma Republican James M. Inhofe's proposal (H Res 134) to make such signatures public. *(Vote 458, p. 112-H)*

Inhofe forced the issue Sept. 8 by getting the 218th name on a discharge petition on H Res 134. He had helped his cause by publicizing the names on his petition; no punishment was attempted. Inhofe and Republicans said the secrecy made it easier for the Democratic leadership to pressure members to withhold signatures for bills it opposed — such as term limits, the line-item veto and the balanced-budget amendment.

Democrats called his proposal a risky step toward plebiscitary democracy — and a direct challenge to their power. "The Inhofe proposal would give the minority a new and powerful tool for forcing House members to take public stands on issues that help the minority," said the Democratic Study Group, a legislative research group for House Democrats. But even after Inhofe succeeded, the discharge process remained flush with ways for the leadership to control the agenda. Any committee faced with a successful petition could report out a bill to its liking — and then refuse to bring even that to the floor, forcing the petitioners to start over. Or the Rules Committee could provide a floor rule giving leaders the advantage.

History of Secrecy

A discharge petition was a procedure designed to enable members to force action on a bill that had stalled in a committee. Once 218 members signed it, their names were made public. After waiting seven legislative business days (with action allowed only on the second or fourth Monday of the month), they could force a floor vote on their discharge motion and then on the bill itself if the motion carried.

The secrecy surrounding discharge petitions stemmed from a decree issued from the chair by Speaker John Nance Garner, D-Texas, on Feb. 23, 1932: "These signatures can not be made public until the required number of members have signed the petition."

At the time, the House was trying to perfect its discharge rule, seeking one that would not be too hard or too easy to invoke. The struggle had begun in 1910 as part of a revolt against the dictatorial Republican Speaker, Joseph G. Cannon of Illinois. Debate over versions of the rule continued for years with the majority party — sometimes Republican, sometimes Democratic — usually successfully arguing for more stringent discharge rules.

The threat of a discharge often was enough to force floor action on a measure — succeeding in enactment in 1983, when Congress repealed the withholding of taxes from interest and dividend payments. The last time before Inhofe's effort that a committee was discharged was in 1992, when the balanced-budget constitutional amendment was freed from the Judiciary Committee — the first discharge in more than a decade. The measure narrowly failed to get the required two-thirds majority.

Discharge petitions were kept in a locked drawer at the clerk's desk on the House floor. Disclosing the names was "strictly prohibited under the precedents of the House," said an "important notice" shown to signatories. "The prerogative of individual members to determine when and whether to sign a discharge petition is in the nature of a private and serious agreement." A message from Speaker Thomas S. Foley, D-Wash., added: "The chair trusts that all members will comply with this time-honored principle on their own responsibility."

Inhofe's Successful Defiance

Inhofe introduced his bill March 18. "This is the first step," he said, "in eliminating yet another congressional

the elimination of as many as 16 subcommittees. The change inspired little controversy for two reasons: Many full committee chairmen eagerly awaited the chance to reshuffle subcommittee jurisdictions, and the departure of many senior members meant no subcommittee chairmen would be ousted.

So many vacancies were created that several midlevel members got gavels for the first time. On Banking, for instance, four new subcommittee chairmen took over, including two who had not chaired any subpanel before. Joseph P. Kennedy II, D-Mass., became chairman of a new and powerful subcommittee on consumer credit. Floyd H. Flake, D-N.Y., headed the newly organized General Oversight subcommittee.

On Education and Labor, no new subcommittee chairmen were installed, but committee Chairman William D. Ford, D-Mich., redesigned the turf. In killing off two sub-

committees, he said he tried to give the remaining panels pieces of the desirable job-training pie.

The Agriculture Committee also used the requirement that it eliminate two subcommittees to change the way the committee functioned. Rather than divide the subcommittees according to similar commodities or regions — for instance, wheat and corn in one place, rice and cotton in another — all of the major commodities were bundled according to similarities in federal support programs. The minor commodities, peanuts and tobacco, were grouped under the Specialty Crop Subcommittee.

Nearly the entire leadership changed at Public Works — a popular committee in 1993. In addition to getting a new chairman, Norman Y. Mineta, D-Calif., and ranking Republican, Bud Shuster of Pennsylvania, the panel had four new subcommittee chairmen and five new ranking Republicans.

The Energy and Commerce Committee changed little

censured by the House, caucus members would choose a permanent replacement.

During the closed-door caucus session, McDade told colleagues that he would accept any decision they made. While grateful for the exemption, he said, he disagreed with the policy.

"My preference would be the presumption of innocence on both sides of the aisle," he said, adding that the rules might tempt the executive branch to level charges against members to silence them.

House Bank Redux

In a footnote to the House bank affair, the General Accounting Office (GAO) conducted a final audit of the since-closed facility showing that some members continued to write insufficient-funds checks on their accounts after the matter had become a full-blown scandal. The report was issued April 28.

It was a GAO audit in 1991 that first had generated controversy about the House bank, disclosing that members had routinely been allowed to overdraw their accounts without penalty. *(Bank, 1992 Almanac, p. 23)*

The new audit covered the 18 months before the bank was closed at the end of 1991. It found no losses related to the bank's closing, but it criticized bank employees for the way they implemented Speaker Foley's Sept. 25, 1991, order that henceforth, without exception, "checks with insufficient funds to cover them will be returned at the close of business on the day they are received."

The GAO said 97 insufficient-funds checks were presented to the bank after that day. Only one was returned, and that was done at the request of the member who wrote it. Of the 96 that were not returned, 69 worth a total of $36,313 were dated after Sept. 25, 1991. All were honored because the members covered them with new deposits after they were called by the bank, which told them they would be returned the next morning if not made good.

"This practice did not appear to be consistent with the guidance provided by the Speaker," the GAO concluded.

House leaders of both parties disagreed, saying the practice was "consistent with both the Speaker's statement . . . and regular banking practice."

Changing Faces

House Counsel Steven R. Ross would resign May 14 to take a job with a law firm, Foley announced May 6. As the top legal adviser to three Speakers, Ross defended the constitutionality of laws and went to court in behalf of members in legal hot water — and was sometimes accused by Republicans of working too closely with Democrats. He was not replaced by the end of the year.

A longstanding vacancy was filled Oct. 27, when House leaders named John W. Lainhart IV, an assistant inspector general for the Transportation Department, to the post of House inspector general, a year and a half after the House created the job. Lainhart started Nov. 14.

The job was created in April 1992, in the midst of controversy over members' overdrafts at the House bank, as part of the package of reforms that created the post of director of non-legislative and financial services filled by Leonard P. Wishart III. *(1992 Almanac, p. 55)*

Lainhart was given a more limited mandate than Congress had extended to the executive branch's cadre of quasi-independent inspectors general. House rules specified that he be responsible only for: conducting periodic financial audits of Wishart's office, the clerk, the sergeant at arms and the doorkeeper; informing them of his findings and suggestions; notifying the Speaker and party leaders of "any financial irregularity" he discovers; and giving them all audit reports he produces.

The rules made the inspector general "subject to the policy direction and oversight of the Committee on House Administration," as was Wishart, who abruptly resigned in early 1994.

END OF SESSION

Clinton, who had begun the year in a weak position as a president elected with a minority of the vote and who had suffered through numerous mishaps, ended the year with major victories on trade, budget policy and gun control.

The often fractious House closed in remarkably civil fashion considering that members voted on a number of controversial measures, such as campaign finance, the Brady bill and the final financing for the savings and loan bailout.

When the House began its final marathon workday on Monday, Nov. 22, at 9 a.m., it was the eighth straight day it had been in session. Members worked through until they finished their business on Nov. 23 at 2:03 a.m., and most left town for the year. The only raucous moment came Nov. 22 after the House rejected, 213-219, an ambitious budget-cutting plan offered by Timothy J. Penny, D-Minn., and John R. Kasich, R-Ohio. As the outcome became clear, Republican members began shouting, "Spend! Spend! Spend!" Democrats yelled back, "Borrow! Borrow! Borrow!" *(Vote 609, p. 148-H)*

In the Senate, Mitchell threatened to bring senators back after Thanksgiving before he and Minority Leader Bob Dole, R-Kan., reached agreement Nov. 24 on the Brady bill to require a waiting period for handgun purchases. But senators already had begun scattering to the four winds or were preparing to do so. Once the accommodation on the Brady bill was reached, the Senate moved quickly to conclude its business. The chamber adjourned Nov. 24 at 3:07 p.m. The House then convened for five minutes Nov. 26 and adjourned at 10:05 a.m., concluding the first session of the 103rd Congress. ∎

103rd Congress: Diversity and Power

Even before it convened, the 103rd Congress was assured a place in the history books for its diversity. It had record numbers of women, blacks and Hispanics in its ranks. And the freshman class that carried this tide represented a quarter of the House, the largest proportion since 1949. The changes they made in Congress — and the acclimatization of each group to the realities of legislative power — were among the most reported stories of 1993.

FRESHMEN TOE PARTY LINE

From the time they stepped on Capitol Hill, the 114 first-term House members (110 elected in 1992, four winners of special elections) were under heavy scrutiny. While they were elected on a broad theme of change, they were mostly political veterans (72 percent previously held office), and most settled into the business of learning the legislative ropes.

With the exception of the class photo shoot and a few other brief occasions in December, Democrats and Republicans never got together as a group. Leaders in both parties tacitly encouraged a schism early on, and the tensions of running the House only deepened it. Indeed, in voting the freshmen proved remarkably partisan. For the most part, the first-termers voted like their elders — although on fiscal matters, they were more likely to vote against federal projects. *(Freshman vote study, p. 61-C)*

The partisan lines were drawn even before they arrived in Washington, when Democrats stayed away from a late November class meeting in Omaha, Neb., that had been billed as a reformist gathering. GOP organizers said the session would be bipartisan. Democratic leaders told their new troops otherwise and instead flew to three cities to meet with new members, telling them that working with a Democratic president was more important than tinkering with House rules.

Republican leaders matched the Democrats in encouraging the class fissure. When it came time for the traditional freshman orientation conducted by Harvard University, GOP chiefs put out the word that the "Harvard boutique" — as George Bush once referred to the school — was no place for Republicans, and they did not attend.

The Democrats' willingness to heed their elders was clear at the beginning of the year when they adopted the leadership position in favor of reauthorizing the four House select committees. The Jan. 26 vote on the first of the four was 180-237 against reauthorization. Seventy percent of the Democratic freshmen voted to preserve the panel, compared with 63 percent of the veteran Democrats. *(Vote 10, p. 2-H)*

Each party's freshman class in March presented a package of suggested reforms in the way the House did its business, but they had little in common. Only on two points did they agree: Both endorsed new legislation to subject Congress to all laws it passes, and the groups came out individually for lower staff funding levels for former Speakers. *(Reform, p. 21)*

Without public dissent, the Republicans quickly united behind their 19-point package, which would limit members' terms, eliminate the Appropriations Committee, lower franking funds, require a three-fifths vote for any tax increase and end proxy voting on committees.

For Democrats, the process of adopting a package was grueling, with nearly 10 hours of meetings the week of March 29 alone. The first two items on the Democrats' agenda were legislative proposals backed by the leadership: a campaign finance bill and lobbying disclosure. They stripped out most controversial elements, including a line-item veto. The most contentious points left in the package were recommendations that members hold only one committee or subcommittee chair (many committee chairmen held top subcommittee posts) and that the legislative branch appropriation be reduced 25 percent over five years.

The freshmen did not depart far from their elders on another issue: financing their campaigns with the help of political action committees (PACs). Only 11 of the 100 members elected in 1992 did not accept PAC funds. According to Federal Election Commission data, first-term members collected nearly $15 million in PAC money in the 1992 election cycle — an average of $149,700 for each who accepted the funds. That compared with an average of $263,500 for incumbents who collected from PACs. Even before they were sworn in, the freshmen began raising their totals: between the election and Dec. 31, 1992, $1.2 million flowed from PACs to their committees.

Twenty newcomers took in more than $200,000 each from PACs, with Gene Green, D-Texas, topping the list with $409,700. An additional 55 freshmen collected more than $100,000 each from PACs. For post-election fundraising, Jane Harman, D-Calif., set the pace, with $79,302 from Nov. 4 to Dec. 31.

WOMEN: A MIXED RECORD

Overnight on Election Day 1992, the number of women slated for the House jumped from 29 to 48, and in the Senate from two to six. (A seventh woman came to the Senate in June, after Republican Kay Bailey Hutchison won a Texas special election.)

Women brought new voices to a conversation long monopolized by men, adding the passion of personal experience to debate about such issues as abortion, women's health and child care. But when it came to calling the shots on legislation, women still said they had a hard time being heard. The problem, in part, was political mathematics: Women still constituted only 11 percent of the House and 7 percent of the Senate, and most of them were junior members in an institution where seniority was power.

As the 103rd Congress began, a woman — Barbara A. Mikulski, D-Md. — was appointed to the Senate Democratic leadership for the first time. In the House, both the Democratic and Republican freshmen elected women as class presidents: Eva Clayton, D-N.C., for 1993 and Deborah Pryce, R-Ohio, as interim president until the first session got under way. Women in both the House and Senate got better committee assignments than was usual for first-termers. In the Senate, Patty Murray of Washington and Dianne Feinstein of California got the two open Democratic seats on the Appropriations Committee. In the House, four more women got on Appropriations and three others on the Energy and Commerce Committee.

The seniority system remained a major obstacle for women. Every one of the 40 standing committees in the House and Senate was chaired by a man. Both women in the House and Senate leadership were appointed: Mikulski and Barbara B. Kennelly, D-Conn., one of four chief deputy whips in the House.

Issues of particular concern to women were prominent on the legislative agenda. Family and medical leave was one of the first issues before the 103rd Congress. Women's health issues took on new prominence. When Congress passed a biomedical research bill, it included a new emphasis on research on women. When the House on June 14 passed a bill to authorize new money for preventing breast and cervical cancers, only two members voted against it.

But a wide gap between expectations and the reality of women's power in Congress opened June 30, when the House rejected an effort to allow Medicaid financing for abortions for poor women. The debate made plain that women were not only too few but also too divided to hold sway — even on an issue that was a top priority for national women's groups. Eleven of the 48 women voted to ban funding. *(Abortion, p. 348)*

The outcome was a defeat for the women's caucus, which had tried for the first time to play the major role in an abortion debate.

The caucus dated to 1977, when the 18 women in the House and two in the Senate formed the Congresswomen's Caucus. At that time, all members were expected to support the Equal Rights Amendment (ERA), but the caucus steered clear of other controversial issues, including abortion, because it took positions only on issues about which members were unanimous.

The group reorganized in 1981 as the Congressional Caucus for Women's Issues, began accepting men as members (in 1993 it had 109) and became increasingly involved in legislative issues.

After the ERA died in 1983, the caucus focused on economic issues. Outside Congress, the women's movement mobilized around abortion rights after a 1989 Supreme Court decision weakened previous rulings on the subject. Women in Congress remained, as a group, silent on the issue because there still were two senior Democrats who were anti-abortion: Lindy (Mrs. Hale) Boggs of Louisiana and Mary Rose Oakar of Ohio. But in 1992, Oakar was defeated, Boggs had been retired for two years, and all 24 of the new women elected were abortion rights supporters. At the first meeting of the women's caucus in 1993, the group for the first time went on record in support of abortion rights.

BLACK CAUCUS FLEXES MUSCLES

In the House, Democratic leaders paid special attention to the party's most cohesive force on its left wing: the Congressional Black Caucus, which emerged as a key player in numerous legislative situations. But at the end of the year, its new profile — drawn largely by its activist chairman, Kweisi Mfume, D-Md. — was shadowed by a controversy with the black separatist group Nation of Islam.

The caucus' new strength came from its numbers: There were 38 Democratic members of the black caucus in the House, and when they threatened to withhold their votes, party vote-counters came up short.

The caucus was formed in 1970 with nine members. In the mid-1980s, when it had grown to about 20 members, it was a force principally on civil rights laws and South Africa sanctions. *(Background, 1992 Almanac, p. 18)*

The 1992 elections, which followed a redrawing of district lines, strengthened the caucus from 26 to 38 Democrats in the House (including Eleanor Holmes Norton, who as the District of Columbia delegate was allowed to vote on some but not all issues on the House floor). The group's full membership of 40 counted a Republican, Gary A. Franks of Connecticut, who seldom agreed with the caucus and was often shut out of its meetings, and the lone African-American in the Senate, Carol Moseley-Braun.

To many members, the caucus became as much a part of the House's legislative activity as the Conservative Democratic Forum — conservative Democratic House members, led by Charles W. Stenholm, Texas, who often voted with Republicans on economic issues.

In the end, black caucus Democrats proved to be among the most loyal of Democrats, voting with the party on partisan votes 97 percent of the time — compared with 89 percent for the party as a whole. *(Party-unity vote study, p. 14-C)*

Role in Budget Negotiations

The black caucus first publicly exercised its voting muscle in April. Democratic House leaders wanted to give President Clinton a victory by handing him a modified line-item veto, but caucus members feared that their favorite programs would be the ones to get cut. After caucus members threatened to vote with Republicans against the rule governing floor debate, leaders were forced to pull the bill and negotiate with the caucus before eventually passing it. *(Rescission authority, p. 146)*

Clinton felt the caucus's anger in early June, when he withdrew the nomination of African-American Lani Guinier for assistant attorney general. Clinton invited the caucus to a White House meeting to smooth ruffled feathers, but the caucus refused. *(Guinier, p. 307)*

The caucus took its highest profile on the budget. Caucus members reminded leaders that without their votes in May, the House version of the deficit-reduction bill would not have passed. They demanded, and largely got, a figurative seat at the table as House and Senate conferees hammered out the final form of the wide-ranging budget-reconciliation bill. *(Budget-reconciliation, p. 107)*

Caucus members were angered by budget cuts that the Senate embraced in June when it backed away from a broad-based energy tax Clinton proposed. Those cuts included $8 billion in additional Medicare cuts and $18 billion in cuts from the earned-income tax credit program. The caucus also wanted to restore a House-passed provision creating "empowerment zones" with aid and special tax breaks to spur economic development in depressed urban and rural areas. While support for the zones was somewhat tepid among caucus members, they said that it was the only program in the bill targeted at poor communities.

During the weeks leading up to the final, Aug. 5 House vote on the package, the caucus held news conferences to articulate its position, met with the leadership and with Clinton, and courted Republicans as well as conservative Democrats. After months of holding back, caucus members announced Aug. 2 — as Clinton was in the final push to round up Democratic votes — that the group had decided to back the bill.

The caucus did not get everything it had hoped for, but it got enough to be satisfied. Conferees agreed to provisions that expanded the earned-income tax credit for poor working families, created empowerment zones, expanded eligibility for food stamps, created a program to help keep troubled families together and provided mandatory immunization for poor and uninsured children.

The immunization measure became a bargaining chip when the administration asked the House for deeper Medicare cuts. House health leaders, with Mfume at their side, refused to accept the Medicare cuts unless they got immu-

nizations and other health measures for the poor. Caucus member Charles B. Rangel, D-N.Y., lobbied to ensure that the conference agreement included money for increased social services, in addition to business tax incentives, for the empowerment zones.

Mfume called the conference report a gain for the nation's poor and working families "after 12 years of Robin Hood in reverse."

Bigger Agenda

The caucus also made its presence felt on other major issues in 1993:

● **NAFTA.** On June 24, the caucus announced that it could not support the North American Free Trade Agreement (NAFTA) in its existing form, saying it would cost American jobs. (On the Nov. 17 vote on NAFTA, caucus members voted overwhelmingly against it.) *(NAFTA, p. 170)*

● **Supplemental spending.** In mid-May, House Democratic leaders had to abruptly postpone a scheduled vote on a $1.8 billion supplemental spending bill because liberals, led by the black caucus, wanted it paired with a $920 million bill that included money for summer jobs for urban youths. After a meeting between Mfume and Speaker Thomas S. Foley, D-Wash., the bills were joined and easily passed. *(Spring supplemental bill, p. 710)*

● **Campaign finance reform.** In House backroom discussions over the fate of campaign finance legislation, members of the black caucus led the fight against the Senate's proposal to prohibit fundraising from political action committees (PACs). Together with women and members who came from less affluent districts, they argued that PAC money was essential to running campaigns against Republicans who could draw on a well-heeled national party. *(Campaign finance, p. 37)*

● **Foreign policy.** Caucus members expressed outrage when Clinton reversed a campaign pledge and continued the Bush administration policy of intercepting Haitian refugees and returning them without letting them apply for political asylum. *(Haiti, p. 499)*

● **Banking issues.** The influence of the black caucus was apparent on the House Banking Committee, where seven of its 30 Democratic members served, including Mfume. They succeeded in adding provisions to a thrift bailout bill (S 714 — PL 103-204) aimed at increasing business opportunities for minorities. *(Thrift bill, p. 150)*

Alliances and Seniority

The caucus closely allied itself with the NAACP, which in 1993 elected a new leader, Benjamin F. Chavis Jr., and seemed to be trying to project a more forceful image. Chavis said that whatever positions the caucus took would also be the positions of the NAACP, a civil rights group. Mfume put the relationship this way: The caucus "entered into a covenant the day we met with Ben Chavis. It was a covenant to lock arms to walk together and to work together, and not to let there be even a crack of daylight between our positions."

The caucus's relationship with a more controversial group came back to haunt it later in the year. In September, Mfume invited Louis Farrakhan to address the black caucus's annual legislative conference; Farrakhan led the Nation of Islam, a black nationalist group. Mfume announced a "covenant" between the two groups to work together on strengthening the black community.

But in November, Farrakhan's spokesman, Khalid Abdul Muhammad, gave an inflammatory speech at Kean College in Union, N.J., in which he called Jews "bloodsuckers of the black nation," called the pope a "no-good ... cracker" and urged South African blacks to murder all the country's whites.

The speech did not attract widespread attention until Jan. 16, 1994, when the Anti-Defamation League of B'nai B'rith, a Jewish civil liberties group, printed excerpts in a full-page ad in The New York Times. After a storm of controversy in the media, caucus members demanded in a Feb. 2 meeting that Mfume make clear that the caucus had never formally voted to establish a relationship with the Nation of Islam. He did so at a news conference. ∎

Michel Announces Retirement

It did not take long for House Republicans to begin the changing of the guard after Minority Leader Robert H. Michel, Ill., announced Oct. 4 that the 103rd Congress would be his last.

Three days after Michel's announcement, Newt Gingrich, Ga., became the heir apparent when he launched his campaign, claiming the support of more than 100 members of the 175-member Republican Conference. The post would be decided in late 1994 when Republicans met to organize for the 104th Congress.

Michel's retirement, after 14 years as leader, cleared the way for the party hierarchy to be dominated by Gingrich and others whose confrontational brand of Republicanism was in ascendancy and made Michel's consensus-oriented style seem like an anachronism.

"I believe we can build a team that can fulfill our rendezvous with destiny," said Gingrich.

Gingrich's allies boasted of his widespread support among the GOP ranks. John Linder, R-Ga., said that Gingrich had the backing of 40 of the 48 Republican freshmen.

When Gingrich announced his candidacy Oct. 7, he was flanked by about 75 members representing different GOP factions, from conservative Mel Hancock, Mo., to moderate Olympia J. Snowe, Maine.

It looked at first as if Gingrich, who held the No. 2 job as minority whip, would at least have to compete for the job.

Gerald B. H. Solomon of New York jumped into the race on the day Michel announced he was leaving, saying that Republicans needed a leader who could bridge divisions within the GOP and reach across party lines to conservative Democrats. "We need a Republican leader who can build a coalition of united Republicans and conservative Democrats who can successfully legislate," Solomon said. "I'm a workhorse, not a show horse."

But 10 days later, Solomon gave up the fight, acknowledging that Gingrich had corralled enough votes to assure victory. Solomon said that to continue the race he would have to ask Gingrich supporters to switch sides.

"I could never bring myself to ask committed Republicans to break their promises," said Solomon. "I believe it would be too divisive to our party and far too distracting to our members for me to continue in the race over a protracted 14 months."

Solomon "expected dissatisfaction with Newt's style to be more formidable than it is," said Henry J. Hyde, R-Ill., who had been mentioned as a possible challenger to Gingrich but who declined to get into the race.

Gingrich's Ascent

It was not always so clear that Republicans would trust Gingrich with the job. But Gingrich had come a long way from the shaky base on which he built his first bid for leadership.

In 1989, when he had no experience in leadership and a reputation as a rambunctious bomb-thrower, Gingrich was elected whip by a two-vote margin over then-Rep. Edward R. Madigan of Illinois, a Michel ally. *(1989 Almanac, p. 3)*

Since then Gingrich had taken some steps to tone down his brash image — enough to fit into his role as a leader but not so much as to alienate his base.

As Michel's retirement loomed, Gingrich took a lower profile as GOP point man, often striking a conspicuously less partisan pose than before. He sided with President Clinton and Democratic leaders to support aid to Russia and the North American Free Trade Agreement.

"Newt Gingrich has worked over the last year at changing his image," said John A. Boehner, R-Ohio, a Gingrich supporter. "He's been trying to evolve into a more responsible leader."

But it was not as much Gingrich's changing his style as the Republican Conference veering toward his brand of conservatism.

When Michel took over in 1981, the Republican Conference was dominated by members who shared his idea of what it meant to be a House Republican, namely looking for ways to influence legislation and cooperating with Democrats on institutional matters such as congressional pay raises and administrative chores.

But there was a growing cadre of feistier conservatives — centering on the class of 1978, which included Gingrich and Solomon. They focused more on drawing clear lines between the parties than on finding common ground in legislation. This confrontational school of thought gained more and more adherents among the Republicans elected in the 1980s.

They began a stampede from the back benches to the leadership in 1989 when Gingrich was elected whip. Every Congress after that, more conservative activists joined Gingrich in the leadership. Michel became increasingly isolated, although he was too respected to be pushed from office.

But Gingrich did nudge Michel a bit, quietly talking to colleagues about his aim of becoming leader — leaving the clear impression that he would run in the next Congress whether or not Michel retired.

Michel acknowledged that he probably would have faced a challenge from Gingrich had he stayed in Congress. "I would have come out ahead in that kind of race," Michel said. "But I don't know that we need a fratricidal kind of thing."

Gingrich also had something to do with the kind of Republican that was being sent to Washington. From 1986 to 1992, Gingrich and his political action committee, GOPAC, provided both financial and campaign support to prospective House candidates. During the 1991-1992 election cycle, GOPAC raised more than $4 million, about $1 million of which went to federal candidates in the form of training videos and speeches. "There are a lot of different ways to show leadership," said a Gingrich aide.

Open Whip's Race Looms

While Gingrich faced little opposition for Republican leader, there was no apparent front-runner to replace him as minority whip.

Three members — Tom DeLay, Texas; Bill McCollum, Fla.; and Robert S. Walker, Pa. — announced that they would seek the post. Like Gingrich, DeLay sought to gain enough commitments to clinch the job, but he was unable to do so. The three then settled into the grueling process of member-to-member lobbying to win crucial votes.

All three were considered in the solid right of their party. Moderates had all but disappeared as a force in the leadership after Steve Gunderson of Wisconsin quit as a chief deputy whip and Fred Upton of Michigan stepped down as a deputy whip. The two moderates gave up their posts in January because of philosophical differences with the more conservative leadership.

Leaders for 103rd Congress

SENATE

President Pro Tempore — Robert C. Byrd, D-W.Va.
Majority Leader — George J. Mitchell, D-Maine
Majority Whip — Wendell H. Ford, D-Ky.
Secretary of the Democratic Conference — David Pryor, D-Ark.

Minority Leader — Bob Dole, R-Kan.
Assistant Minority Leader — Alan K. Simpson, R-Wyo.
Chairman of the Republican Conference — Thad Cochran, R-Miss.
Secretary of the Republican Conference — Trent Lott, R-Miss.

HOUSE

Speaker — Thomas S. Foley, D-Wash.
Majority Leader — Richard A. Gephardt, D-Mo.
Majority Whip — David E. Bonior, D-Mich.
Chairman of the Democratic Caucus — Steny H. Hoyer, D-Md.

Minority Leader — Robert H. Michel, R-Ill.
Minority Whip — Newt Gingrich, R-Ga.
Chairman of the Republican Conference — Dick Armey, R-Texas
Chairman of the Republican Policy Committee — Henry J. Hyde, R-Ill.

Gunderson said he hoped at least that moderates could stick together and become a bloc that could affect the leadership race. "No candidate can lock it up without moderate Republicans," he said.

MICHEL'S CAREER

Michel, who announced his retirement at age 70, had the grim distinction of having served in the House minority longer than any other member in history.

Michel won his seat in 1956, the year Dwight D. Eisenhower won his second term as president, and two years after Republicans lost their majority in the House. There were then just 48 states and no major league baseball teams west of Missouri. The geographic center of the nation's population was in Illinois, not far from Michel's district.

Michel was born in Peoria in 1923, the son of a French immigrant factory worker, and he graduated from his hometown Bradley University. He became administrative assistant to Republican Rep. Harold Velde, who was chairman of the old Un-American Activities Committee. When Velde retired in 1956, Michel was elected to succeed him.

In his second term, Michel won a seat on the Appropriations Committee, where he served for a quarter century. Michel said his committee work taught him the importance of detail and the art of collaborative politics.

He served as chairman of the House Republicans' campaign committee in the post-Watergate election of 1974, which produced 75 Democratic freshmen. But his colleagues did not hold that episode against Michel personally, electing him minority whip that year.

In 1980, with the more junior and conservative elements of the House GOP rebelling against Minority Leader John J. Rhodes of Arizona, Michel was elevated to minority leader, beating Guy Vander Jagt of Michigan by 103-87.

Michel's first two years as party leader were almost certainly his most exciting. Ronald Reagan's administration depended on his sense of strategy and timing in moving its budget and tax cuts through the Democratic House. Michel's ties to GOP moderates and Democratic conservatives helped marshal the needed votes.

As he announced his retirement, Michel said he saw "a big generational gap between my style of leadership and my sense of values and my whole thinking processes," and those of the younger, more confrontational leaders. Without naming names, he decried members bent on "trashing the institution," as well as those who chose confrontation before compromise.

"When you're in the minority," Michel said, "you've got to make up your mind: Are you going to be a player or are you just going to be a constant carping critic?" ∎

No Action Taken on Congressional Reform

Faced with continuing public disillusionment with the political process in Washington, lawmakers considered a variety of proposals to improve congressional operations. After a yearlong study, the Joint Committee on the Organization of Congress, a special panel established in 1992 with equal numbers of members from each party and each chamber, recommended a series of changes, including reducing committee assignments, converting to a two-year budget process and reducing the opportunities for Senate filibusters. Neither the House nor the Senate acted on those recommendations before the end of the year.

The final days of the Joint Committee were dogged by partisan bickering, procedural snarls and petty rivalries — the kinds of squabbles that often paralyzed Congress in the face of major legislation.

The Joint Committee's recommendations were issued far later in the year than had been expected. Although the panel had planned to draft its report in September or October, action was postponed until the last weeks of the session in November. Tensions between the House and Senate ran high, and the two chambers ended up reporting separate recommendations, although their proposals had much in common.

Senate members of the Joint Committee approved their recommendations unanimously; the House recommendations were approved 8-4, over loud GOP complaints that they did not go far enough.

Senate members of the Joint Committee deferred action on proposals to revise the ethics process and to make Congress live under the laws it passed because separate task forces in the Senate were studying those issues. *(Exemptions, p. 22)*

Legislation (HR 3801, S 1824) incorporating the Joint Committee's recommendations was introduced Feb. 3, 1994, in the House and Senate.

Many of the Joint Committee's proposals were certain to face stiff opposition from members reluctant to change the status quo. Before going to the House and Senate floor, the recommendations had to be considered by party caucuses and several committees. For the most part, each chamber was left to write the rules for its own procedures, although some proposals could affect both chambers — such as a two-year budget process and a proposal to abolish joint committees — and could require a conference to settle differences.

A few changes in congressional operations were implemented in other legislation in 1993. The House disbanded four select committees that had no authority to write legislation, and it lifted the secrecy that made it difficult to bypass committees and bring legislation directly to the floor. However, separate measures that were considered part of the broader rubric of reform — on campaign finance, gifts to members and lobbying disclosure — remained stalled. *(Select committees, p. 13; discharge petitions, p. 10; campaign finance, p. 37; lobbying disclosure, p. 50)*

In keeping with the resolution creating it, the Joint Committee dissolved as of Dec. 31, 1993.

BACKGROUND

Congress agreed in 1992 to create the Joint Committee, which was modeled on panels that produced significant changes in 1946 and 1970. Under a concurrent resolution (H Con Res 192) approved in August 1992, the panel was to be made up of an equal number of Democrats and Republicans, House and Senate members (28 in all, including four ex officio leaders). *(1992 Almanac, p. 56)*

To win passage of the resolution, its sponsors — Reps. Lee H. Hamilton, D-Ind., and Bill Gradison, R-Ohio, and Sens. David L. Boren, D-Okla., and Pete V. Domenici, R-N.M. — capitalized on the electorate's angry mood caused by scandals in the House bank and Post Office.

Other members, named to the Joint Committee in 1992, were:

● **Senate Democrats:** Harry Reid, Nev.; Jim Sasser, Tenn.; Wendell H. Ford, Ky.; Paul S. Sarbanes, Md.; and David Pryor, Ark.

● **Senate Republicans:** Nancy Landon Kassebaum, Kan.; Trent Lott, Miss.; Ted Stevens, Alaska; William S. Cohen, Maine; and Richard G. Lugar, Ind.

● **House Democrats:** David R. Obey, Wis.; Al Swift, Wash.; John M. Spratt Jr., S.C.; Sam Gejdenson, Conn; and Eleanor Holmes Norton, D.C.

● **House Republicans:** Robert S. Walker, Pa.; Gerald B. H. Solomon, N.Y.; David Dreier, Calif.; Bill Emerson, Mo.; and Wayne Allard, Colo.

Gradison resigned from the House on Jan. 31, 1993. His place heading House Republicans was filled by Dreier; the vacancy on the panel was filled by Jennifer Dunn, R-Wash.

The panel's official mandate did not allow it to begin work until after the 1992 elections, and it put the committee out of business Dec. 31, 1993. But the mandate opened for consideration nearly everything about the way Congress operated.

HEARINGS

The Joint Committee took its first public step Jan. 26 by calling the top five congressional leaders to testify. The Speaker and the House and Senate majority and minority leaders appeared — a first in congressional annals. But even as the panel's patrons suggested that the historic nature of the day could portend historic change, the witnesses warned of the political and constitutional obstacles to overhauling Congress.

"There are limits to what organization and institutional reform can do," Speaker Thomas S. Foley, D-Wash., said. "Fundamentally this will and must remain an institution where there is political dissent, debate and disagreement, and there is nothing that can or should distract us from the character of the institution."

Moreover, familiar patterns quickly emerged. Democrats cited a need for streamlined legislative management that would let the majority achieve its objectives, Republicans a need for fairness that would protect minority rights. And panel members were distracted by scheduling conflicts of the type that they vowed to solve.

As the bells rang late in the day to call members to a floor vote, Emerson groused, "Now we have to unfocus on what we're focused on to go focus on what we're not focused on."

Boren and the other panel heads set an ambitious agenda, with the aim of readying a bill by August. "Nothing should be out of bounds; there are no sacred cows;

Continued on p. 24

Congress Prepares To Apply . . .

Congress moved toward ending a longstanding stalemate over whether it should remain exempt from key workplace laws, but the effort remained in limbo pending floor action on the recommendations of the Joint Committee on the Reorganization of Congress. *(Congressional reform, p. 21)*

In November, the House members of the Joint Committee included in their package of proposed reforms several recommendations to make Congress subject to the laws it passed. The Senate contingent to the panel deferred action because the matter was the subject of a separate Senate task force inquiry. But leaders of the Joint Committee said they expected eventually to bring the task force recommendations into a broader "reform" package on the Senate floor.

Leaders in both chambers signaled that as long as the executive and judicial branches were not given carte blanche to rummage through legislative affairs, congressional reformers could try to find ways to make the congressional workplace conform to the nation's rules.

The aim was to end complaints that when Congress passed laws, the statutes often applied to everyone but Congress itself.

For decades, Congress had exempted itself from certain laws, primarily those affecting congressional staff, citing the Constitution's separation of powers doctrine. Leaders of both parties had argued that neither executive branch agencies nor the courts should be able to interfere with internal operations of the legislative branch. They also worried that members could get dragged into lawsuits designed to create political embarrassment. In recent years, Congress had set up some in-house structures to parallel the agencies that usually enforced the laws. But critics said those procedures were not public or powerful enough.

In his 1992 presidential campaign, George Bush called for "no more special treatment" for the Democratic-dominated Congress, telling a New Hampshire audience in mid-January that "they ought not to exempt themselves from the laws you and I have to honor."

For years, a deadlock existed between critics who called for outright repeal of the exemptions and Democratic leaders who resisted change on constitutional grounds. But consensus grew, largely for political reasons, that Congress should move aggressively to address the situation. House Speaker Thomas S. Foley, D-Wash., sent an important signal in August when he told the Joint Committee in a letter, "I believe that now is the time to develop a workable mechanism to apply and enforce those laws in Congress."

BACKGROUND

Congressional exemptions dated at least to 1935, when Congress took itself out of the National Labor Relations Act, which gave private-sector employees the right to form unions and the right to file charges for unfair labor practices with the National Labor Relations Board.

Leaders said that the exemptions were necessary to prevent intrusion by the other branches of government and that they were required by the Constitution's Speech or Debate Clause, which prevented members from being "questioned in any other place" for their legislative acts.

Leaders also argued that voters would oust members who violated the spirit of the laws, for instance by illegally discriminating in hiring.

Several steps taken by Congress to establish alternative mechanisms for enforcing the law that did not involve the courts or the executive branch came under scrutiny by the Joint Committee and other members.

The House's employee complaint office, the Office of Fair Employment Practices, was established in 1989 to counsel staff, mediate conflicts and render decisions on formal complaints regarding discrimination, harassment or overtime. It had four staff members to hear and mediate complaints, and it could order monetary compensation from a House fund, a member or a committee. It also could decide on injunctive relief, payment of costs and attorney fees, and employment reinstatement or promotion. But its decisions did not have to be publicized, it did not have subpoena power, and unhappy employees could not appeal its decisions to court.

The General Accounting Office (GAO) reported in May that the office had received only seven formal complaints in its four-year existence and awarded $18,000 in damages.

The Senate had its own Office of Fair Employment Practices, created in 1991, with limited judicial review of internal decisions.

A survey of congressional employees conducted for the Joint Committee, released Sept. 17, showed little confidence in the complaint offices. About 40 percent of House workers and 30 percent of Senate workers surveyed said concerns about confidentiality and notification made them unlikely to file complaints.

The Senate in 1991, after heated debate, made senators personally liable for paying fines levied for civil rights violations. But in 1992, the chamber quietly shifted liability to the government. *(1991 Almanac, p. 257; 1992 Almanac, p. 637)*

LAWS AT ISSUE

The laws most often cited in the debate were these:

● **National Labor Relations Act.** This 1935 law (Chapter 372; Section 1, 49 stat. 449) gave private-sector employees the right to form unions and required employers to bargain with them. It also proscribed unfair labor practices by both groups and gave them the right to file charges with the National Labor Relations Board. The Federal Labor-Management Relations Act similarly governed federal employers and employee unions. Neither law applied to Congress, nor could congressional employees be recognized as parties to collective bargaining.

● **Fair Labor Standards Act.** This 1938 law (Chapter 676; Section 1, 52 stat. 1060) required all covered employers to pay the statutory minimum wage and time-and-a-half wages for work in excess of 40 hours in one week. Amendments made in 1989 (PL 101-157) extended minimum wage and overtime protections to House em-

... Workplace Rules to Itself

ployees and set up the House Office of Fair Employment Practices. Professional, executive and managerial employees (as determined by the House Administration Committee) were exempt, as they would be in the private sector. Senate employees were not covered.

● **Occupational Safety and Health Act (OSHA).** This 1970 law (PL 91-596) required non-government employers and federal agency managers to maintain health and safety standards to protect their employees. The law, which focused on plants and factories, also authorized periodic government inspection of other workplaces.

A 1993 GAO report found numerous OSHA violations in Congress with potential liability of up to $1 million — but the rules did not apply to Congress. Instead, it was up to the Architect of the Capitol's office to monitor congressional buildings, shops and furniture. That office had no power to punish violators; it reported to congressional committees.

● **Civil Rights Act.** Title VII of this 1964 law (PL 88-352) barred discrimination in employment, compensation and promotion on the basis of race, color, religion, sex or national origin and established the Equal Employment Opportunity Commission (EEOC) to hear complaints and seek compliance. It also authorized the federal courts to remedy discrimination by such methods as awarding back pay and retirement benefits. Congress was not included.

In the Civil Rights Act of 1991 (PL 102-166), Congress extended to its workers the same restrictions on discrimination, with the House and Senate's offices of Fair Employment Practices handling complaints.

● **Americans with Disabilities Act.** This 1990 law (PL 101-336) gave civil rights-type protections in employment and accommodations to people with mental and physical disabilities. The law also required public transportation systems, public services and telecommunications systems to be accessible to those with disabilities.

Congressional workers could file complaints with their chamber's Office of Fair Employment Practices. Senate staff members could secure limited judicial review, but House employees could not. The Architect of the Capitol had jurisdiction over the accessibility provisions.

● **Equal Pay Act.** This 1963 law (PL 88-38) required equal pay for men and women doing work equal in skill, effort and responsibility. House employees' gender-based complaints went to the Office of Fair Employment Practices. Senate employees were not covered.

● **Age Discrimination in Employment Act.** This 1967 law (PL 90-202) barred job discrimination against applicants or employees age 40 to 65 (later extended to age 70). The Senate gave this protection to its employees in the 1991 Civil Rights Act. A House rule prohibited discrimination on the basis of age. House employees could file complaints with the Office of Fair Employment Practices. Only Senate employees could secure court appeals.

● **Rehabilitation Act.** This 1973 law (PL 93-112) re-

quired all executive departments and agencies to submit to the EEOC and a related agency an affirmative action plan for disabled persons. The Senate extended similar requirements to its employees in 1991. The House had no similar requirement.

● **Family and Medical Leave Act.** Enacted in 1993, PL 103-3 required employers to allow employees to take up to 12 weeks of unpaid leave during any 12-month period to attend to the birth or adoption of a child or placement of a foster child; the serious illness of a child, spouse or parent; or the employee's own serious health condition. It applied to both chambers, with remedies granted through the offices of Fair Employment Practices.

● **Freedom of Information Act (FOIA).** Congressional documents were not governed under this 1966 law (PL 89-487), which required federal agencies to make government information available to the general public. Many members said that under the Constitution's Speech or Debate Clause, they did not have to make public Congress' administrative records and certain correspondence.

● **Privacy Act.** Congressional employees were not considered under this 1974 law (PL 93-579) protecting the privacy of agency employees subject to FOIA. The law prohibited agencies from releasing information in employees' personnel files without their permission.

● **Miscellaneous.** Other provisions that did not apply to Congress included the appointment of independent counsels under the Ethics in Government Act and provisions prohibiting members and congressional staff from getting Social Security and another form of pension.

LEGISLATIVE VEHICLES

The Senate, traditionally jealous of its prerogatives, set up its own bipartisan task force in the fiscal 1993 legislative appropriations bill to examine the situation and report to the Joint Committee. The task force, headed by Sen. Harry Reid, D-Nev., sent its recommendations to Majority Leader George J. Mitchell, D-Maine, the week of Dec. 6, but they were not made public.

In an Aug. 13 letter to Mitchell, Reid said the task force had unanimously voted that the Senate would keep the system for assuring compliance and handling grievances within the Senate rather than using extra-congressional enforcement boards.

On the House side, Speaker Foley recommended HR 2729, called the Congressional Accountability Act, a working draft based on HR 349, sponsored by Christopher Shays, R-Conn., and Dick Swett, D-N.H.

The draft proposed a new Office of Compliance to govern both House and Senate coverage, and proposed to end exemptions gradually, using a board appointed by House and Senate leaders from both parties to study the matter and issue regulations. This approach formed the basis for the Joint Committee's recommendations.

Many Republicans wanted faster action and more concrete limitations than the bill offered and sought to hold members personally liable for violations.

Continued from p. 21
there's nothing we should be unwilling to look at," Boren told colleagues.

The hearings were to take up ethics reform and then turn to the budget, appropriations and authorization process; committee structures; congressional staffing; floor deliberations and scheduling; interbranch government relations; communications and information technology; and public understanding of Congress.

Mitchell Rules Proposals

At the Jan. 26 meeting of the Joint Committee, Senate Majority Leader George J. Mitchell, D-Maine, outlined a plan to streamline Senate procedures. Mitchell said he had no intention of denying senators the right to fully debate or filibuster an issue, but he said he was fed up with "unlimited delay and obstruction." He proposed seven specific changes (S Res 25-32 and 37) that he said would allow the Senate to operate in a "more orderly and efficient manner."

His package contained the following proposals:

• Limit debate to two hours on a motion to proceed.

Before considering most legislation, the Senate was required to approve a motion to proceed. Under the rules in effect, it was possible to filibuster such motions.

• Require a three-fifths vote of the Senate to overturn a ruling of the chair under cloture.

A simple majority was required to overturn such rulings during most Senate debate, except during consideration of certain budget amendments, when a three-fifths vote was needed to overturn a ruling of the chair.

• Allow committee-reported amendments and amendments to the committee amendment to automatically be considered germane after cloture was invoked.

Legislative decisions made during committee markup sessions typically were brought before the Senate as an amendment in the nature of a substitute. Under existing post-cloture rules, that amendment and amendments to the substitute could be ruled non-germane and therefore out of order.

• Count time consumed by quorum calls during cloture against the senator who suggested the absence of a quorum.

Post-cloture rules provided up to 30 hours of debate and guaranteed every senator as much as an hour and a minimum of 10 minutes for debate. The time consumed by quorum calls was counted against the overall limit, but not against the senator who requested the quorum call.

• Allow the Senate to go to conference with the House after passage of a single motion to proceed.

Under the rules in force, if unanimous consent were not achieved, the Senate had to adopt three separate motions to proceed before a conference could be convened: one on whether to agree with House amendments or insist on Senate language; a second on whether to request a conference with the House or to agree to such a request by the House; and a third on naming conferees. Each motion was subject to debate and possible filibuster.

• Dispense with the reading of a conference report.

Under existing rules, before a conference report could be brought up, it had to be distributed to each senator and any senator could demand that it be read aloud in its entirety.

• Provide for a motion to require that amendments be ruled germane.

There were virtually no restrictions on amendments unless cloture were invoked. The change would allow a three-fifths majority to require that amendments be relevant to the underlying legislation. Such a motion would be in order on the third day of a bill's consideration.

Mitchell conceded that making the changes would be difficult, particularly since it was necessary to gather not just 60 votes but a full two-thirds to block a threatened filibuster of any Senate rules change.

Senate Republicans argued that Mitchell's proposals would fundamentally undermine their rights. They "dilute the ability of the minority to function," said minority whip Alan K. Simpson, R-Wyo. Minority Leader Bob Dole, R-Kan., emphasized that the rights of any minority coalition were at stake.

"It's not just a partisan minority," he said.

In defense, Mitchell cited statistics showing that the number of cloture votes to end filibusters had mushroomed over the previous quarter century, and he complained that filibusters were threatened for "reasons as trivial as a senator's travel schedule." He said senators had six chances to filibuster a bill, and his proposals would limit them to two, not eliminate them.

Eventually, most of Mitchell's recommendations — except for those on germaneness and going to conference — were adopted by the Senate panel of the Joint Committee.

Incumbents Offer Proposals

The Joint Committee set aside the week of Feb. 1 to hear from incumbent members about what needed to be done to improve the way Congress functioned. It got an earful.

The panel had a nearly three-hour dialogue Feb. 2 with Senate President Pro Tempore Robert C. Byrd, D-W.Va., on the history, traditions and rationale of the Senate rules. Byrd cautioned the committee against getting caught up in an "obsession with process," which he said put more emphasis on the rules under which legislation was considered than on the quality of debate about it.

From his mastery of Senate lore and his 34 years in the chamber, Byrd drew conclusions that set him apart from many colleagues. Like other Democrats, Byrd complained that debate in the Senate was not as thoughtful or thorough as it should be. But unlike Majority Leader Mitchell, Byrd did not locate the problem in Senate rules that slowed legislation and permitted multiple filibusters. He said the problem was "the people."

"The Senate has lost its soul. But the answer is not to be found in tinkering with the process or in the pursuit of 'efficiency,' whatever that means," Byrd told the panel. "The Senate will improve as an institution only when individual senators become more interested in once again being full-time senators."

Byrd told members that senators need to become less concerned with appearing on television and raising campaign funds and more concerned with studying the issues of the day. "Senate debate is dying as a legislative art," he said.

On Feb. 14, the panel got a litany of recommendations from 14 House Democrats and 27 Republicans who responded in person to the committee's call for testimony. Another half-dozen members submitted written statements. Many were freshmen, several of whom recommended term limits for committee chairmen.

A bipartisan group including Christopher Shays, R-Conn.; Dick Swett, D-N.H.; Jay Dickey, R-Ark.; and David Mann, D-Ohio, told the panel that Congress should no longer exempt itself from laws that other Americans had to abide by.

"Voters are fed up with us being treated like some type of royalty up here," Dickey told the panel.

Perot Offers Sound Bites

The panel heard from one of Congress' most prominent critics on March 2, when it listened to businessman and former independent presidential candidate Ross Perot. "Fairly or unfairly, the people feel that our government is for sale," Perot said.

The panel had invited Perot to make suggestions on overhauling congressional procedures and improving the public image and understanding of Congress. But after an hour hearing exhortations reminiscent of Perot's self-financed presidential campaign, several members clearly had grown weary of his tone and lack of specifics.

Stevens twice tried to get Perot's opinion of campaign finance legislation that included a public subsidy for congressional campaigns, but he got no answer.

Perot's comment on federal budgeting: "People keep track of their pennies. They get really nervous when we round off $50 million in government." On budgetary language: "Cut out all of the strange language of Washington. Let's just call a dog a dog, an elephant an elephant."

This was the type of folksy rhetoric that earned Perot 19 percent of the vote in the 1992 presidential election. But despite their parties' desire to win over the Perot voters, some members took off the kid gloves after a while.

"You've now given us 45 minutes of sound bites and five minutes of material," said Reid, who went on to advise Perot to "start checking your facts a little more and stop listening to the applause as much."

Joined by Pryor, Reid criticized Perot for saying President Clinton did not have any businessmen in his top ranks, pointing out that White House Chief of Staff Thomas F. McLarty III ran a major natural gas company, Arkla Inc., before coming to Washington.

When Perot was asked what the panel's top priority should be, he said, "Standing out all alone is ethics and integrity."

Asked Co-Chairman Hamilton: "Do you believe that most of us here are crooks? . . . are dishonest? . . . are untrustworthy?"

Perot changed course and went on to praise the panel's members and mission. He told the panelists that they each deserved a "medal of courage" for joining the committee.

Freshman Class Proposals

At back-to-back appearances before the Joint Committee on April 1, leaders of the House Democratic and Republican freshman classes offered contrasting prescriptions for reform, although they said they hoped to work together eventually. The 63 Democrats and 47 Republicans arrived at common ground on only two points. Both party groups endorsed new legislation to subject Congress to all laws it passed, and they came out for lower staff funding levels for former Speakers.

But in the process by which they adopted their reform packages and in the content itself, the two segments of the freshman class could hardly have been more different.

Without public dissent, the Republicans quickly united behind their 19-point package, which included limiting members' terms, eliminating the Appropriations Committee, lowering franking funds, requiring a three-fifths vote for any tax increase and ending proxy voting on committees. These were all popular proposals within the Republican Conference.

The process of adopting a package was grueling for the Democrats, with nearly 10 hours of meetings the week of March 29 alone. And the result was a document more vague than many said they had hoped for.

The first two items on the Democratic freshman reform agenda were legislative proposals backed by the leadership: a campaign finance bill and lobbying disclosure. They dropped most controversial elements, including a line-item veto. The most contentious points left in the package were recommendations that members hold only one committee or subcommittee chair (many committee chairmen held top subcommittee posts) and that the legislative branch appropriation be reduced 25 percent over five years.

On campaign finance, the class endorsed the standard Democratic fare of voluntary spending limits, but it ducked the issue of how to generate the public funds needed to entice candidates to participate in the system.

At a March 31 news conference, task force Chairmen Karen Shepherd, D-Utah, and Eric D. Fingerhut, D-Ohio, tried to return the focus to the thematic issues the class agreed on. But reporters refused to drop the public funding question until Shepherd said, "We can't come to agreement on that right now."

Reporters also grilled the freshmen on why they backed away from the more controversial ideas that had been discussed in previous weeks, such as terms limits for chairmen and curbs on perquisites.

The first-term Democrats included two items aimed squarely at the GOP. They recommended that motions to adjourn be considered out of order unless the House had been in session at least five hours (and that no one could make such a motion more than once a day). The Democrats also proposed ending daily votes approving the Journal, a formal record of previous proceedings.

Democrats complained that these procedural motions wasted time. Republicans said the parliamentary devices were the only way they could draw attention to certain issues or protest closed Democratic rules.

Survey of Members

Twenty-two of the panel's 24 congressional members attended an overnight retreat in Annapolis, Md., on June 27-28 to begin reviewing hundreds of proposals. Counting its last witness, former Vice President Walter F. Mondale, who testified July 1, the panel had heard from 243 witnesses during about 114 hours of testimony over 36 days since late January, an aide said.

The committee's leaders conceded at a news conference June 28 that their final proposal was not likely to make it to either chamber's floor until 1994. "It's quite clear to us now that an awful lot of work needs to be done," said Hamilton.

The committee released the results of a survey it had sent to all 535 members of the House and Senate in May. The panel's leaders said the results were a reliable barometer, although only 145 members took the time to answer its 80 or so questions.

The results included these:

● Nearly 90 percent of the respondents agreed that "major improvements are needed in the way Congress conducts its legislative business."

● The respondents' top five priorities for reorganizing Congress were the committee structure, the budget process, floor procedures, ethics and public understanding of Congress. There were partisan splits on some issues, however, with more Republicans than Democrats complaining about the budget process.

● Respondents overwhelmingly supported reducing the number of subcommittees, limiting members' committee assignments and establishing parallel House/Senate com-

Senate Proposals

Following are highlights of proposals approved Nov. 10 by Senate members of the Joint Committee on the Organization of Congress:

Floor Procedures

- **Reduce filibusters.** A motion to proceed to consider a bill no longer could be filibustered. After cloture was invoked, it would take a three-fifths vote to overturn a ruling of the chair, and quorum-call time would count against the member who called for it.

Committees

- **Limits.** Each senator would have three assignments, as follows: One "Super A" committee (Armed Services, Appropriations, Finance, Foreign Relations); one "A" committee (Agriculture, Banking, Commerce, Energy, Environment, Governmental Affairs, Judiciary, Labor); and one "B" committee (Aging, Budget, Indian Affairs, Rules, Small Business, Veterans' Affairs). Ethics and Intelligence committee assignments would not count.
- **Subcommittee limits.** "Super A" and "A" committees, except Appropriations, could have only three subcommittees; "B" committees only two subcommittees.
- **Subcommittee assignments.** Senators could belong to two subcommittees per "A" committee, except Appropriations, and one subcommittee per "B."
- **Waivers.** Members could get extra assignments only if a waiver was offered by both parties' leaders and approved by a recorded vote.

- **Assignments.** Majority and minority leaders would make assignments, subject to caucus rules.
- **Kill joint committees.** All House-Senate joint committees (Economic; Library; Organization of Congress; Printing; Taxation) would be abolished.
- **Kill unpopular committees.** If restrictions on assignments caused a committee's size to fall by more than half, it would be abolished.
- **Meeting days.** "Super A" committees could meet only on Tuesdays, "A" committees on Wednesdays, "B" committees on Thursdays. Appropriations could meet any day.
- **Proxies.** Proxies could not be used if they would affect the outcome of a vote.
- **Attendance.** Records of attendance and voting would be published twice a year in the Congressional Record.

Bureaucracy

- **Staff.** Staffing levels would be cut in line with reductions proposed for the executive branch.
- **Leftover funds.** Unused funds from office or committee accounts no longer would be available for other uses.
- **Detailees.** Congress would have to reimburse the executive branch or agencies such as the General Accounting Office for staff detailed to it.

Budget Process

- **Two-year budget.** Budget resolutions and appropriations bills would cover two years.
- **Multi-year authorizations.** Programs would have to be authorized for at least two years.

---

mittee jurisdictions.

- There was only lukewarm support for allowing outsiders a role in the process for dealing with members' ethics transgressions.
- A large majority favored a two-year budget cycle instead of the existing one-year cycle, and 77 percent favored "sunsetting" entitlement programs after 10 years. About 74 percent favored eliminating one step from the existing three-step budget process (budget resolution, authorization and appropriation); of those, 43 percent thought the appropriations process should be killed.
- While 68 percent of the House respondents said there were too many limits on floor amendments and debate, House Republicans accounted for much of that sentiment, with 98 percent agreeing, compared with 40 percent for House Democrats. In the Senate, 33 percent said that there were too few limits on floor debates, with Democrats more apt to favor greater limits.
- Half the respondents thought Congress was overstaffed, with Republicans much more apt to think so. Relatively few said members' personal staffs should be cut. More popular was cutting the staffs of committees and congressional support agencies, such as the Government Printing Office and the Architect of the Capitol.

'Reform Month' Fades

The Joint Committee planned to produce its recommendations in September, but markups were delayed by lack of consensus. Speaker Foley began promising that the House would bring a slew of "reform" legislation — including the Joint Committee proposals and bills on campaign finance and lobbying disclosure — to the floor in October.

"In concentrating the scheduling of all these measures in one month, I believe that Democrats can underscore dramatically our commitment to making government fairer, more open and more responsive to the public's needs," Foley said in a Sept. 10 letter to Democratic freshmen. "I trust that this October will offer solid proof of congressional earnestness to deliver what we have promised."

But the heralded "reform month" came and went without any of the measures coming before the House. (The campaign finance bill did win House passage Nov. 22, shortly before Congress adjourned.)

SENATE PROPOSALS

With House members of the Joint Committee at loggerheads, Boren and Domenici — chairman and vice chairman, respectively, of the Senate contingent — decided to move ahead separately. They offered a proposal Nov. 4 that called for pruning the Senate's thicket of subcommittees and committees and stripping members of some of their assignments. They proposed a two-year budget, new limits on proxy voting and the use of outsiders to conduct some Senate ethics investigations.

The senators on the panel adopted the recommendations with few changes; the Nov. 10 vote was 12-0. *(Senate proposals, above)*

grandmother and his right hand up in the air, as he was sworn in by Chief Justice William H. Rehnquist.

About 15 minutes earlier, former Tennessee Sen. Al Gore, surrounded by his wife and four children, had been sworn in as the 45th vice president of the United States by Justice Byron R. White.

Clinton used his inaugural speech, delivered in an exceptionally brief 14 minutes, to lay down the themes for his administration: renewal, responsibility and inclusiveness. Although short on details, the speech did what many members had hoped it would do by calling for across-the-board sacrifices in revitalizing the economy and for all Americans to take responsibility for the nation's future.

Echoing the words of John F. Kennedy, who Clinton had said inspired him to public service, he called on Americans "to break the bad habit of expecting something for nothing, from our government or from each other. Let us all take more responsibility, not only for ourselves and our families but for our communities and our country."

And, as Kennedy did, he challenged young Americans to public service, "to act on your idealism by helping troubled children, keeping company with those in need, reconnecting our torn communities."

He made several references to the passing of the baton from one generation to the next. "Today," he said, "a generation raised in the shadows of the Cold War assumes new responsibilities in a world warmed by the sunshine of freedom but threatened still by ancient hatreds and new plagues."

While praising his predecessor for long years of public service, Clinton said the nation had been allowed to drift "and that drifting has eroded our own resources, fractured our economy and shaken our confidence.... Our democracy must be not only the envy of the world but the engine of our renewal. There is nothing wrong with America that cannot be cured by what is right with America."

He called for a revitalized political system, addressing some of the anti-government sentiment that permeated the 1992 election and helped spur the independent campaign of billionaire Ross Perot, who helped hold Clinton to 43 percent of the vote.

Holding his arms over his head, Clinton gestured toward the marble Capitol behind him, calling it a place where "powerful people maneuver for position and worry endlessly about who is in and who is out, who is up and who is down, forgetting those whose toil and sweat sends us here and pays our way," he said. "Americans deserve better.... Let us resolve to reform our politics, so that power and privilege no longer shout down the voice of the people."

The hourlong ceremony included songs by soprano Marilyn Horne and an inaugural poem by Maya Angelou, who echoed Clinton's message of hope and new beginnings in "On the Pulse of Morning." *(Poem, p. 35)*

The inaugural also marked the end of George Bush's 30-year political career. Bush, who sat opposite Clinton on the podium, appeared subdued throughout the ceremony.

After seeing the Bushes and former Vice President Dan Quayle and Marilyn Quayle off in a helicopter, Clinton went inside to the ornate President's Room off the Senate chamber to attend to his first official acts as president. Using a black and gold pen inscribed "Bill Clinton, The White House," the new president used the more formal "William J. Clinton" to sign an executive order detailing new lobbying restrictions for senior administration officials. *(Guidelines, 1992 Almanac, p. 62)*

Clinton then attended a post-inaugural luncheon in Statuary Hall — a tradition among House and Senate leaders for

Clinton Vetoes Nothing

President Clinton did not cast a single veto in 1993. It was the first time a president had abstained from using his power to nullify legislation since either 1969 or 1979, depending on how the congressional year was defined.

"We were able to work on a cooperative agenda," said George Stephanopoulos, a senior adviser to the president. "It's a Democratic president elected to get things done."

Democrat Jimmy Carter, the last president to serve with a Congress controlled by his own party, vetoed only two bills during his first year in office. But he exercised the power more frequently later in his presidency, ultimately vetoing 31 bills in his four-year term.

The last year without a veto was 1979 under Carter. He did, however, veto a bill in 1980 that Congress had passed in 1979. The last time a president didn't veto a whole year's legislation was 1969. President Richard M. Nixon was the accommodating executive then.

George Bush, better known for his ability to thwart override attempts than for how often he vetoed bills, turned down Congress 46 times in his four years as president. He was overridden only once. Ronald Reagan had 78 vetoes in two terms; Gerald R. Ford, 66 in 2½ years; Dwight D. Eisenhower, 181 in two terms; and Harry S. Truman, 250 from 1945 to 1953.

Grover Cleveland was the most prolific veto-wielder in a single term, with 414. Franklin D. Roosevelt set the record of 635, but he served 12 years.

new presidents since 1897. There, Clinton referred to his heavy lobbying as governor of Arkansas, quipping: "With all respect, I can't believe you were fully briefed about my proclivities in lobbying legislators to let me come up here without an invitation. I may be here all the time."

The inaugural week's ceremonies were filled with symbols of the inclusive kind of administration Clinton said he wanted. From a bus trip to Washington from Thomas Jefferson's home, Monticello, to lunch with 53 "average" Americans whose stories had touched him on the campaign trail, to an early morning visit to President Kennedy's gravesite in Virginia, to star-studded parties and "spontaneous" saxophone numbers at inaugural balls, to the post-inaugural open house, he still seemed to be campaigning.

Clinton dismantled a symbol of the previous administration on Jan. 22 when he disbanded the Council on Competitiveness. Headed by Quayle, it had reviewed decisions of executive agencies and been criticized as a pro-business court of review.

Nominations Quickly Approved

The Senate quickly and easily confirmed 18 of Clinton's top appointments on Jan. 20 and 21. *(Nominations, p. 33)*

Just hours after the new president was sworn in, the Senate by voice vote approved Lloyd Bentsen as Treasury secretary, Warren Christopher as secretary of State and Les Aspin as secretary of Defense. The following day, 15 Cabinet and other top officials were quickly confirmed, leaving the attorney general's post the only Cabinet position unfilled.

By week's end, the new administration had more than 1,000 confirmations to go. In all, 1,163 political appointees

The State of the Address

President Clinton originally advertised his Feb. 17 speech to a joint session of Congress as a State of the Union address, but by early February his advisers were calling it an economic policy speech. The difference was one of nomenclature and scope. A State of the Union address typically included a broad-brush look at the problems the nation faced, domestic and foreign; other presidential speeches usually had a specific focus.

Except for President Richard M. Nixon, who waited more than a year after taking office to address a joint session of Congress, every president since World War II who took office in a change of party had made a major speech to Congress within his first few months.

Only Dwight D. Eisenhower and John F. Kennedy called theirs State of the Union addresses. (Kennedy, who delivered a State of the Union address 10 days after his inauguration, liked the format so much that he made what amounted to a second State of the Union address in May.) Jimmy Carter waited until April to make his first address, on energy. Ronald Reagan's February address on the economy was followed by another in April after he recovered from an attempt on his life.

The title came from the Constitution's requirement that the president "shall from time to time give to the Congress information of the state of the Union, and recommend to their consideration such measures as he shall judge necessary and expedient."

By custom, when presidents indicated that they were coming to deliver a State of the Union message, Congress responded by passing a resolution calling "a joint session of Congress to receive a message from the president on the State of the Union.'

The formal title did not become custom until 1947, with Harry S Truman's speech. Presidents George Washington and John Adams delivered "annual messages" in person before joint sessions of Congress, but the practice was too monarchal for Thomas Jefferson. He submitted his message in writing. Not until Woodrow Wilson in 1913 did another president deliver his annual message to Congress in a speech.

required confirmation, according to the Senate Governmental Affairs Committee. An additional 561 political appointees did not.

The Democratic-controlled Senate confirmed the Democratic president's nominees at the same pace that a Republican-controlled Senate dispatched Republican President Ronald Reagan's nominees in 1981. Clinton's nominations moved slightly faster than those of Bush in 1989. Republicans said they saw little reason to hold up the show. "We believe the president is entitled to have his people in place at the earliest possible time," said Dole.

Other than Baird, the only nominees to stir even a whiff of controversy were Ronald H. Brown for Commerce secretary and Bruce Babbitt for Interior secretary.

There had been much speculation that Jesse Helms, R-N.C., would give Christopher a rough ride into office. Christopher had to endure two grueling days of testimony before the Senate Foreign Relations Committee. After that, aides to Helms submitted more than 400 questions to the nominee in writing. But in the end, neither Helms nor anyone else formally objected to the nomination. Christopher was approved on a 19-0 vote by the Foreign Relations Committee on Jan. 19. (Christopher, p. 531)

The Senate on Jan. 21 by voice vote approved Brown as Commerce secretary after the former Democratic National Committee chairman agreed to further sever his relationships with his former clients and law firm, Patton, Boggs & Blow. The Commerce, Science and Transportation Committee had approved him by voice vote earlier the same day.

Sen. Trent Lott, R-Miss., said Brown had answered his concerns by broadening the recusal and severance policies that would govern his separation from the firm. Brown in a Jan. 6 hearing had said he would not contact previous firm clients for a year, but after criticism from Lott he extended that ban to four years. He also specified that he would not return to the firm after he completed his term as Commerce secretary. Brown also withdrew requests that he be allowed to maintain his financial interests in several companies, including the Washington-based Public Employee Benefits Corp. (Brown, p. 236)

Babbitt's Jan. 21 confirmation was the last to be approved. Members of the Senate Energy and Natural Resources Committee had sought more time to stake him out on issues involving public lands, water and the Endangered Species Act. He answered questions for more than six hours in three separate sessions before the committee Jan. 19 and 21. Republicans seemed particularly irritated by Babbitt's saber-rattling statements when he was the head of the League of Conservation Voters, an environmental advocacy group. He spent much of his time assuring the committee that he was not an environmental radical, but an experienced administrator and consensus-builder. (Babbitt, p. 288)

Lobbying Staff Named

On Jan. 14, the Clinton team announced that its chief emissary to Congress would be Howard Paster, who was given the title of assistant to the president and director of legislative affairs. Paster was a former Capitol Hill aide and veteran lobbyist who had pleaded the cases of unions, brewers, broadcasters, oil companies, the National Rifle Association and Major League Baseball before Congress. Paster, 48, had been overseeing the Cabinet confirmation process for the transition.

He had worked for then-Rep. Lester Wolff, D-N.Y., and served as legislative director of the United Automobile Workers of America and as an aide to then-Sen. Birch Bayh, D-Ind., for five years in the 1970s. In 1980, he joined Timmons and Co., a small lobbying firm handling big names such as Amoco, Anheuser-Busch and Morgan Stanley and Co. In 1992, he left to become chairman of Hill & Knowlton Public Affairs Worldwide.

Susan Brophy, who was chief of staff to former Sen. Tim Wirth, D-Colo., was named deputy assistant to the president and deputy director of legislative affairs. She managed the Clinton campaign's Washington office and oversaw congressional relations for the transition. Steve Ricchetti, who was executive director of the Democratic Senatorial Campaign Committee during the 1992 campaign, was named deputy assistant to the president for legislative affairs; he became the top Senate liaison.

(Shortly after the end of the first session, Paster resigned effective Dec. 15, saying he was tired and wanted to spend more time with his family.)

Major Nominations

Here is a summary of action in 1993 on President Clinton's Cabinet nominations, along with newsworthy choices for key spots in his administration and references to stories on the nominees, where applicable.

Department/Agency	Latest Action	Page
Agriculture		
Mike Espy, secretary	confirmed Jan. 21	235
Commerce		
Ronald H. Brown, secretary	confirmed Jan. 21	236
Defense		
Les Aspin, secretary	confirmed Jan. 20	474
William J. Perry, deputy secretary	confirmed March 5	476
Morton H. Halperin, assistant secretary for democracy and peacekeeping	nomination returned to White House	476
Education		
Richard W. Riley, secretary	confirmed Jan. 21	428
Thomas W. Payzant, assistant secretary for elementary and secondary education	confirmed Aug. 3	429
Energy		
Hazel R. O'Leary, secretary	confirmed Jan. 21	287
Health and Human Services		
Donna E. Shalala, secretary	confirmed Jan. 21	385
Joycelyn Elders, surgeon general	confirmed Sept. 7	356
Housing and Urban Development		
Henry G. Cisneros, secretary	confirmed Jan. 21	427
Roberta Achtenberg, assistant secretary for fair housing and equal opportunity	confirmed May 24	428
Interior and related agencies		
Bruce Babbitt, secretary	confirmed Jan. 21	288
George T. Frampton, assistant secretary	confirmed June 30	288
Sheldon Hackney, chairman National Endowment for the Humanities	confirmed Aug. 3	429
Justice		
Zoë Baird, attorney general	withdrawn Jan. 21	303
Janet Reno, attorney general	confirmed March 11	303
Philip B. Heymann, deputy attorney general	confirmed May 28	308
Drew S. Days III, solicitor general	confirmed May 28	308
Webster L. Hubbell, associate attorney general	confirmed May 28	308
Eleanor Acheson, assistant attorney general for policy development	confirmed Aug. 16	
Lani Guinier, assistant attorney general Civil Rights Division	withdrawn June 3	307
Louis J. Freeh, FBI director	confirmed Aug. 6	309
Labor		
Robert B. Reich, secretary	confirmed Jan. 21	427
State and related agencies		
Warren Christopher, secretary	confirmed Jan. 20	531
Clifton R. Wharton Jr., deputy secretary	confirmed Jan. 26 resigned Nov. 8	
Harriet C. Babbitt, permanent representative to the Organization of American States	confirmed March 31	
Lynn E. Davis, under secretary for international security affairs	confirmed April 1	
Winston Lord, assistant secretary for East Asia and Pacific Affairs	confirmed April 21	
Strobe Talbott, ambassador-at-large for the former Soviet republics	confirmed April 2	
Peter Tarnoff, under secretary for political affairs	confirmed March 10	
Tim Wirth, counselor	confirmed April 21	
J. Brian Atwood, administrator Agency for International Development	confirmed May 10	
Transportation		
Federico F. Peña, secretary	confirmed Jan. 21	236
Treasury		
Lloyd Bentsen, secretary	confirmed Jan. 20	185
Roger C. Altman, deputy secretary	confirmed Jan. 21	186
Veterans Affairs		
Jesse Brown, secretary	confirmed Jan. 21	427
Council of Economic Advisers		
Laura D'Andrea Tyson, chairwoman	confirmed Feb. 4	186
Director of Central Intelligence		
R. James Woolsey	confirmed Feb. 3	532
Environmental Protection Agency		
Carol M. Browner, administrator	confirmed Jan. 21	289
Office of Management and Budget		
Leon E. Panetta, director	confirmed Jan. 21	186
United Nations		
Madeline K. Albright, ambassador	confirmed Jan. 27	531
U.S. Trade Representative		
Mickey Kantor, ambassador	confirmed Jan. 21	187

Overcoming a Rough Start

A week into his term, Clinton sparked two controversies that jammed Capitol Hill switchboards. He cut his losses on the first by withdrawing Baird's nomination for attorney general. But the second, over Clinton's campaign pledge to lift the ban on homosexuals in the military, proved harder to shake and persisted throughout the year. *(Gays, p. 454)*

The fallout from the military brass, from Republicans and from congressional Democrats' leading defense authority, Sen. Sam Nunn of Georgia, forced the White House to spend the president's political capital on damage control sooner than expected.

With the Baird and military controversies came public complaints from Sen. Daniel Patrick Moynihan, D-N.Y., who had complained that the administration was paying insufficient attention to his new importance as Finance Committee chairman.

The White House responded with a flurry of consultations. Moynihan got a call from Clinton on Jan. 25. The president met with bipartisan congressional leaders Jan. 26, the Democratic leadership and key chairmen Jan. 27, Democrats from the Senate Armed Services Committee the evening of Jan. 27 and Senate Democratic leaders Jan. 28 and 29.

The buzz of activity reflected Clinton's style of governance. Recent presidents had come to Capitol Hill for speeches and ceremonies and little else. But Clinton paid a pair of visits in the first week of February, soliciting support like a candidate. His wife, Hillary, whom he had put in charge of his health-care efforts — was on the Hill, meeting with leaders of both parties and holding a joint news conference with Senate leader Mitchell.

Clinton's show of interest evoked a positive response in the Capitol. "He spent a lot of time bashing the institution on the campaign trail," said Rep. Tim Valentine, D-N.C. "It's good for him to come down and get acquainted."

As governor of Arkansas, Clinton was notorious for his aggressive pursuit of legislators' support. By law, the governor was not allowed on the chamber floor of the Arkansas General Assembly unless he was invited to address it. But that did not stop Clinton from buttonholing legislators wherever he found them.

"He didn't sit down in the governor's office and send his aides out," said Rep. Tim Hutchinson, a freshman Republican who served eight years in the Arkansas legislature under Clinton. "He'd be in the hallway, peeking in the chamber watching how we were going to vote," said Hutchinson. "Or he would call us into the hallway. He was everywhere he could be. "

ECONOMIC POLICY ADDRESS

On Feb. 17, Clinton came to Capitol Hill to give his first major speech since the inauguration, a forceful address outlining his economic plans for the nation. Speaking to a joint session, he declared an end to 12 years of GOP economics and asked Congress to radically redraw the nation's tax and spending policies. *(Text, p. 7-D; economic package, p. 85)*

Capping weeks of warnings that he was serious about deficit reduction and the need to broadly share the pain, Clinton unveiled a plan that included deep spending cuts but relied overwhelmingly on tax increases to bring the budget closer to balance. As promised, Clinton proposed sharp new levies on the wealthy, but he also asked middle-income taxpayers and Social Security beneficiaries to shoulder part of the load.

At the same time, Clinton proposed to quickly boost short-term job creation and ensure long-term economic growth by pumping billions of dollars in new spending into a wide range of infrastructure, education, health and local development programs that have gotten short shrift from GOP budget drafters for the past decade.

"Our nation needs a new direction," Clinton declared. "It has been too long — at least three decades — since a president has come and challenged Americans to join him on a great national journey, not merely to consume the bounty of today but to invest for a much greater one tomorrow."

Clinton made a rhetorical effort to reach out to Republicans, declaring that the dismal state of the economy was not a partisan matter. But the frequently hostile responses of congressional Republicans signaled that the new president's tough campaign rhetoric and his relentless attacks on Republican "trickle-down" economics had won him serious enemies.

MIDYEAR LESSONS

By the time Clinton reached his 100th day in office on April 29, he had learned some rough lessons.

He had won victories in March on a budget resolution based on his budget plan (without a single Republican vote in either chamber), plus swift passage of a family leave bill. But he also suffered a major legislative defeat with the April 21 death of an economic stimulus package, giving proof that the end of divided government did not usher in unfettered Democratic rule. *(Budget resolution, p. 102; stimulus package, p. 706)*

"I must say, there's a lot I have to learn about this town, as you can tell if you follow events from day to day," Clinton said the day his stimulus bill died in the Senate.

In the Senate, Republicans demonstrated that even when they could not defeat a presidential priority, they could hold it hostage long enough to get something they wanted if they could hold enough of their votes to sustain a filibuster.

Unity enabled Republicans to hold up family leave legislation (HR 1) long enough in early February to force a vote on the issue of gays in the military, even though 16 Republicans voted for the family leave bill on final passage. A few weeks later, when the Senate considered the so-called motor-voter bill (HR 2), the minority repeated the exercise. Again, some Republicans favored the overall bill, but they let their bill manager, Mitch McConnell of Kentucky, keep it on the floor for 10 days and finally won some compromises. *(Family leave, p. 389; "motor-voter," p. 199)*

In the House, the Democratic leadership settled on a tough partisan strategy that virtually shut Republicans out of the process. Time and again, the Democratic leadership denied Republicans the chance to offer amendments on the floor, particularly if they could be adopted. The Democrats stuck the knife deepest March 25 on family planning legislation (HR 670). Republican amendments were permitted, but only if Democrats could offer a second-degree amendment (an amendment to the amendment). The way House rules worked, this meant that the Democratic amendment, once approved, trumped the Republican amendment, and the GOP could never get an up-or-down vote. *(Family planning, p. 352)*

Republicans settled on their own confrontational strategy, leading to such a poisoned House atmosphere that GOP Chief Deputy Whip Robert S. Walker of Pennsylvania accused the majority of fascism. Republicans were influential only twice in the early months: A coalition of 154 Republicans and 83 Democrats rejected the reauthorization of the Select Narcotics Committee and spurred the death of four select committees, and Republicans provided the critical mass April 2 and again April 21 to block legislation

The Struggle for Campaign Finance Reform

With President Clinton committed to signing legislation to overhaul the nation's campaign finance system, both chambers passed Democratic plans over GOP objections in 1993.

Passage of the bills paved the way for the first major rewrite of campaign finance law since the 1974 post-Watergate reforms, but enactment, put off for the second session, did not look easy. The two plans differed substantially, and Senate Republicans threatened to filibuster a conference report if the differences were not reconciled to their satisfaction.

Public interest groups including Common Cause and Public Citizen, which had lobbied for spending limits and partial public funding for years, applauded the progress. But they, too, said major changes were needed in both bills before a conference report could win their seal of approval.

Just a year earlier, Democrats in Congress did clear legislation that the groups hailed. But then, with President George Bush poised to veto any plan that included spending limits — the core tenet of Democratic efforts — Democrats in the House and Senate had little cause to haggle over details. And Senate Republicans had no reason to obstruct the bill with a filibuster. Bush's veto killed the bill.

Throughout 1993, the debate was colored by the recognition that Clinton would sign virtually any campaign finance bill that congressional Democrats approved. This magnified differences among Democrats over public funding of campaigns and shoved to center stage members' quiet resistance to changing the laws that elected them.

The Senate passed its version of the bill (S 3) June 17 after three weeks of mostly dilatory debate and three cloture votes. The bill bore only a passing resemblance to the 1992 plan. It included spending limits, but in lieu of public funding to encourage candidates to comply with them, S 3 called for a new 34 percent tax on campaign receipts for those who opted out of the system. Many critics questioned the constitutionality of the tax.

The House delayed action for months, as leaders said they too lacked the votes for public financing. In the end, the House passed a bill (HR 3) that included spending limits and up to one-third public funding — though separate legislation was required to implement the public funding.

The main differences between the bills involved funding congressional campaigns: The Senate banned PACs; the House did not. The Senate restricted out-of-state fundraising; the House did not. Minor differences on soft money, independent expenditures and other issues looked far easier to reconcile than the campaign language.

BACKGROUND

The debate over campaign finance had been revisited regularly since 1986 but without much progress on the

---

---

fundamental issues that divided the parties.

Although House and Senate Democrats had different perspectives on the role of PACs and a handful of other subjects, on the major campaign finance issues there was broad agreement within the party.

Most Democrats supported spending limits, which they said would allow challengers to spend on a level equal to incumbents. Under the 1976 Supreme Court decision in *Buckley v. Valeo*, spending limits had to be voluntary. The court said that public financing was a legitimate carrot to encourage compliance with those voluntary limits — a concept some Democrats supported anyway, calling public funding "clean money."

Most Republicans strenuously opposed taxpayer financing of congressional campaigns, which they likened to welfare for politicians. Many Republicans also argued that spending limits locked in incumbent advantages. They said challengers needed the option to outspend incumbents to make themselves equally visible to voters.

In 1987, debate over these issues threw the Senate into a virtually unprecedented procedural fit. Consideration of a bill that included spending limits and federal funding stretched over nine months and forced a record eight clotures votes in an effort to break a Republican filibuster. A 53-hour, 24-minute session and a senator injured and dragged to the floor under arrest highlighted the epidsode. In the end, the Senate failed to overcome partisan divisions, and the bill succumbed to the process. *(1988 Almanac, p. 41)*

In the years that followed, with a Republican in the White House pledging to veto any bill approved by the Democratic Congress, neither party had shown much interest in restaging the drama.

Instead, when an ethics scandal broke — such as the Keating Five affair in 1990 and 1991 in which five Senators were accused of accepting favors from a savings and loan magnate — campaign finance legislation was trotted out as a symbol of reform. The two chambers reached agreement on a bill in 1992 after the House came under siege over the House bank scandal.

That bill merely stapled a plan House Democrats had crafted for their campaigns to an entirely different plan Senate Democrats had sanctioned. Both plans, however, included spending limits and public financing. As promised, Bush vetoed the bill. *(1992 Almanac, p. 63)*

During the 1992 campaign, many Democratic challengers and those running in open seats decried the veto and the existing campaign finance system with its escalating spending and interest group money. Though redistricting and a record number of retirements made 1992 unusual, expenditures on congressional campaigns shot up 52 percent. Democratic presidential nominee Bill Clinton also

vowed to overhaul the system. When the votes that many incumbent members had cast for the 1992 campaign finance bill were added to the mix, the 103rd Congress opened with high expectations for enactment of a new law.

THE ADMINISTRATION PLAN

After months of work and countless hours of backroom negotiations, Clinton and Democratic congressional leaders gathered on the White House lawn May 7 to present their proposal to rewrite campaign finance laws.

Their labors — which had ended at 2 the morning of the announcement — produced a bill much like the one Bush vetoed. Centered on limiting spending for congressional candidates, it called for public funds and tighter limits on contributions from political action committees. It included restrictions on the ability of national parties to raise and spend money that did not comply with federal contribution limits (so-called soft money). New for 1993 was a provision that added $11 million in public funds for major party presidential nominees.

The administration estimated the cost of the plan to be approximately $150 million per election cycle — a subject of much criticism, despite Clinton's plan to pay for the bill by taxing lobbying expenses.

Clinton also came under fire for not holding to a campaign promise to lower the maximum PAC contributions to $1,000, from the existing $5,000 limit. House and Senate leaders refused to go along, and the plan set different contribution limits for House, Senate and presidential candidates.

Republicans criticized the Democratic plan from the outset. In addition to their longstanding objections to spending limits and federal funding, they strenuously objected to establishing different campaign finance structures for House and Senate candidates.

The Clinton plan, which formed the framework for the legislation that the House and Senate considered later in the year, included the following elements:

● **Spending limits.** General-election spending limits in the Senate, ranging from $1.2 million to $5.5 million depending on state population. These levels were to rise with inflation after the 1996 election. The $1.2 million limit for small states was increased from $950,000 in the 1992 bill.

In the House, the $600,000 spending limit in the 1992 bill remained, but it was to be indexed for inflation from that year forward to 1996. At the existing 3 percent inflation rate, the spending ceiling was expected to exceed $675,000.

The spending limits would increase if a candidate faced an opponent who exceeded the cap, was the target of a substantial independent expenditure or (for House members only) won a competitive primary.

Some expenses did not count, such as limited spending for fundraising (House) and legal and accounting work to comply with the law (both chambers).

● **Benefits.** Communications vouchers provided to candidates who complied with the spending limits. The vouchers could be used for media advertising, printing costs and postage. Senate candidates would get vouchers equal to 25 percent of the spending limit, up from 20 percent in the 1992 bill. Broadcasters would be obliged to sell Senate candidates discounted advertising time.

House candidates would receive vouchers worth up to 33 percent of the limit, identical to 1992.

● **PAC contributions.** For presidential candidates, a limit of $1,000 from any one PAC. The limit for Senate candidates was $2,500 for a primary, plus another $2,500

for a general election. House candidates could get up to $5,000 for each election.

A complying candidate's aggregate contributions from PACs could not total more than 33 percent of the House spending limit, 20 percent of the Senate limit.

The PAC limits were the same as in the 1992 bill except for the new limits for presidential campaigns.

● **Contributions from lobbyists.** A ban on contributions to a member of Congress from anyone who had lobbied that member or an aide in the previous year. Those who lobbied executive branch officials could not give to the president's campaign for a year, although they could give to party committees. The proposal assumed enactment of new lobbying legislation. *(Lobbying disclosure, p. 50)*

● **Small donors.** A requirement that complying candidates get a portion of their funds from small donations. To get full public benefits, House candidates would have to raise at least one-third of the spending limit in contributions smaller than $200. Senate candidates would have to raise 20 percent of the limit in contributions less than $250.

● **Bundling.** Democrats could not reach full agreement on this issue. Clinton and Senate leaders recommended prohibiting bundling by all lobbyists, PACs, unions and corporations. House Democrats wanted to retain an exemption that allowed PACs that did not lobby Congress to bundle contributions — a carry-over from the 1992 bill designed to help EMILY's List, a donor network that gathered contributions for Democratic women candidates who backed abortion rights.

Based on projections made by the Congressional Budget Office (CBO) in 1992, the White House estimated that public funding of congressional campaigns would cost about $150 million for the first election. But that estimate was based on lower spending limits. Most outside groups set the price closer to $200 million per election cycle.

Clinton expected to finance the bill by increasing the taxpayer checkoff for federal elections from $1 to $5 and by ending the tax exemption for lobbying expenses. The White House said that the higher checkoff would raise $150 million a year and that the change in tax law would add $978 million in new revenue over five years. The budget-reconciliation bill raised the checkoff to $3. *(Budget-reconciliation, p. 107)*

Soft Money

Crafting language to restrict the flow of soft money — money raised outside federal limits — into presidential campaigns was perhaps the most difficult issue for the White House.

In the 1992, Clinton helped the Democratic Party raise more than $30 million in soft money, roughly 30 percent of the national party's total expenses. Yet he pledged to root the unregulated money out of the system.

Clinton settled on a plan aimed at prohibiting state and national parties from spending unregulated money to influence federal elections.

At the same time, it sought to increase the total an individual could give in a two-year election cycle to $60,000 from the existing limit of $50,000. The plan provided for three competing pots of money. Keeping within the overall contribution limit, an individual could donate up to $25,000 per year to federal candidates, $20,000 to national party committees and $20,000 to new state party grassroots funds.

State parties could use the grass-roots funds to finance generic media and coordinated campaigns, which under existing law could be partially funded with soft money.

SENATE ━━ **HOUSE**

Soft Money (cont.)

ity that promotes a federal candidate would have to be paid for with hard money, even if state candidates were also promoted. Any other activity that would "significantly affect" a federal election would also have to be paid for with hard money.

● **Presidential election years.** In presidential election years, all get-out-the-vote activity, even that designed exclusively for state and local candidates, would have to be paid for with hard money.

● **National party committees.** National party committees could raise soft money only to support party building funds used to buy office space and to transfer to state and local parties and candidates for non-federal functions.

National party committees could transfer hard money to state party grass-roots funds for generic party activity and to other state party federal accounts.

● **State party committees.** State and local party committees would be permitted to raise and spend soft money for certain administrative and overhead costs and party activities including meetings, conventions, polling, building funds and, in odd-numbered years, voter-list maintenance.

● **Grass-roots funds.** New state party grass-roots funds would be established and would accept only money raised in compliance with federal guidelines. Generic party activities would be funded by the grass-roots accounts.

● **Fundraising.** Federal candidates and officeholders would be prohibited from raising soft money. Costs associated with raising hard money would have to be paid for with hard money, even if soft money was also raised at the event.

● **Merchandising cards.** No comparable Senate provision.

● **Candidate committee contributions.** No comparable Senate provision.

● **PAC contributions to party committees.** If the PAC ban is struck down in court, PACs could contribute up to $15,000 to grass-roots funds.

funds for state candidate committees and other non-campaign committees.

● **Merchandising cards.** Political party committees could establish relationships with financial institutions that would enable them to profit from "affinity" credit card programs. Similarly, they could establish relationships with merchandisers to profit from the sale of goods bearing the party logo. In both instances, parties would have to be offered terms and conditions identical to other businesses. At the time, the FEC interpreted such activities as illegal corporate contributions.

● **Candidate committee contributions.** Federal candidate committees could contribute up to $10,000 per year to the congressional campaign committees.

● **PAC contributions to party committees.** Political action committees could contribute $25,000 to national party committees per year, up from $15,000 under existing law. PACs could contribute up to an aggregate of $15,000 to a state party committee per year, with up to $15,000 going to grass-roots funds and up to $5,000 to state party federal accounts.

Other Contribution Restrictions

● **Individual contribution limits.** The bill would raise the limit on what an individual could give to candidates, parties and political committees to $60,000 per two-year election cycle from $50,000. Within that two-year limit, individuals could make annual contributions of up to $25,000 to candidate committees, $20,000 to national parties, $20,000 to state party grass-roots funds and $5,000 to other state party federal accounts.

● **Contributions by minors.** No one under the age of 18 could contribute funds to a federal campaign.

● **Cash contributions.** Candidates would be barred from receiving cash contributions aggregating more than $100 from an individual.

● **Party response funds.** Individual contributions to national party response funds of up to $7,500 per year would be exempt from all such limits.

● **Leadership PACs.** Federal candidates and officeholders would be barred from controlling any political committee other than their own campaign committee, party committee or a joint fundraising committee.

● **Executives and administrative personnel.** Such individuals could not make contributions to candidates, parties or political committees under the direction, control or influence of their employer. Contributions from such officials that met that standard could not aggregate more than $5,000 to a candidate or $20,000 to a party or political committee. The bill does not specify

● **Individual contribution limits.** The House bill corresponds to the Senate in that the individual contribution limit would be $60,000 per two-year election cycle. Within that limit, the House bill differs in that individuals could make annual contributions of up to $25,000 to candidate committees, $20,000 to national party committees, $40,000 to state party grass-roots funds and $25,000 to other state party federal accounts.

● **Contributions by minors.** The House bill corresponds to the Senate.

● **Cash contributions.** The House bill corresponds to the Senate.

● **Party response funds.** No comparable House provision.

● **Leadership PACs.** No comparable House provision.

● **Executives and administrative personnel.** No comparable House provision.

who would be responsible for enforcing the provision.

● **Candidate fundraising.** Federal candidates would be prohibited from raising funds for any tax-exempt organization if a significant portion of its mission was voter registration or get-out-the-vote campaigns. A federal candidate or officeholder also would be prohibited from raising funds for other candidates or party committees, state or federal, unless the money was in amounts and from sources permitted by federal law.

● **Intimidation barred.** The bill would prohibit any person from forcing an individual to make a contribution by using or threatening physical force, job discrimination or financial reprisals.

● **Polling data.** A contribution of polling data would be valued at a fair market rate — with no more than 1 percent depreciation per day from the day the poll was completed.

Other Contribution Restrictions (cont.)

● **Candidate fundraising.** No comparable House provision.

● **Intimidation barred.** No comparable House provision.

● **Polling data.** No comparable House provision.

The bill would enhance disclosure of political activity and internal political communications by independent and member organizations, including labor unions, and would provide candidates and parties with the means to respond to adversarial activity. Such organizations were subject to limited disclosure at the time.

● **Disclosure.** Such groups would have to disclose 48 hours in advance any expenditures on political activities adding up to $2,000 or more. In the final 14 days of an election, seven days' advance notice would be required. The reports would be made available to the affected candidates and parties within 48 hours.

● **Party response funds.** National parties would be permitted to set up new response funds to counter such expenditures against the party or any of its federal candidates. Each fund could receive individual contributions of up to $7,500 per year, money that would be exempt from other individual contribution limits.

If a group spent more than $10,000 communicating with its members about an election, an adversely affected party committee could transfer an equal amount to a state grass-roots fund for the state party to counter political activity against it. Funds would be transferred directly to candidate committees if a candidate was detrimentally affected by an independent campaign; the money would not count against a candidate's spending limit.

Non-Party Soft Money

The House bill has no separate section on this issue. There is one related provision that is not in the Senate bill.

● **Corporations and labor unions.** Expenditures by corporations and labor unions for candidate appearances, debates, voter guides and voting records that were directed to the general public would be prohibited unless all candidates were offered the opportunity to participate or were presented equally.

● **State fundraising.** To qualify for federal matching funds in the primaries, presidential candidates would have to raise $15,000 from 26 states, rather than $5,000 from 20 states as provided in current law.

● **Grass-roots funds.** Candidates who agreed to comply with spending limits would receive additional federal funds for use in grass-roots campaigns. The sum would be equal to 2 cents per voting-age person, indexed for inflation beginning in 1997. For the 1996 election, the sum is estimated to be $11 million per candidate.

● **Debates.** Candidates accepting public funds would be required to participate in three debates; vice presidential candidates would have to participate in one.

● **Aggregate primary spending limit.** In the primaries, candidates would be bound only by aggregate spending and fundraising limits rather than the state-by-state limits in existing law.

Presidential Campaigns

No corresponding House provisions.

● **Advertising disclosure.** All federal candidates would have to state clearly their responsibility for their campaign ads.

The bill would set minimum standards for doing so in print, on radio and on television. For example, the

Miscellaneous

● **Advertising disclosure.** House provision corresponds to Senate.

● **Broadcast rates.** Broadcasters would be required to provide all candidates non-pre-emptible time at the lowest unit rate in the last 30 days of a primary and the

SENATE

candidate's image would have to appear on the television screen for at least four seconds.

● **Broadcast rates.** The Senate bill would provide broadcast discounts for candidates complying with spending limits. See benefits section.

No provision on rates similar to House bill for non-complying candidates.

● **Broadcast endorsements.** A broadcast station that endorsed a candidate for federal office in an editorial would be required to notify all other candidates in the election of the date and time of the broadcast and provide them with a taped or printed copy of the editorial and a reasonable opportunity to reply.

Such notification would be required within 24 hours of the broadcast if it were made more than three days before an election; if it were within 72 hours of an election, advance notice would be required.

● **Telephone voting for the disabled.** The FEC would be directed to conduct a feasibility study on whether a system could be established to enable disabled persons to vote by telephone.

● **Closed-captioned ads.** Complying candidates would be required to provide closed-captioning for the hearing-impaired of all TV advertising.

● **Negative mail campaigns.** A candidate, a campaign or any other individual or group that placed in the U.S. mail any communication to the general public that directly or indirectly referred to a candidate, by name or inference, would have to file a copy of the communication with the FEC by noon on the day it was mailed.

● **Personal use.** Campaign contributions could not be used for any "inherently personal purpose," specifically including clothes, home mortgage payments, country club memberships and vacations.

● **Mass mail ban.** Senators and House members would be prohibited from sending franked mass mail in any calendar year in which they would appear on the ballot.

● **Ballot initiative committees.** No comparable Senate language.

● **Foreign nationals.** No comparable Senate provision.

● **Effective date.** The bill would be effective upon enactment for the 1994 election cycle with the following exceptions: expenditures made before Jan. 1, 1994, would not count against the spending limit; PAC money raised before Jan. 1, 1994, could be spent, and an opponent could raise an equal amount after that date.

● **Inflation.** The spending limits would be indexed for inflation with 1996 as the base year.

● **Severability.** If any portion of the spending limits or the benefits sections were held invalid, the entire bill would be invalid. All other provisions would be severable.

● **Expedited review.** An appeal of any court ruling addressing the constitutionality of the act could be taken directly to the Supreme Court, which would be asked to expedite its review.

● **Constitutional amendment.** The bill said that it was the sense of the Senate that an amendment to allow mandatory campaign spending limits be considered.

● **FBI, IRS contact.** The bill stated that it was the sense of the Senate that federal employees should follow official procedures in contacts and dealings with the FBI and the IRS.

Miscellaneous cont'd

HOUSE

last 45 days of a general election.

● **Broadcast endorsements.** No comparable House provision.

● **Telephone voting for the disabled.** The House provision corresponds to the Senate.

● **Closed-captioned ads.** The House provision corresponds to the Senate.

● **Negative mail campaigns.** No comparable House provision.

● **Personal use.** No comparable House provision.

● **Mass mail ban.** No comparable House provision.

● **Ballot initiative committees.** Committees established to support or oppose state initiatives and referendums that involve federal issues — for instance, term limits — would be required to register with the FEC, comply with federal fundraising guidelines and disclose all expenditures to the FEC. Such committees would be barred from making contributions to influence a federal election.

● **Foreign nationals.** Foreign nationals could not participate directly or indirectly in the administration of any local state or federal campaign committee. Under existing law, they were prohibited from contributing to federal election campaigns.

● **Effective date.** None of the provisions of the bill would become effective until separate funding legislation was enacted. The law could become effective no sooner than the 1996 election cycle beginning Jan. 1, 1995.

● **Inflation.** The spending limits, aggregate PAC contribution limits, large donor limits and benefits would be indexed for inflation with 1992 as the base year.

● **Severability.** If any portion of the spending limits or the benefits sections were held invalid, all of those sections would be deemed invalid. All other provisions of the bill are severable.

● **Expedited review.** House provision corresponds to Senate.

● **Constitutional amendment.** No comparable House provision.

● **FBI, IRS contact.** No comparable House provision.

Senate Passes Lobbying Disclosure Bill

After years of failure, Congress' repeated attempts to revamp lobbying disclosure laws nearly bore fruit in 1993.

The Senate overwhelmingly passed its version of the Lobbying Disclosure Act (S 349). A far-reaching overhaul of loophole-ridden laws, the bill required those paid to lobby Congress and the executive branch to register and report their activities. But the House version (HR 823) stalled in a dispute over how to limit the gifts and other financial benefits that lobbyists and their clients could give to members and congressional staff.

As explained by its authors, the measure was meant to ensure that the public knew who was being paid how much and by whom to lobby on what issues by replacing almost all the disclosure requirements in several laws with one sweeping statute.

Drafters tried to define lobbying broadly and limit exceptions to capture the thousands of lobbyists who had not been registering under existing laws. Likewise, new reporting requirements attempted to leave few lobbying dollars undisclosed to prevent registrants from reporting only small portions of their expenditures or income, as many had been doing. Violators would face stiff fines levied by an agency created to enforce the law.

The gift issue dogged the bill's sponsors from the beginning. Under pressure from public interest groups and editorial writers, the Senate approved an amendment that required lobbyists to disclose financial benefits worth more than $20, including meals and entertainment, given to members and staff. Emboldened, critics of such gifts persuaded the Senate to approve a non-binding call for future restrictions, arguing that existing rules were too lax.

Those moves prompted House Democratic freshmen to demand stricter gift limits than senior members from both parties said were necessary. House leaders had planned to bring the lobbying bill to the floor late in the session but did not after the gift dispute dragged on. A bipartisan compromise emerged late in the session to ban gifts from lobbyists and their clients, but with a lengthy list of exceptions. A House Judiciary subcommittee approved it as part of the lobbying bill, but the session ended before the bill moved to full committee. House leaders planned to bring it to the floor by early in 1994.

One of President Clinton's top reform priorities, the bill was expected to become law by the end of the 103rd Congress.

BACKGROUND

Congress had wrestled with lobby disclosure proposals since the late 1800s. Passage of the Foreign Agents Registration Act of 1938 and the Federal Regulation of Lobbying Act of 1946 did little to put the issue to rest; both laws long had been considered ineffective.

As interpreted by the courts, the 1946 law's registration and disclosure requirements applied only to those whose principal purpose was to influence members on the passage

---

BOXSCORE

➡ **Lobbying Disclosure Act (HR 823, S 349).** The bills were designed to close loopholes in lobbying disclosures and to regulate gifts from lobbyists to lawmakers and staff members.

Report: S Rept 103-37.

KEY ACTION

Feb. 25 — **Senate** Governmental Affairs Committee approved S 349 by voice vote.

May 6 — **Senate** passed S 349, 95-2.

Nov. 22 — **House** Judiciary subcommittee approved HR 823, 10-0.

---

of legislation. That left out those who lobbied only some of the time, who mainly lobbied congressional staff and the executive branch and who attempted to influence non-legislative decisions.

The result: The Justice Department in 1983 called the law unenforceable, and the Senate Governmental Affairs Committee said in its 1993 report on the lobbying bill (S Rept 103-37), "Many lobbyists view registration as voluntary." The General Accounting Office (GAO) found that of 13,500 entries in "Washington Representatives" — a sort of lobbyist phone book — only 3,700 had registered. About 90 percent of the reports that were filed were incomplete. Many lobbyists reported receiving or spending little or nothing for lobbying activities. One firm reported that the lobbying salary of one of its employees totaled $1.31, the Senate committee report said.

As for the foreign agents law, its limited exemptions for lawyers and for representatives of domestic subsidiaries of foreign-owned companies had become so elastic over the years that one lobbyist told the Senate committee that compliance was "entirely up to the judgment of the registrant or potential registrant."

History of Failure

The road to reform was strewn with the wreckage of past attempts.

President Harry S Truman appointed a commission to reform lobby laws in 1948. Nothing happened. Likewise, efforts in the 1950s failed. One or both chambers passed lobbying bills in 1967, 1976 and again in 1978, but each time, Congress failed to agree on how much disclosure to require of whom — mainly whether to require registrants to disclose so-called grass-roots activities aimed at drumming up public support and the names of the lobbying groups' big contributors.

In 1989, in response to an influence-peddling scandal at the Department of Housing and Urban Development, Congress enacted two executive branch disclosure laws, creating a set of requirements that the Governmental Affairs Committee later found to provide little meaningful information.

Leading the effort to revamp lobbying disclosure laws in recent years had been Sen. Carl Levin, D-Mich., chairman of the Governmental Affairs Subcommittee on Oversight, which began studying the issue as part of the Wedtech contracting scandal in 1987. The Governmental Affairs Committee approved a lobbying bill drafted by Levin in 1992, but it never made it to the Senate floor. (1992 Almanac, p. 79)

Levin was confident of passing his bill as 1993 began. He had good reason: Government reform had been a big issue during the 1992 campaigns. During his insurgent run for the White House, Ross Perot struck a chord by railing against influence peddlers and foreign lobbyists. Moreover, lobbying disclosure was one of Clinton's top reform priorities.

Vice President Al Gore on Feb. 4 joined Levin, Sen.

William S. Cohen, R-Maine, and Rep. John Bryant, D-Texas, to announce introduction of the lobbying disclosure bill. Gore underscored Clinton's commitment to signing the measure, giving explicit presidential backing to such an effort for the first time in recent history.

From the bully pulpit, Clinton at times railed against lobbyists, depicting them as villains against the forces of change. When he began selling his painful package of tax increases and spending cuts to the American people with a televised speech Feb. 15, he called "high-priced lobbyists" the "defenders of decline" and predicted that they would be out in force to defeat his proposals minutes after they were made public. His package included a special dig at lobbyists: It eliminated the business income tax deduction for lobbying expenses. That provision was later enacted as part of the budget-reconciliation bill (HR 2264 — PL 103-66). *(Budget-reconciliation, p. 107)*

In a speech to Congress on Feb. 17, Clinton called on lawmakers "to deal with the undue influence of special interests" by broadly expanding lobbyist registration and disclosure requirements. When a roar went up from members, Clinton said, "Believe me, they were cheering that last section at home."

For the most part, lobbyists saw the writing on the wall and did not actively fight to kill the bill, as they had in the past. Many grudgingly supported the gist of Levin's bill because they conceded that their stock with the public was at an all-time low.

SENATE ACTION

The Senate Governmental Affairs Committee approved Levin's bill (S 349 — S Rept 103-37) by voice vote Feb. 25. The measure was nearly identical to Levin's 1992 bill. Some argued that it did go far enough in requiring disclosure, but Levin insisted it was an effective "loophole-plugging bill."

Ted Stevens, R-Alaska, said he was disappointed that the bill did not require some lobbying groups to disclose big contributions. He expressed frustration that when approached by lobbyists from such groups as the Audubon Society or the Wilderness Society, he was unable to determine who was backing their efforts financially.

The public interest organization Common Cause, which strongly supported the bill in 1992, came out against committee passage in 1993 because the bill did not require disclosure of gifts or financial benefits that lobbyists could give to lawmakers and their staffs. In a Feb. 25 editorial, The New York Times sided with Common Cause, calling the bill "a giant hoax" because it did not require more detail about lobbying activities.

The Alliance for Justice, an umbrella organization representing civil rights groups, also argued against the measure, saying it would be an unfair burden to small nonprofit organizations.

The bill exempted organizations that spent or received $1,000 or less per half-year for any single client. Nan Aron, the alliance's executive director, proposed raising the threshold to 20 percent of an organization's total budget. Levin rejected the idea, saying it would exempt companies such as General Motors Corp. and Exxon Corp., which he said did not come near to spending 20 percent of their budget on lobbying.

One committee aide said registered lobbyists tended to support the measure because they were losing clients to lobbyists who did not register. Bill supporters predicted that the bill would cause the number of registered lobbyists in Washington to triple or quadruple from the existing total of more than 8,000.

Senate Floor Action

After three days of debate, the Senate on May 6 approved the bill, 95-2. *(Vote 116, p. 16-S)*

Levin said that "public disgust was a welcome motivating factor" in passing the bill after years of effort. The same public sentiment forced senators to accept an unwelcome amendment by Paul Wellstone, D-Minn., requiring lobbyists to disclose any gifts worth more than $20 — including meals, trips, entertainment and fundraising help — given to a member of Congress or a staff member.

Levin and Cohen vigorously resisted the idea that their narrowly crafted bill should be expanded to require lobbyists to disclose gifts to members of Congress and their staffs. Time and again, Levin said he did not want the bill to become an all-purpose vehicle for reform, arguing that past efforts to strengthen lobbying registration had been sunk by such extraneous amendments.

Levin and Cohen also criticized the mechanics of the Wellstone amendment. They said it was inconsistent with Senate rules, shifted the burden of disclosure from members of Congress to lobbyists and fell short of their goal of eliminating such gifts. Levin called the amendment "a weak response to a weak rule."

But the very mention of the existing gift rules seemed to strengthen Wellstone's hand.

The rules had last been tightened in 1989 as part of a bill that also raised members' pay. But in 1991, Congress angered public interest groups by easing the rules to their current state: Members could accept unlimited gifts worth $100 or less from anyone, but they could not accept more than $250 worth of $100-plus gifts a year from anyone but relatives without permission from their ethics committee. Reimbursements for travel related to speaking engagements, fact-finding trips, charity golf tournaments and similar events, as well as meals and drinks, did not count as gifts. On annual financial statements, members were required to disclose only a limited amount of information about their trips and nothing about meals unrelated to travel or gifts worth less than the $250 limit. *(1989 Almanac, p. 51; 1991 Almanac, p. 22)*

The Senate was in abeyance for hours on May 5 as opponents of the Wellstone amendment tested the waters for a vote on it and tried to persuade Wellstone to drop the matter. When it became clear that Wellstone would not budge and few were willing to vote against the amendment, Levin proposed a few minor changes to it.

The Levin changes provided exemptions for gifts from family members and for gifts that were returned, as well as for attendance at large receptions that were not for the benefit of particular members — for instance, the popular annual ice cream socials sponsored by the dairy industry.

All other meals, gifts, entertainment or other financial benefits to a member or staff member worth more than $20 each or an aggregate of $50 annually were to be reported by the lobbyist on a member-by-member or staffer-by-staffer basis.

Both Levin's alterations and Wellstone's amendment were approved by voice vote May 5.

Frank R. Lautenberg, D-N.J., subsequently offered a non-binding amendment that said gifts from lobbyists to members should be further restricted. The amendment said Congress should pass a gift rule "substantially similar" to the executive branch's before the end of the session.

The executive and the legislative branch each based its

gift rules on the same 1989 ethics reform law, but the executive branch drafted much more stringent standards. Executive branch employees could not accept gifts worth more than $20 per occasion or totaling more than $50 per source a year from anyone interested in their agency's work unless the giver was clearly motivated by family relationship or personal friendship.

Lautenberg's amendment was approved 98-1 on May 6. *(Vote 115, p. 16-S)*

The lobbying bill had seemed a likely vehicle for heated rhetoric on separate campaign finance legislation, but that never happened. With Democrats accusing Republicans of gridlock and a floor debate on campaign finance likely soon, Larry Pressler, R-S.D., dropped an amendment that would have banned political action committee contributions. *(Campaign finance, p. 37)*

The Senate accepted by voice vote an amendment by Paul Simon, D-Ill., to require enhanced disclosure from government-sponsored enterprises, including the Student Loan Marketing Association, which benefited from federal loan guarantees and was lobbying against a Clinton proposal for direct student loans.

An amendment by Stevens to require duplicate filing with the Senate Secretary and the Clerk of the House until a computer hookup was established with the new lobbying office was also approved by voice vote.

Stevens also had hoped to amend the bill to require disclosure of contributors to lobbying entities, an effort environmentalists said was aimed at them. Levin and Cohen said the amendment was unconstitutional, and Stevens eventually relented. Instead, he offered a non-binding amendment calling on an eventual House-Senate conference committee on the bill to require disclosure of all foreign contributions to lobbying organizations.

Bill Highlights

In general, the Senate-passed bill required registration by anyone who received or spent money to contact members, their non-clerical staff or a wide array of senior executive branch officials in connection with bills, regulations, policies or programs. Organizations with in-house lobbyists were to register for their employees, as were lobbying firms, though with separate registration for each client.

The bill included the following requirements:
• Registrants were to disclose the names of their employee-lobbyists and their clients, connections to foreign entities, the issues to be lobbied and whether their lobbyists had served in the previous two years in key government positions. They had to update their initial filing and disclose various aspects of their activities twice a year — rather than quarterly as required under existing law.
• Registrants were required to disclose the "specific issues" on which they lobbied and why any foreign connections were interested. They had to specify which committee or chamber of Congress or agency they lobbied, but not the individual; drafters said they did not want to discourage public officials from talking to lobbyists who might prove controversial.
• Organizations with in-house operations were required to disclose the cost of their lobbying activities. Outside lobbyists had to disclose their lobbying income. The cost of grass-roots support efforts were to be included in the financial totals, but not as a separate line item. Financial disclosures would be "good faith" estimates reported in broad ranges.
• A single office within the Justice Department, the Office of Lobbying Registration and Public Disclosure, would be established to administer and enforce the new law.

Under existing law, lobbyists registered and reported at a variety of places — the House, the Senate, the Justice Department and agency contracting offices.

Agents of foreign political parties and governments, however, still were required to register separately with the Justice Department.

The office's director was subject to Senate confirmation, and the office was required to "maximize public access" to the information filed under the act through a computer system that would allow searches by the names of clients, lobbyists and registering organizations (though not necessarily by issues). The system was to be compatible with the Federal Election Commission's computers so users could check lobbyist-related campaign contributions. The office was to regularly summarize the information it received.

The bill gave the office the power to fine lobbyists up to $10,000 for minor violations and up to $200,000 for major violations, including failure to register and extensive or repeated violations. Lobbyists could contest the fines at administrative hearings and in court.
• Provisions of the so-called Byrd amendment of 1989 that prohibited using appropriated federal funds to lobby for contracts, grants or loans were to be preserved. *(1989 Almanac, p. 736)*

Exceptions

Drafters attempted to keep the legislation free of loopholes that had plagued past disclosure efforts. Still, the bill sought to regulate a right enshrined in the First Amendment, which barred Congress from abridging the people's right "to petition the government for redress of grievances," so lawmakers had to tread lightly.

The result was a series of compromises that of necessity created potential loopholes:

Those who lobbied only occasionally or whose lobbying expenses or incomes were minimal ($1,000 or less per half-year per client or $5,000 or less per half-year for all clients) could avoid registering. So could some lawyers and those who only monitored government activities. Also exempt were journalists and public officials.

Financial reports for the most part were to be based on unitemized estimates. Though the bill required specificity in reporting what issues were being lobbied, a certain amount of obfuscation was likely to pass muster. And the bill explicitly limited the investigative power of its enforcers.

Common Cause said some clients could hide their identities in coalitions that hired lobbyists. Past lobbying bills had faltered amid fights over whether big-money contributors to business and nonprofit lobbying groups should be disclosed. The bill attempted a compromise: It required the disclosure of $5,000-plus contributors but only if they also had a significant amount of control over, and financial stake in, the group's lobbying activities.

The mandate for financial reports on income or expenses related to "lobbying activities" rested on the definition of that phrase. The definition was broad, including not only lobbying contacts but also "efforts in support of such contacts, including preparation and planning activities, research and other background work." But lobbyists said the bill's financial reporting requirements were open to interpretation.

Nonprofit groups that reported lobbying costs to the IRS could use tax rules, which were different from those in the bill, when disclosing expense estimates. The groups had tried to persuade members to let them abide by IRS guidelines for the bill's other requirements.

Supporters said the bill's best chance for success rested

with the new Office of Lobbying Registration and Public Disclosure. While some lobbyists considered the office harmless, others worried that its power would be too great.

While the bill gave the office the power to impose fines, it also explicitly limited the office's power to prevent it from becoming too aggressive. The bill stripped criminal penalties from existing law and denied the office investigative or audit authority. Instead, the office could request information from suspected violators, fine them up to $10,000 for failing to comply with such requests and have the Justice Department ask the courts to order them to comply.

The bill allowed violators to avoid heavy fines if they complied with the law after being informed of a violation. The bill also barred the lobbying office and the courts from telling violators they no longer could lobby.

Gifts Take Center Stage

For a time after Senate passage, it appeared that Levin might attempt to move a separate gift-ban bill. On July 19, Levin's Governmental Affairs Subcommittee on Oversight of Government Management held a hearing on the issue. At it, Levin, Lautenberg, former members, and representatives of several public interest groups urged Congress to put itself on the same footing as the executive branch when it came to the acceptance of gifts. They argued that Congress' gift rules appeared to give well-heeled interests an edge in trying to influence lawmakers.

Lautenberg had introduced a gift bill (S 885) that was based on the allowable levels in executive branch rules. But unlike executive branch rules, which barred $20-plus gifts from anyone interested in the work of a would-be recipient's agency, Lautenberg's rules applied to everyone except family and personal friends. It barred lawmakers and staff from accepting gifts worth more than $20 apiece, or an aggregate of $50 a year, from a single source. It also prohibited members from having speaking fees, which they could no longer legally pocket, contributed to charities on their behalf. And it altered travel rules by requiring that all privately funded trips be approved beforehand by the Ethics Committee and by prohibiting reimbursement beyond what was "reasonably necessary" — a provision Lautenberg said was aimed at barring vacations disguised as business trips.

Lautenberg said the travel restrictions were among the most important provisions of his bill. He said the purpose was to curtail many trips of the kind detailed by the watchdog group Public Citizen in a report titled "They Love to Fly ... And It Shows." The report stated that during the 101st Congress (1989-90), House members went on "nearly 4,000 privately funded trips."

Joan Claybrook, president of Public Citizen, consumer activist Ralph Nader's group, told the panel that "over two-thirds of these trips were paid for by corporations or their trade associations, who were often lobbying lawmakers on specific legislation affecting their economic interests." Claybrook disagreed with the approach in Lautenberg's bill, arguing that any trip deemed important enough should be paid for with public money. Having the Ethics Committee review each trip was not a good idea, she added, because committee members would be pressured by their colleagues to approve trips.

A Levin aide said Lautenberg's bill probably would go to markup soon after the August recess and be on the Senate floor before the end of the session, as specified in Lautenberg's lobbying bill amendment. But two months later, after the House lobbying bill became bogged down

over the gift issue, Levin said the Senate would wait for the House to act next.

HOUSE ACTION

Bryant, the House sponsor and chairman of the Judiciary Administrative Law Subcommittee, held hearings March 31 and planned to mark the bill up soon after the Senate passed its version.

But the Senate's action on gifts prompted freshman Democrats to take up the cause, making gift restrictions a priority issue on their reform agenda. Led by Eric D. Fingerhut of Ohio and Karen Shepherd of Utah, they pressed the leadership to attach the Wellstone amendment and Lautenberg's bill to the House lobbying bill. On Aug. 3, they introduced bills embodying the two approaches (HR 2834 and HR 2835, respectively). Some members wanted to go further, with Jill L. Long, D-Ind., advocating an outright ban on virtually all gifts.

Although House leaders were loath to address the knotty issue, they began to focus on the matter by the fall because they wanted the lobbying bill to be ready for floor action in late October as part of a congressional reform package. They promised that the gift rules would be addressed at the same time, perhaps in the same bill.

In a speech on reform, Speaker Thomas S. Foley, D-Wash., endorsed greater disclosure and indicated that the $20 limit on gifts would be acceptable if there was an exemption for meals — an exception the first-termers were not prepared to embrace.

As the leadership's self-imposed late-October deadline loomed, some members appeared ready to move. The Administrative Subcommittee put the long-stalled lobbying bill on its markup schedule for Oct. 21. Bryant planned to use the bill to limit the financial favors (including meals) that lobbyists could give members to $20 (and no more than $50 a year) and to restrict lobbyist-funded trips.

Foley told reporters Oct. 14 that the House was "tending toward" Bryant's approach. But some members of both parties protested the move. Among them: GOP leader Robert H. Michel, Ill. "To bar someone from having dinner with somebody — jeepers, creepers — or going to a ballgame, or a show. To think our vote is going to be contingent on somebody taking us to dinner just ticks me off," Michel said in an interview.

The markup was indefinitely postponed. "We proceeded with the assumption that there was a groundswell of support" for stricter limits, said Vic Fazio, D-Calif., a key player in past gift debates. "But the more people read about this, they raise questions: What and why? ... There was a feeling, maybe we should rethink this."

Leaders appointed a bipartisan task force to study the issue.

Subcommittee Markup Concludes House Action

In the final days of the session, the task force came up with a sweeping agreement to ban all meals, entertainment, gifts and travel-related expenses from lobbyists and lobbying organizations to members of Congress and their staffs. The agreement — negotiated by a small group of top Democrats and Republicans, Bryant, and several freshman Democrats — also contained a long list of exceptions. The most controversial one would have continued to allow non-lobbyist employees of organizations that lobbied, such as the chairman of a company, to buy meals and entertainment for members.

On Nov. 22, the House Judiciary Subcommittee on Ad-

ministrative Law and Government Relations approved the agreement as part of its lobbying disclosure bill (HR 823). The bill, approved 10-0, was almost the same as the Senate's, except for the gift provisions.

Despite Foley's repeated promises that the House would take up the bill in 1993, however, Congress adjourned for the year without it going to the floor, angering freshman Democrats who wanted to return home with concrete reform results to show their constituents. The Democratic leadership said it would bring the bill to the floor in early 1994.

As the session came to a close Democrats and Republicans blamed each other for stalling the bill.

Gift Provisions

The gift provisions incorporated in the subcommittee bill banned lobbyists and clients from giving members and congressional staffers financial benefits of any kind — gifts, travel, entertainment, meals, loans. House rules would bar members and aides from knowingly accepting such benefactions.

In the fine print, however, was a lengthy list of exceptions:

Gifts motivated by "personal friendship" were exempt, provided there had been a history of reciprocity and that the cost of the gift was paid personally by the lobbyist and not deducted as a business expense. So were items such as baseball caps and T-shirts of "little intrinsic value," potentially costlier books and videos, home-state products of minimal value used for promotional purposes and modest types of food such as coffee and doughnuts.

Though lobbyists could not do so, clients, corporate employees and union representatives could use their expense accounts to pay for meals and entertainment for staffers and bring along their lobbyists.

If they revealed the cost in twice-yearly lobbyist disclosure reports, lobbyists or clients could throw big parties in behalf of members, such as the lavish fetes that were staples at political conventions. They also could pay, subject to disclosure, for "a conference, retreat or similar event" for groups of members, such as the soirees congressional party caucuses had attended.

Also exempt from the ban but subject to disclosure were speaking fees donated to charities on members' behalf and contributions to members' legal defense funds.

Travel reimbursements for speaking engagements and fact-finding trips still were allowed, subject to more detailed disclosure rules. Entertainment on such trips was banned — unless in a "group setting in which all other attendees are invited."

Members also could continue to accept free trips to charity events, such as the corporate-backed golf tournaments various members frequented, or political events, also subject to more detailed disclosure. The rules also exempted meals and attendance fees at charitable or political events.

Other Provisions

The rest of the lobbying bill was similar to the Senate's with some exceptions, including these:

● The House bill included an exemption for certain lobbying activities of religious groups, based on the Constitution's freedom of religion protections. The groups contended that the exception constituted a de facto blanket exemption. The Senate Governmental Affairs Committee's report on the Senate bill said the panel implicitly exempted religious groups, though the bill did not do so explicitly.

● The House bill's definition of "lobbying activities" was somewhat broader than the Senate's. It included some communications, such as public speeches and status requests, that would not trigger the registration requirement but would be considered when reporting lobbying income or expenses.

● For the first three years under the House bill, corporations could use a set of recently drafted IRS guidelines — meant to deny them deductions for lobbying expenses — when filing their financial reports.

● The House bill would have required registrants to say how much they spent on so-called grass-roots campaigns and to name any outside firms hired to run them. The Senate bill required grass-roots expenditures to be included in the reports' financial totals, but not as a separate line item. Common Cause favored the House version.

Grass-roots lobbying activities were a growing and controversial field using phone banks, mailings, advertisements and other techniques to persuade citizens to pressure the government on a given issue. Practitioners argued that they encouraged democracy by getting citizens involved; critics said they sometimes needlessly alarmed people with campaigns aimed at flooding lawmakers with mail and phone calls.

● The House bill reversed a decision by the Senate to place the lobbying office under the Justice Department, which some groups feared would make the office too aggressive. The House bill would have made it an independent agency.

● House drafters also dropped a Senate provision to allow violators to avoid heavy fines if they complied with the law after being informed of a violation. House members reasoned that the Senate provision might encourage lobbyists to wait to get caught before reporting.

● The House bill explicitly excluded those whose lobbying activities constituted less than 10 percent of their working hours for a client; the Senate bill was more vague, excluding those whose lobbying activities were "incidental." The House bill also excluded those with incomes or expenses of $2,500 or less per half-year per client; the Senate bill's exemption covered those with incomes or expenses of $1,000 or less per half-year per client or $5,000 or less per half-year for all clients.

● The House bill required registration for lobbying efforts on nominations and confirmations. ■

Packwood Faces Harassment Charges

Sen. Bob Packwood, R-Ore., spent 1993 embroiled in an ever-expanding ethics investigation that began with reports of unwanted sexual advances toward numerous aides and other women and grew to include evidence of possible corruption and obstruction.

The Senate Ethics Committee began investigating sexual misconduct charges on Dec. 1, 1992, but the probe stalled in late 1993 in a dispute over the panel's subpoena for Packwood's diaries.

The panel initially acted after The Washington Post on Nov. 22, 1992, detailed the first of many allegations concerning Packwood's behavior toward women since joining the Senate in 1969. By the end of 1993, the Post counted more than 40 women accusing Packwood of unwanted sexual advances. At least 21 cooperated with the Ethics Committee, telling the panel they were prepared to testify against the senator publicly. *(Summary of allegations, p. 60; background, 1992 Almanac, p. 52)*

It seemed certain from the beginning that Packwood, who turned 61 in 1993, ultimately would be punished if he did not resign. Some alleged victims and their supporters said he should be expelled, a move requiring a two-thirds majority vote of the full Senate. Packwood supporters argued that he deserved a stern scolding at most.

Under Senate precedents, the Ethics Committee could publicly reprimand him or the full Senate could censure or expel him. The lesser punishments could be made harsher. A committee reprimand, for example, could be delivered on the floor before the assembled Senate. Or a Senate censure could include a recommendation that the Republican caucus strip Packwood of his seniority and post as the top GOP member of the Finance Committee. Some argued that the Senate also had the power to fine members.

Before the Post published its first story in November 1992, Packwood denied the allegations. When the Post ran the story, however, Packwood publicly apologized and declined to dispute any of the allegations. He later called his conduct "just plain wrong" but did not confirm the women's stories. Instead, he requested an ethics investigation and took steps to deal with what he said was a potential alcohol problem.

In 1993, he adopted a more aggressive stance, indicating that he would not let all the allegations go unchallenged but continuing to refuse to discuss specifics.

Dispute Over Packwood's Diaries

A dispute erupted in early October over Packwood's personal diaries after he used them to bolster his version of events during an Ethics Committee deposition. The panel demanded access to the journals. Packwood at first allowed committee aides to see the diaries and have copies of relevant entries. But he balked after they asked for copies of entries unrelated to the sexual misconduct allegations. The committee responded with a subpoena for his post-1988 journals.

The Senate engaged in a wrenching debate Nov. 1-2 before deciding to go to federal court to enforce the committee's subpoena. It acted after learning that two 1989 entries indicated to committee lawyers that Packwood might have broken criminal laws by soliciting jobs for his estranged wife from lobbyists and other associates — possibly in a corrupt exchange for official favors — while he was

in divorce court trying to minimize his alimony payments. Packwood denied doing anything improper.

After months of flatly rejecting calls that he step down, the senator came to the brink of resignation in the closing days of the 1993 session as the Senate prepared to press the subpoena in court. But he changed his mind and renewed his combative stance after the Justice Department subpoenaed his diaries as part of a separate criminal probe.

The court battle for diaries took a dramatic turn when Senate lawyers alleged that Packwood may have tried to obstruct the ethics inquiry by altering audiotapes and transcripts of his journals after realizing that they might be subpoenaed.

In related action on the Packwood case, the Senate Rules Committee rejected petitions challenging Packwood's 1992 re-election on the grounds that he had falsely denied the sexual misconduct allegations to reporters before Election Day. The panel decided that denying members their seats for lying during a campaign would set a bad precedent.

Just beneath the surface in the Packwood case was the memory of the battering the 98-percent male Senate took over its handling of Anita F. Hill's sexual harassment charges against Clarence Thomas during his Supreme Court nomination hearings in 1991. Many in the Senate, including several of the five new female members, said they had to make sure the Senate took the Packwood charges very seriously to redeem the chamber's reputation, but others argued that Packwood was unfairly becoming a scapegoat for the past sins of many men. *(1991 Almanac, p. 274)*

ELECTION CHALLENGE

Among the many tricky questions presented by the Packwood case was this: Should the Senate bar a successful candidate from taking his seat if he lied to win it?

Five groups of Oregon citizens, about 250 in all, claimed in petitions to the Senate that Packwood defrauded voters before his narrow re-election victory by denying that he had made unwanted advances to numerous women and by allegedly trying to discredit and intimidate his accusers to prevent a story about his behavior from appearing before the election. Though they conceded they faced an uphill fight, the petitioners wanted the Senate to declare the election invalid.

Packwood's lawyers denied that he defrauded the voters and argued that in any event the Senate did not have the authority to deny him a seat because he received the most votes and was therefore the rightful winner.

In the end, the Rules Committee rejected the petitions. On Jan. 5, the Senate temporarily sidestepped disputes over the elections of Packwood and another Republican, Paul Coverdell of Georgia. The men were allowed to take their seats, but chamber leaders declared that the Senate reserved the right to investigate the controversies and unseat the two later. Majority Leader George J. Mitchell, D-Maine, and Minority Leader Bob Dole, R-Kan., said the two senators were sworn in "without prejudice," meaning the Senate could later decide that they were not properly elected and exclude them by majority vote, instead of the two-thirds required by the Constitution to expel a member. Packwood and Coverdell then took the same oath in the

The Ethics Inquiry

By the end of 1993, the Senate Ethics Committee inquiry on Sen Bob Packwood, R-Ore., had become sixfold:

● In February, the panel said it would focus on three types of allegations: sexual misconduct, attempts to intimidate accusers and misuse of Senate staff in such attempts.

● The committee developed a fourth line of inquiry in October when its aides read the passages in Packwood's diary about job offers for his estranged wife from lobbyists and other associates. A court document drafted by his lawyer, Jacob A. Stein, suggested that the committee suspected that Packwood's involvement in the job offers might have violated the federal illegal gratuity statute — a felony akin to bribery but less serious.

● After that issue prompted the committee to subpoena Packwood's diary, the staff opened a fifth inquiry — into whether Packwood misused campaign funds to pay his diary transcriber.

● Finally, the committee was investigating whether Packwood committed perjury or otherwise obstructed its probe in altering the diary. Obstruction of a congressional inquiry was a felony punishable by up to five years in prison.

same manner as the other senators seated Jan. 5. *(Congressional overview, p. 5)*

The Rules Committee voted unanimously Jan. 28 to begin considering the Packwood petitions. It appointed the Senate's assistant legal counsel, Claire M. Sylvia, to oversee the case and ordered the petitioners and Packwood to file briefs on a set of legal questions.

The panel decided to address the theoretical questions first: Does the Senate have grounds to set aside an election if the winner is found guilty of "deliberately withholding from the press information material to the voters' assessment of candidates" or of "intimidating individuals by threats of harm to prevent them from supplying to the press" such information?

The basic facts were not in dispute: Days before the Nov. 3 election, the Post confronted Packwood with sexual misconduct allegations. He denied them and asked for time to gather information to discredit the women — information the Post later said included "potentially embarrassing" details "about purported aspects of their sexual histories and personal lives." The Post delayed running the story. On Election Day, Packwood beat his Democratic challenger, Rep. Les AuCoin, 52.1 percent to 46.5 percent. By the time the Post ran its first story on Nov. 22, Packwood had reversed course, apologizing and declining to contest the allegations.

Public Hearings

In a tactical victory for the petitioners, the Rules Committee decided by voice vote April 29 to hold a public hearing on the legal issues before deciding whether to launch a full-blown investigation of the facts. It was to be the first official public airing of any aspect of the matter.

But Packwood's opponents still seemed unlikely to win as one of their most natural would-be allies, Rules member Dianne Feinstein, D-Calif., said she was skeptical about their case.

The questions approved for argument by the Rules Committee focused on whether the Senate could or should exclude someone who lied about "personal, historical facts" to win a seat. At the May 10 hearing, several members of the Rules Committee were clearly troubled by suggestions that it should.

The petitioners' lawyer, Katherine A. Meyer, repeatedly claimed at the televised proceeding in a crowded hearing room that Packwood lied to reporters and threatened to reveal embarrassing information about women who talked to the media about his conduct. "Mr. Packwood stole the Nov. 3, 1992, election," she said.

Packwood's lawyer, James F. Fitzpatrick, denied that Packwood, who was not present for the hearing, lied or intimidated anyone. He had argued in legal briefs that the Senate did not have the power to exclude Packwood because he received about 78,000 more votes than AuCoin. But at the hearing he focused most of his fire on the suggestion that the Senate would want to use that power if it existed. "This proposal would turn elections into a giant game of 'gotcha!'" he said.

Three days after the hearing, ranking Republican Ted Stevens of Alaska told the Associated Press that he would move to dismiss the petitions at the committee's May 20 meeting. Sensing defeat, Meyer on May 17 asked the Rules Committee to delay making a decision until after the Ethics Committee completed its probe; the request was denied. The American Civil Liberties Union opposed the petitions on free speech grounds in a letter dated May 19.

Without debate or dissent, the Rules Committee on May 20 dismissed the petitions. In making the motion, Stevens said that the Senate had the power to probe allegations of fraud but that the committee should not exercise it in the Packwood case. Senators said afterward that even investigating the charges would set a bad precedent that would lead to numerous challenges over campaign rhetoric. As if to prove the point, the Michigan State Republican Party on May 18 said that it wanted Democratic Sen. Donald W. Riegle Jr.'s 1988 election invalidated because, it said, he had lied about his ties to thrift owner Charles H. Keating Jr. *(Keating case, 1990 Almanac, p. 78)*

ETHICS COMMITTEE

The Ethics Committee inquiry got off to a slow start as Senate leaders struggled to find members willing to join the unpopular panel. Some complainants first refused to cooperate with the committee's staff because they wanted assurances that they would be spared questions about their sexual histories — assurances the staff could not give before members were appointed.

The Ethics Committee membership had been in flux. Terry Sanford, D-N.C., its chairman during the previous Congress, lost his re-election bid, and its vice chairman, Warren B. Rudman, R-N.H., retired. All of the other members of the six-member panel — three Democrats and three Republicans — also wanted off. In the end, only Richard H. Bryan, D-Nev., who became the chairman, remained on the committee.

Sensitive to the criticism the Senate received for the all-male Judiciary Committee's handling of sexual harassment charges against Thomas during his Supreme Court confirmation hearings, leaders in both parties looked for

women to appoint to the Ethics Committee to hear the Packwood case.

The committee's members for the 103rd Congress finally were approved by the Senate on Jan. 26: Democrats Bryan, Barbara A. Mikulski of Maryland and Tom Daschle of South Dakota, and Republicans Mitch McConnell, Stevens and Robert C. Smith of New Hampshire. The Republicans tried to get Nancy Landon Kassebaum of Kansas, a former Ethics member, to join, but she refused. Larry E. Craig, R-Idaho, replaced the Rules Committee's Stevens on May 19 when he quit his Ethics Committee seat, saying he was too busy with other matters. The Ethics Committee's chairman in 1983-85, Stevens recently had been an advocate for imposing a statute of limitation on ethics cases, so his departure might have hurt Packwood's cause.

The selection of Mikulski, long a champion of feminist issues, was praised by sexual harassment activists, the alleged Packwood victims and their lawyers.

Meanwhile, Packwood signaled for the first time the week of Jan. 25 that he would present an aggressive defense, a shift from the apologetic stance he adopted when the charges surfaced in 1992. Packwood made his first publicized trip to Oregon that week and was greeted at nearly every stop with protesters calling for his resignation. In interviews, he indicated that he would challenge the stories of some of his accusers and declined to rule out questions about their sexual histories.

The Committee Gets Started

The Ethics Committee moved quickly. The panel announced Feb. 4 that it would prohibit questions about witnesses' sexual pasts in sexual misconduct cases. And it expanded its inquiry to include charges that Packwood attempted "to intimidate and discredit the alleged victims" and misused his staff in doing so. The panel rejected calls for the appointment of an outside counsel to handle the Packwood case but said it would expand its staff.

Ethics Chairman Bryan and ranking Republican McConnell said in a statement that the panel would follow the federal rape shield rule in sexual misconduct cases. The federal rule, enacted by Congress in 1978, prohibited evidence about alleged victims' sexual pasts unless a judge ruled that it was "constitutionally required to be admitted" or was needed to prove consent or to rebut physical evidence of semen or injury. Committee rules would allow exceptions only by a majority vote taken in closed session.

Women activists and alleged victims praised the decision. Fitzpatrick said Packwood had not intended to bring up the women's sexual histories.

Allegations of sexual misconduct against Packwood mounted when the Post reported Feb. 7 that 13 more women said he made unwanted advances toward them. The Post's initial story in November 1992 cited accusations by 10 women, plus one who said Packwood told her sexual jokes, for a total of 24 women claiming impropriety between 1969 and 1990.

Seeking to elicit cooperation from the women, the Ethics Committee reassured their lawyers in a letter March 5 that it would try to protect the women's privacy and to keep the focus on Packwood's conduct.

The probe proceeded quietly through the spring and summer. On Sept. 16, the committee said in a statement that it planned to finish its preliminary inquiry by the end of October. At that point, it planned to decide whether there was reason to believe Packwood had violated Senate rules or standards of conduct and whether to continue the

probe to determine if in fact he had. Also to be decided was whether to hold public hearings, a course advocated by many of the complainants. The committee said it had interviewed or taken depositions from 150 people and sent questionnaires to about 300 women who had worked for Packwood.

THE DIARIES

As the committee's deadline approached, the dispute over Packwood's diaries erupted and indefinitely stalled the investigation.

Though it did not become public until Oct. 21, the dispute began about two weeks earlier. A committee report on the matter (S Rept 103-164) and statements by Chairman Bryan and Packwood lawyer Fitzpatrick gave this version of events:

The committee twice in the previous 10 months had asked the senator for all documents relevant to its sexual misconduct inquiry, but he never turned over anything from his 8,200-page diary, covering his entire time in the Senate, since 1969. The committee said it had heard about the diary but assumed that it contained nothing relevant. On Oct. 5 and 6, Ethics aides began deposing Packwood as the panel wrapped up the first phase of its inquiry. Packwood referred to the diaries to bolster his version of certain events. Asked about them, he explained that he dictated his recollections each morning and then had them transcribed by his secretary.

Once the committee members learned that the diaries contained relevant information, they halted the deposition and demanded to review them. After lengthy negotiations, Packwood and his lawyers agreed to provide them, except for references to legal, medical or private family matters. Bryan said that committee staff warned Packwood's lawyers that the panel would pursue any other misconduct found in the diaries.

Packwood's lawyers masked the privileged passages with so-called redacting tape and then watched committee aides read each page. Each night, the committee informed Packwood of the pages it wanted copied, and he sent them over the next day. Save for dickering over the relevance of some passages, this process went smoothly from Oct. 12 to Oct. 16 as aides plowed through 5,000 pages covering 1969-88.

The agreement collapsed as the staff began reviewing more recent years. When the dispute first surfaced publicly, there was no mention by either side that the committee staff had found evidence of potential wrongdoing unrelated to sexual misconduct in those later diaries. All that was said was that after the staff perused entries from 1989-90, Packwood refused to produce copies of certain entries that the committee said it "determined are directly relevant to the current preliminary inquiry" but that Fitzpatrick said were "wholly unrelated to the sexual misconduct/intimidation issues." Packwood also refused to provide more diaries unless he was allowed to mask additional information.

The committee insisted on access to the diaries as provided by the original agreement. It decided that an independent hearing examiner should review the masked entries to make sure only those covered by the original three exemptions were hidden. Packwood refused.

The Subpoena

Packwood's lawyer offered a compromise Oct. 20, asking the committee to allow him to mask what he called

"collateral issues" unrelated to sexual misconduct. He said the committee could seek those entries after its sexual misconduct inquiry was finished "in connection with any separate investigation it decides to initiate."

The committee refused and on Oct. 20 voted to subpoena the 1989-to-present diaries. Under the subpoena, the diaries were to be turned over to an independent examiner, former Solicitor General Kenneth W. Starr, who would make sure that only matters covered by the three original exemptions had been masked. The subpoena was delivered to Packwood on Oct. 21, but he told the committee that he "simply cannot agree at this point to comply forthwith."

That day, the committee voted unanimously to ask the Senate to go to court to enforce the subpoena. Chairman Bryan introduced a resolution (S Res 153) to that effect, making the matter public for the first time. If the Senate prevailed in such a civil proceeding and Packwood continued defying the subpoena, a judge could find him in contempt and jail or fine him to induce compliance.

Fitzpatrick called the subpoena unprecedented, improper and "a frontal attack on the constitutional right to privacy." He accused the committee of trying to rummage through the diaries for damaging information unrelated to its sexual misconduct investigation of Packwood.

In an Oct. 22 statement, Fitzpatrick said the disputed entries included information about another senator's affair with an aide; an affair between a Democratic congressional leader and a Senate staff member; consensual personal relationships with non-staff having nothing to do with sexual misconduct by Packwood; fundraising activities; Packwood's divorce; and lobbyists' visits to Packwood's office that had nothing to do with sexual activity. (Packwood later said the senator was a former member and the leader was a prominent House member.)

SENATE FLOOR DEBATE

The next week, the diaries were the buzz of the Senate, and angry recriminations over them distracted members as they began the year's final spurt of legislative activity. Many senators viewed the choice this way: Should they vote to set a precedent allowing Ethics Committee aides to paw through their personal ruminations? Or should they cast a vote that could look like a cover-up for a member of the old boys' club?

The week began with Packwood taking to the floor on Oct. 25 to deny that his lawyer's Oct. 22 statement was an implicit threat. "This was not so-called gray mail," he said. "The secrets in that diary are safe with me." Packwood also followed up his lawyer's accusation that the Ethics Committee had demanded entries on the sex lives of other lawmakers with a new charge: That a committee aide, while reading the masked diaries, had peeked at the name of a member involved in an affair.

Packwood signaled that he would try to limit the scope of the subpoena when it came to the floor, declaring himself willing to reveal all entries relevant to the sexual misconduct charges.

The Senate's two party caucuses discussed the case on Oct. 26. Packwood pleaded for support from his caucus, which also heard from the Republican Ethics Committee members. "It was a very powerful, poignant, personal meeting," said GOP whip Alan K. Simpson of Wyoming. Republicans emerged calling for a settlement to avoid a floor fight. Many were sympathetic to Packwood.

Most Democrats expressed support for the committee,

in part because Bryan had told them that the fight over the diaries was sparked by evidence of a previously unknown and serious potential ethical lapse by Packwood. The news spread when Bob Kerrey, D-Neb., and Tom Harkin, D-Iowa, told reporters about Bryan's talk.

Ethics members rejected calls for a negotiated settlement. Majority Leader Mitchell and Minority Leader Dole held several meetings with the principals, but Mitchell put out the word that his aim was to bring the matter to the floor quickly, not to broker a deal. On Oct. 27, he announced that the Senate would begin debating the issue Nov. 1 and barred committee meetings that day so all could be present, a solemn procedure usually reserved for impeachments. Mitchell said that because he could not persuade Packwood to agree to a time limit, the Senate would debate the issue until it was resolved.

Packwood also received some good news Oct. 27 when the American Civil Liberties Union said in a letter to the Ethics Committee that it opposed the subpoena on constitutional privacy grounds.

After quietly seething for days over accusations from Packwood's camp, Bryan fired back Oct. 28. He asserted that on Oct. 17, while reviewing the 1989-90 diaries, "the committee counsel came across information indicating possible misconduct by Sen. Packwood unrelated to the current inquiry. This information raised questions about possible violations of one or more laws, including criminal laws." The next day, Packwood's lawyers "expressed concern that the Ethics Committee might consider additional potential violations" and abrogated the agreement, Bryan said. Bryan and other Ethics members were mum on what had sparked their interest, and Fitzpatrick denied knowing what Bryan was talking about.

Bryan denied that the Ethics Committee was interested in the sex lives of other members. "There is no constitutional right being violated," Bryan said. "There is no witch hunt or fishing expedition under way." He also denied that a committee aide had peeked at masked diary material and demanded an apology from Packwood. Packwood complied shortly thereafter but said nothing about Bryan's comment about a possible crime. Bryan's statement prompted an angry rebuke from Dole, who took to the floor to accuse Bryan of practically prejudging the case.

Two Days of Debate

After a somber two-day debate, the Senate voted overwhelmingly Nov. 2 to go to court to enforce the subpoena after easily defeating an attempt by Packwood's allies to narrow the subpoena to "relevant" entries. On the floor, Bryan and Packwood revealed that the entries that caused the dispute raised questions about whether Packwood had exchanged official favors for job offers for his estranged wife from lobbyists and other associates while he was in divorce court trying to minimize his alimony payments.

After the vote, the Ethics Committee publicly called for Packwood to comply with its subpoena, but he remained defiant.

Senate Legal Counsel Michael Davidson said he would ask the courts for expedited review at each stage, but members fretted that the issue could drag on for years if either side took it all the way to the Supreme Court. Many members called on the committee to push ahead with the evidence it had gathered to date while it fought in court for the diaries. But Ethics members insisted on the floor that they needed the post-1988 diaries to finish their probe — especially of charges that Packwood tried to intimidate his accusers in 1992.

The debate focused on issues of fairness, privacy and precedent as the Senate discussed how far its in-house investigators could go in probing allegations against one of its own. The debate began at 12:25 p.m. on Nov. 1 with 78 members in their seats, obeying the leadership request for sustained attendance. Just before it ended at 9:30 p.m. on Nov. 2, a score remained. The extraordinary colloquy lasted nearly 15 hours over the two days and frayed the institution's nerves like nothing since the 1991 Thomas-Hill contretemps, the last sexual harassment blowup to disrupt the Senate's stately routine.

Charges and countercharges flew. Led by Bryan, Ethics Committee members accused Packwood and his lawyers of being deceitful and spreading misinformation and defended their subpoena with cool resolve. They blamed the mess on Packwood. McConnell called it a "bitter irony" that Packwood could have avoided the sweeping subpoena if he had turned over relevant diary entries months before when he was first asked for relevant documents of any kind.

Looking alternatively depressed and angry, Packwood rambled at times but ultimately focused on the personal insult he felt at being ordered to turn over diaries he previously had shared only with his transcriber. Packwood accused the Ethics Committee of denying him due process and trampling his privacy rights. Only a few GOP colleagues rallied to support Packwood vocally. He and other Republicans, including all three GOP Ethics members, criticized Bryan for saying the previous week that the diaries' new revelations could be criminal. Some accused Bryan of violating committee secrecy rules. Bryan said he wanted to make sure senators knew the matter was serious.

According to his version of events, Packwood was trapped into introducing the diaries during his deposition. He said he had testified that a year after an incident raised by one complainant, he and she were drinking wine in his office when she gave him "a great big kiss and said, 'You are wonderful.' I responded, 'Warts and all?' And she laughed." Packwood said he was asked if he could corroborate the story. "If I say 'no,' I'm guilty of perjury. If I say 'yes,' I have opened up the diaries," he recalled. "So I said 'yes.'"

Many senators expressed fears about the precedent they were being asked to set, but Bryan insisted that it was limited by narrow circumstances: Packwood himself introduced the diaries into the inquiry, then allowed the committee to inspect them and see entries indicating possible unrelated misconduct that required further investigation.

Several members, especially the chamber's freshman Democratic women, attempted to move the focus of the debate away from such legal points and toward the issue of sexual harassment. Other members, including Simpson and Kassebaum, denounced that debating tactic. Simpson traced the matter back to the Thomas-Hill debate, charging that the subpoena was an attempt "to show that this Senate has been properly chastened and baptized in the purest waters of political correctness."

Jobs for Georgie Packwood

Packwood's only hope for narrowing the subpoena required him to offer to turn over everything related to the sexual misconduct charges and the unrelated matter Bryan had mentioned. That way, he could keep everything else to himself. But to make such an offer, he had to admit that he was suspected of corruption and explain why.

The gambit failed, producing only more headlines about his own alleged misbehavior.

News reports and statements on the floor revealed that the dispute over Packwood's diaries was sparked by the entries about job offers for Packwood's estranged wife, Georgie Packwood. "The issue was employment opportunities for my wife and whether there were some quid pro quo on legislation or anything like that," Packwood said Nov. 2, confirming the gist of a story the previous day in the (Portland) Oregonian. The Washington Post and The Associated Press had disclosed additional details Nov. 2.

Packwood said he had "absolutely not" done anything wrong.

According to the news accounts, Bob and Georgie Packwood were in the midst of divorce proceedings in 1990. About that time, Georgie Packwood got several job offers that she had not sought. She suspected her husband was behind the offers. One of her divorce lawyers described the offers as part of an effort by the senator to minimize his alimony payments because he cited them as evidence of her earning potential.

Packwood seemed to acknowledge his role in the offers in a letter to his wife found in court files by the AP. "I will continue to try to steer business your way," Packwood wrote on June 14, 1990. "This business that I steer to you is not to be a gift to you nor a bribe to me." The Oregonian, however, quoted Packwood as testifying in divorce court, "I didn't initiate the calls."

Georgie Packwood got job offers from the following people, according to the senator and news stories based on court papers and interviews with principals:

● Ronald Crawford, a lobbyist for the cable TV industry, a bus association, a Virgin Islands firm and a drug company group. All had business before either the Finance Committee, of which Packwood is the top Republican, or the Commerce Committee, of which Packwood is the top Republican of its main cable TV subcommittee. Crawford said he offered her a $7,500-a-year job as a political consultant because the Packwoods were old friends. Crawford's wife, Carol, used to work for the senator. Georgie Packwood said she was puzzled by the offer because Crawford knows more about politics than she did. She turned it down.

● Lester Pollack, a former law school classmate of Packwood's who was a New York investment banker and a top Packwood fundraiser. He told the AP he offered Georgie Packwood a $5,000-a-year position on a corporate board after speaking to Sen. Packwood about his pending divorce. She turned it down.

● Tim Lee, a former Packwood aide who owned an Oregon trucking company and was active in Packwood's campaigns. He offered to set up Georgie Packwood in an antique business in Oregon that would earn her $20,000-plus a year. She testified in 1990 that Lee told her that he learned from the senator that the couple needed money. She rejected that offer, too.

● Steven R. Saunders, a former Senate aide and trade official. He was a lobbyist for two big Japanese companies and Japan's embassy in Washington. He offered Georgie Packwood more than $20,000 a year to escort the wives of clients on antique shopping trips or to buy and resell American art. Georgie Packwood told the Post she was most interested in Saunders' offer, which she concluded he conceived independent of Sen. Packwood. She told the Oregonian that Saunders shelved the idea, however, after he called the senator to inquire about the ethics of the arrangement and the senator became "coercive and manip-

Continued on p. 62

Hints and Allegations: The List of Accusers

Allegations of sexual misconduct against Sen. Bob Packwood, R-Ore., stemmed mainly from articles in The Washington Post on Nov. 22, 1992, and Feb. 7, 1993, which included accounts from 24 women. Later, the Post and the (Portland) Oregonian published five other women's stories.

Of those 29 women, 15 agreed to be quoted by name, while the names of four others were made available to Packwood by the Post. Several other women, whose allegations were not detailed in newspaper reports, agreed to cooperate with the Ethics Committee probe of Packwood.

The accusers included 13 former aides, three job seekers, three former campaign workers, two former interns, two lobbyists, a baby sitter, a reporter, a Senate elevator operator, two other acquaintances and four women who were strangers at the time of the alleged incidents.

Almost all claimed that Packwood, who turned 61 in 1993, made unwanted advances, sometimes groping at their private parts, forcing his tongue into their mouths or trying to physically maneuver them toward couches. A few described less direct conduct, such as telling ribald jokes. Some also complained of attempts to intimidate them into silence as the Post prepared the first story.

Before its inquiry was sidetracked by the dispute over Packwood's diaries, the Ethics Committee had secured the cooperation of at least 21 women who accused him of sexual misconduct, people following the case said. The women included at least eight whose names were not yet public but who told their stories knowing they would be identified to Packwood and possibly called to testify against him publicly. The Post reported on Dec. 16 that the total number of women accusing Packwood of sexual misconduct had risen to at least 41, including 20 who declined to cooperate with the committee.

For his part, Packwood denied wrongdoing before the Nov. 3, 1992, election, thereby delaying publication of the Post's first story. After the Nov. 22, 1992, story appeared, he apologized for unspecified conduct he called "just plain wrong." Later, in 1993, said he might challenge some of the women's stories before the Ethics Committee, but continued to refuse to discuss his conduct publicly.

Following is a summary of the 29 women's allegations reported by the Post and the Oregonian in roughly chronological order. Descriptions are from the initial two Post stories except where noted. All the women identified by name below were said to be cooperating with the Ethics Committee except Roberta Ulrich and Tiffany Work.

Julie Williamson. Campaign worker in 1968 and Portland, Ore., Senate office aide in 1969, when she was 29; she is now a Democratic consultant. Williamson said Packwood kissed her on the back of the neck while she was talking on the phone in his Portland Senate office. She said she told Packwood not to do that again but that he followed her to an adjoining room and pulled her ponytail, stood on her toes, grabbed at her clothes and tried to remove her girdle. "I kept struggling, and he just gave up," she said, describing herself as "really frightened." She quit within weeks.

Gayle Rothrock. A secretary in another Capitol Hill office in 1969, when she was 23. She said that on a visit to Packwood's office she was asked by Packwood's then-wife, Georgie, to baby-sit that evening. She told the Post that as Packwood walked her to the car to drive her home, he kissed her forcefully and that during the drive he reached over and touched her legs several times. She said she kept talking to signal her lack of interest, and he stopped.

Sharon Grant. Sought a job in Packwood's Washington office in 1969, when she was 28. Grant said that during an interview, Packwood made it clear that he wanted to spend the night with her. "He didn't know me at all, yet he felt he could have what he wanted with impunity," she said. She talked her way out of the office.

Susan Des Camp. A volunteer on Packwood's 1968 campaign. She told the Oregonian that in 1969, when she was 23 and visiting family in Washington, D.C., she was sitting at a table in a bar with her sister, her brother-in-law, Packwood and several others. She said Packwood reached underneath the table and grabbed her leg. Her memory of the evening was vague, but her sister, Anne Kelly Feeney, recalled Des Camp telling her after leaving the bar that Packwood had put his hand up her skirt.

Gail Byler. A dining room hostess in 1970 at a Ramada Inn in downtown Portland where Packwood was a frequent guest. She told the Oregonian that after closing one night, Packwood came from behind her in a dark dining room and ran his hand from her ankle up the inside of her leg and under her skirt. She told him to leave her alone. Looking drunk, Packwood replied, "Do you know who I am?" She told him she did but did not care and never to touch her again. He replied, "Well, you haven't heard the end of this."

Lois Kincaid. Attended a fundraiser at a ranch in Oregon in 1971, when she was 27. She said she had never met Packwood, but he tried to embrace her "out of the blue, without saying a thing" when the two were alone in a room. She stopped him, and he "acted kind of confused and mumbled some kind of apology, like 'excuse me,' like it was inadvertent, which was pretty ridiculous considering the size of the room," she said.

Tiffany Work. A model serving as a hostess at a political gathering in Oregon in 1973, when she was 13 (though she recalled being dressed and made up to look older). Work said he grabbed her buttocks as he walked by her. Packwood, while declining comment on the other stories, has denied Work's accusation.

A woman who had never met Packwood. She said she went to Packwood's office in the mid-1970s to meet the senator. After the meeting, arranged by friends who worked for Packwood, he escorted her to a hallway outside his office and gave her a French kiss, she said.

Employee in Packwood's Portland office. Not otherwise identified. She said Packwood kissed her on the mouth nearly a dozen times, usually "out of the blue," while she worked for him in the mid-1970s. She said she did not consider his conduct serious.

Jean McMahon. She sought a job with Packwood in 1976, when she was about 30. She said that Packwood asked her to draft a sample speech for him during a meeting in a Salem, Ore., motel. Later, after talking about the speech with him several times by phone, she agreed to meet him at a motel on the Oregon coast to discuss it further. "But he had no interest in the speech," she said in a complaint to the Ethics Committee. "Instead, he came after me, sexually. I ran, but he chased me around the table in the motel room, grabbed me and kissed me against my will. I was able to get loose and fled the room."

Paige Wagers. Mail clerk for Packwood's Washington office in 1976, when she was 21. Wagers said Packwood called her to his office, locked the door, embraced her, ran his fingers through her hair and forcefully kissed her. "It was very hard to get him to let go of me," she said. Told that such advances had happened before, Wagers ignored two more invitations to come to Packwood's office and left for another job within months. In 1981, when she was a Labor Department employee, she came across him in a Capitol hallway. The two walked and talked until Packwood suddenly opened a door and ushered her into an unmarked office, shut the door, kissed her and reached out to push some pillows off a sofa, she told the Post. She pulled away and left.

Kerry Whitney. A Senate elevator operator in the late 1970s, when she was in her late 20s. She said that while she was assigned to a lift reserved exclusively for senators from June 1977 through January 1978, Packwood on numerous occasions grabbed her, backed her against a wall and kissed her on the lips against her will.

One night in August 1977, she added, Packwood called her at her home and asked to visit. She said yes, hoping to persuade him to stop kissing her. "During the course of several hours in the apartment, the senator made several efforts to grab Ms. Whitney and kiss her and repeatedly asked to spend the night," her lawyers said in a statement after the Post wrote about Whitney on Dec. 16, 1993. After she declined his advances and persuaded him to leave, "the senator then proceeded to bang on the front door for several minutes, and when that produced no response, to telephone the house, again begging to spend the night. Even after this visit, he continued to grab and kiss her in the elevator."

Packwood staff member. She said she and Packwood were alone in his office one night in 1980, when she was in her early 20s. Packwood had been drinking, she said. She had heard of other incidents, so she did not want to stay in the office alone with him and phoned a friend for a ride home. Before the friend arrived, she said, Packwood put his arms around her and tried to push her onto the couch. She fought him off and left in tears, having felt "extremely vulnerable . . . like I was in danger."

Gena Hutton. Unpaid county campaign chairman for Packwood in 1980, when she was 35. She said that after a visit with him at a Eugene, Ore., hotel restaurant, he grabbed her while walking her to her car, put his arms around her, kissed her "sensuously," attempted to put his tongue in her mouth and invited her to his hotel room. She turned him down. She said when she told the campaign manager about the episode, he told her that "it happens all the time, that they've talked to him over and over about it."

Gillian Butler. Part-time clerk at the Portland Red Lion Inn in 1980, when she was 23. Butler said she mentioned to Packwood as he checked out one day that she had written him a letter complaining about the reinstatement of draft registration. He called her from the airport and suggested that she write again, which she did, prompting another call and an invitation for drinks. She agreed but was wary, so she asked her boyfriend along. Before the boyfriend arrived, Packwood asked her to dance, but she declined. On a later stay, Packwood leaned over the front desk and kissed her on the lips. On another stay, he followed her into a storage area and kissed her again. She said she did not complain to her supervisors because she considered Packwood an important guest and did not consider the incidents serious.

Mary Heffernan. Longtime abortion rights activist and a volunteer coordinator for Packwood's 1980 campaign; she is now executive director of the Women's Foundation of Oregon. Heffernan said that in the early 1980s on a visit to Packwood's office he grabbed her arms and kissed her, but she stopped him.

Packwood clerical employee. Identified to Packwood but not named by the Post. She said she was 21 in 1982, when he invited her into his office one evening and offered her wine. She agreed to sit and talk but declined the wine. "He walked over to me and pulled me out of the chair, put his arm around me and tried to kiss me. He stuck his tongue in my mouth." She said she squirmed away and left, avoiding him in the future and quitting months later.

Packwood staff member. She said Packwood made three unwelcome advances in 1982. Once, he locked the door to his personal office, grabbed her, stepped on her toes, kissed her and motioned toward the sofa. After a second advance, she accelerated her job search. The third advance came while she was typing her résumé after hours. Packwood put his hands on her shoulders and then put one hand down her shirt and tried to touch her breast, she said. She told him to stop, walked away and soon found another job.

High school summer intern, 1982 and 1983. Agreed to be identified to Packwood but not named in the Post. She said that while she was working as a driver for Packwood in 1982, he unnerved her by saying several times that she was pretty and poised and that he considered her a woman despite her age. In the fall of 1983, when she was a 17-year-old senior, she asked Packwood for a written recommendation for college applications. He agreed and called her several times to update her on it. She said he insisted on personally delivering the letter to her suburban Maryland home, arranging to bring it at a time when no one else would be home. Once he was inside, she said, Packwood tried to hug her. "He seemed a little heated," she said. After being rebuffed and shown the door, he "laid a juicy kiss on my lips. I could feel the tongue coming." She pushed him away and escorted him out. She was so "unbelievably shaken" that she double-locked the front door after Packwood left.

A Eugene, Ore., woman. Agreed to be identified to Packwood but was not named in the Post. She said that in 1985, while she was being considered for a campaign post, Packwood asked her to dance at a restaurant in Bend, Ore. "His hands were all over my back, sides and buttock, and he made suggestive movements" and kissed her neck, she said. She blamed the conduct on the fact that he had been drinking and continued to associate with him. Later that year, after she drove him and a top aide to their hotel, he suddenly kissed her. "It turned into a French kiss, and I said, 'I don't appreciate that,' and I pushed him away." She complained to the aide, and Packwood later called to tell her never again to tell anyone about any problems she had with him. She turned down the job.

A campaign worker. Told the Oregonian that while working for Packwood's 1986 campaign for a short time, he leered at her, pushed his body toward her, smacked his lips suggestively and asked what her measurements were. He never touched her, she said.

Maura C. Roche. A college intern in Packwood's Washington office in 1989, when she was 22. She said that while sitting in Packwood's inner office with the senator one day, he pulled out a binder and read several sexually explicit jokes to her. (She said that Packwood earlier had gone around the office offering wine to staff members.) "I couldn't believe it," said Roche, now a Planned Parenthood official in Oregon. "I just sat there and took it" until she eventually excused herself from the room. She called Packwood's comments "tacky" but did not consider them an advance.

Packwood aide. Identified to Packwood but not named by the Post, which based its account on what she told friends, whose recollections she did not dispute. In about 1990, Packwood abruptly kissed her in the office one night after they had been out for dinner and drinks with other staff members. The woman, who had developed a friendship with Packwood, ran out of the building crying but remained on his staff for more than a year.

Roberta Ulrich. A Washington, D.C., reporter for the Oregonian. She told the Oregonian that late one afternoon in March 1992, she went to Packwood's office for an interview with him and his press aide. She accepted one glass of wine; he had at least two but was not drunk, she said. When she rose to leave, Packwood walked around the desk, shook her hand and kissed her on the lips. Ulrich, then about 64, was shocked but did not rebuke Packwood. She considered the kiss inappropriate but not a sexual advance.

Packwood aide. She said she repeatedly rebuffed Packwood and finally left the office because he did not change his behavior, despite warnings from many that his conduct would hurt him some day. No time element given.

Packwood employee in Oregon. She said the senator once chased her around a desk in a back office. No time element given.

Two other Packwood aides and a lobbyist. They said Packwood made unwanted sexual advances. No details given.

Defining Sexual Harassment

A central question in the case against Sen. Bob Packwood, R-Ore., was whether his alleged conduct would constitute illegal sexual harassment.

The precise definition of sexual harassment was not a settled issue in the courts. The Supreme Court ruled in 1986 that sexual harassment was illegal under a federal law barring sex-based discrimination. The law did not cover the Senate, but Senate rules also prohibited sexual discrimination.

The Supreme Court's 1986 decision recognized two types of sexual harassment: "quid pro quo" and "hostile environment."

No one accused Packwood of quid pro quo sexual harassment, where an employer makes submitting to or rejecting unwanted sexual conduct the basis for employment decisions.

The charges against Packwood were more akin to a hostile environment harassment case. That was where unwanted physical or verbal sexual conduct "has the purpose or effect of unreasonably interfering with an individual's work performance or creating an intimidating, hostile or offensive working environment," according to the Equal Employment Opportunity Commission (EEOC).

The Washington Post's initial story on Packwood's conduct said his employees felt his "behavior created an undercurrent of tension and resentment," especially in the late 1970s and early 1980s. In one of his interviews with the Post, Packwood said that "an unwanted approach would be sexual harassment, as I understand it."

But Packwood's supporters said the alleged actions did not constitute harassment because they generally were isolated, one-time incidents where he retreated after being rebuffed. They pointed to EEOC guidelines saying that "a single incident or isolated incidents of offensive sexual conduct or remarks" generally do not create a hostile environment.

But some women alleged that Packwood came after them more than once, and the EEOC said a case could be made if a pattern was established. Moreover, the EEOC said an "unusually severe incident" could create a hostile environment, especially if it involved physical conduct and even more so if it involved touching "intimate body areas" — conduct alleged by some of Packwood's accusers.

Women's advocates generally tried to avoid being drawn into a debate over the legal intricacies of sexual harassment in the Packwood case. Said Holly Pruett, executive director of the Oregon Coalition Against Domestic and Sexual Violence: "I don't even understand the relevance of that because in many cases it was . . . conduct that was more serious than harassment — it could be assaultive. We're talking about grabbing women, restraining them, shoving his tongue into their mouths."

Continued from p. 59

ulative" in inquiring how much she would make.

In a later story, the Oregonian reported that Packwood had asked questions at a 1989 hearing on behalf of one of Saunders' lobbying clients, Mitsubishi Electric Co., which had been accused of unfair trade practices.

The Senate Votes

On the second day of the debate, after Packwood and his lawyers had met with Bryan and McConnell the night before, the senator made his offer: He would turn over "every scintilla of information" related to the sexual misconduct charges and the jobs matter. Arlen Specter, R-Pa., and John C. Danforth, R-Mo., offered an amendment based on Packwood's offer.

Under the amendment, Packwood would have turned the diaries over to Starr, who would have culled them for all relevant entries. The Ethics Committee rejected the idea, arguing that it would require Starr to ignore any other misdeeds noted in the diary and that Starr would not always know what was relevant.

Specter later withdrew the amendment in favor of a more vague proposal by Simpson limiting the subpoena to "relevant" material. The committee opposed Simpson's amendment, too. "Relevant to what?" Bryan asked. Simpson was not specific.

Both sides argued that their proposals treated Packwood the way any other citizen would be treated in similar circumstances.

The Senate defeated the Simpson proposal, 23-77, with Republicans evenly split (22-22). Just one Democrat, Jeff Bingaman, N.M., sided with Simpson. Republicans John

H. Chafee, R.I., and Robert F. Bennett, Utah, initially voted with Simpson but switched sides as the outcome became clear. After supporting the Ethics Committee throughout the debate, one of its three Republican members, Larry E. Craig of Idaho, backed Simpson. (*Vote 347, p. 45-S*)

The Senate then voted 94-6 to go to court. Simpson, Danforth, Specter, Jesse Helms, R-N.C., and Dennis DeConcini, D-Ariz., sided with Packwood. (*Vote 348, p. 45-S*)

During the floor debate, Ethics member Mikulski put down a little-noticed marker on a volatile issue already showing signs of dividing the Senate — whether to hold public hearings on the case once the preliminary inquiry was finished.

"At some point, I would expect the Ethics Committee to hold public hearings," said Mikulski, the committee's one female and its only member to publicize her view on the subject. Many alleged victims and women's groups favored public hearings, but several Republicans off the committee opposed such a move as unnecessary.

THE COURT FIGHT

On Nov. 19, as the committee was about to formally ask the U.S. District Court for the District of Columbia to enforce the subpoena, Fitzpatrick told reporters that Packwood was considering resigning. It later became apparent that Packwood was on the verge of resigning so he could keep the diaries to himself. If he resigned, the Ethics Committee's case and subpoena would become moot because the panel had jurisdiction only over sitting senators. But Packwood changed his mind after the Justice Department served him with a subpoena for the documents to

block him from destroying them. The Justice Department's spokesman, John Russell, said its investigation had begun several weeks before.

On Nov. 22, the Ethics Committee went to court to enforce its subpoena after it became clear that Packwood would not resign. The case was assigned to U.S. District Judge Thomas Penfield Jackson, a Reagan appointee. With the investigation expanded to include the Justice Department, Packwood dismissed Fitzpatrick and hired a defense attorney, Jacob A. Stein, on Nov. 28. Fitzpatrick's expertise involved representing clients before congressional committees; Stein was a well-known criminal lawyer.

In court papers opposing the Ethics Committee's subpoena, Packwood on Dec. 8 invoked the Fifth Amendment for the first time. Packwood also invoked his privacy rights, which previously had been his main argument against the Ethics subpoena. Stein also argued that the subpoena was too broad.

Packwood's legal woes deepened considerably the week of Dec. 13 as the Ethics Committee expanded its investigation and Judge Jackson seized his diaries upon learning that he might have altered them.

The developments prompted Kassebaum, on Dec. 16, to become the first Republican senator to urge Packwood to resign. Democrats Robert C. Byrd of West Virginia, Daniel K. Inouye of Hawaii and Barbara Boxer of California previously had made similar comments.

Packwood's alleged alterations of the diaries came to light almost by accident.

The committee learned of them by questioning Cathy Wagner Cormack, who began transcribing the diaries from Packwood's daily recorded recollections after she became his secretary in 1969. She continued doing so after she left his full-time employ in the early 1980s. The panel first questioned her Nov. 22 to determine what funds Packwood used to compensate her. The committee wanted to determine whether Packwood had violated campaign finance laws or Senate rules barring the use of campaign funds for personal use, court records showed. The panel had another motive.

Packwood had argued that the diaries were personal and therefore protected by his privacy rights. The committee sought to rebut that argument in court papers by showing that Packwood paid Cormack with Senate and campaign funds that could not be converted to personal use. Court records showed that she was paid $4,393 in Senate funds in 1982-83 and $38,666 in campaign funds in 1984-93 for typing the diaries. (Judge Jackson later said he did not care whether Packwood violated laws or rules in preparing the diaries but whether they were essentially personal. Senate Legal Counsel Davidson conceded that they were a "mixed document" but that Packwood probably considered them personal when he wrote them.)

In her initial deposition, Cormack said she never talked to Packwood about the substance of the diaries. But she corrected herself in an affidavit Dec. 10. She said Packwood had retrieved some of his tapes after the Ethics Committee investigation began. Later, she said she noticed that he might have revised some of the tapes. "Subsequently, he confirmed that he had," she swore.

On Dec. 14, the Ethics Committee filed an urgent request asking Jackson to seize the diaries for safekeeping while the case was litigated.

It was not until a second deposition of Cormack on Dec. 15 that the committee learned the details of her disclosure. Cormack told committee lawyers that in September or October, Packwood asked for his latest batch of tapes back,

something he had never done before, according to documents supporting the seizure request.

Q: What did he say?

A: As best I can recall, he said something about the possibility of a subpoena, and he didn't want me to have anything in my possession if that were to occur.

Less than a week later, Cormack said, Packwood returned the tapes for transcribing. Upon hearing them, Cormack said she noticed possible alterations.

Q: Do you recall what you said to him about the tapes?

A: I just asked him if he was making any changes or anything.

Q: And do you remember what he said?

A: He basically confirmed that. We didn't have a long conversation about it. . . . It was sort of a body language thing, but he knew that I knew.

Cormack said Packwood also had ordered her to make some changes to typed transcripts by marking alterations on the pages by hand or by dictating changes on tape. Previously such changes were rare, she said. She said she retyped the pages and threw away the old copies. This happened mostly in mid- to late October, she said — when the committee was reviewing the diaries and was heading toward the dispute that would lead to the subpoena.

Cormack offered no details on the substance of the changes. She said both the transcript changes and the tape changes involved parts of 1992 and 1993. Davidson said in court that the 1992 diaries were key because they might contain evidence of the alleged intimidation campaign.

At a hearing Dec. 16, Davidson told Judge Jackson that when Packwood first mentioned the diary during his deposition, he said he had been "scanning" it. "We now know that 'scanning' is a euphemism. At the very time the senator began his deposition, Oct. 5 and 6 of this year, he was in the process of revising his diaries. But he used the word 'scanning,' " Davidson said. "It is [Cormack's] sworn testimony that he was anticipating a subpoena."

Stein said little about the alterations. In a Dec. 7 letter to the committee, he said that "in discrete instances, the transcripts depart from the original tapes" and that it was "unlikely" that the committee had seen any of those revised transcripts. In court, he said he did not know whether any changes were significant and that he did not think any were made after the subpoena was issued. Stein also said originals of the tapes existed, but it was not clear whether those were tapes Packwood altered.

After the Dec. 16 hearing, Jackson issued an order seizing the diaries — all tapes and transcripts, copies and originals.

During the hearing, Davidson argued that the Ethics Committee's subpoena power was as broad as a grand jury's, if not more so, because the committee was charged with a constitutional duty: disciplining members of Congress under a system of government that made it difficult to prosecute them criminally for certain offenses.

Jackson indicated that he might consider reviewing the diaries for relevant passages himself or having an arbiter do so. But he chuckled out loud at Stein's suggestion that the court should ignore evidence of misconduct unrelated to the committee's inquiry. In the end, Stein seemed to take an all-or-nothing tack, saying he did not want the court "cherry picking" potential violations for the committee and telling the judge he should just reject the subpoena.

On Jan. 24, 1994, Jackson upheld the Ethics Committee's subpoena. "There are a number of issues that we think we will be able to appeal," Stein told reporters. ■

Rostenkowski Investigated in Stamp Scam

A two-year-old federal criminal investigation of the House Post Office turned a harsh spotlight on one of the most powerful members of the House. Federal prosecutors July 19 implicated Dan Rostenkowski, D-Ill., chairman of the Ways and Means Committee, in an embezzlement scheme. Former Rep. Joe Kolter, D-Pa. (1983-93), also was implicated.

Neither was indicted by the end of the year, although a federal grand jury was continuing a wide-ranging examination of Rostenkowski's financial affairs. Both men proclaimed innocence.

Their names had surfaced in 1992 in subpoenas issued in connection with a grand jury investigation of wrongdoing at the post office, in which several former House employees had pleaded guilty to charges including embezzlement and drug-dealing. The case grew more serious when former House Postmaster Robert V. Rota pleaded guilty on July 19, 1993, to conspiracy and embezzlement charges. Rostenkowski and Kolter were tied by prosecutors to a scheme in which Rota helped members illegally convert taxpayer-financed stamps and stamp vouchers to cash. Rostenkowski and Kolter were not named directly, but court documents filed in connection with the charges clearly identified them as alleged participants.

Some House Republicans called for an immediate ethics committee inquiry into the matter, but they did not press the issue because many members were afraid of interfering with the Justice Department investigation.

The recurring rumors of a Rostenkowski indictment did not keep the chairman from leading his committee through negotiations on President Clinton's deficit-reduction package. But members speculated openly about the impact of an indictment on Rostenkowski's future and that of the committee, which would have responsibility in 1994 for major Clinton initiatives including health care, welfare and trade. If indicted, Rostenkowski would have to relinquish his chairmanship while charges were pending, according to Democratic Caucus rules.

BACKGROUND

The federal investigation began in mid-1991. Jay B. Stephens, U.S. attorney for the District of Columbia, began looking into accusations that stamp clerks had been stealing funds from the post office and dealing drugs there. The House Post Office ran its postal operations under contract with the U.S. Postal Service; it was headed by a postmaster who was an elected House official.

Several post office employees eventually pleaded guilty to various charges. Investigations — including one by the House Administration Committee in 1992 — depicted a sloppily run operation where cash and stamps were treated casually and where workers were beholden to political sponsors, not to professional managers. Its status as a House office was ended and its operations turned over to the Postal Service in 1992. *(1992 Almanac, p. 47)*

The first word of the possible involvement of House members came in May 1992, when the House learned that the grand jury had subpoenaed records of Rostenkowski, Kolter and Rep. Austin J. Murphy, D-Pa. Word leaked that a post office supervisor, James C. Smith, had told the grand jury that he helped members get thousands of dol-

lars in cash through false transactions disguised as stamp purchases.

Public records showed that Rostenkowski, Kolter and Murphy all had large amounts of stamp purchases for the 6¼-year period under review by the grand jury. Records of the House clerk showed that Rostenkowski had reported $29,672 in stamp purchases, often in increments of thousands of dollars. Kolter reported $17,374 in purchases; Murphy, $9,244. Because members could send virtually all public business for free using the franking privilege, they seemed to have little need for stamps. More than half of members purchased less than $350 a year, according to records reviewed by Congressional Quarterly. Rostenkowski said he used stamps for overseas mailings; he, Kolter and Murphy denied skimming cash from the post office.

INQUIRIES FOCUS ON FINANCES

Rostenkowski's attorneys went to federal court Jan. 11, asking a judge to bar agents working on the case from leaking information to the media. The action followed by two days a series of media reports that the investigation was now looking into the congressman's taxes.

On Feb. 1, U.S. District Judge John Garrett Penn ruled that some leaks might indeed have occurred. But after examining 74 sworn affidavits from agents involved in the inquiry, Penn ruled Feb. 12 that the government was not the source of leaks.

Republicans suggested that the Clinton administration might be moving to protect a key Democrat when the Justice Department in March ordered the replacement of all U.S. attorneys who were holdovers from Republican administrations, including the District of Columbia's Stephens.

Stephens protested publicly that the administration's move could disrupt his inquiry, although he did not directly accuse the administration of deliberately doing so. "We had been prepared to make a critical decision regarding the resolution of this case within 30 days," Stephens said, contending that the action could delay a decision for months.

Administration officials insisted that their desire to install a Democratic cadre of prosecutors had nothing to do with the probe of Rostenkowski. Attorney General Janet Reno was peppered with questions about the Rostenkowski case at a March 23 news conference announcing the Justice Department action. Reno insisted that there was "no linkage whatsoever" between her decision to replace the attorneys and the probe. Stephens "has not been singled out in any way," Reno said.

In confirmation hearings March 9-10, Reno had repeatedly assured Republicans that she would not allow political considerations to affect such prosecutorial decisions. When asked specifically about Rostenkowski, she said she would not even tell the White House whether an indictment was likely because "I keep politics out of what I do."

Asked at the hearing how she would respond to a request from the president for a description of the evidence in such a case, Reno said: "I would say, 'Mr. President, that is not the way to do it. Let the Department of Justice pursue it in the regular course of business. Let's not mix things up. And if you don't want me to be your attorney general, I will go home.'"

Stephens was replaced in April. The job was taken over

temporarily by J. Ramsey Johnson and then by a new U.S. attorney, Eric Holder Jr., who was appointed by Clinton and sworn in Oct. 8.

Ex-Kolter Aide Pleads Guilty

A one-time top aide to Kolter pleaded guilty March 31 to three felonies related to the post office probe and agreed to cooperate with investigators. Gerald W. Weaver II, Kolter's administrative assistant from 1983 to 1987, was the seventh former House employee convicted in the inquiry, the first from outside the post office.

Weaver admitted obstructing justice, distributing cocaine and conspiring to distribute more than 50 grams of cocaine. Prosecutors said Weaver bought $2,800 worth of cocaine from a postal clerk, financing the deals by cashing checks at the post office. In a failed attempt to mislead the grand jury, they said, Weaver had a former business associate concoct a letter stating that Weaver had been reimbursed for buying a similar amount of postage. At Weaver's plea hearing, prosecutor Thomas J. Motley said Weaver had sold cocaine to lobbyists and congressional aides.

Lifestyle Under Microscope

Throughout the spring, news reports in Chicago and the national media depicted a burgeoning investigation of Rostenkowski's finances. A Congressional Quarterly examination of his public financial records for 1990 and 1991 showed a dizzying lifestyle. Nearly a third of the $358,331 in operating expenditures reported by Rostenkowski's campaign and his political action committee (PAC) in 1990 and 1991 went for items that enhanced his lifestyle or income — travel, chauffeurs, car insurance, cable TV bills, dinner out, a golf caddy and rental payments to himself and his family.

Rostenkowski was on the road more than half the time, almost always at the expense of business and union groups, which also paid him tens of thousands of dollars in speaking fees. He traveled to California five times, Florida and Hawaii twice each and Arizona once, while attending three corporate-sponsored charity golf tournaments. To aid the chairman on his travels, his campaign paid $500 to a caddy and $500 to a chauffeur.

During that period, he charged his campaign account and a PAC he controlled, the America's Leaders Fund, $4,837 for dinners at restaurants in Chicago, Washington and elsewhere.

From his taxpayer-financed House office account, Rostenkowski paid $3,460 to lease two automobiles in his district to supplement another owned by his campaign. Rostenkowski's campaign paid Rostenkowski and his two sisters $3,000 in rent for office space in a building they owned that was connected to his Chicago home. He paid his sisters an additional $2,500 in House funds as rent for his congressional district office.

EX-POSTMASTER PLEADS GUILTY

Rota, the former House postmaster, stunned official Washington on July 19 when he pleaded guilty to embezzlement and misdemeanor charges. In doing so, he said in court that he personally delivered phony stamp proceeds to members whom he called Congressman A and Congressman B.

Rota pleaded guilty to three misdemeanors — one count of conspiracy to embezzle and two of aiding and abetting Congressmen A and B "in willfully and knowingly embezzling" U.S. funds. Prosecutors said there was no evidence that Rota pocketed any money for himself.

Documents related to Rota's plea bargain detailed certain stamp purchases as being fake. The allegedly sham purchases made by Congressman A matched precisely with stamp purchases attributed in public House records to Rostenkowski; Congressman B's purchases matched those of Kolter. The prosecutors alleged that the members regularly gave the House Post Office expense vouchers requesting stamps for official mail and instead received thousands of dollars in cash. *(Rota text, p. 26-D)*

"What Mr. Rota did," prosecutors said in a statement to the court, "was to place the services of his Office, and the United States funds under his control, at the disposal of certain United States Congressmen, knowing full well that he was aiding the embezzlement of money from those funds. What Mr. Rota got in return was to keep his job as an Officer of the United States House of Representatives."

Prosecutors' Case

The scheme, according to the court papers and Rota's account, looked like this:

Congressman A or Congressman B would present Rota with a signed expense voucher requesting from $600 to $2,300 worth of stamps, certifying "that they are for use in or by my office in the discharge of my duties."

Sometimes the member would not have a voucher, and Rota would ask a subordinate to type one from a stack of blanks kept at the post office. One of those occasionally asked to do the typing was Joanna G. O'Rourke, the former post office chief of staff, according to a source with knowledge of the case. O'Rourke agreed to a plea bargain in 1992 in return for cooperation with prosecutors.

Rota would then take the voucher to his supervisor of accounts — either Mary C. Bowman, who held that job until May 1987, or James C. Smith, who held it from May 1989 until mid-1992. Bowman or Smith would take the voucher from Rota and in return give him either cash or stamps.

If it was cash, Rota "then would and did deliver the cash to the members who had signed the vouchers, including Congressman A and Congressman B," prosecutors said in one document. If Rota came back with stamps, the member would return them later to Rota, who would redeem them for cash for the member, again through the supervisor of accounts.

Rota told the prosecutors that he had been supplying members of Congress with cash in exchange for vouchers, stamps and campaign and political action committee checks since shortly after becoming postmaster in 1972. At that time, members were allowed to "cash out" certain unused office expense accounts to supplement their incomes. The House did not specifically allow or prohibit redeeming stamps for cash; some members apparently took advantage of that ambiguity. Reforms implemented in 1977-78 were supposed to end all cash-outs.

As early as 1980, federal prosecutors caught wind of a cash-for-vouchers scam and asked Rota and Bowman about it. Rota admitted that he and Bowman lied to prosecutors on May 5, 1980, when they denied giving members cash.

After this successful cover-up, according to court papers and other public records, Rota said he continued funneling money to several congressmen, including Congressmen A and B, through April 1991. Rota said there was a two-year hiatus in the scheme (May 1987 to May 1989) when another employee, Paul Tomme, held the accounts supervisor

job. Rota resisted Rostenkowski's and Kolter's requests for cash, explaining to them "that he could not trust the new employee to carry out the scheme," prosecutors said. Rota said that after Tomme left in May 1989, he promoted Smith, a patronage employee sponsored by Rostenkowski, following "personal intervention and insistence of Congressman A."

Rota then told Smith that they would give cash to Congressman A "because Congressman A took care of them and they should take care of Congressman A in return," court papers said. Congressman B would get cash "because Congressman B was a close friend of Mr. Rota."

In all, Kolter allegedly received $9,300 over two two-year periods — 1986-87 and 1989-1990 — records show.

Public records show that Rostenkowski's explicitly enumerated take totaled $21,300. But that figure did not include "two other large sums" that Rota said he delivered to Rostenkowski in exchange for stamps shortly after Smith replaced Tomme as accounts supervisor. House records show that in the two years Tomme held the supervisor of accounts job, Rostenkowski reported buying $8,500 worth of stamps.

Identifying 'A' and 'B'

While prosecutors did not directly name Congressmen A and B, they provided clues in court documents that clearly identified Congressman A as Rostenkowski and Congressman B as Kolter.

The principal evidence was the listing of transactions with the House postmaster that the prosecutors said enabled members to procure cash. Court documents listed the date, voucher number, amount and description of services for each transaction. The same details were included in reports of members' expenditures that were published quarterly by the House clerk, except that the clerk used a different numbering system to identify vouchers.

Each of the vouchers cited for Congressman A corresponded, by date, amount and description, with vouchers published in the clerk's reports under Rostenkowski's expenditures, except that a voucher described as "unknown" from December 1990 for $2,000 did not correspond with any for that month in the clerk's report.

Also, court documents declared that "in or about May 1989, with the intervention and support of Congressman A, defendant Rota promoted Employee No. 3, who was a patronage employee of Congressman A, to the position of Supervisor of Accounts." House records showed that Smith was promoted to supervisor of accounts May 22, 1989. In a May 1992 interview, Rostenkowski said that Smith was under his patronage. "I inherited him from another member 20 years ago," he said.

For Congressman B, the vouchers cited corresponded with entries in the clerk's report for Kolter.

No other members had identical entries.

Battle on Floor

Rota's plea sparked a bitter debate on the floor July 22 reminiscent of the bickering that ensued when the House bank scandal erupted in 1991 and 1992. (House bank, 1991 Almanac, p. 39; 1992 Almanac, p. 23)

Republicans, citing Rota's plea, took to the floor and demanded full disclosure of the records of the House Administration Committee task force that in 1992 had examined the case and issued two reports, one by the GOP members and one by Democrats. Republicans suggested on the floor that the documents contained damaging informa-

tion about Democrats.

Speaker Thomas S. Foley, D-Wash., initially said he would support releasing the transcripts after giving the Justice Department 10 days to review whether any of the material would endanger its probe. But he backed off after U.S. Attorney Johnson said in a letter that releasing anything "could have a significant adverse effect on the ongoing criminal investigation."

Republicans pressed for release of the information anyway, with Minority Leader Robert H. Michel, R-Ill., introducing a resolution (H Res 222) ordering the immediate public disclosure of all the transcripts. Members spent three hours debating the issue, much of it yelling at each other.

The most heated moment came when Bill Thomas, R-Calif., charged that Foley had called Attorney General Reno before Johnson sent the letter opposing the release of any documents. Fuming, Foley went to the well. "That is totally and absolutely incorrect," he said, glaring at Thomas, who apologized after the Democrats' cheers subsided.

Democratic leaders used Johnson's letter to rally their troops around an alternative resolution (H Res 223) barring the release at least until the U.S. attorney dropped his objection. The House approved the Democratic resolution by a mostly party-line vote of 244-183 and then rejected Michel's alternative 242-186. (Vote 356, p. 86-H; vote 357, p. 88-H)

ROSTENKOWSKI'S 'CASH-OUTS'

The prosecutors' account revived interest in the former system under which members could draw cash from their official allowances to spend how they pleased. After the practice became controversial, the House ended it in 1977, despite grumbling from members who considered the move a pay cut.

Old public records examined by Congressional Quarterly showed that Rostenkowski had for years legally withdrawn thousands of dollars a year from his stationery account under what was then known as the "cash-out" system.

Prior to 1977, members' office budgets were divided into various allowances. Members could cash out three of them — travel, official expenses outside Washington and stationery — meaning they could pocket the money whether or not they incurred the expense.

At the time, members' salaries were eroding with inflation because many refused to vote for regular pay raises. While members gave themselves only one $2,100 pay increase (to $44,600) in 1969-77, during that time they increased the three cash-out accounts by a total of $5,800 a year to $10,750. Members could keep whatever they did not use for official expenses. Evidence suggested that in addition, some members cashed out some or all of a separate $1,140 stamp allowance, though the rules were silent on whether doing so was allowed.

The biggest of the three explicitly sanctioned cash-outs was the stationery allowance, which the House increased to $6,500 from $3,000 between 1970 and 1974. Members could keep the money in their account at the House stationery store or withdraw some by having the House clerk's finance office issue them a check. If they got a check, the Internal Revenue Service considered the money income, according to a 1978 House Administration Committee history of members' office budgets.

House clerk records from the 1970s show that hundreds of members withdrew money from their stationery ac-

counts. They were listed in the reports under "Commutation of allowance for stationery."

The reports showed that some members took out small, uneven amounts, suggesting that they were collecting for specific expenses. But others — including some of Congress' most prominent current and past members — withdrew hundreds or thousands of dollars at a time in round figures.

Between 1970 and 1976, Rostenkowski increasingly drew on his stationery account, records show. In 1970-73, Rostenkowski withdrew $1,716 to $2,500 a year. His cash-outs increased to $5,000 to $5,403 a year in 1974-76.

This longstanding practice became controversial after it was disclosed that Rep. H. R. Gross, R-Iowa, who had a reputation as a fiscal watchdog, pocketed $23,612 from his stationery account when he retired in 1975. Facing voter outrage, the House in 1976 prohibited cash-outs as of January 1977.

The proposal "deeply angered many members," the reform's chief author, David R. Obey, D-Wis., told reporters at the time. Doing most of the grumbling were senior members who considered themselves underpaid to begin with. Some members defended their large cash-outs by saying they were reimbursing themselves for unspecified job-related expenses.

In 1978, the year after the House stopped allowing cash-outs, some members' postage purchases began to rise sharply.

Before 1977, members' office budgets had a $1,140 stamp allowance. Implementing the Obey reforms, the House killed the stamp allowance, reasoning that members needed few stamps because they could mail virtually anything with their franking privilege.

But the House also did away with the whole allowance system and gave members consolidated budgets so each could decide how much to spend on what — without capping how much they could spend on stamps.

Numerous members then began to report buying more stamps than ever. Some bought thousands of dollars' worth right before leaving office.

In 1978, the first full year that members' individual spending habits were detailed, Rostenkowski reported buying $4,670 worth — more than four times what the old stamp allowance gave him.

That was also the year, prosecutors asserted in court documents, that the stamp scam began.

About that time, Rostenkowski and other members also were angry over new rules that would soon trim their ability to supplement their pay with speaking fees. Rostenkowski earned $25,000 in honoraria in 1978 but would be limited a year later to about $9,000.

Rostenkowski actively opposed those limits; a Chicago Sun-Times report from 1979 said he "rants and raves about the inherent unfairness of the limitation and doesn't give up trying to get it changed."

In 1979 and 1980, Rostenkowski's annual stamp purchase total dipped below $2,000, but by 1986, it had jumped to $6,900; the chairman's total peaked at $8,000 in 1988. A 1992 CQ survey of stamp purchases found that Rostenkowski reported buying more by far than any other member in 1986-92.

ROSTENKOWSKI STATEMENT

Rostenkowski ended nearly a week of silence on the matter July 24 by calling a rare Saturday news conference to deny that he had done anything wrong, to promise to push his legislative agenda and to announce that he had hired one of Washington's most aggressive defense lawyers, Robert S. Bennett. Bennett had served as special counsel to the Senate Ethics Committee in the cases of Harrison A. Williams Jr., D-N.J.; Dave Durenberger, R-Minn.; and the five senators rebuked for dealings with thrift operator Charles H. Keating Jr. He had also represented former Defense Secretary Caspar W. Weinberger, whom President George Bush pardoned in 1992 for his role in the Iran-contra affair, and Democratic insider Clark Clifford, implicated in a banking scandal.

Rostenkowski made the following statement:

"Because of the many unfair, false and baseless allegations that have been made recently about me, I felt it was the appropriate time to make a brief public statement.

"Since there is a pending criminal investigation, I have been advised by my counsel that I am limited in what I can appropriately say. However, I want to make it absolutely clear that I have committed no crime and have engaged in no illegal or unethical conduct.

"This has been a very difficult time for me and my family. I am frustrated and angry with these false allegations.

"For 41 years, I have honestly and proudly served my country, my state and the city of Chicago. Those who know me best would agree.

"While there are a few who are trying to take political advantage of the present situation and others who may be trying to settle old scores, my family and I want to thank our many friends, constituents and colleagues on both sides of the aisle who know I have been an honest public servant and who are supporting us. I want to assure all of them that I will not allow the current situation to interfere with the important legislative work that I and others are presently engaged in and which is so important to the American people.

"Last night I spoke with Bob Bennett, an attorney who is experienced in matters of this kind. Mr. Bennett and his partner, Carl Rauh, will be representing me in this matter. I am presumed innocent. I have been charged with nothing. But most importantly, I am, in fact, innocent of any wrongdoing."

Rostenkowski did not answer questions.

CALLS FOR MORE INVESTIGATIONS

Some House Republicans, over the objections of their party's leader on the House ethics committee, began agitating for an immediate ethics investigation of Rota's allegations. The proposal's chief sponsor, freshman Ernest Jim Istook Jr., R-Okla., with 17 cosponsors, on Aug. 4 introduced H Res 238, which would require such an inquiry.

The ethics committee's top Republican, Fred Grandy of Iowa, had tried to persuade Istook to abandon the idea. The committee had agreed to a Justice Department request that it delay an ethics inquiry until the local U.S. attorney's office finished its criminal probe. Grandy argued that it would be inappropriate and probably fruitless to begin an ethics investigation until federal prosecutors dropped their objection.

As a resolution dealing with the rights and integrity of the whole House, Istook's measure could be called up on the floor with two days' notice. Istook said he would demand a vote on the resolution after the House returned from a break Sept. 8, but he did not do so by the end of the session.

On Oct. 20, House Administration Committee leaders called for an ethics inquiry of the House Finance Office after employees told them that the office violated its rules in overseeing Rostenkowski's payroll. The move came after House employees discovered they could not locate Rostenkowski payroll records that had been subpoenaed.

At a hearing on the matter before the House Administration Oversight Subcommittee on Oct. 20, the employees admitted that the Finance Office had violated its own rules in doing favors for Rostenkowski. He was allowed to have the same payroll overseer for years, though office policy required a switch every two years, Finance Office Chief Michael Heny Jr. told the panel. Heny did not know who had granted the exception but said he allowed it to continue until 1993, when his office was put under the House's administrator, Leonard P. Wishart III.

After the documents turned up missing, Wishart fired Rostenkowski's payroll counselor, Harrison Bruce Avner, because he was found to have altered his own tax withholding amount. Avner said he complained "quite a few times" about being forced to handle Rostenkowski's payroll because "he's a hard person to work with." He admitted keeping signed blank payroll forms in his desk — another violation. He did not explain why documents were missing.

Wishart said a spot check of other files found only one document missing. Rostenkowski's file had 210 documents missing, all forms used to alter employees' pay. "I don't know whether you could characterize it as just sloppy record-keeping, because it's isolated to one counselor and one single account," Wishart said.

U.S. Attorney Holder decided not to seek an indictment before the grand jury's term expired Oct. 29. Holder wanted to continue probing unspecified new allegations, officials said. ∎

Indictments, Convictions Plague Congress

Amid a continuing swirl of bad publicity about members' behavior, both chambers changed leadership of their ethics committees. But the focus of activity was in the courts. Two senators were indicted on criminal charges; a House member was acquitted after a volatile trial; two of the House's former officers pleaded guilty to crimes stemming from their service; and three former House members were convicted and sentenced to prison.

The Senate, meanwhile, spent two agonizing days in November debating allegations of sexual harassment and improper involvement with lobbyists against Bob Packwood, R-Ore., before deciding to enforce a subpoena for Packwood's diaries. *(Packwood investigation, p. 55)*

The two indicted senators were Dave Durenberger, R-Minn., and Kay Bailey Hutchison, R-Texas. They were the first senators indicted in office since 1980, when Harrison A. Williams Jr., D-N.J., was charged with taking bribes in the FBI's Abscam sting operation. He was convicted in 1981 and resigned in 1982. Durenberger was the ninth and Hutchison the 10th sitting senator to be indicted. *(Williams, 1982 Almanac, p. 509)*

After an arduous recruitment by party leaders, the new membership of the Senate Ethics Committee was approved by the chamber Jan. 26. The new chairman was Richard H. Bryan, D-Nev., the only member of the panel who had served on it in the previous Congress. The vice chairman was Republican Mitch McConnell of Kentucky. Other Democrats named to the panel were Barbara A. Mikulski of Maryland and Tom Daschle of South Dakota. The other Republicans were Ted Stevens of Alaska and Robert C. Smith of New Hampshire. (Stevens later quit the panel and was replaced by Larry E. Craig of Idaho.)

The committee's two leaders in the 102nd Congress had left the Senate, and three other senators quit the panel, which was evenly divided between three Democrats and three Republicans.

Bryan, a former public defender and prosecutor, was once Nevada's attorney general. McConnell, a deputy assistant attorney general in the Ford administration, was best known as the GOP's point man against Democratic campaign finance proposals.

In the House, Jim McDermott, D-Wash., was named chairman of the Committee on Standards of Official Conduct on Feb. 4. McDermott replaced Louis Stokes, D-Ohio, who had agreed to serve as chairman during the 102nd Congress provided he could leave the panel afterward. McDermott, a psychiatrist, was on the subcommittee that investigated the House bank overdraft scandal. For Republicans, Fred Grandy of Iowa took over the ranking spot.

DURENBERGER INDICTED

A grand jury on April 2 indicted Sen. Durenberger on two felony counts for charging the Senate thousands of dollars in rent for staying in a Minneapolis condominium he secretly owned.

On Dec. 3, a federal judge dismissed the charges, declaring that the Justice Department, in presenting the case to the grand jury, violated a constitutional provision barring prosecutions of members of Congress based on what lawmakers said during official speeches and debates.

New indictments against Durenberger on the same charges were announced by the Justice Department on Feb. 25, 1994. Meanwhile, Durenberger announced Sept. 16, 1993, that he would not seek re-election in 1994.

Background of Indictment

Federal prosecutors had been investigating the condo arrangement since 1990, when the Senate formally denounced Durenberger for that and other financial actions found to be "clearly and unequivocally unethical." Durenberger did not dispute the findings of the Ethics Committee, accepted the Senate's punishment and asked forgiveness. *(1990 Almanac, p. 98)*

The April 2 indictment said Durenberger made $3,825 in false claims for stays at the condo — $85 a night for 45 nights from April to August 1987. He was indicted on one count of conspiring to make the false claims and one count of actually making them.

Indicted along with Durenberger were Michael C. Mahoney, the Minnesota attorney who advised him on the matter, and Paul P. Overgaard, the senator's friend and 1978 campaign manager. Overgaard's Minnesota company purportedly bought Durenberger's condo in the main

transaction under scrutiny in the indictment.

Rick Evans, Durenberger's top aide, said the indictment came after Durenberger refused to plead guilty to misdemeanor charges during months of negotiations with the Justice Department.

"What they have said is that if Sen. Durenberger would plead guilty to two misdemeanors . . . they would not prosecute him, they would not prosecute his two friends and would not insist on any plea from his two friends," Evans said before the indictment was announced. Durenberger accused the Justice Department of "trying to coerce me into a false confession."

The charges against Durenberger carried possible penalties of 10 years in prison and $500,000 in fines. His associates, who were charged with perjury and making false statements to the Senate Ethics Committee during its investigation of the matter, faced 20 years and $1 million in fines.

Prosecutors apparently declined to pursue the broader case against Durenberger that was outlined in the Ethics Committee findings on the condominium transaction. The committee found that from 1983 to 1989, Durenberger had billed the Senate $40,055 for lodging in the condominium — "essentially his personal residence in Minneapolis." He was ordered to repay the money.

The Ethics Committee's special counsel, Robert S. Bennett, concluded that Durenberger had engaged in a series of transactions transferring ownership of the condo "wholly as a means of permitting the senator to claim Senate per diem reimbursements."

But Bennett also declared that there was "insufficient evidence supporting a finding that Sen. Durenberger acted with criminal intent" — a finding Durenberger said prosecutors should not have ignored.

The indictment focused on several months in 1987 after a partnership Durenberger had formed in 1983 to collect condo reimbursements dissolved and the senator sought ways to continue collecting reimbursements.

It said that Durenberger and his two friends "did devise and carry out a scheme by which the cost of defendant Durenberger's condominium would continue to be paid by the Senate." They allegedly "hid defendant Durenberger's ownership interest in the condominium by making it appear he was renting his condominium from defendant Overgaard's company, ISC, at a time that ISC did not own the property." When the company later did buy the condo, the indictment said, Overgaard agreed Durenberger could eventually buy it back at the same price — "effectively allowing him to 'park' the property with ISC," the Justice Department said in a statement.

The indictment quoted a "totally confidential" 1989 letter from Overgaard to Durenberger in which Overgaard expressed fear that he would be accused of "participating in a sham transaction by which you collect per diem from the Senate for a residence you actually own. That is certainly a conclusion that could be reached as things stand now."

Durenberger was indicted in Washington; on May 19, a judge agreed with his motion to move the trial to Minnesota.

Paternity Suit

Durenberger dodged one of the shadows clouding his political career when a Minnesota judge on Aug. 24 dismissed a civil suit filed against him in 1992 by a Minnesota woman who accused him of raping her and fathering her child in 1963 when he served as her divorce attorney. On Aug. 3, Durenberger said that blood tests by two independent Minnesota laboratories showed that he was not the father. Durenberger had repeatedly denied the charges.

Indictment Quashed

In a ruling dated Dec. 3 and released Dec. 6 in St. Paul, Minn., U.S. District Judge Warren K. Urbom threw out the indictments of Durenberger on grounds that Justice Department lawyers had violated a constitutional provision barring prosecutions of members of Congress based on what they said during official speeches and debates. By then, Durenberger had announced his plans to retire.

Urbom acted after finding that 11 pages from the Ethics Committee's report and the report of its special counsel had been presented to the grand jury — material that Urbom said was inadmissible under the Constitution's provision that members "shall not be questioned" outside Congress "for any speech or debate in either house."

"The defendant contends and I agree," Urbom wrote, "that if a member of the Senate believes that his statements to the committee or the findings of the committee and its special counsel could be introduced as evidence against him one day in a grand jury proceeding, then the intimidation caused by the prospect of criminal liability will chill senators and severely undermine the ability of the committee to effectively investigate and discipline members."

Lawyers involved in the case said the decision did not greatly expand members' constitutional immunity. Instead, it merely followed past rulings that members' statements to the ethics committees could not be used against them.

Durenberger had argued the case in August on broader grounds, contending that prosecutors violated the "speech or debate" clause by presenting to the grand jury witness affidavits submitted to the Ethics Committee by Durenberger. On Aug. 6, the Senate had agreed to join Durenberger's motion. A federal magistrate rejected that argument, and Urbom did not disturb that ruling, said Thomas C. Green, the senator's attorney.

But Urbom did grant Durenberger's request that the court review the grand jury record to make sure the jurors saw no privileged material from the Ethics Committee reports. Urbom acted even though two prosecutors from Justice's Public Integrity Section "emphatically denied that the grand jury had been exposed to . . . the reports."

But, Urbom found, 11 pages from the reports had been presented "as part of a larger exhibit not prepared by the government or ever referred to by the government" — apparently material turned over in response to a subpoena.

The judge rebuked the two prosecutors, Robert P. Storch and Raymond N. Hulser, for what he said was either unethical "overzealous prosecution" or "repeated inadvertence bordering on recklessness." The Justice Department said its Office of Professional Responsibility would investigate the prosecutors' conduct.

Durenberger called on the Justice Department to drop the case. "Concluding this case immediately would be an act of justice and fairness," he said. But Justice did not agree. "We read [the judge's opinion] as an invitation to re-indict," said Justice Department spokesman John Russell. On Dec. 29, the indictments against Mahoney and Overgaard were dismissed at the request of the Justice Department.

HUTCHISON INDICTED

Less than four months after Republican Hutchison was elected to fill a Senate vacancy, a Texas grand jury indicted her on charges that she had misused state government resources for her own purposes. In a saga that lasted into

1994, the charges were dismissed and reinstated twice. Finally, on Feb. 11, 1994, Hutchison was exonerated of all charges on orders of the judge in the case.

Hutchison defeated Bob Krueger in a June 5 special election with 67 percent of the vote. Krueger had been appointed in January to fill the vacancy created when Democrat Lloyd Bentsen became President Clinton's Treasury secretary. *(Hutchison, p. 6-A)*

A grand jury in Austin indicted Hutchison and two former aides Sept. 27 on five felony charges of misconduct stemming from her 2½-year tenure as Texas state treasurer. The indictment charged that Hutchison used state employees, facilities, equipment and supplies for political and personal errands, then ordered the destruction of incriminating computer tapes and records.

The charges were brought to light in 1992 when the Houston Post quoted documents and sources saying Hutchison used state computers to keep fundraising records and to write thank-you letters to major contributors. Other news reports said she used state phones to make political calls, and former employees said she ordered them to help decorate her home.

The charges were aired during the campaign, but Travis County District Attorney Ronnie Earle had declined to acknowledge that an investigation was under way.

On June 10, five days after the election, Earle's staff entered the treasurer's office, seized boxes of documents and subpoenaed employees. Hutchison appeared before the grand jury but would not say whether she testified or invoked the Fifth Amendment.

The charges carried possible penalties of 61 years in prison and $43,000 in fines.

Hutchison immediately denounced the indictment as "another chapter in the sleazy campaign tactics employed by Democrats." At a news conference in Washington on Sept. 27, she said, "This indictment is designed solely to damage my re-election effort next year, by trying to tarnish my reputation and encourage challengers."

Earle quickly denied any partisan motive. "Had we intended to be political, we would have conducted this investigation publicly during the campaign," he said.

Indictments Dismissed, Reinstated

The indictments against Hutchison were thrown out Oct. 26 by a state judge in Austin because one of the grand jurors had an outstanding warrant for his arrest relating to a years-old misdemeanor charge and thus was not qualified to sit on the grand jury.

On Dec. 8, a grand jury reindicted Hutchison on four felony counts and one misdemeanor count similar to the original charges. But those counts, too, ran into trouble.

Visiting Judge John Onion Jr., named to handle the politically sensitive case, dismissed four of the new indictments Dec. 29, saying they were too vague. But he gave prosecutors time to redraw the indictments, and they did so. The charges were reinstated, and Hutchison pleaded innocent to the first counts Jan. 7.

The case did not go to the Senate Ethics Committee because it involved actions taken before Hutchison was a senator.

HATCH PROBED, CLEARED

The Senate Ethics Committee announced Nov. 20 that it had ended a seven-month probe of Sen. Orrin G. Hatch, R-Utah, with a unanimous finding that Hatch had acted neither illegally nor unethically in his dealings with the scandal-ridden Bank of Credit and Commerce International (BCCI). The committee said it had found "no credible evidence" that Hatch had violated any laws or Senate rules. The committee also said it found no "reason to believe that Sen. Hatch engaged in any [illegal] conduct."

BCCI was closed in 1991 in a global crackdown after investigators of various governments uncovered widespread fraud involving billions of dollars and various other crimes, including bribes to leaders around the world, arms trafficking, income tax evasion, smuggling and illicit bank acquisitions.

Contacts between Hatch, one of his aides and key insiders of BCCI had been the subject of numerous news reports since 1991. Hatch called for an ethics probe in August 1992 after denying wrongdoing. The Ethics Committee announced April 7 that it had opened a "preliminary inquiry" into the matter.

Hatch had released a report in August 1991 detailing links between Democratic lawmakers and a failed Miami thrift with ties to BCCI. News organizations later began focusing on links between Hatch and BCCI. The news reports cited several connections:

● Hatch on Feb. 22, 1990, made a speech on the Senate floor defending a Justice Department plea bargain with BCCI in a Tampa, Fla., money laundering case — a settlement under attack by other lawmakers as too lenient. The speech was based on drafts supplied to Hatch by lawyers working for BCCI, including Robert A. Altman, a Washington power-broker and former president of First American Bancshares Inc., which had been secretly controlled by BCCI. Altman was indicted and later acquitted for his ties to BCCI.

● Shortly after his BCCI floor speech, Hatch called a top BCCI official seeking a loan for a friend, Monzer Hourani, a Texas developer who in 1988 began administering a trust in which Hatch invested $10,000. Hourani never got the loan.

● Hatch had several meetings with a Lebanese national, Mohammad Hammoud, who was later found to be a key front man for BCCI. BCCI lawyers later said that it was Hammoud who pressured them to meet with Hatch, who had known him since the early 1980s. Hatch said he did not know of Hammoud's connection to BCCI and had talked to him only about investing in Utah and about Middle East political issues.

● A former Hatch aide, Michael Pillsbury, had numerous contacts with BCCI officials and provided them with public relations and lobbying advice while Hammoud was paying him to write a book.

The committee said it had "subpoenaed and reviewed documents of eight individuals and entities and conducted 10 depositions." But it did not include any details to support its decision. Hatch responded to the committee's decision by saying: "I respect their hard work and am pleased that their finding is unequivocal."

Altman and his mentor in Democratic politics, former Defense Secretary Clark M. Clifford, in 1993 escaped criminal charges for their roles as officers of First American. They had been indicted in federal and New York state courts. In March, Clifford, 86, was found to be too ill to stand trial.

The Justice Department on April 7 announced that it would drop federal charges against both men in deference to the state charges. Altman went to trial in state court in New York on March 30. The judge dismissed several charges July 29, and a jury acquitted him Aug. 14.

INOUYE PROBED, CLEARED

The Senate Ethics Committee announced April 7 that it had decided against pursuing sexual misconduct allegations against Sen. Daniel K. Inouye, D-Hawaii.

A complaint against Inouye had been lodged in 1992 by the Women's Equal Rights Legal Defense and Education Fund, whose complaint about Packwood led to an Ethics Committee inquiry into sexual misconduct allegations against him. (1992 Almanac, p. 55)

The committee decided against pursuing the Inouye case because, unlike the Packwood case, no alleged victim would cooperate.

The charges against Inouye surfaced during his 1992 campaign for election to a sixth term. His opponent aired a television ad in which Inouye's longtime hairstylist, in an audiotape made without her knowledge, said the senator had forced himself on her 17 years earlier. The woman, Lenore Kwock, declined to call the incident a rape but said she submitted only after he grabbed her, removed her clothing and ignored her protests. Kwock repeated the allegation to reporters but said she had forgiven Inouye. She successfully demanded that the ad be pulled.

After Kwock's allegations were aired, Hawaii state Rep. Annelle Amaral, a Democrat, told reporters that nine other women had contacted her with sexual harassment allegations about Inouye, ranging from improper touching to demands for sex through intimidation. She said she knew the identity of two of the women, but neither wanted to be publicly named.

Inouye denied the charges but said he welcomed the Ethics Committee review of the matter.

The committee's statement said Kwock declined to "voluntarily participate" in an inquiry of Inouye. Amaral told the panel that the women she had talked to "were unwilling to be identified to the committee or the public."

The panel also asked Amaral about reports that she had been denied a committee chair because of her remarks about Inouye, but she "informed the committee she had no indication that her loss of any legislative committee assignment was due to any action on the part of Sen. Inouye."

LEGAL CLOUD LIFTED FROM ROBB

A federal grand jury in Virginia voted Jan. 12 not to indict that state's Democratic senator, Charles S. Robb, on charges of conspiracy and obstruction of justice.

A 19-month investigation had damaged Robb's straight-arrow image, and even he expressed surprise at the jury's decision. Appearing with his wife, Lynda Bird Johnson Robb, at a packed news conference, he vowed to rebuild the coalition that had elected him governor in 1981 and senator in 1988 in time for 1994 elections. "I know it will take a long time to get over," Robb said.

Robb maintained his innocence throughout the investigation, even after three aides implicated him in plea agreements they made to criminal charges. The case centered on the release of an illegally recorded cellular phone call involving the state's Democratic governor, L. Douglas Wilder. (1992 Almanac, p. 54)

Robb himself had predicted he would be indicted after a repeat appearance before the grand jury Dec. 17, 1992.

Robb's testimony may have helped convince the grand jurors that he was innocent, but it did not stop them from indicting an associate of his, Virginia Beach businessman Bruce Thompson, on three felony charges, including witness tampering, related to the case. Issued Jan. 12, the

Thompson indictment included allegations that Robb declined to listen to the tapes, although he knew their contents, in order to maintain "plausible deniability." Thompson pleaded guilty March 17 to a misdemeanor count.

The case involved an alleged scheme to disclose a taped phone conversation that Robb aides perceived as damaging to Wilder, a longtime rival. In the tape, recorded in October 1988, Wilder speculated that rumors about Robb's attendance at Virginia Beach parties where cocaine was used would ruin his career. The tape was leaked to the media more than two years later, when rumors about Robb's private life were refueled by a beauty queen's claim that she had had an affair with Robb.

Robb's aides apparently believed that the rumors would be discounted if they could be traced to a rival, particularly when they seemed so inconsistent with the image of the square-jawed former Marine.

On Jan. 12, 1994, Wilder gave Robb another surprise when he announced that he would not challenge Robb in 1994 for his Senate seat.

FORD ACQUITTED

Rep. Harold E. Ford, D-Tenn., was acquitted April 9 of charges that he traded his political influence for sham loans, ending a decadelong legal odyssey that had stripped Ford of his power base in Congress and strained race relations in Memphis. The case also drew the fledgling Clinton administration into an imbroglio involving allegations of racism and political favoritism.

Ending three days of deliberations after a five-week trial in federal court in Memphis, a jury of 11 whites and one black found Tennessee's first black congressman not guilty of one count of conspiracy, three counts of bank fraud and 14 counts of mail fraud. The jury also acquitted two co-defendants.

U.S. District Judge Jerome Turner earlier in the week had thrown out one mail fraud count against Ford and 11 counts against the other two.

Since he was indicted in 1987, Ford had accused prosecutors of pursuing a racist vendetta because he was a politically successful black. He was repeatedly re-elected by healthy margins despite the charges. He initially was tried in 1990, but that case ended in a hung jury, with eight blacks voting to acquit and four whites voting to convict. (1987 Almanac, p. 32; 1990 Almanac, p. 107)

The final acquittal allowed Ford to resume his chairmanship of an important subcommittee, the Ways and Means Subcommittee on Human Resources, which had jurisdiction over welfare. Under Democratic Caucus rules, he had to give up that post when he was indicted.

Ties to Butcher Brothers

Ford's legal troubles stemmed from the 1983 failure of a system of Tennessee banks controlled by two politically connected brothers, Jacob F. and C. H. Butcher Jr. The two brothers pleaded guilty to crimes connected to the failures and served multi-year prison terms.

On trial in 1993 were Ford and two Butcher bank insiders. The three were accused of conspiring with the Butchers to defraud several Butcher banks by obtaining bogus loans to finance Ford's "extravagant and lavish lifestyle" while Ford "would use his political influence as a United States congressman to further the political and business goals" of the Butchers. The loans totaled more than $1 million, but the exact amount was unclear because some

were used to pay off others. After the banks failed, Ford settled the largest debt, $350,000, for $25,000.

Ford insisted that the loans were legitimate business transactions related to his family funeral home. He admitted using some of the money to pay off personal debts because he said the funeral home owed him the money. Ford said he was only a friend of the Butchers'. "At no time, at no time, have I been a congressional liaison or anything else but a friend," he said.

Black Pressure on Clinton

The judge who oversaw the first trial, Odell Horton, who was black, later concluded that the black jurors had been subjected to direct and indirect pressure to acquit Ford, including Ford's charges of governmental racism, according to a Justice Department summary of the case.

Acting on a prosecution request that the second jury be protected from intimidation, Horton in 1991 ordered the jury to be selected from the Jackson area, which was less than 20 percent black, instead of the Memphis area (about 40 percent black), and bused 75 miles to Memphis for the trial. Ford appealed Horton's decision to the 6th U.S. Circuit Court of Appeals but lost, and the Supreme Court declined to review the case.

Jury selection for the retrial began Feb. 1 and took until Feb. 10. After extensive questioning about potential biases, a panel of 11 whites and one black was chosen, along with six white alternates.

The Congressional Black Caucus pressured the Clinton administration to reverse the Justice Department's stance in support of the jury selection process. In a letter Feb. 3, caucus Chairman Kweisi Mfume, D-Md., asked Clinton to help "correct an injustice that is about to occur to our colleague" and called the jury selection process "a dangerous precedent, particularly for trials of minority political and public figures."

Black Caucus members took the issue to the House floor, delivering 15 one-minute speeches between Feb. 4 and Feb. 17.

The White House, responding to personal entreaties from Ford and his allies, including Jesse L. Jackson, referred the matter to the Justice Department, where it was handled by Webster Hubbell, the president's liaison to Justice.

Hubbell — a friend of Clinton's and a former law partner of first lady Hillary Rodham Clinton's — arranged for Ford's lawyer, William McDaniels, to argue before a top Justice official that the Jackson jury be replaced with one from Memphis. Hubbell also arranged for 26 members of the black caucus to meet for 45 minutes Feb. 18 with him and Stuart M. Gerson, a political appointee from the Bush administration whom Clinton named as acting attorney general.

Prosecutors on the case met with Hubbell and Gerson on Feb. 19 to argue against changing Justice's position.

On Feb. 19, Gerson announced that he was backing Ford's motion to select another jury from Memphis. "I am not willing to say on behalf of the United States that justice cannot be served from a Memphis jury or, indeed, from the jury in any city," Gerson said in a five-page statement. He denied that prosecutors were racially motivated in their handling of the case or jury selection. At the same time, he called the evidence against Ford and the others "factually overwhelming." Gerson apologized to Judge Turner for "this unusual and late Justice Department intercession."

The prosecutors in Tennessee were stunned. Clancy and

his partner on the case, Gary Humble, asked to be taken off the case (although they later agreed to rejoin it). The U.S. attorney in Memphis, Edward G. Bryant, a Bush administration appointee, quit. "I saw an exception being made for a congressman," Bryant said.

Officials at the White House and the Justice Department insisted that Gerson acted on his own without pressure from Clinton or his inner circle.

Turner did not take kindly to the Justice Department's stance, presented in his court Feb. 22 by a government lawyer flown in from Washington. "It is a sad day, in my view, when the acting attorney general and a representative of the White House give in to a demand that a jury ... must be selected by race," he said. "Perhaps just as disturbing is the appearance that the Department of Justice has created by this motion that justice in the courts of the United States can be handled differently if one is a member of the United States Congress."

His decision: "It is unlawful to exclude jurors because of their race, and that is what the court is being asked to do, regardless of the gloss that is being placed on this request. This the court will not do."

Turner initially refused a defense request for a short delay, but then Ford, who previously had been hospitalized with chest pains, "began wincing and holding his chest," according to a story in the Memphis Commercial Appeal. He was taken to a local hospital, where he remained until Feb. 25, his office said.

Ford's lawyers appealed Turner's decision to the 6th Circuit, but the Justice Department on Feb. 23 refused to back him. The trial began March 1.

Cleared in House Bank Scandal

In the meantime, Ford on Nov. 4 became the last sitting member to receive a letter from the Justice Department exonerating him from wrongdoing in its investigation of the House bank. Ford had 388 overdrafts.

In 1992, Attorney General William P. Barr appointed a special counsel, retired federal judge Malcolm R. Wilkey, to investigate the scandal at the defunct House bank. The scandal had broken after a GAO audit in 1991 disclosed that members had routinely been allowed to overdraw their accounts without penalty. *(Bank, 1992 Almanac, p. 23)*

Wilkey's investigators reviewed records relating to overdrafts and sent letters to members informing them when they were no longer under scrutiny. *(House bank, 1992 Almanac, p. 23)*

McDADE

A federal judge upheld a 1992 indictment on corruption charges against Joseph M. McDade of Pennsylvania, the ranking Republican on the House Appropriations Committee. McDade, who denied wrongdoing, appealed the May ruling, maintaining that the indictment violated the limited immunity afforded members of Congress by the Constitution.

After a four-year investigation, McDade had been indicted May 5, 1992, by a federal grand jury on charges of enriching himself with more than $100,000 worth of illegal gratuities, bribes and favors extorted from defense firms seeking federal contracts.

The indictment connected the allegedly illicit gains — mostly subsidized trips, campaign contributions, speaking fees, scholarship money for his son and assorted gifts — to official favors McDade provided to the contractors both when he was the top GOP member of the Small Business

Delegates Get 'Symbolic' Floor Vote

House Republicans lost a legal challenge to a new House procedure that allowed the delegates from the U.S. territories and the District of Columbia to participate in some floor votes. But they won a larger point, as federal judges agreed that the delegates' votes could never determine the outcome of legislation. And they exploited rules giving them opportunities to wipe out the delegates' votes in many cases.

The controversy concerned an amendment to the rules of the House, first adopted by Democrats in December 1992 and then, with a significant modification, approved by the full House on Jan. 5. It allowed the resident commissioner of Puerto Rico, the delegate from the District of Columbia and the delegates from the U.S. territories and possessions (Puerto Rico, Guam and American Samoa) to vote whenever the House was considering legislation in the Committee of the Whole — a parliamentary framework under which the entire House met to debate and amend important legislation.

The delegates already had the right to vote in the House's regular committees. *(Rules changes, p. 8; background, 1992 Almanac, p. 14)*

The new rule was the brainchild of Delegate Eleanor Holmes Norton of the District of Columbia, who convinced her Democratic colleagues that there was no legal distinction between voting in committees, which delegates were already allowed to do, and voting on the floor in the Committee of the Whole.

Leaders made a key modification shortly before the rule was formally adopted by the full House. Designed to placate members who were nervous about giving equal voting privileges to delegates who often represented fewer citizens or areas that did not pay federal taxes, it required an automatic revote if the delegates' votes made the difference between winning and losing. With the exception of D.C. residents, voters represented by delegates did not pay federal income taxes. Their populations varied from 47,000 on American Samoa to 3.6 million on Puerto Rico. Most congressional districts had more than 550,000 constituents.

Republicans were not assuaged. All five of the new votes would come from Democrats — effectively halving the 10-vote gain the GOP won in the 1992 elections.

"It's a joke. It's an abuse of power," said Minority Whip Newt Gingrich, R-Ga.

Republicans ridiculed the provision requiring automatic re-votes. "When they vote when it counts, it does not count," Robert S. Walker, R-Pa., said of the delegates, "and when it does not count, it counts."

GOP COURT CHALLENGE

House Minority Leader Robert H. Michel, Ill., joined by a dozen other GOP members and three citizens, challenged the constitutionality of the new voting procedure in a suit filed Jan. 7 in U.S. District Court in Washington.

At a Feb. 9 hearing, they argued that the rule violated the Constitution's first article by granting delegates legislative power. Article I stipulated that all legislative power was vested in the House and Senate and those bodies were "composed of members chosen ... by the people of the several states."

Republicans offered three main arguments at the hearing:

● The Committee of the Whole was not a committee, as the Democrats claimed. It was, they said, tantamount to the full House and should be governed by the Constitution's provisions detailing House powers.

● A vote in the Committee of the Whole effectively franchised citizens of the territories and the District of Columbia at the expense of state citizens and their representatives, whose voting power was diminished by the greater vote totals.

● Delegates were granted committee voting privileges by law, not House rule, and the House could not expand those powers without statutory authority granted by the full Congress and the president.

Democrats' arguments in support of the rule were presented in a brief submitted by House General Counsel Steven R. Ross and by Deputy General Counsel Charles Tiefer, who represented House Clerk Donnald K. Anderson and the delegates in the case.

Tiefer, whose 1989 book "Congressional Practice and Procedure" was cited in both briefs, said at the hearing that the Constitution allowed the House to "determine the rules of its proceedings." Furthermore, he said, the delegates' role in Congress had been open to interpretation.

According to the defendants' brief, the Northwest Ordinance of 1787 gave the first territory delegate "a seat in Congress." The next delegate, William Henry Harrison, also from the Northwest Territory, forged the passage of the Land Act of 1800 and chaired several committees. Other delegates gave up their committee vote to secure other congressional privileges. Delegates secured the vote in standing committees in the early 1970s.

Ross and Tiefer also argued that the Committee of the Whole's actions were "merely advisory" and did not determine the outcome of legislation.

U.S. District Judge Harold H. Greene ruled on March 8, in *Michel v. Anderson,* that the rule was constitutional, but only because of the provision requiring an immediate, members-only revote on any issue decided by delegate participation.

The decision gave a technical victory to Democratic leaders who backed the rule, but one that the court said was legislatively hollow.

"The bottom line is that a delegate's vote can never make the difference between winning and losing," Greene wrote. He declared that delegate votes would be "plainly unconstitutional" without the provision for automatic re-votes.

With the provision, he said, delegate votes were "symbolic" and worth "nothing" in the give-and-take of legislative drafting.

While hailing the judge's decision to hear their challenge and his warnings about the unconstitutionality of full voting privileges, Michel and several other Republicans appealed the decision, filing briefs July 26.

On Jan. 25, 1994, the U.S. Court of Appeals for the District of Columbia Circuit reaffirmed Judge Greene's ruling. As Greene had, the appeals court issued a preemptive warning to those who might want to expand delegate voting privileges.

Republicans said they were unlikely to appeal.

EXTRA VOTES IN HOUSE

As soon as the delegates cast their first votes, the Republicans began a parliamentary counterattack. On Feb. 3, the House took up the family and medical leave bill (HR 1) and considered amendments in the Committee of the Whole. Delegates helped vote down two Republican amendments.

But after two amendments were approved, Republicans were able to take advantage of a House rule that allowed members to demand a new vote on any amendment adopted in the Committee of the Whole. On those votes, taken by the full House, the delegates could not vote. *(Votes 19, 20, p. 6-H)*

Republicans kept up the pattern throughout the year, almost always demanding a second vote on an amendment adopted in the Committee of the Whole. On occasion they would allow an amendment to be approved by voice vote, then demand a roll call after the Committee of the Whole procedure was finished.

This enabled the GOP to wipe out the delegates' votes even when they did not determine the outcome, as required to trigger the automatic revote. The discretionary opportunity to call for a second vote did not apply, however, to any amendments rejected in the Committee of the Whole.

Republicans said the repeat votes underscored for voters the unjust Democratic autocracy in the House. Democratic leaders maintained that the ploy made the GOP look dilatory and on the side of gridlock.

No vote was automatically retaken in 1993, because the delegates' votes never determined the outcome of a vote. But revotes demanded by Republicans were common, and they contributed to an extraordinary number of House roll calls. In 1993, the House took 597 votes (excluding quorum calls), 26 percent more than in 1992, and the highest number of recorded votes since 1979. Sixty-nine were revotes or separate votes on amendments that had been approved in the Committee of the Whole.

(The outcome changed in four of the 69 times a second vote was taken.)

Delegates Defend Votes

Delegates said the GOP was unfairly singling them out for partisan reasons. They called the floor tactics annoying, mean-spirited, even harassment. "If the 435 members have to be protected from the wiles of five delegates . . . then the country's in trouble," said Delegate Robert A. Underwood of Guam.

The delegates maintained that the votes were worth the fight. Norton insisted that the voting privilege increased the delegates' participation in the legislative process. "It has made me more effective because of the many kinds of interaction I now have with my colleagues on the House floor," Norton said.

But GOP members said the improved ties and some votes were evidence that the delegates had more power than they should.

For example, Gerald B. H. Solomon of New York, the GOP's leader on the Rules Committee, said delegates could be responsible for a House vote to kill the Selective Service System. On June 28, delegates contributed four "nays" to a 202-207 vote trying to preserve funding for the military draft office during consideration of the VA-HUD appropriations bill. Had the vote been 202-203, Solomon said, "I would have been able to turn that around" before the vote closed. *(Vote 278, p. 68-H)* ∎

Hill Representatives Barred From FEC

A federal appeals court Oct. 22 held that the composition of the Federal Election Commission (FEC) was unconstitutional. The court ruled that Congress exceeded its authority when it put representatives of the House and Senate on the independent commission as non-voting *ex officio* members.

In *Federal Election Commission v. the National Rifle Association*, a panel of judges from the U.S. Court of Appeals for the District of Columbia Circuit struck down the provision of the Federal Election Campaign Act of 1974 (PL 93-443) that empowered the *ex officio* members. *(1974 Almanac, p. 611)*

"The mere presence of agents of Congress on an entity with executive powers offends the Constitution," wrote the court.

Citing a clause in the Federal Election Campaign Act making any provision severable, the court said the elimination of the *ex officio* members would remedy the situation.

On Oct. 26, the six FEC commissioners appointed by the president voted unanimously to exclude the *ex officio* members from all non-public hearings. They also reclaimed all confidential documents, which had been accessible to the congressional representatives.

On Nov. 2, the FEC voted to appeal the decision to the Supreme Court.

Technically, the clerk of the House and the secretary of the Senate served as the *ex officio* members. But by tradition, they named "special deputies" who were accorded full privileges, offices and support staff at the FEC.

Prior to the court ruling, the special deputies could participate in all commission deliberations and then brief congressional leaders. The special deputies also counseled members on election law. All of these actions were supposed to be bipartisan.

The special deputy "provides information in two directions between the House and the FEC," said Clerk Donnald K. Anderson. But Jan Baran, a Republican election lawyer, offered a different description: "They are spies. They sit there like brooding task masters."

On a practical level, the only employee directly affected by the court decision was Douglas J. Patton, who represented Anderson for the House. The Senate post had been vacant since Sept. 30 when David G. Gartner retired. Former Sen. Wyche Fowler Jr., D-Ga. (1987-93), served in the post for six months in 1993.

FEC Decisions in Doubt

Election lawyers in both parties said the future of the FEC was thrown into question. Those involved in legal action with the agency began seizing on the court decision to have FEC complaints past and present tossed out.

"The commission is whistling in the dark if they think this is behind them," said Kenneth A. Gross, a Democratic election lawyer and former associate general counsel at the FEC.

"Under Supreme Court precedent, this decision could be applied retroactively to any FEC decision," said Baran. On Oct. 26, he filed the first of possibly innumerable motions for dismissal of another case citing the Oct. 22 decision. The test case was *FEC v. the National Republican Senatorial Committee*, in which the NRSC was charged with illegally bundling contributions in the 1986 Nevada Senate race.

Election lawyers said that pending decisions were most vulnerable to challenge. Past decisions appeared safer. "One thing that we are absolutely clear on is that it does not affect closed cases," said Lawrence M. Noble, general counsel to the FEC. In the weeks after the decision, the FEC re-ratified its regulations, actions and forms.

The NRA case involved a FEC finding that the group had illegally used $415,000 in prohibited corporate funds to influence a federal election. The appeals court did not address the merits of the case except to rule that the FEC had decided the case improperly because of the *ex officio* members.

Appointments Under Cloud

Some public interest groups contended that the court decision affected the standing of the other commissioners, who served staggered six-year terms. Though officially nominated by the president, they were handpicked by congressional leaders. Elizabeth Hedlund, project director of FEC Watch, a project of the nonpartisan Center for Responsive Politics, had been leading an effort to get President Clinton to select nonpartisan commissioners without congressional input.

Prior to 1976, Congress directly appointed commissioners without going through the White House. But the Supreme Court struck down the practice in a 1976 decision, *Buckley v. Valeo*. In response, Congress reconstituted the commission, informally establishing the practice that had been in force until the court decision.

For years, the political nature of the appointments and the presence of the *ex officio* members contributed to criticism that the FEC was ineffectual. Cases were backlogged for years, and the toughest ones often fell away on 3-3 votes along partisan lines.

On Dec. 13, the FEC dismissed 137 pending enforcement cases in an attempt to clear its docket. It said the cases were either trivial or old, and it announced a new system for prioritizing cases. The action did not appear to be directly tied to the court decision. ∎

Congress Puts Off High-Tech Library

Hopes that the Library of Congress would recast itself in a few years as a library without walls that could be accessed by personal computer were dashed, at least temporarily, when Congress failed to fund most of the library's "information age" budget or authorize the library to provide cost-recovering information services.

Citing harsh budget realities, appropriators cut the library's forward-looking science and technology programs and special projects out of the fiscal 1994 legislative branch appropriations bill (HR 2348 — PL 103-69). The library ended up with $250.8 million, a cut of $2 million from the previous year. And authorizers were unable to push through a bill (S 345) to expand the library's authority to charge for services for the first time since 1902.

BACKGROUND

In February, Librarian of Congress James H. Billington requested an increase of nearly $30 million in funding for the main library and several related programs, including the Congressional Research Service and the Books for the Blind Program. Testifying before the Senate Legislative Branch Appropriations Subcommittee on Feb. 25, Billington offered a vision of what the world's largest library might be in the 21st century.

Billington's seven-year plan included overcoming a backlog of 32 million uncataloged materials, securing and translating vast collections into digital format, and introducing computerized document searches and deliveries to Congress, the private sector, and the scientific and technical research community.

To help pay for the modernization, he proposed that the library offer specialized fee-based services. That stirred some controversy, with appropriators responding that the library was established to help Congress, not provide non-congressional customers with costly high-tech information services. Many on the committee said the library was moving too hastily into the electronic age.

Blueprint for the Future

The blueprint for an expanded library was drawn by an Electronic Library Working Group, which began in 1992 to prepare bibliographies, exhibits and public information notices for on-line circulation. Their seven-year plan envisioned the library becoming a high-tech drive-through in the nation's information superhighway.

They identified five potential audiences for the new services: Congress, U.S. citizens, education specialists, the scientific and technical research community, and the private sector. The library would increase Congress' links to constituents, provide citizens with remote access to reference assistance, give training and consultation to libraries and teachers, facilitate access to experts in various fields, and provide online searches of congressional research products, electronic guides to specific topics and documents on demand for the technical research community.

The Critics

But lawmakers also offered or heard a variety of arguments against expanding library services.
● Appropriators warned that the technology was costly and said they could not support new ventures into automation when they were cutting agency budgets across the board. They said they would need to determine how to make the technology available to the general public before they could commit funding for pilot projects such as American Memory — a history project that brought original cartoons, photographs, audio recordings, manuscripts and full motion video to hundreds of children in its two years of testing.
● Some librarians feared that a national library focused on electronically based resources could exclude the hundreds of local libraries that had no equipment to receive information from fiber-optic networks. They also worried that all the attention on electronic information services would diminish investments in traditional services such as cataloging, reference and interlibrary loans.
● Publishers of print and information services feared that a more service-oriented, technological library could snuff out their document search businesses.

LEGISLATIVE ACTION

The Senate Rules and Administration Committee gave voice vote approval May 20 to a bill (S 345 — S Rept 103-50) that would have enabled the library to charge for new

services, putting the money into a revolving fund. But that bill never got to the Senate floor. A series of meetings could not forge a compromise between industry and members on copyright protections.

The bill would have allowed the library to offer and charge for costly, technologically advanced services that appropriations or philanthropy could not support. The library would have had to recover costs for 11 types of specialized research services frequently requested, such as detailed legal analysis and document delivery. Recovered fees would have been deposited in a revolving U.S. Treasury fund.

The bill divided library information products and services into three categories — core, national and specialized — and preserved free access to core services.

The panel swiftly approved S 345 after Chairman Wendell H. Ford, D-Ky., coaxed reluctant agreement from Sens. Dianne Feinstein, D-Calif., and Dennis DeConcini, D-Ariz., who also served on the Judiciary Committee, promising to postpone floor action until their questions were satisfactorily answered.

At issue were industry concerns about copyright protection, competition and retransmission of information.

Less than three weeks later, House appropriators in need of savings eliminated American Memory's budget along with two other "information age" initiatives. Senate appropriators did the same. The appropriators said other library programs already serviced science and technology needs.

However, on July 23, Harry Reid, D-Nev., and Mark O. Hatfield, R-Ore., got the full Senate to approve by voice vote an amendment to restore the last $1 million for American Memory. Conferees said the money would go to complete the project's report.

In their conference report they warned the library not to "extend its role in the creation or assembly of educational materials" beyond its core services; staff from American Memory and special projects could be used in arrearage, automation or human resources core programs.

Public/Private Ventures

The library did get help from the private sector. On Nov. 18, the Bell Atlantic Corp. announced that it would distribute American Memory as part of its Northern Virginia technology test. The library supplied the digitized primary source material from its collections, and Bell Atlantic provided the system for delivering the material to home computers. Bell Atlantic also announced plans for marketing the collection to the general public in 1994.

Bell Atlantic was one of 18 corporations, including GTE, Microsoft Corp., IBM and Simon & Schuster, that had donated money, software and equipment to the library's National Demonstration Laboratory, a multimedia demonstration center that contained much of the technology needed to create a library capable of allowing worldwide remote access.

Another joint venture between the library and a private company was an on-line exhibits program. America Online, which made library exhibits part of a free introductory offer to its commercial network, paid the costs of setting up "Revelations From the Russian Archives" on-line to entertain current subscribers and entice new ones to hook up. The arrangement enabled the library to be the first such institution to make electronic versions of its exhibits.

Other Problems

Library officials also were forced to deal with some down-to-earth realities. The previous half-dozen years had brought mandated reductions in services and heightened criticism of library management — all of which made big funding increases harder to justify.

At the same time, William L. Clay, D-Mo., chairman of the House Administration Subcommittee on Libraries and Memorials, criticized the library for its hiring and promotion practices. In August of 1993 U.S. District Judge Norma Holloway Johnson ruled that the library had illegally discriminated against its black administrative and professional employees. And severe security problems forced the library to close its stacks to scholars in 1992. ■

Chapter 2

ECONOMICS & FINANCE

The Democrats' Economic Agenda

*Clinton proposes tax increases and spending cuts,
targets deficit reduction and new spending priorities*

Less than a month after taking office, President Clinton went before a joint session of Congress to outline his ambitious economic agenda. In sharp contrast to the priorities that guided his two Republican predecessors, Clinton called for pairing deficit reduction with a renewed role for the government in promoting economic recovery and growth. Where Republicans had called for cutting taxes and government spending in an effort to unleash private investment, Clinton called for tax increases and spending cuts, with the proceeds devoted to a combination of deficit reduction and new spending priorities. He called for targeting federal spending in ways that would leverage far greater private investment.

In his Feb. 17 speech to Congress, Clinton called for an immediate $30 billion stimulus program to give a quick, job-creating boost to the economy; nearly $160 billion in tax breaks and spending initiatives over four years to spur long-term investment; and a $473 billion deficit-reduction package, split almost evenly between spending cuts and tax increases.

Just how difficult it would be to juggle these seemingly contradictory goals quickly became clear when Clinton sent to Capitol Hill the first piece of his package — a $16.3 billion fiscal 1993 supplemental appropriation (HR 1335) to pay for his short-term stimulus proposals.

Republicans denounced the move as more "tax and spend" policies by Democrats. But many Democrats also resisted starting the year by voting for more spending before they had gotten a chance to go on record for reducing the deficit.

To address those concerns, the Democratic leadership stepped up work on the fiscal 1994 budget, which included Clinton's deficit-reduction proposals.

The Democrats' starting point was a baseline budget left by outgoing President George Bush, which showed what the budget for the next five years would be if existing tax and spending policies remained unchanged.

Although Clinton outlined the changes he planned to make in his Feb. 17 speech, it took him until April 8 to submit the full-blown details of his $1.52 trillion fiscal 1994 budget to Congress.

Meanwhile, Democrats in Congress wrote a fiscal 1994 budget resolution (H Con Res 64), a congressional document that would guide House and Senate tax and spending policies for the year. While Congress made some adjustments, the resolution generally embraced Clinton's proposals. Not a single

---

FISCAL 1994 BUDGET

➡ **Bush's Budget.** Before leaving office, Bush issued a "baseline budget" largely devoid of policy prescriptions............ p. 82

➡ **Clinton's Economic Package.** Clinton outlined his ambitious economic agenda in a February speech to a joint session of Congress............... p. 85

➡ **Clinton's Budget Details.** In April, Clinton filled in the details of his $1.52 trillion budget. p. 89

➡ **Budget Resolution.** Congress approved a set of fiscal guidelines for the year that largely followed Clinton's script........ p. 102

➡ **Budget-Reconciliation Bill.** Congress cleared a massive five-year deficit-reduction bill by the barest of majorities.......... p. 107

➡ **One Last Try.** Before leaving for the year, the House passed a $37 billion package of additional spending cuts......... p. 140

Republican in either chamber voted for the resolution in the Budget Committee or on the floor, leaving Democrats to provide the votes from among their own ranks. The final version of the budget resolution was approved April 1.

The vote was a relatively easy one; the real test lay ahead, when members would vote on specific tax increases and program cuts.

In the House, where members cast back-to-back votes on the budget resolution and the stimulus bill, the supplemental appropriation passed by a healthy margin. But it foundered in the Senate when Republicans called for spending cuts to offset most of the new spending and the White House refused. In the end, Clinton had to settle for a bill that was trimmed of every provision save $4 billion for extended unemployment benefits.

The episode demonstrated lawmakers' growing preoccupation with deficit reduction. It also raised questions about the White House's ability to work effectively to get Clinton's programs enacted, and it consumed valuable White House energy and resources that otherwise might have been devoted to the far more challenging task of shepherding a huge deficit-reduction bill through Congress.

The key test of Clinton's economic policies was the 1993 budget-reconciliation bill (HR 2264), so named because it was intended to reconcile existing law with Congress' deficit-reduction goals. Congress cleared the $496 billion, five-year bill Aug. 6, but only after the administration had conducted an extraordinary lobbying campaign and accepted major changes in the bill — including the elimination of Clinton's proposal for a broad-based energy tax. Even then, the bill made it through by the barest possible majorities in both chambers. Still, passage was a major, if hard-fought, victory for Clinton, reviving his image as a politician who was uncommonly skilled at overcoming the odds and getting what he wanted from legislators.

Congress took one more crack at cutting spending before the session ended. In November, the House passed a bill (HR 3400) to cut spending by $37 billion over five years. In so doing, members narrowly rejected much stronger anti-deficit medicine, a measure that would have cut spending by $90 billion over five years. The year ended with the House-passed bill stalled in the Senate. Senate Appropriations Committee Chairman Robert C. Byrd, D-W.Va., who opposed further cuts, said his committee would not consider it until 1994. ∎

Bush Leaves Clinton a Budget Surprise

On Jan. 6, outgoing President George Bush sent Congress what was described as a "plain vanilla" fiscal 1994 budget. Devoid of any policy prescriptions, the document showed what the budget for the next five years would be if existing tax and spending policies remained unchanged. But tucked away in the document were several time bombs for the incoming Clinton administration, the most significant of which was a sharp increase in the projected deficit for fiscal 1994-97. Democrats also said the White House had underestimated the cost of existing defense programs.

The baseline budget, prepared by the Office of Management and Budget (OMB), showed $1.5 trillion in outlays and $1.2 trillion in receipts in fiscal 1994, leaving a projected deficit of $292.4 billion. It assumed the continuation of existing programs, adjusted for inflation and for changes in demographics.

White House budget director Richard G. Darman insisted that the budget was nothing more than a neutral benchmark exercise that was intended to be "helpful" to the incoming administration. But some Democrats painted it as proof that Darman could not resist manipulating the numbers one more time, just to make life difficult for them.

Deficit Numbers Made Clinton's Job Tougher

At issue were Darman's 1994-97 deficit projections, which were much worse than what OMB had forecast the previous summer in the middle of the presidential campaign. Democrats were particularly worried about the numbers for fiscal 1997. That was the budget that would be under consideration as the 1996 presidential campaign heated up, and that would test a pledge that Clinton had made to cut the deficit in half by the end of his first term.

In July 1992, OMB projected a deficit of about $237 billion for 1997. The final Bush budget revised that to $305 billion, some $68 billion higher. (Despite the surprise expressed by the incoming administration, the Congressional Budget Office had published a revised estimate in August 1992 that showed the 1997 deficit climbing as high as $290 billion.)

Democrats, including Clinton, insisted the real number was higher yet — as much as $350 billion to $360 billion — due in part to a controversial assumption by Darman that appropriated spending would be frozen after 1995.

Senate Armed Services Committee Chairman Sam Nunn, D-Ga., said the Bush budget underestimated the cost of existing defense programs by a cumulative $50 billion, which meant that the actual deficit would be even higher.

Cutting a 1997 deficit of $360 billion in half would require putting the budget on a fiscal diet radical enough to produce savings of about $180 billion in the fourth year — potentially tough medicine for a shaky economy. To get a reduction that big that quickly, spending cuts or revenue increases would have to start almost immediately.

Although Clinton did not abandon his pledge to halve the deficit, his allies on Capitol Hill quickly tried to give him space to change his position. "The president-elect is going to have a very difficult, if not an impossible task, in cutting the deficit in half by 1997," Senate Budget Committee Chairman Jim Sasser, D-Tenn., told reporters. "Much of President-elect Clinton's strategy for putting America on the road to recovery was based on deficit projections supplied by the Bush administration. We now know that these deficit estimates were wrong, despite what the Bush OMB was saying, and despite [its] best efforts to hide it."

But Pete V. Domenici of New Mexico, ranking Republican on the Senate Budget Committee, made it clear that Republicans were not prepared to let Clinton off the hook. Domenici conceded that he did not think it was realistic to try to cut the deficit in half over five years. But, he added, "I didn't make the commitment.... You don't just say ... we aren't going to get there and c'est la vie. We've got to get there some time.... I'd like to see how he intends to get to half. And if he can't, I'd like his explanation."

A Budget Glossary

Appropriations: The process by which Congress provides budget authority — usually through the passage of 13 separate appropriations bills.

Budget authority: The authority for federal agencies to obligate money.

Budget outlays: The money that is actually spent in a fiscal year, as opposed to the money that is appropriated. One year's budget authority can produce outlays over several succeeding years, and the outlays in any given fiscal year can result from a mix of budget authority in that year and prior years. Appropriators provide only budget authority; outlays, until they occur, are simply estimates from the Congressional Budget Office and the White House's Office of Management and Budget (OMB).

The easiest way to distinguish between budget authority and outlays is to use this analogy: Budget authority is when the money is put into a checking account; outlays are when a check is written.

Discretionary spending: Programs that Congress can fund as it chooses through appropriations.

Entitlements: Programs that have eligibility requirements written into the law. People who meet the requirements are entitled to benefits, and the money must be provided, either through appropriations or direct spending.

Fiscal 1994: Oct. 1, 1993, through Sept. 30, 1994.

Mandatory spending: Programs for which money must be spent every year, due primarily to laws mandating that money be made available (see entitlements). Interest on the national debt is also considered mandatory spending.

Reconciliation: The procedure for bringing existing tax laws and entitlement spending into conformity with the congressional budget resolution. Authorizing and tax-writing committees produce sections of the bill, based on instructions in the budget resolution, and the Budget committees package them for floor action.

Rescission: The cancellation of previously appropriated budget authority.

Revenues: Taxes, user fees and other receipts to the federal government.

Sequester: Automatic spending cuts triggered under the Gramm-Rudman anti-deficit law to penalize spending above preset limits.

Bush Economic Assumptions

In developing its baseline budget estimates, the Office of Management and Budget worked from the following economic assumptions, which came not from the administration but from the Blue Chip Economic Indicators, a consensus of 51 private sector forecasters.

(Calendar years; dollar amounts in billions) [1]

	Actual 1991	Projections						
		1992	1993	1994	1995	1996	1997	1998
Gross domestic product								
Dollar levels:								
Current dollars	5,678	5,936	6,254	6,647	7,050	7,467	7,911	8,380
Constant (1987) dollars	4,821	4,910	5,037	5,189	5,324	5,457	5,594	5,734
Implicit price deflator (1987 = 100), annual average	117.8	120.9	124.2	128.1	132.4	136.8	141.4	146.2
Percent change, fourth quarter over fourth quarter:								
Current dollars	3.5	4.9	6.0	6.3	6.0	5.9	6.0	5.9
Constant (1987) dollars	0.1	2.3	3.0	2.9	2.5	2.5	2.5	2.5
Implicit price deflator (1987 = 100)	3.3	2.6	2.9	3.3	3.4	3.3	3.4	3.3
Percent change, year over year:								
Current dollars	2.8	4.6	5.4	6.3	6.1	5.9	5.9	5.9
Constant (1987) dollars	−1.2	1.8	2.6	3.0	2.6	2.5	2.5	2.5
Implicit price deflator (1987 = 100)	4.0	2.7	2.7	3.2	3.4	3.3	3.4	3.3
Incomes, billions of current dollars:								
Personal income	4,828	5,056	5,369	5,693	6,012	6,359	6,730	7,126
Wages and salaries	2,812	2,920	3,101	3,297	3,497	3,704	3,924	4,156
Corporate profits before tax	335	367	403	449	485	516	548	582
Consumer Price Index (all urban) [2]								
Level (1982-84 = 100), annual average	136.2	140.3	144.7	149.8	155.3	160.9	166.7	172.6
Percent change, fourth quarter over fourth quarter:	3.0	3.0	3.3	3.6	3.7	3.6	3.6	3.5
Percent change, year over year	4.2	3.0	3.2	3.5	3.7	3.6	3.6	3.5
Unemployment rate, civilian [3]								
Fourth-quarter level	6.9	7.6	7.0	6.1	6.0	5.8	5.8	5.7
Annual average	6.7	7.5	7.2	6.4	6.1	5.9	5.8	5.7
Federal pay raise, January (percent)	4.1	4.2	3.7	2.2	2.5	2.9	3.2	3.2
Interest rate (percent) [4]								
90-day Treasury bills	5.4	3.4	3.4	4.6	5.0	5.1	5.2	5.1
10-year Treasury notes [5]	7.9	7.0	7.0	7.2	7.3	7.3	7.3	7.2

[1] Based on Blue Chip data for the months of October and November

[2] CPI for urban consumers. Two versions of the CPI were published. The index shown here is that used, as required by law, in calculating automatic adjustments to individual income tax brackets.

[3] Percent of civilian labor force, excluding armed forces residing in the United States

[4] Average rate on new issues within period

[5] Based on the Blue Chip forecast for Aaa corporate bonds adjusted downward to account for the expected spread between corporate bonds and Treasury notes

SOURCE: President's fiscal 1994 budget

Darman Suggested Other Savings

Sasser also complained about Darman's assumption that outlays for discretionary programs would be frozen at $539.1 billion a year through fiscal 1998, despite the fact that existing budget caps adopted as a result of the 1990 budget summit were set to expire after fiscal 1995.

Sasser charged that the freeze allowed Darman to take credit for billions of dollars "in savings that are never specified at all." He also criticized Darman for assuming that Congress would stick to the discretionary spending caps in fiscal 1994-95 without proposing where the necessary cuts should come from. He said holding to the caps would require Congress to come up with cuts of $68 billion over the following two years.

The Bush budget also implied that Clinton could save $65.2 billion if he had the nerve to return to the harsh fiscal medicine of Gramm-Rudman spending cuts. Under the terms of the 1990 budget deal, Clinton was required to decide the day after he took office whether to stick with flexible deficit targets in fiscal 1994-95 or return to old-style Gramm-Rudman fixed deficit targets, which carried the threat of huge across-the-board spending cuts. For the previous two years, Congress had lived under a scheme that allowed OMB to adjust the deficit targets to account for inflation and other "technical" changes.

That let Congress off the hook for factors beyond its immediate control, such as a weak economy or misestimates of revenues or program spending levels. What Congress did have to do was to abide by strict caps on appropriations bills and a pay-as-you-go regime for tax cuts or changes in mandatory spending programs such as Medicare.

Returning to fixed targets raised the threat of a $22.4 billion spending cut, or sequester, in the fall and a $42.8 billion cut in 1994. Those were the differences between the fiscal 1994-95 deficit targets provided in Bush's fiscal 1993 budget and what spending levels were likely to be. The differences were due entirely to what budget estimators call "economics and technicals" — weaker-than-forecast economic performance, incorrect revenue estimates and so on.

(Clinton announced Jan. 21 that the White House would stick with the floating deficit targets, a move that House and Senate Republicans quickly denounced.)

Some Good News

There was some good news for Clinton in the budget: The projected costs of bailing out failed lending institutions were dramatically lower than what OMB had projected the previous summer. The lower estimates were due largely to a "favorable interest rate environment" that had improved earnings by banks and savings and loans and reduced both the number and the size of lending institutions likely to fail. OMB lowered the projected 1993-94 bailout costs from the $86.1 billion it had predicted in July to $31.7 billion.

Finally, in what Darman characterized as an effort to produce credible economic projections, OMB put aside the administration's own estimates and based the budget instead on the so-called Blue Chip projections, a consensus of 51 private forecasts. (Table, p. 83)

Those figures showed modestly healthy growth of 3 percent in the gross domestic product in 1993, tapering off slightly to 2.9 percent in 1994 and then settling at 2.5 percent a year through 1998. Inflation was expected to stay low, rising from 2.9 percent in 1993 to 3.3 percent in 1994 and hovering at or near that figure through 1998.

By contrast, OMB's own "mid-growth" projection showed slightly faster real growth, slightly lower inflation, a steeper decline in unemployment rates and lower short-term and long-term interest rates. ∎

Baseline Budget Estimates

The following table shows what the Office of Management and Budget (OMB), in January, said federal receipts, outlays and deficits would be through fiscal 1998 if no changes were made to spending and tax policies. Critics charged that some of OMB's assumptions led to unrealistically low deficit projections. A case in point was OMB's assumption that discretionary spending would be frozen when the existing discretionary spending caps expired after 1995, a prospect that congressional observers said was politically unlikely.

The two different fiscal 1994-95 deficit numbers reflected two different scenarios, one a continuation of the existing system of flexible deficit targets and the other a return to pre-1990-style Gramm-Rudman fixed targets, which OMB predicted could force substantial across-the-board spending cuts in 1994 and 1995. President-elect Clinton decided Jan. 21 to stick with the flexible targets. Amounts are by fiscal year, in billions of dollars.

	1992 Actual	1993	1994	1995	1996	1997	1998
Receipts	1,091.6	1,147.6	1,230.3	1,305.6	1,378.5	1,439.7	1,523.4
Outlays:							
Discretionary	534.3	548.1	537.4	539.1	539.1	539.1	539.1
Mandatory							
Deposit Insurance	2.6	15.5	16.2	−7.1	−14.9	−11.3	−6.9
Medicaid	67.8	80.5	92.9	107.8	122.7	138.8	156.4
Federal Retirement	74.9	77.4	81.5	83.9	88.6	94.1	98.2
Means-tested entitlements	75.0	83.4	89.8	95.6	98.5	106.2	112.4
Medicare	116.2	129.9	147.8	166.3	188.5	211.4	235.8
Social Security	285.1	302.2	318.7	336.2	355.1	374.8	395.6
Unemployment compensation	37.0	32.7	24.7	24.4	25.5	26.3	27.4
Undistributed offsetting receipts	−39.3	−37.2	−39.0	−40.3	−41.5	−43.5	−46.0
Other	28.7	39.6	32.7	27.9	20.7	22.9	22.9
Subtotal, mandatory	648.0	724.1	765.2	794.9	843.2	919.6	995.7
Net Interest	199.4	202.8	220.1	244.1	262.5	286.0	308.4
Total outlays	1,381.8	1,474.9	1,522.7	1,578.0	1,644.8	1,744.7	1,843.2
Deficit (continuation of flexible deficit targets)	−290.2	−327.3	−292.4	−272.4	−266.4	−305.0	−319.8
Deficit (return to Gramm-Rudman fixed deficit targets)	−290.2	−327.3	−269.9	−229.6	−266.4	−305.0	−319.8

SOURCE: President's fiscal 1994 budget

Clinton Throws Down the Gauntlet

In a forceful speech that had Democrats leaping to their feet in giddy approval and some Republicans openly heckling from their seats, President Clinton outlined his economic proposals to a joint session of Congress on Feb. 17. Capping weeks of warnings that he was dead serious about deficit reduction and the need to broadly share the pain, Clinton unveiled a plan that included deep spending cuts but relied overwhelmingly on tax increases to bring the budget closer to balance. As promised, Clinton proposed sharp new levies on the wealthy, but in a reversal of a campaign pledge, he also asked middle-income taxpayers to shoulder part of the load. Social Security beneficiaries were asked to help as well. *(Text, p. 7-D)*

At the same time, Clinton proposed to quickly boost short-term job creation and ensure long-term economic growth by pumping billions of dollars in new spending into a wide range of infrastructure, education, health and local development programs that had gotten short shrift from Republican budget drafters for the past decade.

"Our nation needs a new direction," he said. "It has been too long — at least three decades — since a president has come and challenged Americans to join him on a great national journey, not merely to consume the bounty of today but to invest for a much greater one tomorrow."

Clinton made a rhetorical effort to reach out to Republicans, declaring that the dismal state of the economy was not a partisan matter. "There is plenty of blame to go around — in both branches of the government and both parties," he said. "The time has come for the blame to end."

But the frequently hostile responses of congressional Republicans signaled that the new president's tough campaign rhetoric and his relentless attacks on Republican trickle-down economics had won him serious enemies and the promise of tough, partisan fights over his economic proposals.

While Democrats seemed galvanized by the address, repeatedly interrupting the president with standing ovations, they could not disguise their anxiety over the sheer magnitude of the tax increases and spending cuts Clinton asked them to approve.

"It's going to be hard to sell," said Sen. Joseph R. Biden Jr., D-Del.

Federal Reserve Board Chairman Alan Greenspan strongly endorsed the outlines of Clinton's plan, saying that "it is a serious proposal; its baseline economic assumptions are plausible, and it is a detailed program-by-program set of recommendations as distinct from general goals." Greenspan refused to promise that the central bank would further cut interest rates to help underpin the recovery. But he declared that the Fed "recognizes that it has an important role to play in this regard," a comment that was interpreted as willingness to help offset any economic fallout if Clinton's deficit cuts were implemented.

Deficit hawk and former independent presidential candidate Ross Perot went on ABC's "Nightline" shortly after the speech and called Clinton's address "a good first step." However, he added, "the devil is always in the details."

In a plea that would be sounded frequently as Congress began debating various pieces of the package, Clinton asked "all those who say we should cut more [to] be as specific as I have been" and warned Congress against dismantling the plan piece-by-piece rather than treating it as a package.

Deficit Reduction

Clinton's budget-cutting plan was the largest in history, proposing to save $704 billion over five years — $200 billion more than the 1990 budget summit agreement was supposed to save over the same number of years. Of that amount, however, only two-thirds was intended for reducing the deficit; the other third was to be used to pay for increased job creation and long-term investment spending. Net deficit reduction at the end of five years of the plan was estimated to be about $473 billion.

At the heart of the plan was a five-year proposal to raise $357 billion in new taxes, chiefly by raising the top rates for individuals and businesses, imposing a broad new tax on energy, uncapping the Medicare payroll tax and increasing the tax bite on better-off Social Security beneficiaries.

Clinton administration officials argued that the total tax package was marginally smaller than the huge tax increase Congress approved in 1982, but that was true only if the increased Social Security tax bite was counted as a benefit cut rather than a tax increase, a scorekeeping distinction that made sense to budget analysts but not necessarily to politicians.

The Pieces of the Plan

Overall, Clinton's plan included three distinct pieces, only one of which focused on the deficit.

● **Stimulus package.** This jobs-creation proposal involved more than $30 billion, split between $16.3 billion in spending, roughly $12 billion in business tax incentives, and other funds in the form of loans and construction obligation authority. The money, most of it to be spent over two years, was intended to quickly reinforce the ongoing economic recovery by creating 500,000 new jobs. Office of Management and Budget (OMB) Director Leon E. Panetta said 200,000 of those would be permanent, 150,000 would be summer jobs and the remaining jobs would be created indirectly by the package. Spending targets included highway construction, summer jobs, extended unemployment benefits and Community Development Block Grants.

Clinton sought to counter a Republican argument that the stimulus proposal was needless pork barrel spending that would make little difference in creating jobs or boosting an economy that was already in the midst of a sustained recovery.

"Some people say, well, we're in a recovery and we don't have to do that," he said. "Well, we all hope we're in a recovery, but we're sure not creating new jobs. *(Stimulus, p. 706)*

● **'Investment' spending.** Clinton proposed more than $230 billion over five years for a combination of spending programs and tax breaks designed to continue stimulating business investment and simultaneously correct an "investment deficit" that Clinton argued had shortchanged infrastructure, education, child care, job training and health-care spending over the previous decade.

"The heart of this plan deals with the long term," he said.

Key items included $69 billion for spending on infra-

A Look at the Highlights . . .

President Clinton's economic proposal relied heavily on a package of $357 billion in tax increases during the period 1993-98. For the four-year period from 1994 to 1997, the increase was expected to be $267 billion. Those figures included Clinton's proposal for increasing taxes paid by better-off Social Security recipients.

Clinton's key tax proposals included:

Individual Income Taxes

A new top rate of 36 percent for taxable income above $140,000 for couples and $115,000 for individuals. The tax on capital gains income would remain capped at 28 percent, although Clinton also proposed a break for investments in small companies. People with taxable incomes above $250,000 would be subject to a 10 percent surtax, giving them a marginal tax rate of 39.6 percent. Clinton wanted the new rates retroactive to the beginning of 1993 but without any penalties for those who did not withhold enough in 1993. Under existing law, there were three income tax brackets: 15 percent, 28 percent and 31 percent.

The cap on itemized deductions and the phaseout of the personal exemption, scheduled to expire in 1995 and 1996 respectively, were made permanent in Clinton's plan. Both affected higher income taxpayers. The personal exemption was not available for single people with adjusted gross incomes over $105,250 and couples with incomes of more than $157,900. The limit on itemized deductions applied to taxpayers making more than $105,250.

Clinton proposed increasing the alternative minimum tax (AMT), which was supposed to ensure that high-income taxpayers with many deductions and exemptions paid some taxes. The increase was from 24 percent to 26 percent for qualified income of less than $175,000 and to 28 percent for income above $175,000. Clinton proposed increasing the level of exemption allowed before the AMT was triggered to $45,000 for couples and $37,500 for individuals.

Individual Deductions

A prohibition on claiming meals and real estate expenses as part of the moving-expense deduction.

Earned-Income Tax Credit

Broader eligibility for the earned-income tax credit, which was created to assist poor working families. The expanded credit was intended to help offset other tax increases for families making up to $30,000. In 1992, families with incomes of less than $22,370 qualified. Under Clinton's plan, families with two children making up to $30,000 would qualify, as would one-child families with income up to $28,500 and childless couples making up to $9,000.

Social Security

A tax increase for higher-income Social Security recipients. Clinton proposed taxing up to 85 percent of benefits, rather than the existing 50 percent. As under existing law, beneficiaries would be subject to the tax if their income, including half their Social Security, exceeded $32,000 for couples and $25,000 for individuals.

Energy Taxes

A new, comprehensive energy tax based on the heat output, or British thermal units (Btu), of various forms of energy, such as coal, oil, natural gas and nuclear power. The tax was to be phased in over three years beginning in 1994. Different tax rates were proposed for various forms of energy to minimize the price advantage that would have resulted from a flat levy.

Clinton proposed making permanent a 2.5-cents-per-gallon addition to the federal gas tax that was scheduled to expire in 1995. The result would be a 14-cents-per-gallon federal gas tax until 1999; dropping to 11.5 cents after that.

Corporate Income Tax

A new top 36 percent rate for corporations with taxable income above $10 million, and a 3 percent surtax on corporations with taxable income above $15 million, effectively giving such companies a flat 36 percent rate on all their taxable income.

Under existing law, the corporate income tax had three brackets: 15 percent on the first $50,000 of taxable income, 25 percent on the next $25,000 and 34 percent on income above $75,000. Corporations with taxable income between $100,000 and $335,000 paid an additional 5 percent surtax that phased out the benefits of the lower marginal rates, making the effective top marginal rate 39 percent. Above $335,000, the tax rate was a flat 34 percent.

Corporate Deductions

A new, $1 million cap on deductions for an individual executive's pay with an exception for executive pay linked to productivity. Clinton also proposed lowering to $150,000 from $235,840 the amount of compensation that could be taken into account in 1994 in determining the amount an employee could deduct for contributions to a retirement plan and for determining benefits.

Clinton also proposed a ban on the deduction for expenses associated with lobbying legislatures, as well as lobbying executive branch officials for the purpose of affecting legislation.

---

structure, environment, housing and technology; $56 billion for education, job training, child nutrition and preschool programs and efforts to convert from a defense-oriented to a peacetime economy; $32 billion to extend unemployment benefits, expand the earned-income tax credit for low-income workers and combat crime; $36 billion for a variety of health, drug treatment and nutrition initiatives; and $28 billion in tax cuts and other incentives for business.

Besides meeting Clinton's loftier goals for society, the short-term stimulus package and the long-term investment proposal were designed to get both Congress and the nation to swallow the bitter pill of deficit reduction.

● **Deficit-reduction plan.** Clinton proposed to cut $704 billion over five years, $375 billion of it coming from spending cuts and $328 billion from tax increases, almost a 1-to-1 ratio. That was much less than the 2-to-1 ratio Panetta had advocated during his Senate confirmation hearings in January, however. And if the $29 billion in increased taxes

... Of Clinton's Tax Proposals

Other Corporate Taxes

A scaling back of a tax credit designed to stimulate economic activity in U.S. possessions and in Puerto Rico that allowed many companies to operate virtually tax-free. Phased in over several years, the new credit would, in most cases, be limited to 65 percent of the wages paid to employees.

An end to the "double dip" under which investors who purchased failed thrifts from the federal government, mostly in 1988, got tax-exempt federal assistance that they also were able to deduct from their income for tax purposes.

Clinton also proposed taxing securities dealers on the full market value of their portfolios and reducing the deductible portion of business meals and entertainment from 80 percent to 50 percent.

Foreign and Multinational Businesses

Improved enforcement of regulations aimed at preventing tax avoidance by making companies provide documentation at the time they transferred assets between units at home and abroad.

Clinton also proposed:
- Changing the foreign tax credit for multinational oil companies to prevent firms from receiving a U.S. tax break on income that was taxed at a low rate abroad. The credit had been established to ease the burden of double taxation.
- Raising taxes on companies that developed intellectual property abroad by restricting treatment of resulting royalties under the foreign tax credit.
- Ending tax incentives that encouraged U.S. subsidiaries of foreign corporations to capitalize through debt financing, rather than equity.
- Requiring U.S. companies to pay taxes on large amounts of passive income accumulated in foreign subsidiaries. Under the plan, if passive income constituted more than 25 percent of the assets of a foreign subsidiary, the excess would be taxed.

Payroll Taxes

Making all wages subject to the Medicare payroll tax, repealing the existing $135,000 cap. The proposed increase applied to both employers and employees, who split payment of the 2.9 percent tax.

Estate Taxes

An increase in the top tax rate on estates (property transferred at death) and gifts (property transferred during the owner's lifetime) to 53 percent and 55 percent, retroactive to Jan. 1, 1993. Those rates had been in effect in 1992, but the top rate in 1993 was 50 percent.

Investment Tax Credit

A two-year, 7 percent investment tax credit. To avoid rewarding a company for investments it would have made anyway, Clinton proposed that the credit apply only to spending above a firm's base level. Businesses with gross receipts of less than $5 million would receive a permanent investment tax credit (7 percent in the first two years, 5 percent in subsequent years) on their entire qualified investment spending.

Treasury officials said they expected the rules on qualifying investments to be similar to those in force before the investment tax credit was eliminated in 1986. Those rules allowed a broad range of investments to qualify, including heavy equipment, office furniture and fixtures, recreational equipment and gambling machines.

Capital Gains

A 50 percent capital gains exclusion for profits on newly issued stock held for five years and issued by companies with paid-in capital of $25 million or less.

Enterprise Zones

The creation of 50 enterprise zones in economically distressed areas of the country that would qualify for tax breaks and other federal assistance including:
- A 25 percent tax credit for zone employers on the first $15,000 in wages paid to zone residents.
- In addition, eligibility for a less generous incentive known as the targeted jobs tax credit for employers who hired zone residents.
- A writeoff of up to $75,000, rather than $10,000, in the first year for assets purchased by businesses within a zone.

Real Estate

Partial restoration of the so-called passive loss deduction, allowing real estate developers and others in the industry to write off losses on rental property against other real estate income.

Other Tax Provisions

Permanent extension of the research and development tax credit, the low-income housing tax credit, the tax exemption for small issue manufacturing bonds and for mortgage revenue bonds, the 25 percent deduction for health insurance costs of the self-employed, the targeted jobs tax credit and the tax break for employer-provided educational assistance. Under the plan, the appreciated value of all charitable gifts would be exempt from the alternative minimum tax.

---

that Clinton expected to receive from Social Security beneficiaries was shifted from the spending cut side to the tax side of the ledger, as many insisted should be done, bringing taxes to $357 billion, the ratio was almost exactly 1-to-1.

Further, after all Clinton's spending increases and tax cuts were counted, the ratio plummeted dramatically. Under those conditions, the plan added up to net five-year spending cuts of $193 billion and tax increases of $280 billion, a ratio of nearly 1-to-1.5. *(Budget-reconciliation, p. 107)*

'No Magic'

The deficit plan's heavy reliance on tax increases testified to the difficulties the Clinton economic team had coming up with acceptable spending cuts. Panetta, who led the effort, said Clinton and his advisers looked at the same options Congress had had for years and encountered many of the same problems that had made the deficit problem insoluble for so long.

"There's no magic here, folks," Panetta said. "You've

Clinton's Program

(by fiscal year; in billions of dollars)

President Clinton's aides said his four-year budget gradually built to more than a 1-to-1 ratio of spending cuts to tax increases. But if his proposal to increase the amount of taxes paid by better-off Social Security beneficiaries was scored as a tax increase instead of a spending cut, and all spending and tax changes were netted out, the ratio at the end of four years was nearly 1-to-2.

	1993	1994	1995	1996	1997	1998	1994-98
Baseline deficit	$319	$301	$296	$297	$346	$390	$1,630
Spending changes							
Defense		−7	−12	−20	−37	−36	−112
Non-defense discretionary	1	−4	−10	−15	−20	−23	−73
Entitlements	−*	−6	−12	−24	−34	−39	−115
Social Security		−3	−6	−6	−7	−8	−29
Debt service	*	−*	−3	−7	−14	−22	−46
Total spending cuts	1	−20	−43	−73	−112	−128	−375
Revenues †	−3	−46	−51	−66	−83	−82	−328
Stimulus and investments							
Stimulus program outlays	8	6	2	1	*	*	9
Investment program outlays		9	20	32	39	45	144
Tax breaks	6	13	17	15	15	17	77
Total stimulus/investment	15	27	39	47	55	62	231
Deficit reduction	13	−39	−54	−92	−140	148	−473
Resulting deficit	332	262	242	205	206	241	1,157

* $500 million or less
† Shown as minus because they reduce the deficit

SOURCE: Office of Management and Budget

got to do defense, non-defense, entitlements and revenues."

Panetta said that the president made all the final decisions about the package after hearing options from his advisers.

Clinton chose to cut defense by $112 billion over five years. He elected to save even more than that — about $144 billion over five years — from entitlement programs, including the controversial $29 billion tax increase on Social Security beneficiaries. The entitlement savings also included substantial trims in Medicare, much of it from payments to doctors, and another big chunk from extending the Medicare premium increase that was enacted in 1990 but set to expire after 1995.

The smallest contribution — $73 billion over five years — came from a wide range of non-defense programs, an area that Democrats argued had been hard hit during successive Republican administrations.

Long-Term Investment Proposals

While Clinton saved many of the details of his long-term investment strategy until he sent Congress the full fiscal 1994 budget, his Feb. 17 package targeted more than 70 programs for spending increases, including the following:

• **Technology.** As part of his theme of closer ties between government and industry, Clinton proposed to increase funding for the National Institute of Standards and Technology, a one-time Commerce Department backwater that he hoped would play a central role in helping U.S. industry gain and retain an edge in manufacturing and research. Clinton wanted to triple the agency's funding to

$2.1 billion by fiscal 1998.

To promote basic research Clinton sought to add $3 billion over five years to existing funding for National Science Foundation grants to universities, including money for "strategically targeted research" into environmental technologies, advanced computers, biotechnology and materials processing.

• **Transportation.** Clinton proposed to increase spending on highways, bridges, railroads, transit and airports by more than $11.5 billion over five years. The largest component was an additional $7 billion for highways; the remaining initiatives focused largely on mass transit, high-speed railways and magnetic levitation trains, programs targeted to receive almost $3 billion over five years under his plan.

• **Housing.** The plan included increases of $1.4 billion over five years for programs to preserve and maintain the existing stock of low-income housing and $430 million to expand programs under the Community Development Block Grant.

• **Energy and environment.** Clinton asked Congress to provide $1.2 billion in fiscal 1994 and $2 billion annually thereafter to create a Clean Water State Revolving Fund program that would make low-interest loans to help municipalities build better water treatment and sewage plants. He also requested about $1.5 billion over four years for the Interior and Agriculture departments to invest in environmental restoration. Interior Secretary Bruce Babbitt said that he planned to put priority on wetlands restoration and on revitalizing habitats of animals such as the Pacific Northwest salmon, which were nearing endangered status.

Clinton's proposal included $4.6 billion for renewable energy, conservation and cleaner, futuristic sources of energy. Almost one-third of the money was earmarked for solar and other forms of renewable energy, conservation research and development, electric vehicles and other "clean" technology programs authorized by the Energy Policy Act of 1992 (PL 102-486). *(1992 Almanac, p. 231)*

• **Education and welfare.** The plan called for investing more than $17 billion a year by 1998 in such education and training programs as apprenticeships, summer jobs, infant nutrition and preschool education. The rationale was that a small amount of spending would lead to substantial savings as Americans became healthier, better-educated and more skilled. The request included increased spending of $3.8 billion over five years on Head Start, a program that offered schooling, food and health services for 3- to 5-year-olds from low-income families.

Besides expanding existing programs, Clinton planned new ones, including spending $9.4 billion over five years on a National Service program, which would allow students to borrow money for college, then pay it back by working in their communities.

• **Crime.** During the campaign Clinton pledged to put

100,000 additional police officers on the nation's streets. As president, he proposed a crime initiative to help meet that goal, including grants to states and localities to recruit officers and a police corps program to provide assistance for education in exchange for a commitment to work as a police officer. The package, which included money to help states upgrade their crime records, was expected to cost $2.3 billion over four years.

Hints of Trouble in Congress

The ratio of tax increases to spending cuts quickly emerged as the flash point in congressional reaction to the plan. Republicans harshly denounced Panetta's failure to reach the 2-to-1 goal, and even Democrats expressed worries that they would have trouble living with the plan unless it contained more spending cuts.

Panetta argued that the plan slowly built toward a larger than 1-to-1 ratio as it went along. "That's the sort of sweet-bye-and-bye approach to budgeting that I have grown weary of under both Democrats and Republicans," said Sen. Phil Gramm, R-Texas. "This is a bad package, and I intend to fight it hard."

"I'm really disappointed," said Pete V. Domenici, N.M., ranking Republican on the Senate Budget Committee and a budget moderate who had sent early signals that he would work with Panetta and the Clinton administration if asked. "This is not a program to create jobs; this is a pro-

gram to dramatically increase taxes," he said.

The reaction of Senate Republicans was potentially critical to Clinton's economic plan. But there were signs that the plan could face trouble in the House, too. In an appearance before the House Budget Committee, which he had chaired until Clinton brought him to head OMB, Panetta heard conservative Democrats warn that they, too, wanted more spending cuts. In an often testy session, Panetta hotly defended the administration's package and challenged anyone else to do better, saying he would welcome further cuts as long as the suggestions were specific.

"I'm more than anxious to hear specifics — I've heard a lot of talk," said the budget director, who demanded that members not come to him with "gimmicks" such as across-the-board freezes, balanced-budget amendments or fixed deficit targets. "The time has come to put up or shut up when it comes to spending reductions," Panetta said.

The Budget Committee's new ranking Republican, John R. Kasich of Ohio, ripped Clinton's heavy reliance on taxes and insisted that Panetta produce more spending cuts before asking members to swallow tax hikes. "I want to make spending reductions now and worry about taxes later," he said.

Panetta, who insisted that the problem could not be solved without a mix of spending cuts and tax increases, momentarily appeared to lose his temper. "You are now the perfect example, through your arguments, of the kind of gridlock people are tired of," he told Kasich. ∎

Clinton Details $1.52 Trillion Budget

After presenting the broad outlines of his economic program in February, President Clinton filled in the details April 8 when he sent the House and Senate a $1.52 trillion budget proposal for fiscal 1994. Except for the voluminous program-by-program details and a few minor policy alterations, however, there was little in the nearly 6-pound volume that Congress had not already seen.

In the meantime, Congress had completed its own outline for tax and spending decisions in the form of a congressional budget resolution that generally followed Clinton's February outline. *(Budget resolution, p. 102)*

Clinton's five-year budget provided about $678 billion in gross deficit cuts, sharply reducing defense spending, making more modest cuts in domestic spending and levying huge new taxes, much of them on upper-income Americans and corporations.

At the same time, the president proposed spending about a third of those savings — roughly $230 billion — on a variety of new spending and tax-relief initiatives, including wide-ranging "investment" spending on domestic targets such as highways, housing, education, child nutrition, AIDS research, job training, crime prevention and subsidies for the working poor. He also proposed targeted tax incentives for businesses, particularly small ones.

Clinton's request for $1.52 trillion in outlays, or actual spending, was up just 3.3 percent from 1993, or about the rate of inflation. (The request was for $1,517.2 billion in budget authority, which translated into $1,513.3 billion in outlays.) The budget anticipated revenues of $1.25 trillion, a 9.2 percent increase, reflecting the effect of Clinton's proposed tax increases. The 1994 deficit was pegged at $264.1 billion, down sharply from what was expected to be

a record-setting 1993 deficit of $322 billion. Altogether, Clinton proposed to cut the deficit by a net $447.5 billion over five years, down from the $473 billion in deficit reduction projected in his February budget plan.

The budget resolution that Congress had already approved outdid the president's proposed deficit cuts, and administration officials gladly piggybacked those extra reductions, virtually all of them unspecified, onto their own plan in a White House briefing April 8. The combined five-year deficit reduction from both plans totaled $514 billion, according to White House scorekeeping. White House budget director Leon E. Panetta said the effect would be to cut the annual deficit to $205 billion or less by 1997; with no change in policy, the number was expected to be roughly $347 billion. "It's a courageous budget," Panetta said. "It asks every American to contribute to our economic future.... We have taken the first major step in changing the direction of this country."

In the thoroughly polarized political atmosphere that surrounded Clinton's economic proposals on Capitol Hill, however, Republicans found the budget something less than bold. "It's pretty much what they promised us: more taxes and more spending," said Senate Minority Leader Bob Dole of Kansas. "But that's not what the American people voted for last November."

Congress Sought Bigger Cuts

The arrival of the president's detailed budget proposal a week after Congress completed work on the budget resolution (H Con Res 64) stood the usual procedure on its head. Usually, the president would have delivered his full budget proposal in early February, and Congress would

Clinton's Own Budget Cuts

In announcements Feb. 9 and 10, Clinton outlined plans to initiate his own federal spending cuts by reducing White House personnel by 25 percent, trimming 100,000 jobs from the civilian side of the federal government and making a significant cut in federal overhead spending. *(Text, p. 5-D)*

On Feb. 9, Clinton said he had begun a reorganization of the White House that would cut 350 jobs from the 1,394 positions that existed under President George Bush. The government, too, Clinton said, "must do more and make do with less." Clinton left hundreds of jobs out of the mix by not counting the Office of Management and Budget (OMB), the Office of the U.S. Trade Representative or the military communications personnel detailed to the White House. White House Chief of Staff Thomas F. McLarty III said that OMB and the trade representative's office would be included in other, governmentwide personnel cuts.

More than a third of the staff cuts came from reducing personnel at the Office of National Drug Control Policy from 146 people to 25. McLarty also announced that salaries of senior White House staff would be cut 6 percent to 10 percent below the levels of their predecessors and that door-to-door car service would be limited to those few officials who could justify it on a national security basis. Finally, McLarty said, the White House mess would be open for meals to all White House personnel, not just senior staff. Taken together, the changes were expected to save about $10 million a year, about 5 percent of the overall $200 million White House budget, excluding the costs of OMB and the trade representative's office.

On Feb. 10, Clinton signed an executive order requiring a cut of 100,000 positions from the federal bureaucracy over the next four years, at least 10 percent of which were to come from senior management. Clinton said the cuts would be made through attrition rather than by layoffs.

A second executive order required all federal departments and agencies to reduce their overhead costs for equipment, travel and the like by 14 percent over four years. A third order mandated the abolishment of hundreds of what Clinton said were "unproductive and duplicitous advisory commissions." He said that henceforth, the White House budget office would have to approve the creation of new commissions by federal departments and agencies.

In related moves, Clinton also ordered a 50 percent reduction in the number of government limousines, tightened the rules for use of government aircraft and ordered the elimination of perks such as below-cost executive dining rooms and free memberships in private health clubs.

still be lingering over its budget (a set of guidelines for later tax and spending decisions), on its way to missing the nominal April 15 deadline it almost never met.

But in early February, Clinton had been in office barely two weeks, hardly long enough to work up the enormously detailed document he finally delivered. Panetta and other administration officials took pains to point out that most incoming presidents simply reworked the detailed proposal submitted by their immediate predecessors. But President George Bush had declined to submit his own line-by-line budget, instead offering a compilation of what federal spending would have been in 1994 if existing programs continued unchanged. That forced Clinton to start from scratch.

Meanwhile, Congress had accelerated its usual budget schedule to get a quick vote on the budget plan and its promise of broad deficit reduction before turning to Clinton's controversial stimulus spending plan.

One serious clash was already apparent between what Clinton was seeking and what Congress had said it was willing to provide. The White House wanted $5.7 billion more in actual spending from appropriations in 1994 than the budget resolution permitted. While the Clinton request fell within an overall cap for 1994 discretionary spending that had been set by the 1990 budget agreement, Congress had set a lower ceiling in the budget resolution.

With defense spending already slated for cuts that had some defense-hawk Democrats near rebellion, it was clear that the White House would have to scale back its domestic shopping list and fight for its spending plans throughout the appropriations process, matching its new investment spending against existing programs with strong congressional support.

"We're prepared to do that," Panetta said, "but it needs to be pointed out that we'll have a difficult time and a difficult battle in fighting for those investments that we care about."

Cutting the Deficit in Half

Both Clinton's budget and the congressional budget resolution were designed to produce their lowest deficit numbers in 1996-97, bringing Clinton close to his campaign promise of cutting the deficit in half in four years. It also meant that in 1996, when Clinton would presumably be running for re-election, Congress and the White House would be implementing one low-deficit budget (fiscal 1996) and debating another (fiscal 1997).

"Low" was a relative term when discussing deficits, however. The $205 billion deficit the White House was predicting for 1997 seemed substantially smaller than the record $332 billion deficit — or 5.2 percent of the gross domestic product (GDP) — that was anticipated for 1993. But at 2.7 percent of GDP, it was still triple or more the level that economists regarded as acceptable by historical standards — somewhere between 0.5 percent and 1 percent of GDP.

And projections showed the deficit climbing sharply again after 1996-97, driven largely by the increasing costs of the twin health-care entitlements, Medicare and Medicaid, and by the rising costs of interest on the nation's accumulated debt. "We are going to be back at the end of Clinton's first term with projections of a growing deficit," said Barry Bosworth, an economist at the Washington-based Brookings Institution. Bosworth called the net effect of the Clinton-Congress deficit reduction trivial when measured against long-run trends in spending for health care

and debt interest. "This program should be looked at as a one-shot deficit reduction," he said, adding that something more would have to be done to reverse the long-term trend.

Democrats were banking on Clinton's yet-to-be-announced health-care reform plan to be that something else. Panetta said enactment of health-care cost controls would "continue this deficit line on a downward trend." Others were extremely skeptical, however. Robert D. Reischauer, director of the Congressional Budget Office (CBO), repeatedly warned that Clinton's plans to extend health coverage to millions of uninsured Americans and otherwise improve the nation's health-care system would cost more money, not less.

"In the short run — say, over the next 10 years — it will be exceedingly difficult to realize any significant budgetary savings," Reischauer said in CBO's evaluation of the president's budget.

Economic Assumptions

The White House based the budget on relatively conservative economic projections developed by CBO. In years past, Democrats had criticized Republican Presidents Bush and Ronald Reagan for building their budgets on "rosy scenarios" — OMB estimates that were more optimistic than those of most private economists.

CBO projected 3.0 percent growth in real GDP in 1994, slowing to just 1.8 percent in 1998, unemployment falling from 7.3 percent in the fourth quarter of 1992 to 5.7 percent in the fourth quarter of 1998, and inflation falling slightly from 2.5 percent in 1993 to 2.2 percent in 1997. ∎

Function-by-Function Highlights

The following is a summary of the spending proposals in President Clinton's fiscal 1994 budget. They are organized by broad program categories, known as functions. The budget presented spending in terms of budget authority (authority for federal agencies to commit money) and outlays (the actual spending that would result in fiscal 1994). In some cases, the two numbers were the same; in others, they differed significantly. For example, some of the fiscal 1994 outlays were the result of budget authority appropriated in prior years. Unless noted otherwise, the numbers in this summary are outlays and are for fiscal 1994 (Oct. 1, 1993, to Sept. 30, 1994).

AGRICULTURE

Clinton requested $17.2 billion for federal agriculture programs in fiscal 1994, $4.7 billion less than estimated for 1993. Over the following five years, he planned to save an additional $5.8 billion in farm subsidies by cutting some longtime commodity programs and improving the economic climate for farmers.

The numbers represented the Agriculture Department's best guess at how much the programs, which included price-support payments for farmers and agriculture marketing programs, would cost the Treasury. But other factors — including the weather and world market prices — were sure to change the cost.

Clinton projected that spending for farm subsidies would drop from an estimated $17.1 billion in 1993 (a number that was driven up by unexpected drops in prices for corn, wheat and cotton) to $12.2 billion in 1994 with no changes in existing programs, and fall to $10 billion by 1997.

He sought additional savings from potentially controversial changes in longtime farm programs, such as eliminating the federal subsidy for beekeepers and lowering the combined subsidies for producers of wool and mohair to $50,000 per person, down from $125,000 for each program. The Agriculture Department said getting rid of the bee subsidy would save $12 million in fiscal 1994 and $32 million over four years. Estimated savings from the wool and mohair proposal were $10 million in fiscal 1994 and $212 million from fiscal 1994-1997.

Clinton also wanted to cut off income-support payments to farmers who made more than $100,000 in income outside their farms, for an estimated savings of $75 million in fiscal 1994 and $470 million over four years.

Most of the agriculture savings came from budget-cutting proposals that were not slated to take place until fiscal 1996 — after a new farm bill had gone into effect. The White House said that would allow U.S. farmers to adjust to changes in the world market that would result from the completion of world trade talks under the General Agreement on Tariffs and Trade. Those talks had

been stalled for years, however.

In fiscal 1996-1997, Clinton planned to save $2.5 billion by, among other things:
● Cutting off payments to farmers to idle their land.
● Cutting 10 percentage points off the amount of acreage eligible for federal price-support payments, on top of the 15 percent made ineligible for payment in the 1990 budget agreement. This was to affect growers of wheat, feed grains, cotton and rice.
● Increasing fees on growers of non-grain crops, such as tobacco, that were protected by government price-support loans.

Clinton also planned to save an estimated $59 million in fiscal 1994 and $723 million over four years by consolidating three large agencies within the Agriculture Department into a new unit called the Farm Service Agency. The three were: the Agriculture Stabilization and Conservation Service, which ran commodity programs; the Soil Conservation Service; and the Farmers Home Administration, which ran farm and rural housing loan programs. Each agency operated its own network of field offices in nearly every county in the nation.

COMMERCE, HOUSING CREDIT

The largest slice of spending in this function went to bank and thrift deposit insurance programs. Other programs covered in the function included housing credit programs, regulatory agencies and several science and technology programs at the Commerce Department.

● **Deposit insurance.** The budget assumed congressional approval of the administration's $45 billion request to finish the savings and loan cleanup. The request included $28 billion for the thrift bailout agency, the Resolution Trust Corporation (RTC), and $17 billion to capitalize the thrift industry's new insurance fund, the Savings Association Insurance Fund (SAIF). The $45 billion in budget authority for the bailout was credited to fiscal 1993.

The impact of deposit insurance on the deficit tended to fluctuate as the government received proceeds from sales of assets it had taken over from failed banks and thrifts. As a result, outlays showed a different story. The largest item was $7.9 billion for the SAIF, which was to assume responsibility for thrifts that failed after fiscal 1993. The SAIF was expected to have a balance of $2.4 billion in 1994.

Net outlays from the Bank Insurance Fund in fiscal 1994 were expected to drop to $2.8 billion, from $4 billion in 1993. The fund was expected to spend $18.6 billion to buy failed bank assets and pay off depositors, but $15.8 billion of that was expected to be offset by asset sales, bank premiums and new fees.

Clinton proposed to raise $1.3 billion over 1994-98 by extending FDIC examination fees to state-chartered banks. Under existing

law, state-chartered banks were not assessed fees for their federal examinations; they instead paid lower fees to state regulators. The administration said that federally chartered banks had been converting to state charters to save money. Under Clinton's proposal, which was unpopular with the industry, bankers were to receive credit for the fees they paid to state regulators.

● **Housing credit.** Clinton assumed a significant boost — from $77.7 billion to $85 billion — in the amount of securities guaranteed by the Government National Mortgage Association (Ginnie Mae), the federal secondary market for home loans pooled by the Federal Housing Administration and the Department of Veterans Affairs. The administration also wanted to raise $146 million a year by allowing Ginnie Mae to charge fees for issuing $50 billion in a new form of security called Real Estate Mortgage Investment Conduits (REMICs). The private Federal National Mortgage Association (Fannie Mae) and the Federal Home Loan Mortgage Corporation (Freddie Mac) already had the authority to issue such securities.

● **Federal Communications Commission.** Clinton proposed raising $4.4 billion over 1995-98 from auctioning licenses for the rights to the additional radio spectrum frequencies transferred from the federal government to the private sector. This was a departure from the existing lottery system.

● **Securities and Exchange Commission (SEC).** The budget also assumed $593 million over fiscal 1994-98 in higher SEC user fees for the registration of new stock issues. Under existing law, corporations paid 1/32 of 1 percent of the value of new securities to the SEC; the administration wanted to raise that to 1/24 of 1 percent.

● **Postal Service.** The Postal Service's subsidized mail program was expected to continue operating at a big loss, though the budget assumed further tightening of eligibility requirements on the types of mail that nonprofit groups could send at subsidized rates. Clinton requested that the Postal Service receive a $91 million appropriation for the subsidy, a $30 million cut from the fiscal 1993 budget.

● **Applied research.** Clinton sought to bolster the activities of the Commerce Department's National Institute of Standards and Technology, the government laboratory devoted to civilian research with commercial applications. He requested $535 million in budget authority for the agency, a 7 percent increase over the fiscal 1993 level of $498 million.

● **Information networks.** The budget included $95 million in new budget authority for the Commerce Department's National Telecommunications and Information Administration, which was expected to play the lead role in developing the nation's computer and communications networks.

COMMUNITY DEVELOPMENT

Clinton sought an increase in spending for community and regional development to $10.1 billion in fiscal 1994, from $9.9 billion the year before. He requested:

● **Community Development.** An increase in budget authority for Community Development Block Grants (CDBG) from $4 billion originally appropriated in fiscal 1993 to $4.2 billion in fiscal 1994.

● **Economic Development Administration (EDA).** $279 million in outlays for the EDA, which provided technical aid to domestic firms and industries adversely affected by foreign trade. The Reagan and Bush administrations had routinely proposed no funding for the program, which had received $240 million in fiscal 1993.

● **Disaster relief.** A decrease in outlays for disaster relief from $2.5 billion in fiscal 1993 to $1.3 billion in 1994, as the need for emergency help to relieve the consequences of Hurricane Andrew and other natural disasters declined.

DEFENSE

For defense-related programs, Clinton requested $263.4 billion in new budget authority, a $9.6 billion cut from the amount

Congress appropriated for fiscal 1993 and $12 billion less than President George Bush had projected for fiscal 1994. Taking account of the cost of inflation, Clinton's budget amounted to a 5 percent reduction from fiscal 1993. It meant total defense outlays in fiscal 1994 of $276.9 billion.

Of the $263.4 billion in new budget authority, $250.7 billion was for military programs in the Defense Department. Most of the remainder — $11.5 billion — was for defense-related work conducted by the Energy Department, which developed, tested and manufactured nuclear weapons and bought nuclear fuel for warships.

Of that amount, $3.8 billion was for the nuclear weapons development and production complex, a reduction of $735 million from the fiscal 1993 appropriation. This cut reflected plans to curtail weapons production and to defer construction of a new reactor to produce tritium, a perishable gas used in U.S. nuclear warheads.

However, Clinton sought an increase of nearly $634 million — to $5.5 billion — in Energy Department funding to clean up toxic and hazardous waste at the nation's nuclear weapons factories.

Preserving Options

Overall, the Clinton defense budget marked time on most major weapons programs in an effort to preserve the administration's options pending a sweeping review of U.S. defense requirements in the post-Cold War world. In broad categories, however, the Clinton request looked this way:

● Funding for research and development remained essentially constant at $38.6 billion, up from $38.2 billion in fiscal 1993.

● Funding for procurement was reduced from $53.6 billion in 1993 to $45.5 billion, but no major weapons program was killed to achieve the reduction. Nearly $2 billion of the cut resulted from the fact that the 1993 budget included the final four of a planned fleet of 20 B-2 stealth bombers.

In addition, the budget sought to continue the existing tempo of training by reducing the number of personnel and disbanding some units:

● Operations and maintenance funding was slightly increased to $89.5 billion, from $86.4 billion in fiscal 1993;

● Spending for military personnel, meanwhile, was to drop from $76.3 billion to $70.1 billion.

Slightly less than 1 percent of Clinton's total request was earmarked to meet the international and domestic challenges of the post-Cold War world. Of that total, $888 million was for the Pentagon's share of the cost of international operations, including:

● $300 million for the cost of U.S. participation in multilateral peacekeeping operations, such as in Somalia.

● $50 million for natural disaster relief operations, in the wake of hurricanes or earthquakes.

● $48 million for other humanitarian assistance missions.

● $400 million, on top of $800 million previously appropriated, to help Russia and other former Soviet republics dispose of nuclear, chemical and biological weapons.

To cushion the impact of defense cutbacks on companies, communities and individuals, the request included $1.66 billion allocated as follows:

● $964 million to encourage small and medium-size defense contractors to invest in "dual-use" technologies — that is, products and manufacturing techniques that would be militarily useful while also helping contractors become more commercially competitive.

● $519 million to help military personnel, civilian Pentagon employees and defense industry workers facing dislocation because of budget cuts.

● $178 million for programs to assist communities hit by layoffs at military bases or by defense contractors.

People and Operations

Clinton's $70.1 billion military personnel request assumed the number of active-duty service members would be trimmed by

108,000 to 1.62 million and the number of National Guard and reserve members would be reduced by 60,000, to 1.02 million.

In line with the personnel cutback, the budget also anticipated a reduction in the "force structure" — the number of combat units in the field — through the following steps:

• Disbanding two of the Army's 14 combat divisions.

• Reducing the number of Navy ships in service from 443 to 413, as retirements of older vessels outstripped the commissioning of new craft.

• Dropping the number of active-duty Air Force fighter wings, which typically consisted of three squadrons of 24 planes each, from 16.1 to 13.3.

But most units were expected to continue training at the existing "operational tempo:" Army battalions would drive their tanks and troop carriers about 800 miles annually in exercises; fleets in the Mediterranean and Western Pacific would be at sea an average of 50.5 days per quarter, compared with an average of 29 days per quarter for ships operating out of U.S. ports; the average monthly flying time would remain 14.5 hours for Army helicopter pilots and 24 hours for Navy fighter pilots; and the average flying time for Air Force pilots would drop slightly to 19.5 hours per month.

Procurement and Research

Strategic weapons. Major requests included:

• $3.76 billion for the Strategic Defense Initiative, the Pentagon's anti-missile defense program. Nearly half of that was earmarked for defenses against short-range (or theater) ballistic missiles.

• $1.13 billion for 24 additional Trident II submarine-launched ballistic missiles.

Ground combat hardware: Major requests included:

• $94 million to upgrade older M-1 tanks and $192 million to modernize older Bradley troop carriers.

• $367 million to continue developing the Comanche armed helicopter.

• $278 million to equip Apache attack helicopters with the new Longbow radar.

• $217 million for MLRS artillery rocket launchers.

Aircraft. The budget funded six major programs:

• $796 million to buy 24 F-16 Air Force fighters.

• $1.75 billion for 36 Navy F/A-18 fighters.

• $2.25 billion to continue developing the new F-22 fighter for the Air Force.

• $1.41 billion to develop a larger version of the F/A-18.

• $399 million to develop the A/F-X carrier-based bomber.

• $2.32 billion for six C-17 cargo jets.

Shipbuilding. Major requests included:

• $2.64 billion for three destroyers equipped with the Aegis anti-aircraft system;

• $894 million to complete construction of a large helicopter carrier to haul up to 2,000 Marines and the helicopters to fly them ashore.

EDUCATION, LABOR

Clinton proposed to reduce spending for job training and higher education in fiscal 1994 and modestly increase elementary, secondary and vocational education.

Outlays for the Labor Department were slated to drop $9.2 billion, to $37.6 billion in fiscal 1994. Training and employment services were cut to $4.9 billion, from $5.2 billion the year before. The administration wanted to combine job-training programs to create one-stop career centers that would provide counseling, job referrals and training in one place. The Labor and Education departments sought $135 million each in fiscal 1994 to create a school-to-work transition program for students who did not move on to higher education. But the money first had to be authorized.

Higher education. Clinton requested $11.5 billion in budget authority for Pell grants, guaranteed student loans, direct loans and the work-study program, down from $12.7 billion in fiscal 1993. Actual dollars available to students were expected to rise

from $27 billion to $28 billion when the federal money was combined with bank loans, school aid and state aid. Finally, outlays for higher education declined to $13 billion in Clinton's budget, from $13.6 billion in 1993.

To phase out the guaranteed student loan program, formally known as Federal Family Education Loans, Clinton requested $3.9 billion in budget authority for 1994, down from $5.2 billion the year before. He asked for $149 million in budget authority, up from $10 million the previous year, for direct loans, which were expected to be the successor to student loans.

Particularly hard hit was the Pell grant program, which provided grants for needy students to attend college. Clinton wanted to freeze the maximum Pell grant at $2,300 per year. Appropriators had cut the maximum grant from $2,400 in 1993 to fund all the students who qualified for the program. Although Clinton requested an increase of about $200 million in 1994 for Pell grants, the actual amount of Pell money available to students was expected to drop to $6.3 billion from $6.4 billion the year before, because of a previous shortfall. And for the first time, the administration wanted students to come up with matching funds up to $800, depending on family income.

Under Clinton's plan, campus-based aid was slated to decline to $1.2 billion from $1.4 billion in 1993. This aid included the work-study program, set to drop to $527 million from $617 million the year before. Supplemental Educational Opportunity Grants, awarded by colleges to students according to need, would decline to $500 million from $585 million in fiscal 1993.

Elementary and secondary education. Clinton requested a slight increase for elementary, secondary and vocational education, with outlays of $15.3 billion in 1994, up from $14.7 billion the year before. He proposed four initiatives totaling $585 million in budget authority to fund his "Goals 2000" program, which included a continuation of Bush's efforts at school reform; a school-to-work transition program; an urban-rural program to help communities integrate education and social services; and professional development for teachers.

Outlays for vocational and adult education went up to $1.4 billion, from estimates of $1.3 billion in spending the year before.

The administration also asked for a slight increase in the Chapter 1 compensatory education program, which provided extra help in basic skills to poor children. Clinton requested $7.1 billion in budget authority, up from $6.7 billion in 1993. Chapter 1 was the largest federal education program aimed at elementary and secondary students.

Finally, Clinton requested $2.2 billion in budget authority in 1994 to help states pay for special education for 5 million children. Actual spending was expected to rise from $2.8 billion in 1993 to $3.5 billion in 1994.

ENERGY

Clinton's budget shifted the focus of energy programs, making sharp cuts in civilian nuclear power research while funneling greater resources into conservation and environmentally friendly energy sources. He called for trimming energy programs overall by $163 million, to $4 billion in budget authority for fiscal 1994.

The Energy Department also was responsible for the nuclear weapons complex, which was accounted for in the defense and science portions of Clinton's budget, where the administration proposed deep cuts and more spending to clean up mothballed facilities.

In energy-related spending, Clinton sought to scale back federal research and development on civilian nuclear power. He requested $267 million in new budget authority for those programs in fiscal 1994, $32 million less than fiscal 1993, according to the Energy Department. Moreover, $85 million of the fiscal 1994 request was for closing ongoing programs.

Much of the savings was slated to come from phasing out the bulk of the Energy Department's advanced reactor program, which had been pursuing designs for two rival reactor technologies. Re-

search and development on fossil fuels — coal, oil and natural gas — also was expected to drop from existing levels. The program aimed to decrease air pollution caused by burning coal to generate electric power.

The budget included $250 million in new budget authority for fiscal 1994 to carry out the fourth and fifth rounds of demonstration projects on technologies to burn coal more cleanly and efficiently. However, it did not include money to continue the so-called clean coal program beyond that round.

Instead, Clinton wanted to shift resources into new energy sources, such as renewables and natural gas, that were generally favored by environmentalists. For example, he requested a jump in budget authority for solar and other renewable energy from $251 million to $327 million, the department said. He also called for a significant boost in programs to increase energy efficiency in homes, businesses, industry and transportation, including a program to promote vehicles powered by alternative fuels.

The budget also proposed to curb federal subsidies to the five regional power administrations that were responsible for developing and marketing power from federal hydroelectric facilities. Clinton called for ensuring regular debt repayment by the power authorities and imposing new conservation requirements.

Clinton also wanted to slow oil purchases to fill the Strategic Petroleum Reserve to 13,300 barrels a day.

ENVIRONMENT

Clinton sought to reduce spending for environmental and natural resources programs by 5 percent in fiscal 1994, to $20.8 billion.

But by shifting funds within the function and adding some from others, an administration that pledged to guard the environment put the best face on those figures. For example, Clinton called for increased spending for the Interior Department and the Environmental Protection Agency (EPA), the government's two central environmental agencies.

Interior Secretary Bruce Babbitt said his agency's budget would increase by almost 6 percent to $9.5 billion over fiscal 1993 spending.

EPA Administrator Carol M. Browner said her agency's funding would increase by 6 percent to $7.3 billion, a figure that included fiscal 1994 funds called for in the president's stimulus package. Without those funds, the EPA budget was $470 million below 1993 funding.

The Interior Department planned to shift its focus to maintaining existing federal lands and facilities. The budget recommended a substantial reduction in federal land acquisition spending, with outlays for such purchases falling 12 percent from fiscal 1993 spending, to $244 million.

Conservation and land management spending by the Forest Service, an arm of the Agriculture Department, dropped to $2.9 billion in Clinton's budget, a 4 percent cut from 1993. The budget was silent about the volume of the government's timber sale program, which was at the center of a controversy over the threatened northern spotted owl and Northwest forest jobs.

Clinton asked Congress to revive the Wetlands Reserve Program, which Congress had refused to fund in 1992. The program, part of the 1990 farm bill, was designed to encourage farmers to take 1 million fragile acres out of production. Clinton's budget called for $370 million for the program in fiscal 1994, enough to enroll 450,000 acres.

Clinton requested $6.9 billion for pollution control initiatives, a 3 percent increase. This included new spending for regulatory, enforcement and research programs; water treatment facilities; and a new revolving fund to help states comply with federal drinking water standards.

The budget assumed that grazing fees on federal lands would go up and that mining royalties on federal lands would be imposed, despite an administration decision not to use the congressional budget process to overhaul these programs. *(Mining reform, p. 261; grazing fees, p. 273)*

Clinton also called for boosting fees paid by visitors to federal parks, forests and recreation areas by 15 percent, bringing receipts to $106.2 million in fiscal 1994, $30 million more than 1993.

HEALTH, MEDICARE

The budget avoided any discussion of the sweeping health-care changes Clinton had promised to unveil later in the year, but it introduced many of the themes that were expected to be writ large in health-care reform.

There were spending increases for preventive care and for women's and children's health, and an increased emphasis on primary care. Clinton also requested almost double existing spending for his highly publicized vaccination program, which aimed to immunize all children before they entered school. Spending for basic science research was restrained, but research on AIDS and women's health was slated for increases.

The most far-reaching proposals were the savings Clinton proposed to achieve in the Medicare and Medicaid programs. These were largely the same cuts detailed in his February deficit-reduction plan.

However, because of recalculations and new economic assumptions, the savings were expected to be $2.9 billion — about $300 million less than the $3.2 billion projected in February. Over five years, the savings in Medicare and Medicaid were $9 billion less than in the February projections.

Donna E. Shalala, the secretary of Health and Human Services, had repeatedly described the budget as a "down payment on health-care reform," and one goal of the budget proposal seemed to be to begin the transition to a national health-care system through additional spending on preventive care and spending limits for Medicare and Medicaid.

Nearly one in four Americans — 65 million elderly, disabled or poor people — were expected to receive either Medicare or Medicaid payments in fiscal 1994. That was a 3 percent increase in recipients above fiscal 1993. Despite efforts to curb the growth in spending for Medicare and Medicaid, spending was expected to climb by 12.5 percent in 1994.

Medicare

The Medicare program, projected to spend $147.4 billion in 1994, served nearly 36.5 million elderly and disabled people. The program covered both hospital expenditures (Part A) and outpatient costs, primarily doctors' bills (Part B).

Clinton estimated spending $101.2 billion for Medicare payments to hospitals, $1.9 billion less than if the program continued at the existing level, adjusted for inflation. Most of the proposed savings were to be achieved by cutting the annual increase for hospital reimbursements to 1 percentage point less than the health-care inflation rate. Clinton also sought to defer the inflation update for three months by putting it on a calendar year.

Hospitals that trained physicians were asked to experience cuts both in the rates of reimbursement for the cost of training and in the salaries of residents and interns. Under the Clinton proposal, salaries were to be based on a national average rather than reflecting geographic differences.

To replenish the dwindling Medicare hospital insurance fund, Clinton proposed using general fund revenues that would be raised by subjecting 85 percent of the Social Security benefits of affluent retirees to the income tax, up from 50 percent. That was expected to raise at least $2.8 billion in fiscal 1994.

Clinton requested $63.6 billion for Part B of Medicare, which paid for physicians' services. That represented a $742 million savings, to be achieved in part by slowing the annual rate of increase in doctors' fees. Primary care physicians, however, could receive a full fee increase. Clinton also proposed reducing Medicare payments for clinical laboratory services.

Medicaid

The joint state-federal program that funded health care for 34 million poor people had a projected cost in fiscal 1994 of $92

billion. To slow the dramatic increase in the cost of the program — which had risen at an annual rate of 22 percent in recent years — Clinton proposed $285 million in spending reductions.

One cost-cutting proposal — a reduction in the federal share of Medicaid's administrative costs — had been a favorite remedy of former Presidents George Bush and Ronald Reagan. The government reimbursed the states for 50 percent of most administrative costs, but 75 percent to 90 percent of selected programs. Clinton wanted to set the federal share at 50 percent for all administrative services.

Clinton also wanted to allow states to continue the optional provision of personal care services, and he proposed closing loopholes that allowed non-poor individuals to qualify for Medicaid's long-term care services.

Discretionary Spending

Spending at the National Institutes of Health, the government's premier health research establishment, barely kept pace with inflation under Clinton's proposal. It was slated to rise just 3 percent in fiscal 1994, to $10.7 billion. However, spending for AIDS research was to rise 21 percent, to $227 million. Clinton also allotted $416 million for research on breast cancer, up from $205 million in 1993. Part of the added funding was to come from a transfer of $216 million from the Department of Defense.

Clinton requested a 20 percent increase in funding for federal family planning programs, bringing spending to $208 million in fiscal 1994. The budget did not include any money to cover abortions for poor women, although Clinton had said he would not ask Congress to ban spending federal dollars for abortions as Bush and Reagan had done.

Clinton boosted proposed spending for maternal and child health programs by $40 million, a 6 percent increase, which was in keeping with his emphasis on women's and children's health. He also sought a $21 million increase (25 percent) in Healthy Start, an infant mortality prevention program begun under Bush. The program, which aimed to cut infant mortality in half over five years in 15 communities with especially high infant mortality rates, received $79.3 million in fiscal 1993.

INCOME SECURITY

Clinton asked for an increase in spending on income security — the social safety net provided by housing, nutrition, unemployment and other programs — from $209.2 billion in fiscal 1993 to $215 billion in fiscal 1994. Social Security spending was expected to increase from an estimated $304.9 billion in 1993 to $320.7 billion in 1994. The increase included a projected 3 percent cost of living adjustment.

• **Housing.** The budget called for gradually eliminating the HOPE program, strongly advocated by Bush administration Housing and Urban Development Secretary Jack F. Kemp. HOPE — Homeownership and Opportunity for People Everywhere — helped public housing and other low-income tenants buy apartments and houses. The budget included $109 million in budget authority for HOPE in fiscal 1994, down from $321 million in 1993 and provided for HOPE grants only to those recipients whose plans were already under way.

At the same time, Clinton sought to reinvigorate a Democratic housing initiative, the HOME Investment Partnerships program, which provided grants to build or renovate affordable housing to localities that provided matching funds. HOME's budget authority was increased from $1.1 billion in fiscal 1993 to $1.6 billion in 1994.

Clinton called for an increase in outlays for Section 8 subsidies for private low-income housing from $3.1 billion in fiscal 1993 to $4.1 billion in 1994. However, the spending level requested for several other major low-income housing programs, including those that funded the development and modernization of public housing for families, the elderly and the disabled, was relatively unchanged from 1993 spending.

Clinton envisioned a reorganized public housing program that focused on renovating the most run-down units, especially in large

developments. He requested $483 million in 1994 budget authority for the program. He requested $320 million in budget authority, up from $150 million in 1993, for the Supportive Housing Program, which provided shelter and support services for the homeless. And he asked for $48 billion, up from $40 billion in 1993, for a reorganized version of a program called Youthbuild, which enabled school dropouts to learn construction skills.

The budget included $265 million in budget authority, up from $175 million in fiscal 1993, for Community Partnership Against Crime (COMPAC), which was to replace the Drug Elimination Grants program, focusing on anti-crime efforts in and near low-income housing developments.

• **Unemployment compensation.** The budget assumed a decline in spending for unemployment compensation to $29 billion in fiscal 1994, from $38 billion in 1993. The administration proposed $9 million in budget authority to improve state profiling systems that identified workers most likely to be unemployed for a long time. The program was supposed to help these workers find jobs when they began collecting unemployment compensation, enabling them to leave the program faster.

• **Nutrition.** With people signing up for food aid programs in record numbers, the administration assumed $25.1 billion in outlays for the food stamps program in fiscal 1994, up from $23.5 billion in 1993. About 27 million people were expected to qualify for food stamps in fiscal 1994.

The budget included increased aid for children, from food to immunizations. Outlays for the supplemental food program for Women, Infants and Children (WIC) was slated to increase from $2.9 billion in 1993 to $3.3 billion in 1994. The program helped low-income women buy food for themselves while they were pregnant and for their children up to age 5.

• **Low-Income Home Energy Assistance Program (LIHEAP).** Clinton sought increased outlays of $2.1 billion in fiscal 1994, up from $1 billion in 1993, for LIHEAP, a program that gave states grants to help low-income households with heating and cooling costs, weatherization and emergency energy assistance. He requested additional increases in subsequent years to offset the impact of his proposed broad-based energy tax.

• **Other income security.** The Supplemental Security Income (SSI) program, which aided the aged, blind and disabled, was slated to increase from $23.6 billion in fiscal 1993 to $27.3 billion in 1994. The increase included a projected 3 percent cost of living adjustment. Outlays for the earned-income tax credit, a refundable tax break for the working poor, were to increase from $8.4 billion in fiscal 1993 to $9.8 billion in fiscal 1994.

INTERNATIONAL AFFAIRS

The budget included $19 billion in outlays for foreign affairs in fiscal 1994 — an increase of $700 million over 1993. The function covered foreign assistance, the State Department's operations, and voluntary and assessed contributions for a host of international organizations.

A technicality in the budget process made it difficult to reconcile White House and State Department estimates of international spending. The State Department calculated foreign affairs outlays at $21.3 billion and new budget authority at $21.6 billion.

Secretary of State Warren Christopher described the spending plan as a "transitional budget" that would begin redirecting foreign policy for the post-Cold War era. Because the State Department was still reviewing assistance levels for most countries, the budget provided only the broad outlines of its initiatives.

But the administration gave a clear signal of the importance it attached to international peacekeeping, requesting nearly $700 million in new budget authority for U.N. peacekeeping operations, an increase of more than $200 million over fiscal 1993. That included $175 million for a new peacekeeping contingency fund to assist the United Nations in meeting unanticipated global crises.

Christopher had highlighted the need for "robust peacekeeping capabilities" to stem regional and ethnic conflicts, such as the war

that had devastated the former Yugoslavia. The defense budget also set aside $300 million to underwrite U.S. military participation in peacekeeping missions.

The budget also included a huge boost in economic aid for Russia and the other republics of the former Soviet Union — $704 million in fiscal 1994, $287 million more than was appropriated in 1993. The administration requested $50 million to establish a new "nonproliferation and disarmament fund" to stem the spread of weapons of mass destruction in the former Soviet Union and elsewhere. The initiative appeared to be modeled on a program for dismantling Soviet nuclear weapons proposed by Sens. Sam Nunn, D-Ga., and Richard G. Lugar, R-Ind., which was first enacted in 1991.

The budget also included increased funding for programs to foster "sustainable development" — a catchall term embracing a host of objectives such as reducing population growth and stemming environmental degradation.

Clinton sought $663 million for family planning programs, an increase of about $100 million over fiscal 1993. And in keeping with administration intentions to overturn Reagan-era restrictions on population aid, the budget included $50 million for the U.N. Population Fund. The Reagan and Bush administrations had denied aid for the U.N. agency because it operated in China, which had been condemned for its policy of coerced abortions.

The administration sought a $371 million increase for the international banks, including $190 million more for the International Development Association, which extended credit to the poorest nations.

As in previous years, Israel and Egypt dominated funding in the security assistance account, which provided military and economic support for key allies. Clinton requested $3 billion for Israel and $2.1 billion for Egypt, the same amount that Congress annually earmarked for the pair of Middle Eastern allies.

Overall, the administration trimmed about $400 million from the $6 billion security assistance account. But most of those savings came from a decision to terminate the obscure Special Defense Acquisition Fund, a revolving fund for purchasing military equipment in advance of its sale to U.S. allies.

To fund its new initiatives, the administration proposed freezing most other international programs — including salaries for State Department employees.

Clinton also requested:

● $30 million to establish Radio Free Asia, fulfilling a pledge he had made during the presidential campaign.

● $409 million in economic assistance for countries in Central and Eastern Europe, a modest increase of $11 million over fiscal 1993.

● $45 million for debt restructuring under the Enterprise for the Americas program, a plan developed by the Bush administration to help stimulate private enterprise in Latin America.

JUSTICE

Clinton requested overall increases for law and judicial programs, but the hikes were not as big as the ones the Bush administration had sought. Outlays for justice programs were slated to increase by $783 million (5.1 percent) to $16.2 billion; Bush, who had stressed anti-crime themes, raised justice programs by 9.5 percent in his last budget.

The biggest increases in Clinton's fiscal 1994 budget were for the courts and the corrections system, which were each slated to receive nearly 20 percent more than in the previous year. The judiciary branch budget was submitted unchanged by the administration.

Overall, outlays for federal law enforcement programs dropped slightly, with border enforcement programs taking the biggest hit. Money for criminal investigations by the FBI, the Drug Enforcement Administration and other agencies went up 8.6 percent.

New spending for Clinton's "investment proposals" included:

● $100 million in budget authority for his federal/state partnership program. The budget called for $50 million to promote local community policing efforts with grants to state and local governments; $25 million to provide scholarships to students pursuing law enforcement careers who promised to serve as police officers; and $25 million to upgrade federal criminal recordkeeping systems.

The Justice Department said the records improvements were partially designed to accommodate the proposed Brady bill, which required waiting periods for handgun purchases. The administration said the money would help create a "national criminal background check system" that police could use to prevent convicted felons from buying handguns.

● $151 million in budget authority for the overbooked Federal Prison System to provide money for 4,620 beds in several new and expanded prisons. Budget documents said the government expected to house an average of 82,717 offenders in 1994, up from 75,320 in 1993. Clinton also requested an extra $88 million in budget authority to pay state and local jailers for keeping federal prisoners.

● $6.6 million in budget authority for resettling Cuban and Haitian refugees in the United States.

● $25.5 million in budget authority for the Immigration and Naturalization Service to pay for new inspectors in the Southwest and other program improvements aimed at detecting illegal aliens and deporting aliens convicted of felonies after they completed their prison sentences.

SCIENCE, SPACE, TECHNOLOGY

While Clinton wanted to add billions of dollars to technology programs with marketplace appeal, he essentially proposed to freeze spending on basic research programs with lesser commercial promise. And "big science" initiatives such as the space station and superconducting super collider were to be cut dramatically.

Outlays for the science, space and technology portion of the budget overall rose about 4 percent to $17.8 billion, up from $17.1 billion in fiscal 1993.

Of that amount, $13.3 billion was for space flight, research and related space programs — a 3 percent increase over fiscal 1993. The remainder was for the National Science Foundation and science programs at the departments of Energy and Defense.

The science function was only one part of the overall federal research effort. Research initiatives also were included in defense, commerce, health and energy programs.

Governmentwide, Clinton proposed to increase budget authority for federal research and development to $76 billion, a 3 percent increase over fiscal 1993 — about the same increase that Bush proposed the previous year.

Shifting Research

Clinton hoped to shift more overall federal science research from its concentration on defense-related applications toward commercial uses. For fiscal 1994, civilian research programs were slated to get $30 billion in budget authority, or 42 percent of the total federal research funds.

● **NASA.** Clinton requested $15.3 billion in budget authority for the space agency, a 6.6 percent increase over fiscal 1993. But NASA's bid to put a space station laboratory into orbit by the turn of the century faced a steep budget challenge. About $9 billion had already been spent on the project, which critics called high on cost and low on merit.

The space station, which the administration had ordered drastically scaled back and redesigned, was slated to get $2.3 billion in budget authority for fiscal 1993, slightly more than the $2.1 billion appropriated in 1993.

But that money was not solely for the space station. Also included were unspecified "new technology investments" that NASA Administrator Daniel S. Goldin described as short-term space technology projects to be funded through savings expected from the redesign effort. The administration was promoting those

projects — totaling as much as $1 billion in fiscal 1993 — as a way to replace any jobs that would be lost after the space station was redesigned.

Clinton also sought to eliminate programs aimed at eventually sending astronauts to the moon and Mars and helping to make the United States more competitive in the commercial space launch industry.

The budget included $313 million in budget authority for the Advanced Solid Rocket Motor favored by many in Congress, down from $360 million in fiscal 1993.

● **Superconducting super collider.** In keeping with Clinton's campaign pledges, the budget included funding for the controversial superconducting super collider that was being built in Waxahachie, Texas. But Clinton planned to stretch out the construction schedule for the atom smasher, a move that had the potential to lower immediate costs but raise the overall price tag, which stood at $8.3 billion.

The budget allotted $640 million in budget authority for the collider in fiscal 1994. Former Energy Secretary James D. Watkins had said $1.2 billion (including foreign contributions) would be required to keep the project on schedule.

● **National Science Foundation.** The budget included $3 billion for the agency, up from $2.9 billion in fiscal 1993. Funding was to be cut for general grants in all research areas, including the life and earth sciences, engineering and mathematics. But $167 million in new spending was earmarked for "strategic" research areas such as the earth's climate, science education, biotechnology and advanced manufacturing.

TRANSPORTATION

All but a fraction of this spending fell within the Department of Transportation, which was slated to receive $40.6 billion in budget authority for 1994 under Clinton's budget — up $789 million from 1993. That total included $21 billion for the Federal Highway Administration, $9.2 billion for the Federal Aviation Administration, $4.6 billion for mass transit, $3.8 billion for the Coast Guard and $1 billion for the Federal Railroad Administration.

The biggest winners in the proposed transportation budget were highway construction, with a $2.7 billion increase over the 1993 budget, and mass transit systems, with a $700 million increase. Unlike the Bush and Reagan administrations, which tried to cut operating assistance for urban transit systems, Clinton sought to continue such funding at existing levels. He also proposed a $41 million increase in aid for rural transit systems.

Even with the increase, funding for mass transit was still a half-billion dollars below the amount that had been authorized by the 1991 surface transportation law (PL 102-240). The highway program, by contrast, was to receive its full authorization under the budget.

Transportation Secretary Federico F. Peña said the budget went "an extraordinary part of the way" toward satisfying the country's transit needs. Clinton's proposal for transit was more than 50 percent higher than Bush's 1993 budget and more than 20 percent above what Congress appropriated for the year, Peña said.

Other proposed increases in budget authority or trust fund spending included:

● $135 million more for the High-Speed Ground Transportation Development program to support high-speed rail and magnetic levitation trains. The program received only $5 million in fiscal 1993, although Congress also appropriated $13 million to study magnetic levitation trains.

● $119 million more to improve the air traffic control system and $30 million more for airport improvements.

● $70 million more for Intelligent Vehicle Highway Systems, a program to reduce traffic congestion without pouring more concrete. It received $31 million in 1993.

● $71 million more for research and development efforts throughout the Transportation Department, an increase of 11 percent.

● $35 million more to improve the Coast Guard's navigational facilities and pollution-control equipment.

● $32 million more for highway safety grants to states, most of it aimed at reducing drunken driving.

To offset some of the increase in highway spending, the administration proposed to stop funding for more than $350 million worth of projects that Congress included in the 1993 transportation appropriations bill.

Clinton proposed to slash the Maritime Administration from $615 million to $430 million, a cut of 30 percent. Most of the cut came from the Ready Reserve Force, a fleet of vessels that supported U.S. troop deployments. Despite the cut, the budget still included enough money to buy four new vessels.

Funding for Amtrak was down slightly, with a $9 million cut in operating grants; $8 million in local rail freight assistance was to be eliminated, along with $7 million in aid for commuter trains in Philadelphia.

The budget assumed that the department would reduce its work force by the equivalent of 1,765 full-time civilian jobs, mainly at the Federal Aviation Administration. Peña said he expected the cuts to be made through attrition, rather than layoffs.

The budget also assumed that the Airport and Airway Trust Fund would be increased by $18 million. The money was to come from increasing the registration fee on private airplanes from a one-time charge of $5 to an annual fee of $90, increasing to $210 by 1996, Peña said.

VETERANS

Clinton assumed an increase in outlays of $37.9 billion for veterans programs, up $2.3 billion, or nearly 6.5 percent, from fiscal 1993.

The bulk of this was an estimated $20.2 billion for mandatory spending programs, an increase of nearly 8 percent. The funds were chiefly disability compensation payments for disabled veterans or their survivors; the payments were set to rise by $1.4 billion to $14.6 billion.

The budget also included discretionary outlays of $17.4 billion in fiscal 1994, an increase of 5.5 percent. The money was mainly earmarked to administer the Department of Veterans Affairs health-care system, whose costs were expected to rise by $836 million.

The picture was reversed when the budget was viewed in terms of new budget authority — an indication of where the administration wanted to go. Budget authority for discretionary programs was slated to rise 5 percent to $17.5 billion; for mandatory programs, it rose at a lower 2 percent rate.

The new health-care spending included $287 million to equip and staff new facilities. The chief long-term savings proposed by the department came from continuing an expiring program that required insurers to reimburse the VA for treating veterans with injuries related to their service.

In the department's housing program, three fee increases were expected to capture $939 million worth of new revenue in five years. The bulk, $763 million, was to come from increasing the fee veterans paid for VA mortgages from 1.25 percent to 2 percent of the value of the mortgage. ■

Clinton Economic Assumptions

(Calendar years; dollar amounts in billions) [1]

	Actual 1991	Projections						
		1992	1993	1994	1995	1996	1997	1998
Gross domestic product								
Dollar levels:								
Current dollars	5,678	5,943	6,254	6,594	6,942	7,288	7,626	7,952
Constant (1987) dollars	4,821	4,918	5,054	5,204	5,354	5,497	5,628	5,740
Implicit price deflator (1987 = 100), annual average	117.8	120.8	123.8	126.7	129.7	132.6	135.5	138.5
Percent change, fourth quarter over fourth quarter:								
Current dollars	3.5	5.1	5.4	5.4	5.2	4.9	4.5	4.1
Constant (1987) dollars	0.1	2.7	2.8	3.0	2.8	2.6	2.2	1.8
Implicit price deflator (1987 = 100)	3.3	2.4	2.5	2.4	2.3	2.2	2.2	2.2
Percent change, year over year:								
Current dollars	2.8	4.7	5.2	5.4	5.3	5.0	4.6	4.3
Constant (1987) dollars	-1.2	2.0	2.8	3.0	2.9	2.7	2.4	2.0
Implicit price deflator (1987 = 100)	4.0	2.6	2.4	2.4	2.3	2.3	2.2	2.2
Incomes								
Personal income	4,828	5,050	5,308	5,617	5,952	6,282	6,602	6,913
Wages and salaries	2,812	2,912	3,055	3,226	3,404	3,576	3,737	3,891
Corporate profits before tax	335	376	432	457	480	509	534	551
Consumer Price Index (all urban) [2]								
Level (1982-84 = 100), annual average	136.2	140.3	144.6	148.5	152.5	156.6	160.8	165.2
Percent change, fourth quarter over fourth quarter:	3.0	3.1	2.8	2.7	2.7	2.7	2.7	2.7
Percent change, year over year	4.2	3.0	3.0	2.7	2.7	2.7	2.7	2.7
Unemployment rate, civilian (percent) [3]								
Fourth-quarter level	6.9	7.3	6.9	6.4	6.1	5.9	5.7	5.7
Annual average	6.7	7.4	7.1	6.6	6.2	6.0	5.8	5.7
Federal pay raise, January (percent)	4.1	4.2	3.7	0.0	2.0	1.7	1.6	2.3
Interest rate (percent) [4]								
91-day Treasury bills	5.4	3.5	3.2	3.7	4.3	4.7	4.8	4.9
10-year Treasury notes	7.9	7.0	6.7	6.6	6.6	6.5	6.5	6.4

[1] *Based on data available as of December 1992, except proposed pay raises*

[2] *CPI for urban consumers. Two versions of the CPI were published. The index shown here is that used, as required by law, in calculating automatic adjustments to individual income tax brackets.*

[3] *Percent of civilian labor force, excluding armed forces residing in the United States*

[4] *Average rate on new issues within period*

SOURCE: President's fiscal 1994 budget

Budget Authority, Outlays by Agency

(Fiscal years; in millions of dollars †)

AGENCY	BUDGET AUTHORITY			OUTLAYS		
	1992 actual	1993 estimate	1994 proposed	1992 actual	1993 estimate	1994 proposed
Legislative Branch	$2,641	$2,716	$3,132	$2,677	$2,847	$3,134
The Judiciary	2,445	2,661	3,257	2,308	2,635	3,141
Executive Office of the President	202	243	178	186	241	187
Funds Appropriated to the President	13,449	23,661	11,641	11,113	11,829	12,123
Agriculture	66,288	68,146	67,548	56,437	66,915	63,021
Commerce	3,023	3,418	3,516	2,567	3,179	3,259
Defense — Military	281,883	259,072	250,745	286,632	277,304	264,227
Defense — Civil	28,415	29,539	30,538	28,268	29,496	30,660
Education	28,833	33,110	30,668	26,047	30,907	31,016
Energy	17,206	17,342	17,301	15,522	17,522	17,005
Health and Human Services, except Social Security	276,265	298,206	324,631	257,332	292,788	325,943
Health and Human Services, Social Security	283,365	300,707	315,727	281,418	298,943	314,121
Housing and Urban Development	24,966	29,231	26,086	24,470	26,018	28,876
Interior	7,110	7,234	7,181	6,549	7,544	7,200
Justice	9,977	10,380	10,408	9,802	10,554	10,348
Labor	48,161	47,879	40,399	47,163	46,812	37,565
State	5,194	5,751	5,560	5,007	5,545	5,538
Transportation	36,224	40,762	40,627	32,491	36,464	39,073
Treasury	295,677	302,512	319,971	292,960	301,663	318,897
Veterans Affairs	33,933	35,453	36,382	33,894	35,406	37,732
Environmental Protection Agency	6,461	7,599	6,089	5,950	6,516	6,745
General Services Administration	359	835	329	469	1,350	839
National Aeronautics and Space Administration	14,317	14,322	15,266	13,961	14,082	14,673
Office of Personnel Management	35,765	39,283	39,688	35,596	37,163	38,743
Small Business Administration	1,891	1,153	867	581	840	700
Other independent agencies	59,698	71,178	34,858	18,572	22,042	25,836
Allowances	—	—	−838	—	—	−747
TOTAL	**$1,466,635**	**$1,533,429**	**$1,517,217**	**$1,380,860**	**$1,467,639**	**$1,515,318**
On budget	1,210,811	1,261,553	1,233,084	1,128,521	1,200,409	1,235,895
Off budget	255,824	271,876	284,133	252,339	267,230	279,423

† Excludes comprehensive health reform; figures may not add to totals due to rounding; undistributed offsetting receipts not included above.

SOURCE: President's fiscal 1994 budget

Fiscal 1994 Budget by Function

(Figures for 1993 and 1994 are estimates; in millions of dollars †)

	BUDGET AUTHORITY			OUTLAYS		
	1992	1993	1994	1992	1993	1994
NATIONAL DEFENSE						
Military defense	$ 282,127	$ 258,869	$ 250,745	$ 286,892	$ 277,185	$ 264,152
Atomic energy defense activities	11,980	12,067	11,536	10,619	11,664	11,505
Defense-related activities	964	1,831	1,082	839	1,768	1,212
TOTAL	295,070	272,768	263,363	298,350	290,617	276,869
INTERNATIONAL AFFAIRS						
International security assistance	6,682	5,586	5,441	7,490	7,915	6,777
International development/humanitarian assistance	6,655	7,125	8,245	6,133	6,316	7,347
Conduct of foreign affairs	4,063	4,598	4,377	3,894	4,449	4,343
Foreign information and exchange activities	1,303	1,373	1,468	1,280	1,438	1,465
International financial programs	2,523	12,312	43	−2,689	−1,769	−970
TOTAL	21,227	30,994	19,574	16,107	18,348	18,963
GENERAL SCIENCE, SPACE AND TECHNOLOGY						
General science and basic research	4,125	4,380	4,736	3,571	4,276	4,503
Space flight, research and supporting activities	13,199	13,062	13,669	12,838	12,856	13,255
TOTAL	17,324	17,442	18,405	16,409	17,133	17,758
ENERGY						
Energy supply	4,789	3,232	2,752	3,226	4,366	2,684
Energy conservation	511	664	763	468	546	648
Emergency energy preparedness	282	60	182	319	360	296
Energy information, policy and regulation	513	235	332	486	184	276
TOTAL	6,095	4,192	4,029	4,499	5,455	3,904
NATURAL RESOURCES AND ENVIRONMENT						
Pollution control and abatement	6,605	7,778	6,268	6,075	6,716	6,937
Water resources	4,768	4,856	4,499	4,559	5,081	4,666
Conservation and land management	4,652	4,503	3,976	4,581	4,688	3,794
Recreational resources	2,690	2,825	2,650	2,378	2,854	2,762
Other natural resources	2,575	2,628	2,761	2,432	2,608	2,635
TOTAL	21,290	22,590	20,154	20,025	21,947	20,793
AGRICULTURE						
Farm income stabilization	19,651	17,757	14,145	12,666	19,176	14,517
Agricultural research and services	2,725	2,703	2,622	2,539	2,682	2,637
TOTAL	22,376	20,460	16,767	15,205	21,858	17,154
COMMERCE AND HOUSING CREDIT						
Mortgage credit	4,514	2,968	2,420	4,320	2,471	1,436
Postal Service subsidy (on budget)	511	161	130	511	161	130
Postal Service (off budget)	2,198	4,509	4,679	659	1,627	1,574
Deposit insurance	36,961	50,476	12,704	2,518	2,839	7,558
Other advancement of commerce	2,575	2,906	2,663	2,111	2,666	2,472
TOTAL	46,759	61,020	22,596	10,118	9,763	13,170
(On budget)	(44,561)	(56,511)	(17,917)	(9,459)	(8,136)	(11,596)
(Off budget)	(2,198)	(4,509)	(4,679)	(659)	(1,627)	(1,574)
TRANSPORTATION						
Ground transportation	23,290	27,180	26,995	20,347	22,786	25,531
Air transportation	10,043	10,466	10,863	9,313	10,081	10,306
Water transportation	3,320	3,253	3,722	3,430	3,746	3,913
Other transportation	277	288	323	244	296	318
TOTAL	36,929	41,186	41,904	33,333	36,909	40,068
COMMUNITY AND REGIONAL DEVELOPMENT						
Community development	3,788	7,437	5,174	3,643	4,475	5,858
Area and regional development	3,285	3,202	3,214	2,315	2,705	2,791
Disaster relief and insurance	5,223	601	565	881	2,714	1,432
TOTAL	12,296	11,241	8,952	6,838	9,894	10,081
EDUCATION, TRAINING, EMPLOYMENT, SOCIAL SERVICES						
Elementary, secondary and vocational education	14,230	14,890	15,350	12,402	14,729	15,299
Higher education	12,166	15,759	12,675	11,268	13,649	13,048
Research and general education aids	2,082	2,184	2,237	1,996	2,138	2,249
Training and employment	7,252	8,144	9,896	6,479	7,744	7,500
Other labor services	894	933	942	884	920	930
Social services	12,041	13,873	15,924	12,221	14,192	14,576
TOTAL	48,665	55,783	57,025	45,250	53,372	53,602

Fiscal 1994 Budget by Function

(Figures for 1993 and 1994 are estimates; in millions of dollars †)

	BUDGET AUTHORITY			OUTLAYS		
	1992	1993	1994	1992	1993	1994
HEALTH						
Health-care services	$ 80,087	$ 96,060	$ 102,765	$ 77,719	$ 92,943	$ 105,299
Health research and training	10,703	11,161	11,377	10,021	10,557	10,851
Consumer and occupational health and safety	1,764	1,818	1,626	1,757	1,816	1,617
TOTAL	92,554	109,039	115,767	89,497	105,317	117,768
MEDICARE	133,599	134,698	147,328	119,024	132,678	147,432
INCOME SECURITY						
General retirement and disability insurance	5,989	6,214	6,551	5,483	5,405	5,557
Federal employee retirement and disability	58,301	61,067	63,646	57,572	59,714	62,411
Unemployment compensation	39,534	38,234	29,068	39,466	38,196	29,088
Housing assistance	19,746	21,402	21,215	18,914	21,292	24,082
Food and nutrition assistance	33,459	39,147	43,164	32,622	35,405	37,964
Other income security	43,618	49,716	55,104	42,901	49,194	55,875
TOTAL	200,649	215,779	218,748	196,958	209,205	214,977
SOCIAL SECURITY	289,532	306,669	322,274	287,585	304,905	320,668
(On budget)	(6,167)	(5,963)	(6,547)	(6,166)	(5,963)	(6,547)
(Off budget)	(283,365)	(300,707)	(315,727)	(281,418)	(298,943)	(314,121)
VETERANS' BENEFITS AND SERVICES						
Income security	17,412	17,754	18,261	17,296	17,578	19,243
Education, training and rehabilitation	600	700	769	783	759	1,051
Housing	815	745	594	898	1,055	678
Hospital and medical care	14,256	15,421	15,918	14,091	15,097	15,933
Other benefits and services	1,070	1,037	1,019	1,065	1,130	1,013
TOTAL	34,152	35,657	36,561	34,133	35,620	37,918
ADMINISTRATION OF JUSTICE						
Federal law enforcement activities	6,690	6,731	6,838	6,462	6,676	6,579
Federal litigative and judicial activities	5,130	5,558	6,212	5,054	5,490	6,143
Federal correctional activities	2,101	2,035	2,313	2,114	2,268	2,692
Criminal justice assistance	872	856	960	795	965	767
TOTAL	14,793	15,179	16,322	14,426	15,399	16,182
GENERAL GOVERNMENT						
Legislative functions	2,137	2,114	2,450	2,124	2,227	2,442
Executive direction and management	212	256	296	188	245	275
Central fiscal operations	7,022	7,452	7,614	6,612	7,461	7,594
General property and records management	508	995	514	692	1,653	1,066
Central personnel management	171	439	177	206	162	163
General-purpose fiscal assistance	1,893	2,198	2,277	1,865	2,205	2,266
Other general government	1,712	1,576	1,123	1,782	1,573	1,112
Deductions for offsetting receipts	−524	−677	−709	−524	−677	−709
TOTAL	13,131	14,352	13,743	12,945	14,849	14,211
NET INTEREST						
Interest on the public debt	292,330	294,658	309,673	292,330	294,658	309,673
Interest received by on-budget trust funds	−54,193	−54,834	−56,604	−54,193	−54,834	−56,604
Interest received by off-budget trust funds	−23,637	−26,967	−29,542	−23,637	−26,967	−29,542
Other interest	−15,025	−11,314	−11,435	−15,061	−11,321	−11,435
TOTAL	199,475	201,544	212,091	199,439	201,536	212,091
(On budget)	(223,112)	(228,511)	(241,633)	(223,076)	(228,503)	(241,633)
(Off budget)	(−23,637)	(−26,967)	(−29,542)	(−23,637)	(−26,967)	(−29,542)
ALLOWANCES	—	—	−838	—	—	−747
UNDISTRIBUTED OFFSETTING RECEIPTS	−39,280	−37,165	−37,546	−39,280	−37,165	−37,546
(On budget)	(−33,179)	(−30,793)	(−30,815)	(−33,179)	(−30,793)	(−30,815)
(Off budget)	(−6,101)	(−6,373)	(−6,731)	(−6,101)	(−6,373)	(−6,731)
TOTAL	$ 1,466,635	$ 1,533,429	$ 1,517,217	$ 1,380,860	$ 1,467,639	$ 1,515,318
(On budget)	(1,210,811)	(1,261,553)	(1,233,084)	(1,128,521)	(1,200,409)	(1,235,895)
(Off budget)	(255,824)	(271,876)	(284,133)	(252,339)	(267,230)	(279,423)

† Figures may not add due to rounding.

SOURCE: President's fiscal 1994 budget

Revenue and Receipts Proposals

(In billions of dollars)

	Estimate			Estimate	
	1994	**1994-1998**		**1994**	**1994-1998**
REVENUE RAISING PROPOSALS:			OTHER RECEIPTS:		
Raise top individual tax rate to 36%	27.5	123.2	IRS initiative	−0.1	1.5
Repeal HI taxable wage base [1]	2.8	29.2	Commodity Futures Trading Commission fee	0.1	0.3
Increase top income tax rate on large corporations to 36%	7.5	28.1	Harbor maintenance tax[1]	*	0.1
Broad-based energy tax [1, 2]	2.0	72.8	Inland waterway tax[1]	*	0.9
Cap possessions tax credit (sec. 936) at 60% of compensation	0.2	7.2	SEC registration fee	0.1	0.4
Service industry non-compliance initiative	0.1	6.2	FDIC assessment fee (receipt effect)	0.1	0.3
Modified substantial understatement penalty	0.3	1.9	General aviation registration fee	*	0.3
Restrict deduction for business meals and entertainment to 50%	1.8	16.1	Federal pay raise (receipt effect)	−0.1	−1.3
Reduce pension compensation cap	0.3	3.6	Federal FTE levels (receipt effect)	−*	−0.1
Mark to market for security dealers	1.0	5.0	**Subtotal, other provisions**	**—**	**2.3**
Disallow moving deductions for meals and real estate expenses	0.1	1.7			
Extend 2.5 cents per gallon gas tax [1]	—	7.8	Addendum:		
Extend 53% and 55% estate tax rate	0.5	2.7	Tax 85% of Social Security benefits for beneficiaries making $25,000 or more ($32,000 for couples)	1.7	23.2
Deny deduction for club dues	0.1	1.2	Corporate estimated tax rules	—	4.7
Bar double-dip for thrift buyers	0.4	0.7			
Deny lobbying deductions	0.1	0.9	**Total, revenue and receipts proposals**	**36.0**	**296.2**
Deny deduction for executive pay over $1 million	0.1	0.6			
International tax provisions	1.3	11.0			
Miscellaneous revenue-raising provisions	0.2	0.7			
Subtotal, revenue-raising proposals	**46.4**	**320.7**			
INVESTMENT/STIMULUS [3]	−12.1	−54.7			
TOTAL, NET REVENUE PROPOSALS	**34.3**	**266.0**			

* *$50 million or less*

[1] *Net of income tax offsets*

[2] *The impact of this proposal was offset for low-income families by increases in the low-income home energy assistance program and food stamps that were reflected elsewhere.*

[3] *The estimates excluded the refundable portion of the earned income tax credit. The proposal was estimated to increase outlays by the following amounts: 1994, $0.3 billion; 1995, $3.4 billion; 1996, $6.7 billion; 1997, $6.9 billion; and 1998, $7.2 billion.*

Budget Resolution Embraces Clinton Plan

Congress' fiscal 1994 budget resolution marked a sharp departure from the prior two years, when House and Senate budget writers largely followed the outlines of a five-year budget-summit agreement enacted in 1990.

This time, they were working from an ambitious, five-year deficit-reduction package put together by a new Democratic president. The White House plan, outlined by President Clinton in a speech to Congress on Feb. 17, included sharply higher tax rates on upper-income taxpayers, a broad-based tax on virtually all forms of energy and a wide range of spending cuts in programs from Medicare to defense. *(Clinton's package, p. 85; text, p. 7-D)*

While Congress made small adjustments, its final budget resolution left Clinton's plan largely intact, preserving most of the president's tax increases, spending cuts and proposed "investment" spending in areas such as education, children's nutrition and health programs. The key difference was that the compromise plan wound up adding roughly $50 billion in spending cuts to Clinton's original package, reflecting conservative pressure for more deficit reduction and leading some to speculate that Clinton might have underestimated Congress' appetite for an even tougher plan.

It was perhaps the easiest budget vote Democrats took all year: The budget resolution, a congressional blueprint that did not go to the president for his signature, simply provided the broad guidelines for tax and spending decisions. Controversial details, such as how and whether to adopt an energy tax, were left for later legislation.

The $1.5 trillion budget resolution (H Con Res 64) provided for about $496 billion in net deficit reduction over five years. By administration accounting, the cuts were almost evenly divided between tax increases and spending cuts, a ratio that would have been all but unthinkable under anti-tax Republican Presidents George Bush or Ronald Reagan. (Republicans and even some Democrats argued that a more accurate accounting showed that the plan actually tilted heavily toward taxes). Equally dissimilar to past GOP budgets was the more than $140 billion to be "invested" in high-priority domestic spending initiatives by 1998.

Republicans bailed out at the outset, charging that the plan was far too heavy on taxes and too light on spending cuts. Not a single Republican in either chamber voted for the budget in committee or on the floor. That forced Democrats to get the votes solely from their own party, which

gave moderate and conservative Democrats leverage to force more spending cuts into the package.

Final passage — the House approved the conference report March 31 and the Senate followed suit April 1 — marked the first time since the congressional budget act was written in 1974 that Congress had met the law's April 15 deadline for producing a budget. Ironically, Clinton's full, formal budget did not arrive on Capitol Hill until April 8.

Targeted for Cuts

The budget resolution bound Congress to reduce the anticipated deficit in two ways:

● **Appropriations.** About a third of the deficit cuts were assigned to the appropriators, who were required to hold discretionary spending to an overall limit for fiscal 1994 that was about $12 billion below the amount of budget authority available under the budget caps set in 1990. The appropriators were free to divide that pot of money among their 13 subcommittees as they saw fit, ignoring the function-by-function recommendations made by the budget resolution. But total discretionary spending could not exceed the limit in the budget resolution, and once the appropriators divided up the money, none of the 13 bills could exceed its individual share.

● **Taxes, entitlements.** The other two-thirds — $343 billion out of the $496 billion — was slated to come from legislation known as a "reconciliation bill," a massive measure rolling together hundreds of changes in taxes and entitlement programs (Medicare, Social Security, food stamps and the like) to "reconcile" them with deficit-reduction requirements in the budget resolution. The budget resolution contained tough instructions requiring 13 tax-writing and authorizing committees in the House and 12 in the Senate to come up with the necessary savings. Again, committees could ignore specific directions about how to achieve the savings, but they had to meet the gross targets set in the resolution. *(Committee instructions, p. 112)*

BACKGROUND

Democratic leaders had expected the budget resolution to be the second stage in the process of enacting Clinton's economic package. The first was to be the fiscal 1993 supplemental spending bill aimed at stimulating the economy. But an outcry, particularly from conservative Democrats who were determined to vote first on spending cuts, forced the leadership to revise the schedule, allowing a vote first on the budget resolution. *(Stimulus package, p. 706)*

Republicans were quick to attack the Clinton package, but they found it difficult to close ranks around an alternative. Senate Minority Leader Bob Dole of Kansas displayed the frustration Republicans felt at being badgered for a coherent plan and backed into a corner by Democrats, who insisted that any GOP proposal be specific. "We're asked almost every five minutes by the media, 'Where's the Re-

BOXSCORE

➡ **Fiscal 1994 Budget Resolution (H Con Res 64, S Con Res 18)** The $1.5 trillion budget resolution, Congress' fiscal blueprint for the year, provided an overall limit for fiscal 1994 appropriations bills, along with deficit-reduction instructions to tax and authorizing committees, which were required to produce provisions for a budget-reconciliation bill.

Reports: H Rept 103-31; S Rept 103-19; conference report H Rept 103-48.

KEY ACTION

March 18 — **House** passed H Con Res 64, 243-183.

March 25 — **Senate** passed S Con Res 18, 54-45.

March 31 — **House** approved the conference report on H Con Res 64, 240-184.

April 1 — **Senate** approved the conference report, 55-45.

publican plan?' Well, we're not the government," Dole said.

Complaining that Clinton had not yet submitted his full budget and desperate for more time to work out their substitutes, Republicans sought in vain to slow action. On March 3, Pete V. Domenici, R-N.M., failed, on a vote of 44-55, to postpone action on the budget resolution until after Clinton had sent his full budget to Capitol Hill on April 8. *(Vote 22, p. 4-S)*

The Democrats' own job grew slightly more difficult in early March when the Congressional Budget Office (CBO) released estimates showing that Clinton's package would produce $61.4 billion less in deficit reduction over five years than Clinton had originally claimed. After scrubbing the administration's tax and spending numbers, CBO and the Joint Committee on Taxation found what they said were a variety of errors, incorrect estimates and dubious policy prescriptions that reduced the White House's claimed net deficit reduction by roughly 13 percent.

The good news for the administration was that CBO's simultaneous re-estimate of underlying economic and policy trends all but offset the shortfall in the Clinton package. Overall, CBO's bottom-line deficit reduction was virtually the same as predicted by the White House. The bad news was that the only part of the CBO estimate that mattered from a political standpoint was the shortfall CBO found in Clinton's plan.

BUDGET COMMITTEES

Rigid Democratic Party discipline rolled over united Republican opposition in back-to-back markup sessions March 10-11 that saw the House and Senate Budget committees approve slightly modified versions of Clinton's 1994 budget on straight party-line votes. In effect, Democrats on both committees restored what the CBO's new estimates had taken away in deficit reduction and added net new savings of roughly $25 billion to $30 billion to the original Clinton plan. Both proposals met or exceeded Clinton's target of at least $140 billion in deficit reduction in 1997.

House Committee

The House Budget Committee voted 27-16 to approve a Democratic budget resolution (H Con Res 64) March 10 after committee leaders added about $63 billion in deficit reduction — all of it from spending cuts — to mollify conservative Democrats who had complained that the package did not cut spending enough. About $55 billion of the new cuts was from appropriated spending, and about $8 billion was from entitlement programs, chiefly from a reduction in cost of living adjustments (COLAs) for federal retirees. Overall, the measure provided for $510 billion in deficit reduction over five years.

The committee's ranking Republican, John R. Kasich of

Ohio, came with a GOP-crafted package of detailed spending cuts that he said would produce $429 billion in deficit reduction over five years without any of Clinton's tax increases. The plan lost on a 15-27 vote that saw only Rick A. Lazio, R-N.Y., cross party lines to vote against the proposal.

Kasich was openly contemptuous of Democrats for modifying Clinton's original budget with a detail-free proposal for more cuts in discretionary spending. Turning to the cameras televising the markup, Kasich said, "Mr. President, if you are watching, will you please give us your specifics? We're getting tired of generalities. . . . Shame on you, Mr. President." Kasich's attacks on Democrats eventually provoked even the nearly imperturbable committee Chairman, Martin Olav Sabo, D-Minn., but Kasich was unrepentant. "We didn't come here to be potted plants," he said. "We came to shake things up."

The unity shown by Budget Committee Democrats — they blocked every GOP attempt to make significant changes to the basic Clinton plan — was a departure from the party's liberal-conservative split of recent years. It left Republicans frustrated but impressed, especially when Democrats held their noses and voted against amendments many of them obviously preferred to support. After some Democrats broke ranks to praise a GOP attempt to cut funds for the controversial superconducting super collider — but then voted against the amendment anyway — Alex McMillan, R-N.C., paid his adversaries a grudging compliment. "I don't admire your vote," he said, "but I admire your discipline."

Senate Committee

The Senate Budget Committee voted 12-9 on March 11 to pass that panel's version of Clinton's proposal. Like the House measure, it contained $63 billion in extra deficit reduction. But unlike their House counterparts, Senate Democrats relied on tax increases for about a third of the additional deficit reduction. The rest came in spending cuts, including similarly tight limits on discretionary spending through 1998. Senate budget drafters suggested postponing more than $30 billion of Clinton's $144 billion in investment spending until after 1998 to get discretionary spending down.

As approved by the committee, the Senate measure trimmed the deficit by a net $516 billion over five years, virtually identical to the House's bill when measured on an equivalent basis. It contained net new taxes of $295 billion.

Although there were complaints, particularly over the recommendation that Congress go along with Clinton's call for an increase in taxes paid by upper-income Social Security recipients and for a broad energy tax, Budget Chairman Jim Sasser, D-Tenn., tranquilized restive Democrats with reminders that the budget resolution was only a blueprint, and a purposely vague one at that. He pointedly reminded J. Bennett Johnston, D-La., who opposed Clinton's energy tax, that voting for the measure did not mean endorsing the tax. The budget only bound the tax-writing Senate Finance Committee to come up with a gross amount of money. How they did it, Sasser noted, was their business. The message to Johnston and other Democrats with problems: Vote for the budget now and get your problem fixed in the relevant committee later.

HOUSE FLOOR ACTION

On March 18, House Democrats steamrolled Republicans and dissenters in their own party, adopting the budget

resolution on a largely party-line vote of 243-183. "You acted with unbelievable dispatch," Clinton told House supporters at a celebratory White House breakfast the next morning. "It is a wonderful beginning, but it is just the beginning." *(Vote 85, p. 22-H)*

Outvoted and outmuscled by the House's overwhelming Democratic majority, Republicans were limited to just two amendments that they had no chance of passing. "You on the Democratic side have the votes to beat us down today," said Minority Leader Robert H. Michel, R-Ill., "but this isn't the end of the fight. We have a long, long way to go."

The budget contained some binding overall tax and spending numbers, but with few of the specifics at stake and party leaders urging them to stand behind the president, only 11 Democrats defected to join Republicans, who voted unanimously against the package.

The daylong floor debate changed not a penny in the measure as it was approved by the Budget Committee.

Republicans Divided on Response

Republicans, at the short end of the House's 255-175 Democratic majority, were divided over how best to counter the Clinton juggernaut. With the Democrats enforcing a rule that any substitute had to present detailed cuts, some Republicans worried that a GOP plan would take the focus off Clinton's proposals and make Republicans vulnerable to the same criticism over specifics that they were giving the Democrats. But other Republicans were convinced that they would have no credibility if they did not respond in kind. Neither of the two alternatives that Republicans were allowed to offer won unanimous GOP support.

Kasich and Budget Committee Republicans had drafted a detailed package of spending cuts to match Clinton's roughly $500 million in deficit reduction but with no tax increases. The five-year proposal contained nearly 160 specific cuts, many of them in areas so sensitive — Medicare, veterans' benefits and federal employees' COLAs, for instance — that some Republicans were afraid to go along. The measure failed on a 135-295 vote. *(Vote 81, p. 20-H)*

On the eve of the floor debate, another group of Republicans upped the ante by accepting all of Kasich's cuts, adding more of their own and risking GOP heresy by accepting some of Clinton's taxes on the wealthiest taxpayers while dropping others aimed at the middle class. Republican Gerald B. H. Solomon of New York, who led that effort, insisted that he was strongly anti-tax, but said he felt that the only way to reduce the deficit even more than Clinton had proposed was to include some targeted tax increases in the plan. Solomon's package would have cut $682 billion over five years — far beyond Clinton's or Kasich's proposals.

But the House Republican Conference decided it would rather opt out than lend its support to any taxes. In an early morning, closed-door meeting before the budget debate got under way March 17, Republicans endorsed by voice vote a resolution that reaffirmed the House GOP's antipathy toward any tax increases. "The official position of the Republican Conference is no new taxes," said freshman Richard W. Pombo, R-Calif., author of the resolution.

The amendment failed on a 20-409 vote. *(Vote 82, p. 20-H)*

Black Caucus Alternative Defeated

A budget drafted by the Congressional Black Caucus and the Progressive Caucus also failed, 87-335. The plan would have cut defense spending and raised taxes substan-

go to Congress, his economic stimulus bill. The White House had hoped to win quick passage for the relatively small $16.3 billion bill, allowing it to focus on the far bigger challenge of winning support for reconciliation. Instead, the administration lost control of the debate on the stimulus bill, leaving the impression that it lacked the ability to appreciate, or perhaps to manage, challenges in the Senate. House Democrats were left bruised and wary of again backing an unpopular measure only to see it unravel in the Senate. *(Stimulus bill, p. 706)*

If the president failed this time, he faced the prospect of losing control of the economic agenda and spending the rest of the year negotiating from weakness with a muscular Republican minority or renegade blocs of his own party.

Leaders on both sides knew the stakes were high, and Democrats and Republicans, alike, geared up for a showdown that Senate Minority Leader Bob Dole, R-Kan., warned would be fought with "real bullets."

With their numbers giving them limited influence in Congress, Republicans conducted an intense public campaign, focusing on the effects of the energy tax on the middle class and seeking to mobilize the elderly against the proposed tax increase on Social Security benefits.

The Assignments

The job of drafting the bill fell to 13 tax-writing and authorizing committees in the House and 12 in the Senate. The House Ways and Means Committee and the Senate Finance Committee had by far the biggest assignments. Lawmakers worked from instructions contained in the fiscal 1994 budget resolution (H Con Res 64), which set deadlines of May 14 for the House committees and June 18 for the Senate panels. Under rules set in the 1974 budget act, the committees could ignore the budget resolution's detailed recommendations, but they were required to reach their assigned deficit-reduction targets. *(Rules, p. 110)*

HOUSE WAYS AND MEANS COMMITTEE

The House Ways and Means Committee was responsible for drafting the core of the bill — nearly $300 billion in tax and spending changes. The panel approved its portions of the measure on a 24-14 party-line vote May 13, after making several crucial modifications to shore up business and congressional support. Clinton told reporters the next day that the bill contained "significantly everything that I presented to the Congress, even though there were some changes. In fact, some of the changes I think made the bill better."

The committee preserved Clinton's proposals for massive income tax increases on wealthy Americans, a broad-based energy tax, and higher taxes on upper-income retirees receiving Social Security benefits. But lawmakers cut in half Clinton's proposed increase in the corporate tax rate, refined the collection points for the energy tax and made several other changes — all of them aimed at easing the burden on businesses. That was in keeping with the strategy of Chairman Dan Rostenkowski, D-Ill., to create a corporate coalition that backed the bill — or at least did not fight it aggressively — in turn attracting conservative Democratic support.

The committee legislation included Medicare spending controls that were expected to save $50.4 billion over five years — the largest chunk of the spending savings in the reconciliation bill. Ways and Means also approved a series of trade-related provisions, a change in the threshold at which Social Security taxes had to be paid for domestic

workers and a new entitlement program aimed at helping keep children out of foster care.

Every Republican attempt to amend the plan in committee was voted down in an unwavering display of Democratic Party discipline.

"We just completed the biggest tax increase in the history of the world, and we did it in 45 minutes," fumed Bill Archer of Texas, the top Republican on the Ways and Means committee.

The committee began marking up the bill May 6 and immediately retreated into closed session, over the objections of all 14 GOP members. Democrats then defeated on a 24-14 party-line vote an amendment by Archer that would have dropped the Btu tax and offset the revenue loss by dropping the investment tax credit and the proposed $28.3 billion expansion in the earned-income tax credit. By the same vote, Democrats rejected an amendment offered by Jim Bunning, R-Ky., that would have dropped the Social Security tax increase and used part of the revenue to extend a 25 percent deduction for the health insurance costs of the self-employed. Clinton had proposed to extend the deduction, which expired in 1992, through the end of 1993.

Most of the tax changes to the Clinton plan, however, were hashed out in a series of closed-door meetings between Rostenkowski and committee Democrats. Rostenkowski, who made it clear from the outset that he intended to stick closely to the White House blueprint, invited Democrats to air their complaints. But he also warned that, if accommodated, they were expected to endorse the plan and help drum up votes on the floor.

Modifying the Proposed Btu Tax

Much of the negotiation focused on efforts to protect specific regions and industries from the effects of the proposed Btu tax. The administration agreed to a number of changes and exemptions, although it rejected a suggestion that electric utilities across the country pay a uniform tax on every kilowatt-hour of energy sold. The White House insisted that the tax vary depending on the mix of fuels the utility used as an incentive for companies to burn the cleanest fuels.

Bill Brewster of Oklahoma won agreement that the tax would be collected directly from the consumer. Clinton originally planned to impose the tax on energy producers and distributors, assuming they would pass it along to consumers, but utilities had complained that state regulators might prevent them from passing the tax along. Under Brewster's plan, the utilities could make the energy tax a separate line on customers' electric and gas bills, bypassing state regulators entirely.

To shore up farm-state support, the committee added a partial exemption — worth 34.2 cents per million Btu — for diesel fuel and gasoline used in farming operations. However Democrats also took away another exemption important in farm country, for ethanol and methanol, which the administration had endorsed previously under pressure from several Democratic senators. Other committee changes included an exemption worth roughly $700 million a year for electricity used as a feedstock in the production of aluminum, chlorine and similar industrial products. The Northeast won an expanded exemption for heating oil used commercially. (The administration had previously agreed to an exemption for exported fuels, which primarily applied to the coal industry.)

To pay for the exemptions, the committee boosted the basic energy tax rate to 26.8 cents per million Btu, 1.1 cents higher than Clinton had proposed, and added a new

Reconciliation Rules

Enacted as part of the 1974 budget act, the reconciliation process was Congress' single most powerful deficit-reduction tool.

The law gave the House and Senate Budget committees extraordinary clout to require authorizing and tax-writing committees to draft deficit-reduction legislation. To ensure that the resulting bill got through Congress — particularly the unpredictable Senate — it provided procedural protections that made the bill immune to filibusters and highly resistant to killer amendments.

● **Binding orders.** Although they did not do so every year, the House and Senate Budget committees could include a section in the annual budget resolution instructing virtually every major committee but Appropriations to make changes in tax or mandatory spending laws (chiefly entitlements such as Medicare, Medicaid and farm subsidies). The committees had wide latitude to decide how to reach their targets, but they were required to get there. The Budget committees then packaged the various provisions into a single bill for floor consideration.

● **House rules.** The majority party controlled the House debate on reconciliation bills, as it did on other bills, through the powerful Rules Committee. Like any other rules, the rule for considering a reconciliation bill was subject to floor debate and a vote.

● **No filibusters.** In the free-wheeling Senate, where time limits for major legislation were rare, the reconciliation bill came to the floor with a limit of 20 hours of debate; any amendments left when that limit expired could be voted on but not debated. That meant no filibusters, and it guaranteed passage by a simple majority vote.

● **No non-germane amendments.** Senate rules also barred amendments that failed to meet a strict germaneness test; the Senate could overturn a ruling that an amendment was not germane only with 60 votes.

● **The Byrd rule.** Additionally, the so-called Byrd rule, named for its author, Sen. Robert C. Byrd, D-W.Va., barred "extraneous" provisions from a reconciliation bill. Any senator could bring a point of order on the grounds that a provision violated the Byrd rule; if the Senate parliamentarian agreed and the presiding senator went along, as always happened, the provision was struck unless supporters could muster 60 votes to save it.

Under the Byrd rule, a provision was extraneous if it:
● Did not produce a change in outlays or revenues.
● Increased outlays or cut revenues and the committee reporting the provision failed to meet its deficit target.
● Was outside the jurisdiction of the committee responsible for that section of the bill.
● Produced changes in outlays or revenues that were "merely incidental" to the provision.
● Led to a net increase in outlays or decrease in revenues beyond the years covered by the bill.
● Changed Social Security.

● **Deficit-reduction requirements.** A section of the bill that did not meet the responsible committee's deficit target was subject to a floor motion to recommit, calling on the committee to report back something that did meet the target. But there was no procedural prohibition against passage of an entire reconciliation bill that failed to meet its target. The only stricture was a political one.

---

tax equivalent to the domestic Btu rate on imported goods if more than 2 percent of their value was due to energy costs.

Other Ways and Means Changes

In other changes to the Clinton tax plan, Ways and Means Democrats decided to:

● **Corporate rate.** Raise the corporate income tax rate from 34 percent to 35 percent, instead of to 36 percent, as Clinton proposed.

● **Investment incentives.** Drop the investment tax credits, which had virtually no support on the committee or in the business community. To satisfy the administration's demand for some investment incentives to help the economy, the committee substituted provisions to increase to $25,000 from $10,000 the amount that small businesses could write off for the cost of machinery and equipment in the year it was purchased.

● **Social Security.** Require that the $32 billion in new revenue from Clinton's proposed increase in the portion of Social Security benefits subject to taxation be deposited into general government coffers, instead of the Social Security Trust Fund. The administration had said that the Social Security revenues would be earmarked for the trust funds to prevent future shortfalls.

● **Real estate.** Expand several tax incentives proposed for the real estate industry. Democrats adopted a provision pushed by Michael A. Andrews, D-Texas, to allow real estate developers and others working full time in the industry to write off losses on rental property ("passive losses") against ordinary income. Clinton had proposed allowing the write-off, but only against real estate income.

● **Luxury taxes.** Repeal luxury taxes on boats, furs, airplanes and jewelry that were enacted in 1990. In addition, the committee agreed that the luxury tax on automobiles costing more than $30,000 would be indexed for inflation.

● **Empowerment zones.** Expand the tax incentives and other government benefits that Clinton proposed for impoverished urban and rural areas, bringing the total cost of the zones to $5.2 billion over five years. (Enterprise zones, p. 422)

● **Intangibles.** Attach a Rostenkowski plan to require businesses that acquired intangible assets, such as customer lists and franchise rights, to write off the cost of the purchase over a period of 14 years. Existing law specified no write-off period for intangible assets.

HOUSE FLOOR ACTION

With House Democrats teetering uneasily between fear of their constituents and fear of abandoning a Democratic president early in his term, Democratic leaders used everything from sweet persuasion to bare knuckles to assemble

the slimmest of majorities behind the bill May 27. The razor-thin 219-213 vote was enough to avert what many feared would have been a politically devastating loss for the president. A grateful Clinton appeared in the White House Rose Garden shortly after the vote to thank Democrats who stuck with him. "Tomorrow we go on to the Senate," he said. (Vote 199, p. 48-H)

The bill (HR 2264), assembled by the Budget Committee, combined the Ways and Means package with provisions submitted by the 12 other committees. Altogether, the five-year House bill contained $496 billion in deficit reduction — about $250 billion in tax increases and $87 billion in entitlement cuts, along with $102 billion in cuts in appropriated spending and $57 billion in reduced interest payments on the national debt.

House leaders and White House officials had to work into the first minutes of the vote to pick up wavering Democrats, 38 of whom ended up voting against the plan. Clinton himself worked the phones incessantly, calling one declared "no" vote after another to make a personal plea. Vice President Gore camped out in his Senate office and summoned members in small groups for face-to-face lobbying. Cabinet members buttressed the effort with repeated phone calls of their own.

Several House members said a key turning point came in the last minutes before the vote, when the White House faced what one participant in the eleventh-hour talks called a "near-death experience." With its vote count still coming up short, the White House finally gave in to long-standing demands from moderate and conservative Democrats to make major reductions in Clinton's energy tax and substantial new cuts in entitlement programs when the Senate took up the measure in June.

Dave McCurdy of Oklahoma, a leader of moderate Democrats and an adamant "no" until the last-minute White House concession, said details on the size of the cuts would be revealed after the Memorial Day recess, but sources said the understanding with the White House contemplated reductions of about $25 billion to $35 billion in the $71.5 billion energy tax, paired with specific, new cuts in entitlements of $40 billion or more. (Chief White House lobbyist Howard Paster insisted, however, that the administration had agreed only to faithfully represent House sentiments for deeper spending cuts and changes in the energy tax when the Finance Committee took up its bill.)

One Eye on the Senate

In trying to secure a majority for the bill, House Democratic leaders were caught squarely between the two wings of their party, squeezed by conservatives who were demanding more spending cuts and, in some cases, fewer taxes, and liberals who thought the mix in the bill was about right and warned that they would object to any significant change. "There is an incredible amount of nervousness about this bill," said one Democratic aide, who said many House members felt that they were risking their political careers on a bill with much in it for voters to hate and little guarantee that the Senate would go along or that the measure, if passed, would actually make a serious dent in the deficit.

Democratic strategists were worried enough that Clinton himself made a lobbying visit to the House on May 19, promising to provide political cover for the tough vote to support the tax-heavy measure. "You go out on that limb and I'll go out with you," Clinton reportedly told the Democrats. Leaders appeared reassured; Speaker Thomas S. Foley, D-Wash., said he thought prospects for the bill were

"very good indeed."

But just one day later, a bipartisan group of four senators raised a new complication for House Democratic leaders. Led by Senate Finance Committee members David L. Boren, D-Okla., and John C. Danforth, R-Mo., the group proposed an alternative reconciliation package that eliminated Clinton's energy tax and imposed a cap on entitlement spending to produce substantial new spending cuts. Boren and Danforth were joined by J. Bennett Johnston, D-La., and William S. Cohen, R-Maine.

The sudden, high-profile opposition to the energy tax in the Senate fanned the fears of House members from energy-producing states, who already were worried about supporting the tax. Charles Wilson, D-Texas, said he did not want to vote for a tax that could hurt his district and then have Texas Republican Sen. Phil Gramm get a chance to play the hero by killing the tax in the Senate. "We don't want to be in a position of walking the plank and then have them go over and make a compromise in the Senate," he said.

Boren raised the stakes again a few days later, announcing that he would vote against the Btu tax in the Finance Committee; with an 11-9 party breakdown in the committee and all the Republicans expected to vote no, Boren's rejection threatened to kill the tax. Speculation mounted that the House would put off voting until the Senate had clarified its position. But Foley insisted he would press ahead. "The House has the constitutional prerogative and the responsibility of dealing first with issues that involve spending reductions and revenue adjustments," he said. "If we had to wait every time in the House for the Senate to complete action, the process wouldn't work."

Hard Sell

Throughout the day of the House vote, Democratic leaders worked with increasing desperation behind the scenes to win over Democratic opponents. When many members proved impervious to the argument that a defeat for the huge package might wound or cripple Clinton's presidency, loyalists turned to hardball and threatened some senior members with loss of their committee or subcommittee chairmanships if they voted against the plan. "Nobody got a pass on this," said Barney Frank, D-Mass.

In an emotional plea to a packed House chamber shortly before the balloting the evening of May 27, Speaker Foley acknowledged that the vote he was asking Democrats to make was not an easy one. "But we seldom do important, valuable and lasting things by taking easy votes, comfortable votes, politically popular votes.... This is a time to stand and deliver; this is a time to justify your election," he said.

Republicans without exception opposed the plan, but their numbers and their sharp opposition to tax increases made them virtually irrelevant. At the losing end of the House's 256-176 Democratic margin, they could do little more than register their view that the Clinton plan had too many tax increases and too few spending cuts. John R. Kasich of Ohio, the ranking Republican on the Budget Committee, offered a substitute reconciliation package that sought to more than match the deficit reduction in the Democratic plan without tax increases. Forty Republicans voted against the proposal, and it failed, 138-295. (Vote 198, p. 48-H)

Deals and Threats

There were a dozen facets to the Democrats' lobbying campaign, but in addition to the last-minute deal with

House, Senate Take Different Paths ...

The budget resolution (H Con Res 64 — H Rept 103-48) included instructions to 13 House and 12 Senate committees to come up with a total of $343 billion in deficit reduction in fiscal 1994-98 through a combination of tax increases and cuts in mandatory spending.

The House Ways and Means and Senate Finance committees were responsible for the bulk of the savings.

The amounts assigned in the House and Senate were difficult to compare because committee jurisdictions differed and because in each chamber some panels' jurisdictions overlapped. At bottom, however, the two chambers were in agreement on the deficit-

(The following amounts are in millions of dollars.)

House Committee Instructions

Committee	1994	1995-98	Committee	1994	1995-98
Agriculture	−$98	−$2,950	**Merchant Marine**	0	−205

Agriculture

Unspecified deficit reduction. Panel also was asked to authorize increased funding for food stamps ($7.2 billion over five years) and to reduce spending for the Rural Electrification Administration.

Merchant Marine

Instructed to make permanent tonnage duties on vessels entering U.S. ports from foreign ports.

Armed Services —128 —2,361

Unspecified savings. In addition, committee was asked to authorize a reduction in military pay ($2 billion in 1994, $20.3 billion over five years) in line with Clinton's federal pay freeze.

Natural Resources —131 —1,991

Instructions included increasing recreation fees; imposing a permanent, annual fee to keep a mining claim active; making permanent a formula for sharing receipts from mineral programs with the states; imposing a surcharge on irrigation water from federal projects in the West; reauthorizing the NRC user fee; and scaling back federal funding for the Northern Marianas Islands.

Budget negotiators eliminated instructions to impose grazing fees and hard-rock mining royalties for the use of public lands.

Banking —338 —2,792

Recommendations included extending Federal Deposit Insurance Corporation examination fees to state-chartered banks and boosting the secondary market for home mortgages.

Education and Labor 118 —5,817

Instructed to achieve savings in college loans in 1997-98, presumably through a new, government-run direct-loan program. Additional savings were to come from requiring employers to report health coverage provided to employees, thereby helping Medicare and Medicaid avoid duplicate coverage.

Post Office and Civil Service —77 —10,643

Savings were to come mainly from eliminating the option for federal employees to take lump-sum retirement benefits. In addition, the committee was asked to authorize a reduction in federal civilian pay in line with Clinton's pay freeze plan, saving an estimated $2.9 billion in 1994 and $28.7 billion over five years.

Energy and Commerce —4,342 —64,518

Instructions included overall savings in Medicare ($48.4 billion over five years) and Medicaid and other health programs ($7.8 billion over five years). Additional savings from auctioning Federal Communication Commission spectrum licenses and reauthorizing Nuclear Regulatory Commission user fees.

Public Works and Transportation —31 —2,580

Instructed to increase recreation fees on Army Corps of Engineers land as well as aircraft registration fees.

Foreign Affairs 0 —5

Savings from foreign service retirement.

Veterans' Affairs —266 —2,580

No specific instructions.

Judiciary 0 —345

Asked to increase patent and trademark fees.

Ways and Means —29,441 —299,771

Unspecified deficit reduction.

moderates and conservatives, three stood out:

● **Controlling entitlements.** Leaders brought several unhappy conservative Democrats into the fold by working out a deal to control spending for entitlement programs, whose automatic spending was not limited by budget rules. Under a compromise worked out less than 24 hours before the vote, if entitlement spending exceeded a preset annual target by more than half a percent, the president would have to propose a way to pay for some or all of the overspending or propose to change the target. Congress would have to vote on the proposal.

Though some deficit hawks derided the plan as too weak to be meaningful, it got strong backing from two of the conservative Democrats who forced the White House and House leaders to insert it in the bill. Charles W. Stenholm of Texas and Timothy J. Penny of Minnesota both lined up behind the bill after the deal was done. "This is a very tight cap," Penny insisted.

The limit on entitlement spending, along with provisions to freeze discretionary appropriations at or below fiscal 1993 levels through fiscal 1998 and to create a deficit-reduction trust fund, were automatically added to the bill

... To Same Deficit-Reduction Target

reduction targets, which reflected President Clinton's priorities.

The chief differences were that the House showed an increase for food stamps and called for cost-cutting changes in authorizations for other programs; those amounts were not included in the following House committee totals. The Senate assumed that the changes would be made when appropriators got to the point of actually funding the programs.

The committees could ignore the specific advice on how to achieve their assigned savings, but they had to match the total dollar amount set in the budget resolution.

(The following amounts are in millions of dollars.)

Senate Committee Instructions

Committee	1994	1995-98	Committee	1994	1995-98
Agriculture	−$98	−$2,950	**Environment and Public Works**	−13	−1,254

Agriculture

Instructions included putting a limit on crop subsidies for farmers, increasing recreation fees in national forests, eliminating subsidies to honey producers and instituting a Commodity Futures Trading Commission fee on all futures exchanges.

Environment and Public Works

Asked to increase recreation fees and to extend NRC fees.

	1994	1995-98
Armed Services	−128	−2,361

Armed Services

Same as House Armed Services.

Finance −29,639 −307,262

Given a lengthy list of Clinton revenue proposals and health-care entitlement program savings, including expanding the earned-income tax credit, achieving a variety of savings in Medicare and Medicaid, increasing the top individual and corporate tax rates, instituting a broad energy tax and increasing Social Security benefits subject to taxation for better-off recipients.

Banking −401 −3,131

Instructed to extend FDIC examination fees to state-chartered banks, impose a Securities and Exchange Commission registration fee and boost the secondary market for home mortgages.

Foreign Relations 0 −5

Same as House Foreign Affairs.

Governmental Affairs −77 −10,638

Savings were to come primarily from eliminating the option for federal employees to take lump-sum retirement benefits.

Commerce −1,700 −7,405

Asked to permanently extend patent and trademark fees, auction FCC spectrum licenses and permanently extend tonnage fees.

Judiciary 0 −345

Same as House Judiciary.

Labor and Human Resources 118 −4,571

Instructed to achieve big savings in college loans, same as the House Education Committee.

Energy −118 −737

Instructed to increase recreation fees on public lands, impose a permanent, annual fee to keep a mining claim active, impose a surcharge on irrigation water from federal projects in the West, make permanent a formula for sharing receipts from mineral programs with the states and scale back federal funding for the Northern Mariana Islands.

Budget negotiators eliminated instructions to impose grazing fees and hard-rock mining royalties for the use of public lands in the West.

Veterans' Affairs −266 −2,580

Instructions included savings from making permanent the Department of Veterans Affairs' ability to recover the costs of medical care and from raising housing loan fees.

when the House adopted the rule governing consideration of the reconciliation measure. The rule (H Res 186) was adopted 236-194. *(Vote 196, p. 48-H)*

● **Energy tax promises.** Several energy-state Democrats who bitterly opposed Clinton's energy tax won assurances that the plan would be changed, either in the Senate or during the House-Senate conference. One specific change sought by members with petrochemical plants in their districts was a rebate in the tax for energy-intensive or energy-dependent products such as petrochemicals or aluminum. The promised changes were aimed at lawmak-

ers from energy states such as Texas, but it was not foolproof. Wilson remained a "no" vote. Other Texans had either received more concrete commitments or were more willing to trust the administration. Democrat Jack Brooks of Texas held off endorsing the bill until the day before the vote and only did so after lining up commitments from Clinton and Treasury Secretary Lloyd Bentsen to push in the Senate for an exemption to the energy tax for intermediate products in steel production, such as coke and residual fuels.

● **Pressure from the ranks.** In a startling display of

brashness, rank-and-file lawmakers led by freshman Leslie L. Byrne, D-Va., circulated a petition on the day of the vote demanding that committee and subcommittee chairmen who failed to vote for the bill be stripped of their positions by the House Democratic Caucus. In the tense hours before the vote, support for the petition spread rapidly among junior members, particularly freshmen, who were irritated that they were under such intense pressure to vote for the bill when party leaders, some in relatively safe districts, were refusing to do the same. Ike Skelton, D-Mo., the chairman of the House Armed Services Subcommittee on Military Forces and Personnel, responded with defiance. "I don't know what pressure is," said Skelton, who voted no. But petition supporters claimed that the threat of quick and severe retribution was responsible for influencing subcommittee Chairmen Bob Carr, D-Mich., and Douglas Applegate, D-Ohio, to change their minds and vote for the bill. Another 10 subcommittee chairmen ignored the threat as well and voted against the bill. Every committee chairman voted yes.

SENATE FINANCE COMMITTEE ACTION

Democrats on the Senate Finance Committee approved a package of tax increases and spending cuts June 18 that, at least temporarily, bridged the party's deep divisions over deficit reduction and seemed to salvage hopes for the bill in the Senate.

Approved on an 11-9 party-line vote, the bill retained the basic thrust of Clinton's plan to concentrate the tax increases on upper-income earners and, to a lesser extent, on corporations. But major changes cut more from Medicare costs, saved additional money by trimming tax breaks for businesses and the poor and dropped Clinton's unpopular Btu tax in favor of a regressive increase in the tax on gasoline and other fuels.

For Clinton, the details were less important than simply getting the bill out of committee and to the full Senate. With 11 Democrats and nine Republicans on the committee — and no GOP support for the bill — a single Democratic defection would have crippled the measure.

Grueling Negotiations

The compromise approved by the Finance Committee was the product of two weeks of grinding negotiations during which committee Chairman Daniel Patrick Moynihan, D-N.Y., and Majority Leader George J. Mitchell, D-Maine, worked to patch together a bill that included deeper spending cuts and fewer tax increases than either the House version or Clinton's plan. With Boren's defection making committee approval of the Btu tax impossible, Senate leaders agreed to drop the levy. But that left a gaping revenue hole and sharp division within the committee over how to fill it.

Adopting a new strategy for dealing with the rebellion among conservative Senate Democrats, Clinton withdrew from the battle over details of the plan. Instead, he enunciated a set of broad principles and left the job of working out the specifics to Senate Democratic leaders. "I'm promoting the principles. These guys are going to work it out," he told reporters June 7 as he sat down to meet with Mitchell and Moynihan. Clinton's bottom line, which seemed to shift from day to day, generally included about $500 billion in deficit reduction over five years, with a greater burden on upper-income earners, some form of regionally balanced energy tax and "investment" provisions giving tax breaks and other assistance to businesses, needy families and urban areas.

The administration also tried to quell an uproar from House members who had voted for the unpopular Btu tax after Clinton personally promised that it would not be dropped in the Senate. Insisting that House members "didn't walk the plank on the budget for nothing," Clinton said June 10 that whatever problems emerged with the bill in the Senate could be smoothed out when House and Senate conferees crafted the final version. "The Senate and House will naturally have some disagreements, but when we wind up in conference, we can perhaps get the best bill of all," he said.

The Committee Compromise

The compromise bill pleased the conservatives more than the liberals. But it spread the pain broadly enough to unify the 11 Democrats on the committee.

In place of Clinton's proposed energy tax, Democrats agreed on a 4.3-cents-per-gallon increase in the tax on gasoline and other transportation fuels. The fuels tax was expected to bring in $24.2 billion over the next five years, compared with $71.5 billion for the Btu tax. Most of the hard bargaining focused on what rate to set for the fuels tax and and where to find additional revenue and spending cuts so that the bill achieved at least as much deficit reduction as Clinton's original plan.

Boren and John B. Breaux, D-La., early opponents of the Clinton plan, proved not to be the main obstacles once they won assurances that the Btu tax would be removed and additional spending cuts substituted. Instead, the leadership had to overcome opposition from Max Baucus, D-Mont., who insisted that Democrats hold the increase in the fuels tax below 5 cents a gallon. To make up part of the revenue, Baucus and Kent Conrad, D-N.D., favored raising the top corporate income tax rate another percentage point above the 35 percent the House had approved.

But that ran into opposition from senators who wanted lower taxes. So Democrats reluctantly turned to a money-saving approach suggested by Bill Bradley, D-N.J. — cutting back Clinton's proposals for tax breaks to help businesses, urban areas and the poor. Boren, Breaux and others had pressed for deeper reductions than the House had approved in mandatory programs, particularly Medicare. But they were partly rebuffed by John D. Rockefeller IV, D-W.Va., and other liberals who managed to limit the additional Medicare cuts to $19 billion over five years. That was in addition to the $48 billion Medicare cut in Clinton's plan.

To shore up support on the Senate floor and to mute opposition from the elderly, committee Democrats reduced the impact of Clinton's proposed tax increase on Social Security benefits by applying it to individuals who made $32,000 and to couples who made $40,000 (as opposed to $25,000 and $32,000 under Clinton's plan).

Desperate for revenue, the committee made several other changes, including:

● **Business breaks.** Much of what remained of Clinton's plan for stimulating the economy through business tax breaks was scaled back or dropped. While the House had increased the small-business write-offs for equipment purchases to $25,000, for example, the panel provided $15,000.

Democrats also rejected Clinton's campaign promise to make the research and development tax credit permanent, opting instead to extend it until July 1994, which "saved" $8.4 billion under government accounting rules, even though Congress was likely to keep extending the popular

credit. Also gone was a Clinton proposal to give a capital gains tax break to investors in certain small companies.

● **EITC.** The committee reduced the proposed increase in the earned-income tax credit by $10 billion. The move angered advocates for the poor, who contended that the credit would no longer be generous enough to fulfill Clinton's pledge to raise above the poverty line a family of four that earned the minimum wage.

● **Empowerment zones.** Clinton's plan to establish so-called empowerment zones in depressed urban and rural areas was dropped.

● **Capital gains.** The committee made capital gains subject to the new 10 percent surtax on income above $250,000 a year.

GOP Amendments

During the markup, Democrats turned back a succession of Republican amendments. Republicans, who knew the votes were immutably stacked against them, saw the exercise largely as a chance to score political points.

"You are at liberty to do anything you wish, sir," Moynihan said at one point when committee member Dole asked if he could offer an amendment.

"Except win," Dole shot back.

Republican proposals included:

● A motion by Danforth to have the committee meet before bringing the bill to the floor to discuss controlling the growth of entitlements, something he said the bill utterly failed to do. Democrats said the matter should be considered as part of health-care reform. The motion was defeated, 8-12, with Charles E. Grassley, R-Iowa, voting against.

● An amendment by John H. Chafee, R-R.I., to strike the transfer of 2.5 cents a gallon in motor fuels taxes to the Highway Trust Fund, which was defeated on a show of hands.

● An amendment by Chafee to strike the provision prohibiting businesses from deducting executive salaries above $1 million in the absence of explicit performance standards approved by an outside board of directors and stockholders. The amendment was defeated, 9-11.

● An amendment by Chafee to replace the provision limiting the executive salary deduction with one limiting deductibility for all individuals who were paid more than $1 million, including, for example, professional athletes. The amendment was defeated, 2-16.

● A Danforth amendment to exempt jet fuel used in commercial airliners and cargo planes from the new fuel tax if such a tax would adversely affect the airline industry's financial health. The amendment was defeated, 8-12.

● An amendment by William V. Roth Jr., Del. (on behalf of Malcolm Wallop, Wyo.), to exempt small businesses such as sole proprietorships, partnerships and subchapter S corporations from the increase in individual income tax rates. The amendment was defeated, 8-12, with Chafee voting against.

● A Roth amendment to sunset all tax increases in the bill at the end of 1998, which was defeated, 9-11.

● An amendment by ranking Republican Bob Packwood, Ore. (on behalf of Orrin G. Hatch, Utah), to strike a provision reducing the business meals deduction, which was defeated, 9-11.

● A Dole amendment to increase the percentage of amortizable intangibles to 100 percent, which was defeated, 9-11.

● An amendment by Grassley to set the Medicare re-

imbursement rate for nurse practitioners and physician assistants at 85 percent of the physician fee schedule amount as a way of helping rural areas retain such medical services. Grassley wanted to offset the increase by reducing Medicare payments for CAT scans and MRIs. Democrats said the amendment would more properly be considered as a part of health-care reform. The amendment was defeated, 9-11.

SENATE FLOOR ACTION

The enormous difficulty of getting fractious Democrats on the same policy page was made clear shortly after 3 a.m. on June 25 when Gore cast the tie-breaking vote — the first in the Senate since 1987 — to save the Senate's version of Clinton's deficit-reduction plan (S 1134). Gore broke a 49-49 tie to pass the bill on a 50-49 roll call vote. *(Vote 190, p. 25-S)*

The deals that had brought a slim majority of House Democrats together in May were not the same as those that eked out the bare win in the Senate, and already members were angrily threatening to kill the package if they did not get what they originally voted for.

But Clinton remained upbeat. "What this means is incalculable," he said at a news conference several hours after the vote. "It means we can now move on to a conference committee with a clear signal to the financial markets that [their] interest rates should stay down and people should be able to refinance their homes and finance their businesses at lower interest rates."

Gore had been on hand throughout the day and into the night, frequently presiding during 18 hours of debate and votes that occasionally saw Republicans come close to gutting key sections of the bill.

The Senate measure combined the Finance proposals with provisions submitted by the 11 other committees.

No Republican voted for the measure, and Democrats lost six of their own, three of whom were up for re-election in 1994: Richard H. Bryan of Nevada, Dennis DeConcini of Arizona and Frank R. Lautenberg of New Jersey, where taxes had become a lightning-rod issue.

Three more Democrats wandered for other reasons: Johnston, Sam Nunn of Georgia and Richard C. Shelby of Alabama. Shelby had consistently voted against the Clinton economic plan.

It was not expected to be quite that dramatic. After the Finance Committee had reshaped the heart of the House-passed bill more to the liking of Senate moderates and conservatives, it looked as if the fix was in. The near-universal prediction early in the week of June 21 was that Democrats' numerical superiority and the unthinkable prospect of embarrassing a president of their own party made the outcome a foregone conclusion.

But individual senators found much to oppose and felt free to do so. Pro-business moderates were upset that business investment incentives had been dealt away to help pay for the downsizing of the energy tax. Liberals were angry that Medicare cuts had been increased for the same reason. "It's not the president, it's the class of '94," said Breaux, referring to the Democrats running for re-election in 1994.

Forced to rely solely on their own party in the face of virtually lock-step Republican opposition, Democratic leaders gave up $17 billion in deficit reduction to buy allegiance from the potential renegades, shrinking the $516 billion package that had come to the floor June 23 down to the $499 billion package that finally passed June 25. Among other things, the money bought smaller Medicare

A History of Reconciliation

The reconciliation process — in which tax laws and entitlement programs were changed, or reconciled, to achieve deficit-reduction targets set in the congressional budget resolution — was established by the 1974 Congressional Budget Act. It was first used in 1980 and became a mainstay of deficit-reduction efforts in the next decade. Prior to 1993, the last reconciliation bill was a five-year plan passed in 1990 that grew out of a White House congressional budget summit.

The job of passing a reconciliation bill typically was an exhausting one that kept Congress in session well beyond its expected date of adjournment.

The following is a capsule history of each year's action, the dates on which the House and Senate completed work on the reconciliation bill and the date the bill was cleared. Also included are the amount of deficit-reduction provided by the bill and the years it covered.

1980

In the face of soaring inflation and election-year politics, Congress scrambled in the spring to pass a budget resolution that showed a balance between revenues and outlays. To that end, the resolution for the first time included reconciliation instructions to tax-writing and authorizing committees. Although hopes of balancing the budget were later abandoned, the reconciliation bill provided $8.2 billion in savings and set a precedent. *(1980 Almanac, p. 124)*

HOUSE: Sept. 4

SENATE: June 30, July 23 *(Two bills, later combined)*

FINAL: Dec. 3

AMOUNT: $8.3 billion *($4.6 b spending cuts; $3.6 b revenue)*

PERIOD: FY 1981

1981

A key element in President Ronald Reagan's sweeping reorientation of the federal budget, the bill relied exclusively on spending cuts and included no tax increases. Driven by Republicans and conservative Democrats, and over the objections of the Democratic leadership, Congress passed an administration-backed reconciliation bill in tandem with a bill that cut taxes by $37.7 billion in fiscal 1982. *(1981 Almanac, p. 256)*

HOUSE: June 26

SENATE: June 25

FINAL: July 31

AMOUNT: $130.6 billion (all spending cuts)

PERIOD: FY 1982-84

1982

With the deficit threatening to exceed $200 billion, lawmakers increasingly agreed that taxes would have to go back up. Still reeling from the previous year's defeats, the House Democratic leadership held back and let the Republican-controlled Senate take the heat for a tax-reconciliation bill, which included cuts in Medicare, Medicaid and welfare programs. A second reconciliation bill made cuts in food stamps, dairy price supports and other entitlements. *(1982 Almanac, p. 199)*

HOUSE: Aug. 10 *(Four bills combined)*

SENATE: Aug. 4

FINAL: Aug. 18

AMOUNT: $13.3 billion *(all spending cuts)*

PERIOD: FY 1983-85

HOUSE: No action

SENATE: July 23

FINAL: Aug. 19

AMOUNT: $115.8 billion *($17.5 b spending cuts; $98.3 b revenue)*

PERIOD: FY 1983-85

1983

The budget resolution called for $85 billion in deficit reduction, most of it from additional taxes. Lawmakers tried a variety of reconciliation proposals, but with Reagan pledging to veto any tax increase, they made little headway and failed to clear a deficit-reduction bill. *(1983 Almanac, p. 231)*

HOUSE: Aug. 25

SENATE: Suspended action

AMOUNT: $10.3 billion

PERIOD: FY 1984-86

1984

Based on a three-year, $140 billion deficit-reduction agreement reached by Senate GOP leaders and the Reagan White House in March, Congress reversed its traditional process, with both chambers approving deficit-reduction bills before completing action on a budget resolution. The deficit-cutting measure included $50 billion in tax increases, the first real rollback of the 1981 cut. The Senate also approved a small tax increase approved by the House in 1983. *(1984 Almanac, p. 143)*

---

cuts and bigger investment incentives for small business.

While many Democrats were obviously reluctant to go along, the outcome was a significant victory for Democratic leaders, who managed to find and hold a center of gravity between party extremes that repeatedly threatened to wreck the bill.

Republican Strategy

Republicans repeatedly denounced the measure as a job-killer, insisting the huge tax increases would further weaken an already staggering economy. Although they conceded early on that they could not hope to win in the Senate, Republicans did their best to make things agonizingly difficult for the Democrats.

Special rules barred them from filibustering the reconciliation bill, but they had free rein to isolate controversial provisions and force Democrats to vote to defend them. Dole and his colleagues used that tactic repeatedly to put Democrats on record in support of some of the most politically painful features of the package, a tactic obviously designed to provide campaign material for 1994.

Save for a $2.3 billion exemption that protected the troubled airline industry from the transportation fuels tax, a change Democrats supported strongly enough to accept on a voice vote, Republicans failed to make a single significant change in the bill. But in the course of considering more than two dozen amendments June 23-25, Senate Democrats skated about as close to the edge of losing significant pieces of the bill as they could go without falling off. For example, Democrats hung on to the measure's

HOUSE: April 11, 12 *(Two bills combined)*

SENATE: April 13, May 17 *(Two bills combined)*

FINAL: June 27

AMOUNT: $63.0 billion *($13.0 b spending cuts; $50 b revenue)*

PERIOD: FY 1985

1985

Congress adjourned in late December deadlocked over the conference report on a $74 billion three-year reconciliation package, after the House rejected a Senate provision for a toxic-waste cleanup tax. Collapse of work on the bill underscored the difficulties members would face in trying to implement the newly passed Gramm-Rudman-Hollings bill, which promised future cuts to balance the budget in five years. *(1985 Almanac, p. 498)*

HOUSE: Oct. 24

SENATE: Nov. 14

FINAL: None

AMOUNT: $74 billion

PERIOD: FY 1984-86

1986

Congress quickly cleared the bill left over from 1985, which had shrunk to $18.2 billion in deficit reduction. In October, lawmakers cleared a second reconciliation measure, but the $11.7 billion bill relied heavily on one-shot asset sales and accounting gimmicks to reach its deficit-reduction goals, rather than more direct spending cuts or revenue increases. *(1986 Almanac, pp. 555, 559)*

HOUSE: Oct. 24

SENATE: (1985)

FINAL: April 1

AMOUNT: $18.2 billion *($12.1 b spending cuts; $6.1 b revenues)*

PERIOD: FY 1986-88

HOUSE: Sept. 24

SENATE: Sept. 19

FINAL: Oct. 17

AMOUNT: $11.7 billion

PERIOD: FY 1987-89

1987

Budget procedures broke down as Democrats spent much of the year trying to force Reagan into negotiating a bipartisan budget deal. Congress and the White House nearly accepted automatic across-the-board spending cuts instead. It took a historic stock market crash in October to prod administration and Hill budget-makers to convene an economic summit, which produced a two-year, $76 billion deficit-reduction plan. More than half the savings were achieved through a two-year, $39.6 billion reconciliation bill (the remainder came in appropriations cuts). *(1987 Almanac, p. 615)*

HOUSE: Oct. 29

SENATE: Dec. 11

FINAL: Dec. 22

AMOUNT: $39.6 billion *($16.4 b spending cuts; 23.2 b revenues)*

PERIOD: FY 1988-89

1988

Peace prevailed on the budget front. Thanks to the 1987 budget summit and the resulting two-year reconciliation bill, there was no need for a deficit-reduction bill.

1989

A bipartisan deficit-reduction agreement reached in April between newly elected President George Bush and congressional leaders seemed to promise another year of budget peace. But a bitter fight over Bush's proposed capital gains tax cut erupted in the fall, stalling final action on reconciliation until late November. The delay triggered across-the-board spending cuts under the Gramm-Rudman deficit-reduction law; more than $4 billion in Gramm-Rudman cuts were retained in the reconciliation bill. *(1989 Almanac, p. 92)*

HOUSE: Oct. 5

SENATE: Oct. 13

FINAL: Nov. 22

AMOUNT: $17.8 billion ($6.9 b spending cuts; $5.6 b revenue)

PERIOD: FY 1990

1990

With the deficit soaring, Congress and the White House faced crippling Gramm-Rudman cuts, and with Bush resisting new taxes, Congress spent the year locked in a seemingly endless budget battle. A drawn out budget summit finally produced a deal that promised to cut the deficit by $496.2 billion over five years. The cornerstone was the reconciliation bill, passed by an exhausted Congress in late October. The bill provided nearly half the five-year savings and included a new, five-year budget process that introduced caps on discretionary spending and pay-as-you-go rules for taxes and entitlements. *(1990 Almanac, p. 138)*

HOUSE: Oct. 16

SENATE: Oct. 18

FINAL: Oct. 27

AMOUNT: $236 billion *($99 b spending cuts; $137 b revenue)*

PERIOD: FY 1991-95

1991-92

The five-year plan enacted in late 1990 spared Congress from the traditional last-minute ordeal of passing a reconciliation bill in 1991 or 1992.

---

controversial fuels tax by only two votes. The equally difficult provision raising taxes paid by better-off Social Security beneficiaries survived by a five-vote margin. Thirteen Democrats joined Republicans in a nearly successful attempt to carve out an expensive exemption from higher taxes for certain small businesses.

A key fight came over a GOP substitute offered by Dole that was designed to achieve roughly $411 billion in deficit reduction over five years but with none of the Democrats' tax increases. Instead, Republicans relied on a mix of unspecified cuts in appropriations and entitlements such as Medicare and Medicaid. Their plan included a lid on appropriations similar to the mechanism proposed by Democrats, but one that would cut spending far more deeply. It also included a controversial cap on entitlement spending that would make no specific cuts but would institute a tough limit on the growth of those programs beginning in 1997.

Mitchell derided the proposal as "more of the same: nothing specific . . . no fingerprints on a specific spending cut that our colleagues will stand up and say they are for." The GOP plan fell on a 43-55 vote that saw Democrat Shelby cross over to back the alternative and Republican James M. Jeffords of Vermont cross the other way to vote against it. *(Vote 165, p. 22-S)*

Other Amendments

The following are some of the more than two dozen amendments considered during floor debate:

● **Business tax incentives 1.** In an effort to appease

Dale Bumpers, D-Ark., and other moderates, Mitchell proposed to add $3.6 billion in tax breaks to benefit small business, including a targeted capital gains tax cut and a bigger write off for equipment purchases.

Bradley, who argued that the proposal was a giveaway and would have little economic benefit, joined Howard M. Metzenbaum of Ohio and three other Democrats in voting with the Republicans to kill the amendment. The amendment required a three-fifths majority because of a procedural motion. It was defeated on a 54-44 vote. *(Vote 164, p. 22-S)*

• **Business tax incentives 2.** Mitchell was back later with a redesigned amendment that dropped the capital gains break and substituted a $3.6 billion provision to expand to $20,500 the amount that small businesses could write off their taxes for purchases of equipment and machinery. (Existing law allowed $10,000; the original Senate bill had allowed $15,000.) No longer subject to the procedural hurdle, the amendment passed the second time around by a vote of 93-5. *(Vote 166, p. 22-S)*

• **Medicare cuts.** The leadership's negotiations with the conservative wing of the party angered liberal Democrats, and a small but critical group that included Metzenbaum, Tom Harkin of Iowa, Barbara A. Mikulski of Maryland and Paul Wellstone of Minnesota threatened to vote against the bill because of the $19 billion in extra Medicare cuts approved by the Finance Committee.

Digging in their heels as the vote drew closer, the liberals were able to cut the increase to $10 billion, prompting Harkin and others to declare support for the package. Rockefeller offered a floor amendment to eliminate a series of specific Medicare reductions in a move tilted in part toward easing the cuts on inner-city and rural areas. The amendment, which brought total Medicare cuts down to $58 billion, passed on a voice vote.

• **Limit on entitlement spending.** Senate Budget Chairman Jim Sasser, D-Tenn., tried to amend the bill to include a mechanism, similar to that in the House bill, to monitor and control spending for entitlement programs. He lost on a 54-43 vote that fell short of the 60 votes needed to waive the Budget Act. *(Vote 168, p. 22-S)*

• **Tax exemption for small business.** Roth offered an amendment to exempt small businesses and family farms from a portion of the higher taxes in the bill. But Roth failed to win even the unanimous support of his fellow Republicans, many of whom objected to the complicated exemption.

Although 13 Democrats voted for the amendment, it needed a two-thirds majority for a waiver of the budget rules, and it fell short, 56-42. *(Vote 171, p. 23-S)*

• **Transportation tax.** Republicans held Democrats' feet to the fire on a series of amendments that would have eliminated the most politically dicey tax increases in the bill — those that fell on middle-income earners and senior citizens. The closest call came on an amendment offered by Don Nickles, R-Okla., to drop the 4.3-cents-per-gallon increase in fuel taxes, which was narrowly defeated 50-48 on a tabling motion. *(Vote 167, p. 22-S)*

Lawmakers approved by voice vote an amendment by Slade Gorton, R-Wash., to give the airline industry a $2.3 billion exemption from the tax on jet fuel beginning after 1993.

• **Taxes on Social Security.** Trent Lott, R-Miss., offered an amendment to eliminate the increase in taxes on Social Security benefits for upper-income recipients. Lott questioned whether retirees slated to pay the extra tax —

individuals with incomes above $32,000 and couples above $40,000 — actually qualify as upper-income earners. But Moynihan contended that the average net worth of those affected was more than $1 million, and he told colleagues that 92 percent of those affected had annual incomes of more than $50,000. Although four Democrats voted with Lott, the leadership was able to defeat the amendment 51-46 on a tabling motion. *(Vote 169, p. 23-S)*

HOUSE-SENATE CONFERENCE

More than 200 House and Senate conferees gathered July 15 to begin the arduous task of crafting a compromise bill. To succeed, they had to satisfy two chambers that had passed separate deficit-reduction bills by the barest of margins, found each other's legislation unacceptable — and probably would have had trouble passing their own bills a second time.

Negotiators had just three weeks to accomplish this. By Aug. 6, the scheduled start of the summer recess, Democratic leaders expected to reach a deal, pass it in both bodies and send it to Clinton. Had Democrats and their president not staked their political futures on success, they might have been tempted to give up. "I don't see how we're going to get 218 votes to do anything," said Rep. Stenholm, citing the minimum victory margin in the House. "But we are. We have to."

The Real Work

After the initial, public meeting, which lasted little more than a half-hour, the real work began behind closed doors. Scores of senior lawmakers from 13 committees in the Senate and 16 in the House broke into subgroups to work on sections of the massive package. But most of the hard bargaining on taxes and spending was done by Mitchell, Moynihan and Rostenkowski.

With the votes so close in both chambers and Republicans hardened into adamant opposition to any Democratic plan, there was hardly a Democrat in Congress who was not consulted, cajoled and in many cases accommodated by the time conferees produced the final bill Aug. 2. "Clinton is dealing with 258 Democrats in the House and 56 in the Senate," said Rep. John P. Murtha, D-Pa. "Every single group has something they're interested in."

The conflicting priorities that had brought the bill close to defeat in the House and Senate were only magnified in the conference. The 38 House Democrats in the Congressional Black Caucus, for example, warned that they might align with Republicans to sink the bill if conferees did not restore items for poor Americans, such as the the earned-income tax credit and the new empowerment zones, that had been cut or trimmed in the Senate version.

"We have to look out for our own best interests," said Chairman Kweisi Mfume, D-Md., noting that caucus members' votes likely would hinge on "principle items that, quite frankly, are more important than whether or not we . . . are able to claim a party victory.

In the Senate, conservative and moderate Democrats, who had threatened to kill the package unless they got lower taxes and higher spending cuts, signaled that they would tolerate little or no backsliding in conference.

Democratic leaders clearly had to do some creative deal-cutting to avoid losing more votes on the conference report than they did on the original bill.

Just as the negotiations were getting off the ground, the pre-eminent deal-cutter, Rostenkowski, was implicated in

an alleged embezzlement scheme at the House Post Office. Democrats were stunned, but Rostenkowski declined to comment on the matter and as the week progressed his role as a linchpin in the ongoing talks seemed unaffected. *(Post Office investigation, p. 64)*

Energy Tax Was Centerpiece

The pivotal question for the leadership was what form of energy tax to impose and how much revenue it would raise. Until that was decided, it was impossible to determine how far the conferees could go in restoring Senate cuts in spending for Medicare and social programs.

The far more lucrative House-passed Btu tax appeared dead; a large contingent of Democrats wanted to drop the idea of an energy tax altogether, arguing that the Senate version was too small and not worth the political pain. It was the one tax in the bill that was aimed at the middle class, and Republicans were using it to bash the Democrats. But Democratic leaders said that killing the tax would make it almost impossible to reach a compromise that fulfilled Clinton's goal for deficit reduction and paid for the many expensive tax breaks sought mainly by the House. In a maneuver that foiled those seeking to scrap the energy levy, Rostenkowski and Moynihan eliminated the main option for replacing much of the lost revenue: They won early approval for a 35 percent top corporate rate, killing energy tax opponents' hopes of tapping a bigger, 36 percent top rate.

Rostenkowski and Moynihan tried without success to come up with a compromise energy tax that split the difference between the revenue raised by a Btu tax and that raised by the Senate's fuels tax. That became impossible when several key Senate Democrats, including Herb Kohl of Wisconsin, began digging in their heels against anything higher than the Senate tax.

With nowhere else to go for the money, conferees adopted the Senate plan for a 4.3-cents-a-gallon increase in the fuels tax. That cleared the way to finish other parts of the package, though it left conferees without enough money to make all factions happy.

The Power of the Byrd Rule

Meanwhile, on a separate track, Democratic aides were working to minimize the chances that the conference report would fall prey to an arcane Senate rule barring "extraneous" matter from reconciliation bills. Republicans hoped to use the Byrd rule, named for author Robert C. Byrd, D-W.Va., to strip or gut key items in the bill. But the trick in utilizing the complex rule lay in defining exactly what items were extraneous. Any senator could bring a point of order on the grounds that a provision violated the rule; it was up to Senate Parliamentarian Alan S. Frumin to agree or disagree. If he agreed, it would take 60 votes to save the provision.

So as the conference proceeded, aides trekked to Frumin's office trying to persuade him that their provisions did not violate the rule or to work out alternative language that passed muster. Aides said some items that had seemed vulnerable, such as the earned-income tax credit, empowerment zones and even an expansion of food stamps, would be allowed. However, the review mechanism to limit entitlement spending, which had been so crucial to House approval of the bill, was dropped because of the Byrd-rule threat, as were scores of other lower-profile non-budgetary provisions sprinkled through the bill. A separate rule that barred Senate consideration of a reconciliation bill that

How Democrats Voted

Voted yes on original bill, no on final bill:

Senate:
Boren, Okla.

House:

Thornton, Ark.	Brewster, Okla.
Dooley, Calif.	McCurdy, Okla.
Hutto, Fla.	Lloyd, Tenn.
Tauzin, La.	Stenholm, Texas
Peterson, Minn.	Inslee, Wash.
Montgomery, Miss.	

Voted no on original bill, yes on final bill:

Senate:
DeConcini, Ariz.

House:

Skelton, Mo.	McHale, Pa.
Maloney, N.Y.	Johnson, S.D.
Holden, Pa.	Sarpalius, Texas
Margolies-Mezvinsky, Pa.	Wilson, Texas

Voted no both times:

Senate:

Shelby, Ala.	Bryan, Nev.
Nunn, Ga.	Lautenberg, N.J.
Johnston, La.	

House:

Browder, Ala.	Swett, N.H.
Coppersmith, Ariz.	Andrews, N.J.
Condit, Calif.	Klein, N.J.
Lehman, Calif.	Pallone, N.J.
Deal, Ga.	Mann, Ohio
Rowland, Ga.	Traficant, Ohio
Lipinski, Ill.	English, Okla.
Long, Ind.	Clement, Tenn.
Roemer, Ind.	Chapman, Texas
Baesler, Ky.	Edwards, Texas
Hayes, La.	Geren, Texas
Minge, Minn.	Hall, Texas
Parker, Miss.	Laughlin, Texas
Taylor, Miss.	Orton, Utah
Danner, Mo.	Pickett, Va.

NOTE: Reps. Farr, D-Calif., and Barca, D-Wis., were not elected until after the first vote; they voted "yea" for the conference report.

contained changes in Social Security caused conferees to strip provisions that would have raised the threshold for paying Social Security taxes on domestic employees. The changes in the tax rate on Social Security benefits escaped the killer rule because they were deemed to be changes to the tax code, not to Social Security. *(Domestic worker taxes, p. 378)*

Other Conference Decisions

In addition to the energy tax, the following conference decisions were central to completing the bill:

● **$500 billion package.** While many Democrats had agitated for a smaller package, arguing that that would reduce the political cost and ease final passage, Clinton,

Continued on p. 122

Evolution of Tax Proposals . . .

ISSUE	CLINTON	HOUSE
Individual Income Taxes	Imposed a fourth bracket, increasing the top marginal rate to 36 percent for couples with taxable income above $140,000 ($115,000 for individuals). Imposed a 10 percent surtax on income above $250,000 (except capital gains), resulting in an effective top rate of 39.6 percent. Effective Jan. 1, 1993.	Same as Clinton.
Capital Gains Income Tax	Kept existing top rate of 28 percent on capital gains income. A 50 percent exclusion from income was allowed on five-year investments in certain small businesses.	Same as Clinton.
Social Security, Medicare Taxes	Tax 85 percent (rather than the existing 50 percent) of Social Security benefits for couples earning more than $32,000 ($25,000 for individuals). Eliminated the cap on wages subject to Medicare tax ($135,000 in 1993). Effective Jan. 1, 1994.	Same as Clinton.
Corporate Income Taxes	Imposed a fourth bracket, increasing the top marginal rate to 36 percent for taxable income above $10 million. (Corporations with income well in excess of $15 million were to be taxed at a flat 36 percent rate.)	Same as Clinton, except the top rate was 35 percent.
Energy Tax	Imposed a broad new tax on most forms of energy based on heat content, or British thermal units (Btu), with a surtax on petroleum products.	Imposed a similar broad Btu tax with a surtax on petroleum products. Exemptions were granted to heating oil, diesel fuel used on farms and energy for certain other uses.
Luxury Tax	No provision.	Repealed the 10 percent excise tax on airplanes, yachts, furs and jewelry; indexed for inflation the price at which the tax kicked in on automobiles.
Investment Incentives	Created a two-year investment tax credit of 7 percent; created a permanent tax credit (7 percent for two years, 5 percent thereafter) for small businesses.	Allowed small business to write off up to $25,000 in equipment purchases in the year they were made (existing write-off was $10,000).
Intangible Assets	No provision.	Allowed a 14-year depreciation period for most newly acquired intangible assets, including good will.
Passive Losses	Allowed real estate professionals to deduct passive losses but only against real estate income.	Allowed real estate professionals to deduct passive losses against ordinary income.
Earned-Income Tax Credit	Expanded the EITC for the working poor; included families without children.	Expanded the EITC: Families with two or more children got up to $2,685 in 1994, $3,460 thereafter. Low-income individuals with no children could receive up to $306.
Empowerment Zones	Created 110 zones in poor urban and rural communities and provided tax breaks and other incentives to attract investment.	Created 10 zones in poor urban and rural communities and provided tax breaks and other incentives to attract investment; provided smaller incentives in 100 other communities.

...From Clinton Through Conference

SENATE	CONFERENCE	ISSUE
Generally the same as Clinton and the House, except imposed the surtax on capital gains, and for 1993 only the fourth bracket rate was 33.5 percent, and the effective rate imposed by the surtax was 35.3 percent on ordinary income and 29.4 percent on capital gains.	Same as Clinton and House, except most individuals had until at least April 15, 1996, to pay the tax increase imposed by this bill.	**Individual Income Taxes**
Increased top rate on capital gains to 30.8 percent for taxpayers with taxable income above $250,000. No exclusion for investments in small business.	Same as Clinton and House. Effective date for small business exclusion was date of enactment.	**Capital Gains Income Tax**
Same as Clinton and House, except the threshold for taxing 85 percent of Social Security benefits was $40,000 for couples ($32,000 for individuals).	Same as Clinton and House, except the threshold for taxing 85 percent of Social Security benefits was $44,000 for couples ($34,000 for individuals).	**Social Security, Medicare Taxes**
Same as House.	Same as House and Senate.	**Corporate Income Taxes**
Increased the tax on gas, diesel and other transportation fuels by 4.3 cents per gallon. Effective Oct. 1, 1993.	Same as Senate, except also applied a similar new tax to compressed natural gas used as a highway or motorboat fuel.	**Energy Tax**
Same as House.	Essentially the same as House and Senate.	**Luxury Tax**
Same as House, except one-year write-off was limited to $20,500.	Same as House and Senate, except one-year write-off was limited to $17,500.	**Investment Incentives**
Allowed a 14-year depreciation period for 75 percent of the value of most intangible assets, with some modifications in definitions and a special nine-year depreciation period for purchased mortgage servicing rights.	Generally the same as House, except set a 15-year depreciation period; followed Senate on purchased mortgage servicing rights.	**Intangible Assets**
Essentially same as Clinton.	Essentially same as House.	**Passive Losses**
Generally same as House, except the maximum credit was somewhat less. No provision for individuals with no children.	Generally same as House and Senate, except provided families with two or more children about $3,554 in 1996 and thereafter. Families with no children could receive up to $300.	**Earned-Income Tax Credit**
No provision.	Generally same as House, except created nine empowerment zones and aided 95 other communities. Part of the assistance was in the form of grants, not tax incentives.	**Empowerment Zones**

Continued from p. 119

Bentsen, White House budget director Leon E. Panetta and a host of congressional leaders insisted that $500 billion was a non-negotiable goal. Federal Reserve Chairman Alan Greenspan warned a House Banking subcommittee on July 20 that trimming the package would have grave consequences for interest rates.

With the reduced energy tax, conferees appeared to fall short, but only slightly. Democrats said the bill would produce $496 billion in deficit reduction over five years, virtually the same as the five-year deficit-reduction plan approved in 1990.

● **Individual tax rates.** Both chambers had approved a new top marginal rate of 36 percent, along with a 10 percent surtax on taxable income above $250,000. In a last-minute move that maximized revenue collections but provoked intense controversy, negotiators kept a House-passed provision making the increases retroactive to Jan. 1, 1993. Republicans pointed out that the retroactive effective date meant that Democrats were reaching back into the final days of George Bush's presidency for additional revenue, and they denounced the move as unfair, unprecedented and even unconstitutional. Sensing trouble, the Treasury Department announced Aug. 4 that taxpayers would have up to three years to pay any back taxes resulting from the change and would face no late penalties. In addition, the White House released a list of 13 retroactive tax increases stretching back to 1917 to bolster their case that this was not unusual.

● **Medicare.** The compromise restored some, but not all, of the extra Medicare cuts approved by the Senate. Conferees agreed to trim the growth in Medicare spending over the next five years by $55.8 billion, compared with $58 billion in the Senate bill and $50 billion in the House measure.

● **Social Security.** The conferees adopted Clinton's proposal to raise the portion of Social Security benefits subject to taxation from 50 percent to 85 percent for upper-income retirees. But they set a higher threshold than was found in either the House or Senate bill. The change applied to individuals earning at least $34,000 a year and couples making $44,000 a year.

● **Corporate income tax.** Conferees stuck with the new 35 percent top corporate rate approved by both chambers, resisting calls from the black caucus and others to go to 36 percent to help offset added social spending or replace the energy tax. Both chambers had made the new corporate rate retroactive to Jan. 1, 1993.

● **Small-business incentives.** The final bill limited the increased write-off for equipment and machinery purchased by small businesses to $17,500. Both chambers originally were more generous: the House had approved a $25,000 write-off; the Senate had reduced that to $20,500.

● **Empowerment zones.** Conferees scaled back Clinton's empowerment zone proposal, providing $1 billion in grants and $2.5 billion in tax incentives. The bill authorized nine empowerment zones that would qualify for federal tax breaks and other assistance and awarded lesser benefits to 95 other communities. Clinton had asked for $4.1 billion for 10 empowerment zones and 100 additional communities. The House had increased the funds to $5.2 billion.

● **EITC.** The compromise expanded the earned-income tax credit for low-income families, including some families with no children, at a cost of $20.8 billion over five years. Clinton had requested and the House had approved a larger, $28.3 billion expansion.

● **Food stamps.** Negotiators agreed on a $2.5 billion expansion of the food stamp program, down from the $7.3 billion approved by the House.

Gearing Up For the Final Votes

Even as congressional Democratic leaders were negotiating the details of the conference report, a White House lobbying army arrived on Capitol Hill to sell the package. With the votes coming up short in both chambers, Clinton counted on a prime-time TV speech Aug. 3 to boost public support for the plan. But Clinton was followed by Dole, who gave a withering critique of the plan and asked voters to call Congress and demand that it be voted down. Callers overwhelmingly opposed the plan, and while some Democrats charged that many of the calls were rigged or orchestrated, the phenomenon seemed to make the vote count even shakier.

The administration went into overdrive. Clinton went to the Capitol to meet with Democrats, and he and top White House officials were everywhere, working members and even reporters from news outlets in the home states of wavering senators and House members.

FINAL HOUSE ACTION

Plainly worried and reluctant to take the leap, the House voted 218-216 on Aug. 5 to pass the package, as close as the vote could get and still have the bill pass. Forty-one Democrats voted no; one more would have killed the plan. *(Vote 406, p. 98-H)*

"Tonight is the time for courage," Speaker Foley shouted shortly before the vote in a final appeal to Democrats, who had been bludgeoned by Republican attacks and pressured by constituent phone calls complaining about the plan.

Powerless to change the bill, Republicans slammed it over and over again.

"This plan is not a recipe for more jobs," said Dick Armey, R-Texas. "It is a recipe for disaster . . . . Taxes will go up. The economy will sputter along. Dreams will be put off, and all this for the hollow promise of deficit reduction and magical theories of lower interest rates."

House Minority Whip Newt Gingrich, R-Ga., predicted that the package would lead directly to "a job-killing recession."

In a last-minute effort to win over wavering moderate and conservative Democrats, congressional leaders and Clinton agreed to give Congress another crack at cutting spending. Clinton promised that in the fall he would send Congress a bill to cut fiscal 1994 appropriations further. House leaders agreed to allow at least two floor amendments to that bill, and Penny predicted that one rider aimed at further appropriations cuts and another aimed at cuts in entitlement programs could produce "tens of billions of dollars" more in additional spending cuts over the next several years. *(Budget cuts, p. 140)*

It also looked as if there would be votes in the Senate and the House on a constitutional amendment to require a balanced federal budget and a vote in the Senate on a House-passed plan (HR 1578) to implement an "expedited rescission" procedure to require Congress to vote on presidential proposals to rescind previously appropriated spending. *(Balanced-budget amendment, p. 145)*

Leaders also held out the possibility that Congress would vote on a plan to apply pay-as-you-go procedures to spending for disasters such as the Midwest flood. And

leaders pledged that they would revive the entitlement review provision that had been stripped from the budget package. The idea survived in diminished form in an executive order signed by Clinton on Aug. 4 and in a change in House rules agreed to as part of the rule for considering the conference report on the bill (H Res 240). Those actions set up a complex process that in effect bound the White House and the House to take some action but let the Senate off with no requirement to vote. Conservative Democrats wanted a statute that would bind both the House and Senate to vote on a presidential proposal to offset any spending above targets for entitlement programs.

Intense Lobbying

Despite all the deal-cutting, by late in the day Aug. 5, vote-counters in the House were still coming up short. As the vote neared, grim-faced House leaders kept insisting they would make it, but they admitted the going was slow. As the 15-minute nominal limit on the vote expired, the count was tied at 210-210. For several more moments, the tally seesawed back and forth, with Democrats winning one moment and losing the next. Finally, all attention centered on freshman Marjorie Margolies-Mezvinsky, D-Pa., who had announced to the largely Republican constituents in her suburban Philadelphia district that she would oppose the plan, just as she had the first time in May.

But leaders told her they would lose without her, and, with the struck demeanor of someone being marched to her own hanging, she walked into the well of the House and signed one of the green cards required to register a yes vote after time had expired and the electronic voting apparatus had been shut off.

"The margin was close, but the mandate was clear," Clinton said shortly after the late-night House vote in comments aimed at shoring up Senate support.

FINAL SENATE ACTION

Twenty-four hours later in the Senate, it took Vice President Gore to break the tie and make the final tally 51-50. *(Vote 247, p. 32-S)*

An air of uncertainty hung over the chamber until shortly before the final balloting, when Bob Kerrey, D-Neb., announced that he would vote for the bill. Kerrey had voted yes when the Senate passed the bill in June, but he had criticized the final measure and declined throughout the day to reveal his intentions. When he finally announced his decision, a hushed chamber hung on his every word.

Speaking into the TV cameras and directly to Clinton, Kerrey said, "I could not and should not cast the vote that brings down your presidency." Kerrey said the bill "challenges America too little," and he derided the notion that the 4.3-cents-a-gallon gasoline tax increase would hurt the middle class. "If they notice, I'll be surprised; if they complain, I'll be ashamed," he said.

When Minority Leader Dole rose to close the Republican side of the debate, he recalled one of President Bush's most effective lines from the 1992 campaign against Clinton, warning viewers watching the debate on TV to "put down your remote control and grab your wallet." Majority Leader Mitchell shot back that Republicans opposed the bill because they wanted to protect the rich.

"We've had enough speeches; the time has come to act," Mitchell urged Democrats. "Tonight we're going to deliver change."

Raising the Federal Debt Ceiling

A small but critically important provision in the 1993 reconciliation bill raised the ceiling on the public debt to $4.9 trillion. The increase, which drew virtually no debate, was calculated to allow for all federal government borrowing needs through fiscal 1995. Congress cleared the reconciliation bill Aug. 6; President Clinton signed it Aug. 10 (HR 2264 — PL 103-66). *(Budget-reconciliation, p. 107)*

Treasury Secretary Lloyd Bentsen warned in March that federal borrowing — the accumulation of annual budget deficits — would exceed the existing ceiling of $4.145 trillion by April 7. Congress, which was in the midst of work on Clinton's economic package, temporarily increased the ceiling to $4.37 trillion, good through Sept. 30. As the leadership hoped, the short-term bill (HR 1430 — H Rept 103-43) passed with little fanfare. The House approved the stopgap debt bill by a vote of 237-177 April 2. The Senate cleared the debt measure by voice vote April 5, and Clinton signed it April 6 (PL 103-12). *(Vote 133, p. 34-H)*

Avoiding Controversial Riders

In previous years, bills raising the debt ceiling had attracted controversial amendments and been subject to lengthy debate. That was because an increase in the limit on federal borrowing was must-pass legislation: When the Treasury reached the statutory debt ceiling, Congress had no choice but to raise it; the alternative was to see the federal government run out of cash, fail to pay Social Security benefits to retirees or interest payments to the holders of government bonds, and eventually default on its obligations. *(1989 Almanac, p. 110; 1987 Almanac, p. 604)*

Sen. Phil Gramm, R-Texas, and others warned that in 1993 they would offer major budget-related riders, such as a balanced-budget amendment to the Constitution.

But the Democratic leadership got around those threats by incorporating the debt-limit increase in the reconciliation bill, which was protected by special Senate rules barring filibusters and non-germane amendments.

First, early passage of the fiscal 1994 budget resolution (H Con Res 64 — H Rept 103-48) gave leaders the chance to protect the short-term bill. The budget, completed April 1, included the debt-limit bill as part of the instructions directing congressional committees to craft a reconciliation bill.

Before the short-term bill expired, Congress approved the long-term increase as part of the omnibus reconciliation bill.

A decade earlier, in August 1982, the ceiling on the debt had stood at $1.389 trillion. In November of that year, it was increased to $1.49 trillion. On 20 occasions since, Congress had acted to increase the debt limit either temporarily or permanently. However, lawmakers had not had to contemplate such a vote since 1990, when it set the ceiling high enough to carry the government for more than two years. *(1990 Almanac, p. 165)*

As expected six Democrats voted against the bill: Boren, Bryan, Johnston, Lautenberg, Nunn and Shelby.

GOP Procedural Gambit Fails

The daylong debate that preceded the vote followed lines familiar since Republicans and Democrats first squared off over the Clinton plan in February. In the only substantive action of the day besides the final vote, Republicans tried and failed three times to strike items from the bill by using points of order.

Citing the Constitution, they sought to strip provisions making the tax increases retroactive, but lost on a 44-56 vote. If the motion had passed, Senate rules would have required pulling the entire conference agreement from the floor. *(Vote 244, p. 32-S)*

Republicans lost twice when they tried to remove provisions they said violated the Byrd rule. Democrats had redrafted or removed more than 100 provisions to make the measure immune to GOP challenges. By a 43-57 vote, the Senate declined to overturn a ruling by the chair that a provision to expand childhood immunizations did not violate the Byrd rule. Republicans failed by an identical vote to overturn a ruling that found no Byrd rule violation in a provision requiring that U.S.-manufactured cigarettes contain 75 percent domestic tobacco. *(Votes 245, 246, p. 32-S)*

Boren and DeConcini

Boren, whose intransigence helped force major changes in the bill when it first came to the Senate, had announced Aug. 1 that he would vote no. That meant that to save the bill, leaders had to convert one of the six Democrats who voted no in June.

"We haven't counted on Sen. Boren's vote for quite some time," Gore said icily.

But the scramble was on, and strategists quickly focused on DeConcini as the most likely candidate to save the plan.

After four days of feverish wooing from party leaders and Clinton himself, DeConcini finally announced his switch from no to yes on Aug. 4, a move that appeared to lock in success for Clinton and the package.

"Both my arms feel twisted," said the Arizonan, who faced an uphill re-election battle in 1994. (A little more than a month later, DeConcini announced that he would not seek another term.)

DeConcini made sure that voters knew he had driven a tough bargain.

To mollify his concern about the bill's effect on Arizona's many retirees, negotiators recalibrated the increase in taxes on some Social Security recipients. Conferees had previously agreed on thresholds of $40,000 for couples and $32,000 for individuals; that was changed to $44,000 and $34,000.

In addition, Clinton signed an executive order Aug. 4 creating a so-called deficit-reduction trust fund that he said would ensure that all the new revenues and spending cuts achieved by the bill would go for deficit reduction, not new spending. ∎

1993 Budget-Reconciliation Act

By White House accounting, the 1993 Omnibus Reconciliation bill (HR 2264 — PL 103-66) was to cut the deficit by $504.8 billion in fiscal 1994-98. It included $250.1 billion in net revenue increases and $254.7 billion in spending cuts.

Most of the package's tax revenue came from the wealthiest taxpayers. The spending cuts came mostly from cutbacks in defense, limits on appropriated spending and reduced Medicare payments to doctors and hospitals.

As enacted, the bill:

AGRICULTURE

Commodity Programs

● **Cotton: reauthorization.** Reauthorized certain provisions of the price support programs for upland cotton through the 1997 crop year. The reauthorization excluded cotton skip-row practices, extra-long staple cotton, cottonseed and cottonseed oil support, preliminary allotments for the 1998 cotton crop, suspension of marketing quotas and acreage allotments, and the suspension of parity-based price supports, which had to be addressed in 1995. Other commodity programs also had to be reauthorized in 1995.

● **Cotton: deficiency payments.** Pared a program that paid farmers to limit their crops to help the government control supply. The so-called 50/92 and 0/92 programs guaranteed farmers 92 percent of their annual deficiency payments or subsidies when producers opted to set aside all or half of their acreage for some alternative crops or conservation steps. As a cost-saving measure, the program was trimmed to guarantee farmers only 85 percent of their deficiency payments when they devoted all or half their land to such other uses. The revised programs, to be known as the 50/85 and 0/85, applied to 1994 and 1995 crops.

The 92 percent deficiency payment was maintained for specified cases: Farmers who certified early in the summer that weather or other factors had killed their crop, or who opted to plant alternative crops such as sunflowers on their acreage, would still receive 92 percent of their deficiency payments.

● **Cotton: surplus crops.** Required the Agriculture secretary to reduce the amount of cotton planted by setting a lower surplus stock target. To do so, the secretary was required to change the acreage reduction program under which farmers were required to idle land in order to qualify for price supports. Surplus stock targets were part of the formula used by the Agriculture secretary to determine how much land farmers had to idle to qualify for deficiency payments. Under the bill, the surplus stock target fell from 30 percent to 29.5 percent for the 1995 and 1996 crop years and 29 percent for the 1997 crop year.

● **Wheat and feed grains: deficiency payments.** Reduced the so-called 0/92 program for wheat and feed grains so that farmers were paid 85 percent of their deficiency payments, rather than 92 percent, if they opted to devote none of their acreage to wheat and feed grains.

● **Rice: deficiency payments.** Cut the so-called 50/92 program for rice, so that farmers were paid 85 percent of their deficiency payments, rather than 92 percent, when they planted rice on less than 50 percent of their land.

● **Dairy: butter.** Continued the system of government purchases of surplus milk products in order to guarantee a minimum price to producers during periods of oversupply. But the provision lowered the price the government could pay to purchase surplus butter from 76 cents per pound to a maximum of 65 cents per pound. The move was expected to boost commercial butter sales and thus reduce butter surpluses and government costs.

● **Dairy: nonfat dry milk.** Increased the minimum price the government could pay for surplus nonfat dry milk to $1.03 per pound from 97 cents per pound.

● **Dairy: assessments.** Continued assessments levied on milk producers to help offset the cost of the dairy price support program and lower the federal deficit. Under the 1990 budget-reconciliation act, the assessment was collected by lowering by 11.25 cents per hundredweight the price milk producers received from the federal government for their milk. The assessment was slated to expire in 1995, but the provision extended it through 1996 at a lower rate. It required that dairy producers get 10 cents per hundredweight less from the federal government for their milk.

● **Dairy: reauthorization.** Reauthorized certain provisions of the dairy price support program through 1996. Reauthorization excluded programs relating to transfer of dairy products to military and veterans hospitals, the dairy indemnity program, the dairy export incentive program, and provisions dealing with the export sales of dairy products.

● **Dairy: bovine growth hormone.** Prohibited the sale of bovine growth hormone for 90 days after the date on which the Food and Drug Administration first approved the sale of the hormone. The hormone, an artificial drug that increased milk production in cows, was expected to be approved for sale within the following 12 months. During the 90-day moratorium, marketing assessments on milk producers were to be reduced by 10 percent.

● **Tobacco: import fees.** The 1990 budget-reconciliation act required that producers of domestic tobacco pay a fee equal to 1 percent of their government loans, with the revenue going to deficit reduction. This law imposed a similar assessment on purchasers of imported tobacco. The new assessment was calculated by multiplying the number of pounds of imported tobacco by the sum of the per pound marketing assessment imposed on purchasers of domestic tobacco.

● **Tobacco: domestic content.** Required domestic cigarette manufacturers to certify the total amount of U.S. produced tobacco used in their cigarettes.

● **Tobacco: import curbs.** Imposed a penalty on cigarette manufacturers who used less than 75 percent domestically grown tobacco in their tobacco products. The provision also required that such manufacturers purchase from tobacco cooperative marketing associations an amount of domestic tobacco equal to the amount they imported. The associations were industry groups that aided in marketing domestic tobacco.

● **Tobacco: tracking imports.** Required U.S. tobacco manufacturers to keep adequate records to help officials determine the amount of foreign grown and domestically grown tobacco used in cigarette manufacturing. Manufacturers who failed to provide required information faced federal criminal sanctions.

● **Tobacco: assessment.** Imposed a fee on tobacco importers to go toward the tobacco marketing associations or to the federal government to make the tobacco program a no-cost program to the Treasury.

● **Tobacco: user fees.** Imposed user fees on tobacco importers to pay for inspection of foreign-grown tobacco that was used in U.S. manufactured tobacco products.

● **Tobacco: quota floors.** Extended floors on reductions that could be made in burley and flue-cured tobacco marketing quotas for the 1995 and 1996 crop years. Flue-cured and burley tobacco were the most common types of tobacco grown in the United States. Growers were limited in the amount they could produce by government-imposed quotas. The provision gave the secretary the right to waive the floors if the tobacco stocks were excessive.

● **Sugar: marketing fees.** Increased the marketing fee that sugar growers paid in fiscal years 1995 through 1998. For raw cane sugar the fee was an amount equal to 1.1 percent of the loan level for raw cane sugar and 1.1794 percent of the loan level per pound of beet sugar. The bill authorized penalties against sugar producers who knowingly violated the marketing allocations set by the 1990 farm law.

● **Sugar: price supports.** Continued the sugar price support program through the 1997 crop year.

● **Oilseeds: soybeans.** Reduced the loan rates for soybeans to $4.92 per bushel from $5.02 per bushel through 1997. The provi-

sion lowered the loan rates for minor oilseeds to 9 cents per pound from $4.09 per pound through 1997.

● **Oilseeds: loan origination fees.** Eliminated the fees loan applicants had to pay for oilseed crop loans in the 1994 crop year. The provision also required that such loans matured nine months after the application was made, or in no case later than the last day of the fiscal year in which they were made.

● **Peanuts: marketing fees.** Increased the marketing fees paid by peanut producers by 10 percent beginning with the 1994 crop. The provision raised the marketing fee by an additional 10 percent in each of the 1996 and 1997 crop years.

● **Honey: loan rate.** Racheted down the minimum price-support loan rate for honey beginning in the 1994 crop year and extending through 1998. The existing rate was 53.8 cents per pound. It dropped to 50 cents in 1994 and 1995, 49 cents in 1996, 48 cents in 1997 and 47 cents in 1998. The provision also tightened limits on the total amount of payments an individual honey producer could receive under the program from $125,000 in the 1994 crop year to $100,000 in 1995, $75,000 in 1996 and $50,000 in 1997 and 1998.

● **Honey: reauthorization.** Reauthorized the honey price support program through the 1997 crop year.

● **Honey: user fees.** Eliminated user fees paid to honey marketing associations.

● **Wool and mohair: incentive payments.** Limited the amount of incentive payments for individual wool and mohair producers to $125,000 per farmer in the 1994 marketing year, $100,000 in the 1995 marketing year, $75,000 in the 1996 marketing year, and $50,000 in the 1997 marketing year.

● **Wool and mohair: producer prices.** Altered the way the Agriculture Department calculated the average price producers got for their wool in an effort to trim the cost of the program. The provision prohibited the Agriculture secretary from deducting certain marketing charges when determining net sales proceeds for shorn wool and shorn mohair.

● **Wool and mohair: reauthorization.** Reauthorized the price support program through the 1997 marketing year.

Rural Electrification

● **Loan programs.** Amended the Rural Electrification Act of 1936 to allow borrowers of funds from the Federal Financing Bank, which coordinated federal agency borrowing, to refinance their loans at existing interest rates or prepay the loans. The provision authorized certain penalties to be assessed on borrowers who opt for refinancing or prepayment.

Agricultural Trade

● **GATT.** Eliminated the authority of the Agriculture secretary to waive minimum levels of acreage that had to be retired by wheat and corn producers under the so-called GATT trigger provisions of the 1990 budget-reconciliation act. The waiver authority had been included in the 1990 budget agreement to give the Agriculture secretary more leverage in negotiations as part of the Uruguay Round of the General Agreement on Tariffs and Trade (GATT). This provision was a savings device: Removing the GATT trigger eliminated its potential for increasing government payments to producers.

● **Sorghum.** Abolished minimum acreage reduction requirements for grain sorghum and barley set by the 1990 budget-reconciliation law.

● **Market promotion.** Amended the Agricultural Trade Act of 1978 to limit spending on the market promotion program, which subsidized overseas marketing of U.S. agricultural product, to $110 million a year beginning in fiscal 1994 through fiscal 1997. The provision capped fiscal 1993 spending at $148 million.

● **Unfair trade practices.** Directed the Agriculture secretary to provide marketing assistance to counter or offset unfair trade practices of a foreign country. Redirected spending for the market promotion program to small-sized firms.

● **Brand-name promotion.** Limited promotion assistance for

any brand name to five years. The provision banned the use of the market promotion program to promote foreign sales of U.S. tobacco.

BANKING & HOUSING

● **Depositor preference.** Required the Federal Deposit Insurance Corporation (FDIC) and the Resolution Trust Corporation (RTC) to give preference to depositors over general creditors and shareholders when they were distributing assets from failed banks or thrifts that had been taken into receivership. The provision increased the amount of money that the FDIC and RTC — which stood in for insured depositors — recovered from failed institutions. Existing law gave the FDIC and the RTC, uninsured depositors and general creditors equal rights.

● **Federal Reserve surplus.** Required the Federal Reserve to transfer $213 million from its surplus account to the Treasury in 1997-98.

● **IRS income check.** Authorized the Department of Housing and Urban Development (HUD) to use IRS income data to verify applicants' and participants' eligibility for rental assistance programs. HUD provided rental assistance to 4.4 million low-income households. A 1992 GAO study estimated that one in five understated their incomes and therefore were receiving too much in rent subsidies. Recipients had the right to a hearing to contest any benefit reduction.

● **REMIC guarantee fees.** Authorized the Government National Mortgage Association (Ginnie Mae) to charge guarantee fees on a new class of mortgage-backed securities known as real estate mortgage investment conduits (REMICs). The provision allowed Ginnie Mae to charge a slightly higher annual fee for guaranteeing mortgage-backed securities. The existing limit was the equivalent of 6/100 of a percent of the value of the securities.

● **FHA premium refunds.** Required the Federal Housing Administration (FHA) to speed up amortization of mortgage insurance premiums. Under existing law, homeowners paid an upfront premium for mortgages insured by the FHA. If they paid off the mortgage before it came due, they received a partial refund (the portion of the premium that the FHA had not yet earned). The provision accelerated the rate at which HUD earned the premium payment and limited the time frame for premium refunds to seven years.

STUDENT LOANS & ERISA

Direct Student Loans

● Created a new Federal Direct Student Loan program that gradually replaced the existing Federal Family Education Loan program, which guaranteed student loans. Direct loans were to be phased in on a schedule of 5 percent of new loan volume in academic year 1994-95; 40 percent of new loan volume in academic year 1995-96; 50 percent in academic years 1996-97 and 1997-98; and 60 percent in academic year 1998-99.

Under the new program, students applied to the federal government for loans through their schools, cutting out the middle-man role of banks and guarantee agencies.

Under the guaranteed loan program (the largest was called the Stafford program), students borrowed money from banks. The federal government paid the interest on the loan until the student left school and assumed the payments. Guarantee agencies reimbursed the banks if a student defaulted on a loan, and the federal government then reimbursed the guarantee agencies. The Student Loan Marketing Association, known as Sallie Mae, generally bought loans from banks and got Wall Street to invest in bonds backed by the loans.

Any school that wanted to participate in the direct loan program beginning in 1996-97 could do so regardless of the fixed percentage. That meant that all schools potentially could participate in direct loans despite the 50 percent benchmark set by conferees.

Other Student Loan Provisions

● **Repayment options.** Students had several options in repaying both their direct and guaranteed loans, including a standard 10-year repayment schedule, graduated repayment, extended repayment and income-contingent repayment. Under graduated repayment, a student could pay back a small amount initially with payments increasing over the years. Under extended repayment, the time allowed to repay the loan was longer than usual.

● **Consolidation loans.** Imposed a monthly fee on holders of consolidation loans — several loans that had been combined — equal to 1.05 percent of the outstanding loan principal. This applied only to new loans.

● **Consolidation of programs.** Combined the Supplemental Loans for Students program and the unsubsidized Stafford Loan program — both guaranteed loan programs — so that students needed to apply for only one rather than two programs. The unsubsidized Stafford program was for students whose family incomes were too high to qualify for subsidized Stafford loans. It was created in the 1992 reauthorization bill so that anyone who wanted a loan could get one.

● **Guarantee agency.** Lowered the amount of money that guarantee agencies could keep from default collections from 30 percent to 27 percent on guaranteed loans.

● **Reduction in borrower interest rates.** Lowered caps on interest rates for guaranteed student loans from 9 percent to 8.25 percent under both direct loans and guaranteed student loans. The interest rates paid by students was to be cut by 0.6 percent beginning in 1998.

● **Reduction in loan fees.** Reduced students' origination and insurance fees from a maximum of 8 percent to a maximum of 4 percent for all new direct and guaranteed loans.

● **Loan fees from lenders.** Imposed a user fee on lenders of 0.5 percent of their new guaranteed loan volume.

● **Fees from Sallie Mae.** Imposed a fee on the Student Loan Marketing Association (Sallie Mae), which bought loans and used them to back bonds it sold on Wall Street. The fee was 0.3 percent of Sallie Mae's outstanding loan volume, based only on new loans issued after the legislation went into effect.

● **Elimination of tax-exempt floor.** Eliminated the 9.5 percent floor on yields on loans made with tax-exempt bonds.

● **Reinsurance fees and administrative cost allowance.** Eliminated the guarantee agency administrative cost allowance and reinsurance fees charged to the federal government. Defaulted loans were reimbursed to banks and guarantee agencies at varying rates, depending on such factors as when the bank requested reimbursement and whether the bank tried to collect on the loan. The bill reduced the federal reinsurance — or reimbursement — on guaranteed loans from 100-90-80 percent to 98-88-78 percent, except for lender-of-last-resort loans, loans made when there were no others available.

● **PLUS loan disbursements.** Required that PLUS loans (Parent Loans for Undergraduate Students) be disbursed in multiple payments rather than in single lump sums.

● **Supplemental preclaims assistance.** Changed the terms for government preclaims payments to collectors of defaulted guaranteed loans from $50 per claim to 1 percent of the total collection.

● **Cost sharing by states.** Required states to cover a portion of the default costs of schools with default rates greater than 20 percent. States could decide to pass on all or some of the cost to the schools.

ERISA Provisions

● Added several new standards for group health plans governed by the Employee Retirement Income Security Act (ERISA). Federal courts had interpreted ERISA as pre-empting state laws concerning employee benefits; the following provisions provided exemptions from pre-emption.

● **Third-party liability laws.** Specified that private group health plans had to comply with state laws requiring them to

reimburse the states in cases in which Medicaid was the primary payer but should have acted as a secondary payer because the beneficiary also was covered by a private insurer.

Group health plans also were prohibited from taking individuals' Medicaid eligibility or enrollment into account in enrolling them or paying claims.

Separate provisions in the Medicaid section of the bill required states to enact such laws covering group health plans.

● **Medical child support orders.** Required group health plans to extend coverage to a child in a case where a parent was required to provide medical child support.

● **Coverage in cases of adoption.** Required group health plans that covered dependent children to extend coverage to adopted children, even if the adoption was not final. The change was intended to ensure that state court orders enforcing this extended coverage in adoption and child support cases were not pre-empted by federal law.

● **Medicaid coverage data bank.** Required group health plans to supply data needed by employers to comply with a separate provision in the bill that established a Health Coverage Clearinghouse to identify third parties that may have been liable as primary payers for Medicaid beneficiaries.

COMMUNICATIONS

Radio Spectrum Transfer

● **Planning.** Required the chairman of the Federal Communications Commission (FCC) and the assistant Commerce secretary for telecommunications to meet at least biannually to plan the management of the radio spectrum. On the agenda: the auctioning of spectrum licenses to raise revenue, the future requirements for private and public use — including state and local government public safety agencies, and any actions needed to promote the efficient use of the spectrum.

● **Identification of frequencies.** Required the Commerce secretary within 18 months to submit a report recommending which radio frequencies used by the federal government could be turned over to the private sector.

The selected frequencies were to have the largest potential for public benefit and productive use. The secretary was to choose at least 200 megahertz of radio spectrum for reassignment, all located below 5 gigahertz (which represents the highest end of the usable spectrum). Of that amount, 100 megahertz was to reside in the portion of the spectrum below 3 gigahertz.

The secretary was required to consider the following factors when identifying which government frequencies should be offered to the private sector: whether the frequency was commercially available; whether reassigning the frequency promoted sharing of frequencies and the development of new communications technologies; and whether the shift would seriously harm federal services, impose excessive federal costs or disrupt the use of government frequencies by amateur radio licensees.

The assignments were to be made within 15 years.

● **Power agency exemptions.** Exempted the Tennessee Valley Authority, the Bonneville Power Administration and the Western, Southwestern, Southeastern and Alaska power administrations from having the radio band they used offered for use by the public sector. Those agencies were required to share their frequencies with commercial users where possible.

● **Procedures for identifying spectrum.** Required that, within six months, the Commerce secretary submit a preliminary list of radio bands that met the criteria for reassignment. The public was to be given 90 days to comment, and the FCC was then to have 90 days to analyze the recommendations. The secretary was urged to encourage discussions among commercial users and government users. The secretary then was to issue a timetable. No less than 50 megahertz was to be reassigned immediately after the preliminary report was issued.

● **Presidential review.** Allowed the president, within six months of receiving the secretary's report, to make changes in the plan. The president could substitute an alternative frequency, while stating the reasons for doing so to the FCC and Congress. The president could retain the frequencies for government use when the reallocation stood to jeopardize national defense or public health or safety, result in excessive costs, eliminate a use uniquely suited to the government or disrupt the use of a government-held band of frequencies by amateur radio licensees.

● **Distribution.** Required the FCC, within 18 months, to issue rules to allocate the frequencies. The agency was to allocate the frequencies gradually over a 10-year period. A "significant" portion of the frequencies was reserved for allocation after the end of the 10-year period. The law did not preclude the FCC from allocating additional frequencies not included in its original plan, nor from altering the plan in the future.

● **Presidential authority.** Allowed the president to reclaim frequencies allocated to the private sector in the future, as long as the president allowed for an orderly transition. The provision required the president to estimate the cost of displacing spectrum users should the government take back control of the frequencies.

● **Transfer authority.** Declared that nothing in the law prevented shifting more of the radio band from the government's use to the private sector.

Competitive Bidding

● **Competitive bidding.** Gave the FCC authority to use competitive bidding to grant some radio licenses. The administration hoped to raise $7.2 billion over five years through such auctions. The initiative overturned a longstanding policy of awarding radio licenses free through lottery or merit review.

The provision affected only businesses that sold direct access to the airwaves, such as cellular phone companies. Other radio licensees, such as broadcasters and cable systems, were not affected.

● **Fair auctions.** Required the FCC to design a competitive bidding system for each class of radio license or permit affected. The agency was required to design and test alternative ways of conducting the auctions. The provision put in place safeguards to protect the public interest and to achieve the following objectives:

● Spur the development of new communications services, including those for people living in rural areas;

● Promote economic opportunity and competition by disseminating licenses among a variety of applicants, including small businesses, rural telephone companies and businesses owned by minorities and women;

● Require that auctions earn for taxpayers a portion of the value of the radio band being put up for auction and that the auctions avoid "unjust enrichment"; and

● Ensure the efficient use of the electromagnetic spectrum.

● **Content of regulations.** Required the FCC to include the following when devising auction regulations:

● Alternative payment schedules for those who won bids for licenses, including lump-sum or installment payments, royalty payments or other methods that would promote competition and economic opportunity;

● Performance requirements, such as deadlines and penalties, to ensure prompt delivery of service to rural areas, to prevent the hoarding of spectrum by licensees and to promote investment in and rapid deployment of new technologies;

● Equitable geographic distribution of spectrum assignments that also provided the widest possible economic opportunity to small businesses, rural telephone companies and businesses owned by minorities and women.

● Assurances that small businesses, rural telephone companies, minority groups and women were given a chance to participate in the auctions. This could come in the form of tax certificates, bidding preferences and other means.

● Requirements for disclosure of license transfers, anti-trafficking rules and payment schedules to prevent the unjust enrichment of bidders as a result of the auction system.

● **Public interest.** Barred the FCC from citing the government's

need to raise revenues as a rationale for granting a license or permit. The provision did not, however, bar the FCC from considering consumer demand for spectrum-based services.

●**Treatment of revenues.** Required that all receipts from auctions be deposited in the Treasury. Revenues also were to be used to offset the FCC's costs of carrying out the auctions.

●**Auction timetable.** Stated that the FCC's authority to grant a license or permit by competitive bidding would expire Sept. 30, 1998. The commission was required to issue a report to Congress examining the auction program no later than Sept. 30, 1997.

Mobile Communications

●**Commercial mobile services.** Stated that any person engaged in a commercial mobile communications service be treated as a "common carrier." The designation meant that the FCC could require that competitors be allowed to connect with the service. The FCC had to list in its annual report the number of competitors in various mobile commercial services, determine whether there was effective competition and whether any competitors had a dominant share of the market.

The FCC could ease some of these requirements and drop the common-carrier status only if they were unnecessary to ensure that the service's rates, practices and rules were reasonable, non-discriminatory and protect consumers.

●**Private mobile services.** Stated that private mobile services, such as radio dispatch services used by delivery companies, should not be treated as common carriers, nor should companies provide dispatch service on any frequencies allocated for common carriers, except those already licensed as such before Jan. 1, 1982.

●**State pre-emption.** Prohibited state or local governments from regulating the rates or entry of any commercial or private mobile service. States could regulate other terms and conditions of commercial services, however. The provision did not affect any state requirements that aimed to ensure telecommunications services at affordable rates and widespread availability.

A state could petition the FCC for authority to regulate the rates for any commercial mobile service. Within nine months, the FCC was to grant the petition if a state demonstrated that market conditions failed to protect subscribers from unjust, unreasonable or discriminatory rates, or that wireless services were replacing a "substantial portion" of the land-based telephone exchange. In the interim, the state retained its rate-setting powers.

States that had in effect on June 1, 1993, any regulation concerning the rates of any commercial mobile service could within one year ask the FCC to continue the regulations. The agency had to act on the petition within one year. Should the rate-setting authority be allowed to continue, private parties could later petition the agency to reverse the decision.

●**Communications fees.** Directed the FCC to collect regulatory fees from all licensees to recover the costs of the agency's activities. The law set exact fees for each type of licensee for fiscal 1994. They ranged from $6 for a small-sized satellite television programmer to $600 for a medium-sized FM radio station and $18,000 for a large-market VHF television station. The provision directed that future fees be based on a combination of factors, including the number of FCC workers it took to perform various duties and the public benefit of those duties.

The total amount collected annually should equal the amount appropriated for that fiscal year for those FCC activities. The schedule of fees was to be revised annually. Licensees who did not pay in time faced a 25 percent penalty. The money was to be used to offset appropriations used to carry out the functions of the commission.

NATURAL RESOURCES

Recreation Fees

●**Admission fees.** Allowed the Interior and Agriculture secretaries to levy entrance fees at conservation and recreation areas,

national monuments, scenic areas and 21 other areas the Agriculture Department managed for outdoor recreation.

●**Golden age passports.** Assessed a one-time fee of $10 for "golden age passports" for those 65 or older. The passports allowed holders unlimited entrance to national parks for one year.

●**Recreation user fees.** Allowed the Interior and Agriculture secretaries to charge visitors for use of such facilities as swimming pools, boat ramps and parking lots at recreation areas the departments managed. The provision did not allow fees to be charged solely for the use of picnic tables. An overnight camping fee also could be charged if the site offered any five of the following: tent space, trailer space, drinking water, access roads, garbage containers, toilet facilities, fee collection, visitor protection or campfire facilities.

●**Collection costs:** Permitted the Interior and Agriculture secretaries to keep 15 percent of the cost of collecting recreation or admission fees. The National Park Service collected about $9 million in fees each year, and the Forest Service collected about $2 million, according to a Senate staff aide.

●**Commercial tours.** Charged commercial tour companies entrance fees at national parks. Tour vehicles with capacities of up to 25 people were to be charged $25 per vehicle, and those with capacities of 26 people or more were to be charged $50 a vehicle. The fees applied to aircraft used for commercial tours that flew over the Grand Canyon National Park in Arizona, the Haleakala Volcanoes National Park in Hawaii and other national parks that had such tour activities.

●**Golden eagle passports.** Allowed businesses, nonprofit groups and other private organizations to sell annual passes to national parks for $25 per person. Such organizations could retain 8 percent of the gross receipts. The Interior and Agriculture departments were to use the remaining 92 percent of the receipts to pay for resource protection, rehabilitation and conservation projects.

●**Communication fees.** Boosted by 10 percent fees charged for the use of radio, television and commercial telephone transmission sites in Forest Service and Bureau of Land Management lands in fiscal 1994. The government expected to collect about $1 million in additional revenue from the change in fiscal 1994.

Hard-Rock Mining

●**Maintenance fees.** Extended a $100 fee in fiscal 1994-98 for maintaining claims to mine such hard-rock minerals as silver and gold from federal lands. The Interior secretary had the discretion to waive the $100 fee for claimants who held 10 or fewer hard-rock mining claims.

●**Location fees:** Levied a $25 location fee for new hard-rock mining claims in fiscal 1994-98.

●**Adjustments:** Directed the Interior secretary to adjust maintenance fees at least every five years. The adjustment was based on the Consumer Price Index, which measured shifts in the retail prices of a set marketbasket of goods and services.

Mineral Receipts

●**States' share of administrative costs.** Doubled to 50 percent the states' share of the administrative cost of collecting royalties from the onshore mineral leasing program. The change was expected to generate $174 million over five years.

GOVERNMENT WORKERS

Civil Service

●**Cost of living adjustments.** Delayed cost of living adjustments (COLAs) for civilian federal retirees until March 1 in fiscal years 1994, 1995 and 1996. Under existing law, COLAs were effective Dec. 1 of each year. The COLA delay applied to the Civil Service, Federal Employees', Foreign Service and Central Intelligence Agency retirement systems.

●**Lump-sum retirement payments.** Prohibited civilian fed-

eral retirees, including former State Department and Central Intelligence Agency officials, from taking their retirement benefits in lump-sum payments as of Oct. 1, 1994. Employees with a life-threatening affliction or other critical medical condition could still get a lump-sum payment.

● **Limitation on physician fees.** Limited fees for physician and outpatient care for select retirees. Affected were the 220,000 retirees 65 and older who did not participate in the optional portion of Medicare (Medicare Part B) but who were covered by the Federal Employees' Health Benefits Program, the nation's largest health insurance program. The Medicare Part B program underwrote part of the costs of physician and outpatient care for some 34 million elderly and disabled beneficiaries. The limits were to be enforced in the way hospital fees limits were enforced under existing law. The Office of Personnel Management and the Department of Health and Human Services were to administer compliance with the provision.

● **Premium payments.** Extended the law setting the procedure for calculating the government's health insurance premium payment, for five years to 1998. At the time, the government paid a monthly maximum of $139, or 75 percent of the premium if that was smaller, for a single person.

● **Benefits for newly wed retirees.** Required the government to automatically adjust (with a roughly 9 percent reduction) the retirement benefits of those who married after retirement and elected to receive their spouse's survivor benefits. The law previously required retirees who were newly wed to pay a lump-sum refund to the government for the extra benefits they would receive as a single person with no survivors.

Postal Service

● **Replenishing Civil Service Retirement and Disability Fund.** Required the Postal Service to pay, over fiscal years 1996-98, $693 million into the Civil Service Retirement and Disability Fund. The Postal Service was required to pay another $348 million into the Employees' Health Benefits Fund. The payments represented what the Postal Service owed for past retiree cost of living adjustments and health benefits.

Armed Services

● **COLA delay.** Delayed the annual COLA payments to non-disabled retirees in 1994-98. The 1994 COLA was delayed until April 1. COLAs in 1995, 1996, 1997 and 1998 were to be paid Oct. 1. Under existing law, COLAs were paid on Jan. 1 of each year.

VETERANS AFFAIRS

● **Copayments for health-care benefits.** Extended for one year, to Sept. 30, 1998, a requirement that veterans other than those who were poor or who had major service-connected disabilities pay the Department of Veterans Affairs (VA) $2 for each 30-day supply of medication furnished on an outpatient basis. This requirement was due to expire Sept. 30, 1997.

● **Medical care cost recovery.** Extended until Sept. 30, 1998, the VA's authority to bill private insurers for the reasonable cost of treating veterans for non-service-connected disabilities. This authority was due to expire Aug. 1, 1994.

● **Income verification authority.** Extended for one year, until Sept. 30, 1998, the VA's authority to use income data from the Internal Revenue Service and the Social Security Administration to verify the eligibility of recipients of, or applicants for, benefits that were based on need. This authority would have expired Sept. 30, 1997.

● **Pension limitations.** Extended until Sept. 30, 1998, a $90-per-month limit of the need-based pension paid to veterans and surviving spouses with no dependents who were in nursing homes that participated in the Medicaid program. This authority would have expired Sept. 30, 1997.

● **Defaults on VA-guaranteed home loans.** Extended until Sept. 30, 1998, a provision that allowed the VA to choose the less expensive of two options when a lender foreclosed on a VA-guaranteed mortgage: acquiring and reselling the property or simply paying the amount of the loan that was guaranteed. The authority for this procedure, which saved money, would have expired Oct. 1, 1993.

● **Loan origination fees.** Increased the fee charged to most veterans who obtained low-interest VA-guaranteed home mortgages. The existing fee was 1.25 percent of the amount of the loan; it was to increase to 2 percent for loans closed between Oct. 1, 1993, and Sept. 30, 1998. Veterans who previously obtained guaranteed home loans would pay a 3 percent fee for any additional VA-guaranteed loans closed in the same period.

● **COLA adjustment in compensation rates.** Provided that when the new cost of living adjustment (COLA) for compensation to disabled veterans and survivors was determined for fiscal 1994, the VA would round down each monthly payment to the nearest dollar. For example, if someone was to receive $235.28 per month after the COLA was calculated, the person would be paid $235 per month.

● **Parity in rates of DIC benefits.** Sought to create parity in rates for dependency and indemnity compensation (DIC) to surviving spouses and children of veterans who died from service-related causes. Before the enactment of changes in 1992, survivors received benefits based on the rank of the deceased veteran. Under the new law, most survivors of veterans dying Jan 1, 1993, or after received the same amount — $750 per month — regardless of the rank of the deceased. "Old law" DIC beneficiaries would have their fiscal 1994 COLA halved. "New law" beneficiaries would receive the full COLA, bringing their monthly payments up to $772 per month in fiscal 1994. No DIC beneficiaries, regardless of the date of a veteran's death, would receive less than $772 per month.

● **COLA limitation for Montgomery GI Bill benefits.** Eliminated the fiscal 1994 COLA in higher education assistance provided under the Montgomery GI Bill. The COLA was halved for fiscal 1995.

REVENUE

Individual Taxes

● **Individual rates.** Imposed a fourth tax bracket, increasing the top marginal rate to 36 percent for individuals with taxable income above $115,000, joint filers with taxable income above $140,000, and heads of households with taxable income above $127,000. A 10 percent surtax was imposed on taxable income above $250,000, creating an effective top rate of 39.6 percent for these taxpayers.

These provisions took effect retroactively, beginning Jan. 1, 1993. Taxpayers could choose to pay additional taxes for 1993 that were attributable to the rate increase in three annual installments, beginning on the due date for the taxpayer's 1993 taxes. Taxpayers were not subject to penalties for underpaying estimated taxes attributable to these changes.

The law made permanent the limitation on itemized deductions and the phase-out of the personal exemption for upper-income taxpayers, which were scheduled to expire in 1996 and 1997, respectively.

● **Alternative minimum tax.** Created a two-tier rate structure for the alternative minimum tax (AMT), which was designed to ensure that individuals who claimed numerous deductions and other tax breaks paid a minimum tax. Under the new structure, a 26 percent rate applied to the first $175,000 of a taxpayer's income subject to the AMT, and a 28 percent rate applied above $175,000.

The law increased the amount of income exempt from the AMT from $40,000 to $45,000 for married couples filing jointly, and from $30,000 to $33,750 for individuals.

● **Anti-conversion rules.** Imposed rules to prevent taxpayers from converting ordinary income to capital gains income in order to take advantage of the lower, 28 percent top rate on capital gains. With certain exceptions, capital gains, or profits, earned from the

sale or trade of appreciated property that was part of a so-called conversion transaction were taxed as ordinary income. The law authorized the secretary of the Treasury to issue regulations defining such transactions.

● **Payroll taxes.** Subjected all wages and self-employment income to the hospital insurance payroll tax, which went to finance Medicare. Under existing law, only the first $135,000 earned was subject to the tax. The provision was effective Jan. 1, 1994.

● **Estate taxes.** Made permanent the top tax rates on estates (property transferred at death) and gifts (property transferred while the owner was alive). The rates were 53 percent for taxable transfers worth $2.5 million to $3 million, and 55 percent for taxable transfers over $3 million. The provision was retroactive to Jan. 1, 1993.

● **Business meals.** Reduced the deductible portion of business meals and entertainment expenses from 80 percent to 50 percent.

● **Club dues.** Eliminated the existing deduction for dues in any club organized for business, pleasure, recreation or other social purpose.

● **Moving expenses.** Scaled back the existing deduction for moving expenses associated with taking a new job. The law barred taxpayers from claiming the deduction for non-transportation costs, such as meals, the cost of selling a residence and house-hunting trips.

Taxpayers could exclude moving expenses from gross income for tax purposes if the expenses were paid by an employer. Moving expenses could be deducted if they were not paid for by an employer.

The law also required that, to claim a moving expense deduction, a taxpayer's new principal place of work had to be at least 50 miles farther from his former residence than was his former place of work. The previous minimum was 35 miles.

● **Estimated taxes.** Liberalized estimated tax rules. Under prior law, individual taxpayers were subject to a penalty in some cases if they underpaid their estimated taxes. To avoid the penalty, taxpayers had to pay in advance (by such means as withholding or quarterly estimated payments) either 100 percent of their previous year's tax or 90 percent of what they owed for the current year. However, for taxpayers whose adjusted gross income exceeded $75,000 and was $40,000 more than it was the previous year, paying 90 percent of their current tax was the only way to avoid penalty.

The law allowed those taxpayers to use the 100 percent of previous-year taxes option, though it required individuals whose adjusted gross income in the previous year exceeded $150,000 to pay 110 percent, rather than 100 percent, effective Jan. 1, 1994.

● **Social Security.** Raised the portion of Social Security benefits subject to taxation from 50 percent to 85 percent for some upper-income retirees. Beginning in 1994, individuals making more than $34,000 a year and couples making more than $44,000 a year were to be subject to the provision. The definition of income included adjusted gross income, tax-exempt interest, foreign-source income and one-half of the taxpayer's Social Security benefits. The provision also applied to Railroad Retirement Tier 1 benefits.

● **Travel expenses.** Prohibited taxpayers from deducting travel expenses associated with a spouse, dependent or other person accompanying them on business travel, unless the person's presence was business related.

● **Bonuses.** Increased the withholding rate on wages paid as bonuses from 20 percent to 28 percent.

Business Taxes

● **Corporate income tax.** Imposed a new fourth bracket, increasing the top marginal rate to 35 percent for corporate taxable income in excess of $10 million. A corporation with taxable income of more than $15 million was required to pay an additional amount — either $100,000 or 3 percent of the amount by which its taxable income exceeded $15 million, whichever was lower. The provision was designed to phase out the benefits of the 34 percent rate for

affected corporations. The rate increase was retroactive to Jan. 1, 1993.

● **Lobbying expenses.** Prohibited companies from taking a deduction for lobbying expenses. The provision, effective Jan. 1, 1993, specified that no deduction was allowed for any amount paid in connection with an attempt to influence federal or state legislation or any communication with certain covered federal executive branch officials, including the president, vice president, Cabinet members and other senior White House officials.

The law also prohibited a deduction for the portion of membership dues paid to a tax-exempt organization that went toward funding lobbying activities.

● **Executive pay.** Limited the ability of companies to deduct compensation, including benefits, paid to top executives. Publicly traded companies could not deduct salaries in excess of $1 million for each of their top five executives. Exceptions were provided for pay earned from commissions and other performance-based compensation and for pay provided under a contract that was in effect Feb. 17, 1993. In addition, companies could continue to claim a deduction for benefits paid to executives if the employee could deduct the benefit from gross income.

● **Retirement plans.** Reduced the amount of compensation that could be taken into account under a qualified retirement plan to $150,000 from $235,840 for 1994. The limit was used in determining the amount the employer could deduct for contributions to the plan as well as determining the participant's benefits. The limit was indexed to increase with inflation in $10,000 increments. The limit could force employers to re-examine defined contribution plans to ensure they did not discriminate against lower-paid employees.

● **'Mark-to-market' securities rules.** Revised rules governing the tax treatment of securities held by dealers for sale to customers. Under the so-called mark-to-market rules in the law, a security that was held as inventory by a securities dealer had to be reported at its fair market value. In addition, a security that was not in inventory and was held at the end of a taxable year was treated as sold for its fair market value; any gain or loss was to be reflected in gross income. The law specified several exceptions. For example, the mark-to-market rules did not apply to any security that was held for investment.

● **Special savings and loan tax benefit.** Clarified that a special tax benefit that had been granted to purchasers of failed savings and loan institutions, and repealed effective May 10, 1989, could no longer be used for transactions completed before that date. Prior to 1989, buyers of failed thrifts often received guarantees of tax-exempt cash payments from the Federal Savings and Loan Insurance Corporation to cover losses on bad assets acquired in the purchase of failed institutions. The tax code also permitted deductions from income for those same losses. Following repeal of this "double dip," the Treasury Department ruled that assistance payments from thrift sales that were concluded before the repeal would no longer be tax exempt, but it asked Congress to clarify whether that indeed had been the intent of the 1989 repeal. The provision was effective for income on losses recorded after March 4, 1991, the date of the Treasury ruling.

● **Estimated taxes.** Tightened corporate estimated tax rules. Under prior law, corporations could avoid the penalty for underpaying their estimated taxes if they made timely estimated payments totaling 97 percent of their tax liability for the current year (91 percent after 1996). The provision required corporations with taxable income of more than $1 million to make estimated payments that fully covered their current year taxes. Corporations with less than $1 million in taxable income had the option of paying 100 percent of their prior-year tax, as they did under prior law.

● **Debt provisions.** Repealed the so-called stock-for-debt exception, which provided favorable tax treatment for bankrupt companies that gave creditors stock to retire debt.

● **Puerto Rico.** Scaled back an existing credit, called the Section 936 tax credit, which was intended to attract jobs to Puerto Rico.

As under prior law, the provision allowed companies in Puerto Rico to claim a tax credit based on their profits, but in 1994 the credit was to be limited to 60 percent of what was allowed under existing law, declining to 40 percent in 1998. The law also gaves companies the option of claiming a scaled-back credit based on investment and wages, rather than on profits.

● **Foreign taxes.** Repealed parts of a provision of the tax code allowing companies to defer paying taxes on earnings accumulated in foreign subsidiaries. In general, the new law required U.S. shareholders to include the undistributed earnings of a foreign subsidiary in its income to the extent that the subsidiary sheltered its income in "excess passive assets."

● **Research and experimentation.** Required that U.S. multinational companies allocate 50 percent of their research and development expenses to U.S.-source income for tax purposes; the other half was to be allocated to foreign-source income. The provision was effective only in 1994.

● **Intangibles.** Allowed companies to write off over 15 years the cost of acquiring most intangible assets, including the value of the company as an ongoing concern, work force know-how, licenses and permits, covenants not to compete and other similar arrangements, and franchises, trademarks and trade names. The law provided more generous tax treatment for purchased mortgage servicing rights, which could be written off over nine years.

Energy Taxes

● **Transportation fuels.** Imposed a permanent 4.3-cents-per-gallon excise tax beginning Oct. 1, 1993, on most transportation fuels, including motor fuels, aviation gasoline, diesel fuel used in trains, fuels used in inland waterway transportation, compressed natural gas used in highway motor vehicles and jet fuel used in non-commercial aviation. Gasoline and jet fuel used in commercial aviation were subject to the tax beginning Oct. 1, 1995. Revenue raised by the tax was to be deposited into the general fund of the Treasury.

The law also extended through 1999 a 2.5-cents-per-gallon increase in the motor fuels tax that was enacted in 1990 and was scheduled to expire in 1995. The revenues were to go into the Highway Trust Fund. The provision included a 1.25-cents-per-gallon tax on diesel used in trains, with those revenues going into the general fund.

● **Motorboat fuel.** Imposed a new tax of 20.1 cents per gallon on non-commercial use of diesel fuel in boats. Revenues were to go to the general fund.

Training and Investment

● **Educational assistance.** Extended until Dec. 31, 1994, a provision that allowed employees to exclude from their taxable income up to $5,250 in educational assistance provided by their employer. The provision, which expired July 1, 1992, was renewed retroactively to that date.

● **Targeted jobs.** Extended the targeted jobs tax credit, which gave employers a tax break — generally up to $2,400 per employee — for hiring certain hard-to-employ individuals. The provision, was made effective retroactively for individuals who began work after June 30, 1992, and on or before Dec. 31, 1994. The credit had expired June 30, 1992.

● **Research and development.** Extended for three years the research and development tax credit, beginning retroactively on July 1, 1993, through June 30, 1995. The credit provided a tax break equal to 20 percent of the amount by which a company's qualified research expenditures exceeded a base amount determined by its previous expenditures on R&D. It also applied to university basic research. The law contained new rules for calculating the R&D base for new companies without a history of R&D expenditures.

● **Orphan drugs.** Extended until Dec. 31, 1994, a 50 percent tax credit for qualified clinical testing of certain drugs for rare diseases, generally referred to as orphan drugs. The extension was retroactive to July 1, 1992, when the provision expired.

● **Capital gains.** Allowed investors who purchased newly issued stock in small companies to exclude from their income 50 percent of the gain when they sold the stock as long as it was held for at least five years. The amount of the gain eligible for the break was limited to $10 million per shareholder or 10 times the taxpayer's basis in the stock, whichever was greater.

For stock to qualify for the break, the company had to have less than $50 million in gross assets, meaning the cash and other assets held by the company.

● **AMT relief.** Gave capital intensive companies relief tax by eliminating the so-called adjusted existing earnings test, which required them to add back in certain deductions when calculating what they owed under the alternative minimum tax.

● **Small-business incentives.** Beginning Jan. 1, 1993, increased from $10,000 to $17,500 the amount that small businesses could write off on the cost of equipment and machinery in the year it was purchased. The maximum was available only to businesses that invested less than $210,000 in depreciable property a year.

● **Tax-exempt bonds.** Permanently extended authority for state and local governments to issue qualified small-issue bonds, which were used to finance purchases of manufacturing facilities and farm property. The law also contained an exclusion from state volume caps for bonds issued to finance high-speed rail projects, as long as the property was to be owned by a government entity.

● **Mortgage revenue bonds.** Permanently extended authority for local housing agencies to issue qualified mortgage bonds, which are used to finance the purchase or rehabilitation of single-family, owner-occupied residences through subsidized mortgages. The law made the bond authority retroactive to July 1, 1992. It had expired June 30, 1992. The same was true for mortgage credit certificates, which provided income tax credits based on interest paid on mortgage loans.

● **Low-income housing.** Made permanent the low-income housing tax credit, which gave developers a tax break for rehabilitating rental housing for the poor. The credit, which expired the previous year, was made permanent beginning on July 1, 1992. It had expired June 30, 1992.

● **Real estate incentives.** Allowed real estate developers and others in the industry to deduct so-called passive losses on rental property against ordinary income. To qualify for the deduction, an individual had to spend at least 750 hours a year in real estate activities, and more than half the personal services performed by the taxpayer had to involve real estate transactions.

The law also modified the tax code to permit pension funds to invest in real estate.

The law increased the depreciation period for non-residential real estate from 31.5 years to 39 years, a change that would increase federal revenue.

Earned-Income Tax Credit

Expanded the earned-income tax credit (EITC), a program to help poor working families, including those who owed no taxes and could receive the credit as a check from the government. For eligible families with one child, the EITC was 26.3 percent of the first $7,750 of earned income in 1994, for a maximum credit of $2,038. For 1995, the credit rate increased to 34 percent on earned income of up to $6,170.

For eligible families with two or more children, the credit was increased to 30 percent of the first $8,425 of earned income in 1994, for a maximum credit of $2,527. The credit rate increased to 36 percent in 1995 and 40 percent in 1996 and thereafter.

Taxpayers earning more than $11,000 a year were eligible for a partial credit. The EITC was not available to families with one child that were making more than $23,760 or to families with two or more children making more than $27,000.

Childless workers over age 25 and below 65 qualified for a modest credit of 7.65 percent of the first $4,000 in income, for a maximum credit of $306 in 1994. No one making more more than $9,000 a year qualified for the childless worker credit.

Empowerment Zones

● **Creation of zones, communities.** Provided for the creation of nine enterprise zones in economically distressed areas of the country — six in urban areas and three in rural areas. The zones were eligible for special tax benefits and other federal assistance aimed at creating jobs and encouraging economic development. The secretary of Housing and Urban Development was to select the urban areas and the secretary of Agriculture was to select the rural areas, based on size and other criteria.

In addition, 95 other areas — 65 of them urban and 30 rural — were to be designated as enterprise communities and would be eligible for more limited tax benefits.

● **Tax incentives.** Created a 20 percent tax credit for the first $15,000 of wages and certain training that a business provided to each employee who lived and worked in an empowerment zone. Businesses within the zone were also allowed to write off a maximum of $37,500 in investments in depreciable property in the first year, compared with $17,500 elsewhere.

The law created a new category of tax-exempt bonds to promote economic development within the zones and communities. An enterprise zone business was limited to issuing bonds with an aggregate face value of $3 million per zone or community, and $20 million for all zones and communities.

● **Block grant.** Created a new social services block grant worth $1 billion over two years. The urban zones would get $100 million each, the rural zones would get $40 million each, and the enterprise communities would get $2.95 million each.

● **Indian reservations.** Provided certain tax incentives for Indian reservations, although no reservations were designated as enterprise zones. Businesses qualified for a shorter depreciation period for property used in connection with a trade or business on an Indian reservation. A 20 percent credit against income tax liability was provided to reservation employers for wages and health insurance costs paid to members of Indian tribes living on or near a reservation. The credit was available for the first $20,000 in wages or benefits paid to each qualified employee.

Miscellaneous Tax Provisions

● **Luxury taxes.** Repealed the 10 percent excise tax on yachts, aircraft, jewelry and furs that was enacted in 1990. The tax on the portion of the price of an automobile that exceeded $30,000 was retained, but the threshold above which the tax applied was to increase with inflation in $2,000 increments.

● **Charitable donations.** Made permanent an exemption from the alternative minimum tax (AMT) for gifts of appreciated tangible property, such as artwork, and extended it to real estate and securities. Donors could deduct the market value of contributions from their taxable income without having to add the appreciated value back in when calculating their liability under the AMT. The provision was retroactive to July 1, 1992.

● **Self-employed health benefits.** Extended the 25 percent deduction for the cost of health insurance for self-employed workers and their spouses and dependents. The provision, which expired July 1, 1992, was extended retroactively to that date through Dec. 31, 1993.

● **Vaccine excise tax.** Made permanent the excise taxes imposed on certain vaccines, which were used to finance the Vaccine Injury Compensation Trust Fund.

● **Disaster relief.** Provided tax breaks for individuals whose homes and property were damaged in a presidentially declared disaster zone. Taxpayers would have an additional two years to use insurance proceeds to purchase a replacement home without incurring tax on any gain. In addition, tax treatment of insurance proceeds was liberalized.

● **Presidential campaign checkoff.** Increased from $1 to $3 the amount individual taxpayers could earmark for the presidential campaign fund on their tax returns. The amount for joint filers was increased from $2 to $6. The change was intended to ensure that the fund did not run out of money before the 1996 campaign.

● **Tips.** Provided restaurant owners and other taxpayers with a dollar-for-dollar credit for federal payroll taxes paid on tips earned by their employees.

● **Group health plans.** Required that, as a condition of an employer's tax deduction for health-care expenses, group health plans continued to reimburse for inpatient hospital services provided in the state of New York at the rate required under New York's all-payer system.

Dropped from the bill were five states' waivers from the requirements of the federal Employee Retirement Income Security Act (ERISA). The waivers would have allowed New York, Oregon, Maryland, Hawaii and Minnesota to proceed with health-care reform plans.

MEDICARE

● **Hospital payments/payment updates.** Adjusted annual inflation increases for hospitals under Medicare's Prospective Payment System as follows:

● Urban hospitals in fiscal 1994 and 1995 would receive increases equal to the percentage increase in the "marketbasket" (a measure of goods and services purchased by hospitals) minus 2.5 percentage points. The fiscal 1994 marketbasket increase was 4.2 percent, so beginning Oct. 1, 1993, urban hospitals were to receive inflation increases of 1.7 percent.

● Rural hospitals, scheduled to receive increases of 6.7 percent in fiscal 1994 (marketbasket plus 1.5 percentage points), were to be subject to a 1 percentage point cut, for a total update of 5.7 percent. As under existing law, rural hospitals were to receive updates in fiscal 1995 sufficient to close the gap between the rates they received and the higher rates paid to urban facilities.

● Both urban and rural hospitals were to receive updates in fiscal 1996 that were equal to the marketbasket amount minus 2 percentage points. In fiscal 1997 the update would be marketbasket minus 0.5 percentage points, and in fiscal 1998 hospitals would receive the full marketbasket update.

● Specially designated sole community hospitals and Medicare-dependent small rural hospitals (which had been receiving specially augmented rates) were to receive updates of marketbasket minus 2.3 percent in fiscal 1994 and marketbasket minus 2.2 percent in fiscal 1995. Beginning in fiscal 1996, these hospitals were scheduled to receive the same rate of increase as other hospitals.

● Hospitals exempt from Medicare's Prospective Payment System (including children's hospitals, psychiatric hospitals, rehabilitation hospitals and cancer treatment centers) were to receive increases of the marketbasket percentage minus 1 percentage point for each of fiscal 1994 through 1997 and the full marketbasket update in fiscal 1998. No reduction was to be applied to hospitals whose operating costs exceeded a preset limit in fiscal 1990 by 10 percent or more.

● **Hospital payments/capital costs.** Beginning in fiscal 1994, reduced by 7.4 percent payments to hospitals for capital-related costs (including depreciation, leases and rentals, interest and property taxes). The existing 10 percent reduction was set to expire at the end of fiscal 1995. Medicare capital payments were in the second year of a 10-year phase-in to be fully included in the Prospective Payment System.

● **Hospice payments.** Increased payment rates for hospice services by the hospital marketbasket increase minus 2 percentage points in fiscal 1994, by marketbasket minus 1.5 percentage points in fiscal 1995 and 1996, by marketbasket minus 0.5 percentage points in fiscal 1997 and by the full marketbasket rate in fiscal 1998.

● **Skilled nursing facility payments.** Delayed inflation updates for skilled nursing facilities until fiscal 1996. Beginning Oct. 1, 1993, special payments for "return on equity" for private nursing homes would be eliminated. (Similar payments for hospitals were phased out in the mid-1980s.) The bill also eliminated special payments for excess overhead costs for hospital-based facilities, beginning Oct. 1, 1993.

Deficit-Reduction Highlights

(Amounts in billions of dollars)

	1994	1994-98
OUTLAYS		
Entitlement changes		
Expand earned-income tax credit	$ 0.1	$18.3
Expand food stamps program	*	2.7
Extend formula for federal employee health benefits	0.3	2.8
Aid family preservation, child welfare	0.3	1.4
Expand social services block grants	0.1	1.0
Create childhood immunization entitlement	——	0.9
Reduce Medicare payments to hospitals, physicians	-1.9	-49.1
Auction radio spectrum	-0.5	-12.6
End lump-sum retirement, delay retirees' COLAs	-0.4	-11.5
Reduce Medicaid spending	*	-7.2
Alter student loan program	-0.4	-3.6
Revise veterans' benefits	-0.3	-3.5
Permanently extend customs fee	——	-1.8
Extend Nuclear Regulatory Commission fee	——	-1.1
Revise agriculture price supports, crop insurance	-0.1	-1.7
Pay off postal liabilities	——	-1.0
Other	-0.2	-5.3
Subtotal, entitlements	-$2.9	-$71.3
Caps on discretionary spending	-10.2	-107.7
Shorter debt maturities	-1.6	-16.4
Debt service	-1.3	-59.6
Other	-3.2	0.2
Total Outlays	-$19.3	-$254.7
REVENUES		
Revenue-losers (add to the deficit)		
Extend R&E tax credit	$ 2.1	$ 4.3
Extend low-income housing credit	0.2	4.3
Increase depreciation for small business	1.6	4.0
Expand earned-income tax credit	*	2.9
Modify passive-loss rules	0.3	2.4
Modify alternative minimum tax depreciation rules	0.1	2.1
Establish empowerment zones, enterprise communities	0.2	2.0
Extend employer-provided education assistance	0.9	1.0
Provide capital gains break for investment in small business	*	0.8
Extend targeted jobs tax credit	0.2	0.6
Other investment incentives	1.9	1.9
Revenue-gainers (reduce the deficit)		
Increase taxes on upper-income individuals	-17.0	-124.5
Subject all wages to hospital insurance payroll tax	-2.7	-29.2
Increase transportation fuels tax	-4.5	-24.0
Increase taxable portion of Social Security benefits	-1.5	-18.3
Reduce deduction for business meals	-1.8	-15.9
Increase top corporate income tax rate	-3.8	-14.3
Extend 2.5-cents-per-gallon motor fuels tax	——	-8.0
Modify corporate estimated tax rules	-1.9	-7.1
Require securities dealers to mark to market	-0.9	-4.3
Limit Puerto Rico tax credit	-0.2	-3.8
Reduce pension compensation cap	-0.3	-3.8
Reinstate top estate tax rates	-0.5	-2.8
Limit moving expense deduction	-0.1	-2.3
Revise certain foreign tax provisions	-0.6	-6.0
Extend unemployment insurance surtax	——	-2.1
Modify individual estimated tax rules	2.2	-1.5
Other	-1.4	-8.7
Total Revenue	-$27.4	-$250.1
Total Deficit Reduction	**-$46.8**	**-$504.8**

SOURCE: Office of Management and Budget

* $50 million or less

• **Medicare hospital payments/regional referral centers.** Reinstated through Sept. 30, 1994, the 180 large rural hospitals that were designated as regional referral centers as of Sept. 30, 1992. Referral centers were paid at a higher rate than other rural hospitals. The provision also made the facilities eligible for back payments.

• **Medicare hospital payments/small rural Medicare-dependent hospitals.** Continued through fiscal 1994 special payments, on a phased-down basis, for certain small rural hospitals whose caseloads were at least 60 percent Medicare patients.

• **Medicare hospital payments/regional floor.** Extended through fiscal 1996 a special payment adjustment for hospitals in areas of the country with costs higher than the national average.

• **Part A premium.** Reduced the premium charged to people 65 and older who did not qualify for Part A benefits but wanted to purchase Part A coverage. The premium was based on the actuarial value of Part A benefits ($221 monthly in 1993). It was to be reduced, on a phased-in basis, for people with credits for 30 or more quarters of taxes paid into the Social Security system and for surviving or divorced spouses of those people. The premium was to be reduced by 25 percent in calendar 1994, and by 45 percent in 1998 and thereafter.

Part B

• **Physician fees: payment update.** Reduced the scheduled inflation adjustment in Medicare fees for physician services in fiscal 1994 and 1995. Under the Medicare fee schedule enacted in 1989, physician payments had to be adjusted each year for inflation and for the amount by which all physicians exceeded or failed to reach an aggregate target for the volume of services provided to Medicare beneficiaries. Because physicians remained far below the volume targets in 1992, under the formula 1994 fees for surgical services would have risen by 12.2 percent, while fees for all other services would have risen by 6.6 percent.

Instead, fee increases in 1994 were to be reduced by 3.6 percentage points for surgical services (resulting in an increase of 8.6 percent) and by 2.6 percentage points for all other services except primary care (resulting in an increase of the full 6.6 percent for primary care and 4 percent for all other services.)

For 1995, increases for all services except primary care were to be reduced by 2.7 percentage points. Primary care services were to receive the full scheduled update.

• **Physician fees: primary care, anesthesia services.** Beginning in fiscal 1994, put primary care in a separate category for the purpose of determining annual increases in physician fees; anesthesia services were put in the surgical services category.

• **Physician fees: practice expenses.** Gradually reduced payments from 1994 to 1997 for the practice expense (overhead) component used to determine fees for individual physician services.

• **Physician fees: anesthesia teams.** Gradually reduced payments to anesthesia care teams (a physician anesthesiologist supervising one or more certified registered nurse anesthetists) so that by 1998, payments to teams would not exceed those that would be made to an anesthesiologist practicing alone in the same locality.

• **Physician fees: EKG interpretations.** Repealed a provision of the 1990 reconciliation bill that prohibited separate payments for interpretation of routine electrocardiograms (EKGs) in conjunction with an office visit or consultation. The bill required the Health and Human Services (HHS) secretary to establish fee schedule amounts for such interpretations.

• **Physician fees: new physicians.** Repealed provisions in the 1987 and 1990 reconciliation bills that reduced fees for physicians in their first four years of practice.

• **Payment for allergy antigens.** Beginning Jan. 1, 1995, provided that payment for antigens used in allergy treatment and related services be made under the Medicare physician fee schedule.

• **Outpatient hospital services.** Extended through fiscal 1998

the 10 percent reduction in Medicare payments for capital-related hospital outpatient costs. The reductions were set to expire at the end of fiscal 1995. Sole community hospitals and primary care hospitals remained exempt from the cuts. The bill also continued through fiscal 1998 the 5.8 percent reduction in operating costs payments for hospital outpatient services.

• **Ambulatory surgical centers.** Froze the level of fees paid to ambulatory surgical centers for fiscal 1994 and 1995.

• **Intraocular lenses.** Beginning Jan. 1, 1994, reduced the $200 maximum payment for intraocular lenses used in cataract surgery to $150. The limit was to expire on Jan. 1, 1999.

• **Laboratory services.** Froze most Medicare payments for laboratory fees for fiscal 1994 and 1995. Beginning in fiscal 1994, the maximum fee was to drop from 88 percent of the national median amount to 76 percent over three years.

• **Durable medical equipment.** Set national payment limits for durable medical equipment based on the median of local payment amounts, similar to the limits for laboratory services (see above). For fiscal 1994 and 1995, the bill froze payment levels for orthotics and prosthetics and enteral and parenteral supplies. Payments for transcutaneous electrical nerve stimulation (TENS) devices were reduced by an additional 30 percent.

• **Alzheimer's demonstration projects.** Reauthorized for one additional year demonstration projects to provide comprehensive services to Medicare beneficiaries with Alzheimer's disease.

• **Cancer drugs.** Beginning Jan. 1, 1994, extended Medicare coverage to oral cancer drugs if they were the same chemical entity as anti-cancer drugs that were covered by Medicare when they were administered intravenously. (Generally, Medicare did not pay for drugs that can be self-administered.) The bill also extended Medicare coverage to off-label uses of anti-cancer drugs (uses other than those for which a drug originally was approved) in certain specific circumstances.

• **Municipal health service demonstration projects.** Extended through 1997 four municipal health service demonstration projects.

• **Indian health programs.** Extended Medicare coverage to certain programs and facilities operated by Indian tribes under the Indian Self-Determination Act.

• **Certified nurse midwife services.** Clarified that Medicare coverage of certified nurse midwife services was not limited to services provided during pregnancy.

• **Outpatient physical and occupational therapy.** Beginning Jan. 1, 1994, increased from $750 to $900 the annual limit on outpatient physical and occupational therapy services.

Parts A and B

• **Graduate medical education.** Froze for fiscal 1994 and 1995 the level of Medicare payments made to hospitals to offset the costs of training physicians who treated Medicare patients. Residents in obstetrics and gynecology were exempt from the freeze, as were those in primary care fields, including family medicine, general internal medicine, general pediatrics, preventive medicine, geriatric medicine and osteopathic general practice. Beginning July 1, 1995, the period of eligibility for such "direct" medical education payments was redefined as the minimum number of years before a resident was eligible for board certification in his or her field of specialization.

• **Home health services.** From July 1, 1994, to July 1, 1996, eliminated the annual inflation adjustment for the maximum Medicare reimbursement for home health services. Beginning Oct. 1, 1993, special payments to hospital-based home health agencies were eliminated.

• **Medicare secondary payer provisions.** Extended through Sept. 30, 1998, authority for Medicare officials to gain access to the records of the Social Security Administration and the Internal Revenue Service to identify Medicare beneficiaries with other sources of health insurance. By law, Medicare was supposed to be the "secondary payer" for many beneficiaries with other insurance, covering only those costs that were not covered by the primary insurer.

The bill also extended through Sept. 30, 1998, a provision making Medicare the secondary payer for disabled Medicare beneficiaries who were covered by employer health plans in businesses with more than 100 employees, as well as beneficiaries who qualified for Medicare as a result of end-stage renal disease.

● **Physician referrals.** Extended a ban imposed in the 1989 reconciliation bill on physicians' referring patients to clinical laboratories in which they or their immediate family members had an ownership or investment interest. Beginning Dec. 31, 1994, such self-referrals also were to be banned for physical and occupational therapy services; radiology or other diagnostic services; radiation therapy services; durable medical equipment; parenteral and enteral nutrients, equipment and supplies; prosthetics, orthotics and prosthetic devices; home health services; outpatient prescription drugs; and inpatient and outpatient hospital services.

The bill revised and added a series of exceptions to the ban, including ones for services provided to rural residents in rural areas, those provided by group practices and those provided by or under the direct supervision of a physician or group of physicians. It also clarified circumstances in which ownership of investment securities constituted a relationship that triggered the referral ban, and it clarified permissible compensation arrangements and definitions of group practices.

● **Immunosuppressive drugs.** Extended Medicare coverage of outpatient immunosuppressive drugs that were used to prevent rejection in organ-transplant patients. At the time, Medicare covered such drugs for one year following a transplant. Beginning Jan. 1, 1995, coverage was extended to 18 months; beginning Jan. 1, 1996, coverage would continue for 24 months; beginning Jan. 1, 1997, coverage would continue for 30 months; and beginning Jan. 1, 1998, and thereafter, coverage would continue for 36 months.

● **Erythropoietin payments.** Beginning Jan. 1, 1994, reduced payments for Erythropoietin (an anti-anemia drug used by dialysis patients in Medicare's end-stage renal disease program) by $1 per 1,000 units. The bill also permitted dialysis patients to administer the drug themselves.

● **Social health maintenance organization demonstrations.** Continued for two additional years, through Dec. 31, 1997, authority for demonstration programs to offer Medicare beneficiaries integrated health and long-term care services on a prepaid basis.

● **Timing of claims payments.** Set new "floors" and "ceilings" for payment of Medicare claims by insurance companies that processed Medicare paperwork. Beginning Oct. 1, 1993, stipulated that "clean" claims (those properly submitted with all necessary information) submitted electronically could not be paid until the 14th day after receipt. (The federal government benefited because it could earn interest on the money in the interim.) Clean claims submitted on paper could not be paid until the 27th day after receipt. However, interest was to be paid to recipients for clean claims not paid within 30 days of receipt.

● **Part B premium.** Extended through 1998 the requirement that the Medicare Part B premium be calculated to recoup 25 percent of the program's costs. The Treasury would continue to subsidize the remaining 75 percent. Without the change, after 1995 the Part B premium could not rise by more than the Social Security cost of living adjustment.

● **Medicare and Medicaid coverage data bank.** Required the HHS secretary to establish a data bank to help identify and collect from private insurers appropriate reimbursement for services provided to Medicare and Medicaid beneficiaries. Beginning in 1994, employers were required to provide information regarding employee health insurance coverage.

MEDICAID

● **Personal care services.** Repealed a mandate requiring states to provide personal care services for Medicaid beneficiaries outside the home and clarified that such services could be provided as a state option. (This corrected a drafting error in the 1990 reconciliation bill.)

● **Medicaid prescription drug discount program.** Permitted states to establish prescription drug formularies (restrictive lists of approved drugs that were to be covered by Medicaid) under certain circumstances. States were allowed to subject drugs to "prior authorization" before they were dispensed to Medicaid recipients — even in the first six months after they were approved by the Food and Drug Administration. Such drugs had been barred from inclusion in prior authorization programs during the first six months.

● **Optional coverage of TB-related services.** Beginning Jan. 1, 1994, allowed states to cover prescribed drugs, directly observed therapy and other services for low-income individuals infected with tuberculosis not otherwise eligible for Medicaid.

● **Emergency services for illegal aliens.** Stipulated that services related to organ transplant procedures did not qualify as emergencies covered by Medicaid for illegal aliens.

● **Certified nurse midwife services.** Beginning Oct. 1, 1993, clarified that Medicaid coverage of certified nurse midwife services was not limited to services provided during pregnancy.

● **Transfer of assets to facilitate Medicaid eligibility.** Required a delay in granting eligibility for Medicaid nursing home coverage for institutionalized individuals (or their spouses) who disposed of assets for less than fair market value 36 months before the date they applied for benefits or the date they were institutionalized, whichever was later. Penalties could not be applied to transfers to spouses, to minor or disabled children, or to trusts solely for the benefit of disabled individuals under age 65.

● **Medicaid estate recoveries.** Required states to establish programs to recover the cost of long-term care services provided to Medicaid beneficiaries from their estates after their death. Recovery could be waived in cases in which "undue hardship" would result.

● **Disproportionate share hospitals.** Tightened conditions under which states could designate hospitals as serving a disproportionate share of low-income individuals (and hence qualifying for higher federal payments). A hospital could not be designated unless at least 1 percent of its inpatients were Medicaid beneficiaries. Special payments were limited to no more than the costs of providing inpatient and outpatient services to Medicaid and uninsured patients, less the amount the hospital received for those patients either from Medicaid or the patients themselves. The bill allowed a transition for high-volume public hospitals.

● **Third-party liability laws.** Required states to enact laws that prohibited insurers, including group health plans under ERISA, from taking an individual's Medicaid eligibility or enrollment into account in enrolling them or paying claims. States also were required to enact laws making it possible to collect payments from group health plans and other private insurers of Medicaid beneficiaries.

● **Medical child support laws.** Beginning April 1, 1994, required states to enact and implement laws to ensure that insurers and employers carried out court or administrative orders for medical child support.

● **Physician referrals.** Beginning December 1994, applied to Medicaid the rules barring physicians from referring patients to facilities in which they had a financial interest (see Medicare, above).

● **State Medicaid fraud control.** Beginning Jan. 1, 1995, required states to operate "effective" Medicaid fraud control units that met requirements established by the HHS secretary, unless the state could demonstrate that operating such a unit would not be cost-effective and that the state could otherwise protect Medicaid beneficiaries from fraud and neglect.

● **Federal Medicaid payments to U.S. territories.** Beginning in fiscal 1994, increased the limit for federal matching payments to Medicaid programs in Puerto Rico, the Virgin Islands, Guam, the Northern Mariana Islands and American Samoa. Beginning in fiscal 1995, the new ceilings were to be adjusted for inflation.

OTHER HEALTH PROVISIONS

● **Permanent extension of Vaccine Injury Compensation Trust Fund.** Made permanent the federal program to compensate families of children injured or killed by adverse reactions to vaccines to prevent childhood illnesses. The bill also made permanent the manufacturer's excise tax on certain vaccines that funded the compensation program. Both the tax and the program had expired as of Jan. 1, 1993, but the law provided that children affected after the expiration date would be eligible as if the coverage lapse had not occurred.

● **Immunization entitlement.** Created a new program under Medicaid designed to guarantee availability of free childhood vaccines to all children eligible for Medicaid, all uninsured children, and all Native Americans. Children with health insurance but whose insurance did not cover the cost of vaccines could receive free vaccines at certain federally supported clinics, such as community health centers.

The program entitled each state to receive at no charge from the federal government a sufficient supply of vaccine to cover the designated class of children. The state in turn was required to make the vaccines available to all public and private health-care providers who were willing to participate in the program and were authorized under state law to administer vaccines. Neither the state nor providers could charge patients for the vaccines, although providers could assess a limited fee for the actual administration.

The Health and Human Services secretary was ordered to negotiate with vaccine manufacturers for a bulk purchase price, which also was to be the price at which states could purchase additional amounts of vaccine for children not covered by the mandate.

The federal government also was to purchase an emergency stockpile of recommended vaccines as protection against unexpected shortages, such as manufacturing disruptions, or sudden needs, such as an epidemic.

HUMAN RESOURCES/INCOME SECURITY

Child Welfare, Foster Care, Adoption

● **Family preservation.** Created a new capped entitlement for family preservation and family support services in the child welfare services program under Title IV-B of the Social Security Act. The entitlement was authorized to be funded at $60 million in fiscal 1994, $150 million in fiscal 1995, $225 million in fiscal 1996, $240 million in fiscal 1997, and $255 million in fiscal 1997.

Of those amounts, $2 million in fiscal 1994 and $6 million in the four years beginning in fiscal 1995 was to be set aside for research, training, technical assistance and evaluation of family preservation and support programs. In addition, $5 million in fiscal 1995 and $10 million in each of the following three years was to be reserved for a grant program for state courts. Also, 1 percent of the family preservation and support service entitlement was reserved for American Indian tribes.

Allocation of the funds to states was to be based on their relative share of children receiving food stamps. States had to match 25 percent of the federal government's contribution. States could spend no more than 10 percent of their allocation on administrative costs.

Eligible programs were those targeted at families at risk or in a crisis. They included programs that provided help in reuniting children with their biological parents or placing them for adoption, help in avoiding placing children in foster care, follow-up care to families to whom a child had been returned following foster care placement, respite care to provide temporary relief to parents and other caregivers, and services to improve parenting skills.

Family support services included community-based activities to promote the well-being of children and families, and to prevent crises, such as abuse or neglect.

The law required the secretary of the Department of Health and Human Services (HHS) to evaluate the effectiveness of various family support and preservation programs.

● **Funding for state courts.** Provided $5 million in fiscal 1995 and $10 million in each of the following three years from the new capped entitlement for a grant program for the highest state courts involved in foster care and adoption. The grants would enable the courts to assess their effectiveness in carrying out laws that required court proceedings in foster care placement, ending parental rights, and adoptions. The federal grant had to be matched with 25 percent from states or localities from fiscal 1996 through 1998.

● **Automated data systems.** Authorized a 75 percent federal matching rate for state expenses to develop or install a foster care and adoption data collection system. The data system was to be used to provide national information on foster care and adoption. The 75 percent federal matching rate was applicable from fiscal 1994 to 1996; the rate would be 50 percent thereafter.

● **Independent living program.** Permanently extended the authorization for the federal-state entitlement program designed to help foster children age 16 and older ease into independent living. The program's authorization expired at the end of fiscal 1992.

● **Training agency staff and foster and adoptive parents.** Permanently extended a provision providing 75 percent federal reimbursement to states for training child welfare agency staff as well as foster and adoptive parents. This provision expired at the end of fiscal 1992. The new authorization was effective Oct. 1, 1993.

● **Moratorium on collection of disallowances.** Imposed until Oct. 1, 1994, a moratorium preventing the federal government from collecting penalties from states under Title IV-B or IV-E based on reviews of state compliance with foster care protections or financial reviews and audits of foster care and adoption payments. Title IV-B covered child welfare services; Title IV-E covered foster care and adoption.

● **State paternity establishment.** Increased the standards states were required to meet in establishing paternity. The new standards required states to establish paternity in 75 percent of out-of-wedlock births, and it set interim improvements that states with lower rates had to meet.

States also were required to have laws that promoted voluntary acknowledgement of paternity in hospitals.

Supplemental Security Income (SSI)

● **Federal administration fees.** Required the HHS secretary to charge states fees for the federal cost of administering SSI payments. The fees started at $1.67 for each monthly supplemental payment in fiscal 1994, increasing to $3.33 in fiscal 1995 and to $5 by fiscal 1996. The fee in subsequent years would be $5 or an amount determined by the secretary.

● **State relocation assistance.** Permanently excluded from consideration as income or resources any state or local relocation assistance received by SSI beneficiaries. Relocation assistance was paid when a government required individuals to move from their dwellings.

● **Absence due to active military service.** Prevented SSI benefits from declining when the spouse or parent of a beneficiary was absent from home solely because of active military service. Certain hazardous-duty pay was also excluded from income.

● **Children of Armed Forces personnel.** Assured that children who were U.S. citizens would remain eligible for SSI when they accompanied their parents on U.S. military assignments to Puerto Rico or to U.S. territories and possessions. The SSI benefits previously continued only if the parents were on military assignments to foreign countries.

● **In-kind support and maintenance.** Altered the method for determining the value of in-kind support and maintenance received by SSI recipients.

SSI benefits were generally reduced by one-third (plus $20 a month) for recipients who received in-kind support and maintenance from others, usually in the form of food, clothing or shelter.

The amount of the reduction was figured on the benefits standard that was paid two months before. For example, January's SSI benefit were reduced by one-third of the standard that applied the previous November.

However, this two-month lag led to an unintended increase in January and February, after the year's cost of living (COLA) increases were provided. That occurred because the one-third reduction was based on the benefits provided in November and December — before the COLA increase — and applied against the benefits in January and February, which had been adjusted for the cost of living.

The new law eradicated this unintended benefit by requiring that the value of the one-third reduction be figured on the existing month's benefits. The change was effective for benefits paid after calendar year 1994.

• **Income exclusions for American Indians.** Excluded from determination as income up to $2,000 received by American Indians that came from leases on individually owned trust or restricted American Indian lands. Previously, only income received by American Indians from tribally owned trust lands had been excluded as income. The change was effective Jan. 1, 1994.

Aid to Families With Dependent Children

• **Federal match rate.** Reduced the federal match rate to 50 percent for certain administrative costs for Aid to Families With Dependent Children (AFDC).

While the federal government had generally provided a 50 percent match rate for AFDC administrative expenses, it had made exceptions. It had provided 100 percent of expenses to verify the immigration status of aliens, 90 percent for information management and 75 percent for fraud control. The law extended the 50 percent match rate to these three categories, effective with calendar quarters beginning on or after April 1, 1994.

Delays in the effective date could be granted to states where the legislature was not scheduled to meet in 1994.

• **Stepparent income.** Increased the monthly earnings of a stepparent that were excluded from income for purposes of determining eligibility and benefits of AFDC applicants and recipients. The amount to be excluded increased from $75 a month to $90 a month, effective Oct. 1, 1993.

Other Provisions

• **Federal unemployment surtax.** Extended the 0.2 percent federal unemployment surtax for an additional two years, through fiscal 1998. The temporary surtax, on the first $7,000 of wages paid annually to an employee, paid for certain unemployment insurance costs. It was in addition to a permanent 0.6 percent tax.

• **Enterprise zone block grants.** Made available $1 billion in grants to empowerment zones and enterprise communities. The money, provided under Title XX of the Social Security Act, could fund a variety of social services in poor communities targeted for increased federal funding and tax breaks.

Each of the six urban empowerment zones to be set up under provisions in the revenue section of this law was eligible for $100 million over two years. Each of the three rural empowerment zones was eligible for $40 million over two years. And each of the 95 enterprise communities was eligible for $2.95 million.

CUSTOMS AND TRADE

• **Customs user fees.** Extended through fiscal 1998 the existing level of fees that the Customs Service charged air and sea passengers, commercial vessels, barges, trucks, rail cars and mail packages. The provision also extended through fiscal 1998 the merchandise processing fee charged on cargo imported from any country other than Canada.

• **Generalized System of Preferences.** Extended through fiscal 1994 the president's authority to grant duty-free treatment to certain products from developing nations under the General System of Preferences (GSP) program. The previous authorization expired July 4, 1993, five weeks before the extension was signed into law, causing some products to be temporarily subject to duties. The provision authorized refunds of those duties, if a request was made by February 1994.

The law also eliminated a provision that banned the Union of Soviet Socialist Republics and its successor nations from duty-free treatment under the GSP.

• **Trade Adjustment Assistance.** Extended the Trade Adjustment Assistance Program, which assisted workers and companies hurt by imports that result from trade liberalization, for five years, through fiscal 1998. The program provided cash, job training, moving expenses and other aid to workers displaced by imports, as well as technical assistance to affected companies. The law authorized appropriations for the program for fiscal 1994-98 but reduced the amount that could be used for training programs in fiscal 1997 by $10 million, to $70 million.

• **Customs officers' pay and benefits.** Reduced some overtime payments, increased the compensation for working the night shift, raised the retirement benefits for officers who worked overtime, and authorized a bonus for officers who used foreign-language skills on the job. To pay for these changes in pay and benefits, the Treasury secretary was authorized to take up to $18 million from the user fees collected by the Customs Service.

FOOD STAMPS

Eligibility and Benefits

• **Students' earnings.** Excluded the income of elementary and secondary school students 21 years of age or under when calculating food stamp eligibility and benefits levels under the food stamps program. Prior law excluded students' earnings only until their 18th birthday. The change was effective Sept. 1, 1994.

• **High shelter expenses.** Increased the amount households could deduct for high shelter expenses in calculating their income for food stamp purposes. High shelter expenses were housing costs that exceeded 50 percent of a family's net monthly income after other deductions had been taken. For households with elderly or disabled members, there was no dollar limit on the deduction. However, the deduction for other households was capped (at $200 a month at the time). The provision increased the cap to $231 on July 1, 1994, and to $247 on Oct. 1, 1995. The cap was to be eliminated on Jan. 1, 1997.

• **Earned-income tax credits.** Disregarded from food stamp resource calculations any earned-income tax credits received by low-income working families for one year, effective Sept. 1, 1994. The provision applied to families that were continuously enrolled in the food stamps program during the year. The new law was designed to discourage families from spending their tax credits too quickly. Prior law disregarded the tax credits only in the month they were received and in the following month.

• **Homeless families.** Disregarded from homeless families' income the payments states made to house them in transitional quarters, effective Sept. 1, 1994. Previously, states were able to count part of the value of these payments as income, reducing the amount of food stamps that homeless families were eligible to receive.

• **General assistance.** Excluded from calculations of households' income certain payments made through state or local General Assistance funds. Such payments for energy or utility costs were to be excluded as income, though payments for general housing expenses could be considered income. The provision was effective Sept. 1, 1994.

• **Continuing benefits.** Prohibited states from prorating food stamp benefits when a household reapplied after having been off the program for less than one month. Since 1981, new food stamp applicants' first month of benefits had been reduced based on the number of days that had already elapsed in the month. In 1982, this requirement was extended to households reapplying after

brief interruptions. The law repealed the 1982 measure, effective Sept. 1, 1994.

● **Puerto Rico.** Increased funding for the block grant that provided nutrition assistance to Puerto Rico in lieu of food stamps. The funding increases were beyond those annually provided for inflation. The law increased funding by $6 million (to $1.096 billion) in fiscal 1994 and by $10 million (to $1.143 billion) in fiscal 1995.

● **Child support payments.** Gave non-custodial parents a deduction for legally obligated child support payments when determining income for food stamp eligibility and allotment levels. This provision was designed to encourage parents to make child support payments by increasing their food stamp allotment to compensate for the lost income.

● **Child care.** Increased the limit that certain families with dependent care expenses could deduct from their income when determining food stamp benefits. The $160 monthly deduction was raised to $200 per month for children under 2 and $175 per month for older children, effective Sept. 1, 1994. States also were to be permitted to set the limit for dependent care reimbursements for those participating in food stamp employment and training programs. However, the reimbursement rate could not be above the local market rate as determined for Aid to Families with Dependent Children (AFDC) employment and training programs.

● **Vehicle resource limit.** Increased the limit above which the value of a vehicle was counted as a household asset when determining food stamp eligibility. Since 1977, the fair market value of most vehicles in excess of $4,500 had been counted as a resource. This threshold was to be raised to $4,550 on Sept. 1, 1994, and to $4,600 on Oct. 1, 1995. After that, the threshold was to be indexed to changes in the Consumer Price Index for new cars each Oct. 1, with the first adjustment calculated from a base of $5,000 on Oct. 1, 1996.

The law excluded any vehicle used to transport water or heating fuel as a household resource if the household lacked piped-in fuel or water. This provision was effective Sept. 1, 1994.

● **Demonstration projects.** Authorized the Agriculture secretary to conduct demonstration projects that would permit food stamp recipients to save up to $10,000 without losing their food stamp eligibility. The law stipulated that these savings would be for later use to improve the education or training of household members or to purchase or renovate a home. The demonstration project was to be available to up to 11,000 households over four years.

● **Household definition.** Revised the definition of a household in determining food stamp eligibility and benefits. Effective Sept. 1, 1994, the law generally permitted people who lived together, but purchased food and prepared meals separately, to apply for food stamps separately. However, separate applications were not permitted from spouses, parents and their children 21 years or younger (unless the children had spouses or children of their own), and children 18 years or younger who lived with and were under parental control of a person other than their parent. The conference report stipulated that minor children under parental control were prohibited from establishing separate households under the food stamps program.

● **Drug and alcohol treatment.** Extended food stamp benefits to children living with their parents in residential treatment centers for drug or alcohol abuse. Previously, the adults entered in such programs were eligible for food stamps, but no provisions were made for their children. The change was effective Sept. 1, 1994.

Program Integrity

● **Claims collection.** Authorized an additional means of recouping overpayments of food stamps resulting from beneficiary error: the reduction of federal pay or pensions. This provision would typically be used after a household had left the food stamps program. The usual way of collecting for overpayments — reducing future food stamp benefits — was not applicable if a household

had left the program.

● **Trafficking in food coupons.** Strengthened the penalties for trafficking in food stamps. Effective Sept. 1, 1994, those found by a court of law to be trading drugs for food coupons were disqualified from the program for one year; a second violation would draw permanent disqualification. The law also permanently disqualified from the program anyone who was found on the first offense to be trading firearms, ammunition or explosives for food coupons. The existing penalty for trafficking in food stamps was six months disqualification for the first violation, one year for the second violation and permanent disqualification for the third offense.

● **Civil penalties on businesses.** Removed the two-year ceiling on civil financial penalties that could be imposed on retailers and wholesalers found to be trafficking in food stamps, including selling firearms, ammunition, explosives or drugs for food coupons.

The Agriculture Department could impose a financial penalty in lieu of disqualification on a business that trafficked in food stamps if the ownership and management were unaware of the violation and there was an anti-fraud policy in place. Previously, the penalty was up to $20,000 per violation, not to exceed $40,000 in a two-year period. The law removed the time limit from the cap, stipulating that a civil money penalty could not exceed $40,000 for all violations occuring during a single investigation. This change ensured that repeated violations were punishable with penalties of up to $40,000 each.

● **Quality control penalties.** Modified the food stamps program's quality control system, which conducted annual surveys of state caseloads to determine erroneous payments. A state paid a financial penalty if its combined error rate was above a "tolerance level" — previously defined as the lowest-ever national average error rate plus 1 percentage point. The law changed the definition to the average combined error rate for that particular year, beginning with fiscal 1992. The penalties were revised to create a sliding scale so that the penalty assessment reflected the degree to which a state's error rate exceeded the tolerance level.

This change responded to state concerns about the accuracy and fairness of the quality control system and the penalties it imposed. In addition, the law gave an administrative law judge the ability to determine whether to waive all or part of a state's quality control liability. The Agriculture secretary previously had this authority.

● **Uniform reimbursement rates.** Extended the federal government's practice of reimbursing 50 percent of the state and local costs related to administering the food stamps program. The federal government previously increased its 50 percent reimbursement in some instances; for example, paying 63 percent of the costs related to automated data processing systems, 75 percent of the cost of investigating and prosecuting fraud and 100 percent of the cost of verifying the immigration status of aliens applying for benefits.

The law reduced the federal share of these activities to 50 percent, beginning with calendar quarters that started on or after April 1, 1994. This provision was part of the Clinton administration's plan to institute a more uniform 50 percent federal matching rate for public assistance programs.

Delays in the effective date could be granted to states in which the legislature was not scheduled to meet in 1994.

● **Nutrition programs.** Provided $230,000 per year in each of the next three fiscal years beginning in 1994 for demonstration projects in two states to assess the impact of making more nutritious foods available through the Emergency Food Assistance Program. Each state was to receive $110,000 worth of commodities each year and $5,000 for state and local expenses to store and distribute the food. The secretary of Agriculture was to select the two states. The program primarily provided food commodities to nonprofit entities that served the poor.

BUDGET PROCESS

● **Discretionary spending caps.** Extended caps on discretionary spending, which were set in the 1990 budget agreement for

fiscal 1991-95, through fiscal 1998. The bill spelled out the following limits for discretionary spending and continued existing procedures for periodically adjusting those limits and enforcing them through across-the-board spending cuts and points of order:

(amounts in billions of dollars)

	1994	1995	1996	1997	1998
Budget authority	$509.9	517.4	519.1	528.1	530.6
Outlays	$537.3	538.95	547.3	547.3	547.9

● **Pay-as-you-go restrictions for entitlements and tax cuts.** Extended through 1998 the existing pay-as-you-go discipline, which required that any tax cuts, new entitlement programs or expansion of existing entitlement benefits be offset by an increase in taxes or a cut in entitlement spending.

The bill extended existing enforcement procedures and related points of order through 1998, and it "reset" the pay-as-you-go score card to zero to prevent Congress from spending any of the entitlement savings or tax increases it achieved in the reconciliation bill.

● **Entitlement review program for the House.** As part of the rule adopted for floor debate on the reconciliation bill, the House agreed to change its rules to establish an entitlement review process to mesh with a procedure set up by an executive order issued by President Clinton. That order required the White House to take action if entitlement spending exceeded pre-set targets. Overall, the new process bound the president and the House but not the Senate.

Under the process, the Office of Management and Budget (OMB) was required to submit to Congress within 30 days of enactment of the reconciliation bill the projected entitlement spending levels for fiscal 1994-97 expected to result from the bill. OMB could adjust these four annual targets for increased caseloads but not for inflation that exceeded existing projections.

The president was required to report to Congress if entitlement spending in the preceding year, existing year or next year exceeded the targets by more than 0.5 percent, and he had to recommend either offsetting the excess with spending cuts and/or revenues or simply changing the targets and in effect adding the excess to the deficit.

The House budget resolution had to incorporate at least the amount of offsets proposed by the president, and if the resolution called for adding the additional spending to the deficit by raising the targets, the House had to agree to do that in a separate vote. If the House then rejected the increase in the targets, it could not proceed to consider the budget resolution.

And, until Congress adopted a budget resolution dealing with the excess entitlement spending above the targets, the House could not take up any of the 13 regular appropriations bills for the next fiscal year.

DEBT-LIMIT INCREASE

Increased the permanent limit on the federal debt to $4.9 trillion, an amount estimated to suffice through the end of fiscal 1995.

The bill also repealed the temporary debt-limit increase to $4.37 trillion, which was approved by Congress earlier in the year.

MISCELLANEOUS PROVISIONS

● **Entry fees at Army Corps of Engineers recreation facilities.** Authorized the Army Corps of Engineers to charge entry fees at certain recreation areas, including campsites, swimming beaches and some boat launching ramps. The law set a maximum fee of $3 per day for vehicles carrying no more than eight passengers, including the driver. It barred fees for restrooms, picnic tables, water fountains and boat launching facilities that were equipped only with a dock and a ramp.

The law also eliminated a previous requirement that all Army Corps camping facilities provide one free campground.

● **NRC fees.** Extended through fiscal 1998 the requirement that the Nuclear Regulatory Commission (NRC) charge fees high enough to cover 100 percent of its budget. The change was to cost companies regulated by the NRC, particularly the electric utilities that operated nuclear reactors, almost $1.2 billion.

Under prior law, the commission's fees would have dropped to about one-third of their existing level after 1995.

● **Patent and trademark fees.** Increased the fees charged by the U.S. Patent and Trademark Office to people who wished to register for and maintain a trademark or patent. The provision was to raise $345 million through fiscal 1998.

● **Merchant Marine tonnage duties.** Extended through fiscal 1998 the existing level of duties paid by cargo vessels entering U.S. ports from foreign ports or places. The duties, which were raised 250 percent to 350 percent as part of the 1990 budget agreement, had been scheduled to drop to their original levels after fiscal 1995.

Vessels arriving from places in the Western Hemisphere were required to pay 9 cents per ton of cargo capacity; the maximum for a single vessel in a given year was to be 45 cents per ton. Vessels from other foreign countries paid 27 cents per ton, up to a maximum of $1.35 per ton per year.

● **Timber sales.** Set aside 85 percent of the receipts from the sale of timber on federal lands in Washington, Oregon and Northern California counties in fiscal 1994.

Counties in those states included large swaths of old-growth forests critical to the survival of the threatened spotted owl and were likely to be hard hit by legal decisions regarding the owl. The pot of funds was to be available to the federal government, the three Northwest states and the affected counties.

The amount set aside was to drop by 3 percent each year thereafter until fiscal 2003. To make up for the loss of revenue to the Treasury, the provision eliminated an export subsidy credit for foreign sales of unprocessed logs, which generated about $390 million annually. Northwest timber counties were expected to receive $270 million under the set-aside program and $120 million would go to deficit reduction. ■

Congress Wrangles Over More Budget Cuts

The bruising battle over the budget-reconciliation bill, enacted in August, did not end congressional efforts to reduce the deficit. The House returned to the subject in November, voting to cut another $37 billion over five years by reducing the federal work force, reversing some fiscal 1994 spending decisions and taking steps to streamline the federal government. Before passing the bill (HR 3400), however, the House bowed to intense lobbying from the White House and Appropriations subcommittee chairmen and narrowly defeated a far more ambitious, $90 billion deficit-reduction plan offered by conservative Democrat Timothy J. Penny of Minnesota and Republican deficit firebrand John R. Kasich of Ohio.

Though Penny and Kasich lost, they fell just four votes short of victory, showing they could forge a robust coalition of fiscally conservative Democrats, Republicans and first-term lawmakers. "What it means," said White House budget director Leon E. Panetta, "is that a lot of what you saw in these proposals will make it into the [fiscal] '95 budget."

House action on HR 3400 marked the end of the budget wars for 1993. Worried that a deficit-spooked Congress would end up approving a large package of aggressive cuts that the White House said would be too big and too dangerous for the economy, Democratic leaders managed to put off final votes on the bill until Congress reconvened in 1994. Senate Appropriations Committee Chairman Robert C. Byrd, D-W.Va., who made it clear that he believed spending already had been cut to the bone, said his committee would not consider the bill until 1994, and Senate Majority Leader George J. Mitchell, D-Maine, said any Senate action on spending cuts hinged on prior committee approval.

As approved by the House, HR 3400 cut federal spending by an estimated $37.1 billion in outlays through fiscal 1998. The bulk of the savings — $32.5 billion in outlays — came from a plan Clinton had announced months before to cut 252,000 positions from the federal work force, though the bill did not specify how that would be achieved. The other key components were $1.9 billion in cuts (rescissions) from fiscal 1994 appropriations and $2.7 billion over five years in modified savings from a proposal by Clinton and Vice President Al Gore to streamline the federal government. The bill did not require that the savings go to deficit reduction, which meant that Congress could use the funds for other programs.

BACKGROUND

Congress already had gone through one major round of deficit reduction in 1993, clearing a $496 billion package of tax increases and spending cuts in August (PL 103-66). But to win the desperately needed votes of Penny and other conservative House Democrats for that bill, the House leadership and the White House had promised another round of votes on spending cuts in the fall. *(Budget-reconciliation, p. 107)*

To fulfill that pledge, Clinton on Oct. 26 outlined roughly $11 billion in additional spending cuts over six years. The two-part initiative was made up of cuts in just-passed fiscal 1994 appropriations and proposals drawn from the Clinton-Gore plan to streamline the federal government.

● **Reinventing government.** Clinton proposed $9 bil-

lion in cost-cutting steps taken from the National Performance Review, a wide-ranging collection of money-saving ideas that Clinton and Gore had announced with much fanfare on Sept. 7. All told, the administration said, the so-called reinventing government plan would save $108 billion over five years by making the federal government leaner and more customer-oriented. *(Reinventing government, p. 191)*

Clinton's Oct. 26 proposal did not include one major element of the reinventing government package — the reduction of 252,000 federal jobs.

The White House hoped to be able to act on its own to direct federal agencies to cut their payroll by 12 percent through attrition, buyouts and relocation — steps the administration said would save $40.4 billion over five years. The cuts ultimately were included in HR 3400, however.

● **Rescissions.** Waiting until most of the fiscal 1994 appropriations bills had cleared, Clinton on Nov. 1 gave Congress a list of 37 specific rescissions that the administration said would save $1.9 billion in budget authority and $392 million in outlays, or actual fiscal 1994 spending.

The Penny-Kasich Plan

The White House argued that Clinton's two-pronged attack should be sufficient to address lawmakers' concerns about deficit reduction.

"We made clear that we would come back with an additional proposal with regard to spending cuts and savings," said Panetta. "This package fulfills that commitment."

But a bipartisan group of House deficit hawks upped the ante Oct. 27 with a vastly more ambitious proposal. Led by Penny and Kasich, the group of 30 fiscal conservatives proposed a package of cuts that they said would trim the deficit by $103 billion over five years. The plan broke down into three parts: $26 billion in savings from discretionary accounts, $50 billion from mandatory accounts that paid for Medicare, Social Security and other entitlement programs, and $27 billion from Clinton's plan to trim 252,000 workers from the federal payroll.

In addition, to ensure that the savings would be applied to deficit reduction, the plan automatically reduced the existing spending caps for appropriations by the amount of any discretionary savings achieved through the legislation.

Some of the strongest opposition came from those who objected to the $34.2 billion Penny and Kasich proposed to cut from Medicare, the government's health program for the elderly and the disabled. The plan included increases in fees and premium charges for most beneficiaries.

The Clinton administration was counting on using savings from Medicare to help finance its upcoming health-care overhaul.

Other large cuts in the Penny-Kasich plan included deferring the cost of living adjustment for military retirees until they reached age 62 ($5.5 billion over five years); reorganizing the Agriculture Department ($1.6 billion over five years); requiring European and Asian allies to pay more of the cost of stationing U.S. military forces overseas ($5 billion over five years); and putting a moratorium on the purchase of new federal buildings ($2 billion over five years).

Deficit hawks hoped to gain momentum for the plan from the Nov. 2 off-year elections, in which voters favored candidates and ballot initiatives that promised reduced spending.

made good on his promise to allow a vote on more spending cuts in 1993. "Sort of," Penny responded. "At the time, I did not [foresee] how much energy the president would expend to defeat our package. We'll know better to ask next time."

SENATE ACTION

In the Senate, Bob Kerrey, D-Neb., and Hank Brown, R-Colo., were waiting with an amendment to cut federal spending by $109.2 billion — more than any of the three House plans. They proposed cuts in federal entitlement programs, such as Medicare, as well as in appropriated spending such as congressional cost of living adjustments and military hardware.

The package's drafters borrowed some cuts included in the Penny-Kasich plan but rejected others that CBO had not confirmed, such as requiring European and Asian allies to chip in $5 billion in defense burden-sharing contributions.

Like their House counterparts, Kerrey and Brown both said they would like to take the controversial step of lowering appropriations spending limits to lock in savings for deficit reduction. But the senators had a procedural problem: Passing the package itself required a simple majority vote; but changing budget law to lower the appropriations limits was subject to a Budget Act point of order, and defeating that challenge required 60 votes. To overcome this, Brown and Kerrey said they would employ a two-step process, trying first to get the package approved and then separately proposing to lower discretionary spending limits. Lowering the limits was bitterly opposed by appropriators, most notably by Byrd, who argued that the limits already were so restrictive that Congress would have to find substantial cuts just to meet existing requirements.

Byrd saw to it that Kerrey and Brown did not get a chance to offer their amendment in the first session. By declining to mark up the bill before Congress adjourned, Byrd blocked Senate action in 1993. ■

Balanced-Budget Amendment Held Until Second Session

Facing a protracted debate with little floor time before adjournment, Senate leaders postponed until early 1994 a vote on a balanced-budget amendment to the Constitution. House leaders had said all year that they would wait for the Senate to act first.

The amendment (S J Res 41, H J Res 103) — sponsored by Paul Simon, D-Ill., in the Senate and Charles W. Stenholm, D-Texas, in the House — required that Congress and the president adopt a balanced budget two years after the amendment was ratified by the states or in 1999, whichever came later. Thereafter, deficit spending could be approved only in time of war or imminent war, or by a vote of 60 percent of both the House and Senate.

Most observers rated the amendment's prospects better than they had ever been, in part because of the large numbers of freshmen who had campaigned for fiscal responsibility in general and the balanced-budget amendment in particular. "If the vote were today, I'd win," Simon said Nov. 10.

Background

Proposed balanced-budget amendments had been kicked around Congress for years. In 1992, a resolution identical to the Simon-Stenholm proposal fell nine votes short in the House and was blocked by a filibuster in the Senate. The high-water mark was in 1982, when the Senate passed a balanced-budget amendment, only to see it fall 46 votes short in the House. Similar proposals made it to the Senate floor in 1986 and the House floor in 1990, but in both cases, failed to win a two-thirds majority. *(1992 Almanac, p. 108)*

Supporters insisted that Congress would never balance the nation's budget without a fiscal gun to its head, while opponents argued that such an amendment meant nothing if politicians lacked the political willpower to make tough budget and tax decisions.

President Clinton opposed the Simon-Stenholm amendment, warning that eradicating the deficit by 1999 would require "some combination" of "huge increases in taxes on working families, massive reductions in Social Security benefits for middle-class Americans, and major cuts in Medicare and Medicaid that would make it impossible to pass meaningful health-care reform legislation."

A constitutional amendment had to be approved by a two-thirds majority of each chamber and then win approval of three-fourths, or 38, of the state legislatures. (Amendments also could be drafted by a constitutional convention petitioned by two-thirds of the states, but that procedure had never been used.)

Senate Action

In what had become an annual exercise, the Senate Judiciary Committee on July 22 approved Simon's balanced-budget amendment (S J Res 41 — S Rept 103-163) by a vote of 15-3. Democrats Edward M. Kennedy of Massachusetts, Patrick J. Leahy of Vermont and Howard M. Metzenbaum of Ohio voted against the proposal.

Majority Leader George J. Mitchell, D-Maine, had promised that the Senate would vote on the measure before adjournment, but as time grew short at the end of the session, Simon agreed to the delay for fear that some supporters might leave town in the holiday rush before the final vote. The amendment's key Senate opponent, Appropriations Chairman Robert C. Byrd, D-W.Va., was an acknowledged master of parliamentary procedure who was likely to pull out all the stops to defeat the proposal.

Not waiting for the committee or the Democratic leadership, Phil Gramm, R-Texas, had threatened early in the year to bring the balanced-budget amendment to the Senate floor by linking it to a vote Congress had to take to raise the ceiling on the federal debt. However, Democratic leaders cut off that path by making the debt-limit extension part of the budget-reconciliation bill; special rules prohibited amendments on reconciliation bills. *(Debt Ceiling, p. 123)* ■

House Ways and Means Approves Tax Code Bill

The House Ways and Means Committee approved a bill designed to simplify the tax code and make technical corrections to recent tax bills, but Congress took no further action on the measure in 1993.

The bill (HR 3419 — H Rept 103-353), which won voice vote approval from the committee Nov. 3, contained hundreds of individual provisions, many of them recycled from past legislative attempts to streamline tax laws and others brand-new efforts to correct or clarify recent tax law. Com-

mittee members and their aides described the measure as non-controversial, and Chairman Dan Rostenkowski, D-Ill., was at pains to keep it free of the sort of add-ons tax bills often attracted.

Many of the measure's tax simplification ideas had been bundled into two major tax bills that Congress had passed in 1992 but that ultimately had died when then-President George Bush vetoed them in unrelated fights over Congress' insistence on increasing some taxes in order to cut others. *(1992 Almanac, pp. 133, 140)*

The Joint Committee on Taxation estimated that the new bill would generate about $1 million in net tax revenue from 1994 to 1998 after all the losers and gainers were taken into account.

The tax simplification provisions ranged from allowing taxpayers to use credit cards to pay their taxes to changing some of the rules that governed pensions, large partnerships, foreign corporations, so-called Subchapter S corporations, regulated investment companies, tax-exempt bonds, taxable estates and various excise taxes.

The technical corrections fixed or clarified tax-related provisions in the 1990 and 1993 deficit-reduction laws and other tax measures. They ranged from clarifying restrictions on tax credits for wine producers to coordinating estate tax credits with U.S. treaties with foreign governments.

Taken together, these provisions stood to lose the government $467 million over five years, according to Joint Tax. But the bill also included four revenue-raising provisions that slightly more than offset the loss by:

● Imposing tax withholding on gambling winnings from bingo and keno when the winnings exceeded $10,000, raising $208 million over five years.

● Eliminating (with narrow exceptions) an exemption that permitted owners who rented homes or apartments for less than 15 days to avoid declaring the proceeds as taxable income. This was expected to raise $97 million over five years.

● Changing the rules for tax-exempt entities such as charities or pension trusts to treat certain income from foreign corporations as unrelated business taxable income, bringing in $98 million over five years.

● Requiring thrift institutions to take net operating loss carry-overs into account when calculating bad debt reserves under the percentage taxable income method, raising $64 million over five years.

Amendments

Bill Brewster, D-Okla., won voice vote approval for a minor technical amendment to preserve a special tax treatment that Congress created in 1987 for retirement plans for football coaches. Because the provision was placed in the wrong section of the tax code, Brewster said, the Internal Revenue Service planned to end the tax preference at the end of 1993.

The committee also sparred over a provision in the budget-reconciliation bill (PL 103-66) that granted restaurants a tax credit for the payroll taxes they paid on their employees' tip income; the budget bill left the effective date unclear. Gerald D. Kleczka, D-Wis., urged the committee to clarify that restaurants could use the credit only for tips earned beginning in 1994. Although the committee declined to make the change, Kleczka said after hearing from a Treasury Department official during the markup that when Treasury implemented the provision, it would apply only to income beginning in 1994. ■

'Expedited Rescissions' Bill Stalls in Senate

It took three attempts and some of the tougher arm-twisting seen on the House floor during the year, but Democratic leaders managed to pass an "expedited rescissions" measure to increase the president's authority to cut individual items from already enacted spending bills.

House sponsors, led by Charles W. Stenholm, D-Texas, thought they had enough momentum to force a vote on the bill in the Senate. But Senate Appropriations Committee Chairman Robert C. Byrd, D-W.Va., a strong foe of anything that might infringe on the role of the appropriators, indicated that he would seek to amend or otherwise stall the bill. That was enough to put off any Senate action in 1993.

The House-passed bill (HR 1578) required Congress to vote within a specified period on presidential proposals to rescind, or cancel, specific spending items in appropriations bills that had already been signed. Appropriators could offer their own substitute rescissions, but only if the president's proposal failed. No spending could be canceled unless both the House and Senate concurred; failure of

> **BOXSCORE**
>
> ➡ **Expedited Rescission Authority (HR 1578).** The bill provided for a slight increase in the president's authority to cancel, or rescind, individual items from previously enacted appropriations bills.
>
> **KEY ACTION**
>
> April 2, 21 — **House** debate on HR 1578 canceled.
>
> April 29 — **House** passed HR 1578, 258-157.

either chamber to pass the proposal would kill the rescission.

Under existing law, presidential rescission proposals expired after 45 days unless both chambers approved them. While appropriators often felt politically compelled to more than match the president's spending cuts, they usually did so by crafting their own cuts and letting the president's proposal languish. Backers of the bill argued that the president deserved a vote on his cuts. The bill was good only for what backers called a two-year "test drive," after which Congress could either renew it or junk it.

The controversy over the bill caught House Democratic leaders off guard. An almost identical bill had sailed through the House on a 312-97 vote in late 1992, raising expectations that it would have a similarly easy ride in 1993. *(1992 Almanac, p. 114)*

But much had changed since then. While President Clinton had called for some form of line-item veto authority, he was not a presence during much of the debate.

In the meantime, many of the Republicans who appeared

satisfied with the bill's minor increase in presidential power in 1992, now viewed it as an unacceptably weak compromise. On the other side of the debate, liberal members rallied colleagues to the notion that the bill would give the president too much power to meddle in congressional spending decisions.

BACKGROUND

For years, Congress had wrestled inconclusively with the idea of increasing the president's power to undo congressionally approved appropriations. The expedited rescission proposal was a relatively weak approach — much weaker than a line-item veto, which would allow the president to veto specific line items in appropriations bills; Congress could restore that spending only by mustering a two-thirds majority in both chambers. Under the expedited rescission proposal, a majority vote in both chambers would be required to rescind the spending.

Many Republicans argued that the expedited rescission idea was a pale, virtually worthless imitation of the line-item veto, while some Democrats said it would give the president far too much power to interfere in spending decisions that were appropriately shared by Congress and the White House.

Although the line-item veto and its various permutations had often been advocated as deficit-reduction tools, most proponents conceded that the proposals were not likely to save much money. For one thing, they applied only to discretionary spending, about a third of the federal budget and an area that was already fairly rigidly controlled by the spending caps agreed to in the 1990 budget deal.

In its 1993 compilation of options for reducing the deficit, the Congressional Budget Office's (CBO) dismissed the savings potential of the line-item veto and its legislative cousins as virtually negligible. Instead of reducing spending, the CBO study said, such proposals would probably just shift spending around by substituting some of the president's priorities for those supported by Congress.

Those advocating a line-item veto or its relations as serious deficit-reduction tools often cited a January 1992 study by the General Accounting Office (GAO) that predicted the line-item veto could save $7 billion to $17 billion a year, or as much as $70 billion over six years. But that study proved to be highly controversial. At Byrd's request, the Congressional Research Service evaluated the study, declaring its premises highly questionable and estimating the likely six-year savings not as $70 billion but as $2 billion to $3 billion "and probably less." In a subsequent letter to Byrd, Comptroller General Charles Bowsher, who headed the GAO, acknowledged that the savings from a line-item veto might actually be "close to zero."

But advocates continued to press for a rescissions bill, in part to deflect criticism that Congress was not serious about controlling wasteful spending. Passage of the bill would get the issue "off the table," said Rep. Bob Wise, D-W.Va. In addition, said one congressional aide, backers wanted to give the president the power to do what they could not do for themselves — cut spending projects that wound up embarrassing the institution. With the president armed with increased authority to target spending projects, the aide said, "a lot of the things that are embarrassing won't get in there in the first place."

HOUSE ACTION

Twice — on April 2 and again on April 21 — House Democratic leaders hastily pulled the expedited rescissions bill from a scheduled floor debate lest they suffer an embarrassing defeat on the rule for debate and possibly on the bill itself. Both times, they backed off in the face of opposition from an unlikely combination of House Republicans, the Congressional Black Caucus and appropriations chairmen.

Republicans had grown increasingly angry about what they said was a pattern of "tyrannical" behavior by the Democratic leadership in sharply limiting floor amendments on controversial bills. In this case, Republicans wanted among other things, a chance to offer an amendment by Minority Leader Robert H. Michel, R-Ill., to give the president unprecedented authority to propose rescissions in tax expenditures — tax breaks that reduced government revenue. The idea was bitterly opposed by Ways and Means Committee Chairman Dan Rostenkowski, D-Ill.

Although Republicans had supported the expedited rescissions bill overwhelmingly in 1992, voting 154-5 for it, they declared that the 1993 bill was not nearly tough enough. Minority Whip Newt Gingrich, R-Ga., called it "line-item voodoo," a "silly sham that's designed to give cover to Democrats who don't want to vote for the line-item veto."

The chief Republican substitute was an "enhanced rescission" bill offered by Gerald B. H. Solomon, R-N.Y., that was viewed as the strongest authority the president could have over spending bills, even stronger than the line-item veto conservatives had advocated for years.

Like the line-item veto, Solomon's measure provided that any proposal by the president to cancel spending would automatically go into effect unless both the House and the Senate voted to disapprove it. The Solomon measure would almost certainly force Congress to muster two-thirds effectively required votes of both chambers to overturn the White House since the president could simply veto any congressional disapproval bill.

What analysts said made the Solomon measure so powerful was that it would allow the president to reach inside the line items in spending bills to cut all or part of even the smallest projects, a surgical touch that was beyond the scope of the clumsier line-item veto. The president's existing rescission authority and the authority contained in the House bill allowed the same surgical intervention. But they were much weaker than the line-item veto or enhanced rescission because no spending could be canceled unless both chambers voted to uphold the president's proposal.

The leadership bill also drew bitter opposition from House appropriators, who complained that it targeted their shrinking piece of the budget while promising to do virtually nothing to cure the real causes of deficit spending, which they contended were tax expenditures and spending for entitlement programs such as Medicare.

To spread the pain, the appropriators tried to force House leaders to extend the president's rescission authority to tax expenditures and spending from the highway, mass transit and aviation trust funds. But that triggered equally furious opposition from Rostenkowski and Public Works Chairman Norman Y. Mineta, D-Calif. The leadership ultimately refused to make the change, agreeing only to give appropriators the right to offer an alternative rescission package after the president's proposal had been considered.

But it was the black caucus' unexpected decision to oppose the bill that forced leaders to pull it down. With many of the 37 Democrats on the House Appropriations Committee opposing the measure, leaders could ill afford to lose a bloc of votes as large as the 38 House Democrats in the black caucus. Kweisi Mfume, D-Md., chairman of the Congressional Black Caucus, announced shortly before floor debate was to begin April 21

Options for Presidential Powers

	President	Congress	Comment
Enhanced Rescission	If granted this authority, the president could propose to rescind all or part of any spending in an appropriations bill after he had signed the bill.	The rescission would go into effect if Congress failed to overturn it. Congress could overturn it if both the House and the Senate, by majority votes, passed a motion of disapproval. The president could veto that motion; Congress could override that veto only with two-thirds votes of the House and the Senate.	Considered to be the strongest form of veto authority. Like a line-item veto, it would ultimately allow the president to force Congress to mount a two-thirds vote of both chambers to override a rescission. What would make it more powerful than a line-item veto was that it would allow the president to cancel any spending, not just entire line items.
Line-Item Veto	If granted this authority, the president could veto line items in an appropriations bill after he had signed the bill.	The veto would go into effect unless Congress overrode it with two-thirds votes of both the House and the Senate.	As with enhanced rescission authority, the line-item veto would give the president substantial new power to control the congressional spending process as long as he maintained a one-third-plus-one minority of either the House or the Senate.
Expedited Rescission	If granted this authority, the president could propose to rescind all or any part of spending in an appropriations bill after he had signed the bill.	The rescission would go into effect only if both the House and the Senate approved it by majority votes. As opposed to existing law, Congress would be required to vote on the president's rescission proposal. The Appropriations committees could offer their own proposals but not until after the vote occurred on the president's proposal.	Offered as a less potent alternative to enhanced rescission or the line-item veto. The only significant change in existing law would be the requirement that Congress vote on the president's proposal, which it previously could ignore. Unlike the other two proposals, it would preserve majority rule on spending matters to which the president objected.
Rescission (Existing Law)	The president had this authority. He could propose to rescind all or part of any spending in an appropriations bill after he signed the bill.	The rescission took effect only if both chambers approved it by majority votes. If Congress failed to vote on the proposal, it expired after 45 days, and the money had to be spent. A rarely used rule allowed one-fifth of either chamber to move to discharge the president's proposal from the Appropriations Committee and bring it to the floor if the committee did not act on it within 25 days of continuous session.	Although Congress was free to ignore presidential rescission proposals, in practice it usually felt compelled to respond with its own proposals, which almost always sought to rescind even more spending than the president did, although usually from different programs.

that his group was sticking to its earlier decision to oppose the measure because it would diminish Congress' authority over appropriations bills. "We feel very strongly on principled grounds that we should not be ceding power to the executive branch," Mfume said April 21.

Third Try Succeeds

When the leadership finally brought up the bill April 29, it passed by a comfortable 258-157 margin. But the key vote came the day before, when House Speaker Thomas S. Foley, D-Wash., had to work the floor for several minutes after the official voting period expired to salvage the controversial rule governing floor debate on the bill. *(Vote 150, p. 38-H)*

With all time to vote expired, the rule was losing by at least three votes, done in by the same unlikely coalition of House Republicans and Democratic members of the black caucus. But in a rare display of political hardball, Foley stalked the floor, cornering wavering Democrats and persuading them to switch their votes. With the vote clock stopped at zero, Republicans occasionally bellowing for the vote to be finalized and the chamber alternating between an expectant hush and chaotic hubbub, Foley gradually turned a 206-209 defeat into a 208-208 tie and then into a 212-208 victory. *(Vote 144, p. 36-H)*

"It was so quiet in there you could hear a shoulder break," cracked Gary L. Ackerman, D-N.Y. Asked what he had done to turn members around, a satisfied Foley said simply, "Sweet persuasion." It was a rare show of power for a Speaker who often had been criticized as too diffident to lead the House effectively.

Clinton made a last-minute attempt to lobby for the bill, sending a letter to Foley endorsing it and plugging it before the National Association of Realtors on April 27.

Republicans tried to toughen the bill by providing that a rescission would go into effect unless both chambers passed a resolution of disapproval — a measure the president could veto, ultimately forcing Congress to overturn any rescission with a two-thirds vote of both houses. That amendment failed, 198-219. *(Vote 146, p. 36-H)*

Republicans had better luck with an amendment to add targeted tax provisions to the items that the president could propose to rescind. Democratic leaders feared the allure of that proposal and forced Republicans to offer it only as an amendment to their own foredoomed substitute. The tax amendment carried 257-157, apparently buoyed by the conviction of some members that it was a free vote. It subsequently died when the underlying GOP substitute failed. *(Vote 145, p. 36-H)*

One top GOP aide said House Republicans were opposing the bill largely for tactical reasons. "Any chance that we can sweat them, we're going to do that," said the aide. "We're trying to use this as leverage." What Republicans wanted to prevent, he said, was Democrats' refusing to vote for tough GOP-backed fiscal measures later in the year, insisting they had already done their duty on the deficit by passing something close to a line-item veto. ∎

Treasury Announces Drop in Deficit

The deficit fell to a surprisingly low $254.9 billion in fiscal 1993, a drop that was part tribute to the power of lower interest rates and part proof of just how hard it was to accurately estimate numbers this high.

The 1993 figure, released by the Treasury Department on Oct. 28 for the fiscal year that ended Sept. 30, marked the first time since 1989 that the deficit had gone down instead of up.

The deficit had set record highs in each of the previous three fiscal years, culminating in an all-time high of $290.3 billion in fiscal 1992.

But a series of factors combined to shrink the final 1993 deficit to a figure nearly $70 billion lower than the $322 billion that the Clinton administration predicted it would be in April and some $30 billion less than the $285 billion the White House forecast in September.

Although it conceded it could not take credit for all the good news, the administration said its policies were responsible for at least some of the reduction, insisting the announcement and subsequent enactment of its big deficit-reduction package helped persuade financial markets to knock interest rates down to record lows. *(Budget-reconciliation, p. 107)*

Combined with an improving economy, those lower rates helped banks and thrifts do better, which translated

---

Fiscal 1993 Deficit Projections

(In billions of dollars)

Bush, January 1992	$ 351.9
Bush, January 1993	327.3
Clinton, April 1993	322.0
Clinton, September 1993	285.3
Congressional Budget Office, September 1993	266.0
Actual, October 1993	**254.9**

SOURCE: Office of Management and Budget, Congressional Budget Office

---

into $16 billion less spending to bail out failed institutions. When added to $3 billion less spending for interest on the national debt — also courtesy of lower interest rates — that meant a drop of $19 billion in the deficit.

Other factors the administration said helped lower the deficit were:

● Defeat of the administration's jobs stimulus plan, which stripped $11 billion from the April estimate. *(Stimulus bill, p. 706)*

● Congress' failure to provide funding before the end of fiscal 1993 for the Resolution Trust Corporation, the agency that bailed out failed savings and loans. Some of the $15 billion the administration said would otherwise have been spent in fiscal 1993 was simply deferred into later years.

● Slightly higher-than-expected tax receipts, which subtracted some $9 billion from the April number, and slightly lower-than-expected spending, which took some $17 billion out of the April deficit estimate.

Congressional Budget Office (CBO) director Robert D. Reischauer said deficit estimates were almost inevitably subject to seemingly large swings, even when they were made only a month before the end of the fiscal year. CBO's estimate in September month put the 1993 figure at $266 billion — $11 billion high.

"The trouble is that you're estimating differences between two very large numbers," Reischauer said of the $1 trillion-plus each in revenues and outlays that made up the federal budget. ■

Treasury To Mint Several Commemorative Coins

The Senate cleared a bill (HR 3616) by voice vote Nov. 24 authorizing the Treasury Department to mint several new commemorative coins. The House had passed the bill by voice vote Nov. 22. President Clinton signed it into law (PL 103-186) on Dec. 14.

The House began by approving two separate commemorative coin bills.

On Nov. 21, by a 428-0 vote, the House passed HR 3548 authorizing the minting of coins to commemorate Thomas Jefferson and several veterans groups, including prisoners of war, Vietnam veterans and women in the military. *(Vote 596, p. 146-H)*

On Nov. 22, at the behest of Senate President Pro Tempore Robert C. Byrd, D-W.Va., the House passed HR 3616 by voice vote. That bill included the provisions of HR 3548, plus one for a U.S. Capitol commemorative coin that Byrd backed.

"The Capitol coin will be used for a very worthy cause, to preserve and maintain the U.S. Capitol, the center of our democracy," said bill sponsor Joseph P. Kennedy II, D-Mass.

Money from sales of the coins was to go to maintenance

of Jefferson's historic home, Monticello, outside Charlottesville, Va.; construction of the Andersonville Prisoner-of-War Museum in Georgia; upkeep of the Vietnam Veterans Memorial; construction of a new Women in Military Service for America memorial; and activities of the U.S. Capitol Preservation Commission.

Even as they voted to authorize the new coins, lawmakers expressed concern that they were flooding coin collectors with too many commemoratives and that revenue from anticipated sales was lagging. ■

SEC Registration

A bill aimed at making it easier for small businesses to raise capital on the securities markets passed the Senate Nov. 2 by voice vote.

The most significant provision in the bill (S 479 — S Rept 103-166) raised from $5 million to $10 million the amount of money that a company could raise through securities offerings without having to register with the Securities and Exchange Commission. The bill, sponsored by Christopher J. Dodd, D-Conn., also contained provisions aimed at making it easier for investors to form venture capital pools that invest in small businesses. ■

Hill Votes More Funds for Thrift Bailout

Congress wrote what it hoped would be the final taxpayer check to close the books on the savings and loan debacle of the 1980s. On Nov. 23, lawmakers gave final approval to a bill (S 714) appropriating $18.3 billion for the Resolution Trust Corporation (RTC), the thrift salvage agency. That amount was expected to be enough to allow the agency to pay off depositors and sell the assets of 64 failed thrifts under its control plus a limited number of future failures.

The bill headed to President Clinton's desk eight months after Treasury Secretary Lloyd Bentsen came to Congress to ask for $45 billion to finish the bailout and capitalize the thrift industry's new deposit insurance fund, the Savings Association Insurance Fund (SAIF).

As the legislation moved through Congress, members proved unwilling to finance the full request, which represented the amount of money needed under Treasury's worst-case projections of failures. In addition to cutting back funds for the RTC, Congress refused to appropriate any of the $17 billion that the administration requested for the SAIF, and it scaled back the SAIF's existing $32 billion authorization to $8 billion.

The bill appropriated the $18.3 billion for the RTC by lifting an April 1, 1992, deadline for use of $25 billion that had been appropriated in November 1991. It required the RTC to close down by Dec. 31, 1995, one year earlier than under existing law. On that date, all assets seized from failed thrifts that remained unsold were to be turned over to the SAIF. At the same time, the bill extended the period during which the agency could take control of failed thrifts. Under prior law, the RTC had ceased taking over thrifts on Sept. 30, 1993, and the SAIF had taken over the job Oct. 1. The bill restored the RTC's role and canceled the SAIF's operations. It required the RTC to stop taking over thrifts by July 1995, with the exact date to be set by the Treasury secretary. The SAIF was to take over after that.

The bill included provisions that increased the number of RTC contracts awarded to businesses owned by minorities and women and restricted capitalizing the SAIF with leftover RTC appropriations.

Clinton signed the bill into law (PL 103-204) on Dec. 17.

BACKGROUND

Although Congress had acted three times in prior years to fund the RTC, lawmakers found the job so distasteful

---

BOXSCORE

➡ **Thrift Cleanup Financing — S 714, HR 1340.** The bill, which the administration hoped would bring a close to the savings and loan debacle of the 1980s, appropriated $18.3 billion for the Resolution Trust Corporation (RTC), the bailout agency; cut back the existing authorization for the new thrift deposit insurance fund; and shortened the RTC's life while extending the period during which the agency could take over new thrifts.

Reports: H Rept 103-103, Pts. 1, 2; S Rept 103-36; conference report, H Rept 103-380.

KEY ACTION

March 25 — Senate Banking Committee approved draft bill, 16-3.

May 6 — House Banking Committee approved HR 1340, 36-16.

May 13 — Senate approved S 714, 61-35.

Sept. 14 — House passed HR 1340, 214-208; it then approved S 714 by voice vote after substituting the text of HR 1340.

Nov. 18 — Conferees unanimously approved report.

Nov. 20 — Senate adopted the conference report, 54-45.

Nov. 23 — House adopted the conference report 235-191, clearing the bill.

Dec. 17 — President signed the bill into law (PL 103-204).

---

that they had left the agency without new funds for almost two years.

The RTC — which was created in 1989 under the Financial Institutions Reform, Recovery and Enforcement Act — began life with an initial grant of $50 billion ($18.8 billion of it from taxpayers). Congress voted twice in 1991 to replenish the agency's coffers with taxpayer money: $30 billion in the spring and up to $25 billion in November. But the November grant had a catch: The RTC had until April 1, 1992, to spend the money; $18.3 billion remained unspent on that date, and it reverted to the Treasury.

Lawmakers tried but failed to provide new money in 1992. The Senate passed a $43 million funding bill by a vote of 52-42. But the bill died in a partisan standoff in the House, where Democratic leaders and the Bush administration had agreed that a majority from each party would vote for the bill. But when it became clear that Republicans were not going to deliver their votes and that the White House was not willing to prod them, Democrats, too, abandoned ship. *(1989 Almanac, p. 117; 1991 Almanac, p. 98; 1992 Almanac, p. 115)*

Without funding, the RTC could take over dead and dying thrifts and continue to operate them at a loss, but it could not "resolve" them by paying off depositors and selling their assets. Treasury Secretary Bentsen told members in March 1993 that Congress' unwillingness to approve further funding had added about $1.1 billion to the cost of the cleanup.

ADMINISTRATION REQUEST

Bentsen appeared before the House and Senate Banking committees March 16-17 to deliver the administration's request for $45 billion — $28 billion to fund the RTC and $17 billion to capitalize the SAIF.

"I know from personal experience that a vote to fund the RTC is a tough vote. I've been there. I've got the scars to show for it," Bentsen said. "But I also know that this is a vote for depositors, for the safety of our financial institutions, and that if we fail to meet this obligation, we will pay a far higher price, and deservedly so." Bentsen told members he was fairly certain that this was the last time they would be asked to vote for the cleanup.

Bentsen received immediate support from the chairmen and ranking Republicans on both the House and Senate committees, who promised to act quickly.

He asked lawmakers to pass a clean bill free of congres-

sionally mandated changes in RTC operations, but he pledged that the new administration would significantly improve the much-criticized management of the RTC. "I know that many of you cannot vote to fund the RTC unless dramatic improvements are made in its operations. I buy that," Bentsen said. "We intend to make such improvements."

Complaints About the RTC

In addition to their reluctance to vote for anything that cost $45 billion and evoked images of government bungling, committee members were extremely critical of the way the RTC had managed the thrift cleanup.

Many complained that the agency was freezing out small investors by bundling assets from failed thrifts into large packages. In the process of trying to sell off its huge asset portfolio, the RTC had been accused of making fire-sale deals that provided the private sector with huge profits — at taxpayer expense.

And black and Hispanic members on the House Banking Committee decried what they said was the RTC's poor performance in contracting with minority businesses.

News stories about bonuses paid to RTC executives and seemingly excessive payments to agency contractors did not make it any easier for members to vote for funds.

Bentsen eased some of those concerns by accepting the resignation of RTC chief Albert Casey on March 15, one day before coming to Capitol Hill to make his pitch for the funding. Bentsen said Deputy Treasury Secretary Roger C. Altman would run the agency temporarily.

Costs

The Congressional Budget Office (CBO) calculated that $50 billion was needed to finish the cleanup and fund the SAIF, but it said the administration's request was "well within the range of uncertainty" inherent in calculating the bailout's cost.

The administration's request was $13 billion higher than the $32 billion figure assumed in Clinton's preliminary budget issued in February. Officials wanted to err on the high side, especially in capitalizing the new insurance fund, to avoid having to come back to Congress for additional money.

Thus far, the RTC had resolved 654 institutions and taken control of an additional 83. The Office of Thrift Supervision estimated that 35 more thrifts would fail before the Sept. 30 deadline. The RTC had taken possession of about $438 billion in assets from failed thrifts and gotten rid of about $337 billion of them. The remainder consisted largely of hard-to-sell assets such as failed real estate ventures and non-performing loans.

SENATE COMMITTEE ACTION

The Senate Banking Committee acted first, voting 16-3 on March 25 to appropriate $28 billion for the RTC and $17 billion to capitalize the SAIF.

Despite Bentsen's plea, the panel was unwilling to provide the money without attaching some strings. Under pressure from committee Democrats, Chairman Donald W. Riegle Jr., D-Mich., amended the bill (S 714) to require the Treasury to certify that its package of administrative improvements was in place and showing results. He negotiated the changes after committee freshmen Barbara Boxer, D-Calif., and Patty Murray, D-Wash., told him they could not vote for a clean bill. Ranking Republican Alfonse M.

D'Amato of New York joined in sponsoring the amendment.

Under the revised bill, the RTC was to get $10 billion immediately; the next $10 billion was to be released after Bentsen (acting in his role as chairman of the RTC's oversight board) certified that his management plan was in place; the remainder of the $28 billion would be released after a second certification.

While the change enabled Riegle to get the measure out of committee, it did not satisfy the bill's Democratic critics. John Kerry, D-Mass., said the self-certification made the language toothless. "They can certify to most of this by next Monday," Kerry said.

The bill included Republican language, sponsored by Connie Mack of Florida, requiring the RTC to set up an appeals process for borrowers whose loans were called in by the agency after it took over an institution.

SENATE FLOOR ACTION

Giving Clinton a half-victory, the Senate on May 13 passed a slimmed-down version of the bill. The measure passed on a bipartisan 61-35 vote after the administration and Banking Committee leaders from both parties agreed on a substitute version that cut $15.2 billion from the administration's $42 billion funding request. *(Vote 121, p. 17-S)*

Senators approved the substitute, crafted by Riegle and D'Amato, by voice vote on May 12. The revised bill appropriated $18.3 billion for the RTC, compared with the $28 billion approved by the Banking Committee. It authorized $16 billion for the SAIF and appropriated $8.5 billion, as opposed to the $17 billion appropriation included in the committee-approved bill.

Although the administration had wanted to err on the high side — its original request was $45 billion, revised to $42 billion after the RTC was found to be in better financial shape than had been thought — the slimmed-down bill was in line with the administration's best guess of how much money actually would be needed for the bailout, barring a new downturn in the economy or other unforeseen problems.

Altman, acting as interim RTC chief, said the administration's revised midrange estimate of funding needs for the bailout was $18 billion for the RTC and $11 billion for the SAIF.

The Senate bill contained several new provisions aimed at improving the RTC's performance in selling off assets from failed thrifts, preventing fraud and abuse by agency contractors and giving more business opportunities to women and minorities. The bulk of the new language mirrored provisions in the House version of the bill.

Several Banking Committee Democrats — including Boxer, Murray, Kerry and Carol Moseley-Braun of Illinois — insisted that such changes be made when the bill came to the floor.

Christopher S. Bond, R-Mo., successfully pressed for language to close down the RTC by Dec. 31, 1995, one year earlier than under existing law.

The Senate bill also required that the RTC try to sell assets from failed thrifts on an individual basis for 90 days before packaging them in one of the agency's bulk sales.

Other changes included limiting bonuses paid to RTC executives, giving federal employees additional whistle-blower protections when they reported mismanagement at the RTC and the Federal Deposit Insurance Corporation

(FDIC), and improving the RTC's performance in setting uniform contracting and enforcement standards.

The bill included language by Howard M. Metzenbaum, D-Ohio, aimed at rebuilding the RTC's professional liability section, which he said fell into disarray under the Bush administration. The section was responsible for suing owners who caused thrift failures through negligence, fraud or breach of fiduciary duty. Under the bill, a new assistant general counsel was to be named to head up the liability section.

Statute of Limitations Extension

The only significant floor battle occurred on an amendment by Metzenbaum to extend from three to five years the time the RTC had to sue thrift officials after it had taken over a failed institution. The Senate had adopted identical amendments by large margins during previous consideration of RTC bills, but D'Amato and Christopher J. Dodd, D-Conn., said the provision would allow the RTC to continue to pursue frivolous lawsuits against directors of failed thrifts.

After Metzenbaum rebuffed a request by D'Amato to make the provision apply only to cases of outright fraud — instead of including less egregious offenses such as negligence — the Senate adopted the amendment on a 63-32 vote. Metzenbaum said the administration was "not particularly supportive" of the addition. *(Vote 119, p. 16-S)*

The only other roll call vote occurred on an unrelated budget amendment by Phil Gramm, R-Texas, which was defeated, 43-53, on a procedural motion. *(Vote 120, p. 16-S)*

The Senate adopted, by voice vote, an amendment by Murray and Paul Wellstone, D-Minn., to require a report from the General Accounting Office (GAO) on whether the thrift industry could bear the cost of capitalizing the SAIF through increased premium payments.

HOUSE SUBCOMMITTEE ACTION

The House Banking Financial Institutions Subcommittee approved its version of the bill (HR 1340) by voice vote April 29, but only after cutting the administration's request to $30.3 billion — $18.3 billion for the RTC and $12 billion for the SAIF.

The funding cut came on an amendment by freshman Herb Klein, D-N.J., to lift the existing April 1, 1992, moratorium. Because the money for the RTC was equivalent to the amount that had reverted to the Treasury in April 1992, members were quick to assert that they had eliminated new RTC money altogether.

"You mean if we adopt this amendment we don't have to vote any more money?" asked Floyd H. Flake, D-N.Y., with a hint of faux amazement. When subcommittee Chairman Stephen L. Neal, D-N.C., answered "yes," Flake immediately called for a vote. The amendment was approved by voice vote.

Shifting Cost Estimates

Much of the pressure to reduce the bill's price tag was prompted by new GAO estimates that, under favorable economic conditions, the RTC might need as little as $7 billion to finish its job.

Given the uncertainty inherent in bailout cost projections, the RTC estimated that its funding needs ranged from $9 billion to $28 billion. The administration requested the higher amount to guarantee that it would not have to come back to Congress.

While subcommittee Democrats agreed on the lower, $18.3 billion figure for the RTC, they resisted calls to cut the SAIF funding. Jim Leach of Iowa, ranking Republican on the full committee, tried to strike the administration's $17 billion request from the bill. Leach argued that using taxpayer money to fund the SAIF amounted to a subsidy of the thrift industry.

The Democrats countered with $12 billion and added significant restrictions on the circumstances under which the money could be tapped. The language, adopted 18-11, said that the SAIF would receive taxpayer money only if thrift regulators certified that the industry could not support the fund on its own through premium payments.

The Treasury Department made a strong pitch to keep the SAIF funding in the bill and to limit statutory mandates on RTC operations. But in the end, it was forced to accept political reality. "We are happy to see the process move forward," said a tight-lipped Treasury Department official. "Their preference would have been the higher figure," said Neal, who conceded that the votes were not there for the full administration request.

Other Amendments

In a skirmish between senior committee Democrats, Bruce F. Vento of Minnesota and Charles E. Schumer of New York clashed over a Vento amendment that would have created a new division at the FDIC to take over the RTC's responsibility to sell off assets of failed thrifts starting July 1, 1994. The amendment was opposed by the Treasury Department. Schumer said it made no sense to create a new entity just as the RTC was finishing up its job and as the agency's management was "finally getting the hang of it."

Congressional Black Caucus Chairman Kweisi Mfume, D-Md., and Maxine Waters, D-Calif., offered a package of amendments on minority contracting that was adopted on a 14-10 party-line vote. The language set specific quotas for distributing contracts among women and minorities.

The panel rejected two Republican-sponsored amendments. The first, offered by Rod Grams, Minn., would have required bailout funding to be offset by spending cuts elsewhere. It was rejected on a party-line 11-18 vote.

Members also rejected, 7-23, a McCollum amendment that would have allowed thrift regulators to buy back so-called supervisory good will, an intangible asset that some thrift institutions had acquired in the mid 1980s when they bought failing thrifts from the government. The thrifts originally were entitled to count the good will toward their minimum capital requirements, but the 1989 thrift bailout law revoked that privilege. McCollum argued that if the government had replaced the good will with cash, these thrifts would have been profitable, and that without it, they would fail at a much higher cost to taxpayers.

The House Rules Committee had barred McCollum from offering a similar amendment on the floor the previous year, triggering the GOP defections that sunk the RTC bill in 1992.

HOUSE COMMITTEE ACTION

Before approving the bill on a 35-16 vote May 6, the full House Banking Committee eliminated the $12 billion direct appropriation for the SAIF. That left a bill that provided $18.3 billion — all of it for the RTC (H Rept 103-103, Pt. 1).

The committee agreed to authorize the SAIF funds and set much stricter conditions before the money could be provided through a separate appropriation. Committee staff aides said many panel Democrats, including Chair-

man Henry B. Gonzalez, D-Texas, agreed with Republicans that the SAIF appropriation would amount to a subsidy of the thrift industry.

As approved by the full committee, the bill allowed the SAIF to get taxpayer money only if the FDIC certified that raising deposit insurance premiums on the thrift industry would cause too many institutions to fail. Next, before any new money was appropriated, the FDIC would have to tap into a $30 billion line of credit that was established in 1991 to pay for possible bank failures.

The Compromise

The cut in SAIF funding was a key part of a compromise amendment worked out between Gonzalez and Leach and adopted by voice vote. The compromise scaled back slightly the minority contracting amendments added in subcommittee.

The minority contracting issue was particularly hot because the remedies that had been proposed were attacked as quotas. And anything that smacked of quotas was a potential bill-killer. As approved by the committee, the bill required companies that contracted with the RTC and received fees in excess of $500,000 to hire minority subcontractors. It also gave preference to minorities in bidding for failed institutions located in black and Hispanic neighborhoods.

One controversial provision required the agency to establish guidelines to try to achieve greater parity in the distribution of contracts among subgroups of businesses owned by minorities and women. The bill also made minority contracting a factor to be considered when granting conflict of interest waivers that allowed firms involved in lawsuits with the government to continue doing business with the RTC.

The bill represented a slight retreat by minority members from the provisions adopted in the subcommittee. "We have all, I think, taken a step backward on this in order that we might be able to take two steps forward," said Mfume.

"I think we got most of what we wanted," said Albert R. Wynn, D-Md., another member of the black caucus.

The compromise also made changes in RTC and FDIC Affordable Housing Programs to raise limits on the value of properties eligible for the programs, gave homeless families preference in obtaining homes and gave tenants the right of first refusal to buy the homes they were renting.

Finally, the compromise amendment included language by Vento requiring the FDIC to meet standards that already were set for the RTC, including employee ethics standards, whistleblower protections for employees and a ban on selling property to unsavory buyers. The language was a small piece of a much more ambitious proposal (HR 1713) by Vento, who chaired a congressional task force on the RTC in 1989-91.

Statute of Limitations Fight

One of the few significant fights at the Banking Committee markup involved an amendment by Joseph P. Kennedy II, D-Mass., to extend the statute of limitations for RTC suits against officials of failed thrifts from three to five years. The amendment applied to any offense for which a lawsuit could be brought, except for simple negligence.

Because Kennedy's amendment gave the RTC the right to sue in cases in which the statute of limitations already had expired, it generated significant opposition from committee members, including Schumer and Barney Frank, D-Mass., both of whom also served on the Judiciary Committee. The amendment earned the provision a referral to Judiciary.

With the support of Gonzalez, the committee adopted Kennedy's amendment on a 25-24 vote; a subsequent at-

tempt by committee Republicans to revisit the issue was turned back on a 23-24 vote.

The House bill required the RTC to carry out a variety of "management reforms" that the administration preferred not to have written into the law. Much of this language was added by committee freshmen, who were very reluctant to vote for the bill.

The Banking Committee rejected a series of Republican-sponsored amendments, offered by:

- McCollum, to allow thrift regulators to use funds in the bill to buy back supervisory good will. Rejected on a 9-40 vote.
- Grams, to require that the president propose a plan to fund the bailout on a pay-as-you-go basis. Rejected 13-35. Another amendment, offered by John Linder, R-Ga., to require only spending cuts was voted down 17-32.
- Richard H. Baker, R-La., essentially to strike the SAIF authorization from the bill. Rejected 18-30.

House Judiciary Committee Weighs In

The House Judiciary Committee approved the bill by voice vote on June 10 after modifying the controversial statute of limitations provision (H Rept. 103-103, Pt. 2). The committee agreed to extend from three to five years the time the RTC had to sue thrift officials after it had taken over a failed institution — but only in cases of fraud or "intentional misconduct" in which savings and loan officials unjustly enriched themselves.

The committee rejected a bipartisan proposal worked out by Chairman Jack Brooks, D-Texas, McCollum and several other committee members, that would have extended the statute of limitations in the narrow circumstances of fraud or intentional misconduct but would not have imposed the liability retroactively in cases in which the statute had expired.

Instead, the committee voted 21-13 to adopt an amendment by David Mann, D-Ohio, to extend the statute for the same narrow set of offenses but impose it retroactively in cases involving such wrongdoing.

"The revival of expired claims sets a very dangerous precedent for other agencies, other persons seeking special statute of limitations treatment, as well as raising serious constitutional questions," Brooks said.

But critics of the RTC argued that the thrift bailout agency had bungled the task of suing savings and loan wrongdoers and needed more time. "Given the truly extraordinary circumstances here, which involve the biggest rip-off of taxpayers in American history, I believe the least Congress could do is provide prosecutors with all the available tools necessary to prosecute and recover moneys form all those involved in looting the S&Ls," John Conyers Jr., D-Mich., said during the markup.

The committee rejected, 10-24, an attempt by Conyers to significantly broaden the types of offenses to which the statute extension would apply to include any tort action, including negligence.

Insurance companies were particularly opposed to extending the statute to negligent activities, which typically were covered by insurance policies purchased for thrift officers and directors. The House language limited the liability for insurance companies because they were not liable in cases of fraud.

HOUSE FLOOR ACTION

After repeated delays, the House on Sept. 14 narrowly passed a modified version of the bill by a vote of 214-208. (The House then passed S 714 by voice vote after substitut-

ing the House-passed bill.) *(Vote 434, p. 106-H)*

With a Democrat in the White House, Republicans felt no responsibility for the bill, and only 24 GOP members joined with 190 Democrats to back the measure. In the last previous recorded House vote on the RTC, taken in March 1991 when George Bush was president, 119 Republicans had voted for RTC financing. Without GOP support in 1993, scores of reluctant Democrats had to be cajoled into changing their position on providing money for the politically unpopular bailout.

"This is a dose of castor oil that this House, the Senate and the administration must take," said Chief Deputy Whip Butler Derrick, D-S.C. "No one wants to vote for this bill. . . . No one likes the idea of getting up here and defending it. But you know, there is a certain responsibility that goes with the right we have been given to govern."

At one point in the tally, the bill appeared to be losing by 20 votes. But Democratic whip counts proved accurate, and the outcome, while close, was not as close as it looked. For one thing, several Republicans were ready to vote for the bill if their support was critical for passage. Among them were California Republicans Al McCandless and David Dreier, whose state was home to a powerful thrift industry that actively lobbied for the bill. The two waited until passage was assured before registering their "no" votes.

A New House Compromise

The bill had been ready for House floor consideration since late June and was listed on the floor schedule for several weeks. Despite vote counts that indicated the bill would pass, House leaders had pressed members of the Banking Committee to revise the measure to accommodate Republicans. GOP members had remained skeptical of the provisions on SAIF financing and on boosting opportunities for minority- and women-owned businesses at a cost to taxpayers.

Those concerns were addressed in a bipartisan compromise crafted by Neal, Gonzalez, Leach and Baker. Adopted by a vote of 406-15, the amendment cut the amount authorized for the SAIF to $8 billion, compared with $16 billion in the Banking Committee version of the bill. *(Vote 432, p. 106-H)*

At the same time, the amendment postponed the date when the SAIF was to take over failed-thrift salvage operations from the RTC from Sept. 30, 1993, to March 31, 1995. The change was intended to give the SAIF 18 additional months to build up its capital using thrift deposit premiums. In the interim, the RTC would continue to use taxpayer money for institutions that failed.

In addition, the compromise modified the minority contracting provisions to make them budget-neutral. CBO had estimated that the original provisions would cost the government $36 million in 1993-94.

CONFERENCE

After a two-month delay, an end-of-session deal produced the final version of the thrift cleanup bill (H Rept. 103-380). House and Senate conferees sealed their agreement Nov. 18 during a 30-minute meeting where they unanimously endorsed a compromise that had been worked out by House and Senate Banking committee staff aides.

Two sticking points — the minority contracting language and the statute of limitations extension — had held up final action. Senate Republicans objected so strongly to

the minority contracting provisions that they blocked Senate leaders from naming conferees until the compromise was struck. Conferees were named Nov. 16.

The final bill made modest changes to the House-passed language that required subcontracts with minority firms on all RTC contracts worth more than $500,000. The House bill would have required the RTC to establish guidelines for "reasonably even distribution" of such contracts to minority subgroups, including blacks, Hispanics and women. The final version made such parity a "goal" and said that the guidelines could take into consideration differences in minority demographics across various regions of the country.

"The heart of what we want to do remains intact," said Mfume, who had crafted the House provisions.

The contested statute of limitations provision was the only issue that aides were not permitted to negotiate. Both the House and Senate bills extended the statute from three to five years and applied to some cases in which the statute already had lapsed. But the House language applied only to more egregious offenses such as fraud and gross negligence, while the more sweeping Senate provisions also covered negligence.

Senate conferees accepted the House position.

Metzenbaum was not a member of the conference, but he showed up anyway, and Senate Banking Committee Chairman Riegle gave him the opportunity to make his case. Metzenbaum circulated an Oct. 31 GAO estimate that he said showed that the RTC needed less than one-fourth of the amount to be appropriated under the bill. The GAO estimated that the RTC's remaining liabilities totaled about $11.2 billion. Because the RTC had $6.8 billion in cash on hand, Metzenbaum said, the agency needed only an additional $4.4 billion.

But bill sponsors responded that any money not needed by the RTC would revert to the Treasury. And they continued to insist that Congress should appropriate enough money to ensure that lawmakers would not have to revisit the politically difficult issue.

"The bottom line," said Sen. Phil Gramm, R-Texas, "is we're obligated to pay off depositors, and it makes absolutely no sense to keep on pretending that that's not the case. I think we ought to provide the money, do it efficiently and get it over with."

The Final Compromise

The final bill generally hewed to the House position on the most important provisions. As cleared, the bill:

● Appropriated $18.3 billion for the RTC by lifting the April 1, 1992, deadline for using $25 billion that Congress approved two years earlier.

● Provided no direct appropriation for the SAIF, run by the FDIC. Conferees also scaled back the existing $32 billion authorization for the SAIF to $8 billion.

The conferees generally accepted House language requiring that, before the money could be appropriated, the FDIC chairman had to certify that financial conditions in the thrift industry required the use of taxpayer funds to capitalize the SAIF rather than the use of increased deposit insurance premiums to do the job.

The agreement also urged the FDIC to look first to tapping a $30 billion line of credit available to the SAIF before using taxpayer funds.

● Required the RTC to close by Dec. 31, 1995, one year earlier than under existing law, but extended the period during which the RTC could be able to take in failed

thrifts. The bill gave the Treasury secretary the authority to set the cutoff any time between Jan. 1, 1995, and June 30, 1995. The change was intended to give thrift institutions more time to capitalize the SAIF through deposit insurance premiums, and remove the need for taxpayer money to finance the SAIF during its initial years of operation.

Senate, House Approval

In the Senate, which had passed thrift bailout bills with relative ease, the final vote on Nov. 20 vote proved to be a squeaker. The conference report came to the Senate floor on short notice, and as the roll call progressed, it was apparent the bill was in trouble. After a wave of Republicans voted no and it appeared the bill might fail, Democratic support began to soften. Majority Leader George J. Mitchell, D-Maine, then prevailed upon several of his Democratic colleagues to switch their votes to yes. The conference report was adopted 54-45. *(Vote 393, p. 51-S)*

By contrast, the House, usually reluctant to vote for RTC money, had a relatively easy time. It adopted the conference report on a 235-191 vote in the early morning hours of Nov. 23, thus clearing it for the president. *(Vote 613, p. 150-H)*

With 208 Democrats voting for the measure — 18 more than when it first came to the floor in September — the bailout bill seemed to lose some of its reputation as a vote that made members squirm. "Nobody who voted for it the first time got any flak over it," said Frank, a senior Banking Committee member and leader in rounding up votes to pass the measure.

House leaders had been skittish throughout the year about bringing the bill to the floor. Without a Democrat in the White House, GOP members essentially considered themselves off the hook, and only 27 Republicans voted for the conference report. That meant scores of reluctant Democrats had to be cajoled into voting for the unpopular bill.

Democratic leaders took no chances, insisting on an impenetrable whip count of 200 Democratic yes votes before bringing the conference report to the floor. The day before the vote, Banking Committee leaders had counted only 134 Democrats committed or leaning to vote yes.

Those whipping the bill said a major selling point was the promise that they would never — ever — have to vote again for the bailout.

"We drove a stake through it," Frank said. ■

Thrift Cleanup Financing Provisions

After a lengthy delay and a congressional rewrite, President Clinton on Dec. 17 signed into law a bill to conclude the government's salvage operation for the savings and loan industry (S 714 — PL 103-204). The bill provided $18.3 billion to the Resolution Trust Corporation (RTC) and nothing immediately to the Savings Association Insurance Fund (SAIF), the thrift industry's new insurance fund, which was to assume responsibility for thrift failures in 1995. As enacted, the bill:

RTC Financing

● Appropriated $18.3 billion to the RTC to cover depositor losses in failed thrifts. The money was provided by removing the April 1, 1992, deadline for using $25 billion appropriated in 1991 (PL 102-233). Only $6.7 billion of that appropriation had been spent by the prior deadline. *(1991 Almanac, p. 98)*

Only $10 billion could be used immediately; the remaining $8.3 billion could be used after the secretary of the Treasury certified that the RTC was complying with "management reforms" mandated under the bill.

The money could be used only to protect insured depositors or for the administrative expenses of the RTC and not to benefit shareholders of insured institutions in any manner.

RTC Termination

● Set Dec. 31, 1995, as the termination date for the RTC, instead of Dec. 31, 1996, as under prior law. The Federal Deposit Insurance Corporation (FDIC) was to assume responsibility for all RTC activities, including sales of remaining thrift assets.

At the same time, the period during which the RTC was to be appointed conservator or receiver of failed thrifts was extended. The agency's responsibility for such institutions had expired Sept. 30, 1993; it was extended to a date between Jan. 1 and July 1, 1995, to be determined by the secretary of the Treasury. The extension was to provide additional time for deposit insurance premiums to flow into the undercapitalized SAIF, before it would be responsible for resolving failed institutions.

Savings Association Insurance Fund

● **SAIF financing.** Reduced the authorization for future SAIF appropriations from $32 billion to $8 billion and limited the use of

such money to losses incurred by the SAIF in fiscal 1994-98. The SAIF was the thrift industry's new insurance fund and was operated by the FDIC. The SAIF was to assume from the RTC responsibility for thrifts that failed after the RTC's authority to take institutions into conservatorship or receivership had lapsed in the first half of 1995.

The requirement under prior law that the Treasury capitalize the SAIF to $8.8 billion by fiscal 1999 was repealed. In the unlikely event that the SAIF's reserves were equal to or greater than 1.25 percent of insured deposits before 1998, no further appropriation was allowed.

Any money transferred to the SAIF that was not needed to pay off depositors was to revert to the Treasury.

Any RTC money remaining after that agency finished its portion of the cleanup could be turned over to the SAIF, starting at the end of 1995. The money would be subject to certification requirements outlined below.

● **Certification.** Required the chairman of the FDIC to certify to Congress each fiscal year that several conditions had been met before any appropriated money could flow to the SAIF. Among the conditions were requirements that the money would be needed to cover losses expected in the coming year and that an increase in thrift deposit insurance premiums would be detrimental to the industry's financial health and lead to more, costly thrift failures.

The FDIC was given flexibility to extend the 15-year schedule under which the SAIF was to be fully capitalized, thereby allowing the FDIC to reduce deposit insurance premiums. Such action could be taken only if the FDIC determined that such a move would, over time, increase SAIF revenue by allowing more institutions to remain viable to pay premiums. The change was aimed at easing a potential "premium differential" that would result if, as expected, the Bank Insurance Fund (BIF) became fully capitalized before the SAIF, and that bank deposit insurance premiums thereby were reduced.

RTC Management Reforms

Required the RTC to adopt a series of management reforms, including:

● Developing a comprehensive business plan for the balance of the cleanup.

● Creating a small-investor program under which the RTC was required to sell real property assets on an individual basis for 120 days after acquiring such assets. An exception was allowed in cases in which a buyer purchased a thrift and took over its asset portfolio, while assuming the thrift's liabilities.

● Requiring real property assets valued at $400,000 or less or non-performing real estate loans of $1 million or less to be analyzed to maximize recovery of government money and to allow broader participation by qualified bidders. The bill required that assets be analyzed on an individual basis and that the analysis be accompanied by a management and disposition plan.

● Appointing a chief financial officer, deputy chief executive officer and assistant general counsel for the agency.

● Strengthening its system for awarding and overseeing contracts, including those for legal services. The agency was required to appoint a new executive senior officer to set uniform standards for contracting and enforcement. The RTC also was required to issue uniform procurement guidelines to prevent the acquisition of goods and services at widely different prices.

● Submitting to additional oversight by a new audit committee established by the Thrift Depositor Protection Oversight Board. The committee was to oversee the RTC's improvement of internal controls.

● Responding better to problems brought to RTC management's attention by auditors, the inspector general, the General Accounting Office (GAO) and the RTC audit committee, or certifying that no action was necessary.

● Maintaining an effective management information system and strengthening internal controls against waste, fraud and abuse.

● Including in its annual report an itemization of agency expenditures, a disclosure of the compensation of executives of thrifts in conservatorship or receivership and a semiannual comprehensive litigation report of all professional liability cases.

● Reducing the cost of the RTC's legal services by using staff attorneys whenever they could provide the same quality legal services as outside counsel at the same or lower cost. Outside counsel could be hired only if it would be practicable, efficient, cost-effective and under a negotiated fee, contingent fee or competitively bid fee agreement.

● Creating a "client responsiveness" unit at every RTC regional office.

● Establishing a process for business and commercial borrowers to appeal lending decisions made by the RTC when it is managing failed thrifts.

● Submitting to an evaluation by the GAO, which was to make two reports — one within six months and another within one year — on the progress made by the RTC in complying with the management reforms. The reports were to include information on the sale of performing assets by the RTC.

● Notifying the General Services Administration (GSA), which managed federal buildings, and providing specific information about commercial office buildings the RTC acquires. The GSA could bid on such buildings, which otherwise would be subject to a competitive bidding process.

Minority Contracting

Required the RTC to implement provisions designed to improve the agency's record in providing business opportunities to minorities and women when issuing RTC contracts or selling assets. In implementing these provisions, the RTC was required to continue to conduct the bailout in a manner that resulted in the least cost to taxpayers. The RTC was required to:

● **Division of Minority and Women's Programs.** Create and maintain a Division of Minorities and Women's Programs, to be headed by a vice president of the RTC who also was a member of the RTC's executive committee.

● **Basic ordering agreements.** Take greater steps to ensure that lists of eligible contractors (basic ordering agreements) contained as many minority- and female-owned businesses as possible. This provision was aimed at providing greater allocation of

RTC contracts to minority- and female-owned businesses. In addition, the RTC was to revise its procedure for reviewing applicants for future contracts to ensure that small businesses, minorities and women were not inadvertently excluded.

● **Parity guidelines.** Establish guidelines — which were not to have the force of law — for achieving the goal of a reasonably even distribution of contracts awarded to minority- and female-owned businesses and law firms among various subgroups such as women, blacks, Hispanics and Asian-Americans. The provision came in response to complaints by minority groups that businesses and law firms owned by white women received contracts at the expense of minorities.

● **Subcontracting requirements.** Require any contractor that received an RTC contract worth $500,000 or more for services (such as accounting or legal services) to subcontract with minority- or female-owned businesses unless no such subcontractor was available. This provision was not to apply if such subcontracting would significantly increase the cost of the contract or hinder the ability of the contractor to fulfill the contract.

● **Sanctions.** Draft sanctions, including contract penalties and suspensions for contractors who did not comply with joint venturing and minority subcontracting requirements.

● **Minority preference in acquisition of institutions.** Give priority to minorities and minority-owned businesses that bid for thrifts in RTC conservatorship or receivership that were in minority neighborhoods — provided that such a sale would not result in greater cost to the taxpayer than would non-minority offers.

RTC-FDIC Transition

Extended to the FDIC a series of RTC regulations concerning management practices. These regulations reflected lessons learned from the RTC and were to be applied to the FDIC because that agency — in its role of managing the SAIF — would assume a much larger asset disposition workload than it previously had. The provisions:

● **Conflict of interest.** Required the FDIC to issue regulations governing agency employees or contractors regarding conflict of interest, ethical responsibilities and the use of confidential information by independent contractors.

● **Restrictions on asset sales.** Barred those who had engaged in questionable or illegal practices from buying assets from the FDIC. The agency was given flexibility to write such rules, but at a minimum the rules had to bar those who had defaulted on debts of $1 million or more to a failed thrift and engaged in fraud from buying FDIC assets, particularly through credit extended by the FDIC or FDIC-seized thrifts. In addition, directors or officers of failed thrifts who had "materially participated" in transactions that produced large thrift losses, had been barred by federal regulators from participating in the business affairs of failed institutions or had engaged in embezzlement were to be barred from buying FDIC-controlled assets.

● **Asset Disposition Division.** Established a new and separate Division of Asset Disposition within the FDIC, effective July 1, 1995, to conduct the agency's liquidation of insured banks and thrifts and disposition of their assets. The provision merged the asset disposition functions of the SAIF and the BIF.

Affordable Housing

● **Housing stock.** Expanded the existing affordable housing programs of the RTC and the FDIC by broadening the potential affordable housing stock of the two agencies. Under the programs, the RTC and the FDIC sold such housing at market or below-market prices and provided loans at market or below-market rates to individuals and groups to purchase housing stock from failed thrifts and banks.

The limit for RTC-eligible single-family properties was raised from $67,500 to $101,250, but money to cover the cost had to be separately appropriated.

● Expanded the FDIC affordable housing program to include properties owned by real estate subsidiaries of institutions in conservatorship or receivership. Under prior law, properties were

eligible only if title was held directly by the FDIC.

● **Information.** Required the FDIC and RTC to provide additional information on the availability of residential properties to agencies and housing groups through clearinghouses, including information about suitable properties not within the statutory scope of the housing programs.

Required the RTC and the FDIC to provide information periodically on the availability and terms of seller financing under their affordable housing programs to minority- and women-owned businesses and to minority-controlled nonprofit organizations.

● **Advisory board.** Established an Affordable Housing Advisory Board to advise the RTC's oversight board and the FDIC board of directors about the affordable housing program and other policies regarding the provision of affordable housing.

● **Joint management.** Unified the management of the RTC and FDIC affordable housing programs to run the programs more efficiently and save administrative costs.

● **Property sales.** Gave tenants of residential properties acquired by the RTC and the FDIC right of first refusal to purchase the properties.

Gave groups that housed the homeless preference in buying RTC and FDIC properties, provided that the revenue from such sales was substantially similar to other sales under the affordable housing program.

Authorized the RTC and the FDIC to conduct expedited sales of commercial real estate to public agencies and nonprofit groups involved in providing low-income housing and shelter for the homeless. The properties were to be used as administrative offices.

● **Housing opportunity hotline.** Required each of the Federal Home Loan Banks to establish a toll-free hotline to provide information on federally owned and controlled single-family homes to prospective buyers. Properties held by the Farmers Home Administration, the FDIC, the Federal National Mortgage Association, the Federal Home Loan Mortgage Corporation, the GSA, the Department of Housing and Urban Development (HUD), the RTC and the Department of Veterans Affairs were to be covered.

● **GAO study.** Required the GAO to conduct a study of the effectiveness of the RTC Affordable Housing Program.

Legal Liabilities

● **Statute of limitations.** Increased the statute of limitations on RTC civil lawsuits from three years to five, or to the period provided in state law, whichever was longer, to give agency lawyers additional time to sue thrift officials for negligence and fraud.

In cases in which the statute of limitations already had expired, claims could be revived for fraud and intentional misconduct resulting in unjust enrichment or substantial loss to the thrift. Such offenses typically were not covered by liability insurance policies purchased for thrift officers and directors.

If the statute of limitations had not yet expired, it was extended for a wider set of offenses, including gross negligence or any offense more egregious than gross negligence.

● **Due process protections.** Modified the authority of bank regulators to seize assets of financial institutions. Under the 1990 crime bill (PL 101-647), bank regulators (Office of the Comptroller of the Currency, Office of Thrift Supervision, Federal Reserve and the FDIC) were given sweeping authority to freeze the assets of banks and thrifts involved in fraud. Under law, such prejudgment attachments generally were allowed only when authorities could show that they were likely to win in court; that the assets were at risk of being dissipated; and that a failure to seize assets would cause immediate and irreparable harm to the government.

The 1990 crime bill relaxed this standard, giving bank regulators broad authority to seize assets without having to prove that each of the three conditions existed. But the RTC and the FDIC,

in their roles as conservators or receivers of failed institutions, were not given the same sweeping authority. Instead, they were only exempted from the requirement to show immediate and irreparable harm. The measure scaled back the authority of bank regulators to make it equal to the standard for the RTC and FDIC.

Miscellaneous

● **Bonus limits.** Barred bonuses to FDIC employees working for the RTC or SAIF that exceeded those paid other federal officials. No bonuses could be paid to employees who announced their intention to take private-sector jobs. No RTC employee could receive total compensation in excess of the compensation provided to the chief executive officer of the RTC.

● **Whistleblower protection.** Expanded whistleblower protections to include RTC employees and contractors who reported agency problems to authorities. The measure protected those who reported possible violations of laws or regulations by RTC officials, gross mismanagement and abuses of authority. In addition, it relaxed the burden of proof and broadened the scope of such protections to include FDIC contractors. Prior law applied whistleblower protections only to those who reported "violations of law or regulation." Whistleblower protections extended to RTC contractors were also extended to FDIC contractors.

● **BIF moratorium.** Continued an existing moratorium on SAIF members converting to BIF membership until the SAIF had attained its designated reserve ratio of 1.25 percent. This provision reflected concerns that thrifts might be tempted to convert to banks in order to elude higher deposit insurance premiums. Any FDIC borrowing for the SAIF would be repaid by SAIF members; any borrowing for the BIF would be repaid by BIF members.

● **Shareholder protection.** BIF and SAIF money could be used only to protect insured depositors and not to benefit shareholders of insured institutions in any manner.

● **RTC contracting.** Prohibited RTC employees from executing a contract unless the employee was a warranted contracting officer or the managing agent in charge of a thrift in conservatorship. Contracts not meeting this requirement were invalid. The RTC was required to award all contracts in excess of $100,000 on a fixed-price basis or to provide an explanation of why a cost estimate of the contract was impractical.

● **Final reports on RTC, SAIF financing.** Required the secretary of the Treasury to issue a final report detailing how RTC money was used. The chairman of the FDIC was required to issue a comparable report on how the SAIF spent its money.

Required the RTC to include in its annual report an itemization of agency expenditures, a disclosure of the compensation of executives of thrifts in conservatorship or receivership and a semiannual comprehensive litigation report of all professional liability cases.

● **GAO study.** Required the GAO to study the feasibility and effectiveness of establishing a single federal agency responsible for selling and otherwise disposing of real property owned or held by HUD, the Farmers Home Administration, the FDIC and the RTC.

● **FDIC inspector general.** Required that the inspector general of the FDIC be appointed by the president rather than by the agency.

● **Justice Department report.** Required, no later than 90 days after enactment, that the Justice Department submit to Congress a report on the status of efforts to monitor and improve the collection of fines and restitution in cases involving fraud and other criminal activity in and against the financial services industry.

● **Auctioneers.** Required the RTC to provide semiannual reports to detail procedures for selecting auctioneers for RTC asset sales with anticipated gross proceeds of $1.5 million or less. ∎

New Laws Enacted To Aid Depositors, Flood Victims

Congress worked on several relatively small banking bills in 1993.

PROTECTING UNCLAIMED DEPOSITS

The House on June 9 cleared a bill (HR 890) giving depositors more time to claim federally insured funds from a failed bank or thrift.

Under existing law, depositors could get their funds only if they filled out the necessary paperwork within 18 months after an institution failed. That posed a problem primarily for holders of long-term certificates of deposit in failed institutions who were unaware of the need to claim their funds. These depositors were able to recover only a portion of their money — usually about two-thirds — after the assets of the institution had been sold. About $40 million in lost deposits were at stake.

The bill authorized the Federal Deposit Insurance Cor-

poration (FDIC) and the Resolution Trust Corporation to turn over such unclaimed deposits to the states after the 18-month claim period expired. The states could hold the deposits under state abandoned property law for 10 years while they tried to find the owners. If the money still remained unclaimed, it would revert to the FDIC.

The House originally passed the bill on March 2 by a vote of 409-1; the Senate made minor modifications before approving the bill May 27, necessitating a quick trip for the bill back to the House. President Clinton signed the bill into law (PL 103-44) on June 28. *(Vote 43, p. 12-H)*

EASING LENDING IN FLOOD AREAS

The Senate on Aug. 5 cleared a bill (S 1273) easing Truth in Lending Act rules for banks in areas affected by the nation's flood disaster, allowing them to speed up loan applications. The measure also allowed banks to exclude big infusions of deposits that resulted from insurance payments when calculating their capital requirements.

The Senate passed an earlier version of the bill July 30; the House passed it with slight modifications Aug. 3. President Clinton signed the bill Aug. 12 (PL 103-76). ∎

Plan Seeks To Bolster Development Banks

A plan by President Clinton to provide federal subsidies to a new network of community development banks won backing from the House, after the House Banking Committee sweetened the measure with a sizable and widely backed set of "regulatory relief" proposals. The House passed the two-part bill (HR 3474) by voice vote Nov. 21.

The Senate Banking Committee approved a companion bill (S 1275 — S Rept 103-169), which included regulatory reforms and several unrelated banking provisions. But the full Senate did not act on the measure before adjourning for the year.

The centerpiece of Clinton's community development bank proposal was a $382 million federal fund that would provide grants and other subsidies to community development banks and other non-traditional lenders that filled a niche generally avoided by mainstream banks.

BACKGROUND

Saying that too many inner cities and poor rural communities were cut off from the money they needed to create jobs and rebuild decaying neighborhoods, Clinton on July 15 sent Congress his plan to give federal support to a fledgling network of community development lenders.

Impressed by the example of Chicago's South Shore Bank, a successful for-profit institution with a community development mission, Clinton vowed during the 1992 presidential campaign to create a network of 100 such banks. But the administration subsequently decided that the 100-bank goal was not realistic in the near-term and pared back its plan to seek just $60 million for fiscal 1994.

Clinton called for the creation of an independently managed fund — the Community Development Banking and Financial Institutions Fund — to provide financial and other assistance to community development banks and other alternative lenders.

Most of the money was directed at an existing group of

alternative institutions, such as credit unions and about 40 community development funds that made loans to non-profit groups and small businesses that were considered "unbankable" by traditional lenders.

Under Clinton's plan these lenders could receive up to $5 million apiece over three years in federal grants, loans and equity investments. Insured institutions would have to match the federal funds with private capital on at least a dollar-per-dollar basis. Loan funds and community development corporations receiving aid also would have to attract private money, but not necessarily on a one-to-one basis. In addition, the fund could provide outright grants for technical assistance to help start community development financial institutions or expand existing ones.

Only institutions whose "primary mission" was community development would be eligible for the federal help, which would rule out participation by conventional banks. In addition, community development subsidiaries owned by large banks could not receive the federal subsidy.

At the same time, Clinton pledged to revamp the way the government enforced the Community Reinvestment Act, a 1977 law that sought to prohibit traditional lenders from discriminating against economically disadvantaged communities. Clinton promised to develop new "performance based" CRA standards, requiring banks to document their activities in three categories: lending in their service area; investing in community projects and in institutions that financed community development; and providing banking services.

SENATE COMMITTEE ACTION

The Senate Banking Committee strongly endorsed Clinton's plan, voting 18-1 on Sept. 21 in favor of a bill providing $382 million to a fledgling group of community lenders. The vote came after the committee leadership added several unrelated provisions aimed at drawing bipar-

tisan support. These included provisions to encourage a secondary market for small-business loans, to curb abusive treatment of minority borrowers by finance companies and to ease banks' paperwork burdens.

The Treasury Department was pleased with the outcome, despite the inclusion of the extraneous provisions.

In a modest concession to Republicans who had complained that traditional banks would be shut out of the Clinton program, the bill allowed non-profit community development subsidiaries owned by a partnership of several banks or thrifts to receive subsidies. But wholly owned bank subsidiaries remained ineligible.

The bill also specified that the lending fund be managed by an administrator, rather than an advisory board.

Committee Chairman Donald W. Riegle Jr., D-Mich., succeeded — with the aid of ranking committee Republican Alfonse M. D'Amato of New York — in deflecting more sweeping banking provisions that might have jeopardized the bill's chances of enactment.

For example, Christopher J. Dodd, D-Conn., wanted to include language allowing banks to open branches across state lines. Coupled to that were provisions sought by the insurance industry to scale back the ability of banks to sell insurance. *(Interstate banking, p. 161)*

What the Committee Added

The chief banking measures added to the bill were:

● **Small-business loans.** Language from a bill (S 384) aggressively pushed by D'Amato to relax regulations that he said hindered the formation of a secondary market for small-business loans.

As approved, the provisions made it easier for banks to sell small-business loans to private firms that issued securities backed by the loans. The bill included language — the subject of difficult negotiations between D'Amato and the Treasury Department — to allow banks to hold less in capital reserves on loans that they had sold. Existing law required banks to retain an 8 percent capital reserve on loans they sold, even if they transferred most of the loan risk to the buyer. The bill required banks to hold 8 percent capital only against the portion of the risk they retained, subject to the approval of regulators. *(Loans, p. 160)*

● **Home equity loans.** A provision drawn from a bipartisan bill (S 924) intended to curb abuses by non-bank home equity lenders. The language targeted "high cost mortgages," defined as those with an interest rate 10 percentage points above comparable Treasury notes or upfront fees of either $400 or 8 percent of the loan amount, whichever was greater. The bill made such loans subject to increased disclosure requirements, including a statement to borrowers listing the loan's annual interest rate, the monthly payment and a warning that borrowers could lose their houses should they default. Lenders were required to provide this information three days before settlement on loans, allowing the borrower extra time to back away.

BOXSCORE

➡ **Community Development Banks (HR 3474, S 1275).** Bills to create a $382 million federal fund to provide grants and other assistance to community development banks and other non-traditional lenders. The House bill would use part of the funds to reward traditional lenders that made loans in poor and distressed neighborhoods.

Reports: S Rept 103-169.

KEY ACTION

July 15 — **President** sent Congress his community development bank plan.

Sept. 21 — **Senate** Banking Committee approved S 1275, 18-1.

Nov. 10 — **House** Banking Committee approved HR 3474 by voice vote.

Nov. 21 — **House** approved HR 3474 by voice vote.

The bill banned several practices, including large end-of-loan "balloon payments" and loans in which high interest rates actually resulted in increases in the amount of principal owed. It also barred penalties on early repayment. Borrowers would be entitled to sue lenders that violated the new law.

● **Regulatory burden.** A requirement that the four federal banking regulatory agencies conduct a review of their regulations within two years, with the goal of eliminating outmoded, duplicative and unnecessary regulations. In addition, the agencies were required to coordinate bank examinations; within two years, banks would be examined by a single regulator and no longer would face examinations by more than one agency.

The bill also required the regulators to set up an appeals process for banks to contest decisions made by bank examiners.

Regulatory relief was the banking lobby's top legislative priority for the year. Bankers argued that streamlining the regulations with which they had to comply, especially some established by the 1991 deposit insurance law, would reduce the cost of credit to borrowers. The language in the bill was a fraction of what the banks wanted.

On March 10, Clinton had unveiled a package of regulatory relief initiatives that the administration hoped would eliminate the pressure for congressional action, but many in Congress argued that changes in bank regulations should be enacted into law. *(Text, p. 17-D)*

HOUSE COMMITTEE ACTION

The House Banking Committee approved Clinton's proposal by voice vote on Nov. 10, after giving it a makeover that the previously indifferent banking industry liked. The committee agreed to a change crafted by Floyd H. Flake, D-N.Y., and Tom Ridge, R-Pa., that set aside a third of the money in the bill for use in rewarding commercial banks and thrifts that made loans in distressed communities. The White House objected, but Flake outlobbied Clinton's team and won a 36-14 vote to make the change.

The committee sent the community development plan to the floor attached to a new bill (HR 3474) designed to ease some regulatory mandates on banks.

Committee Chairman Henry B. Gonzalez, D-Texas, had indicated disappointment with the limited scope of Clinton's community development plan, and he moved the bill only after much prodding from the administration. To ease its way, he linked it with the regulatory relief bill and gained Republican support for the combined measure.

The combined bill retained the centerpiece of Clinton's community development bank plan — the new federal fund to provide financial and technical help to banks, loan funds and credit unions that made loans in poor neighborhoods and had community development as their primary mission. Insured institutions such as banks, thrifts and credit unions could receive up to $5 million in assistance;

Hill Looks at Ways To Boost Lending to Small Businesses

With the nation's small businesses complaining that they were being hobbled by a credit crunch, members of Congress looked for ways to boost lending by creating a secondary market in small-business and commercial loans.

A variety of proposals — none approved by Congress in 1993 — sought to encourage lending to small businesses by making it easier for banks to sell their small-business loans at a profit to Wall Street firms or perhaps to a new quasi-government entity. The idea was for the buyer to sell securities backed by the loans to big investors, funneling the money to credit-starved small, medium and large businesses, which played a critical role in creating jobs.

Such proposals spread the risk of making small-business and commercial loans among a wider number of players in the marketplace, including government-chartered corporations, investors and, ultimately, taxpayers.

Options before Congress included:

D'Amato/Dodd. A plan principally backed by Sen. Alfonse M. D'Amato, R-N.Y., to make it easier for private firms to issue securities backed by small-business loans. The provisions, which the Banking Committee appended to the Senate community development bank bill (S 1275), would allow banks to significantly reduce the amount of capital they held on loans that they sold on the secondary market. It also would simplify paperwork requirements, allowing firms to file a single registration form with the Securities and Exchange Commission instead of separate ones with the individual states. Pension funds could purchase such securities, and new, favorable tax rules would encourage pooling of small-business loans.

Velda Sue. A plan to create a new government-sponsored enterprise, the Venture Enhancement and Loan Development Administration for Smaller Undercapitalized Enterprises. The corporation, Velda Sue, could purchase an 80 percent portion of all qualifying small-business loans held by banks.

As a government-chartered corporation, Velda Sue could borrow from the Treasury at below-market rates and would benefit from an implicit guarantee that the federal government would back its obligations if it defaulted. That would make securities sold by Velda Sue a very safe investment and reduce the interest rates that the enterprise would need to offer to attract investors. The leading sponsor was House Small Business Committee Chairman John J. LaFalce, D-N.Y.

Kanjorski: A proposal drafted by Paul E. Kanjorski, D-Pa., which — unlike the others — was not limited to small-business loans. The House Banking Subcommittee on Economic Growth and Credit Formation approved the measure (HR 2600) on Nov. 3. It required the Federal National Mortgage Association and the Federal Home Loan Mortgage Corporation — cash-rich government-sponsored enterprises that financed much of the U.S. housing market — to form subsidiaries to buy and package business and commercial loans of all sizes.

Other government-sponsored enterprises such as Sallie Mae and Farmer Mac would be authorized to set up such subsidiaries, but would not be forced to. And in a twist from both Velda Sue and the D'Amato-Dodd approach, private firms could apply for the special charters.

uninsured loan funds could get up to $2 million.

Money for Traditional Lenders

Before approving the bill, the committee gave a big win to Flake and Ridge, who had been trying for several years to change the way federal law tried to encourage lending in low-income communities. They were supported by Jim Leach of Iowa, the ranking committee Republican.

In 1991, Flake and Ridge won passage of a measure that authorized rebates on deposit-insurance premiums for banks that made loans in poor and distressed neighborhoods. It was enacted as part of a bigger bill overhauling the deposit-insurance system (PL 102-242), but Congress had never appropriated money to implement it. *(1991 Almanac, p. 75)*

The Flake-Ridge amendment required that one-third of whatever amount was appropriated for the community development bank program, up to $127 million, be earmarked for deposit-insurance premium rebates authorized under the 1991 law.

The two congressmen argued that their initiative would prod mainstream banks to lend more money in poor communities than alternative lenders possibly could. "If we're going to use public dollars, let's figure out a way that we can maximize their use to leverage as best possible the amount of private dollars from mainstream institutions," Ridge said.

But opponents of the amendment, including the administration and a coalition of community lenders, argued against diverting any of the limited money authorized in the bill to traditional banks, which were earning record profits. Commercial banks and thrifts were already required under federal law to make loans to underdeveloped communities. "We should not have to pay them to do what they should be doing anyway," said Maxine Waters, D-Calif.

The Regulatory Package

Gonzalez, Leach and others — chiefly Jim Bacchus, D-Fla., Doug Bereuter, R-Neb., and Stephen L. Neal, D-N.C. — negotiated the regulatory relief language in HR 3474, including provisions to ease examination requirements for healthy small banks, lower auditing costs for big banks and require bank regulators to appoint ombudsmen. The negotiators incorporated about 40 provisions drawn from HR 962 — a more ambitious bill that had the backing of the banking industry and was cosponsored by Bacchus, Bereuter and 270 other House members. The results were similar to provisions approved as part of the Senate Banking Committee bill.

A coalition of consumer groups opposed the regulatory package — but to no avail. They particularly disliked a provision to relax "insider lending" restrictions that limited the ability of some banks to make loans to their own officers and directors. Consumer groups argued that such loans had been a major cause of bank and thrift failures.

Unlike the Senate bill, the House measure did not include provisions aimed at promoting a secondary market for small-business loans, although the Economic Growth Subcommittee had approved such a bill (HR 2600). If the small-business provisions had been incorporated, the bill might have been referred to other committees. ■

Interstate Branching Bill Put Off Until '94

Late in the session, the Clinton administration endorsed a hotly contested proposal to give banks authority to create nationwide networks of branch offices. Despite a core of ardent supporters on Capitol Hill, however, neither Congress nor the administration was ready to tackle the issue in 1993.

An attempt by the Senate Banking Committee to mark up an interstate branching bill was blocked by a GOP boycott. In the House, Stephen L. Neal, D-N.C., chairman of the Banking Committee's Financial Institutions Subcommittee, said he would heed the administration's wishes and hold off until 1994.

Almost every state allowed out-of-state holding companies to own separately chartered and capitalized banks within their borders, subject to each state's banking laws. But interstate branching — allowing an out-of-state bank to open a deposit-taking branch without setting up an in-state bank — was essentially prohibited.

"We currently have a de facto system of interstate banking. But it's a patchwork system, and it's clumsy," Treasury Secretary Lloyd Bentsen said Oct. 25 in a speech laying out the administration's banking priorities. "We must change our banking system in a careful, deliberate manner, to get it ready for the next century. We're operating with laws and regulations made for another time in America."

Background

On the surface, interstate branching was a fairly simple concept. But it drew the interest of a variety of groups — big and little banks, consumer advocates, insurance agents and state bank regulators — and there were many layers of disagreement.

Congressional supporters of nationwide branching were quick to point out its potential benefits: increased bank profitability and efficiency, and protection — of both banks and the federal deposit insurance fund — against regional economic downturns.

On the other side, consumer advocates said the proposal would lead to too much consolidation, which could lead to reduced lending and fewer banking services in poor neighborhoods. Small banks feared that huge, nationwide banks would put them out of business.

The Bush administration pushed hard for interstate branching in 1991, and both chambers approved it that year as part of a bill overhauling deposit insurance. But the branching provisions were dropped in conference. *(1991 Almanac, p. 75)*

The most significant obstacle to a free-standing bill was the high-powered insurance agents' lobby, which had linked the fate of interstate branching to its effort to scale back the ability of banks to sell insurance. But if insurance issues were tied to a branching bill — as they were in 1991 — many of the banks themselves would oppose it and the measure almost certainly would bog down.

Meanwhile, banks were moving toward interstate branching with or without congressional action, aggressively using existing provisions of banking law to advance their agenda.

In one high-profile case, North Carolina-based NationsBank Corp. was seeking to merge its Washington, D.C., and Maryland subsidiaries into a single bank by employ-

ing a loophole in the Civil War-era National Bank Act. That law, as amended in 1959, allowed a federally chartered bank to move its headquarters 30 miles, even across state lines. NationsBank wanted to move its Washington subsidiary's main office to the Maryland suburbs. It then would operate the bank's Washington offices as branches of the Maryland-based bank, effectively evading other provisions of law intended to bar interstate branching.

If approved by the Office of the Comptroller of the Currency, the arrangement could have been repeated by other banks that had headquarters near state borders.

The Administration's Proposal

In his Oct. 25 speech, Bentsen backed interstate branching but urged a go-slow approach, asking that Congress first complete work on bills to conclude the savings and loan cleanup (S 714) and to create a system of community development banks (S 1275). The next day, Bentsen's top lieutenants — including Treasury Under Secretary Frank Newman — appeared before the House Banking Subcommittee on Financial Institutions to provide additional details of the administration position.

The Clinton plan contemplated repeal of the Douglas amendment to the 1956 Bank Holding Company Act, thus permitting a banking company to acquire banks anywhere nationwide. Under the law, acquisitions were permitted only where states had enacted reciprocal arrangements permitting them. Under the plan, an acquired bank could be converted to a branch of an out-of-state bank, and the bank could add new branches to the extent allowed under state banking laws. Any state that wanted to block interstate branching could enact a law to do so; in industry parlance, this was known as an "opt-out" approach.

Members of the House subcommittee said they were pleased with the administration's position, which was similar to a bill (HR 2235) sponsored by Bruce F. Vento, D-Minn., and backed by subcommittee Chairman Neal and top panel Republican Bill McCollum of Florida. But they made it clear they were frustrated by the administration's deliberate pace.

Senate Banking Committee Action

The Senate Banking Committee met Nov. 18 to mark up a draft interstate branching bill modeled largely on the provisions that had passed the Senate in 1991. But Republicans boycotted the meeting, and, without a quorum, Chairman Donald W. Riegle Jr., D-Mich., was forced to adjourn the markup.

"I just don't think we're ready to go forward with interstate," said Christopher S. Bond, R-Mo.

Riegle had scheduled the markup to fulfill a promise to committee member Christopher J. Dodd, D-Conn., who hoped to attach an amendment rolling back the power of certain banks to sell insurance. Dodd was eager to reverse existing law, which allowed federally chartered banks based in towns with fewer than 5,000 residents to sell insurance. In 1986, bank regulators interpreted the so-called town-of-5,000 exemption to allow those banks to sell insurance anywhere nationwide. Dodd had the powerful backing of the insurance agents' lobby, and he had rounded up enough votes in the committee to link the amendment to the interstate bill — as he had done in 1991. ∎

Bentsen Outlines Plan for Bank Regulatory Change

Sparking a confrontation with the Federal Reserve, Treasury Secretary Lloyd Bentsen on Nov. 23 unveiled the outlines of an administration plan to overhaul the government's system for regulating the nation's banks and thrifts.

Bentsen proposed the creation of a single Federal Banking Commission that would merge the supervisory functions of four regulatory agencies — the Federal Reserve, the Federal Deposit Insurance Corporation (FDIC), the Office of the Comptroller of the Currency and the Office of Thrift Supervision (OTS). The plan was similar to bills (S 1633, HR 1214) backed by Henry B. Gonzalez, D-Texas, and Donald W. Riegle Jr., D-Mich., the respective chairmen of the House and Senate Banking committees.

Bentsen said the purpose of the plan was to streamline the system and eliminate a "spider's web of overlapping jurisdictions" that required most banks to answer to more than one regulator.

Under the proposal, the FDIC and the Federal Reserve would largely lose their supervisory roles. The FDIC would continue to provide deposit insurance to banks and thrifts, and the Fed would continue to conduct monetary policy. The functions of the Office of the Comptroller of the Currency and the OTS would be melded into the new agency.

The plan immediately attracted opposition from the Fed, which issued a statement saying that keeping a "hands-on role in banking supervision is essential to carrying out the Federal Reserve's responsibilities for the stability of the financial system."

The proposed Banking Commission would be run by a five-person board: three presidentially appointed members, including a chairman whose four-year term would coincide with the president's, plus the secretary of the Treasury and a member of the Federal Reserve Board. ∎

Financial Services Bill Seeks To Open Markets

As the session drew to a close, lawmakers started work on widely backed legislation to pressure foreign governments to open their financial services markets to U.S. firms.

The House Banking Committee's International Finance Subcommittee gave easy voice vote approval to the Fair Trade in Financial Services Act (HR 3248) on Nov. 19. The Senate Banking Committee tried to mark up a virtually identical bill (S 1527) on Nov. 18 but was unable to assemble a quorum due to a GOP boycott over an unrelated bill.

The Senate measure was cosponsored by a bipartisan majority of the Banking Committee, including Chairman Donald W. Riegle Jr., D-Mich., and ranking Republican Alfonse M. D'Amato of New York. The principal House sponsors were Jim Leach of Iowa, the top Republican on the Banking Committee, and senior committee Democrat Charles E. Schumer of New York.

As approved by the House Banking subcommittee, the bill gave the Treasury Department authority to block foreign banks and securities firms from expanding existing operations in the United States or starting new ones if their home countries discriminated against U.S. banks and securities firms.

The measure was aimed principally at Japan, which had imposed a series of legal and informal barriers that prevented U.S. firms from gaining a niche in the lucrative financial services market. At the same time, Japanese banks controlled about 15 percent of U.S. banking assets. Other countries, including Korea, Indonesia, the Philippines, Taiwan and Brazil, also would be affected.

The Clinton administration urged passage of the legislation, hoping it would give the United States additional leverage in the Uruguay Round of global talks aimed at strengthening the General Agreement on Tariffs and Trade. Those negotiations included a financial services component. Under a new provision of the bill added by the Banking subcommittee in consultation with Treasury, sanctions could not be applied to firms from nations that had entered into a binding commitment to provide full access to their market.

The administration, however, wanted Treasury to have the authority to impose the sanctions, rather than banking and security regulators as the bills required.

Versions of the legislation passed both chambers in the 101st and 102nd Congresses as part of unrelated bills to extend the Defense Production Act. But the provisions fell in the face of resistance from the State Department, the Federal Reserve and free-traders in Congress. *(1992 Almanac, p. 131; 1990 Almanac, p. 189)* ∎

New Law Aims To Curb 'Roll-Up' Abuses

Almost three years after first looking into horror stories of investor losses, Congress cleared legislation aimed at curbing abusive limited-partnership "roll-ups." Such deals occurred when limited partnerships were reorganized into publicly traded corporations. The bill, which was attached to an unrelated measure (S 422), codified and went beyond recently issued Securities and Exchange Commission (SEC) rules that required a roll-up prospectus to be written more clearly and eased proxy rules to allow limited partners to communicate with one another to fight a roll-up. President Clinton signed the bill Dec. 17 (PL 103-202).

BACKGROUND

Limited partnerships typically were long-term, non-traded investments that allowed smaller players to invest in industries such as real estate and oil and gas. They were designed to be held for a fixed term and then liquidated. Investors pooled their money under the control of managing or general partners, who were required under the deal to put the entire partnership's interests before their own.

As the real estate and oil and gas industries faltered, many general partners crafted roll-ups combining several partnerships into a single, publicly traded company with the investors getting stock in exchange for their partnership shares. In the process, critics said, the general partners often enriched themselves, while the new stock issued to the limited partners plummeted from its promised value.

But some members of Congress, particularly Sen. Phil Gramm, R-Texas, argued that roll-ups offered a way for limited partners to cut their losses in a failing venture. Without a restructuring, Gramm said, individual investors would have no other way to get out, except to sell their shares to what he called "predator funds," which bought such shares at steep discounts.

More than 1,800 limited partnerships worth more than $7 billion had been restructured since 1985.

Congress first began to look at the issue in 1991, when the House passed a bill to require that roll-up prospectuses be written more clearly, ease proxy rules to allow limited partners to communicate with one another to fight a roll-up, and bar the practice of paying proxy solicitors only for votes in favor of a roll-up. However, Gramm held up action by the Senate Banking Committee, and the bill was not enacted. *(1991 Almanac, p. 113; 1992 Almanac, p. 131)*

Pressed in part by the congressional effort, the SEC and the National Association of Securities Dealers (NASD), a self-regulatory organization that included most of the nation's securities broker-dealers, subsequently instituted many of the reforms on their own.

LEGISLATIVE ACTION

Bill sponsors wanted to codify the SEC and NASD changes and extend them to broker-dealers who were not members of the NASD and were therefore still free to put together abusive deals. In addition, they wanted to offer partners who opposed a roll-up so-called dissenters' rights, or the option to demand alternative compensation such as cash or a bond, instead of the stock issue.

House Action

The House passed HR 617 (H Rept 103-21) on March 2 by a vote of 408-6. The bill was almost identical to the measure the House passed in 1991. *(Vote 47, p. 12-H)*

The Energy and Commerce Committee had approved HR 617 by voice vote Feb. 23; the Telecommunications and Finance Subcommittee had marked up the bill five days earlier, also approving it by voice vote.

As passed by the House, the bill required roll-up sponsors to provide investors with an independent evaluation of the fairness of the proposed deal and to offer them the option of demanding alternative compensation to the stock issue. It also codified SEC rules requiring that a roll-up prospectus be written more clearly and concisely and that proxy rules make it easier for limited partners to communicate with one another to fight a proposed deal.

The bill effectively imposed a moratorium on roll-ups of up to 18 months from the date of enactment while the SEC drew up rules to enforce the measure.

Senate Action

The Senate passed S 424 (S Rept 103-121) by voice vote Aug. 6., after a deal between the main adversaries —

BOXSCORE

➡ **Limited Partnership Roll-Ups (S 422, S 424, HR 617)** The bill was aimed at protecting investors in limited partnerships from abusive restructuring of their holdings.

Reports: S Rept 103-121, H Rept 103-21.

KEY ACTION

March 2 — **House** passed HR 617, 408-6.

Aug. 6 — **Senate** passed S 424 by voice vote.

Nov. 22 — **Senate** passed S 422, amended to include the roll-up compromise, by voice vote.

Nov. 23 — **House** cleared S 422 by voice vote.

Dec. 17 — **President** signed S 422 into law (PL 103-202).

Gramm and Christopher J. Dodd, D-Conn. — broke a two-year logjam that had kept the bill bottled up in committee.

The Senate's bill was similar to the House measure in some respects, but it did not require that investors receive an independent evaluation of the fairness of the roll-up, and it included compromise provisions to make it easier for roll-ups that were not abusive to go forward.

Gramm had adamantly opposed the dissenters' rights provisions, which he said would allow a minority of the limited partners to kill a roll-up by draining resources from the partnership, giving them rights that they would not have had under the original deal.

The Gramm-Dodd compromise exempted certain types of roll-ups from the bill, making it easier for them to go forward. Most significantly, roll-ups that were proposed by an independent third party, were approved by two-thirds of the investors and did not involve special compensation to the general partners were to be exempt. In such cases, no dissenters' rights were required.

The bill also made exceptions for certain roll-ups — typically those involving research partnerships such as biotechnology ventures — in which investors assumed at the outset that the partnership eventually would be restructured. In addition, any roll-up approved by 75 percent of the limited partners was exempt.

"Our job is to take the steps necessary to curb the abusive transactions but to permit the good deals to continue," Dodd said. "Where investor rights are protected, these transactions may go forward."

The Banking Committee approved the compromise between Gramm and Dodd on an 18-0 tally June 29. The Senate bill also explicitly rejected the 18-month moratorium on new roll-ups that the House had approved.

FINAL ACTION

While Gramm allowed the bill to proceed through the Senate, he refused to allow it to go to conference. That tactic strengthened his position, because it meant the House had to pass S 424 if it wanted to see a bill enacted in 1993.

The result was a House-Senate compromise that included key elements of the Dodd-Gramm deal. The Senate incorporated the compromise into an unrelated bill (S 422) aimed at improving oversight of the government securities market, which it passed by voice vote late Nov. 22. The House cleared the measure by voice vote in the early hours of Nov. 23. *(Government securities, p. 163)*

As cleared, the bill:

● **Fairness opinion.** Did not require roll-up sponsors to provide a so-called fairness opinion, as the House bill add, but it contained language aimed at encouraging them to do so. A roll-up sponsor who did not provide such an opinion was required to disclose why. A sponsor who did provide a fairness opinion had to disclose certain information to help investors determine whether the opinion was reliable. For

example, if the preparer of a fairness opinion did not have access to all the relevant books or had a financial stake in the roll-up, that information was to be disclosed.

● **Exemptions.** Included Senate language exempting several types of non-abusive roll-ups from the bill. For example, certain "arms-length" roll-ups that were proposed by third parties, were approved by two-thirds of the investors and did not involve special compensation to general partners were exempt. Also exempted were roll-ups in which investors were offered seasoned securities whose value was easily ascertained. Deals approved by 75 percent supermajorities of the limited partners were also exempted.

● **Dissenters' rights.** Allowed investors opposed to a roll-up to receive dissenters' rights, which could include requiring compensation such as cash or retention of the original security as an alternative to the stock issue.

● **Regulatory changes.** Wrote into law several rules changes already implemented by regulatory bodies, including the SEC and the NASD. These included changing proxy rules to make it easier for investors to communicate with other investors to fight a roll-up and to make it illegal to pay proxy solicitors only for obtaining votes in favor of a roll-up. ■

SEC Oversight Legislation Runs Out of Time

The House and Senate each approved bills to provide additional resources for the Securities and Exchange Commission (SEC) for use in improving the agency's oversight of the financial planning industry. The Senate action came at the end of the session, and there was no time to resolve differences between the two measures before adjournment.

Both bills provided for an increase in SEC registration fees collected from the nation's 18,400 investment advisers, with the money to be used to hire additional SEC enforcement staff. Under existing law, financial planners paid a one-time $150 fee when registering with the SEC; the bills raised that to annual fees of $300 to $7,000, depending on the value of assets managed by an adviser.

But the House measure (HR 578 — H Rept 103-75) also included new rules for the industry. As passed, the bill required financial planners to reveal their qualifications to their clients, disclose how much they charged in fees and periodically provide reports that summarized all charges incurred by a customer. It required advisers to take into account a client's financial position and recommend only investments that were "suitable," given the client's investment needs. The financial planner had to keep records of how such a determination was reached. The bill also required the SEC to set up a toll-free telephone service for investors to find out whether the agency had taken disciplinary action against their financial planners.

By contrast, the narrower Senate bill (S 423 — S Rept 103-177) included none of the new regulatory language, other than requiring that investment advisers purchase fidelity bonds.

Background

The legislation came in response to revelations of fraud in the industry, including a case in which a California-based adviser was found guilty of bilking clients, about a

dozen California city governments among them, of $174 million.

Unlike stock exchanges and securities firms, which had self-regulatory organizations to police their industries, investment advisers reported only to the SEC.

But the financial planning industry had grown rapidly, and the SEC did not have the resources to adequately enforce industry regulations. The number of investment advisers registered with the government had more than tripled in the past decade, and the value of assets under their management had risen by about 1,700 percent to $8 trillion over the same period. Yet the SEC had fewer than 50 inspectors to oversee the booming industry.

Both chambers passed bills to increase SEC scrutiny of the industry in 1992, but, as in 1993, the Senate bill was significantly narrower. In the short time that remained at the end of the 1992 session, the House and Senate were unable to reconcile differences between the two measures. One of the main reasons was the fact that the House had tacked on a bill (HR 4313) that would have required corporate accountants to report to the SEC when they detected fraud in the course of audits. (1992 Almanac, p. 126)

House Action

The House Energy and Commerce Telecommunications and Finance Subcommittee approved the bill by voice vote April 1, after amending it to give the SEC more latitude to determine what information advisers had to report.

The full Energy and Commerce Committee gave voice vote approval April 20 to the bill, which was a high priority for Chairman John D. Dingell, D-Mich.

"There are a tremendous number of incompetents, rogues, fools, knaves, scoundrels and opportunists entering this business," said Dingell.

The House approved the bill by voice vote on May 4.

Senate Action

The Senate Banking Committee approved S 423 by voice vote Oct. 19. The bill, introduced by Christopher J. Dodd, D-Conn., was identical to the version the Senate had passed in August 1992.

The Senate approved the bill by voice vote on Nov. 20. ■

Bill Tightens Regulation of Government Bond Market

Congress cleared a bill to strengthen regulation of the nation's $2.8 trillion market in government securities after the Clinton administration and key House members reached a compromise that ended a fight among the Treasury Department, the Securities and Exchange Commission (SEC) and several House committees over how much new authority to give the SEC.

The bill (S 422) permanently extended the 1986 Government Securities Act, which gave Treasury the authority to issue rules on government bond auctions and the capital levels of bond traders.

In addition, it gave the SEC access to the transaction records of securities dealers to make it easier for the agency to investigate allegations of illegal trading activity. But it did not give the SEC rule-making authority over banks. The bill also authorized the Treasury to require that deal-

ers with large holdings of federal debt report such positions in an effort to improve oversight of the market.

House-Senate staff negotiations produced the final compromise in the weeks leading up to adjournment, and the bill came to the House and Senate floors coupled with a measure aimed at curbing abusive limited partnership "roll-ups," which often occurred when limited partnerships were reorganized into publicly traded corporations. The Senate approved the bill Nov. 22; the House cleared it Nov. 23. President Clinton signed the measure into law Dec. 17 (PL 103-202).

BACKGROUND

The 1986 Government Securities Act, which expired Oct. 1, 1991, had been on its way to routine reauthorization when the loosely regulated market in government securities was hit that year by revelations of a bid-rigging scandal involving Salomon Brothers Inc. The Wall Street firm, which at the time was the largest of about 40 so-called primary dealers in government bonds, admitted to disguising purchases of larger-than-permitted stakes at auctions. Primary dealers, an elite group of firms, purchased government securities directly from the Federal Reserve Bank of New York, which acted as the government's agent in federal bond sales, and resold them to investors.

After the Salomon scandal broke, the Treasury Department took steps to open the primary market to more participants and limit the potential for abuses. But the affair also led to an ambitious effort — headed by House Energy and Commerce Committee Chairman John D. Dingell, D-Mich., and Telecommunications and Finance Subcommittee Chairman Edward J. Markey, D-Mass. — to expand the authority of the Securities and Exchange Commission (SEC) over the secondary market, where the securities were sold to investors.

The committee reported a bill (HR 3927) in 1992 that would have given the SEC new authority to collect information on government securities dealers and brokers and to step in if it believed that price information in the resale market for bonds was not complete or widely distributed. Because commercial banks were the biggest dealers in government bonds, the Banking Committee asserted its jurisdiction and wrote a version of the bill giving such regulatory authority to the bank regulators.

The fight spilled onto the House floor, where Dingell attempted to pass the bill without the Banking Committee's contribution. Furious, Banking Committee Chairman Henry B. Gonzalez, D-Texas, called the move "nothing more than another insatiable grab for jurisdiction by this power-hungry, insatiable committee known as the Energy and Commerce Committee." The Treasury and Federal Reserve also opposed the bill. Members rejected the measure by a vote of 124-279. *(1992 Almanac, p. 122)*

The Senate had passed a much narrower, administra-

BOXSCORE

➡ **Government Securities Act (S 422, HR 618).** The bill renewed and broadened regulation of the market in federal government bonds.

Reports: S Rept 103-109, H Rept 103-255.

KEY ACTION

May 27 — **Senate** Banking Committee approved S 422, 19-0.

July 29 — **Senate** approved S 422 by voice vote.

Sept. 14 — **House** Energy and Commerce Committee approved HR 618 by voice vote.

Oct. 5 — **House** approved HR 618 by voice vote; it then passed S 422 after substituting the language of HR 618.

Nov. 22 — **Senate** approved a revised S 422 by voice vote.

Nov. 23 — **House** cleared the bill by voice vote.

Dec. 17 — **President** signed the bill into law (PL 103-202).

---

tion-backed version of the bill in 1991. But the standoff in the House marked the end of work on the issue in the 102nd Congress. *(1991 Almanac, p. 114)*

SENATE ACTION

The Senate gave voice vote approval July 29 to a bill (S 422 — S Rept 103-109) that was identical to the measure that passed the Senate in 1991. The Banking Committee had approved the bill by a vote of 19-0 on May 27.

As passed by the Senate, the bill, sponsored by Christopher J. Dodd, D-Conn., permanently extended the Treasury Department's regulatory authority over the market. It also required federal banking regulators to develop and implement sales practice rules for banks that dealt in government securities; it required the National Association of Securities Dealers (NASD) to write the rules for securities brokers, subject to approval by the SEC.

In addition, the bill clarified that it was illegal under federal securities law to make false or misleading statements regarding government securities offerings.

And it required the Treasury, the SEC and the Federal Reserve to study the effectiveness of private sector efforts to disseminate price and volume information on government securities.

The Senate bill was silent on the issue of expanding SEC regulation of the secondary bond market.

HOUSE COMMITTEE ACTION

Without debate, the House Energy and Commerce Subcommittee on Telecommunications and Finance gave voice vote approval July 22 to a bill (HR 618) identical to the one the full committee had reported in 1992. At the time, subcommittee Chairman Markey was negotiating with the Treasury Department and the SEC to craft a new, compromise bill, which he said he hoped would be ready by the time the full committee acted.

Full Committee Endorses Compromise

The House Energy and Commerce Committee easily backed a revised version of the bill Sept. 14, approving it on a bipartisan voice vote (H Rept 103-255).

The bill was the outcome of a deal announced in early August between Treasury, the SEC and bipartisan leaders of the committee. The agreement gave bank regulators authority over banks that marketed securities; the SEC retained authority over broker-dealers. A key part of the compromise was the elimination of a provision authorizing the SEC to require securities dealers to make transactions records available electronically to the agency.

Sponsors insisted that the bill would not impose overly burdensome regulations that could impede the smooth financing of the federal debt. "The purpose of the govern-

ment securities market is to finance the national debt at the lowest possible cost to all the taxpayers," said Jack Fields of Texas, ranking Republican on the Telecommunications and Finance Subcommittee. "Any changes imposed upon this critical market must be managed with utmost care and understanding. In this legislation we have accomplished that goal."

Bill Highlights

The key provisions of the committee-approved bill:

● Permanently extended Treasury's regulatory authority over capital and recordkeeping requirements for dealers of government securities.

● Authorized the SEC to demand the records of securities brokers to make it easier for the agency to reconstruct trades when conducting an investigation. But the SEC was not given rule-making authority over commercial banks.

● Authorized the Treasury Department to require banks, Wall Street firms and others with large positions in government securities to report their holdings to the Federal Reserve Bank of New York to make it easier for regulators to monitor the market. The information would have to be provided to the SEC.

● Required securities brokers and dealers to establish internal policies to prevent and detect fraud and market manipulation by their employees, subject to oversight by Treasury and the SEC.

● Authorized the appropriate regulatory agency to write rules governing sales practices for financial institutions that dealt in government securities, and authorized the NASD to regulate its members' transactions in government securities.

The compromise paved the way for the bill to head to the House floor; the Banking Committee did not ask for a sequential referral as it had in 1992.

HOUSE FLOOR ACTION

With the backing of the Energy and Commerce, Banking, and Ways and Means committees, the scaled-back bill (HR 618) won easy voice vote approval from the floor Oct. 5.

The House then took up the narrower Senate-passed bill (S 422), substituted the language of HR 618 and passed it as well.

A few changes were made to the bill between the time it left the Energy and Commerce Committee and when it reached the floor. The additions — provisions from the Banking and the Ways and Means committees — were incorporated into the bill through a chairman's amendment not subject to a separate floor vote.

The Banking Committee, which had jurisdiction over the primary market for government bonds, added provisions barring special treatment for primary dealers, such as being able to submit bids for customers and being exempt from deposit requirements.

Such practices, which gave primary dealers a competitive advantage over other firms that wished to participate in the primary market, were barred under new Treasury rules that took effect in March 1993.

To further help smaller bidders, the bill incorporated another Banking provision allowing anyone who met a minimum creditworthiness standard to bid in Treasury's newly automated auction system by the end of 1995.

The Ways and Means Committee contributed provisions that required Treasury to make an annual report to Ways and Means and to the Senate Finance Committee on

public debt-related activities. It also required Treasury to report to Congress on its reforms to the auction process.

FINAL ACTION

The House and Senate worked out their differences without holding a conference on the bill. The Senate approved the measure by voice vote late Nov. 22, after amending the House-passed version to reflect House-Senate agreements on it and on the bill regulating limited-partnership roll-ups. The House cleared S 422 by voice vote in the early hours of Nov. 23.

The cleared bill stuck closely to the compromise approved by the House, with mostly small changes.

Major provisions of the bill, as cleared:

● Permanently reauthorized the Government Securities Act.

● Gave the SEC access to the transaction records of securities dealers to make it easier for the agency to investigate allegations of illegal trading activity.

● Gave Treasury the authority to require dealers with large holdings of federal debt to report such positions to the Federal Reserve Bank of New York.

The final bill included the language authorizing banking regulators and the NASD to write rules to prevent fraud and manipulation in government securities sales and to promote fair trading practices. It also included the Banking and Ways and Means provisions. ■

House Panels Move Rival Anti-Redlining Bills

Two rival House committees approved separate versions of controversial legislation to combat insurance "redlining" — the practice of refusing to sell insurance to individuals and businesses in inner-city and poor areas. There was no companion Senate bill in 1993.

The bills (HR 1188, HR 1257) moved forward despite opposition from the powerful insurance industry, propelled by a turf battle between the panels — the Energy and Commerce Committee and Banking. At the end of the session, Energy and Commerce appeared to have gained the upper hand.

Both committee bills required property and casualty insurance companies to report data on where they sold insurance. Bill supporters said the information would help determine the extent of redlining and pressure insurance companies to curb the practice.

But the bills differed significantly in scope. The Energy and Commerce version required insurance companies to supply data by ZIP codes for 25 metropolitan areas. It was set to expire after five years.

The Banking bill was much more strict, requiring the industry to supply data by census tracts, which were typically smaller than ZIP codes and promised to yield more precise comparisons with data on family income and other economic measures. The bill applied to 150 metropolitan areas and 50 rural areas, and it made the reporting requirement permanent.

Consumer groups strongly preferred the Banking version, but it drew powerful industry opposition.

Energy and Commerce gave enforcement responsibility

to the Commerce Department, over which the panel had jurisdiction. The Banking Committee preferred to give the job to the Department of Housing and Urban Development, over which it had jurisdiction.

BACKGROUND

Redlining generally occurred when property and casualty insurance companies refused to sell policies in poor black and Hispanic inner-city neighborhoods. Sponsors said difficulty in getting reasonably priced insurance was a severe economic impediment in such neighborhoods.

The legislation was patterned after the Home Mortgage Disclosure Act, a 1975 anti-redlining law that required mortgage lenders to provide data about loan applicants and recipients. That law had proved effective in documenting patterns of lending discrimination and spurring federal banking regulators to crack down.

Consumer groups and grass-roots community organizations, such as Consumers Union and the Association of Community Organizations for Reform Now (ACORN), were leading the fight for anti-redlining legislation. ACORN had released a study earlier in the year on redlining in 13 cities; it found that insurance companies were five times more likely to refuse quotes on policies to residents of low-income neighborhoods than to those from high-income areas.

"The significance of insurance in our society cannot be overstated," said House Banking Committee Chairman Henry B. Gonzalez, D-Texas. "Without insurance, you can't own a home or car. You can't start a business. Individuals and entire communities suffer."

Republicans generally opposed both bills and were vehemently against the Banking Committee version. They said the legislation would impose significant new costs on the industry that would be passed on to consumers. Some Republicans said they remained unconvinced that the problem was severe enough to warrant federal action.

The Banking Committee bill was opposed by the insurance industry and endorsed by consumer and community groups. The Energy and Commerce bill was grudgingly accepted by parts of the industry as the lesser evil, while consumer groups said it had been gutted to make it acceptable to the industry.

HOUSE SUBCOMMITTEES

The Energy and Commerce Subcommittee on Commerce, Consumer Protection and Competitiveness approved HR 1188 by voice vote July 28. But subcommittee Chairwoman Cardiss Collins, D-Ill., had to make significant concessions to the insurance industry.

Before the scheduled morning markup, Collins circulated a version that required companies to disclose how many policies they sold and the number of agents in each city. The information was to be broken down by census tract and was required of the 150 largest cities. The bill also required companies to reveal how much they paid in

---

BOXSCORE

➡ **Insurance Redlining (HR 1188, HR 1257).** The rival bills sought to combat discrimination in the sale of insurance, but they differed significantly in scope.

Reports: H Rept 103-270, H Rept 103-302, Pts I, II.

KEY ACTION

Sept. 14 — **House** Energy and Commerce Committee gave voice vote approval to HR 1188.

Sept. 22 — **House** Banking Committee approved HR 1257, 30-19.

Oct. 26 — **House** Energy and Commerce approved its version of HR 1257 by voice vote.

---

claims to specific neighborhoods, information that would allow analysts to determine whether higher premiums in inner-city neighborhoods were merited.

But two of Collins' Democratic colleagues — Jim Slattery of Kansas and J. Roy Rowland of Georgia — signaled their intention to join Republicans in supporting an industry-backed amendment making several substantial changes to the bill. By the time the subcommittee reconvened that afternoon, Collins had agreed to accept the changes, which were then offered by Slattery and adopted by voice vote.

The amendment significantly scaled back the bill's data-reporting requirements. Companies were required to report information by ZIP code. Insurance companies claimed it would be too expensive to collect the data by census tract; consumer activists countered that information provided by ZIP code would be too broad to pinpoint redlining.

The Slattery amendment also reduced the bill's scope to the nation's 25 largest metropolitan areas. The amendment removed reporting requirements for commercial insurance and provided that the law would expire after five years.

Banking Subcommittee Weighs In

The following day, the Banking Subcommittee on Consumer Credit and Insurance approved HR 1257, a bill that was considerably tougher on the insurance industry. The party-line vote July 29 was 19-21, with Bernard Sanders, I-Vt., siding with the Democrats.

"It is based on a very simple premise," said subcommittee Chairman Joseph P. Kennedy II, D-Mass. "Sunlight is the best cleanser. Those insurers who have nothing to hide will have nothing to fear."

Kennedy, whose subcommittee was filled with liberal urban Democrats who represented many of the areas in which redlining was a big concern, had no trouble staving off some of the same industry-backed amendments that the Energy subcommittee had adopted.

Ranking subcommittee Republican Al McCandless of California offered an amendment to have the data collected by ZIP code but withdrew it in the face of certain defeat. Michael N. Castle, R-Del., offered and withdrew an amendment to cut the number of cities covered from 150 to 25.

The subcommittee adopted 10 Democratic amendments, including one by Cleo Fields, La., restoring language requiring insurance companies to tell rejected applicants why they were denied insurance. The subcommittee approved the amendment 15-14, with Spencer Bachus, Ala., casting the deciding — and sole Republican — vote in favor of the amendment.

Kennedy's bill, backed by Chairman Gonzalez, extended the reporting requirement to commercial and small-business insurance.

HOUSE COMMITTEES

In a race to get its bill to the House floor first, the Energy and Commerce Committee gave voice vote approval to HR 1188 on Sept. 14 (H Rept 103-270).

Although Republicans disliked both bills, some committee members said the Energy and Commerce revisions made the bill acceptable. "Because there is a much more onerous redlining bill riding its way through the Banking Committee, I intend to support the bill before the committee today," said Alex McMillan, N.C.

"While it would be easy to oppose HR 1188, I would rather be in the game on the playing field rather than sitting on the sidelines while the Banking Committee parades the bill before the full House."

As approved by the committee, HR 1188:

● Required larger insurance companies to report annually to the Commerce Department on their sales of automobile and property insurance, broken down by ZIP code, in the nation's 25 largest metropolitan areas. Companies also would have to report the number of agents serving an area and the number of policy cancellations and non-renewals.

● Required Commerce to study whether the reporting requirements should be extended to commercial and small-business insurance.

● Expired after five years, though the secretary of Commerce could extend the law for two more years.

Banking Approves Its Bill

Bolstered by what it regarded as backing from the Clinton administration, the House Banking Committee on Sept. 22 approved HR 1257 on a party-line 30-19 vote (H Rept 103-302, Part 1).

The administration gave a boost to the Banking Committee bill when the Office of Management and Budget (OMB) sent a letter Sept. 20 to both committees endorsing several elements of the Banking version. The administration embraced the provisions requiring that insurance companies report policy data by census tracts rather than ZIP codes. In addition, it endorsed requiring insurance companies to disclose how much they paid in claims.

"The administration believes that insurance redlining is an important issue that deserves immediate attention and welcomes your committee's action on this matter," said the letter, signed by Associate OMB Director Christopher Edley Jr.

"I think it's enormously helpful to have the White House coming out and indicating the stipulations in the bill that they required ... that happen to be contained in this version and are not contained in the Energy and Commerce version," Kennedy said later.

Energy and Commerce Chairman John D. Dingell, D-Mich., was not pleased. He immediately asked for an audience with House Speaker Thomas S. Foley, D-Wash., and called up OMB Director Leon E. Panetta to complain that the administration was taking sides in the jurisdictional fight.

Committee Democrats' unanimous support of the bill belied significant misgivings by moderate members. Several were concerned that the legislation went too far and would impose too great a cost on the industry.

To shore up support, Kennedy and Gonzalez crafted an amendment that scaled back some of the bill's burdens. The amendment, adopted by voice vote, delayed implementation to give insurance companies at least three years to prepare for reporting information by census tract. In addition, it changed the claims data requirement to mask the information so that it could not be traced to individual insurance companies. Insurance companies argued that such information would reveal trade secrets and undermine competition.

Finally, the amendment pared significantly a provision requiring that data be collected on commercial insurance for small businesses. In the original draft, small-business insurance data would have been collected just as it would for individuals. The amendment substituted a study conducted in the nation's 25 largest cities of a sample group of insurance companies.

Bill Orton, D-Utah, was prepared to offer several amendments — similar to language in the Energy and Commerce bill — to further cut the reporting requirements. But Orton had to leave the markup for another meeting and missed the chance to offer his amendments.

The Banking Committee bill also included a provision aimed at solving problems associated with foreign insurance companies that wrote policies and collected premiums in the United States but did not live up to their obligations when claims were made. This problem had been particularly acute in the area affected by the 1992 Los Angeles riots, where only about $700 million of approximately $2 billion in insured losses had been paid.

The provision, which was not included in the Energy and Commerce bill, required foreign insurance companies wishing to issue policies in the United States to be certified by the Treasury Department. To receive such a certification the company had to have a minimum net worth of $15 million and maintain a U.S.-based trust fund to ensure that claims were paid.

Before approving the bill, the committee rejected, 18-30, a substitute by ranking committee Republican Jim Leach of Iowa and freshman Rick A. Lazio, R-N.Y. The GOP substitute essentially mirrored provisions in the Energy and Commerce bill.

Energy and Commerce Gets an Edge

The Energy and Commerce Committee appeared to gain the upper hand when the House parliamentarian agreed to give the panel a chance to rewrite the Banking Committee bill. Each committee had asked to have the other's bill sequentially referred to it, but the parliamentarian denied Banking's request.

Energy and Commerce gave voice vote approval Oct. 26 to its version of the Banking bill (HR 1257 — H Rept 103-302, Part 2). Before approving the bill, the panel amended it to make it identical to its own bill (HR 1188).

Turf-conscious Energy and Commerce Chairman Dingell had long maintained that his committee had primary jurisdiction over insurance issues, and the parliamentarian's ruling appeared to back him up. Even supporters of the Banking Committee bill acknowledged that the ruling meant that the Energy and Commerce bill — either HR 1188 or its version of HR 1257 — would be the "base text" for floor consideration. Foley promised Kennedy an opportunity to offer his bill or parts of it as amendments, but Kennedy was expected to face an uphill battle on the floor, with the industry offering stiff opposition and the Republicans nearly unanimously opposed.

The rivalry between the two committees put the Clinton administration in an awkward spot. On the day Energy and Commerce acted on HR 1257, Dingell released a letter from top White House congressional lobbyist Howard G. Paster saying the administration would not take sides in the jurisdictional fight. "We are happy to support HR 1188 and other constructive legislation to begin to combat insurance redlining," Paster's letter said.

Dingell received the letter almost three weeks after OMB Director Panetta declined Dingell's request that he rebuff the Edley letter. ■

Credit Report Correction Effort Put on Hold

Members of the House and Senate Banking committees began work on bills to protect consumers from errors in privately compiled credit reports. But the legislation (S 783, HR 1015) did not get to the floor in either chamber, and the real battles were put off until 1994. Fights were anticipated over whether new federal standards on credit reporting should pre-empt tougher state laws, whether credit bureaus would be required to provide consumers with free copies of their reports, and whether consumers should be allowed to sue creditors who supplied inaccurate information.

BACKGROUND

Beefing up the Fair Credit Reporting Act, the law that regulated the credit reporting industry, was a high priority for consumer groups, which said that inaccurate information in credit reports had caused millions of consumers to be turned down for loans, credit cards or jobs.

Since the law was enacted in 1970, the credit reporting industry had grown enormously, and technology made electronic transfers of consumers' credit information a simple matter. The industry's growth was accompanied by horror stories of consumers who learned belatedly of serious errors in their credit reports and had great difficulties in correcting them.

In one widely publicized case, 1,500 residents of Norwich, Vt., were mistakenly labeled as tax deadbeats by TRW Inc., one of the nation's "big three" credit bureaus. According to a U.S. Public Interest Research Group study, one of every five complaints to the Federal Trade Commission was against credit bureaus.

A dispute over pre-empting state laws killed an earlier version of the bill in 1992.

The House Banking Committee approved a credit reporting bill that year, which included pre-emption language that had been added over the objections of the bill's sponsors, Banking Committee Chairman Henry B. Gonzalez, D-Texas, and Esteban E. Torres, D-Calif. When the sponsors failed to strip out the provision on the floor, they killed the bill. The Senate committee did not act on the issue in 1992, primarily because members could not resolve their differences over the pre-emption language. *(1992 Almanac, p. 130)*

SENATE COMMITTEE

In drafting the Senate bill (S 783), sponsors Richard H. Bryan, D-Nev., and Christopher S. Bond, R-Mo., agreed to demands by consumer groups to drop the pre-emption provision. In exchange, they also eliminated language to mandate free reports for consumers, a provision that credit bureaus strongly opposed.

The Senate Banking Committee approved the bill (S Rept 103-209) by a 15-4 vote Oct. 28, with conservative Republicans casting the "nays."

The committee bill contained provisions to make it easier

BOXSCORE

➡ **Fair Credit Reporting (S 783, HR 1015).** The bills sought to give consumers greater protection from errors in their privately compiled credit reports.

KEY ACTION

Oct. 28 — **Senate** Banking Committee approved S 783, 15-4.

Nov. 19 — **House** Banking Subcommittee on Consumer Credit approved HR 1015, 17-12.

---

for consumers to correct errors in their credit reports and to require credit agencies to maintain toll-free telephone numbers for consumers to use to challenge erroneous reports.

It sought to place banks, retailers and other creditors under the law for the first time. It required businesses that supplied information to credit bureaus to clean up their files so that erroneous information was not repeatedly inserted into credit reports. That provision, in particular, generated resistance from banking and business lobbying groups. Conservatives on the committee said the bill would impose yet another layer of federal regulation on the private sector.

Before approving the bill, the committee adopted by voice vote a further compromise drafted by the sponsors. The amendment allowed consumers to demand a free credit report every two years. It also pre-empted stricter state credit reporting laws in some limited cases.

States could not require credit bureaus to provide information to consumers beyond that required under S 783. That included information provided consumers regarding their rights, as well as the form of notices that had to be sent to consumers denied a loan on the basis of a credit report.

The compromise also significantly scaled back restrictions on companies that offered credit based on pre-screened mailing lists derived from credit information. Under existing law, such solicitations had to include "firm offers" of credit that could be revoked only under narrow circumstances. The amended bill allowed the withdrawal of such offers if the consumer's application did not meet the lender's established credit standards. This provision, too, pre-empted stiffer state laws.

HOUSE SUBCOMMITTEE

The House Banking Subcommittee on Consumer Credit gave party-line approval to a companion bill (HR 1015) on Nov. 19. The bill, which included no pre-emption language, passed by a vote of 17-12.

The measure sought to make it easier for consumers to dispute errors in their credit reports and have them corrected. It required credit bureaus to provide free reports on request and blocked employers from obtaining a worker's credit report without his or her permission. And it allowed consumers to sue banks, retailers and other creditors that negligently provided inaccurate information to credit bureaus.

Larry LaRocco, D-Idaho, had been prepared to offer the significantly narrower Senate version of the bill (S 783) as a substitute amendment. He said that while the Senate bill was not perfect, it had a chance of becoming law. LaRocco's initiative, which reportedly was within one vote of prevailing, got the attention of subcommittee Chairman Joseph P. Kennedy II, D-Mass., who agreed to draw up an amendment that made several generally modest changes to the bill. The amendment was approved by voice vote.

The most significant change concerned curbs on the use of credit report data by direct marketers. As drafted, the

bill would have allowed marketers limited use of such information, but only if the consumer explicitly agreed. As amended, the measure required consumers to "opt out" if they did not want to be solicited. The information available to marketers was to be limited to name, address, telephone number and type of credit cards possessed by a consumer.

Ranking committee Republican Al McCandless of California offered a substitute amendment identical to the 1992 Banking Committee bill. The substitute, which included a pre-emption provision and did not require free reports, failed by voice vote. ■

Bill Tells Accountants To Report Fraud

The House Energy and Commerce Committee gave voice vote approval April 27 to a bill (HR 574) requiring independent accountants to blow the whistle when they detected fraud in the course of examining a corporation's books. The Telecommunications and Finance Subcommittee had endorsed the measure by voice vote March 18.

Floor action in the House was held up pending negotiations with the Banking Committee, which was uneasy with the bill because it required that audits of publicly held banks be reported to the Securities and Exchange Commission (SEC) instead of to bank regulators. The Senate did not act on the legislation in 1993.

The bill sought to codify and go beyond existing standards in the accounting profession. It required an accountant who uncovered fraud to report it immediately to company management and, if management did nothing, report the criminal activity to the SEC.

"What is really important about this legislation is that for the first time, auditors would have to report directly to the SEC specifically and quickly when there are major uncorrected frauds at a firm," said bill sponsor Ron Wyden, D-Ore.

Under the existing system, an accountant who discovered fraud reported it to management. If management did not correct the problem, the accountant was supposed to resign. When an auditor quit, the company was required by law to tell the SEC why, but auditors and corporations sometimes skirted the truth when filing such reports. The accountants themselves were not legally required to come out and tell regulators.

The bill required a more substantive explanation of the reasons why an auditor resigned. It also codified existing industry standards that required accountants to conduct audits that "reasonably assured" that they would find fraud if it occurred.

Congress had considered similar bills in the past, but the provisions never made it into law. Versions were tacked on to the 1990 crime bill and the Energy and Commerce version of the 1991 bank overhaul bill. The bill passed the House in 1992 as part of a measure to beef up federal regulation of the financial planning industry, but that measure did not clear. *(1990 Almanac, p. 486; 1991 Almanac, p. 75; 1992 Almanac, p. 130)*

The accounting industry did not oppose the bill; like most finance-related bills emanating from the Energy and Commerce Committee, the measure had been carefully massaged through extensive negotiations and had bipartisan support. ■

Banking, Securities Bills

Congress worked on several relatively small securities and banking bills in 1993.

LIFTING STOCKBROKER LAW

The Senate on July 29 cleared a non-controversial bill (HR 616 — H Rept 103-76) allowing money managers to use stockbrokers with whom they were affiliated to execute trades. The House Energy and Commerce Committee had approved the bill on April 20. The full House followed suit on May 4. President Clinton signed it on Aug. 11 (PL 103-68).

The measure eliminated a 1975 provision of securities law that required the use of independent brokers. That provision was designed to prevent possible conflicts of interest in which a money manager might be tempted to "churn" accounts for brokerage commissions. But bill sponsors said that changes in the market, including the elimination of fixed commission rates and expanded access to exchange membership, substantially eliminated the need for the provision.

The bill protected investors by requiring prior customer authorization before an affiliated broker was used and requiring full disclosure of the fees paid to such brokers.

The securities industry eagerly sought the bill, saying it would save money and improve the execution of trades for managed accounts such as those for pension funds, insurance companies and other institutions.

Supporters hoped the measure would reduce the incentive to execute transactions in the over-the-counter markets or in foreign securities markets instead of on national exchanges such as the New York Stock Exchange merely to avoid the additional costs of an independent broker.

SEC AUTHORIZATION

The House on July 20 gave voice vote approval to a bill (HR 2239) aimed at substantially boosting the budget of the Securities and Exchange Commission (SEC) and making it a self-funding agency. The Senate did not take the measure up in the first session.

The bill authorized $282 million for the SEC in fiscal 1994 and $318 million in fiscal 1995; the commission's fiscal 1993 budget was about $255 million.

The SEC took in much more than that, however. In fiscal 1993, it expected to receive $440 million from user fees — mostly from registering securities. The fees were deposited into the Treasury as general revenues, and appropriators did not take them into account when they decided what to provide each year for the commission. The bill provided for SEC fees to be adjusted annually so that the revenue would offset the agency's budget. The aim was to make the SEC a self-funding agency with the resources necessary to manage a burgeoning workload that had resulted from the expansion of the securities markets over the previous decade.

The House Energy and Commerce committee approved the bill by voice vote June 29 (H Rept 103-179).

CURBING CFTC EXEMPTIONS

The House Agriculture Subcommittee on the Environment, Credit and Rural Affairs marked up a bill (HR 2374) aimed at preventing the Commodity Futures Trading Commission (CFTC) from exempting certain exotic futures con-

tracts from anti-fraud and price-fixing regulations. But the legislation did not move any further in the first session.

The bill, which the subcommittee approved by voice vote June 30, required that all contracts regulated by the CFTC comply with anti-fraud and price-manipulation provisions in the Commodities Exchange Act, which governed futures trading. The CFTC had waived the regulations for some energy contracts and some hybrid futures contracts.

In reauthorizing the CFTC in 1992, Congress gave the agency authority to exempt instruments known as swaps and hybrids from the Commodities Exchange Act, but subcommittee Chairman Glenn English, D-Okla., said at the time that the authority was "to be used sparingly." English said June 30 that lawmakers had had no intention of exempting the instruments from fraud and price manipulation rules. *(1992 Almanac, p. 127)*

MINORITY-OWNED BANKS

The Senate on Nov. 19 passed a bill (S 1685) to allow the Energy Department to continue a program under which department funds were deposited in minority-owned banks. The house did not act on the bill.

Since 1980, the department had made such deposits from its Petroleum Pricing Violation Escrow Fund. But a 1991 banking law (PL 102-242) limited a customer's deposit insurance to $100,000 at any individual bank, which could have forced the department to withdraw monies over that amount from its accounts at minority-owned banks.

S 1685, sponsored by Sen. Carol Moseley-Braun, D-Ill., sought to allow the department to continue making such large deposits.

The bill also contained a section, drafted by Pete V. Domenici, R-N.M., to authorize sewer and water projects for minority communities with "special needs." Money for these projects was provided by the fiscal 1994 VA-HUD appropriations bill (PL 103-124) but only if Congress authorized the money before May 31, 1994. Domenici, who was seeking funds for a sewer and water project in a poor community of Bernalillo County, N.M., included identical language in a housing and community development bill (S 1299), also passed by the Senate on Nov. 19. ∎

Congress OKs North American Trade Pact

At 10:26 p.m. on Nov. 17, 1993, the House of Representatives cast a vote that seemed destined to be long remembered, as much for its political impact as for its effect on U.S. trade policy.

By a comfortable 234-200, the House passed a bill (HR 3450) to approve and implement the North American Free Trade Agreement (NAFTA). The 234-vote majority was well in excess of the 218 required for passage and provided a margin of victory that had appeared unattainable only a week or so before. For months leading up to the House vote, many supporters and opponents thought the pact was in peril.

Three days after the House vote, the Senate provided an anticlimactic finish to the battle, easily passing HR 3450 by a vote of 61-38. NAFTA had always enjoyed stronger support in the Senate than in the sharply divided House, and Senate approval was widely expected. President Clinton signed the bill Dec. 8 (PL 103-182), allowing the historic trade pact to take effect — as planned — Jan. 1, 1994.

The tripartite trade agreement provided for eliminating all tariffs between the United States and Mexico over 15 years and for dropping most other trade barriers. The bill made numerous changes in U.S. law to conform with the trade pact, which President George Bush had signed in December 1992. The law did not, however, include the full text of the agreement.

The bill also made some changes to the U.S.-Canada Free Trade Agreement, approved by Congress in 1988 (PL 100-449), and extended the principles embodied in that accord to the entire North American continent. *(Bill highlights, p. 174; trade agreement highlights, p. 180; U.S.-Canada pact, 1988 Almanac, p. 222)*

Fast-Track Consideration

Because HR 3450 was a bill approving a trade agreement, it was subject to special rules and did not take the typical route to enactment.

It came to Congress under so-called fast-track procedures designed to protect the president's ability to negotiate trade agreements with the confidence that they would not later be undone by Congress. The rules barred amendments and required an up-or-down vote within 90 days of the bill's introduction. They also set precise deadlines for the president to meet in negotiating and signing trade pacts.

In recent years, Congress had kept the president on a tight leash, renewing his fast-track negotiating authority for short periods to ensure that he kept Congress informed about ongoing talks and involved members in the negotiating process as much as possible.

Because Congress could not amend these bills, a quirky process had been devised that involved informal committee markups and even mock conferences to craft trade accord implementing bills before they were formally introduced. Although the president did not have to incorporate all the congressional proposals into the bill he sent to Capitol Hill, failure to do so could cost him votes of potential supporters.

In the case of NAFTA, the mock drafting process had a limited direct impact on the implementing bill. But it gave administration officials time to negotiate with concerned members — in blocs and individually — and to make changes to win their votes. Opponents of the trade pact decried this as an excess of deal-making at the expense of U.S. workers and others who the accord would affect, but supporters said it was no different from the horse-trading over any significant and controversial bill.

International Trade Fallout

By endorsing NAFTA, Congress moved beyond the debate of the previous decade, when free trade forces found themselves on the defensive, parrying efforts to protect particular industries from foreign competition. This time, a powerful concept — a continent-wide trading alliance — enabled the free-traders to triumph after a wrenching national debate.

It was the first time the United States had agreed to take down all economic walls guarding it from a country whose economy was as poor and as different from its own as Mexico's. Bringing Mexico into the alliance with the

United States and Canada was projected to create a huge, tariff-free, $6.5 trillion market with 358 million consumers.

NAFTA also was expected to have a strong effect on trade worldwide, displaying the virtues of continuing to remove the barriers to free trade.

The administration argued persuasively that a NAFTA defeat would cripple Clinton at a crucial juncture. The day after the House vote, the president traveled to Seattle for a meeting on trade issues with Asian leaders. Clinton was seeking help from Japan and other Pacific countries in reviving talks on expanding the General Agreement on Tariffs and Trade (GATT), which governed most world commerce. "It cannot be overstated how damaged he would have been if it had failed," said Jim Leach, R-Iowa.

Three weeks after NAFTA's passage, in time to meet a separate fast-track deadline, Clinton added a feather to his trade cap with the successful conclusion of the GATT talks. (GATT agreement, p. 182)

Domestic Political Fallout

Clinton placed his prestige and political bargaining clout on the line to win passage of the NAFTA bill. Pleading, pushing and bargaining his way, he won a historic, bipartisan come-from-behind victory that had looked nearly impossible when he began the battle in September. Clinton called the victory "a defining moment for our nation," and he lauded Congress for deciding "not to retreat" and recognizing that "change is the only constant."

While economists generally expected the pact to have slight, though generally positive, overall consequences in the United States because of Mexico's small economy, Clinton and other NAFTA supporters clearly exposed themselves to political risks by backing NAFTA to the hilt.

Some jobs and some factories inevitably would pick up and move to Mexico — as opponents of the agreement warned — and, whether or not NAFTA was the direct cause, those who backed the agreement would likely be held to account at the polls.

"There will be three votes on this agreement. This is the first one. The second vote will be in '94, and the third one will be in '96," warned NAFTA foe Ross Perot, a multibillionaire entrepreneur who was an independent candidate for president in 1992.

The issue scrambled political alliances in ways rarely seen. Perot joined with conservative Republican Pat Buchanan and liberal crusader Ralph Nader in opposing the agreement. Organized labor and some environmental groups, which rarely agreed on anything, opposed it as well. Farmers in the Midwest were avidly for it, but growers in Florida, California and North Dakota were against it.

To win over uncommitted House Democrats, Clinton argued that the agreement was an important leg of his plan to create more high-skill, high-wage jobs. But as the vote neared, Clinton also issued dire warnings about the consequences of rejecting free trade with Mexico: Illegal immigration from Mexico would rise, he said, adding that Japan

---

BOXSCORE

➡ **NAFTA Implementing Bill — HR 3450, S 1627.** The bill changed U.S. laws to conform with the North American Free Trade Agreement and in effect gave Congress' approval to the trade pact.

Reports: H Rept 103-361, Parts 1-3; S Rept 103-189.

KEY ACTION

Nov. 4 — Bills formally introduced.

Nov. 17 — **House** passed HR 3450, 234-200.

Nov. 20 — **Senate** cleared HR 3450, 61-38.

Dec. 8 — **President** signed HR 3450 — PL 103-182.

---

and Germany were poised to infiltrate the Mexican market if the United States declined.

Labor groups were bitterly disappointed in Clinton's decision to push NAFTA to a vote. Relations between the White House and the AFL-CIO, which endorsed Clinton during the 1992 presidential election campaign, became acrimonious as the vote neared, and Clinton denounced labor for threatening to defeat members who voted for the trade pact.

When Clinton triumphed, it provoked an angry outpouring. "We won't forget what happened here," Teamsters President Ron Carey told The Associated Press. "We're the folks who went out there and worked for a president who talked repeatedly about jobs, and here what we've done is export jobs."

Minority Whip Newt Gingrich, R-Ga., said the turning point in the effort to round up GOP votes came when Clinton denounced labor for its "muscle-bound" tactics. "It said to a lot of our guys that, if he's going to take that kind of risk in taking on labor unions, how can I turn my back on him?" he said.

Though Perot's opposition to NAFTA had loomed large in many members' minds, his influence waned after a less than stellar performance in a televised debate Nov. 9 with Vice President Al Gore. Perot's poor performance was particularly important for winning over Republicans, who had been concerned about a backlash from Perot supporters in the group United We Stand America.

Peter T. King, R-N.Y., said he noticed an immediate change in Perot's supporters following the debate: "They started by saying they were going to drive me out of office," he said. After the debate, "they ended up saying that NAFTA is only one issue and we can work together."

Canada Hesitates

In the weeks following Congress' approval of the pact, it was unclear whether Canada would sign on. Newly elected Prime Minister Jean Chrétien had called for formal side agreements to resolve several long-running trade disputes before he gave his final approval to NAFTA. The most delicate of those issues involved Canadian complaints about the United States' use of trade laws designed to prevent "dumping" of goods at below-market prices and U.S. efforts to counter Canadian subsidies. But Clinton rejected the possibility of agreements that would require congressional approval. By the time Clinton signed HR 3450 into law, Chrétien had agreed to put the agreement into effect while Canada and the United States continued to discuss their differences.

BACKGROUND

Though politicians in the United States credited — or blamed — Bush for originating NAFTA, the trade pact came to fruition only because of extraordinary changes in Mexico. In less than a decade, first under President Miguel de la Madrid and from late 1988 under President Carlos Salinas de Gortari, Mexico had transformed its econ-

In agency briefings, Labor Department officials said that as many as 22,500 workers could lose their jobs in the 18 months after NAFTA went into effect — half of whom would qualify for benefits under the program. The Labor Department's chief economist, Lawrence Katz, testified Oct. 20 that the agreement would result in at most 10,000 to 15,000 additional unemployed workers through 1995.

The administration proposed to provide the average worker with benefits of roughly $8,000. The administration said the plan would cost an estimated $90 million, but the Congressional Budget Office (CBO), Congress' budget scorekeeper, had a higher estimate. The agency contended that retraining NAFTA workers, factoring in the administration's proposal, would cost $141 million. Extending it for five years would cost $36 million more, according to CBO.

Half the funds were to be for training and half for income-support payments. The plan sought changes in existing worker retraining programs, including Trade Adjustment Assistance and the Economic Dislocation and Worker Adjustment Assistance Program, which had been criticized for being bureaucratic and ineffective.

To address those problems, Clinton sought to require workers who received income support and job placement to be enrolled in training within 16 weeks of initially drawing unemployment. Under the existing program, many workers received waivers that enabled them to receive income payments without enrolling in a training program.

The administration was not counting on its proposal to change many minds: Those who were inclined to vote against NAFTA were apt to consider the retraining benefits too paltry to ameliorate what they argued would be widespread job loss. But Labor Secretary Robert B. Reich told reporters that the plan might be sufficient to solidify votes that the administration was counting on.

● **Financing.** On Oct. 26, the administration sent Congress a $2.7 billion financing package to cover the worker training program and the tariff revenue that would be lost under NAFTA. Under congressional budget rules, the implementing bill had to contain spending cuts or revenue increases to offset the revenue loss for the five years after enactment.

This was the administration's second financing proposal, and it came out of extensive negotiations with a bipartisan group of supporters. The White House originally had proposed to offset lost tariffs by doubling the customs fees charged to individuals and commercial vehicles arriving at U.S. ports of entry. The proposal would have increased fees for international airline and cruise passengers and commercial trucks from $5 to $10. It would have increased the fee for trains from $7.50 to $15.

But this caused quavering within the all-important bloc of Republican NAFTA supporters, 27 of whom — including House Minority Whip Gingrich — signed a letter to Clinton threatening to withdraw their support if the increases were retained. So the administration scaled back its proposed increase in the airline and cruise fee to $6.50, with an estimated return of nearly $1.1 billion over five years. The truck and train fees were dropped.

The remaining $1.6 billion in needed revenue was to be derived over five years from a trio of administrative and bookkeeping changes:

● Requiring banks to transfer employers' withholding tax payments one day earlier by electronic means, which the administration said would enable the government to claim $1.4 billion in additional interest.

● Giving the Customs Service access to Internal Revenue Service records to enable it to step up its anti-fraud

---

NAFTA Boosters Win in Court

A federal appeals court ruled Sept. 24 that the Clinton administration did not have to prepare an analysis of the environmental impact of the North American Free Trade Agreement (NAFTA), saving the White House from a time-consuming process that could have blocked the pact from taking effect at the beginning of 1994.

The unanimous opinion by a three-judge panel of the U.S. Court of Appeals for the District of Columbia Circuit cleared the way for a congressional vote on the trade agreement.

The ruling was a victory for the White House and a blow to environmental groups and others opposing NAFTA who had brought suit to force the administration to conduct an environmental impact study to determine what pollution and other environmental damage would be caused by expanding trade with Mexico. The appeals court overturned a June 30 ruling by U.S. District Judge Charles R. Richey requiring the analysis.

In its ruling, the appeals court did not rule on the specific issue of whether the failure to complete an environmental review of NAFTA violated the National Environmental Policy Act, which required such studies for major federal actions. Instead, the ruling dealt with whether the courts had authority to review the president's actions under the Administrative Procedure Act, which allowed relief through the courts to people who were harmed by the action of a federal agency, once the agency's action was deemed final.

"The president is not obligated to submit any agreement to Congress, and until he does there is no final action," wrote Judge Abner Mikva, adding that "the president's actions are not 'agency action' and thus cannot be reviewed."

Richey had issued the original ruling in a case brought by three environmental and consumer groups — the Sierra Club, Friends of the Earth, and Public Citizen — which contended that a 1970 law requiring environmental impact studies of major federal actions should apply to trade agreements. Both the Bush administration, which negotiated the pact, and the Clinton administration argued that the law did not apply to trade agreements.

Completion of environmental impact studies often took years because the law required highly detailed analysis and gave outside groups the opportunity to challenge government findings.

---

and enforcement efforts, which the administration predicted would bring in about $150 million.

● Assuming increased sales of U.S. farm commodities to Mexico, which would raise prices and reduce by $182 million the amount of income-support payments that the Commodity Credit Corporation would be expected to make to U.S. farmers.

● **Environmental cleanup.** A key element needed to win votes for the NAFTA bill was the administration's plan for financing pollution cleanup and the building of infrastructure along the U.S.-Mexican border, where water treatment facilities were woefully inadequate. The admin-

istration had proposed spending $8 billion, of which $2 billion was to come from existing U.S.-Mexico programs, $2 billion from multilateral lenders and $4 billion from government loans and guarantees.

At a news conference Oct. 27, Treasury Secretary Lloyd Bentsen proposed creating a North American Development Bank and a Border Environment Cooperation Commission to carry out environmental improvement and economic adjustment efforts spurred by NAFTA.

The development bank, referred to as NADBank, was to receive $450 million over four years in start-up capital — half from the United States, half from Mexico. The money was to be used in the international money markets to leverage at least $2 billion for loans and guarantees to borrowers in both countries.

Most NADBank loans would be used for environmental improvement projects, such as wastewater-treatment plants along the border. But NADBank would devote 10 percent of its lending capacity to investments aimed at the economic recovery of communities in the United States or Mexico that were adversely affected by NAFTA.

This provision was sought by Rep. Esteban E. Torres, D-Calif., and other members of the Congressional Hispanic Caucus who had been wavering on NAFTA. Many of their Hispanic constituents were industrial or farm workers who feared NAFTA would spur an outflow of working-class U.S. jobs to Mexico. Torres joined in the news conference to offer his support of the pact. The Ways and Means Committee gave informal approval to the financing and NADBank provisions at a closed session Oct. 27. The Finance Committee followed suit Oct. 28.

While the flurry of activity seemed to add to the momentum for NAFTA's approval, it did not weaken the optimism of NAFTA opponents. Bonior, who was leading the opposition in the House, claimed at week's end to have 209 solid votes against the pact, just nine short of the number needed to defeat it.

Congress Gets the Bill . . . and Some Sweeteners

Following weeks of negotiations and hard-sell lobbying, Clinton sent the long-awaited bill to Congress on Nov. 3. Ways and Means Committee Chairman Dan Rostenkowski, D-Ill., introduced the measure (HR 3450) the following day, starting a statutory fast-track clock that ensured a floor vote Nov. 17.

Clinton acted only after he had wrung last-minute concessions from Mexico in an effort to win more votes. Clinton's transmittal included the implementing bill, on which Congress would vote, a statement laying out the actions the administration would take on its own to put the agreement into effect, and the separate side agreements on environmental, labor and other subjects.

To attract support from lawmakers from sugar-producing states, the administration extracted a commitment designed to prevent Mexico from exporting sugar to the United States in the future. U.S. producers were worried that Mexico would substitute corn sweeteners in domestic products and export its surplus sugar to the United States. Mexico agreed not to do so under the last-minute deal negotiated by Kantor. Louisiana lawmakers and others from sugar-producing states had withheld support, awaiting such assurances from Mexico.

To attract Florida lawmakers, the administration worked out a system under which the price of orange juice concentrate would be tracked on the New York Commodity Exchange, and, if it fell below a certain level, tariffs could be reimposed on imports from Mexico. Similarly, the ad-

ministration agreed to an expedited procedure for reinstating tariffs on Mexican vegetables, including tomatoes, in case of a flood of imports.

Mexico also agreed to begin negotiations soon after NAFTA took effect on more quickly phasing out its remaining tariffs on such products as flat glass, wine, appliances and bedding. U.S. producers of those products had complained that the agreement retained Mexican tariffs on them for as long as 10 years.

Rep. Bill Richardson, D-N.M., a leader of the pro-NAFTA forces, said Nov. 4 that 14 to 18 previously uncommitted members had decided to support the pact because of the agreements on sugar, citrus and vegetable imports. He said Clinton remained 30 to 40 votes short of the 218 needed in the House; roughly 60 of the 258 Democrats in the House were said to remain undecided.

HOUSE ACTION

During the week of Nov. 8, three House committees with jurisdiction over aspects of the trade agreement formally acted on HR 3450 (H Rept 103-361, Parts 1-3).

Ways and Means, which oversaw most of the agreement, approved the measure Nov. 9 by a vote of 26-12, although several members who voted for it said they were not committed to doing so on the floor. The Energy and Commerce Committee agreed by voice vote the same day to send the bill to the floor without recommendation. The following day, the Banking Committee agreed by voice vote to send the bill to the floor with an unfavorable recommendation. Five other House committees with jurisdiction did not act formally on the measure.

Committee consideration was pro forma, given that the fast-track rules prohibited amendments and the full House had to vote on the bill regardless of what the committees did.

House Floor

After intense lobbying and fierce debate, the House passed HR 3450 by a surprisingly comfortable vote of 234-200 the evening of Nov. 17. *(Vote 575, p. 140-H)*

The complex politics of NAFTA were best demonstrated by Clinton's owing his House floor victory more to Republicans than to his own party. In the dramatic House showdown, Democrats supplied only 102 votes for NAFTA, while 156 Democrats and the one independent voted no. With organized labor strongly opposed, it was no surprise that most Democrats — particularly those from hard-hit industrial areas — were in that camp. Republicans voted 132-43 in favor, far surpassing the 110 votes the party leadership had promised.

Because the House's chief vote counter, Bonior, opposed the pact, pro-NAFTA Democrats set up their own ad hoc whip organization to help the administration and its chief NAFTA salesmen — Kantor and William M. Daley, a Chicago lawyer hired by Clinton to head the White House NAFTA lobbying effort. Coordinating the in-house effort were Robert T. Matsui of California, who headed a special House task force on NAFTA, and Richardson, one of Bonior's four deputy whips. Republicans worked separately with their own NAFTA whip operation led by Gingrich.

By the end of an 11-hour floor debate, there was little mystery or passion left: Both sides knew the White House had won, and it showed in different ways.

Marcy Kaptur, D-Ohio, who had crusaded against NAFTA, wiped away tears listening to Bonior give one of the closing speeches. Minority Leader Robert H. Michel, R-Ill., brought down the House when he referred to

NAFTA foes Perot, Buchanan and Nader as the "Groucho, Chico and Harpo of NAFTA politics."

Despite his reliance on Republicans for his victory margin in the House, Clinton also went all out to get Democratic votes. When Tennessee Democrat Bart Gordon decided to switch from opposing to supporting NAFTA, the White House sent Gore to join him in a live news conference beamed back home to defend his vote.

The White House left little to chance. Peter Hoagland, D-Neb., said he had received two lobbying calls — one from a Cabinet member and another from an ambassador — even after promising his support. Both asked Hoagland to cast his vote immediately after the roll call began to create momentum and decide the matter as quickly as possible.

Last-Minute Deals

The White House was able to sway many uncommitted members by offering last-minute deals on a range of issues, some relating to the Mexico trade agreement and some not.

Florida provided a crucial bloc of votes that helped swing the momentum in the administration's direction. In the days before the vote, only four of the delegation's 23 members were committed to vote yes. Many refrained from taking a position or opposed the agreement in order to wring concessions out of the administration for the state's citrus, sugar and vegetable growers. When it was over, the pro-NAFTA forces were able to swing nine more votes from Florida.

The administration worked intensively for months to get the Floridians on board. But negotiations were not finished until the day preceding the vote. At a delegation meeting with industry lobbyists Nov. 16, lawmakers received a letter from Clinton laying out the commitment to toughen safeguards for tomato growers, in case Mexican tomatoes flooded the U.S. market. In the end, "we got almost everything we asked for," said Tom Lewis, R-Fla., a senior member of the Agriculture Committee. The time came, he said, "to declare victory." When Lewis switched from no to yes, it brought along many in the delegation.

Some delegations reached too high. Lawmakers from North Carolina tried to win a reduction in a proposed 75-cents-a-pack tax on cigarettes that the administration wanted to use to finance its health-care overhaul bill, slated for action in 1994. "The White House knew all along that's what we wanted, but they pretty much shot that down," said Charlie Rose, D-N.C. Eight out of 12 North Carolina members voted for the agreement anyway. (Health care, p. 335)

Members received other rewards for their votes. After announcing his support, Floyd H. Flake, D-N.Y., got a call from Clinton, who told him that a Small Business Administration pilot program would be located in his Queens district.

NAFTA supporter King was dismayed to discover the week before the vote that the Army Corps of Engineers was blocking a dredging project at Jones Beach in his Long Island district. He later explained that he called the White House and said: "I asked for nothing for my vote. Now you're taking something away from me. You're making me look like a schmuck." The White House quickly responded with a letter stating that the project would go forward.

The spate of deals infuriated NAFTA opponents, who accused the White House of buying off the opponents. But the White House responded that most of the deals involved trade issues and represented concessions to satisfy lawmakers with legitimate concerns about NAFTA. The deals, officials said, were a substitute for amendments to the trade deal, which the fast-track rules did not permit.

Lawmakers on the receiving end took a more pragmatic view of the deal-cutting. "It's not a question of buying votes," said Glenn English, D-Okla. "This is the only way we could have supported the agreement."

SENATE ACTION

As in the House, Senate committee action on the measure was routine and largely inconsequential. Six different Senate panels met formally Nov. 18 to consider S 1627, the chamber's number for an identical version of the bill. S 1627 had been introduced by Majority Leader George J. Mitchell, D-Maine, the same day as the House bill. When it came time for floor action, however, the Senate voted on the House-passed bill.

The Finance Committee approved S 1627 by a vote of 16-3. The Agriculture and Foreign Relations committees approved the bill by voice votes. The Commerce, Governmental Affairs and Judiciary committees agreed by voice votes to send the measure to the floor without recommendation. The bill was reported jointly (S Rept 103-189).

Senate Floor

Although Clinton's Nov. 20 victory in the Senate was expected, the 61-38 vote reflected the same divisions that had made NAFTA such a tough sell in the House — particularly strong opposition from organized labor. Again, Clinton owed the victory more to Republicans than to members of his party. Thirty-four of 44 GOP senators voted for the agreement, as did 27 of the 55 Democrats casting ballots. (Vote 395, p. 51-S)

Opponents argued that the agreement would lead to job losses and downward pressure on U.S. wages. Supporters took a more long-range view. "This agreement will define the American role in the global economy and in world affairs well into the 21st century," said Mitchell.

The margin of victory in the Senate was larger in part because senators were less susceptible to the pressures that caused many House members to vote no. Most states were expected to derive some benefit from free trade with Mexico; that was certainly not the case with every House district.

Two Democrats with strong union ties — Edward M. Kennedy of Massachusetts and Tom Harkin of Iowa — backed the agreement after delaying an announcement until the very end. Both explained their break with labor by saying Mexico offered their states export opportunities — high-tech exports for Massachusetts and farm products for Iowa. "All of the problems that working families face . . . will be even worse if NAFTA is defeated," Kennedy said.

Senate opponents included the same unusual mix of liberal Democrats and conservative Republicans that characterized House opposition. Many were from states with severe manufacturing job losses or industries that could be subjected to fiercer competition if trade barriers with Mexico came down. "This is a jobs program for Mexico, and, my Lord, we need a jobs program for America," said Riegle.

Some conservative opponents said they feared that the pact would erect a powerful trinational bureaucracy. "The United States should seriously reconsider any agreement which gives up sovereignty to any multinational group that will place the needs of international trade over the interests of the American people," said Dirk Kempthorne, R-Idaho.

An effort by opponents to amend the agreement — a step prohibited under fast-track rules — was rebuffed on a procedural ruling. Ted Stevens, R-Alaska, sought to strike provisions relating to side agreements with Mexico, but the attempt was blocked on a 73-26 vote. (Vote 389, p. 50-S) ∎

NAFTA Provisions

What follows is an overview of the key elements of the North American Free Trade Agreement (NAFTA). The tripartite trade pact provided for the elimination of all tariffs between the United States and Mexico over 15 years and extended the principles embodied in the U.S.-Canada Free Trade Agreement to the entire North American continent.

Tariffs

NAFTA ultimately was to eliminate all tariffs on goods produced and sold in North America. Some of the tariffs were to be eliminated immediately, but most were to be phased out gradually over 10 years. Other tariffs were to be reduced over five years, and a few were to be phased down over 15 years.

The same product could be treated differently depending on which country produced it, reflecting each country's desire to protect specific industries from increased imports.

U.S. tariffs on Mexican goods already were relatively low, and Mexico was to gain duty-free access to U.S. markets fairly rapidly for most goods. However, the United States was given 15 years to phase out tariffs in several import-sensitive sectors, including glassware, footwear and ceramic tile. The tariff reductions could be accelerated if the two countries involved agreed.

Supporters said tariff reductions and other provisions in the agreement would enable U.S. manufacturers to increase their sales in Mexico and, over the long term, increase employment in the United States, as well as raise the Mexican standard of living. But critics contended that Mexico had undertaken a systematic strategy of suppressing wages to lure U.S. companies to Mexico, resulting in a loss of jobs.

Investments

Businesses that made investments in plant and equipment in other NAFTA countries received several specific protections under the agreement. NAFTA guaranteed foreign investors national treatment, meaning that each country pledged to treat investors from other countries as favorably under its laws as it did its own investors (and no less favorably than investors from non-NAFTA countries).

The pact barred governments from imposing special requirements on foreign investors, such as requiring a U.S. company located in Mexico to buy from a local parts supplier or make a product that had a certain amount of Mexican content. Existing restrictions of this sort were to be phased out.

NAFTA did not specifically bar expropriation or nationalization of a business or investment in Mexico, but it set guidelines, such as requiring immediate compensation at fair market value. In addition, unlike the U.S.-Canadian free trade agreement, NAFTA allowed foreign investors targeted for government takeover to seek monetary damages through binding international arbitration, rather than through the host country's court system. This was an important victory for U.S. businesses, which had concerns about corruption in the Mexican court system.

There were exceptions to these rules for each country. The United States reserved the right to bar foreign acquisition or mergers of certain companies for national security reasons. Mexico maintained some restrictions on foreign investment in several sectors, including the oil-drilling and petrochemical industries, which were protected by the Mexican Constitution.

Opponents contended that investment protections provided by NAFTA would encourage relocation of factories and jobs to Mexico by U.S. companies that previously might have worried about the security of investments there. Backers of the treaty contended that the investment provisions eliminated requirements in Mexican law that forced some U.S. companies to move to Mexico in order to sell their products there.

Rules of Origin

NAFTA included rules designed to prevent countries outside the pact from using a NAFTA country as a so-called export platform from which products could be assembled and sold in North America, taking advantage of the open market. The rules were generally stricter than those adopted in the U.S.-Canada free trade agreement.

In general, goods assembled from parts or components from outside the NAFTA region would qualify for low tariff treatment only if the end product was different enough to require a change in tariff classification. That meant, for example, that wood molding manufactured in North America from imported Indonesian logs would be deemed a North American product and thus could be moved duty-free among NAFTA countries.

▶ **Cars, footwear, chemicals.** Automobiles, footwear and chemicals were subject to even stricter rules. Parts or components going into these products had to have at least half and in some cases more than 60 percent North American content in order to move duty-free in the NAFTA region. The content requirement for cars, light trucks, transmissions and engines was to rise gradually to 62.5 percent. Even a part made in North America would not count completely as a North American good if it contained some imported components.

Foreign companies' operating subsidiaries in North America were to receive the benefits of the agreement. For example, U.S. subsidiaries of Japanese auto companies could transport their vehicles duty-free as long as they were in compliance with the regional content requirements.

▶ **Textile and apparel.** The rules governing textile and apparel products were as follows: To qualify for duty-free treatment, a textile or apparel product had to be manufactured in North America with both fabric and yarn that were made in the United States, Canada or Mexico. Only the fiber that went into making yarn could be imported. In the case of cotton and certain other products, even the fiber could not be imported. The rules provided exceptions for fabrics not made in North America, such as silk.

Health and Environmental Standards

NAFTA obligated the three countries to work toward common standards to protect the food supply and the environment, but there was intense debate about what that pledge meant.

Free-market critics contended that NAFTA would bring an onslaught of new federal regulation in the areas of health and environmental protection. Environmental critics made precisely the opposite charge — that working toward common laws would create pressure for countries to weaken tough standards, opening avenues for health and safety laws that were especially strict to be challenged as unfair trade barriers. State and local laws were particularly at risk, environmentalists argued.

Supporters said the pact was the most environmentally sensitive yet negotiated and that failure to adopt it would have reduced pressure on Mexico to improve its environmental enforcement.

Neither the agreement nor the accompanying side deals actually required the countries to harmonize their standards either upward or downward, although there was nonbinding language calling for harmonization to the "highest standard." NAFTA contained a pledge by the three countries "to pursue equivalence" in standards governing preparation and processing of food products "to the extent feasible." And it stated that an effort to make laws equivalent should not force a reduction in a country's level of protection. But there was no enforcement mechanism if a country failed to pursue harmonization.

The agreement explicitly stated that each country, including states and localities, retained the right to set its own standards in food safety and other areas. It barred countries from adopting standards that were less stringent than those accepted by the General Agreement on Tariffs and Trade. And NAFTA specified that it was inappropriate for a country to relax standards to attract foreign investment. But, again, it contained no means of enforcement.

While NAFTA allowed each country to choose the level of protection it considered appropriate, it required that all laws relating to health and food safety be based on scientific findings. It also recognized that different countries could achieve the same level of protection with different standards. So when an exporting country could demonstrate that it had equivalent protection from health dangers, the importing country would have to let the goods enter.

A country was to be subject to penalties only if it discriminated against another NAFTA country and applied its standards in a way that unfairly put imports at a disadvantage. Then, fines could be levied against the government unless it altered its law or enforcement practice, but only after a long administrative procedure.

The burden of proof was to be placed on the party challenging a particular standard.

Safeguards

If imports of a particular product did flood the U.S. market, the agreement made it possible, but not likely, for governments to reimpose tariffs temporarily to protect domestic industries. This so-called snapback provision was deliberately designed so that NAFTA governments would employ it only as a last resort.

Certain U.S. industries whose products competed directly with imported from Mexico contended that the agreement did not contain adequate safeguards in case the U.S. market was deluged with imports. Complaints were loudest from the sugar industry and vegetable and fruit producers in Florida and elsewhere.

In one sense, the NAFTA safeguards were easier to trigger than those in the U.S.-Canada trade agreement. Under that accord, temporary safeguards could be invoked only if a domestic industry proved that it actually had been injured. Under NAFTA the safeguards could be applied to protect an industry that proved it was merely threatened by imports. And the higher tariffs could be maintained for as long as four years for import-sensitive products, including orange juice and sugar. But NAFTA also required a government that resorted to the tariff snapback to compensate all countries whose imports were affected — a feature intended to make it less likely the safeguard would be used.

For agricultural goods, the tariff snapback could be triggered when imports of certain commodities reached certain levels, but that did not satisfy domestic producers who wanted the safeguard triggered if the price of a good dropped below a specified level.

Some U.S. agricultural commodities, including sugar products, cotton, dairy and peanuts, were eligible for special protection. During a phase-in period lasting up to 15 years, these commodities were to get some protection from Mexican imports through the imposition of a quota system that allowed only a certain volume of imports from Mexico (based on prior import levels) to enter duty-free. Imports above the quota were to be assessed a significantly higher tariff. The quota was to increase gradually.

Services

One of the more noteworthy concessions obtained by the United States was Mexico's commitment to open its market for services. That included areas such as banking, telecommunications, transportation and government procurement. Restrictions in certain sectors could be retained by each country, including maritime shipping for the United States, film and publishing for Canada and oil and gas drilling for Mexico.

With certain limitations, each country's service companies were guaranteed the right to equal treatment with domestic firms under any new laws or regulations, the right to invest in other NAFTA countries and the right to sell services across the border.

▶ **Telecommunications.** In the area of telecommunications, the agreement greatly expanded U.S. companies' ability to use public telecommunications services in Mexico. NAFTA permitted providers and users to move information across national borders. But each country could deny foreign firms the right to compete to provide basic telecommunications services.

▶ **Trucking.** The agreement was to relax gradually restrictions that prevented U.S. truckers from operating in Mexico and Mexican

truckers from operating in the United States. U.S. trucking companies would be able to operate in Mexican border states using their own drivers three years after the agreement went into effect and throughout the country after six years. Mexican truckers were to receive access to the United States according to the same schedule.

▶ **Financial services.** The financial service provisions covered banking, securities, insurance and other areas. While NAFTA permitted each country to establish its own regulatory rules governing financial services, it also laid out principles for liberalizing trade, such as allowing citizens of one country to purchase services in another. However, the agreement did not give one country's firms the right to solicit business in either of the other two countries.

Mexico agreed to phase out restrictions on U.S. firms operating in Mexico over 13 years for the banking and securities sectors, and over six years for insurance and other non-bank financial services.

If existing state or regional laws in any country discriminated against foreigners, they were allowed to stand under the agreement, but new restrictions could not be enacted.

Caps on market share were to be imposed on U.S. and Canadian banks and securities firms operating in Mexico until 2000. For example, U.S. and Canadian firms initially were limited to an 8 percent share of the Mexican market. Caps also were to apply to the insurance industry.

Though prohibited from doing so in the United States, U.S. firms were allowed to offer both banking and securities services in Mexico and Canada. Existing U.S. limits on financial institutions owning both banking and securities firms were allowed to remain.

Mexico agreed to allow U.S. financial service firms to operate in Mexico without having to establish banks. That would allow non-bank financial service firms to provide services such as consumer lending, commercial lending, mortgage lending or credit cards.

Intellectual Property

To prevent piracy of intellectual property, NAFTA provided protection throughout North America for copyrights, sound recordings, satellite transmissions, pharmaceuticals, plant breeder's rights, trademarks, industrial designs and similar items.

Specifically, NAFTA required each country to provide effective protection for intellectual property, primarily by requiring the parties to adhere to several international agreements. This provision was directed primarily at Mexico, which had not endorsed these agreements. NAFTA required protection of at least 50 years for copyrights, 20 years from the date of filing a patent or 17 years from the date of a patent grant, and 10 years for trademarks, which could be renewed.

Each country could adopt more extensive protections as long as they did not violate provisions of the agreement.

Side Agreements

The United States, Canada and Mexico signed three side agreements to broaden provisions in the areas of environmental cleanup and enforcement, labor rights and protections against a rapid increase in imports. While the Clinton administration went into the talks with the goal of securing tough provisions to enable one country to impose trade sanctions against another for failure to enforce its environmental and labor laws, the final agreements did not go that far.

The side accords established a Commission for Environmental Cooperation and a Commission for Labor Cooperation, on which each country was to be represented, to be responsible for monitoring compliance with labor and environmental. They could also appoint special panels to investigate complaints and recommend fines or sanctions if a country refused to enforce its own laws.

Fines or sanctions could be imposed only if a long process of consultation failed to resolve the dispute. Moreover, the panels would have no power to compel a government to pay fines, although they could authorize the other two countries to raise tariffs against the third country's goods. Fines would be levied against the government — not against businesses or individuals.

The agreements specified that no fines could be imposed if a government failed to enforce its environmental or labor laws because of a decision to expend its resources on other priorities. ■

GATT Deal Reached; Fast Track OK'd

Following close on the heels of his victory in winning approval of the North American Free Trade Agreement (NAFTA), President Clinton claimed a second sweeping trade success. On Dec. 15, he embraced a long-sought expansion of the General Agreement on Tariffs and Trade (GATT), the global accord that governed most world trade.

Acting under a congressionally imposed deadline, U.S. trade negotiators, their European counterparts and the rest of the 117 participants in the marathon Uruguay Round of the GATT reached agreement at the last minute, capping seven years of difficult talks.

The agreement significantly scaled back tariffs and placed service industries and agriculture under GATT for the first time. The accord, which was initialed but not set to be formally signed until April 1994, still had to be approved by Congress and by the governments of the other signatories before it could take effect.

The administration planned to submit a bill to Congress in 1994 that would bring U.S. laws into conformity with the GATT accord — a task that was expected to be relatively easy, at least compared with the NAFTA battle.

The United States had negotiated under special "fast track" rules that guaranteed that Congress would take an up-or-down vote on the huge deal once it was submitted.

THE GATT AGREEMENT

In a Dec. 15 news conference, Clinton praised the GATT accord, saying it would produce expanded trade and "add as much as $100 billion to $200 billion per year to our economy once it is fully phased in" while creating "hundreds of thousands of good-paying American jobs."

But Clinton acknowledged that the United States had been unable to win concessions in several key areas. The highest-profile disappointment was an attempt to open European markets to the U.S. film and television industries, one of the country's most lucrative areas for export.

In general, the agreement was intended to reduce worldwide tariffs by more than one-third, cut agricultural subsidies and phase out quotas on textile imports. At the same time, the pact preserved the right of the United States to use U.S. laws designed to block imports "dumped" on domestic markets at unfairly low prices.

For the United States, the pact was expected to lead to increased exports of agricultural products and greater copyright and patent protections for high-tech industries, such as computers and semiconductors. Some sectors, particularly manufacturers of textiles and drugs, suffered setbacks. And for the first time, GATT was to apply to trade in services, including banking, accounting and insurance, although the agreement on services was much less sweeping than U.S. negotiators had sought.

The pact also was designed to transform the GATT, set up in 1947 as a temporary entity, into a permanent trade body called the World Trade Organization. The new organization was to have greater authority than GATT to enforce trade agreements.

The Uruguay Round, so-named because the talks had begun in that country seven years earlier, was considered the most ambitious set of negotiations since GATT was established. The talks originally were slated to end in 1990, but they had been hung up for years over several thorny issues, especially a big battle between the United States and Europe over farm subsidies.

A Difficult Fight Ahead

Both Clinton and members of Congress predicted that Congress would have an easier time approving the GATT accord than it had with NAFTA. But they noted that selling the agreement would still be a struggle. (NAFTA, p. 170)

The biggest battle was expected to concern provisions to preserve U.S. anti-dumping laws. Although the accord's language was aimed at protecting steel and other domestic industries from unfairly priced imports, free traders feared that an overly broad anti-dumping provision might allow foreign countries to restrict U.S. exports.

While specific U.S. industries stood to benefit from the accord, others expected to lose; those effects were likely to weigh on individual members as they considered the bill.

U.S. negotiators, for example, had been unable to secure agreement from Asian and developing countries to allow broader entry of U.S. financial services businesses into their markets.

Hollywood was bitterly disappointed that an attempt to get trade in audiovisual materials covered by the pact was scrapped at the last minute; U.S. negotiators were therefore unable to break a European quota system that limited foreign programming.

The biggest U.S. loser appeared to be the textile industry, which benefited from quotas imposed through bilateral agreements negotiated under the Multi-Fiber Arrangement. Those protections were to be phased out over 10 years under the GATT accord. Textile lobbyists had pushed hard for a 15-year phaseout. Consumers, however, were expected to gain from lower prices.

On the whole, farmers fared well, as U.S. negotiators won much-desired cuts in agriculture subsidies that had harmed U.S. exports. In addition, the agreement was likely to produce domestic budget cuts as comparable U.S. subsidies declined. Rice farmers were pleased that Japan and South Korea agreed to buy a portion of that most important dietary staple from overseas suppliers for the first time. Heavily protected sugar, peanut and cotton growers, however, expected more competition as their quotas were to be eliminated and replaced with tariffs.

FAST-TRACK AUTHORITY

In an effort to encourage the completion of the long-stalled GATT talks, Congress in June agreed to a short-term extension of the president's fast-track negotiating authority. The bill (HR 1876) extended through April 15, 1994, the president's authority to enter into a GATT agreement and provided that an agreement so negotiated would receive fast-track treatment. The bill made Dec. 15, 1993, the deadline for the president to inform Congress that he intended to sign the pact.

Fast-track rules, written specifically for bills implementing trade agreements, required that once the bill was introduced, Congress had 90 legislative days to approve or disapprove it. Amendments were not allowed.

The bill's short time frame created a window of opportunity for countries to complete the GATT talks. Without a guarantee that Congress would not alter the agreement,

U.S. trading partners would be unwilling to conclude a pact with U.S. negotiators.

Congress could still have some input into the accord before Clinton signed it in April 1994. Afterward, there would be a period of informal "mock" markups by the committees with jurisdiction over the implementing bill. Those meetings, as well as behind-the-scenes compromising, also would give members a limited opportunity to fine-tune the implementing bill before it was formally introduced. There was no deadline after the signing of the pact for the introduction of the implementing bill.

The fast-track extension bill, which the administration had requested, differed from past practice in that it applied only to the GATT agreement and did not cover any future bilateral trade deals. Usually, fast-track rules covered all trade agreements negotiated while they were in force. The last extension, enacted in 1991, expired May 31, 1993. *(1991 Almanac, p. 118)*

In addition to pressuring foreign negotiators, the focus on GATT also allowed the administration to sidestep a potential fight with Congress over broader renewal of the fast track, which trade officials said they planned to seek, perhaps in 1994. Organized labor and environmental groups had opposed previous extensions of the fast track, arguing that it amounted to a surrender of sovereignty because it forced Congress to choose between rejecting entire trade agreements or accepting wholesale changes to U.S. laws. President George Bush had to fight hard to win the 1991 extension. But with a Democrat in the White House, opposition was muted.

Legislative Action

The House Ways and Means Committee approved HR 1876 by voice vote June 9. The measure had been introduced by committee Chairman Dan Rostenkowski, D-Ill. The House Rules Committee, which shared jurisdiction over the bill, followed suit June 16 (H Rept 103-128, Parts 1-2). The House passed the bill, 295-126, on June 22.

The Senate Finance Committee voted 18-2 for an identical bill (S 1003 — S Rept 103-66) on June 23. The Senate cleared HR 1876 by a vote of 76-16 on June 30 after opponents opted not to delay action. The administration wanted the measure enacted before Clinton headed to Tokyo for the annual summit of the seven leading industrial nations, which began July 7. *(House vote 247, p. 60-H; Senate vote 192, p. 25-S)*

"We are voting to permit the Uruguay Round negotiations to go forward. That is all we are doing," said Finance Committee Chairman Daniel Patrick Moynihan, D-N.Y.

Clinton signed the bill July 2 (PL 103-49). ∎

Highlights of GATT Accord

The Uruguay Round of negotiations to revise the General Agreement on Tariffs and Trade (GATT) that concluded in Geneva on Dec. 15, 1993, began in September 1986 in Punta del Este, Uruguay. The agreement was the seventh renegotiation of GATT, which was created at the end of World War II and governed most world trade.

The pact, which had to be approved by Congress and the governments of the 116 other participants in the negotiations, was intended to sharply reduce trade barriers, including tariffs, import quotas and export subsidies. Key elements of the 550-page agreement, which was to be fully in force July 1, 1995, included changes in the following areas:

Tariffs. Tariffs were to be cut on approximately 85 percent of world trade and eliminated or significantly reduced on a broad range of products, including construction and agricultural equipment, pharmaceuticals, paper, steel, beer and liquor. Tariffs on industrial goods were to drop from an average of about 5 percent to an average of 3 percent.

Generally, tariff cuts were to be implemented in equal annual increments over five years, though they were to go into effect over 10 years in some sensitive industries such as textiles.

Agriculture. Trade in farm commodities was to be covered under GATT for the first time. Governments were to reduce the amount of money they spent on agriculture subsidies by an average of 36 percent; the total volume of agricultural products exported with the help of subsidies was to be reduced by 21 percent.

In addition, government-paid income support payments to farmers were to be cut by 20 percent, a commitment the United States already had met under broad farm bills enacted in 1985 and 1990 (PL 99-198, PL 101-624). *(1985 Almanac, p. 517; 1990 Almanac, p. 323)*

Non-tariff barriers, including quotas, were to be replaced by tariffs. Countries that completely barred imports of certain agricultural products, such as Japan, which banned rice imports, had to provide market access equal to 3 percent of domestic consumption, rising to 5 percent over a six- to 10-year implementation period.

Textiles. The Multi-Fiber Arrangement, under which industrial nations had imposed quotas on textile imports from developing countries for more than 30 years, was to be phased out over 10 years. To protect the U.S. textile industry, tariff reductions on textile and apparel imports were to be significantly less than those required for other industrial goods. On the whole, U.S. textile and clothing tariffs were to be cut by about 12 percent; for all industrial goods, U.S. tariffs were to be reduced by 34 percent.

Protections against dumping. The United States and Europe were allowed to preserve existing authority to use domestic anti-dumping laws to impose fines or countervailing duties against countries that exported goods at prices below cost. Disputes arising on dumping matters were to be settled under a new, binding multilateral dispute-settlement mechanism.

Subsidies. In a big win for the U.S. aerospace industry, the pact included civil aircraft products — a leading U.S. export — under new rules restricting government industrial subsidies. That paved the way for lower subsidies to the European Airbus consortium, a major competitor of the Boeing Co. The agreement permitted subsidies for development of new products.

Services. Applying GATT rules to the world market in services — valued at almost $1 trillion annually — was a key goal of U.S. negotiators. In large part, the pact extended GATT rules governing trade in goods to services for the first time. But multilateral agreements to open markets in specific service sectors, such as shipping, banking, securities and insurance, proved elusive.

Intellectual property. GATT rules were extended to protect from piracy intellectual property, such as computer programs, semiconductor chip designs, books, films and music. Developing countries were to have 10 years before they would have to honor patents on drugs.

World Trade Organization. The Geneva-based GATT organization was to be replaced by the World Trade Organization, a permanent body with greater authority to force member nations to comply with Uruguay Round agreements. This broad authority was strongly opposed by some environmental groups that feared the organization could force the U.S. government to reverse environmental laws that inhibited trade. ∎

China's Trade Status Tied To Human Rights Record

A three-year congressional effort to restrict trade with China until that country improved its human rights record came to a halt in 1993 after President Clinton announced that the administration would act on its own to insist that China make such reforms. But Capitol Hill's leading critics of the Chinese government warned Beijing to respond or face renewed legislative efforts the following year.

Clinton officially informed Congress on May 28 that he planned to renew China's most-favored-nation (MFN) status for the year beginning July 3, thereby allowing that country to continue to export goods to the United States at the low-tariff levels available to nearly all countries.

At the same time, he signed an executive order tying the next renewal to China's performance on human rights and other issues. Specifically, the order directed the secretary of State to recommend whether China's MFN status should be renewed in July 1994. To make a positive recommendation, the secretary was required to determine that Beijing was complying with a 1992 agreement that prison labor would not be used to produce goods for export to the United States and that China was making "overall significant progress" on human rights, releasing and providing an accounting of Chinese citizens detained for their political or religious beliefs, ensuring humane treatment of prisoners, protecting Tibet's religious and cultural heritage, and permitting international radio and television broadcasts into China.

The executive order also stipulated that the United States would vigorously enforce laws barring unfair trading practices and weapons proliferation — two areas where China's actions had been sharply criticized. But Clinton did not explicitly tie renewal of MFN to evidence that China was opening its markets or refraining from shipments of missile and other technology to third countries.

In deciding not to cut off low-tariff trade with China immediately, Clinton echoed the refrain repeatedly heard from President George Bush, who argued that continued trade with China provided the best opportunity to change that nation's behavior. "I don't want to isolate China," Clinton said. "I want to do what's good for the Chinese people." Implicit was an acknowledgment that trade with China was also important to many U.S. business interests.

But in setting human rights goals that China would have to meet before he would consider a further grant of MFN, Clinton departed from Bush's absolute opposition to placing conditions on trade with China. "Starting today, the United States will speak with one voice on China policy," Clinton said in a statement. "We no longer have an executive branch policy and a congressional policy. We have an American policy."

Background

China had gained MFN status with the United States as part of a trade agreement completed in 1990. Under the Jackson-Vanik amendment to the 1974 trade law, which governed U.S. trade relations with communist countries, the president had to renew that status annually. The renewal came due each July 3 and went through automatically unless Congress voted to reject it. (1974 Almanac, p. 553)

While Congress had never rejected the president's decision, lawmakers had tried three times since 1989 to pass bills restricting future extensions. Once, in 1990, only the House acted. Twice in 1992, Congress cleared bills and sent them to Bush, who vetoed them. Although the House was able to summon large margins to override the vetoes, the Senate failed both times to muster the necessary two-thirds majority.

In each of the previous three years, the House had also narrowly supported a separate bill to revoke China's MFN status; the Senate did not act on those measures, however, and the votes were seen as largely symbolic. (1992 Almanac, p. 157; 1991 Almanac, p. 121; 1990 Almanac, p. 764)

Legislative Action

Senate Majority Leader George J. Mitchell, D-Maine, and Rep. Nancy Pelosi, D-Calif., had led the charge on Capitol Hill to restrict the annual MFN renewal for China during the Bush administration. On April 22, they introduced a new bill that would have linked extension of China's MFN status the following year to improvements on human rights, trade policies and missile proliferation. Like the second measure vetoed by Bush in 1992, the restrictions were limited to goods produced by Chinese state-owned companies.

But once Clinton announced his plans, the two lawmakers said congressional action would be unnecessary. Mitchell called Clinton's order "fair, reasonable, responsible." He and Pelosi said it would achieve the same aims as the bill they introduced in April.

"These conditions are calibrated to be met," Pelosi said, acknowledging that other members "would like much, much tougher conditions" on trade with China.

An Unsuccessful Attempt To Revoke MFN

Clinton's action may have satisfied Mitchell and Pelosi, but Gerald B. H. Solomon, R-N.Y., who had sponsored the previous efforts to revoke China's MFN status, vowed to try again. Most members of the Ways and Means Committee, which had jurisdiction over trade in the House, opposed such a move. But under the 1974 Jackson-Vanik amendment, Solomon could have forced a floor vote on revoking MFN within 90 days of Clinton's announcement, whether or not Ways and Means acted.

So, in an unusual parliamentary move June 30, the committee voted 35-2 to report Solomon's legislation (H J Res 208 — H Rept 103-167) but recommended that it be voted down by the full House. "We need to give the president's policy a chance to work before we lose the leverage that MFN affords us," Ways and Means Committee Chairman Dan Rostenkowski, D-Ill., said. "We need to give the Chinese a chance to show they are now willing to play by the rules of the open, free-market, civilized world."

The Ways and Means Trade Subcommittee had taken similar action on June 15.

In an about-face for many members who had backed Solomon's bill in prior years, the House rejected the bill by a wide margin July 20. The 105-318 vote effectively gave a nod to Clinton's decision to renew China's MFN status. "It's very important to get a big vote behind the president so a very clear message is sent to the Chinese government that unless these conditions are met, no kidding, next year MFN is revoked," Pelosi said. (Vote 347, p. 60-H) ∎

Congress Grants Romania Favored Trade Status

The Senate on Oct. 21 cleared by voice vote a measure (H J Res 228 — H Rept 103-279) granting low-tariff treatment, called most-favored-nation (MFN) status, to products imported from Romania. Romania was the only country in Eastern Europe that did not yet have MFN status. President Clinton signed the bill Nov. 2 (PL 103-133).

The Senate Finance Committee approved MFN for Romania on Oct. 14 by voice vote. The House passed the resolution by voice Oct. 12, six days after the Ways and Means Committee gave its voice vote approval.

Romania had had MFN status until 1988, when then-President Nicolae Ceausescu renounced it just as Congress was moving toward revoking it in response to human rights violations.

"Romania is a country that suffered for years under a crushing dictatorship," said Ways and Means Chairman Dan Rostenkowski, D-Ill. "The new leadership of Romania deserves any leg up that the United States can provide them in their long climb back to the community of democratic, free-market societies."

The resolution put into effect a U.S.-Romania trade agreement that had been signed in 1992 by President George Bush but which Congress delayed approving because of concern over the pace of economic and democratic reforms in Romania. *(1992 Almanac, p. 161)*

Under the measure, the president had to renew Romania's MFN status each year after certifying to Congress that the Romanian government was assuring free emigration and other human rights. ∎

Congress Clears Stop-Gap Export Control Bill

The Senate cleared a bill by voice vote March 11 reauthorizing the Export Administration Act through June 30, 1994. The bill (HR 750), a short-term reauthorization with no policy changes, was aimed at giving Congress time to work out a comprehensive overhaul of U.S. export control law in 1994. The Export Administration Act set U.S. export policies and placed restrictions on the export of high-tech equipment. The House passed the bill Feb. 16 by a vote of 330-54. President Clinton signed it into law March 27 (PL 103-10). *(Vote 31, p. 8-H)* ∎

Bentsen, Panetta Head New Economic Team

As part of the effort to allow the new president to get his core team in place quickly, Senate committees began hearings on President Clinton's top economic nominees the week of Jan. 11. In synchronized testimony, the nominees signaled that the administration was likely to place greater emphasis on deficit reduction than Clinton had indicated during his presidential campaign. In his economic plan, "Putting People First," released in June 1992, Clinton had given center stage to other issues, particularly the health-care crisis and what he called the "other deficit," a lack of public and private investment that he said stifled economic growth.

While Clinton's economic advisers provided reassurance to senators looking for a serious attack on the deficit, they did not clarify how that goal could be reconciled with the administration's spending priorities.

LLOYD BENTSEN

The Senate confirmed Lloyd Bentsen as Treasury secretary by voice vote on Jan. 20. Bentsen, whose nomination had breezed through the Senate Finance Committee with unanimous support, was one of three Cabinet members approved on Inauguration Day.

None of Clinton's nominees had an easier ride than his choice for the Treasury post. Until he was confirmed, Bentsen, 71, kept his Senate seat and remained the chairman of the Finance Committee, the same panel that reviewed his qualifications. Daniel Patrick Moynihan, D-N.Y., who was taking over as Finance chairman, held a roll call on Bentsen's nomination 20 minutes into the Jan. 12 hearing, before questioning had even begun. The committee approved the nomination by a 19-0 vote.

In his testimony before the Finance panel, Bentsen stressed that trimming the deficit topped Clinton's list of priorities, although he noted that it was possible to "overdo it" by cutting the deficit too quickly — a course that he said could "put the economy back into a serious recession." He indicated that if unemployment remained high, a modest deficit-widening stimulus package might be necessary to promote job growth. His warnings about the fragility of the economic recovery reflected a modest difference in emphasis from Budget Director-designate Leon E. Panetta, who soft-pedaled the the notion of a short-term stimulus package, suggesting that there might be no need for it at all.

Bentsen refused to rule out tax increases on the middle class and made it clear that the administration expected to make cuts in entitlement spending. "I think you have to address entitlements along with taxes and along with fiscal restraint," he said. "It will be a tough package." Bentsen floated a gasoline tax increase, higher estate taxes and cuts in Medicare as deficit-reduction options. All of these ultimately ended up in the administration's deficit-reduction package that was passed by Congress in August.

Bentsen emphasized a point frequently made by Clinton, that efforts to limit federal spending for Medicare and Medicaid, the nation's fastest growing entitlements, would only be successful if accompanied by an overhaul of the nation's health-care system. "You have to address the underlying cost of health care. It's not enough to say you're going to make some limitations on entitlements. You have to go beyond that," Bentsen said.

While Finance panel members generally applauded Bentsen's hard line on the deficit, there were early glimpses of the difficulties that Clinton would have in convincing Congress to go along with specific proposals. When Bentsen mentioned that cuts in Social Security benefits were

being considered to help balance the budget, Moynihan bristled. "I hope we don't get into the mistake of thinking that it is the Social Security System . . . that has brought us to this condition. It's not," Moynihan said. *(Nomination, 1992 Almanac, p. 147-A)*

LEON PANETTA

The Senate on Jan. 21 confirmed former California Democratic Rep. Leon E. Panetta by voice vote to be director of the Office of Management and Budget. The Senate Governmental Affairs Committee had approved Panetta's nomination by voice vote on Jan. 13.

Panetta, who chaired the House Budget Committee from 1989 to 1992, told the committee Jan. 11 that deficit reduction would be the new administration's highest priority — ahead of a middle-class tax cut or a short-term economic stimulus package. Panetta, 54, had panned Clinton's economic plan when it was released in 1992, complaining that it was not a sufficiently serious attack on the deficit. "Obviously I think all of us are interested in trying to improve the progressivity of the tax system, in trying to improve its fairness," Panetta said. "But I think our first priority right now is to do deficit reduction and to do the investments that need to be made."

Panetta also said that Clinton's commitment to a long-term investment in education, infrastructure and the like was not incompatible with the goal of reducing the deficit.

At the same time, in keeping with the new White House economic team's effort to lower expectations of how much deficit reduction actually could be achieved, Panetta announced a new long-term deficit-cutting goal, that of reducing the ratio of the deficit to the gross domestic product (GDP) from 4.9 percent to less than 1 percent, a level that had not been reached since 1974. By linking the deficit to the GDP, a measure of the size of the economy, Panetta set a goal that could be met by reducing the size of the deficit, enlarging the economy or some combination of the two. One obvious implication of the 1 percent target was that there would always be a deficit of some size. Panetta told the committee that he was not sure that bringing the deficit all the way down to zero was "an absolute essential."

Panetta did promise that the Clinton team would deliver a "bold" deficit-reduction package, and he argued strongly that increased taxes of some kind would have to be part of the mix. He said that he favored a ratio of two-thirds spending cuts to one-third increased revenues — a goal that the administration later would find it was unable to reach.

During his hearing, Panetta got a hint of the difficulty the administration would face in the Senate. Noting that Senate Republicans had the power to frustrate Clinton's economic plans, Pete V. Domenici, R-N.M., warned, "You're not going to get the kind of deficit reduction that is required to really get the deficit under control if you expect one party to do it."

Panetta agreed, but he also issued a warning of his own. "It's a two-way street," he told Domenici. "If we come forward and present a tough plan to the country . . . then it's important that the respected members on the minority side are willing to say he's made the tough choices and [are] willing to try to work with us. But if the first reaction is to kick the hell out of us . . . that makes it very difficult then to try to build that kind of bipartisan relationship."

Fair enough, Domenici said, adding: "If you want Republican support, then you have to get Republicans in-

volved in helping with the deficit-reduction package. . . . If you want to be bold enough to put all the entitlements in unilaterally, and not talk to any of us, I admonish against it, because you're inviting disaster." *(Nomination, 1992 Almanac, p. 148-A)*

ALICE RIVLIN

The Senate confirmed Alice M. Rivlin as deputy director of the Office of Management and Budget by voice vote Jan. 21. Rivlin, a senior fellow at the Brookings Institution and the first director of the Congressional Budget Office when that agency was formed in 1975, was approved by the Governmental Affairs Committee earlier that day on a voice vote.

In her testimony, she amplified Panetta's comments by calling the deficit the "greatest long-term threat to the health of our economy" and predicting that "we will make a lot of people mad at us by reminding them of [its] importance."

She also agreed with Panetta's pronouncement that "everything will be on the table" in the administration's discussions of how to get the deficit under control, including such politically touchy programs as Social Security and Medicare. "We shouldn't rule out some adjustment in non-means-tested entitlements," she said, referring to programs such as Social Security that distribute benefits regardless of a recipient's other income. *(Nomination, 1992 Almanac, p. 148-A)*

ROGER ALTMAN

The Senate approved Clinton's choice for deputy Treasury secretary, Roger C. Altman, by voice vote on Jan. 21. The Finance Committee had recommended his confirmation by voice vote on Jan. 19. Altman, who served as assistant Treasury secretary during the Carter administration, was vice president of a Wall Street investment firm, The Blackstone Group, where he was responsible for its worldwide mergers and acquisitions business.

Echoing the other nominees' attention to the deficit, Altman told the Finance Committee on Jan. 13, "We have been consuming too much and investing too little," and called for a combination of spending cuts and tax increases to control the deficit. Questioned about the need for higher gasoline taxes, he said, "I do think that one form or another of new tax on consumption is necessary. I'm in the midst, together with a variety of other people, of course, of evaluating various alternatives."

LAURA TYSON

Clinton's choice to head the Council of Economic Advisers (CEA), Laura D'Andrea Tyson, won voice vote approval in the Senate on Feb. 4, one day after the Senate Banking Committee had approved her nomination by a vote of 18-0.

Tyson, an economist at the University of California at Berkeley, went before the Senate Banking Committee on Jan. 21 determined to counter critics who questioned her commitment to free markets and her credentials for the job. Tyson emphasized her adherence to free-market principles, but she also offered glimpses of the pragmatic streak on economic matters that led her to champion a greater role for government in helping U.S. industry compete against subsidized and protected foreign competitors. "We need to recognize that the kind of international competition that we are engaged in is not simply a market phenomenon," she said. "Let's understand what foreign com-

panies are doing, and let's think about what we can do, consistent with our own system."

Clinton's choice of Tyson, a microeconomist who had concentrated on trade and competitiveness issues, for a position usually filled by a macroeconomist had raised questions about the role of the CEA in the new administration. There were also doubts about how much influence Tyson would wield, because Clinton has created another entity for giving economic advice, the National Economic Council, headed by Robert E. Rubin.

Describing herself as a "cautious activist," Tyson hewed close to the Clinton line on economic policy, saying the federal government would have to become more involved in opening markets abroad, expanding civilian research and development, training workers and assisting U.S. industry. But she denied being an advocate for an industrial policy under which the government would pick strategic industries to subsidize.

"It's not the government choosing which things to promote and which not to promote," Tyson said, adding that she would like to see policies that encouraged investment, training, and research and development to "help all industries."

Panel Democrats praised Tyson, who earned a doctorate in economics from the Massachusetts Institute of Technology in 1974, for being pragmatic on trade and economic issues. She had just published a book on high-technology trade and competitiveness titled "Who's Bashing Whom" that outlined an aggressive trade policy to assist U.S. companies hurt by trade barriers and subsidized foreign competition.

"The competitiveness of the American economy has exhibited continuing and disturbing signs of erosion," Tyson said. "During the past decade our trade imbalances have totaled over a trillion dollars. Our producers have lost key market shares in several key international industries — computers, automobiles, commercial aircraft, telecommunications products, machine tools — to name a few." ■

Senate Confirms Kantor as Trade Representative

The Senate on Jan 21 confirmed former Los Angeles lobbyist and Clinton campaign operative Mickey Kantor as U.S. Trade Representative by voice vote, two days after the nominee won unanimous approval from the Senate Finance Committee. Kantor, 53, met little difficulty, despite criticism about his lack of experience in the international trade arena and the deep division that beset Democrats on trade issues.

The major faultline, which came into sharp focus with the North American Free Trade Agreement (NAFTA) looming, was between old-time free-traders and those who wanted a more aggressive, protectionist posture. During the campaign, Clinton had identified himself as a free-trader. But during his Jan. 19 appearance before the Senate Finance Committee, Kantor acknowledged that the new administration had yet to make key strategic decisions regarding imminent trade issues.

Kantor's supporters said that his talents as a negotiator would more than compensate for his inexperience. They pointed out that previous trade representatives, including his widely lauded predecessor, Carla A. Hills, came to the job without much background in international trade.

"Prior trade experience is not a prerequisite for this job. Rather, it's intelligence, it's [having] very good negotiating skill," Max Baucus, D-Mont., chairman of the International Trade Subcommittee, told the nominee. "And I can tell . . . you're a tough negotiator."

During his testimony, Kantor reiterated that Clinton did not want to reopen negotiations with Mexico and Canada on NAFTA, but he signaled there was room for changes to the pact through supplemental accords. He expressed support for continuing negotiations on strengthening the General Agreement on Tariffs and Trade, which had dragged on inconclusively throughout the Reagan and Bush administrations. Kantor indicated that the Clinton administration would seek to extend so-called fast-track procedures, which barred Congress from amending trade agreements submitted for its approval. The fast-track rules were set to expire May 31. He also indicated that the administration would likely seek renewal of the so-called Super 301 section of U.S. trade law. The law, which lapsed in 1990, authorized trade sanctions against nations that failed to eliminate import barriers identified by the trade representative in an annual report. *(Nomination, 1992 Almanac, p. 153-A)* ■

New Chairmen Chosen For SEC, FDIC

Later in the year, President Clinton nominated a new chairman for the Securities and Exchange Commission (SEC) and a new head for the Federal Deposit Insurance Corporation (FDIC).

ARTHUR LEVITT

On July 26, the Senate easily confirmed Arthur Levitt Jr., the former chairman of the American Stock Exchange, to become SEC chairman, the nation's top securities regulator. Levitt, 62, took over from Richard C. Breeden, a Republican who was popular on Capitol Hill.

A New Yorker who helped raise big money for Clinton's presidential campaign, Levitt had broad experience in the markets. He built a small brokerage house into the giant that later became Shearson Lehman Bros. Inc. He guided the American Stock Exchange through the 1987 stock-market crash.

The Senate Banking Committee had approved Levitt's nomination, 19-0, on July 22.

RICKI TIGERT

On Nov. 17, Clinton nominated Ricki R. Tigert to chair the FDIC. A partner in the Washington law firm Gibson, Dunn and Crutcher, Tigert was associate general counsel at the Federal Reserve Board from 1985 to 1992 and a senior counsel at the Treasury Department from 1983 to 1985.

If confirmed, Tigert would become the first woman to head the FDIC, the federal agency charged with administering federal guarantes for bank deposits. The FDIC chairmanship had been vacant since the death of William Taylor in August 1992.

The Senate Banking Committee recommended Tigert's confirmation 16-1 on Feb. 10, 1994.

But the nomination became hung up when Republicans vowed to block it over an unrelated fight with the Democrats. Republicans were angry because Democrats had refused to hold hearings to look into President and Hillary Rodham Clinton's investment in the Whitewater land deal and their ties to a failed Arkansas thrift, Madison Guaranty Savings and Loan.

During the Banking Committee vote, Lauch Faircloth, R-N.C., opposed Tigert's nomination, citing the nominee's acquaintance with Clinton. He said their relationship posed a potential conflict of interest, noting that the FDIC was to be one agency investigating allegations of financial impropriety at Madison.

Earlier, Tigert wrote panel members and promised to recuse herself from any involvement in the FDIC's investigation of Madison.

Robert F. Bennett, R-Utah, said he agreed with Faircloth, but he cast his vote for Tigert. "This otherwise qualified and competent nominee has been caught in the cross-fire of circumstance," he said. ∎

GOVERNMENT/ COMMERCE

'Better Government' Plan Unveiled

White House report offers ways to save billions, make government more responsive

President Clinton and Vice President Al Gore on Sept. 7 unveiled a sweeping proposal that they said would make the federal government work better and cost less. The report, prepared by a multiagency review team headed by Gore, became widely known as the "reinventing government" plan.

Clinton and Gore presented the proposal in a ceremony on the White House lawn that poked fun at the government's regulatory excesses by featuring two forklifts carrying thousands of pounds of regulations.

The promise of "better government" embodied in the plan was Clinton's answer to former Republican President Ronald Reagan's call for "less government."

On Capitol Hill, the grumbling from members of Congress began immediately. The amount of claimed savings quickly came under attack, and lawmakers, who had spent years defending some of the programs that Gore wanted reinvented, signaled their reluctance to cede legislative ground or to give up pet projects without a fight.

Most of the suggestions in the report, which ranged from cutting the federal work force by 12 percent — 252,000 workers — to overhauling procurement laws, were expected to take years to enact. The plan called for updating information systems, eliminating select programs and subsidies, and cutting red tape.

It proposed, for example, to end subsidies for wool, mohair and honey production. It vowed to slash regulations by half and transform the culture of the federal work force to put taxpayers first. *(Highlights, p. 194)*

The report — entitled "From Red Tape to Results: Creating a Government That Works Better and Costs Less" — outlined four broad purposes: making government services more responsive to the public; cutting red tape; giving rank-and-file government employees more flexibility and responsibility; and making programs more efficient.

Clinton promised to accomplish at least half of what Gore proposed by the stroke of his pen. Still, Congress had the power to undo any presidential order by enacting legislation or failing to fund an initiative. By the time his fiscal 1995 budget blueprint was released Feb. 7, 1994, Clinton had issued 16 executive orders in the name of reinventing government. Some other recommendations that required congressional action were written into Clinton's fiscal 1995 budget.

On Nov. 22, the House approved a large chunk of the reinventing government plan when it passed a $37 billion, five-year package of spending cuts (HR 3400) that included $35.2 billion in savings culled from the reinventing government report. The Senate did not act on HR 3400. *(Budget cuts, p. 140)*

Most of the savings included in HR 3400, $32.5 billion, were to be achieved through the plan to reduce the federal work force by 252,000 over five years. Other savings included trimming the number of field offices at the departments of Agriculture and Housing and Urban Develop-

ment, canceling the Energy Department's advanced liquid metal reactor program and farming out executive branch printing duties to private companies.

Other recommendations were adopted in some form in fiscal 1994 spending bills, including the proposals to bar subsidies for honey and phase out those for wool and mohair.

Other proposals — including plans to reform government procurement practices and to offer federal employees cash incentives to retire — were broken off and began to move through Congress as separate bills. One measure, to require the use of performance standards, became law.

BACKGROUND

While some of the Gore report — the 12th plan in a century to streamline the government — recycled old ideas, the plan's premise was new. It was drawn largely from the 1992 corporate self-help book "Reinventing Government" by David Osborne and Ted Gaebler.

Past efforts at reform, such as the Grace Commission of 1982-84, focused on less government, a central tenet of Republican ideology. Gore's plan hewed to the conservative Democratic doctrine of making government more entrepreneurial, lean and responsive to customers' needs.

Clinton and Gore had made reinventing government a campaign issue during the 1992 presidential race, borrowing the phrase from public policy guru Osborne, who helped Gore craft the plan. The effort started in earnest in early March, when Gore launched a six-month National Performance Review.

The report's main theory was that the federal government's management style had long been abandoned by even the most rigid companies. The government remained a large, top-down bureaucracy that fostered loyalty only to bloated chains of command and adherence to procedure. The information-age economy, in which products changed and data flowed at lightning speed, required a decentralized government with power and accountability distributed among the lower echelons of the federal work force, the report said.

Gore's plan aimed to adopt corporate management techniques such as rewarding performance and innovation rather than fealty to rules.

The report was filled with examples of waste: The Defense Department owned more than $40 billion in unnecessary supplies. The Agriculture Department operated an average of nearly four field service offices for every county in the nation. Managers at one national forest in Oregon had 53 separate budgets.

"The federal government seems unable to abandon the obsolete," the report concluded. "It knows how to add, but not to subtract."

Some of Gore's recommendations rehashed old fights in the endless power struggle between the executive and legis-

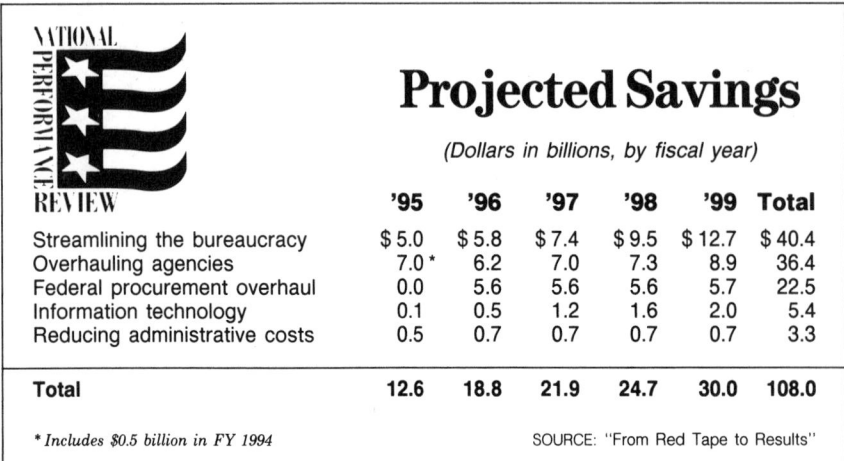

Projected Savings

(Dollars in billions, by fiscal year)

	'95	'96	'97	'98	'99	Total
Streamlining the bureaucracy	$ 5.0	$ 5.8	$ 7.4	$ 9.5	$ 12.7	$ 40.4
Overhauling agencies	7.0 *	6.2	7.0	7.3	8.9	36.4
Federal procurement overhaul	0.0	5.6	5.6	5.6	5.7	22.5
Information technology	0.1	0.5	1.2	1.6	2.0	5.4
Reducing administrative costs	0.5	0.7	0.7	0.7	0.7	3.3
Total	**12.6**	**18.8**	**21.9**	**24.7**	**30.0**	**108.0**

Includes $0.5 billion in FY 1994   SOURCE: "From Red Tape to Results"

lative branches. Others were more novel.

The report proposed such perennials as a two-year budget cycle and modified line-item veto powers, as well as such broad new approaches as scrapping the entire Federal Personnel Manual and allowing midlevel managers to shop for the best retail prices when buying laptop computers.

Weeks before Gore's report was even released, lawmakers launched a number of pre-emptive strikes against moves that Gore's staff was considering.

For example, when Sen. Ernest F. Hollings, D-S.C., learned that a Gore aide had recommended deregulating the maritime industry, he quickly introduced a bill (S 1432) to hold off such a move until another special commission studied the industry. *(Study, p. 214)*

Other lawmakers inserted provisions in various appropriations bills to prevent the Bureau of Alcohol, Tobacco and Firearms from being consolidated with the FBI and to bar the Agriculture Department from closing Forest Service field offices — two proposals considered by the vice president.

ACTION

The president's first round of executive orders to carry out the plan were released with the report Sept. 7. Other orders continued to trickle out of the White House throughout 1993.

The initial orders set "customer service" standards for agencies that dealt directly with taxpayers. For example, the Internal Revenue Service promised to return tax refunds within 40 days, or 14 days if the return was filed electronically and 21 days if the refund was deposited into the taxpayer's bank account electronically. Clinton ordered federal agencies to eliminate half their internal regulations within three years.

On Oct. 1, he signed an executive order that created a layer of bureaucracy — the National Partnership Council — which the report said was to smooth relations between management and labor in the federal work force. Because rank-and-file workers were promised a larger voice in management issues, the three largest federal employee unions supported the "reinventing government" plan.

In releasing the reinventing government report, the White House also directed all federal agencies to cut their payroll by 12 percent through attrition, buyouts and relocations — actions the administration said would save $40.4 billion over five years.

Congressional Action

The package of spending cuts passed by the House in November was by far the biggest of the bills that began moving through Congress.

The House did not act on a procurement reform bill (HR 2238) before the first session ended. The Government Operations Committee approved HR 2238 on July 28 by voice vote. The bill, among other things, required federal agencies to purchase, when possible, off-the-shelf products and raised the limit for small-order purchases from $25,000 to $50,000 to reduce paperwork requirements. The bill was also referred to the Armed Services Committee, which took no action. The Senate took no action on its version of procurement overhaul (S 1587), which awaited action in the Governmental Affairs, Armed Services and Small Business committees. *(Procurement, p. 197)*

To help shrink the federal payroll, House and Senate committees marked up separate bills (HR 3345, S 1535) to provide eligible federal workers with cash incentives to resign or retire early. The bills also provided for workers to be trained at taxpayer expense in areas not directly related to their jobs if the training was in the government's interest. Both bills awaited floor action. *(Buyouts, p. 197)*

Congress cleared legislation (S 20) requiring federal agencies to develop performance standards and use them to measure and account for progress on specific programs by March 31, 2000. Clinton signed the bill into law Aug. 3 (PL 103-62). *(Performance standards, p. 196)*

SELLING THE PLAN

Clinton and Gore quickly launched a campaign to sell the reinvention by heading for town halls and talk shows, recognizing that they had to marshal robust political forces outside the Beltway to develop a formidable coalition within it. By pitching a new "customer service contract" with American taxpayers, the administration hoped to create a populist movement to propel Capitol Hill to accept numerous government changes that had been shelved several times before.

The vice president appeared on David Letterman's "Late Show" Sept. 8 to dramatize wasteful tests required for government-issued products. Gore wore goggles and used a hammer to shatter an ashtray built to government specifications.

In Congress, Clinton and Gore saw allies in the 114-member freshman class, which was swept into office in 1992 largely on a tide of voter anger against government. And the White House rallied Republicans who viewed Gore's promise of "better government" as at least close to their call for "less government." Within their own ranks, they hoped to win over vulnerable veteran Democrats pressured by voters eager to realize 1992 independent presidential candidate Ross Perot's call for better government.

The administration needed Republican votes for the plan to overcome opposition from powerful Democratic committee chairmen who opposed many of Gore's proposals. "He can't succeed without Republican support — and a lot of it," said Sen. Trent Lott, R-Miss.

Republican lawmakers said they would work with the

What To Do With Work Force Savings?

In a rare display of budgetary harmony, the Clinton administration and bipartisan majorities of the House and Senate agreed that forcing the federal bureaucracy to shed a quarter of a million workers by 1999 was a great idea.

What they could not agree on, however, was what to do with the savings.

The amount was estimated to be as much as $40 billion or as little as $20 billion, depending on the speed with which jobs were eliminated and the possibility of extending buyouts to existing employees.

In the Senate, lawmakers passed a crime bill (HR 3355) Nov. 19 that fenced off much of the money to pay for the federal war on crime. The House did not take up the crime bill in 1993. *(Crime bill, p. 293)*

For its part, the House approved a package of spending cuts (HR 3400) on Nov. 22 that required the personnel cuts and left the savings unassigned. The money could be used to help Congress meet statutory limits on discretionary spending. Or it could create spending room under the limits for other priorities. *(Budget cuts, p. 140)*

Meanwhile, a strong bipartisan minority in the House and a group of unknown size in the Senate wanted to devote the savings to deficit reduction. The groups argued that the cuts were pointless if the savings were not locked in for deficit reduction by lowering the limits on discretionary spending by a like amount. Opponents said the spending limits already assumed that personnel cuts would be used to help meet them. Forcing down the limits would require much more in unanticipated spending cuts from other programs, opponents contended.

Reduction Certain

Whatever the outcome, one thing was virtually certain: The federal work force would shrink. Even if Congress did not mandate the reductions and claim the savings, the Clinton administration already had begun the process.

In a February executive order, President Clinton required federal agencies to eliminate 100,000 federal jobs by 1995 from a total civilian, non-postal work force of more than 2 million.

In September, Clinton upped the ante by moving to implement the recommendations of Vice President Al Gore's government-streamlining National Performance Review. To do so, he ordered federal agencies to submit plans to eliminate 252,000 non-postal jobs by 1999 (the Postal Service already had implemented its own work force reduction).

The target was middle management, not rank-and-file workers. The plan was to trim the existing ratio of one manager for every five to seven workers down to the 1-15 ratio that was common in the private work force.

And, although the administration planned to achieve most of the cutbacks through attrition, it hoped to offer buyouts of up to $25,000 apiece to help speed the process. Separate bills (HR 3345, S 1535) were moving in the House and Senate to authorize that process.

An initial analysis by the Congressional Budget Office (CBO) projected that the largest share — about 160,000 jobs — probably would come from Defense Department civilian workers, with the balance coming from other agencies. That estimate was hotly disputed, however.

White House, but with at least one condition: that any savings from the proposal go directly toward deficit reduction — a commitment the White House did not make.

By emphasizing that savings should not be used for other federal programs but only to help lower the deficit, Republicans hoped to crystalize the difference between Republicans and Democrats.

At the same time, the White House faced pressure from traditional Democratic interest groups to steer any savings back into the programs from which those savings were to be gleaned. And the administration had to persuade entrenched old-guard Democratic committee chairmen to weigh a prevailing public disgust with government against their instincts toward turf preservation. From the start, though, powerful lawmakers geared up to battle the most controversial proposals.

For example, key appropriators fought efforts to alter the budget process and end congressional earmarks of individual spending items; opponents included Appropriations Chairmen Sen. Robert C. Byrd, D-W.Va., and Rep. William H. Natcher, D-Ky., and House Budget Committee Chairman Martin Olav Sabo, D-Minn. Sen. Wendell H. Ford, D-Ky., opposed Gore's plan to open the Government Printing Office to competition by allowing federal agencies to use commercial printers if they cost less. Ford co-chaired the Joint Printing Committee, which oversaw the agency. Don Edwards, D-Calif., chairman of the House Judiciary Civil and Constitu-

tional Rights Subcommittee, was skeptical about merging the Drug Enforcement Administration with the FBI.

The administration also faced an uphill fight to sustain the momentum needed to keep those forces in Congress interested in the plan. Impending battles over the North American Free Trade Agreement and health-care reform commanded the legislative spotlight.

One Package

Gore considered empaneling a commission to be a conduit for shipping a single reinventing government proposal to Congress, but he ultimately discarded the idea. Proponents of the commission said the best way to handle the recommendations was to put them into a single bill, rather than carving them up according to congressional jurisdiction.

The Senate Governmental Affairs Committee endorsed that approach Aug. 5, approving by voice vote a bill that included pieces of three reinventing-government measures introduced earlier in the year by committee Chairman John Glenn, D-Ohio, ranking member William V. Roth Jr., R-Del., and member Joseph I. Lieberman, D-Conn. The bill provided for a commission to review any legislative package offered by Gore.

House Democratic leaders also came under pressure from fiscal conservatives in their party to put Gore's myr-
Continued on p. 196

The Nuts and Bolts of Reinvention

The White House hoped to carry out at least half of the hundreds of recommendations in its "reinventing government" plan by executive order or other administrative steps. The remainder required congressional action. The following is an overview of the proposals and the challenges they faced from the outset:

● **Budget process.** Lengthen the budget and appropriations process from one year to two.

Because this required changes in budget law and congressional rules, Congress had to take the lead.

Historically, Congress made significant changes to the budget process only with great difficulty and usually as part of a larger package, such as the radical overhauls of the process in 1985 (Gramm-Rudman anti-deficit law) and 1990 (spending caps and pay-as-you-go rules). While biennial budgeting had substantial congressional support, it also had detractors — chiefly the appropriators, who were reluctant to give up their opportunity to scrutinize and change spending totals every year.

● **Congressional restrictions.** Minimize congressional restrictions on agencies, such as line items and earmarks.

Executive branch agencies long had chafed under the directives Congress frequently wrote into appropriations bills and other legislation, but only Congress could change this practice.

Appropriators, in particular, jealously guarded their prerogative to order certain agency activities or direct specific spending as a condition of continued funding. Congressional reformers had crusaded against earmarking money for favored projects, with only limited success. It was unlikely that Congress would voluntarily give up its ability to shape executive branch actions.

● **Agency spending ceilings.** Establish an executive budget process to set spending ceilings for each agency before the budget was finalized.

The Office of Management and Budget (OMB) said it was already doing this. In what it characterized as a departure from the practice of past administrations, OMB said the White House was conducting a more "collaborative" budget process that began by working with agencies and departments to establish priorities and spending ceilings within which agencies could then develop their budgets.

No congressional action was needed.

● **Consolidating law enforcement.** Transfer law enforcement functions of the Drug Enforcement Administration (DEA) to the FBI, a Justice Department agency. If that was successful, combine the enforcement functions of the Bureau of Alcohol, Tobacco and Firearms (ATF) into the FBI and merge the ATF's revenue functions into the Internal Revenue Service.

Attorney General Janet Reno was ambivalent and was reviewing the suggestion. It was unclear whether the administration needed legislation to merge the DEA into the FBI. It took congressional action to consolidate ATF, which was part of the Treasury Department.

Reaction to the DEA consolidation proposal was skeptical at best among key legislators on the House and Senate Judiciary committees. Meanwhile, appropriators moved to pre-empt the administration by including a provision in the fiscal 1994 Treasury-Postal Service appropriations bill (HR 2403) that barred any transfer of ATF to the FBI. *(Appropriations, p. 679)*

● **Agriculture Department.** Close 1,200 Agriculture Department field offices to save $1.6 billion and trim 7,500 employees.

Most of the closures affected selected field offices of the Agricultural Stabilization and Conservation Service, the Soil Conservation Service, the Farmers Home Administration, the Cooperative Extension Service and the Federal Crop Insurance Corporation. The closures could be accomplished by administrative action. However, Agriculture Department officials had to navigate around laws that required field offices to be maintained to serve a limited geographic area. Department officials were using a six-point rating system to develop a list of offices to be closed or combined.

While no congressional action was required, local interests spurred some members to try to block particular closures. However, they had to go up against strong political sentiment to cut government waste. The consolidation plan promised to offer "one-stop shopping" for farmers for such separated federal services as crop support payments, rural housing loans and crop insurance — a convenience that could soften constituent opposition.

Influential supporters included Sen. Richard G. Lugar, R-Ind., whose 1992 proposal to close some field offices spurred a Bush administration study of Agriculture Department reorganization. The Gore plan also included a proposal by supporter Rep. Dan Glickman, D-Kan., that combined several Agriculture Department bureaus into a single Farm Services Administration.

● **Farm subsidies.** Eliminate federal subsidies for wool, mohair and honey. The fiscal 1994 Agriculture appropriations bill (HR 2493) ended the honey subsidy. Congress cleared a separate bill (S 1548) phasing out the wool and mohair subsidies and eliminating them in fiscal 1997. *(Appropriations, p. 546)*

● **Food safety consolidation.** Eliminate the Food Safety and Inspection Service (FSIS) by consolidating all food safety responsibilities under the Food and Drug Administration (FDA).

Legislative authorization was required to shift regulatory functions from one agency to another. Majorities on the House and Senate Agriculture committees resisted such a shift because it would give the House Energy and Commerce and Senate Commerce committees jurisdiction over the issue. Appropriators had less of a turf concern: Both the Agriculture Department and the FDA were funded by the annual agriculture spending bill.

In addition, Agriculture Secretary Mike Espy said he "agreed to disagree" with Gore on shifting food safety and inspection responsibilities from his department to the FDA, an arm of the Health and Human Services Department. Although he embraced most of the reorganization proposals, Espy said that food safety could be achieved "with our current structure."

● **Agency field offices.** Submit a report to Congress within 18 months on closing or consolidating 28,800 other federal civilian facilities.

Each agency was to develop plans to close, cut back or consolidate field offices. They were to submit these plans to the President's Management Council, which was to submit them to Congress for approval.

While many lawmakers agreed in principle that closing field offices was an admirable goal, each office employed and served constituents nationwide. Attempts to close specific offices were likely to run into resistance in Congress.

● **Paying taxes by credit card.** Allow the Internal Revenue Service to develop a system that would let people pay taxes by credit card.

Congressional action was required to make the change. The Ways and Means Committee included it in a tax simplification bill (HR 3419) that it approved Nov. 3.

The idea had not advanced in the past, in part because of potential problems involving bankruptcy law. Tax debts could not be erased through bankruptcy, but credit card debts could. Bankrupt individuals could evade their tax liabilities by putting the charges on their credit cards. The Senate Judiciary Committee sought to solve that problem as part of a bill to overhaul bankruptcy law (S 540) approved Sept. 15.

● **Private collection agencies.** Allow federal agencies, such as the IRS, to use private collection agencies to collect debts.

The proposal required a potentially controversial change in tax law regarding the privacy of tax return information. Under existing law, such information could be used only by the IRS. Allowing private bill collectors to collect debts was something the Education

Department had done with some success. But Congress had resisted giving such companies access to sensitive tax information.

• **Personnel manual.** Simplify and decentralize personnel policy by phasing out the voluminous Federal Personnel Manual.

Lawyers at the Office of Personnel Management were going through the manual to see how much could be dropped by the administration and how much could only be excised by Congress. Lawmakers wanted to cut back on personnel regulations, but there had been little discussion of junking the entire personnel manual.

• **Air traffic controllers.** Restructure the Federal Aviation Administration's (FAA) overworked and underfunded air-traffic control system into a government-owned corporation supported by user fees and governed by a board of directors.

An interagency task force was studying this idea, which was recommended by a special commission studying the aviation industry. The Transportation Department and the FAA were reviewing the proposal, too, as a potential way to upgrade the air-traffic control system.

The House and Senate Aviation subcommittees had explored the idea of making the FAA independent, but not splitting off the air-traffic control system. Either move required congressional approval. Aides said air-traffic control was so intertwined with other FAA functions that it was very difficult to segregate them. There also was concern that user fees would have to be raised significantly to support the system.

• **Energy labs.** Consolidate and redirect the Energy Department's laboratories and weapons facilities.

The Energy Department had been working for several years on proposals to consolidate its weapons research, production and testing facilities. Energy Secretary Hazel R. O'Leary had continued this effort with a new emphasis: using the department's laboratories to help develop technology for U.S. industries. The wide-ranging functions of the weapons labs overlapped in many areas. O'Leary had cautioned against eliminating this duplication, however, as had the White House science adviser, John H. Gibbons.

Senate Energy Committee Chairman J. Bennett Johnston, D-La., and House Science Committee Chairman George E. Brown Jr., D-Calif., had been pushing bills to redirect the Energy Department labs with an eye toward boosting U.S. industrial competitiveness. The Senate included much of Johnston's bill (S 473) in the fiscal 1994 defense authorization bill (S 1298), but it was dropped in conference. Brown's bill (H 1432), which put more emphasis on consolidating federal laboratories, was still in Brown's committee. *(Federal energy labs, p. 248)*

• **User fees.** Allow agencies more freedom to set user fees and spend the revenue raised.

User fees gained popularity in Congress in the 1980s as an alternative to higher income taxes. Letting the agencies set and spend their own fees, however, was another matter. Congress overhauled the budget process in 1921 to unify it, rather than having agencies pursuing funds independently. And members of the Appropriations committees had resisted efforts to let agencies spend money that had not been appropriated.

• **HUD offices.** Eliminate all regional offices of the Department of Housing and Urban Development (HUD), pare its system of 80 field offices and cut field staff by 1,500 positions.

HUD Secretary Henry G. Cisneros was among the first in the Clinton administration to seek to "reinvent" his department, which had been rife with scandals and inefficiencies. HUD could streamline its ranks through attrition and buyouts, without congressional action.

Cisneros was likely to consult with key members of Congress before launching a major redesign. He generally had been careful to court Congress.

• **Federal benefits.** Create a system for paying federal benefits electronically.

This idea had been bubbling up to the federal level from states and localities. Some federal agencies, especially the Agriculture Department and, to some extent, Health and Human Services, had approved experiments in certain states and localities to allow electronic distribution of food stamps and Aid to Families With Dependent Children payments. The Clinton administration wanted to broaden the program, encompassing federal retirement, Social Security and unemployment insurance benefits.

Much of the work could be done administratively by coordinating computer systems among federal agencies and with states and localities. However, the move raised several controversial issues that required congressional action. For example, the Federal Reserve Board could find that participants with electronic benefit cards deserved the same sort of protection from fraud or loss that users of credit cards had. This was expected to spur calls for congressional action to limit the liability of federal agencies, states and localities.

• **AID missions.** Reduce the number of U.S. Agency for International Development (AID) overseas missions from 150 to perhaps 50.

Long criticized as poorly managed and inefficient, AID was a favorite target of lawmakers and executive branch officials seeking to overhaul the federal bureaucracy. Indeed, some lawmakers criticized the administration's proposal — which rejected calls for merging AID with the State Department — as too minor.

After the administration ran into delays in drafting legislation to revamp the foreign aid program, Congress began taking steps in that direction. The Senate Foreign Relations Committee approved a foreign aid authorization bill (S 1467) that required AID to reduce the number of countries in which it operated by 20 percent by the end of fiscal 1994. Later in the year, AID Administrator J. Brian Atwood took administrative action to streamline AID, announcing plans to close 21 overseas missions during the next three fiscal years. *(Foreign aid authorization, p. 502)*

• **Corps of Engineers.** Reduce the number of Army Corps of Engineers regional offices from 11 to six.

The Bush administration unveiled a $215 million reorganization plan for the Army Corps of Engineers in November 1992. It included reducing the number of division offices from 11 to six and eliminating overlap. A corps spokesman said the plan was to result in annual savings of $115 million. The reorganization was put on hold in January, pending a review by the Defense Department.

Funding for the reorganization required congressional approval. Several members of the House Appropriations and Armed Services committees had opposed the move in 1992.

• **Water pollution.** Promote market-based approaches to reducing water pollution.

Environmental Protection Agency Administrator Carol M. Browner backed the proposal. It was similar to market-based provisions in the 1990 Clean Air Act amendments that allowed industries with low sulfur dioxide emissions to trade their pollution permits with companies that spewed more pollution into the air than limits allowed. Extending the proposal to water pollution required legislation.

Some business groups were pressing lawmakers to include the trading of water pollution permits in a rewrite of the nation's clean water law (S 1114), but the bill did not advance in 1993.

• **Inspectors general.** Redirect the inspectors general, concentrating on collaborative efforts to improve management systems instead of adversarial compliance audits.

A separate executive order was required to direct each agency head to make this change. Inspectors general then would focus on evaluating programs for efficiency and cost-effectiveness. Although no legislation was needed, members were expected to keep a close eye on the offices of inspectors general to ensure that the new focus did not change or diminish their statutory role as watchdogs for fraud and abuse.

• **Davis-Bacon.** Raise from $2,000 to $100,000 the threshold for federal contracts covered under the Davis-Bacon Act, which required that workers be paid the prevailing local wage.

Congressional action was needed to implement the proposal. A House Education and Labor subcommittee Nov. 16 approved a bill (HR 1231) to raise the threshold as the Gore report proposed. Many Republicans wanted to raise it even higher. *(Davis-Bacon, p. 399)* ∎

Performance Standards

Congress cleared legislation (S 20) requiring federal agencies to develop performance standards and use them to measure and account for progress on specific programs by March 31, 2000. The administration adopted the bill as part of its plan to "reinvent government." President Clinton signed it into law Aug. 3 (PL 103-62). *(Reinventing government, p. 191)*

The measure required that by Sept. 30, 1997, each agency that spent more than $20 million annually had to submit to the Office of Management and Budget (OMB) a five-year plan setting out its strategic goals. Agencies had to update the plan at least every three years. Beginning with fiscal 1999, OMB was required to submit a governmentwide performance plan with the annual budget.

Each agency in turn was required to submit to OMB an annual performance plan covering all the programs in its budget, with indicators for measuring success or failure. Beginning March 31, 2000, agency heads were required to submit to the president and Congress annual reports on actual performance for the previous year.

The bill provided for OMB to start the process by selecting 10 agencies to carry out pilot performance review projects in fiscal 1994-96.

Federal employees opposed to the bill argued that it would require agencies to revamp their budgeting systems and result in unnecessary and time-consuming paperwork. Supporters said the measure, which allowed managers to waive some administrative requirements with the approval of OMB and the Office of Personnel Management, gave federal managers and other employees more autonomy, along with recognition for making programs successful.

"Federal program managers will for the first time be asked to document the successes of their programs and, eventually, tie their programs' success to their annual budget," said William F. Clinger, R-Pa., a leading cosponsor. "In these days of tighter budgets, managers will have to figure out how to do more with less."

House. The House Government Operations Committee Subcommittee on Legislation and National Security approved a performance standards bill (HR 826) on May 18, after amending it to make it essentially identical to the companion Senate measure (S 20). On May 20, the full committee — chaired by bill sponsor John Conyers Jr., D-Mich. — approved the measure by voice vote (H Rept 103-106, Part 1). The House passed it by voice vote May 25.

Senate. In the Senate, the Governmental Affairs Committee approved S 20 by voice vote March 24 (S Rept 103-58). The Senate passed the measure, sponsored by William V. Roth, R-Del., by voice vote June 23.

Roth had introduced similar legislation twice before, in 1990 and 1992. The Senate passed Roth's bill in 1992, but the measure never became law.

Final. The bill had to make one last stop in the House, where lawmakers approved provisions covering the U.S. Postal Service; the provisions had been left out of the House version because the Government Operations Committee did not have jurisdiction over that agency. The House cleared S 20 by voice vote July 15.

Continued from p. 193

iad proposals into one big package. HR 3400 was the closest Congress came to doing that, however.

In a Sept. 13 letter to Clinton, 34 Democrats, led by Dave McCurdy, Okla., and Timothy J. Penny, Minn., urged the administration and the House leadership to gather all legislation dealing with the Gore proposal into a single "Reinventing Government Act" to be subject to amendments and considered on both floors prior to adjournment for the year. They also asked House Speaker Thomas S. Foley, D-Wash., to form an ad hoc committee to coordinate the legislative package's course through the dozens of committees with jurisdiction over the various components of the bill. McCurdy said Foley reacted positively to the suggestion — though he never followed through with their idea.

Debating the Numbers

As the recommendations in the final report of the National Performance Review began moving on several tracks in Congress, estimates of the amount of money the effort was expected to save came under attack.

Roughly one-third of the proposal's projected savings, $36.4 billion, came from actual cuts in agency programs. The rest came from broad government overhauls — mostly through changes in personnel and procurement policies, which together accounted for $62.9 billion of Gore's projected savings.

The goal of reducing civilian personnel by 12 percent, or 252,000 employees, over five years was estimated to save $40.4 billion, the report said, though it did not specify how the figure was calculated. The report also estimated that changes in government purchasing policy would yield $22.5 billion in savings.

Republicans called Gore's savings estimates exaggerated. House Minority Leader Robert H. Michel, R-Ill., and Rep. John R. Kasich, R-Ohio, on Sept. 14 asked Congressional Budget Office (CBO) Director Robert D. Reischauer to analyze Gore's savings claims. Pete V. Domenici, R-N.M., ranking member of the Senate Budget Committee, made a similar request of the budget office.

A House Budget Committee analysis dramatically downgraded the claimed savings from the plan. It said the administration's estimated $108 billion in savings actually would provide just $37 billion in immediately usable savings from key discretionary accounts to meet the budget caps set by the 1994-98 budget agreement.

The analysis found that $30 billion in savings was to come in 1999, outside the 1994-98 time frame covered by the caps; that $25 billion had already been incorporated in defense cutbacks in the five-year deficit-reduction plan; that an additional $10 billion was to come from a 100,000-person reduction in the federal work force already assumed in the deficit plan; and that $6 billion was to come in the form of entitlements, user fees or revenues that could not be used to offset appropriations.

The Clinton-Gore initiative took another hit Nov. 15, when CBO downgraded the savings from the portion of the plan that had been included in HR 3400. Looking just at the savings from 1994 through 1998 (the administration plan also included savings for 1999), CBO knocked the likely deficit reduction down from the $5.9 billion claimed by the White House to only $305 million. Nervous House leaders and the administration then beefed up the bill by incorporating the plan to cut the federal work force — an element that was not originally part of HR 3400. ■

Early-Out Cash Incentives Approved by Committees

House and Senate committees approved separate bills to provide eligible federal workers with cash incentives to resign or retire early. The measures were designed to help the Clinton administration implement a key element of its "reinventing government" proposal. The bills awaited floor action when Congress adjourned for the year.

President Clinton and Vice President Al Gore had called Sept. 7 for reducing the federal work force by 252,000 slots by 1999 as a central part of their proposal to streamline government. The White House moved immediately to implement the recommendation by executive order. The bills (HR 3345, S 1535) that began moving through Congress promised to give the recommendation the force of law. *(Reinventing government, p. 191)*

The House on Nov. 22 passed a separate, five-year package of spending cuts (HR 3400) drawn largely from the reinventing government proposal. Most of the savings, $32.5 billion, came from implementing the administration's planned reduction in the federal work force. The House-passed bill did not authorize the cash incentives or specify how the cuts in the federal work force were to be achieved — though earlier versions of the bill had. It did, however, contain some of the other provisions included in the House and Senate versions of the employee buyout bills. Among them, HR 3400 allowed federal workers to be trained at taxpayer expense in areas not directly related to their jobs as long as the training benefited the federal government.

HOUSE COMMITTEE

The House Post Office and Civil Service Committee approved HR 3345 (H Rept 103-386) by a vote of 17-2 on Oct. 27.

The bill, introduced by committee Chairman William L. Clay, D-Mo., gave employees holding jobs targeted for elimination by the administration up to $25,000 to resign. Agency heads were given a 90-day period in which to offer the incentives, up until Dec. 31, 1994. Bill supporters said the measure would facilitate the administration's plan to reduce the federal work force, while minimizing the need for layoffs. Government officials wanted to avoid involuntary layoffs because they posed high costs for the government, including severance payments and unemployment compensation.

The full committee rejected, by voice vote, two amendments by Dan Burton, R-Ind., including one that would have permitted the executive branch to fill only one of every two job openings during the buyout process.

The bill loosened restrictions on the federal bureaucracy, allowing workers to be trained at taxpayer expense in areas not directly related to their jobs if the training was in the government's interest. It also limited to 90 days the amount of annual leave that members of the Senior Executive Service (SES), the top management level of the federal government, could accumulate. Without the provision, employees could earn unlimited annual leave.

The bill also authorized federal agencies to pay 9 percent of the salary of each person who took a buyout into the civil service retirement fund. It required agencies that planned to offer cash incentives to have a written policy

about the program and make it available to employees.

Subcommittees. A week earlier, two Post Office subcommittees approved an earlier version of the bill (HR 3218).

The Subcommittee on Compensation and Employee Benefits approved the measure, 5-0, on Oct. 21. The subcommittee added the requirement that federal agencies compile a written plan explaining the cash incentive program and make that available to employees.

On Oct. 20, the Civil Service Subcommittee also approved HR 3218.

SENATE COMMITTEE

The Senate Governmental Affairs Committee on Nov. 9 approved, 11-0, a companion bill (S 1535) that also allowed eligible federal workers to get cash incentives to leave their jobs early. The bill was sponsored by panel Chairman John Glenn, D-Ohio.

Like the House bill, S 1535 allowed some federal managers to offer cash bonuses of up to $25,000 to certain workers as an incentive for them to leave their jobs. Managers also were given more latitude in retraining workers, with the goal of having a smaller but more efficient federal staff.

Members approved, 7-5, an amendment that wrote into the bill the requirement that 252,000 positions — or 12 percent of the government work force — be cut by fiscal 1999.

By voice vote, the panel approved an amendment to prohibit federal workers who took the money from working for the federal government for five years. That provision stood to cause problems with the Defense Department, which wanted only a two-year hiatus.

HR 3400

The House Post Office Committee included the incentives for early retirement in the House version of the larger bill (HR 3400) that mandated the elimination of 252,000 federal jobs. The provisions, which were essentially the same as in HR 3345, allowed agency heads to offer employees holding jobs targeted for elimination by the administration up to $25,000 to resign. The agency heads had a 90-day period in which to offer the incentives, until Dec. 31, 1994.

But the final version of HR 3400, which the House approved Nov. 22, did not include the buyout provisions; opponents argued that they could cost more than they would save. *(Budget cuts, p. 140)* ∎

Procurement Revision Plan Never Makes It Off Shelf

The House Government Operations Committee on July 28 approved legislation to overhaul government procurement practices. The drive to simplify government buying was a key component of the Clinton administration's plan to streamline government. The full House took no action on the measure.

The bill (HR 2238), introduced by Government Operations Chairman John Conyers Jr., D-Mich., included a requirement that federal agencies buy off-the-shelf products when possible to save money. It also raised the limit

for small-order purchases from $25,000 to $50,000 — and in some cases $100,000 — to reduce paperwork requirements. The bill was jointly referred to the Armed Services Committee, where it awaited action when Congress adjourned for the year.

A companion Senate bill (S 1587) by Governmental Affairs Committee Chairman John Glenn, D-Ohio, awaited action in the Governmental Affairs, Armed Services and Small Business committees.

Background

Overhauling the way the government purchased products was a central element of a six-month study of ways to "reinvent" government led by Vice President Al Gore. *(Reinventing government, p. 191)*

The push for procurement reform came as much from economic necessity as from the desire to cut red tape. U.S. companies were tiring of layers of regulations and paperwork. They were beginning to say no to Uncle Sam's $200 billion in annual procurement requests, 70 percent of which were defense purchases. As post-Cold War era cuts continued, the Pentagon was losing the power it once had over its contractors. By the end of the 1990s, the Defense Department was expected to buy less than 5 percent of the manufacturing sector's $1 trillion output, down from 15 percent in 1986.

The administration estimated that overhauling procurement rules would yield savings of $22.5 billion over five years. But White House budget director Leon E. Panetta conceded that most benefits were so hard to quantify that the Congressional Budget Office likely would confirm only $3 billion to $5 billion in savings from the proposal.

The companion procurement overhaul bills offered by Conyers and Glenn differed in several ways, but their core components were similar. They encouraged:

● **Buying more off-the-shelf items.** Under existing law, any government contracts below $25,000 were considered "small purchases," requiring far less paperwork and cost-tracking measures. Both bills raised the threshold to $50,000 — or $100,000 when a federal entity completed the transaction by computer. This provision was intended to encourage electronic commerce.

● **Reducing paperwork.** Both bills encouraged the use of "electronic commerce" systems that allowed contractors to track their bids by computer networks. The bills also required simplified contracts that more closely resembled those in the commercial sector. Contractors on jobs worth less than $500,000 could bypass special accounting systems and avoid providing lengthy cost and pricing data to the government; under existing law, the cap was $100,000.

● **Keeping contractors informed.** Contractors often spent millions of dollars to place a bid, only to wait months without hearing about its status or why it was rejected. The bills aimed to improve the flow of information.

Legislative Action

House. The House Government Operations Committee on July 28 gave voice vote approval to HR 2238. The Legislation and National Security Subcommittee had approved the measure earlier the same day. The bill included language authorizing certain operations of the General Services Administration, the government's landlord, for unspecified sums through fiscal 1996. The provision replaced the permanent authorization for the agency with a cyclical authorization to give Congress regular opportunities to monitor the agency's work more closely.

Senate. Two key sponsors in the Senate came out against the legislation. Republicans William V. Roth Jr. of Delaware

and William S. Cohen of Maine, who had worked well with Democrats Glenn, Carl Levin of Michigan and Jeff Bingaman of New Mexico on the chamber's bill, dropped off the sponsor list just before the measure was introduced Oct. 26.

They were upset that Democrats, at the apparent behest of the administration and labor unions, dropped a long-sought provision to exempt contractors on jobs worth $100,000 or less from complying with the Davis-Bacon Act, which required contractors to pay prevailing regional minimum wages to all workers. ■

Senate Rejects Fellowship

The Senate Governmental Affairs Committee on June 9 refused to approve a measure that would have established a Mike Mansfield Fellowship Program for intensive training in the Japanese language, government and economy. The bill (S 587), rejected on a 4-5 vote, would have awarded two-year grants to federal workers to study the Japanese language and political system.

Mansfield, D-Mont. (House 1943-53; Senate 1953-77), was a former Senate majority leader who served as ambassador to Japan under presidents Jimmy Carter, Ronald Reagan and George Bush.

Democratic panel members, who had approved budget-reconciliation cuts of $10.7 billion over five years, argued against starting a program when others had to be cut. ■

Census Numbers Stand

A federal judge in New York declined April 13 to order an adjustment of the 1990 census to correct its undercount of racial minorities, even though he said an adjustment was probably in order. Judge Joseph M. McLaughlin let stand the Census Bureau's head count as the official basis for apportioning House seats, drawing district lines and distributing federal funds.

In 1991, the Census Bureau estimated the net undercount at 5.3 million people. Census officials, including Director Barbara E. Bryant, recommended adjustment. But then-Commerce Secretary Robert A. Mosbacher, in one of his last decisions before leaving the Cabinet to become chairman of President George Bush's re-election campaign, reversed the recommendation. *(1991 Almanac, p. 180)*

McLaughlin said Mosbacher probably erred when he refused to adjust that count. But he said there was no evidence that Mosbacher's July 1991 decision to use the head count was "arbitrary and capricious." As a result, he said, it could not be overturned. But he added: "Plaintiffs have made a powerful case that [Mosbacher's] discretion would have been more wisely employed in favor of adjustment. Indeed, were this court called upon to decide this case [from the start], I probably would have ordered the adjustment."

Mosbacher's decision was protested by big cities, big states, many minority group leaders and most congressional Democrats. It also revived an old lawsuit, filed in the 1980s by several of the nation's largest cities, challenging the Census Bureau count of urban populations. The case had been pending in McLaughlin's U.S. District Court since 1988. McLaughlin decided to take it with him when he was elevated to the 2nd U.S. Circuit Court of Appeals in New York. ■

'Motor Voter' Bill Enacted After 5 Years

After a five-year odyssey, backers of so-called motor-voter legislation aimed at boosting voter registration nationwide prevailed over Senate Republicans who argued that the measure would be too expensive for states to implement and would open the doors to new forms of vote fraud.

The bill (HR 2) required states to provide all eligible citizens the opportunity to register to vote when they applied for or renewed a driver's license. It also required states to allow mail-in registration and to provide registration forms at certain agencies that supplied public assistance, such as welfare checks or help for the disabled. The costs were to be borne by the states. Backers estimated that the changes, which were to take effect in 1995, would would add 50 million citizens to the voting rolls.

"Voting is an empty promise unless people vote," President Clinton said as he signed the bill into law (PL 103-31) at a White House ceremony May 20. "Now there is no longer the excuse of the difficulty of registration."

Republicans had used Senate procedures to block votes on the bill since 1990. But in 1993, sponsors attracted the votes of six Senate Republicans — more than enough to break a filibuster. To secure the GOP votes, sponsors agreed to drop a key provision that would have required registration sites at unemployment offices. Sponsors also added language designed to ensure that recipients of public benefits would not be pressured by agency employees into registering for a particular party.

BOXSCORE

➡ **National Voter Registration (HR 2, S 460).** The law required states to allow citizens to register to vote when applying for a driver's license, permit mail-in registration and provide registration forms at certain public assistance agencies.

Reports: H Rept 103-9; conference report, H Rept 103-66.

KEY ACTION

Feb. 4 — **House** approved HR 2 by a vote of 259-160.

March 9 — **Senate** voted 62-38 to invoke cloture and proceed to S 460; a cloture vote March 5 failed 52-36.

March 17 — **Senate** passed HR 2 by a vote of 62-37, after substituting the text of S 460. The Senate failed to invoke cloture the day before by 59-41.

May 5 — **House** adopted the conference report, 259-164.

May 11 — **Senate** cleared the bill, 62-36, after agreeing 63-37 to cut off debate.

May 20 — **President** signed HR 2 — PL 103-31.

---

offices, arguing that Democrats were trying to register inner-city residents who tended to vote Democratic. Democrats roundly denied the charge.

Efforts to increase voter registration had begun in a handful of states by the mid-1980s, with state legislatures ordering motor vehicle departments to provide voter registration forms. By 1992, 27 states had some type of so-called motor-voter practices in place. But state programs varied in their degree of sophistication and in their effect on turnout.

Lawmakers debated motor-voter legislation at length in the 101st and 102nd Congresses. In 1990, the House passed a motor-voter bill, only to see it die in the Senate after Republicans blocked floor consideration. *(1990 Almanac, p. 71)*

In 1991, Senate Republicans again held off a floor vote, as supporters were unable to muster the 60 votes necessary to break off debate and take up the measure. In 1992, Senate sponsors were able for the first time to round up enough votes to limit debate and pass a motor-voter bill; the House agreed to the Senate bill and sent it to the White House. But President George Bush vetoed the measure, saying it amounted to an "open invitation to fraud and corruption," and the Senate sustained the veto. *(1991 Almanac, p. 48; 1992 Almanac, p. 75)*

During the 1992 presidential campaign, Clinton said he would have signed the bill. With his election, Democratic leaders put the measure on a short list of items to complete in the first weeks of the 103rd Congress.

BACKGROUND

Virtually every politician and political scholar subscribed to the tenet that a legislative body was made more representative and more wholly democratic when voter participation was highest. Yet, according to the Federal Election Commission, only about 50 percent of those eligible to vote in the United States typically went to the polls on Election Day. That figure had remained largely unchanged since World War II, despite the fact that the voting age population had been steadily increasing.

While civic leaders and lawmakers were dismayed at the voter turnout, when it came to finding a way to increase registration nationwide, partisan politics took over.

Republicans had been effective for a number of years in blocking enhanced registration bills, which they warned would lead to a new wave of voter fraud, cost too much for states to implement and fail to have any ultimate effect on turnout. They also objected to proposed requirements that states make voter registration forms available at welfare

HOUSE ACTION

The House Administration Committee moved swiftly, approving the bill by a vote of 9-3 on Jan. 27. Opponents on the panel vowed to fight the bill on the floor, but they conceded that it likely would become law after all parliamentary tactics were exhausted.

As approved by the committee, the bill was nearly identical to the one Bush had vetoed in 1992. It required states to make registration forms available not only at motor vehicle departments but also at numerous state offices, including unemployment compensation offices, welfare offices and agencies that served the disabled.

The bill also elevated voting fraud to a federal offense punishable by as much as five years in prison.

It allowed, but did not require, states to use information from change-of-address forms filed with the Postal Service to update voter lists. The committee rejected, by voice vote, a package of amendments by Robert L. Livingston, R-La., that would have placed a cap on how long a registered

voter who failed to vote could be kept on an active list.

The committee also rejected, 4-10, an amendment by Pat Roberts, R-Kan., that would have made the bill voluntary until money was provided to states to pay for implementation.

The committee rejected, by voice vote, a series of other amendments by Livingston that he said would have strengthened anti-fraud sections of the bill. One rejected amendment would have removed mandates for mail-in registration.

Tempers flared when John A. Boehner, R-Ohio, suggested that the bill was being pushed by Democrats solely for "political advantage" to register more Democratic voters in the inner cities. "We all know what's going on here," Boehner said.

The comment brought a strong reaction from bill sponsor Al Swift, D-Wash., who said the "only aim" of the bill was to "remove the roadblocks" to voter registration put in place to stop immigrants and minorities from voting.

The Subcommittee on Elections, which Swift chaired, had approved the bill by voice vote Jan. 26.

House Floor Action

The House easily approved the bill by a vote of 259-160 on Feb. 4. *(Vote 26, p. 6-H)*

But first, lawmakers rejected, 166-253, a procedural move by Republicans to send the bill back to committee with instructions. Republicans wanted the committee to include language to delay implementation of the bill until state election officials notified the Justice Department that "sufficient procedures" were in place to prevent non-citizens from voting. *(Vote 25, p. 6-H)*

Republicans argued that non-citizens applying for drivers licenses might automatically be put on the voter rolls unless more checks were put in place. But Democrats said the states already had procedures to prevent such illegal registration and charged that the GOP language was an attempt to gut the bill by allowing states to avoid implementing motor-voter systems.

SENATE ACTION

The Senate Rules Committee approved a nearly identical companion bill Feb. 18 on a 7-5 vote that fell largely along party lines. The vote sent the bill (S 460) to the Senate floor, where Committee Chairman and Majority Whip Wendell H. Ford, D-Ky., was in a position to get early action. Republican opponents vowed to use all the parliamentary tactics available to kill the measure.

Senate Floor Action

After two weeks of floor debate and backdoor meetings that produced key concessions for Republican opponents, the Senate passed HR 2 by a vote of 62-37 on March 17, after substituting the text of S 460. *(Vote 38, p. 6-S)*

Republican opponents, led by Mitch McConnell, R-Ky., had succeeded in using parliamentary tactics and extensive floor debate to slow the bill's advance and to win substantive changes in the measure.

Final passage came hours after Democratic and Republican leaders agreed to a compromise that removed from the measure provisions that would have required states to provide registration forms at public assistance agencies, such as welfare and unemployment offices. The compromise version said states "may" provide registration forms at public assistance offices. The earlier version required them to do so. The one-word change cleared the way for passage.

Mitchell said the leadership's desire to turn to Clinton's

budget package helped propel the compromise. One day earlier, Senate Democrats had failed to limit debate on the bill. The March 16 vote was 59-41, one short of the 60 needed to invoke cloture. *(Vote 33, p. 6-S)*

Republicans had begun their delaying tactics March 5, when McConnell, with considerable help from Minority Leader Bob Dole, R-Kan., rounded up the votes needed to prevent the Senate from taking up the bill for consideration. With low attendance on a Friday morning, members voted 52-36 on a motion to cut off debate and proceed to the bill; supporters needed at least 60 votes, and Mark O. Hatfield, R-Ore., the principal cosponsor of the bill, was the only Republican to vote for cloture. *(Vote 25, p. 5-S)*

However, on March 9, bill supporters mustered two more than the 60 votes needed to invoke cloture. The vote was 62-38, with five Republicans voting with Democrats to end the debate. In addition to Hatfield, the Republicans who cleared the way for Senate consideration of the bill were Arlen Specter of Pennsylvania, Dave Durenberger of Minnesota, Bob Packwood of Oregon and James M. Jeffords of Vermont. *(Vote 26, p. 5-S)*

Once the Senate turned to the bill, Republican opponents continued efforts to slow its advance.

John McCain, R-Ariz., offered an amendment to give the president line-item veto authority, which would enable him to veto individual provisions of spending bills. After a long debate, the Senate on March 10 rejected the amendment, 45-52. *(Vote 27, p. 5-S)*

On March 11, the Senate tabled, or rejected, 55-42, another McCain amendment that would have barred any agency that dispensed public benefits, such as welfare checks, from registering citizens who received such benefits. McCain and other Republicans argued that welfare recipients might feel pressured into registering to vote when they picked up checks. Democrats said the amendment was a veiled attempt to prevent poor people from voting. *(Vote 30, p. 5-S)*

The same day, the Senate killed, 53-43, an amendment by Don Nickles, R-Okla., that would have required Congress to provide funds to pay for implementation of the measure. *(Vote 31, p. 5-S)*

On March 16, prior to final passage, the Senate approved by a vote of 99-0 a package of amendments by Ford that included provisions requiring states to provide voter registration forms at military recruitment centers and requiring driver's license applicants to fill out a separate form for registering to vote. Under the original bill, a driver's license application automatically would have registered those eligible to vote unless the applicant checked a box declining registration. Ford's amendments were intended to answer concerns of some GOP members and to shore up support for passage. *(Vote 32, p. 5-S)*

CONFERENCE

The largest outstanding difference between the House and Senate versions of the bill was the Senate's decision to drop the requirement that voter registration be provided at unemployment and welfare offices. Key GOP backers in the Senate threatened to withdraw their all-important support for the bill if the House version, which included the welfare, unemployment and disabilities office registration requirement, prevailed in conference.

Conferees decided to accept the House provision but agreed to add new language requiring public agencies to make it clear to beneficiaries that registering to vote was

optional and that not registering would not affect the amount of assistance they received. Durenberger crafted the so-called "non-coercion" language. Durenberger was not a conferee, but his vote was critical to breaking a Senate filibuster against the conference report.

House conferees also agreed to drop the requirement that registration forms be made available at unemployment offices. And conferees dropped Senate language crafted by Alan K. Simpson, R-Wyo., that would have allowed states to require a registrant to produce documentation of citizenship upon request by election officials. Opponents of the Simpson language said it would lead to discrimination against people who appeared foreign or who had foreign-sounding names.

FINAL ACTION

The House approved the conference report (H Rept 103-66) by a vote of 259-164, on May 5. Before final adop-

tion, the House rejected, 170-253, a GOP attempt to send the bill back to conference and require the inclusion of Simpson's language. *(Votes 154, 153, p. 38-H)*

The Senate followed suit, adopting the conference report and clearing the legislation on a 62-36 roll call vote May 11. Six Republicans joined 56 Democrats who voted for the final bill. *(Vote 118, p. 16-S)*

The key Senate vote came earlier May 11 on a motion to shut off debate. Six Republicans joined all 57 Democrats as the cloture motion prevailed, 63-37. *(Vote 117, p. 16-S)*

The six were Durenberger, Hatfield, Specter, Jeffords, Pete V. Domenici of New Mexico and William S. Cohen of Maine. Cohen subsequently voted against the conference agreement, while Packwood, who voted against cloture, voted for final adoption. Most said they supported the concept of the bill all along but had held out in order to force changes in certain parts of the bill that had troubled them. ∎

Hatch Act Restrictions Revised

After trying for nearly two decades, Congress succeeded in revamping a law that limited the political activity of nearly 3 million federal workers. With backing from President Clinton, lawmakers cleared a bill (HR 20) to revise and simplify the 1939 Hatch Act by tightening on-the-job restrictions while easing off-duty limits on most federal and postal employees.

The bill barred federal employees from engaging in political activity while on duty — including wearing a campaign button on the job, a form of political expression that had been permitted under the old Hatch Act.

While off duty, federal employees could hold office in a political party, participate in campaigns and political rallies, publicly endorse candidates and raise political funds from within their agency's political action committee. But the law barred them from running for partisan elective offices or soliciting contributions from the general public.

Existing Hatch Act restrictions were maintained for certain high-level employees and sensitive agencies.

Previous efforts to revise the law had stalled after three Republican presidents vetoed or threatened to veto the bills.

But with Clinton's support, bill sponsors Rep. William L. Clay, D-Mo., and Sen. John Glenn, D-Ohio, steered measures through the House and Senate respectively. House members initially approved a relatively lenient bill, but they ultimately accepted a more restrictive Senate version in order to win passage.

BOXSCORE

➡ **Hatch Act Revisions (HR 20, formerly S 185).** The bill revised the 1939 Hatch Act restricting political activities by federal and postal employees. It tightened on-the-job restrictions, while easing limits on off-duty political activities.

Reports: H Rept 103-16; S Rept 103-57.

KEY ACTION

Feb. 24 — **House** voted to pass the bill, 275-142, three votes shy of the two-thirds needed to approve a bill under suspension of the rules.

March 3 — **House** passed HR 20 on a vote of 333-86.

July 20 — **Senate** passed HR 20 by a vote of 68-31, after substituting the text of S 185.

Sep. 21 — **House** cleared the Senate version of HR 20 on a vote of 339-85.

Oct 6 — **President** signed HR 20 — PL 103-94.

Clinton signed the bill into law (PL 103-94) Oct. 6.

BACKGROUND

Named for former Sen. Carl A. Hatch, D-N.M., (1933-1949), the act originally was written to shield elections from spoilers who pressed workers to contribute to campaigns in exchange for federal job protections. Hatch acted after a Senate panel found that political appointees in the Works Progress Administration had coerced employees into contributing to political campaigns to protect their jobs. At the time, less than 32 percent of the 950,000-member federal work force were career public servants; the rest were political appointees.

For years, proponents of revising the law had argued that the Hatch Act denied federal workers the right to political expression that was guaranteed to other citizens, that it was outdated because the federal work force was comprised mostly of career professionals, and that the jumble of rules and restrictions was confusing and contradictory.

Under the original law, federal employees could not actively participate in partisan campaigns, although there was no restriction on participation in nonpartisan elections, such as those for local school boards or town councils. While federal employees were allowed to contribute money to candidates, they could not stuff envelopes or work on a get-out-the vote effort for a particular candidate or party. However, federal employees were allowed to sport buttons during work and have bumper stickers on their cars.

Bill opponents argued that revising the Hatch Act would politicize the federal work force and pointed out that the Supreme Court had twice upheld the constitutionality of the 1939 Hatch Act, in 1947 and in 1972.

Efforts to revise the law had been blocked repeatedly by Republican presidents. Gerald R. Ford vetoed an effort in 1976. Ronald Reagan prevented a bill from ever reaching his desk in 1988 by threatening a veto. When George Bush vetoed an attempt to revise the Hatch Act in 1990, he said it would have destroyed the political neutrality of civil servants. Bush used a similar veto threat to prevent any action in the 102nd Congress. *(1976 Almanac, p. 490; 1988 Almanac, p. 620; 1990 Almanac, p. 408; 1992 Almanac, p. 222)*

HOUSE ACTION

Even before its membership was settled, the House Post Office and Civil Service Committee gave voice vote approval Jan. 27 to a bill revising the Hatch Act (HR 20).

But the bill stumbled off its fast track Feb. 24, when the full House failed to muster the two-thirds vote needed to push the measure through under an expedited procedure that barred amendments. The 275-142 tally was three votes shy. The attempt failed in part because Republican support was weaker than it had been in the past. *(Vote 42, p. 10-H)*.

On March 3, under normal procedures, the House passed the bill with bipartisan support on a 333-86 vote. *(Vote 52, p. 14-H)*

The bill allowed federal and Postal Service employees to participate in a full range of political activities on their own time, while prohibiting on-the-job political activity. It permitted employees to solicit political contributions, with prohibitions on job-related requests, including seeking money from fellow workers on the job. It barred federal employees from using official influence or information for partisan political purposes. And it prohibited them from wearing political campaign buttons while in government buildings and on duty.

Lawmakers gave voice-vote approval to two Republican-sponsored amendments. One, by Nancy L. Johnson of Connecticut, tightened a provision that allowed federal workers to run for any partisan political office; the amendment permitted them to run only for local offices such as town council. The second amendment, by Fred Upton of Michigan, maintained existing restrictions on the political activities of Federal Election Commission workers.

Several GOP opponents still maintained that the bill would result in government corruption. Frank R. Wolf, R-Va., a longtime opponent of the effort, said it would increase the potential for conflicts of interest among federal workers. For example, he said, an Internal Revenue Service auditor could chair a county Democratic or Republican committee on his own time, or a U.S. attorney preparing a case against a politician could work for the politician's opponent at night.

SENATE ACTION

The Senate Governmental Affairs Committee approved a more restrictive version of the bill (S 185) by a vote of 9-3 on May 13. The vote followed a series of skirmishes between Chairman Glenn and ranking Republican William V. Roth Jr. of Delaware, who had crossed swords over the Hatch Act in previous years.

Unlike the House version, the Senate bill did not allow federal employees to run for local partisan elective office,

and it prohibited federal workers from soliciting the general public for political contributions. It did provide for unionized federal workers to solicit non-subordinate union members for political contributions for that group's political action committee.

The panel included an amendment incorporating language (S 253) that allowed wage garnishment, or court-ordered payments for a legal debt taken from an employee's wages, for all federal employees. Previously, wage garnishment laws had applied only to private-sector and postal employees.

The markup got off to a rocky start May 11 when Glenn and Roth began debating the measure but could not sustain a quorum to vote. Before adjourning, the panel gave voice vote approval to a Glenn amendment to prohibit the use of recommendations from political officeholders in hiring or promoting civil service employees.

When the panel resumed work May 13, Roth offered a string of amendments designed to maintain tighter federal employee restrictions, all of which were defeated by voice vote. One Roth amendment would have exempted a number of employees from the bill, including those at the IRS, the Justice Department and the Central Intelligence Agency. Glenn's bill exempted only Federal Election Commission employees.

Although Glenn insisted that the law already prohibited the misuse of confidential information by employees, Roth said that political activity "could harm the public's perception of impartiality of these agencies."

Roth also tried unsuccessfully to exempt employees such as supervisors and administrative law judges and to retain the president's right to issue an executive order limiting political activity by federal workers.

Senate Floor

In a landmark for supporters of the bill, the Senate approved the bill by a vote of 68-31 on July 20, with 13 Republicans joining 55 Democrats in support of the measure. Unlike the House where Hatch Act revision sentiment was always stronger, the Senate had been unable to muster the 67 votes needed to override past vetoes or veto threats. *(Vote 201, p. 27-S)*

Senators began debate on the bill July 13. Glenn repeatedly emphasized that S 185 would tighten as well as loosen restrictions on federal workers' political activity. Roth maintained that any easing of existing law would damage the public's impression of a nonpartisan civil service.

Roth introduced an amendment to express the sense of the Senate that federal employees could not solicit political contributions from the general public or run for a local partisan political office, two provisions allowed under the House bill. Roth said he wanted to ensure that the Senate sent a message that it strongly opposed the House-approved provisions. "We have not made it very clear that S 185 could be a lot worse — it could be HR 20," said Roth. The amendment passed, 92-4. *(Vote 194, p. 26-S)*

Another Roth amendment, approved 88-7, clarified that an employee would be dismissed for the first violation of the Hatch Act unless the Merit Systems Protection Board voted unanimously instead to suspend the employee's pay for 30 days. Roth tried unsuccessfully to give federal employees a referendum on whether they wanted to be covered under the Hatch Act or under S 185. The amendment was tabled, or killed, by a vote of 62-34. *(Votes 193, 195, p. 26-S)*

After extensive negotiations, Roth and Glenn then announced a compromise amendment to retain existing

Hatch Act restrictions for members of the Senior Executive Service, administrative law judges, members of boards of contract appeals, and employees of sensitive agencies such as the FBI, the Secret Service and the CIA. Senators agreed to the amendment by voice vote.

On July 20, senators accepted by voice vote another Roth amendment to maintain existing Hatch Act restrictions on employees of the Justice Department's criminal division. The amendment was accepted after senators voted 43-56 against tabling it. *(Vote 199, p. 26-S)*

Further attempts to tighten the bill's restrictions failed. A Roth amendment to maintain restrictions on IRS examiners and auditors was killed, 51-48, on a tabling motion. And senators voted 58-41 to kill an amendment by Nancy Landon Kassebaum, R-Kan., that would have barred federal employees from soliciting political funds. *(Votes 198, 200, p. 26-S)*

Senators also agreed by voice vote to an amendment by John McCain, R-Ariz., expressing the sense of the Senate that further U.S. aid to Nicaragua should be halted pending an investigation into the involvement of the Sandinista National Liberation Front in international terrorist activities.

Obstacle to Conference

The victory for supporters in the Senate was short-lived, as GOP opponents quickly moved to set up a last-minute procedural roadblock. Roth objected to the normal ritual following bill passage, the appointment of Senate conferees to negotiate with their House counterparts over the conflicting versions of the bill. Roth said he wanted to see whether the House would accept the language approved by the Senate.

FINAL ACTION

Despite Roth's move, members of both chambers began gearing up for a contentious House-Senate conference. But in September, Clay recommended to the Rules Committee that the House accept the Senate version. Waiting for the bill to move through a conference, he said, would cause even further delays. Clay's recommendation paved the way for speedy action on the bill. The Rules Committee on Sept. 14 agreed to allow the House to debate and then vote on the Senate version. On Sept. 21, the House cleared the bill on a 339-85 vote. *(Vote 437, p. 106-H)* ∎

Hatch Act Provisions

As enacted, the rewrite of the Hatch Act (HR 20 — PL 103-94) contained the following provisions:

Political Activities

● **Policy.** Stated that federal employees should be encouraged to exercise, fully and freely and without fear of reprisal, their right to participate or to refrain from participating in the political process.

● **Federal employees.** Defined employees covered under the bill to be any individual, other than the president or vice president or General Accounting Office workers, employed or holding office in an executive agency or in a competitive civil service position that was not in an executive agency.

● **Postal workers.** Covered United States Postal Service and Postal Rate Commission workers.

● **Other workers.** Covered employees of the District of Columbia government other than the mayor, city council members and the recorder of deeds. It excluded members of the armed forces. Military personnel fell under separate Defense Department rules governing the political activities of the military.

● **Partisan political office.** Defined a partisan political office as one for which a candidate was nominated or elected as representing a party that received electoral votes in the last presidential election. The definition did not include any office or position within a political party or affiliated organization.

● **Political contribution.** Defined a political contribution as a gift or contribution made for any political purpose.

● **Off-duty political activities.** Allowed federal employees to manage political campaigns or take an active role in political parties and groups, including:

● Seeking and holding positions in local and national political parties.

● Stuffing envelopes, organizing and participating in phone banks and participating in voter registration drives.

● Carrying posters at a political rally, distributing campaign material and soliciting votes off the job.

● Organizing and participating in political meetings.

● Publicly endorsing candidates.

● Soliciting contributions for the political action committee of a federal employees' organization from other members of that employees' organization who did not work under the person soliciting funds.

Federal employees had been prohibited from any kind of solicitation of funds. Under the new law, employees could solicit or receive political contributions only from an employee who was a member of the same agency's political action committee. However, federal employees were barred from soliciting funds from a member of the political action committee when the targeted employee was a subordinate worker.

● **Off-duty limits.** Prohibited the following activities by federal employees while on or off the job:

● Running for partisan political office.

● Using official authority to interfere with or affect the result of an election.

● Soliciting or discouraging the political activity of any person with business pending before the employee's office. Such business included an application for any compensation, grant, contract, ruling, license, permit or certificate. Federal employees also were barred from soliciting or discouraging political activity by any person who was the subject of an ongoing audit, investigation or enforcement action.

● **Exceptions for sensitive posts.** Kept in place the original Hatch Act restrictions, forbidding active participation in political management or political campaigns for certain federal employees in sensitive positions.

Such employees included employees at the Federal Election Commission; Federal Bureau of Investigation; Secret Service; Central Intelligence Agency; National Security Council; National Security Agency; Defense Intelligence Agency; Merit Systems Protection Board; Office of Special Counsel; Office of Criminal Investigations of the Internal Revenue Service; Office of Investigative Programs of the U.S. Customs Service; Office of Law Enforcement of the Bureau of Alcohol, Tobacco and Firearms; Criminal Division of the Justice Department; administrative law judges, career Senior Executive Service employees and Contract Appeal Board members.

● **On-duty political activity.** Barred federal employees from engaging in political activity while on duty, in any room or building used by government employees for official business. Such activities also were barred when a government employee was wearing a uniform or official insignia identifying his or her office or position or using any U.S. government vehicle. The law prohibited a federal employee from wearing a campaign button on the job, a

form of political expression that had been permitted under the old Hatch Act.

● **Exceptions.** Made exceptions for employees whose duties continued outside usual hours and away from the usual post, and whose jobs were paid for by an appropriation for the Executive Office of the President or were subject to presidential appointment and Senate confirmation, and involved determination of U.S. foreign policy.

● **Areas with many federal workers.** Permitted the Office of Personnel Management to write rules making exceptions for the local political involvement of federal employees who lived in certain areas such as Maryland, Virginia, the District of Columbia, or areas in which the majority of voters were federal employees.

● **Coercion.** Made it illegal for any person to intimidate, threaten, command or coerce any federal employee to engage in or not engage in a political activity. The law made it illegal to threaten federal workers to vote or not vote for any particular candidate, to make or not make a political contribution for any candidate or to work or not work for a particular candidate.

● **Violations.** Allowed employees who violated the law to be fired. Any person who intimidated, threatened or coerced a federal employee to participate in political activity also could face fines of up to $5,000 or up to three years in jail.

● **Other Penalties.** Stated that a minimum penalty of 30 days' suspension without pay could be imposed if the Merit Systems Protection Board, a quasi-judicial agency that safeguarded the civil service against political partisanship and other unfair practices, found by a unanimous vote that a violation did not warrant firing.

● **Prohibited recommendations.** Specified that a federal manager making a personnel decision such as a hiring, promotion or transfer had to make that decision without regard for any recommendations by a member of Congress or congressional employee, state elected official or official of a political party; or any recommendations made on the basis of the party affiliation of the prospective employee. Those politically affiliated individuals could not make such recommendations, and agencies or employees could not solicit or accept such recommendations. The head of each

agency had to ensure that employees and applicants were aware of these restrictions.

● **Permitted recommendations.** Allowed an agency or manager to solicit and accept recommendations regarding a prospective federal employee only if the recommendation was furnished by a former employer and addressed only the work performance and ability or security standards of the job candidate.

● **Effective date.** Took effect 120 days after enactment.

Garnisheeing Wages

● **Garnisheeing wages.** Allowed creditors to garnishee wages of federal employees through the same legal process that they followed with a private citizen. Garnisheeing wages, a legal remedy for taking a part of the regular pay of an employee, had been used by creditors to recoup debts from a financially delinquent private individual. Previously, federal employees had been exempted from having wages garnisheed.

● **Garnishment limitations.** Limited the percentage of wages that could be garnisheed to 25 percent or the amount by which the disposable earnings for the week exceed 30 times the federal minimum wage, whichever was less. It required that child support and alimony judgments against a federal employee be given precedence over other legal garnishment orders.

Nicaragua

● **Nicaragua.** Stated that it was the sense of the Senate that no further aid should go to Nicaragua until there was an investigation of the potential involvement of the Sandinista National Liberation Front in any terrorist activities that threatened U.S. security or the political stability and economic prosperity of the Western Hemisphere. The non-binding resolution stated that an explosion in Managua, Nicaragua, on May 23 exposed a cache of weapons and 310 passports from 21 countries including the United States. It also said that documents in the possession of those apprehended in connection with the Feb. 26 bombing of the World Trade Center in New York had been traced to Nicaragua. The provision questioned the ability of the Nicaraguan government to stop the export of terrorism by the Sandinista National Liberation Front. ∎

Federal Workers Feel Deficit-Reduction Pinch

The drive to cut the deficit took its toll on federal workers, as Congress froze pay for civilian employees in fiscal 1994 and found several other ways to trim federal benefits.

However, congressional appropriators preserved a scheduled locality-based pay increase for workers who lived in areas with relatively high wages, and the defense appropriations bill provided funds for a pay increase for military personnel.

BACKGROUND

In February, President Clinton called on Congress to save money by eliminating a scheduled 2.2 percent pay increase for federal workers in fiscal 1994, limiting increases in 1995-97 to 1 percent below the rise in the cost of living, and postponing a locality-based pay raise scheduled begin in 1994.

Enacted in 1990, locality pay was an effort to close the gap between federal and non-federal white collar pay levels by giving pay increases to federal employees in high-wage areas of the country. The program was supposed to be

phased in over nine years.

Clinton also proposed several other changes, including an end to the lump-sum retirement option, under which retiring federal workers could choose to get a lump-sum refund of their retirement contributions in exchange for a permanently reduced annuity.

Like most of Clinton's other deficit-reduction proposals, the federal pay changes were taken up when Congress put together the 1993 budget-reconciliation bill. In preparing the bill, three House and three Senate committees with jurisdiction over federal employees were instructed to come up with a total of more than $50 billion in savings by trimming federal pay and retiree benefits.

Although the initial House-passed reconciliation bill included the pay freeze, the companion Senate measure did not, and the freeze was dropped from the final bill (HR 2264 — PL 103-66), which cleared Aug. 6 and was signed Aug. 10.

Later in the year, however, Congress cleared an appropriations bill for the Treasury, Postal Service and general government (HR 2403 — PL 103-123) that contained no funds for the 2.2 percent civilian raise in 1994. As a trade-

off, the bill provided for the increase in locality pay.

Other changes in the 1993 reconciliation bill affecting federal workers included:

• **Lump-sum retirement payments.** Most retiring federal workers permanently lost the option of getting lump-sum retirement benefits. The change applied to civilian federal retirees, including former State Department and Central Intelligence Agency officials.

• **COLA delay.** Cost of living adjustments (COLAs) for civilian federal retirees in fiscal 1994-96 were delayed for three months. Instead of taking effect on Dec. 1, COLAs were delayed until March 1. The delay applied to the Civil Service, Federal Employees', Foreign Service and CIA retirement systems.

• **Limitation on physician fees.** The law limited fees for physician and outpatient care for the 220,000 retirees 65 and older who did not participate in the optional portion of Medicare (Medicare Part B) but who were covered by the Federal Employees' Health Benefits Program, the nation's largest health insurance program.

• **Armed services COLA delay.** Annual COLA payments to non-disabled armed services retirees, which typically were paid on Jan. 1, were delayed until April 1 for 1994 and until Oct. 1 for 1995-98.

RECONCILIATION BILL

The federal pay and benefit provisions in the reconciliation bill were the work of several House and Senate committees. The House and Senate each approved their respective committees' provisions without amendment.

Federal Civilian Employees

House. The House Post Office and Civil Service Committee approved its contribution to the deficit-reduction package May 13 by a vote of 17-5. The committee, which had jurisdiction over the Postal Service and federal civil service, was instructed to come up with $10.6 billion in savings from direct spending programs over five years. The panel proposed to achieve most of that — $8.8 billion — by ending the lump-sum retirement option effective Jan. 1, 1994. The committee also agreed to the COLA delay for civilian retirees, saving $788 million, and approved the limit in physician fees and several other provisions.

In addition, the panel authorized the federal pay freeze, estimated to save $28.7 billion over five years. The provisions repealed the 2.2 percent raise for federal and Foreign Service employees in 1994, extended the freeze to other pay systems in the executive branch and reduced by 1 percent the federal pay adjustments scheduled to take effect in 1995, 1996 and 1997.

The panel gave voice vote approval to an amendment by Delegate Eleanor Holmes Norton, D-D.C., to allow locality pay adjustments to begin in July 1994. The locality pay increase was seen as partially offsetting the effect of Clinton's freeze in regular pay. Norton's amendment funded the locality pay increase by cutting, through attrition, the number of civilian employees in the executive branch by 150,000 over five years. Beginning in 1995, it delayed annual pay adjustments from January until July. It also capped the amount of leave that Senior Executive Service employees could build up and ended bonus awards to employees through fiscal 1998.

Dan Burton, R-Ind., blasted Norton's plan as "bringing home the pork" to her constituents while hurting other federal workers and said that the changes would pit "rural and urban federal workers against one another."

Senate. By a vote of 7-4, the Senate Governmental Affairs Committee on June 9 approved $10.7 billion in spending cuts over five years. The plan included the three month delay in retiree COLAs in fiscal 1994-96 and repeal of the lump-sum retirement option. But the Senate committee was not instructed to authorize a one-year pay freeze, and it did not do so.

The panel added a requirement that the District of Columbia begin Oct. 1, 1993, to pay the employer share of Federal Employee Health Benefit premiums for district retirees. It also required a permanent reduction in a federal retiree's annuities if the retiree married after retirement and opted for survivor coverage, and it required that the Postal Service make payments for COLAs and health benefits for its past retirees.

Conference agreement. Conferees agreed on the COLA delay, the lump-sum benefit repeal and the limit on physicians' fees. They dropped the fiscal 1994 pay freeze approved by the House, along with the reduction in future raises; they also decided against the delay in locality pay increases. They dropped the House-passed provisions limiting accumulated leave for senior executives, prohibiting cash bonuses in fiscal 1994-98 and reducing the government's total number of civilian employees by 150,000 over five years.

The House accepted the Senate requirement that the Postal Service make payments for COLAs and health benefits for its past retirees. Conferees also kept the Senate-drafted permanent reduction in federal annuities for a retiree who later married and opted for survivor coverage.

Conferees dropped Senate provisions requiring that the District of Columbia begin paying the employer share of Federal Employee Health Benefit premiums for its retirees.

Military Personnel

House. The budget resolution instructed the Armed Services committees to authorize a reduction in military pay in line with Clinton's pay freeze for other federal workers.

The House Armed Services Committee voted 32-22 on May 12 to freeze pay for active-duty military in fiscal 1994 and maintain pay increases at 1 percent below inflation for fiscal 1995-98, saving an estimated $11.6 billion over five years.

Rather than reducing or capping retiree COLAs as the Budget Committee suggested, the Armed Services panel accepted a provision by Ike Skelton, D-Mo., to provide a full COLA on a delayed schedule; rather than taking effect Jan. 1, the payments were to be made May 1 in 1994, and Aug. 1, in 1995-98. The delay saved an estimated $2.36 billion over five years.

Senate. The Senate Armed Services Committee agreed by voice vote to delay payment of the retiree COLA to Oct. 1 in fiscal 1994-97, and to Sept. 1 in fiscal 1998. The committee did not approve a pay-freeze provision.

Conference agreement. Conferees dropped Clinton's plan to freeze military pay in fiscal 1994 and scale it back in the following four years. The conference report included a delay in the annual COLA for military retirees to April 1 in fiscal 1994 and to Oct. 1 in fiscal 1995-98.

Foreign Service

House. The House Foreign Affairs Committee came up with $9 million in three-year savings by delaying COLAs for retired Foreign Service officers. The plan approved by May 12 was in line with the legislative proposal of the Post Office and Civil Services Committee, which curbed retirement benefits for all federal workers.

Senate. The Senate Foreign Relations Committee gave voice vote approval June 10 to a package that promised to achieve $61 million in savings over five years, mainly by

eliminating the lump-sum retirement option for participants in the Foreign Service retirement system who retired after September 1995 (except individuals who were critically ill). The Budget Committee had instructed the panel to save $5 million.

The Foreign Relations Committee also approved the delay in COLAs for retired Foreign Service officers.

Conference agreement. Conferees agreed to both the COLA delay and the repeal of the lump-sum retirement option for foreign service employees.

APPROPRIATIONS BILLS

While the reconciliation bill left both the 2.2 percent pay raise for civilian workers and the locality pay increase in place, appropriators chose to drop the regular pay raise for all but military personnel.

● **Civilian workers.** Despite negative signals from the administration, conferees on the spending bill for the Treasury, Postal Service and general government (HR 2403 — PL 103-123) agreed to include 1994 locality pay increases for about 60 percent of federal white-collar workers. Under the 1990 law, a maximum of $1.8 billion could be spent on the program in its first year. Since there was not enough money in the bill both to start the locality pay program and provide the 2.2 percent pay raise in 1994, the conferees decided to eliminate the general pay raise, saving $1.3 billion. Clinton signed the bill Oct. 28. *(Appropriations, p. 679)*

● **Military personnel and Foreign Service.** Active-duty military personnel, members of the National Guard and reserve personnel got their 2.2 percent pay raise as part of the annual Pentagon spending measure (HR 3116 — PL 103-139).

The House version of the bill, approved by the Appropriations Committee on Sept. 22, included an unrequested $1.06 billion to provide military personnel with a 2.2 percent pay raise in 1994. The House approved the measure on Sept. 30, by a vote of 325-102. *(Vote 480, p. 118-H)*

The Senate appropriators followed suit on Oct. 4, giving voice vote approval to a defense appropriations bill that included $1.05 billion for the pay raise. The Senate approved the measure by voice vote Oct. 21.

Conferees settled on the $1.05 billion figure in the Senate measure. Both chambers approved the conference report by voice vote on Nov. 10. Clinton signed the bill Nov. 11. *(Appropriations, p. 569)*

Foreign Service employees were not so lucky; appropriators did not include a pay raise for them in the annual spending measure (HR 2519 — PL 103-121) for the departments of Commerce, Justice, State and the Judiciary. ■

Federal Operations Bills

The committees charged with overseeing federal government administration — Governmental Affairs, Government Operations, and Post Office and Civil Service — acted on several measures in 1993 dealing with federal employees and employer work policies. While two bills became law, others were left pending at the end of the year.

FLEXIBLE LEAVE

Congress cleared legislation (S 1130) extending programs that allowed federal employees to either donate an-

nual leave to a pooled leave bank or transfer it directly to co-workers who were facing personal or family medical emergencies. President Clinton signed the bill into law Oct. 8 (PL 103-103).

The bill made permanent a five-year experimental program that was due to expire in October. More than 23,000 employees facing unpaid absences from work received donations of leave time in 1991 and 1992, according to an Office of Personnel Management report. Delegate Eleanor Holmes Norton, D-D.C., said the bill should save money because higher paid employees typically donated to lower paid employees while the government paid for time at the salary rate of the lower paid employees.

The Senate passed the bill, sponsored by David Pryor, D-Ark., by voice vote July 14.

On July 22, the House Post Office Compensation and Employee Benefits Subcommittee added a provision limiting to five days the accrual of more annual or sick leave while on extended leave for a medical emergency. The full House Post Office and Civil Service Committee reported the bill as amended Sept. 21 (H Rept 103-246), and the full House passed the bill by voice vote that day. The Senate cleared S 1130 by voice vote two days later.

WHISTLEBLOWER BILL

A bill to continue protections for federal workers who exposed corruption and gross mismanagement in the workplace was left pending in the House at the end of the first session. HR 2970, which also reauthorized the Office of Special Counsel through fiscal 1995, was pulled from an Oct. 27 House Post Office Committee markup agenda because the Clinton administration opposed many of its proposed rules changes.

The Post Office Subcommittee on Civil Service had approved the bill on a 5-0 vote Oct. 20.

Established in 1979, the Office of Special Counsel was an independent agency within the executive branch charged with investigating allegations of abuse and mismanagement at federal agencies and contractors. The office also was charged with protecting and representing federal employees who felt they had been punished for exposing violations where they worked.

The bill included provisions to change the rules for disclosing information about employees under investigation, add decisions regarding security clearances and psychiatric testing to the statutory list of personnel practices and change the final appeal court for federal whistleblower cases from the federal circuit court system to the U.S. Court of Appeals for the District of Columbia. It also included an amendment, approved on a voice vote, to maintain exemptions from the law for the FBI and intelligence agencies. The original bill would have lifted the exemptions.

EQUAL OPPORTUNITY COMPLAINTS

A bill to revise the process for addressing discrimination and harassment complaints in the federal workplace was left pending in the Senate at the end of the session.

The Senate Governmental Affairs Committee gave voice vote approval to the bill (S 404 — S Rept 103-167) on June 24, but the full Senate did not act on it.

Under the existing process, federal workers filed complaints of on-the-job harassment or discrimination within their departments.

Bill sponsor and committee Chairman John Glenn, D-

Ohio, said the system often led to abuses, as federal officials tried to protect fellow employees or the department's reputation.

Under S 404, all complaints were to be dealt with by the Equal Employment Opportunity Commission (EEOC), an independent agency. Federal departments and agencies were to shift resources and personnel to the EEOC so that the commission could meet its new responsibilities.

To ensure that no decision was rushed, the bill extended, from 30 to 180 days, the time an employee had to file a complaint.

The Congressional Budget Office said the bill would save the government about $25 million annually. Similar bills to revamp the federal complaint process died in the 102nd Congress. *(1992 Almanac, p. 226)*

BONUS RESTRICTIONS

The Senate passed a bill by voice vote Nov. 24 to ban bonuses for political appointees during presidential election years and bar highly paid federal employees from receiving bonuses. The House did not act on the measure.

The bill (S 1070), barred bonuses to non-career political appointees from June 1 of a presidential election year to Jan. 20 of the following year. It also prohibited career appointees who made more than $108,200 from receiving bonuses at any time.

The bill sprang from a controversy in late 1992 as the Bush administration prepared to leave office. The Office of Personnel Management found that the number of bonuses awarded to political appointees and other highly paid federal workers during the November to January transition period rose to 133 from just 49 in the same period in 1991.

The Senate Governmental Affairs Committee approved the bill by voice vote Nov. 18. The measure was sponsored by Carl Levin, D-Mich.

HONORARIA BAN

On March 30 an appeals court struck down a law barring federal employees from accepting writing or speaking fees. Supporters hoped the ruling would increase pressure for a bill (HR 1095) to allow most government employees, including congressional staff, to accept so-called honoraria while imposing restrictions aimed at preventing influence peddling and conflicts of interest. But the measure stalled in the face of opposition in the Senate and the Clinton administration.

Congress barred House members and all government employees except those working for the Senate from accepting honoraria as part of the Ethics Reform Act of 1989, which also sharply increased House members' salaries. The Senate followed suit two years later, when senators voted themselves a pay raise and barred honoraria in that chamber. *(1989 Almanac, p. 51; 1991 Almanac, p. 22)*

Congress' main aim was to stop its own members from accepting speaking fees from special interest groups, but the law swept all employees in the government's three branches into the honoraria ban.

Lower-level executive branch employees howled in protest, complaining that they could not accept speaking and writing fees even if their subjects or honoraria sources had no connection with their jobs. The employees sued in federal court and won at the U.S. District Court level March 19, 1992.

The U.S. Court of Appeals for the District of Columbia Circuit upheld that decision on a 2-1 vote, declaring the ban an overly broad restriction on free speech.

On Nov. 18 the House Judiciary Subcommittee on Administrative Law approved HR 1095 by voice vote. The measure, sponsored by Barney Frank, D-Mass., provided that all federal employees in the executive, legislative and judicial branches making less than $108,000 annually would be allowed to accept honoraria. Federal workers still could not accept honoraria related to their official duties or payments in excess of $2,000.

REWARDING NON-DRIVERS

The Senate on Nov. 20 cleared, by voice vote, a bill aimed at encouraging federal workers to commute via mass transit, bicycles and other alternatives to driving alone.

The bill (HR 3318 — H Rept 103-356), sponsored by Delegate Eleanor Holmes Norton, D-D.C., authorized federal agencies, courts and Congress to establish programs that would provide transit passes, bicycle facilities or other, non-monetary incentives to those who avoided driving. Unlike existing law, these programs did not have to be offered in conjunction with state or local transit agencies — a requirement that deterred some agencies.

The House Post Office and Civil Service Committee reported the bill Nov. 10. The House passed it Nov. 15, also by voice vote. President Clinton signed the bill into law Dec. 2 (PL 103-172).

COMPETITIVENESS COUNCIL

The House on Nov. 21 voted to rename the independent Competitiveness Policy Council and reauthorize it for four more years. As passed by the House on a voice vote, the bill (HR 2960) renamed the council the National Competitiveness Commission and cut authorization for the council in half, from $5 million annually to $2.5 million. It was introduced by John J. LaFalce, D-N.Y.

The Competitiveness Policy Council was created as part of an omnibus trade law in 1988 (PL 100-418) and was charged with recommending policies to restore U.S. competitiveness in the world economy. It was a 12-member, bipartisan body whose members were chosen by Congress and the president from industry, government, labor and public interest groups.

President Clinton already had adopted many of the goals suggested by the council, including emphasizing the development of dual-use technologies for defense and civilian industries and providing a research and development tax credit. *(1988 Almanac, p. 212)* ∎

House Rejects D.C. Statehood Bill

Delegate Eleanor Holmes Norton, D-D.C., rolled the dice in engineering a Nov. 21 House floor vote she knew would fail on a bill to grant statehood to the District of Columbia.

Although the House soundly defeated the measure (HR 51), Norton said her gamble to boost the cause of statehood paid off and the vote "surpassed my greatest expectation."

But statehood opponents, such as Thomas J. Bliley Jr., Va., the ranking Republican on the House District of Columbia Committee, said the vote sounded the death knell for the statehood movement. Bliley called the vote "an overwhelming defeat" for statehood.

The bill would have created an enclave of government buildings and monuments to remain under the control of the federal government. The remaining areas of the city were to become the 51st state, New Columbia, represented by two senators and one representative.

The debate marked the first time that lawmakers debated on the floor whether the District should become a state, although District statehood bills had been introduced in the House since 1965.

BOXSCORE

➤ **District of Columbia Statehood (HR 51).** The bill would have made the District of Columbia the nation's 51st state.

Report: H Rept 103-371.

KEY ACTION

Aug. 5 — **House** District of Columbia Subcommittee on Judiciary and Education approved HR 51, 5-2.

Nov. 3 — **House** District of Columbia Committee approved the bill, 7-4.

Nov 21 — **House** defeated the bill, 153-277.

BACKGROUND

A bill to make the District the 51st state died in the 102nd Congress without full House action. Statehood supporters were unwilling to take up House floor time to debate the measure, knowing that they could not override a threatened veto by then-President George Bush. The House District of Columbia Committee reported a similar measure in 1987, but, as in 1992, the bill never saw floor action. *(1992 Almanac, p. 223)*

Statehood supporters contended that District residents deserved statehood because they were being taxed but did not have equal representation in Congress. District residents voted for one delegate to represent their interests in the House.

Beginning in 1993, the four delegates in the House, including the D.C. delegate, could vote on questions before the Committee of the Whole. But if their votes were decisive in the outcome, the matter was automatically revoted, with their votes excluded. The delegates could not vote on final passage of bills. Previously, the delegates could not vote in the House. The District had no representation in the Senate.

Republicans generally opposed D.C. statehood. For one thing, the District's residents traditionally voted Democratic. Moreover, many Republicans, and some Democrats, questioned whether it would be constitutional to grant the area statehood given that the Founding Fathers had designated it the nation's capital area.

Article 1, Section 8, Clause 17 of the U.S. Constitution said it was in the power of Congress "to exercise exclusive legislation in all cases whatsoever, over such District (not exceeding 10 miles square) as may, by cession of particular

states, and the acceptance of Congress, become the Seat of Government of the United States."

The Bush administration argued that a constitutional amendment was required before Congress could give back control over the lands ceded to it by Maryland and Virginia more than 200 years earlier.

The Clinton administration supported the statehood effort.

HOUSE COMMITTEE ACTION

On Aug. 5, the House District of Columbia Subcommittee on Judiciary and Education voted 5-2 to send the legislation to full committee.

Subcommittee Chairwoman Norton, who had introduced the bill Jan. 5, acknowledged that "what you see is a state that has no characteristics of any other state." But she added that something had to be done about the fact that D.C. residents did not have full representation. "There are 600,000 people left in the nether world of democracy," she said.

The panel's ranking Republican, Dana Rohrabacher of California, said D.C. residents should get beyond the idea of statehood because it "is not a reality" and focus on other solutions. He said he supported the idea of retrocession, under which D.C. would be returned to the state of Maryland.

Full Committee Action

The full House District of Columbia Committee approved the measure Nov. 3 on a party-line 7-4 vote (H Rept 103-371).

Bliley, the committee's ranking Republican, said D.C. statehood should be put to a vote as a constitutional amendment and be decided by all Americans, not Congress. "Congress is usurping power it does not have," Bliley told the committee. "The power to change the status of the nation's capital is reserved to the people in their right to amend their Constitution."

Norton offered several amendments during the markup, most of which, she said, addressed technical or constitutional issues.

The committee adopted a Norton amendment, by voice vote, to allow that a state constitution — approved by the D.C. Council in 1987 — be considered ratified once statehood was granted.

The panel had rejected, also by voice vote, a substitute amendment offered by Bliley that would have required that D.C. residents vote on the state constitution before statehood could be granted.

The committee also agreed to a Norton amendment providing for a study within two years after enactment on how to deal with District prisoners housed in the Lorton Correctional Complex in Virginia.

Bliley offered a substitute, rejected 4-7, that would have given the new state two years to wind down operations at Lorton and other correctional facilities in Maryland. Bliley

said the prison issue should be resolved at the "front end of the statehood process."

The committee rejected, 4-7, an amendment by Rohrabacher that would have required that the state of New Columbia receive a payment in lieu of taxes in the same manner as any other state.

Rohrabacher said that under the bill the new state would be given a special status to get federal funds beyond what other states with federal facilities received, which, he said, showed that "this state cannot function economically on its own."

Norton opposed the amendment, saying the new state still would have a significant federal presence within its boundaries and that federal property could not be taxed. She said the bill did not create any special status but only spelled out why the new state might be eligible for a federal payment.

In any case, Norton said, any payment would have to be approved by Congress.

HOUSE ACTION

The House on Nov. 21 soundly defeated the measure on a vote of 153-277. Voting for the bill were 151 Democrats, Independent Bernard Sanders of Vermont and Republican Wayne T. Gilchrest of Maryland; 105 Democrats and 172 Republicans voted against the bill. *(Vote 595, p. 146-H)*

Statehood supporters had hoped to win at least 120 "yeas" to ensure that they would make a respectable showing. When the vote reached 150, supporters packed in the gallery broke into applause and those on the House floor embraced.

Although a week earlier Norton had appeared to be wavering on whether to push for a vote, she said afterward that the vote turned the spotlight on the 600,000 District residents, who paid federal taxes without full representation.

Added Rep. Cass Ballenger, R-N.C., "This is dressing up a federal payment for New Columbia in new clothes, and they are trying to pretend that it does not exist."

In deciding to go for a floor vote, Norton said the vote would give statehood supporters a baseline and a working list of members whom they needed to bring into the fold.

Norton took the long view on the effort, citing the more than 40 years it took for Alaska and Hawaii to become states.

Jesse Jackson, the District's so-called shadow senator, who was elected in 1990 by residents to lobby for statehood, sounded a note of pessimism after the vote, complaining that the White House and House Democratic leaders had not pushed hard enough for statehood.

Norton, however, praised the White House lobbying effort, saying President Clinton had called 15 members at her request. Clinton also wrote Norton a letter stating his strong support for statehood and urging House members to vote for the bill.

Norton said that all House members of the Congressional Black Caucus voted for the bill, as did most of the House Democratic leadership, including Speaker Thomas

S. Foley, D-Wash., who rarely voted on bills. One notable exception was House Democratic Caucus Chairman Steny H. Hoyer, whose suburban Maryland district bordered the District.

All other suburban Maryland or Virginia House members, with the exception of Albert R. Wynn, D, who represented a black-majority Maryland district, also voted against the bill. Most lawmakers representing jurisdictions neighboring the District opposed statehood because it would have allowed the District to enact a "commuter tax" on suburban residents who worked in the city.

Looking Ahead

Statehood supporters turned their attention next to the Senate, which failed even to hold a hearing on District statehood in 1993. Sen. Edward M. Kennedy, D-Mass., introduced a statehood bill (S 898) on May 5. Jackson asked in a Nov. 19 letter to Senate Majority Leader George J. Mitchell, D-Maine, that the Senate Governmental Affairs Committee "set a date certain" for a hearing on District statehood.

When the dust settled from the House debate, a number of questions about the bill remained unresolved, including:

● **State boundaries.** Bliley argued on the floor that the boundaries of New Columbia were drawn so that a number of federal and congressional buildings would belong to the new state. But District of Columbia Committee Chairman Pete Stark, D-Calif., said he failed to understand why it mattered that some of the federal agencies would be in New Columbia, noting that the Pentagon and the Central Intelligence Agency were in Virginia and the Social Security Administration and the National Institutes of Health were in Maryland.

● **Building height limitation.** The bill included a complex arrangement to retain the District's building height limitations, which involved the federal government claiming the airspace above the new state before it officially joined the union. Bill opponents, such as Rohrabacher, said limiting the height of buildings in that way exposed the federal government to potential liability suits from chagrined private landowners and set a dangerous precedent that threatened private property rights.

● **Economic viability.** Probably the touchiest question facing statehood supporters was whether the new state could generate enough revenue to stand on its own economically. Opponents said it could not, pointing to the city's projected $194 million deficit in fiscal 1995.

Norton said the new state could stand on its own because the city hosted more businesses than 30 states; more legal services than 41 states; more hotels and lodging than 27 states; and 21 million tourists per year. She also said the District boasted a population larger than that of the states of Alaska, Vermont or Wyoming.

The bill did include a provision requiring a statehood transition commission to recommend to Congress a way of determining an annual payment to the new state as compensation for the federal property the state could not tax.

House-Passed Bill Imposes Smoking Restrictions

Tobacco foes in Congress achieved their biggest legislative victory in five years with House passage Nov. 15 of a bill (HR 881) restricting smoking in most federal buildings to separately ventilated rooms.

Both supporters and critics agreed that the bill would effectively ban smoking in all federal buildings — including the Capitol and congressional office buildings — except for military installations and Department of Veterans Affairs (VA) health-care facilities, which were exempt because of the cost of separately ventilated smoking areas.

The bill was passed late in the year, however, and the Senate did not consider it or a similar Senate bill (S 262) in 1993.

Background

Anti-smoking advocates had sought federal restrictions on smoking for years without much success. Their biggest victory came in 1989, when Congress voted to permanently ban smoking on all but a handful of domestic airline flights. The ban was enacted as part of the fiscal 1990 transportation spending bill (PL 101-164). *(1989 Almanac, p. 749)*

Tobacco opponents suffered a setback in 1992, when lawmakers overturned a VA directive banning smoking in VA hospitals as part of a bill to improve medical care for veterans (PL 102-585). *(1992 Almanac, p. 381)*

But an Environmental Protection Agency (EPA) report released in January changed the political climate. The report blamed the lung-cancer deaths of 3,000 non-smokers a year on environmental tobacco smoke, and it linked the smoke to numerous other health problems. Environmental tobacco smoke, also known as secondhand smoke, included both the mainstream smoke exhaled by smokers and the sidestream smoke emitted from cigarettes, cigars and pipes.

Supporters said the bill was necessary because the EPA report could make the federal government liable for the poor health of workers exposed to secondhand smoke. The report prompted some federal agency chiefs to unilaterally ban smoking in buildings under their jurisdiction. Opponents said the legislation would infringe on the rights of smokers.

Lawmakers who sought a ban on smoking in federal buildings first opted for a back-door approach. Illinois Democrat Richard J. Durbin, chairman of the House Appropriations Agriculture Subcommittee, successfully added language to the fiscal 1994 agriculture spending bill (HR 2493 — PL 103-111) that banned smoking in offices of the Women, Infants and Children nutrition program. *(Appropriations, p. 540)*

However, anti-smoking advocates failed to win approval of more sweeping language included in the fiscal 1994 Treasury-Postal Service appropriations bill (HR 2403 — PL 103-123). The Senate adopted an amendment, offered by Frank R. Lautenberg, D-N.J., chairman of the Transportation Appropriations Subcommittee, to restrict smoking in most federal buildings to separately ventilated areas. But House and Senate conferees quietly dropped the language. House Appropriations Committee Chairman William H. Natcher and Senate Majority Whip Wendell H. Ford, both Democrats from Kentucky, a leading tobacco-producing state, made certain the provisions disappeared. *(Appropriations, p. 679)*

Subcommittee Action

On June 16, the House Public Works Subcommittee on Public Buildings approved HR 881 by voice vote.

Bill sponsor James A. Traficant Jr., D-Ohio, was known for his impassioned defense of the American worker and the non-binding "Buy American" amendments that he regularly offered to legislation, not as a defender of non-smokers' rights. But Traficant had moved into the chairmanship of the Public Buildings Subcommittee at the beginning of the 103rd Congress, and it was from that bully pulpit that he launched the latest challenge to the tobacco industry.

Traficant initially sought to ban smoking in all federal buildings, with no exceptions. But he lowered his sights when opposition to an all-out ban threatened to kill the initiative before it got off the ground. Hours before the June 16 markup, Traficant and his allies crafted a compromise that exempted military installations and VA hospitals from the legislation and allowed separately ventilated smoking areas. "This amendment provides a fair manner by which there will be some latitude granted to smokers," he said at the markup.

Tobacco-state lawmakers tried unsuccessfully to further weaken the bill. Freshman James E. Clyburn, D-S.C., offered a substitute amendment to require the General Accounting Office (GAO) to study whether the government would in fact be liable for health claims made by non-smokers exposed to secondhand smoke and assess the costs to the government of lost productivity due to smoking restrictions.

Clyburn said there was not enough information available to justify the smoking ban. But New York Democrat Jerrold Nadler, a freshman colleague of Clyburn's, said Americans had known the hazards of smoking for nearly three decades, and Congress was behind the curve in imposing restrictions. The subcommittee rejected Clyburn's amendment, 3-8.

House Committee Action

The full Public Works Committee approved the bill by voice vote June 17 (H Rept 103-298).

Tim Valentine, D-N.C., offered a substitute to require federal agency heads to set aside special smoking areas, including zones within cafeterias and other dining facilities. The bill itself only offered separately ventilated smoking areas as an option to agency chiefs, and Valentine and others said no bureaucrats would be willing to use the limited funds they had available to establish those smoking areas unless required by law to do so.

The committee rejected Valentine's amendment, 23-39. Clyburn offered the same amendment he had proposed in subcommittee and was defeated by voice vote. Chairman Norman Y. Mineta, D-Calif., ruled out of order a second Valentine amendment that would have banned alcoholic beverages in all federal buildings.

House Floor Action

The House took up the bill Nov. 15, a little more than a week before members left town for the year; by then passage was a foregone conclusion. In a testament to the dwindling clout of the tobacco lobby in the House, lawmakers passed the bill by voice vote.

Valentine made one last appeal for a compromise that would have required designated smoking areas. "It seems to me that we should be able to accommodate both smokers and non-smokers and protect the legitimate rights of each," he said. But even Valentine was resigned to defeat. He left the floor immediately after making his speech and did not return before the vote.

Lawmakers considered the bill under suspension of the rules, which meant that no amendments could be offered and that two-thirds of the members voting had to vote "yes" for the bill to pass. ∎

More Funds Earmarked for National Museum System

Congress took up two bills to expand the Smithsonian Institution:

AFRICAN-AMERICAN MUSEUM

The House gave voice vote approval June 29 to a bill (HR 877) authorizing the establishment of a National African-American Museum; the Senate did not act on the measure in the first session.

The museum, which African-American lawmakers and others had advocated for years, was to be housed in the Smithsonian Institution's Arts and Industries Building and modeled on that of the National Museum of the American Indian. Rep. John Lewis, D-Ga., was the main sponsor of the bill, which authorized $5 million for fiscal 1994.

The House Administration Subcommittee on Libraries and Memorials approved the measure by voice vote March 17 with the full committee giving its approval, also by voice vote, March 31 (H Rept 103-140, Part 2).

The Public Works and Transportation Subcommittee on Public Buildings and Grounds approved an amended version of the bill June 16, and the full Public Works Committee passed the bill by voice vote June 17 (H Rept 103-140, Part 1).

The subcommittee amendment specified that money appropriated for the project could be used only for costs directly related to establishing and operating the museum, primarily to preclude the use of the funds to support regional and local African-American museums.

In the Senate, Paul Simon, D-Ill., introduced a similar measure (S 277), but no action occurred.

Bills to create an African-American museum (HR 1246, S 523) were introduced in the 102nd Congress but not enacted.

While the earlier bills would have provided for construction of a new facility, HR 877 sought to house the museum in an existing building. The new bill also required that most of the board of trustees be appointed by the Smithsonian's Board of Regents, rather than by the president as the earlier bills had required.

AIR AND SPACE ANNEX

Congress cleared and the president signed legislation that authorized an extension of the Smithsonian Institution's National Air and Space Museum at Dulles International Airport in Virginia.

The measure (HR 847) authorized $8 million in fiscal 1994 for the planning and design of the annex, which was to serve as an additional site to restore and display aeronautical and space flight equipment. Some said the equipment was at risk of deterioration at the Garber Facility in Suitland, Md., where it was being stored.

Past attempts at passing similar legislation were stymied by a dispute over whether the Smithsonian should be required to subject the project to competitive bidding rather than assign it to the Dulles location. *(1991 Almanac, p. 564)*

The House Administration Committee's Libraries and Memorials Subcommittee approved the bill March 17 after hearing testimony from Virginia lawmakers and Smithsonian officials in support of the measure. The full committee approved the measure June 16, and the House followed suit, passing the bill by voice vote June 29. On July 22, the Senate approved the measure by unanimous consent.

President Clinton signed HR 847 into law Aug. 2 (PL 103-57). ∎

Bills Seek To Jump-Start Shipping Industry

Lawmakers in 1993 considered a variety of approaches to revitalizing the U.S. shipping and shipbuilding industries — from subsidies, to tax incentives and loan guarantees, to penalties on foreign-subsidized vessels. Without Congress' help, supporters of those industries said, U.S. companies would either fold or move their operations to foreign flags.

The House Merchant Marine Committee took the lead, advancing a slew of proposals, although only a portion of a single bill made it into law by the end of the year.

The most far-reaching bill (HR 2151) was an authorization for more than $1 billion worth of new programs for both the shipping lines and the shipyards. The measure won overwhelming approval in the House on Nov. 4.

At year's end, Gerry E. Studds, D-Mass., who chaired the House Merchant Marine Committee, and John B. Breaux, D-La., who headed the Senate Commerce Subcommittee on the Merchant Marine, were negotiating with the White House over how to pay for the subsidies. The administration eventually proposed to increase the tax on cargo vessels entering U.S. ports by roughly two-thirds, a move that would affect both U.S. and foreign shipping lines. At the end of the session the bill remained on hold in Breaux's subcommittee.

In separate action, the House Merchant Marine Committee used a routine reauthorization bill for the Maritime Administration (HR 1964) to advance part of its maritime-revitalization agenda. That bill passed the House July 29 but was not acted on by the Senate.

Other committees weighed in on the effort as well. At the initiative of the House Armed Services Committee, money for U.S. shipyards was included in the fiscal 1994 defense authorization bill. The House and Senate Defense Appropriations subcommittees followed up with $80 million in budget authority in the fiscal 1994 defense appropriations bill.

Subcommittees of two other House committees also pushed bills to give U.S. shipyards and shipping lines a boost against their foreign competitors. Those measures did not make it through committee in 1993, however.

BACKGROUND

Supporters of the U.S. merchant marine fleet said it was on the verge of extinction. Building a vessel in the United States cost at least twice as much as building one overseas. Keeping it registered in the United States also carried a high price tag in terms of labor costs, taxes and regulations. Roughly 80 oceangoing vessels received federal subsidies to offset these competitive disadvantages, but those subsidies began to expire in 1993.

As of March 1, 217 privately owned, U.S.-flag vessels carried cargo domestically and 155 carried cargo internationally. The total number of vessels ranked 16th in the world.

Lawmakers from coastal and Great Lakes states had been calling for a new federal maritime initiative for several years, and those calls reached a crescendo in the 103rd Congress. The nation's two leading shipping lines — Sea-Land Service Inc. and American President Lines Ltd. — added urgency to the lawmakers' efforts midyear when they sought permission from the Transportation Department to shift 20 of their vessels to foreign registries.

U.S. shipyards had declined, too, since their heyday in World War II. One factor was Congress' decision in 1981 to end the "construction differential subsidy" as part of the budget-reconciliation bill (PL 97-35) that enacted President Ronald Reagan's initial efforts to cut the budget. The subsidy covered the price gap between U.S. yards and their subsidized foreign competitors. *(1981 Almanac, p. 570)*

Sixteen major construction yards and 27 major repair yards closed in the 10 years after the subsidies ended, according to the Shipbuilders' Council, a private group representing the yards. Employment dropped by 60,000 as orders from private industry all but evaporated. The shipyards became heavily dependent on the Navy for business, and the shrinking defense budget promised more lean times.

In trying to respond to these problems, lawmakers had to grapple with the competing interests among the shipping lines, their customers (the shippers) and the shipyards. For example, the lines and the shipyards took opposing sides on the question of which ships to subsidize.

The lines wanted the federal government to subsidize all their ships, even those built outside the United States. Ships built in foreign yards, most of which were heavily subsidized by their own governments, tended to be far less expensive than ones built in the United States.

But the U.S. yards argued strongly against subsidizing foreign-built ships, saying that would reward a practice that U.S. trade negotiators were trying to eliminate. Instead, they backed the idea of imposing penalties on ships built with foreign subsidies.

For their part, the shippers called for the government to deregulate the lines, arguing that they would be healthier if they were exposed to more competition. That argument was echoed in a preliminary staff report for Vice President Al Gore's National Performance Review, the "reinventing government" effort. The shipping lines opposed such a move, arguing that it would remove whatever protections they had against foreign competitors.

MERCHANT MARINE COMMITTEE

With bipartisan support, the House Merchant Marine Committee promoted a three-pronged initiative for the maritime industries.

● **Shipping subsidies.** In HR 2151 (H Rept 103-251), the committee proposed a subsidy program for shipping lines costing roughly $2 billion over 10 years. The committee bill, approved by voice vote July 29, authorized the government to pay U.S. shipping lines more than $2 million annually per oceangoing ship in exchange for their pledge to aid the military in times of war or national emergency.

The proposal, sponsored by Studds, differed from the existing program in two significant ways. The existing subsidy for shipping lines, which averaged more than $3 million per year, was tied to the difference in labor costs between U.S. and foreign lines. The subsidy in the committee bill was smaller and was not flexible, which would force the lines and their employees to economize.

The existing subsidy also was limited to U.S.-built vessels. The committee bill, on the other hand, allowed subsidies for ships built in foreign yards whose prices could not be matched in the United States.

The shipping lines had long argued in favor of extending subsidies to foreign-built vessels, saying that the existing program forced them to make a painful choice: They

could hold onto their aging U.S.-built ships, which required crews far larger and costlier than new, foreign-built vessels did. Or they could build new ships in U.S. yards, assuming more debt and higher interest payments than their competitors with foreign-built ships had.

To pay for the shipping-line subsidy, the chairman of the Merchant Marine Committee's Subcommittee on the Merchant Marine, William O. Lipinski, D-Ill., introduced a bill (HR 2380) June 10 to raise taxes on ship passengers and impose a new tax on cargo containers. The ticket tax was to increase from $3 to 5 percent of the purchase price, with a new cargo tax of $15 per 20-foot equivalent unit.

Lipinski held a hearing on his bill Oct. 20, but the measure did not advance after that.

● **Tax incentives.** In a second bill (HR 2152 — H Rept 103-194, Part 1), the Merchant Marine Committee approved tax breaks to encourage shipping lines to buy new ships and to put them on more equal footing with their competitors. The committee approved the bill by voice vote May 26. The bill was referred to the House Ways and Means Committee, which took no action on it in 1993.

● **Shipyard subsidies.** The other major piece pushed by the Merchant Marine Committee was HR 2547, which called for federal subsidies and loan guarantees for U.S. shipyards. The House Armed Services Committee incorporated three parts of the measure — loan guarantees for ship purchases, loans for shipyard modernization and a program to develop shipbuilding technology — into the defense authorization bill (HR 2401 — PL 103-160). The fiscal 1994 defense appropriations bill (HR 3116 — PL 103-139) provided $50 million for the loan programs and $30 million for technology development.

The defense committees balked, however, at a fourth provision in HR 2547 — subsidies to shipyards to lower the cost of their products. The subsidies were proposed as a way to help U.S. shipyards move from building highly customized vessels for the Navy, where they competed only among themselves, to building price-conscious cargo vessels, a market that they had all but conceded to Asian and European yards. Unlike the old construction differential subsidies, the new subsidies would be available only for orders of two or more vessels built from the same design. The subsidies would cover the difference in cost between U.S. vessels and comparable ones made overseas, with one restriction: The government could not pay more than half the cost of the vessel.

When the Armed Services committees left this provision out of the defense authorization bill, the Merchant Marine Committee inserted it into HR 2151.

HOUSE FLOOR ACTION

The House on Nov. 4 voted overwhelmingly in favor of HR 2151. The final tally was 347-65, with 54 Republicans and 11 Democrats dissenting. *(Vote 547, p. 134-H)*

After the Merchant Marine Committee approved the bill, Studds had set about negotiating for the White House's backing. Studds and Breaux eventually won the administration's support for roughly $1 billion worth of subsidies for shipping lines over 10 years. That sum would support about 52 of the 72 active oceangoing vessels that were receiving subsidies in mid-1993, although at a lower rate than the existing subsidy program.

The negotiations did not resolve the questions of how to pay for the subsidies or what to do for the shipyards. Nevertheless, Studds took HR 2151 to the House floor armed with

a statement from the White House in support of the bill.

During floor debate, not a single lawmaker spoke against the bill's premise — that private shipping lines and shipyards required the taxpayers' help to keep their operations going. Republicans and Democrats alike stressed how important the maritime industry was to national defense, trade and jobs. The only disagreements concerned the proposed subsidy for U.S.-owned but foreign-built ships and the tangential issue of cargo preference.

Gene Taylor, D-Miss., offered an amendment to delete the provision allowing subsidies for certain U.S.-owned but foreign-built ships, arguing that U.S. taxpayers should not subsidize foreign shipyards. Studds countered that rather than resulting in more ships being built in U.S. yards, Taylor's amendment would push more U.S. vessels to switch to foreign flags. The House defeated Taylor's amendment, 64-362. *(Vote 545, p. 134-H)*

Timothy J. Penny, D-Minn., and Fred Grandy, R-Iowa, offered an amendment to limit spending on programs that reserved some military and food-aid cargo to U.S.-flag vessels (so-called cargo preference programs). The amendment would have limited the rate paid for shipping the cargo to no more than twice the world market rate.

Jack Fields of Texas, the top Republican on the Merchant Marine Committee, argued that the amendment did not take into account how much more expensive it was to operate a ship under the U.S. flag. The House defeated the amendment by a vote of 109-309. *(Vote 546, p. 134-H)*

OTHER BILLS

Other attempts to find ways to revitalize the maritime industry included:

● **Maritime Administration reauthorization.** The House voted on one other measure in 1993 that was related to the failing health of the maritime industry, a bill (HR 1964 — H Rept 103-182) to authorize $621 million in spending on the Maritime Administration and related programs in fiscal 1994. The House passed the bill July 29 by a vote of 372-48. *(Vote 386, p. 94-H)*

The Merchant Marine Committee, which approved the bill by voice vote May 26, had included a proposal to revive a federal loan guarantee program for new vessel purchases. The bill authorized $54 million for loan guarantees and administrative expenses. According to Studds, that amount could translate into the construction of about $1 billion worth of commercial vessels in U.S. shipyards.

When the bill reached the House floor, a provision of major consequence to U.S. shipping lines was added as part of a wide-ranging Studds amendment. That provision barred any line from moving its vessels to foreign registries in 1993 or 1994. The Studds amendment was adopted by a vote of 388-41. *(Vote 384, p. 94-H)*

Studds' main targets were Sea-Land Service Inc. and American President Lines Ltd., the two lines that had sought permission to shift 20 of their vessels to foreign registries.

In addition to providing the loan guarantees and restricting reflagging, the House-passed bill called for improving the maintenance of the Ready Reserve Force, a fleet of government-owned cargo ships held in reserve for wars or emergencies.

The bill quickly ran into trouble in the Senate, however. Breaux said in August that he shared Studds' concern but did not like the proposed restrictions on the shipping lines. He added that the bill would not move forward in his

committee with the amendment on it; the subcommittee took no action on the bill before the Senate adjourned for the year.

● **Combating foreign subsidies.** The House Ways and Means Subcommittee on Trade gave voice vote approval Nov. 9 to a bill that sought to impose high duties and entry restrictions on vessels built in subsidized foreign shipyards. Subcommittee Chairman Sam M. Gibbons, D-Fla., who introduced the bill, argued that the best way to help the U.S. shipyards was to pressure foreign governments to drop their subsidies, rather than providing new subsidies to the U.S. yards. Gibbons, who was a vocal advocate of free trade, had pushed a similar measure through the House in 1992, but the bill died in the Senate. *(1992 Almanac, p. 203)*

Gibbons reintroduced the bill in 1993, but he eventually removed one of its most controversial sections to answer complaints from the Clinton administration and shippers. That section would have imposed heavy duties on companies that bought or leased ships built in foreign-subsidized yards or had ships repaired there.

The penalties that remained in the bill ranged from denying the offending vessels entry into U.S. ports to imposing a fee of $500,000 to $1 million per voyage. The bill gave subsidizing countries six months to negotiate an agreement phasing out their subsidies before the first penalties would be imposed.

Gibbons said that his main goal was to give the United States more leverage in international negotiations to end shipbuilding subsidies. U.S. officials had been seeking such an agreement for several years, but their clout had been limited by the United States' unilateral termination of its own shipbuilding subsidies.

Gibbons delayed taking the bill to the full Ways and Means Committee while he monitored one more round of international negotiations over the subsidies. Those negotiations continued into early 1994 without yielding any agreement.

A similar Senate bill (S 990), sponsored by Breaux, remained idle in the Senate Finance Committee at the end of 1993. Like Gibbons, Breaux had introduced an anti-subsidy measure in 1992 that had failed to advance. *(1992 Almanac, p. 204)*

● **Extending U.S. labor laws.** The House Education and Labor Committee's Labor Standards Subcommittee on Oct. 28 voted 7-3 to approve a bill (HR 1517) to discourage cargo, cruise and fishing companies from registering their vessels in other countries to avoid U.S. labor laws. At year's end, the bill — sponsored by William L. Clay, D-Mo. — was awaiting action by the full committee.

One advantage enjoyed by many foreign-flag vessels was the ability to hire crews from developing countries, where wages were a fraction of those in the United States and Europe. Vessels flying the U.S. flag had to employ U.S. citizens and comply with U.S. wage and benefit laws.

As approved by the subcommittee, the bill required that any ship that "regularly engaged" in business at U.S. ports, or that made or processed goods on board for sale in the United States, pay its crew the minimum U.S. wage and overtime. The crew members also were to have a right to bargain collectively. The measure did not apply to ships registered in the country where their owners were based and on which at least half of the crew members were citizens of that country.

● **Study commission.** The Senate Commerce Committee approved a bill (S 1432 — S Rept 103-196) to create a commission that would examine the economic problems facing the maritime industry.

It was the only measure related to maritime-industry revitalization that the committee acted on during the year. Chairman Ernest F. Hollings, D-S.C., had insisted that any bill proposing new spending also provide a way to pay for it; as a result, Breaux's Merchant Marine Subcommittee remained quiet through must of 1993.

S 1432 emerged after aides to Gore, working on the "reinventing government" report, floated a proposal in August to deregulate the maritime industry. They later suggested a blue-ribbon panel be created to study industry ills. Hollings and other industry supporters denounced deregulation, saying it would kill the industry. They also argued that the commission would be stacked in favor of deregulation. Instead of waiting for a formal proposal from the administration, the Commerce Committee approved a bill by voice vote on Oct. 6 to create a commission of its own design, called the National Committee To Ensure a Strong and Competitive United States Maritime Industry. *(Reinventing government, p. 191)*

Modeled after a commission Congress created on the airline industry, the maritime committee was to investigate impediments to the competitiveness of U.S.-flagged commercial vessels and examine problems that had caused the domestic shipbuilding industry to shrink. The commission also was to examine whether the merchant marine could fulfill the demand for cargo hauling in wartime. It would have 60 days after appointments were made to report recommendations to the president and Congress. *(Airline commission, p. 220)*

The Senate adjourned without taking up the bill.

On Sept. 22 the House Merchant Marine Committee's Subcommittee on the Merchant Marine gave voice vote approval to a similar proposal (HR 3103) by its chairman, Lipinski, but the bill was not taken up by the full committee in 1993. Studds, for one, did not support the idea of a commission, saying that it would only delay Congress from tackling the industry's problems. ■

Coast Guard Reauthorized; Fishery Bills Included

The House on Nov. 23 cleared a bill reauthorizing the Coast Guard for fiscal 1994 after the Senate attached the contents of several House-passed bills dealing with fishery management, vessel safety and ship memorials. President Clinton signed the bill into law Dec. 20 (PL 103-206).

The bill (HR 2150) authorized $3.6 billion for the Coast Guard in fiscal 1994, including $2.6 billion for operations and $418 million to buy vessels, aircraft and other equipment. The total was about 4 percent higher than the fiscal 1993 spending level and $40 million more than the amount provided in the transportation spending bill for fiscal 1994 (HR 2750 — PL 103-122).

Sponsored by Rep. W. J. "Billy" Tauzin, D-La., the bill raised the limit on the number of commissioned, active-duty Coast Guard officers from 6,000 to 6,200. It allowed the Coast Guard to acquire family housing units, such as condominiums, and to enter long-term leases for high-level antenna sites and other aids to navigation.

A number of provisions in the bill dealt with establishing new facilities or improving existing ones. These included provisions authorizing the acquisition and placement of oil-spill response equipment at Port Arthur, Texas,

and Helena, Ark., as requested by Reps. Jack Brooks, D-Texas, and Blanche Lambert, D-Ark.; the construction of new offices, living quarters, a pier and a boat ramp at the Coast Guard station in Little Creek, Va., as requested by Rep. Owen B. Pickett, D-Va.; the acquisition of a marine oil-spill management simulator at the State University of New York Maritime College, as requested by Rep. Thomas J. Manton, D-N.Y.; the establishment of fisheries law enforcement training centers in southeastern Louisiana, as proposed by Tauzin, and in South Carolina, as proposed by Sen. Ernest F. Hollings, D-S.C.; and the transfer of lighthouses in Washington and Maine to preservation groups, as requested by lawmakers from those states.

The bill also gave 49 vessels exemptions from the Jones Act, which barred vessels not built, owned and registered in the United States from doing business between U.S. ports. Two other vessels received waivers for Great Lakes trade as well, and one vessel received a waiver for a single shipment in the Gulf of Mexico.

Legislative Action

The House passed its version of the bill (H Rept 103-146) by voice vote July 30, but the Senate did not take up the measure until Nov. 22, the last full day of its 1993 session. Before approving the bill by unanimous consent, the Senate attached to it the contents of several maritime bills and one resolution, all of which had been approved by the House or the House Merchant Marine and Fisheries Committee.

● A bill (HR 2134 — H Rept 103-202) giving the federal government and the states more power to regulate fishing along the Atlantic coast. Modeled after the Striped Bass Act of 1984, the language allowed the federal government to place a moratorium on fishing in any state that did not comply with an interstate plan to preserve depleted fish stocks. The Atlantic States Marine Fisheries Commission and the states would jointly develop management plans for each dwindling species of fish. The House had passed HR 2134 by voice vote Aug. 2. *(Atlantic coast marine protection, p. 285)*

● A bill (HR 58 — H Rept 103-370) giving three nonprofit organizations two obsolete ships each from the National Defense Reserve Fleet. The fleet was established in 1945 to help meet shipping needs during emergencies and to support the military in times of war.

The nonprofit groups planned to make the ships seaworthy in time to commemorate the 50th anniversary of the Normandy invasion. The House Merchant Marine Committee had approved the bill Oct. 21. The House passed it Nov. 20 by voice vote.

● A bill (HR 3509 — H Rept 103-382) extending until May 1, 1994, an agreement between the United States and Russia allowing fishermen from each nation access to waters controlled by the other. The House Merchant Marine Committee had approved the bill Nov. 18.

● A resolution (H Con Res 135 — H Rept 103-317) calling for an international agreement to limit fishing in an area of the Bering Sea between waters controlled by the United States and Russia. The area, called the "Donut Hole" in the House resolution, was referred to as the "Doughnut Hole" in the bill. The House had approved the resolution by voice vote Nov. 2.

The Senate's expanded version of HR 2150 was sent back to the House, which cleared it by voice vote.

Congress also took the following action on related legislation:

CHARTER BOAT SAFETY

Congress cleared legislation establishing tougher safety standards for chartered passenger boats.

The provisions, which were attached to the Coast Guard reauthorization bill (HR 2150 — PL 103-206), closed a loophole in marine safety laws that allowed some boat owners to charter their vessels to groups without complying with U.S. Coast Guard safety regulations. Such arrangements were known as "bareboat charters," referring to boats that were provided without a crew.

By "bareboating" their vessels, owners temporarily relinquished ownership and responsibility of their boats to the renting party. Yet many renters were not aware that they were fully responsible and liable for anything that happened on the boat while it was in their possession, or that the boat probably had never been inspected by the Coast Guard.

The new law gave the Coast Guard the right to inspect any bareboat charter, as well as larger boats chartered with crews and submersible vessels that carried passengers. Supporters of the law said it would force 500 to 700 boat operators to upgrade their vessels' structures, lifesaving features and firefighting equipment.

For passenger vessels not subject to inspection, the law called for new regulations within two years to require additional safety equipment. The law also gave the Transportation Department the authority to write special rules for individual excursion or research vessels that needed less stringent treatment than typical passenger vessels.

Action on the bareboat charter provisions began in the House Merchant Marine Committee, which approved them as a separate bill (HR 1159 — H Rept 103-99), sponsored by Tauzin, by voice vote May 5. The House passed the bill June 9 by a vote of 409-4, after adopting by voice vote an amendment by Peter Deutsch, D-Fla., allowing the Coast Guard to extend the deadline for compliance to two years. *(Vote 202, p. 50-H)*

On Oct. 6, the Senate Commerce Committee attached the provisions to its version of the bill reauthorizing the U.S. Coast Guard (S 1052 — S Rept 103-198), which the committee approved by voice vote. In the waning moments of the session, the contents of the Coast Guard bill were combined with four other House measures into a broad maritime package (HR 2150 — H Rept 103-146). That bill passed the Senate on Nov. 22 by unanimous consent, and the House cleared it in the early morning hours of Nov. 23.

CRUISES TO NOWHERE

Despite objections from some coastal lawmakers, the House gave voice vote approval Nov. 20 to a bill barring foreign-flag vessels from offering "cruises to nowhere," excursions that began and ended at the same U.S. port. The Senate did not act on the bill before adjournment.

The bill (HR 1250 — H Rept 103-307) was an amendment to an 1886 law requiring that any passenger vessel traveling from one point in the United States to another be built, owned and registered in the United States.

The law did not apply to trips from a U.S. port into international waters and back. Foreign vessels used this exception to launch the "cruise to nowhere" business in the 1980s, offering short trips on casino-equipped vessels. They had little U.S. competition until 1992, when Congress repealed a 1952 law forbidding U.S.-flagged vessels to carry gambling equipment in U.S. waters.

The sponsor of HR 1250, Gene Taylor, D-Miss., con-

tended that foreign vessels still enjoyed an unfair advantage because they did not have to comply with U.S. labor laws. His bill let foreign vessels stay in the market for up to 15 years on three conditions: that they had no competition from comparably sized U.S. vessels, that they hired a U.S. crew and that they did not change ownership.

A similar bill by Taylor passed the House by voice vote late in the 1992 session, but it died in the Senate. At the end of 1993, HR 1250 was in the hands of the Senate Commerce Committee. *(1992 Almanac, p. 205)* ∎

Changes in Taxes, Fees For Boat Owners

As part of the broad 1993 deficit-reduction bill (HR 2264 — H Rept 103-213), Congress agreed to several fee and tax changes affecting private and commercial boats. The House included an increase in registration fees for non-commercial aircraft in its version of the measure, but that provision was dropped in the final bill.

The House passed its version of the reconciliation bill (H Rept 103-111) by a vote of 219-213 on May 27. The Senate approved its bill (S 1134) on June 25 by a vote of 50-49. The bill cleared Aug. 6, and President Clinton signed it (PL 103-66) on Aug. 10. *(Budget-reconciliation, p. 107)*

CARGO TONNAGE FEES

The budget-reconciliation bill extended until fiscal 1999 the existing level of duties being paid by cargo vessels entering U.S. ports. The duties, which were raised 250 percent to 350 percent as part of the 1990 budget agreement, had been scheduled to drop to their original levels after fiscal 1995. The extension was expected to raise an additional $205 million.

Vessels arriving from places in the Western Hemisphere were required to pay 9 cents per ton of cargo capacity; the maximum for a single vessel in a given year was 45 cents per ton. Vessels from other foreign countries paid 27 cents per ton, up to a maximum of $1.35 per ton per year.

The House Merchant Marine Committee approved the duty-extension as its contribution to the reconciliation bill May 12. The committee abandoned two other provisions — both proposed by Chairman Gerry E. Studds, D-Mass. — after the Ways and Means Committee objected. The first would have expanded the Capital Construction Fund — a tax shelter that helped U.S. shipping lines save money to buy American-built ships — to cover ship leases as well as purchases. It also would have allowed U.S. shippers to depreciate a new vessel over three years instead of 10 years. The second provision would have modified the funding formula for the federal Boat Safety Account so that grants not spent by state boat safety programs would not be counted against the account's $70 million cap.

The Senate Commerce, Science and Transportation Committee agreed June 15 to include the $205 million duty extension in the Senate version of the bill.

BOAT FUEL TAX

The reconciliation bill extended the 20.1-cents-per-gallon tax on diesel fuel used in highway transportation to

recreational boaters. In addition, beginning Jan. 1, 1994, recreational boaters were subject to the 4.3-cents-per-gallon increase in the transportation fuels tax that was included in the bill. Fuel used by boats for commercial fishing, transportation for hire, or business uses other than recreation remained exempt.

Many recreational boaters used gasoline, not diesel fuel, and already paid an excise tax on their fuel. Still, the government expected the extension to raise $148 million over five years, covering a little more than half the cost of a separate provision in the bill that eliminated the luxury tax on boats, aircraft, jewelry and furs. That tax had been added as part of the 1990 budget agreement.

The extension of the diesel fuel tax to recreational boaters was approved by both chambers in their original versions of the bill.

AIRCRAFT FEES

The House-passed version of the reconciliation bill contained a provision that would have increased registration fees for the owners of non-commercial aircraft. The increase would have raised an estimated $140 million through annual fees of $40 to $1,000, depending on the weight of the aircraft. The existing fee was a one-time charge of $5. The Senate bill did not include the provision, and it was dropped in the conference report on the bill. ∎

House Passes Seamen, Panama Canal Bills

Congress took action on the following bills:

SEAMEN RE-EMPLOYMENT

The House on March 16 passed a bill (HR 1109) by a vote of 403-0 that gave re-employment rights to workers who left their regular jobs to serve on merchant marine ships. The Senate did not act on the measure. *(Vote 72, p. 18-H)*

The bill, sponsored by William O. Lipinski, D-Ill., was virtually identical to provisions in the Maritime Administration reauthorization bill that the House passed in 1992. Similar language also was included in the Maritime Administration authorization bill in 1991. Both of those bills died in the Senate.

Gerry E. Studds, D-Mass., chairman of the House Merchant Marine and Fisheries Committee, said the Persian Gulf War focused attention on a problem that merchant sailors faced in times of war: If they volunteered to serve in the Ready Reserve Force, hauling military cargo overseas, there was no guarantee that their regular jobs would be waiting for them when they returned.

HR 1109, the Merchant Seamen Re-employment Rights Act of 1993, gave civilian sailors "substantially equivalent" re-employment rights as U.S. military reservists. The rights also extended to civilians who served on a government-owned or -controlled vessel during a war, an armed conflict, a national emergency or maritime mobilization.

Studds told the House that many civilian sailors decided not to participate in the sealift during Operation Desert Shield/Desert Storm for fear of losing their jobs. "Because of the lack of re-employment rights, the United

States had to use, in some cases, volunteer pensioners who were in their 60s, 70s and even 80s," Studds said.

Civilians who participated in the Persian Gulf sealift and lost their jobs were eligible for re-employment under HR 1109.

Rep. Herbert H. Bateman, R-Va., listed a number of things that the bill did not do, such as conveying veterans benefits on merchant mariners, compelling participation in a sealift or setting salary levels. "HR 1109 solves the problems facing our war planners without the attendant cost of a large, expensive and bureaucratic Merchant Marine reserve," he said.

PANAMA CANAL COMMISSION

The House on July 13 passed by voice vote a bill to reauthorize the Panama Canal Commission for one more year. The Senate did not take up the bill before Congress adjourned for the year.

The bill (HR 1522 — H Rept 103-154) made three minor changes in the commission's powers and duties. It allowed employees of the commission who were not U.S. citizens to accept employment with the government of Panama; it allowed commission employees to resolve grievances through binding arbitration; and it permitted the commission to buy up to 35 U.S.-built vehicles to replace ones it was using to transport its staff.

The commission was established by the Panama Canal Treaty of 1977 to operate and maintain the canal until 2000, when the United States finished transferring ownership of the canal to Panama. It was funded by the tolls collected from vessels passing through the 51-mile-long canal. *(1977 Almanac, p. 403)*

House Merchant Marine Committee Chairman Gerry E. Studds, D-Mass., said that the commission expected to collect $542 million in tolls in fiscal 1994. The bill authorized the panel to spend as much money as it collected to fulfill its duties. ∎

High-Speed Rail Plan Runs Out of Track

Committees in both chambers approved bills, sought by the Clinton administration, to greatly expand the nation's high-speed rail program. Administration officials promoted the plan as a way to create jobs and develop technology.

The legislation (HR 1919, S 839) ran into trouble, however, when transportation unions argued that the new routes would result in layoffs or wage cuts for workers on conventional rail and bus lines. Republicans objected to a provision in the amended House version that applied the Davis-Bacon Act to contracts that would be funded by the high-speed rail program. Davis-Bacon required federal contractors to pay the prevailing wage in a community or, if more than half the work force was unionized, the union wage.

Neither bill made it to the floor in the first session.

Without the authorization, appropriators were willing to fund only a small slice of the plan. The fiscal 1994 transportation appropriations bill (HR 2750 — PL 103-122) included $20 million for research into high-speed trains that rode above magnetized rails on a cushion of air. *(Transportation appropriations, p. 663)*

BACKGROUND

Transportation Secretary Federico F. Peña on April 28 unveiled a five-year plan to develop high-speed rail routes and technology, with states, cities and private organizations carrying a major portion of the costs. In his budget, President Clinton proposed spending $140 million on the program in fiscal 1994 and $1.3 billion over five years.

The proposed legislation amended the Railroad Revitalization and Regulatory Reform Act of 1976 to establish a National High-Speed Rail Assistance Program. The 1976 law authorized the country's only operating high-speed rail route, the multibillion-dollar Northeast Corridor from Washington to Boston, which remained several years away from completion. The Transportation Department had designated five other high-speed rail corridors in 1992, and all were in the early stages of planning.

Under the Peña proposal, new corridors linking at least two major metropolitan areas were to be eligible for federal aid if they met certain criteria. State governments, in addition to committing a substantial amount of funding, had to demonstrate that their routes would not require federal operating or maintenance subsidies once they were developed.

The General Accounting Office estimated that a single 200-mile corridor would cost $2 billion to $12 billion — the higher the speed, the higher the cost. The bill limited the federal high-speed rail program's share to 50 percent of the public expenses, which were defined as those costs that could not be borne by private investors.

State and local governments were still allowed to dip into other federal pots to help pay for their corridors, however. For example, high-speed routes required underpasses and overpasses to eliminate all the highway crossings, and the federal highway program provided money for those projects.

The bill also listed several factors that the Transportation Department had to consider when deciding which corridors to fund. Those included the potential reduction in congestion on the roads and at airports, the amount of local financial support, the potential reduction in air pollution, the anticipated number of riders and the effect on other transportation systems.

At a hearing April 29 of the House Energy and Commerce Subcommittee on Transportation and Hazardous Materials, Peña said his department planned to invest only in corridors that would complement the airlines, not compete with them. Commuter airlines, led by Texas-based Southwest Airlines, had argued against a major public investment in high-speed rail, maintaining that it would be more costly than the service they already provided.

Amtrak President W. Graham Claytor Jr. warned the subcommittee that it would be "virtually impossible for any high-speed system at the outset to fully cover its cost of capital ... without substantial public assistance." Amtrak operated the Northeast Corridor.

HOUSE COMMITTEE

HR 1919 received quick approval May 27 on a voice vote from the Transportation and Hazardous Materials Subcommittee. But the railroad unions' objections forced lengthy negotiations between the unions and aides to subcommittee Chairman Al Swift, D-Wash., full committee Chairman John D. Dingell, D-Mich., and Peña.

The unions argued that the bill should provide at least as much protection for their members as they got through

the mass transit program. For transportation workers who lost their jobs when a federally subsidized high-speed route moved in, the unions asked the U.S. government to pay up to six years of severance pay, medical benefits and moving expenses.

They also wanted to have the Davis-Bacon Act cover any construction work financed by the bill and a provision added to protect union employees from being displaced by low-wage subcontractors. Finally, they wanted the secretary of Labor, not the secretary of Transportation, to decide whether the labor arrangements on a proposed high-speed corridor were adequate.

House Full Committee

The full Energy and Commerce Committee took up the bill July 27, approving it by a vote of 28-16 (H Rept 103-258) — but only after adding several provisions to protect railroad workers from career-ending layoffs.

The bill authorized $1.2 billion over five years to help states design, acquire and/or build high-speed rail corridors and the signaling systems needed to operate them. It authorized an additional $75 million over five years to support research and technology development.

No money was available for the trains or a corridor's operation expenses. Nor could the high-speed rail program contribute more to the cost of a corridor than did state and local governments.

At the markup, Swift, a chief sponsor of the bill, proposed a substitute amendment with eight pages of protections for railroad workers other than those employed by Amtrak, who were guaranteed expanded unemployment benefits when Amtrak was created. The proposal included 18 months of pay and benefits for workers displaced by a subsidized high-speed rail route.

The unions, however, continued to seek stronger language and a greater role for the secretary of Labor. Swift said only modest protections were needed because most of the affected workers were likely to be Amtrak employees and because the program would create far more jobs than it terminated.

Republicans on the Energy and Commerce Committee attacked the provision applying Davis-Bacon to contracts funded by the high-speed rail program. Carlos J. Moorhead, Calif., the committee's top Republican and an original bill cosponsor, offered an amendment to delete the Davis-Bacon provision from Swift's substitute amendment. Moorhead said applying Davis-Bacon to high-speed rail would be a fiscal disaster for job-starved California because it would raise the cost of every construction project on a high-speed route.

Swift responded that Davis-Bacon simply prevented the federal government from driving down local wages. It protected both construction workers and local contractors from having to compete with contractors from lower-wage areas, he said.

The committee voted largely along party lines to defeat Moorhead's amendment, 19-24. Swift's substitute amendment then was adopted by voice vote.

SENATE COMMITTEE

The Senate Commerce, Science and Transportation Committee approved its version of the bill (S 839 — S Rept 103-208) by voice vote Nov. 9.

The bill authorized $982 million over five years in grants to public agencies to do engineering, conduct environment studies, acquire rights of way, and build or improve tracks or signals. The grants could cover up to 80 percent of the cost of a specific improvement, but no more than half the cost of all the improvements on that high-speed corridor. The bill also authorized $15 million annually for five years in grants to businesses, universities and public agencies involved in high-speed rail technology development.

As approved by the committee, the bill included provisions requiring that applicants for high-speed rail grants obtain $500 million in liability insurance for themselves, the operator of the high-speed service and the owners of the track. For trains using existing tracks, the insurance was to pay any claims resulting when trains exceeded the maximum speed allowed. On new tracks, the insurance was to cover any claim, regardless of the conduct that caused it.

The freight railroads had said they supported high-speed rail and would share their tracks with the new passenger service. In exchange, their representatives had asked Congress to protect them against lawsuits in the event of a high-speed wreck.

The provisions won the support of the freight railroads' trade association, the Association of American Railroads, a spokesman for the group said. They posed a financial hurdle, though, for states that wanted to launch high-speed routes.

The committee bill also added a requirement that federally subsidized high-speed routes comply with existing railroad labor and retirement laws. The provision, sought by the transportation unions, aimed to help the unions organize employees on the new routes by giving them the right to collective bargaining.

The unions wanted more, however — particularly, protection for other types of transportation workers who might lose their jobs if high-speed rail proved to be popular. They also wanted the Davis-Bacon Act provision that was put in the House version. ∎

FAA Authorization Crashes in Senate

Congress let lapse the authorization for the Federal Aviation Administration (FAA) and a program to improve the nation's airports at the end of fiscal 1993, preventing the FAA from issuing any more grants for airport improvement projects. The reauthorization bill became ensnared in a Senate dispute over setting limits on lawsuits against the manufacturers of small planes.

The House on Oct. 13 passed a three-year reauthorization that renewed funding for airport improvement grants. The House bill (HR 2739) authorized $14.1 billion for FAA operations, $6.5 billion for the airport improvement program, $7.9 billion for FAA facilities and equipment and $827 million for FAA research and development through fiscal 1996.

The Senate Commerce Committee on Nov. 9 approved a one-year, $2.1 billion reauthorization of the airport improvement program (S 1491). The bill bogged down before reaching the Senate floor, however, when Nancy Landon Kassebaum, R-Kan., demanded a vote on her separate proposal to limit liability lawsuits against the manufacturers of small planes.

The Clinton administration preferred a one-year bill to give Congress and the administration more time to consider changes in the FAA's structure. Among the possible changes were turning over the air-traffic control functions of the FAA to an independent public agency.

HOUSE ACTION

House action began in the Public Works and Transportation Subcommittee on Aviation. The panel approved HR 2739 by voice vote July 29 after resolving a lengthy dispute over labor protections included in the measure.

The subcommittee voted, 20-16, to delete from the bill a provision that would have applied the 1931 Davis-Bacon Act to construction work at Washington National Airport and Washington's Dulles International Airport. The Davis-Bacon Act required that prevailing local wages be paid to construction workers hired under federal contracts.

The subcommittee rejected, 13-23, a separate amendment to delete a proposed expansion in the airport employees' bargaining rights. The disputed provision gave employees at the two airports the right to bargain collectively over wages and benefits, although they were not permitted to strike. "It's benign, it's reasonable, it's fair," panel chairman and bill sponsor Democrat James L. Oberstar of Minnesota, said of the collective-bargaining provision. He said employees at 35 of the nation's 45 largest airports had collective bargaining rights.

Full Committee Action

The House Public Works and Transportation Committee approved the bill on a voice vote Aug. 5. The bill (H Rept 103-240) authorized:

• **FAA operations.** $4.6 billion for the FAA in fiscal 1994, $4.7 billion in fiscal 1995 and $4.8 billion in fiscal 1996. Authorization for the program expired Sept. 3.

• **Airport improvements.** Up to $2.1 billion for airport infrastructure improvements for fiscal 1994 and about $2.2 billion each for fiscal years 1995 and 1996. Airport infrastructure projects included expenditures such as runway repairs and extensions and purchases of heavy terminal equipment.

• **Airway improvements.** $2.5 billion in fiscal 1994 and nearly $2.7 billion each in fiscal 1995 and 1996 for "airway" improvement projects. As opposed to airport improvement projects, these projects included such things as state-of-the-art control tower electronics.

After lengthy debate, members rejected, 19-41, an amendment by William O. Lipinski, D-Ill., to clarify that discretionary airport grants could be made to airports even if airport revenues were used for other purposes by the city in which the airport was located.

Opponents said it was unfair for some cities to divert airport revenues to city projects when other cities did not. They also said the practice threatened to spread as cities looked for innovative ways to raise more revenue. Bill sponsor Oberstar opposed the amendment, saying it threatened to result in more costs being passed on to airline

---

BOXSCORE

➡ **FAA Reauthorization (HR 2739, S 1491).** HR 2739 was a three-year, $30.5 billion reauthorization for the Federal Aviation Administration and airport improvement programs. The Senate bill reauthorized airport improvements at $2.1 billion for one year.

Reports: H Rept 103-240, S Rept 103-181.

KEY ACTION

Aug. 5 — **House** Public Works and Transportation Committee approved HR 2739 by voice vote.

Oct. 13 — **House** passed HR 2739, 384-42.

Nov. 9 — **Senate** Commerce Committee approved S 1491 by voice vote.

---

passengers. He said most cities did not siphon revenues from airports to pay for unrelated city projects.

Lipinski argued that many large airports that received federal grants already had funding diverted to host cities for non-airport uses, including Chicago, Baltimore, Boston and San Francisco. Lipinski said the amendment would clarify that such airports should not be penalized for having their host cities divert airport revenues.

The bill included language that called on the Transportation Department to consider the diversion of airport revenues, such as local taxes on aviation fuel, as a "factor militating against" the distribution of discretionary improvement grants.

Members also approved, by voice vote, an amendment by Oberstar to require the Transportation Department to study whether improvements in technology and wider use of quieter aircraft made it reasonable to lift limitations on hourly operations at some busy airports.

House Floor Action

The House passed HR 2739 on Oct. 13 by a vote of 384-42. Floor debate had begun Oct. 7. *(Vote 492, p. 120-H)*

The biggest change recommended by the House bill was to give the FAA administrator a fixed, five-year term. Under the system of political appointees, the average FAA administrator had remained in office only two years. Other policy changes included prohibiting airport surcharges on passengers who used frequent-flier coupons and discouraging local governments from tapping airport revenues for non-airport uses. The bill also required taxpayers to pay a larger portion of the FAA's costs, a provision that drew protests from House appropriators.

The bill required the FAA to reconsider limits placed on flights to and from John F. Kennedy and La Guardia international airports in New York, Washington National Airport and O'Hare International Airport in Chicago. James P. Moran, D-Va., offered an amendment Oct. 7 that would have exempted National Airport from that study, but it failed on a vote of 110-294. *(Vote 489, p. 120-H)*

Frank R. Wolf, R-Va., tried unsuccessfully to knock out the provision that gave certain employees of the Metropolitan Washington Airports Authority the right to bargain collectively over their pay and benefits. The provision applied to firefighters, police officers and other employees at Washington National and at Dulles International airports who already were represented by labor organizations. The amendment was rejected, 167-259, on Oct. 13. *(Vote 490, p. 120-H)*

The House agreed to an amendment requiring airlines to provide child-safety seats but stopped short of requiring passengers to put children in them.

Jim Ross Lightfoot, R-Iowa, offered an amendment Oct. 7 to require child restraint systems on commercial airlines. Although adults, baggage and pets were required to be restrained during much of a flight, Lightfoot said, children younger than age 2 were permitted to sit in an adult's lap.

The FAA opposed Lightfoot's amendment on the grounds that it threatened to increase the cost of flying for

families, who would have to purchase tickets for infants, prompting many to drive instead of fly. The same argument was made by Oberstar, who noted that far more people died in highway accidents than on airplanes. Oberstar offered a substitute amendment to require the airlines to provide child-safety seats for parents who bought separate tickets for their infants; parents would still have the option of holding their children in their laps.

The House voted 374-48 to approve the Lightfoot amendment, after accepting Oberstar's modification, 270-155. *(Votes 488, p. 120-H; 487, p. 118-H)*

SENATE ACTION

Wendell H. Ford, D-Ky., chairman of the Senate Commerce Committee's Aviation Subcommittee, supported the administration's position and produced a simple, one-year reauthorization. The full committee approved the $2.1 billion fiscal 1994 airport improvement bill by voice vote Nov. 9 (S 1491 — S Rept 103-181).

The committee first approved an amendment by Byron L. Dorgan, D-N.D., to require that airlines give 60 days' notice to local authorities and the Transportation Department if they planned to cut off service to small markets.

In related action, the committee also approved the bill (S 1458 — S Rept 103-202) by Kassebaum to protect the makers of small planes against certain liability lawsuits. The bill made manufacturers immune from liability for incidents involving airplanes that were more than 15 years old.

The production of small planes had plummeted in the United States in the previous 15 years, and analysts put at least part of the blame on liability lawsuits. The chief executive of one manufacturer told The Wall Street Journal that liability insurance was the second most expensive component of his planes, after the engine.

Kassebaum's state was home to the top two small-plane manufacturers, Cessna and Beech. Cessna had stopped making anything but jets but had pledged to reopen production of piston-engine planes if a bill like Kassebaum's passed. ∎

Airline Commission Sends Report to the Hill

The House on March 23 cleared a bill (HR 904) to expand and accelerate the work of a commission created by Congress to study the financial woes of the airline and airplane manufacturing industries.

The measure increased the membership of the National Commission to Ensure a Strong Competitive Airline Industry and shortened its deadline from six months to 90 days. President Clinton signed the bill into law April 7 (PL 103-13).

The commission released its report Aug. 19, calling for the government to quickly modernize the air-traffic control system, limit the cost of federal regulations and negotiate more landing rights overseas. It also urged Congress to cut the taxes on airlines, roll back the tax on airplane tickets and allow greater foreign investment in U.S. air carriers.

The commission's report landed with a thud in Congress. No committee hearings were held on it, and no legislation was introduced. Aides said Congress was waiting for the administration to release a formal response to the commis-

sion's report, and many lawmakers expected Congress to deal with the recommendations in separate bills in 1994.

BACKGROUND

The airlines had posted $10 billion in losses from 1990 to 1992, and their hard times continued in the first half of 1993. They turned a $375 million profit in the third quarter, but industry officials still expected to lose roughly $1 billion by the end of the year.

Congress created the commission in 1992 under a bill reauthorizing the Federal Aviation Administration (PL 102-581). The panel was to study the financial condition of the airline industry, the adequacy of competition, legal and regulatory burdens on carriers, international aviation policy and the condition of the aircraft manufacturing industry. Congress gave itself six seats to fill; the president was allowed one.

The panel was given six months to produce a set of recommendations, but it was grounded almost immediately by political and financial problems. Congress never filled its six seats, and when Transportation Secretary Federico F. Peña took over the Transportation Department he asked that the administration be given a greater voice in the study. *(1992 Almanac, p. 198)*

HOUSE ACTION

The House Public Works Committee approved HR 904 (H Rept 103-22) on Feb. 23. It enlarged the commission to 15 voting members instead of seven and gave it only 90 days to finish its work. Bill sponsor James L. Oberstar, D-Minn., said the shorter time frame would cut the cost from an estimated $2 million to an estimated $750,000.

The bill removed President George Bush's appointee — Albert V. Casey, the head of the Resolution Trust Corporation — and allowed Clinton to appoint five new members, plus one non-voting member. The Speaker and Senate majority leader each could appoint three voting and two non-voting members, while the minority leaders each could appoint two voting members and one non-voting member.

The 1992 law called for elected officials to be included on the commission, and a number of lawmakers had sought seats in the hope of advancing their own agendas. HR 904 made no mention of elected officials and instead called for the voting members to be experts in aviation economics, finance and trade. The 1992 law also called for one of the members to be a representative of a grass-roots group opposed to airport noise. The new bill dropped that provision, and the committee rejected an attempt by Bob Franks, R-N.J., to restore it.

The law enacted in 1992 made no provision for funding the commission, which was one reason the panel had remained dormant. Peña pledged to finance the new version of the commission out of his department's budget for operations.

The House on March 2 quickly passed HR 904 by a bipartisan vote of 367-43. The dissenting votes came from conservative Republicans who objected to the bill's $750,000 price tag. *(Vote 44, p. 12-H)*

SENATE ACTION

On March 17, the Senate passed its version of HR 904 by voice vote, after substituting the text of a slightly different Senate bill (S 366).

The Senate bill expanded the commission to 26 mem-

bers, including 11 non-voting advisers. The House-passed bill provided for 22 members, including seven non-voting advisers.

S 366 originally had provided for nine non-voting members. But Sen. John C. Danforth, R-Mo., won voice vote approval for an amendment increasing the number to 11. Danforth withdrew a second amendment to move the deadline for the commission's final report from 90 days to 30 days.

FINAL ACTION

The House on March 23 accepted the Senate amendments, clearing HR 904.

The commission's report was expected to influence the outcome of a pending legislative battle over the limits on foreign investment in U.S. airlines. Key players in this battle were expected to be supporters and opponents of an attempt by USAir Group Inc. to forge a global airline operation with British Airways.

The congressional allies of USAir and other cash-strapped airlines saw foreign investment as the means to gain competitive muscle internationally. They wanted Congress to increase the foreign ownership limit from 25 percent to 49 percent to attract more investment from the likes of British Airways. The so-called Big Three airlines — American, United and Delta — said any change should wait until foreign governments allowed more landing rights to U.S. carriers. ∎

Foreign Investment Debate

Senate passage of HR 904 came on the heels of a decision announced March 15 by Transportation Secretary Federico F. Peña not to block the first phase of a British Airways' deal with USAir Group Inc., a $300 million investment that gave British Airways 19.9 percent of USAir's voting stock.

There were indications that some senators who supported the USAir deal had been holding up HR 904, which Peña was eager to see passed, until Peña announced his decision on the investment deal.

Peña's decision set the stage for a legislative battle over the limits on foreign investment in U.S. airlines. Peña made it clear he would not approve British Airways' plan to invest an additional $450 million in USAir within five years because that investment would give British Airways more than the legal limit of 25 percent of USAir's voting stock.

The so-called Big Three U.S. airlines — Delta, United and American — argued that the USAir deal gave British Airways virtually unlimited access to the U.S. market.

This kind of arrangement should not be allowed, they contended, unless the British government gave U.S. carriers the same access to British airports, which it had refused to do.

Most of the Big Three's congressional allies seemed resigned to accepting Peña's decision, however. Peña said the law gave him no choice but to approve almost all the elements of the deal's first phase, which called for the two airlines to share their ticket-reservation systems and to coordinate flights. The ultimate goal of the two airlines was to create a unified, global airline operation.

House Passes Bill To Fund NTSB

The House on Nov. 8 voted to reauthorize the National Transportation Safety Board (NTSB) for three years. The Senate Commerce, Science and Transportation Committee on Nov. 9 approved a companion measure (S 1588 — S Rept 103-85), sponsored by Wendell H. Ford, D-Ky. The Senate took no further action on the bill in 1993.

The House bill (HR 2440), sponsored by James L. Oberstar, D-Minn., authorized $37.6 million in fiscal 1994 for the NTSB, which investigated airplane accidents and conducted transportation research. The amount was to rise to $44 million in fiscal 1995 and $45.1 million in fiscal 1996 to allow the NTSB to hire additional employees.

Action began in the House Public Works Subcommittee on Aviation, which approved HR 2440 on June 23 by voice vote. Subcommittee Chairman Oberstar said the authorization level would hold NTSB employment steady in fiscal 1994 and allow for 17 additional full-time employees in fiscal 1995-96. Funding in fiscal 1993 was $36 million.

President Clinton had requested $37.1 million in fiscal 1994, which would have required the elimination of nine NTSB jobs. But Oberstar noted that the board's jurisdiction had expanded in recent years. While he emphasized the need for deficit reduction, Oberstar argued that the NTSB served a "vitally important" role in transportation safety. Ranking Republican William F. Clinger Jr., Pa., agreed: "I don't think you can really economize with safety."

The full Public Works Committee approved the bill (H Rept 103-239, Part 1) by voice vote Aug. 5.

Action then turned to the Energy and Commerce Subcommittee on Transportation and Hazardous Materials, which approved the bill by voice vote on Oct. 21. The full Energy and Commerce Committee approved HR 2440 on Oct. 26 (H Rept 103-239, Part 2). The House passed HR 2440 Nov. 8 by a vote of 353-49 without changing the authorization levels. *(Vote 549, p. 134-H)* ∎

Hazardous Materials Act Awaits Senate Passage

After dropping two controversial provisions on billboards and radar detectors, the House passed a bill reauthorizing the federal programs for transporting hazardous goods for four years. In the Senate, a similar measure won committee approval but did not reach the floor.

The House bill (HR 2178) authorized a gradual increase in spending on the programs established by the Hazardous Materials Transportation Act (PL 101-615), starting at $18 million in fiscal 1994 and increasing to $19.7 million in fiscal 1997. Those programs included inspections, research, training and emergency preparedness. *(1990 Almanac, p. 380)*

Legislative Action

The legislation began as a one-paragraph, straightforward reauthorization measure introduced by Nick J. Rahall, D-W.Va., on behalf of the bipartisan leadership of the Public Works and Energy and Commerce committees and their surface transportation panels. But as the bill moved

through the two committees, it grew in size and controversy, largely due to changes made by Public Works.

The House Energy and Commerce Subcommittee on Transportation and Hazardous Materials approved the measure by voice vote Oct. 21, after adopting an amendment by panel Chairman Al Swift, D-Wash. His provision exempted foreign shippers from certain registration fees as long as they transported hazardous materials only as far as a U.S. port and did not ship goods between states.

The full Energy and Commerce Committee approved the bill Oct. 26 by voice vote (H Rept 103-336 Part 1).

The Public Works Subcommittee on Surface Transportation switched strategy and folded the measure into a larger bill (HR 3460) introduced by panel Chairman Rahall. Both the Surface Transportation Subcommittee and the full committee passed Rahall's expanded bill Nov. 9 by voice vote.

As approved by Public Works, the new bill watered down an existing prohibition on billboards along state-designated scenic highways and authorized a study of the ban on radar detectors in trucks and other commercial vehicles. Congress adopted both prohibitions in 1991 as part of the surface transportation law (PL 102-240) and the fiscal 1992 transportation spending law (PL 102-143). *(1991 Almanac, pp. 137, 603)*

Dick Swett, D-N.H., and Sherwood Boehlert, R-N.Y., attempted to strike the billboard provision, which allowed billboards along scenic highways in commercial and industrial areas. Swett's amendment was defeated by a voice vote in the Surface Transportation Subcommittee on Nov. 9, and the full committee defeated Boehlert's amendment 12-50 later the same day.

Tim Valentine, D-N.C., tried to remove the radar detector study, but he was defeated 16-20 in subcommittee and 19-41 in full committee. A second Valentine amendment to shift the study from radar detectors to "microwave technology" was defeated on a voice vote.

The new bill also stretched the $75.3 million four-year authorization in the original bill to $95.6 million over five years. HR 3460 also authorized $10 million in grants to certain firefighters for hazardous materials training and equipment, and $1 million for fiscal years 1995 and 1996 for a demonstration project and a study on how advanced communications equipment could improve the transportation of hazardous materials.

But members of the Energy and Commerce Committee balked at two provisions in HR 3460, temporarily stalling the reauthorization efforts. The committee objected to the study of the proposed radar detector ban, which had been pushed by William F. Clinger, R-Pa. And it found the easing of billboard restrictions, which had been supported by Rahall and Public Works ranking Republican, Bud Shuster, Pa., disagreeable.

Ultimately, the two committees agreed on a four-year, $75.3 million version of HR 2178 that did not include those provisions.

The Energy and Commerce Committee did agree to add several provisions. One, sought by Rahall, authorized up to $1.25 million in annual grants to train firefighters for incidents involving hazardous materials. A second, pushed by Douglas Applegate, D-Ohio, authorized up to $1 million in fiscal 1995 and 1996 for an experiment in computerized tracking of hazardous shipments.

The bill also ordered the Transportation Department to study safety considerations for transportation of hazardous goods near prisons, as requested by Clinger. And it re-

quired the department to determine whether drums made of fibers could safely transport hazardous liquids, a provision sought by James E. Clyburn, D-S.C.

The House passed the compromise bill by voice vote Nov. 21.

The Senate Commerce, Science and Transportation Committee gave voice vote approval Nov. 9 to similar legislation (S 1640, S Rept 103-217). The bill, introduced by committee member Jim Exon, D-Neb., was a three-year version that authorized $5.4 million to $5.5 million less each year than the House bill. ∎

Drunk Drivers Targeted in Highway Safety Bill

In a bid to reduce highway deaths, the Senate on Nov. 20 passed legislation aimed at getting high-risk drivers off the road. Teenagers who drank and drove were the principal target of the bill. The legislation (S 738), sponsored by John C. Danforth, R-Mo., offered special grants to prod states to crack down on repeat traffic offenders and drivers 16 to 20 years old.

In the House, Frank R. Wolf, R-Va., sponsored a similar bill (HR 1719), which was pending before the Public Works and Transportation Committee at year's end.

Bill backers cited statistics showing that teenagers, who held only 7.4 percent of all driver's licenses, were responsible for 15.4 percent of all fatal highway accidents.

Bill Highlights

Under the bill, states that granted only provisional licenses to drivers under age 18 were eligible for incentive grants totaling $100 million over five years, beginning in fiscal 1994. Provisional licenses typically imposed restrictions on the times of day a teenager could drive without adult supervision and required a license holder to maintain a clean record for one year before receiving a permanent license.

To win the grants, states had to adopt an increasing number of requirements over a five-year period, including:

● Establishing a blood alcohol content of 0.02 or less as the measure of intoxication for drivers under age 21 — in effect, a zero tolerance level. Twelve states and the District of Columbia already met this standard.

● Setting a mandatory minimum fine of $500 for anyone who sold or provided alcohol to a minor.

● Requiring all passengers in a car, including those in the back seat, to use seat belts.

● Suspending for at least six months the driver's license of anyone under age 21 convicted of purchasing or possessing alcohol.

● Prohibiting possession of an open alcoholic beverage container or consumption of such a beverage in a car.

● Enforcing a minimum penalty for driving through a railroad crossing while the gate was closed.

● Participating in an interstate compact for prompt electronic exchange of information on individual driving records.

● Creating statewide traffic safety enforcement, education and training programs aimed at high-risk drivers.

● Confiscating the vehicles of drivers convicted two or more times in five years of driving under the influence of drugs or alcohol.

States were eligible for supplemental grants if they required licenses of drivers under age 21 to be clearly distinguishable through profile photographs or other special markings, and if they used Social Security numbers as the license identification number for all drivers to facilitate transfer of driving records between states.

While the bill pushed states to impose tight restrictions and tough sanctions on teenage drivers and repeat offenders, it took a more gingerly approach to the problem of elderly drivers, expressly recognizing their need for access to transportation. The bill required the Department of Transportation to conduct detailed studies of the abilities of older drivers and various options for restricting their licenses without forbidding them to drive.

BACKGROUND

Since the 1960s, Congress had enacted a number of laws designed to reduce traffic accidents and fatalities. Those laws, which forced improvements in highway design and new safety features in motor vehicles, brought a steady decline in the rate of traffic fatalities, even as the numbers of licensed drivers and of cars on the road increased.

According to the U.S. Department of Transportation, motor vehicle fatalities in 1992 dropped to a 30-year low of 39,200 deaths. That figure represented a fatality rate of 1.8 per 100 million vehicle miles traveled, down from 5.1 in 1962.

Congress' first major attack on traffic safety came in 1966, with the passage of two related measures, the National Traffic and Motor Vehicle Safety Act (PL 89-563) and the Highway Safety Act (PL 89-564). These laws required establishment of safety standards for vehicles, tires, highways and drivers. *(1966 Almanac, p. 266)*

Ironically, however, the law (PL 93-239) that had the most dramatic impact on highway safety was intended to save gasoline rather than lives. Enacted in 1973 at the height of the Arab oil embargo, it required states to set a maximum speed limit of 55 mph or lose their federal highway aid. The following year saw the nation's biggest single-year drop in the rate of highway deaths, from 4.1 per 100 million miles traveled to 3.5. *(1973 Almanac, p. 637)*

In 1987, after years of widespread defiance of the 55 mph standard, Congress authorized the states to raise their speed limits to 65 mph outside urban areas. Most states had done so by 1993, although the 55 mph limit remained in effect in a number of densely populated East Coast states.

After several false starts, Congress in 1977 allowed the Department of Transportation to require installation of air bags or other passive restraints in all new-model cars by 1984. Although the deadline was repeatedly pushed back under pressure from the auto industry, seat belt use was up and manufacturers were scrambling to install air bags in response to public demand for them. *(1977 Almanac, p. 531)*

The last major step Congress took to address highway safety came in 1984, when it ordered states to raise their minimum legal drinking age to 21 or lose portions of their highway aid. By 1993, all states and the District of Columbia had a minimum drinking age of 21. *(1984 Almanac, p. 283)*

SENATE ACTION

The Senate Commerce Committee approved S 738 by voice vote Nov. 9, nearly six months after it held hearings on the measure May 26 (S Rept 103-199).

At the May 26 hearing, Danforth said state experiments proved the effectiveness of some of the steps outlined in S 738. California, Maryland and Oregon were among nine states that already had a provisional license system in place, and they had "experienced as much as a 16 percent reduction in accidents and a 15 percent reduction in traffic convictions for 16- to 17-year-old youths," Danforth said.

Senate Floor

The full Senate approved S 738 by voice vote Nov. 20. Only Danforth spoke on the measure.

He told his colleagues that if existing trends continued, more than 400,000 people would be killed on U.S. highways over the coming decade and more than 5 million would be hospitalized. "We can prevent a substantial portion of the loss by reducing the number of crashes experienced by high-risk drivers," he said.

While the bill primarily targeted teenagers, Danforth noted that elderly drivers also were "disproportionately involved" in fatal traffic accidents. "According to a 1993 study, drivers 75 years and older were involved in 11.5 fatal crashes per 100 million miles driven, as compared to two fatal crashes per 100 million miles for drivers aged 35 to 59," he said.

"In light of the aging American population and the higher propensity of accidents, the concerns of older drivers need to be addressed." ∎

Panels OK Protection For Gas Stations

The House Energy and Commerce Committee approved legislation (HR 1520) aimed at protecting privately operated gasoline stations. Although the bill reflected a compromise hammered out by representatives of the gas stations and the oil companies, it was sidetracked by a continuing power struggle between the two groups. The House bill got no further in 1993, and a companion Senate bill (S 338) did not even get out of committee.

BACKGROUND

The dispute between the operators and the companies was rooted in the 1973 oil embargo, which caused a shake-up in the gasoline business. Companies competed for larger shares of the market by switching to self-service stations with numerous pumps. And when convenience stores started competing for gasoline sales, the major franchises responded by putting small-scale groceries at their stations.

The net result was a drastic decline in the number of traditional service stations — franchises run by small-business men that offered repairs as well as fuel — and a corresponding rise in the number of stations operated by the oil companies themselves.

Station operators contended that the oil companies hastened their decline by improperly terminating or refusing to renew their franchise agreements in order to force them out of the market. Representatives of independent dealers said the oil companies used tactics such as raising their dealers' rent, requiring 24-hour service in areas with no late-night business or setting a price for gasoline that the market could not bear.

A number of state legislatures stepped in, passing a variety of laws to regulate the relationship between the oil companies and their dealers. Congress intervened in 1978 with the Petroleum Marketing Practices Act (PL 95-297), which set a single set of rules for oil companies wishing to terminate a franchise. *(1978 Almanac, p. 748)*

Disputes between the station owners and the oil companies continued, however, and more state laws were enacted to restrict what the companies could demand from their dealers. The companies and the dealers often wound up in court, battling over whether the Petroleum Marketing Practices Act invalidated the protections offered by state law.

The station operators appealed to Congress again in the late 1980s, hoping to get more protections written into federal law. Pressed by the House Energy and Commerce Committee to work out a compromise solution, the station operators, the oil companies, the oil distributors and the independent gasoline marketers negotiated for almost two years before striking a deal in February 1992. *(1992 Almanac, p. 262)*

Although the compromise — which was embodied in the 1993 House and Senate bills — was backed by every segment of the oil industry, three powerful oil companies opposed it. Those three — Texaco, Shell Oil Co. and Mobil Corp. — controlled about a fourth of the U.S. gasoline market, according to Donald M. Smith, editor of National Petroleum News, a trade magazine. Their chief concern, according to officials at Texaco and Mobil, was preventing their franchise operators from buying gasoline from another company.

LEGISLATIVE ACTION

House subcommittee. The House Energy and Commerce Subcommittee on Energy and Power gave voice vote approval May 19 to HR 1520, a bill designed to give gas station operators a more secure grip on their franchises.

The bill attempted to clarify the scope of the Petroleum Marketing Practices Act, which barred state and local governments from regulating the termination or renewal of gasoline franchises. The bill left that restriction in place but added that state and local governments could regulate "any specific provision of a franchise."

All sides agreed that states and local governments should have the power to stop companies from setting abusive requirements on their dealers as a pretext to reclaim a franchise. There was sharp disagreement, however, over how to accomplish that goal without making the companies relinquish too much control over their brands.

Several members of the subcommittee said they were unhappy with the bill's language, and Chairman Philip R. Sharp, D-Ind., called for more negotiations before the bill reached the full committee.

The subcommittee defeated two amendments proposed by Joe L. Barton, R-Texas. One, rejected by a vote of 2-6, would have eliminated all the disputed language regarding what states and local governments could do. The other, which failed on a 4-4 vote, attempted to clarify the limits on state and local regulations, but was opposed by the oil companies, dealers and distributors.

The bill, sponsored by Ron Wyden, D-Ore., was identical to one that Wyden introduced in April 1992. That bill was reported by the Energy and Commerce Committee but not voted on by the House.

House committee. Members of the full Energy and Commerce Committee tried unsuccessfully for about a month to answer the companies' concerns without straying too far from the compromise. Spokesmen for Mobil and Texaco said they accepted most of the elements of the legislation, such as the right of a station operator's survivors to hold on to the franchise. What they could not accept, they said, was the section allowing states to regulate "any specific provision of a franchise."

To bill supporters, the provision clarified the states' power to regulate any franchise terms other than those dealing with termination or non-renewal, such as the hours of operation and sales quotas. But opponents said it was so poorly worded that it could give states the power to wreak havoc on the oil companies' relationship with their dealers.

On June 8 the committee made one slight modification aimed at clarifying the intent of HR 1520, then agreed by voice vote to report the bill to the full House. At the end of the year, House supporters said they did not expect floor action unless the Senate Energy and Commerce Committee approved its version of the legislation.

Senate. Wendell H. Ford, D-Ky., sponsored a similar bill in the Senate (S 338). The Energy and Natural Resources Committee held hearings Feb. 25 but took no further action. The bill ran into opposition not only from Texaco, Mobil and Shell but also from a group of gas station operators who argued that it was too favorable to the oil companies.

Ford tried a different tack in early March with a second bill (S 539) requiring any proposed changes in franchise agreements to be fair, reasonable and economically necessary to the operation of the franchise. It, too, awaited action in Senate Energy. ∎

Bankruptcy, Gun Permits Among Bills Considered

Congress acted on a number of bills related to road transportation in 1993.

LIMITING BANKRUPT TRUCKERS' CLAIMS

Rolling over the objections of organized labor, Congress on Nov. 19 cleared a bill (S 412) aimed at stemming a flood of litigation between bankrupt trucking companies and former customers over shipping rates. President Clinton signed the bill into law Dec. 3 (PL 103-180).

Many trucking companies had offered discounted rates following the deregulation of the industry in 1980, but they often did not file the discounts with the Interstate Commerce Commission. When a number of these companies went bankrupt, trustees tried to collect the difference between the higher rates on file and the lower prices the companies originally charged.

The U.S. Supreme Court had ruled in 1990 that the trustees could seek such reimbursement from the customers. The bill's sponsor, Sen. Jim Exon, D-Neb., tried to reverse the ruling during the 101st Congress, sponsoring a nearly identical bill that passed the Senate but died in the House under pressure from the Teamsters union. *(1992 Almanac, p. 206)*

"It is as if you bought a discount airplane ticket from Washington to Omaha for $200 and several years later were sued by a bankruptcy trustee for an additional $200 be-

cause the airline failed to file the discount rate with the appropriate authorities," Exon said during the 1993 debate on the bill.

As cleared, the 1993 bill barred any claims by bankrupt trucking firms to recoup undercharges for shipments made before October 1990. For goods moved after that date, the customers had the option of settling eligible undercharge claims for 15 percent or 20 percent of the amount sought, depending on the type of shipment. Small businesses, charities and recyclers were exempt, and the bill did not apply to previously settled claims.

The Senate Commerce, Science and Transportation Committee on May 25 gave voice vote approval to a version of the bill (S 412 — S Rept 103-79) that did not include the ban on pre-October 1990 claims. The Senate approved the bill July 1 by voice vote.

The House version of the bill (HR 2121 — H Rept 103-359) included the pre-October 1990 ban. The Public Works and Transportation Committee approved it Nov. 9. During the markup, William O. Lipinski, D-Ill., attempted to raise the percentages to 20 percent and 25 percent and to remove the ban on claims made before October 1990. The committee rejected the amendment, 16-48.

The House passed HR 2121 by a vote of 292-116 on Nov. 15; it then inserted its language into S 412 and approved the Senate bill. *(Vote 566, p. 138-H)*

The Senate agreed Nov. 19 to accept the House-passed version of the bill, clearing it for the president's signature.

The Teamsters and the AFL-CIO particularly opposed the provision that eliminated any chance of collecting pre-October 1990 claims. Lipinksi argued on the House floor that the bill effectively eliminated 90 percent to 95 percent of all undercharge claims, money that was needed if truck drivers and other employees of bankrupt trucking companies were to get some of the wages and benefits they had lost. Proponents of the bill argued that little of the money collected through undercharge claims made it into the workers' hands.

ARMORED CAR GUARDS

Congress cleared a bill by voice vote July 13 that eased gun permit requirements for armored car guards. On July 28, President Clinton signed the bill into law (PL 103-55).

The legislation (HR 1189) was prompted by complaints from armored car guards, who said that obtaining gun permits for every state they passed through during delivery or pickups was a bureaucratic hassle that caused delays and elevated costs.

Under the law, gun permits from the state in which armored car guards were primarily employed were declared valid for other states as well. The state issuing the permits had to meet several safeguards, including checking the criminal background of the guards and certifying that the guards underwent yearly gun-safety training. The provisions applied only when an armored vehicle crew was on duty.

The House bill was sponsored by Cardiss Collins, D-Ill., chairwoman of the Energy and Commerce Subcommittee on Commerce. Her panel approved the bill by voice vote March 10; the full Energy and Commerce Committee followed suit April 20 (H Rept 103-62). The House passed the legislation May 18, also by voice vote.

The Senate Commerce Committee approved a companion bill (S 608 — S Rept 103-67) on May 25 by voice vote. The Senate passed HR 1189 by voice vote June 30, after substituting the text of S 608. The House cleared the bill July 13 by unanimous consent.

AUTO TITLES

In a bid to crack down on automobile "title washing," the Senate on Nov. 20 passed, by voice vote, legislation to require that auto titles disclose all previous major damage to the car.

Title washing referred to the practice of selling cars that had been extensively rebuilt after an accident without noting the repair history on the title.

The bill (S 431 — S Rept 103-197), sponsored by Jim Exon, D-Neb., was approved Nov. 9 by the Senate Commerce Committee. The panel ordered the measure reported on a voice vote after adopting two amendments.

One amendment, by Larry Pressler, R-S.D., required the Transportation Department to study whether all used-car purchases should be accompanied by a report of prior damage, no matter how small.

A second amendment, by Slade Gorton, R-Wash., required that the titles of used cars bought back by dealers as "lemons" reflect that information.

The House took no action on the measure.

ADJUSTMENTS TO 1991 TRANSPORT LAW

The House on Nov. 8 passed a bill to make clarifying changes and adjust the locations or routes of certain demonstration projects in the 1991 surface transportation law (PL 102-240). The Senate took no action on the bill.

The so-called technical corrections bill (HR 3276 — H Rept 103-337), which passed on a voice vote, was not purely technical. For example, lawmakers from Kentucky and West Virginia inserted a provision dictating that the "East-West Transamerica Corridor" authorized by the 1991 law pass through or near 13 specific towns in their states. The 1991 law included no description of the route.

The most significant change concerned state laws requiring use of seat belts and motorcycle helmets. The bill extended by one year — from Sept. 30, 1993, to Sept. 30, 1994 — the deadline for states to enact such laws or face loss of highway construction money. According to safety advocacy groups, 44 states and the District of Columbia had some seat-belt requirements. While all but three states had some helmet use laws, only 25 required all motorcycle riders to wear helmets.

The bill also waived new weight limits for trucks on sections of highway in Wisconsin and, if the federal Transportation Department wished, in Ohio. Instead, trucks on those roads would have to comply with the higher limits in effect before the 1991 law.

The House Public Works and Transportation Subcommittee on Surface Transportation approved the measure by voice vote Oct. 21. The full Public Works and Transportation Committee followed suit Oct. 26. ∎

$3.2 Billion Cut From Agriculture Programs

Lawmakers included $3.2 billion in cuts to Agriculture Department programs in the 1993 budget-reconciliation bill (HR 2264 — H Rept 103-213) cleared on Aug. 6. President Clinton signed the bill Aug. 10 (PL 103-66). *(Budget-reconciliation bill, p. 107)*

The most controversial agriculture provisions proved to be the ones that saved the least money — particularly a plan to overhaul the Rural Electrification Administration (REA) and provisions to impose a new tax on cigarette manufacturers who relied on imported tobacco and to delay the marketing of a controversial growth hormone for cows.

Big-ticket items did not spur as much debate. The single largest agriculture savings — $586 million over five years — stemmed from a provision limiting the ability of the Agriculture secretary to boost price-support payments as a bargaining chip in negotiations aimed at strengthening the General Agreement on Tariffs and Trade (GATT).

In addition, lawmakers agreed to reform crop insurance to reduce fraud and abuse, and to reduce participation in the conservation reserve program, which paid farmers not to plant on erodible land.

CLINTON'S PROPOSAL

In outlining his economic program in February, President Clinton recommended $3.8 billion in cuts over four years from programs that protected and subsidized the incomes of major commodity producers.

Clinton called for an end to government subsidies for farmers who earned more than $100,000 in non-farm income — effectively converting farm programs from universal "entitlements" to "means-tested" welfare programs, an idea that was anathema to independent-minded farmers. The administration said the change would save $470 million by fiscal 1997.

Clinton also proposed lopping $2 billion from the $10 billion to $13 billion annual cost of farm subsidies, including:

● The biggest savings — $1 billion over four years — came from a plan to cut by 10 percent the amount of acreage eligible for some crop subsidies for wheat, feed grains, cotton and rice.

● Clinton also proposed eliminating a program that paid farmers to idle most or even all of their land, saving $937 million over four years.

● Another $900 million in savings under Clinton's plan came from a proposed increase in the assessments on farmers of non-grain crops, such as soybeans, sugar and tobacco, which did not qualify for subsidies but were protected through price-support loans.

Many of Clinton's cost-savings proposals hewed closely to ideas that were proposed during the Reagan and Bush administrations — and that were routinely ignored by Congress. For example, he wanted to revamp the REA loan program for rural communities so that the REA would charge its borrowers usual Treasury Department interest rates. The REA charged interest rates as low as 2 percent. The administration said the change would bring in an estimated $374 million by fiscal 1997.

HOUSE ACTION

When the House Agriculture Committee marked up the legislation May 13, members rejected the most controversial cost-cutting suggestions in Clinton's plan and opted instead for a $3 billion deficit-reduction package designed to avoid hitting farmers' pocketbooks directly. The committee approved the package by a vote of 26-17.

The House later approved the agriculture provisions, unchanged (H Rept 103-111), when it passed the budget-reconciliation bill, 219-213, on May 27. *(Vote 199, p. 48-H)*

Agriculture Committee members decided to look for the bulk of their savings by expanding a program known as triple-base, which limited the land on which farmers could grow the major subsidized crops of wheat, corn, cotton and feedgrains, while still protecting a farmer's "base acreage" for future planting decisions.

Under triple-base, farmers could plant a portion of the idled land ("flex-acres") with other non-subsidized crops that were in demand at no penalty if they wanted to return the flex-acres to subsidized crops in future years. (Crop subsidies were paid on a rolling-year average of acres planted to a particular program crop.) The flex-acre option was expected to induce farmers to forgo planting subsidized crops on those acres, thus reducing the subsidy cost to the government.

Members approved a plan to increase the existing 15 percent set-aside for flex-acres to 20 percent, beginning in 1994. The Congressional Budget Office (CBO) estimated that reducing the land available for subsidized crops would save $1.96 billion over five years.

The second-largest savings came in the Conservation Reserve Program, which paid farmers not to plant crops on land vulnerable to erosion. By limiting federal payments to a total of 36 million acres through 1995 and 38 million acres after that, as well as increasing the amount of acres included in a related program for wetlands, the committee projected savings of $469 million over five years.

The committee approved policy changes to the REA, including higher loan costs, that had been worked out earlier with House lawmakers and the National Rural Electric Cooperative Association.

The Agriculture panel also approved a Clinton administration proposal to increase spending for the federal food stamp program by $7.29 billion over five years.

Farm Act Reauthorization

Although little noted at the time, the Agriculture Committee package also included the first major revision of the 1990 farm bill (PL 101-624), the five-year law that governed most federal farm and nutrition programs. *(1990 Almanac, p. 323)*

House members took the step of reauthorizing all commodity programs through fiscal 1998. The move went unremarked during the committee markup. Soon after, however, farm program critics pointed out the reauthorizations as a behind-the-scenes way to avoid producing a 1995 farm bill.

The farm bill always had proved to be a lightning rod in the House for debates over agriculture subsidies. Fiscal conservatives and urban liberals regularly teamed up — with limited success — in efforts to gut commodity support programs, which they viewed as an extravagant benefit for a dwindling number of commercial farmers.

House Agriculture Committee staff said there was nothing unusual about the extension — they were required to

change the statute's expiration to get credit for $3 billion in farm program savings over the next five years.

SENATE COMMITTEE

Taking a somewhat different route June 16, the Senate Agriculture Committee, by voice vote, approved a $3.2 billion package of spending cuts. The committee did not reauthorize commodity programs through fiscal 1998, nor did it expand the food stamp program.

The Senate incorporated the provisions into its version of the bill (S 1134); on June 25, the Senate passed HR 2264, 50-49, after substituting the text of S 1134. *(Vote 190, 25-S)*

Alongside cuts in existing programs, the Senate panel agreed to require cigarette manufacturers to report their use of imported tobacco and to institute a fee for cigarette manufacturers who used more than 25 percent imported tobacco in their products.

At the request of dairy state lawmakers, the panel also voted to impose a one-year moratorium on sales of milk from cows that had been injected with bovine somatotropin (bST), a synthetic growth hormone. The Senate stripped the bovine hormone provision from the bill by a vote of 38-40 on a procedural motion; a shorter version was restored in conference. The Food and Drug Administration (FDA) approved bST for use later in the year.

The panel also approved most of the policy changes to the REA, including higher loan costs.

But Senate lawmakers rejected changes to the flexible-acreage program. Instead, the largest single component of the Senate committee's savings came from eliminating a provision of law that permitted the Agriculture secretary to boost price support payments to grain farmers should European and other nations refuse to cooperate on reducing farm subsidies as part of the GATT talks.

According to a committee aide, CBO estimated that if the Agriculture Department used such authority once in the following four years, it would cost $586 million in additional corn subsidies.

The committee achieved savings in commodity programs by reducing the size of payments to farmers who agreed not to plant certain subsidized grain crops. Under the so-called 0/92 program — designed to control the supply of grains — farmers were paid 92 percent of their allotted subsidies if they decided not to plant.

The Senate measure reduced payments to wheat and feed grain farmers to 85 percent of their expected subsidies. The panel also approved changes to the crop insurance program, which required more complete farm histories from applicants, saving approximately $501 million over five years.

Like the House version, the Senate measure proposed capping participation in the conservation reserve program, which took fragile farmland out of production for 10 years. It would have increased enrollment in the related wetlands reserve program. It included recreation fees for Forest Service parkland, limited subsidies to beekeepers and required states to pay more of the costs of food stamp administration.

CONFERENCE, FINAL ACTION

House and Senate conferees on the agriculture portion of the reconciliation bill agreed to cut $3 billion from agriculture programs, adopted parts of the controversial House language to aid rural electric cooperatives and approved Senate provisions to protect tobacco farmers.

House members generally acceded to the Senate's savings provisions, which reduced payments to wheat and feed grain farmers under the 0/92 program, saving an estimated $300 million over five years. Conferees opted against the House-passed changes to the triple-base program.

They adopted the Senate proposal to eliminate the so-called GATT trigger that permitted the Agriculture secretary to boost grain subsidies if the GATT negotiations failed, saving $586 million.

And they achieved an estimated $501 million in savings over five years by adopting a Senate-backed plan to tighten fraud controls and administrative oversight of the Federal Crop Insurance Program. An additional $469 million in savings came mainly from limiting enrollment in the Conservation Reserve Program.

Despite objections of conferees representing the House Ways and Means Committee, House and Senate Agriculture committee lawmakers agreed to the Senate language instituting a fee for cigarette manufacturers who used more than 25 percent imported tobacco in their products. Sam M. Gibbons, D-Fla., chairman of the Ways and Means Subcommittee on Trade, said the provision violated the GATT.

One of the toughest battles came over House changes to the REA. In the end, conferees adopted a compromise designed by Glenn English, D-Okla., the REA's strongest supporter in the House. The compromise allowed rural electric cooperatives to continue providing utility service to rural areas even if those areas were annexed by a nearby municipality that ran its own utility. The annexation provision, which was strongly opposed by local government officials, was to take effect in February 1994.

The language was later stripped out of the conference report, however, because of concern that it would spark a procedural challenge in the Senate. Later in the year, Congress cleared a separate REA bill (HR 3123 — PL 103-129). *(REA, below)*

At the urging of Senate Agriculture Committee Chairman Patrick J. Leahy, D-Vt., lawmakers also added language barring manufacturers of bST from marketing the hormone for 90 days after any FDA approval of the chemical. The 90-day moratorium was considerably shorter than the one-year ban initially included in the Senate bill.

In the final reconciliation bill, a few of the commodity programs were authorized through 1998, though many were not because of fears that the reauthorization provisions would violate the same Senate procedural rules at issue in the REA language. ∎

Restructuring the REA

Congress cleared a bill making far-reaching changes in the Rural Electrification Administration's (REA) lending programs for rural electric and telephone cooperatives.

Under the bill, low-cost loans, formerly available to some rural electric cooperatives at 2 percent interest were eliminated. But communities that demonstrated some hardship were made eligible for loans at a subsidized interest rate of 5 percent. The remainder of the co-ops could borrow money at the same rate available to municipalities up to a maximum rate of 7 percent. Rural telephone cooperatives were eligible for similar rates.

Rural electric cooperatives were given additional access

to water and sewage improvement loans, and states were required to submit plans to modernize rural telephone systems if they wished to be eligible for REA loans.

The changes were largely the result of work that had been done earlier in the year on the budget-reconciliation bill (HR 2264) but was stripped out at the last minute because of procedural complications.

House and Senate lawmakers then moved quickly to pass a version of the language as a stand-alone bill (HR 3123). The House passed the bill Sept. 28; the Senate cleared the measure Oct. 4. President Clinton, who had called for cuts in the REA, signed the bill into law Nov. 1 (PL 103-129).

BACKGROUND

Critics had argued for years that the REA had outlived its usefulness. When President Franklin D. Roosevelt created the agency in 1935, just 10 percent of America's rural areas had access to electricity. By 1993, the Agriculture Department reported that 99 percent of the country's 2.3 million farms had electricity, and 97 percent had telephones.

In outlining his economic package in February, Clinton called for cutting $545 million from the REA budget over five years, mostly by charging borrowers Treasury Department interest rates.

Recognizing that the agency could not avoid some cuts, REA supporters and rural cooperatives began negotiating with the administration. The White House Office of Management and Budget and the National Rural Electric Cooperative Association took part in the talks and signed off on a compromise.

Over four months, Rep. Glenn English, D-Okla., and Sen. Howell Heflin, D-Ala., put together a plan to increase the rates for REA loans and fold the agency into the Agriculture Department's Rural Development Administration. Lawmakers envisioned the agency as becoming a main source of funding for rural water and sewer systems, many of which were in need of renovation and modernization. The change promised to give rural electric cooperatives, the main recipients of REA loans, the chance to play a larger role in rural development.

"We enhanced the overall utility effort . . . and we were able to bring about some savings," said English. "We made lemonade from lemons."

RECONCILIATION BILL

When the House Agriculture Committee approved its contribution to the omnibus budget-reconciliation bill May 13, it adopted the interest rate proposal that had grown out of the negotiations. The Senate Agriculture Committee followed suit with similar language June 16. The committee provisions were included without change in the House- and Senate-passed versions of the bill.

As approved by both chambers, the REA provisions eliminated all loans offered at a 2 percent interest rate and replaced them with a new three-tiered interest rate system.

• In the first tier, rural cooperatives that had electric rates 20 percent higher than the statewide average and whose consumers earned less than the state average income were given access to a pool of $125 million in lending authority; the interest rate was 5 percent.

• The second tier included most other rural cooperatives that had more than 5.5 people per mile of electric utility line or whose electric rates and local income were lower than the state average. These cooperatives and other borrowers were to pay interest rates equal to the average rate for municipal bonds — at the time, just under 6 percent. But the rural cooperatives' rate would be capped at 7 percent. About $600 million was to be available for these borrowers, most of whom had paid a fixed interest rate of 5 percent.

• The third tier — those utilities, local government groups and rural cooperatives that did not fit into the first tiers — could borrow from the Treasury with an REA guarantee of repayment, but at the same rate as the government's cost of borrowing.

Staff members with the House Agriculture Committee said the new criteria for participating in the lending tiers would weed out organizations that did not need the subsidized loans. In the past, the REA had come under attack for giving low-interest loans to larger utilities serving suburban areas.

Other Provisions in Conflict

On several other important provisions, the House and Senate Agriculture committees did not see eye to eye.

The House bill included a committee provision allowing electric cooperatives to retain the right to provide electric service to areas even after a municipality voted to annex the land.

Supporters said that if cooperatives recruited and helped establish new businesses or residential and industrial development for rural areas, they should be able to retain the customers rather than surrender the new business to cities that might see it as a fertile new revenue source.

But the municipalities cried foul, arguing that the provision pre-empted state and local agreements and that prohibiting such annexation of rural utility rights would result in a checkerboard of utility service in rural towns and cities.

The Senate bill had no comparable provision.

The House bill also included the language incorporating the REA in the Agriculture Department's Rural Development Administration; the Senate bill did not.

Conference Action

The fiercest fight was over the House-passed limitation on the ability of cities and towns to annex territory served by rural electric cooperatives. In the end, conferees agreed to allow rural electric cooperatives to continue to provide utility service to rural areas even if those areas were annexed by a nearby municipality that ran its own utility.

The annexation provision, which was strongly opposed by local government officials, was to take effect in February 1994. Co-ops could only have opted to continue to provide utility service to clients that were recruited after the enactment date of the reconciliation package.

As part of the compromise, House conferees agreed to drop language making the REA part of the Agriculture Department's Rural Development Agency. Senate members argued that the law already allowed rural cooperatives to participate in water and sewage lending programs. Senate Agriculture Committee Chairman Patrick J. Leahy, D-Vt., also said that any restructuring of the Agriculture Department should wait until a review of the entire department had been completed.

REA Provisions Dropped

Despite the lengthy debate that went into the REA restructuring, all provisions relating to the REA were

stripped from the final reconciliation bill before the conference report was sent to the floor.

The language was eliminated because of fears that it would be subject to the so-called Byrd rule when the conference report was taken up on the Senate floor. Named for its author, Sen. Robert C. Byrd, D-W.Va., the rule barred "extraneous" provisions from a reconciliation bill.

Senate Agriculture Committee members were especially concerned that Alan K. Simpson, R-Wyo., a longtime foe of REA loans, would raise a point of order on the floor that could have endangered the full reconciliation bill.

STAND-ALONE BILL

Action on the separate REA bill (HR 3123) started with a House Agriculture Committee markup Sept. 23. The committee approved the legislation by voice vote.

The bill adopted the lending structure that had been worked out by conferees on the reconciliation bill for both rural electric and rural telephone cooperatives. It also required that, to be eligible for federal loans, states must submit plans to modernize rural telephone systems. The purpose was to encourage the states to provide the kind of high-tech phone services to their rural areas that were available in urban settings, such as fiber optic links between junior colleges in rural areas and universities, video information to be passed between academic medical diagnostic centers and local clinics and teaching links between rural elementary schools and suburban classes.

The committee approved an amendment by English that allowed rural electric cooperatives to participate in the water and sewer development grant and loan programs administered by the Rural Development Administration.

The bill did not contain the two most controversial provisions that came up during work on the reconciliation bill — restraints on the ability of municipalities to annex neighboring territory and language incorporating the REA into the Agriculture Department.

The full House passed the bill under suspension of the rules Sept. 28. Without debate, the Senate cleared the legislation Oct. 4. Because of some wording differences, a concurrent resolution (H Con Res 160) was introduced and subsequently passed by both chambers. ∎

Legislation Clarifies REA Regulatory Authority

The Senate on Nov. 22 cleared by voice vote a bill clarifying the regulatory role of the Rural Electrification Administration (REA) over certain borrowers. The House Agriculture Committee approved the bill, sponsored by Chairman E. "Kika" de la Garza, by voice vote Nov. 17 (HR 3514 — H Rept 103-381). The House passed the bill Nov. 19, also by voice vote. President Clinton signed it Dec. 17 (PL 103-201).

REA officials had sought the change to clarify language in a bill (HR 3123 — PL 103-129) enacted earlier in the year establishing a new interest rate system for REA loans. A provision in that bill prohibited the REA from imposing restrictions on or delaying a loan to any borrower with a net worth exceeding 110 percent of the outstanding principal of all loans made or guaranteed to the borrower by the REA.

REA officials complained that the provision was too

broad. As rewritten, it allowed the REA to issue regulations on such borrowers based on the practices of private lenders, while meeting the original provision's goal of minimizing regulatory controls.

HR 3514 also authorized the REA administrator to ensure that adequate security was provided for any loan or guarantee made by the agency and stated that nothing in the provision limited the authority of the REA administrator to invoke terms and conditions relating to how the borrower might use the lent money. ∎

No Action Taken on Pesticide Regulation

Pressure grew in 1993 to rewrite the nation's major pesticide laws — the 1947 Federal Insecticide, Fungicide and Rodenticide Act (FIFRA), which regulated the sale and use of pesticides, and the 1958 Food, Drug and Cosmetic Act, which set health standards for raw and processed foods. But Congress took no action on pending pesticide bills.

A report released in June on toxicity in children's diets and the announcement in September of an administration blueprint for reforming pesticide law both garnered widespread publicity. But as the year drew to a close, two of the key panels with jurisdiction over the Food and Drug law and parts of FIFRA — the House Energy and Commerce Subcommittee on Health and the Environment and the Senate Education and Labor Committee — became embroiled in health-care reform proposals, and efforts to sort out the morass of competing pesticide regulations fell by the wayside.

Background

Revamping pesticide legislation was complicated by the fact that the two laws had separate and distinct problems to be worked out.

The last major change in pesticide law had been in 1988, when Congress rewrote FIFRA and set a 1997 deadline for the Environmental Protection Agency (EPA) to review existing pesticide licenses based on new scientific standards and information. But the mammoth task, known as "reregistration," caused its own problems. Because of the industry costs associated with the lengthy review, some chemical companies had decided not to market their pesticides and had taken them off the market. That caused problems for fruit and vegetable farmers who depended on the chemicals to grow their crops. (1988 Almanac, p. 139; 1992 Almanac, p. 212)

Meanwhile, significant problems had arisen surrounding the interpretation and enforcement of a section of the 1958 Food, Drug and Cosmetic Act known as the Delaney clause. The clause specifically prohibited chemical residues in processed food when the chemicals had been shown — at any dosage — to cause cancer.

The rigid language was intended to safeguard against the fact that some chemicals tended to concentrate in processed food, giving consumers a more intense dose. But scientific tests for pesticide residues had gotten more sensitive since the 1958 law was passed. Because it had become possible to detect minute levels of pesticides, federal regulators contended that strictly enforcing the Delaney clause would mean virtually banning pesticide use.

In addition, the Food, Drug and Cosmetic Act allowed

the use of carcinogenic chemicals on fresh foods if the benefit derived from having an adequate and low-cost food supply outweighed the public health risk. But EPA regulators could not easily track where the fresh produce went after harvest, making it almost impossible to carry out the letter of the law regarding processed foods.

As a result, the EPA permitted pesticides linked with cancer to be used on all foods, as long as the cancer risk was found to be negligible.

But the EPA lost its flexibility Feb. 22, when the Supreme Court decided to let stand a lower court ruling requiring the agency to strictly enforce the wording of the Delaney provision. In July 1992, the U.S. Court of Appeals for the 9th Circuit had ruled that the Delaney clause clearly prohibited the use of any carcinogenic chemicals on processed foods. *(Supreme Court, p. 325)*

As a result, the EPA was required to begin proceedings that were expected to remove more than 30 pesticides from the market. Most were important for foods that concentrated the raw produce substantially, such as tomato sauce or raisins.

Study Provides 'Wake Up' Call

On June 28, the National Academy of Sciences released a highly publicized study of toxicity levels in children's diets that raised the hopes of those seeking to update pesticide regulations.

The report's primary conclusion was that because children had different metabolisms and diets than adults, pesticide tolerances should be measured separately and adjusted for them. Existing regulatory tests for toxicity applied the same standard for children and adults. The panel recommended that instead of just measuring the residues of chemicals on single items, scientists should take into account that children were exposed to a cumulative amount of pesticides from a variety of sources, including everything from drinking water to lawn-care products or fruit juices.

Rep. Henry A. Waxman, D-Calif., called the report a "wake up call" and appeared before a Senate Agriculture Committee hearing to support regulation to sort out the questions about enforcement of the Delaney clause.

The report also spurred White House and EPA officials to promise new regulations for pesticides.

Legislative Proposals

Waxman and Sen. Edward M. Kennedy, D-Mass., were proposing legislation (HR 872, S 331) to allow toxic pesticides in raw and processed foods if the chance was one in a million — considered negligible — that consumption of the chemical residue over a lifetime would cause cancer. The bills set somewhat stricter standards for foods that made up a significant portion of children's diets, such as bananas, peaches and potatoes. They also required the EPA to measure the cumulative amount of pesticides consumed.

In addition, the bills sought to simplify the procedures for phasing out pesticides and to delete language from FIFRA that required regulators to weigh the benefits of pesticide use against the possible health risks when determining whether to permit a chemical on the market. The legislation made health risk the only consideration.

The agricultural community opposed this last provision. Instead, farmers and chemical producers were supporting legislation (HR 1627) introduced by Rep. Richard H. Lehman, D-Calif., that allowed the EPA to set its own tolerance standards, based on the best existing scientific methods and taking into account the economic and agricultural benefits of the chemical as well as potential health risks.

Clinton Administration Proposal

On Sept. 21, the Clinton administration presented its recommendations for simplifying pesticide law, proposing to marry the two statutes governing pesticide use and food safety and to ground both in public health, rather than in economic, concerns.

In a show of lawmakers' eagerness to tackle the issue, the Senate Labor and Human Resources Committee and the House Energy and Commerce Health Subcommittee held a joint hearing on the package the same day. The hearing was the centerpiece of a weeklong session of briefings and news conferences.

The key element of the president's proposal was language to do away with the Delaney clause, instead allowing chemical residues on both raw and processed foods if the residues posed a "reasonable certainty of no harm."

While making rules for pesticide residues less strict than Delaney, the plan also required that scientists use tolerance levels of children, not adults, as the baseline to determine whether a chemical was safe to use. This was considered a tougher standard.

Some environmental groups complained that easing the Delaney standard would turn the clock back on food safety and environmental safeguards. They also said the administration had not gone far enough in pushing farmers toward alternative farming practices.

Farm-state lawmakers and the agriculture industry also were somewhat cool to the package. During a hearing on the proposal Sept. 22, House Agriculture Committee members argued that the agricultural benefits of an abundant food supply ought to be considered when deciding whether to take farm chemicals off the market.

In addition, the administration proposal said Congress should:
● Expedite the removal of older pesticides from the market and speed the registration of safe chemicals.
● Allow the EPA to temporarily remove pesticides thought to pose a health hazard while they were being reviewed.
● Require that pesticides be reregistered every 15 years.
● Provide education programs aimed at helping farmers develop regional pest management plans using natural predators, crop rotation and other methods to control insects and parasites on the food.
● Prohibit the export of pesticides banned for health reasons in the United States. ■

Grain Inspection Fees and Market Promotion Ok'd

Congress considered several other agriculture-related bills in 1993:

GRAIN INSPECTION FEES

The Senate on Nov. 11 cleared a bill (S 1490) extending the authority of the Federal Grain Inspection Service to collect fees for weighing and inspecting marketed grain through Sept. 30, 2000. President Clinton signed the bill into law Nov. 24 (PL 103-156).

The Senate yielded on the most controversial issue in the bill, agreeing to drop a proposed ban on the use of

water on stored grain. Some companies used water to suppress grain dust, which could explode if allowed to accumulate in high concentrations. But foreign importers of U.S. grain complained that some exporters added water to increase the weight, and therefore the price, of the grain.

In the House, the Agriculture subcommittees on General Farm Commodities and on Foreign Agriculture and Hunger endorsed a ban on watering grain when they approved the House version of the bill Sept. 9. But the provisions's sponsor, Dan Glickman, D-Kan., withdrew the language in response to opposition when the full Agriculture Committee approved the bill (HR 2689 — H Rept 103-265) by voice vote Sept. 22.

As a result, the House bill, sponsored by E. "Kika" de la Garza, D-Texas, contained no water ban. In a compromise, the committee asked the U.S. Office of Technology Assessment and the Agriculture Department to study the issue further and report back to Congress.

The House approved the bill, which reauthorized the inspection service for five years, by voice vote Sept. 28.

On Sept. 29, the Senate passed a 10-year reauthorization (S 1490), which included a system to allow grain handlers to use water to suppress grain dust.

On Nov. 4, the House passed S 1490 after substituting a compromise text that reauthorized the inspection service for seven years and dropped the Senate provision on watering grain. The Senate accepted the compromise.

MARKET PROMOTION

Congress cleared several bills Nov. 21 that tinkered with Agriculture Department market-promotion programs — industry-financed programs through which growers and producers collectively promoted their specific products. The boards were operated out of the Agriculture Department, but producers paid for advertisements. Market-promotion boards covered a variety of products, including dairy products, beef, pork, cotton and wine.

All four bills were passed by the Senate on Nov. 20 and cleared by the House on Nov. 21. The president signed the bills Dec. 14. The bills cleared included:

● **Flowers.** S 994, which established a program to promote sales of fresh-cut flowers and greenery. The bill set up the ProFlor Council to administer the marketing program (PL 103-190).

● **Eggs.** S 717, which increased the cost for participants in the existing egg research and marketing program. The assessment rate for participants in the program was bumped from 10 cents per case of eggs to a maximum of 20 cents per case of eggs. The Egg Board was also required to allocate a proportion of future funds for research (PL 103-188).

● **Watermelons.** S 778, which expanded the watermelon marketing program to Alaska, Hawaii and the District of Columbia; they had not been covered by the previous authorizing law. Exemptions from program assessments were provided to watermelon growers with 10 acres or less (PL 103-189).

● **Limes.** S 1766, which changed the lime marketing program so that it applied to seedless limes and not seeded limes. The bill provided for exemption from assessments for producers of up to 200,000 pounds of limes a year (PL 103-194).

VEGETABLE OIL-BASED INK

The Senate on Nov. 19 passed by voice vote a bill to require that federal agencies, the Government Printing Office and federal contractors use vegetable oil-based ink for lithographic printing when such ink was commercially available and economically feasible.

The bill (S 716), sponsored by Christopher S. Bond, R-Mo., and cosponsored by a bipartisan group of farm state senators, was aimed at expanding markets for such agricultural products as soybeans, corn, sunflowers, rapeseeds and cotton, whose oils were used in the manufacture of printing inks. Advocates also said these inks were friendlier to the environment than the main alternative, petroleum-based inks, and were produced from renewable rather than nonrenewable resources.

The bill began in the Senate Rules and Administration Committee, which approved it Nov. 4 by voice vote (S Rept 103-178).

In the House, Richard J. Durbin, D-Ill., introduced a similar bill (HR 1595), but no action was taken on it.

ENVIRONMENTAL OFFICES

A House Agriculture subcommittee on Aug. 4 approved legislation (HR 1440) to consolidate the Agriculture Department's many environmental planning assistance programs under the aegis of the Soil Conservation Service. The House took no further action on the bill.

HR 1440, approved by voice vote by the Environment, Credit and Rural Development Subcommittee, gave the agency primary responsibility for helping develop site-specific plans for agricultural land and ensuring compliance with federal environmental regulations.

The department ran 15 programs to help farmers develop plans to comply with water and soil conservation rules and other environmental regulations. Farmers were not compelled to use these services.

The purpose of the measure, according to bill sponsor and subcommittee Chairman Glenn English, D-Okla., was to make it easier for farmers to develop environmental plans by turning to one office for assistance.

The subcommittee gave voice vote approval to an amendment by English that directed the Soil Conservation Service to give top priority to farmers in areas that had water-quality problems. ■

Senate Panel Approves Bankruptcy Bill

The Senate Judiciary Committee on Sept. 15 approved by voice vote a bill (S 540 — S Rept 103-168) to overhaul federal bankruptcy law, give judges more flexibility when trying bankruptcy cases and speed up the resolution of these often lengthy civil procedures. But despite the optimism of bill sponsor Sen. Howell Heflin, D-Ala., no additional progress was made on the legislation before the end of the year.

Heflin said the bill was needed, in part, because after the federal Bankruptcy Code was amended in 1978, the number of individual and corporate bankruptcies increased rapidly, hitting a high of nearly 972,000 cases in 1992. *(1978 Almanac, p. 179)*

The legislation gave judges more flexibility to resolve both individual bankruptcies, covered by Chapter 7 and Chapter 13 of the bankruptcy code, and corporate bankruptcies, which fell under Chapter 7 and Chapter 11. The bill also created a filing — Chapter 10 — for small businesses.

The bill encouraged individuals to file for bankruptcy under Chapter 13 rather than Chapter 7. Chapter 13 allowed the typical debtor to work out a pay-back scheme with creditors, an arrangement that was considered better for the debtor and the creditor alike because it could lead to quicker resolution, more money for creditors and a better credit rating for the debtor.

For Chapter 11 debtors — corporations that were bankrupt and trying to reorganize so they could pay off their creditors and regain their economic footing — the bill set limits on how long they could delay reorganization and still receive Chapter 11 protection from creditors.

The committee approved a substitute version that accelerated the resolution of both individual and corporate bankruptcies and established a two-year commission to recommend ways to overhaul the system.

One change, requested by Committee Chairman Joseph R. Biden Jr., D-Del., ensured that if taxpayers were allowed to use credit cards to pay their taxes, they would not be able to evade their tax liabilities. Under existing law, tax debts could not be erased through bankruptcy but credit card debts could be. *(Tax simplification, p. 145; "reinventing government," p. 191)*

Congress came close to clearing a similar bill (S 1985) in 1992, but the House did not take action on the conference report before adjournment. *(1992 Almanac, p. 227)* ∎

Toy Warning Measure Poised To Clear

In an effort to stem the tide of accidents and choking deaths of young children, Congress in 1993 neared final action on legislation (HR 965) to require standardized "plain English" warning labels on certain toys, games and balloons.

The House passed the bill on March 16; the Senate approved a slightly different version on Nov. 20. Lawmakers were expected to clear the measure in 1994 after working out minor differences. The Clinton administration supported the legislation.

In addition to requiring a series of "choking hazard"

warning labels on balloons and toys with detachable small parts intended for use by children ages 3 to 6, the bills required that balls intended for children ages 3 and under meet minimum choke-proof size requirements, increasing the minimum size from 1.25 inches to 1.75 inches in diameter. The measures also required the Consumer Product Safety Commission to set minimum safety standards for bicycle helmets. And, at the urging of Sen. Howard M. Metzenbaum, D-Ohio, they required labels on buckets in the five-gallon size range warning that toddlers could drown in even small amounts of liquids.

Background

Sen. Slade Gorton, R-Wash., chief sponsor of the Senate version of the bill, noted that the Consumer Product Safety Commission found that in each year between 1980 and 1988, "3,200 children were rushed to hospital emergency rooms for toy-related ingestion and aspiration injuries. And in the years between 1980 and 1991, 186 children choked to death on balloons, marbles and small balls."

Despite such statistics, the commission during the Bush administration rejected the recommendations of its own staff and decided against requiring warning labels on toys. The commission, Gorton said, contended that most choking accidents occurred because "parents allow their children to play with toys that are intended for older children."

Gorton and other supporters of the bill said it was often difficult for parents to know when a toy might be dangerous to a toddler. "When small children reach for a fire engine whose ladder is removable, or a small ball that looks like candy, that seemingly harmless toy may end up seriously injuring or killing the child. Too often, it is hard for a parent to tell if a toy, in its sealed package, has small pieces that are potentially dangerous," said Gorton.

Many toy manufacturers voluntarily placed age requirement labels on toy packages, but parents often misinterpreted those labels. Sen. John D. Rockefeller IV, D-W.Va., chairman of the National Commission on Children and a cosponsor of Gorton's bill, said parents often believed "that the words 'for ages 3 and up' refer solely to the child's intellectual development, and not to the physical dangers presented by small toys."

Both the House-passed legislation and the Senate bill required warning labels to specifically state that a particular toy posed a "choking hazard." The warning was to be placed in a rectangular "Surgeon General"-style box to ensure that the message did not get lost in a clutter of package designs. Toy manufacturers opposed boxing the labels on packages, although they did support a universal labeling procedure to preempt differing state labeling requirements.

Sen. Richard H. Bryan, D-Nev., sponsored the provision requiring the Consumer Product Safety Commission to set minimum standards for bicycle helmets. Such helmets were not previously subject to government safety requirements, although most did meet voluntary industry-set standards. According to the bill's findings, 2,985 bicyclists in the United States died between 1984 and 1988 from head injuries, and another 905,752 suffered head injuries serious enough to require hospital emergency room treatment. Bill sponsors estimated that 85 percent of all head injuries suffered by cyclists could be prevented by proper helmet use.

In 1992, Cardiss Collins, D-Ill., tied the child safety provisions to a bill that would have reauthorized the Consumer Product Safety Commission. The bill passed the House by voice vote but died when the Senate Commerce Committee failed to act on it. *(1992 Almanac, p. 209)*

To put the child-safety bill on a fast track in 1993, Collins drafted the separate bill, HR 965.

House Action

With little debate, the House Energy and Commerce Subcommittee on Commerce, Consumer Protection and Competitiveness approved HR 965 by voice vote Feb. 24. The full Energy and Commerce Committee followed suit March 2, approving the bill by voice vote. It was formally reported (H Rept 103-29) on March 10.

The measure was brought to the House floor March 16 under suspension of the rules and passed by 362-38. *(Vote 71, p. 18-H)*

The bill provoked only scattered opposition, nearly all from Republicans. Cliff Stearns, R-Fla., voted for the measure but criticized it for imposing rules that the Consumer Product Safety Commission had considered unnecessary.

Even supporters of the labeling requirement conceded that it would not prevent all choking accidents. "No warning label, no matter how well drafted or visible, will save the life of a child if the purchaser does not read it, understand it and act upon it," said Marjorie Margolies-Mezvinsky, D-Pa., during House debate on the bill.

Still, advocates of the labels said every little step helped. "If there is an old adage that may be quoted to describe this bill, it is: An ounce of prevention is worth a pound of cure," said Patsy T. Mink, D-Hawaii.

Senate Action

S 680 was introduced in the Senate March 31 by Gorton. The bicycle helmet provisions were introduced separately by Bryan as S 228.

The Consumer Subcommittee of the Commerce, Science and Transportation Committee held hearings on the legislation July 1, and the full committee approved the measure Nov. 9 (S Rept 103-195). The Senate approved HR 965 on Nov. 20, after substituting the text of S 680. ∎

Congress Looks at Various Commerce-Related Bills

Congress took up a variety of smaller bills aimed at facilitating commerce or improving its regulation. These included the following:

SMALL-BUSINESS LOANS

Congress cleared a bill aimed at providing small businesses greater access to guaranteed loans without increasing the cost of the loans to the government. The bill (S 1274) cut the Small Business Administration (SBA) loan guarantee rate for certain long-term loans and imposed a new fee on certain loans.

The Senate passed the bill July 30; the House cleared it Aug. 4. President Clinton signed the measure into law Aug. 13 (PL 103-81).

The SBA's popular 7(a) program made it easier for small businesses to get commercial bank loans by guaranteeing that the loans would be repaid. Demand for the loan guarantees had increased rapidly in recent years, outstripping the funds available to the SBA. In fiscal 1992 and 1993, Congress approved supplemental appropriations to continue the program. The program had to close down for 10 weeks in 1993 because it ran out of funds.

The bill reduced SBA guarantees on real estate loans of more than $155,000 to 75 percent from 80 percent; it reduced to 70 percent from 80 percent the maximum loan guarantee on loans made under the preferred lenders program, which allowed certain lenders to make guaranteed loans without SBA's prior approval.

The bill also imposed a new fee of two-fifths of 1 percent on SBA loans that were sold in the secondary market to private investors.

The bill authorized the SBA to guarantee $7.2 billion in loans in fiscal 1993 and $8.5 billion in fiscal 1994.

Sen. Dale Bumpers, D-Ark., prime sponsor of the Senate bill, said lowering the SBA guarantee was unlikely to drive banks out of the small-business loan market, but instead would result in more loans being available.

Legislative Action

The Senate Small Business Committee approved the bill, 22-0, on July 28. The Senate passed the bill by voice vote July 30.

The House passed the Senate bill Aug. 4 after amending it to include several provisions taken from other bills passed by the House on Aug. 2, including:

● HR 2766, a House bill reducing the loan guarantees and imposing a fee on guaranteed loans sold on the secondary market.

● HR 2747, a bill increasing by a total of $1 billion the authorizations for various other loan guarantee programs administered by the SBA.

● HR 2746, a measure that delayed a White House conference on small business scheduled for the first quarter of 1994. Sponsor John J. LaFalce, D-N.Y., said the Bush administration had not set in motion the necessary preparations. The bill required that the conference be held between May 1 and Sept. 30, 1994.

● HR 2748, a bill making technical changes in the Small Business Act.

The Senate agreed to the House amendments by voice vote Aug. 5, clearing the bill.

PATENT OFFICE REAUTHORIZATION

The Senate on Nov. 20 cleared a measure that reauthorized the Patent and Trademark Office for fiscal 1994 at a level of $103 million. The bill (HR 2632 — H Rept 103-285), approved by voice vote, also increased the trademark application fee from $210 to $245.

The agency's budget was entirely generated by fees and surcharges paid by those who applied for or wished to maintain trademarks or patents.

President Clinton signed the bill into law (PL 103-179) on Dec. 3.

The House had passed HR 2632 by voice vote Oct. 12. William J. Hughes, D-N.J., chairman of the Judiciary Subcommittee on Intellectual Property and Judicial Administration, said the increase in the trademark application fee was necessary because the agency no longer could rely on a longtime surplus to make up for cost increases.

COPYRIGHT ROYALTY TRIBUNAL

Congress agreed to do away with the Copyright Royalty Tribunal, an independent agency of the legislative branch that was set up in 1978 to disburse cash and settle disputes

arising from the collection of artistic royalty fees.

The panel mediated between those who held copyrights — including movie studios, broadcasters, sports teams and the recording industry — and those who used copyrighted material to make a living, such as cable and satellite television operators and record stores.

Critics complained that the tribunal's thin workload did not justify the $111,800 salary paid to each of its three commissioners.

In a bill (HR 2840 — H Rept 103-286) cleared Nov. 23, Congress replaced the tribunal with ad hoc arbitration panels, chosen by the librarian of Congress, that would settle future disputes about the disbursement of royalty payments.

Minor modifications were made to the bill before it cleared. The members of the ad hoc panels had to be members of professional arbitration associations and have experience in dispute resolution procedures. Previous language would have given the parties in the dispute a role in choosing panelists, which critics said could lead to deadlocked decisions and biased arbitrators. The revised bill also set standards of conduct for such panels.

About 85 percent of the tribunal's $1 million annual budget was supported by those who paid copyright fees into various royalty pools. The bill made the administration of the copyright royalties 100 percent financed by those who paid royalties.

The House Judiciary Subcommittee on Intellectual Property and Judicial Administration approved the bill Aug. 5. The full committee agreed Oct. 6 by voice vote to report the bill, and the House passed it Oct. 12 by voice vote. The Senate approved the bill by voice vote Nov. 20, after adding an unrelated amendment on longshore work by foreign crew members in Alaska. The House accepted the amendment Nov. 23, clearing the bill. President Clinton signed the bill Dec. 17 (PL 103-198).

COPYRIGHT PROCEDURES

The House on Nov. 20 passed a bill to eliminate most of the need to formally register a work for copyright. The Senate did not take up the bill in the first session.

The bill (HR 897), sponsored by William J. Hughes, D-N.J., allowed owners of copyrightable works to bring suits against copyright infringers and collect damages even if the copyrights were not registered.

Under existing law, completed works were automatically considered to be copyrighted in the eyes of the law. Owners of all copyrights could sue to recover any monetary losses that resulted from copyright infringement. But specific statutory damages of up to $20,000 per work also existed for copyright infringement. To collect those additional damages owners were required to have registered their copyrights with the Library of Congress.

The bill was a response to complaints from photographers and industries such as software producers that existing registration requirements were time-consuming and expensive. Photographers, for example, had to register each photo individually.

After making some modifications to accommodate the Library of Congress, the Judiciary Subcommittee on Intellectual Property and Judicial Administration approved the bill by voice vote Nov. 4. Hughes, who chaired the subcommittee, modified his original bill to address the concern that without the registration requirement, owners of copyrighted works no longer would deposit them at the Library of Congress. Under the existing system, the library received

three free copies of every registered work, allowing the institution to continually update its collection of books, periodicals and other works at no cost.

The new language enhanced a separate and rarely invoked law that required the producers of published works to deposit two copies at the library. The amendment gave the library authority to charge the copyright owner for the legal costs associated with collecting works that had not been deposited.

However, because the library did not keep every work it received, library officials would have to publish a list of the types of works they wanted deposited. Producers of copyrighted material would refer to this list in determining whether to deposit a work with the library.

The full Judiciary Committee approved the bill by voice vote Nov. 17 (H Rept 103-388).

PRODUCT LIABILITY

The Senate Commerce Committee on Nov. 9 approved a bill (S 687 — S Rept 103-203) designed to provide greater protection to manufacturers and sellers who were accused of selling faulty products. But the legislation, sponsored by John D. Rockefeller IV, D-W.Va., advanced no further in the first session.

The Senate committee approved Rockefeller's bill by a vote of 16-4. The version was similar to one that was narrowly blocked from Senate consideration in the 102nd Congress.

The bill sought to encourage buyers and sellers to arbitrate rather than use legal means to settle product liability complaints. It allowed federal courts to penalize a party that refused to settle suits during negotiations and subsequently lost its case. Defendants were to be exonerated from liability in cases where the plaintiff was drunk or under the influence of drugs at the time of an accident and was more than 50 percent responsible.

For 13 years, members trying to change the product liability law had engaged in annual struggles to move a bill through the Senate, with only incremental successes. In late 1992, the Senate came within two votes of moving to consideration of the measure. Majority Leader George J. Mitchell, D-Maine, who argued that the floor calendar could not accommodate such a controversial issue, persuaded enough lawmakers to switch their votes to kill the measure for the year. (1992 Almanac, p. 210)

ECONOMIC DEVELOPMENT

The House Public Works Committee on Nov. 9 approved a bill (HR 2442 — H Rept 103-423, Part 1) to authorize a major increase in economic development programs, including projects at closed military bases. The bill, which the committee approved by voice vote, did not advance further in the first session.

The committee bill reauthorized the Economic Development Administration (EDA) and the Appalachian Regional Commission for the first time since fiscal 1982. In addition to increasing the funding levels, the bill sought to streamline the EDA so that projects would receive funding more quickly.

EDA was to be authorized at $312.6 million for fiscal 1994 and $325 million each in fiscal years 1995 and 1996. The Appalachian Regional Commission was authorized at $249 million for fiscal 1994 and $239.6 million each in fiscal 1995 and 1996.

The Public Works Subcommittee on Economic Development had approved the bill Aug. 5 by voice vote after

adopting an amendment, also by voice vote, by Sherwood Boehlert, R-N.Y. Boehlert's amendment provided that the EDA could fund projects in the community around a closed military base, not just on the base itself.

The Clinton administration wanted the EDA to play a key role in helping communities hurt by Defense Department cutbacks, as well as in assisting after such emergencies as the Mississippi River flooding. The committee-approved bill went much further, however, authorizing more than twice the amount per year that the administration requested.

Bill sponsor Bob Wise, D-W.Va., said that some of the subcommittee's Republican members did not want to authorize more than the administration requested, and new levels were negotiated before the bill reached full committee.

The House had passed bills to reauthorize the EDA and the Appalachian Regional Commission in each Congress since their authorizations expired, but the bills never made it to the Senate floor.

FEDERAL TRADE COMMISSION

Both chambers passed legislation (HR 2243, S 1179) to reauthorize the Federal Trade Commission (FTC), but they did not agree on a compromise version in 1993. The FTC monitored domestic and international trade activities and investigated complaints of unfair business practices. The FTC also was responsible for protecting consumers from deceptive marketing practices and for promoting competition in the marketplace by enforcing antitrust laws.

The FTC had operated without an authorization since 1982 because of a dispute between the House and Senate over whether the agency should have the authority to restrict advertising that it deemed misleading or unfair. The same dispute stalled the 1993 bill. The Senate version barred the FTC from regulating advertising on such grounds, while the House wanted the agency's authority to be unrestricted.

The House bill began in the Energy and Commerce Subcommittee on Transportation, which approved it by voice vote May 27. The bill authorized $88 million in fiscal 1993, $92 million in fiscal 1994 and $99 million in fiscal 1995. The FTC had gotten about $87 million in fiscal 1993. The legislation clarified the effective dates for FTC cease and desist orders, which the agency issued to stop anti-competitive business dealings. The bill also eliminated the agency's authority to monitor agricultural cooperatives. Subcommittee Chairman Al Swift, D-Wash., said that the Agriculture Department adequately oversaw the cooperatives.

The full House Energy and Commerce Committee approved the bill by voice vote June 8 (H Rept 103-138). The House passed HR 2243 by voice vote June 21.

The Senate Commerce, Science and Transportation Committee approved its version of the bill (S 1179 — S Rept 103-130) on Aug. 3. The Senate passed HR 2243 by voice vote Sept. 22, after substituting the text of its own bill.

The bill was slated to go to conference, and lawmakers said they were determined to work out some compromise on the advertising issue, but they were unable to do so before the close of the first session.

LIMITING LEAD LEVELS

The Senate Environment and Public Works Committee on July 30 gave voice vote approval to a bill to restrict lead levels in products such as paint, pesticides and plumbing solder fixtures. The Senate did not vote on the bill. The measure, S 729 (S Rept 103-152), sponsored by Harry Reid,

D-Nev., exempted paint used by artists and paint on collectible toys, such as models. The bill required states to inspect schools and day-care centers for lead hazards and required that all lead-acid batteries be recycled. It authorized $71 million over three years for the program.

The committee approved a similar bill in August 1991, but it went no further. *(1991 Almanac, p. 234)*

BASEBALL ANTITRUST BILL

Congressional action on legislation to repeal baseball's antitrust exemption, which allowed baseball owners to legally conspire on a broad set of baseball business matters, saw little committee action in 1993. But backers attempted to keep debate on the subject alive and looked to 1994 for movement on the legislation.

The Senate Judiciary Committee on Sept. 30 put off action on the measure (S 500), sponsored by Howard M. Metzenbaum, D-Ohio. Committee Chairman Joseph R. Biden Jr., D-Del., requested the delay in order to hold more hearings on the bill. Biden said that lifting the exemption likely would affect a host of issues, including television rights and the status of minor league teams.

The Supreme Court in 1922 ruled that baseball was exempt from federal antitrust laws, deciding that the sport was a game, not a business. Since that decision, team owners had had a virtual monopoly, something not legally enjoyed by any other professional sport.

Metzenbaum's bill aimed at prohibiting team owners from colluding on many issues. Under the bill, a baseball club would be able to move to another location without the approval of other team owners. Such approval was required at the time.

Metzenbaum said that lifting the exemption would force baseball to be more responsive to fans by allowing old teams to move and new teams to be created.

Metzenbaum and others argued that as a legally protected cartel, baseball had the ability to force states fearful of losing a popular team to spend millions of taxpayers' dollars on stadium improvements.

Team owners opposed the bill, claiming that it would bring on a long period of uncertainty that would result in expensive litigation.

Biden said action was not likely to occur until 1994. ■

Former Rep. Mike Espy To Head Agriculture

The Senate confirmed former Democratic Rep. Mike Espy of Mississippi as the nation's first black Agriculture secretary by voice vote Jan. 21. The Senate Agriculture Committee had approved the nomination by voice vote two days earlier.

Espy, 39, the first Agriculture secretary from the Deep South, glided through a Jan. 14 Senate confirmation hearing, promising to make restructuring the department a top priority. Most of the panel's questions centered on upcoming international trade agreements, federal farm subsidies and downsizing the U.S. Department of Agriculture (USDA).

The committee's top concern was the planned USDA restructuring, which had prompted concerns that farmers would have to drive farther to reach department field offices. Espy promised to emphasize reducing the depart-

ment's central bureaucracy in Washington before closing or consolidating field offices.

Tom Daschle, D-S.D., Max Baucus, D-Mont., and Kent Conrad, D-N.D., expressed concern that Espy would tilt agricultural policy toward the cotton and sugar cane farmers of the South at the expense of wheat and feed-grain farmers of the upper Midwestern states.

Espy assured senators that he intended to be an Agriculture secretary for the nation and that while crops differed from one region to another, the nation's agricultural interests overlapped. Increasing farm income, cutting regulation, opening world markets and reducing government overhead would help farmers nationwide and allay concerns of any regional bias, Espy said.

Of special concern to some members was Espy's stance on the North American Free Trade Agreement and on the stalled international effort to strengthen the General Agreement on Tariffs and Trade. Espy said he would follow President Clinton's lead on both and promised that as a proponent of free trade, he would "stand toe to toe" with the European Community and other trading competitors to negotiate a fair trade package.

The only hint of controversy came when ranking Republican Richard G. Lugar of Indiana asked Espy about a Justice Department investigation into accounting irregularities in campaign finance reports that Espy filed with the Federal Election Commission during his four congressional races. Espy said the problem stemmed from a misunderstanding about the reports and had been resolved to the Justice Department's satisfaction.

In his opening statement, Espy pledged to tackle many of the problems facing rural America, stressing his expertise in the area. Committee Chairman Patrick J. Leahy, D-Vt., applauded Espy's role in the formation of the Lower Mississippi Delta Commission, which Clinton had chaired during his tenure as governor of Arkansas.

Espy said his goal of boosting farm income would increase the standard of living for farmers and other rural residents. But he also stressed the need to focus on hunger and the lack of services for rural Americans.

"Individuals of America who live in rural areas don't have access to the same things that others take for granted," Espy said. He said that as Agriculture secretary he would make improving nutrition and decreasing hunger high priorities.

During his tenure in the House, Espy served on the Agriculture Committee for six years and was an active member of the House Select Committee on Hunger. *(Nomination, 1992 Almanac, p. 155-A)* ■

Transportation Nominee Peña Easily Confirmed

Former Denver Mayor Federico F. Peña won Senate voice vote approval Jan. 21 as secretary of Transportation. Earlier the same day, the Commerce and Transportation Committee approved the nomination by voice vote.

At a smooth two-hour confirmation hearing Jan. 7, Peña, 45, showed his political skills as he fielded questions from the Senate Commerce Committee, committing himself only to study concerns and seek compromises despite numerous attempts to pin him down on an array of transportation issues.

Peña, one of two Hispanics nominated to the Cabinet, promised to help Congress revitalize the ailing domestic airline and maritime industries. He endorsed the idea of having a special commission study airline industry problems, and he cited three steps that the new administration would take to help the airlines: strengthening the domestic economy, paring unnecessary regulations that drove up costs and seeking more landing rights for U.S. airlines in foreign countries.

Some consumer groups blamed deregulation for the woes in the airline industry, but Peña disagreed. Instead, he pointed to the weak economy, poor management, leveraged buyouts, high fuel prices and price-undercutting by bankrupt carriers. Asked about his general views of deregulation, Peña said he favored a free-market approach, with some caveats, including safety, competition, service to rural areas and employment issues.

Peña also said that the amount of foreign investment in U.S. airlines should be linked to the access U.S. airlines had overseas.

He promised to work quickly with Congress to resuscitate the maritime industry, and he called for more spending on infrastructure improvements, a continuation of the laws limiting certain cargo to U.S. ships and more investment in high-technology transportation.

On particularly controversial issues, Peña voiced sympathy with both sides. For example, when Trent Lott, R-Miss., asked him about the proposal to raise corporate average fuel economy standards, he said, "I support the notion of increased CAFE standards. . . . At the same time, we all understand the importance of the auto industry to our nation."

Committee members handled Peña with a light touch, asking no questions about his limited experience in transportation issues. Peña served as mayor of Denver from 1983 to 1991 and later was an investment adviser and lawyer in Denver. According to his financial disclosure forms, his two biggest legal clients were communications companies: Western Union and U.S. West, a regional Bell Telephone company.

As mayor, he helped assemble a series of major building projects to boost the economy at a time of regional recession. The largest of these, a $2.7 billion regional airport, gave Peña his introduction to the Transportation Department. *Nomination, 1992 Almanac, p. 152-A)* ■

DNC's Brown Is Confirmed As Commerce Secretary

The Senate confirmed Ronald H. Brown as secretary of the Department of Commerce by voice vote on Jan. 21. The former Democratic National Committee chairman secured unanimous approval from the Senate Commerce Committee the same day, after earlier fending off questions about his past lobbying activities.

Brown, 51, the man widely credited for keeping Democrats unified in the 1992 presidential election, was the first of President Clinton's nominees to appear before a Senate committee. In three hours of testimony on Jan. 6, the longtime partner in the prominent Washington law firm of Patton, Boggs & Blow promised to work in "close partnership" with industry to strengthen the economy and protect

U.S. trade interests. Brown vowed to obey strict ethics rules and refrain from dealing directly with former clients for one year. (Brown resigned from partnership in the firm the day before his confirmation.)

Both Democratic and Republican members of the Commerce Committee focused on his lobbying activities, which included representing the former Haitian dictator Jean-Claude "Baby Doc" Duvalier and U.S. subsidiaries of Japanese electronics firms.

Committee Chairman Ernest F. Hollings, D-S.C., attempted to put to rest conflict of interest questions, saying he had examined Brown's record and was "satisfied that [he] acted properly."

The most intense grilling came from Mississippi Republican Trent Lott, who was tapped by the GOP to examine Clinton's nominees. Lott told Brown that the combination of his lobbying and fundraising for the Democratic Party "convey at least the appearance that your nomination is at odds" with the ethical standards set by Clinton.

At every turn, Brown easily defused questions and presented himself as a formidable negotiator primed to advocate American business interests. He defended his work with the Duvalier regime by saying he was trying to persuade the Haitian government to bring about changes in labor laws and human rights in exchange for trade preferences from the United States. He said his work for Japanese electronics firms would help him in his new role as chief advocate for U.S. business interests. "Those of us who are lawyers know that some of the best lawyers in the criminal defense bar come from the offices of prosecutors," he said.

Brown also called "totally false" news reports that he helped a Louisiana-based company called Chemfix Technologies Inc., on whose board of directors he served, secure a sludge-hauling contract with New York City in exchange for his influence in selecting New York as host of the 1992 Democratic National Convention. He said the city had always been the front-runner to host the convention.

Brown said he would work to fulfill Clinton's goal of elevating the stature of the Commerce Department as the key coordinating agency to create jobs and strengthen the nation's manufacturing and export base. While Brown said he anticipated no large-scale restructuring of the department, he added that the administration would push for increased funding for the National Institute of Standards and Technology, a Department of Commerce agency charged with helping U.S. manufacturers develop civilian technologies and improve manufacturing processes. *(Nomination, 1992 Almanac, p. 150-A)* ∎

SCIENCE & TECHNOLOGY/ COMMUNICATIONS

House Passes Competitiveness Bill

President Clinton proposes plan for high-tech business and government partnership

The House on May 19 endorsed an initiative by President Clinton to forge a new partnership between government and industry aimed at making U.S. companies more competitive in the global marketplace. The Senate Commerce, Science and Transportation Committee approved a companion bill that did not make it to the Senate floor.

The House bill (HR 820) authorized $1.5 billion over two years for grants, loans and research assistance to small- and medium-size businesses. The money was to be distributed through programs in the Commerce Department and the National Science Foundation.

The Senate bill (S 4) provided $2.3 billion over two years. Unlike the House bill, it also included funding for federal high-performance computing and communications programs. It authorized $380 million over two years for such programs.

Both the House and Senate measures proposed helping small manufacturers learn new manufacturing processes.

Commerce, Science and Transportation Committee Chairman Ernest F. Hollings, D-S.C., remained hopeful that the Senate would pass S 4 early in 1994, after having ironed out conflicts with rival committees. The Small Business Committee eyed a $52 million pilot program to spur private sector investment capital in new technologies, and the Energy and Natural Resources Committee wanted to weigh in on the high-performance computing provisions.

BACKGROUND

National science and technology policy had been formulated in the shadow of World War II. First articulated in a 1945 report by former presidential adviser Vannevar Bush, the policy stated that federal funding should be directed toward basic science — such as cancer research — and so-called mission-oriented defense and space projects — such as the nuclear weapons program. "Applied" civilian research — to generate new American-made products — was to be left to the marketplace.

But decades of White House reluctance to mix government with private enterprise ended Feb. 22, when Clinton and Vice President Al Gore unveiled a $17 billion, four-year proposal to spur cooperation to boost high technology.

BOXSCORE

➡ **Competitiveness Bill (HR 820, S 4).** Authorization for Commerce Department and National Science Foundation programs to provide grants, loans and research assistance to small and medium-size businesses. The Senate bill included funding for federal high-performance computing and communications programs.

Reports: H Rept 103-77; S Rept 103-113.

KEY ACTION

Feb. 22 — **President** unveiled $17 billion competitiveness plan.

March 30 — **House** Science Subcommittee on Technology, Environment and Aviation approved HR 820 by voice vote.

April 28 — **House** Science, Space and Technology Committee approved HR 820, 20-10.

May 19 — **House** passed HR 820, 243-167.

May 25 — **Senate** Commerce, Science and Transportation Committee approved S 4 by voice vote.

Clinton's plan included new tax breaks for joint private-sector and government research projects. It proposed to more than triple funding for research to help spur new technology applications and greatly expand manufacturing "extension" centers to help small businesses modernize.

Key elements of the plan simply expanded upon much of what Congress already had put in place with the assistance of a hesitant Bush administration. Still, the program telegraphed a sea change in attitude at the White House.

President George Bush had balked at promoting research cooperation between business and government, warning — as had his predecessor Ronald Reagan — that such links amounted to an "industrial policy," a term that raised the specter of government dictating to industry what to produce and how.

Clinton hoped to avoid that label by selling his plan as a new policy designed to help nascent high-tech industries expand and revive the nation's economic base.

To justify the switch toward aiding applied research, Clinton's 36-page technology policy cited a swiftly changing international marketplace in which access to cheap labor and natural resources was less important than being able to adapt to market needs — for example, by being able to respond with new product lines within months rather than years.

Highlights of Clinton's Plan

Clinton called for redirecting more federal research away from the Pentagon and toward the marketplace. The key components of the plan included:

• Tripling funding for the National Institute of Standards and Technology (NIST), the chief federal research laboratory devoted to helping the private sector develop new technologies and manufacturing processes. Created in 1901, the agency (formerly the Bureau of Standards) long had concerned itself almost exclusively with weights and measures. But by 1992, it also had come to play a leading role in civilian research.

The funding boost was to expand NIST's fledgling Advanced Technology Program. A grant program launched by

Congress in 1988 to help companies more quickly commercialize new technologies, the Advanced Technology Program carried out research projects with private companies in such areas as machine tool manufacturing, biotechnology, optics and materials engineering.

Congressional Democrats and the Clinton administration hailed the program as a model of successful government-industry cooperation, largely because the private sector took part in choosing projects and because grant recipients typically paid more than half the costs of the research conducted. Companies were eligible for up to $2 million each in government funding for research projects over three years. Joint ventures had five years to spend the money. In fiscal 1993 alone, Clinton hoped to finance about 60 new grants.

Clinton also proposed:

● Creating 100 manufacturing research "extension" centers to be modeled after the successful Agriculture Department centers that brought farming advances to rural areas.

● Increasing funding for "information superhighways" to connect businesses, schools, hospitals and local governments with federal computer data base networks as well as each other. The money also was to go toward research into the use of supercomputer networks to help solve problems in the fields of health care, education and manufacturing.

● Making the symbolic change of dropping the word "defense" from the Defense Advanced Research Projects Agency. In 1993, defense accounted for about 56 percent of all federal research.

The nation's 726 federal laboratories also were encouraged to engage in joint ventures with private companies "wherever possible."

Drawing Criticism

From the beginning, the proposal faced criticism. Some said the plan did not go far enough in shifting defense research to civilian applications. The Advanced Research Projects Agency was to remain part of the Pentagon, for instance, where, critics said, it was subject to pressures from the defense establishment.

Critics also said the plan positioned defense contractors to take advantage of Clinton's proposed tax credits for research and development, giving them a "double subsidy," since most of their research and development activities and procurement already was underwritten by taxpayers.

Some of the program built on defense conversion legislation that was enacted in 1992 as part of the fiscal 1993 defense authorization and appropriations bills (PL 102-484 and PL 102-396). *(1992 Almanac, p. 483)*

HOUSE SUBCOMMITTEE

The House Science Subcommittee on Technology, Environment and Aviation approved HR 820 on March 30 by voice vote, after rejecting attempts by Republican freshmen to cut authorized spending levels and make Congress more accountable for the new programs.

The bill authorized up to $840 million in fiscal 1994 and $1.2 billion in fiscal 1995 for programs to help manufacturers develop new processes and technologies, set up joint research ventures with government agencies and provide low-interest loans to small and medium-size businesses.

Democratic sponsors had the votes to move the bill forward, and backers such as Norman Y. Mineta, D-Calif., said it would "move ideas from the lab to the marketplace."

But providing a helping federal hand to private business did not sit well with many Republicans who said it amounted

to too much government interference in the marketplace, and the panel markup dragged over five days. Robert S. Walker of Pennsylvania, ranking Republican on the full Science Committee, said emerging high-tech companies would be better served through less regulation, more tax incentives and changes in product liability and antitrust laws.

Key provisions of the bill authorized:

● $650 million through fiscal 1995 for the Commerce Department's Advanced Technology Program, which provided grants to companies and institutions for research into technologies that had yet to reach the marketplace.

● $550 million over two years for research into new technologies at NIST.

● $100 million through fiscal 1995 for a manufacturing outreach program to extend state-of-the-art processes and technology to U.S. businesses.

● $1 million in fiscal 1994 and $20 million in fiscal 1995 for a "civilian technology loan program" to provide low-interest loans to help businesses upgrade their manufacturing facilities or conduct research.

● $1 million in fiscal 1994 and $50 million in fiscal 1995 for a "civilian technology development program" to offer venture capital grants to small and medium-size businesses.

GOP Amendments

The first effort by freshman Republicans to cut the bill came from Ken Calvert of California, who proposed killing the civilian loan and grant programs. His amendment was rejected by a party-line vote of 10-11.

Next came Peter I. Blute of Massachusetts, who wanted to delay setting specific authorization levels for all the bill's programs until Clinton presented his budget to Congress in April. The amendment failed by a vote of 12-19.

Members defeated, also by a 12-19 vote, an amendment by Roscoe G. Bartlett, R-Md., to freeze authorized funding levels at the fiscal 1993 appropriated levels. The bill's authorization level was 239 percent higher than fiscal 1993 funding of $284 million.

The subcommittee then switched course, complying easily with a veteran Republican's request for more funds for her district. Constance A. Morella of Maryland won, by voice vote, an amendment to authorize $62 million in fiscal 1994 and $106 million in fiscal 1995 for a long-planned modernization of research facilities at NIST, located in Gaithersburg, Md.

Lawmakers also compromised on an effort by a Republican freshman to make Congress more accountable for spending in the bill. Rod Grams, R-Minn., offered an amendment to make each of the bill's programs expire on Sept. 30, 1995.

Grams argued that too often programs outlived their usefulness, with no mechanism in place for Congress to reconsider them. Opponents of the amendment argued that industry would be loath to enter into contracts with the government for programs that expired after only two years.

The panel then agreed to a compromise crafted between Grams and Subcommittee Chairman Tim Valentine, D-N.C., stating that no funds could be appropriated for fiscal 1996 and 1997 without first being authorized — an amendment that members said carried more weight than the standing House rule against appropriating without an authorization.

The committee also debated the value of government-financed joint research projects with private industry.

Martin R. Hoke, R-Ohio, had hoped to delete from the bill a provision setting up a large-scale, industry-led research and development consortium. The bill authorized

the program at $50 million for fiscal 1994 and $100 million for fiscal 1995.

Hoke withdrew the amendment after agreeing to wait to offer it in the full committee. Hoke said Sematech — a government-industry consortium set up in 1987 to spur the U.S. semiconductor industry — illustrated that such government-sponsored ventures did not work. Because only a handful of the hundreds of U.S. computer chip makers ever joined Sematech, the government-subsidized consortium ended up competing with private chip makers.

George E. Brown Jr., D-Calif., chairman of the full committee, acknowledged that there were initial problems with the way Sematech was structured, but he defended the concept of a large-scale consortium.

HOUSE FULL COMMITTEE

After several days of partisan wrangling, the Science, Space and Technology Committee approved the bill by a vote of 20-10 on April 28 (H Rept 103-77), but only after Republicans injected the gay rights issue into the debate.

The bill authorized $541 million in fiscal 1994 and $1 billion in fiscal 1995.

The price tag of the bill, which had drawn Republican objections, had been pared when members by voice vote approved an amendment by Valentine to make the measure conform with spending targets in Clinton's fiscal 1994 budget. Until amended, the bill had authorized $2 billion over two years.

The committee began marking up the bill April 21-22, but the session fell apart when Republicans refused to proceed. The GOP boycott came after committee Chairman Brown defeated two Republican amendments that were aimed at gutting key portions of the bill.

One amendment, to strike the bill's civilian technology loan and grant programs, by California Republicans Calvert and Ed Royce, was defeated 13-29. Another Royce amendment to kill training partnership programs was voted down 10-29.

Brown used the proxy votes of absent Democrats to defeat those amendments, leading ranking Republican Walker to protest by urging lawmakers on his side of the aisle to boycott the committee when it resumed after a midday break. When it became clear that Republicans were boycotting the April 22 markup, Brown postponed action until April 28, saying it was "essential to have the cooperation of the minority" to do business.

Preceding the breakdown in comity, the panel accepted every Democratic amendment offered and rejected every Republican attempt to modify the bill — all by party-line votes.

The amendments adopted included those by:

● Xavier Becerra, D-Calif., to encourage the director of the National Science Foundation to steer training programs toward women and "socially and economically disadvantaged individuals," by a vote of 15-10.

A Walker attempt to broaden the scope of the amendment to include the "middle class" and "disabled" was rejected, 11-16.

● Herb Klein, D-N.J., to require the Commerce secretary to encourage businesses in areas that had "a depressed economy, or a significant concentration of defense-related industries, or chronically high unemployment" to take advantage of the bill's programs, by voice vote.

● James A. Traficant Jr., D-Ohio, requiring goods purchased as a result of the bill to be made in the United States, by voice vote.

GOP attempts to strike key provisions of the bill included a Walker effort to remove $100 million authorized over two years for additional regional Manufacturing Technology Centers, which provided local technical support to industries at low cost. The amendment was rejected by a vote of 12-14.

The panel also rejected, by a vote of 9-10, an amendment by Bartlett that would have stripped all provisions aimed at helping U.S. manufacturers and states to develop and adopt advanced manufacturing technologies.

Walker fired a couple more salvos at the measure before final committee approval. He shifted the debate from what was best for U.S. industrial policy to questions of social policy as the panel sparred over whether homosexuals qualified for a $21 million civilian technology loan program.

By a vote of 24-13, the panel adopted an amendment by Becerra that required the Commerce secretary to ensure "to the fullest extent possible" that at least 10 percent of the amounts lent under the program be given to businesses owned and controlled by "socially and economically disadvantaged individuals."

Walker and fellow Republicans Dana Rohrabacher of California and Hoke of Ohio said the amendment might be construed by the Commerce Department to include homosexuals as a class of people to whom loans could be targeted. Two of the panel's senior Democrats, Valentine and Ralph M. Hall of Texas, echoed the concern.

But both dropped their objection after being told by committee counsel that the amendment comported with the Small Business Administration's (SBA) definition of "disadvantaged," which did not include gay people as a preferred group.

On another front, Walker won an ideological point when the panel accepted his amendment expressing the sense of Congress that other actions — such as deficit reduction, tax incentives, regulatory relief and revisions in antitrust and liability laws — promised to do the most to improve U.S. competitiveness. The amendment was approved by voice vote.

Key Provisions

After Valentine's amendment reducing spending, the bill's key provisions included:

● $578 million through fiscal 1995 for grants from the Commerce Department's Advanced Technology Program.

● $539 million over two years for internal research conducted at the NIST laboratory.

● $236 million through fiscal 1995 for National Science Foundation engineering research, manufacturing training and fellowship programs.

● $186 million through fiscal 1995 for manufacturing extension programs, including $50 million for local and regional centers that offered low-cost technical support to manufacturers.

The committee also gave voice vote approval to amendments by:

● Walker, to ensure that the Commerce Department inspector general was authorized to perform audits on the bill's programs, as well as private-sector auditing firms.

● Eddie Bernice Johnson, D-Texas, to ensure that minorities and women were represented on a private-sector Technology Advisory Board that was to advise the government on how to carry out the bill's provisions.

HOUSE FLOOR

After three weeks of intermittent debate, the House passed HR 820 on May 19 by a vote of 243-167. (Vote 173, p. 42-H)

The two-year, $1.5 billion bill included up to $731.5 million through fiscal 1995 for the Commerce Department's Advanced Technology Program, $722 million for research sponsored by the NIST and $50 million for the National Science Foundation. The NIST authorization included $186 million to create about 100 technical outreach centers.

From the start of the House debate on the bill May 5, it was clear that it would take weeks to complete action on a host of controversial amendments.

On the opening day, Republicans applauded the Democratic leadership for allowing an open rule for floor debate, thus allowing all germane amendments.

But the Democratic majority on May 6 easily turned back two Republican amendments. One by Rohrabacher of California proposed cutting off federal funding for the Manufacturing Technology Centers after six years. It was rejected 201-221. (Vote 156, p. 38-H)

A second amendment, by Bartlett of Maryland, proposed eliminating all National Science Foundation manufacturing programs from the bill. It was rejected 170-248. (Vote 157, p. 38-H)

Manufacturers — particularly those affiliated with the Japanese-dominated electronics industry — were dismayed when the House on May 6 adopted an amendment by Thomas J. Manton, D-N.Y., that barred foreign-owned U.S. companies from taking part in the bill's programs unless the nation of the parent company offered similar programs.

But sponsors reportedly accepted the Manton amendment to appease Energy and Commerce Committee Chairman John D. Dingell, D-Mich., who backed Manton and threatened to request that the bill be referred to his committee — a signal that Dingell could seriously delay the bill further.

Bill Inspired Little Interest

Amid very little interest from the outside world, debate on the bill inched forward. The House resumed action May 12, only to put it off a day later until May 19 after lawmakers rejected a handful of Republican amendments and compromised on two others.

The reasons for the lack of interest were several:

• The House had passed a practically identical bill in 1992, which died in the Senate for lack of time. Lobbyists had had enough. (1992 Almanac, p. 301)

• The bill was the first in the 103rd Congress — indeed, since September 1992 — to go to the House floor under an "open rule," with no limit to the number of germane amendments allowed and no time limit for debate on each amendment. As a result, tedium ensued, leading even sponsors to complain that the bill was occupying too much of the House's time.

• The bill dealt with obscure, complex loan and grant programs that few observers found intellectually or politically captivating. Most amendments were simply variations of the ongoing "industrial policy" debate between the parties over whether the government should play any role at all in helping the private sector compete.

While the bill's backers hoped it would aid 350,000 small and medium-size businesses, enabling them to compete more effectively in the global marketplace, Republican opponents said, few if any private-sector companies cared about HR 820. Most business groups instead focused their efforts on more direct pocketbook issues such as reducing taxes on capital gains and fighting Clinton's plans to raise corporate taxes.

There was at least one group that eagerly supported the bill: the U.S. fastener industry, which made nuts, bolts and washers. Walker and Dingell work out a compromise to relieve manufacturers and distributors of fasteners of much of the regulatory burden imposed by a 1990 law (PL 101-592) aimed at tightening quality standards for nuts and bolts. (1990 Almanac, p. 19-A)

Redundant and unworkable regulations caused by the 1990 law cost the fastener business about $1 billion annually, the industry maintained. Agreements were reached on two issues: Making manufacturers, not distributors, responsible for certifying the chemical composition of their product, and allowing buyers to purchase slightly imperfect fasteners as long as the imperfection did not affect the performance of the product.

Republicans Rebuffed

Apart from such rare compromises, most Republican attempts to pare the bill's scope and price tag were rebuffed, including those by:

• Calvert of California, to eliminate $2 million in fiscal 1994 and $70 million in fiscal 1995 for civilian technology loan and grant programs. It fell on May 12 on a 180-239 vote. (Vote 159, p. 40-H)

• Jan Meyers, R-Kan., to cut funding for the civilian grant program to $10 million in fiscal 1995 and shift management of the program to the SBA, which managed a similar program. The House rejected it on May 12, 194-224. (Vote 161, p. 40-H)

• Walker, to include the "middle class" as a group of people that should be singled out — along with women and minorities — for special attention in receiving grants and loans. Walker defined middle class as any business with at least 51 percent of its ownership earning $15,000 to $85,000 individually. Members on May 13 rejected the amendment, 181-231. (Vote 162, p. 40-H)

• Hoke of Ohio, to eliminate a $100 million authorization for the creation of large-scale industrial research and development joint ventures. It failed May 13 on a 176-234 vote. (Vote 163, p. 40-H)

A surprising exception to the string of GOP failures came when freshman Republican Mac Collins of Georgia not only managed to win easy approval of an amendment but also had Democrats scurrying to switch their votes.

Collins sought to prevent the funds from having a "direct financial benefit to any person who is not a citizen or national of the United States" or a legal alien.

"If we are going to expend this kind of money or these tax dollars, we ought to expend them on people who are citizens of the United States of America," Collins said in support of his first floor amendment as a House member.

When voting time ran out, Collins was prevailing with the support of most Republicans and several Democrats. Many more Democrats, perhaps sensing their vote might be perceived as unpatriotic, then lined up to change their votes. As Republicans applauded, 37 Democrats switched their votes from "nay" to "yea." They included party Caucus Chairman Steny H. Hoyer of Maryland and Judiciary Committee Chairman Jack Brooks of Texas. The final tally on the amendment was 263-156. (Vote 171, p. 42-H)

When Jim Kolbe, R-Ariz., subsequently made a procedural request for another vote on the Collins amendment, even more Democrats switched over, approving it by a vote of 288-127. (Vote 172, p. 42-H)

Some Democratic Concessions

Other Republican shots at the bill failed to get House approval, though they did force Democrats to make some

concessions on the overall funding level.

On an amendment by Valentine, lawmakers agreed by voice vote to reduce the bill's Commerce Department authorization level for fiscal 1995 from $1.2 billion to $950 million, to bring it in line with budget projections of the Clinton administration.

Before approving that language, members rejected an amendment to Valentine's provision by Walker to cut $88 million in grant and loan programs not requested by the administration but added by the Science Committee. That amendment fell by a vote of 187-222. *(Vote 165, p. 40-H)*

Democrats also turned back an amendment by GOP Conference Chairman Dick Armey of Texas to freeze the authorization total at the fiscal 1993 level. It failed 199-217. *(Vote 166, p. 40-H)*

The closest Republicans came to affecting the bill's spending levels was on an amendment by John J. "Jimmy" Duncan Jr., R-Tenn., to make an across-the-board reduction of 10 percent.

The National Taxpayers Union had been lobbying hard for Democrats to cast at least one vote in favor of trimming the bill's funding, a Science panel aide said. After rejecting the more severe GOP attempts, many Democrats viewed the Duncan amendment as a vote for fiscal conservatism. The outcome was close, as the amendment fell on a 208-213 vote. That tally included the "nay" votes of four congressional delegates, who under new rules were allowed to vote even though those votes could later be nullified if they determined the outcome of any amendment. *(Vote 167, p. 40-H)*

Though the Duncan amendment still would have failed by one vote if the delegates' votes were not counted, GOP Whip Newt Gingrich of Georgia argued that the appearance of the delegates' votes cast a "psychological impression" that the margin was wider than it actually was. Without those votes appearing on the chamber scoreboard, Republicans argued, they might have been able to whip more support for the amendment.

Unable to force another vote on Duncan's amendment, Cliff Stearns, R-Fla., offered a similar amendment except that it sought to cut $100,000 beyond the 10 percent. But Democrats were in no mood to give Republicans another victory, and Stearns' amendment failed, 203-225. *(Vote 168, p. 42-H)*

SENATE COMMITTEE

The Senate Commerce, Science and Transportation Committee easily approved the companion $2.3 billion mea-

sure (S 4 — S Rept 103-113) by voice vote on May 25. The Senate bill authorized $837 million in fiscal 1994 and $1.5 billion in fiscal 1995.

The major difference between the House and Senate versions was that the Senate measure contained $380 million for Gore's proposal to link public libraries, schools, health-care facilities and manufacturing centers to the nationwide network of computer "information highways." The House planned to deal with that issue separately. *(Information highways, below)*

The Senate measure focused much of its funding on the Commerce Department's NIST, authorizing $668 million for NIST's Advanced Technology Program. The bill boosted funding for the program fivefold in two years, from a fiscal 1993 level of $68 million to $200 million in fiscal 1994 and $468 million in fiscal 1995.

Whereas Republicans in the House were vocal in their opposition to the competitiveness bill, the only Senate Republican to speak against the measure was John McCain of Arizona. He called it "another attempt by the government to pick winners and losers" in the private sector.

One part of the bill that stirred some controversy was a $52 million pilot program that aimed to improve the investment climate for technology-based companies. The money was to supplement private sector investment capital in new technologies.

The program, modeled after an SBA Small Business Investment Company program, sought to use government funds as leverage to encourage investors to put their money into fledgling high-technology companies. The new program was to be administered by the Commerce Department, a distinction that rankled Dale Bumpers, D-Ark., chairman of the Senate Small Business Committee. Bumpers argued that the program duplicated SBA efforts and, in any case, should be run by that agency rather than the Commerce Department.

John D. Rockefeller IV, D-W.Va., said Bumpers was "completely and spectacularly wrong" for opposing the Commerce Department's involvement. He said the SBA was not equipped to provide the amount of capital needed for high-technology companies and had little history of helping that sector.

In an attempt to compromise, the Commerce Committee bill allowed the department at first merely to study ways to administer the venture capital program, authorizing $2 million for that purpose in fiscal 1994. But in fiscal 1995, the bill authorized $50 million to begin the program. ∎

House Bill Supports 'Information Highways'

The House on July 26 passed a measure to coordinate the completion of a nationwide grid of "information highways." The bill (HR 1757) authorized $1 billion in fiscal 1994-98, half what the administration had sought, for a multiagency effort to expand the availability and applications of the nation's high-speed computer networks.

The money was to be used to set standards; finance research and development for faster, higher-capacity computer links; and help schools, libraries, health-care facilities and government agencies hook up to the networks.

The Senate Commerce, Science and Transportation Committee voted to authorize $380 million over two years

for high-performance computing and networking programs as part of a broader competitiveness bill (S 4), but the Senate took no further action on that measure. *(Competitiveness, p. 241)*

The House-passed high-performance computing bill was expected to be added to the Senate's competitiveness measure in conference in 1994.

BACKGROUND

The term "national information infrastructure" became part of the congressional vernacular in 1993, in part be-

cause of Vice President Al Gore's interest in the subject. Such information "highways" were to link public and private institutions — and eventually households — to computer networks capable of transmitting vast amounts of text and video data at lightning speeds.

Many of the networks already had been built by telephone and cable companies, although they operated at slower speeds. Supporters of data networks insisted that the government role be limited to funding cutting-edge research and providing grants to give more users access to the data networks.

Clinton's Proposal

President Clinton, in his first foray into telecommunications policy, used his fiscal 1994 budget to propose a modest government initiative aimed at spurring major investments by private industry. The administration also included the plan in a comprehensive technology policy statement issued Feb. 22.

Clinton called for linking more schools, libraries, hospitals and businesses through a nationwide computer network — a kind of "information superhighway." Just as the Interstate Highway System had fostered decades of economic growth, ranging from neighborhoods and roadside industrial parks to hotel and fast-food chains, Clinton's plan was intended to spawn a new era in technology to be driven by state-of-the-art information networks.

The Clinton plan had a $2 billion price tag over five years. About $1 billion was to go toward finding better ways for doctors, educators and manufacturers to use computer networks. Another $1 billion was to go toward grants to help schools, libraries and other public institutions tap into the 10,000 computer networks that already were linked worldwide.

Administration planners believed that the more users were directed to the on-ramps of the information highway, the greater the incentive for private companies to invest in building and expanding the networks themselves. The government investment was intended as a beginning step to spur industry involvement in completing the network — a task that private companies estimated would ultimately cost an additional $100 billion to $400 billion.

While the Clinton-Gore plan focused on linking computer networks to local public institutions, the administration remained silent on how to bring these networks across the "last mile" — into people's homes.

Government Role

The federal government had played a role in computer networking since 1969 — the year the Defense Department first linked two distant computers over telephone lines.

By 1993 that network had grown into an unregulated worldwide web of computer data bases known as the Internet.

BOXSCORE

➡ **National Information Infrastructure (HR 1757, S 4).** Authorization for a multiagency effort to boost access to the nation's high-speed computer networks and to coordinate completion of a nationwide grid of "information highways."

Reports: H Rept 103-173; S Rept 103-113.

KEY ACTION

May 25 — **Senate** Commerce, Science and Transportation Committee approved broad competitiveness bill, S 4, by voice vote.

June 17 — **House** Science, Space and Technology Subcommittee approved HR 1757 by voice vote.

June 30 — **House** Science, Space and Technology Committee approved HR 1757 by voice vote.

July 26 — **House** passed HR 1757, 326-61.

Its "backbone" was the National Science Foundation's network, known as NSFNET, which linked about 1,000 colleges and universities.

An estimated 15 million people used the Internet and NSFNET each day, communicating by electronic mail, tapping into a trove of data bases or borrowing supercomputing power from a distant university.

But it was not until 1991 that Congress passed a law (PL 102-194), sponsored by then-Sen. Al Gore of Tennessee, to merge the patchwork of agency initiatives into one high-performance computing and networking program.

The 1991 law was limited in scope; it focused on linking high-performance supercomputers to sophisticated research projects at universities and did little to foster wider public access. But it quickly illustrated how small amounts of federal spending promised to leverage significant private-sector investment. *(1991 Almanac, p. 244)*

Clinton's follow-on plan emphasized bringing computer networks to communities.

HOUSE ACTION

The House Science, Space and Technology Subcommittee on Science approved HR 1757 by voice vote on June 17.

By voice vote, the panel set authorization ceilings for the five-year bill of $129 million in fiscal 1994, rising to $250 million by fiscal 1998.

The full House Science, Space and Technology Committee approved the measure by voice vote June 30 (H Rept 103-173).

The House approved HR 1757 by a vote of 326-61 on July 26. The bill authorized $1 billion from fiscal 1994 through 1998 for the multiagency effort. *(Vote 365, p. 90-H)*

Bill sponsor Rick Boucher, D-Va., emphasized that the measure did not commit the federal government to building, managing or operating information networks. "That will be a private sector responsibility," he said.

But he said the bill did define a clear government role. Part of the money was to go toward setting computer protocols and standards for the private sector as it worked to link more people to the Internet. The bill also continued the federal role in research and development to build faster, higher-capacity networks, a goal established in the 1991 law.

The measure aimed to bring four specific areas more quickly into the information age: schools, libraries, healthcare facilities and government offices. It proposed to do this by helping schools link via computer for "distant learning" sessions; helping libraries put their holdings into digital form for remote computer users; developing healthcare applications such as distant diagnoses; and making it easier to retrieve government information through computer networks. ∎

Telecommunications Bills in Both Chambers

The House on Nov. 8 passed by voice vote a bill to set up pilot projects to promote the application of advanced telecommunications in rural areas and in hospitals, museums and libraries.

A companion Senate bill was pending in the Commerce, Science and Transportation Committee when the session adjourned.

The bills (HR 2639, S 1086) were part of the Clinton administration's drive to spur the private sector to build a national information infrastructure.

Such information "highways" were to link public and private institutions — and eventually households — to computer networks capable of transmitting vast amounts of text and video data at lightning speeds. *(Information highways, p. 245)*

LEGISLATIVE ACTION

The House took the following action on the bill:

House Subcommittee

The House Energy and Commerce Subcommittee on Telecommunications easily approved HR 2639 by voice vote on Oct. 14.

The legislation authorized federal grants for projects to connect health-care providers, schools, libraries, museums, research facilities, social service agencies, and state and local governments to a national information network.

The bill left the job of building the information superhighway — a high-speed, high-volume network for data, analogous to the network of telephone or cable television wires — to private companies.

Its grants covered up to half the cost for most connections to that network, with $150 million authorized for the grants in each of fiscal years 1995 and 1996.

The subcommittee's action came a day after two telecommunications giants, Bell Atlantic Corp. and Tele-Communications Inc., announced a $26 billion megamerger plan. The two companies said that by merging assets they planned to become the trailblazers in establishing information superhighways that promised to allow consumers to use new hybrids of computers, telephones and televisions to provide entertainment, business transactions, education, customized news and even groceries for delivery.

Bill sponsors said the measure would promote the application of advanced telecommunications in rural areas and in hospitals, museums and libraries.

"As events of the last few weeks have made plain, the private sector is gearing up rapidly to meet the challenge of building the information superhighway," said subcommittee Chairman Edward J. Markey, D-Mass. "It is our mission to ensure that the promise of the electronic future is kept for all Americans and that we not become a nation divided into the information rich and the information poor."

Markey said that without government oversight, information superhighways might cater only to the wealthy, leaving nothing more than "video-on-demand for everyone else."

Under the subcommittee bill, the federal grants could amount to no more than 50 percent of the construction cost of a project.

The bill authorized additional grants to encourage public broadcasting stations to expand their reach into traditionally underserved areas, with the aim of expanding the reach of public television and keeping it at the forefront of delivery service technology.

The grants were designed to be used to extend delivery of public broadcasting using all types of available technology, including fiber-optic cable, coaxial cable, and satellite and microwave broadcasting.

House Full Committee

The House Energy and Commerce Committee on Oct. 26 approved HR 2639 (H Rept 103-325) by voice vote. The committee bill authorized $135 million for fiscal 1995 and $185 million for fiscal 1996.

The panel approved, by voice vote, an amendment by Mike Kreidler, D-Wash., to create a clearinghouse for information on programs that enabled schools to share information and educational services through computer or video networks.

Members also approved, by voice vote, an amendment by Mike Synar, D-Okla., to create a clearinghouse for information on telecommunications programs that linked rural hospitals with larger, advanced medical facilities.

House Floor

The House passed HR 2639 by voice vote Nov. 8. The bill authorized $250 million in grants for local governments, universities, medical centers and other nonprofit organizations to tap into the emerging "information superhighway." The grants were expected to cover up to half the cost for most connections to that network, with $100 million authorized in fiscal 1995 and $150 million in fiscal 1996.

The bill also included a new grant program to help governments and nonprofit organizations build public television and radio stations. An additional $70 million was authorized for that purpose. The grants could pay up to 75 percent of the construction costs of new or expanded stations. Up to $35 million in grants were to be available annually in fiscal 1995 and 1996, but only to existing public broadcasting stations, nonprofit groups or government agencies.

The bill also included the creation of government clearinghouses on "distance learning," a method of teaching students remotely through video or computer connections, and on "telemedicine" projects, in which advanced medical centers were to help doctors in other areas diagnose and treat their patients' illnesses.

The bill reauthorized the National Telecommunications and Information Administration (NTIA), which helped the president set telecommunications policy, for two years at $28 million per year. It also moved the National Endowment for Children's Television into the NTIA and authorized $6 million annually for the endowment in fiscal 1995 and 1996. The endowment made grants to support educational television programs for children.

A final section of the bill mandated a feasibility study of a satellite-based educational television network for children in Africa. The section was written by Rep. Jack Fields, R-Texas, in memory of his former Democratic colleague from Texas, the late Mickey Leland. ∎

Law Enacted To Encourage Joint Production Ventures

Congress on May 28 cleared a bill to encourage more joint ventures among the nation's manufacturers. President Clinton supported the legislation as part of his drive to make the United State more competitive in world markets.

The measure (HR 1313), sponsored by Rep. Jack Brooks, D-Texas, protected companies from being liable for triple damages in lawsuits contending that a joint research or production venture was anti-competitive.

Courts were allowed to use a less stringent standard in antitrust cases involving joint manufacturing ventures under the legislation. Courts could rule that such activities were reasonable given the existing competitive climate, rather than being forced to rule that all such ventures were illegal.

Such protections previously had been granted, through a 1984 law, only to joint research and development ventures between companies. The new law extended such protections to joint production ventures as well. *(1984 Almanac, p. 258)*

The legislation required that companies receiving the protection be located in the United States and that they be owned by U.S. residents or people from countries whose own laws did not discriminate against U.S. companies seeking to form joint ventures abroad.

Similar legislation passed the Senate by a vote of 96-1 in 1992, but the measure died in the House amid a dispute over foreign participation in joint ventures. *(1992 Almanac, p. 306)*

Clinton signed the bill June 10 (PL 103-42).

CONGRESSIONAL ACTION

House and Senate committees the week of March 22 began moving this component of Clinton's competitiveness agenda. The House Judiciary Committee on March 24 gave voice vote approval to HR 1313 (H Rept 103-94). The Senate Judiciary Committee, on a voice vote, approved a similar bill (S 574 — S Rept 103-51) March 25.

Both bills relaxed antitrust restrictions against joint ventures involving cooperative research, development and production agreements among competing companies. The aim was to encourage more joint ventures between rival companies to produce innovative goods and services.

This time, House sponsor Brooks and the Senate sponsors, Patrick J. Leahy, D-Vt., Strom Thurmond, R-S.C., and Joseph R. Biden Jr., D-Del., reached a compromise requiring that production facilities be in the United States and participants be either U.S. companies or foreign companies whose antitrust laws treated U.S. companies fairly.

The House passed HR 1313 by voice vote under expedited procedures May 18. During the floor debate, Brooks said, "There is a widely held misperception in the business community that even legitimate cooperative activity is likely to result in substantial legal liability." Mike Synar, D-Okla., the only lawmaker to speak against the measure, called it "a remedy in search of a problem" and said there was no evidence that existing antitrust laws inhibited the creation of joint ventures.

With the compromise between the House and Senate backers already worked out, the Senate cleared the House-passed bill by voice vote on May 28, bypassing the Senate Judiciary Committee. ∎

Senate Bill Clears the Way For Energy Lab Ventures

The Senate on Nov. 20 passed a bill (S 473) aimed at making it easier for Energy Department laboratories to forge new partnerships with private industry. The House took no action on the bill in 1993.

The Senate acted on the bill after it included most of the provisions in its version of the fiscal 1994 defense authorization bill (HR 2401, formerly S 1298), but saw the move rejected by the House.

Legislative Action

The Senate Energy and Natural Resources Committee approved S 473 (S Rept 103-69) on May 26 by a vote of 19-0. The bill, sponsored by Chairman J. Bennett Johnston, D-La., required some Energy Department laboratories to set aside 20 percent of their budgets for partnerships with industry.

The legislation served as a jurisdictional marker for Johnston, who wanted to ensure that the department labs remained in his committee's domain despite their increasingly commercial mission. So far, the labs had entered into more than 500 cooperative research and development agreements worth more than $700 million.

On Sept. 9, the Senate voted by voice to add most of the provisions of S 473 to its version of the defense authorization bill (S 1298).

The amendment expanded the mission of the laboratories to include research, development and commercial application of industrial technologies. It also removed paperwork roadblocks that often inhibited partnerships between government and the private sector and took steps to encourage a range of partnership arrangements.

However, the House rejected the addition of the language to the defense authorization bill, and it did not appear in the final version of that measure.

The Senate then took up S 473 and approved it by voice vote Nov. 19.

In separate action, the Senate Commerce, Science and Transportation Committee on May 25 approved a broader competitiveness bill (S 4 — S Rept 103-113) that included provisions to increase cooperation between federal laboratories and industry. That bill awaited Senate floor action when the first session adjourned. *(Competitiveness, p. 241)* ∎

House Passes NASA Authorization Bill

The House on July 29 passed a two-year NASA authorization bill (HR 2200), after waging yet another funding battle over the controversial — and once again redesigned — space station.

The Senate Commerce, Science and Transportation Committee took no action on a companion measure. As a result, the fiscal 1994 funding and policy decisions for the National Aeronautics and Space Administration (NASA) were largely in the hands of appropriators, who provided money for the agency through the fiscal 1994 spending bill for veterans and housing programs.

The House bill was most noteworthy for a June 23 vote in which members narrowly defeated an attempt to kill the space station, NASA's beleaguered $31 billion manned orbiting laboratory project. A core group of space station backers remained loyal despite yet another impending redesign and a renewed determination by lawmakers to achieve budget savings.

The bill did call for the cancellation of the Advanced Solid Rocket Motor (ASRM), a NASA project aimed at creating a rocket motor for the space shuttle program that could carry heavier payloads into space more efficiently. The program had come under attack for being unnecessary and too costly.

The space station survived in the final VA-HUD appropriations bill (HR 2491 — PL 103-124), getting a total of $2.1 billion in fiscal 1994. But Congress killed the ASRM project, providing $100 million to terminate it. *(Appropriations, p. 691)*

As passed by the House, the NASA authorization bill contained $14.8 billion in fiscal 1994 and $15.6 billion in fiscal 1995 for NASA programs. In addition, the bill authorized $1.9 billion in fiscal 1994 and $10.8 billion through fiscal 2000 for the space station. The bill included:

• **Space shuttle production.** $1.1 billion in fiscal 1994 and $979 million in fiscal 1995, of which $185 million was to cover the cost of terminating the ASRM program.

• **Space shuttle operations.** $3 billion for fiscal 1994 and $2.8 billion for fiscal 1995.

• **Research and program management.** $1.65 billion for fiscal 1994 and $1.6 billion for fiscal 1995.

• **Space Transportation Capability Development programs.** $751 million in fiscal 1994 and $819.3 million in fiscal 1995. Of that, $61 million over two years was directed toward the development of improved expendable launch vehicles and $67.4 million toward development of advanced rocket technologies.

The bill also authorized $2.5 billion for Mission to Planet Earth, a series of Earth-observing satellites to monitor the environment; $1.3 billion for planetary exploration; $911.7 million for life sciences and microgravity research, including women's health programs; $2.3 billion for physics and astronomy programs; and $160 million for the National Aerospace Plane, which would take off like an airplane and achieve orbit.

The bill also authorized $22 million in fiscal 1994 and $40 million in fiscal 1995 for a new "technology investment program." The aim was to encourage industry-led consortia to develop advanced space technologies that would improve U.S. competitiveness, and to encourage new industrial contractors not typically associated with the federal contracting base to bid for NASA projects.

BACKGROUND

When President Clinton took office, the space station — originally billed in 1984 as an $8 billion project with numerous scientific missions — had ballooned into a $31 billion project. Critics derided it as a boondoggle with little or no scientific value; defenders called it critical for the future of manned space research and stressed its importance for local jobs. Clinton did what past leaders had done: He ordered NASA back to the drawing table.

In early March, NASA Administrator Daniel S. Goldin announced that a team of as many as 35 officials from NASA and participating foreign space agencies would completely redesign the space station. After a 90-day cram session at an office suite in the Washington suburb of Crystal City, Va., NASA officials presented an independent blue-ribbon panel with three design options. It was, by various counts, the fifth or sixth such redesign since the project's inception in 1987; the last one had been ordered by Congress in 1991. *(1991 Almanac, p. 240)*

After reviewing the team's work, Clinton announced June 17 that he had chosen a variation of the middle-priced option — a modular design that amounted to a smaller version of the previous *Freedom* blueprints. New components could be added to the station over time, culminating in 2001 with the capability of sustaining five astronauts for up to 30 days in space. The crew would perform research on life sciences, advanced materials and microgravity. The space station was temporarily renamed *Alpha*.

Other options presented to Clinton included one favored by many lawmakers that hewed even more closely to the existing *Freedom* design and a much less expensive option that effectively would have scrapped most of the work already done. Or he could have chosen to kill the station entirely.

In choosing a new configuration for the space station, Clinton combined aspects of the other options. The building-block approach came from one design. Clinton borrowed components from another option that more closely resembled a scaled-back version of *Freedom* to maximize the ongoing work, and political support, of that previous design.

But Clinton also borrowed the budget numbers of the lowest-cost option, the one that effectively would have scrapped most of the work already done. He dismissed NASA's estimates that the redesign option he chose would cost $2.6 billion per year for the next five years, or $18.2 billion. Clinton proposed to spend $2.1 billion a year from

Early Retirement Urged

Congress neared completion of an administration-backed bill (HR 2876) aimed at giving the National Aeronautics and Space Administration authority to offer buyouts to employees in order to achieve personnel reductions associated with the space station redesign.

Minor differences between the House and Senate measures over budgeting language remained to be worked out at the close of the first session.

The House Science, Space and Technology Subcommittee on Space kicked off action on the measure, approving a draft version July 28. The bill authorized NASA to offer "buyout" options to encourage more than 1,000 employees left out of the space station redesign plan to take early retirement. The measure, approved by voice vote, allowed NASA to offer eligible employees up to $25,000 in severance pay.

NASA officials said the bill promised to help the agency avoid imposing agencywide furloughs or permanent staff cuts in light of a June 17 decision by President Clinton to redesign the orbiting laboratory, the space station *Freedom*. Gen. Spence M. Armstrong, NASA's associate administrator for human resources, gave the agency an Oct. 1 deadline to eliminate 1,100 of the 1,300 full-time positions allocated for the space station in the fiscal 1994 budget. *(Space station, p. 251)*

The full House Science Committee approved HR 2876 (previously HR 2800) on Aug. 4, and the leaders of the House Post Office and Civil Service Committee, where it had been jointly referred, discharged it the same day.

The House, acting quickly, passed the bill Aug. 6 by voice vote.

The Senate passed HR 2876 by voice vote Nov. 22, after amending it to include a stipulation by Governmental Affairs Committee Chairman John Glenn, D-Ohio, that the incentive money "should be subject to the availability of appropriations" for that purpose. If, by Sept. 30, 1994, not enough civil service employees had retired or resigned, NASA was required to implement furloughs to achieve reductions in personnel.

a longtime trend of downsizing the orbiting laboratory into irrelevance in the name of preserving jobs. "We are now going into the fifth or sixth redesign, and we're not getting more science, we're getting less," said Tim Roemer, D-Ind.

Later in the year, NASA said the space station could be built for $19.4 billion from fiscal years 1994 to 2003.

Clinton also brought the Russians into the process. On Sept. 2, Vice President Al Gore and Russian Prime Minister Victor S. Chernomyrdin signed an agreement that called for a joint effort to design and construct *Alpha* as an international space station. More immediately, Soyuz crew rescue vehicles would be used under the redesigned plans. And NASA pondered the merits of using an orbit that would be more compatible with other Russian space hardware.

In November, Clinton met with key space station backers and won their support for Russian involvement in exchange for his commitment to more actively promote the project. However, lawmakers continued to harbor concerns about the impact of the Russian agreement on U.S. jobs.

HOUSE COMMITTEE ACTION

On May 20, a month before Clinton had announced his decision on the redesign, Science Committee Chairman Brown introduced a $31 billion, two-year NASA authorization bill that called for $1.9 billion a year in funding for the space station, for a total of $9.5 billion over the next five years. It was Brown's way of making it known, before the design options were announced, that he favored salvaging the existing plan for the orbiting space station.

The Science Subcommittee on Technology, Environment and Aviation gave voice vote approval May 20 to a $2.5 billion portion of the NASA bill that authorized the space agency's research and development and aeronautics programs for fiscal 1994 and 1995.

House Full Committee

On June 9 the full Science, Space and Technology Committee approved HR 2200 by voice vote, after defeating two attempts to kill the space station (H Rept 103-123). As approved, the bill authorized $15 billion in fiscal 1994 and $15.6 billion in fiscal 1995 for NASA programs, as well as $1.9 annually billion for the space station through fiscal 1999 and $1.3 billion in fiscal 2000.

The committee turned back an amendment by Tim Roemer, D-Ind., to cancel the space station and authorize $825 million in fiscal 1994 to carry out the program's termination. The vote was 10-30. The panel also rejected, by a vote of 6-27, an amendment by Dick Zimmer, R-N.J., to cancel both the space station and the ASRM program.

But members did agree by voice vote to another amendment by Roemer, discontinuing just the ASRM program. The amendment provided $150 million for fiscal 1994 and $35 million for fiscal 1995 to cover the cost of terminating the program and transferring the production of the space shuttle and other solid rocket motor nozzles, as well as the refurbishment of redesigned solid rocket motor cases, to a new production site located near Yellow Creek, Miss.

A subsequent amendment, by Brown, agreed to by voice vote, directed 50 percent of the savings from canceling the ASRM program to research and development programs.

The committee approved a number of amendments by voice vote, including those by:

• Dana Rohrabacher, R-Calif., to authorize research into single-stage-to-orbit rocket technologies as part of the space transportation capability development program.

fiscal 1994 through 1998 on the new design. That was $10.5 billion over the next five years, more than the $9 billion cap that Clinton demanded when he ordered the station redesigned in March, but less than the $14 billion to $17 billion that NASA said space station *Freedom* would cost without being redesigned. These estimates were in addition to the $9.8 billion spent on the program through the end of fiscal 1993.

Space station supporters in Congress breathed sighs of relief at the news, though they conceded the going would be rough. "This decision preserves good science, saves money, maintains programmatic and political continuity and — with enhancements — will honor our international commitments," said George E. Brown Jr., D-Calif., chairman of the House Science, Space and Technology Committee.

But House lawmakers who opposed the space station were resolute, saying Clinton's plan simply would continue

Space Station Struggles To Survive

The space station *Freedom* was conceived in 1984 as an $8 billion orbiting manned laboratory in which astronauts would live and conduct experiments for prolonged periods. A major redesign in March 1991 made the station smaller, less powerful and capable of handling four instead of eight crew members. Yet another redesign, ordered by President Clinton in 1993, reduced its cost but also threw the project's scientific merits further into question.

The program had been attacked annually on the House and Senate floors for being light on scientific merit. In early 1993, it already was headed for trouble again amid news of cost overruns topping $500 million.

Before Clinton ordered the new redesign, the project was expected to cost $30 billion to $40 billion by the year 2000. Canada, Japan and nine European countries had promised to contribute $8 billion. So far, the United States had spent nearly $9 billion; other countries had spent an additional $2 billion.

Proponents argued that the space station would preserve a U.S. role in human space exploration. They said the station could determine how humans would react to being in space for long periods and that it would provide advances in space-based biomedical and advanced materials research. Moreover, research and construction contracts reached into 37 states and 151 congressional districts and already provided about 75,000 jobs.

Critics said almost every justification for the space station had run its course: Competition with the former Soviet Union was no longer a priority; exploration of deep space could more safely and effectively be conducted by unmanned spacecraft; and satellites could handle national security needs. Most scientists also repeatedly stated that little, if any, unique science would come from the space station. Clinical researchers argued that the money would be more wisely spent at earth-bound laboratories.

Legislative History

The space station had survived almost annual challenges since 1987, but support for the project had gradually declined. The following is a summary:

● **1987.** The Senate voted 84-12 to reject (table) an amendment that would have transferred $118 million from

NASA funds for a proposed space station to the Veterans Administration for medical care programs. The amendment was on the fiscal 1988 spending bill for Veterans Affairs, Housing and Urban Development and Independent Agencies. *(1987 Almanac, vote 329, p. 57-S)*

● **1989.** The House rejected, 125-291, an amendment on the 1990 VA-HUD appropriations bill to transfer $714 million from NASA to veterans, housing and other agencies. *(1989 Almanac, vote 146, p. 52-H)*

The Senate voted 97-0 for a sense-of-the-Senate resolution that the chamber should provide NASA's budget request for the space station. *(1989 Almanac, vote 137, p. 27-S)*

● **1991.** The House rejected, 122-296, an amendment to the fiscal 1992 VA-HUD appropriations bill that would have blocked the proposed transfer of $217 million from HUD public housing operation subsidies to the space station. *(1991 Almanac, vote 140, p. 34-H)*

The House then voted 240-173 to fund the space station at its fiscal 1991 level of $1.9 billion by cutting HUD programs and freezing all NASA programs to the fiscal 1991 level. *(1991 Almanac, vote 141, p. 34-H)*

The Senate rejected, 35-64, an attempt to reduce funding for the space station from $2 billion to $100 million and transfer $182 million to other federal science programs, $431 million to veterans programs and about $1.3 billion to deficit reduction as part of the fiscal 1992 VA-HUD bill. *(1991 Almanac, vote 132, p. 18-S)*

● **1992.** The House rejected, 159-254, an amendment to the fiscal 1993-95 NASA reauthorization bill that would have cut $2.3 billion to terminate the space station, transferring $1.1 billion of the funds to other NASA programs and using the rest to reduce the deficit. *(1992 Almanac, vote 90, p. 22-H)*

The House also rejected, 181-237, an attempt to cut $1.2 billion of the $1.7 billion for the space station in the fiscal 1993 VA-HUD bill, leaving $525 million for costs associated with closing down the program. *(1992 Almanac, vote 334, p. 82-H)*

The Senate rejected, 34-63, an attempt to amend the VA-HUD bill to provide $500 million to terminate the space station and transfer from its account $262 million for veterans health programs. *(1992 Almanac, vote 194, p. 26-S)*

● Jennifer Dunn, R-Wash., to set aside $2 million for fiscal year 1994 and $2 million for fiscal year 1995 for women's health and cancer research.
● Space Subcommittee Chairman Ralph M. Hall, D-Texas, to increase the authorization for Mission to Planet Earth from $1 billion to $1.1 billion for fiscal 1994, among other things.
● James A. Traficant Jr., D-Ohio, to encourage recipients of grants under the bill to purchase U.S.-made equipment and products when available and cost-effective.

HOUSE FLOOR ACTION

The House passed the $30.4 billion NASA authorization bill by voice vote July 29, after voting by a razor-thin

margin to save the space station.

As passed, the bill authorized up to $14.8 billion for fiscal 1994 and $15.6 billion for fiscal 1995. The space station *Freedom* was authorized at $1.9 billion annually from fiscal 1994 through fiscal 1999 and $1.3 billion in fiscal 2000.

Because of the need to act on more pressing legislation and the unlikelihood of any Senate action on a companion measure in 1993, the bill had languished on and off the House floor for weeks before being passed.

Space Station Vote

The vote on the space station came on June 23 during initial consideration of the bill. By a vote of 215-216, members rejected an amendment by Roemer and Zimmer to kill

the project. The vote was not quite as close at it looked: The 215 votes in favor of the amendment included four delegates who, under new House rules, were allowed to cast votes only so long as doing so did not determine the outcome. Still, it was the closest the project had ever come to cancellation. *(Vote 263, p. 64-H)*

Space station supporters got some encouragement a week later, when the House on June 28 rejected, 196-220, an attempt to cut $2.1 billion for the project as part of the fiscal 1994 appropriations bill for VA-HUD and related agencies. *(Vote 282, p. 68-H)*

During the authorization bill debate, proponents touted the space station's potential for spurring medical advances, materials research and retaining a U.S. presence in manned space exploration. Critics said it held little potential for curing cancer or other diseases and said the project's main purpose was as a pork barrel jobs program mainly of benefit to Texas, Florida, California and Alabama.

The Clinton administration was under pressure to prove its commitment to the space station by helping turn votes toward the program. The White House did its part, but not without stumbles. A hastily arranged meeting the morning of the vote between Democratic freshmen and Vice President Al Gore was sparsely attended, forcing Gore to seek out wavering lawmakers on the floor. "Not the most satisfying setting to do some serious arm-twisting," Brown lamented.

Because Democrats were divided on the issue, the House leadership kept a low lobbying profile. However, space station supporter Speaker Thomas S. Foley, D-Wash., who typically refrained from voting, was prepared to cast a vote if needed. The space station was saved in large part because of a successful vote-whipping job by the GOP leadership: Voting Republicans sided with *Freedom*, 112-173.

Just 63 of 114 freshman members voted to kill the project. California Democrats, whose state was among the biggest beneficiaries of the space station, also were evenly split on the amendment, 15-15.

Other traditionally soft blocs of support for the space station, including most Northeastern and Midwestern members and black and Hispanic lawmakers, remained largely opposed because the project competed for funds against housing and other programs on the VA-HUD spending bill. "It was hard for me to justify voting for the space station when I came here to address the lack of dollars appropriated for inner cities, jobs and communities," said Bobby L. Rush. A freshman Democrat from Chicago, Rush said he was undecided until just before he cast his vote against the space station.

Also on June 24, the House approved an amendment by Hall of Texas to limit the fiscal 1994 authorization to no more than 3.1 percent above the amount authorized in fiscal 1993, reducing the total in the bill by $264 million. It passed by a vote of 411-11. *(Vote 262, p. 64-H)*

Solid Rocket Motor Facilities

With the battle over the space station behind it, the House did not resume floor debate on the bill until July 23.

In the most significant action, lawmakers approved, 276-139, an amendment by F. James Sensenbrenner Jr., R-Wis., to cancel $35 million in fiscal 1995 for completing work on the solid rocket motor facility in Mississippi, as well as $25 million slated for relocation of rocket motor facilities to Yellow Creek, Miss. *(Vote 360, p. 88-H)*

Sensenbrenner argued that the physical plant was no longer needed because the bill already canceled the ASRM program, the reason for building the facility. (The VA-HUD bill, passed by the House on June 29, terminated ASRM but left the facility construction funds in place.)

Science Committee Chairman Brown argued that the new plant, which was 90 percent complete, should be used to build the more traditional solid rocket motors that propelled the space shuttle. The contractor that built the motors, Thiokol Corp., wanted to shift its solid rocket motor facilities — and roughly 1,000 jobs — from Utah to the Mississippi plant.

Helium Vote

On a 326-98 vote, members adopted an amendment by C. Christopher Cox, R-Calif., and Barney Frank, D-Mass., to allow NASA to buy helium from private sources. *(Vote 380, p. 92-H)*

The space agency had been required to purchase its helium, an inert gas used for spacecraft and space missions, from a government reserve established for national security reasons in the 1920s, when it was believed that natural sources of helium were rapidly depleting. The gas since had been found to be naturally abundant. By 1993, 90 percent of the helium in the United States was produced by private industry and sold at prices lower than NASA paid for helium from the stockpile.

Lawmakers also adopted, by voice vote, an amendment by Mac Collins, R-Ga., to allow the president to request that 1 percent of the NASA authorization bill be set aside to help offset the costs of a federal Midwest flood relief program. ∎

House Approves Marine Biotechnology Program

The House on July 13 passed a bill by voice vote to establish a marine biotechnology program at selected colleges and universities.

The bill (HR 1916) authorized $90 million in grants over four years to support research into genetically modified marine organisms. Those grants were in addition to the roughly $44 million being spent each year under an existing federal program for marine biotechnology.

The grants were to be made through the National Sea Grant College Program, with applications considered by a new Marine Biotechnology Review Panel, made up of 15 experts in marine biotechnology or related fields.

To address concerns about the release of genetically altered organisms, the House Merchant Marine and Fisheries Committee amended the bill to require researchers to abide by federal safety standards or lose their grants. The committee adopted the legislation May 13 by voice vote (H Rept 103-170).

Earlier, the Subcommittee on Oceanography, Gulf of Mexico and the Outer Continental Shelf had amended the measure to clarify that the new program was contingent on the availability of new appropriations.

The bill's sponsor, House Merchant Marine Committee Chairman Gerry E. Studds, D-Mass., said the research held great promise for food production, pharmaceuticals, industry and environmental cleanups. Lynn Schenk, D-Calif., warned that the United States needed to increase such research to keep pace with efforts by Japan and other Pacific Rim competitors.

Sen. Ernest F. Hollings, D-S.C., introduced a similar measure (S 1517), and the Commerce, Science and Transportation Committee, which Hollings chaired, approved an amended version of his bill Nov. 9. But no further action occurred in the Senate. ■

Senate Bill Sets Stage for Magnetic Fusion Research

The Senate June 29 approved by voice vote a bill (S 646) to require the Energy Department to devise a research plan for harnessing magnetic fusion energy. The House did not take up the bill.

The Senate Energy and Natural Resources Committee approved the bill, 18-0, on May 19 (S Rept 103-62). Committee Chairman J. Bennett Johnston, D-La., the bill's sponsor, said the measure would help the department prepare for its next big science project — the international thermonuclear experimental reactor. Backers of the bill said they hoped the reactor, which was in its infancy, eventually would let scientists sustain magnetic fusion reactions long enough to produce power that could be used commercially.

Scientists were studying the use of magnetic fields to contain hot gases that reacted to produce energy. At the time, the Energy Department spent about $350 million on its fusion research program, focused primarily on magnetic fusion. S 646 authorized the same amount for fiscal 1994 but required the Energy secretary to direct all research

toward development of the new reactor.

A floor amendment, requested by Johnston and passed by the Senate, transferred some of the responsibility for the plan from the Energy Secretary to an International Fusion Negotiator provided for in the amendment. The amendment also specifically linked the Tokamak Physics Experiment at the Princeton Plasma Physics Laboratory to the legislation. ■

National Science Foundation Funding Clears Committee

By voice vote Oct. 6, the House Science, Space and Technology Subcommittee on Science approved a draft bill to reauthorize the National Science Foundation (NSF) for three years. The bill, formally introduced Oct. 12 by the subcommittee's chairman, Rep. Rick Boucher, D-Va., was not taken up in full committee by session's end.

As approved by the subcommittee, the bill authorized $2 billion in fiscal 1994, about 8 percent more than the fiscal 1993 appropriation; $2.62 billion in fiscal 1995; and $2.88 billion in fiscal 1996.

Sherwood Boehlert of New York, ranking Republican on the subcommittee, offered and then withdrew an amendment to cut more than $400 million from the fiscal 1994-95 authorization and eliminate the fiscal 1996 authorization. He said he would offer the amendment in full committee.

The measure included $250 million in each of the three years to modernize academic research facilities. That was a fivefold increase from fiscal 1993. ■

Both Chambers Pass Bills Targeting Arson

The House and Senate passed similar bills aimed at helping states deter arson, but they did not agree on a compromise bill in 1993.

The bills authorized $4.8 million in fiscal 1994 and $6.3 million in fiscal 1995, most of it for grants to states for demonstration programs aimed at reducing arson, including one to establish juvenile fire-starter counseling programs. The bills included $2 million in fiscal 1995 to expand arson investigator training programs at the National Fire Academy and federal law enforcement training centers.

The House Science, Space and Technology Subcommittee on Science approved its version of the bill (HR 1727) by voice vote on June 17. The panel had amended the bill to encourage the purchase of U.S.-made equipment and products, to promote cardiopulmonary resuscitation training for firefighters and to sunset the bill at the close of fiscal 1995. The full committee approved the bill (H Rept 103-172) by voice vote June 30, after rejecting, 12-17, an amendment by Bill Baker, R-Calif., to fund the programs established by HR 1727 from otherwise authorized funds. The House passed the measure July 26, also by voice vote.

The Senate approved HR 1727 by voice vote Nov. 22 after substituting the text of S 798, which was identical to the original House bill. ■

Radio Spectrum Allocation Policy Revised

As part of the budget-reconciliation bill (HR 2264) enacted in August, Congress voted to put a portion of the public radio spectrum on the auction block for commercial users. The decision, which was expected to bring in $7.2 billion over five years, overturned a longstanding policy of awarding radio licenses free through lottery or merit review. Under the new law, cellular phone companies and other businesses that sold direct access to the airwaves were required to bid for any new licenses. Other license holders, such as broadcasters and cable systems, were not affected.

In addition, the law required broadcasters and other spectrum users to pay yearly fees to raise an estimated $100 million annually to pay for Federal Communications Commission (FCC) expenses. The law set exact fees for each type of licensee for fiscal 1994, ranging from $6 for a small-sized satellite television programmer to $600 for a medium-sized FM radio station and $18,000 for a large-market VHF television station.

The law also required the FCC to shift 200 megahertz of radio spectrum from government use to the private sector. That was roughly half the amount of radio frequencies that had been allotted to the cellular telephone industry 10 years earlier. The newly released frequencies, along with others that the FCC already had slated for private use, were to be allocated through competitive bidding.

The measure also set rules to govern how new mobile telephone service licenses should be allocated and regulated. States largely lost their right to set rates for cellular service, although 19 states that already set such rates retained those rights at least temporarily. Other states did not regulate cellular service because most markets had at least two competing cellular companies.

The House approved the radio spectrum provisions as part of the reconciliation bill conference report (HR 2264 — H Rept 103-213) adopted Aug. 5 by a vote of 218-216. The Senate cleared the bill Aug. 6 by a vote of 51-50, and President Clinton signed it (PL 103-66) on Aug. 10. (Budget-reconciliation provisions, p. 127; House vote 406, p. 98-H; Senate vote 247, p. 32-S)

BACKGROUND

Traditionally, except for a routine filing fee, those who met FCC application standards used the airwaves free of charge. The FCC assigned licenses either by "comparative review" for broadcasters — a kind of merit process — or by lottery for most other users. Lotteries had begun as a way to grant rights to the new cellular telephone industry, but they turned out to create a bazaar of private sector speculators who bought out other license applicants and then resold the spectrum rights to the highest bidder.

By the early 1990s, much of the usable radio band was committed, with the most valuable space around the center of the spectrum held by TV and radio broadcasters. The lack of available radio frequencies was threatening the commercial viability of new wireless technology.

Pressures for Change Grow

In the 102nd Congress, lawmakers tried to increase the portion of the radio spectrum that was available to commercial users. The House approved a bill in 1991 that would have transferred 200 megahertz controlled by various government agencies to civilian use. But President Bush threatened a veto because the bill contained no proposal to auction the airwaves. The Bush administration argued that the best way to manage access to the airwaves was through auctions that would recoup some of the private sector profits.

House Energy and Commerce Chairman John D. Dingell, D-Mich., accused Republicans of grabbing for money with little concern that only those with the deepest pockets would win rights to the airwaves.

In 1992, Senate Commerce Communications Subcommittee Chairman Daniel K. Inouye, D-Hawaii, and Ted Stevens, R-Alaska, crafted a compromise that would have required the FCC to auction off up to 30 megahertz in an experimental program. But lawmakers ran out of time before they could complete work on the bill. (1991 Almanac, p. 157; 1992 Almanac, p. 193)

As part of his Feb. 17 economic package, newly inaugurated President Clinton called on Congress to approve the transfer of 200 megahertz to private use and to grant the FCC authority to use auctions to assign the new spectrum and make all future license assignments. Noting that "many multimillion-dollar industries — including television and radio — are built around the free use of a scarce and valuable federal resource," the administration concluded that "an 'auction' of these rights already occurs today: The question is whether the taxpayer will benefit." (Text, p. 7-D)

Congress Sidesteps Industry Conflicts

In opting for a spectrum auction, lawmakers sidestepped a controversy over who would be allowed to bid for the new frequency licenses, an issue that pitted the cellular phone industry, which was barely 10 years old, against the even newer "personal communications services" industry that was developing the newest generation of wireless telephones and computers.

On one side was PCS Action, a newly formed lobbying group that included small upstart companies as well as communications giants, such as long-distance carrier MCI and cable industry titan Time Warner Inc. PCS Action hoped to limit the ability of the $15 billion cellular telephone industry, 80 percent of which was controlled by the regional Bell telephone companies, to gain an early market advantage in the wireless communications arena. The group's lobbyists argued that well-established cellular interests would quash any newcomers to the wireless market.

The cellular industry, meanwhile, worked hard to persuade lawmakers to include an "open market" provision in the auction legislation that would guarantee them a full piece of the new action. The cellular representatives had a powerful argument: Allowing them free rein to bid up the price of the newly available frequencies was likely to mean more revenues for the U.S. Treasury.

In the end, while the law gave guidelines for developing regulations, it left it up to the FCC to resolve such questions as whether to limit cellular industry access to the airwaves, how many licenses to allow in each market, what size of band width to allow for each license holder and whether there should be regional and nationwide "long distance" licenses as well as hundreds of local rights.

Each of those issues carried huge consequences for the cellular industry and its would-be competitors.

HOUSE SUBCOMMITTEE ACTION

The House Energy and Commerce Subcommittee on Telecommunications and Finance agreed May 6 to authorize the FCC to auction radio frequencies through fiscal 1998 as the panel's contribution to the budget-reconciliation bill.

The proposal, approved by voice vote, applied only to new licenses for businesses such as cellular telephone, paging or other communications networks that planned to directly sell use of the airwaves to subscribers. Others who did not depend on the airwaves directly for subscriptions, such as broadcasters, cable operators, electrical utilities or land-based telephone companies, were exempt. Radio and television broadcasters had fought hard to keep their frequencies exempt from auction, arguing that their mandate to use the airwaves in the public interest was payment enough for the use of the spectrum.

The bill required the FCC to help small businesses that feared being outbid by wealthier rivals, allowing for innovative ways to pay for winning bids, such as paying them off over time or promising payment in the form of royalties or a percentage of earned profit. The bill left intact a recent FCC rule granting "pioneers' preferences," which reserved a few licenses for entrepreneurs who wanted to test new communications technologies over the airwaves.

To avoid the problem of private-sector trafficking of new auctioned licenses, the bill required the FCC to make sure bidders were qualified to build and operate a communications system within a limited time.

The measure required the FCC to begin issuing licenses for personal communications services within nine months. The FCC had been accused of foot-dragging on its decision to carve out a new slice of the spectrum for those technologies.

In an effort to put the cellular industry and the nascent personal communications services industry on the same regulatory plane, the measure treated both technologies as "common carriers" not unlike land-based local telephone services. The designation meant that the FCC could require a carrier to allow competitors to connect with its service. But the committee bill made the wireless industry (unlike telephone services) exempt from state or local rate regulation. Under that provision, which was later changed, states that already set rates for cellular companies no longer would have been able to do so.

HOUSE COMMITTEE ACTION

The full House Energy and Commerce Committee approved the radio spectrum provisions by voice vote May 11 with the support of all the panel Republicans, despite concerns expressed by some members that the measure might hurt rural areas and prematurely deregulate the cellular telephone industry. The House approved the provisions May 27 when it passed the reconciliation bill.

Before the full committee approved the bill, Markey amended it to incorporate a separate bill (HR 707), previously approved by the House, that directed the FCC to transfer to the private sector 200 megahertz of unused or underutilized radio spectrum that was reserved for government use. The House had passed that bill by a vote of 410-5 on March 2. *(Vote 46, p. 12-H)*

The Energy and Commerce Committee rejected, 8-36, an amendment by Mike Synar, D-Okla., to guarantee that each rural telephone company would get at least one license for new communications services, for which the company would pay a market rate. The amendment also would have retained the regulatory role of state governments over the new generation of pocket-size wireless telephones, computers and other communications advances that were expected to bid for the newly available frequencies.

Historically, telephone companies had had to be forced by the FCC and state utility commissions to develop service in rural areas with few customers. Phone rates in urban areas were regulated to subsidize rural service.

Markey's auction legislation specifically mentioned rural areas in a provision that directed the FCC to "promote" rapid deployment of new technologies in a way that benefited all the public. But Synar argued that this would have little effect because another part of the bill removed the right of states to regulate the rates for wireless communications services. Synar said the bill would remove any control states might have to ensure that rural areas were served. "Certain rural areas are still trying to get Touch-Tone phone service," Synar said.

Markey sought to mollify Synar by adding a provision to allow states to petition the FCC to regulate rates if competition did not develop. The FCC would have to rule on such a petition within nine months. But Synar said such petitions easily could get bogged down in court battles.

SENATE ACTION

The Senate Commerce, Science and Transportation Committee approved a slightly different auction plan by voice vote June 15. The Senate approved the provisions June 25 as part its deficit-reduction bill.

The Senate measure included language authorizing the FCC to transfer 200 megahertz of electromagnetic radio spectrum from government use to the private sector. The bill authorized the FCC to conduct auctions through fiscal 1998 or until the auctions raised $7.2 billion, whichever occurred first.

The bill explicitly stated that broadcasters, public safety agencies and government users would be exempt from auctions. That wording was good news to broadcasters, who planned to use more radio spectrum over the coming decade to upgrade their equipment for the arrival of high-definition television.

The bill barred states from regulating rates for the wireless telephone industry if three or more companies competed in any market area of a state. States still could set terms and conditions of cellular service, and they could petition the FCC for the right to set prices if market conditions failed to protect consumers.

Richard H. Bryan, D-Nev., won voice vote approval for an amendment that allowed 19 states and territories, including Nevada, California and New York, that already exercised rate-setting authority to continue doing so. But those states had to apply to the FCC within a year of enactment to show why they should be allowed to continue doing so. The FCC would have one year to accept or reject the petition. Any interested party, such as a cellular company, could later petition the FCC to lift the state rate regulations on the grounds that competition existed.

The rural-oriented committee kept small-town interests in mind by including a provision that assured each rural telephone company access to at least one wireless communications license at an undefined market rate. The lan-

guage was similar to an amendment rejected by the House Energy and Commerce Committee. The Congressional Budget Office estimated that the rural set-aside would subtract $100 million to $200 million from the projected revenues earned from auctions. The provision authorizing the FCC to continue auctions until it raised $7.2 billion was an attempt to address that dispute.

FINAL ACTION

House and Senate conferees on the commerce portion of the deficit-reduction bill approved the competitive bidding plan through fiscal 1998, along with the transfer of 200 megahertz for new private sector licenses. Conferees agreed to retain the Senate provision, written by Bryan, to keep intact the abilities of states that already set rates for mobile telephone services. The conferees noted that their intent was to establish a federal regulatory framework to govern all commercial mobile services such as cellular telephones and wireless laptop computers.

Also during the conference, Dingell won approval of the language setting new fees for all spectrum license holders — a provision that did not exist in either chamber's original legislation. ∎

Both Chambers Take Aim At Telephone Fraud

Legislation to crack down on telemarketing scams — fraudulent sales pitches made over telephone lines to unwitting consumers — passed in both chambers. Differences between the two measures were considered minor, and sponsors expected to finish the bill in (HR 868) 1994.

The legislation aimed to widen the regulatory scope of the Federal Trade Commission (FTC) to assist in snaring more offending telemarketers. It also sought to give state prosecutors more authority to track down fraudulent telemarketers who skipped across state lines to avoid capture.

BACKGROUND

The incidence of telemarketing fraud increased in the 1980s and 1990s, in part because U.S. consumers were making more purchases over the telephone using credit cards. While many telephone sales businesses were legitimate, some telemarketing practices were built purely on deception with the intent to defraud consumers. In such cases, consumers purchased products or services over the telephone only to find that the product was never delivered or was of inferior quality.

Schemes including phony credit card offers, bogus charities, fake gem stones, job scams, deceptive travel promotions and pyramid sales schemes cost consumers as much as $40 billion annually, according to a report by the House Government Operations Committee.

Similar legislation passed the Senate and died in the House in an end-of-session legislative crush in the 102nd Congress. *(1992 Almanac, p. 191)*

LEGISLATIVE ACTION

The House Energy and Commerce Subcommittee on Transportation and Hazardous Materials gave voice vote

approval Feb. 17 to a bill (HR 868) to expand the powers of the FTC and state law enforcement officials to go after those who engaged in illegal telemarketing activities. The subcommittee had jurisdiction over the FTC.

"The telephone has become a powerful weapon in the hands of those with a persuasive message and a desire to steal," said the bill's sponsor, subcommittee Chairman Al Swift, D-Wash. "From a boiler room operation thousands of miles away, a long hand can reach out and into a consumer's pocket."

As approved by the subcommittee, the bill expanded the FTC's authority to combat fraudulent, deceptive or abusive telemarketing schemes, mostly by focusing on criminals who skipped across state lines to avoid prosecution. It also attempted to coordinate multistate investigations and prosecutions, and allow state attorneys general to pursue suspects in other states.

Under existing law, criminals who fled state prosecution faced federal prosecution only if they used the U.S. mail with intent to defraud or they violated other federal laws. The bill gave victims who lost $50,000 or more from telephone fraud crimes the right to sue the perpetrators in federal court.

The bill also required telephone marketers to offer refunds to consumers when the promised service or merchandise was not delivered in a reasonable amount of time. And it required telemarketing companies to cancel orders when consumers changed their minds within a certain period.

The measure included a nationwide clearinghouse to keep law enforcement officials aware of fraudulent activities.

With little debate, the full Energy and Commerce Committee approved the bill on Feb. 22 (H Rept 103-20).

The House followed suit, overwhelmingly passing HR 868 on March 2 in a 411-3 roll call. *(Vote 45, p. 12-H)*

Before floor action, Swift settled a turf dispute between Energy and Commerce and the Agriculture Committee, which had jurisdiction over the Commodity Futures Trading Commission (CFTC). Swift and Agriculture Chairman E. "Kika" de la Garza, D-Texas, agreed to amend the bill to require the CFTC, the Securities and Exchange Commission (SEC) and the FTC to craft similar telemarketing fraud enforcement rules. The CFTC regulated telephone commodity transactions, and the SEC regulated telephone securities transactions.

Senate Action

The Senate Commerce, Science and Transportation Committee approved a companion bill (S 568 — S Rept 103-80) on May 25. Like its House counterpart, the Senate bill sought to expand the FTC's regulatory role and strengthen the ability of state prosecutors to track down telemarketing fraud artists who skipped over state lines.

The bill outlined several possible rules for the FTC to consider, including requiring telemarketers to promise a shipping date for goods sold over the phone or granting a "cooling off" period during which consumers could rescind an order after the call was made.

The bill also sought to expand the ability of the FTC to crack down on long-distance telephone fraud, allowing victims who lost $50,000 or more from telephone fraud crimes to sue in federal court. And it included the nationwide clearinghouse on telemarketing fraud.

The Senate bill, which was nearly identical to the measure the Senate passed in 1992, was sponsored by Richard H. Bryan, D-Nev.

The Senate approved S 568 by voice vote on June 30; it then passed HR 868 after substituting the Senate language.

RELATED BILLS

Two related bills progressed in the Senate but saw no action in the House.

Combating Fraud Against Older People

The Senate gave voice vote approval July 30 to a bill (S 557) authorizing additional federal penalties and law enforcement resources to combat telemarketing fraud, especially when it was aimed at people over age 55, and it created a new federal statute criminalizing such fraud.

It provided up to an additional five years imprisonment for telemarketing fraud and up to 10 additional years for cases aimed at older citizens. It provided for fines of up to $250,000 and required that offenders repay losses to the victims.

Under the bill, the attorney general could offer a reward of up to $10,000 to any person who provided information leading to the conviction of a telephone scam artist. S 557 authorized $23.5 million to train federal agents to discover and investigate deceptive, abusive and fraudulent marketing schemes carried out over the telephone. And it provided for the creation of a national toll-free hotline to report instances of fraudulent marketing.

The Senate Judiciary Committee approved the bill by voice vote on July 22.

The House Judiciary Committee did not act on the measure in 1993.

Limiting Caller ID

The Senate Judiciary Committee on Aug. 3 approved a bill to allow telephone customers to block new devices that revealed a caller's telephone number. The measure (S 612) was approved by voice vote without debate.

As approved, the bill amended federal wiretapping laws to clarify that so-called caller ID was legal in the states where it was provided, but also to require that telephone companies provide customers with the option of preventing their numbers from appearing on the receiving machines.

Bill backers suggested a variety of situations in which callers might wish to have their phone number kept private, such as victims of domestic violence calling home from a shelter or police performing undercover work.

Similar legislation stalled in the Senate in 1992 after Republicans tried to attach a controversial anti-crime measure to it. The most controversial aspect of the bill in 1992 was the pre-emption of state laws that did not allow customers to block caller ID devices. *(1992 Almanac, p. 191)* ■

House Bill Seeks To Aid Satellite Carriers

The House Judiciary Subcommittee on Intellectual Property and Judicial Administration gave voice vote approval Aug. 5 to legislation (HR 1103) aimed at allowing satellite carriers to transmit network programming with or without the expressed permission of the networks.

The Satellite Home Viewer Act of 1988 granted transmission rights through 1994 to carriers — companies that leased space on a satellite in order to beam programming to viewers with satellite dishes. Many of those viewers were in rural areas.

The subcommittee bill would have extended such rights through 1998, but the panel gave voice vote approval to an amendment by Hamilton Fish Jr., R-N.Y., to extend the transmission rights until 1999.

The bill required arbitration to set the cost to satellite carriers of transmitting network signals. Under existing law, carriers paid broadcasters for each person they served in an area where the broadcast signal was not received.

Satellite carriers expressed concerns about the arbitration provision, saying it might put them in competition with cable operators that were continuing to expand into rural areas. But the generally popular bill was expected to become law in the second session of the 103rd Congress. ■

Chapter 5

ENVIRONMENT/ ENERGY

Overhaul of Mining Law Advances

Western senators had previously outmuscled House colleagues, thwarting efforts to change 1872 law

Congress came close to overhauling the 1872 Mining Law, enacted during the administration of Ulysses S. Grant to attract settlers to the Western frontier. The mining legislation awaited action by a joint House-Senate conference committee when Congress adjourned in November.

The House gave a major boost to supporters of the overhaul by passing a tough mining bill (HR 322) on Nov. 18 by a lopsided vote that was expected to give the House leverage in negotiations with the Senate. The Senate had passed a much leaner version (S 775) by voice vote on May 25.

The House bill was written by Nick J. Rahall II, D-W.Va., with the aid of Natural Resources Committee Chairman George Miller, D-Calif., and Energy and Mineral Resources Subcommittee Chairman Richard H. Lehman, D-Calif.

The measure imposed an 8 percent royalty on the extraction of hard-rock minerals but allowed miners to deduct the costs of smelting and shipping. It also required miners to pay a $25 location fee for each claim, a $100 annual fee to maintain existing claims and a $200 annual fee for new claims. The size of a mining claim increased from 20 acres to 40 acres under the bill.

Small mining operations with 10 claims or less were exempt from the maintenance fees, although they were required to perform $100 worth of work annually to keep their claims active.

All revenue from royalties and fees was to be placed in a new fund to pay for the cleanup of abandoned mines damaged by past mining operations. The bill included stricter rules for mining operations, aimed at making them more environmentally sensitive. And it gave the Interior secretary the authority to declare certain federal lands "unsuitable" for mining operations.

The House also approved July 15 a one-year moratorium on the processing of new mining claims as part of the Interior appropriations bill (HR 2520). But House-Senate negotiators dropped the provision in conference. *(Appropriations, p. 618)*

In a sharp departure from previous years, the Senate passed a mining bill sponsored by Larry E. Craig, R-Idaho, to provide what Energy and Natural Resources Committee Chairman J. Bennett Johnston, D-La., called a "ticket to conference" with the House. Johnston moved the industry-supported bill swiftly through committee and onto the

---

BOXSCORE

➡ **Mining Royalties (HR 322, S 775).** The bills amended the 1872 Mining Law and imposed royalties for the first time on extraction of hard-rock minerals from federal lands. The House approved an 8 percent gross royalty, the Senate, a 2 percent net royalty. The House bill imposed strict environmental rules; the Senate bill required miners to abide by state laws governing reclamation.

Reports: H Rept 103-338, S Rept 103-45.

KEY ACTION

May 6 — **Senate** Energy and Natural Resources Committee approved S 775 by voice vote.

May 25 — **Senate** passed S 775 by voice vote.

Nov. 3 — **House** Natural Resources Committee approved HR 322, 28-14.

Nov. 18 — **House** passed HR 322, 316-108.

Senate floor without amendments. Arkansas Democrat Dale Bumpers, the Senate's most ardent advocate of mining reform, agreed with Johnston's strategy and stopped pushing his own tougher bill (S 257).

Craig's bill (S 775) included a 2 percent royalty on the extraction of hard-rock minerals but allowed miners to deduct most development, exploration and production costs. The bill eliminated the practice of selling federal lands cheaply and required miners to pay the fair market value of the land's surface — not including the value of the underground minerals.

S 775 also required a $25 location fee, but it limited annual maintenance fees to $100. The maintenance fee was to be waived for miners with 10 claims or less, and miners with 10 to 50 claims were to pay $25 a year to maintain each claim.

Unlike HR 322, Craig's bill did not include any new federal environmental standards for the repair of public lands damaged by mining. Instead, the bill required miners to comply with state laws for reclamation, which varied widely in their stringency. It did not set up a fund to pay for the repair of abandoned mines.

In preparation for sending the bill to conference, the Senate on Nov. 22 appointed its negotiating team, headed by Johnston and senior members of the Natural Resources Committee. It also passed HR 322 after substituting the text of S 775. House negotiators were not appointed before Congress adjourned in November.

BACKGROUND

Efforts to overhaul the 1872 Mining Law had become a perennial battle, pitting Western mining-state lawmakers against policy advocates passionate about reaping more money from those who used federal land for commercial enterprises.

The 121-year-old law did not charge royalties for the extraction of gold, silver, copper, platinum, zinc and other hard-rock minerals from federal lands. Miners were allowed to buy or "patent" claims on federal lands for as little as $2.50 an acre. The law also had few requirements for the restoration of lands damaged by hard-rock mining.

Lawmakers had tried since 1987 to revamp the law, among the last "homesteading" measures enacted to en-

courage development of the West. But as with other natural resource and public lands issues, Western senators had long managed to outmuscle their House colleagues, and the effort to change the law remained in a virtual stalemate.

But the terrain in 1993 was different. Mining overhaul legislation was propelled in part by the fact that the Clinton administration came into office with a stronger environmental agenda than previous Republican administrations. Interior Secretary Bruce Babbitt had emphasized that preservation of federal land was as important as allowing mining or grazing on those lands.

The soaring budget deficit, too, prompted a review of what industry was charged to use federal resources.

In his fiscal 1994 budget proposal, Clinton called for increases in grazing fees, an end to below-cost timber sales from federal lands and the imposition of a surcharge on federally subsidized water.

Industry Arguments

The mining industry argued that overhauling the law threatened to force mines to close, put thousands of workers out of jobs and encourage U.S. mining companies to set up operations overseas — where the environmental laws were looser and royalty payments less burdensome.

In particular, industry officials and mining-state lawmakers opposed efforts to impose a royalty on hard-rock mineral extractions, arguing that they had little control over world mineral prices and that the royalties threatened to cut profits.

Industry officials said that without the ability to convert federal land to private property, they faced difficulty in getting banks to extend loans to finance mining operations. They also said there were plenty of environmental protections in place, even if they were not spelled out in the 1872 law.

The industry had commissioned several studies, including one conducted for the Gold Institute by a University of Nevada economist, which concluded that an 8 percent royalty would cost nearly 7,000 jobs in Nevada alone and "threaten the economic viability" of 20 percent of U.S. gold mines. Advocates of the overhaul legislation said those predictions were exaggerated.

Clinton Backs Down

The level of any new royalty charge attracted heated debate early in the year and briefly became entangled in the budget debate. In the early version of the administration's budget proposal, the Office of Management and Budget (OMB) called for instituting a 12.5 percent royalty on hard-rock mineral sales. The administration estimated that the tax would bring in $748 million in new revenues through fiscal 1998.

The House Budget Committee included that expectation in the budget resolution that the House passed March 18, though it used different assumptions about mine production and came up with a lower overall figure: $380 million in additional revenue over five years.

Johnston expressed concern that his committee was to be held to the 12.5 percent revenue estimate even if there was little chance of passing a bill with such a royalty level. Babbitt also had said he was feeling some pressure from OMB Director Leon E. Panetta to meet those revenue estimates. But Babbitt indicated March 16 that he planned to support a lower royalty level in order to keep the budget resolution on track. "I think you can hear me edging away from 12.5 percent," Babbitt said.

Eventually the administration caved in. Under pressure

from Sen. Max Baucus, D-Mont., and other Western members, the budget that Clinton submitted to Congress in April dropped the proposed 12.5 percent royalty. Clinton promised to push the fee as part of separate legislation. Although the administration never proposed a separate bill, Babbitt voiced support of Bumpers' bill and of the House measure.

Costly Cleanup

Cleaning up abandoned hard-rock mines was estimated to cost as much as $71.5 billion, according to a study released July 20 by the Mineral Policy Center, a conservation group based in Washington. The report expanded the debate on revising the 1872 Mining Law to include environmental as well as economic concerns.

Lawmakers who had tried for years to change the mining law praised the report's findings immediately. But the mining industry and one of its chief Senate supporters, Republican Craig of Idaho, denounced the report's findings as flawed and baseless.

According to the report, the vast majority of the nation's nearly 558,000 abandoned mines posed little or no public health or environmental threat. However, 52 mines, all on the national "superfund" priority list, represented a serious public health threat. Each of these sites, such as the Summitville mine in Colorado, threatened to cost as much as $350 million to repair, the study said.

The report was based on information provided by the Environmental Protection Agency (EPA), the General Accounting Office, the Interior Department's inspector general and on-site interviews by the policy center.

Environmentalists said they viewed House votes on mining royalties during the 102nd Congress as a favorable indicator for mining law overhaul. That year, lawmakers killed an attempt by Barbara F. Vucanovich, R-Nev., to get rid of mining royalties altogether, though opponents also fought off an attempt by Peter A. DeFazio, D-Ore., to impose a 12.5 percent royalty. (1992 Almanac, p. 114-H)

SENATE ACTION

Senate committee debate on the issue began the week of March 15 when the Energy and Natural Resources Subcommittee on Mineral Resources held its first hearing on Bumpers' tough mining overhaul bill (S 257).

Bumpers said the 1872 Mining Law amounted to a valuable giveaway of public land. Since 1989, his effort to change the law had run up against the political clout of Western senators whose states were heavily dependent on the mining industry. "Time is running out," Bumpers said at a March 16 hearing packed with mining industry representatives. "The president and secretary [of the Interior] favor reform, the American people favor reform."

As introduced by Bumpers, S 257 barred miners from patenting or converting federal land to private property and required them to rent the lands. Like the House bill, it also required miners to pay an 8 percent royalty on the gross value of their mineral sales and restored the environment to its original condition.

Babbitt expressed support for the Bumpers bill. Repeating what he told a House Natural Resources subcommittee March 12, Babbitt told the Senate panel four days later that taxpayers should get a fair return for the development of public resources and that mining companies should be forced to adhere to new federal environmental standards. Babbitt said the patent law should be altered so that public lands did not

unnecessarily move into private hands.

The panel chose, however, not to deal with Bumpers' bill in an attempt to avoid a protracted battle in committee and on the Senate floor. Bumpers, a member of the committee, did not object to that strategy.

Senate Committee Action

Instead, the full Energy and Natural Resources Committee on May 6 approved the industry-backed mining bill (S 775 — S Rept 103-45) by voice vote. The bill called for a 2 percent net royalty on hard-rock minerals extracted from federal lands. That meant the government was to receive 2 percent of the mineral's value after subtracting the cost of mining, exploration, development and processing.

Committee Chairman Johnston said the bill represented "a ticket to conference committee." At his urging, the committee reported the measure to the Senate floor with no amendments and little discussion of its substance.

The bill fell far short of mining law reforms supported by the Clinton administration and by Bumpers, who wanted royalties to be based on the mineral's gross value — or how much it was worth when it came out of the ground. Bumpers said net royalty was "unacceptable" because minerals still could be extracted from public lands without the government sharing in the bounty.

In addition to the 2 percent net royalty provision, the Senate bill also required a $25 location fee for each mining claim and a $100 annual fee for maintaining the claim. Miners with 10 or fewer claims had their fees waived.

Two-thirds of the royalties and fees were to be deposited in the federal Treasury and one-third was to go to the state where the minerals were extracted. The bill also required that reclamation work be done according to state law.

The American Mining Congress, the largest industry group, supported the Craig bill and contended that it was the only mining reform bill that did not threaten to significantly decrease jobs. At the time of the markup, a coalition of mining groups stepped up its opposition to the Bumpers bill with a full page ad in The Washington Post on May 4.

An industry-sponsored study released May 3 said that under the Bumpers bill 47,000 jobs and $433 million in federal revenue were to be lost. The Craig bill stood to cost 4,900 jobs and pump $53 million into the government, according to the study, by the accounting firm Coopers & Lybrand and the law firm Morrison & Foerster.

A Bumpers aide said that industry analysis was biased and cited testimony May 4 before a Senate Energy subcommittee, where the Congressional Budget Office said the Bumpers bill promised to generate $164 million in revenue over five years, while the Craig bill created no revenue.

Senate Floor

Less than a month later, the Senate on May 25 quickly passed S 775 by voice vote. While the Senate stalemate may have ended, the issue was far from resolved, however. Senate passage was merely a continuation of Johnston's strategy of speeding the bill to conference. "The Craig bill neither represents a Senate position or a limitation on what we can do in conference," Johnston said.

Interior Secretary Babbitt said in a statement that the Craig bill did not represent "true reform."

HOUSE SUBCOMMITTEE

The summer passed before House lawmakers took any action toward rewriting the much-criticized mining law.

The House Natural Resources Subcommittee on Energy and Mineral Resources approved HR 322 by voice vote Oct. 28. The bill instituted a royalty on hard-rock minerals extracted from federal lands and increased fees paid by miners for their land claims. It also set up an extensive regulatory regime aimed at protecting the environment from mining-related damage.

With the blessing of bill sponsor Rahall, the subcommittee agreed by voice vote to use a substitute bill by panel Chairman Lehman as the markup vehicle. Lehman's bill generally followed the contours of Rahall's measure, but it provided miners more flexibility by easing limits on the types of land that were to be closed to hard-rock mining and by loosening restrictions on mining activities.

The bill was the result of negotiations between the committee's Democratic leaders, key Republicans and Western Democrats, such as Vucanovich and Larry LaRocco, D-Idaho. The goal was to write a bill that imposed royalties, eliminated the fewest mining jobs and still met tough environmental standards. Rahill said the negotiations took six months.

By the time of the markup, Lehman had made enough changes in the bill to win over leery Democrats such as LaRocco and Pat Williams of Montana — both from states with large mining interests.

"Either side can kill this bill," Lehman said. "The hard thing to do is pass it."

Key elements of the bill included:

● **Royalties.** A royalty of 8 percent on miners' gross revenue from selling minerals extracted from federal lands, minus the costs of smelting (a figure known as "net smelter return"). The royalty provision was expected to remain a key point of contention between the House and Senate versions of the legislation.

● **Patents.** Eliminating the controversial practice of giving miners title, or "patent" to public lands for as little as $2.50 per acre. HR 322 maintained federal ownership over these lands, allowing miners only to rent the land through the payment of annual claim fees.

● **Claim fees.** A $25 location fee for each claim. The bill also made permanent a provision in the budget-reconciliation law (PL 103-66) that required miners to pay an annual $100 fee to maintain an existing mining claim, instead of an earlier requirement that miners do at least $100 worth of work each year to keep their claims active. HR 322 imposed an annual $200 fee for new claims, although the bill increased the size of a claim from 20 acres to 40 acres. Small mine operations with 10 claims or less were exempted from the maintenance fees, although they were required to perform $100 worth of assessment work on each claim per year. *(Budget-reconciliation, p. 107)*

● **Reclamation.** Strict standards governing the cleanup of abandoned mines, which were considered an environmental hazard because the toxic remnants of mineral extraction threatened to leach into groundwater supplies.

HR 322 required miners to file detailed operations and reclamation plans with the federal government and to pay for the government's administrative and environmental review costs. The Interior secretary was to establish standards for soils, erosion, hydrologic conditions and surface lands. The new federal standards were similar to measures enacted for the coal industry in the Surface Mining Control and Reclamation Act of 1977.

HR 322 also placed all revenues from royalties and fees into a newly created Abandoned Locatable Minerals Mine Reclamation Fund to be administered by the Interior De-

partment. Proceeds were to be used to repair lands damaged by past mining operations.

In one of the bill's most controversial elements, the Interior secretary was authorized to declare certain lands as "unsuitable" and off-limits for mining, based on potential adverse environmental impacts.

HOUSE COMMITTEE

A week after the subcommittee acted, the Natural Resources Committee on Nov. 3 approved HR 322 (H Rept 103-338) on a party-line vote of 28-14.

Western Republicans, already under pressure from the Clinton administration to end subsidies for ranchers who grazed livestock on federal land, vowed to fight the bill. They said the measure threatened to cripple the domestic mining industry and forced companies to move abroad.

In the end, the bill approved by the full committee came closer to the the goals of environmentalists and those eager to reap revenues from Western land users than did the companion Senate bill.

Westerners' Amendments

During the nearly five-hour committee markup, LaRocco, Vucanovich and other Western lawmakers offered a host of amendments aimed at easing restrictions on miners. Although several technical changes were accepted, Western lawmakers lost their bids to loosen environmental standards and reduce the financial burden on mining companies.

Williams offered an amendment to further ease the financial burden of the bill on small mining companies by halving the $100 annual maintenance fee for any company or individual with as few as 11 claims but no more than 25 claims a year. The amendment was defeated, 18-24.

In an attempt to protect mining companies that might lose money or shut down trying to comply with HR 322, LaRocco offered an amendment to give the Interior secretary authority to waive, suspend or reduce the royalty payment for financially ailing companies. LaRocco eventually withdrew the amendment after Miller and Lehman noted that the royalty provisions stood to change dramatically during House-Senate negotiations.

LaRocco said his amendments were not aimed at gutting the legislation. Rather, he said lawmakers from states such as Nevada, Idaho, Montana and Utah were only trying to cushion the financial blow they considered inevitable under the bill.

Vucanovich, whose state of Nevada was home to some of the nation's largest gold mines, tried to ease reclamation standards in the bill by simply requiring companies to do "the maximum extent practicable" in cleaning up the lands scarred by mining. The amendment was defeated by voice vote.

Williams said Western Democrats were "caught in the middle" between environmentalists and the mining industry. But even before the contentious markup began, ranking Republican Don Young of Alaska lashed out at Williams and LaRocco and other Western Democrats for supporting any move to overhaul the 1872 Mining Law. "I hope each of you Western congressmen goes back home and tells your people you put them out of work," Young said.

HOUSE FLOOR

The House on Nov. 18 passed its mining reform bill by a vote of 316-108, despite strong opposition from Republi-

cans from Western states. *(Vote 577, p. 140-H)*

Only six Democrats voted against the measure, while nine Republicans from Western, Rocky Mountain or Plains states voted for it, including New Mexico's Steven H. Schiff and Joe Skeen, who hailed from a state with large copper mines.

Proponents of the bill said the existing law was grossly outdated and constituted a giveaway of federal lands and mineral rights — mainly to corporations that long ago supplanted the pickax-and-mule settler as the norm in Western mining. They were led during floor debate by Miller, Energy and Mineral Resources Subcommittee Chairman Lehman and Rahall.

Bill opponents were led by a trio of Western Republicans: Vucanovich of Nevada, James V. Hansen of Utah and Craig Thomas of Wyoming.

They argued that the royalties, fees and regulatory costs that were to result from the bill promised to render many mining operations unprofitable and force them to close. The provisions of HR 322 "will bring about an end to jobs and destroy a viable U.S. industry," Hansen said. "This entire debate on the 1872 law is simply another follow-up on the Babbitt-Clinton assault of the West," said Thomas.

But such arguments swayed few votes in the House. The bill received key support from several Democrats from Western mining districts. Williams of Montana, LaRocco of Idaho and Karan English of Arizona said in floor speeches that they had serious reservations about some provisions in the bill but viewed it as a reasonably balanced vehicle to take to conference with the Senate.

Despite the opponents' charges of draconian fees and overregulation, many Republicans were not interested in being identified with the existing law. Among the 70 Republicans voting for the bill were Minority Whip Newt Gingrich of Georgia and veteran "pork buster" Harris W. Fawell of Illinois.

Floor Amendments

In debate that began Nov. 16, bill opponents questioned whether miners would be able to meet the bill's requirement that they restore their parcels to the uses they were capable of supporting prior to the mining. A Vucanovich amendment to add the phrase "to the maximum extent practicable" to this provision was defeated on a 149-278 vote. *(Vote 570, p. 140-H)*

But Lehman, who described the bill as "very finely balanced" between the goals of protecting the land and preserving a viable mining industry, also beat back an attempt by DeFazio to allow the Interior secretary to declare lands unsuitable for mining if "significant" damage occurred (the bill specified "significant, permanent and irreparable" damage). Lehman said DeFazio's amendment threatened to "lock up far more land than is necessary." It was defeated, 199-232. *(Vote 569, p. 140-H)*

The House did accept, by voice vote, an en bloc amendment by Lehman that required the Interior Department to consult with the EPA before issuing a mine operating permit and confirmed the EPA's continued authority to apply to miners a variety of existing environmental laws.

The House also accepted by voice vote an amendment by Skeen to require that once there was a judicial ruling that the federal government had taken control of private property as a result of the legislation, the owner be reimbursed from the Abandoned Locatable Minerals Mine Reclamation Fund, and not by the Justice Department. The change allowed for a more rapid settlement.

Also approved was an amendment by James A.

Subsurface Mining Rights Law Amended

The Senate on April 1 cleared by voice vote a bill to keep federal rangelands from being mined without the approval of ranchers. The 102nd Congress had failed to pass similar legislation.

The bill (HR 239) amended the 1916 Stock Raising Homestead Act to ease tensions between miners and ranchers that had developed over the years after mining operators disturbed farming and ranching operations in exercising their rights to subsurface minerals.

The bill required mining companies eyeing or holding subsurface mineral rights to notify ranchers and farmers who used the same land of their intention to prospect the area. Miners also were required to take additional steps before developing such mining claims when ranchers and farmers opposed the mining or mineral exploration.

President Clinton signed the bill into law April 16 (PL 103-23).

Background

Under the 1916 Stock Raising Homestead Act, subsurface minerals such as gold and silver remained federal property, subject to claim, even after ranchers obtained title to the surface lands. The surface rights to 68 million acres of Western lands were transferred to private hands under the 77-year-old law.

But the law gave miners precedence over ranching and farming operations, and throughout the years this had sparked tensions.

HR 239 required miners to notify ranchers of their intent to prospect on such lands. In the event a miner decided to develop and mine a claim, he first had to seek permission of the surface owner. If permission was denied, an operator had to submit to the Interior Department a plan aimed at minimizing disruption of grazing and farming operations.

The bill also required mining companies to restore the land to approximately its original condition and pay a fee to the surface owner for damage or any income lost due to the mining or mineral exploration.

Similar legislation was defeated under expedited floor procedures in July 1992; it later passed under regular floor rules in September 1992. A compromise was then reached late in the session, but supporters were unable to clear the bill before the 102nd Congress adjourned. *(1992 Almanac, p. 293)*

Committee Action

The Senate Energy and Natural Resources Committee approved its version of the bill (S 336 — S Rept 103-21) by a 20-0 vote March 3. No amendments were offered.

A day later, the House Natural Resources Subcommittee on Energy and Natural Resources approved HR 239 by voice vote after incorporating a bloc of technical amendments. The legislation required miners with federal mineral rights to notify the ranchers who held the surface rights at least 30 days in advance that they planned to prospect for minerals. The bill encouraged miners to get ranchers' consent before prospecting and established an approval procedure to broker disputes.

The full Natural Resources Committee approved the bill March 17 (H Rept 103-44).

The scope of HR 239 was limited to "locatable minerals," such as gold, silver and copper. The federal government had discretionary authority over the availability of other minerals.

Both cattle raisers and the mining industry supported the bill. "Neither the surface owners nor mining interest groups get everything they seek," said Barbara F. Vucanovich, R-Nev.

FLOOR ACTION

The House on March 30 passed HR 239 on a vote of 421-1 under suspension of the rules, an expedited procedure that required a two-thirds majority. *(Vote 118, p. 30-H)*

The vote came a day after a brief House debate on the bill. Bill sponsor Richard H. Lehman, D-Calif., said the measure struck a balance between the rights of surface owners and those interested in underlying minerals by setting a procedure for gaining access to and undertaking mining activities on lands used to graze livestock.

Vucanovich praised the legislation, calling it the "unadulterated product of the fruitful negotiations" at the end of 1992. She also said the key to her support was that the bill did not foreclose the federal government from developing minerals deposits under public lands.

With no debate, the Senate on April 1 cleared HR 239 by voice vote and then indefinitely postponed action on its companion bill (S 336).

Traficant Jr., D-Ohio, requiring that any equipment or products purchased under HR 322 be American-made and that the Interior secretary report to Congress on the percentage of each mining claim held by a foreign company.

The House defeated, on a 193-238 vote, an amendment by Hansen to authorize the Defense secretary to waive all requirements under the bill to ensure a sufficient supply of critical and strategic minerals. *(Vote 571, p. 140-H)*

The House also defeated, 183-250, an amendment by Williams to waive administrative and environmental review fees for a miner with a claim of fewer than 10 acres. Williams said the proposal was to benefit only small entrepreneurial mine operations. But Miller argued that it provided a blanket waiver without any consideration of a miner's ability to pay. *(Vote 568, p. 138-H)*

At the end of the debate, opponents of HR 322 fell back on the jobs argument, citing findings by the Interior Department and a pair of independent accounting firms that the bill threatened to cost jobs. Michael D. Crapo, R-Idaho, offered a motion to recommit the bill to the Natural Resources Committee with instructions to develop royalty schemes that resulted in no net loss of jobs.

However, Lehman responded with a Congressional Budget Office study that projected a net job gain if the bill was enacted. The motion to recommit was defeated, 148-270. *(Vote 576, p. 140-H)*

■

Action Delayed on Elevating EPA's Status

Legislation to elevate the Environmental Protection Agency (EPA) to Cabinet-level status passed in the Senate but stalled after committee action in the House.

The Senate version (S 171) approved May 4 made a number of changes in EPA programs, such as abolishing the White House Council on Environmental Quality and transferring its responsibilities for compiling environmental statistics to a bureau within the department.

A companion House bill (HR 3425) won approval from the House Government Operations Committee on Nov. 4. House members later pulled the measure from the floor schedule after bill opponent William F. Clinger, R-Pa., was hospitalized at the end of the session and could not attend the debate. That ended action on the bill for the year.

BACKGROUND

Cabinet status for the EPA had enjoyed bipartisan congressional support for several years. President George Bush favored the change as a way to give the United States greater clout with foreign countries during negotiations about environmental problems.

But lawmakers had used the widespread appeal of the bill to try to reinvent the agency through a vast array of provisions that went beyond granting the EPA a formal seat at the Cabinet table.

The Senate passed a bill in 1991 that had Bush's support, but the House did not act on the measure. In 1990, the House passed an EPA Cabinet bill, but the measure died when Bush and Congress could not agree on how much power the agency should wield. *(1991 Almanac, p. 221; 1990 Almanac, p. 291)*

Clinton made elevating the EPA to Cabinet level a top legislative priority when he nominated Carol M. Browner, a former aide to Vice President Al Gore and a former director of the Florida environmental agency, to the post of EPA administrator. Browner said the bill would ensure that environmental concerns were at the center, not the margins, of all policy decisions.

Bill supporters also said that a federal Department of the Environment would increase compliance with environmental laws already on the books and heighten the clout of federal environmental officials.

But while many Republicans supported elevating the status of the EPA, they opposed any language that would add new offices or mandates to the department.

Much of the debate on the measure centered on a proposal to move the Council on Environmental Quality, a White House agency charged with reviewing federal compliance with environmental statutes and publishing an annual study on environmental trends, to the new department.

The council had long ensured compliance with laws such as

BOXSCORE

➡ **Department of the Environment (S 171, HR 3425).** The bills would have elevated the Environmental Protection Agency (EPA) to Cabinet-level status. The Senate bill made a number of changes in EPA programs.

Reports: S Rept 103-38, S Rept 103-39, H Rept 103-355.

KEY ACTION

March 24 — **Senate** Governmental Affairs Committee approved S 171 by voice vote.

April 2 — **Senate** Environment and Public Works Committee approved provisions by voice vote.

May 4 — **Senate** approved S 171, 79-15.

Nov. 4 — **House** Government Operations Committee approved HR 3425, 31-11.

Nov. 17 — **House** Rules Committee approved restrictive rule.

the 1969 National Environmental Policy Act (PL 91-190), which required federal agencies to conduct environmental impact studies before launching projects. Clinton set the stage for the debate Feb. 8 when he proposed transferring the council's functions to the Department of the Environment. He also called for establishing a smaller White House Office of Environmental Policy to advise the president on environmental issues.

Eleven leading environmental groups, including the Sierra Club and the Natural Resources Defense Council, complained in a March 3 letter to Clinton that shifting the council's duties to the new department threatened to weaken the administration's ability to effectively enforce environmental initiatives.

SENATE COMMITTEE ACTION

The Senate Governmental Affairs Committee on March 24 approved by voice vote a bill (S 171 — S Rept 103-38) to transform the EPA into the Department of the Environment, making it the 15th Cabinet department.

Bill sponsor and committee Chairman John Glenn, D-Ohio, had long advocated elevating the agency to increase its clout and its standing in international environmental negotiations.

The committee-approved bill, which included the controversial provision to abolish the Council on Environmental Quality, gave the president final authority to resolve turf disputes among federal agencies in complying with environmental requirements — a duty that had been carried out by the council.

Environmental groups contended that effective government-wide coordination could be carried out only by the White House. But Glenn defended the provision and dismissed claims that the language would attract additional, and perhaps crippling, amendments.

The bill also established a Bureau of Environmental Statistics in the new department to compile and publish statistical data on the environment.

The committee also cut the two-year authorization from about $15 million to $5 million. The bulk of the reduction came after lawmakers said there was no need to provide funding for the new statistics bureau established by the bill.

The committee defeated a substitute amendment offered by ranking Republican William V. Roth Jr. of Delaware, which would have simply elevated the agency without according it any new duties. The amendment was rejected, 8-5.

Environment Committee

On April 2, the Senate Environment and Public Works Committee gave voice vote approval to the provisions of the bill that were under its jurisdiction, namely those abol-

ishing the White House Council on Environmental Quality (S Rept 103-39).

SENATE FLOOR ACTION

After several days of debate and a handful of amendments, the Senate approved S 171 by a vote of 79-15 on May 4. *(Vote 114, p. 16-S)*

In addition to eliminating the Council on Environmental Quality, the Senate bill also designated one assistant secretary to oversee environmental concerns on Indian lands, created an ombudsman for small business and local government concerns, and created an Office of Environmental Justice to document the extent of environmental problems in poor and minority neighborhoods.

Although some senators grumbled about the Cabinet's size, both Republicans and Democrats generally agreed that a department was necessary to give the EPA more clout, especially in international negotiations. Bob Kerrey, D-Neb., was the lone Democrat to vote against the bill, saying he supported protecting the environment but not enlarging the government.

The Senate began its debate on the $5 million bill on April 22. Bill sponsor Glenn said a new department would help establish a more coherent set of environmental policies for the government. Authority for environmental regulation had been scattered throughout most government departments. But Glenn disputed Republican assertions that the bill was designed to take away powers from the Interior Department or other departments.

Amendments Debated

On April 27, Senators voted 54-42 to table, or kill, a Roth substitute amendment after Democrats argued that Roth's pared-down version would not go far enough in addressing concerns about EPA management and organization. *(Vote 106, p. 15-S)*

Roth's substitute would have retained the Council on Environmental Quality. He said the provision to eliminate the council, along with provisions establishing the advisory commission and requiring annual reports, would open the door for other amendments that would detract from the main objective of creating a Cabinet-level department.

The Senate also voted 70-26 to table an amendment by Orrin G. Hatch, R-Utah, that would have required the new department to offset any "reasonably anticipated costs" of regulations. *(Vote 112, p. 15-S)*

A much closer, 50-48 vote to table came on a proposal by Don Nickles, R-Okla., to require an accounting of dollars spent and jobs lost on all legislation being considered by Congress or regulations imposed by federal agencies. Although Nickles said his amendment would exempt legislation and regulations that affected less than $100 million or 10,000 jobs, Democrats said that additional reports would cause unnecessary and costly delays. *(Vote 109, p. 15-S)*

The Senate also approved an amendment by Paul Wellstone, D-Minn., to create an "environmental justice" office in the new department to document the extent of problems in poor neighborhoods that might be disproportionately affected by toxic waste sites, pollution and other environmental hazards.

Completing Senate Action

On April 29, Majority Leader George J. Mitchell, D-Maine, reached an agreement with Republicans that limited further debate. The agreement eliminated a major threat to the bill — a proposed amendment by Minority Leader Bob Dole, R-Kan., that would have required the government to compensate private property owners for land taken from them through new land-use regulations.

A similar proposal by then-Sen. Steve Symms, R-Idaho, won Senate approval in the 102nd Congress, but it contributed to the EPA bill's demise in the House, which never voted on the legislation. *(1991 Almanac, p. 222)*

Before final passage, the Senate approved a watered-down version of an amendment by Christopher S. Bond, R-Mo., who wanted to designate the Agriculture Department's Soil Conservation Service as the sole agency responsible for determining whether protectable wetlands existed on agricultural land.

Democrats argued against the Bond amendment and cited a letter from EPA Administrator Browner, who said it would make wetlands designations even more complicated and costly. John H. Chafee, R-R.I., also spoke against the amendment.

Max Baucus, D-Mont., chairman of the Environment and Public Works Committee, superseded Bond's proposal with a substitute directing the president to merely recommend to Congress within 90 days how to streamline the wetlands designation process under a single agency. Bond's effort to kill Baucus' substitute failed, 40-54, on a tabling motion. The Senate subsequently approved the modified Bond amendment by voice vote. *(Vote 113, p. 16-S)*

HOUSE ACTION

After the Senate passed its bill, key House members signaled that the EPA Cabinet legislation faced an uphill battle in that chamber, where lawmakers wanted to use the legislation to strengthen the agency's civil rights protections and management structure — and even to try to correct abuses by contractors throughout the government.

John Conyers Jr., D-Mich., chairman of the House Government Operations Committee, was interested in adding language to refocus EPA's attention on what he said was the disproportionate number of environmental problems in minority and poor communities.

Conyers also said he wanted to substantially change EPA management, including limiting the use of outside contractors, more effectively linking the agency's computerized information systems and ensuring that EPA fairly enforced environmental laws in poor communities.

Proponents of EPA elevation who thought the House version of the bill might sail through to final passage were also sobered by criticism from John D. Dingell, D-Mich., chairman of the House Energy and Commerce Committee, as well as from leading environmentalists, such as Henry A. Waxman, D-Calif., chairman of the House Energy Subcommittee on Health and the Environment.

Dingell insisted that the bill include provisions that ensured accurate environmental data from the new department and a cleanup of abuses by contractors.

Waxman criticized provisions in the Senate version that required health and environment risk assessments of all government regulations. He believed such exercises undermined existing health and environment laws.

On the other side of the aisle, Clinger of Pennsylvania, the ranking Republican on the Government Operations Committee, argued for a substitute that would do nothing more than designate the EPA as a full department of the government.

Committee Action

House Democrats finally reached agreement the week of Nov. 1 to move the legislation forward. But lawmakers had

to abandon desires to overhaul the agency and broadly rewrite environmental policy.

The House Government Operations Committee on Nov. 4 voted 31-11 to approve a bill (HR 3425 — H Rept 103-355) that did little more than designate the EPA as a Cabinet-level department and correct some management problems.

The only additions were provisions to overhaul the agency's contracting procedures, create a Bureau of Environmental Statistics to coordinate far-flung data collection functions and create an Office of Environmental Justice to advise the new secretary on ways to reduce the impact of environmental laws on minorities.

During the markup, Republicans tried to broaden the new department's authority to make it more responsive to the financial concerns of state and local governments that had to carry out expensive federal environmental mandates. But Conyers, Waxman and Mike Synar, D-Okla., fought them by employing a procedural tactic that prohibited any amendments on a bill from going beyond the measure's original scope.

The committee, however, approved by voice vote an amendment by Dick Zimmer, R-N.J., to create an Office of Environmental Risk, which would merely advise the new secretary and not mandate new regulations. Conyers, Waxman and Synar said they needed more time to review the amendment before deciding whether the risk office would create new powers for the department.

An amendment by John L. Mica, R-Fla., that would have delayed creation of the new department for one year also was defeated by voice vote. Mica, a frequent EPA critic, sought the postponement until Clinton could certify that Browner had overhauled the agency's contracting and management policies.

On a voice vote, the committee rejected a substitute bill by Clinger that simply would have elevated the agency to Cabinet status.

Under a tentative agreement among the Clinton administration, Conyers and two other House committee chairmen, the panel delayed action on the proposal to abolish the Council on Environmental Quality and transfer its responsibilities to the new Cabinet-level department.

The agreement, reached with Merchant Marine and Fisheries Committee Chairman Gerry E. Studds, D-Mass., and Energy and Commerce Chairman Dingell, called for the Clinton administration to keep a smaller version of the council in the White House.

Studds, a leading House environmentalist whose committee had jurisdiction over the council and the environmental policy law, and Dingell, who was a prime sponsor of the environmental policy law in 1969, were two of council's main protectors. Both lawmakers withheld support for the EPA Cabinet bill until the issue was resolved. Even then, Dingell did not include himself as a co-sponsor of the compromise bill as rewritten by Conyers.

House Floor

The House Rules Committee cleared a legislative path for the bill Nov. 17, only to see further action blocked. The Rules panel barred 18 of 27 amendments, declaring them beyond the bill's scope of providing the Cabinet-level department with a new organizational structure.

The Rules Committee rejected two amendments favored by Republicans and conservative Democrats to require the new department to examine the costs and benefits of new environmental regulations — a potentially costly and time-consuming requirement.

The committee also barred an amendment favored by

the Clinton administration to resolve the fate of the Council on Environmental Quality, and left bill proponents looking beyond House action to a House-Senate conference committee to resolve the issue.

When Clinger, the ranking Republican on Government Operations and the point man for the opposition, suffered a detached retina and could not attend the debate, the House took no further action on the bill before adjourning.

Separate Bill on White House Council

Studds crafted a separate bill (HR 3512) incorporating the Council on Environmental Quality compromise and pushed it through his Merchant Marine Committee on Nov. 18. The measure won House voice vote approval Nov. 20.

Studds' bill authorized $4.7 million over four years for the White House compliance office and authorized a staff of seven professionals. ■

Environmental Research

The House on Nov. 20 passed by voice vote a bill (HR 1994) that reauthorized the Environmental Protection Agency (EPA) research and development programs. The Senate failed to act on the bill or a companion measure (S 1545) by Sen. Harry Reid, D-Nev., before Congress adjourned in November.

The House bill authorized $475.4 million in fiscal 1994 for programs at the agency's Office of Research and Development. The bill was intended to improve the quantity and quality of the EPA's scientific research projects.

The Office of Research and Development had been operating without an authorization since 1982, but it had continued to receive annual appropriations. The office employed about 1,900 people and administered 17 laboratories nationwide.

The measure required the EPA administrator to support research programs that ensured that the agency's environmental regulations were based on sound science. For example, bill supporter Tom Lewis, R-Fla., said during floor debate Nov. 20 that the EPA had determined after spending billions of dollars that a $20 billion program to remove asbestos from public buildings created more health risk from asbestos dust than was caused by leaving the material in place. Lewis said more rigorous scientific risk assessment promised to avoid such policy decisions.

Legislative Action

The House Science, Space and Technology Committee approved HR 1994 (H Rept 103-376) on June 30 by voice vote. Under the bill, the agency's research and development office was directed to focus on the areas of ecological, health and risk-reduction research.

The EPA administrator was directed to establish a program to develop new technologies for detecting and removing lead found in soil, water and paint.

The committee defeated, 16-16, an amendment by Rod Grams, R-Minn., to freeze the authorization at the existing funding level of about $418 million.

Months later, the House passed the bill under special expedited procedures after bill supporters worked out largely technical problems with the Energy and Commerce and the Merchant Marine and Fisheries committees.

The bill was referred to the Senate's Environment and Public Works Committee, which took no further action. ■

House Approves Biological Inventory

After lengthy debates on property rights issues, the House passed legislation to authorize an inventory of all plant and animal species in the United States.

The National Biological Survey was a priority of Interior Secretary Bruce Babbitt, who envisioned it as a way of heading off conflicts in the implementation of the 1973 Endangered Species Act (PL 93-205).

The House bill (HR 1845) provided for the creation of an office within the Interior Department to undertake the survey and supply information on all species. The measure also authorized the creation of a policy board to advise the survey's director and a science council to work with other governmental agencies and private groups.

But the bill encountered strong opposition from conservatives who argued that it would inspire regulatory decisions that would trample the rights of private property owners. House conservatives won a key amendment requiring that the federal government obtain written permission before entering private property. The same language ended up in the fiscal 1994 Interior appropriations bill (HR 2520 — PL 103-138) at the behest of House Republican conferees. The spending bill, signed into law Nov. 11, provided $163.5 million for the survey. *(Appropriations, p. 618)*

A companion Senate authorization bill (S 1008), introduced by Environment and Public Works Chairman Max Baucus, D-Mont., was not marked up, and the Senate took no action on the House-passed bill.

BACKGROUND

President Clinton formally announced plans for the National Biological Survey during an address on Earth Day, April 22. The idea was to pull together far-flung biological research within the Interior Department and related agencies for the purpose of counting and monitoring every species of plant and animal in the nation.

Interior Secretary Bruce Babbitt hoped the project would allow the government to anticipate and head off endangered species disputes, such as the protracted battle in the Pacific Northwest, where efforts to protect the threatened northern spotted owl had collided with the needs of the timber industry. By taking inventory of the nation's biological resources, he said, the government would have a better chance of preventing a species from becoming endangered. "I would hope 10 years from now the Endangered Species Act is virtually forgotten ... that there is so little controversy that it just sits there, and there aren't any endangered species anymore," Babbitt said.

Babbitt had the administrative authority to conduct the survey, but he wanted to make it permanent and sought help from some of Congress' key environmentalists to pass authorizing legislation.

At a joint hearing of House Merchant Marine and

BOXSCORE

➡ **National Biological Survey (HR 1845).** The bill was to authorize a survey of all the plant and animal species in the United States.

Reports: H Rept 103-193, Pts 1, 2.

KEY ACTION

July 27 — **House** Merchant Marine and Fisheries Committee approved by voice vote.

July 28 — **House** Natural Resources Committee approved by voice vote.

Oct. 26 — **House** passed HR 1845, 255-165.

House Natural Resources subcommittees on July 15, Babbitt criticized the government for being passive in endangered species controversies, often leaving it up to federal judges to be the final arbiters of scientific issues.

Supporters said the survey would act as a good warning system, because disputes such as the one over the spotted owl might not surface until a species was on the brink of extinction and there were few options to try to save it.

But some critics feared that in practice, the survey would create even more endangered species controversies. During the July 15 hearing, some Republicans said they envisioned the new Interior division evolving into a regulatory agency that would make decisions on controversial issues such as wetlands policy.

Babbitt said researchers would not enter private property unless ordered by a judge, and he emphasized that the survey would stick to science — not regulation.

As of June 1992, 1,245 species of plants and animals had been listed as endangered or threatened. The government had been under court order to list another 450 species in four years.

Implementation of the survey involved the reorganization of research functions that existed principally in the U.S. Fish and Wildlife Service, National Park Service and the Bureau of Land Management. The survey was also to include researchers from the Bureau of Reclamation, the Minerals Management Service, the Office of Surface Mining, the Geological Survey and the Bureau of Mines.

The Interior Department estimated that about 1,400 scientists — 1,700 workers altogether — would be transferred into the new Interior division. The survey's director would be appointed by the president and confirmed by the Senate.

HOUSE COMMITTEE ACTION

After contentious debate, the Environment and Natural Resources Subcommittee of the House Merchant Marine and Fisheries Committee approved the measure by voice vote July 22.

The full Merchant Marine Committee approved the bill by voice vote July 27 (H Rept 103-193, Part 1).

Opposition came from some Republicans and conservative Democrats who argued that the bill did not go far enough in protecting individual property rights or directing the survey to study the conflicts between biological resources and humans. Subcommittee chairman and bill sponsor Gerry E. Studds, D-Mass., responded that the concerns were not germane to establishing the survey, which would only conduct scientific research.

To allay some concerns, the full committee gave voice vote approval to a compromise amendment by Charles H. Taylor, R-N.C., requiring government officials working on

the survey to get written consent to enter private property and requiring them to divulge information gathered on that property if the landowner requested it.

Bill opponent W. J. "Billy" Tauzin, D-La., offered two amendments during the Merchant Marine Committee markup that were struck on the grounds that they were not germane to the bill. One would have explicitly stated that HR 1845 would not authorize any action that resulted in the "taking" of private property; another would have guaranteed compensation through the Land and Water Conservation Fund, the nation's primary land purchase account, for property owners who lost 50 percent or more of the value of their land.

The next day, July 28, the Natural Resources Committee followed suit by giving voice vote approval to its version of the bill (HR 103-193, Part 2). The committee's bill — written by Bruce F. Vento, D-Minn., chairman of the National Parks, Forests and Public Lands Subcommittee — left out the Taylor language. Instead, a Vento amendment stating that survey employees would comply with federal and state laws "including laws relating to private property rights" was approved 32-0.

Panel member Richard W. Pombo, R-Calif., tried to include the Taylor amendment but was defeated by a 17-26 vote. Vento suggested that Pombo was trying to rewrite the trespass laws of all 50 states.

The committee also had a lengthy debate about the validity of the scientific information to be gathered by the survey. Cal Dooley, D-Calif., wanted to require three "independent referees" to review the data, but some members said that could lead to more lawsuits. A proposal by Vento to allow the survey's director to set up "appropriate peer review" was approved 22-20.

HOUSE FLOOR ACTION

After two days of debate, the House approved the National Biological Survey legislation Oct. 26. The measure passed by a vote of 255-165 after supporters had only partial success in fighting off amendments aimed at watering down the legislation. *(Vote 530, p. 130-H)*

When the bill first came to the House floor Oct. 6, members argued about it for six hours. Studds and Natural Resources Committee Chairman George Miller, D-Calif., were on the losing end of votes on two amendments backed by conservatives who said the survey would cause landowners to be blocked from using their land as they wished.

The first vote was on whether to include Taylor's language requiring that survey workers obtain written permission from landowners before entering private property. The House adopted the amendment by 309-115. *(Vote 485, p. 118-H)*

On a closer 217-212 vote, the House adopted a Tauzin amendment barring the survey from enlisting the support of volunteers to help collect information. Tauzin argued that untrained or overly pro-environment volunteers would produce tainted data. *(Vote 484, p. 118-H)*

While the Taylor and Tauzin amendments did not cripple the bill, they served as significant portents for more ambitious environmental bills, such as rewrites of the Endangered Species Act and the clean water act.

The Oct. 26 debate was a continuation of the earlier disagreements, with bill supporters trying to fight off opponents' attempts to brand the bill an infringement of private property rights.

Studds managed to deflect two other weakening

amendments on the grounds that the provisions were not germane because they strayed outside the purview of the biological survey.

One, by Tauzin, would have prohibited the government from taking private property without compensation. It also would have compensated owners of private property that had been devalued by environmental restrictions and ensured that the federal government gave top priority to buying such lands.

The second, also by Tauzin, would have authorized the director of the National Biological Survey to consider the impact of the work on citizens, private property, employment and state and local government revenues. The move was an attempt to ensure that the government would weigh the economic effects of protecting plants and animals along with any environmental benefit before imposing restrictions on regions.

One Tauzin amendment that did win voice vote approval prohibited other federal agencies from using information collected under the survey pertaining to private land unless the landowner had access to the information, a detailed description of the manner in which it was collected and an opportunity to dispute its accuracy. ∎

No Big Fix Found for Logging Standoff

Although timber harvests in the Pacific Northwest had come to a virtual standstill because of a legal dispute over how to protect the threatened northern spotted owl and its old-growth forest habitat, a specific legislative solution continued to elude lawmakers in 1993. However, Congress did take several steps to boost the area's timber-dependent economy and employment prospects.

President Clinton unveiled his own long-awaited forest management plan on July 1, aimed at ending the stalemate pitting jobs against the environment. Clinton called for a dramatic reduction in timber harvests in the Pacific Northwest forests that were home to the threatened owl. At the same time, he promised to pump $1.2 billion in economic assistance over five years into the timber communities in Oregon, Washington and Northern California. Most of the money was to go to retrain workers and to spur business and forestry-related programs such as repairing watersheds.

Although Northwestern lawmakers were generally unhappy with Clinton's plan, they were not able to agree on an alternative strategy of their own. That left Clinton to carry out his program, much of which could be implemented administratively. The part of Clinton's plan that fell in Congress' purview was the financing. Lawmakers agreed to provide the money and took several other steps in 1993:

• Congress approved a long-term funding mechanism to provide economic development money for the Pacific Northwest as part of the fiscal 1994 budget-reconciliation bill (HR 2264).

• Lawmakers provided $69.5 million for various forestry, wildlife and park programs in the Pacific Northwest in the fiscal 1994 Interior Department spending bill (HR 2520).

• Congress also cleared a bill (HR 2343) by Washington Democrats Sen. Patty Murray and Rep. Jolene Unsoeld to shore up employment in the timber-processing industry by restoring a ban on exporting raw logs from state-owned and

other public lands; the ban had run into trouble in the courts.

● And lawmakers cleared a bill (S 1508) to extend eligibility for economic development assistance to the rural communities that faced economic hardships caused by restrictions on timber harvesting in adjacent national forests.

BACKGROUND

The federal government had been caught in the protracted legal battle over the timber harvests since 1989. The issue became more divisive in 1990 when the spotted owl was declared threatened under the Endangered Species Act. The habitat of the northern spotted owl was in the old-growth forests west of the Cascade Mountains in Washington, Oregon and Northern California. Most old-growth forests were on federal land. An estimated 3,602 pairs of the birds remained in 1993. *(1990 Almanac, p. 296)*

U.S. District Judge William Dwyer of Seattle halted logging on public lands in 1991, ruling that the government was violating environmental laws by overharvesting. The Bush administration convened a high-level committee known as the "God squad," which voted in May 1992 to suspend the Endangered Species Act and allow logging on 13 of 44 disputed tracts of timberland that were home to the spotted owl. Court injunctions prevented the action from taking effect, and Congress in 1992 failed to enact any compromise logging plan. *(1992 Almanac, p. 277)*

Environmental groups, meanwhile, sued the government for violating the laws that protected wildlife.

Fulfilling a campaign pledge to intervene directly in the impasse that had stymied the Bush administration, Clinton hosted a so-called timber summit in Portland, Ore., on April 2. The president called the conference after he and Vice President Al Gore met with the Pacific Northwest congressional delegation and key committee chairmen. Clinton ordered the development of his comprehensive forest management plan following the conference.

CLINTON'S PLAN

Clinton submitted his forest plan to Judge Dwyer as the federal government's environmental impact statement to show how logging could continue without further endangering the owl. The federal court took the plan under review but made no final decision in 1993. However, the Clinton administration and environmental groups reached an agreement Oct. 7 to allow some cutting in the old-growth forests to ease the economic impact on the region's economy pending a final legal resolution of the dispute.

Clinton's proposal called for the annual timber harvest to be reduced to 1.2 billion board feet per year, about half the amount cut before the federal court imposed the logging ban. The region harvested more than 5 billion board feet per year in 1987 and 1988. A board foot was one foot square by one inch thick. A single-family house typically used about 10,000 board feet of lumber.

The plan reserved areas for the spotted owl in which logging was to be greatly restricted. It also set aside 10 areas for ecological experiments and watershed protections. The 10 "adaptive management areas" were to consist of 78,000 to 380,000 acres each for ecological experiments. The plan also called for protecting entire watersheds in an attempt to head off controversies over endangered salmon and other fish species.

To help workers and families in the region, Clinton proposed $270 million in new funding for fiscal 1994 or $1.2

billion over five years for a new Northwest Economic Adjustment Fund. The fund was to support retraining or related logging activities such as cleaning up logging roads and streams.

In releasing his plan, Clinton admitted it was more difficult than he had envisioned to create a fair and balanced approach. But he portrayed his proposal as the only solution that was "scientifically sound, ecologically credible and legally defensible."

The plan was immediately assailed from all sides.

Environmentalists said it did not go far enough to block logging activity or preserve fragile ecosystems. They hinted at filing other lawsuits.

Meanwhile, timber groups contended that the plan threatened the future of their industry, estimating that as many as 85,000 jobs were on the line directly and indirectly. The White House countered that only 6,000 jobs were threatened. Home builders warned that fewer new houses would be built, since less timber would be available.

Timber industry groups also questioned whether Clinton ever intended to live up to his promise to reach a balanced compromise. Black wreaths were sent to the White House by groups representing Oregon workers before the plan was announced. "The Clinton administration has spent 90 days developing a solution to the crisis that will leave us exactly where we were when it began: in court-ordered gridlock," said Mark Rey, a vice president for the American Forest & Paper Association.

Many of the region's lawmakers said the timber-cutting levels in Clinton's plan were too low, but they conceded that there was no agreement within the Pacific Northwest delegation on how to proceed. To increase the logging levels, they would have had to win changes in laws such as the National Forest Management Act and the Endangered Species Act, encountering strong opposition from environmentalists. The administration also warned that it intended to fight any congressional efforts to sidestep federal environmental laws.

RECONCILIATION

Congress agreed in the budget-reconciliation bill (HR 2264 — H Rept 103-213) to set aside 85 percent of the receipts from the sale of timber on federal lands in the Pacific Northwest in fiscal 1994 for economic development in the region. After fiscal 1994, the amount dropped by 3 percent per year until fiscal 2003. The receipts were to be shared by the federal government, the three Northwest states and the affected counties. The provision was included at the insistence of Peter A. DeFazio, D-Ore., whose district included many of the most affected timber communities. Under existing law, the amount set aside for the region from the timber receipts had fluctuated. *(Budget-reconciliation, p. 107)*

To make up for the loss in revenue to the Treasury, the reconciliation bill eliminated an export subsidy credit for foreign sales of unprocessed logs, generating about $390 million in savings annually. Of that amount, $270 million was earmarked for timber communities in the Pacific Northwest; the remainder was to go for deficit reduction. Max Baucus, D-Mont., chairman of the Environment and Public Works Committee, included the proposal in the Senate's version of the reconciliation package, and lawmakers retained it in the final bill.

The House on May 27 passed the reconciliation bill, 219-213. The Senate followed suit June 25, passing the bill 50-49.

The House approved the conference report on the bill Aug. 5 by a vote of 218-216; the Senate cleared the bill the next day on a vote of 51-50. Clinton signed the bill into law (PL 103-66) Aug. 10. *(House votes 199, p. 48-H, and 406, p. 98-H; Senate votes 190, p. 25-S, and 247, p. 32-S)*

INTERIOR APPROPRIATIONS

House appropriator Norm Dicks, D-Wash., helped win $69.5 million in the fiscal 1994 Interior spending bill (HR 2520 — H Rept 103-158) for Pacific Northwest programs. *(Appropriations, p. 618)*

In the Senate, veteran appropriator Mark O. Hatfield, R-Ore., and freshman Murray pressed for the money for the Pacific Northwest (S Rept 103-114). The two helped ensure that the Senate version of the Interior bill also included money to repair damaged watersheds and help replenish dwindling salmon stocks in the region and to provide direct community assistance. But Hatfield and Murray lost a battle to provide financial incentives to U.S. Forest Service employees who wanted to retire early. The retirement provisions were considered important because the Forest Service was expected to lay off more employees as the federal timber harvest program continued to shrink.

The House adopted the conference report (H Rept 103-299) on Oct. 20. The Senate passed it Nov. 9, 91-9, and sent it back to the House, which cleared the bill the same day by voice vote. Clinton on Nov. 11 signed the Interior spending bill into law (PL 103-138). *(House vote 339, p. 82-H; Senate vote 359, p. 46-S)*

EXPORT BAN

The House on June 14 gave voice vote approval to the bill (HR 2343) by Sen. Murray and Rep. Unsoeld to boost employment in the timber-processing industry. The House Foreign Affairs Committee had approved the bill June 10. The Senate cleared the measure by voice vote June 17, and Clinton signed it July 1 (PL 103-45) when he announced his timber plan.

The bill sought to create jobs in the timber industry by restoring an export ban on raw logs from state-owned and other public lands included in the 1990 Customs and Trade Act (PL 101-382).

A provision in the 1990 law that required governors to come up with plans to implement part of the log ban had been struck down by the 9th U.S. Circuit Court of Appeals. The court ruled that the provision was unconstitutional because it required states to regulate trade, a power that the Constitution delegated to Congress.

HR 2343 circumvented the problem by making the Commerce secretary responsible for implementing regulations, though states could voluntarily submit their own plans. Bill sponsor Unsoeld said June 14 that before the original law was passed, raw log exports from the United States were booming. She said that it made no sense to export unprocessed timber when there was a shortage of logs for mills in the Northwest — a situation that had caused job loss in the industry.

COMMUNITY ASSISTANCE

The House on Oct. 6 cleared legislation (S 1508) amending the 1990 farm bill to provide economic development assistance and diversification programs for communities in the region that were economically dependent on tim-

ber from national forests. The bill clarified that unincorporated areas — as well as the towns, townships and municipalities specifically provided for in the 1990 bill — were eligible for the aid, which was administered by the U.S. Forest Service. The Senate passed the measure by voice vote Sept. 30. Clinton signed it Oct. 26 (PL 103-115).

S 1508 changed a statutory standard to provide that residents in "any county that is not contained within a Metropolitan Statistical Area" was eligible for the development aid. Previously, only counties with fewer than 22,550 residents were eligible for the aid. Supporters of the change said that whole counties were unfairly excluded from the program because of the presence of a single small city.

The bill also made nonprofit corporations and institutions that were organized to promote economic development eligible for the aid, along with government agencies. ∎

House BLM Renewal Bill Sidesteps Controversy

The House on Sept. 13 approved a two-year renewal for programs under the Interior Department's Bureau of Land Management (BLM), but the Senate failed to take up the measure in the first session.

The bill (HR 2530) reauthorized the agency's activities but remained silent on a trio of controversial issues targeted in earlier versions of the bill — grazing fees, timber clear-cutting in the Pacific Northwest and access for aircraft over federal parks.

Although the BLM authorization had expired at the end of fiscal 1982, the land agency had continued to receive funding through annual appropriations bills. But on July 14, the House stripped funding for the agency from its version of the fiscal 1994 Interior appropriations bill (HR 2520) after lawmakers objected that the agency was not authorized. That move added to House momentum to pass the BLM reauthorization bill.

As the nation's chief landlord, the Bureau of Land Management received $1 billion a year to oversee about 270 million acres of federal land, mostly in the West. The bureau's vast terrain covered about 13 percent of the United States. The bureau also leased more than 300 million acres that contained a wealth of hard-rock minerals, such as gold and silver, beneath their surface. About 4.3 million head of cattle grazed on bureau lands, and timber was harvested from 4 million acres of its forests. The lands also were home to more than 50,000 wild horses and burros. Bureau-managed lands included recreation spots that drew an estimated 71 million visitors annually.

The House had passed bills reauthorizing BLM during the previous two Congresses, but the Senate failed to act on the legislation. *(1989 Almanac, p. 688; 1992 Almanac, p. 294)*

HOUSE COMMITTEE ACTION

The House Natural Resources Committee approved HR 2530 by voice vote June 30 (H Rept 103-171). The bill authorized "such sums as may be necessary" for the bureau for two years and was free of virtually all controversial provisions, including language on grazing fees. *(Grazing fees, p. 273)*

A Yearlong Struggle Over Grazing Fees

Critics had long contended that federal grazing fees amounted to a subsidy for 27,000 Western ranchers — dubbed the "welfare cowboys" by Rep. Mike Synar, D-Okla. Environmentalists warned that years of grazing had damaged once-verdant ranges and grasslands.

President Clinton vowed early in 1993 that he would charge Western ranchers more money for grazing their livestock on federal lands. But Clinton pulled back in March after Western senators complained that higher grazing fees would drive ranchers out of business. Since congressional approval was not needed to implement higher grazing fees, Clinton instead vowed to pursue grazing policy changes by executive order.

Interior Secretary Bruce Babbitt on Aug. 9 announced administrative steps to impose higher grazing fees and tough environmental standards for the management of the federal rangeland. He said grazing fees would increase to $4.28 over three years from $1.86 per animal unit month — the amount of forage needed for one cow and calf, five sheep or one horse. That was still lower than rates charged on private lands, which often topped $10 per animal unit month. The Bureau of Land Management (BLM) was to retain the rights to water, even after ranchers built water facilities on public lands, making its policy consistent with U.S. Forest Service standards. Babbitt also proposed levying steep fees to discourage subletting of grazing permits and tying the duration of a grazing permit to a rancher's environmental stewardship.

House Renews Support for Higher Fees

Even before Babbitt's announcement in August, the House tried to reassert its longstanding position on higher grazing fees. Synar and Ralph Regula, R-Ohio, introduced a bill (HR 643) to change the formula from which grazing fees were calculated. The bill, which was never acted on, eventually would have increased grazing fees to more than $5 a month. Synar and Regula had planned to offer the same language as an amendment to a bill (HR 2530) reauthorizing the BLM, but they held off after Babbitt's announcement. The House passed the BLM reauthorization bill Sept. 13 under special expedited procedures. The Senate never acted on it. *(BLM reauthorization, p. 272)*

Regula also won an amendment to the fiscal 1994 Interior appropriations bill during House subcommittee markup June 15 that would have increased grazing fees 33 percent. However, the amendment was killed on the House floor July 14 in a procedural move.

The only House vote on grazing came Oct. 20 when lawmakers accepted, 317-106, a compromise included by House and Senate negotiators in the final version of the Interior spending bill (HR 2520 — H Rept 103-299). The compromise was negotiated by Synar, House Natural Resources Committee Chairman George Miller, D-Calif., Rep. Bruce F. Vento, D-Minn., and Sen. Harry Reid, D-Nev. *(Vote 525, p. 128-H; appropriations, p. 618)*

Efforts to raise grazing fees had prevailed in the House by overwhelming margins in the past, only to be blocked by strong opposition from Westerners in the Senate. In July 1991, the House passed a BLM authorization bill that would have increased the fees to $8.70 per animal each month. The Senate did not act on the measure. Smaller grazing fee increases had regularly been included in the House versions of the annual Interior appropriations bill but had been stripped out in conference. *(1991 Almanac, p. 214)*

Senate Avoids Increase

The Senate on Sept. 14 defined its opposition to grazing policy overhaul, voting 59-40 for an amendment by Pete V. Domenici, R-N.M., to the Interior appropriations bill that would have barred Babbitt from spending any money to implement his grazing proposals for one year. Senate opponents contended that Babbitt's land management proposals amounted to an assault on the West. Domenici was assisted on the Senate floor by Reid. But Reid, mindful of the longstanding House support for higher grazing fees, quickly began crafting a compromise with House Democrats to end a stalemate. *(Vote 266, p. 35-S)*

Reid's compromise amendment would have increased grazing fees to $3.45 over three years and codified most of Babbitt's land management proposals. Senate negotiators approved the compromise on a party-line vote. But when the final version of the spending bill came back to the floor, Domenici and the Western senators balked at Reid's amendment, saying the proposed land management changes were far too sweeping.

After three attempts to cut off Senate debate failed, Reid agreed to drop all grazing language from the final version of the Interior spending bill. Domenici agreed to drop the one-year moratorium, and the conference report was approved, 91-9, on Nov. 9. *(Vote 359, p. 46-S)*

The agreement left Babbitt free to pursue his grazing proposals.

However, committee Chairman George Miller, D-Calif., and Bruce F. Vento, D-Minn., chairman of the Subcommittee on National Parks, Forests and Public Lands, acknowledged that they viewed the brief, two-page BLM bill as an alternative vehicle for provisions to raise the amount ranchers and herders were required to pay to graze their animals on public lands.

The Clinton administration had proposed an increase in grazing fees in its fiscal 1994 budget, but it dropped the matter from the budget package in March to mollify Western members. The fee under existing law was $1.86 per animal unit month, a measure of the amount of forage needed to feed one cow and calf, five sheep, or one horse.

The House Appropriations Committee included a provision increasing the fee to $2.48 per animal unit month in the fiscal 1994 Interior Department spending bill (HR 2520). But on June 30 — despite pleas for open debate from Mike Synar, D-Okla., and other supporters — the House Rules Committee decided not to protect the provision when the spending bill went to the House floor. That meant that any member could raise a point of order to strike the provision on the basis that it was authorizing language, not appropriate on a spending bill. It was at that point that Miller and Vento readied the BLM authoriza-

tion bill for floor action. *(Appropriations, p. 618)*

Miller said the move was "an attempt to remove the [grazing] issue from the appropriations cycle. This is an attempt to put it back into the policy committee and proceed under an open rule on the floor."

James V. Hansen of Utah, ranking Republican on Vento's subcommittee, said Republicans supported a "clean bill" simply reauthorizing the BLM, as Vento had written HR 2530, and were not in favor of legislation filled with "extraneous" amendments such as the one anticipated on grazing fees.

Previous House bills to reauthorize the BLM contained rights-of-way changes to the federal Land Policy and Management Act and other items that some lawmakers said weighed it down. But Vento, who favored the rights-of-way changes, said he streamlined the reauthorization bill to give BLM Director Jim Baca time to develop administration proposals to change the land policy law.

HOUSE FLOOR ACTION

The House swiftly passed HR 2530 on Sept. 13 by voice vote; the grazing-fee amendment was never offered. Though the grazing fee debate was still raging on the Interior bill, the Clinton administration had announced Aug. 9 that it would raise the fees administratively to $4.28 per animal unit month over a three-year period.

The BLM bill had been scheduled for floor action more than a month earlier, but Vento had pulled it, saying its passage was jeopardized by pending amendments on timber clear-cutting in the Pacific Northwest and access for aircraft overflights.

When the House finally took up the bill and approved it, it was under special procedures that allowed no amendments.

In the end, the grazing fee language was dropped from the Interior bill; Interior Secretary Bruce Babbitt said he would consult with Western senators and ranchers before publishing new grazing regulations in 1994. ∎

Infighting Holds Up Drinking Water Aid

Two House committees began the year trying to respond to a public health problem in Milwaukee, where an estimated 300,000 people became ill from bacteria in the city's drinking water supply. But efforts to help cities such as Milwaukee rebuild rickety drinking water facilities quickly bogged down in a turf battle between the Energy and Commerce and Public Works and Transportation committees.

The two panels approved competing bills in April, but neither bill reached the House floor before Congress adjourned. The Energy and Commerce bill (HR 1701) called for a new revolving loan fund to assist states in helping cities and local governments to prevent and detect drinking water contamination. The Public Works Committee approved a narrower measure (HR 1865), which included a revolving fund to be used only for the "construction, rehabilitation and improvement of water supply systems."

In the Senate, a related reauthorization bill (S 1547) by Environment and Public Works Committee Chairman Max Baucus, D-Mont., did not advance beyond the hearing stage.

The Clinton administration stepped in Sept. 8, calling for legislative and administrative changes to the Safe Drinking Water Act aimed at giving states and local governments more flexibility. The administration proposed establishing a $4.6 billion revolving loan fund over five years to help states pay for improvements to water systems.

The administration also proposed scrapping a provision in the clean drinking water law that required the Environmental Protection Agency (EPA) to set standards for 25 contaminants every three years. Instead, the administration said EPA should be required to regulate only those contaminants that posed the greatest risk to drinking water quality.

Congress provided money for the administration's proposed revolving fund in the fiscal 1994 appropriations bill for Veterans Affairs, Housing and Urban Development and Independent Agencies (HR 2491 — PL 103-124), pending separate authorization. *(Appropriations, p. 691)*

Rep. Henry A. Waxman, D-Calif., chairman of the Energy and Commerce Health Subcommittee, said he wanted to write a comprehensive drinking water reauthorization bill to incorporate the administration recommendations, but the legislation never materialized.

A separate bill (HR 3392) introduced by Jim Slattery, D-Kan., to do just that attracted wide support from states and localities because it did not require strict standards for contaminants. Waxman and many environmental groups opposed Slattery's bill, but groups such as the National League of Cities supported it. The bill did not advance in the first session.

The 1974 Safe Drinking Water Act (PL 93-523) set standards for removing contaminants from the nation's drinking water and required states to protect their groundwater supplies. Local governments and smaller water systems had long complained that the law was too cumbersome and costly to comply with. The law was reauthorized in 1986 (PL 99-339) and expired in 1991. It had been kept alive through annual appropriations. *(1986 Almanac, p. 134)*

LEGISLATIVE ACTION

The House Energy and Commerce Subcommittee on Health gave voice vote approval April 21 to HR 1701, sponsored by full Committee Chairman John D. Dingell, D-Mich., and Waxman. The bill provided for a new, federally financed revolving fund that states could draw on to issue loans to local communities to build drinking water treatment plants or to make improvements to older plants. As the communities repaid the loans with interest, states could make additional loans to other communities.

As approved, the measure authorized $3.6 billion over four years: $599 million in fiscal 1994 to help set up the state funds and $1 billion each year thereafter through fiscal 1997. The authorization was permanent, though the amounts were unspecified after fiscal 1997.

Waxman said the General Accounting Office found that poor drinking water quality was directly connected to a lack of resources at the state and local levels.

The subcommittee approved a technical amendment allowing investor-owned public water systems that showed financial need to get loan assistance from the revolving fund.

Republicans Thomas J. Bliley Jr., Va., and Alex McMillan, N.C., questioned how the bill was to be financed. McMillan said many communities might be reluctant to take the loans knowing that the money was adding to the nation's deficit. Waxman vowed to work with the Republicans before the full committee markup to find ways to pay for the bill.

Competing Committee Bills

On April 27, the full House Energy and Commerce Committee approved the Dingell-Waxman bill (HR 1701 — H Rept 103-114) by voice vote.

The committee approved, also by voice vote, an amendment offered by Mike Synar, D-Okla., and Gerry E. Studds, D-Mass., to set aside 15 percent of the revolving fund, about $90 million, to be available solely to small public water systems that served fewer than 10,000 people. Studds said that 92 percent of the public water systems that had failed to comply with the Safe Drinking Water Act fell into such a category.

The funding issue had not been resolved, and McMillan offered an amendment, which he later withdrew, proposing to make federal loans to the states instead of grants. The states were to be required to pay back the loans over 30 years at an interest rate of 75 percent of the rate the U.S. government paid on similar long-term loans. McMillan said his proposal promised to reduce the bill's cost to $150 million in fiscal 1994 and to $250 million, rather than $1 billion, in each of the following years. McMillan said he realized it was unusual to suggest lending money to the states, because "we prefer to give it away."

But the bill quickly became entangled in a turf fight. HR 1701 amended the Safe Drinking Water Act, which was under Energy and Commerce's jurisdiction. But because the bill authorized money for the building of new public water treatment plants, Public Works Committee Chairman Norman Y. Mineta, D-Calif., argued that his committee also had jurisdiction.

Not waiting for a parliamentary ruling on the referral issue, Public Works met April 28, one day after the Energy and Commerce markup, to approve its own bill (HR 1865 — H Rept 103-115). The committee's bill provided for a state-run revolving fund for the purpose of financing the construction of new water supply systems and improvements to existing systems. While the Energy and Commerce bill provided a permanent authorization, the Public Works bill authorized funding for three years at the same levels as the Energy and Commerce bill.

The Public Works bill also covered loans for the treatment of pollutants from "navigable waters" in order to make such water usable by water supply systems. That language sounded more like a provision from the clean water act, which was under Public Works' jurisdiction. HR 1865 stated that nothing within it should be construed as affecting the Safe Drinking Water Act. (Clean water, p. 275)

Panel Republicans praised HR 1865, calling its quick introduction another example of how well the committee worked on a bipartisan basis.

Senate

In the Senate, the Environment and Public Works Committee held a hearing Oct. 27 on Baucus' reauthorization bill (S 1547), but no further action was taken.

The bill, which mirrored the Clinton administration's proposals, authorized $6.6 billion over seven years to help states and local governments pay for drinking water treatment plants. It reauthorized the 1974 Safe Drinking Water Act and required the EPA to regulate 15 contaminants and evaluate each one within three years. It also gave smaller water systems more flexibility to comply with the law.

Don Nickles, R-Okla., introduced a related bill (S 767) that required the EPA to balance the costs and benefits of drinking water regulations. It did not authorize any money and did not set specific standards for contaminants. ■

Clean Water Rewrite Fails To Advance

Congress took preliminary steps toward renewing the nation's clean water law, the 1972 Federal Pollution and Water Control Act (PL 92-500), but no bills advanced in the first session.

The clean water law required states to establish limits on the amount of pollutants discharged into surface waters by industrial facilities, factories and municipal sewage treatment plants. The law authorized federal funds to help state and local governments pay for the construction of sewage treatment facilities — a provision that was set to expire in 1994. Lawmakers said a rewrite of the clean water law should continue that funding, as well as deal with the issue of "non-point" sources of pollution, such as irrigated water from farms, that were difficult to trace.

Lawmakers also vowed to use the rewrite to address wetlands policy. There were an estimated 104 million acres of wetlands in the lower 48 states and 170 million acres in Alaska. In the mid-1980s, those wetlands were disappearing at a rate of nearly 300,000 acres each year. Environmentalists wanted to protect the fragile ecosystems, citing their role as a critical habitat for wildlife. Wetlands also were used to control floods and maintain water quality. At the same time, developers and farmers were seeking more flexibility in managing wetlands.

The Clinton administration on Aug. 24 offered a series of administrative and legislative recommendations aimed at protecting wetlands and ending a dispute sparked during the administration of President George Bush over the definition of a wetland. The plan was designed to give farmers and developers more flexibility to comply with federal regulations. The proposal called on Congress to give states and local governments financial incentives to protect entire watersheds and to close loopholes that had allowed developers to build on wetlands.

Bills Introduced

Two key bills were introduced in the House (HR 2255, HR 2199) and one in the Senate (S 1114) to reauthorize the clean water act. Several other bills introduced in 1993 sought to protect wetlands (HR 3465, HR 350, HR 1330, S 1304). None of the bills advanced.

In the House, Public Works Committee Chairman Norman Y. Mineta, D-Calif., introduced HR 2255 to rewrite the clean water act. The bill addressed funding for anti-pollution programs and wetlands policy and sought to exert his committee's jurisdiction over clean water issues. Merchant Marine and Fisheries Committee Chairman Gerry E. Studds, D-Mass., introduced HR 2199, which called for new taxes on pesticide and fertilizer manufacturers, a group targeted by environmentalists as a major source of water pollution. HR 2199 authorized $6 billion for anti-pollution activities each year, with $4 billion of that to come from polluters.

Three other House bills addressed wetlands policy. HR 3465, sponsored by Studds and Agriculture Committee Chairman E. "Kika" de la Garza, D-Texas, mirrored the administration's plan. HR 350, sponsored by Don Edwards, D-Calif., was supported by environmentalists. HR 1330, introduced by Jimmy Hayes, D-La., was supported by farmers and developers.

In the Senate, Environment and Public Works Commit-

tee Chairman Max Baucus, D-Mont., and the committee's ranking Republican, John H. Chafee of Rhode Island, introduced a bipartisan bill (S 1114) to renew the clean water act. The committee held hearings on the measure but took no legislative action.

The bill included an increase in the annual authorization for pollution control projects from about $2 billion to $2.5 billion for fiscal 1995-2000. The levels were to rise by increments of $500 million a year if Congress met deficit-reduction goals set in 1993 — up to a maximum of $5 billion in 2000. The legislation also limited "non-point" pollution — pol-

luted water flowing from farmlands, urban streets and construction sites. It required the Environmental Protection Agency to set guidelines to control polluted runoff. States were to use these guidelines to improve their existing non-point pollution control programs.

The Environment and Public Works Committee held a hearing Sept. 15 on the administration's wetlands policy and a bill by Baucus and Chafee (S 1304) to give farmers more flexibility to comply with wetlands regulations. Baucus said he wanted to incorporate S 1304 into the clean water bill in 1994. ■

California Desert Bill Advances

Legislation to protect huge stretches of California desert cleared a major hurdle in 1993, winning the approval of the Senate Energy and Natural Resources Committee Oct. 5. Senate floor action was expected in 1994. The House did not act on a companion measure in 1993.

As approved by the committee, the bill (S 21) created 71 separate wilderness areas and protected about 6.4 million acres of desert land.

The centerpiece of the bill was the creation of a 1.2 million-acre Mojave National Park in the state's southeast corner. The measure also expanded and upgraded the 794,000-acre Joshua Tree and 3.27 million-acre Death Valley national monuments to national parks.

The bill won the panel's approval after three weeks of delay in which senators narrowly defeated amendments that would have speeded up government purchases of private desert property and allowed hunting in parts of the proposed Mojave National Park. Dianne Feinstein, D-Calif., the bill's chief sponsor, was not a member of the Energy Committee, but she attended all three of its markups. She said the amendments would have weakened the legislation.

Feinstein, however, did make some concessions to miners, ranchers, off-road vehicle operators and others who had adamantly opposed the legislation from the time of its inception in 1986. Among the pre-markup changes were boundary revisions and less restrictive land designations.

Feinstein also agreed to make changes to the bill to address the concerns of Senate Armed Services Committee Chairman Sam Nunn, D-Ga., and the Pentagon, allowing the military to continue military flights over the desert. And, to allay concerns raised by the Justice Department, Feinstein included language to allow Border Patrol activities to continue in the desert.

Mojave Desert

A major stumbling block in the bill was the creation of the Mojave park and the transfer of the land's management authority from the Bureau of Land Management (BLM), generally more protective of traditional land users, to the National Park Service. The National Park Service's mandate was to maintain and preserve lands for future generations. BLM was directed to administer public lands under multiple-use programs, which allowed a variety of activities such as hunting and grazing while prohibiting certain types of development.

Environmentalists contended that national park status gave greater protection to the desert, which was home to

scenic terrain and endangered species such as bighorn sheep and the desert tortoise.

But Energy Committee Ranking Republican Malcolm Wallop, Wyo., and other opponents said the National Park Service already was overburdened and could not afford to add another park to the system, much less the three parcels proposed under the bill.

The bill also curbed commercial and recreational activities in the 71 wilderness areas, except in specific tracts where some grazing, mining, military overflights and off-road vehicle use were permitted.

BACKGROUND

Legislation to protect the California desert had been hotly debated since 1986, when then-Sen. Alan Cranston, D-Calif., introduced a measure to include California desert land in the nation's park and wilderness system. Every year until 1993, however, the bills had been stalled in the Senate Energy Committee by California Republicans who opposed the legislation as too sweeping.

Desert protection legislation passed the House in 1991. But then-Sen. John Seymour, R-Calif., blocked action in the Senate, and the bill died at the end of the 102nd Congress. *(1991 Almanac, p. 228; 1992 Almanac, p. 282)*

The legislation's fortunes improved dramatically in 1992 with the election of two Democratic senators from California, Feinstein and Barbara Boxer, and President Clinton, effectively ending partisan squabbling among California senators and giving the measure White House backing for the first time.

Compensating Landowners

From the beginning, one of the most controversial aspects of the bill had to do with the acquisition of private property, particularly the two land parcels needed to create the Mojave National Park. Included in these parcels were 355,000 acres owned by Catellus Development Corp., a San Francisco company in which the California retirement system for state employees owned a substantial stake, and more than 200,000 acres owned by the California State Lands Commission.

Feinstein's original draft, like Cranston's version, would have allowed Catellus to purchase surplus federal property through a special credit account, which opponents argued would give the company special privileges unavailable to other private property owners.

The federal government's public land agencies typically

acquired private property for national parks through land swaps or legal condemnation proceedings. Private property owners were paid for their land through the Land and Water Conservation Fund, created by Congress in 1964 to acquire public lands for national parks, federal wildlife refuges and other federally protected areas. In 1993, however, the conservation fund was strained, and there was a backlog of about $3 billion in desired, but unacquired, properties.

As introduced, the bill would have required Congress to approve land swaps between the government and Catellus that involved federal property outside California. On Oct. 1, 1998, Catellus would have received credit equal to the value of any remaining acreage, which the company could use to buy other federal parcels.

Wallop and Pete V. Domenici, R-N.M., objected to the credit provision, arguing that it would set a costly precedent for failed or stalled land exchanges.

Wallop said he was concerned that it ultimately could cost the government up to $1 billion to acquire the private tracts.

But William C. Matheson, vice president for sales and land management at Catellus, took issue with the $1 billion price tag Republicans put on the 615,000 acres of private land targeted for exchange. He said the Catellus parcel was worth no more than $188.9 million.

Ultimately, the committee agreed to eliminate the special financing mechanism from the bill. The committee-approved measure still allowed Catellus to swap its land for any undesignated federal parcels, but the bill provided no special financing for the deal.

To head off further controversy over the issue of private property, Feinstein reached an agreement with Senate Energy Committee Chairman J. Bennett Johnston, D-La., and House Natural Resources Committee Chairman George Miller, D-Calif., to ensure that the special financing mechanism for Catellus was kept out of the final bill.

The rights of private property owners who held smaller parcels of desert land affected by the bill also were debated. Committee Republicans tried but failed to amend the bill to create an expedited process for compensating land owners, whereby all private desert property would have been immediately turned over to the federal government and landowners would have been compensated through a Justice Department fund. Opponents said the proposal sidestepped the appropriations process and violated deficit-reduction rules.

The committee-approved bill still allowed the government to buy or swap private parcels within the desert, but not under any expedited measures.

Hunting Rights

An issue that had long threatened the bill was whether to allow hunting in the Mojave Park. This debate went hand in hand with the question of how to designate and protect the area.

The National Rifle Association (NRA) wanted the Mojave, at the time a scenic area overseen by the BLM, to become a national preserve, a designation created by Congress in the 1970s to allow hunting on federal lands within the national park system. Environmentalists said the Mojave's diverse attributes qualified it as a national park, which would bar hunting.

Environmentalists contended that the NRA was using the bill as a test case in a drive to open all national parks to hunting. But the NRA said its efforts were directed only at the Mojave, home to bighorn sheep, quail, rabbits and

other game. At the time, some hunting was allowed by permit in the area.

The committee turned back efforts by hunting proponents on the panel to designate some areas of the park a national preserve. At an earlier markup, members of the committee also rejected an attempt to redesignate the area as a national monument to be overseen by the BLM.

In the House, a separate bill (HR 2379) was introduced by Jerry Lewis, R-Calif., that would have kept the Mojave a national scenic area. That bill saw no action in 1993.

SENATE COMMITTEE ACTION

The Senate Energy Committee approved the bill (S 21 — S Rept 103-165) by a vote of 13-7 on Oct. 5.

Committee action had stretched over three weeks, as markups were delayed to allow Feinstein and panel members to work out differences, particularly over land exchange provisions.

But even with the behind-the-scenes negotiations, the measure faced strong opposition in committee. The panel defeated two Republican amendments that would have allowed hunting in the Mojave, but only by very narrow margins.

On Sept. 29, the panel rejected, 9-10, a Wallop amendment to designate the Mojave as a national monument to be overseen by the BLM. And, on Oct. 5, the committee rejected, 9-11, an amendment by Frank H. Murkowski, R-Alaska, that would have designated some areas of the park a national preserve.

The panel on Sept. 29 did agree to make some modifications to the measure. Members adopted, by voice vote, a Johnston amendment that struck from the bill the controversial credit account that would have allowed Catellus to buy undesignated federal lands.

The committee on that day also approved Republican amendments that reduced the bill's acreage and clarified that the bill allowed border patrols and military overflights.

On a 10-9 vote, the panel approved an amendment by Wallop that stripped up to 250,000 acres of land in the Lanfair Valley of San Bernardino County from the proposed Mojave National Park.

The amendment also killed a provision that would have given Interior Secretary Bruce Babbitt authority over land-use zoning in the valley, which Wallop opposed. The valley was home to some property owners who would have faced condemnation had their property been included in the park designation.

Compromises Pay Off

Feinstein's compromises earned her the surprise support in the committee of Robert F. Bennett, R-Utah. "She is willing to solve the problem rather than trumpet the issue, which is more than her predecessor did," Bennett said.

Going into the Oct. 5 markup, bill supporters were counting on Mark O. Hatfield, R-Ore., to provide the crucial vote needed to get the bill out of the committee, which was split between 11 Democrats and nine Republicans. Hatfield, an original cosponsor of Cranston's desert bill, was considered pivotal because Feinstein expected Democrat Richard C. Shelby of Alabama to vote against the bill.

But when it came time to vote, Feinstein not only won Hatfield and Bennett but also got Shelby's vote, even though he had voted against committee Democrats on key amendments.

At the Oct. 5 markup, Murkowski revisited the issue of private property rights. But the committee rejected, 7-13, his amendment that would have immediately turned over all private desert property to the federal government and compensated landowners through a Justice Department fund.

The committee also voted, 12-8, to accept an amendment by Larry E. Craig, R-Idaho, that would have removed four roads from the desert protection area to facilitate access in and out of the wilderness areas.

HOUSE ACTION

Although Feinstein won bipartisan praise in the Senate for her willingness to negotiate with miners, ranchers and others opposed to the bill, her accommodations still did not satisfy Lewis, whose district encompassed much of the affected desert area. Lewis, who attended the Senate markups, said the legislation did not protect the interests of Californians who lived in the desert or used it for recreation.

The House Natural Resources Committee held a hearing on a companion bill (HR 518), similar to Feinstein's, sponsored by Richard H. Lehman, D-Calif., but the House measure was not marked up in 1993.

Still, the House already had gone on record that it supported the effort when it passed a more expansive version of the bill in 1991.   ■

Congress Clears Protection Of Colorado Wilderness

Congress cleared legislation (HR 631) to protect more than 600,000 acres of Colorado wilderness, ending a 13-year impasse over the issue of water rights on the lands. The bill designated 611,730 acres as wilderness and set aside 174,510 acres in a less protective management area. The bill had the support of both Colorado senators, Democrat Ben Nighthorse Campbell and Republican Hank Brown. President Clinton signed the bill into law Aug. 13 (PL 103-77).

Attempts to create the Colorado wilderness area had been stalled for over a decade by fights over access to Colorado water, about 85 percent of which was used by other states.

In the past, House leaders had strongly opposed Senate water-rights language because it differed from wilderness laws that gave the federal government the right to water found within wilderness areas. Key House lawmakers and environmentalists feared that if water rights were not given to the federal government, state water authorities would be more likely to rule in favor of the water claims of landowners or municipalities, possibly threatening preservation of wilderness areas dependent upon scarce water resources.

Those opposed to federal control included property owners living upstream from the wilderness areas, who were concerned that they might lose their access to water.

In 1992, the House and Senate differed sharply over language in a House Colorado wilderness bill that reserved an explicit federal water right to nourish the wilderness areas. The companion Senate bill, passed in 1991, retained jurisdiction for Colorado. *(1991 Almanac, p. 231)*

A Senate compromise ironed out late in the 1992 session banned the construction of new or expanded water projects on the lands, but Congress adjourned before the House had time to act on the Senate amendment, and the bill died. *(1992 Almanac, p. 292)*

HR 631 did not assert any federal water rights in the protection area; the bill was silent on the controversial issue, but it did not allow anyone to claim a reserved water right in court or through any administrative proceeding. The bill also prohibited construction of new or expanded water projects on the lands.

Lawmakers pointed out that the water rights issue might no longer be a serious concern because the land designated as wilderness in HR 631 was limited to headwaters areas. Headwaters were the streams that were the sources of a river, and in most wilderness areas they originated on federal lands. Previous versions of Colorado wilderness legislation had included a wilderness area that received its water from a stream that began outside the area.

The bill also prohibited mining, mineral leasing, timber harvesting, developed campgrounds and new roads or trails in most of the lands set aside in the less protective management areas.

Legislative Action

The House Natural Resources Subcommittee on National Parks, Forests and Public Lands approved HR 631 by voice vote June 17.

Bill sponsor David E. Skaggs, D-Colo., said the compromise on water rights was not perfect but was "the first language that enjoys enough support to be enacted." The subcommittee also approved changing the name of the proposed Wren and Tim Wirth Wilderness Area to the Fossil Ridge Wilderness Area. Wirth, a former Democratic senator from Colorado who had pushed the issue for years, requested the change.

The full Natural Resources Committee approved the bill by voice vote June 30, after making a series of technical changes (H Rept 103-181). The House passed the bill July 19.

The Senate Energy Committee approved the House bill, 20-0, on Aug. 3 (S Rept 103-123). The full Senate cleared the measure by voice vote the next day.   ■

Hill Approves Land Swap

Congress agreed to use land exchanges to acquire about 80,000 acres north of Yellowstone National Park in Montana, consolidating ownership of private land into federal hands to protect parts of the Gallatin National Forest from development. The land was home to the nation's largest elk herd and the endangered grizzly bear.

The House approved its version of the bill (HR 873 — H Rept 103-82) by a vote of 317-101 on May 20. The House bill authorized a series of exchanges and purchases that had the support of environmental groups and the Big Sky Lumber Co., the landowner. The bill, sponsored by Pat Williams, D-Mont., also authorized $3.4 million to pay for the acquisitions. *(Vote 175, p. 42-H)*

Republicans opposed the bill, citing Congressional Budget Office estimates that the land could cost as much as $20 million if the exchanges were not successful. Dan Burton, R-Ind., called the bill a "quasi-pork barrel project" that threatened to burden the government with unnecessary

land. But a procedural motion by Tom DeLay, R-Texas, to send the bill back to committee to remove provisions allowing land purchases was rejected 128-287. *(Vote 174, p. 42-H)*

A week earlier, an attempt to pass HR 873 under expedited procedures failed; the House rejected the bill May 11 by a vote of 262-140, six short of the two-thirds majority needed under suspension of the rules. The House Rules Committee then granted a one-hour open rule for consideration of the bill under normal procedures, but no amendments were offered. *(Vote 158, p. 38-H)*

The Senate amended and passed HR 873 (S Rept 103-122) by voice vote Aug. 4. Among the key changes, the Senate eliminated the $3.4 million authorization, leaving the Big Sky lands to be acquired only through land swaps. The House cleared the bill by voice vote Sept. 13, accepting the Senate change. The House also accepted the Senate's removal of nonprofit land trusts from having a role in facilitating the land exchanges authorized in the bill.

President Clinton on Oct. 1 signed the bill into law (PL 103-91). ■

Various Wilderness Bills Considered by Congress

Congress took up a host of park and wilderness bills, ranging from a measure to protect the nation's deepest cave from oil and mineral exploration to a bill to conserve nearly a half-million acres around Idaho's Snake River. The following is a rundown of key action:

Alaskan Park Fishing

The House Merchant Marine Committee gave speedy approval May 12 to a bill by Rep. Don Young, R-Alaska, that allowed fishing in Glacier Bay National Park to continue at its existing level. The bill never made it to the House floor before adjournment.

The National Park Service had proposed prohibiting all commercial fishing in the park after 1997. Young's bill (HR 704 — H Rept 103-201, Part 1) allowed such fishing to continue with these restrictions: no new types of equipment, no fishing in wilderness areas, and for each species, no catches larger than the average number of fish or crabs caught per season over the previous 10 years.

The committee approved the bill by voice vote, with no debate and no dissent. The next stop for the measure was the Natural Resources Committee, where it was opposed by at least one leading Democrat, Bruce F. Vento, D-Minn., the chairman of the National Parks, Forests and Public Lands Subcommittee. The Natural Resources Committee did not take up the bill in 1993. The Merchant Marine Committee approved an identical bill in 1992; the bill died in Natural Resources (then named the Interior Committee).

The Clinton administration and some environmental groups that wanted to reduce the amount of fishing in the bay, opposed the bill. Roughly 400 boats were licensed to fish commercially in the bay, with the primary catches being salmon and crabs.

New Mexico Cave Protection

A bill to protect the nation's deepest cave from oil and

mineral exploration cleared its last hurdle Nov. 21 when the House sent it to the president on a voice vote.

The bill (HR 698), sponsored by Bruce F. Vento, D-Minn., chairman of the House Natural Resources Subcommittee on National Parks, Forests and Public Lands, increased protection of Lechuguilla Cave in Carlsbad Caverns National Park in New Mexico. Proposals to drill for oil and gas on federal lands next to the national park had raised concerns about Lechuguilla, which extended for more than 60 miles. The cave contained such rare features as gypsum "chandeliers."

Under the bill, the Interior secretary was prohibited from issuing new leases for drilling or allowing new mineral exploration on federal lands. Development was restricted on existing leases in the Dark Canyon area of Lechuguilla Cave, along the northern boundary of Carlsbad Caverns National Park.

The House first passed HR 698 (H Rept 103-86) on May 11 by voice vote under suspension of the rules. The Senate passed the measure by voice vote Nov. 19 with some amendments, sending it back to the House for final approval. The key Senate amendments clarified access to rights of way and the authority of the Interior secretary to cancel any existing mineral or geothermal lease. The Senate amendments were agreed to by Vento and Joe Skeen, R-N.M., whose district included the Lechuguilla Cave and Carlsbad Caverns. The House cleared the bill Nov. 21 and President Clinton signed HR 698 on Dec. 2 (PL 103-169).

New Mexico Recreation Area

The House on Sept. 29 cleared by voice vote a bill (HR 38) that established the Jemez National Recreation Area in New Mexico to protect one of the nation's richest ancient Indian settlements.

The bill created a 57,000-acre recreation area for the 300,000 visitors who trekked to the lands each year for sightseeing, camping, hunting and other activities.

The House passed a similar bill during the 102nd Congress, but it languished in the Senate because Pete V. Domenici, R-N.M., objected to the number of acres set aside for recreation. HR 38 reflected a compromise worked out by Domenici and Rep. Bill Richardson, D-N.M., that reduced the number of acres set aside for recreation and eased mining restrictions in those areas. President Clinton signed HR 38 into law on Oct. 12 (PL 103-104).

The House first passed the bill (H Rept 103-58) April 21, 363-57. The Senate passed the bill (S Rept 103-139) on Sept. 22, after making largely technical changes, and sent it back to the House. *(Vote 141, p. 34-H)*

Also on April 21, the House approved directing the Forest Service to transfer control of Old Taos Ranger Station and Warehouse to Taos, N.M. The bill (HR 328 — H Rept 103-60) was passed 420-0. The city was to pay $18,000 each year for 20 years for the land. *(Vote 140, p. 34-H)*

The Senate cleared HR 328 by voice vote Oct. 20, and President Clinton signed it into law (PL 103-132) on Nov. 2.

Bird Refuge in Idaho

The Senate on July 28 cleared a compromise bill that set aside nearly a half-million acres around Idaho's Snake River as a federally protected conservation area.

The bill (HR 236 — S Rept 103-108) protected lands that stretched about 30 miles south of Boise and supported one of North America's densest populations of eagles,

hawks and owls. The Snake River Birds of Prey Natural Area had been a refuge since 1980, but that status had been scheduled to expire in 2000. The bill established new standards for compatible use of the area by visitors, the military and ranchers.

Although both the House and Senate passed similar bills in the 102nd Congress, the final version died in 1992. HR 236 reflected the compromise hammered out in 1992 that allowed several groups, including the National Guard, ranchers and tourists, to use the area, but prohibited private companies from using it as a dump site.

The House Natural Resources Committee approved HR 236 (H Rept 103-80, Part 1) by voice vote on March 17. The committee also approved by voice vote a package of technical amendments to clarify that existing users — visitors, the military and ranchers — could continue to use the land. The full House passed the bill May 11 by voice vote.

President Clinton on Aug. 4 signed the bill into law (PL 103-64).   ■

Law Urges Flood Victims To Build Elsewhere

In the aftermath of the summer floods that inundated 17,000 square miles and destroyed thousands of homes in the Midwest, Congress cleared legislation (S 1670) aimed at encouraging flood victims to move out of danger rather than rebuild in the flood plain; the aim was to reduce the likelihood that they would need disaster assistance again. The bill's provisions applied to victims of future floods as well as to those hit by the 1993 disaster.

President Clinton signed S 1670 into law Dec. 3 (PL 103-181).

In separate action, the House approved a bill (HR 3583) to make it easier for individuals to obtain federal assistance to repair flood-damaged levees that were not built by the federal government. The Senate did not act on the measure in the first session.

Neither bill authorized the expenditure of any new disaster aid funds by the federal government. Each placed new claims, however, on a $5.7 billion pool of disaster assistance funds that Congress approved in a supplemental appropriations bill (HR 2667 — PL 103-75) enacted in August. (Disaster supplemental, p. 714)

Relocation Aid

The House version of the relocation bill (HR 3445) began in the Public Works Subcommittee on Water Resources and Environment, which approved it by voice vote Nov. 3. The full Public Works Committee followed suit Nov. 9 (H Rept 103-358). The House passed HR 3445 by voice vote Nov. 15.

The House bill allowed the Federal Emergency Management Agency (FEMA) to use 15 percent of all its appropriated disaster assistance funds to aid people who wished to relocate outside flood plains.

Under existing law, FEMA was limited to using 10 percent of only the portion of its funds dedicated to community assistance disaster funding for relocation, or "hazard mitigation," activities.

The bill also increased from 50 percent to 75 percent the share of relocation activity costs that the federal government would pick up.

The bill required the Army Corps of Engineers to report to Congress by June 30, 1995, on flood control policy. The study was to include analysis of alternatives to levees and other flood-control structures, such as preservation of wetlands areas. The bill also allowed the corps to offer aid for relocation or other options such as flood-proofing or elevating buildings. Under existing law, the corps could use funds only for construction or repair of flood-control structures.

The bill combined proposals made in separate bills by two House members from districts hit heavily by flooding: Richard J. Durbin, D-Ill., and Harold L. Volkmer, D-Mo.

The Senate passed its version of the bill (S 1670) by voice vote on Nov. 20. The bill included the FEMA provisions, specifying that the agency could pay for relocations only if the local governments involved in the purchase of flood plain properties guaranteed that the properties were to be used in perpetuity for such non-residential purposes as a public park or a wetlands area.

The Senate bill dropped the Army Corps of Engineers provisions, although funding for the studies was provided in the fiscal 1994 appropriations bill for energy and water development (HR 2445 — PL 103-126).

The House accepted the changes and cleared S 1670 by voice vote Nov. 20.

Levee Repair

The House on Nov. 23 gave voice vote approval to HR 3583, a bill to expand the Army Corps of Engineers' role in repairing levees destroyed by the Midwest floods. Under existing law, the corps was authorized to repair non-federal levees only if the owners had obtained state or local governmental sponsorship before the flood damage occurred.

HR 3583 sought to change that by giving owners of flood-damaged levees until Sept. 30, 1994, to obtain public sponsorship that would make them eligible for retroactive federal assistance. Eligible levees had to have met all of the corps of engineers' construction and maintenance standards prior to the flooding.

The bill also set the federal share of repair costs at 75 percent, as opposed to the 80 percent provided for those levees that had obtained prior public sponsorship under existing law in 1993.

The bill was sponsored by Rep. Pat Danner, D-Mo., for a bipartisan group of Missouri and Illinois members from flood-affected districts.   ■

Exemption Extended for Marine Mammal Kills

Congress on Sept. 22 cleared legislation (HR 3049) that gave commercial fishermen a six-month extension of an exemption from the ban on killing marine mammals. The action was necessary to give lawmakers more time to overhaul the 1972 Marine Mammal Protection Act, which prohibited the harassment, capture or killing of dolphins, sea lions, walruses and other marine mammals without special permits.

On Nov. 9, the Senate Commerce Committee approved a five-year reauthorization bill (S 1636 — S Rept 103-220) to revise the government's system for monitoring and controlling the impact of commercial fishing operations on

marine mammal stocks.

The House Merchant Marine and Fisheries Committee did not act in 1993 on its version of the reauthorization bill (HR 2760), introduced July 27 by Chairman Gerry E. Studds, D-Mass., and cosponsored by senior committee Republican Don Young of Alaska, among others. The Subcommittee on Environment and Natural Resources held hearings on the proposal Aug. 4 but took no further action.

The Temporary Extension

The Senate cleared HR 3049 by voice vote Sept. 22, and President Clinton signed the bill into law Sept. 30 (PL 103-86). The House had passed it 421-6 on Sept. 21. *(Vote 444, p. 108-H)*

The measure extended, until April 1, 1994, what had been a five-year exemption for the commercial fishing industry from the law's ban on "incidental takings" of dolphins, sea lions and other marine mammals.

Congress passed the five-year exemption in 1988, after a 1987 federal court decision prevented the National Marine Fisheries Service from issuing permits that allowed the incidental killing of marine mammals. The exemption expressly permitted incidental takings by U.S. commercial fishing operations while government agencies studied the problem and came up with a long-term solution. *(1988 Almanac, p. 168)*

The five-year exemption from a ban on incidental takings was set to expire Oct. 1, which is why Congress had to adopt the six-month extension once it realized it would not have time to act on a full reauthorization bill. Without action, commercial fishing operations, which invariably snagged a few animals accidentally, could have been all but shut down.

BACKGROUND

The Marine Mammal Protection Act was passed in 1972 to ensure that marine mammals such as whales, dolphins, sea otters, seals, walruses, manatees and polar bears stayed at or returned to healthy population levels. The act barred the intentional harassment or killing of marine mammals and prohibited the importation of products made from them, although it allowed the incidental taking, or killing, of animals from non-depleted species during commercial fishing operations.

The 1988 amendments to the law ordered the National Marine Fisheries Service (NMFS) to collect data during the five-year period on marine mammal stocks and the impact of commercial fishing operations on those stocks. The law required the NMFS and other agencies to propose a new regulatory scheme by Jan. 1, 1992.

The NMFS did not actually send its proposal to Congress until November 1992, 11 months late. The plan's goal was to achieve optimum sustainable populations of all marine mammal stocks and to limit allowable takings to numbers compatible with that goal. The specifics of the proposal, however, drew criticism from the fishing industry and the scientific and environmental communities.

As a result, a coalition of animal welfare groups, commercial fishing industry representatives, Alaska natives and environmental groups drafted a compromise plan that was released June 10 with endorsements from 31 fishing organizations and seven environmental groups.

The Studds Bill

Studds introduced legislation (HR 2760) on July 27 that incorporated much of that compromise. It also addressed concerns expressed by the NMFS, the Marine Mammal Commission and various animal welfare organizations that were not involved in the industry-environmentalist coalition.

The Studds bill, as introduced, would have:
● Required the secretary of Commerce to establish a Scientific Working Group to help assess marine mammal stocks and determine how many animals could be killed in a given period without depleting those stocks.
● Required expedited conservation plans for endangered, threatened or depleted species.
● Allowed incidental takings of non-endangered species during commercial fishing operations as long as the total lethal takes did not adversely affect stocks of the marine mammal.
● Required fishermen to obtain a separate authorization to incidentally take endangered species.
● Established regional conservation teams to assist the secretary in reducing incidental takes.
● Established a Pinniped Interaction Task Force to determine the extent, if any, to which seals and sea lions were affecting salmon stocks and salmon aquaculture operations.
● Authorized funding of $15 million annually for the program through 1999.

Praise and Brickbats

Studds had bipartisan support within his committee. Young said the bill would provide "a permanent mechanism to conserve marine mammals while allowing commercial fishermen to continue their livelihood."

But some environmental groups said the legislation would do little more than extend the five-year exemption from a ban. For conservationists, the point of an incidental-take program was to allow the mammals to regain healthy population levels, said Suzanne Iudicello, counsel for the Center for Marine Conservation. "The House bill appears to be a quota-based regime that does little more than continue the current exemption program with the addition of increased observer coverage and draconian penalties for administrative violations," she said.

Government agencies and fishing industry representatives also were not satisfied with the bill as it was introduced.

Captive Mammals

A July 28 hearing before the Senate Commerce Committee explored the Marine Mammal Protection Act's effectiveness in ensuring humane treatment of captive animals. "Free Willy," a hit summer movie about a boy's efforts to help a killer whale escape from a marine park, gave the topic added currency.

John W. Grandy, the Humane Society's vice president for wildlife and habitat protection, testified on behalf of the Marine Mammal Protection Coalition, made up of 17 animal rights and environmental groups. Grandy urged Congress to impose new restrictions on the display of captive mammals by aquariums and marine parks such as Sea World, and to prohibit their capture for public display in the future.

Groups such as the American Association of Zoological Parks and Aquariums and organizations such as Sea World vigorously opposed the demands. They said that captive marine mammals were used for educational purposes and for scientific research that benefited animals in the wild.

They wanted the right to continue to capture mammals from the wild, but asked Congress to streamline the federal statute.

"Clarification is needed to end duplicative regulatory demands, codify existing practices and avoid the costly and unnecessary court challenges," John H. Prescott, executive director of Boston's New England Aquarium, told the Senate committee.

Under the existing law, anyone who held an exhibitor's license could apply for a public display permit. However, to display the animals, exhibitors had to provide either an educational or a conservation program that met the standards set by the act and the secretaries of Interior and Commerce.

The Humane Society said the four small whale species in captivity around the United States (killer whales, false killer whales, belugas and pilot whales) suffered extremely high mortality rates, reduced life spans and low birth rates compared with whales in the wild.

"Cetacean species may travel up to 50 to 100 miles a day, dive several hundred feet deep, and spend only 20 percent of their time at the surface of the water," Grandy testified. "The transition from their natural environment to captivity in a small concrete tank can only be unimaginably traumatic."

Naomi A. Rose, a Humane Society scientist who specialized in whales, said efforts to create captive breeding programs for whales had been unsuccessful. "In 25 years, only six killer whale calves have survived past one year. No pilot whales have been born at all. The dream of captive breeding for these animals is only a dream — a dead dream."

However, marine parks and aquariums had been able to establish successful captive breeding programs for dolphins. Therefore, Grandy testified, "wild captures of individuals from these groups are no longer necessary for public display or captive breeding."

Grandy urged Congress to prohibit petting pools, swim-with-the-dolphins programs and other activities that permitted contact between the public and marine mammals. "Such programs pose unacceptable levels of risk both to the animals and to the humans participating," he said.

Education and Conservation

Prescott, of the New England Aquarium, testified on behalf of the 26 members of the Alliance of Marine Mammal Parks and Aquariums and the 159 institutions and 6,000 individuals in the American Association of Zoological Parks and Aquariums.

He said that more than 115 million people visited marine mammal parks, aquariums and zoos in 1991, gaining significant education about, and appreciation for, the animals. "Fully 86 percent agreed in a recent Roper poll that they are more likely to be committed to environmental conservation after visiting a marine park or zoo, just as the congressional drafters of the original Marine Mammal Protection Act intended," he said.

Prescott said that marine mammals in the wild had benefited from research conducted on captive animals, and he noted that members of the organizations he represented had rescued and returned to the wild about 1,500 stranded marine mammals since 1987.

Prescott urged Congress to amend the law to ease regulatory burdens on marine parks and aquariums and to reduce legal challenges by groups such as the Humane Society.

He said bureaucratic delays in processing various applications had caused serious problems. "Breeding seasons have been lost waiting for simple authorization to transport animals. A rehabilitated stranded animal was in isolation for 12 months awaiting an agency decision on its transport. One agency attempted to require transport of seals in wire mesh cages, which is inhumane and a violation of another agency's regulation," he said.

FIVE-YEAR REAUTHORIZATION

The reauthorization bill approved by the Senate Commerce Committee near the end of the session did not address the section of the law dealing with captive marine mammals; the committee said it hoped to develop amendments on that section of the law that could be offered on the Senate floor.

Instead, S 1636 sought to develop criteria for identifying and ranking marine mammal stocks most affected by commercial fishing operations. It called for immediate action to protect animals whose populations were depleted or in decline.

The bill authorized appropriations for the program through fiscal 1998, setting funding levels in fiscal 1994 as follows:

● Department of Commerce, $21.6 million.
● Department of the Interior, $8 million.
● Marine Mammal Commission, $1.35 million.

The measure added a section to the Marine Mammal Protection Act to govern interactions between commercial fisheries and marine mammals. It required the government to issue a stock assessment for each marine mammal and to rank animals in one of five classes based on population size and trend, and on the level of total accidental kills. The first two classes, the mammals most threatened, would be classified as "critical stocks."

For critical marine mammal stocks affected by commercial fishing, the measure required establishment of "incidental take" teams of experts to recommend measures for reducing accidental kills and assisting stock recovery. If necessary, emergency regulations could be issued to protect threatened mammals.

The bill authorized a new vessel registration system to assess fishery efforts and their impact on marine mammals. Fees charged for a registration decal were to be limited to the administrative costs incurred in issuing the decal. Appropriated funds were to be used to cover any costs of maintaining a separate registration system. Only vessels that fished in an area where marine mammals were accidentally killed fairly often would have to register.

The bill required fishing vessels to report all accidental killings or woundings of marine mammals at the end of each fishing trip. A vessel owner or operator could be fined for failing to make the required reports.

All vessels could be required to carry observers who could check on compliance with the law.

Amendments Adopted

At the urging of Sen. Daniel K. Inouye, D-Hawaii, the committee amended the bill to allow whale-watching vessels in Hawaii to come as close as 100 yards from any whale.

And Sen. Slade Gorton, R-Wash., won adoption of an amendment to allow the intentional killing of certain sea lions that returned year after year to feed on salmon stocks in the Columbia River.

Both amendments were adopted by voice vote. ∎

Many Environment Bills Offered; Few Pass

Congress acted on a variety of environment bills in 1993, including the following:

PROTECTING OLD FAITHFUL

The House on Nov. 15 gave voice vote approval to a bill to protect Old Faithful and other geysers at Yellowstone National Park from being developed as energy sources by surrounding landowners. The Senate did not act on the measure.

Under the bill (HR 1137 — H Rept 103-364), future geothermal development was to be banned within a 15-mile area surrounding the park. The Interior secretary was restricted from issuing any leases for tapping into the energy sources on nearby federal land.

The bill, which amended the 1970 Geothermal Steam Act, also clarified the water rights of the federal government and Montana. It directed the Interior secretary to research the potential impact of full development of the geothermal resources.

Yellowstone, the oldest national park, contained the largest intact geyser system and geothermal resources in the world. The measure represented the third attempt by Pat Williams, D-Mont., to restrict the development of the geysers.

Most of Yellowstone was in Wyoming, but portions of the park reached into Idaho and Montana. The three states had different policies regarding geothermal management and regulation. For this reason, the bill required the three states to submit geothermal protection programs to the Interior Department for review.

The Church Universal and Triumphant in Montana owned a well that tapped into La Duke Hot Springs, which fed from the Yellowstone River. Williams called for the church to be banned from using the well if it harmed the Yellowstone geysers.

The House Natural Resources Committee approved HR 1137 by voice vote Nov. 10. To address concerns about private property rights, the committee first approved by voice vote an amendment by Williams to allow citizens to sue the federal government if they believed their property was being taken without compensation. The Natural Resources Subcommittee on Energy and Mineral Resources had approved HR 1137 by voice vote June 10.

GUAM PARK

The Senate on Nov. 22 cleared a bill (HR 1944) authorizing $8 million to develop a national park in the U.S. territory of Guam and build a memorial there. The memorial was to be dedicated to the U.S. forces who liberated Guam during World War II and to the people of Guam who suffered under the Japanese occupation from Dec. 8, 1941, to Aug. 10, 1944. President Clinton signed the bill into law Dec. 17 (PL 103-197).

The War in the Pacific National Historic Park in Guam had been established by Congress in 1978 to honor the people of that island for their loyalty to the United States during the war, but little work had been done to develop it. The goal was to have the monument completed by July 21, 1994, the 50th anniversary of the Marianas Campaign, in which U.S. forces liberated Guam.

The House first passed HR 1944 on June 21 by voice vote under expedited procedures. That version of the bill (H Rept 103-145), which had been reported by the Natural Resources Committee, provided for a monument honoring the people of Guam and commemorating by individual name those who suffered during the Japanese occupation.

The Senate Energy and Natural Resources Committee approved the bill (S Rept 103-98) on an 18-0 vote June 3 after changing it to authorize $8 million each for the completion of visitor centers in the War in the Pacific Park and in the American Memorial Park in Saipan. The Senate passed the bill by voice vote July 21.

The House on Nov. 21 passed a compromise version of the bill by voice vote. The new bill applied only to the Guam park and provided that the memorial be dedicated to U.S. liberation forces as well as to the people of Guam — but without the individual names.

Sen. Daniel K. Akaka, D-Hawaii, said the change did not preclude the Park Service from building a monument that listed the people of Guam who suffered during the occupation. The Senate cleared the compromise bill by voice vote.

MARINE BIOTECHNOLOGY GRANTS

The House on July 13 passed by voice vote a bill to establish a marine biotechnology program at selected colleges and universities. The Senate took no action on the measure.

The bill (HR 1916 — H Rept 103-170), authorized $90 million in grants over four years to support research into genetically modified marine organisms. Those grants were in addition to the roughly $44 million being spent each year under a federal program for marine biotechnology.

To address concerns about the release of genetically altered organisms, the bill was amended to require researchers to abide by federal safety standards or lose their grants.

House Merchant Marine Chairman Gerry E. Studds, D-Mass., said the research held great promise for food production, pharmaceuticals, industry and environmental cleanups. Lynn Schenk, D-Calif., warned that the United States needed to increase such research to keep pace with efforts in Japan and other Pacific Rim competitors.

The grants were to be made through the National Sea Grant College Program. Applications for funding were to be considered by a new Marine Biotechnology Review Panel, made up of 15 experts in marine biotechnology or related fields.

GREEN TECHNOLOGY

The Senate Environment and Public Works Committee on July 30 gave voice vote approval to a pair of bills designed to promote "green" technology and reduce indoor environmental problems. The full Senate did not consider either measure.

● S 978, sponsored by committee Chairman Max Baucus, D-Mont., sought to create a National Environmental Technology Panel under the White House's Office of Science and Technology Policy and a separate environmental technology bureau at the Environmental Protection Agency (EPA). The bill (S Rept 103-156) authorized $236 million

over three years, mostly for matching grants to private industry with an emphasis on small businesses.

The House Merchant Marine and Fisheries Committee on Aug. 4 formally reported a similar bill (HR 2112 — H Rept 103-214, Part 1). The House took no action on it.

• S 729, by Harry Reid, D-Nev., aimed at restricting lead levels in products such as paint, pesticides and plumbing solder fixtures. It exempted collectible toys, such as models, and paint used by artists. The bill (S Rept 103-152) required states to inspect schools and day-care centers for lead hazards and required that all lead-acid batteries be recycled. It authorized $71 million over three years.

The committee had approved a similar bill in August 1991, but it went no further. *(1991 Almanac, p. 234)*

INDOOR AIR

The Senate on Oct. 29 passed by voice vote a bill to expand research into indoor air pollution. The House took no action on the measure.

The bill (S 656 — S Rept 103-161), sponsored by Majority Leader George J. Mitchell, D-Maine, required the Environmental Protection Agency to develop a list of contaminants and to issue health advisories on those pollutants. Studies showed that contaminants such as radon, an odorless gas, could lead to lung cancer and other medical problems. The bill authorized up to $48.5 million each year from fiscal 1994 through fiscal 1998 for research, grants to states and an assessment of "sick" buildings that had a high concentration of indoor air pollutants.

The Senate Environment and Public Works Committee had approved S 656 on July 30 by voice vote.

RADON

Senate and House panels also approved separate bills designed to increase public awareness of radon's potential health risks. Radon, an odorless, toxic gas that could accumulate in buildings, was the second leading cause of lung cancer in the country. The bills did not advance in either chamber.

The Senate Environment and Public Works Committee was the first to act. On July 30, the committee approved a bill (S 657 — S Rept 103-176), sponsored by Frank R. Lautenberg, D-N.J., that required testing for radon gas in federally owned buildings and housing. The bill also required schools in high-risk areas to be tested by 1998.

The House Energy panel's Health Subcommittee on Sept. 29 approved by voice vote a bill (HR 2448) that required real estate salespeople to alert prospective home buyers to potential risks from radon. The bill also required the Environmental Protection Agency (EPA) to initiate a public information campaign on the risks. Lawmakers agreed to drop a provision that would have given purchasers 10 days to have a home tested for radon. Jim Slattery, D-Kan., who offered the amendment to strike the provision, said some members were concerned that it could lead to delays in completing sales transactions.

The bill still required that purchasers or renters be provided with radon warning pamphlets, that sellers disclose any known radon test results and that home purchase contracts contain a radon warning statement.

Slattery said his amendment also allowed states to establish radon information programs that, if certified by the EPA, could then be considered "substantially equivalent" to the government's program.

The subcommittee's ranking Republican, Thomas J. Bliley Jr., Va., said he did not believe the EPA could handle the radon requirements "in a responsible way," saying that the agency had "made a shambles of the superfund and asbestos programs." Subcommittee Chairman Henry A. Waxman, D-Calif., said members were committed to working out problems on the bill before it reached the full committee. The full committee never considered the bill. *(1992 Almanac, p. 291)*

CONSERVATION FOUNDATION

The House voted 368-59 on Nov. 3 to reauthorize the National Fish and Wildlife Foundation, a nonprofit organization that funded natural resources conservation and environmental education projects with a combination of donations from private contributors and federal dollars. The Senate did not act on the bill. *(Vote 539, p. 132-H)*

The bill (HR 2684 — H Rept 103-249) authorized $125 million over five years for the foundation and included provisions to expand the foundation's board of directors and honor the late Merchant Marine Committee Chairman Walter B. Jones, D-N.C.

Passage of the bill had been stalled by Craig Thomas, R-Wyo., who demanded a roll call during debate Nov. 2. Thomas said the reauthorization money could be better used for other things such as the national parks.

The bill included authorization for a fish hatchery in Ohio and conservation centers in Brownsville, Texas, and Columbia, N.C.

The Merchant Marine and Fisheries Committee reported the bill on Sept. 21.

FOUNTAIN DARTER

The House on Nov. 20 passed by voice vote a bill to help boost the population of the endangered fountain darter, an inch-long fish found in the San Antonio, Texas, region.

Under the bill (HR 3402), sponsored by Jack Fields, R-Texas, a captive breeding program was to be established at the San Marcos National Fish Hatchery and Technology Center. Fields said a 1985 federal recovery plan for the San Marcos River called for the fountain darter to be bred in captivity for release into the river or into Comal Springs, its main habitat.

There were an estimated 1,000 fountain darters remaining in the San Marcos River and in Comal Springs, which fed from the Edwards Aquifer, the primary source of water for San Antonio. The aquifer had been drying up rapidly. According to a Fish and Wildlife Service report, there were 100,000 fish in the habitat in 1975.

The House-passed bill authorized $1 million annually during fiscal 1994-1998 for the program. The federal government also was required to work with Texas A&M University on research of the fountain darter.

The Merchant Marine and Fisheries Committee approved the bill by voice vote Nov. 18. The Senate was expected to take up the issue in 1994.

EVERGLADES WATER

The House on Nov. 23 passed by voice vote a bill to improve water flow through the Everglades into Florida Bay. The House bill (HR 3617), sponsored by E. Clay Shaw Jr., R-Fla., authorized the Interior secretary to spend $17.4 million to purchase land needed for the water flow project.

The money was to be transferred from an Army Corps of Engineers flood control and pump station project.

The Florida Bay water-flow project ultimately was expected to cost federal, state and local governments $100 million. The money authorized under Shaw's bill represented the federal portion of the costs.

The tracts to be acquired were primarily agricultural lands located east of Everglades National Park.

Identical language was included in a separate bill (HR 2530) to reauthorize the Interior Department's Bureau of Land Management. The House passed that bill Sept. 13; the Senate did not act on it. *(BLM, p. 272)*

LEASING THE PRESIDIO

The House approved a bill by voice vote Nov. 15 aimed at paving the way for private companies to lease buildings on the grounds of the mothballed Presidio Army Base in San Francisco. Under the bill (HR 3286 — H Rept 103-363), the Interior Department was to be allowed to lease out a 50-building complex at the Presidio. The complex, known as the Letterman-Lair complex, included a hospital and biological research institute.

The Army base at the foot of the Golden Gate Bridge was scheduled to become part of the national park system Oct. 1, 1994. The federal base-closure commission announced in 1988 that it would shut down the 1,400-acre facility, which was considered a prime piece of San Francisco real estate.

Nancy Pelosi, D-Calif., whose district included the Presidio and who sponsored the bill, said leasing out the hospital would help speed up the facility's conversion to a national park.

A pet cemetery, office buildings, golf course, houses and apartments also were located on the Presidio site. The Interior Department was working on a separate plan to determine what parts of the base could best be used as a national park. But some lawmakers were balking at the estimated $1.2 billion conversion cost.

NOAA REAUTHORIZATION

The House on Nov. 20 passed a bill to authorize the National Oceanic and Atmospheric Administration (NOAA) for six years. The Senate did not act on the measure in 1993.

The bill (HR 2811 — H Rept 103-248, Parts 1 & 2) authorized $1 billion in fiscal 1994, $1.2 billion in fiscal 1995 and $543 million in fiscal years 1995-1999 for the weather, satellite and atmospheric research programs of the agency. It was passed by voice vote.

The measure, sponsored by Ralph M. Hall, D-Texas, sought to ensure continued operation of all National Weather Service offices and to help modernize satellites and facilities used by the service. The weather service's flood forecasting system also was to be improved in response to the flooding in the Midwest earlier in 1993.

The House Merchant Marine Committee approved the portion of the bill under its jurisdiction Oct. 21. The House Science Committee approved its portion of the bill Aug. 4. ■

Congress Moves To Protect Oceans, Marine Life

Lawmakers took several efforts to improve the conservation of marine life in the Atlantic and Pacific Oceans:

ATLANTIC COAST MARINE PROTECTIONS

Congress cleared legislation giving federal and state governments more power to regulate fishing along the Atlantic coast. The provisions, aimed at renewing the marine life of several Atlantic coast fisheries, were folded into a bill reauthorizing the Coast Guard (HR 2150). The Senate passed HR 2150 by voice vote Nov. 22, the House cleared it by voice vote Nov. 23, and President Clinton signed the measure into law Dec. 20 (PL 103-206).

The fish conservation provisions began as a separate bill (S 1126 — S Rept 103-201), which won voice vote approval from the Senate Commerce Committee on Oct. 6.

Patterned after the 1984 Atlantic Striped Bass Conservation Act (PL 98-613), the bill established a procedure under which the secretary of Commerce could impose a federal fishing moratorium on Atlantic states that violated coastal fishery management plans. The bill called on the Atlantic States Marine Fishery Commission, an existing interstate commission, to develop management plans for each dwindling species of fish. The federal government could bar fishermen in a state that did not implement or enforce the plan from catching that species until their state came into compliance.

The bill authorized funding for the fisheries commission at $3 million for fiscal 1994, $5 million for fiscal 1995 and $7 million for fiscal 1996.

The bill aimed to protect the populations of striped bass, weakfish, bluefish, lobster and red drum, which populated the coastal waters of the Atlantic states.

The House passed a similar bill (HR 2134 — H Rept 103-202) by voice vote Aug. 2. The House bill authorized $2 million per year for fiscal years 1994-96. Thomas J. Manton, D-N.Y., who chaired the House Merchant Marine Subcommittee on Fisheries Management, said existing law allowed coastal states to ignore plans designed to restore dwindling fish stocks. "While fishermen from neighboring states reduce their catches so as to allow the stocks to grow, fishermen in the non-complying state continue the practices" that led to the shortage of fish, he said.

FISHING LIMITS

The House on Nov. 2 passed three other measures aimed at reviving marine life in the Atlantic Ocean and parts of the Pacific Ocean. The bills pressed U.S. fisheries to stem pollock and bluefin tuna harvests in international waters and encouraged other nations to follow suit. The Senate took no action on the measures.

Bill sponsors said that limiting fishing in the eastern Atlantic Ocean and Bering and Okhotsk seas promised to improve the long-term benefits for all countries that fished in those waters.

The bills were passed by voice vote:
● HR 3188 (H Rept 103-316) added new fishing restrictions to a 1992 law (PL 102-582) that penalized both foreign and U.S. ships that harvested fish in a part of the Bering Sea called the Donut Hole. The bill imposed similar punishments

for U.S.-flag ships in the nearby Peanut Hole in the Sea of Okhotsk, where such fishing had migrated. Bill sponsor Don Young, R-Alaska, said the stock of pollock was in danger of being fully depleted by nations still fishing in the area, which was encircled by the territorial waters of the United States and the Russian Federation. *(1992 Almanac, p. 286)*

Russian fleets had stopped fishing in both areas for pollock, a fish that swam back and forth from Russian and Alaskan coastal waters to the North Pacific seas.

The measure also granted the United States authority to participate in the enactment of a 10-year-old Northwest Atlantic Fisheries Organization treaty governing fishing in international waters near Canada and the United States. The House Merchant Marine and Fisheries Committee formally reported the bill Sept. 29.

● H Con Res 135 (H Rept 103-317), sponsored by Young, expressed congressional support for negotiators urging China, Korea, Poland and Japan to join the United States and Russia in developing permanent limits on pollock fishing in the Central Bering Sea.

● H Con Res 169 (H Rept 103-318), sponsored by Studds, was a non-binding resolution expressing congressional support for Atlantic tuna conservation rules. It urged U.S. delegates to an upcoming meeting of the International Commission for the Conservation of Atlantic Tunas to win pledges from other delegates to comply with international limits on bluefin tuna harvests. "The United States and all coastal states have a responsibility to participate in international management and conservation for shared resources on the high seas," said Studds. The Senate passed it Nov. 16.

Both U.S. commercial fisheries and environmentalists supported limits on foreign fishing because they wanted to help the population multiply. Failure to comply with rules governing bluefin tuna threatened to prompt U.S. trade sanctions on seafood products such as sushi. ■

White House Extends Nuclear Test Ban

Responding to pressure from Congress, the Clinton administration announced July 3 that it would not resume nuclear testing for at least 15 months if no other nation broke the worldwide moratorium on testing.

Three months later, the Chinese government detonated an 80- to 90-kiloton nuclear bomb at the Lop Nur underground test site in northwest China. Lawmakers again urged Clinton not to resume testing, and Clinton agreed, although he ordered the Energy Department to be ready in case he decided to conduct tests in 1994.

Congress had imposed a nine-month testing moratorium in October 1992 as part of the fiscal 1993 energy and water development appropriations act (PL 102-377). The law allowed up to 15 underground detonations of nuclear warheads from July 1, 1993, to Sept. 30, 1996, but none thereafter unless another country conducted tests. The law also required the president to notify Congress 90 legislative days in advance of the first detonation. *(1992 Almanac, p. 659)*

A number of Pentagon and Energy Department officials urged the new administration early in 1993 to resume testing and to continue testing through the end of the century. In addition to the tests specifically allowed by the appropriations act, they wanted to conduct test detonations with

small warheads after 1996.

Supporters of the proposal said it would help test trigger systems and retain valuable nuclear scientists at Energy Department laboratories. Opponents said it would violate the law. Said Sen. Mark O. Hatfield, R-Ore., "It's not a limited ban. It's a ban. B-A-N."

Hatfield was one of 26 senators and 38 House members who sent letters to the administration protesting the proposal. Many of the lawmakers also urged the administration not to resume testing at all, saying that new tests would hurt U.S. efforts to stop nuclear proliferation.

Clinton agreed to continue the moratorium with one caveat. If another country broke the moratorium, Clinton said July 3, "I will direct the Department of Energy to prepare to conduct additional tests, while seeking approval to do so from Congress."

When it became clear that China was planning to detonate a warhead, opponents of nuclear testing again lobbied the White House not to renew the U.S. program. Led by Carl Levin, D-Mich., 24 senators sent a letter to Clinton saying, "Should China conduct a test, we believe that it would be highly inappropriate and counterproductive for the United States to precipitously conduct a test of our own in response." Democratic Reps. Mike Kopetski of Oregon and Martin Olav Sabo of Minnesota circulated a similar letter in the House.

Secretary of State Warren Christopher also was reported to be cool to the idea of resumed testing, saying it could hamper efforts to reduce worldwide proliferation of nuclear arms.

The Chinese broke the moratorium Oct. 5. Later that day, Clinton took only one of the two steps outlined July 3: He instructed the Energy Department to prepare for new tests but did not ask Congress to approve them.

The White House said the president was not committed to the resumption of testing but was keeping options open to allow for a test at a later date. The president's ultimate decision to authorize a detonation would be based on four factors: the safety and reliability of the U.S. arsenal, the number of nations that honored the moratorium, the progress toward a comprehensive test ban treaty and the effect of further U.S. tests on efforts to stem nuclear proliferation. ■

Nuclear Projects Saved

Congress considered bills relating to nuclear research, nuclear regulation and the role of the federal energy laboratories:

NUCLEAR R&D

Fiscal 1994 energy and water appropriations bill (HR 2445 — PL 103-126) conferees came to the rescue of a handful of advanced nuclear research projects that one or both chambers of Congress wanted to nix. *(Appropriations, p. 589)*

● **Advanced liquid metal reactor.** While it did not have the notoriety and media attention provided the superconducting super collider, the advanced liquid metal reactor research program also drew criticism from lawmakers looking for spending cuts. However, the final energy and water bill included $31.9 million for continued research on the reactor, which was supposed to recycle used nuclear

materials, such as plutonium, from atomic weapons and power plants and use them to generate electricity.

Critics said the reactor would pose environmental and proliferation risks. Supporters, notably Senate Energy and Water Appropriations Subcommittee Chairman J. Bennett Johnston, D-La., said the project was worth funding and that ending it would cost almost as much as continuing it.

The House on June 24 voted 267-162 to terminate the project, but the Senate on Sept. 30 rejected a similar amendment by John Kerry, D-Mass., to kill the program. The Senate vote was 53-45. *(House vote 267, p. 66-H; Senate vote 298, p. 39-S)*

● **Space-based nuclear reactor.** The final appropriations bill also included $25 million for a space-based nuclear reactor program, called SP-100. The House had voted 333-98 on June 24 to cancel funding for the project, which aimed to develop a nuclear-based power source for use in outer space. *(Vote 268, p. 66-H)*

● **Gas-turbine helium reactor.** Conferees also kept funds in the bill for more research into a gas-turbine helium reactor, also known as the high-temperature gas reactor, aimed at eventually developing a nuclear reactor impervious to meltdown. The Senate on Sept. 30 agreed by voice vote to an amendment to kill the project.

NUCLEAR REGULATORY RENEWAL

The Senate Environment Subcommittee on Clean Air and Nuclear Regulation on Oct. 28 gave voice vote approval to a bill (S 1162) to reauthorize the Nuclear Regulatory Commission (NRC) and create new penalties for wrongdoing at nuclear facilities. The bill did not advance further in the first session.

The subcommittee bill increased the NRC's funding level by 1 percent per year, to $542.9 million in fiscal 1994 and $546.8 million in fiscal 1995.

Money for the NRC, whose reauthorization ran out in 1985, came entirely from fees paid by its licensees. The nuclear industry had complained about fee increases and was hoping to get Congress to add a provision creating an NRC advisory committee that would give the industry more say about the fees.

The bill included civil penalties for the owners, operators, suppliers or builders of nuclear facilities who failed to report a defect or rule violation to the NRC. And it allowed the NRC to obtain a warrant from a federal judge or magistrate to search unlicensed facilities, such as parts suppliers, without giving notice. Another section of the bill made it a federal offense to sabotage a nuclear plant or nuclear waste storage facility, not only when it was operating but also while it was being constructed.

Alan K. Simpson, R-Wyo., said he had reservations about the search warrant language that he hoped to clear up before the bill was brought up in the full committee.

The subcommittee also adopted by voice vote an amendment by Howard M. Metzenbaum, D-Ohio, increasing the penalty for violating NRC regulations governing some medical uses of radiation from $5,000 to $20,000.

The subcommittee approved a second bill (S 1165) to allow people to petition the NRC for sanctions against an operating nuclear facility. If the NRC denied such a petition, a federal appeals court could overturn that decision if it obtained evidence that the facility was in "significant non-compliance" or presented a "substantial hazard" to public health, safety or security.

The bill was approved on a 4-3 vote, with the committee's four Democrats in favor and its three Republicans opposed. Simpson said the bill would divert some of the NRC's scarce resources from public safety to legal fees. Chairman Joseph I. Lieberman, D-Conn., disagreed, noting that NRC Chairman Ivan Selin had testified that the bill would not have much impact on the NRC's resources.

Lieberman said he did not expect to see full committee action until 1994. ■

O'Leary Easily Confirmed To Top Energy Post

The Senate confirmed Energy Secretary Hazel R. O'Leary by voice vote Jan. 21, after she had won approval in an Inauguration Day telephone poll of Senate Energy and Natural Resources Committee members.

During her confirmation hearing Jan. 19, O'Leary advocated some of the environmental community's top priorities without disparaging the coal, oil and nuclear industries. She appealed to both sides on such controversial issues as nuclear power, nuclear waste and offshore drilling. O'Leary also echoed President Clinton's environmentally oriented pledges on energy, calling several times for more energy conservation and cleaner sources of power. Yet she offered the committee members, who tended to favor the domestic energy industry, reason to support her with comments on the limits to conservation and the need for continued domestic energy production.

Clinton plucked O'Leary, 55, from Northern States Power Co., an electric and gas utility in Minnesota. The company generated much of its electricity from coal and nuclear reactors — the environmental community's least favorite sources of energy — but it also had invested heavily in wind power and energy conservation. O'Leary's prior experience in government included directing the Federal Energy Administration's Office of Consumer Affairs under President Gerald R. Ford and the Energy Department's Economic Regulatory Administration under President Jimmy Carter.

At her confirmation hearing and in her written responses, O'Leary repeatedly struck a balance between conservation and "traditional" sources of energy. "I don't turn away from conservation or alternatives, and I do not turn away from traditional supplies that are on-line and that are economically and environmentally correct," she told the committee. "We've got to do it all."

One traditional supply that was not economical, in O'Leary's view, was nuclear power. "The costs of nuclear power, if you include new construction, are not competitive. Moreover, the long-term waste-storage problems are daunting," she wrote in response to a committee member's question. Still she said nuclear power should be an option.

O'Leary pledged to shift the Energy Department's research budget toward research into renewable energy and anti-pollution technologies, as Clinton had promised during the campaign. She also voiced support for reducing the money spent on nuclear weapons testing, speeding up decisions on natural-gas pipelines and weeding out problems in the department's contracting and procurement.

On the touchy issue of spent fuel rods from nuclear plants, O'Leary promised to stay the course plotted by the Bush administration. She said the department would do an

extensive study of the proposed permanent disposal site at Yucca Mountain, Nev., "as expeditiously as feasible" while treating the residents of that state fairly and complying with all environmental, safety and health laws.

She said the department's nuclear waste negotiator would continue to look for volunteer sites for a temporary facility for the rods, and that testing the Waste Isolation Pilot Plant, a storage site in New Mexico for plutonium-contaminated waste, would be a high priority. *(Nomination, 1992 Almanac, p. 154-A)* ■

Senate Confirms Babbitt

The Senate confirmed Bruce Babbitt as secretary of the Interior by a voice vote Jan. 21, after the nominee had won unanimous committee support.

In two days of hearings Jan. 19 and 21, the former Arizona governor and 1988 Democratic presidential contender reassured the Senate Energy and Natural Resources Committee that he was not a radical and would not toe the environmentalists' line as head of the Interior Department. Babbitt — a committed environmentalist but also a member of one of Arizona's oldest ranching families — noted that he grew up on a Western cattle ranch, was trained as a geologist and a lawyer, and had represented ranchers, small towns, Indian tribes and environmental groups.

"If I'm confirmed," Babbitt, 54, told the committee, "it will be my task . . . to represent not any one of those groups — and I've represented them all at one time or another — but to represent the public interest, to reconcile the conflicts, to find the common ground."

He also pointed to his ability as governor of Arizona to bring opposing groups together on such controversial issues as groundwater protection and wildlife preservation.

After more than six hours of questions and answers, Babbitt won the committee's endorsement on a 20-0 vote. Still, several senators made it clear to Babbitt that they were troubled by his barbed comments from 1991-93 as president of the League of Conservation Voters, the self-described political arm of the environmental movement.

"The secretary is no longer the guardian of narrow Western regional interests," said Chairman J. Bennett Johnston, D-La. "The old days of few users and little or no constraints on the secretary's decisions are gone forever."

And Malcolm Wallop, R-Wyo., the ranking member, said after an opening welcome, "I'm not certain that I'm enthusiastic about what I see coming down the road."

The Interior secretary had responsibility for managing about 442 million acres of public land nationwide, which was open to competing interests — mining, grazing, logging, recreation and wilderness. Babbitt had been a persistent critic of the management of the Interior Department and had called for a new philosophy of public-land management that would downgrade the importance of traditional uses such as mining and ranching to give more weight to environmental and recreational needs.

Western Republicans tried with limited success to have Babbitt support such Western interests as low-cost grazing and mining on public lands, private-property rights, the multiple-use system of managing public lands and a more cautious administration of the Endangered Species Act. Babbitt said he would not back away from the Endangered Species Act but promised to listen to suggestions for im-

proving it. On most other topics, though, Babbitt remained noncommittal. *(Nomination, 1992 Almanac, p. 154-A)*

Babbitt's popularity among environmental groups was underscored a little more than four months later, when his name briefly made the short list of potential appointees to fill the Supreme Court slot being vacated by Justice Byron R. White. The news provoked an outcry from environmental groups alarmed at the thought of getting a new Interior secretary so soon — possibly someone without Babbitt's political acumen or experience. The Environmental Defense Fund and the Defenders of Wildlife strongly urged President Clinton to look elsewhere for a court nominee. "His best contribution to the country is as secretary of Interior, more so than on the Supreme Court," said Rodger Schlickeisen, president of Defenders of Wildlife. *(Supreme Court, p. 325)* ■

Frampton's Controversial Nomination Approved

George T. Frampton Jr., President Clinton's controversial nominee to head the Interior Department's fish, wildlife and national parks programs, won voice vote approval from the Senate on June 30.

The Senate Energy and Natural Resources Committee had delayed voting on Frampton's nomination twice before finally approving him June 16 on a vote of 13-5. Frampton, who had served as president of The Wilderness Society from 1986-1993, had drawn criticism from Western lawmakers, who considered him to be a blunt, outspoken environmentalist. Several senators said they were especially concerned about how he would administer the Endangered Species Act. But the immediate cause of the delay was a charge that the former assistant Watergate prosecutor had overstepped his authority as a consultant to Interior while awaiting confirmation.

Senate Energy was first scheduled to vote before the Memorial Day weekend. But the panel's Western senators objected, saying Frampton had violated a federal management policy that prohibited consultants from directing the activities of federal employees. At issue was a May 18 memo in which Frampton wrote, "I want to assign the following tasks and deadlines" to Interior employees responsible for implementing the National Biological Survey. The project had created controversy among Westerners who believed it would expand the reach of the Endangered Species Act.

The Office of Personnel Management (OPM) ruled June 7 that Frampton did not break the policy, arguing that he was carrying out orders from Interior Secretary Bruce Babbitt's chief of staff. The Energy Committee had scheduled a vote June 9, but ranking Republican Malcolm Wallop of Wyoming, asked for a second delay until the week of June 14 because OPM's written explanation had not yet circulated among panel members.

When the committee finally voted, three Western Republicans — Mark O. Hatfield of Oregon, Pete V. Domenici of New Mexico and Robert F. Bennett of Utah — joined the panel's 10 Democrats to recommend the nomination. Domenici said the Senate ultimately would hold Clinton and Babbitt responsible for public lands policy, not Frampton.

The Senate Environment Committee, which also had jurisdiction, had approved Frampton's nomination by voice vote May 25. ■

Browner OK'd for EPA

The Senate confirmed Carol M. Browner as administrator of the Environmental Protection Agency (EPA) by voice vote on Jan. 21, two days after she received the committee's approval on a 15-0 vote.

Browner, 37, promised a regulatory climate that would not be hostile to business but revealed few specifics about her plans for EPA at her Jan. 11 hearing before the Senate Committee on Environment and Public Works. Members of both parties greeted her with enthusiasm.

"I would urge you to look upon the members of this committee as your allies," said John H. Chafee, R-R.I. But Chafee cautioned the Florida environmental regulation chief not to bend too far to placate the needs of business: "You are an advocate for the environment . . . the word 'balance' is in the eye of the beholder." Max Baucus, D-Mont., the incoming committee chairman who ran the $3\frac{1}{2}$-hour confirmation hearing, presaged many of the committee members' comments when he said, "For the past several years, Congress and the administration have been paralyzed by gridlock, particularly when it comes to environmental policy. . . . Now the American people expect all that to change."

In general, Browner was careful not to tip the hand of President-elect Clinton. Repeating a refrain often sounded by Clinton and Vice President Al Gore during the 1992 presidential campaign, she said, "We can ease the regulatory burden on business without compromising the environment."

Browner was a close ally of Gore, an ardent environmentalist, and worked as legislative director of his Senate office from 1989 to 1991. But her comments suggested that she had taken heed of the more pragmatic, cost-conscious brand of environmentalism practiced by Clinton.

She gave noncommittal answers to questions on the environmental components of the North American Free Trade Agreement, on the planned opening of a controversial hazardous waste incinerator in Ohio and on reformulated gasolines that use ethanol as an additive. She said that while she supported laws giving communities the right to know what types of pollutants local factories and businesses might be releasing into the air and water, she was sensitive to business concerns, such as the disclosure of trade secrets, sometimes raised by such requirements.

Before she was confirmed, Browner spent two years as secretary of the Florida Department of Environmental Regulation. There, she clashed with business and agricultural interests, including the state's powerful sugar cane industry, which had been linked to pollution in the Everglades.

At the same time, she was credited with working with business. A case in point was an agreement the state brokered in which the Walt Disney Co. agreed to spend $40 million to buy 8,500 acres of wetlands in central Florida. Disney agreed to turn the land over to the Nature Conservancy, a national conservation organization, in exchange for being allowed to destroy several hundred acres of wetlands on its property at Walt Disney World in Orlando. *(Nomination, 1992 Almanac, p. 148-A)* ■

LAW & JUDICIARY

Anti-Crime Bill Chronology

The bulk of crime legislation that came before Congress in 1993 had been under consideration in some form since 1988 or earlier. Democratic and Republican bills had shared similar provisions, but conservatives generally favored tougher penalties for criminals while liberals supported tougher gun control. The following is an overview:

1988: Congress cleared an anti-crime package (PL 100-690) that included the death penalty for drug-related felonies. The bill initially contained a seven-day waiting period for handgun purchases — a proposal known as the Brady bill, a reference to President Ronald Reagan's press secretary, James S. Brady, who was wounded in a 1981 assassination attempt on the president. The waiting period provision died on the House floor before the bill reached the Senate. Gun lobbyists succeeded in replacing the Brady language with an identity-check system, requiring the Justice Department to develop a plan for gun dealers to identify criminals. *(1988 Almanac, p. 85)*

1989: Democrats and Republicans introduced crime legislation, but no omnibus bill reached either floor. The plans called for more law enforcement funding, stricter penalties for criminals and the death penalty for more federal crimes. Both parties also called for reform of habeas corpus appeals, petitions filed by death row inmates challenging their sentences as unconstitutional. Democrats in both chambers introduced the Brady bill as separate legislation. A Senate Judiciary subcommittee held hearings in 1989,

but the bill went no further. *(1989 Almanac, p. 259)*

1990: Congress cleared a watered-down anti-crime bill (PL 101-647) after abandoning more sweeping legislation. The bill included increased penalties for child abuse and more funding for local law enforcement agencies and for alternatives to prison, such as house arrest. The House Judiciary Committee approved a Brady bill with a seven-day waiting period, but it never reached the floor. *(1990 Almanac, p. 486)*

1991: A Democratic bill became the main anti-crime vehicle, with the House approving its conference report in November. The Senate waited until 1992 to consider — and block — the conference report. The bill would have authorized the death penalty for additional federal crimes, restricted habeas corpus appeals and granted more money for prisons and law enforcement. It also included a Brady provision with a five-day waiting period. Although the omnibus bill stalled short of enactment, the year marked a milestone for the Brady bill: For the first time, both chambers passed bills including a five-day waiting period. *(1991 Almanac, p. 262)*

1992: Senate Republicans blocked approval of the conference report on the 1991 anti-crime bill in March and again in October. They argued that the bill failed to adequately reform the habeas corpus process and safeguard defendants' rights. They also stopped floor consideration of a separate Brady bill calling for a five-day waiting period. *(1992 Almanac, p. 311)*

---

and action ground to a halt as Senate leaders began backroom negotiations on how to proceed. Those talks continued throughout the next day, scuttling hopes of completing work on the bill before the Veterans Day recess.

A week later, after a series of other obstacles had been cleared away, the Senate on Nov. 17 approved Feinstein's amendment, 56-43. Five Republicans switched sides to support the ban: Hank Brown, Colo.; Daniel R. Coats, Ind.; James M. Jeffords, Vt.; Richard G. Lugar, Ind.; and Bob Packwood, Ore. *(Vote 375, p. 48-S)*

Gun control opponents considered filibustering the entire bill over the amendment but gave up, apparently in hope of gutting or narrowing it in conference with the House, which had rejected an assault gun ban in 1991.

Biden, a supporter of the ban, said it faced "an uphill fight." DeConcini said he would not be surprised if it died in conference, given the still-considerable influence of the National Rifle Association in the House.

Guns, Mandatory Sentencing

Senators also took another tack against gun violence, approving tougher mandatory sentences for federal crimes involving firearms.

Phil Gramm, R-Texas, a gun control opponent, offered an amendment Nov. 9 to impose stiff minimum penalties for using a gun during a violent crime or drug felony: 10 years for gun possession, 20 years for discharging it during a crime and life imprisonment or death for murders involv-

ing firearms. Hatch praised the amendment as a superior approach to gun control. "We want to get tough on crime, not get tough on honest, decent, law-abiding citizens who happen to want to own their own guns," he said.

Alfonse M. D'Amato, R-N.Y., attached an amendment to Gramm's proposal specifying that the federal gun penalties — including the death penalty — could apply to state offenses involving a gun that had crossed state lines. State prosecutors could decide whether to seek federal jurisdiction for such cases. Biden warned that the D'Amato proposal would flood the federal courts with tens of thousands of handgun crimes. But senators approved it nonetheless, 58-42. Gramm's underlying amendment was adopted by voice vote. *(Vote 362, p. 47-S)*

Senators approved several additional gun restrictions by voice vote Nov. 10 barring gun sales to people convicted of domestic abuse or under a restraining order, and tightening rules for firearms dealers.

On Nov. 8, the Senate approved an amendment by Trent Lott, R-Miss., to require life imprisonment for criminals convinced of a third felony with a maximum penalty of more than five years. The amendment was adopted 91-1, with Packwood voting no. *(Vote 357, p. 46-S)*

Breaking the Logjam

Besides the assault weapons issue, other amendments still threatened to hold up the bill midway through the debate. Edward M. Kennedy, D-Mass., was determined to

offer his proposal to make it a federal crime to bar access to abortion clinics. Arlen Specter, R-Pa., meanwhile, resisted proposals to abandon the contentious issue of limiting habeas corpus petitions. A former prosecutor, Specter said he had drawn up a series of changes to speed up the time frame for considering such appeals.

Talks continued throughout the day Nov. 10. Finally, close to midnight, Majority Leader Mitchell emerged with a complex agreement to move ahead. Under that accord, senators agreed to take up the clinic access bill (S 636) and Specter's proposal to overhaul habeas corpus petitions (S 1657) as separate bills. Biden agreed to drop his own habeas corpus proposal from the overall crime bill. With those issues resolved, senators would go back to the crime bill, with votes scheduled on Feinstein's assault weapons ban and a fixed number of additional amendments.

On Nov. 16, the Senate passed the clinic access bill, 69-30. The next day, senators voted 65-34 to table, or kill, Specter's habeas corpus bill, putting off for another year a nettlesome issue that had long evaded compromise. *(Votes 373, 374, p. 48-S)*

A Flood of Amendments

In addition to approving Feinstein's assault-ban amendment, senators used the final days of debate to tack a host of additional amendments on to the crime bill.

● **State and local criminal justice systems.** On Nov. 16, senators gave voice vote approval to an amendment by Howell Heflin, D-Ala., to set aside up to $100 million a year through fiscal 1998 for state and local governments to expand their criminal justice systems with more prosecutors, public defenders and judges to handle additional defendants arrested by the new police officers.

● **Death penalty.** The following day, the Senate approved, 74-25, an amendment by D'Amato to extend the death penalty to so-called drug kingpins — the leaders of criminal enterprises that dealt in large amounts of illegal drugs. The bill already extended the federal death penalty to include about 50 new crimes, most of them involving murder. *(Vote 377, p. 49-S)*

And in a blow to death penalty opponents, the Senate rejected, 25-74, an amendment by Carl Levin, D-Mich., to replace capital punishment penalties in the bill with life in prison without parole. *(Vote 379, p. 49-S)*

From Nov. 16-18, the Senate also:

● Approved an amendment by Jesse Helms, R-N.C., to limit the power of federal courts to impose population caps in prison overcrowding cases, bar class-action lawsuits in such cases and retroactively apply the new limits to existing court-ordered caps. The Senate rejected a move to kill the proposal, 31-68, and passed it by voice vote. *(Vote 376, p. 48-S)*

● Approved by voice vote an amendment by Bob Graham, D-Fla., to allow the federal government to take custody of criminal aliens or to pay states for housing them.

● Approved by voice vote an amendment by Kay Bailey Hutchison, R-Texas, to bar prisoners from getting federal Pell grants for higher education. Hutchison said that Congress in 1992 barred death row and life-imprisonment inmates from getting Pell grants, but she wanted to extend the provision to other prisoners.

● Approved by voice vote an amendment by Barbara Boxer, D-Calif., to bar states from releasing personal information from motor vehicle records. Aimed at stalkers who used such public records to track their victims, the proposal was opposed by media groups that said it would dry up an important source of information. Hatch, the

crime bill's main Republican sponsor, said he would seek to alter the proposal to address those concerns in conference.

● Rejected, 26-73, an amendment by Robert C. Smith, R-N.H., to halve certain federal grants to states that did not stiffen their sentencing laws. *(Vote 378, p. 49-S)*

After 1 a.m. on Nov. 19, senators approved about 50 amendments by voice vote, including steps to deport criminal aliens more quickly and to provide hundreds of millions of dollars in grants for programs such as after-school activities to keep juveniles out of crime.

Further Action Delayed

Biden predicted that the Senate measure would end perennial partisan fights over crime by embracing ideas from both sides. Others were not so sure. Gramm, a conservative, called the bill "the toughest crime bill ever passed in American history." But, he added, "the gun control provision in this bill is basically a cop-out."

The big crime bill's ultimate fate, however, was delayed until 1994, when congressional negotiators would try to reconcile the Senate's bill with a much more limited set of House proposals, including one that would put 50,000 more police officers on the street.

Biden promised to fight in the conference to eliminate what he called "the wacko amendments" — the most stringent proposals adopted on the floor, including those to federalize state gang and gun crimes, try youths accused of serious violent crimes as adults and imprison for life without parole anyone convicted of three violent crimes. He also criticized proposals to condition federally funded prison space for state prisoners on stiffer state sentencing laws, to loosen evidence rules in sex crime cases and to limit federal court power in prison crowding cases.

Republicans warned that they would attempt to sink the bill, as they had in 1992, if it came back from conference without touchstone conservative law-and-order proposals: the provision pressuring states to stiffen their sentencing laws, strict federal minimum mandatory sentences and life in prison for "three-time losers."

Attorney General Janet Reno indicated that the administration supported the Senate bill. "This package is going to have a tremendous impact on crime," she said. Asked about some of the tougher measures added on the floor, including death penalty provisions, she said tersely and without elaboration, "The administration supports those very definitely." Reno opposed the death penalty; Clinton favored it.

HOUSE ACTION

Unable to persuade liberals on his committee to swallow the omnibus anti-crime bill, which they found too harsh, House Judiciary Committee Chairman Brooks broke out the more popular and digestible pieces in a series of separate bills. His strategy ended hopes that Congress would enact a sweeping crime bill in the first session.

The biggest piece — the Brady bill — was enacted at the end of the session. Ten other smaller bills won House approval in 1993.

Brooks deferred action on other hot-button issues, such as extending the federal death penalty to more crimes and overhauling habeas corpus procedures. He said both liberal and conservative lawmakers had sought more time to debate those issues. "But I am not willing to see important, innovative crime prevention programs like cops on the beat be deferred at a time when the American public is clamoring for us to provide more protection against violent acts," Brooks said.

Democratic members of the Judiciary Committee had long been more liberal on average than the House Democratic Caucus as a whole, and that tilt had been reinforced in the 103rd Congress. Two of the five new Democrats on the committee — Robert C. Scott of Virginia and Melvin Watt of North Carolina — were members of the Congressional Black Caucus. Another, Xavier Becerra of California, was on the Hispanic caucus.

Backed by senior committee Democrats Don Edwards of California and John Conyers Jr. of Michigan, the liberals had introduced their own bill (HR 3315) that focused more on crime prevention and criminal rehabilitation and included certain legal protections for prisoners on death row as well as numerous gun control initiatives.

Brooks' strategy generally suited the liberals, who supported the smaller bills and were happy to put off action on more controversial issues until the next session. Craig Washington, D-Texas, sponsor of HR 3315, said the approach would allow for a substantive debate on crime-fighting strategies in 1994, rather than a quick "sound-bite" war in the fall of 1993.

Judiciary Committee Republicans, who were backing their own omnibus anti-crime bill (HR 2872), complained that Brooks was thwarting their attempts to debate critical initiatives such as money for new prisons and tougher sentencing laws.

F. James Sensenbrenner Jr., R-Wis., called Brooks' strategy the result of "excessive partisanship," reflecting an unwillingness to negotiate with Republicans on a broad bill. He warned that Brooks might circumvent concerns of both the left and right on the death penalty and other issues by negotiating a broad crime bill directly with the Senate when House and Senate conferees sought to meld the broader Senate bill with the separate House pieces. Brooks sidestepped a question about whether he would consider such a move, saying he would await Senate action on a crime bill before making any decision about his strategy for conference.

Small Bills — First Round

Having assuaged his left flank, Brooks was able to move quickly to mark up the smaller bills.

On Oct. 28, the full Judiciary Committee voted 34-1 in favor of five new bills; Sensenbrenner cast the sole no vote. A sixth measure won voice vote approval. Republicans tried to attach some of their death penalty provisions and, at one point, the entire GOP crime bill. But Brooks ruled the amendments out of order as non-germane.

Five of the bills came to the House floor Nov. 3 amid finger-pointing over just who had blocked consideration of the broader anti-crime package. While most lawmakers agreed that the bills before them would do some good, they argued fiercely over how much. Charles E. Schumer, D-N.Y., said the programs represented the heart of anti-crime legislation. He said the community policing grants would do far more to reduce crime than proposals to reduce death row appeals, which would affect criminals already in jail. But Newt Gingrich, R-Ga., called them "pygmy bills" without the force of GOP proposals.

The House approved four of the bills Nov. 3 under suspension of the rules; a fifth bill passed Nov. 19.

● **Community policing.** The most expensive and arguably the most important of the measures approved by the committee Oct. 28 was HR 3355 (H Rept 103-324), a new grant program to boost community policing. The House approved the bill by voice vote Nov. 3.

The bill authorized $3.5 billion over six years to help states and localities hire about 50,000 additional police

officers. The aim, which had bipartisan support, was to send more police into neighborhoods — on foot, horse, bicycle or other means — where they would be more visible and could develop closer ties to the community.

During the committee markup, some Republicans questioned the impact of the proposed authorization without a corresponding cost-cutting mechanism to ensure that the grant program was funded in the appropriations process. House Republicans, in their crime bill, proposed paying for anti-crime programs with across-the-board cuts in federal administrative expenses.

But Schumer responded angrily to the criticisms, saying that Clinton had fought to target some of the newly announced budget savings for anti-crime programs. And in a letter to Brooks, White House budget director Leon E. Panetta said the administration already had begun budgeting for the community policing program.

● **Drug treatment for prisoners.** The committee approved a bill (HR 3354 — H Rept 103-323) authorizing $300 million over three years to help states provide drug treatment to inmates. A second measure (HR 3350 — H Rept 103-320) required drug treatment in federal prisons. The House passed the bills Nov. 3 by votes of 394-32 and 373-54 respectively. *(Votes 543, 540, p. 132-H)*

● **Juvenile gangs and drug trafficking.** A fourth bill approved by the committee (HR 3353 — H Rept 103-322) authorized $200 million over two years to help states fight juvenile gangs and drug trafficking. The House passed the bill, 413-12, Nov. 3. *(Vote 542, p. 132-H)*

● **School crime prevention.** A bill (HR 3375) to authorize grants to support local school initiatives for preventing crime and violence won committee approval only.

● **Alternative sentencing.** The committee approved the sixth bill (HR 3351 — H Rept 103-321) by voice vote. It provided for state grants of up to $200 million a year for three years to develop alternative sentencing for youthful offenders age 22 or younger. One alternative to prison would be boot camp. Youths would not be eligible if convicted of sexual assault, a crime involving a firearm, or any crime punishable by one year or more in prison.

The House first took up the bill Nov. 3, voting 235-192, less than the two-thirds majority needed to pass it under expedited procedures. Republicans objected to grants for alternative punishments when, they said, the government was not doing more to support traditional incarceration. The House subsequently passed the bill, 336-82, on Nov. 19. *(Vote 541, p. 132-H; vote 590, p. 144-H)*

Small Bills — Second Round

The Judiciary Committee marked up five more anti-crime bills Nov. 17. All but HR 1237 had been approved the previous day by the Judiciary Subcommittee on Crime. The House approved all five on Nov. 20.

● **Crimes against women.** The committee voted 34-1 to approved a measure (HR 1133 — H Rept 103-395) to establish new laws aimed at reducing domestic violence against women. The Violence Against Women Act, sponsored by Patricia Schroeder, D-Colo., contained provisions prodding states to toughen laws against domestic violence, providing grants for law enforcement efforts to prosecute and prevent crimes such as rape, and making interstate stalking and domestic violence federal crimes.

The committee approved, by voice vote, an amendment to provide education programs for judges dealing with sexual assault and domestic violence. After lengthy procedural debate, George E. Sangmeister, D-Ill., withdrew an amend-

ment that would have allowed the victim in a sexual assault case to make a statement at the sentencing hearing. The panel also discussed an amendment by Edwards that would have eliminated language requiring a mandatory minimum sentence of three months for crimes against women. Edwards eventually withdrew the amendment but said he might try to offer it on the floor.

The House passed the bill, 421-0. *(Vote 593, p. 144-H)*

● **Youth handgun ban.** The committee approved, by voice vote, a bill (HR 3098 — H Rept 103-389) prohibiting the sale of handguns or ammunition to minors. The bill, sponsored by Dan Glickman, D-Kan., made it a federal crime to sell or transfer a handgun to a person under 18, or for the minor to possess the gun. The bill included some exceptions, such as allowing minors to use guns under limited circumstances with proper parental supervision.

The measure, which was similar to language in the big Senate crime bill, had won support from gun control and gun rights advocates alike. It passed the House by a vote of 422-0. *(Vote 592, p. 144-H)*

● **Crimes against minors.** A third bill (HR 324 — H Rept 103-392), approved by voice vote, required people convicted of a crime such as sexual assault against a minor to notify police of their addresses for 10 years following their release from prison or their parole. The bill, sponsored by Jim Ramstad, R-Minn., included penalties for states that did not create such registries within three years.

The House approved the measure by voice vote.

● **Kidnapping by parents.** The Judiciary Committee approved a bill (HR 3378 — H Rept 103-390) that made it a federal crime for parents to kidnap their children and take them out of the United States. The bill, sponsored by George W. Gekas, R-Pa., allowed the federal government to have the parents extradited to the United States for prosecution. The House and Senate each passed the bill by voice vote Nov. 20, and Clinton signed it Dec. 2 (PL 103-173).

● **Child-care providers.** The committee also approved a bill sponsored by Schroeder (HR 1237 — H Rept 103-393) to establish a national system for carrying out criminal background checks on people applying for jobs as child-care providers. The House passed the bill by voice vote Nov. 20. The Senate cleared the bill by voice vote the same day, and Clinton signed it Dec. 20 (PL 103-209).

● **'Black talon' bullets.** The Judiciary Crime Subcommittee approved another bill (HR 3398), sponsored by Thomas M. Barrett, D-Wis., that did not get approval from the full committee. The bill sought to restrict the use of particularly dangerous new bullets, known as black talons, that opened on impact to reveal spikes that tore flesh. The subcommittee approved the bill, 8-5, on Nov. 16. Opponents said some hunters used similar bullets to ensure that animals were killed when shot and not just wounded, but bill backers said the bullets were used primarily for crimes.

Brooks predicted that his panel would take up additional crime proposals in 1994, including some regarding the death penalty, though not necessarily the full range of matters addressed in the Senate bill. "We'll have enough in common," Brooks said. ■

President Signs 'Brady' Gun Control Law

After seven years of debate and a harrowing final week of political maneuvering, the Senate on Nov. 24 cleared the so-called Brady bill (HR 1025) requiring a five-day waiting period for the purchase of a handgun. It was the first major gun control legislation to pass Congress since 1968, when lawmakers approved restrictions in response to urban violence and the assassinations of Robert F. Kennedy and the Rev. Dr. Martin Luther King Jr.

The Senate acted only after pulling back from an escalating standoff between gun control advocates and opponents that had imperiled Congress' plans to adjourn by Thanksgiving. President Clinton signed the Brady bill into law Nov. 30 (PL 103-159).

The bill instituted a waiting period of five business days for all handgun purchases, providing a cooling-off period for impetuous gun buyers as well as time to check the purchaser's background. The bill also raised licensing fees for gun dealers and required that police be notified of any multiple gun purchases. House-Senate conference negotiators agreed to phase out the waiting period within five years and replace it with a national "instant-check" system that would scan computerized criminal records to prevent the selling of weapons to felons.

The bill was named for former White House press secretary James S. Brady, who was permanently disabled in the 1981 assassination attempt on President Ronald Reagan. The legislation became a crusade for Brady and his wife, Sarah.

Many on both sides described the bill as a modest measure that at best would make only a small dent in crime. But the well-publicized legislation took on gigantic political dimensions, as evidenced by an exhausting week of brinkmanship in the final days of the session. The vote was the first major setback for the National Rifle Association (NRA), which had thwarted past gun control efforts and had endorsed the instant-check system.

Two factors helped advocates win passage in 1993: Lawmakers separated the Brady bill from the more complicated and controversial omnibus crime bill making its way through Congress, and public sentiment in support of gun control reached a crescendo that politicians were afraid to ignore.

Yet, even Brady acknowledged that the watered-down version of the initial legislation was only a first step in ridding the country's streets of violence. And to prevent a GOP filibuster in the Senate, Democratic leaders agreed to consider changes in the law when Congress returned in 1994.

BACKGROUND

With a sympathetic Democrat in the White House, gun control proponents began 1993 optimistic that they finally would see the Brady bill become law. They were right, though just barely. It had been an arduous, seven-year fight.

In 1988, Congress cleared an anti-drug package, but a handgun waiting period provision — named that year after Brady — died on the House floor. In 1989, Democrats in both chambers introduced the Brady bill as separate legislation, but it got no further than Senate Judiciary subcommittee hearings. In 1990, the House Judiciary Committee approved a

Brady bill with a seven-day waiting period, but it never reached the House floor. *(1990 Almanac, p. 500)*

In 1991, both chambers passed crime bills that included a five-day handgun waiting period, and the House narrowly approved the conference report on the bill at the end of the year. But in 1992, the conference report languished in the Senate, blocked by the Republicans. Gun control advocates tried but failed to bring up a separate bill providing for a seven-day handgun waiting period. *(1992 Almanac, p. 311)*

1993 Bill

Making good on pledges to help Clinton win new federal anti-crime initiatives, the leaders of the House and Senate Judiciary committees — Rep. Jack Brooks, D-Texas, and Sen. Joseph R. Biden Jr., D-Del. — introduced parallel crime bills Sept. 23. While not identical, both bills reflected an anti-crime package that Clinton had announced in August. The bills, and Clinton's proposal, were based on the conference agreement for the anti-crime bill that died in the 102nd Congress. *(Crime bill, p. 293)*

However, Brooks and Biden parted ways over how to handle gun control. Clinton supported the Brady bill, and Brooks included the five-day waiting period for gun purchases in his crime bill, even though he opposed gun control. During the five-day period, local police would check whether the applicant was prohibited by federal or state law from buying a handgun. The bill provided for the waiting period to be phased out once the attorney general certified that there was a viable, nationwide instant background check system in place to block sales to felons or other unqualified buyers. The bill authorized $100 million a year, beginning in fiscal 1994, to help states set up such a system.

The Senate bill contained no Brady language. Biden planned to move the handgun waiting period as a separate bill (S 414).

HOUSE COMMITTEE ACTION

In late October, Judiciary Committee Chairman Brooks agreed to disentangle the Brady bill provisions from his overall anti-crime proposal (HR 3131), which appeared to have little chance of getting enacted before the end of the first session. The Crime Subcommittee promptly approved the resulting free-standing bill (HR 1025) by a vote of 10-3 on Oct. 29.

Supporters had been seeking such an opportunity all year, because they feared that the issue could become stalled as part of the omnibus crime bill, as it had in 1992.

Full Committee

The House Judiciary Committee approved the Brady bill, 23-12, on Nov. 4 (H Rept 103-344). The vote split largely along partisan lines, but two Democrats — Brooks and Rick Boucher of Virginia, voted against the bill. Four

---

BOXSCORE

➡ **Handgun Waiting Period (HR 1025, S 414).** The legislation, known as the Brady bill, required a five-day waiting period for the purchase of a handgun, to give local police time to do a background check on the would-be purchaser.

Reports: H Rept 103-344; Conference Rept 103-412.

KEY ACTION

Nov. 4 — **House** committee approved HR 1025, 23-12.

Nov. 10 — **House** passed HR 1025, 238-189.

Nov. 20 — **Senate** passed HR 1025, 63-36, after substituting text of S 414.

Nov. 23 — **House** adopted conference report, 238-187.

Nov. 24 — **Senate** adopted conference report by voice vote.

Nov. 30 — **President** signed bill, PL 103-159.

Republicans supported the bill: Hamilton Fish Jr., N.Y.; Henry J. Hyde, Ill.; Jim Ramstad, Minn.; and F. James Sensenbrenner Jr., Wis.

Clinton met with key backers Nov. 2 and emerged urging speedy passage. Crime and Criminal Justice Subcommittee Chairman Charles E. Schumer, D-N.Y., who attended the meeting, said Clinton might call on Congress to stay in session past Thanksgiving, if needed, to pass the measure.

Although the outcome of the committee markup was not in doubt, lawmakers took almost four hours to sift through numerous amendments, eventually rejecting almost all of them as unfriendly.

Bill McCollum, R-Fla., said state waiting periods should be eliminated once the nationwide instant-check system kicked in. Schumer replied that states had the right to maintain a waiting period if they chose, to offer a cooling-off period for potential crimes of passion. McCollum's amendment was rejected 16-19.

Lawmakers also rejected, 16-19, an amendment that would have required police officials to supply a written reason, within five days, for denying a handgun purchase. But Schumer agreed to let would-be gun purchasers sue to clear their record if they were wrongly denied a gun.

Robert W. Goodlatte, R-Va., sought to replace the Brady bill with a Republican-sponsored proposal for an instant-check system. But members rejected that plan as well as efforts to set a date to phase out the waiting period.

No one was certain how soon states could bring their criminal records up to speed, but Schumer said it would probably take five to 10 years.

HOUSE FLOOR ACTION

The House approved the five-day waiting period for handgun purchases Nov. 10 by a vote of 238-189. *(Vote 564, p. 138-H)*

It was a victory for gun control advocates, but not an unequivocal one. Opponents waged close fights over amendments that sponsors said would undermine the bill, and lawmakers approved one to phase out the waiting period in five years.

The NRA and other gun rights advocates seized on the Nov. 2 elections as evidence that voters had little faith in gun control initiatives and preferred getting tough on criminals. In Virginia, the pro-gun-control Democratic nominee for governor lost to a Republican who stressed getting tough. But others said voters were hungry for any and all measures to combat crime. Both sides lobbied fiercely during the week of Nov. 8, working the halls outside the House chamber.

Advocates said the measure could prevent thousands of homicides and suicides by keeping handguns away from criminals and providing a cooling-off period for agitated gun buyers.

Critics skewered such claims, saying the law would in-

convenience lawful gun owners and police while criminals obtained their guns on the black market.

But the bill's substance had in some respects become secondary to its symbolic importance.

Uncertainty Over Amendments

Lawmakers on both sides went into the debate knowing there were almost certainly enough votes to pass some version of the bill. They voted 238-182 for the rule allowing the measure to come to the floor. *(Vote 557, p. 136-H)*

But neither side was certain who would prevail on a series of amendments sponsored by Republican opponents and bearing the endorsement of Judiciary Committee Chairman Brooks.

Bill sponsor Schumer agreed to accept one of those, a proposal by Jim Ramstad, R-Minn., requiring that police provide a reason within 20 days for denying a handgun purchase. It subsequently was adopted 431-2. *(Vote 558, p. 136-H)*

But there was little bipartisanship on two other GOP amendments.

The first, offered by George W. Gekas, Pa., provided that the five-day waiting period would end five years after enactment — regardless of whether the instant-check system was up and running. Schumer said five years was an unrealistic deadline, given that some states still had criminal data in shoeboxes. But proponents of the cutoff said many states had implemented instant-check systems quickly, and the sunset provision would encourage the Justice Department to put the national system in place promptly. Gekas prevailed on a 236-198 vote. *(Vote 559, p. 136-H)*

The stakes were higher on the next amendment, sponsored by McCollum, to pre-empt state waiting periods once the instant-check system was in place. As written, the Brady bill set a national minimum waiting period of five days but did not affect states that had adopted longer waiting periods. McCollum said his proposal would make the bill more balanced. Because the bill imposed a waiting period on states that did not have such laws, he said, it would be fair to pre-empt all waiting periods once the instant-check system was in place.

McCollum said the amendment would not affect other state gun laws, such as Virginia's limit of one gun purchase per month. But Schumer and others disagreed, saying such restrictions would be prohibited because they required purchasers to wait to obtain guns. As debate continued, Schumer produced a letter from Attorney General Janet Reno siding with his interpretation of the amendment.

Off the floor, Brady bill strategists debated whether to urge a "no" vote on the overall bill if the amendment prevailed or approve a flawed bill with the hope of killing the pre-emption language in conference. But they were spared that decision when members rejected the amendment, 175-257. *(Vote 560, p. 136-H)*

SENATE PASSAGE

With Congress pressing to close up shop for the year, the Senate took up its version of the bill on Nov. 19, after senators agreed to forgo a debate on the handgun waiting period as part of the broader crime bill approved earlier that day. After two failed attempts to limit debate, the Senate passed the Brady bill Nov. 20, 63-36. The Senate voted on HR 1025 after substituting the text of its own bill (S 414). *(Vote 394, p. 51-S)*

Floor consideration began under the terms of a complex agreement concluded early on Nov. 19. Under the agreement, Majority Leader George J. Mitchell, D-Maine, and Minority Leader Bob Dole, R-Kan., offered a substitute for the original version of S 414.

Like the original, sponsored by Sen. Howard M. Metzenbaum, D-Ohio, the substitute established a five-day waiting period for handgun purchases to give local law enforcement agencies time to conduct a background check on would-be buyers. The Mitchell-Dole version authorized $200 million per year to help create a national computerized network of criminal records; the waiting period would phase out once this instant-check system was in place.

But the substitute also included two new provisions sought by the NRA and its allies.

The first, and most controversial, pre-empted state and local waiting periods once the national instant-check system was in place. Proponents said waiting periods would be unnecessary at that point. Mitchell promptly offered an amendment to strike that provision, saying it was an affront to states' rights and that he had included it only to let debate move forward. His amendment prevailed, 54-45. *(Vote 385, p. 50-S)*

But senators did not heed Mitchell's call to delete a second provision to phase out the five-day waiting period five years after enactment, regardless of whether the instant-check system was completed. His amendment failed 43-56 and the provision stayed in the bill. *(Vote 386, p. 50-S)*

GOP Filibuster

Senators next clashed over whether to block a planned filibuster by gun rights advocates, including Larry E. Craig, R-Idaho, who said the bill should not go forward without the language to pre-empt state and local waiting periods.

The first vote Nov. 19 to impose cloture and end debate on the Dole-Mitchell amendment was 57-42, three short of the three-fifths, or 60, needed to limit debate. Nine Republicans broke ranks to support cloture, while seven Democrats crossed their majority to oppose it. A second cloture vote at 11 that night also failed, 57-41. Several senators said Dole girded Republicans to vote against cloture a second time, saying he needed more time to negotiate additional changes. *(Votes 387, 390, p. 50-S)*

Metzenbaum and Sarah Brady attacked the move in a midnight news conference. "I think the Republicans now find themselves in the position ... of having killed the Brady bill," Metzenbaum said.

The Nov. 20 morning papers pronounced the bill dead for the year, and many thought it was. But Assistant Minority Leader Alan K. Simpson, R-Wyo., said a handful of Republicans, unhappy with the outcome, wanted a straight vote on the matter before leaving town. William S. Cohen, R-Maine, for example, said he voted against cloture on the second vote to support Dole, but with the expectation and desire that the bill ultimately would move ahead.

That discontent sent Dole back to the negotiating table. Although he tried for a better deal, Dole had to settle for a version only superficially different from the one Republicans had filibustered the night before. The change was a four-year sunset for the waiting period, with the attorney general getting the authority to extend it one more year if necessary — in contrast to a five-year sunset in the original Dole-Mitchell compromise.

With that change, the Senate passed the substitute by voice vote, and then passed the bill easily, with 16 Republicans joining 47 Democrats to support it. Eight Democrats voted against it.

Nevertheless, the mistrust that had fermented all week lingered in the chamber Nov. 20. Biden announced prior to the vote that he would not fight for the four-year sunset in conference. In dueling news conferences after the vote, Dole cried foul, saying Republicans had negotiated in good faith on the new expiration language. But Biden said he would try to advance the wishes of the 57 senators who had sought to end the filibuster. "I'm prepared to be mildly autocratic to get this done," he said.

CONFERENCE/ FINAL ACTION

Those tensions set the stage for a difficult conference. Brooks led the five-member House delegation. Although Brooks opposed the Brady bill, he appeared resigned to seeing it pass and opened with a compromise proposal.

Biden, the chief Senate negotiator, led fellow Democrats Metzenbaum and Kennedy along with Republicans Ted Stevens of Alaska and Dirk Kempthorne of Idaho. Stevens, a member of the NRA board of directors and no fan of the Brady bill, put his challenge bluntly to House conferees: "Do you want a bill or not? Do you want a bill this year?" If so, Stevens advised, the House should accept the Senate terms on when to end the waiting period.

The Senate-passed bill had said the waiting period could phase out as early as 24 months after enactment as long as the computerized background check system met certain specifications for completeness. But House negotiators called those standards too weak.

The conferees eventually agreed to a deal Nov. 22, with Stevens and Kempthorne casting dissenting votes.

Compromise Bill

The compromise bill established a waiting period of five business days to let police check criminal records. It authorized $200 million per year to help states computerize their records. The waiting period was to end five years after enactment, with no provisions for the attorney general to replace it with the computerized instant-check system before then.

Negotiators agreed to drop several Senate-passed fire-arms provisions unrelated to the core of the bill. One would have expanded the definition of antique firearms, which were exempt from regular gun restrictions, to incorporate thousands of functioning World War I era rifles. Conferees also dropped a provision allowing face-to-face gun sales between dealers from different states. House negotiators did agree to several less controversial changes in firearms rules, such as requiring that police be notified of multiple purchases.

Final Passage

Shortly after the conference ended, Biden went to the Senate floor to request that the deal be accepted. Dole objected, saying he reflected opposition among 18 Republicans and two Democrats. Their exchange became increasingly hostile, with Dole accusing Biden of selling out the Senate position in conference. "I don't think that under these conditions, cloture will be invoked this year or next year," Dole said.

Later that night, the House passed the conference report, 238-187, with little debate and votes to spare. That left Mitchell, Dole and a handful of senators in town to approve the deal by voice vote, craft an alternative or declare an impasse. *(Vote 614, p. 150-H)*

The final flurry of action was punctuated by frequent news conferences as each side sought to blame the other for killing a popular bill. Talks, which continued throughout the day Nov. 23, appeared to break down by early evening. Mitchell and other Brady bill supporters said Dole rejected an offer to pass a separate bill containing modifications to the conference report. But Dole eventually agreed to a similar configuration, and he submitted a separate proposal as part of the final agreement.

His bill, to be considered and voted on promptly when the Senate returned in January 1994, would adopt the four-year sunset, set standards to replace the waiting period with the instant-check system as soon as 24 months after enactment and require that states submit mental health records for the national registry.

With that, the Senate cleared the bill by voice vote on Nov. 24. ∎

Reno Named First Woman Attorney General

It took President Clinton three tries to find an attorney general who could win Senate confirmation, but after he finally named Janet Reno to head the Justice Department, she quickly became his most popular Cabinet member.

Reno, a veteran Florida prosecutor, was the first woman to serve as attorney general. She was confirmed 98-0 on March 11, one day after the Senate Judiciary Committee had unanimously endorsed her. *(Vote 29, p. 5-S)*

Judiciary Committee members, like Clinton, were eager to get an attorney general in place. Clinton's first selection, corporate attorney Zoë Baird, was forced to withdraw amid controversy over her hiring of two illegal aliens as household help and her failure to pay Social Security taxes for them. A second leading candidate, federal Judge Kimba M. Wood, dropped out over a similar, albeit less severe, "nanny problem."

That left the Justice Department in the hands of a Bush administration holdover, Stuart M. Gerson, for nearly two months — scarcely what the White House had wanted.

It also proved a harbinger; several prospective Clinton appointees for other administration positions also had failed to pay Social Security taxes for household employees. With the spotlight on such omissions, these men and women lost their shot at coveted appointments. The controversy over a little-known section of the tax code led to efforts to revise the filing and payment requirements for domestic workers. *(Domestic worker taxes, p. 378)*

Baptism of Fire

Reno, 54, had 15 years' experience as top prosecutor for crime-ridden Dade County, which included Miami. She had garnered national attention as an innovator in the criminal justice field, and her appointment drew praise from many in Congress.

Reno had little time to bask in the praise, however. She had to cope with a series of crises, including investi-

gations into a Feb. 26 terrorist bombing of the World Trade Center in New York City, questions about the ethics of FBI Director William S. Sessions, and a deadly standoff between federal law enforcement agents and a religious cult, the Branch Davidians, headed by David Koresh.

Four agents of the Bureau of Alcohol, Tobacco and Firearms (BATF) were killed and 16 injured on Feb. 28 in an ill-advised raid on the cult's compound near Waco, Texas. All efforts to persuade cult members to surrender thereafter had failed.

On April 19, the FBI, with Reno's authorization, injected non-lethal tear gas into the compound in an effort to drive out the cult members. Instead, fire erupted at several points in the compound, immolating 85 cult members, including at least 25 children, while television cameras rolled and a horrified nation watched.

Reno took full responsibility for the decision. "I approved the plan, and I'm responsible for it. I advised the president, but I did not advise him as to the details," she said at a news conference that day.

"I made the decision, I'm accountable, the buck stops with me," she said.

In a government culture where top officials usually hid behind circumlocutions such as "mistakes were made," Reno's readiness to accept personal responsibility was seen as heroic. Overnight, she became a public idol.

THE FIRST TRY: BAIRD

Baird, Clinton's first choice for attorney general, was a surprise pick. The 40-year-old corporate attorney was little known in Washington political circles. The first woman nominated as attorney general, Baird had no experience in law enforcement and had taken few public positions on the key legal issues she was tapped to oversee, including civil rights and criminal justice. Judge Patricia M. Wald of the U.S. Court of Appeals for the District of Columbia Circuit, an early favorite, had taken herself out of the running.

Baird's nomination, which came Dec. 24, 1992, during Clinton's final round of Cabinet selections, fulfilled early predictions that he would choose a woman to run the department.

Baird's only government experience came early in her career. During the Carter administration, she spent two years in the Justice Department's Office of Legal Counsel. Her work came to the attention of White House Counsel Lloyd Cutler, and at his instigation she moved to the White House legal office as an associate counsel.

After the White House changed hands in 1981, Baird went to the Washington firm of O'Melveny and Myers, where she worked with Clinton's nominee for Secretary of State, Warren Christopher.

Baird married Paul Gerwirtz, a constitutional law professor at Yale University Law School, and then accepted a top legal job at the Connecticut-based General Electric Co. In 1990 she became general counsel for Aetna Life & Casualty Co., an insurance giant based in Connecticut.

Her corporate background troubled Congress Watch, a consumer advocacy group that criticized her nomination. "It's of great concern," said Pamela Gilbert, the organization's acting director, "when the next leader of our Justice Department comes from a corporate community that's been denigrating the justice system for so many years."

Many lawmakers and colleagues, on the other hand, hailed Baird's private-sector experience as an asset that forged the managerial skills needed to run an agency.

The Nanny Problem

As it turned out, what sank Baird was not her professional background but her personal life — in particular, her child-care arrangements.

In July 1990, Baird and her husband illegally hired a Peruvian woman to take care of their son and the woman's husband to work as a driver. Neither had papers allowing them to work in the United States, and under a 1986 immigration law, it was unlawful to hire undocumented workers.

In addition, Baird and Gerwirtz did not pay Social Security or unemployment taxes on the couple's wages. According to Baird, a lawyer told them they could not pay those taxes until the couple had Social Security numbers. They did, however, apply to sponsor the couple and to win them special certification to work legally.

Baird said a lawyer for the Clinton transition team explained that it was possible to pay the Social Security taxes, which she and her husband then did. And just days prior to her confirmation hearing before the Senate Judiciary Committee, Baird paid a $2,900 fine for violating immigration laws.

Judiciary Committee Hearing

Clinton transition officials and several key senators initially downplayed the likely impact of the nanny issue. But it erupted with a vengeance at the Senate Judiciary Committee confirmation hearings Jan. 19 and 21, fueled by angry calls that flooded Senate switchboards.

Baird apologized repeatedly during two long days of testimony. "The hiring of this couple and our failure to pay the appropriate taxes at the time was wrong, and I take full responsibility for it," she said.

But that did not assuage a public that showed little sympathy for the child-care difficulties of a corporate attorney with a $500,000 annual salary. In their calls, said Sen. Herb Kohl, D-Wis., voters told official Washington: "Regular people do not do this."

Judiciary Committee Chairman Joseph R. Biden Jr., D-Del., quickly put to rest any speculation that Democrats would dismiss the matter to avoid embarrassing a Clinton nominee. He marched Baird through a lengthy and detailed recital of the facts surrounding the illegal workers.

Baird was composed and matter-of-fact throughout the questioning, only occasionally offering a joke or digression. She repeatedly asserted her culpability but also tried to explain why she had hired the Peruvians.

Baird noted that she and her husband had told the federal government that they had already hired the couple when they applied to acquire working papers for them. "I allowed myself to think that the processes set up by the Labor Department ... gave tacit approval to this sort of situation, which I can't condone now," she said.

Baird said she had been unable to find a legal baby sitter and needed good, reliable care for her son. "Quite honestly, I was acting at that time really more as a mother than as someone who would be sitting here designated to be attorney general," she said.

That generated little sympathy from Biden. "There are tens of thousands, millions of Americans out there who have trouble taking care of their children, both couples required to work or single parents, with one-fiftieth the income that you and your husband have, and they do not violate the law," Biden said.

Baird found her strongest advocate in Orrin G. Hatch of Utah, ranking Republican on the Judiciary Committee. Hatch pledged to support her and said it would be "hyper technical"

to disqualify her. "Sometimes these laws are very difficult to comply with," Hatch said, noting that neither Baird nor her husband was an immigration law specialist.

But most senators were much harsher, and several noted constituent anger over the nomination.

Senators reported calls running against Baird in staggering proportions: 305 to 4 in the office of Dennis DeConcini, D-Ariz., and 1,987 to 217 at Paul Simon's, D-Ill.

When the hearings resumed Jan. 21 following Clinton's inauguration, senators asked Baird point-blank if she should withdraw. But Baird again urged senators to consider her entire record, saying she would still be a good attorney general. By the end of Baird's second day of testimony, about a dozen Democratic and Republican senators were publicly urging her to withdraw.

Baird Withdraws

As the wave of public anger bore down, few countervailing pressures emerged to buoy Baird's nomination. Her record as a corporate attorney appealed more to conservatives than to liberals. The prospect of the nation's first woman attorney general did appeal to liberals, but civil rights organizations, women's groups and other liberal associations did not rally on her behalf.

Baird asked Clinton to withdraw her nomination late Jan. 21, the day after his inauguration. She said the controversy had damaged her ability to lead the Justice Department.

Clinton did so, faulting himself and his transition team for not fully analyzing the significance of the issue before nominating Baird. The withdrawal, which was greeted with relief on Capitol Hill, sounded a jarring note during an otherwise upbeat inaugural week and cast some doubt on the judgment and political skills of the Clinton team. But lawmakers said Clinton spared himself serious political damage by pulling the nomination before it went to a committee vote or to the Senate floor.

THE SECOND TRY: WOOD

Clinton consulted repeatedly with Biden after Baird's withdrawal as he sought a new nominee. Although women's groups continued to urge the president to name a woman to the Justice Department, Clinton made no such commitment in public.

On Feb. 5, U.S. District Court Judge Kimba M. Wood was reported to be Clinton's top choice. But that afternoon Clinton said no decision had been made, and several hours later Wood withdrew because her baby sitter had been an illegal alien — a problem similar to the one that forced Baird to withdraw.

In a statement, Wood said a woman she employed was an illegal alien for seven years, including one year in her employ. But at the time she hired the woman, it was not illegal to employ an undocumented alien. Wood said she had paid all applicable Social Security and taxes.

"I have fulfilled every legal requirement with respect to the employment of our baby sitter," Wood said. "Nevertheless ... I have concluded that in the current political environment proceeding further ... would be inappropriate."

President Ronald Reagan named Wood, 49, a Democrat, to the bench in 1988. She was best known for presiding over the trial of junk-bond financier Michael Milken.

Some women's groups were furious that both Baird and Wood were disqualified over issues that male nominees for other positions had not faced.

The administration denied that a double standard was

at work, saying it had begun screening all job candidates on such issues as taxes and immigration status of domestic help. At least one male candidate for attorney general reportedly dropped out of consideration on those grounds after Baird withdrew.

Nevertheless, some women's advocates continued to complain that the issue would work most strongly against women, who were disproportionately responsible for selecting household help.

THIRD AND FINAL CHOICE: RENO

In turning to veteran Florida prosecutor Reno as his third choice, Clinton finally found a nominee who could win confirmation. The Feb. 11 selection drew bipartisan praise.

Reno, who had a strong reputation for integrity, had been the Dade County state's attorney for 15 years. She managed an office of 900 workers and supervised thousands of criminal cases.

Accepting the nomination, Reno said she would strive to create a partnership between federal and local law enforcement agencies. She also pledged to put the department's muscle behind civil rights, the needs of children and environmental protection.

Reno was single and had no children. "I've never hired an illegal alien. And I think I paid all my Social Security taxes," she said in one of the few light moments of her initial remarks.

Women's groups, which had pressed Clinton to name the nation's first female attorney general, were quick to toast the selection.

Reno's Record

The daughter of two newspaper reporters, Reno grew up in Miami and graduated from Cornell University and Harvard University Law School.

She joined the Dade state's attorney's office in 1973. She spent three years there and another two in private practice before then-Gov. Reubin Askew, D, appointed her to fill out the Dade prosecutor's term in 1978. Reno, a Democrat, held the position thereafter, running for the office five times.

Dade County's criminal caseload was challenging: The area was a hot spot for drug activity, violent crime and racial conflict. Reno generally won high marks for her work.

Early on, many blacks criticized Reno's Dade County record on such concerns as police brutality against minorities. In 1980, her office lost a high-profile case against police officers who had fatally beaten a black man. The verdict set off race riots.

But Reno won over many of these skeptics through subsequent cases and diligent community outreach.

Reno pioneered alternative strategies to fight crime, such as a special court designed to deter young drug offenders. She aggressively prosecuted sexual and child abuse cases. A local rap star made the music charts with a song praising Reno's efforts to crack down on parents who did not pay child support.

However, Reno was criticized for not being equally assertive in pursuing corrupt public officials. Reno disputed that charge during a White House news conference, saying she sometimes transferred such cases to the federal system because different legal rules made it easier to obtain convictions there.

Reno said she personally opposed the death penalty,

but she had sought it as a prosecutor. She supported abortion rights.

Smooth Sailing in Senate

Clinton's most troubled Cabinet search ended in one of his smoothest confirmations. The Senate Judiciary Committee voted unanimously in support of Reno on March 10, following two full days of testimony. The next day, the full Senate confirmed her on a 98-0 vote after many glowing tributes. (Vote 29, p. 5-S)

"She is an intelligent, innovative thinker with a distinguished legal background," said Howard M. Metzenbaum, D-Ohio. "Best of all, Janet Reno has hands-on street level experience fighting crime."

She faced no real opposition from Judiciary Committee members, who, like Clinton, were eager to get an attorney general in place.

"What you're hearing up here is a collective sigh of relief," Judiciary Committee Chairman Biden told reporters during a break in the first day's testimony. "We finally got one like other committees get."

Sen. Carol Moseley-Braun, D-Ill., praised Clinton for persevering in his effort to name a woman to head the Justice Department. She said that in addition to sending a strong message about the capability of women in legal fields, Reno's selection would bring overdue changes to the Justice Department. "She does bring a perspective that's new: cooperation, coordination," Moseley-Braun said. "Feminist perspectives if you will."

Reno's opening statement reflected what had been considered her greatest strength: her character.

With a row of relatives behind her, Reno spoke of her modest upbringing in Florida as the daughter of newspaper reporters. When the family outgrew their house, Reno said, her mother set out to build a larger one on the edge of the Everglades. "That house is a symbol to me that you can do anything you really want to if it is the right thing to do and you put your mind to it," said Reno, who still lived in the home her mother built.

An Emphasis on Law Enforcement

At Justice, as in Dade County, Reno said she would seek to abandon traditional turf battles and forge a cooperative system of law enforcement. "I want to do what is best for the case ... not to say, 'That's my turf, you can't be involved,'" Reno said. "I want to do what is right."

She said her priorities would be tackling public corruption, prosecuting drug traffickers and investigating complex economic crimes that were difficult to prosecute locally.

Most of the Senate questioning focused on Reno's area of expertise: fighting crime. Reno repeatedly cited her philosophy of combining tough, certain punishment for criminals with opportunities for diversion or rehabilitation where appropriate.

She was most forceful and impassioned in denouncing the growing incidence of serious crimes by juveniles.

Some conservatives had complained that Reno's inclinations ran more to social work than to fighting crime. Reno took issue with that assessment, saying she had been tough on hardened criminals and believed many should serve more time in jail than they did.

But she also stressed the need for early intervention and education to wean children from a culture of violence. At times, her statements sounded like testimony that might be heard from a candidate to head the Department of Health and Human Services. She cited the debilitating

influences of poverty and the importance of prenatal care and nurturing crack babies.

Some senators raised questions about Reno's prosecution record, citing statistics that suggested her office lagged behind others in the state. But Reno said her overall effort — including diversion, plea bargains and prosecutions — showed a strong and effective use of resources to fight crime.

During the hearings, Reno reiterated Clinton administration positions in support of a ban on assault weapons and a waiting period for handgun purchases. She opposed an outright ban on handgun purchases, saying she had seen handguns save innocent lives in Dade County.

Reno said she personally opposed the death penalty, but she went out of her way to assure senators that her opposition had not deterred her from using the death penalty in Dade County, nor would it hamper her willingness to pursue it at the federal level.

In response to questioning from Strom Thurmond, R-S.C., Reno said that lengthy delay in carrying out some death sentences "makes a mockery" of capital punishment. She said the time frame should be shortened without gutting defendants' legal rights.

Her remarks were strong enough to alarm Metzenbaum, who reminded Reno of a recent case involving a man who was wrongly sentenced to death. Metzenbaum called for balance on the push to restrict death row appeals.

Cautious Replies

Reno acknowledged having limited direct experience with many legal issues — particularly those involving civil law — that she would face at the Justice Department. She generally was unwilling to speculate on what views she might adopt if confirmed.

Senators' forays into federal issues such as antitrust or civil rights law typically met with a succinct promise to look into the matter. Among the issues Reno pledged to give priority: immigration, terrorism and revision of the civil justice system.

Reno supported reauthorizing a law that required the attorney general to seek an independent counsel to investigate alleged wrongdoing by top executive branch officials. The law expired in December 1992. But she was noncommittal about whether independent counsels should necessarily handle investigations involving members of Congress. (Independent prosecutors, p. 309)

The most divisive exchanges came over allegations that the Clinton administration or members of the Congressional Black Caucus may have improperly influenced Gerson, the Bush administration holdover who was the acting attorney general, in the ongoing trial of Rep. Harold E. Ford, D-Tenn. (Ford case, p. 71)

Charles E. Grassley, R-Iowa, questioned Reno closely on the incident, which he said gave the appearance of impropriety. But Reno said Gerson had assured her that he acted on his own initiative, and she said she saw no need for further action on the matter.

Reno promised she would resist any high-level efforts to influence the department's actions on particular cases, even if it meant showing senators to the door or resigning. However, Reno said she would try to be accessible to lawmakers and others to discuss policy issues.

Moseley-Braun later attacked Republicans for pressing the issue of the Ford trial, saying the black caucus had done nothing improper.

Many police organizations, as well as many women's groups enthusiastic about the prospect of the nation's first

female attorney general, supported Reno's nomination.

But she faced some criticism going into the hearing.

The conservative Free Congress Foundation issued a 12-page report criticizing Reno as a lackluster prosecutor with inadequate experience in federal legal issues. "She was chosen because of her gender and her politically correct views, not because of her law enforcement," said Thomas Jipping, director of the foundation's Center for Law and Democracy.

There also had been scattershot allegations of personal misconduct, some of which Jipping and a lobbyist for the National Rifle Association (NRA) had passed on to staff aides on the Judiciary Committee.

But Biden and ranking GOP member Hatch of Utah both stressed that Reno had come through extensive committee and FBI investigations with a clean bill of ethical health.

During the hearings, Sen. Patrick J. Leahy, D-Vt., attacked the rifle association for apparently mounting a backdoor attack on Reno. Wayne LaPierre, executive vice president of the NRA, said the lobbyist who raised the charges was acting on his own initiative. Before the hearings were over, the lobbyist had resigned. ∎

President Withdraws Guinier Nomination

Facing a bleak decision on the beleaguered nomination of his friend Lani Guinier, President Clinton chose a messy political amputation that pleased conservatives, angered black lawmakers and civil rights groups and left the top civil rights post in the Justice Department vacant through the end of his first year in office.

Attorney General Janet Reno announced Guinier's nomination to head the civil rights division April 29. The announcement came at a ceremony where Reno appeared with Clinton to present the names of most of her top management team for the department.

Guinier immediately came under attack from conservatives, who accused her of holding dangerously radical views on minority rights. Even some moderate Democrats expressed doubts and urged Clinton not to send her before an uneasy Senate for confirmation.

Clinton's decision spared senators a difficult vote, but it enraged members of the Congressional Black Caucus as well as leaders of civil rights and women's groups who had argued strenuously for letting Guinier proceed.

Lobbying for and against the appointment intensified the week of May 31, culminating in a meeting between Guinier and Clinton.

Clinton called an evening news conference June 3 to announce that he was withdrawing Guinier's name. He praised Guinier's qualifications as a civil rights lawyer and said he held her in high esteem. "The problem is that this battle will be waged based on her academic writings," Clinton said at the conference, noting that he had difficulty with some of those views. "And I cannot fight a battle that I know is divisive ... if I do not believe in the ground of the battle."

Clinton rejected charges that the move was part of an overall political strategy to reach out to Republicans and Democratic conservatives. "This has nothing to do with the political center; this has to do with my center," he said.

Senate Majority Leader George J. Mitchell, D-Maine,

released a statement supporting Clinton's decision. "While Ms. Guinier has a distinguished record as a civil rights litigator, the controversy around her writings would have been divisive and counterproductive to the goal of civil rights enforcement," Mitchell said.

But it clearly cost Clinton among some liberal allies, who accused the president of weak leadership. Rep. Kweisi Mfume, D-Md., chairman of the Congressional Black Caucus, had warned Clinton earlier that a decision to abandon Guinier could erode what had been a loyal bloc of votes among the 40-member caucus. On June 4, Mfume said that did not mean the caucus was poised "to go from staunch allies to archenemies." But he said black lawmakers would reassess their relationship with Clinton and review their options.

"I respect the president," Guinier said at a news conference June 4. But she added, "I disagree with his decision to withdraw my nomination.... I think that the president and many others have misinterpreted my writings, which were written in an academic context." Guinier had fought to go forward, saying she deserved a chance to defend her writings before the Judiciary Committee and saying she could win over her critics.

Attacks Focus on Guinier's Writings

Guinier's civil rights experience included more than seven years at the National Association for the Advancement of Colored People's Legal Defense and Educational Fund. She also served as special assistant to Drew S. Days III when Days headed the civil rights division under President Jimmy Carter; Days had joined the Justice Department under Clinton as the solicitor general. Guinier was widely regarded as a bright, skilled attorney more than suited for the intellectual demands of the civil rights post.

What got Guinier into trouble were academic writings that spoke to some of the most difficult and volatile issues of race and political power. Clinton said he had not read Guinier's legal writings prior to selecting her — and would not have nominated her if he had.

Guinier had argued that voting rights initiatives must go beyond simply increasing the number of black elected politicians, and instead should seek to truly enhance political influence for blacks and other minorities. She suggested a range of potential options to meet that goal — including cumulative voting, which allowed individuals to target their voting strength.

Guinier also suggested re-examining electoral rules and legislative procedures, saying, for example, that it might be appropriate to require supermajorities for some votes, or to grant minorities a veto on certain issues.

Those ideas went considerably beyond what some lawmakers considered the proper parameters for enforcement of the Voting Rights Act, as Senate Minority Leader Bob Dole, R-Kan., made clear in a May 20 floor speech. "The key concept has always been access, not proportionality," said Dole, who said Guinier's ideas undermined the principle of "one person, one vote."

Sen. Orrin G. Hatch, R-Utah, called her views "frightening to many, even in the civil rights community."

Some observers saw these criticisms as payback for the failed 1987 Supreme Court nomination of Judge Robert H. Bork, who sank in the Democrat-led Judiciary Committee in part because of his extensive and controversial academic writings. *(1987 Almanac, p. 271)*

But Republicans were not the only critics.

At least two Democrats on the Senate Judiciary Commit-

tee, Chairman Joseph R. Biden Jr. of Delaware and Patrick J. Leahy of Vermont, had raised a warning flag on Guinier.

When the Leadership Conference on Civil Rights held a May 26 news conference to support Guinier, several member groups refused to sign on — among them the American Jewish Congress and the Anti-Defamation League.

Jess N. Hordes, the Anti-Defamation League's Washington representative, said his group was extremely troubled by some of her writings. "She seems to view politics through a racial prism," he said.

Guinier's defenders complained of unfair distortions in the attacks. Guinier stressed that cumulative voting was an attempt to enhance the political power of groups with common interests without resorting to fixed racial lines, as in legislative districts drawn specifically to create a minority seat.

But some allies also sought to explain her writings as the theoretical work of an academic. And the White House stressed that Guinier would be working under Attorney General Janet Reno and would not have the final word on setting civil rights policy. Those arguments added to the impression that Guinier's writings were indeed problematic — even before Clinton on June 2 said he disagreed with some of her work.

Guinier's Last-Minute Lobbying Fails

Guinier spent considerable time on Capitol Hill the week of May 24, meeting with Judiciary Committee members. Those meetings reportedly went well, and allies said they felt Guinier would acquit herself well during confirmation hearings. But uneasiness continued to settle around the nomination over the Memorial Day weekend, and on June 1 Biden was quoted giving slim odds to confirmation.

Guinier struggled to save her prospects, appearing on ABC-TV's "Nightline" June 2 to make a public pitch for senators and others to examine her more closely.

"I believe in fairness, I believe in democracy, and I think that fairness requires that I be given an opportunity to present my views to the Senate," Guinier said. "My own mother does not recognize me in terms of the press and the media that I've been receiving."

Meanwhile, Guinier's allies turned up the heat on Clinton to stand by his nominee. Prominent black and women's group leaders held their own Capitol Hill news conference as they set grass-roots networks in motion. They tried to defer debate over Guinier's writings and instead focus on her right to be heard before the Senate.

The White House struggled with the controversy, mounting a sluggish defense of Guinier, then engaging in public hand-wringing over whether to continue to seek confirmation. The episode recalled the public deflation and then withdrawal of Clinton's first nomination for attorney general, Zoë Baird. But while Baird went down without real protest from political interest groups, Guinier enjoyed the active support of prominent groups voicing disappointment and anger. *(Baird, p. 304)*

"I hope that we are not witnessing the dawning of a new intellectual orthodoxy in which thoughtful people can no longer debate provocative ideas without denying the country their talents as public servants," Guinier said June 4.

Leahy said Clinton may have made the proper calculation to save his strength for larger political battles such as deficit reduction. But Leahy was troubled that Guinier did not get a chance to address the Judiciary Committee. "I think we're reaching too much this idea that nominations are determined by which special interest group gets a chance to frame the debate," he said. ∎

Justice Department Appointments

The Senate on May 28 confirmed three top Justice Department officials, filling out the department's anemic upper ranks. By voice vote, the Senate approved Philip B. Heymann as deputy attorney general, Webster L. Hubbell as associate attorney general and Drew S. Days III to be solicitor general. The Senate Judiciary Committee approved the nominations May 24.

Two controversial nominees were confirmed late in the session — those of Walter E. Dellinger III to lead the Justice Department's Office of Legal Counsel and Janet Ann Napolitano to be U.S. attorney for Arizona.

Hubbell

Hubbell, 45, a Little Rock, Ark., lawyer and a close friend of President Clinton, had been a controversial nominee. But he defused concerns that he might be too closely tied to the White House, as well as criticism over his past membership in a virtually all-white country club.

Hubbell announced his resignation from the Little Rock Country Club at the outset of his May 19 confirmation hearing before the Senate Judiciary Committee, saying he wanted to avoid any perception of racial insensitivity.

That decision pleased committee member Carol Moseley-Braun, D-Ill., the Senate's only African-American. "His resignation is no admission of guilt. It is a demonstration of sensitivity," she said. But Chairman Joseph R. Biden Jr., D-Del., and several other senators said the resignation was unnecessary, citing Hubbell's efforts to integrate the club — which recently had approved its first black member.

Republicans generally did not criticize Hubbell's membership in the club, but several did fault Democrats for allegedly applying a double standard on the issue to Republican and Democratic nominees.

Hubbell took the No. 3 slot at the Justice Department where he was to oversee many of the department's subsections, including the civil rights division, the Immigration and Naturalization Service and the Office of Legal Counsel.

(Hubbell abruptly resigned March 14, 1994, amid charges that he had overbilled the Arkansas law firm where he and Hillary Rodham Clinton had once been partners.)

Heymann and Days

Heymann and Days, both former Carter administration officials, had little trouble at their confirmation hearings on May 18 and 20, respectively.

Heymann, 60, a Harvard University law professor, was assistant attorney general in charge of the criminal division from 1978 to 1981. His confirmation made him Attorney General Janet Reno's top deputy, with responsibility for the day-to-day operation of the large department. (Heymann resigned abruptly the week of Jan. 24, 1994, citing differences with Reno over management styles. He left office in mid-February.)

Days, 51, a Yale University law professor, was assistant attorney general for civil rights during the Carter presidency. He had been active in several civil and human rights organizations, but at his confirmation hearing he said he would resign from those groups to avoid the appearance of a conflict of interest.

As solicitor general, Days was to represent the U.S. government before the Supreme Court.

The House Judiciary Subcommittee on International Law, Immigration and Refugees took the lead, endorsing a bill to tighten the rules for asylum proceedings. The bipartisan measure called for pre-inspection posts in several overseas airports, an expedited hearing process at U.S. airports and a requirement that all asylum applicants file requests within 30 days of arriving in the United States. Refugee advocacy groups opposed the legislation, saying it could send refugees back to their persecutors.

The Clinton administration called for a series of administrative, rather than legislative, changes to allow the government to screen and potentially deport ineligible asylum seekers directly from airports and other points of entry; it also proposed legislative changes to crack down on smugglers who trafficked in illegal aliens.

Edward M. Kennedy, D-Mass., chairman of the Senate Judiciary Subcommittee on Immigration and Refugee Affairs, introduced a bill (S 1333) generally reflecting the administration's proposal; at year's end the bill was pending before the full committee.

BACKGROUND

The Immigration and Naturalization Service (INS) had a backlog of more than 300,000 asylum cases, and it was not closing the gap.

Acting Commissioner Chris Sale projected that the agency would decide 50,000 cases in 1993 — fewer than the number of predicted new claims. "We're falling further and further behind," she said.

The INS detained only a fraction of those applicants. Most were released into the community, often with work authorizations, and were told to return months later for an asylum hearing. If they did not, the INS had few resources for tracking them.

Critics traced the INS overload to the 1980 Refugee Act (PL 96-212) and subsequent regulations. Before 1980, political asylum was largely restricted to those fleeing communist countries.

In the three years before that law took effect, annual asylum applications averaged about 4,000. But the 1980 law expanded the definition of refugees to those fleeing persecution or the well-founded fear of persecution based on factors such as race, religion or political opinion. *(1980 Almanac, p. 378)*

In 1990, the INS issued permanent regulations for carrying out the 1980 law. Advocates for refugees, who previously had accused the INS of making politically biased asylum determinations, generally praised the changes as more fair.

But as the asylum system was winning over some of its critics, it acquired new detractors reacting to the backlogs and perceived abuse. Domestic terrorism provided the latest impetus for new restrictions. The most highly publicized case was the Feb. 26 bombing of the World Trade Center in New York, which killed at least five people and injured 1,000. Sheik Omar Abdel-Rahman, some of whose followers were charged with carrying out the bombing, entered the country on a visa but delayed deportation by filing for asylum.

LEGISLATIVE ACTION

The House Judiciary Subcommittee on International Law, Immigration and Refugees on Oct. 20 approved a bill (HR 2602) to make it more difficult for foreigners who claimed to be fleeing persecution to be granted political asylum. The panel approved the measure, sponsored by Democratic subcommittee Chairman Romano L. Mazzoli of Kentucky, by voice vote.

The Subcommittee Bill

Drawing on a previous bill (HR 1153) introduced by Democrat Charles E. Schumer of New York, the asylum legislation called for pre-inspection posts in several overseas airports. Inspectors there would seek to block foreigners without proper documentation from ever boarding U.S.-bound jets.

On U.S. soil, the bill provided for a new "expedited exclusion" process at airports, modeled on legislation (HR 1355) proposed by Bill McCollum of Florida, ranking Republican on the subcommittee. The new system would provide for an asylum officer to hear a new arrival's case as quickly as possible and order prompt deportation if the claim was found wanting.

The bill also set new limits on applications for asylum from immigrants already in the United States. For instance, the bill required asylum seekers to initiate their claims within 30 days of entering the country. And the bill cut out some existing layers of review for applicants whose claims were denied.

After the subcommittee markup and in preparation for full committee action, Mazzoli introduced a clean bill (HR 3363) on Oct. 26. While his initial bill had called for doubling the number of INS asylum officers by Oct. 1, 1996, the revised bill doubled that number by April 1, 1994. The INS had only about 120 asylum officers to hear claims, although the number of people applying for asylum had risen from about 25,000 annually in the mid-1980s to about 75,000 per year by 1993.

The new bill also specified that applicants for "provisional asylum" — those with pending asylum cases — could not work in the United States without special permission from the attorney general. Administration officials and others said that giving work authorizations to asylum applicants created a magnet for bogus claims.

The legislation also included less controversial provisions, such as increasing criminal penalties for smuggling aliens and authorizing additional money for the Immigration and Naturalization Service's corps of asylum officers and Border Patrol.

McCollum praised the bill as a bipartisan response to a pressing problem. But Mazzoli was at odds with the Clinton administration, which favored narrower changes in existing procedures.

And two freshman Democrats on the subcommittee, Xavier Becerra of California and Jerrold Nadler of New York, complained that some provisions could punish legitimate political refugees. Nadler said that while abuses occurred, there was no flood of bogus asylum seekers.

Among the issues that concerned refugee advocates was a critical definitional change from existing law. The bill required an asylum applicant to show that he "more likely than not" would face persecution if deported, rather than that he had a "well-founded fear of persecution" if sent home.

But Schumer, another key sponsor of the bill, warned against inaction, saying that existing law had created a situation such that "if you cheat, you do better than if you don't." Schumer warned panel members that they must approve sensible changes in the system, "or it will be reformed for us, irrationally and devastatingly." ∎

Citizenship Rules Eased

The House and Senate passed separate versions of a bill (HR 783) aimed at making it easier for some older resident aliens and others to become U.S. citizens. They did not have time to reconcile minor differences before the session ended.

The bill, sponsored by Rep. Romano L. Mazzoli, D-Ky., waived the citizenship test requirement for resident aliens older than 65 who had lived in the United States for 20 years. It also waived the requirement for resident aliens who could not be expected to pass the test because of physical, mental or developmental disabilities. Under existing law, resident aliens were required to pass an exam that tested their knowledge of history and government before they could become citizens. Supporters of the bill said that elderly residents who had been in the United States for two decades or more should not be barred from citizenship merely because they failed a test.

The bill also made it easier for U.S. citizens to confer citizenship upon their children born in foreign lands. And it made retroactive a six-decade-old change in the law that allowed children born abroad of a non-citizen father and a citizen mother to receive citizenship through the mother. The 1934 law had covered only those born abroad after 1934.

The House bill, approved by voice vote Nov. 20, originated in the Judiciary Subcommittee on International Law, Immigration and Refugees, which approved it May 19. The full Judiciary Committee approved the bill Nov. 17 (H Rept 103-387).

The Senate approved HR 783 on Nov. 20 by voice vote, after including the text of S 1197, a bill sponsored by Edward M. Kennedy, D-Mass., which the Senate passed July 1. Kennedy's bill made a series of technical changes to immigration law. ■

Panel OKs Torture Treaty

The House Judiciary Committee's Subcommittee on International Law, Immigration and Refugees approved a bill (HR 933) by voice vote May 19 to implement the Convention Against Torture and Other Cruel, Inhuman or Degrading Treatment or Punishment.

Treaty codification language also was contained in the omnibus anti-crime bill (HR 3355) that passed the Senate Nov. 19.

The United Nations General Assembly had unanimously approved the torture treaty in 1984. President Ronald Reagan signed the pact in 1988, and the Senate ratified it in 1990. *(1990 Almanac, p. 806)*

But legislation to change U.S. law and implement the treaty, which made torture a criminally punishable offense under international law, had yet to be approved by both the House and Senate. Codifying the treaty would have given the United States jurisdiction over foreign nationals present in the United States who committed acts of torture abroad.

Lawsuits Against Foreign Governments

On Sept. 8, the subcommittee gave voice vote approval to a separate bill (HR 934) allowing civil damages lawsuits in federal court on behalf of U.S. citizens tortured or killed by foreign governments.

A similar measure failed to pass in the 102nd Congress after the Justice and State departments warned of possible retaliatory action by foreign governments. Ranking subcommittee Republican Bill McCollum of Florida opposed the bill, citing similar concerns. But sponsor Romano L. Mazzoli, D-Ky., who chaired the panel, said he wanted to defend U.S. citizens who were "lured" to jobs in other countries, only to face torture or extrajudicial execution.

The bill permitted lawsuits only after plaintiffs had exhausted legal avenues in the country where the torture or wrongful death took place. Charles E. Schumer, D-N.Y., amended the bill to specify that it included victims of genocide. ■

Group Loses Patent for Confederate Insignia

Prodded by the Senate's only African-American, senators twice rejected efforts to renew a design patent for the emblem of the United Daughters of the Confederacy because it featured the Confederate flag.

In the first round, on May 6, Carol Moseley-Braun, D-Ill., successfully lobbied her colleagues on the Judiciary Committee to reject the patent extension, invoking the sensibilities of African-Americans whose ancestors "were held as human chattel under the flag of the Confederacy."

She stressed that she was not trying to shut down the group or censor its emblem, only deny special congressional protection for the design.

The debate came on consideration of a bill (S 409) to extend several patents. Members approved the bill by voice vote after voting 12-3 for the amendment excluding the United Daughters of the Confederacy patent extension.

The confrontation pitted Moseley-Braun against Strom Thurmond, R-S.C., the Senate's most senior member. Thurmond said the Senate had reauthorized the design patent numerous times and that the group did charitable work.

"Why raise this question now?" asked Thurmond. "Why not find things that unite us rather than things that divide us?"

The United Daughters of the Confederacy sponsored educational efforts on Confederate history as well as a range of charitable activities.

A Second Round

Sen. Jesse Helms, R-N.C., raised the issue again in July, attempting to renew the group's patent in a floor amendment on an unrelated bill, the National and Community Service Act (S 919). Debate over the amendment July 22 produced a highly personal discussion of race and slavery in America. Helms argued that the 24,000 "delightful ladies" of the United Daughters of the Confederacy were engaged in historical, educational and patriotic endeavors. Thurmond added that "this group has nothing to do with discrimination or radical ideas."

Moseley-Braun tried but failed to kill the amendment. The Senate defeated her tabling motion 48-52. *(Vote 206, p. 27-S)*

Galvanized by the vote, Moseley-Braun vowed to filibuster "until this room freezes over" to reverse the decision. "The issue is whether or not Americans such as myself who

believe in the promise of this country . . . will have to suffer the indignity of being reminded time and time again that at one point in this country's history we were human chattel," she said. "We were property. We could be traded, bought and sold." The Confederate flag, she said, "is something that has no place in our modern times . . . no place in this body . . . no place in our society."

Ben Nighthorse Campbell, D-Colo., the Senate's only American Indian, added his support. "Slavery was once a tradition, and killing Indians like animals was also a tradition. It didn't make it right," he said.

Perhaps the turning point in the debate occurred when Howell Heflin, D-Ala., a self-described son of the Confederacy, choked up as he described his family's roots in the Confederate struggle and his decision to switch his vote against the group's symbol. Heflin said his great-grandfather was one of the signers of the Declaration of Secession and his grandfather was a surgeon in the Confederate army. While he revered his ancestors, Heflin said, "we live today in a different world."

Other senators said they still had to honor their ancestors' memories. Mitch McConnell, R-Ky., said his great-grandmother's first husband was killed in the Civil War, even though he was not a slaveholder. And, he said, his grandmother belonged to the United Daughters of the Confederacy, though she did not support slavery. McConnell said he intended to stick with Helms.

The Senate voted 76-24 to reconsider the initial Helms vote. It then voted 75-25 to table, and thus kill, the Helms amendment. Two Democrats voted with Helms: Sam Nunn of Georgia and Robert C. Byrd of West Virginia. *(Votes 207, 208; p. 27-S)* ■

Religious Freedom Bill Wins Quick Passage

Congress easily cleared a bill (HR 1308) to make it harder for government to infringe on religious practices. The bill reversed a controversial 1990 Supreme Court decision that made it easier for states or the federal government to pass laws that restricted individual religious rights.

The bill enjoyed wide bipartisan support, but only after sponsors included language to ensure that it would not be used to challenge state abortion restrictions. Similar legislation introduced in 1990, 1991 and 1992 had become mired in the abortion debate. *(1992 Almanac, p. 332)*

President Clinton signed the measure (PL 103-141) on Nov. 16.

Background

The Supreme Court held in *Employment Division v. Smith* that states could impose laws that incidentally limited religious freedom as long as the laws served a "valid" state purpose and were not aimed at inhibiting religion.

Previously, state laws restricting religion had to meet a stricter legal standard of serving a "compelling" government interest in a way that posed the least possible burden on religious freedom. Federal courts could strike down a law if the state could not prove such a compelling interest.

The *Smith* decision involved two American Indians who were fired from their jobs at a drug rehabilitation clinic for using the illegal hallucinogenic drug peyote during a reli-

gious ceremony. Oregon refused to grant the men unemployment compensation benefits because they were fired for illegal behavior. The men sued, claiming the state's interest was not compelling enough to warrant infringement on their religious rights. But the Supreme Court ruled against them, effectively eliminating the compelling interest test.

Legislative Action

The House approved HR 1308, which restored the pre-*Smith* compelling interest standard, by voice vote on May 11. The Judiciary Committee had approved the measure (H Rept 103-88) by 35-0 on March 24; the Subcommittee on Civil and Constitutional Rights endorsed it by voice vote March 17.

The Senate passed the bill by 97-3 on Oct. 27 after substituting the text of its own version (S 578). Senators rejected, 41-58, an amendment by Harry Reid, D-Nev., that would have excluded prisoners from the bill's protections. *(Votes 331, 330, p. 43-S)*

The Senate bill clarified that the government need not justify every law or action that might affect a person's religious rights, but only those that placed a "substantial burden" on the free exercise of religion.

The Senate Judiciary Committee had approved S 578 by 15-1 on May 6, with Alan K. Simpson, R-Wyo., casting the lone dissenting vote.

Orrin G. Hatch, R-Utah, said the legislation was sorely needed because courts, acting under standards outlined in *Smith,* recently had upheld dozens of laws restricting religious freedom. Edward M. Kennedy, D-Mass., the lead sponsor of the Senate bill, underscored the broad support from groups such as Baptist and Roman Catholic organizations and the American Civil Liberties Union. "These organizations don't agree on much, but they do agree on the need to pass [this]," he said.

Attorney General Janet Reno also backed the bill.

Simpson and several other senators voiced concerns, however, particularly about whether prison administrators would be forced to accommodate myriad dietary and other demands from inmates in the name of religious freedom.

The House on Nov. 3 agreed to accept the Senate language, including the substantial burden language, and cleared the bill by voice vote. ■

Other Crime, Judiciary Matters Considered

Congress considered a long list of smaller crime and judiciary matters in 1993. They included:

FBI PHONE ACCESS

The Senate on Nov. 4 cleared a bill (HR 175) giving the Federal Bureau of Investigation easier access to telephone records of people suspected of spying or of terrorist activities.

Under existing law, the FBI could get access to phone records in terrorism and counterintelligence cases without seeking a subpoena or court order — but only if the telephone subscriber was believed to be an agent of a foreign power. The FBI wanted the scope of the law expanded to cover any subscriber who was in contact with foreign pow-

ers or a suspected agent of foreign powers.

Sen. Patrick J. Leahy, D-Vt., working with Rep. Don Edwards, D-Calif., agreed on compromise language granting the broader powers, but only in cases where the FBI believed that the communications concerned terrorism or clandestine intelligence activities that might involve a violation of U.S. criminal laws.

The House Judiciary Subcommittee on Civil and Constitutional Rights approved the bill March 17. The full Judiciary Committee followed suit March 24 (H Rept 103-46). The House passed the measure under expedited procedures March 29 by a vote of 367-6. *(Vote 111, p. 28-H)*

The Senate cleared the bill by voice vote Nov. 4, and President Clinton signed it into law Nov. 17 (PL 103-142).

DNA ANALYSIS

The House voted 374-4 on March 29 to approve a bill aimed at helping police use genetic analysis to catch criminals. The measure (HR 829 — H Rept 103-45) sought to promote genetic identification technology while protecting against possible abuses. The Senate did not act on the bill. *(Vote 112, p. 28-H)*

Each person has a unique genetic "fingerprint" carried in biological material known as DNA. Using DNA analysis, police could match the genetic code of hair or blood samples from a crime site with that of a suspect.

The bill authorized $10 million annually in fiscal years 1994-98 to help states establish or improve DNA analysis labs. State labs would have to meet proficiency and privacy standards to be established by the FBI director.

The bill also authorized the FBI director to set up a national index of DNA records of convicted criminals, as well as DNA samples recovered from crime scenes or unidentified human remains. The legislation restricted access to such records to law enforcement officials or, where relevant, criminal defendants.

The House Judiciary's Civil and Constitutional Rights Subcommittee approved the bill March 17. The full Judiciary Committee approved it by voice vote March 24. The House had passed a similar proposal at the end of the 102nd Congress, but the Senate did not take up that bill. *(1992 Almanac, p. 334)*

CIVIL PROCEDURE

The House approved a bill (HR 2814 — H Rept 103-319) to block pending changes in the rules governing federal civil trials, but the effort failed when the Senate did not act on the bill. As a result, the new rules took effect Dec. 1.

Under the 1934 Rules Enabling Act, the Judicial Conference of the United States periodically reviewed and recommended changes to the rules governing civil trials in the federal courts. Such changes became law in seven months unless Congress acted first. The Supreme Court transmitted the latest changes to Congress on April 22; they were due to become law Dec. 1.

HR 2814 would have rejected two of the proposed changes. The first required all parties in a civil case to automatically reveal background information that pertained to specific allegations. Previously, parties seeking such information had to request it through a more time-consuming and costly process of pretrial "discovery."

The bill also would have blocked a less controversial change that allowed parties to record depositions by non-

stenographic means, such as audio recording.

The House passed the bill by voice vote Nov. 3. The bill had been approved by the House Judiciary Committee on Oct. 6.

CIVIL ARBITRATION

The Senate backed away from a plan to require all federal district courts to offer arbitration in lieu of lawsuits for civil cases. Instead, it cleared Nov. 24 an alternate bill (S 1732) that simply extended for another year a five-year-old pilot arbitration program in 20 of the nation's 94 federal district courts. That program had expired Nov. 19.

The more ambitious plan (HR 1102 — H Rept 103-284), a response to a backlog of civil cases, passed the House by voice vote Oct. 12. It would have required district courts to offer arbitration in most civil cases and would have let the courts require non-binding arbitration in cases involving $150,000 or less.

But Sen. Howell Heflin, D-Ala., citing a request by the Judicial Conference of the United States for further study, persuaded his colleagues to delay any Senate vote on the expansive arbitration program.

S 1732, which reauthorized the pilot program through the end of 1994, passed the Senate by voice vote Nov. 19. The House passed the bill, with a technical amendment to revive the program with funds as needed, Nov. 23. The Senate accepted that version the next day. President Clinton signed the bill into law Dec. 14 (PL 103-192).

ADMINISTRATIVE LAW JUDGES

The Senate on Nov. 19 passed a bill (S 486 — S Rept 103-154) aimed at eliminating agency influence on the findings of administrative law judges. The House did not act on the bill.

The bill sought to establish an independent administrative law judge "corps" in the executive branch to resolve complaints against all federal agencies. Under existing law, administrative law judges were employed by specific federal agencies, which provided their offices and staff and determined which cases they decided.

Sponsor Howell Heflin, D-Ala., a former chief justice of the Alabama Supreme Court who had advocated the changes for a decade, said such a close working relationship pressured the administrative law judges to rule in favor of agencies. He also cited a Congressional Budget Office report estimating savings of as much as $22 million a year under the bill.

But opponents argued against removing the judges from a single agency assignment.

Administrative law judges worked as fact-finders and appliers of agency regulations and policies. They were not federal judges in the constitutional sense. Under the bill, agency heads retained final authority to reverse their decisions.

A companion bill, HR 2586, was introduced in the House on July 1 by Dan Glickman, D-Kan.

DRUNKEN DRIVING

The House on Sept. 21 passed a bill (HR 1385 — H Rept 103-245) to amend the Omnibus Crime Control and Safe Streets Act of 1968 to let states use existing federal grant money to prosecute drunken drivers.

The bill, sponsored by Steven H. Schiff, R-N.M., authorized no new spending. It made drunken driving enforcement the 22nd option open to states for spending

funds already available through the Bureau of Justice Assistance Edward Byrne Memorial State and Local Enforcement Assistance Program.

The House Judiciary Subcommittee on Crime and Criminal Justice approved the bill by voice vote July 28; the full committee did the same Sept. 14.

A companion bill was introduced in the Senate (S 604) on March 17 by Pete V. Domenici, R-N.M.

WARDS COVE

A House Judiciary subcommittee gave voice vote approval March 17 to a bill aimed at applying employment discrimination law to Wards Cove Packing Co. workers in Alaska. The bill (HR 1172) went no further.

In 1971, the Supreme Court ruled that employment practices that had a disparate impact on women and minorities, such as tests and height requirements, violated the 1964 Civil Rights Act — unless employers could justify the practice as a business necessity. But in 1989, the Supreme Court in *Wards Cove Packing Co. v. Atonio* shifted the burden of proof to the employees, making them show that no business necessity existed. *(1989 Almanac, p. 295)*

The 1991 Civil Rights Act reversed the Wards Cove ruling, returning the burden of proof to employers. But Alaska members added an amendment exempting Wards Cove. *(1991 Almanac, p. 251)*

The bill, sponsored by Rep. Jim McDermott, D-Wash., and approved by the Subcommittee on Civil and Constitutional Rights, was aimed at ending the exemption, allowing the Wards Cove workers to be judged by the 1991 standard.

However, the fate of the Wards Cove workers — and other workers whose cases were filed before the 1991 law — would still hinge on a Supreme Court ruling expected in 1994 on whether the 1991 law could be applied retroactively.

WHITE HOUSE TRAVEL OFFICE

After heated partisan debate, the House Judiciary Committee on July 14 rebuffed a Republican effort to force a congressional inquiry into allegations of misconduct at the White House travel office.

The committee voted 20-15 almost along party lines to recommend that the full House defeat a resolution (H Res 198 — H Rept 103-183) requesting documents from the Clinton administration regarding the firing of seven travel office employees. Only Romano L. Mazzoli, D-Ky., sided with the Republicans. The measure went no further.

Seven employees of the travel office, which made travel arrangements for the White House news corps, were fired May 19 for alleged mismanagement and possible financial wrongdoing. In a report issued July 2, White House Chief of Staff Thomas F. McLarty III acknowledged that the dismissals were mishandled. These mistakes, the report said, were based on bad judgment. Five of the seven fired employees were reinstated in different positions, and four aides involved in the dismissal were reprimanded.

But Republicans called for more details and stronger punishments, saying the incident demonstrated cronyism in the Clinton administration.

Republicans alleged that President Clinton's longtime friend Harry Thomason, who was part owner of an airline charter company, pressured administration staff members to investigate possible irregularities at the travel office.

Thomason, according to a report by the House Republican Conference, also had complained that the office was excluding his travel company from bidding on White House travel business.

Republicans also said the FBI and IRS were "politicized" when they were inappropriately brought into the investigation in order to create the impression that the administration was concerned about possible criminal activity at the travel office.

The resolution, sponsored by Rep. Henry J. Hyde, R-Ill., would have made 26 document requests from the White House concerning nearly all aspects of the affair.

The panel voted along strict party lines to reject, 14-21, an amendment by Bill McCollum, R-Fla., requesting additional documents and expanding the inquiry to include questions about first lady Hillary Rodham Clinton's role in the matter and the procedures the White House used in its internal review.

COLLINS IMPEACHMENT

The House was poised in June to begin impeachment proceedings against Louisiana federal Judge Robert F. Collins, who was serving a six-year prison sentence for bribery and related offenses.

House Judiciary Committee Chairman Jack Brooks, D-Texas, introduced the impeachment resolution June 24, two days after the Judicial Conference of the United States officially recommended that Congress consider such action. The conference set administrative policy for the federal judicial system. But Collins resigned before the committee acted.

President Jimmy Carter appointed Collins to the federal bench in 1978.

In 1991, Collins was convicted of taking a $100,000 bribe. But he did not resign from the court and continued to receive his full salary. Because federal judges were appointed for life, congressional impeachment proceedings were the only way to force them from the bench.

Under the Constitution, the House was charged with investigating Collins' alleged wrongdoing and approving the official charges against the judge, known as articles of impeachment. The Senate would then hold a trial and vote on whether to convict on those charges.

In the nation's history, seven federal judges had been impeached and convicted — three of them during the 1980s. One of the three, Democrat Alcee L. Hastings, represented Florida's 23rd District in the House in 1993.

All three judges challenged the Senate procedures used to convict them, but in January the Supreme Court upheld those procedures.

OFFICE OF DRUG CONTROL POLICY

The House on Nov. 21 passed by voice vote a bill (HR 1926) to reauthorize the Office of National Drug Control Policy through fiscal 1998 and strengthen the hand of its director. The Government Operations Committee had given voice vote approval to the bill Nov. 19. The Senate did not act on the measure in 1993.

The bill, sponsored by Government Operations Chairman John Conyers Jr., D-Mich., provided that the office's director would become a member of the National Security Council, giving him or her more leverage when dealing with interagency disputes. ∎

Ginsburg Easily Wins Seat on High Court

Ruth Bader Ginsburg, a federal appeals court judge regarded as a trailblazer in securing equal rights for women, was sworn in Aug. 10 as the 107th justice of the Supreme Court, just seven weeks after President Clinton selected her.

The Senate easily confirmed Ginsburg on Aug. 3, following a pro forma debate the day before. The vote was 96-3. Republicans Jesse Helms, N.C., Don Nickles, Okla., and Robert C. Smith, N.H., opposed Ginsburg. Donald W. Riegle Jr., D-Mich., was absent but had expressed support. *(Vote 232, p. 30-S)*

Ginsburg's smooth trip through the Senate confirmation process was a stark contrast to the rough and raucous 1991 ride of President George Bush's second and final nominee, Clarence Thomas. *(Thomas nomination, 1991 Almanac, p. 274)*

Ginsburg, 60, succeeded Justice Byron R. White, who retired June 28 after 31 years on the high court.

She was expected to carry on his centrist tradition but with a somewhat more liberal tilt. The sharpest distinction between the two was on abortion rights. Ginsburg supported a constitutional right to seek an abortion, while White was one of two justices dissenting from the landmark 1973 *Roe v. Wade* decision legalizing abortion nationwide.

Ginsburg's appointment came at a time when a woman's right to have an abortion was hanging by a legal thread; the court upheld it by a scant 5-4 in a 1992 decision, *Planned Parenthood of Southeastern Pennsylvania v. Casey.*

Ginsburg was the first justice appointed by a Democratic president since Thurgood Marshall was named to the high court in 1967 by President Lyndon B. Johnson. She was only the second woman ever to serve on the Supreme Court, and its first Jewish member since the resignation of Justice Abe Fortas in 1969.

JUSTICE WHITE RETIRES

White, 75, announced his decision to step down on March 19, giving Clinton ample time to have his successor confirmed before the start of the 1993-94 court term in October. White's retirement was effective at the conclusion of the court's 1992-93 term.

After notifying Clinton of his plans to retire, White issued a brief statement on his lengthy tenure: "It has been an interesting and exciting experience to serve on the court," he said, but after 31 years, he and his wife, Marion, "think that someone else should be permitted to have a like experience."

White, a former Rhodes scholar and noted athlete, was appointed in 1962 by his friend, President John F. Kennedy. A pragmatic, non-ideological jurist, he was aligned most often with the conservative camp during his final years on the court — particularly on issues such as church-state relations and restrictions on abortion rights, affirmative action and the rights of criminal defendants.

Yet he left no distinctive judicial legacy. "He has not left his stamp on the court in a doctrinal sense," said A. E. Dick Howard, a constitutional law professor at the University of Virginia. "There are no monuments that bear his name."

Columbia University law Professor Henry P. Monaghan said White was a practical judge who sought sensible legal solutions rather than strict adherence to the words of the Founding Fathers. "He was a person who lived very much in the present," Monaghan said.

In the early 1970s, White was once called a "one-man Supreme Court" because he cast numerous swing votes that put the four justices appointed by President Richard M. Nixon in the majority. When it came to balancing law enforcement requirements and defendants' rights, he almost always sided with the government. He joined the majority in the 1970s in decisions to pare back the 1966 *Miranda* ruling, which required that people be read their rights at the time of arrest and upheld the right of law enforcement officials to conduct certain searches without warrants.

Yet White also cast the critical vote in several cases that aligned him with court liberals. In 1990, for instance, he sided with the majority in a decision allowing a federal judge to order the Kansas City School District to raise taxes to pay for desegregation.

Over time, White's approach to the law was described as more pragmatic than ideological. His frequently narrow view of legal issues often led to seemingly contradictory stands. For example, he provided the decisive vote in the court's 1990 decision upholding the so-called exclusionary rule, which prohibited the use of illegally obtained evidence in a criminal trial — even though he wrote the majority opinion for a 1984 decision that limited the scope of the rule for the first time in 70 years.

Plenty of Advice for Clinton

There was no shortage of advice for Clinton on whom he should select for his first court appointment — nor on how he should go about the process.

George Kassouf, director of the judicial selection project at the liberal Alliance for Justice, said it was critical that Clinton consider female and minority candidates as well as those from fields such as public interest law.

Sen. Arlen Specter, R-Pa., promptly wrote Clinton to recommend three circuit court judges for the job. Numerous senators said they hoped Clinton would restore meaning to the first half of the Senate's constitutional "advice and consent" role.

Sen. Paul Simon, D-Ill., cited the example of President Gerald R. Ford who, according to Simon, sought reactions to potential nominees before choosing Justice John Paul Stevens. "George Bush, by contrast, consulted with no members of the Senate," Simon said.

Several Republicans said they would scrutinize Clinton's nominee for competence and integrity but did not expect to fight the candidate on ideological grounds.

"Clinton is going to appoint someone to the court that I don't like, but he was elected, and the people knew . . . what he was going to do," said Sen. Phil Gramm, R-Texas. "If the person is competent . . . we shouldn't be trying to win on the Senate floor what we couldn't win at the ballot box."

Although many Democrats were heartened at the chance to begin reversing the court's conservative drift, some Democrats were among those urging Clinton not to choose a nominee likely to incite Republicans.

"We don't need any bruising confirmation battles at the moment," said Sen. David Pryor, D-Ark. "The president is fighting enough battles with the budget and the health-care plan."

Breyer, Babbitt Passed Over

Clinton took his time choosing a nominee, and he raised the hopes of two men in particular before he turned to Ginsburg.

By the second week in June, the president appeared to have narrowed his choice to Interior Secretary Bruce Babbitt or federal appeals court Judge Stephen G. Breyer, chief judge of the New England-based 1st Circuit.

Breyer, as a sitting judge, was more typical of recent candidates for the court. But in the past, appointees with political backgrounds were far more common, and many of them had a profound impact on the court.

"The people who have really made their stamp on the court have been political types," said Dennis Coyle, a politics professor at Catholic University in Washington. He cited Chief Justices Earl Warren and John Marshall as examples.

Of the 106 justices who had served on the court since 1789, 27 were alumni of Congress. Six were former governors, and one — William Howard Taft — was a former president. Twenty-three former Cabinet members were put on the court, including 13 who moved directly from the Cabinet to the court.

But in the mid-20th century, the trend changed. The last member of Congress to serve was Indiana's Sherman Minton, named to the court by Harry S Truman in 1949. Arthur Goldberg was the last Cabinet member named to the Supreme Court. He was Labor secretary in 1962 when John F. Kennedy gave him the nod.

Breyer, who had been hospitalized for several days following a bicycling accident, met with Clinton for about two hours on June 11, amid reports that he was the presumptive choice. Afterward, White House spokeswoman Dee Dee Myers said that the meeting went well but that Clinton had made no decision.

The public dithering prompted furious lobbying. Some environmentalists pleaded that Babbitt be kept at the Interior Department, while certain conservatives criticized the former Arizona governor's lack of judicial experience and suggested that he would be harder to confirm. Several senators lobbied hard for Breyer, who had served as chief counsel of the Senate Judiciary Committee in 1979-80.

The delay and subsequent politicking disquieted several senators, including some who participated in the jockeying. "That's the problem with waiting so long," said Orrin G. Hatch of Utah, ranking Republican on the Judiciary Committee, who had publicly touted Breyer while raising some concerns about Babbitt. "It's a big mess from what I can see."

But Judiciary Committee Chairman Joseph R. Biden Jr., D-Del., brushed.off the notion that such lobbying was unseemly. "This is like an election," Biden said. "This appointment will have more effect on their lives than anything we do short of declaring war."

Biden said it was wise to keep the Republicans in the process, saying that the Constitution gave the full Senate and the president equal roles in selecting a new justice. "It doesn't say seek the advice of Democrats. It says seek the advice of the Senate."

As the administration closed in on a decision, it seemed determined to avoid the kind of embarrassment it faced over the failed nomination of two attorney general candidates and of Lani Guinier to head the Justice Department's civil rights division. *(Appointments, pp. 307, 308)*

Sen, Dennis DeConcini, D-Ariz., said he had received detailed inquiries on Breyer far beyond any he could recall

---

Ruth Bader Ginsburg

Born: March 15, 1933, New York

Home: Washington, D.C.

Education: Cornell U., B.A. 1954; Harvard Law School, 1956-58; Columbia Law School, LL.B. Kent Scholar, 1959

Occupation: Federal judge

Family: Husband, Martin D. Ginsburg; two children

Religion: Jewish

Career highlights: Law clerk to U.S. District Judge Edmund L. Palmieri, Southern District of New York, 1959-61; assistant professor, Rutgers University School of Law, 1963-66; associate professor, Rutgers University School of Law, 1966-69; professor, Columbia University Law School, 1972-80; general counsel, American Civil Liberties Union (ACLU), 1973-80; U.S. circuit judge, U.S. Court of Appeals for the District of Columbia Circuit, 1980-present.

Other distinctions: One of nine women enrolled in her Harvard Law School class of 400; tied for first place in her Columbia Law School class, 1959; won five out of six women's rights cases that she argued before the Supreme Court as counsel for the ACLU, 1973-76.

---

for a nominee. DeConcini's prediction: "They are going to take the absolutely least problematic."

GINSBURG'S NOMINATION

Despite the public clues that he would choose Breyer or Babbitt, Clinton announced his selection of Ginsburg on June 14. His choice immediately won praise from Democrats and Republicans alike.

Announcing his choice in the Rose Garden, Clinton said he had been swayed by Ginsburg's reputation as a talented judge, her role as one of the foremost legal advocates for women's rights during the 1970s and her potential to build consensus on the Supreme Court.

During more than 12 years on the U.S. Court of Appeals for the District of Columbia Circuit, Ginsburg had earned a reputation as a non-ideological moderate who eschewed judicial activism. "Ruth Bader Ginsburg cannot be called a liberal or a conservative," Clinton said. "She has proved herself too thoughtful for such labels."

Ginsburg responded with a speech that touched heavily on her family, women's rights and the obstacles she had faced as a female lawyer. She said her nomination "contributes to the end of the days when women, at least half the talent pool in our society, appear in high places only as one-at-a-time performers." *(Texts of Clinton, Ginsburg remarks, p. 19-D)*

Ginsburg said little about her judicial views beyond citing Chief Justice William H. Rehnquist and Justice Sandra Day O'Connor, the court's first woman member, on the virtues of judicial integrity and self-restraint.

The selection triggered palpable relief on Capitol Hill, where senators began dispensing praise even before the official announcement. "I cannot speak highly enough of this woman," DeConcini said shortly before the White House ceremony. "I'd be surprised if anyone's against her."

Republicans were also effusive in their praise. "She's going to make a very excellent judge," said Hatch.

The bipartisan acceptance reflected not only Clinton's ultimate selection but also his decision to consult with key senators in both parties during the search. And it broke sharply with the recent tradition of hostile, partisan relations between Republican presidents and a Democratic-controlled Senate on Supreme Court nominations.

Outside the Senate as well, the nomination met with broad if not overwhelming support. Liberals generally praised Ginsburg's advocacy for women's rights prior to her becoming an appeals court judge in 1980. Conservatives praised her judicial restraint since joining the court.

After a run of 10 Republican Supreme Court appointees, some liberal activists were aching for a nominee with a bolder judicial vision. But Clinton and his advisers made it clear from the outset that they were inclined to pick a centrist, not a liberal crusader. "I think he operated within a grid, and within that grid he chose very well," said Henry P. Monaghan, a constitutional law professor at Columbia University.

Losers Left Hanging

Clinton met Ginsburg for 90 minutes June 13 and called late that night to offer her the appointment.

That left some lawmakers, many of whom had publicly praised or lobbied for Babbitt or Breyer, feeling that the two men had been badly treated because their names had been so prominently played in the press.

"I think we've got to get away from this process of appearing to send up trial balloons," Senate Judiciary member William S. Cohen, R-Maine, told a television reporter, even as he praised Ginsburg.

Clinton mentioned the two by name in his Rose Garden speech, saying they were worthy candidates who might well find themselves on the court one day.

But environmentalists had beseeched Clinton to keep Babbitt at the Interior Department. And Breyer's fortunes appeared to decline after news reports recounted his initial failure to pay Social Security taxes for a part-time cleaning woman — an issue that had toppled two attorney general candidates — although Clinton aides later insisted that Breyer had not been rejected on that basis.

Ginsburg: Breaking Ground

At age 60, Ginsburg belonged to a generation of women who cut the trail into professional schools and careers.

She was born in Brooklyn, N.Y., and graduated from Cornell University. She married Martin D. Ginsburg soon after graduation. She then entered Harvard Law School, becoming one of fewer than a dozen women in a class of hundreds. Ginsburg stayed long enough to become the first woman editor of the Harvard Law Review but transferred to Columbia Law School when her husband took a job in New York.

After graduating from Columbia in 1959, she clerked for New York federal Judge Edmund L. Palmieri.

Ginsburg began a teaching career at Rutgers University, and in 1972 she became the first tenured woman professor at Columbia Law School. While teaching at Columbia and raising two children, Ginsburg served as counsel to the American Civil Liberties Union, and it was in that role that she made history before the Supreme Court.

She argued six gender discrimination cases, winning five of them. Those cases represented an escalating assault on laws that treated men and women differently, ranging from benefit policies to jury selection rules. Collectively, the rulings established unprecedented legal protection against sex discrimination under the Equal Protection Clause of the Constitution.

On the Bench

But Ginsburg, whom many described as shy and somewhat formal, appeared more naturally suited for her subsequent role as a judge. President Jimmy Carter nominated her to the U.S. Court of Appeals for the District of Columbia Circuit in 1980.

Ginsburg was known as a restrained and fair-minded judge who did her homework, and then some. "She was always, always, always thoroughly prepared," recalled Barbara Flagg, a former Ginsburg clerk who taught constitutional law at Washington University in St. Louis.

Most observers credited her with a keen intellect, though she was not generally viewed as a notably bold or creative legal thinker. The University of Virginia's Professor Howard said Ginsburg was more likely to refine an existing legal doctrine than to chart a new one.

Associates who had worked with Ginsburg noted her close eye to detail and said she was not afraid to put lawyers on the spot. "Any litigant [who appears before her] has to take very seriously their obligation to understand their case," said Marcia Greenberger of the National Women's Law Center.

Legal analysts predicted Ginsburg would be a relatively progressive justice on issues such as free speech, religious freedom and separation of church and state. Clinton called attention to her 1984 Court of Appeals dissent in which Ginsburg defended a military officer's right to wear a yarmulke while on duty.

With less certainty, some law professors also predicted a fairly liberal stance on civil rights and access to the courts.

By contrast, Ginsburg was considered moderate to conservative on criminal issues and business law. For example, in 1986 she joined then-colleague Robert H. Bork on two antitrust opinions that liberals later attacked in Bork's Supreme Court confirmation hearings during the Reagan administration.

In one noteworthy separation-of-powers case, Ginsburg in 1987 dissented from the majority opinion and upheld the constitutionality of the independent counsel statute. Her view was upheld the following year, 7-1, by the Supreme Court in *Morrison v. Olson.* (1987 Almanac, p. 363; 1988 Almanac, p. 123)

She was known for giving relatively generous weight to legislative intent, and she sometimes cited legislative floor debate or reports to bolster her rulings.

Hugh Baxter, a Boston University law professor who had clerked for Ginsburg, said she was not wont to search out avenues to bypass Supreme Court precedents. "For her, there are very strong limits on what judges can do," Baxter said. "She took very seriously that she was a judge on a lower court."

Ginsburg had good relations with justices of all ideologies — including former Justice William J. Brennan Jr., a staunch liberal, and Justice Antonin Scalia, an ardent conservative who once sat on the D.C. Circuit with Ginsburg.

But by most accounts, Ginsburg was not an active coalition-builder on the D.C. Circuit, and some legal analysts were skeptical that she would play that role on the fragmented Supreme Court.

If Ginsburg were to assume such influence, said How-

ard, "it's likely to be through quiet persuasion ... rather than force of personality."

Abortion Rights

Ginsburg was certain to be a stronger voice for abortion rights than White, who was one of only two justices to dissent from the benchmark 1973 *Roe v. Wade* decision that upheld a constitutional right to abortion. Yet Ginsburg had criticized the *Roe* decision, on both political and legal grounds.

In *Roe*, the Supreme Court ruled that abortion rights were guaranteed under a constitutional right to privacy and, in so doing, struck down a plethora of state laws restricting abortion.

Ginsburg argued that the *Roe* decision went too far too fast, creating a political backlash that actually set back the abortion rights movement. She also critiqued it on legal grounds, suggesting that abortion rights should be upheld as a matter of gender equality.

Unlike Bush's two nominees, David H. Souter and Clarence Thomas, Ginsburg had written extensively on the 1973 court decision. She laid out her basic critique of *Roe* in a 1984 speech at the University of North Carolina and a subsequent law review article. She restated her view in a March 1993 lecture at New York University.

The *Roe* decision grounded the legal right to abortion in an established constitutional doctrine of privacy, drawing from earlier cases concerning issues such as the right to use contraceptives. Those rights were traced in part to the 14th Amendment's guarantees of liberty and due process.

The decision set up a legal framework to evaluate governmental restrictions on abortion. During the first two trimesters of a pregnancy, the woman's privacy rights took priority over the state's interest in potential human life, namely the fetus. Only in the third trimester would the state's interest in the fetus become controlling. Yet even at this stage, the state's interest would be overridden if the woman's life or health was endangered.

In the years since *Roe,* the court had reaffirmed the privacy or liberty basis for abortion rights, although it lowered the standard for justifying abortion restrictions.

In the North Carolina lecture and elsewhere, Ginsburg did not reject the privacy argument but saw it as an incomplete justification for abortion rights. She sought to cast access to abortion additionally, and perhaps primarily, as a matter of equality.

Thus, Ginsburg would ground abortion rights in the Constitution's equal protection guarantees, found in the Fifth Amendment and the 14th Amendment, which said that a state could not "deny to any person within its jurisdiction the equal protection of the laws."

"The conflict ... is not simply one between a fetus' interests and a woman's interests, narrowly conceived, nor is the overriding issue state versus private control of a woman's body for a span of nine months," Ginsburg said in her North Carolina address. "Also in the balance is a woman's autonomous charge of her full life's course."

Unlike the idea of privacy, the guarantee of equal protection is explicit in the Constitution (although the 14th Amendment was first written to address discrimination against blacks rather than women). And some legal analysts believed that it could offer a more straightforward framework for defending abortion rights.

Under an equal protection framework, the state would have to offer a significant justification for laws that treated women differently from men — in this case abortion regulations. Guiding this legal argument was the view that, particularly in a society in which women carried the primary burdens of rearing children, women could not operate as equal players unless they could control when and if to bear children.

Several high court justices gave a nod in the direction of Ginsburg's equality argument in the 1992 decision *Planned Parenthood of Southeastern Pennsylvania v. Casey.* In that case, three of the justices made several references to the link between abortion and women's rights, in particular: "The ability of women to participate equally in the economic and social life of the nation has been facilitated by their ability to control their reproductive lives." *(Casey decision, 1992 Almanac, p. 398)*

Some analysts said that language could indicate an opening for Ginsburg to integrate some equality standard into the court's abortion reasoning, perhaps alongside an ongoing privacy analysis. "This is not an either-or proposition," said Marcy Wilder, a senior staff attorney at the National Abortion Rights Action League.

In the *Casey* decision, the court rejected the trimester framework laid out in *Roe*, and instituted a new — but as yet ill-defined — standard for reviewing abortion restrictions: States should not place an "undue burden" on a woman's right to abortion before the fetus is viable.

SENATE HEARINGS, CONFIRMATION

The most striking thing in the weeks leading up to Ginsburg's July 20 confirmation hearing before the Senate Judiciary Committee was the utter lack of controversy surrounding her nomination.

One reason senators gave for the lack of controversy was Ginsburg's extensive record of writings and speeches, reflecting years of teaching and advocacy and more than a decade on the U.S. Court of Appeals for the District of Columbia Circuit. Senators said they felt they knew a good deal about her legal thinking — and most were comfortable with what they saw. "No one is going to not know who they're voting for," said Herb Kohl, D-Wis.

The American Bar Association, which rated all federal judicial nominees, deemed Ginsburg "well qualified" — its highest rating. Several outside groups that routinely scrutinized Supreme Court nominations issued detailed reports on Ginsburg, highlighting areas of concern. The conservative Judicial Selection Monitoring Project concluded that she held a more activist judicial philosophy than her "moderate" label suggested.

At the other end of the spectrum, the liberal Alliance for Justice praised Ginsburg's early career as a legal crusader for women's rights but had some qualms about her more restrained approach to civil liberties on the bench.

However, several liberal interest groups that aggressively researched and sometimes lobbied against controversial Republican nominees chose not to expend resources poring over Ginsburg's record. Her views appeared acceptable if not always ideal, they said.

Even with the aura of inevitability, no one treated the confirmation hearings casually. White House officials helped Ginsburg prepare, including showing her tapes of prior confirmation hearings. In the Senate, members and staff of the Judiciary Committee scoured her writings and consulted with constitutional law scholars.

The Public Hearings

Ginsburg testified publicly before the committee July 20-23, offering a solid oral performance to accompany her impres-

Continued on p. 324

In Her Words: Ginsburg on Abortion . . .

Abortion Rights

In a speech March 9 to the New York University School of Law, Judge Ginsburg argued that the Supreme Court had ruled too broadly in Roe v. Wade, *the 1973 decision that legalized abortion. Following are excerpts of her address:*

The idea of the woman in control of her destiny and her place in society was less prominent in the *Roe* decision itself, which coupled with the rights of the pregnant woman the free exercise of her physician's medical judgment. The *Roe* decision might have been less of a storm center had it both homed in more precisely on the women's equality dimension of the issue and, correspondingly, attempted nothing more bold at that time than the mode of decision-making the court employed in the 1970s gender-classification cases. . . .

No measured motion, the *Roe* decision left virtually no state with laws fully conforming to the court's delineation of abortion regulation still permissible. Around that extraordinary decision, a well-organized and vocal right-to-life movement rallied and succeeded, for a considerable time, in turning the legislative tide in the opposite direction. . . .

I do not suggest that the court should never step ahead of the political branches in pursuit of a constitutional precept. *Brown v. Board of Education*, the 1954 decision declaring racial segregation in public schools offensive to the equal-protection principle, is the case that best fits the bill. Past the midpoint of the 20th century, apartheid remained the law-enforced system in several states, shielded by a constitutional interpretation the court itself advanced at the turn of the century — the "separate but equal" doctrine. . . .

But without taking giant strides and thereby risking a backlash too forceful to contain, the court, through constitutional adjudication, can reinforce or signal a green light for a social change. In most of the post-1970 gender-classification cases, unlike *Roe*, the court functioned in just that way. It approved the direction of change through a temperate brand of decision-making, one that was not extravagant or divisive.

Roe v. Wade, on the other hand, halted a political process that was moving in a reform direction and thereby, I believe, prolonged divisiveness and deferred stable settlement of the issue. The most recent *Planned Parenthood* decision, although a retreat from *Roe*, appears to have prompted a renewed dialogue, a revival of the political movement in progress in the early 1970s. That renewed dialogue, one may hope, will, within a relatively short span, yield an enduring resolution of this vital matter.

Senate Confirmation

Following are excerpts from a Jan. 27, 1988, speech Ginsburg made on the Senate confirmation process. She delivered the speech at the University of Illinois College of Law shortly after the Senate rejected the Supreme Court nomination of Robert H. Bork.

Are senators ill-equipped to engage in all inquiry into a nominee's judicial philosophy because they are too much occupied with domestic and foreign policy matters of the moment to think grandly, if at all, about constitutional theory? And if that is so, shouldn't senators confine themselves to less complex questions concerning the nominee's professional competence, integrity and general deportment?

Taking into account the system of mutual restraints the framers put in place, and the historical record, I agree with those who hold that sauce for the goose must serve for the gander as well. The president, too, is occupied with multiple issues, and may not himself have thought rigorously about the tension between judicial supremacy and democratic theory. Judicial confirmation is the extraordinary moment in which the three branches of government intersect. . . .

Will the performance of judges or legal scholars be chilled by negative campaigns of the . . . anti-Bork character? . . . Chief Justice [William H.] Rehnquist said some years ago that a judge steps out of the proper judicial role most conspicuously and dangerously when he or she flinches from a decision that is legally right because the decision is not the one "the home crowd wants." I believe most of my colleagues on the federal bench are strong enough generally to resist the temptation to vote the politically popular way or to toss out *in dicta* sops for particular groups. And my experience on law faculties suggests to me that professors too are not an easily intimidated breed. Still, campaigns against judges that spread misinformation, turn complex issues into slogans, and play on our fears are worrisome. I have no magic formula for making the interest groups involved act more responsibly, for keeping their comment fair. I believe, however, that, if the president seeks more "advice" from the Senate prior to a nomination — for the Senate's role encompasses both "advice and consent" — such campaigns may be kept within more tolerable bounds.

Equal Rights

During her 1980 confirmation hearings for a judgeship on the U.S. Court of Appeals for the District of Columbia Circuit, Ginsburg was questioned about her views on equal rights for men and women:

Sen. Howard M. Metzenbaum, D-Ohio: Ms. Ginsburg, for a number of years after you commenced teaching law, you devoted yourself to the classroom and traditional legal scholarship. What motivated you to engage in advocacy — particularly to place yourself on the firing line — with respect to equal rights for men and women? And you might in answering that question indicate, rather briefly, the degree or the manner in which you are involved, and the results, if you care to comment on those.

Ginsburg: The stimulation came from two sources. The first, my students at the end of the '60s at Rutgers Law School [in Newark, N.J.] sought the introduction of a seminar on the legal status of women. In response to that request, I spent some weeks in the library looking at statutes, cases and commentaries. At the same time, women complaining about sex discrimination began coming into

...Confirmation Process, Equal Rights

the ACLU affiliate in New Jersey, and their complaints were referred to me. It was that combination — research in the lawbooks and confrontation with the genuine grievances of women who had been denied jobs or other opportunities — that combination engaged my interest both as an attorney and as a woman.

The legal research persuaded me that for the first time in history, for the first time certainly since women had achieved the vote, their claims to more encompassing equality of opportunity would attract sympathetic listeners. Congress had taken a lead role by that time; it had enacted the Equal Pay Act in 1963, and it had included sex in Title VII in the Civil Rights Act of 1964. And the lower courts had begun to apply the equal protection principle to overturn some obsolete, gender-based laws. I found those developments heartening. They encouraged me to devote my hand to the cause of equal justice for men and women under the law. For the next 10 years I engaged in litigation that I hope helped to solidify that principle: Equal justice for men and women under the law. . . .

Metzenbaum: You have urged in speeches and in articles the ratification of the Equal Rights Amendment. Why do you think it a desirable amendment? Why do you support it? And do you think that it would dissolve all problems of sex discrimination?

Ginsburg: I would like to start with the last inquiry. No; I surely do not think it would solve all problems. That will be evident to anyone who understands our Constitution, its structure and the history of its application. The First Amendment guarantees free speech, press and religion. That amendment has been around a long time, but questions of interpretation arise today as they did yesterday and as they will tomorrow. Similarly, the Equal Rights Amendment, if it is adopted, will require interpretation. No; I do not see the Equal Rights Amendment as a measure that would provide certain answers to every question that might arise under it. Still, I regard it as a highly desirable measure and for this principal reason: We do have an Equal Protection Clause phrased broadly enough to cover the same territory, but it is historic fact that the framers of that clause — the framers of the 14th Amendment — were not thinking about the legal equality of men and women. And that is part of our history, and we cannot revise it. So, I see the Equal Rights Amendment essentially as the front-door way, the clear, clean means of establishing a national commitment, of acknowledging our national belief in the equal status and dignity of every woman and every man.

Independent Counsel

On Jan. 22, 1988, Ginsburg dissented when the U.S. Court of Appeals for the District of Columbia Circuit struck down the independent counsel law In Re Sealed Case *(which later became* Morrison v. Olson*). Following are excerpts of her dissent:*

The core of the constitutional issues presented in these consolidated cases is whether the independent counsel provisions of the Ethics in Government Act . . . violate the doctrine of separated government powers. There is an irony in the majority's holding that the act is constitutionally infirm, for the measure strives to maintain the structural design that is the genius of our Constitution — the system of mutual checks and balances; the act's sole purpose is to curb or avert abuses of executive branch power. Because I conclude that the Ethics Act neither impermissibly transfers an executive function to another branch nor orders an undue displacement of executive prerogatives, I would hold that the legislation withstands appellants' separation-of-powers challenges.

Appellants advance two less encompassing constitutional claims: that the act contravenes the Appointments Clause [of the Constitution], and that it also violates the case or controversy requirement of Article III. These challenges are intertwined with the overarching separation-of-powers question; I find neither claim persuasive, whether considered separately or in conjunction with the larger challenge. . . .

The Ethics Act is designed to function as a control against abuse of executive branch power. It implements the checking aspect of the separated powers. The independent counsel provisions of the act were developed in response to the Watergate-era abuses of executive branch powers, abuses which themselves threatened the balance between the three branches of government. The act is rooted in the principle that "no man can be a prosecutor or judge in his own case". . . . It is similarly unreasonable to expect an individual to investigate or prosecute his superiors. . . .

The Ethics in Government Act is a carefully considered congressional journey into the sometimes arcane realm of the separation-of-powers doctrine, more particularly, into areas the framers left undefined. The act is designed to prevent Congress' own appropriation of the functions it insulates from executive supervision, and it implements a fundamental control essential to our Constitution's doctrine of separated powers: the control of mutual checks. It is a measure faithful to the 18th century blueprint, yet fitting for our time. I find the Ethics Act constitutional, and would affirm the judgments of the district court.

Continued from p. 321

sive record of professional achievements. She maneuvered carefully through three long days of questioning, offering steady, informed and polite responses with occasional spurts of humor or digression. *(Hearing excerpts, p. 30-D)*

With family and friends arrayed behind her, Ginsburg spoke of a personal history of discrimination and perseverance. She stressed her dedication to impartial judging and to the system in which each branch of government plays its appointed role. There were no bombshells, and senators learned little new about her opinions on critical matters of constitutional law.

Advocate in Judge's Clothing?

If there was any tension surrounding Ginsburg's nomination, it was the effort to reconcile her path-breaking role in the 1970s as an advocate for women's equality with her restrained record as a federal judge.

Liberal Democrats yearned to see in Ginsburg the broad legal vision of her advocacy days. Republicans, meanwhile, sought reassurances that Ginsburg would continue to display the judicial restraint that characterized her work as an appellate judge. Many of Ginsburg's answers on this theme offered comfort to conservatives.

In her opening statement, Ginsburg said that she was neither liberal nor conservative but rather committed to an independent and restrained judiciary. She said judges should decide the issue before them, "without reaching out to cover cases not yet seen."

Later Ginsburg stressed the difference between advocacy and judging and sought to reassure senators that she would not pursue a personal political agenda on the bench. Legislators, not the courts, are key to setting policy and even safeguarding rights, Ginsburg told the committee, and she emphasized the restraints on judges, such as legal precedent.

When Chairman Biden argued July 20 that courts must sometimes lead society, Ginsburg remained skeptical. "Judges must be mindful of what their place is in this system and must always remember that we live in a democracy that can be destroyed if judges take it upon themselves to rule as Platonic guardians," she said.

At the same time, Ginsburg distinguished herself from some Republican nominees in her approach to constitutional rights and the role of judges.

She told Biden that she would look beyond the strict text of the Constitution in determining rights worthy of the court's protection, to encompass the broad liberty guarantees embodied in the Declaration of Independence.

She noted that the Constitution was structured as a check on government power and specifically guaranteed unenumerated rights — rights not explicit in the text. "I think the Framers are shortchanged if we view them as having a limited view of rights," she said. For Ginsburg, that included a constitutional right to privacy that she traced to two constitutional principles: the right to be left alone and the right to make personal decisions.

Ginsburg also said judges must at times set policy, when cases before them exposed legal gaps that legislators had not addressed and constitutional rights were at stake. And she said the court on occasion must move ahead of the legislative branch, particularly when the political process offered no viable resolution — as on racial segregation prior to the 1954 *Brown v. Board of Education* decision.

On voting rights and civil rights, for example, Ginsburg stressed the importance of diversity and said she had been sensitized by her own encounters with discrimination as the daughter of Jewish immigrants. She recalled traveling with her parents and seeing signs stating: "No Dogs or Jews Allowed."

Abortion Rights

Ginsburg erased any doubts about her support for abortion rights, clarifying her critique of the landmark abortion rights decision and underscoring her belief in a woman's right to choose whether to continue a pregnancy.

She defended her analysis that the *Roe* decision had pre-empted or distorted an ongoing political dialogue on abortion — with the effect of galvanizing the anti-abortion camp. "One side seemed to relax its energy while the other side had a single target around which to rally," she said, while acknowledging that others could properly disagree with that political analysis.

But in an exchange July 21 with Hank Brown, R-Colo., Ginsburg clarified her legal critique and emphasized her support for abortion rights. She explained that she was not challenging the privacy basis for abortion rights but rather seeking to add another, and perhaps dominant, underpinning — equality.

She explained her equality argument in forceful terms. "This is something that is central to a woman's life, to her dignity," Ginsburg said. "It's a decision that she must make for herself. And when government controls that decision for her, she's being treated as less than a fully adult human."

Tight-Lipped

Like all nominees, Ginsburg sparred with senators over which questions she could properly answer. In her opening statement, she cautioned that it would be improper for her to comment on matters likely to come before the Supreme Court, and she urged senators to rely foremost on her written record. She held to those attitudes, to the frustration of some.

At the outset of the third day of testimony, Biden chastised her for putting too many areas of questioning off limits. "You have given us less than I would like," Biden said, although he conceded that Ginsburg probably was offering about as much as some recent nominees.

In the July 22 session, Hatch pushed Ginsburg to state her views on the constitutionality of the death penalty — an issue she had sidestepped earlier in the week — particularly given her straightforward remarks on abortion rights. "I think you ought to tell us where you really come down on this thing," he said.

Ginsburg resisted, reiterating that she could not prejudge a legal issue that could come to the Supreme Court.

Hatch eventually let the matter go, but Ginsburg soon ran afoul of Arlen Specter, R-Pa. on the same grounds. At the same time, Specter commented that "nominees answer about as many questions as they have to for confirmation."

Biden said Ginsburg's guarded responses probably reflected a combination of political strategy and natural temperament. "This is obviously not a person who throws caution to the wind very often," he said.

Sex Discrimination

Ginsburg was most expansive and passionate when discussing her personal and legal experiences regarding sex discrimination. She explained her inherent skepticism toward laws that treated women differently than men, even those presumably intended to "protect" women. Ginsburg said she had encountered many such laws during her life and believed their real purpose was usually "protecting men's jobs from women's competition."

Ginsburg acknowledged that some feminists advocated making legal distinctions on the basis of gender to assist women. She said she remained unconvinced but might feel different if such laws were passed by legislatures with far more women.

Ginsburg, who had been a strong proponent of the Equal Rights Amendment (ERA) to the Constitution during the 1970s, said there was no longer a compelling legal need for the amendment given that the Supreme Court had recognized equal rights for women under the 14th Amendment's Equal Protection Clause — due in part to cases Ginsburg successfully argued before the court.

Nevertheless, Ginsburg continued to advocate the ERA as an important symbolic marker. The 14th Amendment was written with African-Americans rather than women in mind, she said, and she would like the country to put an explicit guarantee of women's equality into the Constitution.

Gay Rights

Ginsburg had far less to say about a more controversial discrimination issue — gay rights — although she stood by a statement she made in 1979 deploring "rank discrimination" on the basis of sexual orientation.

Patrick J. Leahy, D-Vt., approached the issue July 21, asking Ginsburg whether the constitutional right to free association continues in the military. "It doesn't mean you have the same rights of association in the military that you would have in civilian life," Ginsburg replied. "But our constitutional rights don't end. They are fitted to the setting in which you are placed."

Cohen, a member of the Armed Services Committee, pressed the matter explicitly the next day. He connected it to a circuit court case in which Ginsburg had suggested that the military should relax its uniform code to accommodate a Jewish soldier's desire to wear a yarmulke while in service. But Ginsburg did not respond, calling it a "burning question" that would undoubtedly come before the courts.

Separation of Powers

For all her caution, Ginsburg provided glimpses into her reasoning on constitutional law — often in the context of past writings or cases that had come before her on the U.S. Court of Appeals for the District of Columbia.

While reaffirming her friendship with Justice Scalia, a former colleague on the appeals court, Ginsburg disassociated herself from Scalia's view that judges should hew to statutory text to determine legislative intent.

Ideally, Ginsburg said, laws would be precise enough to give judges a clear notion of how to apply them. But because statutes are often vague, Ginsburg said she turned to committee reports and other legislative history with "hopeful skepticism" that they would reveal how legislators meant the law to be applied.

On First Amendment issues, she emphasized the need for religious freedom. And she voiced support for a controversial Supreme Court precedent that set strong restrictions on government involvement with religious activities — despite criticism of that standard from some sitting justices.

Closed-Door Session

Biden announced he was going ahead with several reforms — first outlined in a June 1992 floor speech — inspired by the messy public investigation of sexual harassment allegations against Clarence Thomas in 1991.

On July 23, after three days of public testimony, the Judiciary Committee held a closed-door session with Ginsburg to review any ethical allegations that might have emerged — a practice that Biden said would be standard for all Supreme Court nominees.

Biden said the private session would not deal with matters of political or judicial philosophy but rather any concerns raised about a nominee's background or integrity. Biden said the practice could spare senators and nominees a public airing of frivolous charges. He said a transcript of the private session would go into the nominee's confidential file, which was available to any senator but not the media or public.

Final Approval

The committee approved Ginsburg's nomination unanimously, 18-0, on July 29, less than a week after the conclusion of its hearings.

The full Senate followed suit in short order, conducting a pro forma debate on Aug. 2 before approving the nomination 96-3 on Aug. 3. ∎

High Court Stays Its Conservative Course

The Supreme Court on June 28 ended a relatively quiet 1992-93 term that featured no groundbreaking decisions and only a handful of rulings with broad ramifications.

The court continued to follow the conservative course it had pursued in the Reagan-Bush era, taking a narrow view of civil rights laws, siding with prosecutors and police in criminal cases and lowering a bit the wall separating church and state.

Its 107 signed opinions showed little appetite for judicial activism, as the justices largely deferred to legislators and the executive branch in setting policy.

The big news of the term came in late March, when Justice Byron R. White announced he would retire. He stepped down at the end of the term, concluding a 31-year career on the high court. President Clinton nominated Ruth Bader Ginsburg, a federal appellate judge in Wash-

ington, to replace him, and she was confirmed by the Senate on Aug. 3.

Ginsburg was expected to pull the conservative-leaning court a bit more toward the center. But she was the only justice appointed by a Democratic president, and she had built a record as a centrist rather than a liberal during her years on the U.S. Court of Appeals for the District of Columbia Circuit. (Ginsburg appointment, p. 318)

MINORITY DISTRICTS

One of the term's most significant rulings came on the final day, June 28, as a 5-4 majority held that congressional districts that appeared to have been drawn solely on racial lines were subject to constitutional attacks by white voters, even if the districts were designed to comply with the

Voting Rights Act.

"We believe that reapportionment is one area in which appearances do matter," said Justice Sandra Day O'Connor, writing for the majority. "A reapportionment plan that includes in one district individuals ... who may have little in common with one another but the color of their skin bears an uncomfortable resemblance to political apartheid."

O'Connor's opinion signaled dissatisfaction with the broad interpretation of the Voting Rights Act's mandate, as expressed in the court's 1986 ruling in *Thornburg v. Gingles*, that states should create minority districts wherever possible. She was joined by Chief Justice William H. Rehnquist and Justices Antonin Scalia, Anthony M. Kennedy and Clarence Thomas.

The court's ruling invited a new wave of lawsuits challenging the constitutionality of districts drawn to ensure the election of minorities.

The ruling in the case of *Shaw v. Reno* reinstated a suit by five white North Carolinians who contended that the state's new congressional district map, which created two sinuous majority-black districts, violated their 14th Amendment right to "equal protection under the law" by diluting their votes. Freshman Democratic Reps. Eva Clayton and Melvin Watt in 1992 became the first African-Americans elected to represent North Carolina in Congress since 1901.

In her majority opinion, O'Connor decried the creation of districts based solely on racial composition, as well as map-drawers' abandonment of traditional redistricting standards such as compactness and contiguity.

Many Districts Potentially Affected

The ruling's implications extended well beyond the narrow action taken in *Shaw*. By calling into question the constitutionality of amorphous computer-generated entities that wriggled through areas to collect a majority of minority voters, the court gave legal standing to challenges to any congressional map with an oddly shaped majority-minority district that might not be defensible on grounds other than race (such as shared community interest or geographical compactness).

The 1990s round of redistricting produced a record number of majority-minority districts. Of the 52 districts with a majority black or Hispanic population, some of the most extreme examples of the type of gerrymandering the court found fault with included:

● **Florida's 3rd District (black population: 55 percent).** Likened in appearance to a gnawed wishbone, the 3rd twisted narrowly through 14 counties along its 250-mile path. Democrat Corrine Brown was elected in 1992.

● **Illinois' 4th District (Hispanic population: 65 percent).** The "earmuff" district — it resembled a headset placed on its side — the 4th was created in 1991 redistricting to include two Hispanic blocs of Chicago. Democrat Luis V. Gutierrez was elected in 1992.

● **Louisiana's 4th District (black population: 66 percent).** Dubbed by a state redistricting staff member as "the 'Z' with drips," the 4th followed the state's northern, eastern and northeastern borders, with forays into central Louisiana. Democrat Cleo Fields was elected in 1992.

● **New York's 12th District (Hispanic population: 58 percent).** To collect a majority of Hispanics, the 12th followed a meandering path through parts of three New York City boroughs: Queens, Brooklyn and Manhattan. Democrat Nydia M. Velázquez was elected in 1992.

● **Texas' 30th District (black population: 50 percent).** As chairman of the state Senate's redistricting committee, Democrat Eddie Bernice Johnson tailored the downtown Dallas 30th to suit her political needs. The district, which a panel of federal judges said resembled a "microscopic view of a new strain of a disease," elected Johnson in 1992.

Mixed Reactions

The ruling triggered a debate among constitutional scholars, civil rights advocates and minority-group representatives about the use of majority-minority districts to carry out the Voting Rights Act and help minorities attain equal representation.

"This is a fairly dramatic decision," said Michael A. Hess, chief counsel for the Republican National Committee, which filed a "friend of the court" brief in the case on behalf of the white plaintiffs. "It raises the question of [whether] the automatic creation [of such districts] is in the best interest of the democratic process."

In a written joint statement, Watt and Clayton said: "We believe this Supreme Court decision will have little, if any, value in terms of establishing a precedent for other cases."

But North Carolina Attorney General Michael F. Easley, a white Democrat and one of the defendants in the case, foresaw greater implications: "Any way you slice it, it opens up every district to judicial attack and review based on the lines."

For some, *Shaw* established a contradictory set of criteria for a Voting Rights Act-controlled state to meet to win federal approval of its map. While the Justice Department or a federal court had to approve a state's redistricting plans, *Shaw* raised the possibility that Justice Department insistence on creating the maximum number of minority districts could be challenged on constitutional grounds.

"It's almost as if you had a speed limit sign saying, 'Maximum speed 55, minimum speed 65,'" said one North Carolina redistricting expert.

Race-Based Districts Deplored

In her opinion, O'Connor lamented the practice — mandated by the Justice Department in its enforcement of the Voting Rights Act — of creating congressional districts solely on the basis of race.

"Racial gerrymandering, even for remedial purposes, may balkanize us into competing racial factions ...," she wrote. "Racial classifications of any sort pose the risk of lasting harm to our society. They reinforce the belief, held by too many for too much of our history, that individuals should be judged by the color of their skin."

"I would like to be on the side of the majority of the Supreme Court," said Watt, whose serpentine 12th District became a national symbol for opponents of racial gerrymandering. "I would hope that we would have a race-neutral society. But I have to say ... it hasn't happened yet."

North Carolina was one of 14 states that, because of past racial discrimination, were required by the Voting Rights Act to submit any election-law changes to the Justice Department for approval, or "preclearance. Section 5 of the law prohibited states from eroding minorities' gains. The 1982 amendments to the act and later court decisions added a broader mandate: Section 2 of the act barred any state law that weakened minority voting strength — regardless of the state legislature's intent.

North Carolina was the first state in 1991 to approve a new black-majority district, but in December 1991, the Justice Department rejected the map, ruling that one majority-black House district out of 12 was not sufficient. The department ordered North Carolina to add a second majority-black district to accommodate the state's 22 percent black population. That map won Justice Department approval in February 1992.

Unresolved Cases, Questions

The court left unresolved most of the larger questions about the constitutionality of race-based redistricting. It did not invalidate North Carolina's map or rule in favor of the plaintiffs' 14th Amendment complaint. Rather, it reversed the decision of a three-judge federal panel that had granted a motion to dismiss the complaint, returning the case to the state.

In *Shaw*, the court asserted that the plaintiffs were entitled to raise a question of constitutionality under the 14th Amendment because the state legislature "adopted a reapportionment scheme so irrational on its face that it can be understood only as an effort to segregate voters into separate voting districts because of their race, and that the separation lacks sufficient justification."

But, O'Connor wrote, the justices "express no view" as to whether the simple creation of majority-minority districts "always gives rise to an equal protection claim." Nor did the court choose to answer the defendants' contention that "the creation of majority-minority districts is ... the only effective way to overcome the effects of racially polarized voting."

The court said that even if a map was unquestionably a racial gerrymander, it might still pass constitutional muster if a lower court determined that it was "narrowly tailored to further a compelling governmental interest." Nevertheless, the court said, the fact that a redistricting plan was drawn to comply with the Voting Rights Act did not automatically shield it from a challenge on constitutional grounds. And the court added that the question of whether Section 2 was unconstitutional if it required the adoption of North Carolina's second plan remained "open for consideration."

The Dissent

The majority opinion was sharply criticized in separate dissents by Justices Byron R. White, David H. Souter, Harry A. Blackmun and John Paul Stevens. Blackmun and Stevens also joined White's dissent.

Stevens rejected O'Connor's recoil at the North Carolina map's "bizarre and uncouth district boundaries," contending: "There is no independent constitutional requirement of compactness or contiguity, and the court's opinion ... does not suggest otherwise."

Stevens defended districts designed to elect minorities: "If it is permissible to draw boundaries to provide adequate representation for rural voters, for union members, for Hasidic Jews, for Polish Americans, or for Republicans, it necessarily follows that it is permissible to do the same thing for members of the very minority group whose history in the United States gave birth to the Equal Protection Clause. A contrary conclusion could only be described as perverse."

The notion that North Carolina's plan might have violated the white plaintiffs' "constitutional rights is both a fiction and a departure from settled equal protection principles," wrote White.

White castigated the majority for misinterpreting a 1977 decision in the case of *United Jewish Organizations of Williamsburgh Inc. v. Carey (UJO)*, which affirmed the constitutionality of creating majority-minority districts. He singled out a passage in O'Connor's opinion that said: "Nothing in the *[UJO]* decision precludes white voters ... from bringing the analytically distinct claim that a reapportionment plan rationally cannot be understood as anything other than an effort to segregate citizens into separate voting districts on the basis of race without sufficient justification."

White rebutted: "As I understand the theory that is put forth, a redistricting plan that uses race to 'segregate' voters by drawing 'uncouth' lines is harmful in a way that a plan that uses race to distribute voters differently is not, for the former 'bears an uncomfortable resemblance to political apartheid.' The distinction is untenable."

CLINIC ACCESS, ABORTION RIGHTS

In a blow to abortion rights advocates, the Supreme Court on Jan. 13 ruled that a Reconstruction-era federal civil rights law enacted to protect blacks could not be used to guarantee women access to abortion clinics.

The 6-3 ruling dismayed abortion rights advocates, who had used the law to obtain federal court injunctions barring blockades of abortion clinics. In Congress, abortion rights supporters immediately announced plans to push legislation that would undo the effects of the court decision and make it a federal crime to impede access to an abortion clinic.

But some abortion opponents were just as quick to attack those proposals, saying anti-abortion activists should not be singled out for penalties that did not apply to other protesters. By year's end, the bill had passed both chambers of Congress but in slightly different form. *(Clinic access, p. 354)*

The court case, *Bray v. Alexandria Women's Health Clinic*, was a test of whether abortion clinics could use existing laws to protect themselves against disruptive protests by Operation Rescue and other anti-abortion groups. Although such protesters could be prosecuted under local laws against such infringements as trespassing, some abortion advocates had appealed to federal judges to issue broader injunctions under the 1871 civil rights law, known as the Ku Klux Klan Act.

That law, designed to protect blacks, had been held to offer protection against discrimination aimed at a class of people. But the Supreme Court ruled that women seeking abortions did not qualify for this class-based protection because anti-abortion protesters were not targeting them on the basis of their gender.

Justice Antonin Scalia wrote the majority opinion, joined by Chief Justice Rehnquist and Justices White, Kennedy and Thomas. Justice Souter agreed with the core of that ruling but disagreed in part and wrote a separate opinion.

Justices Stevens, Blackmun and O'Connor dissented. Stevens said applying the 1871 law to the clinic blockades was wholly consistent with its congressional purpose "to protect this Nation's citizens from what amounts to the theft of their constitutional rights by organized and violent mobs across the country."

Other Abortion Cases

On March 8, the court refused to review a Louisiana law that sought to outlaw most abortions. The action effec-

A Summary of Major Rulings, 1992-93 Term

Bray v. Alexandria Women's Health Clinic, 6-3, Jan. 13, 1993. An 1871 Reconstruction-era civil rights law originally enacted to help blacks cannot be used to guarantee women access to abortion clinics.

Nixon v. United States, 9-0, Jan. 13. The courts have no standing to review impeachment proceedings because the Constitution grants the Senate the "sole power" to try impeachments. The court upheld the Senate's 1989 conviction of then-U.S. District Judge Walter L. Nixon Jr. of Mississippi, who had challenged his conviction because the Senate used a 12-member panel, rather than the full body, to gather evidence for his trial.

Herrera v. Collins, 6-3, Jan. 25. New evidence suggesting that an inmate facing execution for murder might be innocent does not entitle him to a new federal court hearing.

Lamb's Chapel v. Center Moriches Union Free School District, 9-0, June 7. A school district may not ban a religious group from using school facilities for a film presentation when other groups are allowed to use the premises for such presentations.

Church of the Lukumi Babalu Aye Inc. v. City of Hialeah, 9-0, June 11. Communities may not selectively prohibit practices, such as animal sacrifice, motivated by religious belief.

Wisconsin v. Mitchell, 9-0, June 11. States may impose longer prison terms on people convicted of "hate crimes" without violating their rights to free speech.

Zobrest v. Catalina Foothills School District, 5-4, June 18. Public schools may provide a sign-language interpreter to a deaf student who attends parochial school without breaching the wall between church and state.

Sale v. Haitian Centers Council Inc., 8-1, June 21. Nothing in U.S. or international law limits the president's authority to repatriate Haitian boat people or other aliens interdicted beyond the territorial seas of the United States without first screening them to see if they qualify for political asylum.

St. Mary's Honor Center v. Hicks, 5-4, June 25. It is not enough for a person claiming to be the victim of illegal job discrimination to prove that an employer gave a false reason for an adverse action against the person. Instead, the worker must produce direct evidence that the unfavorable treatment stemmed from illegal bias.

TXO Production Corp. v. Alliance Resources Corp., 6-3, June 25. A punitive damages award in a civil case that is hundreds of times bigger than the actual damages does not necessarily violate the due process clause of the 14th Amendment.

Shaw v. Reno, 5-4, June 28. Congressional districts that appear to have been drawn solely on racial lines are subject to constitutional attacks by white voters, even if the districts were designed to comply with the Voting Rights Act.

Austin v. United States, 9-0, June 28. Civil forfeitures of property seized under federal drug laws are subject to the Eighth Amendment's constitutional protection against excessive fines, and thus such confiscations must stand in some proportion to the crime at issue.

---

tively killed the law in question and reaffirmed that states could not go so far in restricting abortion as to make it virtually unavailable. A federal appeals court had already invalidated the 1991 Louisiana law, which banned most abortions and mandated prison terms for doctors who performed them. State officials, including Democratic Gov. Edwin W. Edwards, appealed the ruling, but to no avail.

On the other hand, the court voted April 2 to let a North Dakota law restricting access to abortion take effect despite a pending constitutional challenge to the statute. Justice Blackmun had granted an emergency appeal March 31 to block the law while a federal appeals court decided whether it violated women's legal rights to obtain abortions. But the full court reversed that decision, 7-2, with Blackmun and Stevens dissenting.

The case concerned a North Dakota law requiring women to wait 24 hours for an abortion after being told about risks, alternatives and fetal development. The Supreme Court upheld similar restrictions in Pennsylvania in a landmark 1992 ruling. In that opinion, the court upheld abortion restrictions that do not impose an "undue burden" on women seeking abortions. But lawyers for the Fargo Women's Health Organization said the North Da-

kota waiting period posed an unreasonable burden because the Fargo clinic was the only abortion provider in the state. Some women traveled long distances to use it.

HAITIAN REFUGEES

On June 21, the court upheld the U.S. policy of picking up Haitian refugees on the high seas and summarily returning them to Haiti. The 8-1 ruling in *Sale v. Haitian Centers Council Inc.* allowed the Clinton administration to continue to intercept and return Haitian boat people without first screening them to see if they qualified for political asylum.

Clinton had harshly criticized this Bush administration interception policy during the presidential campaign, but he announced Jan. 14 that he would continue it to deter Haitians from undertaking the risky sea journey to the United States.

The Clinton administration accepted the court victory quietly, reiterating promises to help Haitians apply for political asylum without leaving their country.

But the decision was a blow to Haitians seeking to flee to the United States. And some refugee groups feared it

would send a bleak message to the international community.

In Congress, some Florida lawmakers and others had supported the interdiction policy as necessary to ward off a potential mass exodus from Haiti. But the policy was criticized by the Congressional Black Caucus.

"The tragedy is not in the court's ruling, but rather in the ongoing practice of this administration," Rep. Kweisi Mfume, D-Md., chairman of the black caucus, said after the ruling. *(Haiti policy, p. 499)*

The Court's Reasoning

Advocates for the Haitian refugees said the U.S. interdiction policy violated a 1967 U.N. treaty, which the United States had signed, and a 1980 U.S. law, both of which stipulated that the government could not return refugees to a place where they would face danger.

However, Justice Stevens said the interdiction policy might violate the spirit of the 1967 treaty but not its text. "While we must, of course, be guided by the high purpose of both the treaty and the statute, we are not persuaded that either one places any limit on the President's authority to repatriate aliens interdicted beyond the territorial seas of the United States," he wrote.

Justice Blackmun dissented, saying the refugee law and the U.N. treaty clearly sought to protect people fleeing persecution regardless of where they were found. "What is extraordinary in this case is that the Executive, in disregard of the law, would take to the seas to intercept fleeing refugees and force them back to their persecutors."

Refugee advocates had argued that the United States was not obligated to take in the Haitians, only to offer them temporary safe haven or transport to a third country — anything, in short, but returning them to Haiti if they would be in danger of being persecuted there.

To determine which intercepted Haitians had such fears of persecution, the United States would have had to screen the boat people before returning any to Haiti — as it had done before May 1992.

In February 1992, the government directed embassy staff in Port-au-Prince to allow Haitians to apply for political asylum from within their own country — an unusual step. However, refugee advocates said many Haitians were unable or afraid to seek help in Port-au-Prince.

An array of political, humanitarian and civil rights groups had urged the Supreme Court to strike down the interdiction policy. And about two dozen members and former members of Congress submitted an amicus curiae brief on behalf of the Haitians. They said Congress had intended the 1980 Refugee Act to apply to situation like that of the Haitians.

But the question of whether the law applied outside the United States was not closely examined during debate on the 1980 refugee law. Stevens took that silence as evidence that there was no clear congressional intent to extend the protections beyond U.S. borders. "It would have been extraordinary for Congress to make such an important change in the law without any mention of that possible effect," he wrote. *(1980 Almanac, p. 378)*

IMPEACHMENTS

The court on Jan. 13 affirmed the Senate's authority to carry out impeachment trials as it saw fit, voting 9-0 to uphold the Senate's 1989 conviction of then-U.S. District Judge Walter L. Nixon Jr. of Mississippi. Nixon had challenged his conviction because the Senate used a 12-member panel, rather than the full body, to gather evidence for his trial.

The Supreme Court ruled that the courts had no standing to review impeachment proceedings because the Constitution granted the Senate the "sole power" to try impeachments. Two justices, White and Blackmun, argued separately that courts should have an oversight role in impeachment trials, but they nonetheless upheld Nixon's conviction.

The decision, *Nixon v. United States*, appeared applicable as well to Rep. Alcee L. Hastings, D-Fla., a former U.S. District Court judge who was impeached and convicted by Congress in 1989 under the same procedures. U.S. District Judge Stanley Sporkin overturned that conviction because the full Senate did not gather the evidence. But Sporkin had stayed his own ruling pending appeal, predicting that the matter would be settled by the Supreme Court.

With the *Nixon* ruling in hand, the appeals court appeared to have ready grounds to reverse Sporkin. *(Nixon, Hastings impeachments, 1989 Almanac, p. 229)*

The ruling did not affect Hastings' status as a new member of Congress (he had been elected in 1992). A federal judge on Jan. 4 rejected a lawsuit claiming that Hastings' Senate conviction disqualified him from holding office.

Historically, the Senate had held separate votes to convict an impeached official and to disqualify him from another office. In Hastings' case, the Senate took no vote on disqualification.

Checks and Balances

Nixon's case centered on a 1935 Senate rule that allowed the Senate to use a 12-member committee to gather evidence in impeachment trials and report its results, but not recommendations, to the full Senate. The rule was first used during the 1986 impeachment trial of U.S. District Judge Harry E. Claiborne, and then again for Nixon and Hastings. *(Claiborne impeachment, 1986 Almanac, p. 75)*

David O. Stewart, Nixon's lawyer, argued that the committee rule violated the constitutional directive that the Senate "try" impeachment cases. Stewart said a fair trial required that all the "jurors" hear the evidence. And his brief noted that in all three modern impeachment trials, members of the evidence panel were generally less likely to vote to convict than were senators who had not heard the evidence directly.

A federal district court and then an appeals court rebuffed Stewart's argument, but the Supreme Court agreed to examine two aspects of the case: first, whether the courts had a right to review impeachment proceedings and, second, whether the use of an evidence panel represented an unconstitutional shortcut.

The case marked the first time the high court had ruled directly on Congress' impeachment powers. By concluding that impeachment proceedings were basically off-limits to judicial review, the court passed up a chance to enlarge the judiciary's powers over the legislative branch.

Chief Justice Rehnquist wrote the majority opinion, which had the backing of five other justices. In separate opinions, Blackmun, White and Souter said they felt the courts could review impeachments in certain cases.

Rehnquist wrote that the Constitution's directive that the Senate "try" impeachment cases did not carry with it specific requirements for such proceedings. And he said

judicial oversight of impeachment trials would upset the system of checks and balances among the branches of government. "Judicial involvement in impeachment proceedings, even if only for purposes of judicial review, is counter-intuitive because it would eviscerate the 'important constitutional check' placed on the Judiciary by the Framers," he wrote.

Rehnquist also noted practical obstacles to allowing courts to review impeachment proceedings, saying it could create political disorder by throwing impeachment convictions into question indefinitely.

White and Blackmun, in a separate opinion, said the judiciary did have a role in ensuring the fairness of Senate impeachment proceedings. "In a truly balanced system," White wrote, Senate impeachment trials would serve as a check on the judicial branch "even as judicial review would ensure that the Senate adhered to a minimal set of procedural standards." However, White and Blackmun rejected the substance of Nixon's appeal, writing that the Senate was within its rights to use a special panel to gather evidence.

Souter offered a more limited qualification to the main opinion. He agreed that the courts had no grounds to review Nixon's impeachment trial but argued that judicial scrutiny might be warranted in extreme cases: for example, if the Senate resorted to a coin toss to decide an impeachment charge.

Michael Davidson, the Senate's legal counsel, said he was pleased the majority opinion affirmed the Senate's independence on impeachment proceedings, while White and Blackmun endorsed its specific methods.

Two other federal judges had been convicted of crimes since the Nixon and Hastings cases, and the *Nixon* decision meant the Senate could continue to use a special panel to hear evidence if either of those cases eventually reached it. *(Collins impeachment charges, p. 317)*

OTHER CASES

The court disposed of a number of other cases in its 1992-93 term that had potential ramifications for Congress. In some instances, lawmakers already were acting on the issues addressed by the justices. In others, the court in effect invited Congress to respond.

Death Penalty

The court on Jan. 25 continued to shut the door on death row appeals, ruling against inmates in three separate cases.

The most dramatic ruling, *Herrera v. Collins*, involved a Texas inmate who was sentenced to death for the murder of two police officers. Herrera wanted the courts to review his case in light of new evidence suggesting that his brother was responsible for the murders.

But the Supreme Court ruled, 6-3, that new evidence did not entitle an inmate to a new federal court hearing. Chief Justice Rehnquist, who wrote the majority opinion, said federal courts were intended to review possible constitutional violations, not to correct factual errors of a state trial.

Rehnquist said executive pardons were a more appropriate route for reversing the conviction of an innocent person. However, his opinion left open the possibility that the federal courts would review death row cases in which the defendant offered "truly persuasive" evidence of innocence.

Justice Blackmun, joined by Justices Souter and Stevens, dissented. Blackmun said the Constitution forbade executing a person who could prove his innocence with new evidence, even if he was sentenced to death after a valid trial. Blackmun wrote that a death row prisoner should be entitled to a federal court hearing if he had new evidence showing "he probably is innocent."

However, Souter and Stevens did not sign the final portion of the dissent, in which Blackmun wrote: "The execution of a person who can show that he is innocent comes perilously close to simple murder."

Howard M. Metzenbaum, D-Ohio, a member of the Senate Judiciary Committee, promptly introduced legislation (S 221) aimed at overturning the *Herrera* decision. "Whether you support or oppose the death penalty, surely we all agree that an innocent person should not be executed," Metzenbaum said. But his bill did not advance during the year.

Two additional rulings also turned away death row appeals.

In *Graham v. Collins*, another Texas case, the court voted 5-4 to uphold the death penalty for an inmate sentenced at age 17. The defendant argued that the jury had not been able to give sufficient weight to his youth when sentencing him. But the court majority refused to order a federal review, saying it did not believe his sentencing proceedings were seriously flawed. Blackmun, Souter, Stevens and O'Connor dissented.

In a third case involving an Arkansas inmate, the court rejected the man's claim of faulty representation and reinstated his death sentence. That case, *Lockhart v. Fretwell*, was decided 7-2. Blackmun and Stevens dissented.

Pesticides and Cancer

In a move that caught the notice of both Congress and the executive branch, the Supreme Court on Feb. 22 let stand a lower court ruling that required the Environmental Protection Agency (EPA) to enforce a law prohibiting pesticide use when there was any evidence that the chemical could cause cancer.

The decision set into motion EPA action that could remove dozens of commonly used pesticides from agricultural production. The action also thrust the issue into the lap of Congress.

The sticky issue of pesticide regulation rallied both the environmental and chemical lobbies. The Natural Resources Defense Council brought the suit against EPA, arguing that department rules, which allowed farm-chemical use on processed food when the cancer risk to human health was "negligible," violated the so-called Delaney clause of the 1958 Food, Drug and Cosmetic Act (PL 85-929).

The U.S. Court of Appeals for the 9th Circuit in July 1992 agreed with the environmental group, saying the law was "clear and mandatory." The court said the Delaney clause expressly prohibited the use of any carcinogenic chemicals on processed foods.

But the law allowed using pesticides on raw foods even if the pesticide was known to cause cancer as long as the benefits outweighed any public health risk. Because it was impossible to track where all fruits and vegetables ended up — on the produce shelf or in processed food — EPA rules had allowed the use of chemicals linked to cancer on processed foods as well as long as they posed a "negligible" risk to human health.

Anticipating the Supreme Court's action, EPA Admin-

istrator Carol M. Browner in early February released a list of more than 30 chemicals that could be affected by the appeals court decision.

Despite concern over the court's ruling, Congress did not act in 1993 to rewrite either the 1958 food and drug law or the Federal Insecticide, Fungicide and Rodenticide Act (PL 100-532). *(Pesticide regulation, p. 229)*

Church-State

The Supreme Court acted on three cases the week of June 7 and a fourth the following week that involved the delicate relationship between government and religion. In all four, it relaxed government restraints on religious activity.

The court ruled unanimously June 7 that a New York school district had violated free speech guarantees when it banned a religious group from using school facilities for a film presentation. If other groups were allowed to use the premises for such presentations, the majority ruled in an opinion signed by six justices, the school could not exclude a religious group from doing so. The other three justices signed concurring opinions.

The New York school district dispute, *Lamb's Chapel v. Center Moriches Union Free School District*, was one of the term's pivotal cases on the separation of church and state. Following a policy based on a state law, the school district refused to allow a church pastor to use school facilities to show a religiously oriented film series on family values, even though other outside groups were permitted to use the facilities in off-school hours. A federal district and appeals court both upheld the refusal.

But Justice White, writing for the court, said the policy violated free speech guarantees. White suggested that it "discriminates on the basis of viewpoint to permit school property to be used for the presentation of all views about family issues and childrearing except those dealing with the subject matter from a religious standpoint." White said the use of school facilities after hours by the church group would not be taken as an official endorsement of that religion.

Justices Scalia and Thomas signed a concurring opinion offering different reasons for reaching the same conclusion, and Justice Kennedy wrote his own concurring opinion.

Also on June 7, the court refused to take up the case of a Texas student who challenged her school's policy of allowing prayer at graduation ceremonies. That action upheld an appeals court ruling, which said the school's custom of student-led prayer did not violate constitutional mandates about separating government from religion. In 1992, however, the high court ruled that public schools could not arrange for religious officials to deliver prayers at graduation.

In a third case, *Church of the Lukumi Babalu Aye Inc. v. City of Hialeah*, the court ruled unanimously June 11 that the sacrifice of animals for religious purposes is protected under the First Amendment. The case involved a challenge by a Florida church to local ordinances banning animal sacrifices in the Miami suburb of Hialeah. The church practiced the African-based religion Santeria, in which animal sacrifice was a central ritual.

In 1990 the court, in *Employment Division v. Smith*, established a test that upheld the constitutionality of statutes that barred religious practices as long as the laws advanced a valid purpose and were not enacted to inhibit religious freedom. *(1990 Almanac, p. 514)*

Writing for the court, Kennedy said that the laws in question did not meet the standard, stating that "each of Hialeah's ordinances pursues the city's governmental interests only against conduct motivated by religious belief."

The *Smith* ruling was about to be scrapped, in any event. The decision had provoked widespread protest from religious organizations, and Congress had struggled ever since it was issued to draft an acceptable bill overruling it.

Lawmakers finally succeeded in 1993. Legislation (HR 1308 — PL 103-141) cleared by Congress on Nov. 3 imposed a tougher standard on states than the one enunciated in *Smith*, requiring that any law inhibiting religious practices advance a "compelling governmental interest." *(Religious freedom bill, p. 315)*

In a fourth ruling on religion and government, the court on June 18 held 5-4 that public schools could provide a sign-language interpreter to a deaf student who attended parochial school without breaching the wall between church and state.

The majority, led by Chief Justice Rehnquist, said that "the service at issue in this case is part of a general government program that distributes benefits neutrally to any child qualifying as 'handicapped' under the Individuals with Disabilities Education Act." It did not matter whether the child was attending a public or sectarian school, the court said. Because the law provided "no financial incentive for parents to choose a sectarian school, an interpreter's presence there cannot be attributed to state decision-making," Rehnquist said in *Zobrest v. Catalina Foothills School District*.

Hate Crimes

The Supreme Court ruled June 11 that states may impose longer prison terms on people convicted of "hate crimes" without violating their rights to free speech.

The decision cleared the way for consideration of legislation (HR 1152) that instructed the U.S. Sentencing Commission to set guidelines for increasing federal sentences for hate crimes. The House passed the bill by voice vote Sept. 21, sending it to the Senate. Although the Senate did not act on the House-passed bill, it adopted a similar measure (S 1522), sponsored by Dianne Feinstein, D-Calif., as an amendment to an omnibus crime bill, S 1607. The amendment was adopted Nov. 4, and the crime bill was passed Nov. 19. *(Hate crimes, p. 311; Crime bill, p. 293)*

The court case, *Wisconsin v. Mitchell*, involved a Wisconsin law allowing judges to impose longer sentences on people convicted of violating existing laws if the crimes were motivated by racial, religious or other prejudice. The defendant, a black man, was convicted of exhorting a group of youths to beat a white passerby.

The court ruled that the defendant's motivation was one of several factors that a judge could legitimately consider when determining a sentence. Chief Justice Rehnquist wrote that the First Amendment "does not prohibit the evidentiary use of speech to establish the elements of a crime or to prove motive or intent."

The unanimous decision came just one year after the court overturned a Minnesota law banning cross-burnings and other expressions of bigotry as a violation of First Amendment rights. In that case, *R.A.V. v. City of St. Paul*, the court held that the city ordinance had unconstitutionally singled out certain types of offensive expression for punishment. *(1992 Almanac, p. 326)*

Job Discrimination

Victims of illegal job discrimination suddenly found it harder to prove their case as a result of a June 25 ruling in

St. Mary's Honor Center v. Hicks. The court stiffened the standards for proving illegal discrimination on the basis of race, sex, religion or national origin under Title VII of the 1964 Civil Rights Act.

Dividing 5-4, the high court said it was not enough for workers who alleged such bias to prove that an employer gave a false reason for his or her action. Instead, workers had to produce direct evidence that their unfavorable treatment stemmed from illegal bias.

Justices Souter, Blackmun, Stevens and White dissented, saying that such a stiff standard of proof placed an unfair burden on employees.

In another job rights case, the court ruled 9-0 that the federal law against age discrimination was not necessarily violated because a company fired someone age 62 within weeks of the time his pension rights would have vested. Pension rights were based on years of service, regardless of age. The plaintiff might have a cause of action under the Employee Retirement Income Security Act (ERISA) but not under the Age Discrimination in Employment Act, the court held in the case of *Hazen Paper Co. v. Biggins.*

Asset Forfeiture

The Supreme Court curbed the government's power to seize suspects' homes and other assets, ruling that such confiscation could violate constitutional guarantees against excessive fines.

On Feb. 24, the court ruled 6-3 that the government could not use the forfeiture provisions of the 1970 Drug Abuse Prevention and Control Act to seize the home of a woman who did not know that the money she used to buy the property had come from drug trafficking. The money had been given to her by a friend who did not tell her the source of the funds. Justices Kennedy, White and Rehnquist dissented in this case of *United States v. A Parcel of Land.*

In the past, the government had argued successfully that the Eighth Amendment prohibition on undue fines did not apply to civil forfeiture proceedings. But the court contradicted that view in a 9-0 ruling June 28, a move that could chill prosecutors' heightened reliance on forfeiture to deter crime and help finance law enforcement.

The case, *Austin v. United States,* involved the government's efforts to seize the mobile home and auto body shop of a South Dakota man, Richard Lyle Austin, who pleaded guilty to one count of cocaine possession. The Supreme Court agreed with Austin's claim that the Eighth Amendment applied to the seizure, and therefore such confiscations must stand in some proportion to the crime at issue.

The court reiterated the need for proportionality in a second case, *Alexander v. United States,* in which the government seized and destroyed books and other materials belonging to a man convicted of selling obscene material. By 9-0, the justices said forfeiture of a business under federal racketeering law was subject to the Eighth Amendment's prohibition against excessive fines. But by 5-4, the court held that destroying all of the materials — including some that had not been found obscene — did not violate the defendant's free speech rights.

Punitive Damages

For the second time in five years, the court refused to find any constitutional bar to punitive damages in civil cases that were many times greater than the actual damages. In the case of *TXO Production Corp. v. Alliance Resources Corp.,* the court on June 25 upheld, 7-2, a $10 million punitive damages award in a case involving actual damages of $19,000. The petitioner had claimed that the huge punitive damage award was so excessive that it violated the due process clause of the Constitution's 14th Amendment. A majority of the court disagreed, although the justices splintered in their reasons. The only two dissenting throughout were O'Connor and White.

The *TXO* ruling was the second setback in a row for companies looking for some constitutional protection against huge punitive damage awards. In 1989, the court ruled in the case of *Browning-Ferris Industries Inc. v. Kelco Disposal Inc.* that the Eighth Amendment prohibition against excessive fines did not apply in civil damage suits. *(1989 Almanac, p. 325)*

The combined effect of the two cases was to leave up to Congress and the state legislatures the task of crafting limits on the size of punitive damage awards available in civil cases.

Unclaimed Funds

A March 30 high court ruling governing the distribution of unclaimed dividends and interest payments set the stage for a likely congressional battle pitting Delaware and New York against other states.

In a 6-3 decision, the court backed distribution rules that favored Delaware over New York — while rejecting a formula that would have disbursed the money throughout more states.

At issue were arcane laws governing which state could claim millions of dollars in unclaimed dividends, interest and other money held by banks and other brokers on behalf of owners who could not be identified or located. New York, home to many financial houses, had been collecting tens of millions of dollars in unclaimed funds held by brokerages within its borders. But Delaware said it was entitled to much of that money because many of those brokerage firms were chartered in Delaware.

The Supreme Court referred the dispute, *Delaware v. New York,* to a special master, who recommended that the money go to states based on the principal location of the entity that issued the securities rather than the brokerage firm that handled them. That would have distributed the money more broadly among the states.

But the Supreme Court rejected that formula, saying precedent dictated that the money go to the state in which the brokerage firms were incorporated.

However, Justice Thomas, who wrote the opinion, essentially invited legislation to undo it. "If the states are dissatisfied ... they may air their grievances before Congress," Thomas wrote.

"I have a draft of the legislation on my desk," said Bernard Nash, who represented 31 states seeking a broad distribution of the money. Nash said the legislation would address the money at issue, as well as the future distribution of such funds — an amount he estimated at $100 million a year.

Justices White, Blackmun and Stevens dissented, saying the master's recommendation offered a fairer result. ∎

HEALTH/
HUMAN SERVICES

Health Reform 335
   Background 336
   Clinton's Proposal. 340
   Benefits. 342
   Rival Plans 344
   Middle-Ground Health Plans. 346
Abortion 348
Clinic Access. 354
Elders Appointment 356
National Institutes of Health 357
   Breast Cancer Research 360
   Provisions. 363
Health Changes in the Budget Bill. 366
   Childhood Immunizations. 368
Centers for Disease Control 369

Other Health-Related Legislation 370
Dietary Supplements 371
Welfare Reform. 373
   Child Support Enforcement. 374
Food Stamps. 375
   Eligible Stores 376
Family Preservation 377
Domestic Worker Taxes 378
Social Security Administration 380
Adoption Bias, Energy Aid, Poverty Data. 381
Other Human Services Legislation. 382
American Indian Legislation 383
Deer Appointment. 385
Shalala Appointment 385
Chater Appointment. 385

Health-Care Debate Takes Off

Congress gets up to speed on the complex economics and policies driving the U.S. health-care system

The year 1993 turned out to be Act I in the national health-care reform drama. Much of the action took place not on Capitol Hill but at the other end of Pennsylvania Avenue, where the White House worked feverishly for much of the year to craft its legislative proposal. Congress played a supporting role.

The scope of Clinton's health reform proposal, the process he set up to draft it — including the appointment of his wife to spearhead the administration's effort — and Congress' response made it a historic endeavor, unlike any other legislative overhaul in the 20th century.

Although Congress did not become actively involved until Clinton introduced his legislation near the end of the session, the subject loomed large in congressional calculations throughout the year — especially in the crafting of the 1994 budget. And while Clinton had hoped to have Congress pass his bill in 1993, he underestimated the time it would take to draft the proposal and the difficulty he would have focusing Congress on it when lawmakers had other controversial legislation on their agenda, such as the North American Free Trade Agreement.

In the end, 1993 was the year that Congress and much of the nation's elite got up to speed on the complex economics and policies that drove the U.S. health-care system. The subject dominated the pages of the nation's newspapers; it was on prime time television; and it was the chief topic of conferences and seminars held not only by health groups, but by teachers, churches, unions and corporations. *(Background, p. 336)*

From early on, Clinton's drive to revamp the nation's health-care system was likened to the New Deal policies of President Franklin D. Roosevelt. Its effect was projected to be at least as sweeping, and like Roosevelt's programs, its economic and social impact was expected to touch every American.

But unlike the New Deal, the Clinton proposal — when it finally arrived — bore the marks of an era when even Democrats had become reluctant to support programs that carried high government costs. The plan always aimed to pay for itself without a broad-based tax — a sharp contrast to past Democratic social programs, such as Medicare and Social Security, both of which were financed by an earmarked payroll tax.

Clinton's proposal, released in September, had three guiding themes: that all Americans should be guaranteed access to affordable health-care services; that the rate of growth in health-care costs should slow; and

that government and the market should work together to achieve those goals.

THE MAKING OF THE PLAN

During the 1992 presidential campaign, the promise of health-care reform had been part of Clinton's standard stump speech, but his ideas were vague at best. Almost immediately after the election, however, he became convinced of the need for a comprehensive overhaul and at the end of January optimistically proclaimed that he would send Congress a proposal within 90 days. He said he expected Congress to complete its work on his bill by the end of the year.

To meet that ambitious goal, Clinton convened a health-care task force of Cabinet members and White House staffers to draft the administration's overhaul proposal. On Jan. 25, five days after his inauguration, he announced that his wife, Hillary Rodham Clinton, would oversee the group.

The first lady's appointment caused a flurry of controversy that resurfaced throughout the year. Critics argued that her imprimatur on the plan might make people reluctant to criticize it. Some argued that she had no health-care experience, and others said Clinton was abdicating power to someone who had not been elected.

Hillary Clinton had headed up the task force that overhauled the Arkansas school system when Clinton was governor, one of his most widely noted initiatives. Her position as chairwoman of the health-care task force was a clear signal that health care would have the highest priority in the Clinton administration.

Others appointed to the task force included six Cabinet members and a key player on the White House's domestic policy staff, Ira Magaziner, a friend of the president's from his days at Oxford University. In addition, the White House set up 15 working groups on different health-care topics. Members included more than a hundred congressional staffers who dealt with health-care policy, health-care experts from federal agencies and experts from across the country with both public- and private-sector backgrounds.

The goal of the Task Force on National Health-Care Reform was to fashion a system that met two seemingly contradictory ends: expanding health care to all Americans — about 38 million Americans were uninsured — and reducing the rising rate of health-care spending. Health care made up about

---

HEALTH-CARE REFORM

➤ **Background.** There was broad agreement that the existing health-care system was out of control. . . . . p. 336

➤ **Wide Reach.** A snapshot of the way Clinton's plan would affect everything from antitrust laws to workers' compensation. p. 340

➤ **Benefits.** A summary of what was to be covered under Clinton's plan. . . . . p. 342

➤ **Competing Plans.** By the time Clinton's plan reached Capitol Hill, lawmakers had offered other proposals. . . . . p. 344

➤ **Clinton's Speech.** Clinton outlined his plan in a televised address to a joint session of Congress. . . . . p. 48-D

The One Thing Everyone Agreed Upon . . .

As President Clinton set out to overhaul the nation's health-care system, there was broad agreement that it was out of control. Health-care costs had skyrocketed: The money spent on health care in the United States reached $832 billion in 1992 — one-seventh of the U.S. economy — and it was projected to rise to $1.6 trillion by 2000. Yet more and more Americans were being put at risk. Nearly 38 million of the U.S. population of 250 million had no health insurance, and 100,000 more lost their insurance every month.

Insurance companies and doctors, consumers and unions agreed on the magnitude and gravity of the health-care system's problems.

Most Americans also felt strongly about the system's failings. A Wall Street Journal/NBC News poll published March 12 showed that 74 percent believed an overhaul was needed. Nearly as many — 66 percent — said they would pay higher taxes to fix it.

"The degree of consensus that it's time to do something is truly extraordinary," said Harris Wofford, D-Pa., who ran his 1991 Senate race on a health-care reform platform. "A year ago we were nowhere close to this."

While there was broad agreement that something needed to be done, however, disputes quickly arose when the topic turned to what trade-offs to make and how to pay for a new system.

Constituencies for Change

For most workers and their employers, the system was a web of costs over which they had no control. In addition to out-of-pocket expenses, there were invisible costs: For example, the cost of every U.S.-built car included $700 for workers' health insurance; 19 cents of every federal tax dollar went for health care.

When the health insurance business first appeared on the scene in the 1930s, insurance was affordable and widely available. But that began to change in the 1960s when advances in medical technology drove up costs. For the previous 10 years, private insurance premiums had galloped ahead of inflation. Some people could not get insurance at all, and others avoided switching jobs because they feared losing their benefits.

Nevertheless, 85 percent of all Americans still had insurance most of the time. Whether they would embrace fundamental change was apt to depend on how much they trusted the government to fashion a system that would be affordable and dependable.

Health-care providers, meanwhile, had resisted change for more than 60 years. Almost every sector of the health-care industry was immensely profitable. Doctors' average net incomes grew by about 6.6 percent annually from 1982 to 1990 — from $98,000 to $164,000 — in contrast to the average full-time worker's pay, which grew at a 4.3 percent rate, from $18,500 to $25,900.

Hospitals prospered, even in the face of government cutbacks, by sending higher bills to private insurers. Their profit margins had grown 4 percent to 5 percent a year on average since the late 1980s. Pharmaceutical firms posted record earnings during the 1980s, and the health insurance business also had done well.

Still, many physicians, burdened by an explosion of paperwork, had reached a level of disgust with both the government and the private insurance industry. They especially resented the detailed and sometimes irrational measures used to review every aspect of their practice, and many were eager for reform.

Philip Sumner, a New York rheumatologist, said half his patients were covered by Medicare, which reimbursed him at half the rate of his privately insured patients. Yet Medicare paid the least for the work he considered most significant: a patient's medical history and a careful examination. If he did an X-ray or a more expensive medical test, his reimbursement rate more than doubled. "Ninety percent of what you need to know comes from

14 percent of the U.S. economy and close to 14 percent of the federal budget.

Throughout the spring, Hillary Clinton and Magaziner met with the congressional subcommittees and committees that were expected to be most involved in working on the legislation. In addition, members with a longstanding interest in health care met privately either with Mrs. Clinton or Magaziner. At the same time, more than 500 different interest groups met with the White House health-care staff to discuss concerns about the overhaul.

Challenging Task Force Secrecy

Within a month of the task force's formation, the Association of American Physicians and Surgeons filed suit seeking to make the group's meetings and records public. Invoking the 1972 Federal Advisory Committee Act, they charged that because Hillary Clinton was neither a public official nor a federal employee, the task force was forbidden to close its meetings to the media and the public. On March 10, Federal Judge Royce C. Lamberth issued a ruling that made a distinction between the Cabinet members and senior White House staff, who made recommen-

dations to the president, and the working groups that were gathering information and formulating alternative policies.

Lamberth enjoined the working groups from meeting in private without complying with the requirements of the act. But he permitted the task force to continue to meet privately to formulate and pass on its recommendations to the president. The administration appealed the decision to the United States Court of Appeals for the D.C. Circuit.

In the meantime, Republican members asked the General Accounting Office to report on the legality of the meetings and, through the GAO, requested that the White House release a list of task force participants.

As the court case was moving forward, members of Congress alternately expressed frustration with the White House and praise for Hillary Clinton's efforts to brief them about what was going on. The frustration came predominantly from Republicans, none of whose staff members had been asked to participate in the working groups.

Nonetheless, most said they approved of Hillary Clinton's work and felt the White House was listening to their views. A group of House Republicans met weekly with Ira Magaziner.

... The Health-Care System Needed a Cure

the history, the physical exam and thinking through the diagnosis," Sumner said. "But Medicare gives you no reward for thinking."

The other constituency for change was the U.S. government. Health spending was growing faster than any other part of the federal budget, squeezing out funding for education, public works, environmental safety and other favored causes, including cutting the federal deficit.

The health system's devastating impact on the federal balance sheet had not been anticipated 30 years earlier when the government entered the health business. Until then, it had played only a bit part in the health marketplace — paying bills for veterans and federal employees. But Medicare and Medicaid, part of President Lyndon B. Johnson's Great Society program, transformed the government into a major force in the health market. These two programs — which provided government health insurance for the elderly and disabled and for the poor, respectively — had come to account for nearly 30 percent of the nation's health-care spending.

Sources of Money

The existing health-care system, which had evolved over many years, drew on 10 basic sources of money. Roughly half the funds came from the government; the other half came from private insurance and consumers. In designing a new system, Clinton and Congress had to decide how many of those sources — or what ingredients in them — should be tapped. (The numbers in parentheses are spending figures for fiscal 1991; spending was higher in fiscal 1992 and was expected to be higher still in 1993.)

Medicare. ($118 billion) The program served about 35.6 million elderly and disabled Americans in fiscal 1992. It was popular and ran relatively efficiently, with only 2 percent of its budget spent on administration. If Medicare were incorporated into a new system, many elderly people were likely to be forced into managed-care programs such as health maintenance organizations.

Medicaid. ($110.4 billion) The federal-state Medicaid program provided much of the health care available to the poor. It served 31.6 million people in 1992. Medicaid had too few doctors and a high proportion of patients with AIDS and drug abuse problems. Nearly 30 percent of Medicaid dollars went for long-term care and care for the mentally retarded.

Indian Health Service. ($1.2 billion) The service operated hospitals, health centers and clinics for Indians, most of them on reservations.

Veterans. ($12.2 billion) The veterans health system had been plagued with problems, but it had a strong lobby that wanted to see it remain autonomous.

Department of Defense. ($12.8 billion) Included base hospitals and the Civilian Health and Medical Program of the Uniformed Services (CHAMPUS). Base hospitals were likely to remain autonomous. But CHAMPUS, which covered families of active and retired military personnel, could easily be folded into a new program.

Other federal spending. ($17.6 billion) Included funding for such agencies as the National Institutes of Health, not likely to be greatly affected by an overhaul.

State and local government health spending. ($107 billion) About $45 billion went to Medicaid; the rest was scattered and would not be affected by the overhaul.

Private insurance and consumer spending. ($388 billion) Changes in the private insurance system were the heart of Clinton's health overhaul.

Workers' compensation. ($30 billion) Coverage for injured workers could be difficult to transfer from the states to the federal system.

Auto insurance. ($13 billion) This money, paid through private insurance, could fit into a new system.

On June 22, a three-judge panel overturned the district court's ruling that Hillary Clinton's involvement in the task force triggered the advisory committee act and affirmed that the task force was free to make its recommendations to the president in private. The court went on, however, to say that it had insufficient information to determine the status of the working groups and remanded the case to the district court for discovery about the membership and tasks of the working groups.

On Nov. 9, in a sharply worded order, Judge Lamberth threatened to hold the administration in contempt of court unless, within 20 days, it produced documents, payroll records, travel vouchers, meeting agendas and notes of the working groups that were needed in order to comply with the appeals court decision. He accused the White House of producing "dribbles and drabs of information at its convenience" and ordered Hillary Clinton and the Cabinet members named in the suit to pay the legal fees of the three groups who had filed suit in February.

On Nov. 30, the White House responded to the district court order with the list of the people who served on the working groups. In addition, it submitted schedules of meetings, records of travel reimbursements and financial disclosure forms.

Deadlines Slip

By early May it was apparent that the White House's self-imposed 90-day deadline to complete work on the health-care plan had been too tight, and while officials refused to admit that they were behind, they intimated that the plan was unlikely to be released before the end of May. Several officials said publicly on May 20 that key decisions were still being made. By that time, the congressional Democratic leadership was in no hurry to see the health-care bill. Worried about their ability to pass Clinton's deficit-reduction package (HR 2264 — PL 103-66), they asked the White House to delay submitting the health-care plan until after the budget vote, which was not scheduled in the Senate until June. *(Budget-reconciliation, p. 107)*

The deep cuts proposed for Medicare as part of the deficit-reduction bill — which at one point in the negotiations topped $60 billion — alarmed the White House health-reform team, which was relying on reductions in Medicare spending to pay for health-care reform. They

feared that if the savings were too high, it would be politically and practically difficult to make any further cuts later. Hillary Clinton along with administration lobbyists contacted several senators to discuss the reform team's concerns. The amount ultimately dropped to $55.8 billion — still more than the White House felt comfortable with.

The task force disbanded in May, and over the summer the Clintons, working with Cabinet members and top policy advisers, assumed the task of filling in the plan's details.

The bruising battle over the reconciliation bill finally came to an end Aug. 6, and Clinton turned his full attention to the coming health-care fight. The budget battle had signaled a number of problems awaiting him, including lawmakers' reluctance to push for the broad new taxes that most economists said would be needed to meet the administration's goal of offering comprehensive health insurance to all Americans. Lawmakers made it clear they would reject any general tax, or anything that looked like one.

Clinton's razor-thin margin of victory on the budget package also underscored the need for Republican help in getting a health reform proposal through Congress.

THE PROPOSAL

Clinton unveiled his long-awaited proposal Sept. 22 in a nationally televised speech to a joint session of Congress. The 245-page draft, which had been leaked nearly two weeks earlier, outlined a health-care system whose financing and organization was guided by "new Democratic" principles but whose reach resembled that of an old fashioned liberal social program.

"Let us agree on this," Clinton said. "Whatever else we disagree on, before this Congress finishes its work next year, you will pass, and I will sign, legislation to guarantee ... security to every citizen." *(Text, p. 48-D)*

The symbolic high point of the speech came when Clinton waved a prototype of a "Health Security Card" and promised that the plastic credit card would guarantee everyone access to health insurance and health care. His speech outlined six goals that he wanted to see in any final plan: security of health-care coverage that could not be taken away, simplicity, savings, choice, quality and responsibility.

Clinton's vision was to have the government set up new market mechanisms and regulations but then allow the system to run on its own. The framework of Clinton's health-care system drew on aspects of a health policy known as managed competition — in which doctors, insurers and hospitals competed for patients. Clinton added to that a regulatory structure to control costs and quality.

Underlying the Clinton plan was an economic analysis — shared by a number of academics who espoused the managed competition approach — that consumers lacked the necessary market power to bargain with health insurers. Gathering consumers into large groups, known as health-care alliances, was supposed to enable them to drive a better bargain with insurance companies, theoretically receiving more services for less money. The key to Clinton's system was the requirement that all Americans buy health insurance as part of large groups to maximize their market power.

Funding for the plan was to come through a combination of private and public sources. In the private sector, all employers would be required to pay for about 80 percent of their employees' health-care costs. Employees would pay the balance. However, employers of low-wage employees would be eligible for subsidies, as would their workers. Employers with more than 5,000 workers would be allowed

to opt out of the government organized purchasing system but would have to pay an additional 1 percent tax on payrolls to help fund health care for the unemployed or underemployed. And smokers would pay a tax on tobacco equivalent to about an additional 75 cents per pack of cigarettes, bringing the total federal cigarette tax to about $1.00 a pack.

At the same time, Clinton sought to reduce the rate of growth in health-care spending nationwide by capping the rate of increase in health insurance premiums and by making cuts totaling $238 million over six years in Medicare and Medicaid, the government's health insurance for the elderly and the poor, respectively.

Health-care delivery would change in two ways under Clinton's plan. Almost everyone would join a local health alliance. The alliance, a new quasi-governmental entity, would buy health insurance on behalf of everyone in a region. States would set up as many alliances as they felt they needed. A small state, such as Vermont, might have one, and a big state, such as New York, might have four or more.

The alliance would play the role that health insurers played under the existing system: It would negotiate with health plans (groups of doctors and hospitals) for the best insurance price for the people in the alliance and then offer the plans to everyone in the region. The money collected from employers and employees would be sent to the health alliance, which would then pay the plans. The state could opt for a government-run system, in which the state ran the alliance. Whatever option they chose, states would have extensive day-to-day enforcement powers.

Most doctors would have to join health-care networks with hospitals and other providers to be part of a health plan and have access to patients.

CONGRESS REACTS

In the absence of many of the plan's details, members on both sides of the aisle felt free to enthuse about the prospect of reform. For the first time in years, it seemed as if Congress was filled with a sense of the possibility of enacting a piece of sweeping social legislation. "The public wants us to work something out. Of the six goals the president laid out, I don't think any Democrat or any Republican disagrees with any of them. It is how you get from A to B that there is disagreement on," said Thomas J. Bliley Jr., R-Va., a key player on the Republican side on the House Energy and Commerce Committee.

Over the following week, Hillary Clinton testified before the five key committees that would have jurisdiction over the plan: the House committees on Ways and Means, Energy and Commerce, and Education and Labor, and the Senate committees on Finance and on Labor and Human Resources. The hearings gave the administration and the health overhaul's proponents a week of unparalleled media exposure.

Although Hillary Clinton was not the only first lady to testify before Congress, none had testified at such length or exhibited such depth of knowledge. She answered hundreds of questions about the plan over the course of the week, and while it was the first time that she had appeared publicly before Congress, her responses to members' questions made it clear that she knew many of the lawmakers well. She filled her testimony with references to specific districts, hospitals and members' backgrounds.

While she told every committee that the administration was open to adjustments in the plan's details, she also tried

to draw a bottom line: guaranteed health insurance coverage for all Americans, a decline in the rate of increase in health spending, and a cigarette tax.

Clinton's Bill Goes to Congress

Clinton formally submitted his health-care reform bill to congressional leaders on Oct. 27. The ceremony in the historic Statuary Hall of the U.S. Capitol marked the end of the first act of the national debate.

For the preceding nine months, the health-care comments of the president and Hillary Clinton had regularly topped the evening news and made the front page. But as Clinton acknowledged, the drama was about to shift to Congress. On stage with Clinton were the key players who would share top billing with him from then on: Senate Republican leader Bob Dole of Kansas, Senate Democratic leader George J. Mitchell of Maine, House Speaker Thomas S. Foley, D-Wash., House Democratic leader Richard A. Gephardt of Missouri, and House Republican leader Robert H. Michel of Illinois.

Despite lawmakers' generally complimentary tone as they began to discuss the plan, the hot-button issues as well as the points of consensus began to emerge.

The Hot-Button Issues

The areas of Clinton's bill (HR 3600, S 1757) that came under attack increasingly throughout the autumn included the health alliances, the cap on insurance premiums' annual increase, the mandate that employers' pay for 80 percent of the cost of their employees' health insurance, and the cap on the amount the government would spend on subsidies for small businesses and the poor.

● **Health alliances.** The health alliance rapidly came to stand for many members' fear that the program would be "big government" at its most bureaucratic and restrictive. Indeed, Clinton's bill gave the alliances the power to negotiate doctors' fees, limit the plans that consumers' could subscribe to and monitor the plans' performance.

● **Premium caps.** The Clinton plan proposed caps on how much insurance premiums could increase annually. Health alliances would have to adhere to state budgets. For the health-care industry, this was the most onerous part of the proposal.

Hospitals, doctors, pharmaceutical companies, health maintenance organizations and insurers were concerned that their profits would be sharply reduced. But their arguments against the cap were also rooted in the experience under President Richard M. Nixon, when prices were artificially suppressed, only to leap up after the lid was off. In addition, they underscored that the caps would give them no leeway to respond to exceptional situations, such as an outbreak of disease or a disaster, that would require them to spend more to care for additional patients.

● **Employer mandate.** The requirement that employers pay for their employees' health insurance was a call to arms for small businesses, which protested that the additional expense could force them to cut their work forces or even shut their doors. At the time, many businesses with fewer than 100 employees were not paying for their employees' health insurance.

By contrast, larger companies that already paid for their employees supported requiring all businesses to pay. They hoped such a change would stop the cost shifting that occurred when doctors and hospitals raised prices for insured patients to pay for care given to patients who were uninsured or underinsured, in turn causing insurance companies to increase their rates.

● **Subsidy cap.** Liberal Democrats criticized the bill's cap on subsidies, which the administration added to its proposal at the last minute to protect the government from the flood of red ink that followed its other health-care entitlement programs, Medicare and Medicaid.

The provision would mean that programs for the poor and the fund to cover small businesses' subsidies could run out of money.

Underlying those concerns, and in some measure larger than all of them, was Congress' criticism that the bill was too complicated. The legislation, 1,342 pages long, was simply too difficult for most members to understand themselves, let alone explain to constituents. Moreover, it began to be clear that the bill's effect on the health-care industry would be so deep and complex that it would be impossible to predict. Every interest group's assessment of the plan laid out a new set of concerns for lawmakers and raised previously unconsidered questions.

Points of Consensus

Most members of Congress expressed agreement with four elements of the president's bill — or wrote similar proposals of their own.

● **Insurance reform.** Lawmakers generally agreed that insurance companies should be stopped from denying coverage to people who had health problems. The companies would be required to renew coverage annually, basing premium rates on the health-care costs for everyone in the community, or risk pool.

● **Malpractice reform.** Most lawmakers also wanted to respond to longstanding complaints from physicians that the fear of lawsuits prompted them to do extra tests and procedures. All members' proposals discouraged lawsuits, but only the Republican plans put a clamp on punitive and non-economic damages. Clinton and moderate Republicans required that patients go through a "dispute resolution" process before seeking legal remedies.

● **Purchasing cooperatives.** The formation of purchasing cooperatives for health insurance was a fundamental element of most proposals, including Clinton's. The idea was to allow businesses to join together to purchase insurance so that they could get the discounts that previously were available only to very large companies. Clinton's plan required all individuals and companies with fewer than 5,000 employees to join a local purchasing pool, or health alliance.

● **Streamlining.** There also was wide agreement with Clinton's proposal to streamline the health-care claims procedure and require electronic billing and a single claims form for paying medical bills. The Clinton plan went further than many by other members in requiring electronic mechanisms for exchanging information about treatment, outcomes and risks.

Alternative Proposals

By the time Clinton brought his legislation to Congress, a host of other health-care reform bills had already been introduced and were gathering support. *(Alternatives, p. 344)*

● **Cooper-Grandy (HR 3222).** Reps. Jim Cooper, D-Tenn., and Fred Grandy, R-Iowa, introduced a bipartisan bill that emerged as the chief rival to Clinton's plan. They had 56 cosponsors, an almost even split of Democrats and Republicans. The plan favored managed competition, in which providers would form networks to compete for patients; it would encourage, but not require, people to join managed-care plans; and it would limit tax deductions for health care and make employer participation optional.

● **McDermott (HR 1200).** Jim McDermott, D-Wash.,

The Wide Reach of Clinton's Proposal

President Clinton's goal of insuring all Americans and bringing down the rate of growth in health-care costs entailed a radical restructuring of the U.S. system of buying and delivering health-care services and health insurance. The crux of his social and economic philosophy was that only when everyone was insured would it be possible to control the entire system's cost. His plan sought to do that by creating health alliances, which were designed to allow everyone to buy insurance as part of a large group so that they would have more bargaining power with insurers. But that was only one piece of the new and complex structure that Clinton sought to put in place. The following is a look at the potential reach of Clinton's 1993 proposal.

Antitrust Laws

Insurance companies would be subject to federal antitrust laws for the first time in more than 50 years. However, the laws would be relaxed for doctors who would be able to create informal bargaining groups to negotiate fees with the new health-care purchasing groups known as health alliances.

Auto Insurance, Workers' Compensation

Consumers and employers would continue to get coverage for auto-related and work-related injuries, but insurers would pay the portion of the premium related to health costs directly to the alliances. Consumers would receive care through their own health plans.

Choosing a Physician

A consumer in an urban area would be able to choose among several health plans — including the plan his or her doctor joined. The type of plan, however, would determine its price. If the doctor worked on a fee-for-service basis, the consumer could stay with that doctor but would pay a higher premium. If a doctor joined a health maintenance organization, the consumer could join that plan and pay the standard premium. Otherwise, the consumer would have to choose another plan and another doctor.

Cost Controls

Once the new system was in place, there would be a cap on the annual increase in insurance premiums. No one's insurance could rise at more than the rate of inflation plus population growth, about half the existing annual rate of increase in health-care costs. Under the existing system, insurance rate increases varied rose at different rates, sometimes exceeding 20 percent per year, depending on the plan and whether individuals or employers bought insurance on their own or as members of a small or large group.

Employer-Employee Contributions

Employers would be required to pay 80 percent of the average cost of a health plan offered in the local area; employees would pay the balance. The employee would pay extra to join a plan that was more expensive than the average. The projected average annual cost of a plan for an individual would be about $1,800, with the employer paying about $1,440 and the employee, $360.

For a two-parent family, the employer would pay 80 percent of the average family premium divided by the average number of workers per family in the region. Family premiums were estimated to cost about $4,200. Thus, for a two-worker family in a region where the average number of workers per family was 1.5 and 80 percent of the average premium was $3,360, the per worker contribution for each employer would be $2,240. The rationale here was to raise money from all workers and their employers to help cover families in which one spouse did not work. However, individual and family insurance payments would be capped at 3.9 percent of income.

Working individuals who earned $11,040 or less a year (below 150 percent of poverty) would receive government subsidies to cover their share of the premium.

Employers with fewer than 75 workers would have their contributions capped at a percentage of payroll — with the cap ranging from 3.5 percent to 7.9 percent, depending on average salaries. Regardless of size, no employer would be required to spend more than 7.9 percent of total payroll on health insurance.

Large employers who could not afford to pay for their employees' premiums would become eligible for federal subsidies over an eight year phase-in period.

Health Insurance, Health Alliances

Instead of buying health insurance from an insurance agent or receiving it through an employer, a consumer would obtain coverage through a new entity, a local health alliance that would act as a purchasing agent. All plans in an alliance would be required to offer at least a federally mandated package of health benefits. The alliance plans would have to include at least one fee-for-service arrangement.

Insurance companies could be involved in setting up the health plans, which would be made up of networks of doctors and hospitals.

All firms of fewer than 5,000 employees would buy health insurance through an alliance. Companies with more than 5,000 employees could bypass the local alliance and form a "corporate alliance" to bargain with health plans, as long as the plans met national standards.

Part-time workers would be covered on a prorated

---

gathered more than 90 cosponsors for a proposal to set up a single-payer system similar to the one that existed in Canada.

● **Michel (HR 3080).** The House Republican leader got 137 Republicans to cosponsor a proposal to make incremental changes in the existing system but do nothing to make coverage more available to the working poor and little to contain the system's costs.

● **Chafee (S 1770).** A bill introduced by Sen. John H.

Chafee, R-R.I., with 19 Republican cosponsors, shared many features of the Clinton plan, but it had no cost controls and no employer mandate. It included purchasing pools but made them voluntary.

● **Wellstone (S 491).** A handful of Democratic senators led by Paul Wellstone, D-Minn., cosponsored a single-payer bill similar to McDermott's.

● **Nickles (S 1743).** Sen. Don Nickles, R-Okla., intro-

basis. The government would cover the employer share of premiums for early retirees from age 55 to 65. Either the retirees themselves or their employers would be responsible for the balance, or about 20 percent of the cost.

When people made an emergency doctor's visit while traveling, the bill would be sent to their health plan.

Malpractice

All health plans would have to have an alternative dispute resolution arrangement, which members would be required to use first if they believed they had been injured by a doctor, nurse or other health-care provider. The consumer would have the right to appeal in a court of law. The plan made no mention of punitive damages awarded by juries. Several lawmakers who supported changes in federal tort laws wanted to limit the discretion of juries to award punitive damages.

Medicaid

The joint state and federal health insurance program for the poor would continue to subsidize the costs of poor families with dependent children and those who received Supplemental Security Income: the aged, blind or disabled. That accounted for about 60 percent of the total Medicaid population. The government would pay the employer share of the health alliance premium and subsidize the employee share.

The remaining 40 percent of Medicaid recipients, who included pregnant women and children and people needing institutional care, would go into the local health alliance. Virtually all special payments to hospitals that cared for large numbers of the uninsured and Medicaid patients would be dropped on the basis that everyone had insurance, so no additional payments were necessary.

The patients' employers would be required to pay a share of the premium; unemployed patients would receive subsidies from the federal government.

Overall, Medicaid would be cut an estimated $114 billion over the years 1996-2000.

Medicare

The government's health insurance program for the elderly would remain intact, but individuals with incomes in excess of $90,000 and couples earning more than $115,000 would pay higher premiums for the voluntary "Part B" side of the program, which paid for outpatient physician services.

Medicare would offer two broad new benefits: prescription drugs and some long-term care, including extended home health care. From 1996 to 2000, the federal government would attempt to slow growth in the program's cost, saving an estimated $124 billion.

Prescription Drugs

All health plans would automatically cover the cost of prescription drugs. However, health plans would be free to establish a list of drugs that they would pay for — for instance, using only generics where available, instead of more expensive brand-name products.

Patients would have to pay a $250 deductible for prescriptions, after which they would pay a 20 percent copayment up to a maximum out-of-pocket cost of $1,000 a year.

The elderly, who received their insurance through the federally funded Medicare program, would be covered in the same way. However, the government would require pharmaceutical manufacturers, who would be paid through Medicare, to give a 17 percent discount on drugs bought by Medicare beneficiaries.

The government could review the prices for new drugs and request that they be reduced.

Self-Employed

Self-employed and unemployed individuals would have to pay both the employer and employee share of the premium unless they were eligible for government assistance based on their incomes. The premium payment would be 100 percent tax-deductible.

People who were self-employed were considered small businesses and thus would be eligible for federal subsidies on the employer share just as a small business would be.

Tax-Deductibility

Employers and employees would be able to deduct the premiums they paid for the standard benefits package, but they would be taxed for benefits that went beyond the national standard package.

Under existing law, employers could deduct all health premium payments.

Clinton's plan made an exception for benefits that were in place in January 1993, which would be tax-exempt for 10 years; this was an issue of special importance to unions that had negotiated contracts with generous health benefits in lieu of pay increases.

Uninsured

Everyone who qualified for health coverage — "American citizens, nationals, legal residents and long-term immigrants," as listed in the Clinton plan — would have to enroll in a health plan through a local health alliance.

Individuals or families would be required to pay 20 percent of the average premium for the plans offered by that alliance.

Families and individuals with incomes below 150 percent of the federal poverty level would be eligible for federal subsidies. The poverty line in 1993 for a family of three was $11,890; 150 percent of that was $17,835.

Illegal immigrants with no regular employment would be prohibited from enrolling in a health-care alliance. However, they still could go to hospitals or outpatient clinics for emergency treatment.

---

duced a version of a plan drafted by the conservative Heritage Foundation that avoided government controls. Nickles had the support of 24 Republicans.

THE SALES EFFORT

Well before Clinton's plan was released, the administration had begun mounting a public relations effort aimed at setting the agenda before others could do so, although it was not clear that it would be able to control the debate.

The administration began scheduling Hillary Clinton to speak at numerous conventions of health-care professionals, and the president held several town meetings, including a late-night one Sept. 23 that was broadcast live from Tampa, Fla.

Originally, the Democratic National Committee (DNC)

Clinton's Plan: What Would Be Covered

Service Covered	Definition of Service	Limitations
General	Generally, patients in a low-cost-sharing plan such as a health maintenance organization would have to pay a $10 co-payment for each visit to a health-care provider. The maximum an individual would have to pay a year was $1,500; the maximum a family would have to pay was $3,000.	
Hospital and emergency services	Inpatient, outpatient and emergency room services at a hospital, including room and board; therapeutics; and lab, diagnostic and radiology services. $25 co-payment for use of an emergency room in a non-emergency; no other fees.	No private room accommodations.
Physicians and other health professionals	Inpatient and outpatient medical and surgical services, including consultations, in-home, office, ambulatory care or institutional settings. $10 co-payment per visit.	No private-duty nursing, cosmetic or sex-change surgery, or custodial care. No investigational treatments, but routine medical expenses incurred during an approved research trial would be covered.
Clinical preventive services	Physicals every three years for those age 20-39, every two years for those age 40-65 and annually thereafter. Checkups for young children. Mammograms every two years for women 50 and older. Pap smears and pelvic exams every three years until age 50, then every two years. Cholesterol screenings every five years beginning at age 20. A range of immunizations, including hepatitis B vaccine for children and annual flu shots for the elderly. More frequent tests for high-risk patients. No deductibles or co-payments.	
Inpatient mental health and substance abuse services	Comprehensive inpatient mental health services by 2001. Inpatient care for psychiatric and substance abuse disorders at hospitals and other residential treatment centers. No deductibles or co-payments.	Initially, patients would be limited to 30 days per episode, with an annual maximum of 60 days. Health plans could grant more time for patients deemed dangerous. By 1998, the maximum would rise to 90 days. Inpatient care available only when non-residential or less restrictive residential services were inadequate.
Non-residential and outpatient mental health and substance abuse services	Partial hospitalization, psychiatric rehabilitation, ambulatory detoxification and home-based services; professional psychiatric and substance abuse services, diagnosis and medical management; substance abuse counseling and relapse prevention; outpatient psychotherapy. Co-payments of $10 for medical management, $25 for each psychotherapy session. After 2001, psychotherapy co-payments would drop to $10. No other fees.	Extent of the benefit's reach would depend on the approval of the patient's health plan. Greater cost-sharing than with other benefits; this would be phased out by 2001. Initially, outpatient psychotherapy visits limited to 30 per year.
Family planning and pregnancy-related services	Prenatal and well-baby services. Abortions covered. No deductibles or co-payments specified.	No in-vitro fertilization coverage.
Hospice	Same as Medicare benefit: nurses' and doctors' care, social services, short-term inpatient care, medical supplies, physical or occupational therapy and speech-language pathology. No deductibles or co-payments.	Limited to the terminally ill; available only as an alternative to hospitalization.

had hoped to start a semi-independent, bipartisan group to lobby at the grass roots for health-care reform. But the idea quickly fizzled when potential participants backed away, fearful that the group would always be viewed as an arm of the party. Instead, the party, working closely with Clinton's political shop, formed the National Health Care Campaign, a group within the DNC working exclusively on reform and chaired by former Ohio Gov. Richard F. Celeste. The group planned to spend $3 million in 1993.

Still sensing a vacuum at the grass-roots level, Sen. John D.

Rockefeller, IV, D-W.Va., an ardent proponent of the Clinton plan, called together the groups that would most benefit from the administration proposal to suggest that they form their own grass-roots campaign. Within a few weeks the Health Reform Project had been formed. Backed by groups such as the American Association of Retired Persons and a number of unions and physician groups, it collected more than $3 million to fund its lobbying efforts.

At the same time, the plan's opponents were at work. Most visible was the Health Insurance Association of

Service Covered	Definition of Service	Limitations
Home health care	Nurses' care, social services, medical supplies, physical or occupational therapy and speech-language pathology. The plan would also cover prescribed home infusion therapy and outpatient prescription drugs and biological products. No deductibles or co-payments.	Patient re-evaluated after 60 days. Available only as an alternative to hospitalization.
Extended-care services	Inpatient services in a skilled nursing or rehabilitation facility.	Available only after an acute illness or injury, as an alternative to hospitalization. Limited to 100 days per calendar year. Custodial care not covered.
Ambulance services	Ground or air ambulance services. No deductibles or co-payments.	Cover air transport only when other means were inadvisable.
Outpatient laboratory and diagnostic services	Prescribed laboratory and radiology services, including diagnostic services, to those who are not patients of a hospital, hospice or extended care facility. No deductibles or co-payments.	
Outpatient prescription drugs and biologicals	Drugs, biological products and insulin. $5 co-payment per prescription; with higher cost plans, a $250 deductible.	For outpatient use only; no special limits on quantities. Health plans would be free to establish a list of drugs that physicians could prescribe, and to set up systems of substituting generic drugs, mail-order programs and drug utilization reviews.
Outpatient rehabilitation services	Occupational and physical therapy and speech-pathology services. $10 co-payment per visit.	To be used only to restore capacities or minimize limits on physical or cognitive functions after an illness or injury. Must be re-evaluated after 60 days.
Durable medical equipment, prosthetic and orthotic devices	Durable medical equipment; prosthetics that replaced internal organs, eyes or limbs; braces for legs, arms, backs and necks; training for these items. No deductibles or co-payments.	Custom devices not covered. Items had to improve functional abilities. No cosmetic orthodontia.
Vision and hearing care	Routine eye and ear exams; diagnosis and treatment for vision defects. Eyeglasses and contact lenses for children under 18. $10 co-payment per visit or per pair of children's glasses.	No eyeglasses or contact lens coverage for adults; routine eye exams limited to one every two years for people 18 or over. No hearing aids.
Dental services	Initially, services only for children, including treatment for prevention of dental disease and injury, maintenance of dental health and emergency dental treatment after an injury. Adult preventive care added by 2001. $10 co-payment per visit. After 2001, $20 per visit for dental restoration and medically necessary orthodontia.	No cosmetic orthodontia.
Health education classes	Education or training to reduce behavioral risk factors and promote healthful activities. May include: smoking cessation, nutrition counseling, stress management, skin cancer prevention, physical training classes. No deductibles or co-payments listed.	Had to be offered by a health plan.

SOURCE: President Clinton's draft proposal

America. Most experts agreed that the nation's 1,500 insurance companies would be reduced by at least half if the Clinton proposal became law. The organization, led by a highly respected former member of Congress, Bill Gradison, began running a series of ads featuring a pleasant looking couple named Harry and Louise. The ad's tag line was, "There's got to be a better way."

Also working at the grass-roots level was the Health Care Leadership Council, which represented the 50 biggest health companies in America, including Cigna Insurance and Humana hospitals. The organization also started an anti-Clinton campaign, although it endorsed Clinton's aim of preventing insurance companies from refusing to insure those who had pre-existing conditions.

VYING FOR JURISDICTION

The first real congressional battle in the health-care wars was an internecine fight among committees for jurisdiction over the bill. Weeks before Clinton even sent the

legislation to Capitol Hill, the disputes emerged. Some committees drafted memoranda listing each section of the bill that they thought belonged in their bailiwick; others met in closed-door meetings with the leadership and the parliamentarian.

At stake was not just the excitement of working on and amending the legislation but also oversight of the new system in future years. In general, the committees that shaped a bill ended up with responsibility for overseeing its implementation and for altering it if the policy did not work. Moreover, members serving on committees involved in health-care legislation were likely to receive large campaign contributions from health-care interest groups, which were contributing more generously than ever before. The rules on jurisdiction differed in the House and Senate.

Competing House Committees

Eager to avoid arguments, the House Democratic leadership opted to refer the entire bill to all three House committees with major jurisdictional claims. Those committees were Ways and Means, Energy and Commerce, and Education and Labor. Chaired respectively by Dan Rostenkowski, D-Ill., John D. Dingell, D-Mich., and William D. Ford, D-Mich., the panels encompassed a broad spectrum of House members. The chairmen were among the old-time barons of the House, and they had real gifts for dealmaking.

On Nov. 20, when the bill was introduced, the leadership also gave sequential referral to those committees with smaller portions of the bill, including the Veterans' Committee, the Judiciary Committee, the Post Office and Civil Service Committee, and the Armed Services Committee. It also went to the Government Operations and Natural Resources committees.

It was clear that the Rules Committee, whose role ordinarily was limited to determining the terms for debate on the House floor, would be responsible for melding the different versions of the bill into a single piece of legislation for floor action. Rules Committee members said they were hopeful that the committee chairmen would reconcile their differences before dumping the legislation in their lap. But most players expected Rules to shape the bill with the help of the leadership and the caucuses.

Senate Scramble

The looser Senate rules allowed any senator to offer an amendment on the floor to any bill. Indeed, the Senate had been known to write entire bills on the floor. Thus, while committee jurisdiction was important on some legislation, on a subject as sprawling as health care, it was unlikely that any committee could retain control over the floor debate.

As in the House, the real battle was not over the clear-cut jurisdictional questions, such as control over the veterans program or health care for federal employees, but over the grand sweep of the entire bill. Two committees vied for the prize: Finance, and Labor and Human Resources.

The Finance Committee (like Ways and Means) claimed jurisdiction because it was the committee in charge of taxation — a crucial element of the bill. The Labor and Human Resources Committee (like House Energy and Commerce) based its claim on its jurisdiction over health issues generally.

In the Senate, one committee had to have primary jurisdiction. Neither Finance Committee Chairman Daniel Patrick Moynihan, D-N.Y., nor Labor and Human Resources Chairman Edward M. Kennedy, D-Mass., was willing to let the other have the prime position. The Senate leadership's solution was to leave the bill on the calendar instead of referring it to one or the other committee. That meant the leadership would take the original Clinton bill to the floor in 1994 and allow both committees (and any other senators) to amend it.

1993 Denouement

Despite the repeated drum rolls about the Clinton's proposal and the imminence of reform, by the end of the session, the health-care debate had been subsumed. The administration was feverishly working to pass the North American Free Trade Agreement, and most members were talking of little else. Although lawmakers with specific jurisdiction over health-care matters held hearings on many aspects of the president's proposal through the fall, they were in the minority. To most members, it was clear that although they would have to confront the task of overhauling health-care policy, they would not have to do it or even think much more about it in 1993. ∎

Alternative Health-Care Proposals

The locus of the health-care debate shifted in the fall from the White House to Capitol Hill, where lawmakers were already discussing a range of contending plans. On the left, liberal Democrats supported a single-payer plan, under which the government would run the health insurance system, putting private insurers out of business. At the other end of the spectrum, conservative Republicans put forward incremental plans that relied on limited insurance reforms.

Occupying the middle ground were several proposals that sought to move toward universal coverage without necessarily achieving it. Unlike Clinton's plan, these proposals did not include a cap on insurance premiums, nor did they require employers to pay for their employees' health insurance. They also downsized Clinton's proposed health alliances, which were designed to gather consumers into large groups to purchase insurance.

The two leading middle ground proposals were the Health Equity and Access Today Reform Act (S 1770, HR 3704) sponsored by Sen. John H. Chafee, R-R.I., and the Managed Competition Act (HR 3222, S 1579) sponsored by Rep. Jim Cooper, D-Tenn. Chafee's plan had only Republican support. Cooper had bipartisan support. For details of the Chafee and Cooper plans, see p. 346.

Single-Payer Plan

Rep. Jim McDermott, D-Wash., and Sen. Paul Wellstone, D-Minn., sponsored bills (HR 1200, S 491) aimed at creating a Canadian-style single-payer system offering universal coverage. Under their plan, the government would take the place of private insurance companies, collecting premiums and paying health-care providers. The plan entailed price controls, a massive new tax program and a severe reduction in the medical industry's profits.

The idea was relatively simple. Relying primarily on a

new payroll tax, the government would collect hundreds of billions of dollars to pay for medical care for every American. State and local governments would administer the program, receiving an annual budget for all health-care expenses and dispensing the money to certified providers. Patients would be free to choose their own doctors and would not be charged copayments or deductibles.

The single-payer approach also promised big administrative savings. The Congressional Budget Office estimated in December that McDermott's bill would reduce national health expenditures by about 6 percent in 2003.

Yet the bill faced enormous obstacles. "Something about the single-payer system is highly egalitarian in nature," said John Sheils, an economist with Lewin-VHI Inc., a medical consulting group based in Fairfax, Va. "For better or worse, it isn't the way Americans think; it's very contrary to our culture."

In one scenario, the government would collect a payroll tax that would take the place of existing health insurance premiums; it would allocate money to states, which would negotiate fees with doctors and hospitals. Medical decisions would be left to doctors and patients. Doctors would not work directly for the government.

Most physicians could expect to see their profit margins dwindle under the single-payer plan. But some were willing to trade profits for fewer forms and less red tape. "We don't have for-profit fire departments, and we don't have for-profit police and military," said David Himmelstein, a doctor with Physicians for a National Health Program, a single-payer advocacy group. "Vital community functions have long been declared not in the realm of for-profit corporations; this is clearly another one."

Perhaps the greatest political liability for McDermott's bill was its reliance on enormous new taxes, which were anathema to most elected officials.

The simple math of passing legislation, however, convinced single-payer advocates that Clinton would need them to enact any major health-care bill in 1994. While supporting their own plan, they sought to use their leverage to fight for items that would make the Clinton bill more palatable to them.

Virtually all members who supported the single-payer bill indicated that they would oppose any legislation that did not at least guarantee states the right to test the approach. Single-payer supporters believed that eventually others would see the value in such a system and that it would sweep across the country. The other feature they insisted on in any health-care bill was the guarantee of health coverage for all Americans.

Medical Savings Accounts

Meanwhile, conservatives, led by Sen. Phil Gramm, R-Texas, put forward a plan to minimize government involvement in health care and instead encourage consumers to put aside savings for health-care expenses. It relied on the existing health system but was designed to reduce expenditures by using a carrot-and-stick approach.

The linchpin of Gramm's plan was a medical savings account known as "medisave," a relatively new and untested concept. Consumers would continue to use private health insurance, but they would be encouraged to set aside money to pay for deductibles and uncovered costs. Contributions to the account and the interest on it would be tax-free if used within the year for medical expenses. Taxes would be deferred if the money was used for something else.

The Gramm proposal had its roots in two conservative articles of faith: that individuals were the best arbiters of their needs and means, and that taxes should be levied on consumption, not savings.

Philosophically, Gramm's proposal was virtually the opposite of Clinton's: It was likely to require people to pay more out of pocket for health care, and it encouraged them to use fewer services, not more — as the Clinton plan would through its emphasis on preventive care.

It also was anchored by the belief that insurance insulated people from understanding the true cost of health care. "The bottom line is that when somebody goes to the hospital in America today, somebody else pays 95 percent of the bill," said Gramm. "If I bought groceries like I buy health care, I would eat differently.... I'd buy steaks; I would buy lobster; I would feed my dog at least hamburger."

Gramm's proposal was not aimed at universal coverage, and it did not require employers to offer health insurance to their employees. But if employers chose to provide it, they would be required to offer a catastrophic plan with a medical savings account, in addition to whatever other health insurance plan they offered. Catastrophic plans, which had low premiums, generally covered health-care costs above $3,000 but required the policyholder to pay up to that amount out of pocket. Since the catastrophic premiums were lower, Gramm's plan would require employers to open a medical savings account for each employee with the balance of what they would have paid had they given the employee a comprehensive health insurance plan.

Critics, including some conservative health policy experts, said that at best, only a minority of Americans — those with extra disposable income — would want to use a medical savings account.

Besides providing for a medisave account, Gramm's plan included provisions to:

● Allow employers and organizations such as clubs and associations to voluntarily form groups to buy insurance.

● Give tax credits to people who earned less than the federal poverty level.

● Subsidize those who were uninsured because of pre-existing medical conditions so they could buy catastrophic coverage, if the cost exceeded 7.5 percent of their income.

● Penalize people who earned more than 200 percent of the poverty level and who failed to buy at least a catastrophic plan.

● Reward preventive medicine and healthful lifestyles by allowing insurers to charge different amounts depending on lifestyle. People who smoked, drank, overate or engaged in other harmful activities would receive lower subsidies.

● Leave intact the existing Medicaid program, the joint federal-state health insurance program for the poor. But Medicaid spending would be cut $101 billion over five years. The annual rate of increase would be cut to the medical inflation rate.

● Leave intact the federal Medicare program, which provided health insurance for the elderly and the disabled. But Medicare spending would be cut $62 billion over five years. Beneficiaries could opt to receive government assistance up to the expected cost of their annual Medicare coverage; they could use the money to enroll in a health maintenance organization (HMO) or to buy a medical savings account.

● Reform the medical malpractice system. The loser in a malpractice case would have to pay court costs. Any claim of negligence not justified or improperly advanced would result in an automatic judgment against the plaintiff. Non-economic damages would be capped at $250,000. Punitive damages would not be allowed against a manufacturer of a drug or medical device if the device had been approved by the Food and Drug Administration. ■

Middle Ground Health Plans

Three plans dominated the middle ground in the health-care debate — those of President Clinton (HR 3600, S 1757), Rep. Jim Cooper, D-Tenn. (HR 3222, S 1579) and Sen. John H. Chafee, R-R.I.(S 1770, HR 3704).

The three plans had several key elements in common. All three would change the insurance market to force insurers and health providers to compete for consumers' business on the basis of price and quality. The proposals differed, however, in their financing, government regulation and whether they would provide universal coverage.

Clinton's plan was the only one that would guarantee universal health insurance and that would require employers or the government to cover most costs. Under the Chafee and Cooper plans, universal coverage was a goal — but not a requirement; also, consumers would pay for more of the costs than under Clinton. The bills would:

Issue	Clinton	Cooper	Chafee
Universal Coverage	Guarantee health insurance coverage for all Americans by 1998. Coverage would include a specified package of benefits covering routine doctor visits, hospitalization, preventive care and limited mental health coverage.	Rely on reorganizing the health insurance market to increase coverage. No mandate for universal coverage. Estimates by the Congressional Budget Office on an early version of the Cooper bill found that it would leave at least 20 million Americans uninsured. Everyone who bought insurance would be required to purchase a comprehensive package of benefits.	Require that all Americans have health insurance by 2005. All plans would have to offer a nationally defined, comprehensive package of benefits. Individuals who lacked health insurance would pay a penalty (the local average yearly insurance premium plus 20 percent). People could select a comprehensive or a catastrophic plan, which generally would cover costs only after the beneficiary had spent $1,500 to $3000.
Health Alliances	Require that states set up large consumer purchasing groups called "health alliances" to collect premiums, bargain with health plans and pay them based on their number of subscribers. The idea was to organize consumers into large blocs to give them bargaining clout. The alliances could refuse to offer plans that charged more than 20 percent above the nationally set premium target price for that region. The alliances also would collect information about the plans' quality and prepare consumer reports.	Require that each state set up "health care purchasing cooperatives" through which individuals and employers with fewer than 100 workers who paid for employee health insurance would have to buy insurance if they wanted tax advantages. All workers in such small firms would have access to all plans offered by the cooperative. Larger employers could offer workers just one health plan. States could have several cooperatives; none could overlap. Cooperatives would provide consumer information about the quality of plans.	Require each state to designate geographic areas in which individuals and employers with fewer than 100 workers could form one or more purchasing groups. The groups would have to contract with any plan that wanted to offer its services. Groups and all health plans would be required to offer enrollment to all employees and individuals in the area. States would supply consumer information on the cost and quality of health plans.
Insurance Reforms	Require insurance companies and health plans to accept all applicants regardless of health status. Coverage could not be delayed because of a pre-existing medical condition. Premium costs would be based on the average cost per capita of covering everyone within the alliance area. Premium payments would differ depending on whether the enrollment was for a single person, a couple, a single-parent family or a two-parent family. Plans would be paid based on the health status of enrollees.	Require insurance companies to accept all applicants, regardless of pre-existing medical conditions. If a person failed to sign up for insurance within several years of the bill's enactment, insurers could refuse to cover a pre-existing condition for six months. The same rule would apply to individuals who dropped and later renewed their coverage. Insurance companies and health plans could consider only age and geographic location in setting premium prices for members of purchasing cooperatives.	Require all plans in a local area to accept all individuals regardless of health status. Reduce to six months the time that an uninsured individual with a pre-existing condition, who then purchased insurance, would have to pay for coverage while being ineligible for benefits. All plans would have to offer the nationally mandated benefits package. Premium rates for small employers and individuals would vary only by age, family configuration, benefit plan and geographic area. Plans would be paid based on the health status of enrollees. States would have to provide consumers with information needed to compare plans.

Financing and Taxes	Pay for subsidies for small businesses and the poor through Medicare cuts ($103 billion by 2001), a 75-cent-a-pack increase in cigarette taxes ($54 billion by 2001), a 1 percent payroll tax on employers of more than 5,000 workers who did not join health alliances ($8 billion by 2001) and an eventual limit on the business tax deductibility of health insurance benefits.	Combine Medicare cuts ($40 billion over five years) and a limit on the business deductibility of health benefits to pay for insurance subsidies for the poor and for allowing individuals and self-employed people to deduct all health insurance costs up to the lowest priced plan. Employers would pay a 34 percent excise tax on contributions that exceeded the cost of the lowest priced plan, raising $79 billion over five years.	To subsidize health insurance for the poor, cut Medicare and Medicaid by $213 billion over six years. Allow employers to deduct the cost of health insurance only up to the average cost of the lowest-priced half of qualified health plans offered in the area. The employee would be taxed on employer-paid premiums in excess of that amount. States would continue to pay most of their share of Medicaid costs to cover the needy.
Employer Mandate	Require employers to pay 80 percent of the cost of the average health plan offered in a region for all full time employees. Employees would pay the difference between the employer share and the plan they chose. Businesses with fewer than 75 employees and average wages below $24,000 a year would be eligible for subsidies; their insurance costs would be capped at 7.9 percent of payroll. Self-employed individuals would be considered small businesses, eligible for subsidies on the 80 percent employer share of premium costs.	Not require that employers pay for their employees' health insurance. However, employers of fewer than 100 workers who did buy insurance would have to buy it through the local purchasing cooperative. Such employers would have to allow employees to pay for health insurance through payroll deductions.	Not require that employers pay for their employees' health insurance. However, they would be required to make information about area plans available and allow employees to pay for health insurance through payroll deductions.
Cost Containment	Set a national health-care budget based on existing costs, and divide it up among the states. The bill would limit the rate of increase in health insurance costs to the annual rate of inflation (about 3 percent), taking into account population shifts.	Set no limits on health insurance prices or the rate of increase in health-care costs. To hold down costs, the plan would rely on reorganization of the market: competition among health plans, insurance reforms and the formation of purchasing cooperatives.	Set no limits on private sector health insurance prices or the rate of increase in health-care costs. To hold down costs, rely on reorganization of the market: competition among health plans, insurance reforms and the formation of purchasing cooperatives. Hold down federal spending through cuts and caps in Medicare and Medicaid spending, plus a spending cap on the new voucher program for the poor. Phase out the $16 billion to $17 billion spent annually to compensate hospitals serving large numbers of Medicaid and uninsured patients.
Low-Income Programs	Require that Medicaid beneficiaries be covered through health alliances. Their care would be paid for with state and federal funds, adjusted annually to reflect inflation. Other low-income people also would obtain coverage through alliances and receive subsidies based on income. However, Medicaid beneficiaries who worked would no longer be subsidized for copayments — the patient's share of doctor visit costs. The bill would not cover supplemental services such as transportation to health clinics, translation and rehabilitation therapy for beneficiaries not on welfare.	Abolish Medicaid, replacing it with a subsidy program that would pay the medical costs of the 36 million Americans earning poverty wages. Those earning up to 200 percent of the poverty level would receive subsidies on a sliding scale. States would be required to take over the long-term care portion of Medicaid. The government would subsidize enrollment in an area's lowest priced plan. Supplemental services that were provided to Medicaid beneficiaries, such as transportation to clinics, would continue only for those below the poverty line.	By 1997, make vouchers available to fully subsidize health costs for those earning up to 90 percent of the federal poverty level. Vouchers would be phased in by 2005 on a sliding scale to help cover those who earned up to 240 percent of the poverty level. But subsidies would be available only if the federal government cut Medicare and Medicaid. States could contract with health programs to serve the poor exclusively.

Limited Change Made to Abortion Policy

Despite the election of abortion rights backer Democrat Bill Clinton and a record number of women lawmakers, Congress in 1993 took only limited steps toward assuring abortion rights for all women.

Late in the year, both the House and Senate passed legislation to prohibit anyone from intimidating by force or threat of force a woman seeking to obtain an abortion or an abortion clinic worker. The measure was expected to go to the White House in early 1994. *(Clinic access, 354)*

However, lawmakers in both chambers refused to approve more than a slight relaxation of the longstanding ban on the use of federal Medicaid funds to finance abortions for poor women. And the House only narrowly agreed to allow the federal government's health insurance plans to cover abortions for federal employees.

While President Clinton and Congress did eliminate a half dozen restrictions, abortion foes were able to point to victories, too. Most notably, Congress did not act on the so-called Freedom of Choice Act, the bill that led the priority list for advocates of a woman's right to choose an abortion.

Also unresolved at year's end was the question of whether abortion would be covered under a new national health plan that Congress was expected to devise in 1994. The health-care reform plan submitted by Clinton in 1993 begged the question by including a reference to coverage of "reproductive health services," essentially leaving the matter to interpretation by states and individual health plans. But few expected the matter to be left so vaguely defined.

BACKGROUND

As in previous years, the abortion fight was a multi-front war, with skirmishes on a wide variety of both spending and other bills. But while some of the controversies were old ones, 1993 was a watershed, with several issues put to rest, at least for the time being, and new ones popping up.

Clinton resolved many of the abortion-related fights of the previous four years on his second full day in office. In a series of executive orders issued Jan. 22, the new president:

• Ended enforcement of the so-called gag rule, which prohibited abortion counseling and referrals in federally

---

Legislative Roundup

As in previous years, the abortion fight was a multi-front war, with skirmishes on a wide variety of both spending and other bills. Following are the major bills in which abortion issues were resolved or fought out:

• **Freedom of Choice Act** (HR 25, S 25) sought to codify a woman's fundamental right to end her pregnancy prior to fetal viability, as spelled out in the 1973 Supreme Court ruling, *Roe v. Wade*. Congress did not complete work on the bill.

• **Family Planning Reauthorization** (HR 670) sought to codify language requiring that clinics counsel women with unintended pregnancies about all their options, including abortion. Congress did not complete work on the bill.

• **National Institutes of Health Reauthorization** (S 1 — PL 103-43) included language codifying the end of the ban on using federal funds for fetal tissue research. *(NIH, p. 357)*

• **Fiscal 1994 Labor-HHS Appropriations** (HR 2518 — PL 103-112) banned the use of most federal funds to pay for abortions for women on Medicaid, but permitted abortion funding in cases of rape and incest, as well as when the pregnancy endangered the woman's life. *(Appropriations, p. 632)*

• **Fiscal 1994 Foreign Operations Appropriations** (HR 2295 — PL 103-87) included funds for the United Nations Population Fund but sought to limit the fund's spending in China. *(Appropriations, p. 603)*

• **Fiscal 1994 D.C. Appropriations** (HR 2492 — PL 103-127) lifted the ban on the use of locally raised tax funds to pay for abortions for poor District women. *(Appropriations, p. 585)*

• **Fiscal 1994 Treasury-Postal Appropriations** (HR 2403 — PL 103-123) for the first time since 1981 did not include a provision barring health plans for federal workers from covering abortions. *(Appropriations, p. 679)*

See also the Supreme Court's 1993 ruling on Bray v. Alexandria Women's Health Clinic, p. 328.

---

funded family planning clinics. Congress and former President George Bush had sparred repeatedly over the regulations since they were upheld by the Supreme Court in the 1991 decision *Rust v. Sullivan. (1991 Almanac, p. 286)*

• Rescinded a ban on funding research using tissue from aborted fetuses, thus freeing long-delayed legislation reauthorizing portions of the National Institutes of Health. Clinton signed the NIH bill, including codification of the end of the fetal tissue research ban, in June. *(NIH, p. 357)*

• Ordered the lifting of a 1988 ban that prohibited abortions in overseas military medical facilities even if the woman paid for the procedure herself.

• Directed the Department of Health and Human Services to study whether to lift the "import alert" that prevented even small amounts of the abortion pill RU 486 from being brought into the country.

• Overturned the so-called Mexico City policy that since 1984 had banned U.S. aid to international organizations that performed or "actively promoted" abortions.

Abortion rights forces thought Clinton's Jan. 22 actions would be the first in a long list of accomplishments for the year. In the end, however, they proved to be the high-water mark.

Small Shifts in Congress

Congress did loosen some of the abortion-related restrictions imposed since the mid-1970s. Although abortion rights backers counted it as a loss, the fiscal 1994 spending bill for the departments of Labor, Health and Human Services, and Education permitted the use of federal Medicaid funds to pay for abortions for poor women whose pregnancies were the result of rape or incest. For the preceding 12 years, such funding had been allowed only if the pregnancy endangered the woman's life. Similarly, the fiscal 1994 spending bills for the Treasury Department, the Postal Service and General Government, and the District of Columbia lifted bans on abortion coverage in health plans for federal employees and use of locally raised tax funds to pay for abortions for poor District women, respectively.

Despite the end of the controversy over the "gag rule," Congress failed to complete action on legislation to reauthorize the federal family planning program, Title X of

---

House Action

The change was partly due to Clinton's presence in the White House. But the initial impetus came from the new Treasury-Postal Appropriations Subcommittee chairman and abortion rights supporter, Steny H. Hoyer, D-Md. Subcommittee ranking Republican Jim Ross Lightfoot of Iowa sought to restore the language at the subcommittee markup May 26, but he failed on a voice vote.

For both political and parliamentary reasons, abortion foes opted not to fight to reinstate the language at committee or during House floor debate, choosing instead to focus their efforts on the higher-profile spending bill for the Labor, and Health and Human Services departments.

Senate Action

Abortion foes in the Senate tried to add the ban back, with some initial success. The Treasury-Postal Appropriations subcommittee July 20 approved an amendment by Christopher S. Bond, R-Mo., to reinstate the previous language. But at the full committee markup July 22, members voted 15-14 to strip the language. The vote, a procedural one, was engineered by abortion rights supporter Barbara A. Mikulski, D-Md.

Mikulski won a second procedural victory, this one on the Senate floor. Members on Aug. 3 voted 48-51 against allowing abortion opponent Don Nickles, R-Okla., to offer an amendment to reinstate the ban — voting, in effect, that the amendment amounted to inappropriate legislating on a spending bill. Nickles' amendment would have allowed female federal workers to receive abortions through their health plans, but only if they paid a separate premium for the coverage. (Vote 235, p. 58-H)

Conference, Final Action

Although dropping the ban was not negotiable during conference because both the House and Senate bills had identical provisions, abortion opponents in the House came within a hairbreadth Sept. 29 of pulling off a sneak attack on the bill.

The abortion question was not mentioned when the Treasury-Postal conference report came back to the House Sept. 29, in deference to Appropriations Committee Chairman Natcher, who asked opponents not to stir up the issue through a contentious floor debate. But abortion opponents, led by Congressional Pro-Life Caucus Chairman Christopher H. Smith, R-N.J., quietly lobbied colleagues throughout the day. Their efforts almost sank the bill. The conference report was ultimately adopted by a vote of 207-206. (Vote 476, p. 116-H)

Abortion foes made no further attempts to reinstate the ban, and Clinton signed the bill into law without the abortion ban Oct. 28 (PL 103-123).

DISTRICT OF COLUMBIA APPROPRIATIONS

As with so many bills in 1993, the spending bill for the District of Columbia (HR 2492 — H Rept 103-303) relaxed restrictions imposed in previous years. But the final version disappointed abortion rights backers and elated abortion foes by not going as far as both thought it might have.

As signed into law by Clinton Oct. 29 (PL 103-127), the measure allowed the city to use locally raised funds to pay for abortions for poor women through the joint federal-state Medicaid program, lifting a ban that had been in place since 1988. But it maintained restrictions on the use of federal funds appropriated in the bill.

Both the House and Senate had approved versions of the bill with no abortion restrictions, and a conference

committee approved a final bill that was silent on the issue. Had that version become law, it would have been the first D.C. bill without abortion related restrictions since 1979. But in a debate dominated by abortion foes, the House rejected the conference report Oct. 20 by a vote of 206-224. (Vote 518, p. 126-H)

Sent back to the drawing board, bill sponsors quickly produced a new version that permitted federal funds to be used for abortion only in cases of rape, incest or when the pregnancy endangered the life of the woman — tracking the language in the 1994 spending bill for the departments of Labor, Health and Human Services, and Education. Like the previous version, the bill was silent on use of city-raised funds, allowing abortions to be funded without restriction.

House abortion foes cried foul when they were not permitted to offer an amendment to restrict locally raised funds to cases of rape, incest and life endangerment, but the new version passed relatively easily, 225-201, on Oct. 27. The Senate approved the new version by voice vote later that day. (Vote 534, p. 130-H)

FOREIGN OPERATIONS APPROPRIATIONS

Reports of brutality and coercive practices by China in enforcing its one-child-per-family goal, spurred controversy over the Clinton administration's desire to restore funding to a United Nations agency that had long had ties to Beijing's population control program.

U.S. aid to the U.N. Population Fund was cut off during the Reagan administration because of the agency's involvement with the China program. Since 1985, the annual Foreign Operations spending bill had explicitly barred funds from going to any organization that supported or participated in the "management of a program of coercive abortion or involuntary sterilization," which the Reagan and Bush administrations interpreted to include the U.N. Population Fund.

The administration asked for a $50 million appropriation for the population fund. But in April, The New York Times reported that Chinese family planning authorities had again undertaken a draconian nationwide crackdown — including the forced sterilization of numerous women — to sharply reduce the nation's birthrate.

The brutal picture painted by The Times story prompted even some of the fund's strongest supporters to urge that it shut down its China operation. "It cannot be disputed any more that the Chinese policy has been coercive," said David R. Obey, D-Wis., chairman of the House Appropriations Subcommittee on Foreign Operations. "The problem now is how best to change the policy."

As passed by the House June 17, the fiscal 1994 spending bill (HR 2295) provided $36.2 million for the population fund. But in order to spend the aid before March 1, 1994, it required the president to certify that the U.N. agency had terminated its activities in China.

The Senate version, passed Sept. 23, provided the full $50 million Clinton requested.

A House-Senate conference committee ultimately agreed to provide $40 million for the population fund, $10 million less than the administration's request. The bill also required the administration to report to Congress on the agency's budget for its activities in China in 1994. Any amount above $10 million that the agency intended to spend in China was to be deducted from the U.S. contribution. President Clinton signed the bill Sept. 30 (PL 103-87). ∎

Bills Seek To Ensure Abortion Clinic Access

In one of the few major wins in 1993 for abortion rights supporters — and a major setback for abortion foes — the House and Senate each passed bills to make it a federal crime to intimidate by force or threat of force abortion clinic workers or women seeking to obtain abortions.

In the crush of end-of-the-session action, however, Congress did not settle on a compromise version of the two bills (HR 796, S 636). But backers expressed confidence that the legislation would be enacted early in 1994.

The bills were propelled in part by the arrival of abortion rights backer Bill Clinton in the White House, and in part by a January Supreme Court decision ruling that abortion clinic blockaders could not be restricted or prosecuted under a Reconstruction-era federal civil rights law. But a bigger reason was the escalation of violence surrounding abortion protests in 1993. On March 10, Dr. David Gunn, who performed abortions at a Pensacola, Fla., clinic, was shot to death at close range; an abortion protester from the group Rescue America went on trial for the murder in 1994. In August, an abortion doctor in Wichita, Kan., was also shot, but survived.

"This was not so much about policy based on pro-life or pro-choice," said Rep. Olympia J. Snowe, R-Maine, an abortion rights supporter. "This year, with the murder of Dr. Gunn, the violence reached a level that is way unacceptable. It's just gone beyond the pale of reason."

BACKGROUND

A major spur for the legislation was the Supreme Court's Jan. 13 ruling in *Bray v. Alexandria Women's Health Clinic*. The case tested the constitutionality of allowing federal judges to use a Reconstruction-era civil rights law, the Ku Klux Klan Act, to issue injunctions barring anti-abortion protesters from harassing women as they entered clinics. *(Supreme Court, p. 325)*

The law originally was framed to protect blacks trying to exercise their constitutional rights to vote and to travel. Abortion rights advocates argued that women, like blacks, were a protected class of citizens whose constitutional rights were being violated.

But the court disagreed, striking down the use of the civil rights law to issue injunctions against clinic protesters.

The bill's drafters faced three challenges. They wanted to show that state laws were insufficient to deal with anti-abortion protests. They needed to protect protesters' right to picket, leaflet and shout slogans. And they needed to ensure that the bill did not discriminate on the basis of viewpoint. The key was to punish violent or intimidating action, not words, bill supporters said.

"If someone stands up outside an abortion clinic and says 'Abortion is wrong — you're killing your baby,' that is not force or intimidation," said Burt Neuborne, a New York University law professor and First Amendment specialist. "But if what you do is shout in somebody's face and don't go away, and physically thrust yourself upon them, then you've reached the point of intimidation."

The distinction was a fine one, and the Supreme Court had struggled with it repeatedly, including in two hate crime cases in 1992 and 1993. In 1992, the court struck down a St. Paul, Minn., law that made it a crime to burn a cross on a lawn or commit other racially motivated acts that intimidated or angered others. The court ruled that

the law selectively silenced speech on the basis of its content. *(1992 Almanac, p. 326)*

But in June 1993, the court upheld a Wisconsin law that increased penalties for crimes that were racially motivated, on the grounds that the statute was aimed at conduct, not freedom of expression.

Provisions

Most of the provisions of the House and Senate bills were identical. Among other things the bills sought to:

● Prohibit the use of force, threat of force or physical obstruction — such as sit-ins — to interfere with, injure or intimidate clinic workers or any woman attempting to obtain an abortion. The ban applied both at the clinic door and at women's and workers' homes, which had been targeted by protesters. It covered both abortion clinics and pregnancy counseling centers run by anti-abortion groups. The Senate bill extended the protections to places of worship, as well.

● Allow civil and criminal actions to be brought by the U.S. attorney general, state attorneys general and persons whose rights under the statute were violated.

● Authorize injunctive relief, and compensatory and punitive damages, for civil actions under the law.

● Set criminal penalties for destroying or damaging a clinic because it provided abortions. For a first offense, the House version authorized fines up to $100,000 and one year in prison; for subsequent offenses, fines up to $250,000 and up to three years in prison. If someone was injured, the maximum penalty would be 10 years in prison. The Senate version made a distinction between violent and non-violent protests, punishing the latter with six months in jail and a $10,000 fine for a first offense, and 18 months and a $25,000 fine for a second offense.

HOUSE COMMITTEE ACTION

During consideration March 25 by the House Judiciary Subcommittee on Crime and Criminal Justice, many members — including several who opposed legal abortion — condemned the behavior of radical anti-abortion activists, but they also expressed concern about approving a bill that might limit the First Amendment right to freedom of expression. The subcommittee ultimately approved the measure by a vote of 9-4.

Amendments to narrow the bill's scope were offered by Romano L. Mazzoli, D-Ky., Lamar Smith, R-Texas, and George E. Sangmeister, D-Ill.

The subcommittee approved by voice vote Sangmeister's amendment, which sought to clarify that peaceful demonstrations would not be affected.

The two Mazzoli amendments, one of which would have narrowed the list of plaintiffs qualified to sue under the bill, were rejected 6-7.

Smith's amendment, which carried 7-6, said that only protesters who were blocking clinic access, and not those who were merely "hindering" a woman's entrance, would be subject to penalties.

Full Committee

The full House Judiciary Committee approved the bill (H Rept 103-306) by a vote of 24-11 on Sept. 14, after

rejecting several amendments offered by its opponents.

At the urging of Sangmeister, an abortion foe who nevertheless supported the bill, sponsor and subcommittee Chairman Charles E. Schumer, D-N.Y., made several adjustments to the measure between subcommittee action and the full committee markup. The changes were aimed at narrowing the bill's language to ensure that it did not violate protesters' constitutional right of free expression.

The revised measure won the support not only of the committee but also of Attorney General Janet Reno. In a letter to House Judiciary Committee Chairman Jack Brooks, D-Texas, Reno said the bill was "essential to curb an escalating pattern of interference with the access of women to abortion services."

But anti-abortion groups and their allies took a different view.

F. James Sensenbrenner Jr., R-Wis., denounced the violence and shootings at some abortion clinics, but he said state and local authorities should be left to handle such crimes. He also said the bill would stifle legitimate protest against abortion.

"Its purpose is to put a chilling effect on demonstrations in front of abortion clinics," he said.

On voice votes, the committee defeated two amendments offered by Henry J. Hyde, R-Ill., one of the House's leading anti-abortion activists.

One amendment would have blocked the federal law from being used until a court determined that state or local authorities had not adequately enforced local statutes pertaining to clinic violence or blockades.

The other would have extended the bill to cover union protests outside work sites. Hyde called the proposal an "anti-hypocrisy" amendment, but Schumer labeled it a "poison pill" aimed at bringing down the underlying bill.

Bob Inglis, R-S.C., sought to eliminate language allowing private citizens affected by clinic blockades or violence to bring suit under the bill. Inglis said clinic operators might initiate groundless suits to harass anti-abortion protesters and that the right to sue under the bill should be left solely to the U.S. attorney general or state attorneys general. Inglis's amendment was defeated 13-22.

The final tally on the bill reflected increased support since the March subcommittee markup. Two Democrats who voted against the bill in subcommittee supported it during full committee markup — Mazzoli and David Mann of Ohio. Three Republicans joined all 21 Democrats to endorse the bill: George W. Gekas of Pennsylvania, Steven H. Schiff of New Mexico and Jim Ramstad of Minnesota.

HOUSE FLOOR ACTION

The House approved the bill by voice vote Nov. 18 after rejecting, 182-246, a motion to recommit the bill to committee. *(Vote 582, p. 142-H)*

Much of the criticism of the bill during the floor debate centered on 'questions about its constitutionality. Opponents charged that it singled out one point of view for censure, in effect punishing those who expressed opposition to abortion.

"You apply this bill to any other movement — antinukes, AIDS activists, civil rights activists — and it would be laughed right out of Congress. This is the felonization of viewpoint differences," said Christopher H. Smith, R-N.J., a leader of anti-abortion forces in the House.

Proponents, however, insisted that the bill was narrowly tailored to discourage violent, intimidating conduct while not inhibiting free speech protected under the First Amendment.

SENATE COMMITTEE ACTION

Backers of the bill got an important boost when Attorney General Janet Reno gave the measure the administration's official endorsement at a hearing of the Senate Labor and Human Resources Committee May 12.

"This is a problem that is national in scope," Reno told the committee. "Some anti-abortion activists have increased the intensity of their activities from picketing to physical blockades, sabotage of facilities, stalking and harassing abortion providers, arson, bombings," she said. In the process they have shut down clinics and otherwise made it "impossible for women to exercise their right to choose."

The committee approved the bill (S Rept 103-117) on June 23, by a vote of 13-4, over the objections of some Republicans who said it could impede the free speech rights of abortion protesters. Dave Durenberger, R-Minn., an abortion opponent, joined abortion rights Republicans Nancy Landon Kassebaum of Kansas and James M. Jeffords of Vermont and all the panel's Democrats in supporting the bill.

Bill sponsor and Labor Committee Chairman Edward M. Kennedy, D-Mass., reworked his original bill to accommodate suggestions from the Justice Department and others. One change allowed state attorneys general, as well as the U.S. attorney general, to press for civil penalties against violators.

Several other adjustments were attempts to win over Republicans who saw the bill as tilted toward an abortion rights agenda.

For example, Kennedy broadened the bill's protections to cover facilities that provided counseling on alternatives to abortion. And the substitute bill carved out an exception for the actions of a parent or legal guardian directed solely at a minor child.

But even those changes did not go far enough for some. Daniel R. Coats, R-Ind., an abortion foe, offered his own version of the bill that included numerous changes, the most significant of which sought to extend penalties to anyone who, through force or threat of force, obstructed a peaceful protest regarding abortion services.

Orrin G. Hatch, R-Utah, another abortion foe, said that without such protections, abortion advocates could use the clinic access bill to harass anti-abortion protesters. "History shows us you don't achieve peace by disarming only one of the combatants," Hatch said.

But Kennedy replied that lawful speech was amply protected under the bill and the Constitution. Coats' substitute was rejected, 6-11, with Jeffords joining all the committee Democrats to oppose it.

Hatch subsequently offered a narrower amendment, dealing only with the protection for lawful protesters, which was rejected by the same margin.

Two other Hatch amendments also went down to defeat.

Members rejected, 8-9, his proposal to change the term "lawful abortion related services" to refer to abortion, pregnancy and childbirth services. Kennedy said the change would not affect which facilities were covered. But the amendment was backed by committee Republicans and by Harris Wofford, D-Pa., who said it would insult anti-abortion groups to refer to childbirth counseling as a subsidiary of abortion.

Another Hatch amendment, to specify that the bill's

protections applied only to "lawful" abortion services, was rejected 5-12.

SENATE FLOOR ACTION

The Senate passed its bill by a vote of 69-30 on Nov. 16, but not before making some changes that ultimately prevented a quick agreement with the House. *(Vote 373, p. 48-S)*

Proponents argued that the bill was necessary to protect women's ability to secure abortions. "The Constitution guarantees the right of a woman to end a pregnancy, but the violence and blockades are designed to make it impossible for women to exercise that right," said Kennedy.

But opponents said the bill went too far. "It is my concern that this narrowly drafted legislation, if enacted, will suppress non-violent political demonstrations because of the subject matter of the conduct," said Strom Thurmond, R-S.C. "Unfortunately, this legislation would elevate the right to abortion above the First Amendment."

The key amendment — offered by Hatch and adopted by voice vote — extended the bill's reach to protect "any person lawfully exercising or seeking to exercise the First Amendment right of religious freedom at a place of worship." The amendment also called for penalties for those who intentionally damaged property of a place of religious worship. Hatch cited a series of attacks and demonstrations at a number of churches and synagogues, including New York City's St. Patrick's Cathedral.

By a vote of 56-40, members also adopted a Kennedy amendment to lower monetary penalties in the bill for those convicted of offenses not involving force or threat of force. The original version included fines of up to $100,000 for a first offense and $250,000 for a subsequent offense; the amendment lowered those thresholds to $10,000 and $25,000, respectively. The amendment was offered as a substitute to an amendment offered by Robert C. Smith, R-N.H., who complained that the penalties for non-violent offenses were too severe. *(Vote 369, p. 48-S)*

Other amendments adopted included:

● One by Kennedy, to stipulate that nothing in the bill was intended to interfere with an individual's First Amendment rights of free speech and peaceful assembly. The amendment — adopted by voice vote after the Senate failed to table it by a vote of 36-63 — was a substitute to an amendment offered by Coats. Coats' original amendment would have provided a legal cause of action for clinic protesters who were intimidated or interfered with during a peaceful and lawful protest at or near an abortion clinic. *(Vote 370, p. 48-S)*

● One by Kennedy and Barbara Boxer, D-Calif., to stipulate that the bill neither expanded nor limited states' rights to regulate the performance or availability of abortions. The Senate adopted the amendment by voice vote after rejecting a motion to table it by a vote of 35-64. The Kennedy-Boxer amendment was a substitute to language offered by Hatch that would have applied the bill's protections only to those performing legal abortions. Kennedy and others argued that the bill as written did not protect those performing illegal procedures and that Hatch's amendment would subject all abortion facilities to harassing searches of their records to ensure the legality of all services provided. *(Vote 371, p. 48-S)*

By a vote of 38-61, members rejected a full substitute to the bill offered by Hatch. The substitute included several of the previously defeated amendments, including differentiating between violent and non-violent demonstrations and stipulating that those performing illegal abortions would not be protected. *(Vote 372, p. 48-S)* ∎

Elders Is Confirmed as Surgeon General

After two months of acrimonious opposition from conservatives, the Senate on Sept. 7 voted 65-34 to approve Dr. Joycelyn Elders, a black Arkansas pediatrician, as surgeon general of the United States. She was sworn in the next morning. *(Vote 248, p. 60-H)*

The Senate Labor and Human Resources Committee had recommended Elders' confirmation by a vote of 13-4 on July 30. Elders won the support of all 10 committee Democrats, along with Republicans Nancy Landon Kassebaum, Kan.; James M. Jeffords, Vt.; and Dave Durenberger, Minn.

The Clinton administration wanted Elders confirmed before the monthlong August recess. But a handful of Republicans successfully blocked the Senate from taking up the matter until the Senate returned Sept. 7.

When the Senate voted, 13 Republicans backed Elders, some saying they did so because of her moving personal history or because of her ability to raise awareness about pressing issues such as teenage pregnancy. Four Democrats opposed Elders: Robert C. Byrd, W. Va.; Wendell H. Ford, Ky.; John B. Breaux, La.; and Jim Exon, Neb.

During her confirmation hearing July 23, Elders, 59, pledged to be "the voice and the vision for the poor and the powerless" and said she "would like to make every child born in America a planned, wanted child."

A sharecropper's daughter who did not visit a physician until she entered college, Elders attended medical school on the GI Bill after serving in the Army. She wrote extensively on children and the treatment of hormone-related illnesses, and in 1992 was selected as president of the Association of State and Territorial Health Officials.

Critics attacked Elders for her fiery rhetoric and firm views on politically charged issues such as abortion and teenage sex. They depicted her as a radical abortion rights proponent, labeled her the "condom queen" and recounted some of her most dramatic statements, including a suggestion that drug-addicted prostitutes use the birth control device Norplant, advice to teenage girls to carry condoms on dates, support for the use of marijuana for medicinal purposes and a remark that anti-abortion activists should get over their "love affair with the fetus."

"She continues to make a lot of statements that I find intolerant, radical, clearly out of the mainstream and offensive to hundreds of Americans," said Oklahoma Republican Don Nickles, who led the attack on Elders. Even some of the nominee's supporters expressed concerns that her personal style was more divisive than unifying. Kassebaum, ranking Republican on the Labor Committee, said she hoped Elders "builds consensus and will not be lost in controversy over the messenger."

Dale Bumpers, D-Ark., responded that Elders' forthrightness and no-nonsense manner would be an effective tool for the nation's top medical spokesperson. "Dr. Elders does not deal with niceties, and the reason is that the problems she has dealt with are not nice," he said.

The confirmation was also delayed by the administration's need for more time to clarify issues, including Elders' husband's failure to pay Social Security taxes for a nurse, Elders' role on the board of directors in the alleged mismanagement of the National Bank of Arkansas, and whether Elders exceeded state payroll limits as Clinton's Arkansas health director. ∎

NIH Bill Focuses on AIDS, Women's Health

After years of contention centering on fetal tissue research, Congress in 1993 finally reauthorized selected programs at the National Institutes of Health (NIH), the nation's premier biomedical research establishment.

President Clinton signed the three-year, $6.2 billion reauthorization measure (S 1 — PL 103-43) into law on June 10, closing another chapter in the fight over abortion policy that had raged between Congress and his Republican predecessors, Presidents George Bush and Ronald Reagan.

A year earlier, Bush had vetoed a similar measure because it would have lifted a 1988 Reagan administration ban on federal funding of research using fetal tissue from elective abortions. The House fell 14 votes short of the two-thirds majority needed to override that veto. *(1992 Almanac, p. 413)*

Clinton did not wait for Congress to reverse the Reagan-Bush policy. On Jan. 22, two days after his inauguration, he issued a memorandum to lift the funding ban. Bush and other opponents had argued that fetal tissue research might encourage women to have abortions. But Clinton sided with biomedical researchers and others who said transplants of fetal tissue offered great hope in finding treatments or even cures for such diseases as diabetes, Parkinson's disease and Alzheimer's disease.

S 1 codified Clinton's decision to permit federal funding of fetal tissue research and included rules designed to prevent abuses. *(Provisions, p. 363)*

BACKGROUND

The measure was the first full-scale NIH reauthorization to make it through Congress since 1988, although a limited version had cleared in 1990. Annual appropriations bills had kept the affected institutes operating in the meantime. *(1988 Almanac, p. 296; 1990 Almanac, p. 600)*

Most of NIH — a sprawling complex of 17 institutes — was covered by a permanent authorization that required no renewal by Congress. But periodic reauthorizations were required for the National Cancer Institute and the National Heart, Lung and Blood Institute, the two largest, plus the National Institute on Aging.

Highlights of Bill

Besides reauthorizing 16 institutes and creating a 17th, the National Institute of Nursing Research, S 1 included the following provisions:

● **AIDS Research.** The bill centralized AIDS research, planning and evaluation activities in the Office of AIDS Research. Previously, each of NIH's research institutes had

---

BOXSCORE

➡ **National Institutes of Health Reauthorization (S 1, HR 4).** The three-year, $6.2 billion reauthorization included provisions codifying President Clinton's decision to permit federal funding of fetal tissue research and banning permanent immigration by foreigners infected with the AIDS virus.

Reports: S Rept 103-2, H Rept 103-28; conference report, H Rept 103-100.

KEY ACTION

Jan. 26 — **Senate** Labor and Human Resources Committee approved the bill 16-0.

Feb. 18 — **Senate** passed S 1, 93-4.

March 2 — **House** Energy and Commerce Committee approved HR 4, 34-10.

March 11 — **House** passed HR 4, 283-131.

May 25 — **House** approved the conference report on S 1, 290-130.

May 28 — **Senate** cleared the bill by voice vote.

June 10 — **President** signed the bill into law (PL 103-43).

---

determined on its own which AIDS research to pursue. The AIDS office director — not the NIH director — was to make funding decisions for AIDS research at the various institutes. The bill also created a $100 million AIDS discretionary research fund to be distributed by the AIDS office for unfunded or underfunded projects.

The bill also gave the secretary of Health and Human Services authority to deny funding for a $2 million study at the University of Washington at Seattle seeking to determine whether telephone counseling could help homosexual men learn how to have safe sex. The researchers were required to show that the data being collected through the survey could not be obtained through any other procedure.

● **Cancer.** The measure authorized $3.2 billion in fiscal 1994 for the National Cancer Institute, including $2.7 billion for the cancer institute in general; $325 million specifically for breast cancer research; $75 million for research on other reproductive cancers; and $72 million for prostate cancer research. *(Breast cancer research, p. 360)*

It authorized unspecified sums for a breast cancer study in Nassau and Suffolk counties in New York and two other counties in the Northeast with high breast cancer rates. It also authorized a study of malnutrition in the elderly — those in hospitals and long-term care facilities as well as those living independently.

● **HIV, Immigration Ban.** Finally, the measure acknowledged in law that HIV, the virus that causes AIDS, was a communicable disease with significant implications for public health and specified that infection with HIV could be grounds for excluding immigrants and travelers from entering the United States. The provision applied to HIV-infected refugees, such as a group of Haitians who were held for nearly 20 months at Guantánamo Bay Naval Base in Cuba.

Just before Clinton signed the bill, a federal judge ruled June 8 that the government had to release the Haitian refugees and allow them to apply for asylum in the United States. The attorney general continued to have discretion to grant waivers from the HIV exclusion, particularly for short-term visits.

Congress had adopted an HIV immigration ban before, in 1987. The Senate had voted 96-0 for that provision, and the House had accepted it as part of a supplemental appropriations bill. *(1987 Almanac, p. 403)*

But in a 1990 immigration law, Congress decided that the secretary of Health and Human Services should decide which diseases posed a health threat and should be grounds for keeping out immigrants. Louis W. Sullivan, secretary of

Health and Human Services under President George Bush, subsequently moved to limit such exclusions to would-be immigrants with infectious tuberculosis. But Bush intervened to keep the HIV ban intact. *(1990 Almanac, p. 480)*

The ban applied to refugees as well as would-be immigrants. Many of those affected by the provision already were in the United States and were seeking legal residence.

Many public health officials challenged the exclusion policy because HIV was not spread by casual contact. During the presidential campaign, Clinton denounced the policy as "cynical politicization" and pledged to change it.

SENATE COMMITTEE ACTION

Freed from the politics of the abortion debate, the NIH bill won 16-0 approval from the Senate Labor and Human Resources Committee on Jan. 26 with none of the Republican dissent that had stalled the measure in past years.

"This is a different political climate," said Orrin G. Hatch of Utah, the chief opponent of lifting the fetal tissue ban. "My most significant concern . . . is now largely moot."

The bill codified Clinton's Jan. 22 action allowing fetal tissue research but also required the secretary of Health and Human Services to set up safeguards governing the conduct of such research. For example, the purchase or sale of human fetal tissue was prohibited, along with the direct donation of such tissue.

The Senate bill made no attempt to eliminate or sanction a tissue bank that Bush had ordered created in May 1992. The bank was to continue collecting tissue samples from miscarriages and ectopic, or "tubal," pregnancies. But, in a departure from a compromise crafted after the 1992 veto, researchers no longer had to turn to the bank first as a source of fetal tissue. Scientists generally had found it difficult to obtain usable tissue from miscarriages because most miscarriages occurred outside sterile hospital settings. Although tissue from ectopic pregnancies was usable, such pregnancies were rare.

New Additions to the Bill

The Senate bill was very similar to the vetoed 1992 version. But it contained a new provision designed to improve the coordination of AIDS research activities among NIH institutes.

The director of the Office of AIDS Research was given responsibility for overseeing all such agency research. The director also was to prepare a long-term plan to evaluate existing efforts toward a thorough AIDS research program. The director was to retain 25 percent of new research money for high-priority initiatives.

The bill also required the NIH to include more women, and racial and ethnic minorities in federally funded research. The Office of Research on Women's Health was authorized to ensure that women's health needs were addressed in research conducted or supported by NIH.

The committee-approved bill authorized $5.5 billion for expiring NIH programs for fiscal 1994, including $2.2 billion for the National Cancer Institute and $1.5 billion for the National Heart, Lung and Blood Institute. The bill included unspecified amounts for fiscal 1995 and 1996.

For fiscal 1994, the cancer institute also was authorized to spend $400 million for research on breast cancer and other gynecological cancers and $72 million for prostate cancer research.

Other Provisions

In other provisions, the committee bill:

● **Health-care costs.** Required the NIH to study the costs of health care during the last six months of patients' lives.

● **Science fraud.** Authorized the Office of Scientific Integrity to address charges of scientific misconduct.

● **Whistleblowers.** Required regulations to protect those who reported or cooperated in investigations concerning scientific misconduct.

● **Protection of health facilities.** Made it a crime to enter a federally funded health facility to alter or destroy records, release or injure laboratory animals, or damage property.

● **Contraceptive and infertility research.** Authorized $30 million in fiscal 1994 to operate research centers to study contraceptives and infertility.

● **Research facility construction.** Authorized $150 million in fiscal 1994 for the construction, expansion or renovation of public and nonprofit private research facilities.

● **Senior Biomedical Research Service.** Expanded from 350 to 750 the number of people who could serve at any one time in the Senior Biomedical Research Service. The service permitted senior clinical or biomedical research scientists to earn salaries higher than otherwise allowed under federal rules.

SENATE FLOOR ACTION

The Senate passed S 1, the NIH reauthorization bill, on Feb. 18 by a vote of 93-4. *(Vote 15, p. 3-S)*

For Democratic sponsors, the price of passage was an amendment by Don Nickles, R-Okla., codifying rules that prevented immigrants from taking up U.S. residence if they carried HIV.

Abortion Politics

Although the fetal tissue question was basically settled, the bill did not escape abortion politics altogether.

Jesse Helms, R-N.C., unsuccessfully sought to eliminate a provision to establish "ethics advisory boards" at NIH. The temporary boards were to be convened whenever the secretary of Health and Human Services decided to withhold research funds based on ethical grounds, such as banning fetal tissue research. The advisory board could overrule such a decision by majority vote.

Helms complained that yet another advisory panel would be unnecessary, could undermine the president's powers over agency decisions and most likely would be staffed by political appointees who would rubber-stamp a president's views.

But bill sponsor Edward M. Kennedy, D-Mass., chairman of the Labor Committee, said that what Helms really wanted was to ensure that a future president who might oppose fetal tissue research would not be stymied by an ethics advisory board. "This isn't about how many advisory panels there are. This is about fetal tissue transplantation," Kennedy said.

Nancy Landon Kassebaum, R-Kan., also defended the ethics boards, saying it would be wrong to "prejudge which way a panel is going to go" on future ethical issues.

Senators rejected Helms' amendment, 23-74. *(Vote 14, 3-S)*

Women's Health, AIDS Controversy

A major focus of the bill was a new emphasis on health research involving women and minorities.

The bill required increased participation of women in

clinical studies, ordered NIH to employ more women scientists, and increased funding for research on breast cancer, ovarian and cervical cancer, osteoporosis and reproductive health.

Children's health also got more attention. One initiative focused on the search for more affordable, improved vaccines, including study into an HIV vaccine for women, infants and children. Other provisions established new programs for study of children's cardiovascular disease and juvenile arthritis.

Inside NIH corridors, the most controversial provision was one bolstering the authority of the Office of AIDS Research, which Congress had created in 1987 to better coordinate research among the 21 NIH institutes, centers and divisions. Some lawmakers, as well as many NIH institute directors, complained that the AIDS office would have too much power, hinder the decision-making ability of the separate institutes and add an unneeded layer of bureaucracy.

Under a compromise that Kennedy and Kassebaum crafted, the secretary of Health and Human Services, rather than the president, was to appoint the director of the AIDS research office. The office was not set up to conduct its own research and was to directly control only the flow of new AIDS research, not existing studies.

HIV-Positive Immigrants

Most of the Senate debate over the NIH bill involved the Nickles amendment to bar entry into the United States of HIV-infected immigrants.

Within days of becoming president, Clinton had pledged to rescind the existing entry ban on people who had HIV, and administration officials in early February indicated that he was proceeding with plans to alter the policy. To pre-empt him, Nickles on Feb. 17 offered an amendment to keep the ban in place, saying it had prevented a potential influx of foreigners infected with HIV who might burden the health-care system and put Americans at risk.

His amendment won overwhelming approval, 76-23, with all but one Republican and 22 Democrats voting for it. *(Vote 13, p. 3-S)*

The vote came after senators defeated an alternative amendment by Kennedy, who sought to keep the ban in place for 90 days while the administration studied the cost and health implications of rescinding it. Kennedy's compromise fell, 42-56, when 19 Democrats joined 37 Republicans in voting against it. *(Vote 12, p. 3-S)*

The immigration debate took place against the grim backdrop of an ongoing hunger strike by HIV-infected Haitian refugees at Guantánamo. About 260 Haitians who had been cleared for political asylum hearings in the United States were being held at the naval base because they or their relatives tested positive for HIV.

Senators on both sides of the debate invoked the image of those refugees and other Haitians who might enter if the ban were lifted. Nickles said the cost of treating each AIDS patient was generally $100,000 or more, with at least some of that cost falling on the government.

"Why should we take on the medical expenses of Haiti?" agreed J. Bennett Johnston, D-La.

Existing law allowed the government to keep out immigrants who were likely to become a "public charge" or to deport any who became dependent on state support within five years. Opponents of the HIV immigration ban said this provision was sufficient to protect against a potential drain on public resources.

But Nickles said he did not trust the Clinton administration to enforce that provision. Other senators stressed the risk of HIV-infected immigrants spreading the disease.

Clinton's supporters, led by Kennedy, said public health officials did not see a medical basis for the HIV-exclusion rule. Kennedy noted that senators who backed the exclusion had not voiced the same concerns about the financial burden posed by immigrants with cancer or with other costly diseases.

Instead, Kennedy suggested, it was racism and anti-homosexual sentiment that motivated support for Nickles' amendment, as well as a possible desire to "get a hit in on the president."

Nickles denied that was the case.

The vote on the amendment came just two weeks after Senate Democrats blocked a similar assault on Clinton's controversial plan to let homosexuals serve in the military. *(Gays in the military, p. 454)*

This time, however, Democrats appeared less willing to brave political fire, and the White House did not press them. Several Democratic senators said administration officials had not contacted them, generating no extra pressure to vote against Nickles' amendment.

The Nickles amendment notwithstanding, the administration retained authority to grant various exemptions. In addition, Nickles' amendment specifically allowed the attorney general to grant waivers to those entering the country for medical treatment, tourism or other short-term visits.

HOUSE SUBCOMMITTEE ACTION

The NIH reauthorization began moving through the House less than a week after it passed the Senate.

On Feb. 24, the House Energy and Commerce Subcommittee on Health and the Environment voted 20-6 to approve HR 4, a bill reauthorizing NIH, increasing its funding, streamlining AIDS research and emphasizing research involving women and minorities.

As in the Senate, subcommittee members barely mentioned the once-divisive issue of fetal tissue transplants.

Members sparred, however, over an amendment offered by subcommittee Chairman Henry A. Waxman, D-Calif., that authorized the Office of AIDS Research to distribute research dollars among NIH's institutes and write an overall AIDS research plan. Under existing law, each of the 21 NIH institutes, centers and divisions got its own AIDS research money, and no entity within NIH set AIDS spending priorities.

A substitute amendment, offered by ranking minority member Thomas J. Bliley Jr., R-Va., failed 12-13. It would have stripped the AIDS office of its power to distribute funds, leaving it with far less leverage over the institutes' research decisions. Bliley, with the backing of NIH institute directors, argued that the AIDS office would add bureaucracy and remove knowledgeable scientists from decisions about what research should be done.

Bliley also failed in an effort to attach a provision to the bill similar to the Nickles amendment in the Senate banning immigration by people infected with the AIDS virus.

The House bill authorized $472 million for breast, ovarian and prostate cancer research and $30 million for contraception and infertility research. It created an Office of Research on Women's Health and mandated that women and minorities be involved in clinical trials of drugs and

Funding Levels Soar 160 Percent . . .

The enactment of a bill (S 1) reauthorizing the National Institutes of Health (NIH) marked another in a string of victories for advocates of increased spending for breast cancer research.

Congress agreed to authorize an additional $325 million specifically for such research at the National Cancer Institute, the premier government-funded cancer research facility. That was about a 160 percent increase over the fiscal 1993 appropriation. While appropriations rarely matched authorizations, the boost did indicate the depth of support for higher spending. Indeed, over the preceding five years, total appropriations for breast cancer had grown 450 percent. No other cancer research received such increases.

Joanne Howes, a lobbyist for the National Breast Cancer Coalition, said of the increases, "You can directly attribute the success to the grass-roots advocacy of the women, and most of them are breast cancer survivors."

Even some who criticized the coalition's exclusive focus expressed admiration. "They have been phenomenally successful," said Stacey Beckhardt, who represented the American Society of Clinical Oncology.

A Skewing of Priorities?

However, the infusion of earmarked money gave pause even to some researchers who specialized in breast cancer, not to mention those who worked on other cancers and saw their funding levels remain virtually flat. Spending at the National Cancer Institute overall had increased 25 percent over the past several years, a fraction of the increase for breast cancer — which meant that breast cancer's gain was a loss for other cancer research.

Several cancer and biomedical research groups, including the clinical oncologists, supported additional spending for all cancer research but opposed the earmarking of research funds for particular cancers.

The continuing increase for breast cancer research also disturbed some scientists who said it might be out of kilter with statistics on which cancers were most deadly. While both breast and lung cancer were leading cancer killers of women, more women died annually of lung cancer. And while breast cancer mortality rates had remained steady for more than a decade, lung cancer mortality rates for women had risen 71.7 percent since 1973.

Behind the controversy lay a longstanding philosophical debate: Should politicians earmark dollars for the study of specific diseases, or should they leave the decision to scientists?

When politicians decided, they often did so based on political pressure or personal experience with a disease.

On the other hand, when the decisions were left to scientists, research into diseases that afflict women and minorities often got short shrift. A 1990 study by the General Accounting Office found that NIH did not require the inclusion of women or minorities in clinical trials of new treatments. As a result, research often failed to reflect their specific problems.

"Historically, there has never been enough money to fund everything, and somebody has always made the decision to fund X instead of Y, and those decisions were always made at the expense of women," said Fran Visco, coalition president.

Research Outcomes Hard to Predict

But scientists said the civil rights concepts used to remedy inequalities in the workplace did not readily apply to medical research.

"Many of the major discoveries in breast cancer have come from research that wasn't targeted towards any particular cancer," said Dr. Daniel C. Ihde, deputy director of the National Cancer Institute.

For instance, Ihde pointed out, scientists discovered a gene that suppressed tumors while doing research on viruses that caused pneumonia. When the gene mutated in breast cancer patients, their prognosis was worse — information important in treatment, Ihde said. "There would have been no way to predict at the time of the

treatments. Those provisions were lifted from the research title of the Women's Health Equity Act, first introduced in 1990 with the backing of the Congressional Caucus for Women's Issues. Portions of the act had been included in various pending bills.

The bill also mandated a study on adolescent health, a particular interest of Patricia Schroeder, D-Colo., and authorized $50 million to develop children's vaccines.

HOUSE FULL COMMITTEE ACTION

Despite some partisan infighting over an effort to channel breast cancer study funds to New York, the House Energy and Commerce Committee on March 2 approved HR 4 by a vote of 34-10. The measure was similar in most respects to the Senate-passed S 1.

Committee members offered several amendments to the bill, including one by Cliff Stearns, R-Fla., that was similar to Nickles' Senate amendment barring HIV-infected immigrants. However, Stearns' proposal was ruled non-germane

to the NIH bill, which dealt primarily with biomedical research.

An unexpected and bitterly partisan spat broke out between Waxman and Bliley over an amendment that Waxman had added to the bill in subcommittee earmarking funds for a breast cancer study for Nassau and Suffolk counties on Long Island in New York. The amendment did not set aside new money but did require that some of the $225 million authorized for breast cancer research nationwide in fiscal 1994 be spent on the Long Island study.

In arguing against the earmark, Bliley pointed out that Waxman's administrative assistant, Philip Schiliro, ran unsuccessfully in 1992 for the House seat that encompassed much of Nassau County. (The seat was captured by Republican David A. Levy.) Armed with information from NIH, Bliley argued that there were other counties in New York and nationwide with higher breast cancer rates. He offered an amendment requiring that the study be done in the two counties in the nation with the highest breast cancer rates.

Waxman, also waving information from NIH, countered

...For Breast Cancer Research At NIH

virus research that it would have a major clinical application in breast cancer, and certainly it would never have been labeled as breast cancer research," he said.

Breast cancer researcher Dr. Larry Norton underscored that pouring money into specific research did not necessarily mean scientists would find a cure.

"You can't legislate creativity in science any more than you can in art," said Norton, chief of the Breast and Gynecological Cancer Medicine Service at Memorial Sloan-Kettering Cancer Center in New York. "But the one thing we know for sure is that if the field is unfunded, no advance occurs at all."

Norton noted that scientists made one of their most exciting breast cancer discoveries while researching brain tumors in rats. They found a gene that also turned out to be present in breast cancer tumors. The research would not have been funded by dollars earmarked for breast cancer studies, he said. "You want to really support the best research no matter where it is because all of science is so interrelated," he said.

Ihde said scientists should continue intense research into breast cancer because its cause was unknown. In contrast, the incidence of lung cancer in women could be traced to the increasing number of women who smoked cigarettes.

More money, however, should be going into the treatment of lung cancer, Beckhardt said. Americans who had lung cancer had a 13 percent chance of survival, while women who had breast cancer had a 78 percent chance of survival. "Lung cancer is pretty much a death sentence. Breast cancer we're doing better with," Beckhardt said. "We get dismayed by the lack of attention to treatment research."

A Relatively New Lobby

The breast cancer lobby, a relative newcomer to Capitol Hill that drew much of its strength from breast cancer survivor groups, was well-known among lawmakers. Congressional staff members described the lobbyists with a mixture of admiration and frustration as "tenacious" and "persistent."

Their campaign began in earnest in 1991, when the Breast Cancer Coalition hired Bass and Howes, a Washington firm with a successful record lobbying on women's health issues. The firm also worked on ending the ban on fetal tissue research and educating members and the public about RU-486, also known as the French abortion pill.

One of the coalition's first goals was to deliver to Congress and the White House 175,000 letters — a number reflecting the projected diagnoses that year — requesting more research dollars for breast cancer. Success was overwhelming: 600,000 letters went to lawmakers. Appropriations for fiscal 1992 increased to $145 million, up about $52 million over fiscal 1991, a 55 percent increase.

In 1992, the coalition convened a conference of breast cancer researchers in Washington. "We asked them, 'How much money could you spend this year?'" Howes recalled. Said the researchers: $300 million.

Howes and coalition members set to work. They got only about $50 million added to the appropriations bill that funded NIH. So they turned to Sen. Tom Harkin, D-Iowa, whose two sisters had died of breast cancer. With help from him and Sen. Alfonse M. D'Amato, R-N.Y., both members of the Appropriations Committee, $210 million was added to the Defense Department appropriations bill for breast cancer research to be done by the Army. *(1992 Almanac, p. 601)*

Several observers attributed the success to the coalition's ability to make breast cancer funding a way for members of Congress — especially men — to show their commitment to women's health even if they opposed abortion rights.

"The men are afraid to vote against money for breast cancer," Beckhardt said. "It has become such a powerful issue that to vote against breast cancer research is to vote against women."

---

that while other counties had higher rates in recent years, none had such high rates for the period from 1953 to 1987. Bliley replied that 16 counties, according to his research, had higher rates than Nassau during the period cited by Waxman. Waxman said the other counties had not done studies in the past, so comparisons could not be made. Several committee Democrats jumped in to defend Waxman, including Craig Washington, D-Texas, who said that his mother had died of cancer.

The argument went on for 20 minutes, until committee Chairman John D. Dingell, D-Mich., after describing his mother's death from cancer, said he was troubled by the "differences" between "two such valuable members of the committee."

After Dingell's remarks, Bliley offered to withdraw his amendment and Dingell asked staff members to work matters out. Dingell made clear he was not convinced that Waxman's earmark was appropriate. "I am troubled that ... we may end up with a bill that skews breast cancer research," he said.

Fetal Tissue Banks

By voice vote, the committee approved a Waxman amendment that nullified the Bush administration's executive order requiring NIH to create fetal tissue banks to collect tissue from ectopic pregnancies and miscarriages instead of elective abortions. The effect of the amendment was to leave it up to NIH to decide whether to continue such tissue banks.

In another action, the committee rejected, 17-27, an amendment by Bliley that would have required that only doctors, not other health professionals in an abortion clinic, inform women about fetal research regulations. The effect of this amendment would have been to slow the collection of fetal tissue.

HOUSE FLOOR ACTION

The House passed HR 4 on March 11 by a vote of 283-131. The bill authorized $6.6 billion in fiscal 1994 and unspecified sums through 1996. *(Vote 69, p. 18-H)*

In most respects, the three-year reauthorization was similar to the Senate-passed bill. Much of the content of the measure was never discussed — even though the bill marked a turning point in NIH funding for women's health research and increased attention to AIDS research.

In the $3.7 billion House authorization for cancer research, $325 million was designated for breast cancer and $72 million for prostate cancer.

The House bill also authorized $100 million for special projects in the Office of AIDS Research and $30 million for contraception and infertility research. The bill authorized $500 million for the Institute on Aging.

These specific authorizations, strongly supported by the Congressional Caucus for Women's Issues, drew criticism from some Republicans, who charged that the bill's Democratic authors were substituting their research opinions for those of scientists.

The Immigrant Issue

House leaders barred consideration of a floor amendment similar to the Senate amendment banning HIV-infected immigrants. But many members wanted to accept the Senate ban. The House by 356-58 approved a nonbinding motion by Bliley to instruct House conferees on the bill to accept the Senate's provision. *(Vote 70, p. 18-H)*

"The issue is a lot more complicated than some people think it is," said Waxman, who nonetheless supported the motion to instruct conferees. "How would you implement such a policy?" he said. "Do you intend to stop business travelers and tourists? Would we intend to send refugees back to dictator governments just because the refugees are HIV-positive?"

Supporters of the ban offered three points in its favor: AIDS was always fatal, treatment was costly, and it was dangerous to add to the pool of infected people who could spread the disease.

Several Republicans who backed proposals to add the AIDS restrictions to the bill cited medical costs as a primary concern.

Proponents of the ban also cited health risks. "Why take the risk of adding one more possible person who could spread that disease to an innocent victim?" said Bill McCollum, R-Fla., ranking member of the Judiciary Committee's immigration panel.

Opponents of the ban pointed out that the government already had the authority to exclude immigrants likely to become public charges. And they cited numerous public health officials who argued that AIDS should not be singled out for immigration purposes, distinct from other diseases not spread through casual contact.

Mike Synar, D-Okla., who opposed the immigration restriction, said the votes reflected anti-homosexual sentiment as well as legitimate concern about medical costs.

But Charles B. Rangel, D-N.Y., said he saw something else at play in the vote: racism toward the black Haitians being held at Guantánamo. Rangel said the prospect of admitting those refugees guided many to vote to codify the HIV ban. By contrast, 27 of the 58 votes against codifying the ban came from black lawmakers.

The fate of the Haitians was also on the minds of some people supporting the ban. Gerald B. H. Solomon, R-N.Y., spoke on the floor about the cost of providing health care for the refugees. And several Republican lawmakers from Florida, which had absorbed many of the Haitian immigrants, were among those speaking in favor of the ban.

But McCollum said proponents of the ban were concerned primarily about immigration and health policy, not the Haitians specifically.

By taking pre-emptive action to codify the HIV ban, the Republicans caught Democrats without a well-prepared response. The immediate reaction of most was to oppose a change that might allow more HIV-infected people into the country. And the administration did not appear prepared to expend political capital on the volatile issue. There was no evident White House lobbying before the Senate or House votes, and White House Press Secretary Dee Dee Myers said Clinton was unlikely to push the issue over strong congressional objections.

Project Aries

A minor but perhaps symbolic fight over how the country viewed homosexuality surfaced when the House voted 278-139 to strip NIH funding from a little-known study at the University of Washington involving gay and bisexual men. The amendment was sponsored by Sam Johnson, R-Texas. *(Vote 68, p. 18-H)*

Known as Project Aries, the $2 million, three-year telephone counseling project offered homosexuals a way to discuss safer sex habits without having to walk into an AIDS center or other public place, where they might feel uncomfortable. The project had a toll-free telephone number, and men who called were screened before being accepted into the counseling program, which consisted of several months of conference calls with other gay men and the researchers.

Johnson credited the strong support he got to budget-cutting sentiment and distaste for a program in which homosexual men discussed their sexual habits on the telephone.

"Members said to me they didn't think taxpayer money should be used for that type of thing," he said.

Others said the amendment was a slap at Clinton and his efforts to ease discrimination against homosexuals. "My sense is that coming after the matter of the gays in the military, some say, 'Here's a chance to give the president a hard time around issues connected to gays,'" said Ron Wyden, D-Ore.

Other Amendments

The House approved 250-161 an amendment by Bliley that had been modified substantially by Waxman. The modified amendment dealt with the donation of fetal tissue, requiring that physicians certify that abortions in which fetal tissue was donated were performed in accordance with state law. *(Vote 64, p. 16-H)*

In an earlier vote March 10, including delegates from territories and the District of Columbia, the same language was approved 261-162. Before it was modified by Waxman, Bliley's amendment had included other constraints. *(Vote 61, p. 16-H)*

The House also approved, 350-67, a Waxman amendment requiring that an ongoing study of breast cancer in New England include a study of environmental causes of breast cancer in Nassau and Suffolk counties on Long Island, N.Y., as well as two other counties in the Northeast that had high breast cancer rates, as determined by NIH. The amendment also established an Office of Alternative Medicine within NIH. *(Vote 65, p. 16-H)*

Also approved, 305-109, was an amendment offered by Benjamin A. Gilman, R-N.Y. requiring NIH to study back pain and back injuries. *(Vote 66, p. 16-H)*

An amendment by Doug Bereuter, R-Neb. to freeze

NIH spending at the fiscal 1993 level failed 193-234. *(Vote 62, p. 16-H)*

CONFERENCE/FINAL

House and Senate negotiators on May 20 filed a conference report (H Rept 103-100) on the final version of S 1, including the ban on permanent immigration by foreigners infected with the AIDS virus.

The issue of excluding HIV-infected foreigners was the key sticking point in the conference. The administration did not fight to keep the HIV provision out of the conference report, although some conferees opposed it. Waxman and Kennedy sought at least to tone down the ban in conference.

What negotiators adopted was a modification of the Nickles language offered by McCollum. It banned permanent immigration by HIV-infected foreigners, including refugees, but left policy details to the attorney general. Under existing guidelines, the government generally did not test or restrict entry of short-term visitors.

The final bill included the House provision — which was not in the Senate version — codifying Clinton's order lifting the Reagan-Bush ban on fetal tissue research. The conference report included rules designed to prevent abuses, such as banning the sale of fetal tissue.

Final Action

The House on May 25 adopted the conference report on S 1 by a vote of 290-130. The Senate cleared the bill for the president by voice vote on May 28. *(Vote 178, p. 44-H)*

Although some House members opposed the House-Senate conference report because it codified Clinton's fetal tissue research decision, the issue no longer had the potency to stymie the bill. It did, however, account for many of the "nay" votes against the conference report.

The ban on permanent immigration by HIV-infected foreigners was the major point of conflict in the final bill.

On the House floor, Waxman denounced the immigration language as "a simple question of discrimination." But he said he would not block the NIH bill on that basis, because the HIV-exclusion had broad support and doubtless would pop up elsewhere.

Some Republicans also complained that Congress was seeking to micromanage the health institutes with overly detailed requirements about which illnesses to research and how.

Bliley said the bill would "impede, not enhance" work at NIH.

But mostly the bill drew praise, particularly from female lawmakers and others who said it would redress past discrimination against the health concerns of women. ∎

NIH Reauthorization Bill Provisions

Congress on May 28 cleared legislation (S 1) reauthorizing portions of the National Institutes of Health, the nation's premier biomedical research establishment. President Clinton signed the bill into law (PL 103-43) on June 10. Following are the measure's major provisions:

Ethics

● **Ethical review boards.** Permitted the secretary of Health and Human Services (HHS), after public notice, to convene an ethics advisory board to examine the ethical implications of any NIH project. The board was to be made up of 14 to 20 people, none of whom could work for the federal government. Members were required to have expertise in biomedical and behavioral ethics and were to include at least one lawyer, one physician, one ethicist and one theologian. The board was to report within six months to the secretary, to the Senate Committee on Labor and Human Resources and to the House Committee on Energy and Commerce. The secretary could withhold funding for a project only if a majority of the board recommended doing so.

Fetal Tissue Research

● **Fetal tissue transplant moratorium.** Stipulated that neither the secretary nor any executive branch official could prohibit research on the transplantation of fetal tissue. The secretary could withhold funds only in the case of a violation of fetal tissue research guidelines.
● **Research on transplantation of fetal tissue.** Authorized funding for research on "the transplantation of fetal tissue for therapeutic purposes." Scientists hoped to learn more about Alzheimer's, Parkinson's and other diseases through research using transplanted fetal tissue. The tissue could be obtained from induced abortions, as well as from stillbirths and miscarriages.
● **Safeguards for use of fetal tissue.** Required the woman providing the tissue to sign a statement declaring that she was donating fetal tissue for research, that she understood she could

not designate the recipient of the tissue and that she was not aware of the recipient's identity. The physician performing the abortion was to certify that the woman gave her consent to have an abortion before she was asked about the fetal tissue donation. The physician also had to disclose any financial or other interest in the subsequent research as well as any known medical risks.
● **Prohibitions on the use of fetal tissue.** Prohibited the sale or purchase of human fetal tissue from induced abortions and any donation intended for a specific person, including a relative of the donor. This was intended to prohibit a woman from getting pregnant in order to have an abortion and donate the tissue to a family member, for instance. Violators could be imprisoned for up to 10 years.

Women's Health Research

● **Inclusion of women and minorities in clinical research funded by NIH.** Generally required that women and members of racial and ethnic minority groups be included as subjects in NIH-funded research projects. Exceptions were permitted if, for example, such inclusion would threaten the health of the research subjects. The bill stipulated that the cost of including women and minorities was not a permissible reason to exclude them from a research project. Women and minorities could be excluded if there were scientific reasons to assume the variables being studied did not affect women or minorities differently than white men.

The NIH director, in consultation with the director of the Office of Research on Women's Health and the Office of Research on Minority Health, was to create a program to recruit women and minorities as research subjects. Guidelines were to be published within 180 days of enactment.
● **Office of Research on Women's Health.** Authorized a women's health research office within the office of the NIH director. The office — which was created in 1990 but had never been formally authorized — was to ensure that women's health issues were identified and addressed in research activities.
● **Biennial report.** Beginning Feb. 1, 1994, required that a

report on the progress made in women's health research and treatment conducted or supported by the NIH be included in the NIH's biennial report to the president and Congress.

● **Data system and clearinghouse on research on women's health.** Required the creation of a single data system to collect and disseminate information regarding research on women's health conducted or supported by the NIH.

NIH-Wide Programs

● **Children's vaccine initiative.** Required the HHS secretary, in consultation with the director of the National Vaccine Program and the directors of other institutes and public and private programs, to develop affordable and improved vaccines. The vaccines were to provide long-lasting protection, require fewer contacts to deliver, not require refrigeration, needles or syringes, and protect against a large number of diseases. Authorized $20 million in fiscal 1994.

● **NIH director discretionary fund.** Authorized $25 million in fiscal 1994 and unspecified sums for fiscal 1995 through fiscal 1996 for a fund that the NIH director could use for such purposes as research that did not fit clearly into the assignment of any existing institute or to respond to scientific emergencies and new issues.

● **Plan for use of animals in research.** Required the NIH director to prepare a plan to study research methods that did not require the use of animals, methods that could reduce the number of animals needed in research and methods that reduced the amount of pain and distress for animals used in research.

● **Surveys of sexual behavior.** Stipulated that surveys of human sexual behavior to be funded by the NIH had to meet the same ethical and peer-review requirements as other research using human subjects, and that information to be obtained had to be expected to assist in reducing the incidence of sexually transmitted diseases, including AIDS, and in improving reproductive health or other health conditions.

● **Office of Alternative Medicine.** Established an Office of Alternative Medicine within NIH, responsible for the evaluation of alternative medical treatment including acupuncture, Oriental medicine, homeopathic medicine and physical manipulation therapies. The bill required the office director to establish an information clearinghouse to exchange information with the public about alternative medicine. The office had existed for several years but did not have statutory authority, which gave it more permanence.

● **Program of research on osteoporosis and related bone disorders.** Authorized $40 million in fiscal 1994 and unspecified sums through fiscal 1996 for research on osteoporosis, Paget's disease and related bone disorders. These conditions afflicted about 27 million Americans.

● **Interagency Program for Trauma Research.** Required establishment of a comprehensive program to conduct and support research on all aspects of trauma, the leading cause of death and disability in children and young adults.

● **National Research Service Awards Program.** Authorized $400 million for the National Research Service Awards for fiscal 1994 and unspecified sums for fiscal 1995 and fiscal 1996. The program provided funds for individuals and institutions for the training of research scientists. The bill authorized grants for programs to recruit women, underrepresented minorities and people from disadvantaged backgrounds into biomedical or behavioral research.

● **Senior Biomedical Research Service.** Redesignated the Senior Biomedical Research Service as the Silvio Conte Senior Biomedical Research Service, honoring the late Massachusetts representative. Conte was the ranking Republican on the Appropriations subcommittee that oversaw NIH and an ardent backer of biomedical research funding. The provision also raised from 350 to 500 the number of researchers who could participate in the service at one time. The service allowed high-level researchers to be paid higher salaries than otherwise would be allowed under federal guidelines.

● **Loan repayment program.** Required establishment of a program to repay up to $20,000 per year in student loans for health professionals who agreed to conduct research at NIH on contraception and infertility, AIDS, or in a research area of demonstrated need. A separate program established a similar, $20,000-per-year loan repayment program for minorities or people from underprivileged backgrounds who agreed to conduct clinical work at NIH.

National Foundation for Biomedical Research

● **Purpose.** Created a foundation to advance NIH collaboration with biomedical researchers in universities, industry and nonprofit organizations. The foundation could solicit and accept gifts, grants and other donations, and spend the money to support scientific research.

● **Supplementary programs.** The foundation was to hire or recruit foreign scientists to do research in the United States and support scientists working on international projects. The foundation also was to support science education in elementary, secondary and postsecondary schools.

● **Authorization.** Authorized $200,000 for fiscal 1994 and 1995.

National Cancer Institute

● **Authorization.** Authorized $2.73 billion for fiscal 1994 and unspecified sums for fiscal 1995 and 1996.

● **Breast cancer.** Authorized $225 million for research on the causes of and cures for breast cancer, and $100 million for prevention, detection and treatment in fiscal 1994, and unspecified sums for fiscal 1995 and 1996. This was the first time that the bill had earmarked an authorization for a particular cancer.

● **Female reproductive system cancers.** Authorized $75 million for research on the cause, detection and cure of ovarian and other reproductive system cancers in fiscal 1994 and unspecified sums for fiscal 1995 and 1996.

● **Prostate cancer.** Authorized $72 million for research on the cause, prevention, detection and treatment of prostate cancer in fiscal 1994 and unspecified sums in fiscal 1995 and 1996.

National Heart, Lung and Blood Institute

● **Authorization.** Authorized $1.5 billion for fiscal 1994 and unspecified sums for fiscal 1995 and 1996.

National Institute on Aging

● **Authorization.** Authorized $500 million for fiscal 1994 and unspecified sums for fiscal 1995 and 1996, the institute's first separate authorization. The provision authorized research on the aging processes of women, with special concentration on the effects of menopause and the physiological and biological changes that accompany menopause.

National Institute on Allergy and Infectious Diseases

● **Chronic fatigue syndrome.** Authorized the development of centers to conduct basic and clinical research on the condition known as chronic fatigue syndrome.

National Institute on Child Health and Human Development

● **Research centers on contraception and infertility.** Authorized $30 million in fiscal 1994 and unspecified sums in fiscal 1995 and 1996 to establish research centers to study improved methods of contraception and infertility treatment.

● **Child health research centers.** Authorized existing child health research centers established by the National Institute on Child Health and Human Development. Most of the centers were at universities.

National Library of Medicine

● **Authorization.** Authorized $150 million for the National Library of Medicine, including grants to medical libraries and nonprofit biomedical publications for fiscal 1994, and unspecified sums for fiscal 1995 and 1996.

● **National Information Center on Health Services Research and Health-Care Technology.** Established a center for the collection, storage, analysis and dissemination of information on clinical practice guidelines, health-care technologies and health-services research.

AIDS and AIDS Research

● **Office of AIDS Research.** Created an Office of AIDS Research to oversee and evaluate all AIDS research within the NIH. The office's director was to be the primary federal official responsible for AIDS research and was to represent NIH at all executive branch task force and other committee meetings on AIDS research. This provision augmented the authority of the AIDS office, giving it more power to coordinate AIDS research activity.

● **AIDS plan and budget.** Required the office to write a plan setting priorities for AIDS research throughout the NIH by June 1994 and to revise the plan annually. The AIDS director was to submit a budget for carrying out the plan to the president as well as to the NIH director.

● **AIDS emergency discretionary fund.** Authorized the creation of a $100 million fund each year from fiscal 1994 through fiscal 1996 for unanticipated research projects. The fund was designed to allow the AIDS office to respond to the rapid pace of AIDS research, augment funding for existing research or fund promising new projects.

● **Exclusion of aliens infected with HIV.** Codified existing policy that AIDS was a public health threat and that infection with the HIV virus was a basis for excluding immigrants from entering the United States. The provision was aimed particularly at immigrants seeking permanent residence and refugees. The attorney general continued to have discretion to grant waivers from the HIV exclusion, particularly for short-term visits.

Other Agencies

● **National Institute for Nursing Research.** Redesignated the National Center for Nursing Research as the National Institute for Nursing Research, giving it additional prestige and potentially more clout in dealing with Congress. The nursing center thus became NIH's 17th institute.

● **National Center for Human Genome Research.** Authorized the National Center for Human Genome Research, which since 1989 had been coordinating and supporting efforts to map all human genes. The bill stipulated that at least 5 percent of available funding be reserved for projects to examine the ethical issues associated with the genome project. Official authorization as a center was its first step toward becoming an institute.

● **National Eye Institute.** Authorized research grants to one or more diabetes eye research institutions. Diabetes, which afflicted 14 million Americans, was the leading cause of new cases of blindness.

● **Division of Research Resources.** Redesignated the Division of Research Resources as the National Center for Research Resources. The agency oversaw the provision of equipment, laboratory animals and other supplies needed for research.

● **Research facility construction.** Authorized $150 million for fiscal 1993 and unspecified sums through fiscal 1996 for competitive matching grants to expand or renovate existing biomedical or behavioral research facilities or to construct new facilities. Up to $5 million was reserved for renovation of regional primate centers, where the most sophisticated animal research was done on AIDS and other diseases.

● **Toxicological research and testing.** Required the National Institute of Environmental Health Sciences to establish a program on the health effects of environmental agents, including selected chemicals. The program already existed but had not been authorized. The provision also required research on ways to reduce and eventually eliminate the use of animals in testing the toxicity of chemical agents such as pesticides.

● **Multiple sclerosis research.** Required the National Institute of Neurological Disorders and Stroke to conduct and support research on multiple sclerosis, including research on the effects of genetics and hormonal changes on the progress of the disease.

Scientific Integrity

● **Office of Scientific Integrity.** Authorized the Office of Scientific Integrity outside NIH and under the secretary of Health and Human Services. The office, which already existed, was to monitor investigations carried out by universities and other recipients of NIH funding, as well as conduct independent investigations of potential scientific misconduct.

● **Whistleblower protection.** Required regulations to protect those who reported or cooperated in investigations of scientific misconduct.

● **Financial conflicts of interest.** Required regulations establishing criteria to prevent scientists from having financial interests that might be in conflict or appear to be in conflict with their federal research or administrative responsibilities. The regulations were to guard against situations in which a researcher would have a bias in favor of obtaining a certain result or situations that could "be reasonably expected" to create such a bias.

Studies

● **Adolescent study.** Authorized a study of adolescent health, and the behaviors and environments that promote or detract from good health in this age group.

● **Chronic pain conditions.** Authorized a study of chronic pain, including back injuries, and the effect of such cases on the cost of health care.

● **Life-threatening illnesses.** Authorized a study of the policies of insurance companies regarding coverage of clinical trial medications for terminally ill patients, including those with cancer or AIDS.

● **Malnutrition in the elderly.** Authorized a three-year study of the nutritional status of the elderly and of efforts to provide the elderly with appropriate nutrition.

● **Breast cancer study.** Authorized a study of environmental causes and other potential risk factors contributing to breast cancer frequency in Nassau and Suffolk counties in Long Island, N.Y., and in two other counties in the Northeast with high mortality rates from the disease.

● **Cost of care in last six months of life.** Authorized a study of the average health-care expenditures incurred during the last six months of life.

● **Conditional prohibition against funding for Project Aries.** Authorized the termination of funding for a study at the University of Washington that used telephone counseling to help gay men learn about safe sex, provided that another way could be found to accomplish the same results.

● **Biological warfare.** Required the HHS secretary to report to Congress on "the appropriateness and impact" of giving NIH responsibility for research on the medical aspects of developing defenses for biological warfare. ■

Health-Care Reform Begins in Budget Bill

In what the Clinton administration described as a "down payment" on health reform, the budget-reconciliation bill that squeaked through Congress in August included a raft of health-related changes, most notably provisions to trim nearly $63 billion over five years from Medicare and Medicaid, the two principal federally funded health programs.

Spiraling health costs made the two big health entitlements obvious targets for deficit cutting. And indeed, one of every four dollars of the $255 billion in spending cuts in the bill (HR 2264) came from health accounts. But the bill also included provisions redirecting some of the nation's health-care dollars toward preventive and primary care and toward improving children's health — two major administration themes for health reform. Key among them was the creation of a new $1.5 billion entitlement to pay for immunizations to protect children against preventable diseases. President Clinton signed the bill into law (PL 103-66) on Aug. 10

The deepest cuts in the bill were made in Medicare, the federal health insurance program for the elderly and disabled. Under the bill, Medicare was projected to grow by $55.8 billion less than it would have without the cuts. The bill also sought to slow the rising costs of Medicaid, the joint federal-state health plan for the poor, by $7.1 billion over five years.

Unlike many of the previous deficit-reduction bills, the cuts this time were deep enough to be felt by Medicare beneficiaries as well as doctors, hospitals and other providers of care. The bill, for example, made it more difficult for the elderly to "spend down" their savings and qualify for long-term care services under Medicaid. Some analysts predicted that doctors might take fewer Medicare patients because of reduced payments.

During the 1980s, the almost annual deficit-reduction measures were the primary vehicle not only for spending changes to Medicare and Medicaid but also for important policy changes, such as the 1990 overhaul of federal rules regarding the sale of private "Medigap" policies to supplement Medicare coverage. *(1990 Almanac, p. 572)*

New Senate rules, however, made such non-spending changes more difficult to include in the budget-reconciliation bill. As a result, a raft of House-passed provisions, including several waivers of the federal Employee Retirement Income Security Act (ERISA) sought by states trying to enact their own health-reform plans, were dropped from the final bill.

One far-reaching non-spending change that did make it into the final bill clamped down hard on "self-referrals," recommendations doctors made to patients to go to facilities offering X-rays, physical therapy or medical equipment — facilities in which the doctors had a financial interest. The 1989 budget bill (PL 101-239) banned Medicare and Medicaid payments for physician self-referrals to clinical laboratories in which the doctors had an interest. The 1993 bill continued that ban and extended the self-referral prohibitions to a variety of other services. *(1989 Almanac, p. 167)*

BACKGROUND

The 1993 budget battle began in February, when Clinton presented his economic plan to a joint session of Congress.

Health and Human Services Secretary Donna E. Shalala described the health cuts proposed in the plan as "the first down payment on health-care reform," designed to complement the more far-reaching changes that ultimately would be included in the president's health-reform bill. Indeed, many of the proposals in the initial budget package were familiar ones, having been proposed in earlier years by Presidents Ronald Reagan and George Bush, but never adopted by Congress.

Due to recalculations and new economic assumptions, the Clinton budget sent to Congress in April called for fiscal 1994 savings of $2.9 billion, about $300 million less than the $3.2 billion projected in February. Over five years, the package contained projected savings of $9 billion less from Medicare and Medicaid than the February projections. *(February speech, p. 7-D; Clinton budget, p. 89)*

The Clinton budget called for cuts of $1.9 billion in fiscal 1994 in Medicare payments to hospitals. Most of the proposed savings were to be achieved by cutting the annual increase in hospital reimbursements to one percentage point lower than the health-care inflation rate. Teaching hospitals were to be subjected to cuts both in their rates of reimbursement for the cost of training and in the salaries of residents and interns. Under the plan, salaries were to be based on a national average rather than reflecting geographic differences.

To replenish the dwindling Medicare hospital insurance fund, Clinton proposed using general fund revenues that he wanted to raise by subjecting 85 percent of the Social Security benefits of affluent retirees to the income tax, up from 50 percent.

The budget called for $742 million in fiscal 1994 savings in Medicare's Part B, which paid for physician and other outpatient services. Much of those savings were to be realized by lowering inflation increases for doctors, although primary care services were to be reimbursed at the full rate, reflecting the administration's desire to raise traditionally lower payments for such services. The budget also proposed reducing Medicare payments for clinical laboratory services.

One of Clinton's cost-cutting proposals for Medicaid — reducing the federal share of payments for administrative costs — had been a perennial in the budgets of Reagan and Bush. Clinton's budget also proposed closing loopholes that were allowing certain individuals who were not poor to qualify for long-term care under Medicaid.

HOUSE COMMITTEE ACTION

The first committee action on the health elements of the Clinton budget was not what the president had in mind.

On April 27, the House Ways and Means Subcommittee on Health ignored the administration's detailed proposals for making cuts in Medicare and substituted its own $50.6 billion, five-year package that would have simply frozen inflation adjustments for payments to doctors and hospitals. Subcommittee Chairman Pete Stark, D-Calif., said the package, approved by voice vote, was a "placeholder" for the Clinton health-care reform plan, which was expected to make major changes to Medicare. "Why should we go through this twice?" asked Stark.

The full committee approved the Health Subcommittee package in closed session May 6.

Energy and Commerce Subcommittee Bill

The House Energy and Commerce Committee, which shared partial jurisdiction over Medicare with Ways and Means and oversaw all of Medicaid, took a different approach. The panel's subcommittee on Health and the Environment approved a package of cuts by voice vote May 6 that was expected to save $28 billion over five years. (The total was lower than the Ways and Means total because Energy and Commerce was not responsible for savings from the hospital portion of Medicare, which was solely under Ways and Means jurisdiction.)

Many of the subcommittee's cuts differed from those the administration proposed. They included limiting inflation increases for physicians, although, like the administration, the subcommittee proposal preserved payments for primary care services. The panel also limited payments for anesthesia, clinical laboratory services and durable medical equipment.

For Medicaid, the proposal included provisions to save $8.9 billion in federal spending over five years. Most of the savings were achieved by reducing payments to hospitals that treated large numbers of Medicaid patients and by eliminating a mandate that states provide personal care services, such as nurses, to Medicaid beneficiaries. The committee avoided cutting Medicaid reimbursements, as Clinton had proposed, and made up the money elsewhere.

As it had in previous years, however, the subcommittee also added provisions costing about $744 million over five years, reducing the total net savings to $8.2 billion. That was still higher than the committee's deficit-reduction target for Medicaid of $7.8 billion.

The change in the rules for reimbursing hospitals that treated a high number of low-income patients — known as disproportionate share hospitals — represented the committee's third attempt since 1989 to close loopholes in the law governing how states financed Medicaid. Previous provisions were attached to the 1990 reconciliation bill (PL 101-508) and a separate bill in 1991. *(1990 Almanac, p. 147; 1991 Almanac, p. 358)*

The otherwise routine markup took a sudden controversial turn when Alex McMillan, R-N.C., offered an amendment to require wealthy Medicare beneficiaries to pay a larger portion of the premiums for the optional Part B coverage of physician and outpatient services. Under existing law, Medicare beneficiaries paid premiums equal to 25 percent of the program's cost, with the federal Treasury picking up the rest.

McMillan's amendment, similar to a proposal first put forward by President Bush, would have reversed that for couples earning between $125,000 and $200,000 annually, requiring that they pay premiums equal to 75 percent of the program's per capita cost. The government subsidy would have been ended entirely for couples with annual incomes higher than $200,000.

Health and the Environment Subcommittee Chairman Henry A. Waxman, D-Calif., spoke against the amendment, but it drew support from some other panel Democrats. "This is an idea whose time has come," said Jim Slattery, D-Kan. Other Democrats supporting the proposal included Mike Kreidler of Washington and J. Roy Rowland of Georgia.

The subcommittee, however, rejected the amendment by voice vote, along with two other McMillan amendments that would have required beneficiaries to pay part of the costs of home health care and laboratory services.

The subcommittee bill also included the creation of a $1.8 billion entitlement program for childhood immunization. *(Childhood immunizations, p. 368)*

Energy and Commerce Committee Action

The full Energy and Commerce Committee approved the package with few changes by voice vote May 11.

One amendment, adopted 26-18, called for a one-year program to help states with large numbers of undocumented immigrants pay for their emergency health care, including the delivery of babies. The program, which was to be capped at $300 million, would have benefited border states such as Arizona, California, Florida, Texas and Washington, whose hospitals each year delivered babies of undocumented immigrants who crossed the border so that their children could be born in the United States and thus qualify for U.S. citizenship. Two Californians, Democrat Waxman and Republican Carlos J. Moorhead, ranking minority member of the full committee, crafted the amendment.

The panel also agreed by voice vote to soften slightly language making it more difficult for the elderly to transfer assets in an effort to qualify for Medicaid coverage of their long-term nursing home care. Advocates for the elderly had condemned the original measure as "draconian." The new language added a provision allowing states to waive the penalties for asset transfer if they would cause an undue hardship. Among the more controversial penalties was one requiring that elderly people pay the full cost of nursing home care until they had spent the same amount of money that they had transferred to a relative.

HOUSE FLOOR ACTION

The House approved HR 2264 (H Rept 103-111) by a vote of 219-213 on May 27. *(Vote 199, p. 48-H)*

Although members made no specific changes to the health provisions during House floor consideration May 27, the administration did agree to add language to control entitlement spending, including funding for Medicare and Medicaid, to the Senate version of the bill in order to get it through the House. Under a compromise worked out less than 24 hours before the House floor vote, if entitlement spending exceeded a preset annual target by more than half a percentage point, the president would have to propose a way to pay for some or all of the overspending or propose to change the target. Congress would have to vote on the proposal.

SENATE COMMITTEE ACTION

On the other side of the Capitol, the zeal for deficit reduction was far greater than in the House. Indeed, while the House-passed bill called for Medicare reductions of $50 billion over five years, the deficit-reduction package the Senate Finance Committee approved June 18 anticipated $67 billion in Medicare reductions. In addition, the Finance package, approved 11-9, transformed the House's $1.8 billion immunization entitlement into a money-saver.

To achieve the additional Medicare cuts, the committee further cut physician reimbursements to all but primary care doctors and hospital reimbursements for outpatient services. It also reduced payments to teaching hospitals for

Childhood Immunization Program Expanded

While the fiscal 1994 budget-reconciliation bill (HR 2264 — PL 103-66) included few provisions that spent rather than saved money, one notable exception was the creation of a new program to help pay for immunizations to prevent common childhood diseases. *(Health provisions, p. 136)*

The immunization program, set to take effect in fiscal 1995, was expected to cost $1.5 billion over five years. However the net cost to the federal Treasury was estimated at only $585 million, because the program was expected to save money for shots that otherwise would have been spent under Medicaid, the joint federal-state program for the poor.

Under the new entitlement program, the federal government was to purchase vaccines for an estimated 11 million children, including children on Medicaid, American Indian children and children with no other health insurance coverage. Children with insurance but whose plans did not cover the costs of the shots could get free vaccines at federally funded community health centers.

Parliamentary problems caused several provisions to be dropped from the bill that would have increased access to vaccine services. Among them were a $250 million outreach program to lengthen clinic hours, creation of a vaccine registry for tracking a child's immunizations and a bonus program to reward states that improved their vaccination rates.

Just days after taking office, President Clinton highlighted the immunization issue — particularly the low rates of immunization for preschool age children — in a visit to a suburban Virginia clinic. He charged that vaccine manufacturers were price-gouging and floated the idea of having the federal government purchase and distribute all vaccines. Drug companies criticized the proposal as an attempt to nationalize their business. They said it would cut into their profits so much that they would be forced to stop doing research.

The controversy involved three issues: Who should pay for immunizing children whose insurance plans did not cover vaccinations (only about half of policies did, according to the federal Centers for Disease Control); how to make parents take their children in for vaccinations; and whether the government should become the primary buyer of vaccines or should regulate the prices charged by pharmaceutical companies.

Both the House and Senate versions of the reconciliation bill attempted to address the problem of immunization rates that lagged far below those of many other Western countries. Overall, at age 2, only about 58 percent of American children were fully immunized against polio, measles, rubella, mumps, diphtheria, pertussis and tetanus, according to the Centers for Disease Control.

But the two chambers addressed the problem in different ways.

The House proposal, which originated in the Energy and Commerce Subcommittee on Health and the Environment and most closely incorporated Clinton's proposals, provided for the creation of an entitlement program that would use tax dollars to pay for vaccines for all children not covered by insurance. The Secretary of Health and Human Services was to negotiate the price with vaccine manufacturers and purchase a bulk amount to be distributed to the states. States would be able to purchase additional vaccine at the government-negotiated price. Critics charged that the program, costing $2.1 billion over five years, meant the government would pay for shots even for children from well-to-do families.

The Senate plan, rewritten on the Senate floor by longtime immunization advocate Dale Bumpers, D-Ark., was designed to limit the free vaccine to children whose families were covered by Medicaid. While such children already were eligible for free vaccines, Bumpers' plan involved changing the reimbursement system to give more incentives to doctors to provide the vaccines themselves instead of sending children to clinics. The Senate plan included provisions to freeze the price that states paid for vaccines at the then-current federal government price plus inflation for the next five years, and to withhold payments for mothers on welfare who failed to have their children immunized.

Although Senate negotiators were set against the House version because of its expense, a coalition of liberals led by Rep. Henry A. Waxman, D-Calif., ultimately held out for a final product much closer to their — and the president's — proposal.

In separate action, the Senate on Nov. 4 passed a bill (S 732) to establish registries across the country that could be used by doctors to determine the immunization history of a particular child. The bill, approved by voice vote authorized $152 million in fiscal 1994, $125 million in fiscal 1995 and $35 million annually from fiscal 1996 through 1999 to establish immunization registries. It also authorized $250 million in fiscal 1994 for states to expand immunization services by, for example, expanding clinic hours and educating parents about the importance of vaccines.

The Senate gave voice vote approval to an amendment by Jesse Helms, R-N.C., to allow parents to opt out of the registry program and bar the use of information in the registry against a parent in criminal proceedings.

The House did not act on the bill.

training interns and residents.

Over the two weeks preceding the markup, two conservative Democrats on the panel, David L. Boren of Oklahoma and John B. Breaux of Louisiana, had been pushing a compromise version of the reconciliation bill, including a controversial increase in the premiums paid by wealthy Medicare beneficiaries for the optional coverage of physician and outpatient costs. But after a storm of criticism from members of the powerful American Association of Retired Persons (AARP), backed by a White House that feared a political backlash from the elderly, the committee left out the increase.

Groups affected by the cuts the committee did propose responded with sharp criticism as the package took shape, and they embarked swiftly on grass-roots lobbying campaigns, attempting to reach lawmakers both in Washington and at home. "We are obviously very disturbed by the level of cuts," said Mary Elizabeth Bresch White, a lobbyist for the Association of American Medical Colleges, whose 400 teaching hospitals included many of the nation's top research institutions.

The AARP was not happy either. "Touching Social Security causes a conflagration," said legislative director Martin Corry. "And Medicare is just as hot; it just burns a little slower." The AARP was running a grass-roots campaign urging senators to resist the additional Medicare cuts.

The American Hospital Association also criticized the cuts. "This is not the time to do it when you're going to health-care reform, because it will weaken the very institutions that the administration is looking towards to be leaders," said Rick Wade, vice president of communications.

SENATE FLOOR ACTION

The Senate approved its version of the reconciliation bill by a vote of 50-49 on June 25, with Vice President Al Gore casting the tie-breaking vote. *(Vote 190, p. 25-S)*

The leadership's negotiations with the conservative wing of the party had angered liberal Democrats, and a small but critical group that included Howard M. Metzenbaum of Ohio, Tom Harkin of Iowa, Barbara A. Mikulski of Maryland and Paul Wellstone of Minnesota threatened to vote against the bill because of the additional Medicare cuts the Finance Committee added.

The liberals wanted no more than $10 billion in added Medicare cuts; leaders insisted they needed something closer to $19 billion. But when the June 25 vote drew closer and the liberals dug in their heels, leaders agreed to lower the cuts by the full $9 billion, prompting Harkin and others to declare support for the package.

John D. Rockefeller IV, D-W.Va., chairman of the Finance Subcommittee that oversaw Medicare, offered a floor amendment to eliminate a series of specific Medicare reductions in a move titlted in part toward easing the burden of the cuts on inner-city and rural areas. The measure, which brought total Medicare cuts down to $58 billion, passed on a voice vote.

CONFERENCE, FINAL ACTION

Early in the House-Senate conference on the reconciliation bill, negotiators agreed to $54 billion in Medicare cuts — splitting the difference between the $50 billion House figure and the $58 billion passed by the Senate.

But then negotiations pushed tax revenues down, and the Senate sought to increase Medicare cuts to $56 billion.

The outcome hinged on a new coalition among House liberals, progressives and the Democrats in the Congressional Black Caucus, who worked together to ensure that no deal would go through without additional money for inner-city needs such as tuberculosis care and immunizations for poor children. "The condition for me to support the bill was that we had to get a lot of items back in, and we had to make sure the additional Medicare cuts didn't hurt beneficiaries," said Waxman.

Among the items Waxman held out for were: $205 million for treatment of impoverished tuberculosis victims, an additional $293 million for Medicaid payments to Puerto Rico and other U.S. territories, and the $1.5 billion immunization program.

With those items included, the coalition agreed to support the $55.8 billion in Medicare cuts that were included in the final bill.

The House passed the conference report on the bill (H Rept 103-213) by a vote of 218-216, on Aug. 5. The Senate approved the report and cleared the bill, 51-50, on Aug. 6; Gore again cast the tie-breaking vote. *(House vote 406, p. 98-H; Senate vote 247, p. 32-S)* ∎

Congress Reauthorizes CDC Programs

Congress cleared a bill (HR 2202) on Nov. 22 reauthorizing several programs at the Centers for Disease Control (CDC), including $150 million in fiscal 1994 for early detection of women's reproductive and breast cancers. The bill authorized $50 million for a program on domestic violence, $85 million for research on sexually transmitted diseases and $6 million to study regional trauma centers.

In addition, the bill authorized $250 million in fiscal 1994 to fight tuberculosis — $200 million for grants to states for research, demonstration projects and training on the control and prevention of TB, and $50 million to the National Institute of Allergy and Infectious Diseases for research on the cause, diagnosis, prevention and treatment of the disease.

HR 2202 also included provisions to allow the Department of Health and Human Services to issue temporary quality standards for mammography; final regulations were to be ready by Oct. 1, 1995.

In addition to the specific amounts for fiscal 1994, the bill authorized "such sums as may be necessary" through fiscal 1998. President Clinton signed the measure into law Dec. 14 (PL 103-183).

House Action

The final version of HR 2202 incorporated a series of health bills. All of the House measures were approved May 20 in the House Energy and Commerce Health Subcommittee. The full Energy and Commerce Committee approved two of the bills May 25 and two more June 8. All four passed the House separately. The following are the House-passed bills:

● **HR 2202 — H Rept 103-120.** The bill, sponsored by Henry A. Waxman, D-Calif., originally provided $100 million for early detection of reproductive and breast cancer; that amount was increased to $135 million in the full committee. The program provided grants to states to pay for mammograms and pap smears for poor women. The House approved the bill, 365-2, on June 14. *(Vote 219, p. 54-H)*

● **HR 2201 — H Rept 103-119.** The bill authorized $50 million in fiscal 1994 for CDC grants for data collection and education programs on domestic violence. "For too long, the medical profession has had its own 'don't ask, don't tell' policy on violence against women," said Mike Kreidler, D-Wash., the bill's sponsor. "But it is time to break the silence." The House passed the bill, 305-61, on June 14. *(Vote 218, p. 54-H)*

● **HR 2203 — H Rept 103-131.** The bill, which the House passed by voice vote June 21, authorized $80 million in fiscal 1994 for block grants to states to develop and carry out "innovative" approaches to the prevention and control of sexually transmitted diseases. Waxman sponsored it.

● **HR 2205 — H Rept 103-122.** The bill, also sponsored by Waxman, authorized $45 million over three years for programs related to trauma care. The House approved it June 14 by voice vote.

Senate Action

The Senate Labor and Human Resources Committee gave voice vote approval July 30 to a bill (S 1318 — S Rept 103-135) that was an amalgam of several draft bills aimed

at detecting and preventing a host of diseases. On Nov. 2, the Senate passed HR 2202 by voice vote — after substituting the text of S 1318.

The Senate-passed bill authorized $200 million in fiscal 1994 to fight breast and cervical cancer, $132 million to prevent sexually transmitted diseases and $60 million for the CDC for research on violence and injuries.

It authorized $226 million for the CDC's TB control programs; $46 million for the National Institute of Allergy and Infectious Diseases for research on the disease; $25 million for a grant program to renovate facilities devoted to the prevention and control of TB, and $5 million for a tuberculosis drug research program at the Food and Drug Administration.

"In the 1950s, science thought it had TB under control," said Sen. Edward M. Kennedy, D-Mass., chairman of the Labor and Human Resources Committee. "Today we face an epidemic of TB resisting every drug we have."

In addition to the amounts for fiscal 1994, the bill authorized unspecified sums through fiscal 1997.

In separate action, the Senate approved HR 2205 by voice vote June 29 after substituting the text of a Senate bill on trauma care (S 1113).

Final Action

Conferees on HR 2202 melded all the bills into a single measure (H Rept 103-397) that was reported Nov. 20. Where the House and Senate numbers conflicted, they struck compromises.

The House adopted the conference report on the bill Nov. 21, by a vote of 420-0. The Senate cleared it by voice vote the next day. (House vote 598, p. 146-H) ∎

Various Health Bills Considered in 1993

Congress worked on several smaller health-related bills in 1993, including the following:

EPHEDRINE SALES

By voice vote, the Senate on Nov. 24 cleared for the White House a bill (HR 3216) expanding the Drug Enforcement Administration's (DEA) control over chemicals used in the manufacture of illegal substances. The House had approved the bill by voice vote Nov. 21. President Clinton signed the measure into law (PL 103-200) Dec. 17.

The bill was aimed at an illegal stimulant called methcathinone, commonly known as CAT, a relatively new, cheap amphetamine that was easy to manufacture from household ingredients and ephedrine, the active ingredient in numerous legal over-the-counter drugs. CAT, which looked like but was more potent than crack cocaine, had become popular in the Upper Peninsula of Michigan and other areas of the Midwest.

Under the bill, sponsored by Rep. Bart Stupak, D-Mich., companies that manufactured the pure form of ephedrine were required to register with the DEA and submit records of the drug's sales. That information could be used to track those who bought the drug.

More broadly, the legislation gave the attorney general the power, on a case-by-case basis, to subject other legal chemicals to the sort of record-keeping requirements applicable to controlled substances.

The House Energy and Commerce Subcommittee on Health and the Environment approved HR 3216 by voice vote Nov. 10; the full committee approved it Nov. 16 (H Rept 103-379, Part 1). "This legislation will greatly increase our ability to deny clandestine laboratory operators access to the chemicals which they need to synthesize illicit controlled substances," the DEA said in a letter to the committee.

The Senate passed a similar bill (S 1767) on Nov. 20 but agreed to the House version.

FOOD LABELING

The Senate on Aug. 6 cleared a bill that broadened small-business exemptions from food-labeling requirements that were scheduled to become effective in May 1994. The House had approved the bill earlier the same day; both chambers acted by voice vote. President Clinton signed the bill into law Aug. 13.

The bill (HR 2900 — PL 103-80) amended the 1990 Nutrition Labeling and Education Act, giving some small businesses up to three more years to comply with its labeling requirements. It was sponsored by John D. Dingell, D-Mich.

The 1990 law (PL 101-535) required nutritional information on almost all food labels by May 8, 1994, granting exemptions only to small retailers. The bill extended the exemptions to small manufacturers. It also based the exemptions on the number of products sold and the number of employees from year to year, not on the level of net earnings. Moreover, the bill set up a simpler process for getting an exemption from the Food and Drug Administration.

Henry A. Waxman, D-Calif., chairman of the House Energy and Commerce Subcommittee on Health and the Environment, said many small businesses would be hit hard financially if they were forced to adhere to labeling regulations by the following May.

Nancy Landon Kassebaum, R-Kan., a leading Senate supporter of the bill, said on the floor, "If the original exemption remains unchanged, a number of small specialty food and confectionary manufacturing and retail businesses may be forced to reduce their product lines or go out of business, and it will be very difficult to establish new businesses. Many of these businesses are family owned and started by women working out of their homes."

DISABILITIES ASSISTANCE

The House and Senate passed separate versions of a bill (S 1284) aimed at funneling federal funds to states to help provide support services to people with disabilities and their families. But the two chambers were unable to reconcile the differences in their bills before Congress adjourned for the year.

The bill, sponsored by Sen. Tom Harkin, D-Iowa, authorized four state grant programs to help people born with disabilities affecting their emotional, intellectual or physical development. The Senate version authorized $131 million in grants to individuals, universities and disability councils in fiscal 1994. The House bill authorized $117

million for the same programs.

Most of the money in both versions, $70 million in the House bill and $77 million in the Senate version, was designed for state developmental disabilities councils, which provided support services and served as advocates for the disabled.

The Senate Labor and Human Resources Committee acted first, approving the legislation (S 1284 — S Rept 103-120) by voice vote July 30. The Senate passed the bill by voice vote Aug. 5.

The House Energy and Commerce Committee marked up its version (HR 3505 — H Rept 103-378) on Nov. 16, passing it by voice vote. During the markup, the committee approved by voice vote an amendment by Henry A. Waxman, D-Calif., clarifying that Guam was eligible for funding in the bill under the provisions that supported university disability programs.

On Nov. 21, the House stripped the Senate language from the bill, substituted the text of its own bill (HR 3505) and passed S 1284 by voice vote.

MINORITY HEALTH

The Senate Labor and Human Resources Committee approved a non-controversial draft bill by voice vote Oct. 20 to authorize at least $144 million in fiscal 1994 to improve the health of minorities.

The bill included authorizations of $37.8 million in scholarships to minority students who pursued health studies (and designated those students as Cesar Chavez Primary Care Scholars) and $26 million to establish an Office of Minority Health in several federal agencies.

DISABILITY TECHNOLOGY GRANTS

The House and Senate passed separate versions of a measure aimed at assisting people with disabilities, but they did not complete work on the bill in 1993.

The legislation (S 1283, HR 2339) authorized grants to help states fund a host of projects — from increasing public awareness to expanding training — aimed at improving technology assistance for the disabled.

The House Education and Labor panel on Select Education and Civil Rights gave quick voice vote approval to the disability technology legislation June 30. The full Education and Labor Committee approved the bill (HR 2339 — H Rept 103-208) by voice vote July 28.

The committee bill renewed the state grant program through 2002 and authorized $50 million in fiscal 1994, an increase over the fiscal 1993 appropriation of $34.1 million for the programs.

Some of the funds were to be used to help states establish low-interest consumer loan programs to help the disabled buy state-of-the-art devices and services to assist them, such as automated wheelchairs.

The House passed the measure by voice vote Aug. 2.

The Senate Labor and Human Resources Committee approved a companion bill (S 1283 — S Rept 103-119) by voice vote July 30. When the full Senate took it up Aug. 5, it inserted the text of its bill into the House measure and approved HR 2339 by voice vote.

ORGAN TRANSPLANTS

The House on Oct. 5 agreed to reauthorize for three years the major federal law facilitating organ transplants.

The Senate took no action on the measure.

The House bill (HR 2659) authorized $20 million for organ and bone marrow transplants in fiscal 1994 and unspecified amounts in fiscal 1995 and 1996. It also included changes to the law aimed at better assuring that organs were provided to patients with the greatest medical need.

The House Energy and Commerce Subcommittee on Health approved the bill by voice vote July 1.

Ranking Republican Thomas J. Bliley Jr., Va., said he had "serious reservations" about language that might cause potential donors to feel coerced into participating in the voluntary programs. And Michael Bilirakis, R-Fla., complained that some patients were dying while waiting for transplants because organs were given to other patients who ranked lower on priority lists. The discrepancy occurred because patients were ranked by region, rather than nationally.

The full Energy and Commerce Committee approved the bill July 27 by voice vote (H Rept 103-272). The committee approved an amendment by Health Subcommittee Chairman Henry A. Waxman, D-Calif., that called for the Department of Health and Human Services to study the feasibility of establishing a national priority list for patients awaiting organ transplants.

Bilirakis praised a study as "helpful" but said he was concerned that more patients might die while it was being conducted. But Waxman said a study was necessary. "These are difficult decisions," he said. "We are deciding who is going to live and die. And if we are going to make such decisions, we ought to do it with as much information as possible."

The bill included language intended to discourage foreigners from traveling to the United States for organ transplants. It required that U.S. citizens receive a higher priority on transplant lists.

The legislation also authorized grants to organizations seeking to recruit more minority donors for organ and bone marrow transplants. Cardiss Collins, D-Ill., said that minorities had a "significantly reduced chance" of finding compatible bone marrow for transplants because so few minorities were donors. ■

Senate Tries To Delay Diet Supplement Rules

The Senate passed a bill (S 1762) by voice vote Nov. 20 aimed at postponing plans by the Food and Drug Administration (FDA) to impose new labeling rules on dietary supplements. The bill was sent to the House Energy and Commerce Committee the next day, but the committee failed to act before the end of the year.

The Senate bill, sponsored by Orrin G. Hatch, R-Utah, sought to extend a moratorium on the labeling regulations for four months, to April 15, 1994. The moratorium expired Dec. 15, 1993. Without the extension, the FDA could put its regulations in place in the spring.

The FDA rules required manufacturers of dietary supplements such as vitamins and herbal remedies to back up health claims made on their labels with evidence supported by "significant scientific agreement" — the same standard that foods such as breakfast cereals and orange juice had to uphold.

An earlier attempt by Hatch to require the FDA to use separate labeling and safety standards for dietary supplements bogged down in committee.

Background

The legislation was the latest effort by supporters of dietary supplements to keep the $4 billion market free from what they called overzealous regulation by the FDA.

In the 1970s, Sen. William Proxmire, D-Wis., was the driving force behind a bill that curbed the FDA's power to regulate traditional vitamins and minerals.

The dispute in 1993 stemmed from the 1990 Nutrition Labeling and Education Act (PL 101-535), which instructed the FDA to develop labeling instructions and guidelines for dietary supplements, among other products.

But in 1992, during work on a bill to impose user fees on prescription drug makers, Hatch successfully lobbied for language placing a moratorium on FDA rules for dietary supplements through Dec. 15, 1993. *(1992 Almanac, p. 420)*

Senate Action

On Nov. 17, senators shelved a tougher Hatch bill (S 784) after a Senate committee scrambled unsuccessfully for a compromise and then delayed action on the legislation.

Hatch, the ranking Republican on a Labor and Human Resources subcommittee, was unable to work out a compromise with committee Chairman Edward M. Kennedy, D-Mass., who opposed the bill.

Kennedy, however, left open the possibility that the committee could send a compromise bill directly to the floor without a markup, but only if all members agreed to the bill language. That is the way S 1762 later made it to the floor.

Under S 784, Hatch's original bill, dietary supplements would not have been considered foods or drugs under the Food, Drug and Cosmetic Act of 1938, which regulated product safety and labeling. Instead, they would have been given special treatment, subject to new labeling and safety standards.

The bill would have blocked FDA's proposed standard for labeling claims. Instead of "significant scientific agreement," the bill would have allowed claims on labels unless the FDA determined through studies and the "totality of scientific evidence" that the claim was invalid.

Products that had been on the market for years without negative health effects would have been considered safe for use.

The bill would have required the FDA to prove that products were unsafe before removing them from health-food store or supermarket shelves. Under existing law, the FDA had to prove that a product was unsafe, but the standard was tougher to meet under Hatch's bill.

House

On the House side, staff aides to Henry A. Waxman, D-Calif., chairman of the Energy and Commerce Subcommittee on Health and the Environment, said no markup would be scheduled on the House version of the bill (HR 1709), sponsored by Bill Richardson, D-N.M. Waxman opposed the measure.

Some lawmakers were deluged by mail campaigns in support of extending the moratorium, largely organized by supplement manufacturers and health-food stores. During an Agriculture Appropriations Subcommittee hearing in October, Ed Pastor, D-Ariz., said that he heard more from his constituents about vitamins than he had about the North American Free Trade Agreement.

But consumer groups such as the American Association of Retired Persons and the Center for Science in the Public Interest pointed to products that claimed to help arthritis or boost the immune systems as fraudulent and victimizing. ∎

Clinton, Congress Talk of Welfare Reform

Although he vowed during his campaign to "end welfare as we know it," President Clinton sent no legislative proposal on the subject to Congress during 1993. Instead, Republicans came out with their own plan in an effort to steal a bit of the president's thunder.

At year's end, a 27-member working group within the administration was preparing to present its welfare recommendations to Clinton. But it was not clear how soon he would decide on the details of a legislative package or when he would push it on Capitol Hill. The White House had made clear that a health-care overhaul would be its top priority once the president's economic initiatives were enacted. As a practical matter, that made it unlikely that the 103rd Congress could make much headway on welfare reform. The same committees had jurisdiction over both health and welfare, and they could not work on two complex issues at once.

The underlying purpose of Clinton's anticipated proposal was to transform welfare into a temporary safety net instead of a permanent way of life. The president was expected to offer more education, training and social services to beneficiaries to prepare them for entry into the work force, while at the same time imposing a two-year limit on welfare payments to most able-bodied recipients of Aid to Families With Dependent Children (AFDC).

As part of his plan to make work more rewarding than welfare, Clinton did succeed in 1993 in pushing through an increase in the earned-income tax credit for low-income families. The budget-reconciliation bill (HR 2264 — PL 103-66) boosted the maximum credit for the working poor to $3,554 for families with two or more children and to $2,050 for those with one child. The credit, which was reduced as a family's income rose, was to be eliminated for those making more than $23,760 (with one child) or $27,000 with two or more children. *(Reconciliation provisions, p. 124)*

Separate provisions of the reconciliation bill also set stricter federal guidelines for establishing paternity of children born out of wedlock — a crucial precursor to obtaining a court order for child support payments. *(Child support enforcement, p. 374)*

The GOP welfare-reform proposal (HR 3500), which was cosponsored by 160 of the 175 House Republicans, was more punitive than Clinton's, threatening stiff penalties for AFDC recipients who refused to work within two years and punishing beneficiaries who did not establish the paternity of their children. It also sought to deny welfare to most immigrants.

One major problem with any welfare overhaul was cost. The added education, training, child care and job placement costs involved in pushing recipients off the dole within two years were likely to be substantial. And the White House did not say whether or how it would finance public-service jobs for welfare mothers who could not find work on their own.

"If the goal is to promote self-sufficiency rather than reducing the welfare rolls, there's no way to do that without additional revenues," said A. Sidney Johnson III, executive director of the American Public Welfare Association, which represented state human service departments and local public welfare agencies.

BACKGROUND

There was nothing new about any of the welfare reform concepts bandied about in 1993. The Family Support Act of 1988 (PL 100-485) contained many of the elements under discussion, from stricter child support enforcement to improved job training for welfare mothers. Clinton helped draft that 1988 law while he was governor of Arkansas, serving as the point man for the National Governors' Association. *(1988 Almanac, p. 349)*

The 1988 law required states to start providing education, training and work programs for welfare mothers, and it extended child-care and medical benefits to families in which parents left the welfare rolls for jobs. "In return for having a work requirement and work as a goal, the government would provide support for education, training, health care and child care," said Johnson of the American Public Welfare Association. "There was a concept of a reciprocal agreement."

Conservatives and liberals alike hailed the compromise legislation as the most sweeping package of changes since the creation in 1935 of the program that became AFDC.

President Ronald Reagan signed the package into law Oct. 13, 1988. He said it responded "to the call in my 1986 State of the Union message for real welfare reform — reform that will lead to lasting emancipation from welfare dependency."

The new law ordered states to operate a Job Opportunities and Basic Skills (JOBS) program to provide recipients with work, remedial education and training. The bill provided $1 billion a year for JOBS programs in fiscal 1992 and 1993, rising to $1.1 billion in fiscal 1994 and $1.3 billion in 1995. States were required to put up matching funds to claim their share of the federal pot. One parent in two-parent welfare families was required to perform at least 16 hours per week of community service or other unpaid work.

But the law was never designed as a quick fix. States were not required to start phasing in education and training programs until October 1990, and the programs did not have to be fully operational until 1995.

Moreover, the bill's success was undercut by the double whammy of a recession. First, a weakened economy contributed to an explosion of welfare rolls. From 1989 to 1992, the number of families on AFDC rose 25 percent to 4.76 million families representing 13.6 million people. About one in seven children was on welfare. Second, the economy's drain on state revenues left states unable to provide matching funds and fully participate in the education and training programs. For example, states claimed about $750 million of the $1 billion in federal JOBS funds available for fiscal 1992, according to Department of Health and Human Services estimates.

In fact, fiscal constraints and a lack of public support for welfare prompted six states to cut AFDC benefits in 1992 and 38 others to freeze them, according to the Center on Budget and Policy Priorities, a liberal Washington policy research group.

The House Ways and Means Committee found that in January 1992, the median state AFDC benefit for a family of three was $372 a month. The benefit increased to $647 when food stamps were included.

The Center on Budget and Policy Priorities also reported that eight states reduced or eliminated general assistance welfare programs for poor people who did not qualify for AFDC or Supplemental Security Income (SSI) for the low-income aged, blind and disabled.

To work, experts said, welfare reform needed more of everything: more work requirements, more social supports and more federal money to make it happen.

Douglas Besharov, a resident scholar at the American Enterprise Institute, a Washington think tank, wrote that the 1988 law might yet be seen as an important stepping-stone — depending on what happened next.

"We can now see that the act codified a fundamental shift in public and professional attitudes: It legitimized discussions of behavioral poverty and of government's right (and obligation) to do something about it," he said. "By doing so, the act opened the door to a second, much more ambitious wave of reform. Whether or not Clinton comes up with a workable plan, it's a tale that could give incrementalism a good name."

INITIAL PLANNING

The complexity of reforming welfare became obvious as the 27-member Clinton task force began holding hearings around the country. The task force was led by Bruce Reed, deputy assistant to the president for domestic policy; David T. Ellwood, assistant secretary for planning and evaluation at the Department of Health and Human Services (HHS); and Mary Jo Bane, HHS assistant secretary of Administration for Children and Families.

At an Aug. 19 hearing in Washington, representatives of more than three dozen interest groups and several current or former welfare recipients detailed the existing system's shortcomings, from the Byzantine and ineffective child support network to the legal and financial disincentives to work.

Clinton's campaign proposal to limit welfare recipients to two years of benefits, after which they would be required to work, drew the most controversy. Several speakers urged the administration's working group on welfare reform to approach the idea cautiously.

Delegate Eleanor Holmes Norton, D-D.C., a critic of the two-year limit, also questioned the administration's ability to follow through on its promise to overhaul the system. "I believe you've overpromised," she said, suggesting that Clinton had raised expectations about a radical change "that you can't deliver on."

Reorienting welfare was more complicated than improving health care, Norton said, because welfare involved other deep-seated problems, such as intense poverty, unemployment and the lack of child care. Requiring people to work after two years did not take into account the difficulties that low-income people already had obtaining jobs, especially when military cutbacks were sending more people into the civilian labor market, she said. "You completely underestimate the straight-out prejudice against people on welfare," she said.

Several members of a panel representing states and localities also urged caution in developing a two-year limit. Barry Van Lare, deputy executive director of the National Governors' Association, said time limits ought to be handled on an individual basis. Ohio state Rep. Jane L. Campbell, representing the National Conference of State Legislatures, said the conference would not take a position on time limits until it knew what would happen to welfare recipients who could not find jobs.

Later, Lee A. Saunders, representing the American Federation of State, County and Municipal Employees, cautioned that creating a public jobs program for former welfare recipients could displace public sector jobs. Mark

Child Support Enforcement

Both the White House and Republicans wanted to force more fathers to support their children, and Congress took some limited steps to beef up enforcement in this area as part of the budget-reconciliation bill (HR 2264 — PL 103-66). *(Provisions, p. 124)*

Although states operated their own programs for establishing paternity, locating absent parents and issuing child support orders, they did so under federal guidelines imposed by 1975 amendments to the Social Security Act and modified thereafter.

Congress stiffened requirements for state efforts to establishing the paternity of children born out of wedlock — a crucial precursor to obtaining a court order for child support payments. The reconciliation bill required states to establish the paternity of 75 percent of children born out of wedlock who were receiving welfare or child-support enforcement services. States with paternity establishment rates between 50 percent and 75 percent had to increase their success by 3 percentage points per year; those with rates below 50 percent had to improve by at least 6 percentage points per year.

States were also required to provide a simple civil procedure for voluntary acknowledgments of paternity, including a plan for obtaining such acknowledgments in the hospital just before or after the birth of a child.

The reconciliation bill also contained a provision requiring states to force health insurers to provide coverage to a child born out of wedlock if the non-custodial parent was eligible for family coverage at a reasonable cost. The private insurance would be first recourse before the child could receive Medicaid coverage.

Greenberg, representing the liberal Center for Law and Social Policy, argued that welfare recipients were more likely to have difficulty getting jobs because they lacked education, child care and appropriate skills than because they were dependent on handouts.

Several speakers said that the welfare system discouraged work by reducing benefits as outside income increased.

Any changes in welfare law ran the risk of having unintended consequences. For instance, if AFDC recipients got more support when entering the job market than other poor people, that would create an incentive to have a child and get on welfare. Minneapolis Mayor Donald M. Fraser, representing the National League of Cities, noted that welfare was more generous to unmarried women with children than to parents who stayed together. "I think the general perception is, if there's a man in the house, you won't get any help," he said.

A panel on child support spun a series of stories about bureaucratic incompetence and indifference in trying to get money from non-custodial fathers. "We must make child support as important in this country as paying taxes," said Geraldine Jensen, president of the Association for Children for Enforcement of Support, based in Toledo, Ohio. And Robert Greenstein, director of the liberal Center for Budget and Policy Priorities, offered a final caution: "We can't

assume," he said of the welfare system, "that it can't be made even worse than it already is."

HOUSE REPUBLICAN PLAN

While the administration struggled to put together its welfare proposal, House Republicans sought to stake out a piece of the action with their own plan. The GOP proposal (HR 3500), unveiled Nov. 10, sought to impose stiff penalties on recipients who refused to work within two years of receiving benefits. The legislation, sponsored by Minority Leader Robert H. Michel, R-Ill., also proposed to sanction welfare beneficiaries who did not establish paternity for their children, deny any AFDC benefits to most non-citizens, and combine 10 food programs into one block grant, cutting costs by 5 percent.

Leaders of the effort said net savings from the bill would be $19.5 billion over five years.

Although the bill had little chance of passage in the Democrat-controlled House, it nonetheless laid down an early marker for Clinton. With some liberal Democrats likely to balk at imposing a two-year limit on welfare benefits, Clinton was expected to need bipartisan support for his plan.

Clinton's chief welfare advisers said they welcomed the Republican initiative, but they expressed concern about such elements as across-the-board cuts in nutrition programs.

Clinton's plan was expected to include less severe penalties for welfare recipients who did not work and more social services to help them enter the job market. The Democratic view on denying benefits to foreigners was less clear.

But anti-immigrant sentiment was running fairly high in Congress. To help finance an extension of emergency unemployment benefits for the long-term unemployed, the House voted Oct. 15 to restrict the ability of recent legal immigrants to collect Supplemental Security Income payments, which went to poor people who were aged, blind or disabled. *(Unemployment, p. 392)*

The Two-Year Plan

The GOP bill permitted recipients to collect AFDC for two years — or less at states' option — while participating in education and training programs. The two-year limit was cumulative throughout one's lifetime. Recipients who could not find a private sector job in two years would be required to participate in a community service assignment or a government-subsidized private sector job to earn their benefits.

The first time that a participant failed to meet the training and work criteria, the combined value of the family's AFDC and food stamp benefits would be reduced 25 percent. By the third violation, the parents and children would lose AFDC benefits, though they still would be eligible for food stamps and Medicaid, which provided health insurance for the poor.

Short-term exemptions from these sanctions would be granted when a child was born and if recipients were deemed incapacitated.

The bill would provide about $10 billion to assist states in providing mothers with jobs, including aid for child care. States could drop AFDC benefits to anyone who had participated in a work program for three years and had not found a private sector job.

Parental Responsibility

To promote parental responsibility, the bill would require mothers who applied for welfare to identify the child's father in order to receive benefits. Mothers would receive a reduced AFDC benefit until paternity was legally established.

Rep. Nancy L. Johnson, R-Conn., stressed the importance of compelling welfare mothers to make fathers take partial responsibility for a child. Under the bill, Johnson said, "you will not have the right — nor will you be supported in the irresponsible action — of not naming the father."

In addition, states would be required to stop increasing welfare checks when recipients had more children and to stop paying welfare benefits to parents under 18 years old.

All welfare benefits — other than emergency Medicaid assistance — would be eliminated for non-citizens, except for refugees and certain permanent resident aliens.

The bill would combine 10 food and nutrition programs — including food stamps and the program for Women, Infants and Children (WIC) — into a single block grant to states.

To further control anti-poverty costs, the bill would also cap the annual outlay growth at 2 percent plus inflation for the following programs: AFDC, SSI, public housing and subsidized private housing, food stamps and the earned-income tax credit, which provided tax rebates for the working poor. ∎

Leland Act To Expand Food Stamp Program

In legislation known as the Mickey Leland Childhood Hunger Relief Act, Congress agreed to expand the nation's food stamp program, primarily by allowing more families to qualify for benefits. The food stamp provisions, cleared in August as part of a massive deficit-reduction bill (HR 2264 — H Rept 103-213), were named for the first chairman of the House Select Committee on Hunger; Leland died in a 1989 airplane crash during a hunger relief mission to Ethiopia. The changes were expected to cost $2.5 billion over five years.

The original House-passed measure would have provided considerably more money — $7.3 billion — and included an increase in benefit levels as well as changes in eligibility requirements. The Senate did not include the food stamp expansion in its version of the bill.

The final measure dropped a House provision that would have raised overall food stamp benefits by a maximum of $4 per month for a family of four. However, other changes in the law served to increase benefits, depending on one's circumstances. For example, a household could deduct more for housing costs in determining its income for food stamp purposes, and it no longer had to count money earned by members who were still in high school. *(Provisions, p. 137)*

The House adopted the conference report on the deficit-reduction bill by a vote of 218-216, on Aug. 5. The Senate cleared the bill, 51-50, on Aug. 6, and President Clinton signed it (PL 103-66) on Aug. 10. *(Budget-reconciliation, p. 107)*

BACKGROUND

President John F. Kennedy began the food stamp program as a pilot project in 1961; it was established as a permanent federal-state program in 1964 to provide coupons that low-income households could use to purchase enough food for a minimal, nutritious diet. The program was overseen by the federal government but administered by the states using national guidelines.

In the early 1980s, conservatives led by President Ronald Reagan and then-Senate Agriculture Chairman Jesse Helms, R-N.C., succeeded in reducing the funds for food stamps, but in 1985, reports of increased poverty prompted Congress to restore some of the money. In 1990, then-Rep. Leon E. Panetta, D-Calif., introduced a version of the Leland bill, but his attempts to widen the reach of the food stamp program foundered over a lack of money.

In 1992, the House passed a child welfare bill that included provisions to increase food stamps to families with children, but the language was dropped in conference. (The entire child welfare initiative died when President George Bush vetoed a tax bill to which it had been attached.) Prospects brightened in 1993, when the Agriculture Committee included the food stamp expansion in its package for the deficit-reduction bill, a major Democratic effort to reconcile taxes and entitlement spending with deficit-reduction efforts. *(1992 Almanac, p. 462; 1991 Almanac, p. 389; 1990 Almanac, p. 354)*

LEGISLATIVE ACTION

The food-stamp provisions were written in the House Agriculture Committee and modified by House-Senate conferees who put together the final reconciliation bill.

House Action

Acting on a recommendation in the fiscal 1994 budget resolution, which gave committees guidelines for crafting portions of the deficit-reduction bill, the House Agriculture Committee on May 13 approved the $7.3 billion food stamp expansion. The vote was 26-17. The House passed the overall bill May 27.

As approved by the House, the legislation:

● **High shelter expenses.** Enabled more families to qualify for food stamps by allowing them to deduct more housing costs from the income figure used to determine food stamp allocations. Under existing law, most households were allowed to deduct shelter expenses (including rent and utilities) that exceeded 50 percent of their incomes, up to $200 per month. The House bill eliminated the $200 cap. (The final bill established interim caps until 1997, after which the cap was eliminated.)

● **Maximum benefit level.** Increased food stamp benefits from 103 percent to 104 percent of the Thrifty Food Plan, a government estimate of how much money a family of four needed to provide nutritional meals. (This provision was later dropped.)

● **Exclusions from income.** Excluded from consideration as income the first $50 a month that a household member received as child support, and excluded all support payments by household members for a child outside the home. The bill also excluded income of elementary and secondary school students 21 or younger, as well as earned-income tax credits, which were available for the working poor. And it increased the amount that could be excluded for child-care expenses. (The proposed exclusion for child support payments received by household members was later dropped, but the exclusion for those who paid child support remained.)

● **Automobile limit.** Raised the existing $4,500 limit on the fair market value of automobiles that food stamp recipients could own to $5,500 in fiscal 1994, then indexed it to the inflation rate for new cars. (The final bill had a less generous increase in the limits.)

The Agriculture Committee rejected two Republican amendments. One by Pat Roberts of Kansas that would have shifted nearly $3 billion from food stamp to commodity programs was rejected 17-27. Another by Bill Emerson of Missouri that would have delayed changing the food stamp program until President Clinton submitted his welfare reform proposal to Congress was rejected 19-25.

Senate Action

The Senate Agriculture Committee, which received no comparable instructions in the budget resolution, did not include the food-stamp expansion in its reconciliation provisions. Had the food-stamp increases been included, they would have been subject to an arcane Senate procedure for handling budget legislation known as the Byrd rule.

Named for author Sen. Robert C. Byrd, D-W.Va, the rule barred reconciliation bills from including "extraneous matter," broadly viewed as any provision that did not reduce the deficit. The rule could only be waived with 60 votes. An attempt to add the food-stamp language on the floor would have been subject to the Byrd rule because it would have added to outlays, causing the Agriculture Committee to miss its deficit-reduction target.

Final Action

The food-stamp expansion was one of several House-passed social spending initiatives that were dropped or reduced in the Senate bill. The Senate provided no money for enterprise zones in distressed neighborhoods, for example, and cut back funds for expanding the earned-income tax credit. At the same time, to secure the votes needed to get the overall bill through the Senate, Democratic leaders cut back on a major source of revenue (eschewing a broad House-passed energy tax in favor a much smaller increase in the gas tax).

That set up a fierce intraparty conflict, with conservative Democrats stressing spending cuts and deficit reduction, and urban and minority members insisting that spending for food stamps and other social programs was their price for supporting the tax increases and spending cuts that made up the bulk of the bill.

In the end, the compromise on food stamp funds, along with other changes, won the support of the Black Caucus, whose 38 House Democrats unanimously backed the conference report on the bill. In the Senate, GOP threats to invoke the Byrd rule in an effort to strip the food stamp provisions from the conference report did not materialize. ■

Defining a Food Store

Worried that many low-income families could lose easy access to groceries, the House by voice vote passed legislation Nov. 10 to allow most convenience stores to continue accepting food stamps. The Senate did not act on the measure prior to adjournment.

The House Agriculture Committee approved the bill (HR 3436 — H Rept 103-352) by voice vote one day before the House acted on it. The committee's Department Operations and Nutrition Subcommittee had endorsed the bill on Nov. 4. The measure was sponsored by subcommittee Chairman Charles W. Stenholm, D-Texas.

In a review that began in 1992, the Agriculture Department found that thousands of convenience stores no longer qualified to accept food stamps because they did not meet

the definition of "retail food stores." Under existing law, that designation was limited to outlets in which at least 50 percent of food sales were made up of staples: meat, poultry and fish; bread or cereals; vegetables or fruits; and dairy products. The requirement was intended to encourage good nutrition.

Unless that definition was refined, however, about half of the 56,000 convenience stores authorized to accept food stamps no longer would qualify, department reviewers found. And if those stores no longer accepted food stamps, the bill's supporters said, poor residents of rural areas and inner-city neighborhoods lacking supermarkets would have trouble buying food. "In many areas of concern, those are the only stores available," said Agriculture Committee Chairman E. "Kika" de la Garza, D-Texas, during the panel's markup Nov. 9.

The department postponed revoking the authorization for the convenience stores, pending the legislative changes.

Provisions

The bill permitted stores to continue participating in the food stamp program if they met one of two conditions. The first was that they continually offered for sale a variety of foods in each of the four categories of staples. The stores also had to sell perishable foods in at least two of the four categories. Alternatively, at least 50 percent of the outlet's total store sales — not just food sales — had to consist of staples.

The legislation also:
● Directed the Agriculture secretary to issue regulations providing for periodic reauthorization of stores.
● Permitted information from stores about the food stamp program to be used by federal and state investigators.
● Required the Agriculture Department to conduct demonstration projects to enable state or local police to investigate food stamp trafficking.

What Is a 'Retail Food Store'?

Ellen Haas, the Agriculture Department's assistant secretary for Food and Consumer Services, told the House committee that the existing definition of a "retail food store" had kept pace neither "with changing retailer practices over the years nor consumer shopping practices."

Such entities as gasoline stations, bars and party stores had little trouble meeting the definition, she noted, even though they primarily sold non-food items. That was because such outlets sold the required proportion of staple foods in relation to their total food sales. "The participation of such stores has harmed the program's image," Haas said.

By requiring that at least half of a store's total sales come from food staples, she said, the legislation would restrict the number of gas stations and other non-food outlets that qualified to accept food stamps.

Stores such as doughnut shops, coffee shops and ice cream vendors still would be prohibited from taking food stamps under the new definition.

Thomas W. Ewing, R-Ill., wondered if a museum food stand could simply put an apple on the counter and qualify to accept food stamps. Haas said it could not.

Other members raised concerns about the price and nutritional content of convenience store foods. Haas told Bill Sarpalius, D-Texas, that she was "appalled there has been virtually no nutrition education and consumer education" for food stamp recipients, and she promised to do something about it.

Dan Glickman, D-Kan., wondered if convenience stores were appropriate places to accept food stamps because they were more expensive than supermarkets. Haas said that the department had not done a price comparison, although she acknowledged that other surveys had shown convenience stores to be more expensive.

But the real issue, Haas insisted, was that many residents of inner-city neighborhoods and rural areas had few alternatives to shopping at convenience stores. ■

New Entitlement Program For Troubled Families

Lawmakers agreed to create an entitlement program aimed at keeping troubled families together and giving early help to children who were at risk of being put into foster care. The legislation, approved as part of the 1993 reconciliation bill (HR 2264 — H Rept 103-213), provided $930 million for the program through fiscal 1998. The initiative sprang from concern that while states received considerable federal aid for programs to remove children from troubled homes and place them in foster care, there was relatively little federal assistance devoted to helping families overcome a crisis and stay together.

The program, which expanded the child welfare sections of the Social Security Act, provided the states with money to help keep families together. Such programs, which existed in more than 30 states, provided intense temporary counseling at home to troubled families whose children faced the possibility of being placed in foster care. States were allowed to use the money for community services such as programs to improve parenting skills, temporary assistance to parents and other child guardians, activities to improve relationships between parents and children, information and referral services, and early developmental screening of children.

The program was a "capped" entitlement, with a set amount of money available to the states each year; the money was not subject to annual appropriations. (By contrast, unlimited entitlement programs provided whatever money was needed to cover all those eligible for benefits.) The law authorized $60 million for family preservation services in fiscal 1994, $150 million in 1995, $225 million in 1996, $240 million in 1997 and $255 million in 1998.

The House on Aug. 5 adopted the conference report on the reconciliation bill, which was designed to reconcile taxes and entitlement spending with deficit-reduction goals, by a vote of 218-216. The Senate cleared the bill, 51-50, on Aug. 6, and President Clinton signed it (PL 103-66) on Aug. 10. (Budget-reconciliation, p. 107)

BACKGROUND

There was widespread agreement in Congress that the existing child welfare law gave states an incentive to rely on the expensive and overburdened foster care system, rather than investing in preventive services. Under an existing, unlimited foster care entitlement, states were to receive about $2.6 billion from the federal government in fiscal 1993. By contrast, the federal government expected to pay only about $295 million in fiscal 1993 for child welfare services aimed at preventing children from needing foster care. The need for preventive services was clearly growing. According to child

welfare advocates, child abuse and neglect cases had increased from 1.1 million in 1980 to 2.7 million in 1991.

The Bush administration and many GOP lawmakers had favored expanding services for abused and neglected children. But they balked at raising taxes for the purpose and objected to creating a new entitlement, preferring instead to reorient money within the foster care program.

The House had passed a $7 billion overhaul of the child welfare system in 1992 that included a capped entitlement to help states pay for services designed to keep troubled families together; the program was to be paid for with a 10 percent surtax on millionaires. But the measure was incorporated into a larger tax bill that President George Bush vetoed. *(1992 Almanac, p. 462)*

Unlike his GOP predecessors, Clinton endorsed the idea of a capped entitlement for family support and preservation services and requested $60 million in fiscal 1994 for the program, increasing to $600 million by fiscal 1998.

LEGISLATIVE ACTION

House Approves Entitlement

The House Ways and Means Subcommittee on Human Resources approved the capped entitlement by voice vote April 27, authorizing $1.4 billion for the program over five years. The provisions were among several that the subcommittee recommended for inclusion in the House reconciliation bill.

Subcommittee Republicans objected to the costs and expressed skepticism that family preservation programs could be efficient. Fred Grandy, R-Iowa, offered several unsuccessful amendments, including one that would have combined some foster care and adoption programs under a capped entitlement, using Congressional Budget Office (CBO) estimates of future program costs. That would have put a ceiling on costs but would have given states broad flexibility to use the money for purposes that could have included family preservation. Democrats opposed putting foster care into a capped entitlement, saying that it would be difficult to predict each state's needs. The amendment was defeated 4-7 in a party-line vote.

Grandy offered another amendment that would have used CBO estimates but added $1.3 billion over five years. But Democrats still objected to putting a ceiling on foster care spending, and the amendment was defeated by the same 4-7 margin.

The full Ways and Means Committee agreed May 11 to include the family preservation provisions in the reconciliation bill, and the House approved the overall bill, 219-213, on May 27.

Senate, Final Action

John D. Rockefeller IV, D-W.Va., and Christopher S. Bond, R-Mo., introduced a family preservation bill (S 596) in the Senate early in the year, but the Senate did not include any family preservation provisions in its reconciliation bill. The $2.2 billion Rockefeller-Bond measure would have offered a more comprehensive overhaul of child welfare laws by creating three capped entitlements for family preservation and related programs. Some of the money would have been targeted for children in families beset by drug or alcohol abuse.

House and Senate conferees agreed to include the House-passed entitlement in the final reconciliation bill but scaled back the funding to $930 million over five years. ∎

Lawmakers Fail To Revise Domestic Worker Taxes

Despite the uproar caused by the discovery that President Clinton's first choice to be attorney general had failed to pay Social Security taxes for domestic workers, Congress made only moderate progress toward changing the wage threshold for requiring such payments.

Under existing law, employers were supposed to pay Social Security and Medicare taxes for housekeepers, baby sitters, gardeners, lawn mowers and other domestic workers if those individuals earned more than $50 per quarter. The wage threshold had not been changed since the Social Security law was expanded to include household workers in 1950. The tax requirement, which also involved the filing of quarterly tax forms, was unknown to many household employers and widely ignored by others.

Lawmakers in both the House and Senate agreed that the $50 wage threshold was outdated and virtually invited non-compliance. But they could not agree on an acceptable new figure.

The House version of the budget-reconciliation bill (HR 2264) increased the threshold to $1,800 per year in 1994 and indexed it thereafter to the average increase in wages. It also adjusted the threshold retroactively, to $1,750 in 1993, for example. But the provisions were dropped in conference, falling victim to a little-known budget rule that blocked Senate consideration of any reconciliation bill that contained provisions that changed Social Security.

Senate Finance Committee Chairman Daniel Patrick Moynihan, D-N.Y., argued that the House-passed increases in the tax threshold were too steep and would jeopardize retirement coverage for many workers. Moynihan introduced his own bill (S 1231) to raise the threshold to $610 annually. He was eyeing the possibility of packaging that measure with a separate proposal to make the Social Security Administration an independent agency. *(Social Security, p. 380)*

BACKGROUND

The Social Security tax question exploded into public view with the disclosure that corporate attorney Zoë Baird of Hartford, Conn., Clinton's first choice for attorney general, had employed an illegal alien as her baby sitter and failed to pay either Social Security taxes or unemployment taxes for the woman and her husband, who worked for Baird as a driver. The revelation prompted a public outcry, and members of the Senate Judiciary Committee were swamped with calls and letters opposing Baird's nomination. She asked that it be withdrawn Jan. 21, after two grueling days of testimony before the committee. *(Attorney general nomination, p. 303)*

According to the Internal Revenue Service, as few as 25 percent of household employers were complying with the law's quarterly reporting and tax payment requirements. Under the Federal Insurance Contributions Act (FICA), employers and their workers were each required to pay taxes of 7.65 percent of the worker's pay (6.2 percent for Social Security and 1.45 percent for Medicare). Many employers of domestic workers paid both shares of the tax.

To earn credits toward Social Security coverage, domestic workers had to meet a two-part earnings test. They had to earn $50 per per quarter per employer to have their

wages reported and be subject to Social Security taxes. They also had to earn at least $590 a year to get a quarter of coverage from Social Security, which was a measurement of work used to determine Social Security eligibility. Workers could earn up to four quarters a year and generally needed 40 quarters to qualify for retirement benefits.

Unless household employers paid the required Social Security and Medicare taxes, the workers involved could not qualify for retirement and health benefits when they reached age 65.

Even raising the threshold and relaxing the filing requirements was unlikely to gain full compliance from employers and their workers, however. Many household workers preferred to be paid "off the books" — either to avoid paying income taxes on their earnings or to continue meeting restrictive income eligibility requirements for other federal benefits such as welfare or housing programs. And illegal aliens often were afraid of exposing their immigration status.

Also, raising the threshold meant that some domestic workers would no longer qualify for Social Security coverage or would have their benefits reduced.

Although the Baird nomination highlighted the tax threshold question, it was not the first time the issue had drawn attention in Congress. Provisions to increase the threshold had been included in two tax bills (HR 4210, HR 11) that President George Bush vetoed in 1992.

HOUSE ACTION

Two House Ways and Means subcommittees examined the tax issue at a well-attended hearing March 4. Members considered a variety of proposed new thresholds and reporting requirements.

"Single-handedly, Ms. Baird has done more to publicize the law which provides Social Security coverage for domestic employees than the IRS or the Social Security Administration have ever managed to do," declared Jim Bunning, R-Ky., ranking Republican on the Social Security Subcommittee. The Human Resources Subcommittee also participated in the hearing.

Carrie Meek, D-Fla., a former domestic worker, warned the Ways and Means members that they should not concentrate solely on providing relief for employers. "The goal of this legislation is not merely to make life easier for those who can afford to hire domestic help," she said. "It is rather to encourage compliance with the law and thereby ensure the economic well-being of domestic workers when they retire or are suddenly out of work."

Subcommittee Markup

On April 28, the House Ways and Means Social Security Subcommittee recommended raising the wage threshold to $1,750 a year, from $50 per quarter. Subcommittee Chairman Andrew Jacobs Jr., D-Ind., noted that the Baird case would not have been affected by the proposed changes because Baird's employees worked full-time and earned more than $1,750 per year.

The proposed new threshold was figured by calculating what the $50 quarterly threshold would have been in 1993 if it had been subject to an annual percentage increase equivalent to the average percentage increase in wages since 1950. Under the bill, the threshold was to increase to $1,800 annually in 1994 and be indexed in subsequent years to the average increase in wages.

The bill also adjusted the threshold retroactively. Employers no longer would be liable for retroactive taxes on domestic workers whose incomes fell short of the new thresholds.

The Joint Committee on Taxation estimated that increasing the threshold would lower revenues by $114 million over five years. Jacobs questioned that estimate, alluding to previous predictions by Joint Tax that a higher threshold actually could raise revenue by encouraging more employers to comply with the law.

Under the subcommittee proposal, domestic workers who earned less than $1,750 per employer in 1993 would no longer qualify for any credits toward Social Security coverage that year. According to the Social Security Administration, about 16 percent of the estimated 733,000 domestic workers covered by Social Security in 1993 would no longer qualify for credits toward Social Security coverage under the proposal. About 41 percent might lose some earnings posted to their Social Security record, possibly reducing their benefits.

Full Committee Markup

The full House Ways and Means Committee approved the threshold increase May 11, despite objections by Barbara B. Kennelly, D-Conn., that the committee was raising the threshold too sharply, denying Social Security coverage to many domestic workers. The measure was included in the Ways and Means legislative package for the huge budget-reconciliation bill (HR 2264).

Committee members rejected Kennelly's amendment to impose a less dramatic increase in the threshold by a 19-19 vote. Kennelly's amendment would have set the threshold at $1,000. It would not have indexed the figure to future wage increases or adjusted it retroactively, as the committee's proposal did. Under Kennelly's amendment, about 8 percent of domestic workers would no longer qualify for Social Security credits, and 27 percent might lose some earnings posted to their record.

"I'm not going to drop the issue," Kennelly said later. "This really is egregious. The Social Security standards over the years have really been inequitable to women, and we can't continue to allow this," she said, noting that most domestic workers were women. Kennelly noted that a housekeeper who earned $50 a day working every other week for 10 employers would no longer qualify for Social Security under the committee plan.

Kennelly said she planned to urge Sens. Barbara A. Mikulski, D-Md., Carol Moseley-Braun, D-Ill., and Barbara Boxer, D-Calif., to try to change the provision in the Senate.

The committee accepted an amendment to enable employers of domestic workers to file Social Security payments on their income tax returns and adjust tax-withholding from their own wages, a change that Rostenkowski had repeatedly suggested.

The modified Social Security provision was then approved by the House May 27 as part of the reconciliation bill. *(Budget-reconciliation, p. 107)*

SENATE ACTION

Although the Social Security tax threshold was addressed in the House version of reconciliation, Senate Finance Committee Chairman Moynihan said July 21 that procedural concerns constrained the Senate from including the issue in the deficit-reduction bill. He said he preferred to handle the matter in separate legislation.

In addition to increasing the threshold to $610 from a single employer in a year, Moynihan's bill exempted from Social Security taxes the earnings of baby sitters, yard workers and other domestic employees under age 18.

Moynihan noted that in the 1950s, the test for coverage of domestic workers and for qualifying for a quarter of Social Security coverage were the same. He said his proposal would restore that relationship by eliminating the separate $50 per quarter per employer figure for domestic workers and merely setting an annual $610 threshold.

His approach drew praise at a Finance Committee hearing on the issue July 21.

Rep. Meek of Florida warned that the House-backed increase could cause as many as 300,000 domestic workers to lose some Social Security benefits. "We need to encourage better compliance with the law, not provide tax relief for employers," Meek said.

Although she introduced a bill (HR 1114) that would set an annual earnings threshold of $300, Meek described Moynihan's bill as "very reasonable."

Representatives from the National Women's Law Center, Older Women's League and National Council of Senior Citizens, as well as the Clinton administration, generally echoed her comments.

David T. Ellwood, assistant secretary for planning and evaluation at the Department of Health and Human Services, said, "There is no magic number" to use as a threshold. But Ellwood said that a threshold "above $1,000 is very hard to justify," and that it would not "protect domestic workers who desperately need Social Security coverage."

Randolf Hurst Hardock, acting benefits tax counsel for the Treasury Department, suggested that a $1,000 threshold would be particularly appealing because it would be easier for taxpayers to remember. Hardock also recommended that the threshold be indexed periodically in even dollar amounts. For instance, he said the $1,000 threshold could be indexed to $1,200 after five years or to $1,500 after 11 years, assuming a 4 percent annual increase in wages.

The Parliamentary Hang-Up

The parliamentary problem Moynihan cited was a budget act provision stipulating that a reconciliation bill in the Senate could not contain any provisions affecting Social Security benefits. If a point of order was upheld on this issue, the entire reconciliation bill would be at risk.

Andrew Jacobs Jr., D-Ind., chairman of the House Ways and Means Subcommittee on Social Security, said he was disappointed at the prospect of delays, along with "millions of American families who are kind of up in the air now on what the law is or could be."

Moynihan said that his committee could address the issue separately later in the 103rd Congress. "I think we have the makings of a bipartisan measure here," he said. Sen. Bob Packwood, R-Ore., agreed. "If we can't solve this one," Packwood said, "we can't solve anything."

One possibility, the chairman indicated, was to package the tax threshold provisions with proposals to make the Social Security Administration an independent agency and to respond to growing concern about the financial health of the Social Security-administered disability fund. The latter measure would reallocate 0.275 percent of the employer and employee Social Security payroll tax from the Old-Age and Survivors Insurance Trust Fund to the disability fund. The overall 7.65 percent Social Security payroll tax would remain unchanged. ∎

Moynihan Pushes To Alter Social Security's Status

The Senate Finance Committee approved legislation Nov. 19 to make the Social Security Administration an independent agency. But the action came just days before adjournment, and the full Senate did not consider the measure.

The bill (S 1560 — S Rept 103-221), sponsored by committee Chairman Daniel Patrick Moynihan, D-N.Y., was sent to the floor on a voice vote. It was the third time in five years that the Finance Committee had approved legislation to separate the agency from the Department of Health and Human Services (HHS). Previous bills died on the Senate floor.

Asked why its fate would be any different in the 103rd Congress, Moynihan said, "The idea's matured." He indicated that the Clinton administration's emphasis on health care had relegated Social Security to a lesser role within HHS, to the displeasure of many in Congress.

The Clinton administration opposed the legislation, as had the Bush administration. However, Moynihan said that early drafts of Clinton's plan to reorganize government had included a proposal to make Social Security independent. *(Reinventing government, p. 191)*

Although S 1560 dealt only with the issue of independence for the Social Security Administration, Moynihan indicated that he might combine it with proposals to reallocate payroll taxes to help out the agency's disability fund and to increase the threshold for payment of Social Security taxes for domestic workers. *(Domestic workers, p. 378)*

Background

Social Security had been an independent entity for four years after it was first created in 1935. Interest in returning it to independent status began soon after the federal budget was "unified" in fiscal 1969 to reflect all federal spending, including the Social Security trust fund.

Efforts toward independence intensified in the 1980s, when the Reagan administration cut the agency's staff by 21 percent and tossed 265,000 recipients of disability benefits off the rolls. Many beneficiaries were later reinstated.

The House passed legislation to make Social Security independent in 1986, but the measure died in the Senate. Similar legislation reached the House floor again in 1989, as part of the Omnibus Budget Reconciliation Act. The Senate Finance Committee went along, but the measure died on the floor. *(1989 Almanac, p. 221; 1986 Almanac, p. 594)*

The initiative's supporters geared up again in 1992, when the House passed a measure by a 350-8 vote. The Senate Finance Committee approved a companion bill, but it died on the Senate floor once more. *(1992 Almanac, p. 472)*

More than 100 interest groups supported giving Social Security its independence, including the American Association of Retired Persons (AARP). "If someone wants a good Social Security vote, this is a good one to take home to the folks," said Evelyn Morton, an AARP legislative representative.

Moynihan's Crusade

Moynihan had argued for years that the Social Security Administration was too big and too important to be just another agency of HHS. At a Sept. 14 Finance Committee hearing, he said the agency had about 65,000 workers, an annual budget of more than $300 billion and outlays that

were larger than those of 11 federal departments combined. He contended that independence would heighten Social Security's visibility and isolate it somewhat from the party in control of the White House, giving it more autonomy to direct and protect the Social Security trust fund, which paid Social Security benefits.

But HHS Secretary Donna E. Shalala, like her predecessors under GOP administrations, said there was no need to split off the Social Security Administration. The public might be clamoring for some sort of change, she said, but it had little to do with independence. Rather, people were reacting to "whether they think the Social Security system will be there for them and whether the trust fund will be solvent or not."

In testimony to Moynihan's committee, Shalala insisted that Social Security should remain within her purview. "It is here that Social Security and its beneficiaries are assured the top Cabinet-level leadership, attention and support that they need and deserve," she said. Distancing the program from HHS "would seriously dilute the attention and support it will receive at the highest level of our government." She spoke of her determination to "make the tough decisions necessary to restore the public's waning confidence in Social Security." And she said making Social Security independent would have no bearing on the trust fund's fiscal soundness.

Phil Gambino, an agency spokesman, said making Social Security independent "doesn't change how the trust funds are invested, nor would it change the financial solvency of the program. It would be purely administrative."

Moynihan drew support for his proposal during the hearing from Sens. Donald W. Riegle Jr., D-Mich., David Pryor, D-Ark., and Charles E. Grassley, R-Iowa.

The effort also was endorsed by Bob Packwood of Oregon, the Finance Committee's ranking Republican. Another Finance Committee member, John H. Chafee, R-R.I., reaffirmed his opposition to the plan, however. "If it ain't broke, don't fix it," Chafee had said in 1992.

Debate Over Structure

Moynihan also had the support of Andrew Jacobs Jr., D-Ind., chairman of the House Ways and Means Social Security Subcommittee, who was sponsoring his own version of the bill (HR 647). "I will do everything in my capacity to push it along in the House when it comes over," Jacobs said.

However, the two differed over the structure of an independent agency. Moynihan favored having the agency governed by a single commissioner, appointed by the president and advised by a seven-member board. Jacobs was just as committed to establishing a bipartisan three-member board to make policy while an executive director ran the agency.

Several experts at the Sept. 14 hearing endorsed the idea of a single commissioner, saying it was the only way to effectively manage such a large and diverse organization. These experts included Robert J. Myers, the agency's former chief actuary for 23 years and executive director of the 1982-83 National Commission on Social Security Reform, as well as Elmer B. Staats, who served as the commission's chairman.

Those who favored administration by a board said that approach would minimize partisanship within the agency by presenting alternative points of view. They also said a board would be a check on any future president who sought to cut people from disability rolls. The board approach had

the support of Arthur S. Flemming, a secretary of the Department of Health, Education and Welfare (predecessor to HHS) under President Dwight D. Eisenhower. Flemming represented the Save Our Security Coalition and Education Fund, an organization of labor and other groups concerned with Social Security and health care.

Jacobs said he was convinced that having a single administrator running an independent Social Security agency was a bad idea. "A Social Security czar strikes me as bizarre," he said. "Our whole system is based on a separation of power, legislative and executive. The board should set broad policy; the director or commissioner carries out those policies." ∎

Adoption Bias, Energy Aid, Poverty Issues Considered

Congress took the following action on bills that dealt with adoption discrimination, energy assistance to low-income families and the distribution of poverty data:

ADOPTION DISCRIMINATION

The Senate Labor and Human Resources Committee on Oct. 6 gave voice vote approval to a bill (S 1224) to bar adoption agencies that received federal funding from discriminating against people who wanted to adopt a child of another race. Luis V. Gutierrez, D-Ill., introduced a companion House bill (HR 3307). Neither bill advanced further in the first session.

The Senate committee bill allowed agencies to consider the race, color or national origin of the prospective parents but not to use those factors as the only criteria in denying an adoption.

The bill's sponsor, Howard M. Metzenbaum, D-Ohio, introduced a substitute for his original bill, laying out more clearly that the bill favored "transracial or multiethnic" adoptions over long-term foster care. It said such adoptions could not be denied or delayed. Metzenbaum offered the new bill to get support from Daniel R. Coats, R-Ind.

The bill also prohibited the disqualification of any person "from initial consideration" based on race.

ENERGY ASSISTANCE

The Senate cleared legislation (HR 3321) on Nov. 22 that gave states more flexibility in determining how much energy assistance to give residents of federally assisted housing. President Clinton signed the measure into law on Dec. 14 (PL 103-185).

The House had passed the bill Nov. 15. Both chambers acted by voice vote.

The Low Income Home Energy Assistance Program (LIHEAP) provided federal grants to states to help low-income people pay their heating and cooling bills and to weatherize their homes. Some federally assisted housing programs — such as public housing and federally subsidized private housing — also provided allowances to individuals to help pay their energy bills.

The legislation allowed states to reduce LIHEAP benefits for these residents by the amount they received from other programs to pay heating or cooling costs. Under

existing law, states were not allowed to reduce or eliminate LIHEAP to people receiving utility allowances through these other programs. As a result, states were paying full LIHEAP benefits to individuals who also were receiving utility allowances through the housing programs.

POVERTY DATA

The House passed a bill by voice vote Nov. 21 that required the Census Bureau to develop poverty data every two years for states, counties, cities and school districts. The Senate did not act on the measure.

The bill (HR 1645 — H Rept 103-401), known as The Poverty Data Improvement Act of 1993, was aimed at helping Congress target more than $20 billion in annual spending on federal programs such as the Chapter 1 education program for disadvantaged children, the Job Training Partnership Act, community development block grants and rural housing programs. It was sponsored by Tom Sawyer, D-Ohio, chairman of the House Post Office and Civil Service Subcommittee on Census, Statistics and Postal Personnel. Sawyer's subcommittee reported the bill Nov. 20.

Under existing law, poverty data was released after each decennial census. Sawyer said the data quickly became outdated.

For example, he noted that until the spring of 1993, the government had used 1980 data — which relied on 1979 income — to distribute Chapter 1 education funds. Yet the number of poor school-age children increased by as much as 67 percent in some states during that decade, while it decreased as much as 34 percent in others, Sawyer said.

Under the bill, the Census Bureau was to begin distributing the biennial poverty figures in 1996. The bureau estimated that such an exercise would cost about $1 million annually. To develop the data, the bureau was to use administrative records, such as federal tax returns and enrollment records in such anti-poverty programs as Aid to Families With Dependent Children and the food stamps program. ∎

Health, Welfare Changes Approved by Panel

The Senate Finance Committee approved draft legislation Nov. 17 consisting of more than 120 health and income security provisions described as no-cost items that dealt, in part, with child welfare, rural hospitals and health insurance for the elderly. The bill (S 1668) went no further.

Some of the measures had been included in an omnibus 1992 tax bill (HR 11), which President George Bush vetoed. Others had been dropped from the 1993 budget-reconciliation bill (HR 2264 — PL 103-66) under the so-called Byrd rule.

The rule, named for its author, Sen. Robert C. Byrd, D-W.Va., barred "extraneous" matter from reconciliation bills. S 1668 prompted little discussion and won voice vote approval.

Income Security

The nearly three dozen income security provisions included one that clarified a citizen's right to sue a state for enforcement of programs under the federal Social Security Act, which included Aid to Families with Dependent Children, foster care programs and Medicaid, the federal-state health insurance program for the poor.

The language was a compromise agreed to by organizations representing state officials as well as child advocacy groups. It had been part of the 1992 tax bill as well as the House version of the 1993 reconciliation bill.

The provision responded to a recent Supreme Court decision focusing on child welfare laws. The ruling dealt with the Adoption Assistance and Child Welfare Act of 1980 (PL 96-272), which required states to make a "reasonable effort" to save a child from being placed in foster care and, if placed, returned home. The court, in its 1992 *Suter v. Artist M.* decision, turned down a citizen suit based on this "reasonable effort" clause, and called into question whether individuals had the right to bring suit to enforce the Social Security Act provisions.

The committee-approved language ensured that individuals who had been damaged by state failures to comply with federal mandates would generally have standing to sue. However, the measure still restricted a person's right to sue under the "reasonable efforts" clause.

Other income security provisions:
● Required state child support enforcement agencies to periodically report to credit bureaus the names of people who were at least two months delinquent in child support payments and the amount of their delinquency.
● Required the secretary of Health and Human Services (HHS), working with the Agriculture Secretary, to provide an annual report on the characteristics of families that depended on welfare programs and the duration that they collected welfare.
● Established federal rules for awarding child welfare training grants for social workers.
● Required the HHS secretary to issue regulations guiding the withholding of federal funds when state child welfare and foster care programs did not comply with state requirements.

Health Provisions

The committee also approved health provisions that clarified existing law and strengthened consumer protections. The bill included provisions to:
● **Community hospitals.** Extend the Essential Access Community Hospital program through fiscal 1995. The program primarily helped rural hospitals that were in financial trouble. The bill authorized a $25 million annual grant program to help hospitals and encourage them to focus on primary care services, and it expanded the program from seven states to nine. Under a separate program, rural primary care hospitals were to be eligible for grants from the Rural Health Transition Grant program, authorized at $30 million annually through fiscal 1997.
● **Changes in billing policies.** Extend further protections to elderly patients who were subject to overcharges by physicians. Under existing law, physicians who did not accept Medicare reimbursement rates as full payment for their services were allowed to charge patients part of the difference between their price for a service and the Medicare rate. However, some physicians tried to make up the full amount.

In the mid-1980s that practice cost Medicare beneficiaries nearly $3 million a year. The amount dropped to $1.3 million in 1992, after a 1989 law (PL 101-239) limited the amount doctors could bill patients over and above the Medicare-approved charge. S 1668 gave additional enforcement powers to the Department of Health and Human

Services, and it required that the policy be explained on the Explanation of Medicare Benefits forms that were sent to all beneficiaries. *(1989 Almanac, p. 157)*

● **Clarification of Medigap policies**. Reduce the penalties on the sale of Medigap insurance to the elderly. Medigap policies covered medical costs not covered by Medicare, such as coinsurance and deductibles. At the time, stiff penalties could be imposed on any insurer who sold additional health insurance policies to those elderly beneficiaries who already had a Medigap or similar policy.

The goal had been to ensure that elderly beneficiaries were not tricked into buying multiple policies with the same benefits.

But the penalties were so severe that companies often refused to sell policies even to beneficiaries who needed them to cover gaps in their coverage. The reduction in penalties was intended to facilitate the sale of the policies. However, the bill also required that all policies include a clearly displayed statement disclosing whether they duplicated Medicare benefits. ■

American Indian Bills Advance in 1993

Congress in 1993 considered a number of bills related to American Indians.

LAND CLAIMS

Congress resolved a 153-year-old land dispute between the Catawba Indian tribe and 62,000 South Carolina landowners Oct. 12, when the House cleared legislation (HR 2399) by voice vote authorizing a settlement. President Clinton signed the bill Oct. 27 (PL 103-116).

The dispute stemmed from an 1840 treaty under which the state of South Carolina purchased 144,000 acres from the Catawbas. The tribe called the sale invalid because Congress never ratified it. The Catawbas had tried in court since 1980 to regain the land and threatened to sue roughly 62,000 private landowners.

Early in 1993, the tribe reached a settlement with the landowners under which the Catawbas would relinquish their land claim. Congressional approval and the president's signature were the final steps in ratifying the agreement.

In exchange for giving up its land claim, the tribe received $50 million over five years. The federal government contributed $32 million; the remaining $18 million was raised from state, local and private sources. The bill earmarked $7.5 million to be spread among 1,400 members of the Catawba tribe. Each member was expected to receive an average of $5,700.

The agreement restored the Catawbas' status as a federally recognized Indian tribe, making members eligible for additional federal assistance. In 1959, Congress had stripped the Catawbas of their official status as part of a federal effort to assimilate American Indians into mainstream society.

The House Natural Resources Committee took the first step, approving the legislation Sept. 22, by voice vote (H Rept 103-257, Part 1). The House approved the measure five days later by voice vote. The Senate approved its version of the bill Oct. 5 by voice vote. On Oct. 12 the House agreed to the amended Senate bill, clearing the measure for the president.

TRIBAL COURTS

Underfunded tribal court systems got a boost when the Senate cleared legislation (HR 1268) on Nov. 20 to funnel technical and financial resources to the struggling courts. President Clinton signed the measure (PL 103-176) on Dec. 3.

The bill authorized $58 million annually through fiscal 2000, more than four times the amount provided to tribal

courts in fiscal 1993. The bulk of the money was to be used to create an Office of Tribal Justice Support within the Bureau of Indian Affairs (BIA), supplanting the bureau's Branch of Judicial Services.

Many Indian tribes, recognized as quasi-independent nations, operated judicial systems outside the jurisdiction of U.S. courts. Under federal law, Indian tribes were accorded authority over any tribal governance that was not specifically given to Congress. A 1968 Indian civil rights law ensured that Indian tribes had the right to exercise legal jurisdiction over their affairs. Traditionally, the tribal courts suffered from a lack of financial and technical support.

Legislative efforts to shore up tribal courts had been hung up for the previous three years over Senate provisions that would have given tribal judicial conferences some say in the administration of Indian justice programs.

The House Natural Resources Committee acted first on the 1993 measure, approving it by voice vote July 28 (H Rept 103-205). The House quickly followed suit, passing the bill by voice vote Aug. 2.

The Senate Committee on Indian Affairs took up the legislation Aug. 6, approving it by voice vote. The Senate passed its version of the bill later in the day by voice vote.

But the Senate and House versions still differed over granting tribal judicial conferences control over aspects of justice programs. In the last days of the 1993 session, House-Senate conferees agreed to a compromise that allowed the judicial conferences to administer certain functions of the programs (H Rept 103-383).

Conferences could contract with the BIA to employ judges and judicial staff, develop standards of conduct, train personnel, construct law libraries and develop innovative projects for victims services, alternative dispute resolution and child abuse.

Both chambers approved the final version of the bill by voice vote on Nov. 19.

LUMBEE TRIBE

Revisiting a century old debate over the status of the Lumbee tribe of Cheraw Indians in eastern North Carolina, the House approved a bill (HR 334) Oct. 28, making the tribe eligible for federal social services. But the Senate did not act on the bill in the first session.

The House-passed bill amended a 1956 law that recognized the Lumbees as an Indian tribe but prohibited its members from receiving federal funds through the Bureau of Indian Affairs (BIA) and the Indian Health Service. The 1956 law also forbade the Lumbee tribe from seeking for-

mal recognition, and thus federal benefits, through the process administered by the BIA. The Lumbee tribe first sought federal recognition in 1890, but it had been routinely denied for economic and political reasons.

Against Republican opposition, the House Natural Resources Committee approved the bill, 27-14, June 16 (H Rept 103-290). Republicans opposed HR 334 because of its cost — $80 million to $100 million a year, according to the Congressional Budget Office — and precedent. If the bill was enacted, said Craig Thomas, R-Wyo., other tribes would be encouraged to seek recognition legislatively rather than administratively.

When the bill reached the floor, Thomas offered an amendment that would have set up a process for the Lumbees to apply for recognition through the Interior Department, instead of extending federal recognition to the tribe. But the House rejected the change, 178-238.

The last action of the year on the bill occurred when the House passed the measure Oct. 28, 228-184. *(Votes 537, 538, p. 132-H)*

INDIAN LANDS

Lawmakers cleared legislation Nov. 20 that was designed to improve the management of Indian farmlands and ranches. President Clinton signed the bill Dec. 3 (HR 1425 — PL 103-177).

The bill encouraged tribes to develop their own programs, tailored to the specific needs of their reservations, to manage Indian farmlands. The bill represented the fourth major legislative effort since 1986 aimed at improving farming and ranching opportunities on Indian lands.

This time, the legislation had a fairly easy ride. On Sept. 22 the House Natural Resources Committee approved the bill by voice vote (H Rept 103-367). The House quickly approved the legislation on Nov. 16, also by voice vote.

The Senate made quick work of the measure, with the Indian Affairs Committee sending the bill to the floor by voice vote Nov. 18 (S Rept 103-186). The the Senate cleared the bill by voice vote Nov. 20.

INDIAN DAMS

The Senate passed legislation (S 442) to repair unsafe dams in Indian country on July 20, but the bill stopped at the House Natural Resources Committee.

The Senate-passed measure directed the Interior secretary to fix and maintain dams on Indian lands, including 53 dams that were considered dangerous. Proponents of the measure said the Bureau of Indian Affairs had not complied with a 1980 dam safety program.

The Senate Indian Affairs Committee approved the measure, by voice vote, June 16 (S Rept 103-86). The House took no action on the legislation.

INDIAN ENVIRONMENTAL LAWS

On Nov. 11, Congress cleared legislation aimed at simplifying the implementation of federal environmental laws on Indian lands. President Clinton signed the bill on Nov. 24 (S 654 — PL 103-155).

The bill extended the authorization for the 1992 Indian Environmental General Assistance Program Act, at $15 million per year, through fiscal 2003. The act allowed the Environmental Protection Agency (EPA) to provide "omnibus" grants to Indian tribes to administer environmental laws, reducing paperwork and federal spending. Without the program, EPA would have had to issue separate grants for each federal environmental statute.

The Senate Indian Affairs Committee agreed to the bill by voice vote on June 16 (S Rept 103-87). On July 20, the full Senate passed the bill by voice vote.

The bill was stuck in the House until Nov. 8, when Bruce F. Vento, D-Minn., offered to suspend the rules, forgoing consideration of the bill by the House Natural Resources Committee, and the House amended and approved the measure by a voice vote. Three days later the Senate cleared the measure for the president by voice vote.

TRIBAL SELF-GOVERNANCE

The Senate on Nov. 24 approved a bill (S 1618) granting some Indian tribes permanent control over their federal programs and funds. The House did not act on the bill.

The bill sought to create a permanent tribal self-governance program and allow up to 20 new tribes to join the program every year.

In 1988, Congress established a demonstration project within the Bureau of Indian Affairs that allowed some tribes to take over the administration of federal programs for their tribes.

As the session wound down, supporters moved the bill quickly through the Senate. The Senate Indian Affairs Committee approved it Nov. 18 (S Rept 103-205), by voice vote, two weeks after it was introduced by Sen. John McCain, R-Ariz. Six days later, on the final day of the session, the Senate passed the bill by voice vote.

FEDERAL BENEFITS

The House failed to complete work on legislation to exclude from federal benefit formula calculations all income earned from the use of land owned by individual Indians.

Many Indian landowners earned royalties by opening their land to grazing, mining, logging or farming. The bill was aimed at letting them keep that income without fear of losing supplemental security income and other federal benefits. The only action on the bill (HR 1367) occurred May 3, when the House Natural Resources Subcommittee on Native American Affairs approved it on a voice vote.

OTHER INDIAN BILLS

The Senate also passed the following bills; the House did not act on them in the first session:

• **Menominee Tribe.** The Senate approved a bill (S 1335) by voice vote Aug. 6 to allow the Menominee Tribe of Wisconsin to sue the federal government for damages resulting from elimination of the tribe's federal recognition in 1954.

Tribes with federal recognition were eligible for federal benefits. The federal government restored the tribe's recognition in 1973.

• **Indian trade.** The Senate on Nov. 20 passed, by voice vote, a bill (S 1501 — S Rept 103-190) to repeal the 1834 Trading With Indians Act, which prohibited federal employees from engaging in trade with Indians.

The 159-year-old law was designed to prevent federal employees from taking advantage of Indians. But supporters of the bill said the law placed impractical restrictions on federal employees. For example, some federal employees were barred from selling a car to an Indian, according to bill sponsor Sen. John McCain, R-Ariz. ∎

Senate OKs Deer To Head Bureau of Indian Affairs

The Senate embraced Ada Deer, President Clinton's nominee to head the Bureau of Indian Affairs (BIA), easily approving her nomination by voice vote July 16. The Senate Indian Affairs Committee had approved Deer's nomination a day earlier, also by voice vote.

As the Interior Department's assistant secretary for Indian affairs, Deer was in charge of the bureau's annual $2.4 billion budget and 12,000 employees. The bureau served more than 500 recognized tribal governments.

Deer, an unsuccessful candidate for Congress in 1992, inherited a troubled federal agency that often was criticized by tribal governments and faced internal and external pressures to change its management practices.

Throughout its 169-year history, the BIA had been plagued by complaints, including allegations of corruption. Tribal leaders alleged that the bureau was inefficient and insensitive to the inadequate health care and failing economies found on many Indian reservations. A top priority for Deer was to determine whether changes at the BIA would be handled internally or mandated by Congress.

In Deer, Clinton chose an Indian activist widely respected, both on Capitol Hill and Indian reservations, as a passionate and experienced advocate for Indian rights. Indian leaders hoped that Deer, a social worker and former chairman of the Menominee Tribe, would be sympathetic to Indian concerns.

During her confirmation hearing, Deer pledged to improve the BIA by giving tribal governments more independence and control over their federal programs and funds.

Deer made unsuccessful bids in 1978 and 1982 for Wisconsin secretary of state. In 1992 she ran for Congress, scoring an upset over the favorite in the Democratic primary. She went on to lose to incumbent Republican Scott L. Klug in November. *(1992 Almanac, p. 43A; 1992 Weekly Report, p. 3288)* ∎

HHS Pick Shalala To Focus On Health-Care Reform

Donna E. Shalala, the first woman to head a Big Ten school as chancellor of the University of Wisconsin at Madison, won voice vote approval from the Senate on Jan. 21 as President Clinton's secretary of Health and Human Services (HHS). The Finance Committee, which had jurisdiction over the nomination, approved Shalala by voice vote Jan. 19.

The Jan. 14 Finance Committee hearing on the nomination was dominated by health-care issues familiar from the 1992 presidential campaign. "No problem afflicts families around the kitchen table more than the radical escalation of health-care costs," Shalala said, "and no problem demands our greater attention as policy-makers and public servants."

She said the government had to ensure health coverage for the roughly 35 million Americans who had no health insurance and another 35 million with inadequate coverage.

Senators pressed Shalala about when Clinton's health-care reform bill would arrive on Capitol Hill. Clinton previously had said he wanted to put together a plan during his first 100 days in office. Shalala said the president would not back away from his commitment to revamp the country's health-care system, but that the new administration needed to take over the department and determine program costs before sending a bill to the Hill.

Shalala also pledged to make the first four years of the Clinton administration the "years of the woman" in health care, with continued research to find cures and treatment for ovarian, cervical and breast cancers, and osteoporosis. For children, she said the department would increase immunizations to combat polio, rubella, mumps and measles. She also called for a strengthened commitment to Head Start, the education and health program for low-income preschoolers.

Shalala said the department had to develop a more comprehensive, aggressive program to deal with AIDS, including education, treatment and research to find a vaccine and a cure. "Silence and bigotry combined to slow our nation's response to this dread disease," she said.

While Finance Chairman Daniel Patrick Moynihan, D-N.Y., did not take issue with any of Shalala's pledges, he pointed out that most of her testimony was devoted to health issues. "Most of your budget goes to Social Security, and that wasn't mentioned," he said. And while Clinton had promised during the campaign to overhaul the welfare system, Moynihan said, Shalala made only a single reference to the subject.

Shalala responded, "While I didn't dwell as long on the president's welfare reform promises, you can be assured that from the moment, if I'm confirmed, we move into the department, we will have a task force at work to fill out the president's welfare reform pledges."

The Senate Labor and Human Resources Committee held a separate hearing on the nomination Jan. 15.

Shalala, 51, was a surprise pick to head HHS. She was mentioned as a possible secretary of Education because of her involvement in higher education, and as secretary of the Department of Housing and Urban Development because she served as an assistant secretary under President Jimmy Carter. Shalala had little experience in health policy but had been involved in children's programs as chairman of the board of the Children's Defense Fund, a children's advocacy group, succeeding Hillary Rodham Clinton in that post. *(1992 Almanac, p. 149-A)* ∎

Social Security Gets New Administrator

Shirley Sears Chater was sworn in as the new head of the Social Security Administration on Oct. 8, one day after the Senate approved her nomination. The Senate Finance Committee recommended her confirmation by voice vote on Sept. 30.

President Clinton announced Aug. 3 that he intended to nominate Chater to the post, but he delayed formally sending her name to the Senate. Administration officials said routine FBI background checks slowed the nomination. Chater had failed to pay Social Security taxes for part-time baby sitters from 1969 to 1975. She paid the taxes earlier in 1993, however. The issue of non-payment of Social Security taxes

had received national attention during the January confirmation hearings for Attorney General nominee Zoë Baird, who subsequently asked Clinton to withdraw her nomination. *(Attorney General appointment, p. 303)*

The top Social Security post had been vacant since Oct. 1, 1992, when Gwendolyn S. King resigned. In the interim, Lawrence H. Thompson served as acting commissioner. With 65,000 workers and 1,300 regional offices, the agency ran the federal government's largest domestic program and was expected to disburse more than $300 billion in retirement, survivors' and disability benefits in 1993.

The lengthy delay in filling the post prompted frequent criticism from Daniel Patrick Moynihan, D-N.Y., chairman of the Senate Finance Committee, which oversaw the Social Security system. "It's disgraceful," Moynihan said during a Sept. 14 hearing. "It indicates a lack of concern." His thoughts were echoed by David Pryor, D-Ark., usually a reliable ally of the Clinton administration. "I'm embarrassed that we don't have a commissioner," Pryor said.

During Chater's Sept. 29 confirmation hearing, Moynihan warned that the nominee had her work cut out for her. Calling the Social Security Administration "an agency in crisis," Moynihan painted a bleak picture of an organization that once was run well but which had "lost its internal energy." He said the agency was "disappearing from view," and cited recent surveys showing that a majority of working Americans did not believe they would receive the Social Security benefits that they had earned once they retired.

Chater agreed. "We must work to turn public opinion around before eroding public confidence . . . is transformed into popular support for measures that could diminish the system's effectiveness and endanger the financial security of millions of Americans," she said.

Chater had served as president of Texas Woman's University, where she was credited with increasing enrollment and restoring the institution's credibility with the state Legislature. She also had served as chairman of the Texas governor's Health Policy Task Force. ∎

Chapter 8

LABOR/
EDUCATION/
VETERANS/
HOUSING

Clinton Signs Family Leave Act

Democrats put long-stymied bill at front of the list; president declares end of congressional gridlock

President Clinton won his first legislative victory Feb. 4, when Congress cleared family and medical leave legislation.

The Family and Medical Leave Act required businesses with 50 or more employees to grant unpaid leave of up to 12 weeks to all but their top employees for the birth or adoption of a child or the illness of a close family member. The bill, designated HR 1, was the Democrats' first legislative priority in the new session, and Clinton and his allies in Congress heralded its passage as the end of gridlock on Capitol Hill after 12 years of divided government. Clinton signed the bill in a Rose Garden ceremony Feb. 5 (PL 103-3).

But the new era of Democratic control in the White House and Congress had not meant an effortless ride for the measure. GOP senators held up the bill for three days as they tried to gut it and use it as a vehicle for an unrelated goal: getting a floor vote on an amendment to ban homosexuals in the military. In addition, pro-business groups fought hard to kill the measure, arguing that it would hurt U.S. competitiveness and cost jobs.

As enacted, HR 1 was nearly identical to a bill that President George Bush had vetoed the year before. It allowed 12 weeks of unpaid leave during any 12-month period for employees who had worked for the same employer for at least one year and for at least 1,250 hours that year. Employers could deny leave to a worker who fell among the highest paid 10 percent of workers if that person was considered a key employee whose leave would result in "substantial and grievous economic injury" to the business. *(Provisions, p. 390)*

BACKGROUND

Congressional Democrats had been pushing family-leave legislation for years but had been stymied, mainly by the Republican White House. The first bill was introduced in 1985; some early versions would have applied to companies with as few as 15 employees and to employees who had worked only three months. Republicans killed a 1988 version with a Senate filibuster. By 1990, supporters mustered majorities for family-leave legislation in both chambers, but the House sustained a veto by Bush.

In 1991, Christopher J. Dodd, D-Conn., and Christopher S. Bond, R-Mo., brokered a compromise that earned

---

BOXSCORE

➡ **Family and Medical Leave (HR 1, S 5).** The law required employers with 50 or more employees to provide workers with up to 12 weeks of unpaid leave for the birth or adoption of a child or the illness of a close family member.

Reports: H Rept 103-8, Pts 1, 2; S Rept 103-3.

KEY ACTION

Feb. 3 — **House** passed HR 1 by a vote of 265-163.

Feb. 4 — **Senate** passed HR 1, 71-27, after the text of S 5 was inserted.

Feb. 4 — **House** cleared HR 1 by adopting a rule (H Res 71) that accepted the Senate amendments. The vote was 247-152.

Feb. 5 — **President** signed the bill — PL 103-3.

---

strong bipartisan support in the Senate. They made several changes — such as exempting key employees — to appease business interests. Conservatives, including Daniel R. Coats, R-Ind., who had felt uncomfortable opposing "pro-family" legislation but did not want to hurt businesses, then signed on.

The bill cleared in 1992, but once again Bush vetoed it, saying he did not want to place another government mandate on business; the House sustained his veto. *(1992 Almanac, p. 353; 1991 Almanac, p. 311; 1990 Almanac, p. 359)*

With Clinton's election, the dynamics suddenly changed. Clinton had made family leave one of his lead campaign issues and had promised to sign a bill quickly. Vice President Al Gore spoke frequently during the campaign about how fortunate he had been to take time off from work when his young son lay critically ill in the hospital after he was hit by a car. When the 103rd Congress convened, family and medical leave became the first legislative priority for the new administration.

Objections From Business

Because the law applied to businesses with 50 or more workers, about 95 percent of all employers were exempt. But the 5 percent subject to the law employed about 60 percent of all workers.

During the debate, business organizations such as the U.S. Chamber of Commerce and the National Federation of Independent Business vigorously fought the unpaid leave mandate.

Just before the bill went to the Senate floor, the National Retail Federation broke away from the anti-leave coalition to support the measure. President Tracy Mullin said the bill would no longer pose "an administrative nightmare" for retailers. "This bill has gone through an evolution," she said.

But the other groups maintained that the government had no right to impose mandates that might increase business costs. In addition, they feared that Congress would revisit the issue in a year or two and require them to give their workers paid leave.

On Feb. 3, House Speaker Thomas S. Foley, D-Wash., was emphatic: "There is no plan that I am aware of which treats this family leave bill as a staged development toward a legislative paid leave. None."

But some House members sharply disagreed, calling the

Provisions of the Family Leave Law

HR 1 (PL 103-3), signed on Feb. 5, required employers to give all but their top employees up to 12 weeks of unpaid leave a year to take care of a new baby or an ill family member. It went into effect six months after Clinton's signature. As enacted, the law:

● **Unpaid leave.** Required employers to allow employees to take up to 12 weeks of unpaid leave during any 12-month period because of the birth of a child; the adoption of a child or the placement of a foster child; the serious illness of a child, spouse or parent; or the employee's own serious health condition.

● **Eligibility.** Covered people who had worked for the employer for at least 12 months and for at least 1,250 hours during that period.

● **Exclusions.** Excluded employees who worked for a business with fewer than 50 employees within a 75-mile radius.

● **Intermittent leave.** Allowed employers to require workers who took intermittent leave for planned medical treatment to transfer temporarily to an available alternative position for which the worker was qualified, provided the position had equivalent pay and benefits and better accommodated the worker's schedule.

● **Accrual of leave.** Allowed workers who received paid leave for fewer than 12 weeks to take the additional weeks of leave up to the 12 weeks but without pay.

● **Substitutions.** Allowed workers to substitute any accrued paid vacation leave, personal leave or family leave for any part of the unpaid 12-week leave. Or, employers could require the employee to substitute paid leave for the unpaid portion. In other words, if a company already granted six weeks of paid leave, it had to grant six weeks of unpaid leave to reach the 12 weeks. The company did not have to offer 12 weeks' unpaid leave after paid leave was used up.

● **Employer notice.** Required employees to provide their employers with 30 days' notice when the leave was foreseeable, such as for the expected birth or adoption of a child.

● **Married employees.** Limited the aggregate number of weeks of leave to 12 when both spouses were employed by the same employer.

● **Certification.** Allowed employers to require that a request for leave be supported by a health-care provider's certification of the medical condition of the employee's child, spouse or parent, including the date on which the serious health condition began; the probable duration of the condition and other appropriate medical facts; a statement that the employee was needed to care for the child, spouse or parent, and an estimate of the amount of time that the employee was needed.

If the employee was ill, the certification was required to include a statement that the employee was unable to perform his or her job. When the certification was for intermittent leave for planned medical treatment, it was supposed to include the dates and duration of the treatment.

● **Second opinion.** Allowed the employer to require, at its expense, that the employee obtain the opinion of a second health-care provider when certifying the need for a leave of absence.

● **Third opinion.** Allowed the employer to require, in cases in which the second opinion differed from the first, that the employee obtain a third opinion from a health-care provider at the expense of the employer. The law required that the opinion of the third health-care provider be the final opinion, binding upon the employer and the employee.

● **Equivalent position.** Required that employers restore any employee who had taken leave to the position held by the employee when the leave began or restore the employee to an equivalent position with equivalent employment benefits, pay and other conditions.

● **Benefits.** Prohibited a leave of absence from causing the loss of any employment benefit accrued before the leave began.

● **Periodic reports.** Allowed the employer to require employees on leave to report periodically on their status and intention to return to work.

● **Top employees.** Allowed employers to deny leave to the highest-paid 10 percent of workers if such denial was necessary to prevent substantial and grievous economic injury to the business.

● **Health care.** Required the employer to maintain health-care benefits for employees on leave.

● **Congressional employees.** Applied to employees of the House and Senate.

---

bill a first step that would primarily benefit "yuppie" workers who did not live from paycheck to paycheck.

HOUSE ACTION

The House Education and Labor Committee approved HR 1 by a vote of 29-13 on Jan. 27, after Democrats fought off more than a dozen GOP amendments designed to mitigate what Republicans said would be the measure's negative impact on the business community.

Several amendments would have granted businesses more time to comply with the mandate. Ranking Republican Bill Goodling, Pa., sought to allow businesses to offer other benefits in lieu of unpaid leave. But with Chairman William D. Ford, D-Mich., under orders from Democratic

leaders to keep the bill clean, all the GOP amendments were rejected, mostly along party lines.

The only amendment adopted was a Democratic substitute incorporating mostly technical changes recommended by the Department of Labor. The amendment, approved by voice vote, also revised a Labor Department rule that prohibited businesses from giving professional employees unpaid leave for part of a day without eliminating their exemption from overtime pay under the Fair Labor Standards Act. Under the act, employers were not required to pay overtime to salaried employees; to keep this overtime exemption, employers were prohibited from docking salaried employees for taking part of a day off. Businesses had complained that the rule discouraged them from adopting flexible-leave policies. Instead of allowing a professional

worker to take part of a day off without pay, they said, it forced them to require those employees to take a full day without pay.

The amendment allowed employers to give salaried employees unpaid leave for part of a day without losing their general exemption under the act.

The House Post Office and Civil Service Committee — which had jurisdiction over a section of the measure that guaranteed leave for federal civil service and postal workers — approved the bill by voice vote, also on Jan. 27.

House Floor Action

The House passed HR 1 on Feb. 3 by a vote of 265-163. *(Vote 22, p. 6-H)*

During floor debate, bill opponents uniformly stressed that they supported family leave policies but argued that such arrangements were a private matter between worker and employer.

Goodling offered an amendment that would have allowed employers to offer their workers a "cafeteria" plan of benefits that included family and medical leave. Under the amendment, workers could have chosen which benefits they wanted. The House rejected the language 187-244. *(Vote 15, p. 4-H)*

The House did adopt, 223-209, another amendment offered by Goodling to allow a worker to take part of a day's leave only upon agreement with the employer. The provision had been included in the 1992 legislation. *(Vote 17, p. 4-H)*

SENATE ACTION

The Senate Labor and Human Resources Committee got a head start, marking up the legislation the day before the House committee acted. The committee voted 13-4 on Jan. 26 to approve a bill (S 5) that was identical to HR 1. Because everyone believed that S 5 would shoot through the legislative process, the committee debate was brief.

"It is unfair to force working parents to abandon their jobs to care for a newborn child," said committee Chairman Edward M. Kennedy, D-Mass.

Ranking Republican Nancy Landon Kassebaum, Kan., declined to offer any amendments, saying that she would "save my ammunition for the floor."

Senate Floor Action

The Senate passed HR 1 by a vote of 71-27 on Feb. 4, after inserting the text of its bill, S 5, into the House vehicle. The Senate vote occurred one day after the House passed its version of HR 1. *(Vote 11, p. 3-S)*

The vote had been delayed for three days while the Senate wrangled over the ban on homosexuals in the military. Clinton, who favored lifting the ban, had announced a compromise with centrist Senate Democrats on Jan. 29. Under the deal, most Senate Democrats who opposed removing the ban agreed not to block Clinton's steps toward suspending the prohibition on homosexuals. In exchange, Clinton promised to narrow the scope of any changes and, in effect, retain some restrictions.

But Republicans, led by Minority Leader Robert Dole of Kansas, pressed the matter, trying to use S 5 as a vehicle for imposing a congressional ban on gays in the military. The issue came to a head when the Senate voted 62-37 to table, or kill, a Dole amendment that would have required Clinton to seek congressional approval before lifting the ban by executive order. This allowed S 5 supporters to move ahead and pass the bill. *(Vote 9, p. 3-S; Gays in the military, p. 454)*

The Senate did approve by voice vote a non-binding amendment offered by Majority Leader George J. Mitchell, D-Maine, calling on the Pentagon and Congress to review existing policy regarding homosexuals in the military.

Like their colleagues in the House the day before, bill opponents went to great lengths during the Feb. 4 debate to express their support for the concept of family leave. But, they argued, S 5 would impose too great a burden on businesses.

During debate, senators tabled, or killed, a slew of unfriendly amendments. For example, the Senate voted 67-31 to table a Dole amendment that would have allowed employers to ignore the law until the federal government paid all costs or certified that the law would not cost them any money. *(Vote 7, p. 2-S)*

The Senate rejected by voice vote a Dole amendment that would have capped the cost of the legislation to employers at $7.30 per worker per year. Proponents frequently said the measure would not cost businesses more than 2 cents a day per worker.

In addition, the Senate voted 63-36 to table an amendment by Kassebaum that would have allowed workers to choose family and medical leave as part of a menu of benefits offered by an employer. The language was identical to that offered unsuccessfully by Goodling in the House. *(Vote 4, p. 2-S)*

The Senate also voted 59-39 to table an amendment offered by Hank Brown, R-Colo., to restrict the availability of partial day leaves. The Brown language was a companion to the amendment that Goodling had successfully added to the House bill. *(Vote 10, p. 3-S)*

FINAL ACTION

Later on Feb. 4, the House accepted the Senate version of the bill, clearing it for the president. Using a procedure that avoided a direct vote, the House voted 247-152 to adopt a rule that included automatic agreement with the Senate version. As a result, the bill included the non-binding language on homosexuals in the military and excluded Goodling's amendment, which would have limited partial-day leave. The Senate bill also contained a number of minor technical additions not in the House measure. *(Vote 29, p. 8-H)*

With the exeption of the Goodling language contained in the original House measure, the bills were almost identical in substance. In light of this, Ford, who had opposed the Goodling amendment, and other House Democratic leaders gladly moved to adopt the Senate language as an easy way to clear the bill. ∎

Jobless Benefits Get Two Extensions

Congress acted twice in 1993 to extend a temporary program that provided emergency federal benefits to the long-term unemployed, after it became clear that a 1992 effort to avoid further extensions had failed.

The Clinton administration sought the extensions because tens of thousands of people were exhausting their 26 weeks of state-paid basic benefits without finding jobs. The federally financed emergency program, which had been in place in various forms since November 1991, allowed the long-term unemployed to receive additional cash assistance.

The first extension (HR 920), which expired Oct. 2, provided an extra 20 to 26 weeks of emergency benefits to an estimated 1.5 million workers who had exhausted their state unemployment compensation. Although Republicans objected, President Clinton and congressional Democrats agreed to count the cost — $5.7 billion — as emergency spending not subject to pay-as-you-go budget rules that required offsetting tax increases or spending cuts.

The second extension (HR 3167) gave unemployed workers who had used up their 26 weeks of basic benefits an additional seven or 13 weeks and was good through Feb. 5, 1994. The $1.1 billion bill included provisions to offset the cost of the extension.

BACKGROUND

Congress had extended emergency federal unemployment compensation three times in the previous two years. The most recent extension, enacted in July 1992, was to expire March 6, 1993. In both 1991 and 1992, congressional Democrats had tried to designate the money as emergency spending, which did not have to be offset by other spending cuts or tax increases and was instead added to the deficit. But, faced with veto threats from President George Bush, they backed down and found ways to offset the costs, mainly by increasing revenues. *(1991 Almanac, p. 301; 1992 Almanac, p. 346)*

The 1992 emergency benefits extension also overhauled an existing state-federal "extended benefits" program that was supposed to cover long-term unemployed workers in states with higher-than-average unemployment rates, but was effectively not being used. The 1992 law changed the rules to make it more likely that workers would be eligible for those benefits — and thus eliminate the need

---

BOXSCORE

➡ **Emergency Unemployment Benefits (HR 920, S 382).** The $5.3 billion bill extended a federally financed emergency unemployment program through Oct. 2, 1993.

Report: H Rept 103-17.

KEY ACTION

Feb. 24 — **House** passed HR 920, 254-161.

March 3 — **Senate** passed HR 920, 66-33, after substituting text of S 382.

March 4 — **House** cleared HR 920, 247-156.

March 4 — **President** signed HR 920 — PL 103-6.

➡ **Emergency Unemployment Benefits (HR 3167).** The $1.1 billion bill extended the program through Feb. 5, 1994.

Reports: H Rept 103-268; conference reports H Rept 103-333, H Rept 103-404.

KEY ACTION

Oct. 15 — **House** passed HR 3167, 302-95.

Oct. 28 — **Senate** passed HR 3167, 76-20.

Nov. 9 — **House** rejected conference report, 226-202.

Nov. 20 — **Senate** adopted conference report, 79-20.

Nov. 23 — **House** adopted conference report, 320-125.

Nov. 24 — **President** signed HR 3167 (PL 103-152).

---

for further renewals of the federally financed emergency benefits program. But most states had not put the new system into effect. And even if they had, most long-term unemployed workers would still not have qualified for the program. *(How the system worked, p. 394)*

Labor Secretary Robert Reich told a Ways and Means subcommittee Sept. 22 that while the overall unemployment rate for the country had fallen to about 6.7 percent from a high of 7.7 percent a year before, the number of long-term unemployed workers was 1.7 million. A year before, the number had been 2.1 million. Reich said that 250,000 workers were expected to exhaust their basic benefits each month.

FIRST ROUND: HR 920

With the expiration date for the previous extension looming, Congress cleared a bill (HR 920) on March 4 extending the period for new claims for federal emergency benefits from March 7 through Oct. 2, 1993. Clinton signed the bill the same day (PL 103-6).

Although no new claims could be processed after Oct. 2, unemployed workers who had started collecting benefits would continue to receive them until they had gotten the full 20 or 26 weeks of federal benefits, or until Jan. 15, 1994. The extension was expected to cost $3.3 billion in fiscal 1993 and $2.4 billion in fiscal 1994, all of it designated as emergency spending that would be added to the deficit. Congress appropriated $4 billion for the extension in a separate supplemental spending bill.

House Ways and Means

The Ways and Means Committee approved the extension by voice vote Feb. 18 (H Rept 103-17), despite objections from Republicans who said the cost should be offset by cuts in federal spending. Amo Houghton, R-N.Y., offered an amendment to extend the benefits only until June 7.

Houghton said his proposal would cost $1.2 billion and would be paid for by reversing a change in income tax withholding rates that Bush had ordered in January 1992. Panel Democrats countered that the cost of HR 920 would be offset as part of Clinton's overall economic package. Houghton's amendment was defeated by voice vote.

The committee also defeated by voice vote an amendment offered by Dave Camp, R-Mich., to allow more states with declining unemployment rates to qualify for extended

benefits. The additional benefits would have been paid for by reducing the number of weeks workers received benefits.

Also rejected by voice vote was an amendment by E. Clay Shaw Jr., R-Fla., to allow people who were temporarily displaced from their jobs because of a federally declared natural disaster and who had exhausted their unemployment benefits to receive extended benefits for up to 13 weeks.

House Floor Action

The House took up the bill the following week, approving it Feb. 24 by a vote of 254-161. Members considered the measure under a restrictive rule that barred amendments, but Republicans were still able to draw attention to the cost of the bill. Bill Archer of Texas, ranking Republican on the Ways and Means Committee, offered a motion to recommit the bill with the intent of requiring that the cost be offset. The motion was defeated 186-229, but it enjoyed unanimous GOP support. *(Votes 41, 40, p. 10-H)*

Senate Action

On Feb. 24, the day of the House vote, the Senate Finance Committee approved a companion measure (S 382) by voice vote.

The full Senate passed the bill March 3 by a vote of 66-33, with 10 Republicans joining the 56 Democrats who were present and voting. The Senate passed HR 920, after substituting the text of S 382. A provision added by the Senate abrogated a scheduled cost of living adjustment (COLA) for members of Congress in 1994. *(Vote 24, p. 4-S)*

During the floor debate, Republicans tried unsuccessfully to offset the cost of the bill. "If this program is worthwhile — and it is — we should pay for it," said Bob Packwood of Oregon. Packwood offered an amendment that would have cut administrative services for the executive branch by 0.5 percent across the board. Packwood said that would save $3.3 billion, enough to cover the fiscal 1993 cost of the bill.

But, citing estimates by White House and congressional budget experts, Senate Majority Leader George J. Mitchell, D-Maine, maintained that Packwood's plan would not cover the full $3.3 billion. And he questioned how Packwood's amendment would work, asking whether it would require firing federal workers. Mitchell argued that since the unemployment bill was part of Clinton's total economic package, which included spending cuts, Packwood's amendment was an attempt to torpedo the president's broader economic plans. The Senate tabled, or killed, Packwood's amendment on a straight party-line vote, 57-43. *(Vote 21, p. 4-S)*

Hank Brown, R-Colo., then offered an amendment to help pay for the bill by eliminating COLAs for federal employees and members of Congress. But Mitchell preempted Brown's amendment by offering language to drop the COLA only for members of Congress. The Senate agreed to Mitchell's amendment by voice vote before voting 58-41 to kill Brown's amendment. *(Vote 23, p. 4-S)*

Final Action

The House passed the bill in a pair of votes March 4. It agreed to the bulk of the bill, 247-156, and accepted the Senate's COLA freeze, 403-0. *(Votes 53, 54, p. 14-H)*

Clinton asked Congress to appropriate funds to pay for the bill as part of his ill-fated $16.3 billion economic stimulus package. By the time that bill was enacted, the only surviving element was $4 billion for the emergency unemployment benefits. Congress cleared that bill (HR 1335) on April 22; Clinton signed it into law April 23 (PL 103-24).

SECOND ROUND: HR 3167

The emergency benefits enacted in March 1993 expired Oct. 2 with Democrats still locked in a battle over how to pay for yet another extension. The dispute had delayed action on the new extension for several weeks as the administration scrambled to come up with a way to offset the cost of the bill. Ways and Means Committee Chairman Dan Rostenkowski, D-Ill., had made it clear from the outset that he would not mark up another emergency benefits bill without a financing mechanism.

The bill (HR 3167), which did not clear until the end of the session, extended the emergency program for four months. Unemployed workers who had exhausted their 26 weeks of basic benefits and who lived in a state with at least 9 percent total unemployment qualified for 13 weeks of emergency benefits. Those living in states with less than 9 percent total unemployment were eligible for seven weeks. The program was made retroactive to Oct. 2, when the previous program expired. Workers could qualify for benefits through Feb. 5, 1994.

To pay the $1.1 billion cost of the new program, the bill required each state agency that administered an unemployment insurance program to profile all new applicants for basic unemployment benefits. The idea was to identify people most likely to remain unemployed for long periods and provide them with job search assistance in hopes of getting them off the unemployment rolls sooner. The Congressional Budget Office estimated that the profiling system would save $764 million over five years.

The bill also changed the Supplemental Security Income (SSI) program by limiting the eligibility of recent legal immigrants to receive SSI benefits, which went to poor people who also were aged, blind or disabled.

House Ways and Means Committee

The Ways and Means Committee approved the $1.1 billion four-month extension by voice vote Sept. 29 (H Rept 103-268).

Initially, the administration had proposed to extend the program for six months at a cost of $1.7 billion, but officials scaled it back to four months to reduce the cost. The administration proposed a two-part financing plan. First, it wanted to require states to identify those most likely to remain jobless for a long time and give them job search assistance. The Labor Department hoped to cover costs associated with the profiling requirement by using existing appropriations. In addition, the administration proposed to raise about $140 million over five years by accelerating a planned fee increase on the federal administration of state SSI payments.

The Ways and Means Committee agreed to go along with the first idea, but it rejected the second one, replacing it with a provision aimed at saving $331 million by delaying the eligibility of new, legal immigrants for SSI payments. Ordinarily, when a U.S. citizen sponsored an immigrant, the sponsor's assets were considered to be available to the immigrant for three years. After that, the immigrant could apply for SSI payments if he or she met eligibility criteria. The Ways and Means Committee proposed to lengthen to five years the period during which an immigrant would be considered dependent. The change was to be in effect temporarily from Jan. 1, 1994, until Oct. 1, 1996.

A Flawed but Vital System

Unemployment compensation was a complicated system run by the states, overseen by the U.S. Department of Labor and paid for by both state and federal taxes. Approximately 106 million people were covered by the system — 98 percent of all wage and salary workers.

The system was created in 1935 as part of the Social Security Act (PL 74-271) to provide temporary assistance to workers who had lost their jobs involuntarily and, more broadly, to help stabilize the economy during recessions.

States paid basic benefits to the unemployed — an average of $179 per week per worker — for approximately 26 weeks or until the worker found a new job. States paid for the benefits by taxing employers; the states set both the tax rates and the benefits to workers.

A second, "extended benefits" compensation system existed for long-term unemployed workers when a state's economy and rate of unemployment were in particularly bad shape. When circumstances caused the extended benefits program to kick in, workers could collect an extra 13 or 20 weeks of benefits, financed half by the federal government and half by the states.

The federal share of the extended program was paid out of a trust fund supported by the Federal Unemployment Tax Act of 1939 (PL 76-379), which imposed a net 0.8 percent tax on the first $7,000 paid annually to each eligible employee.

Although the extended benefits program was on the books during the 1990-91 recession, it was of no help in many states. The program was triggered by a state's insured unemployment rate — the percentage of unemployed workers eligible to receive benefits, not the total number of unemployed. A state qualified only if its insured unemployment rate reached at least 5 percent for 13 consecutive weeks and was 20 percent higher than it had been for the same period in the previous two years.

As a consequence, many unemployed workers were cut off from assistance when they exhausted their basic state benefits. Congress responded by passing a succession of bills creating — and then extending — a federal emergency benefits program. The first of those bills was enacted in November 1991, providing 3 million jobless workers either 13 or 20 extra weeks of benefits, and costing $5.3 billion. The federal government picked up the tab. Congress passed two more extensions in 1992. *(1991 Almanac, p. 301; 1993 Almanac, p. 346)*

1992 Attempt To Revise System

In mid-1992, in the third measure authorizing the emergency program, Congress changed the triggering formula for the largely unused state-federal extended benefits program so that it would be based on the total unemployment rate.

The new formula triggered 13 weeks of extended benefits when a state had a total unemployment rate of 6.5 percent for the most recent three months, and that rate was at least 10 percent higher than during the same period in either of the two previous years. In states in which the total unemployment rate was at least 8 percent, workers could receive 20 weeks of extended benefits.

However, states had to make their own legislative changes to allow the new extended benefits program to work. They also had to pay half the cost of the benefits, and many states were already having difficulty financing basic unemployment benefits. Only Washington, Oregon and Puerto Rico had changed their laws. Moreover, under the new trigger, unemployed workers in only eight states plus Puerto Rico qualified for the extended benefits.

As a result, many in Congress preferred to continue the federally financed emergency program to ensure that long-term unemployed workers were not left without a safety net.

House Floor Action

The House passed the emergency unemployment bill, 302-95, on Oct. 15 after a two-week delay caused by a dispute over the financing plan. *(Vote 509, p. 124-H)*

The bill was scheduled for floor action Sept. 30, two days before the existing program was set to expire. But it was abruptly pulled from the calendar when the Congressional Hispanic Caucus objected to limiting the availability of SSI payments to new immigrants.

"I don't see why we're denying benefits to people who are aged, blind or disabled to give them to the unemployed," said Xavier Becerra, D-Calif., a member of the Hispanic caucus who took the lead on the issue. "It's robbing Peter to pay Paul."

Speaker Thomas S. Foley, D-Wash., tried but failed to foster a compromise. Rostenkowski, whose aides said they were out of additional ideas for financing the bill, refused to drop the provision; Hispanic members remained flatly opposed to it. Foley eventually decided to send the bill to the floor under a "self-executing rule" (H Res 273 — H Rept 103-287) that automatically dropped the SSI provision and scaled back the unemployment program by five weeks so it would end New Year's Day. But when the measure came to the floor Oct. 14, the House defeated the rule by a vote of 149-274. *(Vote 505, 124-H)*

Republicans generally opposed rules that limited their ability to offer amendments; in this case they also wanted to keep the SSI provisions. Many Democrats opposed the rule because they did not want the unemployment program to expire at the end of the holiday season when Congress would be in recess. The vote left Hispanic members angry and upset, however. "I found the tone of the floor debate on this bill offensive, misleading and antithetical to everything this country stands for," said Jose E. Serrano, D-N.Y., chairman of the Hispanic caucus.

After the vote, Foley said he thought he had the votes when debate began. He blamed the defeat on Rostenkowski, who spoke against the rule on the floor. "When a chairman of a committee takes the unusual position of opposing a rule, members are cautious," he said. Rostenkowski said he did not solicit a single member's vote. Rostenkowski said that far fewer Hispanics would be hurt by the SSI provision than by cutting off unemployment benefits, but he noted that the debate pointed up the hard fact that "there is no place to find revenue.... The cupboard is bare."

After the first rule was rejected, the House dropped the self-executing procedure and adopted a new rule the morning of Oct. 15 that left the SSI provision in the bill.

Before passing the bill, the House rejected, 128-277, an amendment by Nancy L. Johnson, R-Conn., to prohibit workers in states with unemployment rates below 5 percent from collecting emergency benefits. The amendment would have affected workers in 10 states.

Senate Action

The Senate, which appeared in no hurry to vote on the bill, passed the measure 76-20 on Oct. 28. Much of the debate was devoted to unrelated issues, such as taxes, the superconducting super collider and the space station. Many members said they had not heard many complaints from constituents about being unable to get unemployment benefits. *(Vote 342, p. 44-S)*

Don Nickles, R-Okla., raised a parliamentary objection to the bill, pointing out that the program's cost was to be incurred over four months, while the offsetting revenues would take five years to accrue. Budget rules required offsets in the same year as the expenditures. Daniel Patrick Moynihan, D-N.Y., moved to waive the budget rules, which required 60 votes. He failed on the first try Oct. 26 by a vote of 59-38, but he succeeded the following day, 61-39. *(Vote 328, p. 42-S; vote 334, p. 43-S)*

Moynihan and Nickles tried unsuccessfully to come up with an alternative financing mechanism that did not violate the budget rules. But Senate Democrats did agree Oct. 27 by voice vote to a non-binding sense-of-the-Senate resolution (S Res 156) offered by Nickles, indicating that the Senate did not expect to pass additional extensions of the emergency benefits program.

The Senate made a potentially historic change to the unemployment program, adopting an amendment by Brown to prohibit people with taxable incomes above $120,000 in 1992 from receiving the federal benefits. The restriction did not apply to the basic system of state unemployment benefits. Brown estimated that his amendment — adopted 52-43 on Oct. 27 — would save $2 million. Throughout the history of the unemployment compensation system, which dated to 1935, most people who worked were eligible for benefits. Earnings had never disqualified a person from collecting. *(Vote 336, p. 43-S)*

The Senate took the following action on a series of unrelated amendments:

● **Retroactive taxes.** In a replay of the budget battle earlier in the year, the Senate spent much of the debate on the unemployment bill arguing over the fairness of retroactive tax increases that were included in the 1993 budget-reconciliation bill (HR 2264). *(Budget-reconciliation, p. 107)*

Kay Bailey Hutchison, R-Texas, offered an amendment to rescind an income tax increase for wealthy individuals that was made retroactive to Jan. 1, 1993. Hutchison said she raised the issue anew because she continued to hear complaints, particularly from small-business owners who filed their business taxes as individuals. Her amendment allowed a new, higher marginal tax rate of 36 percent for wealthy taxpayers and a 10 percent surtax for the wealthiest to take effect Aug. 10, the day the bill was signed. It left the previous top rate of 31 percent in place until then and accommodated the change by assessing a "blended" rate of 32.97 percent for the entire year. The surtax was to be assessed at a blended rate of 34.39 percent.

Her amendment also allowed the top rate on estate and gift taxes to revert downward to 50 percent as of Jan. 1,

1993, as previously scheduled. The reconciliation bill had rescinded that rate cut. She proposed to pay for the lost revenue by cutting administrative spending.

Mitchell and other Democrats blasted Hutchison's amendment, arguing that it could derail the unemployment bill. Mitchell's point was that the Constitution required tax bills to originate in the House; typically, when the Senate added a tax amendment to a non-tax bill, the House informed the Senate that it would not consider the bill further, essentially killing the measure.

To defeat Hutchison, Mitchell raised a parliamentary objection that the amendment violated budget rules by not saving as much money as it would lose in the same year. Hutchison asked the Senate to waive the rules, an action that required 60 votes. Her motion failed Oct. 26 on a 50-44 vote. *(Vote 327, p. 42-S)*

After criticizing nearly every aspect of Hutchison's proposal, Dale Bumpers, D-Ark., then offered an almost identical amendment to repeal the retroactive tax increases — paying for the move by killing the space station project, which had a large number of Texas contractors. Bumpers' motion to waive the budget rules failed Oct. 27, 36-61. *(Vote 335, p. 43-S)*

With the tough talk on both sides of the aisle about the unfairness of retroactive tax increases, Nickles offered an amendment to change Senate rules to require a three-fifths majority roll-call vote on any future bills increasing taxes retroactively. The Senate rejected it Oct. 28, 40-56. *(Vote 339, p. 44-S)*

● **Super collider savings.** Phil Gramm, R-Texas, tried to waive congressional budget rules to apply to the deficit the savings from a recent decision to kill the superconducting super collider. He proposed to reduce statutory caps on discretionary spending for fiscal years 1995 through 1998 to prevent the savings from the big science project from being spent elsewhere. The motion was rejected, 58-39, on Oct. 27. Waiving the budget rules required 60 votes. *(Vote 337, p. 44-S)*

● **Social Security.** John McCain, R-Ariz., sought to waive budget rules and adopt an amendment to change the Social Security Act. McCain wanted to eliminate a provision of existing law that limited outside earnings of Social Security recipients. The Senate rejected the motion, 46-51, on Oct. 27. *(Vote 338, p. 44-S)*

● **Reducing federal payroll.** In a move that had support in both chambers, Gramm offered an amendment to reduce the number of federal employees by 252,000 over five years as proposed by the Clinton administration in its so-called reinventing government plan. The administration wanted to make the cuts without having Congress write them into law. The Senate agreed to the amendment, 82-14, on Oct. 28. *(Vote 341, p. 44-S; reinventing government, p. 191)*

Conference, Final Action

The House cleared the conference report Nov. 23, the last day of the session — but only after the bill survived several additional perils.

The final saga began Nov. 4, when House and Senate conferees took six minutes to kill two controversial Senate amendments (H Rept 103-333).

House conferees refused to accept Brown's amendment barring people with taxable incomes of more than $120,000 in 1992 from receiving the benefits.

More important to the fate of the bill, conferees rejected Gramm's amendment to cut the federal work force

by 252,000 — even though the House had voted 275-146 earlier in the day to instruct its conferees to accept the amendment. Democratic leaders in both chambers opposed giving the proposal the force of law, arguing that it would lead to wholesale firings rather than well-thought-out reductions. *(Vote 544, p. 132-H)*

Angry at being ignored, the House refused Nov. 9 to take up the conference report, voting 226-202 to send it back to conference with instructions to restore the Gramm amendment. At that point, Foley said it appeared the bill might not become law in 1993. *(Vote 552, p. 134-H)*

The conference report then went to the Senate, where Gramm refused the entreaties of Majority Leader Mitchell and tried to recommit it to conference with instructions to restore his amendment. Gramm said the potential savings of $21.8 billion were the impetus for holding out. "We're on the goal line, and I'm reluctant to walk away from a bill that I know would become law," he said.

But senators eager to adjourn before the Thanksgiving holiday were not willing to cooperate, and Gramm's motion was rejected 36-63 on Nov. 20. The Senate then adopted the conference report, 79-20. *(Votes 391, 392, p. 50-S)*

The next day, Rostenkowski and Moynihan filed a new conference report (H Rept 103-404). It was identical to the first report, despite House support for Gramm's amendment. With the Senate already having approved the conference report, the House was blocked procedurally from trying again to recommit the bill. Forced to vote the measure up or down, the House adopted the conference report, 320-125, on Nov. 23. It was the last recorded House vote of the year. *(Vote 615, p. 150-H)* ■

Striker Replacement Bill Stalls in Senate

Legislation (HR 5) to prohibit companies from permanently replacing striking workers easily passed the House for the second time in two years. But, much to the chagrin of organized labor, the presence of a pro-union Democrat in the White House was not enough to push a companion bill (S 55) through the Senate.

Despite early and decisive House action, the bill never reached the Senate floor due to a credible Republican filibuster threat. At year's end, Democratic leaders were still unsure about the legislation's fate.

Background

Banning the permanent replacement of striking workers was a top priority for the AFL-CIO and its 14 million union members, who largely supported President Clinton's candidacy during the 1992 presidential election. Although Clinton did not express much enthusiasm for the bill during the campaign, he did promise labor leaders that if Congress passed the "striker replacement" measure, he would sign it.

The legislation was fiercely opposed by major business organizations, including the U.S. Chamber of Commerce, the National Association of Manufacturers and the National Federation of Independent Business.

Employers already were barred from hiring permanent replacement workers in strikes involving unfair labor practices, such as an employer's refusal to bargain in good faith. But that prohibition did not apply to replacing workers

who went on strike for economic reasons, such as higher pay or other benefits. The bills eliminated that distinction.

At issue was the balance of power between unions and employers as they negotiated contracts and weighed the possibility of a strike.

Labor groups and their allies said that businesses upset this balance during the late 1970s and 1980s, exploiting the supposed loophole in existing law to replace some striking workers and to intimidate others into accepting inadequate contracts. They argued that the striker replacement bill would restore a healthier balance of power and make the right to strike a meaningful, rather than illusory, option for workers. They said that, in turn, could strengthen labor-management relations and productivity.

But Republicans and many business groups argued that the unions already held substantial leverage in contract negotiations. In their view, the striker bill would hand too many cards to labor, encouraging more strikes and ultimately costing jobs.

In July 1991, the House passed identical legislation by 247-182, falling 39 votes short of the two-thirds necessary to override President George Bush's promised veto. A year later, threats of a GOP filibuster derailed the measure in the Senate, which failed twice to invoke cloture. Democrats were never able to muster more than 57 votes to cut off debate, three votes shy of the 60 required. *(1991 Almanac, p. 314; 1992 Almanac, p. 361)*

House Action

The House Education and Labor Committee approved HR 5 (H Rept 103-116, Part 1) by a 28-15 party-line vote on May 5. On May 25, the House Energy and Commerce Committee gave voice vote approval to the bill (Part 2). And two days later, on May 27, the House Public Works and Transportation Committee — which had jurisdiction over airline employees — followed suit (Part 3).

The House voted 239-190 on June 15 to pass HR 5. *(Vote 224, p. 54-H)*

During the floor debate, members rejected two amendments, including one by Chet Edwards, D-Texas, that would have exempted non-union workers — thereby allowing employers to permanently replace workers who struck to create a union shop. The House voted it down, 94-339. *(Vote 222, p. 54-H)*

Tom Ridge, R-Pa., offered a substitute amendment that would have prohibited employers from hiring permanent replacements for 10 weeks, starting when the employer hired temporary workers. Democrats argued that employers would drag out strikes until the 10 weeks expired and then permanently replace their workers. The amendment was rejected, 58-373. *(Vote 223, p. 54-H)*

Many Republicans voted against the two amendments in the hope that the bill would be "as bad as possible" when it arrived in the Senate, giving opponents of the

measure no reason to reconsider their position.

The House debate took an emotional turn when members recalled growing up watching their fathers go on strike. To those who predicted that the bill would cause more strikes, they offered personal memories of just how miserable a strike could be. "The Kildee household really suffered in 1946," recalled Dale E. Kildee, D-Mich. Kildee, a junior in high school at the time, said he had no money for new clothes or a class ring. The family, he said, ate cornmeal mush to get by.

But not all Democrats were eager to debate the striker replacement issue. Pete Geren, D-Texas, tried to convince the Democratic Caucus that the bill was too tough a vote coming immediately after the vote on the budget-reconciliation bill. Geren submitted a petition, signed by about 50 Democrats, asking the leadership to hold off on the striker bill. He also argued that it was the Senate's turn to vote first on the bill — particularly because the Senate did not seem to have the votes to pass the measure.

But the Democratic leadership dismissed Geren's effort, pointing out that he would oppose striker replacement legislation regardless of when the vote occurred. "The only people complaining are the same people who voted against reconciliation," said Mike Synar of Oklahoma, chairman of the Democratic Study Group. "If you don't like voting, don't be a congressman."

Senate Action

On May 5, the Senate Labor and Human Resources Committee backed companion legislation (S 55 — S Rept 103-110) by a 10-7 margin. The vote fell along party lines, with Democrats supporting the proposal.

But S 55 advanced no further. Democrats still did not have the 60 votes needed to invoke cloture.

In 1992, five Democratic senators had voted against cloture: David L. Boren of Oklahoma, Dale Bumpers of Arkansas, Ernest F. Hollings of South Carolina, David Pryor of Arkansas, and Terry Sanford of North Carolina. Of those, only Sanford was gone in 1993, replaced by Republican Lauch Faircloth. ∎

House OKs Legislation To Scale Back ERISA

Legislation aimed at giving states more latitude to regulate employee benefit programs passed the House late in the year, but the Senate did not take up a companion measure in 1993. Lawmakers did clear, as part of unrelated legislation, provisions clarifying that federal law did not pre-empt certain state health-insurance regulations.

BACKGROUND

Enacted in 1974, the Employee Retirement Income Security Act (ERISA) governed most private pensions and other worker benefits. The law established a system designed to ensure that workers would actually receive their retirement income. To protect employee benefits from simultaneous state and federal regulation, it contained a clause stating that ERISA pre-empted state laws.

But bill supporters claimed that federal appeals court decisions had broadened the scope of the ERISA pre-

emption beyond congressional intent. House Education and Labor Committee Chairman William D. Ford, D-Mich., who served on the panel when ERISA was drafted, said during floor debate Nov. 9 that he was "confounded with how the courts have managed to construct out of whole cloth an intention that was never any place in the record of our consideration of the bill."

The 1993 legislation, sponsored by Howard L. Berman, D-Calif., specified three kinds of state laws that would be permitted:

- Laws requiring employers to meet certain standards regarding the employment and training of apprentices.
- "Prevailing wage" laws that required private contractors on publicly funded projects to pay their workers the equivalent of locally prevailing wages and benefits.
- Laws allowing employees to acquire a lien on the property of an employer delinquent in its payment to a multi-employer pension plan. These laws were intended to protect contract workers — particularly in the construction industry — who moved frequently from one employer and project to another.

Opponents of the bill, including many business groups and most House Republicans, argued that scaling back the ERISA pre-emption clause would hurt businesses by forcing them to consider different employee benefit laws in each state in which they operated. Pre-empting state statutes, they said, mitigated that regulatory burden, lowering administrative costs.

The House approved a similar bill in 1992, but the Senate did not take up the legislation because of an administration veto threat. *(1992 Almanac, p. 362)*

LEGISLATIVE ACTION

With little debate, the House Education and Labor Committee approved HR 1036 (H Rept 103-253), 30-12, on June 23.

The committee rejected by voice vote an amendment by Harris W. Fawell, R-Ill., that would have continued ERISA pre-emption for state apprenticeship standards. Fawell complained that without the ERISA pre-emption, states could override the National Apprenticeship Act of 1937 — also known as the Fitzgerald Act — which established federal standards for state programs. But Pat Williams, D-Mont., countered that Fawell's concerns should be addressed by overhauling the Fitzgerald Act, not ERISA.

The House passed the bill Nov. 9 by a vote of 276-150. *(Vote 554, p. 136-H)*

Members rejected, 174-255, an amendment offered by Bill Goodling, R-Pa., that would have prohibited states from denying employers the right to create apprenticeship programs, so long as the programs met state standards.

States would not have been able to discriminate against a program for any other reason. Goodling and others feared that some programs could be prohibited because they competed with nearby programs or because trainees were not union members. The amendment would have left intact bill language allowing states to set apprenticeship standards without being subject to federal pre-emption. *(Vote 553, p. 136-H)*

In the Senate, Arlen Specter, R-Pa., introduced a related measure (S 1580), but no action was taken on the bill.

Health Insurance Regulation

Congress did clear, as a small part of the massive 1993 budget-reconciliation act (HR 2264 — PL 103-66), provi-

Pension Benefits Protection

On Oct 28, the Senate passed, by voice vote, legislation (S 1312) that was targeted at helping 84,000 retirees and employees whose pension benefits were threatened as a result of the insolvency of the Executive Life Insurance Company. The measure gave those retirees and workers greater latitude in seeking redress from their employers. However, the House took no action on the measure in the first session.

Bill sponsor Howard M. Metzenbaum, D-Ohio, maintained that the legislation was needed to counter a June 1 Supreme Court decision, *Mertens v. Hewitt Associates*, that he said had stripped away many of the protections that had covered workers under the Employee Retirement Income Security Act (ERISA), the 1974 federal law that governed most private pension plans.

Metzenbaum and others argued that the court in *Mertens* read ERISA too narrowly and took away the previous right of workers to sue their employers for monetary damages in cases where pension benefits had been lost as a result of an ERISA violation. Under ERISA, employers had a fiduciary duty to act in their employee's best interests in managing their pension plans.

During the 1980s, many employers terminated their pension plans and replaced them with cheaper annuities offered by Executive Life. Under those annuities, Executive Life took responsibility for paying covered beneficiaries. According to Metzenbaum, most of the employers benefited financially from this transfer. But when regulators seized control of Executive Life in 1991, beneficiaries had payments reduced for a year. In litigation against employers, retirees had failed to recover the lost benefits.

Metzenbaum argued that future pension benefits were still in danger of being reduced or eliminated. In addition, he claimed, many employers purchased Executive Life annuities with the knowledge that the company was not on sound financial footing and were hence in violation of their fiduciary duty to their workers and retirees.

S 1312 clarified that beneficiaries could receive monetary damages from those employers who bought Executive Life annuities in violation of this duty.

Language more extensive than the provisions in S 1312 had originally been included in the Senate version of the budget-reconciliation bill. That provision would have allowed monetary damages for all persons wrongfully denied pension benefits, regardless of whether Executive Life was involved. An attempt by Sen. Nancy Landon Kassebaum, R-Kan., to strike the provision failed, 8-9, when the Senate Labor and Human Resources Committee took up the provisions as part of its contribution to the deficit-reduction bill on June 16. Kassebaum argued in committee that Metzenbaum was moving too soon after the *Mertens* decision and could potentially prompt some businesses to stop offering pension plans. But the provision was later removed from the Senate bill, after Metzenbaum and Kassebaum agreed to sponsor the narrower S 1312.

sions ensuring that ERISA did not pre-empt certain state laws regarding health insurance. *(ERISA provisions, p. 126)*

One provision amended federal pension law to clarify that ERISA did not pre-empt states from seeking reimbursements from private insurers in cases in which a claim had been unnecessarily paid by Medicaid, the government health insurance program for the poor. Under HR 2264, states were required to seek such reimbursements. Under existing law, insurance companies were the primary payers for people covered both privately and by Medicaid. This provision simply stated that ERISA was not an obstacle in a state's attempt to recover money from insurers.

Another provision in HR 2264 clarified that ERISA did not pre-empt state authority to force non-custodial parents to provide health insurance to their children.

The Senate Labor and Human Resources Committee approved the provisions June 16; the House Education and Labor Committee followed suit May 12. HR 2264 cleared Congress on Aug. 6 and was signed by President Clinton on Aug. 10. ∎

Benefits for Miners Among Stalled Labor Bills

Congress took up a variety of smaller labor bills in 1993, including the following:

AGE DISCRIMINATION

The House by voice vote Nov. 8 passed a bill (HR 2722 — H Rept 103-314) to allow state and local public safety agencies to consider age in their hiring and retirement policies. The bill was not considered in the Senate.

Sponsored by Major R. Owens, D-N.Y., HR 2722 allowed a mandatory retirement age as low as 55. It applied only to public safety agencies in which service to the public required a firefighter's or police officer's physical ability. The bill also allowed elected judges who reached the state age of compulsory retirement to complete their terms.

The bill permanently exempted state and local public safety agencies from the Age Discrimination in Employment Act. The law, enacted in 1967 and amended in 1986 (PL 99-592), set a seven-year exemption to allow mandatory retirement ages for firefighters, law enforcement officers and employees at colleges and universities. *(1986 Almanac, p. 581)*

The House Education and Labor Subcommittee on Select Education and Civil Rights reported the bill by voice vote Aug. 5. "We are keenly aware that age discrimination continues to plague older workers," said Subcommittee Chairman Owens. But he said that the legislation was necessary because the public had to have the best and most able public safety officers.

The House Education and Labor Committee approved the bill by voice vote Oct. 19.

The committee adopted by voice vote an amendment by Tom Sawyer, D-Ohio, to authorize $5 million over the following four years to develop guidelines for performance testing of public safety officers in lieu of setting a mandatory retirement age. The amendment also urged cities to develop wellness programs to help determine ways of evaluating the fitness of older employees.

DAVIS-BACON REVISION

Legislation aimed at updating a Depression-era labor law won approval Nov. 16 from a House Education and Labor subcommittee but went no further in 1993.

By a 6-3 vote, the Labor Standards Subcommittee approved a bill (HR 1231) to raise from $2,000 to $100,000 the contract value threshold for coverage under the 1931 Davis-Bacon Act. The Davis-Bacon Act required contractors on federally funded construction projects to pay the prevailing local wage, usually a union rate. The statute was intended to prevent big construction companies from hiring low-wage, itinerant workers and underbidding local companies for coveted government contracts during the Depression.

Republicans protested that the bill would extend the reach of the act to businesses that were not covered and would impose added paperwork on winners of federal contracts.

Opponents saw the Davis-Bacon Act as an icon of another era when there were hardly any federal labor standards, such as a minimum wage, and worker exploitation was common. Harris W. Fawell, R-Ill., said the act drove up the cost of public works projects by 5 percent to 15 percent because the prevailing local wage rate was usually a union rate that was higher than non-union private sector pay rates.

Proponents, led by bill sponsor Austin J. Murphy, D-Pa., said raising the threshold for coverage under Davis-Bacon to $100,000 would ease paperwork and other requirements for small public works projects.

The panel rejected, by voice vote, a GOP amendment that would have raised the threshold to $1 million.

Members also rejected, by voice vote, a GOP amendment that would have exempted contracts in which 25 percent or less of the money came from federal funds.

Fawell said the measure would create "hassles and headaches" for small businesses because the prevailing wage rate requirement would be expanded to cover off-site contractors and suppliers. The existing law restricted coverage to on-site workers. "Nobody would dream of ever building their house under Davis-Bacon, because it would cost more. But if it's taxpayers' money and if it's a construction project, then Congress says it's OK," Fawell said.

BLACK LUNG

The House Education and Labor Subcommittee on Labor Standards voted 6-3 on Sept. 21 to approve a bill (HR 2108) to make it easier for coal miners suffering from black lung disease to win benefits. A similar bill passed the House in 1992 but was not considered by the Senate. *(1992 Almanac, p. 365)*

Under the Black Lung Benefits Act of 1969, miners suffering from the disease were entitled to payments from coal companies. Those who worked for companies no longer in existence were paid from a trust fund financed by a coal excise tax. But deficits were common, and the trust fund had had to borrow money regularly to make up the shortfall.

According to the National Black Lung Association, roughly 200,000 people had the condition, which was caused by long-term exposure to coal dust, resulting in serious respiratory problems similar to emphysema.

All claimants denied benefits were guaranteed a hearing before an administrative law judge. Under existing law, each side could present an unlimited amount of evidence supporting its case. Proponents for victims of the disease argued that this was unfair to miners because companies had much greater resources for building a case.

In what bill supporters contended was an effort to bring more equity to the claims process, HR 2108 allowed miners to present three medical exams as evidence at a claims hearing. Opponents — a coal company or the trust fund — could present only one such exam.

In addition, the bill required the administrative judge presiding over the case to give substantial weight to the opinion of the miner's doctor. The bill also allowed the 90,000 claimants denied benefits since 1981 to refile claims with the Labor Department.

Ranking subcommittee Republican Harris W. Fawell, Ill., and his GOP colleagues opposed the bill, arguing that taxpayers and the coal industry would bear the burden of paying for legions of new beneficiaries. The Congressional Budget Office estimated that the measure would cost the federal government $185.5 million over five years. Fawell said the trust fund already owed $3.5 billion to the federal government.

But subcommittee Chairman Murphy countered that the Treasury Department, which held the debt, was charging the trust fund a "usurious" interest rate of 10 percent. He said the fund would be on better financial footing if it could refinance this debt, paying interest more in line with market rates.

Republicans also were concerned that new standards of evidence would prove unfair to coal companies. In addition, they said that by limiting the number of medical exams that could be used at the hearing, the bill violated the fundamental judicial principle that all relevant evidence was admissible.

MINERS' BENEFITS

The House Ways and Means Committee on Oct. 6 rejected, 15-22, a bill that would have delayed for one year the premium payment by certain coal companies for retired miners' health benefits.

Under provisions in the 1992 National Energy Strategy Act, companies that signed the Bituminous Coal Operators Association Agreement were required to help pay retiree benefits for coal miners whose companies had gone out of business. The troubled retiree health fund was facing financial difficulties, and West Virginia Democratic Sen. John D. Rockefeller IV dedicated himself to rescuing it.

The compromise plan that emerged on the energy bill called for using a "reach back" formula that would trace as many retired miners as possible to their previous employers or, if those companies had gone out of business, to related companies. Such companies were required to pay their first premiums Oct. 25, 1993. *(1992 Almanac, p. 231)*

The legislation (HR 3211) that the Ways and Means panel rejected would have given Congress time to review the 1992 energy bill and decide whether the miners' fund needed the additional revenue that the reach-back companies would have to pay, said J. J. Pickle, D-Texas, the bill's sponsor.

Pickle said that some companies had been assigned by the Department of Health and Human Services to pay premiums for miners who had been dead for years and that these payments would force smaller companies into bankruptcy. He said health benefits for retired coal miners should be addressed in a national health-care plan.

But Pete Stark, D-Calif., argued against the bill, saying the courts had upheld the obligation of coal companies to pay these premiums and the companies were "trying to wriggle out" of paying.

The committee's ranking Republican, Texan Bill Archer, agreed with Pickle and said the energy bill picked up companies that had no idea they had to pay into the retirement fund. "There is no way that can be considered fair," he said. ∎

National Service Paired With Student Aid

President Clinton scored a win on a domestic initiative that delivered on a 1992 campaign promise when Congress cleared his National Service program Sept. 8. Clinton signed the bill (HR 2010 — PL 103-82) on Sept. 21.

The National Service program was designed to send young people from across the country into communities to serve others. In return, participants would receive limited financial assistance for their education.

But the final version of the legislation was pared significantly from Clinton's original vision, and from the original House and Senate bills. When the legislation reached the House and Senate floors, it ran into a wall of Republicans concerned about spending too much money. Many worried that the funding would come at the expense of federal student aid programs that awarded money based on need.

As enacted, the bill offered awards of up to $4,725 a year for no more than two years to individuals age 17 or older who performed community service before, during or after their postsecondary education. That was trimmed from the $5,000 awards the House and Senate originally envisioned; Clinton initially hoped to give students $10,000 a year.

Under the measure, national service programs were to be run locally by nonprofit organizations, including institutions of higher education, local governments, school districts and state or federal agencies. Young people could work in positions such as nurse's aides in hospitals or helpers in police departments, or in environmental jobs in national parks.

Local programs were to offer stipends of up to $7,400 a year, with the federal government providing 85 percent of the stipend and up to 85 percent of the cost of health- and child-care benefits.

The Senate cleared the bill over the objections of some Republicans that the plan did nothing to streamline the federal bureaucracy or save money. "It's another almost open-ended new spending program," said Slade Gorton, R-Wash.

But pared funding sped the bill's passage.

Rather than including an unlimited authorization to finance the program, the final bill capped spending at $300 million in fiscal 1994, $500 million in fiscal 1995 and $700 million in fiscal 1996. That limited the number of participants to about 100,000.

BACKGROUND

When Clinton stood on the Capitol's marble steps to give his inaugural address Jan. 20, he called out to young

BOXSCORE

➡ **National Service program. (HR 2010, S 919).** The bill provided education awards of up to $4,725 a year for two years to individuals who performed community service before, during or after high school. Local programs were to offer stipends of up to $7,400 a year, with the federal government providing 85 percent of the stipend and up to 85 percent of the cost of health- and child-care benefits.

Reports: H Rept 103-155; S Rept 103-70; conference report: H Rept 103-219.

KEY ACTION

June 16 — **House** Education and Labor Committee approved HR 2010 by voice vote: the **Senate** Labor and Human Resources Committee approved S 919, 14-3.

July 28 — **House** passed HR 2010, 275-152.

Aug. 3 — **Senate** amended and passed HR 2010, 58-41.

Aug. 6 — **House** adopted the conference report on HR 2010, 275-152.

Sept. 8 — **Senate** adopted the conference report on HR 2010, 57-40, clearing the bill.

Sept. 21 — **President** signed HR 2010 — PL 103-82.

Americans to give "a season of service."

But many questions remained: What did Clinton mean? Who would be eligible? How would he pay for it?

On the campaign trail and in his campaign book, "Putting People First," Clinton said he would scrap the existing student loan program and establish a national service trust fund. People who borrowed money from the fund to cover the cost of college or job training programs could repay their debt either by remanding a percentage of their earnings over the years — or by serving their communities doing work the country needed.

Friends of Clinton said he believed the program could be the highlight of his presidency — the equivalent of President John F. Kennedy's request to "ask not what your country can do for you; ask what you can do for your country."

"The concept of service and citizenship can become a defining element of his administration," said Rep. Dave McCurdy, D-Okla.

The Philosophy

Before candidate Clinton began talking about national service, President George Bush talked about "points of light." Almost every day during his four years in office, Bush's own national service team issued a news release touting a person or organization doing good deeds. It was the bully pulpit approach. It also was based on volunteerism, rather than an organized plan for serving the country.

Clinton's plan was rooted in the moderate Democratic Leadership Council's (DLC) notion that Americans had to start giving before they could receive. "We think national service has the potential to change the ethos of the nation," said Will Marshall, president of the Progressive Policy Institute, the think tank arm of the DLC. "We want to reinforce the notion that there really is no free lunch."

Eli Segal, assistant to the president and director of the Office of National Service, said national service and the trust fund made up a perfect model for linking responsibility and opportunity.

Not everyone believed that the Clinton philosophy was sound, however. Doug Bandow, a senior fellow at the libertarian Cato Institute, said national service in exchange for student aid would not eliminate the "entitlement" mentality but would reinforce it. And Bandow questioned whether the service performed by young people would be of much value.

That also was a concern of people who supported the

notion of national service. "We have to be careful these do not become make-work projects and the program becomes a laughingstock," said Richard F. Rosser, president of the National Association of Independent Colleges and Universities.

HOUSE COMMITTEE ACTION

The House Education and Labor Committee approved its version of the bill (HR 2010 — H Rept 103-155) by voice vote June 16.

The committee bill included education awards of $5,000 a year to people age 17 or older who performed community service before, during or after their postsecondary education. The bill authorized $394 million in fiscal 1994 and unspecified sums for the following four years. At the time, Segal hoped to start with about 25,000 participants and grow to about 150,000 in four years.

Republican Critique

The bill ran into opposition from Republicans who said that National Service would come at the expense of higher education programs that helped students pay for college and trade school. The Clinton administration had proposed several cuts in aid programs in fiscal 1994, and appropriators were expected to follow suit. In one case, the House Appropriations Subcommittee on Labor, Health and Human Services, and Education was expected to go further than the administration had recommended, cutting the maximum Pell grant available to students by $100 to $200 from its existing $2,300-a-year level, already down from $2,400 the year before. Pell grants helped poor students pay for college. (The fiscal 1994 grant eventually was set at $2,300 a year.) *(Appropriations, p. 632)*

Bill Goodling, R-Pa., the Education and Labor Committee's ranking minority member, said he could not support a program that provided education aid to students who did not need the assistance. He proposed that the program only provide education awards to students who were eligible for financial aid, and that the $5,000 service award, when combined with other aid, could not exceed the student's financial need.

But Committee Chairman William D. Ford, D-Mich., said Goodling's amendment would hurt poor students by forcing them to take all available financial aid and loans before getting the national service money.

The committee rejected Goodling's amendment in a 12-29 vote.

Susan Molinari, R-N.Y., tried unsuccessfully to require better funding for several financial aid programs slated to be cut in the fiscal 1994 budget before money was made available for National Service. Molinari wanted work-study, Supplemental Educational Opportunity Grants and Perkins loans to be funded at fiscal 1993 levels. She also wanted the State Student Incentive Grant Program to be funded at its fiscal 1993 level. And she wanted Pell grants to return to the maximum award level of $2,400 provided in fiscal 1992.

Several Democrats said that money for the National Service program would come out of the Appropriations bill that funded veterans, housing and space programs, not out of the Labor-HHS bill that funded education. Therefore, they argued, National Service would not be funded at the expense of education.

The committee rejected Molinari's amendment, 17-26. Pat Williams, D-Mont., and Patsy T. Mink, D-Hawaii,

joined Molinari, while Steve Gunderson, R-Wis., voted against her amendment.

HOUSE FLOOR ACTION

After several weeks of debate, the House passed the measure July 28 by a vote of 275-152. *(Vote 379, p. 92-H)*

Before approving the bill, the House voted to scale back the education award that National Service participants could get so that youths would not get as much education money for National Service as they did for military service.

Bob Stump, R-Ariz., ranking minority member of the Veterans' Affairs Committee, initially offered an amendment to provide National Service workers with education awards equal to 80 percent of the GI benefit. That would have cut the amount from $5,000 to $3,840 for each year of service. "Military service warrants a higher education benefit than civilian service because of its unique dangers, hardships, separation from home and family, restrictions on civil liberties and mandatory time in service commitment," he said.

Stump also said that the GI bill's education benefit was one of the military's most important recruiting tools, and unless it was substantially more than the benefit received for National Service, the armed forces could have difficulty signing up recruits. The GI bill provided $4,800 per year for three years with a mandatory service commitment of three years. Service members had to put in $1,200 of their own money from military pay during their first year of service.

The administration strongly opposed the amendment, but Stump had the votes to win. So Veterans' Affairs Committee Chairman G. V. "Sonny" Montgomery, D-Miss., suggested compromising at 90 percent of the GI benefits. That put the education benefit for National Service at $4,725.

Stump agreed, and the amendment was adopted July 28 by voice vote.

Immigration and Racism

The House spent the bulk of its time on the bill July 28 embroiled in an emotional debate about illegal immigrants and racism. Bill Baker, R-Calif., offered an amendment that would have required charities and other groups participating in the National Service program to have a written policy stating that they provided no services to illegal aliens and would report illegal aliens to the Immigration and Naturalization Service. Otherwise, they would not qualify for federal funds. Baker said taxpayers should not be forced to subsidize illegal aliens through the service program.

The amendment, which was modified to let illegal aliens obtain religious instruction and services, sparked an outcry among Democrats and minority lawmakers.

Jose E. Serrano, D-N.Y., chairman of the Congressional Hispanic Caucus, called Baker and the amendment "mean." He said, "This doesn't strengthen the country, it just makes us look like really bad people."

But Republican lawmakers took Serrano's statement to mean he was calling them racists. Other lawmakers said immigration policies should be debated and decided on immigration bills, not on National Service.

The House agreed to the perfecting amendment regarding religious services by a vote of 270-163. Then it rejected the Baker amendment by 180-253. *(Votes 374, 375, p. 92-H)*

The House also agreed to an amendment by John Edward Porter, R-Ill., that required states to enact laws pro-

tecting service participants and volunteers from personal liability for any injury or damage if they were acting in good faith while performing their work. The vote was 239-194. *(Vote 372, p. 90-H)*

Republicans Try Again

During the floor debate, Republicans repeated objections they had raised in committee that Congress and the administration ought to adequately fund existing college student aid programs before creating and funding a new program.

Goodling again tried, without success, to scale back the National Service initiative by limiting the education awards to those who were financially needy. The House rejected the amendment 156-270. *(Vote 349, p. 86-H)*

Goodling said that with a limited amount of money available for student aid, it was not right to give money to children who did not need help. But opponents said means-testing the awards would limit the program to a corps of poor young people, eliminating the advantage of a common bond among diverse participants. Goodling directed his remarks to members who represented low-income, low-middle income and middle-income Americans. The money for National Service, he said, was going to come out of the pockets of low-income people who qualified for need-based student aid.

But McCurdy, a longtime champion of National Service, said it was not a student loan program.

"I believe National Service is one of the ways to help bring together people from less-privileged homes, less-privileged conditions and those who are from the very privileged," he said.

Molinari repeated her effort to help student aid programs by delaying the funding of National Service. She offered an amendment that would have prevented Congress from funding National Service until other financial aid programs were funded at least at fiscal 1993 levels. "It is crystal clear that we are in a zero sum game when it comes to funding for education programs," Molinari said. The American Council on Education and other higher education groups supported Molinari's amendment.

But Ford said he did not believe that imposing a funding trigger for National Service on the Appropriations Committee would work.

The amendment was rejected 184-247. *(Vote 351, p. 86-H)*

SENATE COMMITTEE ACTION

The Senate Labor and Human Resources Committee acted simultaneously with the House committee, voting 14-3 on June 16 to approve National Service legislation (S 919 — S Rept 103-70). Republicans Orrin G. Hatch of Utah, Nancy Landon Kassebaum of Kansas and Strom Thurmond of South Carolina voted against the measure.

Like the original House bill, the committee bill provided for education awards of $5,000 a year to people who performed community service.

As in the House, the legislation ran into opposition from Republicans, who argued that it would come at the expense of other student aid programs.

Said Kassebaum, ranking minority member on the Senate Labor and Human Resources Committee: "At a time when programs such as Pell grants are receiving far lower levels of support than any of us would like to see, it simply does not make sense to devote substantial resources to loan forgiveness plans and educational awards which may or

may not have any bearing on an individual's participation in service programs."

SENATE FLOOR ACTION

After being snarled for a time by Republican delaying tactics, the Senate voted 58-41 on Aug. 3 to pass the National Service bill. The Democratic leadership won the votes of seven Republicans and lost those of four Democrats. *(Vote 231, p. 30-S)*

To win passage, Democrats pared the measure by placing caps on spending of $300 million in fiscal 1994, $500 million in fiscal 1995 and $700 million in fiscal 1996. Senate aides said that would cut the maximum number of service workers to about 100,000 from 150,000.

Supporters said the slower rate of growth would not harm the initiative. "National Service is what the effort to reinvent America is all about," said Edward M. Kennedy, D-Mass., chairman of the Labor and Human Resources Committee. "The passage of this legislation marks the end of the 'me' era in American life."

Republicans Object to Cost

Floor debate began on July 20, and like the House, the Senate wrestled with setting priorities for scarce funds.

Pete V. Domenici, R-N.M., offered an amendment similar to Molinari's in the House. He said he wanted to ensure that the financial soundness of the Pell grant program was a higher priority than funding a National Service program.

Under Domenici's amendment, funds would not have been available for National Service unless the College Work-Study program, the Supplemental Educational Opportunity Grants, the State Student Incentive Grants and the Perkins Loan Program received the same amount of funding that they got in fiscal 1993. In addition, Pell grants would have had to be funded at $2,300 a year for the maximum grant.

Democrats defended the National Service program and said the Clinton administration was committed to funding student aid programs. The Senate tabled, or killed, the Domenici amendment by a vote of 55-44. *(Vote 205, p. 27-S)*

The Senate also rejected two Kassebaum amendments. Kassebaum argued repeatedly that the National Service program was too big, too bureaucratic and would cost too much money. Her first amendment would have combined all existing service-type programs, including VISTA and the Peace Corps, into one program. Her amendment would not have guaranteed the $5,000 post-service benefit to participants. The Senate rejected the amendment, 38-59. *(Vote 202, p. 27-S)*

Kassebaum tried again, offering an amendment to limit spending to $100 million in the first year, down from $394 million. She also wanted to limit the authorization to two years from five years. The Senate rejected this amendment, 42-57. *(Vote 210, p. 28-S)*

On other GOP amendments, the Senate:

• Voted 56-42 on July 21 to kill an amendment by John McCain, R-Ariz., that would have made veterans eligible for National Service education awards. *(Vote 203, p. 27-S)*

• Rejected, 46-53, a July 21 amendment by Paul Coverdell, R-Ga., to delay funding National Service until the portion of the deficit caused by fiscal 1993 emergency spending was eliminated. *(Vote 204, p. 27-S)*

• Voted 64-35 on July 22 to kill an amendment by Larry E. Craig, R-Idaho, to deny family and medical leave benefits to National Service participants. *(Vote 209, p. 28-S)*

Highlights of the Bill

The National Service bill (HR 2010 — PL 103-82) gave education awards for community service. As enacted, the measure:

A New Corporation

● Created a Corporation for National and Community Service to administer the program by combining two existing independent federal agencies, the Commission on National and Community Service and ACTION.

● Required the corporation to administer all programs authorized under the National and Community Service Act and Domestic Volunteer Service Act, including VISTA and the older Americans volunteer programs.

● Required each state to establish a commission on National Service to receive a federal grant. Commissions were to include 15 to 25 citizens or community service experts to be appointed by the governor on a bipartisan basis.

● Required state commissions to form plans for National Service and prepare applications to the corporation for funding. Commissions could not operate programs, though they could fund state agencies that did. Commissions were required to allocate at least 60 percent of funds to non-state groups.

Participants

● Allowed people to serve before, during or after post-secondary education. Participants could be age 17 or older; they had to be high school graduates or agree to achieve general equivalency diplomas.

● Required that participants be chosen on a non-discriminatory basis, without regard to political affiliation. Information about National Service was to be available through high schools, colleges and other placement offices. Recruiters were required to pay special attention to the needs of disadvantaged youths.

● Required that to earn an education award, a participant could serve one year of full-time service, two years of part-time service or three years of part-time service if the person were in school. A person could serve up to two terms and earn up to two education awards.

● Set education awards at $4,725 for one term of service. The awards had to be used within five years of completing a term of service.

● Set stipends at 85 percent of a minimum wage stipend equivalent to benefits received by VISTA volunteers. Programs could provide additional stipends up to twice this amount, with no federal match.

● Required that all participants without health insurance receive coverage, with federal funds paying up to 85 percent of the cost. Full-time participants were to receive child-care assistance if they needed it.

Funding

● Distributed the funds according to the House plan, giving one-third to the states based on population, a minimum of one-third to the states based on competition, and whatever was left up to one-third, to participating federal agencies and national not-for-profit organizations.

● Required that all participants receive education awards.

● Authorized the program for three years with funding set at $300 million in fiscal 1994, $500 million in fiscal 1995 and $700 million in fiscal 1996.

● Required programs to pay 15 percent of the stipend and health-care benefits in cash, and 25 percent of other program costs receiving federal support. The 25 percent match could be in cash or in kind from any source other than programs funded under the national service act.

Cloture Fight

Debate on the National Service bill was interrupted the week of July 26 when a threatened GOP filibuster forced Democrats to pull the bill while they scrambled to get the 60 votes to invoke cloture, a parliamentary step to stop debate and bring the measure to a vote. It took Senate Democrats a full week to obtain the votes.

The first cloture attempt failed July 29 on a 59-41 vote. Three Republican senators joined the Democrats in the vote — James M. Jeffords of Vermont, Dave Durenberger of Minnesota and John H. Chafee of Rhode Island. *(Vote 224, p. 29-S)*

Finally, on July 30, Democrats had the votes they needed to break the logjam. (William S. Cohen of Maine and Mark O. Hatfield of Oregon were slated to join the three who had voted with the Democrats the first time.) But at that point, Republicans allowed them to forgo the balloting and proceed to wrapping up the last amendments on the bill.

The main hang-up had been the program's cost. The original bill authorized $394 million in fiscal 1994 and unspecified sums for the next four years. Republicans, aware of administration plans to jump from 25,000 participants to 150,000 participants in four years, feared that the program would spiral out of control.

To placate the Republicans, Kennedy offered an amendment to restrict the spending to $1.5 billion over three years, with caps specified for each year. Republicans countered by saying they could live with a two-year authorization, but not three years; they said they wanted a chance to review the program in two years.

Administration officials said that was unacceptable because the program would take at least six months to get off the ground and participants would not know whether it would be reauthorized, allowing them to complete a two-year term.

The Senate accepted Kennedy's proposal by unanimous consent July 30. An attempt by Arlen Specter, R-Pa., to require a reauthorization after two years failed, 41-52. *(Vote 228, p. 30-S)*

Although the measure passed, the conflict left bruised feelings between Democrats and Republicans. Majority Leader George J. Mitchell, D-Maine, called the Republican opposition "unfortunate obstructionism on a measure which has broad support among the American people and is favored by a majority of the Senate." Mitchell also said he believed Republicans resisted the bill principally because National Service was an important part of the president's agenda.

Kassebaum, who led the opposition, said that might be true for some Republicans but not all. "There's a general desire to get the funding down as low as possible," she said.

Minority Leader Bob Dole, R-Kan., said Republicans were simply trying to negotiate a better bill. "It's not a filibuster; it's not gridlock," Dole said.

CONFERENCE/FINAL ACTION

Once the Senate passed the bill, the measure moved rapidly toward enactment. House and Senate conferees

resolved their differences and approved a final version Aug. 4 (H Rept 103-219). The House adopted the conference report by a vote of 275-152 on Aug. 6, the last day before the August recess. The Senate followed suit Sept. 8, voting 57-40 to adopt the conference report and clear the bill. *(House vote 408, p. 100-H; Senate vote 249, p. 33-S)*

The conferees' job was relatively simple; there were only a few key differences between the bills:

● **Funding.** The House would have started the program at a faster rate, authorizing $394 million in fiscal 1994 and unspecified sums in the next four years to provide 150,000 people with service jobs. The Senate voted to start slower and set annual caps ($300 million for the first year, $500 million for the second and $700 million for the third).

Conferees agreed to adopt the Senate's slower approach.

● **Distributing funds to states.** The House and Senate also took different approaches in distributing funds to states for service programs. The House originally voted to give one-third of the money to the states based on population and one-third by competitive grants, with the remaining one-third going to federal agencies, national parks or national nonprofit groups to provide service opportunities.

The Senate would have given more money to the states automatically.

Conferees agreed to adopt the House language but modified it so that at least one-third of the money would go for competitive grants and whatever was left over would be used for federal agencies and national nonprofit groups. ■

House Advances Education Reform Bill

The House on Oct. 13 easily passed President Clinton's Goals 2000 education reform bill, aimed at encouraging states to adopt national goals, standards and tests for their elementary and secondary education systems. The Senate Labor and Human Resources Committee approved a companion Senate bill (S 846, later reintroduced as S 1150), but S 1150 did not make it to the Senate floor in 1993.

The House-passed bill (HR 1804) authorized $427 million in fiscal 1994 for competitive grants to states to finance their visions of what it would take to improve public schools.

The legislation, which closely tracked an initiative that Clinton sent to Capitol Hill in April, identified a set of eight national education goals — the first six proposed by Clinton, and the final two added in the House. The goals prescribed that by the year 2000:

● All children would start school ready to learn.

● At least 90 percent of students would finish high school.

● Students would leave grades four, eight and 12 with demonstrated competence in English, math, science, foreign languages, arts, history and geography.

● The United States would be first in the world in math and science achievement.

● Every adult American would be literate and possess the skills to compete in a global economy.

● Every school would be free of drugs and violence.

● More parents would participate in their children's schooling.

● All teachers would have access to good teacher training.

The administration hoped that if Congress spelled out what was expected of all students and schools, both groups

---

BOXSCORE

➡ **Goals 2000: Educate America Act (HR 1804, S 1150, formerly S 846).** The authorization bills included $427 million in the House and about $420 million in the Senate for school improvement, with most of the money to be awarded to states. The bills laid out a framework for what was expected of all students and schools through voluntary national standards, tests and goals.

Reports: H Rept 103-168; S Rept 103-85.

KEY ACTION

May 6 — **House** Subcommittee on Elementary, Secondary and Vocational Education approved HR 1804, 17-9.

May 19 — **Senate** Labor and Human Resources Committee approved S 846, 14-3.

June 23 — **House** Education and Labor Committee approved HR 1804, 28-15.

Oct. 13 — **House** passed HR 1804, 307-118.

---

would rise to the challenge, ultimately contributing to a high-skill, high-wage economy. States were encouraged to adopt the national goals, but they did not have to do so to qualify for grants.

The bulk of the money authorized by the bill was to be awarded to states to improve their elementary and secondary schools. Participating states were to develop and adopt plans for restructuring and improving their education systems, including setting standards of content — or what children should know in English, math and other subjects at certain points in their schooling; devising a way to assess or test what students had learned; and developing ideas for teacher training.

The states also were required to develop opportunity-to-learn standards prescribing what a school needed — such as competent teachers or up-to-date textbooks — to give children the opportunity to meet the goals and standards.

It was the opportunity-to-learn standards that created partisan ill will during early consideration of the House bill. Republicans, including Bill Goodling of Pennsylvania, the ranking minority member of the House Education and Labor Committee, feared that those standards would become an onerous federal mandate, requiring school districts and states to spend billions of dollars to comply. Republicans also feared that if the plans were not effective, parents would sue school systems and states.

Meanwhile, the fiscal 1994 appropriations bill for the departments of Labor, Health and Human Services, and Education (HR 2518 — PL 103-112) included $155 million for the grants and other costs of putting the national goals program in place.

BACKGROUND

Bills aimed at improving public schools died in both the 101st and 102nd Congresses, after President George Bush and congressional Democrats failed to agree on the basic elements of the legislation. The most volatile issue was Bush's proposal to use federal funds to give parents more choice over whether to send their children to public or private schools. But there also was disagreement over national student testing, state and federal regulation of education, and the amount of federal money to spend on improving elementary and secondary education.

Bush had signaled his interest in reform during the 1988 presidential race, promising to be the education president. He started a national dialogue about what needed to be done to improve education and what role the federal government should play. In 1989, he convened a meeting of the nation's governors in Charlottesville, Va., where they developed the original six education goals.

In 1991, Education Secretary Lamar Alexander, an aggressive former Tennessee governor, crafted a $690 million "America 2000" plan that included voluntary national testing for fourth-, eighth- and 12th-graders; merit pay for teachers; creation of non-traditional schools; and a school choice proposal — an administrative priority. But the Senate Labor and Human Resources Committee wrote a bill (S 2) allowing choice only among public schools. In the waning days of the 1991 legislative session, Republicans blocked the Senate from taking up the bill.

The measure, which won Senate approval in early 1992, would have provided $800 million in block grants to states and schools, leaving specific reforms up to local officials. The bill that emerged contained no mention of the America 2000 proposals, no non-traditional schools and no school choice.

Neither Democrats nor Republicans expressed much support for the conference report. Republicans disliked it because it did not include Bush's initiatives. Democrats disliked it because they thought it did not go far enough and did not authorize enough money. Still, they moved it along because they did not want to appear to be thwarting Bush's education efforts. The House approved the bill, but Senate Republicans blocked consideration of the conference report. *(1991 Almanac, p. 377; 1992 Almanac, p. 455)*

CLINTON'S PROPOSAL

The school reform train had come full circle since 1989 when Bush began pushing the notion of national goals, standards and tests. During that time, Democrats roundly denounced him for not putting enough money into education. House Democrats had to swallow those words as they praised Clinton's new school reform bill brought to Capitol Hill on April 22 by Education Secretary Richard W. Riley.

Clinton's bill contained the concept of voluntary national goals, standards and tests. But the cost was estimated at $420 million in fiscal 1994, well below Bush's second education proposal of $690 million, and about the same as Bush's first education plan, which many Democrats then called "a Band-Aid."

The Clinton plan, formally called the "Goals 2000: Educate America Act," included six national education goals that the president wanted written into law.

At the national level, Clinton wanted to create three panels to work with the states:

• The National Education Goals Panel, which already existed but was to be written into law, to report on state and national progress toward achieving the national goals.

• The National Education Standards and Improvement Council to develop criteria for certifying content standards, opportunity-to-learn standards and state assessments. The Department of Education already had awarded grants to universities and other groups to develop content standards, which the states could later use as models. Because all standards and testing were to be voluntary, the certification was merely a "Good Housekeeping seal of approval," as Riley put it.

• A National Skills Standards Board to identify major occupations and develop standards and tests for people to show they were qualified to work in a particular field.

Democratic Dissonance

The initial draft of the bill that Riley sent to Congress made many House Democrats unhappy. It did not emphasize the opportunity-to-learn standards. Such "school delivery" standards had been controversial features of recent school reform legislation. Democrats argued that it was not fair to test students when no one knew whether the children were failing or the schools were failing the children.

After the chilly reaction, Riley became a fixture in the Rayburn House Office Building, meeting repeatedly with the Education and Labor Committee Democrats as a group and individually. "I think he got beat up pretty badly by the majority," said ranking minority member Goodling.

In their talks with Riley, House Democrats also said they were concerned that provisions for testing children might turn into barriers to disadvantaged children. Riley agreed that the testing would not be "high-stakes" — that is, it would not be used to determine a child's future, such as whether the student would be admitted to college. Rather, the testing would be a way for schools and states to evaluate schools' progress in reaching educational goals.

William D. Ford, D-Mich., chairman of the House Education and Labor Committee, was disappointed that the Clinton plan did not include more money for education and school reform. But by April, he had dropped that criticism in reaction to the successful Senate filibuster of Clinton's economic stimulus plan — which included more than $3 billion for summer jobs, college tuition grants and the Chapter 1 supplemental education program for disadvantaged students. "After what happened in the Senate, I could see he'd be wasting his time," Ford said. "We're going to take what we can get." *(Stimulus, p. 706)*

HOUSE COMMITTEE ACTION

The Elementary, Secondary and Vocational Education Subcommittee of the Education and Labor Committee voted 17-9 on May 6 in favor of Clinton's $420 million bill.

Democrats and Republicans agreed on several technical amendments. Republicans also agreed to accept the opportunity-to-learn standards, although Goodling said he still worried that those standards would encourage parents to sue a school that did not meet them. "If, five years from now, all the money goes to court rather than children, I want to be able to say 'I told you so,' " Goodling said.

Bipartisan cooperation broke down, however, when Jack Reed, D-R.I., won committee approval for an amendment requiring states, before they could get any federal money, to list specific "corrective action" to be taken if a school or school system did not meet the states' delivery standards. "Many states will take the money, do the plan-

ning and shrug when schools don't make it," Reed said.

Steve Gunderson, R-Wis., called the amendment a "deal breaker" because it required states to take certain actions — making the standards no longer voluntary. Gunderson later said that Democrats had promised not to offer any controversial amendments if the Republicans agreed to go along with the opportunity-to-learn standards.

Education Secretary Riley opposed the Reed amendment.

Subcommittee Chairman Dale E. Kildee, D-Mich., said he believed both sides acted in good faith and could work something out before the full committee markup.

The subcommittee also approved an amendment by Tim Roemer, D-Ind., to add a seventh national goal, namely that all teachers should have access to good teacher training programs by 2000.

With little discussion, the subcommittee rejected an amendment by John A. Boehner, R-Ohio, to allow states to use federal funds to promote private as well as public school choice.

The subcommittee left for the full committee a controversial section of the bill creating a board to help develop standards for training workers.

Full Education Committee Action

The House Education and Labor panel divided along party lines June 23, voting 28-15 to approve the bill (H Rept 103-168).

Ranking Republican Goodling was so upset with Democratic amendments that he called the bill "a disaster."

It was the opportunity-to-learn standards that forced the partisan breach. After weeks of discussion, Reed had agreed to tone down the language of his subcommittee amendment requiring states to identify specific "corrective action" to take if a school did not meet the state's standards. But Republicans were dissatisfied and were losing patience.

The amendment asked each state to describe how it would monitor its progress toward putting the state and local education plans in place, and it asked states to describe the procedures they would use to ensure that schools and school districts met state opportunity-to-learn and content standards. Reed called it intellectually dishonest to set standards but not think about what should be done if schools did not meet them.

Goodling pointed out that the language was opposed by Clinton and by Al Shanker, president of the American Federation of Teachers. He said the amendment created more unfunded mandates for state and local governments. But Reed said that without the language, "what we're essentially saying is 'Take the money and run.'"

Goodling predicted that states would hesitate to apply for reform money knowing that they would be expected to try to meet opportunity-to-learn standards. After listening to George Miller, D-Calif., speak for the amendment, Goodling blew up, banging his fist on the table and shouting, "We aren't helping anyone anywhere."

The committee agreed to the Reed amendment 28-15, on a party-line vote.

In an effort to wave the previous GOP administration's flag, Dick Armey, R-Texas, offered a substitute amendment to provide $393 million to state and local agencies for public, private and parochial school choice, merit schools, model schools and site-based management. The committee, which had repeatedly voted down school-choice proposals in the past, rejected the amendment 7-35.

The bill's last title provided for a National Skills Standards Board to set qualifying standards for trades. The panel voted 22-21 to exempt about 200 trades that had apprenticeship programs. Some members argued for including all trades, but subcommittee Chairman Kildee said those groups could "opt in." The panel rejected, 15-28, a Goodling amendment to require that a majority of board members come from the business community.

HOUSE FLOOR ACTION

In contrast to the partisan fights that marked committee consideration of the bill, the measure sailed through the House on Oct. 13 on a 307-118 vote. The only tussle occurred when a cadre of Republicans raised anew their longstanding call for federal support of private school choice. *(Vote 496, p. 122-H)*

To win Republican support, Democrats agreed to accept a floor amendment by Goodling stating that nothing in the bill should be interpreted to give the federal government control over local prerogatives. "This should put to rest the concern that we were going to dictate from the federal government," Goodling said.

Kildee said the bill's language still would ensure that opportunity-to-learn standards would help show whether a student was failing or a school was failing that student. The House adopted the Goodling amendment by a vote of 424-0. *(Vote 495, p. 120-H)*

School Choice Rejected

The most controversial floor amendment was a proposal by Armey to provide $400 million for model schools, merit schools, school choice and decentralized management. It would have eliminated all commissions, standards and testing systems in the underlying bill.

Armey said he offered the amendment "for the children of our country" who were forced to stay in public schools because their parents could not afford better private schools.

"Rich people already have school choice," he said. "It is the poor people who are trapped in failing schools."

Armey argued that providing vouchers — or some means to pay for alternatives — would force public schools to improve to keep their students.

But Kildee maintained that education was a local function, a state responsibility and a federal concern — a balance that he contended was preserved in HR 1804. Democrats argued that the federal government should use its limited resources on public, rather than private, schools. The House rejected Armey's amendment 130-300. *(Vote 494, p. 120-H)*

Other Amendments

The House also agreed by voice vote to the following amendments:

● By George E. Brown Jr., D-Calif., to include use of the metric system in the stated objectives for math and science education and standards for teachers of math and science.

● By Melvin Watt, D-N.C., to authorize money to plan and pay for activities that coordinated children's education with other federal programs that served children or their families.

● By Dave McCurdy, D-Okla., to add increased parental participation in schooling to the list of national education goals.

● By Donald M. Payne, D-N.J., and Ronald K. Machtley,

R-R.I., adding objectives to another national education goal that called for access to physical and health education.

SENATE COMMITTEE ACTION

The Senate Labor and Human Resources Committee voted 14-3 on May 19 to its version of the bill (S 846), pending resolution of one snag.

The committee hit the snag when it took up the section of the bill aimed at creating a board to identify major trades and develop standards and tests for people to show they were qualified to work in a particular field. Some civil rights groups were concerned that businesses could use those standards to justify not hiring minorities. And some members questioned why a labor provision was in an education bill. The committee deferred action on that section of the bill until the week of May 24.

Ranking Republican Nancy Landon Kassebaum of Kansas said she thought the bill dictated too much to states, but she supported it anyway. The three opponents were Republicans Daniel R. Coats of Indiana, Judd Gregg of New Hampshire and Orrin G. Hatch of Utah.

As approved by the committee, the bill authorized $420 million for school improvement and wrote into law Clinton's six national education goals.

The key difference between the Senate and House bills was in the opportunity-to-learn standards. The Senate bill did not include a provision comparable to the Reed amendment requiring states to list specific corrective action to be taken if a school did not meet standards.

Several Democratic senators said they remained concerned about wide disparities in school funding from one district to another within states. Jeff Bingaman, D-N.M., proposed that the committee authorize a commission to study whether the federal government should provide state incentives to equalize spending.

But other senators said that by the time a commission was funded, it would be too late to act on its recommendations in the upcoming reauthorization of the Elementary and Secondary Education Act (HR 6). Senators agreed to hold hearings on the issue and to ask the Office of Technology Assessment to conduct a study. *(Chapter 1, below)*

Training Standards Approved

On May 26, the committee agreed by voice vote to create a national skills standards board to be made up of representatives of business, organized labor and educational institutions in roughly equal strength.

By a 10-7 party-line vote, the committee rejected an amendment by Kassebaum that called for the board to be made up of 12 business representatives and eight others. Kassebaum said the board should include a business majority because businesses would be using the skills standards for their employees.

Democrats said labor should have an equal say in the development of standards. ∎

Congress Looks to Chapter 1 Rewrite

A huge political fight was brewing in 1993 over the pending reauthorization of the Elementary and Secondary Education Act, a Johnson-era law that contained the main federal aid program for the nation's elementary and secondary schools. The law was due to be reauthorized by the end of fiscal 1994.

Most of the money in the act went to the Chapter 1 remedial program for disadvantaged children, which provided about $6.3 billion a year to give more than 5 million students extra help in reading, math and other areas in which they had fallen behind. The act also included bilingual education, Drug-Free Schools grants to prevent and treat alcohol and drug abuse, and Eisenhower grants to improve the teaching of math and science.

A version of the reauthorization bill (HR 6) was introduced in the House at the beginning of 1993, but it was not expected to provide more than a few elements of whatever measure was enacted in 1994, and it was not expected to take care of the biggest trouble spot in the reauthorization: the financing formula for the Chapter 1 program.

Neither the House Education and Labor Committee nor the Senate Labor and Human Resources Committee acted on a reauthorization bill in 1993, but both were expected to move early in 1994, particularly after the Clinton administration produced a draft rewrite of the Chapter 1 program in September 1993.

Under the existing program, the government based Chapter 1 allocations both on a county-by-county census of poor children and on the amount that states spent per pupil on education. Chapter 1 grants went to 95 percent of all school districts, a degree of distribution that had existed since the program began in 1965 and was in part intended to build broad political support for it.

Critics complained that the formula spread the available money too thin, thwarting the program's intent to benefit economically and educationally disadvantaged students. They cited the use of county-by-county numbers, which had the effect of muting the needs of small school districts within large metropolitan counties, and the reliance on per pupil expenditures, which tended to direct more Chapter 1 money to wealthier states. Critics also complained that the 10-year census caused the formula to react too slowly to population changes.

Clinton Proposal

In its draft reauthorization bill presented Sept. 14, 1993, the Clinton administration proposed several changes to Chapter 1, mostly aimed at sending more Chapter 1 money to counties and school districts with the highest poverty rates.

At the time, 10 percent of Chapter 1 money was earmarked for so-called concentration grants that went to the most impoverished areas. The administration proposed to increase the allocation for concentration grants to 50 percent and shift about $500 million from lower-poverty to higher-poverty counties.

In allocating the aid, the administration proposed to discount the first 2 percent of children in a school district who were poor. That meant that areas with low poverty levels would lose a substantial amount of money. However, the plan included a "hold harmless" provision that would prevent an area from losing more than 15 percent of its

money in a single year, despite changes in the formula or census figures.

Clinton's reallocation proposal was in line with contemporary studies but was highly controversial. There was strong political support to continue the allocation formula that had been in place since Chapter 1 was created as part of President Lyndon B. Johnson's War on Poverty.

Dale E. Kildee, D-Mich., chairman of the House Subcommittee on Elementary, Secondary and Vocational Education, cautioned that lawmakers would have to see what sort of resources were available before they signed on to the administration's reallocation plan. Many communities that were receiving Chapter 1 money provided effective programs, he said, but might not qualify for aid under the proposed formula. Kildee preferred simply to get more money for the whole program.

To ensure that children receiving assistance under the Chapter 1 program got high-level instruction, the draft bill also proposed that states be required to submit plans to the Department of Education outlining content and performance standards of what children were expected to know and be able to do.

States would have to do this to receive any Chapter 1 money. Such standards were an integral part of Clinton's Goals 2000 school reform bill (HR 1804, S 846), which saw some action in 1993. Because the Goals 2000 program was to be voluntary, the administration wanted to have states develop the standards under the Chapter 1 program if they wanted Chapter 1 money and chose not to participate in Goals 2000. *(Education reform, p. 404)*

Another Clinton proposal in line with Goals 2000 was to expand the Eisenhower Mathematics and Science Education program to focus on upgrading teacher skills in core subjects.

Education officials proposed to expand the Eisenhower program by wiping out Chapter 2 block grants, which traditionally had gone to school districts to support innovative programs or school reform efforts. In fiscal 1993, the program received $473.9 million.

Highlights

The Clinton plan included the following proposals:

● Change the name of the Chapter 1 program back to Title I — as it was originally known. President Ronald Reagan got Congress to rename the program in 1981. *(1981 Almanac, p. 499)*

● Require states, in order to receive Chapter 1 money, to develop performance and content standards describing what all children were expected to know and be able to do. The standards could be the same ones developed under the administration's Goals 2000 school reform measure (HR 1804, S 846), or they could be developed under the Chapter 1 program if the state was not participating in Goals 2000.

● Replace existing multiple-choice basic skills tests for Chapter 1 students with a set of assessments designed to find out if children were meeting the state content standards. The administration wanted to eliminate multiple-choice testing in favor of more sophisticated assessments.

● Expand the number of schools providing Chapter 1 enrichment to the entire school rather than to a few "pullouts" from the classroom. The proposal would reduce the minimum poverty threshold, allowing schoolwide programs in 1995-96 where 65 percent of a school's students met a poverty test, instead of 75 percent as under existing law. In later years the threshold was to be 50 percent. That would allow 12,000 more of the poorest schools to develop schoolwide programs, bringing the total to about 20,000 schools.

● Prohibit schools from using Chapter 1 money to teach only low-level skills through repetitious drills. Instead, the administration wanted Chapter 1 programs to focus on more creative, higher-level concepts and skills. The Chapter 1 program had come under intense scrutiny, with three major studies released in 1992 severely criticizing its focus on low-level rote learning, among other things.

● Require local school districts to give Chapter 1 money first to all schools where 75 percent of the students met a poverty test.

● Require districts to screen children for health and nutritional problems in elementary schools where at least 50 percent of the children met a poverty test. The administration also planned to ask the school districts to coordinate Chapter 1 programs with Head Start, school-to-work programs, and health and social services.

● Allocate 50 percent of Chapter 1 money — up from 10 percent — to high-poverty areas, resulting in a shift of about $500 million away from counties and districts with lower poverty rates.

● Require school districts to distribute Chapter 1 dollars to schools based on poverty, rather than the achievement of their students. The change reflected a concern that sending money to schools with the lowest achievement rates had created a disincentive for schools to raise their students' performance, because improvements could cause the schools to lose money. ∎

House Passes High School Job-Training Bill

The House passed a "school-to-work" bill (HR 2884) by voice vote Nov. 15. The bill was aimed at helping students who were not bound for college to move from high school into skilled jobs. The Senate Labor and Human Resources Committee approved a similar bill (S 1361) on Nov. 3, but the full Senate did not consider it before the end of the first session.

The school-to-work bill was a Clinton administration priority and the result of a collaboration between the Education and Labor departments. It also had the support of labor and business groups.

At the time, about 75 percent of all high school students did not receive college degrees, but few programs existed to help them obtain the skills and work experience needed for a career.

The two bills authorized grants for educators, employers and labor representatives to develop partnerships to allow high school juniors and seniors to go to school part time and to work part time. Students who finished the program would receive a high school diploma, a certificate or diploma from a postsecondary school and an occupational skill certificate.

The legislation gave the states flexibility to design programs the way they thought was best. The federal govern-

ment was to provide a one-year planning grant and one five-year grant to inaugurate the partnerships. After that, states would be on their own. While programs could vary, each had to provide job training, paid work experience and workplace mentoring, along with academic training.

Congress already had set aside $100 million under existing authority for a school-to-work program in its fiscal 1994 appropriations bill (HR 2518 — PL 103-112) for the two departments. *(Appropriations, p. 632)*

BACKGROUND

The Clinton administration sent its school-to-work legislative proposal to Capitol Hill on Aug. 5 as part of its effort to raise education standards and the quality of the nation's work force. The package attracted bipartisan support from members involved in education and labor issues. Secretary of Labor Robert B. Reich and Secretary of Education Richard W. Riley worked together to develop and promote the initiative.

The administration bill authorized $300 million in fiscal 1995 for federal grants to states to develop systems to help students who were not going to college to acquire work skills. School-to-work programs would vary from state to state, but each one would have to provide: learning about work with job training, paid work experience and workplace mentoring; learning at school with career counseling that could involve at least one year of postsecondary education and evaluations to identify students' academic strengths and weaknesses; and coordination among employers, schools and students, along with the training of teachers, mentors and counselors.

"We are the only major industrialized nation with no formal system for helping our young people ... make the transition from the classroom to the workplace," Riley said in a statement. "That translates into lost productivity and wasted human potential."

The administration's bill included:
● Development grants for all states to create school-to-work systems.
● Five-year implementation grants to states that had developed plans.
● Waivers allowing other federal funds to be used with school-to-work programs.
● Grants to localities that were ready to put a school-to-work program in place even if their state had not yet received an implementation grant.
● Direct grants to high-poverty areas.

At the National Association of Manufacturers, Phyllis Eisen, the senior policy director for education and work force readiness, said her organization supported the administration's proposal and planned to urge its members to participate. "It probably will be made or broken by how much the business community is brought into this," Eisen said. "Ultimately, the jobs have to be there."

Eisen said that small and medium-size businesses would

---

need some incentives from government to participate: "That's where the job growth is. It all can't come from IBM and Xerox and Texas Instruments and Motorola. Many of them are already involved in these programs."

Calvin Johnson, a legislative representative at the AFL-CIO labor organization, said that the proposal was a good effort but that he wanted to make sure it was an education program and did not turn into a jobs program.

LEGISLATIVE ACTION

On Nov. 3, two committees approved similar school-to-work bills, both by voice vote. The House Education and Labor Committee approved HR 2884 (H Rept 103-345), and the Senate Labor and Human Resources Committee approved S 1361 (S Rept 103-179).

Both bills authorized $300 million for fiscal 1995 and unspecified amounts through 2002. The Senate bill allowed the secretaries of Labor and Education to reserve up to $30 million in fiscal 1995 for high poverty areas, while the House bill required 10 percent of the appropriation in each fiscal year to go for programs in high-poverty areas.

The House bill, unlike the Senate measure, also reauthorized through fiscal 1995 the job training for the homeless demonstration program created under the Stewart B. McKinney Homeless Assistance Act (PL 101-645). *(1990 Almanac, p. 665)*

When Clinton forwarded his school-to-work proposal to Congress, many Republicans said they were concerned that Democrats would diminish the role of business and put too much emphasis on organized labor. But members had no complaints about the role assigned to business groups in either bill.

In the Senate, Nancy Landon Kassebaum, R-Kan., ranking member of the Labor and Human Resources Committee, said she remained concerned that the federal government had too many job training programs and that too much money was spent administering duplicative activities. She voted against reporting the bill but said she hoped it would be changed so she could support it on the floor.

In the House Education and Labor Committee, ranking Republican Bill Goodling, Pa., agreed that duplication was a problem. But he noted that the bill would require states to coordinate their training programs, especially vocational education programs and so-called "tech-prep" programs designed to help students move from high school to postsecondary vocational programs.

Goodling's main concern was that some Democrats would try to target the program to disadvantaged students, rather than helping all students who did not move on to college. He noted that the bill contained about 30 references to meeting students' special needs. He said Congress should leave that to the Chapter 1 compensatory education program, which was to be reauthorized in 1994. *(Chapter 1, p. 407)* ■

The Direct Approach to Student Loans

Congress approved an overhaul of the nation's student loan program, creating a new system of direct federal loans that cut out the banks, guarantee agencies and secondary markets that traditionally had supplied student loan funds.

Supporters said the new program, which was expected to account for at least half the new student loans within five years, would lower interest rates for students and save the government up to $2 billion a year by cutting out federal subsidies to banks.

On Nov. 15, Education Secretary Richard W. Riley released a list of 105 colleges selected to take part in the initial phase of the operation.

Lawmakers created the program as part of the 1993 budget-reconciliation bill (HR 2264 — H Rept 103-213). Congress cleared the bill Aug. 6, and President Clinton signed the measure into law (PL 103-66) on Aug. 10. *(Budget-reconciliation, p. 107)*

Under the bill, the federal government was authorized to supply 5 percent of all new student loans in the 1994-95 academic year, with the existing system providing the rest. The following year, up to 40 percent of all new loans could come directly from the federal government. In the third and fourth years, the government was authorized to supply 50 percent or more of all new loans, and by the fifth year, the percentage could hit 60 or more.

Under the existing system, the federal government guaranteed student loans issued by private banks. If the student defaulted, a state guarantee agency reimbursed the bank, and eventually the federal government reimbursed the guarantee agency. While the student remained in school, the government paid the bank the interest on the loan, calculated at the 91-day Treasury bill rate plus 3.1 percent.

When students graduated, banks frequently sold their loans to secondary markets, such as the Student Loan Marketing Association, known as Sallie Mae. Sallie Mae then collected monthly payments from the students and sold loan-backed bonds on Wall Street.

The new direct lending system dispensed with the banks, guarantee agencies and secondary markets. Instead, students were to apply for federal loans through their schools. Students also were given a choice of repayment options: They could make fixed monthly payments over 10 years, make lower fixed payments over a longer term, or they could use a graduated repayment system in which they paid a small amount initially with payments increasing over the years. There was also a repayment system tied to income. *(Budget-reconciliation provisions, p. 126)*

BACKGROUND

The student loan program, which was created in 1965 to help young people get a college education, had spawned an entire industry that included most of the nation's banks, thrifts and credit unions; a network of state and private guarantee agencies that insured the loans; and the highly profitable secondary market for student loans, led by the federally chartered Sallie Mae.

The Bush administration briefly floated the idea of converting to direct federal loans as a way of eliminating the fees and subsidies that the government paid to these institutions. But by time the House approved a direct loan plan in 1992 as part of a bill rewriting the Higher Education Act, the administration had rejected the idea, arguing that it would add to the debt and that the Education Department could not handle such a huge program. With a veto threat hanging over the bill and a companion Senate bill that included no direct loan plan, proponents settled for creating a direct loan demonstration project. *(1991 Almanac, p. 365; 1992 Almanac, p. 438)*

When Clinton came into office, he called for turning the demonstration into a full-fledged program that would replace guaranteed student loans by 1997; the administration estimated that the change would save $1.3 billion annually when it was fully phased in.

HOUSE ACTION

The House Education and Labor Committee agreed by voice vote on May 12 to scrap the existing guaranteed student loan program and replace it within four years with direct government loans. Direct loans were to constitute 4 percent of new loans in the 1994-95 academic year, 25 percent in 1995-96, 60 percent in 1996-97 and 100 percent in 1997-98. The change, projected to save $4.3 billion over five years, covered the bulk of the $5.8 billion in savings the committee had been instructed to achieve as part of the 1993 budget-reconciliation bill. Committee Democrats argued that the switch was the only way to save that much money.

The House approved the program without change when it passed the reconciliation bill, 219-213, on May 27. *(Vote 199, p. 48-H)*

In general, Republican committee members opposed the switch to direct loans, arguing that it was untested and might not be properly administered by the Education Department. They also said that a direct loan system would add to the national debt because private banks would no longer be providing the capital to students and that many jobs would be lost.

Bill Goodling, R-Pa., the ranking minority member, blasted the committee for moving ahead with direct loans but declined to offer a substitute amendment that he had been working on to save money from the existing student loan program. Asked why he had not offered the amendment in committee, Goodling said, "Did you ever see us win anything here?"

The only amendment offered and accepted on direct loans came from Tom Petri, R-Wis., who for 10 years had pushed for students to be able to pay back their loans based on their incomes. His non-binding amendment stated that members would like to see the Internal Revenue Service develop a mechanism to collect loan payments from students.

Hordes of lobbyists for bankers, guarantee agencies, secondary markets and others with a stake in the existing system attended the committee markup. Deputy Education Secretary Madeleine Kunin and other representatives of the Education Department, the Office of Management and Budget, and higher education groups backing the new proposal also attended.

Robert E. Andrews, D-N.J., who had been pushing for direct loans for a decade, called the existing system "a billion-dollar hemorrhage in the federal budget." He com-

plained about the "special interests" trying to hang on to guaranteed student loans. "We are shifting from an entitlement to banks to an entitlement for students," Andrews said.

Education Secretary Riley said he was in the process of pulling in the most knowledgeable people in the country to help design the technology needed to run a direct-loan system. "We can absolutely make the system more streamlined, more simple, more easy to work with as far as the student is concerned," Riley said.

Proponents of direct loans said the savings from eliminating big subsidies to banks would go to reduce the interest rates that students paid on their loans. Committee Chairman William D. Ford, D-Mich., said interest rates could drop from 8 percent to as low as 3.65 percent with the new system and that the government eventually could save $2 billion a year after getting out of the loan business.

SENATE ACTION

Acknowledging that a direct student loan program was untested, the Senate Labor and Human Resources Committee voted 15-2 on June 10 to phase in the new system slowly. The committee stipulated in its contribution to the reconciliation bill that direct lending account for 50 percent of new student loans made during the 1997-98 academic year. The full Senate left the language unchanged when it approved the bill 50-49 on June 25. *(Vote 190, p. 25-S)*

The legislation was a compromise forged by Claiborne Pell, D-R.I., chairman of the Education Subcommittee. Pell said he had "deep reservations" about using direct loans without first testing the program. He proposed that direct loans account for "at least" 50 percent of new student loans by the fourth year, 1997-98.

Several Republicans suggested that such a phase-in would be too hasty and that there ought to be a maximum percentage of loans provided directly to students, not just a minimum. "A minimum could easily mean 100 percent in the fourth or fifth year," said Nancy Landon Kassebaum, Kan., the full committee's ranking Republican. "We need to approach this carefully."

Unless banks were assured of getting access to at least half of the student loan market, agreed James M. Jeffords, R-Vt., "it won't be a fair test" of the two approaches.

But Paul Simon, D-Ill., a strong supporter of direct lending, said placing a 50 percent ceiling on direct loans would merely ensure that interest groups would continue to lobby lawmakers for several years.

Committee Democrats agreed to remove the words "at least" before 50 percent, ensuring that conventional loans would account for half of new student loans in 1997-98. The change persuaded all committee Republicans to vote for the measure.

Committee Chairman Edward M. Kennedy, D-Mass., tried to assure members that the compromise still "puts us irrevocably down the road of direct loans" and noted that the issue would be reviewed in 1998, when Congress reauthorized the higher education program. But the change disenchanted several Democratic supporters of direct lending, two of whom — Tom Harkin of Iowa and Paul Wellstone of Minnesota — voted against the compromise. Although Simon voted for the compromise, he said he hoped the conference report would more closely approach the House version.

The Senate bill said the secretary of Education should make sure that direct loans accounted for 5 percent of new student loans for the 1994-95 academic year, rising in successive years to 30 percent, 40 percent and 50 percent.

FINAL ACTION

Meeting four times on the last day of negotiations and at least seven times during the week, conferees from the House and Senate committees agreed July 29 on a plan that left the existing guaranteed student loan system in place while partially phasing in the new direct loan program at a pace faster than the Senate had wanted. The change was expected to save $4.6 billion over five years.

Conferees agreed to start the Federal Direct Student Loan program at 5 percent of new loan volume in 1994-95; 40 percent the next year; 50 percent of new loan volume in 1996-97; 50 percent in 1997-98; and 60 percent in 1998-99. Any school that wanted to participate could do so beginning in 1996-97, regardless of the fixed percentage. That meant that all schools potentially could participate in direct loans despite the 50 percent benchmark set by conferees.

Philosophically, the House and Senate positions had been far apart. The Senate viewed its approach as setting up two systems to compete against each other and allow the market to decide which was more efficient. But the House feared that by cutting so deeply into the banks' profits, most of the small and medium-size banks would pull out and many of the guarantee agencies would collapse. Members worried that would eliminate access to loans for many students.

Another key difference between the House and Senate measures was the treatment of the banks, guarantee agencies and secondary markets that ran the existing guaranteed student loan system. The House would have continued to subsidize interest on the bank loans at the rate of the 91-day Treasury bill plus 3.1 percent while a student was attending school. The Senate, on the other hand, wanted to cut that subsidy to the 91-day Treasury bill plus 2.5 percent in order to reap savings needed to make up for not moving completely to direct loans. Conferees agreed to the Senate approach. ■

Arts Funding Avoids Obscenity Debate

The House in October approved a two-year reauthorization for the National Endowment for the Arts (NEA), the National Endowment for the Humanities (NEH) and the Institute of Museum Services. Identical legislation won committee approval in the Senate but made it no further in 1993. The House bill, introduced by Pat Williams, D-Mont., authorized appropriations of $381 million in fiscal 1994 — $174.6 million for the NEA, $177.5 million for the NEH and $28.8 million for the Institute of Museum Services.

The bill made no policy changes on the controversial issues of what was art and what was obscenity, topics that were dealt with in 1990.

BACKGROUND

Funding for the agencies had been a perennial war over art and obscenity, but lawmakers avoided fighting over this issue in the 1993 reauthorization. The bill maintained language worked out in 1990 in the House's reauthorization bill and on the fiscal 1991 spending bill for Interior appropriations (PL 101-512), which included a permanent change to the NEA's charter. *(1991 Almanac, p. 555; 1990 Almanac, p. 430)*

That language specified that the NEA chairman would award grants based on artistic merit and artistic excellence and would take into consideration "general standards of decency and respect for the diverse beliefs and values of the American public." If a project was funded and a court later ruled that the art was obscene, the NEA could recoup the grant money from the artist, the law said.

In grappling with the obscenity issue in 1990, House members decided to reduce the amount of money that the NEA distributed directly to artists and increase to 35 percent from 20 percent the amount it gave states to distribute to artists.

LEGISLATIVE ACTION

The House Education and Labor Subcommittee on Labor-Management Relations approved the two-year reauthorization (HR 2351) by voice vote June 22, sending it to the full committee.

Steve Gunderson, R-Wis., tried to amend the bill to bar the federal government from increasing a state's arts funding if the state reduced arts spending from the previous year. Although previous reauthorization legislation had forbidden states from using increases in federal money in place of state money, Gunderson said that was exactly what had been happening. He said that in fiscal 1991, 24 states or territories reduced arts funding from the previous year's level by an average of 16 percent. At the same time, NEA "basic grants" to states increased almost 22 percent, from $21.5 million to $26.2 million. In fiscal 1992, Gunderson said, 36 states and territories cut arts funding from the fiscal 1991 level.

BOXSCORE

➡ **NEA, NEH Reauthorization (HR 2351, S 1218).** Two-year reauthorization for National Endowment for the Arts, National Endowment for the Humanities and Institute of Museum Services.

Report: H Rept 103-186, S Rept 103-182.

KEY ACTION

June 29 — **House** committee approved HR 2351 by voice vote.

Oct. 14 — **House** approved HR 2351, 304-119.

Nov. 3 — **Senate** committee approved S 1218 by voice vote.

Chairman Williams, however, did not like the idea of holding back federal dollars, noting that the states were struggling with their own budget problems. Although Williams was the only member to vote against the Gunderson amendment on a voice vote, he asked for a roll call vote and defeated the amendment 7-13 with the use of proxy votes. Gunderson received support from liberal Democrats such as Major R. Owens of New York and Matthew G. Martinez of California, who said he would rather see arts funding used for children in Head Start than for artists.

The full committee took up and passed the bill June 29 by voice vote, but with more rancor than during subcommittee action (H Rept 103-186).

Gunderson pressed the issue of state arts spending. To address the concerns of Williams and Marge Roukema, R-N.J., the subcommittee's ranking minority member, Gunderson had modified his amendment since losing in subcommittee. Originally, he proposed that if a state cut its funding for arts programs in a previous fiscal year, then the federal government would not increase its art funding to that state. In full committee, Gunderson proposed that if a state cut its funding for state art programs by a percentage that was larger than cuts to non-art programs, the state would not receive an increase in federal arts money.

The amendment was rejected, 18-24, with three Democrats joining Gunderson: Martinez, Ron Klink of Pennsylvania and Ted Strickland of Ohio.

Besides rejecting the Gunderson amendment, the committee turned down two amendments offered by Dick Armey, R-Texas. Armey first proposed repealing the NEA, NEH and the Institute for Museum Services. That plan was rejected 3-37, with Tom Petri, R-Wis., and Peter Hoekstra, R-Mich., voting with Armey. The committee then rejected, 11-32, an Armey amendment to restructure the NEA and increase the percentage of its funding that went to the states to 65 percent from 35 percent.

House Floor

On Oct. 14, the bill went to the House floor, where it passed 304-119, withstanding conservative assaults aimed at slashing the NEA budget or abolishing the agency outright. *(Vote 503, p. 122-H)*

Roukema, who supported the bill, told members that the key to success for the NEA and the NEH would be their two new directors: noted actress Jane Alexander and former University of Pennsylvania President Sheldon Hackney, respectively. "We will have someone to answer questions about suspect projects," Roukema said. *(Hackney, p. 429; Alexander, p. 430)*

Numerous members gave tributes to the arts, including Jerrold Nadler, D-N.Y. "The arts are an essential element in our way of life," he said. "It's ridiculous to allow an intolerant few to set our agenda." Nevertheless, a core of legislators continued their effort to kill or seriously wound the NEA.

Philip M. Crane, R-Ill., offered an amendment to abolish the arts endowment. He argued that it was not a legitimate function of government to supply money for the arts, particularly when private donors spent $9.3 billion a year on arts activities, compared with the $174 million provided to the NEA in fiscal 1993. The House rejected the Crane amendment, 103-326. *(Vote 500, p. 122-H)*

The House also rejected, 151-281, an amendment by Robert K. Dornan, R-Calif., to cut the fiscal 1994 authorizations for all three agencies by 40 percent. Under Dornan's amendment, the NEA would have lost almost $70 million of its $174.6 million authorization; the NEH would have lost $71 million of its $177.5 million authorization; and the Institute of Museum Services would have lost $11.5 million of its $28.8 million authorization. *(Vote 501, p. 122-H)*

By voice vote, the House adopted an amendment by Gunderson, and Louise M. Slaughter, D-N.Y., to freeze a state's NEA allocation at the previous year's level if the state's current year arts spending was less than the average amount it had spent annually during the three most recent years.

The House rejected a motion by Randy "Duke" Cunningham, R-Calif., to send the bill back to committee. It would have had the effect of reiterating an existing ban on NEA grants to illegal aliens. Cunningham's motion failed on a vote of 210-214. *(Vote 502, p. 122-H)*

Senate Committee

The Senate Labor and Human Resources Committee agreed by voice vote Nov. 3 to reauthorize the agencies (S 1218 — S Rept 103-182). The bill, introduced by Sen. Claiborne Pell, D-R.I., on July 14, was identical to the House-passed measure. ∎

Several Education Bills See Action in Congress

Congress worked on a variety of smaller education bills during the year:

EDUCATIONAL RESEARCH OFFICE

The House passed a bill (HR 856) on Aug. 2 to reauthorize the Education Department's Office of Educational Research and Improvement (OERI). A companion Senate measure (S 286) won committee approval but went no further in 1993. The office directed research for the Department of Education by giving grants to nonprofit organizations to study all aspects of education policy. Both bills sought to reorganize the office along the lines of the National Institutes of Health by creating five institutes or directorates to oversee different areas of research.

Major R. Owens, D-N.Y., chairman of the House Education and Labor Subcommittee on Select Education and Civil Rights, said the changes would play an important role in school-reform efforts. "If we are to achieve the ambitious national educational goals, OERI must be moved from the periphery to the center of educational reform and innovation in America," Owens said.

House Action

The House passed the OERI authorization by voice vote Aug. 2. The Education and Labor Committee had approved

the bill by voice vote July 28. (H Rept 103-209) after the Subcommittee on Select Education gave its approval June 30.

The four-year bill authorized a total of $156 million in fiscal 1994 and $219 million in fiscal 1995. In an effort to create a better framework for directing research dollars, the bill restructured OERI into five institutes focusing on specific education goals: educating at-risk students; education governance, finance and management; early childhood learning, communities and families; student achievement; and postsecondary education, libraries and lifelong learning. Each institute was authorized at $20 million in fiscal 1995.

The bill established an 18-member board to oversee the office and set research priorities. The board was to consist of educational researchers and representatives of teachers, parents, school administrators and others.

The bill also established a computer network (SMART-LINE) designed to help schools across the country share information on successful school reforms.

Senate Committee

The Senate Labor and Human Resources Committee approved a similar bill (S 286 — Rept 103-183) by voice vote Nov. 3.

S 286 was a six-year authorization; it included $217 million in fiscal 1994, compared with $156 million in the House bill. The Senate bill called for a nine-member advisory board to oversee the office.

The Senate measure called for five national directorates to support basic and applied research, apply research to schools and serve as a national data base on model programs. The five directorates would be: curriculum, instruction and assessment; early childhood development and education; educational achievement of historically underserved populations; elementary and secondary educational governance, finance, policy-making and management; and adult education and literacy.

SERVICES FOR THE DISABLED

The House and Senate passed separate versions of a bill (HR 2339) to provide technology related assistance for people with disabilities. The House bill, passed Aug. 2 by voice vote, reauthorized for nine years a 1988 law that provided federal support for state programs. Appropriations had risen from $5 million in 1988 to $34 million in fiscal 1993. The bill included a provision phasing out the federal dollars in the ninth and 10th years.

The measure authorized $50 million for grants in fiscal 1994 and unspecified amounts through fiscal 2002. The money also could be used to help states establish low-interest consumer loan programs to aid the disabled in purchasing technology devices and services.

The House Education and Labor Committee approved the bill by voice vote July 28 (H Rept 103-208); the Education Subcommittee on Select Education had approved it by voice vote June 30.

The Senate Labor and Human Resources Committee approved a companion measure (S 1283 — S Rept 103-119) on July 30. On Aug. 5, the Senate approved HR 2339 by voice vote, after substituting the text of S 1283.

NEW MATH, READING TESTS

Congress cleared a bill (S 801) allowing the Department of Education to develop new tests in reading and math to be conducted in states across the country. The Senate

passed the bill by voice vote April 21. The House approved it, also by voice vote, on May 11, clearing the bill for President Clinton, who signed it May 25. (PL 103-33).

The legislation authorized the National Assessment of Educational Progress (NAEP) to administer tests in math to fourth-grade and eighth-grade students and in reading to fourth-graders. It also authorized the development of tests for 12th-grade math and eighth- and 12th-grade reading.

Congress created NAEP in 1969 to measure the country's progress in education. The new tests were to be conducted in states on a voluntary basis. In the spring of 1993, close to 40 states had volunteered. In past years, the NAEP test results were issued nationally and regionally without singling out individual states. The bill authorized unspecified sums to fund the project.

SCHOOL SAFETY

The Senate Labor and Human Resources Committee approved a bill by voice vote Nov. 3 aimed at helping local school districts make schools safer. School safety was one of the six national education goals first endorsed by President George Bush and then supported by President Clinton. The bill — which had been approved Oct. 21 by the Senate Subcommittee on Education, Arts and Humanities — went no further in the first session.

The committee bill (S 1125 — S Rept 103-180) authorized $75 million in fiscal 1994 and $100 million in fiscal 1995 to provide competitive grants to school districts with a high rate of homicides committed by people under 18, referrals of young people to juvenile court, expulsions and suspensions of students, young people under court supervision, and victimization of young people by violence, crime or abuse.

The grants, which could not exceed $3 million a year and could not last longer than two years, could be used several ways, including:
- Training school employees to deal with violence.
- Setting up conflict resolution programs.
- Providing alternative after-school programs as safe havens for students.

- Educating students and parents about the dangers of guns and other weapons.
- Buying and installing metal detectors and hiring security guards.

Appropriators set aside $20 million for Safe Schools Grants, provided the bill was authorized by April 1, 1994. If it was not, the money was to go to the Drug-Free Schools program, which provided drug-abuse prevention education. The money was in the fiscal 1994 spending bill for the departments of Labor, Health and Human Services, and Education (HR 2518 — PL 103-112).

The House Education and Labor Committee did not consider its companion bill (HR 2455) in 1993.

GENDER EQUITY

A group of women lawmakers and the chairman of a key House education panel bundled nine bills into omnibus legislation to help girls who might be shortchanged by sex discrimination during the course of their education. The bill, called the Gender Equity in Education Act (HR 1743), was introduced April 20 by Reps. Patricia Schroeder, D-Colo., Olympia J. Snowe, R-Maine, Patsy T. Mink, D-Hawaii, and Dale E. Kildee, D-Mich., chairman of the Education and Labor Subcommittee on Elementary, Secondary, and Vocational Education. It was not marked up in 1993.

The legislation would set up an Office of Gender Equity at the Department of Education. It would create teacher training programs to identify and eliminate inequitable classroom practices — such as paying more attention to boys or taking them more seriously. It would encourage the recruitment of women math and science teachers as role models, and it would call on school dropout prevention programs to focus on pregnant teenagers and teen mothers. It also called for research addressing sexual harassment and abuse at school.

The package came on the heels of a 1992 study by the American Association of University Women about how sex discrimination affected all areas of American schools, including student testing, teachers' interactions with students and textbooks' portrayals of women. *(Reauthorization, p. 412)*
■

Vets Health Package Stalls Over Abortion

Legislation to expand health-care services for veterans, particularly women, advanced in Congress, passing the House and winning the approval of the Senate Veterans' Affairs Committee. But differences over abortion and other issues in the House and Senate versions stalled the bills (HR 3313, S 1030).

BACKGROUND

The attempt to expand health services for female veterans was evidence that many in Congress had recognized a new demographic reality: The steady increase in the number of women in the armed forces would lead to a steady increase in the number of female veterans.

According to the Department of Veterans Affairs (VA), there were nearly 1.2 million female veterans in 1993, compared with 959,000 in 1970.

To improve care for female veterans, both measures:

● Required the VA to offer Pap smears, breast exams and mammography, and treatment for osteoporosis, sexually transmitted diseases and conditions arising from menopause.

● Required counseling for sexual trauma and treatment of physical conditions resulting from that trauma.

● Prohibited the VA from performing mammograms unless the test met federal quality standards.

● Ensured that the VA conduct medical research related to the health-care needs of female veterans.

In addition, both measures required the VA to continue guaranteeing treatment of veterans suffering from conditions linked to exposure to Agent Orange — a chemical defoliant used during the Vietnam War — or radiation.

But each bill also included provisions not in the companion measure. For example, S 1036 included pilot programs to begin providing hospice care to terminally ill veterans and to better provide health services to veterans in rural areas.

HR 3313 authorized the VA to offer limited medical treatment at Vet Centers — which generally provided counseling to Vietnam War veterans.

But the most important and controversial difference concerned abortion and certain pregnancy-related services. Unlike its House counterpart, S 1036 required the VA to provide female veterans with abortions and other reproductive services as well as pre- and post-natal and delivery care.

SENATE ACTION

On July 15, the Senate Veterans' Affairs Committee approved S 1030 (S Rept 103-136) by a vote of 11-0.

But the unanimous vote belied divisions over the abortion issue. Frank H. Murkowski, R-Alaska, tried unsuccessfully to amend the bill to bar the VA from using taxpayer

---

BOXSCORE

➡ **Women Veterans Health (S 1030, HR 3313, formerly HR 3082).** The bills sought to expand health services for female veterans and guarantee treatment for patients suffering from conditions linked to Agent Orange.

Reports: S Rept 103-136; H Rept 103-349

KEY ACTION

July 15 — **Senate** Veterans' Affairs Committee approved S 1030, 11-0.

Oct. 26 — **House** Veterans' Affairs Committee approved HR 3313, 26-0.

Nov. 16 — **House** passed HR 3313 by voice vote.

---

money for abortion services at VA hospitals, except in cases of rape, incest or to save the life of the woman.

Committee Chairman John D. Rockefeller IV, D-W.Va., and Tom Daschle, D-S.D., strongly opposed the amendment, saying it was far too restrictive. Murkowski said that a vote to kill his amendment would be a vote to "provide abortion on demand." Still the committee rejected the amendment, 5-6.

The committee approved, 8-3, an amendment by Daschle to provide inpatient and outpatient care for about 4,000 Persian Gulf War veterans who claimed to have acquired physical ailments related to their service in the gulf. Opponents said the amendment would give Persian Gulf veterans a higher priority for outpatient care than veterans from other wars. *(Persian Gulf veterans, p. 416)*

HOUSE ACTION

The House Veterans' Affairs Subcommittee on Hospitals and Health Care gave voice vote approval Oct. 6 to HR 3082. The bill, sponsored by subcommittee Chairman Roy J. Rowland, D-Ga., was later re-introduced as HR 3313.

Attempts to expand the women's health language led to a long and acrimonious debate over fiscal responsibility and abortion.

The subcommittee rejected several attempts by Rep. Luis V. Gutierrez, D-Ill., and others to further enlarge the list of guaranteed services to include birth control, prenatal care, delivery services, postnatal care and gynecological services. These services were guaranteed in S 1036.

Pointing to the steady increase in the number of female veterans, Gutierrez argued that the additional services listed in his amendment were "basic" for adult women. "Our female veterans have a right to equitable care," he said.

Gutierrez originally had planned to offer an amendment adding full reproductive services — including abortion — to the list. He eliminated the abortion language, he said in an effort to make his proposal less divisive.

But subcommittee ranking Republican Christopher H. Smith of New Jersey said that unless abortion was specifically excluded, courts could interpret even the revised amendment to authorize the VA to end pregnancies.

Also, many subcommittee members worried about the cost of providing the extra services, estimated by the Congressional Budget Office to be $430 million over the next five years. Joseph P. Kennedy II, D-Mass., said he supported the amendment's goals, but he reminded his colleagues that the money would have to come from other VA programs, which already were strapped.

Kennedy argued that the case for expanding VA services would be raised again soon when Congress took up President Clinton's health-care plan, which required the VA to compete for patients with private health-care providers. He

said Gutierrez's limited proposal would be "overwhelmed by the debate" and should be put aside for now.

The amendment was defeated 7-12.

Bob Filner, D-Calif., then attempted to allay the fears of Smith and other abortion opponents by offering Gutierrez's amendment with one key difference. The Filner amendment would have specified that veterans were "limited to" the services listed, to guard against a broad reading of the law.

But Smith successfully offered a substitute to Filner's amendment, specifically excluding abortion and in vitro fertilization from the Gutierrez language. It was approved 10-9.

Filner, Gutierrez and their supporters then voted against the Filner amendment, because of Smith's changes. The amendment was defeated 7-12, leaving the original bill intact.

The subcommittee also gave voice vote approval to the Agent Orange language and to the Vet Centers provisions, which at the time were contained in separate bills (HR 3081 and HR 3108).

Full Committee, Floor

Rowland introduced a clean bill (HR 3313) containing the provisions on women and other health issues as well as the agent orange provision. The full Veterans Affairs Committee approved the measure, 26-0, on Oct. 26 (H Rept 103-349).

The panel gave voice vote approval to an amendment, offered by Maxine Waters, D-Calif., to include treatment for cardiac disease in the list of services offered to women.

But the committee rejected several amendments, including one by Gutierrez that was similar to the language he offered during the subcommittee markup. Seven Democrats joined a solid Republican phalanx to kill Gutierrez's amendment, 10-20.

Lane Evans, D-Ill., offered an amendment that would have expanded Agent Orange treatment to cases in which a connection between the herbicide and a given illness had not been shown but had not been ruled out either. It was rejected 5-22, with most committee members arguing that such language would have defeated the purpose of commissioning research into the effects of Agent Orange.

The bill then moved to the House floor, where it passed by voice vote Nov. 16. ■

VA Authorized To Treat Sick Persian Gulf Vets

Late in the session, Congress cleared a measure that authorized the Department of Veterans Affairs (VA) to treat sick veterans whose conditions could have been linked to their service in Operations Desert Shield and Desert Storm — the deployment and operational phases of the 1991 Persian Gulf War. The bill also extended an existing treatment guarantee for victims of sexual trauma and for veterans with illnesses that might have been caused by exposure to Agent Orange or radiation.

The bill (HR 2535 — PL 103-210), signed by President Clinton on Dec. 20, was intended only as a temporary solution. Unlike the original House-passed version of the bill, the final measure did not offer extensive coverage for those suffering from this new syndrome. Supporters pre-

dicted that Congress would clear a more comprehensive "Persian Gulf" measure in 1994.

BACKGROUND

The so-called Persian Gulf syndrome referred to a multitude of ailments reported by a growing number of military personnel who served in the gulf during the 1990-91 confrontation with Iraq over its invasion of Kuwait. While no one was sure of causes or long-term effects, gulf veterans had experienced such symptoms as fatigue, nausea, hair loss and diarrhea.

Preliminary investigations indicated that exposure to smoke from oil fires, desert parasites, vehicle paints and the depleted uranium used to reinforce tank and artillery shells all could have contributed to these ailments. Others suggested that the problem could be a condition known as "multiple chemical sensitivity," in which exposure to a variety of chemicals could cause illness.

Bill supporters argued that Congress should avoid repeating the mistakes it made in ignoring for years the illnesses suffered by Vietnam veterans who were exposed to Agent Orange, a chemical defoliant widely used during the war in Southeast Asia.

In the case of Agent Orange, legislation (PL 97-72) that gave victims priority treatment was not enacted until 1981, more than 10 years after the herbicide was last sprayed in Vietnam. In addition, the effects of Agent Orange were still being discovered, as evidenced by the July 27 release of a National Science Foundation report adding two ailments — Hodgkin's disease and a skin disorder — to the three already linked to the herbicide. *(1981 Almanac, p. 481)*

And so while the VA and other government agencies in 1993 were only just beginning to study Persian Gulf syndrome, there was substantial political momentum in Congress to ensure that no potential victim was denied care in the meantime.

LEGISLATIVE ACTION

The House Veterans' Affairs Subcommittee on Hospitals and Health Care gave voice vote approval to HR 2535 on June 29. The bill, sponsored by subcommittee Chairman Roy J. Rowland, D-Ga., required the VA to give "priority" treatment to eligible gulf veterans for roughly five years. In the complex web of VA eligibility requirements, "priority" status virtually guaranteed that no patient legitimately seeking treatment would be turned away. The bill did not offer any monetary compensation to those afflicted.

On July 27, the full House Veterans' Affairs Committee approved the bill (H Rept 103-198) by a vote of 30-0. The House followed suit Aug. 2, passing the bill by a vote of 411-0. *(Vote 388, p. 94-H)*

The Senate did not take up HR 2535 until late in the session. Senators passed the bill by voice vote Nov. 20, but only after approving a substitute amendment offered by Wendell H. Ford, D-Ky. The substitute, approved by voice vote, provided the Persian Gulf priority treatment for roughly one year only, until Dec. 1, 1994. The House passed bill had authorized treatment until late in 1998.

In addition, Ford's amendment, offered on behalf of Sen. John D. Rockefeller IV, D-W.Va., extended the authorization for a number of unrelated VA programs that were about to expire. These included priority treatment for veterans with conditions that could have been linked to exposure to Agent Orange and radiation (until June 30,

1994) and counseling for sexual trauma (until Dec. 31, 1994). These provisions, in a more extensive form, were also part of the female veterans health legislation (HR S 1030) that failed to clear Congress in 1993. *(Women veterans' health benefits, p. 415)*

The bill was then sent back to the House, which cleared it by voice vote Nov. 22. ■

Cost of Living Increases

Congress cleared legislation (S 616) that provided a 2.6 percent increase in the cost of living adjustment (COLA) for benefits received by veterans and their survivors.

The change applied to compensation paid to approximately 2.2 million disabled veterans. In addition, it applied to most payments to the roughly 300,000 spouses and dependent children of veterans who died as a result of service related injuries, known as dependency and indemnity compensation (DIC).

The COLA increase took effect Dec. 1, 1993. The bill also set a flat $9 per month increase to DIC beneficiaries who, under the pre-1992 system, received monthly payments that were higher than the $750 minimum set that year for all subsequent beneficiaries.

The measure was signed by President Clinton on Nov. 11, Veterans Day (PL 103-140).

Background

Unlike veterans' pension benefits, payments to disabled veterans and their survivors were not automatically indexed to inflation. Each year, Congress had to pass legislation to adjust the COLA.

No controversy surrounded S 616, but that had not always been the case with COLA bills. In 1990, the COLA bill stalled after members divided over whether to attach a provision ensuring compensation to some veterans suffering from cancer as a result of exposure to Agent Orange. *(1990 Almanac, p. 418)*

In a less controversial, though more important, action, Congress in 1992 provided that all new DIC beneficiaries would receive $750 per month. Previously, DIC payments were based on the deceased veteran's rank. Payments to beneficiaries who already were receiving more than $750 per month were not reduced. *(1992 Almanac, p. 378)*

LEGISLATIVE ACTION

On May 19, the Senate Veterans' Affairs Committee gave voice vote approval to S 616 (S Rept 103-55). The measure, introduced by committee Chairman John D. Rockefeller IV, D-W.Va., did not contain a specific rate increase, which was based each year on the rate of inflation as measured by the Consumer Price Index (CPI). At the time of the bill's introduction, the CPI for 1993 had not been estimated. The Senate approved the bill by voice vote July 14.

In the House, the Veterans' Affairs Subcommittee on Compensation, Pension and Insurance gave voice vote approval Oct. 21 to HR 2341, introduced by subcommittee Chairman Jim Slattery, D-Kan.

The bill originally had authorized a 3 percent COLA based on the estimated CPI at the time of its introduction in June. The estimate proved high, and the CPI was later revised to 2.6 percent for the year.

By voice vote, the subcommittee approved an amendment by Slattery to set the COLA at 2.6 percent.

The amendment also reinstated death payments for surviving spouses of deceased veterans whose subsequent marriages had ended.

Spouses of veterans who died of service-related injuries were not eligible for compensation payments if they remarried. And under a provision of the 1990 Omnibus Budget-Reconciliation Act (PL 101-508), remarried spouses of veterans also were ineligible for benefits if their subsequent marriage ended due to death or divorce. Slattery's substitute allowed those no-longer-married spouses to resume receiving benefits.

Finally, George E. Sangmeister, D-Ill., added language to the bill restoring burial eligibility for surviving spouses of deceased veterans whose subsequent marriages had ended because of death or divorce. The 1990 reconciliation bill also barred a remarried spouse's burial at a national cemetery, even if the veteran was interred there.

After subcommittee action, a clean bill (HR 3340) was introduced incorporating the changes made by the panel. The full committee approved the new measure (H Rept 103-312) by voice vote Oct. 26.

The committee also voted to remove the provisions reinstating death payments for veterans' surviving spouses whose subsequent marriages had ended.

The Congressional Budget Office (CBO) originally estimated that the cost of restoring these benefits would be $100 million over five years. Bill sponsor Slattery had found $100 million in savings to offset the expense, but CBO later revised its estimate to $158 million, requiring, under budget rules, that more savings be found.

The provisions removed from the measure were later introduced as a separate bill (HR 3313). *(Spousal benefits, p. 420)*

House Floor Action

On the House floor, members voted to insert the entire text of HR 3340 into S 616, the bill that had passed the Senate before specific rates could be set. The House then passed S 616 by voice vote Nov. 2.

The bill was returned to the Senate, which cleared it Nov. 4 by voice vote. ■

Increases on Home Loans For Veterans Considered

Both chambers passed legislation (HR 949, S 843) to increase the amount veterans could borrow under a government guaranteed home loan program. But a number of unresolved issues stalled the bills late in the year, forcing members to put off further action on the legislation until 1994.

The Department of Veterans Affairs (VA) guaranteed home loans for all former service personnel, which allowed veterans to obtain mortgages without having to make a down payment. The bills increased — from $184,000 to $203,000 — the maximum amount that could be borrowed under the program.

But the House bill also allowed the VA to extend bridge loans of up to $10,000 to veterans who, because of job loss

or underemployment, were facing foreclosure on their VA guaranteed home mortgages. The extra money could only be used to make payments on the outstanding mortgage, and the granting of these loans was to be entirely at the discretion of the VA.

In addition the House bill increased the federal matching share — from 50 percent to 65 percent per plot — to states that owned and operated veterans cemeteries.

The bridge loan and cemetery provisions were not part of the Senate measure.

Legislative Action

On April 29, the House Veterans' Affairs Subcommittee on Housing and Memorial Affairs gave voice vote approval to HR 949. Originally set out in three separate bills (HR 949, HR 950 and HR 951), the provisions were rolled together in a substitute amendment, which also was approved by voice vote. The full committee followed suit, approving the bill by voice vote on July 27 (H Rept 103-222). On Sept. 21, the House passed the bill, also by voice vote.

In the Senate, the Veterans' Affairs Committee considered a related measure (S 1510) on Oct. 28. But final vote was put off due to lack of a quorum.

The following week, the Senate approved the text of S 1510 as an amendment to S 843, a bill aimed at clarifying a 1940 law that guaranteed comparable re-employment for military personnel returning from duty. The home loan provision was added to S 843 because the Congressional Budget Office calculated that it would save enough money to offset the estimated $2 million cost of implementing the re-employment legislation. Pay-as-you-go budget rules required that newly authorized mandatory spending be offset with corresponding savings.

As the year ended, two unresolved issues stood in the way of final passage. First, members had not decided whether to include the bridge loan and cemetery provisions that were contained in the House bill but not in its Senate counterpart. In addition, a difference existed between House and Senate versions of the re-employment bill, effectively stalling the home loan language until this unrelated issue was resolved. *(Job protection, below right)* ∎

National Cemetery Burials Opened to Reservists

The House and Senate passed slightly different versions of a bill (HR 821) aimed at allowing people who never served on active duty but spent 20 or more years in the Reserves or the National Guard to be buried in national cemeteries.

The measure was a recognition of the military's increased reliance on reservists due to the downsizing of the armed forces.

With minor exceptions, only veterans who had served on active duty, their spouses and their dependent children were eligible for national cemetery burial under existing law.

More than 2 million people — both veterans and family members — had been interred in 114 VA-operated cemeteries nationwide. The VA estimated that its existing cemeteries would accommodate an additional 1.7 million people,

with roughly 270,000 spaces available for immediate use.

In urging support for the legislation, George E. Sangmeister, D-Ill., chairman of the House Veterans' Affairs Subcommittee on Housing and Memorial Affairs, argued that reservists deserved the benefit. "The requirement that they be prepared to report within 24 hours of notification underscores the fact that today's selected reservists are members of the total force," he said.

But the VA worried that the measure might greatly add to the short- and long-term cost of maintaining national cemeteries, while limiting future space for active-duty veterans.

At a June 10 Housing subcommittee hearing, Jerry Bowen, director of the VA's national cemetery system, testified that with more than 1.5 million people in the reserves, "we cannot estimate the long-term costs since we do not know the percentage of reservists who would seek burial in national cemeteries."

Supporters argued that the bill would result in no more than 800 additional burials a year. In addition, they pointed to a Congressional Budget Office annual cost estimate of less than $400,000.

But the VA was also concerned that cemeteries with limited space might be closed prematurely because of an influx of reservists. If a cemetery closed, all eligible veterans in the surrounding area probably would have to go to a distant cemetery.

A similar measure passed the House in 1992 but went no further.

Legislative Action

In the House, the Veterans' Affairs Subcommittee on Housing and Memorial Affairs gave voice vote approval to HR 821 on July 22. The full committee followed suit on July 27 (H Rept 103-197). The bill passed the House by voice vote on Aug. 2.

The Senate Veterans' Affairs Committee approved a related bill (S 1620) on Nov. 3. Unlike HR 821, S 1620 included provisions allowing a newly eligible veteran's spouse and dependent children to be buried at a veterans cemetery. On Nov. 11, the Senate passed HR 821 by voice vote, after inserting into the measure the entire text of S 1620.

At year's end, members were predicting that differences between the two versions would be worked out early in 1994. ∎

Veterans Job-Protection Legislation Stalls

The House and Senate each passed legislation (HR 995, S 843) to clarify and expand a 53-year-old law guaranteeing that soldiers returning from military duty would be hired back at their old firms in positions comparable to the ones they left. But differences between the two bills, primarily concerning pension benefits, stalled the legislation late in the year.

The bills reaffirmed the obligation of employers, regardless of the size of their business, to rehire any veteran who returned within five years of his or her last employment. Returning veterans were entitled to the same or a comparable job as well as any promotions that would have

accrued had they not left for military service. Employers were to use several factors in determining those promotions, such as company policy and the current positions of those who held the returnees' jobs when they left.

The measure was a response to longtime complaints that the 1940 Soldiers' and Sailors' Civil Relief Act was confusing and difficult to interpret. After the 1991 Persian Gulf War, many employers and veterans were unsure of their obligations and rights under the act.

Sponsors of the measure explained that the existing law contained different rules for different types of service personnel. It distinguished between those on active duty and those in active training. HR 995 aimed to sweep away those layers, applying the same rules to all military personnel, regardless of their status.

The bill also reaffirmed provisions in the existing law that required veterans coming home after 31 to 180 days of military service to return to work within two weeks to be guaranteed re-employment. Those serving in the armed forces more than six months had up to 90 days to return to work.

While the bills included few substantive changes to existing law, they extended — from four years to five years — the amount of time a person could serve and still retain a job.

In addition, the bill included provisions requiring departing service personnel to give reasonable notice to employers before leaving.

Legislative Action

The House Veterans' Affairs Subcommittee on Education, Training and Employment gave voice vote approval to HR 995 on March 25.

The subcommittee also approved by voice vote an amendment by bill sponsor G. V. "Sonny" Montgomery, D-Miss., chairman of the subcommittee and the full committee, guaranteeing that any pension benefits would continue to accrue during the veteran's time of service.

HR 995 won the voice vote approval of the full committee April 1 (H Rept 103-65, Part 1). On May 4, the House passed the measure by voice vote.

In the Senate, the Veterans' Affairs Committee approved a related bill (S 843 — S Rept 103-158) by a vote of 11-0. On Nov. 2, the Senate passed the measure by voice vote after amending it to include the text of S 1510, a bill to increase the amount veterans could borrow under the Department of Veterans Affairs' home loan guarantee program.

The home loan language was added because the Congressional Budget Office estimated that S 1510 would save the federal government enough money to offset the $2 million that it would cost to implement S 843. Pay-as-you-go budget rules required that newly authorized mandatory spending be offset with corresponding savings. The Senate passed HR 995 by voice vote Nov. 8 after substituting the text of S 843. *(Veterans home loans, p. 417)*

A number of differences existed between the House- and Senate-passed bills, the most important of which concerned pension benefits. Both measures allowed employees to retroactively pay contributions into a pension fund upon their return from duty. In addition, both bills required employers to pay their share of the pension contribution as if the veteran had never left. But, unlike S 843, the House bill also required employers to pay interest on those contributions.

The year ended with members in both chambers predicting that a deal would be worked out in 1994. ■

$157.6 Million Authorized For VA Construction

On Aug. 6, Congress cleared legislation that authorized the Department of Veterans Affairs (VA) to spend $157.6 million for major construction projects in fiscal 1994. President Clinton signed the bill (HR 2034 — PL 103-79) on Aug. 13.

In previous years, VA construction projects were not individually authorized. But a law (PL 102-405) enacted in 1992 required Congress to authorize the VA's major medical construction projects and leases, beginning in 1993.

In addition to the authorization, the House attempted unsuccessfully to attach to the bill a set of criteria for future VA construction.

Legislative Action

The House Veterans' Affairs Subcommittee on Hospitals and Health Care gave voice vote approval to HR 2034 on April 28. The full committee did the same on May 11 (H Rept 103-92), sending the measure to the floor, where it passed by voice vote on May 18.

With one exception, the House-passed bill authorized all the large VA construction projects that Clinton had requested in his fiscal 1994 budget. These included $41.7 million for a psychiatric care facility in Lyons, N.J., and $33.2 million for a replacement bed building at the VA Medical Center in Muskogee, Okla. The measure also included a project not requested by the White House: $46 million for an outpatient care building in San Juan, Puerto Rico. In addition, the bill authorized $50.1 million for major VA medical leases.

But the House bill did not authorize the administration's $14.5 million request for a nursing home in Baltimore. In explaining the omission, bill sponsor J. Roy Rowland, D-Ga., did not question the need for nursing home beds in the Baltimore area. Instead, he expressed concern that the project had not been properly planned or prioritized. The House bill took most of the money intended for the nursing home ($13 million) and used it to authorize three smaller projects.

The House-passed bill also contained language directing the VA to assess its health-care needs to promote better planning of future hospital construction. To this end, the VA was required to review the mission of each of its facilities so as to avoid duplicating services when determining the allocation of resources.

The VA also was directed to make long-term care and ambulatory care priorities when building new hospitals or expanding existing facilities. Supporters maintained that the VA would need to stress long-term and ambulatory care in the future to cope with an aging veterans population.

The Senate passed HR 2034 on July 14 by voice, but only after John Glenn, D-Ohio, had successfully amended the House bill, replacing its language with the text of a very different Senate companion measure. That bill (S 1079) authorized the president's entire request, including the Baltimore nursing home omitted from the House bill.

In addition, the Senate version contained none of the construction planning criteria included in the House bill.

The measure was then sent back to the House, which approved it by voice vote Aug. 6 after members accepted a substitute amendment offered by Veterans' Affairs Com-

mittee Chairman G.V. "Sonny" Montgomery, D-Miss. The Senate cleared the bill on the same day by voice vote.

The final version, as amended by the House, reflected a compromise worked out between members of the Veterans' Affairs committees in both chambers. Like the original Senate-passed version, the final bill had none of the required planning criteria first contained in HR 2034.

As for the $14.5 million nursing home in Baltimore, the measure authorized the VA to build such a facility to serve veterans in that region of the country. But first, the bill required the VA to conduct a thorough study to assess the best location for the project. ∎

Congress Advances Other Veterans Bills

In addition to action on bills dealing with issues such as women's health and the Persian Gulf Syndrome, Congress addressed many other veterans matters.

Veterans Education Outreach

The House on May 24 gave voice vote approval to a bill (HR 996) establishing a program that would assist colleges and universities in providing services to veterans who attended those institutions. The bill authorized $3 million for the program in fiscal 1994. The Senate did not act on the measure.

As approved by the House, the bill authorized the Department of Veterans Affairs (VA) to grant money to colleges with offices that provided counseling and outreach to veterans on campus. Only those institutions with 50 or more veterans receiving VA educational assistance were eligible for the money, which came to $100 per veteran served.

The bill won voice vote approval April 29 from the House Veterans' Affairs Subcommittee on Education, Training and Employment. The full committee followed suit on May 11 (H Rept 103-98).

Court of Veterans Appeals

On Nov. 3, the Senate Veterans' Affairs Committee gave voice vote approval to a bill (S 1546) aimed at making a number of administrative and procedural changes at the Court of Veterans Appeals. The court, which was established under the Veterans' Judicial Review Act of 1988 (PL 100-687), heard appeals concerning veterans' benefits claims.

The committee bill required nominees for the position of chief judge to be confirmed by the Senate. In addition, it required the VA to pay attorney's fees for successful appellants at the court if the veteran's attorney was working on a contingency fee.

Discrimination Complaints

Legislation aimed at revamping the system for dealing with discrimination and harassment claims at the Department of Veterans Affairs passed the House by voice vote April 27.

But the measure advanced no further, as reform advocates began pushing, unsuccessfully, for a government-wide overhaul.

The House bill (HR 1032) called for the establishment of a VA office to resolve discrimination and harassment cases. Complaints were to be handled by a permanent staff of Equal Employment Opportunity (EEO) counselors and trained

investigators. The measure provided for a corps of independent administrative law judges to resolve complaints.

Supporters argued that the bill was needed because the VA's system for handling complaints lacked safeguards against conflicts of interest. For example, complaints were filed with part-time EEO counselors who reported to the same boss as the person filing the claim.

The House Veterans' Affairs Committee approved the measure (H Rept 103-64) by a vote of 32-0 on April 1.

Lockerbie Memorial

Congress cleared legislation (S J Res 129) that authorized a memorial in Arlington National Cemetery to the 270 victims of the 1988 terrorist bombing of an airliner over Lockerbie, Scotland.

The resolution won the voice vote approval of the Senate Veterans' Affairs Committee on Nov. 3. It passed by voice vote in the Senate on Nov. 8 and in the House on Nov. 16. President Clinton signed the measure into law on Nov. 24 (PL 103-158).

Spousal Benefits

The House on Nov. 16 approved by voice vote a bill (HR 3456) to reinstate death benefits for certain veterans who were affected by a 1990 change in the law; the Senate did not act on the measure.

The 1990 budget-reconciliation bill (PL 101-508) had expanded an existing law that prohibited surviving spouses from receiving compensation if they remarried to include those whose subsequent marriages ended due to death or divorce. *(1990 Almanac, p. 111)*

The bill won the voice vote approval of the House Veterans' Affairs Committee on Nov. 9. The committee also approved, by voice vote, an amendment offered by George E. Sangmeister, D-Ill., to allow these spouses and their dependent children to be buried in a national cemetery (H Rept 103-350).

Vet Center Expansion

On Nov. 3, the Senate Veterans' Affairs Committee gave voice vote approval to a draft bill to expand the mandate of veterans centers, which provided counseling and other services to veterans of the Vietnam War and post-Vietnam conflicts. The measure required the centers to serve all combat veterans, including those who fought in World War II and Korea. In addition, it authorized a two-year pilot program to provide limited health-care services, such as blood pressure screening and other medical tests, at 10 or more centers. Congress took no further action on the bill.

Health Administration

Both chambers passed versions of legislation changing a requirement that the head of the Veterans Health Administration (VHA) be a physician.

The Senate passed a bill repealing the requirement (S 1534) by voice vote Oct. 7. The House passed the bill by voice vote Nov. 16 after amending it to require that two of the top three VHA officials be medical doctors. In addition, the amendment required that the Department of Veterans Affairs give priority to physicians when hiring for all three VHA positions. This same language was included in a bill (HR 3400) to cut government spending that passed the House on Nov. 22.

Date Line

The House approved legislation (HR 2647) to retroactively set the International Date Line as the base for deter-

mining when service personnel became eligible for new life insurance benefits. The House passed the bill by voice vote Aug. 2, but the Senate did not take it up. The bill was drafted to extend life insurance coverage to the families of 11 servicemen killed just hours before they were eligible for new benefits.

The Servicemen's Group Life Insurance (SGLI) program automatically provided $100,000 in life insurance coverage to military personnel. The Veterans Benefit Act of 1992 gave service members the opportunity to apply to purchase an additional $100,000 in life insurance taking effect Dec. 1, 1992.

On Nov. 30, 1992, two air accidents killed 17 people. One crash in Texas occurred at 11 p.m. CST; the other over Montana at 8:20 p.m. MST. Eleven of the servicemen who were killed had opted for the additional coverage, but their families were denied the extra benefits.

The Uniform Time Act of 1966 required officials to use the time zone in which the beneficiary died. But under HR 2647, eligibility was retroactively and prospectively based on the International Date Line — a change that would make the servicemen eligible for the additional benefits. The date line runs roughly through the middle of the Pacific Ocean at 180 degrees longitude marking the beginning of the calendar day.

The bill won the voice vote approval of the House Veterans' Affairs Committee on July 26 (H Rept 103-199).

Medal of Honor

Congress cleared legislation (HR 3341) increasing the monthly stipend to living veterans who had won the Medal of Honor. The stipend increased from $200 to $400. The Medal of Honor was the highest U.S. military decoration, awarded by Congress for gallantry at the risk of life beyond the call of duty.

The bill won the voice vote approval of the House Veterans' Affairs Subcommittee on Compensation, Pension and Insurance on Oct. 21 and the full committee on Oct. 25 (H Rept 103-313). The House passed the bill by voice vote

Nov. 2. The Senate followed suit Nov. 17. President Clinton signed the bill Nov. 30 (PL 103-161).

Veterans Reconciliation

After lengthy negotiations, conferees on veterans issues reached agreement Aug. 3 on provisions that contributed $2.6 billion in revenue increases and tax cuts over five years to the 1993 budget-reconciliation bill (HR 2264 — H Rept 103-213).

The original House and Senate bills had both included a cut in pensions for veterans in Medicaid-approved nursing homes and an increase — from 1.25 percent to 2 percent — in the fee veterans paid for guaranteed home loans. These provisions were included in the final bill, which cleared Congress on Aug. 6 and was signed by Clinton on Aug. 10 (PL 103-66).

But the House and Senate had differed over two issues: GI Bill fees and the cost of living adjustment (COLAs) for veterans' survivors.

House Veterans' Affairs Committee Chairman G. V. "Sonny" Montgomery, D-Miss., successfully fought against a Senate proposal that would have raised the fees that service personnel paid to participate in the GI Bill program. The fee increases, from $100 per month for a year to $137 per month for a year, would have generated an estimated $444 million. Montgomery argued that raising the fee for the program, which provided education assistance to veterans, would hamper the program's effectiveness as a recruiting tool.

Conferees agreed to drop the fee increase and make up part of the money by freezing the COLA on benefits in fiscal 1994 and holding it to 50 percent in fiscal 1995 to save an estimated $229 million over five years.

Negotiators also agreed to halve the COLA on benefits to many spouses and dependent children of veterans who died of injuries related to their service. Under the plan, only those beneficiaries who were receiving the minimum payment were given a full COLA. The cut was expected to produce $74 million in savings over five years. *(Budget-reconciliation provisions, p. 124)* ■

Congress Votes To Create Enterprise Zones

Thirteen years after the first enterprise zone legislation was introduced, President Clinton signed a bill that included $3.5 billion for tax breaks and other federal assistance to selected zones in poor communities.

Republicans generally had been the chief proponents of enterprise zones, calling for capital gains tax breaks and other tax and regulatory relief to spur investment in poor communities. President Clinton offered a variation on the GOP plan, putting more emphasis on wage credits and staking out a federal government role in coordinating resources in the targeted neighborhoods.

Congress cleared the enterprise zone provisions Aug. 6 as part of the omnibus budget-reconciliation bill (HR 2264 — H Rept 103-213). Clinton signed the measure into law (PL 103-66) on Aug. 10. *(Budget-reconciliation, p. 107)*

The original House version of the bill included $5.2 billion for the zones over five years, most of it for wage-related credits. The House-Senate conference agreement pared that back to $3.5 billion over five years, including $1 billion in new spending.

Generally following Clinton's lead, the law created nine so-called empowerment zones — six urban and three rural — to get most of the federal spending and tax incentives. In addition, 95 enterprise communities — 65 in urban areas and 30 in rural areas — were to be eligible for lesser benefits.

The law also created a new social services block grant worth $1 billion over two years to provide $100 million to each of the urban empowerment zones, $40 million to each of the rural empowerment zones and $2.95 million to each of the enterprise communities. Businesses were eligible for a 20 percent tax credit on the first $15,000 of wages and certain training expenses for employees who lived and worked within an empowerment zone. Lawmakers dropped a requirement that some of the zones be on Indian reservations, but businesses there were made eligible for wage credits and accelerated depreciation for investment in buildings and equipment.

BACKGROUND

Congress had debated enterprise zones annually since 1982, when President Ronald Reagan first presented a plan to provide federal tax and regulatory relief to businesses that invested in economically depressed inner cities and rural towns. For several years, either the House or the Senate adopted a variation of enterprise zone legislation, only to see the other chamber balk at the provisions.

Finally, in December 1987, Congress cleared an authorization bill for housing and community development programs that included enterprise zones. Reagan signed the bill into law Feb. 5, 1988. *(1987 Almanac, p. 682)*

The (PL 100-242) law authorized the Department of Housing and Urban Development (HUD) to designate 100 zones in which state and local governments would reduce taxes, fees and bureaucracy while increasing public services to encourage economic development. Two-thirds of the zones were in cities; one-third were in rural areas. But the law provided no federal tax breaks and little federal money — $1 million a year for administrative expenses.

HUD developed regulations for the zones and accepted almost 300 applications from areas seeking designation. But Jack F. Kemp, who became HUD secretary in 1989, believed the law was flawed, especially because it lacked federal tax

incentives. No federal enterprise zones were ever declared.

Congress agreed on a more comprehensive plan in 1992 as part of a broad tax bill, but George Bush vetoed the bill for other reasons. *(1992 Almanac, pp. 140, 345)*

Action in the States

While the federal government debated the merits of zones in the 1980s, many states were putting them to a test. About 40 states authorized enterprise zones, and the 30 most active states named about 800. Typical incentives include loans and loan guarantees, reductions in sales and local property taxes for businesses that located in depressed areas, and tax credits for hiring local employees.

Proponents argued that new federal legislation was still necessary, mainly because a federal presence could lend more energy and influence. Federal tax breaks were in demand because federal taxes generally were higher than state and local taxes. Proponents also hoped that federal legislation would bring needed attention to depressed areas.

Originally, the state efforts were seen by some as a way to cut back the government's role in poor areas by reducing or eliminating taxes and regulations. But states and localities gradually became more involved in the zones, improving roads and sewers, enhancing social services, helping finance businesses and marketing the zone itself.

Clinton Weighs In

Taking a page from state efforts, Clinton emphasized the coordination of government aid to distressed areas, rather than tax breaks for businesses that located there. The tax incentives he did recommend were mostly credits for education and training.

Clinton's plan severely restricted the number of zones. Previous bills would have designated as many as 300. Clinton proposed creating 10 "empowerment zones" slated to receive most of the tax breaks and 100 "enterprise communities" eligible for smaller benefits. Administration officials said focusing the incentives on 10 areas would enhance their effectiveness.

Clinton called for $4.1 billion in new tax breaks over five years. About $3 billion of that was for employment and training wage credits for businesses in the 10 empowerment zones, applicable to new and existing employees; the remaining $1 billion was to fund other tax incentives. The plan included the creation of an Enterprise Board of domestic agency Cabinet secretaries to coordinate the program.

Conservatives warned that Clinton's plan raised the specter of federal control over local activities and criticized the lack of incentives for capital — Clinton's proposal did not include a capital gains tax break for investment in the zones. "We need to let the marketplace work," Kemp said. He argued for more broad-based incentives for capital formation, including eliminating the capital gains tax on anyone who worked, saved or invested in enterprise zones.

Rep. Charles B. Rangel, D-N.Y., and others who represented low-income areas initially criticized the plan as not potent enough to revitalize impoverished communities. "We want to get some juice into those zones," Rangel said in May. But their disappointment was tempered after they won a hard-fought battle to preserve much of the plan in the final bill. Rangel also succeeded in including money for increased social services in the zones — though others

Jesse Brown Confirmed As VA Secretary

The Senate confirmed Jesse Brown, a lobbyist for disabled veterans and a Purple Heart recipient who lost partial use of his right arm as a Marine in Vietnam, as secretary of Veterans Affairs (VA) on Jan. 21. Brown was confirmed by voice vote; to expedite the confirmation process, the Veterans' Affairs Committee agreed to allow floor consideration without a committee vote on the nomination.

During his Jan. 7 appearance before the Veterans' panel, Brown said his background as a veterans' advocate gave him "an intimacy with veterans' issues that can only come from hard work, every day, year in, year out, in a single field." Brown, 48, had lobbied repeatedly for more funding for veterans as the executive director of the Disabled American Veterans (DAV) and spent more than half his life with the organization before being nominated.

But Brown's 26-year affiliation with the DAV also brought questions from Alan K. Simpson, R-Wyo., concerning a substantial pension provided to him by his former employer. Simpson, long a critic of veterans' advocacy groups, asked if the DAV pension — which Simpson said amounted to $41,000 per year or $960,000 if paid in one lump sum — would create the wrong perception.

Brown defended his association with the organization and argued that the pension was "not an unreasonable amount" for someone with his experience and years of service. He also disputed Simpson's figures, saying the lump sum would total $500,000 to $600,000. On his financial disclosure form, Brown checked off a box saying his pension was worth $500,000 to $1 million.

Simpson also warned that Brown could never satisfy what Simpson called the unreasonable demands of veterans' groups. "I hope you'll run them into their holes when they start to harass you, and they will," Simpson said.

Brown promised to go directly to the president to press for funding increases if budget woes led to unfair cuts in veterans' programs. Brown spoke of broad goals for the VA such as increasing the department's efficiency while providing higher quality health care. He said that could be done in tandem with President Clinton's proposed overhaul of the nation's general health-care system. *(Nomination, 1992 Almanac, p. 150-A)* ∎

Clinton Taps Reich To Head Labor

The Senate confirmed Robert B. Reich, 46, as secretary of Labor by voice vote on Jan. 21. Two days earlier, on Jan. 19, the Senate Labor and Human Resources Committee reported the nomination also by voice vote.

During the committee's confirmation hearing Jan. 7, Reich kept his answers terse but polite, as senators made numerous attempts to draw him out. His testimony pleased labor interests but caused some worries for business advocates.

Reich reiterated President Clinton's desire to sign a family and medical leave bill, require businesses to set aside 1.5 percent of their payrolls for job training and sign a striker replacement bill to prohibit companies from permanently replacing striking workers.

In his prodigious writings on the economy, Reich (who was not an economist) had stressed the need not just for more jobs but for higher-wage jobs. Businesses performed best, he argued, when they viewed their workers as their most "precious asset," involving them in decision-making about products and the workplace. "If you confirm me," Reich told the committee, "I will ensure that the Department of Labor is the department of the American work force."

Reich had written and spoken extensively about job training, a top Clinton priority, and he told senators that non-college-bound students needed a school-to-work transition program. With that, he said, went a need for certification and standards for people in fields that did not require university degrees.

Labor groups hesitated little in backing Reich. The AFL-CIO expressed delight in having a Labor secretary who was close to the president and intimately involved with economic planning. Reich had been a close friend of Clinton's since their days as Rhodes scholars, and he headed Clinton's economic policy-planning group during the presidential transition period.

Advocates for business stressed concern about Reich's desire for higher wages and more benefits. Small-business groups were worried about the possibility of a 1.5 percent payroll tax to fund job training. Business groups also expressed uncertainty over what Reich would actually do at the Labor Department since he was known more for his economic theories than for his plans regarding the agency's programs and policies.

To those who saw the Labor Department under the Bush and Reagan administrations as being lackadaisical in enforcing wage and hour laws, along with safety and health regulations, Reich pledged, "If confirmed, I will see that the laws are enforced."

Before being tapped to be Labor secretary, Reich was a lecturer at Harvard University's Kennedy School of Government, a director of policy planning at the Federal Trade Commission under President Jimmy Carter and an assistant solicitor general in the Justice Department under the Ford administration. *(Nomination, 1992 Almanac, p. 149-A)* ∎

Cisneros Easily Confirmed As HUD Secretary

Henry G. Cisneros, a Hispanic former mayor of San Antonio with extensive experience in urban renewal programs, won voice vote approval Jan. 21 as President Clinton's secretary of Housing and Urban Development. His confirmation came one day after the Senate Banking, Housing and Urban Affairs Committee reported the nomination by a vote of 19-0.

During a Jan. 12 confirmation hearing, Cisneros, 45, received praise from both Democratic and Republican panel members, as well as a startling show of support from the outgoing head of the department. "If there is one man who was born to be HUD secretary, it is Henry Cisneros," former Secretary Jack F. Kemp, a Republican, said at the start of the hearing.

Cisneros said HUD's mission under his leadership would be to restore "safety and prosperity" to communities

and to "ensure a livable and steady supply of affordable housing."

"I come to this assignment as an advocate of cities, a skeptic of the status quo and a believer in experimentation, federalism and the need to provide people with hope," he said. Specifically, Cisneros said he would seek accelerated spending of $2.5 billion appropriated in fiscal 1992 and 1993 for the HOME Investment Partnership Act, a federal block grant program aimed at helping state and local governments solve housing needs. He also said he would seek a permanent extension of popular tax credits for investment in low-income rental housing and for mortgage revenue bonds.

Cisneros said he would support inner-city investment proposals similar to so-called enterprise zones to lure corporate investment into depressed parts of the nation's inner cities.

About the only challenging questions for Cisneros came from freshman Lauch Faircloth, R-N.C., who suggested that HUD has too many programs for the homeless and that the deficit could be reduced if Cisneros proposed cuts in the department's budget. But Chairman Donald W. Riegle Jr., D-Mich., interrupted Faircloth, saying, "No agency in the 1980s was marched to the chopping block more than [HUD]."

While generally liberal on social issues, as mayor of San Antonio from 1981-89, Cisneros placed an emphasis on economic development through innovative government and industry partnerships to revitalize urban areas. He was touted as a rising national star, mentioned as a potential senator or governor, and seriously considered as Walter F. Mondale's vice presidential running mate in 1984.

However, he became tainted by a highly publicized extramarital affair with a campaign supporter. The affair and his son's medical problems contributed to Cisneros' decision not to seek re-election as mayor in 1989. He spent the next four years prior to becoming secretary of HUD running a financial consulting company, Cisneros Asset Management, as well as a health and benefit planning company and a communications firm. During Clinton's 1992 presidential campaign, Cisneros was instrumental in focusing on Hispanic voters. ∎

Divided Senate Confirms Achtenberg Appointment

After three days of impassioned floor debate, the Senate voted 58-31 on May 24 to confirm Roberta Achtenberg, the first avowed lesbian appointed to such a high federal office, as assistant secretary for Fair Housing and Equal Opportunity at the Department of Housing and Urban Development. The Banking, Housing and Urban Affairs Committee had approved the nomination May 9 by a vote of 14-4 after hearings on April 29. (Vote 122, p. 17-S).

Opponents, led by Jesse Helms, R-N.C., described Achtenberg as unqualified for the post and eager to impose her own social agenda on the agency and extend fair housing laws to cover homosexuals as a class. Supporters said she was being subjected to unfair personal attacks, many of them related to her sexual orientation.

Helms spoke directly to the issue of her being a lesbian, saying the Senate would be "crossing the threshold" by confirming her. He described Achtenberg, a member of the San Francisco Board of Supervisors, as a "militant activist" who wanted society to accept as normal "a lifestyle that most of the world's religions consider immoral and which the average American voter instinctively finds repulsive." Helms denied that he was engaging in "gay-bashing" and said he was simply "standing up for America's traditional family values."

Many of the GOP attacks centered on Achtenberg's actions as a supervisor and as a local United Way board member in pressuring the Boy Scouts to reverse its policy of excluding homosexuals. She tried to remove city money from the Bank of America because it contributed to the Boy Scouts.

Achtenberg's defenders, mostly Democrats, suggested that the tenor of the debate was demeaning and that the nominee was unfairly characterized. Donald W. Riegle Jr., D-Mich., chairman of the Senate Banking, Housing and Urban Affairs Committee, described as "distasteful" a newspaper quotation in which Helms had said he opposed Achtenberg because she was a lesbian and had added, "If you want to call me a bigot, fine." Carol Moseley-Braun, D-Ill., said she was "frightened to hear the politics of fear and divisiveness and of hatred rear its ugly head on this Senate floor."

The debate took an emotional turn on May 21 when Claiborne Pell, D-R.I., told a hushed chamber that his daughter, Julia, was a lesbian and the president of the Rhode Island Alliance for Gay and Lesbian Civil Rights. "I would not want to see her barred from a government job because of her orientation," he said.

Five Democrats voted against the nomination: Richard C. Shelby, Ala.; Ernest F. Hollings, S.C.; Harlan Mathews, Tenn.; Jim Sasser, Tenn.; and Robert C. Byrd, W. Va. Thirteen Republicans voted for it. ∎

Education Nominee Riley Gets High Marks

On Jan. 21, the Senate confirmed by voice vote the nomination of Richard W. Riley to be secretary of Education. Two days earlier, the Senate Labor and Human Resources Committee had given voice vote approval to the nomination.

At his confirmation hearing Jan. 12, Riley, 60, reassured Democratic members of the Senate Labor and Human Resources Committee by reaffirming his support for direct student loans and his opposition to private school choice. He opened his remarks by stating his support for the direct student loan pilot program established in the 1992 reauthorization of the Higher Education Act. This program bypassed the banks as middlemen in the issuance of student loans and allowed loan recipients to pay the government a percentage of their income over a period of years. (1992 Almanac, p. 440)

Riley told the committee that the direct loan program, which President Bush had opposed, could lead to great savings. Chairman Edward M. Kennedy, D-Mass., a supporter of direct loans, said he was "encouraged" by the nominee's response.

Riley also mollified Claiborne Pell, D-R.I., assuring him that his namesake, the Pell grant program, which provided money for low-income college students, would not be eliminated in favor of the new administration's national service proposal.

Riley supported a national testing system for elementary and secondary school students to "determine what's working and not working." But he warned that he favored testing only "to help students, not label them."

On alternative certification for teachers and increasing the number of days students spent in the classroom, Riley was noncommittal. But he promised to examine these and any other proposals that might improve the nation's schools.

Democrats at the hearing could hardly contain their glee at the prospect of one of their own setting the country's education agenda after 12 years of Republican rule. "The nation's long nightmare in education nonsense is over," said Ernest F. Hollings, D-S.C. Even Republicans, though they disputed Hollings' "nightmare" scenario, seemed genuinely pleased with Riley's credentials and demeanor.

The only hint of tension in an otherwise cordial hearing came when several Republicans pressed the nominee on school choice — a plan long favored by conservatives to establish a voucher system giving some federal money to parents to help them pay private school tuition. Reiterating earlier statements, Riley unequivocally opposed private school choice, arguing that funneling public money to private schools would undermine the public education system.

"I am absolutely sure," Riley said, "that the bottom half of the population would be de-served by full choice." Instead, Riley expressed support for choice within the public school system.

Riley had served as governor of South Carolina from 1979 to 1987. During his tenure in the state house, he acquired a reputation as an innovative education reformer, leading the fight in 1984 to enact sweeping changes in the state's school system. The resulting law included initiatives — paid for by a 1 percent sales tax — to upgrade teacher and principal training and to increase academic standards.

After retiring as governor, Riley joined the large South Carolina law firm of Nelson, Mullins, Riley & Scarborough as a full partner in 1987. The firm represented companies that disposed of nuclear and other hazardous wastes, leading some environmental groups to oppose the nominee as someone who had profited from representing polluters. But Riley effectively dismissed these charges, saying that he had built a strong environmental record during his years in the state house. In addition, he said that he had not been directly involved in any environmental litigation while at the firm. *(Nomination, 1992 Almanac, p. 155-A)* ∎

Senate Confirms Payzant For Education Post

The Senate on Aug. 3 voted 72-27 to confirm Thomas W. Payzant to be assistant secretary for elementary and secondary education at the Department of Education. One Democrat, Robert C. Byrd of West Virginia, voted against Payzant, along with 26 Republicans. *(Vote 233, p. 31-S)*

The Senate Labor and Human Resources Committee had endorsed Payzant's nomination on July 14 by a vote of 13-4.

Payzant's confirmation ran into some difficulty when senators learned that as superintendent of San Diego schools, he had banned the Boy Scouts from conducting a special program in the schools during school hours. Payzant said it was because the Boy Scouts discriminated

against homosexuals and the San Diego School Board had just adopted a non-discrimination policy regarding sexual orientation. Payzant allowed the regular after-hours Boy Scouts program to continue.

At a July 1 Labor Committee hearing on his nomination, Payzant defended himself against charges from the Traditional Values Coalition, a conservative grass-roots lobby on family issues, that he was a liberal extremist.

Secretary of Education Richard W. Riley urged the Senate to confirm Payzant quickly, calling him "the best possible choice for this important post."

In addition to serving as superintendent of San Diego schools from 1982 to 1993, Payzant had worked as superintendent in Oklahoma City and Eugene, Ore., and as administrative assistant to the superintendent in New Orleans. He had been listed as one of the 100 best school administrators by Executive Educator magazine in February 1993.

Riley noted that in San Diego, Payzant had reduced central office staff by 31 percent, saving $13.5 million a year; reduced dropouts while improving student achievement; instituted a rigorous core curriculum; and expanded the district's magnet program to promote voluntary racial integration.

Payzant also received glowing recommendations from both Democratic and Republican congressmen from San Diego and from Sen. Dianne Feinstein, D-Calif. ∎

Hackney OK'd for NEH Despite Controversy

On Aug. 3, the Senate confirmed Sheldon Hackney on a 76-23 vote to be chairman of the National Endowment for the Humanities (NEH), which provided federal research grants to academics. The Senate Labor and Human Resources Committee had voted on July 14 to endorse the nominee, 17-0. *(Vote 234, p. 31-S)*

Before his confirmation, Hackney's nomination had become embroiled in controversy. Some Senate Republicans had expressed a fear that Hackney, who had served for 12 years as president of the University of Pennsylvania, might use his position to advance a liberal or "politically correct" agenda within the academic community at the expense of free speech.

Much of the concern stemmed from the attention given to a hate speech code at the University of Pennsylvania.

Hackney had also been criticized for his recent handling of two racially charged incidents at the university. In both cases, conservatives and First Amendment advocates said the nominee had ignored free speech principles to appease minority students.

The first incident involved a white student who yelled "water buffalo" at five black women. The student, a native of Israel, said that in Hebrew slang "water buffalo" referred to a rude person and had no racial connotations. The women eventually dropped their complaint.

During his June 25 confirmation hearing before the Senate Labor and Human Resources Committee, Hackney said the case had led him to reverse his position on speech codes. "I don't think that a speech code backed up by punishments . . . is a good thing."

In the other cited incident, black students had destroyed about 14,000 copies of the campus newspaper to

protest its editorial policy. Critics said that instead of condemning the action, Hackney legitimized it by casting it as a conflict "between open expression and diversity."

But the nominee said that his words had been taken out of context and that his full statement recognized the primacy of free speech. He also said the students involved would "face disciplinary proceedings."

During his confirmation hearing, Hackney appeared to satisfy the concerns of Senate Labor Committee Republicans regarding his commitment to free speech and fairness.

He told members that free speech is a "paramount" right and that the "NEH should not have a social agenda."

Still, Orrin G. Hatch, R-Utah, had some concerns. "I would have preferred you to have said that this [behavior] was abominable. Your statement could have been better," he said, referring to the newspaper incident.

But others seemed satisfied.

"Balance is not easy," said Daniel R. Coats, R-Ind. "In the academic community, there is a strong pull toward political correctness." ■

Airline Pension Bill Passes

The House on March 16 cleared by voice vote a Senate bill (S 400) designed to guarantee retirees of troubled airlines their pension benefits and to preserve a Continental Airlines plan to reorganize in the wake of financial woes. President Clinton signed the bill the next day (PL 103-7). The Senate had passed the bill March 11 by voice vote.

The measure, which applied generally to all airline bankruptcy cases, arose when embattled Continental Airlines officials, trying to dig out of bankruptcy, hit a snag in negotiating a reorganization plan.

The proposal clarified the legal status of leased aircraft equipment and defined Continental's relationship with the Pension Benefit Guaranty Corporation (PBGC). The PBGC, a federal agency, was established to help retirees obtain pensions they were promised by companies that no longer could deliver them because of financial troubles.

Continental was liable for almost $694 million in pension funds when it filed for Chapter 11 protection in 1990. It gave 15 aircraft to the PBGC in an effort to resolve the liability claims. Continental agreed to lease the planes back from the PBGC, drawing concern that the agreement would diminish special protections that the bankruptcy law gave equipment leasing companies and discourage similar

Senate Affirms Alexander

The Senate on Sept. 29 confirmed, by voice vote, Jane Alexander to be director of the National Endowment for the Arts (NEA). Alexander had received the Labor and Human Resources Committee's unanimous, 17-0, approval Sept. 22.

Panel members praised Alexander for setting aside a successful stage and movie career to devote four years to head the beleaguered arts agency. The endowment had come under criticism for providing grants to artists whose work some considered indecent.

While backing Alexander's nomination, Orrin G. Hatch, R-Utah, said, "When the NEA funds works of art that are blatantly offensive or obscene, it flouts its principal purpose, which is to bring the arts to all Americans."

Alexander told the panel that her main goal would be to turn around the image of the NEA. "We need to let the American people know of all the good the NEA has done in the past few years." ■

financial arrangements that might be beneficial to airlines. The bill ensured that such arrangements were protected.

The bill defined the PBGC as a lessor in the agreement, allowing the company to foreclose on the planes if Continental went bankrupt. ■

Checking Security Guards

The House Education and Labor Subcommittee on Human Resources approved a bill Sept. 30 that allowed more stringent background checks for security guards. The bill went no further in 1993.

The bill (HR 1534), approved by voice vote, called on states to develop minimum standards for security guards employed in the private sector. The bill also allowed private employers, with FBI help, to check the criminal backgrounds of their security guards or applicants.

The measure required the Labor Department to study ways to provide incentives for states to adopt the minimum standards. Supporters said the measure was needed to address the increase in the number of security guards being hired around the country and to prevent the hiring of felons. ■

Chapter 9

DEFENSE

$261 Billion Authorized for Defense

Lawmakers trim president's numbers but grant most of his defense requests

The $261 billion defense authorization bill for fiscal 1994 (HR 2401) backed the essentials of President Clinton's budget request, from his efforts to revamp research into anti-missile defenses to his proposals to continue work on a new generation of combat planes.

The Senate cleared the bill Nov. 17, and Clinton signed it Nov. 30 (PL 103-160).

Lawmakers sliced about $2.6 billion from the Clinton request, which in turn was $12 billion less than former President George Bush had projected in a skeletal budget request for the year that he had prepared before leaving office.

But Congress also asserted its own priorities, spurning Clinton's request for a governmentwide wage freeze to approve a 2.2 percent pay raise for military personnel.

Although liberal lawmakers argued for deeper defense cuts to reflect the end of the Cold War arms race, other members in both chambers expressed concern that Clinton's long-range defense plans would cut too fast and too deep and would risk the nation's military capabilities. Those warnings were conveyed by leaders of the Armed Services committees and the Defense Appropriations subcommittees in both chambers.

The net reduction of $2.6 billion from Clinton's spending proposal was made to comply with budget limits and technical assumptions made by the Congressional Budget Office (CBO). Accounts for operations and maintenance (cut $2 billion) and for research and development (cut $4 billion) took the heaviest hits.

BACKGROUND

The defense measure was shaped by familiar players, some of them in new roles. Les Aspin, Clinton's new Defense secretary, had for years been an architect of the bill as a Democratic representative from Wisconsin and chairman of the House Armed Services Committee.

Aspin saw the authorization bill move to enactment, but, after a tumultuous year of controversies over his leadership of the Pentagon, he announced on Dec. 15 that he would resign effective Jan. 20, 1994. *(Aspin, p. 474)*

He was succeeded by his deputy, William J. Perry, who

THE MAJOR ISSUES

See also the following stories on major issues that were addressed in the Defense bill:

➤ **Combat Aircraft.** Agreement on plans for a new generation of planes included canceling the A/F-X. .... p. 446

➤ **Strategic Defense.** The anti-missile program was renamed and scaled back to $2.8 billion for the year. .... p. 448

➤ **C-17s Troubles.** Lawmakers backed continued funding for the C-17 cargo jet but attached schedule and testing standards that the plane would have to meet. .... p. 450

➤ **Bottom-Up Review.** The administration maintained it could scale back the military but preserve the capacity to fight two wars at a time. .... p. 452

➤ **Gays in Military.** Despite Clinton's campaign promise to drop the military's ban on gays, the bill locked the prohibition into law. .... p. 454

➤ **Women in the Military.** The measure repealed legislation that had prevented women from serving on combat ships. p. 463

---

was swiftly confirmed Feb. 3, 1994. *(Successor, p. 476)*

Meanwhile, Aspin's successor as House Armed Services Committee chairman was Ronald V. Dellums, D-Calif., known as one of the most liberal members of Congress.

An opponent of many major weapons systems and of most U.S. military intervention abroad, Dellums had never voted for passage of the defense authorization bills that he helped craft as a committee member and subcommittee chairman. Yet he was also widely respected by committee members of both parties for his courtly manner and willingness to serve as an honest broker of compromises within the panel.

The Senate Armed Services Committee continued to be chaired by Sam Nunn, D-Ga., who shared Aspin's centrist views on defense issues but had in the past been viewed as a frequent rival for influence.

Action on the defense authorization bill was delayed for months beyond the customary congressional schedule to avoid embroiling the measure in a fierce dispute over Clinton's campaign promise to eliminate the military's longstanding ban on homosexuals. Ultimately, Clinton settled for a slight easing of the ban, but lawmakers, led by Nunn, insisted on adding a provision to the authorization bill that attempted to assure the ban's permanence by sealing it into law. *(Gays in the military, p. 454)*

Other controversial issues, including congressional resistance to U.S. involvement in U.N. peacekeeping operations in Somalia and elsewhere, played out partly on the companion $240.5 billion defense appropriations bill (HR 3116 — PL 103-139). *(Peacekeeping, p. 483; Appropriations, p. 569)*

PRESIDENT'S BUDGET

For defense-related programs, Clinton's fiscal 1994 budget request, formally submitted on April 8, called for $263.4 billion in new budget authority. That was a $9.6 billion cut from the amount Congress appropriated for fiscal 1993. Taking account of the cost of inflation, it amounted to a 5 percent reduction from fiscal 1993. *(Clinton's budget, p. 89)*

Clinton's request translated into total defense outlays

in fiscal 1994 — money that could actually be spent that year — of $276.9 billion.

Of the $263.4 billion in new budget authority, $250.7 billion was slated for military programs of the Defense Department.

Most of the remainder — $11.5 billion — was for defense-related work conducted by the Energy Department, which developed, tested and manufactured nuclear weapons and bought nuclear fuel for warships.

Priorities

The Clinton defense budget marked time on most major weapons programs in an effort to preserve the administration's options pending a review of U.S. defense requirements in the post-Cold War world. In broad categories, the Clinton request followed this outline:

● **R&D.** Funding for research and development was essentially constant at $38.6 billion, up from $38.2 billion in fiscal 1993.

● **Procurement.** Funding for procurement dropped from $53.6 billion in 1993 to $45.5 billion, but no major weapons program was killed to achieve the reduction. Nearly $2 billion of the cut resulted from the absence of the B-2 stealth bomber. The fiscal 1993 budget had included the final four of a planned fleet of 20 of the bombers.

In addition, the budget held steady the tempo of training by reducing the number of personnel and disbanding some units:

● **Operations and Maintenance.** Operations and maintenance funding was increased slightly to $89.5 billion, from the $86.4 billion in fiscal 1993;

● **Personnel.** Spending for military personnel dropped from $76.3 billion to $70.1 billion.

Clinton's military personnel request trimmed the number of active-duty service members by 108,000 to 1.62 million. It reduced the number of National Guard and reserve members by 60,000, to 1.02 million.

In line with the personnel cutback, the budget also envisioned a reduction in the "force structure," the number of combat units in the field. Under Clinton's plan:

● The Army was to disband two of its 14 combat divisions.

● The number of Navy ships in service was to drop from 443 to 413, as retirements of older vessels outstripped the commissioning of new craft.

● Active-duty Air Force fighter wings, which typically consisted of three squadrons of 24 planes each, was to drop from 16.1 to 13.3.

Post-Cold War Challenges

Slightly less than 1 percent of Clinton's total request was earmarked to meet the international and domestic challenges of the post-Cold War world.

Of that total, $888 million was for the Pentagon's share of the cost of international operations, including:

● $300 million for the cost of U.S. participation in multilateral peacekeeping operations, such as in Somalia;

● $50 million for natural disaster relief operations, in the wake of hurricanes or earthquakes;

● $48 million for other humanitarian assistance missions; and

● $400 million, on top of $800 million previously appropriated, to help Russia and other former Soviet republics dispose of nuclear, chemical and biological weapons.

To cushion the impact of defense cutbacks on companies, communities and individuals, the request included

$1.66 billion for "defense conversion," allocated as follows:

● $964 million to encourage small- and medium-size defense contractors to invest in "dual-use" technologies — that is, products and manufacturing techniques that would be militarily useful while also helping contractors become more commercially competitive;

● $519 million to help military personnel, civilian Pentagon employees and defense industry workers facing dislocation because of budget cuts; and

● $178 million for programs to assist communities hit by layoffs at military bases or by defense contractors.

Major Weapons Systems

Major weapons requests included:

● $3.76 billion for the Pentagon's anti-missile defense program, which had been called the Strategic Defense Initiative but would soon be renamed the Ballistic Missile Defense program;

● $1.13 billion for 24 additional Trident II submarine-launched ballistic missiles;

● $94 million to upgrade older M-1 tanks and $192 million to modernize older Bradley troop carriers;

● $367 million to continue developing the Comanche armed helicopter;

● $278 million to equip Apache attack helicopters with the new Longbow radar; and

● $217 million for MLRS artillery rocket launchers.

The budget called for funding six major aircraft programs:

● $796 million to buy 24 F-16 Air Force fighters;

● $1.75 billion for 36 Navy F/A-18 fighters;

● $2.25 billion to continue developing the new F-22 fighter for the Air Force;

● $1.41 billion to develop larger versions of the F/A-18;

● $399 million to develop the A/F-X carrier-based bomber; and

● $2.32 billion for six C-17 cargo jets.

Major requests in shipbuilding included:

● $2.64 billion for three destroyers equipped with the Aegis anti-aircraft system and

● $894 million to complete construction of a large helicopter carrier to haul as many as 2,000 Marines and the helicopters to fly them ashore.

EARLY DEBATE

Even before Clinton formally submitted the budget in April, key members of the Armed Services committees questioned the cuts that Clinton had promised in his presidential campaign and that Aspin set out to impose as Pentagon chief.

On Feb. 17, the president announced he would seek to cut defense spending by at least $88 billion from Bush's projected budgets for fiscal 1994-97. This included the $60 billion that Clinton had pledged during his presidential campaign to cut, plus $18 billion that would be saved from the defense payroll by freezing federal pay in fiscal 1994 and limiting raises thereafter. *(Text, 7-D)*

Additionally, Aspin held out the prospect of deeper cuts — $10 billion or more — if needed to compensate for what some Pentagon officials viewed as unrealistic assumptions of costs and savings in Bush's plan. The new Defense secretary appointed a panel to study those assumptions. Additionally, administration officials spoke of cutting $42 billion, based on the assumption that inflation would prove lower than Bush's plan had anticipated. Such cuts could

bring the total in reductions to $130 billion from Bush's projections, more than twice the cuts Clinton had promised in his campaign.

Even the broad-brush strokes of the Clinton budget disturbed some conservative Democrats. "Whenever they needed money for anything, they took it out of the defense budget," said Jim Exon, D-Neb., a member of the Senate Armed Services Committee.

Nunn's Bottom Line

As the Senate geared up to debate Clinton's budget proposals, Armed Services Chairman Nunn called on administration and congressional budget writers to buffer the Pentagon from unanticipated increases in costs.

"The Pentagon ought to be held harmless against things they have no control over," Nunn said March 4, previewing the argument he made in a major Senate floor speech the next morning.

With his expertise on military affairs and his centrist politics, Nunn typically played a pivotal role in Senate debates on defense policy. In this case, he essentially accepted the new Democratic administration's planned cuts in defense spending — but signaled his resistance to any deeper cuts that would be imposed either by Congress or by changing economic circumstances.

In the March 5 speech, Nunn focused on Clinton's proposed cuts beyond the $60 billion pledged in his campaign. The senator portrayed the added cuts as reasonable, if somewhat optimistic.

However, Nunn insisted that future Pentagon budgets should be increased if the projected cost reductions did not materialize. Otherwise, Nunn argued, the Defense Department would have to make unacceptably large cutbacks in the number and readiness of its forces.

Nunn said he had administration assurances that the Pentagon would be protected against some of the potential cost increases. But for others, Nunn could say only that he "hoped and expected" that future costs increases would be allowed for.

For example, Nunn cited Clinton's plan to cut $18 billion from defense on the assumption that Congress would agree to his proposal that there be no federal pay raise in fiscal 1994 and that pay in the following three years be increased by 1 percent less than the rate of inflation. Nunn argued that the Pentagon budget should be increased if Congress rejected the proposed pay restraints. The Clinton administration concurred, Nunn said, provided that Congress rejected the pay caps for all government employees and not just for defense personnel.

Aspin Prodded

Although Congress seemed likely from the start to go along with the basics of Clinton's fiscal 1994 defense budget, even some staunch Pentagon allies on Capitol Hill rebelled at the administration's intention to postpone tough decisions on which expensive weapons programs to winnow out.

BOXSCORE

➤ **Fiscal 1994 Defense Authorization (HR 2401, S 1298).** The $261 billion bill backed the essentials of President Clinton's budget request, from efforts to redirect research into anti-missile defenses to continuing work on a new generation of combat planes.

Reports: S Rept 103-112, H Rept 103-200; conference report H Rept 103-357.

KEY ACTION

Sept. 14 — **Senate** approved S 1298, 92-7.

Sept. 29 — **House** passed HR 2401, 268-162.

Nov. 15 — **House** adopted the conference report, 273-135.

Nov. 17 — **Senate** cleared the bill, 77-22.

Nov. 30 — **President** signed the bill into law (PL 103-160).

Defense Secretary Aspin told reporters on March 27 that Clinton's defense budget was built around a strategy of "treading water" on major weapons issues, while paying for a high tempo of training and maintenance by disbanding some units. Aspin argued that more far-reaching changes should await a sweeping "bottom-up" review of U.S. defense requirements that he had initiated.

But that strategy of marking time met strong criticism when Aspin and Joint Chiefs of Staff Chairman Gen. Colin L. Powell Jr. appeared before the House and Senate Armed Services committees the week of March 29.

So on April 1, Aspin told the Senate committee that he would try to recommend some specific weapons cuts before Senate and House conferees finished work on the annual defense authorization bill in the fall.

"I don't think that the Congress is willing to wait on some of the major issues you are reviewing," Nunn told Aspin.

In the House committee, Chairman Dellums told his predecessor Aspin, "To 'tread water' would be to go back on hard-won understandings and policy positions reached by this committee and the Congress last year."

SENATE COMMITTEE ACTION

The Senate Armed Services Committee moved July 23 to radically cut back the Pentagon's plans for a new generation of combat jets as the panel approved a $262 billion defense authorization bill for fiscal 1994 (S 1298 — S Rept 103-112). The committee marked up the bill in closed session and did not announce the vote by which it approved the measure.

Rejecting the plans for new tactical aircraft as too expensive, the committee ordered the Air Force and Navy to scrap two costly aircraft programs. The committee denied $399 million requested to develop a long-range Navy ground attack plane designated A/F-X, ordering the service instead to adapt the Air Force's new F-22 fighter to carry bombs. And it ordered the Air Force to drop plans to develop a small fighter (designated MRF) to replace existing F-16s early in the next century.

The fighter plane decisions were among the most significant elements of the bill. For some other controversial weapons programs — including the C-17 cargo plane, the B-2 stealth bomber and the anti-missile defense program formerly known as the Strategic Defense Initiative — the committee approved all or most of the funds that Clinton requested.

But in each case, the panel stipulated that the funds could not be spent unless the program satisfied various criteria.

The committee incorporated into the bill a modified version of the policy on gay military personnel that Clinton announced July 19. The committee bill also provided for repeal of the statutory ban on the assignment of women to combat ships.

Rejecting Clinton's recommendation of a pay freeze for civilian and military federal employees, the committee approved a 2.2 percent pay increase for military personnel.

But to fit the spending within the limit on defense outlays set by the congressional budget resolution, the panel had to make offsetting cuts. These resulted in a cut of $1 billion from the total defense budget authority that Clinton had requested and that the congressional budget resolution allowed. *(Budget resolution, p. 102)*

Committee Chairman Nunn warned that a technical dispute between the Clinton administration and the Congressional Budget Office (CBO) might force a much larger cut in budget authority.

CBO estimated that the bill would result in outlays nearly $2 billion higher than the administration and the Armed Services Committee had projected — and thus $2 billion higher than the budget resolution, which set Congress' spending guidelines, allowed. Nunn said that if CBO's view prevailed and Congress had to cut $2 billion in outlays from the bill, it would require an additional cut in budget authority of $7 billion to $9 billion.

The committee combined in a single $2.7 billion fund the amounts the administration had requested to build C-17 long-range cargo planes and new cargo ships. It ordered Aspin to evaluate possible trade-offs between air and sea transport for delivering U.S. forces to distant trouble spots.

The panel approved the $604 million requested to continue production of the fleet of 20 B-2 bombers previously authorized. However, as had been true of all B-2 funds approved by Congress since fiscal 1992, none of this money could be spent until the administration demonstrated that the plane met various cost and performance requirements. Moreover, the committee added two additional requirements that would have to be met before the B-2 money could be spent, bringing to 30 the total number of legislative "fences" around those funds.

For the program to develop anti-missile defenses, the committee approved $3.2 billion of the $3.75 billion requested. Of that reduction, $300 million was a real cut. The remaining $253 million resulted from consolidating funds for the Brilliant Eyes missile detection satellite with funds requested for several other missile-detection satellites.

Of the $1.2 billion requested for all of these missile-detection devices, the committee approved more than $900 million and directed the Pentagon to spend the money on less expensive ways to detect attacking missiles.

HOUSE COMMITTEE

The defense authorization measure approved July 27 by the House Armed Services Committee followed the Clinton administration's lead, both in its major decisions and its overall caution. After a drafting session that lasted nearly 15 hours, the committee voted 46-9 to send the bill (HR 2401 — H Rept 103-200) to the House floor.

The committee's bill included provisions to:
● Cancel development of the stealthy A/F-X, a carrier-borne bomber for the Navy, slicing $399 million from the fiscal 1994 budget;
● Repeal the statutory ban against assigning women to combat vessels; and
● Deny $206 million of the $428 million requested for the underground nuclear test program.

But in each of those instances, the House panel either was tracking a decision that Clinton previously had announced or — in the case of the A/F-X cancellation —

anticipating a decision that was expected to surface shortly.

And most significant, the bill followed the administration's lead by marking time. It sought to whittle down the size of the U.S. defense establishment while deferring any radical change in its shape until Aspin and senior military planners hammered out a military strategy for the post-Soviet era.

"This bill does not go as far as I would like in adapting the military budget to the needs of the post-Cold War era," said Chairman Dellums. But the longtime critic of Pentagon spending also supported the bill with the argument that it took some significant first steps away from Cold War defense policy.

Ranking committee Republican Floyd D. Spence, S.C., was less concerned with those first steps than with the slope down which they could lead. "The fiscal year 1994 budget represents only a small down payment on the Clinton administration's five-year plan to cut at least $127 billion from the defense budget," he said, comparing Clinton's program disapprovingly with the Bush administration's projections.

The bill's highest profile provision used language borrowed from the Senate Armed Services version of the defense bill codifying the Pentagon's ban on homosexual conduct.

Committee Amendments

For the anti-missile defense program, the Armed Services Subcommittee on Research and Technology, chaired by Patricia Schroeder, D-Colo., had recommended cutting Clinton's $3.76 billion request to $2.59 billion. Of the $1.2 billion reduction, $253 million resulted from shifting the Brilliant Eyes satellite project to another program.

By a vote of 29-27, the full committee adopted an amendment by John M. Spratt Jr., D-S.C., boosting anti-missile funds to $2.74 billion. Seven Democrats joined all 22 Republicans in voting "yea."

The committee debated two amendments on aspects of Clinton's defense program that dealt with new, post-Cold War defense missions.

By a 33-22 party-line vote, it adopted an amendment by Oversight and Investigations Subcommittee Chairman Norman Sisisky, D-Va., earmarking $111 million for the cost of U.S. forces engaged in peacekeeping, disaster relief and other international multilateral operations.

The administration had requested $300 million for this purpose. Without such a contingency fund, Aspin noted, the services raided their training funds and other readiness-related budget accounts to cover the costs when such international operations were undertaken on short notice until Congress approved supplemental funding.

But some senior Republicans objected that the lump sum amounted to a blank check for overseas entanglements. "How do we know where and when such funds will be used?" asked James V. Hansen, R-Utah. "It takes away from Congress the power of the purse."

The committee also adopted, 33-23, a Dellums substitute amendment that authorized the use of $979 million in fiscal 1993 defense funds for aid to Russia and other former Soviet republics. The House had approved the expenditure in a supplemental appropriations bill (HR 2118 — PL 103-50).

Dellums' substitute gutted an amendment by Duncan Hunter, R-Calif., that would have authorized the funding but required that the Defense Department manage the

expenditure. Hunter contended that his amendment would ensure that the money would be used for defense priorities, especially dismantling the nuclear missiles of the former Soviet Union.

But several Democrats insisted that supporting the fragile Russian experiment with democracy was a vital U.S. interest. "If the [former] Soviet experiment fails," said Schroeder, "we'll be back into defense expenditures like you never saw."

Hunter's was one of several amendments aimed at dramatizing GOP objections to the use of Pentagon funds for arguably non-defense purposes. The only committee member to depart from a straight party line on the Soviet aid vote was Florida Democrat Earl Hutto, who opposed the Dellums substitute.

By a vote of 36-17, the committee in effect turned down a proposal by its Readiness Subcommittee that would have slowed efforts to build a dozen large cargo ships to carry tanks, other heavy equipment and supplies for Army divisions. Routinely anchored at overseas bases, these "pre-positioning ships" could steam to a trouble spot where troops flown in from U.S. bases would link up with the equipment.

In 1990, a similar 13-ship fleet enabled heavily armed Marine Corps units to deploy within days after President Bush ordered U.S. forces to Saudi Arabia. Drawing on that lesson, the Joint Chiefs of Staff decided to create an Army pre-positioning fleet. But some partisans of the Marine Corps opposed the move as an Army ploy to find new turf after the prospect of a massive land war in Europe evaporated.

Marine Corps officials asserted that, with a few additional ships, their existing fleet could take care of the small Army airborne force that typically was the thin end of the wedge of a major U.S. deployment.

Freshman Paul McHale, D-Pa., vigorously advocated the subcommittee's proposal, which would have required a comparative analysis of the Army and Marine approaches.

McHale, a 20-year veteran of the Marines, most of it in reserve status, resigned from his seat in the Pennsylvania legislature to join a Marine unit that served in the Persian Gulf War. He opposed the Army pre-positioning plan as "a $3.1 billion redundancy."

But the Marine Corps partisans were outgunned in the political arena. There was a particularly large caucus of Army backers among House Armed Services Democrats.

BILL COMPARISONS

As the House and Senate versions of the defense authorization bills headed toward floor debate, the following were key similarities and differences in the measures:

Tactical aircraft. Anticipating a decision that the Clinton administration would soon announce, both committees denied the $399 million requested by the Navy to develop the carrier-based bomber designated A/F-X. Both panels ordered the Pentagon to scrap that program.

(Aspin announced the plans to scrap the A/F-X on Sept. 1, as an element of the Pentagon's "bottom-up" review of policies and strategy.)

Both Armed Services panels also approved the $2.25 billion requested to continue developing the Air Force's F-22, the stealthy, long-range fighter plane intended to replace the 1970s vintage F-15. Ordering the Navy to use the F-22 as a substitute for the A/F-X, the Senate panel added $50 million to the defense bill to adapt the fighter to

operate from carriers and to attack ground targets.

To replace A-6E carrier-based bombers slated for retirement, both committees approved the $1.41 billion requested to develop enlarged "E" and "F" models of the existing F/A-18.

Both committees approved the $1.49 billion requested for 36 of the F/A-18 model that was already being flown. But the Senate panel rejected the $725 million requested for 24 additional F-16s.

Anti-missile defense. The House committee sliced $1 billion from the administration's $3.76 billion request to develop defenses against missile attack, approving $2.74 billion. The Senate panel cut the program by $553 million, to $3.2 billion.

In each case, the reduction included the $253 million requested to develop the Brilliant Eyes missile detection satellite. Contending that the Pentagon was trying to fund too many similar systems, each committee lumped funding for several systems — including Brilliant Eyes — into one fund and ordered the Defense Department to thin out the field.

But the two panels laid out different policy maps for the anti-missile program. House Armed Services sought to dilute provisions enacted in 1991 that committed the government to deploy a ground-based defense of U.S. territory. The Senate committee directed the Pentagon to begin reviewing several programs designed to protect against short-range missiles to determine whether they were consistent with the 1972 treaty limiting anti-ballistic missile weapons.

C-17 cargo plane. Both committees approved substantial additional funding for the C-17 wide-body cargo jet but ordered the Pentagon to consider alternatives before spending more on a project with a history of cost increases and technical problems.

Of the $2.56 billion requested to continue testing the plane and to build six, the House panel approved $2.11 billion. The committee stipulated that the funds could be spent only after the Pentagon reviewed alternative long-range cargo planes, including C-5s and commercial aircraft.

Senate Armed Services lumped into one sum the $2.4 billion earmarked for C-17 procurement and the $291 million requested for fast cargo ships. The panel approved the entire $2.7 billion request but ordered the Pentagon to determine the most cost-effective mix of C-17s, other planes and ships for long-range transport.

Trident II missile. Both committees approved the $983 million requested for 24 Trident II submarine-launched missiles.

The House panel also approved the $145 million requested for components that would be used to continue Trident II production in future years, but it ordered the Navy to review alternatives before spending the money. By contrast, the Senate committee boosted funding for components to $170 million and told the Navy to speed up Trident II production.

Aegis destroyers. Both committees approved three additional *Arleigh Burke*-class destroyers for which the Navy requested $2.64 billion. But the Senate panel trimmed the request by $30 million, and the House panel by $96 million.

Budget add-ons. Additions to Clinton's request that were agreed on by both committees included:
● A 2.2 percent pay raise for all military personnel, to take effect Jan. 1, 1994. Clinton had proposed a pay freeze for civilian and military federal workers.

● Extra funds to continue building Apache missile-armed anti-tank helicopters at a slow rate. The goal was to keep the assembly line operating after the Army bought its last new Apache and before those already in service were brought in to be upgraded.

The House committee added $150 million; the Senate committee added $160 million.

● $195 million more than the $409 million requested for JSTARS planes equipped with radar to detect ground targets at long range. The added funding was to buy two of the converted jetliners instead of one. Both committees approved the $295 million requested to continue JSTARS development.

SENATE FLOOR ACTION

After five days of debate that lacked much of the intensity and drama that permeated defense debates in the 1980s, the Senate approved a $261 billion version of the defense authorization bill Sept. 14 by a vote of 92-7. *(Vote 265, p. 35-S)*

Only the issue of homosexuals in the military stirred much emotion, and that fight had been all but settled before the bill reached the Senate floor. The bill basically sought to codify the existing prohibition against openly gay armed services personnel.

Senators defeated, 33-63, an amendment by Barbara Boxer, D-Calif., that would have struck provisions on gays drafted by Armed Services Committee Chairman Nunn. Boxer's amendment, sought by gay rights advocates, would have explicitly ceded the issue to the president. *(Vote 250, p. 33-S)*

The Senate's most dramatic departure from the administration's funding proposals came Sept. 9, when senators voted 50-48 to approve only $2.8 billion for anti-missile defenses; not including the separate funding for the Brilliant Eyes satellite, $400 million less than Senate Armed Services had recommended. Clinton had requested $3.8 billion for the former SDI program, including Brilliant Eyes. *(Vote 251, p. 33-S)*

In a move indicative of growing congressional unease over the continued deployment of U.S. troops in Somalia, the Senate also voted, 90-7, to add to the bill on Sept. 9 a non-binding amendment urging Clinton to obtain congressional authorization for the deployment by Nov. 15. *(Vote 252, p. 33-S; Somalia, p. 486)*

Base Closings, Conversion

The largest single group of amendments on the defense bill dealt with the base-closing process, which called for another round of politically agonizing cutbacks in 1995.

On Sept. 10, the Senate brushed aside, 18-79, an amendment by Dianne Feinstein, D-Calif., that would have delayed the 1995 round of closings until 1997. *(Vote 254, p. 33-S; 1993 base closings, p. 465)*

Six amendments approved by voice vote Sept. 13 were relatively minor and non-controversial. They were:

● By Arlen Specter, R-Pa., requiring the Pentagon to report to Congress the cost of closing bases under the expedited procedure adopted in 1990 and to highlight cases in which the actual cost exceeded by more than 50 percent the estimate that was the basis of the decision to close the base. Specter contended that the 1991 decision to close the Philadelphia Navy Yard — which he and others were trying to block in court — was based on a low-ball estimate of closing costs.

● By Specter, requiring that, when a base was slated for closure, local governments, chambers of commerce and ci-

vilian employees of the installation be consulted about potential uses for the facility.

● By Boxer, allowing the Pentagon to train the civilian employees displaced by closure of a base to perform environmental cleanup work at the site.

● By George J. Mitchell, D-Maine, providing that the legal ban on contracting out fire protection services at military bases could be waived to allow the Pentagon to contract with a local government for protection at a base in the last six months before the installation closed.

● By Donald W. Riegle Jr., D-Mich., requiring the Pentagon specifically to justify the selection for closure of any base it previously had targeted, if the earlier recommendation was rejected by the independent commission that drew up the final list of sites to be closed.

● By Carl Levin, D-Mich., urging the Pentagon to make available to communities suffering economic hardship because of a base closure any surplus military equipment that could be useful in economic redevelopment.

Also by voice vote, the Senate on Sept. 13 adopted two amendments dealing more generally with the process of converting the defense establishment to commercial work:

● By Mitchell, setting a goal of ensuring that small businesses participated in partnerships that received at least 15 percent of the funds provided to foster dual-use technologies, those with both military and commercial application.

● By Bob Dole, R-Kan., requiring the Environmental Protection Agency to establish a program to train military personnel and civilian Pentagon employees in the management of hazardous and radioactive waste.

By a vote of 63-37, the Senate tabled, or killed, an amendment by Jeff Bingaman, D-N.M., that would have deleted from the bill a provision earmarking $25 million to guarantee up to $1 billion in loans to foster arms sales to U.S. allies. *(Vote 262, p. 34-S)*

A Mitchell amendment requiring the National Security Council to review proposed arms sales was adopted by voice vote.

European Concerns

By voice vote, the Senate adopted an amendment by Levin codifying economic sanctions on Serbia that Clinton had imposed by executive order in retaliation for Serbian attacks on Bosnia.

Also by voice vote, the Senate adopted a Dole amendment requiring the Pentagon to turn over to the Agency for International Development 500,000 cases of military field rations for distribution in Bosnia-Herzegovina and Armenia as humanitarian assistance.

Another Levin amendment adopted by voice vote was designed to pressure Germany to pay for U.S. military facilities that were being shut down in that country as the U.S. force in Europe diminished. Levin said Germany had paid only $3 million of the $2.5 billion it owed for installations the Pentagon decided to give up.

Levin's amendment barred transfer of the U.S. Embassy to Berlin — where the German government was moving from Bonn — until Germany paid at least half the residual value of the former U.S. bases. Funds to build a new embassy complex in Berlin would come only from additional German payments.

Arms Control

The Senate approved two non-controversial arms control initiatives Sept. 14. The first, by Patrick J. Leahy, D-Vt., adopted 100-0, continued for one year the moratorium

on the export of land mines enacted by Congress for fiscal 1993. *(Vote 258, p. 34-S)*

The other, by Pete V. Domenici, R-N.M., approved by voice vote, required the president to inform Congress of any indications that weapons in the U.S. nuclear stockpile were becoming unreliable or unsafe.

Clinton extended a moratorium on underground nuclear tests that had been imposed by Congress in 1992 as part of the fiscal 1993 energy and water appropriations bill (HR 5373 — PL 102-377). Like the House version of the defense authorization bill, the Senate bill sought to terminate a 30-year-old program intended to preserve the option of resuming above-ground tests that were banned by a 1963 treaty. *(1992 Almanac, p. 517; nuclear test ban, p. 286)*

Tom Harkin, D-Iowa, offered an amendment to delete from the bill $10 million that the Armed Services Committee earmarked to develop an anti-satellite (ASAT) missile. By a vote of 90-10, the Senate gutted Harkin's amendment by adopting a modification by Richard C. Shelby, D-Ala., providing that the ASAT funds could be spent once the Pentagon adopted a formal statement of requirements for the program. And then, by 40-60, the Senate rejected even that watered-down version of the Harkin amendment. *(Votes 260, 261, p. 34-S)*

The Senate also adopted by voice vote an amendment to cut the amount authorized for the Energy Department to maintain its capability to conduct nuclear testing. The bill as sent to the floor had included $428 million for the mothballed testing sites.

Harkin offered an amendment that would have cut the testing funds to $222.4 million, the same amount included in the House bill. But senators approved by voice vote a substitute amendment offered by Exon, setting the funding at $375 million.

Budget Matters

By a 57-43 vote, the Senate on Sept. 14 tabled (killed), an amendment by Charles E. Grassley, R-Iowa, that would have abolished the Defense Business Operations Fund (DBOF) at the end of 1994, unless auditors gave the fund a clean bill of health for fiscal 1993. *(Vote 259, p. 34-S)*

DBOF was a revolving fund through which unit commanders bought supplies, equipment overhauls and certain other goods and services. It was intended to make commanders more cost-conscious but was plagued by inadequate financial controls.

John Glenn, D-Ohio, who oversaw DBOF as chairman of both the Armed Services Military Readiness Subcommittee and the Governmental Affairs Committee, said the best way to gain control of Pentagon costs was by reforming DBOF rather than abolishing it.

Four amendments adopted by voice vote highlighted other facets of the Pentagon's budget:

● By David Pryor, D-Ark., requiring an annual report to Congress on Pentagon recruiting costs, which were running about $2 billion.

● By Robert C. Byrd, D-W.Va., requiring that all federal agencies with secret programs report annually to Congress on their budgets and activities, as the Defense Department and the intelligence agencies already were required to do.

● By John McCain, R-Ariz., giving the secretary of Defense discretion to scrap any of more than 1,000 annual reports mandated by Congress if the secretary deemed them superfluous.

● By William V. Roth Jr., R-Del., urging the Pentagon to designate one major procurement program as a pilot pro-

gram to test the savings that might result from greatly simplifying the rules that governed such purchases. Congress authorized such test programs in 1990, but none had been implemented.

Other Amendments

In amendments that were rejected, the Senate tabled (killed):

● By 61-32, an amendment by Dennis DeConcini, D-Ariz., that would have authorized the transfer of $50 million in unspent fiscal 1993 defense funds to drug rehabilitation programs for women and children. Members of the Armed Services and Appropriations committees banded together to kill the amendment Sept. 9, arguing that the transfer would violate spending allocations set by the appropriators even though the budget law no longer barred the transfer of funds from defense to domestic programs. *(Vote 253, p. 33-S)*

● By 63-34, an amendment by Paul Simon, D-Ill., authorizing the secretary of the Army to pay the full cost of repairing levees damaged by the summer's floods on the Mississippi and Missouri rivers. Generally, localities were required to pay 20 percent of such costs. *(Vote 264, p. 34-S)*

● By 66-33, an amendment by Domenici to authorize $75 million to develop a reusable rocket that could fly into orbit without using disposable, auxiliary engines. *(Vote 263, p. 34-S)*

The Senate adopted by voice vote the following amendments:

● By McCain to allow retired members of the U.S. armed services to serve in the military of newly democratic nations such as the Baltic Republic of Estonia. The secretaries of Defense and State would have to agree that the state in question was an emerging democracy.

McCain said that Col. Alexander Einseln, an American citizen whose family had fled Estonia during World War II, had been asked by the Estonian government to head its nascent military. Einseln spent 35 years in the Army, serving in the Korean and Vietnam wars.

● Striking a provision of the bill that would have earmarked an annual $20 million grant for the American Metalcasting Consortium. Instead, the bill authorized an additional $10 million for technology reinvestment projects and would direct the Defense secretary to give "serious consideration" to the problems of the U.S. metalcasting industry when deciding how to spend that funding.

● By Ted Stevens, R-Alaska, authorizing $150 million for cargo and VIP planes for the National Guard.

● By Phil Gramm, R-Texas, providing that the Pentagon buy small VIP and cargo planes only by competitive bids.

● By Dole, earmarking $2 million for research on the use of lasers for burn treatment.

● By Dole, requiring the Pentagon to notify school districts with a particularly high concentration of students from local military bases that they were entitled to special federal funds.

● By Robert C. Smith, R-N.H., urging the Navy to award a medal to veterans of the fleet that launched Jimmy Doolittle's 1942 raid on Tokyo.

● By John W. Warner, R-Va., expressing the sense of the Senate that no Iraqi POWs taken during the 1991 Persian Gulf War be admitted to the United States as refugees unless the president certified that they collaborated with the U.S.-led coalition against Iraq and that they committed no war crimes.

● By Smith, providing — in effect — that 11 U.S. military personnel killed in two aircraft accidents on Nov. 30, 1992, whose government life insurance policies had been slated to double in value the following day, be awarded the higher payment. The rationale was that, though the two crashes occurred on the evening of Nov. 30 local time, the day of Dec. 1 had begun as calculated by Greenwich Mean Time — the time zone encompassing the Greenwich Observatory, near London, which was used as a standard time by military forces.

Smith's amendment, which was retroactive, provided that the effective date of changes in GI life insurance policies be determined by the first time zone west of the International Date Line.

HOUSE FLOOR ACTION

The House on Sept. 29 passed a $263 billion version of the bill by a vote of 268-162. (Vote 474, p. 116-H)

Chairman Dellums of the Armed Services Committee voted "yea" on a defense bill for the first time in his 23 years in the House.

The bill included language identical to that in the Senate version to codify the military's ban on gay personnel. The provision, sponsored by Ike Skelton, D-Mo., was adopted by the House on a vote of 301-134. (Vote 462, p. 112-H)

It rejected 144-291 an amendment by Hunter that would have made the ban tougher by ordering the Pentagon to resume the practice — suspended by Clinton in January — of asking recruits to disclose whether they were homosexual. (Vote 461, p. 112-H)

Also rejected, by a vote of 169-264, was an amendment backed by opponents of the gay ban. Like a similar amendment that was rejected in the Senate, it would have deleted from the defense bill any reference to the issue, explicitly leaving the policy in the hands of the president. (Vote 460, p. 112-H)

Votes on Intervention

The House also debated a number of amendments that reflected congressional concern about the budgetary costs and military risks of growing U.S. involvement in international peacekeeping missions.

Reflecting widespread congressional frustration over the continued deployment of U.S. troops in Somalia, the House on Sept. 28 added to the defense bill a non-binding amendment requesting that Clinton obtain congressional authorization by Nov. 15 if he wanted to continue the deployment in Somalia. The resolution was adopted 406-26. (Vote 463, p. 112-H)

Just before the bill was passed, Republicans offered a motion to recommit the measure to the Armed Services Committee with instructions that it add a provision to limit future deployments of U.S. troops under foreign commanders. The provision would have allowed such an operation only if the president certified to Congress 30 days in advance that such a deployment would protect vital U.S. security interests and accompanied that certification with a detailed report on the size, cost and withdrawal timetable for the U.S. force.

The motion was rejected 192-238. (Vote 473, p. 116-H)

In previous debate on the bill, Republicans on Sept. 13 spearheaded the defeat of two amendments that would have provided defense funds for peacekeeping efforts.

The first would have set aside $30 million as a "Defense Response Fund" to cover the cost of deploying U.S. forces for international peacekeeping operations, foreign disaster relief or other unforeseen missions requiring large-scale action on short notice. The amendment, by Sisisky, was rejected 199-211. (Vote 426, p. 104-H)

A second amendment by Sisisky would have earmarked $10 million to create a U.N. peacekeeping command post and to train other nations' troops in peacekeeping operations. It also would have set aside $23 million for efforts to instill deference to civil authority in the military personnel of emerging democracies. That amendment was rejected 199-210. (Vote 427, p. 104-H)

Strategic Defense

The House stuck with the $3 billion in funding for antimissile defenses — including the separate but related funding for the Brilliant Eyes satellite — that the Armed Services Committee had approved. Lawmakers rejected two liberal amendments to cut deeper and a conservative effort to match the Senate Armed Services Committee's recommended figure of $3.46 billion, including the funding for Brilliant Eyes.

The deepest cut, to $1.5 billion, was proposed by Dellums, demonstrating that he had not abandoned the liberal views of his Berkeley constituents. Dellums' amendment was defeated 160-272. (Vote 412, p. 100-H)

An amendment by Schroeder to cut missile defense funding by $229 million, shifting the funds to defense conversion efforts, failed more narrowly, 202-227. (Vote 414, p. 100-H)

Republicans fared no better. The House soundly rejected, 118-312, an amendment by Joel Hefley, R-Colo., that would have increased the funding to the level sought by Senate Armed Services. (Vote 413, p. 100-H)

Top Concerns

House action also focused on:

● **Trident II missiles.** Members seeking to cut funding for Trident II missiles questioned the need to buy more strategic ballistic missiles that were originally designed to destroy "hard targets" such as missile silos and bunkers deep in the former Soviet Union.

Dellums offered an amendment to eliminate $1.1 billion for the procurement of the missile after fiscal 1993, with half of the savings going to defense conversion programs. "The Cold War is over," he said. "To talk about fighting a nuclear war is madness."

Opponents, led by ranking committee Republican Spence, countered that canceling plans for new Trident II missiles would force a choice between two unacceptable options: "One, send submarines to sea with empty launch tubes, or two, conduct costly modifications to the new Atlantic Ocean Trident submarines so as to permit them to employ the aging and less capable C-4 missile."

Dellums' amendment was rejected 183-240. Also rejected, 188-240, was an amendment by Neil Abercrombie, D-Hawaii, to eliminate funding for the missiles after fiscal 1994. (Vote 415, p. 100-H; vote 416, p. 102-H)

The House adopted by voice vote an amendment by Norm Dicks, D-Wash., to allow older Trident I submarines to be fitted with the new missiles and direct the Defense Department to study that option.

● **Defense conversion.** Many Democrats pushed to expand funding for programs to help businesses and workers convert from defense to civilian work, while many Republicans complained of big-government solutions to economic problems.

Spence argued that defense conversion "has come to mean too many things to too many people," resulting in "today's grab bag of unfocused conversion programs covering the spectrum from job retraining to health care, from community assistance to dual-use technologies."

With Spence's backing, Hansen offered an amendment to transfer $40 million from the Pentagon's conversion programs for industry to its Office of Economic Adjustment, which helped communities absorb the blow of losing military bases. The amendment failed, 171-251. *(Vote 421, p. 102-H)*

Also rejected, 151-261, was an amendment by Robert S. Walker, R-Pa., to reduce the Defense Technology Reinvestment Grant program by $300 million to $275 million. *(Vote 423, p. 102-H)*

Adopted, however, was an amendment banning the use of conversion funds to finance foreign arms sales. The measure, sponsored by Thomas H. Andrews, D-Maine, passed, 256-160. *(Vote 422, p. 102-H)*

● **'Burden sharing.'** As in previous years, the House debated "burden sharing" amendments that sought to force allies to contribute more toward the cost of U.S. troops stationed abroad.

"It is clear that the most widely read book in Western Europe is 'Tom Sawyer,'" said Barney Frank, D-Mass. "Not only have we been painting their fences, we pay for the privilege of doing it."

The administration opposed Frank's amendment, which would have cut funding for U.S. forces in Europe by $1 billion, reducing troop levels unless allies picked up the tab. In a joint letter to Congress, Aspin and Secretary of State Warren Christopher warned that such measures would "force the withdrawal of U.S. troops from Europe and with them would go our leadership position in European affairs."

Frank's amendment was narrowly rejected, 210-216. Also rejected, 195-231, was an amendment by John Bryant, D-Texas, to withdraw all U.S. troops from NATO countries, Japan and Korea unless those countries assumed the costs of stationing them abroad by the end of fiscal 1996. *(Votes 417, 420, p. 102-H)*

But the House adopted, 424-0, an amendment by Marilyn Lloyd, D-Tenn., to reduce operating and maintenance funding for overseas bases by $580 million. And members adopted, 286-137, an amendment by Schroeder requiring the 1995 Base Closure and Realignment Commission to include foreign bases in its closure recommendations. *(Votes 418, 419, p. 102-H)*

Other Amendments

In other action, the House rejected 149-263 an amendment by Hunter that would have reduced by $300 million the amount earmarked to help dismantle the former Soviet Union's nuclear arsenal. The funds would have been added to the amounts authorized for the services' maintenance budgets. *(Vote 429, p. 104-H)*

By a vote of 156-256, the House rejected an amendment by David E. Bonior, D-Mich., that would have granted certain employee rights to civilian technicians in the National Guard. *(Vote 428, p. 104-H)*

FINAL ACTION

The final version of the bill authorized $261 billion for defense programs of the Pentagon and Energy Department in fiscal 1994, cutting $2.6 billion from Clinton's budget request.

The House adopted the conference report Nov. 15 by a vote of 273-135; the Senate approved it Nov. 17 by a vote of 77-22, thus completing action on the bill. *(House vote 565, p. 138-H; Senate vote 380, p. 49-S)*

Debating Cuts

The House-Senate conference committee on the bill, which completed its work Nov. 5, did not have to address the emotional issue of homosexuals in the military because the chambers had passed bills with identical language codifying the longstanding ban on gay military personnel.

But the mostly pro-Pentagon members of the Armed Services Committee had the uncomfortable task of cutting Clinton's request even though they generally argued that the president already was cutting defense too deeply.

In large measure, the cuts in the bill resulted from a technical disagreement between CBO and the Office of Management and Budget over how to estimate the fiscal 1994 outlays that would result from Clinton's defense budget request.

The upshot was that the conferees had to slice the defense bill's projected outlays by $2 billion from the level Congress had approved in its annual budget resolution.

Beyond the reductions forced by that esoteric dispute, some Republicans and centrist Democrats warned that defense spending was being cut too much by the bill — and by Clinton's long-range defense plan, on which the bill was to be a first installment.

The conference report on the measure conveyed a warning on that score from many Republicans and centrist Democrats on the Armed Services committees. It came in the form of a provision barring any further reduction in the Army's personnel ceiling below the level of 540,000 set by the bill. Though the administration had not announced how much more it planned to cut the Army, there were reports that its goal was a force of about 500,000 soldiers.

The conference provision was sponsored by Skelton, chairman of the House Armed Services Subcommittee on Military Forces and Personnel. In an unusual move, Skelton set the stage by holding a hearing on Army manpower levels Oct. 27, in the midst of conference negotiations on the authorization bill.

He warned that the Clinton team's plan would leave the Army too small to meet the administration's standard of being able to fight two "nearly simultaneous" major regional wars in areas such as the Persian Gulf and Korea. The shortfall was exacerbated, he argued, by the increasing commitment of Army units to peacekeeping deployments.

In an unusual display of political solidarity, senior members of the House Defense Appropriations Subcommittee joined Armed Services members at Skelton's hearing to inveigh against cuts in the Army roster.

Administration officials insisted that Skelton was too pessimistic. A second war likely would not start for "several weeks" after the first one, they argued, allowing time to shift forces and to mobilize National Guard and reserve units.

They also contended that neither Iraq, North Korea nor any other plausible enemy could field a force by 1999 that was as powerful as Iraq's army had been in 1991. And dramatic increases in the number of fast cargo ships and in the amount of U.S. combat gear stored near potential hot spots since the Persian Gulf War would let the Pentagon get a larger force to the scene in a shorter time.

When the conference report came to the Senate floor

for approval, Armed Services Committee Chairman Nunn warned, "Readiness ... is beginning to be threatened by disproportionate cuts in the defense budget. We must either adjust our defense resources or our expectations of what our military will be able to do because the two are going in opposite directions."

Senate Minority Leader Dole carried his objections one step further, casting what he acknowledged would be a symbolic vote against the conference report. "This bill codifies a defense plan that is ... both inadequate and dangerous," he said, "... especially when the administration seeks to expand America's military involvement ... in these so-called peacekeeping and nation-building efforts."

Bill Summary

The final bill supported — or made only minor reductions in — the major elements of Clinton's budget request, including funding three new Navy destroyers ($2.8 billion) and continuing development of the Army's Comanche helicopter ($367 million) and the Air Force's F-22 fighter ($2.3

billion).

It authorized $2.8 billion for anti-missile defenses, not including $253 million for the Brilliant Eyes satellite.

For the controversial C-17 cargo jet, the bill left open the possibility of ultimately providing as much as $2.2 billion of the $2.4 billion Clinton requested to buy six of the planes. However, the bill earmarked only $1.9 billion exclusively for C-17s, enough to buy four planes.

An additional $300 million could go to buy two more C-17s if the program met certain requirements, but otherwise the money would be used to begin buying another wide-body, long-range cargo jet.

In either case, the bill authorized $100 million to start work on a modified version of a wide-body jet as a potential competitor to the C-17.

The bill authorized $2.55 billion for defense conversion efforts; a ceiling on active-duty personnel of 1,623,500; a ceiling on National Guard and reserve units of 1,039,400, a reduction of 55,580; a 2.2 percent increase in military pay; and $87.4 billion for operations and maintenance. ∎

Defense Authorization Provisions

HR 2401 (PL 103-160) authorized $261 billion in defense spending for fiscal 1994. Following are the bill's major provisions, including comparisons with President Clinton's budget request and with the versions of the bill passed by the House and Senate:

Economic Conversion

The bill authorized $2.55 billion for programs aimed at helping government and private sector defense workers, defense contractors and their communities adapt to a long-term retrenchment in defense spending.

The lion's share ($2.22 billion) was to help defense firms reorient themselves toward finding commercial markets. This included $624 million — $300 million more than Clinton requested — for "dual use" partnerships to help small- and medium-size firms develop technologies that had military applications but also could give companies a foothold in the commercial arena.

The bill also included $197 million to help domestic shipbuilding companies become competitive in the construction of commercial ships. And it had several provisions intended to speed the search for new job-producing uses for abandoned military bases.

Personnel Policy

Clinton recommended a ceiling of 1.62 million active-duty personnel in fiscal 1994, a reduction of 107,700 from the fiscal 1993 ceiling. Each chamber approved a slightly smaller cut, and the conferees agreed on a ceiling of 1,623,500, which allowed the services to keep 2,900 more members on the rolls than Clinton proposed.

Rejecting Clinton's call for a freeze on all federal pay in fiscal 1994, both chambers approved a 2.2 percent military pay raise to take effect Jan. 1, 1994.

Reconciling minor differences between the Senate and House, the conference report extended the Pentagon's expiring authorization to pay various bonuses intended to encourage the enlistment or re-enlistment of personnel in certain essential job specialities.

The conference report also expanded the pool of service members eligible to receive either a lump-sum payment or a multiyear annuity if they left the service after completing more than 15 years of duty but less than the 20 years that was needed to qualify for a military pension.

Both versions of the bill had backed Clinton's proposal to repeal the statutory ban on assigning women to combat vessels. The conference report also required the Pentagon to give Congress 90 days' notice before announcing a change in the ban on assigning women to ground combat units and 30 days' notice before opening to women any combat unit or ship from which they had been barred.

Navy Secretary John Dalton told reporters Dec. 1 that in 1994 the service would put 400 to 500 women — 8 percent of the crew — on each of three aircraft carriers.

The bill added to Clinton's research and development request $20 million to establish a center for medical research related to women in the services. Another provision expanded the definition of medical services to which women in the military and female dependents were entitled to include mammograms, treatment for pregnancy and infertility and other gynecological procedures.

The conferees rejected a Senate provision earmarking $2 million to study the claims of some veterans that they might have been exposed to chemical or biological weapons during the Persian Gulf War in 1991. Although insisting they did not take those claims lightly, the conferees contended it would be unwise to focus on suspected chemical and biological weapons effects while ignoring the possibility that the symptoms resulted from the troops' exposure to other toxic substances, such as the pervasive smoke from thousands of sabotaged oil wells in Kuwait.

Following the lead of the House, the conference report included $1.2 million to study the possible health effects on gulf war veterans of exposure to low levels of oil smoke and other chemicals. The report also included $1.7 million for a five-year-study of the medical effects of contact with depleted uranium "darts" fired by U.S. tank guns. The mildly radioactive metal was used because its great density helped penetrate enemy tank armor.

Both versions of the bill included a provision sealing into law, with only slight modifications, the Pentagon's longtime ban on homosexual conduct by military personnel. The definition of "conduct" was sufficiently broad to include the private disclosure to a friend of one's homosexual orientation.

Guard and Reserves

The conference report trimmed 55,580 members from National Guard and reserve units, setting the ceiling at 1,039,400. Clinton

had proposed a cut of nearly 68,000.

The bill did not include two Clinton proposals intended to make it easier to mobilize Guard and reserve units in conflicts short of all-out war. The proposed provisions would have:

• Increased from 180 days to 360 days the period for which the president could mobilize up to 200,000 Guard and reserve personnel without having to declare a state of national emergency.

• Allowed the president to delegate to the secretary of Defense authority to call up as many as 25,000 people.

The conferees balked at expanding the president's call-up authority without first studying the impact of any change on employers' support for the reserves.

The bill authorized $990 million, not requested by the administration, for equipment to be allocated to Guard and reserve units.

The conferees accepted a House provision ordering the Army to test a new approach to the "round-out" policy that used National Guard units to bolster active-duty combat forces. In several active-duty Army divisions, a Guard brigade had been designated since the mid-1970s as one of the three brigades forming the unit. But when three of these divisions were deployed to the Persian Gulf in 1991, they left behind the round-out brigades, contending they were not ready for combat.

The conferees ordered the Army to test the round-out idea on a smaller scale, by assigning a Guard unit as one of the three battalions — each with several hundred members — in an active-duty brigade and assigning a Guard company as one of the several companies constituting some active-duty battalions.

To further bolster the combat-readiness of Guard and reserve units, the bill included provisions requiring the Army to:

• Establish two units to provide training support to reserve forces.

• Demonstrate, in effect, that active-duty officers assigned to duties in support of the reserves had at least as good a chance of promotion as officers assigned to other duties.

The bill also elevated the status of the Army Reserve Command in the Army's hierarchy. And it required the secretary of Defense to report to Congress on Air Force plans to turn over some B-1 bombers to Air National Guard and Air Force Reserve units.

Operations and Maintenance

The $87.4 billion authorization for operations and maintenance programs was $2.1 billion less than Clinton's request. As usual, the conferees added funds intended to boost the combat-readiness of forces in the field, including:

• $300 million for major overhauls of ships, planes and vehicles in military depots;

• $500 million to increase the forces' operating tempo, boosting the amount of time spent training; and

• $100 million to accelerate the return to U.S. bases of equipment in Europe.

But those additions to Clinton's budget request were more than offset by reductions. As always, the conferees made hundreds of millions of dollars' worth of cuts that, they contended, reflected economic changes and thus would not affect Pentagon operations. These reductions included:

• $289 million because of declining fuel prices;

• $232 million because of vacancies in the Pentagon's civilian work force; and

• $400 million because U.S. units stationed abroad would not have to spend as much as anticipated to buy local supplies and services due to the dollar's increasing value compared with foreign currencies.

The bill ordered the Pentagon to spend nearly $600 million less than the $17.5 billion it requested to operate overseas bases. The withheld funds were to be channeled instead toward covering the operating costs of bases in the United States. However, the secretary of Defense could waive this requirement if he gave Congress 15 days' notice.

The provision was intended to beef up the administration's effort to get host countries to pick up a larger share of the cost of stationing U.S. forces abroad.

Another section of the bill was intended to reduce the pressure on the services to skimp on training and maintenance in order to fund unanticipated operations such as the deployment of forces to Somalia. This provision let the Pentagon designate such missions as "national contingency operations," thus exempting the services from having to reimburse other Pentagon agencies for transportation, supplies and services worth up to $300 million.

In such cases, however, the secretary of Defense was required to submit a plan to pay the deferred costs through reprogramming, supplemental appropriations or allied contributions.

The bill also authorized:

• $400 million, as requested, to help Russia and its neighbors dismantle the former Soviet nuclear arsenal and

• $1.96 billion to clean up toxic and hazardous waste on current or former military bases. This was $347 million less than Clinton requested.

Strategic and Nuclear Weapons

Both chambers approved Clinton's request for $604 million in procurement funds related to the 20 B-2 stealth bombers that were previously authorized.

Congress had previously barred the Air Force from paying for the last five planes until the Pentagon certified that prototypes had passed certain tests. That certification was made, and the conference report lifted the restriction. But it also reaffirmed the statutory provisions allowing deployment of no more than 20 B-2s at a total cost of no more than $29 billion in fiscal 1981 dollars.

The conferees had to reconcile diametrically opposite approaches to equipping the long-range bomber fleet for non-nuclear missions. The House insisted that the older B-1s be modified, while the Senate insisted the upgrades be limited, at least initially, to the B-2.

At issue were two types of bombs designed to be dropped from high altitudes and to use extremely precise data from satellites to steer themselves toward preselected targets. In contrast to many "smart" bombs used during the 1991 war with Iraq, the new systems would not require that a laser be kept trained on the target by the bomber pilot.

While imposing a variety of funding restrictions, the conference report authorized the Air Force to equip the B-2 with the first of the new bombs — an interim system designated GATS/GAM — and to test the feasibility of installing that system on the B-1. The report also authorized modifying the B-1 to carry the second, more sophisticated system, designated JDAM, which was originally intended for B-2s.

The bill also included a provision requiring the Air Force to test under realistic conditions its claim that B-1 squadrons could keep 75 percent of their planes mission-ready for several months, provided they were given larger stocks of spare parts and maintenance equipment.

Both Armed Services committees had approved the $983 million requested for 24 additional Trident II submarine-launched missiles. The conferees also approved the $145 million requested for components that would be used in missiles requested in future budgets. The Senate had recommended an additional $25 million for these "long lead time" components to provide the option of accelerating missile production.

The conferees accepted a modified form of a House provision requiring the Pentagon to report on alternative ways of meeting a limit on sub-launched missile warheads that would be set by the U.S.-Russian START II arms control treaty, which awaited ratification.

To meet the limit, the Pentagon planned to deploy Trident IIs carrying only four warheads apiece, instead of the eight they could carry. Some critics favored buying fewer missiles but loading them with eight warheads.

Reflecting Clinton's decision to continue a moratorium on underground nuclear tests, the bill authorized only $211 million of the $428 million requested to keep the nuclear testing infrastruc-

ture ready to resume testing. The measure also ended a 30-year-old program intended to preserve the capability of testing nuclear weapons in the atmosphere.

Anti-Missile and Space Programs

The bill authorized $2.8 billion of the $3.8 billion requested for anti-missile defenses being developed by the Ballistic Missile Defense program, previously called the Strategic Defense Initiative.

The $2.8 billion did not include $253 million requested to develop the Brilliant Eyes satellite, intended to detect and track incoming missiles. The conferees treated this issue separately.

The $2.8 billion included:
- $1.45 billion to develop defenses against relatively short-range (theater) ballistic missiles, such as the Soviet-designed Scuds fired by Iraq in 1991;
- $121 million to buy Patriot missiles modified to intercept theater missiles;
- $650 million to develop a system to defend U.S. territory against a small number of missile warheads; and
- $538 million to develop more sophisticated defenses for possible future deployment and to cover overhead costs.

The bill also ordered the administration to determine whether several key anti-theater missile devices were consistent with the 1972 U.S.-Soviet treaty limiting anti-ballistic missile (ABM) systems.

Weeks after the conferees wrote that provision, the administration reportedly proposed easing ABM Treaty standards to allow tests of an anti-theater missile designated THAAD. Arms control advocates warned that the new standard would dangerously blur the line between permitted and prohibited weapons.

In their report, conferees complained that the anti-missile effort remained too unfocused: "Future program plans, timetables for deployment, testing plans and missile defense architectures are incompletely defined, providing little basis thus far for congressional support of higher funding levels," they said.

Separate from the Ballistic Missile Defense budget, the conferees approved $3.8 million requested by the Air Force to test the effectiveness of laser-armed airplanes to intercept theater missiles.

The bill authorized $10 million to develop an anti-satellite weapon. However, the companion defense appropriations bill denied the funds.

For the Brilliant Eyes satellite, the conference report combined that request with three other programs to develop and procure missile attack warning systems for which the administration had requested a total of $1.05 billion. The conferees authorized $802 million, which the Pentagon was permitted to allocate among the four programs.

The bill authorized $1 billion to develop and purchase satellite launch rockets: $801 million, as requested, for the large Titan IVs and $202 million — $2 million less than was requested — for the smaller Atlas IIs and Delta IIs.

But the conferees turned a skeptical eye toward Pentagon plans to develop an array of future launch vehicles. "The administration must stop trying to keep multiple space launch programs alive despite ever dwindling resources," they complained. "The administration must focus scarce resources to achieve any success at all."

The bill authorized:
- None of the $54 million requested for a "National Launch System" for heavy payloads.
- None of the $43 million requested to continue developing an experimental prototype of a hypersonic "aerospace plane" designed to take off like an airplane and soar into orbit. Instead, the bill provided $40 million to experiment with hypersonic technology, but without building the so-called X-plane.
- $35 million for "space launch modernization," including the $5 million requested to develop a single-stage, reusable launch vehicle.

Ground Combat

To accelerate modernization of early model M-1 tanks into "A2" models, with larger cannons and nightvision electronics, the

bill authorized $97 million for the program instead of the $80 million requested.

The conferees also approved the $192 million requested to begin upgrading early model Bradley armored troop carriers. But they rejected a House initiative to add $33 million to the bill to develop still more sophisticated electronics for the Bradley.

As requested, the bill authorized $8 million to continue buying a small number of lightweight tanks for air-mobile Army divisions.

It added to the request $150 million for 10 Apache missile-armed attack helicopters, intended to keep that production line humming until its scheduled use for a major upgrade of the Apache fleet.

The bill also authorized:
- $278 million to continue developing the Longbow modification, a program to equip Apaches with target-finding radar;
- $258 million to modernize 18 scout helicopters with missiles and target-finding electronics; and
- $367 million to continue developing the new Comanche scout helicopter.

Both chambers had added to the bill funds to accelerate the Army's plan to achieve "horizontal integration" of combat units by digital data links that could transmit among its units information about the location of both U.S. and enemy units.

In the final bill, the conferees approved $8 million for the project. But they complained that the Army's plan would install the data links only in several thousand tanks, armored troop carriers and attack helicopters, and only gradually, as part of more extensive upgrades of those vehicles that were scheduled to stretch well into the next century.

Citing the importance of such equipment to prevent accidental "friendly fire" attacks by U.S. units against their own side, the conferees urged the Army to install the data links in all air and land vehicles likely to wind up near the front lines and to complete the project in half the planned time.

The bill authorized $547 million of the $629 million requested to develop and gear up for production of a 300-mile-range stealth missile designated TSSAM, canceling the Army's participation in the triservice project. But the conferees approved $146 million — only $7 million less than requested — to continue production of the ATACMS bombardment missile, with a range of less than 100 miles.

They rejected the Army's plan to shut down for two years the production line for smaller, 20-mile-range MLRS rockets and then reopen the line to build a longer-range version of those missiles. To keep the factory running — and thus, the conferees argued, to save money in the long run — they added $45 million to buy 12,000 additional rockets.

The conference report authorized $110 million of the $117 million requested to continue developing BAT warheads, intended to be scattered from TSSAM, ATACMS and MLRS missiles and to home in on enemy tanks.

Rather than the $282 million requested for a single JSTARS radar-plane, the bill authorized $477 million for two of the converted jetliners, intended to find targets for bombardment rockets far behind enemy lines.

To modernize the Army's artillery, the bill authorized:
- $172 million, as requested, to upgrade existing self-propelled cannons;
- $19 million, as recommended by the House, to equip those artillery vehicles with a cannon that could shoot much farther; and
- $148 million, as requested, to develop a new self-propelled cannon and an armored ammunition carrier to accompany it.

Tactical Air Combat

On the blueprint to develop a new generation of combat jets for the Navy and Air Force, the House and Senate versions of the bill agreed with the administration. The bill authorized:
- $2.25 billion to continue development of the Air Force's F-22 fighter, intended to supplant the 1970s-vintage F-15 as the service's most sophisticated fighter. The conferees dropped $50 mil-

lion the Senate had added to begin work on a variation of the F-22 to operate from aircraft carriers.

● $1.46 billion, only $27 million less than requested, to develop enlarged "E" and "F" models of the Navy's F/A-18. The new planes were to replace aging A-6E carrier-based bombers, though they could not fly as far.

● None of the $399 million requested to develop the stealthy, carrier-based A/F-X, which the Navy had planned as a replacement for the A-6E. The Clinton administration scrapped this project midyear.

In the effort to keep U.S. air squadrons up to date for the following 10 to 15 years, before new planes entered service in large numbers, the conferees approved:

● $400 million for 12 Air Force F-16s plus $71 million to terminate that contract. This was half the number requested, but the administration had planned to buy no more after fiscal 1994.

● $1.49 billion for 36 of the current model F/A-18s, as requested, plus $113 million for components to be used in future production, a cut of $139 million from the request.

● $130 million, as requested, to refurbish and upgrade four Harrier vertical takeoff jets, used by the Marines as a bomber.

The administration had requested $188 million to upgrade the Navy's F-14 fighter. But the conferees approved $315 million for that project and ordered the Navy to reorient the program so that at least some of the F-14s — which could fly farther than the enlarged F/A-18 models that were being developed — could attack ground targets with "smart" bombs.

Naval Combat

The bill authorized $2.64 billion, as requested, for three *Arleigh Burke*-class destroyers, equipped with the Aegis long-range anti-aircraft system. It provided $373 million — $19 million more than requested — for a program intended to link the radars of several types of ships and aircraft so a fleet could protect itself more effectively against high-speed missiles.

The conferees turned down a House initiative that would have added to the bill $20 million to test a large blimp as an airborne radar station that could detect approaching missiles much sooner than ship-borne radars. But the conference report urged the Navy to study how a radar blimp might fit into the new fleet radar network.

To provide the teeth for fleet air defense, the bill approved, as requested, $215 million for 220 Standard long-range missiles and $58 million for 240 short-range RAM missiles.

The bill authorized $25 million — $7.5 million more than requested — to test methods of equipping warships with either guns or missiles that could bombard distant shore targets to support ground troops. One option being studied was equipping ships to launch Army ATACMS missiles.

The bill authorized $240 million, as requested, to develop a new nuclear submarine, designated *Centurion*, which was intended to be less expensive than the two *Seawolf*-class ships under construction. The administration planned to buy only one more *Seawolf* because of the ship's high cost.

The conference report adopted some House initiatives intended to accelerate a change in focus of the Navy's sub-hunting efforts from finding Soviet nuclear-powered subs in the ocean depths to finding the smaller, non-nuclear-powered subs operated by other countries in relatively shallow water.

In some respects, the new problem was more complex: Modern conventional subs running submerged on battery power were quieter than some nuclear ships. And shallow seas often had high levels of background noise.

Following the House's lead, the bill included $50 million to adapt for existing *Los Angeles*-class subs a sonar system designed for the new *Seawolf* class.

It also added to the budget $10 million to test the ability of powerful computers to make existing sonars on some older ships more effective in detecting subs in shallow water.

But the bill authorized $125 million of the $134 million requested to develop a portable network of listening gear that could be deployed quickly near a distant trouble spot. The reduction was intended to slow the project pending the completion of certain tests.

The conferees approved $100 million requested for large Mark 48 homing torpedoes, carried by submarines. But they also added $21 million to begin adapting for shallow water operation the smaller Mark 46 homing torpedoes that were already in the inventory.

Air and Sea Transport

Clinton requested $2.32 billion for six C-17 long-range cargo jets. The conference report authorized that amount and stipulated that it could be used to buy as many as six C-17s. But that would happen only if the trouble-plagued plane satisfied certain schedule and testing requirements.

In any case, the bill required the Air Force to come up with an "off-the-shelf" alternative — either modified commercial cargo jets or newly built Air Force C-5 planes — that could replace some of the 120 C-17s that were planned. Later, Defense Secretary Les Aspin announced that the Pentagon was considering buying only 40 C-17s.

Specifically, the bill approved:

● $1.9 billion for four C-17s.

● $100 million to buy alternative planes.

● $300 million that could be used either for two additional C-17s or for additional alternative planes.

The bill also authorized the $894 million requested for a helicopter carrier the size of a medium-size aircraft carrier. The ship was designed to carry 2,000 Marines plus helicopters and barges to haul them ashore. ∎

Budgetary Flak Downs the A/F-X

The Clinton administration and the Appropriations and Armed Services committees of the House and Senate agreed in 1993 on the basic outline of a pared-down program to develop a new generation of combat planes for the Navy and Air Force.

Despite the broad accord, there were lingering differences over the specific goals and funding of some of the programs. And the agreement came only after Congress prodded the new administration to begin making some tough choices.

That pressure contributed to the Pentagon's decision to abandon plans for a new carrier-based stealth bomber that would have been called the A/F-X.

BACKGROUND

Officially, Pentagon plans inherited by the Clinton administration at the start of 1993 called for spending more than $150 billion over the next 20 years — and tens of billions more thereafter — to buy more than 4,000 new combat planes.

The menu of planned aircraft ranged from enlarged versions of existing F/A-18s to the futuristic A/F-X attack plane that was still on the drawing boards.

But most defense specialists across the political spectrum contended that these planes were too expensive for the shrinking defense budgets that were in prospect after the Cold War.

Some critics argued that the Pentagon was pushing too hard at the frontiers of combat aircraft technology, considering that no opponent was on the horizon who could rival the prowess displayed by U.S. air squadrons during the 1991 war with Iraq. In particular, some skeptics questioned the price the Pentagon was willing to pay for planes that were "stealthy" — built of expensive and exotic materials and with carefully calibrated contours so that they would be hard to spot and shoot down.

The military services responded that they needed to develop the planes that they would buy in 10 years and fly for 20. Given the rapid proliferation of high-technology equipment, they warned, it would be dangerous to count on maintaining the U.S. advantages in air power without such new aircraft.

"Sophisticated weapons are available for sale ... to anyone with the hard currency to pay for them," Adm. David Jeremiah, Joint Chiefs of Staff vice chairman, told the Senate Armed Services Committee on June 11.

Competing Service Plans

There was also debate over the competing — and some said redundant — plans of the various services. As the Cold War was ending in 1990, the Air Force and Navy had different needs to fill in their modernization programs.

The Air Force was equipped with the "high-end" F-15 fighter; the smaller, much less expensive F-16 that could be used as either a fighter or an attack plane; and three types of long-range attack planes packed with target-finding electronics for "all-weather" combat: the F-15E, the stealthy F-117 and the Vietnam War-era F-111.

The Air Force's priority was to develop a top-of-the-line fighter that would give U.S. pilots early in the 21st century the unquestioned aerial supremacy that the F-15 guaran-

teed at the start of the 1990s. In particular, the Air Force wanted to stay ahead of Soviet fighters that were expected to come off the drawing boards and go into the international marketplace.

The Navy, too, already had a high-end fighter — the F-14, with its powerful radar and long-range Phoenix missiles, designed to fend off swarms of Soviet anti-ship missiles. It also had a smaller "swing" fighter, the F/A-18, designed to handle both fighter and attack missions. And it had a major, imminent problem: the aging A-6Es that made up its force of long-range, all-weather attack planes.

The wings of these 1970s-vintage planes literally were wearing out, requiring a costly and technically difficult effort to replace them. More fundamentally, the design, dating from the late 1950s, made the plane relatively slow and anything but stealthy, compared with other front-line jets.

By the mid-1990s, each branch intended to have a new plane ready to enter service. The Air Force held a competition between two advanced fighters, picking the Lockheed F-22 in 1991. The Navy was committed to the McDonnell Douglas Corp.'s A-12, a stealthy "flying wing" design, reminiscent of the larger B-2 stealth bomber.

Bush Cancels A-12

That plan started to come apart on Jan. 7, 1991, when Defense Secretary Dick Cheney canceled the A-12, citing rising costs, slipping schedules and technical difficulties with the design. *(1991 Almanac, p. 431)*

The Bush administration's fiscal 1993 defense budget, sent to Capitol Hill a year later, included a four-part tactical air modernization program:

● The Air Force would continue with the F-22, though at a slower pace.

● In lieu of the A-12, the Navy would solicit contractors' proposals for an attack plane with a shorter range and a smaller bomb load. This project would come to be designated the A/F-X.

● Because the A/F-X would enter service more than a decade after the planned deployment of the A-12, the Navy would buy an enlarged version of the F/A-18 — the "E" and "F" models — to fill the spots on carrier decks as A-6Es and F-14s wore out.

● And sometime before 2010, the Air Force would choose a Multi-Role Fighter, a relatively inexpensive plane to replace F-16s.

While the total cost of all four programs would be a fraction of projected defense budgets, the Senate and House Armed Services and Appropriations committees objected that the Bush plan would require that tactical aircraft programs be allocated a much larger share of annual budgets than had been the norm.

To underscore these warnings, Congress ordered Cheney to conduct studies about the expected weapons cost crunch. But lawmakers also shied away from the tough decisions themselves, making only relatively minor cuts in the funds requested for the F-22, A/F-X, and F/A-18 E and F. *(1992 Almanac, p. 506)*

Clinton's Request

The fiscal 1994 Pentagon request that President Clinton sent to Congress on March 27 essentially continued the

Bush plan for combat aircraft, earmarking $4.1 billion to develop the new planes.

Clinton's budget requested $2.25 billion to develop the F-22 fighter for the Air Force as a replacement for the 1970s-vintage F-15. It also requested $1.49 billion to develop the Navy's F/A-18 E and F. And it sought $188 million to upgrade the F-14, partly to adapt the plane as an interim replacement for the A-6E.

The budget request also included $399 million for the new A/F-X.

Clinton's plan included two changes made by Bush at the last minute: It dropped the Air Force's Multi-Role Fighter, and it accelerated the timetable for retiring A-6Es, slating the last squadron to leave service in 1999. To provide the carriers with long-range attack planes on an interim basis, the plan was to begin equipping F-14s for ground attack.

The administration's failure to cut back the services' array of combat aircraft caused grumbling in Congress when Defense Secretary Les Aspin appeared before the House and Senate Armed Services Committees the week of March 29.

With characteristic candor, Aspin had told reporters that the administration was "treading water" on the combat planes and other key defense issues until the completion of a comprehensive "bottom-up review" of defense policy. (Bottom-up review, p. 452)

Ronald V. Dellums, D-Calif., who succeeded Aspin as House Armed Services chairman, singled out the plans to build or develop five types of Navy and Air Force combat jets. "These programs together are widely known to cost more than could have been afforded even within the Bush budget," Dellums said. "Two or three . . . are unlikely to survive the bottom-up review in their current form."

Though Dellums was among the most energetic congressional proponents of deeper defense cuts, his point was echoed by more conservative members, such as House committee member Dave McCurdy, D-Okla., and Senate Armed Services Chairman Sam Nunn, D-Ga.

"I don't think that the Congress is willing to wait on some of the major issues you are reviewing," Nunn told Aspin on April 1, also citing the new combat aircraft as examples.

Aspin promised to try to come up with recommendations, particularly regarding the naval aircraft, before Senate-House conferees concluded action on the fiscal 1994 defense authorization bill.

By June, there were published reports that the Pentagon would recommend canceling the A/F-X and proceeding with the other aircraft. It was a stark turnaround for Aspin.

In 1992, as chairman of House Armed Services, Aspin had argued that a new, long-range attack plane for the Navy was the most urgent priority in tactical air modernization. For fiscal 1993, he had proposed authorizing five times as much for the A/F-X as the Bush administration requested. And he had sought to pay for that increase by cutting the amount authorized for the F/A-18 E and F.

The cancellation of the A/F-X was not formally announced until the release of the bottom-up review on Sept. 1. But lawmakers were well aware of that outcome when they crafted the defense authorization and appropriations bills, leaving out funds for the plane.

LEGISLATIVE ACTION

The House and Senate expressed their priorities for the new generation of combat aircraft in their respective versions of the fiscal 1994 defense authorization bill (HR 2401) and the companion defense appropriations bill (HR 3116.)

Both chambers deleted any funding for the A/F-X, anticipating its cancellation. Both authorized and appropriated essentially the $1.49 billion requested for the F/A-18 E and F.

To develop the Air Force's F-22, the House bills authorized and appropriated the $2.25 billion requested. The Senate authorized the F-22 request — even adding $50 million to develop modifications so that the plane could be operated from aircraft carriers and attack ground targets — but the Senate appropriations bill contained only $1.93 billion for the project.

The House bills authorized $266 million and appropriated $159 million — compared with the $72 million requested — to modify the Navy's F-14s to serve as long-range ground-attack planes to replace some of the aging A-6Es aboard carriers. But the House appropriations bill rejected the $107 million that the administration had sought for a less extensive upgrade of F-14s.

The Senate bills authorized $363 million and appropriated $327 million to accelerate the F-14 modification project.

But the Senate vigorously objected to the administration's request for $725 million to buy one last batch of 24 F-16s for the Air Force, which the House had approved. Senators contended that the Air Force had far more F-16s than it needed for a new era of smaller forces.

The defense authorization bill was approved by the Senate Armed Services Committee in closed session July 23 and by the Senate, 92-7, Sept. 14. The bill was approved by the House Armed Services Committee, 46-9, July 27 and by the House, 268-162, Sept. 29. (Senate vote 265, p. 35-S; House vote 474, p. 116-H)

The defense appropriations bill was approved by the House Appropriations Committee by voice vote Sept. 22 and by the full House, 325-102, Sept. 30. It was approved by the Senate Appropriations Committee by voice vote Oct. 4 and by the Senate by voice vote Oct. 21. (Vote 480, p. 118-H)

Final Action

The final versions of the defense authorization and appropriations bills for fiscal 1994 reflected the fundamentals of the administration's plans for combat planes:

● **A/F-X:** The bills provided no funds for the A/F-X. The administration had canceled the project.

● **F-22:** The authorization bill backed the administration's full $2.25 billion request to develop the Air Force's F-22 fighter to replace the F-15 as the service's most sophisticated fighter. The appropriations bill funded the F-22 program at $2.09 billion.

Conferees on the authorization bill dropped the $50 million that the Senate had added to begin work on a variation of the F-22 that could operate from aircraft carriers.

● **F/A-18 E and F:** Of the $1.49 billion requested, Congress authorized $1.46 billion and appropriated $1.47 billion to develop the enlarged "E" and "F" versions of the Navy's F/A-18.

● **F-16s:** The final version of the authorization bill approved $400 million for 12 final Air Force F-16s plus $71 million to terminate that contract. This was half the number requested for the last batch.

● **F-14s:** The biggest unresolved difference concerned im-

provements for the Navy's F-14 fighter.

Congress agreed to appropriate the $188 million requested to develop and install modifications to the F-14. But the appropriators objected to the emphasis of the Navy's upgrade program, arguing that it was more important to equip the plane with more powerful engines than to equip it to serve as a bomber.

By contrast, the final defense authorization bill contained $315 million for F-14 upgrades, insisting that the program be focused on equipping the planes — which could fly faster than the enlarged F/A-18s — to drop "smart" bombs.

• **Future plans:** The debate over combat aircraft in 1993 did not directly address two additional planes that were on Pentagon drawing boards as eventual complements to the F-22 and the F/A-18 E and F. One of these was a relatively low-cost fighter to replace the F-16, just as the F-22 was slated to replace the larger F-15. The other plane was a long-range, carrier-based bomber as a full replacement for the A-6E.

The Clinton administration had under consideration a single project (designated JAST) to develop technologies that might serve both purposes. But skeptics, including conferees on the defense authorization bill, expressed concern that a common project might not be feasible in meeting the distinct requirements of the two missions.

The House adopted the conference report on the defense appropriations bill by voice vote Nov. 10. The Senate cleared the bill, 88-9, Nov. 10. *(Vote 368, p. 47-S)*

The House adopted the conference report on the defense authorization bill, 273-135, Nov. 15. The Senate cleared that bill, 77-22, Nov. 17. *(House vote 565, p. 138-H; Senate vote 380, p. 49-S)*

The president signed the appropriations bill (PL 103-139) on Nov. 11 and the authorization bill (PL 103-160) on Nov. 30. ■

Clinton Team Gives SDI New Name and Mission

The Clinton administration renamed the Strategic Defense Initiative, endorsed a less ambitious focus for the anti-missile defense program and dramatically reduced its projected funding.

But the rechristened Ballistic Missile Defense program was not scaled back enough for the Senate. In a floor vote on the fiscal 1994 defense authorization bill (HR 2401, formerly S 1298), senators voted to reduce funding for the program to $2.8 billion, significantly less than the average annual budget of $3.6 billion that Defense Secretary Les Aspin had outlined for the Clinton administration's approach to anti-missile defenses.

The action was also a rebellion against the Senate Armed Services Committee, which had recommended $3.2 billion. The Senate action essentially settled the funding issue; the House-passed bill authorized $2.74 billion, nearly the same amount.

The $2.8 billion in the final version of the defense authorization bill (HR 2401 — PL 103-160) did not include $253 million that was authorized for the satellite known as Brilliant Eyes, which Congress removed from the Ballistic Missile Defense program and placed in a separate funding category.

The fiscal 1994 defense appropriations bill (HR 3116 — PL 103-139) adopted nearly the same funding levels, with $2.64 billion for the Ballistic Missile Defense.

BACKGROUND

President Ronald Reagan founded the Strategic Defense Initiative (SDI) in 1983 with a vision of rendering nuclear missiles "impotent and obsolete." The program's original goal was to deploy a shield of anti-missile defenses, including futuristic space-based weapons, that could make the United States impregnable to an all-out attack by the Soviet Union.

The program was embraced by conservatives as the key to future defense policy, ridiculed by liberals as "Star Wars" and accepted with caveats and some skepticism by many centrists.

Through 1986, most congressional debate over the anti-missile defense program centered on funding, with Congress routinely slicing Reagan's requests but rejecting calls for even deeper cuts that would have limited the effort to laboratory research.

From 1987 to 1991, the SDI debate turned largely on the role of space-based weapons, which conflicted with the 1972 treaty limiting anti-ballistic missile (ABM) systems.

Republican conservatives fought for a network of space-based interceptor missiles that could destroy attacking Soviet weapons in the first few minutes of flight, before they could swamp the defense with multiple warheads and swarms of decoys. But prominent centrist Democrats — such as Senate Armed Services Chairman Sam Nunn, D-Ga., and Aspin, who was then chairman of the House Armed Services Committee — challenged that goal as technically dubious and gratuitously provocative.

The two Democrats proposed a more modest goal of protecting U.S. territory, allies and forces abroad against "limited" missile attacks by a Third World country such as Iraq or a renegade military unit. From 1987 onward, Congress repeatedly insisted that the anti-missile program be subordinated to the ABM Treaty.

Without abandoning the long-term goal of a defense of the continental United States, President George Bush in 1991 made SDI's priority a program called GPALS, or "global protection against limited strikes." It was envisioned as a combination of space-based Brilliant Pebbles missile interceptors and ground-based defensive missiles.

The same year, Congress went further by ordering that SDI be recast to focus on near-term, ground-based defenses and anti-theater (shorter-range) missile programs.

New Stance on SDI Goals, ABM Treaty

In 1993, President Clinton reined in SDI, eliminating large budget increases that Bush had planned for the program. For fiscal 1994, Clinton requested $3.8 billion — including $121 million for procurement — instead of the $6.3 billion that Bush had projected.

Clinton also reshaped the anti-missile work along the lines mandated by Congress in 1991, placing more emphasis on early deployment of ground-based defenses against attacks by a small number of intercontinental-range ballistic missiles or theater missiles.

Aspin announced that he had changed not only the Strategic Defense Initiative's priorities but also its name, which became the Ballistic Missile Defense program.

In another move away from Reagan's vision of the Stra-

tegic Defense Initiative, the Clinton administration told Congress in July that it would not support Reagan's loose interpretation of the ABM Treaty.

The Reagan administration in 1985 had proposed a broad interpretation of the ABM Treaty that would have allowed testing of space-based ABM weapons for SDI. But Congress later blocked the Reagan and Bush administrations from acting on that new interpretation. *(1985 Almanac, p. 132)*

Thomas Graham, the acting director of the Arms Control and Disarmament Agency (ACDA), notified Congress that the Clinton administration would hew to a "traditional" or "narrow" interpretation of the U.S.-Soviet treaty of 1972, which sharply limited the testing and deployment of anti-missile defenses. In a July 13 letter to Senate Foreign Relations Committee Chairman Claiborne Pell, D-R.I., Graham emphasized that the ABM Treaty "prohibits the development, testing and deployment of sea-based, air-based, space-based and mobile land-based ABM systems."

HOUSE ACTION

The Armed Services Subcommittee on Research and Technology approved a version of the defense authorization bill July 23 that recommended cutting Clinton's $3.76 billion anti-missile request to $2.59 billion. Of the $1.2 billion reduction, $253 million resulted from shifting the Brilliant Eyes surveillance satellite project to another program.

The shift of the Brilliant Eyes project reflected the subcommittee's concern that the Pentagon was spending too much on duplicative projects to detect missiles. The panel consolidated requests totaling more than $1 billion for Brilliant Eyes and related programs, then approved $822 million for the combined efforts. The intent was to force the Pentagon to winnow out some of the competing projects.

The subcommittee, chaired by Patricia Schroeder, D-Colo., also included a provision in the bill to dilute the goals of the anti-missile program.

The provision was aimed at a 1991 law, which had declared that the program's goal was to deploy a defense of U.S. territory. That act stipulated, for instance, that the program would seek to deploy a ground-based system in compliance with the ABM Treaty. And it also directed the president to try to negotiate amendments to the treaty to allow testing and deployment of more robust defenses.

The subcommittee recommended changing the goal to require developing only the "option" to deploy a U.S. defense. And it dropped the requirement to seek a loosening of the ABM Treaty.

When the bill reached the full committee, members voted 29-27 to adopt an amendment by John M. Spratt Jr., D-S.C., boosting funds for the Ballistic Missile Defense program to $2.74 billion, still not including Brilliant Eyes. Seven Democrats joined all 22 Republicans in voting "aye."

By a nearly straight party-line vote of 23-33, the committee rejected an amendment by Jon Kyl, R-Ariz., that would have overturned the subcommittee recommendation to alter the goals of the missile defense program.

House Floor Debate

In floor debate on the bill, members stuck with the missile defense funding approved by the Armed Services Committee. Lawmakers on Sept. 8 rejected two liberal amendments to cut deeper and a conservative effort to

match the Senate Armed Services Committee's recommended figure of $3.2 billion, not including the separate but related funding for Brilliant Eyes satellites.

The deepest cut, to $1.5 billion, was proposed by Armed Services Chairman Ronald V. Dellums, D-Calif., demonstrating that he had not abandoned the liberal views of his Berkeley constituents since ascending to the chairmanship in 1993. Dellums said that, with the collapse of the Soviet Union, the idea of a nationwide defense "makes even less sense now than it did $30 billion ago."

Republicans, and some moderate Democrats, countered with visions of despots armed with dreams of the power offered by attaining Soviet technology on the black market. "Right now we cannot defend against one single nuclear device coming at this country. Not one," said Robert K. Dornan, R-Calif. "If one single missile hits this country, people will be marching on this place like Victor Frankenstein's castle to burn it down because we let other Americans die."

Dellums' amendment was defeated 160-272. *(Vote 412, p. 100-H)*

An amendment by Schroeder to cut missile defense funding by $229 million, shifting the funds to defense conversion efforts, failed more narrowly, 202-227. *(Vote 414, p. 100-H)*

Republicans fared no better. The House soundly rejected, 118-312, an amendment by Joel Hefley, R-Colo., that would have increased the funding to the level sought by Senate Armed Services. *(Vote 413, p. 100-H)*

Subsequently, the House accepted by voice vote an amendment to the defense appropriations bill (HR 3116) that called for reducing funding for the Ballistic Missile Defense program by an additional $150 million. The amendment was offered by Elizabeth Furse, D-Ore. The House passed the underlying bill, 325-102, Sept. 30. *(Vote 480, p. 118-H)*

SENATE ACTION

The Senate Armed Services Committee completed work July 23 on its version of the fiscal 1994 defense authorization bill. Acting in closed session, the panel authorized $3.2 billion for the Ballistic Missile Defense program.

Following the approach taken by its House counterpart, the committee separated the $253 million requested for the Brilliant Eyes satellite and combined that program with similar missile detection efforts. The Senate committee's bill approved $822 million for this consolidated funding.

Floor Action

The full Senate on Sept. 9 narrowly approved an amendment to cut funding for the Ballistic Missile Defense program by $400 million to $2.8 billion, not including the Brilliant Eyes satellite program.

Budget Committee Chairman Jim Sasser, D-Tenn., led the surprisingly effective effort to cut funding over the opposition of the usually influential Nunn. Sasser won a 50-48 vote to impose the cut. *(Vote 251, p. 33-S)*

The Senate went on to pass the $261 billion authorization bill, 92-7, on Sept. 14. *(Vote 265, p. 35-S)*

Two stalwart supporters of the anti-missile defense program — Malcolm Wallop, R-Wyo., and Frank H. Murkowski, R-Alaska — did not vote on Sasser's amendment. The decision came down to freshman Dianne Feinstein, D-Calif., who was lobbied on the floor by both Sasser and Nunn over a vote that concerned defense jobs in her eco-

nomically hard-hit state. In the end, Feinstein voted for the Sasser cut.

Defending the full amount allocated by the Armed Services Committee, Howell Heflin, D-Ala., said that although the Soviet Union was gone, "we are still without any means of defending against attacks from hostile and possibly irrational Third World leaders."

"How long will it be before our luck runs out and we lose thousands of troops to a ballistic missile attack with chemical, biological or nuclear warheads?" he asked. "How long before we are blackmailed by a fanatical Third World leader with the threat of ballistic missile attack against one of our major cities?"

Sasser retorted, "We're not talking about emasculating the program." He argued that the biggest threat to U.S. national security was no longer ballistic missiles but a federal budget deficit that "threatens the very survival of our nation."

In another action on anti-missile defenses, the Senate passed by voice vote an amendment by Wallop to write into law an interpretation of the 1972 ABM Treaty.

The amendment stated that anti-missile prohibitions in the treaty did not apply to theater missile defenses even as those weapons grew more sophisticated.

On Oct. 21, the Senate gave voice vote approval to its version of the companion defense appropriations bill (HR 3116). As crafted by the Senate Appropriations Committee and its Defense Subcommittee, the appropriations bill mirrored the authorization measure's funding level for anti-missile defenses.

FINAL ACTION

The final version of the defense authorization bill authorized $2.8 billion of the $3.8 billion requested for anti-missile systems being developed by the Ballistic Missile Defense program.

The amount authorized did not include the $253 million requested for Brilliant Eyes. The House and Senate conferees consolidated this project with other missile-tracking satellites, as had the initial House and Senate versions of the bill.

The House adopted the conference report on the bill (H Rept 103-357), which authorized $261 billion for defense-related programs, 273-135, on Nov. 15. The Senate approved it, 77-22, on Nov. 17, clearing the measure for the president. *(House vote 565, p. 138-H; Senate vote 380, p. 49-S)*

Clinton signed the bill (PL 103-160) on Nov. 30.

The $2.8 billion for the Ballistic Missile Defense program included:

● $1.45 billion to develop defenses against theater ballistic missiles, such as the Soviet-designed Scuds fired by Iraq in the 1991 Persian Gulf War;

● $121 million to buy Patriot missiles modified to intercept theater missiles;

● $650 million to develop a system to defend U.S. territory against a small number of missile warheads; and

● $538 million to develop more sophisticated defenses for possible future deployment and to cover overhead costs.

The bill also ordered the administration to determine whether several key anti-theater missile devices were consistent with the ABM Treaty.

(It was subsequently reported in December that the administration planned to seek an easing of the ABM Treaty's standards to allow tests of an anti-theater missile

designated THAAD. Arms control advocates warned that the new standard would dangerously blur the line between permitted and prohibited weapons.)

In their report, conferees complained that the anti-missile effort remained too unfocused: "Future program plans, timetables for deployment, testing plans and missile defense architectures are incompletely defined, providing little basis thus far for congressional support of higher funding levels," they said.

Separate from the Ballistic Missile Defense budget, the conferees approved $3.8 million requested by the Air Force to test the effectiveness of laser-armed airplanes to intercept theater missiles.

The bill also authorized $10 million to develop an anti-satellite weapon. However, the companion defense appropriations bill denied the funds.

As for the Brilliant Eyes satellite, the conference report combined that request with three other programs to develop and procure missile attack warning systems for which the administration had requested a total of $1.05 billion. The conferees authorized a total of $802 million, which the Pentagon could allocate among the four programs.

The final version of the companion defense appropriations bill (HR 3116) provided $2.64 billion for the Ballistic Missile Defense program. The House approved the conference report on the spending bill by voice vote on Nov. 10. The Senate cleared the measure for the president, 88-9, Nov. 10. *(Vote 368, p. 47-S)*

Clinton signed the defense appropriations bill (PL 103-139) on Nov. 11. ∎

Strings Attached to Funds For Troubled Cargo Jet

Even as U.S. military strategy placed increased emphasis on deploying troops and equipment rapidly to distant trouble spots, the administration and Congress faced continuing problems with the C-17 cargo jet, which was intended to be the new workhorse of the military's airlift fleet.

Costs for the plane had increased and schedules had slipped, partly due to design flaws revealed by prototype planes and partly because McDonnell Douglas Corp. had problems managing the program and manufacturing the aircraft. The company was expected to lose $1.1 billion on its $6.7 billion contract to develop the plane and build the first seven copies.

Although some lawmakers called in 1993 for canceling the wide-body plane, the House and Senate Armed Services Committees and Defense Appropriations Subcommittees accepted Defense Secretary Les Aspin's argument that the C-17 was too important to the nation's mobilization plans to abandon.

Ultimately, Congress authorized the $2.32 billion that President Clinton requested for fiscal 1994 for six of the jets and appropriated $1.94 billion for the planes.

But the defense authorization measure set schedule and testing standards that the plane would have to meet, and both measures prodded the Pentagon to develop alternatives in case the C-17 continued to falter.

In December, in his last major decision before announcing that he was resigning, Aspin said that the Defense

Department would buy no more than 40 of the planes unless McDonnell Douglas conquered the C-17's problems within two years. The deal also required the aircraft manufacturer to drop $1.2 billion in claims against the government concerning the C-17 in return for a $237 million settlement.

Background

The C-17 was designed to carry objects as heavy as an M-1 tank into primitive airstrips close to a battle front. The Air Force had originally planned to buy 120 of the big planes, both to replace some older cargo jets and to expand its transoceanic (or "strategic") airlift fleet.

The C-17 was designed to meld features of two Air Force cargo haulers already in service: Like the bigger C-5, it could carry cargo that was both heavy and very wide, such as tanks and other ground combat gear. Like the smaller C-130 Hercules, it could land on a field only slightly more than a half-mile long.

The C-17 was 174 feet long compared with the C-5's 248 feet. And the new plane's jet engines were rigged so the craft could back up on the ground, making it more maneuverable. Therefore, the C-17 was supposed to be able to land on airfields that could not handle the C-5.

Compared with a contract specification that the plane carry 80 tons of payload for 2,400 nautical miles on a specified flight plan, in 1993 it could carry about 75 tons for the specified distance. The plane also had trouble with fuel leaks, an understrength wing and its landing gear.

In a review of budget-cutting options published in February 1993, the Congressional Budget Office estimated that resuming production of the C-5 would cost about $200 million apiece compared with the C-17's cost of $240 million apiece.

But the newer plane was designed to cost much less to operate, partly because it was to have a crew of three, compared with the C-5's six-member crew.

Congressional Hearings

Some of the Pentagon's staunchest political allies warned Air Force officials March 10 that problems besetting the C-17 could undermine political support for the multibillion-dollar program — and for defense spending generally.

The warnings came on the second day of a House Armed Services subcommittee hearings on the effort to develop the wide-body, long-range aircraft, one of the largest single items in the weapons procurement budget.

Lt. Gen. John E. Jaquish said changes in McDonnell Douglas' management of the C-17 and in the schedule for testing and building the planes had solved the problems. "The fixes are in place to keep the program on track," he said.

But some committee members objected that those assurances sounded all too similar to Air Force assurances, repeated in each of the prior several years, that the program had "turned the corner" as a result of some change in its budget, schedule or organizational chart. "How many corners are there in this program?" asked Gene Taylor, D-Miss.

Other Pentagon supporters on the panel contended that the program's travails would make it harder for them to lobby their colleagues to support defense requests. "When we can't convincingly [explain] to people what we're trying to get them to vote for ... this is a very serious matter," said John Tanner, D-Tenn. "I'm about out of ammunition

on this one."

On March 9, retired Air Force Col. Kenneth Tollefson, who formerly supervised Pentagon contracts at the McDonnell Douglas plant in Long Beach, Calif., where the C-17 was being built, told House Armed Services that the company had been swamped trying to develop the C-17 and three other new planes while undergoing a wrenching company reorganization. Tollefson said that Pentagon superiors, including a former Air Force chief of staff, had ignored his warnings that the program was in trouble.

But David O. Swain, the McDonnell Douglas vice president in charge of the project, told reporters March 8 that the program's problems stemmed from the Pentagon's insistence on signing a fixed-price contract to develop the new plane.

Touted as a way to put Pentagon programs on a more businesslike level, that approach assumed the contractor would accept the risk of development, while the government would relax the oversight and second-guessing it applied to major weapons programs.

But Pentagon officials interfered repeatedly with the program, Swain said. He noted that the government effectively conceded that the fixed-price approach was unworkable by abandoning it in 1990.

In April, Aspin fired Maj. Gen. Michael J. Butchko Jr., a former C-17 program manager, and imposed lesser sanctions on three other Air Force officials who he contended had not been candid with top Pentagon officials about the plane's troubles. "The story of the C-17 program reflects an unwillingness on the part of some high-ranking acquisition professionals to acknowledge program difficulties and to take decisive action," Aspin said April 30.

On May 11, the Pentagon's chief of weapons procurement, Under Secretary of Defense John Deutch, warned that the Clinton administration might cancel production of the C-17 unless McDonnell Douglas acted quickly to correct technical problems and get a handle on its increasing costs. In testimony to House Armed Services, Deutch said that McDonnell Douglas had been "exceedingly slow to devote the managerial, technical and financial resources necessary to successfully develop and build this aircraft."

CONGRESSIONAL ACTION

In crafting the fiscal 1994 defense authorization and appropriations bills, members indicated they felt compelled to continue funding the C-17 as a badly needed element of the nation's military hardware. But they sought ways to signal their dissatisfaction with the troubled plane and to keep open alternatives.

Defense Authorization

Both the House and Senate versions of the defense authorization bill (HR 2401, S 1298) backed substantial additional funding for the C-17 but ordered the Pentagon to consider alternatives before spending more on the project.

Of the $2.56 billion requested to continue testing the plane and to build six, the House approved $2.11 billion. But it stipulated that the funds could be spent only after the Pentagon reviewed alternative long-range cargo planes, including C-5s and commercial aircraft.

The Senate bill took a slightly different tack, lumping into one sum $2.4 billion earmarked for C-17 procurement and $291 million requested for fast cargo ships. The measure approved the entire $2.7 billion request but ordered

the Pentagon to determine the most cost-effective mix of C-17s, other planes and ships for long-range transport.

The final version of the authorization bill crafted by House-Senate conferees approved Clinton's full request for C-17s and stipulated that the administration could buy as many as six of the planes.

But the bill specified that the administration could do so only if the trouble-plagued plane satisfied certain schedule and testing requirements. In any case, the bill required the Air Force to come up with an "off-the-shelf" alternative — either modified commercial cargo jets or newly built Air Force C-5 planes — that could replace some of the planned C-17s.

Specifically, the bill approved:

● $1.9 billion for four C-17s.
● $100 million to buy alternative planes.
● $300 million that could be used either for two additional C-17s or for additional alternative planes.

The House adopted the conference report on the defense authorization bill, 273-135, on Nov. 15. The Senate cleared the bill, 77-22, on Nov. 17. *(House vote 565, p. 138-H; Senate vote 380, p. 49-S)*

Clinton signed the measure (PL 103-160) on Nov. 30.

Defense Appropriations

The companion defense appropriations bill (HR 3116) provided $1.94 billion — a reduction of less than 7 percent from Clinton's request — for six C-17s. It also included the $246 million requested for components that would be used in the eight C-17s slated for inclusion in the next budget request.

To put competitive pressure on McDonnell-Douglas, the bill also provided $100 million to begin buying a modified version of an existing wide-body cargo jet, either a plane in commercial service or the Air Force's C-5.

The House adopted the conference report on the defense appropriations bill by voice vote Nov. 10. The Senate cleared the bill, 88-9, on Nov. 10. *(Vote 368, p. 47-S)*

Clinton signed the appropriations bill (PL 103-139) on Nov. 11.   ■

Pentagon Examines Its Post-Cold War Role

Les Aspin began his tenure as Defense secretary in January 1993 by announcing that the Defense Department would re-examine its mission in a world that had grown uncertain since the Cold War ended and the Soviet Union broke up, leaving the United States without the main target of its strategic defenses.

From January through August, teams within the Pentagon examined every facet of their operations — from rules governing weapons purchases to the number and structure of the troops.

On Sept. 1, Aspin released the results of his "bottom up" review of the Pentagon's mission and machinery. The plan cut less than experts had expected, but administration officials said the changes in defense programs would reduce defense spending enough to meet President Clinton's budget targets while still allowing for a more flexible fighting force.

The plan was intended as a blueprint for the new administration's defense policy, a set of decisions and priorities that would guide year-to-year defense spending and provide broad outlines for military strategy in the aftermath of the Cold War.

Key lawmakers began to use the report as a frame of reference as well, questioning whether the spending, force levels and weaponry sought by the administration were sufficient to meet the announced standard: the ability to simultaneously fight and win two major regional wars. Many of the immediate steps recommended by Aspin were incorporated in the fiscal 1994 defense authorization bill (HR 2401 — PL 103-160). *(Defense authorization, p. 433)*

Key Elements of the Plan

The plan was designed to cut active-duty forces by 300,000, while allowing the United States to fight and win nearly simultaneous wars in regions such as Asia and the Middle East, Aspin said. It also kept alive some Pentagon-dependent defense industries by buying additional — though apparently unneeded — weaponry and by cutting only one aircraft carrier from the existing fleet of 13.

Other key elements of the Aspin plan included:

● Killing the Navy's attempt to build a long-range carrier-based bomber, called the A/F-X, as well as the Air Force's Multi-Role fighter program. Lawmakers had anticipated the demise of the futuristic A/F-X and had left it out of their defense budgeting for fiscal 1994. No funding was provided in the defense authorization or appropriations bills.

● Delaying deployment of a national ballistic missile defense system, the offspring of the Strategic Defense Initiative. Congress backed the idea of a scaled-down anti-missile defense system, reducing funding below the administration's request. *(Strategic defense, p. 448)*

● Reconfiguring both the B-1B and the new B-2 stealth bombers to be used in non-nuclear conflicts.

Aspin did not release a cost analysis, but deputy Defense Secretary William J. Perry said Sept. 2 that the cost estimates were "in the ballpark" of the $123 billion that Clinton had planned to cut from the defense budget through fiscal 1998.

"We're comfortable on that point now," Perry said.

In outlining the plan, Aspin and Joint Chiefs Chairman Gen. Colin L. Powell Jr. said the most likely danger for the United States in the new global environment would come from regional conflicts that involved U.S. strategic interests, such as the Iraqi invasion of Kuwait, which led U.S. forces into the Persian Gulf War in 1991.

Powell said he and the heads of the armed services believed the United States had to be prepared to deal with two such local conflicts breaking out in separate parts of the world at the same time.

For example, the Aspin force structure was designed to allow the United States to deploy troops rapidly to the Middle East in the event of an Iraqi invasion of Kuwait and still have sufficient troops and weapons to begin deploying to the Korean Peninsula if North Korea prepared to invade South Korea at roughly the same time.

The plan anticipated cutting troop strength to 1.4 million soldiers, down from the existing level of about 1.7

lowing acknowledged homosexuals to serve would compromise military effectiveness.

Rep. G. V. "Sonny" Montgomery, D-Miss., the longtime chairman of the Veterans' Affairs Committee, urged proponents of lifting the ban to moderate their position. "Don't push us to the wall," Montgomery said. "I'm not sure you could win an up-or-down vote."

Like Nunn's committee, the House panel extensively debated whether allowing gays to serve would be analogous to Truman's decision in 1948 ordering the racial integration of the services.

Dellums, a veteran civil rights activist, said that many of the same arguments made against allowing gays to serve were once used against blacks. "There are parallels here, and very strong parallels if you approach the questions as a civil rights question," he said.

But Chuck Jackson, a black former Navy petty officer who headed the 160,000-strong Non-Commissioned Officers Association, disagreed. "Many of my brothers and sisters are offended and incensed" by the comparison between the civil rights and gay rights movements, he said.

Seeking Agreement

Convinced that Congress would block any effort by Clinton to eliminate the ban on gays, Rep. Barney Frank — one of two openly gay members of Congress — shook up the debate by proposing a variation on the "don't ask, don't tell" compromise.

Frank, D-Mass., said May 18 that the policy on gays and lesbians in the military should be: "Don't ask, don't tell, don't listen and don't investigate." In essence, homosexuals in the military would be allowed to be open about their orientation — but only when they were off duty and off base.

The compromise was criticized as a capitulation by some gay leaders and as unacceptable by conservatives.

However, Frank's acquiescence to the military's insistence that gays keep their orientation private on base was a significant turning point. "The majority community appears to be convinced that members of the military are not ready, overnight, to fully accept the presence of openly gay men and lesbians holding hands and dancing among them," Frank said. "I wish that weren't the case ... but the perception is a very real fact."

Unlike Nunn's version of a compromise, however, Frank's approach would have expressly barred investigations of the private, off-base behavior of discreetly gay personnel, provided they did not run afoul of civilian law enforcement agencies.

"Gay men and lesbians who are willing to restrain and restrict themselves on base and on duty and in uniform should be allowed off duty, off base to live their lives in a reasonable fashion as gay men and lesbians without that being held against them," Frank told reporters.

Frank's compromise was challenged by gay rights groups and by Rep. Gerry E. Studds, D-Mass., the other openly gay member of Congress, who previously had taken a lower profile on gay rights issues.

Frank, however, insisted that lawmakers already were locking themselves into public positions against lifting the ban. "Those who insist on no compromise at all are very likely to see the enactment into law of the current policy of a total and complete ban," he said. "I'm talking about freeing people from the need to live in the closet most of the time."

Clinton took an increasingly conciliatory tone on the issue, insisting he was seeking a compromise and not intending to put the military's imprimatur on homosexuality. In a "town meeting" televised by CBS on May 27, Clinton emphasized that he had no intention of changing the Uniform Code of Miitary Justice, the body of federal criminal law that governed the military. It prohibited sodomy, whether homosexual or heterosexual.

"Should you be able to acknowledge, if asked, that you are homosexual?" Clinton asked. "And, if you don't do anything wrong, should you be booted from the military?" A compromise should be reached "so our country does not appear to be endorsing a gay lifestyle," Clinton added. But in a Senate speech hours later, Nunn flatly rejected Clinton's proposal that homosexuals be permitted to acknowledge their sexual orientation so long as they did not engage in prohibited acts. The senator said a gay soldier could disrupt his platoon just as severely by declaring his sexual orientation as by engaging in homosexual conduct — and as much by making that orientation known off base as by doing so on base.

But Nunn agreed with Frank — and Clinton — that military officials should not spend their time hunting down gays. "I do not believe we should have sex squads looking for ways to investigate service members' private, consensual behavior," he said.

CLINTON'S DECISION

On July 19, Clinton announced his long-promised policy in the form of a Pentagon directive. It was intended to take effect Oct. 1, although that was later delayed by court rulings.

Clinton's plan barred the Pentagon from asking gays to disclose their sexual orientation. And it reeled in the dragnets sometimes cast by Pentagon investigators in an effort to catch closeted homosexuals.

At the same time, however, the new policy reaffirmed the Pentagon's strict proscription of homosexual conduct, forbidding even the disclosure to a friend in private conversation that one was gay or bisexual. "From the point of view of homosexuals who wish to serve honorably," Clinton said, "I think it was a substantial advance." *(Speech text, p. 23-D; Pentagon text, p. 25-D)*

But as Defense Secretary Aspin told the Senate Armed Services Committee on July 20, "Homosexual members will have to play by the rules." And the burden of rules that precluded any sexual self-expression was compounded by an institutional culture that remained unapologetically hostile. "If a person is homosexual, they would be much more comfortable pursuing a different profession," Aspin said.

Clinton announced his decision before an audience of senior officers in an auditorium on a military base in Washington. While he lauded the efforts of gay rights advocates, none of them were invited. He touted the policy as an illustration of his willingness to take on tough, uphill fights: "I'm the first president who ever took on this issue," he said during a July 20 interview. "It may be a sign of madness, sir, but it is not a sign of weakness."

Clinton's compromise evoked powerful — and largely hostile — reactions:

● Gay rights advocates, contemptuous of Clinton's assertion that the policy opened a new "zone of privacy" for military personnel, blasted the move as a betrayal of his campaign pledge to a constituency that generously supported him with votes and cash.

Congress' Ban on Gays Allows Little Leeway

The language on gays in the military that Congress adopted as part of the fiscal 1994 defense authorization bill (HR 2401 — PL 103-160) was stern in rejecting homosexual conduct in the armed forces. Unlike the Clinton administration's regulations issued in the name of Defense Secretary Les Aspin, the congressional version offered no words of tolerance toward homosexuals.

"It is clear on the people who would not be able to serve in the military," Senate Armed Services Committee Chairman Sam Nunn, D-Ga., said of the legislative language that his panel drafted. He added, "We don't try to define the people who would be able to serve."

The provisions, which the Armed Services committees wrote into both chambers' versions of the fiscal 1994 defense authorization bill, superseded the Clinton-sponsored Pentagon rules wherever the two versions conflicted. Mostly, however, the congressional language allowed the specifics of the Clinton plan to take effect while locking into law a broad policy statement rejecting the notion of accepting gays in the military.

Highlights of the congressional language follow:

● **Congress' authority.** In a matter that the White House had sought to resolve solely by executive order, the provisions reasserted that "it lies within the discretion of the Congress to establish qualifications for and conditions of service in the armed forces." The measure cited Article I, Section 8 of the Constitution, which gave Congress exclusive power to "make rules for the government and regulation of the land and naval forces."

● **The rationale.** Setting forth a rationale — and a legal defense — for continued rejection of gays in the military, the provisions maintained that "there is no constitutional right to serve in the armed forces." The bill asserted that "the conduct of military operations requires members . . . to make extraordinary sacrifices, including the ultimate sacrifice," and that "the military society is characterized by its own laws, rules, customs and traditions, including numerous restrictions on personal behavior, that would not be acceptable in civilian society."

"The prohibition against homosexual conduct is a longstanding element of military law that continues to be necessary in the unique circumstances of military service," the provisions said. They added, "The presence in the armed forces of persons who demonstrate a propensity or intent to engage in homosexual acts would create an unacceptable risk to the high standards of morale, good order and discipline and unit cohesion that are the essence of military capability."

● **The ban.** The provisions stated that the armed forces, under regulations set out by the secretary of Defense, were to dismiss a member who was found to have engaged in, attempted to engage in or solicited a homosexual act; married or tried to marry a person of the same sex; or stated that he or she was homosexual, unless such a member could show that "he or she has not engaged in or attempted to engage in homosexual acts and did not have a propensity or intent to engage in such acts."

● **A one-time exception.** The provisions revived from past Pentagon policy an exemption that appeared aimed at protecting "straight" soldiers who might give in just once to a passionate urge or to youthful experimentation. It provided that a service member who committed a homosexual act need not be dismissed if he or she could demonstrate that "such conduct is a departure from the member's usual and customary behavior" and "under all the circumstances, is unlikely to recur."

● **Asking recruits.** In a "sense of Congress" statement, the provisions gave a cautious go-ahead to the military's practice since January of no longer asking applicants to military service whether they were homosexual. It said the suspension "should be continued, but the secretary of Defense may reinstate that questioning . . . if the secretary determines that it is necessary to do so."

● **What was missing.** The congressional measure did not address — and thus left intact — the portion of Aspin's order that curbed dragnet-style investigations of suspected gays. Under Aspin's order, a commanding officer could begin an inquiry or request a criminal investigation of a service member only on the basis of "credible information" of homosexual conduct.

The congressional codification did not extend any words of support or tolerance for homosexuals who stayed chaste or in the closet. By contrast, Aspin's directive said that the Department of Defense "recognizes that individuals with a homosexual orientation have served with distinction in the armed services" and specified that "homosexual orientation is not a bar to service entry or continued service unless manifested by homosexual conduct."

Also conspicuously missing from the congressional language was Aspin's order that commanders "will investigate allegations of violations of the Uniform Code of Military Justice in an even-handed manner without regard to whether the conduct alleged is heterosexual or homosexual or whether it occurs on-base or off-base."

Gay political strategist David Mixner, a longtime Clinton friend and political adviser, contended that administration officials deliberately sabotaged efforts by gay activists to weigh in on the administration's deliberations. "We were purposely misled in an effort to keep us quiet," he said. "White House political operations determined that we, as a community, had nowhere else to go and that even our anger would work in favor of the president by showing the country that he could stand up to the queers."

Frank and Studds also rejected Clinton's policy, but they gave him high marks for trying. "He is the first president of the United States to deal seriously with the prejudice against gay men and lesbians," Frank said. "Bill Clinton was quite courageous in taking it on."

● Social conservatives, including many congressional Democrats from southern and border states, were disturbed by one of several administration moves — including the nomination of openly gay officials to domestic policy posts — that appeared to weaken traditional moral sanctions against homosexuality.

"I want to support the president," said Ike Skelton, D-Mo., chairman of the House Armed Services Military

Forces and Personnel Subcommittee, "but my family background is deeply rooted in traditional, religious values, and my constituents have sent a clear signal that they believe the president is off track."

● Some Republicans cited Clinton's initiative as one more indicator that he did not understand the armed forces, a failing they linked to his vigorous efforts to avoid military service in Vietnam.

"If President Clinton had gone through basic training at Parris Island [the Marine Corps' South Carolina boot camp] ... do you think we'd be here today discussing this question?" said Lauch Faircloth, R-N.C.

Although Clinton's plan drew few enthusiastic backers and a bevy of critics, it gained considerable political momentum, largely because it carried the endorsement of the Joint Chiefs of Staff. Repeatedly, in hearings before the Senate and House Armed Services committees, the nation's six highest-ranking officers averred that Clinton's policy was workable and would not erode combat readiness.

Joint Chiefs Chairman Gen. Colin L. Powell Jr. called Clinton's July 19 policy "an honorable compromise" and praised the administration's extensive consultations with the chiefs.

The chiefs' endorsement frustrated and angered GOP conservatives such as House Armed Services member Randy "Duke" Cunningham, Calif., who was highly decorated as a Navy combat pilot in the Vietnam War. "I can't believe that you support this," Cunningham told the chiefs July 21. "My mind may, but my heart doesn't."

"Your heart should," Powell said, "because I'm speaking with my heart and mind. My heart always is speaking for the best interests of the services."

After committee hearings on July 21 and 22, Nunn said the chiefs had been "effective and persuasive" in arguing that Clinton's policy could be implemented. But Nunn also insisted that lawmakers had a constitutional duty to act on the issue, despite Clinton's stated preference that they not lock provisions on gays into law.

CONGRESSIONAL ACTION

Not content to let the president have the last word, the Senate Armed Services Committee wrote Nunn's own, tougher-toned version of the ban into its fiscal 1994 defense authorization bill (HR 2401). An identical provision was adopted by the House Armed Services Committee in the companion House bill.

The provision withstood challenges on the floor of both chambers and became law when Clinton signed the defense authorization bill Nov. 30 (PL 103-160).

Senate Committee Action

On July 23, only four days after Clinton announced his plan, the Senate Armed Services Committee voted 17-5 to include a policy on gays in the military in its version of the defense authorization bill (S 1298). The provision did not directly overturn any element of Clinton's plan, but it sealed what had been a military regulation into the law — and framed it in tough terms intended to provide a clear rationale for the inevitable court challenges.

Ignoring Clinton policy's statement that "homosexual orientation is not a bar to service," the provision stated that those who "demonstrate a propensity or intent to engage in homosexual acts would create an unacceptable risk" to military standards and morale.

Nunn told reporters that the bill's language "incorpo-

rates the essential features and is consistent with" Clinton's policy and that "the president and the secretary of Defense approve this."

Significantly, however, all of the committee's Republicans voted for Nunn's language. Republican Coats portrayed it as a significant improvement on the "ambiguous political deal" that Clinton had presented. "One advantage ... is that some future president won't be tempted to try to lift the ban," said Thurmond.

The Democratic opponents objected that the measure was a step backward from Clinton's plan and that it would block future liberalization.

House Committee Action

On July 27, the House Armed Services Committee approved a provision identical to the one drafted by its Senate counterpart to codify the Pentagon's long-running ban on gays.

The committee folded the language into the House defense authorization bill by voice vote, as part of a package of provisions drafted by its Subcommittee on Military Forces and Personnel.

The panel handily rejected amendments to make the ban stricter or eliminate it.

Dellums offered an amendment to eliminate the ban on homosexual service members. "We should only ask of our soldiers, sailors and airmen that they be the best they can be, not that they be celibate saints without human dignity or emotion," Dellums said. "We should remove off-duty, consensual sexual acts from the reach of [military law]."

Dellums' amendment was rejected 12-43. Peter G. Torkildsen of Massachusetts was the lone Republican to support it; 22 Democrats, most of them from Southern or border states, voted "nay."

Duncan Hunter, R-Calif., tried to amend the bill to require the Pentagon to ask incoming recruits if they were homosexual or bisexual. The question had not been asked since January, and the Nunn-crafted language sought to leave the secretary of Defense discretion as to whether to resume asking it, although the provision required that recruits be specifically informed of the prohibition on homosexual conduct.

The amendment was rejected 18-28; seven conservative Democrats voted "aye" and 11 Republicans voted "nay."

Senate Floor Action

The Senate stood by Nunn's provision, rebuffing an effort Sept. 9 to cede the explosive issue to the president. Senators defeated, 33-63, an amendment by Barbara Boxer, D-Calif., that would have struck the Nunn language from the defense authorization bill. *(Vote 250, p. 33-S)*

The Senate passed the defense bill, 92-7, on Sept. 14.

Boxer's amendment would have written into the bill a non-binding opinion of Congress that federal policy on the issue should be left to the president to decide with the advice of his military advisers.

Nunn countered that under Boxer's amendment Congress would give up its right to have a say in the matter as well as its constitutional duty to act. "This amendment basically says the Congress is not part of this. It's up to the president," Nunn said. "There's no doubt whatsoever that we not only have the right to legislate in this area, we have the responsibility."

Howard M. Metzenbaum, D-Ohio, said the Boxer amendment was "as important as any civil rights legislation that has come before this body."

Opponents, led by Republican Coats, contended that the matter was a privacy issue for heterosexual military personnel who were segregated by gender. "No one would advocate having men and women live together on a 24-hour basis," Coats said.

But conservatives such as Jesse Helms, R-N.C., appeared satisfied with Nunn's resolution of the issue. They did not respond to Boxer's amendment with verbal broadsides or with legislative counterproposals.

House Floor Action

The House closed the book on the year's fractious congressional debate over gays in the military Sept. 29, voting 268-162 to pass a defense authorization bill that codified the prohibition. *(Vote 474, p. 116-H)*

The gay ban in the bill, sponsored by Skelton, was adopted Sept. 28 on a vote of 301-134. *(Vote 462, p. 112-H)*

The same day, the House rejected 144-291 an amendment by Hunter that would have made the ban tougher by ordering the Pentagon to resume the practice — suspended by Clinton in January — of asking recruits to disclose whether they were homosexual. *(Vote 461, p. 112-H)*

Also rejected that day, by a vote of 169-264, was an amendment backed by opponents of the gay ban: Like Boxer's amendment in the Senate, it would have deleted from the defense bill any reference to the issue, leaving the policy in the hands of the president. *(Vote 460, p. 112-H)*

Many members may have been drawn to Skelton's amendment at least partly because they wanted no more of the emotionally charged battle that had raged since Clinton took office. "Enough is enough," Skelton told the House. "The issue ... has been far too divisive, has consumed far too much of the nation's energy and has robbed this body of far too much of our legislative agenda. We must put this issue behind us."

Asked Sept. 30 whether the Nunn-Skelton language would alter the application of the administration's policy on gays in the military, Pentagon spokeswoman Kathleen deLaski said, "We don't think so."

DeLaski also told reporters that the administration would delay for "a few weeks" implementing Clinton's new policy, which had been scheduled to take effect Oct. 1.

Final Action

Because the House and Senate versions of the defense authorization bill included identical language on gays in the military, the issue was not debated in the conference committee that crafted the final version of the bill.

The House adopted the conference report Nov. 15 by a vote of 273-135. The Senate approved the report Nov. 17 by a vote of 77-22, clearing the measure for the president. *(House vote 565, p. 138-H; Senate vote 380, p. 49-S)*

THE COURTS WEIGH IN

Despite the action, the gay ban — and Clinton's effort to reformulate it — were left in limbo at year's end by a series of court rulings.

Even before the congressional debate on the issue was over, civil liberties and gay rights advocates went to court to block the policy that Clinton sought to put into effect. Acting on behalf of six reservists and one active-duty soldier, the American Civil Liberties Union and the Lambda Legal Defense and Education Fund on July 27 asked the U.S. District Court for the District of Columbia to block the new policy. The plaintiffs argued that the ban was a violation of free speech and association and of the Equal Protection Clause of the 14th Amendment.

Then, in October, the Pentagon suspended enforcement of its ban on homosexuals in the military while preparing to appeal a California judge's ruling against the ban.

Acting in the case of Meinhold, the gay sailor in California, U.S. District Judge Terry Hatter Jr. of Los Angeles issued a sweeping order Sept. 30 banning discrimination against homosexuals in the military. The U.S. Court of Appeals for the Ninth Circuit declined to block the decision.

On Oct. 29, the Supreme Court granted a request from the Clinton administration for an emergency stay of Hatter's ruling ordering the military to lift its ban on homosexuals. "The barrier erected by the district court to implementation of the president's new policy and the pending legislation is all the more egregious," the administration argued in its brief, "in light of the enormous amount of time and attention that the political branches devoted to developing that policy."

On Nov. 16, another ruling against the gay ban came from a panel of the U.S. Court of Appeals for the District of Columbia. In a unanimous decision, a three-judge panel headed by Chief Judge Abner J. Mikva ordered the Navy to give an officer's commission to Joseph C. Steffan.

After disclosing that he was gay, Steffan was forced to resign as a midshipman in 1987, just six weeks before he would have graduated from the U.S. Naval Academy, where he had compiled an impressive record. He was accused of no homosexual conduct beyond revealing his sexual orientation.

Mikva's ruling applied specifically to the Pentagon policy on homosexuals that was in effect in 1987. It had been suspended in January and was to be supplanted by Nunn's language in the defense authorization bill.

However, Mikva's opinion was a legal broadside against the fundamental premise of both the old and new policies. Noting that Steffan was accused of no misconduct, Mikva wrote that the policy that drove the midshipman from the service was based on the assumption that other military personnel would be offended by having to serve with homosexuals.

"The Constitution does not allow government to subordinate a class of persons simply because others do not like them," Mikva wrote. "The government cannot discriminate in an effort to avoid the effects of others' prejudices."

In the past, federal courts had given the armed services wide leeway to depart from generally applicable standards of civil liberties in deference to the requirements of military life. They also had held that the services need not assume that an avowed homosexual would abstain from disruptive conduct.

But Mikva argued that the gay ban went too far. "There is no 'military exception' to the Constitution," he said.

With the broader issue of the military treatment of homosexuals evidently headed to the Supreme Court for resolution, Nunn maintained that the legal case against homosexuals was strengthened by the language defending the ban that lawmakers wrote into the defense authorization law.

"The courts generally defer to the Congress if we have findings that justify treating people differently," Nunn said on NBC's "Meet the Press" on Oct. 10, "and I think those findings, assuming we get the law passed and it's signed in the next few weeks, will play a major role in any Supreme Court deliberations." ∎

Combat Roles for Women a Step Closer

In actions that affected the future of women in the military, Congress repealed legislation that had prevented women from serving on combat ships, and Defense Secretary Les Aspin took steps to get women into the cockpits of combat planes.

The Pentagon also issued a report concerning assaults on women during the 1991 Tailhook Association convention. While the report concluded that more than 100 members of the military had been involved in assaults on women at the Las Vegas gathering, attempts to prosecute the cases ran into problems of evidence and witnesses. By the end of 1993, none of the people involved had been court-martialed, and many of the cases had been dropped for lack of evidence.

WOMEN IN COMBAT

Congress repealed the combat exclusion for women on ships as a part of the fiscal 1994 defense authorization (HR 2401 — H Rept 103-357). The conference report accompanying the bill required the Pentagon to notify Congress 90 days before announcing a change in the ban on assigning women to ground combat units and 30 days' notice before allowing women to join any combat unit or ship from which they had been barred. President Clinton signed the bill into law Nov. 30 (PL 103-160).

Background

While Aspin had the authority to open the doors to women pilots, he needed congressional action to put women on combat vessels.

Inspired by the role of women just behind the front lines of the Persian Gulf War, Congress in 1991 repealed a law that had prevented women in the military from flying combat missions. The change, part of the fiscal 1992 defense authorization bill (PL 102-190), did not force the armed services to open combat pilot positions to women; rather it left the military with discretion on whether to maintain the ban. The bill also established a commission to study the issue of women in combat. *(1991 Almanac, p. 414)*

Women had gone to sea since 1978, when Congress relaxed a blanket prohibition to allow women on non-combat vessels, including hospital and ammunition ships. However, women still were barred by law from being assigned permanently to combat warships. *(1978 Almanac, p. 321)*

The congressionally created commission proposed in November 1992 that women be permitted to serve on warships but that the military continue to ban them from ground combat. After fierce ideologically charged debate, the 15-member commission also voted, 8-7, to continue the ban on female combat pilots and flight crews. *(1992 Almanac, p. 519)*

Aspin Opens Doors

On March 30, Defense Secretary Aspin told the House Armed Services Committee that he would lift the Pentagon's ban on women serving in combat on ships and perhaps on flight crews as well.

"We're probably going to accept the commission's report . . . with the possible exception of the combat aircraft," Aspin told the committee. "We may be back to you and

recommend that in fact we do something different than they recommended with the combat aircraft." Referring to a bloc of staunch conservatives whom President George Bush had appointed to the panel, Aspin said: "There are some people who are pretty locked into their position appointed to this commission, which was not what Congress had in mind."

On April 28, Aspin followed up by ordering the military services to allow women aviators to compete for coveted assignments to fly fighters, bombers and armed helicopters in combat squadrons. He also directed the Navy to draft for Congress a bill to repeal the law barring women from serving on combat vessels. And he instructed the Army and Marine Corps to look for jobs that women could be assigned to in combat-related roles then closed to them, such as in field artillery and air defense units.

"We know from experience that women can fly our high-performance fighter aircraft," Aspin said. "We know from experience that they can perform well in assignments at sea. And we know from Operation Desert Storm . . . that women stand up to the most demanding environments. So we're acting on what we know."

"For the wonderful women who sat for years and could train the fighter pilots but couldn't be a fighter pilot, this is terrific," said House Armed Services Committee member Patricia Schroeder, D-Colo., who had led in the effort to allow women in combat roles.

Aspin's recommendations were greeted with widespread approval at the Capitol, even from some members who had opposed the 1991 repeal. For instance, Sen. John McCain, R-Ariz., a retired Navy pilot, said the recommendations were "clearly appropriate."

On May 12, military brass came before the House Armed Services Military Forces and Personnel Subcommittee to discuss their efforts to comply with Aspin's order. They told members that standards for combat pilots would not change — except that the best person for the job now could be a woman.

Aspin's changes were most enthusiastically endorsed by a representative of the Navy, which was struggling to repair its damaged reputation after the Tailhook scandal, in which naval aviators were accused of sexually harassing women during a convention. "The debate over whether women can do the job should have ended long ago," Navy Vice Adm. Ronald J. Zlatoper told the subcommittee. He said his only regret was that many Navy men had never had the chance to serve with women.

He promised that Navy standards would not be compromised in making the historic change: "No quotas, no double standards and no slack for anyone, man or woman, who can't hack it," Zlatoper said.

Some lawmakers were skeptical. Jon Kyl of Arizona, the ranking Republican on the panel, said he was concerned that many aspects of the plan had not been fully thought out, such as whether women should serve on submarines.

Freshman Republican Roscoe G. Bartlett of Maryland said, "I don't want my daughter or granddaughters to be in a position" to become prisoners of war.

But freshman Jane Harman, D-Calif., noting that the military panel testifying before the subcommittee was all-male, said that it was time women had an equal chance to advance. Military women have "not had the same opportu-

nities for performance and have not had the same opportunities for promotion," she said.

Elaine Donnelly, a member of the Presidential Commission on the Assignment of Women in the Armed Forces, told the panel there still was a "body of evidence that [shows that] assignment of women to combat positions would adversely affect military readiness, cohesion and effectiveness." Donnelly also said her task force's work was being "brushed aside."

Moving Quickly

The Navy and the Air Force, which already had trained female pilots, moved quickly to implement Aspin's decision to allow women to fly combat aircraft.

Zlatoper told the subcommittee that the Navy's first three women combat pilots were scheduled to take on their new jobs by July. He said as many as 25 women could be flying Navy combat missions within a year. Lt. Gen. Billy J. Boles told the panel that by May 19 the Air Force's first woman pilot would have begun her fighter training. And the Air Force was looking into the qualifications of its women pilots to compete for the 10,000 jobs from which they previously were barred.

The Army and the Marine Corps were expected to move more slowly because aircraft training in those branches was directed mostly at readiness for combat. Army Lt. Gen. Thomas P. Carney said that women had begun training on Army tank-hunting helicopters, with one assigned to Cobras and two to Apaches. But Lt. Gen. Matthew T. Cooper said it would take the Marine Corps more than three years to train its first active-duty women combat pilots and up to six years for the reserve forces.

The Navy's representatives at the subcommittee hearing urged Congress to repeal the law barring women from being assigned permanently to combat warships. Kyl objected that he needed "to know what the policy is before we lift the ban."

Kyl said he was concerned that when the Navy refitted its ships, the reconfigured living quarters would effectively mandate "gender-specific quotas to sail." Zlatoper said it could cost $800,000 to $1 million per ship to redo the living quarters and bathrooms.

TAILHOOK SCANDAL

The Pentagon completed a report on the Tailhook sexual harassment scandal in February, but Aspin refused to release it, saying he would wait for the appointment and confirmation of a Navy secretary or a Pentagon general counsel who could take responsibility for responding to the investigation by the Pentagon's inspector general.

"Certainly, discipline in terms of the military system is going to be appropriate in some cases, maybe even criminal charges in some cases," Aspin said March 30. "But in order to do that, I need somebody who can follow through on that thing and do it well."

On April 28, the Pentagon's inspector general finally released the report, which found that 83 women and seven men had been subjected to "indecent assaults" during the

Tailhook Association's three-day meeting in Las Vegas in September 1991. The Tailhook Association was a private club of naval aviators that had worked closely with the Navy hierarchy. The report was based on interviews with more than 2,900 of an estimated 4,000 people who attended the rowdy convention that became a military scandal.

The report concluded that 117 officers were "implicated in one or more incidents of indecent assault, indecent exposure, conduct unbecoming an officer or failure to act in a proper leadership capacity.... Some of the Navy's most senior officers were knowledgeable as to the excesses ... and, by their inaction, these officers served to condone and even encourage the type of behavior that occurred," said the report.

A Navy vice admiral and a Marine Corps lieutenant general, neither of them aviators, were designated to supervise all disciplinary actions, whether criminal or administrative, resulting from the investigation.

Rep. Schroeder said the real lesson of the scandal was that "so long as women are excluded from combat roles and cannot participate as full partners, they will be seen as second-class citizens."

In a letter to Navy Secretary-designate John H. Dalton, Schroeder urged approval of a proposal by Chief of Naval Operations Adm. Frank B. Kelso II to gradually open to women all Navy job specialities.

News accounts on Oct. 1 disclosed that Navy Secretary Dalton had urged Aspin to dismiss Kelso, the Navy's top-ranking admiral, for failing to exercise leadership in dealing with the Tailhook scandal; Kelso was slated to retire in July 1994. Dalton also informed Aspin that he intended to reprimand a dozen other admirals and Marine generals who attended the Tailhook convention.

Then-Navy Secretary H. Lawrence Garrett III, Kelso and dozens of others had attended the convention but said they witnessed no improper behavior. However, Dalton reportedly argued to Aspin that Kelso should have cracked down on Tailhook meetings, which had benefited from considerable Navy support and had become notoriously freewheeling. Moreover, Dalton reportedly contended that Kelso should have come down hard on officers who stonewalled the initial investigation.

Garrett and two admirals who had conducted the initial probe of the incident had resigned, and dozens of other officers had been fined or disciplined. However, the Navy dropped charges against dozens of others for lack of sufficient evidence. *(1992 Almanac, p. 520)*

On Oct. 4, Aspin rejected Dalton's recommendation, saying it would unfairly subject Kelso to a different standard than the one applied to other senior officers at the meeting.

Kelso had offered to resign in 1992, but the Bush administration had rejected the offer.

Dalton issued letters of censure Oct. 15 to three senior officers who "failed to exercise active leadership" to prevent the Tailhook scandal despite "ample signals that trouble could arise." The three were retired Vice Adm. Richard Dunleavy, the former assistant chief of naval operations for air warfare, and his top deputies, Rear Adms. Riley Mixson and Wilson Flagg. ∎

Hill Again Votes To Close Military Bases

For the third time in five years, Congress voted to close unneeded domestic military bases. The 1993 list contained 35 major military installations and 95 minor ones.

On July 1, the Defense Base Closure and Realignment Commission recommended closing the facilities. President Clinton quickly accepted the closures, which the commission estimated would save $2.3 billion annually after 1999, and forwarded the list to Congress. On Sept. 20, the Senate defeated a resolution that would have blocked the closures. The House never took up the matter because any action it took would have been moot under a base closure law that required both chambers to act in order to block the closing list from taking effect. The closures were scheduled to take place over the following five years.

The base closing commission made its recommendations after months of considering an original list submitted by Defense Secretary Les Aspin. The commission spared five installations that were on Aspin's list and voted to close three facilities that Aspin had wanted to keep open — Plattsburgh Air Force Base in upstate New York, Agana Naval Air Station in Guam and the Portsmouth Naval Electronics Systems Engineering Center in Virginia.

Among the bases to be closed were the huge Navy complexes in Charleston, S.C., and Alameda, Calif., and K.I. Sawyer Air Force Base in Michigan.

BACKGROUND

It was the second round of closures to take place under a 1990 law that established the base closing process (PL 101-510). In 1991, members voted to close 25 major military bases. Under slightly different procedures, Congress had voted in 1989 to close or cut back operations at 91 bases. *(1991 Almanac, p. 427; 1990 Almanac, p. 693; 1989 Almanac, p. 470)*

Lawmakers designed the base-closing system to limit their own ability to interfere and block the closure of facilities that created local jobs but contributed little to defense operations.

Under the 1990 law, the Pentagon first drew up a list of bases it considered superfluous. The list was then reviewed by an independent commission, appointed by the president in consultation with Congress. President George Bush appointed the eight-member commission for the 1993 round on Jan. 8, sparing Clinton the task. The Senate confirmed the eight on March 4; after Arthur Levitt Jr., was nominated to head the Securities and Exchange Commission, he resigned from the commission and was not replaced.

Once the panel completed its review, it sent its list of recommended closings to the president. The president could have rejected the list and sent it back to the commission for revisions. Congress could only vote up or down on the entire list; there was no opportunity to make changes. The 1990 law provided for the process to be repeated in 1995. *(Key dates, p. 466)*

ASPIN'S LIST

The process began March 12, when the Pentagon put out a politically explosive list of 31 major domestic military bases which Aspin recommended for closure. The Defense Department said the closures — combined with scaled-

back operations that it was recommending at 134 bases — would save $3.1 billion annually after 2000.

The list, like those issued in previous years, brought cries of anguish and charges of unfairness from lawmakers whose home states or hometowns stood to lose a local shipyard or Air Force base. "It's an economic disaster," said Sen. Ernest F. Hollings, D-S.C., whose state was positioned to lose the Charleston Naval Shipyard and Station.

Attempting to take some of the sting out of the painful process, Clinton promised on March 11 to spend $20 billion over five years to help workers and communities ravaged by major cutbacks in defense spending.

And Aspin, aware that members facing potential base closings at home frequently called for cutbacks abroad instead, also announced the planned closure of 29 facilities overseas.

Bracing for Hits

California was far and away the biggest loser on Aspin's list; the state was slated to lose 10 bases and a combined total of almost 32,000 military and civilian jobs by Defense Department calculation. South Carolina stood to lose up to 19,000 jobs if its naval complex was closed, and Florida was slated to lose 10,591 jobs with the closure of the Orlando Naval Training Center and surrounding facilities.

But the possible closure of the Florida training center and its sister facility in San Diego was good news for Illinois, where the Great Lakes Naval Training Center stood to pick up more than 8,000 jobs. That made Illinois the biggest winner, with a net gain of more than 9,000 jobs. Washington state was slated to gain 5,600 jobs, and North Carolina 5,453.

The target list was dominated by Navy installations — 23 of the 31 major bases in 15 states — including sprawling facilities such as the Charleston shipyard and the Alameda Naval Air Station in Northern California. The Navy also planned to close its just-completed homeport in New York, even though it was in the process of building another homeport in Everett, Wash., in the district of Democrat Norm Dicks, a member of the House Defense Appropriations Subcommittee.

The Navy had come under heavy criticism in the two previous rounds of base closings for holding on to as many facilities as possible, while the Army and Air Force had volunteered more bases to close.

In 1993, the only large base that the Army proposed to close was Fort McClellan in Anniston, Ala., which included a center where the military trained with live chemical weapons. The Army tried to close McClellan in 1991, but that year's base-closing commission took it off the list.

The Air Force put four installations on the list, including Homestead Air Force Base in Florida. Bush had made a campaign-year promise to rebuild Homestead, which was nearly destroyed by Hurricane Andrew in 1992.

The chagrin among California lawmakers was tempered by the realization that the proposed cuts were not quite as bad as they had expected. Three California bases that were on a widely publicized preliminary list were not on Aspin's final version: McClellan Air Force Base in Sacramento, the Long Beach Naval Shipyard and the Monterey Presidio. And March Air Force Base, earlier reported to be closing, was instead scheduled to be cut back. But the San Diego

Dates and Decision-Makers

Jan. 8 — President George Bush appointed the members of the Defense Base Closure and Realignment Commission, charged with deciding which military bases should be closed.

March 12 — Defense Secretary Les Aspin released a list recommending 31 major domestic military bases for closure.

March 15 — The base closing commission began hearings.

July 1 — The commission recommended closing 35 major military installations and 95 minor ones.

July 2 — President Clinton accepted the closures and forwarded the list to Congress.

Sept. 20 — The Senate voted against a resolution that would have blocked the closures; the House did not act, thus allowing the process to move forward and the bases to be closed.

The following are the members of the 1993 Defense Base Closure and Realignment Commission:

● **James A. Courter**, former Republican House member from New Jersey. He chaired the commission in 1993 as he had in 1991.

● **Peter B. Bowman**, vice president for Gould Shawmut Inc. From 1987 until his retirement in 1990, he commanded the Portsmouth Naval Shipyard in New Hampshire.

● **Beverly B. Byron**, former Democratic House member from Maryland. She was on the Armed Services Committee when it drew up the base-closing law.

● **Rebecca Gernhardt Cox**, vice president for governmental affairs for Continental Airlines. She was married to Rep. C. Christopher Cox, R-Calif.

● **Hansford T. Johnson**, chief of staff for the Automobile Association.

● **Arthur Levitt Jr.**, chairman of the board of Levitt Media Co. Levitt served on the 1991 commission. Levitt resigned after being nominated to head the Securities and Exchange Commission; he was not replaced.

● **Harry C. McPherson Jr.**, partner with Verner, Liipfert, Bernhard, McPherson & Hand. He served as deputy under secretary of the Army for international affairs.

● **Robert D. Stuart Jr.**, president of Conway Farms. He served on the 1991 panel.

Naval Training Center, not on the early list, was on Aspin's final list.

The district of House Armed Services Committee Chairman Ronald V. Dellums, D-Calif., was one of the hardest-hit on the base list issued by Aspin, Dellums' predecessor as committee chairman. Dellums said it was "no coincidence" that the Pentagon had listed five bases in or near his district, including the Alameda air station, and charged that the military had retaliated for his efforts over 22 years to cut defense spending.

Strom Thurmond of South Carolina, the ranking Republican on the Senate Armed Services Committee, saw politics of a different sort at play. "It is obvious that changes were made to the list of bases in California, which supported President Clinton in the recent elections and which has two Democratic senators," he said in a statement. "This suggests that politics played some part in a decision which should be totally separate from any whisper of partisanship."

While California was slated to lose the greatest number of facilities and jobs, the proposed closures in Charleston were likely to have an even greater impact on a much smaller state.

The sprawling naval complex, which had been in operation since 1901, was the third-largest Navy station in the country, behind Norfolk, Va., and San Diego. Nearly 19,000 direct military and civilian jobs were slated to be lost by the recommended closure of the Naval Shipyard, Naval Station, and the attendant supply center and defense depot. Charleston County, with a population of 304,840, was also going to lose its modern 348-bed Naval hospital.

"The Navy, or any arm of the government, ought to bear the burden of proving why it makes sense to walk away from billions of dollars in investment, much of it made in the last 15 years," John M. Spratt Jr., D-S.C., a member of the House Armed Services Committee, said.

THE COMMISSION BEGINS

Aspin made no effort to hide his relief as he handed off the task of shutting military bases to the eight-member commission crafted to weather the political storm. "This is now your baby," Aspin told the panel at its opening hearing March 15, noting that the easy closures had already occurred.

The 1993 list of closings was based on the structure of military forces that was planned by the Bush administration's Defense Department. Aspin said he expected to come before another base-closure commission in 1995 with another list of bases to close after he completed a bottom-up review of defense policy. *(Bottom-up review, p. 452)*

Aspin said that the process of choosing bases to vacate was "an art, not a science" and that the current list was "probably not enough." With that in mind, Aspin urged the commission to maintain the level of reductions anticipated in his list, which projected cutting 24,000 military and 57,000 civilian jobs and saving $3.1 billion annually after the year 2000. If the commission subtracted a base from his list, Aspin said, it should find a replacement to add.

Aspin cited concern over the "cumulative impact" of pending and proposed shutdowns on communities and regions that had built their economies around a formidable military presence. He said that was the reason he removed McClellan Air Force Base from the preliminary closure list that the service branches had offered up. Targeting McClellan, he said, would have looked "like we were piling on in that Northern California area." Aspin said he also removed the Monterey Presidio from the preliminary list because intelligence agencies had opposed plans to move the Defense Language Institute from the Monterey facility.

After those adjustments, Aspin said, "No one state can claim, I think, to be picked on."

Commissioner Robert D. Stuart Jr. questioned Aspin closely about how the Defense Department had reached its conclusions on the cumulative economic impact of base closings. Aspin said each of the services had considered its

own recommendations in isolation; his staff then reviewed the cumulative impact of past rounds and of all the cuts proposed in this round. Stuart asked if Aspin had taken into account other factors, such as a depressed economy in northern Michigan or the effects of Hurricane Hugo on Charleston, S.C.

Aspin said he had not weighed those factors. But, referring to the Charleston complex, he invited the commissioner to do so. "It's your choice, sir," he said.

Joint Chiefs of Staff Chairman Gen. Colin L. Powell Jr., testifying with Aspin, said that fewer bases were needed because of plans for a smaller Navy, with less than 400 ships compared with the previous plan for 600 ships. "They have to abandon that concept of many, many homeports," he said.

The Commission's Criteria

The 1990 law required the base commission to use eight criteria in evaluating whether the Defense Department had properly chosen its shutdown targets. Only if the commissioners determined that the Pentagon significantly deviated from these standards could they add or delete a base.

The first and most important factors dealt with the military value of the base.

The commission was to evaluate:

● How the base affected mission requirements (both existing and future) and the readiness of U.S. forces.

● How easily the base could expand into adjacent land if needed and the condition of that land.

● How the base could accommodate mobilization and other future force structure requirements.

● The cost and manpower implications of closing the base.

The commission was to consider:

● How much money could be saved by closing the base.

● The economic impact on local communities, including the cumulative economic impact.

● The ability of bases receiving additional forces to accommodate them in terms of schools, roads and other facilities.

● The environmental impacts.

Environmental problems at U.S. domestic bases were enormous. Cleaning up the 42 bases slated for closure in the 1989 and 1991 rounds was estimated to cost at least $3 billion. For all of the Defense Department's facilities, environmental cleanup was expected to cost at least $35 billion over the next 20 years.

Many communities got hit twice as a result of the polluted bases: They lost their local base, and they could not convert it to other economically or socially productive uses until the Defense Department had cleaned it up, which could take years.

Aspin acknowledged March 15 that "there has been an enormous delay, for reasons that are not entirely clear to me, in cleaning up bases." Commission Chairman James A. Courter said he was concerned that bases that were very polluted were not put on the list because they would be too costly to clean. "The system would be very perverse," he said, if it prevented the closure of the most tainted bases.

Commission Hearings

To allow communities to plead their cases for local bases, the commission held a series of regional hearings.

On April 20-21, the commission held two days of hearings in Northern Virginia to listen to local leaders discuss Aspin's proposal to move many naval headquarters offices from rented space in Arlington, Va., to government-owned space elsewhere.

California got its say on April 25, 26 and 27 during commission hearings in Oakland and San Diego. Charleston was next on May 1-2, followed by Orlando, Fla., on May 3 and Birmingham, Ala., on May 4. Commissioners held their final field hearings in the Northeast on May 9 and 10 in New York, May 11 in Boston and May 12 in Detroit.

In addition to the field hearings, every major military base that was on the list received a visit by at least one commission member.

COMMISSION ACTION

The commission added 47 bases to the Pentagon's list of candidates for closure. Most of the bases were added during a 15-hour session May 21 and were offered as alternatives to those selected by the Pentagon.

The members planned to review not only the merits of closing a particular base but also the Pentagon's underlying assumptions: Which shipyard should be closed on the East Coast? Should one of the Strategic Air Command bases be shut down? What Army training base should go? How could the Pentagon merge operations at its supply depots to cut costs?

Many community groups with bases on the Pentagon list had done their homework and offered an alternate base with a similar mission that could be closed instead.

"Communities obviously have come up with competing scenarios," Commission Chairman Courter said during the May 21 session.

Many of those arguments needed to be studied, he said, so the alternative bases were added to the list.

While some lawmakers who suddenly found their hometown bases at risk attempted to minimize the development — Senate Armed Services Committee Chairman Sam Nunn, D-Ga., called the commission's work an "opportunity to illuminate the many strong features of our Georgia bases and their important role in the overall defense structure" — others were not so sanguine.

Sen. John W. Warner, R-Va., said the commission was supposed to take the politics out of the process and warned that if this "fire wall had been breached and any decision has been influenced by politics, then a 'civil war' is going to break out between the states and congressional delegations." The commission had added several bases in Virginia, including the Norfolk Naval Shipyard, the Navy's second-highest-rated ship repair facility.

Such exhortations were all that was left to members of Congress, however, since they had deliberately excluded themselves from the commission process when they crafted the base closure law. Reps. Arthur Ravenel Jr., R-S.C., and G. V. "Sonny" Montgomery, D-Miss., spent most of May 21 sitting in the huge House Ways and Means Committee room in the Longworth House Office Building watching the commission debate. Ravenel wanted to make sure that the commission added all the bases that could be alternatives to his district's huge naval complex in Charleston. Montgomery was concerned about the Meridian Naval Air Station in his district. Both men left satisfied with the commission's actions.

Some lawmakers were caught off-guard as the May 21 session droned on. Sometime after 9 p.m., the commission began discussing adding large aircraft bases to the list. Sen.

Continued on p. 470

The Target List

Following are the major military bases closed by the Defense Base Closure and Realignment Commission, the lawmakers who represented the home communities and the Pentagon's estimate of the number of military and civilian personnel employed at each facility:

State, Senators	Base	Representatives	Military	Civilian
Alabama Howell Heflin, D; Richard C. Shelby, D	Mobile Naval Station	Sonny Callahan, R	524	126
California Barbara Boxer, D; Dianne Feinstein, D	Mare Island Naval Shipyard	George Miller, D	1,963	7,567
	Alameda Naval Aviation Depot	Ronald V. Dellums, D	376	2,672
	Alameda Naval Air Station	Dellums	10,586	556
	Treasure Island Naval Station	Nancy Pelosi, D	637	454
	Oakland Naval Hospital	Dellums	1,472	809
	San Diego Naval Training Center	Lynn Schenk, D	5,186	402
	El Toro Marine Corps Air Station	C. Christopher Cox, R	5,689	979
	Port Hueneme Naval Civil Engineering Lab	Elton Gallegly, R	17	384
	Public Works Center	Dellums	10	1,834
Florida Bob Graham, D; Connie Mack, R	Orlando Naval Training Center	Bill McCollum, R	8,727	753
	Pensacola Naval Aviation Depot	Earl Hutto, D	297	3,107
	Pensacola Naval Supply Center	Hutto	20	245
	Cecil Field Naval Air Station	Cliff Stearns, R	6,833	995
	Orlando Naval Hospital	McCollum	759	352
Hawaii Daniel K. Inouye, D; Daniel K. Akaka, D	Barbers Point Naval Air Station	Patsy T. Mink, D	3,534	618
Illinois Paul Simon, D; Carol Moseley-Braun, D	Glenview Naval Air Station	John Edward Porter, R	1,833	389
	O'Hare Airport Air Force Reserve Station	Henry J. Hyde, R	5	757
Michigan Donald W. Riegle Jr., D; Carl Levin, D	K. I. Sawyer Air Force Base	Bart Stupak, D	2,354	788
	Detroit Naval Air Facility	John Conyers Jr., D	523	24

| Dellums | McCollum | Stupak | Molinari | Ravenel | Pickett |

State, Senators	Base	Representatives	Military	Civilian
New Jersey Bill Bradley, D; Frank R. Lautenberg, D	Trenton Naval Air Warfare Center	Christopher H. Smith, R	8	448
New York Daniel Patrick Moynihan, D; Alfonse M. D'Amato, R	Staten Island Home Port Plattsburgh Air Force Base *	Susan Molinari, R John M. McHugh, R	1,773 2,009	1,001 304
Ohio John Glenn, D; Howard M. Metzenbaum, D	Newark Air Force Base Defense Electronics Supply, Dayton	Douglas Applegate, D Tony P. Hall, D	92 93	1,760 2,804
Pennsylvania Arlen Specter, R; Harris Wofford, D	Philadelphia Defense Clothing Factory Philadelphia Defense Personnel Support	Thomas M. Foglietta, D Foglietta	2 78	1,235 3,878
South Carolina Strom Thurmond, R; Ernest F. Hollings, D	Charleston Naval Station Charleston Naval Shipyard	Arthur Ravenel Jr., R Ravenel	8,634 74	1,194 4,837
Texas Phil Gramm, R; Kay Bailey Hutchison, R	Dallas Naval Air Station	Eddie Bernice Johnson, D	1,374	268
Virginia Charles S. Robb, D; John W. Warner, R	Vint Hill Farms Station (defense intelligence) Norfolk Naval Aviation Depot Portsmouth Naval Electronic Systems Engineering Center *	Frank R. Wolf, R Owen B. Pickett, D Norman Sisisky, D	407 104 12	1,472 4,295 413
District of Columbia	Naval Electronic Security Systems Engineering Center	Del. Eleanor Holmes Norton, D	515	636
Guam	Agana Naval Air Station *	Del. Robert A. Underwood, D	2,920	391

* This base was added by the commission to those originally proposed by Defense Secretary Les Aspin.

NOTE: This list is based on the commission's definition of a major base, which differed from the definition used in Aspin's initial list.

SOURCES: Defense Base Closure and Realignment Commission; Defense Department

Continued from p. 467

Kent Conrad, D-N.D., walked into the hearing room wearing a jogging suit, sneakers and a New York Mets baseball cap, and listened to the discussion, nodding at some points. But there was nothing he could do — the commission added Grand Forks Air Force Base in North Dakota to its review list.

Courter repeatedly reminded those watching the deliberations that nothing had been decided. "Our job as an independent commission is to render a fair and informed judgment of the [Defense] secretary's recommendations," Courter said. "I don't think we can do that in some cases without making direct comparisons between bases that are on the secretary's list and similar bases that are not."

Navy Choices

Just as the Navy had the bulk of bases on Aspin's original list, naval bases dominated the commission's list of added starters. Perhaps the most difficult choice for commissioners was what shipyards to close, particularly on the East Coast. "All the commissioners are wrestling with" it, said panel member Beverly B. Byron, a former Democratic House member from Maryland.

Responding to Aspin's plan called for closing the Charleston shipyard, the neighboring community argued that the Navy would get rid of even more of its excess capacity if it closed the far bigger Norfolk Naval Shipyard in Virginia.

To keep their options open, commissioners put all three East Coast shipyards at risk. The panel added to its list both Norfolk and Portsmouth Naval Shipyard, which was in Maine and next to Portsmouth, N.H. The vote to add Norfolk was one of the closest of the day: 4-2. Commissioner Peter Bowman recused himself from voting on the East Coast shipyards because he owned property close to Portsmouth.

The commission also expanded its West Coast options. Representatives of the community surrounding the Mare Island shipyard in the San Francisco Bay Area argued that their local facility was capable of repairing nuclear ships but that Long Beach Naval Shipyard, which escaped Aspin's list, was not. Commissioners voted 6-1 to add Long Beach to the list. Commissioner Rebecca Gernhardt Cox, who was married to Rep. C. Christopher Cox, R-Calif., dissented.

With that vote, the commission had put on the list of potential shutdowns all but one of the nation's six shipyards. The exception was the Navy's top-rated facility at Puget Sound in Washington state.

The commission added naval stations in Ingleside, Texas, and Pascagoula, Miss., as alternates to Charleston's naval station. And members agreed to study the not-yet-completed naval station in Everett, Wash., as a substitute for the Alameda Naval Air Station.

Montgomery and his constituents scored a minor success in the deliberations when the commission added the naval air training station in Corpus Christi, Texas, as a potential substitute for the Meridian training center in Mississippi.

Air Force Surprises

One of the biggest surprises was the commission's decision to add three large aircraft bases to the list as potential alternatives to closing K. I. Sawyer in Michigan, which was on Aspin's original list. K. I. Sawyer, home to B-52 bombers and KC-135 tankers, was in the Upper Peninsula of Michigan, where the average yearly snowfall was 137.6 inches. It was the only major military installation left in Michigan; in 1991 the commission's predecessor voted to close the state's Wurtsmith Air Force Base.

The commission voted unanimously to add to the endangered list Plattsburgh Air Force base in upstate New York and Grand Forks Air Force Base in North Dakota. And only Byron voted against a motion to add Fairchild Air Force Base in Washington.

The Air Force had conceded that it had four more large aircraft bases than it would need once terms of the Strategic Arms Reduction Treaty between the United States and the former Soviet Union were fully in place. But with the volatility in Russia and the other republics, the Air Force had wanted to wait to close the bases.

Grand Forks was a Strategic Air Command base that was home to aircraft including B-1 bombers and KC-135s. Plattsburgh, a tanker base, was used mostly for refueling. The addition of Plattsburgh was also seen as a boon for neighbors of McGuire Air Force Base in New Jersey, who had recommended that the commission close Plattsburgh instead of their own base. McGuire was slated to lose all its active-duty functions and up to 8,000 jobs, while keeping its reserve and National Guard roles. The base, the largest aerial port of embarkation on the East Coast, functioned primarily as a cargo-loading depot. Courter, a former Republican House member from New Jersey, smiled as he observed sympathetically that the Plattsburgh base had "been a victim of a double team" attack by advocates of both K. I. Sawyer and McGuire.

The commission also expanded its options for Army base closures. It added a training base at Fort Lee in Virginia as a possible substitute for Fort McClellan in Alabama and added Fort Monroe in Virginia as an alternative to cutting back operations at Fort Belvoir, also in Virginia.

Too Many Depots

The commission also took on the huge task of reviewing most of the services' 29 depots, which functioned as repair and storage centers. According to a report by the Joint Chiefs of Staff, these depots had up to 50 percent more capacity than the services needed.

But efforts over the preceding 15 years to consolidate the depots had met strong resistance. The services did not want to share facilities, and the depots enjoyed strong political support because they had large civilian payrolls.

According to the commission staff, the depots cost about $13 billion each year and employed 130,000 civilians and 2,000 military personnel. The staff estimated that as many as 10 of the depots could be closed without losing any repair ability.

Of the six Air Force depots, one, Newark Air Force Base in Ohio, was already on the closure list. The commission added California's McClellan Air Force Base on March 29; on May 21, it added the remaining four facilities: Hill Air Force Base in Utah, Kelly Air Force Base in Texas, Robins in Georgia and Tinker in Oklahoma.

Aspin had put three of the Navy's six aviation depots on the closure list: Norfolk, Va., Pensacola, Fla., and Alameda, Calif. The commission added the remainder: Cherry Point, N.C., Jacksonville, Fla., and North Island in San Diego.

After adding so many bases to the original list, the commission held a weeklong marathon of hearings to listen to concerned members. Over three days during the week of June 14, 209 members of Congress trooped into the Hart

Senate office building to make cases for their bases. Some lawmakers were friendly, chatting warmly with commissioners they had come to know well.

Others sternly warned the panel about the consequences of approving Aspin's list — or, in some cases, of adding their hometown bases to it.

Members borrowed time from their other duties to plead for local installations. Senate Finance Committee Chairman Daniel Patrick Moynihan, D-N.Y., interrupted crucial negotiations on the budget-reconciliation bill to ask the commission to spare New York Naval Station at Staten Island. And GOP Sen. Kay Bailey Hutchinson, in her first official appearance as a senator, made a plea for the various Texas installations on the list.

Members of Congress with bases in jeopardy were aware of the heavy burden of proof they had to take to the commission to overturn Aspin's choices. That was one reason why so many took the opportunity to testify one last time before the commission.

THE COMMISSION VOTES

From the start, the commission had vowed not to be a "rubber stamp" for the Pentagon, and it showed its long-promised independence when it came time to make the final decisions. Although the commissioners accepted many of Aspin's recommendations, including his call to close the Charleston shipyard, they also saved bases that Aspin wanted closed and voted to close some that he wanted to retain.

The commission began its final deliberations June 23 and worked for the next four days straight.

Air Force

One of its boldest moves was the vote June 24 on which facility to recommend as the Air Force's East Coast air mobility base. That base was to be the primary location for refueling tankers and cargo planes on the East Coast.

Two New York bases — Plattsburgh and Griffiss — were competing with McGuire in New Jersey for that designation. The Air Force had picked Plattsburgh, which sat on the shore of Lake Champlain and had an 18-hole golf course, and recommended cutting back operations at the other two bases. But commissioners contended that McGuire was the better choice. Commissioner and former Air Force Gen. Hansford T. Johnson led the charge for McGuire, arguing that while facilities were much nicer at Plattsburgh, "the location of McGuire" made it a better a pick, because it was "much closer" to the other bases it would serve. Commissioners then voted 6-1 to give the mobility mission to McGuire.

That left Plattsburgh without a mission. The commission voted 6-1 to close the base, the first time in two rounds of closures that commissioners had voted to close a base that was not on the Defense Department's original list. Commissioner Byron was the dissenter on both votes.

Panel members voted unanimously to approve the Pentagon recommendation to cut back operations at Griffiss.

Commissioners struggled with another Air Force decision on June 24 — the vote to close K. I. Sawyer in Michigan. Panel members spent much of the afternoon searching for a way to spare the facility in the sparsely populated Upper Peninsula. The commission staff estimated that the 2,700 jobs lost due to the closure could result in 24 percent unemployment for that part of Michigan.

But after hours of discussion, the commissioners agreed

that the Air Force had too many bases for its force structure and voted unanimously to close the base. Commissioners were subdued during the vote. Chairman Courter, who appeared distracted, almost forgot to cast his ballot; he called for a five-minute recess after the vote and immediately left the room.

Most of the Air Force facilities the commission had added to its list for study May 21 were spared. Members declined to close the Grand Forks base because arms control treaties specified it as a prime location for anti-missile defenses and Fairchild Air Force Base in Washington state because it was too costly to close.

Florida's Homestead Air Force Base got a small reprieve. Although the Air Force had recommended closing the base and relocating its functions, commissioners voted unanimously to keep two Air Force reserve divisions at Homestead.

Members unanimously approved, with little discussion, the Air Force's realignment plan for Southern California's March Air Force Base. March was to become primarily a reserve base and would lose about 4,000 jobs.

The commission voted, 6-1, to save McClellan Air Force Base, which the panel had added to Aspin's list. Commission members also removed from the target list three other Air Force logistics centers.

Army

For the second time, the base-closure commission rejected an attempt by the Army to close Fort McClellan in Alabama. When the Pentagon tried to close the base in 1991, the commission took it off its list, arguing that the country needed the chemical training functions performed by the base. Two years later, its successor commission said the situation had not really changed.

The Pentagon had recommended closing the fort and keeping open just a part of the chemical training facility — the only known place where soldiers could learn how to decontaminate equipment that had been exposed to chemical weapons. The commission voted 6-1 to take Fort McClellan off the closure list.

Commissioners also decided not to close 175-year-old Fort Monroe in Virginia, which it had added to the Pentagon list. Members agreed that the facility was still a necessary part of the Army training command. The commission agreed with the Defense Department's recommendations to cut back operations at Virginia's Fort Belvoir and to close Vint Hill Farms Station, also in Virginia. Vint Hill Farms collected top-secret information for various government agencies.

Navy

The panel voted, 6-0, to close the shipyard in Charleston, despite the local community's ambitious lobbying effort to save the complex that had been central to its economy and history. The commission voted 5-2 to close the Charleston Naval Station, another key part of the complex. When a commission aide spoke of the economic havoc that closing the complex would cause, Courter waved aside further discussion of that concern. "We know the recommendation is nuclear warfare on Charleston," he said.

The commission voted 6-0 to keep open the shipyard in Norfolk, Va., which the panel had added to its list as a possible alternative to Charleston. "I had hoped that Norfolk would be the solution" to the Navy's problem of excess shipyard capacity in an era of reductions," said commission member Harry C. McPherson Jr., who said he found no

support within the commission. "I struck out," he added.

The commission also spared Portsmouth Naval Shipyard in Maine, which it had also considered as an alternative to Charleston.

To dull the pain of closing Charleston's Naval shipyard and station, the commission decided to concentrate the Navy's electronics systems and repair centers there. The Navy had wanted to consolidate its scattered electronics shops in Portsmouth, Va. But the commission chose to move the operations to Charleston, where they could be located in buildings that would be vacated once the naval station closed.

Commissioner Bowman attempted to console Thurmond with the argument that the decision could prove the best solution for Charleston. Even if the commission had voted to keep open the shipyard or naval station, it almost certainly would have been on the Defense Department's next hit list for closure in 1995. "Charleston is stronger now with what we put there," Bowman said. The move promised to leave at least 3,000 jobs in Charleston, a fraction of the 16,000 jobs the community stood to lose.

The panel voted 4-3 to close Alameda Naval Air Station and unanimously to close Mare Island Naval Shipyard in the San Francisco Bay Area. "My family history to Mare Island goes back almost 50 years" said Bowman, a retired Navy officer. Moved to tears, Bowman reminisced that he was married in the base chapel.

The commission also endorsed the Pentagon recommendation to close the Treasure Island Naval Station in San Francisco Bay.

Forces stationed at the three facilities were to be transferred mainly to the megaport in San Diego. To soften slightly the blow to the Bay Area, the commission voted unanimously to keep open the Oakland Naval Supply Center.

One of the closest votes came when the panel decided to keep open Long Beach Naval Shipyard in Southern California, which it had added to Aspin's original hit list. A motion to close that shipyard failed, 3-4, with Courter casting the deciding vote.

The commission rejected two major elements of the Navy's plan. The Defense Department wanted to close the South Weymouth Naval Air Station in Massachusetts and move its mission to several other bases, including two facilities not yet built. Commissioners voted unanimously to keep South Weymouth as the last naval reserve station in the Northeast, choosing instead to scrap partially constructed bases in Johnstown, Pa., and Martinsburg, W.Va.

Finding that the Defense Department had miscalculated how much space it needed for air-to-ground attack training, commissioners voted unanimously to retain Meridian Naval Air Station in Mississippi, to the delight of Rep. Montgomery, who had invested so much of his time lobbying the commissioners to save his local base.

The panel cited economic hardship in Philadelphia in voting to merge two Navy facilities there. Aspin had called for closing the Aviation Supply Office and the Defense Personnel Support Center. But the commission voted to close the personnel office and move its function to the aviation center, thus keeping nearly 6,400 jobs in the Philadelphia economy. The area was hard hit in 1991 by the commission's predecessor, which voted to close the Philadelphia Naval Shipyard.

Happy Losers

At least two communities were pleased to lose their bases. After years of lobbying the Pentagon unsuccessfully, leaders of Guam persuaded the commission to close the Agana Naval Air Station, which was not on Aspin's list.

Courter said that the 1991 commission had told the Navy and the Air Force to try sharing Anderson Air Force Base on the island so that Agana could be used to expand a neighboring commercial airport. "I guess we weren't taken seriously," Courter said.

The commission also responded to pleas from Hawaii in voting to close the Naval Air Station at Barbers Point, freeing prime waterfront real estate for development.

Perhaps the most complicated scenario tackled by the commission involved closing El Toro Marine Corps Air Station in California. After debating alternative scenarios urged by California Republican Reps. Randy "Duke" Cunningham and Duncan Hunter, the commission accepted a game of musical aircraft urged by the Pentagon.

To accommodate planes and helicopters coming out of El Toro, F-14 fighter planes at Miramar Naval Air Station were to be moved to Lemoore Naval Air Station, also in California.

Arlington, Va., across the Potomac River from Washington, took a big hit when the commission approved the Pentagon plan to move six naval headquarters out of the Crystal City high-rise development. The plan would result in the loss of about 6,000 jobs beyond the 5,300 positions at the headquarters that were to be eliminated though layoffs and attrition. The Pentagon said it could save money by moving from rental space to government-owned buildings.

Courter said the commission could not take into consideration a plan, proposed by Arlington, for the Navy to buy the building it rented. But he called that an attractive alternative and noted that the Navy would have time to study the alternative before the closure, slated to begin in 1996.

PRESIDENT'S ACTION

Less than 24 hours after receiving the commission's list, Clinton announced July 2 that he had accepted the panel's recommendations. The list identified 35 major military bases and 95 smaller ones across the country to be shut down, along with 27 major bases and 18 minor facilities slated for cutbacks. The panel estimated that its recommendations would require a one-time expenditure of $7.4 billion, then would save about $2.3 billion each year after 1999.

Clinton promised that he would also take steps to reduce the economic pain of the closings. He said the moves would include: appointing a single federal coordinator to work with each affected community, offering grants averaging $1 million to help plan new uses for bases, speeding the cleanup of pollution that taints many of the bases and changing federal rules so that closed bases could be sold at a discount for new commercial uses that create jobs.

"Compared to the past," he said, "we will respond more quickly, cut red tape more aggressively, and mobilize resources more assertively to help these communities, so that when they lose their bases they do not lose their future."

Clinton spoke of a $5 billion program over five years, half of it for environmental cleanup; Aspin confirmed that the money would come mostly from previously proposed spending.

With timing that appeared aimed at underscoring the need for military belt-tightening, Aspin on July 1 announced plans to close or reduce 92 overseas bases. These closures did not require congressional approval.

CONGRESSIONAL ACTION

The Senate on Sept. 20 dealt the final blow to the 35 major military installations slated for closure by the De-

fense Base Closure and Realignment Commission. By a vote of 12-83, the Senate rejected a resolution (S J Res 114) that would have overturned the work of the seven-member panel and kept the bases open. *(Vote 271, p. 35-S)*

"We don't need all these bases, and, basically, we can't afford to pay for them," said Sen. John Glenn, D-Ohio.

Most of the opposition came from senators whose states would bear the brunt of the closings. "I cannot support something that will destroy the lives of so many of my people," said Thurmond.

Barbara Boxer, D-Calif., spoke of the pain the proposed closings would cause to her home state. Of the 35 major bases slated for closure, nine were in California. "No one state should be disproportionately hit," she said. "Is it fair to take 48 percent of the personnel reductions from one state?" asked California's other senator, Democrat Dianne Feinstein.

But Armed Services Committee Chairman Nunn said the process was a fair one, though, he said, "fair does not mean perfect." ∎

Senate Defers Ratification Of START II Treaty

President George Bush and Russian President Boris N. Yeltsin signed START II, the second Strategic Arms Reduction Treaty, on Jan. 3.

The treaty, which fleshed out a broad agreement signed by Yeltsin and Bush the previous June, called for slashing the number of U.S. and Russian nuclear warheads to no more than 6,500. The treaty thus promised to remove from service more than two-thirds of the nearly 24,000 warheads that had been deployed as of 1990 by the United States and the Soviet Union.

That cutback would eliminate from service all weapons carried by multiple-warhead, land-based missiles, which U.S. officials long had regarded as the most threatening type in the former Soviet arsenal. And the reduction could be achieved as early as the year 2000, provided the United States helped Russia bear the cost of demobilizing its large nuclear force.

But the Senate did not take up the treaty during 1993 because former Soviet republics — Ukraine in particular — had failed to conclude action under the previous START I treaty.

START I

The initial Strategic Arms Reduction Treaty was ratified by the Senate on Oct. 1, 1992, only to become stalled by the complexities of post-Soviet geopolitics. *(1992 Almanac, p. 513)*

START I, negotiated between the United States and the Soviet Union, was supposed to reduce strategic warhead inventories by about one-third. But after the Soviet Union disintegrated, that pact had to be recast with a series of negotiated appendices to bind the four former Soviet republics that controlled parts of the former Soviet nuclear force.

START I, in its final form, required that the three republics other than Russia — Ukraine, Belarus and Kazakhstan — eliminate all nuclear weapons under their control and seal that commitment by signing the 1968 nuclear non-proliferation treaty. The Russian government an-

nounced that it would not begin implementing START I reductions until the other three republics followed through on those requirements.

Ukrainian President Leonid M. Kravchuk promised to carry out the terms of START I. But Kravchuk and the Ukrainian parliament sent contradictory and wavering signals throughout 1993 as to their willingness to do so and the price they would demand in Western aid and security guarantees.

The Clinton administration initially took the stand that the Senate should move ahead with START II, rather than await resolution of the conflicts over its predecessor treaty. "I believe that delay on START I is no reason for us to defer action on START II," Secretary of State Warren Christopher told the Senate Foreign Relations Committee on May 11. "START II, after all, reduces the threat to all of Russia's neighbors by reducing Russian nuclear forces. Thus, prompt Senate action to approve START II will encourage rapid action on the part of Kazakhstan and Ukraine."

But the START II treaty did not advance, and the administration did not continue to lobby for action.

Final Negotiations

The START II agreement was confirmed by Bush on Dec. 30, 1992, after three final issues were resolved in a series of phone conversations between Bush and Yeltsin and in face-to-face negotiations between U.S. Secretary of State Lawrence S. Eagleburger and Russian Foreign Minister Andrei V. Kozyrev. Those end-game agreements would:

● Allow Russia, which was required by START I to scrap 154 of its giant 10-warhead SS-18 missiles, to retain some of the armored launch silos for the remaining 154 SS-18s, though the missiles themselves would have to be scrapped. The remaining silos would have to be partly filled with concrete, so that they no longer could contain SS-18s.

● Allow Russia to avoid the cost of developing a new, single-warhead missile by keeping a certain number of its multiwarhead SS-19s, from which it would have to remove all but one warhead.

● Allow the United States to exempt from treaty limits some of its bombers by assigning them solely to conventional missions. However, the United States retained the right to reassign those planes to a nuclear role, as older, nuclear-armed B-52s were retired. ∎

Senate Approves Foreign Reconnaissance Flights

The Senate on Aug. 6 approved a pact, known as the Open Skies Treaty, which allowed the United States, Canada, Russia and 24 European countries to fly unarmed reconnaissance planes over each other's territories.

The pact (Treaty Doc. 102-37), approved by the requisite two-thirds of senators on a standing vote, assigned each country an annual quota of overflights that it had to accept. After giving 72 hours' notice, the planes could use photography and infrared devices to look for troop or equipment movements.

U.S. and Russian satellites routinely provided more detailed information than did the sensors that the Open Skies treaty mandated for these overflights. But the Bush

and Clinton administrations, in mutual support of the treaty, argued that the pact would reassure other European countries.

The Senate Foreign Relations Committee had approved the Open Skies Treaty by voice vote May 20 with no discussion.

The treaty was signed March 24, 1992, by President George Bush, along with the leaders of the 15 other NATO countries, five members of the former Warsaw Pact and four republics of the former Soviet Union. Congress did not act on the treaty in 1992. *(1992 Almanac, p. 516)*

The pact assigned each signator country a quota of overflights that it must allow. The United States had by far the biggest quota — 42 flights — which was the same amount designated for both the Russian Republic and the Republic of Belarus. The smallest quota, two annual over-flights, went to Portugal.

The treaty did not mean that the overflights would actually take place, only that the signator countries had the right to fly them if they chose.

The resolution of ratification approved by the Senate required the president to:

● Give the Senate 30 days' notice of any proposed change in the aerial sensors.

● Estimate, after the treaty had been in effect for one year, the annual number of U.S. flights to be conducted under the treaty and the number of specially equipped planes required. ■

Chemical Arms Ban

During a three-day meeting in Paris that began Jan. 13, the United States, Russia, China and more than 120 other countries signed a treaty that sought to eliminate chemical weapons within 20 years.

The Senate took no action on the treaty during 1993.

The agreement banned the development, production, use or stockpiling of such weapons. It required that chemical weapons be destroyed and their production facilities destroyed or converted to other uses within 10 years, although a country could request a five-year extension.

The treaty was to take effect two years after the Paris ceremony or six months after 65 countries ratified it, whichever came first.

Iraq, Libya, Syria and North Korea, which were suspected of covertly developing chemical weapons, declined to sign the chemical weapons treaty.

The treaty did not permit countries to dispose of chemical weapons and lethal chemicals by dumping them at sea, burying them or burning them outdoors. All weapons were to be destroyed at designated sites that would be subject to on-site monitoring by observers from other countries.

To deter cheating, the treaty allowed any signatory to demand a spot inspection of any facility in another country on five days' notice. To prevent contraband from being spirited away, the site was to be cordoned off by international inspectors within 48 hours of the demand.

But critics, such as Frank J. Gaffney Jr., argued that the verification system was inadequate to prevent cheating by pariah states such as Iraq. Gaffney, a Pentagon official during the Reagan administration, contended that the treaty would deprive U.S. forces of the opportunity to deter chemical attacks by threatening "in kind" retaliation. ■

Les Aspin Serves One Year As Defense Secretary

A few hours after President Clinton took the oath of office Jan. 20, the Senate Armed Services Committee approved Wisconsin Democratic Rep. Les Aspin's nomination as Defense secretary. The full Senate gave voice vote approval to the Aspin nomination the same day, after Armed Services Committee Chairman Sam Nunn, D-Ga., lavishly praised Aspin's mastery of defense-related issues.

To ensure a smooth transition at the Pentagon, Aspin was sworn in two hours later at a small ceremony at the House Armed Services Committee, which Aspin chaired from 1985 until he stepped down to head the Defense Department. He was sworn in again Jan. 22 with other confirmed Cabinet and Cabinet-level officers in a White House ceremony.

Although Aspin was one of the first members confirmed to Clinton's Cabinet, he also was the first to leave. After a troubled tenure, Aspin announced Dec. 16 that he would resign Jan. 20, 1994, exactly a year after becoming Defense secretary.

From a congressional vantage point on the sidelines of defense policy, Aspin, 54, had been instrumental in devising guiding principles for an active U.S. military in the post-Cold War era. During his Jan. 7 confirmation hearing before the Senate Armed Services Committee, the always opinionated Aspin tried to sidestep tough policy questions. However, he could not avoid the implications of his past pronouncements or the urgency of current events. One message that came through was his conviction that U.S. force could and should be used — even for limited objectives with uncertain outcomes.

As Aspin testified, about 20,000 U.S. troops were trying to safeguard relief shipments against marauding clans in Somalia. And at the United Nations, diplomats were drafting a Security Council resolution that would mandate military action to enforce a ban on flights by Serbian aircraft over the former Yugoslav republic of Bosnia-Herzegovina.

Bosnia Central to Testimony

U.S. response to the carnage in Bosnia, where Serbian forces ravaged Muslim-populated areas, was a focal point of Aspin's confirmation hearing and a case study of his views on the U.S. military after the Cold War.

Aspin agreed with Clinton's calls for stronger U.S. action in Bosnia. "If the world does nothing about what's going on in Bosnia," Aspin asked, "what kind of signal does that send to other places, in the former Soviet Union and other places, where similar things might erupt? And if the world does nothing about Bosnia, what message does it send about a willingness to sit back and let these things happen also?"

A key congressional backer of war with Iraq in 1991, Aspin advocated the use of precision-guided weapons to conduct finely calibrated attacks on targets chosen for the leverage they provided against an adversary. He also argued that, in the wake of the disintegration of the Soviet Union, the United States could afford interventions that might not end in triumph because the balance of influence was no longer at stake everywhere.

"During the Cold War," he said, "every instance of the use of force was watched by our friends and enemies to see if we had resolve. So if we went into an operation . . . and it didn't work, we couldn't back off because it would be read [as a sign of weakness] in Moscow or in Jerusalem or in Taipei."

"Maybe that's different now . . . . Maybe you can use

force not to achieve something, but to punish people for doing certain things."

Liberal Democrats, some of whom had urged stronger action to save lives in the former Yugoslavia, did not question Aspin's views on the use of force in regional conflicts. But Aspin's penchant for the limited use of force was questioned by some conservative Republicans who worried that limited interventions might turn into Vietnam-style quagmires. "If force is used imprecisely and out of frustration rather than clear analysis, the situation can be made worse," said Robert C. Smith, R-N.H. "I think that applies to Bosnia."

Aspin touched on a number of other issues during the confirmation hearing. He reiterated Clinton's campaign pledge to trim at least $60 billion from President George Bush's projected defense budgets over five years. But he warned senators that deeper cuts were likely because the Bush long-term plan had anticipated $70 billion in savings as a result of improvements in the Pentagon's contracting systems. Pentagon officials had since written those estimated savings off as overly optimistic.

Aspin pointed out that he had supported the successful 1991 effort to repeal the law banning the assignment of women to fly combat aircraft. But he declined to commit to recommending a change in the Pentagon's continuing policy against women in combat. Aspin rambled in response to a question about Clinton's campaign promise to drop the controversial ban on homosexuals in the armed services, but he made no suggestion that Clinton would fail to uphold the pledge. *(Nomination, 1992 Almanac, p. 151-A)*

Aspin's Resignation

On Dec. 16, Aspin appeared in the Oval Office to announce that he would resign. "I have been working continually for over 20 years to help build a strong American military," Aspin said. "It's time for me to take a break and to undertake a new kind of work, so I have asked the president to relieve me of this duty as secretary of Defense as of January 20th."

Clinton responded that he greeted Aspin's decision with "real sadness," praising the "razor-sharp mind" Aspin had applied to tough defense issues. "I have told him that after he takes the break he has requested," Clinton added, "I very much hope he will consider other assignments for this administration."

But the carefully orchestrated show of good will did little to mask the reality that Clinton and his aides had been planning for weeks to prod Aspin out the Pentagon door. That was demonstrated when only a day later Clinton nominated retired Adm. Bobby Ray Inman as Aspin's successor. Inman later withdrew his nomination, and Aspin's successor turned out to be his deputy, William J. Perry. *(Successor, p. 476)*

Aspin had been faulted for his lack of executive acumen and had been frequently bogged down in controversies that ranged from gays in the military to peacekeeping in Somalia. Early in his tenure, Aspin was sidelined for weeks with a heart ailment, although he insisted that the problem had not held him back since doctors implanted a pacemaker.

During his years in Congress, Aspin had established himself as one of the most influential voices in public debate on U.S. defense policy, frequently willing to breast the political current. Until Clinton chose him as Defense secretary, however, he had never run anything larger than the staff of the House Armed Services Committee.

Removed from his familiar environs on Capitol Hill, Aspin's lack of administrative experience became a chronic problem. "Aspin could get some of the big substance right, but style and implementation were problems," said one close adviser. "He was better at working through the question of why we need a military than at running the military day-to-day."

At the Pentagon, as during his sometimes turbulent tenure heading the House Armed Services Committee, Aspin's quest for the political clout to implement his views was handicapped by his penchant for prolonged — and sometimes public — rumination before he reached a decision. "He dances around problems intellectually," said House Foreign Affairs Committee Chairman Lee H. Hamilton, D-Ind., a longtime friend. "He doesn't fit into the military spit-and-polish mentality."

Aspin's hopes of using his grasp of the issues to come out of the blocks running were thwarted by Clinton's own agenda: For six months, the secretary and his senior aides were occupied trying to salvage some shard of Clinton's fiercely disputed campaign pledge to lift the armed services' ban on gay and lesbian members. *(Gays, p. 454)*

Although some experts also criticized the foreign policy leadership of Secretary of State Warren Christopher and National Security Advisor Anthony Lake, Aspin became the chief lightning rod for broader dissatisfaction with Clinton's difficulty in defining U.S. security needs in the post-Cold War world.

On Aspin's watch, this ambivalence played out most dramatically in the U.S. involvement in Somalia, a mission inherited from the Bush administration that became transformed into efforts to tamp down murderous clan warfare. *(Somalia, p. 486)*

After 18 U.S. soldiers were killed in a firefight in October, it was revealed that Aspin had denied requests to reinforce the U.S. contingent in Somalia with tanks and other equipment. He became the focal point of angry critics, including some Republican lawmakers who demanded his resignation.

His backers, including House Speaker Thomas S. Foley, D-Wash., contended that the criticism was unjustified because military planners wanted to use the tanks for purposes different from the deadly firefight. But Aspin acknowledged he regretted failing to send the armor, and the issue became one more item on the list of his political liabilities. "The tanks were a very, very serious problem politically," conceded the Aspin aide.

In the days before his resignation, Aspin was embroiled in a dispute with budget director Leon E. Panetta over Pentagon spending for the following several years.

Aspin insisted that additional funds were needed to pay for higher-than-anticipated inflation and for a military pay raise that Congress enacted for fiscal 1994 over Clinton's objections. On Dec. 17, senior officials from the White House and the Pentagon told reporters that revised inflation estimates had reduced the disputed amount from about $47 billion to about $31 billion.

Despite the funding dispute, Lake pledged that Clinton "remains committed to the strategy and force structure in the bottom-up review." That review set the military's goal as the ability to fight two major regional wars nearly simultaneously. To do so, the review called for an active-duty force of 10 Army divisions, 12 aircraft carriers and 13 Air Force fighter wings. *(Bottom-up review, p. 452)*

The bottom-up review was quintessential Aspin — typical of his success over the previous decade in shaping debate on defense policy and in pushing the Democratic Party toward more hawkish stands. Fittingly, it also may have been the most enduring legacy of his troubled year at the Pentagon. ∎

Clinton Has Trouble Finding Successor for Aspin

Only a day after Les Aspin announced his resignation as Defense secretary, President Clinton on Dec. 16 nominated retired Adm. Bobby Ray Inman to fill the post.

Aspin resigned after months of criticism for his inexperience as a manager and controversy over issues that ranged from homosexuals in the military to the intervention in Somalia. *(Aspin, p. 474)*

But Inman abruptly withdrew his nomination on Jan. 18, 1994. Aspin's deputy, William J. Perry, was soon named to the post.

Clinton had presented Inman at a White House ceremony Dec. 16, emphasizing his experience in a string of positions in the Navy and in key intelligence posts. "Admiral Inman was one of our nation's highest-ranking and most respected military officers," Clinton said. "He was a four-star admiral, whose career in the Navy, in our intelligence community and in private business has won him praise from both Democrats and Republicans who admire his intellect, his integrity and his leadership ability."

An intelligence specialist held in high regard across the political spectrum, Inman boasted a gilt-edged résumé that included significant experience as a manager of complex programs.

Inman was born April 4, 1931, in Rhonesboro, Texas. He joined the Navy in 1951, advancing to the rank of admiral in 1981. He was director of Navy intelligence in 1974-76; director of the Defense Intelligence Agency in 1976-77; director of the National Security Agency in 1977-81; and deputy director of the CIA in 1981-82.

The super-secret National Security Agency reportedly had more than 20,000 employees and a budget of about $3 billion. The Texas native served in corporate management after retiring from the military in 1982. "I am an operator, hopefully with a strategic view," Inman said after Clinton's announcement.

Inman's personal stature on defense issues also appeared likely to give him particularly strong leverage in administration tussles over budget levels and other defense issues. He had a reputation for flinty independence, underscored by his remarks Dec. 16. "I did not seek the job. In honesty, I did not want the job," he said.

He volunteered that he had voted for George Bush for president over Clinton and even made it sound as if Clinton was auditioning during their private discussions about the defense job. "I had to reach a level of comfort that we could work together, that I would be very comfortable in your role as the commander in chief while I was secretary of Defense," Inman told Clinton, "and I have found that level of comfort."

Inman's abrupt decision to withdraw his nomination left members of Congress stunned and perplexed.

In a news conference in Austin, Texas, Inman blasted several newspaper columnists who had criticized him, calling them practitioners of a "new McCarthyism." Most commentary on Inman's nomination had been laudatory.

At least as startling was Inman's unsubstantiated contention that Senate Minority Leader Bob Dole, R-Kan., was planning a partisan attack on the nomination, perhaps in collusion with New York Times columnist William Safire. "I've already given 30 years of service to my country," Inman said at his news conference. "And I don't wish

or intend to subject myself to that on a daily basis as the cost of trying to produce change."

Dole and Safire each dismissed as ridiculous Inman's allegation that they were conspiring against him, and Inman later retracted his charge.

Some members of Congress expressed sympathy for Inman's unease with the harsh glare of the spotlight. But others called his rambling performance "bizarre" — as Sen. Trent Lott, R-Miss., put it — and noted that he had been expected to win confirmation easily in the Senate.

On Jan. 24, Clinton named Deputy Secretary Perry to take over the Pentagon's top civilian post. The Senate voted to confirm Perry, 97-0, on Feb. 3. ∎

Halperin Withdraws From Pentagon Nomination

A Clinton administration nominee for a top post in the Pentagon revived old feuds about Vietnam, the 1970s and the Cold War even as his nomination became entangled in new disputes over peacekeeping and the United Nations.

In the end, the nomination of Morton H. Halperin to become assistant secretary of Defense for peacekeeping and democracy was sent back to the White House when the Senate adjourned for the year without acting on it.

And while the Clinton administration vowed to renominate him for the position in 1994, Halperin removed himself from consideration on Jan. 10, 1994. He did not cite resistance in the Senate but instead the expectation that Bobby Ray Inman, Clinton's nominee to succeed Les Aspin as Defense secretary, would want to map his own organizational structure for the Pentagon.

Inman had expressed respect for Halperin but reportedly had questioned the need for the post he had been nominated to fill. Inman later withdrew his own nomination. *(Successor, left)*

Conservatives headed the effort to block Senate confirmation of Halperin, an outspoken opponent of government secrecy and former Washington director of the American Civil Liberties Union. The new post reportedly was tailor-made for him by Aspin.

John W. Warner, R-Va., expressed "grave concerns" over Halperin's past writings criticizing government policies on defense and intelligence. "As a senior member of the Armed Services Committee, I will intensely examine Mr. Halperin's complete record," Warner said in a floor speech Aug. 6. "I believe the president and the secretary of Defense should carefully reconsider this nomination. . . ."

Beyond Halperin's writings, many lawmakers were wary of U.S. involvement in U.N.-run peacekeeping operations, such as the one in Somalia. The creation of the assistant secretary's office reflected the administration's intention to stay in the peacekeeping business. *(Somalia, p. 486)*

Opponents also said the new position put too much power in the hands of one assistant secretary. Under a July 6 Pentagon directive, the assistant secretary was to be Aspin's principal adviser on "policy and planning for the promotion of democracy and the defense of human rights throughout the world." He was to be responsible for "U.S. participation in international peacekeeping" activities and for the Pentagon's role in "humanitarian assistance, refu-

476 — 1993 CQ ALMANAC

gee affairs and U.S. international information programs." And he was to be the Pentagon's drug policy czar.

Halperin's Background

Halperin, 55, had garnered an impressive résumé. After receiving his doctorate in international relations from Yale University when he was 22, the New York native became an assistant professor at rival Harvard University. In 1966, he became a deputy assistant secretary of Defense responsible for international security affairs. By 1969, he had risen to the position of senior staff member of the National Security Council (NSC) in the Nixon administration.

Eight months later, the young star quit his job in a disagreement over the administration's bombing of Cambodia. The FBI tapped Halperin's phone for 21 months at the request of national security adviser Henry A. Kissinger on the suspicion that Halperin was involved in leaking the secret Pentagon Papers on the Vietnam War. Halperin waged a 20-year court battle, charging that the tap was illegal and that Kissinger was personally responsible.

"As I have stated publicly and at my deposition, nothing that came to my attention from the surveillance or otherwise cast doubt on your integrity or your loyalty to the country," Kissinger wrote in a letter to Halperin that was part of a secret settlement in the lawsuit.

As head of the ACLU's Washington office — one of the few non-lawyers to hold that position — Halperin became widely known for building coalitions among a mixed bag of politicians, think tanks, policy-makers and human issues groups.

On July 1, the former chairman of the Senate Select Intelligence Committee, David L. Boren, D-Okla., took to the Senate floor to vouch that Halperin's work at the ACLU "gained not only my respect and that of other committee members but also the respect of many executive branch officials with responsibility for intelligence law and policy."

Gaffney's Assault

The nomination fight was also a fight between two strong-willed veterans of Washington's policy wars. Conservative Frank J. Gaffney Jr., director of the Center for Security Policy, waged a media war against Halperin for weeks.

Gaffney had never met Halperin and said he declined an invitation from the nominee to do so. Instead, he concentrated on decades of writings. Portraying the nominee as an unrelenting critic of intelligence agencies, Gaffney quoted from an October 1975 edition of "First Principles," the Center for National Security Studies' newsletter: "The CIA should be limited to collating and evaluating intelligence information, and its only activities in the United States should be openly acknowledged actions in support of this mission."

Halperin's supporters said that such comments were made against the backdrop of Senate investigations that had revealed abuses in covert operations. They said that Halperin supported past covert operations in Afghanistan, Angola and Nicaragua because they were consistent with public policies at the time.

Gaffney also criticized Halperin as an opponent of U.S. military intervention, quoting from a summer 1993 article in Foreign Policy magazine. Halperin wrote: "The United States should explicitly surrender the right to intervene unilaterally in the internal affairs of other countries by overt military means or by covert operations. Such self-

restraint would bar interventions like those in Grenada and Panama, unless the United States first gained the explicit consent of the international community acting through the Security Council or a regional organization. The United States would, however, retain the right granted under Article 51 of the U.N. Charter to act unilaterally if necessary. . . . "

Supporters said that Halperin raised this idea as a way the United States could gain international support for collective efforts to protect democracy.

Intelligence Bill Held

Republicans escalated their opposition to Halperin late in the session by blocking Senate action on the fiscal 1994 intelligence authorization bill (S 1301). The Republicans said they took the action to protest the CIA's failure to produce an intelligence report that Halperin's critics maintained would have provided damaging evidence about his past activities. (Intelligence authorization, p. 522)

Senate Intelligence Committee Chairman Dennis De-Concini, D-Ariz., said in remarks on the Senate floor Oct. 27 that the CIA had twice searched its records and failed to find any such report. But Warner, the Intelligence panel's vice chairman, said he had a secret source who confirmed that the alleged document on Halperin existed. "In fact, this particular individual indicated to me that he saw the document," Warner said, "and has since that time indicated to me a second individual who corroborated the fact. . . ."

DeConcini said the impasse could have been resolved if the White House had not vetoed a meeting he had arranged with Republicans and CIA Director R. James Woolsey. The administration blocked Woolsey from participating in the session on grounds that all inquiries concerning the background of nominees should be handled through the FBI, he said. The Republicans later settled for assurances that the CIA files would be searched again. No CIA report about Halperin was disclosed.

Joseph R. Biden Jr., D-Del., told the Senate on Oct. 28 that Halperin's reputation "should not be sullied" by old ideological grudges from the Cold War era.

The Confirmation Hearing

At his confirmation hearing Nov. 19, Halperin vigorously defended what he called his "pointed and provocative views."

"A number of charges have been made about my beliefs and activities, which are simply false," Halperin told the Senate Armed Services Committee. "They are, in some cases, made up out of whole cloth. In others, they result from wrenching sentences out of context and building tales around them."

Sharp attacks by GOP committee members underscored the difficulty that Clinton and Aspin faced in getting their pick through the Senate. "We are convinced he already has, and will in the future, put American lives and interests in jeopardy," said Strom Thurmond of South Carolina, the committee's ranking Republican. Thurmond charged that Halperin's statements during the Cold War "suggested that the U.S. government, and not the Soviet empire, was the enemy of peace and freedom."

Halperin also had fierce defenders. Senators who came to the confirmation hearing to praise him included Republican Mark O. Hatfield of Oregon and Democrats Biden and Boren.

Flanked by stacks of brown files and silver folders

stamped "secret," Halperin spoke softly of his boyhood desire to serve in government and of regrets for writings during the 1970s in which he called for abolishing the CIA's covert operations. "Some of the views I expressed then I have long since abandoned," he said. "Others have become irrelevant...."

Halperin also apologized for acting in an official capacity at the Pentagon before being confirmed, which angered senators of both parties. "I can only assure you that it was not done with any intention of presuming on the Senate's right to confirm nominees," he said. "We were all eager to begin to do what the secretary of Defense wanted done."

But Halperin offered a vehement litany of denials to other allegations made by his critics. He said: "I have been accused of advising the secretary of Defense not to send armor to Somalia. That is false.... I have been accused of believing that the United States should subordinate its interests to the United Nations, never using force without its consent, and putting American forces at its disposal. That is false.... Most recently, I have been accused of traveling abroad for secret meetings with terrorists. That is false."

Republicans focused much of their attention on Halperin's trip to London in the 1970s to testify at the deportation hearing of renegade CIA agent Philip Agee, who published the names of covert CIA agents. Richard Welch, the agency's station chief in Athens, Greece, later was assassinated. Halperin said he made the trip as an employee of the ACLU sent to aid the defense as an expert on national security issues and not to aid Agee in his endeavors to expose agency operatives. "I do not support what Mr. Agee did," Halperin said. "I condemn it."

Halperin said that, like an attorney, he did not always agree with those whose civil liberties he defended as an ACLU official. Halperin noted that he also faced harsh criticism when he acted on behalf of the ACLU in defending the constitutional rights of Reagan administration officials Oliver L. North and John M. Poindexter during the Iran-contra affair.

Senate Action

On Nov. 20, the Senate returned Halperin's nomination to the White House when supporters failed to win unanimous consent to carry it over into next year. Senate rules required such agreement whenever the body recessed for longer than 30 days. For Halperin's nomination to be considered in 1994, Clinton would have had to resubmit it to Congress. ∎

Shalikashvili Confirmed as Joint Chiefs Chairman

Army Gen. John M. Shalikashvili won Senate confirmation by voice vote Oct. 5 to serve as chairman of the military's Joint Chiefs of Staff.

In nominating the general Aug. 11, President Clinton called him "a soldier's soldier, a proven warrior, a creative and flexible visionary who clearly understands the myriad of conflicts — ethnic, religious and political — gripping the world." The Polish-born Shalikashvili, 57, had been commander in chief since June 1992 of U.S. forces in Europe and of NATO's military forces.

The Senate Armed Services Committee held up his nomination briefly, but only because it was unwilling to see him leave the important NATO post until his successor in that job was named.

Shalikashvili succeeded Gen. Colin L. Powell Jr., an extraordinarily popular leader of the Joint Chiefs who made history as the first black to hold the military's top post. The charismatic Powell's tour of duty as chairman ended Sept. 30.

Background

Shalikashvili (pronounced sha-lee-kash-VEE-lee and frequently shortened to "Shali") had firsthand experience in the military's changing role in the post-Cold War era.

In 1991, he was head of a multilateral force that provided humanitarian aid and military cover to Kurds in northern Iraq after the Persian Gulf War. As NATO commander, he was responsible for planning the airstrikes and other military options that the Clinton administration considered for use in strife-torn Bosnia.

Powell had brought to the job political skills that were well-honed in positions that included national security adviser to President Ronald Reagan. Although Shalikashvili had a much more conventional string of military assignments, he was exposed to high-level policy debates as an assistant to Powell from August 1991 to June 1992.

The chairman's assistant routinely acted as the military's representative to the secretary of State. In that capacity, Shalikashvili was involved in matters such as delicate negotiations aimed at dismantling nuclear weapons in Russia and Ukraine.

In naming Shalikashvili, Clinton focused on the only-in-America aspects of his family roots and immigrant youth. Born in Warsaw in 1936, Shalikashvili was the first foreign-born Joint Chiefs chairman. His grandfather was a general in czarist Russia. His father was a Georgian army officer who emigrated to Poland and married a Polish woman. The family moved to Germany in 1944 to escape the advancing Soviets.

At 16, Shalikashvili moved to Peoria, Ill. In 1958, he graduated from Bradley University with a mechanical engineering degree and was drafted into the Army. He was commissioned through Officer Candidate School as an artillery officer.

But the immigrant success story was clouded soon after the nomination, when it was revealed that Shalikashvili's father served under Germany's dreaded Waffen SS corps during World War II.

Confirmation Hearing

When the Senate Armed Services Committee held its confirmation hearing on Sept. 22, the general read an opening statement emphasizing that he had never known of the Nazi skeleton in his family closet.

"To me, he was a kind and gentle man, and I loved him very much," he said of his father.

"He was a man who, perhaps, loved his native Georgia too much — certainly a man caught up in the awful tragedy of World War II."

Senators dismissed as irrelevant the revelation about Shalikashvili's father. They said they were touched by the general's statement on the matter.

The only hangup at the hearing was the committee's refusal to recommend Shalikashvili's confirmation until the selection of his successor as NATO commander. Committee Chairman Sam Nunn, D-Ga. argued that the NATO post was too important to be left vacant even temporarily.

Fielding questions for more than two hours on administration policy around the world, Shalikashvili proved not only an experienced soldier but also an adept political player. He supported administration policy while soothing the panel's concerns about the risks of peacekeeping operations and of placing troops under foreign command.

On Bosnia, the general bolstered the administration's promise to participate in enforcement of a proposed peace plan, which later crumbled. Shalikashvili said such an operation would require 50,000 NATO peacekeeping troops at a first-year cost of $4 billion. He acknowledged that many of the troops and much of the funding would be American.

In weighing the costs and risks of such a mission, he said, "The alternative of not doing so is also very expensive." As winter approaches in Sarajevo, he said, "women and children and old people will pay an awful price if there is not a peace settlement."

On Somalia, Shalikashvili said a U.S. presence was necessary to keep the country from sliding back into anarchy and to maintain U.S. credibility.

"The prospect of leaving a task undone is never easy, and you cannot totally wash your hands of it," he said. "And that's true of us, perhaps, much more so than of nations that have less global responsibility than we do."

But when pressed by John McCain, R-Ariz., a proponent of removing the troops, to outline the criteria for deployment, Shalikashvili noted the wavering public and congressional support for the mission. "I think the jury is probably out in my mind right now on this issue," he said. "I cannot tell you now how to bridge the dilemma" of persevering in the unfinished mission in Somalia while "articulating to the nation" the reasons for continued involvement.

Shalikashvili supported Secretary of Defense Les As-

pin's "bottom up" review of defense requirements and reinforced the report's conclusions that a reduced military would still be able to fight in two regions at once. However, he said a problem occurred on "the margins" because the military's involvement in peacekeeping operations in addition to fighting the "win-win" scenario could spread forces too thin. "It's this margin of safety or this margin of tolerance to handle additional missions in addition to the two major contingencies, that you no longer have," he cautioned.

Shalikashvili also loyally defended the Clinton administration's decision to emphasize development of anti-missile defenses for troops in battle rather than the more ambitious defense of the U.S. mainland that was envisioned in Reagan's Strategic Defense Initiative.

Challenging that shift in priorities, Richard C. Shelby, D-Ala., asked, "Do you believe that we should defend our troops and allies but not defend the American people?"

"No, I certainly don't mean that," the general replied. "But I think that the most immediate threat and the most vulnerability — as we have seen, for instance, in Desert Storm — are our troops."

Final Action

The Senate confirmed Shalikashvili as chairman of the Joint Chiefs of Staff by voice vote on Oct. 5.

Nunn lifted his hold on the nomination when Clinton nominated Gen. George A. Joulwan to succeed Shalikashvili as commander in chief of U.S. European forces and supreme allied commander of NATO.

Joulwan, an Army officer who had been commander in chief of the U.S. Southern Command, was confirmed by the Senate by voice vote on Oct. 7. ∎

FOREIGN POLICY

U.N. Peacekeeping Proves Risky

Congress, Clinton administration grow cautious about providing troops for multinational efforts

The Clinton administration's policy of expanding U.S. participation in U.N. peacekeeping operations triggered widespread criticism and eventually resistance on Capitol Hill. At the beginning of 1993, many in the administration and Congress had looked forward to a more assertive United Nations that could shoulder more of the burden of making and keeping the peace around the world. By year's end, the administration and Congress had pulled back from what were seen as the risks of turning over funds, foreign policy decision-making and control over troops to the international organization.

The policy debate was dramatized by the failure of international peacekeeping efforts in three regional trouble spots:

● **Somalia.** The U.S. role in the U.N. peacekeeping mission in Somalia spurred congressional outrage after 18 Army soldiers were killed Oct. 3 in a bloody battle with the forces of Gen. Mohammed Farah Aidid, a local warlord. Under congressional pressure, President Clinton agreed to withdraw most U.S. forces from the East African nation by March 31, 1994.

Fending off calls for a faster withdrawal, the Senate and House supported provisions effectively endorsing that timetable. But the compromise, which was attached to the fiscal 1994 defense appropriations bill, also asserted Congress' power of the purse, its ultimate control over overseas intervention, by explicitly cutting off funding for the Somalia mission after the March 31 deadline. *(Somalia, p. 486; appropriations, p. 569)*

● **Bosnia-Herzegovina.** After moving to the brink of military intervention in Bosnia several times, the Clinton administration adopted a far more cautious approach.

Congress, like the administration, grew increasingly wary of any direct military involvement in the brutal ethnic conflict over the former Yugoslavia. After repeatedly calling on the administration to arm the Bosnian government, Congress adopted non-binding language in the defense appropriations bill urging the administration not to send U.S. forces without first obtaining congressional approval. *(Bosnia, p. 493)*

● **Haiti.** The military rulers of Haiti defied a U.N.-backed agreement that called for the return of ousted President Jean-Bertrand Aristide by Oct. 30. Congress divided — largely along partisan lines — over Clinton's efforts to pressure Haiti's rulers to permit Aristide to retake power. The U.S. actions included sending a flotilla of naval ships to enforce U.N. economic sanctions against the impoverished island.

Lawmakers put non-binding language in the defense appropriations measure urging Clinton to seek congressional authorization before dispatching any U.S. troops to intervene in Haiti. *(Haiti, p. 499)*

The year's debate on intervention did nothing to resolve the perennial questions over the respective powers of the executive and legislative branches to commit U.S. troops abroad. Congressional leaders promised to offer proposals

in 1994 to revamp the largely ignored provisions of the War Powers Resolution of 1973. *(War powers, p. 485)*

Limiting Funds for Peacekeeping

While most of the attention was focused on direct involvement by U.S. forces in dangerous U.N. missions in countries such as Somalia, lawmakers also balked at the administration's request for a large increase in funding for peacekeeping operations.

The Commerce, Justice, State appropriations bill (HR 2519 — PL 103-121) provided $402 million in contributions for U.N. peacekeeping activities, a reduction of $240 million from the administration's $642 million request. Because the appropriations bill actually set the funding level for peacekeeping, it was more significant than the companion State Department authorization bill. The authorization bill included $598 million in the version passed in 1993 by the House and $423 million in the bill as it passed the Senate on Feb. 2, 1994. *(Appropriations, p. 555; State Department, p. 505)*

During debate on the fiscal 1994 defense authorization bill (HR 2401 — PL 103-160), the House rejected two amendments to set aside Pentagon funds for U.N. peacekeeping missions even though the sponsors had argued that the purpose was to prevent such operations from diverting funds that would otherwise go to readiness programs such as troop training. *(Defense authorization, p. 433)*

In floor action on the fiscal 1994 defense appropriations bill (HR 3116 — PL 103-139), the House adopted by voice vote an amendment eliminating an Appropriations Committee proposal to provide $383 million in defense funds for "humanitarian operations" such as peacekeeping. House Defense Appropriations Subcommittee Chairman John P. Murtha, D-Pa., sought to strip the funds to short-circuit a fight over the money and over an Appropriations Committee requirement that the administration give 15 days' notice to Congress before spending money on an overseas intervention.

BACKGROUND

With the end of the Cold War, the United Nations appeared ready and able to step into a power vacuum. No longer stalemated at every turn by the U.S.-Soviet competition for power and influence, the world organization could attempt to become the exemplar and enforcer of world peace that some of its founders envisioned after the Second World War.

Many on Capitol Hill initially welcomed the prospect of a more muscular United Nations as a way to ease the burdens that the United States had inherited as the sole surviving superpower.

But there were concerns as well: That the United States would have to give up a good measure of its authority in international affairs. That Americans would have to con-

tinue to pay nearly a third of the rapidly growing bill for U.N. operations around the world. And, perhaps most emotional of all, that U.S. troops might have to serve under U.N. command, a break with tradition.

There also was something of a role reversal in Congress. Some liberal Democrats who had objected to U.S. military intervention during the Cold War and had opposed the Persian Gulf War formed the core of congressional support for strong multinational action to stem violence and lawlessness in Somalia and Bosnia-Herzegovina. *(Gulf war, 1991 Almanac, p. 437)*

Some of those Democrats urged that ad hoc arrangements for peacekeeping be formalized by contributing U.S. troops to a standing U.N. force that could intervene in world trouble spots. The benefits, said Sen. Joseph R. Biden Jr., D-Del., would come in "burden sharing and risk sharing. . . . We would draw other nations into the obligation of military responsibility."

But others questioned whether a militarily formidable U.N. would really lighten the burden of U.S. global leadership — or merely exact a cost in U.S. independence. "Do you think we are on a slippery slope [toward] becoming the world's police force — under the auspices of the United Nations?" Jim Exon, D-Neb., asked a Pentagon appointee at a Senate Armed Services Committee hearing March 4.

Many lawmakers of both parties were uncomfortable with anything other than what Sen. Mitch McConnell, R-Ky., called "the Persian Gulf model — where we're in charge and other countries send in troops to help us."

In fact, the idea of a standing U.N. force had been around as long as the world organization. Under Article 45 of the U.N. charter, signed in 1945, the United States and other nations committed themselves to negotiate "special agreements" to make troops available to the Security Council for "maintaining international peace and security." Equally important, Congress authorized the president to negotiate such arrangements in the United Nations Participation Act of 1945.

But over the years, no standing force was created. Member nations contributed troops to peacekeeping forces when and if they chose, and the lightly armed U.N. troops in baby blue helmets primarily monitored peace agreements that had already been reached between rival forces.

The end of the Cold War and the ensuing outbreak of regional conflicts revived the idea of more aggressive operations that some called "peacemaking" rather than solely peacekeeping. And in 1992, U.N. Secretary General Boutros Boutros-Ghali wrote an essay that broached the possibility of a standing U.N. force.

As a presidential candidate in 1992, Bill Clinton said the United States should explore the possibility of establishing a "standby, voluntary U.N. rapid deployment force" to deter international aggression. But his administration drew back from that idea in its first year.

The effort to define the extent and limits of U.S. involvement began before Senate committees at confirmation hearings for Clinton's Cabinet in January.

At his confirmation hearing, Defense Secretary Les Aspin endorsed the formation of "peacemaking organizations" for a new era. Nonetheless, he seemed to reject putting U.S. troops under U.N. command. "The president is commander in chief. . . . Congress has war powers. And if you second these forces to the U.N., how do you maintain the Constitution?" Aspin said. "We couldn't be part of that option."

Warren Christopher attempted to define a middle ground on U.S. intervention at his confirmation hearing for secretary of State. Christopher, a deputy secretary of State in the Carter administration, seemed determined to erase the Democratic Party's longstanding image of weakness in national security matters as well as his own reputation as an advocate of negotiation over confrontation. In crises from Iraq to Bosnia, he said, the Clinton administration would not shrink from using force to buttress diplomacy.

"While there is no magic formula to guide such decisions," he told the Foreign Relations Committee, "I do believe that the discreet and careful use of force in certain circumstances — and its credible threat in general — will be essential to the success of our diplomacy and foreign policy."

At the same time, the Los Angeles corporate lawyer said there were limits on what the United States would be able to achieve as the world's lone surviving superpower. And he indicated that U.S. strategic and moral interests in this new age — particularly those that might warrant a military defense — had yet to be fully defined.

"We cannot respond to every alarm," he said, assuring Americans that "we will not turn their blood and treasure into an open account for use by the rest of the world."

In its early months, the administration promoted "assertive multilateralism" as a pillar of its foreign policy. But by September, Clinton outlined a policy that was neither boldly assertive nor consistently multilateral.

The shift was most clearly signaled Sept. 27, when Clinton used his first speech to the U.N. General Assembly to circumscribe the limits of U.S. support for international peacekeeping missions.

"The United Nations simply cannot become engaged in every one of the world's conflicts," Clinton said. "If the American people are to say yes to U.N. peacekeeping, the United Nations must know when to say no." *(Text, p. 54-D)*

PEACEKEEPING FUNDS

Clinton had sought $642 million for fiscal 1994 as the U.S. contribution to international peacekeeping efforts, but the appropriations bill for the departments of Commerce, Justice and State and the federal judiciary cut that to $402 million.

When House-Senate conferees hammered out the final version of the bill in October, lawmakers complained that the administration was committing the country to an increasing number of peacekeeping efforts with open-ended risks and costs. At the urging of Rep. Harold Rogers, R-Ky., the legislative negotiators added report language calling on the administration to notify Congress of new or changed peacekeeping missions whenever possible.

The lawmakers also signaled in the conference report (H Rept 103-293) that the United Nations had better look to other countries for more money: "The conferees expect that the administration will notify the U.N. that the United States will not accept an assessment of more than 25 percent of peacekeeping costs for any new or expanded peacekeeping commitments." The United States had been paying almost 32 percent of the cost per mission.

The reluctance to foot the bill for the U.N.'s expanding missions also was demonstrated on the House floor Sept. 13 in action on two amendments to the defense authorization bill (HR 2401). In spearheading defeat of the amendments, House Republicans tapped into growing concern about the administration's willingness to commit U.S. forces to U.N. operations.

The first of the amendments would have set aside $30 million as a "Defense Response Fund" to cover the cost of deploying U.S. forces for international peacekeeping opera-

The Powerful War Powers Conflict

As the first president elected in the post-Cold War era, Bill Clinton arrived in office confident that he could avoid the clashes with Congress over the power to commit U.S. troops abroad that had bedeviled his Republican predecessors. Indeed, the administration briefed Congress so regularly and solicited guidance so deferentially on intervention abroad that in some cases lawmakers questioned whether the administration had a position of its own.

After a generation of ideological conflict with GOP presidents, congressional Democrats eagerly accepted Clinton's pledge of cooperation.

At first, the White House and Congress brushed aside longstanding, unresolved questions over the validity of the War Powers Resolution of 1973, which purported to set deadlines for presidents to obtain congressional approval whenever troops were sent into likely conflict.

But before the end of his first year in office, Clinton found himself replicating battles with Congress that President Ronald Reagan had waged a decade earlier.

This time, some Republicans abandoned their previous defense of presidential prerogatives, demanding advance congressional approval for U.S. deployments to Haiti and Bosnia and for any dispatch of combat forces under the U.N. flag. In November, some House Republicans even invoked provisions of the War Powers law, which they had long rejected as unconstitutional, to force House action on an amendment that would have required U.S. forces to be withdrawn from Somalia more quickly than the administration had planned. *(Somalia, p. 486)*

For his part, Clinton protected his powers as fiercely as had Reagan and President George Bush.

In the end, Clinton survived a series of votes in the Senate over intervention abroad with his executive powers intact. As previously, lawmakers ultimately proved reluctant to impose statutory restrictions on the president. But the experience reminded lawmakers that changes in the world had done nothing to resolve the constitutional struggle between the White House and Congress over who should have war-making authority.

Senate Majority Leader George J. Mitchell, D-Maine, announced Oct. 22 that the Armed Services, Foreign Relations and Intelligence committees would review Congress' role in decision-making on military intervention and issue a report in 1994.

Decrying "piecemeal" reactions to U.S. intervention in crises, Mitchell said, "We must devise standards or criteria by which we can measure such requests, to be able to say 'no' when appropriate and be able to say 'yes' when necessary."

House Armed Services Committee Chairman Lee H. Hamilton, D-Ind., also pledged that his panel would review the issue.

Many lawmakers were skeptical.

"We will never be able to specifically craft a set of rules to cover these gray areas," said Mitch McConnell, R-Ky. "But as a political reality, when the president puts troops on the ground in another country, he will need a congressional resolution indicating support."

Background

The War Powers Resolution (HJ Res 542 — PL 93-148), which grew out of the conflicts over the Vietnam War, passed over President Richard M. Nixon's veto on Nov. 7, 1973. But it came to be so widely regarded as unworkable that it was seldom invoked even by those lawmakers who demanded a greater voice in foreign policy. *(1973 Almanac, p. 905)*

The law provided that in the absence of a formal declaration of war, the president had to report to Congress within 48 hours of introducing U.S. forces "into hostilities or into situations where imminent involvement in hostilities is clearly indicated by the circumstances."

The troops had to be withdrawn — generally within 60 days, although the president could extend the period for as much as 30 days — unless Congress voted to extend the period or "declared war or enacted a specific authorization for such use of United States armed forces."

But Clinton's predecessors had resisted sharing the responsibility for sending troops into battle, questioning the constitutionality of the law, and most lawmakers seemed relieved to hand such politically explosive decisions to the executive branch.

In January 1993, during confirmation hearings for Defense Secretary Les Aspin, Senate Armed Services Committee Chairman Sam Nunn, D-Ga., questioned the law's relevance and its requirement that the president withdraw troops from hostile action.

"It's never going to work," Nunn said, adding that he had voted for the legislation. "It's never worked in the past; it's never going to work. That automatic trigger makes any president reluctant to acknowledge that hostilities are imminent."

Aspin doubted that revamping the law would be worth the effort.

"It's always been assumed that to try to amend it would be such a humongous fight and raise such enormous hackles, and in the end it's not clear whether you'd get anything much better," he said.

The Clinton administration wavered. Asked about Clinton's position, presidential spokesman George Stephanopoulos said Feb. 26, "I don't want to get into a long philosophical discussion beyond saying that he does support the War Powers act. He believes it's an appropriate act, and he intends to abide by it."

By May 5, Clinton was dismissing a question about the constitutionality of the act by telling a reporter, "Ask my lawyer." But the president added that the law has "worked reasonably well."

Ultimately, the administration adopted the same linguistic straddle used by its predecessors: In an Oct. 20 report to congressional leaders describing the situation in Haiti, Clinton described the report as "consistent with" the law — a phrase chosen to indicate that he was not seeking a confrontation over the statute but neither was he conceding its constitutionality.

tions, foreign disaster relief or other unforeseen missions requiring large-scale action on short notice.

Norman Sisisky, D-Va., who offered the amendment, contended that such a fund would spare the Pentagon from having to cancel training exercises and other important activities to pay for such emergencies.

But Utah Republican James V. Hansen denounced the proposal as a source of "blank checks to pay for unspecified peacekeeping adventures throughout the world." Hansen said the administration seemed bent on advancing "global multilateralism . . . by the United States' shouldering the burden of military peacekeeping operations."

The amendment to create the peacekeeping fund was rejected 199-211. Jim Leach of Iowa was the only GOP member to support the amendment, while 166 Republicans opposed it, as did 45 Democrats scattered across the party's spectrum. (Vote 426, p. 104-H)

Sisisky also sponsored the second amendment, which would have earmarked $10 million to create a U.N. peacekeeping command post and to train other nations' troops in peacekeeping operations. It also would have set aside $23 million for efforts to instill deference to civil authority in the military personnel of emerging democracies.

That amendment was rejected 199-210, with 161 Republicans and 49 Democrats voting against it. Six GOP members, 192 Democrats and independent Bernard Sanders, Vt., voted "yea." (Vote 427, p. 104-H)

CROSSCURRENTS

The crosscurrents of opinion in Congress were complex, with some leading members taking different positions in different crises, not only about the wisdom of sending U.S. forces but also about the appropriateness of Congress' imposing its views on the administration.

That was illustrated in particular by Minority Leader Bob Dole, R-Kan., who bounced awkwardly between the roles of partisan critic and unexpected Clinton ally.

Dole, the often acerbic leader of the congressional opposition, found an opportunity to cooperate with the president during the Senate's debate on Somalia the week of Oct. 11. He angered many conservative Republicans — and put himself at odds with a majority of his 44-member Republican Conference — when he opposed an amendment to cut off funding immediately for the Somalia operation.

"It ties the president's hands," said Dole, one of only 16 Republicans to vote against the cutoff. "I have been scolded by some for supporting the president in this instance."

But Dole won praise from others. "He was a statesman," said Robert C. Byrd, D-W.Va.

Days later, Dole proposed strict limits on the president's ability to deploy troops in Haiti and Bosnia.

Having himself accused Democrats in Congress of trying to "micromanage" foreign policy during the Republican administrations of Ronald Reagan and George Bush, Dole was accused of doing just that. "If it were a Democrat doing that to Bush or Reagan, we'd be outraged," said a fellow Republican, Nancy Landon Kassebaum of Kansas.

Denying any inconsistency, Dole said he was trying to find "some balance between the Congress and the president" in foreign policy.

"I don't believe we should tie the president's hands, but I don't think Congress should sit on its hands either," Dole said after agreeing to water down his Haiti and Bosnia amendments to the defense appropriations bill.

Even before agreeing to dilute those amendments, Dole maintained that the proposed restrictions were not inconsistent with his arguments against congressional meddling in Somalia. In Somalia, he said, the president needed more flexibility because U.S. troops already were on the ground and at risk; U.S. troops had not yet been committed to Haiti and Bosnia. "I think Congress has a right to be heard," he said.

As with the Somalia amendment, Republicans were divided over Dole's approach. "I have very grave constitutional concerns," said John McCain, Ariz. "I don't see how you can prospectively tell the commander in chief what he can or cannot do."

Dole acknowledged that if he were president, he too probably would oppose his amendments as originally drafted. "If I were the executive," said Dole, who had run for president before and was thought to be interested in doing so again, "I would probably object to any perceived encroachment." ∎

Hill Demands Early '94 Somalia Withdrawal

The United States' leading role in the U.N. peacekeeping mission in Somalia spurred congressional outrage after 18 Army soldiers were killed Oct. 3 in a bloody battle with the forces of Gen. Mohammed Farah Aidid, a local warlord. Under congressional pressure, President Clinton agreed to withdraw most U.S. forces from the East African nation by March 31, 1994.

Fending off efforts to force a faster withdrawal, the Senate and House effectively endorsed that timetable. But the compromise also asserted Congress' power of the purse, its ultimate control over overseas intervention, by explicitly cutting off funding for the Somalia mission after the March 31 deadline.

Although Clinton and his aides defended the continued involvement of U.S. forces in the Somalia mission, they ruefully acknowledged that during 1993 they had allowed the operation to drift from its ostensible focus as a humanitarian aid operation to far riskier direct involvement in Somalia's domestic infighting.

The congressional compromise — offered by Senate Appropriations Committee Chairman Robert C. Byrd, D-W.Va. — came as an amendment to the fiscal 1994 defense appropriations bill (HR 3116 — PL 103-139). It was the culmination of an off-and-on debate in Congress that lasted throughout the session as lawmakers grew increasingly jittery about the risks and uncertainties of the Somalia mission.

Earlier in the year, the House and Senate approved different versions of a resolution (S J Res 45, H Res 173) authorizing U.S. participation in the Somalia mission, but members never took final action on that measure.

On July 1, Congress cleared a fiscal 1993 supplemental appropriations bill (HR 2118 — PL 103-50) that included $750 million to cover the Somalia mission. The bill cut, or

being dragged through the streets of Mogadishu by an angry mob.

The political impact of the botched raid played out for months, becoming a factor in the forced resignation in December of Defense Secretary Aspin.

Aspin became the target of fierce criticism when it was learned he had denied a request in September from U.S. commanders in Somalia for armored reinforcements. Such forces might have been able to rescue the Ranger unit that was pinned down by Somali guerrillas. Aspin told reporters that there had been "mixed" views in the Pentagon over the request for more armor. But he acknowledged that "had I known at that time what I knew after the events of Sunday, I would have made a very different decision." *(Aspin, p. 474)*

Congressional opposition to the Somalia mission continued to grow. A group of 142 House Republicans sent Clinton a letter Oct. 6 insisting that he pull out U.S. forces. The United States, they said, could not afford an "indecisive and naive" foreign policy.

Initial administration efforts at damage control only seemed to make matters worse.

Aspin and Secretary of State Warren Christopher were dispatched to Capitol Hill on Oct. 5 to provide a closed-door briefing with the underlying objective of buying the administration more time to develop a new approach.

Members described it as "an unmitigated disaster." The basement briefing room at the Capitol was packed with more than 200 members demanding answers, but Aspin and Christopher appeared more interested in soliciting the views of the assembled lawmakers. Liberals and conservatives were unsparing in their criticism. Rep. Patricia Schroeder, D-Colo., described the session as the Clinton team's version of the "Five O'Clock Follies" — the rosy news briefings by U.S. military officials during the dark days of the Vietnam War.

With the policy in danger of unraveling, congressional leaders from both parties sought to cool the overheated atmosphere.

Senate leaders provided breathing space for the administration by delaying consideration of the defense appropriations bill. Nunn — who had opposed Clinton on issues such as the president's effort to permit gays in the military — weighed in to help the president at a critical moment by calming the frenzy for immediate withdrawal. "We expect our troops in Somalia to remain calm and collected under fire," he told the Senate on Oct. 6, "and we owe them nothing less than equal composure back here in Washington as we decide what to do next in Somalia."

Clinton's Announcement

Facing calls from Capitol Hill for an immediate withdrawal from Somalia, Clinton pledged in a nationally televised address Oct. 7 that most U.S. forces would be pulled out by March 31. "Our mission from this day forward," Clinton said, "is to increase our strength, do our job, bring our soldiers out and bring them home." *(Text, p. 58-D)*

Yet in the effort to ensure that U.S forces could leave "on our terms," the president ordered an additional 1,700 Army troops to Somalia and announced that 3,600 more Marines would be stationed offshore. The U.S. forces deployed in support of the U.N. operation in Somalia were more than doubled, to approximately 10,600.

In a bow to congressional critics who charged that the United Nations had become preoccupied with capturing the warlord Aidid, Clinton said U.S. forces were not there to "personalize the conflict." And administration officials did not rule out striking a bargain with Aidid.

The president's new stand led to a de facto truce with Aidid, who soon freed Durant, the captured airman.

Nonetheless, some key senators, including Democrat Bill Bradley of New Jersey and Republican McCain of Arizona, rejected Clinton's retooled policy. "President Clinton has provided a deadline for withdrawal without providing a clear reason for staying in Somalia," Bradley said after the Oval Office speech. "If our goal is to pressure and defeat the guerrillas or to capture Gen. Aidid, the new approach does not provide enough troops. If our goal is establishment of a government and political stability, the new approach does not provide enough time."

Yet the opposition to Clinton's policy, while broad and bipartisan, was also divided. There was no consensus as to whether the United States should pull out instantly or within months.

One aspect of the new approach that drew broad support was Clinton's decision to dispatch Ambassador Robert Oakley to negotiate with the leaders of neighboring states to help build stability in Somalia. Oakley, who was the Bush administration's envoy to Somalia, was widely respected in Congress.

Senate Action

On Oct. 15, the Senate endorsed Clinton's decision to sharply narrow the mission of U.S. forces in Somalia and to remove them from that country by March 31, 1994.

The Senate vote was a tarnished trophy for Clinton, however, in part because it embraced the narrowed mission that the president had accepted only a week earlier in the face of congressional outrage.

The Senate language — a compromise sponsored by Byrd — was adopted as an amendment to the fiscal 1994 defense appropriations bill (HR 3116). The Senate endorsed the amendment, 76-23. *(Vote 314, p. 41-S)*

Before voting on the Byrd amendment, the Senate voted by a seemingly solid margin of 61-38 to table (kill) an amendment by McCain that would have repudiated Clinton's Somalia plan and instead required a "prompt" withdrawal of U.S. forces. "The mission which the American people supported . . . has been accomplished," McCain said in arguing for his amendment. "We didn't say we would feed those people forever." *(Vote 313, p. 41-S)*

Clinton said he was "gratified by the margin" of a victory that crossed lines of party and ideology. But the results belied the unresolved tensions over U.S. participation in multinational interventions. The debate reflected unease — bordering on contempt — toward the administration's performance in international peacekeeping.

Even among senators who backed the successful amendment, there was derisive criticism of the Clinton team's handling of Somalia. "This is not a policy. It is gibberish," John C. Danforth, R-Mo., said of a 33-page report summarizing U.S. aims and plans that the administration submitted to Congress on Oct. 13. But Danforth said he backed the amendment "because our troops are in place, and [Clinton] is our commander in chief, and we're headed out [of Somalia]."

Byrd initially had talked of stopping funding for operations in Somalia after Jan. 1, 1994. On Oct. 13, he offered an amendment setting a cutoff date of Feb. 1 — two months earlier than Clinton's deadline.

Byrd was a fierce protector of congressional prerogatives. He also had been sharply skeptical of U.S. intervention abroad since the 1960s, when he had doggedly defended what he later

The Somalia Compromise

The compromise provision on U.S. intervention in Somalia that was attached to the fiscal 1994 defense appropriations bill (HR 3116 — PL 103-139) included:

● Findings that "the United States entered into Operation Restore Hope in December of 1992 for the purpose of relieving mass starvation in Somalia" but that "neither the expanded United Nations mission of national reconciliation, nor the broad mission of disarming the clans, nor any other mission not essential to the humanitarian mission has been endorsed or approved by the Senate."

● A requirement that U.S. forces in Somalia were to be used only for "the protection of United States personnel and bases" and "the provision of assistance in securing open lines of communication for the free flow of supplies and relief operations...."

● A cutoff of funds that generally permitted the Defense Department to pay "for expenses incurred only through March 31, 1994, for the operations of United States Armed Forces in Somalia."

● An exception to the funding cutoff providing that U.S. forces should remain deployed "in or around Somalia until such time as all American service personnel missing in action in Somalia are accounted for and all American service personnel held prisoner are released."

● An exception providing that funds could be spent after March 31 "to support a limited number of U.S. military personnel sufficient only to protect American diplomatic facilities and American citizens and noncombat personnel to advise the United Nations commander in Somalia."

● A requirement that U.S. "combat forces in Somalia shall be under the command and control of United States commanders under the ultimate direction of the president of the United States."

● An instruction that "the president should ensure that, at all times, United States military personnel in Somalia have the capacity to defend themselves and American citizens."

came to view as President Lyndon B. Johnson's disastrous determination to prosecute the war in Vietnam.

A group of Senate heavyweights — including Dole, Mitchell and Nunn — quickly began seeking an amendment that could win the support of Byrd and a majority in the Senate while also acquiescing in the essentials of Clinton's retooled Somalia mission.

In a letter Oct. 14, Clinton assured Byrd that he would complete the pullout before March 31 "if at all feasible.... It remains our common goal," he wrote, "to use no more time than absolutely necessary to complete our tasks in Somalia and bring our troops home."

At a news conference the same day, Clinton emphasized that the Somalia operation "would make me more cautious about having any Americans in a peacekeeping role where there was any ambiguity at all about what the range of decisions were which could be made by a commander other than an American commander."

Within hours of Clinton's news conference, Mitchell,

Dole, Nunn, Byrd and other members of the bipartisan Senate leadership had worked out a common amendment.

In his Oct. 13 report to Congress, Clinton named four missions for U.S. forces pending their withdrawal by March 31: self-defense; keeping open the communication routes needed for U.N. officials and relief operations; "keeping the pressure" on local forces who had attacked U.S. personnel; and "through that pressure and the presence of our forces, help making it reasonably possible for the Somali people, working with others, to reach agreements among themselves so they can solve their own problems."

But the Byrd amendment authorized only self-defense and keeping open communications routes as legitimate U.S. military aims. And Byrd insisted that the final compromise include an explicit cutoff of funding for the Somalia mission after the March deadline.

"I got 80 percent of what I wanted," Byrd said in an interview after the vote. "We put an end to this business of the appearance of the U.N. leading us around by the nose. And we put Congress in the front seat and on the front row as it should be under the Constitution."

Mitch McConnell, R-Ky., who supported Byrd's amendment, said, "Creeping multilateralism died on the streets of Mogadishu. This is not just about Somalia. This is about how we should operate in the post-Cold War world."

But some senators who voted for Byrd's amendment lamented the backlash against U.S. participation in collective military actions.

"The mishandling of the U.S. involvement in Somalia and Haiti and serious mistakes by U.N. leaders, especially in Somalia, have done grave damage to the idea of coping with regional conflicts and crises through multilateral action," said Patrick J. Leahy, D-Vt. "This is the greatest cost of these botched operations."

House Action

As the Clinton administration had hoped, the compromise Senate language on Somalia effectively became Congress' final word on that conflict in 1993.

The House accepted the Somalia provisions as part of the conference report on the defense appropriations bill, which was approved by voice vote Nov. 10. The Senate cleared the measure for the president, 88-9, the same day. The president signed the bill Nov. 11 (PL 103-139). *(Vote 368, p. 47-S)*

A FINAL SKIRMISH

But there was one more skirmish. House Democratic leaders had to use their powers of persuasion and their parliamentary domination to defeat a Republican-backed non-binding resolution calling on Clinton to remove all troops by Jan. 31, 1994.

The Republicans forced the issue by making use of the 1973 War Powers resolution, a law that many of them had denounced when their party held the White House as an unconstitutional infringement on the president's authority as commander in chief.

House Committee

On Oct. 22, Gilman introduced a non-binding resolution (H Con Res 170) urging Clinton to bring U.S. troops home two months before the deadline the president had accepted. Concerned that Democratic leaders would block the measure, Gilman invoked in his resolution a section of the War Powers law providing for expedited consideration

of such a measure whenever forces "are engaged in hostilities outside the territory of the United States." It required action on the resolution by the Foreign Affairs Committee within 15 days of its introduction and a House vote within three days after that.

When the Foreign Affairs Committee took up the matter Nov. 3, the administration narrowly averted embarrassment. The panel voted 22-21 to endorse the March 31 deadline, which was offered as a substitute to Gilman's resolution. The committee then approved the underlying resolution, as modified, by voice vote.

Three Democrats — Robert E. Andrews of New Jersey and Sherrod Brown and Eric D. Fingerhut of Ohio — joined unanimous Republicans in opposing the substitute, which was sponsored by Foreign Affairs Chairman Hamilton.

The outcome of the committee's vote was in doubt until the end, despite a frantic scramble by the administration and its Democratic allies to beat back the Republican challenge.

"Let's face it," Gillman said, "the U.S. mission in Somalia has changed from saving lives to saving face. . . . I am prepared to state with total conviction that it is not worth one American life to help the authors of a failed policy save face."

Hamilton, too, played hardball, eliciting statements from administration officials that it might be risky for U.S. forces to withdraw too rapidly from Somalia. The officials insisted the March 31 deadline would give the administration a "reasonable chance" to line up replacements for the departing U.S. forces from countries such as Egypt and Pakistan.

Arguing that Gilman's resolution would undercut Clinton's ability to run the nation's foreign policy, Hamilton invoked a favorite phrase used in similar circumstances by President Ronald Reagan and congressional Republicans. "If that's not micromanagement," Hamilton said of Gilman's resolution, "I don't know what is."

Before taking up Gilman's resolution, the committee defeated by voice vote an amendment by Bill Goodling, R-Pa., calling on the president to withdraw U.S. forces within 30 days of the resolution's adoption.

House Floor

Venting discontent over a U.S.-backed military operation that by that time had cost the lives of 35 U.S. troops, the House on Nov. 9 voted 224-203 in favor of Gilman's non-binding language calling for a withdrawal of U.S. forces by Jan. 31. *(Vote 555, p. 136-H)*

But the administration escaped more serious embarrassment when the House reversed course and adopted an amendment supporting Clinton's March 31 pullout date, 226-201. Under the "king of the hill" procedures that the Rules Committee set for the debate, that amendment prevailed. Lawmakers went on to approve the underlying resolution (H Con Res 170) by voice vote. *(House vote 556, p. 136-H)*

The White House launched an intensive last-minute effort on behalf of its embattled Somalia policy. House Democratic leaders delayed consideration of the resolution for several hours to allow the administration to lobby wavering members.

Despite those efforts, 55 Democrats bucked the administration in supporting the Jan. 31 deadline. All but three of the 171 Republicans voting supported Gilman's amendment.

The GOP remained solid in opposing Hamilton's superseding amendment. But 24 Democrats who backed the Jan. 31 deadline — including such senior lawmakers as Charles E. Schumer, N.Y., and G. V. "Sonny" Montgomery, Miss. — turned around and supported Clinton's pullout date, providing the margin of victory.

Republicans faced their own dilemma. While sharply opposing the administration on Somalia, few wanted to be accused of tying Clinton's hands or undercutting the carefully crafted compromise on the March 31 deadline that had been embraced by many leading GOP senators.

Several Republicans, including Hyde, said they probably would not have supported Gilman's resolution had it been binding.

Yet Republicans were torn by a desire as well to send what Minority Whip Newt Gingrich, R-Ga., said was "a signal that says to the president there is not support in this Congress for a muddled, confused and unexplained policy which risks the lives of Americans for no purpose."

House Speaker Thomas S. Foley, D-Wash., and other leading Democrats countered that the wrong signal would be sent if the House went on record opposing the president's support for an "orderly withdrawal" from Somalia. "It would be a tragic moment for American resolve, American principle and American position around the world," said Foley. "Do not do this to the president of the United States. We should not do this to any president, Republican or Democrat." ∎

Administration Struggles With Bosnia Policy

After moving to the brink of military intervention in Bosnia-Herzegovina on several occasions in 1993, the Clinton administration adopted a far more cautious approach to the ethnic warfare that devastated the former Yugoslavia.

In the face of opposition from European allies who had peacekeeping troops on the ground and at risk, President Clinton abandoned a proposal to launch multilateral airstrikes against Bosnian Serb positions and to arm the Muslim-led government forces.

The administration tentatively offered U.S. troops for a NATO peacekeeping force in Bosnia, but only if the warring parties reached an enforceable peace. The unrelenting conflict left that plan in limbo at year's end.

Congress, like the administration, grew increasingly wary of any direct military involvement in the complex, three-sided war among Bosnia's Muslims, Serbs and Croatians. Although there was brutality and aggression on all sides, most lawmakers shared the administration's view that the Muslim population in Bosnia was the outgunned victim of aggression and of "ethnic cleansing." That was the term some Serbian forces had used for systematic murder and rape to displace Muslims from wide portions of Bosnia.

The support for the Muslims was reflected in a non-controversial provision in the fiscal 1994 foreign operations appropriations bill (HR 2295 — PL 103-87) allowing Clinton to provide $50 million in arms and materiel to the Bosnian government if an international arms embargo that applied to all of the warring parties was lifted. A similar provision had been included in the fiscal 1993 foreign operations bill (PL 102-391). *(Appropriations, p. 603; 1992 Almanac, p. 532)*

A provision urging Clinton to break the arms embargo

unilaterally to arm the Bosnians was included in a foreign aid authorization bill that was approved in the House (HR 2404) and by the Senate Foreign Relations Committee, but that measure stalled short of passage.

Although some lawmakers argued passionately for direct U.S. action against what they viewed as attempted genocide against the Muslims, most argued against risky intervention in a murky regional conflict. On Oct. 20, the Senate voted 99-1 for a non-binding amendment to the defense appropriations bill (HR 3116 — PL 103-139) urging the administration not to send U.S. forces to Bosnia without first obtaining congressional approval. The House backed the Senate language by adopting the conference report on the defense appropriations bill Nov. 10.

SEEKING A POLICY

After the fall of communism, Yugoslavia broke into feuding republics riven by ancient ethnic rivalries. What remained of Yugoslavia was controlled by Serbia, which fought for dominance and territory with neighboring Croatia and Bosnia-Herzegovina.

As a presidential candidate in 1992, Democrat Clinton had urged his rival, Republican President George Bush, to consider multilateral airstrikes as a means of ensuring the delivery of humanitarian aid to Bosnia's besieged Muslims. Clinton was so insistent in raising the issue of military intervention that Bush's White House spokesman, Marlin Fitzwater, once called Clinton "reckless." Fitzwater sought to raise doubts about Clinton's competence to handle national security matters.

Once Clinton took office, his administration attempted in its early weeks to develop a clear policy toward the warfare in Bosnia. Its efforts resulted in a six-point plan announced by Secretary of State Warren Christopher on Feb. 10 that sought to bolster international mediation efforts. But the administration's ambivalence toward the prospect of intervention in Bosnia was displayed from the outset, when Clinton's nominees to Cabinet-level positions mixed expressions of moral outrage with imprecise suggestions about the course to be taken.

Christopher was pressed on Bosnia at his confirmation hearing before the Senate Foreign Relations Committee Jan. 13. Joseph R. Biden Jr., D-Del., who had urged military intervention to halt Serbian aggression, told Christopher that the West cannot "allow the rape of Bosnia to continue." Comparing Serbia's actions to Hitler's annexation of Czechoslovakia before World War II, Biden laid out a menu of possible options the new administration might consider — including a U.S. role in a multilateral force to liberate Bosnian cities.

Christopher sounded cool and detached even as he echoed Biden's outrage over shocking reports that beleaguered Bosnians might resort to cannibalism to avoid starvation during the winter. "It's the most horrifying situation in recent memory for me," he said. "This is not just unpleasantness; this is slaughter and murder for purposes of ethnic cleansing."

But aside from reiterating Clinton's support for enforcement of a "no-fly zone" that the United Nations had declared over Bosnia, Christopher declined to outline any actions to address the crisis. "You look at Bosnia and you can see the horror of it, but the next part of the analysis is very difficult," he said. He added that enforcement of the no-fly zone probably would amount to little more than a symbol of the West's desire to "level the playing field" among warring factions in Bosnia.

Madeleine K. Albright, Clinton's nominee as permanent representative to the United Nations, said at her confirmation hearing Jan. 21 that the administration would have little patience if U.S. allies in Europe continued to shrink from aggressive efforts to halt the bloodshed in Bosnia. "I must say that I have watched with some amazement the fact that the Europeans have not taken action on this," she said. "The coalition is very important to us, but we have to lead it."

Christopher's Plan

On Feb. 10, Christopher outlined a plan to build on a controversial peace process spearheaded by former Secretary of State Cyrus R. Vance, representing the United Nations, and Lord Owen, the former British foreign secretary, representing the European Community.

Christopher said the administration's objective was to bring a "just, workable and durable solution" to the conflict and to ensure the survival of Bosnia as a state.

The plan committed the administration to:
- Bring "the full weight of American diplomacy to bear" on the negotiations being led by Vance and Owen.
- Communicate "to the Bosnians, Serbs, and Croatians that the only way to end this conflict is through negotiation" in which each party must "accept a resolution that falls short of its greatest goals."
- Work "to tighten the enforcement of economic sanctions, increase political pressure on Serbia and deter Serbia from widening the war." In particular, the United States warned that it would "respond against the Serbians in the event of a conflict in Kosovo caused by Serbian action."
- Take steps "to reduce the suffering and bloodshed as the negotiations proceed." Clinton called on all parties to stop the violence, urged enforcement of the "no fly" zone over Bosnia, set up a U.S. team to urgently assess humanitarian needs and pledged to seek a "war crimes tribunal at the United Nations."
- "Do its share to help implement and enforce an agreement that is acceptable to all parties." If such an enforceable agreement was reached, the administration said, "the United States would be prepared to join with the United Nations, NATO, and others, in implementing and enforcing it, including possible U.S. military action."
- Consult with allies, particularly Russian President Boris N. Yeltsin, many of whose countrymen felt historic and religious ties to the Serbs.

Although Christopher declined to provide specifics on possible military intervention, some senators said they had been told that the U.S. contribution to a multilateral force might ultimately involve as many as 10,000 troops.

Aware of the sensitivity of that issue, Clinton said at a "town meeting" near Detroit on Feb. 10 that the plan envisioned the United States becoming "more involved in what is going on in Bosnia, not in committing our ground troops now or anything like that."

The secretary of State emphasized that the administration inherited an immense challenge in trying to develop a coherent policy toward the former Yugoslavia. The Bush administration had come in for considerable criticism for failing to address the crisis until the country had virtually disintegrated. "Because those actions were not taken," Christopher said, "we face a much more intractable situation with vastly more difficult options."

Congressional Reaction

Broad congressional backing for Christopher's diplomatic initiative masked the concern of many lawmakers

that the plan ultimately would achieve too little even as it committed the United States to do too much.

Yet there was a widespread sense that because of past U.S. inaction on Bosnia and the complex nature of the crisis, the president had few alternatives for action.

Lee H. Hamilton, D-Ind., chairman of the House Foreign Affairs Committee, said the president and his top advisers "had made a very important choice: They've decided to engage U.S. power and diplomacy in support of the peace effort."

Biden, who had previously urged much more aggressive steps, enthusiastically supported the administration's plan. He called it "a clear-cut rejection of appeasement" and praised Clinton for a "much-needed act of American leadership."

Hamilton, who had consulted closely with Christopher on the proposal, insisted that "this is not a commitment of American military power to fight in the Balkans; it's a commitment to enforce an agreement that the parties themselves have consented to."

But the prospect of sending ground forces touched a nerve with some Republicans. "I'm deeply and gravely concerned — first, about what they will do and, second, under whose command they will serve," said Sen. John McCain, Ariz. "Are they to be stationed at the airport like the Marines at Beirut?" In 1983, 241 U.S. Marines on a peacekeeping mission in Lebanon were killed in a terrorist bomb attack.

At the same time, other Republicans criticized the administration for backing away from the muscular approach to Bosnia that Clinton had advocated during 1992.

Senate Minority Leader Bob Dole, R-Kan., said he was disappointed with Clinton's plan "because it is far less than the tough action he promised during the campaign. . . . His plan won't be near enough to stop the bloodshed and ethnic cleansing, so I doubt the Serbs will back off."

The administration's acceptance of the negotiating process begun by Vance and Owen worried Bosnia's Muslims and their U.S. supporters. The two diplomats had proposed that the country be divided along communal lines, which many U.S. officials said would reward Serbian aggression.

Identical measures introduced in the House (H Res 35) and Senate (S Res 11) in January urged the president to seek the immediate lifting of the U.N. arms embargo against Bosnia so that the Muslims could obtain defensive arms. The resolutions also supported the use of airstrikes to neutralize Serbian mortars and other heavy weapons. The Senate measure, which was referred to the Foreign Relations Committee, won the backing of Dole and Majority Leader George J. Mitchell, D-Maine.

But Christopher said that the administration, after consulting with U.S. allies, had ruled out both proposals.

Three countries with peacekeeping forces in the former Yugoslavia — France, the United Kingdom and Canada — "felt that their troops would be gravely endangered if we lifted the embargo on weapons to the Bosnians," the secretary said. Similar considerations were involved in the decision not to press for multilateral airstrikes against Serbian gun emplacements.

ADDING AIRDROPS

The fighting and humanitarian suffering in Bosnia only worsened in the weeks following the administration's new initiative.

In late February, the administration decided to initiate airdrops of desperately needed humanitarian aid to Bosnia-Herzegovina. The airdrops began after some lawmakers be-

came increasingly outspoken in criticizing the administration.

Sen. Richard G. Lugar of Indiana, a leading Republican spokesman on the issue, expressed frustration with the heavy reliance on diplomacy. Lugar, who called for the establishment of a huge, multinational military force for Bosnia, said he feared that the negotiations would drag on "for months and years" and that the administration was "kibitzing around the situation."

A particularly harsh assessment of the administration's initiative came from Christopher's colleague from the Carter administration, former national security adviser Zbigniew Brzezinski, who testified Feb. 18 before two subcommittees of the House Foreign Affairs Committee.

"The powerful rhetoric used by Secretary Christopher to justify the U.S. engagement was, much to my regret, refuted by the toothless and essentially procedural steps that then emanated from the rhetoric," Brzezinski said.

In the House, Rep. Frank McCloskey of Indiana emerged as the sharpest Democratic critic of the Clinton plan. Appearing Feb. 19 at a news conference with Bosnia's visiting foreign minister, Haris Silajdzic, McCloskey said that the United States and its allies had responded to Serbian atrocities with "hypocritical diplomacy." "To the people of Bosnia," McCloskey said, "the message has been . . . stay where you are and reach some compromise with the thugs who are slaughtering you and raping you and starving you."

After meeting with British Prime Minister John Major on Feb. 24, Clinton confirmed reports that U.S. aircraft would begin dropping humanitarian supplies. The president said that the planes would fly at high altitudes, beyond the range of hostile ground fire, to "virtually assure the complete safety" of participating military personnel.

Under the plan, which was formally announced Feb. 25, U.S. C-130 transport planes were to parachute food and other assistance to isolated villages, including 200,000 Muslims who had been cut off from U.N. ground convoys by Serbian militias.

Most members of Congress accepted the president's assurances that the proposal would provide some aid and moral support for the besieged Bosnians while limiting the danger faced by American pilots. "It's the minimum that we should be doing," said Rep. Henry J. Hyde, R-Ill., "and it can be done with minimal risk."

Clinton acknowledged that the aircraft would be dropping their supplies with less precision than if they flew at lower altitudes: "We know that . . . a percentage of the packages we drop will be outside the more-or-less half-mile circle we would be trying to hit."

But Clinton's commitment to what he called a "temporary measure" stoked the concerns of some Republicans that the administration had started down a path that would result in full-scale U.S. military intervention in Bosnia.

"The first question I have is: Why are we doing this?" asked Doug Bereuter, R-Neb., a member of the House Intelligence Committee. "There are some people over there who would like to bring the United States into the war. One way to do that would be to bring one of our planes down."

The administration won politically crucial support from Senate Armed Services Committee Chairman Sam Nunn, D-Ga., but only after some scrambling.

After Nunn complained Feb. 25 that a scheduled military briefing on the operation had been canceled, the White House dispatched the Pentagon's A-team — including Defense Secretary Les Aspin and Gen. Colin L. Powell Jr., chairman of the Joint Chiefs of Staff — to the Hill to

meet with the committee. Aspin had been released hours earlier from a hospital, where he had been treated for a heart ailment.

Nunn called the airdrops "more symbolic than it is the ultimate answer." He said that while the missions involved some risk, "this is not an operation where we expect people to shoot at our airplanes."

The president insisted that the United States was not taking sides in the conflict, although the plan originally had been conceived to aid only the trapped Muslims. "We're prepared to help anybody who needs food and medicine," he said, including Serbians.

In the weeks that followed, lawmakers grew increasingly polarized in their views, with some members angry that the administration was not taking more direct action to intervene in Bosnia and others warning that the airdrops alone could draw the administration deeply into the conflict.

Old lineups of military hawks and doves had little relevance. For example, Floyd D. Spence, S.C., the senior Republican on the House Armed Services Committee, fired one of the strongest salvos against involvement at a committee hearing March 4. "Why should we get involved?" Spence asked. "Who appointed us designated hitter? . . . Are we putting ourselves in a position where we will have little alternative but escalation if the conflict widens?"

On the other hand, Rep. Charles Wilson, a conservative Democrat from Texas, told Christopher at a March 25 hearing of the House Appropriations Subcommittee on Foreign Operations that only a NATO force including as many as 15,000 U.S. troops could end "the ethnic horrors" in Bosnia. "We're going to have to face that," Wilson said, "or we're going to have to be willing to endure . . . the worst human rights abuses that have occurred in the world since 1942."

A CACOPHONY OF VIEWS

The administration was subjected to a cacophony of criticism throughout the spring and summer from those members of Congress in both parties who wanted more aggressive action in Bosnia and those who thought Clinton had already made too great a commitment to use U.S. forces.

McCain, one of the nation's most famous prisoners of war from the conflict in Southeast Asia, said he was unwilling to "risk another Vietnam" in the Balkans.

But McCain's view about intervention in Bosnia was hardly unanimous, even among fellow Republican conservatives. "What's taking place there is worse than what Hitler did," said Strom Thurmond of South Carolina, the ranking Republican on the Senate Armed Service Committee, at a panel hearing April 28. "Can we do nothing?"

Hyde, a member of the House Foreign Affairs Committee, said lawmakers were groping for the correct analogy. "People now are trying to figure out," he said, "whether this is Germany 1942 or Vietnam 1975."

Calls for Action

During most of April, the criticism came largely from those who urged a more combative strategy.

The Serbian push for control of eastern Bosnia made a significant advance April 16, as the Muslim enclave of Srebenica appeared ready to fall to the forces that had besieged it for months.

"At this point," Clinton told reporters April 16, "I would not rule out any option except the option that I have never ruled in, which was the question of American ground troops." He added, "We have to consider things which at least previ-

ously have been unacceptable to some of the [U.N.] Security Council members and some of those in NATO."

Earlier that week, Senate Minority Leader Dole issued his strongest criticism of the administration to date, saying, "No matter how you spin it, this policy has been a failure."

And an implicit rejection of the administration policy came from a team of midlevel officials from several agencies that assessed the humanitarian crisis in the war-ravaged country. The 26-member team recommended "robust military and/or renewed diplomatic means to silence heavy weapons systems," which were controlled by the Serbs, in Bosnia. It also called for establishing "safe havens" for civilian populations, which would be protected by international forces.

Senior Democrats in Congress expressed frustration with the administration after The New York Times reported that the humanitarian aid team had been under orders not to mention the recommendations concerning military force in briefing congressional aides on its draft report.

Leading members of Congress renewed their calls to end the U.N. arms embargo for Bosnia. "Lifting the arms embargo won't be easy," Dole said, "but it's the right thing, the moral thing, to do."

In the House, a bipartisan coalition of more than 40 lawmakers signed a letter to Clinton urging the use of air power against the Serbs, saying "The United States cannot acquiesce in genocide in Bosnia."

Emphasizing the lack of good options in the Bosnia crisis, Clinton told reporters at a news conference April 23, "This is clearly the most difficult foreign policy problem we face and that all of our allies face."

But Biden, complaining that the United States and its allies were not doing "a damn thing" to prevent Serbian shelling of Srebenica, said, "The time has come for us — the world — to stop bemoaning the fact that all our options are bad ones. They are all bad ones. We've got to pick a couple."

Calls for Caution

The approaching possibility of military action sharpened differences over the war in Bosnia-Herzegovina during the week of April 26.

Clinton and his senior aides consulted in hours of meetings with members of Congress on several options: limited airstrikes by the United States and its allies on Bosnian Serb artillery emplacements; airstrikes on other economic or military targets in Bosnia or in Serbia; and pressing the United Nations to lift the embargo that prevented Bosnia's Muslim-led government from obtaining weapons.

After an exhaustive 2½ -hour White House meeting attended by a group of about 20 senior lawmakers April 27, Republicans and Democrats said they were equally impressed with the president's willingness to hear them out.

But if Clinton, a new president lacking in foreign policy experience, was hoping for a consensus from Congress, he was to be disappointed. Beyond their strong resistance to deploying ground forces, the lawmakers disagreed on most other points.

Some supporters of airstrikes argued that the president would face little significant opposition if he carefully limited the scope of the mission to calm fears of an open-ended intervention. Clinton's "strong pitch should be that it's limited," said Rep. Barney Frank, D-Mass.

A diverse group of lawmakers — including Rep. Richard J. Durbin, D-Ill., and Sen. John W. Warner, R-Va. — urged the president to seek congressional authorization for any military action in Bosnia. Durbin rounded up signatures

from 91 House members for a letter making that case. But lawmakers appeared uncertain as to whether Clinton needed to obtain such authorization before any intervention began.

But others predicted that the House could reject a resolution authorizing such a course. "I think that it is a loser," said Robert G. Torricelli, D-N.J., a member of the House Foreign Affairs Committee who opposed any U.S. military involvement in the former Yugoslavia. He warned that the administration "should know that there are limits to partisan loyalty."

The rising congressional opposition to airstrikes stemmed partly from pessimistic assessments in the Pentagon. A panel of senior military officers told the Senate Armed Services Committee on April 28 that multilateral attacks — without the deployment of large-scale ground forces — could not halt the Serb advance. "My gut instinct is that in the larger sense there is no military solution to this," said Lt. Gen. Barry McCaffrey. The officers also warned that Serbian gunners would respond to air attacks by moving artillery pieces to populated areas, raising the possibility that U.S. bombing could cause civilian casualties.

Like Congress, however, the Pentagon appeared divided. Gen. Merrill A. McPeak, the Air Force chief of staff, insisted that Serb positions could be effectively attacked with very little risk to U.S. pilots.

By May, when the self-styled parliament of the Bosnian Serbs rejected a U.N.-backed peace plan, lawmakers were united only in urging Clinton to provide a clear case to the American people for any action in Bosnia. "He has to spell out our interests in the region and the importance of the mission," said House Foreign Affairs Chairman Hamilton. "Up to this point it's been an inside discussion — inside the White House and inside congressional cloakrooms."

Europe Resists

Christopher failed to sell European allies on Clinton's proposals for arms sales to Bosnia coupled with airstrikes on Serbian positions. European allies objected to supplying new arms to any of the parties in the conflict and protested that, unlike the United States, they had peacekeeping forces already on the ground that could face retaliation for airstrikes.

Clinton expressed frustration with critics who accused the administration of vacillating. "I have gotten more done on this than my predecessor did," the president said, "and maybe one reason he didn't try to do it is because [of such criticism] if you can't force everybody to fall in line overnight."

But the administration also began to temper its talk of a moral imperative to play a role. Christopher told the House Foreign Affairs Committee on May 18 that the Bosnian war had become a bloody free-for-all in which no side was blameless.

"It's been easy to analogize this to the Holocaust," he said, "but I never heard of any genocide by the Jews against the German people."

On May 22, setting aside its moribund plan for airstrikes and arms, the administration joined Great Britain, France, Russia and Spain in endorsing an interim plan to contain Bosnia's war by creating six Muslim enclaves that the five powers would protect. U.S. air power would be committed to protecting allied peacekeeping forces — but not the enclaves themselves.

"Of all the bad solutions . . . this is the best one," House Majority Leader Richard A. Gephardt, D-Mo., told CNN on May 23. But Senate Foreign Relations Committee member Daniel Patrick Moynihan, D-N.Y., savaged the proposal, saying the administration was "legitimating genocide."

VOTES FOR ARMS

In the first congressional action on Bosnia in Clinton's term, the House Foreign Affairs Committee voted, 24-15, on June 8 to authorize the president to spend up to $200 million arming Bosnia's Muslim-dominated government forces — even if the United Nations declined to lift the international embargo on arms to any of the parties in the former Yugoslavia. The provision was added to the fiscal 1994 foreign aid authorization bill (HR 2404), which won voice vote approval from the committee the same day. The House passed the bill by voice vote June 16.

The Senate Foreign Relations Committee voted, 14-5, for a non-binding amendment to the same effect Sept. 8. It then approved its version of the foreign aid bill, 16-4. But the measure stalled at that point. *(Foreign aid authorization, p. 502)*

House Action

The Foreign Affairs Committee's action June 8, calling on the administration to act alone if necessary to arm Bosnia's government, reflected members' frustration at the failure of multilateral efforts to resolve the conflict.

The 24-15 vote came over administration objections even though the committee amended the proposal so that the action would not be forced on the president: It would be up to the president whether to provide as much as $200 million in military equipment to Bosnian government forces in defiance of the U.N. embargo against weapons shipments to the region.

Hyde, who sponsored the amendment, argued that maintaining the weapons embargo had only served to benefit the better-armed Serbian forces. "You don't have much of a war when one side has the weapons and all the other side can do is die and suffer," he said.

Hamilton warned his colleagues of grave consequences if the United States were to arm the Bosnian government forces without the imprimatur of the United Nations and Europe. "At that point this conflict becomes an American conflict," he said.

Assistant Secretary of State Wendy Sherman told the committee that by ignoring the U.N. embargo the United States would set a precedent for actions "that we could later regret." Other nations could use similar rationales to evade U.N. arm embargoes against Serbia or Iraq, she said.

Hyde's amendment directly challenged one of the central tenets of administration policy: that the United States had to work in concert with the United Nations and allies in Europe to resolve the Bosnian crisis.

The debate demonstrated anew that the congressional fault lines over Bosnia ignored partisan and ideological lines. Hyde's amendment drew the support of 10 Democrats; 11 others joined Hamilton in opposition.

Many of the Democrats who backed the amendment, such as Tom Lantos of California, had called for tougher steps to counter Serbian aggression but had mostly refrained from criticizing the administration.

But Lantos rejected the allied policy of establishing six "safe havens" in Bosnia to protect hundreds of thousands of Muslim refugees. "The policy has now been reduced to a pathetic attempt, on paper, to claim safe havens," Lantos said. Serbian attacks on Muslims in some of the designated safe areas made a mockery of that strategy, he said.

Opponents of Hyde's amendment included all four committee members who belonged to the Congressional Black

Caucus. Freshman Cynthia McKinney, D-Ga., warned of becoming bogged down in a Vietnam-style "morass."

Perhaps sensing a low-cost opportunity to highlight differences with the administration over foreign policy, Republicans voted 14-3 in favor of Hyde's amendment.

Two days after the committee vote, the administration announced June 10 that it planned to send a small contingent of U.S. troops to the former Yugoslav republic of Macedonia in an effort to prevent a potentially explosive widening of the regional warfare.

Officials feared that Serbia could move against the ethnic Albanian majority in the province of Kosovo and that fighting then could spread to neighboring Macedonia. A broader conflict could draw in NATO allies such as Turkey and Greece.

Senate Action

After months of inaction on the conflict, the Senate Foreign Relations Committee on Sept. 8 followed the House in urging Clinton to provide arms to Bosnia's Muslim forces despite the U.N. embargo.

As Clinton met with Bosnian President Alija Izetbegovic, the panel provided the Bosnian leader with a symbolic boost by voting, 14-5, to authorize up to $200 million in military equipment and training for his government's military forces.

The vote came on a non-binding amendment to the foreign aid authorization bill (S 1467 — S Rept 103-144).

Lugar, who offered the amendment, called the committee's action "a very strong statement and a very strong vote on an issue that the committee has evaded for 1½ years."

But the panel significantly modified Lugar's original proposal, which would have required Clinton to act alone to end the U.N.'s embargo on all of the warring factions in the former Yugoslavia. Instead, the committee voted 11-8 to leave to the president the decision on terminating the arms ban, as had the House.

Reflecting the broad range of congressional views on Bosnia, many Democrats backed the idea of providing weapons to the Muslims but voiced concerns over contravening the U.N. Security Council resolution that established the embargo. Some also objected to tying the president's hands in foreign policy.

Opponents of Lugar's amendment argued that it would endorse a broader and potentially dangerous U.S. role in the Bosnian conflict by authorizing U.S. troops to train Bosnian government forces. Colorado Republican Hank Brown expressed skepticism that Congress had the staying power to support such a mission. When the U.S. peacekeeping operation in Lebanon turned deadly a decade earlier, he said, "I saw all of those heroes who voted for the mission turn around and cut off support."

The committee's action came as Clinton emphasized that he would seek the assent of Congress before deploying U.S. forces to enforce any peace agreement in Bosnia. That would be a far more difficult issue for Congress than recommending that the president lift the arms ban, Lugar said. U.S. military officials "envision extensive ground forces in Bosnia" if an agreement is reached, he said.

The foreign aid authorization bill died after committee approval, as Senate leaders declined to schedule floor time for a measure that had repeatedly stalled short of passage in previous years.

CONGRESSIONAL SHOWDOWN

By autumn, it became clear that good news for Bosnia could become bad news for lawmakers and an administra-

tion wary of military ventures abroad: Progress in winning an enforceable peace agreement between Bosnia's warring Muslims, Serbs and Croats could force the administration to make good on its pledge to contribute troops to the international effort to police such a pact.

At a news conference while he was in New York to address the U.N. General Assembly on Sept. 27, Clinton set out more specific — and restrictive — criteria for U.S. participation in such a multinational force for Bosnia:

"I would want a clear understanding of what the command and control was, and I would want the NATO commander [to be] in charge of the operation. I would want a clear timetable for first review and ultimately for a right to terminate American involvement so that we — I would want a clear political strategy along with the military strategy. After all, there will be more than soldiers involved in this. And I would want a clear expression of support from the U.S. Congress.

"Now, there are 20 other operational things I would want, but those are the big policy issues."

When asked about the financing for such an operation, Clinton added: "We would have to know exactly what our financial responsibilities are, and, of course, under our budget law, which is very strict now, we have to know how we're going to fund it, and then we'd have to know that others were going to do their part as well and that, at least for the period of the operation that we were responsible for, that we were going to do it properly."

But those conditions were not enough to forestall the congressional debate over involvement in Bosnia — as well as Somalia and Haiti — that erupted during Senate consideration of the fiscal 1994 defense appropriations bill (HR 3116).

Senate Floor Action

Institutionally, the executive branch came out ahead in the debate over U.S. intervention abroad during the week of Oct. 18. Instead of requiring advance authorization by Congress, the Senate settled for non-binding resolutions that were negotiated with the White House.

Politically, however, Clinton and his foreign policy team were forced to acknowledge — and in some measure accommodate — congressional concerns about projected peacekeeping deployments. And they were battered by portrayals of their approach to trouble spots, such as Somalia and Bosnia, as confused and inept.

Senate Minority Leader Dole led the unsuccessful push for binding restrictions on the president's power to intervene. But the criticism of the administration's foreign policy performance came from both sides of the aisle during four days of debate.

Senators on Oct. 20 adopted 99-1 a non-binding amendment urging the president to seek congressional authorization before sending troops into Bosnia, as Clinton previously had promised to do. *(Vote 320, p. 41-S)*

Dole and Mitchell cosponsored the amendment, which stated the sense of Congress that no funds in the defense bill should be used for deployments to enforce a peace settlement in Bosnia unless Congress authorized the intervention in advance.

The prohibition did not apply to U.S. participation in multilateral operations that were already under way, including the airlift of humanitarian supplies to Sarajevo and NATO aerial patrols that were intended to enforce a flight ban on Serbian aircraft.

Bosnia's brutal factional warfare was not much discussed in the two weeks of Senate debate on intervention

policy. But the strong warnings against committing U.S. troops in uncertain circumstances appeared to reflect deep opposition to Clinton's offer to participate in a multilateral peacekeeping force if Bosnia's warring parties ever agreed to an enforceable peace.

Mitch McConnell, R-Ky., said of the prospect that the White House would seek authorization to send troops to Bosnia, "I don't think they'll ever ask for it, given the trouble they've had with Haiti and Somalia."

More broadly, senators on Oct. 19 rejected 33-65 an amendment by Don Nickles, R-Okla., that would have required prior approval to place troops under a foreign officer in any conflict. They then adopted 96-2 an amendment urging the same course of action. *(Votes 317, 318, p. 41-S)*

Nickles' amendment would have barred the president from assigning U.S. combat troops to U.N. control under command of a foreign officer unless he gave Congress 30 days' notice and Congress then adopted a joint resolution approving the arrangement. The amendment also would have barred the assignment of U.S. forces to a standing U.N. army. The president could have waived the require-

ment for prior congressional approval if he determined that national security interests required placing U.S. troops under foreign command. In that case, the arrangement could continue only if Congress approved it within 30 days.

The non-binding alternative to Nickles' amendment, sponsored by Democrat Nunn and Republican Warner, said that the president "should consult with Congress before placing [U.S.] combat forces . . . under the operational control of foreign commanders," outside of NATO. It also stated that the president should report to Congress within 48 hours of making such an assignment.

Final Action

The conference committee on the defense appropriations bill accepted the Senate's non-binding amendments on peacekeeping intervention in Bosnia and other regional trouble spots. The House accepted the amendments by approving the conference report (H Rept 103-339) by voice vote Nov. 10. The Senate cleared the bill for the president, 88-9, the same day. Clinton signed the measure (PL 103-139) on Nov. 11. ∎

Attempts Fail To Reinstate Haiti's Aristide

President Clinton struggled unsuccessfully throughout 1993 to end the long history of totalitarian rule in Haiti, one of the Western Hemisphere's poorest nations.

The United States was instrumental in imposing an international embargo on oil, arms and financial dealings in an effort to force Haiti's military rulers to restore Jean-Bertrand Aristide, the democratically elected president they had ousted in 1991.

The coup leaders signed an agreement with Aristide that promised to permit his return by Oct. 30. But on Oct. 11, armed Haitians chased off U.S. and Canadian military engineers who were supposed to aid in rebuilding efforts in keeping with that agreement. On Oct. 15, Clinton announced the deployment of Navy ships to the waters off Haiti to enforce the embargo. The Oct. 30 deadline passed with Aristide still living in the Washington area and the military rulers still firmly ensconced in Haiti.

Although some members of Congress, especially members of the Congressional Black Caucus, urged intervention to restore Aristide, some conservatives denounced him as an unstable radical. Most members of Congress appeared opposed to armed intervention.

Lawmakers put non-binding language in the fiscal 1994 defense appropriations bill (HR 3116 — PL 103-139) urging Clinton to seek congressional authorization before dispatching any U.S. troops to intervene in Haiti.

BACKGROUND

Haiti, which shared the island of Hispaniola with the Dominican Republic, knew much poverty and little democracy throughout its history. The island won independence from French colonial rule in 1804 after a series of bloody uprisings by the black population, most of whom were former slaves.

U.S. Marines occupied Haiti from 1915 to 1934. Francois Duvalier, a physician known as Papa Doc, was elected president in a plebiscite in 1957. Duvalier and then his son

Jean-Claude, known as Baby Doc, ruled with the help of their brutal extralegal force, the *tontons macoutes*.

Jean-Claude Duvalier fled into exile in 1986. The next year, the first free elections in 30 years were canceled after pro-Duvalier forces murdered at least 34 voters waiting in line to cast ballots. On Dec. 16, 1990, Aristide, a leftist Roman Catholic priest, was elected president. He was ousted by a military coup Sept. 30, 1991.

Although opposing the coup, President George Bush expressed concern that the instability in Haiti was leading to a flood of Haitian "boat people" arriving on U.S. shores and at a makeshift refugee center that was opened at the U.S. Guantanamo Bay Naval Station in Cuba. On May 24, 1992, Bush issued a directive that Haitians rescued or intercepted at sea should be summarily returned without hearings on their claims of political persecution.

CLINTON'S REVERSAL

As a presidential candidate in 1992, Bill Clinton denounced Bush's policy as inhumane and promised to reverse it. But on Jan. 14, 1993, confronted by reports that thousands of Haitians were preparing to set sail for the U.S. on rickety boats as soon as he took office, President-elect Clinton went on the Voice of America, the government's international radio service, to announce that he would continue the controversial interception policy.

Clinton told reporters that he still believed that summary repatriation was wrong but now viewed the practice as necessary in the short term to help political negotiations advance and to protect the Haitians. "I will end the practice . . . when I am fully confident I can do so in a way that does not contribute to a humanitarian tragedy," said Clinton, who promised in the meantime to improve the processing of claims for U.S. asylum that were filed in Haiti.

Clinton's announcement came amid a flurry of unprecedented diplomatic activity concerning Haiti that involved Bush and Clinton aides, Aristide, the Organization of

American States and the United Nations. As a result of those negotiations, Aristide on Jan. 11 made a radio address urging Haitians not to flee the country. And Aristide later rescinded a statement calling on Clinton to halt forced repatriations.

Refugee advocacy groups sharply criticized Clinton's reversal, saying the policy of forced repatriation violated international and U.S. refugee law. However, Rep. Charles B. Rangel, D-N.Y., who had been a leading critic of the policy under Bush, praised the new drive by the outgoing and incoming administrations to restore democracy to Haiti. Noting that Haiti's deposed president had endorsed Clinton's approach, Rangel said, "I'm not going to be more Haitian than Aristide."

But black members of Congress became more critical after the administration on March 2 defended the repatriation policy against a challenge before the Supreme Court, putting its legal stamp on the Bush-era practice.

Arguing that he was driven largely by the fear of Haitians drowning on the high seas, Clinton said, "If we did what the plaintiffs in the court case want, we would be consigning a very large number of Haitians . . . to some sort of death warrant."

Clinton conceded that he might have been "too harsh" in his campaign criticism of Bush but maintained that his policy was different because he had improved opportunities for Haitians to apply for asylum in their country and was pushing more vigorously for a return to democracy there.

But black leaders said the policy amounted to racism against Haitians. Indicating that an initial period of patience with Clinton was ending, Rep. Kweisi Mfume, D-Md., chairman of the Congressional Black Caucus, said, "The time has passed for this kind of grace period."

Appearing on Capitol Hill on March 4, Aristide urged Clinton to issue an ultimatum to Haiti's military by setting a "date certain" for the ousted president's return. Clinton gave a show of support for Aristide by welcoming him to the White House on March 16, but he did not offer to take such a step.

On June 21, the Supreme Court upheld the U.S. policy of picking up Haitian refugees on the high seas and summarily returning them to Haiti. The 8-1 ruling in *Sale v. Haitian Centers Council* allowed the Clinton administration to continue to intercept and return Haitian boat people without first screening them to see if they qualified for political asylum. *(Political asylum, p. 312)*

THE TROOP QUESTION

On June 16, the U.N. Security Council unanimously adopted an oil, arms and financial embargo against Haiti to pressure the military regime to step down. At the insistence of Brazil, however, a provision allowing member states to inspect cargo ships bound for Haiti was deleted. On July 3 at Governors Island in New York, the Haitian coup's leader, Lt. Gen. Raoul Cedras, signed an agreement with Aristide that promised the president's return to power by Oct. 30.

The Clinton administration expressed cautious optimism, although prospects for a peaceful transition in Haiti were clouded by an outbreak of attacks and killings of Aristide's supporters in Haiti.

William L. Swing, Clinton's nominee for ambassador to Haiti, said Sept. 29 that the administration was "confident" the Haitian military would comply with the final steps in the Governors Island Agreement.

At his confirmation hearing before the Senate Foreign Relations Subcommittee on Western Hemisphere and

Peace Corps Affairs, Swing seemed eager to distance the U.N. mission that was planned to implement the Governors Island agreement from events unfolding in Bosnia and Somalia. "The term peacekeeping is imprecise and misleading," Swing said, because the U.S. troops would be only lightly armed and would not be operating under the section of the U.N. charter authorizing peacekeeping intervention.

But Sen. Paul Coverdell, R-Ga., gently pressed his concerns about troop safety and mission goals. "I would hope that you would match the task with the timetable," he said, "so that we don't get backed into a plan" as open-ended as the intervention in Somalia.

House Republicans expressed similar concerns. "I think we should be sending more [troops] than we are," said Benjamin A. Gilman, N.Y., the ranking Republican on the Foreign Affairs Committee. "It could be a trouble spot."

Rangel disagreed that such backup forces would be needed. Referring to those behind Haiti's violence, Rangel said, "This cowardly, ragtag, thug operation has never been involved in the shooting of someone who is armed. Most of the victims have been powerless, poor Haitians."

Rangel's optimism proved misplaced.

The agreement calling for Aristide's return to Haiti also anticipated international efforts to help restore the impoverished and violence-torn island. About 600 U.S. military construction troops were to deploy as part of a U.N. reconstruction effort.

On Oct. 11, armed Haitians prevented the USS *Harlan County* from landing with about 200 U.S. and Canadian engineers. While threatening and chasing away U.S. diplomats, the pro-military Haitian protesters had their eyes on the debate in Washington: They chanted warnings of another Somalia if U.S. troops came to Haiti. Then, on Oct. 14, assassins killed Justice Minister Guy Malary, a leading Aristide supporter, in a daylight public shootout in Port-au-Prince, the Haitian capital.

On Oct. 15, responding to the political violence and defiance by Haiti's military rulers, Clinton ordered a flotilla of Navy warships to waters off the Haitian coast to enforce U.N. economic sanctions. "These destroyers are going there to enforce the sanctions and to do it very strongly," he said.

The president also put an infantry company on alert at Guantanamo Bay in Cuba in case they were needed to protect the 1,000 U.S. citizens in Haiti. Proclaiming that "there are important American interests at stake," the president said, "The military authorities in Haiti simply must understand that they cannot indefinitely defy the desires of their own people as well as the will of the world community."

In Congress, no one pushed for direct U.S. military intervention to restore Aristide to power. But there was an undercurrent of debate about how deeply U.S. interests were at stake in Haiti.

"I don't understand why the president seems determined to use American military power in regions where it is not clearly applicable," Sen. Phil Gramm, R-Texas, said Oct. 14 on CNN. "I think if you watched what happened when we tried to send our troops ashore, it was clear that there were people there who didn't want us there and that the authorities that were supposed to be there to help didn't do anything to stop it."

Appearing on the same program, Mfume responded that presidents Ronald Reagan and Bush saw strategic interests in the hemisphere to justify intervention in Grenada and Panama. "The difference in Haiti is that we have a democratically elected government, one that we did not have in those other

two nations," Mfume said. "We also have a situation that desperately cries out for an honest broker."

IMAGES OF ARISTIDE

No one in the Senate had a kind word for Haiti's military rulers or its history of brutal dictators. But there was bitter disagreement during floor debate Oct. 20 over the politics, the intentions and even the aphorisms of Aristide.

The debate capsulized growing disagreement in Washington about the ousted president and the extent of the U.S. responsibility to return him to power. Supporters, such as Congressional Black Caucus members, honored him as the soft-voiced worker-priest who won more than two-thirds of the vote in his country's first democratic election. Critics, citing leaked intelligence reports, portrayed him as an unstable radical.

Jesse Helms, R-N.C., denounced Aristide as a leftist who had urged mobs of his supporters to kill opponents with "necklaces" of burning tires doused in gasoline. Helms displayed an oil painting of Aristide beaming on a crowd bearing tires, a scene that Helms asserted had hung in Aristide's presidential office. "In my judgment, this man is a psychopath," Helms said. "I do not think we have any business whatsoever . . . risking the life of one soldier or one sailor or other American to put Aristide back into office."

Even as he was being damned by the ranking Republican on the Foreign Relations Committee, Aristide was meeting with Democratic senators in a room in the Capitol. They came back to the floor with tributes to Aristide's character.

"President Aristide has unequivocally denied the allegations that have been raised against him personally," said Christopher J. Dodd, Conn.

Carol Moseley-Braun, D-Ill., added, "He spoke about his love for Haiti and his love for non-violence as an approach to resolution of issues."

Tom Harkin, D-Iowa, argued that critics mistranslated a Creole aphorism in which Aristide urged supporters to give an enemy "what he deserves," telling them the "tool is in your hands" and it "smells good." Harkin said the fragrant tool of retribution that Aristide had in mind was not a burning tire but Haiti's constitution.

The debate over Aristide's character soon became a debate over the character of information being spread by the CIA.

Conservative opponents of supporting Aristide had cited classified CIA reports portraying the Roman Catholic priest as mentally unbalanced and inclined to support mob violence. Liberal supporters of Aristide accused the CIA of a campaign to favor Haiti's military rulers and smear the democratically elected president.

The chairman of the Senate Intelligence Committee charged Nov. 4 that the CIA was being badly served by those in Congress attempting to shape U.S. policy. "I think the CIA may be getting a bad rap," Intelligence Committee Chairman Dennis DeConcini, D-Ariz., said in a prepared statement. "We have no evidence that the CIA sought to prevent Mr. Aristide from coming to power. Similarly, we have no information suggesting any concerted effort by the CIA to weaken or discredit President Aristide since he was elected."

DeConcini disputed Helms' assertion that intelligence sources had branded Aristide a "psychopath," saying information in closed-door CIA briefings had "been taken out of context. And I'm not one who sits around here defending the CIA."

On Oct. 31, the Los Angeles Times reported that in the late 1980s the Senate Intelligence Committee forced the CIA to abandon a covert program aimed at support of candidates opposed by Aristide. On Nov. 1, The New York Times, also citing anonymous sources, reported that the CIA had made payments to a number of Haitian military leaders for information from the mid-1980s until their overthrow of Aristide in 1991.

FLOOR ACTION

On Oct. 21, during debate on the defense appropriations bill (HR 3116), the Senate rejected 19-81 an amendment by Helms that would have required prior congressional authorization to send U.S. forces into Haiti except to protect and evacuate U.S. citizens. *(Senate vote 321, p. 42-S)*

The Senate next adopted, 98-2, a non-binding amendment sponsored by Majority Leader George J. Mitchell, D-Maine, and Minority Leader Bob Dole, R-Kan. It expressed the "sense of Congress" that the U.S. military should not operate in Haiti unless Congress granted prior approval or the president sent Congress a detailed report before the deployment. *(Senate vote 322, p. 42-S)*

The report was to summarize the national security interests the deployment would serve; the steps that would be taken to protect U.S. personnel; an assessment of the mission the forces were to carry out and of whether the force was large enough for the job; an "exit strategy" for withdrawing the force; and a projection of the operation's cost.

The Dole-Mitchell limitation did not apply to U.S. personnel deployed in Haiti to protect diplomatic facilities, to collect intelligence or "to counter emigration from Haiti."

The House accepted the non-binding Haiti amendment by approving the conference report (H Rept 103-339) by voice vote Nov. 10. The Senate cleared the bill for the president, 88-9, the same day. *(Senate vote 368, p. 47-S)*

Clinton signed the measure (PL 103-139) on Nov. 11. ■

Foreign Aid Bill Stalls in Senate

For the eighth year in a row, Congress failed to enact a bill to authorize U.S. foreign aid programs. Although the House passed its version of the fiscal 1994 foreign aid blueprint (HR 2404), the Senate bill never saw floor action.

In the House, the foreign aid bill originally was attached to the fiscal 1994-95 State Department authorization (HR 2333). But Democratic leaders separated the bills at the insistence of House Foreign Affairs Committee Republicans, who were concerned that the unpopular aid bill would drag down the State Department legislation. *(State Department authorization, p. 506)*

Congressional efforts to put together a foreign aid authorization bill also were hampered because the Clinton administration did not produce a promised legislative proposal to rewrite the 30-year-old law governing the nation's foreign aid program until very late in the process. The draft version of that proposal was left for debate in 1994.

The legislation languished because Senate leaders apparently did not want to risk a divisive floor debate over a bill that was no longer viewed as indispensable. In a time of considerable resistance to spending scarce funds abroad, the leaders concentrated on winning enactment of the annual foreign operations appropriations bill that actually provided foreign aid funds. *(Appropriations, p. 603)*

The final version of the appropriations bill included a blanket authorization of the programs funded by the measure.

BACKGROUND

In a determined effort to win passage of the fiscal 1994 foreign aid authorization bill, the new House Foreign Affairs Committee Chairman, Lee H. Hamilton, D-Ind., established a task force of senior members to prevent the legislation from becoming a magnet for controversial policy amendments. Congress had not passed a foreign aid bill since 1985, and the relevance of the committee — and its Senate counterpart, the Foreign Relations Committee — had slipped as a result.

In 1991, for example, after a grueling battle, the House defeated the conference report on the fiscal 1992 foreign aid bill in a vote that was an expression of strong America-first sentiment. The bill's future had been clouded even before the House vote, because President George Bush objected to foreign family planning funding and threatened to veto it. In 1992, neither chamber acted on an authorization bill. *(1991 Almanac, p. 470)*

Over the years, the Foreign Affairs subcommittees frequently produced contentious proposals that made it more difficult to gain votes for the unpopular foreign aid bill. With each panel acting more or less on its own, the draft bill grew dramatically and became more complex by the time it was considered by the full committee. Hamilton's task force was devised to streamline that process, a com-

---

BOXSCORE

➡ **Fiscal 1994 Foreign Aid Authorization (HR 2404, formerly HR 2333; S 1467).** The bills contained one-year authorizations for U.S. foreign aid programs; both bills included $904 million for the former Soviet republics.

Reports: H Rept 103-126; S Rept 103-144.

KEY ACTION

June 8 — **House** committee passed HR 2333 by voice vote.

June 16 — **House** approved HR 2404 by voice vote.

Sept. 8 — **Senate** committee approved S 1467, 16-4.

---

mittee aide said, though members were free to offer any amendments during the full committee's markup.

HOUSE COMMITTEE ACTION

The House Foreign Affairs Subcommittee on Economic Policy marked up a section of the foreign aid bill May 12, authorizing by voice vote several trade and development programs under its jurisdiction.

The panel approved a $300 million pilot program for the Trade and Development Agency to support so-called capital projects in developing countries. The goal was to expand U.S. business opportunities by directing more aid toward infrastructure projects.

The draft bill gave the Agency for International Development (AID) permanent authority to establish "conservation trust funds" in developing countries. In addition, it rewrote authorizing language for the Overseas Private Investment Corporation. Panel members acceded to a request from Chairman Sam Gejdenson, D-Conn., to hold off on amendments until the full Foreign Affairs Committee considered the legislation.

On May 19, the Foreign Affairs Africa Subcommittee marked up its portion of the draft bill, backing a $200 million increase in economic assistance for Africa by voice vote. The subcommittee approved the draft bill by voice vote. The panel recommended $1 billion for the Development Fund for Africa — the primary source of U.S. assistance for scores of African countries — saying Africa had consistently been shortchanged in foreign aid. The Clinton administration had sought $800 million for the fund, the same level provided in fiscal 1993.

Full Committee Action

The Foreign Affairs Committee approved the fiscal 1994 foreign aid authorization by voice vote June 8. Hamilton had combined the foreign aid bill with the less controversial State Department authorization (H Rept 103-126) in an effort to overcome traditional congressional hostility to foreign assistance.

The bill authorized $904 million in economic aid for Russia and the other former Soviet republics for fiscal 1994 — the full administration request. That was a portion of the administration's $2.5 billion request for those countries, the remainder of which was to come from fiscal 1993 funds. *(Russian aid, p. 509)*

The panel earmarked $3 billion in military and economic aid for Israel and $2.1 billion for Egypt — the same levels as in previous years. It also authorized $400 million in economic aid for Eastern Europe and $900 million for the Development Fund for Africa.

To deliver on Hamilton's objective of avoiding controversy, the legislation approved by the committee contained few new initiatives and thus bore little resemblance to the massive, complex authorization bills from years past. In most

instances, it merely authorized spending at the approximate levels requested by the administration or included in the foreign operations appropriations bill (HR 2295) that passed the House on June 17. *(Appropriations, p. 603)*

The committee's consideration of the bill also reflected a dramatically different political environment from the one that existed during the previous 12 years: Committee Democrats found themselves in the unfamiliar position of defending an administration's foreign policy.

Democrats prevailed in a series of party-line votes on issues ranging from restrictions on aid to India to international family planning. In most instances, Democrats sought to maintain greater flexibility for their president — just as Republicans had done when they controlled the White House.

Democrats used their numerical advantage to defeat several policy amendments proposed by Republicans:

● Christopher H. Smith of New Jersey was rebuffed in a bid to strip about $36 million in aid for the U.N. Population Fund from the bill. Smith opposed the funding because the U.N. agency continued to operate in China, where coercive population control efforts had come under new criticism. The amendment was defeated, 11-23.

● Dan Burton, D-Ind., a longtime critic of human rights abuses in India, tried to reduce economic development assistance to that country unless the Indian government repealed laws used to persecute dissidents in Punjab and Kashmir. Though many Democrats were sympathetic to Burton's arguments, they followed the administration's lead in opposing the proposal, and the amendment was defeated on a voice vote.

● Smith also failed in an effort to impose stiff restrictions on economic assistance to Nicaragua. Smith's amendment would have conditioned aid on Nicaragua's progress in reducing the control of leftist Sandinistas over its military forces and in settling property claims brought by U.S. citizens. The chairman of the Western Hemisphere Subcommittee, Robert G. Torricelli, D-N.J., bluntly warned that attaching restrictions to the Nicaraguan aid would trigger attempts to condition aid to El Salvador and other countries that Republicans long had favored. Smith's amendment was defeated, 14-19.

Democratic initiatives also were sacrificed. At the behest of the administration, Howard L. Berman of California agreed to drop a provision included in the original State Department bill that would have lifted restrictions on cultural and educational exchanges with Cuba and other nations subject to U.S. economic embargoes.

Prodding Clinton on Bosnia

Before approving the bill, members frustrated at the failure of multilateral efforts to resolve the conflict in Bosnia-Herzegovina called on the Clinton administration to act alone if necessary to arm Bosnia's Muslim-led government forces. Over administration objections, the panel voted 24-15 to authorize the president to provide up to $200 million in military equipment to Bosnian government forces, despite a U.N. embargo that barred weapons shipments to any of the warring parties in the former Yugoslavia. Amendment sponsor Henry J. Hyde, R-Ill., argued that maintaining the weapons embargo had only served to benefit the better-armed Serbian forces. "You don't have much of a war when one side has the weapons and all the other side can do is die and suffer," he said.

The vote marked the first congressional action on Bosnia since President Clinton took office. *(Bosnia, p. 493)*

HOUSE ACTION

The foreign aid authorization legislation arrived on the House floor as a separate, $9.3 billion bill (HR 2404). After overwhelmingly defeating an attempt to delete $704 million in economic and technical assistance for Russia, lawmakers easily passed the measure by voice vote June 16.

Although eager to keep the foreign aid bill moving, the administration expressed concern over several aspects of the legislation, in particular objecting to the provision recommending that the United States unilaterally lift the U.N. arms embargo against Bosnia-Herzegovina.

The attempt to strip all but $200 million in assistance to Moscow from the bill came from Jon Kyl, R-Ariz. Kyl opposed the aid on the grounds that billions of dollars in economic assistance previously committed to Moscow by the United States and its allies had not been spent. Other conservative Republicans objected to Russia's continued support for communist governments, such as the regime of Cuban leader Fidel Castro.

But Kyl's amendment drew strong opposition from his own party's leadership. House Minority Leader Robert H. Michel, R-Ill., argued that the amendment could undercut the efforts of Russia's democratic reform movement. Kyl's amendment was defeated 118-317, as Michel, Minority Whip Newt Gingrich, Ga., and 81 other Republicans opposed the proposal. Ninety-one Republicans and 27 Democrats supported it. *(Vote 229, p. 56-H)*

The House adopted a less contentious amendment offered by Richard J. Durbin, D-Ill., to condition aid to Russia on a presidential certification that Moscow had made "significant progress" in withdrawing thousands of troops still stationed in the Baltic countries. The amendment was approved by voice vote.

Other Amendments

In other floor action, Democrats accepted a proposal by Benjamin A. Gilman, R-N.Y., to reduce the overall authorization level in the bill by $360 million.

But Hamilton strenuously opposed another Republican amendment that would have shut down AID by the end of fiscal 1994. The amendment, offered by Gilman and budget firebrand John R. Kasich, R-Ohio, came in response to continuing allegations of corruption and mismanagement at AID. "The time has come for tough love" at the agency, Gilman said.

While acknowledging that the criticisms of AID were on target, Hamilton said Congress should not prejudge the outcome of a review by the administration of foreign assistance and AID. With lawmakers largely split along party lines, the House voted 246-186 in favor of a substitute amendment by Hamilton to continue AID but terminate the $1.3 billion development assistance account by the end of fiscal 1995. *(Vote 227, p. 56-H)*

The House also rejected another attempt by Burton to attach stiff restrictions on development assistance to India. The House, which had narrowly backed a similar provision in 1992, reversed course and defeated Burton's amendment, 201-233. *(Vote 230, p. 56-H; 1992 Almanac, p. 612)*

But lawmakers vented their concerns over alleged human rights violations and adopted by voice vote an amendment by Vic Fazio, D-Calif., to set human rights conditions on military training assistance for India.

Torricelli had hoped to offer a controversial cargo preference amendment, but the Rules Committee barred the amendment as part of the rule governing floor debate on

the bill. Torricelli's amendment would have required that a certain percentage of foreign aid be carried on U.S. ships. Torricelli warned members who voted for the rule that they might face retaliation from organized labor, which supported cargo preferences. "This will be a critical vote in the record of the AFL-CIO," he said. But the administration firmly opposed the amendment, and the rule was adopted 294-129. (Vote 226, p. 56-H)

SENATE SUBCOMMITTEE ACTION

The Senate Foreign Relations Subcommittee on International Economic Policy approved its version of the foreign aid bill (S 1467) by voice vote Aug. 3. In an effort to prod the administration to complete a long-delayed plan to revamp foreign assistance, it required AID to cut back its operations and instructed the administration to consult with Congress on its administrative and legislative proposals for foreign aid within 60 days after the bill's enactment.

The subcommittee approved the measure in an amicable session lasting barely an hour. At the request of panel Chairman Paul S. Sarbanes, D-Md., senators held off on offering potentially contentious foreign policy amendments until the full Foreign Relations Committee worked on the bill.

Like its House counterpart, the Senate bill fully authorized the administration's $904 million aid request for the republics of the former Soviet Union. It included $3 billion for Israel and $2.1 billion for Egypt, the same levels as in the House bill. And it authorized the administration-requested level of $409 million in aid for Eastern Europe.

The panel generally followed the lead of the House Foreign Affairs Committee in trying to keep the legislation free of detailed policy provisions.

Revamping AID

The Foreign Affairs Committee and Sarbanes' panel had refrained from offering proposals to reorganize the aid bureaucracy out of deference to the administration, which had promised to submit its own plan to revamp the aid program by the end of 1993. But like its predecessors, the Clinton team found it unexpectedly difficult to tame the vast foreign aid bureaucracy. Deputy Secretary of State Clifton R. Wharton Jr. had difficulty completing his review of AID, the lead agency in delivering U.S. foreign aid, and the administration did not submit promised legislation incorporating Wharton's recommendations.

So the subcommittee bill, which bore the strong imprint of ranking Republican Nancy Landon Kassebaum of Kansas, put the issue of reforming the program squarely before Congress. The bill required AID to reduce the number of countries in which it operated by 20 percent by the end of fiscal 1994.

AID Administrator J. Brian Atwood said that to be effective, the agency should focus on about 50 countries. Yet because of factors having little bearing on the agency's effectiveness — including foreign policy considerations — AID had operations in 108 countries in 1993. Atwood said the number of countries could be reduced to about 70 within the next year. (Later in the year, Atwood took administrative action to streamline AID, announcing plans to close 21 overseas missions during the next three fiscal years.)

At the same time, the subcommittee endorsed the four objectives outlined by Wharton for the development assistance program, which provided aid to the poorest countries. Those were: promoting sustainable economic growth, building democratic participation, addressing global issues and responding to humanitarian needs.

The legislation gave the administration greater flexibility to shift funds within accounts. It also repealed a host of outdated laws and executive branch reporting requirements that were no longer considered necessary.

Subcommittee Amendments

The panel adopted by voice vote an amendment by Russell D. Feingold, D-Wis., to bar U.S. arms manufacturers who engaged in so-called offset agreements with foreign governments from making cash payments. Under such arrangements, arms manufacturers agreed to help foreign governments pay for weapons by finding those governments lucrative business opportunities. But Feingold charged that Northrop Corp. went too far by offering a payment of $1.5 million to another U.S. company as an inducement to do business with its Finnish client.

Feingold said he became aware of the practice, which apparently was not barred by law, when a Wisconsin company nearly lost a sale to the company that had received the $1.5 million payment.

The panel also adopted by voice vote an amendment by Hank Brown, R-Colo., to withhold aid to Jordan unless that country was found to be "substantially" complying with U.N. sanctions against Iraq. The issue took on new urgency with the release in June of a General Accounting Office report alleging that Jordan shared intelligence information with Iraq during the Persian Gulf crisis.

Brown initially proposed conditioning aid for Jordan on a determination by the secretary of State that the kingdom had been in compliance with the sanctions. But at the request of the administration, he modified the provision to require only that Jordan be in "substantial" compliance.

The committee also adopted the following amendments by voice vote:
● By Sarbanes and Kassebaum to trim $165 million from the original $12.2 billion bill. Most of the money came from security assistance programs.
● By Jesse Helms, R-N.C., to require the administration to halt aid to a government if it was found to be in "substantial violation" of a bilateral agreement covering the use of that assistance. The amendment did not allow the secretary of State or the AID administrator the option of waiving the provision.

SENATE COMMITTEE ACTION

The Senate Foreign Relations Committee approved the $12 billion bill (S Rept 103-144) by a vote of 16-4 on Sept. 8, using the opportunity to urge Clinton to provide arms to Bosnia's Muslim forces despite the U.N. embargo.
● **Bosnia.** As Clinton met with Bosnian President Alija Izetbegovic, the panel provided the Bosnian leader with a symbolic boost by voting, 14-5, to authorize up to $200 million in military equipment and training for his government's military forces. Richard G. Lugar, R-Ind., author of the non-binding amendment, called the committee's action "a very strong statement and a very strong vote on an issue that the committee has evaded for 1½ years."
● **South Africa.** The legislation also contained provisions repealing most of the economic sanctions that Congress had imposed on South Africa seven years before to force that nation's government to abandon its policy of forced racial segregation. Although the Bush administration lifted

the sanctions in 1992, the committee approved by voice vote an amendment by Kassebaum to wipe most of the anti-apartheid laws from the books. Congress later cleared another measure that lifted all U.S. sanctions against South Africa. *(South Africa, p. 529)*

● **Russian aid.** As expected, conservatives launched a concerted effort to impose stiff terms on the administration's aid package for the former Soviet Union. But after hours of debate, the Senate committee modified or defeated several amendments aimed at attaching conditions to the aid.

Helms proposed to link assistance to Russia to its termination of subsidized trade with Cuba. Helms said he was disturbed by Moscow's recent pledge of credits to Cuba and by reports that Russian advisers had assisted Cuba in constructing a nuclear energy facility.

Assistant Secretary of State Wendy Sherman said that "to our knowledge" Moscow had only extended market-based credits to Havana. She told the committee that about a dozen Russian advisers had been helping Cuba to "mothball" the nuclear facility at Cienfuegos. The panel defeated Helms' amendment, 5-13.

Helms modified a second amendment on Russian aid, which would have barred assistance to governments that sold military equipment to nations identified by the State Department as supporting international terrorism.

Kassebaum argued that under the proposal "we would not be able to extend any kind of aid to Russia and Eastern Europe," which had been linked to arms sales to Iran and other nations on the terrorist list. Helms subsequently modified the proposal to allow the president to waive the provision if he determined that doing so was in the national interest.

In the same vein, Larry Pressler, R-S.D., agreed to substantially weaken his amendment to condition aid to Moscow upon its withdrawal of the remaining Russian forces in the Baltic nations. After his original amendment was criticized in unusually blunt terms by committee Democrats, Pressler dropped the conditions in favor of sense-of-the-Senate language.

● **Vietnam.** Pressler came closer to success with a nonbinding proposal calling on Clinton to lift the longstanding U.S. trade embargo against Vietnam. The sense-of-the-Senate resolution was narrowly defeated, 7-9.

The embargo was intended to pressure Hanoi to come forward with information about U.S. service personnel missing from the Vietnam War. But Pressler and other advocates of lifting the embargo argued that it only served to harm U.S. corporations. "I have two major corporations in Illinois that want to sell to Vietnam, and they can't do it," said Paul Simon, D-Ill. But other Democrats were wary of forcing Clinton's hand.

● **Indonesia.** The committee also approved an amendment by Feingold urging the president to consult with Congress about human rights abuses in Indonesia before approving arms sales to that country. Congressional criticism of Indonesia increased after the 1991 massacre of unarmed civilians by Indonesian security forces on the island of East Timor. Feingold said that Indonesia was still preventing international human rights organizations from visiting the island, which had been occupied by Indonesia since 1975.

The amendment, approved by voice vote, called on the president to determine whether the Indonesian government was "taking steps to curb human rights violations by its security forces."

The committee also adopted the following amendments:

● A modified cargo preference amendment by Sarbanes to increase the percentage of aid under the Economic Support Fund that was provided in the form of U.S. commodities rather than cash. The amendment, approved by voice vote, stood to benefit U.S. shipping interests because half of the commodities were to be transported on U.S. vessels. The administration had no position on the amendment, though it generally opposed cargo preference provisions.

● An amendment by Helms that sought to punish foreign embassies for what Helms said were $6 million worth of past-due parking fines owed to the District of Columbia. Despite administration protests that the amendment violated the principle of diplomatic immunity, the panel voted 12-4 to reduce foreign aid for foreign governments by the amounts that they owed in parking fines.

● Another Helms amendment to limit the State Department's inspector general to a six-year term. The proposal, similar to an amendment that Helms added to the State Department authorization bill (S 1281), could have forced out the inspector general, Sherman M. Funk, who had been in the post since 1987. ■

State Department Authorization Held Over

Lawmakers began work on legislation to authorize State Department programs for fiscal 1994 and 1995, but they did not complete the job in the first session.

The House passed its bill (HR 2333) on June 22; the Senate Foreign Relations Committee approved its version (S 1281) on July 15. While the full Senate did not take up the bill before adjourning, senators agreed to do so in 1994.

The bills authorized funding for State Department activities, such as the upkeep of U.S. embassies and diplomatic missions, along with several independent agencies including the U.S. Information Agency (USIA) and the Arms Control and Disarmament Agency (ACDA).

In the House, the bill originally incorporated the foreign aid reauthorization bill, but Democratic leaders separated the measures before they went to the floor at the insistence of House Foreign Affairs Committee Republicans, who were

concerned that the unpopular aid bill would stall the reauthorization of the State Department. *(Foreign aid, p. 502)*

HOUSE COMMITTEE ACTION

The House Foreign Affairs Subcommittee on International Operations approved its draft version of the authorization bill, 7-6, on May 26. The panel's Democrats scrambled to beat back a GOP challenge to a provision lifting restrictions on cultural and educational exchanges with Cuba and other nations that were subject to U.S. economic embargoes.

That was the most contentious item during the subcommittee's consideration of the bill, which authorized about $15 billion in funding for the State Department, the U.S. Information Agency and several smaller agencies in fiscal 1994 and fiscal 1995.

Republicans attacked a proposal by subcommittee Chairman Howard L. Berman, D-Calif., to facilitate international cultural contacts — which he called the Free Trade in Ideas Act — charging that such exchanges would provide Fidel Castro's regime with desperately needed hard currency. "It is that money that will continue to prop up the Cuban government," said Robert Menendez, D-N.J., a Cuban-American.

But Berman argued that his proposal would weaken Castro's rule by exposing the Cuban people to democratic ideas. Insisting that he had no sympathy for Castro, he said that he had backed legislation enacted in 1992 as part of the fiscal 1993 defense authorization bill that tightened economic sanctions against Cuba. *(1992 Almanac, p. 557)*

Lincoln Diaz-Balart, R-Fla., withdrew an amendment that would have eliminated Berman's provision, opting instead to try to defeat the overall measure. With Menendez joining the Republicans, the effort fell short by one vote.

Much of the State Department bill focused on the nuts and bolts of U.S. foreign policy. Berman sought to write the bill broadly to provide the administration with maximum flexibility for its plans to reorganize the State Department.

Reflecting a general desire to cut spending for international affairs, the bill limited the number of deputy assistant secretaries to 63 — a cut of about 30 — in line with the administration's goal of streamlining the State Department.

But the subcommittee backed other proposals to maintain the status quo or establish new positions, for example, expanding the role of ACDA. There had been proposals to merge ACDA with the State Department in light of the collapse of the Soviet Union and the declining relevance of nuclear arms control treaties. But Berman urged that the arms control agency become more active in controlling the proliferation of conventional weapons.

The committee provided all but $2 million of the $50 million requested for the National Endowment for Democracy, a nonprofit organization that was almost totally dependent on the government for its funding. The organization had received $30 million in fiscal 1993.

The bill authorized $1.2 billion for the USIA in fiscal 1994 — the full administration request. As had become customary, the portion of the bill that authorized USIA grants for private institutions and scholarship programs tended to reflect the parochial concerns of lawmakers.

It authorized $23 million, $3 million less than the administration had requested, for the East-West Center, a think tank associated with the University of Hawaii that had long been championed by Sen. Daniel K. Inouye, D-Hawaii.

The report accompanying the bill also offered strong support for the North-South Center at the University of Miami, the legislative legacy of former House Foreign Affairs Chairman Dante B. Fascell, D-Fla. As part of its deficit-reduction plan, the administration had proposed terminating funding for the center. Though the bill did not authorize funding for the think tank — the center had a permanent authorization of $10 million annually — the

---

BOXSCORE

➡ **Fiscal 1994-95 State Department Authorization includes (HR 2333, S 1281).** Bills authorizing funds for the State Department, the U.S. Information Agency and other agencies that carried out U.S. foreign policy.

Reports: H Rept 103-126, S Rept 103-107.

KEY ACTION

June 8 — **House** committee approved HR 2333 by voice vote.

June 22 — **House** passed bill, 273-144.

July 15 — **Senate** committee approved its version, 19-0.

---

report called on the Appropriations Committee to fund the institution at that level.

The legislation included a new fellowship program in the name of former Sen. Mike Mansfield, D-Mont., to enable government workers to study in Japan. Mansfield was a longtime ambassador to Tokyo.

As approved by the subcommittee, the State Department bill also:

● Provided $36.2 million a year for two years for the U.N. Population Fund. Responding to criticisms of the U.N. agency's activities in China, which had a coercive abortion policy, Berman trimmed $13.8 million from the administration's annual request, unless the fund withdrew from China.

● Authorized nearly $700 million for contributions to U.N. peacekeeping activities in fiscal 1994 — the full administration request — with a slight increase in fiscal 1995.

Full Committee Action

The full House Foreign Affairs Committee marked up the joint State Department-foreign aid authorization bill (HR 2333 — H Rept 103-126) on June 8, approving the measure by voice vote.

In the only action on the State Department portion of the omnibus bill, Berman agreed with Clinton administration requests to drop the provision lifting restrictions on Cuba and other nations subject to U.S. economic embargoes.

HOUSE FLOOR ACTION

The House approved the State Department bill on June 22 by a vote of 273-144. But first, with strong backing from Republicans and freshmen from both parties, the House voted 243-181 to cut off funding for the National Endowment for Democracy, dealing a blow to President Clinton's plans to expand financial support to promote democracy abroad. *(Vote 252, p. 62-H; vote 249, p. 60-H)*

In a June 16 letter to House leaders, Clinton had made a strong pitch for the endowment, calling it "one of our most effective means for supporting grass-roots, trade union, business and citizen groups, which form the basis for democratic reform."

But a cross section of lawmakers supported an amendment offered by Paul E. Kanjorski, D-Pa., which struck all funding for the organization. Republicans voted by nearly a 2-1 margin to cut off the funds, which had been established in 1983 with the backing of President Ronald Reagan. Tailoring his pitch to the freshmen, Kanjorski, who had tried to cut or kill the funding for years, said the organization had evolved into a "welfare fund" for the two political parties, the AFL-CIO and the U.S. Chamber of Commerce because it bankrolled pro-democracy projects managed by those groups. The argument swayed first-term lawmakers, who voted 75-36 in favor of Kanjorski's amendment.

Berman said the amendment drew backing from lawmakers who had become weary of supporting international programs. In addition, the administration, which appeared to underestimate the strength of that sentiment, had scaled back its lobbying presence on the State Department bill.

The House disposed of the remainder of the bill smoothly. Lawmakers defeated, 184-235, an effort by Republican Gerald B. H. Solomon of New York to require random drug testing for State Department employees. Solomon said he was going to offer similar amendments to other bills to force every government agency to require such tests. *(Vote 248, p. 60-H)*

SENATE SUBCOMMITTEE ACTION

By voice vote, the Foreign Relations Subcommittee on Terrorism, Narcotics and International Operations on June 29 approved its bill (S 1099, later S 1281) authorizing funds for the State Department, the USIA and related agencies.

The bill was largely free of policy recommendations and of the foreign policy controversies that some senators believed had contributed to a steady decline in the effectiveness and influence of the Foreign Relations Committee.

The subcommittee bill authorized international programs only for fiscal 1994. Subcommittee Chairman John Kerry, D-Mass., said fiscal 1995 authorization levels would be added in the full committee, bringing the measure in line with the two-year House version.

In addition, Kerry said, an administration proposal to reorganize the government's far-flung international broadcasting operations would be attached. In a cost-saving move, Clinton had announced plans June 14 to phase out the quasi-independent board that funded the major government-backed broadcasting networks — the Voice of America, Radio Free Europe and Radio Liberty. Clinton proposed to put them under a single board but retain them as separate services.

The fiscal 1994 authorization levels backed by the Senate subcommittee were similar to those in the House bill. But the Senate subcommittee bill fully funded the administration's request for $50 million for the National Endowment for Democracy, which the House bill had eliminated.

The only point of contention during the markup was an amendment offered by Christopher J. Dodd, D-Conn., urging that the Clinton administration work in the United Nations to establish an international criminal court.

Though the amendment required no action by the administration — and had been approved by the Foreign Relations Committee on May 20 as a free-standing resolution (S J Res 32) — Republicans opposed it on procedural and philosophical grounds. Larry Pressler of South Dakota, the subcommittee's ranking Republican, read a letter from GOP colleagues raising possible jurisdictional problems. Conservatives had warned that such a court could undermine the sovereignty of the United States. They also complained that Foreign Relations had held only one subcommittee hearing on the issue.

Dodd argued that the amendment was merely advisory and not intended to endorse specific jurisdictional arrangements. An international court would not only help in the prosecution of alleged war criminals, Dodd said, but also would be able to adjudicate cases of international narcotics trafficking. The subcommittee approved the language, 5-4.

The subcommittee also approved potentially controversial language requiring the USIA to establish an office in the Tibetan capital of Lhasa for the purpose of "promoting discussions on conflict resolution and human rights." The Chinese government was particularly sensitive to persistent allegations from human rights organizations that it had engaged in widespread violations in Tibet. The bill also required the administration to make periodic reports on

the state of "bilateral" relations between the United States and the "Tibetan government in exile," led by the Dalai Lama. The Clinton administration, like its predecessors, considered Tibet part of China, but raised concerns over the reports of human rights abuses.

Aside from Dodd's resolution, the amendments considered by the subcommittee were handled smoothly. The following were approved by voice vote:

● An amendment by Daniel Patrick Moynihan, D-N.Y., to establish a bipartisan commission to reduce the volume of government classified information. Moynihan said the government classified more than 6 million documents each year and that the defense industry spent $14 billion a year to fulfill government regulations on secrecy.

● Three amendments offered by Pressler requiring the president to notify Congress before committing troops to U.N.-sponsored operations and before providing contributions to U.N. peacekeeping missions and seeking improved budgetary management at the United Nations.

● An amendment by Foreign Relations Chairman Claiborne Pell, D-R.I., to strike provisions in existing law referring to the former Soviet Union and East European countries as "captive nations."

SENATE COMMITTEE ACTION

The full Senate Foreign Relations Committee defended the Clinton administration's plan to reorganize overseas broadcasting against a determined challenge July 15, then approved the $12 billion State Department authorization bill (S 1281 — S Rept 103-107) by a vote of 19-0. As had become customary, the legislation afforded senators the opportunity to weigh in on both high-profile and obscure international issues.

● **International broadcasting.** The most heated debate occurred on the administration's complex proposal to overhaul government-sponsored broadcasting programs. Joseph R. Biden Jr., D-Del., bitterly attacked Clinton's plan, arguing that it would compromise the journalistic integrity of a pair of radio networks that dated to the Cold War — Radio Free Europe and Radio Liberty.

The administration wanted to preserve those "surrogate" radio services, whose primary mission was to broadcast local news to the former Warsaw bloc nations. But to save money, the administration proposed to phase out the independent board that funded them and place them instead under the USIA.

Biden argued that the radio services had played a significant role in the triumph over communism. He insisted that their status as independent corporations had been critical to that success, enabling the surrogates to operate at arm's length from the government. "If it ain't broke, don't fix it," Biden said. "Why are we doing this?"

Joseph D. Duffey, USIA director, and Gordon Adams, associate director of the Office of Management and Budget (OMB), led a spirited defense of the administration's proposal. Adams told the committee that retaining the existing structure would jeopardize an estimated $240 million in savings from the reorganization through fiscal 1997.

Adams' pitch for frugality proved persuasive to the committee, although Biden denied that retaining the existing arrangement would cost money. His amendment, which would have maintained Radio Liberty and Radio Free Europe as independent corporate entities, failed 4-15.

Biden warned that the issue might be raised once again on the Senate floor. While Biden's primary concern was for

the two Europe-based services, he also apparently wanted to set a precedent for the new Radio Free Asia, a proposal that he had championed from its inception. The legislation authorized broadcasts to Asian countries "where communications media are not fully developed or free." But like the Europe-based radio operations, under Clinton's plan, Radio Free Asia would be placed under the USIA.

● **United Nations.** The committee dealt a new setback to the administration's efforts to win increased support for U.N. peacekeeping operations, eliminating a proposed $175 million contingency fund for that purpose. The cutback was a result of a cost-cutting move initiated by Jesse Helms of North Carolina, the committee's ranking Republican.

Helms' initial proposal would have taken an ax to the whole bill, forcing an across-the-board reduction of about $500 million in each fiscal year. Under pressure to keep spending in check, Democrats agreed to accept the approximate level of Helms' cuts but insisted that the reductions be targeted.

A modification offered by Kerry and Pressler eliminated the peacekeeping money and drew the rest of the savings from a variety of accounts, including State Department salaries and expenses. Kerry acknowledged that the United States could fall well short of meeting its assessments for peacekeeping in 1993, which administration officials estimated could amount to $1 billion. "The money is not going to be appropriated anyway," Kerry said. The panel approved the changes offered by Pressler and Kerry, 19-0, then adopted the Helms amendment by voice vote.

As approved by the committee, the bill authorized $423 million for peacekeeping activities in fiscal 1994.

Pressler also seemed to be on a crusade to punish the United Nations over reports of mismanagement. He proposed an amendment targeting 38 specific "desk warmers" whom he alleged received U.N. paychecks although they had no formal jobs. The amendment would have withheld 50 percent of the U.S. contributions to specialized U.N. agencies in fiscal 1995 unless the United Nations established an advisory committee to institute management changes.

While there was a consensus that the U.N. needed to shape up, many senators worried that the funding reduction would hurt popular programs such as the United Nations Children's Fund. The amendment was defeated 6-13.

● **National Endowment for Democracy.** The committee lent strong support to the administration's request for $50 million for the National Endowment for Democracy.

Hank Brown, R-Colo., proposed to cap funding for the organization at $17.5 million in fiscal 1994 — the level provided in the House version of the Commerce, Justice and State appropriations bill. Brown charged that groups receiving grants from the agency had taken advantage of the endowment's loose budgetary oversight to finance first-class trips and have expensive parties. The main target of Brown's ire was the International Republican Institute, a GOP-affiliated organization.

Carl Gershman, National Endowment president, and Lorne Craner, a vice president of the Republican Institute and a former Republican staff aide, stepped forward to rebut the allegations. But the most compelling support

probably came from Richard G. Lugar, R-Ind., who sat on the board of the endowment. Lugar, among the Senate's most influential voices on foreign policy, said he reviewed endowment grants. "We are minding the store and doing it very carefully," he said.

Brown's amendment was rejected by voice vote.

● **Taiwan.** Like its Republican predecessors, the Clinton administration tried to block any amendment that it feared might tie the president's hands or complicate diplomacy.

A case in point was an amendment on U.S. relations with Taiwan offered by Frank H. Murkowski, R-Alaska. Murkowski said he wanted to end the "fiction" that had grown out of a 1982 communiqué with China stipulating that arms sales to Taiwan should decline over time. Murkowski's amendment affirmed that the communiqué was superseded by an earlier law that set no conditions on sales of defensive weapons to Taiwan.

Many senators agreed with Murkowski that the Bush administration's huge sale of F-16 fighters to Taipei in 1992 had dashed any illusions that the terms of the communiqué still served as a basis for U.S. policy. But the State Department, apparently concerned over upsetting Beijing, asked Murkowski to hold off on the amendment.

The committee did not share those concerns, and the amendment was adopted 20-0.

The committee also took the following action on amendments offered by Helms:

● Rejected an amendment to limit the number of assistant secretaries of State to 16, instead of the 20 provided for in the legislation. The amendment was defeated on a vote of 8-11.

● Approved by voice vote an amendment to force State Department Inspector General Sherman M. Funk to leave office by the end of the year. Funk, appointed to the nonpartisan post in 1987 by President Reagan, led a highly publicized investigation into circumstances surrounding a State Department search of Bill Clinton's passport records during the 1992 presidential campaign.

● Approved by voice vote an amendment aimed at ensuring "easy access" for lawmakers visiting the State Department on official business. It called on the Office of Diplomatic Security to "make available a reasonable number of parking permits" to congressional foreign policy committees.

Prying the Bill Loose

The Senate committee-approved bill languished for months, largely because of the dispute over the administration's plans to revamp international broadcasting.

Just before the end of the session, the bill was pried loose after the administration reached a compromise with Biden, acquiescing in the senator's demand that Radio Free Europe and Radio Liberty retain their status as independent, government-funded contractors.

Under this compromise, their funding would come through a bipartisan board that would also oversee the Voice of America and other international broadcasting operations.

The Senate then agreed to make the bill its first order of business when it returned in 1994. ■

Congress Backs Massive Aid to Russia

With President Clinton making support for Russian President Boris N. Yeltsin a foreign policy priority in 1993, Congress overwhelmingly approved Clinton's request for $2.5 billion in aid for the former Soviet republics.

Clinton and Congress stood by Yeltsin as democracy's best hope in Russia even after he dissolved the conservative-dominated Russian legislature on Sept. 21 and then ordered an assault on the parliament building by troops to oust the hard-liners Oct. 4. It was the worst political violence in Russia in 70 years.

The $2.5 billion in aid was approved as part of the fiscal 1994 foreign operations appropriations bill (HR 2295 — PL 103-87), although the bulk of it was in the form of a supplemental appropriation of unused funds from fiscal 1993.

Altogether, Clinton pledged $4.5 billion to the newly independent states within months of taking office. In addition to the $2.5 billion provided in the foreign aid spending bill, the total included $1.6 billion in previously appropriated funds and $400 million for a continuing effort to help dismantle the Soviet nuclear arsenal and other weapons of mass destruction.

The aid to dismantle weapons was provided through the annual defense appropriations (HR 3116 — PL 103-139) and authorization bills (HR 2401 — PL 103-160). *(Defense appropriations, p. 569; authorization, p. 433)*

Lawmakers also cleared the "Friendship Act," legislation (HR 3000 — PL 103-199) that removed statutory restrictions affecting relations with the former Soviet Union, such as condemnations of communist aggression and requirements for the registration of communist front organizations in the United States. *(Cold War laws, p. 512)*

BACKGROUND

In 1991, President George Bush faced criticism from some quarters for failing to offer enough U.S. aid to support the reform efforts of Soviet President Mikhail S. Gorbachev and from others for depending too much on Gorbachev as the champion of change. In 1992, Democratic presidential candidate Clinton was among those who prodded Bush to move more quickly in providing aid to Yeltsin's fledgling post-Communist regime. *(1991 Almanac, p. 463; 1992 Almanac, p. 523)*

By 1993, Clinton was being urged by some foreign policy experts to stand by Yeltsin as Russia's best hope for democracy and by others to be skeptical of Yeltsin's commitment to democratic values. But Clinton and Congress remained committed to Yeltsin and managed to forgive, or at least look beyond, the undemocratic means he invoked to crush unrepentant ex-communists, far-right-wing forces and other opponents of Russia's painful economic, social and government transition.

Urging Support

Clinton signaled his commitment to assist in that transition by naming a close friend, former Time magazine columnist Strobe Talbott, to coordinate U.S. policy toward the former republics.

Early in the new administration, Clinton was compelled to reaffirm his support for Yeltsin. At the time, the Russian president was under pressure from the conservative parliament, which was elected before Communism fell at the end of 1991. Richard L. Armitage, coordinator of humanitarian and technical assistance to the ex-Soviet republics, raised widespread concern by predicting during a speech in Tennessee that Yeltsin's "days are somewhat numbered." Armitage, a Bush administration holdover, later called his remarks "injudicious."

At a news conference Feb. 24 with British Prime Minister John Major, Clinton vouched for Yeltsin. "I think it is a grave error to assume that he cannot continue and do well," Clinton said. "I believe that he can."

Appearing the same day before the Senate Armed Services Committee, Armitage said that he had intended to make the point that it was extremely difficult for Yeltsin to govern and that the United States should "keep our eye firmly on the forces of democracy and reform." Armitage added that Yeltsin remained "the most popular political figure today in Russia" despite his political difficulties with parliament.

Appearing with Armitage, Retired Maj. Gen. William Burns, who supervised an existing $800 million U.S. program to help dismantle the nuclear arsenal of the former Soviet Union, told the committee that the effort was essential for compliance by Russia and the other republics with arms-reduction treaties.

Burns added that failing to provide U.S. assistance when the republics were undergoing extraordinary social and political upheaval would be "extremely dangerous" for stability in Russia and ultimately could threaten U.S. national security.

Earlier in the day, three experts on Russia and the other former Soviet republics delivered a similar message to the House Foreign Affairs Committee, calling for expanded U.S. economic assistance to a Russia that they said was on the verge of hyperinflation and economic chaos.

Stephen F. Cohen, a Russian studies professor at Princeton University, told the committee that failure to help Moscow quickly could mean the re-emergence of an unfriendly regime and a return to the arms race that ate up vast U.S. resources during the Cold War. Proposals that the United States invest $3 billion or more a year in the former Soviet Union would be "the cheapest national security we could buy," he said.

Like Burns and Armitage, Cohen was preaching to the choir. Members of the House and Senate Armed Services committees, as well as of House Foreign Affairs and Senate Foreign Relations, were among the most ardent backers of continued U.S. assistance to the former republics.

The problem faced by those committees and those in the new administration who sought more aid was skepticism among rank-and-file members, as well as the public, that it was vital to spend limited government funds on a former enemy.

Among the biggest obstacles to selling U.S. lawmakers on additional aid in 1993 was widespread confusion about what had been done with previously approved assistance.

Burns told Armed Services members that of the $800 million authorized in 1992 for weapons dismantlement — all of which was to come from the defense budget — agreement had been reached with the republics to spend about $300 million, and $500 million was committed by the United States to particular projects.

Nevertheless, congressional aides had identified only

about $1 million of the funds that actually had been spent.

Armitage said that he had spent or committed about $97 million to transport humanitarian aid and that $238 million had been committed for technical and economic assistance projects.

Harvard economist Jeffrey D. Sachs told the Foreign Affairs Committee that only about $11 billion of a $24 billion multilateral aid package announced in 1992 had been delivered, mostly in the form of short-term loans that were coming due and burdening the Russian economy. "Probably the single most corrosive thing we did last year," Sachs said, was to announce an aid package "and then not follow through." He said the failure by Western nations to provide real aid was breeding cynicism in Russia.

Meanwhile, in Russia, the parliament voted March 11 to strip Yeltsin of many of his executive powers. Yeltsin sought tangible signs of U.S. support before an April 11 referendum that he had called on the structure of the Russian government.

Nixon Lobbies

In Washington, Clinton gained an influential, if unlikely, ally in calling for more U.S. aid: former President Richard M. Nixon. In an opinion piece published in The New York Times on March 5, Nixon warned that the Yeltsin government would not survive without a substantial increase in Western aid. "If Boris Yeltsin's democratic government collapses and is replaced by an aggressive, hard-line nationalist government, this will have a far greater impact on the American economy than all the Clinton domestic programs combined," Nixon said. "The peace dividend will be down the tubes. The defense budget will have to be increased by billions of dollars rather than cut."

The former president, who met privately with Clinton at the White House on March 8, took his message to Capitol Hill the following day at Clinton's request.

In 1992, Nixon had been instrumental in prodding the Bush administration to support the reform effort in the former Soviet republics, and his participation in the 1993 debate was seen as critical in attracting reluctant Republicans. Sen. Richard G. Lugar, R-Ind., an early advocate of Russian aid, said Nixon's address to Senate Republicans on March 9 was "very worthwhile" in building a consensus.

Nixon spoke the following day to the House Republican conference, where opposition to foreign aid traditionally had run deep. According to those present, the former president was well-received as he urged GOP lawmakers to use him as a "blocking back" to cover them politically for casting a difficult vote to send Russia more money.

Lawmakers began to offer their own plans. In a speech on the Senate floor March 4, Patrick J. Leahy, D-Vt., chairman of the Agriculture Committee and the Foreign Operations Appropriations Subcommittee, called for an ambitious aid package including $1 billion in direct bilateral assistance. Leahy said the money could come from other foreign aid programs and could be used to provide food and other aid to the neediest Russians. Leahy said such bilateral aid was preferable to what he called the backdoor assistance of extending agricultural credits to Russia, an approach that was popular with many farm-state lawmakers.

Other lawmakers demanded that U.S. allies, such as Japan, be pressed to do more. "It's unrealistic to expect major contributions from the United States, but not unrealistic to expect major leadership from the United States," said Rep. Tom Lantos, D-Calif. Others said the United States should exert pressure on multilateral financial institutions to be more flexible. The International Monetary

Fund, for example, had been unwilling to grant loans to Russia until the republic brought down its budget deficit and controlled the soaring inflation rate.

Many experts argued that Russia's government was powerless to achieve such results unless it got Western assistance. "We've got conditions that basically say the inflation rate ought to be completely under control, and everybody knows they're in hyperinflation," said Senate Armed Services Committee Chairman Sam Nunn, D-Ga. "I think we need a more realistic set of conditions."

A Face-off in Moscow

Events in Moscow forced the administration and Congress, which had been equally determined to concentrate on the domestic economy rather than international affairs, to shift their focus.

On March 20, Yeltsin made the startling announcement that he planned to assume emergency presidential powers. Members of the Congress of People's Deputies, many of them Communist holdovers, threatened to oust him from office.

Ruslan Khasbulatov, the speaker of parliament, countered that "a direct threat of the return to the worst times of neo-totalitarianism is looming over the country."

But Clinton stood by Yeltsin, telling a news conference March 23, "Boris Yeltsin is the elected president of Russia, and he has shown a great deal of courage in sticking up for democracy and civil liberties and market reforms, and I'm going to support that."

Some lawmakers quickly agreed that, as Lugar put it, "Yeltsin had to move as he did." But others expressed concern that the United States not be locked into support of Yeltsin no matter what he might do.

"We have to state the national interests of the United States in terms of encouraging the move toward democracy and market reform," said House Foreign Affairs Committee Chairman Lee H. Hamilton, D-Ind. "Now Yeltsin happens to be the leader of that reform, and so we support him. But there are many other reformers; there are many other democrats in Russia, and we must be prepared to support them."

As events unfolded, Clinton delivered on a promise to consult closely with Congress. The president invited groups of House and Senate leaders to the White House on March 25-26 to solicit their suggestions.

Taking the tack urged by congressional leaders, Clinton and other administration officials repeatedly stressed that providing aid to bolster Russian democratic and economic reforms was as much in the United States' interest as in Russia's. "It will save the American people billions of dollars in money we don't have to spend maintaining a nuclear arsenal," Clinton told reporters March 24. "It will make the American people billions of dollars in future trade opportunities. And it will make the world a safer place."

By March 26, the crisis in Moscow was defused but not resolved. The emergency decree Yeltsin issued did not include his threatened assertion of "special powers" that effectively would have stripped the Congress of authority. And, despite hours of speeches denouncing Yeltsin, the Congress did not move to oust him, apparently lacking the votes to do so.

CLINTON'S PROPOSALS

Clinton offered his proposals for a total of $4.5 billion in aid to Russia and its neighbors in a series of announcements in April:

● At a summit with Yeltsin in Vancouver, British Columbia, on April 3-4, Clinton offered a $1.6 billion package of food credit and aid, all of it from previously appropriated funds.

● In the fiscal 1994 budget submitted to Congress on April 8, Clinton proposed $703.8 million in new grants and other aid. He also proposed using $400 million to be included in the defense appropriations bill — in addition to the $800 million previously set aside — to help dismantle the nuclear arsenal of the former Soviet Union.

● At a meeting of the Group of Seven (G-7) industrial nations in Tokyo on April 15, Clinton announced the final element: an additional $1.8 billion in new economic aid.

Cold-War Era Laws

Clinton said the administration also would review with congressional leaders a list of Cold War-era laws and regulations that restricted trade and other relations with Russia to determine if they should be revised. *(Cold War laws, p. 512)*

However, he stopped short of promising changes in two of the restrictions that Yeltsin said Russians found most troublesome: the Jackson-Vanik amendment to the 1974 trade act, which denied most-favored-nation trading status to Russia unless the president certified that it allowed free emigration, and restrictions against exporting certain Western high-technology items to former Soviet bloc nations.

Jewish groups favored yearly waivers of Jackson-Vanik because of loosened restrictions on Soviet emigration but were reluctant to back its abolition. Clinton, in a meeting with Russian journalists April 4, said he believed that there would "be an openness to change the law if the Congress is convinced there are in fact no more refuseniks, no more people who wish to emigrate who are not being allowed to."

There was also some concern among national security experts about lifting the export-control restrictions, designed to limit the spread of dual-use technologies.

Yeltsin raised the trade restrictions April 7 in a meeting in Moscow with a House delegation. Majority Leader Richard A. Gephardt, D-Mo., and Minority Leader Robert H. Michel, R-Ill., said in a statement afterward that they had assured the Russian leader that "when our delegation returns we will begin a review of any outmoded legal restrictions. . . . This is an important first step in forging our new economic partnership with the Russian people."

Vancouver Package

The $1.6 billion aid package presented to Yeltsin in Vancouver included $700 million in low-interest food credits as well as a repackaging of the assistance approved by Congress in 1992 as part of the Freedom Support Act.

Many of the programs authorized by that legislation had been slow in getting off the ground, but Clinton pledged that his new initiative was designed to spend the money quickly and in ways that would be felt immediately by the Russian people. The funds were to be devoted to an array of programs to promote private enterprise, ease U.S. investment in Russia, provide basic medical and food assistance, and offer student and other exchange opportunities for Russians.

The package announced by Clinton and Yeltsin included:

● $204 million in direct food aid and $20 million in medical assistance;

● $700 million in food credits. This assistance was to be provided under the Food for Progress program, which allowed for a far more generous repayment schedule than the regular commodity credit program. That assistance had

been stopped late in 1992 because of Russia's failure to make payments on $5 billion in outstanding loans.

● $148 million to help develop private enterprises in Russia. A $50 million Russian-American Enterprise Fund was to be created to lend money to start-up businesses and support joint ventures with U.S. companies "that disseminate Western business know-how and practices." Technical assistance, at an estimated cost of $60 million, was to be provided to accelerate Russia's effort to privatize its state-owned enterprises. Another $20 million was to be used to provide technical assistance and training to Russian farmers.

● $48 million to establish a so-called Democracy Corps of U.S. citizens to help the Russian people learn the basics of democracy.

● $6 million for a demonstration project to build 450 housing units and to provide job training for Russian military officers to help them with the transition to civilian life. The program was intended to allow quicker withdrawal of Russian troops from surrounding republics.

● $38 million to help improve the efficiency and environmental soundness of Russia's energy system, including oil and gas pipelines, nuclear power plants and coal mines. Gas and oil exports provided a crucial source of much-needed hard currency for Russia.

● $215 million to help dismantle the nuclear arsenal of the former Soviet Union. Most of the money was to dismantle nuclear delivery vehicles, such as ballistic missiles, submarines and heavy bombers; $75 million was for construction of a nuclear warhead storage facility in Russia. These funds were part of the $800 million approved by Congress in 1991 and 1992.

● Encouraging U.S.-Russian trade through Export-Import Bank loans, Overseas Private Investment Corporation backing of U.S. investments, support of Russia's membership in the General Agreement on Tariffs and Trade, and extension of duty-free status for certain Russian products under the U.S. Generalized System of Preferences.

Tokyo Summit

At their meeting in Tokyo on April 15, the G-7 nations pledged more than $30 billion in new loans and grants for Russia, including the $1.8 billion in aid announced there by Clinton and a similar amount from Japan.

But other nations refused entreaties from U.S. officials to expand their direct aid to Russia, so the bulk of the new package was to come from international financial institutions. The announcement was timed to bolster Yeltsin in advance of an April 25 referendum in Russia. Yeltsin scored a strong victory in the referendum.

Congressional Concerns

Leaders in Congress remained generally supportive of Clinton's aid proposals, echoing the administration's rationale that the United States had a huge stake in seeing democracy take hold in Russia. But key members expressed anxiety about the difficulties of winning passage of so much aid — particularly since they assumed it would require passage of a separate supplemental appropriations bill.

"I am worried when people talk about doing a supplemental and a regular foreign aid bill just months apart — neither of which would be popular," said Leahy, the chairman of the Senate Appropriations Foreign Operations Subcommittee. "What I'm afraid of is that we're looking at two bills, each of which could take a week [of Senate floor debate], when we've got economic stimulus, taxes and

Cold War Language Wiped From Books

Congress handed President Clinton a modest victory as members wrapped up work for 1993 by clearing legislation (HR 3000) that eliminated scores of largely symbolic Cold-War era constraints on relations with Russia and the other former Soviet republics. Clinton wanted the law in hand before meeting with Russian President Boris N. Yeltsin in Moscow in January 1994.

The bill removed or modified numerous restrictions and critical references to the Soviet Union. At an April summit in Vancouver, Yeltsin had complained to Clinton that such laws showed that the United States was still treating Russia "as though we are a communist country."

Some of the anti-Soviet provisions dated back four decades. For instance, the bill repealed most sections of the Internal Security Act of 1950, which required registration of communist front organizations and created the Subversive Activities Control Board.

But the bill left on the books several trade restrictions that Yeltsin had urged the United States to lift — in particular, the Jackson-Vanik amendment to the 1974 trade act, which denied most-favored-nation trading status to Russia unless the president certified that its government allowed free emigration. U.S. Jewish organizations continued to view Jackson-Vanik as a tool to ensure that Moscow lived up to its commitment to free emigration for Jews.

Nor did the bill loosen restrictions on high-technology exports to the former Soviet bloc. The administration was reviewing those rules.

Nonetheless, House Majority Leader Richard A. Gephardt, D-Mo., and other supporters said passage represented a breakthrough. "This is a matter of building confidence among the reformers in Russia that we believe what they are doing is the right thing to do," Gephardt said.

Legislative Action

The House Foreign Affairs Committee reported the bill Oct. 15 (H Rept 103-297, Part 1). The full House followed suit Nov. 15, approving HR 3000 by voice vote.

In the Senate, the Foreign Relations Committee approved a nearly identical measure (S 1672) by voice vote Nov. 18. The Senate approved HR 3000 by voice vote Nov. 22, after substituting the text of its own bill.

The Senate measure included an amendment by Jesse Helms, R-N.C., authorizing a privately funded but official memorial in Washington to the victims of communism. The amendment said that "the rulers of empires and international communism" had been responsible for the deaths of more than 100 million victims "through conquests, revolutions, civil wars, purges, wars by proxy, and other violent means." Some Republicans had demanded the authorization in return for dropping historical references to Soviet misdeeds, and the Foreign Relations Committee had approved it.

Senate action came after Dale Bumpers, D-Ark., lifted his hold on the bill. Bumpers, a senior member of the Energy and Natural Resources Committee — which had jurisdiction over the authorization of memorials — had expressed concerns that the Washington Mall was becoming cluttered with statues and monuments.

Final action on the bill came in the House, which approved the Senate version by voice vote Nov. 23, clearing the measure for the president. Clinton signed it Dec. 17 (PL 103-199).

health care ahead."

David R. Obey, D-Wis., chairman of the corresponding House subcommittee, said, "Wherever I go, people ask me — is this necessary? What about needs here at home?" But Obey said that when he asked constituents if they were willing to risk a return to Cold War tensions, "I usually get grudging acceptance."

The concerns in Congress were underscored April 21, when Talbott, Clinton's coordinator of aid to the former Soviet republics, appeared before Leahy's subcommittee.

"I intend to support assistance to Russia and the other republics, but it must be paid for," said Mitch McConnell of Kentucky, the ranking Republican on Leahy's panel. "We simply cannot afford to drive up our deficit and damage our economy."

Leahy told Talbott the administration should "forget all about" seeking a major foreign aid supplemental after the Senate had rejected Clinton's economic "stimulus" proposal for a supplemental to fund domestic programs. (*'Stimulus' supplemental, p. 706*)

At a news conference April 23, Clinton acknowledged that Russian aid had become entangled in debate over the domestic economy. "Can we get any more aid for Russia that requires a new appropriation by the U.S. Congress? ... That, I think, will be resolved in the weeks ahead in part by what happens to the American workers and their jobs and their future," Clinton said. "I think the two things will be tied by many members of Congress."

HOUSE ACTION

With a strong push from the leadership of both parties, Clinton's proposal for $2.5 billion in aid to Russia and its neighbors sailed through the House on June 17 as part of the $13 billion fiscal 1994 foreign operations appropriations bill. The foreign aid spending bill passed, 309-111. (*Vote 240, p. 58-H; appropriations, p. 603*)

To finesse congressional resistance to passing a separate bill to make use of unspent fiscal 1993 funds, the single measure incorporated two ways of funding the aid to the former Soviet republics: about $900 million in regular fiscal 1994 foreign aid funds, and about $1.6 billion from unspent fiscal 1993 funds ($630 million from foreign aid and $979 million from defense) provided through a supplemental appropriation that was attached to the foreign aid bill.

The appropriations measure proved to be the key House action. A day earlier, the House had passed by voice vote a foreign aid authorization bill (HR 2404) that also backed the aid to Russia. Members voted overwhelmingly, 118-317, against an amendment to strip $704 million in fiscal 1994 aid from the authorization bill. But that proved to be a symbolic debate because the foreign aid authoriza-

tion bill was never taken up in the Senate. *(Vote 229, p. 56-H; foreign aid authorization, p. 502)*

Committee Action

The House Appropriations Committee gave voice vote approval June 10 to a $13 billion foreign aid appropriations measure that included the $2.5 billion for the Soviet republics. The panel turned aside by voice vote an amendment to strip the bulk of the funding, the $1.6 billion supplemental appropriation.

The funding formula had been devised in negotiations between House leaders and appropriators and the administration and was incorporated into the bill by the House Appropriations Subcommittee on Foreign Operations, which approved the bill May 26.

Subcommittee Chairman Obey, who played a central role in negotiations with the administration, said the plan achieved an important foreign policy objective while conforming with fiscal reality. "It's a whole lot easier to provide a Marshall Plan when the economy is expanding and everyone is feeling good," he said after the panel's action. "It's a lot more difficult when everything is getting cut."

Though lawmakers had been worried for weeks about how the administration intended to pay for its promised aid to Yeltsin, they were equally concerned over delays in detailing the specific projects that the aid would support. In an effort to address those concerns, Talbott, the ambassador-at-large for the former Soviet republics, offered an unusual briefing for the subcommittee before its markup.

He said that about $1 billion of the aid would support projects aimed at modernizing Russia's energy sector, fostering the development of a private sector and expanding housing for Russian troops. The housing proposal, which proved controversial in Congress, was intended to facilitate the withdrawal of Russian troops from the Baltic republics. About $300 million of the aid would back programs in the non-Russian republics; $500 million would underwrite the U.S. contribution to a special private sector development fund in Russia. Talbott said he envisioned those funds serving as a "challenge grant" to induce other industrialized nations to provide as much as $1.5 billion for the fund.

Republican Sonny Callahan of Alabama told the subcommittee that he had "great disdain" for the notion of voting aid to Russia "during a week when we're voting a multibillion-dollar tax bill."

Obey countered by citing data that every American family had spent the equivalent of $80,000 for defense expenditures during the Cold War. He recalled the thousands of troops — including a friend — who were killed during conflicts in Vietnam and Korea.

Callahan remained opposed, but Obey won over the subcommittee's ranking Republican, Robert L. Livingston of Louisiana. "I believe you're on the right track," Livingston, a bedrock conservative, told Obey.

Floor Debate

On June 17, Callahan took his opposition to the aid to the House floor, introducing an amendment to strip the $1.6 billion in supplemental funding.

His amendment drew support from a disparate alliance of some conservative Republicans and some members of the Congressional Black Caucus.

"To defeat the domestic stimulus package in April and then somehow mysteriously pass Russian aid in June will create the perception that our priorities are in the wrong place," said Kweisi Mfume, D-Md., chairman of the Congressional Black Caucus, who complained that Clinton appeared to be moving to the political right to placate critics.

But House leaders stood united behind the president's request. Majority Leader Gephardt argued that failing to help the former communist states could necessitate a return to Cold War defense budgets. "This is the most important issue of our lifetime," he said.

The key to the convincing victory was clearly the strong backing leading Republicans provided. That more than offset opposition to the Russian aid from 17 of the Congressional Black Caucus' 38 House members.

Conservatives, such as Minority Whip Newt Gingrich of Georgia and Livingston echoed Gephardt's argument that the aid package served U.S. interests. Gingrich remarked that it had been a "very interesting day" of scrambled political alliances.

Many Republicans previously had backed Bush administration requests for the former republics, and Gephardt had bolstered support for a new package by arranging for a delegation of senior members from both parties to visit Russia and Ukraine in April. In the end, 210 Democrats and 79 Republicans joined in the 140-289 vote to defeat Callahan's amendment. *(Vote 237, p. 58-H)*

SENATE ACTION

Acting despite the uncertainty caused by a constitutional showdown in Moscow, the Senate passed its version of the fiscal 1994 foreign operations bill — including the $2.5 billion in aid for Russia and its neighbors — by an 88-10 vote on Sept. 23. *(Vote 287, p. 37-S)*

The appropriators were facing a serious time crunch because the $1.6 billion that was to come from unspent fiscal 1993 funds could not be captured unless the bill became law by Sept. 30, the last day of the fiscal year. The measure moved in the Senate only after intervention by Clinton and some creative bookkeeping finessed problems with the aid formula that had been devised during House consideration of the bill.

Committee Action

The Senate Appropriations Committee had approved the foreign aid spending bill, with its $2.5 billion for the former Soviet republics, by a vote of 28-0 on Sept. 14. The Foreign Operations Subcommittee had backed it by voice vote the previous day.

After personal lobbying by Clinton, Defense Appropriations Subcommittee Chairman Daniel K. Inouye, D-Hawaii, signed on to the deal to provide the Russian aid despite his concerns about the use of unspent defense funds. Inouye had warned that tapping the unexpended balances would put a further strain on a taut Pentagon budget by soaking up available outlays. Other senators who had raised objections, such as Ted Stevens, R-Alaska, also fell into line.

In marking up the foreign aid appropriations bill, the Foreign Operations Appropriations Subcommittee first had to get around a funding snag. When the full Appropriations Committee allocated spending for fiscal 1994, it provided Foreign Operations with $97 million less in outlays than its House counterpart received. The problem was solved by circumventing a requirement of the Congressional Budget Office that $170 million in outlays be set aside to protect against a possible default by Israel in the program enacted

in 1992 that provided guarantees for up to $10 billion in loans over five years. *(1992 Almanac, p. 539)*

With the consent of Senate Budget Committee Chairman Jim Sasser, D-Tenn., and Appropriations Committee Chairman Robert C. Byrd, D-W.Va., the panel declared that costs associated with the loan guarantees would not count against the discretionary spending limits established under the 1990 budget agreement or the Foreign Operations Subcommittee's funding allocation for fiscal 1994.

In spite of Leahy's insistence that the president be given "maximum flexibility" in providing aid for the former Soviet Union, most of the $2.5 billion in assistance was earmarked or specified for individual programs in the Senate bill.

The bill included a proposal by McConnell, the subcommittee's senior Republican, stating that "not less than $300 million should be provided to Ukraine from this or any other act." McConnell said he was concerned that Ukraine might receive short shrift because of the intense focus on Russia.

The bill also required that $18 million in assistance be provided for Armenia, which was locked in a brutal territorial dispute with neighboring Azerbaijan. Armenia had long been a favored country of many key lawmakers, including Senate Minority Leader Bob Dole, R-Kan.

In addition, the bill included a general breakdown of how the aid should be spent:

● $50 million in the form of agricultural commodities, an earmark with obvious appeal for farm-state lawmakers.

● $895 million for private-sector development through bilateral and multilateral enterprise funds.

● $125 million to support a multilateral fund to convert state-owned enterprises into private concerns, a central aspect of the administration's initiative.

● $185 million to enhance trade with the former Soviet Union through assistance for exports of energy and environmental commodities.

● $295 million for pro-democracy initiatives, including expanded exchange programs.

● $190 million to support more housing for former Russian troops in an effort to facilitate their withdrawal from the Baltic nations and other countries.

● $285 million in aid for energy and the environment;

● $239 million for humanitarian assistance;

● $300 million in backing for loan guarantee programs administered by the Export-Import Bank.

Floor Action

The Senate began consideration of the foreign operations bill Sept. 22, just one day after Yeltsin threw his nation into turmoil by disbanding the parliament and calling for December elections. Yeltsin's move prompted the opposition to impeach Yeltsin and establish a parallel government under the hard-line vice president, Aleksandr V. Rutskoi. The opposition forces hunkered down in the parliament building — the so-called White House.

Clinton moved quickly to express his full support for Yeltsin while attempting to put the Russian president's actions — which clearly violated the existing Soviet-era constitution — in a broader context. "There is no question that President Yeltsin acted in response to a constitutional crisis that had reached a critical impasse and had paralyzed the political process," Clinton said in a Sept. 21 statement.

A few senators raised concerns over Yeltsin's decision. "It goes without saying that the means do not justify an end," said Arlen Specter, R-Pa. Yeltsin's actions "could be very damaging in the long run."

John McCain, R-Ariz., said of Yeltsin, "The problem is that we want him to succeed, but he's violated his own constitution — no matter how flawed the constitution is."

But the administration argued that the crisis only added to the urgency of Senate action on the aid request. And although Leahy expressed concern that bringing up the bill in the midst of the Russian crisis would set off a messy public debate over U.S. policy toward Russia, senators followed Clinton's lead in rallying around the Russian president.

By a 97-1 vote, the Senate on Sept. 23 adopted an amendment by Byrd requiring the president to certify that Moscow had made "substantial progress" in withdrawing its remaining forces from the Baltic nations before providing aid to Russia. *(Vote 283, p. 37-S)*

Byrd's proposal was not nearly as restrictive as his amendment to the fiscal 1993 foreign operations bill (PL 102-391), which gave Russia one year to pull all of its forces from the Baltics or set a firm timetable for withdrawal. Byrd said the earlier provision, which was to take effect Oct. 6, probably would force a cutoff of a small amount of fiscal 1993 aid because Moscow had yet to agree to a timetable for withdrawing about 20,000 troops from the Baltic nations of Latvia and Estonia. *(1992 Almanac, p. 612)*

Byrd acknowledged that Yeltsin's government had reduced substantially the number of Russian forces in the Baltics, which at one time numbered more than 100,000.

The Senate adopted by voice vote an amendment by Connie Mack, R-Fla., reducing aid for Moscow by $380 million unless the president certified that Russia was not supporting Cuba. Mack used the $380 million figure because Russia extended a loan for that amount to Cuba earlier in 1993.

And the Senate by voice vote backed a proposal by McConnell barring aid for any of the former Soviet republics that violated the "territorial integrity or national sovereignty" of neighboring states.

FINAL ACTION

The House voted overwhelmingly on Sept. 29 to adopt the conference report on the legislation, 321-108. On Sept. 30 — just hours before $1.6 billion of the $2.5 billion in aid to the former Soviet republics would have been unavailable — the Senate approved the conference report, 88-11, clearing the bill for the president. Clinton signed it into law the same day (PL 103-87). *(House vote 467, p. 114-H; Senate vote 297, p. 39-S)*

The final action on the aid bill came as Russia's political crisis grew more ominous and nationalist violence intensified elsewhere in the former Soviet empire.

In spite of the turmoil, the dominant sentiment in Congress seemed to be that the United States had little choice but to extend strong support for the political and economic changes being pursued by the Russian president. "God help this nation; God help this world if they revert to another form of communism, fascism, totalitarianism or any other form of dictatorship," Republican Livingston said during the brief House debate.

Conference Committee

Much of the conference was devoted to resolving differences that arose from the Senate's penchant to earmark specific spending levels for programs. The House bill was free of earmarks.

While senators offered only mild opposition to Obey's proposal to eliminate most of the spending mandates, they

satellite. They noted that in 1992 Congress cut $744 million from the Air Force's contribution to the NRO for a new satellite. This time, the NRO reportedly was seeking the satellite funds through the CIA.

Members of the Legislation Subcommittee also put their fingerprints on the bill. They met June 9 in a rare open session to approve by voice vote three proposals that extended various benefits to divorced spouses of intelligence officers; raised annual bonus pay to $1,200 for reserve personnel proficient in a foreign language; and authorized up to $5,000 a year for the CIA to make awards in high school science contests.

After spirited debate, George W. Gekas, R-Pa., withdrew a proposal that would have limited any award and subsequent tour of the CIA to high school students who were U.S. citizens. "It occurs to us," he said, "that the recipient of one of these awards may be a foreign national."

Full Committee Action

The House Select Intelligence Committee approved the bill in closed session June 17. The panel reportedly agreed to freeze intelligence spending at $28 billion (H Rept 103-162, Part 1).

Glickman said intelligence spending should not increase during a time of belt-tightening throughout the government. He said the committee conducted "the most exhaustive set of budget reviews we've had [in intelligence] since World War II."

Despite vigorous lobbying by Woolsey, even the influential NRO apparently did not get all that it sought for a new generation of spy satellites. Woolsey pushed hard for full funding, reportedly arguing that the satellites would cost more to build later. Advocates for the satellites included several big defense contractors who argued for the contracts — and ultimately for the jobs they would create — in an era of declining Pentagon budgets.

In a telling sign of the new political pressures facing the Intelligence Committee, Glickman said it was the first time the committee had to consider the domestic economic fallout of intelligence budget decisions.

The chairman said the panel focused budget resources on efforts to track contraband nuclear materials and hidden efforts to develop nuclear weapons. "The nuke search is something you would have human beings do," said one analyst. "That's basically a bribery and blackmail intelligence activity, rather than a technological overhead one."

Faced with the budget crunch, the House Intelligence panel also went after a favorite project of former Senate Intelligence Committee Chairman Boren, voting unanimously to eliminate a $150 million CIA program for language studies at American University, which Boren had pushed through two years before. "We had to set an example," Glickman said. The chairman denied that the move was intended as a slap at Boren but acknowledged that some House Democrats were angry at him for his leading role in challenging Clinton's economic plan. *(Clinton budget, p. 89)*

The bill also included language endorsing the administration's efforts to review the way the government classified secret documents. "We spend, historically, billions and billions of dollars on classifying documents," said committee member David E. Skaggs, D-Colo. "All of that needs a fresh look."

Clinton's Response

In a July 27 letter to Glickman, Clinton reluctantly accepted the cuts from his request but vowed to fight moves to cut deeper. "I will oppose any amendment on the House floor which seeks to reduce intelligence spending beyond the reductions already proposed by the committee," Clinton wrote. He said the bill already would "test our ability to manage prudently the reduction of the intelligence budget while we simultaneously seek to meet the new challenges which confront our country."

Woolsey, who had lobbied members heavily for the administration's budget request, renewed his case publicly July 28 at a hearing of the House Foreign Affairs Subcommittee on International Security, International Organizations and Human Rights. Woolsey used as an analogy the money that was being spent to close obsolete military bases in the interest of long-term savings. He argued that the CIA and other intelligence agencies needed to spend money to restructure their operations to meet new threats. "Our effort with whatever share of that budget Congress ends up approving will be to use those funds and conduct our planning in such a way that we do end up saving substantial resources for the country over the period of the next five to 10 years," he said.

HOUSE FLOOR ACTION

After soundly defeating proposals for deeper cuts, a bipartisan coalition in the House passed the fiscal 1994 intelligence authorization bill Aug. 4 by a vote of 400-28. *(Vote 398, 98-H)*

Members also rejected an amendment that would have made public the supposedly classified total budget for the nation's network of intelligence-gathering agencies. But they repeatedly alluded to the bill's reported $28 billion total.

During two days of debate, most Democrats backed the committee budget in a show of confidence in Glickman and support for the new era of openness promised by Woolsey.

Republicans found themselves in the unaccustomed position of championing Clinton's original budget request and quoting his warnings that the cuts in the House bill would "test our ability" to reduce spending over the long run while meeting intelligence challenges. But the Republicans did not attempt to restore the committee's trims, concentrating instead on helping Glickman fend off deeper cuts.

The question was how fast to cut intelligence programs, and the answers offered by members turned largely on the threats to national security since the the the end of the Cold War. Glickman cited CIA estimates that as many as 25 countries had "either the real power or the capability to develop nuclear weapons."

"When you combine that nuclear threat with the terrorist threat, [and] the ability to transport nuclear devices around the world," he said, "we have a problem in this country, in this world."

Lawmakers defended the committee bill by repeatedly invoking enemies such as Iraqi leader Saddam Hussein and the terrorists who bombed the World Trade Center in New York.

But Barney Frank, D-Mass., ridiculed the notion that intelligence agencies could not track such threats while shedding some of the massive costs of past intelligence struggles against the Soviet Union. "What threat exists today that did not exist five years ago?" asked Frank. "There were no terrorists? What was Iran, a theme park five years ago? There was no North Korea nuclear program? It started yesterday?"

An amendment by Frank to cut the bill's authorization level by $500 million was rejected, 134-299, on Aug. 4.

Nancy Pelosi, D-Calif., was the only Intelligence Committee member to support the cut. *(Vote 393, p. 96-H)*

A day earlier, the House rejected, 104-323, a far deeper, 10 percent cut proposed by Bernard Sanders, I-Vt. *(Vote 391, p. 96-H)*

Opponents of the 10 percent cut raised the ghosts of past intelligence blunders as a warning. But conservatives acknowledged that actual intelligence spending was likely to be cut somewhat deeper by appropriators. Most intelligence funding was buried in classified sections of the annual defense appropriations bill.

Arguing for Openness

Glickman's support from Democrats came in part from his moves to make intelligence matters less secret and more accessible to members. The House bill formalized the new openness by requiring the CIA director to submit an annual unclassified report describing the intelligence "community's successes and failures for the preceding fiscal year."

"This report will make intelligence a little less mysterious and a little more understandable to the average American," Glickman said. Praising such moves, Jane Harman, D-Calif., told the House, "These are important departures from past practice. I think this information will go a long way toward increasing public understanding of the intelligence community."

Like its Republican predecessors, however, the Clinton administration opposed proposals to make public the total spending in the bill. The House rejected, 169-264, an amendment by Frank to reveal the total. "I think it is essential for those engaged in debate to know the gross number," said committee member David E. Skaggs, D-Colo. "We ought to be in a position to defend the number," he said. Like Skaggs, Glickman voted to make the budget public, but the chairman remained discreetly silent during the debate. *(Vote 396, p. 96-H)*

Porter J. Goss, R-Fla., revived a GOP proposal from 1991 to require House members to sign an oath promising not to disclose classified intelligence information and acknowledging that a violation could bring censure or expulsion. His amendment passed, 341-86, but only after Glickman won approval, 262-171, of language expanding the oath-taking requirement to all members of the Senate and executive branch. *(Vote 395, p. 96-H; vote 394, p. 96-H; 1991 Almanac, p. 482)*

A Circumspect Debate

The bulk of the intelligence bill remained secret. Members were invited to read the classified text in a secure room at the Capitol that was off-limits even to their top aides. Some of those who sought to cut the bill, including Sanders and Rep. Major Owens, R-N.Y., declined on principle to read the secret provisions of the measure they were debating. And conservative advocates of more intelligence spending made circumspect but revealing comments about the bill's classified programs.

"One of the great innovations of the president's budget was a proposed overhaul of our intelligence satellite architecture by which a modest current expenditure will yield huge savings in the future," said Combest. "That innovation has barely survived this bill. In this case a further cut will most definitely be penny-wise and pound-foolish."

Analysts speculated that the proposed system combined optical and listening functions of previous generations. The move would save money by allowing a number of ground stations to be closed in the process.

Attempting to rebut the arguments for intelligence cuts, Richardson of New Mexico huddled for five minutes with a committee aide, then strode to the podium armed with a doomsday list of programs that he said would be harmed by any additional cuts: photo and signal intercepter satellites, computer communications equipment, research and development and military tactical unit deployments.

For their part, liberal advocates of deeper cuts argued that the intelligence agencies had room to cut if they had budget enough to launch expanded programs on issues such as environmental protection. Don Edwards, D-Calif., a former FBI agent who headed the Judiciary Subcommittee on Civil and Constitutional Rights, questioned the propriety of intelligence agencies playing an expanded role in such topics, for which they previously gathered data only "incidentally" in the course of their regular duties.

Other Provisions

Two amendments were agreed to by voice vote. The first, offered by Glickman, struck a provision in the bill that would have increased a monthly stipend for military linguists in the reserves. Glickman said Armed Services Committee members had raised a question of jurisdiction.

The second was non-binding language asking for establishment of a National Task Force on Counterterrorism, an amendment proposed by Bill McCollum, R-Fla.

Other provisions of the bill were to:

● Abolish the Central Imagery Office, a clearinghouse for analyzing imagery collected by myriad defense and government intelligence agencies. The office was created 14 months earlier in an effort to save money after an interagency organizational review. The move to eliminate the office was criticized as "premature" by the Armed Services Committee in its committee report on the fiscal 1994 defense authorization bill (HR 2401 — H Rept 103-200).

● Provide about $18 million in retirement and survivor benefits to approximately 400 former spouses of CIA agents who were divorced before Dec. 4, 1991. The entitlement modified eligibility requirements. It provided an average of $15,500 per person for 1995, the first year benefits could be paid.

● Repeal the National Security Educational Trust Fund, Boren's pet program, which provided language scholarships to college and graduate students. About $100 million of the trust's $157 million fund was obligated through 1998. The balance was to be returned to the Treasury Department.

● Authorize the CIA to sponsor science fair competitions for high school students in the United States and award cash prizes totaling not more than $5,000 annually.

● Permit the CIA director to exceed personnel levels by 2 percent on a temporary basis to correct gaps created between new hires and those about to retire.

SENATE COMMITTEE ACTION

The Senate Intelligence Committee moved to cap spending at existing levels as it drafted a fiscal 1994 intelligence authorization bill July 16. The panel, torn over how deeply to cut intelligence programs, approved the bill (S 1301 — S Rept 103-115) by a vote of 11-6.

"It's a freeze," committee Chairman DeConcini said after the closed session. "Spending levels are the same as last year."

The bill, DeConcini's first as chairman, bore the mark of his determination in the aftermath of the Cold War to hold down the costs of the nation's sprawling intelligence

Bill Urges Early Retirement From CIA

The Senate cleared legislation May 26 to provide lump-sum payments of up to $25,000 to unneeded CIA employees who took early retirement. The House had passed the bill (HR 1723) two days earlier. Both chambers acted by voice vote. President Clinton signed the bill into law June 8 (PL 103-36).

The early retirement incentive was to be offered to CIA employees in certain specialties or locations that were designated as overstaffed by the director of Central Intelligence. The House Intelligence Committee had approved the bill by voice vote May 12 (H Rept 103-102); the Senate Intelligence Committee approved a similar measure (S 647 — S Rept 103-43) on March 30.

During House floor debate, Intelligence Committee Chairman Dan Glickman, D-Kan., said the bill was backed by the administration and would be "a tool in not only shrinking the size of the CIA but in reorienting it from its Cold War focus and methods."

"The end of the Cold War has brought to the intelligence community, as it has to other parts of the national security establishment, a need to re-examine the mix of skills in its work force," he said. "Employees whose expertise is no longer in demand must either be retrained, if possible, or be encouraged to retire or resign so that those with the skills necessary for the future can be recruited."

Glickman said the payments were needed to help the intelligence agency reach a 17.5 percent reduction in its work force by 1997, as mandated by Congress in the fiscal 1993 intelligence authorization bill (PL 102-496). The size and cost of the CIA payroll remained secret. *(1992 Almanac, p. 564)*

The measure's advocates also made it clear that the incentive payments were devised in part to reduce the risk of forced layoffs that could produce disgruntled — and disloyal — former spies.

During the Senate debate, John W. Warner, Va., senior Republican on the Intelligence Committee, said that CIA Director R. James Woolsey had "raised delicately the difficult subject of the counterintelligence impact of involuntary separations, expressing concern that forcing out large numbers of CIA employees involuntarily would increase the risk that an employee who had access to sensitive intelligence secrets might fail to maintain his or her obligation to protect those secrets."

The measure prohibited a CIA employee who took the early retirement bonus from being rehired by the agency or working for it under contract for a year.

---

network. As a committee member in 1992, DeConcini had been an unusually vocal advocate for significant spending cuts in intelligence.

The conservative Democrat said he could not justify authorizing the Clinton administration's request for an intelligence budget increase of more than $1 billion "when you're facing a $300 billion deficit." The committee included language in the bill specifically directing that savings be applied to the deficit.

The vote did not fall solely along party lines. An aide to Democrat John Glenn of Ohio confirmed that he joined most committee Republicans in opposing the intelligence spending freeze. Several Republicans reportedly broke ranks to support the measure.

Woolsey lobbied vigorously against any cuts in the president's request, buttonholing senators in one-on-one meetings and frequent telephone calls. "One time he called right while I was sitting there talking to a senator," DeConcini said.

The affairs of the supersecret committee also became public the morning of the meeting, as several newspapers printed stories on the budget dispute that were attributed to intelligence officials chagrined at the prospect of cuts in Clinton's request. "I don't know what Jim's problem is," DeConcini said of Woolsey's lobbying efforts. "This causes no rifts. I didn't touch any of his people. I already gave him authorization for $25,000 bonuses for early retirements, and they're already maxed out."

According to the published reports, intelligence officials were particularly upset that the Intelligence committees were forcing significant cuts in the administration's plans for a new generation of satellites. "The strategy is to cut the NRO because it's all procurement money," said Robert J. Kohler, vice president and general manager of TRW Inc.'s Avionics and Surveillance Group.

"We created no gap" in satellite coverage, DeConcini said. He did say, however, that his committee had denied "two big budget outlays," forcing the intelligence agencies to stretch out their time line to develop and launch the costly surveillance equipment.

In other provisions, the panel adopted a Glenn proposal to create an office of legal counsel to the director of intelligence, a position that would require Senate confirmation. It also voted to cut $25 million from Boren's language studies program. The House bill eliminated the $150 million program.

SENATE FLOOR ACTION

The Senate approved HR 2330 by voice vote Nov. 10, after substituting the text of the Senate bill (S 1301). The measure froze spending at fiscal 1993 levels and carried the same price tag as the House-passed version.

The supposed secrecy surrounding the budget total was the only issue remaining in debate by the time the measure reached the Senate floor, where members inserted their bill into House-passed version and sent it to a House-Senate conference committee.

Debate Over Secrecy

Howard M. Metzenbaum, D-Ohio, offered a non-binding provision asking the executive branch to make public the aggregate amount spent to fund the spy agencies. "I wish I could offer something stronger," said Metzenbaum, "but I regret to say that anything stronger than this would be opposed by the administration." Metzenbaum quoted from a March 27 letter in which Clinton had promised to "take seriously your suggestion that our administration disclose the aggregate amount." Like its Republican predecessors, however, the Clinton administration ultimately

came out against making the intelligence total public.

Metzenbaum's amendment nearly failed. Conservatives led by Select Intelligence Committee Vice Chairman John W. Warner, R-Va., narrowly lost, 49-51, on a motion to table (kill) the amendment. Metzenbaum's resolution was adopted, 52-48. *(Votes 366, 367, p. 47-S)*

Opponents argued that revealing the number could start the government down a slope that eventually would lead to making public an agency-by-agency breakdown of spending. Such details, they said, would aid foreign spy agencies in their efforts to figure out the U.S. intelligence community's programs and objectives.

Supporters of Metzenbaum's amendment countered that excess secrecy acted as a shield to protect agencies from public scrutiny and proper congressional oversight. Arguing that the intelligence agencies needed closer scrutiny, Daniel Patrick Moynihan, D-N.Y., who previously had proposed abolishing the CIA, said, "Two years before the Berlin Wall came down, the CIA estimated that the per capita gross domestic product in East Germany was higher than in West Germany. Any taxi driver in East Berlin could have told you it was not so."

Other Amendments

DeConcini offered three amendments that were approved by unanimous consent. They required the CIA director and the secretary of Defense to prepare a joint report detailing gaps between intelligence needs and capabilities; preserved pay levels of FBI employees who participated in a demonstration project, since ended, in the New York office; and authorized funds to restructure the nation's satellite program.

The Senate bill also included provisions to:

• Amend the Fair Credit Reporting Act to allow the FBI access to credit records of a consumer the bureau suspected of past, present or imminent contact with a foreign power or spy.

• Cut $25 million from the $150 million National Security Education Trust Fund, the Boren-sponsored scholarship program for college and graduate-level students. It created a more modest annual grant of $5,000 for high school science competitions in its place.

• Raise language proficiency bonus pay for the 9,000 military reservists serving in intelligence to a maximum annual salary bonus of $1,200. The pay would be equal to that received by their active-duty counterparts.

• Create a National Intelligence Officer for Proliferation to coordinate intelligence activities aimed at stopping the spread of nuclear, chemical and biological weapons.

• Require Senate confirmation for future nominees to the job of CIA general counsel.

FINAL ACTION

House and Senate conferees completed work on the fiscal 1994 intelligence authorization bill the week of Nov. 15. The House approved the conference report (H Rept 103-377) by voice vote Nov. 20; the Senate cleared the measure for the president hours later, also by voice vote.

Conference Decisions

Conferees deleted several contentious Senate-passed amendments, including Metzenbaum's language urging the administration to make public the amount spent annually on intelligence activities. According to the conference report, members removed the provision because the House had defeated an attempt to make the number public earlier in the year. But the report warned that both the House and Senate Intelligence committees would hold hearings on the disclosure in 1994.

Conferees included a provision requiring the head of the intelligence community to release an unclassified annual report detailing intelligence successes and failures during the previous year.

They authorized $120 million for Boren's National Security Education Trust Fund, $5 million less than the Senate had approved. The House had sought to cancel the program.

Conferees also dropped the House-passed provision requiring members of Congress and the executive branch to sign an oath promising not to disclose classified intelligence information.

They included the House provision providing retirement and survivor benefits to former spouses of CIA employees who were divorced before Dec. 4, 1991.

But they dropped from earlier versions of the bill:

• A sense-of-Congress provision that asked for the establishment of a national task force on terrorism. Instead, the measure required the secretary of State, the attorney general and the CIA director to give members a report on terrorism by the following May 1.

• A Senate provision requiring the CIA's general counsel to be confirmed by the Senate.

• A Senate provision allowing the FBI to obtain credit reports without a court order. ■

U.S. Suspects North Korea Of Nuclear Arms Capacity

North Korea, which the U.S. government believed was developing nuclear arms, announced March 12 that it intended to withdraw from a 1968 treaty intended to limit the spread of such weapons.

The communist government in Pyongyang repudiated the pact after the United Nations' nuclear oversight agency insisted on exercising its right under the treaty to examine two sites suspected of being nuclear waste dumps.

North Korea insisted that its nuclear research program was conducted for peaceful purposes, as allowed by the treaty. But R. James Woolsey, director of Central Intelligence, told the Senate Governmental Affairs Committee on Feb. 24 that North Korea was rapidly gaining the ability to assemble a nuclear weapon. "We have every indication that the North Koreans are hiding some evidence of some nuclear weapons-related activities," Woolsey said.

Making his first appearance before Congress as director of Central Intelligence, Woolsey painted a bleak picture of a world where — despite the end of the Cold War — threats to the United States and its allies lurked around every corner.

While West European countries were limiting weapons sales to the Third World, Woolsey added, both North Korea and China leapt into the vacuum. North Korea posed the bigger risk, said Woolsey, because it apparently had "no threshold governing its sales. It is willing to sell to any country with the cash to pay."

The dispute with North Korea carried into 1994, with North Korea eventually allowing international inspectors back into the country but severely limiting their access. ■

POW-MIA Issue Clouds Vietnam Relations

Congress and the Clinton administration edged warily toward reconciliation with Vietnam in 1993, but the relationship was haunted by unanswered questions over the fate of U.S. soldiers who never returned from the Vietnam War that had ended two decades earlier.

On Jan. 13, the Senate Select Committee on POW-MIA Affairs issued a report concluding 15 months of investigation. The panel said it found "no compelling evidence" that any American prisoners remained alive at that point in Southeast Asia. But its 1,000-page report held open the possibility that some soldiers had languished in enemy hands after the war ended.

On Sept. 13, President Clinton renewed the long-running U.S. embargo on trade with Vietnam. But he relaxed it slightly to allow U.S. companies to bid on multimillion-dollar contracts in Vietnam that were financed by international lending institutions.

Prodded by U.S. businesses that saw trading opportunities in a rapidly growing economy, some lawmakers argued that Vietnam was cooperating fully in the frustrating hunt for information about more than 2,200 Americans who had been listed as prisoners of war (POWs) or missing in action (MIAs) since the Vietnam War.

But many other lawmakers insisted that Vietnam knew far more than it shared. They championed the view, advanced by families of the missing soldiers and some veterans' organizations, that the United States should not lift the trade embargo because it provided leverage to force far greater cooperation.

SENATE REPORT

The report released Jan. 13 by the Senate Select Committee on POW-MIA Affairs conveyed a delicately crafted balance of judgments, reflecting the debate that occurred within the committee. The report, which was signed by all 12 members of the committee — six Democrats and six Republicans — concluded: "There is, at this time, no compelling evidence that proves that any American remains alive in captivity in Southeast Asia."

But it also said, "We acknowledge that there is no proof that U.S. POWs survived, but neither is there proof that all of those who did not return had died. There is evidence, moreover, that indicates the possibility of survival, at least for a small number, after Operation Homecoming," the official repatriation of prisoners from North Vietnam in April 1973.

The committee criticized top U.S. government officials for dismissing the possibility that some soldiers remained in custody in Vietnam and neighboring countries at the end of the war but rejected charges that the officials possessed any "certain knowledge" that prisoners were abandoned.

Committee Chairman John Kerry, a Massachusetts Democrat, said at a news conference Jan. 13 that the continued cooperation of Vietnam, Laos and Cambodia was essential to obtain the fullest possible accounting for missing Americans. "This report does not close the issue," he said. "It is not meant to. This report provides the reality base from which we can now make real judgments about probabilities and possibilities."

Vice Chairman Robert C. Smith, R-N.H., said, "There's evidence that some POWs may have survived to the present, and some information still remains to be investi-

gated. However, at this time, there's no compelling evidence that proves that. And that's a fact, and we all agree to that."

In 1992, Smith had said that while he could not speak for others on the panel, he believed there was strong evidence to suggest U.S. prisoners had been held in Southeast Asia well into the 1980s. *(1992 Almanac, p. 560)*

In a footnote in the committee's report, Smith and Charles E. Grassley, R-Iowa, dissented from a majority view that neither "live sighting" reports nor other sources of intelligence provided any grounds for encouragement that POWs may still have been alive. They wrote that they believed there was "evidence that POWs may have survived to the present."

Committee Background

As part of the Paris peace accords signed in January 1973, Hanoi agreed to release all U.S. prisoners. Vietnam ultimately returned 591 prisoners. The fate of others who disappeared in the dense Vietnam countryside left a lingering controversy from a war that had bitterly divided Americans.

The Senate created its select committee Aug. 2, 1991, following news reports about photographs purporting to show live American prisoners from the Vietnam War. The committee also investigated military personnel unaccounted for from the Korean War, World War II and the Cold War. *(1991 Almanac, p. 491)*

But Vietnam became the focus of the most attention and debate. The Defense Department listed 2,264 Americans as unaccounted for from the war, but the committee said the number of Americans whose fate was "truly unknown [was] far smaller."

The committee's authorization expired Jan. 3. Kerry and other members said they would continue to press for more answers to the POW issue in permanent committees of the Senate.

Committee members detailed the extraordinary efforts that went into their investigation. Smith said members and staff "spent hours and days and weeks — man-hours, five or six investigators, full time — investigating every single available lead that we could find."

"The result of the committee's efforts has been the most rapid and comprehensive declassification of materials on a single subject in American history," the report said.

The committee held 22 days of public hearings, with testimony from 144 witnesses, including former secretaries of Defense and State, former North Vietnamese military officials and members of POW families and activist groups.

Committee members also made numerous trips of varying length and success to Vietnam, Laos and Cambodia, the Soviet Union and Korea in attempts to track down prisoners or any artifacts that could help determine their fate.

Some passages of the voluminous report reflected the frustrations the senators felt in attempting to determine the fate of men who had long since vanished.

"The POW issue is alive today because of a fundamental conflict between the laws of probability and the dictates of human nature," the report said. "On the subject as personal and emotional as the survival of a family member, there is nothing more difficult than to be asked to accept the probability of death when the possibility of life remains . . . .

"We knew at the outset that we could never answer all the questions that exist."

Kerry said that through investigation with the cooperation of the Defense Department, the committee determined that 135 "discrepancy cases" remained in which there was reason to believe that governments in Southeast Asia may have known the fate of the individual.

For the remainder of the 2,264, the committee said the government determined that, in most cases, death was considered almost certain but that it could not be proved because bodies were unrecoverable from crash sites, especially ones at sea or in areas of heavy combat where ground had been lost to the enemy.

Reaction

Representatives of Vietnam veterans groups said they were disappointed with the final report, calling it inadequate and written to meet an arbitrary deadline.

J. Thomas Burch, the chairman of the National Vietnam Veterans Coalition, said the report "was basically filled with syrupy congratulatory notes" and failed to give veterans "one straight shot at the truth."

Burch criticized the committee for letting current and former administration officials review drafts of the report.

Former Secretary of State Henry A. Kissinger was allowed to read an advance copy of the report. According to news accounts, he got a chance to rewrite language that was critical of his handling of the Paris Peace Accords.

Panel member John McCain, R-Ariz., himself a former POW in Vietnam, denied that the committee watered down any of its conclusions to protect the image of administration officials, current or former.

Regarding Kissinger's role in negotiating the accords, the final report said, "The record does indicate that efforts to gain accountability were made. Dr. Henry Kissinger personally raised the issue and lodged protests with [North Vietnamese negotiator] Le Duc Tho and leaders of the Pathet Lao. . . . Ultimately, the Nixon administration proceeded with the withdrawal of troops in return for the release of prisoners on the lists provided by the North Vietnamese and the Viet Cong."

Smith said Kissinger "tried his best to negotiate an agreement and implement accords with an intransigent enemy who exploited the American political situation. And they did it well."

RENEWED QUESTIONS

The Senate committee's voluminous report on the Vietnam War's missing soldiers did not resolve the issue.

The discovery in Moscow of a 20-year-old military document inflamed passions in April; in June, lawmakers of both parties came back from a visit to Southeast Asia with word of new cooperation from Vietnam.

The Soviet Report

The Soviet military report indicated that Vietnam had lied about the number of U.S. prisoners it was holding.

The document that caused the stir purported to be a Russian translation of a Vietnamese general's 1972 intelligence briefing that had been given to Soviet military officials. Publicity surrounding the report, retrieved from dusty Soviet military archives, put a cloud over the Clinton administration's strategy of inching toward normalized relations with Vietnam.

Sen. Smith told reporters April 13 that U.S. and Russian

investigators found the classified document in February. Smith said it indicated that even though Vietnamese officials told the United States in September 1972 that they held 368 American POWS, they actually held more than 1,200.

Smith said the U.S.-Russian team unearthed the document independently from Harvard University researcher Stephen Morris. Morris made the document public in early April, saying he had discovered it in Moscow's military archives while doing research in January.

If the Russian document proved accurate, Smith said, 614 Americans were never returned.

Organizations led by the families of POWs joined Smith in calling on the administration to put off any steps toward normalizing relations with Vietnam until the new report was explained.

Smith said he was convinced of the authenticity of the newly discovered document, noting that it had been signed by former high-level Soviet officials, as had an official summary of the report.

But Kerry, the former chairman of the Senate Select Committee on POW/MIA Affairs, was more skeptical. Appearing April 12 on ABC's "Nightline," Kerry said: "This document clearly smacks of authenticity, but there's a distinction between authenticity and accuracy. It is a secondhand translation — Russian from Vietnamese, second-person, you don't really know all the nuances."

Noting that the report purported to list numbers of U.S. prisoners by military rank, Kerry said the numbers cited "far exceed the numbers of actual American colonels, lieutenant colonels and majors who were lost, raising the question of whether or not they are not mixing South Vietnamese majors, Thai majors or Lao majors."

In news reports from Hanoi on April 12, Vietnam denounced the Moscow report found by the investigators as a fake.

Retired Gen. John W. Vessey, the administration's envoy to Vietnam on POW questions, returned from Vietnam convinced that the 20-year-old Russian document was authentic — but thoroughly inaccurate. "There are two points," Vessey told reporters April 21. "One is: Is it an authentic Russian document? And I think we've fairly well come to the conclusion that it is. And the second thing is: Is the information accurate in it? And we know that a great deal of the information is inaccurate."

Lawmakers' Trip

A congressional delegation looking for fresh leads in the search for missing U.S. servicemen returned from Southeast Asia on June 2 with more documents from the Vietnamese and renewed commitments of assistance.

But lawmakers were careful not to suggest that the United States should move yet to lift its trade embargo.

Led by Kerry, the delegation spent two full days in Hanoi in meetings with key Vietnamese officials, including Communist Party chief Do Muoi.

The delegation pored over archival materials and read transcripts of oral history interviews of former Vietnamese officials. On Memorial Day, May 31, Vietnam provided the delegation with 12 new documents, including a once-secret list of U.S. servicemen and others taken prisoner during the war and the medical records of some of the prisoners. Hanoi also showed the lawmakers footage of POWs said to be filmed during the war.

At a news conference at Travis Air Force Base in Northern California on June 2, Kerry said, "We arrive back . . . with a feeling of more than just hope — of expectation,

really — that the system put in place in Vietnam to do the job of accounting for our missing servicemen is working effectively."

But Sen. Smith, who did not go on the trip — expressed skepticism toward the pace of Vietnam's release of information. "It continues to dribble out," he said. "The Vietnamese can provide much more than they have. And that's why it is so frustrating. They should unilaterally provide us with everything, whether it be live Americans, remains of their bodies or explanations about what happened to them."

In addition to Kerry, Sens. McCain and John Glenn, D-Ohio, and Reps. Pete Peterson, D-Fla., Lane Evans, D-Ill., and Dana Rohrabacher, R-Calif., were in the delegation that made the trip. Like McCain, Peterson was a military pilot who was shot down during the war and held by the Vietnamese.

While in Hanoi, McCain and Peterson visited the notorious "Hanoi Hilton," the nickname of the Vietnamese prison where they were held. McCain said the tour through the prison was not an occasion for bitterness but "a trip down memory lane" that reminded him of "many friendships forged there" with fellow prisoners.

McCain said he was "surprised at how primitive" Vietnam's record-keeping was but was pleased that Hanoi was setting up new procedures to better collate its scattered archives.

Peterson discounted theories that Vietnam continued to hold back secrets. "Was it a token process earlier? Of course," Peterson said. "It was clear Vietnam did not want to get on board. But there has been a major change."

Although McCain said a "full accounting" of the missing should remain the U.S. priority, he added: "The United States has to look at the issue of what is in its interest in this region in a post-Cold War era — the relationship with the emerging economic and military powers there."

PRESIDENT'S ACTIONS

Clinton tried to reassure Vietnam veterans and the families of the missing that he was sensitive to their plight even as he moved incrementally to improve relations with Vietnam.

Declassifying files. On Memorial Day, Clinton ordered the declassification by Veterans Day, Nov. 11, of the government's remaining files relating to the POWs and those missing in action.

Defense Department spokesman Bob Hall said the executive order bolstered one issued in 1992 by President George Bush by setting a deadline for release of the material. Hall said the government had already declassified about 800,000 pages of documents out of about 1.5 million that were expected to be made public.

In a speech at the Vietnam Veterans' Memorial, Clinton said the demand for a full accounting of the missing Americans remained "the central outstanding issue in our relationship with Vietnam."

Supporting loans. On July 2, Clinton announced that the United States was dropping its longstanding opposition to international loans to Vietnam.

The action made it possible for Vietnam to seek loans from institutions such as the World Bank and International Monetary Fund. But Clinton emphasized that relations with Hanoi remained clouded by questions about the fate of the POWs and MIAs.

"Any further steps in U.S.-Vietnamese relations will strictly depend on further progress by the Vietnamese on the POW/MIA issue," Clinton said. "Progress to date is simply not sufficient to warrant any change in our trade embargo or any further steps toward normalization."

Senate Minority Leader Bob Dole, R-Kan., objected to any easing of U.S. policy. "It's not right to reward Vietnam for their non-answers," said Dole.

Easing the embargo. On Sept. 13, Clinton renewed the embargo against trade with Vietnam, but he relaxed it slightly to allow U.S. companies to bid on multimillion-dollar contracts in Vietnam financed by the World Bank and the Asian Development Bank.

Clinton's decision to further ease the trade embargo with Vietnam was greeted with general approval on Capitol Hill by lawmakers who said that U.S. businesses should be able to profit from the large-scale redevelopment projects planned in Vietnam. But some members warned that with each step the White House took toward normalizing relations, leverage was lost in the search for long-missing U.S. soldiers.

Clinton's decision "returns a measure of fairness to U.S. exporters," said Sen Richard G. Lugar, R-Ind. "And we've not lost leverage on the POW issue. The pressure is still on."

But Sen. Smith said Clinton "made a serious mistake. He sent a mixed signal when instead he could have drawn a line in the sand and said to Vietnam, 'Look, you either cooperate fully or we're not going to budge.'"

On Feb. 3, 1994, Clinton announced he was lifting the trade embargo against Vietnam "because I am convinced it offers the best way to resolve the fate of those who remain missing and about whom we are not sure."

The Senate had given the president political cover to lift the embargo action on Jan. 27, 1994. In debate on a State Department authorization bill (S 1281), the Senate voted 62-38 for an amendment urging that he lift the embargo. Kerry and McCain, the former Vietnam POW, were among key supporters of the amendment. The leading opponents included Smith and Dole. ∎

Law Lifts Last Sanctions Against South Africa

President Clinton signed legislation Nov. 23 (HR 3225 — PL 103-149) that observed the dramatic change in South Africa's political landscape by repealing the remaining sanctions of the 1986 Anti-Apartheid Act.

"Today the Congress sends a signal to South Africans: We welcome you back into the international community," said Sen. Nancy Landon Kassebaum of Kansas, who had provided a key Republican vote for the 1986 bill. "The days of isolation and sanctions are over, and we stand ready, as partners, to support your efforts to create a new, democratic and non-racial nation."

Several days earlier, on Nov. 18, South African President F. W. de Klerk and African National Congress President Nelson Mandela signed an agreement calling for a multiparty transitional government that would rule for five years, based on an election to be held April 27, 1994. It was to be the first general election in which the black majority in South Africa was to be permitted to vote.

Earlier in 1993, Mandela and de Klerk shared the Nobel Peace Prize for their efforts to bring about change peaceably in South Africa.

The bill repealed bans on the import of products from South Africa and removed South Africa from a list of nations that were ineligible for most-favored-nation status.

Background

Congress passed the Anti-Apartheid Act in 1986 over the veto of President Ronald Reagan in protest over apartheid, South Africa's institutionalized system of racial discrimination. *(1986 Almanac, p. 359)*

The law imposed a series of sanctions, such as barring importation of South African coal, steel and agricultural products, and it ended landing rights in the United States for the government-owned South African Airways.

Supporters argued that the only way to break the system of apartheid was to isolate South Africa and its economy from the rest of the world. Opponents countered that the sanctions would hurt the very people they were designed to help by making the poor in South Africa even poorer.

Changes in South Africa led President George Bush to lift some of the sanctions in 1991. *(1991 Almanac, p. 478)*

House Action

The House passed HR 3225 on Nov. 19 by voice vote. The measure had been put together by four House committees: Banking, Foreign Affairs, Public Works, and Ways and Means (H Rept 103-296, Parts 1-4).

● **Foreign Affairs.** The Foreign Affairs Committee was the first to take up the measure, approving HR 3225 on Oct. 7 by voice vote. The committee bill authorized the president to make foreign aid available to support the transition to a democracy in South Africa.

Members rejected 14-15 an amendment by Dan Burton, R-Ind., that would have prohibited any U.S. funds from going to the South African Communist Party. "I do not believe the South African Communist Party should be a beneficiary of these funds," Burton said. But Harry A. Johnston, D-Fla., chairman of the Africa Subcommittee, said South Africa's communists had implicitly renounced violence. "What we want to do here is entice everybody into the democratic process," he said.

Committee members accepted by voice vote an amendment by Donald Manzullo, R-Ill., that barred U.S. aid to any organization that previously had engaged in violence and had not renounced the use of violence.

● **Public Works.** The Public Works Committee was the next to consider the bill. The committee approved HR 3225 by voice vote Oct. 26, after amending it to give 179 nonfederal entities until October 1995 to repeal their anti-apartheid ordinances or face a possible cutoff of transportation aid.

Scores of local and state governments still had their own anti-apartheid laws on the books, precluding U.S. companies based in those jurisdictions from dealing with South Africa.

The committee had jurisdiction over two sections of the bill — one that formally restored U.S. airport landing rights for South African aircraft and a second that repealed permission for states and municipal governments to institute local sanctions against South Africa.

● **Banking.** The Banking Committee approved the legislation Nov. 4 with no debate and by voice vote.

The Banking Committee's portion of the legislation repealed the requirement that U.S. representatives to the International Monetary Fund and the World Bank vote against projects to aid South Africa.

● **Ways and Means.** Finally, the Ways and Means Committee considered the bill Nov. 17. The committee had jurisdiction over sections that repealed bans on the import of products from South Africa and which removed South Africa from a list of nations that were not eligible for most-favored-nation trade status.

The committee approved the bill by voice vote.

Senate Action

On Nov. 20, the day after the House vote, the Senate approved the sanctions bill (HR 3225) by voice vote, clearing it for Clinton.

Two months earlier, the Senate had passed its own bill (S 1493) repealing the remaining U.S. economic sanctions against South Africa. The Senate passed that measure by voice vote Sept. 24, hours after Mandela urged the international community to drop all sanctions in recognition of South Africa's progress toward democracy.

The legislation, sponsored by Kassebaum and Paul Simon, D-Ill., provided for an end to U.S. restrictions on loans to South Africa by the International Monetary Fund. It also called on local and state governments to remove their sanctions in consideration of South Africa's move toward a multiracial democracy. ■

Clinton Restores Fund Aid

In one of his first acts in the White House, President Clinton on Jan. 22 signed an executive order overturning the so-called Mexico City policy, a Reagan-era prohibition on funding for international organizations that promoted abortion as a means of family planning.

Soon after, the administration lifted an 8-year-old ban on U.S. assistance for the U.N. Population Fund, which provided family planning aid in more than 100 developing nations.

The Reagan administration had cut off support for the international organization because of its involvement in China, where the government reportedly used coercion — including forced abortions — to enforce its goal of one child per family. Democrats had attached language to the fiscal 1993 foreign aid bill lifting the funding ban on the Population Fund, but they dropped the provision in the face of a veto threat from the Bush administration. *(1992 Almanac, p. 397)*

The Clinton administration followed through and requested $50 million for the U.N. fund as part of the fiscal 1994 foreign operations appropriations bill (HR 2295).

But renewed reports of brutality in China's population control program spurred controversy even among supporters of the U.N. agency, and Congress cut $10 million out of the $50 million requested, the estimated amount that would have been spent in China.

The provision also required reducing the $40 million for the U.N. agency by any amount in excess of $10 million that it budgeted for activities in China. *(Appropriations, p. 603)*

The funding was part of $392 million that Congress appropriated for the Agency for International Development's population program in fiscal 1994, an increase of $42 million over the previous year's level.

Congress retained longstanding restrictions that barred direct use of U.S. funds for abortion. ■

Warren Christopher OK'd As Secretary of State

Despite early speculation that conservative Republican Sen. Jesse Helms, N.C., would give President Clinton's Secretary of State-designate Warren Christopher a rough ride into office, the Senate Foreign Relations Committee easily approved his nomination, 19-0, on Jan. 19. The full Senate approved the nomination by voice vote the next day.

But first, Christopher, who was deputy secretary of State in President Jimmy Carter's administration, had two grueling days of testimony before the committee, after which aides to Helms submitted more than 400 additional questions in writing. In the end, neither Helms nor anyone else formally objected to the nomination.

During the Foreign Relations hearings Jan. 13 and 14, Christopher seemed determined to erase the Democratic Party's longstanding image of ineptitude in national security matters and his own reputation as an advocate of negotiation over confrontation. In crises from Iraq to Bosnia, he told panel members, the Clinton administration would not shrink from using force to buttress diplomacy.

"While there is no magic formula to guide such decisions," he told the committee, "I do believe that the discreet and careful use of force in certain circumstances — and its credible threat in general — will be essential to the success of our diplomacy and foreign policy."

At the same time, the Los Angeles corporate lawyer said there were limits to what the United States could achieve as the world's lone surviving superpower. And he indicated that U.S. strategic and moral interests in this new age — particularly those that might warrant a military defense — had yet to be fully defined. "We cannot respond to every alarm," he said, and assured the American people that "we will not turn their blood and treasure into an open account for use by the rest of the world."

As part of his mission to make sure the hearings did not become, as he put it, a "love-in," Helms exhumed the Carter foreign policy record to question Christopher, 67, at length on everything from the Iranian hostage crisis to the Panama Canal treaties. Helms also initiated a follow-up inquiry into news reports that Christopher might have known more about Army domestic surveillance operations than he told the Senate committee during his 1977 confirmation hearings. Christopher served as deputy attorney general during the Johnson administration when the Army infiltrated anti-war and civil rights groups.

But the deliberate Christopher denied any wrongdoing and managed to avoid serious damage. As the exhaustive hearings wound down, even Helms softened a bit. He told Christopher that "we're going to work with you — there is going to be no problem about that."

Christopher tried to identify himself closely with Clinton's campaign themes of change and heightened emphasis on reviving the domestic economy. He said Clinton would "elevate America's economic security as a primary goal of foreign policy," while maintaining a strong national defense and promoting the spread of democracy abroad.

In characteristically understated fashion, Christopher sought to distance Clinton from certain aspects of the previous administration's foreign policy. He implied that former President George Bush and former Secretary of State James A. Baker III had failed to heed warnings of potential trouble spots, allowing them to deteriorate.

"We cannot afford to career from crisis to crisis," Christopher said. "We must have a new diplomacy that seeks to anticipate and prevent crises like those in Iraq, Bosnia, and Somalia, rather than simply to manage them." Yet he acknowledged that the Clinton administration would be unable to distance itself from the many simmering ethnic conflicts and regional crises.

Joseph R. Biden Jr., D-Del., a proponent of the use of U.S. military force to stem Serbian aggression in Bosnia-Herzegovina, displayed particular interest in eliciting the nominee's views on the situation in that region. But aside from reiterating Clinton's support for enforcement of a "no-fly zone" that the United Nations had declared over Bosnia, Christopher refrained from offering any actions to address the crisis. "You look at Bosnia and you can see the horror of it, but the next part of the analysis is very difficult," he said.

In Bosnia, Somalia and other countries torn by strife, Christopher said he would look to the United Nations and European allies to do more than they had so far. He blasted European nations for the "abysmal way" that they had responded to the Bosnian crisis, a situation that he said cried out for multilateral action.

On the broader question of the future role of the United Nations in such conflicts, he endorsed U.N. Secretary-General Boutros Boutros-Ghali's recommendation that U.N. forces go beyond their traditional peacekeeping missions and engage in peacemaking. But he said that if the United States was to expect more from the United Nations, it would have to deliver more in the way of resources in return, and he backed a proposal to tap the Pentagon's budget for a portion of the U.S. support for such operations. *(Nomination, 1992 Almanac, p. 150-A)* ∎

Albright Approved As U.N. Envoy

The Senate on Jan. 26 gave voice vote approval to the nomination of Madeleine K. Albright as permanent representative to the United Nations, after the Senate Foreign Relations Committee unanimously approved the nomination the same day.

President Clinton boosted the prestige of Albright's post by according it Cabinet-level status. Shortly after his Jan. 20 inauguration, Clinton signed an order making Albright, who served as an aide to national security adviser Zbigniew Brzezinski during the Carter administration, a member of the National Security Council (NSC).

During her confirmation hearing before the Foreign Relations panel Jan. 21, Albright, 55, told senators that the humanitarian tragedy in Bosnia-Herzegovina was "clearly the highest priority" for both the president and the NSC. She also indicated that the administration would have little patience if U.S. allies in Europe continued to shrink from efforts to halt Serbian aggression against Bosnian Muslims. "I must say that I have watched with some amazement the fact that the Europeans have not taken action on this," Albright said. "The coalition is important to us, but we have to lead it."

She repeated Clinton's call for a war crimes tribunal to

try those responsible for atrocities in Bosnia and promised the administration would press for enforcement of the "no-fly zone" that the United Nations had declared for the embattled republic.

Albright also indicated that she would lobby Congress to pay nearly $300 million in arrearages owed to the United Nations — a sensitive issue in Congress in an era when appropriations labeled as foreign aid faced significant opposition.

Albright came to the United States in 1948. Her father, who was Czechoslovakia's ambassador to the United Nations, defected to the United States after communists seized power in their native land. Foreign Relations Committee Chairman Claiborne Pell, D-R.I., commented that Albright had come "full circle" in that she would soon represent her adopted country in the United Nations. *(Nomination, 1992 Almanac, p. 153-A)* ∎

Woolsey Confirmed for CIA

Amid warnings that the U.S. intelligence community would face deep budget cuts along with pressure to provide new services, the Senate easily confirmed President Clinton's choice for director of central intelligence, R. James Woolsey, on Feb. 3 by voice vote. The Senate Select Intelligence Committee approved his nomination on the same day by a vote of 17-0.

During Woolsey's confirmation hearing Feb. 2, Intelligence Committee members applauded the former arms negotiator as someone who would advise them on how to balance the need for budget cuts in the wake of the Cold War against emerging demands for intelligence on a range of issues, from obscure ethnic conflicts to economic and environmental threats.

As with most controversial issues brought up during the confirmation hearing, Woolsey, 51, was noncommittal about the extent and type of cuts he would seek or whether Clinton would carry out his campaign pledge to slice $5.5 billion from the intelligence budget over four years.

Sounding more like committee Republicans than his fellow Democrats, Woolsey cautioned that "the number and complexity of very serious threats" to U.S. interests had grown, not shrunk, in recent years. "In many ways, today's threats are harder to observe and understand than the one that was once presented by the U.S.S.R.," he told the committee. "Yes, we have slain a large dragon. But we live in a jungle filled with a bewildering variety of poisonous snakes."

Woolsey said he thought some savings could be found in restructuring costly intelligence satellite operations and consolidating some intelligence facilities, which were spread throughout more than a dozen agencies. However, he spoke of the need to avoid firing intelligence workers if possible, calling them "a very precious natural resource."

The intelligence director-designate came to the job with close ties to Capitol Hill. He served as general counsel to the Senate Armed Services Committee in the early 1970s and was an undersecretary of the Navy during the Carter administration. He was an arms control negotiator for the Reagan administration and led the U.S. negotiating team for the Bush administration on a treaty to reduce arms and conventional forces in Europe.

The confirmation hearings were held under extremely tight security because of the shooting deaths a week earlier of two CIA workers near the agency's headquarters in McLean, Va. *(Nomination, 1992 Almanac, p. 154-A)* ∎

APPROPRIATIONS

Domestic Spending Agenda Modified

In 1993, Congress provided for future outlays to decline, something that had not happened since the late '60s

President Clinton came into office in 1993 with ambitious plans to "invest" in a domestic policy agenda that ranged from science, commerce and crime-fighting to education, rural development and highway construction.

But he quickly ran up against an inescapable reality: The $1.5 trillion budget universe was no longer expanding — at least, not the sector that the president and his allies in Congress could readily get to from year to year. Strict budgetary limits first enacted in 1990 already were pressing spending downward when Clinton got to the White House, and a Congress with a nervous eye on the 1994 elections accelerated the push.

For fiscal 1993, Democrats managed to find money for much of what they wanted to do — enough, for instance, for above-inflation increases in five of the 13 regular appropriations bills. In the case of the Interior spending bill, for instance, the 9.6 percent bump from fiscal 1993 to 1994 was nearly triple the inflation rate.

Among the beneficiaries were many of Clinton's "investment" programs, the nearly $17 billion in 1994 spending Clinton targeted at the beginning of the year for top priority treatment from Congress. Clinton got about 69 percent of what he asked for, according to the White House's Office of Management and Budget, including money for about 90 separate proposals in education, health, research and development, highways and railroads, housing, environmental protection and other areas.

But increases such as these came only after Congress found offsetting reductions in other bills — mainly from defense and foreign aid, but also from other domestic accounts. Five domestic bills may have gotten healthy increases, but five others were either cut below fiscal 1993 levels or got increases too small to keep up with inflation.

The result was evident in the bottom line: For the first time since appropriations were kept at bay in the post-Vietnam War build-down years of the late 1960s and early 1970s, outlays for discretionary spending — the one-third of the federal budget over which Congress had annual discretion — all but stopped growing. The $541.4 billion that was to move out of the Treasury in fiscal 1994 was just $600 million more than was spent in 1993 — an increase of one-tenth of 1 percent at a time when inflation was running a little more than 3 percent. And decisions Congress made in 1993 provided for future discretionary outlays to decline, something that had not happened since the last budget year of Lyndon B. Johnson's presidency, 1969.

A Hard Freeze

As part of the 1993 budget-reconciliation act (HR 2264 — PL 103-66), Democrats and Republicans agreed to impose a "freeze" on appropriations outlays through 1998. That was a *hard* freeze, not allowing increases to keep up with inflation, which meant there would not be enough money to cover the same value of services in fiscal 1995 that the government provided in fiscal 1994, much less expand them. Clinton and Congress could obligate new money in slightly increasing increments over the following five years, but they had to do so in a way that did not increase year-to-year outlays from the Treasury over the same period.

Backers of Clinton's investment plans hoped that continued deep cuts in other programs, especially defense, would provide enough breathing room under the spending limits to keep overall domestic spending growing at roughly the rate of inflation for the next five years.

But that was a risky bet that depended heavily on the world remaining a relatively stable place. Even with no major conflicts directly involving the United States, the U.S. military was deploying various-sized peacekeeping and humanitarian supply forces to Somalia, Haiti and Bosnia, and the costs were beginning to make defense appropriators extremely uncomfortable.

John P. Murtha, D-Pa., chairman of the House Defense Appropriations Subcommittee, said that if defense spending was to stay on a sharp downward path without eviscerating training and readiness, every deployment should have its own supplemental spending bill to pay for it, with the money designated as emergency funding outside the spending limits. But it seemed doubtful that Congress would agree to that, meaning that funds would generally have to be found somewhere within the appropriations account.

Fiscal 1994 Cuts

Battered by public criticism of their big-spending ways — and driven by freshman members who had campaigned on pledges of fiscal austerity — the House and Senate began to make difficult choices they might never have contemplated even a year before, including ending some programs that had warded off repeated death threats. The result was a tough year for all sorts of spending:

● **Pump-priming.** Clinton's first appropriations initiative — the $16 billion jobs "stimulus" package that was supposed to be the down payment on his investment agenda — died in the Senate when lockstep Republican opposition and a swing group of rebellious Democrats combined to kill it.

● **Emergency spending.** Over the summer, midyear supplemental appropriations bills that would have skated through Congress in previous years suddenly ran into trouble. Lawmakers insisted that the Pentagon find ways to offset part of the cost of the U.S. military deployment to Somalia. And a bill to help victims of devastating Midwestern flooding stalled for five days in the House in a battle over how to pay for it.

● **Big projects.** Congress killed two projects that had avoided the budget knife for years: the $11 billion superconducting super collider, a Texas-based "big science" project, and the $3.7 billion Advanced Solid Rocket Motor, a NASA project based in Mississippi.

● **Last-minute cuts.** Just before adjourning for the year, the House voted 429-1 for a bill (HR 3400) to cut $37 billion over the coming five years, mostly from discretionary ac-

Continuing Resolutions Keep Uncle Sam Afloat

Congress was able to complete action on only two of the 13 regular appropriations bills for fiscal 1994 by the Oct. 1 start of the fiscal year — those for the Legislative Branch (HR 2348) and Foreign Operations (HR 2295).

A variety of disputes slowed action: A disagreement between authorizers and appropriators stalled the Transportation measure (HR 2750) in the House; grazing fees and federal land-use policy held up the Interior bill (HR 2520) until November; Defense (HR 3116) was difficult to complete because the parallel authorization bill was bogged down over the issues of homosexuals in the military and the U.S. roles in Somalia and Haiti.

To keep the government in business, Congress had to act on three continuing appropriations resolutions (CRs):

• The first (H J Res 267 — PL 103-88) kept money flowing to agencies through Oct. 21, by which time three more regular appropriations bills were enacted — for Agriculture (HR 2493), Labor, Health and Human Services, and Education (HR 2518) and Military Construction (HR 2446). The House passed the measure 274-156; the Senate cleared it by voice vote. *(Vote 464, p. 114-H)*

Cleared Sept. 29, the continuing resolution provided funding for agencies and departments at the lowest of three levels: current spending or the figure in either the House- or Senate-passed bill.

The stopgap bill also included a provision designed to enforce the Clinton administration's February executive order to reduce the size of the federal bureaucracy by 4 percent over three years, starting with a 1 percent cutback in fiscal 1993. At least for the duration of the resolution, departments were not allowed to pay for personnel beyond 99 percent of the level they had before the order was issued. An Appropriations Committee aide said the language was intended to signal the executive branch that Congress wanted the downsizing enforced.

• The second continuing resolution (H J Res 281 — PL 103-113) cleared Oct. 21 and was good for a week. The House and Senate each approved the measure by voice vote. Some Republican senators had threatened to load down a second CR with controversial amendments, such as a proposal to repeal retroactive tax increase provisions in the 1993 budget-reconciliation bill that passed in August. But when the time came, Sen. Phil Gramm, R-Texas, said he would instead focus his amendments on an upcoming bill to extend unemployment benefits. *(Unemployment, p. 392)*

• The third CR (H J Res 283 — PL 103-128), was cleared Oct. 28, and provided temporary funding until midnight Nov. 10. The measure was intended to give Congress time to complete the Interior and Defense measures, the only ones then outstanding. The House approved the measure 256-157; the Senate cleared it by voice vote. *(Vote 536, p. 130-H)*

The House approved its last appropriations bill, for defense, on Sept. 30. The Senate cleared the bill Nov. 10.

---

counts. About $33 billion of that was supposed to come from adding the force of law to a Clinton administration plan to force the federal work force to shed 252,000 jobs.

The common thread in almost all of this was the focus on appropriations. Except for the tax increases and entitlement cuts that Congress adopted as part of the five-year reconciliation bill, all of the deficit reduction Congress approved in 1993 came out of the one-third of the budget controlled by the appropriators. That was at least in part because it was so easy to go after discretionary spending and so hard to go after everything else.

The appropriators tried, largely in vain, to shift attention to mandatory spending, which was expected to grow at 6.2 percent a year through 1997. But Clinton was determined to earmark cutbacks in Medicare and Medicaid to fund Clinton's health-care reform plan, which could leave the two biggest engines of entitlement growth effectively off-limits for deficit reduction. That left appropriations as the easiest way for Congress to prove its devotion to deficit reduction. "You've got an austerity mood in the Congress, in the country ... and in the White House," said Allen Schick, a Brookings Institution visiting fellow and an expert on the budget. "Ask members of Congress what they can do about it and they say, 'Appropriations....' "

Savings Not for Deficit Reduction

Deficit hawks wanted to "lock in" the cuts for deficit reduction by simultaneously lowering the spending limits, rather than merely freeing the money to be spent for something else. But Congress elected not to do that, and some of what looked like deficit reduction in 1993 was, in effect, just Congress reordering priorities in domestic spending.

For example, when Congress voted to kill the superconducting super collider and the Advanced Solid Rocket Motor, in neither case did the savings go to reduce the borrowing that created the deficit. In both cases, a substantial part of the money that would have been spent on the project would have to be spent for termination costs.

In the case of the rocket motor, some of the money freed by shutting down the project was immediately shifted to four other programs. And after the super collider's substantial termination costs were paid, the money that otherwise would have gone to fund that project over the next several years was expected to be parceled out to other, smaller-scale programs.

Sen. Phil Gramm, R-Texas, a supporter of the Texas-based atom smasher, tried but failed Oct. 27 to win a procedural vote that would have opened the way to lowering the caps to lock most of the project's savings in as deficit reduction. "When we voted on that project, and when it was killed in the Congress, those who voted against it did not say, 'Let us cut it to fund education,' " Gramm said. "They did not say, 'Let us cut it to fund roads.' They did not say, 'Let us cut it to fund bridges.' They did not say, 'Let us cut it to fund environment.' They said, 'Let us kill the SSC to reduce the deficit.' "

Gramm needed 60 votes to waive congressional budget rules and permit a vote on lowering the spending limits, and while he won a majority, he fell short of the required supermajority. When Gramm's amendment fell, 58-39, Senate Appropriations Committee Chairman Robert C. Byrd, D-W.Va., did not celebrate the victory. "We are going to have more and more and more of these amendments," he said. "I hope the Senate will reject them more and more and more, each time." ∎

Appropriations Mileposts
103rd Congress — First Session

Bill	House	Senate	Final	Story
Agriculture and related agencies (HR 2493 — PL 103-111)	Passed 6/29/93	Passed 7/27/93	Cleared 10/15/93 Signed 10/21/93	540
Commerce, Justice, State (HR 2519 — PL 103-121)	Passed 7/20/93	Passed 7/29/93	Cleared 10/21/93 Signed 10/27/93	555
Defense (HR 3116 — PL 103-139)	Passed 9/30/93	Passed 10/21/93	Cleared 11/10/93 Signed 11/11/93	569
District of Columbia (HR 2492 — PL 103-127)	Passed 6/30/93	Passed 7/27/93	Cleared 10/27/93 Signed 10/29/93	584
Energy and Water Development (HR 2445 — PL 103-126)	Passed 6/24/93	Passed 9/30/93	Cleared 10/27/93 Signed 10/28/93	589
Foreign Operations (HR 2295 — PL 103-87)	Passed 6/17/93	Passed 9/23/93	Cleared 9/30/93 Signed 9/30/93	603
Interior and related agencies (HR 2520 — PL 103-138)	Passed 7/15/93	Passed 9/15/93	Cleared 11/9/93 Signed 11/11/93	618
Labor, Health and Human Services, Education (HR 2518 — PL 103-112)	Passed 6/30/93	Passed 9/29/93	Cleared 10/18/93 Signed 10/21/93	632
Legislative Branch (HR 2348 — PL 103-69)	Passed 6/10/93	Passed 7/23/93	Cleared 8/7/93 Signed 8/11/93	646
Military Construction (HR 2446 — PL 103-110)	Passed 6/23/93	Passed 9/30/93	Cleared 10/19/93 Signed 10/21/93	657
Transportation and related agencies (HR 2750 — PL 103-122)	Passed 9/23/93	Passed 10/6/93	Cleared 10/21/93 Signed 10/27/93	663
Treasury, Postal Service, General Government (HR 2403 — PL 103-123)	Passed 6/22/93	Passed 8/3/93	Cleared 10/26/93 Signed 10/28/93	679
Veterans Affairs, Housing and Urban Development, Independent Agencies (HR 2491 — PL 103-124)	Passed 6/29/93	Passed 9/22/93	Cleared 10/21/93 Signed 10/28/93	691
Fiscal 1993 'Stimulus' Supplemental (HR 1335 — PL 103-24)	Passed 3/19/93	Passed 4/21/93	Cleared 4/22/93 Signed 4/23/93	706
Fiscal 1993 Spring Supplemental (HR 2118 — PL 103-50)	Passed 5/26/93	Passed 6/22/93	Cleared 7/1/93 Signed 7/2/93	710
Fiscal 1993 Disaster-Assistance Supplemental (HR 2667 — PL 103-75)	Passed 7/27/93	Passed 8/4/93	Cleared 8/6/93 Signed 8/12/93	714

APPROPRIATIONS IN PERSPECTIVE

(Fiscal 1994, outlays in billions of dollars)

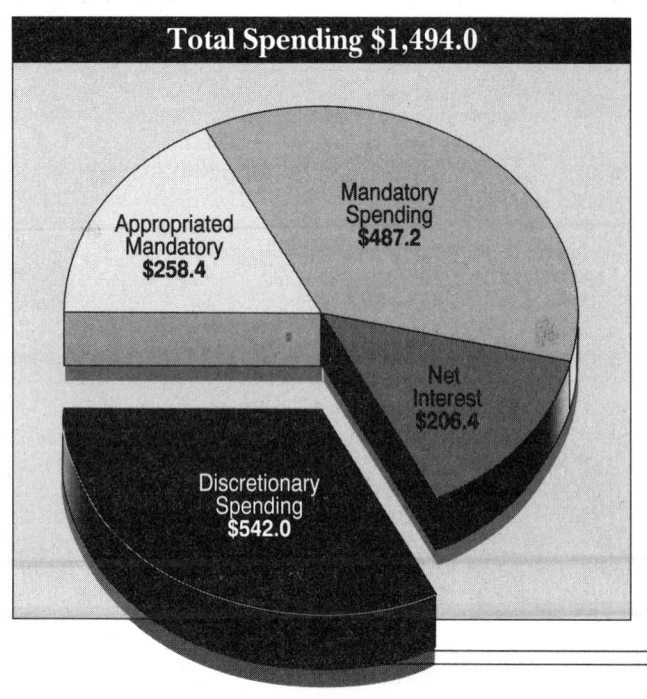

Total Spending $1,494.0

- Mandatory Spending **$487.2**
- Appropriated Mandatory **$258.4**
- Net Interest **$206.4**
- Discretionary Spending **$542.0**

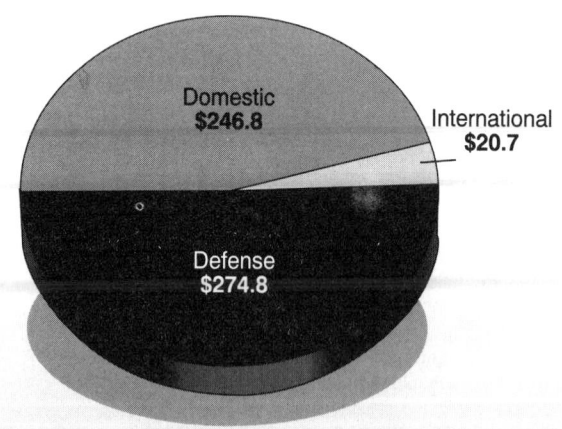

Spending Categories

- Domestic **$246.8**
- International **$20.7**
- Defense **$274.8**

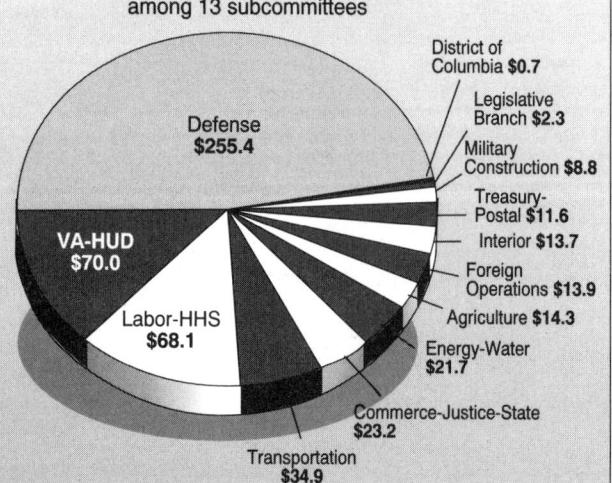

Subcommittee Allocations

Appropriations divide spending among 13 subcommittees

- Defense **$255.4**
- VA-HUD **$70.0**
- Labor-HHS **$68.1**
- Transportation **$34.9**
- Commerce-Justice-State **$23.2**
- Energy-Water **$21.7**
- Agriculture **$14.3**
- Foreign Operations **$13.9**
- Interior **$13.7**
- Treasury-Postal **$11.6**
- Military Construction **$8.8**
- Legislative Branch **$2.3**
- District of Columbia **$0.7**

Total Spending: Only about one-third of the federal budget is "discretionary" spending – money that Congress appropriates every year as it sees fit. About half the budget pie is classified as "mandatory" spending, over which appropriators have little or no control; some of these programs are funded through annual spending bills, but most need no yearly appropriation.

An additional 14 percent of federal spending is consumed by interest payments on the national debt.

Spending Categories: Congress and the White House have taken to dividing discretionary spending into three categories: defense, international and domestic. In the recent past, congressional budget rules prohibited appropriators from taking money from one category to increase another. Those rules no longer apply, and appropriators are looking to defense and foreign aid cuts to help pay for domestic initiatives.

Subcommittee Allocations: The House and Senate Appropriations committees divide the total amount available for discretionary spending among their 13 subcommittees. The allocations do not necessarily coincide with the spending categories. The Defense subcommittees control the bulk of defense spending, but other subcommittees handle some defense-related programs, such as nuclear weapons research (Energy-Water) and base closings (Military Construction).

Conversely, some areas of government can be spread out among several subcommittees. The Energy Department receives funding from three bills – Energy-Water, Interior and Defense – while foreign aid programs can be found in Commerce-Justice-State and Agriculture as well as Foreign Operations.

SOURCE: President's budget, Office of Management and Budget, Appropriations committees

Jamie L. Whitten, D-Miss. — who used supplementals as vehicles for individual members' pet projects — and Presidents Ronald Reagan and George Bush, who wanted to give the CCC open-ended spending authority to obviate the need for supplemental funding.

Whitten was able to parry administration efforts to provide the CCC with such a "permanent" appropriation. But recent improvements in the farm economy had rendered the point moot, as the CCC had not even come close to exceeding its borrowing limit.

Federal Crop Insurance Corporation

The Federal Crop Insurance Corporation (FCIC) existed to help farmers cope financially when natural disasters destroyed their crops. The FCIC made payments to premium-paying policyholders to cover a portion of the dollar value of the lost crops.

To encourage participation, the FCIC paid subsidies to farmers equaling 30 percent of the cost of buying crop insurance. The insurance was provided by private companies and underwritten by the FCIC, which also made payments to the private insurers to cover a portion of their administrative costs. Policy losses were apportioned between private insurers and the federal government.

Crop insurance costs were established through an eligibility formula and thus did not fall within the discretion of appropriators. The bill provided $525.9 million for this program in fiscal 1994.

The FCIC was created in 1938 after catastrophic drought forced farmers off lands in the Midwest's legendary "dust bowl." It was greatly expanded by a 1980 law, which aimed to use crop insurance as a substitute for the deficit-boosting emergency appropriations that Congress usually passed in the wake of natural disasters.

By 1993, the crop insurance program had failed to replace emergency appropriations. Most farmers continued to bet against being hit by a disaster rather than pay insurance premiums. Crop insurance policies covered less than 40 percent of the eligible farm acreage nationwide. This low participation rate had contributed to the program's lack of actuarial soundness: Since its expansion in 1980, the program had lost nearly $1.50 for every $1 that it had earned in premiums.

The non-participants' mind-set was reinforced when Congress rushed in to provide aid payments to farmers — both insured and uninsured — in the event of a natural disaster. This occurred again after the Midwest floods, but it spurred an outcry for reform to increase participation in the program.

Congress did not debate reform in the context of the fiscal 1994 agriculture spending bill. In fact, it acted to limit participation by some farmers, whom critics accused of abusing the crop insurance program.

The effort was led by House Agriculture Appropriations Subcommittee Chairman Richard J. Durbin, D-Ill., who said some farmers purposely planted crops doomed to fail because they were ill-suited to the region or which they had no intention of cultivating, seeking to claim disaster losses under their crop insurance policies.

Durbin obtained a provision in the fiscal 1994 measure that barred participation in the crop insurance program by farmers of particular crops in counties where those crops had failed 70 percent of the time since 1980 and in which the loss ratio exceeded $1.10 for each $1 paid in premiums.

The bill also reduced, from 32 percent to 31 percent, the cap on federal reimbursements to private reinsurance companies to pay for administrative expenses.

Other Agriculture Programs

▶ **Soil Conservation Service.** This New Deal-era agriculture program was created in 1935. It was the first legislation that linked eligibility for federal financial support to a farmer's use of practices that conserved soil and water.

Congress appropriated $916 million for the program in fiscal 1994. The money was funneled through the Soil Conservation Service's 3,000 county field offices, where government experts helped land users design and apply conservation techniques —

dams, windbreaks, terraces, irrigation systems and ponds — that improved water quality, preserved wetlands and topsoil, and reduced flooding.

The service's six programs typically attracted earmarks by members seeking to ensure funding for projects in their states and districts. For example, the watershed and flood prevention operations account included earmarks totaling $11.7 million for six projects in West Virginia, the home state of Senate Appropriations Committee Chairman Robert C. Byrd, D. In the conservation operations programs, the Senate listed 15 earmarks, including four in Arkansas, home state of Senate Agriculture Appropriations Subcommittee Chairman Dale Bumpers, D, and a $500,000 allotment for the Appalachian Soil and Water Conservation Laboratory in Beckley, W.Va. The House put six earmarks in the section.

▶ **Agricultural Stabilization and Conservation Service (ASCS).** The ASCS administered the farm subsidy and price support programs of the Agriculture Department and the CCC. In addition, the agency administered seven of the department's conservation programs.

By far, the largest of these was the Conservation Reserve Program. Under the program, the federal government paid farmers to take erodible land out of production for 10 years and plant cover crops that discouraged erosion. Established by Congress in 1985, it quickly burgeoned into the most expensive of the government's rural conservation programs.

By the end of fiscal 1992, nearly 377,000 contracts were let, temporarily retiring nearly 36.5 million acres of farmland. The fiscal 1994 bill provided $1.7 billion for payments under these contracts, well over half the bill's $3 billion for all conservation programs.

However, Congress in recent years had grown skeptical of the program's cost-effectiveness. The House report to the fiscal 1994 spending bill focused on the fact that the government was spending large sums for what amounted to 10-year rentals of the contracted land — the first of these contracts was due to expire in 1995 — while some of the other conservation programs provided the government with permanent easements. As a result, Congress barred additional sign-ups to the Conservation Reserve Program for fiscal 1994, as it had in fiscal 1993.

The ASCS also administered the Agricultural Conservation Program, for which Congress had provided $194.7 million in fiscal 1994. The program had a variety of cost-sharing arrangements for farmers to help them restore and improve soil fertility, reduce erosion and conserve water on land.

Among the House earmarks for the Agricultural Conservation Program was a $220,000 allotment for a project to reduce levels of the farm chemical atrazine in three lakes in Durbin's House district. The Senate report earmarked $2 million for the Lake Champlain water quality project, a priority of Patrick J. Leahy, D-Vt., chairman of the Senate Agriculture Committee and a member of the Appropriations Committee.

The third-largest ASCS conservation program was the Wetlands Reserve Program. Created as part of the 1990 farm bill, the program, which authorized the government to buy easements that took environmentally fragile wetlands permanently out of farm production, grew by fits and starts. During its first two years, a pilot program retired 50,000 acres in nine states. However, no funding was provided in fiscal 1993.

President Clinton, who campaigned on an environmentalist platform, aimed to change that, proposing in his fiscal 1994 budget to spend $370.3 million on the program, eight times more than its total cost to that date. Congress pared that greatly but still provided the Wetlands Reserve Program with its biggest kitty ever: $66.7 million to purchase easements in 20 states, including the nine in the pilot program.

The Wetlands Reserve Program had eclipsed the older but similar Water Bank Program. Describing it as duplicative, the Senate tried to eliminate the Water Bank Program from the fiscal 1994 bill. Although it ultimately survived, the program was cut to $8 million from the fiscal 1993 $18.6 million.

Congress scrapped the Emergency Conservation Program, which shared the costs of assisting farmers in rehabilitating land damaged by natural disasters. The program received $33 million in fiscal 1993.

▶ **Agricultural Research Service.** The Agricultural Research Service was responsible for conducting basic, applied and developmental research on soil and water conservation, plant and animal productivity and genetics, and human nutrition.

Most of the agency's $692.5 million budget for operations went to federal agricultural research laboratories, as well as to private and state universities conducting the research. Of that amount, $16.8 million was earmarked for specific projects. The agency parceled out the rest of the money based on existing research priorities and on competitive grants.

However, the buildings and facilities fund provided more fertile ground for members' parochial interests. All $32.7 million in this section was dedicated to specific federal and private research facilities.

In most cases in which the House and Senate provided different levels for a fiscal 1994 building project, the conference committee split the difference. There was one major exception, though. Congress approved the House's $1.4 million for a subtropical agriculture lab in Weslaco, Texas, even though the Senate had provided no funding. The lab was in the district of House Agriculture Committee Chairman E. "Kika" de la Garza, a Democrat.

▶ **Cooperative State Research Service.** The CSRS, which supported research projects funded jointly by the Agriculture Department, the states' land grant schools and private-sector agribusiness, received less funding than the Agricultural Research Service. The fiscal 1994 bill provided $453.7 million for program operations and $56.9 million for its buildings and facilities fund.

However, the CSRS carried a much larger load of congressional earmarks than the Agricultural Research Service. The bill provided $72.9 million for earmarked special research grants. The money was divided among 134 specified projects, which filled up 2½ small-type pages in the bill's conference report.

Nearly all of the money in the buildings and facilities fund was earmarked. The Clinton administration had proposed to eliminate this account to provide savings. But the lure of "science pork" proved enduring to members, who increased the program's funding by $4.8 million over fiscal 1993 levels.

▶ **Animal and Plant Health Inspection Service.** A total of $449.7 million in fiscal 1994 went to this agency, which monitored animal and plant health and conducted programs to control and eradicate agricultural pests and diseases. The agency also regulated animal care at research facilities and inspected cargoes coming into the United States to prevent the introduction of exotic diseases.

One of Durbin's first priorities as House Agriculture Appropriations Subcommittee chairman was to defend as necessary the agency's research programs, many of which focused on farm pests with unusual names — such as pink bollworm, scrapie and screwworm — that often were mocked by "deficit hawks" looking for programs to cut from the federal budget.

Although not as earmarked as the Agriculture Research Service and the Cooperative State Research Service, the animal and plant inspection agency had a handful of programs that reflected members' particular interests. For example, the fiscal 1994 bill maintained a $100,000 project to control blackbirds that preyed on sunflower crops in North Dakota, a favorite earmark of the late Senate Agriculture Appropriations Subcommittee Chairman Quentin N. Burdick, D-N.D., who died Sept. 8, 1992. It also provided an additional $100,000 to control blackbird depredation of rice in Arkansas and corn in Illinois.

▶ **Food Safety and Inspection Service.** When he took office in January 1993, Agriculture Secretary Mike Espy was confronted with a food-poisoning outbreak caused by tainted meat served by a fast-food chain in the Pacific Northwest. Subsequently, he made improving the government's meat inspection program one of his top priorities.

Congress cooperated by appropriating $516.7 million, $22.9 million more than in fiscal 1993, for the Food Safety and Inspection Service, which inspected meat and poultry slaughter and processing facilities to make sure meat was free from contamination when it came to market. The extra funds were to be used to hire additional inspectors for the more than 6,000 slaughter and processing plants in the United States.

The food inspection service funding also included $8 million for Espy's Pathogen Reduction Program, which sought to improve scientific measurements of potential illness-causing microbes in meat. Espy sought to improve this science-based approach to replace the traditional visual methods of inspecting meat carcasses. Most bacterial contaminants were too small to be observed by the naked eye. High-speed slaughter technology had reduced the scrutiny given to each animal carcass. It was routine in poultry plants for 40 to 60 carcasses a minute to move down the line, making it difficult, some critics said, for inspectors to do much more than eyeball each bird.

Although Congress provided more money for the food inspection service, it rejected all but $1 million of the Clinton administration's proposal to recoup $104 million through an increase in user fees paid by the inspected meat plants. The bill reports cited the lack of legislative authorization for such fees.

▶ **Extension Service.** The best known of the outreach programs operated by the Agriculture Department, the Extension Service received $434.6 million in fiscal 1994. The nearly 15,000 county extension agents in 3,150 counties across the country taught rural residents everything from how to apply pesticides to how to start a home sewing business.

For decades, the Extension Service was the primary contact farmers in remote rural areas had with the outside world. It provided information on the latest farming methods and on home economics to people who lived far from the hubs of mass communication.

In 1993, however, rural residents had near-universal access to radio and television, and an increasing number had personal computers. This led some members of Congress to question whether the Extension Service needed to be as ubiquitous as it had been. The House report called on the Agriculture secretary to consider merging some county offices into regional offices as part of his effort to reorganize and downsize his department's unwieldy bureaucracy.

▶ **National Agricultural Statistics Service.** The Agriculture Department agency was given $81.8 million in fiscal 1994 to spend on gathering statistics on production, supply, price and other aspects of the agricultural economy. The statistics, which were gathered by employees throughout the country and released in weekly and monthly reports by the agency, were treated as gospel by futures market analysts who used the information to forecast crop yields and market prices. They were also used by farmers, Congress and the Agriculture Department to estimate the size of U.S. crop subsidies.

▶ **Economic Research Service.** Federal budget economics nicked the Agriculture Department's own think tank of economists and academic experts. The Economics Research Service received $55.2 million in the fiscal 1994 bill, down $3.5 million from fiscal 1993.

The agency's experts analyzed economic and other social science information on agricultural prices, world markets, crop production, the rural economy and related issues. The information was disseminated to the general public through technical papers, professional journals, general-readership magazines and direct computer access. An additional $2.6 million went to the World Agricultural Outlook Board, which provided estimates of foreign crop conditions. Those, in turn, allowed government analysts to forecast the impact of world supply on U.S. farm prices and exports. The agency's information came from an array of sources, including the CIA, and was considered a cornerstone of the country's economic intelligence as well as a critical factor in establishing the prices of U.S. commodities.

▶ **Agricultural Marketing Service.** The $73.7 million appropriation for this agency helped promote the sale of U.S. commodities through an array of programs. One of its largest activities involved the distribution of nearly $400 million of food annually for the federally run school lunch program. It also collected information on the supply, inventories and prices of agricultural farm goods for the commodity trade.

The service also ran the program that set the standards that enabled food and fiber products to earn the familiar "USDA Grade A" seal. However, some members questioned whether taxpayer funds should be used to set esoteric standards — such as the size of pickle stems — that mainly benefited the industries that used the Agricultural Marketing Service. The House report called on the agency to develop a program of user fees for such services.

▶ **National Agricultural Library.** Established in tandem with the Agriculture Department in 1862, the National Agricultural Library was one of three national libraries funded by Congress. (The others were the Library of Congress and the National Library of Medicine.) Its headquarters in Beltsville, Md., north of Washington, held 2.2 million volumes. Its fiscal 1994 appropriation was $18.2 million.

RURAL DEVELOPMENT PROGRAMS

Two Agriculture Department agencies, the Farmers Home Administration (FmHA) and Rural Electrification Administration (REA), administered the bulk of the money the government spent on housing and economic development in rural America. Both agencies were rooted in the Great Depression, when farmers, especially in the rural South, could not get credit from financially troubled private banks.

The FmHA's mission was to extend loans to farmers to buy farms and finance their operations. It became known as the "lender of last resort" for farmers who could not get credit from commercial banks or the quasi-governmental Farm Credit System.

The REA's mission was to finance electric and telephone service to rural communities where private companies were reluctant to do business.

During the farm crisis of the early 1980s, the FmHA lost billions when thousands of farmers defaulted on their loans. The Reagan and Bush administrations, to bring the agency's costs under control, wanted Congress to stop making direct loans to farmers and instead to guarantee loans made by private lenders.

Although Congress in the 1985 farm bill and again in the 1990 budget agreement approved a gradual shift in loan policy from direct to guaranteed loans, the Appropriations committees were slow to pursue that course as aggressively as the administrations wanted. However, the ratio of guaranteed loans to direct loans gradually increased.

Farmers Home Administration

The FmHA operated four "revolving loan" accounts for farm lending. The Appropriations committees set limits on the amount of loans that could be issued from each account. In the past, the appropriation for each account reflected the difference between the amount of loans issued each year and the amount repaid from previous years, with Congress making up the losses incurred from subsidizing interest rates or when borrowers failed to repay loans. Critics of these and other credit programs throughout the federal government charged that this procedure never gave an accurate picture of the actual government subsidy in the loan programs, because Congress could (and often did) appropriate less than was actually needed during the fiscal year, forcing the FmHA to use its borrowing authority to cover the remaining losses.

The 1990 Credit Reform Act (PL 101-508) established new accounting practices for revolving loan accounts such as those administered by the FmHA. The 1993 agriculture spending bill continued to establish loan ceilings for each revolving account, but the actual appropriation reflected Congress' estimate of the current and future losses, called the loan subsidy. This was supposed to provide a more accurate reflection of the government's year-to-year liability.

▶ **Agricultural Credit Insurance Fund.** Congress authorized the ACIF in fiscal 1994 to make direct and guaranteed loans of up to $3.6 billion, which required an appropriation of $199 million to cover the estimated loan subsidies. The total appropriation, including salaries and other expenses, was $474.4 million.

The agency's biggest programs helped farmers finance their farm operations and to purchase, improve and maintain ownership of farmland. The fund also provided large loan pools to finance credit sales of government-acquired farm property and to provide emergency disaster aid. Smaller programs included loans for soil and water conservation; Indian tribe land acquisition; watershed protection and flood prevention; and resource conservation.

▶ **Rural Development Insurance Fund.** The bill authorized the fund to finance up to $1.4 billion in loans, requiring an appropriation of $143.6 million to cover the loan subsidy. The total appropriation for this account was $201.8 million.

This fund provided loans to rural communities to improve water and sewer systems and build community facilities such as firehouses, health clinics and centers that provided social and cultural services. This fund authorized $249.4 million in guaranteed loans for industrial development projects.

▶ **Rural Housing Insurance Fund.** This program provided loans to the following entities: low-income rural residents to build and repair homes and rent houses; farm owners, private organizations and public agencies to build farm labor housing; developers of low- and moderate-income, rental and cooperative housing; and credit purchasers of government-acquired property. Loan programs were limited to communities of fewer than 20,000 people. The bill authorized up to $3.3 billion in loans, with an appropriation of $718.6 million for the loan subsidies. The total appropriation was $1.6 billion.

▶ **Rural Development Loan Fund Program Account.** The fiscal 1994 bill authorized the program to lend $100 million to small investment groups, which in turn would relend the money to public and private entities involved in economic development and diversification in rural areas. An appropriation of $56 million was made for loan subsidies. The total appropriation was $57.5 million.

The Senate report requested that fund administrators consider loan applications by Maine cranberry growers, an item of interest to Senate Majority Leader George J. Mitchell, D-Maine.

▶ **Miscellaneous grant programs.** The bill appropriated $639.8 million for a grab bag of FmHA grant programs. By far, the largest was the rural water and waste disposal program, which received $500 million in fiscal 1994, an increase of $75 million over fiscal 1993. This increase was largely offset, however, by a $50 million cut in the emergency community water assistance grant program, which had a $10 million appropriation in fiscal 1994.

Other grant programs included those for home repair for the elderly poor, community fire protection facilities, home rehabilitation for low-income families and outreach for socially disadvantaged farmers. A $42.5 million rural development grant program was another font for congressional earmarks.

Rural Electrification Administration

The REA was created by an executive order of President Roosevelt in 1935 to bring electricity to rural America. Before its creation, many rural residents literally were left in the dark, because utility companies deemed it too costly to wire expansive but sparsely populated regions.

Beginning in 1949, the REA also began subsidizing telephone service for rural communities. Much of the money dispersed by the REA went to electric and telephone cooperatives created to provide such services.

The REA long since had accomplished its mission of providing electricity and telephone service to nearly all rural Americans, raising questions among some members of Congress as to whether the agency was still needed. But REA advocates emphasized that it continued to provide loans to companies that maintained and

replaced aging power lines and helped rural areas keep up with the rapid advances in telephone technology.

REA officials also were trying to gain a lead role in adapting telecommunications technology to connect undercapitalized rural schools and hospitals with major urban centers and universities. In fiscal 1994, Congress doubled the appropriation for the REA's Distance Learning and Medical Link program from $5 million to $10 million.

The REA also provided low-interest loans to companies that conducted rural economic development and job creation activities. Some of its backers wanted to remake the REA as the nation's superagency for rural development.

▶ **Rural Electrification and Telephone Loans.** Interest rates on REA loans were set at 5 percent or pegged to current Treasury rates or municipal bond rates. Under this program, the REA was authorized in fiscal 1994 to make $1.54 billion in loans for electric service and $418 million for telephone service, for a total of $1.96 billion. The $112.4 million appropriation for this account included $82.4 million for the estimated loan subsidies.

▶ **Rural Telephone Bank.** This program, created in 1971, had somewhat different criteria from the REA telephone loan program. It was designed as an incentive for companies that were too well-financed to qualify for the very low-interest loans offered through the REA's Electrification and Telephone Revolving Loan Fund. The loans provided through the Rural Telephone Bank offered less of a subsidy and had been used by such telecommunications giants as General Telephone & Electric.

The bill authorized up to $199.8 million in loans in this account, appropriating $3.1 million to cover the loan subsidies. The total appropriation is $11.9 million.

▶ **Rural Economic Development.** This program allowed some of the unused money in the REA loan account to be used by REA borrowers for rural economic development programs and job creation projects. The bill authorized up to $13 million in loans, with an appropriation of $3.4 million for the loan subsidies.

FOOD AND NUTRITION PROGRAMS

These Agriculture Department programs accounted for $39.5 billion, or 55 percent, of the bill's cost. The biggest item went to pay for the food stamps program. In 1993, about 27.3 million people received food stamps, and that number was expected to stay essentially the same in 1994.

Food stamps and the school lunch program were created as pilot programs in part to dispose of surplus food. Recognizing the potential for political benefits, President Lyndon B. Johnson took what had been a modest demonstration program under President John F. Kennedy and turned it into a pillar of his Great Society. The nutrition programs turned out to be a boon for farm-state legislators, who needed to protect controversial farm programs from an increasingly urban Congress. A new constituency base — the urban poor — joined the traditional farm coalition when farm and nutrition programs were married in the same bill.

The continued expansion of nutrition programs was why farm bills regularly passed the urbanized House by wide margins. The 1990 budget agreement placed the food stamps program under the "mandatory" spending category, joining the school lunch program. That meant that any citizen who met the eligibility criteria could get them, so Congress had little discretion over annual funding levels. However, House Chairman Durbin, like Whitten before him, maintained that appropriators still had the final say and tried to exert some control over spending levels.

Food Stamps

The bill provided $28.1 billion for fiscal 1994, which was $2.5 billion less than the Agriculture Department's request. The difference was that the Clinton administration recommended that $5 billion be set aside as a reserve for unanticipated benefits; Congress only appropriated $2.5 billion for a reserve. The House report noted that the $2.5 billion reserve appropriated for fiscal 1993 was

not used. If the economy performed worse than expected, keeping more people out of work and raising the need for food stamps in fiscal 1994, the reserve would be tapped. If additional funds were still needed, the department would have to seek a supplemental appropriation from Congress.

The recession spurred food stamp appropriations to double between fiscal 1989 and 1993. More than one in 10 United States residents, about 27.3 million people, received food stamps in fiscal 1993. The average benefit in fiscal 1993 was $68.24 per person per month.

Participating households received free food stamps in amounts determined by household size and income. The Mickey Leland Childhood Hunger Relief Act, contained in the 1993 budget-reconciliation bill, broadened eligibility for food stamps and raised some benefits. Since fiscal 1992, states had had the option to provide benefits through electronic transfers.

▶ **Puerto Rico.** Since 1981, Puerto Rico had received a special block grant rather than food stamps. The bill provided $1.1 billion in fiscal 1994. The commonwealth distributed money, not food stamps, directly to eligible individuals. The program's guidelines were looser than those for mainland states, leaving to the discretion of recipients what the money was used for. About 42 percent of the island's population received the cash benefits in fiscal 1993, according to the Agriculture Department. The average monthly benefit was $139 per household, or $56 per person.

The only special condition imposed by Congress was that the department spend $12.5 million from this account on cattle tick eradication on the island, to be carried out by the department's Animal and Plant Health Inspection Service. The House report said it anticipated that the tick would be eradicated by fiscal 1998.

Child Nutrition Programs

Congress appropriated $7.5 billion for supplemental feeding programs such as school lunches and breakfasts, and summer food service. The programs also fed homeless children at shelters, poor children at day-care centers and the elderly poor at adult day-care centers. Schools that served subsidized breakfasts and lunches to poor children were reimbursed through their local school districts. States administered the other child nutrition programs and were reimbursed by the federal government. In fiscal 1993, about 25 million children were served by the school lunch program during an average school day, amounting to 4.2 billion lunches. In addition, about 5.6 million children were served by the school breakfast program, amounting to 942 million breakfasts.

Women, Infants and Children (WIC)

Congress had much more direct control over the funding of this supplemental feeding program, and historically it had been a bone of contention between urban and rural lawmakers. For urban members, it often was the only discretionary item in the agriculture bill that sent money to their districts. But for rural lawmakers, the more money that went to WIC, the less there was for the traditional pork barrel projects that helped farm communities and rural areas. However, the targeted nature of the aid had made it increasingly popular.

The states administered this program, but they were fully reimbursed by the federal government. Women with children younger than age 5 became eligible for WIC vouchers only after a health-care professional certified that the children had nutritional deficiencies and a state WIC caseworker certified that they were financially needy. The vouchers were exchanged at grocery stores for eggs, milk and other dairy products, infant formula, cereal, fruit or vegetable juice, beans, peas and peanut butter. The 1994 appropriations bill prohibited administrative expenses from being used by any clinic that permitted smoking within its confines.

The WIC appropriation was $3.2 billion, up from $2.9 billion in fiscal 1993. The House committee report described WIC as its "highest priority for funding considerations." It noted that WIC's appropriation had increased by more than $1.7 billion over 11 years and that the 1994 increase of $350 million was the largest

for any program in the bill. The Agriculture Department estimated that 6 million individuals would participate in the program in fiscal 1994, at an average cost of $42.46 per person a month.

Even so, the funding increases had not been high enough to keep up with demand. The Congressional Budget Office projected that in fiscal 1994, about 9.6 million mothers and children would be eligible for WIC, and that 7.6 million of them would apply for the program and receive benefits if sufficient funds were available to fully fund the program. The Clinton administration, which requested $3.3 billion in fiscal 1994, sought full funding by 1996.

Other Food and Nutrition Programs

▶ **Commodity Supplemental Food Program.** The $104.5 million appropriated for this program provided food to a targeted poor population similar to that of WIC, but also was available to the elderly and to women with children up to age 6. Instead of the vouchers the WIC program used, the Agriculture Department contracted, through state human services agencies, with nonprofit church and other social service groups to distribute food packages containing approved groceries such as iron-fortified infant formula, rice, cereal, canned juice, evaporated milk or nonfat dry milk, canned vegetables or fruits, peanut butter and dry beans. In fiscal 1993, about 246,000 women and children received an average of $21.66 in food packages per person per month. About 142,000 elderly received an average of $19.93 per person per month.

▶ **The Emergency Food Assistance Program.** Both the name and function of TEFAP had evolved since its creation in 1983, when the "T" in TEFAP stood for "Temporary." The program distributed food commodities and cash subsidies free of charge to soup kitchens, hunger centers, food banks and similar nonprofit food-distribution centers whose goal was to relieve situations of emergency and distress. The bill provided $120 million in fiscal 1994.

When it began, the program strictly used surplus commodities; the only appropriation was for storage and distribution costs. But as the surplus commodities dwindled, Congress had appropriated funds to buy additional commodities. In 1993, twice as much money was appropriated for buying commodities for TEFAP than for distributing surplus food. Critics therefore wondered whether TEFAP had outlived its usefulness. Citing the existence of more targeted anti-hunger programs elsewhere in the bill, Congress appropriated $45 million less than the 1993 appropriation and $87 million less than the Clinton administration's request.

▶ **Food donation programs for selected groups.** The bill provided $258.6 million for selected groups: $150 million for the elderly feeding program, $68.6 million for distributing food on Indian reservations and Pacific Island territories, and $40 million for purchasing commodities for soup kitchens and food banks.

Funds for the elderly program were distributed through state agencies to local meal sites. The program served the elderly at senior citizens centers or in their own homes, where it often was known as "Meals on Wheels." About 247 million such meals were expected to be served in fiscal 1994. State agencies were to be reimbursed by the federal government at about 58 cents per meal.

FOREIGN ASSISTANCE

Commodity Distributions

▶ **Food for Peace (PL 480).** The Food For Peace program, known almost worldwide by its public law number from the 83rd Congress, was the nation's main way of distributing surplus crops to less developed or famine-stricken regions of the world. Created in 1954 and overhauled most recently by the 1990 farm bill, its goal was twofold: to provide humanitarian hunger relief and to develop new markets for U.S. commodities in the Third World. The program was administered jointly by the Agriculture Department and the State Department's Agency for International Development. The food was provided to the countries through low-interest, long-term loans and outright grants.

The PL 480 program was not immune to the growing congressional and public sentiment against foreign aid. Its total fiscal 1994 appropriation, including the grant program, shipping costs and salaries and expenses, was $1.5 billion, $76.4 million less than in fiscal 1993. The "program level" that the government was to regulate was capped at $1.6 billion, a decrease of $100.8 million from the previous year.

Also, Congress barred any funding in fiscal 1994 for a program that provided debt relief to Latin American and Caribbean countries. The Clinton administration had requested $32.2 million; $40 million had been appropriated for debt relief in fiscal 1993.

▶ **CCC Export Loans Program.** The government's largest means for stimulating overseas commodity sales was its program to guarantee repayment of loans made by commercial enterprises to approved foreign buyers. The guarantees were provided to foreign entities that were short on cash or were otherwise perceived as credit risks by private lenders. The U.S. guarantee made it easier for the countries to obtain a loan.

The 1990 farm bill required that the Agriculture Department provide loan guarantees of not less than $5 billion a year. The bill authorized guarantees of short-term and intermediate-term loans and loans made to emerging democracies of up to $5.7 billion in fiscal 1994. The bill provided $403.2 million for loan subsidies as part of a total appropriation of $406.6 million.

▶ **Export Enhancement Program.** This was the government's main program to give U.S. commodity exporters a leg up in international trade competition. The Export Enhancement Program reimbursed exporters who sold such United States commodities as grains, oils and dairy products in selected foreign markets at below the world market price. Exporters became eligible for the program if it had been determined that they were victims of unfair trading practices in the countries where they were attempting to do business.

Under the program, the Agriculture Department covered exporters' losses by giving them certificates that could be traded for government-owned surplus commodities that were worth the amount of the discount. The exporters then could sell those commodities to make up for their losses. The goal of the program was to gain market share in overseas markets by undercutting the prices foreign countries, particularly those in the European Community, charged for their agricultural products.

The program had its critics, who pointed out that it paid a large portion of its proceeds to the nation's three largest grain merchants: Cargill Inc., Continental Grain Co. and Louis Dreyfus Corp.

No appropriation was required for the program because the Office of Management and Budget said it had no net cost to the Treasury. However, in fiscal 1994 the department expected to spend $1 billion on the surplus commodities it would give to exporters in the program.

Foreign Agricultural Service (FAS)

Operating much like a mini-State Department, the service administered $8.7 billion worth of programs, most of which were paid for through the Commodity Credit Corporation. The FAS also administered PL 480 programs. The Appropriations committees had little control over spending for them; however, they did control the salaries and expenses of the service. In fiscal 1994, Congress appropriated $118 million for administration.

▶ **Personnel.** Foreign Agricultural Service officers had worked as agricultural attachés reporting to the State Department until 1954, when their activities were transferred to the Agriculture Department. They reported on agricultural production and trade issues in the 75 countries where they were posted, as well as an additional 58 countries, and their reports sometimes were used by government intelligence agencies. The service also worked with a variety of governmental agencies and private organizations to promote U.S. agricultural sales overseas, and it ran the Cooperator Program, a joint partnership between the FAS and private nonprofit trade and producer organizations that worked to increase

export opportunities.

▶ **Market promotion.** The Market Promotion Program (MPP) was created in 1990 to replace the Targeted Export Assistance program. MPP supporters — mainly members from states and districts that had commodity producers and food processors that benefited from the program — said it had succeeded in boosting sales of U.S. food products overseas.

However, the program had attracted critics who called it a boondoggle that channeled money to a number of large corporations and trade associations to subsidize overseas television and print advertising campaigns that they should be conducting with their own money.

In 1992, for example, the MPP budgeted $7.8 million to the Sunkist fruit company to promote its California citrus products and $3.3 million to Sunsweet to promote its prunes overseas. The Gallo wine company received $4.5 million. Dozens of other well-known brands also received substantial subsidies.

One program singled out during the fiscal 1994 appropriations debate provided subsidies to the McDonald's restaurant chain to market Egg McMuffins in Germany. The program's initiators had justified it on the basis that it increased sales of U.S.-produced eggs.

The criticisms of the MPP took a toll. Congress voted to cut its funding to $100 million, down from $147.7 million in fiscal 1993. The figure was a compromise reached during the House-Senate conference. The House — after rejecting a proposal to bar all funding for the program — initially voted to provide $127 million in fiscal 1994; the Senate came in with a $75 million figure.

The House report also called for the agency to target its funds to small and medium-size companies and new exporters, and to require larger companies participating in the program to provide matching funds of up at least 50 percent.

Food and Drug Administration (FDA)

The FDA's responsibility was consumer protection. An arm of the Department of Health and Human Services, the FDA set standards for food content and cosmetics, tested all new drugs and medical technology before they were marketed, regulated certain health-care technology services and conducted safety studies on a variety of products. The agency also ensured that the nation's blood supply was safe and that products were clearly and accurately labeled. The FDA also investigated consumer product tampering incidents and claims.

Since taking office in 1991, FDA Commissioner David A. Kessler had staged an aggressive effort to enforce FDA regulations and improve its product-testing efforts. In the process, he had become one of the most recognized figures in the federal bureaucracy. Appointed to his position by President George Bush, he was retained by President Clinton.

Clinton showed his support for the FDA by proposing an increase in its budget from $819 million in fiscal 1993 to $924.3 million in fiscal 1994, including $54 million from an authorized prescription drug user fee program. However, he tried to offset some of the expense by calling on the agency to collect $200 million

in new user fees from private-sector users of FDA services.

The House rejected that approach, citing the lack of legislative authorization for such fees. Although the Senate included $175 million in such fees when it passed the fiscal 1994 spending bill, its managers conceded that they were skeptical that the FDA could initiate a user fee system in time to provide revenues to pay for programs in fiscal 1994. In conference, the House position won out. As a result, $870.3 million for FDA spending would come from appropriation funds, with the remaining $54 million derived from the prescription drug user fee.

▶ **Orphan drug program.** Both House and Senate reports directed the FDA to spend $15.2 million on its program to encourage the development of drugs, biologicals, medical devices and medical foods for rare diseases and conditions. About $12 million of that went in the form of new and continuing research grants and contracts.

▶ **Mammography facility inspections.** The House report provided $10 million to assist the FDA in hiring personnel needed to fulfill the mandates of the 1992 Mammography Quality Standards Act. The law required FDA certification of medical facilities that provided mammography breast examinations.

▶ **Medical devices.** The FDA also needed personnel to inspect new medical devices under the mandates of the Safe Medical Devices Act of 1990. The personnel shortage had delayed getting some potentially useful devices to consumers. The House report provided $20 million to try to remedy the situation.

▶ **Generic drugs.** Citing large potential savings to consumers through substituting generic drugs for brand-name products, the House report provided $46.7 million to improve the generic drug evaluation process.

▶ **Immunizations.** The Senate report added $10 million to the FDA's biologics program in response to President Clinton's initiative to increase childhood immunizations.

▶ **Women's health.** The Senate report recommended $2 million to establish an Office of Women's Health in the Office of the FDA Commissioner.

Commodity Futures Trading Commission

The CFTC regulated the commodity futures markets, including the Chicago and Kansas City boards of trade. Its employees did market surveillance analysis and research, enforcement, audits and registrations of futures firms. The agency's $47.5 million appropriation covered the salaries of employees and commissioners, but the majority of its operational costs were covered by fees paid by commodity trading firms.

Farm Credit Administration

The Farm Credit Administration was an independent federal agency that regulated the Farm Credit System, a federally chartered network of agricultural lending institutions. Those institutions included land banks, production credit associations and banks for cooperatives. The regulatory agency's $40.4 million operating budget was paid for by fees on the banks, although Congress set an overall limit on the agency's expenses. ∎

Commerce, Justice, State Bill Takes a Hit

Congress on Oct. 21 approved a $23.4 billion fiscal 1994 appropriations bill for the departments of Commerce, Justice and State and the federal judiciary (HR 2519). Reflecting growing impatience with certain foreign policy expenditures, appropriators curbed spending for the United Nations and cut deeply into President Clinton's request for funds for international peacekeeping activities.

President Clinton signed the bill into law Oct. 27 (PL 103-121).

Allocations for the Justice and State departments, which received $9.6 billion and $4 billion, respectively, declined from fiscal 1993 — although Congress managed to find extra money for the Immigration and Naturalization Service (INS). The Commerce Department received $3.6 billion, up from $3.3 billion the previous year. That included a sizable increase for the National Institute of Standards and Technology (NIST), which conducted research of significance to manufacturing and high-technology industries.

Congressional debate over the bill reflected confusion about the urgency of programs that sent dollars overseas, as well as a heightened sense of the nation's financial and emotional limits. Politicians lashed out at the United Nations and its peacekeeping operations, saying U.S. citizens were being asked to pay too much for international programs that were ill-advised or ill-managed.

The Clinton administration requested $642 million for international peacekeeping missions. Appropriators provided $402 million, and even that stuck in many throats. It did not help the administration's cause that votes on the appropriation came amid public and congressional dismay over a drawn-out peacekeeping mission in Somalia that had claimed some American lives. *(Somalia, p. 486)*

Appropriators complained that they had no control over peacekeeping expenses and, at the urging of Rep. Harold Rogers, R-Ky., pressed the administration to notify them of upcoming votes on new U.N. missions.

Ernest F. Hollings, D-S.C., who chaired the Senate Commerce, Justice, State Appropriations Subcommittee, said it was difficult to accommodate growing peacekeeping expenses within his bill and that it might be appropriate to shift those costs into a defense account.

But his House counterpart, Neal Smith, D-Iowa, said the bottom line was the same no matter where the item was placed in the budget: The United States could not afford to do as much around the world as people expected.

Lawmakers also complained about regular U.S. dues to the United Nations and specified that the administration should withhold 10 percent of those payments until the United Nations appointed an inspector general or similar watchdog against spending abuses.

BOXSCORE

➡ **Fiscal 1994 Commerce, Justice, State and federal judiciary appropriations (HR 2519).** The bill provided $23.4 billion for programs under the Commerce, Justice and State departments, the federal judiciary, and related agencies.

Reports: H Rept 103-157; S Rept 103-105; conference report, H Rept 103-293.

KEY ACTION

July 20 — **House** passed HR 2519, 327-98.

July 29 — **Senate** passed HR 2519, 87-13.

Oct. 13 — **House-Senate** conferees approved HR 2519.

Oct. 19 — **House** adopted conference report, 303-100.

Oct. 21 — **Senate** adopted conference report, 90-10.

Oct. 27 — **President** signed HR 2519 — PL 103-121.

The decline of communism shook the political consensus for other projects as well, particularly the National Endowment for Democracy. Some House members declared the program a welfare measure for political consultants, noting that the endowment channeled money through established political interests. But a majority in both chambers eventually agreed with arguments by the Clinton administration that the endowment still had a vital role to play in strengthening democracy abroad. Congress approved $35 million for the program.

In the same vein, lawmakers tussled over the necessity of having the federal government run Radio and TV Marti, pro-democracy radio and television broadcasting programs aimed at Cuba. Lawmakers ultimately kept the programs alive with a $21 million appropriation but included restrictions and reviews that could lead to their demise. *(Box, p. 559)*

Tight Resources

Overall, the fiscal 1994 bill was $220 million below spending in fiscal 1993 and $1.5 billion below the president's request. *(1992 Almanac, p. 646)*

This was not simply a matter of self-imposed restraint. When the 13 House Appropriations subcommittee chairmen met to divvy up the overall available money for fiscal 1994, Smith received a comparatively small allocation for his bill, forcing him to pare many programs and augment almost none.

House-Senate negotiators received a somewhat larger allocation for the final bill and approved some cuts in existing programs.

This enabled them to fund some new domestic initiatives within the Commerce Department and to allocate increased funds to fight illegal immigration.

The final bill contained $171 million for expanded immigration control programs that Clinton and various lawmakers advocated, along with a mixture of administration and congressional priorities in other policy areas:

Appropriators agreed to most of the administration's proposed increase for the NIST, raising the institute's allocation to $519 million, about $135 million more than in fiscal 1993.

The bill included $1.9 billion for the National Oceanic and Atmospheric Administration (NOAA). Senate appropriators prevailed in boosting spending for fleet modernization, aircraft procurement and construction.

The bill's $2.7 billion appropriation for the federal judicial system included $19.8 million for death penalty resource centers, which provided legal advice to inmates on death row. The administration had requested $30.6 million, but the Senate slashed the appropriation to $11.5 million. Senate negotiators later agreed to the compromise figure,

COMMERCE, JUSTICE, STATE

	Fiscal 1993	Fiscal 1994 Clinton Request	House Bill	Senate Bill	Final Bill
		(In thousands of dollars)			
Department of Justice					
Office of Justice Programs	$ 843,312	$ 696,588	$ 678,936	$ 712,250	$ 708,041
Legal activities	2,555,586	2,295,047	2,255,540	2,254,843	2,269,035
Organized crime drug enforcement	385,248	384,381	384,381	382,381	382,381
Federal Bureau of Investigation	2,007,423	2,060,405	2,024,705	2,038,705	2,038,705
Drug Enforcement Administration	718,684	731,639	718,684	727,161	722,000
Immigration and Naturalization Service	965,000	1,100,052	1,059,000	1,048,538	1,054,538
INS fees and receipts	(608,304)	(614,787)	(627,787)	(627,787)	(677,787)
Federal prison system	1,837,937	2,275,064	2,155,211	2,333,460	2,229,754
Other	350,182	296,036	172,894	170,664	173,941
TOTAL, Justice Department	**$ 9,663,372**	**$ 9,839,212**	**$ 9,449,351**	**$ 9,668,002**	**$ 9,578,395**
Related Agencies					
EEOC	222,000	234,845	230,000	227,305	230,000
Federal Communications Commission	140,000	129,889	129,889	129,889	99,900
Federal Trade Commission	69,650	71,740	69,740	69,740	67,920
Securities and Exchange Commission	115,535	57,856	57,856	57,856	57,856
Other related agencies	39,626	47,373	39,998	40,373	40,726
The Judiciary					
Supreme Court	25,606	27,695	25,025	26,200	25,850
Courts of Appeals, District Courts	2,406,769	3,001,940	2,650,041	2,516,692	2,601,255
Administrative Office of the United States Courts	45,100	57,553	44,612	43,358	44,900
Other	57,362	77,372	71,707	70,228	97,213
TOTAL, Judiciary	**$ 2,534,837**	**$ 3,164,560**	**$ 2,791,385**	**$ 2,656,478**	**$ 2,743,368**
Department of Commerce					
National Institute of Standards and Technology	384,007	535,198	210,000	535,198	518,710
National Oceanic and Atmospheric Administration	1,630,232	1,862,749	1,766,120	1,921,048	1,927,801
Bureau of the Census	297,255	271,716	241,170	248,370	238,286
International Trade Administration	213,851	246,333	221,445	251,103	248,590
Patent and Trademark Office	86,672	103,000	88,329	88,329	88,329
Economic Development Administration	444,118	253,301	26,284	352,793	350,642
Other	231,052	303,639	233,658	275,785	263,356
TOTAL, Commerce Department	**$ 3,287,187**	**$ 3,575,936**	**$ 2,787,006**	**$ 3,672,626**	**$ 3,635,714**
Related Agencies					
Maritime Administration	564,236	380,081	376,423	374,423	374,423
Small Business Administration	922,620	693,061	751,948	684,156	657,687
Legal Services Corporation	357,300	525,515	—	349,000	400,000
Other related agencies	25,555	25,686	25,993	24,672	25,309
Department of State					
Administration of Foreign Affairs	2,927,411	2,788,335	2,666,608	2,710,295	2,699,606
International organizations and conferences	1,379,129	1,769,948	427,962	1,356,262	1,268,492
Other	70,877	65,916	64,157	67,885	66,365
TOTAL, State Department	**$ 4,377,417**	**$ 4,624,199**	**$ 3,158,727**	**$ 4,134,442**	**$ 4,034,463**
Related Agencies					
Arms Control and Disarmament Agency	46,500	62,500	47,279	58,000	53,500
Board for International Broadcasting	220,000	220,000	—	206,000	210,000
Israel Relay Station (rescission)	−180,000	—	−180,000	—	—
U.S. Information Agency	1,164,105	1,228,766	1,058,520	1,144,072	1,142,570
Other related agencies	46,302	46,866	45,841	43,450	44,950
GRAND TOTAL	**$ 23,616,242**	**$ 24,928,085**	**$ 20,839,956**	**$ 23,540,484**	**$ 23,396,781**

SOURCE: House Appropriations Committee

which was meant to keep the centers running at their existing level at a time of rising caseloads.

Clinton, like his Republican predecessors, targeted the State Justice Institute for elimination. But the institute, which sought to improve the operation of state courts, was favored by key appropriators and survived another year at its fiscal 1993 funding level of $13.6 million.

HOUSE COMMITTEE

The House Appropriations Subcommittee on Commerce, Justice, State and the Judiciary approved its version of HR 2519 in a closed session June 16.

Although details were embargoed, panel members said the $23 billion measure eliminated funding for several federal law enforcement initiatives, forcing some personnel layoffs. "There are going to be RIFs [reductions in force], no doubt about it," one Democratic panel member said.

Full Committee Action

The House Appropriations Committee approved a taut, $22.8 billion Commerce, Justice, State spending bill June 24, paring about $2 billion from Clinton's budget request and cutting more than a half billion off the fiscal 1993 appropriation. The bill (H Rept 103-157) was approved by voice vote. Most programs barely kept pace with inflation, if that, although there were increases for select law enforcement and research programs.

Lawmakers had no choice but to scale back Clinton's spending recommendations for the three departments and related agencies. When Appropriations subcommittee chairmen divided up the total pot of available revenue, they set aside $23.5 billion in fiscal 1994 budget authority for the bill — $1.4 billion less than in the administration request.

The bill came in well under that cap on budget authority, although it barely met a $23.7 billion limit on outlays, the dollars actually spent in the fiscal year.

Smith, who chaired the Appropriations subcommittee that wrote the bill, said on average programs received 95 percent of what it would cost to continue their existing level of services. Although some lawmakers had warned of layoffs, Smith predicted that most or all of the savings could be achieved without firing employees.

Some members were disappointed in the cuts, particularly those who wanted more money for law enforcement. Charles E. Schumer, D-N.Y., who chaired the Judiciary Subcommittee on Crime, lamented a $100 million cut in an existing grant program to help state and local law enforcement. But he acknowledged that appropriators had worked within an extremely spare allocation and praised them for finding about $56 million for new anti-crime initiatives, such as putting more police officers on the beat.

• **State Department.** State Department programs absorbed much of the reduction, reflecting lawmakers' unwillingness to invest in international initiatives when they were being asked to cut programs at home. Appropriators allotted $4 billion for the department, about $370 million below its fiscal 1993 appropriation. Many of the accounts, including administrative costs and contributions to international peacekeeping, took cuts.

The bill provided $422.5 million for international peacekeeping; Clinton had requested $642 million.

The subcommittee also cut back international broadcasting, voting to end pro-democracy broadcasting to Cuba, known as Radio Marti and TV Marti. But after much debate at the full committee markup, Carrie Meek, D-Fla.,

won back close to $9 million to continue the radio broadcasts to Cuba.

• **Justice Department.** Justice Department programs, which were the largest chunk of the bill's spending, received varied treatment.

The department got less overall than in fiscal 1993. There were increases for some administration law enforcement priorities, although generally less than Clinton had sought. Lawmakers increased the INS border patrol, although not as much as many lawmakers believed was necessary to stem illegal immigration from Mexico.

The bill included some increases to open several newly built federal prisons. But it did not include money to construct new prisons, and report language accompanying the bill pointedly praised Attorney General Janet Reno's pledge to examine the strains that mandatory minimum sentences were placing on federal prison facilities.

• **Commerce Department.** Some Commerce Department programs received significant increases, reflecting support for technology programs that could enhance the competitiveness of U.S. products in global markets. Appropriators included a $50 million increase over fiscal 1993 spending for the NIST. That increase was still well below Clinton's request, however, and below the levels authorized in a separate competitiveness bill (HR 820) that had passed the House. *(Competitiveness, p. 241)*

Even within the confines of the spending limits, however, appropriators found room to help some of their preferred projects. They approved $752 million for the Small Business Administration, $59 million more than Clinton's request.

And while the overall appropriation for NOAA was below the administration recommendation, lawmakers asserted some of their own priorities within the account, restoring money for various weather and marine research programs.

• **The Judiciary.** Lawmakers trimmed close to $400 million from the judiciary's budget request, partly by eliminating a requested cost of living increase and locality pay for judges and other staff. However, appropriators found $13.6 million for the State Justice Institute, which Clinton had targeted for extinction.

Radio and TV Marti

During the markup, some appropriators voiced strong misgivings about a State Department authorization bill (HR 2333) approved two days earlier by the House that authorized $28 million for Radio and TV Marti while cutting a $48 million authorization for the National Endowment for Democracy. TV Marti could not be seen in many parts of Cuba, and Radio Marti had been criticized for including inappropriate political propaganda. Smith's subcommittee had already voted to end funding for the broadcasts to Cuba while including $35 million for the endowment. *(State Department authorization, p. 505)*

In full committee, Meek accepted their judgment on the television broadcasts but sought to restore most of the funding for Radio Marti. Meek, whose district was home to 18,000 Cuban exiles, said the radio broadcasts played an important role in undermining Cuban leader Fidel Castro. "We don't want to send the wrong message that this country is pulling back in its intent to kill the threat of Castro," she said.

Meek's amendment cut $17.5 million, or half, of the appropriation for the endowment, and allotted $8.75 million for Radio Marti. Because the two programs spent money at a different rate, Meek had to trim more from the

endowment's appropriation than she sought for Radio Marti in order to stay within the bill's annual limit on outlays — the actual dollars spent in a budget year.

Numerous lawmakers argued against the amendment. Some objected to taking money from the National Endowment for Democracy, despite the recent floor vote to kill it. Several cited the endowment's role in helping promote democracy in Eastern Europe and the former Soviet Union. Others said the radio broadcasts to Cuba were unnecessary because commercial stations in Miami already reached many Cubans.

With the backing of eight Democratic colleagues and most of the panel's Republicans, Meek prevailed 26-21 after almost an hour of debate.

Later in the markup, Tom DeLay, R-Texas, sought to cut off funds for any activity that could help HIV-infected foreigners enter the United States. Congress already had banned permanent immigration by people infected with the AIDS virus. But DeLay said lawmakers had to reassert that position in the wake of a court order that the United States admit HIV-infected Haitian refugees who had been detained at Guantánamo Bay Naval Base in Cuba. His amendment would have barred using Justice or State Department funds to process or otherwise facilitate the entry of any alien infected with HIV.

However, other members said the recently passed immigration ban was sufficient and that DeLay's proposal was unduly strict. The amendment was rejected, 15-30.

HOUSE FLOOR ACTION

The House passed its $20.8 billion version of the bill July 20 by a vote of 327-98. The debate began July 1, but members waited until after the July Fourth recess to complete work on the bill. *(Vote 346, p. 84-H)*

As passed by the House, the bill included $9.4 billion for the Justice Department, $2.8 billion for Commerce and $3.2 billion for State.

During debate July 1 and July 20, the House shaved nearly $2 billion from the bill's bottom line. Most of the reductions came as a result of procedural moves as members made points of order against spending for programs that were not authorized. Because the spending bill came to the floor without a rule for floor debate waiving such points of order, the unauthorized line items had to be stricken.

But members expected many of the stricken programs to be restored in conference with the Senate. For example, on July 1, members cut $223 million in funding for the Commerce Department's Economic Development Administration (EDA) because the program had not been authorized by separate enabling legislation. But, in a clear signal that members expected some of the grant money to survive, the House on July 20 rejected, 122-300, an attempt by Joel Hefley, R-Colo., to cut the $26 million in the bill for salaries and expenses at the EDA. *(Vote 340, p. 82-H)*

The House also dropped the $214.6 million in the bill for the Board for International Broadcasting, on the grounds that the agency was not authorized. The board gave grants to Radio Free Europe and Radio Liberty to broadcast news to the countries of Eastern Europe and the former Soviet Union. Clinton had announced June 15 that he intended to reorganize the nation's foreign broadcasting service.

The House also reversed itself on two cost-cutting amendments that were approved by voice vote July 1. One

amendment, by Robert S. Walker, R-Pa., to strike $9.6 million for NOAA facilities, was rejected 70-356 when subcommittee Chairman Smith called for a recorded vote July 20. The second amendment, by Timothy J. Penny, D-Minn., to cut $22 million from the Small Business Administration was rejected, 183-242, on July 20. Penny said he would like to kill the agency outright. He said it affected a minuscule percentage of the nation's small businesses and had a questionable track record. But the program had strong allies in Congress. *(Votes 343, 344, p. 84-H)*

Immigration

The House voted July 1 to add $60 million to the $1 billion that Clinton originally had requested for the INS. The extra funds, approved 265-164, were for the Border Patrol, the INS unit that policed the US.-Mexican border. *(Vote 318, p. 78-H)*

Clinton's request had assumed a reduction in Border Patrol positions. The appropriators had added $6.5 million to keep the border unit at full strength. But some border state lawmakers called for a much larger increase.

Duncan Hunter, R-Calif., offered the amendment to add $60 million to the general INS account, enough to hire 600 new Border Patrol agents. Without more help, Hunter and others argued, immigration officials could not hope to control the flow of illegal immigrants entering on the southwestern border. Hunter said immigrants were putting a crippling burden on his state, citing an estimate that California was spending $3 billion a year on criminal and social services for illegal aliens.

"Please, give us some relief," urged Carlos J. Moorhead, R, one of several California members who spoke on behalf of the amendment. Others cited the risk of terrorism from illegal aliens.

Subcommittee Chairman Smith tried to fend off the amendment, warning that the vote would put the spending bill over its assigned allocation — the first time the House had done so since the 1990 budget agreement established such spending caps and a dangerous precedent for the future. Smith agreed that the Border Patrol was a high priority and suggested that appropriators might be able to win more money for it as the bill moved toward conference. But he and other members also cautioned that money alone would not solve the problem of illegal immigration.

Nevertheless, the amendment passed handily after extended debate.

The tone of the immigration debate troubled Luis V. Gutierrez, D-Ill., who said colleagues had painted a picture of immigrants as sponging off public welfare, when in fact many worked hard and contributed to society and the economy. Gutierrez warned against casting foreigners as the source of the country's many problems: "We're starting to sound a lot like Germany," he said.

SENATE COMMITTEE ACTION

On July 21, the Senate Commerce, Justice and State Appropriations Subcommittee approved its $23 billion version of HR 2519 by voice vote. The full Senate Appropriations Committee approved the bill the following day on a 26-0 vote (S Rept 103-105).

As in the House bill, the Justice Department received most of the funding — $9.4 billion. The State Department got $4 billion — $250 million less than was appropriated for fiscal 1993.

Senate appropriators provided money for many pro-

Radio and TV Marti Avoid Cancellation

Members of Congress had argued about TV Marti — which beamed news reports, situation comedies and sports shows to Cuba — for more than three years. Supporters, led by the influential Cuban émigré community, said that free information had to get through to the island nation to force Cuban President Fidel Castro out of power.

Opponents called TV Marti a waste because Castro had effectively jammed the broadcast signal, preventing most Cubans from seeing it. They said TV Marti's radio counterpart, Radio Marti, carried programs filled with inappropriate political propaganda.

Opponents succeeded in deleting funding for Radio and TV Marti from the House version of the fiscal 1994 spending bill (HR 2519) that paid for the Voice of America, the government agency that ran the Cuba operations. The Senate disagreed, providing the full $28 million that President Clinton had requested.

House and Senate negotiators decided Oct. 13 to give the controversial television and radio broadcasts one last chance to prove themselves. The House-Senate conference agreement required TV Marti to prove to a board appointed by the U.S. Information Agency, which oversaw the Voice of America, that it could actually be seen by Cubans. Radio Marti had to show that its news and information were accurate.

Negotiators gave the programs $21 million — $7 million for TV Marti and $14 million for Radio Marti. Of that, $7.5 million was to be withheld until the board reviewed the programs and reported back to Congress by July 1, 1994. If the problems could not be fixed, Congress would use the $7.5 million to shut down the two programs.

In a Jam From the Beginning

The United States created the radio broadcast to Cuba in 1983 as part of its effort to force Castro from power. Citing the radio program's immense popularity, anti-Castro lawmakers — particularly those from Florida — led the drive for TV Marti in the late 1980s.

Congress had funded the controversial TV undertaking since fiscal 1987. But since virtually the first broadcast in 1990, detractors argued that the United States should stop funding it because the signal was jammed.

In 1991, the House Appropriations subcommittee that funded the departments of Commerce, Justice and State and the federal judiciary cut funding for TV Marti from the fiscal 1992 spending bill. But the funds were restored by the full committee and made it into the final bill. *(1991 Almanac, p. 535)*

The next year, opponents nearly succeeded in killing funding in the House. On a 206-194 vote, the House approved an amendment to strike the $12.7 million in the fiscal 1993 bill for TV Marti. But quick-thinking supporters forced another vote, and the amendment failed 181-215. *(1992 Almanac, p. 646)*

On Oct. 7, David E. Skaggs, D-Colo., who led the 1993 fight to kill TV Marti, released a declassified report by U.S. representatives in Havana. The report, which covered the 27 days from Sept. 3 through Sept. 29, found that the broadcast could be seen only in a few outlying areas. Even then, the reception was sporadic.

TV Marti supporters argued that the U.S. government had the responsibility to keep trying to get past the jam to help the free flow of information into a closed society.

Since fiscal 1987, Congress had appropriated a total of $82.9 million for TV Marti. To avoid criticism for flouting international prohibitions on using foreign television channels, TV Marti aired from 3:30 a.m. to 6 a.m. EST on a channel not used by the Cuban government. It broadcast Spanish-language news shows and translated versions of American sitcoms such as "Kate and Allie."

Although the project survived in fiscal 1994, other factors threatened to render the debate moot. According to a report in the Oct. 12 edition of The Washington Times, enterprising Cubans looking for additional information had begun putting up illegal satellite dishes from which they could get the cable channels available to foreigners in their hotels. As one resident told the Times: "I have HBO and CNN. Why do I need TV Marti?"

---

grams stricken by the House. The subcommittee included $131 million for increased immigration controls, including the hiring of 600 additional border patrols and construction of detention facilities at international airports. Dianne Feinstein, D-Calif., who had been pushing for increased funding for border programs, applauded the panel's action, calling the initiative "extremely important."

The Senate bill also allotted $20 million toward counterterrorism initiatives, including the creation of a second hostage rescue team within the Federal Bureau of Investigation. Numerous lawmakers had called for such a backup hostage team following the fiery ending to the Branch Davidian standoff in April near Waco, Texas.

Senate appropriators provided $445 million for international peacekeeping efforts, more than the House but still below the fiscal 1993 appropriation. Clinton had sought $642 million. The bill set conditions on U.S. contributions to some international organizations, barring back payments on U.N. dues, for example, until the organization established an inspector general office to prevent mismanagement.

The bill provided $28 million for pro-democracy radio and television broadcasts to Cuba.

Like the House committee, Senate appropriators were constrained by budget caps that forced them to keep spending below the administration's request. But subcommittee Chairman Hollings got a somewhat larger allocation than his House counterpart.

Senate appropriators steered that extra money toward fleet and aircraft modernization at NOAA, additional Justice Department grants and technology development at the Commerce Department. They also restored funding for the Legal Services Corporation, the Board for International Broadcasting and the Economic Development Administration, programs that were challenged and cut in the House because they were not authorized.

SENATE FLOOR ACTION

The Senate on July 29 passed a $23.5 billion version of the bill; the vote was 87-13. As in the House, senators signaled

that they wanted to spend more on policing U.S. borders and less on what was going on outside them. *(Vote 225, p. 30-S)*

The bill allotted $4.1 billion for the State Department — substantially more than in the House bill but still well below administration requests — particularly for contributions to the United Nations and international peacekeeping. It provided $3.7 billion for the Commerce Department — more than in either Clinton's request or the House bill — and $9.7 billion for the Justice Department.

Changes made to the bill on the Senate floor included the following:

● **National Endowment for Democracy.** Dale Bumpers, D-Ark., led the fight in the Senate to eliminate funding for the National Endowment for Democracy, saying the organization's mission had melted along with the Cold War. Bumpers said the agency had a poor management track record and enjoyed strong political support only because it channeled money through powerful political interests — including the Democratic and Republican national party organizations. "Everything in this town has a constituency, even waste," agreed Byron L. Dorgan, D-N.D. "If we can't cut this, we can't cut anything."

But many senators leapt to the program's defense. Mitch McConnell, R-Ky., said it would be "national suicide" to abandon such an investment when many former communist nations had only the most fragile democracies in place and could topple back into authoritarianism: "It's not over yet."

After lengthy debate July 28, senators voted 23-74 to defeat Bumper's amendment. *(Vote 223, p. 29-S)*

But the next day, the Senate gave voice vote approval to an amendment by Hank Brown, R-Colo., to bar funds to certain endowment grantees until they reimbursed the government for improper expenditures, such as first-class travel and entertainment.

The Senate also cast a skeptical eye on other foreign policy expenditures.

● **Nicaragua.** Jesse Helms, R-N.C., won restrictions on aid to Nicaragua in the wake of a May 23 explosion in Managua that revealed a formidable cache of weapons, illegal documents and other evidence of a terrorist network. Senators voted 77-23 to cut off aid to the Nicaraguan government until there was proof that officials there had eliminated any links to terrorist groups and had prosecuted certain terrorists. *(Vote 222, p. 29-S)*

Helms' amendment barred all but emergency U.S. aid until the president certified that the Nicaraguan government had prosecuted those who provided Nicaraguan passports linked to the World Trade Center bombing in New York in February 1993 and that no high-ranking Nicaraguan officials were involved in terrorism.

Hollings urged Helms to wait to attach his measure to an upcoming foreign relations authorization bill, as did Foreign Relations Committee Chairman Claiborne Pell, D-R.I. But Christopher J. Dodd, D-Conn., an influential Senate voice on Central America policy, was among those voting with Helms. While taking issue with aspects of the amendment, Dodd said it was important to send Nicaragua a message that it must address the terrorism issue.

● **Terrorism.** The Senate also agreed to allow the death penalty for terrorists whose actions resulted in a death. The amendment, sponsored by Alfonse M. D'Amato, R-N.Y., established procedures to apply the death penalty to terrorists involved in murder.

Several senators who opposed capital punishment argued against the amendment. "Terrorists are ready to die for their cause," said Mark O. Hatfield, R-Ore. "They are not deterred by anything." But D'Amato, who reportedly was the target of a terrorist assassination plot, said nothing less than the death penalty would suffice for acts such as the World Trade Center bombing. Senators supported the proposal, 75-25, on a procedural challenge, then approved it by voice vote. *(Vote 221, p. 29-S)*

FINAL ACTION

House and Senate conferees agreed on a $23.4 billion bill in a quick session Oct. 13 (H Rept 103-293).

The House adopted the conference report, 303-100, on Oct. 19 and finished considering outstanding amendments the next day. The Senate cleared the measure Oct. 21, 90-10. *(House vote 517, p. 126-H; Senate vote 323, p. 42-S)*

Senate subcommittee Chairman Hollings said that to stay within the bill's budget caps, lawmakers had to cut roughly $1.5 billion from Clinton's request, and he chided the administration for offering little guidance in the task. Hollings' House counterpart, Smith, said negotiators struggled to keep agencies at existing funding levels and generally sought to funnel any additional money to law enforcement efforts. Overall, the spending bill was about $220 million less than fiscal 1993 appropriations.

Key conference decisions included the following:

● **International broadcasting.** The final bill included a compromise on U.S.-sponsored broadcasts to Cuba. Appropriators allotted $21 million for Radio Marti and TV Marti but fenced off part of that money pending a review of technical and editorial issues.

But negotiators bowed out of a dispute regarding overseas broadcasting. They included $210 million for the Board for International Broadcasting but reportedly did not issue any policy directives on reorganizing the agency — the topic of intense debate between the administration and Capitol Hill.

● **National Endowment for Democracy.** Negotiators included $35 million for the controversial National Endowment for Democracy. Clinton had requested $50 million, the House had eliminated the funding, and the Senate had restored $35 million for the program.

● **U.N. dues.** Responding to allegations of wasteful U.N. spending, negotiators specified that the United States withhold 10 percent of its dues until the United Nations appointed an inspector general or equivalent watchdog for spending.

● **Peacekeeping.** Conferees included $402 million for international peacekeeping, well below the $642 million initially sought by the administration.

Lawmakers, many of whom criticized the U.N. peacekeeping mission in Somalia, complained that the administration was committing the country to an increasing number of peacekeeping efforts with open-ended risks and costs. At the urging of Rep. Rogers, the House subcommittee's ranking Republican, negotiators agreed to add report language calling on the administration to notify Congress of upcoming votes on peacekeeping missions whenever possible.

● **Immigration.** The final bill included $171 million for expanded immigration control programs advocated by Clinton and several lawmakers. That included $45 million to hire about 600 additional Border Patrol agents and about $40 million to build detention space for illegal aliens.

Negotiators also included $1.9 billion for NOAA and $680 million for Office of Justice Programs, which included grants to state and local law enforcement agencies. And they dropped the provision added by D'Amato on the Senate floor to authorize the death penalty for terrorists. Smith said the issue was better addressed in upcoming crime legislation. ■

Commerce, Justice, State Provisions

Congress' $23.4 billion bill (HR 2519) for the departments of Commerce, Justice and State and the federal judiciary reflected growing impatience with certain foreign policy expenditures. The bill curbed spending for the United Nations and cut deeply into President Clinton's request for funds for international peace-keeping activities.

JUSTICE DEPARTMENT

The Department of Justice, created in 1870 to handle all criminal prosecutions and civil lawsuits in which the United States had an interest, in recent years had one of the fastest growing budgets in the government. Lawmakers had nearly quadrupled the department's budget over the past decade, reflecting worries over crime and a perennial battle between Democrats and Republicans to claim the mantle of "toughest on crime." The department investigated and prosecuted federal violations, carried out immigration law and supervised the federal prison system. The department also interpreted laws under which federal departments acted.

But in 1993, even Justice could not escape the pinch of the federal budget deficit. Lawmakers appropriated $9.6 billion for fiscal 1994, almost $85 million less than the preceding year and $260.8 million below the administration's request.

Lawmakers steered many of the recent increases toward more investigators, prosecutors and prisons, spread throughout the country at the department's discretion.

Fighting illegal immigration became another political priority, and the Immigration and Naturalization Service received $1.7 billion including fees and receipts, a 10 percent increase.

Within each Justice division, most of the money was spent on salaries and related employee expenses. The number of employees directly funded through the appropriations process had grown at Justice from about 54,600 in 1982 to more than 84,000.

Federal Bureau of Investigation

The FBI, which pursued a broad range of wrongdoing from street-gang crime to international terrorism, received a $2 billion appropriation in fiscal 1994, up $31.3 million from the preceding year. Former Director William S. Sessions presented the fiscal 1994 budget request to Congress but was forced out of office in July amid allegations of ethical improprieties. Louis J. Freeh, a former FBI agent and U.S. District Court judge, succeeded Sessions as director. Freeh pledged to work more closely with other units of law enforcement and to continue Sessions' controversial efforts to hire and promote more women and minorities at the bureau.

FBI operations were run out of 56 field headquarters and about 400 local offices throughout the United States, Puerto Rico, Guam, the U.S. Virgin Islands and Saipan. The bureau's national priorities were organized crime, drugs, white-collar crime, counterterrorism and foreign counterintelligence. The FBI also coordinated with state and local law enforcement on a national crime data bank, fingerprinting system and forensic laboratories, including new standards for DNA research.

Most of the bureau's budget was to go to salaries and operating expenses (cars, telecommunications, field office equipment) for about 22,000 employees.

Beyond sustaining the FBI's base operations from from fiscal 1993, the conference agreement provided money for several high-priority programs, including:

▶ **Automated fingerprint identification.** In 1994, $84.4 million was to go toward developing an automated fingerprint identification system, $9 million above the fiscal 1993 appropriation. The administration had requested an additional $16.7 million for continuing the relocation and updating of the fingerprinting headquarters at the new FBI building in Clarksburg, W.Va., but appropriators said the bureau was able to apply fiscal 1993 appropriations toward those costs. A 1990 supplemental appropriations bill (PL 101-302) directed the FBI to move its fingerprinting headquarters to West Virginia, the home state of Senate Appropriations Committee Chairman Robert C. Byrd, a Democrat.

Officials intended to develop an electronic image system by which local law enforcement agencies could take an electronic print of a suspect's finger and transmit it to federal headquarters for potential identification. The goal was a two-hour turnaround, compared with the 22 days it took with fingerprints sent to the FBI by mail.

The funds were to go toward developing a system and prototype. FBI officials predicted they would be able to move into the West Virginia facility in the spring of 1995, with initial operations beginning in the fall of 1996. The facility was supposed to be fully operational in early 1998.

▶ **Counterterrorism.** Negotiators backed a $10 million program to boost the bureau's efforts to combat terrorism, half from fiscal 1993 appropriations and half from fiscal 1994. Some of that money was to be used to add 50 additional agents to the elite Hostage Rescue Team and expand it from two to four units. The team became an issue after the disastrous conclusion of the FBI standoff with the Branch Davidians near Waco, Texas, in April 1993. In that confrontation, administration officials cited the lack of a backup squad to relieve the Hostage Rescue Team as a factor in their decision to step up pressure on cult leader David Koresh rather than simply waiting him out. Koresh and many of his followers died. The money would also pay for improved equipment for the Hostage Rescue Team and other FBI units involved in anti-terrorism.

Prisons

The increased effort to put criminals behind bars, combined with Congress' predilection toward mandatory minimum prison sentences, had put tremendous pressure on the federal prison system and the U.S. Marshals Service, which had to find housing for prisoners awaiting trial and sentencing in often overcrowded state and local jails. Since 1988, the inmate population had grown 95 percent — necessitating parallel increases in staff and budget. The bureau estimated a total inmate population of 88,645 by the end of fiscal 1994, an increase of almost 9,000 over the preceding year. At that growth rate, officials predicted more than 106,000 prisoners by 1997.

As of early 1993, about 62 percent of the inmates were imprisoned on drug-related offenses. Another reflection of the war on drugs was the rise in the number of criminal aliens in federal prisons — to about 26 percent of the inmate population. Administration officials and lawmakers were considering steps to deport criminal aliens more promptly. Even with double-bunking in some facilities, the federal prisons were at about 142 percent of capacity. Prisons in the West were among the most crowded, at about 170 percent of capacity. However, the bureau predicted that overcrowding would decline substantially by 1998, when new facilities opened.

The cost of new buildings was just the first expense, to be followed in future years by the cost of upkeep and care for the additional prisoners. The Bureau of Prisons received $2.2 billion, including $269.5 million for construction and repair of facilities, up from total prison budget authority of $2.1 billion in 1993. Most of the bureau's money was spent on salaries and related expenses, of which about $34 million was to support the projected increase in the inmate population. The Justice Department figured that it cost roughly $22,400 a year to confine an inmate.

▶ **New prisons and expansions.** Appropriators provided $112 million to activate new prison facilities during the 1994 fiscal year: a 640-bed high-security prison and an administrative maximum security prison in Florence, Colo.; a high-security prison in Allenwood, Pa.; medium-security prisons in Pekin and Greenview, Ill., and Cumberland, Md.; and a detention center in Miami. Officials planned to activate expansion projects in Atlanta; Fort

Worth and Big Spring, Texas, and El Reno, Okla.

They also received $75 million to buy and renovate the Fort Devens Medical Facility in Massachusetts, a former military base site being targeted for prison facilities. Prisons were still under construction in Beckley, W.Va.; Taft, Calif.; Butner, N.C.; Oklahoma City; Edgefield, S.C.; Coleman, Fla.; Waseca, Minn.; Carswell AFB, Texas, and George AFB, Calif. Prisons were planned for Elkton, Ohio; Beaumont, Texas; Yazoo City, Miss.; Pollock, La.; and Forrest City, Ark.

▶ **Detention:** Within the total construction funds, the prison bureau received $10.3 million to begin a joint detention facility in Buffalo, N.Y., with the Immigration and Naturalization Service, and $30 million for INS detention facilities in El Paso, Texas ($7.5 million); Dade County, Fla. ($11.3 million); and San Francisco ($11.3 million). Additional detention facilities were planned, or under construction, in Brooklyn, N.Y.; Seattle, Houston, Philadelphia and in Hawaii.

Appropriators also provided $20 million for construction grants to localities in exchange for guaranteed contract space in local jails to house federal detainees.

Immigration and Naturalization Service

The INS enforced immigration laws, oversaw the Border Patrol and investigated, apprehended and deported foreigners who were in the United States illegally. The administration initially requested $1.02 billion for salaries and expenses at the immigration agency, a 5 percent increase over the fiscal 1993 appropriation. But that did not keep pace with public concern about illegal immigration, and the administration later upped its request to $1.09 billion. Appropriators settled on just under $1.05 billion.

That appropriation did not include the agency's fee accounts, which were expected to bring in $683.8 million in fiscal 1994 and give the immigration agency a total budget of $1.7 billion. In recent years, the INS had added user fees to help pay for programs such as airport inspections, adjudication of alien status, naturalization and refugee programs. The fiscal 1994 budget included $171 million for enhanced immigration control initiatives, $129 million of it going directly to the INS.

▶ **Border Patrol.** The Border Patrol monitored the U.S. perimeter, on foot, on horse and by car, helicopter and airplane. Close to 90 percent of its work was on the Southwest border. The division was expected to receive $397.4 million for fiscal 1994, including $45 million to hire more than 600 new agents.

▶ **Detention and deportation.** In coordination with the Border Patrol, the detention and deportation division handled illegal aliens, from the quick-turnaround cases of hundreds of thousands of Mexicans who crossed the border each year and were put on a bus home after a few hours of processing, to criminal aliens who had come through court trials and were awaiting arrangements with home countries. The division was to receive $179.1 million. Included in that amount was $11 million to support roughly 250 new positions at expanded processing centers in Florence, Colo., and El Centro, Calif.

Land-border inspections, which took place at designated ports of entry and made up the third-largest INS section, were to cost $86.3 million under the new budget. That included $17 million to hire 200 additional inspectors.

▶ **Asylum corps.** One of the most highly criticized elements of INS operations was its system for dealing with political asylum applications, made by foreigners who reached U.S. soil and claimed to be fleeing persecution in their home countries. The agency faced a backlog of more than 300,000 pending asylum claims, and critics said the resulting delays invited abuse because applicants were allowed to stay in the country pending resolution of their claims.

In 1993, lawmakers began efforts to tighten the rules for asylum applications. At the same time, administration officials and appropriators agreed to direct more money to the overloaded system — especially with regard to asylum seekers arriving at U.S. airports.

The spending bill included $5.3 million to hire new asylum officers and interpreters, and $10.7 million for pre-inspection at key foreign airports.

▶ **Detention.** At the administration's request, appropriators agreed to more than $65 million to enhance INS' ability to detain and deport illegal immigrants, including $40 million — contained in the Bureau of Prisons budget — to expand or construct four detention facilities.

▶ **User fees.** In conference, appropriators added one dollar to the entry fee charged to individuals arriving at U.S. airports or ports from foreign countries, bringing the fee to $6 per passenger. Lawmakers established the fee in a 1987 appropriations bill. It went into the Immigration User Fee Account at INS, which paid for the costs of inspecting international arrivals. The account was expected to bring in $305 million in fiscal 1994, with an estimated $50 million of that coming from the fee increase. Appropriators directed that much of the additional money be directed at costs associated with the new programs to deter fraudulent asylum claims.

Drug Enforcement Administration

The annual funding tussles over the Drug Enforcement Administration (DEA) took place against a more dramatic debate over the agency's fate; the Clinton administration, as part of its plan to "reinvent" government, in September recommended folding the drug agency into the FBI. Advocates believed the move could save money and reduce counterproductive turf battles between the two agencies. But the reaction among several key lawmakers on crime and drug issues ranged from ambivalence to hostility, and Attorney General Janet Reno subsequently outlined a plan to improve coordination between the two agencies rather than consolidating them.

Congress gave the DEA, the lead agency in the federal government's effort to stop illegal drug trafficking, $722 million — $9.6 million less than the administration requested. But the agency also was allowed to spend an anticipated $42.1 million from fees from doctors and pharmaceutical companies — for a total of $764.1 million, or $33.4 million above the fiscal 1993 appropriation of $730.7 million.

Although the agency may have been best known for its role in the war on drugs, it also regulated the legal use of drugs and worked to prevent their diversion to illicit uses.

DEA's largest section was the domestic enforcement program, which included DEA's 19 field divisions and a staff of roughly 1,800. Using confidential informants, undercover operations and electronic surveillance, DEA agents identified and penetrated national and international drug trafficking organizations. The section received $196 million.

▶ **Special enforcement operations.** The agency ran programs aimed at specific problems or organizations, such as the Colombian Medellin cartel.

DEA officials told Congress that Colombian cartels provided up to 90 percent of the cocaine entering the United States, with primary distribution operations in Miami, New York, Los Angeles and Houston. They said the agency was aggressively fighting these syndicates by assisting Colombian police raids on drug cartels and by destroying distribution facilities in the United States.

The foreign cooperative investigations unit got $115 million toward its coordination of the effort to reduce illegal drugs imports. The unit worked out of 70 offices in 48 countries. It maintained a network of informants and developed intelligence intended to cooperative arrests and diminished drug supply.

The DEA's efforts to stop the diversion of legally produced chemicals and drugs into illegal trafficking got $57 million; a fund for state and local task forces received $73 million.

Additional anti-drug money was included throughout other Justice divisions for the apprehension and prosecution of individuals involved in secondary drug activities such as money laundering, tax evasion and firearms possession. Justice Department officials estimated that overall, $4.5 billion had been spent on anti-drug efforts in 1993.

An Organized Crime Drug Enforcement program, an interagency effort aimed at fighting sophisticated drug trafficking, received $382.4 million, slightly less than the previous year. The

program consisted of 13 regional task forces that sought to combine the resources of 11 federal agencies, as well as local law enforcement, to combat drug cartels. Member agencies, such as the FBI and DEA, were reimbursed for staff and other costs out of the overall Organized Crime and Drug Enforcement appropriation.

Office of Justice Programs

Several programs provided resources for state and local police, including those that generated research and demonstration programs, built criminal justice statistics and fostered juvenile justice and missing children programs. The total appropriation for these was $679.6 million.

Within that appropriation, lawmakers allotted $107 million for juvenile justice and delinquency prevention programs, with most of it distributed among states based on their population under age 18. The money was used to prevent delinquency and to provide community-based alternatives to prison.

The largest share, $475 million, went to an eight-year-old program of anti-drug-abuse grants. The grants were intended for state and local governments to work in partnership with a national drug control approach. A quarter of the funds had to be matched by states.

The grants include funds for the following:
▶ **Community policing.** Clinton came to office with a pledge to place 100,000 new police officers on the nation's streets. His budget request for the Justice Department made a step in that direction, including $50 million for community policing grants designed to reduce crime by increasing police visibility and increasing officers' familiarity with the neighborhoods they were charged to protect. Appropriators halved that to $25 million. However, toward the end of the session, lawmakers were debating proposals to authorize and appropriate as much as $8.9 billion over five years for 100,000 new officers.
▶ **National Crime Information Center.** Appropriators designated $13 million, the full administration request, for the fourth and final year of a project to modernize the National Crime Information Center. This was an FBI-managed system designed to provide state and local police with instantaneous information on wanted people, stolen property and criminal history records. The system was the only one by which local police could quickly identify individuals who had committed a crime in one state and then moved to another state. It ultimately would support speedy background checks on would-be handgun purchasers, as contemplated in federal waiting-period legislation known as the Brady bill (PL 103-159). Appropriators included up to $10 million toward developing this "instant check" system.
▶ **Alternatives to prison.** The conference agreement provided $12 million for grants for correctional options that offered alternatives to traditional modes of incarceration. This grant program would allow for the development and testing of projects such as house arrest and boot camps.

Department Lawyers

Appropriators provided almost $2.3 billion for the lawyers and other resources that made Justice the nation's "law firm." That money included the salaries of U.S. attorneys and marshals, specialized departmental divisions on issues such as antitrust or environmental law, and the Solicitor General's office.
▶ **U.S. attorneys.** Spread through 94 judicial districts, U.S. attorneys were the federal government's principal litigators. Within each office, attorneys pursued criminal and civil litigation, debt collection, organized-crime eradication and drug enforcement. Their funds had been growing steadily in recent years and went up to $813.8 million for fiscal 1994, $5 million more than the administration requested. Senate appropriators, who had approved an additional $10 million above the request, said they wanted to mitigate cutbacks made in the name of deficit reduction.

Most of the resources were directed at criminal litigation, which ranged from white-collar crime such as insurance fraud to prosecution of violent criminals and drug dealers. Administration officials said the office had focused on improving coordination with state and local law enforcement. Two such programs were Operation Weed and Seed, an effort to reclaim troubled neighborhoods through a combination of aggressive law enforcement and social service programs, and Project Triggerlock, a joint federal, state and local program to identify and prosecute the most dangerous criminals within a community.

Related Agencies

▶ **Equal Employment Opportunity Commission (EEOC).** The EEOC was created by the 1964 Civil Rights Act (PL 88-352) to end job discrimination. It enforced the act's prohibition against discrimination on the basis of race, color, religion, sex or national origin by employers of 15 or more workers. The commission most often resolved bias complaints through conciliation or settlement, but in selected cases it went to court to force compliance.

The Clinton administration sought $234.8 million for the agency; appropriators provided $230 million. Administration officials warned that anything less than the full budget request could force the agency to cut staff at a time when its workload was growing because of two new civil rights statutes: the Americans with Disabilities Act (PL 101-336) and the Civil Rights Act of 1991 (PL 102-166). The ADA, which allowed workers who believed they were victims of discrimination because of physical or mental disabilities to seek redress through the EEOC, began to take effect July 26, 1992. The 1991 civil rights law sought to counter the effects of several Supreme Court decisions that made it harder for workers to sue their employers for discrimination, and for the first time allowed women to seek limited money damages for sex discrimination.

The EEOC operated 50 enforcement field offices to receive and handle complaints; these accounted for 75 percent of its costs.
▶ **Securities and Exchange Commission (SEC).** Established by the Securities Exchange Act of 1934, the SEC regulated the sale of securities by requiring traders to disclose financial and other information. It enforced numerous federal laws to prevent fraud and malpractice in the securities markets; its workload had increased markedly in recent years alongside growth in the securities industry.

Congress provided $57.9 million for fiscal 1994. House-Senate conference negotiators ordered fees for issuers of securities to be raised from one-fiftieth of 1 percent to one-twenty-ninth of 1 percent of the total dollar amount of the shares registered. But this increase was to be superseded by legislation authorizing an issuer's fee increase. Such legislation, which was pending when the appropriations bill became law, sought to recover a greater portion of the agency's administrative costs. Conferees said the increased fees would generate $171.6 million for the SEC and, when added to the appropriation, would mean $229.5 million in new spending authority.

House and Senate negotiators agreed to allow the SEC to collect $16.6 million in fees on investment advisers, to hire staff members to oversee these financial counselors. However, the permission was contingent on Congress passing relevant authorizing legislation, which also was pending at the close of the first session.
▶ **Federal Communications Commission (FCC).** The FCC was established by the Communications Act of 1934 to rationalize and manage use of the electromagnetic radio spectrum. By 1993, it controlled licenses for about 3 million companies and individuals who relied on the airwaves for communications, ranging from amateur radio operators to regional Bell telephone companies and cable television systems. Four issues dominated the agency's agenda with Congress in fiscal 1994: new user fees that financed much of the agency's budget; a new plan to raise revenues by auctioning off radio licenses; debate over how to finance the FCC's mandate to carry out the 1992 law (PL 102-385) reregulating cable television; and the push to complete the next generation of nationwide computer networks, also called data "superhighways."

Appropriators agreed to spend $160.3 million, including fees, on the agency, up from $140 million in fiscal 1993 and more than the $146 million administration request. The boost was the result of a provision added to the 1993 omnibus budget-reconciliation law setting new annual user fees for FCC license holders. The fees

were credited to the agency for a net appropriation of $99.9 million.

House-Senate conference negotiators added language to allow the FCC to grant more exceptions, or waivers, to rules barring the cross-ownership of newspapers and broadcast stations.

Appropriators included $16.1 million to carry out the new cable law, which called on the FCC to enforce new rates for basic cable and other cable services nationwide unless local authorities requested the power to do so. Appropriators also included $9.3 million to modernize FCC equipment and $5 million to handle the regulatory workload resulting from Clinton's "information highways" initiative, which sought to link government agencies and other public institutions through computer networks.

▶ **Federal Trade Commission (FTC).** Charged with promoting competitiveness at home and abroad, the commission monitored trade practices and investigated complaints of monopoly, unfair restraints or deceptive practices. The commission's budget was divided roughly between its mission of maintaining competitiveness (through the regulation of mergers and other potential antitrust activities) and consumer protection. The latter division educated consumers on their rights and businesses on their responsibilities under federal law. Congress appropriated $67.9 million but noted that the anticipated collection of $20.8 million in fees from pre-merger notification filings raised the FTC budget to $88.7 million.

▶ **State Justice Institute.** Like his Republican predecessors, Clinton targeted the State Justice Institute for elimination in his budget. But appropriators continued to smile upon the organization, which ran programs to improve the efficiency of state courts. Appropriators gave it $13.6 million for fiscal 1994. The agency continued to attract budget cutters, however — in the fall of 1993, Clinton included it in a package of proposed budget rescissions.

THE JUDICIARY

Unlike other budget requests that came to Capitol Hill, the judiciary request went directly to Congress without first being reviewed by the Office of Management and Budget. The judiciary was in the unique position of constituting the third branch of government but depending on the budgeting process of the other two branches to run its operations. Personnel was the major expense in the federal judiciary, where about 28,000 people worked. The total budget was $2.7 billion for fiscal 1994. That number was well below the overall request of $3.2 billion, but about $208.5 million above 1993.

Appropriators rebuffed the request for a cost of living increase for judges and court personnel, in keeping with the Clinton administration's proposed pay freezes in other arms of the federal government.

▶ **Supreme Court.** The highest court in the country, the Supreme Court interpreted the Constitution, federal legislation and treaties. It received $25.9 million, about $250,000 more than in 1993. The chief justice had a salary of $171,500; associate justices got $164,100.

▶ **Court of Appeals, district courts and other judicial services.** This encompassed all federal trial courts, the 13 circuit courts of appeals and their employees. Their workload had increased because of rising prosecutions for drug-related crimes and the crackdown on financial fraud. The appropriation was increased to $2.6 billion, including $86 million for court security and $77 million for juror fees.

The account also provided $280 million for legal services for indigent defendants, close to 4 percent more than in 1993. Up to $19.8 million of that money could go to death penalty resource centers that provided legal advice to death row inmates. That was a drop from the 1993 allotment for the centers, but an increase over the Senate recommendation of $11.5 million. Some lawmakers opposed the program, because they believed it encouraged prisoners to file numerous appeals.

▶ **Bankruptcy judges and fees:** The courts account also provided money to hire 35 new bankruptcy judges authorized in the Bankruptcy Judgeship Act of 1992 (PL 102-361). To help pay for

them, the spending legislation also increased bankruptcy filing fees as follows: fees to file for Chapter 7 (individual litigation) and Chapter 13 (individual debt adjustment) would rise from $120 to $130, while the fee to file a Chapter 11 (business reorganization) petition would jump from $600 to $800. The new fees were expected to raise $12.8 million in fiscal 1994.

▶ **U.S. Court of Appeals for the Federal Circuit.** This court, which reviewed decisions from the Merit Systems Protection Board, Patent and Trademark Office, Court of International Trade and Claims Court, received $12.9 million, up from $11.6 million.

▶ **U.S. Court of International Trade.** The court, which handled disputes on imports and exports, received $11 million.

▶ **Administrative Office of the U.S. Courts.** This office was the bureaucratic arm of all courts except the Supreme Court. It examined court dockets, prepared statistical data and reported on court business. The office, made up of about 800 workers, coordinated support staff, such as clerks and librarians, for the judges and assisted with the automation of judicial records. It found accommodations for the courts and coordinated the building of any new chambers or courthouses. It received $44.9 million, $200,000 less than the previous year.

▶ **Federal Judicial Center.** The appropriation for this office was $18.5 million. The center conducted research on the operations of the federal court system and provided continuing education programs for judges and court employees.

▶ **United States Sentencing Commission.** It got $8.5 million, down from $9 million, to develop and monitor guidelines for judges to use in sentencing criminal defendants.

COMMERCE DEPARTMENT

Funding for the Commerce Department barely held steady during the 1980s as the Justice Department consumed more and more of the discretionary funds available under this appropriations bill. But the Commerce Department had gotten some fresh attention, as the Clinton administration and lawmakers attempted to revitalize some core programs. The department, established in 1913, was intended to promote economic growth, international trade and technological development. Its contemporary goals included raising the quality of U.S. products and services, directing national export initiatives and making it easier to bring new technologies to market.

The department received $3.6 billion for fiscal 1994, just above what Clinton requested and $348.5 million more than the last year.

NOAA

More than half of the Commerce Department's budget went to the National Oceanic and Atmospheric Administration (NOAA). The total was $1.9 billion for fiscal 1994. This far-ranging agency managed existing and long-term data on the status of the Earth. Its scientists and researchers followed climate and global changes and managed a worldwide series of experiments and data-gathering programs.

▶ **Satellite programs.** NOAA observed the environment, using polar orbiting and geostationary satellites (GOES). The polar satellites' route took them over Earth's entire surface, producing routine data for weather forecasters. The GOES revolved at a speed synchronized to the Earth's rotation so that they always appeared above the same place on the Earth.

NOAA was in the midst of a $1 billion weather satellite modernization, which had been complicated by the increasing age of existing satellites, for which parts were becoming difficult to obtain. Satellite outages made the prediction of violent weather difficult, raising questions for appropriators about the timing of funding and whether the money was well spent.

For 1994, the polar system received $139 million, compared with $148.4 million in 1993. Vice President Al Gore's National Performance Review recommended merging the polar system with those of the Defense Department and another planned by NASA — for an estimated $300 million in savings. Appropriators tentatively endorsed the notion of consolidating NOAA's program

with Defense, but they were skeptical about integrating it with NASA's system.

The GOES observational satellites, mostly intended to monitor severe storms, received $123.7 million.

Funding for storing the data collected from satellites was $37.3 million, bringing the total cost of the satellite systems to $349.5 million, $2.8 million above the previous year.

▶ **National Weather Service.** The weather service maintained stations across the country, providing advance warning on dire conditions such as Hurricane Andrew in Florida or Hurricane Iniki in Hawaii. Its total appropriation for fiscal 1994 was $660.1 million (compared with $532.7 million in 1993), the bulk of which went to local forecasters and warning systems. The Clinton administration had requested $673.1 million, citing ongoing modernization of the weather service as NOAA's highest priority.

House-Senate conference negotiators set aside $189.7 million for systems acquisitions, including equipment for the Next Generation Weather Radar system (NEXRAD). This was intended to replace obsolete weather radar systems and enhance severe weather and flood warnings. The weather service said nationwide implementation of this advanced Doppler radar warning system could increase tornado-warning lead time from the existing average of one to two minutes to 20 to 30 minutes and reduce false warning rates. The NEXRAD project, which in 1993 got $84.5 million, received $120 million.

Conferees specified $75 million for training and staffing for new weather service facilities linked to the modernization, and requested quarterly updates on these facilities.

▶ **NOAA fleet.** The bill included $77.1 million to replace NOAA's aging fleet of ships, more than double the 1993 appropriation of $30 million. The Clinton administration had requested only $23.1 million, citing limited resources, and House appropriators went along. But Senate appropriators approved $77.1 million, warning that the fleet was in perilous condition and modernization could not be delayed. NOAA vessels conducted operations to support programs in nautical charting, fisheries research, resource assessment and marine environment. The fleet consisted of 23 vessels, several of which were inactive and many others of which were obsolete and deteriorating.

Congress began the modernization program in fiscal 1992. It was expected that the fleet would take about 10 to 15 years to replace, with appropriations needed every year. The fiscal 1994 appropriation included money to buy a new oceanographic research vessel.

▶ **Other NOAA funds.** The National Ocean Service, which managed ocean and coastal resources and was responsible for improving the quality and timeliness of ocean observation data, received $163.5 million.

The National Marine Fisheries Service, responsible for making sure fishery stocks continued as a renewable resource and for protecting endangered marine species, got $231 million. The appropriation included numerous small earmarks, such as $300,000 to finish a U.S.-Canada lobster study. Oceanic and Atmospheric Research, which conducted research on global change issues at the heart of NOAA's mission, got $226.8 million. That included $46 million for the Sea Grant program, which helped fund marine research and technology transfer at participating educational institutions; $2.8 million was targeted specifically at research and public education on the problem of zebra mussels.

Census Bureau

The bureau collected and published information including economic, social and demographic data on the U.S. population. It employed more than 4,000 permanent employees, and its major task was the decennial census. The bureau's budget was $238.3 million, down from $297.3 million in 1993 and $33.4 million below the administration request. Of its appropriation, $128.3 million went to salaries and expenses. As in recent years, appropriators earmarked a portion of that — $390,000 — for three census reports on cotton, soybean cotton and sunflower oilseeds.

The bill included $110 million for periodic censuses and other programs, $20.9 million less than requested.

▶ **2000 Census.** The periodic census account included money to pay for early planning and testing for the 2000 decennial census. The primary function of the census was to carry out the constitutional mandate to determine population for congressional and other political districts. But the questionnaire had expanded to provide such information as commuting patterns, income, education and housing patterns. That was valuable information for many federal agencies and businesses. Lawmakers themselves had mandated that the bureau collect demographic data on issues such as age, race and housing accommodations.

But appropriators had complained that the existing form was too long and complicated, discouraging people from filling it out. A key critic was Rep. Neal Smith, D-Iowa, chairman of the House Appropriations subcommittee that oversaw the Commerce, Justice, State bill. Smith and other House appropriators made their displeasure known in the report accompanying the House bill: "The 1990 census was far too costly and inaccurate, and the results were delayed considerably. These problems would only increase unless there were significant changes in the approach to taking the decennial census." And House appropriators slashed requested funding for the 2000 census to $8 million, about $15 million less than the bureau requested. The Senate was more generous, approving $18 million. Conferees did not specify a precise amount, giving administrators flexibility on how much to spend.

However, the conference report reiterated concerns that ongoing planning for the 2000 census was not taking adequate note of congressional concerns regarding cost and scope. Conferees directed the Commerce secretary, along with the Office of Management and Budget, to play a more active role in the planning and to report back to appropriators and the relevant authorizing committees by January 1, 1994.

NIST

The National Institute of Standards and Technology (NIST) was the federal laboratory providing technical research and services to support the competitive objectives of U.S industry. The institute was a key component of the Clinton administration's technology policy; NIST's profile also had risen under the Bush administration as lawmakers grew increasingly concerned that the United States was losing ground to foreign companies in the world marketplace.

For 87 years under its previous name, the National Bureau of Standards, NIST had provided technical support for the nation's companies. But the agency's mission expanded in 1988 under the Omnibus Trade and Competitiveness Act (PL 100-418), which formalized NIST's growing role assisting in the development of cutting-edge technology, through both in-house research and joint development ventures for other government agencies and private businesses.

Areas of NIST research included electronics, chemistry, physics, materials science, optical fibers, supercomputers and microwave communications.

Lawmakers eagerly agreed with the Clinton goal of bolstering NIST, giving the agency $518.7 million, a 35 percent increase over the fiscal 1993 level of $384 million. The administration had requested $535.2 million.

Of NIST's budget, $226 million funded scientific and technical research by staff scientists. In addition, NIST had guest scientists working at its laboratories in Gaithersburg, Md., and Boulder, Colo. Many of those were from industry. The agency also received $232.5 million for external research programs, which included the Advanced Technology Program and the manufacturing extension partnerships.

▶ **Advanced Technology Program.** The program provided seed money to companies that wanted to research generic technologies needed to develop commercially viable products. Authorized in 1988, it promoted the competitiveness of U.S. industry by sharing the cost of high-risk research projects that developed technologies before there was a market for them.

Companies could choose projects they wished; their bids were selected through a competitive review process.

Fiscal 1994 was the fifth year of funding for the program. It received $199.5 million, up from $67.9 million in fiscal 1993. The money would pay for an estimated 120 more joint ventures and single company projects.

▶ **Manufacturing extension partnerships.** Lawmakers included $30.2 million for this category, which combined the Manufacturing Technology Center Program with a State Technology Extension Program. The centers gave small and midsize companies technical assistance and help to accelerate the adoption of advanced technologies by industry. The state program provided grants for technical aid to manufacturers. The partnerships received $18.2 million in fiscal 1993.

Other Department Agencies

▶ **Economic Development Administration.** This agency provided public works and technical assistance grants to state and local governments, public institutions, nonprofit organizations and Indian reservations. Its goal was to stimulate growth and create jobs. It received $350.6 million, down from $444.1 million in fiscal 1993. President George Bush had sought to phase out the program, which critics said was a wasteful giveaway. But the Clinton administration supported its continuation — albeit at $97 million less than Congress provided.

▶ **International Trade Administration.** The agency developed trade policy and put in place programs to promote world trade and strengthen U.S. international trade and investments. It received $248.6 million.

▶ **Patent and Trademark Office.** The office awarded patent protection to qualified inventions and disseminated technological information disclosed in patents. It received $88.3 million.

▶ **Other Commerce programs.** Appropriators also provided for the following programs: National Telecommunications and Information Administration, $70.9 million; Economic and Statistical Analysis, $45.2 million; Export Administration, $34.7 million; and Minority Business Development Agency, $42.1 million.

Related Agencies

▶ **Small Business Administration.** The SBA provided loans and management advice to small businesses, including programs to help victims of floods and other catastrophes rebuild. It provided financial aid to municipalities for development projects and generated economic and statistical data on small businesses. The SBA received $657.7 million for fiscal 1994, down from $922.6 million the previous year. That included $258.9 million for salaries and expenses, with much of the rest going to loan programs.

Most of the funding drop came from a policy change involving the agency's loan guarantee program, which provided billions of dollars in loans. Appropriators allotted $196 million for the loan subsidies, about half as much as in 1993. In keeping with an administration recommendation, lawmakers cleared a separate bill reducing the level at which the government guaranteed certain long-term small-business loans under the SBA's 7(a) program (PL 103-81). That was expected to provide greater access to the loan program without increasing federal costs or, in this case, enable administrators to maintain the same level of loans with a smaller appropriation. Under the program, the government guaranteed loans to preferred banks that lent to small businesses.

▶ **Legal Services Corporation.** This quasi-governmental corporation awarded grants to local agencies providing legal services to the poor. It received $400 million, $125.5 million less than the corporation requested, but only $32 million below Clinton's recommendation. It was a $42.7 million increase over fiscal 1993.

President Ronald Reagan tried to abolish the program because he was concerned that the grantee-lawyers were too ideologically liberal. Although controversy quieted under President Bush, the Legal Services Corporation remained alive only through the appropriations process. The agency had not had a formal authorization for more than 12 years. But the Clinton administration supported the agency, and some lawmakers believed the 103rd Congress might clear a new authorization bill.

▶ **Maritime Administration.** Although this was a division of the Department of Transportation, it was funded in this appropriations bill. The administration received $374.4 million in fiscal 1994. It conducted research on shipbuilding and operations, helped secure financing and tax-deferred funds for shipbuilding and operated the U.S. Merchant Marine Academy in Kings Point, N.Y.

The largest chunk of the appropriation, $298 million, was to go to maintenance and operation of the Ready Reserve Force. But appropriators specified that none of that could be spent on new vessels without first notifying Congress.

▶ **U.S. Trade Representative.** Congress provided $20.6 million for the Office of the U.S. Trade Representative.

STATE DEPARTMENT

The bill provided $4.03 billion in fiscal 1994 for the State Department to conduct the foreign affairs of the United States. That figure was $590 million less than the administration's request and $343 million less than the fiscal 1993 appropriation.

The bill funded the salaries of State Department employees and the maintenance and construction of U.S. facilities around the world.

The bill also funded U.S. obligations to the United Nations and other international organizations. U.S. foreign aid was funded through the separate appropriations bill for foreign operations. That bill was often the subject of intense policy debates, but the State Department appropriation was usually handled in a more routine fashion.

However, two international programs generated heated debate on the 1994 Commerce, Justice, State bill: TV and Radio Marti and the National Endowment for Democracy.

Salaries and Expenses

More than half the funding for the State Department's operations, $2.1 billion, went for the salaries and expenses of the agency's 26,820 employees.

That $2.1 billion was broken down into two accounts: a regular salaries and expenses account ($396.7 million) and a new "Diplomatic and Consular programs" account, which got the bulk of the funds — $1.7 billion.

The new account was an attempt to show how much of the State Department's spending went for overseas programs. No breakdowns of the totals were available.

▶ **Classified documents.** Lawmakers warmly applauded a Clinton administration plan to review the process by which government documents were classified for security purposes. In the conference report accompanying the State Department appropriations bill, members argued that the existing process resulted in "overclassification, which exacts excessive costs both in dollars and in the ability of a democratic society to function."

Members said they expected the review to result in substantial savings, to be reflected in the fiscal 1995 budget request. They also set a deadline of March 31, 1994, for a report from the State Department on fiscal 1993 funds spent to classify documents, including an estimate of how many people spent their time dealing with document classification.

U.S. Buildings Abroad

After salaries and expenses, the second-largest portion of the State Department's budget was for acquisition and maintenance of buildings abroad.

The bill provided $410 million to rehabilitate dilapidated U.S. facilities and construct new embassies and chanceries — significantly less than the $570.5 million appropriated in fiscal 1993. One reason for the drop was that the fiscal 1993 bill included a second and final installment of $140 million for completion of a new embassy in Moscow.

The Clinton administration told members in early 1993 that to save money, it wanted more emphasis on redesigning and updating old facilities, rather than designing and building new chanceries.

▶ **Moscow Embassy.** It appeared that the question of what to do about the Moscow Embassy was not quite as settled as people had thought.

After six years of debate over what to do about the unfinished U.S. Embassy in Moscow, which was riddled with eavesdropping devices, Congress in essence left the matter up to the State Department in 1991. The fiscal 1992 spending bill provided $100 million for construction of an annex to the bugged building; the fiscal 1993 bill provided $140 million for completion of the project.

None of the $240 million had been spent, and the annex had not been built.

In 1993, the Clinton administration said it wanted to review the decision to build the annex, to see whether U.S. security concerns still merited the additional space.

In addition, Congress and the administration still had to resolve the fate of the unfinished, vacant facility, on which construction halted in 1985, when the electronic bugs were discovered.

▶ **New facilities.** In its budget request, the State Department asked for $5.2 million to design two new embassies, one in Kampala, Uganda, and another in Panama City, Panama. Since the United States re-established diplomatic relations with Uganda in 1979, its embassy had occupied a section of the British Embassy. But the British had asked for the space back, so the State Department wanted to build a new facility.

The existing building in Panama had several problems: It was seriously overcrowded and had no fire alarms or sprinklers. And because it was not set back from the street, providing security was difficult.

▶ **Rehabilitation of facilities.** In fiscal 1993, the State Department renovated its Bangkok, Thailand, embassy. In fiscal 1994, the department asked for $2.6 million for "furniture and furnishings for the new chancery."

The department also asked for almost $2.9 million to do environmental surveys of its embassies. Included in this was a request to remove asbestos from the embassies in Belgrade, Yugoslavia; Frankfurt, Germany; and Khartoum, Sudan.

Other State Department Programs

▶ **Protecting foreign missions.** The bill provided $10.6 million for the protection of foreign missions and officials in the United States. Of that, $2.2 million would be used to protect foreign diplomats and their families. The remaining $8.3 million would go to reimburse New York City for costs entailed in providing protection for foreign visitors to the United Nations and other international organizations.

▶ **Representation allowances.** The bill funded the department's $1.3 million request for what were termed "representation allowances." The funds reimbursed U.S. diplomats for entertainment expenses — including tuxedo rentals and the purchase of wine and flowers — incurred in carrying out their official duties.

International Organizations and Conferences

The bill provided $1.3 billion for U.S. payments to international organizations, including $860.9 million in current and past dues to the United Nations and affiliated organizations and $401.6 million for the U.S. share of maintaining several U.N. peacekeeping forces.

▶ **United Nations.** Just as the United States was about to pay off its U.N. debt, lawmakers approved a provision that would begin withholding part of the U.S. contribution to the international organization until a U.N. inspector general was hired.

For years, the United States regularly held back payments to signal displeasure with a program or policy. Beginning in fiscal 1991, the Bush administration made the pitch for fully funding the U.S. contribution and instituted a five-year payback plan for the arrearages.

Congress had appropriated about $275 million to pay the $322.1 million in U.S. debt.

But reports of extravagant spending and mismanagement at the United Nations led lawmakers to impose a new requirement: 10 percent of the U.S. assessment would be withheld until the international body created an independent office with the power to investigate and rein in spending.

Congress appropriated only a portion of the Clinton administration's request for international organizations, and it was difficult to pinpoint exactly how much would go to which organizations.

Under the Clinton budget, most of the U.N. money was to go to three accounts: the general account; the World Health Organization, an affiliated agency that had helped eradicate some diseases worldwide through inoculations; and the Food and Agriculture Organization, which worked on international hunger problems.

▶ **International peacekeeping activities.** This was the fastest-growing and one of the most controversial accounts in the appropriations bill. The $401.6 million in the bill would pay for the U.S. portion of maintaining U.N. peacekeeping troops in countries around the world, from Somalia to the former Yugoslavia. But many lawmakers were uneasy about having U.S. soldiers participate in U.N.-led missions.

Congress expressed its uncertainty with the peacekeeping program in two ways.

First, lawmakers slashed $240 million from Clinton's request. Members also served notice that the United Nations had better look to other countries for more money: "The conferees expect that the administration would notify the U.N. that the United States would not accept an assessment of more than 25 percent of peacekeeping costs for any new or expanded peacekeeping commitments."

The United States was paying for close to 32 percent per mission for U.N. peacekeeping troops.

According to the conference report, existing U.S. commitments far outstripped even the president's request. After the United Nations added — with U.S. support — three new missions for its blue-helmet troops in Haiti, Liberia and Rwanda, the U.S. obligation rose to nearly $1.3 billion for peacekeeping activities in fiscal 1994.

▶ **Other organizations.** The bill provided $40.3 million for the North Atlantic Treaty Organization (NATO). It also included nearly $1 million for the U.S. contribution to the International Coffee Organization, a group of coffee-producing nations that set goals for international coffee prices.

International Commissions and Foundations

The bill provided $46.1 million for the U.S. contribution to other international commissions, including $25.6 million for the International Boundary and Water Commission.

The commission managed water and boundary issues for the U.S.-Mexico border region. In recent years, the commission had been occupied with the increasingly serious environmental problems along the southern border.

Of the total, $2.5 million would go to reimburse the city of San Diego for treatment of sewage from Tijuana, Mexico.

The bill provided almost $20.3 million for international activities, including $16 million for the Asia Foundation, a nonprofit organization that aimed to promote democracy in Asia.

RELATED AGENCIES

United States Information Agency

Founded in 1953 to tell "America's story to the world," according to a former director, the USIA operated the Voice of America, which broadcast worldwide in 46 languages and provided government-sponsored television programs for several countries.

The USIA also managed the government's educational and cultural exchange programs, including the Fulbright Scholarship Program and the National Endowment for Democracy, which attempted to promote democratic values around the world.

With more than 8,000 employees and an appropriation of more than $1 billion, it was by far the largest independent agency involved in foreign policy.

A pending Clinton plan for reorganizing the nation's broadcasting mission sought to expand the USIA's role. Under the plan, Radio Free Europe and Radio Liberty, then under the independent Board for International Broadcasting, would be transferred to the U.S. Information Agency.

Congress provided $1.14 billion for the agency, nearly $86 million less than Clinton's request and more than $22 million less than the fiscal 1993 appropriation.

▶ **Salaries and expenses.** The bulk of USIA's funds — $730 million — went to this category.

▶ **Educational and cultural exchanges.** Few programs were more popular in Congress than USIA's educational and cultural exchanges. The conference committee agreed to fund them at $242 million, almost reaching the administration's request of $242.9 million. Most of that funding was to go toward academic exchanges and international visitor programs. The agency had been shifting funds from programs in Western Europe to expand programs in Eastern Europe, the former Soviet Union and Islamic countries.

The bill also included $26 million for the East-West Center, an institution based in Honolulu that promoted better relations between the United States and Asia. Daniel K. Inouye, D-Hawaii, the second-ranking member of the Senate Appropriations Committee, had been a consistent advocate for the center.

▶ **Broadcasting to Cuba.** Created during the Reagan administration, both Radio and TV Marti had come under increasing scrutiny from Congress.

Supporters, led by the influential Cuban émigré community, said that free information must get through to the island nation to force Cuban President Fidel Castro from power.

Opponents called TV Marti a waste of money because Castro had effectively jammed the broadcast signal, preventing most people from seeing it. TV Marti's radio counterpart, Radio Marti, had been criticized for some of its programs, which opponents said were filled with inappropriate political propaganda.

Opponents got their first break when they successfully deleted funding for Radio and TV Marti from the House version of this bill. The Senate disagreed, providing the full $28 million that Clinton requested.

House and Senate negotiators decided to give the controversial broadcasts one last chance to prove that they worked.

Negotiators gave the programs $21 million, including $7 million for TV Marti and $14 million for Radio Marti. Of that, $7.5 million would be withheld until a new, independent board reviewed the programs and reported back to Congress by July 1, 1994. If the problems could not be fixed, Congress would use the $7.5 million to shut down the two programs.

▶ **National Endowment for Democracy.** To its supporters, the National Endowment for Democracy represented all that was noble about U.S. foreign policy: a valiant champion of dissidents fighting entrenched dictators, of free markets, workers' rights and a free press.

To opponents who worked to cut its federal funds, the endowment was a slush fund for the political establishment, doling out funds to the pet foreign policy projects of insiders and interest groups on both sides of the aisle.

Though the endowment was a private foundation, its funds came almost exclusively from the federal government. The organization then awarded grants to organizations around the world to promote democracy.

Congress had appropriated more than $200 million for the endowment, which in turn had awarded more than 1,500 grants since it was created in 1983.

The House removed all funding for the endowment from its version of the bill; the Senate included $35 million. Clinton had requested $50 million. After a protracted and emotional House battle, the final bill appropriated $35 million.

Board for International Broadcasting

Conferees approved $210 million for the Board for International Broadcasting, the agency that funded radio broadcasts to the countries of the former Soviet bloc. That represented a $10 million cut from the president's request.

But tougher times were ahead for the agency. The Clinton administration unveiled a plan to reorganize the foreign broadcasts of the United States under the U.S. Information Agency, and, in the process, eliminate the Board for International Broadcasting.

The board housed Radio Liberty and Radio Free Europe, two institutions that came to symbolize U.S. propaganda efforts during the Cold War. Their mission was to "provide surrogate or proxy domestic broadcasting to the people of the Soviet Union and Eastern Europe," according to the board's presentation to Congress.

Arms Control and Disarmament Agency

The agency advised the president and members of the Cabinet on arms control issues.

As with many programs in this bill, the end of the Cold War meant that the agency's mission and goals came under scrutiny. After a review, the Clinton administration decided to keep the agency independent, rejecting calls to subsume it under the State Department.

Created during the presidency of John F. Kennedy, the agency was established to give arms control policy an independent voice in the Cabinet. But although the Clinton administration backed an independent arms control agency, it opposed legislation that would have made the agency as powerful in arms control discussions as its big brother agencies: the departments of State and Defense.

The agency got a new mission with the signing on Jan. 13, 1993, of the Chemical Weapons Convention, which banned the use, production and stockpiling of chemical weapons. More than 120 countries, including the United States and Russia, signed the treaty. The arms control agency was to oversee the terms of the pact, including the training of inspectors, creation of chemical inspection equipment and plans to ensure that countries complied.

Congress appropriated $53.5 million for the agency, an increase of $7 million over fiscal 1993. Of that, Congress earmarked $9.5 million for the U.S. portion of the start-up costs for the chemical weapons convention. That resulted in a cut in agency spending for continuing programs, which were funded at about $44 million, compared with $46.5 million in fiscal 1993.

International Trade Commission

The International Trade Commission conducted investigations and research into trade-related issues. The commission's work was used by the Office of the U.S. Trade Representative and the Department of Commerce in formulating trade policy. Its investigations focused on alleged unfair trade practices by other countries. Congress provided $43.5 million in fiscal 1994.

Conferees earmarked $8.4 million to pay for requests by members of Congress for specific country-to-country trade studies. ■

Defense Funding Drops by $12.6 Billion

The $240.5 billion fiscal 1993 defense spending bill, cleared by Congress on Nov. 10, represented the first installment of President Clinton's plan for a relatively modest long-term defense retrenchment. The bill (HR 3116), which generally followed the outlines of Clinton's budget request, only slightly accelerated the cuts in Pentagon spending that had been planned by President George Bush following the collapse of the Soviet military threat.

The House and Senate each adopted the conference report on the bill Nov. 10, sending the measure to the White House and concluding congressional action on the 13 regular appropriations bills for fiscal 1994. Clinton signed the bill the next day (PL 103-139).

Congress ended up cutting $12.6 billion from the amount provided for defense in fiscal 1993 — just $323 million more in cuts than Clinton had requested.

The Pentagon funding bill included additions of $1.04 billion to provide a 2.2 percent pay raise for military personnel that Clinton had sought to postpone and $1.2 billion to buy equipment for National Guard and reserve units.

While appropriators were working within rigid spending ceilings, they still managed to accommodate billions of dollars worth of spending that was of particular interest to individual members of Congress — especially to members of the Defense Appropriations subcommittees. Many of the other add-ons reflected members' direct constituent interests, such as the $60 million that Senate Defense Appropriations Subcommittee Chairman Daniel K. Inouye, D-Hawaii, secured to begin clearing unexploded bombs from an island in his state, or the $65 million that House Defense Subcommittee Chairman John P. Murtha, D-Pa., funneled to a university in his hometown.

The appropriators achieved the spending cuts and paid for the members' add-ons in part by outright cuts from programs requested by the Pentagon. There were a handful of large slashes from individual programs, such as $1 billion from Clinton's request for anti-missile defense research. But most of the cuts were relatively modest reductions made to hundreds of programs, mostly in research and development.

The appropriators displayed their usual prowess in wringing from the budget request hundreds of millions of dollars that the subcommittees insisted reflected outdated economic assumptions and thus could be cut with no impact on Pentagon operations.

For instance, the bill cut more than $500 million from Clinton's request because of declining fuel prices and the possibility of drawing down huge fuel stocks that were amassed during the Cold War as a war reserve. It cut $300 million to prevent the military retirement fund from building up an excessive cash reserve. And it cut $348 million to

BOXSCORE

➡ **Fiscal 1994 appropriations for the Defense Department (HR 3116).** The bill provided $240.5 billion for the Pentagon, a $12.6 billion cut from fiscal 1993.

Reports: H Rept 103-254; S Rept 103-153; conference report, H Rept 103-339.

KEY ACTION

Sept 30 — **House** passed HR 3116 by a vote of 325-102.

Oct. 21 — **Senate** passed HR 3116 by voice vote.

Nov. 10 — **House** adopted conference report by voice vote; **Senate** cleared conference report 88-9.

Nov. 11 — **President** signed HR 3116 — PL 103-139.

mained in the service.

● Maintaining the existing tempo of operations for major combat units. In fact, to pay for those activities, the bill included $205 million more than Clinton requested.

● Continued production of several major weapons, such as the Navy's *Arleigh Burke*-class Aegis destroyer and the Air Force's C-17 cargo plane, that the services contended would be as useful in the future as they would have been in the Cold War world for which they were designed. The bill added funds to continue production of Army combat helicopters and missiles that Clinton's request would have let lapse.

● Continued development of a new generation of high-tech weaponry, including the Army's Comanche scout helicopter, the Navy's *Centurion*-class submarine and enlarged F/A-18 fighter-attack jet, and the Air Force's F-22 fighter jet.

reflect the growing strength against local currencies of the dollars used to pay operating costs of U.S. forces abroad.

The bill actually increased by nearly $2.4 billion the new budget authority Clinton requested for operations and maintenance. But that largely reflected the conferees' rejection of Clinton's plan to fund that account partly with $3 billion drawn from a Pentagon revolving fund that financed maintenance and supply purchases.

The bill met stringent limits on defense outlays set by the congressional budget resolution, largely by cutting more than 9 percent from the $38.6 billion request for research and development (R&D) funds.

A Cautious Cutback

Highlights of the bill included:

● A reduction of nearly 105,000 in active-duty personnel, 97 percent of the cut Clinton proposed. But the bill added to the budget the 2.2 percent pay raise for the 1.6 million who re-

BACKGROUND

Clinton's $240.9 billion defense budget request was tolerable to the two Defense Appropriations subcommittees, but just barely. And they clearly were skeptical of Clinton's projected long-term defense retrenchment.

The outlook of the panels was personified by the four men who led them. House subcommittee Chairman Murtha was a union-oriented liberal on most domestic issues. But he also was a Marine officer decorated for combat duty in Vietnam. Ready as Murtha was to blast fellow Democrats for trying to cut defense too much, he was just as ready to blast the Pentagon brass for shortchanging the welfare of the troops — a willingness underscored by his role in forcing the military pay raise on the administration. Murtha also had been prominent among members questioning the risks and costs of committing U.S. forces to multina-

DEFENSE

	Fiscal 1993 Appropriation	President's Request	House Bill	Senate Bill	Final Bill
	(In thousands of dollars)				
Personnel					
Army	$ 23,238,457	$ 21,206,600	$ 21,571,207	$ 21,212,285	$ 21,296,177
Navy	19,228,564	18,356,900	18,633,383	18,156,982	18,330,950
Marines	5,980,998	5,678,700	5,763,117	5,755,272	5,772,317
Air Force	18,522,963	15,629,630	15,916,937	15,662,809	15,823,030
National Guard and reserves	9,304,043	9,211,940	9,392,876	9,343,012	9,401,570
Subtotal	**$ 76,275,025**	**$ 70,083,770**	**$ 71,277,520**	**$ 70,130,360**	**$ 70,624,044**
Operations and maintenance					
Army	13,442,418	14,966,194	15,221,091	15,706,229	15,802057
Navy	19,108,558	18,139,200	18,097,782	19,845,083	19,860,309
Marines	1,383,138	1,697,000	1,773,889	1,834,495	1,857,699
Air Force	16,009,040	18,582,984	18,305,447	19,107,389	19,093,805
Defense agencies	8,778,004	9,500,581	9,487,133	9,452,165	9,456,801
National Guard and reserves	7,911,476	8,187,411	8,346,623	8,130,715	8,119,478
Environmental restoration	1,199,700	2,309,400	1,716,800	2,207,800	1,962,300
Humanitarian assistance	28,000	—	15,000	48,000	48,000
Global Cooperative Initiatives	—	448,000	—	—	—
Former Soviet Union threat reduction	—	400,000	400,000	400,000	400,000
Other	1,545,629	8,538	14,338	22,538	16,338
Subtotal	**$ 69,405,963**	**$ 74,239,308**	**$ 73,378,103**	**$ 76,754,414**	**$ 76,616,787**
(By transfer)	**(3,454,000)**	**(3,535,300)**	**(3,535,300)**	**(500,000)**	**(500,000)**
Procurement					
Army	7,556,211	6,814,040	7,270,703	6,259,148	6,932,223
Navy	21,380,522	16,435,580	16,851,119	18,765,372	15,880,246
Marines	824,607	483,464	527,754	441,056	441,216
Air Force	22,085,333	19,604,080	18,069,473	15,672,073	18,199,354
National Guard and reserves	1,567,200	—	1,178,100	785,000	1,200,000
Defense agencies	1,962,058	1,730,164	1,557,344	1,602,726	1,810,039
Defense Production Act	—	—	200,000	—	200,000
Transfer to Sealift	(−1,875,100)	—	—	—	—
Subtotal	**$ 55,375,931**	**$ 45,067,328**	**$ 45,654,493**	**$ 43,525,375**	**$ 44,663,078**
Research, development and testing					
Army	6,032,860	5,249,948	5,560,082	5,275,385	5,427,546
Navy	8,930,381	9,215,604	8,604,777	7,925,369	8,365,786
Air Force	13,199,006	13,694,984	12,608,995	11,847,970	12,314,362
Other	10,072,601	10,459,791	9,622,160	8,537,285	9,083,797
Subtotal	**$ 38,234,848**	**$ 38,620,327**	**$ 36,396,014**	**$ 33,586,009**	**$ 35,191,491**
Intelligence programs					
CIA retirement and disability	168,900	182,300	182,300	182,300	182,300
Intelligence community staff	77,700	105,788	114,688	115,788	151,288
National Security Education Trust Fund	—	24,000	—	24,000	10,000
Rescissions	—	—	−150,000	—	—
Subtotal	**$ 246,600**	**$ 312,088**	**$ 146,988**	**$ 322,088**	**$ 343,588**
Other programs					
Economic conversion	472,000	—	—	—	—[1]
General provisions	380,925	—	21,900	−507,936	−569,025
Revolving and management funds	1,737,200	1,451,895	1,581,900	3,830,195	2,643,095
Chemical agents destruction	518,600	433,647	397,561	395,847	389,947
Drug interdiction	1,140,651	1,168,200	757,785	1,080,656	868,200
Inspector general	126,000	127,601	169,801	127,601	137,601
Defense Health Program	9,242,572	9,353,300	9,644,447	9,576,209	9,626,072
GRAND TOTAL [2]	**$ 253,156,315**	**$ 240,857,464**	**$ 239,426,512**	**$ 238,820,818**	**$ 240,534,878**

[1] *An estimated $2.49 billion for defense conversion is in various sections of the bill.*

[2] *Does not include budget scorekeeping adjustments*

SOURCE: House Appropriations Committee

tional peacekeeping efforts such as the one in Somalia.

Murtha and a handful of other defense-minded Democrats combined with a solidly hawkish Republican subcommittee caucus, led by fellow Pennsylvanian Joseph M. McDade, to give the House panel a clear slant in favor of defense spending.

Senate subcommittee Chairman Inouye and senior Republican Ted Stevens of Alaska were veterans of World War II who had drawn from that experience a conviction that it was dangerous for the country to drop its guard in a still-uncertain world.

In addition to the role of the appropriators, the defense spending bill reflected the clout of the House and Senate Armed Services committees. Those panels were solidly established as arbiters of policy, and they used the annual companion authorization bill to set very detailed funding limits.

As usual, the appropriators collaborated closely with the Armed Services panels on contentious issues in the budget request, producing a spending bill that mirrored in most respects the authorization measure (HR 2401). *(Defense authorization, p. 433)*

The $240.5 billion defense appropriations bill that resulted from their combined efforts included 92 percent of the total amount that Congress provided for defense-related activities in fiscal 1993.

An additional $10.1 billion came in the companion military construction bill to build military facilities and to build and maintain military family housing units. Most of the rest of the nation's defense budget was made up of $10.9 billion included in the energy and water development appropriations bill for Energy Department programs to develop and manufacture nuclear weapons and nuclear power plants for warships.

Two-thirds of the funds provided by the defense appropriations bill went to cover recurring costs of day-to-day Defense Department operations, including the military payroll, operations and maintenance and revolving funds used to finance overhauls and the purchase of fuel and other supplies.

Only one-third was for capital investment in the form of procurement of weapons and major equipment (19 percent) and research and development (less than 15 percent).

Although the bill appropriated $240.535 billion for defense programs in fiscal 1994, it was officially scored in the congressional budget system as costing $240.570 billion in new budget authority. The difference of $35 million reflected various technical adjustments.

HOUSE COMMITTEE ACTION

The House Defense Appropriations Subcommittee approved its fiscal 1994 spending bill Sept. 9; as usual, the panel kept much of its closed decision-making secret until the bill went before the full Appropriations Committee.

Chairman Murtha said his subcommittee largely followed the lead of the defense authorization bill, which the House began debating Sept. 8 and 9. That bill authorized about $252 billion for Defense Department spending.

Full Committee

The House Appropriations Committee approved the Pentagon appropriations bill by voice vote Sept. 22 (H Rept 103-254).

On most major issues, the bill conformed with Clinton's program and with the companion defense authorization

bill. Both bills funded requests to continue developing a new generation of combat planes for the Air Force and Navy and a new armed scout helicopter for the Army. Both funded a pay raise for military personnel, rejecting Clinton's proposal for a freeze on military and federal civilian pay in fiscal 1994.

But the markup also underscored lawmakers' increasingly sour mood toward the involvement of U.S. troops in dangerous — and perhaps fruitless — peacekeeping operations, such as the one in Somalia. The bill provided $383 million of the $448 million requested by Clinton to cover some of the costs of unanticipated deployments to help foreign populations cope with natural disasters or to participate in multilateral peacekeeping operations. *(Peacekeeping, p. 483; Somalia, p. 486)*

But HR 3116 also barred use of those funds for "humanitarian interventions" — other than natural disaster relief — unless the president gave Congress 15 days' notice. The notification would have to include a description of the deployment's goals, an estimate of its cost and duration, and an explanation of how the costs were to be covered.

Subcommittee Chairman Murtha, who had vigorously opposed the Somalia deployment, argued that such operations dulled the fighting edge of U.S. combat units because they sopped up time and money that had been earmarked for training and maintenance geared toward their more traditional combat roles. "The only way it can be controlled is through the appropriations process," Murtha told the Appropriations Committee during its brief debate on the bill.

Murtha also contended that senior U.N. officials lacked the know-how to command U.S. troops in complex and dangerous situations, such as the one in Somalia. "They frankly just don't have the skills or expertise," Murtha said. "These deployments worked much better when the United States was in complete control."

There was no formal test of committee sentiment on the provision aimed at limiting Somalia-like deployments. But several members of both parties vigorously endorsed its thrust.

Major Departures

Major departures from Clinton's budget request included the following additions:

● $1.06 billion to provide military personnel with a 2.2 percent pay raise effective Jan. 1, 1994.

● $1 billion to speed work on a new aircraft carrier slated for inclusion in the fiscal 1995 budget request.

● $609 million to allow combat units more operating time in the field.

● $363 million to overhaul tanks, ships and planes. The administration had sought to defer their scheduled maintenance.

Money to pay for these congressional initiatives came mostly from hundreds of relatively small cuts in Clinton's budget. But the committee also took a few big bites out of the administration's request, including:

● Cutting $399 million, the entire amount requested to develop the A/F-X, a stealthy, carrier-based bomber. The administration had abandoned this project in its "bottom up" review of long-term defense plans, released by Defense Secretary Les Aspin on Sept. 1. *(Bottom-up review, p. 452)*

● Cutting $629 million, the entire amount requested to develop a stealthy cruise missile designated TSSAM. It would be intended to carry several "smart" warheads that would home in on tanks, anti-aircraft missile launchers and

other targets far behind enemy lines. In its report on the defense bill, the Appropriations panel blasted the program as "an acquisition horror story," featuring cost overruns, delays and technical glitches.

• Cutting $300 million from the $2.07 billion requested to continue production of the C-17 long-range cargo jet. Citing that program's history of cost increases, delays and technical problems, Murtha called it "one of the most screwed-up programs we've ever seen. . . . Our patience is very thin on this issue," he told reporters.

In its report, however, the committee struck a note of resignation: "Barring substantial unforeseen difficulties, future armed services air transport requirements and sunk costs incurred . . . to date warrant the continued production of the C-17."

Bill Highlights

Personnel. The bill included $71.3 billion for military personnel.

This was to fund the 1.62 million-member active-duty force requested in Clinton's budget as well as a National Guard and reserve force of 1.03 million. The Guard and reserve force included 7,400 more members than Clinton sought. But it trimmed the rolls by more than 53,000 members, compared with the fiscal 1993 Guard and reserve ceiling.

The bill also included $1.18 billion for Guard and reserve equipment not requested by the administration, as well as the $1.06 billion to pay for the 2.2 percent pay raise.

Operations. For operations and maintenance costs, the bill provided $73.8 billion in new budget authority, $468 million less than Clinton requested. It also adopted the administration's proposal to boost the appropriation by $3.5 billion transferred from existing Pentagon funds.

Despite the net reduction, the bill included $609 million more than Clinton requested to allow units more time in the field to hone their training and $363 million more than the administration had planned for the tank, ship and plane overhauls.

Many of the reductions made to offset those expenditures were in keeping with those routinely made by the Appropriations panel on the argument that the readiness of combat forces would not be at risk. For instance, the bill cut from Clinton's request $550 million to reduce inventories and $85 million to reduce the Pentagon's use of outside consultants.

The bill also sliced $593 million from Clinton's $2.3 billion request to clean up toxic and hazardous wastes at existing and former military bases. Even with that reduction, the committee noted, the $1.7 billion that the bill provided was $517 million more than Congress appropriated for this account in fiscal 1993.

Naval forces. The Appropriations Committee backed Clinton's request for $2.64 billion for three *Arleigh Burke*-class destroyers equipped with the Aegis system of powerful radars and defensive missiles. But the committee challenged the administration's decision, announced as part of the bottom-up review, to build a third *Seawolf*-class submarine in order to keep intact General Dynamics Corp.'s sub-building complex at Groton, Conn.

The administration acknowledged that the *Seawolf*, which was designed to take on the huge submarine fleet of the former Soviet Union, was too complex — and thus too costly — for the missions facing the Navy in the post-Cold War world. A less-expensive sub, designated *Centurion*, was being designed, but the first of this new class could not

be funded until late in the decade at the earliest.

Warning that the cost of the two *Seawolf* subs previously funded was increasing, the Appropriations panel contended that a third ship could cost $2 billion. As a less expensive alternative to keep intact the Electric Boat sub complex in Groton, the committee ordered the Navy to study the cost and feasibility of upgrading the 31 oldest *Los Angeles*-class subs, built in the 1970s and early 1980s.

The committee approved the $476 million requested to continue developing the *Centurion* design.

Long-range bombers. The committee added $56 million to the amounts requested to develop improvements for the fleet of B-1 and B-2 bombers. The Pentagon planned to modify the 20 B-2s to carry "smart" bombs designed to use navigation data from satellites to steer to within a few yards of their targets. The panel's funding increase was intended to speed up the B-2 project and develop a similar capability for the 96 B-1s.

The committee also ordered the Air Force to mothball 22 of its 1960s-vintage B-52 bombers, trimming $100 million from the service's operations appropriation.

Strategic and space programs. The appropriators cut Clinton's request for $3.76 billion for the Ballistic Missile Defense program, providing $2.99 billion for the program, which was the Clinton team's pared-down version of the Reagan-era Strategic Defense Initiative (SDI).

The bill provided $6 million more than the $801 million requested to develop and build the huge Titan IV launch rockets needed to hurl into orbit some of the Pentagon's heaviest satellites. But in its report, the Appropriations Committee ordered the Pentagon to develop smaller satellites that could use less expensive launch vehicles. It also added $50 million to the bill to develop such launchers.

Army modernization. The committee added funds to several Army hardware programs, including:

• $386 million to buy 24 new Apache missile-armed attack helicopters to replace two dozen Apaches from the Army's inventory that were given to Israel. The change was also aimed at keeping the Apache production line humming until the Army was ready to begin using the facility to convert existing Apaches to the Longbow version, which was to carry a new target-finding radar. Without that added purchase, the committee warned, the production line faced a 19-month shutdown that would cost $400 million. The bill also included the $278 million requested to develop the Longbow modification.

• $216 million to equip 36 additional scout helicopters with long-range target-finding electronics. The bill also included $367 million, as requested, to continue developing the new Comanche scout helicopter.

• $31 million to begin upgrading "tank recovery vehicles," designed to tow damaged tanks off the battlefield. New M-1 tanks were too heavy for the recovery vehicles then in service.

• $20 million to accelerate development of a new mobile command post to replace older vehicles that were unable to keep pace with new M-1 tanks and Bradley troop carriers.

• $33 million to accelerate development of a new version of the Bradley, equipped with a digital data system that all the combat vehicles in a unit could use to quickly share information about their status and the location of enemy forces.

• $25 million to accelerate development of the intervehicle data system.

• $167 million — $75 million more than was requested — to develop and begin carrying out a program to upgrade early model M-1 tanks with the larger guns and sophisti-

Pay and Benefits

Sorting out what the military personnel appropriation bought was complicated because there was no simple answer to the question, "What does a colonel get paid?" The military's compensation system was built around a backbone of "basic pay," which was pegged to rank and seniority. But that could account for less than two-thirds of a service member's take-home pay, which also included an array of other allowances and bonus payments.

▶ **Basic pay.** In the fiscal 1994 bill, a total of $33 billion was for active-duty basic pay. To illustrate how that sum was parceled out:

—There were 34 four-star generals and admirals at the apex of the largest organization in the industrialized democracies. A general with 26 years' seniority would get slightly more than $108,000 in basic pay. There also was an expense allowance of $4,000 for the six who sat on the Joint Chiefs of Staff.

—There were 13,648 colonels and Navy captains on the top rung of the services' middle management, who might command a billion-dollar warship or a 6,000-man combat brigade. A colonel with 22 years' seniority would receive roughly $66,000.

—There were 97,406 Army, Air Force and Marine Corps captains and Navy lieutenants who might fly a $40 million fighter plane or command a 250-man infantry company. An Army captain with eight years of service would collect nearly $36,300.

—At the top of the enlisted ranks stood 13,338 sergeant majors and master chief petty officers. A master chief with 26 years of experience would collect basic pay of nearly $38,600.

—The most numerous ranks were the 421,597 Army and Marine corporals, Navy third-class petty officers and Air Force sergeants. A corporal with four years' service would receive nearly $14,900 in basic pay.

▶ **Housing allowances.** Traditionally, the government also had provided housing for military personnel as well as meals for all enlisted members and, under some circumstances, for officers. In lieu of those in-kind contributions, service members who obtained housing privately were paid allowances that varied with their rank and whether they were living with dependents.

The bill included $4.4 billion to pay active-duty members their "basic allowance for quarters." For example, a colonel with dependents would receive more than $9,700; a Navy lieutenant without dependents, nearly $5,800; a corporal with dependents, more than $4,300.

An additional $1.2 billion in the bill was for an extra allowance paid to personnel stationed in areas with particularly high local housing costs. Nearly half of these payments were to Navy personnel, who were concentrated in major seaports that typically were high-cost areas.

▶ **Subsistence allowance.** To pay allowances for meals ("subsistence," in Pentagon jargon), the bill provided $2.7 billion. Most of that sum was for enlisted members who did not live on bases and were authorized to dine at their own expense rather than eating in mess halls or aboard Navy ships. Their allowance was $6.80 per day.

▶ **Bonuses.** $1.95 billion was provided for an array of additional payments intended to attract and retain active-duty personnel in job specialties that were particularly hazardous or were highly paid in civilian life.

Nearly 23 percent of that total was the $447 million budgeted for aircraft crew members. Payments varied with seniority, but flight pay for officers with more than six years of flight duty (and less than 18 years as officers) could amount to $7,800 annually. Moreover, experienced pilots who contracted to remain in the service for a certain number of years could receive an additional payment of several thousand dollars annually.

Nearly a quarter of the special pay went to physicians, nurses, dentists and other medical professionals, for whom the bill contained $484 million. A physician might qualify to receive concurrently several different medical bonuses, one of which paid up to $36,000 annually. A nurse anesthetist could receive an additional $6,000 per year.

Also included was $267 million for crew members of Navy ships and $100 million for submarine crews. A Navy captain commanding a nuclear sub would receive annual sea pay amounting to

nearly $3,500 and an additional $7,140 for serving in a submarine. The top-ranking petty officers in his crew would receive $4,933 annually for sea pay and $4,259 for sub duty.

A total of $30 million was included for enlistment bonuses. These could amount to as much as $12,000 for a four-year enlistment, though not more than $7,000 could be paid in an initial lump sum.

For re-enlistment bonuses to encourage trained personnel to stay in hard-to-fill job specialties, the budget included $315 million, with nearly two-thirds earmarked for the Navy. For most personnel, the bonus could not exceed $20,000, though up to 10 percent of bonus recipients could get as much as $45,000.

▶ **'Early-Out' incentives.** The bill also included $1.1 billion to fund three temporary programs Congress created in 1991 and 1992 to encourage the voluntary departure of personnel who had not completed the 20 years of service needed to qualify for the military's relatively generous pension. The programs were intended to facilitate a rapid reduction in the size of the force without recourse to involuntary dismissals.

As requested in the budget, the defense bill included:

—$79 million for a program that paid an annuity for twice the number of years the person had served on active duty.

—$719 million for a program that paid a lump-sum incentive.

—$319 million for a program that allowed personnel with more than 15 years of service, but less than 20, to retire at a reduced pension.

OPERATIONS AND MAINTENANCE

The largest of the major slices in the defense funding pie was the $76.6 billion appropriation for operations and maintenance, referred to simply as O&M. Other than the military payroll, this title of the bill covered most of the day-to-day costs of military operations, including most of the $41.5 billion civilian payroll. It covered everything from the $3.25 billion cost of operating the 28 squadrons of long-range Air Force cargo planes to the $100,000 needed to operate the mailroom at Fort Huachuca, Ariz.

The bill appropriated $2.4 billion more than Clinton requested for O&M, but that apparent increase was largely a matter of bookkeeping: Congress decided to fund some purchases with new budget authority, rather than using money drawn out of Pentagon revolving funds as the administration requested.

The Pentagon broke most of the O&M appropriation into four broad categories of funding for the active-duty force:

—**Operating forces.** $33.8 billion (44 percent of the appropriation) to operate and support combat forces in the field. Forces supported by the bill included 16 ground combat divisions (13 Army and three Marine), 334 warships (including 12 aircraft carriers), 667 intercontinental ballistic missiles, 184 long-range bombers and 52 squadrons of Air Force fighters.

—**Mobilization.** $6.4 billion (8.3 percent) for stockpiles of equipment and supplies to support combat operations abroad and for training air and sea cargo units that would deploy forces from U.S. bases.

—**Training and Recruiting.** $6.4 billion (8.3 percent) for recruiting expenses, including advertising, and for Pentagon education programs, from basic training for recruits to the operation of the National War College, where promising colonels slated for the highest ranks studied strategy and management.

—**Administration and other costs.** $20.8 billion (27 percent) for overhead expenses not directly tied to the operating forces. These included activities conducted by one service for the benefit of all defense agencies.

An additional $8.1 billion (10.6 percent) of the O&M appropriation was for Guard and reserve activities.

Operating Tempo

Since the late 1970s, O&M funding had enjoyed a privileged status on Capitol Hill. At first, conservative critics blasted the Carter administration for tight defense budgets that skimped on training time and spare parts, producing a "hollow force." Then, liberal critics of the high-tech weapons programs of the Reagan years touted O&M

funding as a higher priority, on grounds that it contributed directly to the "combat readiness" of U.S. forces. Then the wheel turned again: As Pentagon spending was ratcheted down, conservatives contended that the Clinton team was undermining readiness, risking a return to the "hollow force" of the late 1970s.

In fact, the appropriation paid for a wide range of activities engaged in by a bureaucracy of nearly 3 million uniformed and civilian members. The portion that related most closely to combat readiness of units in the field was the funding of operating tempo. "Op tempo" was the Pentagon's term for the pace at which combat units practiced their craft, using fuel and other supplies in the process. It was measured crudely by how much vehicles were driven, ships steamed and planes and helicopters flew.

▶ **Army, Marines.** The defense bill included $1.6 billion for operations of active-duty Army combat units and $320 million for Marine forces. For the year, that would permit each Army battalion to log, on average, 800 miles in its M-1 tanks, 889 miles in its Bradley armored troop carriers and more than 4,100 miles in its jeeplike High-Mobility Multipurpose Wheeled Vehicle trucks, nicknamed "hum-vee." Army helicopter pilots would average 14.5 hours per month in flight.

▶ **Navy.** To operate nearly 400 ships manned by active-duty crews or civilian contractors, the Navy would receive $2 billion for "steaming time," which traditionally was measured in terms of the average number of days per quarter of the year that each ship would spend underway. The bill complied with the budget request by allowing ships assigned to the 6th Fleet in the Mediterranean and the 7th Fleet in the Far East to operate an average of 50.5 days per quarter while ships assigned to the U.S.-based fleets would steam an average of 29 days per quarter. More than a quarter of the fleet was nuclear-powered, mostly submarines. The remaining ships would consume nearly 16 million barrels of fuel oil.

▶ **Flight operations.** A total of $4.3 billion was provided for more than 1.6 million hours of flight operations by nearly 4,200 active-duty Navy, Marine Corps and Air Force aircraft. (This did not cover training or cargo hauling operations.)

In the Air Force, bomber crews would fly an average of 19.5 hours monthly and fighter crews 19.1 hours. Navy and Marine fighter crews would average 24 hours per month. The Navy said its higher standard reflected the difficulty its pilots faced in landing on aircraft carriers.

Recruiting and Training

The bill provided $334.8 million for active-duty recruiting costs, including advertising. The active-duty forces planned to take in nearly 184,000 fresh recruits during the year and to sign up an additional 2,050 people with prior military experience.

The bill also included $6 billion for training and educating active-duty personnel.

Base Operating Support

The bill provided $14.8 billion of the $15.1 billion requested to operate 304 active-duty bases and 23 reserve bases in the United States and 172 bases overseas.

The more than 136,000 military personnel assigned to keep the bases humming were paid out of the military personnel account. But the base operations fund in the O&M title paid the nearly 140,000 civilians who held similar jobs.

Revolving Fund

The Defense Business Operations Fund (DBOF) was covered by a separate title of the bill but inextricably connected to O&M funding. This was a revolving fund that bought fuel and other supplies on the commercial market and operated Defense Department maintenance depots. It also operated the Transportation Command, which conducted all long-haul air and sea movement of personnel, equipment and supplies.

In general, the fund was reimbursed by the operating units that "bought" goods and services from it. But the bill appropriated $1.1 billion to make up shortfalls. All but $12 million of this amount was the annual subsidy to cover operating costs of Pentagon commissaries.

▶ **Commissaries.** That $1.1 billion subsidy allowed the worldwide network of more than 350 commissaries to sell groceries and certain personal-care items to active-duty and retired personnel at prices as much as 20 percent lower than those at commercial stores. The stores projected sales in fiscal 1994 totaling $5.7 billion.

▶ **Air transport.** DBOF also would fund about half the $3.25 billion cost of running the Pentagon's long-range air cargo fleet, with the remainder covered by part of the Air Force O&M appropriation. In fiscal 1994, the Transportation Command, which was run as a part of DBOF, planned to charge other Pentagon agencies $1.65 billion for routine peacetime carriage by air of people or goods. But beyond the work needed to serve those customers, the command's long-range cargo planes and maintenance crews would conduct additional operations to sustain their ability to work at a much more rapid tempo in case of war. To cover those added readiness costs, the Air Force budget would pay the Transportation Command an additional $1.6 billion.

Medical

The bill also appropriated $9.6 billion for medical programs serving an eligible population of 8.2 million active-duty personnel, military retirees and their dependents and survivors. Though funded separately from the O&M title of the bill, the medical funding was largely for operating expenses.

Nearly 1.8 million personnel on active duty (including National Guard and reserve members serving on active duty) were entitled to unlimited care in the 140 hospitals and 578 clinics run by the military services.

The 2.37 million military dependents, the 1.74 million military retirees and the 2.29 million dependents and survivors could receive treatment in military facilities if space and time permitted. Otherwise, their treatment in private facilities was covered by the Civilian Health and Medical Program of the Uniformed Services (commonly known as CHAMPUS), which was the Pentagon's medical and hospitalization insurance program for dependents and retirees.

The bill provided $3.9 billion for CHAMPUS benefits, to cover an anticipated 284,000 hospital admissions and 14.4 million outpatient visits.

Other Programs

The Operations and Maintenance title also provided $1.96 billion to remove toxic and dangerous waste from operating and abandoned military installations. And it provided $400 million to assist Russia and other newly independent states in dismantling nuclear weapons formerly deployed by the Soviet Union.

In other parts of the bill, funds were provided for:

▶ **Chemical weapons destruction.** To dismantle existing chemical weapons and neutralize their contents, $390 million.

▶ **Drug interdiction.** Operations by military units, $868 million.

▶ **Office of the department's Inspector General.** $138 million.

PROCUREMENT

The bill's $44.7 billion procurement appropriation covered the purchase of durable goods ranging from Navy destroyers ($2.6 billion for three ships of the *Arleigh Burke* class) to air cargo pallets ($6.6 million).

Slightly less than half of that total was to be used for major weapons — planes, missiles, ships, ammunition and other big-ticket items. The remainder was earmarked for spare parts, so-called support equipment (such as the pallets) and modification of existing weapons.

In principle, Congress appropriated the complete cost of an item in the first year, even though the funds would be doled out to contractors over the several years that were required to build a jet plane or a warship. The chief exception to this "full funding" principle was that Congress appropriated funds to buy so-called long lead-time items a year or more in advance of funding certain ships and planes. These were components such as engines or electronic gear that had to be in hand early in the process of construction.

Aircraft

About 30 percent of the procurement total was devoted to aircraft for active-duty forces. Of this $13.6 billion, nearly 60 percent, was earmarked to buy planes and helicopters, with the rest going for spare parts, modifications and support equipment.

▶ **Cargo planes.** The largest single amount in the bill for purchasing an aircraft was the $2.2 billion earmarked for one of the most controversial programs — the long-range, wide-body C-17 cargo jet, which had faced a string of cost, schedule and technical problems. This amount would buy six planes, plus long lead-time components for future purchases.

To put competitive pressure on the McDonnell-Douglas Corp., builder of the C-17, the bill also provided $100 million to begin buying a modified version of an existing wide-body cargo jet, either a plane in commercial service or the Air Force's C-5.

▶ **Long-range bombers.** The bill included $735 million in procurement funds for the B-1 and B-2 bomber, but no additional planes would be purchased beyond the 96 B-1s already in service and the 20 B-2s previously authorized by Congress. These funds were earmarked largely for equipment used to maintain and operate those planes.

▶ **Tactical combat jets.** $2.2 billion was provided to buy jet fighters and ground attack planes: $1.52 billion for 36 Navy F/A-18s (plus $128 million for long-lead funding); $130 million to rebuild four Harrier vertical takeoff jets used by the Marine Corps (plus $15 million for long-lead funding); and $400 million for a final production run of 12 Air Force F-16s.

▶ **Electronic warfare planes.** The bill included $437 million for two JSTARS radar planes, converted jetliners rigged with powerful radar to detect tank columns and other ground targets more than 100 miles away.

▶ **Helicopters.** Nearly $1.6 billion was provided for helicopters, about half of which was for troop and cargo carriers including:

—$408 million for 60 Blackhawks used by the Army to carry 11-man infantry squads (plus long lead-time items.)

—$131 million for six Blackhawks for the Navy, equipped to rescue downed pilots.

—$292 million for 12 of the much larger CH-53Es for the Marine Corps, designed to carry 55 Marines or a 14-ton armored car (plus long-lead items).

The rest of the helicopter funds were for armed craft, with most of the money — $339 million — earmarked for 15 Navy Seahawks (plus long-lead). These were ship-based versions of the Blackhawk, equipped to launch torpedoes at submarines. The bill included $168 million for 10 missile-armed Apache tank-hunting helicopters for the Army. An additional $144 million was earmarked for a dozen Cobra helicopters, which carried anti-tank missiles, for the Marines.

▶ **Trainers.** The bill included $470 million for training aircraft. The largest piece of this was $290 million for 12 Goshawks (plus long lead-time funding). The Navy used this British-designed plane, which could land on aircraft carriers, as a basic trainer. Also provided was: $141 million for 35 small twin-engine jets used to train pilots who would fly multiengine cargo and tanker planes, $29 million for training helicopters and $10 million for small planes used to screen applicants for pilot training.

▶ **Modifications.** The $2.5 billion appropriated for aircraft modifications would touch on practically every type of aircraft in the Pentagon's fleet. But nine large programs accounted for nearly half the funds.

One of these was the Army's AHIP program, which would rebuild existing scout helicopters to the extent that they became practically new weapons. The $123 million provided for AHIP in this bill would equip 18 helicopters with night-vision equipment and anti-tank weapons. A related program appropriated $104 million to arm AHIPs previously equipped with the night-vision equipment.

Another program provided $116 million to modify Navy F-14 fighters to attack ground targets. But the defense appropriations conferees ordered the Navy to consider shifting its priorities by

using the modification funds instead to equip the planes with more powerful engines.

Amounts appropriated for other large aircraft modification programs were: $112 million to upgrade the electronic intelligence-gathering equipment on the Army's Guardrail planes, $118 million for the Navy's P-3C land-based patrol planes, $124 million for the E-2C radar surveillance planes that operated from aircraft carriers, $268 million for Air Force F-15 fighters, $129 million for C-130 midrange cargo planes and $121 million for F-16 fighters.

Missiles, Satellites and Torpedoes

About one-sixth of the procurement appropriation ($7.7 billion) was for sophisticated "smart" weapons such as guided missiles and torpedoes and for space-related equipment. This included $3.8 billion for combat missiles and $355 million to modify missiles already in the inventory. It included $1.44 billion for space satellites and satellite launch rockets and $234 million for torpedoes and other anti-submarine weapons. It also included almost $1.6 billion for secret projects — the largest pot of money for classified programs in the procurement budget.

▶ **Trident II.** More than half the missile procurement total — $1.14 billion — was for the only long-range, nuclear-armed (or "strategic") weapon then in production in the United States, the Trident II submarine-launched missile. The funds were earmarked to buy 24 of these multiwarhead weapons (plus long lead-time components).

▶ **Tomahawk missiles.** The bill allocated $248 million to the Navy for 216 Tomahawk cruise missiles, which had been deployed in the past decade to greatly extend the reach of most U.S. warships. When equipped with a 1,000-pound conventional warhead, as were the nearly 300 Tomahawks launched against Iraq in the Persian Gulf War, this extremely accurate weapon had a range of more than 300 miles.

▶ **Artillery rockets.** Nearly $370 million was provided for Army artillery rockets: $153 million for 255 ATACMS missiles (plus long lead-time) with a range of more than 60 miles; $75 million for 20-mile-range MLRS rockets, which were fired in salvos of up to a dozen; and $179 million for launchers to accommodate both weapons. Both types of rocket blanketed their targets with hundreds of fist-sized "bomblets" designed to kill troops and damage any vehicles that were not heavily armored.

▶ **Short-range missiles.** More than $400 million was provided for short-range guided missiles designed to punch through tank armor. This included nearly $150 million for more than 3,400 four-mile range Hellfires, carried by helicopters; $73 million for 2,000 shorter-range TOWs, launched from several types of vehicles or from a simple tripod; and $207 million for 1,000 Javelins, small enough to be carried by one soldier.

▶ **Anti-aircraft weapons.** The bill included more than $621 million for anti-aircraft weapons. The largest single amount was $215 million to buy 220 Standard missiles used by the Navy. An additional $121 million was for Patriot missiles adapted to intercept short-range (or "theater") ballistic missiles, such as the Soviet-designed Scuds launched by Iraq during the Persian Gulf War.

The total also included $33 million for three-mile-range Stinger missiles and $154 million for 168 turrets armed with clusters of Stingers to be mounted in the back of Army pickup trucks or Marine Corps armored cars.

▶ **Air-to-ground missiles.** For such missiles (other than the anti-tank Hellfire), the bill provided $339 million. Nearly half ($161 million) was for a stealth missile designated TSSAM, each of which would carry several warheads designed to home in on tanks and other battlefield targets. Also included was $98 million for 75 additional SLAMs, a television-guided version of the Navy's Harpoon missile, with a 570-pound warhead and a 60-mile range. There also was $70 million for 102 TV-guided AGM-130s, with a one-ton warhead and a range of more than 25 miles, designed to be carried by fighter planes; $5 million for the Israeli-designed "Have Nap" missile, a larger TV-guided weapon with a one-ton warhead and a 50-mile range, intended to be carried by B-52 bombers; and $5 million to pay for loose ends of a long-range stealth cruise

missile no longer in production.

▸ **AMRAAM missiles.** The bill included $549 million for nearly 800 AMRAAM radar-guided air-to-air missiles, with a range of more than 30 miles. They were carried by all types of Air Force, Navy and Marine Corps fighters.

▸ **Space satellites.** The nearly $1.44 billion provided to buy space satellites and related equipment included $471 million for Titan IV launch rockets — the largest unmanned ones used by the United States — and $143 million for smaller Atlas-Centaur and Delta launchers. It also included:

—$160 million for Navy communication satellites.

—$28 million for general-use communication satellites.

—$172 million for navigation satellites.

—$360 million for satellites that could detect missile launches.

▸ **Anti-sub weapons.** The bill included $234 million for homing torpedoes and related equipment: $100 million for 108 copies of the 20-mile range Mark 48 (plus long lead-time), a 3,000-pound weapon carried only by submarines; $46 million for 800-pound Mark 50s, carried by aircraft; and $23 million for a missile designed to launch a Mark 50 from a warship toward a submarine up to 15 miles away.

Ships

The bill provided $5.7 billion for Navy vessels and cargo ships, including $300 million to put the finishing touches on ships nearing delivery (for instance, stocking them with spare parts and supplies).

▸ **Warships.** Only three front-line combat vessels were funded: The bill included $2.6 billion for three *Arleigh Burke*-class destroyers. Each of the ships would be equipped with the Aegis anti-aircraft system, an anti-aircraft missile battery controlled by a network of powerful radar and computers.

There was an effort in Congress to add to the bill $3.4 billion for a nuclear-powered aircraft carrier that the Clinton administration planned to request in fiscal 1995. Ultimately, however, that was rejected despite belated administration support for the move. But the bill provided $1.2 billion more than Clinton requested to build high-speed cargo ships to haul U.S.-based combat divisions to distant trouble spots. This extra money could be used to expedite work on the new carrier if Congress passed a supplemental bill authorizing the shift. Otherwise, the entire $1.5 billion "sealift" fund was to be spent on cargo ships.

▸ **Other vessels.** The bill also provided:

—$894 million for a *Wasp*-class helicopter carrier able to carry 2,000 Marines and the helicopters to fly them ashore. It included an additional $50 million for long lead-time funding for another ship of the same type.

—$124 to convert the older helicopter carrier *Inchon* into a headquarters ship for minesweepers.

—$110 million for two oceanographic research ships, to be used for charting the sea bottom.

▸ **Ship equipment.** In addition to the funds for ship construction, the bill provided nearly $2 billion for equipment to be installed in new vessels and in older ships being modernized. This included $58 million for radars, $360 million for weapons-related equipment, and $312 million for sonar and other electronic devices used by submarines and anti-sub vessels.

It also included $289 million for nuclear reactor components and alterations to the propulsion systems of nuclear-powered warships.

Tanks, Guns and Ammunition

The bill included $1.4 billion for ammunition, aerial bombs and munitions production plants and an additional $1 billion to buy or upgrade tanks, combat vehicles, cannons and personal firearms.

▸ **M-1 tanks.** This included $97 million to upgrade 72 older M-1 tanks to M-1A1s, with a larger cannon and sophisticated electronic gear so they could fight in the dark.

▸ **Other.** The bill also included:

—$160 million to modernize self-propelled 155 mm howitzers so that they could shoot farther, more quickly and more accurately, and could be driven at night.

—$192 million to keep warm the production line for Bradley armored troop carriers so it would be available when the Army wanted to begin upgrading its early-model Bradleys with the heavier armor and more sophisticated electronics of later models.

—$8 million to begin buying lightly armored tanks for use by the Army's air-mobile units.

—$66 million for 21 armored cars used by the Marine Corps.

National Guard, Reserve Equipment

Since the early 1980s, it had become routine for Congress to add to the annual defense bills hundreds of millions of dollars for equipment earmarked for National Guard and reserve units, which had considerable clout on Capitol Hill. Though the Guard and reserve had been assigned many high-priority missions, congressional backers insisted that the services routinely shortchanged reserve equipment requirements at budget time.

Congress added to the appropriations bill $1.2 billion for equipment to be issued to Guard and reserve units. The sum was allocated among the reserve branches, but it was not earmarked for specific projects, except that $800 million was set aside to buy unspecified transport and cargo aircraft.

Other Procurement

▸ **Communications.** To buy myriad types of communications and intelligence-gathering equipment and similar electronic devices, the bill provided nearly $3.7 billion. The largest slice of this pie by far was the nearly $400 million appropriated for SINCGARS, a network of battlefield radios designed to foil enemy jamming efforts by rapid changes of frequency.

▸ **Vehicles.** Nearly $1 billion was provided for non-combat vehicles ranging from trucks to fire engines to sedans. This included:

—$243 million for more than 5,800 hum-vees. These boxy, four-wheel-drive vehicles were the more muscular successors to the venerable jeep. They were used by the Army, Marine Corps and Air Force as everything from ambulances to missile-armed tank-hunters.

—$403 million for 945 heavy-duty ammunition trucks, able to carry 16 tons of munitions and equipped with rapid unloading equipment.

—Nearly $10 million for 61 fire engines and crash trucks for Air Force bases.

RESEARCH AND DEVELOPMENT

The $35 billion appropriation for Pentagon research and development accounted for 46 percent of all R&D funding in the federal government's fiscal 1994 budget.

By the Defense Department's accounting, $3.7 billion of the total was for basic research and nearly $3.5 billion was for development of technologies not yet linked to a particular weapons development program. Taken together, these two pots of money — which the Pentagon regarded as investment in its technology base — accounted for more than 21 percent of the R&D total.

An additional $2.6 billion was provided for the anti-missile defense program formerly known as the Strategic Defense Initiative (SDI) and renamed the Ballistic Missile Defense program.

Development programs related to strategic arms consumed $3 billion, conventional weapons programs $13 billion and communications and intelligence programs $4.6 billion.

An additional $4 billion was for overhead and support costs that underwrote the overall defense effort, including the cost of operating military test ranges. This category included $273 million to continue developing the Titan IV satellite launch rocket, designed to orbit 20-ton payloads.

Strategic Programs

The lion's share of the strategic weapons R&D was for the Air Force ($2.9 billion). In turn, nearly two-thirds of that money was to continue development of a handful of major programs: the B-2 bomber ($790 million), the Milstar communication satellite ($932

million) and two programs to develop new types of satellites that could detect attacking missiles ($250 million).

Conventional Weapons

The $13 billion appropriated by the bill to develop conventional arms was parceled out among hundreds of programs. But a dozen major projects — three in the Navy, three in the Air Force, four in the Army and two that cut across service lines — absorbed half the total.

▶ **Army.** The Army's largest program ($367 million) was to develop the Comanche, a missile-armed scout helicopter intended to be smaller, faster and harder to detect than Apaches or the scout helicopters presently in use.

Another of the Army's projects was the Longbow system, a target-finding radar coupled with a radar-guided version of the Hellfire anti-tank missile ($278 million).

The original Hellfire was designed to home in on the reflection of a laser beam bounced off a target by the launching Apache or by a scout helicopter. If the Longbow worked out, it would be able to find targets in smoke and haze that would blind a laser.

Moreover, because the modified Hellfires would be guided to the target by their own tiny radars, the launching helicopter could dodge away from hostile fire as soon as it launched the missiles.

The other major Army programs were:
— $238 million to develop a new self-propelled artillery piece and an armored ammunition carrier to accompany it.
— $120 million to develop the BAT anti-tank warhead, designed to be scattered over enemy forces by artillery rockets and home in on the roofs of tanks, where their armor was relatively thin.

▶ **Navy.** The Navy's largest development program by far was the effort to develop an enlarged version of the F/A-18 fighter. These "stretched" versions — the single-seat "E" and two-seat "F" models — were intended to fly farther than the existing F/A-18 models and to carry a larger bomb load. The bill provided $1.47 billion for that project.

The bill also provided $240 million to continue development of a new nuclear sub, designated *Centurion*, that would be smaller and less expensive than the *Seawolf*-class subs then under construction.

There was $414 million provided for a project that combined several programs — some of them secret — that were aimed at improving the self-defense capability of smaller warships and transports to protect themselves against cruise missile attack. Essentially, the project was intended to let each ship in a task force collect data from all the other ships' radar.

▶ **Air Force.** The $2.1 billion appropriated for fiscal 1994 toward development of the F-22 fighter plane accounted for nearly half the Air Force's conventional weapons development budget. Designed to combine agility and stealthiness, the plane was intended to supplant the F-15 as the service's premier air-to-air fighter.

Two other large appropriations were to continue development of planes slated to enter service in the next few years:
— $180 million for the C-17 wide-body cargo plane.
— $289 million for the JSTARS radar plane.

▶ **Multiservice.** The amount appropriated for the TSSAM missile was secret, but data from various sources suggested that the total was $548 million, including $387 million for development. Designed on "stealth" principles, to evade enemy detection, TSSAM was intended to dispense several BAT anti-tank warheads up to 100 miles from its launcher.

The bill also provided $219 million to develop unspecified types of combat equipment for special operations forces.

ECONOMIC CONVERSION

Scattered through the defense appropriations bill were provisions allocating $2.49 billion for projects to help Pentagon workers, defense contractors, employees of those firms and their localities retool for non-defense business as the defense budget continued to shrink.

Major elements of this defense conversion package funded the following projects:

▶ **Military personnel.** $331 million: This was to induce career-minded members to leave the armed services earlier than they had planned. The bulk of it ($319 million) was for a temporary program to provide pensions — although at scaled-down levels — for personnel who had completed more than 15 years of service but less than the 20 years previously required to collect a pension. The remaining $12 million was to provide transitional health insurance while former service members find civilian jobs.

▶ **Operations and maintenance.** $377 million: This included $100 million to provide severance pay and transitional health insurance for displaced civilian Pentagon employees. Among the other components were: $39 million for the Pentagon's Office of Economic Adjustment, which attempted to help communities find new job sources to replace vanished Pentagon contractors; $15 million to train former military personnel as law enforcement and health-care providers; and $73 million to expand junior ROTC programs in hopes of fostering a sense of discipline in at-risk, urban youth.

▶ **Procurement.** $56 million: The bulk of this amount ($50 million) was to guarantee loans to finance the construction of commercial ships and the modernization of private shipyards that had built Navy ships.

▶ **Research and development.** $1.726 billion: Of this amount, $474 million was to fund the federal government's share of so-called dual-use partnerships. These were projects to develop technologies that promised to be useful both in military applications and in commercial products. By law, they had to be jointly funded by the Pentagon and by consortia of universities, research institutes and corporations. ■

D.C. Abortion Funding Restrictions Eased

In what District of Columbia officials considered a major victory for local autonomy, Congress on Oct. 27 cleared a spending bill (HR 2492) that, for the first time in five years, allowed the District to use local funds to pay for abortions for poor women through the joint federal-state Medicaid program.

Abortions-rights advocates were disappointed nevertheless: With a supporter in the White House, they had hoped the bill would go much further. Indeed, both chambers initially passed versions of the D.C. spending bill that contained no abortion restrictions. But the House rejected the conference report, and bill sponsors wrote a new version that permitted federal funds to be used for abortion only in cases of rape or incest or when the pregnancy endangered the life of the woman — tracking the language in the 1994 spending bill for the departments of Labor, Health and Human Services, and Education.

President Clinton signed HR 2492 (PL 103-127) on Oct. 29.

As cleared, the bill provided $700 million in federal funds to the District, $630.6 million of which was in lieu of property taxes and other revenue that was lost to the city because it could not tax the federal government. The bill also included $17.3 million in federal funds to help the city combat its continually rising crime rate and $52 million as the federal government's contribution to the retirement fund for city employees. In addition, the bill authorized the city to spend its own budget of $3.7 billion.

BACKGROUND

The boost to local autonomy was directly related to having Democrat Clinton in the White House. Republican President George Bush had vetoed every D.C. appropriations bill that failed to place a restriction on the spending of both federal and local funds for abortions. *(1992 Almanac, p. 681)*

In fact, the city had been prevented since 1979 from using federal funds for abortions, and that ban was broadened to include local funds in 1988.

It was indicative of the strange, and often strained, relationship that D.C. officials had with Congress that such a small change as allowing the city to do as it saw fit with its own funds should be regarded as a significant victory.

But Congress often had approached its relationship with the nation's capital with mixed intentions. On the one hand, Congress granted the city home rule in 1973 so that residents could elect a mayor and City Council to run city affairs. But lawmakers also retained control over the city's finances through the annual appropriations bill.

BOXSCORE

➡ **Fiscal 1994 appropriations for the District of Columbia (HR 2492).** The spending bill provided $700 million to the District, including a $630.6 million federal payment, and allowed the city to raise $3.7 billion in local revenue.

Reports: H Rept 103-152, S Rept 103-104; conference reports H Rept 103-291, H Rept 103-303.

KEY ACTION

June 30 — **House** passed HR 2492, 213-211.

July 27 — **Senate** passed HR 2492, 70-29.

Oct. 14 — HR 2492 approved by a **House-Senate** conference.

Oct. 20 — **House** rejected conference report, 206-224.

Oct. 27 — **House** agreed to second conference report, 225-201.

Oct. 27 — **Senate** agreed to conference report by voice vote.

Oct. 29 — **President** signed HR 2492 — PL 103-127.

The requirement that the city's budget be approved by the House and Senate gave lawmakers an annual opportunity to tell city officials what they liked or disliked about the way the city was being run.

Lawmakers had used the D.C. bill to complain about the city's crime rate, to try to protect firefighter jobs slated to be cut by the D.C. government, to criticize the salaries of D.C. council members, to condemn D.C. statehood protests being held outside House office buildings, to direct money to local universities and even to deplore the conditions of bridges coming into the city.

But the presence of a Democrat in the White House did not help District officials move any closer to their ultimate objective: statehood. Clinton had said he supported the idea, but congressional Democrats were deeply divided, and a bill granting statehood was badly defeated when it came to the House floor for a vote on Nov. 21. *(D.C. statehood, p. 208)*

HOUSE SUBCOMMITTEE ACTION

The House District of Columbia Appropriations Subcommittee approved the spending bill by voice vote June 15. The measure allowed the city to pay for poor women's abortions and to implement an ordinance letting unmarried couples register as domestic partners. Both issues had caused angry floor fights on the bill in past years.

The bill gave the city a $630.6 million federal payment, up from the fiscal 1993 payment of $624.9 million; Clinton had requested $653 million. It provided $52 million for city employee retirement funds and $17.3 million to be directed to Mayor Sharon Pratt Kelly's youth and crime initiative, a program aimed at curbing the city's high crime rate; $2 million of that was to be delayed until Oct. 1, 1994, the start of fiscal 1995.

The bill also authorized the city to raise $3.7 billion of its own funds through taxes and the city lottery.

Domestic Partners, Abortion

At the markup, Democrats barely defeated, 5-5, an attempt to prevent the city from implementing its law allowing domestic partners to register.

Under the D.C. ordinance, unmarried couples, including homosexuals, could register with the city as domestic partners. Partners of District government employees were eligible for the group health insurance offered to city employees; the employee was responsible for paying the higher premiums.

In the 1992 D.C. spending bill, Congress prohibited the city from spending any funds to implement the law. D.C.

DISTRICT OF COLUMBIA

	Fiscal 1993 Appropriation	Fiscal 1994 Clinton Request	House Bill	Senate Bill	Final Bill
	(In thousands of dollars)				
Appropriations to D.C.					
Federal payment	$624,854	$653,031	$630,603	$630,603	$630,603
Contributions to retirement fund	52,070	52,070	52,070*	52,070	52,070*
Federal contribution to crime and youth initiative	—	—	17,327	15,327	17,327
Inaugural expenses	5,514	—	—	—	—
Trauma Care Fund	5,562	—	—	—	—
Subtotal, federal funds	**$688,000**	**$705,101**	**$700,000**	**$698,000**	**$700,000**
District-raised funds	3,988,421	3,740,382	3,753,705	3,777,932	3,740,382
Total D.C. budget	**$4,676,421**	**$4,445,483**	**$4,453,705**	**$4,475,932**	**$4,440,382**

* $2 million of this is being deferred until fiscal 1995.

SOURCE: House Appropriations Committee

Appropriations Subcommittee Chairman Julian C. Dixon, D-Calif., had removed the prohibition in the 1993 bill, but Oklahoma Republican Ernest Jim Istook Jr. offered an amendment to keep the ban.

"I look at this as a statement of public policy," Istook said. "We're going to have a government policy that says we don't care about the institution of marriage."

But Dixon argued that Congress should not overrule a local decision approved by the City Council.

Istook's amendment was rejected despite the support of Ohio Democrat Marcy Kaptur, who voted with the subcommittee's three Republicans and Joseph M. McDade, Pa., the ranking Republican on the full committee, who had a vote in the subcommittee.

Dixon's bill also dropped the longstanding ban on the city's using its own money to pay for poor women's abortions. In past years, the D.C. spending bill had explicitly prohibited the city from spending either local or federal funds for the procedure. Dixon's bill was silent on abortion funding, thus allowing the use of local funds while leaving the city subject to a federal ban on spending federal funds for abortions.

Istook offered an amendment to reinstate the ban on local funds. It was rejected on a 4-6 show of hands, with Henry Bonilla, R-Texas, voting with the Democrats.

To let the city raise more revenue, the subcommittee agreed to a McDade amendment to lift an exemption from local taxes that Congress had granted two government-sponsored enterprises, the Federal National Mortgage Association (Fannie Mae) and the Student Loan Marketing Association (Sallie Mae). Lifting the exemption was expected to bring about $25 million to $30 million a year to city coffers, subcommittee staff said.

FULL COMMITTEE ACTION

The House Appropriations Committee on June 23 approved the $700 million D.C. spending bill (H Rept 103-152) by voice vote, after debating Congress' right to overrule decisions made by the City Council.

James T. Walsh, N.Y., the ranking Republican on the D.C. subcommittee, criticized the $17 million added for youth and crime programs as "walking around money" and sought to remove it from the bill. Walsh said the city received a generous federal payment and got additional federal funds through Community Development Block Grants and other grant programs for states and territories.

Dixon argued that no more important issue faced the city than crime prevention. The committee subsequently rejected Walsh's amendment on a 17-24 show of hands.

Debating Local Issues

As often happened with the D.C. spending bill, members used the occasion to argue over city politics and whether they should assert federal prerogatives over local affairs.

At the request of Steny H. Hoyer, D-Md., the bill was amended to require that the city maintain the existing staffing level of 269 firefighters per 24-hour period. City officials wanted to reduce the staffing level to 236 firefighters per 24-hour period, saying it would save the city $3.4 million. Hoyer, whose suburban Maryland district was home to many D.C. firefighters, said public safety would suffer if the number of firefighters were cut.

As he had done during subcommittee consideration, Istook offered an amendment to restrict the city from using any funds to implement the domestic partners law. Istook said he was concerned that the city ordinance would redefine what the "family in America is about."

Dixon opposed Istook's amendment and said that Congress should not block decisions made at the local level. But Istook insisted that the Constitution gave Congress the right to oversee the District. David R. Obey, D-Wis., called the domestic partners act "whacko" but said Congress should not play "national nanny to D.C."

The committee rejected Istook's amendment by voice vote.

In other action, the committee:

● Approved, by voice vote, an amendment by Dixon and McDade striking the language that would have made

Fannie Mae and Sallie Mae subject to local taxes. Dixon said that the Banking Committee objected to the provision because it constituted legislative language on an appropriations bill.

● Defeated, on a 19-22 show of hands, another Walsh amendment that would have precluded the D.C. government from using District funds for payments to the D.C. shadow senators and representatives. The city was already prohibited from making payments to the elected shadow officials, who included Jesse Jackson. The bill removed that restriction.

HOUSE FLOOR ACTION

Expressing its paradoxical relationship with the District of Columbia, the House on June 30 approved the bill on a 213-211 vote, after asserting its right to block a local law but refusing to tell the city not to cut its work force. *(Vote 317, p. 78-H)*

The close vote was probably due to the bill's lack of any prohibition on abortion funding and the failure of a Republican amendment trying to cut its funds.

New Jersey Republican Christopher H. Smith, co-chairman of the Pro-Life Caucus, told members that he opposed the bill because it lacked an abortion ban. He was joined by 160 other Republicans and 50 Democrats in voting against it.

Repeating an attempt made in the full Appropriations Committee, Walsh offered an amendment to strip the $17.3 million for crime prevention from the bill. The amendment was defeated, 200-227. *(Vote 312, p. 76-H)*

Istook again offered an amendment to prohibit the city from using any funds in the bill to implement the domestic partners law. This time he succeeded; the amendment was approved 251-177, *(Vote 313, p. 76-H)*

Although the Istook amendment passed easily, on another local issue, the House voted in favor of letting the city make its own decisions.

The District's lone House representative, Democratic Delegate Eleanor Holmes Norton, offered an amendment to drop Hoyer's language barring the District from reducing firefighter staffing. "Public safety is cited, but the facts are so clearly contrary that the motive is transparent to retain the jobs of firefighters who live outside the District," she said.

Hoyer responded that Congress was responsible for ensuring the safety of the thousands of visitors to the nation's capital and of the federal work force, and a fully staffed city fire department was needed for that protection.

But Norton's amendment prevailed, 270-158, after she received support from a number of Republicans, including Istook and Thomas J. Bliley Jr., Va., the ranking Republican on the House District of Columbia Committee. Bliley said that if Congress prevented the city from cutting its own budget then city officials would come to Congress and say: " 'You won't let us trim the fat. Then give us the money to pay for the fat.' " *(Vote 314, p. 76-H)*

SENATE COMMITTEE ACTION

The Senate Appropriations Committee on July 20 approved its version of the bill (S Rept 103-104) by a vote of 29-0.

Although the $698 million in federal funds essentially tracked what was provided in the House-passed bill, the Senate committee deleted the House provision prohibiting the District from implementing its domestic partners law.

The Senate version of the bill, like the House measure, was silent on whether the city could use local funds to pay for abortions.

The bill included a $630.6 million federal payment to the city and $52 million for city employee retirement funds, the same amounts as in the House bill. It provided slightly less — $15.3 million — for Mayor Kelly's anti-crime initiative. Left out was the $2 million in fiscal 1995 spending.

The five members of the Senate D.C. Appropriations Subcommittee were all serving on the panel for the first time. New Chairman Herb Kohl, D-Wis., said he removed the House provision that would have prevented the city from implementing its domestic partners ordinance because he supported "home rule" and believed that city officials and residents should decide local issues.

The Senate bill included a provision, not in the House measure, directing the city to keep open D.C. Fire Engine Company No. 3, which was four blocks from the Capitol. The city had wanted to close the station for years, but lawmakers wanted it saved because of its proximity to their offices.

Another local issue that was expected to provoke floor debate was report language on a plan by Georgetown University to build a 56-megawatt co-generation power plant on the campus.

The university wanted the plant to help meet campus heating and cooling needs, but the mayor and some City Council members said residents were concerned about the plant being built in a residential neighborhood. The report language directed the city and the university to resolve the dispute "on the merits of the project, at the local level, without frivolous delay."

Norton, who attended the Senate committee markup, said that she appreciated Kohl's first effort at handling the D.C. spending bill, saying, "He produced a very clean bill, in very short order."

SENATE FLOOR ACTION

The full Senate easily approved the $698 million D.C. bill on a 70-29 vote July 27, after a two-hour debate most notable in its restraint on challenging D.C. policies. *(Vote 219, p. 29-S)*

Kohl said after the vote that he was pleased by the fact that the abortion language did not come up during floor debate. "We were not looking for confrontation on the bill," he said. "I wanted to have as civil a tone as possible."

The Senate did, however, seek to modify local will on another issue. Senators rejected, 43-55, the Appropriations Committee's recommendation that they drop the House-passed prohibition on implementing the D.C. domestic partnership law. "We may like it [the domestic partners law], we may not like it," Kohl argued, "but we ought to respect it, and that is what home rule requires." *(Vote 217, p. 29-S)*

But Trent Lott, R-Miss., who led the fight against the domestic partners law, urged his colleagues to reject the committee recommendation and said that dropping the ban would "undermine the family" because "it legitimizes and extends benefits to relationships outside marriage."

CONFERENCE

House and Senate negotiators reached agreement Oct. 14 on a fiscal 1994 spending bill that provided the city $700 million, including a $630.6 million federal payment. The

They also argued that the technology would be easy for terrorists or emerging countries with nuclear ambitions to exploit to build bombs.

● **Gas-cooled reactors.** The subcommittee approved $12 million for the development of the gas-turbine modular helium reactor, also known as the high-temperature gas reactor, which was an attempt to create a reactor impervious to meltdown. The administration had called for the elimination of all funding for the project.

● **Space-based reactors.** The subcommittee also salvaged a remnant of the Cold War — an Energy Department program to develop a high-powered nuclear reactor for civilian and defense use in space.

The program, known as SP-100, was an effort by the Energy Department, the Pentagon and the National Aeronautics and Space Administration (NASA) to develop a nuclear-based power source for outer space. Defense officials early on saw applications for the Strategic Defense Initiative (SDI). And NASA envisioned using such a reactor to provide power for extended moon visits and robotic exploration of Mars and other planets.

But the project was plagued by cost overruns and missed deadlines. When interest in SDI waned with the end of the Cold War, the Pentagon stopped funding its share of the project. Then in 1993, NASA proposed ending its Moon-Mars program.

The Clinton administration had recommended that the program be terminated, but the subcommittee restored $30 million for the project at the behest of two lawmakers whose districts benefited from the jobs created by the project. Norman Y. Mineta, D-Calif., said about 180 employees worked on the project for Martin Marietta Corp. in his San Jose district. An additional 270 employees worked in Valley Forge, Pa., in the district of Republican Robert S. Walker.

● **Renewable energy.** The subcommittee also increased Energy Department research funding for solar and renewable energy to $247.4 million in fiscal 1994, though not to the level that the administration had requested, $248.4 million.

Full Committee Action

The House Appropriations Committee on June 17 approved the $22.2 billion spending bill by voice vote (H Rept 103-135) after making only minor technical changes to the Energy and Water Subcommittee recommendations.

The panel kept intact the $620 million in fiscal 1994 spending for the superconducting super collider. The day before the markup, Clinton reiterated his support for the controversial project in a letter to Appropriations Chairman William H. Natcher, D-Ky. "Abandoning the [super collider] at this point would signal that the United States is compromising its position of leadership in basic science — a position unquestioned for generations," Clinton wrote.

Energy Subcommittee Chairman Tom Bevill, D-Ala., said a tight budget climate limited spending increases in the bill to a total of $182 million over fiscal 1993 levels. For example, Bevill said he received a record number of requests for new Army Corps of Engineer water projects from lawmakers, the bill's traditional forum for sending federal dollars back to congressional districts. But he said the subcommittee had to reject every one to remain within spending limits.

The bill allocated $1.4 billion for general construction of water projects and $352 million for flood control projects in several Southern and Midwestern states.

One of the biggest spending increases in the bill was for environmental cleanup of Energy Department nuclear research facilities. The committee agreed to provide $6.2 billion in fiscal 1994, up $648 million from fiscal 1993. Within that amount, however, the environmental cleanup of defense-related facilities became a victim of the year's budget constraints. The appropriators cut funding for that program to $5.2 billion, down $280 million from Clinton's budget.

The bill also boosted funding for wind and ocean energy and bio-fuels research and development by $60 million to $247 million.

The committee set a level of $404 million for nuclear testing, below the president's request of $462 million.

HOUSE FLOOR ACTION

The House passed the fiscal 1994 energy and water spending bill by a vote of 350-73 on June 24, but only after voting to kill three staple Energy Department programs — the embattled superconducting super collider and two smaller efforts to develop an advanced nuclear reactor and a nuclear power source for space. The result was a slightly slimmer $21.7 billion bill. *(Vote 273, p. 66-H)*

Super Collider

The House adopted, on a 280-150 vote, an amendment by Jim Slattery, D-Kan., and Sherwood Boehlert, R-N.Y., to kill the super collider. *(Vote 269, p. 66-H)*

During floor debate, Slattery, Boehlert and others continued to hammer away at cost overruns and delays in the $11 billion project, the failure of foreign governments to participate as promised and the need for frugality amid budget deficits. The opponents were given fresh ammunition the day before the vote in the form of news accounts of an internal Energy Department draft document alleging that $216 million in subcontractor expenses were unnecessary or excessive. Project managers subsequently rejected the allegations.

Super collider advocates argued that nothing less than the United States' pre-eminence in basic research was at stake and said the project annually represented just a minute fraction of the total $76 billion U.S. research budget.

After the vote, supporters of the project, led by Martin Frost, D-Texas, looked to the Senate to rescue the program as it had done before.

Nuclear Reactors

● **Liquid metal reactors.** The House voted 267-162 to adopt an amendment by Sam Coppersmith, D-Ariz., cutting $31.9 million from the bill to eliminate the Energy Department's advanced liquid metal reactor program. The agency already had spent $1.3 billion on the program, one of several approaches being explored in the search for a safer nuclear power source. *(Vote 267, p. 66-H)*

Coppersmith called the reactor obsolete and too expensive, because newer generations of light-water reactors (so called because they used regular water rather than deuterium-based heavy water) used less costly and more abundant uranium, rather than plutonium and a mix of other radioactive materials. He also echoed concerns of antinuclear groups that the technology was vulnerable to terrorists who could exploit its ability to generate plutonium.

The Clinton administration originally proposed killing the program but reversed itself and restored funding in its fiscal 1994 budget, but only for research into how to recycle fuels for such reactors.

The Super Collider's Final Crash

In a vast stretch of prairie south of Dallas, Texas, $1.6 billion in federal dollars was left to waste in October 1993 — the result of Congress' vote to terminate the controversial superconducting super collider, which would have been the largest, most expensive single scientific experiment ever undertaken.

The Energy Department project was devised as a 54-mile oval underground tunnel, through which atomic particles would collide at nearly the speed of light. Scientists would use high-powered computers to analyze the collisions, in hopes of discovering the smallest particle in the universe — a "God particle," in the words of physicist and author Leon Lederman — that theretofore had existed only in theory.

Vastly more powerful than a rival experiment being built by a consortium of European nations called the Large Hadron Collider, the super collider was viewed by high-energy physicists as having the most potential for unlocking the secrets of matter. But opponents criticized the project's limited focus and highlighted its increasing cost, which started out at $4.4 billion in 1987 and was expected to be $11 billion by completion.

Audits completed in 1993 by the General Accounting Office and the Energy Department's inspector general found examples of mismanagement, cost overruns and unnecessary spending. Defenders of the project dismissed those reviews and hailed the project for meeting or exceeding targets for magnet production and tunnel construction. The project was more than 20 percent completed when Congress voted to kill it.

Before Congress canceled the project, the federal government had spent $1.6 billion on it. Along with $425 million from Texas, the money paid for 14.7 miles of completed tunneling; salaries for 7,000 primary scientific, manufacturing and construction jobs; state-of-the-art physics equipment; and 211,000 square feet of high-tech laboratory facilities in the small farming town of Waxahachie.

Fights were sure to continue through 1994 over how much money it would cost to terminate the project, after paying off salaries and settling inevitable lawsuits by scientists, contractors and the state of Texas. Predictions for ultimate shutdown costs approached $1 billion, although super collider opponents put the costs much lower. Congress agreed to put the full $640 million that was originally slated for the project in fiscal 1994 toward termination costs. But it begged off on decisions about what to do with the existing tunneling, buildings and equipment, leaving those matters to the Energy secretary.

After the termination vote, Congress' science advocates began to reassess the future of U.S. science policy. Many worried that basic research itself was in danger as lawmakers continued to focus on winning immediate fiscal victories at the expense of long-term scientific investment.

"The House of Representatives has dealt a serious blow to the future of high-energy physics and to the future of basic research in the United States," said George E. Brown Jr., D-Calif., chairman of the House Science, Space and Technology Committee.

Energy and Water Appropriations Subcommittee member and super collider advocate Vic Fazio, D-Calif., agreed. "What happened here is far greater than just the super collider," he said. "It really is calling into question all of the major science experiments."

● **Space-based reactors.** Lawmakers also voted to eliminate the space-based reactor program. The amendment, by Edward J. Markey, D-Mass., was approved overwhelmingly by a vote of 333-98. It trimmed $25 million from the program, leaving $5 million for the costs of canceling it. Markey said $420 million had been spent on the program thus far, with an additional $1.6 billion planned to be spent over the next 12 years. "In a time of tough budget decisions, this one is easy," Markey said. *(Vote 268, p. 66-H)*

Other Amendments

The House rejected a handful of amendments, including:
● An amendment by John J. "Jimmy" Duncan Jr., R-Tenn., to strike $5 million for the Kissimmee River ecosystem restoration project in Florida. The amendment failed by a vote of 100-324. Supporters said the project, which was expected to cost $745.5 million to complete, was crucial to preserving Florida wildlife habitat. But opponents called it wasteful spending that protected wildlife that was not endangered. *(Vote 264, p. 64-H)*
● Two amendments by Dan Burton, R-Ind. One, a 3 percent across-the-board cut in the bill's water projects, saving about $117 million, was rejected 96-329. The other, to reduce the Interior Department's funding in the bill by 7 percent, saving about $65 million, was turned back by a vote of 135-287. *(Votes 265, 266, p. 64-H)*

SENATE COMMITTEE ACTION

The Senate Appropriations Committee on Sept. 23 approved its version of the $22.2 billion energy and water bill (S Rept 103-147) by a vote of 29-0, though with barely a word mentioned about the controversial superconducting super collider.

The appropriators agreed to provide $640 million for the atom smasher in fiscal 1994, shrugging off the resounding June 24 House vote against the project and setting the stage for another floor fight over the issue. The collider's opponents in the Appropriations Committee held their fire, acceding to the wish of Chairman Robert C. Byrd, D-W.Va., that controversial issues be settled on the Senate floor.

Nuclear Power Research

The Senate bill also departed from the House position on nuclear energy research. The bill provided $354 million, including more than $30 million for actinide recycling, a nuclear fuel research program, and $27.5 million for space reactors, a project intended for future space missions and defense activities. The House had voted to terminate both of those programs.

The largest piece in the bill was $5.8 billion for cleanups at Energy Department facilities, including $5.1 billion for

its defense laboratories.

Other major features included:

• $3.9 billion for Army Corps of Engineers projects, including $1.9 billion for construction and $2 billion for operations and maintenance.

• $5.7 billion for atomic energy defense activities other than cleanups, including $403.4 million for nuclear weapons testing. That level, $5 million less than the administration requested, recognized a moratorium on nuclear testing that Clinton announced in July.

• $3.3 billion for energy supply, research, development and demonstration programs. This included $343 million for nuclear fusion, $252 million for solar energy and $416 million for biological and environmental projects.

• $1.6 billion for general science and research, a sum that included $613 million for high energy physics and $353 million for nuclear physics.

• $243 million for the Energy Department's technology transfer program, an increase of $102 million over the current year. The program was designed to encourage Energy Department laboratories to form research partnerships with U.S. companies to develop industrial technologies with commercial applications. The committee's report stressed that such partnerships should focus on technologies to clean up the Energy Department's contaminated atomic weapons facilities — one of the federal government's biggest environmental problems.

• $249 million for the Appalachian Regional Commission, up $59 million from fiscal 1993 and up $60 million from the administration's request. The report directed that $60 million be used for a highway corridor in West Virginia.

SENATE FLOOR ACTION

The Senate on Sept. 30 granted temporary reprieves to the super collider and another controversial research program, the advanced liquid metal reactor, before passing its $22.2 billion bill by a vote of 89-10. (Vote 301, p. 39-S)

The chamber voted 57-42 to table an amendment by Dale Bumpers, D-Ark., that would have terminated the troubled super collider. Hours later, senators also turned back an attempt by John Kerry, D-Mass., to kill the advanced liquid metal reactor program. A motion to table the Kerry amendment passed by a vote of 53-45. (Votes 296, 298, p. 72-H)

The Senate did vote to terminate one smaller nuclear reactor research program. Bill Bradley, D-N.J., won his bid to cut $22 million from the bill for the high-temperature gas reactor program. The amendment was approved by voice vote after a motion to table it failed, 41-58. The House version of the bill provided funding for the research program, however, and the project ultimately was revived in conference committee. (Vote 299, p. 72-H)

Super Collider

A visibly frustrated Bumpers, a longtime crusader against the super collider and NASA's space station, complained that the Senate was institutionally averse to cutting spending, no matter how controversial the program or how upset voters were about the budget deficit. Bumpers reminded his colleagues that just 45 days earlier, senators had been calling for spending cuts to offset Clinton's tax increases. "I do not see how anybody can keep a straight face and talk about spending cuts, then walk onto this floor and vote for the super collider," Bumpers said. "I've got a dog with a longer memory than the United States Senate."

But others said the Senate was supposed to take the long view. Johnston, chairman of the Energy and Water Appropriations Subcommittee, in whose state the powerful magnets for the super collider were produced, urged lawmakers not to ride an "emotional wave" of sentiment for austerity. He said such appeals would come at the expense of a project that held potentially significant value to science and already was nearly one-quarter completed. "The super collider should not be a metaphor for a balanced budget or more spending cuts," Johnston said.

Though the Clinton administration nominally supported the super collider, the White House did not mount a major lobbying effort for it, in an apparent effort to avoid helping Texas Republican senators and key super collider backers Phil Gramm and Kay Bailey Hutchison.

Bumpers sought to leave only $220 million to cover the cost of killing the project. But his self-described lone effort to lobby senators against the project bore little fruit. Just eight senators switched their positions from 1992 to vote to kill the project: Max Baucus, D-Mont.; Conrad Burns, R-Mont.; Alfonse M. D'Amato, R-N.Y.; Dennis DeConcini, D-Ariz.; Daniel K. Inouye, D-Hawaii; William V. Roth Jr., R-Del.; Paul S. Sarbanes, D-Md.; and Harris Wofford, D-Pa. However, Hutchison and Johnston said at least two senators, D'Amato and freshman Lauch Faircloth, R-N.C., gave assurances that they would switch their votes to oppose Bumpers if necessary.

Of the Senate's 14 freshman members — who were swept into office, in part, on promises to cut deficit spending — eight voted to kill the super collider and six voted to continue the program. The overall vote was largely bipartisan, though the votes in favor of Bumpers' position to kill the project were weighted toward Democrats, 29-13.

The only senator to switch his vote from 1992 to support the super collider was Joseph R. Biden Jr., D-Del. Biden said he decided the project was too far along to cancel, though opponents of the project accused Biden of switching to ensure funding in the bill for a bridge in his state.

Though he doubted the project's scientific merits, Bumpers' most passionate argument was a fiscal one. He attacked the program as "the most abysmal waste of taxpayers' money I have ever seen" and focused on the project's ever-increasing costs, projected at $8.25 billion in 1991, up from $4.4 billion in 1987. The final price likely would top $13 billion, Bumpers said, considering the cost of stretching out the program's completion date to 2002 — as directed by Clinton — and the added costs identified by the Energy Department in a July review.

Bumpers and other opponents also cited recent audit reports by the General Accounting Office (GAO) and the Energy Department that declared the program behind schedule, over budget and rife with management problems.

But Johnston was largely able to deflect charges of super collider mismanagement by backing an amendment by Hank Brown, R-Colo., that effectively required Energy Secretary Hazel R. O'Leary within 90 days to report how the agency planned to address the concerns raised in the two audits. Failure to do so would terminate the project. The Senate passed the amendment by voice vote.

Liquid Metal Reactors

While the super collider fight was driven by the emotion of budgetary pressures, the advanced liquid metal reactor debate focused on the highly technical issue of dealing with the nation's mounting nuclear waste disposal problem.

Picking a Procedural Lock

In their final bid to kill the superconducting super collider, Reps. Jim Slattery, D-Kan., and Sherwood Boehlert, R-N.Y., had to walk members through a complex parliamentary maneuver — a task they accomplished by peppering the House chamber with sheets of green and pink paper at the right moment.

When the House first voted June 24 to end the big science project, the question was simple: Do you want to kill the super collider? The House responded with a resounding "yes," voting 280-150 to terminate the project. *(Vote 269, p. 66-H)*

But after the Senate voted to restore the super collider, and the House-Senate conference committee agreed, Slattery and Boehlert had no chance to get another stand-alone vote on the issue. Their only option when the conference report on the bill came to the House floor Oct. 19 was to try to ship the bill back to the conferees with instructions to drop the project.

Before members voted on a final adoption of a conference report, House rules allowed the minority to offer one motion — and only one motion — to recommit the conference report to committee for further deliberation. However, Slattery and Boehlert could not offer that motion. House rules and customs gave the nod to John T. Myers, R-Ind., the ranking minority leader of the subcommittee that wrote the bill and a supporter of the super collider.

Myers' motion to recommit had no instructions, and had it prevailed, the final version of the energy and water spending bill would have immediately bounced back to the House with super collider funding intact.

The only way for Slattery and Boehlert to pick the procedural lock was to call for the "previous question" — a step that asked the House to shut off debate on the Myers motion and send the conference report back to committee. In this case, Slattery and Boehlert wanted House members to vote "nay" so they could alter Myers' motion.

To walk lawmakers through this procedural maze, Slattery and Boehlert handed out pink slips to those who had voted against the super collider on June 24 and urged them to vote "no" on the previous question.

They won. Lawmakers defeated the previous question, 159-264. Slattery then amended Myers' motion to instruct conference negotiators to remove super collider funding from the bill. Next, the House voted on the motion to recommit as amended by Slattery to kill the super collider. At that point, collider opponents pulled out green leaflets that told the same lawmakers to vote "yea." They prevailed again, by a vote of 282-143. *(Votes 510, 511, p. 124-H)*

Kerry's unsuccessful amendment was the first attempt to kill a nuclear energy program since the 1983 cancellation of the Clinch River, Tenn., breeder reactor, and for that reason the political fault lines were not easily predictable. A bipartisan coalition of reactor opponents fought the project — including the liberal environmental group Greenpeace and the conservative National Taxpayers' Union — while liberal and conservative senators from Illinois and Idaho, the states where the reactor was under development, argued that it should be continued.

"This is one of those crunch moments in the Senate where we have to pit the local interests of a couple of states against the larger interests of the country. And it's hard to do that," Kerry said.

Clinton's budget included only $15 million for actinide recycling (actinide being the chemical term given to manmade highly radioactive elements such as plutonium). The Senate bill included that amount, plus another $15 million to continue operating the test reactor where the fuel would be burned.

In other action, the Senate approved, by voice vote, an amendment by Jeff Bingaman, D-N.M., to bar funding for grants to search for a temporary nuclear storage facility. Bingaman said Congress should take a closer look at the need for the facility before spending money on the project.

CONFERENCE

A House-Senate conference committee agreed Oct. 14 to report the final fiscal 1994 energy-water spending measure to the House and Senate with $640 million for the collider intact, despite the overwhelming House vote against the atom smasher (H Rept 103-292).

Conferees on the bill — eight members of the House

Energy and Water Appropriations Subcommittee on one side of the room and Senate subcommittee Chairman and super collider champion Johnston on the other — said they felt it was their duty to protect the super collider from the passions in the full House to force an end to the project.

"The emotional tide of the moment should not direct this committee and its responsibility to science," Johnston said at the two-hour conference meeting. "To walk away from this project after $2 billion has been spent would be something this country just cannot do."

Slattery, who had led the charge against the collider in the House, took exception. The vote "was not an emotional outburst," he said. "It was the result of some damned hard work that was done member to member over a three-year period of time. This year, some new members have come in here and have taken their campaign pledges to cut spending seriously."

House-Senate negotiators based their decision to save the super collider on grounds that circumstances had changed since the June House vote to kill the project. Foremost, the Senate had voted 57-42 to finance the project at $640 million, the amount requested by the administration. Johnston stressed at the conference that he had commitments from "four or five" other senators if their votes were needed.

Conferees also cited an Oct. 13 letter in which Energy Secretary O'Leary vowed to correct management, cost and schedule problems detailed in reports issued in early 1993 by the GAO and her own Energy Department. O'Leary also vowed to complete the project by 2002, spending no more than $11 billion — a promise that conferees wrote into the conference report as a formal spending cap. And Clinton weighed in with an Oct. 12 letter to "underscore my con-

Appropriations Lite: Purging 'Earmarks'

If the energy and water development spending bill (HR 2445) felt about $138.2 million lighter than the fiscal 1993 version, it was because lawmakers had cut back on the longtime practice of steering research funds toward their favorite universities.

The 13 fiscal 1994 appropriations bills in general had fewer special "earmarks" for academic research projects at specific colleges than in previous years. But the fiscal 1994 energy and water bill had the biggest decrease of such spending, down 78 percent from $176.8 million in fiscal 1993 to $38.6 million in fiscal 1994.

The reasons were twofold: The new chairman of the House Appropriations Committee, William H. Natcher, D-Ky., had long disapproved of spending for items that had not been approved by authorizing committees. And a longtime foe of earmarking, House Science, Space and Technology Chairman George E. Brown Jr., D-Calif., turned up the heat against the practice considerably in the fiscal 1994 bill.

Over the previous decade, earmarks for academic research had been an increasingly popular way for lawmakers to help out their favorite hometown campus. An example in HR 2445, won by Sen. Mark O. Hatfield, ranking Republican on the Energy and Water Appropriations Subcommittee, directed that $4.6 million be spent on a "statewide high-speed information, education and data gathering network" to be developed by the Oregon Health Sciences University in Portland.

Such line items bypassed the traditional peer review process that forced colleges to compete against one another for research grants from agencies such as the Energy Department and the National Science Foundation. Typically, panels of experts decided who received the grants.

The number of academic earmarks on the 13 appropriations bills grew from seven that totaled $10.7 million in fiscal 1980 to 499 separate line items costing $708 million in fiscal 1992, according to the Congressional Research Service.

But in fiscal 1994, according to a study by Brown's committee, earmarks were reduced by half or more in four major appropriations bills, including the energy and water measure. Brown's Science Committee study could find only 14 line items directed toward specific schools, amounting to $38.6 million in the energy and water spending, down from 40 different earmarks totaling $176.8 million in fiscal 1993.

Of the special research projects that did get funding, Florida got the lion's share — a testament to the two Floridians serving on the House Energy and Water Appropriations Subcommittee, Democrats Pete Peterson and first-term lawmaker Carrie Meek.

The state received $17.6 million, almost 46 percent of the bill's total academic earmarks in fiscal 1994, for three of the bill's most expensive projects — at Florida A&M University, the University of Miami and Florida State University.

Brown's Crusade

Brown's self-styled "minor crusade" against earmarks began as the 102nd Congress was winding down in 1992, when he succeeded on the House floor in stripping almost $100 million in academic earmarks from the fiscal 1993 energy and water appropriations bill.

His ire was raised, however, when the same 10 projects showed up days later on the defense appropriations bill. Eager to go home for the holidays, lawmakers defeated Brown's bid to delete the earmarks.

In 1993, Brown vowed to publicize the practice of academic earmarks as much as possible. He held two hearings and issued a report on the practice. The results were mixed: There was a significant decline in the number of earmarks on most appropriations bills, but his renewed bid to strip earmarked research projects from the fiscal 1994 defense spending bill was again deflected by appropriators.

Energy and Water Appropriations Subcommittee Chairman Tom Bevill, D-Ala., conceded that Brown's crusade had had an impact. "I understand what George is seeking to do. He feels like that is very important," Bevill said.

But Bevill added that the decline in earmarks had at least as much to do with Natcher's ascension as chairman of the full Appropriations Committee. Early in the year, Natcher issued an edict to all subcommittee chairmen that unauthorized appropriations should be avoided as much as possible. Some chairmen ignored the order, but others such as Bevill heeded the mandate.

Lawmakers defended earmarks on the grounds that they redressed agencies' tendency to award grants only to larger, more established universities. But the recipients of earmarks were an elite group themselves: While there were more than 4,000 two-year and four-year colleges in the nation, fewer than 200 had been the recipients of the roughly $2 billion in earmarks over the previous five years, the House Science Committee study revealed.

tinuing support" for the project.

But for super collider critics, nothing had changed. In fact, the conference decision to preserve the collider was simply a reprise of what had happened the previous year, when the project was saved in conference after a House vote to kill it.

After less than an hour of debate, in which several House conferees expressed dismay at ignoring the House position on the collider, House conferees agreed by voice vote to recede to the Senate and retain the full amount for the project.

Other Conference Decisions

Overall, the two chambers' spending levels for other energy and water resource programs were close. Tight budget caps left appropriators little room for new projects. And negotiators agreed to save every other major project killed by either the House or the Senate, including:

● The Energy Department's advanced liquid metal reactor. The conference report provided $31.9 million to continue research on the reactor. Johnston argued that to terminate the program would cost nearly as much as to continue it.

- The space-based nuclear reactor program.
- The high-temperature gas reactor.

FINAL ACTION

In a rebuke to appropriators and a resounding confirmation that lawmakers wanted to at least nominally address grass-roots voter outrage over deficit spending, the House on Oct. 19 struck a death blow to the super collider.

Collider opponents Slattery and Boehlert rallied the House to overcome seemingly insurmountable institutional and political obstacles to again kill the project after it had been rescued by the House-Senate conference committee. A vote on an arcane procedural question had the effect of sending the $22.2 billion fiscal 1994 energy and water appropriations bill back to the conference committee with instructions to kill the project. *(Box, p. 594)*

Because they had no chance for another stand-alone vote on whether to terminate the project, super collider opponents had no other choice but to attack the entire energy and water spending measure. In previous years, conventional political wisdom would have written off the opponents. Most lawmakers would have feared retribution by appropriators and voted to save their own water projects at the cost of salvaging the super collider.

Indeed, at one point in the debate, John T. Myers, R-Ind., hinted that water projects might indeed be jeopardized if the conference report was rejected. "All of the items will be reopened," Myers warned. "Many things will be considered that many members will not want [us] to consider."

Myers' bluff failed, mainly because lawmakers feared their constituents more than the wrath of appropriators. With the session winding to a close, Congress had done little to calm voter outrage over profligate spending and the budget deficit.

In the end, lawmakers largely stuck with their June votes on the super collider. They defeated Myers' attempt to retain funding for the super collider by a vote of 159-264. They then agreed to send the conference report back to the conference committee with orders to kill the super collider, by a vote of 282-143. *(Votes 510, 511, p. 124-H)*

Only 18 lawmakers switched to defend the appropriators. And 81 of the 113 voting freshmen voted against the collider, forming a crucial bloc for opponents.

In the immediate aftermath of the votes, the project's supporters suffered from a temporary bout of denial. Rep. Jim Chapman, D-Texas, a member of the conference committee, told reporters he would push conferees to try to resurrect the project by offering the House a lower funding level for the super collider.

But within hours, reality sank in. Johnston, to whom collider supporters had looked to rescue the project, issued a statement that indicated that the fight was over. "Today is a sad day for science," the statement said. "The House was wrong, but they have a right to be wrong. Their message on deficit reduction and the SSC was clear and unmistakable. The conference must find ways to accommodate this message."

Rewriting the Bill

House and Senate negotiators regrouped Oct. 21, and they invited four members of the Texas delegation, as well as Slattery and Boehlert, to sit in. That was a radical shift from weeks earlier, when the House leadership had rebuffed efforts to include opponents of the collider in the conference.

After some debate, both sides agreed on the exact wording of language that directed the Energy Department to conduct an "orderly" termination of the project and give thousands of contract scientists and workers 90 days of severance pay.

The lawmakers quickly agreed to direct the entire $640 million toward termination costs, even though Slattery and Boehlert later said that figure likely was high. Super collider officials estimated that total shutdown costs would approach $1 billion, counting the cost of restoring the land at the project's site to its original condition and settling inevitable lawsuits from contractors, universities and the state of Texas.

The move marked the largest spending program to be canceled by Congress since urban development action grants were wiped out in 1988.

Final Passage

The House adopted the new conference report (H Rept 103-305) on Oct. 26 by a vote of 332-81. The House also accepted, 227-190, an amendment to the conference report that called on the Energy secretary to submit a plan by July 1, 1994, to terminate the super collider project, while maximizing the value of the $2 billion already invested. *(Votes 527, 526, p. 128-H)*

The Senate sent the bill to the president after approving the conference report Oct. 27 by a vote of 89-11. The Senate approved the House amendment by voice vote. *(Vote 333, p. 43-S)*

Apart from the super collider issue, the final spending bill came in $25 million lower than the enacted level for fiscal 1993, marking the first time in eight years that energy and water programs had been funded at a lower level than during the previous year.

Decreases in the bill's overall funding were attributed to lower spending levels for nuclear weapons testing, production and design. Total nuclear energy defense activities declined by $1.26 billion from fiscal 1993.

Instead, the measure focused on environmental cleanup and restoration of the Energy Department's nuclear energy, weapons and storage facilities. Appropriators spent $4.6 billion, $478 million more than in fiscal 1993, on operating expenses for the environmental restoration of nuclear weapons facilities. ∎

Energy and Water Provisions

The energy and water development spending bill (HR 2445) played varied roles: purveyor of cutting-edge science projects, keeper of the nation's nuclear defense arsenal and wellspring of more than 1,000 water projects for most every congressional district. Following are the provisions of the bill, as enacted:

ARMY CORPS OF ENGINEERS

The Corps of Engineers was a domestic unit of the Army that since 1824 had ensured the navigability of the nation's commercial waterways and since 1936 had built and maintained civil works projects to enhance flood control, storm damage reduction and environmental restoration.

State and local governments had been required to share costs on federal water control projects since 1986, a requirement that corps officials cited as key to ensuring that the water projects with the most merit and accountability got funded.

To lawmakers, this section of the energy and water spending bill provided for bread-and-butter public works projects back home. As a rule, such projects tended to be non-controversial, and the House and Senate authorizing committees had approved most of them. However, lawmakers on the Energy and Water Appropriations subcommittees often earmarked high spending levels for ongoing projects in their states, such as the Red River Waterway in Louisiana or the Passaic River Mainstem in New Jersey. Still, earmarks had been on the decline in recent years due to strict budget limits and the 1986 cost-sharing requirement.

The corps first approved water projects for preliminary study. The studies and subsequent design work showed up as part of the corps' "general investigations" budget. Studies examined the costs, benefits and scope of the projects and the probability of securing local funding. If study results were favorable, projects might later be approved as new construction starts. After the first round of exploratory studies, the cost of subsequent planning and construction work was shared with local groups.

While such studies in the past had focused on more traditional lock, dam and waterway construction projects, corps officials were increasingly mindful of the environmental threats posed by ongoing and new water projects. Lawmakers also were beginning to view corps funding as a way to further environmental goals. House Energy and Water Development Appropriations Subcommittee member Vic Fazio, D-Calif., persuaded colleagues to steer $600,000 toward a study of whether a deep-water shipping channel along the Sacramento River should be modified to allow for the migration of anadromous fish such as trout.

For fiscal 1994, the budget included $3.9 billion for the corps, compared with $3.6 billion requested by President Clinton and $3.9 billion appropriated in fiscal 1993. The total accounted for one year's worth of work on corps projects, some of which was spread over decades.

Surveys, Construction, Maintenance

▶ **General investigations**. Congress agreed to spend $207.5 million on general investigations, $31.8 million more than in fiscal 1993. The money paid for surveys, feasibility studies and preconstruction engineering and design for new projects. State and local governments had to match each dollar of any money appropriated for general investigations. The administration requested $157.8 million for the general investigations account.

The measure provided funding for 356 studies, including 73 added by Congress that the administration did not request.

The appropriations for most of the investigations were in the low hundreds of thousands of dollars, but examples of more expensive general investigations projects that were not requested by the administration included: $17 million for a flood control project along the Passaic River in New Jersey, won by House Energy and

Water Development Appropriations Subcommittee member Dean A. Gallo, R-N.J.; $1 million for the Gillespie Dam along the Gila River near Yuma, Ariz., won by Dennis DeConcini, D-Ariz., of the Senate Appropriations subcommittee and Ed Pastor, D-Ariz., of the House subcommittee; and $3.7 million for a flood prevention project at the White River central waterfront in Indianapolis, for which the administration requested $300,000, won by John T. Myers, R-Ind., ranking Republican on the House subcommittee.

▶ **Construction.** The $1.4 billion general construction budget for fiscal 1994 included $134.6 million for 52 new projects. The Clinton administration requested a construction budget of $1.2 billion, of which $30 million was to go toward new projects.

▶ **New projects.** The administration's request for 16 new construction projects included those in: Charleston (S.C.) Harbor, $5.8 million; Sargent Beach, Texas, $3.9 million; Captiva Island, Fla., $1.8 million; Rio Puerto Nuevo, Puerto Rico, $1.5 million; and along the Brazos River in Texas, $4.6 million, and the Mississippi River in Illinois and Missouri, $1.6 million.

House appropriators agreed to add 44 additional new construction projects. A "new" project was one for which Congress provided money even though it had not received prior funding and was not requested by the administration. Senate appropriators originally agreed to 30 of the House projects, then added nine of their own. In conference committee, the House won all but one of its 44 projects back, which combined with the Senate's nine projects to bring the total of new projects to 52, at a cost of $134.6 million for fiscal 1994. Of those, 27 were in the states of members of the House and Senate Energy and Water Appropriations subcommittees, amounting to $60.6 million or 45 percent of the total.

Such projects included $5 million won by House subcommittee member Carrie Meek, D-Fla., to speed up ecological restoration of the Kissimmee River; $6.3 million by Senate Energy and Water Appropriations Subcommittee Chairman J. Bennett Johnston, D-La., for a levee project along the Ouachita River in Louisiana — an amount increased in conference from the $3.8 million Johnston originally sought; and $10 million won by Bud Shuster, R-Pa., with help from House Appropriations Committee member John P. Murtha, D-Pa., for an environmental restoration project in south central Pennsylvania.

▶ **Ongoing projects.** Of Clinton's $1.2 billion request for construction projects, all but $30 million would have gone toward ongoing projects.

Appropriators added about $200 million to Clinton's request under the construction heading, bringing the total to $1.4 billion. Much of the additional money went toward increased spending levels on various ongoing projects.

Louisiana received the highest-priced construction project, at $145 million, thanks to Johnston. He had long championed funding for the Red River Waterway, a 25-year-old project to construct a commercial channel to the Mississippi River about 75 miles north of Baton Rouge to Shreveport, La. The initial three locks were virtually complete.

The Clinton administration requested $32.8 million to help finish the proposed additional locks, roughly the same annual amount that the Bush administration had requested. But Johnston persuaded fellow congressional appropriators to put $145 million toward the project — an increase similar to those of past years. After fiscal 1994, the project was expected to be roughly $35 million away from completion, according to corps estimates.

Many other big-ticket water projects also were in the states of members of Energy and Water Appropriations subcommittees. Such projects included a flood control project along the Santa Ana River in Rep. Fazio's home state of California ($118.8 million); an Olmsted lock and dam project that lay partly in Illinois and partly in Kentucky, the home state of House Appropriations Committee Chairman William H. Natcher, D ($110.3 million); and two West

Virginia projects, one a lock and dam project in Winfield ($56.6 million) and another a flood control project on the upper Cumberland River ($45.6 million). West Virginia was the home state of Senate Appropriations Committee Chairman Robert C. Byrd, D.

Flood Control

The waterway and flooding problems associated with the lower Mississippi basin were so extensive that the project was in a separate section of the corps' budget. The budget included $348.9 million for this account, $2.3 million less than in fiscal 1993 and $6 million more than Clinton requested.

The money was to pay for projects such as channel dredging, levee construction and erosion-control in appropriators' home states of Arkansas, Illinois, Kentucky, Louisiana, Mississippi, Missouri and Tennessee.

Maintenance

While lawmakers liked to reserve funds for new construction projects, most of the corps' money and attention went toward maintenance, an emphasis made increasingly necessary because 25 percent of the agency's inventory of locks, dams, canals and other projects was more than 50 years old. The average age of corps projects was 35 years. Also, as soon as a project's construction was completed, it transferred into this category, which placed even heavier burdens on the corps' maintenance duties.

Lawmakers agreed to spend $1.69 billion for the operation and maintenance of 714 navigation, beach erosion control and flood control projects across the United States and its territories, compared with a Clinton request of $1.66 billion. The amount in fiscal 1993 was $1.60 billion.

The projects typically ranged from $1 million to $10 million each. Appropriators added 15 projects that were not requested by the administration; 11 of them were located in the home states of House and Senate Energy and Water Appropriations subcommittee members.

Regulation

Appropriators agreed to spend $92 million, an increase of $6 million, to carry out the corps' regulatory duties, which included issuing permits for commercial navigation of waterways and for construction and development on areas designated as wetlands.

Corps Reorganization

Lawmakers barred any funds appropriated in the measure from being used to close or transfer the duties of any Corps of Engineers district offices. In 1993 there were 37 district offices across the country, each of which answered to one of 10 regional division headquarters. Like President George Bush before him, Clinton hoped to streamline corps operations by reducing the number of district offices. Vice President Al Gore's "reinventing government" report estimated that $105 million could be saved over six years by trimming corps operations.

BUREAU OF RECLAMATION

Part of the Interior Department, the Bureau of Reclamation was charged with managing water and related land resources in 17 Western states and trust territories. It was created in 1902 to provide irrigation for the arid West, but since then, its mission had expanded greatly. Projects included irrigation, water supply, hydroelectric power generation, flood control, and recreation area and wildlife habitat protection. For fiscal 1994, the $910 million budget included a $464.4 million construction program, $282.9 million for operation and maintenance of reclamation projects, and special restoration funds of $45 million and $25.7 million, respectively, for two of the bureau's largest irrigation and power projects in central Utah and the Central Valley of California. It also included a $13.8 million general investigations budget to conduct studies of future projects.

In recent years, the bureau had tried to change its mission

toward more environmental concerns, fighting its image as a construction agency that plowed under and poured concrete over Western lands to provide hydroelectric power and irrigation projects. That transition was formalized under Clinton.

On Nov. 1, just four days after the energy and water spending bill was signed into law, Interior Secretary Bruce Babbitt — who in the past had branded the bureau as environmentally destructive and called for its abolition — announced plans to transform the bureau to reflect more environmentally aware water management practices.

The energy and water bill was completed prior to that announcement, but many lawmakers had long promoted a more conservation-oriented approach, and that emphasis was evident in the spending bill.

▶ **Construction.** The bureau's general construction budget for fiscal 1994 was $464.4 million, down from $470.6 million in fiscal 1993. Of the total, $40.7 million went toward construction of California's Central Valley Project, a sprawling water project begun in 1936 that generated hydropower and supplied water to farms and municipalities. An additional $45 million was allocated for a restoration fund for the project that was created in 1992 to address environmental concerns.

Another large appropriation within the bureau's construction budget was for the controversial Garrison Diversion Unit in North Dakota, an irrigation and water supply project first authorized in 1965 and since under fire as unaffordable and environmentally unsound. With previous attempts to abandon the Garrison project having failed, the administration in 1993 requested $30 million toward completing a more limited plan. Senate appropriators added an additional $5 million for the project; conferees compromised on a total of $32 million in the final bill.

▶ **Colorado River storage.** The bureau also ran several large projects in the Colorado River Basin, which were funded from separate accounts. One such project was the Colorado River Storage Project, which sought to secure dependable water supplies for the Upper Colorado Basin. Appropriators provided $62.7 million for the project, the same as the administration request.

▶ **Central Utah Project.** The Central Utah Project limped along without authorization for several years, but Congress again authorized spending for it in 1992 (Titles II-VI of PL 102-575). Appropriators spent $24.7 million in fiscal 1994 to carry out provisions of that law, which included $9.9 million for fish, wildlife and recreation mitigation and conservation programs. The growing water demands of sprawling Salt Lake City were propelling the project. But Utah lawmakers prior to the authorization had battled environmentalists over whether to focus on building an aqueduct or fish and wildlife facilities. The authorization law took project control away from the Bureau of Reclamation and significantly bolstered state and local control over engineering and grant-making powers. The Interior secretary oversaw the project.

▶ **Central Arizona Project.** Appropriators allocated $178.8 million for construction of the Central Arizona Project, which included a hydropower generating facility and a massive aqueduct and pumping system that was to deliver water to farms, municipalities and Indian reservations in central and southern Arizona. When completed, it was to carry Colorado River water as far as Tucson and was meant to ease pressure on the state's groundwater supplies.

ENERGY DEPARTMENT

The Energy Department was created as a Cabinet-level agency in 1977, at the urging of President Jimmy Carter. The department's responsibilities included regulating domestic energy industries, managing nuclear waste, and researching and developing energy technologies and nuclear weaponry. The energy and water spending bill included just under $17 billion for the department, the bulk of the agency's budget. The department's fossil fuel programs were funded in a separate bill, with appropriations for the Interior Department.

Congress and the Clinton administration were aggressively shifting the Energy Department's 700 national laboratories away from their Cold War military orientation toward more cooperative science and technology ventures with private-sector companies and academia.

The agency had entered into more than 500 cooperative research and development agreements with industry, more than five times the number as in early 1992. Those agreements amounted to $700 million worth of research, with the Energy Department contributing less than half that amount.

Still, on average, only 10 percent of a national laboratory's resources had gone toward collaborative activities in 1992-1993, leading appropriators to push labs to shift more of their budgets toward such agreements. But the laboratories instead were fighting for additional funding. Indeed, the competition between the laboratories to prove they had made the post-Cold War transition led some to conclude that the number of laboratories needed to be winnowed down to better reflect existing needs.

Research and Development

The bill provided $3.2 billion for an array of Energy Department programs to promote energy sources, such as solar and nuclear power, and related research and environmental cleanup work at the department's non-military facilities.

▸ **Solar and renewables.** The program promoted the development of various forms of solar energy, as well as photovoltaics, wind, ocean energy and biofuels. Clinton requested $248.4 million for fiscal 1994, the largest budget increase in more than a decade. Appropriators increased that slightly to $252.3 million, up from $187.4 million in fiscal 1993.

The geothermal and hydropower research program received only a slight increase from fiscal 1993, to $24 million from $23.4 million.

▸ **Hydrogen research.** Lawmakers added a new $10 million budget line-item for hydrogen research, which appropriators said might play an important role in U.S. energy security. The money was to go toward accelerating the Energy Department's basic hydrogen research program.

▸ **Electric energy systems and storage.** The bill provided $49.9 million for researching the health effects of electricity transmission, as well as developing improved transmission, distribution and storage systems. In this category, $10 million went toward research into the health effects of electric and magnetic fields, such as power lines over neighborhoods. The program was intended to help carry out a provision of the 1992 Energy Policy Act (PL 102-486) that called for a multi-agency research and a public information program on the health effects of electromagnetic transmissions.

▸ **Superconducting magnet energy storage.** The bill provided $10 million for researching the development of a method of storing electricity in superconducting coils, which offered the ability to discharge electricity as needed with 95 percent efficiency. Utilities could use the technology to store energy for use during peak power periods.

▸ **Environment, safety and health.** The bill provided $158 million in fiscal 1994 for this Energy Department office that was responsible for ensuring that all department programs conformed with environmental laws and safeguarded workers and the public against health and safety hazards. The office conducted assessments, known as the Tiger Team program, of how well Energy Department operating facilities complied with relevant environmental and safety laws.

▸ **Nuclear energy research programs.** Appropriators agreed to spend $341.4 million on research into new ways to produce energy using nuclear power — a decrease from the fiscal 1993 level of $341.9 million. The spending came only after contentious House and Senate floor fights over the Energy Department's three main research projects.

House and Senate conferees on Oct. 14 rescued the controversial advanced liquid metal reactor after the House voted on June 24 to kill it, providing $30.4 million for the advanced liquid metal reactor (also known as the integral fast reactor). In exchange, the House conferees the same day insisted on and won $12 million for the gas turbine-modular helium reactor that the Senate had voted on Sept. 30 to kill.

The advanced liquid metal reactor was designed to develop an environmentally efficient nuclear power source that used nuclear waste as fuel. Advocates said such "actinide recycling" might offer a way to get rid of radioactive waste piling up around the country. Critics, led in the House by Sam Coppersmith, D-Ariz., contended that the advanced liquid metal reactor would be dangerous and could increase nuclear proliferation.

Clinton had proposed phasing out the liquid metal reactor program in 1994, although he also proposed continuing research on actinide recycling. But appropriators were keeping the reactor alive by directing $109 million that Clinton requested to mothball the program toward "shutdown activities for the facility conducted in parallel with reactor operation" through fiscal 1996.

The helium reactor program was to provide a nuclear reactor resistant to a meltdown, a dangerous situation in which a rapid climb in a reactor's power level caused the fuel rods to melt and radiation to escape into the atmosphere. A helium reactor could run at higher temperatures than existing reactors, producing more electricity per unit of fuel. Critics cited little commercial interest in the project and urged the Energy Department to abandon it — a position Clinton supported.

Appropriators also allotted $27.5 million to rescue a research project in space-based nuclear power that the House on June 24 voted 333-98 to kill on an amendment by Edward J. Markey, D-Mass. The project, called SP-100, was a remnant of the Strategic Defense Initiative program and was to provide energy to propel satellites and spacecraft.

▸ **Fusion.** This program was designed to promote magnetic fusion energy, with the goal of running a demonstration plant by 2025 or sooner. Advocates hoped fusion could provide safer and cheaper nuclear power without creating the hazardous waste of nuclear fission.

The total budget for the fusion program was $347.6 million for fiscal 1994, an $8 million increase over fiscal 1993, as requested by the administration.

The Energy Department was nearing the site-selection stage for the "international thermonuclear experimental reactor" that would serve as the testing area for the project. In fiscal 1994, the Energy Department was to begin building a new facility, the Tokamak Fusion Test Reactor, at the Princeton Plasma Physics Laboratory in New Jersey, to carry out reactor testing in advance of the thermonuclear project. House Energy and Water Appropriations Subcommittee member Dean A. Gallo, R-N.J., was its chief defender.

The fusion budget included U.S. participation in an international effort to develop fusion energy in concert with Japan, the European Community and Russia.

▸ **Biological and environmental research.** The bill provided $416.1 million for a program to study the health and environmental impact of energy use and to employ the Energy Department's scientific and technological resources to help solve medical and biological problems. The amount equaled the president's budget request; the fiscal 1993 amount was $356.7 million.

The Energy Department Office of Biological and Environmental Research was created during the formation of the Atomic Energy Commission in 1946 to study the potential health effects of radiation. That "radiobiology" function continued, but the office's duties had expanded to include other subjects of biological research such as global warming and the human genome project.

Much of the funding, $338 million, went toward research grants under the "operating expenses" heading and was spread among all of the Energy Department's 726 national laboratories. Examples included $38.9 million to study health effects of radiation and other chemical reactions; $15.8 million for atmospheric science projects; and $20 million for the study of "terrestrial transport" of

microbes, bacteria and other airborne particles.

Also included in that amount was $11 million for the National Institute for Global Environmental Change at the University of California. Conferees rejected an effort by House lawmakers to give $750,000 to Illinois to conduct a cooperative international study into possible strategies to reduce "greenhouse gases" in the Earth's atmosphere.

The Energy Department and the National Institutes of Health were jointly pursuing the human genome project, which sought to map the genetic coding guiding human development and functioning. However, the institute's budget for the project had been almost twice that of the Energy Department's. The bill provided $68 million for the department's share of the project in fiscal 1994, $11 million more than in the previous year. Energy's genome research took place at three of its national laboratories: the Lawrence Livermore National and Lawrence Berkeley laboratories in California and the Los Alamos National Laboratory in New Mexico.

House and Senate conferees also steered millions of dollars for biological and environmental research to several universities, including: $5.8 million for the Medical University of South Carolina's Cancer/Oncology Center, $4 million for the Environmental Biotechnology program at Florida A&M University, and $4.6 million for the Biomedical Information Communication Center at Oregon Health Sciences University.

▶ **Supporting research and analysis**. The bill provided $975.7 million for Energy Department support in the physical, biological and engineering sciences for basic research that could help produce energy. This spending category supported the government's national energy laboratories and some related efforts at private universities. The amount was $22 million less than the administration requested.

Funding for this category broke into four parts: Basic energy sciences ($801.9 million), which was a broad grant-making category for the national laboratories; a state-of-the-art reactor known as the Advanced Neutron Source that would allow researchers to study radioactive materials with an eye toward cancer therapy and medical advances ($17 million); energy research analysis and university science education programs, ($115 million) and facilities construction and maintenance ($41.6 million).

Earmarks in this section of the bill included: $8.3 million for the Super Computations Research Institute at Florida State University and $3 million for the Midwest Superconductivity Consortium. But conferees dropped a House bid to steer $2 million toward the Dade County, Fla., public school system for a pilot science education program, as well as an effort by House appropriators to give $500,000 to the New York City school system's Queens Hall of Science Discovery lab.

▶ **High-performance computing**. The Energy Department was part of an interagency effort to develop high-performance computing, or supercomputers. Appropriators agreed in report language that the department should spend $106.2 million for programs related to the effort and urged that the department be given a clearer and larger role in the joint effort.

▶ **Non-defense cleanup**. This account allotted $717.5 million for an array of environmental cleanup programs related to the Energy Department's non-military programs.

Of that amount, $230 million went toward operating expenses to clean up non-defense nuclear facilities and sites.

Another $124 million was allotted for a West Valley, N.Y., nuclear waste storage project. The West Valley demonstration project would process high-level nuclear waste, some of it in liquid form, into a solid that was easier to store.

Uranium Supply and Enrichment

This program supplied enriched uranium for use in civilian nuclear power plants, domestic and foreign, and for other governmental needs, including defense. The 1992 Energy Policy Act transferred most uranium enrichment functions from the Energy Department to a new government corporation, the United States Enrichment Corporation, aimed at processing uranium ore more

efficiently and staving off foreign competition. The corporation leased two enrichment facilities from the Energy Department, at Paducah, Ky., and Piketon, Ohio, for at least six years.

Appropriators spent $13 billion on civilian uranium activities in fiscal 1993, but the new privatization left federal spending at $160 million in fiscal 1994, to make a final payment to the Tennessee Valley Authority for the buyout of a utility power contract.

▶ **Uranium enrichment decontamination fund.** The fund, created by the 1992 Energy Policy Act to cover the cleanup of sites leased and operated by the newly created United States Enrichment Corporation, was to receive $286.3 million. Sites included the operating facilities at Piketon, Ohio, and Paducah, Ky., and an inactive enrichment site in Tennessee. The fund was fed by appropriations and a tax on domestic utilities.

General Science and Research

▶ **High-energy physics.** The bill provided $627.8 million for research into particle physics, particularly for studying particle collisions produced by colliders or accelerators.

Included was $36 million to build an "asymmetric B-meson" production facility, known as a B-factory, at the Stanford Linear Accelerator Center in California. Total cost for the project was $237 million. The B-factory accelerator aimed to explain to physicists why the universe consisted of matter, even though shortly after the beginning of the universe matter and anti-matter existed in equal proportion and should have killed each other off.

▶ **Nuclear physics.** Appropriators allocated $353.3 million to investigate the structure and interactions of atomic particles and the possible applications of such particles to astrophysics. This account included money to continue building the Relativistic Heavy Ion Collider at Brookhaven, N.Y., and the Continuous Electron Beam Accelerator Facility at Newport News, Va.

Appropriators also spent $19 million to continue operations at the Los Alamos Meson Physics Facility in Albuquerque, N.M., despite Energy Department attempts to cancel the nuclear physics program.

▶ **Superconducting super collider.** After years of protracted funding battles, Congress killed this project in October, ending the most elaborate physics experiment ever undertaken. House lawmakers dealt the fatal blow on Oct. 19, by rejecting the efforts of negotiators to save the $11 billion Texas-based atom smasher project from a previous June 24 House vote to terminate it. Deficit-conscious lawmakers, who argued that the project was mismanaged and over budget, won out over advocates who said the project's mission — to discover the tiniest atomic particle in matter — was crucial to keeping the United States on the leading edge of science. Senate super collider proponents, led by Energy and Water Appropriations Subcommittee Chairman J. Bennett Johnston, D-La., gave up efforts to save the project after the Oct. 19 House vote. The project was roughly one-fifth complete, leaving to waste $1.6 billion in federal expenditures and $425 million in Texas expenditures.

The Senate had voted on Sept. 30 to put $640 million toward the project in fiscal 1994, an amount equal to the administration's request. Conferees initially ignored the House vote to kill the super collider. But after House lawmakers affirmed their will, conferees met again and agreed to put the entire $640 million toward termination costs.

The bill directed the Energy secretary to conduct an "orderly" termination of the project under specific conditions. Full-time employees of contractors and designated subcontractors could receive, at the secretary's discretion, up to 90 days of termination pay and "reasonable" relocation expenses and assistance. The secretary also was required to submit a report to the president and Congress by July 1, 1994, containing a plan to maximize the value of the investment already made.

Miscellaneous

▶ **Nuclear waste disposal.** The bill provided $260 million to proceed with various projects to store or dispose of nuclear waste

from civilian power plants.

Among the largest expenses was a project to study Yucca Mountain in Nevada as a possible site for a high-level civilian nuclear waste dump. The bill included $12.5 million for Nevada's universities and its state and local governments to monitor the work, which was highly controversial in Nevada.

The disposal fund also covered smaller programs to design and site a temporary waste dump, known as monitored retrievable storage, as well as waste transportation systems.

The Senate added bill language that barred the government from spending money to conduct feasibility studies of possible sites for a future monitored retrievable storage facility, pending agreement among local officials of any proposed site. Such facilities were to serve as a short-term dump site for nuclear waste until the Yucca Mountain site was completed. The sponsor of the language, Jeff Bingaman, D-N.M., said Congress should take a closer look at the need for the facility before spending money on the project.

Bingaman said that when the idea of a temporary facility was conceived in 1982, the idea was to locate the site close to where the waste was produced — on the East or West coasts of the country. But the Energy Department was looking "toward the vast open spaces of the West" such as his state of New Mexico.

▶ **Isotope fund.** The Energy Department supplied radioactive and stable isotope products and services to a range of customers in the United States and abroad. The isotopes could be used in such fields as medical research, manufacturing, agriculture and defense activities. The program operated under a revolving fund, which was granted an initial $16.2 million appropriation in fiscal 1990 and in 1993 operated on the interest earnings of that account. In fiscal 1994, the program received $3.9 million in borrowing authority to finance new medical and industrial product initiatives, that in turn would be repaid through sales.

▶ **Departmental administration.** The bill included a net appropriation of $162 million, after revenues were deducted, to pay for department salaries and other administrative expenses. Such expenses included the cost of international energy activities such as nuclear non-proliferation programs.

▶ **Inspector general.** Appropriators allocated $30.4 million for the department's oversight office, which conducted audits and investigations to correct fraud, waste or mismanagement.

▶ **Power marketing administrations.** The bill provided $345.3 million to operate and maintain four regional power authorities that developed and marketed power from federal hydroelectric facilities. They were the Alaska Power Administration, $4 million; Southeastern Power Administration, $29.7 million; Southwestern Power Administration, $33.6 million; and the Western Area Power Administration, $273 million.

It authorized the Northwest's Bonneville Power Authority, which was self-supporting, to spend its revenues. An effort was under way to sell the Alaska Power Administration's assets to state and local interests.

▶ **Federal Energy Regulatory Commission.** Appropriators set aside $165.4 million to run the Federal Energy Regulatory Commission, which oversaw regulations affecting oil and natural gas, hydroelectric power and electric utilities. Budgeted expenses were entirely offset by projected revenues from license fees and other charges.

Independent Agencies

▶ **Appalachian Regional Commission.** The bill allotted $249 million for infrastructure and other development work in the 13 Appalachian states. Of that money, about $50 million was earmarked for road construction in West Virginia, $38.7 million for roads in Alabama, $13.5 million for roads in Kentucky and $4.6 million for roads in Mississippi.

The Reagan administration repeatedly had tried to eliminate this program, founded in 1965, but House Energy and Water Subcommittee Chairman Tom Bevill, D-Ala., and other congressional supporters kept it alive through the 1980s. For fiscal 1994, appropriators had little problem boosting the Clinton administration's request of $189 million.

▶ **Tennessee Valley Authority.** The authority oversaw an array of public lands and facilities connected with the vast public utility project. Its operations paid for themselves, but the federal agency spent money on environmental management, rural development and a National Fertilizer and Environmental Research Center. Appropriators gave the authority $140.5 million for fiscal 1994, only slightly more than the administration's $139 million request.

▶ **Nuclear Regulatory Commission.** The commission was charged with overseeing the nuclear power industry, particularly by reviewing nuclear power plant license applications and promoting plant safety. Appropriators allocated $542.9 million for commission expenses, most of which would be offset by projected revenues from fees. Lawmakers approved a net appropriation of $22 million.

▶ **River commissions.** The bill also budgeted money for several regional river basin commissions that the federal government helped to support: Delaware River Basin Commission, $821,000; Potomac River Basin, $498,000; Susquehanna River Basin Commission, $606,000.

▶ **Nuclear defense safety board.** The board oversaw the standards governing most nuclear defense facilities and was charged with investigating any health or safety issues at the facilities. It was created in late 1988 as an independent agency that could make recommendations to the Energy secretary but was not under his direction. The board's fiscal 1994 allocation was $16.6 million.

NUCLEAR DEFENSE PROGRAMS

The Energy Department maintained the nation's nuclear arsenal at more than a dozen complexes across the country. But the breakup of the former Soviet Union had halted bomb building and, at least temporarily, the periodic testing of nuclear weapons in the United States. Since the late 1980s, the nuclear weapons program also had been beset by safety, environmental and management problems.

Energy Secretary Hazel R. O'Leary had vowed to increase both the pace of environmental cleanup and the dismantlement of the nuclear arsenal to comply with international treaties. In keeping that pledge, she brought to the Energy Department several members of environmental watchdog groups such as the Natural Resources Defense Council that had for years criticized as slow the pace of the cleanup under previous administrations.

Other goals of the new administration were to dismantle roughly 2,000 warheads in fiscal 1994, to redesign the entire nuclear weapons complex to allow for fewer, safer and more efficient facilities with a smaller nuclear stockpile, and to provide assistance to defense workers who lost their jobs.

Congress put even more emphasis on cleanup than did Clinton in his budget request, trimming funding below administration requests for research, development and stockpile support, and boosting spending for environmental programs.

Critics still believed the budget too strongly favored production, research and testing programs. And they were eager to see whether O'Leary would live up to expectations regarding the pace of environmental restoration.

The Energy Department was receiving public comment for a report, due in late 1994, that would outline how the entire U.S. nuclear weapons complex would be downsized and reorganized.

Until then, research activities continued to take place primarily at four installations: the Lawrence Livermore National Laboratory in California, the Los Alamos National Laboratory in New Mexico, the Sandia national laboratories in New Mexico and California, and the Nevada Test Site.

The Mound Plant in Ohio, the Kansas City Plant and the Pinellas Plant in Florida all manufactured non-nuclear components for nuclear weaponry. O'Leary planned in 1994 to begin consolidating those activities at the Kansas City Plant.

Though no nuclear materials were being produced, the nation's nuclear complex facilities included the Oak Ridge Plant in Tennessee, which handled uranium from dismantled nuclear war-

heads and provided long-term storage of mothballed nuclear weapons; the Savannah River Site in South Carolina, which acted as a reserve for the possible future production of tritium, a perishable gas used in nuclear warheads; and the Pantex Plant in Texas, which disassembled warheads. Three other former facilities — the Hanford Plant in Washington, the Rocky Flats Plant in Colorado and the Idaho National Engineering Lab — were undergoing environmental cleanup.

Appropriators provided $10.9 billion for the Energy Department's nuclear defense program, compared with an administration request of $11.4 billion.

Research, Stockpile Support, Testing

Traditionally, nuclear weapons research and development encompassed designing new weaponry, as well as increasing the safety of nuclear weapons and inventing new design concepts such as reusing explosive warhead triggers. Planners had sought to make the weapons manufacturing more efficient and less wasteful.

But in recent years, the money primarily had been used to accelerate the dismantling, storage and disposal of nuclear warheads and to support the reorganization of the nuclear weapons complex.

Appropriators agreed to spend $3.6 billion on weapons activities relating to research, stockpile support and testing, $973.6 million less than in fiscal 1993. The administration had requested $3.7 billion.

▶ **Research programs.** Research and development programs received $1.3 billion, of which $957 million went toward operating nuclear defense laboratories. The administration had requested $1.4 billion. Research and development in 1993 focused on keeping the United States at the fore of nuclear weapons production, in part to ensure against "technological surprise" by potential threats to national security. The account also included funds to ensure that the nation was prepared for any nuclear emergency. It also was meant to ease the transfer of non-sensitive technology to the private sector.

▶ **Nuclear fusion.** One of the largest projects within the research program was known as "inertial confinement fusion." The project was an attempt to create a controlled thermonuclear explosion through fusion to study the process and consider its potential for weaponry and as an energy source. The bill contained $188.4 million for the fusion project, equal to the administration request. House appropriators earmarked about $25.2 million of that to upgrade the OMEGA laser at the University of Rochester.

▶ **Testing.** The fiscal 1994 level of $403 million for nuclear weapons testing was intended to preserve the option of conducting underground tests. Clinton announced on July 3 that the United States would not conduct any nuclear tests for at least 15 months, provided that no other nation did either. Clinton then reversed that order and called on the Energy Department to prepare for new tests in 1994 after China detonated a nuclear bomb underground on Oct. 5.

▶ **Stockpile support.** This $1.9 billion account provided operating expenses and environmental, safety and health programs for the nation's nuclear weapons facilities. Because no new weapons were being built, this category had been renamed "stockpile support"; it formerly was called "production and surveillance." Still, the stockpile program retained the capability to resume producing uranium and plutonium components should nuclear bomb production resume. The amount was $461.1 million less than fiscal 1993, a reduction that came mostly from lower operating expenses. Less spending meant fewer workers. Energy Department officials complained that the reduced spending conflicted with Congress' goal of accelerating the dismantling of nuclear weapons.

▶ **Program direction.** The bill provided $281 million for "program direction," which provided payments to defense contractors affected by the reduction in nuclear defense activities. Another account, called "weapons complex reconfiguration," was funded at $193.5 million. The money was used to support efforts to redesign the entire nuclear weapons complex to make it smaller and more efficient.

Environmental Cleanup

Nearly half of the spending for the atomic defense program in fiscal 1994 went to clean up nuclear weapons facilities and develop waste management technologies. The account was the fastest-growing item in the program budget, jumping to $5.2 billion in fiscal 1994 from $4.8 billion in the previous fiscal year. But appropriators were beginning to fire warning shots at the Energy Department to step up progress in this area. "There will not be an endless source of funding for this program," the House report stated. "The committee expects to see concrete results from the investment to date."

Environmental restoration work was under way at virtually all of the Energy Department complexes that had been involved in the production of nuclear weapons. Particularly extensive work was under way at Hanford, Rocky Flats, Oak Ridge, Savannah River and the Idaho National Engineering Laboratory.

Most of the funds — $2.84 billion — paid for waste management activities such as treating, storing and disposing of radioactive and hazardous waste. Another $1.54 billion was to go toward operating expenses for programs that sought to reduce and remove potential environmental risks at nuclear weapons facilities, including a number of sites on the Environmental Protection Agency's "superfund" list of the nation's worst toxic dumps.

But the bill also set aside funds for specific cleanup jobs, such as $43.9 million for defense waste processing at Savannah River and $40 million to close the Hanford waste vitrification plant, which processed nuclear waste into a less hazardous solid. The work at Hanford was far from over: Another $35 million also was provided to begin another round of cleanup activities required by a recent agreement with the state of Washington. And $45.7 million more went toward a waste removal facility at Hanford to speed up construction of new storage tanks and develop waste treatment facilities.

Miscellaneous

▶ **Materials support.** The bill provided $1.1 billion to provide nuclear materials to meet national defense requirements that were determined annually by the president. The program also produced and managed nuclear materials for use in federal and civilian research, and commercial and medical applications.

This account — given a new, post-Cold War name rather than its previous heading of "materials production" — had been reduced from $1.6 billion in fiscal 1993, in keeping with overall reductions in the stockpile of materials. The account included $88.97 million for environment, safety and health programs that upgraded facilities and provided training for workers.

▶ **Verification and security.** The bill included $366 million for arms control verification programs and measures to safeguard against the proliferation of nuclear weapons, about $38.3 million more than the previous year. Most of that increase was allocated for non-proliferation activities, particularly research programs that sought to better monitor the movement of nuclear materials. The money also went toward verification of arms control treaties with Russia and other former Soviet states, as well as to prepare for an upcoming Comprehensive Test Ban Treaty, which Clinton hoped to complete by 1996.

▶ **Worker training.** Appropriators allotted $100 million for a new worker training and adjustment program, which was to assist workers at Energy Department defense facilities and sites that were hurt by curtailed mission responsibilities. The program was required as part of the 1993 defense authorization.

▶ **Naval reactors.** The program conducted the research, development and oversight of nuclear propulsion plants and reactor cores for the nation's nuclear naval fleet, predominantly submarines such as the attack submarine *Seawolf*, being built by Electric Boat Co. in Groton, Conn., but also large surface ships. The program also included uranium enrichment to manufacture the fuel needed for the cores in naval ships powered by nuclear reactors.

Appropriators put $759.9 million toward naval reactors, including $689.9 million for the research and development program, and $70 million for uranium enrichment activities. ∎

$2.5 Billion Approved for Ex-Soviet States

Undaunted by the political chaos gripping Russia and its neighbors, Congress handed President Clinton a major foreign policy victory in 1993 by easily clearing legislation funding his $2.5 billion aid request for the former Soviet Union. The aid was part of a $14.6 billion foreign operations appropriations bill cleared by the Senate on Sept. 30; Clinton signed the bill into law the same day (HR 2295 — PL 103-87).

Facing a taut foreign aid budget, lawmakers were forced to draw $1.6 billion of the aid for the former Soviet republics from unexpended fiscal 1993 defense and foreign aid funds. That was attached to the bill as a supplemental appropriation for fiscal 1993.

The regular fiscal 1994 measure provided $13 billion, a reduction of $1.4 billion from the administration's request. But the cuts could have been worse for the White House. The legislation closely followed funding levels included in the more generous House bill, which provided nearly $500 million more than the Senate measure.

More than half the bill's funding — $7.6 billion — went to a handful of recipients. Congress earmarked $3 billion in military and economic aid for Israel and $2.1 billion for Egypt in addition to the $2.5 billion provided for Russia and the other former Soviet republics.

Lawmakers cut almost $480 million from the administration's $2.3 billion request for U.S. contributions to international financial institutions such as the World Bank and International Monetary Fund. The reduction left the United States $819 million behind in its promised contributions to those institutions.

The final action on the aid bill came as Russia's political crisis became more ominous and nationalist violence intensified elsewhere in the former Soviet empire. In spite of the turmoil, the dominant sentiment in Congress seemed to be that the United States had little choice but to extend strong support for the political and economic changes being pursued by Russia's President Boris N. Yeltsin.

"God help this nation; God help this world if they revert to another form of communism, fascism, totalitarianism or any other form of dictatorship," Robert L. Livingston, R-La., said during the brief House debate. *(Russian aid, p. 509)*

BACKGROUND

The foreign operations spending bill was the centerpiece of the U.S. foreign aid program, paying for foreign assistance and for U.S. participation in a variety of international military and economic efforts.

Since the mid-1980s, Congress had steadily cut funding for the bill. Though foreign aid was a tiny fraction of the $1.5 trillion budget, it was unpopular and an easy target when lawmakers were looking for ways to cut the deficit. *(1992 Almanac, p. 612)*

BOXSCORE

➡ **Fiscal 1994 Foreign Operations appropriations (HR 2295).** The $14.6 billion spending bill included $2.5 billion in aid for the former Soviet Union.

Reports: H Rept 103-125, S Rept 103-142; conference report, H Rept 103-267.

KEY ACTION

June 17 — **House** passed HR 2295, 309-111.

Sept. 23 — **Senate** passed HR 2295, 88-10.

Sept. 29 — **House** agreed to conference report, 321-108.

Sept. 30 — **Senate** agreed to conference report, 88-11.

Sept. 30 — **President** signed HR 2295 — PL 103-87.

The creative budgetary maneuvers used to assemble the aid package for the former Soviet republics recalled other recent efforts to finance high-profile diplomatic initiatives on a shoestring.

At the height of the Persian Gulf crisis in 1990, for example, President George Bush forgave about $7 billion in debts owed by Egypt. That proved to be a far less expensive approach than offering Cairo a new assistance program. In 1992, Bush dropped his opposition to Israel's request for guarantees for $10 billion in commercial loans after the moderate government of Prime Minister Yitzhak Rabin was swept to victory in parliamentary elections. Israel sought the aid through guarantees, in apparent recognition that Congress was unlikely to add to the country's $3 billion a year in direct aid. *(1990 Almanac, p. 830; 1992 Almanac, p. 612)*

For the Clinton administration, the international demands continued to mount even after the president signed the foreign operations bill into law. Although the administration sought to back the landmark agreement between Israel and the Palestine Liberation Organization, budget constraints forestalled any significant offers of assistance. *(Middle East peace, p. 516)*

At the same time, pressure to cut foreign aid continued, a fact that was underscored when the administration proposed $290 million in rescissions from previously appropriated foreign assistance as part of an $11 billion package of spending cuts introduced shortly before Congress adjourned. *(Spending cuts, p. 140)*

Assembling the Russian Aid Package

The formula for aiding the former Soviet republics grew out of an intensive series of meetings among senior administration officials and members of the House leadership, as well as House Foreign Operations Subcommittee Chairman David R. Obey, D-Wis., and other members of the Appropriations Committee. Highlighting the importance of the effort to the administration, Office of Management and Budget Director Leon E. Panetta took time out from lobbying for the president's economic plan to work on the package.

Eventually, the administration and lawmakers came up with the following funding plan:

● **Fiscal 1993:** The core of the package was $1.6 billion in unspent fiscal 1993 budget authority — $630 million drawn from foreign aid and $979 million from defense funds.

● **Fiscal 1994:** The remaining $900 million in budget authority came from fiscal 1994 funds — all of it from Economic Support Fund (ESF) assistance that otherwise would have gone to other nations.

By combining the fiscal 1993 and 1994 money in a single bill, the administration avoided having to ask lawmakers to

FOREIGN OPERATIONS

	Fiscal 1993 Appropriation	Fiscal 1994 Clinton Request	House Bill	Senate Bill	Final Bill
(In thousands of dollars)					
Multilateral Aid					
World Bank					
Paid-in capital	$ 62,180	$ 70,126	$ 55,821	$ 27,911	$ 55,821
Global Environment Facility	30,000	30,810	30,000	30,000	30,000
Limitation on callable capital	*(2,010,513)*	*(2,267,418)*	*(1,804,879)*	*(902,440)*	*(1,804,879)*
International Development Association	1,024,332	1,250,000	1,024,332	957,143	1,024,332
International Finance Corp.	35,762	50,000	35,762	17,881	35,762
Inter-American Development Bank	76,738	77,889	76,330	76,330	76,330
Limitation on callable capital	*(2,202,040)*	*(2,235,077)*	*(2,190,283)*	*(2,190,283)*	*(2,190,283)*
Enterprise for the Americas	90,000	100,000	75,000	50,000	75,000
Asian Development Bank	38,014	13,026	13,026	2,000	13,026
Asian Development Fund	62,500	170,000	62,500	62,500	62,500
African Development Fund	103,893	135,000	132,300	135,000	135,000
European Development Bank	60,000	61,000	—	—	—
State Department international programs	310,000	390,000	339,500	360,628	360,628
U.S. quota, International Monetary Fund	12,313,857	—	—	—	—
TOTAL, multilateral aid	**$ 14,207,276**	**$ 2,347,852**	**$ 1,844,571**	**$1,719,392**	**$1,868,399**
Bilateral Aid					
Agency for International Development (AID)					
Development assistance	1,387,480	1,321,480	1,203,900	1,203,900	1,203,900
Sub-Saharan Africa development aid	800,000	800,000	784,000	784,000	784,000
Sub-Saharan Africa disaster aid	100,000	—	—	—	—
International disaster aid	48,965	148,965	145,985	48,965	145,985
AID operating expenses	551,316	551,916	540,878	532,599	540,878
Debt restructuring	50,000	45,427	7,000	7,000	7,000
Economic Support Fund	2,670,000	2,582,000	2,364,562	2,280,500	2,364,562
Multilateral aid for Philippines	40,000	40,000	20,000	20,000	20,000
Assistance for Eastern Europe	400,000	408,951	400,000	380,000	390,000
Assistance for ex-Soviets	417,000	903,820	903,820	603,820	603,820
(1993 supplemental)	—	(1,609,000) [1]	(1,609,000) [1]	(1,609,000) [1]	(1,609,000) [1]
Rescission	—	—	−185,000	−255,100	−208,100
Other	123,099	68,965	68,068	50,468	72,068
Subtotal, AID	**$ 6,587,860**	**$ 6,871,524**	**$ 6,253,213**	**$5,656,152**	**$5,924,113**
State Department					
International narcotics control	147,783	147,783	100,000	100,000	100,000
Migration and refugee aid	669,949	689,949	689,949	719,949	719,949
Anti-terrorism assistance	15,555	15,555	15,244	15,244	15,244
Subtotal, State Department	**$ 833,287**	**$ 853,287**	**$ 805,193**	**$835,193**	**$835,193**
Peace Corps	218,146	219,745	219,745	219,745	219,745
OPIC *(loan levels)*	*(650,000)*	*(375,027)*	*(—)*	*(346,885)*	*(—)*
Other	65,793	65,793	63,828	64,448	64,448
TOTAL, bilateral aid	**$ 7,705,086**	**$ 8,010,349**	**$ 7,341,979**	**$6,775,538**	**$7,043,499**
Bilateral Military Aid (appropriated to president)					
Foreign military financing (grants)	3,300,000	3,231,657	3,175,000	3,123,558	3,149,279
Loan subsidies	149,000	120,263	46,530	46,530	46,530
Estimated loan program	*(855,000)*	*(855,000)*	*(769,500)*	*(769,500)*	*(769,500)*
International military education and training	42,500	42,500	21,250	21,250	21,250
Defense acquisition fund *(obligations limits)*	*(225,000)*	*(—)*	*(—)*	*(—)*	*(—)*
Fund elimination	—	−266,000	−266,000	−266,000	−266,000
Other	27,366	127,860	86,123	73,000	86,123
TOTAL, military aid	**$ 3,518,866**	**$ 3,256,280**	**$ 3,062,903**	**$2,998,338**	**$3,037,182**
Export Assistance					
Export-Import Bank	786,150	751,512	693,586	993,586	993,586
Export assistance *(loan levels)*	*(15,500,000)*	*(16,500,000)*	*(—)*	*(—)*	*(—)*
Trade and development	40,000	60,000	40,000	40,000	40,000
GRAND TOTAL	**$ 26,257,378**	**$ 14,425,993**	**$ 12,983,039**	**$ 12,526,854**	**$ 12,982,666**

[1] *$1.609 billion for the former Soviet republics was drawn from unexpended balances of foreign assistance and defense funds in fiscal 1993.*

SOURCE: House Appropriations Committee

vote more than once on the package. But the strategy also put pressure on Congress to complete work on the measure by midnight Sept. 30, the last day of the fiscal year. After that date, the $1.6 billion would no longer be available.

Obey's Pitch

Though lawmakers were worried for weeks about how the administration intended to pay for its promised aid to Yeltsin, they were equally concerned over delays in detailing the specific projects the $2.5 billion would support.

In an effort to address those concerns, Strobe Talbott, ambassador-at-large for the former Soviet republics, offered an unusual briefing for the Foreign Operations Appropriations Subcommittee before its markup, outlining where the money would go.

Talbott was the administration's point man for the program, but it fell largely upon Obey to sell the idea to his subcommittee colleagues. In an exchange with Sonny Callahan, R-Ala., he offered an impassioned plea to support Russia's democratic reformers.

Callahan said he had "great disdain" for the notion of voting for aid to Russia "during a week when we're voting a multibillion-dollar tax bill."

Obey countered by citing data that every American family had spent the equivalent of $80,000 for defense expenditures during the Cold War. He recalled the thousands of troops — including a friend — who were killed during conflicts in Vietnam and Korea.

"The fact was that each and every one of those people gave a hell of lot more than a few bucks" to fight communism, Obey said. He called the aid package "a gamble" but argued that "we're not, in my view, going to survive as a democratic island in a sea of undemocratic forces."

Callahan remained opposed, but Obey won over the subcommittee's ranking Republican, Livingston of Louisiana. "I believe you're on the right track," Livingston, a bedrock conservative, told Obey.

HOUSE SUBCOMMITTEE ACTION

With the aid formula worked out, the House Appropriations Subcommittee on Foreign Operations on May 26 approved a $14.6 billion bill that combined the $1.6 billion fiscal 1993 supplemental with $13 billion in regular fiscal 1994 appropriations. The subcommittee approved the plan by voice vote.

By drawing down defense funds and other foreign assistance to pay for aid to the former republics, the subcommittee managed to avoid the political pitfalls of raiding domestic accounts or adding to the budget deficit.

But the bill made substantial cuts in the regular fiscal 1994 foreign aid budget, cutting $1.4 billion from the administration's fiscal 1994 request and providing nearly $1 billion less in foreign aid than the fiscal 1993 aid bill. (The 1993 bill totaled $26.3 billion, but $12.3 of that was for the U.S. quota for the International Monetary Fund, an item that did not add to the U.S. deficit.)

Cuts in Security Assistance

The panel reduced the administration's request for virtually every program — with the exception of politically sacrosanct assistance for Israel and Egypt. The bill anticipated providing $3 billion in military and economic aid for Israel and $2.1 billion for Egypt — the same levels as in recent years. For the rest of the world, the bill sharply reduced funding for security-related assistance.

In a departure from his predecessors' policies, Clinton had proposed modest cuts in security assistance — ESF aid and military assistance for key allies. Former Presidents George Bush and Ronald Reagan had annually sought increases for these programs.

But because of a funding shortfall compounded by the unexpectedly large request for the former Soviet republics, Obey's subcommittee was forced to make reductions well beyond those requested by Clinton.

The bill trimmed ESF by $217 million below the administration request and included rescissions of $185 million from previously appropriated funds. It also cut the Foreign Military Financing (FMF) program — the most important source of military assistance — by about $130 million.

With approximately $5.1 billion of the $5.6 billion security assistance program reserved for Israel and Egypt, aid for some important U.S. allies had to be scaled back or abandoned.

There was only about $350 million in the $2.4 billion ESF account available for countries other than the Middle Eastern allies. That was not enough to fund $567 million in administration requests, including $143 million for Turkey and more than $100 million for the war-ravaged Central American countries of Nicaragua and El Salvador.

In the fiscal 1993 bill, Obey had pushed through a proposal to "graduate" Turkey and other NATO allies from a program of military grants to market-based loans. In the fiscal 1994 bill, the Foreign Operations Subcommittee reduced the request for loans to those countries by 10 percent.

The bill provided $405 million in military loans for Turkey, $283.5 million for Greece and $81 million for Portugal. As had become customary, the bill stipulated that Greece receive $7 in loans for each $10 provided to Turkey.

The legislation reduced by half the administration's $42.5 million request for international military and education training assistance. It also retained restrictions on aid to Indonesia because of alleged human rights abuses by its military.

In addition, it cut $47.8 million from the administration's $147.8 million request for international narcotics control activities. In the report accompanying the legislation, Obey's subcommittee was unsparing in its assessment of past anti-narcotics efforts. It said the Bush administration's $2.2 billion "Andean strategy" to stem narcotics trafficking in Peru, Colombia and Bolivia had failed to reduce levels of cocaine reaching the United States from those countries.

Cuts in Economic Assistance

Funding for programs intended to aid developing countries also was frozen or reduced. The legislation trimmed $16 million from the administration's $800 million request for the Development Fund for Africa, which was begun in 1988 to alleviate poverty and foster economic growth in the sub-Saharan region.

It provided $816 million — a $221 million cut from fiscal 1993 — to fund a broad range of projects, including child survival and AIDS prevention and education.

The legislation recommended $392 million in funding for international family planning programs, a $42 million increase over the fiscal 1993 level. But that was still $8 million less than the administration requested.

The bill froze aid to the former communist nations of Eastern Europe at the fiscal 1993 level of $400 million. It also provided $19.6 million to a special fund for Ireland —

long a favorite program of House Democratic leaders.

The Philippines, which ranked near the top of aid recipients during the 1980s, received only $20 million in economic development assistance under the bill. Aid levels declined after the United States shut down its military bases there.

Only a few programs managed to escape the budget cutting. The legislation funded the administration's $219.7 million request for the Peace Corps. It also continued a trend toward higher levels of assistance for international refugee programs. The bill provided $690 million in refugee aid in fiscal 1994, the full administration request and an increase of about $20 million over fiscal 1993. Funding for such programs had grown by 42 percent since fiscal 1991, reflecting the rapidly increasing number of refugees worldwide.

Policy Issues

Overall, the foreign operations legislation was more of a budget blueprint and less of a policy statement than it had been in several years. But the bill and accompanying report did address some foreign policy concerns:

• The bill retained authority for the president to provide $50 million in military equipment to the outgunned government forces of Bosnia-Herzegovina but only if the United Nations lifted its arms embargo against the former Yugoslavia. That proposal did not go as far as a provision in the fiscal 1994 aid authorization bill that allowed the president to act unilaterally to aid the Bosnians.

• The report said the administration should not provide military aid for El Salvador unless its government complied with recommendations of the U.N. Truth Commission, which called for removal of military officers blamed for atrocities in the country's long-running civil war. The administration had frozen fiscal 1993 military aid to El Salvador but sought $2.7 million as part of its fiscal 1994 budget.

• The bill cut about $14 million from the administration's $50 million request for the U.N. Population Fund — the amount that the U.N. agency was expected to spend on its activities in China. In addition, none of the funds could be provided before March 1, 1994, unless the family planning agency withdrew from China. The population fund had come under criticism for operating in China because of renewed reports of coercion in Beijing's population control program.

During the markup, Obey repeatedly stated that he would follow the lead of the House Foreign Affairs Committee on such policy questions. A Foreign Affairs subcommittee had addressed the issue in considering a bill authorizing the State Department's budget. *(State Department authorization, p. 505)*

The subcommittee was particularly rough on Clinton's $2 billion request for international financial institutions, cutting it by nearly $449 million. Outraged by recent news reports that the European Bank for Reconstruction and Development had diverted millions of dollars to build an opulent headquarters, the subcommittee eliminated all of the $70 million that the administration sought for the bank.

"We do not approve appropriations for that bank to keep marble companies in business," said subcommittee Chairman Obey.

The bill also reduced funding for the World Bank to protest its recent loans to Iran.

Even popular programs, such as support for the lending of the Export-Import Bank, took serious hits. The subcommittee cut support for the bank's programs from $757 million to $700 million.

Obey Removes Earmarks

In an effort to provide the new administration with latitude in allocating foreign aid, Obey eliminated earmarks — congressionally mandated spending levels for certain programs favored by lawmakers, including the popular earmarks for Israel and Egypt. In something of a surprise, the subcommittee raised no objections to the proposal, in part because of a tacit understanding that aid for the Middle East allies would be earmarked in the final version of the bill.

Nita M. Lowey, D-N.Y., a strong supporter of Israel, said she was not worried by the elimination of the funding requirements because the subcommittee had received assurances from Secretary of State Warren Christopher that there would be no cuts in 1993 in U.S. aid to the two countries. Equally important, Lowey said, the subcommittee endorsed language in the bill mandating that Israel receive its $3 billion aid allocation in a lump sum at the start of the fiscal year. That provision, which had been included in aid bills for several years, enabled Israel to reap interest income by investing in U.S. government securities.

HOUSE FULL COMMITTEE

The full House Appropriations Committee approved the bill (H Rept 103-125) by voice vote June 10. Foreign Operations Subcommittee Chairman Obey said the legislation "allows us to respond to the No. 1 foreign policy challenge we had in the world" by strongly supporting the former Soviet republics. "But I don't want to kid you," he told his colleagues. "It also requires draconian reductions."

An attempt by Callahan of Alabama to strip the $1.6 billion supplemental appropriation from the measure was easily turned aside by voice vote. Callahan insisted that he was not averse to helping the newly independent states but said he wanted an opportunity to attach stiffer conditions to the aid. Callahan focused his opposition on the administration's plans to use some of the funds to ease a severe housing shortage for Russian troops returning from Warsaw bloc deployments. "We're downsizing 3,000 military people a week in this country," he said, "and we're not giving them any housing."

But Obey and Livingston joined forces to defend the aid proposal. "We are talking about the single most important move this country could make for future generations," Livingston said.

HOUSE FLOOR ACTION

With a strong push from the leadership of both parties, the $2.5 billion aid package for the former Soviet republics sailed through the House on June 17 as part of HR 2295. Overcoming its traditional reluctance to vote for foreign aid, the House approved the $14.6 billion measure, 309-111. Democrats backed the legislation, 202-47, while Republicans supported the bill, 107-63. *(Vote 240, p. 58-H)*

The week of June 14 turned out to be a successful one for supporters of international programs. This came at a time when such spending was widely assumed to be unpopular. The day before the House approved the spending bill, members gave a strong vote of approval to the companion foreign aid authorization measure. *(Foreign authorization bill, p. 502)*

The only challenge to the spending bill came from a disparate alliance of some conservative Republicans and some members of the Congressional Black Caucus. Moti-

vated by an array of cost and foreign policy concerns, they joined forces to back an amendment offered by Callahan to strip the $1.6 billion supplemental from the bill.

"To defeat the domestic stimulus package in April and then somehow mysteriously pass Russian aid in June would create the perception that our priorities are in the wrong place," said Kweisi Mfume, D-Md., chairman of the Congressional Black Caucus, who had complained that Clinton appeared to be moving to the political right to placate critics.

But House leaders stood united behind the president's request. Majority Leader Richard A. Gephardt, D-Mo., argued that failing to help the former communist states could necessitate a return to Cold War defense budgets.

"This was the most important issue of our lifetime," he said. With 79 Republicans joining most Democrats to oppose Callahan's amendment, it was rejected, 140-289. (Vote 237, p. 58-H)

The cuts the committee had made in the bill made it easier for many members to support aid to Moscow at a time when domestic programs were facing the budget ax.

The key to the convincing victory was clearly the strong backing provided by leading Republicans. That more than offset opposition to the Russian aid from 17 of the Congressional Black Caucus' 38 Democratic House members. Conservatives, such as Minority Whip Newt Gingrich of Georgia and Livingston of Louisiana echoed Gephardt's argument that the aid package served U.S. interests. Gingrich remarked that it had been a "very interesting day" of scrambled political alliances.

Many Republicans previously had backed Bush administration requests for the former republics, and Gephardt had bolstered support for a new package by arranging for a delegation of senior members from both parties to visit Russia and the Ukraine in April.

Dispute Over Multilateral Aid, India

The bipartisan spirit evaporated, however, when John R. Kasich of Ohio, the ranking Republican on the Budget Committee, offered an amendment to eliminate the $56 million U.S. contribution to the World Bank. Kasich said the institution had squandered massive sums on ill-considered projects and extravagant perquisites for senior officials. "Their costs are out of control," he said.

The amendment was narrowly rejected, 210-216. But providing funds for international financial institutions was clearly a sensitive issue for many lawmakers. (Vote 238, p. 58-H)

Indiana Republican Dan Burton failed in an attempt to strike $41 million from the bill, which was the administration's request for development assistance for India. Burton had long crusaded against such assistance because of atrocities committed by Indian security forces in Kashmir and Punjab. Though Burton was successful with a similar amendment on the 1992 foreign operations bill, the House unanimously adopted Obey's substitute amendment, which cut only $4.1 million in development aid. The vote was 425-0. (Vote 236, p. 58-H)

SENATE COMMITTEE ACTION

The Senate Foreign Operations Appropriations Subcommittee acted quickly on its $14.1 billion version of HR 2295, approving the bill by voice vote Sept. 13.

With a taut Senate allocation for foreign aid, the subcommittee cut about $500 million from the House-passed bill, reducing the administration's fiscal 1994 foreign aid request by nearly $2 billion.

The bill incorporated the formula devised by the House to provide $2.5 billion in assistance for the former Soviet republics, with $1.6 billion provided as a fiscal 1993 supplemental appropriation and the remainder drawn from fiscal 1994 funds.

The markup was virtually devoid of controversy, reflecting strong support in both parties to aid Russia and its neighbors and to maintain assistance for Israel and Egypt. Like the House bill, the measure provided $3 billion in aid for Israel and $2.1 billion for Egypt.

Acting on the same day that Israel and the Palestine Liberation Organization (PLO) signed a historic agreement, the Foreign Operations Subcommittee supported a modest but symbolically important increase in aid for Israel. The panel adopted by voice vote an amendment by ranking Republican Mitch McConnell, Ky., that increased assistance for Jewish immigrants in Israel from $55 million to $80 million. The money was to be drawn from other international refugee programs.

McConnell's proposal drew criticism from subcommittee Chairman Patrick J. Leahy, D-Vt., who complained that the additional refugee aid for Israel would equal the entire funding in the bill — $25 million — for projects benefiting Palestinians. The Palestinian aid funded an existing program that supported private voluntary organizations in the West Bank and Gaza Strip and represented no increase from the level provided in fiscal 1993. The fund covered only a fraction of the expected monetary requirements of the proposed Palestinian self-governing authority in the area.

Clearing the Way for Russian Aid

For weeks, Leahy had warned that a budget crunch might prevent his panel from funding the $2.5 billion in aid for the former Soviet republics. Yet it seemed inevitable that the panel would somehow find the money to support the aid program, which Clinton and his aides had repeatedly identified as a foreign aid priority.

The funding crunch arose when Daniel K. Inouye, D-Hawaii, chairman of the Senate Defense Appropriations Subcommittee, and other pro-Pentagon senators balked at plans to tap $979 million in unexpended defense budget authority from fiscal 1993 for the aid package. Inouye initially said the defense budget could not afford to absorb the $210 million in reduced outlays required by that shift. But after personal lobbying by Clinton, Inouye signed on to the deal. Other senators who had raised objections, such as Ted Stevens, R-Alaska, also fell into line.

A second funding snag was overcome by evading a requirement of the Congressional Budget Office (CBO) that $170 million in outlays be set aside to protect against a possible default by Israel in a program that provided guarantees for up to $10 billion in loans over five years. (1992 Almanac, p. 539)

With the consent of Senate Budget Committee Chairman Jim Sasser, D-Tenn., and Appropriations Committee Chairman Robert C. Byrd, D-W.Va., the subcommittee included a provision declaring that costs associated with the loan guarantees would not count against the discretionary spending limits established under the 1990 budget agreement or the Foreign Operations Subcommittee's funding allocation for fiscal 1994.

In essence, the legislation treated any costs associated with the loan guarantee program as an off-budget expense.

Other major foreign assistance programs — such as the $12 billion contribution to the International Monetary Fund in fiscal 1993 and the $6.7 billion grant of debt relief for Egypt in 1990 — had been handled in a similar fashion.

The unusual decision to circumvent CBO came without debate. Lawmakers were reluctant to address the politically sensitive issue publicly.

Even with the maneuvering, however, the subcommittee was forced to cut foreign aid more deeply than the House-passed legislation. Not only were most programs reduced, but there were no outlays remaining that could be committed for additional foreign aid spending during fiscal 1994.

The report by Leahy's subcommittee was sharply critical of "the meager results of foreign aid reform in the first year of the new administration." The administration's review of foreign aid had recently been completed by Deputy Secretary of State Clifton Wharton Jr.

Wharton's team focused primarily on the Agency for International Development, the lead agency in delivering foreign aid. By doing so, the subcommittee said, the review had overlooked the critical need to develop a new rationale for security assistance in the post-Cold War era.

Senate Earmarks

In an effort to provide the new administration with latitude in allocating foreign aid, House Foreign Operations Appropriations Subcommittee Chairman Obey had pushed through a bill that eliminated earmarks — congressionally mandated spending levels for specific programs.

In contrast to the House bill, the Senate measure was studded with statutory earmarks, although the report accompanying the bill said the subcommittee reduced the number from past years. In addition, the report included extensive recommendations that the subcommittee made clear it expected to be followed.

In spite of Leahy's insistence that the president be given "maximum flexibility" in providing aid for the former Soviet Union, most of the $2.5 billion in assistance was earmarked or specified for individual programs. The bill included a proposal by McConnell to earmark $300 million in aid for Ukraine. McConnell said he was concerned that Ukraine might receive short shrift because of the intense focus on Russia.

The bill also required that $18 million in assistance be provided for Armenia, which was locked in a brutal territorial dispute with neighboring Azerbaijan. Armenia had long been a favored country of many key lawmakers, including Senate Minority Leader Bob Dole, R-Kan.

In addition, the bill included a general breakdown of how the aid should be expended:

● $50 million to be provided in the form of agricultural commodities, an earmark with obvious appeal for farm-state lawmakers.

● $895 million for private-sector development through bilateral and multilateral enterprise funds.

● $125 million to support a multilateral fund to convert state-owned enterprises into private concerns, a central aspect of the administration's initiative.

● $185 million to enhance trade with the former Soviet Union through assistance for exports of energy and environmental commodities.

● $295 million for pro-democracy initiatives, including expanded exchange programs.

● $190 million to support more housing for former Russian troops in an effort to facilitate their withdrawal from the Baltic nations and other countries.

● $285 million in aid for energy and environment.

● $239 million for humanitarian assistance.

● $300 million in backing for loan guarantee programs administered by the Export-Import Bank.

Cutting Deeper Than the House

Aside from the former Soviet Union, Israel and Egypt, most foreign aid recipients and international assistance programs were also in line for deep reductions.

The legislation provided $1.7 billion for multilateral financial institutions, a cut of $628 million from the administration request and a cut of $146 million from the House bill.

The Senate bill, like the House measure, eliminated funding for the European Bank for Reconstruction and Development. Leahy's subcommittee also reduced the administration's $70 million request for the World Bank by $42 million. The panel approved by voice vote an amendment by Connie Mack, R-Fla., to withhold funds from the World Bank unless the administration certified that the bank was not lending to Iran.

In addition, the Senate rescinded about $255 million in appropriated foreign assistance, about $70 million more than the House. The Senate bill also cut $20 million from the $400 million provided by the House for the Baltic countries and Eastern Europe.

Perhaps the most significant cut came in the area of international disaster assistance, which had become an important program in aiding victims of the world's many raging ethnic conflicts. The Senate bill provided $49 million for such assistance, $100 million below the administration request and $97 million below the level approved by the House.

The legislation also:

● Provided $50 million, the full administration request, for the U.N. Population Fund.

● Earmarked $35 million to assist refugees in the war-torn former Yugoslavia. In addition, the Appropriations Committee approved an amendment by Arlen Specter, R-Pa., providing $3 million to help fund a war crimes tribunal in the former Yugoslavia.

Senate Full Committee Action

Hurrying to commit the unused funds from fiscal 1993 before it ended Sept. 30, the full Senate Appropriations Committee reported the bill 28-0 on Sept. 14, a day after the subcommittee markup (S Rept 103-142).

SENATE FLOOR ACTION

Acting against a backdrop of political upheaval in Russia, the Senate sent a strong signal of support for Yeltsin Sept 23 by overwhelmingly approving the $2.5 billion in aid as part of the annual foreign aid bill. The Senate approved the bill 88-10. *(Vote 287, p. 37-S)*

The Senate began consideration of the bill Sept. 22, just one day after Yeltsin threw his nation into turmoil by disbanding the parliament and calling for December elections. The Clinton administration argued that the crisis only added to the urgency of Senate action on the aid request, which had emerged as a foreign policy priority of the White House.

Foreign Operations Subcommittee Chairman Leahy said it was "a real roll of the dice" to bring the bill to the floor while Yeltsin was struggling with his hard-line rivals from the parliament. But his concern that the bill would

set off a messy public debate over U.S. policy toward Russia proved unfounded. Despite the unresolved struggle for power, senators followed Clinton's lead in rallying around the Russian president.

Middle East

The Senate addressed the changed political environment in the Middle East by adopting a pair of amendments, co-sponsored by Leahy and McConnell, lifting long-standing restrictions on the PLO. The amendments, approved by voice vote, temporarily waived statutory provisions reducing U.S. contributions to international organizations that supported the PLO. Though it was not clear whether the waivers would free more multilateral assistance for the PLO, they represented the first action taken by Congress in support of the agreement. (Middle East Peace, p. 516)

Russia Amendments

Senators easily disposed of several amendments aimed at attaching conditions to aid for Moscow that reflected concerns over various Russian policies.

By a 97-1 vote, the Senate adopted an amendment by Appropriations Committee Chairman Byrd requiring the president to certify that Moscow had made "substantial progress" in withdrawing its remaining forces from the Baltic nations before providing aid to Russia. Byrd said the provision, to take effect Oct. 6, probably would force a cutoff of a small amount of fiscal 1993 aid because Moscow had yet to agree to a timetable for withdrawing about 20,000 troops from the Baltic nations of Latvia and Estonia. (Vote 283, p. 37-S)

The Senate adopted by voice vote an amendment by Mack to reduce aid for Moscow by $380 million unless the president certified that Russia had not been supporting Cuba. Mack used the $380 million figure because Russia had extended a loan for that amount to Cuba earlier in the year.

And the Senate by voice vote backed a proposal by McConnell barring aid for any of the former Soviet republics that violated the "territorial integrity or national sovereignty" of neighboring states.

Other Amendments

For all of the concern over the Russian aid package, the debate was dominated by other issues. The most closely contested vote came on an amendment by Hank Brown, R-Colo., to cut off $28 million in funding for the World Bank. Brown charged that the bank had spent hundreds of millions of dollars to build a lavish new headquarters building in Washington. "The World Bank was out of control," Brown said. Leahy countered that the aid bill already cut the administration's $70 million request for the bank by $42 million. He said it would be counterproductive to reduce U.S. support further, particularly because the bank was expected to play a key role in assisting the proposed Palestinian self-governing authority. Brown's amendment was tabled (killed) 55-44. (Vote 284, p. 37-S)

New Hampshire Republican Robert C. Smith unsuccessfully sought to tap into the unpopularity of foreign aid by proposing to cut $200 million in funding from the bill and use the money to support defense conversion programs. Smith managed to attract the support of some Democrats, such as Dianne Feinstein, Calif., who usually could be counted on to defend foreign aid. Feinstein said that because of the devastating cutbacks in California's defense industry she had no choice but to support the

proposal. Smith's amendment was tabled (killed), 64-35. (Vote 285, p. 37-S)

North Carolina Republican Jesse Helms made several attempts to impose harsh conditions on aid to Russia, Nicaragua and other countries. But he sidestepped confrontation on the amendments by agreeing to allow the president to waive restrictions if he determined that to be in the national interest.

The Senate avoided a full-scale debate over Clinton's policy toward the conflict in Bosnia-Herzegovina when Minority Leader Dole withdrew an amendment calling on the president to seek congressional approval for any deployment of U.S. peacekeeping forces to Bosnia. Clinton had said that he would seek congressional authorization if he decided to dispatch forces to the former Yugoslavian republic. In return for withdrawing his amendment, Dole secured a pledge from Foreign Relations Committee Chairman Claiborne Pell, D-R.I., to hold hearings on the Bosnian crisis. (Bosnia, p. 493)

FINAL ACTION

Rushing to meet the Sept. 30 deadline, House and Senate conferees met into the early hours of Sept. 28 to craft a final version of the bill. The resulting conference agreement (H Rept 103-267) increased the final bill's total by more than $450 million over the Senate version. That required the consent of Senate Appropriations Chairman Byrd, who revised the allocation of discretionary spending to eliminate a discrepancy between the House and Senate Appropriations Subcommittees on Foreign Operations.

Despite the procedural maneuvering, the final version of the legislation reduced funding for virtually all foreign assistance programs other than aid to Israel, Egypt and the former Soviet republics.

The House voted overwhelmingly to adopt the conference report Sept. 29; the vote was 321-108. With little debate, the Senate approved the conference report 88-11 the next day, clearing the bill for the president's signature. (House vote 467, p. 114-H; Senate vote 297, p. 39-S)

Few Substantive Disputes

The conference on the measure went smoothly, unlike previous years when the annual funding bill often became embroiled in foreign policy disputes. The conferees had to resolve more than 100 differences between the two bills, but only a few involved policy concerns.

Most of the four-hour conference was spent in debate over earmarks. The House measure was free of such spending mandates, reflecting Obey's determination to provide broad latitude to Clinton's team in allocating foreign aid. But the Senate had set spending levels for several development accounts as well as for aid to the Middle East and much of the assistance for the former Soviet Union.

Senators offered only mild opposition to Obey's proposal to eliminate most of the spending mandates that did not concern the former Soviet republics, such as $3 million for the World Food Program and $11 million to support the role of women in economic development.

The conference backed Obey's compromise, which spared the politically popular earmarks for aid to Egypt and Israel — as well as $80 million in funding for Jewish immigrants to Israel provided through an international refugee assistance program — and $15 million for Cyprus.

Senate conferees were more aggressive in defending the earmarks on assistance to the former Soviet Union. Mc-

Connell, the ranking Republican on the Foreign Operations Subcommittee, argued strenuously for his amendment requiring the administration to provide at least $300 million to Ukraine.

The conferees eventually agreed on a compromise that called on the administration to provide at least $300 million to Ukraine but allowed some of the money to be drawn from the so-called Nunn-Lugar funds for dismantling weapons in the former Soviet Union. The program was named for its sponsors, Sens. Sam Nunn, D-Ga., and Richard G. Lugar, R-Ind.

The conference committee also eliminated an $18 million earmark for humanitarian aid to Armenia, which had been championed by Dole. Instead, conferees urged the administration to provide at least that level of aid to Armenia.

The lawmakers took a similar tack in modifying a provision in the Senate bill that would have established separate categories of aid — such as support for the energy industry — and would have set funding levels for each.

Cuba Debate

The most hotly contended issue during the late-night conference was Mack's amendment requiring the president to certify that Russia had cut off support to Cuba as a condition of aid to Moscow.

House conferees said the amendment was a sop to conservative Cuban-American organizations that had long sought to bring down Cuban dictator Fidel Castro.

Although many House members wanted to strike the provision, they were hamstrung by the need to move the bill quickly. Under Senate rules, Mack could have held up the legislation past the Sept. 30 deadline, jeopardizing much of the aid for Russia and its neighbors.

McConnell proposed a compromise allowing the president to waive the restriction if he determined it to be in the "national security interest." House conferees demanded that the waiver be allowed if the president determined that it was in the "national interest," an easier standard to meet. After some debate, that language was adopted.

The conference endorsed several other conditions on assistance to the former Soviet Union and other nations, though most provided some sort of waiver authority for the president.

The conferees approved an amendment by McConnell conditioning aid to the former republics on "their respecting each others' national sovereignty and territorial integrity." That provision had the potential to affect aid to Russia, although it too included a presidential waiver. Moscow had indicated that it would take on an assertive peacemaking role in wars involving its neighbors.

The conference committee eliminated an amendment by Helms that would have barred aid to nations that had failed to resolve cases involving properties expropriated from U.S. citizens. But the legislation explicitly barred the former Soviet republics from using U.S. assistance to expropriate private property.

The conferees also backed Byrd's amendment requiring the president to certify that Russia had made "substantial progress" in removing its remaining forces from Estonia and Latvia before providing aid to Moscow.

Peru to Parking

The conferees took up numerous other restrictions on foreign assistance, many of which initially were proposed by Helms. His concerns ranged from weighty policy issues to more mundane tiffs over deadbeat foreign embassies.

The conference committee approved a Helms amendment barring economic aid to Nicaragua unless Secretary of State Christopher could show that the government of President Violeta Chamorro had adequately investigated a May 23 explosion of an arms cache in Managua. The blast uncovered weapons and false passports linking Nicaragua's leftists Sandinistas to international terrorism.

The bill also required Nicaragua to make "significant and tangible progress" in resolving expropriation claims brought by U.S. citizens. At stake was about $29 million in ESF aid that the administration had proposed to provide to Nicaragua in fiscal 1994.

Lawmakers eliminated another Helms proposal that would have prohibited aid to Peru unless it compensated the family of a U.S. Air Force sergeant whose plane was shot down by Peruvian military forces in 1992. Instead, the conferees urged the administration to withhold "an appropriate amount of assistance" until Peru disposed of the matter.

Helms clearly struck a chord with his proposal to force governments receiving U.S. assistance to pay parking fines run up by their embassies in the District of Columbia. The Senate adopted Helms' original amendment to withhold aid to such governments by an amount equivalent to that owed the District until they paid the fines. But the conferees went further by withholding 110 percent of the amount owed the District government.

The conference committee backed $40 million in assistance for the U.N. Population Fund but included a provision reducing funds for the U.N. agency by any amount in excess of $10 million that the agency budgeted for activities in China.

Aid Reductions

The bill provided $1.9 billion in funding for multilateral financial institutions, a cut of nearly $500 million from the administration request. It did not include any funding for the European Bank for Reconstruction and Development.

The legislation included $56 million in "paid in" capital for the World Bank, restoring about $28 million that had been cut by the Senate. The final bill reduced about $14 million from the administration's request to protest approximately $477 million in World Bank loans to Iran.

In an expression of concern over persistent reports of waste and fraud in many of the multilateral banks, including the World Bank, the conferees urged the administration to press for the appointment of independent auditors for those institutions.

The final bill trimmed funding for many popular programs, including about $19 million from the administration's $409 million request for Eastern Europe and the Baltic states, and $16 million from its $800 million budget for African development assistance.

The legislation slashed the administration's $148 million request for anti-narcotics activities by $48 million. The House and Senate had called on the administration to devise an international drug-trafficking strategy to replace the Bush administration's Andean initiative, which relied heavily on military assistance to support interdiction efforts.

Both chambers supported a modest $30 million increase in the administration's $690 million request for migration and refugee assistance. The final version included the Senate's $80 million earmark in aid for Jewish emigrants to Israel.

The conference committee restored nearly $100 million in

tended for exporters who provide their own favorable, short-term credit to foreign buyers. It was administered by the Foreign Credit Insurance Association, which was made up of several insurance companies, but the Ex-Im Bank assumed all the risk.

The bank had suffered annual losses throughout the past decade and began fiscal 1994 with a loss reserve of $4.5 billion — an amount equal to about 47 percent of the bank's outstanding loans, guarantees and insurance.

▶ **Loans, guarantees and insurance financing.** The bill provided $1 billion for the Ex-Im Bank to cover the subsidy cost of its activities for fiscal 1994 (although the money was to remain available to be obligated through the end of fiscal 1995 and may be disbursed through calendar 2008). This represented the estimate of what it would cost the bank to offer in excess of $17 billion in assistance, a calculation required by the Credit Reform Act of 1990 (PL 101-508). Specifically, the subsidy appropriation covered the expected cost to the bank of offering below-market interest rates plus an amount set aside to cover future defaults.

The bill also included a "negative appropriation" of $51.8 million, which resulted from the expectation that in a few cases direct loans, loan guarantees or credit insurance would yield income to the federal government, principally because they were made to very low-risk borrowers. The effect was that the net total Ex-Im Bank appropriation for loan subsidies was less than $1 billion, but the entire $1 billion remains available to leverage loans, guarantees and insurance.

In the past, the foreign aid appropriations bill set caps on the various forms of financing the Ex-Im Bank could offer each year. But the caps constrained the bank's ability to provide financing and were eliminated several years ago.

The $1 billion for fiscal 1994 included $300 million intended for assistance to countries that were formerly republics of the Soviet Union, a sum shifted from Clinton's request for direct aid to those countries. There was no explicit requirement that it be used for that purpose, however.

▶ **Overhead.** The bill also appropriates $45.4 million for administrative expenses, including salaries for the bank's employees, travel and other costs of running the bank.

▶ **Tied aid.** The bill permits the bank to use $50 million for tied-aid grants, which are paired with traditional export financing to encourage foreign purchasers to contract with U.S. companies for construction projects or to buy U.S.-made goods. The purpose of the Ex-Im Bank's so-called tied-aid war chest was to combat the use of tied aid by U.S. competitors. Since fiscal 1992, the tied-aid earmark had been reduced from $150 million, as other industrialized countries had agreed to reduce their use of similar export inducements.

Trade and Development Program

This program, run by the International Development Cooperation Agency, a U.S. government program, helped plan development projects in the Third World, employing staff experts as well as private consultants. The bill provided $40 million, the same amount as in fiscal 1993.

INTERNATIONAL ORGANIZATIONS

The bill provided $361 million for voluntary contributions to a number of international organizations and programs, about $51 million more than in fiscal 1993. The Commerce, Justice, State appropriations bill financed assessed contributions — in effect, dues — for organizations such as the United Nations.

▶ **Population Fund.** Congress backed the first U.S. support for the United Nations Population Fund since 1985. The Reagan administration cut off funding for the agency because of its operations in China, whose coercive family planning program, with reports of forced abortions, had drawn condemnation.

Still concerned over the agency's China program, Congress placed a ceiling of $40 million on the United Nations Population Fund in fiscal 1994 — $10 million less than the administration had requested. The bill also required the administration to report to Congress on the agency's budget for its activities in China. Any amount above $10 million that the agency intended to spend in China was to be deducted from the U.S. contribution.

▶ **UNICEF.** Congress did not earmark funds for the United Nations Children's Fund (UNICEF) but left no doubt about its support for the program. Lawmakers endorsed the administration's plans to provide $100 million for UNICEF in fiscal 1994. It required that 75 percent of the U.S. contribution be provided no less than 30 days after the enactment of the bill. The conference report said, "Few other programs have such widespread support both in Congress and with the American people." ■

Western Issues Hold Sway in Interior Bill

A bloc of Senate Republicans and five Democrats from Western and Plains states ended a filibuster on the fiscal 1994 Interior appropriations bill Nov. 9 after all language on grazing fees was removed from the conference report. That freed the Senate to adopt the Interior conference report, 91-9; the House later cleared the measure by voice vote. President Clinton signed the bill into law Nov. 11 (HR 2520 — PL 103-138).

The $13.4 billion bill generally followed Clinton's requests to devote more funding to energy conservation and to improve operations in the national parks, which had faced a deluge of visitors and a cutback in maintenance and programs. It provided $1.2 billion more in budget authority than was appropriated in fiscal 1993, but $230 million less than Clinton had requested.

The Senate action came only after a somber Harry Reid, D-Nev., agreed to drop a compromise he had brokered and that House and Senate negotiators had included in the Interior bill conference report. The compromise would have imposed a more moderate grazing fee increase than Interior Secretary Bruce Babbitt wanted and codified many of Babbitt's land management proposals.

In the aftermath of the Senate battle, Babbitt said he planned to consult with Western senators and ranchers before publishing draft grazing regulations in April 1994.

A majority of the funds in the bill went to the Interior Department and the Forest Service, which together managed natural resources on public lands spread over 660 million acres. The bill also provided funds for an array of cultural programs, including the Smithsonian Institution, the National Endowment for the Arts (NEA) and the National Endowment for the Humanities.

The bill included $1.1 billion for National Park Service operations, $2 billion for Indian health and education programs and $690 million for energy conservation programs that provided funding for low-income people who faced severe weather conditions, especially in the cold Northeast.

BACKGROUND

The annual spending bill for agencies that managed federal lands, parks and forests was a perennial battleground for two radically different political views.

On one side were the cowboys, lumberjacks, miners and farmers of the Old West who wanted to preserve their way of life, a key tenet of which was being able to take commercial advantage of the natural resources on public lands — be it rangeland, timber or water. On the other side were

---

BOXSCORE

▶ **Fiscal 1994 appropriations for the Interior Department and related agencies (HR 2520).** The $13.4 billion spending measure funded the Interior Department, the Forest Service, Indian health and education, and national cultural programs.

Reports: H Rept 103-158, S Rept 103-114; conference report, H Rept 103-299.

KEY ACTION

July 15 — **House** passed HR 2520, 278-138.

Sept. 15 — **Senate** passed HR 2520 by voice vote.

Oct. 15 — **House-Senate** conferees approved conference report.

Oct. 20 — **House** agreed to amended conference report by voice vote.

Nov. 9 — **Senate** agreed to amended conference report, 91-9; **House** accepted Senate changes by voice vote, clearing the bill.

Nov. 11 — **President** signed HR 2520 — PL 103-138.

---

recreation enthusiasts and conservationists of the increasingly urban New West, who wanted to protect the nation's vast land holdings and precious natural resources for more passive uses.

Perhaps the hottest issue in that fight was grazing fees.

About 27,000 ranchers were renting federal rangeland at one-fifth the cost of leasing private land. In 1993, ranchers paid $1.86 per "animal unit month" to forage on public lands. An animal unit month was the amount of forage required to feed one cow and calf, five sheep or one horse for a month.

Critics said the low fees were a subsidy to ranchers that should be phased out. Western lawmakers countered that higher grazing fees would cripple the cattle and sheep industries and damage the regional economy.

In each of the previous three years, the House had passed a grazing fee increase as part of the Interior appropriations bill, only to trade the fee increase away in conference with the Senate. *(Grazing fees, p. 273; background, 1992 Almanac, p. 686)*

The Clinton administration set out early in the year to increase the grazing fees as part of the deficit-reduction process. But under lobbying from Western senators, Clinton did an abrupt turnaround in March, saying the changes would be made administratively.

Another perennial issue of concern to Western lawmakers was the treatment of mining claims on federal lands. Under the 1872 Mining Law, miners were allowed to gain title, or "patent," to federal land for as little as $2.50 an acre. Critics of the law wanted miners to rent the land and pay royalties on the minerals extracted. The House included a provision to halt the processing of new mining claims for a year while Congress updated the 1872 law, but Senate conferees succeeded in dropping the provision.

Amid talk of an overhaul, miners steadily had been submitting more mining patent applications. Sen. Dale Bumpers, D-Ark., a proponent of the House moratorium, said the Interior Department received an average of 76 patent applications annually from 1985-1988, compared with an average of 104 applications from 1989-1992.

Following the Administration's Guidelines

When Clinton was elected in 1992, he vowed to find a middle ground in the divisive jobs vs. environment debate. For the most part, the fiscal 1994 Interior appropriations bill reflected Clinton's and Babbitt's desire to embark on a new era in resource and land management.

For example, the Interior Department's Fish and Wildlife Service was to continue with its efforts to conserve whole ecosystems instead of individual species. But at Babbitt's insistence, the service also was embarking on a radi-

The increase for national park operations did not include more money for building new visitor centers or other facilities. Construction programs throughout the Interior Department were cut, including cuts of $38.6 million for national parks and $32 million for new forest roads.

One of the largest increases in the bill — nearly $124 million — reflected Clinton's request to steer the nation toward more energy conservation, bringing the total energy conservation budget to $702.8 million.

The Bureau of Indian Affairs and the Indian Health Service also got big increases under the bill.

The bill continued a moratorium on new drilling off the East and West coasts, in Alaska's Bristol Bay and off Florida. *(1992 Almanac, p. 239)*

The committee also approved a one-year moratorium on processing applications for mining "patents," or titles, on federal lands.

Sidestepping another controversy that had stymied lawmakers, appropriators set no target level for timber sales in the Pacific Northwest. But the committee earmarked $187.8 million for sales during fiscal 1994, compared with about $197 million for fiscal 1993, in anticipation of a decline in volume of available timber.

Recognizing the administration's desire to reorganize far-flung federal scientific research activities, the committee reduced the total Fish and Wildlife Service budget by about $38.3 million, to $492.2 million for fiscal 1994.

Part of the decrease was reflected in a separate account to establish the National Biological Survey. But appropriators agreed to increased funding for other endangered species programs throughout the Fish and Wildlife Service. Activities such as species listing and habitat conservation increased by $21 million under the bill. The subcommittee's report made special note of $2 million earmarked for a new habitat conservation program in Southern California for the threatened gnatcatcher songbird. Under a plan announced by Babbitt in March, limited development was to be allowed, and the $2 million would help defray the expenses of local governments that had to implement the plan. *(Biological survey, p. 269)*

HOUSE FLOOR ACTION

The House on July 15 passed a slightly trimmed, $12.7 billion version of the Interior bill by a vote of 278-138 after two days of debate. The lower price tag was due largely to the elimination of more than half the funding requested by Clinton for the Bureau of Land Management (BLM), which was expected to be restored in conference. *(Vote 339, p. 82-H)*

With little fanfare, the House put off the battle over grazing fees. Western lawmakers argued successfully that the increase in fees that had been added to the spending measure by the Appropriations subcommittee violated the House rule against legislating on an appropriations bill. "The correct place for this type of legislation is in the authorizing committee," said Larry LaRocco, D-Idaho.

Lawmakers removed several other provisions on the same grounds, reflecting their intent to depart from the pattern of previous years and play by the congressional rule book on HR 2520. Dan Burton, R-Ind., struck $602 million in funding for BLM land management programs. The authorization for BLM, one of Interior's largest agencies, had expired in 1982, but the agency had continued to receive annual appropriations, which in effect provided a temporary authorization. *(BLM, p. 272)*

Because of its broad spending authority, the Interior

appropriations bill always had the potential for melodrama on the floor — especially as it related to funding for arts and cultural institutions. The NEA attracted attention, but not at the emotional level of previous years when some members criticized the grant program for funding what they claimed was obscene art. Philip M. Crane, R-Ill., tried for a second year to eliminate all funding, about $175 million, for the NEA. But his amendment was defeated July 14 by a vote of 105-322. The next day the House approved, by a vote of 240-184, an amendment by Cliff Stearns, R-Fla., to cut NEA funding by 5 percent to about $166 million in fiscal 1994. *(Votes 326, 330, p. 80-H)*

In a small humanitarian gesture, lawmakers approved by voice vote a one-time $38,400 payment to the widow of James A. Hudson, a caretaker for the Lincoln Memorial. Hudson, a "temporary" National Park Service employee who worked full time for eight years but had no benefits, had died July 5 from a heart attack and apparent heat exhaustion.

The House cut about $55 million from the bill's $438 million appropriation for fossil energy research and development. An amendment by Philip R. Sharp, D-Ind., to eliminate $5 million earmarked for oil shale research was approved by a 395-37 vote. Sharp, chairman of the Energy and Commerce Subcommittee on Energy and Power, said the program was unnecessary. *(Vote 325, p. 80-H)*

In a trade-off of funding, the House approved an amendment by Robert S. Walker, R-Pa., that cut about $50 million from coal research but put about $25 million back into the energy conservation account. The Walker amendment was approved by a 276-144 vote. *(Vote 331, p. 80-H)*

Although the House remained collegial throughout most of the Interior appropriations debate, tempers flared briefly during a bid to eliminate a project often criticized as a prime example of pork barrel spending. Joseph M. McDade, R-Pa., fought off an amendment from Michael A. Andrews, D-Texas, to cut $3.1 million earmarked for the Steamtown railroad history museum in the veteran appropriator's district in Scranton, Pa. *(Steamtown, 1992 Almanac, p. 289)*

Andrews called Steamtown "one of the worst misappropriations of tax dollars in recent memory," citing $66 million that had been spent to date on a collection of steam-era locomotives and railroad equipment that Andrews said had been described as a "second-rate collection of trains in a third-rate site." McDade fumed, calling Andrews' proposal a "destructive" amendment that could lead to the facility's closure. McDade rattled off a list of spending for national parks and recreational facilities in Texas and other states, challenging members that "maybe we should close all these parks and put a fence around" them.

Andrews' amendment was rejected by a 192-229 vote. *(Vote 332, p. 80-H)*

Northern California lawmakers defeated an amendment by John J. "Jimmy" Duncan Jr., R-Tenn., to cut National Park Service operations by $14 million. Duncan was trying to freeze funding for operations at the Presidio Army Base in San Francisco, which was to be turned over to the park service in fiscal 1994. The amendment was rejected 193-230. *(Vote 333, p. 82-H)*

Duncan cited a General Accounting Office report that converting the base to a park could cost up to $1.2 billion, and he said annual operations of the new park could skyrocket into the hundreds of millions each year. But Nancy Pelosi, D-Calif., whose district included the Presidio, argued that the project "represents a remarkable model for military conversion."

SENATE COMMITTEE

The Senate Appropriations Committee voted 20-0 on July 28 to approve a $13.3 billion version of the bill (S Rept 103-114) that restored significant cuts made by the House but temporarily avoided such contentious issues as mining and grazing fees, timber sales and arts funding. The Interior Appropriations Subcommittee had approved the bill by voice vote July 27.

Appropriations Committee Chairman Robert C. Byrd, D-W.Va., who also chaired the Interior Subcommittee, said he had received more than 1,800 requests for new spending from individual senators. The committee bowed to Byrd's wishes that controversial amendments be delayed until the bill went to the floor.

However, the report accompanying the Senate bill recommended that the House-approved moratorium on accepting new mining patents be deleted.

The Senate committee also restored $9.4 million that the House cut from U.S. Forest Service programs, such as road construction and timber sale preparations. But the committee followed the House's lead by making no recommendation on the level of timber harvests in public forests, a highly divisive issue in the Pacific Northwest that Clinton, Interior Secretary Babbitt and Agriculture Secretary Mike Espy were trying to resolve administratively.

According to the Senate committee report, the money was put back into the Forest Service budget in a modest attempt to address the administration's economic and environmental proposals for the Pacific Northwest and the threatened northern spotted owl, as outlined July 1 by Clinton. His forest management plan called for $1.2 billion in economic assistance to the Pacific Northwest over the following five years. Most of the assistance was expected to come through existing programs.

"Unfortunately, expectations have been raised that significant influxes of new funding will be provided, which is not the case given the current budgetary situation," the report said.

The committee earmarked $157 million for the National Biological Survey, compared with $164 million in the House bill.

Dispute Over Oil and Gas Drilling

The major battle between subcommittee and full committee markups involved an amendment by J. Bennett Johnston, D-La., to lift a ban on oil and gas drilling off the coasts of North Carolina and the Florida Keys, as well as a ban on new leasing or pre-leasing off the Florida Panhandle. North Carolina and Florida were part of a larger moratorium placed on drilling and leasing off the West and East coasts, the eastern Gulf of Mexico and Alaska's Bristol Bay.

The Interior Subcommittee approved Johnston's provision, but when the bill moved to full committee, appropriators voted 10-9 in support of an amendment by Connie Mack, R-Fla., to kill it. The moratorium was supported by the Clinton administration, which was trying to form a national energy policy before allowing exceptions to the drilling ban.

Johnston, chairman of the Energy and Natural Resources Committee, said the coasts of North Carolina and the Florida Panhandle were potentially lucrative sources of natural gas. But Mack said the committee should keep the entire moratorium in place until the administration clearly outlined its energy policy.

The committee also restored about $4.4 million in funding cut by the House for the NEA and recommended $170 million for fiscal 1994.

SENATE FLOOR ACTION

The Senate passed the $13.3 billion Interior spending bill by voice vote Sept. 15.

But first, in a serious setback for the Clinton administration, the Senate approved, 59-40, an amendment by Pete V. Domenici, R-N.M., to block the administration from implementing a new plan for higher grazing fees and stricter environmental controls on federal rangelands announced by Babbitt on Aug. 9. The amendment barred the use of fiscal 1994 spending to carry out the plan — including publishing the proposed policy changes or conducting the town meetings that were required by federal rule-making procedures. *(Vote 266, p. 35-S)*

Environmentalists and the White House immediately began to regroup and marshal support from House members who backed the grazing fee increase.

Under Babbitt's grazing proposal, the fee charged to Western ranchers who grazed their livestock on federal land was to increase over three years to $4.28 per animal unit month. After the new fee was fully implemented, increases or decreases were to be limited to 25 percent.

Western senators — and even some from elsewhere — argued on the floor that Babbitt's grazing proposals were more than a simple rent increase and too sweeping to be imposed by executive order without congressional input. "We are saying the government should not do this by fiat," Domenici said.

Senators also criticized many of the particulars of Babbitt's proposal, including a plan to require the government to retain rights to water even when ranchers had paid for water development projects on public land. They also criticized the proposal to expand grazing advisory boards to include environmentalists and others generally opposed to grazing, and they complained about linking the duration of a grazing permit to a rancher's environmental stewardship.

Many Western senators supported a separate bill (S 1326) by Ben Nighthorse Campbell, D-Colo., to limit the grazing fee increase to 25 percent, or $2.33 per animal unit month. The bill, written with the help of the cattle industry, had been criticized by environmentalists and lawmakers concerned that it would not generate a fair return for public land use.

Supporters of the grazing fee increase countered that the existing formula to calculate fees also was established by executive branch edict, having been ordered by President Ronald Reagan in 1985. They called arguments that the administration's plan was too sweeping merely a smoke screen intended to completely block higher fees.

Unlike other issues that often were decided along partisan lines, grazing policy fell along regional lines. In all, 38 Republicans and 21 Democrats supported the amendment, and 23 of them were from the West.

Only three of 11 Democratic senators from Western states — Daniel K. Akaka of Hawaii, Barbara Boxer of California and Patty Murray of Washington — opposed the one-year funding moratorium, overcoming geographic concerns to side with Clinton on a major policy issue.

Some senators known as environmentalists defied conventional wisdom and voted for the Domenici amendment. John H. Chafee of Rhode Island, the ranking Republican on the Environment and Public Works Committee, said he sided with the Westerners because he believed the Babbitt

proposals were too far-reaching. Democrat Dianne Feinstein of California said she voted with Domenici because the plan would hurt ranchers in her home state.

The strong showing by the Westerners was expected to give them additional leverage during conference committee. Domenici, who rounded up Republican votes while Reid worked the Democrats, said even he was surprised by the margin. A 1992 Senate vote to raise the grazing fee by 25 percent was defeated 50-44.

Other Provisions

The Senate bill dropped the House-passed moratorium on spending money to process hard-rock mining patents.

The Senate sidestepped at least one battle with the House over forest programs in the Pacific Northwest with the voice vote approval Sept. 14 of an amendment by Murray and Mark O. Hatfield, R-Ore., to earmark $29 million for communities hit hard by the legal dispute over the northern spotted owl. The amendment was designed to accomplish the same thing as House-approved language to provide $30 million in ecosystem management programs to create new jobs for the timber-dependent region.

As in years past, Republican Jesse Helms of North Carolina continued his assault on federal funding of the arts. The Senate bill restored about $4.4 million cut by the House for the arts, but Helms offered an amendment to eliminate all $170 million earmarked for the NEA. It failed on a 15-83 vote late Sept. 14. *(Vote 268, p. 35-S)*

Another Helms amendment to eliminate funding to individual artists was tabled, or killed, 65-30, while a proposal to shift grant-making authority from the federal government to the states was tabled, or killed, 57-39. *(Votes 270, 269, p. 35-S)*

In the only other amendment to get a roll call vote, the Senate voted 81-17 to table, or kill, a proposal by Bill Bradley, D-N.J., to limit funding for the coal liquefaction program and reduce funds that could be used to prepare timber for sale in the Tongass National Forest in Alaska. Bradley said his amendment was designed to adhere to the president's request on both issues and aimed at reducing the deficit. *(Vote 267, p. 35-S)*

CONFERENCE DELAYED

After weeks of threats and negotiations, and against a backdrop of a pending Senate filibuster, House and Senate conferees agreed on a final version of the Interior spending bill (H Rept 103-299) by voice vote Oct. 15.

The Battle Over Grazing Fees

The dispute over grazing fees had threatened to derail the entire bill. Western senators warned that they were willing to hold up the spending measure to delay Babbitt's plan. Sen Malcolm Wallop, R-Wyo., charged that House members, Babbitt and Clinton were trying to kill small businesses in the West. "We have had this arrogant posture that if ranchers can't make it in ranching then maybe they should make cappuccino for the tourists," Wallop said.

Babbitt met with at least nine Western senators Sept. 21 to listen to their concerns. The scion of an Arizona ranching family and an ardent environmentalist, Babbitt was known for his ability to achieve consensus. But senators said no deals were made to drop the one-year moratorium to block the grazing fee increase. "Nothing got resolved," said Domenici. "There may be a big stalemate brewing."

Meanwhile, at Regula's behest, the House voted 314-

109 on Sept. 29 to instruct House negotiators to reject the Senate's one-year moratorium on the grazing fee increases. *(Vote 465, p. 114-H)*

Rep. Mike Synar, D-Okla., warned that if the conference report came back to the House containing the Senate-approved moratorium, representatives were prepared to argue before the Rules Committee that the Senate language constituted legislating on an appropriations bill — a violation of House rules.

On Oct. 7, Babbitt agreed on a compromise with key Democrats — Reid, Miller, Synar, Vento. Under the compromise, the grazing fee was to increase from $1.86 per animal unit month to $3.45 over three years — less than the $4.28 that Babbitt had proposed in August. After fiscal 1996, any increase or decrease in the fee was to be limited to 15 percent annually.

The agreement preserved key elements of Babbitt's proposal to overhaul the management of federal rangeland. It included:

● Prohibiting those who received new permits to graze cattle on federal land from claiming rights to water and water facilities. Existing permit holders would be allowed to retain rights to water and facilities.

● Allowing permits to be suspended if ranchers violated environmental safeguards.

● Imposing a 20 percent surcharge on ranchers who subleased the land for grazing.

● Abolishing grazing advisory boards dominated by ranchers and herders and replacing them with panels that included environmentalists, wildlife managers and fisheries experts as well as ranchers.

Babbitt agreed to hold off on other rangeland proposals for one year, including a plan to issue comprehensive environmental and management guidelines for federal rangeland.

"A good settlement is when everybody is unhappy," Reid said. But he emphasized that "the offer is fair to everyone involved." Reid, a moderate Democrat, said several lawmakers had asked him to negotiate a grazing deal on behalf of the Senate even though he helped Domenici round up the votes for the pivotal Senate vote Sept. 14 blocking Babbitt's initiatives.

The conferees delayed a vote on the grazing compromise until Oct. 13.

Domenici tried but failed to alter Reid's amendment after arranging for ranching proponents such as Wallop, who was not a member of the conference committee, to make an unusual presentation to the conference. Domenici's alternate would have stretched the fee increase over six years instead of three years and would have delayed the overhaul of rangeland management practices for a year. House negotiators shot down Domenici's amendment 2-5, and Senate negotiators followed suit with a 6-9 vote.

Senate negotiators approved the Reid amendment Oct. 14 on an 8-7 party line vote; the House negotiators adopted the provision, 5-2. Regula was the only House Republican to vote for the amendment.

Other Issues

● **Hard-rock mining moratorium.** In other major action on the Interior bill, House negotiators agreed, with little debate, to drop their moratorium on hard-rock mining patents. Yates simply said the House would bow to the Senate bill, which included no such language.

Environmentalists and lawmakers had expected the mining moratorium to be used as a trading chip for higher grazing fees. But Regula said the issue was dropped be-

cause the Senate passed a bill (S 775) to overhaul the 1872 Mining Law in May and the House Natural Resources Committee was expected to act on another measure (HR 322) soon. Senate Energy and Natural Resources Committee Chairman Johnston, an Interior conferee, argued that the issue should be dealt with as part of the broader mining law overhaul. *(Mining reform, p. 261)*

● **National parks.** In other action, House Subcommittee Chairman Yates sternly rejected pleas to earmark funds for new visitor centers in national parks and a host of other unauthorized projects to rehabilitate housing and deter crime on Indian reservations.

In the end, negotiators agreed to provide funding for any new visitor center if a state, local government or private group could raise 50 percent of the construction costs. The matching requirement sparked complaints from Sen. Conrad Burns, R-Mont., whose attempt to win $1.2 million for the Lewis and Clark Trail Interpretive Center in his home state also was rebuffed. Burns said the requirement was too burdensome for many states without "the population base to get the matching funds."

● **National forests.** Conferees also agreed to spend $56.8 million for construction of new roads in national forests that were used to facilitate logging. The House bill had earmarked $36.9 million for the roads, and the Senate version had called for $71.9 million.

The conferees agreed to accept Senate-approved report language by Bumpers that banned clear-cutting in the Ouachita and Ozark national forests in northern Arkansas except when required to recover from a natural disaster or to help plants and animals thrive.

But Charles Wilson, D-Texas, a House appropriator who did not sit on the conference committee, had difficulty protecting House-approved language that prohibited the sale of unprocessed logs to foreign countries. Negotiators left the issue unresolved.

● **Biological survey.** House conferees lost an attempt to prevent Babbitt from spending any money to carry out the mission of his proposed National Biological Survey until separate legislation was passed that would authorize the new Interior division. The amendment by Ron Packard, R-Calif., was defeated by House negotiators, 2-5.

Instead, Packard and Regula won compromise language requiring federal land managers to gain the written permission of private landowners before surveying plants and animals on their property.

Although Babbitt had the authority to shuffle scientists and programs throughout his department, separate legislation (HR 1845) to make the survey a permanent Interior division was in doubt since it had been pulled from the floor Oct. 7.

● **Retirement incentives.** Conference members also adopted a Senate-approved provision that provided financial incentives to Forest Service employees who wanted to retire early. House Post Office and Civil Service Committee Chairman William L. Clay, D-Mo., wanted to pass separate legislation (HR 3218) to provide buyouts for all federal employees.

FINAL ACTION

House Adopts Conference Report

The House adopted the conference report by voice vote Oct. 20 and approved Reid's grazing amendment, 317-106. *(Vote 525, p. 128-H)*

Voicing concern about the rights of private property owners, conservative House Democrats and Republicans tried to stall action on the bill Oct. 20 by defeating the rule governing floor debate on the conference report. They failed, however, and the rule was adopted, 253-174. *(Vote 522, p. 128-H)*

At the heart of the House dispute was Babbitt's plan to count and monitor all of the nation's plants and animals.

W. J. "Billy" Tauzin, D-La., Charles H. Taylor, R-N.C., and other lawmakers wanted House appropriators to include language in the Interior conference report restricting Babbitt's authority to conduct the survey. Instead, negotiators agreed Oct. 15 to require the Interior Department to obtain written permission from landowners before federal workers could survey any private property.

Survey opponents also wanted appropriators to include language that would ban the Interior Department's use of volunteers for the survey and force the government to disclose survey findings to private property owners. "Getting a bunch of volunteers to run all over private property in America to do this survey creates some real problems for us," Tauzin said.

Yates said the dispute over the biological survey was a sham designed to stall the spending bill and divert attention from the grazing fee dispute.

In other action, Post Office and Civil Service Committee Chairman Clay won his bid to strike an amendment that would have authorized financial incentives to Forest Service employees seeking early retirement. Clay argued that the amendment amounted to legislation on an appropriations bill.

Senate Filibuster

In the Senate, meanwhile, the grazing fee dispute had evolved into a high-risk game of brinkmanship, with neither side willing to blink first. Reid, Byrd and the Clinton administration failed three times in three weeks to get the 60 votes needed to cut off debate on the conference report.

The first try came Oct. 21, when the motion to invoke cloture failed 53-41. Ignoring admonitions that they were holding up public lands projects, Western senators vowed to continue to filibuster HR 2520 until, in Burns's words, "there is no more blood left." *(Vote 326, p. 42-S)*

Domenici said the senators would stop their filibuster if the proposed fee increase was phased in over a longer period of time and Babbitt agreed to hold off on a sweeping series of changes that would determine how ranchers could use federal rangeland. But Reid said the grazing fees and policy changes in the appropriations bill were Babbitt's final offer.

In an effort to convince undecided lawmakers or cajole some of the more defiant senators, Appropriations Committee Chairman Byrd appealed to those who had asked him to include funds in the Interior bill for pet projects in their home states to help him end the filibuster.

"I wonder if every senator who wrote to me believes that the grazing issue is more important than the projects contained therein," said Byrd, who also chaired the Appropriations Subcommittee on Interior.

Lawmakers eager to pass the Interior spending bill also warned that some Western senators could face the wrath of voter outrage over gridlock.

On Oct. 28, Babbitt raised the stakes, announcing that he would bypass Congress and move ahead under federal rule-making procedures with his plan to charge even higher grazing fees and implement more rangeland management

requirements than contained in the Interior bill. "As long as the gridlock persists, the department cannot stand idly by, waiting interminably for reform that never seems to happen," Babbitt said.

During the week of Oct. 25, Byrd made two more attempts to get the 60 votes needed to break the filibuster. The first attempt failed 51-45 on Oct. 26. The second failed 54-44 on Oct. 28. *(Votes 329, p. 43-S; 340, p. 44-S)*

Chagrined that the battle was spilling into November, Byrd vowed not to seek another cloture vote until Nov. 10. That was the expiration date for a third stop-gap funding measure, passed by Congress late Oct. 28, which was needed to continue funding for the Interior and Defense departments.

Byrd also threatened to try to ship the Interior bill back to a conference committee, exposing every item to the whims of the 15 senators and 10 House members on the joint panel. He suggested that all grazing language be struck from the bill, leaving Western interests to duel with Babbitt in the administrative arena.

In a scathing speech, Byrd said he was "sick and tired" of the grazing issue, which had stymied the Senate for the past three weeks and bedeviled his Appropriations Subcommittee on Interior since 1976.

But the coalition of Western senators, led by Domenici, refused to budge. "We are willing to sit down ... but not with a gun to our heads that says, 'Our way or no way,'" Domenici said. "If we lose, we'll go down with every rule of this Senate to protect our people."

The coalition consisted of 41 Republicans — all except John H. Chafee of Rhode Island, William S. Cohen of Maine and William V. Roth Jr. of Delaware — and five Democrats. The Democrats were Max Baucus of Montana, Jeff Bingaman of New Mexico, Campbell of Colorado, and Kent Conrad and Byron L. Dorgan, both of North Dakota.

Compromise Reached

Finally, Reid concluded Nov. 9 that he could not amass the 60 votes needed to pry the bill lose, and he agreed to have his compromise removed from the bill. The Western and Plains states senators then ended their filibuster, and the Senate adopted the conference report, 91-9, on Nov. 9. The House accepted the change and cleared the bill by voice vote. *(Vote 359, p. 46-S)*

Postscript

The maneuverings in Congress had altered the political climate considerably since Babbitt first announced his controversial plan in August to increase grazing fees by 230 percent and impose tough environmental standards on ranchers who grazed their cattle on federal land.

Babbitt appeared far more conciliatory toward the concerns of ranchers and their allies in the Senate than he had been when the legislative tug of war began in June. "We have listened, and we have learned a great deal," Babbitt said. "I am committed to an even more inclusive process — one involving elected officials, ranchers, environmentalists and others." ∎

Interior Provisions

The $13.4 billion spending bill (HR 2520) for the Interior Department and related agencies paid for the upkeep of the nation's vast public lands and cultural resources. Most of the federal land holdings were in the West, but the bill's impact was felt in virtually every state and territory. Following are provisions of the bill, as enacted:

INTERIOR DEPARTMENT

Bureau of Land Management

As the nation's chief landlord, the Bureau of Land Management received about $1.1 billion to oversee about 270 million acres of federal land, mostly in the West. The bureau's vast terrain covered about 13 percent of the United States. The bureau also leased more than 300 million acres that contained a wealth of hard-rock minerals such as gold and silver beneath their surface. About 4.3 million head of cattle graze on bureau lands, and timber was harvested from 4 million acres of its forests. The lands also were home to more than 50,000 wild horses and burros. The bill provided funding for 270,000 acres of wildlife habitat and more than 150,000 miles of streams for fisheries. Bureau-managed lands offered popular spots for recreation, with an estimated 71 million visitors annually.

Under the 1976 Federal Land Policy Management Act, the bureau was directed to manage its property for "multiple uses." But in recent years, that mandate had caused friction among the settlers of the old West. On one side were the cowboys, miners and lumberjacks who built up the Western frontier. On the other side were the recreation enthusiasts and conservationists who had moved into the area and wanted to preserve the land. In addition, laws protecting wilderness and endangered species also compli-

cated the bureau's mission. President Clinton vowed to end federal subsidies that favored timber, mining and grazing on federal land over other uses. Battles in Congress erupted each year over the use of the nation's natural resources.

▸ **Land management.** Appropriators provided $599.9 million for more than 12,000 workers to monitor, inventory and keep up the bureau's lands.

▸ **Firefighting.** House and Senate appropriators set aside $117.1 million for firefighting in fiscal 1994. That included non-emergency firefighting, fire prevention and activities such as planned burns, the stockpiling of firefighting equipment and the rehabilitation of scorched land. A separate "emergency firefighting fund" could be used only if the president declared a budgetary emergency. In 1992, Congress ordered that the emergency fund be used for firefighting only if costs exceeded a 10-year average. The bill allotted $116.7 million for the emergency fund.

▸ **Payments to local governments.** To partially offset revenue losses to local governments, the bureau provided money known as "payments in lieu of taxes" to communities that had non-taxpaying federal lands within their boundaries. The bill provided these communities with $104.1 million, which could be used at the discretion of local governments.

▸ **Land acquisition.** Reflecting Clinton's request to decrease the amount of money spent to buy property rather than maintain the land already owned, the bureau's land acquisition account was cut by more than 56 percent to $12.1 million to purchase 14 parcels nationwide. In general, the government was trying to acquire more property through land swaps. The largest allocation, $1.5 million, was to buy land in northern Idaho to improve access to Lake Coeur d'Alene and the Spokane River. Also on the list: $700,000 to buy land to protect the habitat of the endangered desert tortoise in California; $1 million for the San Pedro National Conservation Area near Sierra Vista, Ariz.; and $2.15 million to buy two Oregon parcels.

▶ **Oregon and California grant lands.** The Oregon and California Railroad Co. was granted about 2.6 million acres in 1866 by the federal government, which reacquired the southern Oregon tracts in 1916. The area, known as O&C lands, was the source of some of the country's best timber. But these lands included large swaths of old-growth forest, the primary home of the threatened northern spotted owl. Timber harvests in the area were at a standstill because of a court injunction issued in a protracted legal dispute over the protection of the owl and the forests. Appropriators provided $83 million to tend, build on and buy land for the O&C forests. The money also would help repair roads and bridges in the area. Because of reduced timber harvests in the area, appropriators instructed the bureau to redirect up to $17.3 million from this account to fund programs designed to restore watersheds that had been damaged by logging.

Through this account, timber communities in the Pacific Northwest were provided a percentage of the receipts from federal timber harvests on O&C tracts. The House tried unsuccessfully to cap those payments, and both chambers wanted to provide in the bill a minimum guaranteed level of timber receipts for those communities. Appropriators scrapped plans to mandate any minimum payments because such minimums were established under the budget-reconciliation law (PL 103-66).

Under the budget law, timber communities were to receive a sum equal to 80 percent of the average amount of timber receipts collected from 1986 to 1990.

▶ **Range improvements.** The bureau's land had to be seeded, fenced and weeded. Breeding grounds for fish and wildlife also had to be restored. Using money from the fees charged ranchers to graze their livestock on lands managed by BLM, appropriators set aside $10 million for this effort.

▶ **Grazing.** Despite the efforts of key House Democrats and Sen. Harry Reid, D-Nev., the bill included no provisions to increase grazing fees on federal lands or impose tough environmental rangeland standards on Western ranchers.

The absence of language left it up to Interior Secretary Bruce Babbitt to pursue higher fees and new rangeland management requirements administratively.

The existing fee was $1.86 per "animal unit month," the amount of forage needed to feed a cow and calf, five sheep or one horse in a month. The federal grazing fee was one-fifth the amount charged on most private lands. The formula used to establish grazing fees had not changed since it was devised under the Public Range Lands Improvement Act of 1978. Grazing fees actually had decreased in recent years because the formula discounted a rancher's production costs, which had gone up.

The House Interior Appropriations Subcommittee on June 15 called for grazing fees to be increased to $2.48, a 33 percent boost. The move came at the request of ranking Republican Ralph Regula of Ohio. But on July 14 the full House stripped the provision from the bill on a procedural motion because it violated rules that barred legislating on a spending bill.

Soon after, Babbitt announced Aug. 9 that he would use his administrative authority to more than double grazing fees and overhaul land management practices on federal lands. Under Babbitt's proposal, federal grazing fees would increase over three years to $4.28 per animal unit month.

Babbitt also proposed such land management changes as tying a rancher's environmental stewardship to the duration of a grazing permit and charging a 20 percent supplementary fee to ranchers who subleased their permits. In addition, Babbitt proposed seizing the ownership of water and water facilities from ranchers using bureau-operated lands, bringing the bureau's policy in line with the Forest Service's practices. He also proposed revamping grazing advisory boards, which were dominated by ranchers, to include environmentalists, business representatives and fisheries experts.

But Western senators, led by Republican Pete V. Domenici of New Mexico and Reid, sought to block Babbitt, approving a one-year moratorium Sept. 15 to prevent the Clinton administration from implementing the grazing fee policy. The House on Sept. 29 affirmed its longstanding position for higher grazing fees, voting to instruct its negotiators to reject the Senate moratorium.

Mindful of House support for higher grazing fees, Reid immediately began to broker a compromise with Babbitt, Reps. George Miller, D-Calif., chairman of the Natural Resources Committee, Mike Synar, D-Okla., and Bruce F. Vento, D-Minn. Although the three House Democrats were not appropriators, they were key advocates for higher grazing fees.

In conference, Reid won his compromise amendment to increase grazing fees to $3.45 over three years and to codify most of Babbitt's land management proposals. Babbitt supported Reid's amendment, preferring the strength of law over federal regulation.

But when the conference report came back to the Senate, Domenici waged a filibuster. Reid and the Democrats failed three times to limit debate and invoke cloture. Appropriations Committee Chairman Robert C. Byrd, D-W.Va., repeatedly threatened the Republicans and five Western and Northern Plains Democrats supporting Domenici with loss of funding for pet projects in the Interior spending bill if they continued to stall the bill.

The dispute ended when Reid agreed Nov. 9 to drop his grazing amendment. Domenici called off the filibuster. Babbitt was free to proceed with his higher grazing fee and tougher rangeland management reforms.

U.S. Fish and Wildlife Service

The Fish and Wildlife Service was charged with the study, conservation, management and protection of fisheries and wildlife resources. It also was responsible for the nation's wetlands and for carrying out the controversial 1973 Endangered Species Act. Overall, the service managed 93.7 million acres that included about 490 national wildlife refuges and 28 districts containing waterfowl sanctuaries and breeding areas. About 6.4 million pounds of fish were available annually at 78 national fish hatcheries.

The service was allotted $682.4 million in fiscal 1994, down from $750.3 million the year before. Much of the decrease was attributed to the reshuffling of accounts needed to pay for Babbitt's separate initiative to survey the nation's plants and animals, known as the National Biological Survey. The service had recently been promoting "biodiversity" and the protection of entire ecosystems instead of individual species.

▶ **Resource management.** Managing natural resources was the main focus of the Fish and Wildlife Service. Appropriators provided $484.3 million to cover operating costs, management of wildlife and endangered species, and the operation and maintenance of wildlife refuges and fish hatcheries. The service's research functions were transferred to the National Biological Survey.

Spending items included: $100,000 for the Port of Philadelphia and $200,000 for the Port of Baltimore to continue weekly inspections of ships and $665,000 to operate wildlife refuges in Alaska. At the request of House Interior Appropriations Subcommittee Chairman Sidney R. Yates, D-Ill., lawmakers provided $353,000 to keep a wetlands advisory office open in Yates' hometown of Chicago.

▶ **Endangered species.** Appropriators earmarked $58.7 million for endangered species activities, $9 million less than Clinton requested. Still, the appropriation represented an increase of $20 million from fiscal 1993. Specific projects included steps to begin the process of protecting the Atlantic salmon, the peregrine falcon, the California condor and the Mexican wolf. The money also went toward the listing of an additional 400 endangered or threatened species by 1996.

▶ **Habitat conservation.** Under the 1982 amendments to the Endangered Species Act, private property owners had to file a plan with the government showing how they intended to protect the habitat of a threatened or endangered species. The department estimated that 357 listed species did not have habitat conservation plans, which had to be approved by the service. A majority of the plans that were in place or being developed were for threatened species in California. Early in 1993, Babbitt took the unprecedented step of allowing limited development in the gnatcatcher songbird's habitat in Southern California. Appropriators set aside

$3 million to assist the state of California and San Diego, Orange and Riverside counties in developing conservation plans for the gnatcatcher and other endangered species.

▶ **Construction.** Negotiators set aside $73.6 million for construction, about $20.4 million more than the House wanted to allocate and $3 million less than the administration's request. Overall, the construction funds went to refuges, hatcheries, research centers, dams and bridges.

The final list of 31 projects reflected not only Interior's attempts to repair facilities but also the wishes of lawmakers. The most expensive project, $21.3 million, was a training facility in West Virginia, home state of Byrd, who also chaired the Interior Subcommittee. Other projects included a $2.6 million road for the Tensas National Wildlife Refuge in Louisiana, home of Senate appropriator J. Bennett Johnston, D-La., and $2.45 million to repair a seawall and build fences for three projects in Hawaii, the home of appropriator Daniel K. Inouye, D-Hawaii.

▶ **Land acquisition.** Negotiators rebuffed Clinton's request to decrease funding for land acquisition, providing $82.7 million to buy 43 tracts in fiscal 1994, $6.1 million more than the previous year. Clinton requested $55.4 million to finance 26 purchases and to reserve money to operate fish and wildlife programs. Land purchases were funded through the Land and Water Conservation Fund, which was established in 1965 to buy land for recreation and to protect wetlands and fish and wildlife habitats. Money for the fund came from offshore oil leasing royalties and a motorboat fuel tax. The largest purchase was $4.5 million to help pay for 6,000 acres needed for an addition to the E. B. Forsythe National Wildlife Refuge in New Jersey. The funding was requested by the Interior Department and several members of New Jersey's congressional delegation, including H. James Saxton, a senior Republican member of the Merchant Marine and Fisheries Committee.

Negotiators allotted $2 million for the Lake Wales Ridge National Wildlife Refuge in Florida, the nation's first refuge created for plants. Rep. Don Edwards, D-Calif., won $2.5 million of the $12 million he requested for the San Francisco Bay National Wildlife Refuge. The additional land was to include habitat for the threatened California clapper rail bird. And at the request of Rep. Glenn Poshard, D-Ill., negotiators set aside $3 million for the Cypress Creek National Wildlife Refuge in southern Illinois.

▶ **Cooperative Endangered Species Fund.** States received money from this fund to assist in the conservation of threatened and endangered species. Appropriators alloted $9 million for this effort, $2.4 million more than the previous year.

▶ **National Wildlife Refuge Fund.** Appropriators set aside $12 million for this fund, which was generated by fees charged to visitors of wildlife refuges. The fund went to reimburse local governments for lost revenues because those federal facilities generated no tax revenues.

National Biological Survey

Babbitt created the National Biological Survey to avert environmental and economic "train wrecks" that, he said, had resulted from enforcement of the 1973 Endangered Species Act. With a budget of nearly $164 million, Interior scientists were to conduct a comprehensive inventory of the nation's plants and animals. Babbitt had shifted funds from an array of programs under eight different branches of the Interior Department to pay about 1,600 workers — 1,400 of them scientists — to conduct the survey.

In conference, House Republican negotiators tried to insert report language aimed at protecting the private property rights of individuals. Reps. Jim Kolbe, R-Ariz., Ron Packard, R-Calif., and Regula also wanted to restrict Babbitt's use of volunteers to conduct the survey. The language was similar to two amendments the House had approved Oct. 6 during consideration of a separate bill (HR 1845) to create the National Biological Survey. Conferees agreed that the Interior Department would have to get written permission from landowners before entering private property to conduct the survey. The provision still allowed volunteers to be used to help conduct the survey.

National Park Service

The National Park Service was founded in 1916 to conserve natural conditions, scenery and wildlife. Since the creation of Yellowstone National Park in 1872, the service had grown to include 367 national parks, monuments and reservations spread over 80 million acres of land. The service's scope ranged from the 0.2-acre Thaddeus Kosciusko National Memorial in Philadelphia to the 13 million-acre Wrangell-St. Elias Park and Preserve in Alaska. The service's goal was to make parks and other facilities easily accessible. In 1992 there were 273 million visitors to Park Service facilities.

Appropriators increased the Park Service's budget by $51.3 million to $1.44 billion for fiscal 1994. Most of the increase was devoted to park operations. But recognizing the need to address the backlog of maintenance requests, appropriators rejected funds for construction of new visitor centers — popular spending perennially sought by lawmakers. House Interior Appropriations Subcommittee Chairman Yates said new visitor centers could be funded only if local, state or private groups paid for half of the costs.

▶ **Operations.** To operate the nation's 367 parks, appropriators provided $1.1 billion in fiscal 1994, a 9 percent increase over the previous year. The additional funds were intended to keep campgrounds open, offer visitors more information and relieve a backlog of park maintenance requests. Byrd and Yates included instructions in the conference report that Yellowstone National Park, the nation's oldest, be given special consideration when operating funds were distributed.

▶ **Workers without benefits.** Lawmakers appropriated $38,400 for the family of James A. Hudson, a temporary Park Service employee who died July 5 while cleaning the Lincoln Memorial. Hudson was considered a temporary worker and received no health or life insurance benefits even though he had worked for the Park Service for eight years. His death of heat stroke and a heart attack spotlighted the problem of some 150,000 temporary employees who had no benefits. The payment equaled the benefits his family would have received from the federal government had he been considered a full-time employee. Hudson's cause was taken up by Delegate Eleanor Holmes Norton, D-D.C., who cosponsored an amendment by Yates to include the one-time payment in the House's version of the bill. The Senate concurred.

▶ **Carlsbad Caverns.** At Domenici's request, the New Mexico park best known for its underground caverns was allocated $150,000 for its care. Domenici also persuaded conferees to include language urging the Interior secretary to revisit the service's decision to remove an underground lunchroom at the park. Domenici asked that a study be conducted to determine whether removing the lunchroom would have an environmental impact on the caverns and affect the experience of park visitors.

▶ **National recreation and preservation.** Negotiators provided $42.6 million for recreation, cultural, international and natural resource programs at the nation's parks in fiscal 1994, $6.7 million more than in fiscal 1993. Byrd won $5.3 million for the Wheeling National Heritage area in West Virginia. Among other projects, $1 million was provided for the National Center for Preservation Technology at Northwestern State University in Natchitoches, La., and $1.7 million for a Native Hawaiian culture and arts program.

▶ **Historic preservation.** Negotiators followed Clinton's request and set aside $40 million for historic preservation programs, about $3.4 million more than was appropriated in fiscal 1993. These projects included $2 million for renovations to the Boston Public Library.

▶ **Construction.** Negotiators set aside $201.7 million for park construction projects, $16 million more than administration requested. The spending funded 64 projects in 36 states, the District of Columbia and Guam. For example, $925,000 was earmarked for the Jean Lafitte Park outside New Orleans in Sen. Johnston's home state of Louisiana. Nine of Georgia's 11 House members lobbied Yates to set aside funding for the Martin Luther King Jr. National Historic Site in Atlanta. Conferees agreed to provide $10 million to upgrade parking and restrooms at the site, which was undergoing renovations for the 1996 Olympics in Atlanta. Some of

the more expensive projects included $11 million for a Washington, D.C., memorial to honor Franklin D. Roosevelt and $15.1 million to repair Independence Hall in Philadelphia.

▶ **Construction costs.** Appropriators urged the service to develop a priority list for projects and consider ways to lower the costs of construction.

▶ **Urban park and recreation fund.** As in previous years, the administration requested no money for the maintenance of urban parks. But negotiators set aside $5 million for these parks, such as San Francisco's Golden Gate National Recreation Area.

▶ **Land acquisition.** Despite Clinton administration appeals to trim land purchases, conferees set aside $95.3 million to buy tracts and make grants to states to do likewise — $17.7 million more than Clinton requested. Still, negotiators noted the final amount was $22.7 million less than appropriated in fiscal 1993. The money went to buy 24 national park or historic sites, including five sought by the administration.

For example, $3 million was to be used to acquire land for the Salt River Bay National Historic Park in St. Croix, Virgin Islands. It was the only site under U.S. jurisdiction that Christopher Columbus had visited. The bill also included $300,000 to purchase tracts for a national park in Samoa.

Negotiators also provided $175,000 to buy a school in Topeka, Kan., to commemorate the landmark school desegregation case *Brown v. the Board of Education,* at the request of Rep. Jim Slattery, D-Kan. The 1992 Civil Rights in Education Historical Act authorized the purchase of the Monroe School, which was the all-black school that Linda Brown attended when she filed the lawsuit.

Following the administration's request, lawmakers set aside $635,000 to buy less than an acre in Washington, D.C., to honor Mary McLeod Bethune, a noted black educator and founder of the National Council of Negro Women. And $6 million was allotted to purchase about 1,668 acres in 12 states to extend the Appalachian Trail. At the request of Senate appropriator Domenici and Rep. Steven H. Schiff, R-N.M., $3.5 million went to buy land for the Petroglyph National Monument project near Albuquerque, N.M.. Domenici also secured $500,000 to buy additional tracts for the Pecos National Monument in Pecos, N.M.

▶ **Presidio Army Base.** The bill provided $25.4 million to convert the Presidio Army Base in San Francisco into a national park. The funds were to be used to pay for maintenance, fire prevention, housing and inspections. A 1972 law stipulated that if the base was ever abandoned, the site would become part of the Golden Gate National Recreation Area. The government agreed in 1988 to close the base. The Interior Department was studying how much of the 1,480-acre site to make part of the park.

▶ **John F. Kennedy Center for the Performing Arts.** Lawmakers provided $20.6 million, the same as in fiscal 1993, for the John F. Kennedy Center in Washington, D.C. The park service was responsible for the center's visitor information, maintenance and security. Funds were to be used to increase accessibility, repair the center's marble facade and upgrade its mechanical systems.

National Geological Survey

As the nation's chief mapmaker, the Geological Survey made more maps than any other government agency. But it also was the nation's largest earth science research agency and the primary source of information on groundwater. Established in 1879, the agency also studied the solar system and issued warnings about earthquakes. The bill provided $584.7 million for surveys, investigations and research.

Negotiators set aside $5 million to build an addition to the Earth Resources Observation System Data Center in Sioux Falls, S.D. When completed, the expansion was to house the equipment needed to process and distribute information expected to be generated by two NASA satellites slated for launch in late 1997. Appropriators said they expected to allot another $4 million in fiscal 1995 to complete the addition.

To conduct marine and coastal geologic surveys, conferees agreed to spend $35.6 million. This category provided money to study coastal erosion and wetland areas in Louisiana, Texas, Florida, South Carolina, the Great Lakes and Northern California. It also funded pollution research in Louisiana's Lake Pontchartrain, Boston Harbor, the Florida Keys and parts of Hawaii.

Minerals Management Service

The Minerals Management Service had two responsibilities: to collect and distribute royalties from mineral leases on federal and Indian lands, and to oversee offshore drilling and exploration. Appropriators earmarked $198.5 million for the minerals service.

▶ **Offshore oil.** The outer continental shelf began three miles from the nation's coastline. Exploration suggested the area was a potential source of oil and gas, which could reduce the nation's dependence on imports. A total of $198.5 million was provided for the service to oversee leasing, royalty collections and oil spill research.

Despite their potential as energy sources, certain shelf areas had been off-limits for leasing and exploration activities because of oil spills and other environmental concerns. Those limits generally had been imposed through annual appropriations bills. Backed by the Clinton administration, conferees extended the ban for another year. It covered Alaska's Bristol Bay, the eastern Gulf of Mexico, the Florida Panhandle and Keys, the North Carolina coast and other areas in the Atlantic and Pacific.

Johnston, chairman of the Senate Energy and Natural Resources Committee and an appropriator, tried to lift the moratorium on drilling along the Florida and North Carolina coasts. He said those two areas offered potential sources of natural gas that posed little risk to explore. The Senate Interior Appropriations Subcommittee on July 27 approved a Johnston amendment lifting the ban, but the full committee reinstated the moratorium the next day at the request of Connie Mack, R-Fla.

Bureau of Mines

The bureau was charged with studying mine safety, disaster prevention and occupational health issues. Appropriators set aside $169.4 million for fiscal 1994, a decrease of about $4.8 million from fiscal 1993. With Byrd and Yates strong supporters of the nation's coal mining industry, mine research, productivity and safety were top priorities of the agency. Although progress had been made in mine safety, conferees noted that the industry still averaged 131 fatalities and 27,181 injuries annually.

Congress also had become increasingly concerned with research into the drainage of acid from active and abandoned mine sites. Negotiators urged the bureau to step up efforts to resolve drainage problems at a mine near Casselman River in Pennsylvania and at the Pitt Creek watershed in Oklahoma.

Surface Mining

The surface mining office regulated 3,600 commercial coal mining operations and oversaw the restoration of mined lands. Appropriators provided $190.1 million for the Abandoned Mine Reclamation Fund, about $2 million more than the previous year. The fund derived its revenues from a tax levied on coal producers and was dedicated to cleaning up abandoned coal mines. Negotiators agreed with a Senate provision to allow the office to lay off 16 workers in Wilkes-Barre, Pa. The House bill included a provision by Yates and veteran appropriator John P. Murtha, D-Pa., that would have required the Wilkes-Barre office to keep 16 full-time employees.

Territories

The United States administered aid to or was associated with the Pacific islands of American Samoa, Guam, Northern Mariana Islands and the uninhabited Palmyra Atoll, and the U.S. Virgin Islands in the Caribbean. It also administered Palau and provided aid to the independent Marshall Islands and Micronesia. The Office of Territorial and International Affairs was allocated $127.8 million in fiscal 1994 to carry out these activities.

Under a longstanding agreement to provide financial aid, $27.7 million was allotted to the Commonwealth of the Northern Marianas Islands. Lawmakers had been concerned about labor prob-

lems, taxes and immigration on the islands and had decreased aid to the Marianas in recent years. Funding for the Marianas could be used only for capital improvement projects, and $3 million was earmarked for a new monument and exhibits at the American War Memorial Park.

Among other projects, conferees allotted $4.5 million to repair buildings at the University of the Virgin Islands damaged by Hurricane Hugo in 1989. American Samoa was granted an additional $500,000 to buy pharmaceutical supplies and $1 million was allocated to help repair a hospital damaged by a typhoon on the island of Ebeye in the Marshall Islands. Appropriators also provided $595,000 to control the brown tree snake, a 5- to 10-foot reptile that attacked birds in Guam and was believed to be spreading to other islands.

Department Offices

Appropriators provided $132.1 million for fiscal 1994, about $9.8 million more than 1993's allocation for the Interior's offices of the secretary, solicitor, inspector general and the National Indian Gaming Commission.

▶ **Timber area restoration.** At the request of House appropriator Norm Dicks, D-Wash., and Senate conferees Patty Murray, D-Wash., and Mark O. Hatfield, R-Ore., a new $7 million account was established to pay for projects aimed at restoring entire ecosystems damaged by logging in the Pacific Northwest. Ecosystem restoration was proposed as a component of a forest management plan for the Pacific Northwest. The plan, first unveiled by the administration in July, was aimed at protecting the northern spotted owl, the marbeled murrelet and their old-growth forest habitat. Funding for the program was established as a line item in the departmental offices account to give the Interior secretary flexibility in directing this money to the Bureau of Land Management, Fish and Wildlife Service or Bureau of Indian Affairs.

AMERICAN INDIANS

Federal programs for American Indians funded under this bill were administered by Interior's Bureau of Indian Affairs, the Department of Health and Human Services' Indian Health Service and the Education Department.

The Bureau of Indian Affairs (BIA) was the largest recipient of Interior dollars, providing social services, education and natural resource development to American Indians. Since its creation in 1824, the bureau had been plagued with complaints of mismanagement and corruption. An intra-agency task force had been examining the agency since 1991 and issued its first set of recommendations in December 1992.

President Clinton, who issued his own list of policy objectives for American Indians during the 1992 presidential campaign, incorporated some of the recommendations in his fiscal 1994 budget. For the first time, Clinton's budget split the BIA request into funds dedicated to tribal programs and money meant for BIA operations.

The administration's budget request was received fairly well by appropriators, who welcomed the administration's requests for a substantial increase in education funding, support for tribally run programs and funds to settle Indian land and water claims. The bill provided $1.8 billion for the bureau.

The Indian Health Service, a division of the U.S. Public Health Service, was charged with providing health and medical services to the approximately 1.3 million American Indians and Native Alaskans. The bill provided $1.9 billion for the service for fiscal 1994.

The 1972 Indian Education Act authorized a series of education programs for American Indian and Alaskan native children, college students and adults that were funded through the Education Department. The Bureau of Indian Affairs also funded Indian education programs. Programs under the Education Department received $83.5 million this year.

▶ **Indian land and water claims.** Clinton called for the creation of a new, separate fund to pay authorized land and water claims to Indian tribes. Appropriators set aside $103.3 billion for the new fund.

▶ **Indian construction.** The bill provided $167 million for the bureau's construction programs, a $17.4 million increase over fiscal 1993. Most of the increase was dedicated to the construction and rehabilitation of schools on Indian reservations.

Appropriators agreed with the administration's request for $13 million to complete the construction of six new schools: Pinon Dormitory, Rock Point and Many Farms in Arizona, Eastern Cheyenne in South Dakota, Tucker in Mississippi and Shoshone Bannock in Idaho. Construction funds were also dedicated to building roads, fish hatcheries, irrigation systems and buildings on Indian reservations.

▶ **Navajo-Hopi land dispute.** Ever since Congress sought to settle a centuries-old land dispute with a 1974 law divvying up disputed land between neighboring Hopi and Navajo tribes in Arizona, the bureau had been attempting to resettle those who ended up on the wrong side of boundary lines. The law guaranteed new housing to resettled Indian families. The Office of Navajo and Hopi Indian Relocation still had to resettle about 708 families into new homes. The bureau also had to provide housing to others who moved before their houses were built. The bill provided $26.9 million for the resettlement program.

▶ **Indian education.** The bill provided $495.7 million for the bureau's Indian education programs in fiscal 1994, a 13 percent increase over fiscal 1993. Much of the increase was to provide for an estimated 5 percent jump in enrollment in the fall at the 181 schools operated by the BIA.

▶ **Indian health facilities.** The bill included $297 million for the repair and maintenance of hospitals to serve Indians, a $37 million decrease from fiscal 1993 levels. The decrease was due to the fact that no new health construction projects were planned in fiscal 1994.

RELATED AGENCIES

Forest Service

The Agriculture Department's Forest Service was allocated $2.4 billion for fiscal 1994 to manage 191 million acres of public lands across the country. Those lands were used to graze cattle and other livestock, harvest timber, protect wildlife, conserve soil and water, and for recreation. More than 10,000 ranchers and farmers grazed their livestock on federal forest land. But the service's primary goal was to conserve forests. Federal forests and grasslands provided about 55 percent of the annual water yields of the Western states.

About 41 percent of the recreational opportunities available on public lands were managed by the Forest Service. Overall, 3,000 species of fish and wildlife and 10,000 plant species were on lands managed by the forest service.

▶ **Research.** Appropriators granted $193.1 million, $10.4 million more than the previous year, to study pesticides and ways to protect forests from fire, disease, beetles and other insects. Included in the funding was $250,000 requested by Byrd to study timber bridges at West Virginia University in Morgantown, W.Va. Appropriators also urged the Forest Service to study the Formosan termite, which had damaged historic properties.

▶ **State and private forests.** Lawmakers allotted $168.1 million to the Forest Service to help manage, protect from pest infestation and preserve 805 million acres of privately owned forests under cooperative programs with local governments, the forest industry and private landowners. The appropriation was $11.9 million more than provided in fiscal 1993.

Within this account, $15 million had been set aside for the Pacific Northwest as part of Clinton's plan to provide financial assistance for the timber communities that had lost jobs during the protracted legal dispute over endangered species. The region's lawmakers, particularly Murray, Hatfield and Dicks, were instrumental in securing this funding. Clinton promised he would direct $1.2 billion over five years to Oregon, Washington and Northern California to offset financial losses stemming from an ongoing legal battle to protect the spotted owl and its old-growth forest habitat. The bill provided $69.5 million

from various accounts for the region.

▶ **Timber sales.** Each year, Congress appropriated funds to harvest and sell timber from federal forests. The timber sale program depended on how much money was provided for such things as logging roads and the planting of new trees. Timber from federal forests was sold to private companies, which harvested the trees.

The Forest Service was allotted $198 million to prepare forests for tree cutting and timber sales. Conferees declined to specify how much timber should be cut and harvested during fiscal 1994. But Forest Service officials said the funding would provide close to Clinton's recommendation that 4.6 billion board feet be sold in fiscal 1994. A board foot was equal to a plank of wood a foot square and an inch thick.

Negotiators provided $128.2 million for road construction, essentially the amount requested by the administration.

Lawmakers urged the administration to review the practice of "below cost" timber sales, which did not cover the government's costs to build the roads needed for the timber harvest and other expenses associated with the sale.

▶ **Watershed restoration.** Lawmakers provided $20 million to restore watersheds in forests west of the Cascade Mountains in Washington, Oregon and Northern California that had been damaged by excessive timber cutting. This provision was pushed by Dicks, Murray and Hatfield. The funds were to be used to remove logging roads, control soil erosion and convert some trails to recreational uses. Watershed restoration were expected to help all of the species in a particular ecosystem, but scientists hoped these projects would specifically protect dwindling salmon stocks.

▶ **International forestry.** About $7 million was set aside for this account, which provided funding for projects such as the Forests for the Future initiative. The project was proposed by the United States during the 1992 "Earth Summit" in Rio de Janeiro, Brazil. Under this program, the United States planned to help foreign countries protect their forest resources and understand ecosystems. The project would focus on major forest ecosystems, including the boreal forests of Russia and the tropical forests of the Amazon, Africa and Southeast Asia.

▶ **Firefighting.** Negotiators followed Clinton's request and appropriated $190.1 million for firefighting.

▶ **Construction.** The total budget of $249 million for construction of roads, trails and facilities represented a decrease of nearly $6.3 million from the fiscal 1993 appropriation. Still, lawmakers cut Clinton's request by $25.2 million. Funding for timber roads was important because there could be no timber cutting without the roads. Appropriators set aside $128.2 million for road construction. Contained in the total allocation was $1.1 million to complete the visitor center in Ketchikan, Alaska, and $3.1 million to replace a visitor center in Seneca Falls, W.Va. Senate appropriator Conrad Burns, R-Mont., fought to get $300,000 for a visitor's center in his home state, and appropriators provided nearly $1.2 million to build a discovery center at the Columbia River Gorge in Washington.

▶ **Land acquisition.** Appropriators set aside $64.3 million to purchase land in 41 areas, about $1.8 million more than the previous year. Included was $2 million to buy tracts in areas such as Kentucky's Daniel Boone National Forest, $3 million for Montana's Gallatin National Forest, $3 million for Vermont's Green Mountain National Forest and $500,000 for Indiana's Hoosier National Forest.

▶ **Tree measurement.** To reduce fraud in timber sales, lawmakers endorsed a change in the way the Forest Service calculated sales. Appropriators mandated that no funds be used to prepare timber sales using the "scaling" method. That method had required an independent third party to estimate the usable wood content of logs to determine what the government should charge for the timber. Under the new "tree measurement" program, payment was based on the volume of timber as it stood in the forest.

Energy Department

Agreeing with Clinton's call for more energy conservation, lawmakers boosted Energy Department accounts to $1.5 billion, up

from $808.3 million in fiscal 1993. That amount — an 82 percent increase from fiscal 1993 and one of the largest in the bill — paid for alternative fuel research, energy conservation and the operation of the Strategic Petroleum Reserve. Appropriators Byrd and Yates supported the president.

▶ **Clean-coal technology.** Appropriators delayed $175 million from these programs until fiscal 1996. Under the programs, the Energy Department shared the cost of industry demonstration projects of innovative coal-burning technologies. The projects looked for ways to reduce air pollutants from coal-burning power plants, with the goal of increasing usage of America's most abundant energy resource. On May 1, 1994, the Energy Department was expected to issue a report, discussing available funding from terminating projects.

▶ **Fossil energy.** Lawmakers provided $430.7 million to continue funding fossil fuels research, including coal liquefaction, flue-gas cleanup and enhanced oil and gas recovery. Some of the beneficiaries included the University of Oklahoma, represented by Senate appropriator Don Nickles, R-Okla., and the Illinois mild gasification facility in Yates' home state. The appropriation represented an increase of $12.3 million compared with fiscal 1993.

▶ **Alternative fuels.** The main project under this account was the Great Plains Gasification Plant near Beulah, N.D. Purchased by the Beulah Electric Power Cooperative from the Energy Department in 1988, it was the only synthetic natural gas plant in the country. Congress instructed that $5.2 million in interest from the sale be transferred to the Treasury Department.

▶ **Naval petroleum and oil-shale reserves.** Appropriators provided $214.8 million for six government-owned oil fields — two in Elk Hills, Calif., one northeast of Casper, Wyo., two in Rifle, Colo., and one in the Utah counties of Carbon and Uintah. The reserves produced 60,400 barrels of oil and liquid products a day and were expected to produce $504 million in revenues in fiscal 1994. The appropriation was $21.3 million less than the previous year. In the past, the oil reserves had been a bone of contention between the Bush administration and Congress: The administration wanted to sell or lease them, while Congress valued them for their revenue-producing capabilities.

▶ **Energy conservation.** Conservation programs received the biggest increase among the energy accounts. The bill allocated $690.4 million — a $111.5 million increase from fiscal year 1993. That included research on waste processing and the efficiency of heating, cooling and lighting in federal buildings. Appropriators urged private industry to develop fuel-efficient clothes washers, similar to fuel-efficient refrigerators. The bill also allotted $254 million for grants to state and local governments to support weatherization programs for homes, schools and hospitals.

▶ **Emergency preparedness.** Appropriators provided the Energy Department $8.9 million to analyze the vulnerability of U.S. energy supplies to sudden disruption because of human and natural disasters. One example lawmakers considered was Hurricane Iniki, which struck Hawaii in 1992 and cut off electrical power in the islands.

▶ **Strategic Petroleum Reserve.** Lawmakers appropriated $206.8 million to operate the Strategic Petroleum Reserve in fiscal 1994. Created in 1975, the reserve could store 750 million barrels of oil in five underground salt domes in Texas and Louisiana and at a ground marine terminal in Louisiana. The government planned to expand capacity by 250 million barrels. The reserve held more than 570 million barrels; lawmakers instructed that it be filled to 1 billion barrels. While no money was appropriated to purchase the oil to boost the stockpile, lawmakers said there was remaining money to do so in fiscal 1994.

CULTURAL PROGRAMS

Smithsonian Institution

To operate 15 museums in Washington and New York, appropriators allocated $342.1 million. The Smithsonian also managed

the National Zoo in Washington, D.C.; an animal conservation and research center in Front Royal, Va.; an aircraft museum in Suitland, Md.; natural wildlife preserves on the Chesapeake Bay and in Panama; an oceanographic research facility in Fort Pierce, Fla.; and astrophysical observatories in Cambridge, Mass. and Mount Hopkins, Ariz. There were more than 100 million art objects, natural history specimens and artifacts in the collection. Nearly 30 million people visited the Smithsonian facilities annually. The spending included $5.4 million for an aquatic trail and grasslands exhibit and other improvements at the National Zoo. Another $700,000 was set aside to clean part of the Museum of Natural History's collection that was stored in Maryland. The objects were contaminated with asbestos when a tornado damaged the facility in the fall of 1992. Appropriators also set aside $6.2 million to design a national museum dedicated to American Indians.

National Gallery of Art

Originally created as part of the Smithsonian in 1937, this independent museum grew out of the private collection of industrialist Andrew W. Mellon. The gallery also was widely known for its East Wing, designed by famed architect I.M. Pei. Appropriators set aside $54.7 million for operation of the museum.

National Endowment for the Arts

Lawmakers appropriated $170.2 million for the endowment, which made grants to individuals and groups in all facets of the arts. In recent years, the endowment had been attacked by Sen. Jesse Helms, R-N.C., and others for funding art they considered obscene.

Helms failed in his attempt to cut funding for individual artists and direct federal grant-making authority to the states. But some lawmakers, such as Rep. Cliff Stearns, R-Fla., said federal arts funding should be cut because it was no longer a top spending priority.

National Endowment for the Humanities

The endowment was granted $177.5 million to support projects in history, literature, foreign languages and other disciplines.

▶ **Cultural panels.** The bill also provided funding for a host of arts and cultural panels. The Woodrow Wilson International Center for Scholars was allotted $6.4 million to extend educational grants for research into international and cultural fields; the Institute of Museum Services was appropriated $28.8 million for educational programs and the renovation of museums; the Commission of Fine Arts was granted $805,000 to advise the government on arts and architecture in the nation's capital; art programs in Washington, D.C. were provided $7.5 million; the Advisory Council on Historic Preservation was appropriated nearly $3 million to support preserving historic and cultural resources; and the National Capital Planning Commission was given $5.9 million for the planning and renovation of federal facilities. The Franklin Delano Roosevelt Memorial Commission was granted $49,000 for salaries and expenses to plan the monument to the 32nd president; the Pennsylvania Avenue Development Corp. was granted $14.2 million to upgrade the street stretching between the White House and the Capitol; and the United States Holocaust Memorial Council was given $21.7 million to complete and oversee the new memorial to Holocaust victims. ■

Huge Bill Funds Labor, HHS, Education

The Senate on Oct. 18 easily cleared the fiscal 1994 appropriations bill for the departments of Labor, Health and Human Services (HHS), and Education. President Clinton signed the measure into law Oct. 21 (HR 2518 — PL 103-112). The massive bill provided $256.3 billion for the three Cabinet departments and 15 related agencies — more money than any other appropriations bill, including Defense.

As in years past, the most controversial issue in the bill concerned the circumstances under which Medicaid, the federal-state health insurance program for the poor, could pay for abortions. After a bitter debate, the issue was settled when the Senate voted Sept. 28 to accept a House provision allowing abortions in cases of rape, incest and when the life of the woman was in danger.

The language was less restrictive than existing law, which allowed the use of federal money to pay for abortions only when the woman's life was in danger. But abortion rights advocates, who had hoped to eliminate the restrictions altogether, were deeply disappointed. Both sides in the abortion debate agreed that the skirmish was only the beginning of a bigger fight over federal funding of abortion expected to take place in 1994 when Congress debated Clinton's health-care reform plan.

Three-fourths of the spending in the Labor-HHS bill went for entitlement programs, such as Medicaid; Medicare, the health program for the elderly and disabled; Aid to Families With Dependent Children, the nation's principal welfare program; Supplemental Security Income for poor elderly and disabled people; and unemployment insurance. For those programs, spending levels were determined by eligibility formulas and other criteria set by law, and appropriators had little or no discretion over how much to provide for them.

The bill contained $67 billion for discretionary programs, such as student financial aid, medical research and job training. That was a 7.8 percent increase over fiscal 1993.

An early concern was that appropriators planned to cut the maximum Pell grant for needy college students. The final bill included $6.3 billion, with a maximum grant of $2,300. That was still a decrease from the 1992-93 maximum grant of $2,400. An increase in the number of students forced the cut in the maximum grant, despite an overall increase in spending for the program.

BACKGROUND

The Labor-HHS bill was one of the most politically complex spending bills because it pitted an array of social programs against each other. Even in the brightest budget years, Labor-HHS appropriators could not hope to find

---

BOXSCORE

➡ **Fiscal 1994 appropriations for the departments of Labor, Health and Human Services, and Education (HR 2518).** The $256.3 billion spending bill provided funding for most federal social programs.

Reports: H Rept 103-156, S Rept 103-143; conference report H Rept 103-275.

KEY ACTION

June 30 — **House** passed HR 2518, 305-124.

Sept. 29 — **Senate** passed HR 2518, 82-17.

Oct. 5 — **House-Senate** conferees approved conference report.

Oct. 7 — **House** adopted conference report, 311-115.

Oct. 18 — **Senate** cleared bill, 80-15.

Oct. 21 — **President** signed HR 2518 — PL 103-112.

---

every dollar requested for the more than 500 programs under their jurisdiction. Head Start and special education programs, for example, routinely got less money than it took to serve all the young people who qualified. Under Head Start, more than half the eligible preschoolers simply were not served. In the case of special education, states were required to offer the program but were left to fill the money gap.

Democratic appropriators hoped the picture would improve under a like-minded Democratic president with priorities that closely matched their own. But when Clinton's budget request reached Capitol Hill, lawmakers discovered they had a new problem: His wish list was too long. Clinton asked Congress to provide $72.9 billion for the discretionary portion of the Labor-HHS bill, $5.9 billion more than was available.

Clinton had counted on a fiscal 1993 supplemental spending bill (HR 1335) to pay for many of the big-ticket "social investment" initiatives that he had advocated during his presidential campaign. But Senate Republicans mounted a successful filibuster that forced Clinton to drop virtually every new project from the bill. Instead, the task of finding ways to pay for new social service programs fell to the House and Senate Labor-HHS Appropriations subcommittees. *(Stimulus bill, p. 706)*

To cope with the disparity, the appropriators went to each of the departments and agencies under their jurisdiction and asked them to be more realistic and to winnow their priorities.

Shunning Earmarks

Unlike other appropriations bills, the Labor-HHS measure did not include earmarks for special projects in the districts of key members. House Appropriations Committee Chairman William H. Natcher, D-Ky., who also chaired the House Labor-HHS Appropriations Subcommittee, had insisted for years that his panel refrain from telling agencies how to spend money, beyond making allocations on a program-by-program basis.

Education programs were based on competitive application processes. The majority of education grant money went through the Chapter 1 program for the disadvantaged. More than $6.9 billion in this program helped 5 million students with reading, math and other academics. It was spread to 95 percent of all school districts in the nation, however, a factor that tended to mitigate the need for lawmakers to dictate where the money went.

Student financial aid provided in the bill went directly to the students or schools based on strict formulas.

For members of the Labor-HHS Appropriations subcommittees, the art of earmarking was reserved for their other subcommittee assignments.

LABOR, HHS, EDUCATION

	Fiscal 1993	Fiscal 1994 Clinton Request	House Bill	Senate Bill	Final Bill
	(In thousands of dollars)				
Labor Department					
Training and employment services	$ 4,396,756	$ 6,867,218	$ 5,083,762	$ 4,958,623	$ 5,013,510
Trade adjustment, allowances	211,250	190,000	190,000	190,000	190,000
Unemployment insurance (advance)	4,665,000	2,556,000	2,556,000	2,556,000	2,556,000
Trust fund	*(3,136,831)*	*(3,367,879)*	*(3,367,477)*	*(3,338,389)*	*(3,376,617)*
Black lung disability	944,783	1,002,331	1,002,331	1,002,931	1,002,931
Occupational Safety & Health	288,250	294,490	294,640	297,244	297,244
Other	1,764,477	1,962,222	1,845,424	1,854,853	2,044,853
Total, Labor Department	**$ 12,270,516**	**$ 12,872,261**	**$ 10,972,157**	**$ 10,859,651**	**$ 10,914,538**
Health and Human Services					
Public Health					
Health resources and services	2,775,252	3,289,068	3,035,726	3,186,979	3,159,019
Centers for Disease Control	1,662,545	2,161,788	1,910,182	2,088,781	2,051,132
National Institutes of Health	10,325,604	10,667,984	10,936,652	10,956,389	10,955,773
Substance Abuse/Mental Health	2,004,803	2,153,480	2,057,167	2,119,205	2,125,178
Health-care policy and research	109,051	139,045	129,051	139,305	135,409
Health-care Financing/Social Security					
Medicaid grants to states	90,095,650	91,077,413	64,477,413	91,077,413	91,077,413
Medicare and other Medicaid	45,962,862	45,731,440	45,731,440	45,731,440	45,731,440
Supplemental Security Income	25,256,771	26,951,775	20,181,775	26,942,775	26,953,775
Public Welfare					
Family support payments (AFDC)	15,695,072	16,115,966	11,915,966	16,115,966	16,115,966
Workfare programs	1,000,000	1,100,000	1,100,000	1,100,000	1,100,000
Low Income Home Energy Assistance	2,783,438	1,474,780	— [1]	1,507,408	1,475,000
Refugee assistance	381,481	420,052	400,000	400,000	400,000
Community Services block grant	440,871	440,871	447,643	472,649	464,224
Child-care grants	892,711	932,711	892,711	892,711	892,711
Social Services block grant (Title XX)	2,800,000	2,800,000	2,800,000	3,800,000	3,800,000
Head Start, family assistance	3,658,392	5,051,477	4,169,806	4,296,796	4,237,050
Programs for the aging	838,676	839,075	841,875	881,863	871,282
Foster care, adoption assistance	2,924,014	2,992,900	2,992,900	2,992,900	2,992,900
Other	1,324,589	1,284,381	1,012,013	1,265,487	1,264,565
Total, HHS	**$ 210,931,782**	**$ 215,624,206**	**$ 175,032,320**	**$ 215,968,067**	**$ 215,802,937**
Education Department					
Elementary and Secondary Education					
Compensatory education (Chapter 1)	6,708,986	7,110,155	6,871,147	6,971,620	6,924,497
Impact aid	820,154	688,800	813,074	748,368	798,208
Education reform	—	585,000	133,750	166,000	155,000
Bilingual, immigrant education	225,745	232,251	242,789	232,251	240,155
Special education	2,965,602	3,124,921	3,039,442	3,134,734	3,108,702
Higher Education					
Pell grants, student financial aid	7,917,109	9,538,166	8,120,366	8,004,293	8,020,160
Guaranteed student loans	2,285,036	2,251,156	2,251,156	2,251,156	2,251,156
Direct loan subsidies	—	22,179	22,179	22,179	22,179
Higher education grants	832,799	873,421	889,855	882,974	893,688
Vocational, adult education	1,474,243	1,447,566	1,474,243	1,483,433	1,481,183
Rehabilitation services	2,182,699	2,251,028	2,251,028	2,316,913	2,296,936
Libraries	146,069	114,749	145,101	147,517	146,309
Education research	280,109	352,579	277,244	301,398	292,592
Other	2,248,869	2,329,658	2,095,946	2,092,574	2,134,427
Total, Education Department	**$ 28,087,420**	**$ 30,921,629**	**$ 28,627,320**	**$ 28,755,410**	**$ 28,765,192**
Action	201,526	206,738	201,526	206,287	205,097
Corporation for Public Broadcasting	292,640	292,640	292,640	320,000	312,000
Other related agencies	794,963	553,639	553,248	318,750	328,499
GRAND TOTAL	**$ 252,578,847**	**$ 260,471,113**	**$ 215,679,211**	**$ 256,428,165**	**$ 256,328,263**

[1] *The House bill did not include money for the Low Income Home Energy Assistance Program, but it would have made available about $1.5 billion from previous and supplemental appropriations.*

SOURCE: House Appropriations Committee

HOUSE COMMITTEE

The House Labor-HHS Appropriations Subcommittee marked up its version of the spending bill in closed session June 8. In what abortion rights supporters hoped would represent a sea change, the subcommittee followed Clinton's policy of allowing the use of federal funds to pay for abortions under Medicaid. A ban on such funding — known as the Hyde amendment for its author, Rep. Henry J. Hyde, R-Ill. — had been attached to appropriations bills since the Carter administration.

"The subcommittee is not representative of the full committee and even less of the House," responded Douglas R. Johnson, a lobbyist for the National Right to Life Committee, an anti-abortion group. "We are going to fight every step of the way."

Full Committee Action

With little debate, the full Appropriations Committee on June 24 voted to restore restrictions on the use of Medicaid funds to pay for abortions — although the restrictions were somewhat looser than the existing language that allowed abortions only to save the life of the woman.

On a 31-14 show of hands, the committee adopted an amendment by Natcher to prohibit the use of Medicaid funds for abortions except in the cases of incest or rape or to save the woman's life. There was no debate on the amendment. Natcher appealed to members, reminding several by name that the bill took care of their particular interests in areas such as AIDS research or library services. Then he asked for their support. "I beg of you to help me . . . help us out, help us out."

The panel rejected, 18-27, a substitute amendment by David R. Obey, D-Wis., that would have allowed the funding of abortions to protect a woman's health, basically leaving the decision to a woman and her doctor. The amendment would have allowed Medicaid to pay for abortions just as it paid for other services related to pregnancy and surgery.

The committee then approved the bill by voice vote (H Rept 103-156).

The measure included partial funding for Clinton initiatives that had not yet been enacted. For example, it provided $68 million, to be split by the departments of Labor and Education, for a school-to-work transition program that would help students who were not going to college to move into the work world. The administration, which had not yet sent the school-to-work legislation to Capitol Hill, had asked for $270 million for the two departments. *(School-to-work bill, p. 408)*

The bill also allocated $100 million to begin funding the Goals 2000: Educate America Act, the president's school reform effort. That was $320 million less than Clinton requested and the education authorization committees had approved. *(Goals 2000, p. 404)*

Members of the Education and Labor Committee complained about the bill's nearly $200 million cut in the Chapter 2 school improvement programs. State and local officials had used Chapter 2, which included the Dwight D. Eisenhower Mathematics and Science Education Act and dropout prevention, to advance reform efforts ahead of the federal government.

The appropriations bill provided $689 million for summer youth employment and training during the summer of 1995 for 513,000 participants. The bill also included $300 million to add to existing funding for the summer of 1994. Part of the administration's plan to revitalize the economy had been to provide summer jobs to young people. Congress had initially shot that down when it defeated Clinton's stimulus package.

One of the areas hardest hit in the measure was student aid for higher education. However, the committee managed to save some programs that the administration had planned to kill and to soften cuts to other programs.

The committee provided a total of $6.3 billion for Pell grants, $546 million more than in fiscal 1993. The Pell grant program, which helped needy students pay for college, was running a deficit of about $2 billion. The administration had tried to make up the shortfall in the stimulus package. When that bill failed, Clinton included the $2 billion in his budget request for the Department of Education. The administration recommended paying off the debt at the expense of other programs, but the committee opted to cover $415 million of the deficit.

Appropriators also cut the maximum Pell grant available to students from $2,300 to $2,250. Congress had authorized up to $4,500 per year per student, but appropriators had never allocated more than about $2,400. In 1992, they cut the grants to $2,300. In their report, the appropriators said that the $2,300 maximum grant could be restored if Education Committee members would change the law to exclude some of the middle-class students who qualified under the 1992 reauthorization of the Higher Education Act. *(1992 Almanac, p. 438)*

The committee cut spending levels for other student aid programs, including Federal Supplemental Educational Opportunity Grants, the federal work-study program, the Perkins loan program and the State Student Incentive Grants program.

Some of the education cuts helped increase funding for the National Institutes of Health (NIH), a committee priority. Clinton had sought to increase NIH funding by 3 percent, although most of that was targeted for breast cancer research and AIDS programs. The committee increased NIH funding by 5.9 percent, omitting earmarks for breast cancer and AIDS.

HOUSE FLOOR

Any thought that Democratic control of the White House would lead to congressional consensus on the abortion issue vanished June 30 when, after an emotional debate, the House handed an unequivocal victory to abortion opponents on the issue of spending federal dollars for abortions. By a vote of 255-178, the House approved an amendment to HR 2518 that effectively banned abortion funding for poor women except to save the life of the woman or in cases of rape or incest. *(Vote 307, p. 74-H)*

The Labor-HHS spending bill then passed 305-124. *(Vote 311, p. 76-H)*

By the end of the turbulent day, it seemed that abortion rights legislators, led by the Congressional Caucus for Women's Issues, had seriously miscalculated their political clout. Although the number of women in the House had increased by 23 in the 103rd Congress, the number of House Republican moderates had declined, narrowing the pool of potential abortion rights supporters. Moreover, abortion foes were willing to compromise to avoid having the ban on abortions lifted altogether.

What emerged was support for an abortion funding position that was only marginally more supportive of abortion rights than in the past.

House leaders tried to minimize the significance of the

vote, pointing out a difference between those who opposed abortion and those who opposed public funding of abortions. "I wouldn't confuse sentiment on the Hyde amendment with freedom of choice. . . . It's a different question," said Majority Leader Richard A. Gephardt, D-Mo.

The acrimonious floor fight on the bill, which turned on rapid-fire parliamentary maneuvers, revealed much about the complexity of the abortion debate: members' deeply held views on abortion; gender and racial politics; and institutional House politics. *(Abortion, p. 348)*

At the beginning of the debate, abortion rights supporters succeeded in striking Natcher's abortion funding restrictions from the bill on the grounds that the language was legislating on a spending bill and therefore violated House rules. That left the measure with no restrictions on the use of federal funds to pay for abortions.

Then it was Hyde's turn to use procedural ploys. Under House rules, his amendment was considered "disfavored" because it set conditions for funding; it could only be offered after lawmakers — meeting as the Committee of the Whole — finished all other amendments and had a chance to report the bill to the House for final approval. Only if the Committee of the Whole turned down the motion to rise and report the bill would Hyde be allowed to offer his amendment. Members acceded to Hyde's wishes, defeating the motion to rise by a vote of 190-244. *(Vote 306, p. 74-H)*

Hyde then offered his amendment — worded in the passive voice, following a 1908 precedent, to avoid the charge that he was legislating on an appropriations bill.

Abortion rights lawmakers, led by Patricia Schroeder, D-Colo., and Nita M. Lowey, D-N.Y., tried to block Hyde from speaking. Hyde struggled for permission to present his amendment and won it with the help of Appropriations Committee Chairman Natcher.

As abortion rights lawmakers saw the tide turn against them, the debate became increasingly bitter. Finally, Natcher, who had looked increasingly uncomfortable through the debate, brought it to a close, asking for the procedural vote needed before Hyde could bring his amendment to a vote.

Afterwards, Don Edwards, D-Calif., an abortion rights advocate, expressed frustration at lawmakers who had pushed for no restrictions at all. "I could have told them they weren't going to win," Edwards said. "People don't want to use federal funds to pay for other people's abortions. They haven't won this vote for 16 years."

Direct Student Loans

While the abortion debate was raucous, an expected fight over direct lending for student loans fizzled on the floor, much to the surprise of direct-lending opponents.

Bart Gordon, D-Tenn., and Bill Goodling, R-Pa., offered an amendment they said would prohibit spending to implement a full-fledged direct-loan program that the administration favored. Instead, only a pilot project approved in 1992 would be funded. The legislation included $22 million to fund the demonstration in fiscal 1994. According to the committee report, the funding could be used either for a pilot program or for the start-up of a direct-lending program.

Gordon and Goodling were hoping that their amendment would give ammunition to Senate conferees on a separate budget-reconciliation bill (HR 2264 — PL 103-66) to reject a House proposal to begin a full-fledged direct student loan program.

But in a surprise move, William D. Ford, D-Mich., chairman of the Education and Labor Committee, agreed to accept the amendment. An aide to Ford said consultations with Education Department lawyers, the Office of Management and Budget and committee lawyers resulted in a consensus that the language would not prevent a total switch to direct loans.

Robert E. Andrews, D-N.J., a key booster of direct lending, called the Gordon-Goodling effort "possibly the most irrelevant amendment in the 103rd Congress." But Goodling said, "I never offered anything I thought was irrelevant in my life." He said he expected that because his amendment was agreed to by voice vote and later by a roll call vote of 397-28, the reconciliation conferees would not accept the House plan on direct lending. *(Vote 308, p. 74-H)*

In the end, the reconciliation bill left the existing student loan program in place but provided for a direct-loan program that was expected to account for at least half the new student loans within five years. *(Direct loans, p. 410)*

Some lobbyists speculated that Ford agreed to accept the amendment because he did not have the votes to oppose it. Both the Conservative Democratic Forum and the Congressional Black Caucus urged their members to support the Gordon-Goodling amendment. The United Negro College Fund had recently announced its opposition to direct lending, saying it was concerned, in part, that the Education Department could not administer the program.

SENATE COMMITTEE

The Senate Appropriations Committee on Sept. 14 approved a version of HR 2518 that did not contain the limit on abortions paid for by Medicaid (S Rept 103-143). The committee approved the $256.7 billion bill 27-1, with Phil Gramm, R-Texas, casting the only dissenting vote.

Tom Harkin, D-Iowa, chairman of the Labor-HHS Appropriations Subcommittee, had removed all abortion-restricting language from the Senate measure before the subcommittee considered and approved it by voice vote earlier the same day.

Don Nickles, R-Okla., considered tackling the abortion issue in committee, but Appropriations Committee Chairman Robert C. Byrd, D-W.Va., suggested that he wait until the bill was on the floor. Byrd said he had the votes in committee to beat Nickles.

Two of the three women senators on the Appropriations Committee — Patty Murray, D-Wash., and Barbara A. Mikulski, D-Md. — said they intended to see that the abortion restrictions stayed out of the bill. "We believe we have enough votes to win our position," Mikulski said. Mikulski would not say how many votes she had, but she needed only a simple majority — 51 — to win.

Financing Social Programs

Harkin noted that Clinton had requested $72.5 billion for the discretionary programs under the subcommittee's jurisdiction — more than $5 billion beyond what the panel had to work with. "It's been a very tough year for us," he said. "We got a size 12 foot in a size 10 shoe."

Harkin said he recommended eliminating 13 Education Department programs by zeroing out their appropriations. But most of them were extremely small, including the Student Literacy and Mentoring Corps, which received $5 million in fiscal 1993; Howard University construction grants, which also received about $5 million in fiscal 1993; and the Blue Ribbon Schools program to reward top

The History of Hyde

In the first years after it was legalized in 1973, abortion was classified as a "medically necessary service." Accordingly, the law required Medicaid to cover the cost of that service. Because Medicaid was jointly funded by the federal government and the states, the states also had to share the cost.

On June 24, 1976, Rep. Henry J. Hyde, R-Ill., first successfully offered an amendment on the House floor forbidding federal dollars from paying for abortions or for promoting or encouraging abortions.

Later, in a House-Senate conference on the appropriations bill that paid for what was then the Department of Health, Education and Welfare (later the Department of Health and Human Services), a compromise was worked out that became known as the Hyde amendment.

At the time, the Hyde amendment prohibited Medicaid, the federal-state health program for the poor, from paying for an abortion except when the woman's life was in danger. But on Oct. 1, 1976, one day after the bill became law, U.S. District Judge John F. Dooling Jr. issued an injunction keeping the Hyde prohibition from taking effect. The injunction was lifted Aug. 4, 1977, following three Supreme Court decisions (*Beal v. Doe, Maher v. Doe* and *Poelker v. Doe*). The number of Medicaid-financed abortions then dropped from about 300,000 a year to a few thousand.

While the courts were deciding whether the Hyde language was constitutional, Congress continued its fine-tuning. After a bruising, months-long battle, the House and Senate agreed on Dec. 7, 1977, to relax the Hyde language by permitting Medicaid abortions not only to save a woman's life but also in cases of rape or incest or when a woman would sustain severe and lasting physical damage by carrying a pregnancy to term.

In 1978, President Jimmy Carter included the Hyde ban in his budget, legitimizing Democratic support for the position despite the party platform supporting abortion rights.

On June 30, 1980, in *Harris v. McRae*, the Supreme Court ruled 5-4 that the original Hyde amendment was indeed constitutional. Under pressure from newly elected President Ronald Reagan, Congress in 1981 went back to the original Hyde language, prohibiting Medicaid abortions except to save a woman's life. That language had been routinely enacted into law every year since.

On June 30, 1993, the House voted to change the Hyde amendment yet again — restoring exceptions for rape and incest. Hyde himself offered the amendment, calculating that the change was necessary to preserve the broader restriction. "I didn't think the votes were there anymore for a straight ban on abortion funding," he said, "but the formulation including rape and incest . . . was the correct one."

On Sept. 28, the Senate voted to accept the House language, which was enacted in the fiscal 1994 Labor-HHS appropriations bill (HR 2518 — PL 103-112). *(1976 Almanac, p. 790; 1977 Almanac, p. 295; 1980 almanac, p. 7-A; 1981 Almanac, p. 331)*

schools, which received $879,000 in fiscal 1993.

Despite the nicks in those programs, education lobbyists said Harkin's bill went a long way toward restoring student aid cuts made by the House.

The House, for example, had cut spending below fiscal 1993 levels for Federal Supplemental Educational Opportunity Grants, the federal work-study program, the Perkins loan program and the State Student Incentive Grant program. All of those student aid programs were campus-based and distinct from the existing guaranteed student loan program — renamed the Federal Family Education Loan program — which was a mandatory spending program available to all students who met the eligibility criteria.

The Senate maintained the fiscal 1993 spending levels for each of those programs except Perkins loans.

The Senate committee recommended covering $188 million of the $1.2 billion shortfall in the Pell grant program. The House had opted to pay off $415 million. Since the House vote, Congress had provided $341 million to help reduce the shortfall as part of a supplemental spending bill (HR 2118 — PL 103-50) that cleared July 1.

The House had cut the maximum Pell grant from $2,300 to $2,250. But the Department of Education told the Senate that it discovered it could maintain $2,300 grants with the $6.3 billion the House proposed to appropriate for fiscal 1994. The Senate also recommended $6.3 billion for Pell grants.

"Given the restrictive funding picture that we're under, we think the Senate did a good job," said Susan Frost, executive director of the Committee for Education Funding, which lobbied Congress for education money.

Chapter 1, the compensatory education program for the disadvantaged, received by far the largest federal appropriation for elementary and secondary education. The Senate recommended $7 billion for fiscal 1994 — below the administration's $7.1 billion request, but above the $6.7 billion provided in fiscal 1993.

The Senate bill also included money for two of Clinton's top legislative initiatives. It provided $116 million for Clinton's Goals 2000 school reform proposal to provide grants to states. The House appropriated $100 million, while Clinton had asked for $420 million. The Senate measure also provided $100 million for Clinton's school-to-work transition program, split between the departments of Labor and Education. The House provided $68 million, while the administration had asked for $270 million.

On the health front, the Senate committee recommended a 6.1 percent increase in spending for NIH, bringing the total to almost $11 billion; the House bill allowed for a 5.9 percent increase.

Clinton had also made a big effort to spotlight his goal to immunize all children against childhood diseases. The Senate bill included $554 million for that program, $213 million more than the fiscal 1993 level.

SENATE FLOOR

The Senate passed the spending bill on Sept. 29 by a vote of 82-17. *(Vote 295, p. 38-S)*

But first, in an embarrassing defeat for the five Democratic women members, senators overwhelmingly refused to allow the federal government to help pay for abortions for poor women in most circumstances.

The vote came Sept. 28 on an Appropriations Committee amendment to strike the House language in the bill

barring Medicaid from paying for abortions except in cases of pregnancy due to rape and incest and when the life of the woman was in danger. Senators rejected the amendment, 40-59. *(Vote 290, p. 38-S)*

The language on Medicaid abortions in both bills was an incremental step forward for supporters of funding for the procedure. But it was a cold shower for abortion rights activists. "It was a rout, it is a disaster," said Susan A. Cohen, a senior associate with the Alan Guttmacher Institute, a reproductive health research group. "It's a disaster for poor women that Congress, on the eve of making real progress on health-care reform, said poor women don't have the same rights as everybody else."

The abortion fight was led by Mikulski and the four new Democratic women in the Senate — Murray, Carol Moseley-Braun of Illinois, and Barbara Boxer and Dianne Feinstein, both of California.

In a meeting at the White House a week before the vote, the five senators told Clinton that they intended to try to eliminate all restrictions on Medicaid abortions. The senators later said they were worried that if they offered a compromise and lost, it would hurt attempts to insure abortion on a universal health-care plan.

"We knew it was a long shot," said Mikulski when the vote was over. She called it a temporary setback.

Altogether, 21 Democrats voted against dropping all Medicaid abortion restrictions. Among Republicans, 38 of 44 voted for restrictions, including both GOP women — Kay Bailey Hutchison of Texas and Nancy Landon Kassebaum of Kansas.

Floor debate on the bill began Sept. 23.

In action not related to the abortion fight, Nickles complained that appropriators had prohibited the Labor Department from putting regulations into effect that would allow the use of "helpers" on federally contracted construction projects covered by the Davis-Bacon Act. The Davis-Bacon Act required that workers on federal construction sites be paid the area's prevailing wage. Nickles said the regulations would allow minorities and other low-skill workers entree into the higher-wage construction jobs. But unions complained that the regulations would result in reduced wages. The Senate voted 60-39 to retain existing law. *(Vote 289, p. 38-S)*

In other action, the Senate agreed, 95-3, to an amendment by Frank R. Lautenberg, D-N.J., to require federally financed child-care facilities to set policies to protect children from secondhand smoke. *(Vote 291, p. 38-S)*

Senators rejected, 25-72, an amendment by John McCain, R-Ariz., to freeze spending for the Corporation for Public Broadcasting by cutting $27.4 million from the bill. *(Vote 292, p. 38-S)*

The Senate agreed, 97-0, to an amendment by Alfonse M. D'Amato, R-N.Y., expressing the sense of the Senate that the Justice Department should conduct a civil rights investigation into the 1991 Crown Heights riots in New York and the related Aug. 19, 1991, murder of Yankel Rosenbaum, a student from Australia. *(Vote 293, p. 38-S)*

Jesse Helms, R-N.C., won adoption of an amendment to prohibit the criminally insane from receiving Social Security benefits while in public institutions. Senators agreed to the amendment, 94-4. *(Vote 294, p. 38-S)*

FINAL ACTION

With both chambers in agreement on the hot-button abortion issue, House and Senate conferees easily wrapped up work on a $256.3 billion Labor-HHS bill Oct. 5 (H Rept 103-275).

The House quickly adopted the conference report Oct. 7 by a vote of 311-115. With almost no discussion, the Senate on Oct. 18 also adopted the conference report, 80-15, clearing the bill for the president. *(House vote 486, p. 118-H; Senate vote 315, p. 41-S)*

The conference report provided $10.9 billion in new budget authority for the Department of Labor, a drop from the $12.3 billion Congress provided in fiscal 1993.

The total for the Department of Health and Human Services was $215.8 billion in fiscal 1994, up from $210.9 billion in fiscal 1993. And the total for the Department of Education was $28.8 billion in fiscal 1994, up from $28.1 billion in fiscal 1993.

Conferees spent the bulk of their time debating how to get the National Cancer Institute to conduct a study of cancer and the environment in two counties on Long Island, New York. D'Amato wanted to require the cancer institute to conduct the study by writing the requirement into bill language — a practice known as earmarking. D'Amato said that the study had already been approved in a bill (S 1 — PL 103-43) reauthorizing the National Institutes of Health. *(NIH, p. 357)*

"We have hysteria on Long Island," D'Amato said, due to reports that pesticides used on potato fields could be causing high cancer rates. "I don't want to wait and see if they do the study; I want to mandate the study."

With House Appropriations Committee Chairman Natcher vigorously opposed to such earmarks, and the conference spent more than an hour discussing whether to require the study or to strongly urge the action through report language.

Sen. Connie Mack, R-Fla., said it was difficult to argue about earmarks and cancer when his brother Michael had died of cancer after a 12-year fight; his mother was a breast cancer survivor; his daughter was a survivor of cervical cancer; his wife was a breast cancer survivor; and he was diagnosed with and treated for melanoma, the same type of cancer that killed his brother.

Despite the emotional shock of Mack's statement, other members were not convinced, and D'Amato ultimately bowed to Natcher's wish for strong report language.

Members also argued strenuously over whether to require the National Collegiate Athletic Association (NCAA) to contribute money to the National Youth Sports program, which financed summer sports programs for disadvantaged children from the ages of 10 to 16 at colleges around the country.

The House bill included $12 million for the program; the Senate bill, as approved in committee, would have provided $5 million. On the Senate floor, Harkin and Dennis DeConcini, D-Ariz., agreed to a compromise, appropriating $9.4 million, the same as in fiscal 1993. The compromise provided that if the NCAA, which helped run the program, contributed $1.3 million, Congress would match that amount, bringing the total to $12 million.

The compromise drew criticism from conferees who said it would impose too great a burden on the NCAA. Rep. Louis Stokes, D-Ohio, said the program had helped many poor children who might never visit a college campus otherwise. Sen. Slade Gorton, R-Wash., said, "We should be thanking the NCAA and helping them in any way we can." Harkin then agreed with Gorton to a second compromise, requiring the NCAA to put up $750,000 for the program to receive $12 million. ■

Labor/HHS/Education Provisions

For the first time, the bill (HR 2518 — PL 103-112) for the departments of Labor, Health and Human Services (HHS), and Education was the largest of the 13 regular appropriations bills. Three-quarters of the $256.3 billion measure funded entitlement programs over which appropriators had little control. As in past years, an issue that had little to do with money — abortion — dominated debate on the bill. Appropriators and other members of Congress had long fought over the circumstances under which Medicaid, the federal-state health program for the poor, should pay for abortions. In the fiscal 1994 bill, abortion rights supporters got the restriction on abortion funding relaxed slightly, allowing funding in cases of rape and incest cases, as well as when a woman's life was endangered.

Following are the provisions of the bill, as enacted:

DEPARTMENT OF LABOR

Employment and Training Services

The Labor Department's Employment and Training Administration oversaw job-training and related skills programs for dislocated and economically disadvantaged workers, mainly through the 1982 Job Training Partnership Act (JTPA) (PL 97-300).

The bill appropriated $5 billion for JTPA, money that paid for a "program year" running from July 1, 1994, through June 30, 1995, rather than the traditional fiscal year that ran from Oct. 1 to the following Sept. 30. The money went to consortiums of business and local governments that acted as private industry councils that planned the job training programs and contracted with job training providers.

Also under JTPA was the Job Corps, established during President Lyndon B. Johnson's War on Poverty in the mid-1960s to provide remedial education and job skills to disadvantaged youths. The bill set aside $1 billion of the JTPA appropriation for the Job Corps, including $126.6 million to build and expand residential Job Corps centers.

JTPA enjoyed bipartisan support, but some lawmakers complained that it had unnecessarily provided assistance to many skilled people who did not need government help to find a job. Labor Secretary Robert B. Reich had said he was rethinking the entire job training system for dislocated workers and for young people who were leaving high school and not moving on to college.

Reich's school-to-work proposal was pending in Congress (HR 2884, S 1361), and appropriators had set aside $50 million for the Department of Labor to spend on the program if it was enacted, as well as $50 million for the Department of Education.

Beyond JTPA, the bill included $410.5 million for the Community Service Employment for Older Americans program, which provided about 65,000 jobs for low-income elderly people in hospitals, libraries and other community facilities.

And it appropriated $888.3 million to pay for grants to states for summer youth employment and training for the summer of 1994 and to augment money previously provided to pay for summer jobs during the summer of 1993. This money was to help about 655,000 young people obtain work experience, remedial education and supportive services. The program was aimed at economically disadvantaged young people between the ages of 14 and 21. Participants received the minimum wage.

Jobless Benefits

The bill appropriated $2.5 billion in discretionary spending for the administration of the state unemployment benefits system. The money went to pay for the equivalent of 50,300 full-time state unemployment workers. State workers expected to handle 6 million employer tax accounts, 22.6 million initial unemployment claims, a total of 170.8 million weeks of claimed benefits and 1.3 million unemployment appeals in fiscal 1994.

Altogether, about $24 billion in regular unemployment benefits — financed by the Federal Unemployment Tax Act of 1939 (PL 76-379) and state unemployment taxes — would be passed out in fiscal 1994.

Under existing law, states provided up to 26 weeks of benefits to unemployed workers, with benefits averaging $176 weekly. The average jobless worker collected benefits for 16.4 weeks.

The federal government also provided emergency unemployment compensation for people who exhausted their state benefits before finding a job.

Appropriators advanced $2.2 billion to a trust fund handling payments for emergency unemployment benefits. The federal government expected to pay $2.6 billion in emergency benefits in fiscal 1994, under the terms of a bill (HR 3167 — PL 103-152) to continue the program through Feb. 5, 1994.

Employment Standards

The bill appropriated $237.2 million for the Employment Standards Administration, charged with administering many of the federal government's laws that protected workers' rights. These included the Fair Labor Standards Act of 1938 (PL 75-718), which set the minimum wage and other working conditions, and the Immigration Reform and Control Act of 1986 (PL 99-603), which governed the employment of foreign workers.

The agency also enforced non-discrimination laws relating to companies that did business with the federal government and oversaw income-maintenance programs for disabled workers not covered by Social Security.

Pension Benefit Guaranty Corporation

Created in 1974, the Pension Benefit Guaranty Corporation (PBGC) was a government-owned corporation that the secretary of Labor chaired. Its mission was to guarantee pension payments for retirees of companies that went out of business or whose plans failed.

The PBGC was financed primarily by insurance premiums paid by covered companies, assets recovered from terminated underfunded plans for which the PBGC had become trustee, investment earnings, and amounts owed to the PBGC by employers who had terminated underfunded plans. The PBGC could borrow up to $100 million from the Treasury.

Appropriators determined the amount the corporation could spend on administrative expenses, a figure set at $34.2 million for fiscal 1994. Appropriators also set an estimate of what was likely to be spent in fiscal 1994 to cover terminated pension plans — $101.5 million — though the estimate did not prohibit more money from being spent.

Occupational Safety and Health

The bill appropriated $297.2 million for the Occupational Safety and Health Administration (OSHA), which set and enforced standards to protect workers from health and safety dangers on the job. It also gathered statistics about on-the-job injuries and illnesses and aided states in administering and enforcing their related programs.

Bureau of Labor Statistics

The bill provided $333.9 million for the Bureau of Labor Statistics, the federal agency that collected and analyzed data, including unemployment rates and the Consumer Price Index, which measured changes in retail prices.

Mine Safety/Black Lung Benefits

The Labor Department was also responsible for ensuring the safety of workers in the nation's mines. The bill appropriated $195 million for the Mine Safety and Health Administration, which set

health and safety standards for, and conducted inspections in, the nation's mines. The department also oversaw the Black Lung Disability Trust Fund, an entitlement program for afflicted coal miners and their families. Financing for the program, estimated to cost $1 billion in fiscal 1994, came from an excise tax on coal, payments made by mine operators and contributions from the U.S. Treasury. Appropriators also advanced $350 million to a trust fund for black lung benefits.

DEPARTMENT OF HEALTH AND HUMAN SERVICES

The Department of Health and Human Services (HHS) administered programs that touched the lives of virtually every American.

Almost 96 percent of the nation's work force contributed a portion of each paycheck for Social Security retirement benefits. And 41.5 million people collected benefits averaging $589 a month from Social Security.

With some overlap, Medicare and Medicaid, health insurance programs for the elderly and the poor, respectively, served about 100 million people. Indirectly, almost everyone was affected by medical research underwritten by the National Institutes of Health or by the Food and Drug Administration's regulation of food and medicine.

HHS also administered programs for the poor, including Aid to Families With Dependent Children, or AFDC, the principal federal-state welfare program, and Head Start, for preschoolers.

With a budget estimated at $708 billion for fiscal 1994, HHS was by far the government's largest single agency, accounting for more than one-third of the total federal budget. HHS' budget was more than twice the Defense Department's budget of $280 billion.

Most of HHS' money, however, was not included in the department's annual appropriations bill. Spending for the Food and Drug Administration (FDA), for example, was by tradition provided in the Agriculture appropriations bill (HR 2493 — PL 103-111). (FDA was part of that department until 1940.)

Spending for most of the department's two largest programs — Medicare and Social Security — did not appear in the Labor-HHS bill either. More than half the department's budget — an estimated $410 billion in fiscal 1994 — was for Social Security retirement and disability benefits. An additional $103 billion was for the hospital portion of Medicare.

Both programs had permanent appropriations and were financed directly from the proceeds of the 7.65 percent payroll tax paid by workers and their employers, which was paid into three special trust funds.

By contrast, three-quarters of the amount needed to finance Medicare's Part B, which covered physician and other outpatient costs, appeared in the bill. For fiscal 1994, that was estimated to require $45.1 billion in appropriations. The remaining 25 percent was financed by monthly premiums that beneficiaries paid for the optional program, which was a permanent appropriation.

MANDATORY PROGRAMS

Most of the $215.8 billion in the fiscal 1994 bill for the department was for "mandatory" programs, over which appropriators had limited authority.

Appropriators, for example, had little leeway over spending levels for "capped entitlements." These were programs in which money was made available, mostly to states, according to an eligibility formula, with limits.

Because state officials knew from year to year exactly how much they were eligible to receive, they could more accurately plan budgets than if they were dependent upon the uncertainty of the regular appropriations process. States generally had to match with their own money what the federal government provided. Matching did not always occur, and in that case, the federal money was not spent.

Under traditional entitlement programs, such as Medicare, the government paid for anyone who qualified, and money was appro-

priated according to eligibility and price estimates. Caps for the programs, as well as basic eligibility requirements, were determined by authorizing committees, primarily the Ways and Means Committee and the Energy and Commerce Committee in the House, and the Finance Committee in the Senate.

Among the major capped entitlements in the bill were:

▸ **Social Services Block Grant, Title XX of the Social Security Act** ($2.8 billion cap). States could use the money for services, including child care and aid to the homebound elderly, that were aimed at helping the poor or disabled become self-sufficient. The money was distributed according to population, and states had great leeway over what services they provided.

▸ **Job Opportunities and Basic Skills Program (JOBS)** ($1.1 billion cap). The 1988 welfare overhaul law (PL 100-485) required states to put into effect JOBS education and training programs in an effort to move adult welfare recipients into full-time jobs. About 500,000 AFDC recipients participated in a JOBS program every month.

▸ **Child care for families** ($300 million cap). Congress created this new program in 1990 as part of an omnibus child-care bill folded into the fiscal 1990 budget-reconciliation bill (PL 101-508). Money was distributed to states to provide child care for families with jobs who would otherwise need welfare without the government-financed child care.

▸ **Family support and preservation** ($60 million cap). The 1993 reconciliation bill (PL 103-66) created a new capped entitlement to help keep troubled families together. The initiative sprang from concern that while the federal government provided considerable financial resources to remove children from troubled homes and place them in foster care, it offered relatively little assistance to help families overcome a crisis and stay together.

The bill also included money for traditional entitlement programs, which required the government to spend as much as it took to assist all those who qualified. Amounts were determined largely according to estimates. Among the biggest:

▸ **Medicare Part B.** The bill appropriated $45.1 billion for the optional part of Medicare, which underwrote some physician and outpatient care for 34 million elderly and disabled beneficiaries. Under law, the federal government paid 75 percent of Part B costs; beneficiary premiums paid the rest.

▸ **Medicaid.** The bill provided $91.1 billion for the federal share of Medicaid, the federal-state health program for the poor. Following tradition, that total included money for the first quarter of fiscal 1995, which amounted to $26.6 billion. Appropriators included money for the start of the following fiscal year for some programs serving the poor in case the appropriations bill was tied up in controversy and Congress was unable to clear the bill before the fiscal year ended. Medicaid was to provide grants to states for the medical care of more than 34 million low-income people in fiscal 1994. Total federal and state Medicaid outlays had increased at an average annual rate of 22 percent per year, from $32.7 billion in fiscal 1989 to a projected $88.9 billion in fiscal 1994, according to HHS.

States were required to provide certain basic services to all Medicaid recipients. Those included inpatient and outpatient hospital care, health screening services to children under 21, physician services and nursing facility services to people 21 and older.

Congress prohibited Medicaid from paying for abortions unless the life of the woman was in danger or the pregnancy resulted from rape or incest. This was a change from existing law that dated to 1981, which allowed Medicaid to pay only for abortions to save the life of the woman. The change was proposed by anti-abortion lawmakers who wanted to undercut abortion rights supporters who were pushing to allow Medicaid to cover all abortions, regardless of the circumstance. Despite the limitations placed on Medicaid abortions by Congress, states that wished to pay the total cost of abortions could spend their own money to do so; currently 13 states paid for most abortions under Medicaid. The 31 states that prohibited Medicaid abortions, except to save the life of the woman, would have to allow them in cases of rape and incest, since federal law set the minimum standard for Medicaid services.

▶ **Aid to Families With Dependent Children.** The bill provided $16.1 billion for the federal share of AFDC, the principal federal-state welfare program. That included spending for the first quarter of fiscal 1995. As of July 1993, nearly 5 million families — more than 14 million individuals — were beneficiaries of the program. The average weekly benefit was $375 per family. The bill provided an additional $2.5 billion for adjunct programs, among them child care for families in the JOBS program, and state and local welfare administration.

▶ **Supplemental Security Income.** The bill appropriated $27 billion for Supplemental Security Income (SSI), the federal welfare program for low-income aged, blind and disabled people. That amount included spending for the first quarter of fiscal 1995. The maximum federal benefit was $447 per month for an individual and $671 per month for a couple as of January 1994; the average benefit was $324 a month. Nationwide, about 43 percent of all SSI recipients also received a state supplement to the federal payment. Payments were to go to an estimated 6.3 million people in 1994, an increase from 5.8 million in 1993.

▶ **Foster care and adoption assistance.** The bill appropriated $3 billion for foster care and adoption assistance programs; the federal government and the states jointly financed both kinds of programs. The federal government helped states pay foster-care costs of more than 245,000 children removed from their homes due to abuse or neglect. These were children who would have qualified for welfare if they lived at home. The adoption assistance program supported efforts to find permanent homes for more than 90,000 difficult-to-place youngsters.

▶ **Child support enforcement.** This program provided services aimed at locating absent parents, establishing paternity, and establishing and enforcing support obligations. For fiscal 1994, the federal government was to pay state and local agencies $896 million to collect overdue child support payments; the federal government paid two-thirds of the cost. In fiscal 1993, these efforts brought in an estimated $8.9 billion in child support. Of that amount, $2.6 billion was collected on behalf of AFDC families and returned to state and federal agencies. The other payments went to custodial parents.

Although they had little say about overall totals for entitlement programs, appropriators had some authority to allocate specific sums for set purposes within those programs. Two of the most prominent examples were:

▶ **Medicare contractors.** The bill allocated $1.6 billion to pay insurance companies that processed claims for Medicare.

▶ **Social Security administrative costs.** The bill allowed the Social Security Administration to spend up to $5.5 billion to run its programs. The money, taken from the Social Security trust funds, paid for operation of Social Security old-age and disability programs and for SSI.

DISCRETIONARY PROGRAMS

Research and Data Programs

By far the largest programs within HHS' discretionary pot paid for research into health and social services. Many programs existed as well to gather, analyze and disseminate data used to made policy and other decisions.

▶ **National Institutes of Health.** The $10.96 billion appropriated for the 21 research establishments that made up the National Institutes of Health (NIH) accounted for more than 15 percent of the bill's discretionary program total. Clinton asked for $10.7 billion, up from fiscal 1993's $10.3 billion.

NIH had many champions in Congress and long had been a bipartisan favorite of the Labor-HHS Appropriations subcommittees; NIH's appropriation was regularly greater than the president's request. But strings often were attached to the congressional largess. The House report on the bill devoted 26 of its 243 pages to directives for NIH to follow; the Senate report's NIH section consumed 53 of its 256 pages.

The directives took the form of recommendations; House Appropriations Committee Chairman William H. Natcher, D-Ky.,

steadfastly opposed statutory earmarks in this bill. In conference committee negotiations on the bill, Sen. Alfonse M. D'Amato, R-N.Y., tried to get money appropriated to the National Cancer Institute that would require it to conduct a study of cancer and the environment in two counties in New York, but he settled for language that "directs" the institute to become "more aggressive" in pursuing such research.

The bill contained $2.1 billion for the cancer institute, a 5.3 percent, $103.9 million increase over fiscal 1993 for the largest of NIH's divisions. Most of the institutes and centers within NIH received an increase of about 5.2 percent over 1993.

The National Center for Human Genome Research, which had provided money for scientists outside NIH to map out the structure of human DNA, got a 21.3 percent increase to $128.7 million. The extra money allowed NIH to bring some scientists in-house and set up its own genome research project — one designed to coordinate efforts and in part to help stem the drain of scientists leaving NIH.

NIH's Office of the Director received a 22.7 percent increase, to $233.6 million. Programs financed by the office that got major boosts included the women's health initiative, with a $20.1 million increase to $61.3 million, and the minority health initiative, with a $15.7 million increase to $56.5 million. Money from the director's office that went to study AIDS increased $11 million to $24.9 million.

The ADAMHA Reorganization Act (PL 102-321) dismantled the Alcohol, Drug Abuse and Mental Health Administration (ADAMHA) as of Sept. 30, 1992, sending its research functions to NIH and its health-care delivery operations to a new agency, the Substance Abuse and Mental Health Services Administration, in HHS.

Fiscal 1994 was the first year reflecting the change. The three ADAMHA components that became part of NIH — the National Institute of Mental Health, the National Institute on Drug Abuse and the National Institute on Alcohol Abuse and Alcoholism — each received 5.2 percent increases, to $613.4 million, $425.2 million and $185.6 million, respectively.

▶ **Centers for Disease Control and Prevention — research activities.** One of the largest data-gathering programs was to receive $543.3 million for AIDS-related research activities in the Public Health Service's Centers for Disease Control and Prevention. CDC, whose epidemiologists investigated and responded to outbreaks of contagious diseases nationwide, had become one of the federal government's leaders in combating AIDS. It used its AIDS money to help track cases of AIDS and HIV, the AIDS virus; to help finance blood testing, counseling and partner notification programs; and to provide information, education and prevention services. CDC's other functions included preventing disability, injury and such non-contagious diseases as lung cancer.

The bill also appropriated $54.5 million for the CDC's National Center for Health Statistics, which collected, analyzed and disseminated statistics on health, illness and disability, in addition to tracking births, deaths, marriages and divorces. The center was also authorized to receive an additional $28.9 million from other Public Health Service agency budgets.

The National Institute for Occupational Safety and Health received $128.3 million to conduct research and set criteria for standards aimed at reducing on-the-job illness and injury.

CDC got $116.8 million to study tuberculosis and $47.8 million to investigate infectious diseases in general. It got $123 million to prevent chronic and environmental diseases, $34.7 million to prevent lead poisoning and $39.3 million to control injuries. In all, the bill appropriated $2.1 billion for the CDC, much of the rest of which went for the delivery of health-care services (see below).

▶ **Agency for Health Care Policy and Research.** This agency was created in the 1989 budget-reconciliation bill (PL 101-239) to study the effectiveness of medical treatments and the organization, financing and delivery of health-care services. It got $135.4 million in the bill, up $26.4 million from fiscal 1993. The agency also received an additional $13 million from other Public Health Service agencies, as well as $5.8 million from the Medicare trust fund, bringing its total fiscal 1994 budget to $154.4 million.

▶ **Office of Rural Health Policy.** The bill provided $9.4 million for this program — up $5.3 million, or 126 percent, over fiscal 1993 levels. The office coordinated public and private sector research on how best to deliver health care to rural areas.

▶ **National Practitioner Data Bank.** The data bank maintained a nationwide list of physicians, dentists and other health-care practitioners who had been found guilty of malpractice, lost their licenses or otherwise had been professionally sanctioned. The bill appropriated no taxpayer money for the data bank; its $7.5 million cost was expected to be covered by user fees.

Health Delivery Programs

HHS operated a series of programs that distributed large block grants to provide or help states offer health-care services.

▶ **Substance Abuse and Mental Health Services Administration.** The part of ADAMHA that administered programs was known as the Substance Abuse and Mental Health Services Administration (SAMHSA). The agency consisted of three centers: the Center for Mental Health Services, the Center for Substance Abuse Treatment and the Center for Substance Abuse Prevention. Overall, SAMHSA received $2.1 billion through the bill, up 6 percent from the spending on these activities in fiscal 1993 by ADAMHA.

The largest parts of SAMHSA's budget were a $277.9 million mental health block grant and a $1.2 billion substance abuse treatment block grant. These provided money to states to help operate prevention, treatment and rehabilitation programs. Money was allocated according to a formula based on each state's relative wealth, the average age of its residents, how many people lived in urban areas and how much the state received in prior years. Rural legislators had complained that the formula was unfair to their districts. The fiscal 1992 military construction appropriations bill (PL 102-136) required states to spend at least 5 percent of their substance abuse block grants annually to expand services to pregnant women and women with dependent children.

▶ **Health Resources and Services Administration.** This agency provided money for a variety of clinics and grants. It also operated the National Health Service Corps (see below).

The bill appropriated $603.7 million for a network of about 1,500 community health centers that provided primary health care to about 6 million individuals annually, most of them with low incomes or living in areas with shortages of health professionals.

The agency also received $59 million for migrant health centers, which served 555,000 migrant and seasonal farmworkers in 364 sites. The amount was $1.7 million higher than fiscal 1993 levels, and Senate appropriators specified that the extra money went to raise the level of services available at existing centers. More than 80 percent of the migrant health centers also received money under the community health centers program.

The bill provided $63 million for health care for the homeless, distributed to 119 centers serving 525,000 adults and children. Black lung clinics received $4.1 million to diagnose, treat and rehabilitate active and retired coal miners with pulmonary impairments.

▶ **Maternal and Child Health Block Grant.** This was the second-largest of the block grant programs, after the SAMHSA substance abuse block grant (see above), with a fiscal 1994 appropriation of $687 million, up $22.5 million from fiscal 1993. The grant helped state and local health agencies provide services to reduce infant mortality and improve the health of young children.

▶ **Healthy Start.** Clinton requested $100.3 million to continue the Bush administration's controversial initiative to test comprehensive child health-care programs in selected areas with high infant mortality rates, and those programs received $97.5 million, up $18.2 million from 1993. The program served 15 urban and rural communities with infant mortality rates 1.5 to 2.5 times the national average, with the goal of reducing infant mortality by 50 percent over five years. The Appropriations committees indicated that the increase was to go to existing centers.

▶ **Emergency Medical Services for Children.** The bill provided $7.5 million for demonstration grants to study how best to deliver effective pre-hospital care to children.

▶ **Transplantations and trauma.** The bill included $2.7 million to support a registry of organ transplant recipients, the National Organ Procurement and Transplantation Network, along with other activities in support of organ transplants. It also included $4.8 million for states to improve the trauma-care aspects of their own comprehensive health-care delivery plans.

▶ **AIDS services.** In addition to the appropriation for AIDS research, the 1990 Ryan White Comprehensive AIDS Resources Emergency Act (PL 101-381) authorized spending for areas hardest hit by the epidemic as well as money to create networks of comprehensive treatment services for those afflicted with the disease and their families.

The bill appropriated $579.4 million for Ryan White AIDS programs, a 66 percent increase over the fiscal 1993 total of $348 million, but well short of the approximately $880 million designated for AIDS treatment activities in 1990. Of the increase, $22 million was for pediatric AIDS demonstration projects that existed outside the bounds of the programs authorized under the Ryan White Act in previous years. Much of the rest was to pay for up to 10 new centers in 1994.

The bill separately appropriated $7 million for dental services for AIDS patients, which was to be spent in the form of grants to dental schools to help pay for free dental care given to AIDS patients. In the past, the money had come from within the Ryan White Act's appropriation.

▶ **Centers for Disease Control and Prevention — health-care delivery.** The bill gave $99.8 million to CDC's program to prevent sexually transmitted diseases. It gave grants to state and local governments and to private facilities and voluntary health agencies that tracked, treated and prevented diseases such as syphilis.

The bill also gave CDC's immunization programs $528.1 million, an increase of $187.1 million (almost 55 percent) over fiscal 1993. The bulk of the program provided grants to states to vaccinate children against preventable diseases, including measles, mumps and polio. Of the increase, $97 million was to go to improve the vaccine delivery infrastructure because of the belief that it was the lack of access to vaccines — not the lack of vaccines themselves — that kept immunization rates low.

CDC also was to receive $78.1 million for a program to screen women for breast and cervical cancer when they were most treatable.

The bill provided $157.2 million as a preventive health services block grant that CDC would distribute to the states for a variety of purposes, including rodent control, in-school water fluoridation and emergency medical services.

▶ **Family planning.** Appropriators approved $180.9 million for the federal family planning program, Title X of the Public Health Service Act. The family planning program had not been authorized since 1985 because of abortion-related controversies. Nevertheless, it had obtained appropriations each year. The administration requested $208 million for the program. The money went not only to states but also to private nonprofit agencies, such as affiliates of Planned Parenthood Federation of America.

▶ **Vaccine Injury Compensation.** The bill provided $197.2 million — $84.2 million of which was from the Vaccine Injury Compensation Program Trust Fund — to pay individuals who were harmed by vaccines administered before Sept. 30, 1992. The money in the trust fund came from a per-dose excise tax on selected vaccines. The bill also provided $3 million from the trust fund to pay administrative expenses.

Education and Training Programs

HHS devoted considerable money and other resources to education and training programs for health and social service professionals. It was impossible to identify a definitive amount, because money for many programs was included within larger appropriations that provided services or paid for research, as well as training. Other programs, such as the National Health Service Corps, accomplished dual purposes: They paid to train health professionals, who then generated services when those professionals paid off their debts by practicing in medically underserved areas.

▶ **Health professions.** The health professions program was the largest of the efforts aimed exclusively at training. The bill appropriated $282.7 million for 21 separate programs for education of doctors, dentists and other health professionals. Most programs were aimed at encouraging health professionals to enter primary care fields, such as family medicine and geriatrics, and at increasing the number of minority professionals.

Included was $750,000 for a demonstration project to study how chiropractors and "so-called traditional schools of medicine" — according to the Senate report — could work together. The Senate had wanted $1 million for the effort, while the House and the Clinton administration had not asked for any money.

The bill appropriated $63.5 million for nurse training programs, which enabled nursing schools to recruit low-income and minority applicants and to offer advanced training in specialties such as anesthesia and obstetrics.

Presidents Ronald Reagan and George Bush had tried to eliminate most spending for the health professions programs (Bush sought $84 million for fiscal 1992, which Congress increased to $235 million). But Clinton showed a decided interest in the programs, recommending $9.6 million more than the bill provided.

▶ **Health Education Assistance Loans Program (HEAL).** The bill provided $26.5 million to HEAL to guarantee repayment of loans non-federal lenders gave to students in the health professions.

▶ **National Health Service Corps.** This program, part of the Health Resources and Services Administration (above), paid for the education of doctors and other health professionals in exchange for their practicing on Indian reservations or in underserved rural and inner-city areas. The corps received $126.7 million in fiscal 1994.

▶ **AIDS education and training.** This program got $16.4 million in fiscal 1994. The 17 projects included in the program were expected to train 85,000 caregivers in 1993.

Social Service Delivery Programs

Although its health programs were considerably larger, HHS also oversaw programs that provided social services to specific groups of people. These were separate from HHS programs aimed at those with low incomes, although beneficiaries generally had to meet other specific requirements, such as being disabled or elderly.

▶ **Administration on Aging.** The largest such programs were those operated by the Administration on Aging under the 1965 Older Americans Act (PL 89-73). The bill appropriated $871.3 million for the programs, which included money to help run 6,000 senior citizen centers, to provide hot meals both in seniors' homes and in group settings, for legal assistance, and to provide homemaker, home-health and other services needed by frail elderly people to continue living at home. Among the services the money provided were more than 250 million meals and more than 50 million rides, plus 700,000 visits and phone calls to the frail elderly.

▶ **Child-care grants.** The bill appropriated $892.7 million for the child-care grant program Congress approved as part of the 1990 budget-reconciliation bill (PL 101-508). States had to use almost 25 percent of their allotment on early childhood development programs, before- and after-school child-care services, and improving the quality of child care. Most of the rest of the money was to be used for direct child-care services for low-income families.

▶ **Family violence.** This program helped states prevent family violence and provide immediate shelter and related assistance to victims. It received $27.7 million; states spent more than twice that amount of their own money on family violence prevention.

▶ **Child abuse.** Several programs designed to identify, prevent and treat child abuse and neglect received a total of $44.4 million in fiscal 1994. The money went for state grants, technical assistance, research and demonstration programs. In calendar 1991, these programs paid to investigate 1.8 million reports of alleged child abuse and neglect involving about 2.7 million children. Evidence of mistreatment was confirmed for about 863,000 children.

▶ **Runaway and homeless youths.** The bill appropriated $62.9 million to address the needs of runaway and homeless youths and their families. The program included $36.1 million to pay for grants to states, localities and nonprofit agencies for runaway and homeless youth centers. It provided $12.2 million to pay for temporary shelter and services for youths age 16 to 20 who had no safe alternatives. The bill allocated $14.6 million for a drug education and prevention program for runaway and homeless youths.

In all, the program helped finance 358 runaway and homeless youth centers and more than 1,000 volunteer host homes nationwide, who helped about 63,000 runaway and homeless youths each year. About 56 percent of the parents of these youths also received services from the program. And a national hotline for runaways received more than 10,000 calls monthly.

▶ **Child welfare services.** This $294.6 million program, Title IV-B of the Social Security Act, which was created in 1968, gave states money for services aimed at keeping troubled families together.

▶ **Developmental disabilities.** The bill included $115.2 million for several programs to promote the independence and protect the rights of those with developmental disabilities, including mental retardation and cerebral palsy. The program was expected to serve nearly 4 million people in fiscal 1994.

▶ **Protection and advocacy for the mentally ill.** This was a $22 million program within the Substance Abuse and Mental Health Services Administration to ensure protection of the rights of mentally ill individuals while they were in institutions and for 90 days after discharge. Money was allocated to states based on population and per capita income.

Low-Income Programs

Among the largest of the HHS discretionary programs were those aimed at helping the poor become self-sufficient.

▶ **Head Start.** The largest, best-known and most politically popular of these programs, Head Start provided low-income preschoolers with early education, health, nutrition and social services. The bill appropriated $3.3 billion for the program, which began in 1965. Spending for Head Start had increased by more than $2 billion since fiscal 1989, including a $550 million increase since fiscal 1993. The program still enrolled fewer than half of all eligible preschoolers, however. About 715,000 participated in the program in fiscal 1993.

The Clinton administration was seeking to add $8 billion over four years to the program, to fully pay for an estimated 1.4 million eligible disadvantaged children by 1999. The hoped-for increase faced difficulty, however. Some experts questioned whether Head Start children gained lasting benefits from the program, and even its defenders were concerned about the poor quality of staff and facilities at some centers.

The Senate committee report expressed concern about the administration's intention to use the fiscal 1994 increase to expand programs to full-day, 12-month schedules, thereby increasing the future cost of financing Head Start for all eligible children.

In fiscal 1993, grants were awarded to about 1,400 public and private nonprofit agencies. Most Head Start centers offered a half-day of preschool five days a week during the school year, primarily serving 3- and 4-year-olds. About 15 percent of the children attended for a full day, and some continued for two academic years. In addition to preparing children for elementary school, Head Start provided medical and dental screenings, including immunizations, and home visits to help parents with parenting skills and social service needs.

▶ **Low Income Home Energy Assistance Program.** LIHEAP, as it was known, helped low-income families pay heating and cooling bills and weatherize their homes. It was a target for elimination by the Reagan administration and for major cuts by the Bush administration; Frost Belt legislators fought every year to maintain it.

Clinton had given it a better reception. The administration recommended $1.4 billion in advance appropriations for fiscal 1995. (The program was paid for a year in advance to give grantees planning time.) The House balked at advance appropriations on the grounds that the coming year's budget allocation was unknown. The Senate recommended $1.5 billion. The conference committee generally agreed with the Senate, providing just under $1.5 billion as an advance appropriation for the 1994-95 program year.

The bill provided an additional $600 million that would be

available only if the president declared the funding to be an emergency expenditure under federal budget law and thus exempt from spending caps; the amount was not included in the appropriation for the program. About 70 percent of LIHEAP money paid for home energy heating and winter crisis assistance such as weather-related and supply shortage emergencies. In fiscal 1992, 6.2 million households received heating and winter-crisis assistance, with an average benefit of $190 each.

▶ **Community Services Block Grant.** This was another budget-cutting target of the Bush administration kept alive by Congress and supported by the Clinton administration. The fiscal 1994 Senate committee report noted with pleasure that "for the first time in nearly a decade, an administration recommended funding" for this block grant. The administration requested $372 million, the amount received in fiscal 1993; the bill provided $385.5 million.

Like Head Start, it was one of President Johnson's Great Society social programs. The block grant primarily provided money to local community action agencies that offered services aimed at helping the poor become self-sufficient. In proposing to end the program, Bush officials had said "basic reforms had been institutionalized" and appropriations increased for other programs with the same goal.

The bill also financed several discretionary programs among community services, including $12 million for the National Youth Sports Program, which provided low-income youth recreation and counseling opportunities through the National Collegiate Athletic Association.

▶ **Refugee and Entrant Assistance Program.** This program helped states offset social service and other costs associated with helping settle refugees during their first months in the United States. About 122,000 refugees were expected to arrive in the United States in fiscal 1994. The program financed cash and medical assistance, preventive health, job-training and English-tutoring programs. The bill provided $400 million.

▶ **Comprehensive Child Development Centers.** Designed to provide continuous support services for low-income children and their families from birth until the children entered school, this program received $46.8 million, the same as in fiscal 1993 and the amount requested by Clinton. About 5,000 families participated in the program in fiscal 1993.

DEPARTMENT OF EDUCATION

The Department of Education was created in 1979 (PL 96-88) as a political reward to the nation's teachers for helping elect President Jimmy Carter. The department had a rocky history, however. President Reagan tried to dismantle it during the 1980s. Some education experts said the department had little impact on the quality or content of children's educational experience — particularly since that responsibility rested with state and local governments that spent more than 90 percent of all money going to education.

Generally, the department's mission was to focus its elementary and secondary programs on children who were economically disadvantaged and needed remedial help, and on physically and mentally disabled children needing expensive training. During the previous few years, higher education programs, which were in the process of being reauthorized, included student loans and grants to help cover the cost of trade schools and colleges for those who could not afford tuition.

Education for the Disadvantaged

▶ **Chapter 1.** This was originally Title I of the Elementary and Secondary Education Act of 1965 (PL 89-10). During the Reagan administration, the name was changed to Chapter 1, though Democrats vowed to change the name back again. The bill appropriated $6.9 billion for Chapter 1 to provide states and local school districts with money to help educate disadvantaged children. A school might use the money to hire an extra teacher to work with children having trouble reading, writing or learning math. Some Chapter 1 money was used to help migrant children.

The money was distributed by formula, based on what a state spent per pupil and on the number of school-age children from low-income families. The money went to 95 percent of all school districts to help 5 million students.

Congress was preparing to reauthorize the Elementary and Secondary Education Act in 1994, and a key decision in that reauthorization would be how to distribute the money so that more of it went to the poorest students and school districts. The Clinton administration had proposed allocating 50 percent of the money — up from 10 percent — to high-poverty areas, resulting in a shift of about $500 million away from counties and districts with lower poverty rates.

▶ **Even Start.** Of the $6.9 billion for Chapter 1, the Even Start program was to receive $91.4 million to teach literacy skills to young children and their parents.

Impact Aid

This program received $798.2 million to compensate school districts for the costs of educating children when federal activities had caused increased enrollment or a loss of revenue. For example, a military base in a school district might send hundreds of children to the local schools, but their parents who lived in base housing would not pay the property taxes that helped finance the schools.

During the 1993-94 school year, federal payments were to be made to about 2,500 school districts with 1.8 million eligible children. Impact aid also helped districts damaged by natural disasters.

School Improvement Programs

The department ran several programs to improve the quality of education, particularly in math and science, and to promote drug-free schools. The Chapter 2 block grant program provided grants to state education agencies to improve elementary and secondary education in public and private schools. The money might be used to buy books, train teachers and finance programs to help students at risk of failing school. Money also went to the Eisenhower mathematics and science education state grant program, which paid to improve teachers' skills and the quality of instruction. The programs were given a combined $1.4 billion.

▶ **Chapter 2.** Of that amount, $369.5 million went to state block grants for Chapter 2. That was a cut from the $435.5 million appropriated in fiscal 1993. Congress and the administration had begun chipping away at the Chapter 2 program in favor of getting states to participate in Clinton's new education improvement program, called Goals 2000.

States received Chapter 2 money according to their share of the population age 5 to 17, and they had to pass 80 percent of the block grant money to local education agencies. Local school districts had complete discretion in using the money for eligible activities.

▶ **Drug-Free Schools.** Appropriators set aside $487.2 million for the Drug-Free Schools program, which financed prevention education. Of that amount, $20 million was to go to a safe-schools initiative, provided it was authorized by April 1, 1994. If it was not authorized, the money would revert to the Drug-Free schools program. The concept of "safe schools" (S 1125, HR 2455) was to provide grants to schools to train school employees to deal with violence; to provide conflict resolution programs; to provide alternative after-school programs; and to buy and install metal detectors and to hire security guards for schools.

▶ **Eisenhower Mathematics and Science Grants.** One of the most popular school improvement programs was the Eisenhower mathematics and science education state grant program, which received $251 million in fiscal 1994. The primary emphasis of the program was on teacher training and improving the quality of instruction in math and science.

Eisenhower grants were awarded by formula on the basis of each state's school-age population and its share of Chapter 1 basic grants. States had to use 75 percent of their grants for elementary and secondary education programs and the remainder for programs conducted by institutions of higher education.

▶ **Inexpensive Book Distribution.** One of the smaller school improvement programs was Inexpensive Book Distribution, which received $10.3 million. It was operated by Reading Is Fundamental, a private nonprofit organization that worked with more than 4,500

local volunteer groups to distribute books to children in low-income families to help motivate them to read. In 1993, about 6.6 million books would be distributed to 2.1 million children.

Goals 2000: Educate America Act

Appropriators provided $155 million for Clinton's school-reform initiative, as well as his school-to-work proposal to help children who did not go on from high school to higher education. The Goals 2000 initiative had to be enacted by April 1, 1994, or the money would be applied to the Pell grant program to reduce its deficit. Of the total amount, $105 million was slated for Goals 2000 and $50 million for the school-to-work program.

The Senate Labor and Human Resources Committee and the House Education and Labor Committee approved the school-to-work bill (HR 2884, S 1361) on Nov. 3, and the House approved it by voice vote on Nov. 15. The House passed the Goals 2000 bill (HR 1804 — H Rept 103-168; S 1150 — S Rept 103-85) on Oct. 13 by 307-118. The Senate had not yet taken it up.

The Goals 2000 bill would write into law seven national education goals and was similar to a program President Bush proposed in 1991. The bill would authorize $427 million, most of which would be awarded to states to improve their elementary and secondary schools.

Each state plan would include a way to create standards of content — or what children should know in English, math and other subjects at certain points in their schooling; a way to assess what students had learned; and ideas for teacher training. States would be encouraged to adopt the national goals but would not have to do so to qualify for grants. The states also would develop "opportunity to learn" standards that would prescribe what a school needed — such as competent teachers or up-to-date textbooks — to expect children to meet the goals and standards.

Bilingual and Immigrant Education

Federal support for bilingual education, at $240.2 million, came in the form of discretionary grants to local school districts to help them pay for the cost of helping students who spoke limited English. In fiscal 1994, bilingual programs would support about 1,080 local projects serving about 357,000 children. Bilingual programs taught English to students and helped them meet grade promotion and graduation requirements. The grants supported a variety of bilingual programs that varied in their use of native language. Within the appropriation, the bill provided $39 million for immigrant education, which provided grants to school districts that had at least 500 immigrant students, or in which those students made up at least 3 percent of current enrollment. The money was to help with the extra costs of educating recently arrived immigrants.

Special Education

This $3.1 billion appropriation went to carry out the Individuals with Disabilities Education Act of 1975 (IDEA) (PL 94-142), which helped states provide all children with disabilities access to a free public education that was appropriate for their needs.
▶ **Grants to states.** The bulk of the money was sent to states in the form of grants, based on the number of disabled children served. Grants to states would total $2.1 billion in fiscal 1994 to help about 5 million children, an increase of about 100,000 children over 1993. The appropriation provided an average of about $437 per child. States had to serve all children age 6 to 17 to be eligible for awards and had to serve all children age 3 to 5 to receive any money for this age group. Youths age 18 to 21 had to be served, except when it would be inconsistent with state law or a court order.
▶ **Chapter 1 handicapped program.** Besides grants to states, the special education appropriation included $116.9 million for the Chapter 1 handicapped program, which was similar to the IDEA program and was in the process of being merged with it.
▶ **Preschool grants.** Another $339.3 million went for preschool grants to help states serve preschool children with disabilities. Under this program, states would receive a combined per-child share of $1,209 for the 3-to-5-year-olds they served.
▶ **Grants for infants and families.** Grants totaling $253.2 mil-

lion in fiscal 1994 would be used to improve school readiness for young children with disabilities. The grants went to states for planning, developing and instituting statewide systems to provide early intervention services to all children with disabilities from birth through 2 years old and their families. States also could use the money to serve infants at risk of developmental delays, such as infants with low birth weights or drug-exposed babies.
▶ **Special purpose programs.** The bill set aside $249.7 million to pay for a variety of research, demonstration, training and technical assistance activities.

Rehabilitation Services, Disability Research

The Rehabilitation Act of 1973 (PL 93-112) included multiple programs to help people with disabilities obtain employment and learn to live independently. Most of the $2.3 billion appropriation went to states in the form of vocational rehabilitation grants. These grants helped pay the cost of job training for people with physical and mental disabilities to help them find work in the future.

Services included vocational evaluation, counseling and guidance, work adjustment, diagnosis and treatment of physical and mental disorders, education and vocational training, job placement, and post-employment services. When a state could not provide services to all eligible people with disabilities who applied, it had to give priority to applicants with the most severe disabilities.
▶ **Supported employment grants.** $34.5 million was set for formula grants to help states develop collaborative programs with public and private nonprofit groups to provide employment services to people with the most severe disabilities.
▶ **Client assistance.** Another $9.5 million was provided to help states inform clients of benefits available to them under the Rehabilitation Act and to ensure the protection of clients' rights in their relationships with the nonprofit groups with which they worked.
▶ **Helen Keller National Center.** Appropriators set aside $6.7 million for the Helen Keller National Center for Deaf-Blind Youth and Adults in Sands Point, N.Y. Tom Harkin, D-Iowa, chairman of the Senate Labor-HHS Appropriations Subcommittee, had a special interest in this field because his brother was deaf.
▶ **National Institute on Disability and Rehabilitation Research.** The bill provided $68.1 million.

Institutions for Persons With Disabilities

▶ **American Printing House for the Blind.** $6.5 million.
▶ **National Technical Institute for the Deaf.** $41.8 million.
▶ **Gallaudet University.** $78.4 million.

Vocational and Adult Education

This $1.5 billion appropriation went to support the Carl D. Perkins Vocational and Applied Technology Education Act of 1990 (PL 101-392) and the Adult Education Act of 1966 (PL 89-750). Most of the money went for basic grants to help states expand and improve vocational education programs. Appropriators ignored Clinton's request to kill two programs that the president said were no longer needed: Consumer and Homemaking Education, which received $34.7 million; and Bilingual Vocational Training, which received $2.9 million.
▶ **Tech-prep.** Of the total, the "tech-prep" program to prepare high school students for postsecondary vocational education received $104.1 million to provide a smooth transition for students between high schools and postsecondary schools.
▶ **Adult Education Act.** States also received $254.6 million in grants under the Adult Education Act to help educationally disadvantaged adults learn basic skills, such as reading and writing, as well as to earn high school equivalency degrees.
▶ **Literacy Training for the Homeless.** The bill set aside $9.6 million to pay for literacy training for the homeless, the amount provided in fiscal 1993.

Student Financial Assistance

The Higher Education Act of 1965, last reauthorized in 1992 (PL 102-325), governed all federal financial aid programs for college, trade

school and graduate students. For fiscal 1994, the bill appropriated $10.3 billion to provide grants, scholarships and loans.

▶ **Pell grants.** The best-known program — financing grants for college and trade school students — was named for Sen. Claiborne Pell, D-R.I., chairman of the Labor and Human Resources Subcommittee on Education, Arts and the Humanities. A total of $6.6 billion was set aside for the program. Eligible students received a maximum $2,300 for the 1994-95 academic year; minimum grants totaled $200. An estimated 4.7 million students would receive grants in 1994-95, most from families earning no more than $20,000 a year.

Over the years, more students had qualified for Pell grants than the Bush administration had expected, primarily because of the 1990-91 recession. The Education Department paid out more money for grants than appropriators had provided, and a shortfall developed. The deficit was estimated at $950 million counting the fiscal 1994 appropriation, which included $270 million intended to reduce it. In fiscal 1993, appropriators provided $671.2 million to reduce the Pell deficit. Congress also included $341 million in a bill cleared July 1 (HR 2118 — PL 103-50), for a total of $611 million to reduce the Pell deficit in fiscal 1994.

▶ **Federal Supplemental Educational Opportunity Grants.** An estimated 994,000 students would receive an average of $745 each to help pay for the cost of college in 1994-95. The bill provided $583.4 million for this program, which required schools to supply at least 25 percent of the cost of all grants. Unlike Pell grants, these grant amounts were determined at the discretion of the school's financial aid administrators. But administrators were required to give priority to students with exceptional need and to Pell grant recipients. Undergraduate students could receive a maximum of $4,000 per academic year.

▶ **Federal work-study.** The bill provided $616.5 million to pay an estimated 714,000 students an average of $1,065 each. This program provided grants to schools to cover as much as 75 percent of the salaries of undergraduate or graduate students working part time, usually in on-campus jobs. The remaining 25 percent was paid by the school or employer.

▶ **Perkins student loans.** Appropriators provided $173 million, down from $180.7 million in fiscal 1993, for this loan program for needy students that was financed jointly by the federal government and participating schools. About 3,127 schools participated, providing a 25 percent match of the appropriation, which went into the school's own revolving Perkins loan fund. The Department of Education determined how much of the total appropriation each school would receive. Each school matched the federal contribution and put all the money into a separate fund that provided the loans to students. Borrowers were charged no interest on these loans while they remained in school, and 5 percent interest after they graduated and began repaying principal. Students repaid their school's loan fund, and the school then recycled the money for other students in later years. In 1993, about 675,000 students borrowed an average of $1,328. The maximum amount a student could borrow in one year was $3,000 for undergraduates and $5,000 for graduate students, with a cumulative loan amount of $30,000. Within the appropriation, $15 million was set aside to cancel loan obligations for people who took jobs teaching in Head Start programs or who worked full time in law enforcement or nursing.

▶ **State student incentive grants.** The Clinton administration proposed to end this program, but appropriators refused. The bill provided $72.4 million, the same as in fiscal 1993, which paid for a dollar-for-dollar federal match to states to provide need-based grants for higher education. The maximum grant was $5,000, although the average grant was about $600 to 242,000 students.

▶ **Direct loans.** The bill provided $22.2 million for the subsidy cost of a new direct student loan program. This was authorized as a demonstration under the 1992 amendments to the Higher Education Act. The demonstration was to allow 500 schools to make direct loans from July 1, 1994, to June 30, 1998. Under direct loans, the federal government would provide the money to the schools for the students.

In academic year 1994-95, direct loans would constitute 4 percent of all federal loans available. The 1993 budget-reconciliation bill (PL 103-66) changed the program beyond a demonstration. In academic year 1995-96, 40 percent of all new student loans would be direct loans, rising to 60 percent in academic year 1998-99.

▶ **Guaranteed student loans.** The federal guaranteed student loan program was designed to give private lenders incentives to provide long-term loans to students. Not only did the government guarantee repayment, for some loans the government also paid interest owed while a student remained in school or until the student could take over the payments.

There were three types of guaranteed student loans. The most popular was the Federal Family Education Loan (formerly known as the Stafford loan), available to needy students at the 91-day Treasury bill interest rate plus 3.1 percentage points — not to exceed 9 percent. Also available were Supplemental Loans for Students (SLS), generally given to graduate and financially independent undergraduate students, and PLUS loans for parents of dependent undergraduates. PLUS and SLS loans were not made based on need, and the federal government did not pay the interest while students were in school. The $2.3 billion fiscal 1994 appropriation covered the cost of subsidies on loans made in 1994 and included the amount expected to be spent over the life of the loans.

▶ **Higher education.** Congress also financed smaller programs designed to improve historically black colleges and universities as well as other postsecondary schools; to improve minority participation in the sciences; to run a student literacy corps promoting community service; and to foster international education and foreign language studies. These programs were to receive $893.7 million in fiscal 1994.

▶ **Howard University.** Congress traditionally provided money to help run Howard University, a historically black university in Washington. For fiscal 1994, the appropriation was $192.7 million.

▶ **Academic facilities loans.** Congress gave colleges loans to help build dormitories and academic facilities. The bill provided $730,000 for fiscal 1994.

▶ **Education research, statistics and improvement.** This appropriation of $292.6 million included money for the Office of Educational Research and Improvement.

▶ **Libraries.** This appropriation of $146.3 million included grants to states to improve and extend library services.

▶ **Departmental management.** The bill appropriated $437.4 million, to cover salaries and benefits, travel, rent, communications, utilities, printing, equipment and supplies. Of that amount, $56.6 million went to the Office for Civil Rights, and $28.8 million went to the Office of the Inspector General.

RELATED AGENCIES

The bill also appropriated $1.1 billion for 15 related independent agencies. Some, like the Physician Payment Review Commission and National Commission on Acquired Immune Deficiency Syndrome, were permanent boards that advised Congress and the administration on policy matters. Others, like the National Commission on the Cost of Higher Education, were created temporarily to produce a single report or study. Still others, like the Federal Mediation and Conciliation Service and Federal Mine Safety and Health Review Commission, performed statutory functions, such as arbitrating disputes.

▶ **Corporation for Public Broadcasting.** The most prominent of the related agencies financed by the bill, the Corporation for Public Broadcasting developed programming and provided money for the nation's public radio and television stations. Because of planning needs, the corporation's money was provided two years in advance; thus the $312 million appropriation was for fiscal 1996.

▶ **ACTION.** The bill appropriated $205.1 million for ACTION, the umbrella agency that oversaw domestic volunteer programs. That included money for VISTA (Volunteers in Service to America), an anti-poverty program, and the Older American Volunteer Programs, which encouraged activities aimed at both children and the elderly.

▶ **National Labor Relations Board.** The bill appropriated $171.3 million for the agency that investigated charges of unfair labor practices made by businesses, labor unions and individuals. ■

Legislative Cuts Go Largely Unnoticed

Although the legislative branch spending bill constituted just 0.15 percent of the $1.5 trillion federal budget, it typically took a pummeling from lawmakers determined to score points by criticizing Congress. But in 1993, the $2.27 billion spending bill (HR 2348) stood in the shadow of the $496 billion budget-reconciliation package, and no one paid it much mind. *(Budget-reconciliation, p. 107)*

Less than 10 minutes after the conference report was brought to the House floor Aug. 6, it was approved by voice vote. Not a soul spoke against any provision. The Senate cleared it by voice vote later the same day. The first appropriations bill to pass each chamber, the legislative branch bill was also the first regular appropriations measure to reach the president. President Clinton signed it Aug. 11 (PL 103-69).

In his brief remarks on the floor, Vic Fazio, D-Calif., chairman of the House Appropriations Subcommittee on the Legislative Branch, said Congress had applied "maximum constraint on spending" in the bill, which he said came in 1.4 percent below fiscal 1993 in budget authority and 4.5 percent below in outlays. The spending bill provided $443.3 million for the Senate and $684.7 million for the House.

The fiscal 1993 bill had provided $2.3 billion, including $451 million for Senate operations and $699.1 million for the House. *(1992 Almanac, p. 633)*

But that bill fell victim to partisan bickering that made it the last of the 13 appropriations bills to clear Congress. The contrasting ease with which the House made the fiscal 1994 bill the first to clear in 1993 surprised the dozen members assembled for the debate. "Hey, Fazio, what is this?" yelled Jerry Lewis, R-Calif., across the floor after the matter was settled quietly. "I can't believe this."

Lewis had been the ranking Republican on the Appropriations subcommittee during past bitter disputes over the bill. In 1993 he turned the reins over to C. W. Bill Young of Florida, who said several factors helped quell old rancor. Young pointed to cuts in spending and to the bill's small size in comparison with the reconciliation bill that was foremost on members' minds. Young also said the House held critics at bay by nipping spending on franked mail. The House appropriated $40 million for mail in fiscal 1994, an election year, nearly $8 million less than in fiscal 1993.

The Senate froze its mail allowance at $20 million.

The bill required a reduction of 900 jobs, but only half were to come from the House and Senate; no particular jobs were specified.

Although the overall cut in appropriations was small, it was the second reduction in two years. At least since World War II, Congress had never cut appropriations for itself twice in a row. Trims in the past were rare, and they were

---

---

always offset by a large increase the following year.

BACKGROUND

The legislative branch appropriations bill did not make it easy to determine how much taxpayer money lawmakers actually spent on their own operations. The bill did not include all the funds appropriated for Congress, and not all the money in the bill was for congressional activities.

The $2.27 billion that showed as the bottom line in the fiscal 1994 bill included spending that bore little relationship to Congress. Congress long ago had attempted to clear up the matter by splitting the spending bill into two titles. The first was for "congressional operations," which included the House, the Senate, and agencies and divisions that worked only for Congress (such as the Congressional Budget Office and the Library of Congress' Congressional Research Service). The second title was for "other agencies" — those with broader purposes (such as the rest of the Library of Congress and the Botanic Garden).

The split, however, made it appear that Congress cost significantly less than it did. The congressional operations title included $1.55 billion in fiscal 1994. But that accounting ignored the fact that more than half of the $724 million in the bill's second title went to the General Accounting Office (GAO) — an agency that said it did 80 percent of its work directly for Congress.

And nowhere in the bill was the money for the legislative branch's most obvious big-ticket item: the salary and benefits of Congress' 535 members, four delegates and resident commissioner. Rank-and-file lawmakers each earned $133,600 a year; leaders earned more. Compensating them cost taxpayers $92 million in fiscal 1994. That money came from a permanent appropriation established in 1981 and aimed, unsuccessfully, at preventing fights over members' pay.

The bill also included no money for the unreported sums the executive branch spent shuttling members aboard military aircraft, money that was tucked into the Pentagon's budget.

The bottom line in fiscal 1994 was that Congress was likely to cost taxpayers close to $2 billion — $1.55 billion for the spending bill's congressional operations title, about $345 million for the GAO (80 percent of its total budget), $92 million for members' pay and benefits, plus an unknown sum for military travel.

HOUSE SUBCOMMITTEE ACTION

The House Legislative Branch Appropriations Subcommittee approved by voice vote May 26 a $1.78 billion fiscal 1994 spending bill. The measure did not include

LEGISLATIVE BRANCH

	Fiscal 1993 Appropriation	House Bill	Senate Bill	Final Bill
	(In thousands of dollars)			
Senate				
Senators' personal office accounts	$ 185,768	—	$ 185,768	$ 185,768
Mileage	60	—	60	60
Leadership, party caucuses	10,360	—	10,360	10,360
Leadership expense accounts	86	—	86	86
Committees	77,000	—	77,000	77,000
Official mail	20,000	—	20,000	20,000
Administrative offices	134,761	—	125,625	125,625
Other	23,416	—	24,416	24,416
Subtotal, Senate	**$ 451,451**	**—**	**$ 443,315**	**$ 443,315**
House of Representatives				
Members' personal office accounts	306,858	301,549	301,549	301,549
Mileage	—	—	—	—
Leadership, party caucuses (including expense accounts)	9,218	9,557	9,557	9,557
Committees	135,870	129,927	129,927	129,927
Official mail	47,711	40,000	40,000	40,000
Administrative offices	53,536	59,920	59,920	59,920
Other (including prior-year rescissions)	145,916	143,743	143,743	143,743
Subtotal, House	**$ 699,109**	**$ 684,696**	**$ 684,696**	**$ 684,696**
Joint Items				
Joint committees	12,076	11,058	10,638	11,025
Office of Attending Physician (partial)	1,509	1,502	1,502	1,502
Capitol Police Board	64,881	64,232	64,232	64,232
Capitol Guide Service	1,644	1,628	1,628	1,628
Special Services Office	366	363	363	363
Office of Technology Assessment	21,025	20,815	21,815	21,315
Congressional Budget Office	22,542	22,317	22,442	22,317
Architect of the Capitol	149,613	103,193	149,914	150,223
Congressional Research Service	57,291	56,718	56,718	56,718
Government Printing Office (congressional printing)	89,591	88,404	88,404	88,404
TOTAL, congressional operations	**$ 1,571,098**	**$ 1,054,926**	**$ 1,545,667**	**$ 1,545,738**
Other Agencies				
Botanic Garden	4,906	3,008	3,008	3,008
Library of Congress (net)	252,808	250,225	250,868	250,813
Architect of the Capitol (library buildings)	9,733	9,543	9,974	9,974
Copyright Royalty Tribunal (net)	130	128	128	128
Government Printing Office (salaries and expenses)	29,082	29,082	29,082	29,082
General Accounting Office (net)	435,167	430,815	434,815	430,815
TOTAL, other agencies	**$ 731,826**	**$ 722,801**	**$ 727,875**	**$ 723,820**
GRAND TOTAL	**$ 2,302,924**	**$ 1,777,727**	**$ 2,273,542**	**$ 2,269,558**

NOTES: Numbers based on Appropriations Committee reports; categories were readjusted to illustrate more precisely how the money was spent, so some figures do not match those in committee charts. The "administration request" category was deleted because the president submitted without change requests forwarded from Congress and the agencies. The House bill included no funding for the Senate because the bill originated in the House and, by tradition, each chamber was solely responsible for its own appropriations.

funding for the Senate, which was added when the bill reached that chamber.

Determining exactly what the panel trimmed or protected, however, was not easy. Though the markup was open to the public, it was shrouded in a secrecy many members found odd and frustrating. According to several members, they were not given the subcommittee "mark" — as the drafting notes were known — until the hearing began, and staff members said they were asked not to take notes during the two-hour session. At its conclusion, even members were asked to turn in all documents; a staff member stood guard at the door to see that none slipped out.

"It was very curious when Fazio asked for all the paper," said Young, the new ranking Republican. "But if I thought they were up to anything, I would have objected." Fazio said he simply wanted to make sure the documents and figures were accurate before circulating them.

Grand Totals

Girding for an anticipated floor fight, Fazio repeatedly said that the cuts in the bill were bigger than they appeared from budget authority figures. Budget authority represented how much would be spent over several years as a result of the bill, as opposed to the outlays, the amount that actually would be spent in fiscal 1994. While the bill fell 1 percent below the $1.8 billion in budget authority approved for fiscal 1993, the Appropriations Committee estimated that it would reduce outlays by $111 million — a 5.8 percent cut.

On paper, the fiscal 1993 bill had cut $23 million from the previous year's budget authority. But that was accomplished with an accounting gimmick that credited the House for returning to the Treasury funds that had been appropriated earlier. Without that, the cut from the 1992 bill was .04 percent.

Fazio also stressed that the measure put Congress on track for a 25 percent reduction in personnel and administrative costs over five years, in keeping with Clinton's directive to executive branch agencies earlier in 1993. "This is a very tough bill," Fazio said time and again.

"We've got serious pneumonia, and we're talking about cough syrup," responded Charles H. Taylor, R-N.C., who offered an amendment to cut 25 percent across the board from the bill. It was rejected on a voice vote.

The subcommittee similarly turned back several other cost-cutting amendments.

The panel did unanimously agree to a Taylor amendment that cut $55,000 from the total (an additional .003 percent). The money had been earmarked for a staff assistant to Librarian Emeritus Daniel J. Boorstin, the former librarian of Congress.

The panel approved without objection a Young amendment to rescind $1.5 million that had been appropriated for the House select committees in fiscal 1993 but remained unspent. The House had allowed the committees' authorization to expire March 31.

The panel also approved a Young amendment that directed the full committee to add report language shifting the financial burden for Government Printing Office (GPO) employees detailed to the House from the agency to the House beginning in fiscal 1995. In 1993 there were 72 printing office detailees assigned to various House entities at an estimated cost to the GPO of $5.8 million, according to a congressional aide.

To achieve staff reductions that Democrats said the bill would require in congressional agencies, the bill provided for an "early out" program designed to eliminate 900 positions at the GPO, the GAO and the Library of Congress.

Modeled on a Defense Department program, it offered senior employees as much as $25,000 to retire early. No such program was offered to congressional employees.

HOUSE COMMITTEE ACTION

The full House Appropriations Committee approved HR 2348 on June 8 by voice vote (H Rept 103-117).

Committee members gave voice vote approval to amendments by Fazio that:

● Ordered the GAO to spend up to $500,000 for an independent "broad-based organizational performance review" of itself. The GAO had come under fire from Republicans who thought its work was biased.

● Repealed a law first passed in 1866 that provided members with a 20-cents-a-mile reimbursement for one trip home a year. Members said the provision was no longer needed because their office accounts included money for regular trips home. The House in 1992 declined to appropriate money to fund the old law; the fiscal 1994 bill permanently did away with the annual payments for the House, which ranged from just a few dollars to more than $2,000. Senators appropriated money for their own payments in 1992, and the House's action did not affect them.

● Barred agencies from filling positions vacated by employees who accepted retirement incentives authorized in the bill. The chairmen of two committees that relied on the GAO for support — John D. Dingell, D-Mich., of Energy and Commerce and John Conyers Jr., D-Mich., of Government Operations — opposed the provision. The subsequent rule governing floor debate on the bill did not protect the provision from a point of order against legislating on a spending bill, a circumstance that Conyers used to knock the provision out of the bill when it reached the House floor.

HOUSE FLOOR ACTION

Responding to presidential calls for shared sacrifice, the House on June 10 approved the bill on a largely partisan vote of 224-187. The big fight of the day came on a restrictive rule governing floor debate, which was approved by another partisan vote of 226-185. *(Vote 217, p. 52-H; vote 205, p. 50-H)*

While offering limited praise to Democrats for some cuts, Republicans called for further reductions, arguing that voters wanted bigger changes. But their proposals were blocked by Democrats, who said that the bill went far enough and accused the GOP of partisan grandstanding. Democratic leaders blocked votes on all but six of 50 proposed amendments, many offered by members of the large 1993 freshman class.

The six amendments had the blessing of the bill's Democratic crafters, and five were approved. They cut less than $10 million from the $1.8 billion bill.

The Republicans' final chance to alter the bill, a motion to order the Appropriations Committee to redraft it by cutting all accounts by 5 percent, was rejected 202-209. *(Vote 216, p. 52-H)*

Not counting floor amendments, the bill appropriated about $19 million less in budget authority than was enacted for fiscal 1993.

The bill required administrative cost reductions of 14 percent by the end of fiscal 1997 and ordered all legislative branch agencies with more than 100 employees to cut their staffs by 4 percent by 1995. The Appropriations committee

estimated that the bill would reduce by 920 the legislative branch's fiscal 1992 employee total of 37,087.

Most of the savings from these provisions, modeled after executive branch cuts ordered by Clinton earlier, were reflected in the committee's bill. But the panel estimated that they would result in an additional $10.9 million in outlay cuts, which would bring the total outlay reduction to 6.4 percent.

While most agencies faced cuts, House leadership offices of both parties received increases ranging from 1 percent ($12,000) for Speaker Thomas S. Foley, D-Wash., to 14 percent ($254,000 in all) for the two parties' whip organizations. Foley said much of the extra leadership money would finance staff for a new leadership position: the Democrats' fourth chief deputy whip, Bill Richardson, N.M. As mandated by tradition, the GOP whip organization, led by Newt Gingrich, Ga., received a similar increase. A leadership aide said the rest of the money would fund raises for leadership staff members.

Fight Over the Rule

Democratic leaders blocked Republicans and maverick Democrats from offering amendments by having the Rules Committee craft a restrictive rule governing floor action. During a June 9 session that lasted 10 1/2 hours, the Rules Committee took testimony from more than 30 members, mostly Republicans, who wanted to offer amendments. On a series of party-line votes, the panel refused to allow votes on all but the six amendments. It was the second year in a row the Democrats used a restrictive rule to limit amendments on the legislative funding bill, breaking a long tradition of open floor consideration.

"You are about to witness one of the most outrageous charades ever attempted on the floor of this House," said Gerald B. H. Solomon, N.Y., the Rules Committee's top Republican, urging colleagues to defeat the rule. He accused Democrats of "continuing on their drunken spending spree."

Only one Democrat spoke against the rule. "This is not democratic, and it is not consistent with the principles of the Democratic Party, of which I am a member," said Timothy J. Penny of Minnesota, who was denied a chance to offer an amendment to cut the bill by 5 percent.

The Amendments

Amendments that were approved by the House:

● Rescinded a total of $1.6 million in unspent money from fiscal 1991 and 1992. Offered by freshman Democrats Karan English, Ariz., and Bart Stupak, Mich., the amendment was approved by a 415-2 vote. *(Vote 208, p. 50-H)*

● Cut $5.8 million from the account that paid for members' mailing privilege, known as the frank. Offered by several freshman Democrats and Penny after negotiations with Fazio, the amendment was approved 418-4. With the amendment, the House appropriated $40 million for franking in fiscal 1994, about $7.7 million less than in fiscal 1993. Fazio said 1994 would mark the first time in recent history that the House reduced franking appropriations for an election year. *(Vote 209, p. 50-H)*

Republicans argued that the cuts should have been deeper. Bill Thomas, R-Calif., was blocked from offering an amendment that would have barred almost all mailings of more than 100 letters.

● Cut off spending for former Speakers' offices in five years. At the time, living former Speakers — there were three in 1993 — received funds annually for an unlimited number of years, a total of $417,000 for nine staff members in fiscal 1994, plus office expenses of about $67,000 each and franking costs.

Porter J. Goss, R-Fla., had been pushing to have the former Speakers, all Democrats, cut off after three years but then agreed to join a bipartisan group of freshmen backing a five-year cutoff. Under the amendment, approved 383-36, former Speakers would be cut off Oct. 1, 1998. Speakers who retired in the future would get office funds for five years after they left office. *(Vote 210, p. 52-H)*

● Directed the House Administration Committee to transfer the financial oversight of members' so-called Legislative Service Organizations (LSOs) to the House clerk.

Members contributed taxpayer funds from their office accounts to these caucuses, which employed staff members to work on particular issues. Offered by John Edward Porter, R-Ill., and Jan Meyers, R-Kan., the amendment came in response to calls by Pat Roberts, R-Kan., to ban the use of taxpayer funds for LSOs. Roberts had complained for years that funds used for LSOs were open to abuse. The amendment was approved by voice vote.

● Barred the use of money in the bill to relocate members' offices. The amendment by Rod Grams, R-Minn., was approved by 340-76. Grams complained that midterm vacancies often prompted a shuffling of offices as members sought better space, costing an estimated $3,000 per move. His amendment put off moves through fiscal 1994. *(Vote 211, p. 52-H)*

John A. Boehner, R-Ohio, withdrew an amendment to require quarterly spending reports by the Architect of the Capitol after learning that the office already issued twice-yearly reports.

SENATE ACTION

Bypassing a formal subcommittee markup, the Senate Appropriations Committee approved HR 2348 by a vote of 29-0 on July 20. Members heeded the request of Chairman Robert C. Byrd, D-W.Va., to refrain from offering controversial amendments that would be revisited on the floor. "There's no point in having two fights," Byrd told colleagues at the start of the brief session. The only amendments offered in committee were a handful of technical corrections recommended by Legislative Branch Appropriations Subcommittee Chairman Harry Reid, D-Nev.

Senate Floor Action

The Senate passed the $2.3 billion measure July 23 by a vote of 85-7. *(Vote 212, p. 28-S)*

Reid attributed the bill's smooth course less to the political environment than to the bill's austerity. After floor amendments, the bill was $34 million below 1993 levels, a 1.5 percent cut. Reid said this represented a 12 percent reduction in outlays over two years. "There are real spending cuts in the bill," Senate Republican leader Bob Dole of Kansas said after the vote.

Senate leaders reached an agreement that would have allowed as many as 15 amendments. But with the Senate beginning consideration of the bill at 8 on a Friday morning, and with many senators holding plane tickets to leave town, only five amendments were offered.

An amendment by ranking subcommittee Republican Connie Mack, Fla., to bar funds from being used for unsolicited mass mailings could have caused a partisan tussle. But it first drew the ire of fellow Republican Ted Stevens of Alaska, who said the amendment would unfairly hurt those from rural states. Stevens complained that Senate newsletters were often the only way to communicate with people in remote villages that did not have daily newspapers.

His anger at a Republican amendment defused any

partisan tension, and a motion to kill the amendment by tabling it carried on a 48-47 vote that defied partisan characterization. *(Vote 211, p. 28-S)*

Stevens also complained that the committee decision to repeal the 1866 law that provided members with a 20-cents-a-mile reimbursement for one trip home a year — similar to the House-passed provision — unfairly hurt senators who lived far from the capital.

Although senators could pay for travel from their official accounts, the Senate went along with Stevens' request and restored the travel reimbursement by unanimous consent.

Hank Brown, R-Colo., discussed an amendment to require Congress to return all unspent funds to the Treasury rather than rolling them into a revolving fund for future use. Brown complained that all other federal agencies were required to return the money. Though the issue had prompted bitter fights in the House, Brown decided not to offer the amendment after Reid promised to review the matter and address it in the future.

The Senate gave voice vote approval to two amendments that increased spending.

One by Mack added $1 million to the Office of Technology Assessment for a study of health-care reform models; another by Reid added $1.2 million for the Library of Congress.

The Senate also approved by voice vote an amendment requiring that most government printing costing more than $1,000 be done by the GPO.

A Squeeze on the Senate

The bill included an $8 million reduction in the Senate's own budget authority, a 1.8 percent cut.

It directed individual senators to reduce their personal office allowance by 2.5 percent. While the savings were modest, they marked a shift from the fiscal 1993 bill, which increased Senate funding by $2 million.

The 1994 bill froze funding for the majority and minority leaders' and whips' offices, as well as for the office of the vice president. For the first time since Byrd became president pro tempore in 1989, his office budget lost funds — $20,000.

The move to squeeze the Senate budget began earlier in the year, when the Senate Rules Committee cut nearly 7.5 percent from committee budgets. Funding for official mail was to be frozen at $20 million, although the committee included language to allow senators to transfer funds between various office accounts without approval by the Appropriations Committee.

Under existing law, such transfers had to be approved by both the Senate Administration and Appropriations committees.

The Senate appropriation for the Architect of the Capitol was $43 million more than the House recommendation because it included funding for maintenance of Senate office buildings. The report noted the "shabby condition" of the furniture in several Senate hearing rooms and directed the architect to survey the situation periodically.

Overall, the differences between the Senate bill and the one passed by the House were slight.

Although the Senate approved somewhat larger cuts for the joint House-Senate committees than the House did, the agency funding levels were almost identical. The Senate specifically concurred with a House amendment directing the GAO to conduct a broad-based organizational performance review.

Library of Congress

The Library of Congress was slated to take a $2 million reduction from the $253 million in budget authority it received the year before. The library had requested an increase of nearly $30 million.

The Senate Appropriations Committee and the full House had approved comparable cuts, although the House exempted the Books for the Blind program; the Senate cut the $43 million program 1 percent.

On the Senate floor, however, Reid's amendment added $1.1 million for the American Memory Program and restored $55,000 for the librarian emeritus, who was to lose an aide under the House bill.

The Senate bill also included language to exempt private gifts to the library from being counted against its annual budget authority. "We're really going to have to do some creative things to keep the library from hemorrhaging," Reid said. *(Library of Congress, p. 77)*

CONFERENCE/FINAL ACTION

It took less than a half-hour Aug. 2 for House and Senate conferees to reconcile their differences on HR 2348 (H Rept 103-210). By tradition, each chamber took a hands-off approach to funding recommendations that affected the other. Easing the process further, the House and Senate had approved similar funding levels for the related agencies.

The final package came in at $33.4 million less in budget authority than was enacted for fiscal 1993, with congressional operations taking a slightly larger hit than the related agencies.

The House and Senate each approved the conference report by voice vote Aug. 6.

The Senate provided $443.3 million for its own operations, a cut of $8 million, or 1.8 percent, from fiscal 1993 funding. The House got $684.7 million in budget authority, a reduction of 1.8 percent, or $14 million.

While all the Senate leaders froze their office budgets at 1993 levels, House leaders in both parties got hikes. Democrats aggregated a 5 percent increase, $161,000, primarily to accommodate the addition of a fourth chief deputy whip. Republican leaders got a 7 percent boost of $149,000, which brought their funding up to a level that was nearly proportionate to their representation in the House.

The House eliminated the travel allowance for members' first trip home and included legislative language to do away with the benefit in the future. The Senate Appropriations Committee had recommended similar language for the Senate, but it was stricken by a floor amendment.

The House instructed its conferees to accept a Senate amendment to require unspent funds to be returned to the Treasury annually. House conferees also approved a Senate transfer of $7 million that was appropriated for Capitol security in the mid-1980s but never spent; it was to be used to replace the roof on the Thomas Jefferson Building of the Library of Congress.

The House went along with the Senate's proposal to provide funding to complete a pilot program on the Library of Congress' American Memory Program.

House conferees rejected a Senate amendment that would have required all executive branch printing to go through the GPO.

Conferees also pledged to review the practice of assigning GPO detailees to congressional committees, warning that they believed significant changes were needed in the existing policy. Often more highly paid than regular committee staff, the detailees assisted in printing committee reports. ∎

Legislative Branch Provisions

The following is a breakdown of where all the money in the fiscal 1994 legislative branch spending bill (HR 2348) went and other significant provisions in the measure. Some of the employee counts and other figures were based on information in a reference book called "Vital Statistics on Congress," as well as various government sources.

THE SENATE

The Senate was to spend $443.3 million on itself under the bill, a 1.8 percent cut compared with fiscal 1993. The chamber employed more than 7,000 people.

Member and Committee Expenses

▶ **Members' offices.** The biggest chunk ($185.8 million) was to pay the salaries of more than 4,000 aides on senators' personal staffs — about one-third in senators' home states and the rest in Washington — and expenses to run their Capitol and home-state offices (except mail costs).

Senators were allowed between about $1.4 million and $2.4 million each from this account, depending mainly on their states' size and distance from the Capitol. A provision of the bill reduced the cap on each member's expenses by 2.5 percent, and the Senate Appropriations Committee warned of a similar reduction in the next year. Many senators did not spend all they were allowed, so there apparently was no need to cut the total amount provided in the bill, which was the same as the year before.

Senators got the bulk of what they spent operating their offices from this account, but they also got help from other accounts. For example, computers, telephone services and the rent for state offices were paid by the sergeant at arms budget, and the Architect of the Capitol provided furniture to senators' personal offices.

▶ **Travel.** Under an 1866 law, Congress every year appropriated a total of $60,000 for 20-cent-per-mile payments to senators to compensate each for one round trip home from the Capitol. Payments to senators (and the vice president) ranged from $4 for a Virginian to $2,076 for a Hawaiian.

House members used to get similar payments, but in 1992 they did not appropriate the usual $210,000 for them. In 1993, they repealed the underlying authorization. The Senate Appropriations Committee decided to repeal it for Senate payments, too, but Ted Stevens, R-Alaska, who got $1,847 a year under the law, persuaded the Senate to restore it with a floor amendment that was approved by voice vote without debate.

Senators also could turn to their office accounts, the committee budgets and other pockets of money to pay for trips. There was a separate $125,000 account for foreign travel. Moreover, the Pentagon frequently shuttled members overseas on military planes, but those trips were covered by the defense appropriations bill. An additional permanent appropriation of $440,000 a year — administered by the State Department and established in a 1987 omnibus spending bill — paid for House and Senate members' trips to international meetings of parliamentary groups. Members of both chambers also took trips at the expense of corporations, interest groups and foundations.

▶ **Franking.** Both chambers appropriated money every year to reimburse the Postal Service for official mail costs, much of which paid for members' franked mass mailings. The bill included $20 million for franked Senate mail, the amount needed to pay for one statewide mailing for each senator and for the mail of committees and Senate officers.

Members' franking rights always had been among the most controversial items in the bill. But past reform efforts had limited members' use of the frank and made the cost of each member's mass mailings public, and this had resulted in lower costs for congressional mailings. The Senate killed, 48-47, an amendment by Connie Mack of Florida, the top Republican on the Legislative Branch Appropriations Subcommittee, that would have barred members from using the frank for most mass mailings.

Senators were allowed to transfer up to $100,000 from their mail accounts to their personal office accounts. They could not transfer office account money to their franking budgets, as House members could.

▶ **Committees.** Another big item was the cost of running the Senate's 19 committees, which employed more than 1,000 people. Most of the committees' operations were funded under the bill's "inquiries and investigations" account, which totaled $77 million, the same as the previous year.

During each Congress, the Senate separately approved budgets for almost all the committees, based on recommendations that the Rules Committee crafted, which in turn were based on requests from the committees. The most recent committee budget measure (S Res 71, approved Feb. 25) reduced total committee funding for 1993 by 7.6 percent. The inquiries account each year approved enough money to fund whatever was in the resolution, as well as funds for the Ethics Committee and committee employees' fringe benefits.

Not counting fringe benefits, the committees' annual budgets ranged from about $1.1 million for Small Business to about $5 million or more each for Labor, Judiciary and Governmental Affairs. Senate rules called for total committee staff to "reflect the relative number of majority and minority members" on each committee.

Administrative Offices

Accounts totaling more than $125 million covered the salaries and expenses of more than 1,000 other Senate employees — those in the chamber's administrative offices.

▶ **Sergeant at Arms.** The biggest of these offices was that of the sergeant at arms, which oversaw the day-to-day operations of most of the Senate's basic support services, sometimes working with the General Services Administration, the executive branch's landlord.

The sergeant at arms — at the time Martha S. Pope, former chief of staff to Majority Leader George J. Mitchell, D-Maine — maintained the Senate's massive computer system; rented home-state offices for members; oversaw the Senate's phone system and public address system; leased cars and provided drivers for the Senate's top five leaders; printed and mailed news releases and other documents for members; provided members with office equipment; furnished the Capitol's Senate side; and ran the Senate's photographic, audio and video studios.

The office also oversaw Senate pages, doorkeepers, hair stylists, parking lot attendants, tour guides, custodians, cabinetmakers, photographers and video operators, telephone operators, post office workers, folding room workers and elevator operators. Pope also helped oversee the Capitol Police, funded elsewhere in the bill. The Senate press galleries fell under the sergeant at arms' budget, although they were basically autonomous.

In all, Pope's office was to employ 908 people in fiscal 1994 at a cost of $32.7 million, not counting benefits. For other expenses, the bill provided $74.9 million, the biggest chunk of which was to be spent on computer items; about $11.9 million was to be spent on renting office space and mobile offices for members in their home states.

▶ **Secretary of the Senate.** The second-biggest office belonged to Walter J. Stewart, who as secretary of the Senate was the chamber's chief administrative officer. He was to employ up to 236 employees at a cost of $11.7 million, not counting benefits, and spend almost $1.4 million more on other expenses.

The office disbursed appropriated funds; kept track of bills; transcribed floor debates for the Congressional Record; maintained public records and documents for inspection and distribution; ran the Senate library, historical office, curator's office and parliamentarian's office; oversaw the office-supply distribution system; provided orientation seminars for members and staff; supplied Senate offices with reference books; contracted with the

District of Columbia for the education of Senate pages; oversaw closed-captioning services for the deaf on C-SPAN; and ran the Senate's gift shop and stationery room.

▶ **Senate lawyers.** The Senate's chief lawyers — the legislative counsel and the legal counsel — were to spend $3.9 million and employ nearly 40 people.

▶ **Chaplain.** The chaplain was to get $172,000 for himself and two employees.

▶ **Office of Fair Employment Practices.** This office, established in the Civil Rights Act of 1991 to handle complaints of Senate workers under major job-bias laws, was to get $825,000, including $286,000 for contract services. It had five employees.

Leadership Offices

The budgets for Senate leadership offices and party organizations totaled more than $10 million; they employed more than 200 people.

▶ **President pro tempore.** Of the leadership offices, perhaps the fastest-growing was that of the president pro tempore — the person who presided over the Senate in the absence of the vice president and was third in the line of succession to the presidency, behind the vice president and House Speaker.

The position, which by tradition went to the senior senator of the majority party, was held by Robert C. Byrd, D-W.Va., who also was the chairman of the Appropriations Committee. The salary budget for his office in 1994 was to be $432,000 — the same as in fiscal 1993 but up from $156,000 when Byrd assumed both positions in 1989, and enough for about nine employees.

▶ **Vice president.** Vice President Al Gore, who served as president of the Senate, had the biggest single leadership office budget — $1.4 million. Earlier in 1993, Gore had nearly 60 people on his Senate payroll, compared with the 40 or so who were on Dan Quayle's Senate payroll when he was vice president. The vice president's office got additional money from the spending bill that funded the White House — an office budget of $3.3 million (for 21 aides) plus $324,000 for running his residence. *(Treasury-Postal Service, p. 679)*

▶ **Democratic leadership.** On the surface, Majority Leader Mitchell's budget seemed much smaller than the vice president's Senate budget. The majority leader's office got about $1 million. But the Democratic leadership's power was consolidated, and Mitchell had control over most of another $2.7 million — the entire budgets of the Democratic Conference ($942,000) and the secretary of the majority's office ($567,000), plus much of the budget of the Democratic Policy Committee ($1.2 million), the chairmanship of which Mitchell shared with Tom Daschle of South Dakota.

Altogether, these offices were to get $3.7 million and employ a staff of more than 60.

There were two other Democratic leadership offices — the whip (Wendell H. Ford of Kentucky), with a budget of $322,000, and the secretary of the conference (David Pryor of Arkansas), with a budget of $181,000.

▶ **Republican leadership.** Among Republicans, who got the same amount as the Democrats for their party leadership offices, power was more diffuse.

Republican leader Bob Dole of Kansas basically controlled two budgets — the minority leader's ($1 million) and the secretary of the minority's ($567,000). The Republican Conference, headed by Thad Cochran of Mississippi, had a budget of $942,000. The secretary of the conference, Trent Lott of Mississippi, got $181,000. The Republican Policy Committee, headed by Don Nickles of Oklahoma, got $1.2 million. And the minority whip, Alan K. Simpson of Wyoming, got $322,000.

Included in both the Democratic and Republican conference budgets was money for radio and television services for members, which supplemented the services offered by the sergeant at arms.

▶ **Consultants.** Various Senate leaders and officers had authority to hire consultants "on a temporary or intermittent basis." The bill allocated $725,000 for this purpose. In effect, the money supplemented the salary budgets of these offices, allowing them to expand their staffs. For example, Republican leader Dole had had a "temporary" consultant on his staff since 1987, Robert B. Dove, the Senate's parliamentarian in 1981-87.

▶ **Expense allowances.** The leaders from both parties, including the vice president, were allowed some tax-free spending money under laws that did little to define which expenses were allowable. According to records, the money paid for food at official meetings, office expenses not funded from other accounts and other expenses. These "expense allowances" totaled $56,000 — up to $10,000 each for the vice president, president pro tempore and the majority and minority leaders; $5,000 each for the majority and minority whips; and $3,000 each for the chairmen of the majority and minority conference committees.

The majority and minority leaders also were allowed a vaguely defined "representation allowance" of $15,000 each for expenses related to "their appropriate responsibilities" to visiting foreign officials and "intergovernmental organizations."

The money was in addition to the leaders' annual salaries, $171,500 for the vice president, $148,400 for the president pro tempore and the two leaders and $133,600 for the others.

▶ **Other accounts.** A variety of other items were to take up the rest of the Senate's money, including: nearly $20 million for employee benefits; $25,000 for receptions for foreign dignitaries; $371,000 for fellowship programs; $77,000 for the Rules Committee to print calendars; and $336,000 for the Senate's Caucus on International Narcotics Control.

THE HOUSE OF REPRESENTATIVES

The House was to spend $686.3 million on itself under the bill, a 1.8 percent cut from fiscal 1993. It employed more than 11,000 people. The bill rescinded $3.1 million in unspent money from prior years.

Member and Committee Expenses

▶ **Members' offices.** Like the Senate, the House spent the biggest chunk of its money on salaries and expenses of its members' offices, which were authorized to spend an average of $752,400 each, not counting mail costs.

The members, delegates and resident commissioner were to be allowed $557,400 each for the salaries of up to 22 staff members. Over the past 2½ years, the House Administration Committee, which oversaw such matters, had increased this "clerk hire" allowance by $82,400 (17 percent). The bill appropriated $225 million for this purpose, which was somewhat less than would be needed if all members used the maximum; some did not.

In all, that money was to pay the salaries of more than 7,000 employees — more than a third of whom were based in district offices.

Members also were allowed temporary helpers from the Lyndon Baines Johnson Congressional Intern program, for which $483,000 was appropriated, down from $1.1 million in fiscal 1993.

About $76.5 million was to be spent on members' official expenses, an average of nearly $174,000 each ($21,000 less than the average allowance). Members' allowances ranged from $152,000 to $334,000, depending on their districts' distance from the Capitol and office rental rates in the districts.

Members were allowed to transfer up to $75,000 a year between the two accounts. They could also transfer a total of up to $25,000 from these accounts to their franking accounts.

More than in the Senate, House members got most of what they spent on running their offices from these two accounts. Some, but not many, other expenses (such as office furniture) were funded by other accounts.

▶ **Legislative Service Organizations.** Various study groups (the Democratic Study Group, the House Wednesday Group, the Congressional Black Caucus, e.c.) were not funded individually in the bill but got funding from members' office accounts. Members of the groups contributed voluntarily and paid fees or dues for their services.

The bill required the House Administration Committee to transfer

to the clerk the job of overseeing the financial activities of the legislative service organizations by Jan. 1, 1994. The House Finance Office was expected to take over this oversight job eventually.

▶ **Travel.** The bill permanently repealed House members' annual 20-cents-a-mile reimbursement for one round trip home, negating the need to appropriate the usual $210,000 for this purpose. As with senators, members got travel subsidies from a host of other sources, including their office expense accounts, which also allowed House members to lease cars.

▶ **Franking.** The bill included $40 million for franked mail in fiscal 1994. Franking limits and disclosure requirements enacted in 1990 to check mass mailings had greatly reduced mail costs, especially in election years, when they usually peaked. In fiscal 1990, the members spent $73 million. In fiscal 1992, the House appropriated $80 million but spent only about $54 million.

All members got a mail budget big enough to send three items to each home in their district, and how much they spent was disclosed quarterly. Members were allowed to transfer up to a total of $25,000 a year from their "clerk hire" and official expenses accounts into their mail accounts.

▶ **Committees.** Four accounts, totaling $129.9 million, provided almost all funding for the House's 23 committees, which employed more than 2,000 people. (Some administrative expenses, such as stenographic services, office supplies and some telephone services, were funded from other accounts.)

It was impossible to tell from the public record how much each committee was to spend in total in fiscal 1994. Records for fiscal 1992 indicated that committee budgets ranged from less than $1 million for the Committee on Standards of Official Conduct to nearly $20 million for the Appropriations Committee, which employed more than 200 people.

The House in 1993 killed its four temporary select committees (Aging; Hunger; Narcotics Abuse and Control; and Children, Youth and Families), panels that were meant to be temporary but that had been allowed to continue for years. Savings from that move constituted much of the $5.9 million (4.4 percent) cut from the committee accounts.

All but two of the House's 23 committees got a base contingent of 30 employees, with up to 10 assigned to the minority in most cases. The Appropriations and Budget committees set their own base staff levels. The biggest of the four accounts paid the salaries of these aides.

The second-biggest account funded the expenses and additional staff of the panels funded by the first account except Budget and Appropriations (which got additional money from the two remaining accounts).

Funding from this second account, though part of the spending bill, was approved separately by the House in annual resolutions crafted by the House Administration Committee.

It was the division of money from this account that often drew the ire of House Republicans because House rules — unlike Senate rules — did not put aside a set amount for the minority party. Thus, funding from the second account was in effect controlled by the majority party.

In the past, House rules for the second account guaranteed minority committee members either "fair consideration" in staffing splits or at least one-third of the staff money. In 1993, minority members were assured only that the ranking minority members of up to six subcommittees of each committee was to get at least one aide.

House Republicans had pushed in recent years for at least 20 percent of the staff funding in the second account, with an eventual goal of one-third. In 1989, they persuaded the House Administration Committee to endorse that goal. When 1993's committee funding resolution (H Res 107) was approved in March, the Republicans complained that they still controlled less than 20 percent.

Pat Roberts, R-Kan., a longtime veteran of such debates, estimated that Republicans controlled 24 percent of all committee aides while constituting more than 40 percent of House membership.

Administrative Offices

There were 12 administrative offices in the House. The bill appropriated almost $60 million for them, roughly the same as in fiscal 1993. These offices employed more than 1,000 people.

▶ **Director of Non-Legislative and Financial Services.** The House created this office in 1992 to oversee most of its administrative functions in response to scandals over overdrafts at its since-closed bank and over embezzlement and drug-dealing at its post office. The bipartisan leadership hired Leonard P. Wishart III for the job.

The House Administration Committee was still in the process of handing over tasks to Wishart that previously had been handled by other offices. The bill established budgets for the different offices based on where that process stood earlier in 1993, giving Wishart a budget of $14.4 million. But the bill also included a provision transferring other funds to Wishart as tasks were handed over to him.

As of the fall, Wishart had or was about to get control over more than 600 employees. They included workers from the old House Post Office (since changed to House Postal Operations); Clerk's Office employees from the Finance Office, the Placement Office, the Department of Office Furnishings, the Office Supply Service, the Child Care Center and Office Systems Management; the barber shop and beauty salon employees from the Doorkeeper Office; the member's paymaster employees from the sergeant at arms' since-closed House bank; and the House restaurant system, a self-sustaining business that had been overseen by the House Administration Committee.

The House Administration Committee was having second thoughts about several tasks that the House voted to turn over to Wishart's office when it created the post in 1992. Exercising its power to reverse decisions made when the House approved the resolution creating the post (H Res 423), the panel rejected turning over the Doorkeeper's Office of Photography, which provided portrait, candid and news photo services for members while they were on Capitol Hill.

The committee had deferred decisions on: the non-legislative functions of the Clerk's Printing Service, Recording Studio and Office of Records and Registration; the Clerk's Employee Assistance, Telecommunications and Telephone Exchange offices; and the House Administration Committee's House Information Systems (the chamber's computer center). The Senate had blocked moves to transfer the jointly funded Capitol Guide Service and Special Services Office to Wishart.

The figures listed below for the House's other administrative offices came from the spending bill, regardless of the existing status of the tasks they funded.

▶ **Clerk of the House.** Donald K. Anderson's budget was $11.9 million. His office oversaw the technical aspects of moving bills through the House; the House library; the transcribing of committee hearings and floor debates; the radio and television recording studios; the printing service; the telephone system; the House's Fair Employment Practices and Employee Assistance offices; and the public records office, which collected financial disclosure, lobbyist registration and campaign documents.

Included in the clerk's budget was money for three leased automobiles that were to cost about $15,000. One was at Anderson's disposal, although he said he usually walked to and from work; the others were used for transporting documents, other House officials and members on official business.

▶ **Sergeant at Arms.** Werner W. Brandt's budget was $1.4 million. Like his Senate counterpart, he helped oversee the Capitol Police (funded elsewhere) but otherwise had very few of the same duties.

His office's most important other job used to be administering the members' payroll and benefits, including insurance and retirement, and running the House bank. He continued to be the House's chief of security and protocol and oversaw deceased members' funeral arrangements.

Brandt's budget included $14,400 for three leased four-wheel-drive vehicles. Brandt, who used one car to get to and from work,

said they were used mostly to take members to official meetings, to drive members home after late-night House sessions and to bring leaders to work during snowy or icy conditions or when their cars broke down.

▶ **Doorkeeper.** James T. Molloy's budget was $10.1 million. His office supervised the doormen who tended the entrances to the House floor and galleries, the pages and the cloakroom workers. He oversaw the document room, which distributed documents to the public, and the members' photography and publications distribution services.

The press galleries fell under his bailiwick, although like the Senate's they were relatively autonomous. Included in his budget was money for two leased automobiles that were to cost $8,800, one for shuttling pages around, the other for Molloy to use for errands.

The clerk, doorkeeper and sergeant at arms were the House's top officers. They were elected by the members of every Congress, traditionally on a party-line vote in which the majority party nominees won. The chaplain also was an elected official. A fifth elective post, the postmaster, was abolished in 1992.

▶ **House Information Systems.** Unlike the Senate, where the sergeant at arms oversaw the computer system, the House's system was run by a standing committee — House Administration, which operated a separate office for that purpose. Called House Information Systems, it employed up to 254 people. Its budget was to total $22.9 million, but only $14.6 million was directly appropriated in the bill; reimbursements from legislative branch agencies for computer services covered the rest.

▶ **Inspector General.** The previous year's administrative reform measure (H Res 423) created an Office of Inspector General, but House leaders did not appoint one until Oct. 27, when they named John W. Lainhart IV, an assistant inspector general for the Transportation Department, to take the job, effective Nov. 14. It was not clear from the bill what Lainhart's total fiscal 1994 budget was to be, though he said in an interview in October that he was to earn at least $115,700 a year and that his office was to have two other employees to start, as well as help from the General Accounting Office.

▶ **Other offices.** The other six administrative offices funded by the bill were the chaplain ($123,000); the parliamentarian ($898,000); the historian ($310,000); the law revision counsel, which codified enacted laws into the U.S. Code ($1.5 million); the Legislative Counsel ($4.1 million); and the Office of General Counsel, the House's top lawyer ($674,000).

Leadership Offices

The five main leadership offices, which employed about 100 aides, were to get about $6.6 million under the bill — $1.4 million for the Speaker (Thomas S. Foley, D-Wash.); $1 million for the majority leader (Richard A. Gephardt, D-Mo.); $2.1 million for the minority leader (Robert H. Michel, R-Ill.); $1.2 million for the majority whip (David E. Bonior, D-Mich.); and $855,000 for the minority whip (Newt Gingrich, R-Ga.).

Not counting the Speaker's budget and $738,000 given to the minority leader for six extra aides to compensate his party for having no control over whom the Democrats picked to be the House's top elected officers, the budgets for the leaders and whips were evenly split between the parties.

The leadership accounts were among the only accounts in the bill to got substantial increases in 1993, averaging 5 percent ($313,000 in all). The reason: The Democrats added a fourth chief deputy whip (Bill Richardson, N.M.) to their team and decided to give him and the Republican leadership extra money for staff. The whips' budgets included money for the Democrats' four chief deputy whips' offices ($539,600) and for the Republicans' single chief deputy whip, Robert S. Walker, Pa. ($97,980).

▶ **Expense accounts.** Each leader's budget included an annual allowance for official expenses — $25,000 for the Speaker; $10,000 each for the two leaders; and $5,000 each for the whips. Bonior did not accept the money, an aide said, because he had almost no unreimbursed official expenses. The money was paid to each of the

others personally in monthly installments, and they did not have to account publicly for how they spent it. However, they were required to declare it as income for tax purposes and pay taxes on any amount not used for official expenses.

The expense money was in addition to their annual salaries (at the time, $171,500 for the Speaker, $148,400 for the two leaders and $133,600 for the whips).

▶ **Other accounts.** The bill elsewhere included money to lease cars for Speaker Foley (1991 Lincoln Town Car, $5,450), Majority Leader Gephardt (1992 Oldsmobile 98 Royale, $3,600) and Minority Leader Michel (1992 Cadillac Fleetwood, $5,100). Foley and Gephardt had Capitol police officers detailed to drive them around; Michel had a civilian chauffeur. Whips Bonior and Gingrich could get cars and drivers but declined them.

▶ **Party caucuses.** The two parties each got a pot of money (almost $1.5 million) for their main House organizations.

Most of the Democrats' money went to the Democratic Steering and Policy Committee (headed by Speaker Foley), the executive arm of the entire Democratic Caucus (headed by Steny H. Hoyer, Md.), which got the rest of the money.

In the bill, the GOP's money was all designated for the Republican Conference (headed by Dick Armey, Texas), but its budget also funded the Republican Policy Committee (headed by Henry J. Hyde, Ill.) and the Republican Research Committee (headed by Duncan Hunter, Calif.)

Other Expenses

▶ **Former Speakers.** The House paid for staffs for the three living former Speakers, for which $417,000 was appropriated. The former Speakers were authorized to spend up to another $67,000 each on other expenses, not counting their office rents or their franking costs. All told, their office budgets likely were to total nearly $200,000 each in fiscal 1994.

The bill included an amendment approved by the House by a 383-36 vote that was to cut off spending for the former Speakers' offices on Oct. 1, 1998. Future former Speakers were to get office expenses for five years.

▶ **Miscellany.** Various other accounts took up much of the rest of the House's money.

More than $115 million was to cover employee benefits.

About $800,000 was to pay for more than a million Capitol Historical Society calendars for members to give away. Incumbent members got 2,500 each, while retiring members each got 200. Committees made do with 200 copies each of a different calendar, the Government Printing Office's two-year version.

Another $27 million was to cover office equipment, telephone expenses, furniture, parking lot rentals, copies of the U.S. Code for members, uniform laundering services, subscriptions, closed captioning of floor proceedings on C-SPAN, photography supplies, employee transportation subsidies, blank video tapes, Federal Express and Wells Fargo services, leadership and committee stationery, stenographic services, death benefits paid to heirs of deceased House employees, automobile repairs and "interparliamentary receptions."

LEGISLATIVE BRANCH AGENCIES

The rest of the money in the bill was divided among agencies and divisions that worked only for Congress (such as the joint committees, the Congressional Budget Office and the Library of Congress' Congressional Research Service) and entities deemed to have broader purposes (such as the rest of the Library of Congress and the General Accounting Office).

Together, the bill appropriated $1.1 billion for these agencies. They employed about 19,000 workers.

Using the panel's breakdown, direct congressional operations were to cost $1.55 billion ($443 million for the Senate and $686 million for the House and $418 million for entities that directly served Congress).

In the descriptions that follow, agencies' total budgets are given

regardless of how they were split up in the bill.

▸ **Joint committees.** The bill funded three committees that had members from both chambers and a total of 145 employees. The Joint Committee on Taxation, Congress' official estimate-producer for revenue measures, was to get $5.7 million. The Joint Economic Committee, which studied the nation's economic health on a continuing basis, was to get $4 million. The Joint Committee on Printing, which oversaw government printing programs, including the Government Printing Office, was to get $1.3 million.

The Joint Committee on the Organization of Congress, which expired at the end of 1993, was funded under each chamber's regular committee budget. Its budget for calendar 1993: nearly $1 million.

▸ **Capitol Police.** The budget was to be $64.2 million, almost all of which was for the salaries of about 1,300 employees. The payroll budget was split between the House ($29.5 million) and the Senate ($32.8 million). The police were controlled by the Capitol Police Board, made up of the two sergeants at arms and the Architect of the Capitol.

The bill required the Treasury Department to cover the cost of basic training for the police.

The bill's House and Senate drafters ordered the police to limit the number of cars available to be taken home by officers to three — one for the chief and two others.

▸ **Capitol Guide Service.** This agency ran tours, showing off the Capitol to more than a million visitors a year. Its budget was to be $1.6 million, enough for 45 employees, including a dozen temporary guides to be hired "during emergencies," according to the bill.

▸ **Special Services Office.** This office, with a budget of $363,000, helped disabled guests, staff members and visitors.

▸ **Office of Technology Assessment** (OTA). With a budget of $21.3 million and up to 143 employees, this was the smallest of Congress' main legislative support agencies (behind the General Accounting Office, the Congressional Budget Office and the Library of Congress' Congressional Research Service). Established in 1972, it studied high-tech issues for Congress.

▸ **Congressional Budget Office (CBO).** This 226-person agency studied a range of budget-related issues for Congress and determined the cost of each bill, providing a counterweight to the White House's Office of Management and Budget. CBO had a budget of $22.3 million.

▸ **General Accounting Office (GAO).** Aside from the House and the Senate, the GAO had the single largest budget in the bill — about $430 million. The GAO investigated and audited government agencies for Congress and had employees scattered in offices across the country and overseas. The bill required the GAO to reduce its staff level to 4,800, a decline of 100 from fiscal 1993.

The bill ordered the GAO to spend up to $500,000 on an independent "broad-based performance review" of its work. The agency had been under fire in recent years from some Western Democrats and Republicans for alleged bias. The Senate approved a similar study the previous year, but it was rejected by the House; in 1993, the House initiated the study. Separately, the Senate Governmental Affairs Committee had asked the National Academy of Public Administration to study GAO.

The Senate Appropriations Committee praised the GAO for reducing the number of offices it maintained around the country but urged it to consider closing more.

▸ **Library of Congress.** The library had a split budget because only the Congressional Research Service (CRS) was considered part of Congress' organization.

The library, with about 5,000 employees, was to have a $432 million budget, but only about $317.5 million was included in the legislative branch spending bill. About $56.7 million was for the CRS, whose 800 employees responded to hundreds of thousands of research requests a year for members. The remaining $260.8 million was for the rest of the library. The money included $42.7 million to provide special books and audio materials to hundreds of thousands of disabled people.

At the Senate's insistence, the bill included $1 million for the library to complete a report on its American Memory project, which for two years enabled children in 30 states to "visit" the library's historical archives via television videodiscs and audio compact discs. But, the conferees warned, "The Library of Congress was to not extend its role in the creation or assembly of educational material." The rest of a $2.9 million library request for "information-age" programs was denied.

An additional $10 million, part of the Architect of the Capitol's budget, paid for maintenance of the library's main buildings in Washington. The bill allowed the library to transfer up to $3.8 million from its budget to the architect's to finish the renovation of the Thomas Jefferson and John Adams buildings. Up to $7 million more in prior-year funds was set aside to replace the Thomas Jefferson Building's roof.

The rest of the library's budget ($115 million) came from fees paid for public services, reimbursements from other government agencies and donations from outside organizations. Included in this figure was overhead money from royalty revenues paid to the Copyright Office by cable television stations, the digital audio device industry and other copyright users. The bulk of the royalties — an estimated $340 million in fiscal 1994 — was distributed to copyright holders by the Copyright Royalty Tribunal.

The bill required the library to help establish a "Great Basin Intergovernmental Center" at the University of Nevada, Senate Subcommittee Chairman Harry Reid's home state, and allowed the center to "accept contributions from federal sources" as well as "non-federal sources." The Senate committee's report said the center "was designed to improve the interface" between the federal and state and local governments in the West's Great Basin. It was to serve as "a meeting and training center" and an "independent research" facility to study public policy issues related to the West.

The bill's House and Senate conferees attempted to settle a dispute between the Library of Congress and the Gettysburg National Military Park in Pennsylvania over where to house the first of five drafts of President Abraham Lincoln's Gettysburg address. One of two drafts of the speech owned by the library had been on loan to the park for about 12 years, and more than 500,000 visitors a year viewed it. The library kept its other draft in a vault where few ever saw it. The library had expressed concern about the preservation of the first draft, but the conferees said they wanted it kept in Gettysburg, a location they said was both secure and altogether fitting. The language was backed by Gettysburg's congressman, Republican Rep. Bill Goodling, who worked the issue with well-placed Pennsylvanians on the Appropriations Committee.

▸ **Architect of the Capitol.** The architect, George M. White, maintained the Capitol and its office buildings, the Library of Congress and the Supreme Court — 12 million square feet. The architect also cared for its grounds and its power plant. The office employed more than 2,000 people and had a budget of $150.2 million, not counting the $10 million for Library of Congress buildings and $2.9 million for the Supreme Court. The office also ran the Senate restaurant (but not the House's), provided custodial services for some parts of the Capitol Hill complex and oversaw the House's 22 elevator operators (but not the Senate's). It also employed the House gym's workers and both chamber's subway operators.

Included in its budget was $100,000 "to meet unforeseen expenses," but the Senate knocked out language that would have allowed the money to remain available for years.

The architect also employed the workers who flew flags over the Capitol so members could send them to constituents. He requested but was denied another $31,000-a-year worker for the program, which he called an "essential service to the Congress." The Flag Office had six employees who ran the operation; laborers from elsewhere actually ran the flags up and down six poles for an hour or two a day. The architect's office expected to fly 150,000 flags in fiscal 1994 at a cost of more than $250,000.

The architect asked for money to begin a seven-year, $24.5

million renovation program to comply with the 1990 Americans with Disabilities Act (ADA) — a program his top lawyer told Congress would make Capitol buildings "a model of compliance with the Act."

But the Senate cut the architect's $700,000 request for ADA improvements to Senate buildings to zero, the House cut the $900,000 request for House buildings to $400,000 and together the two chambers cut the $550,000 request for the Capitol and its grounds to $325,000 and the $750,000 request for the Library of Congress to $200,000.

Also included in the architect's budget was $50,000 for the conservation of wall paintings; $600,000 to modernize elevators and escalators; $4.9 million to relocate the Senate library (except its reading room) from just under the chamber's dome to the Dirksen and Hart buildings; $100,000 for a "lightning protection system" for the Senate's Russell Building; $500,000 to improve the Capitol dome's drainage system; $2 million to continue retrofitting the Capitol complex with low-energy lighting; $200,000 to upgrade X-ray machines and $250,000 to replace sidewalks.

The Senate committee chided the architect for allowing some furnishings in hearing rooms to be "in shabby condition" and ordered him to survey them to make sure "their appearance and function were appropriate to meet the operational needs of the Senate." (The architect was not in charge of House furnishings; Wishart was.)

Funding for the Supreme Court building, $2.9 million, was included in the Commerce, Justice, State spending bill.

▶ **Botanic Garden.** This $3 million, 57-employee agency, founded in 1820 and run by the Architect of the Capitol, collected and cultivated plants for display and offered tours and various classes on plants. It also supplied landscaping plants for the Capitol grounds. Each member's office used to be able to borrow six potted plants, but the House halted that practice in response to the 1992 controversy over members' perks; the Senate still allowed it. The garden provided floral displays for some official functions.

Congress rejected a $7 million request to renovate the garden's conservatory near the Capitol. In 1992, $2 million was appropriated to design the conservatory project, but the Senate subcommittee in 1993 said construction funds might not be available for years.

In a written question to White, the panel asked, "Why not just face facts and close [the] Botanic Garden and transfer its function to, say, the National Arboretum?" White said that would not save much money and noted that it would be difficult to use the conservatory for anything besides plants without "considerable expense."

▶ **Copyright Royalty Tribunal.** This obscure agency, which distributed royalties to various copyright holders, had a budget of $1 million, of which $900,000 was offset by the royalties, which were collected by the Library of Congress' Copyright Office. In the fall of 1993, Congress enacted a bill (HR 2840) that was to abolish the three-member tribunal and its six-person staff and replace them with temporary arbitration panels to settle future copyright disputes.

▶ **Government Printing Office (GPO).** The bill included a total of $117.5 million for the GPO, of which $88.4 million was for congressional printing and binding services, including $25 million for the Congressional Record ($481 a page, on average), $10.7 million for bills and resolutions and $22 million for hearing transcripts.

The GPO was actually a much bigger agency than those figures implied. Employing nearly 5,000 people, it was the federal government's main printer and known as the biggest printing shop in the world — even though more than 75 percent of its work was contracted out to private printers.

The bill also authorized the GPO's revolving fund, which financed its non-congressional printing operations. Nearly $1 billion was to flow through the fund in fiscal 1994. Most of that money was from executive branch agencies and was appropriated through other spending bills. The bill allowed the GPO to start spending receipts from the sale of government publications instead of turning them over to the Treasury.

In their report on the bill, House and Senate conferees requested that the Joint Committee on Printing review the practice of assigning GPO detailees to congressional committees, warning that they believed "significant changes were needed in this practice." The detailees helped print committee reports.

▶ **Office of the Attending Physician.** Based near the Capitol's rotunda, Congress' health clinic employed 32 people, including three doctors, 13 nurses and 10 technicians. Its budget came from three accounts and totaled about $2.4 million. It provided health-care services to the Capitol Hill complex, including members. The bill identified about $1.6 million for the office (including $146,000 in the House budget); more than half reimbursed the Navy for military personnel and equipment. The rest of the physician's budget ($800,000 or so) came from the Architect's budget and paid the salaries of the nurses who staffed first aid rooms in various Capitol Hill buildings.

In the wake of the previous year's controversy over perks, congressional leaders announced that members would be charged an annual fee of $520 if they wanted to take advantage of the office's previously free non-emergency services, including office visits, routine exams and laboratory and X-ray work. Leaders also ended the office's practice of dispensing free prescription drugs to members. (Members paid separate fees for health insurance.)

The $520 figure was based on the average cost of federal group health plans in Washington, D.C. In 1993, the House Administration Committee cut the fee House members paid to $263.19, reasoning that the value of services provided by the physicians' office "amounts to less than 45 percent" of the value of those provided under federal health plans. Senators still paid $520. Most members in both chambers reportedly paid the fees, which did not nearly cover the office's cost.

Emergency care was still provided free of charge to all.

GENERAL PROVISIONS

The bill included several changes in laws and rules related to Congress. The most significant:

Architect of the Capitol, the Capitol Police, the CBO, the GAO, the GPO, the OTA and the Library of Congress were to cut their staffs by at least 4 percent by the end of fiscal 1995. At least 2.5 percent had to be cut by the end of fiscal 1994. Ten percent of the positions had to be higher-pay jobs. The base for calculating the cuts was the number of employees on staff on Sept. 30, 1992, unless the Appropriations Committees approved a later date (up to Sept. 30, 1993) for a particular agency.

In June, the House Appropriations Committee estimated that the provision would reduce the Sept. 30, 1992, employment level of the covered entities by 920 in fiscal 1994 — from 37,087 to 36,167 — for a total savings of more than $50 million. Since that estimate was produced, the Senate decided to exempt positions funded by gifts and trust funds.

The bill also required the same agencies, as well as the Copyright Royalty Tribunal, to cut "administrative expenses" by 14 percent by the end of fiscal 1997. The House committee predicted this provision would cut the cost of the $2.3 billion bill by less than $1 million.

The House and Senate committees said the reductions from these two provisions were modeled after executive branch cuts ordered by President Clinton earlier in the year. It was unclear whether these cuts were to force members themselves to make do with fewer aides, because the bill did not explicitly require them to cut their own staffs.

▶ **Early retirement.** The measure allowed the GAO, the GPO and the Library of Congress to offer early retirement options to their employees in an attempt to cut their staffs. The library said on Oct. 14 that 149 staffers took advantage of the option on the first day it was offered, accepting up to $25,000 each.

▶ **Midsession relocations.** No money in the bill could be used to relocate any House member's office. The provision was designed to stop the musical-chairs shuffle for better offices that traditionally followed midterm vacancies. Relocations were to have to wait until at least the end of fiscal 1994, and perhaps until the end of the 103rd Congress. ∎

Funding for Military Construction Is Up

Although the size of the U.S. military was declining, the price tag on the fiscal 1994 military construction bill — which paid the costs of building and closing U.S. military bases and housing military personnel and their families — was $10.1 billion, $1.7 billion more than was approved for fiscal 1993.

Of the total, $2.68 billion was earmarked for cleaning up and closing surplus military bases in an effort to produce long-term savings.

The bill (HR 2446) cut President Clinton's request by $729 million. It was slightly less than the $10.27 billion the House had passed in June, although it exceeded the $9.8 billion bill the Senate passed in September. Demanding that U.S. allies pay more, lawmakers provided just $140 million of the $240 million that Clinton had requested for the U.S. contribution to building and maintaining NATO's bases and barracks.

Clinton signed the measure Oct. 21 (PL 103-110).

Funding for military construction projects for the Army, Navy, Air Force and Marines totaled almost $3.74 billion for fiscal 1994. The administration had requested $3.77 billion. Big winners were the politically well-connected National Guard and reserve forces, which garnered $752 million, more than twice the requested $352 million.

The Defense Department received $3.5 billion of the $3.76 billion that the administration sought for family housing. The final bill cut requested levels for family housing for all three branches of the military. The Army received $1.30 billion of its requested $1.34 billion; the Navy received $1.10 billion of its $1.21 billion request; and the Air Force received $923 million of its requested $1.03 billion.

W. G. "Bill" Hefner, D-N.C., chairman of the House Military Construction Appropriations Subcommittee, said the bill included $500 million for a Pentagon initiative to upgrade and replace "antiquated World War II barracks" and to "repair and replace housing that is substandard and dangerous to the health of families because of the presence of asbestos and lead-based paint."

The $2.68 billion for base realignment and closing was a cut from the $3.03 billion requested by the administration. The figure was an increase from the $2.03 billion appropriated for fiscal 1993.

BACKGROUND

Until 1958, construction funds for U.S. military bases were included in the annual defense appropriations bill. That year, the House Appropriations Committee created the Military Construction Subcommittee and the first military construction appropriations bill.

The bill covered the annual cost of building U.S. bases

BOXSCORE

➡ **Military Construction Appropriations bill (HR 2446).** The $10.1 billion bill paid for the cost of building U.S. and overseas military bases and housing military personnel and their families.

Reports: H Rept 103-136, S Rept 103-148; conference report, H Rept 103-278.

KEY ACTION

June 23 — **House** passed the bill, 347-67.

Sept. 30 — **Senate** approved the bill by voice vote.

Oct. 13 — **House** agreed to the conference report by voice vote.

Oct. 19 — **Senate** agreed to the conference report, 94-5.

Oct. 21 — **President** signed HR 2446 — PL 103-110.

---

around the world, including everything from houses, shops and recreation centers to infrastructure needs such as roads, utilities, hospitals and schools. Since 1989, the bill also had paid for the cost of closing unneeded military bases.

For a measure that cost the government more than $10 billion and affected about 1.6 million active-duty personnel and their dependents, the bill generated remarkably little controversy.

As in the past, debate in the committees and on the floor rarely lasted longer than a few minutes. But even as the military grappled with the problems of a 25 percent, five-year force reduction and a continually shrinking budget, military construction remained expensive — $3.9 billion for new base facility projects, $3.5 billion to operate and maintain housing and $2.7 billion to close bases. The bill was 20 percent more than its fiscal 1993 counterpart. *(1992 Almanac, p. 623)*

The Clinton administration had little impact on the 1993 bill. An attempt by Pentagon officials to drop Congress' tradition of funding projects over a period of years instead of paying for costs up front was rebuffed in committee. And the administration's effort to be more of a team player in NATO fell flat too when the president's $240 million request for the U.S. share of funding for NATO infrastructure costs was almost halved.

HOUSE COMMITTEE ACTION

The House Military Construction Appropriations Subcommittee marked up HR 2446 in a five-minute closed session May 9, reportedly cutting at least $1.8 billion from the Clinton administration's request. "We cut everything," committee member Carrie Meek, D-Fla., said. "We had to."

Details of the markup were kept secret. Members and staff were instructed to leave all papers on the bill with committee staff. Norm Dicks, D-Wash., said the funding was between $8 billion and $9 billion.

Despite the tight budget, the panel reportedly lifted a suspension imposed the previous year on base construction. Congress had appropriated $3.9 billion for all defense housing programs in fiscal 1993.

With overseas base closures and the resulting troop shifts, "you've got a lot of people coming home and no place to put them — literally," said one source close to the committee.

A Department of Defense spokesman said military personnel returning from Europe to Fort Bragg, N.C., had to wait several years before moving into base housing.

The somber fiscal mood in the subcommittee was a definite about-face from the last time it marked up a funding bill. In 1992, the subcommittee voted out an $8.6

MILITARY CONSTRUCTION

	Fiscal 1993 Appropriation	Fiscal 1994 Clinton Request	House Bill	Senate Bill	Final Bill
	(In thousands of dollars)				
Military construction					
Army	$ 425,270	$ 776,642	$ 837,644	$ 709,605	$ 892,776
Navy	371,887	655,123	575,971	511,081	558,746
Air Force	717,280	906,378	913,297	947,016	991,472
Defense agencies	262,116	1,077,718	618,770	508,665	546,508
NATO infrastructure	60,000	240,000	140,000	—	140,000
Outside U.S. account	—	—	—	300,000	—
National Guard and reserves	584,648	351,769	548,349	764,407	751,765
Subtotal	**$ 2,421,201**	**$ 4,007,630**	**$ 3,634,031**	**$ 3,740,774**	**$ 3,881,267**
Family housing					
Army	$ 1,523,692	$ 1,343,474	$ 1,286,295	$ 1,353,574	$ 1,298,074
Navy	1,044,025	1,208,824	1,149,721	1,164,775	1,101,892
Air Force	1,211,727	1,027,147	998,044	993,845	922,845
Defense agencies	28,400	27,496	25,870	27,496	26,496
Homeowners Assistance Fund	133,000	151,400	151,400	151,400	151,400
Subtotal	**$ 3,940,844**	**$ 3,758,341**	**$ 3,611,330**	**$ 3,691,090**	**$ 3,500,707**
Base realignment and closure	**$ 2,034,300**	**$ 3,028,370**	**$ 3,028,370**	**$ 2,736,140**	**$ 2,683,140**
Appropriations reduction	—	—	—	−$ 414,527	—
GRAND TOTAL	**$ 8,396,345**	**$ 10,794,341**	**$ 10,273,731**	**$ 9,753,477**	**$ 10,065,114**

SOURCE: House Appropriations Committee

billion measure, $290 million more than the Bush administration had requested.

Full Committee

The full House Appropriations Committee approved a $10.3 billion version of HR 2446 by voice vote June 17, cutting the Clinton administration's original request by $520 million (H Rept 103-136).

The markup held the full committee's attention for about five minutes with little discussion and no proposed amendments.

The cost of closing bases continued its upward tick in 1993, increasing by about $994 million to $3 billion. Of that, $582 million was to go to the environmental cleanup of bases that were being closed. The committee's report on the bill emphasized that the cost of closing bases accounted for 30 percent of the bill and had increased 300 percent since fiscal 1992.

Still, members called the funding "reasonable" and a good investment. "It's going to take five to 10 years before we realize any savings on base closures," said subcommittee Chairman Hefner.

The committee imposed a $286 million "general reduction" in anticipation of savings from construction projects that were no longer needed at bases that had been ordered to close. It apportioned the cuts to the different services on the basis of an initial list of recommended closures that Defense Secretary Les Aspin released in March.

Funds in the bill for military construction projects grew by $1.1 billion over fiscal 1993 after a one-year spending "pause" instituted by President George Bush and the Department of Defense.

The committee approved $311.3 million for construction of new family housing, accepting all the projects sought by the administration except a Navy project in Scotland.

Some other items in the administration's family housing budget did not fare as well. The request for operations and maintenance of base housing — utilities, repairs and the like — for active-duty personnel was cut by $160 million to $2.7 billion.

Clinton's request for NATO's infrastructure fund took a big hit, as had become customary. The committee agreed to provide $140 million (Clinton sought $240 million). That was still $80 million more than the fiscal 1993 U.S. contribution.

Funding for overseas programs — long a favorite target of domestic-minded appropriators — emerged unscathed, largely because of the costs of the Navy's relocation from the Philippines to Guam.

Under the bill, Florida's Homestead Air Force Base, heavily damaged in 1992 by Hurricane Andrew, was slated to receive a second life as a reserve military and civilian airfield, paid for with $76 million in unused planning and restoration funds. The funds also were to be used to build a hospital for the area's many retired and reserve personnel.

It still paid for a state to have strong representation on the Appropriations Committee — even when that state had bases slated for closure. The doomed Philadelphia Naval Shipyard — in the home state of three committee members — was allocated $4.5 million beyond the Navy's request for

those operations that were to continue after the rest of the base was closed.

HOUSE FLOOR ACTION

The House passed the $10.3 billion military construction appropriations bill June 23, cutting the Clinton administration's original request by $521 million and adding more than 100 domestic spending projects not requested by the Pentagon. HR 2446 won swift and overwhelming approval, 347-67. *(Vote 261, p. 64-H)*

"I point out that this is a jobs bill," said supporter G. V. "Sonny" Montgomery, D-Miss. "It will put people back to work. It is military construction, and it spreads defense spending around the country in the United States. It gives people jobs in small states building armories and ranges."

Passage of the annual bill had long been fueled by the jobs and other benefits of military base improvements that appropriators spread through favored congressional districts. "The defense budget has become a pot of gold for members of Congress who can't get their programs funded in other budgets," complained Harris W. Fawell, R-Ill.

Fawell led a group of self-styled "porkbusters" who made a botched attempt to eliminate $520 million for 143 projects that the committee had added or expanded in the bill.

The amendment never came to a vote because Fawell made the mistake of leaving the floor in the middle of what turned out to be a brief debate on the measure. "He was not on the floor, and we certainly weren't going to call him," said Barbara F. Vucanovich, R-Nev., ranking member of the Military Construction Appropriations panel.

As usual, the construction bill was laden with projects in the states and districts of Appropriations Committee members. High on the winner's list was Texas, with five committee members and $49.57 million in construction projects over the $259.4 million that the administration requested. California's six committee members boasted of $103.7 million, $36.7 million more than requested.

The power to move money did not always come through numbers. Vucanovich managed to get an extra $11.9 million for five projects in her state — twice as much money for nearly twice as many projects as requested. Four of the projects were in her district.

Vic Fazio, Calif., the No. 2 Democrat on the Energy and Water Development Appropriations Subcommittee, steered an unrequested $50 million to the Pentagon's energy conservation program. Of that, $3 million went to a public/private consortium of California-based power companies researching and manufacturing solar energy products for sale in the commercial market.

Indiana's two Appropriations members funneled to their state about $19.7 million for six unrequested building projects. The administration had sought $4.1 million for four projects.

SENATE COMMITTEE ACTION

The Senate Appropriations Committee approved a $9.8 billion version of the bill (S Rept 103-148) by a vote of 28-0 on Sept. 23, cutting the Clinton administration's original request by $1 billion. The measure was $519 million less than the House had approved.

The markup took about 10 minutes, with Committee Chairman Robert C. Byrd, D-W.Va., telling members to hold back controversial amendments until the bill came before the full Senate.

In a move reflecting reluctance to spend scarce funds on overseas bases, the panel sidestepped the administration's $240 million request for NATO's "infrastructure fund." Instead of trimming the request, as the House had, Senate appropriators voted to establish a $300 million "special account" for both NATO and U.S. overseas bases. The panel said the administration's request for the two items was more than $450 million. The committee report directed the Defense Department to "seek greater burden-sharing payments from our allies."

The committee's preliminary report protested that the Senate Armed Services Committee "added more than $1 billion not included in the president's budget request" for military construction to its version of the annual defense authorization bill (S 1298). Military Construction Subcommittee Chairman Jim Sasser, D-Tenn., wryly told Byrd, "There are no additions for West Virginia, and there are no additions for Tennessee." *(Defense authorization, p. 433)*

To compensate for the Armed Services additions, the appropriators imposed a 4 percent across-the-board reduction on the military construction bill. The move deferred the decision on which projects to fund until a House-Senate conference committee met on the bill.

Sasser offered a $25 million addition for construction of a chemical weapons destruction facility in Indiana. The amendment, adopted by voice vote, also directed the Defense Department to obligate, but not add, funds for five such facilities scattered across the continental United States.

The Senate bill provided for a $1.3 billion increase for military construction over fiscal 1993.

The committee provided $2.7 billion for base closings. On Sept. 20, the Senate rejected an effort to block the closings, guaranteeing that they went into effect. *(Base closures, p. 465)*

The committee report also said that the cost of moving the Agana Naval Air Station on Guam to the Andersen Air Force Base on the same island should be shouldered by the local community because the base was being relocated at the request of Guam's representatives in order to permit new development.

The Navy would be directed to halt payment of funds for Guam from the base-closure account until a civilian financing plan had been submitted and approved by the secretary of the Navy.

SENATE FLOOR ACTION

The Senate approved the $9.8 billion bill by voice vote Sept. 30. The early evening action was handled without roll call votes or debate after a number of senators expressed their desire to leave for events that included a child's birthday party and a back-to-school night.

The Senate adopted without debate an amendment by Frank R. Lautenberg, D-N.J., that held hostage $120 million of the $300 million in the bill for NATO's "infrastructure fund" and for overseas bases. The money was not to be spent until the secretary of Defense certified that negotiations were under way — and making progress — for "host nations" to pick up more of the costs of U.S. military operations overseas.

The Senate also approved by voice vote:

● An amendment by Daniel K. Inouye, D-Hawaii, providing for the transfer of 50 to 70 acres of Navy land to the city of Honolulu.

● An amendment by Sasser earmarking $9.2 million to extend a runway at Maxwell Air Force Base in Alabama.

FINAL ACTION

A House-Senate conference committee agreed by voice vote Oct. 7 to appropriate $10.1 billion in fiscal 1994 for military construction projects.

The House approved the conference report (H Rept 103-278) by voice vote Oct. 13. The Senate cleared the bill, 94-5, on Oct. 19. *(Vote 316, p. 41-S)*

Conferees agreed to the House decision to provide $140 million for NATO's infrastructure fund.

The conference report also expressed "regret" at reducing the administration request of $2.84 billion for operations and maintenance of family housing to $2.66 billion.

Some states emerged as winners in allocations of construction money. Texas, for example, would have received $309 million in the House bill but only $233 million in the Senate's. Conferees compromised at $286 million, more than the administration request of $259 million.

California, which had been hit heavily by domestic base closings, also came out ahead. Conferees approved $150 million in projects for California, well in excess of the administration's request for $117 million and the $129 million that the Senate had approved. The House earmarked $160 million for the state.

Lawmakers trimmed spending for the 1993 round of base closures to $2.7 billion.

Conferees also dropped Inouye's amendment to transfer Navy land to the city of Honolulu. ■

Military Construction Provisions

The military construction appropriations bill, HR 2446, paid for the building of military bases in the United States and around the world, for housing military personnel and their families, and — in an activity that began in 1989 and was certain to become more common — for closing unneeded military bases.

CONSTRUCTION PROJECTS

Loaded into this category — which received $3.9 billion in fiscal 1994 — were many popular construction projects that members of Congress could bring home to their districts. Most of the funds would end up being contracted out to local companies to build structures on military bases.

Barracks

Despite a 25 percent reduction in troop levels expected by 1997, Congress and the Pentagon wanted to spend hundreds of millions of dollars to repair troop housing and build new barracks.

Barracks was housing for "unaccompanied" or single members of the military. Congress appropriated $417.5 million for barracks construction, covering 37 projects in 19 states.

Both House and Senate reports on the legislation emphasized lawmakers' opinion that the quality of life for members of the military constantly needed improvement, even in an era of shrinking forces.

▶ **Major projects.** The costs for barracks projects in fiscal 1994 ranged from $32 million to build a 384-person quarters for Army enlisted personnel at Fort Campbell, Ky., to $1.7 million for modernization of enlisted quarters at Corpus Christi Naval Air Station in Texas.

Reserve and National Guard

Every year the president's request for military construction faced intense scrutiny as members juggled the interests of the administration, individual services and their own concerns for projects they deemed necessary. The part-time soldiers, sailors and airmen of the reserve forces provided lawmakers a particularly tempting opportunity to demonstrate, through base improvements, their influence to voters back home. Fiscal 1994 was no different.

Congress appropriated $751.8 million for non-active-duty forces, more than twice the amount requested by President Clinton. The funds went for construction of training facilities, maintenance shops for on-site weapons and storage buildings.

Of the funding for the National Guard and reserves, $98 million went for new armories at 34 sites across the country, totaling about $7 million. For Guard and reserve troops, an armory functioned as a drill hall and also contained offices.

Facilities for Weapons

To accommodate new military planes, weapons and other hardware, specialized structures frequently were needed. For example, each new airplane called for different types of runways and hangars. To keep up with technology, the military construction bill funded projects to house the new weapons that were purchased through the bigger defense appropriations bill.

▶ **C-17 facilities.** The fiscal 1994 bill included $15.2 million for specialized construction for the C-17 cargo planes to be stationed at Altus Air Force Base in Oklahoma and Kelly Air Force Base in Texas. That money was split almost evenly between the two bases. At Altus the money was used to build a maintenance shop specially designed for the C-17 ($3.3 million), four new bays to house new six-way C-17 flight simulators for rookie crews ($2.9 million) and a fire station ($780,000). At Kelly the money was used to expand and modernize an aircraft inspection hangar constructed in 1942 ($4.9 million), build an engineering test laboratory to investigate mishaps and routine service problems ($2.6 million) and provide alterations to the base's existing avionics facility ($731,000).

▶ **B-2 facilities.** The fiscal 1994 appropriation for B-2 stealth bomber facilities was $43.5 million for eight construction projects at Whiteman Air Force Base in Missouri. The biggest expense ($14.5 million) was the seventh and eighth maintenance docks of a planned 14-dock hangar. The B-2 ground crew work areas were to be specially constructed to withstand the extreme heat from jet blasts as aircraft taxied out, and the area also had to provide specially sized doors for loading trailers carrying bombs and bullets. The money also was used to finance three major road and runway upgrade projects needed to handle the increased traffic and weight of the B-2 and vehicles associated with the bomber ($13.3 million). Funds were also used to increase power and sewerage capabilities ($4.8 million), expand the armory ($3.3 million), construct a two-loop hydrant fueling system ($2.7 million) and build a new maintenance shop ($1.7 million).

▶ **Other projects.** Major new construction to accommodate weapons included:

— $24.4 million for four projects to alter buildings and water and power utilities at Robins Air Force Base, Ga., for JSTARS radar planes.

— $10.2 million to build a research and development engineering facility for ship defenses at Wallops Island, Va. The facility was to be used to install and improve upon the latest technological developments in electronic defenses against missile attack.

— $2.9 million to upgrade a 13-mile target test track at the Army's White Sands Missile Range in New Mexico. The money also was to be used to build six optical instrumentation sites to simultaneously track and record multiple weapons firings during testing.

— $2.7 million to finance construction of a specialized maintenance support facility for a fleet of T-1 planes at Vance Air Force Base, Okla. The T-1 was a jet designed to train college students to become cargo pilots.

Training Facilities

The bill appropriated $241 million for construction of buildings, firing ranges, obstacle courses and battle simulation facilities used to teach military personnel how to do everything from fighting fires to operating weapons and weapon delivery systems such as tanks and planes.

Although the average cost for each of the 74 projects related to training was $3.3 million, the price tag for four projects was significantly higher: $18.5 million for construction of a medical training facility for special forces combat medics at Fort Bragg, N.C.; $14 million to build a school to train Army personnel in supply logistics and chemical weapons handling at the Aberdeen Proving Ground in Maryland; $10 million for construction of a maintenance and training equipment site for the Army National Guard at Fort Knox, Ky.; and $9.7 million for an Air National Guard communications electronics training facility in State College, Pa.

Hospitals

The bill appropriated $160.6 million for hospital construction projects in fiscal 1994. (This did not include funds to improve or replace hospitals that were affected by base closings, which were in a separate base-closings account.)

The Pentagon maintained 140 hospitals and 553 clinics around the world that provided free medical care to members of the military and their dependents and to retired military personnel. Construction of hospitals was one of the big-ticket items in the annual military construction bill. Many of the hospitals were multimillion-dollar projects whose funding was spread over several years.

For example, a replacement for Portsmouth Naval Hospital in Virginia received $20 million in fiscal 1994. But that covered only the fifth phase of the project, construction of an acute care facility. Since fiscal 1990, Congress had appropriated $104.5 million for the first four phases of the hospital replacement. The hospital was to cost $316.4 million over seven years of construction.
▶ **Other projects.** Major hospital projects and their fiscal 1994 funding included $37 million for a new hospital at Elmendorf Air Force Base in Alaska and $50 million for a new hospital complex at the Army's Fort Sam Houston in Texas.

Child-Care Centers

These centers were a relatively new feature on many military bases and a sign of growing concern about the quality of life for military families. The Pentagon requested $55 million for 18 child-care center projects at military bases around the world.

Congress appropriated the funds for each project at the level requested. And for good measure, the domestic-minded lawmakers added $7 million for construction of three more day-care centers at bases in Maryland, Mississippi and New Mexico.

Each center was relatively inexpensive in comparison with other military facilities in the bill. The costs ranged from $5.4 million for a center at Eielson Air Force Base in Alaska to $940,000 to build a 110-child facility at the Marine Corps Logistics Base in Albany, Ga. The Marine Corps' official request to Congress noted that the existing day-care center was adjacent to the brig and 250 feet away from an ammunition storehouse.

Overseas, the government was to spend more than $13 million for new child-care centers. Of this, $3.1 million was to go to Ramstein Air Force Base in Germany, $4.5 million for construction of a center at the naval hospital and naval station in Guam, $3.5 million to Sigonella Naval Air Station in Italy and $2.7 million to Rota Naval Station in Spain.

Physical Fitness Centers

Not surprisingly, the military was concerned with the shape its soldiers and sailors were in, and most U.S. bases had physical training centers.

These gyms had typical health club equipment — stationary bicycles, treadmills and weight-training apparatus. Many centers also had swimming pools nearby.

The bill for fiscal 1994 provided $13.4 million to the military for construction and improvements at three centers: the U.S. Naval Academy at Annapolis, Md. ($6.5 million); Nellis Air Force Base, Nev. ($4.3 million); and the Army's Fort Gillem, Ga. ($2.6 million).

Overseas Construction

For construction projects overseas, the bill provided $135.2 million. Among those projects, $54.7 million was to go to Guam; $21.2 million was to build a sewage plant ($11.2 million) and a housing complex ($10 million) on Kwajalein Atoll; and $11.8 million was to construct a diesel fuel storage facility ($9.6 million) and two storage facilities ($2.3 million) on Diego Garcia. The bill appropriated $10.8 million for classified overseas construction projects.
▶ **Guam.** The biggest overseas construction project — $54.7 million on Guam in the western Pacific — included building a general warehouse and materiel handling facility ($21.2 million); constructing an explosive ordnance disposal operations facility ($12.5 million); renovating and modernizing bachelor enlisted and officer quarters ($7.3 million); and expanding a wastewater treatment plant ($7.2 million). The improvements were needed to accommodate ships and aircraft relocated by the closing of Navy and Air Force bases in the Philippines. Clinton had asked for $78.5 million to ease the transition.
▶ **NATO fund.** The bill was to provide $140 million for NATO's infrastructure fund, the pooled contributions that paid for construction of bases used by the North Atlantic Treaty Organization. Clinton had requested $240 million for the fund, but Congress balked, calling instead for "host nations" to pay more for operating and maintaining bases on foreign soil.

Miscellaneous

The measure appropriated $349.6 million for construction of pollution control measures, including: $95.5 million for waste water plant construction and system improvements; $86.9 million to build or replace fuel storage tanks at 70 locations; $62.3 million for sewage system and plant construction; $40.8 million for industrial waste destruction and storage facilities; $43.6 million to build nine hazardous waste processing facilities and three dump sites; and $3.6 million to seal fuel containment dikes and control fuel spills. The rest was split among smaller projects such as air emission controls, storm drainage repairs, and trash recycling projects.
▶ **By service:** The Army received $892.8 million for military construction in fiscal 1994; the Navy got $558.7 million; and the Air Force received $991.5 million.

FAMILY HOUSING

Because pay for members of the military was relatively low, Congress and the executive branch consistently had supplemented military paychecks with benefits such as imminent danger pay to make serving in the armed forces more attractive. One such perquisite was government aid in finding and paying for housing.

Depending on the location, the military would either provide housing on-base for soldiers and their families or give an allowance to help pay for housing in the surrounding civilian community.

Once on-base housing was full, the services looked first to communities that surrounded bases. But in some cases, renting or buying existing houses was very expensive, and construction of more government-owned buildings was considered a better value.

The Pentagon asked for $3.8 billion for construction of family housing, operations and maintenance costs and rental expenses for fiscal 1994, $183 million more than was appropriated in fiscal 1993.

That amount would have included funds for construction of

3,954 new units of housing. Congress approved $3.5 billion, including funds for 3,454 new housing units.

The military owned a total of 421,300 housing units as of 1992.

Construction

Of the funds for housing, $691 million was to pay for construction of new family housing projects, improvements to existing housing and planning costs.

▶ **Major projects.** Topping the list of major housing construction projects was $50.7 million for 388 units for enlisted personnel at the Navy's Ben Morrell subdivision in Norfolk, Va., and construction of four houses for officers in Little Creek, Va. The Navy's request noted that housing units at Ben Morrell were "structurally unsound" and "failing at a rate of six to eight per month."

Other major projects included:

— $36.6 million for construction of 218 new and 100 replacement homes for Navy junior enlisted families in the Bayview Housing Area in San Diego.

— $27.4 million for construction of 290 units at the Naval Submarine Base in Bangor, Wash.

— $52 million for construction of 348 units at the Army's Schofield Barracks in Hawaii.

— $26 million for construction of 275 Army units at Fort Mead, Md.

— $21.6 million for construction of 188 replacement homes for enlisted personnel at the Navy's Bellevue subdivision in Washington, D.C.

Operation Costs

The government picked up the tab for operating the housing. Military personnel living in on-base housing paid neither rent nor utilities.

For maintenance costs, which made up the bulk of family housing expenditures, Congress appropriated $2.66 billion.

The money went for items such as furniture ($124 million) and management costs ($213.4 million) associated with the base housing. That account also paid for off-base family housing units that the Pentagon leased for military personnel ($522.6 million).

▶ **Homeowners Assistance.** The bill included $151.4 million for the Homeowners Assistance Fund. This account helped personnel who, because of base closings or related activities, had to sell their houses at a loss. Owners were able to recapture as much as 95 percent of the value of their houses through this assistance.

▶ **By service:** The bill appropriated $1.3 billion for Army family housing, $1.1 billion for the Navy and $922 million for the Air Force.

Base Closings

In order to save money, it was necessary to spend money — that remained the prevailing wisdom when the time came to close military bases in the United States.

▶ **1989 closing list.** Congress in 1989 approved a list of 86 military bases for closure or realignment. The fiscal 1994 bill appropriated $12.8 million for continuing expenses in that round of closings.

Lawmakers reduced the $27.9 million the administration requested. Their rationale: Some operations at the bases being closed were gradually being moved to other bases, where new facilities were being built to accommodate the extra people and hardware. The improvements were paid for out of the base-closure account. During the 1993 round of base closures, the commission voted to shut some of the bases that were to be upgraded in the round robin of closures and "realignments." Thus, the appropriators reduced the overall funding level to reflect the deleted projects.

▶ **1991 closing list.** Congress set up a second base closing account in 1990 as part of the fiscal 1991 defense authorization (PL 101-510). This account continued to be used for the closing of 34 bases approved in 1991. In fiscal 1992, Congress appropriated $100 million for this account, and in fiscal 1993 the Pentagon received $1.6 billion for it. Again using the rationale that some bases that were to take over functions from the doomed bases on the 1991 list would instead be closed as well, Congress reduced the level of funding to $1.5 billion from the $1.8 billion sought by the administration.

The conference report earmarked $7.5 million for construction of bachelor enlisted quarters at Everett Naval Station in Washington because of the closure of its sister station at Sand Point. And it required the Navy to submit a proposal to build a second barracks in fiscal 1995.

The bill also was to provide $18.7 million to reconfigure utilities ($16.3 million) and build a hazardous waste handling facility ($2.4 million) that was to continue operating after the Philadelphia Naval Shipyard closed.

▶ **1993 closing list.** Clinton took less than 24 hours to approve the most recent list of 34 major bases and 95 smaller ones recommended for closure by the seven members of the Defense Base Closure and Realignment Commission on July 1. Despite the intense lobbying and controversy surrounding this issue, none of the drama spilled over into the appropriations process. The Pentagon was to get $1.1 billion to begin the job of deactivating these bases in fiscal 1994, nearly $100 million less than the administration requested. ■

Transportation Programs Score Big Gains

Despite the general mood of budget austerity, Congress managed to provide a major boost in federal aid for highways and mass transit programs in fiscal 1994. The appropriations bill for the Transportation Department and related agencies (HR 2750) represented a $2.25 billion increase over fiscal 1993. The total — $13.9 billion from the Treasury plus $24.7 billion from the transportation trust funds — included the highest amount ever for highway programs and a near-record level for mass transit.

The Senate adopted the conference report on the bill by voice vote Oct. 21, clearing it for the president. The House had adopted the conference report earlier that day, also by voice vote. President Clinton signed the bill (PL 103-122) Oct. 27.

The increase reflected the Clinton administration's emphasis on "infrastructure" — roads, bridges, subways, sewers and other capital investments.

Initially, Clinton's budget request for transportation spending exceeded by $3.6 billion the amount that was available to the Transportation subcommittees. The administration eventually cut its request for transportation, bringing it within $1.5 billion of the appropriators' ceiling.

The appropriators made up the difference mainly by lowering the proposed increase in highway spending, cutting the money for the Federal Aviation Administration (FAA) and holding the Coast Guard near its fiscal 1993 levels.

Mass transit. The administration's greatest impact was probably on mass transit. Focused on urban areas, the transit programs had declined during the Reagan years after flourishing under President Jimmy Carter. Clinton asked for and won the largest increase for mass transit since Congress launched the formula grant program for transit systems in 1983: $783 million, or 21 percent. The total — $1.6 billion from the Treasury and $3 billion from the Highway Trust Fund — was just short of the high reached in fiscal 1981 in the final Carter budget.

The increase in transit spending came despite the sluggish demand for mass transit. According to a Transportation Department survey, only about 2 percent of the nation's travelers used public transportation. The percentage of workers using mass transit had declined steadily since 1945. Advocates of mass transit said that low gas prices, a heavy public investment in highways and higher tax subsidies for commuting by car than by mass transit contributed to the decline.

Highways. Congress had authorized a big boost in highway investments in the 1991 surface transportation act (PL 102-240). Appropriators had kept spending capped well below the authorized level, however, in part because the Highway Trust Fund did not have enough to cover that much spending. The same was true in fiscal 1994, as the

BOXSCORE

➡ **Fiscal 1994 appropriations for the Transportation Department and related agencies (HR 2750).** The bill for highway and mass transit programs appropriated $13.9 billion and provided $24.7 billion from the transportation trust funds.

Reports: H Rept 103-190; S Rept 103-150; conference report, H Rept 103-300.

KEY ACTION

Sept. 23 — **House** passed HR 2750, 312-89.

Oct. 6 — **Senate** passed HR 2750, 90-9.

Oct. 15 — **House-Senate** conferees agreed on conference report.

Oct. 21 — **House** approved conference report by voice vote; **Senate** cleared conference report by voice vote.

Oct. 27 — **President** signed HR 2750 — PL 103-122.

appropriators kept trust-fund spending almost $700 million below the authorized level. Nevertheless, the amount of money flowing to state transportation departments was higher than ever before.

Even if they were so inclined, the states were not allowed to spend all of their highway money on highways. Under the 1991 law, states had to put a portion of their federal aid into such things as planning, bicycle facilities, historic preservation, safety improvements and clean-air projects. *(1991 Almanac, p. 137)*

Special projects. The final bill was less of a departure from past practices than either of its prime sponsors had hoped. But some of the changes were significant. There were no new highway or bridge projects, only ones that already had been authorized by law. And on the House side, the special bus and rail projects were judged by new, more objective criteria that required members to justify their proposals.

The bill made few changes in transportation policy. House and Senate conferees agreed Oct. 15 to support only a small portion of Transportation Secretary Federico F. Peña's $140 million high-speed rail initiative, providing $20 million for research into trains that would ride above magnetized rails on a cushion of air. The main reason for rejecting Peña's proposal was the fact that it had not been authorized.

BACKGROUND

The major debate over the transportation bill was not over how much to spend or even where to spend it. It was a struggle between House appropriators and the House Public Works and Transportation Committee over who would have the power to direct money to lawmakers' special road and bridge projects. That struggle over prized turf stalled action on the bill for nearly two months.

The Public Works Committee, which had jurisdiction over transportation policy, funneled money to specific projects every four to six years, whenever it reauthorized the federal surface transportation programs. The appropriators, meanwhile, earmarked money for their own list of projects every year, although usually in consultation with Public Works.

In the fiscal 1994 bill, the House Transportation Appropriations Subcommittee proposed to spend $305 million on 58 highway and bridge projects, plus $1.5 million on three highway studies. The subcommittee chose its projects not by consulting with Public Works, however, but by following a set of "investment criteria" developed by the new subcommittee Chairman Bob Carr, D-Mich.

Carr said the new criteria would enable appropriators to choose projects based on their value as investments rather

TRANSPORTATION

	Fiscal 1993	Fiscal 1994 Clinton Request	House Bill	Senate Bill	Final Bill
(In thousands of dollars)					
Transportation Department					
Office of the secretary	$ 199,484	$ 224,310	$ 150,005	$ 223,005	$ 222,031
Rural airline subsidies (trust fund)	*(38,600)*	*(38,600)*	*(—)*	*(33,423)*	*(33,423)*
Coast Guard					
Operating expenses	2,315,000	2,609,747	2,555,695	2,590,083	2,570,000
Acquisition, construction	340,000	414,000	310,700	354,690	327,500
Other	637,365	706,021	695,564	705,964	703,064
Subtotal, Coast Guard	**$ 3,292,365**	**$ 3,729,768**	**$ 3,561,959**	**$ 3,650,737**	**$ 3,600,564**
Federal Aviation Administration					
Operations	4,530,000	4,576,000	4,568,219	4,584,584	4,580,518
Facilities and equipment	2,301,700	2,524,000	2,142,000	2,162,578	2,120,104
Research, engineering, development	230,000	250,000	240,000	254,000	254,000
Other	150	150	150	150	150
Subtotal, FAA	**$ 7,061,850**	**$ 7,350,150**	**$ 6,950,369**	**$ 7,001,312**	**$ 6,954,772**
Airport Trust Fund limit	*(1,800,000)*	*(1,879,000)*	*(1,500,000)*	*(1,800,000)*	*(1,690,000)*
Federal Highway Administration					
Special road and bridge projects	336,476	—	46,628	125,000	143,562
Baltimore-Washington Parkway	15,000	—	16,000	—	12,800
Other	175,000	—	—	—	—
Subtotal, FHwA	**$ 526,476**	**—**	**$ 62,628**	**$ 125,000**	**$ 156,362**
Highway Trust Fund limit	*(15,401,750)*	*(18,473,000)*	*(17,557,663)*	*(18,095,000)*	*(17,665,000)*
Obligations exempt from limit	*(2,677,000)*	*(2,117,009)*	*(2,117,009)*	*(2,117,009)*	*(2,117,009)*
National Highway Traffic Safety Admin.	128,250	130,024	121,001	128,311	124,145
Highway Trust Fund limit	*(141,650)*	*(177,000)*	*(174,000)*	*(174,000)*	*(174,000)*
Federal Railroad Administration					
Local rail freight assistance	8,000	—	10,000	20,000	17,000
Amtrak	687,000	633,000	568,000	696,580	683,700
Northeast Corridor improvement	204,100	204,100	130,000	250,000	225,000
Other	112,121	113,529	78,958	73,878	94,294
Subtotal, railroads	**$ 1,011,221**	**$ 950,629**	**$ 786,958**	**$ 1,040,458**	**$ 1,019,994**
Federal Transit Administration					
Formula grants	650,975	1,324,916	1,324,916	1,324,916	1,284,916
Highway Trust Fund	*(1,049,025)*	*(1,129,951)*	*(1,079,951)*	*(1,011,084)*	*(1,129,951)*
Discretionary grants					
Highway Trust Fund	*(1,725,000)*	*(1,771,575)*	*(1,707,425)*	*(1,785,000)*	*(1,785,000)*
Washington Metro	170,000	200,000	200,000	200,000	200,000
Other	119,120	115,408	59,807	120,408	117,658
Subtotal, Transit	**$ 940,095**	**$ 1,640,324**	**$ 1,584,723**	**$ 1,645,324**	**$ 1,602,574**
Highway Trust Fund limit	*(2,859,150)*	*(2,961,575)*	*(2,847,425)*	*(2,861,133)*	*(2,980,000)*
Other Transportation Department	350,324	95,795	42,251	90,596	93,549
TOTAL Transportation Department	**$ 13,510,065**	**$ 14,121,000**	**$ 13,259,894**	**$ 13,904,743**	**$ 13,773,991**
Related Agencies					
Architectural and Transportation Barriers Compliance Board	3,300	3,348	3,348	3,348	3,348
National Transportation Safety Board	36,000	37,125	37,105	37,105	37,105
Interstate Commerce Commission	43,930	45,466	44,904	44,960	44,960
Panama Canal Commission (limitation on expenses)	*(530,000)*	*(—)*	*(540,000)*	*(540,000)*	*(540,000)*
St. Lawrence Seaway Toll Rebate	10,250	9,707	9,707	9,707	9,707
Other	51,663	51,664	51,663	51,663	51,664
GRAND TOTAL	**$ 13,386,062 ***	**$ 14,268,310**	**$ 13,382,997 ***	**$ 14,047,902 ***	**$ 13,897,150**
(Trust fund limitations)	*($ 22,933,925)*	*($ 25,766,634)*	*($ 24,210,422)*	*($ 25,197,040)*	*($ 24,674,408)*

* Fiscal 1993 total includes a rescission of $269,146,000. House total includes a rescission of $23,624,140. Senate total includes a rescission of $3,624,140. Conference total includes a rescission of $23,624,140.

SOURCE: House Appropriations Committee

than their importance to a lawmaker. Yet the results fell into a familiar pattern: Almost two-thirds of the $307 million proposed for highway and bridge projects went to states represented by subcommittee members. That percentage was higher than the one in the previous year's House bill.

Norman Y. Mineta, D-Calif., the new Public Works Committee chairman, protested that the earmarks violated a House rule against appropriating money for unauthorized projects. Although some of the projects had been authorized in previous laws, none were authorized for the levels the appropriators were proposing to spend from the Highway Trust Fund.

Carr, in turn, argued that the Public Works Committee authorized so infrequently that appropriators had to be able to respond to the country's changing needs.

After two months spent vainly searching for a compromise, the House Democratic leadership sided with the Public Works Committee. All of the projects were knocked out on the House floor by Mineta; four projects were later restored by dipping into the general Treasury, rather than the Highway Trust Fund.

The episode appeared to give the Public Works Committee veto power over new highway projects, allowing it to block funding for any specific project not included in one of the committee's authorization bills. Still, the committee deferred to Carr on two points: It announced that it would reauthorize projects more frequently, and it adopted a Carr-like set of investment criteria for the projects in its next authorization bill.

Carr's counterpart in the Senate, Transportation Appropriations Subcommittee Chairman Frank R. Lautenberg, D-N.J., also tried to change the way federal transportation dollars were allocated. Lautenberg proposed that no highway or bridge money go to projects that had not been authorized — the same stance, essentially, that Mineta had taken.

Still, 97 percent of the highway money earmarked in the Senate bill was for states represented by members of Lautenberg's panel. By changing the rules of the game, Lautenberg cut the number of projects but increased the advantage held by appropriators.

The final version of the fiscal 1994 transportation bill and the accompanying report, as negotiated by House and Senate appropriators, directed money to 36 projects worth $217.4 million in 19 states. The projects in the report ranged from a computerized traffic-management system in Minneapolis — home of Democratic Rep. Martin Olav Sabo, a member of Carr's subcommittee — to a railroad crossing in Brownsville, Texas, represented by Democratic Rep. Solomon P. Ortiz.

Of the top 10 recipients, nine were represented by members of Carr's or Lautenberg's subcommittee. The 10th was Kentucky, home of House Appropriations Committee Chairman William H. Natcher, D. All told, more than $4 out of every $5 for road and bridge projects went to states represented by transportation subcommittee members; the rest went to states represented by other appropriators.

HOUSE COMMITTEE

The House Appropriations Subcommittee on Transportation marked up the spending bill in a closed session June 10. Almost $800 million was earmarked for lawmakers' pet transit projects. Aviation, railroads and the Coast Guard, meanwhile, were trimmed from the existing spending levels. The adminis-

tration's high-speed rail initiative was slashed, and almost every administrative account in the Transportation Department was to be cut, according to Carr.

Highways. The subcommittee agreed to spend $17.2 billion on federal aid to highways, not including the money for lawmakers' pet projects. That amount was about $1.9 billion more than in fiscal 1993, but about $1.2 billion less than Clinton proposed and the 1991 surface transportation law authorized.

The highway program received $2.1 billion more for safety improvements, congestion projects and supplemental grants to states that received less than the minimum share of highway grants. Carr said the major factor limiting spending on highways was the amount of gasoline-tax revenue flowing into the trust fund. "It's really iffy whether the revenues are there," Carr said, adding, "You can't dip into the general fund to do this."

Mass transit. In mass transit, the bill provided $2.4 billion for formula grants for bus and rail purchases — $700 million more than in fiscal 1993. New subways and rail systems received an additional $593 million, down 18 percent from 1993, while subway and rail modernization received $760 million, up 14 percent.

Carr said he had hoped to leave at least $150 million for new subways and rail systems unattached to any lawmaker's pet projects. By the end of the markup session, however, more than 90 percent of that money had been earmarked, leaving only $50 million for the Federal Transit Administration to distribute on a competitive basis.

Bus facilities. Carr had more success guarding the money for new bus facilities against pork barrel projects. Of the $354 million in the bill for new bus facilities, $101 million remained unattached to any project. The total for bus facilities represented an increase of $17 million, or 5 percent. On the other hand, Carr said, the bill cut operating subsidies by $50 million from the existing $802 million.

Amtrak. For Amtrak, the national passenger rail corporation, the subcommittee proposed a $20 million increase in operating subsidies, to $351 million. The increase was to be offset by the cut in Amtrak's capital budget, from $165 million to $100 million.

An additional $130 million was to go toward completing the Northeast Corridor, the high-speed route that Amtrak was developing between Washington and Boston. Although that amount was well below the $204 million provided in fiscal 1993, it represented a significant change from previous House bills, which had not included any money for the corridor.

High-speed rail. The administration had sought $140 million for high-speed rail and magnetic levitation trains, $135 million more than authorized in the 1991 law. The subcommittee, however, put no money in for magnetic levitation, and no money for high-speed rail beyond the money for the Northeast Corridor.

Carr said the subcommittee decided to defer any additional spending on those projects at least until a new, larger authorization was approved. Bills (S 839, HR 1919) to expand the high-speed rail program had been introduced in both chambers, with the administration's backing. *(High-speed rail, p. 217)*

FAA. The subcommittee proposed to cut the grants for airport improvements from $1.8 billion to $1.5 billion, and for FAA facilities and equipment from $2.35 billion to $2.14 billion. On the other hand, the FAA received a $30 million increase for operations, much of which was to go to salaries for air traffic controllers, and a $10 million increase for research and development.

Coast Guard. The Coast Guard received $3.5 billion under the subcommittee's proposal, $203 million less than Clinton requested.

Full Committee Action

The full House Appropriations Committee approved a $13.8 billion version of the bill by voice vote June 22 (HR 2490 — H Rept 103-149). The bill drew protests for trimming the money for Coast Guard drug interdiction efforts and flight pay, rural airport subsidies, an anti-terrorism office at the Transportation Department and 28 highway projects that had been slow to get started, among other proposed cuts.

The lion's share of the increase was in highway spending, which would rise almost $1.8 billion. Mass transit also climbed, with a proposed increase of $677 million from the existing level of $3.8 billion.

In a letter to Chairman Natcher, Transportation Secretary Peña said the $3.5 billion included for the Coast Guard was less than the amount needed to maintain existing services. But the Appropriations Committee turned back efforts June 22 to restore some of the Coast Guard cuts.

At the full committee markup, Helen Delich Bentley, R-Md., proposed to shift $6.35 million to the Coast Guard's ship repair yard at Curtis Bay, Md., from the subcommittee's proposal for consolidating FAA air traffic control facilities. The committee rejected that proposal on a 10-27 show of hands.

TURF BATTLE

The bill immediately sparked a new round of skirmishing in the long-running turf war between the Transportation Appropriations Subcommittee and the Public Works Committee.

When the bill went to the Rules Committee on June 24, it came under attack from the bipartisan leadership of the Public Works Committee. Chairman Mineta said his panel had found at least 48 violations of the House rule against legislating on an appropriations bill. Mineta asked the Rules Committee to reject Carr's request for a blanket waiver of the rule, citing 20 sections of the bill that Mineta said amounted to the most serious violations.

Mineta and his colleagues focused their complaints on proposals in the bill to:

● Eliminate the Essential Air Service program, which provided subsidies to rural airports. James L. Oberstar, D-Minn., the chairman of the Aviation Subcommittee, said the subsidies were a key part of the compromise when Congress agreed to deregulate the airlines in 1978.

● Terminate the Transportation Department's Office of Intelligence and Security, which was created in the wake of the Pan Am 103 bombing in 1988. The office's purpose was to improve the flow of information about terrorist threats collected by other federal agencies.

● Earmark $305 million for 58 highway projects that had no specific authorization from Congress. Mineta and Bud Shuster, Pa., the Transportation Committee's ranking Republican, noted that more than a third of the money was to go to Carr's home state. Another third of the money was to go to the home states of the other members of Carr's subcommittee.

Carr made one other change from past practice that upset the Public Works Committee. The funding for all 58 highway and bridge projects came out of the Highway Trust Fund, not the general fund. As a result, the earmarks for 22 states came at the expense of highway construction grants for all 50 states.

Carr said afterward that it was a case of the pot calling the kettle black. In the 1991 surface transportation law, Carr said, the Public Works Committee usurped the appropriators' role by channeling money to 539 highway and 73 mass transit projects.

Peña sided with the Public Works Committee on several issues and complained about the "level of micromanagement" in the bill. For example, he noted that the appropriators were seeking to direct several reorganizations within the department and to place caps on the number of attorneys in the FAA. Carr said that what Peña called micromanagement, he called accountability.

On June 28, the Rules Committee sided with Mineta. The proposed rule allowed Mineta to knock out all 20 disputed provisions, reducing the cost of the bill by roughly $240 million. That included eliminating $305 million in special projects and restoring more than $65 million in spending cuts, primarily from the highway projects that lawmakers had inserted in the 1987 surface transportation authorization bill. *(1987 Almanac, p. 331)*

Carr protested, and in the weeks that followed, Speaker Thomas S. Foley, D-Wash., and other members of the Democratic leadership tried unsuccessfully to forge a compromise.

Deal Falls Through

The appropriators thought the dispute had been settled July 20, when Mineta, Carr and Foley agreed on a framework for handling special projects in the future. Under the deal, starting in 1994, Carr would alert Mineta to any provision of the transportation appropriations bill that invaded Mineta's turf. Within a reasonable amount of time, Mineta would come back to Carr with any objections, and the two would negotiate. If they found they could not agree, the Democratic leadership would make the final call.

Mineta pledged to support a new rule for HR 2490 to protect the 58 projects from a procedural challenge, although they still could be eliminated by amendment.

When the rule reached the House floor July 22, however, several leading members of Mineta's committee decried the projects and urged the rule's defeat. The verbal assault took the appropriators and House Democratic leaders by surprise, and the leadership pulled the bill from the floor rather than risk defeat on the rule.

Some appropriators and members of the leadership grumbled that Mineta had reneged on his pledge. Mineta said he had called his committee together the day before to outline the agreement with Carr, and against his advice, the members decided to oppose the rule. "I had a revolt on my hands last night [at the meeting] just by saying, 'I'm going to be voting for the rule,'" he said.

Bob Wise, D-W.Va., said committee members were not happy with the deal and felt compelled to protect their role in approving special projects. The action July 22 showed that, with 63 members, more than any other House committee, Public Works "is in a position to assert itself when it feels it has to," Wise said.

A Revised Bill

The House Appropriations Committee reported a new version of the bill (HR 2750 — H Rept 103-190) by voice vote July 27. The Transportation Subcommittee had rewritten at least six sections of the measure to blunt the Public Works challenge. But there also were some surprises for Mineta and Shuster: The bill scrapped a $28.2 million mass transit grant that Mineta had sought for the San Francisco Bay Area, and it proposed to take back $4.4

million that Pennsylvania had received for a highway project in Shuster's district.

The new bill's bottom line was $13.7 billion in appropriations, or $37.7 billion counting spending from the Highway Trust Fund.

The total was $10 million less than the earlier version and 4 percent higher than the fiscal 1993 bill.

The Coast Guard was slated to receive $35.3 million more in the new version, though it was still $168 million below the administration's request. Amtrak received $20 million less in the new version, putting it $74 million below its existing budget.

In mass transit, the major change was a $500,000 increase for planning and research. The total for transit — $4.48 billion in appropriations and trust fund spending — was almost $680 million higher than in fiscal 1993.

Both versions of the bill directed money to dozens of bus, subway and light-rail projects. The only difference was the elimination of the $28.2 million grant to the Bay Area Rapid Transit system's airport extension project and to the Tasman Corridor light-rail project.

Nancy Pelosi, D-Calif., offered an amendment at the full committee markup to restore funding for those projects. Carr countered that the projects were not economically feasible, costing an estimated $27 to $40 for each rider added. The committee sided with Carr by voice vote.

The original bill had earmarked $305 million for 58 road and bridge projects lawmakers had requested. The new version eliminated one of the 58 — a $21 million highway project in Michigan, one of seven in Carr's home state — and cut another one in half — a $1 million Minneapolis road project.

The new bill described 26 of the projects as authorized and/or in progress, and reclassified five others as studies. The remaining 25 were clumped in one group that clearly violated a House rule that barred appropriators from directing money to unauthorized projects unless the projects already had received money and were in progress.

Included in the latter group were two projects requested by Mineta's colleagues for Northern California, three projects sought by Shuster's colleagues from Pennsylvania, a project requested by Foley and a project sought by House Minority Leader Robert H. Michel, R-Ill. A single member of the House could eliminate all 25 projects from the bill by raising a point of order against them on the floor.

Several Democratic lawmakers — including such veteran members from the San Francisco Bay Area as Pelosi, Ronald V. Dellums, George Miller, Pete Stark, Tom Lantos and Don Edwards — reportedly urged the House leadership to protect those projects. When Foley floated the idea of a rule to shield the projects and restore the Bay Area grant, however, Mineta sent him and the Rules Committee a letter promising the "virtually unanimous" opposition of the 40 Democrats on his committee.

In addition to the special highway projects, the new bill dropped two of the 19 provisions that the Public Works Committee had said violated the rule against legislating on an appropriations bill. It rewrote five others to comply with the rule. The rewritten provisions included ones to eliminate subsidies for rural airports, bar grants to airports that imposed surcharges on frequent-flier discounts, and bar transportation grants of any kind to cities that diverted airport revenues to fund other public services.

Two disputed provisions that were not rewritten rescinded money for 25 highway projects that the Public Works Committee wrote into the 1982 and 1987 surface transportation laws. Most of the money was unspent, Carr

said, and so should be transferred to projects that were ready to be built.

The new version of the bill added to the list of rescisions a $4.4 million highway project in Bedford County, Pa., that was included in the 1987 law. The original bill had rescinded money for that project, too, but Carr had removed the provision at Shuster's request.

Pennsylvania officials said environmental studies delayed work on the Loysburg Bypass project in Bedford County, so the $4.4 million was not tapped until late July. Construction on the project was set to begin in 1995.

HR 2750 also contained a new provision that denied federal aid to any mass transit project that cost more than $20 for each new rider it served. Carr said the provision affected only the two Bay Area projects. Mineta disagreed, saying that the provision blocked a $2 million grant requested by Alan Wheat, D-Mo., for a planned Kansas City light-rail line, and a $70 million grant requested by Elizabeth Furse, D-Ore., to continue construction on a light-rail line in Portland. The provision violated the House rule against legislating on an appropriations bill, Mineta said, so he planned to try and strike it on the House floor.

HOUSE FLOOR

Hoping to avoid a floor fight, Foley suggested July 28 that the appropriators go back to the original transportation bill with a rule protecting the 58 projects. Although Democrats on the Public Works Committee pledged to support the rule, Carr rejected the proposal. In the days that followed, negotiations continued among the interested parties, but no solution was at hand. "If there was a readily foreseeable middle ground," said Steny H. Hoyer, D-Md., "this would have been over two weeks ago."

Finally, on Sept. 23, the House voted on HR 2750, approving it 312-89. *(Vote 456, p. 112-H)*

Before voting on the bill, however, the House handed the Public Works Committee a sweeping victory in its turf battle with the appropriators. The House threw out most of Carr's choices for highway projects, as well as one of the criteria he attempted to set for mass transit projects. Mineta and his 60 colleagues emerged with an apparent lock on the power to spend money out of the Highway Trust Fund.

As passed by the House, the bill included $13.4 billion in new budget authority, $23.6 million in rescissions and $24.2 billion in spending from the federal trust funds for highways and airports. These trust funds were financed through federal taxes on gasoline and airline tickets, respectively.

The bill called for almost $1.5 billion more spending than existing law, mostly in the areas of highways and mass transit. It included a $1.3 billion increase for highways, bringing the amount to $19.8 billion, still roughly $800 million less than the 1991 surface transportation law authorized. Bus, subway and light-rail spending increased $633 million, to $4.4 billion — although that amount, too, was about $170 million less than the administration requested.

The increases came at the expense of the Coast Guard ($3.6 billion, a $23 million cut) and Amtrak ($568 million, a $119 million cut). Airports took the biggest hit, with construction grants falling from $1.8 billion to $1.5 billion and equipment grants falling from $2.3 billion to $2.1 billion.

Carr made one other change from past practice that upset the Public Works Committee. The funding for all 58 highway and bridge projects came out of the Highway Trust Fund, not the general fund. As a result, the earmarks for 22 states came at the expense of highway construction grants for all 50 states.

Open Rule Dooms Projects

The Rules Committee had proposed a virtually open rule for the bill. The only wrinkle to the rule was that, once it was adopted, it would restore the $28.2 million grant for two transit projects near Mineta's district. When the bill reached the floor Sept. 22, Carr and his fellow appropriators opposed the rule while Mineta, his colleagues on Public Works and the bipartisan House leadership supported it. Mineta's side prevailed, 257-163. *(Vote 447, p. 108-H)*

John Linder, R-Ga., took advantage of the rule to bring points of order against 18 unauthorized sections of the bill, including the entire office of the Transportation secretary. Linder's moves cut $180 million from the bill, although even Linder admitted that the money would be restored in conference.

Mineta also capitalized on the rule to bring points of order against 11 sections of the bill that would have spent $284.7 million from the Highway Trust Fund on 59 projects. He argued, and the House parliamentarian agreed, that the appropriators could not spend more out of the trust fund than Public Works had authorized through the transportation laws of 1991, 1987, 1982 and 1956. That limitation was imposed by the 1991 law.

Carr said in an interview that the parliamentarian's ruling changed the nature of the 1991 law. Under the ruling, Carr said, the amount listed for each road project had become a ceiling for federal aid, not a floor.

Several members complained that Mineta was putting procedure ahead of the public interest. Democrat Peter J. Visclosky of Indiana said, for example, that the city of Gary needed $4 million to widen a bridge that was the site of a gruesome train wreck in January, and it should not have to wait for the next highway bill.

Mineta pledged to introduce later a "technical corrections" bill that could authorize new projects. Unlike the transportation appropriations bill, however, a technical corrections bill was not guaranteed to pass.

The House rules appeared to allow only one way around the Public Works Committee: Construction projects on federally owned roads could receive money out of the general fund, as long as the work was in progress. This route was not available for projects that were authorized at a specific level, such as the projects in the 1991 law, Mineta said.

After Mineta's points of order knocked out funding for their projects, three members of the Appropriations Committee offered amendments to use $33.8 million from the general fund to restore three highways and one bridge project. Harold Rogers, R-Ky., proposed to increase funding for a highway widening project in Eastern Kentucky (to $3.8 million, from $1.85 million). All three amendments were adopted by voice vote.

Before striking the $284.7 million in projects, Mineta offered an amendment to increase the pool of money for highway and bridge projects by the same sum. That pool was distributed to each state according to formulas in the 1991 law. The amendment passed by a vote of 281-154. *(Vote 449, p. 110-H)*

Mineta and Oberstar, the chairman of the Public Works Subcommittee on Aviation, successfully brought points of order against 11 more sections of the measure on the grounds that they violated the House rule against legislating on an appropriations bill. Included among these were proposals to rescind $55.6 million in special highway grants from the 1982 and 1987 surface transportation laws that the states had left largely unspent.

Carr defended all but a handful of the sections, fre-quently arguing that they were "good government" provisions. House rules, Carr said several times, should not stand in the way of saving the taxpayers money.

Although Carr and Mineta said their dispute was procedural, the debate sounded like a personal power struggle between the two new chairmen. At one point, Carr said in response to a Mineta point of order, "I know that the chairman from California wants to write our bill. I know that he wants to *be* the Appropriations Committee."

Carr continued to argue, without success, against the California mass transit projects that had been dropped in the second version of the bill. After voting to restore the projects through the rule, the House voted 136-290 to defeat an amendment by Robert S. Walker, R-Pa., that would have deleted them. It later agreed by voice vote to remove a provision that would have made the projects ineligible for federal grants. *(Vote 452, p. 110-H)*

Carr said later that the projects were put in the first bill not on their merit, but as an attempt to curry some support for the bill from Mineta. "We got no points for that," he said, adding, "If we're not going to get points for it, we're not going to do something that lacks merit."

Carr also failed in his attempt to stop the FAA from providing any new letters of intent to fund airport improvement projects. The House voted 317-117 on Sept. 22 to adopt an amendment by Bob Clement, D-Tenn., to remove that prohibition. *(Vote 448, p. 110-H)*

The next day, the House rejected three amendments by Joel Hefley, R-Colo., aimed at cutting spending. One, to cut Amtrak operating assistance by $331 million, was defeated 84-337; a second, to cut Amtrak operating assistance by $33 million, was defeated 153-271; a third, to eliminate $45 million in funding and $7.3 million in fees for the Interstate Commerce Commission and transfer its duties to the Transportation Department, was defeated 207-222. *(Votes 450, 451, 453, p. 110-H)*

SENATE COMMITTEE

The Senate Transportation Appropriations Subcommittee approved a $14 billion version of HR 2750 by voice vote on Sept. 29. The full committee approved the bill later the same day by a vote of 29-0 (S Rept 103-150).

Subcommittee Chairman Lautenberg included no earmarks for bus or highway projects. Rather than follow Carr's lead on "investment criteria," Lautenberg laid down a single rule for highway projects: no money for new projects that had not been previously authorized by Congress. The point, Lautenberg said, was to cut down on earmarks and leave more money to the discretion of state and local transportation authorities. In highways alone, he said, 46 senators had asked for almost $1.4 billion in earmarks.

The shift mirrored the changes made by several other appropriations chairmen in response to the public outcry about pork barrel spending. But it received a chilly reception from Lautenberg's fellow appropriators, particularly among the senior members of the committee.

Republican Alfonse M. D'Amato of New York, ranking member of the Transportation Appropriations Subcommittee, argued that if the House were going to insist on earmarking, Senate appropriators must be ready to do it, too. Otherwise, he said, "we shouldn't be on this committee."

Lautenberg replied that he was responding to public opinion. Still, the bill was far from pure on the earmark front. It directed $672 million to 26 rail projects and $125 million for eight highway and bridge projects. Of the eight,

seven were in the home states of members of the Transportation Appropriations Subcommittee. The largest earmark was $62 million for a highway corridor in West Virginia, home of Democrat Robert C. Byrd, chairman of the full Appropriations Committee.

Lautenberg noted that the House had taken a similar stand, eliminating almost all the unauthorized highway projects Carr had proposed. Byrd, however, pointed out that the Senate was not governed by House rules. And under Senate rules, the appropriators could authorize projects themselves.

Dale Bumpers, D-Ark., agreed. Voicing a sentiment common among members of the committee, Bumpers said that the appropriators should not leave the decisions on allocating money to unelected bureaucrats. "I know what's good for my state better than they do," Bumpers said.

One source of irritation for Bumpers: None of the earmarks he requested made it into the bill. Among the consequences, Bumpers said, was that Arkansas would not receive the money it needed for a bridge that was already under construction but was not authorized.

Lautenberg stood his ground, saying, "I thought it was an appropriate time to [respond to] what I hear is a clamor from the people we represent."

The committee bill appropriated $665 million more than the House-passed version and spent $987 million more from the highway and airport trust funds. These increases affected more than 30 programs, including almost $600 million more for highways, $300 million more for airport improvement projects, $89 million more for the Coast Guard, $74 million more for mass transit and $129 million more for Amtrak.

The bill also differed from the House version on a number of policy issues. The House proposed to kill the Essential Air Service program, which provided $39 million in subsidies to remote rural airports. The Senate appropriators proposed to restore the service — which was a favorite of Byrd's — with two restrictions requested by the White House that cut 11 rural airports and $5 million from the program.

The Senate committee provided almost $28 million from the Highway Trust Fund to start developing a high-speed magnetic-levitation train. It also spent $77 million from the trust fund to continue the high-speed rail program. The House, by contrast, had included no money in its bill for the magnetic-levitation train program and only $3.5 million for high-speed trains outside Amtrak's Northeast corridor.

The Senate appropriators did far more adding to the House bill than they did subtracting, but they did make roughly $95 million worth of cuts. Two-thirds of those cuts related to earmarks for highway and bridge projects, including a $12 million grant to finish a bridge in the district represented by House Appropriations Committee Chairman Natcher.

Most of the Senate appropriators' earmarks were for rail projects that were either recommended by the administration or authorized in the 1991 surface transportation law. In the report that accompanied the bill, however, the Senate appropriators earmarked $61.6 million for 18 "smart highway" projects, none requested by the administration or authorized by the 1991 law.

The Senate bill dropped several restrictions that were in the House bill, including a ban on grants to cities or states that diverted airport revenues to non-airport uses. The measure also extended federal labor-law protections to

U.S. airline pilots and crew members who were sent overseas temporarily.

SENATE FLOOR

The Senate voted 90-9 on Oct. 6 to approve a version of the transportation spending bill that appropriated $14 billion and spent $25.2 billion from the trust funds. In a break from past practice, the bill remained free of earmarks for specific bus programs or for highway projects that had not been authorized. *(Vote 306, p. 40-S)*

White House travel office. The one major amendment adopted by the Senate came from Minority Leader Bob Dole of Kansas and fellow Republican Christopher S. Bond of Missouri, on a topic that Dole called "travelgate." The amendment, adopted by voice vote, appropriated $150,000 to cover the legal expenses of five former employees of the White House travel office who had been dismissed in May.

Dole said the employees, who had since been reinstated and placed on paid leave, hired lawyers when the White House ordered the Federal Bureau of Investigation to conduct a criminal probe of the travel office. They were no longer subjects of the investigation, Dole said, but their legal bills amounted to at least $30,000 each.

The amendment reimbursed the five employees at the expense of the Transportation Department's Office of Public Affairs.

The Senate dropped a pair of potentially controversial amendments that could have caused trouble when the bill went to a House-Senate conference.

Cargo preference. On Oct. 5, the Senate voted 50-49 to kill an amendment by Hank Brown, R-Colo., to put new limits on the so-called cargo preference program, which aided U.S. shipping lines. The program, frequently attacked by farm-state lawmakers, was prized by the maritime industry and its unions. *(Vote 304, p. 39-S)*

Under the cargo preference laws, U.S. ships received first crack at 50 percent to 100 percent of U.S. foreign aid and military cargo. Because U.S. vessels often charged far more than did foreign ships, the cargo preference program inflated the government's shipping costs by more than $500 million a year.

Brown's proposal, which was offered as an amendment to an amendment by Republican Conrad Burns of Montana, would have prohibited federal agencies from paying more than twice the world market rate for shipping contracts.

Federal regulations already barred agencies from paying more than "fair and reasonable" charges under the cargo preference program. Still, Brown's amendment could have cost the U.S. maritime industry dearly in terms of lower payments or lost business.

The Senate had approved a non-binding version of the same amendment June 22, turning aside a tabling motion on a 47-51 vote.

Brown lost the second time because five senators switched their votes — two joining Brown, three leaving him — and two previously absent senators voted against the amendment. *(Vote 162, p. 22-S)*

Immediately after defeating the Brown amendment, the Senate killed, 69-30, Burns' proposal to waive the cargo preference requirements for grain shipments to Russia from Pacific Northwest ports. *(Vote 305, p. 40-S)*

California projects. On Oct. 6, California's two Democratic senators withdrew a proposal to spend $315 million to rebuild a stretch of Interstate 880 destroyed in the 1989

Loma Prieta earthquake. That amendment, backed by Clinton, would have classified the spending as an emergency appropriation not subject to the budget caps.

Pete V. Domenici of New Mexico led the Republican opposition to the amendment, questioning why a four-year-old highway problem should be treated as an emergency. He also noted that $200 million of the cost stemmed from moving the highway, rather than rebuilding the double-deck roadway along its existing path through Oakland. Domenici predicted correctly that the project would be included in a supplemental appropriations bill in 1994. "We're not trying to kill it. We said this is the wrong way to do it and we don't have enough facts," he said.

Barbara Boxer, D-Calif., said officials concluded that it would not be prudent to rebuild a double-deck freeway in an area prone to earthquakes. They decided to move the highway, she said, because it seemed less expensive than widening its path through business and residential neighborhoods or tunneling under them.

Still, she withdrew the amendment after speaking with the Senate leadership and White House officials. In an interview, Boxer said she was assured that she would get a second shot at the money in 1994 and that such a delay in funding would not hurt the project.

Other amendments. Other amendments voted down included a proposal by John C. Danforth, R-Mo., to cut off funding for the Interstate Commerce Commission. The amendment was killed, 52-39, on a tabling motion. Danforth argued that the commission was a waste of money — "615 people sitting around, receiving forms" — because the trucking companies and railroads had been deregulated. Supporters of the commission argued that an independent commission still was needed to resolve disputes and oversee the financial health of those industries. *(Vote 302, p. 39-S)*

The Senate rejected a proposal by John W. Warner, R-Va., to eliminate a provision aimed at slowing the flow of highway dollars to the so-called donor states — states that received less in highway grants than their drivers paid in federal gasoline taxes. Lautenberg said that the provision was needed to keep the bill within its budgetary limits. The amendment fell on a point of order after Warner's motion to waive Senate budget rules failed, 35-63. *(Vote 303, p. 39-S)*

Among the issues remaining to be resolved in a House-Senate conference were whether to subsidize rural airports — the Senate said "yes," the House "no" — and how much to support high-speed rail and high-tech magnetic levitation trains. The Senate also had provided almost $600 million more than the House for highways, $300 million more for airport improvement projects, $89 million more for the Coast Guard, $74 million more for mass transit and $129 million more for Amtrak.

The Senate was more generous than was the House on highway and rail demonstration projects, too. The Senate bill included $130 million for nine highway and bridge projects, compared with $33.8 million for four projects in the House bill, and $675 million for 27 rail projects, compared with $620 million for 19 rail projects in the House bill.

FINAL ACTION

House and Senate appropriators completed work on the conference report (H Rept 103-300) Oct. 15.

The House adopted the conference report by voice vote Oct. 21; the Senate cleared it by voice vote the same day.

The final bill appropriated $13.9 billion — almost $500 million more than the House version of the bill but about $175 million less than the Senate version.

To settle one of the biggest differences in the two bills, the Senate joined the House in directing money to specific bus projects. The final bill contained $357 million for bus projects. Almost $100 million was left to the administration's discretion, and the House and Senate appropriators each earmarked half of the rest.

Originally, the House had proposed $354 million for bus projects, with $253 million earmarked for specific state and local bus systems. The Senate had proposed $357 million with no earmarks. Subcommittee Chairman Carr said House appropriators could not accept that position, in part because they had lost most of their highway earmarks on the House floor.

Carr and Lautenberg worked out the agreement on bus earmarks before the conferees began meeting on the afternoon of Oct. 15. The two chairmen left a number of other issues unresolved, however, including two disputed provisions involving airports.

The conferees agreed to accept a House provision barring the FAA from reducing a U.S. airline's landing rights, or slots, at O'Hare International Airport in Chicago for the sake of a foreign airline's landing rights. Rep. Richard J. Durbin, D-Ill., argued that the United States was the only country that unilaterally took slots away from its airlines to benefit foreign airlines.

Conferees also accepted a House provision that barred highway, aviation and mass transit grants to any state or local government that spent a public airport's revenues on non-airport items.

The conferees agreed to put only $3.5 million into conventional high-speed rail programs, as the House recommended, instead of the $79.2 million recommended by the Senate.

The Senate had more luck winning money for research into magnetic-levitation trains, for which the conferees agreed to provide $20 million. House conferees had objected to funding the conventional high-speed rail program beyond the $3.5 million authorized in the 1991 surface transportation law. A bill to authorize far more spending on high-speed rail had been bottled up.

Many of the differences between the House and Senate bills stemmed from the fact that the Senate appropriators started with $300 million more in budget authority than did the House. The allocation for the conference agreement split the difference between the two sides, forcing the Senate to delete $150 million from discretionary programs.

The conferees agreed to bar the Transportation Department from enforcing the requirement that states use recycled rubber in 5 percent of the asphalt they laid in fiscal 1994. They also banned airports from imposing surcharges on passengers using frequent flier coupons.

The final bill included Dole's amendment providing $150,000 to cover the legal expenses of the employees dismissed from the White House travel office earlier in 1993. The conferees dropped an amendment by Sen. Tom Harkin, D-Iowa, to extend federal labor protections to U.S. airline employees based overseas. ∎

Transportation Provisions

The appropriations bill for the Transportation Department and related agencies (HR 2750) provided annual funding to operate, build and improve the nation's highways, airports and mass transit systems. It also provided procurement and operating funds for the Coast Guard and the Federal Aviation Administration (FAA), subsidized the Amtrak passenger rail corporation and paid for safety programs aimed at all transportation modes. Following are the provisions of the bill, as enacted:

AIR

Federal Aviation Administration

The FAA, established in its existing form in 1958, was responsible for the safety and development of civil aviation and the evolution of a national system of airports. Total funding for FAA activities came to $8.6 billion, a decrease of $217.1 million, or 2.4 percent, from fiscal 1993. The administration had requested $9.2 billion.

FAA got its money from the general Treasury and the Airport and Airway Trust Fund, which was fed mostly by a 10 percent tax on airline tickets. Airport development and planning grants were made from the trust fund, with money available for grants capped at $1.7 billion, down from $1.8 billion in fiscal 1993. Direct appropriations, which totaled $7 billion, paid for operations, facilities and equipment, research and an aircraft purchase loan guarantee program.

In addition to the $1.7 billion in airport grants, $2.1 billion from the Airport and Airway Trust Fund was to be spent to modernize and improve air-traffic control and airway facilities.

▶ **Airport grants.** The money for airport development and planning grants was issued in the form of contract authority, which amounted to a promise to airports that federal funds would be available to reimburse them for construction or improvement projects. Congress pledged up to $1.69 billion for such grants in fiscal 1994. It also provided $2.2 billion in "contract authority liquidation" — money pledged to airports in previous years for construction payments that were coming due.

In prior years, House and Senate appropriators recommended a list of airport projects that should be given priority consideration by the FAA without directing any specific grants. However, the new chairman of the House Transportation Appropriations Subcommittee, Democrat Bob Carr of Michigan, argued that the FAA had used its discretion poorly. At his urging, the conference report directed money to three projects sought by House appropriators: $9.4 million to O'Hare International Airport in Chicago, $10 million for Philadelphia International Airport and $10 million for Luis Muñoz Marin International Airport in San Juan, Puerto Rico. The Chicago and Philadelphia airports were in the home states of members of Carr's subcommittee. The Senate added $14 million for the Clarksburg/Benedum Airport in Clarksburg, W.Va., home state of Senate Appropriations Committee Chairman Robert C. Byrd, D.

The conferees also directed the FAA to give priority consideration to 49 other airports, with no specific funding levels cited. The conference report pledged, however, not to make such lists in the future. Instead, the conferees said they would work with the FAA to develop criteria for airport grants, a task that was one of Carr's pet projects.

The Senate appropriators directed the FAA not to provide any more money to the proposed new airport at Otay Mesa, Calif., until local governing bodies demonstrated their support. Rep. Bob Filner, D-Calif., had tried to cut off funding for the new airport, but the more moderate language suggested by Sen. Dianne Feinstein, D-Calif., prevailed.

Congress also barred any federal aid to plan, design or build an additional runway at the Tulsa, Okla., International Airport. House appropriators sought the provision because of a lack of consensus in Tulsa about the project.

The 1991 act denied airport-improvement grants to any airport that imposed a surcharge on free tickets, such as those obtained through frequent-flier coupons. Congress tried to stop that practice in fiscal 1993, but the FAA applied the ban only to airports that had not already started collecting surcharges.

An even bigger penalty faced any city, county or state that diverted airport revenues to its own uses: the loss of all federal transportation grants. This provision, authored by Carr, was aimed at cities such as Los Angeles that were considering or had already started using airport revenues to pay for city services.

Finally, the House conferees agreed with the Senate's directive that the FAA put a moratorium on letters of intent to fund new airport improvement projects. The moratorium could be lifted on two conditions, the conference report stated: that the outstanding letters tied up less than 50 percent of budget for airport-improvement grants, and that the FAA became more adept at estimating the impact of proposed projects on the capacity of the national aviation system.

▶ **Operations.** The largest portion of the FAA's spending — $4.58 billion — was to go to operate, evaluate and maintain the nation's air-traffic control and navigation systems. Half the money for operations came out of the Airport and Airway Trust Fund. Operations programs included:

Air-traffic control. Congress appropriated $2.1 billion to operate the nation's air-traffic control system, $43.7 million more than in fiscal 1993. The money paid for 17,871 air-traffic controllers, the same number as in fiscal 1993. An estimated 227 of those controllers, however, were to have moved from training into regular operations.

Of the total amount, $1.7 billion went toward air-traffic control centers and towers, and $262.9 million went toward the operation of flight service stations.

The conference report recommended $20.1 million more for the system than the administration requested. More than half of that money was to phase out, instead of simply canceling, an experimental program that offered higher pay to recruit air-traffic controllers. The rest was to be used to convert the control towers at selected small airports to privately run operations.

The conferees rejected a recommendation in the Senate appropriators' report that air-traffic controllers who lost their jobs during the 1981 strike be given priority when the FAA filled vacancies in the control towers. President Clinton made these controllers eligible for rehiring in August.

Logistical support. The conferees recommended $9 million more than the administration requested for the FAA Logistics Center in Oklahoma City, which repaired equipment used in the air-traffic control system. Appropriators said that a backlog of maintenance work at the depot was hurting the system.

Telecommunications services. The conferees objected to the FAA's plan to eliminate subsidies for the Direct User Access Terminal Service, a program that enabled general aviation pilots to file flight plans and obtain weather information by phone. Instead of an $11 million cut, the program was to be cut by $2 million.

Aviation safety inspections. At the insistence of the House appropriators, the conferees restored all but $40,000 of the proposed $2.54 million cut for aviation safety inspectors. They also reduced by half the FAA's proposed $5 million cut in flight inspection flight hours. The FAA had sought the reductions to reflect the efficiencies gained by computerizing the inspections.

Aviation medical examiners. The conferees cut the FAA's budget for registering aircraft and aviation personnel by $400,000. To make up the shortfall, the conferees urged the FAA to raise the registration fee for doctors who certified the health of pilots by roughly $70 per year.

Aviation security. The FAA proposed to cut its civil aviation security work force by the equivalent of 13 full-time employees in

order to hold its budget to $69.2 million, or $602,000 more than fiscal 1993. The conferees, however, directed that spending on this program be reduced to $67 million, a cut of $1.59 million.

Training. Congress added $2 million to the administration's request for training to fund the Mid-American Aviation Resource Consortium in Minnesota, a project championed by House Transportation Appropriations Subcommittee member Martin Olav Sabo, D-Minn.

An additional $750,000 was provided for grants to at least two unspecified technical colleges to acquire or build advanced training facilities for airline maintenance technicians. The money had been sought by the Senate. Only a handful of technical schools met the criteria in the law; among them were schools in Arkansas, Oklahoma and Minnesota.

Miscellaneous. Sen. Frank R. Lautenberg, D-N.J., inserted a provision into the act to spur completion of an FAA environmental impact study on new airline routes over New Jersey. Until a final report was issued, no FAA employee involved in noise abatement policy, aircraft route design or the study itself could receive a raise or a bonus.

The conferees accepted two provisions sought by House Transportation Appropriations Subcommittee member Richard J. Durbin, D-Ill., for home-state Illinois airports. The first forbade the FAA to reduce any U.S. airline's access to O'Hare for the sake of increasing a foreign airline's access. The second, contained in the conference report, directed the FAA to give Illinois transportation officials $250,000 to study air service at small and midsize airports.

The conference report also included a provision sought by a senior member of the Senate Appropriations Committee, Democrat Daniel K. Inouye of Hawaii, directing the FAA to finish preliminary work on a new radar installation on Oahu in fiscal 1994.

Another provision in the conference report ordered the FAA to repay the Grand River Dam Authority in Oklahoma, home state of Republican Senate appropriator Don Nickles, for the costs of removing a transmission line near an FAA installation. The FAA had approved the original location, then reversed its decision.

Congress placed three restrictions on FAA's efforts to consolidate its facilities. It forbade the FAA to remove the radar facility from the Roswell, N.M., airport unless it could demonstrate a significant reduction in costs. It also forbade the FAA to close flight service stations at Red Bluff Airport in Red Bluff, Calif., and Tri-City Airport in Bristol, Tenn., as it had in fiscal 1993.

Congress also recycled from the fiscal 1993 act a provision barring the FAA from requiring U.S. airlines to compile passenger manifests on international flights unless foreign airlines were required to do so. The lists were to include the names of passengers and their closest relatives, as well as a number to call in case of emergency.

▶ **Facilities and equipment.** Congress provided $2.1 billion to buy new equipment and build and modernize facilities. The amount fell $398 million short of what the FAA requested to continue developing its comprehensive "national airspace system" — a master plan to modernize and coordinate all airport activities. More than 70 percent of the shortfall affected programs for the FAA's air-traffic control centers. Spending included:

Air-traffic control. The amount included $470.6 million for upgrading equipment at air-traffic control centers across the country, $360.9 million for equipment for air-traffic control towers and $48.2 million for flight service stations.

Engineering, development, testing and evaluation. The conferees provided $438.5 million to develop and test equipment. The House appropriators proposed to cut $7 million of the $16 million requested for equipment at the FAA Technical Center near Atlantic City, N.J., arguing that it was low-priority spending. Lautenberg defended his home-state program, but the conferees still cut $3 million.

Landing and navigational aids. The conferees agreed to spend $93.2 million on landing and navigational aids, $8.3 million less than the administration requested. They directed that the FAA accelerate its plans to upgrade the instrument landing system at the Des Moines, Iowa, airport, as requested by Senate Transportation

Appropriations Subcommittee member Tom Harkin, D-Iowa.

The Senate appropriators also directed the FAA to speed installation of a new instrument landing system for Newark International Airport in Lautenberg's home state. They further directed the FAA to act promptly on an application for an instrument landing system at Felts Field in Washington, home state of Senate Appropriations Committee members Patty Murray, D, and Slade Gorton, R.

Weather. The FAA was to spend $53.6 million to pay its share of the Next Generation Weather Radar (NEXRAD) program. The FAA shared 20 percent of the costs of the project with the Defense and Commerce departments.

Congress ordered the FAA to install seven NEXRAD stations at different sites in Alaska, and to study the safety effects of not installing nine stations. That provision was a milder version of the one offered by Senate Appropriations Committee member Ted Stevens, R-Alaska, and adopted by the Senate, which would have required the FAA to install nine NEXRAD stations by September 1996.

At Sabo's request, the conferees barred the FAA from developing a new national weather graphics system. The principal supplier for the existing system of color weather graphic terminals was Kavouras Inc. of Minneapolis, one of Sabo's constituents.

Airway sciences program. Congress doled out $30 million in fiscal 1993 to colleges and universities to train the next generation of airways operators, managers and technicians. Citing an unfavorable report by the Transportation Department's inspector general about the program's value, Carr proposed to shut it down. The conferees agreed to put no more money into the program, dipping instead into unspent appropriations from previous years to provide $2.8 million for the University of North Dakota's distance learning program.

▶ **Research, engineering and development.** Congress spent $254 million for research on air-traffic control, advanced computers, navigation, aviation weather, medicine, safety and environment.

The conferees included $4 million above the administration's request for these programs. Half of that increase was to go to improve the safety of aging aircraft, an effort championed by Senate Transportation Appropriations Subcommittee member Pete V. Domenici, R-N.M. Some of that work was done in Domenici's home state by a consortium of public and private groups at Kirtland Air Force Base in Albuquerque.

At the request of House appropriators, the conference report directed that at least $450,000 be spent to continue research on unleaded aviation fuels. The money was sought by the trade association representing the owners and pilots of small planes, who feared that they would run out of the high-octane fuel they needed to power their planes' piston-driven engines. The work was being done at the FAA's technical center in Atlantic City.

▶ **Aircraft purchase loan guarantee program.** This program shut down in 1983, but the taxpayers continued to pay its bills. Created in 1957, it authorized the Transportation Department to guarantee loans for airlines that wanted to buy planes. Twelve airlines that won guaranteed loans — Big Sky, Dorado Wings, Midway, Mid Pacific, Pocono, Continental, Air Florida, Golden West, Excellair, Cascade, Altair and Wheeler — went into bankruptcy, defaulting on their loans and leaving the federal government with the bill.

The Transportation secretary was to be allowed to borrow up to $9.97 million from the Treasury to pay airlines' defaulted loans, the same as the fiscal 1993 level. To repay the Treasury for previous borrowing, Congress provided the Transportation Department an additional $150,000.

ROADS

Federal Highway Administration

The FHwA worked with states to administer the federal-aid highway construction program, which included more than 276,000 bridges, the 45,280-mile Interstate Highway System and 808,546

miles of other federally subsidized roads. It regulated and enforced federal safety requirements for commercial trucks engaged in interstate or international commerce. The agency also governed the safety of moving dangerous cargoes and hazardous materials over the nation's highways.

Most federal aid to state highway programs came from the Highway Trust Fund, which was fed by an 18.4-cents-per-gallon tax on motor fuels. Almost all of this aid was distributed through various highway programs, each using different formulas that included factors such as population, the number of miles of highway in a state and postal route mileage.

Federal funds for highway construction and safety grants were pledged to states through contract authority. States then entered into contracts for road and bridge work and were later reimbursed from the Highway Trust Fund.

Because of budget constraints, the executive branch since 1966 — and Congress since 1976 — had put limits on the amount of new contract authority that could be obligated from the trust fund. This trust fund "ceiling" did not limit the amount of cash available for reimbursement to states. It did limit the amount made available to states for new obligations for future road work during any one fiscal year. In fiscal 1994, Congress set that limit at $17.7 billion, compared with $15.4 billion in fiscal 1993.

Nor was the limit universal — a number of programs were exempted from it by the 1991 surface transportation law (PL 102-240). Congress made an additional $2.1 billion available to the states for those programs in fiscal 1994, compared with $2.7 billion in fiscal 1993. The programs included emergency relief, bonuses for states that received less in highway grants than their drivers paid in fuel taxes and demonstration projects listed in the 1991 law.

About 2 percent of the money flowing out of the trust fund — $468.9 million — was reserved for the operating expenses of the FHwA. Within that total, the conferees recommended that $252.7 million go for administrative expenses, $156.7 million for various research, development, testing and training programs, $47.7 million for the federal truck safety program, $10 million for state programs to help businesses owned by women and minorities compete for highway contracts, $1.25 million for repairs at the Turner Fairbank Highway Research Center in McLean, Va., and $500,000 to collaborate with international transportation groups.

Congress also tapped the trust fund for the following programs: grants to states for truck safety programs, $65 million; highway-related safety grants, $10 million in contract authority. The conferees made available an additional $42.5 million from the trust fund for cash advances to states for acquiring rights of way for highway construction, so that property values did not increase while the states waited for construction to begin. States reimbursed the funds once construction got under way.

In addition to the money from the Highway Trust Fund, Congress dipped into the general Treasury for $156 million in highway spending. Most of that amount was for specific road or bridge projects authorized by previous laws. To offset some of that cost, Congress rescinded $3.6 million that had not been spent for three demonstration projects in previous appropriations acts. Two grants totaling $564,180 had been for purchasing rights of way along interstate highways in Maryland, and a third grant for $3.1 million had been for improving an intersection in El Segundo, Calif.

All told, Congress directed more than $19.9 billion into highways for fiscal 1994, an increase of 7 percent over the fiscal 1993 appropriations act. (A supplemental appropriations act for fiscal 1993 added $175 million from the general Treasury for highways damaged by flooding in the Midwest.)

A final bookkeeping note: The $19.9 billion represented fiscal 1994 decisions on highway priorities. The FHwA was to cut checks for another $18 billion pledged in previous years — a process known as "liquidation of contract authority" — for federal-aid highways, as well as $68 million for truck safety grants and $10 million for highway-related safety grants.

▶ **Demonstration projects.** No aspect of transportation spending was more controversial than the "demonstration projects" that

lawmakers funded to build roads and bridges back home. The fiscal 1994 transportation appropriations bill included the fewest demonstration projects in three years — 13, with a price tag of $126 million. That sum compared with $751 million in fiscal 1991, $589 million in 1992 and $351 million in 1993.

Demonstration projects had been controversial for several reasons. In the past, most were not authorized by House and Senate Public Works committees. In addition, state transportation officials often disliked these projects because they bypassed the traditional highway funding method of lump-sum grants, which let states decide how to spend the money. Critics said the projects rarely "demonstrated" novel road-building techniques and forced states to put up matching funds to pay for work not considered by state officials to be of priority.

Many members of Congress defended the spending, saying they often knew local road needs better than state transportation officials. Still, Congress took a different approach to highway demonstration projects in the fiscal 1994 bill. Pushed by the House Public Works Committee, the House rejected any project that had not been authorized by a previous law. The Senate appropriators followed suit, and the conferees agreed.

One thing did not change: The projects funded were the ones favored by the most powerful lawmakers. All 13 were sought by senior members of the Appropriations committees, either for their own districts or their own states.

Consistent with past practice, conferees agreed to accept all of the projects approved in the House and Senate bills. The conferees also trimmed the proposed grants by almost 15 percent on average. The only projects not cut were $12 million for an ongoing bridge project in House Appropriations Committee Chairman William H. Natcher's district in Kentucky and $7.8 million for a highway project in Mineola, N.Y., sought by Alfonse M. D'Amato, the top Republican on the Senate Transportation Appropriations Subcommittee.

The money for all but one of the demonstration projects was to come out of the general Treasury. The exception was the Mineola grant, which was to come from the Highway Trust Fund.

The largest grant went once again to a West Virginia highway project, whose sponsor was Senate Appropriations Committee Chairman Byrd. In fiscal 1994, the project was known as Corridor "L" on the Appalachian Regional System, and it was to receive $54 million. The same corridor received $24 million in fiscal 1993, second only to the $80 million earmarked for West Virginia Corridors "G" and/or "H."

The other grants were $6 million for the Cumberland Gap Tunnel in eastern Kentucky; $4 million for the Lock and Dam No. 4 bridge in Pine Bluff, Ark.; $1.6 million for a project to ease congestion near Syracuse, N.Y.; $9.8 million for car-pool lanes along Interstate 287 in Westchester, N.Y.; $3.2 million for a bridge in Schenectady County, N.Y.; $2.5 million for the Columbia Gorge Highway between Hood River, Ore., and Mosier, Ore.; $3 million for a new interchange along Interstate 66 near Manassas, Va.; $6.4 million for the border highway in El Paso, Texas; $12.8 million for the Baltimore-Washington Parkway in Maryland; and $3 million for U.S. 23 in eastern Kentucky.

The conferees made two other earmarks in their conference report for eliminating intersections between railroads and highways. Of the $30.3 million provided for these projects, the conferees recommended that $5.5 million go to a project backed by House appropriator John T. Myers, R-Ind., in Lafayette, Ind., and $4.8 million to a project in Brownsville, Texas, backed by Rep. Solomon P. Ortiz, D-Texas.

▶ **'Intelligent vehicles.'** Congress recommended spending $169.8 million on intelligent vehicle-highway systems (IVHS) research, to find new ways to reduce traffic congestion, improve safety and aid motorists through electronic communication. The amount was $44 million less than the administration requested. Examples of these technologies included electronic toll-charging devices, message signs along highways and automobile navigation devices that could "read" road and traffic conditions and suggest alternate routes.

The conference report divided money for these projects into a variety of pots for research, testing and demonstration projects. Most of the recommended projects were in the state or district of a member of the Transportation Appropriations subcommittees; the rest were in states represented by other appropriators.

House appropriators steered $42.5 million toward IVHS projects in six highway corridors in Michigan, Minnesota, North Carolina, Texas, Illinois and the Gary, Ind.,-Chicago-Milwaukee area. They also directed $2 million to the National Center for Regional Mobility at George Mason University in Fairfax, Va., and $950,000 to the University of Minnesota's Humphrey Institute in Minneapolis.

Senators added $35 million for high-technology corridors in California, Maryland, Michigan, New Jersey, New Mexico, New York, Tennessee, and Washington. At the urging of Sen. Harkin of Iowa, the conferees said that they expected $2 million to be made available to the Iowa Department of Transportation's commercial vehicle information system, an effort to track the performance of truck drivers.

▶ **Other highway research.** Congress agreed to spend $49.5 million for other highway research, development and technology, including $7 million to examine how pavement performed in the long term. The conferees recommended that $1.5 million be spent developing the geographic information system in North Carolina, home of House Transportation Appropriations Subcommittee member David Price, D. At the Senate's request, the conferees recommended that $500,000 be used to study the health aspects of mixing recycled tires into asphalt. They also called for $1 million to be spent studying construction techniques and worker safety on bridges. The remainder of funds were to be allocated by the highway administration.

▶ **Crumb-rubber asphalt.** The Senate agreed to accept a provision in the House bill that delayed for one year the requirement that states mix recycled tires into a portion of the asphalt they used. Under the 1991 surface transportation law, states were required to use recycled rubber in at least 5 percent of their asphalt in fiscal 1994.

▶ **Tolls.** The House agreed to accept a provision offered by D'Amato that prohibited tolls from being charged on drivers traveling in New York from Staten Island to Brooklyn on the Verrazano-Narrows Bridge. Drivers had paid a $6 toll on the bridge when traveling from Brooklyn to Staten Island, but the Triborough Bridge and Tunnel Authority (TBTA) was considering proposals to impose tolls both ways or to switch the tolls to the other direction. Congress had blocked such a move since 1986 at the urging of two Staten Island Republicans — former Rep. Guy V. Molinari and his successor, daughter Susan Molinari. The younger Molinari had sued the TBTA to force a reduction in the toll, which subsidized the New York City subways and the Long Island commuter rail system.

National Highway Traffic Safety Administration

Established in 1970, NHTSA had as a main goal to reduce deaths, injuries and economic losses from traffic accidents on the nation's highways. The agency also worked to improve automotive fuel economy and aid consumers who bought automobiles.

Appropriators agreed to boost NHTSA programs by 10 percent, spending a total of $298.1 million — three-quarters of it coming from the Highway Trust Fund. Almost 60 percent of the money was distributed to state and local highway safety programs. NHTSA also was to draw $138.6 million from the trust fund to cover pledges made in previous years to state and local programs.

▶ **Operations and research.** The appropriators trimmed President Clinton's request by $5.9 million, from $130 million to $124.1 million. That represented a $4.1 million cut from fiscal 1993. The conference report recommended cutting all $2 million for the advanced driving simulator being developed at the University of Iowa; halving the program to encourage seat belt use by "high risk/low-use" groups; freezing spending on a program to help police identify drivers who used drugs; and eliminating funds for new crash-test and gas-mileage studies.

The last of these recommendations came from House Transportation Appropriations Subcommittee Chairman Carr, a Democrat from a district in Michigan where automakers were the dominant employer. Starting in fiscal 1994, cars would have to meet a new federal standard for safety when hit from the side. NHTSA had asked for $600,000 to do side-impact tests on 15 models and make the results available to consumers. The Senate appropriators recommended almost twice as much, arguing that NHTSA should be able to test as many vehicles that claimed to meet the new standard as possible. The conference report, however, recommended that NHTSA receive no money for these tests. Carr said that it made more sense for NHTSA to oversee the crash tests that the law required automakers to conduct, rather than doing their own expensive tests.

NHTSA also had asked for $801,000 to study "emerging technologies that appear to have significant potential" to raise the gas mileage of light vehicles. "These studies will assist the agency in establishing reasonable fuel economy standards that result in maximum savings in fuel without adverse effects on financial condition or vehicle safety," NHTSA told the House appropriators. The Senate supported this request, but the conferees recommended that no money be spent on such a study. Carr said that NHTSA should not try to reinvent the wheel with its own tests but should evaluate the tests being conducted by advocates and opponents of higher fuel-economy standards.

▶ **Highway traffic safety grants.** Congress directed $174 million into five grant programs, each with a separate limit on obligations: $123 million for state and community highway safety programs, $35.5 million in two programs to help states combat drunken driving, $12 million to encourage the use of seat belts and motorcycle helmets and $3.5 million for a national registry of drivers with revoked, suspended or canceled licenses.

The total was $3 million less than the administration requested, with the difference coming in the grants to encourage seat belts and helmets. The amount for state and community highway safety programs was $8 million higher than in fiscal 1993, though. The appropriators directed that all $8 million be spent combating underage drinking.

RAILROADS

Federal Railroad Administration

The Federal Railroad Administration (FRA), established as a separate agency in 1967, was responsible for carrying out safety programs for the freight and passenger railroad industries and for providing financial aid programs and grants to Amtrak to rehabilitate and improve passenger railroads. Appropriators agreed to spend $1 billion for such activities, more than half of which was to go to Amtrak. Amtrak got a funding increase, but also an admonishment not to begin any more routes unless a state agreed to cover any losses.

Railroad administration funding also included local rail-freight assistance, railroad safety and research programs, including research into high-speed technologies. Reflecting Carr's reservations about investing in high-speed rail, the conferees rejected most of the president's request in that area. Overall, the appropriation for the railroad administration was $32.1 million less than the president's request but $7.3 million more than was spent in fiscal 1993.

The freight railroad industry, partly deregulated in 1980, was highly dependent on coal, heavy industry and agriculture for much of its traffic base. Like its two predecessors, the Clinton administration attempted to stem the flow of federal dollars to the railroads. The appropriators disagreed, more than doubling the support for local rail lines.

The appropriators did attempt to trim the railroad administration's administrative costs, recommending that four positions be cut, travel spending be frozen and bonuses reduced within the administrator's office.

▶ **National Railroad Passenger Corporation (Amtrak).** Congress created Amtrak in 1971 to take over the unprofitable

passenger services offered by private rail lines. It operated about 250 trains over 24,000 miles of track, most of which was owned by private freight rail lines. About half the trains ran on or around the Northeast Corridor between Washington and Boston. Of the routes outside the Northeast Corridor, almost half were subsidized by the states.

For fiscal 1994, Congress gave $683.7 million for Amtrak operating and capital expenses, down $3.3 million from fiscal 1993 but up $50.7 million from the administration's request.

Included was a $351.7 million operating grant to offset losses expected by the public-private train system in fiscal 1994. The railroad had asked for almost $30 million more to continue its existing intercity passenger services. The action by Congress had led Amtrak to run fewer trains from Chicago to Texas and from Denver to Seattle, and to eliminate a train from Carbondale, Ill., to St. Louis.

The railroad's revenues covered almost 80 percent of its costs, up from 48 percent in 1980. Without a major infusion of cash from Congress, however, Amtrak's high maintenance costs would prevent it from breaking even, Amtrak officials said.

The grant to Amtrak also included $195 million for capital expenses, $5 million more than in fiscal 1993. Most new spending was to go toward purchasing or overhauling locomotives and passenger cars.

The last component of Amtrak's funding was $137 million to cover payments to the Railroad Retirement Trust Fund and the Railroad Unemployment Insurance Account. The amount represented the difference between the benefits received by Amtrak retirees and the contributions made by Amtrak and its existing employees. The $137 million did not go to Amtrak but was paid on Amtrak's behalf by the Federal Railroad Administration.

Congress placed a new restriction on Amtrak's Thruway Bus Service program, which offered bus service from Amtrak stations to cities not served by Amtrak. Under the 1994 appropriations act, no federal funds could support any Amtrak bus route that was not connected to a rail route. The provision originated with Rep. Tom DeLay, a Republican from Texas, where the Greyhound Lines bus company was based.

The House also accepted a provision offered by Sen. Trent Lott, R-Miss., that allowed new state-supported Amtrak routes only if the states involved agreed to cover any losses. At the request of Price, a subcommittee member, the conference report exempted a route in Price's home state of North Carolina from that restriction. The route, which would double Amtrak's service between Raleigh and Charlotte, was ordered and funded by Congress two years earlier but had yet to start operations. The appropriators gave Amtrak an additional $700,000 to cover any losses it might incur on the route.

▶ **Northeast Corridor Improvement Program.** The Northeast Corridor was a high-speed electric-locomotive route that Amtrak was developing between Washington and Boston. It had a powerful advocate in the Senate Transportation Appropriations Subcommittee's chairman, Democrat Lautenberg of New Jersey, who often took the train from his home to the Senate.

The segment between Washington and New York was completed, and the rest was nearly half done. Congress provided $225 million for fiscal 1994, up from $204.1 million in 1993. The administration had proposed no increase, and the House had proposed a $74 million cut.

Much of the money was to be used to extend electrification from New Haven, Conn., to Boston, the only segment where the high-speed electric locomotives could not run. The money also was to provide a down payment on the purchase of 26 high-speed trainsets. The Senate had urged Amtrak to buy at least 80 percent of the equipment from U.S. manufacturers, but the conferees eliminated that goal. Instead, the conference report stated that "Amtrak should seek to maximize the U.S. content of the new trainsets."

▶ **Local rail service assistance.** This program, established for the Northeast in 1973 and expanded to all states in 1976, provided financial support to states to allow continuation of rail-freight service on abandoned lines. Congress provided $17 million, up $9 million from

fiscal 1993. The Clinton administration requested no funding.

The conference report directed that the railroad administration give priority consideration to grant applications from six rail lines suggested by the House in Illinois, Ohio, Michigan, Iowa, New York and Texas, and three lines suggested by the Senate in New York, South Dakota and Pennsylvania.

▶ **Railroad safety.** Congress provided $44.4 million to encourage safe operation of passenger and freight trains, an 8.5 percent increase over fiscal 1993 but $496,000 less than requested by Clinton. The funding paid for federal enforcement, track inspection and safety education programs.

Part of the increase was to be used to hire eight inspectors to improve safety at railroad crossings. These employees were to help monitor the warning devices at about 60,000 crossings across the United States. This task was so monumental, the Senate appropriators urged the FRA to assign some of the work to the existing staff of signal inspectors.

▶ **Research and development.** Congress provided $37.6 million for research activities, up almost 50 percent from fiscal 1993. At the Senate appropriators' request, $20 million from this account was to be spent on research into magnetic levitation trains, which rode at extremely high speeds on a cushion of air above the rails.

The research and development program supported the FRA's efforts to adopt safety-related regulations and to stimulate technological advances. Its work covered such areas as transporting hazardous materials, strengthening tracks and reducing the risks posed by high-speed rail.

At the request of House appropriators, the conference report recommended that the Transportation Test Center in Pueblo, Colo., receive $400,000 more than the president requested for improvements. The center was operated for the government by the Association of American Railroads, the freight railroads' trade association.

Congress instructed the FRA to spend up to $100,000 on non-governmental railroad crossing safety programs, including the industrywide Operation Lifesaver initiative. It also directed that $100,000 be used to support railroad metallurgical and welding studies at the Oregon Graduate Institute in Beaverton, as requested by the administration.

▶ **High-speed rail and magnetic levitation.** Efforts to increase the speed of passenger trains had focused in the short term on high-speed "steel-on-steel" systems, which used electric or diesel turbine locomotives. For the long term, the Federal Railroad Administration was developing a prototype magnetic levitation (maglev) train, which would operate on an electromagnetic field.

The Clinton administration made high-speed ground transportation its top priority in the transportation spending bill, asking for $105 million from the Highway Trust Fund and $35 million from the general Treasury for high-speed rail and maglev. Lautenberg, a strong supporter of both technologies, backed most of the administration's request. The problem for the administration was that Congress had authorized a major investment only in maglev, not high-speed rail.

In the face of House appropriators' opposition to unauthorized spending on high-speed rail, the conferees limited spending on high-speed rail to $3.5 million. The House report directed that the money be spent on the high-speed corridors that passed through the districts of two members of the House Transportation Appropriations Subcommittee: Price of North Carolina and Durbin of Illinois.

The maglev program was to receive $20 million out of the research and development budget. The House appropriators insisted, though, that none of the money be used to build a prototype maglev train. The restriction reflected Carr's wish to move slowly on maglev, rather than committing the government to a major investment in an expensive and unproven technology.

▶ **Railroad rehabilitation and improvement.** Congress provided up to $5 million in loan guarantees, costing the federal government $250,000, to help private railroads finance improvements to major facilities. The conference report recommended that the money be used to guarantee loans for rehabilitating track

between Syracuse and Binghamton, N.Y., owned by the New York, Susquehanna & Western Railway. That provision was requested by two Republican appropriators from New York: D'Amato and Rep. James T. Walsh, who represented Syracuse.

MASS TRANSIT

Federal Transit Administration

The transit administration provided federal financial aid for planning, developing and improving mass-transportation systems in urban and rural areas.

In contrast to the two previous administrations, the Clinton administration proposed a sharp increase in aid for mass transit — to $4.6 billion from $3.8 billion in fiscal 1993. Still, the administration's request was $742 million less than the 1991 surface transportation law authorized.

More than 98 percent of the transit money in fiscal 1994 was to go to state and local mass transit programs, either in the form of formula grants or discretionary grants. Formula grants helped with routine capital and operating expenses and programs for the elderly and handicapped. Discretionary grants were project-specific funds for bus facilities, rail modernization, new rail systems and research at university transportation centers.

Largely following the administration's request, Congress put almost 75 percent of the transit money into formula-driven programs. These programs received the bulk of the increase in funding over fiscal 1993.

Where Congress differed most sharply from the administration was in discretionary programs. The administration had wanted to use its own judgment to distribute more than $1 billion in grants for transit systems, planning and research. Congress earmarked $938 million of the discretionary money, however, leaving the administration in control of only $174 million.

About 46 percent of transit administration funds came from the mass transit account of the Highway Trust Fund, which received 1.5 cents of the 18.4-cents-per-gallon gasoline tax. The remainder came from general revenues.

▶ **Formula grants.** Congress provided $2.4 billion for capital and operating assistance in urban and rural areas, which was $715 million more than fiscal 1993 levels.

Grants could be used to buy and repair buses, modernize bus stations and garages, improve rail service equipment and maintain or expand service for the elderly and handicapped. Congress applied $802 million of the formula grant program toward operating assistance, an amount that had remained the same since the mid-1980s. The money was divided among the nation's transit systems based on formulas using population density, the number of route miles in a transit system and the amount of revenue earned from each vehicle. The conference report directed that rural transit systems receive $130 million, and programs for the elderly and the disabled collect $59 million.

▶ **Discretionary grants.** Congress designated $1.8 billion for discretionary grants, an increase of $60 million from fiscal 1993. Grants went toward building new "fixed guideway" (rail) systems, major bus fleet expansions and rail modernization for existing systems.

For new rail systems and extensions, Congress provided $668 million in appropriations and $76.5 million reclaimed from a mass transit project in Honolulu that had not gotten off the ground. The money, which could be used for preliminary engineering, right-of-way acquisition, project oversight and construction, was divided among 29 cities or urban corridors: Los Angeles, $170 million; St. Louis, $15.2 million; San Francisco, $28.2 million; Houston, $40 million; Dallas, $44 million; Cleveland, $800,000; New Jersey urban core, $62.5 million; Chicago, $32.6 million; Salt Lake City, $3 million; Pittsburgh, $41.7 million; Portland, Ore., $83.5 million; New York, $65 million; Boston, $20 million; Orlando, Fla., $3 million; Boston to Portland, Maine, $9.5 million; Cincinnati, $1.4 million; Miami, Dade County and Broward County, Fla., $10 million; Hawthorne, N.J., to Warwick, N.Y., $6.7 million; Lakewood, N.J., to Matawan, N.J., $3 million; new

routes to Washington, D.C. from Waldorf, Md., and Frederick, Md., $23.5 million; Memphis, $500,000; New Orleans, $3.6 million; northeast Ohio, $1 million; Orange County, Calif., $15.5 million; Sacramento, Calif., $1 million; southern New Jersey, $500,000; Minneapolis-St. Paul, $2.8 million; suburban Chicago, $8 million; the Milwaukee Interstate 94 corridor in Milwaukee, $3 million. The remaining $45 million was to be distributed at the discretion of the Federal Transit Administration.

The conference report specified that $760 million of the total was to be distributed by formula to upgrade commuter rail systems. Funding went primarily to seven areas: New York, Chicago and its suburbs, Philadelphia and its suburbs, northeastern New Jersey, Boston, San Francisco and southwestern Connecticut.

Bus facilities received $357 million, including $257 million for 60 specific state or local transportation authorities. Those cities could use the funds to buy or improve buses and to build or upgrade bus facilities. The remaining $100 million was to be distributed at the transit administration's discretion.

▶ **Administrative expenses.** At the behest of Senate appropriators, Congress gave the transit administration the $39.5 million it requested to cover administrative costs. The transit administration planned to cut the number of full-time equivalent employees to 466, down from the 478 allowed by Congress in the fiscal 1993 appropriations act.

Noting that Congress had helped support the cities sponsoring major international sporting events, the conferees urged the transit administration to support the nine cities that were to play host to the 1994 World Cup soccer games. They were Washington, Boston, Chicago, Dallas, Detroit, Los Angeles, New York, Orlando and San Francisco.

The bill included the full amount the administration requested for expansion of the Washington, D.C., Metrorail system.

▶ **Planning and technical studies.** Congress spent $92.3 million for planning and technical studies. Of that amount, $56.3 million was to be distributed by formula to state, county and local planning, research and training programs. Industry research projects were to receive $8.8 million, and technology development projects picked by the transit administration were to receive $14.25 million. The rest was to be divided among projects specified in the conference report: $3 million for training programs at the National Transit Institute at Rutgers University in New Jersey; $500,000 for the "team transit" program in Minneapolis; $2.3 million to develop fuel cell bus technology, a project managed by Georgetown University in Washington but done largely in New Jersey, California and Chicago; $1 million for research in Pittsburgh into inertial navigation systems for buses, which would help bus companies keep track of their vehicles as they made their rounds; and $6.3 million to build a high-technology bus, which was being done in Los Angeles. Only the money for the National Transit Institute had been requested by the administration.

▶ **Interstate transfer grants.** States that canceled interstate segments in favor of mass transit projects received $45 million, the amount requested by the administration. The money, distributed by formula, was to go to 15 cities and one state, led by New York City ($24 million), Baltimore ($10.5 million), Portland, Ore., ($3 million), Cleveland ($1.6 million), San Francisco ($1.3 million), Providence, R.I., ($1.3 million) and Chicago ($1 million).

▶ **Grants to university centers.** Congress provided $6 million for transportation research and education programs at 13 universities in 13 states. Regional centers were at the Massachusetts Institute of Technology, City University of New York, Pennsylvania State University, the University of North Carolina, the University of Michigan, Texas A&M University, Iowa State University, North Dakota State University, the University of California at Berkeley and the University of Washington. National centers were at the New Jersey Institute of Technology, Morgan State University in Maryland and the University of Arkansas. The centers were chosen by the Transportation Department.

▶ **Washington, D.C., Metro.** The bill included $200 million for expansion of the Washington, D.C., Metrorail system, the amount

Hoyer's concern for his district was evidenced through the $27.9 million included in the bill for a Census Bureau computer center in Bowie, 16 acres of free federal land for a subway station in Suitland and the transfer of 55 acres of federal land in Queen Anne's County to Maryland for a "Chesapeake Bay Study Site."

The main player in the Senate was Dennis DeConcini, D-Ariz., who had chaired the Treasury-Postal Appropriations Subcommittee since 1987. DeConcini was a major supporter of the Treasury Department law enforcement agencies funded under the bill. He also was adept at channeling money to Arizona, including a $120 million federal courthouse in Phoenix.

HOUSE COMMITTEE

The House Appropriations Treasury-Postal Service Subcommittee on May 26 gave voice vote approval to a $22.7 billion version of the bill that trimmed the budgets of several agencies and gutted the Office of National Drug Control Policy. The bill, marked up behind closed doors, exceeded Clinton's request by about $720 million, but most of that was accounted for by a change in the calculations used to determine the government's cost for the health plans of federal employees and retirees.

Overall funding for the Treasury Department was $10.2 billion, a $100 million increase over fiscal 1993. Within Treasury, the IRS budget went to $7.3 billion. The IRS got a $235 million increase for processing tax returns and enforcing tax laws, but the increase was partially offset by cutting $85 million from the $1.5 billion Clinton requested for IRS information systems and slightly paring a proposed increase for tax law enforcement.

Other Treasury agencies faced budget freezes or funding cutbacks. The subcommittee provided $1.4 billion for the Customs Service, $457 million for the Secret Service and $366 million for the Bureau of Alcohol, Tobacco and Firearms (ATF).

In keeping with Clinton's request to cut the White House staff by 25 percent, the measure appropriated $268 million for the Executive Office of the President, nearly $60 million less than in fiscal 1993. Most of the savings were produced by a huge cut that Clinton requested in the budget of the Office of National Drug Control Policy, which was reduced from $101.2 million to $5.8 million. Democrats had long criticized the office of the so-called drug czar for being stocked with political appointees, and they had been critical of the leadership of the most recent Republican drug czar, former Florida Gov. Bob Martinez.

The bill included $86 million in new spending requested by Clinton for extra assistance to federal, state and local law enforcement officials in areas especially hard-hit by drug trafficking: New York, Los Angeles, Miami, Houston and the Mexican border.

With an abortion rights supporter in the White House and the ascent of strong abortion rights backer Hoyer to the subcommittee chair, the panel dropped the language in force since 1984 that effectively banned federal employee health plans from offering abortion services. Ranking Republican Jim Ross Lightfoot of Iowa sought to restore the language, but his attempt failed on a voice vote.

The gun control lobby also claimed some victories. Hoyer dropped a longstanding provision backed by the National Rifle Association (NRA) that barred the ATF from "consolidating or centralizing" 48 million records of firearms transactions on file at the agency. Gun control

advocates said the provision, in force since 1978, kept ATF record-keeping in the "stone age" because it prevented the records from being computerized for easy use by law enforcement officials.

In addition, the bill allowed the ATF to require the "tagging" of explosives with microscopic bits of plastic to help track down the sources of illegally used explosives. The bill also continued a prohibition that barred the ATF from giving gun licenses to convicted felons.

While Hoyer's bill generally followed the administration's requests closely, there were some exceptions, including an extra boost for GSA construction projects. The bill included $829.3 million for construction and acquisition of federal facilities, $203 million more than fiscal 1993 and $82 million more than the Clinton request.

The subcommittee also dropped a $2.3 million request for the Administrative Conference of the United States, which was the main advisory body on improving the government's administrative and rulemaking processes.

The subcommittee complied with Clinton's request for further cuts in Postal Service subsidies for nonprofit groups. The bill included $130 million for such subsidies, a $30 million cut from existing funding. The appropriators also tightened eligibility requirements for nonprofit mail. In general, subsidies were to be cut off or reduced for nonprofit mail that contained certain levels of advertising or included political advocacy material. Commercial publishers that had been mailing material at fourth-class library rates also were to be affected by the change.

Full Committee Action

The full Appropriations Committee approved the bill by voice vote June 14 (H Rept 103-127).

The only significant action at the markup was an agreement by Hoyer to restore the language favored by the NRA barring the ATF from consolidating records on gun owners.

The committee report also encouraged agencies to develop plans to prevent wasteful spending at the fiscal year's end.

The committee also weighed in on a big fight among private sector contractors concerning the controversial FTS 2000 telecommunications program, a governmentwide long-distance telecommunications system. In 1988, AT&T and Sprint had won exclusive 10-year contracts worth up to $25 billion to provide the service, but other long-distance carriers were trying to get a crack at the lucrative government business. The General Accounting Office (GAO) said in 1991 that the federal government was paying more than comparable commercial long-distance prices, although that record later improved.

Appropriators for years had included language requiring every government agency to use the FTS 2000 system. The belief was that the government's huge buying power would increase its bargaining power with vendors. AT&T and Sprint lobbied hard to keep the language in the bill; the committee complied, but the provision was to expire if a study due in July 1994 did not show a cost savings to the government.

HOUSE FLOOR ACTION

The House finished work June 22 on its $22.7 billion Treasury-Postal bill, approving it 263-153 with many of the "nays" coming from Republicans apparently miffed by tactics Hoyer used to control floor action. *(Vote 260, p. 64-H)*

Hoyer said the bill did "not fund all of the agencies at

the levels that I would like to see them funded." But, he said, "Congress needs to show the American people that we can control spending and that we can do it in a responsible way." Hoyer's Republican counterpart, Lightfoot, seemed to agree. "Any way you describe it," he said, "this is a very tight bill."

Abortion opponents did not attempt to restore the anti-abortion language that had been stripped in committee.

During floor consideration June 18, members cut $21 million from the bill. Almost $13 million came on an amendment by Earl Pomeroy, D-N.D., adopted 339-50, to pare 2 percent from each of the new courthouse projects in the bill. *(Vote 245, p. 60-H)*

Another amendment, by Joel Hefley, R-Colo., adopted by voice vote, saved $1.9 million by eliminating the Advisory Commission on Intergovernmental Relations. The commission examined the relations of federal, state and local governments and issued recommendations on how to improve cooperation among the various levels of government.

The House also adopted amendments:

● By a group of freshmen, including Karen Shepherd, D-Utah, and Peter G. Torkildsen, R-Mass., to eliminate clerical staff for former presidents five years after they had left office. Adopted 247-127. *(Vote 246, p.60-H)*

● By Timothy J. Penny, D-Minn., to cut $4 million from the Customs Service, in keeping with the administration's request. Adopted 298-104. *(Vote 241, p. 58-H)*

● By Nathan Deal, D-Ga., to cut $2 million from the ATF, in line with Clinton's request. Adopted 333-65. *(Vote 242, p. 58-H)*

The House on June 22 rejected, 180-235, a motion to require the Appropriations Committee to make an additional 2 percent across-the-board cut. *(Vote 259, p. 64-H)*

Several provisions were stripped out of the bill on points of order because they constituted legislating on an appropriations bill, including:

● Language that would have allowed federal employees to use sick leave to take time off after adopting a child.

● A program to give cash awards to IRS employees who saved the agency money by suggesting ways to streamline IRS operations.

● Imposing Treasury Department user fees for processing requests for approving warning labels on alcoholic beverages.

Republicans offered or were prepared to offer several amendments to make cuts in Clinton's staff over the course of debate June 18 and 22. None was adopted, and for the most part Republicans were content to take a few shots at the administration.

But the debate grew testy June 22, when Hoyer used a procedural move to block Jim Kolbe, R-Ariz., from offering an amendment to limit the staff for the White House office to 306 full-time employees — a 25 percent reduction from fiscal 1993. "That is what President Clinton promised that he would do," said Kolbe.

Hoyer said it was inappropriate for Congress to try to play around with the White House budget because presidents traditionally had allowed Congress to write its own budget. "Clearly the president ought to have some flexibility to manage the office to which he is constitutionally elected," he said.

To prevent Kolbe from offering his provision, Hoyer employed a procedural move to cut off further amendments to the bill. Republicans challenged the move but lost on a party-line vote of 241-171. *(Vote 254, p. 62-H)*

Republican unanimity did not extend to the broader notion of cutting the White House budget, however. "You don't want to tie any president's hands so they can't do their job," Lightfoot said in an interview. Chief Deputy Minority Whip Robert S. Walker, R-Pa., said that Republicans generally deferred to Lightfoot's judgment and that little time was spent preparing for a big floor fight over the White House budget. "It was a great opportunity that we could have done better with," said John A. Boehner, R-Ohio.

Republicans also took shots at Vice President Al Gore, who recently had tapped a Navy Department fund usually reserved for emergency repairs to barracks to pay for $1.2 million in renovations to the vice president's residence. An attempt June 18 to cut $1.2 million from the vice president's budget failed by voice vote.

SENATE COMMITTEE

The Senate Treasury, Postal Service and General Government Appropriations Subcommittee approved a $22.3 billion version of the spending bill by voice vote July 20. In contrast to the House bill, the measure included the language barring federal employee health plans from covering abortions. Subcommittee Chairman DeConcini said he had honored a request from Appropriations Committee Chairman Robert C. Byrd, D-W.Va., to exclude the restriction. But Christopher S. Bond, R-Mo., moved to add the language, and DeConcini, an abortion opponent, voted with him. The vote was 3-2.

Like its House counterpart, the bill generally hewed to the administration's budget, with a few changes.

The biggest difference between the House and Senate bills was $688 million for federal retirees' health-care coverage, required by a change in how the plan's cost was calculated. The House bill included the money, which was not part of the Clinton budget. The Senate bill did not contain the funding, but the final version would, a committee staff member said, because the spending was an entitlement. The staff aide said the committee had not received an administration request for the money.

In other changes from the House bill, the Senate subcommittee:

● Restored $64 million in administration-proposed cuts in the Customs Service, mostly for salaries and administrative expenses to pay for almost 500 Customs employees not funded under the House bill.

● Added $120 million for IRS information systems and tax law enforcement. That money, requested by the administration, was not included in the House bill, but the Senate subcommittee had $200 million more to work with and was able to fund the request.

● Provided double the administration's $5.8 million request for the drug czar's office, funding 35 more staff positions than the House-passed bill.

● Added more money for the construction of federal courthouses and other projects cherished by members. The Senate added $187 million to the Clinton request for such projects, $113 million more than the House passed. The projects included:

● $200 million for the U.S. courthouse project in Phoenix that DeConcini sought.

● $162 million for a U.S. courthouse and federal building in Sacramento, Calif., and $84 million for a federal building and courthouse in Santa Ana, Calif., at the request of Democrat Dianne Feinstein of California.

● $45 million for a courthouse in Wheeling, W.Va., supported by Byrd.

- $96 million for a courthouse project in Portland, Ore., backed by committee ranking Republican Mark O. Hatfield of Oregon.

The subcommittee dropped the language requiring all federal agencies to use the FTS 2000 long-distance system.

Full Committee Action

The full committee approved the $22.3 billion bill July 22 by a vote of 26-0 (S Rept 103-106). But first, in a controversial move, the panel reversed the subcommittee's decision to include the anti-abortion language.

On a 15-14 vote, the committee approved a move by Barbara A. Mikulski, D-Md., to strip the language from the bill, which meant that taxpayers would partially pay for abortions for women who worked for the federal government. In a savvy parliamentary maneuver, Mikulski moved to table the amendment that Bond had added in subcommittee. Byrd said that under Senate rules, a motion to table an amendment was in order even after the amendment had been adopted. Because a motion to table was not debatable, Mikulski avoided a lengthy fight over the abortion language. That may have won Byrd's vote, which proved to be decisive.

"I believe we were able to pick up a substantial number of votes because I chose a procedural tool," Mikulski said after the vote. Republicans Ted Stevens of Alaska and Arlen Specter of Pennsylvania joined 13 of the committee's 16 Democrats in backing Mikulski. Democrats J. Bennett Johnston of Louisiana and Harry Reid of Nevada joined DeConcini in voting to retain the ban.

Mikulski said the issue should be decided on the floor and that she was "cautiously optimistic" that she would prevail.

SENATE FLOOR ACTION

The Senate passed a $22.2 billion version of the Treasury-Postal spending bill on a 73-27 vote Aug. 3. As passed, the Senate bill was $550 million less than the $22.7 billion version passed by the House. But the conference report on the bill would have to include the $688 million in mandatory spending for federal retiree health-care plans that was in the House bill but not the Senate version. *(Vote 236, p. 31-S)*

In a narrow victory for abortion rights supporters, the Senate did not restore the anti-abortion language. But the win, on a 48-51 vote, may have hinged on procedure, not substance. *(Vote 235, p. 31-S)*

The vote came on a procedural move by Mikulski to block an amendment by Don Nickles, R-Okla. The Nickles amendment would have modified the ban to allow women to receive abortions through their federal health-care plans only if they paid a premium for the coverage. After a brief debate, Mikulski raised a point of order against the amendment, saying it amounted to legislating on an appropriations bill. A point of order was not debatable; Nickles demanded a recorded vote on whether his amendment was germane.

The procedural move may have picked up enough votes for abortion rights supporters to win. "It's hard to know, but a couple" of votes turned on procedure, said Barbara Boxer, D-Calif. One of those may have been that of Byrd, who, while not an enthusiastic supporter of abortion rights, was a stickler for Senate rules. "I was concerned that it would be very close," Boxer said. "I was hopeful, but I wasn't sanguine that we were going to win."

The victory resulted from a cohesive effort by the Senate's five Democratic women, who had vowed to fight to keep abortion restrictions off appropriations bills. This was Senate abortion opponents' first attempt to continue such restrictions.

Other Amendments

On July 29, the first day of floor consideration, the Senate adopted an amendment to cut approximately $325 million from the bill. The amendment, by Trent Lott, R-Miss., imposed an across-the-board reduction of 1.5 percent on programs covered by the bill, bringing it in line with Clinton's overall request. The managers of the bill, DeConcini and Bond, accepted the amendment, which was adopted on a voice vote.

Howard M. Metzenbaum, D-Ohio, offered an amendment to bar any of the money in the bill from being used for new federal building projects that had not been approved by the Environment and Public Works Committee by Feb. 1, 1994.

Before acting on the Metzenbaum amendment, senators tabled (killed), 65-34, an amendment by John McCain, R-Ariz., to strike the unauthorized projects from the bill. Metzenbaum's amendment then carried on a voice vote. *(Vote 226, p. 30-S)*

The following day, the Senate voted down, 30-68, an attempt by Paul Simon, D-Ill., to attach a provision that would have raised the fee to become a gun dealer from $10 per year to $375. Simon said the amendment would raise enough money to hire 300 additional Bureau of Alcohol, Tobacco and Firearms inspectors to supervise the nation's gun dealers.

On Aug. 3, the Senate adopted an amendment by Frank R. Lautenberg, D-N.J., to ban smoking in all federal office buildings, except in designated ventilated areas. The amendment, vigorously opposed by Wendell H. Ford, D-Ky., passed by voice vote. Ford had agreed not to call for a recorded vote; Lautenberg said afterward that Ford would have prevailed had he requested a vote. The smoking ban did not extend to buildings that served primarily as living quarters, such as retirement homes for veterans.

Other amendments adopted by the Senate included those by:

- John H. Chafee, R-R.I., to require the IRS to institute policies and procedures to safeguard the confidentiality of taxpayer information. The amendment came on the heels of revelations that numerous IRS employees had been electronically browsing through tax returns — a violation of agency rules.
- Jeff Bingaman, D-N.M., to bar the sale of cigarettes and other tobacco products in federal buildings and on property accessible to minors.
- DeConcini, to shift $19 million in courthouse construction money from the project he promoted in Phoenix to Feinstein's favored project in Santa Ana, Calif. The move was made to accommodate Feinstein.

CONFERENCE

House and Senate negotiators reached agreement Sept. 23 on a $22.5 billion version of HR 2403 (H Rept 103-256).

The conferees had no big-ticket items in dispute, and members spent about seven hours endorsing and fine-tuning an agreement that had been worked out in advance by DeConcini and Hoyer in consultation with their Republican counterparts.

● **Abortion ban.** The most controversial aspect of the bill — overturning the 10-year ban on allowing women who were federal workers to receive abortions through their taxpayer-subsidized health-care plans — was non-negotiable because both the House and Senate took identical positions to drop the ban.

● **Courthouse construction.** For new courthouse construction, traditionally one of the highest priorities for members eager to bring federal money back home, conferees managed to provide at least some money for almost every project included in either version of the bill. The final version of the bill provided $925 million for new courthouse construction projects — $178 million more than the Clinton request.

To make room for member-initiated projects, the conferees dumped one project sought by the administration: $50 million for an Army Corps of Engineers headquarters in Washington. Also, Hoyer was forced to abandon a $20 million project in his district. The project, a building that would have stored research samples at the Agricultural Research Center in Beltsville, Md., normally would have been financed by the Agriculture appropriations bill.

Underscoring how important projects were to members, the negotiators spent considerable time haggling over about $6 million — a portion of the cost of the Portland, Ore., courthouse that was of paramount concern to Sen. Hatfield. The Senate had provided $96 million for the project; the House had provided $85 million. A tentative conference deal essentially would have split the difference. But Hatfield insisted on getting the full amount, saying the project was ready to go and that anything less would delay it.

Bond suggested taking the money from a controversial Environmental Protection Agency (EPA) building in North Carolina — EPA projects belonged in the VA-HUD spending bill — eagerly sought by House Democrat David Price, N.C., and strongly opposed by North Carolina's two Republican senators.

"This project will not be dropped from this bill," said Hoyer, who said he had made a promise to Price.

After much back-and-forth on the issue, conferees agreed to use a portion of the extra budget authority that was made available by the bill's final allocation to pay for Hatfield's courthouse.

● **Smoking ban.** Conferees quietly dropped the Senate-passed provision to ban smoking in federal office buildings. A ban on cigarette vending machines in federal buildings was also dropped. House Appropriations Committee Chairman William H. Natcher and Senate Majority Whip Ford, both Kentucky Democrats, made certain the provisions disappeared.

● **Independent agencies.** Conferees restored spending for two independent agencies that would have been eliminated by the House bill. The Administrative Conference of the United States received $1.8 million. The Advisory Commission on Intergovernmental Relations was given $1 million. The Senate bill had included the money.

● **FTS 2000.** The conference agreement adopted House language to continue to require each federal agency to use the controversial FTS 2000 governmentwide, long-distance telecommunications system. In doing so, members weighed in on the side of AT&T and Sprint. "We've had more political contact on this than on anything in this bill," said DeConcini.

● **Reinventing government.** For the most part, appropriators tried to help Clinton keep his pledge to overhaul the federal bureaucracy, but conferees also decided that

reinventing government should only go so far. *(Reinventing government, p. 191)*

Conferees agreed to drop most of the member earmarks in the bill that would have set minimum staffing levels for law enforcement positions at the Customs Service, ATF and IRS, giving federal managers a little more flexibility when implementing the president's pledge to cut the federal work force by 252,000 over five years.

But DeConcini drew the line at cuts in the office of the drug czar. He insisted that there be a floor of 40 positions at the 112-person office; Clinton had proposed to cut 87 employees, bringing it down to 25.

In another rebuke to Clinton, the conferees moved to preserve their own turf and that of the Treasury Department by retaining Senate provisions barring any transfer of the Bureau of Alcohol, Tobacco and Firearms to the Federal Bureau of Investigation. The FBI was a Justice Department agency.

The conferees also added a provision aimed at giving federal managers incentives to avoid wasteful end-of-year spending. Under the provision, backed by Hoyer and Frank R. Wolf, R-Va., agencies funded by the bill were allowed to carry over 50 percent of such unobligated funds for an additional year; the other half would revert to the Treasury.

● **Locality pay.** Conferees also added language that gave so-called locality pay increases to about 60 percent of federal white-collar workers in fiscal 1994. Under existing law, a maximum of $1.8 billion could be spent on the program, which was supposed to help close the gap between federal and private-sector wages.

As a deficit-reduction device, Clinton had requested delaying both locality pay and a 2.2 percent pay increase for federal workers. But Congress decided not to include the cuts in the final budget-reconciliation bill. Without further congressional action, both pay increases would have gone forward as required under existing law, but that would have forced agencies to fire or furlough employees to meet their budgets. To solve the problem, the conferees provided for the locality pay and eliminated the general pay raise, saving $1.3 billion. *(Budget reconciliation, p. 107)*

● **Postal Service.** The final bill also included language worked out by the Post Office and Civil Service Committee to tighten eligibility rules for nonprofit mailers, which qualified for reduced mailing rates subsidized by the federal government. Clinton urged Congress to cut such postal subsidies from $122 million to $91 million in fiscal 1994.

The bill required the Postal Service to bar commercial use of nonprofit third-class mail, restrict advertising in nonprofit mailings and limit publishers' use of library-rate mail to shipments to schools and libraries.

FINAL ACTION

The conference report barely survived an eleventh-hour attack by abortion foes when it came to the House floor Sept. 29. The House adopted the report on a 207-206 vote, over the opposition of 48 Democrats and all but 11 Republicans. *(Vote 476, p. 116-H)*

Abortion opponents had held their fire when the bill first came to the floor in June because they were concentrating their attention on the spending bill for the departments of Labor, Health and Human Services and Education (HR 2518). That bill included much more sweeping language — subsequently overturned on the House floor — to permit the federal Medicaid program to pay for abortions for the first time since 1976. Because health-care coverage was an

earned benefit for federal employees, the Treasury-Postal issue was a less clear-cut example of using federal funds to pay for abortion. *(Labor-HHS bill, p. 632)*

Indeed, the abortion question was never mentioned when the Treasury-Postal conference report came back to the House on Sept. 29, in deference to Appropriations Committee Chairman Natcher, who asked opponents not to stir up the issue through a contentious floor debate. Instead, Christopher H. Smith, R-N.J., and other abortion foes quietly lobbied like-minded colleagues throughout the day. Their efforts almost sank the bill. "If we'd had a real straight shot at this, I'm sure we would have won," said leading abortion opponent Henry J. Hyde, R-Ill.

Senate Delay

The bill then went to the Senate for final approval, but it hit a snag there when leaders of the Environment and Public Works Committee, which had jurisdiction over federal building construction, expressed displeasure at the number of projects in the spending bill that had not been fully authorized. They kept the conference report from coming up on the floor before the Senate recessed Sept. 30, pushing final approval past the Oct. 1 start of fiscal 1994.

The Treasury Department and other agencies covered by the bill had to operate temporarily under a 21-day continuing resolution that Congress cleared Sept. 29. *(Continuing resolution, p. 536)*

Then, in a step that set up an unusual legislative labyrinth for the final bill, the Senate on Oct. 21 adopted the conference report — but made that action contingent on the House's adopting a relatively minor change embodied in a separate concurrent resolution (S Con Res 48).

The extra step became necessary after members of the Senate Environment panel objected to a provision in the conference report allowing Congress to block unauthorized lease, construction, repair or alteration projects financed by the GSA's federal buildings fund. Under the conference agreement, it took both the House and Senate Public Works committees to waylay a project. S Con Res 48 instructed congressional clerks to make a one-word change in the bill — from "and" to "or" — which allowed either committee to nix a project if it did so before Feb. 1, 1994.

After adopting S Con Res 48, the Senate agreed by voice vote that upon House adoption of the concurrent resolution, the Senate would be deemed to have adopted the conference report on HR 2403, thus clearing the bill.

The House took the final turn Oct. 26, passing S Con Res 48 by voice vote. ■

Treasury/Postal Service Provisions

The most important thing that HR 2403 did was finance the activities of the Treasury Department, which was responsible for a host of critical functions for the federal government. The $22.5 billion bill also included funds to run the office of the president, the Office of Personnel Management and the General Services Administration; it included some money for the Postal Service. Following are provisions of the bill as enacted:

TREASURY DEPARTMENT

The Treasury Department was responsible for the financial workings of the nation. It collected taxes, issued bonds to finance the national debt and disbursed all monies appropriated by Congress. Under its umbrella were several agencies that regulated the country's financial affairs. The main Treasury Department offices set and carried out economic policy; other principal divisions were the IRS, the Customs Service, the Bureau of Alcohol, Tobacco and Firearms, and the U.S. Secret Service.

Appropriators provided about $10.3 billion for the department, slightly more than the president's request. Of that, $105.2 million went to the departmental offices account, which paid much of the cost of the Treasury Department's headquarters, as well as the salaries and expenses of almost 1,100 employees.

About $33 million of the money for departmental offices went for the activities of the International Affairs division. The division provided staff analysis for the Treasury secretary and other senior officials responsible for determining and implementing economic and financial policies overseas. The staff handled issues that included relations with the oil-producing countries of the Middle East, international monetary affairs and economic analysis, international trade, and investment policy. In a departure from prior years in which the division had a separate budget line, appropriators merged this function into the main departmental offices account.

One large Treasury expense — in fact the second largest single expenditure by the government next to Social Security — was interest on the federal debt. Paid to private investors as well as government trust funds that invested in government bonds, interest amounted to $292.5 billion in fiscal 1993. That money was permanently appropriated, however, and not a part of this bill.

Bureau of Alcohol, Tobacco and Firearms

The bureau, frequently referred to by its initials, BATF, had broad responsibility for reducing the criminal use of firearms (including trafficking in illegal firearms and explosives) and combating arson-for-profit schemes.

The agency also combated illegal trade practices in the alcoholic beverage industry as well as the manufacture and sale of untaxed alcoholic beverages. It assured collection of more than $13 billion in excise taxes on alcohol and tobacco, and tried to prevent organized crime from entering the alcohol and tobacco industries.

Lawmakers provided $366.4 million for the agency. The money paid the salaries of about 4,200 full-time employees. In response to President Clinton's pledge to "reinvent government," members — who liked BATF's law-and-order functions — departed from their traditional practice of mandating agency staff levels.

After bureau agents botched a February 1993 raid in Waco, Texas, of the compound of Branch Davidian cult leader David Koresh, the agency came under additional scrutiny and criticism. Clinton at first proposed merging the agency into the Justice Department. But BATF had a strong supporter in Dennis DeConcini, D-Ariz., chairman of the Senate Treasury-Postal Service Appropriations Subcommittee. DeConcini insisted that the bill include a provision that blocked a merger during 1994. Finding little congressional support for the merger, the administration reversed itself in November 1993 and dropped the idea.

▶ **Armed Career Criminal Apprehension Program.** The program was created under the 1984 Armed Career Criminal Act (PL 98-473) and later expanded by the Anti-Drug Abuse Act of 1986 (PL 99-570). It was designed to facilitate the capture, prosecution and conviction of repeat offenders, especially those involved with drugs. Program-sponsored "Achilles" task forces in 21 cities helped capture suspects and confiscate illegal weapons and paraphernalia.

▶ **Operation Alliance.** The bureau participated in this ongoing multiagency effort to combat drug smuggling along the Southwest border. The BATF initiated 243 Operation Alliance investigations in 1992.

▶ **Anti-gang efforts.** The bureau was also stepping up its anti-gang efforts, focusing on Jamaican "posses," the Crips and Bloods, outlaw motorcycle gangs and Asian gangs. The Senate Appropriations Committee earmarked $3 million to continue three pilot gang activity prevention task forces in Phoenix, Albuquerque, N.M., and Honolulu. The task forces were financed by the Gang Resistance Education and Training (GREAT) program.

U.S. Customs Service

The Customs Service was the watchdog over the nation's borders. It was mandated by Congress to enforce U.S. border laws governing international traffic and trade and to collect tariffs and duties. The Customs Service was divided into seven regions with 44 districts and was responsible for about 300 ports of entry into the United States.

Customs agents' duties included protecting Americans and the environment against hazardous products. In addition, the service was directed to safeguard U.S. industries and workers from unfair competition from foreign manufacturers.

Money was used for investigation and interdiction of all contraband, including illegal drugs, arms and toxic products. It was the lead agency for drug interdiction in territorial waters, with an authorized fleet of 200 vessels. It also had major forces directed at combating drug smuggling in air and on land, including a fleet of six sophisticated P-3 surveillance aircraft that operated in Central and South America and provided host countries with information on drug laboratories and clandestine airfields.

The service received $1.45 billion, including salaries and expenses, construction and drug interdiction costs. The president had requested $1.4 billion. The agency was expected to bring in $21.3 billion in fiscal 1994 from its collections of import duties and other fees.

Most of the Customs budget — $1.35 billion — paid the salaries of almost 18,000 agency employees. About 41 percent of Customs personnel were dedicated to anti-drug and other law enforcement operations, with 59 percent devoted to commercial operations such as Customs facilities at the nation's ports, airports and border crossings. To restore 642 proposed job cuts, appropriators provided $38.8 million more than the president's request. The P-3 program received $28 million.

Treasury Forfeiture Fund

Established under the fiscal 1993 Treasury-Postal bill (PL 102-393), the Treasury forfeiture fund account provided for spending from the proceeds of cash and other assets seized by Treasury during criminal prosecutions. In short, it provided a means to finance Treasury law enforcement activities without direct infusions of taxpayer dollars.

The fund had two accounts, one permanently appropriated and the other an annual "limitation on the availability of deposits" in which Congress annually determined how much could be appropriated from the fund.

The permanent appropriation was available for activities directly related to producing seizures, including investigation costs. The annual appropriation financed a broader set of enforcement-related activities, including payments to informants, new equipment and overtime payments to state and local law enforcement agencies.

Appropriators settled on $32.5 million; the administration requested $14.8 million. Fiscal 1994 was the first year that money from the fund was to be spent.

Internal Revenue Service

The federal government's tax collector received the largest single appropriation of any agency financed by the bill. And because each federal dollar provided to the IRS — particularly for enforcement efforts — yielded many more in taxes collected, the IRS typically made a strong case for its budget. For fiscal 1994, the agency received $7.34 billion; it had requested $7.4 billion.

▶ **Administration and management.** Appropriators provided $167.8 million to administer and manage the operations of the agency. The money paid the salaries and expenses of about 2,400 employees, including senior IRS staff and policy-makers who managed the mammoth bureaucracy. Important operations included internal audits and security activities designed to combat bribery, fraud and extortion by IRS employees.

▶ **Tax returns.** For processing tax returns, providing assistance to taxpayers, and issuing refunds and notices, lawmakers included $1.7 billion. Of that figure, $3.7 million was designated for tax counseling for the elderly.

▶ **Tax law enforcement.** Appropriators included $4 billion for tax law enforcement, including tax return examinations and taxpayer audits, tax fraud and financial investigations, appeals and tax litigation. This money financed about 69,000 IRS jobs. For investigation of money laundering, especially high-level schemes, tax fraud and drug-related crimes, the appropriators earmarked $350 million.

▶ **Computer systems.** The bill provided almost $1.5 billion for IRS information systems, including an ongoing overhaul of the agency's computers. Because of their age and outmoded technology, the IRS' existing computer systems were extremely complex, costly to maintain and ultimately at risk of collapse. Such "tax systems modernization" were to receive $570 million; the project was expected to cost $7.8 billion through 2008. But the agency said the expenditure would produce a $4.8 billion net benefit to the government because of reduced long-term costs and increased savings and revenues.

U.S. Secret Service

The Secret Service's most important — and most visible — job was to protect the president. But it also was responsible for multiple other law enforcement jobs, including investigating and apprehending those engaged in counterfeiting or forging U.S. currency and U.S. and foreign securities, credit card fraud, computer fraud, food stamp fraud and fraudulent use of government identification.

The agency was charged with protecting the president, vice president and their immediate families, visiting heads of state and their families, former presidents and their spouses, and spouses of deceased presidents until they remarried. Its uniformed division protected the White House and grounds, and it patroled neighborhoods heavily populated by diplomats.

For salaries and expenses, the bill provided $461.9 million, $4.5 million more than requested. The extra money was to allow the service to employ 4,570 full-time staff; that was 46 fewer than 1993 but 69 more than proposed by the administration.

Under the bill, Clinton was allowed to designate one "nongovernmental property" — meaning his private residence — to receive up to $300,000 in security improvements. Having lived most of the previous decade in the Arkansas governor's mansion, however, Clinton did not own a home.

Other Divisions

▶ **Bank and thrift regulators.** Treasury bore responsibility for two of the nation's four financial institution regulators — the Office of the Comptroller of the Currency and the Office of Thrift Supervision. Both were permanently appropriated under the nation's banking laws and received their financing through assessments paid by banks and thrifts.

The comptroller's office supervised about 3,600 federally chartered banks — most of the nation's largest — which together held assets of more than $2 trillion. Its budget for 1994 was $373 million, which paid the salaries of about 2,800 bank examiners.

The Office of Thrift Supervision was created in 1989 by the Financial Institutions Reform, Recovery and Enforcement Act (PL 101-73), the thrift bailout law. The office was responsible for supervising all state- and federally chartered savings and loans — about 2,000 institutions. Its budget for 1994 was $190 million.

▶ **Office of Foreign Assets Control.** This office administered economic sanctions against foreign countries in the interest of national security. Its staff implemented trade and economic sanctions against several countries, including Iraq, Cuba, North Korea, Cam-

bodia, Libya, Panama and the former Republic of Yugoslavia.

The office was financed through the general departmental offices account. Conferees on the bill removed a Senate earmark that would have mandated $3 million for office operations and salaries for 46 full-time employees.

▶ **Office of the Inspector General.** This office was the Treasury's internal watchdog, auditing and investigating department activities. Its mission was to promote efficiency and economy in departmental programs and operations and to prevent and investigate waste, fraud and abuse. It was charged with keeping the secretary and Congress informed of whatever problems it discovered.

The office received $28.9 million for salaries and expenses for 330 full-time staff members, 14 more than in fiscal 1993. As much as $2 million was earmarked for official travel expenses and as much as $100,000 for "unforeseen emergencies of a confidential nature." Unforeseen emergencies included cash-for-drug and other sting operations.

▶ **Financial Crimes Enforcement Network (FinCEN).** The network was created by administrative order in 1990 as a component of the administration's national drug control strategy to fight money laundering. It was a multiagency network that helped coordinate investigations of federal, state, local and foreign law enforcement, and regulatory agencies. Lawmakers provided $18.3 million for FinCEN operations, including salaries for 147 employees. In 1992, the network assisted more than 3,700 investigations.

▶ **Federal Law Enforcement Training Center.** The center provided facilities, equipment and support services for basic training of federal law enforcement personnel at three sites. State and local governments could use the facilities if space was available.

Appropriators provided $47.4 million for the center's operations, $250,000 more than requested by the administration. The additional money was to go to the GREAT anti-gang program, which was especially favored by DeConcini.

Appropriators approved $12.7 million for construction and improvements, including a DeConcini-sponsored $6 million to build classrooms, automobile driving ranges, a "burn building" and student buildings at Davis Monthan Air Force Base in Tucson, Ariz. The base was to permanently house a training facility.

▶ **Financial Management Service.** The service was the government's central bookkeeper, managing and monitoring the movement of all federal government receipts and expenditures. It served Congress, the agencies, financial institutions and the public. The service oversaw the government's daily cash flow of more than $10 billion.

Appropriators provided $209.9 million for salaries and expenses for the service, compared with $214.1 million in fiscal 1993. The money paid for 2,194 employees, a slight decrease from fiscal 1993.

▶ **U.S. Mint.** The Bureau of the Mint was headquartered in Washington, D.C., and four Mint facilities — located in Philadelphia, Denver, San Francisco and West Point, N.Y. — made the nation's coins. In addition, the legendary Fort Knox in Kentucky was the heavily fortified repository of the bulk of U.S. gold bullion reserves. The money appropriated in fiscal 1994 allowed production of 15 billion coins. Members provided $54.8 million to pay the salaries of 862 full-time staff members and expenses for the Mint. That was an increase of $1.8 million over fiscal 1993, the same as the president's request.

▶ **Bureau of Engraving and Printing.** This agency, which printed the nation's currency and stamps, was self-financing and did not receive an annual appropriation. Its $487.6 million budget was provided through a revolving fund that received payments from the Postal Service and Federal Reserve banks, which purchased stamps and currency from the bureau. The fund was established in 1950; bureau operations yielded a revenue surplus in the range of $50 million a year.

The bureau produced about 8 billion bills per year and more than 31 billion stamps.

▶ **Bureau of the Public Debt.** The bureau carried out the federal government's debt financing activities. Its major focus was the

issuing, servicing and retiring of government bills, notes and bonds. Appropriators provided $187.2 million, $2 million less than the president's request. The money paid operating costs of the bureau (including salaries for 1,853 full-time positions, a cut of 102 from fiscal 1993) and the U.S. Savings Bonds Division. That division promoted the sale of Savings Bonds to individuals to reduce government borrowing by institutional investors. The bureau also had a permanent appropriation under which it paid the Federal Reserve Banks about $100 million a year to provide services as fiscal agents for the federal government.

Appropriators included $2.5 million to continue an agency consolidation effort. Two years earlier, the bureau, which already had located about 60 percent of its employees in an office in Parkersburg, W.Va., decided to move all Washington, D.C.-based activities to West Virginia, home of Senate Appropriations Committee Chairman Robert C. Byrd, a Democrat. The consolidation was expected to be complete by 1995. By that time, 700 Washington area positions were to be moved to West Virginia; about 140 employees were expected to make the move, though those who chose not to were entitled to other government jobs.

U.S. POSTAL SERVICE

The quasi-private postal agency had financed most of its own operations since the Postal Reorganization Act of 1970 (PL 91-375) converted the 141-year-old Post Office Department into the U.S. Postal Service. The bulk of the postal appropriation was an annual payment to subsidize free or discounted delivery for qualified organizations, particularly nonprofit groups. The rest covered pre-1972 workers' compensation claims.

Over the previous few years, Congress had cut payments for subsidized mail. The fiscal 1994 subsidy appropriation was $91.4 million; the figure for 1993 was $121.9 million. For fiscal 1994, the bill provided $38.8 million for old claims.

For three straight years prior to 1994, Congress declined to appropriate enough money to reimburse the Postal Service for the cost of reduced-rate mailings. At the same time, however, Congress blocked the Postal Service from increasing rates for nonprofit groups and other subsidized mailers. By 1993, the resulting shortfall had ballooned to $360 million, which the Postal Service was forced to pay out of operating revenues.

In 1993, appropriators directed the Postal Service to rewrite rules for such so-called revenue-forgone mail and increase rates for it. Under a compromise worked out between appropriators and the House Post Office and Civil Service Committee, there was to be a six-year phase-in of higher rates for nonprofit groups' mail. Similar provisions to scale back postal subsidies were included in the House version of the budget-reconciliation bill (HR 2264) but were dropped in conference with the Senate. Unless changes in subsidized mail rates were made for fiscal 1994, the Postal Service believed it would have to raise rates on other mail to finance the loss. So Congress took the relatively unusual step of legislating on an appropriations bill.

On average, affected groups would pay 2 percent more each year for six years on second-class mail such as magazines. Third-class rates for mailed advertising would increase between 1 percent and 3 percent the first year and an average of 4 percent annually thereafter. Fourth-class library rates would increase an average of 1 percent each year. Commercial use of nonprofit third-class mail had been prohibited. And the use of the library rate by commercial publishers had been limited to matter ordered by libraries or schools. Mailings for the blind and absentee ballots for Americans overseas would continue to be free.

The Postal Service had already acted, putting the new rates into effect Nov. 21.

As they had done routinely in previous years, appropriators protected rural and other small post offices from the budget ax by including language specifying that none of the money provided by the fiscal 1994 bill could be used to "consolidate or close" small post offices.

EXECUTIVE OFFICE OF THE PRESIDENT

This portion of the fiscal 1994 bill generated considerable controversy, as Clinton struggled to fulfill a promise to cut the White House staff by 25 percent. Republicans and reporters delighted in pointing out the creative arithmetic used to account for the staff cuts — several large executive offices such as the Office of Management and Budget were exempted, for example — and the actual staff within the White House barely shrank at all.

For accounts listed under the Executive Office of the President, appropriators included $298.3 million.

▶ **President's salary and compensation.** The president received a yearly salary of $200,000 and $50,000 for official expenses. Any unused money in the expense account reverted to the Treasury.

The bill also provided $2.8 million to pay for pensions, office staff and travel for the five living former presidents: Richard M. Nixon, Gerald R. Ford, Jimmy Carter, Ronald Reagan and George Bush. The figure was up from $2.4 million in fiscal 1993.

▶ **White House Office.** Appropriators provided $38.8 million for the White House Office, which employed about 400 full-time employees, ranging from top presidential advisers to administrative and support staff. Peak levels under Bush reached 408 aides; Clinton's promised staff cuts were being implemented mostly through cuts in other offices and not the immediate White House staff.

▶ **Office of Administration.** Appropriators included $24.9 million to provide common services (such as personnel management, recruitment, training, payroll, printing and graphics) to all White House agencies. Congress heeded Clinton's request to cut 45 employees from the office; 189 remained. Almost half the money — $11.5 million — paid for computer systems for the Executive Office of the President.

▶ **White House residence.** Appropriators provided $7.9 million for care, maintenance and repair, heating, lighting, and other necessities at the White House. That amount was requested by the president. The money paid the salaries of 89 people who maintained the 132-room residence and grounds. The maintenance staff included domestic workers such as cooks and housekeepers; skilled laborers, including plumbers, carpenters and painters; as well as a specialized staff including curators, florists and calligraphers.

▶ **Office of the Vice President.** Appropriators provided $3.3 million for the vice president's staff under a budget line titled "special assistance to the President." The money paid the salaries and expenses of 21 aides.

▶ **Vice president's residence.** For the operation of the vice president's official home on the grounds of the U.S. Naval Observatory in Washington — including heating, lighting, furniture and furnishings — the bill included $324,000.

▶ **Council of Economic Advisers.** Appropriators provided $3.4 million for salaries and expenses for the council and its 35 full-time employees. The council was a group of economists who provided economic advice to the president, including assistance in preparation of official administration economic assumptions that helped guide budget decisions.

▶ **Office of Policy Development.** The bill provided $5.1 million for this office, which advised the president on long-range economic and domestic policy. It also paid for the salaries of 40 employees for fiscal 1994, a cut of 11 from 1993. The appropriation was a $1.4 million increase over fiscal 1993. Clinton reorganized the office into three distinct policy clusters: the National Economic Council, the Domestic Policy Council and the Office on Environmental Policy.

▶ **National Critical Materials Council.** Appropriators followed Clinton's request and eliminated money for this office and its two employees. The council was established in 1984 (PL 98-373) to help coordinate federal policy, programs and research on critical materials such as manganese, cobalt and platinum. The fiscal 1993 appropriation was $235,000.

▶ **National Security Council (NSC).** The NSC advised the president on domestic, foreign and military policies dealing with national security. It also coordinated defense and intelligence activities of the departments of State and Defense. Appropriators provided $6.6 million, the amount requested by the president, for operations and salaries of 60 staff members.

▶ **Office of Management and Budget (OMB).** OMB wrote the president's budget and helped implement it. It also had sweeping authority to coordinate administration policy goals, and the agency insisted on signing off on policy decisions reached by Cabinet heads. In that regard, the agency provided the administration's official positions on congressional actions.

OMB was exempted from Clinton's 25 percent staff cut, and appropriators provided $56.5 million to pay for 526 full-time staff members and other operating expenses. In addition, appropriators melded a $3.1 million appropriation for the Office of Federal Procurement Policy into the OMB account. That office was responsible for promoting improvements in procurement policies throughout the executive branch.

▶ **Office of National Drug Control Policy.** Established by a 1988 anti-drug law (PL 100-690) amid public fear of the spread of illegal drugs and violence in American communities, the "drug czar" was responsible for developing an annual national drug-control strategy and coordinating all federal anti-drug programs and policies.

The office bore the brunt of the pledge to cut the White House staff; Clinton recommended cutting the number of full-time employees from 112 to 25. The administration's budget request would have cut the appropriation from $101.2 million to $5.8 million. Democrats had long criticized the office under the Bush administration for being stocked with too many political employees. They focused their objections on the most recent drug czar, Bob Martinez, a former Republican governor of Florida, who was given the job after losing his 1990 re-election campaign. At Sen. DeConcini's insistence, appropriators mandated that the drug czar's office have 40 employees.

The bulk of the nation's anti-drug efforts were financed outside the drug czar's office; appropriators reshuffled the programs that fell under the Treasury-Postal bill, creating a new appropriations account titled "Federal Drug Control Programs" that included the following:

▶ **High Intensity Drug Trafficking Areas Program.** This program directed federal money to federal, state and local law enforcement entities operating in areas where drug trafficking was particularly severe. There were five such designated areas: New York, Miami, Houston, Los Angeles and the Southwest border. Appropriators fully met the president's $86 million request for the program; one half of the money was to go to states and localities, the rest was to be transferred to federal agencies.

▶ **Special Forfeiture Fund.** The 1988 anti-drug law created a special forfeiture fund for anti-drug efforts. Spending on programs authorized under the law were expected to total $52.5 million; $28 million (the amount of the Clinton request) was to come from forfeited assets received by the Justice and Treasury departments. Appropriators earmarked how the forfeiture fund's receipts would be spent, including:

▶ $25 million for the Substance Abuse and Mental Health Services Administration. The money was to be divided three ways: community partnership grants would total $10 million; $10 million would be spent on state bloc grants; and $5 million would be available for a residential program for women and children.

▶ $7.5 million for the Counter-Drug Technology Assessment Center, which was the center of anti-drug enforcement research and development for the federal government.

▶ $5 million to BATF for anti-gang programs.

▶ $6 million to be transferred to the IRS for tax law enforcement.

▶ $4 million to improve the Drug Enforcement Administration's Intelligence Center in El Paso, Texas.

▶ $5 million left at the drug czar's discretion.

▶ **Contingency account for the president.** Congress annually provided $1 million to the president for "unanticipated needs." The money could be spent only to advance the national interest, national security or national defense. The last time any of this money was spent was in 1989, when the National Space Council received $189,000.

INDEPENDENT AGENCIES

U.S. Tax Court

The court, an independent judicial body of the legislative branch, decided cases involving federal estate, income and gift tax problems of individuals and corporations, and excise tax cases involving public charities, qualified pension plans and private foundations. The court was made up of a chief judge and 18 other judges. The bill included $33.7 million for the court, $1.7 million less than the president requested. The court handled about 95 percent of all major tax litigation in the federal courts, exclusive of IRS collection actions.

Unlike tax cases decided in federal district courts, taxpayers could litigate their cases in the U.S. Tax Court without first paying liabilities determined by the IRS.

Federal Election Commission

The agency was responsible for enforcement of the Federal Election Campaign Act, which governed the financing of election campaigns for federal office. Its mission included: promoting public disclosure of financial activities of campaigns for federal office and helping the public, press and campaigns understand campaign finance laws. It also ran the program that provided taxpayer money to presidential candidates.

The commission enforced compliance with the act through investigations, audits and litigation if necessary. Appropriators included $23.6 million for its operations and a staff of 320. The appropriation was $2.4 million more than the Clinton request, but unlike most other federal agencies, the Federal Election Commission had authority to make a budget request independent of the administration. One reason the commission said it needed more money than Clinton requested was to implement the "motor voter" bill (PL 103-31) enacted in May.

General Services Administration

The GSA supported the logistical needs of other federal agencies. It served as the government's landlord, provided automobile and truck fleets and managed job-related travel and lodging for federal employees. It also made bulk purchases of supplies — from paper and paper clips to computers to paint and other maintenance items.

▶ **Federal Buildings Fund.** GSA's major spending account was the Federal Buildings Fund. It paid for the government's Public Buildings Service, which provided office space and services to federal agencies in a relationship similar to landlord and tenant. Created in 1975, the fund received rent payments from federal agencies and used the money to design, construct and purchase new facilities, repair existing federal buildings and lease privately owned space. Rental payments financed the bulk of the fund's activities; the rest came from direct appropriations.

Members traditionally had tapped this GSA account to bring home projects, especially courthouses, for their individual districts or states.

The total amount of money that could be spent out of the Federal Buildings Fund was capped at $5.25 billion. Almost all of that amount was derived from rent and other payments by federal agencies for GSA services; appropriators added $288.5 million.

As usual, appropriators had ambitious plans for construction and acquisition of federal buildings, and the bill provided $925.0 million for those activities — $178.1 million more than the president's request. Appropriators included $2.1 billion for agencies to rent office space from the private sector. And the bill provided $1.2 billion for routine upkeep of both federally owned and leased facilities, including maintenance, cleaning services, and fuel and utility costs. To repair and make alterations to federal buildings, appropriators allocated $523.8 million. For design and other preconstruction activities for new federal buildings, they provided $184.1 million.

▶ **Unauthorized projects.** The bill allowed the financing of projects for which Congress had not passed a separate authorizing law. But no money for such projects could be released until Feb. 1, 1994, unless the House Public Works and Senate Environment and Public Works committees approved bills to authorize the projects. This included new construction, repairs, alterations and leases. In addition, either committee would be able to veto unauthorized projects by voting to disapprove them.

National Archives, Records Administration

Appropriators included $195.5 million, $2.3 million more than requested by the president, for operations and management of the federal government's records and archives, grants for historical publications, operating expenses for presidential libraries and reviews necessary to declassify classified material. The Archives had about 2,600 employees.

Office of Government Ethics

The office, established in 1978 as part of the Office of Personnel Management, became an independent agency of the executive branch when reauthorized in 1988 (PL 100-598). The office was established to help prevent conflicts of interest in the executive branch and to promote public confidence in federal officials. The office developed regulations on such issues as post-government employment restrictions, conflicts of interests and financial disclosure requirements. It also provided guidance to officials to help them comply with ethics rules, determined whether violations had occurred and recommended corrective action. The office referred possible violations of law to the Justice Department. The bill provided the administration's request of $8.3 million.

Office of Personnel Management

The Office of Personnel Management (OPM) was the government's personnel office. It helped recruit federal civilian workers and oversaw health and retirement plans. The office also developed job qualifications for all personnel as well as standards and policies for pay and leave.

Appropriators included $118.5 million for salaries and operations of the office; the total appropriation, most of which was mandated by law and not subject to the whims of appropriators, was $11.0 billion. The bulk of that money went to pay federal contributions to pension and health plans for federal government retirees.

The agency also ran the Federal Employee Health Benefits Program, which provided health-care benefits to federal workers, financed in part by about $13 billion in health insurance premiums collected from employees.

▶ **Office of Inspector General.** The office was responsible for preventing and investigating waste, fraud and abuse at OPM. Appropriators provided $4.3 million for salaries for 120 staff members and operations of the office. The fiscal 1993 appropriation was $4.2 million.

▶ **Health benefits for retirees.** Appropriators provided $3.8 billion for the government's share of payments for health benefits for 1.7 million retirees, administered through two trust funds. This was mandatory spending, over which appropriators had no control. The appropriation covered the government's share of health benefit costs for annuitants and survivors who no longer had an agency to contribute the employer's share.

▶ **Life insurance for early retirees.** This account paid for the federal government's contribution toward the life insurance benefits of a small group of federal retirees: those who retired after Dec. 31, 1989, but who had not yet reached 65. Because the pool of such annuitants was shrinking, so too was the federal government's payment. The fiscal 1993 appropriation was $12.4 million; for 1994, the figure was $1.6 million.

▶ **Civil Service Retirement and Disability Fund.** The fund was created in 1920 to administer the financing and payment of annuities to retired federal workers and their survivors. The fund would serve about 1.7 million retirees and 609,000 survivors in fiscal 1994, providing benefits of more than $36 billion. Appropri-

ators provided $7.1 billion for the fund. This was another mandatory account to cover unfunded liabilities that resulted from pay raises, new benefits and increases in existing benefits. It was in addition to amounts contributed for employee retirement benefits through agency budgets.

The fund covered the government's two civilian retirement systems: the Civil Service Retirement System (CSRS) and the Federal Employees Retirement System (FERS). The CSRS was a defined benefit plan, covering federal employees hired prior to 1984. The FERS was a three-tiered pension program that used Social Security as a base, provided an additional basic benefit and included a thrift savings plan; it covered employees hired after 1983 and pre-1983 employees who elected to transfer to the FERS.

Merit Systems Protection Board

The board was an independent agency responsible for safeguarding the federal civil service against political partisanship and other unfair practices. The board, a quasi-judicial agency, also protected employees from management abuse and required federal agencies to hire and promote based on merit. It received $24.7 million.

▶ **Office of Special Counsel.** This office, located within the Merit Systems Protection Board, was established to investigate and prosecute government personnel involved in activities prohibited by law, including illegal personnel practices and politics. The office also gave federal employees a protected confidential means of disclosing information about wrongdoing within the agencies. The bill included $8 million for operations for the office, including salaries for 98 staff members.

Other Agencies

▶ **Federal Labor Relations Authority.** This office was created in 1978 to resolve disputes among unions, employees and federal agencies. It had 245 employees, who handled more than 16,000 cases per year. Appropriators provided the $21.3 million that Clinton requested.

▶ **Administrative Conference of the United States.** This agency was responsible for improving administrative procedures for all government agencies, the president and Congress. It conducted studies, issued recommendations and encouraged their implementation through congressional, agency or judicial action. The administrative conference barely survived the budget ax. Steny H. Hoyer, D-Md., chairman of the House Treasury-Postal Appropriations Subcommittee, excised its appropriation when drafting his version of the fiscal 1994 bill. But the agency was resurrected by the Senate and survived in conference. It received a $1.8 million appropriation, $514,000 less than the administration's request.

▶ **Advisory Commission on Intergovernmental Relations.** The House voted to kill the commission, an independent bipartisan body whose mission was to identify and analyze the causes of intergovernmental conflicts between federal, state and local governments and suggest ways to improve the system. The Senate restored $1 million for the agency, $859,000 less than requested by the president. In doing so, Senate appropriators said they believed the commission had been "virtually ineffective" and put it on notice that they would vote to kill it in fiscal 1995, unless its performance improved.

▶ **Citizens' Commission on Public Service and Compensation.** This commission was created in 1992 to review and recommend to the president the appropriate pay levels for senior federal employees. Commission members were never named, however, and

Vice President Al Gore headed a similar review board. Appropriators declined the administration's $254,000 request for the commission and rescinded a $250,000 fiscal 1993 appropriation.

▶ **Committee for Purchase From People Who Are Blind or Severely Disabled.** The committee was established in 1971 to increase the employment opportunities for the blind and others with severe physical or mental disabilities. The federal government purchased at fair market rates many of the products made and services offered by the blind and severely handicapped.

The committee published a procurement list of services available and supervised the selection of new goods and services and helped set pricing guidelines. Appropriators provided $1.7 million for committee operations and salaries for 18 employees.

OTHER PROVISIONS

▶ **Abortion.** For the first time since fiscal 1984, the bill did not contain a provision that previously had blocked federal employees from receiving abortions through their taxpayer-subsidized health-care plans. The ban had been in force because of language that barred the Office of Personnel Management from using any of its money for administrative expenses associated with including abortion services in federal health-care coverage. The administration supported reversing the ban.

▶ **Locality Pay.** The bill included language to modify the Federal Employees Pay Comparability Act of 1990 (PL 101-509), which authorized two pay raises for federal workers: "locality pay" increases for white-collar workers in the nation's 27 largest Metropolitan Statistical Areas and other areas where federal pay lagged behind the private sector, and a general Employment Cost Index (ECI) adjustment for all federal workers. The 1990 law essentially capped the raises for 1994 at $1.8 billion.

Without further congressional action on the issue, both pay increases would have gone forward as required under existing law, but if their cost exceeded $1.8 billion, the president would have had the discretion to scale them back. The cost of both was estimated at $3.1 billion; conferees determined that covering locality pay increases was more important, and they feared that allowing both raises to go forward might force agencies to fire or furlough employees to meet their budgets. The bill permitted locality pay increases, but not the ECI adjustment. As a budget savings device, Clinton had requested delaying both.

▶ **Unobligated appropriations.** The bill included a provision that gave federal managers incentives to avoid wasteful, end-of-year spending by agency bureaucrats who hustled to justify their budgets by spending money that otherwise would have reverted to the Treasury. Under a provision backed by Hoyer and Frank R. Wolf, R-Va., agencies financed by the bill would be allowed to carry over 50 percent of such unobligated money for an additional year; the other half would revert to the Treasury.

▶ **FTS 2000.** FTS 2000 was a controversial governmentwide long-distance telecommunications system. Appropriators included a provision that required every government agency to use the system.

By including such "mandatory use language," appropriators weighed in on the side of two long-distance carriers — AT&T and Sprint — which in 1988 won exclusive 10-year contracts worth as much as $25 billion to provide the governmentwide service. MCI and other long-distance carriers eager to get a crack at the lucrative market had pressed appropriators to drop the mandatory use language, which had been included in the bill for years. ∎

VA-HUD: A Study in Diversity

No appropriations bill served more diverse needs — or made up a larger share of Congress' annual spending decisions on domestic programs — than the spending bill for the departments of Veterans Affairs (VA), Housing and Urban Development (HUD) and related agencies.

Altogether the $87.8 billion fiscal 1994 VA-HUD bill (HR 2491) accounted for about one-third of all federal domestic discretionary spending. It funded nearly two dozen separate departments, agencies and commissions. The two largest were the VA, which received $35.9 billion, and HUD, which received $25.2 billion. The other major agencies were NASA, with $14.6 billion, the Environmental Protection Agency (EPA), which received $6.7 billion, and the National Science Foundation (NSF), which got $3 billion.

The fiscal constraints that limited what members could provide for these programs also hit lawmakers where they lived. Special purpose projects — known as pork — had become a scarce commodity in a spending bill long known for being filled with it.

The catchall bill was originally intended to cover all non-Cabinet agencies. But Congress elevated Veterans Affairs to the Cabinet in 1989; HUD had been transformed in 1965 under President Lyndon B. Johnson. Bills also had been introduced in Congress to raise the EPA to Cabinet level as well. The bills's wide reach ensured a clash between priorities as diverse as space exploration, public housing and veterans benefits. As in years past, most of the debate focused on the space program.

● **Space station.** The space station *Freedom* escaped the budget ax, but only after undergoing yet another design overhaul. The newly scaled-back orbiting laboratory, renamed *Alpha*, picked up votes with its promise of a lower price tag and its new role as part of a U.S.-Russian joint space program. The bill provided $1.9 billion for the manned orbiting space laboratory. *(Space station, p. 251)*

● **ASRM.** The bill terminated another NASA project, the development of the Advanced Solid Rocket Motor (ASRM). ASRM was designed after the 1986 explosion of the space shuttle *Challenger* as a safer rocket motor that could carry heavier cargoes into space and attain higher-latitude orbits.

Critics had long derided ASRM as a wasteful pork barrel project whose first mission was to provide jobs in the Mississippi district of Democrat Jamie L. Whitten, the former House Appropriations Committee chairman. Opposition stiffened as the program's total cost rose from $1.5 billion to $3.7 billion.

● **Housing.** Reversing the direction of his Republican predecessors, HUD Secretary Henry G. Cisneros put more emphasis on improving and expanding public housing than

BOXSCORE

➡ **Fiscal 1994 VA-HUD Appropriations (HR 2491).** The $87.8 billion bill provided funds for the departments of Veterans Affairs and Housing and Urban Development, as well as for NASA, the Environmental Protection Agency and the federal disaster assistance agency.

Reports: H Rept 103-150, S Rept 103-137; conference report, H Rept 103-273.

KEY ACTION

June 29 — **House** approved bill, 313-110.

Sept. 22 — **Senate** passed bill, 91-9.

Oct. 6 — **House** defeated rule for debate on conference report, 123-305.

Oct. 19 — **House** adopted conference report, 341-89, and voted to terminate ASRM, 401-30.

Oct. 21 — **Senate** adopted conference report and ASRM amendment by voice votes.

Oct. 28 — **President** signed bill (PL 103-124).

on selling it, priorities that were reflected in the VA-HUD bill.

Congress agreed with the administration to phase out the Home Ownership and Opportunity for People Everywhere (HOPE) program. HOPE, promoted by former President George Bush's HUD secretary, Jack F. Kemp, provided grants to public housing tenants to help them buy the units they lived in. The HOME Investment Partnership program, a block grant favored by Democrats that helped build and renovate low-income housing, got $1.3 billion — less than President Clinton requested, but an increase over the $1.2 billion provided in fiscal 1993. The bill provided $778 million for a program to improve some of the nation's most dilapidated public housing, more than double the amount in fiscal 1993.

In its quest for greater efficiency, Congress — at the Senate's behest — stripped funding for the $900,000 Interagency Council on the Homeless. The Senate VA-HUD Appropriations Committee report said that shifting the independent agency's responsibilities to HUD was a first step in consolidating homeless programs.

● **Selective Service.** Congress opted to continue the Selective Service System, which registered young men for a potential military draft. The bill included $25 million for the agency. Many veterans groups lobbied Congress to reject an effort by the House to terminate the program.

● **EPA.** Dogged by criticism of high administrative costs and abuse of federal money by contractors, the EPA absorbed its first budget cut in nearly a decade. Nevertheless, there were new EPA initiatives; the bill provided $599 million for grants to states to improve drinking water, pending reauthorization of the Safe Drinking Water Act.

HOUSE SUBCOMMITTEE

The House VA-HUD Appropriations Subcommittee approved its version of the spending bill by voice vote May 27 during a closed-door markup that lasted nearly three hours.

Reflecting the wishes of its new chairman to remain "flexible" on the beleaguered space station *Freedom*, the panel approved $1.9 billion in fiscal 1994 spending for the NASA project. Subcommittee Chairman Louis Stokes, D-Ohio, said he wanted the spending bill to remain open to what the Clinton administration ultimately recommended for *Freedom*. The president had given NASA until June 7 to come up with new options for a redrawn space station.

Although the space station funding was less than the original $2.1 billion Clinton request, it tracked closely with the $1.9 billion-a-year recommendation of George E.

VA, HUD, INDEPENDENT AGENCIES

	Fiscal 1993	Fiscal 1994 Clinton Request	House Bill	Senate Bill	Final Bill
	(In thousands of dollars)				
Veterans Affairs					
Compensation and pensions	$ 16,969,239	$ 16,828,446	$ 16,828,446	$ 16,828,446	$ 16,828,446
Readjustment benefits	814,010	947,400	947,400	947,400	947,400
Insurance and indemnities	22,730	15,370	15,370	15,370	15,370
Loan funds	681,243	620,792	620,792	620,792	620,792
Health-care reform contingency fund	—	—	—	500,000	—
Medical care	14,645,723	15,642,452	15,522,452	15,637,452	15,622,452
Medical research	232,000	206,000	252,000	252,000	252,000
Construction projects	688,620	563,508	524,008	570,215	570,215
Other	998,336	1,004,662	1,004,578	1,024,578	1,008,078
TOTAL, VA	**$ 35,051,901**	**$ 35,828,630**	**$ 35,715,046**	**$ 36,396,253**	**$ 35,864,753**
Housing and Urban Development					
HOPE grants	271,000 [1]	109,190	119,190 [1]	109,190 [1]	109,190 [1]
HOME program	1,172,500	1,600,000	1,325,000	1,275,000	1,275,000
Assisted housing	8,861,665	8,423,000	9,192,900	9,334,900	9,312,900
Expiring Section 8 subsidies	6,796,135	6,358,106	6,358,106	4,558,106	5,358,106
Low-income housing projects	2,282,436	2,520,808	2,620,808	2,620,808	2,620,808
Severely distressed public housing	300,000	483,240	483,240	803,240	778,240
Drug elimination grants	175,000	—	265,000	265,000	265,000
Federal Housing Administration	262,149	231,990	231,990	231,990	231,990
Limitation on guaranteed loans	*(100,000,000)*	*(64,564,645)*	*(64,564,645)*	*(64,564,645)*	*(64,564,645)*
Ginnie Mae (receipts)	−322,500	−269,300	−269,300	−269,300	−269,300
Limitation on guaranteed loans	*(107,700,000)*	*(85,000,000)*	*(85,000,000)*	*(130,000,000)*	*(130,000,000)*
Homeless assistance	571,550	752,900	702,900	728,747	722,747
Community development grants	4,240,000	4,223,675	4,273,675	4,400,000	4,400,000
Other HUD accounts	195,885	833,220	603,767	528,619	534,000
TOTAL, HUD	**$ 24,805,820**	**$ 25,266,829**	**$ 25,657,276**	**$ 24,336,300**	**$ 25,208,681**
NASA					
Research and development	7,080,000	7,690,400	7,475,400	7,544,400	7,529,300
Space station	(2,122,500)	(1,946,000)	(2,100,000)	(1,946,000)	(1,946,000)
Space flight	5,058,800	5,333,800	4,878,400	4,892,900	4,853,500
Administration	1,635,014	1,675,000	1,637,500	1,635,508	1,635,508
Construction of facilities, other	535,062	565,800	528,091	555,691	565,691
TOTAL, NASA	**$ 14,308,876**	**$ 15,265,000**	**$ 14,519,391**	**$ 14,628,499**	**$ 14,551,399**
Environmental Protection Agency					
Research and development	323,000	353,565	353,565	328,565	338,701
Abatement, control and compliance	1,337,215	1,367,535	1,367,535	1,352,535	1,352,535
Superfund	1,573,528	1,496,400	1,416,100	1,496,400	1,480,853
Water infrastructure	2,550,000	1,528,000	2,477,000	2,500,000	2,477,000
Program, research, other	1,139,631	1,617,982	1,018,383	994,213	1,009,838
TOTAL, EPA	**$ 6,923,374**	**$ 6,363,482**	**$ 6,632,583**	**$ 6,671,713**	**$ 6,658,927**
Other Independent Agencies					
FEMA	2,827,270	796,846	792,119	1,190,329	788,289
Disaster relief	(2,292,000)	(292,000)	(292,000)	(292,000)	(292,000)
Disaster relief contingency fund	—	—	—	(400,000)	—
Limitation on direct loans	*(40,000)*	*(25,000)*	*(25,000)*	*(25,000)*	*(25,000)*
Planning and assistance	(253,243)	(222,960)	(212,960)	(215,000)	(212,960)
Food and shelter program	(129,000)	(123,000)	(130,000)	(130,000)	(130,000)
National Science Foundation	2,733,548	3,180,200	3,021,297	2,981,997	3,027,797
Research, facilities	(1,909,000)	(2,259,800)	(2,100,000)	(2,065,000)	(2,108,500)
Education	(487,500)	(556,100)	(569,600)	(569,600)	(569,600)
Selective Service System	28,616	29,012	5,000	25,000	25,000
National Service program	—	394,000	—	370,000	370,000
Other independent agencies	217,018	778,542	236,363	125,856	128,112
FSLIC resolution, RTC	2,661,510	1,365,842	1,367,046	1,205,582	1,212,314
GRAND TOTAL	**$ 89,557,933**	**$ 89,268,383**	**$ 87,946,121**	**$ 87,931,529**	**$ 87,835,272**

[1] *The bill would rescind $250 million of fiscal 1992 and fiscal 1993 funds for the HOPE program.*

SOURCE: House Appropriations Committee

Brown Jr., D-Calif., chairman of the House Science, Space and Technology Committee.

The HOME program got $1.3 billion in the committee bill, $350 million less than the administration request.

That program fared better than the HOPE initiative. Following Clinton's request, the subcommittee funded HOPE at $109 million, $552 million less than originally appropriated for fiscal 1993.

The subcommittee restored a $26 million cut that Clinton sought for Veterans Affairs medical research. The proposal followed the wishes of G. V. "Sonny" Montgomery, D-Miss., chairman of the Veterans' Affairs Committee.

The subcommittee set aside $500 million for wastewater projects and $599 million for a new drinking water state revolving fund, pending legislative authorization. (Drinking water, p. 274)

The subcommittee also acted to end the Selective Service System, funding it at $5 million, compared with the $29 million funded in fiscal 1993 and requested by the administration. (Selective Service, above)

Full Committee Action

The space station was the most divisive issue during the four-hour full Appropriations Committee markup of the bill June 22. The committee approved the $87.9 billion fiscal 1994 VA-HUD bill by voice vote (H Rept 103-150).

Five days earlier, Clinton had ended months of speculation about his intentions for the massive orbiting space lab by endorsing a slimmed down version of the *Freedom* program. Clinton proposed to spend $2.1 billion a year on the program for fiscal 1994 through 1998. (Space station, p. 251)

"I believe we should give the space station one more chance," Stokes told the panel. The appropriators agreed, voting 31-22 in favor of an amendment by Stokes adding $250 million to the amount that the subcommittee had recommended for the space station funding, bringing the total to $2.1 billion, exactly what Clinton had requested. The committee also added $200 million to the National Aeronautics and Space Administration's budget for technology initiatives.

Most of the additional money for the NASA programs — $365 million — came from within NASA's budget, including a $165 million reduction for the space shuttle.

The amendment also shifted into NASA's budget $55 million from the HOPE program and $30 million from housing subsidies for certain financially troubled projects. Jim Kolbe, R-Ariz., objected to cutting the HOPE program. "We ought to have hope here on Earth as well as in space," Kolbe said. Stokes dismissed Kolbe's complaint, saying that HOPE "has not worked at all."

Stokes said that as part of trimming plans for the space station, NASA would cut project management costs by 30 percent, eliminating 2,000 contract jobs and 650 civil service positions. Several members expressed concern over the loss of jobs. But other station supporters, including Jerry Lewis, R-Calif., and Tom DeLay, R-Texas, said a smaller space station was better than none: Fewer jobs would be lost under the redesign and under the Stokes amendment than if the station were killed. "I'm willing to risk some of the loss of jobs in my area to continue the space station," DeLay said.

The committee also accepted an amendment by Stokes that shifted HUD money to provide more funds to victims of 1992 natural disasters. Members set aside $75 million in the HOME housing block grant program and $50 million in Community Development Block Grant funds for areas affected by Hurricanes Andrew and Iniki and Typhoon

The Selective Service

The Selective Service was best known for conducting a military draft each year from 1940 to 1973, except for 1947. Registration was suspended in 1975, and the agency shrank to a skeletal staff. President Jimmy Carter reinstated registration in 1980 during the Iranian hostage crisis, and the agency grew.

Men were required to register with the Selective Service within 30 days of their 18th birthday, filling out the forms at a post office or by mail. They were dropped from the active rolls when they turned 26.

The system's supporters argued that for a rather modest expense, Selective Service gave the United States a hedge in an unstable world. The agency said it could have the first draftees in uniform within 13 days. Even without registration, the agency said that if fully staffed, it could get the first men in uniform in 42 days.

Opponents said that registration and a well-staffed Selective Service System were wasteful in light of the breakup of the Soviet Union and the Warsaw Pact. A 13-day mobilization was an unnecessary luxury when any sort of massive military buildup by an enemy would give the United States ample time to react, they said.

Failing to register was a felony punishable by up to five years in prison, a fine of up to $250,000 or both. Violators were also ineligible for Pell grants, which helped pay for college or trade school, Job Training Partnership Act benefits and jobs within the federal executive branch.

An attempt in 1992 by then-Rep. Chester G. Atkins, D-Mass., to delete money for the agency from the fiscal 1993 VA-HUD bill was rejected, 96-310. (1992 Almanac, Vote 336, p. 82-H)

Omar. The amendment also increased HUD's policy development and research budget to $85 million and VA medical research to $252 million.

Offsetting these increases were a $195 million rescission in HOPE funds and a $20 million cut in VA medical care.

Stokes stressed that he resisted requests to fund projects that were unauthorized or specific to one location. In recent years, the House had initially refrained from including such earmarks in its bill but added them once the Senate did so. These "special purpose" grants amounted to $260 million in fiscal 1993. Stokes said he had agreed with Barbara A. Mikulski, D-Md., chairwoman of the Senate VA-HUD Appropriations Subcommittee, not to include such projects in the fiscal 1994 bill.

It was partly on those grounds that Stokes opposed an amendment by Ronald D. Coleman, D-Texas, to designate $80 million for wastewater construction grants in the "colonias," poverty-stricken communities near the Mexican border. Stokes said the issue should be addressed by the EPA, which had not endorsed the grants. The bill included a $500 million EPA fund to help distressed communities meet water quality standards.

But Coleman pressed his case: He displayed a color photograph of the squalor and said he had tried for 10 years to get the projects authorized. The committee approved the amendment by voice vote, giving $50 million in

grants to Texas colonias; the remaining money was to be distributed in Arizona, New Mexico and California.

HOUSE FLOOR

Fending off suggestions that building the space station was less important than reducing the federal budget deficit, the House on June 28 rejected an attempt to terminate the program by a 196-220 vote. The House then went on to approve the $87.9 billion VA-HUD spending bill by a vote of 313-110 on June 29. *(Vote 281, p. 68-H; vote 290, p. 70-H)*

Less than a week earlier, the space station had come within a vote of being killed in the NASA reauthorization bill. Members on June 23 had rejected an amendment to kill the project, 215-216. *(Vote 263, p. 64-H; NASA authorization, p. 249)*

After the appropriations vote, the relief of space station supporters was etched on NASA administrator Daniel S. Goldin's face as he stood beaming outside the House chamber, vigorously shaking the hands of members who passed by. But space station opponents portrayed the fight as an insurgency that nearly succeeded. "If it's not killed this year, it'll be next year," predicted Dick Zimmer, R-N.J., who sponsored the amendment to kill it with Tim Roemer, D-Ind. "And if not next year, then the year after."

The votes on the space station reversed the pattern set the year before, when opponents picked up votes as they moved from the authorization to the appropriations bill. A similar Roemer-Zimmer amendment to the NASA authorization bill in 1992 was defeated by a 95-vote margin. The margin slid to 56 votes when the VA-HUD spending bill came to the floor three months later. *(1992 Almanac, pp. 296, 639)*

Roemer and Zimmer noted that in 1993, they had less than one week to persuade members who had voted for space station authorization to change their mind in the appropriations vote. The Clinton administration and House leadership successfully lobbied some space station opponents to switch; other opponents abstained from voting.

The political equation also had changed. The fight to kill the space station in the fiscal 1993 appropriations bill was waged by Bob Traxler, D-Mich., and Bill Green, R-N.Y. — who were the chairman and ranking member, respectively, of the VA-HUD Appropriations Subcommittee. Traxler had retired, and Green was defeated for re-election. Their successors, Stokes and Lewis, led the fight to save space station funding in the fiscal 1994 bill.

Stokes, who opposed the space station in 1992, said his switch was motivated by a desire to support Clinton as well as to shepherd a spending bill that would not be overturned on the House floor. Stokes cautioned, however, that if NASA, the Clinton administration and Congress "do not have the political will to fix this program, then there is no way I can support it."

Other members said that NASA still lacked credibility. They said the agency repeatedly had underestimated the project's cost and overestimated its scientific worth, and that NASA could not be trusted to fix matters through the redesign. "NASA has led this Congress around by the nose for a decade on this issue, and it is time we get the ring out of our nose," said David R. Obey, D-Wis.

Most of the space station's opponents argued that the project ought to be killed in the name of deficit reduction. "This is a clean cut," Roemer said as the debate began, insisting that all savings from eliminating the space station would be used to reduce the deficit. But Roemer was unable to include language to that effect in his amendment.

He said later that such an effort would have been subject to a parliamentary point of order for legislating on an appropriations bill, quashing the amendment.

The space station vote cut across partisan lines. Democrats voted for the amendment to kill the program by a 140-108 margin. The Republican vote was 55-112. Differences among states were more evident. The program received lopsided support from Texas and the southern half of California, which voted a combined 45-13 against the Roemer-Zimmer amendment. By contrast, New York, Illinois and Minnesota voted a combined 45-13 for the amendment.

Other Issues

The House took the following action on other issues in the VA-HUD bill:

● **ASRM.** Members voted to reduce funding in the bill for the advanced rocket motor. The committee bill provided $104.5 million in termination fees for ASRM. It also provided $32.6 million to complete a facility at Yellow Creek, Miss. — originally designed for ASRM — to handle some activities from the space shuttle solid rocket motor program.

An amendment by Scott L. Klug, R-Wis., reduced the termination fees by $4.5 million and deleted funding to complete the Mississippi facility. "There is absolutely no need whatsoever to go on with this project," he said. The amendment was adopted initially by voice vote and then on a revote, 379-43. *(Vote 288, p. 70-H)*

● **Selective Service.** The House turned back an effort to restore money for the Selective Service System. By a vote of 202-207, members rejected an amendment by Gerald B. H. Solomon, R-N.Y., that would have restored $20 million to keep the agency operating. *(Vote 278, p. 68-H)*

Supporters of registration and the Selective Service System said that, given the continuing instability in the world, both were needed in the post-Cold War era. Opponents said the 1991 Persian Gulf War proved the United States could rely on an all-volunteer military.

● **Colonias.** Stokes succeeded in eliminating the designation of $80 million for wastewater construction grants in poverty-stricken communities near the U.S.-Mexican border. Stokes obtained a parliamentary ruling that the provision was not properly authorized.

● **Housing.** One housing issue that drew attention during the debate was an amendment Kolbe proposed to shift $10 million into HOPE grants from HUD's policy development and research account. The amendment was approved 214-199. *(Vote 280, p. 68-H)*

SENATE COMMITTEE

The Senate VA-HUD Appropriations Subcommittee approved its version of the $87.9 billion measure by voice vote Sept. 8, and the full Appropriations Committee endorsed it Sept. 9 by a vote of 26-0 (S Rept 103-137). The Senate version of HR 2491 provided $1.9 billion for space station development. That was comparable to the $2.1 billion the House approved because, at the administration's request, the Senate shifted $154 million in certain space station-related costs to other NASA program areas.

In giving the space station their blessing, appropriators included several provisions to deal with questions surrounding the project's design, rocket motor and relationship with Russian space efforts.

The Senate bill barred NASA from spending more than $1 billion of the space station's appropriations before Jan. 31, 1994, enabling Congress to assess the final design plan

ASRM: A $100 Million Burial

Even in its passing, the cost of NASA's proposed Advanced Solid Rocket Motor (ASRM) was large.

The program's total cost had grown from $1.5 billion in the mid-1980s to an estimate of $3.7 billion. But shutting down the rocket motor — which the House insisted on doing Oct. 19 — still cost $100 million in fiscal 1994 appropriations.

Some House members questioned why it should cost so much to kill a program. But a spokesman for the agency said NASA figured that if it handled the shutdown by the book, the costs actually would approach $200 million. NASA had about $130 million to cover termination costs, including $30 million in unobligated money. Additional amounts had to come from within NASA's budget.

The termination paid for 60 days of personnel costs for certain employees on the project. Many NASA contractors and subcontractors were covered by the Worker Adjustment and Retraining Notification Act of 1988, a federal law that required 60 days of notice to employees before large-scale business closings or substantial layoffs. Those likely to be affected by the 60-day notice included about 300 employees at Lockheed Missiles and Space Co., the project's prime contractor, and about 400 employees at Aerojet Co., which was designing the rocket and the manufacturing facility.

The approximately 200 NASA employees working on the project did not have to get 60 days' notice and could be reassigned.

NASA also had to reimburse some companies for their project costs. For example, Babcock & Wilcox Co. built and financed a facility to construct metal cases for the rocket motor. A spokesman said reimbursement for the facility could cost nearly $20 million.

Termination costs also covered disposing of unneeded material. NASA had to dispose of about $450 million in equipment and $415 million in facilities scattered across the country. Each aspect of the program was to be examined to determine whether it ought to be sold, scrapped or used for other NASA purposes.

NASA's ground rules for terminating a program generally required that any construction be finished if it was 90 percent complete. NASA said it might waive the rule in this case to save money.

Although the agency originally estimated that termination would take two years, a spokesman later said NASA hoped to finish in one.

before agreeing to release the balance. Although Clinton had selected a new design, NASA had not completed work on the details of the project, renamed *Alpha*.

Appropriators were also somewhat wary of an agreement Sept. 2 by Vice President Al Gore and Russian Prime Minister Victor S. Chernomyrdin to combine the U.S. and Russian manned space programs. The Senate spending bill prohibited any space station appropriation from being used to pay Russia. The legislation did set aside $50 million to expand joint activities with the Russian *Mir* space station and another $50 million for space science activities with the Russians. "We support a cooperative effort with Russia, but we believe the space station effort, if approved by Congress, must be an American space station," said subcommittee Chairwoman Mikulski.

Senate appropriators provided $162 million for the ASRM, which was only about half of what the project needed in fiscal 1994 to meet the space station construction schedule. The committee report said that if NASA wanted more money to continue the ASRM, it would have to identify offsetting reductions from within its fiscal 1994 appropriation and submit these reductions to Congress by Sept. 30, 1993. Otherwise, the $162 million could be used for ASRM termination costs, development of an aluminum lithium tank, and completion of the facility at Yellow Creek, Miss., to handle some activities from the existing space shuttle solid rocket motor program.

The committee appropriated $25 million to continue the Selective Service System. Mikulski said that decisions on the nation's capability to organize a draft should not be made through "a back-door cut" in appropriations. Instead, she said, the Pentagon and congressional Armed Services committees should consider the question. The Senate committee report on the bill noted that the $25 million appropriation was $4 million less than the Clinton administration requested, reflecting concerns that the agency was overstaffed.

The bill also provided $391 million for the newly authorized National Service program, enabling about 20,000 youngsters to receive education awards for performing community service. The bill limited administrative expenses to $25 million, which was $15 million below the program's authorized level. And it set aside $400 million as a contingency fund for future national emergencies within its $1.2 billion appropriation for the Federal Emergency Management Agency (FEMA). Release of the money would be contingent on the president's designation that an emergency existed. Mikulski praised FEMA for its relief efforts during the summer's Midwestern floods. Mikulski, a former critic of the agency, said, "We say hats off to FEMA. They have been quick to respond to American disasters."

SENATE FLOOR

The space station sailed over its final 1994 appropriations hurdle Sept. 21 when the Senate voted decisively to dispense with an amendment to kill the program. The action put the House and Senate in agreement that the space station should receive about $1.9 billion in fiscal 1994. The Senate passed the $87.9 billion VA-HUD spending bill Sept. 22 by a vote of 91-9. *(Vote 281, p. 37-S)*

The space station dominated most of the three-day floor debate. The amendment to kill the program was offered by Dale Bumpers, D-Ark., Jim Sasser, D-Tenn., and John W. Warner, R-Va., who proposed to apply the $1.4 billion in savings to reducing the budget deficit. They said it was hypocritical for senators to decry the size of the deficit but refuse to terminate the space station, which they derided as a pork barrel project. "Have you no shame?" Sasser asked his colleagues. "Either vote for the projects and be quiet about it, or do not make these long, lengthy speeches saying, 'I am for cutting spending,' and then not voting to do it."

The program's defenders were led by Mikulski and Phil

Gramm, R-Texas. Noting that the program had been slimmed down by the Clinton administration, Mikulski said, "We have cut the cost of the space station without cutting its ability to do significant science."

Supporters concentrated on the potential scientific advances that could come from the space station — Kay Bailey Hutchison, R-Texas, said it offered the potential to find a cure for cancer. Others hailed the agreement to cooperate with Russian space efforts. Advocates circulated letters from Clinton and Gore backing the space station, employed NASA administrator Goldin for last-minute lobbying and held a State Department briefing for senators on the Russian agreement.

The administration's decision to scale back the space station's cost won over John D. Rockefeller IV, D-W.Va., the new chairman of the Commerce Subcommittee on Science, Technology and Space. Rockefeller had voted against the program in 1992. The Russian deal persuaded another former opponent, Tom Harkin, D-Iowa, to change his vote. Harkin said the Russian agreement would focus missions more on civilian than military uses and speed up the timetable for the manned space station.

Bumpers argued that the agreement was of little value because Russia's space program as well as its economy was in shambles. And he noted that Russian President Boris N. Yeltsin had dissolved the country's parliament even as the Senate debated the VA-HUD bill, calling into question whether the space agreement would even be honored.

Space station opponents also warned that the project could end up costing more than $100 billion. "This space station in my judgment is the engine that can pull this nation over the cliff in terms of economic disaster," Warner said.

Bumpers said that NASA had learned a lesson from the Pentagon in spreading space station-related jobs across 47 states to enhance its pull. "The political clout is always with spending, not spending cuts," he said, adding later that Texas Gov. Ann W. Richards, a Democrat, was particularly persuasive in calling senators to support the project, which heavily benefited her state.

The vote to table, or kill, the amendment to terminate the space station program was 59-40. Republicans provided much of the support, voting 36-8 to table the amendment; Democrats voted 23-32 to table. (Vote 272, p. 35-S)

Other Amendments

Two other attempts to slice the space budget also failed on the floor. An amendment by Warner to require full congressional approval before NASA could spend more than $1 billion in fiscal 1994 funds for the space station was tabled, 55-39. And senators voted 53-47 to kill a Bumpers amendment to terminate spending for ASRM, which left $162 million for the proposed rocket motor in the Senate bill. That set up a confrontation with the House, which had voted June 23 to terminate ASRM. (Votes 274, 275, p. 36-S)

The Senate did adopt an amendment by Richard H. Bryan, D-Nev., to eliminate spending for a NASA program that tried to determine whether there was life elsewhere in the universe. A motion to table Bryan's amendment was rejected, 23-77. The amendment was then adopted by voice vote. (Vote 276, p. 36-S)

Though NASA and the space station drew most of the attention on the floor, many other amendments were considered.

Bill Bradley, D-N.J., tried and failed to terminate the Selective Service System and, with it, registration for a potential military draft. He called the system "a dinosaur

in the post-Soviet world made obsolete by two welcome developments: the creation of an all-volunteer armed forces and the end of the Soviet threat." The Senate voted against Bradley's amendment, 58-41, leaving $25 million for the agency in the bill. (Vote 273, p. 36-S)

Senators also:

● Adopted an amendment by Paul Simon, D-Ill., to provide $30 million to remove asbestos from schools. The amendment was adopted by voice vote after a motion to table it was rejected, 31-68. (Vote 278, p. 36-S)

● Adopted an amendment by Don Nickles, R-Okla., to reduce spending for Clinton's National Service program by $21 million, to $370 million. The amendment was adopted by voice vote after a motion to table it was rejected, 45-55. (Vote 277, p. 36-S)

● Rejected an amendment by Frank H. Murkowski, R-Alaska, to cut Department of Veterans Affairs construction projects by $97.1 million, to $271.9 million. The amendment was tabled (killed), 73-27. (Vote 280, p. 37-S)

● Rejected, 48-51, an amendment by Hank Brown, R-Colo., to reduce spending for the Community Development Block Grant program by $176.3 million, to $4.2 billion. (Vote 279, p. 36-S)

FINAL ACTION

With the fate of the space station largely resolved, House and Senate conferees agreed to spend $1.9 billion on the space station, plus $154 million in space station-related costs through other NASA programs. But NASA could not spend in excess of $1.1 billion on the station before March 31, 1994, without the approval of the House and Senate Appropriations committees, a provision that grew out of uncertainty over the program's design and relationship with Russian space efforts.

The conferees took the following action on other key issues in conflict:

● **ASRM.** ASRM was more problematic. The House had voted to stop spending on the launch system, providing $100 million to cover termination costs. But the Senate resisted an attempt to kill the project. Conferees followed the Senate's lead, agreeing to appropriate about $157.5 million for the new rocket motor and to modify the Yellow Creek, Miss., production site; they indicated that if NASA wanted more money to continue the ASRM, the agency had to identify offsetting reductions from within its fiscal 1994 appropriation before Nov. 15.

Mikulski said after the conference meeting, "We think the future of the ASRM will be determined by what comes out of the final decision involving the Russians." ASRM would make it cheaper to build the space station in an orbit that passed over Russia, which would be beneficial under terms of a new U.S. and Russian space alliance.

● **Search for life in the universe.** Conferees agreed with the Senate's position to eliminate $11.3 million in spending for a NASA program to determine whether there was life elsewhere in the universe. Mikulski said that, while the program had merit, "there was no ambiguity" in the Senate's 23-77 vote against saving the program.

● **National Service.** Conferees also agreed with the Senate's position in paying for Clinton's National Service Initiative. The Senate had reduced spending to $370 million.

● **Selective Service.** Conferees were unable to agree on whether to continue paying for the Selective Service System, sending the matter back to both chambers to see if they could concur on the issue.

House Balks at ASRM

The decision to restore partial funding for the expensive ASRM program infuriated the House, enabling opponents to block consideration of the conference report on the VA-HUD spending bill. By a vote of 123-305, the House on Oct. 6 rejected a rule for floor debate that would have protected various aspects of the spending bill from points of order. *(Vote 482, p. 118-H)*

During the Oct. 6 floor debate, members spoke of their frustration in voting to kill projects only to have them return intact in conference committees. "People are getting fed up around here," said Timothy J. Penny, D-Minn., who voted against the rule. "People are getting tired of the games. Cuts aren't cuts."

"Old pork barrel projects never die. They just come back in appropriations bills," said F. James Sensenbrenner Jr., R-Wis. "This is our last shot to kill the ASRM completely."

Roemer urged his colleagues to vote against the rule not just to oppose the rocket motor, but to support "the institutional integrity of what the House of Representatives wants and what they vote on." He said members ought to stand firm "to make sure that these inefficient projects, these unscientific projects, do not stay in these legislative bodies."

As members filed in to vote, rocket motor opponents distributed a flier that asked, "Are we utterly powerless to stop wasteful spending around here? Can't we finally succeed in killing an obvious pork barrel program?" It listed the 379 members who had voted June 29 to reduce ASRM funding. "Don't give up now!! Be consistent. Defeat the VA/HUD conference report," it said.

While Republicans opposed adoption of the rule by an overwhelming 9-165 margin, it was not a partisan outcome: 139 Democrats opposed the rule; 114 voted for it.

The vote temporarily stymied action on the bill while appropriators assessed their options. The rocket program's supporters, meanwhile, scurried to see if there was any chance to keep it alive. But even some of those backers acknowledged that persistent opposition in the House appeared to have doomed the new engine.

A senior aide to Gore, a strong advocate of the new rocket motor, said the effort would turn to having NASA complete construction at the rocket motor's planned production site in Yellow Creek, Miss., so that it could handle some activities from the existing solid rocket motor program. The House previously had rejected even those efforts to complete the Mississippi facility.

Transferring parts of the rocket motor program to Mississippi would have created 600 to 1,000 jobs there while draining a comparable number from its previous home of Utah, said a spokesman for Rep. James V. Hansen, R-Utah.

Another Try

The House took up the conference report Oct. 19, after the Rules Committee had agreed to permit a floor vote on terminating the ASRM program. The House voted 341-89 to adopt the conference report before turning to the rocket motor issue and the fate of the Selective Service. The final bill appropriated a total of $87.8 billion. *(Vote 513, p. 126-H)*

As allowed under the rule, Stokes offered an amendment to provide $100 million in termination costs for ASRM and to shift $57.5 million to other program accounts within the VA-HUD bill. The House adopted the amendment, 401-30. *(Vote 514, p. 126-H)*

The House then voted 236-194 to accept the Senate's appropriation of $25 million for Selective Service. Republicans and Southern Democrats allied in favor of the agency, 199-60; Northern Democrats opposed it, 37-133. *(Vote 515, p. 126-H)*

During the debate, Stokes argued that Selective Service ought to be abolished because it was unnecessary and penalized inner-city youths who did not register. But the agency's supporters tried to instill doubt that the United States was more secure in the post-Soviet era.

Solomon, the agency's leading advocate, noted that since the House first voted in June "there has been a near revolution in Russia. Members do not realize how close that attempted coup came to putting hard-line communists back in power, with their finger on the triggers of nuclear weapons."

In the Senate, ASRM supporters conceded that strong House opposition made it fruitless to continue the battle. "As much as I hate to admit it, ASRM is dead," said Howell Heflin, D-Ala. Both Heflin and Thad Cochran, R-Miss., said they hoped NASA still could use the ASRM production site in Mississippi. Although the House had resisted attempts to complete construction of the facility for $32.6 million and transfer other work there, Heflin noted that the conference report did not prohibit that action.

The Senate adopted the conference report and the rocket motor amendment by voice votes Oct. 21, clearing the bill for the president. ∎

VA, HUD, Independent Agencies Provisions

Appropriators putting together the spending bill for Veterans Affairs (VA), Housing and Urban Development (HUD) and independent agencies (HR 2491) generally disdained the time-honored practice of stuffing the measure with special projects for members' districts.

Lawmakers still provided some help for local priorities. But the bill was a far cry from the measures that had been routinely pummeled by the authorizing committees and by congressional watchdogs for being filled with special projects. Following are provisions of the bill as enacted:

VETERANS AFFAIRS

First established in 1930 and elevated to Cabinet status in 1989, the VA touched the lives of nearly one-third of the total population of the United States. Its principal mission was to provide the nearly 27 million veterans of U.S. armed forces — and their families — medical care, education loans and grants, discount home mortgages, and pensions and compensation for service-related disabilities. Essentially, the department was split into two branches — the Veterans Benefits Administration and the Veterans Health Administration. Just over half of all veterans spending was mandatory, such as funding for pensions, disability benefits and aid for education, which meant funding was determined by eligibility requirements of permanent law and economic fluctuations not controlled by Congress. Congress controlled the rest through annual discretionary appropriations.

Veterans Benefits Administration

Funded at $18.4 billion in fiscal 1994, this part of the VA covered all non-medical benefits to veterans and their families.

Most of this money, $16.8 billion, was allocated for pensions and compensation benefits, including monthly payments for the surviving spouses and dependents of service personnel who died as a result of injuries connected with their active duty service. In addition, needy veterans who were permanently disabled or older than 65 qualified for pensions, which could go to their families after they died.

▶ **Readjustment benefits.** The VA also got $947.4 million to finance the education and training of peacetime veterans and for dependents of veterans who died from service-related causes, were missing in action or had a permanent service-related disability. Veterans also could get vocational rehabilitation training and grants to adapt their homes and cars to accommodate their disabilities. Other non-medical benefits included: vocational rehabilitation, education loans and training assistance. These programs, authorized under the Montgomery GI Bill in 1987, had 357,000 participants in fiscal 1993. Given efforts to downsize the military, the VA anticipated the same or a greater number of GI Bill participants in fiscal 1994.

▶ **VA home loan guarantees.** The bill included $619.6 million to finance a program in which the VA partially guaranteed and subsidized home loans for veterans. This allowed veterans to acquire a home mortgage without making a down payment. This program was very popular, with 3.7 million veterans participating. The VA guaranteed 383,000 new loans in fiscal 1993 and expected to back a similar number in fiscal 1994.

Veterans Health Administration

Funded at $16 billion, this part of the VA maintained a national health-care delivery system for veterans. It included 171 medical centers, 371 outpatient clinics, 131 nursing homes and 36 soldiers' homes — the nation's largest government-funded health-care system. The bulk of VHA funding was used to staff and maintain this system, which served about 3 million veterans annually. But part of the funding was channeled to related activities, such as $252 million for medical and prosthetic research.

In report language over the years, appropriators had repeatedly criticized the quality of health care provided to veterans. This year was no different, with both House and Senate reports calling for improvement. The Senate language urged the VA to "improve its tarnished image" as a low-quality care provider and to prepare for an expected overhaul of the nation's health-care system. Under President Clinton's health-care reform proposal, the VA would have to compete with other providers for those veterans who paid for their own medical care.

Departmental Administration

Of the nearly $1.5 billion in this account, $826.7 million went for such general operating expenses as determining eligibility and adjudicating claims for veterans benefits. Congress provided $3.5 million more than the administration requested, directing the VA to pay for training and staff overtime to reduce a backlog of veterans benefits claims that, according to the Senate report, would reach 1 million by the end of 1994. The VA employed 4,736 people to help process claims.

▶ **National cemeteries.** The bill allocated $70.5 million to operate the national cemetery system, which provided burial for veterans and their spouses and maintained their graves in 147 cemeteries across the country.

▶ **Construction projects.** Squirreled away in this section of the bill was $523.9 million to fund large and small construction projects of veterans hospitals, clinics, nursing homes and parking lots. Congress earmarked $369 million largely for 12 construction projects, including $41.7 million for a new psychiatric building in Lyons, N.J., and $16 million for a nursing home care unit in Honolulu. The Lyons facility was in the district of Dean A. Gallo, R-N.J., who sat on the House Appropriations Subcommittee on VA, HUD and Independent Agencies.

Another $153.5 million was to go to small construction projects, which were alterations to existing VA facilities and estimated to

cost less than $3 million per project.

In addition, appropriators earmarked $41.1 million to help states establish new veterans nursing homes or extended care facilities, or improve existing ones.

HOUSING AND URBAN DEVELOPMENT

HUD encompassed a wide variety of programs. It was charged with ensuring fair housing opportunities and combating discrimination against home buyers through enforcement of fair housing laws. It provided mortgage credit in order to make more money available to lenders, generally for the benefit of middle-class home buyers. It was responsible for carrying out programs to aid the homeless as well as for providing rental subsidies and other housing assistance for low-income families. For many years, HUD was the principal agent for construction of low-income housing.

During the Reagan administration, Democrats were so preoccupied with protecting existing programs from GOP budget-cutters that they were unable to get new housing legislation. Under President George Bush, who was more amenable to housing issues, the time was ripe for the first two major housing bills enacted since Community Development Block Grants were created in 1974. The 1990 legislation (PL 101-625) created programs with two seemingly contradictory proposals: one to expand the supply of affordable housing, the other to sell off the existing stock. The 1992 Omnibus Housing Bill (PL 102-550) resolved the difficult issue of mixing the elderly and the disabled in public and subsidized housing, as well as starting several new initiatives.

Housing groups still complained that Bush was not willing to spend enough money on the agency. Nor did all applaud his successor's first effort. Clinton proposed spending 2 percent more on housing programs than in fiscal 1993; conferees provided less than that. Congress generally was more receptive to funding increases for public housing in fiscal 1994 than to subsidized private housing.

Recognizing the scarcity of federal dollars, HUD Secretary Henry G. Cisneros quickly sought a departmentwide re-evaluation to make the most of funds that were available. The Senate Appropriations Committee report cheered on Cisneros in his quest for greater efficiency. It noted that the department operated 162 programs and used 315 different handbooks, perpetuating "the maze of cumbersome and costly regulations." Along those lines, conferees bowed to the Senate's desire to consolidate programs to help the homeless and opted to cease funding an independent agency on homelessness, shifting the responsibilities to HUD.

▶ **New housing programs.** Much of the controversy over federal housing programs during the past several years had focused on two aspects of the National Affordable Housing Act of 1990: Home Ownership and Opportunity for People Everywhere (HOPE) and HOME Investment Partnerships. The HOPE grants, promoted by Bush's HUD secretary, Jack F. Kemp, had several dimensions, but the best known gave grants to public housing tenants to help them buy the units in which they lived.

Kemp argued that home ownership could help stabilize blighted urban areas, giving families a stake in their communities. Many Democrats protested that the government should not give away its public housing stock and that very poor public housing tenants were not financially able to become homeowners. Congress funded HOPE considerably below Kemp's request. HOPE lost its prime benefactor when Bush lost the 1992 election to Clinton, who recommended that no further planning grants be offered. Congress concurred, funding HOPE at $109.2 million, $161.8 million below the 1993 appropriation.

Though the HOME Investment Partnerships program had suffered from a slow start-up, it had fared better in the appropriations process. The Senate devised HOME to provide grants to states and local governments to expand affordable housing through construction, rehabilitation and rental assistance to low-income families. The idea behind the program was to leverage private and local funds with federal dollars, letting state and local

governments set local priorities. HOME required participating jurisdictions to provide from 25 percent to 30 percent of a program's cost.

The Clinton administration initially suggested consolidating several other programs into HOME. Congressional opposition quickly surfaced, and the notion was scratched. One of the congressional objections was that funds were being distributed too slowly; as of June 30, 1993, only 5 percent of the $2.5 billion appropriated in fiscal 1992 and 1993 had been dispersed.

The fiscal 1994 appropriation for HOME was $1.3 billion, $102.5 million more than the 1993 appropriation but $325 million less than Clinton requested.

Assisted Housing

This was an umbrella account for federally assisted housing. It generally contained programs that added to or changed federal subsidies for affordable housing. These programs primarily fell into two categories — public housing owned and operated by government authorities and federal subsidies to private entities. The benefits of many of these programs were measured in "incremental units," which referred to net additions to the federally assisted low-income housing stock.

Total spending for assisted housing was $9.8 billion in fiscal 1994 in the annual contribution account: $5.6 billion to subsidize private housing and $4.2 billion to finance publicly owned units. Of the $9.8 billion, lawmakers approved $9.3 billion in new budget authority.

▶ **Incremental Section 8 Rental Assistance.** The largest subsidized private housing program was Section 8 rental assistance, which provided people with vouchers and certificates to be paid to their landlords. Typically, HUD vouchers were "tenant based," to be used wherever the tenant chose to live. Vouchers were set at a figure designed to reflect a "fair market rent standard" for a community. If a family's rent was higher than the voucher, the family paid the difference. Housing certificates, by contrast, were "project based," available to tenants in designated apartment buildings. Tenants with certificates could not spend more than 30 percent of their monthly income to make up the difference between HUD's contribution and rent. More than 3 million units were under the Section 8 program.

The bill included $1.3 billion to provide Section 8 rental assistance for five years to 39,703 individuals or families who did not previously receive federal rental aid. An additional $900 million was earmarked for Section 8 contracts that had spent their federal subsidies faster than expected. This additional money was supposed to be able to carry the existing contracts to term.

▶ **Mortgage prepayment subsidies.** The bill set aside $541 million to preserve low-income housing units threatened by the prepayment of subsidized federal mortgages. The 1990 housing bill established new rules for owners who wanted to pay off their mortgages and stop renting to low-income families. The federal money was used as an incentive for owners to continue renting to low-income families. These funds would help maintain 33,330 affordable housing units in fiscal 1994.

▶ **HUD foreclosure subsidies.** Appropriators earmarked $555 million as subsidies to dispose of government-insured apartment buildings that had fallen to HUD through foreclosure. The mortgages on these buildings were insured by the Federal Housing Administration. In order to dispose of many of the buildings, HUD was required to provide 15-year rent subsidies to prospective buyers as a condition of the sale. The funds provided for fiscal 1994 would permit subsidizing 5,325 units. But that hardly met the need — HUD owned 190 foreclosed projects representing 31,225 housing units as of June 30, and the number was expected to grow. The department was seeking legislation (S 1299, HR 3400) to give HUD more flexibility to dispose of the units.

▶ **Elderly and disabled assistance.** Separate programs assisted housing aimed at the elderly and handicapped. The Section 202 program provided grants directly to groups to develop housing for the elderly. This used to be a loan program but was changed

because the government provided subsidies to pay off the loans, making the program more expensive in the long run. The projects also qualified for Section 8 rental assistance. The bill provided $521 million in grants and $637 million in 20-year rental assistance, enough for 9,000 net additions to the affordable housing stock. A similar program that helped build housing for the disabled, Section 811, received $180 million in grants and $207 million in 20-year rental assistance, enough to fund 3,000 incremental units.

▶ **AIDS housing assistance.** The bill designated $156 million for a program to house people with AIDS, enough to finance 888 housing units. Another $150 million was to go to states and local governments to help eliminate lead-based paint in low- and moderate-income rental units.

▶ **Public and Indian housing.** The assisted housing account also included $4.2 billion for public and Indian housing. Most of this money, $3.2 billion, was designated for modernizing public housing developments, such as replacing roofs, boilers and kitchens. The bill also included $478.8 million to build or acquire 5,746 additional units of public housing and $263 million to build or acquire 2,785 units of Indian housing. Another $119.2 million was earmarked for major reconstruction of obsolete public housing, enabling 1,255 housing units to undergo more extensive repairs than was available under the modernization program.

Other Housing Subsidies

▶ **Section 8 renewals.** Besides the new money for "incremental" or additional vouchers and certificates, the bill included $4.6 billion to renew expiring Section 8 contracts that provided subsidies to families who had been receiving vouchers or certificates. An additional $800 million was listed as an advance appropriation for fiscal 1995.

▶ **Public housing subsidies.** The bill also provided public housing authorities with operating subsidies to maintain about 1.4 million housing units in more than 10,000 public housing developments nationwide. The operating subsidies generally were the difference between the tenants' rent and what it actually cost to maintain the buildings. Public and Indian Housing Authorities received $2.6 billion to operate existing housing, $100 million more than the administration requested and $338.4 million more than appropriated in fiscal 1993.

▶ **Severely distressed public housing.** This program provided grants to large public housing developments to improve some of the nation's most dilapidated public housing units, an effort that was expected to cost $7 billion over 10 years. These funds could be used for extensive reconstruction projects as well as some economic development activities and social services. The bill appropriated $778.2 million, an increase of $478.2 million over fiscal 1993.

▶ **Anti-drug programs.** The bill provided $265 million for grants to public housing agencies to fight drug-related crime in low-income housing, an increase of $90 million over the fiscal 1993 appropriation. The money was used for security guards at public housing projects as well as for drug education programs. The Clinton administration had proposed replacing this program with a broader anti-crime effort called the Community Partnership Against Crime (COMPAC). However, Congress had not yet approved authorizing legislation for the new program.

Housing Loans

▶ **Federal Housing Administration (FHA).** The FHA mutual mortgage insurance program had backed loans for more than 15 million homes since Congress first authorized the program in 1934. The program was intended to spur home ownership and stimulate the housing industry by encouraging banks to make loans to people who did not have the money for a traditional 10 percent to 20 percent down payment. FHA loans required down payments of 3 percent on the first $25,000 and 5 percent on the remainder.

FHA's budget was divided into two accounts. The mutual mortgage insurance program covered basic single-family homes

and cooperative housing. Appropriators prohibited the FHA from making commitments to guarantee loans exceeding a total of $64.6 billion in fiscal 1994. The bill provided $262.8 million to cover administrative expenses, which would be covered by $267 million in offsetting receipts from the insurance program.

The other FHA program was known as the general and special risk program account. The bill limited loan guarantees in this account to $13.4 billion and provided $192.3 million in new spending authority for administrative expenses. The bill also set aside $147.4 million to cover the projected losses from the loan guarantees.

▶ **Government National Mortgage Association (Ginnie Mae).** Ginnie Mae was a federally run secondary loan market that guaranteed privately issued securities backed by pools of mortgages. The mortgages involved were backed by the FHA, the VA and the Agriculture Department's Farmers Home Administration (FmHA). The bill limited the amount of loans that Ginnie Mae could guarantee to $130 billion and provided $8 million for administrative costs. Ginnie Mae was expected to recoup $269 million in offsetting receipts.

Homeless Assistance

The Stewart B. McKinney Homeless Assistance Act of 1987 (PL 100-77) authorized a number of small programs to provide temporary and transitional housing for homeless people. Rep. McKinney, R-Conn., was one of the original sponsors of the legislation, though he died in 1987 before it passed.

The fiscal 1994 funding bill included a total of $822.7 million for these programs, $251.2 million more than the fiscal 1993 appropriation.

▶ **Emergency shelters.** The bill provided $115 million in grants to communities to help pay for emergency shelters. Grants could be used to renovate or convert buildings to homeless shelters or to operate emergency shelters and provide social services. Communities were required to provide matching funds to participate. Grants went to all 50 states and the District of Columbia, plus 116 metropolitan cities and counties.

▶ **Transitional and supportive housing.** This demonstration program, funded at $334 million, was designed to encourage local groups to develop new approaches to helping homeless people move into temporary housing. Money was targeted particularly to people who were disabled, homeless families and people who had been released from mental institutions. The money went for acquiring and renovating housing for the homeless; additionally, it covered the costs of operating the housing and providing support services for the people living there.

▶ **Single-room occupancy.** Part of the Section 8 program, this was an effort to provide permanent housing for the homeless. Many housing advocates believed that the ranks of the homeless had increased over the years due to the elimination of "flophouses," or single-room occupancy units in old boardinghouses and hotels, as redevelopment projects overtook seedier parts of the inner cities. This $150 million program, for development and renovation of single rooms, was designed to reverse that trend.

▶ **Shelter Plus Care.** This was a new program developed in the 1990 housing act to aid homeless people not only with housing but also with social services. The bill used rental assistance and single-room occupancy programs as a way for HUD to enter into contracts with states and local governments. In turn, these governments contracted with nonprofit organizations to provide services such as job training and day care. The bill included $123.7 million, down $142.8 million from fiscal 1993, to offset additional expenses for the emergency shelter grants program. The Senate committee report indicated that the decrease was precipitated by its desire to consolidate homeless programs, concentrating on efforts that permitted local flexibility and long-term solutions to homelessness.

▶ **Interagency Council on the Homeless.** Conferees, at the behest of the Senate, opted not to fund the council and to transfer its responsibilities to HUD. The council was an independent organization composed of 17 federal agencies that reviewed federal programs to help the homeless. The Senate committee report suggested that terminating the council would help streamline the number of homeless programs and save money. The council received $900,000 in fiscal 1993.

Community Planning and Development

The Community Development Block Grants (CDBG) program had been popular among lawmakers for sending money back to the states and local governments. The states and communities were given discretion over what to do with the money, but Congress intended it to be used for economic development, affordable housing and eradicating urban blight. Recent Republican administrations frequently requested far less money than Congress ultimately appropriated. The differences were less pronounced for fiscal 1994, when the Clinton administration recommended $4.2 billion, and the conference settled on $4.4 billion. That represented a $160 million increase over fiscal 1993 spending.

At least 70 percent of the money was supposed to go to programs benefiting low- and moderate-income people. Critics said the funds were not carefully distributed and were all too frequently used to build golf courses, swimming pools and other nonessential projects. Those criticisms held sway during debate over Clinton's proposed $16.3 billion economic stimulus plan, which included $2.5 billion in supplemental CDBG funds for fiscal 1993, helping to doom the proposal.

NASA

Founded in 1958 to do space and aeronautical research for peaceful purposes, the National Aeronautics and Space Administration (NASA) came of age with the Apollo program, which landed American astronauts on the moon in 1969. Apollo, begun in 1962 by President John F. Kennedy, marked the zenith of Americans' love affair with space exploration. For nearly a quarter of a century the agency was the golden child of Congress and the country, receiving hefty annual increases in its budget as its spacecraft ranged farther into the solar system, sending back pictures of Mars, Venus and Saturn.

The golden era ended with the 1986 explosion of the space shuttle *Challenger*, which killed seven astronauts and shocked the nation. Since then NASA had had a succession of mishaps leading to flawed missions, hundreds of millions of dollars in cost overruns and a widespread perception that the agency was adrift.

Since the tragedy of 1986, no year had been harder on NASA than 1993. Congress came closer than ever — by a one-vote margin in the House — to killing the agency's flagship program, the manned space station *Freedom*. In what had become an annual ritual, floor debate over the future of the space station dominated debate on the fiscal 1994 VA-HUD bill. But Congress did manage to kill the NASA Advanced Solid Rocket Motor program, an attempt to find a more powerful, safer way to boost the space shuttle into orbit and a longtime pet project of former House Appropriations Committee Chairman Jamie L. Whitten, D-Miss.

The year's budget constraints alone would have dealt NASA a heavy blow. Congress held the agency to just short of a $300 million increase from its fiscal 1993 funding level, for a total agency budget of $14.6 billion — hardly enough to cover inflation. By contrast, NASA grew by nearly 15 percent in 1989 and 12 percent in 1990. About 80 percent of its budget went to pay the contractors who built its spacecraft, launch vehicles, computers, telescopes and other gear.

But on top of its budget problems and Congress' appetite for killing the space station and solid rocket motor, NASA, headed by Bush administration holdover Daniel S. Goldin, met with greater criticism in Congress than in any previous year. Even the agency's staunchest supporters blasted it as a mismanaged, bloated bureaucracy hobbled by infighting and a lack of purpose and direction. Senate appropriators came down particularly hard on the agency in the conference report. As a result, the agency was again in the midst of a massive reorganization, with emphasis on shorter, less

costly missions that had more highly defined and specific goals.

NASA's work was divided into two high-profile areas: space research, which included the space station, and space flight, which included the shuttle program. Within its space research activities the agency had three main missions: conceptualizing space projects, doing the research necessary to design and build them, and getting them into space. In addition, the agency had programs whose goal was to transfer technology learned through the space program to private industry.

The reports of House and Senate VA-HUD subcommittees consisted mainly of NASA projects and activities listed in no particular order or budget structure. Neither the legislation nor reports said much about where the money went or how the agency functioned. The following description of NASA programs was a synthesis of information from NASA officials, Appropriations Committee hearings, the agency's budget documents and the appropriations conference report.

Major Projects

Every major NASA program except the space shuttle was funded through the $7.5 billion fiscal 1994 appropriation in the research and development account. Some of the major projects under way:

▶ **Space station *Alpha*.** After squeezing past narrow voting margins in the House on amendments to kill the space station, the would-be manned orbiting laboratory in 1993 got a new name, yet another complete design overhaul, some new Russian friends and a new lease on life.

Space station *Freedom*'s moniker was changed to *Alpha* after the Clinton administration and NASA finished a top-to-bottom redesign of the project in June 1993, trimming its work force and operations costs by 30 percent and moving its completion date to 2000. NASA said the revised space station would be built for $19.4 billion from fiscal 1994 to 2003, in addition to the $9.8 billion spent on the program through the end of fiscal 1993. Management of the project was consolidated from four NASA space centers to one, the Johnson Space Center in Houston, and a Reston, Va., NASA space station headquarters was ordered closed. The administration in October also formalized plans to work with the Russians toward linking the space station with the next-generation Russian *Mir* space station and its rescue vehicles, a move intended to help cut costs and improve scientific collaboration between the two countries.

The station's fiscal 1994 cost was put at $1.95 billion, down from $2.1 billion as proposed by the House. But lawmakers also agreed to spend $150 million on space station activities from other accounts, bringing total activities for the project to $2.1 billion. From a separate account, appropriators also earmarked $100 million to develop the joint U.S./Russian space relationship.

▶ **Mission to Planet Earth.** This was a series of environmental research satellites, components of which were already sending volumes of environmental information on the oceans, atmosphere and the land to scientists. The centerpiece of the system and the largest of the satellites, the Earth Observing System, was scheduled for launch in 1998. In 1993 NASA scaled back the project from an $11 billion total development cost to $8 billion through 2000.

The entire Mission to Planet Earth program received $1.1 billion in fiscal 1994, compared with an administration request of $1.2 billion. The Earth Observing System received $320.7 million, while the administration requested $322.7 million.

Fiscal 1994 promised to be a big year for Mission to Planet Earth. NASA planned nine space shuttle flights that included the mission's payloads or related experiments aboard the shuttle. Flight agendas included studying land surfaces, the sun, the oceans and the atmosphere.

▶ **Cassini.** This was a joint United States-European Space Agency program to send a large spacecraft in 1997 to descend to the surface of Titan, a moon of Saturn, for environmental research. The project received $266.6 million, within a broader planetary exploration account of $625.3 million, the same as the Clinton

administration request.

▶ **National Aero Space Plane (NASP).** A joint project with the Defense Department, NASP was an attempt to build an orbiting aircraft with horizontal takeoff and landing capability. Budget constraints led to the termination of the plane in fiscal 1992 and 1993. But the Clinton administration had attempted to revive the program. Appropriators were disappointed, however, with the low amount requested by the Pentagon ($43 million) compared with the NASA request ($80 million), and the House recommended only $8 million until funding could be resolved. The Senate favored canceling the project. Appropriators ultimately steered $20 million to the program from the canceled ASRM project.

▶ **Mars Observer.** The loss in late August 1993 of the Mars Observer — a space probe that fell out of contact with Earth on its way to Mars and was presumed lost — capped a year of setbacks for the agency. "The recent, apparent loss of the Mars Observer mission is a serious blow to NASA's credibility with the Congress," Senate VA-HUD appropriators wrote in their report. They cited the program's problems as emblematic of the agency's recent troubles: It was a large, ill-defined mission that overpromised its capabilities and understated the costs.

Appropriators removed $24 million from the program's mission operations and data analysis account. But they still hoped to salvage the mission and agreed to spend $10.2 million toward a new Mars mission. The launch, likely in 1996, would best utilize the investment already made, they said.

▶ **Hubble Space Telescope and other space observatories.** NASA had four space-based "Great Observatories" — powerful scientific instruments that could "see" light in different parts of the light spectrum, including infrared and gamma rays, all of which gave scientists new information about the heavens.

Of these, the best known and most troubled was the nearly $2 billion Hubble Space Telescope, launched in 1990. It was designed to pick up faint visible light and ultraviolet. But its mirror was flawed, and it could see only half of what it was designed to discern. Conferees directed that NASA put "high priority" on a Hubble repair mission, which lifted off Dec. 2.

The Gamma Ray Observatory, launched in April 1991, was able to pick up gamma rays, the highest energy particles in the universe. They usually emanated from the area inside quasars, black holes and supernovas. There had been little controversy over the project's cost.

The Advanced X-Ray Astrophysics Facility (AXAF), scheduled for launch in 1998 and 1999, was designed to pick up X-rays that would help astronomers study large-scale galactic phenomena such as black holes, the contribution of hot gases to the mass of the universe and clusters of distant galaxies. Facing budget constraints, NASA broke the program into two components with separate launch dates. Senate appropriators had proposed terminating the second phase of the program, called AXAF/S, in its report. But conferees agreed to spend $16.9 million for fiscal 1994, $19 million less than the administration request. Lawmakers hoped to save money by mounting the AXAF/S instrument on an existing satellite.

▶ **Discovery Planetary Program.** As part of its reorganization, NASA was shifting emphasis toward smaller, lower-cost missions that could be carried out in a short time period. The Discovery program aimed to achieve this by choosing missions with smaller spacecraft and highly focused scientific objectives that could take better advantage of state-of-the-art instruments.

The first two of 11 upcoming projects received $66.2 million each, at a combined $64.3 million increase over Clinton's budget. The Near Earth Asteroid Rendezvous (NEAR) was a probe that would orbit around a near-Earth asteroid. The Mars Environmental Survey Pathfinder (MESUR) program was a spacecraft that would land on Mars. It included a rover vehicle that would survey the Martian surface and take soil samples. Both projects were scheduled for 1996 launches, and each program's total cost was capped at $150 million.

▶ **Search for Extraterrestrial Intelligence.** This program, re-

named the Towards Other Planetary Systems/High Resolution Microwave Survey Program, made headlines when the Senate voted to kill it on Sept. 22. Begun in fiscal 1989, the project involved using high-performance computers to send and track microwave radio signals into the outer reaches of space, in hope of detecting signs of life. NASA pegged the program's completion cost at about $135 million over 10 years. The administration had requested $12.3 million for fiscal 1994. Conferees agreed to spend $1 million for termination costs.

Before the program's demise, NASA was able to collect one year's worth of data from the scanner. The SETI Institute, a private organization partially funded by NASA and the University of California, had expressed interest in analyzing the data for signs of intelligence and possibly reviving the program.

Ongoing Research and Development

▶ **Space science and applications.** Appropriators spent $1.8 billion for NASA's Space Science division. The division's observation systems conducted scientific investigations of the Earth, sun, other planets and the galaxy. Its research also included development of some space technology. Included in this account was funding for the AXAF, Discovery, Hubble, Cassini and Mars Observer programs as well as $50 million for joint U.S.-Russian space science research.

▶ **Life and microgravity science and applications.** Appropriators spent $474.8 million on this account, which funded experiments aboard the space shuttle and other scientific inquiry.

▶ **Space transportation capability and development.** For fiscal 1994, appropriators approved $680.6 million for development, testing and procurement of hardware to deploy spacecraft into higher orbits than the shuttle could achieve. This was nearly $24.4 million less than the agency requested, and about $30 million more than the fiscal 1993 appropriation. The space shuttle was developed using funds from this account.

Within this program was $50 million for the second part of NASA's joint Russian-U.S. activities and $139 million for Spacelab, the observatory-laboratory that rode inside the cargo bay of space shuttles.

▶ **Commercial programs.** Appropriators spent $135.7 million on NASA's cooperative ventures with industry, down from $173 million requested by the administration. Within this account were two programs, the commercial development of space (for which NASA requested $145 million) and technology transfer (for which NASA requested $28 million). The agency would decide how to apportion the reduced funding among the two programs.

NASA's commercial programs took off in the early 1980s in the wake of the first flights of the space shuttle. Congress hoped that once space was accessible, private companies would develop space-based industry.

However, that proved more difficult than expected. Companies wanted to experiment with manufacturing in space, but the cost of getting there was too high unless the government continued to pay for it. In an effort to get the program off the ground, Congress in 1985 gave partial funding to 15 Centers for the Commercial Development of Space; two more were added in fiscal 1992. The balance of the funding was provided by private industry and universities that worked in the fields of space propulsion and systems, materials, pharmaceuticals and communications.

NASA also funded seven "technology transfer centers" scattered across the country, where businesses worked with NASA scientists to learn applications for aerospace technologies.

The seventh center was a project sponsored annually by Senate Appropriations Committee Chairman Robert C. Byrd, D-W.Va. The National Technology Transfer Center at the Wheeling Jesuit College in West Virginia, was among the government's largest technological data bases. The scope of the center's reach went beyond NASA and included software and data — all available to industry free of charge — from such areas as the Strategic Defense Initiative and other defense research facilities. The center received $3.5 million for fiscal 1994.

▶ **Space research and technology.** Since NASA's beginnings,

the Space Research division had been NASA's think tank, charged with dreaming up new projects for the agency. The division's work was largely theoretical and rarely focused on near-term missions. Appropriators gave this account $303.5 million, down from an administration request of $348.2 million.

The division had been the lead player in the effort to return to the moon and then go on to Mars, a mission favored by former President George Bush. But the moon-Mars expedition was canceled by NASA early in 1993 for budgetary reasons.

In 1993, NASA Administrator Goldin created a new office called Advanced Concepts and Technology, which served as the focal point for innovations such as space robotics, miniature new-generation satellites and "telepresence" — whereby scientists on Earth would use virtual reality techniques to manipulate instruments in space. It also sought to forge closer ties with industry to keep NASA focused on missions that had maximum commercial value.

Goldin put this office in charge of both the commercial programs and space, research and technology budgets, though appropriators did not recognize the new structure in their bill.

▶ **Aeronautical research and technology.** The bread and butter of NASA's work was its research on aeronautics — the science of flight. Nearly half a century before there was a space agency, the National Advisory Committee on Aeronautics coordinated government and industry research in flight dynamics. Its research was folded into NASA when the agency was created. For fiscal 1994, the category received a big boost to $1.13 billion, up from $865.6 million in fiscal 1993. The administration request was $1.2 billion. Most of the new money was to go toward developing high-speed flight systems, high-performance computing and advanced subsonic flight technology.

Space Flight

The space flight control and data communications account, which paid for shuttle operations and production, got $4.9 billion, $480.3 million less than the administration's request and $205.3 million less than in fiscal 1993. The cuts were mostly from Congress' termination of the Advanced Solid Rocket Motor. This account also included the space shuttle and space and ground-based data and tracking satellites that transmitted data gathered by spacecraft and directed it to computer storage facilities on Earth.

▶ **Space shuttle.** Appropriators spent $2.8 billion for shuttle launches and operations to pay for NASA's schedule of nine missions during fiscal 1994. An account called launch services received $313.5 million. Space communications received $761.3 million. The space shuttle was the first reusable space vehicle and was designed to carry astronauts, scientific experiments and Defense Department projects. Its annual costs were driven largely by the need for a standing army of 2,500 engineers, aeronautics experts and support staff at Cape Canaveral, Fla., where the shuttle and other spacecraft were launched. NASA's four shuttles — *Columbia*, *Atlantis*, *Discovery* and *Endeavour* — were made by Rockwell International Corp., the agency's largest contractor.

▶ **Expendable launch vehicles.** The Space Flight Control division also got a $313.5 million appropriation for one-time-only rockets to launch spacecraft carrying scientific projects that did not require special handling by astronauts. The administration sought $316.9 million. These expendable vehicles largely burned up when they re-entered the atmosphere.

▶ **Advanced Solid Rocket Motor project (ASRM).** Congress voted to kill this project in fiscal 1994, ending years of debate over whether NASA really needed a new rocket motor to carry heavier cargoes and attain higher-latitude orbits.

The House fired the first shot on June 28, when it voted 379-43 to kill the rocket motor, a favored project of former Appropriations Chairman Whitten. Critics said the current generation of rocket motors had an excellent success record and that the ASRM was not needed. But the Senate rescued the project, and conferees agreed to go with the Senate's position. But the House stiffened its resistance on Oct. 6, when members rejected a rule permitting

floor debate on the VA-HUD bill because it protected the ASRM.

Conferees met again and dropped the program, while providing $100 million to shut it down. The amendment also shifted $57.5 million to other program accounts within the VA-HUD bill.

The conference report left open the possibility that NASA could use the ASRM production site in Yellow Creek, Miss., for future rocket motor production that would be transferred from Utah — where prime contractor Thiokol Corp. had been making the rockets that lifted the shuttle. The House and Senate accepted the new wording.

Construction and Administration

The appropriation of $517.7 million for construction at NASA included modernization, repair and renovation at the agency's eight space flight centers across the country and at other NASA-funded facilities. The administration had requested $550.3 million; for the previous year construction received $520 million.

This typically was a fertile budget account for lawmakers seeking special projects for back home, but appropriators largely resisted the temptation for earmarks.

The personnel and administration account was funded at $1.6 billion, the same as in fiscal 1993 and $39.5 million less than the administration request. It paid salaries, benefits and travel for NASA employees as well as the overhead for agency facilities. Appropriators directed NASA to cap fiscal 1994 employment at 22,900 people at its Washington headquarters and at the eight centers.

NATIONAL SCIENCE FOUNDATION

The National Science Foundation (NSF) was established in 1950 as an independent agency to support basic and applied research, science and technology policy research, and science and engineering education programs.

The NSF awarded grants, contracts and other forms of aid such as cooperative agreements to more than 2,000 colleges and universities and other nonprofit research organizations. It also supported international science ventures such as the U.S. Polar Research Programs. The foundation's own facilities included laboratories for astronomy, atmospheric research and four national university-based supercomputing research centers at the University of California at San Diego, the University of Illinois, Cornell University and the University of Pittsburgh.

The NSF provided almost 25 percent of federal support for basic research going to academic institutions. In some fields, such as astronomy, ocean sciences, environment sciences and biology, mathematics and engineering, the agency provided the dominant share of funding.

The foundation was slated to provide roughly 22,000 grants in fiscal 1994, averaging between $50,000 and $100,000.

After an early-year funding scare that had NSF officials worried that basic research would be gored by the new Clinton administration and Congress, appropriators agreed to give the NSF more than a 10 percent increase to $3 billion.

There was a renewed push, however, by Senate appropriators to get the NSF to focus more on joining forces with industry for more "applied" research that had a specific, presumably commercial, goal in mind.

Senate VA-HUD Appropriations Subcommittee Chairwoman Barbara A. Mikulski, D-Md., and her colleagues wrote that the agency could join the Clinton administration's push for "science and technology policy in pursuit of specific national goals, or it can diminish into becoming nothing more than a national endowment for science."

In their report, Senate appropriators warned the NSF to set specific performance goals by the time Clinton's fiscal 1995 budget was submitted, or risk losing much of its funding to agencies such as the National Institute of Standards and Technology, NASA, the national energy labs or the National Institutes of Health. The agency also was told to assure that no less than 60 percent of its

research was "strategic," rather than "of a generic nature."

The NSF was preparing a response to the appropriators' demands. An NSF spokesman said the agency's shift toward applied research was continuing and was a priority of new Director Neal F. Lane, who came aboard in mid-October.

Within the NSF budget, conferees agreed to spend $2 billion on research and related activities and $569.6 million on education programs, which included science instruction programs for pre-college students and fellowships and equipment for college-level students.

The agency, whose advocates had long complained that big-science projects such as NASA's space station drained funding from traditional science coffers, won an extra $22.5 million when Congress killed NASA's Advanced Solid Rocket Motor, which would have been used to launch station components into orbit.

ENVIRONMENTAL PROTECTION AGENCY

The EPA, founded in 1970 during the administration of President Richard M. Nixon, combined the functions of nine programs spread throughout five agencies. As a regulatory agency, it was chiefly responsible for overseeing an alphabet soup of laws dealing with air, water, drinking water, and hazardous and toxic wastes. Among those laws were the 1980 Comprehensive Environmental Response, Compensation and Liability Act — commonly known as the "superfund" law — its 1986 follow-up, the Superfund Amendments and Reauthorization Act and the 1990 revision of the Clean Air Act. The agency also provided grants to help build sewage treatment plants across the country and assisted in getting rid of leaky underground petroleum storage tanks.

Despite a steady increase of environmental mandates over the last decade, the EPA's budget had not kept pace. As a result, states and cities were shouldering much of the financial burden of carrying out these federal laws. The Senate Appropriations Subcommittee on VA-HUD and Independent Agencies called for elimination of "unnecessary" environmental mandates, in an attempt to ease that financial burden.

Still, the EPA budget was cut for fiscal 1994 by 3.8 percent to roughly $6.7 billion. It was the first time the EPA's budget had been cut since 1983 and only the third time in its 23-year history. Clinton, who was swept into office partly on his promise to do more for the environment than his predecessor, endorsed the cut.

In an attempt to put environmental issues on the front burner, Clinton had made elevating the EPA to Cabinet status a top legislative priority. As the 15th department in the Cabinet, the proposed Department of Environmental Protection was to have an increased role representing the United States' position on environment in the international arena. The Senate passed a bill to elevate the EPA in May, and a companion measure awaited action in the House.

▶ **Research and development.** Congress allocated $338.7 million for all outside research programs, excluding the superfund and leaking underground storage tank account. EPA Administrator Carol M. Browner had emphasized obtaining credible scientific information as a cornerstone of environmental protection. Appropriators provided $15.7 million more than in fiscal 1993 but $14.9 million less than Clinton requested.

In addition to the administration's request, appropriators earmarked $500,000 for the study of air pollutants at the Mickey Leland National Urban Air Toxics Research Center in Houston (named after the late Texas representative) and $2 million to improve air quality along the U.S.-Mexican border.

Lawmakers also provided $1.8 million for research into the environmental problems faced by low-income and minority communities. Browner had said she would try to mitigate what some lawmakers, civil rights activists and environmentalists believed was an unequal burden on the poor and minorities in the application of environmental laws.

▶ **Operating programs.** Appropriators limited EPA's operating expenses to $50.6 million for fiscal 1994. These funds were used to

buy laboratory equipment and supplies and pay for the operations of research and development activities. The House tried to reduce operating expenses to $10.2 million by changing the definition of "operating expenses" and eliminating funds for laboratory equipment and supplies. But conferees agreed not to change the definition because of the difficulty in separating administrative expenses.

▶ **Anti-pollution programs.** Lawmakers provided nearly $1.4 billion for the abatement, control and compliance account, which paid for most of the EPA's anti-pollution programs. Standards were set through these programs for air quality, water quality, safe drinking water, hazardous wastes and radiation exposure. The EPA monitored these anti-pollution standards and enforced the regulations.

The amount provided was $15.3 million more than allocated in fiscal 1993 but $15 million less than the administration request.

Appropriators generally followed the administration's request for anti-pollution funding for each medium. They provided about $308.4 million for the EPA's air program, $85.2 million for the drinking water program, nearly $230 million for the water quality program, $21.6 million for radiation activities, $54.1 million for the pesticides program, $198.8 million for hazardous waste regulation, $67.6 million for the control of toxic substances and $50 million for the "multimedia" program, which reviewed federal environmental impact statements.

Conferees said they did not specifically include funds for asbestos control because of tight fiscal constraints and the need to devote resources to other high-priority environmental problems. They noted that $350 million had been provided through fiscal 1993 for asbestos abatement in schools.

Congress added $5 million to study the nation's lakes, $8 million for grants to rural communities to help comply with the 1974 Safe Drinking Water Act (PL 93-523), $4 million for efforts to reduce lead poisoning, $2 million to improve the EPA's supercomputer and $1.5 million for environmental education grants to minority colleges and institutions.

▶ **Buildings and facilities.** To correct unsafe conditions at EPA-owned facilities and construct new buildings, Congress adhered to the administration's request and provided only $18 million for these functions. By comparison, $134.3 million was appropriated for buildings and facilities in fiscal 1993. The bill included $3 million for the planning and design for an EPA laboratory in Research Triangle Park in North Carolina. Congress also included $3 million requested by the EPA to help find a new headquarters building in Washington, D.C.

▶ **Superfund.** Appropriators allocated about $1.5 billion for the superfund, which provided money for the cleanup of hazardous and toxic materials that had been released into the ground or water. The superfund program also was responsible for emergency response to chemical accidents and the research and development of new cleanup technologies.

The fiscal 1994 appropriation was $92.7 million less than allocated in fiscal 1993 and $15.5 million less than Clinton requested.

The superfund was created in 1980, and its authorization would expire Sept. 30, 1994. The superfund trust fund, which collected most of its revenue from taxes, was extended through 1995 through the 1990 budget-reconciliation act. Appropriations and taxes on petroleum, hazardous chemicals and an environment tax on corporations financed the trust fund.

The EPA had identified nearly 2,600 sites requiring some form of cleanup. But 1,202 sites were listed on the superfund's priority list of facilities posing the highest health and safety risk. As of May 1993, only 54 sites had been totally cleaned up.

▶ **Leaking Underground Storage Tank Trust Fund.** This fund was created in 1986 to help with the cleanup of thousands of corroding and leaking underground tanks that seeped gasoline, oil and toxins into the ground. The responsibility for cleaning up the tanks laid with the owners, but the EPA provided grants to states and local agencies to assist them with devising the best cleanup strategy. Appropriators provided $75.4 million for this trust fund

in fiscal 1994, about $7.6 million less than fiscal 1993 and the same amount as requested by Clinton.

▶ **Oil spills.** EPA was responsible for directing the cleanup and removal of oil and other petroleum products that spilled into the nation's waterways. A total of $21.2 million was provided for EPA's response to oil spills.

▶ **Construction grants/state revolving funds.** The EPA provided below-market rate loans to states and local governments to build sewage and wastewater treatment plants. The long-range goal was to eliminate the discharge of treated or untreated pollutants into the nation's waters. Appropriators provided $2.5 billion for these grants and revolving loans.

The bill stipulated that $500 million was not available until May 31, 1994, to pay for projects not yet authorized in communities with special needs. If those projects were authorized through separate legislation on or before May 31, 1994, the money could be used by communities with high sewer rates and by the poverty-stricken areas along the Mexican border.

▶ **Drinking water grants.** Conferees set aside $599 million for grants to states and local governments to improve the quality of drinking water, provided Congress authorized the money in a rewrite of the Safe Drinking Water Act. A drinking water reauthorization bill (S 1547) had been introduced by Senate Environment and Public Works Committee Chairman Max Baucus, D-Mont. It largely followed recommendations by Browner to make the law more flexible to help small water systems comply with federal mandates.

▶ **Administrative provisions.** Congress stipulated that none of the funds provided in the bill could be used by the EPA to develop new mandates on radon, an odorless gas, in drinking water. The Senate said it would be too costly for small cities to comply with any new standards regarding radon.

Negotiators also accepted language adopted by the Senate that classified dried hops as a raw agricultural commodity. Hops, used as a flavoring agent in beer, were grown in Washington state. The provision was pushed by lawmakers in the Pacific Northwest, including Washington's two senators, Republican Slade Gorton and Democrat Patty Murray, Sen. Mark O. Hatfield, R-Ore., House Speaker Thomas S. Foley, D-Wash., and Rep. Jay Inslee, D-Wash.

The lawmakers complained that the EPA had been misclassifying dried hops as a processed agricultural commodity. Because of that designation, dried hops had been subject to twice as much regulation as nuts, grains, alfalfa or hay.

SAVINGS AND LOAN BAILOUT

A total of $1.17 billion was provided to cover costs previously incurred when the since-closed Federal Savings and Loan Insurance Corporation (FSLIC) closed 200 failed thrifts in 1988. The appropriation added $7 million for a program enabling the Federal Deposit Insurance Corporation (FDIC) to provide rebates and discounts to low- and moderate-income households to help them afford to own or rent properties from an inventory retained from failed banks.

OTHER INDEPENDENT AGENCIES

▶ **American Battle Monuments Commission.** The commission was responsible for administering, operating and maintaining cemetery and war memorials commemorating armed forces achievements that had occurred since 1917. The bill provided $20.2 million for this purpose.

▶ **Chemical Safety and Hazard Investigation Board.** This board, authorized by the Clean Air Act Amendments of 1990, investigated accidental releases of hazardous substances into the air. The bill provided $2.5 million.

▶ **Consumer Product Safety Commission.** The commission was an independent regulatory agency responsible for protecting the public against unreasonable risks of injury from consumer

products and developing uniform safety standards for consumer products — $42.3 million.

▸ **U.S. Court of Veterans Appeals.** The court was established to review decisions of the Board of Veterans Appeals. It had the authority to decide all questions of law and all statutory and regulatory provisions under the Department of Veterans Affairs — $9.2 million.

▸ **Department of Defense.** This portion of the bill funded the Pentagon's upkeep for Civil Cemeterial Expenses, Arlington National Cemetery and the Soldier's and Airmen's Home National Cemetery — $12.7 million.

▸ **Executive Office of the President — Council on Environmental Quality and Office of Environmental Quality.** The council's main responsibility was to advise the president on national and international policies promoting environmental protection — $375,000.

▸ **Office of Science and Technology Policy.** The office was created to advise the president on science and technology policies — $4.5 million.

▸ **Office of National Service.** The office helped form and coordinate executive branch policy on national service — $160,000.

▸ **Federal Emergency Management Agency (FEMA).** FEMA was responsible for coordinating federal efforts to anticipate and respond to a range of major civil emergencies, such as hurricanes and earthquakes — $788.3 million for emergency management planning. The total included $292 million for the disaster relief fund.

▸ **General Services Administration's Consumer Information Center.** The center was designed to help federal departments and agencies promote and distribute consumer information collected from government programs. The center also distributed catalogs of information to the general public through its distribution center in Pueblo, Colo. The center distributed 11.6 million publications in fiscal 1992 — $2.1 million.

▸ **Department of Health and Human Services Office of Consumer Affairs.** This office was designed to make sure consumers' views were heard throughout federal agencies — $2.2 million.

▸ **National Credit Union Administration.** The administration provided funds to help credit unions meet emergency financial needs. Credit unions were required to invest in the capital stock of the administration in order to benefit, and those funds ultimately were available to the individual credit unions. The bill limited those loans to $600 million.

▸ **National Service initiative.** The federally owned Corporation for National and Community Service was created by the National and Community Service Trust Act of 1993. The corporation made grants to states and localities as well as public and private agencies in order to enhance community service opportunities for youths and adults. Participants could receive financial rewards for further education. The conference agreed to $370 million, $24 million less than the administration requested. It also imposed a $14 million limit on the corporation's administrative expenses.

▸ **Neighborhood Reinvestment Corporation.** This corporation assisted local communities in creating partnerships between residents and representatives of the private and public sectors. The partnerships were independent, tax-exempt, nonprofit groups known as NeighborWorks, promoting affordable housing. A national network of 183 NeighborWorks organizations in 151 cities produced more than 6,500 units of affordable housing in 1992. The bill provided $32 million for this purpose in fiscal 1994.

▸ **Selective Service System.** The system's mission was to be prepared to supply the armed forces with manpower during a national emergency. It did so in part by registering young men for a potential military draft. The House said that the system was obsolete in the post-Cold War era and sought to appropriate $5 million for the agency's termination costs. The Senate insisted that the agency was a cheap insurance policy in an unstable world. Conferees were unable to compromise on the issue.

The House finally settled on the Senate's recommendation of $25 million, $3.6 million less than appropriated in fiscal 1993 and $4 million less than the administration requested. ∎

Fiscal 1993 Stimulus Bill Killed

Senate Republicans killed President Clinton's first piece of fiscal legislation — an economic stimulus package — in April, refusing to accept a multibillion-dollar increase in the deficit in exchange for several hundred thousand temporary jobs.

The package took the form of a $16.3 billion supplemental appropriations bill for fiscal 1993 (HR 1335). It was a blend of diverse elements: public works projects to create jobs and spur economic development, summer jobs for youths and unskilled laborers, social programs for the poor and high-technology purchases for the federal government.

The House approved the president's proposal quickly and with little alteration. In the Senate, however, the measure was slowed by dissident conservative Democrats, then stopped by a united Republican bloc. After failing on four tries to limit Senate debate, Democratic sponsors deleted everything from the package but a $4 billion emergency appropriation for extended unemployment benefits. The truncated measure quickly passed, and Clinton signed it into law on April 23 (PL 103-24).

BACKGROUND

The defeat amputated one of the three legs of Clinton's economic plan. That plan, which Clinton outlined in a speech to Congress on Feb. 17, consisted of a short-term stimulus bill, followed by a combination of deficit reduction and long-term "investment" to revitalize the economy. Administration officials said the stimulus bill would not only provide a booster shot to help offset the belt-tightening of the deficit-reduction plan, but it would also make a down payment on the investment program. *(Text, p. 7-D)*

Rather than pay for the supplemental appropriations by cutting already appropriated spending for fiscal 1993 or raising taxes, the administration proposed to treat the bill as emergency spending not subject to the budget caps that limited discretionary spending for fiscal 1993. That decision eventually spelled doom for the package, however, as Congress proved more eager to cut spending than to increase it, even for the sake of creating jobs.

Critics of the bill argued that the only emergency was the deficit. They also took issue with the elements of the package, particularly a proposed $2.5 billion increase in block grants to cities. While Democrats tried to focus the debate on what they called the "jobless recovery" from the recent recession, Republicans shifted it to a discussion of seemingly frivolous projects that cities had proposed for

BOXSCORE

➡️ **Emergency Supplemental Appropriations — HR 1335.** The original version of the bill would have made $16.3 billion in emergency appropriations for fiscal 1993. The so-called stimulus package was designed to spur the economy by creating temporary jobs. A Senate filibuster forced sponsors to delete virtually all of Clinton's proposals; the final version of the bill made a $4 billion emergency supplemental appropriation for extended unemployment benefits.

Report: H Rept 103-30.

KEY ACTION

March 9 — **House** Appropriations Committee approved HR 1335 by voice vote.

March 19 — **House** passed HR 1335, 235-190.

March 23 — **Senate** Appropriations Committee approved HR 1335, 19-10.

April 2, 3, 5, 21 — Motions to limit **Senate** debate were defeated.

April 21 — **Senate** cut all provisions from HR 1335 save a $4 billion emergency appropriation for unemployment benefits. It then passed the revised bill by voice vote.

April 22 — **House** cleared HR 1335, 301-114.

April 23 — **President** signed the bill — PL 103-24.

their block-grant money.

The episode was a lesson in the limits of presidential power for Clinton. He was able to steamroll Republicans in the House, where the rules allow the Democratic majority to pass bills without GOP votes. But in the Senate, where the rules were far more generous to the minority party, the Republicans were determined not to suffer the same fate as their House colleagues. Clinton's team later admitted miscalculating the strength of the Senate Republicans. Rather than negotiating, the administration and the bill's manager, Appropriations Chairman Robert C. Byrd of West Virginia, tried to play hardball. They assumed that the Republicans could not filibuster a jobs bill, but they were wrong.

The biggest problem for Clinton and the Democratic leadership may have been the wide-ranging nature of the bill. Although they portrayed it as a jobs bill, much of the spending had no clear relationship to creating jobs. On the whole, it was a grab-bag of spending increases with no unifying theme.

Contents of the Package

As initially proposed, the package was divided somewhat equally between construction projects and other types of spending. Money was targeted for about 75 public works, environmental, energy, technology and social programs in 12 federal departments, seven agencies or commissions and the District of Columbia.

Spending authority in the bill included the following major elements:

- $4 billion to extend unemployment benefits for jobless Americans who were about to reach the end of the benefits provided by their states. *(Unemployment, p. 392)*
- $3 billion in spending from the Highway Trust Fund for highway and bridge repairs that were ready to go to contract.
- $1.2 billion for public bus systems, subway and light-rail projects, airport improvements and capital investments by Amtrak, the national passenger rail service.
- $2.5 billion in Community Development Block Grants, which cities and counties used for repairs, economic development projects and public services, and $133 million for economic development projects in rural areas and on Indian reservations.
- $1.2 billion in grants and loan subsidies to build water and wastewater treatment plants.
- $1 billion for maintenance and construction at federal parks, forests, water projects and buildings.
- $1.9 billion to make up an accumulated shortfall in the

budget for Pell grants, which provided money for college for low- and middle-income students.

• $1 billion for summer school programs for poor children, and $284 million for other educational programs for disadvantaged and Indian children.

• $1 billion to expand the Job Training Partnership Act summer program to provide jobs and educational programs for youths.

• $1.1 billion to expand programs providing housing, immunization, AIDS treatment and food.

• $528 million for research and high-technology equipment purchases by government agencies and federally funded universities.

• $291 million to guarantee loans for small businesses and create more joint ventures between federal Energy Department laboratories and private industry.

• $143 million for a variety of energy conservation projects.

• $30 million to cover budget shortfalls in the District of Columbia and at the Minority Business Development Administration, and $13 million to add staff at the Equal Employment Opportunity Commission and the Food Safety and Inspection Service.

The package added up to $16.3 billion in new budget authority — not coincidentally, the same amount that the appropriators had left unspent from the fiscal 1993 budget. Most of the savings had been in the areas of defense and foreign aid, while the stimulus package was entirely in domestic programs. In effect, Clinton was proposing a transfer from defense and foreign operations to domestic programs, something that the 1990 budget law prohibited. That is why the package had to be treated as an emergency appropriation, even though the spending did not exceed the overall budget cap.

The budget authority translated into outlays — money actually spent in a given year — of $8.3 billion in fiscal 1993 and $9.3 billion in fiscal 1994-97. In addition, the bill included $3.2 billion in spending from federal trust funds. All in all, it amounted to roughly $19.5 billion in deficit spending.

HOUSE COMMITTEE ACTION

At Clinton's request, House Appropriations Committee Chairman William H. Natcher, D-Ky., persuaded his subcommittee chairmen to move Clinton's proposal to the House floor rapidly and without change. The procedure caused grumbling among some appropriators, who had not been consulted much about the bill in advance. They argued that they were being reduced to rubber stamps.

Upset by the pace and lack of bipartisanship, Republicans demanded more hearings on the president's proposal so that they could call their own witnesses. Still, they succeeded only in pushing the subcommittee markups back one day, from Feb. 23 to Feb. 24.

A more serious problem for the bill came from outside the Appropriations Committee. Numerous Democrats complained to the House leadership that they were being asked to vote for increased spending before they had a chance to vote for spending cuts. To address these concerns, the leadership put HR 1335 on hold while the House and Senate Budget committees rushed to complete the fiscal 1993 budget resolution (H Con Res 64 — H Rept 103-48), which embodied Clinton's five-year budget plan and included substantial deficit reduction. The change in tactics stalled the stimulus bill for two weeks. *(Budget resolution, p. 102)*

Full Committee Moves Quickly

On March 9, the House Appropriations Committee approved HR 1335 by voice vote with only three significant changes. The committee deleted Clinton's request for $5.5 million to improve energy efficiency at the Defense Department, largely because the Pentagon had more than $50 million in unspent appropriations for that purpose.

The appropriators also rejected a request for $5.6 million to guarantee loans for nine Indian businesses, putting the money instead into repairs at Indian schools. David R. Obey, D-Wis., objected to the loans because some of the money would have been used to build casinos in his state. Finally, the appropriators gave states and local governments 90 days to spend their highway and mass-transit grants, not 60 days as the administration proposed.

Democrats voted as a bloc to defeat every Republican attempt to amend the bill. These included an amendment by Ron Packard of California to require up to $12.3 billion in spending cuts to offset the appropriations, defeated by a vote of 21-38, and one by Joe Skeen of New Mexico to reclaim any money not spent by the end of fiscal 1993, defeated by a vote of 19-30.

Frank R. Wolf, R-Va., offered amendments to prohibit overtime on projects funded by the bill and eliminate the requirement that highway grants be spent within 90 days. These were defeated by votes of 20-30 and 19-31, respectively.

Tom DeLay, R-Texas, proposed to waive the Davis-Bacon law, which required federal contractors to pay the prevailing local wage, for projects funded by the bill. That amendment was rejected by a vote of 17-34. And Dean A. Gallo, R-N.J., tried in vain to require quarterly reports on the number of new jobs created by the bill, losing once by a vote of 21-30 and again later by voice vote.

HOUSE FLOOR ACTION

House Democrats on March 19 handed Clinton a victory on the bill over the opposition of a united Republican Party and scattered Democrats. The supplemental was approved by a vote of 235-190, with three Republicans and Independent Bernard Sanders of Vermont joining 231 Democrats in support. *(Vote 88, p. 22-H)*

Before the bill reached the floor, conservative Democrats lobbied the Democratic leadership and the White House to scale back the stimulus package and limit it to spending that was clearly related to creating jobs or stimulating the economy. But liberals, still smarting from spending limits that conservatives had won in the budget resolution, objected to any further reductions. They also wanted to send the Senate as big a bill as possible, given the noises that conservative Democratic senators were making about cutting the stimulus package.

Rule Decides Outcome

At the Rules Committee on March 16, Charles W. Stenholm of Texas, who led the Conservative Democratic Forum, sought permission to offer an amendment slashing the amount of deficit spending in HR 1335. His amendment would have required any outlays after fiscal 1993 to be offset by spending cuts, a proposal that would have reduced what the bill added to the deficit by at least $11 billion.

Republicans also asked for the chance to propose cuts in funding for Community Development Block Grants, summer jobs for youths, equipment modernization at the Internal Revenue Service, computer equipment at the National

Library of Medicine, a fish-mapping program at the U.S. Fish and Wildlife Service, capital improvements at Amtrak and the energy efficiency grants to industry.

Natcher and the Democratic leadership were concerned that Republicans and conservative Democrats could come up with the votes to make some of those cuts. After two days of lobbying and head-counting by the leadership and the administration, the Rules Committee proposed a rule allowing only one amendment: an unspecified proposal by Natcher to remove potentially embarrassing projects from the bill. That amendment was to be offered only if needed to shore up support.

Conservative Democrats did get one thing they wanted: The leadership agreed to schedule back-to-back votes on the budget resolution and the stimulus package. That way, Democrats could make a better case to their constituents that the spending increases were part of an overall economic plan that included large cuts in the deficit.

Republicans vehemently protested the proposed rule, noting that amendments had been allowed on every "urgent" or "dire emergency" supplemental since 1977. Joined on the floor by Stenholm, they argued that the bill was rife with pork barrel projects. Said Gerald B. H. Solomon, R-N.Y., "I really don't think the American people want to break gridlock with ham hock." Still, a heavy behind-the-scenes lobbying campaign by the administration won the support of all but 13 Democrats, enabling the rule to pass on March 18 by a vote of 240-185. *(Vote 86, p. 22-H)*

The debate over the bill stretched into the early morning hours of March 19, but the outcome was effectively decided by the passage of the rule. The top Republican appropriator, Joseph M. McDade of Pennsylvania, offered a motion to recommit the bill with instructions to cut enough spending in other areas to offset all but the $4 billion for extended unemployment benefits. That motion failed by a vote of 181-244. *(Vote 87, p. 22-H)*

SENATE COMMITTEE ACTION

Like Natcher, Senate Appropriations Committee Chairman Byrd urged his troops to move HR 1335 to the floor without changes or delay. Byrd did not even give his subcommittees a chance to amend the bill, bringing it straight to the full committee instead.

On March 23, the committee voted 19-10 in favor of the House bill, with one minor change in the distribution of money for youths' summer jobs. The House had proposed to give more money to the 100 cities with the largest number of disadvantaged youths, but the Senate committee opted to keep the distribution formula already written into the Job Training Partnership Act.

The divided vote in the Appropriations Committee — a panel that typically presented a united bipartisan front — signaled that the bill was in for a tough time on the Senate floor.

The first hurdle for Byrd was posed by fellow Democrats David L. Boren of Oklahoma, John B. Breaux of Louisiana and Richard H. Bryan of Nevada. Boren and Breaux had been saying for several weeks that Congress should make actual spending cuts before it approved the entire stimulus package. They proposed to cut the bill in half, leaving only the most urgent, job-related projects; the remainder of the bill would wait until after Congress enacted the tax increases and spending restraints called for by the budget resolution.

Meanwhile, Herb Kohl, D-Wis., was floating Stenholm's

House proposal to offset all of the bill's outlays with spending cuts after fiscal 1993. This proposal, unlike the Breaux-Boren plan, was strongly supported by Senate Republicans.

SENATE FLOOR ACTION

When the bill reached the floor March 25, Byrd moved quickly to protect his flanks. He offered an amendment prohibiting any money in the bill from being spent on projects that the House Republicans had ridiculed, such as fish atlases. The amendment was adopted by voice vote.

Byrd then set up a parliamentary obstacle course, offering two slightly different versions of Clinton's entire stimulus package as substitute amendments. This "amendment tree" established a procedural framework under which amendments could be offered, debated and voted upon, but then wiped out just before a vote on the original package. The tactic, unusual but not unprecedented, left the bill's opponents only two choices: either round up the 51 votes needed to defeat the package, or muster the 40 votes needed to sustain a filibuster.

The tactic bought Byrd time, allowing the White House to negotiate a compromise with Boren, Breaux and Bryan. The three dropped their attempt to postpone half the bill's spending after they received a letter March 29 from Clinton, who pledged to propose more spending cuts if Congress did not meet the deficit-reduction targets in the budget resolution.

The maneuver brought the Democrats into line, but it provoked an angry response from Republicans. Early on, Republicans had seemed less interested in killing the stimulus package than in scoring political points against it. They planned to offer a series of amendments highlighting what they felt was wasteful spending in the bill. When Byrd cut them off with his amendment tree, however, Republicans started talking about a filibuster.

Byrd offered March 29 to remove the tree if Republicans would submit a list of their amendments, set a limit on the debate and allow a final vote on the supplemental March 30. Republicans rejected the proposal, saying they did not want to play the game by Byrd's rules.

That evening, Republican Hank Brown of Colorado offered the first of nine GOP amendments that attacked spending, even if there was only a slim connection between that spending and the bill. Brown proposed to cut $103.5 million from the Community Development Block Grants and bar funding for 54 recreation, housing and commercial projects proposed by local officials in 19 states and Puerto Rico.

Byrd failed on his first attempt to kill the amendment when his tabling motion fell by a vote of 44-48 on the night of March 29. The next day, with eight absent Democrats back on the floor, Byrd's motion to table the amendment was approved by a vote of 52-48. *(Votes 84, 86, p. 12-S)*

Down Comes the Tree

Brown's proposal was more symbolic than substantive, given that Byrd's amendment tree was still in place. Once Brown was defeated, Byrd removed the tree and invited Republicans to try to change the bill for real. They did, offering eight more amendments on March 30-31. Forty-two of the 43 Republicans also signed a letter to Senate Minority Leader Bob Dole of Kansas, pledging to filibuster the bill unless changes were made.

Like their counterparts in the House, the Senate Republicans took issue with the very premise of the bill. They

gative agencies" in the so-called Travelgate matter and report back to Congress by Sept. 30. There had been charges that the White House improperly manipulated the FBI in the aftermath of the firing of White House travel staff amid charges of financial impropriety.

In action on June 22, the Senate agreed to language offered by Alfonse M. D'Amato, R-N.Y., to cut federal welfare aid to states that did not, within a year, require at least 10 percent of their "able-bodied" welfare recipients without dependents to work for their benefits. The "workfare" participation rate would be increased by 2 percent a year until 50 percent of recipients were working.

The amendment was approved by voice vote after a motion to kill it by Finance Committee Chairman Daniel Patrick Moynihan, D-N.Y., failed, 34-64. *(Vote 163, p. 22-S)*

The Senate rejected, 39-59, an amendment by William V. Roth Jr., R-Del., to enact numerous tax breaks and spending cuts. GOP leaders called the proposal their job-creation alternative. *(Vote 160, p. 21-S)*

FINAL ACTION

The House approved the conference report on the bill by a vote of 280-138 on July 1. The Senate cleared the bill by voice vote the same day. *(Vote 321, p. 78-H)*

The final bill was worked out in a frequently heated House-Senate conference June 29-30. The key issue was what to do about the Pentagon money.

House Defense Appropriations Subcommittee Chairman Murtha argued that forcing the Pentagon to find offsets would risk eroding the military. "We feel very strongly in the House that we will have a hollow force if we continue to take this out of the hide of the military," Murtha said. But Byrd insisted that the Senate's 95-0 vote on the issue locked his side into offsetting the military spending.

Inouye offered the compromise that was ultimately accepted: Rescind enough spending from lower-priority defense programs to cover $973.5 million of the Pentagon money while allowing an additional $326 million to count against the spending available under the cap. Senators rejected Murtha's offer to provide about $650 million in offsets, and the House conferees ultimately gave in.

Inouye himself ran into trouble when he tried to use some of the defense money remaining under the cap. Citing the new recommendation by the base-closure commission to shut down dozens of military bases around the country, Inouye proposed spending $700 million to help maintain those bases until communities could claim them for local use. But Lautenberg, who had led the charge in the Senate to force the Pentagon to offset its new spending in the bill, protested that the money would simply be added to the deficit, and Inouye withdrew the proposal. *(Base closures, p. 465)*

Conferees dropped the D'Amato amendment requiring increasing numbers of welfare recipients to work for their benefits.

Congress' growing anti-deficit fever also affected other items in the bill:

● **U. N. peacekeeping.** Conferees provided none of the $293 million the Clinton administration had requested to help pay the U.S. share of U.N. peacekeeping forces around the world. Some members complained that the administration had made no formal suggestions for where to find the money; others said they were stymied because the program was not authorized. Byrd and Murtha both sent strong warnings to the administration to consult closely with Congress if it wanted peacekeeping money in the future.

● **Remains of the "stimulus" bill.** The measure resurrected only about $1 billion worth of items from the original bill and a subsequent Clinton request. Chief among those items was $220 million in funding for summer jobs, $100 million less than the House had provided, but $20 million more than the Senate originally voted. Of that money, $50 million was earmarked for the Youth Fair Chance program to help the long-term unemployed; the maximum eligibility age under that program was raised from 21 to 30.

Other key elements in the conference report included:

● $150 million to help communities hire more police.

● $341 million toward a shortfall in Pell grants for college students.

● $175 million for an SBA business loan program.

● No money for Environmental Protection Agency waste-water-construction grants, for which the White House sought $400 million and the House $290 million.

● $475 million for a cost of living adjustment for veterans. ■

$5.7 Billion Earmarked for Disaster Victims

On the last day before its summer recess, Congress cleared a $5.7 billion supplemental appropriations bill (HR 2667) to provide financial assistance to the victims of massive floods in the upper Midwest and other 1993 natural disasters.

Although the bill moved through Congress quickly — it took less than four weeks from President Clinton's initial proposal to final enactment Aug. 7 — its ride was unusually bumpy for a disaster-aid measure.

HR 2667 was briefly derailed in the House, largely because of concerns about the bill's designation as emergency spending, which allowed Congress and the president to add its full cost directly to the federal budget deficit rather than having to find offsetting spending cuts.

Most recent disaster-aid bills had sailed through Congress. An emergency supplemental providing $11.1 billion in aid to victims of hurricanes Andrew and Iniki faced no obstacles and moved through Congress in 10 days after being introduced by President George Bush in September 1992. *(1992 Almanac, p. 583)*

However, the 1993 flood-aid measure came up at a time when Congress was embroiled in a debate over Clinton's controversial budget-reconciliation legislation, which contained nearly $500 billion in spending cuts and tax increases over five years. *(Budget-reconciliation, p. 107)*

Concerns over the budget impact of the disaster-aid bill were piqued by its price tag, which escalated rapidly as the immensity of the disaster — caused by persistent heavy rains that began drenching the upper Mississippi and lower Missouri river basins during the spring and continued well into the summer — became evident.

On July 4, Clinton promised Midwest officials about $900 million in aid. When he sent his proposal to Congress on July 14, the cost was $2.25 billion. By the time the bill reached the House floor, it contained $2.77 billion.

A fierce House debate over offsetting the spending, which stalled the bill briefly, appeared to exhaust congressional interest in making the measure "pay as you go," however. Although the cost of the bill as cleared had swollen to $5.7 billion, there were no further serious efforts to avoid adding it to the deficit.

Clinton signed the bill into law on Aug. 12 (PL 103-75).

BACKGROUND

A stationary weather front that stalled over the upper Midwest for weeks beginning in the late spring brought a series of torrential downpours to the region. By the onset of summer, local residents and emergency management experts were describing the flooding of the Mississippi, Missouri and dozens of tributary rivers and streams as the nation's worst in at least a century, perhaps even 500 years

---

BOXSCORE

➡️ **Fiscal 1993 Disaster-Aid Supplemental (HR 2667).** The bill provided $5.7 billion in aid for victims of massive river flooding in the upper Midwest and other presidentially declared 1993 natural disasters.

Report: H Rept 103-184.

KEY ACTION

July 27 — **House** passed, 400-27.

Aug. 4 — **Senate** passed amended bill by voice vote.

Aug. 6 — **House** passed compromise bill by voice vote.

Aug. 7 — **Senate** cleared the bill by voice vote.

Aug. 12 — **President** signed the bill — PL 103-75.

---

in some of the affected places.

The floods caused widespread damage to thousands of homes, farms, businesses, roads, bridges, railways and public facilities. Clinton ultimately declared all 99 counties in Iowa as disaster areas, along with portions of eight other states: Illinois, Kansas, Minnesota, Missouri, Nebraska, North Dakota, South Dakota and Wisconsin.

With estimates of total damage topping $10 billion, Clinton, who was en route to an economic summit in Japan, made a July 4 stop in the Mississippi River city of Davenport, Iowa, where he promised to ask Congress to pass disaster-aid legislation. Cutting short a brief vacation in Hawaii following the summit, Clinton on July 14 visited Des Moines, Iowa, which temporarily lost its water supply after flooding damaged the city's water treatment plant.

While in Des Moines, Clinton released his initial proposal for a disaster-aid supplemental spending bill appropriating $2.24 billion. The largest portions were $945 million for the Agriculture Department to cover crop losses suffered by flood-stricken farmers and $800 million to the Federal Emergency Management Agency (FEMA) to provide immediate financial assistance to individuals and businesses dislocated by the floods.

Other agencies slated to receive funds were: the Small Business Administration, $70 million, mainly to subsidize loans to flood-affected businesses; the U.S. Army Corps of Engineers, $65 million for flood-control efforts; the Transportation Department, $105 million for road repairs and Coast Guard expenses; the Department of Housing and Urban Development (HUD), $153 million for disaster-related housing and community development needs; the Commerce Department, $100 million for the emergency programs of the Economic Development Administration; and the Department of Health and Human Services (HHS), $4 million for the Public Health Emergency Fund.

But some flood-state members of Congress were dissatisfied. Sens. Tom Harkin, D-Iowa and Dave Durenberger, R-Minn., in separate statements, described the amount of money in the draft bill as "woefully inadequate." The Clinton administration responded July 19, on the eve of the House Appropriations Committee markup, with a late-night request for an additional $501 million, raising the total to $2.74 billion.

HOUSE APPROPRIATIONS COMMITTEE ACTION

In the interest of speeding the bill along, House Appropriations subcommittees held no hearings or markups. However, the chairmen of seven subcommittees were made responsible for those sections of HR 2667 that fell under their jurisdiction.

The bill moved directly to the full Appropriations Committee, which approved it without objection July 20.

First, however, the committee passed by voice vote an amendment, sponsored by committee Chairman William H. Natcher, D-Ky., and ranking Republican Joseph M. McDade of Pennsylvania, incorporating most of the administration's add-ons.

These included: $1 million to the Commerce Department's National Oceanic and Atmospheric Administration to repair damaged weather equipment; $43.5 million to the Labor Department to hire workers, including people dislocated by the floods, for flood-cleanup efforts; $16 million to the Transportation Department for rail-line repair; $2 million for the Commission on National and Community Service to enlist youth corps participants in disaster relief services; and $33.1 million to the Interior Department for flood-repair efforts of the Fish and Wildlife Service, the National Park Service and the U.S. Geological Survey; plus additions of $250 million to Agriculture to cover crop losses; $85 million to the Army Corps of Engineers; $15 million to FEMA; $50 million to HHS; and $5 million to Transportation for Coast Guard expenses.

Although McDade complained about the last-minute nature of the administration's request, there was no dissent from any committee member concerning the added expense. Nor was there any mention in the Appropriations markup of offsetting the costs of the bill with cuts in other programs or tax increases.

Other Amendments

The committee gave voice vote approval to an amendment by Richard J. Durbin, D-Ill., modifying the formula for crop-loss payments to farmers. The provision was aimed at increasing disaster aid to farmers who suffered catastrophic losses.

Originally, the bill would have applied a 50 percent cut to a long-established formula for crop-loss payments to individual farmers. Under the formula, the federal government was expected to pay 65 percent of the assessed market value on 65 percent of a farmer's destroyed crops, or about 42 cents on the dollar. But farmers complained that the 50 percent cut, or pro rate, would reduce their crop-loss assistance to just about 21 cents on the dollar.

Durbin's amendment increased the aid amount to 90 percent of the formula for farmers whose losses were greater than 75 percent of normal yield, with the practical result of raising aid payments to nearly 40 cents on the dollar for these farmers.

The committee also gave voice vote approval to amendments by Neal Smith, D-Iowa, providing $300 million to the Legal Services Corporation to supply legal aid to low-income flood victims, and Bob Carr, D-Mich., providing an additional $5 million to the Transportation Department for rail repair.

Helen Delich Bentley, R-Md., proposed and then withdrew an amendment barring disaster-aid payments under the bill to illegal aliens. The proposal drew strong criticism from Ed Pastor, D-Ariz., a Hispanic member of the committee.

Marcy Kaptur, D-Ohio, asked that consideration be given to action discouraging people from building homes and businesses in flood-prone areas. However, committee leaders dissuaded her from offering an amendment in exchange for the promise of a colloquy on the issue during floor debate.

W. G. "Bill" Hefner, D-N.C., asked for and received assurances that victims of other presidentially declared disasters in 1993 would be eligible for aid under the bill. Crops in Hefner's home state and other parts of the Southeast were damaged by a severe drought, the flip side of the stalled weather pattern that brought the flooding rains to the Midwest.

HOUSE RULES COMMITTEE ACTION

The atmosphere was sharply different on July 21 when the Rules Committee wrote a rule governing House floor action on HR 2667. After heated debate, the committee's Democratic majority beat back Republican efforts — led by ranking Rules Committee Republican Gerald B. H. Solomon of New York and supported by McDade, the ranking Republican on the Appropriations Committee — to bring the bill to the floor with an open rule allowing for unlimited amendments. That would have allowed consideration of GOP-backed "pay as you go" proposals. The Rules Committee also rejected, on party-line votes, specific amendments proposing offsetting cuts, as well as several that would have created additional claims to the money in the bill.

The committee rejected an amendment by Timothy J. Penny, D-Minn., and Jim Nussle, R-Iowa, to pay for the disaster-aid supplemental with offsetting cuts in dozens of other federal programs, rather than by adding its costs to the deficit.

The committee also blocked a proposal by Jim Slattery, D-Kan., to offset the costs by cutting discretionary funding for the fiscal 1994 appropriations bills.

While barring these amendments, however, committee Democrats stirred controversy by including within the rule a self-enacting clause, not subject to amendment. Referred to as the "Waters clause," after its sponsor, Maxine Waters, D-Calif., the provision authorized the payments of stipends of about $100 a week to participants in the Youth Fair Chance Program, which provided job training and counseling services for low-income individuals age 14 to 30.

The rule allowed for floor consideration of only one amendment, sponsored by Harold L. Volkmer, D-Mo., to provide an additional $25 million to the Transportation Department for road repair.

The following proposed amendments also were rejected:
● By Richard H. Baker, R-La., to make price gouging in presidentially declared disaster areas a federal crime.
● By Fred Grandy, R-Iowa, to expand the availability of "prevented planting" coverage under the Federal Crop Insurance program.
● By Rod Grams, R-Minn., to relax federal lending regulations on financial institutions that made loans to farmers in disaster areas.
● By Rick A. Lazio, R-N.Y., to add $14 million for the Army Corps of Engineers to address flood-control problems in coastal areas of New York's Long Island.

After voting all these proposals down, the committee briefly debated the Waters clause. Committee Republicans, who largely opposed the stipends on their substance, argued that including them contradicted Appropriations Committee Chairman Natcher's strongly stated preference for a "clean" bill.

However, Democratic backers of the provision noted that the House had voted to authorize the stipends as part of an earlier supplemental spending bill, but that the disbursements had been dropped during a conference with the

Senate. They described their inclusion of the clause as a "correction."

HOUSE FLOOR ACTION

The $2.74 billion supplemental bill came to the House floor July 22, but it was quickly derailed by an uprising of fiscal conservatism and GOP opposition to the Waters clause. To the leadership's surprise, the rule went down to defeat. With heavy lobbying, leaders turned enough votes to pass the rule five days later, leading to swift passage of the bill.

Rule Defeated on First Try

To the surprise of just about everybody, including the leaders of the rebel coalition, the rule was defeated July 22 by a roll call vote of 205-216. Of the 45 Democrats who joined with all 171 voting Republicans voting against the rule, 11 were first-term members. Most of the Democrats voting "nay" were from the South and the West. *(Vote 355, p. 86-H)*

The Democratic House leadership was blindsided by the uprising. So certain did the rule's passage appear that no organized whip operation had been applied to the vote. The outcome immediately sparked a bitter round of finger-pointing over who was responsible for delaying aid to the flood victims.

A bipartisan coalition of House "deficit hawks" was angry that the rule barred debate on the Penny-Nussle and Slattery proposals to pay for the aid. Republican opposition was further stoked by the House Democratic leadership's inclusion in the rule of the Waters language. Porter J. Goss, R-Fla., a Rules Committee member and the GOP manager for the rule debate, set the tone by scoffing at providing stipends for "youths up to 30 years of age." He continued, "I fail to see a rational connection between that subject and the emergency flood relief bill we are supposed to be focused on."

Republicans also put the issue in the context of their grievance against the Democratic leadership's frequent use of closed rules early in the 103rd Congress.

Bill supporters responded that it was unfair to the flood victims to delay the aid bill in order to establish a new funding procedure. This emotional argument, combined with the specter of flood-district members having to go home for the weekend and explain why the aid bill had stalled, seemed to boost the rule's chances. Even Penny, in his floor speech, did not envision defeating it.

Second Try Succeeds

Stunned by their earlier defeat, Democratic leaders did not make the same mistake twice. Lobbying and leaning on a number of Democrats who had voted against the first rule, they felt confident enough to push a nearly identical rule through the Rules Committee on July 23. In the process, they rejected a Republican proposal to drop demands for an open rule in exchange for the removal of the Waters clause.

With none of the contentious issues resolved, the floor debate on the second rule July 27 was nearly a replay of the first. But the outcome this time was different. The rule passed by a 224-205 vote, with just 32 Democrats joining with all 173 voting Republicans in voting against it. Of the 45 Democrats who had voted against the first rule, 15 supported the second; two Democrats who supported the first rule voted against the second. *(Vote 368, p. 90-H)*

However, the deficit dissidents exacted a promise from House Speaker Thomas S. Foley, D-Wash., to establish a bipartisan task force to examine ways to fund future disaster relief efforts.

Republicans took one more shot at the Waters clause, with a motion by John Edward Porter, R-Ill., to recommit the bill to the Appropriations Committee with orders to strike the stipend provision. The motion was defeated on a 201-226 vote. *(Vote 369, p. 90-H)*

Quick Passage

Even at the height of the debate, there was never any real doubt that the House would pass a disaster-aid bill. Most of the deficit hawks — including Nussle, Penny and others who represented Midwest districts that were hit hard by flooding — insisted they were committed to passing a bill. So when the rule passed, opposition to the bill evaporated. After accepting an amendment that added an additional $25 million, bringing the total to $2.77 billion, the House approved HR 2667 by a 400-27 vote July 27. All 254 Democrats voting backed the bill. *(Vote 370, p. 90-H)*

SENATE COMMITTEE ACTION

Predictions that the funding in the original bill would be insufficient quickly proved prescient. Two days after the House vote, Clinton requested an additional $1.94 billion, bringing the total to $4.7 billion.

As in the House, Senate appropriators eschewed subcommittee markups and took the bill directly to the full Appropriations Committee July 30. The appropriators quickly approved, by voice vote, an en bloc amendment proposed by Chairman Robert C. Byrd, D-W.Va., embodying the administration's new request.

The amendment provided: $100 million to the Department of Education to provide assistance to student-aid recipients and local school districts adversely affected by the floods; $34 million to the Environmental Protection Agency for pollution control, abatement and compliance activities in the flood zone; and additions of $1.2 billion to FEMA; $359 million to Agriculture; $97 million to HUD; $85 million to the Army Corps of Engineers; $21 million to HHS; $13 million to Interior; and $45 million to Transportation.

The bill approved by the Senate committee differed from the House-passed bill in three significant ways. It struck the Waters clause, reduced rail repair spending by $5 million and eliminated the $300,000 the House had provided for the Legal Services Corporation.

Appropriations Committee members complied with a request from Byrd to save time by holding off on amendment proposals until floor debate.

A Warning on Farm Payments

However, Iowa Democrat Harkin and Missouri Republican Christopher S. Bond signaled that they would fight hard to increase the size of federal payments to farmers to cover crop losses. They expressed strong opposition to the 50 percent cut applied to the crop-loss formula that had been proposed by Clinton and adopted by the House.

Harkin and Bond argued that the 1990 farm bill had established the 42-cents-on-the-dollar formula as the standard for crop-loss payments. The Bush administration, citing fiscal restraints, applied the 50 percent cut to a disaster aid program in 1991 and in the wake of the catastrophic hurricanes of 1992. But the Midwest senators said

the widespread financial impact of the floods made it incumbent for Congress to return to 100 percent of the formula.

Thad Cochran, R-Miss., and Connie Mack, R-Fla., warned they could not support such an amendment unless the bill provided additional payments to their constituents who had been victimized by Hurricane Andrew but received just 50 percent of the formula under the 1992 disaster-aid supplemental.

SENATE FLOOR ACTION

The Senate approved a $5.7 billion version of the bill by voice vote Aug. 4.

The Harkin-Bond effort to increase payments to farmers was the central issue during two days of floor debate.

Most flood-state members backed their proposal to provide full funding of the crop-loss formula. But Byrd argued that the amendment would add $900 million to the bill's cost and undercut the Clinton administration's request for expeditious passage of a "clean" bill.

Amendment supporters initially tried to broaden support by meeting the concerns voiced by Cochran and Mack. Harkin and Bond tried to provide full formula funding not only for 1993 crop losses, but retroactively for 1991 and 1992 as well. Byrd countered that additional funds for victims of past disasters hardly qualified as emergency funding, and he challenged the germaneness of the amendment. The amendment survived one attempt to kill it when a motion to table the question of germaneness received a 50-50 vote. But the Senate then voted, 46-54, to rule the amendment as non-germane. *(Votes 237, 238, p. 31-S)*

The Senate then passed a Byrd amendment, requested by the administration, adding another $123 million to the bill, including $100 million for Commerce, $10 million for the Small Business Administration, $11 million for Labor and $2 million for the Commission on National and Community Service. Byrd agreed to a secondary amendment by Harkin raising the maximum for small-business disaster loans to individuals from $500,000 to $1.5 million. The Byrd amendment passed, 86-14. *(Vote 239, p. 31-S)*

Harkin and Bond then took another shot at increasing the crop-loss formula, this time limiting it to 1993 disaster losses. Byrd continued to insist that the bill be kept free of amendments not requested by Clinton. But Harkin — who had been lobbying the White House for intercession — received help just in the nick of time.

As debate on the amendment was winding down, Harkin produced a letter from Office of Management and Budget Director Leon E. Panetta, stating administration support for 100 percent funding of the formula. Although Byrd complained that Harkin and the White House had pulled the rug from under him, he dropped his objection to the amendment, which then passed, 68-32. *(Vote 240, p. 31-S)*

The additional $900 million was counted as fiscal 1994 borrowing authority for the Commodity Credit Corporation (CCC), which made payments to farmers under federal crop programs. That left a total of $4.8 billion in appropriated spending.

Little Interest in Offsets

Attempts to offset the bill's spending with cuts in other programs created only a minor stir, a far cry from the spirited debate that took place in the House. Durenberger proposed to offset the bill with cuts in discretionary spend-

ing for fiscal 1994. Only a handful of senators spoke up, and a motion to table, or kill, the amendment passed on a 54-45 vote. *(Vote 241, p. 32-S)*

Durenberger later offered an amendment to offset the spending with non-specific rescissions, sequesters and taxes. However, the provision would have required a waiver of the 1974 Budget Act; a motion to approve such a waiver failed, 35-64. *(Vote 243, p. 32-S)*

A third amendment by the Minnesota Republican, to increase federal crop insurance coverage for farmers who were prevented from planting by natural disasters, was tabled on a 68-31 vote. *(Vote 242, p. 32-S)*

The Senate did pass, by voice vote, an amendment by Bond to increase Transportation Department funding for rail repair by $5 million, equaling the amount approved by the House.

FINAL ACTION

With floods continuing to ravage wide areas of the Midwest, the disaster-aid measure became one of the "must-pass" bills as Congress rushed toward its August recess.

When the House took up HR 2667 as amended by the Senate on Aug. 6, the Waters clause stood out as the only potential sticking point. Waters remained adamant that the language remain in the bill, and the Democratic leadership said it would stand by its commitment. But the Clinton administration stepped in to remove the potential roadblock. Labor Secretary Robert B. Reich sent letters to Appropriations Committee Chairmen Byrd and Natcher stating that he would implement the stipend program through administrative action. The stipend clause was then dropped from HR 2667 with Waters' assent.

Eager to finish work, members acceded to the increased spending in the Senate-passed bill, despite some members' qualms about the crop-loss formula change. The House restored the $300,000 for the Legal Services Corporation that the Senate had dropped, then approved the bill by voice vote.

During the early morning hours of Aug. 7, the Senate accepted the House changes and cleared the bill, also by voice vote.

Key Provisions

As cleared, the bill provided the following amounts to federal departments and agencies to fund disaster-relief efforts:

- Agriculture Department, $2.45 billion.
- Federal Emergency Management Agency, $2 billion.
- Department of Housing and Urban Development, $250 million.
- Army Corps of Engineers (Defense Department), $235 million.
- Transportation Department, $206 million.
- Commerce Department, $201 million.
- Education Department, $100 million.
- Small Business Administration, $90 million.
- Department of Health and Human Services, $75 million.
- Labor Department, $54.6 million.
- Interior Department, $41.2 million.
- Environmental Protection Agency, $34 million.
- Commission on National and Community Service, $4 million.
- Legal Services Corporation, $300,000. ∎

POLITICAL REPORT

Ballots Again Cast for Change

GOP sees climate 'mighty good for Republicans' following Bush's defeat in 1992 election

Out with the in; in with the out. That simple message continued to reverberate across the political landscape in 1993 as several states filled local and state-wide offices and voted on ballot measures.

Much as they did in 1992, voters signaled their dissatisfaction with incumbents in general and with governmental business as usual. In 1993, however, the main victims of the house-cleaning impulse were the Democrats, who lost governorships in New Jersey and Virginia as well as the mayor's office in New York City.

Republicans Say They See a Trend

Republican officials were swift to see national implications in the results. Haley Barbour, the chairman of the Republican National Committee, connected the November outcomes to earlier GOP triumphs in the Los Angeles mayoral race, the June special Senate election in Texas and the November 1992 runoff Senate election in Georgia.

"We have won all six of the biggest elections in the country in the last 12 months," said Barbour, adding that since his party lost the White House in November 1992, the political climate had changed and become "mighty good for Republicans."

In all five special elections held to fill House vacancies in 1993, however, the party that had held the seat retained it. Democrats won all three of the seats vacated by House members joining the Clinton administration: California's 17th (budget director Leon E. Panetta's district), Mississippi's 2nd (Agriculture Secretary Mike Espy's district) and Wisconsin's 1st (Defense Secretary Les Aspin's district).

Republicans held onto the seats in Ohio's 2nd District and Michigan's 3rd District that were vacated by the departure of Bill Gradison for a private-sector job and the July 31 death of Rep. Paul B. Henry, respectively.

The most closely watched contest among political professionals was the New Jersey gubernatorial race. Democrats had hoped that a win for incumbent James J. Florio, who had pushed through a big tax increase in 1990, would prove that such moves need not be politically fatal. Both President Clinton and first lady Hillary Rodham Clinton campaigned personally for Florio, indirectly helping the GOP cast the vote as a referendum on the administration.

With her victory, Christine Todd Whitman translated her "don't raise taxes without doing the cutting [of spending]" into a national theme on the networks' morning-after programs.

"We'd have loved to have won," said David Wilhelm, chairman of the Democratic National Committee, striving to remind reporters that Florio had lifted his hopes for re-election from oblivion to the threshold of victory.

"It's a big, big defeat for the White House," Senate Minority Leader Bob Dole, R-Kan., said, seeing portents for future elections and struggles on Capitol Hill.

In electoral terms, the 1993 results indicated that the pressure felt by congressional incumbents in the 1990 and 1992 electoral cycles would continue through the midterm elections of 1994. But it was not so clear what immediate effect those political winds might have on legislation.

Such congressional issues as health care and the North American Free Trade Agreement were not salient in the November elections. Voters expressed high anxiety over crime in several states, but there were contradictory messages on gun control. And there were mixed signals for anti-tax advocates and deficit hawks in the results of ballot initiatives on taxes and spending.

A Desire for Change

The most convincing Democratic statement of reaction may have come from David Axelrod, who ran the successful Detroit mayoral campaign of Dennis Archer. Axelrod said voters "want police on the streets, their garbage picked up, other basic services and someone to fight for their quality of life."

That someone turned out to be a Republican in the three most eye-catching contests of the day. Whitman became the first woman to be elected governor of New Jersey, narrowly defeating Florio, 50 percent to 48 percent.

In Virginia, voters ended a dozen-year Democratic reign in the governor's office by delivering a decisive victory for George F. Allen, a Republican former House member. Just as important, Allen carried Republicans to virtual parity in the state House, bringing the GOP within sight of majorities in both chambers of the historically Democratic state legislature.

And in New York City, where voter registration favored Democrats 5-to-1, Republican Rudolph W. Giuliani ousted Democratic Mayor David N. Dinkins.

The inclination to change showed up in various guises in the various local elections, not all of which had the same partisan dimension. In Pittsburgh, voters turned to an unconventional state legislator who campaigned for mayor door-to-door, sometimes carrying his son on his shoulders. The new mayor, Thomas J. Murphy, won 66 percent of the vote with a plan to make city government "customer friendly."

In Boston, voters chose their first non-Irish mayor in 64 years, electing Thomas Menino the city's first Italian-American mayor. Minneapolis elected its first black woman mayor, Sharon Sayles Belton. And as if to demonstrate that not everyone was unhappy with incumbents, Cleveland, Houston and Seattle re-elected mayors Michael White, Bob Lanier and Norman Rice, respectively, with overwhelming majorities.

House Special Elections

CALIFORNIA — 17TH

Leon E. Panetta resigned his 17th District California seat early in the year to become director of the White House Office of Management and Budget, but he proved to be a force in the choice of his successor. Most of the candidates regularly invoked his name and reputation as a budget hawk.

In the end, the mantle descended upon state Rep. Sam Farr, a veteran local official and legislator whose state Assembly district covered much of Panetta's congressional district.

Sam Farr (D)	53,675	51.5%
Bill McCampbell (R)	43,774	42%

Farr's path was far from smooth, however. In the April 13 Democratic primary, he finished second at the polls, some 1,600 votes behind Bill Monning, a Salinas lawyer. But Farr got the Democratic nomination on the strength of more than 10,600 absentee ballots that had been cast on or before Election Day under California's increasingly popular vote-by-mail program.

Absentee ballots accounted for about one-third of the total vote in the all-party primary, and nearly half of Farr's votes came on those ballots, giving him an overall winning plurality of 25.7 percent. Monning had 18.5 percent and Monterey County Supervisor Barbara Shipnuck 14.3 percent.

The fourth-place finisher, and top Republican, was Bill McCampbell, a Pebble Beach attorney who had received less than one-fourth of the vote as Panetta's GOP challenger in 1992. McCampbell's 12 percent of the total April primary vote eclipsed the 10.3 percent collected Jess Brown, an executive with the Santa Cruz County Farm Bureau and the choice of the Republican Party. Farr entered the campaign with several advantages. A Monterey County supervisor for five years, he then represented much of Monterey and Santa Cruz counties for nearly 12 years in Sacramento. Voters in those two counties had cast nearly 95 percent of the district's vote in 1992.

Farr also had the most organized campaign staff and was the best financed. Farr's workers blanketed the district with phone calls and door-to-door visits, telling voters Farr would protect the coastline, serve farm interests and push for federal funds for low- and moderate-income housing.

Monning, a former executive director of International Physicians for the Prevention of Nuclear War, gained momentum late in the campaign. But by that time, Farr's $240,000 treasury dwarfed Monning's $71,000 — and Farr had rendered Monning's late surge inconsequential by getting in his absentee ballots.

Shipnuck raised more than $200,000 — much of it with the aid of EMILY's List, an influential Democratic fundraising group, but was unable to compete with Farr's head start.

McCampbell had little chance in the general election. Democrats enjoyed a 20 percentage point registration advantage in the 17th, and nearly 65 percent of the primary ballots counted April 13 were cast for Democrats. In 1992, voters in the 17th had supported Bill Clinton and both of California's Democratic Senate candidates.

McCampbell painted the contest as a referendum on some of President Clinton's policies, however, and managed to make the race tight in Monterey County, where the bulk of the district's vote was cast. McCampbell, who also lived in the county, came within 1,500 votes of beating Farr there. But Farr ran away with the election in Santa Cruz County, which cast the remainder of the district vote and gave the Democrat nearly 60 percent.

In the end, Farr won 52 percent of the vote to McCampbell's 42 percent. Three minor-party candidates and two independents divided another 5 percent.

MICHIGAN — 3RD

In a contest many considered little more than a formality, Vernon J. Ehlers, a Republican state senator and former physics professor, easily won the Dec. 7 special election to replace the late Paul B. Henry in Michigan's 3rd District.

Vernon J. Ehlers (R)	57,484	66.4%
Dale R. Sprik (D)	19,993	23.1%
Dawn Ida Krupp (I)	8,759	10.1%

Ehlers, 59, was considered a front-runner from the beginning in this heavily Republican district, where his political career had shadowed Henry's for a decade — following him in the state House, the state Senate and finally to Congress.

Henry, who had been elected in 1984, died July 31 of brain cancer.

Ehlers took 66 percent of the vote to conservative Democrat Dale R. Sprik's 23 percent. Independent Dawn Ida Krupp, a supporter of independent 1992 presidential candidate Ross Perot, received 10 percent.

Official returns showed Ehlers with 57,484 votes to Sprik's 19,993 and Krupp's 8,759.

Sprik, 56, was a lawyer who specialized in personal injury cases, but in this campaign his ads showed another side of him, picturing him on his buffalo farm.

Given the nearly 3-1 ratio of Ehlers' victory, attention turned to Krupp's somewhat surprising vote. A lawyer from Grand Rapids Township, Krupp, 51, spent $15,000 of her own money and raised $5,000 more. Krupp, a member of Perot's United We Stand America, said the group did not provide direct support for her campaign.

Ehlers had been on track to win the seat since the Nov. 2 primary, when he received nearly one-third of the GOP vote in a field of eight.

The entire GOP primary field espoused views that were nearly identical on issues from abortion to taxes. Only Marge Byington, chief deputy director of the state Commerce Department, had her credentials challenged by the local media and by her opponents over her stance on abortion. Byington said she was personally against abortion but that she was troubled by government intervention in the lives of citizens.

In the end, as expected, the primary contest was between Ehlers and his friend and legislative colleague Ken Sikkema, a Republican state representative from Grand Rapids. Unofficial vote totals showed Sikkema taking second place with 25 percent of the vote. Byington placed third with 19 percent.

In personal style, Ehlers resembled the physics professor he was educated to be more than the politician he became. He vowed to bring to Congress his keen interest in issues related to science, the environment and health care. "There are just so precious few scientists in Congress," he said.

And, like Henry, Ehlers was public about his devotion to Christianity. He was the co-author of several books that melded theology and science as guides to managing the environment: "I've always believed that any Republican should be concerned about the environment, because a true conservative should be a preservationist. If you think just using resources and discarding them is good then you're not using common sense," he wrote.

MISSISSIPPI — 2ND

In 1986, Democrat Mike Espy made history by becoming the first African American elected to the House from Mississippi since Reconstruction. Seven years later, Demo-

crat Bennie Thompson made history by becoming the first African American in Mississippi to be elected on the strength of a district's black majority. Thompson based his campaign explicitly on the black vote, rather than stressing a biracial appeal as Espy had done.

Bennie Thompson (D)	72,561	55.2%
Hayes Dent (R)	58,995	44.8%

Thompson, a Hinds County supervisor, six other Democrats and one Republican qualified for the special, all-party ballot to replace Espy, who resigned in January 1993 to become U.S. Agriculture secretary. With no candidate in the large field approaching a majority in the March 30 special election, state law required a runoff between the two top finishers.

The leader in the first vote was the lone Republican, Hayes Dent, an adviser to GOP Gov. Kirk Fordice, who took 34 percent. Thompson was second, leading all Democrats with 28 percent of the vote. Espy's brother, Clarksdale Mayor Henry Espy, finished third with 20 percent.

Despite Dent's first-round showing, Thompson was the favorite in the April runoff in the state's most distinctly black and Democratic district. African Americans constituted 63 percent of the 2nd District population, 58 percent of the voting-age population. The seven Democrats on the March 30 ballot had collected more than 65 percent of the vote among them.

Unlike Espy, Thompson had not been viewed as a candidate with strong appeal across racial lines. His participation in the state's civil rights battles made him less attractive to some whites, and he emphasized turning out the black vote over courting the white.

The runoff leg of the race was brief but intense. Both candidates were plagued by unfavorable publicity. Dent had to answer for a simple assault conviction stemming from a tavern incident in 1983. And stories were revived from the 1980s questioning whether Thompson's friendship with a state official had helped to prevent an investigation into Thompson's practices as a Hinds County supervisor.

But the latter stories did not gain much momentum through retelling in 1993, nor did they prevent Thompson from uniting and galvanizing blacks. Turnout in the runoff was even higher than it had been for the March 30 vote, with more than 130,000 votes cast. Thompson prevailed with 55 percent of the vote (the same percentage Bill Clinton received in the district in 1992).

Thompson was educated in segregated elementary and secondary schools in the state. As a student at Tougaloo College, he met civil rights activist Fannie Lou Hamer, who inspired him to pursue a career in politics.

Thompson began his political career at a time when black officeholders were few and the discouragements many. He ran for alderman in his native Bolton at age 20. He won but was denied a seat by white officials until a court order forced the town to relent. Four years later, Thompson was elected mayor of Bolton. And at 32, he took a seat on the Board of Supervisors for Hinds County, which includes the state's capital city of Jackson.

With the election behind him, Thompson said he planned to emphasize the concerns of the majority in the district. He also vowed to work to unify the district. "I hope to bridge that gap, but right now it's still very much divided," he said.

OHIO — 2ND

When 18-year veteran Ohio Republican Bill Gradison resigned his 2nd District seat early in the year to become

president of a health insurance industry group, the thought of losing the district to Democrats in a special election never entered the minds of Ohio Republicans.

Their confidence was justified when Republican Rob Portman, a Cincinnati lawyer and political neophyte, easily won the May 4 race.

Rob Portman (R)	53,020	70.1%
Lee Hornberger (D)	22,652	29.9%

Portman and his staff appeared just as confident going into the contest with Democrat Lee Hornberger, also a Cincinnati lawyer.

Portman cast his first vote on the House floor just 18 hours after the polls closed; his staff denied that he had bought tickets for Washington before the polls closed. However, his campaign spokesman, Barry Bennett, conceded: "I knew what the flight schedule was."

The Qualifying Round

The real battle in Ohio's single most Republican district — in which George Bush beat Bill Clinton by 24 percentage points in 1992 — was between Portman and former Rep. Bob McEwen (1981-93) in the March 16 GOP primary.

In that race, Portman took 36 percent, outdistancing McEwen, who received 30 percent, and Cincinnati home builder Jay Buchert, who surprised many by finishing close to the leaders with 25 percent.

Hornberger, a first-time congressional candidate, collected 46 percent of the vote in a field of five Democratic candidates. He swept past his nearest competitor, hospital technician Thomas R. Chandler, by 18 percentage points. Chandler had been Gradison's Democratic opponent in 1992.

But the district's political history, reinforced by turnout on primary day, left Hornberger little hope for victory. Eighty-six percent of the primary votes were cast on the Republican side.

Hornberger's chances might have been better against McEwen, who had represented the neighboring 6th District. McEwen lost that seat in 1992, in part because of his 166 overdrafts at the since-closed House bank. That issue was revived in the primary, when McEwen was also accused of using his congressional office equipment for his 1992 campaign and of spending more time abroad at public expense than he spent in Ohio.

Portman was criticized in the primary because he had worked for a Washington law firm that had represented such clients as Haiti's autocratic Duvalier family, but that issue was too obscure to be of benefit to Hornberger.

In the campaign against Hornberger, Portman recycled television advertisements from his primary campaign that bashed President Clinton rather than Portman's GOP rivals or Hornberger.

Portman carried each of the five counties that make up the 2nd District. His vote share was biggest (74 percent) where it mattered most, in populous Hamilton County, which accounted for more than half the votes. His share was smallest (53 percent) where it mattered least, in Brown County, source of just 6 percent of the overall tally.

(Portman had also won 45 percent of the primary vote in the Hamilton County portion of the 2nd District, which included part of Cincinnati in addition to its suburbs and accounted for 60 percent of the GOP primary total.)

The financial investment in the two races indicated which contest Portman took more seriously: He spent about $650,000 in the primary and just $81,000 against

Hornberger. Portman nonetheless spent about twice as much as the Democrat, who did not run TV ads.

WISCONSIN — 1ST

The contest between Democrat Peter W. Barca and Republican Mark W. Neumann in Wisconsin's 1st District lived up to its billing as the most competitive House special election of the year: Barca prevailed with a margin of just 675 votes in the May 4 race. By so doing, he spared his party some embarrassment by holding the seat vacated by Defense Secretary Les Aspin.

Peter W. Barca (D)	55,605	49.9%
Mark W. Neumann (R)	54,930	49.3%
Edward J. Kozak (L)	375	0.3%
Gary W. Thompson (I)	327	0.3%

Both Barca and Neumann easily won their primaries April 6. Neumann's victory in the Republican primary over state Rep. Charles W. Coleman (whom he defeated by a ratio of more than 3-to-1) had been expected. Neumann was well-known after spending nearly $1 million in 1992 in an aggressive campaign against Aspin. While he got just 41 percent of the vote against the incumbent, his full-dress ad campaign established him as a household name across the southeast Wisconsin district.

Not expected, however, was the ease of Barca's victory over former state Democratic Chairman Jeff Neubauer. The race had been considered too close to call, but Barca cruised to a winning ratio of more than 3-to-2.

Barca, a state representative from 1985 to 1993, had the support of a number of prominent state legislators in the district as well as most elements of organized labor, including the state AFL-CIO and the United Auto Workers. Neubauer relied more on his clout in Washington, highlighted by a friendship with President Clinton that began when Neubauer endorsed Clinton well before the 1992 Wisconsin presidential primary.

Endorsements and connections aside, the primary became a battle of home bases. Neubauer carried his base in Racine County, the district's main population center, by about 3,000 votes. But Barca rolled up a 13,000-vote margin in Kenosha County, where a strong union presence and Barca's personal popularity were amplified by hometown pride and a robust turnout. Barca and Neumann offered contrasting styles in the general election. Neumann presented himself as an energetic political novice and jogged across the district to prove it. Barca, by contrast, stressed his support within the state political establishment and the legislation he had helped fashion in the state Assembly, where he chaired the Democratic Caucus for two years.

By edging out Neumann, Barca followed the same route to victory as he did in defeating Neubauer. He rolled up a big lead in Kenosha County, held down his deficit in Racine County and won Rock County, Neumann's home base.

Neumann fashioned the vote as a test of the popularity of Clinton's proposed tax increases. The significance of the race brought several big-name Republicans, such as Senate Minority Leader Bob Dole, R-Kan., former President Gerald R. Ford and former Housing and Urban Development Secretary Jack F. Kemp, to the district to campaign on Neumann's behalf.

But Barca detailed his differences with Clinton policy. He campaigned with Wisconsin's two Democratic senators, Herb Kohl and Russell D. Feingold, but kept national Democrats at a distance. Barca repeatedly emphasized that the special election was a contest to choose the candidate who best fit the Aspin model of constituent service.

On the attack through much of the campaign, Neumann found himself on the defensive as the vote neared. He denied that his campaign was closely tied to national religious groups and downplayed the role of anti-abortion activists as well.

After the vote, Neumann delayed Barca's swearing-in by requesting a recount. The new tally confirmed the original result.

As a politician, Barca defied easy labeling. The product of a middle-class Italian-American upbringing, he indicated he would support the Freedom of Choice Act pending in Congress. Still, he proudly depicted himself as a reflection of his hometown, and his political concerns in the state Legislature often were unmistakably local.

Senate Election

Republican Kay Bailey Hutchison proved her political mettle — and Texas voters confirmed their trend toward the GOP — in the 1993 special election to replace Lloyd Bentsen, who retired to become President Clinton's Treasury secretary.

Hutchison flattened appointed Democratic Sen. Bob Krueger in a June 5 runoff election, running up a two-thirds share of the vote — the largest vote share any challenger had ever achieved against an incumbent senator.

Krueger, a state railroad commissioner at the time of his January appointment over a handful of better-known Democrats who declined the opportunity, had served in the House from 1975 to 1979 and had run unsuccessfully for the Senate twice before (in 1978 and 1984).

Political analysts expected him to enter the runoff as the front-runner because Hutchison had been busy fending off several Republican rivals, including GOP Reps. Joe L. Barton and Jack Fields. But instead, it was Hutchison, then the state treasurer, who headed into the final weeks with momentum, money and the all-important conservative mantle.

She topped the 24-person field in the all-party May 1 primary and then went on to defeat Krueger in the head-to-head contest, 67 percent to 33 percent.

Hutchison carried 239 counties, Krueger just 15. She won every county in every metropolitan area, rolling up a margin of more than 100,000 votes in Harris County (Houston) alone.

Krueger's counties, by contrast, lay mostly in the state's impoverished southern extreme, along the Mexican border. And even where he won, Krueger did not pile up many votes. His combined margin in all the counties he carried was fewer than 7,600 votes.

However, the victory was tarnished only a few days after the votes were tallied, when a grand jury in Travis County (Austin) on June 10 issued subpoenas for 14 members of Hutchison's state Treasury staff and two of her campaign aides to investigate whether state records had been tampered with after inquiries about the use of state office staff and equipment for campaign purposes. Then on Sept. 27, Hutchison and two former aides were indicted on five counts of using her state office and equipment for political purposes. *(Legal woes, p. 7-A)*

Hutchison and her aides depicted the investigation and indictment as a political assault. They said it had been orchestrated by high-level state Democrats interested in

Texas' Hutchison Entangled in Legal Woes

Within a week of her landslide victory in a special Senate election, Kay Bailey Hutchison found herself embroiled in a controversy that threatened to damage her reputation as one of the GOP's rising stars.

During the fall of 1993, she was indicted on charges of misusing her state office for political and personal gain, saw the indictment dismissed because of a flawed grand jury and was re-indicted by a second grand jury on the same charges. In late December, the judge hearing the case tossed out four of the five charges against her, ordering prosecutors to be more specific. Prosecutors complied, and a grand jury indicted her for the third time. The trial was to begin Feb. 7, 1994, in Fort Worth.

An Ineligible Juror

A Travis County grand jury in Austin charged Hutchison Sept. 27 with five counts of using state employees and other resources for political and personal errands during her years as Texas state treasurer. She was accused of using state personnel and equipment for political and personal gain and of tampering with official records to hide evidence. If convicted of all charges, Hutchison faced up to 61 years in prison and $43,000 in fines.

The discovery of an ineligible juror on the first grand jury forced Travis County District Attorney Ronnie Earle to dismiss the indictments against Hutchison. But Earle presented the evidence on Hutchison to another grand jury, and she was re-indicted on Dec. 8. The third indictment came Jan. 7, 1994.

The timing of the indictments and trial were of concern to Hutchison and others interested in the 1994 campaign cycle (when Hutchison had to defend the seat she won in the June 5 special election). The filing deadline for candidates was Jan. 3, with the primary on March 8.

Hutchison had pushed for a quick trial and had been given an initial trial date of Nov. 29, before the discovery of the problem juror. David Beckwith, the senator's spokesman, said she had hoped to minimize the disruption of her 1994 re-election effort. Hutchison characterized the entire case as "sleazy campaign tactics employed by the Democrats."

But Earle, a Democrat, pointed out that any trial delay might be laid to Hutchison's own defense attorneys, who raised the issue of the problem juror in a series of pretrial motions. "Sen. Hutchison has raised a legal technicality, which could result in the dismissal of her indictment and a delay in her trial," Earle said in a statement in October. "In that event, the state will present its evidence against Mrs. Hutchison to another grand jury and fully prosecute this case."

In some of the verbal parrying that accompanied the case from the beginning, Beckwith said the filing of the motions "will delay the trial only if the district attorney wants it to delay the trial." He said Hutchison's attorneys felt compelled to point out the ineligible juror in the first case because they were certain it would have come to light eventually. "All we did was speed up the process," Beckwith argued.

After the second indictment, Hutchison again stressed her interest in a quick trial. But Assistant District Attorney Mark Lane said the state needed time to respond to a 1-inch-thick stack of motions that Hutchison's attorneys filed. "We're not even going to try to guess" when the case might go to trial, he said.

Hardly Helping

It was hard to see how any delay would benefit the defendant. "The longer this drags out, the more Kay Bailey Hutchison has to lose," said Robert Bezdek, a political science professor at Texas A&M University-Corpus Christi.

A protracted legal struggle threatened to consume much of Hutchison's time and energy, dampen her fundraising and lend opponents powerful ammunition. It also heightened interest in the Democratic nomination against her. Former state Attorney General Jim Mattox, Rep. Michael A. Andrews of Houston and businessman Richard Fisher, a former adviser to Ross Perot, all signaled their intent to run by the end of the year.

By year's end, no Republican had made a move toward an intraparty challenge. State Republican Chairman Fred Meyer said, "If you had your druthers, you'd rather it be over and done with. But we're not going to let the Democrats kill a Republican senator."

A survey conducted by the Public Policy Research Institute of Texas A&M University on Oct. 8-16 found Hutchison's public approval rating to be 34 percent, a 25-point decline since her initial indictment. Analysts also said 38 percent of the 1,019 Texans interviewed said they did not know enough about Hutchison's legal problems to hold an opinion.

challenging Hutchison's re-election in 1994, when Bentsen's term expired and Hutchison had to face the voters again to win a full term of her own.

A Texas Breakthrough

Hutchison's special-election victory in June 1993 was a breakthrough both for her sex and for her party. Like many of the women beginning their Washington careers in the 103rd Congress, Hutchison was the first woman from her state to occupy her office. And her triumph was a significant boost for Republicans, giving the GOP control of both Texas Senate seats for the first time since Reconstruction.

Hutchison also helped her party counteract the Democratic dominance of the "Year of the Woman" phenomenon in 1992, when all the women elected to the Senate and most of those elected to the House were Democrats.

Even before she was sworn in, however, Hutchison highlighted the differences between herself and the four Democratic women who were newly elected to the Senate in 1992. For starters, Hutchison's candidacy had little relation to the contentious 1991 Supreme Court nomination hearings of Clarence Thomas. Only when pressed on the matter did Hutchison concede the Judiciary Committee hearings "showed the panel was out of touch."

Her feminist pitch on the campaign trail was hardly radical; she told voters she hoped to create a society that

was "better for our sons and open for our daughters."

Her own assessment of her place in the Senate was on point: "I am not philosophically in touch with the women that won in '92. But on some issues we will come together."

Like the only other Republican woman in the Senate, Nancy Landon Kassebaum of Kansas, Hutchison supported abortion rights.

She said during the spring campaign, however, that she opposed using government funds for abortion and supported some restrictions on abortion — such as requiring parental consent for minors. Her mixed positions prompted Krueger to label her not "pro-choice" but "multiple choice."

Hutchison expected to team up with other women in Congress on legislation benefiting children and on crime bills dealing with female victims. While serving in the state House in 1975, Hutchison cosponsored legislation with then-state Rep. Sarah Weddington that gave added protections to victims of sexual offenses, including a ban on the publication of the names of rape victims. Weddington, a Democrat, was the lawyer for the plaintiff in the landmark Supreme Court case legalizing abortion, *Roe v. Wade.*

Hutchison advocated establishing gender equity in Individual Retirement Accounts. She hoped to eliminate discrepancies that limited non-working spouses to setting aside $250 annually for their retirement, while working people could set aside up to $2,000.

With the exception of the abortion issue, Hutchison was a solid conservative rooted in the anti-regulatory, pro-entrepreneurial beliefs that represented the core philosophies of the Texas GOP.

"I see three enemies of small business," she said frequently on the campaign trail, "taxation, regulation and litigation."

She supported the presidential line-item veto, a balanced-budget constitutional amendment and pay freezes for members of Congress. Although she advocated slashing government spending and reducing the federal deficit, Hutchison defended two expensive, Texas-based projects — the superconducting super collider (which was sent to a highly publicized death in 1993) and the space station *Freedom* — as good science that could benefit the entire nation.

But Hutchison was a pragmatic politician who realized she would be in the minority on Capitol Hill as she fought for the two programs. Because of that, Hutchison said early on that she would cross party lines and accept program reductions if that would preserve the projects.

If Hutchison's ideology was tried and true Texas conservative, her style was anything but. In a state where male and female politicians often ran boisterous campaigns, Hutchison worked her way up in the system quietly. A soft-spoken woman, she had trouble rousing a large crowd but charmed people one on one.

While that style seemed likely to prove successful in the Senate, it was clear that Hutchison would need some time to matter as much in that chamber as Bentsen. A silver-haired Tory Democrat who held the seat for 22 years, Bentsen became something of an elder statesman after running a respectable campaign as the party's vice presidential nominee in 1988.

Hutchison also had to contend with the presence of the state's senior senator, high-powered, high-energy Republican Phil Gramm. And she had to move quickly to be prepared to defend her seat in 1994. ∎

Whitman Defeats New Jersey's Gov. Florio

Surviving early miscues, a steady assault from Democratic Gov. James J. Florio's camp and a late drop in the polls, Republican Christine Todd Whitman hung on to win the Nov. 2 gubernatorial race in New Jersey.

But her election turned less on Whitman herself and her plans for the state than on Florio and his record. Just six months into his term in 1990, Florio raised taxes by $2.8 billion, including a deeply unpopular increase in the state sales tax. Florio's approval ratings plunged into the teens and never fully recovered.

Florio made enough of a comeback in the latter half of his term — largely by stressing toughness on crime and guns — to give him a lead over Whitman in most of the autumn polling. But a close look at these polls revealed potential problems for the Florio campaign. Steve Salmore, a political science professor at Rutgers University and a former Republican consultant, said a majority in most polls gave Florio poor ratings on his handling of taxes and job creation.

For much of the campaign, however, Whitman seemed unable or unwilling to capitalize on the anyone-but-Florio sentiment. She took a long summer vacation and did not come up with an economic plan until Sept. 21. And when Whitman released her proposal to cut income tax rates by 30 percent over three years, she encountered deep voter skepticism.

But in the final days of the campaign, Whitman gave Republican consultant Edward J. Rollins the reins. He reordered her priorities, focusing her stump speeches on Florio's record and playing down her own promises. Soon the momentum seemed to shift.

About a week after the election, Rollins prompted a firestorm of criticism when he told a group of reporters about spreading $500,000 around to suppress the black voter turnout. Rollins later retracted his statement about "walking around" money, but an investigation was continuing at year's end. *(Vote suppression, p. 9-A)*

The Early Going

Whitman's inexperience left her vulnerable to mistakes — and jabs from the Florio forces about those mistakes. And after winning the primary in June, she spent most of her time on the defensive. The daily barrage of attacks from the Florio camp, run in part by Democratic Party consultant James Carville, kept her off balance.

When the Whitman campaign tried to go on the offensive, the message sometimes backfired. For example, Whitman attacked Florio's welfare overhaul proposal by comparing some of the plan's requirements to conditions endured by Holocaust survivors. "What is the governor's next idea in his headlong rush to embrace right-wing radicalism? . . . A program of tattoos for welfare mothers? A badge sewn onto their clothing identifying them as welfare recipients?" her statement said.

The Florio campaign turned that comment into a public relations bonanza, releasing reactions from Jewish leaders who condemned Whitman's statement, arguing that the

Claims of Vote Suppression Tarnish Whitman Victory

Alleged efforts to suppress black voter turnout in New Jersey's Nov. 2 gubernatorial election prompted state and federal investigations and turned a spotlight on the role of "street money" in electioneering.

Democrats in New Jersey and Washington filed complaints and letters with a federal judge, the Department of Justice's Civil Rights Division and Attorney General Janet Reno after GOP consultant Edward J. Rollins bragged to reporters about spreading $500,000 around to hold down the black vote. In addition, a group of black ministers, led by Jesse Jackson, filed a slander suit against Rollins.

Despite a retraction by Rollins and denials by Gov.-elect Christine Todd Whitman, Rollins' verbal shocker cost him clients, lawyers' fees and, perhaps, his reputation as a pre-eminent political strategist and operative. It also cast a cloud over Whitman, who, rather than basking in her come-from-behind victory over Gov. James J. Florio, had to try frantically to scrub the tarnish off her victory.

A Flurry of Denials

There was no immediate evidence that Rollins' allegations, if true, would account for the election's outcome. But much of the heat Rollins generated radiated from his reference to "street money" or "walking-around money," which he averred was common currency in black precincts. "We played the game the way the game is played in New Jersey," Rollins told a breakfast gathering of reporters in Washington on Nov. 9.

That prompted a flurry of denials. Many who responded to Rollins' remarks hotly insisted that he did not know what he was talking about. These included Rollins' own candidate in the New Jersey race, Whitman: "It did not happen," she announced. Flat denials also came from her campaign staff — including Rollins himself, who on Nov. 10 issued a statement saying his own remarks had been "inaccurate" and "not true."

But New Jersey newspapers on Nov. 11 and 12 reported remarks made right after the Nov. 2 vote by a Whitman spokesman who referred to "vote suppression" and by Whitman's brother, Webster Todd Jr., who spoke of "keeping the vote light in other areas."

The puzzling turn of events left some GOP officials worrying that they would be tarred as a party willing to employ questionable tactics. "I don't know what would possess him to do that," said Dave Carney, deputy executive director of the National Republican Senatorial Committee. Whether Rollins lied in the first instance or

in the latter, "it all seems pretty weird to me."

Disbelief was also voiced by many black ministers, who Rollins had said accepted "contributions to their favorite charity" from Republican operatives and, in exchange, soft-pedaled their pre-election exhortations to African-American voters. The objections from clerics were echoed by many members of the Congressional Black Caucus who found the implication offensive.

"I don't really believe that he did pay off ministers to keep the vote down," said Rep. Charles B. Rangel, D-N.Y. "I think he should be made to identify his co-conspirators. It's unfair to broad-brush an entire community."

David Bositis, a senior research associate at the Joint Center for Political and Economic Studies in Washington, said the indignation of black ministers and officials involved a certain amount of "posturing." At the same time, he said, "street money" was by no means exclusive to black precincts. "I think it's stretching it and somewhat unfair to talk about it in terms of minority communities," he said. "It's more disguised in white suburban places."

In the suburbs, he said, the money went to poll watchers and campaign workers. In the black community, he said, where candidates used little television advertising, "walking-around money" was crucial. In black communities get-out-the-vote drives were particularly important, and those who ran them often were students, housewives and others with little income. "To those people, getting $50 or $75 or $100 is very much a part of politics," he said. "It's not spent on media, so where do you think it goes?"

Bositis objected to what he called a double standard being applied to the black community. "Why is it that all black people have to be involved for pristine motives?" he asked. "I really hate these people who want to take politics out of politics," he said. "To hear these people talk, no one's involved in politics but saints and virgins."

Who Shrank Florio's Vote?

Also subject to contention was the actual effect of any vote-suppression effort. Janice Ballou of the Eagleton Institute at Rutgers University said exit polling showed that about 8 percent of the Nov. 2 vote was cast by blacks, a drop of about one-third from the 12 percent in 1989. Ballou said black turnout had been about 10 percent of the total New Jersey vote in the 1992 presidential election.

But Florio had another problem besides the lowered turnout. He appeared to have received a solid majority of the black vote but well under the 90 percent that other Democrats typically received. "If Jim Florio had paid a little bit more attention to black voters this time around, this wouldn't have happened," said Bositis. "Ed Rollins took the black vote seriously, which Jim Florio didn't."

comparison belittled the enormity of the Holocaust. In the flurry, Whitman's principal points were largely overlooked: that the Florio proposal went too far in requiring a woman to name a child's father in order to become eligible for public assistance and in funneling welfare checks to a minor mother through her parents.

Whitman's personal wealth also provided fodder for her opponent. After she released her most recent tax returns — which showed that she and her husband earned $3.7 million in 1992 — the Florio team emphasized the deductions

the Whitmans took for two farms they owned.

Playing the class card for all it was worth, the Florio campaign questioned whether one of the properties was a real working farm. They released a booklet filled with caustic suggestions about the farm's use. Florio campaign workers stood outside the Whitman farm to distribute the packet to journalists going to tour the farm. The issue came to a head when Whitman chased off Florio campaign people who were videotaping her farm for use as a backdrop for one of their political television ads.

Invoking a Memory

Later, however, Whitman refocused on the central goal of her campaign — hammering home the governor's record. Rep. Marge Roukema, R-N.J., said Whitman "began to remind voters how angry, how bitterly angry they were at Florio. She just rekindled that anger, at the last moment."

Whitman also exploited the outsider theme that had worked well for candidates in both parties thus far in the 1990s. "I think as a woman and not a professional politician, people wanted a change and were willing to give her a chance," said Roukema.

Whitman's political résumé was slim for a would-be governor. She was a member of the Somerset County Board of Chosen Freeholders, the county's governing body, for five years. She also was appointed to the New Jersey Board of Public Utilities under Florio's predecessor, Republican Thomas H. Kean. She served until 1990, when Florio came to office.

That was the year Whitman found the limelight. She was the "sacrificial" Republican chosen to oppose Democrat Bill Bradley, New Jersey's popular senior senator, in that fall's general election. But by running not against Bradley but against Florio and his tax increase, Whitman won a stunning 47 percent of the vote and became the front-runner to oppose Florio in 1993.

Rumors of Revival

Even before Bill Clinton won the presidency, reporters had become fascinated with the possibility of a Florio comeback. A May 1992 story in The New York Times was headlined: "Bruised But Not Out: Florio's Comeback Bid With Voters." The (Bergen) Record ran a poll in March 1993 with a headline: "Florio Ahead."

Florio had pressed the Legislature for tough crime legislation and a ban on assault weapons, provoking a confrontation with the National Rifle Association and winning national attention.

For a time, it appeared that Florio would have one final triumph attributed to his stubborn persistence. He had won his first term as governor after 12 years of hard fighting for the job. Elected to Congress with the "Watergate babies" class of 1974, he had soon turned his attention to statewide office. He ran for governor in 1977 and lost in the primary. Winning the nomination four years later, he lost narrowly in the 1981 general election to Kean.

But after Kean had finished two terms, Florio stormed into office in 1989, crushing his fellow House member, GOP Rep. Jim Courter (1979-91), with more than 60 percent of the vote.

In his 15-year tenure in Congress, Florio had been active in environmental causes, earning much of the credit for the federal "superfund" program. But the superfund fight illustrated a problem that plagued Florio throughout his career.

While respected for his intelligence, he paid a price for the abrasive and intense personality that often made him difficult to work with. Because he would not yield on several provisions of the superfund law, for example, he was denied a leading role in the final formation of the bill.

Florio's stubborn streak was on display again in the 1990 tax controversy. At his insistence, the Legislature rushed the tax increases through with little public debate. Florio seemed unable to explain to voters just why the increases were needed; in fact, he seemed to "enthusiastically back the tax increases," said Janice Ballou, director of Rutgers University's Eagleton poll.

As Salmore of Rutgers summed it up: "He raised taxes, he lied about it, and he smiled when he was doing it."

Low Urban Turnout Hurts

While the election tally was close — roughly 33,000 votes separated the two candidates — Florio lost in at least two counties usually considered Democratic strongholds. He got just 47 percent of the vote in Mercer County, home to Trenton, the state capital. He also lost Passaic County, which included Paterson, the state's third-largest city.

In addition, he had much smaller margins of victory than he needed in some of the state's traditionally Democratic urban areas. Ballou said that strong voter participation overall (more than 60 percent statewide) was attributable to higher turnout in the suburbs; urban turnout was low. Florio held Whitman to slim majorities in Bergen and Ocean counties, suburban areas that usually were bedrock Republican. But Whitman came closer than expected in the Democratic-leaning counties of Cumberland, Cape May and Burlington. ∎

GOP's Allen Takes Virginia In Surprise Landslide

When the 1993 election season opened in Virginia, Democratic state Attorney General Mary Sue Terry was widely expected to cruise to an easy gubernatorial victory over former U.S. Rep. George F. Allen, a Republican.

An air of inevitability surrounded Terry's campaign, attracting a steady flow of campaign contributions. Allen, however, campaigned vigorously throughout the summer while Terry was criticized for failing to capitalize on her early lead.

On Nov. 2, Allen scored a landslide victory over Terry, ending 12 years of Democratic control of the governor's office. It was Allen's first statewide bid. Terry's 41 percent showing was the worst by a Democrat since Virginia began popular elections for governor in 1851.

Allen scored crushing majorities in nearly every region of the state. He carried all but 16 of the state's 136 counties and independent cities. In 21 municipalities, he received 70 percent or more of the vote.

Democrats won only one of the state's three statewide constitutional offices: Lt. Gov. Donald S. Beyer Jr. was re-elected, defeating the GOP's controversial nominee, Michael Farris, a home-schooling advocate and former Moral Majority activist. Republican James Gilmore prevailed over Democrat William Dolan to become state attorney general.

Different Campaign Styles

The featured issues included crime and gun control. Allen's vow to end parole for violent offenders proved more compelling than Terry's call for a five-day waiting period for handgun purchases.

Overriding any issue, however, was the difference between Allen's and Terry's campaign styles. Terry was no match for the indefatigable Allen, who appeared genuinely to relish each encounter with voters. Terry was criticized for a manner that many found aloof, while Allen was admired for his "aw-shucks" affability.

Allen got more than 1 million votes and 58 percent of the total, a showing all the more remarkable for the amount of

ground he had to make up in the race. In early 1993, polls had shown Terry with a 29 percentage-point lead.

The most compelling theme offered by Allen was change, the same cause heralded by candidates in both parties across the country in 1992.

Allen campaigned less against Terry than against the Virginia Democratic establishment. Democrats had held the governorship and the attorney general's office since 1982 (and the lieutenant governor's office since 1978). In recent years, however, the party's united front had been riven by a high-profile feud between the state's two leading Democratic officeholders, Gov. L. Douglas Wilder and Sen. Charles S. Robb, which damaged both men's careers. The Democrats also benefited little from having one of their own in the White House. President Clinton was not popular in the state, having lost there to George Bush in 1992 with even less of the vote (40.6 percent) than Terry would get in 1993.

For her part, Terry, a moderate from conservative Southern Virginia, repudiated some of Clinton's policies and largely distanced herself from Wilder and Robb. But having twice been elected to statewide office, she found it difficult to convince voters that she did not belong in the same tent with her party's best-known leaders.

Prior to the campaign year, relatively few Virginians were familiar with Allen, 41, except as the son of the late George Allen Sr., who had coached the Washington Redskins football team in the 1970s. But the younger Allen, who played football and received his law degree at the University of Virginia, capitalized on Virginians' recent disillusionment with Democrats. He labeled his opponent a "Robb-Wilder-Terry" Democrat.

Role of Religion

Much of the Democrats' effort was aimed not at Allen but at Farris. Farris, a Baptist minister as well as a lawyer, represented the conservative Christian movement within the state GOP. He became the focal point for the Demo-crats, who viewed his nomination as a providential opportunity to label the entire GOP ticket extremist.

In Farris' case, the label stuck. But Terry and Dolan failed in their attempts to paint their rivals as tools of Christian conservative leaders such as Pat Robertson, the religious broadcaster and 1988 presidential candidate, and the Rev. Jerry Falwell, former head of the Moral Majority, both of whom had their headquarters in Virginia.

While Farris did not win, his presence on the ballot was credited with energizing many Christian conservatives, who came to the polls and boosted the GOP ticket.

David Wilhelm, chairman of the Democratic National Committee, called the Virginia results "an impressive performance" by religious conservatives who "obviously turned their voters out."

Weak in the North

Unlike in 1989, when Wilder cobbled together a bare majority to become the state's first black governor, Terry was unable to generate excitement among Virginia voters as she sought to become the commonwealth's first female governor. She did better among women than among men, but an exit poll by Mason-Dixon Political/Media Research found 52 percent of the women surveyed voted for Allen.

Wilder had won largely by scoring in the vote-rich Northern Virginia suburbs of Washington, where he ran up a margin of 15 percentage points. His support for abortion rights was considered a crucial issue in this swing region.

But in 1993, Terry was unable to capitalize on the abortion issue. Despite her haranguing of Allen as "multiple choice," she could not convincingly brand him an opponent of abortion rights. (Allen said the only changes in state law that he would seek would be restrictions such as a waiting period and parental notification.)

In the end, Allen edged Terry in Northern Virginia by one percentage point. ∎

Perot Tries To Hold On to Influence

For a presidential candidate who failed to carry a single state or congressional district in 1992, Ross Perot continued to command a lot of attention on Capitol Hill in 1993.

From marshaling grass-roots support on congressional reform to playing a lead role in opposing the North American Free Trade Agreement (NAFTA), Perot kept himself in the center of national debate as no recent independent or third-party candidate had.

He did it because he had a base from which to speak. In drawing the highest vote share in 1992 (19 percent) of any independent or third-party candidate in 80 years, Perot demonstrated a broad-based appeal that stretched across regions and voting blocs. He may not have won any sizable constituency, but he drew a respectable 10 percent to 30 percent almost everywhere.

With Perot choosing to remain on the scene, the two major parties were unable to co-opt his following as they had those of major third-party movements in the past. And Perot tried to use his supporters' anger with government and the political process to sustain himself as an independent political force.

Some of that force seemed to have been spent, and fruitlessly, on opposition to NAFTA, which passed despite Perot's vigorous opposition. Perot's standing in public opinion polls, already eroding, dropped perceptibly after his televised NAFTA debate with Vice President Al Gore on Nov. 9.

Nevertheless, Perot remained a factor that members of Congress had to consider as they cast votes in Washington and prepared for re-election bids. He represented a threat to members from both parties, but Republicans may have had the greater concern because most Perot voters came out of a GOP heritage of presidential voting.

Republicans and Perot shared common ground on a number of issues — from opposing President Clinton's budget plan to urging widespread reform of the Democratic-controlled Congress, although Perot and many free-trading Republicans parted company on NAFTA.

There was considerable concern within the GOP that Perot was stealing the party's thunder as the leading opposition voice to the Clinton administration.

He was a "shrill demagogue," GOP Sen. Thad Cochran of Mississippi was quoted as saying by The Boston Globe. "Getting too close to him is like getting on the back of a tiger."

While many members of both parties expressed ambivalence about Perot, few could afford to ignore his supporters: More than half the House members (220) repre-

sented districts in which Perot drew at least 20 percent of the vote. Roughly one of every six (75) members represented districts in which Perot drew at least 25 percent, including at least a dozen members from each region — 35 from the West alone.

In addition, more than half the 1994 Senate races (20 of 34) would be contested in states in which Perot drew at least 20 percent of the vote, including five of the six states — Arizona, Minnesota, Missouri, Ohio and Wyoming — in which Senate seats had been opened by retirements.

Perot Voters and Congress

Perot voters split almost evenly between the two parties in 1992 congressional voting. According to exit polling in 1992 by the network consortium Voter Research and Surveys, 51 percent preferred the Republican House candidate; 49 percent, the Democrat. There was a pattern, though, to the results. The higher Perot's percentage in a district, the more apt that district was to elect a Republican to Congress. Perot ran poorly in Southern minority districts and urban areas of the Rust Belt, which almost exclusively elected Democrats to the House.

But in many areas of the country where Perot ran best — the West, New England, the Plains states, around his Dallas base, in economically distressed parts of the Rust Belt and in high-growth districts on Florida's coasts — Republicans had long done well in congressional voting.

Perot also tended to run well in places where there was identifiable anti-incumbent sentiment. He ran above his 19 percent nationwide share in 13 of the 14 states that passed congressional term-limit measures. The exception was Clinton's home state of Arkansas. And in nearly two-thirds of the districts (15 of 24) in which House incumbents were beaten, Perot drew at least 20 percent of the vote.

When members of Congress talked about Perot, they often tried to separate the man from the movement.

GOP Rep. Bill Paxon of New York said the members of Perot's nonpartisan United We Stand America (UWSA), whom he had met often, emphasized that they were involved in politics because they "want to effect change," not further the political ambitions of Ross Perot. "I don't look at this [movement] as monolithic or blindly loyal to Perot," said Paxon.

Yet members of Congress were not able to step between Perot and his supporters. In the past, the two major parties had been able to slide left or right after an election to absorb the followers of an independent or third-party movement. But a study released in July by the Democratic Leadership Council (DLC) found that three-fourths of 1992 Perot voters would vote for the Texas billionaire again in 1996.

One of the DLC study's major findings was that Perot voters distrusted large, established institutions, whether big business or labor unions or, by implication, political parties. And they had a particular distaste for Congress, viewing it as a living embodiment of the evils of the political process — greed, gridlock, privilege and special-interest influence.

"Indeed," wrote Clinton pollster Stanley B. Greenberg, who conducted the survey of Perot voters, "Congress and Perot are defined in direct opposition to one another: the Congress, self-seeking and deadlocked; Perot, honest, for people and results-oriented."

Republicans and Perot

Several Republican members of Congress, including House Minority Whip Newt Gingrich of Georgia and Texas' new senator, Kay Bailey Hutchison, joined UWSA. And Perot frequently appeared on Capitol Hill in 1993 in the company of Republican members.

In May, he met with House GOP freshmen, applauding their agenda for congressional reform. In June, eight Republican senators accompanied him as he presented millions of petition signatures urging Congress to cut spending before raising taxes. In early September, he showed up at the Capitol to lend support for Oklahoma GOP Rep. James M. Inhofe's fight to make public the names of members who signed House discharge petitions. The change, which Inhofe won, made it easier to force floor votes on bills opposed by the Democratic leadership.

UWSA members even held a vigil outside the district office of House Rules Committee Chairman Joe Moakley, D-Mass., to protest his resistance to the Inhofe initiative.

Paxon, who chaired the National Republican Congressional Committee, encouraged GOP House members to establish ties with UWSA chapters at home, and he said he hoped that Perot and the UWSA would embrace GOP candidates as the best vehicles for congressional change in 1994. Republicans and the Perot movement "are together on about 80 percent of the issues," said Paxon. "I don't look at this [UWSA] with fear and trepidation as some folks do in the party."

A Variety of Views

While some members made an appeal to Perot and his followers, others — even in districts where Perot ran well — were considerably less enthusiastic.

Eight-term Democratic Rep. Al Swift lumped Perot with conservative radio talk-show host Rush Limbaugh as a public figure who mouthed generalities about the nation's ills but failed to offer specific solutions. Swift represented a district in northwest Washington in which Perot drew 26 percent of the vote.

Swift, who had announced his plan to retire, saw Perot as a manifestation of a "grumbly, disenchanted public that doesn't think government works." And Perot's continued presence on the political scene, Swift said, only worsened what was already a difficult environment in which to govern. "It makes it harder to debate solutions that will work."

Swift, however, tried to speak to areas of Perot's agenda during the campaign, such as the need for an aggressive industrial policy. But he was aware that he could not always be in agreement with Perot. You can't "shave what you believe [in] that much," he said.

Freshman Democratic Rep. David Minge of Minnesota shared some of Swift's concerns about Perot's backers. They come to meetings wanting "100 percent answers," he said. "They don't want to hear the problems about making changes. They want action."

However, Minge stressed his empathy with Perot backers. A self-described "country lawyer," Minge said he felt much of the same frustration with government before he ran for Congress. But as a member, he said, he became aware of the need to focus his attention on a handful of issues and came to appreciate the value of compromise.

Rep. Pat Danner, a freshman Democrat from a Missouri district that offered marginal support for the party, seemed less concerned than Minge with the impact of Perot and his movement.

Perot drew 27 percent of the presidential vote in Danner's district. But since she defeated GOP Rep. Tom Coleman by nearly 30,000 votes, she thought she would have been victorious with or without Perot on the ballot.

Danner, who opposed NAFTA and the Clinton budget, said she did not feel much pressure from Perot backers.

And she did not see why the presidential results in her district should affect her voting behavior in Congress. "Maybe we're all egomaniacs" in Congress, she said, "but we think our future depends on our own performances."

The Third-Party Option

In most parts of the country, Perot supporters rallied under the UWSA banner. But in Pennsylvania, a group of Perot backers took a step that Perot so far had declined to take. They formed a third party. Known as the Patriot Party, it made an early impact: Its candidate finished second in a special state Senate election in the Philadelphia suburbs in July — ahead of the Democratic entry. The party fielded about two dozen candidates in Pennsylvania in the fall, including one for the state Supreme Court, but it failed to score any breakthroughs.

Perot's Dallas headquarters had contact with the Patriot Party but had not yet embraced it. In a swing through Pennsylvania in August urging opposition to NAFTA, Perot appeared under the auspices of UWSA. He talked of his followers as a vital swing vote in 1994 that could spell defeat for NAFTA's congressional supporters.

Yet Patriot Party state Chairman Nicholas R. Sabatine III saw little prospect for change in Congress if the Perot forces simply moved from district to district supporting either a Democrat or a Republican. He argued that it would take a new third party fielding candidates to offer voters a real alternative in 1994. ∎

Congressional Departures

(as of Dec. 31, 1993)

RETIRING

Senate	Date Announced	Office Since	Age	House	Date Announced	Office Since	Age
John C. Danforth, R-Mo.	Feb. 1, 1993	1976	57	Mike Kopetski, D-Ore. (5)	Oct. 19, 1993	1991	44
Dennis DeConcini, D-Ariz.	Sept. 16, 1993	1977	56	Marilyn Lloyd, D-Tenn. (3)	Oct. 1, 1993	1975	64
Dave Durenberger, R-Minn.	Sept. 16, 1993	1978	59	Romano L. Mazzoli, D-Ky. (3)	Sept. 3, 1993	1971	61
Howard M.				Alex McMillan, R-N.C. (9)	Nov. 29, 1993	1985	61
Metzenbaum, D-Ohio	June 29, 1993	1976 [1]	76	Robert H. Michel, R-Ill. (18)	Oct. 4, 1993	1957	70
Donald W.				Timothy J. Penny, D-Minn. (1)	Aug. 6, 1993	1983	42
Riegle Jr., D-Mich.	Sept. 28, 1993	1976	55	J. J. Pickle, D-Texas (10)	Dec. 3, 1993	1963	80
Malcolm Wallop, R-Wyo.	Sept. 9, 1993	1977	60	George E.			
				Sangmeister, D-Ill. (11)	Oct. 19, 1993	1989	62
				Bob Smith, R-Ore. (2)	Nov. 24, 1993	1983	62
				Al Swift, D-Wash. (2)	Oct. 25, 1991 [2]	1979	58
				Tim Valentine, D-N.C. (2)	Nov. 16, 1993	1983	67

RESIGNING

	Date Announced	Office Since	Age
Glenn English, D-Okla. (6)	Dec. 10, 1993	1975	53

ANNOUNCED FOR OR LIKELY TO SEEK OTHER OFFICE

House	Office Since	Age	Office		Office Since	Age	Office
Michael A. Andrews, D-Texas (25)	1983	49	Senate	Ronald K. Machtley, R-R.I. (1)	1989	45	Governor
Helen Delich Bentley, R-Md. (2)	1985	70	Governor	Arthur Ravenel Jr., R-S.C. (1)	1987	66	Governor
Jim Cooper, D-Tenn. (4)	1983	39	Senate	Tom Ridge, R-Pa. (21)	1983	48	Governor
Rod Grams, R-Minn. (6)	1993	45	Senate	Rick Santorum, R-Pa. (18)	1991	35	Senate
Fred Grandy, R-Iowa (5)	1987	45	Governor	Jim Slattery, D-Kan. (2)	1983	45	Governor
Michael Huffington, R-Calif. (22)	1993	46	Senate	Don Sundquist, R-Tenn. (7)	1983	57	Governor
Jon Kyl, R-Ariz. (4)	1987	51	Senate	Alan Wheat, D-Mo. (5)	1983	42	Senate

[1] *Metzenbaum also served January to December 1974.*
[2] *Swift announced in 1991 that he would not seek re-election after 1992.*

1992 ELECTION
District Vote for President

Listed below are the 1992 presidential election vote tallies for Bill Clinton, George Bush and Ross Perot within each congressional district in the 50 states.

The results, computed by Polidata with the assistance of Congressional Quarterly, were based on records provided by state, county and municipal election officials nationwide.

In some jurisdictions, precincts were split between two or more congressional districts and official records did not break out the presidential vote within the precincts. In those split precincts, the presidential vote was estimated, extrapolated from each precinct's House election vote. Also, in some

jurisdictions with more than one House district, official records did not break out the absentee presidential vote by district. In those jurisdictions, the absentee presidential vote for each district was estimated, extrapolated from the jurisdiction's total House absentee vote.

The entry for each district includes its existing representative, the total number of votes cast for Clinton, Bush and Perot, and the vote tally and percentage for each candidate. The winner's percentage is in **boldface.** Due to rounding, percentages may not add to 100. Votes cast for other presidential candidates are not included in these computations.

District, Member	Votes cast	Clinton vote	Clinton %	Bush vote	Bush %	Perot vote	Perot %
Alabama							
1. Sonny Callahan, R	229,420	84,202	37	118,421	**52**	26,797	12
2. Terry Everett, R	234,199	82,550	35	124,272	**53**	27,377	12
3. Glen Browder, D	220,948	92,142	42	105,034	**48**	23,772	11
4. Tom Bevill, D	240,209	104,557	44	107,087	**45**	28,565	12
5. Robert E. "Bud" Cramer, D	249,298	102,124	41	110,256	**44**	36,918	15
6. Spencer Bachus, R	284,539	77,506	27	180,798	**64**	26,235	9
7. Earl F. Hilliard, D	218,801	146,955	**67**	58,365	27	13,481	6
Alaska							
AL Don Young, R	253,775	78,294	31	102,000	**40**	73,481	29
Arizona							
1. Sam Coppersmith, D	262,174	88,247	34	105,784	**40**	68,143	26
2. Ed Pastor, D	145,112	74,588	**51**	41,757	29	28,767	20
3. Bob Stump, R	269,256	86,060	32	109,840	**41**	73,356	27
4. Jon Kyl, R	276,531	86,922	31	118,927	**43**	70,682	26
5. Jim Kolbe, R	276,712	115,986	**42**	104,301	38	56,425	20
6. Karan English, D	239,092	91,247	38	91,477	**38**	56,368	24
Arkansas							
1. Blanche Lambert, D	222,861	131,585	**59**	71,160	32	20,116	9
2. Ray Thornton, D	234,705	130,435	**56**	84,922	36	19,348	8
3. Tim Hutchinson, R	252,453	109,111	**43**	107,351	43	35,991	14
4. Jay Dickey, R	232,260	134,692	**58**	73,891	32	23,677	10
California							
1. Dan Hamburg, D	255,248	119,491	**47**	74,597	29	61,160	24
2. Wally Herger, R	262,626	93,823	36	101,505	**39**	67,298	26
3. Vic Fazio, D	243,903	99,781	**41**	90,799	37	53,323	22
4. John T. Doolittle, R	287,716	97,501	34	117,155	**41**	73,060	25
5. Robert T. Matsui, D	236,705	120,577	**51**	73,562	31	42,566	18
6. Lynn Woolsey, D	301,785	169,301	**56**	71,564	24	60,920	20
7. George Miller, D	230,553	140,159	**61**	51,356	22	39,038	17
8. Nancy Pelosi, D	247,777	187,201	**76**	39,396	16	21,180	9
9. Ronald V. Dellums, D	237,315	186,714	**79**	29,394	12	21,207	9
10. Bill Baker, R	300,821	127,450	**42**	107,191	36	66,180	22
11. Richard W. Pombo, R	195,757	79,432	**41**	75,319	38	41,006	21
12. Tom Lantos, D	242,336	139,244	**57**	64,967	27	38,125	16
13. Pete Stark, D	214,955	116,829	**54**	55,100	26	43,026	20
14. Anna G. Eshoo, D	268,505	143,727	**54**	71,736	27	53,042	20
15. Norman Y. Mineta, D	274,553	127,060	**46**	83,301	30	64,192	23
16. Don Edwards, D	164,993	86,418	**52**	44,693	27	33,882	21
17. Sam Farr, D	212,244	111,937	**53**	57,990	27	42,317	20
18. Gary A. Condit, D	181,900	74,357	**41**	67,898	37	39,645	22
19. Richard H. Lehman, D	223,225	85,049	38	97,124	**44**	41,052	18
20. Cal Dooley, D	119,184	55,942	**47**	44,674	37	18,568	16
21. Bill Thomas, R	204,027	66,284	32	94,727	**46**	43,016	21
22. Michael Huffington, R	259,890	106,815	**41**	92,045	35	61,030	23

District, Member	Votes cast	Clinton vote	Clinton %	Bush vote	Bush %	Perot vote	Perot %
23. Elton Gallegly, R	214,896	82,613	**38**	74,106	34	58,177	27
24. Anthony C. Beilenson, D	265,925	128,572	**48**	79,728	30	57,625	22
25. Howard P. "Buck" McKeon, R	230,690	83,305	36	89,987	**39**	57,398	25
26. Howard L. Berman, D	127,853	72,673	**57**	31,013	24	24,167	19
27. Carlos J. Moorhead, R	221,114	98,057	**44**	80,986	37	42,071	19
28. David Dreier, R	219,225	82,958	38	90,644	**41**	45,623	21
29. Henry A. Waxman, D	276,374	183,233	**66**	55,924	20	37,217	13
30. Xavier Becerra, D	89,970	56,378	**63**	21,750	24	11,842	13
31. Matthew G. Martinez, D	115,315	59,616	**52**	37,250	32	18,449	16
32. Julian C. Dixon, D	189,140	147,623	**78**	23,956	13	17,561	9
33. Lucille Roybal-Allard, D	53,398	33,642	**63**	12,607	24	7,149	13
34. Esteban E. Torres, D	155,014	78,889	**51**	48,181	31	27,944	18
35. Maxine Waters, D	129,067	100,432	**78**	16,685	13	11,950	9
36. Jane Harman, D	269,118	111,014	**41**	95,646	36	62,458	23
37. Walter R. Tucker III, D	122,727	90,523	**74**	19,299	16	12,905	11
38. Steve Horn, R	198,971	88,728	**45**	66,647	33	43,596	22
39. Ed Royce, R	229,808	78,305	34	100,669	**44**	50,834	22
40. Jerry Lewis, R	216,771	76,363	35	86,453	**40**	53,955	25
41. Jay C. Kim, R	184,680	64,666	35	78,902	**43**	41,112	22
42. George E. Brown Jr., D	167,770	76,964	**46**	54,978	33	35,828	21
43. Ken Calvert, R	201,074	76,040	38	76,837	**38**	48,197	24
44. Al McCandless, R	214,819	87,180	**41**	76,772	36	50,867	24
45. Dana Rohrabacher, R	250,148	80,646	32	105,893	**42**	63,609	25
46. Robert K. Dornan, R	119,583	44,352	37	47,689	**40**	27,542	23
47. C. Christopher Cox, R	278,206	86,279	31	127,700	**46**	64,227	23
48. Ron Packard, R	246,182	71,621	29	108,581	**44**	65,980	27
49. Lynn Schenk, D	262,771	114,081	**43**	82,834	32	65,856	25
50. Bob Filner, D	142,643	69,546	**49**	42,830	30	30,267	21
51. Randy "Duke" Cunningham, R	268,920	86,870	32	108,470	**40**	73,580	27
52. Duncan Hunter, R	219,510	74,913	34	81,421	**37**	63,176	29
Colorado							
1. Patricia Schroeder, D	241,822	135,372	**56**	63,207	26	43,243	18
2. David E. Skaggs, D	272,882	123,341	**45**	82,991	30	66,550	24
3. Scott McInnis, R	266,845	107,330	**40**	92,314	35	67,201	25
4. Wayne Allard, R	254,386	93,922	37	97,062	**38**	63,402	25
5. Joel Hefley, R	253,785	70,671	28	125,664	**50**	57,450	23
6. Dan Schaefer, R	268,823	99,045	37	101,613	**38**	68,165	25
Connecticut							
1. Barbara B. Kennelly, D	267,926	133,686	**50**	82,086	31	52,154	19
2. Sam Gejdenson, D	265,445	113,553	**43**	79,110	30	72,782	27
3. Rosa DeLauro, D	271,395	121,163	**45**	96,085	35	54,147	20
4. Christopher Shays, R	259,996	109,122	42	110,072	**42**	40,802	16
5. Gary A. Franks, R	266,184	93,966	35	111,327	**42**	60,891	23
6. Nancy L. Johnson, R	278,456	110,828	**40**	99,633	36	67,995	24
Delaware							
AL Michael N. Castle, R	287,580	126,054	**44**	102,313	36	59,213	21
Florida							
1. Earl Hutto, D	230,245	59,247	26	117,712	**51**	53,286	23
2. Pete Peterson, D	240,191	101,623	**42**	91,760	38	46,808	19
3. Corrine Brown, D	162,927	93,384	**57**	49,288	30	20,255	12
4. Tillie Fowler, R	248,368	75,323	30	131,930	**53**	41,115	17
5. Karen L. Thurman, D	264,800	110,058	**42**	90,598	34	64,144	24
6. Cliff Stearns, R	238,644	74,349	31	113,029	**47**	51,266	21
7. John L. Mica, R	236,157	81,312	34	105,263	**45**	49,582	21
8. Bill McCollum, R	213,710	67,724	32	102,514	**48**	43,472	20
9. Michael Bilirakis, R	273,837	93,626	34	112,832	**41**	67,379	25
10. C.W. Bill Young, R	269,457	107,685	**40**	97,492	36	64,280	24
11. Sam M. Gibbons, D	201,820	82,898	**41**	79,126	39	39,796	20
12. Charles T. Canady, R	196,616	67,802	34	89,585	**46**	39,229	20
13. Dan Miller, R	290,518	100,950	35	124,271	**43**	65,297	22
14. Porter J. Goss, R	280,610	87,856	31	129,605	**46**	63,149	23
15. Jim Bacchus, D	271,113	83,679	31	117,685	**43**	69,749	26
16. Tom Lewis, R	274,499	97,621	36	108,426	**39**	68,452	25
17. Carrie Meek, D	133,734	99,539	**74**	24,721	18	9,474	7
18. Ileana Ros-Lehtinen, R	166,496	54,252	33	94,963	**57**	17,281	10
19. Harry A. Johnston, D	294,440	158,752	**54**	88,829	30	46,859	16

District, Member	Votes cast	Clinton vote	Clinton %	Bush vote	Bush %	Perot vote	Perot %
20. Peter Deutsch, D	249,018	116,547	**47**	83,626	34	48,845	20
21. Lincoln Diaz-Balart, R	146,404	45,561	31	85,342	**58**	15,501	11
22. E. Clay Shaw Jr., R	258,220	114,938	**45**	98,148	38	45,134	17
23. Alcee L. Hastings, D	153,255	96,629	**63**	34,659	23	21,967	14
Georgia							
1. Jack Kingston, R	193,275	75,066	39	89,692	**46**	28,517	15
2. Sanford D. Bishop Jr., D	161,616	97,077	**60**	47,171	29	17,368	11
3. Mac Collins, R	218,492	80,954	37	105,426	**48**	32,112	15
4. John Linder, R	251,634	101,990	41	116,418	**46**	33,226	13
5. John Lewis, D	207,571	140,270	**68**	52,087	25	15,214	7
6. Newt Gingrich, R	279,991	82,355	29	155,760	**56**	41,876	15
7. George ''Buddy'' Darden, D	200,375	77,103	38	93,175	**47**	30,097	15
8. J. Roy Rowland, D	209,440	83,332	40	94,018	**45**	32,090	15
9. Nathan Deal, D	201,959	70,969	35	98,184	**49**	32,806	16
10. Don Johnson, D	205,630	81,014	39	95,164	**46**	29,452	14
11. Cynthia McKinney, D	183,617	118,708	**65**	48,026	26	16,883	9
Hawaii							
1. Neil Abercrombie, D	183,226	87,632	**48**	72,156	39	23,438	13
2. Patsy T. Mink, D	185,823	91,630	**49**	64,635	35	29,558	16
Idaho							
1. Larry LaRocco, D	244,963	75,499	31	101,787	**42**	67,677	28
2. Michael D. Crapo, R	225,090	61,514	27	100,858	**45**	62,718	28
Illinois							
1. Bobby L. Rush, D	263,868	214,045	**81**	32,628	12	17,195	7
2. Mel Reynolds, D	243,494	194,796	**80**	31,730	13	16,968	7
3. William O. Lipinski, D	263,729	108,211	**41**	102,626	39	52,892	20
4. Luis V. Gutierrez, D	126,980	82,497	**65**	29,091	23	15,392	12
5. Dan Rostenkowski, D	243,729	124,437	**51**	80,139	33	39,153	16
6. Henry J. Hyde, R	261,041	86,444	33	121,863	**47**	52,734	20
7. Cardiss Collins, D	235,772	184,383	**78**	35,437	15	15,952	7
8. Philip M. Crane, R	249,310	76,327	31	118,714	**48**	54,269	22
9. Sidney R. Yates, D	253,302	155,503	**61**	68,485	27	29,314	12
10. John Edward Porter, R	261,269	108,149	41	112,401	**43**	40,719	16
11. George E. Sangmeister, D	248,732	108,447	**44**	90,085	36	50,200	20
12. Jerry F. Costello, D	244,597	132,556	**54**	69,850	29	42,191	17
13. Harris W. Fawell, R	275,076	88,324	32	128,627	**47**	58,125	21
14. Dennis Hastert, R	241,719	83,107	34	105,698	**44**	52,914	22
15. Thomas W. Ewing, R	253,593	107,962	**43**	98,372	39	47,259	19
16. Donald Manzullo, R	260,220	95,102	37	108,949	**42**	56,169	22
17. Lane Evans, D	265,292	124,173	**47**	95,553	36	45,566	17
18. Robert H. Michel, R	277,510	116,864	**42**	113,656	41	46,990	17
19. Glenn Poshard, D	277,820	131,483	**47**	95,672	34	50,665	18
20. Richard J. Durbin, D	280,739	130,383	**46**	94,532	34	55,824	20
Indiana							
1. Peter J. Visclosky, D	222,665	117,126	**53**	68,403	31	37,136	17
2. Philip R. Sharp, D	233,680	81,915	35	101,341	**43**	50,424	22
3. Tim Roemer, D	215,549	82,483	38	91,708	**43**	41,358	19
4. Jill L. Long, D	221,636	69,292	31	102,779	**46**	49,565	22
5. Steve Buyer, R	226,365	70,893	31	103,118	**46**	52,354	23
6. Dan Burton, R	269,169	61,171	23	153,280	**57**	54,718	20
7. John T. Myers, R	223,502	70,699	32	103,700	**46**	49,103	22
8. Frank McCloskey, D	243,948	103,697	**43**	97,070	40	43,181	18
9. Lee H. Hamilton, D	240,377	98,063	**41**	97,441	41	44,873	19
10. Andrew Jacobs Jr., D	196,201	92,514	**47**	70,458	36	33,229	17
Iowa							
1. Jim Leach, R	277,298	128,655	**46**	95,660	34	52,983	19
2. Jim Nussle, R	270,512	120,228	**44**	95,005	35	55,279	20
3. Jim Ross Lightfoot, R	264,038	120,495	**46**	96,515	37	47,028	18
4. Neal Smith, D	273,443	117,863	**43**	107,745	39	47,835	17
5. Fred Grandy, R	259,421	99,112	38	109,966	**42**	50,343	19
Kansas							
1. Pat Roberts, R	290,095	81,526	28	123,019	**42**	85,550	29
2. Jim Slattery, D	273,126	98,527	36	98,999	**36**	75,600	28
3. Jan Meyers, R	306,557	116,729	**38**	114,220	37	75,608	25

District, Member	Votes cast	Clinton vote	Clinton %	Bush vote	Bush %	Perot vote	Perot %
4. Dan Glickman, D	282,965	93,652	33	113,713	**40**	75,600	27

Kentucky
1. Tom Barlow, D	244,108	116,637	**48**	96,602	40	30,869	13
2. William H. Natcher, D	239,486	98,955	41	107,339	**45**	33,192	14
3. Romano L. Mazzoli, D	285,246	143,824	**50**	105,520	37	35,902	13
4. Jim Bunning, R	241,468	94,335	39	106,695	**44**	40,438	17
5. Harold Rogers, R	229,310	109,591	**48**	95,831	42	23,888	10
6. Scotty Baesler, D	246,608	101,762	41	105,191	**43**	39,655	16

Louisiana
1. Robert L. Livingston, R	276,802	86,886	31	155,422	**56**	34,494	12
2. William J. Jefferson, D	221,710	153,342	**69**	54,555	25	13,813	6
3. W. J. "Billy" Tauzin, D	257,595	115,406	**45**	105,989	41	36,200	14
4. Cleo Fields, D	220,705	150,000	**68**	54,230	25	16,475	7
5. Jim McCrery, R	258,719	95,048	37	127,134	**49**	36,537	14
6. Richard H. Baker, R	263,628	92,040	35	135,915	**52**	35,673	14
7. Jimmy Hayes, D	261,673	123,248	**47**	100,140	38	38,285	15

Maine
1. Thomas H. Andrews, D	363,716	145,191	**40**	115,697	32	102,828	28
2. Olympia J. Snowe, R	313,028	118,229	**38**	90,807	29	103,992	33

Maryland
1. Wayne T. Gilchrest, R	249,392	93,165	37	109,039	**44**	47,188	19
2. Helen Delich Bentley, R	272,022	98,267	36	121,087	**45**	52,668	19
3. Benjamin L. Cardin, D	254,296	136,829	**54**	82,494	32	34,973	14
4. Albert R. Wynn, D	201,138	149,262	**74**	37,716	19	14,160	7
5. Steny H. Hoyer, D	240,415	107,618	**45**	95,356	40	37,441	16
6. Roscoe G. Bartlett, R	260,066	88,196	34	125,494	**48**	46,376	18
7. Kweisi Mfume, D	204,631	159,191	**78**	32,431	16	13,009	6
8. Constance A. Morella, R	295,119	156,043	**53**	103,477	35	35,599	12

Massachusetts
1. John W. Olver, D	271,098	130,311	**48**	72,246	27	68,541	25
2. Richard E. Neal, D	263,918	121,750	**46**	76,244	29	65,924	25
3. Peter I. Blute, R	271,207	122,900	**45**	84,711	31	63,596	23
4. Barney Frank, D	282,472	144,352	**51**	75,080	27	63,040	22
5. Martin T. Meehan, D	268,610	112,959	**42**	85,260	32	70,391	26
6. Peter G. Torkildsen, R	307,174	134,424	**44**	96,857	32	75,893	25
7. Edward J. Markey, D	299,499	150,102	**50**	87,432	29	61,965	21
8. Joseph P. Kennedy II, D	201,369	136,582	**68**	39,284	20	25,503	13
9. Joe Moakley, D	274,129	131,539	**48**	85,981	31	56,609	21
10. Gerry E. Studds, D	316,503	133,776	**42**	101,936	32	80,791	26

Michigan
1. Bart Stupak, D	285,215	118,879	**42**	100,997	35	65,339	23
2. Peter Hoekstra, R	280,608	95,342	34	127,008	**45**	58,258	21
3. Paul B. Henry, R	276,177	94,721	34	128,677	**47**	52,779	19
4. Dave Camp, R	276,046	104,709	**38**	103,464	37	67,873	25
5. James A. Barcia, D	264,214	118,699	**45**	84,525	32	60,990	23
6. Fred Upton, R	253,550	100,683	**40**	97,200	38	55,667	22
7. Nick Smith, R	255,949	96,940	**38**	96,336	38	62,673	24
8. Bob Carr, D	289,362	117,654	**41**	103,725	36	67,983	23
9. Dale E. Kildee, D	265,211	117,872	**44**	92,262	35	55,077	21
10. David E. Bonior, D	277,363	100,587	36	115,849	**42**	60,927	22
11. Joe Knollenberg, R	317,058	117,274	37	149,109	**47**	50,675	16
12. Sander M. Levin, D	283,639	119,055	**42**	115,065	41	49,519	17
13. William D. Ford, D	255,557	125,913	**49**	86,769	34	42,875	17
14. John Conyers Jr., D	221,544	180,007	**81**	28,937	13	12,600	6
15. Barbara-Rose Collins, D	178,791	144,092	**81**	26,421	15	8,278	5
16. John D. Dingell, D	269,010	118,079	**44**	97,968	36	52,963	20

Minnesota
1. Timothy J. Penny, D	283,440	109,829	**39**	98,384	35	75,227	27
2. David Minge, D	281,072	103,447	**37**	98,015	35	79,610	28
3. Jim Ramstad, R	327,023	129,171	**39**	117,975	36	79,877	24
4. Bruce F. Vento, D	287,097	148,046	**52**	79,690	28	59,361	21
5. Martin Olav Sabo, D	288,387	167,941	**58**	68,072	24	52,374	18
6. Rod Grams, R	303,250	119,847	**40**	101,495	33	81,908	27

District, Member	Votes cast	Clinton vote	Clinton %	Bush vote	Bush %	Perot vote	Perot %
7. Collin C. Peterson, D	271,593	104,359	**38**	103,624	38	63,610	23
8. James L. Oberstar, D	289,482	138,357	**48**	80,586	28	70,539	24
Mississippi							
1. Jamie L. Whitten, D	204,426	84,555	41	101,889	**50**	17,982	9
2. Bennie Thompson, D	181,207	105,052	**58**	66,350	37	9,805	5
3. G.V. "Sonny" Montgomery, D	200,489	67,645	34	116,689	**58**	16,155	8
4. Mike Parker, D	203,499	84,089	41	102,666	**50**	16,744	8
5. Gene Taylor, D	183,974	58,905	32	100,128	**54**	24,941	14
Missouri							
1. William L. Clay, D	236,360	161,794	**68**	44,980	19	29,586	13
2. James M. Talent, R	314,628	114,792	36	126,788	**40**	73,048	23
3. Richard A. Gephardt, D	272,783	120,866	**44**	87,406	32	64,511	24
4. Ike Skelton, D	256,934	94,951	37	96,752	**38**	65,231	25
5. Alan Wheat, D	258,198	134,932	**52**	67,503	26	55,763	22
6. Pat Danner, D	274,254	110,064	**40**	89,005	32	75,185	27
7. Mel Hancock, R	264,262	96,621	37	118,817	**45**	48,824	18
8. Bill Emerson, R	240,654	109,858	**46**	89,238	37	41,558	17
9. Harold L. Volkmer, D	265,696	109,995	**41**	90,669	34	65,032	24
Montana							
AL Pat Williams, D	405,939	154,507	**38**	144,207	36	107,225	26
Nebraska							
1. Doug Bereuter, R	247,771	80,700	33	107,092	**43**	59,979	24
2. Peter Hoagland, D	242,593	78,697	32	115,244	**48**	48,652	20
3. Bill Barrett, R	244,282	57,467	24	121,342	**50**	65,473	27
Nevada							
1. James Bilbray, D	225,445	98,801	**44**	70,586	31	56,058	25
2. Barbara F. Vucanovich, R	272,111	90,347	33	105,242	**39**	76,522	28
New Hampshire							
1. Bill Zeliff, R	267,639	101,415	38	104,653	**39**	61,571	23
2. Dick Swett, D	265,222	107,625	**41**	97,831	37	59,766	23
New Jersey							
1. Robert E. Andrews, D	244,312	118,060	**48**	78,095	32	48,157	20
2. William J. Hughes, D	250,284	101,718	**41**	97,696	39	50,870	20
3. H. James Saxton, R	283,075	114,503	**40**	113,583	40	54,989	19
4. Christopher H. Smith, R	266,010	105,335	40	109,907	**41**	50,768	19
5. Marge Roukema, R	294,403	99,733	34	146,004	**50**	48,666	17
6. Frank Pallone Jr., D	250,864	110,821	**44**	98,397	39	41,646	17
7. Bob Franks, R	282,146	115,846	41	125,592	**45**	40,708	14
8. Herb Klein, D	235,075	107,304	**46**	99,974	43	27,797	12
9. Robert G. Torricelli, D	256,781	122,676	**48**	102,578	40	31,527	12
10. Donald M. Payne, D	176,706	125,922	**71**	35,930	20	14,854	8
11. Dean A. Gallo, R	297,846	97,697	33	153,731	**52**	46,418	16
12. Dick Zimmer, R	302,575	121,447	40	130,651	**43**	50,477	17
13. Robert Menendez, D	174,782	95,144	**54**	64,727	37	14,911	9
New Mexico							
1. Steven H. Schiff, R	209,755	95,677	**46**	81,046	39	33,032	16
2. Joe Skeen, R	171,182	70,646	**41**	68,754	40	31,782	19
3. Bill Richardson, D	185,399	95,294	**51**	63,024	34	27,081	15
New York							
1. George J. Hochbrueckner, D	252,178	96,890	38	101,160	**40**	54,128	21
2. Rick A. Lazio, R	228,795	91,430	40	92,762	**41**	44,603	19
3. Peter T. King, R	287,738	126,112	**44**	121,176	42	40,450	14
4. David A. Levy, R	256,439	119,947	**47**	106,016	41	30,476	12
5. Gary L. Ackerman, D	250,156	131,095	**52**	88,586	35	30,475	12
6. Floyd H. Flake, D	152,443	115,253	**76**	27,855	18	9,335	6
7. Thomas J. Manton, D	164,704	91,803	**56**	57,783	35	15,118	9
8. Jerrold Nadler, D	218,835	169,005	**77**	37,614	17	12,216	6
9. Charles E. Schumer, D	205,601	121,110	**59**	66,917	33	17,574	9
10. Edolphus Towns, D	150,094	125,206	**83**	19,177	13	5,711	4
11. Major R. Owens, D	120,303	104,678	**87**	11,709	10	3,916	3
12. Nydia M. Velázquez, D	97,857	67,114	**69**	25,622	26	5,121	5

District, Member	Votes cast	Clinton vote	Clinton %	Bush vote	Bush %	Perot vote	Perot %
13. Susan Molinari, R	209,874	82,796	39	100,761	**48**	26,317	13
14. Carolyn B. Maloney, D	229,844	159,750	**70**	53,675	23	16,419	7
15. Charles B. Rangel, D	144,909	124,594	**86**	15,589	11	4,726	3
16. Jose E. Serrano, D	123,478	100,602	**81**	18,834	15	4,042	3
17. Eliot L. Engel, D	158,364	120,286	**76**	30,133	19	7,945	5
18. Nita M. Lowey, D	234,710	117,937	**50**	94,754	40	22,019	9
19. Hamilton Fish Jr., R	260,003	104,950	40	109,965	**42**	45,088	17
20. Benjamin A. Gilman, R	260,412	116,294	**45**	107,107	41	37,011	14
21. Michael R. McNulty, D	290,431	140,251	**48**	99,094	34	51,086	18
22. Gerald B. H. Solomon, R	278,759	99,988	36	116,238	**42**	62,533	22
23. Sherwood Boehlert, R	247,948	92,549	37	99,497	**40**	55,902	23
24. John M. McHugh, R	225,972	85,078	38	86,357	**38**	54,537	24
25. James T. Walsh, R	262,049	108,334	**41**	95,476	36	58,239	22
26. Maurice D. Hinchey, D	261,036	116,525	**45**	91,625	35	52,886	20
27. Bill Paxon, R	273,347	90,194	33	115,432	**42**	67,721	25
28. Louise M. Slaughter, D	271,066	119,055	**44**	103,544	38	48,467	18
29. John J. LaFalce, D	260,491	103,528	**40**	86,732	33	70,231	27
30. Jack Quinn, R	260,620	119,115	**46**	68,172	26	73,333	28
31. Amo Houghton, R	242,731	82,959	34	97,447	**40**	62,325	26
North Carolina							
1. Eva Clayton, D	182,464	111,398	**61**	53,026	29	18,040	10
2. Tim Valentine, D	214,701	85,542	40	98,516	**46**	30,643	14
3. H. Martin Lancaster, D	191,900	74,639	39	89,038	**46**	28,223	15
4. David Price, D	271,025	126,616	**47**	105,555	39	38,854	14
5. Stephen L. Neal, D	227,468	97,821	43	99,087	**44**	30,560	13
6. Howard Coble, R	234,784	75,652	32	120,684	**51**	38,448	16
7. Charlie Rose, D	163,016	70,664	43	70,136	**43**	22,216	14
8. W. G. "Bill" Hefner, D	194,474	81,697	42	85,758	**44**	27,019	14
9. Alex McMillan, R	248,994	80,953	33	131,335	**53**	36,706	15
10. Cass Ballenger, R	238,634	76,021	32	127,067	**53**	35,546	15
11. Charles H. Taylor, R	244,093	105,064	**43**	104,383	43	34,646	14
12. Melvin Watt, D	193,982	127,941	**66**	49,105	25	16,936	9
North Dakota							
AL Earl Pomeroy, D	306,496	99,168	32	136,244	**44**	71,084	23
Ohio							
1. David Mann, D	243,364	104,494	**43**	104,339	43	34,531	14
2. Rob Portman, R	277,061	78,957	28	146,098	**53**	52,006	19
3. Tony P. Hall, D	259,824	107,798	**41**	104,414	40	47,612	18
4. Michael G. Oxley, R	254,963	77,918	31	118,088	**46**	58,957	23
5. Paul E. Gillmor, R	263,551	87,883	33	109,020	**41**	66,648	25
6. Ted Strickland, D	248,726	98,768	40	100,162	**40**	49,796	20
7. David L. Hobson, R	250,678	84,111	34	112,517	**45**	54,050	22
8. John A. Boehner, R	255,973	75,189	29	120,847	**47**	59,937	23
9. Marcy Kaptur, D	250,854	118,818	**47**	81,881	33	50,155	20
10. Martin R. Hoke, R	258,404	107,460	**42**	92,849	36	58,095	22
11. Louis Stokes, D	231,180	169,877	**73**	37,880	16	23,423	10
12. John R. Kasich, R	259,748	104,187	40	108,618	**42**	46,943	18
13. Sherrod Brown, D	266,379	101,104	**38**	94,651	36	70,624	27
14. Tom Sawyer, D	261,085	119,144	**46**	81,603	31	60,338	23
15. Deborah Pryce, R	267,395	95,627	36	119,355	**45**	52,413	20
16. Ralph Regula, R	254,970	95,193	37	98,953	**39**	60,824	24
17. James A. Traficant Jr., D	266,566	133,213	**50**	68,417	26	64,936	24
18. Douglas Applegate, D	256,501	110,494	**43**	87,429	34	58,578	23
19. Eric D. Fingerhut, D	287,736	114,357	**40**	106,950	37	66,429	23
Oklahoma							
1. James M. Inhofe, R	247,772	73,495	30	122,189	**49**	52,088	21
2. Mike Synar, D	226,992	96,510	**43**	81,375	36	49,107	22
3. Bill Brewster, D	227,791	94,763	**42**	77,054	34	55,974	25
4. Dave McCurdy, D	217,001	72,613	33	90,467	**42**	53,921	25
5. Ernest Jim Istook Jr., R	250,988	61,842	25	129,465	**52**	59,681	24
6. Glenn English, D	215,328	73,843	34	92,379	**43**	49,106	23
Oregon							
1. Elizabeth Furse, D	309,068	136,630	**44**	99,304	32	73,134	24
2. Bob Smith, R	279,050	97,672	35	106,839	**38**	74,539	27
3. Ron Wyden, D	278,073	146,835	**53**	72,338	26	58,900	21
4. Peter A. DeFazio, D	291,723	123,387	**42**	93,889	32	74,447	26

District, Member	Votes cast	Clinton vote	Clinton %	Bush vote	Bush %	Perot vote	Perot %
5. Mike Kopetski, D	293,248	116,790	**40**	103,387	35	73,071	25
Pennsylvania							
1. Thomas M. Foglietta, D	205,762	149,699	**73**	39,042	19	17,021	8
2. Lucien E. Blackwell, D	230,630	184,284	**80**	31,836	14	14,510	6
3. Robert A. Borski, D	240,035	124,944	**52**	75,474	31	39,617	17
4. Ron Klink, D	245,541	118,701	**48**	76,193	31	50,647	21
5. William F. Clinger, R	215,515	78,049	36	89,373	**41**	48,093	22
6. Tim Holden, D	218,324	78,326	36	89,791	**41**	50,207	23
7. Curt Weldon, R	285,274	111,518	39	123,954	**43**	49,802	17
8. James C. Greenwood, R	257,160	101,630	**40**	99,269	39	56,261	22
9. Bud Shuster, R	204,905	66,929	33	97,772	**48**	40,204	20
10. Joseph M. McDade, R	230,848	88,150	38	95,820	**42**	46,878	20
11. Paul E. Kanjorski, D	218,834	91,671	**42**	84,203	38	42,960	20
12. John P. Murtha, D	220,300	102,777	**47**	72,671	33	44,852	20
13. Marjorie Margolies-Mezvinsky, D	271,133	119,042	**44**	107,811	40	44,280	16
14. William J. Coyne, D	249,895	145,419	**58**	66,016	26	38,460	15
15. Paul McHale, D	221,452	92,363	**42**	81,349	37	47,740	22
16. Robert S. Walker, R	225,035	72,719	32	109,037	**48**	43,279	19
17. George W. Gekas, R	230,355	73,654	32	115,598	**50**	41,103	18
18. Rick Santorum, R	265,056	137,507	**52**	80,795	30	46,754	18
19. Bill Goodling, R	222,462	74,445	33	104,258	**47**	43,759	20
20. Austin J. Murphy, D	239,866	121,815	**51**	69,802	29	48,249	20
21. Tom Ridge, R	234,464	105,538	**45**	81,003	35	47,923	20
Rhode Island							
1. Ronald K. Machtley, R	216,446	107,702	**50**	61,011	28	47,733	22
2. Jack Reed, D	233,499	105,597	**45**	70,590	30	57,312	25
South Carolina							
1. Arthur Ravenel Jr., R	191,418	62,513	33	102,194	**53**	26,711	14
2. Floyd D. Spence, R	227,678	82,964	36	119,122	**52**	25,592	11
3. Butler Derrick, D	198,432	69,365	35	102,458	**52**	26,609	13
4. Bob Inglis, R	197,211	65,092	33	107,983	**55**	24,136	12
5. John M. Spratt Jr., D	190,605	81,197	43	85,971	**45**	23,437	12
6. James E. Clyburn, D	190,515	118,394	**62**	59,799	31	12,322	6
South Dakota							
AL Tim Johnson, D	334,901	124,888	37	136,718	**41**	73,295	22
Tennessee							
1. James H. Quillen, R	206,850	75,681	37	106,939	**52**	24,230	12
2. John J. "Jimmy" Duncan Jr., R	226,194	92,889	41	108,109	**48**	25,196	11
3. Marilyn Lloyd, D	220,446	97,296	44	97,361	**44**	25,789	12
4. Jim Cooper, D	208,052	100,292	**48**	83,922	40	23,838	11
5. Bob Clement, D	213,724	112,795	**53**	79,398	37	21,531	10
6. Bart Gordon, D	231,082	109,895	**48**	93,036	40	28,151	12
7. Don Sundquist, R	228,674	91,644	40	114,544	**50**	22,486	10
8. John Tanner, D	210,189	101,328	**48**	89,533	43	19,328	9
9. Harold E. Ford, D	229,348	151,590	**66**	68,358	30	9,400	4
Texas							
1. Jim Chapman, D	220,760	85,745	**39**	84,516	38	50,499	23
2. Charles Wilson, D	215,237	91,698	**43**	76,372	35	47,167	22
3. Sam Johnson, R	276,247	58,352	21	133,807	**48**	84,088	30
4. Ralph M. Hall, D	230,424	65,617	28	95,181	**41**	69,626	30
5. John Bryant, D	175,036	70,766	**40**	59,237	34	45,033	26
6. Joe L. Barton, R	275,495	67,131	24	125,693	**46**	82,671	30
7. Bill Archer, R	239,243	52,501	22	137,541	**57**	49,201	21
8. Jack Fields, R	245,256	55,330	23	134,583	**55**	55,343	23
9. Jack Brooks, D	227,190	98,959	**44**	80,813	36	47,418	21
10. J. J. Pickle, D	267,677	128,813	**48**	84,560	32	54,304	20
11. Chet Edwards, D	184,537	66,521	36	75,651	**41**	42,365	23
12. Pete Geren, D	203,568	75,792	**37**	71,212	35	56,564	28
13. Bill Sarpalius, D	202,135	73,454	36	87,492	**43**	41,189	20
14. Greg Laughlin, D	212,051	78,776	37	86,178	**41**	47,097	22
15. E. "Kika" de la Garza, D	152,237	80,085	**53**	52,080	34	20,072	13
16. Ronald D. Coleman, D	129,760	65,614	**51**	45,367	35	18,779	14
17. Charles W. Stenholm, D	215,712	73,388	34	86,490	**40**	55,834	26

District, Member	Votes cast	Clinton vote	Clinton %	Bush vote	Bush %	Perot vote	Perot %
18. Craig Washington, D	178,881	118,349	**66**	40,150	22	20,382	11
19. Larry Combest, R	217,522	50,815	23	130,639	**60**	36,068	17
20. Henry B. Gonzalez, D	168,320	81,380	**48**	57,974	34	28,966	17
21. Lamar Smith, R	277,398	70,402	25	143,720	**52**	63,276	23
22. Tom DeLay, R	230,521	63,175	27	116,614	**51**	50,732	22
23. Henry Bonilla, R	171,875	72,452	**42**	70,577	41	28,846	17
24. Martin Frost, D	179,850	73,019	**41**	60,020	33	46,811	26
25. Michael A. Andrews, D	182,710	85,325	**47**	64,896	36	32,489	18
26. Dick Armey, R	252,883	52,771	21	118,610	**47**	81,502	32
27. Solomon P. Ortiz, D	164,684	78,491	**48**	58,802	36	27,391	17
28. Frank Tejeda, D	172,605	94,112	**55**	51,293	30	27,200	16
29. Gene Green, D	104,728	54,424	**52**	31,864	30	18,440	18
30. Eddie Bernice Johnson, D	156,623	98,031	**63**	33,514	21	25,078	16
Utah							
1. James V. Hansen, R	235,133	50,622	22	115,627	**49**	68,884	29
2. Karen Shepherd, D	258,323	81,233	31	101,169	**39**	75,921	29
3. Bill Orton, D	216,005	51,574	24	105,836	**49**	58,595	27
Vermont							
AL Bernard Sanders, I	287,705	133,592	**46**	88,122	31	65,991	23
Virginia							
1. Herbert H. Bateman, R	241,264	81,826	34	120,131	**50**	39,307	16
2. Owen B. Pickett, D	179,306	62,946	35	85,773	**48**	30,587	17
3. Robert C. Scott, D	190,479	124,857	**66**	48,843	26	16,779	9
4. Norman Sisisky, D	228,500	90,641	40	106,392	**47**	31,467	14
5. Lewis F. Payne Jr., D	221,983	90,769	41	104,236	**47**	26,978	12
6. Robert W. Goodlatte, R	224,649	84,037	37	111,405	**50**	29,207	13
7. Thomas J. Bliley Jr., R	282,656	85,357	30	154,575	**55**	42,724	15
8. James P. Moran, D	258,949	133,183	**51**	96,799	37	28,967	11
9. Rick Boucher, D	219,448	99,099	**45**	93,673	43	26,676	12
10. Frank R. Wolf, R	249,225	83,214	33	124,783	**50**	41,228	17
11. Leslie L. Byrne, D	241,347	102,721	**43**	103,907	**43**	34,719	14
Washington							
1. Maria Cantwell, D	274,068	112,353	**41**	88,456	32	73,259	27
2. Al Swift, D	266,270	109,438	**41**	87,957	33	68,875	26
3. Jolene Unsoeld, D	249,008	104,748	**42**	82,647	33	61,613	25
4. Jay Inslee, D	205,096	71,848	35	87,996	**43**	45,252	22
5. Thomas S. Foley, D	246,442	99,676	**40**	90,294	37	56,472	23
6. Norm Dicks, D	244,489	106,373	**44**	77,538	32	60,578	25
7. Jim McDermott, D	291,426	191,781	**66**	54,478	19	45,167	15
8. Jennifer Dunn, R	267,659	102,857	**38**	92,276	34	72,526	27
9. Mike Kreidler, D	221,594	93,963	**42**	69,592	31	58,039	26
West Virginia							
1. Alan B. Mollohan, D	245,743	113,756	**46**	86,131	35	45,856	19
2. Bob Wise, D	231,445	104,257	**45**	90,375	39	36,813	16
3. Nick J. Rahall II, D	204,616	112,988	**55**	65,468	32	26,160	13
Wisconsin							
1. Peter W. Barca, D	266,967	109,790	**41**	94,712	35	62,465	23
2. Scott L. Klug, R	296,260	149,340	**50**	94,368	32	52,552	18
3. Steve Gunderson, R	278,126	120,261	**43**	90,731	33	67,134	24
4. Gerald D. Kleczka, D	283,774	116,048	**41**	108,463	38	59,263	21
5. Thomas M. Barrett, D	251,120	142,047	**57**	76,935	31	32,138	13
6. Tom Petri, R	281,398	97,248	35	114,698	**41**	69,452	25
7. David R. Obey, D	277,999	117,203	**42**	93,238	34	67,558	24
8. Toby Roth, R	285,994	101,493	35	115,128	**40**	69,373	24
9. F. James Sensenbrenner Jr., R	295,302	88,176	30	142,582	**48**	64,544	22
Wyoming							
AL Craig Thomas, R	198,770	68,160	34	79,347	**40**	51,263	26

Redrawn Minority Districts Face Challenges

The Supreme Court on June 28 invited a new wave of lawsuits challenging the constitutionality of districts drawn to ensure the election of minorities. The 5-4 ruling in the case of *Shaw v. Reno* reinstated a suit by five white North Carolinians who contended that the state's new congressional district map, which created two majority-black districts, violated their 14th Amendment right to "equal protection" by diluting their votes. *(Supreme Court, p. 325)*

By year's end, a Louisiana court became the first to apply the *Shaw* opinion, using it to invalidate the congressional district map used in Louisiana in 1992.

Louisiana in January 1994 began the formal process of appealing the decision to the Supreme Court. And later, discussions began among members of the congressional delegation and among state legislators over drawing a new map.

The Dec. 28 Louisiana ruling came from a special panel of three federal judges appointed to consider *Hays v. Loui-*

siana, a challenge to the 1992 district map, which included two majority-black districts.

The judges indicated that the lengths the Louisiana Legislature went to in creating the second of two black districts exceeded the limits implicit in the *Shaw* ruling. In that decision, the Supreme Court had suggested that race-conscious district-drawing could be unconstitutional if the districts created had no common interest other than race.

Shaw did not actually invalidate any of the maps used in North Carolina in 1992; it merely returned that case to a lower court for further proceedings. The ruling in *Hays* took the next step, becoming the first to incorporate and act on the terminology, methodology and philosophy embodied in *Shaw* to strike down a redistricting plan.

The *Hays* ruling let stand the results of the 1992 elections but prohibited the use of the same district lines in 1994. If that decision stood, it threatened to affect dramati-

Majority-Minority Districts

Following is a list of the congressional districts created for the 1992 election that had a majority population of blacks or Hispanics, along with the total percentage of minorities in the district.

Black-Majority Districts (32)

District	% of Blacks	Total % of Minorities	Representative
N.Y. 11	74.0	84.2	Major R. Owens, D
Md. 7	71.0	73.1	Kweisi Mfume, D
Mich. 15	70.0	75.1	Barbara-Rose Collins, D
Ill. 1	69.7	74.1	Bobby L. Rush, D
Mich. 14	69.1	71.2	John Conyers Jr., D
Ill. 2	68.5	75.4	Mel Reynolds, D
Ala. 7	67.5	68.0	Earl F. Hilliard, D
La. 4	66.4	67.6	Cleo Fields, D
Ill. 7	65.6	72.8	Cardiss Collins, D
Va. 3	64.1	66.6	Robert C. Scott, D
Ga. 11	64.1	65.9	Cynthia McKinney, D
Miss. 2	63.0	63.6	Bennie Thompson, D
Ga. 5	62.3	65.1	John Lewis, D
S.C. 6	62.2	62.9	James E. Clyburn, D
Pa. 2	62.2	65.9	Lucien E. Blackwell, D
La. 2	61.0	66.5	William J. Jefferson, D
N.Y. 10	60.7	79.0	Edolphus Towns, D
N.J. 10	60.2	73.6	Donald M. Payne, D
Tenn. 9	59.2	60.7	Harold E. Ford, D
Ohio 11	58.6	60.7	Louis Stokes, D
Md. 4	58.5	68.9	Albert R. Wynn, D
Fla. 17	58.4	80.2	Carrie Meek, D
N.C. 1	57.3	58.6	Eva Clayton, D
N.C. 12	56.6	58.6	Melvin Watt, D
Ga. 2	56.6	58.7	Sanford D. Bishop Jr., D
N.Y. 6	56.2	77.2	Floyd H. Flake, D
Fla. 3	55.0	58.3	Corrine Brown, D
Pa. 1	52.4	64.0	Thomas M. Foglietta, D
Mo. 1	52.3	54.2	William L. Clay, D
Fla. 23	51.6	60.7	Alcee L. Hastings, D
Texas 18	50.9	68.7	Craig Washington, D
Texas 30	50.0	68.6	Eddie Bernice Johnson, D

Hispanic-Majority Districts (20)

District	% of Hispanics	Total % of Minorities	Representative
Calif. 33	83.7	91.9	Lucille Roybal-Allard, D
Texas 15	74.5	76.1	E. "Kika" de la Garza, D
Texas 16	70.4	75.0	Ronald D. Coleman, D
Fla. 21	69.6	74.5	Lincoln Diaz-Balart, R
Fla. 18	66.7	70.8	Ileana Ros-Lehtinen, R
Texas 27	66.2	69.3	Solomon P. Ortiz, D
Ill. 4	65.0	73.2	Luis V. Gutierrez, D
Texas 23	62.5	66.4	Henry Bonilla, R
Calif. 34	62.3	73.3	Esteban E. Torres, D
Calif. 30	61.5	84.8	Xavier Becerra, D
Texas 20	60.7	67.8	Henry B. Gonzalez, D
Texas 29	60.6	72.2	Gene Green, D
Texas 28	60.4	69.6	Frank Tejeda, D
N.Y. 16	60.2	95.8	Jose E. Serrano, D
Calif. 31	58.5	82.5	Matthew G. Martinez, D
N.Y. 12	57.9	86.0	Nydia M. Velázquez, D
Calif. 20	55.4	67.4	Cal Dooley, D
Calif. 26	52.7	65.8	Howard L. Berman, D
Ariz. 2	50.5	61.8	Ed Pastor, D
Calif. 46	50.0	64.4	Robert K. Dornan, R

NOTE: *There are two districts with a majority-Asian population. The total minority population is based on 1990 census data, subtracting non-Hispanic white population from the total population in the district.*

SOURCES: Polidata with assistance from Congressional Quarterly; Census Bureau data.

cally the districts of at least half the Louisiana delegation in the House. But beyond that, *Hays* offered the potential for the Supreme Court (or other federal courts) to set guidelines for all the states that were trying (in response to earlier court mandates) to create the maximum number of congressional districts with a majority of minorities.

Louisiana's congressional district map contained one of the most eye-catching examples of racial gerrymandering in the nation: the Z-shaped 4th District. The 4th, where the population was 66 percent African-American, elected black Democrat Cleo Fields in 1992. The district traced the state's northern, eastern and northeastern borders and swayed into central and south-central Louisiana.

State redistricting struggles in the early 1990s grew not only from the 1990 census but from a decade of congressional action, Supreme Court decisions and Justice Department regulations on how to comply with the Voting Rights Act in drawing congressional districts to accommodate minority voters' rights.

The court had given a broad interpretation of the Voting Rights Act's mandate in a 1986 ruling in *Thornburg v. Gingles*, saying that states should create minority districts wherever possible.

In some legislatures, including Louisiana's, white Republicans joined black Democrats to ensure the creation of new majority-minority districts — at least in part because doing so created corresponding districts that were whiter and more Republican.

In Louisiana, four Lincoln Parish voters (three white and one black) filed suit in July 1992 challenging the new map. They said it created racial voting blocs that disenfranchised the racial minority (black or white) in each of the state's seven districts by establishing racial supermajorities in each. ∎

CONGRESS AND ITS MEMBERS

Characteristics of Congress

Following is a compilation of information about individual members of the 103rd Congress — their birth dates, occupations, religions and seniority.

The average age of members of the new Congress was 52.9, slightly younger than in the previous Congress.

As in other years, the biggest single occupational group in Congress was lawyers. Nearly half the members — 238 — listed law as their profession. Businessmen and bankers made up the next-largest category, with 155 members falling into those groups.

Roman Catholic members made up the largest religious group, followed by members of the Methodist, Baptist and Episcopal faiths.

The data below, and the composition of Senate and House committees, reflect the information received as of Dec. 31, 1993.

Senate — Birth Dates, Occupations, Religions, Seniority

(Seniority rank is within the member's party.)

ALABAMA
Heflin (D) —June 19, 1921. Occupation: judge, lawyer. Religion: Methodist. Seniority: 24.
Shelby (D) —May 6, 1934. Occupation: lawyer. Religion: Presbyterian. Seniority: 37.

ALASKA
Stevens (R) —Nov. 18, 1923. Occupation: lawyer. Religion: Episcopalian. Seniority: 3.
Murkowski (R) —March 28, 1933. Occupation: banker. Religion: Roman Catholic. Seniority: 22.

ARIZONA
DeConcini (D) —May 8, 1937. Occupation: lawyer. Religion: Roman Catholic. Seniority: 16.
McCain (R) —Aug. 29, 1936. Occupation: Navy officer, Senate Navy liaison, beer distributor. Religion: Episcopalian. Seniority: 28.

ARKANSAS
Bumpers (D) —Aug. 12, 1925. Occupation: lawyer, farmer, hardware company executive. Religion: Methodist. Seniority: 11.
Pryor (D) —Aug. 29, 1934. Occupation: lawyer, newspaper publisher. Religion: Presbyterian. Seniority: 20.

CALIFORNIA
Feinstein (D) —June 22, 1933. Occupation: public official. Religion: Jewish. Seniority: 49.
Boxer (D) —Nov. 11, 1940. Occupation: congressional aide, journalist, stockbroker. Religion: Jewish. Seniority: 52.

COLORADO
Brown (R) —Feb. 12, 1940. Occupation: tax accountant, meatpacking company executive, lawyer. Religion: Congregationalist. Seniority: 37.
Campbell (D) —April 13, 1933. Occupation: jewelry designer, rancher, horse trainer, teacher. Religion: Unspecified. Seniority: 53.

CONNECTICUT
Dodd (D) —May 27, 1944. Occupation: lawyer. Religion: Roman Catholic. Seniority: 27.

Lieberman (D) —Feb. 24, 1942. Occupation: lawyer. Religion: Jewish. Seniority: 44.

DELAWARE
Roth (R) —July 22, 1921. Occupation: lawyer. Religion: Episcopalian. Seniority: 6.
Biden (D) —Nov. 20, 1942. Occupation: lawyer. Religion: Roman Catholic. Seniority: 8.

FLORIDA
Graham (D) —Nov. 9, 1936. Occupation: real estate developer, cattle rancher. Religion: United Church of Christ. Seniority: 39.
Mack (R) —Oct. 29, 1940. Occupation: banker. Religion: Roman Catholic. Seniority: 34.

GEORGIA
Nunn (D) —Sept. 8, 1938. Occupation: farmer, lawyer. Religion: Methodist. Seniority: 6.
Coverdell (R) —Jan. 20, 1939. Occupation: financial executive, Peace Corps director. Religion: Methodist. Seniority: 40.

HAWAII
Inouye (D) —Sept. 7, 1924. Occupation: lawyer. Religion: Methodist. Seniority: 4.
Akaka (D) —Sept. 11, 1924. Occupation: elementary school teacher and principal, state official. Religion: Congregationalist. Seniority: 46.

IDAHO
Craig (R) —July 20, 1945. Occupation: farmer, rancher. Religion: Methodist. Seniority: 37.
Kempthorne (R) —Oct. 29, 1951. Occupation: public affairs manager, securities representative, political consultant, building association executive. Religion: Methodist. Seniority: 40.

ILLINOIS
Simon (D) —Nov. 29, 1928. Occupation: author, newspaper editor and publisher. Religion: Lutheran. Seniority: 31.
Moseley-Braun (D) —Aug. 16, 1947. Occupation: lawyer. Religion: Roman Catholic. Seniority: 54.

INDIANA
Lugar (R) —April 4, 1932. Occupation:

manufacturing executive, farm manager. Religion: Methodist. Seniority: 11.
Coats (R) —May 16, 1943. Occupation: lawyer. Religion: Presbyterian. Seniority: 33.

IOWA
Grassley (R) —Sept. 17, 1933. Occupation: farmer. Religion: Baptist. Seniority: 21.
Harkin (D) —Nov. 19, 1939. Occupation: lawyer. Religion: Roman Catholic. Seniority: 31.

KANSAS
Dole (R) —July 22, 1923. Occupation: lawyer. Religion: Methodist. Seniority: 4.
Kassebaum (R) —July 29, 1932. Occupation: broadcasting executive. Religion: Episcopalian. Seniority: 15.

KENTUCKY
Ford (D) —Sept. 8, 1924. Occupation: insurance executive. Religion: Baptist. Seniority: 10.
McConnell (R) —Feb. 20, 1942. Occupation: lawyer. Religion: Baptist. Seniority: 27.

LOUISIANA
Johnston (D) —June 10, 1932. Occupation: lawyer. Religion: Baptist. Seniority: 7.
Breaux (D) —March 1, 1944. Occupation: lawyer. Religion: Roman Catholic. Seniority: 34.

MAINE
Cohen (R) —Aug. 28, 1940. Occupation: lawyer. Religion: Unitarian. Seniority: 19.
Mitchell (D) —Aug. 20, 1933. Occupation: judge, lawyer. Religion: Roman Catholic. Seniority: 26.

MARYLAND
Sarbanes (D) —Feb. 3, 1933. Occupation: lawyer. Religion: Greek Orthodox. Seniority: 15.
Mikulski (D) —July 20, 1936. Occupation: social worker. Religion: Roman Catholic. Seniority: 35.

MASSACHUSETTS
Kennedy (D) —Feb. 22, 1932. Occupation: lawyer. Religion: Roman Catholic. Seniority: 3.

Kerry (D) —Dec. 11, 1943. Occupation: lawyer. Religion: Roman Catholic. Seniority: 30.

MICHIGAN

Riegle (D) —Feb. 4, 1938. Occupation: business executive, professor. Religion: Methodist. Seniority: 14.

Levin (D) —June 28, 1934. Occupation: lawyer. Religion: Jewish. Seniority: 23.

MINNESOTA

Durenberger (R) —Aug. 19, 1934. Occupation: lawyer, adhesives manufacturing executive. Religion: Roman Catholic. Seniority: 14.

Wellstone (D) —July 21, 1944. Occupation: professor. Religion: Jewish. Seniority: 47.

MISSISSIPPI

Cochran (R) —Dec. 7, 1937. Occupation: lawyer. Religion: Baptist. Seniority: 16.

Lott (R) —Oct. 9, 1941. Occupation: lawyer. Religion: Baptist. Seniority: 31.

MISSOURI

Danforth (R) —Sept. 5, 1936. Occupation: lawyer, clergyman. Religion: Episcopalian. Seniority: 9.

Bond (R) —March 6, 1939. Occupation: lawyer. Religion: Presbyterian. Seniority: 29.

MONTANA

Baucus (D) —Dec. 11, 1941. Occupation: lawyer. Religion: United Church of Christ. Seniority: 19.

Burns (R) —Jan. 25, 1935. Occupation: radio and television broadcaster. Religion: Lutheran. Seniority: 35.

NEBRASKA

Exon (D) —Aug. 9, 1921. Occupation: office equipment dealer. Religion: Episcopalian. Seniority: 21.

Kerrey (D) —Aug. 27, 1943. Occupation: restaurateur. Religion: Congregationalist. Seniority: 41.

NEVADA

Reid (D) —Dec. 2, 1939. Occupation: lawyer. Religion: Mormon. Seniority: 38.

Bryan (D) —July 16, 1937. Occupation: lawyer. Religion: Episcopalian. Seniority: 41.

NEW HAMPSHIRE

Smith (R) —March 30, 1941. Occupation: real estate broker, high school teacher. Religion: Roman Catholic. Seniority: 36.

Gregg (R) —Feb. 14, 1947. Occupation: lawyer. Religion: Congregationalist. Seniority: 39.

NEW JERSEY

Bradley (D) —July 28, 1943. Occupation: professional basketball player, author. Religion: Protestant. Seniority: 23.

Lautenberg (D) —Jan. 23, 1924. Occupation: computer firm executive. Religion: Jewish. Seniority: 28.

NEW MEXICO

Domenici (R) —May 7, 1932. Occupation: lawyer. Religion: Roman Catholic. Seniority: 7.

Bingaman (D) —Oct. 3, 1943. Occupation: lawyer. Religion: Methodist. Seniority: 29.

NEW YORK

Moynihan (D) —March 16, 1927. Occupation: professor, writer. Religion: Roman Catholic. Seniority: 16.

D'Amato (R) —Aug. 1, 1937. Occupation: lawyer. Religion: Roman Catholic. Seniority: 22.

NORTH CAROLINA

Helms (R) —Oct. 18, 1921. Occupation: journalist, broadcasting executive, banking executive, congressional aide. Religion: Baptist. Seniority: 7.

Faircloth (R) —Jan. 14, 1928. Occupation: farm owner. Religion: Presbyterian. Seniority: 40.

NORTH DAKOTA

Conrad (D) —March 12, 1948. Occupation: management and personnel director. Religion: Unitarian. Seniority: 40.

Dorgan (D) —May 14, 1942. Occupation: public official. Religion: Lutheran. Seniority: 50.

OHIO

Glenn (D) —July 18, 1921. Occupation: astronaut, soft drink company executive. Religion: Presbyterian. Seniority: 9.

Metzenbaum (D) —June 4, 1917. Occupation: lawyer, newspaper publisher, parking company executive. Religion: Jewish. Seniority: 13.

OKLAHOMA

Boren (D) —April 21, 1941. Occupation: lawyer. Religion: Methodist. Seniority: 21.

Nickles (R) —Dec. 6, 1948. Occupation: machine company executive. Religion: Roman Catholic. Seniority: 22.

OREGON

Hatfield (R) —July 12, 1922. Occupation: professor, college administrator. Religion: Baptist. Seniority: 2.

Packwood (R) —Sept. 11, 1932. Occupation: lawyer. Religion: Unitarian. Seniority: 5.

PENNSYLVANIA

Specter (R) —Feb. 12, 1930. Occupation: lawyer, professor. Religion: Jewish. Seniority: 22.

Wofford (D) —April 9, 1926. Occupation: lawyer, college president, Peace Corps official, White House official. Religion: Roman Catholic. Seniority: 48.

RHODE ISLAND

Pell (D) —Nov. 22, 1918. Occupation: investment executive. Religion: Episcopalian. Seniority: 2.

Chafee (R) —Oct. 22, 1922. Occupation: lawyer. Religion: Episcopalian. Seniority: 10.

SOUTH CAROLINA

Thurmond (R) —Dec. 5, 1902. Occupation: lawyer, teacher, coach; education administrator. Religion: Baptist. Seniority: 1.

Hollings (D) —Jan. 1, 1922. Occupation: lawyer. Religion: Lutheran. Seniority: 5.

SOUTH DAKOTA

Pressler (R) —March 29, 1942. Occupation: lawyer. Religion: Roman Catholic. Seniority: 20.

Daschle (D) —Dec. 9, 1947. Occupation: congressional aide. Religion: Roman Catholic. Seniority: 36.

TENNESSEE

Sasser (D) —Sept. 30, 1936. Occupation: lawyer. Religion: Protestant. Seniority: 16.

Mathews (D) —Jan. 17, 1927. Occupation: public official. Religion: Protestant. Seniority: 51.

TEXAS

Gramm (R) —July 8, 1942. Occupation: professor. Religion: Episcopalian. Seniority: 26.

Hutchison (R) —July 22, 1943. Occupation: broadcast journalist, banking executive, candy manufacturer. Religion: Episcopalian. Seniority: 44.

UTAH

Hatch (R) —March 22, 1934. Occupation: lawyer. Religion: Mormon. Seniority: 11.

Bennett (R) —Sept. 18, 1933. Occupation: management consultant. Religion: Mormon. Seniority: 40.

VERMONT

Leahy (D) —March 31, 1940. Occupation: lawyer. Religion: Roman Catholic. Seniority: 12.

Jeffords (R) —May 11, 1934. Occupation: lawyer. Religion: Congregationalist. Seniority: 32.

VIRGINIA

Warner (R) —Feb. 18, 1927. Occupation: lawyer, farmer. Religion: Episcopalian. Seniority: 18.

Robb (D) —June 26, 1939. Occupation: lawyer. Religion: Episcopalian. Seniority: 41.

WASHINGTON

Gorton (R) —Jan. 8, 1928. Occupation: lawyer. Religion: Episcopalian. Seniority: 30.

Murray (D) —Oct. 11, 1950. Occupation: educator. Religion: Roman Catholic. Seniority: 54.

WEST VIRGINIA

Byrd (D) —Nov. 20, 1917. Occupation: lawyer. Religion: Baptist. Seniority: 1.

Rockefeller (D) —June 18, 1937. Occupation: public official. Religion: Presbyterian. Seniority: 33.

WISCONSIN

Kohl (D) —Feb. 7, 1935. Occupation: businessman, professional basketball team owner. Religion: Jewish. Seniority: 44.

Feingold (D) —March 2, 1953. Occupation: lawyer. Religion: Jewish. Seniority: 54.

WYOMING

Wallop (R) —Feb. 27, 1933. Occupation: rancher, meatpacking executive. Religion: Episcopalian. Seniority: 11.

Simpson (R) —Sept. 2, 1931. Occupation: lawyer. Religion: Episcopalian. Seniority: 17.

House — Birth Dates, Occupations, Religions, Seniority

(Seniority rank is within the member's party.)

ALABAMA

1 Callahan (R) —Sept. 11, 1932. Occupation: moving and storage company executive. Religion: Roman Catholic. Seniority: 65.

2 Everett (R) —Feb. 15, 1937. Occupation: newspaper executive, construction company owner, farm owner, real estate developer. Religion: Baptist. Seniority: 128.

3 Browder (D) —Jan. 15, 1943. Occupation: professor. Religion: Methodist. Seniority: 161.

4 Bevill (D) —March 27, 1921. Occupation: lawyer. Religion: Baptist. Seniority: 17.

5 Cramer (D) —Aug. 22, 1947. Occupation: lawyer. Religion: Methodist. Seniority: 171.

6 Bachus (R) —Dec. 28, 1947. Occupation: lawyer, manufacturer. Religion: Baptist. Seniority: 128.

7 Hilliard (D) —April 9, 1942. Occupation: lawyer, insurance broker. Religion: Baptist. Seniority: 195.

ALASKA

AL Young (R) —June 9, 1933. Occupation: elementary school teacher, riverboat captain. Religion: Episcopalian. Seniority: 14.

ARIZONA

1 Coppersmith (D) —May 22, 1955. Occupation: lawyer, foreign service officer. Religion: Jewish. Seniority: 195.

2 Pastor (D) —June 28, 1943. Occupation: teacher, gubernatorial aide, public policy consultant. Religion: Roman Catholic. Seniority: 191.

3 Stump (R) —April 4, 1927. Occupation: cotton farmer. Religion: Seventh-day Adventist. Seniority: 17.

4 Kyl (R) —April 25, 1942. Occupation: lawyer. Religion: Presbyterian. Seniority: 79.

5 Kolbe (R) —June 28, 1942. Occupation: real estate consultant. Religion: Methodist. Seniority: 65.

6 English (D) —March 23, 1949. Occupation: public official. Religion: Unspecified. Seniority: 195.

ARKANSAS

1 Lambert (D) —Sept. 30, 1960. Occupation: government affairs specialist, congressional aide. Religion: Episcopalian. Seniority: 195.

2 Thornton (D) —July 16, 1928. Occupation: lawyer. Religion: Church of Christ. Seniority: 169.

3 Hutchinson (R) —Aug. 11, 1949. Occupation: minister, college instructor, radio station executive. Religion: Baptist. Seniority: 128.

4 Dickey (R) —Dec. 14, 1939. Occupation: lawyer, restaurateur. Religion: Methodist. Seniority: 128.

CALIFORNIA

1 Hamburg (D) —Oct. 6, 1948. Occupation: teacher. Religion: Jewish. Seniority: 195.

2 Herger (R) —May 20, 1945. Occupation: rancher, gas company executive. Religion: Mormon. Seniority: 79.

3 Fazio (D) —Oct. 11, 1942. Occupation: journalist, congressional and legislative consultant. Religion: Episcopalian. Seniority: 61.

4 Doolittle (R) —Oct. 30, 1950. Occupation: lawyer. Religion: Mormon. Seniority: 110.

5 Matsui (D) —Sept. 17, 1941. Occupation: lawyer. Religion: Methodist. Seniority: 61.

6 Woolsey (D) —Nov. 3, 1937. Occupation: personnel service owner. Religion: Presbyterian. Seniority: 195.

7 Miller (D) —May 17, 1945. Occupation: lawyer, legislative aide. Religion: Roman Catholic. Seniority: 35.

8 Pelosi (D) —March 26, 1940. Occupation: public relations consultant. Religion: Roman Catholic. Seniority: 140.

9 Dellums (D) —Nov. 24, 1935. Occupation: psychiatric social worker. Religion: Protestant. Seniority: 22.

10 Baker (R) —June 14, 1940. Occupation: budget analyst. Religion: Roman Catholic. Seniority: 128.

11 Pombo (R) —Jan. 8, 1961. Occupation: rancher. Religion: Roman Catholic. Seniority: 128.

12 Lantos (D) —Feb. 1, 1928. Occupation: professor. Religion: Jewish. Seniority: 73.

13 Stark (D) —Nov. 11, 1931. Occupation: banker. Religion: Unitarian. Seniority: 26.

14 Eshoo (D) —Dec. 13, 1942. Occupation: legislative aide. Religion: Roman Catholic. Seniority: 195.

15 Mineta (D) —Nov. 12, 1931. Occupation: insurance executive. Religion: Methodist. Seniority: 35.

16 Edwards (D) —Jan. 6, 1915. Occupation: title company executive, lawyer, FBI agent. Religion: Unitarian. Seniority: 8.

17 Farr (D) —July 4, 1941. Occupation: state legislative aide. Religion: Episcopalian. Seniority: 258.

18 Condit (D) —April 21, 1948. Occupation: public official. Religion: Baptist. Seniority: 162.

19 Lehman (D) —July 20, 1948. Occupation: legislative aide. Religion: Lutheran. Seniority: 86.

20 Dooley (D) —Jan. 11, 1954. Occupation: farmer. Religion: Protestant. Seniority: 171.

21 Thomas (R) —Dec. 6, 1941. Occupation: professor. Religion: Baptist. Seniority: 21.

22 Huffington (R) —Sept. 3, 1947. Occupation: film production executive. Religion: Episcopalian. Seniority: 128.

23 Gallegly (R) —March 7, 1944. Occupation: real estate broker. Religion: Protestant. Seniority: 79.

24 Beilenson (D) —Oct. 26, 1932. Occupation: lawyer. Religion: Jewish. Seniority: 49.

25 McKeon (R) —Sept. 9, 1939. Occupation: clothing store owner. Religion: Mormon. Seniority: 128.

26 Berman (D) —April 15, 1941. Occupation: lawyer. Religion: Jewish. Seniority: 86.

27 Moorhead (R) —May 6, 1922. Occupation: lawyer. Religion: Presbyterian. Seniority: 10.

28 Dreier (R) —July 5, 1952. Occupation: real estate manager and developer. Religion: Christian Scientist. Seniority: 32.

29 Waxman (D) —Sept. 12, 1939. Occupation: lawyer. Religion: Jewish. Seniority: 35.

30 Becerra (D) —Jan. 26, 1958. Occupation: lawyer. Religion: Roman Catholic. Seniority: 195.

31 Martinez (D) —Feb. 14, 1929. Occupation: upholstery company owner. Religion: Roman Catholic. Seniority: 84.

32 Dixon (D) —Aug. 8, 1934. Occupation: legislative aide, lawyer. Religion: Episcopalian. Seniority: 61.

33 Roybal-Allard (D) —June 12, 1941. Occupation: nonprofit worker. Religion: Roman Catholic. Seniority: 195.

34 Torres (D) —Jan. 27, 1930. Occupation: international trade executive, autoworker, labor official. Religion: Unspecified. Seniority: 86.

35 Waters (D) —Aug. 15, 1938. Occupation: Head Start official. Religion: Christian. Seniority: 171.

36 Harman (D) —June 28, 1945. Occupation: lawyer, White House aide, congressional aide. Religion: Jewish. Seniority: 195.

37 Tucker (D) —May 28, 1957. Occupation: lawyer. Religion: Baptist. Seniority: 195.

38 Horn (R) —May 31, 1931. Occupation: professor, college president. Religion: Protestant. Seniority: 128.

39 Royce (R) —Oct. 12, 1951. Occupation: tax manager. Religion: Roman Catholic. Seniority: 128.

40 Lewis (R) —Oct. 21, 1934. Occupation: insurance executive. Religion: Presbyterian. Seniority: 21.

41 Kim (R) —March 27, 1939. Occupation: civil engineer. Religion: Methodist. Seniority: 128.

42 Brown (D) —March 6, 1920. Occupation: management consultant, physicist. Religion: Methodist. Seniority: 25.

43 Calvert (R) —June 8, 1953. Occupation: real estate executive. Religion: Protestant. Seniority: 128.

44 McCandless (R) —July 23, 1927. Occupation: automobile dealer. Religion: Protestant. Seniority: 48.

45 Rohrabacher (R) —June 21, 1947.

Occupation: White House speechwriter, journalist. Religion: Baptist. Seniority: 97.

46 **Dornan (R)** —April 3, 1933. Occupation: broadcast journalist and producer. Religion: Roman Catholic. Seniority: 64.

47 **Cox (R)** —Oct. 16, 1952. Occupation: White House counsel. Religion: Roman Catholic. Seniority: 97.

48 **Packard (R)** —Jan. 19, 1931. Occupation: dentist. Religion: Mormon. Seniority: 48.

49 **Schenk (D)** —Jan. 5, 1945. Occupation: lawyer. Religion: Jewish. Seniority: 195.

50 **Filner (D)** —Sept. 4, 1942. Occupation: public official, college professor. Religion: Jewish. Seniority: 195.

51 **Cunningham (R)** —Dec. 8, 1941. Occupation: computer software executive. Religion: Christian. Seniority: 110.

52 **Hunter (R)** —May 31, 1948. Occupation: lawyer. Religion: Baptist. Seniority: 32.

COLORADO

1 **Schroeder (D)** —July 30, 1940. Occupation: lawyer, law instructor. Religion: United Church of Christ. Seniority: 26.

2 **Skaggs (D)** —Feb. 22, 1943. Occupation: lawyer, congressional aide. Religion: Congregationalist. Seniority: 124.

3 **McInnis (R)** —May 9, 1953. Occupation: lawyer. Religion: Roman Catholic. Seniority: 128.

4 **Allard (R)** —Dec. 2, 1943. Occupation: veterinarian. Religion: Protestant. Seniority: 110.

5 **Hefley (R)** —April 18, 1935. Occupation: community planner, management consultant. Religion: Presbyterian. Seniority: 79.

6 **Schaefer (R)** —Jan. 25, 1936. Occupation: public relations consultant. Religion: Roman Catholic. Seniority: 62.

CONNECTICUT

1 **Kennelly (D)** —July 10, 1936. Occupation: public official. Religion: Roman Catholic. Seniority: 83.

2 **Gejdenson (D)** —May 20, 1948. Occupation: dairy farmer. Religion: Jewish. Seniority: 73.

3 **DeLauro (D)** —March 2, 1943. Occupation: political activist. Religion: Roman Catholic. Seniority: 171.

4 **Shays (R)** —Oct. 18, 1945. Occupation: real estate broker, public official. Religion: Christian Scientist. Seniority: 94.

5 **Franks (R)** —Feb. 9, 1953. Occupation: real estate investor. Religion: Baptist. Seniority: 110.

6 **Johnson (R)** —Jan. 5, 1935. Occupation: civic leader. Religion: Unitarian. Seniority: 48.

DELAWARE

AL **Castle (R)** —July 2, 1939. Occupation: lawyer. Religion: Roman Catholic. Seniority: 128.

FLORIDA

1 **Hutto (D)** —May 12, 1926. Occupation: advertising and broadcasting executive, high school teacher, sportscaster. Religion: Baptist. Seniority: 61.

2 **Peterson (D)** —June 26, 1935. Occupation: educational administrator. Religion: Roman Catholic. Seniority: 171.

3 **Brown (D)** —Nov. 11, 1946. Occupation: college guidance counselor, travel agency owner. Religion: Baptist. Seniority: 195.

4 **Fowler (R)** —Dec. 23, 1942. Occupation: White House aide, congressional aide, lawyer. Religion: Episcopalian. Seniority: 128.

5 **Thurman (D)** —Jan. 12, 1951. Occupation: teacher. Religion: Episcopalian. Seniority: 195.

6 **Stearns (R)** —April 16, 1941. Occupation: hotel executive. Religion: Presbyterian. Seniority: 97.

7 **Mica (R)** —Jan. 27, 1943. Occupation: government consultant. Religion: Episcopalian. Seniority: 128.

8 **McCollum (R)** —July 12, 1944. Occupation: lawyer. Religion: Episcopalian. Seniority: 32.

9 **Bilirakis (R)** —July 16, 1930. Occupation: lawyer, restaurateur. Religion: Greek Orthodox. Seniority: 48.

10 **Young (R)** —Dec. 16, 1930. Occupation: insurance executive, public official. Religion: Methodist. Seniority: 7.

11 **Gibbons (D)** —Jan. 20, 1920. Occupation: lawyer. Religion: Presbyterian. Seniority: 8.

12 **Canady (R)** —June 22, 1954. Occupation: lawyer. Religion: Presbyterian. Seniority: 128.

13 **Miller (R)** —May 30, 1942. Occupation: businessman. Religion: Episcopalian. Seniority: 128.

14 **Goss (R)** —Nov. 26, 1938. Occupation: businessman, newspaper founder, CIA agent. Religion: Presbyterian. Seniority: 97.

15 **Bacchus (D)** —June 21, 1949. Occupation: lawyer, journalist. Religion: Presbyterian. Seniority: 171.

16 **Lewis (R)** —Oct. 26, 1924. Occupation: real estate broker, aircraft testing specialist. Religion: Methodist. Seniority: 48.

17 **Meek (D)** —April 29, 1926. Occupation: educational administrator, teacher. Religion: Baptist. Seniority: 195.

18 **Ros-Lehtinen (R)** —July 15, 1952. Occupation: teacher, private school administrator. Religion: Roman Catholic. Seniority: 108.

19 **Johnston (D)** —Dec. 2, 1931. Occupation: lawyer. Religion: Presbyterian. Seniority: 145.

20 **Deutsch (D)** —April 1, 1957. Occupation: lawyer, nonprofit executive. Religion: Jewish. Seniority: 195.

21 **Diaz-Balart (R)** —Aug. 13, 1954. Occupation: lawyer. Religion: Roman Catholic. Seniority: 128.

22 **Shaw (R)** —April 19, 1939. Occupation: nurseryman, lawyer. Religion: Roman Catholic. Seniority: 32.

23 **Hastings (D)** —Sept. 5, 1936. Occupation: lawyer. Religion: African Methodist Episcopal. Seniority: 195.

GEORGIA

1 **Kingston (R)** —April 24, 1955. Occupation: insurance broker. Religion: Episcopalian. Seniority: 128.

2 **Bishop (D)** —Feb. 4, 1947. Occupation: lawyer. Religion: Baptist. Seniority: 195.

3 **Collins (R)** —Oct. 15, 1944. Occupation: trucking company owner. Religion: Methodist. Seniority: 128.

4 **Linder (R)** —Sept. 9, 1942. Occupation: financial executive, dentist. Religion: Presbyterian. Seniority: 128.

5 **Lewis (D)** —Feb. 21, 1940. Occupation: civil rights activist. Religion: Baptist. Seniority: 124.

6 **Gingrich (R)** —June 17, 1943. Occupation: professor. Religion: Baptist. Seniority: 21.

7 **Darden (D)** —Nov. 22, 1943. Occupation: lawyer. Religion: Methodist. Seniority: 116.

8 **Rowland (D)** —Feb. 3, 1926. Occupation: physician. Religion: Methodist. Seniority: 86.

9 **Deal (D)** —Aug. 25, 1942. Occupation: lawyer. Religion: Baptist. Seniority: 195.

10 **Johnson (D)** —Jan. 30, 1948. Occupation: lawyer. Religion: Baptist. Seniority: 195.

11 **McKinney (D)** —March 17, 1955. Occupation: professor. Religion: Roman Catholic. Seniority: 195.

HAWAII

1 **Abercrombie (D)** —June 26, 1938. Occupation: educator. Religion: Unspecified. Seniority: 170.

2 **Mink (D)** —Dec. 6, 1927. Occupation: lawyer. Religion: Protestant. Seniority: 167.

IDAHO

1 **LaRocco (D)** —Aug. 25, 1946. Occupation: stockbroker. Religion: Roman Catholic. Seniority: 171.

2 **Crapo (R)** —May 20, 1951. Occupation: lawyer. Religion: Mormon. Seniority: 128.

ILLINOIS

1 **Rush (D)** —Nov. 23, 1946. Occupation: insurance broker, political aide. Religion: Protestant. Seniority: 195.

2 **Reynolds (D)** —Jan. 8, 1952. Occupation: professor. Religion: Baptist. Seniority: 195.

3 **Lipinski (D)** —Dec. 22, 1937. Occupation: parks supervisor. Religion: Roman Catholic. Seniority: 86.

4 **Gutierrez (D)** —Dec. 10, 1954. Occupation: teacher, social worker. Religion: Roman Catholic. Seniority: 195.

5 **Rostenkowski (D)** —Jan. 2, 1928. Occupation: insurance executive, public official. Religion: Roman Catholic. Seniority: 5.

6 **Hyde (R)** —April 18, 1924. Occupation: lawyer. Religion: Roman Catholic. Seniority: 15.

7 **Collins (D)** —Sept. 24, 1931. Occupation: auditor. Religion: National Baptist. Seniority: 32.

8 **Crane (R)** —Nov. 3, 1930. Occupation: professor, author, advertising executive. Religion: Protestant. Seniority: 6.

9 **Yates (D)** —Aug. 27, 1909. Occupation: lawyer. Religion: Jewish. Seniority: 11.

10 **Porter (R)** —June 1, 1935. Occupation: lawyer. Religion: Presbyterian. Seniority: 31.

11 **Sangmeister (D)** —Feb. 16, 1931. Occupation: lawyer. Religion: United Church of Christ. Seniority: 145.

12 **Costello (D)** —Sept. 25, 1949. Occupation: law enforcement official. Religion: Roman Catholic. Seniority: 143.

13 **Fawell (R)** —March 25, 1929. Occupation: lawyer. Religion: Methodist. Seniority: 65.

14 **Hastert (R)** —Jan. 2, 1942. Occupation: teacher, restaurateur. Religion: Protestant. Seniority: 79.

15 **Ewing (R)** —Sept. 19, 1935. Occupation: lawyer. Religion: Methodist. Seniority: 127.

16 **Manzullo (R)** —March 24, 1944. Occupation: lawyer. Religion: Baptist. Seniority: 128.

17 **Evans (D)** —Aug. 4, 1951. Occupation: lawyer. Religion: Roman Catholic. Seniority: 86.

18 **Michel (R)** —March 2, 1923. Occupation: congressional aide. Religion: Apostolic Christian. Seniority: 1.

19 **Poshard (D)** —Oct. 30, 1945. Occupation: educator. Religion: Baptist. Seniority: 145.

20 **Durbin (D)** —Nov. 21, 1944. Occupation: lawyer, congressional and legislative aide. Religion: Roman Catholic. Seniority: 86.

INDIANA

1 **Visclosky (D)** —Aug. 13, 1949. Occupation: lawyer. Religion: Roman Catholic. Seniority: 118.

2 **Sharp (D)** —July 15, 1942. Occupation: professor. Religion: Methodist. Seniority: 35.

3 **Roemer (D)** —Oct. 30, 1956. Occupation: congressional aide. Religion: Roman Catholic. Seniority: 171.

4 **Long (D)** —July 15, 1952. Occupation: professor. Religion: Methodist. Seniority: 160.

5 **Buyer (R)** —Nov. 26, 1958. Occupation: lawyer. Religion: Methodist. Seniority: 128.

6 **Burton (R)** —June 21, 1938. Occupation: real estate and insurance agent. Religion: Protestant. Seniority: 48.

7 **Myers (R)** —Feb. 8, 1927. Occupation: banker, farmer. Religion: Episcopalian. Seniority: 4.

8 **McCloskey (D)** —June 12, 1939. Occupation: lawyer, journalist. Religion: Roman Catholic. Seniority: 86.

9 **Hamilton (D)** —April 20, 1931. Occupation: lawyer. Religion: Methodist. Seniority: 12.

10 **Jacobs (D)** —Feb. 24, 1932. Occupation: lawyer, police officer. Religion: Roman Catholic. Seniority: 34.

IOWA

1 **Leach (R)** —Oct. 15, 1942. Occupation: propane gas company executive, foreign service officer. Religion: Episcopalian. Seniority: 17.

2 **Nussle (R)** —June 27, 1960. Occupation: lawyer. Religion: Lutheran. Seniority: 110.

3 **Lightfoot (R)** —Sept. 27, 1938. Occupation: radio broadcaster, store owner, police officer, flight instructor, charter pilot, farmer. Religion: Roman Catholic. Seniority: 65.

4 **Smith (D)** —March 23, 1920. Occupation: lawyer, farmer. Religion: Methodist. Seniority: 5.

5 **Grandy (R)** —June 29, 1948. Occupation: actor, congressional aide. Religion: Episcopalian. Seniority: 79.

KANSAS

1 **Roberts (R)** —April 20, 1936. Occupation: journalist, congressional aide. Religion: Methodist. Seniority: 32.

2 **Slattery (D)** —Aug. 4, 1948. Occupation: real estate broker. Religion: Roman Catholic. Seniority: 86.

3 **Meyers (R)** —July 20, 1928. Occupation: homemaker, community volunteer. Religion: Methodist. Seniority: 65.

4 **Glickman (D)** —Nov. 24, 1944. Occupation: lawyer. Religion: Jewish. Seniority: 49.

KENTUCKY

1 **Barlow (D)** —Aug. 7, 1940. Occupation: sales director, conservation consultant. Religion: Methodist. Seniority: 195.

2 **Natcher (D)** —Sept. 11, 1909. Occupation: lawyer. Religion: Baptist. Seniority: 3.

3 **Mazzoli (D)** —Nov. 2, 1932. Occupation: lawyer, professor. Religion: Roman Catholic. Seniority: 22.

4 **Bunning (R)** —Oct. 23, 1931. Occupation: investment broker, sports agent, professional baseball player. Religion: Roman Catholic. Seniority: 79.

5 **Rogers (R)** —Dec. 31, 1937. Occupation: lawyer. Religion: Baptist. Seniority: 32.

6 **Baesler (D)** —July 9, 1941. Occupation: lawyer, farmer. Religion: Independent Christian. Seniority: 195.

LOUISIANA

1 **Livingston (R)** —April 30, 1943. Occupation: lawyer. Religion: Episcopalian. Seniority: 20.

2 **Jefferson (D)** —March 14, 1947. Occupation: lawyer. Religion: Baptist. Seniority: 171.

3 **Tauzin (D)** —June 14, 1943. Occupation: lawyer. Religion: Roman Catholic. Seniority: 72.

4 **Fields (D)** —Nov. 22, 1962. Occupation: public official. Religion: Baptist. Seniority: 195.

5 **McCrery (R)** —Sept. 18, 1949. Occupation: lawyer, congressional aide, government relations executive. Religion: Methodist. Seniority: 95.

6 **Baker (R)** —May 22, 1948. Occupation: real estate broker. Religion: Methodist. Seniority: 79.

7 **Hayes (D)** —Dec. 21, 1946. Occupation: lawyer, real estate developer. Religion: Methodist. Seniority: 124.

MAINE

1 **Andrews (D)** —March 22, 1953. Occupation: association director, political activist. Religion: Unitarian. Seniority: 171.

2 **Snowe (R)** —Feb. 21, 1947. Occupation: public official. Religion: Greek Orthodox. Seniority: 21.

MARYLAND

1 **Gilchrest (R)** —April 15, 1946. Occupation: high school teacher. Religion: Methodist. Seniority: 110.

2 **Bentley (R)** —Nov. 28, 1923. Occupation: international trade consultant, journalist. Religion: Eastern Orthodox. Seniority: 65.

3 **Cardin (D)** —Oct. 5, 1943. Occupation: lawyer. Religion: Jewish. Seniority: 124.

4 **Wynn (D)** —Sept. 10, 1951. Occupation: lawyer. Religion: Baptist. Seniority: 195.

5 **Hoyer (D)** —June 14, 1939. Occupation: lawyer. Religion: Baptist. Seniority: 82.

6 **Bartlett (R)** —June 3, 1926. Occupation: teacher, engineer. Religion: Seventh-day Adventist. Seniority: 128.

7 **Mfume (D)** —Oct. 24, 1948. Occupation: professor, radio station program director, talk show host. Religion: Baptist. Seniority: 124.

8 **Morella (R)** —Feb. 12, 1931. Occupation: professor. Religion: Roman Catholic. Seniority: 79.

MASSACHUSETTS

1 **Olver (D)** —Sept. 3, 1936. Occupation: professor. Religion: Unspecified. Seniority: 190.

2 **Neal (D)** —Feb. 14, 1949. Occupation: public official, college lecturer. Religion: Roman Catholic. Seniority: 145.

3 **Blute (R)** —Jan. 28, 1956. Occupation: public relations director. Religion: Roman Catholic. Seniority: 128.

4 **Frank (D)** —March 31, 1940. Occupation: lawyer. Religion: Jewish. Seniority: 73.

5 **Meehan (D)** —Dec. 30, 1956. Occupation: lawyer. Religion: Roman Catholic. Seniority: 195.

6 **Torkildsen (R)** —Jan. 28, 1958. Occupation: public official. Religion: Roman Catholic. Seniority: 128.

7 **Markey (D)** —July 11, 1946. Occupation: lawyer. Religion: Roman Catholic. Seniority: 48.

8 **Kennedy (D)** —Sept. 24, 1952. Occupation: energy company executive. Religion: Roman Catholic. Seniority: 124.

9 **Moakley (D)** —April 27, 1927. Occupation: lawyer. Religion: Roman Catholic. Seniority: 26.

10 **Studds (D)** —May 12, 1937. Occupation: high school teacher. Religion: Episcopalian. Seniority: 26.

MICHIGAN

1 **Stupak (D)** —Feb. 29, 1952. Occupation: lawyer, state trooper, patrolman. Religion: Roman Catholic. Seniority: 195.

2 **Hoekstra (R)** —Oct. 30, 1953. Occupation: furniture company executive. Religion: Christian Reformed. Seniority: 128.

3 Vacancy

4 **Camp (R)** —July 9, 1953. Occupation: lawyer. Religion: Roman Catholic. Seniority: 110.

5 **Barcia (D)** —Feb. 25, 1952. Occupation: congressional aide. Religion: Roman Catholic. Seniority: 195.

6 **Upton (R)** —April 23, 1953. Occupation: congressional aide, budget analyst. Religion: Protestant. Seniority: 79.

7 **Smith (R)** —Nov. 5, 1934. Occupation: dairy farmer. Religion: Congregationalist. Seniority: 128.

8 **Carr (D)** —March 27, 1943. Occupation: lawyer. Religion: Baptist. Seniority: 85.

9 **Kildee (D)** —Sept. 16, 1929. Occupation: teacher. Religion: Roman Catholic. Seniority: 49.

10 **Bonior (D)** —June 6, 1945. Occupation: probation officer, adoption caseworker. Religion: Roman Catholic. Seniority: 49.

11 **Knollenberg (R)** —Nov. 28, 1933. Occupation: insurance broker. Religion: Roman Catholic. Seniority: 128.

12 **Levin (D)** —Sept. 6, 1931. Occupation: lawyer. Religion: Jewish. Seniority: 86.

13 **Ford (D)** —Aug. 6, 1927. Occupation: lawyer. Religion: United Church of Christ. Seniority: 12.

14 **Conyers (D)** —May 16, 1929. Occupation: lawyer. Religion: Baptist. Seniority: 12.

15 **Collins (D)** —April 13, 1939. Occupation: public official. Religion: Shrine of the Black Madonna (Pan-African Orthodox Christian). Seniority: 171.

16 **Dingell (D)** —July 8, 1926. Occupation: lawyer. Religion: Roman Catholic. Seniority: 4.

MINNESOTA

1 **Penny (D)** —Nov. 19, 1951. Occupation: sales representative. Religion: Lutheran. Seniority: 86.

2 **Minge (D)** —March 19, 1942. Occupation: lawyer. Religion: Lutheran. Seniority: 195.

3 **Ramstad (R)** —May 6, 1946. Occupation: lawyer, legislative aide. Religion: Protestant. Seniority: 110.

4 **Vento (D)** —Oct. 7, 1940. Occupation: science teacher. Religion: Roman Catholic. Seniority: 49.

5 **Sabo (D)** —Feb. 28, 1938. Occupation: public official. Religion: Lutheran. Seniority: 61.

6 **Grams (R)** —Feb. 4, 1948. Occupation: contractor, television journalist. Religion: Lutheran. Seniority: 128.

7 **Peterson (D)** —June 29, 1944. Occupation: accountant. Religion: Lutheran. Seniority: 171.

8 **Oberstar (D)** —Sept. 10, 1934. Occupation: language teacher, congressional aide. Religion: Roman Catholic. Seniority: 35.

MISSISSIPPI

1 **Whitten (D)** —April 18, 1910. Occupation: elementary school teacher and principal, lawyer, author. Religion: Presbyterian. Seniority: 1.

2 **Thompson (D)** —Jan. 28, 1948. Occupation: teacher. Religion: Methodist. Seniority: 256.

3 **Montgomery (D)** —Aug. 5, 1920. Occupation: insurance executive. Religion: Episcopalian. Seniority: 17.

4 **Parker (D)** —Oct. 31, 1949. Occupation: funeral director. Religion: Presbyterian. Seniority: 145.

5 **Taylor (D)** —Sept. 17, 1953. Occupation: sales representative. Religion: Roman Catholic. Seniority: 164.

MISSOURI

1 **Clay (D)** —April 30, 1931. Occupation: real estate and insurance broker. Religion: Roman Catholic. Seniority: 19.

2 **Talent (R)** —Oct. 18, 1956. Occupation: lawyer. Religion: Presbyterian. Seniority: 128.

3 **Gephardt (D)** —Jan. 31, 1941. Occupation: lawyer. Religion: Baptist. Seniority: 49.

4 **Skelton (D)** —Dec. 20, 1931. Occupation: lawyer. Religion: Christian Church. Seniority: 49.

5 **Wheat (D)** —Oct. 16, 1951. Occupation: legislative aide, federal economist. Religion: Church of Christ. Seniority: 86.

6 **Danner (D)** —Jan. 13, 1934. Occupation: congressional aide, federal official. Religion: Roman Catholic. Seniority: 195.

7 **Hancock (R)** —Sept. 14, 1929. Occupation: security company executive. Religion: Church of Christ. Seniority: 97.

8 **Emerson (R)** —Jan. 1, 1938. Occupation: government relations executive, congressional aide. Religion: Presbyterian. Seniority: 32.

9 **Volkmer (D)** —April 4, 1931. Occupation: lawyer. Religion: Roman Catholic. Seniority: 49.

MONTANA

AL **Williams (D)** —Oct. 30, 1937. Occupation: elementary and secondary school teacher. Religion: Roman Catholic. Seniority: 61.

NEBRASKA

1 **Bereuter (R)** —Oct. 6, 1939. Occupation: urban planner, professor, state official. Religion: Lutheran. Seniority: 21.

2 **Hoagland (D)** —Nov. 17, 1941. Occupation: lawyer. Religion: Episcopalian. Seniority: 145.

3 **Barrett (R)** —Feb. 9, 1929. Occupation: real estate and insurance broker. Religion: Presbyterian. Seniority: 110.

NEVADA

1 **Bilbray (D)** —May 19, 1938. Occupation: lawyer. Religion: Roman Catholic. Seniority: 124.

2 **Vucanovich (R)** —June 22, 1921. Occupation: congressional aide, travel agency owner. Religion: Roman Catholic. Seniority: 48.

NEW HAMPSHIRE

1 **Zeliff (R)** —June 12, 1936. Occupation: hotel owner. Religion: Protestant. Seniority: 110.

2 **Swett (D)** —May 1, 1957. Occupation: architect. Religion: Mormon. Seniority: 171.

NEW JERSEY

1 **Andrews (D)** —Aug. 4, 1957. Occupation: professor. Religion: Episcopalian. Seniority: 168.

2 **Hughes (D)** —Oct. 17, 1932. Occupation: lawyer. Religion: Episcopalian. Seniority: 35.

3 **Saxton (R)** —Jan. 22, 1943. Occupation: real estate broker, elementary school teacher. Religion: Methodist. Seniority: 63.

4 **Smith (R)** —March 4, 1953. Occupation: sporting goods executive. Religion: Roman Catholic. Seniority: 32.

5 **Roukema (R)** —Sept. 19, 1929. Occupation: high school government and history teacher. Religion: Protestant. Seniority: 32.

6 **Pallone (D)** —Oct. 30, 1951. Occupation: lawyer. Religion: Roman Catholic. Seniority: 144.

7 **Franks (R)** —Sept. 21, 1951. Occupation: newspaper owner. Religion: Methodist. Seniority: 128.

8 **Klein (D)** —June 24, 1930. Occupation: lawyer. Religion: Jewish. Seniority: 195.

9 **Torricelli (D)** —Aug. 26, 1951. Occupation: lawyer. Religion: Methodist. Seniority: 86.

10 **Payne (D)** —July 16, 1934. Occupation: community development executive. Religion: Baptist. Seniority: 145.

11 **Gallo (R)** —Nov. 23, 1935. Occupation: real estate broker. Religion: Methodist. Seniority: 65.

12 **Zimmer (R)** —Aug. 16, 1944. Occupation: lawyer. Religion: Jewish. Seniority: 110.

13 **Menendez (D)** —Jan. 1, 1954. Occupation: lawyer. Religion: Roman Catholic. Seniority: 195.

NEW MEXICO

1 **Schiff (R)** —March 18, 1947. Occupation: lawyer. Religion: Jewish. Seniority: 97.

2 **Skeen (R)** —June 30, 1927. Occupation: sheep rancher, soil and water engineer, flying service operator. Religion: Roman Catholic. Seniority: 32.

3 **Richardson (D)** —Nov. 15, 1947. Occupation: business consultant. Religion: Roman Catholic. Seniority: 86.

NEW YORK

1 **Hochbrueckner (D)** —Sept. 20, 1938. Occupation: aerospace engineer. Religion: Roman Catholic. Seniority: 124.

2 **Lazio (R)** —March 13, 1958. Occupation: lawyer. Religion: Roman Catholic. Seniority: 128.

3 **King (R)** —April 5, 1944. Occupation: lawyer. Religion: Roman Catholic. Seniority: 128.

4 **Levy (D)** —Dec. 18, 1953. Occupation: lawyer, radio journalist, legislative aide, utility company executive. Religion: Jewish. Seniority: 128.

5 **Ackerman (D)** —Nov. 19, 1942. Occupation: teacher, publisher and editor, advertising executive. Religion: Jewish. Seniority: 115.

6 **Flake (D)** —Jan. 30, 1945. Occupation: minister. Religion: African Methodist Episcopal. Seniority: 124.

7 **Manton (D)** —Nov. 3, 1932. Occupation: lawyer. Religion: Roman Catholic. Seniority: 118.

8 **Nadler (D)** —June 13, 1947. Occupation: city official, lawyer. Religion: Jewish. Seniority: 193.

9 **Schumer (D)** —Nov. 23, 1950. Occupation: lawyer. Religion: Jewish. Seniority: 73.

10 **Towns (D)** —July 21, 1934. Occupa-

tion: professor, hospital administrator. Religion: Independent Baptist. Seniority: 86.

11 Owens (D) —June 28, 1936. Occupation: librarian. Religion: Baptist. Seniority: 86.

12 Velázquez (D) —March 22, 1953. Occupation: professor. Religion: Roman Catholic. Seniority: 195.

13 Molinari (R) —March 27, 1958. Occupation: political aide. Religion: Roman Catholic. Seniority: 109.

14 Maloney (D) —Feb. 19, 1948. Occupation: legislative aide, teacher. Religion: Presbyterian. Seniority: 195.

15 Rangel (D) —June 11, 1930. Occupation: lawyer. Religion: Roman Catholic. Seniority: 22.

16 Serrano (D) —Oct. 24, 1943. Occupation: public official. Religion: Roman Catholic. Seniority: 166.

17 Engel (D) —Feb. 18, 1947. Occupation: teacher, guidance counselor. Religion: Jewish. Seniority: 145.

18 Lowey (D) —July 5, 1937. Occupation: public official. Religion: Jewish. Seniority: 145.

19 Fish (R) —June 3, 1926. Occupation: lawyer. Religion: Episcopalian. Seniority: 5.

20 Gilman (R) —Dec. 6, 1922. Occupation: lawyer. Religion: Jewish. Seniority: 10.

21 McNulty (D) —Sept. 16, 1947. Occupation: public official. Religion: Roman Catholic. Seniority: 145.

22 Solomon (R) —Aug. 14, 1930. Occupation: insurance executive. Religion: Presbyterian. Seniority: 21.

23 Boehlert (R) —Sept. 28, 1936. Occupation: congressional aide, public relations executive. Religion: Roman Catholic. Seniority: 48.

24 McHugh (R) —Sept. 29, 1948. Occupation: city official, legislative aide, insurance broker. Religion: Roman Catholic. Seniority: 128.

25 Walsh (R) —June 19, 1947. Occupation: marketing executive, social worker. Religion: Roman Catholic. Seniority: 97.

26 Hinchey (D) —Oct. 27, 1938. Occupation: state employee. Religion: Roman Catholic. Seniority: 195.

27 Paxon (R) —April 29, 1954. Occupation: public official. Religion: Roman Catholic. Seniority: 97.

28 Slaughter (D) —Aug. 14, 1929. Occupation: market researcher, gubernatorial aide. Religion: Episcopalian. Seniority: 124.

29 LaFalce (D) —Oct. 6, 1939. Occupation: lawyer. Religion: Roman Catholic. Seniority: 35.

30 Quinn (R) —April 13, 1951. Occupation: teacher. Religion: Roman Catholic. Seniority: 128.

31 Houghton (R) —Aug. 7, 1926. Occupation: glassworks company executive. Religion: Episcopalian. Seniority: 80.

NORTH CAROLINA

1 Clayton (D) —Sept. 16, 1934. Occupation: consulting firm owner, nonprofit executive, state official, university official. Religion: Presbyterian. Seniority: 193.

2 Valentine (D) —March 15, 1926. Occupation: lawyer. Religion: Baptist. Seniority: 86.

3 Lancaster (D) —March 24, 1943. Occupation: lawyer. Religion: Presbyterian. Seniority: 124.

4 Price (D) —Aug. 17, 1940. Occupation: professor. Religion: American Baptist. Seniority: 124.

5 Neal (D) —Nov. 7, 1934. Occupation: publisher. Religion: Presbyterian. Seniority: 35.

6 Coble (R) —March 18, 1931. Occupation: lawyer, insurance claims supervisor. Religion: Presbyterian. Seniority: 65.

7 Rose (D) —Aug. 10, 1939. Occupation: lawyer. Religion: Presbyterian. Seniority: 26.

8 Hefner (D) —April 11, 1930. Occupation: broadcasting executive. Religion: Baptist. Seniority: 35.

9 McMillan (R) —May 9, 1932. Occupation: food store executive. Religion: Presbyterian. Seniority: 65.

10 Ballenger (R) —Dec. 6, 1926. Occupation: plastics company executive. Religion: Episcopalian. Seniority: 78.

11 Taylor (R) —Jan. 23, 1941. Occupation: tree farmer, banker. Religion: Baptist. Seniority: 110.

12 Watt (D) —Aug. 26, 1945. Occupation: lawyer. Religion: Presbyterian. Seniority: 195.

NORTH DAKOTA

AL Pomeroy (D) —Sept. 2, 1952. Occupation: lawyer. Religion: Presbyterian. Seniority: 195.

OHIO

1 Mann (D) —Sept. 25, 1939. Occupation: lawyer. Religion: Methodist. Seniority: 195.

2 Portman (R) —Dec. 19, 1955. Occupation: lawyer, White House aide, congressional aide. Religion: Methodist. Seniority: 175.

3 Hall (D) —Jan. 16, 1942. Occupation: real estate broker. Religion: Presbyterian. Seniority: 61.

4 Oxley (R) —Feb. 11, 1944. Occupation: FBI agent, lawyer. Religion: Lutheran. Seniority: 47.

5 Gillmor (R) —Feb. 1, 1939. Occupation: lawyer. Religion: Protestant. Seniority: 97.

6 Strickland (D) —Aug. 4, 1941. Occupation: professor. Religion: Methodist. Seniority: 195.

7 Hobson (R) —Oct. 17, 1936. Occupation: financial executive. Religion: Methodist. Seniority: 110.

8 Boehner (R) —Nov. 17, 1949. Occupation: plastics and packaging executive. Religion: Roman Catholic. Seniority: 110.

9 Kaptur (D) —June 17, 1946. Occupation: urban planner, White House aide. Religion: Roman Catholic. Seniority: 86.

10 Hoke (R) —May 18, 1952. Occupation: cellular phone company president, lawyer. Religion: Protestant. Seniority: 128.

11 Stokes (D) —Feb. 23, 1925. Occupation: lawyer. Religion: African Methodist Episcopal Zion. Seniority: 19.

12 Kasich (R) —May 13, 1952. Occupation: legislative aide. Religion: Christian. Seniority: 48.

13 Brown (D) —Nov. 9, 1952. Occupation: teacher. Religion: Presbyterian. Seniority: 195.

14 Sawyer (D) —Aug. 15, 1945. Occupation: teacher. Religion: Presbyterian. Seniority: 124.

15 Pryce (R) —July 29, 1951. Occupation: judge, lawyer. Religion: Presbyterian. Seniority: 128.

16 Regula (R) —Dec. 3, 1924. Occupation: lawyer, businessman. Religion: Episcopalian. Seniority: 10.

17 Traficant (D) —May 8, 1941. Occupation: county drug program director, sheriff. Religion: Roman Catholic. Seniority: 118.

18 Applegate (D) —March 27, 1928. Occupation: real estate broker. Religion: Presbyterian. Seniority: 49.

19 Fingerhut (D) —May 6, 1959. Occupation: lawyer. Religion: Jewish. Seniority: 195.

OKLAHOMA

1 Inhofe (R) —Nov. 17, 1934. Occupation: real estate developer, insurance executive. Religion: Presbyterian. Seniority: 79.

2 Synar (D) —Oct. 17, 1950. Occupation: rancher, real estate broker, lawyer. Religion: Episcopalian. Seniority: 61.

3 Brewster (D) —Nov. 8, 1941. Occupation: pharmacist, rancher, real estate executive. Religion: Baptist. Seniority: 171.

4 McCurdy (D) —March 30, 1950. Occupation: lawyer. Religion: Lutheran. Seniority: 73.

5 Istook (R) —Feb. 11, 1950. Occupation: lawyer. Religion: Mormon. Seniority: 128.

6 English (D) —Nov. 30, 1940. Occupation: petroleum landman. Religion: Methodist. Seniority: 35.

OREGON

1 Furse (D) —Oct. 13, 1936. Occupation: community activist. Religion: Protestant. Seniority: 195.

2 Smith (R) —June 16, 1931. Occupation: cattle rancher, businessman. Religion: Presbyterian. Seniority: 48.

3 Wyden (D) —May 3, 1949. Occupation: lawyer, professor. Religion: Jewish. Seniority: 73.

4 DeFazio (D) —May 27, 1947. Occupation: congressional aide. Religion: Roman Catholic. Seniority: 124.

5 Kopetski (D) —Oct. 27, 1949. Occupation: advertising executive. Religion: Unspecified. Seniority: 171.

PENNSYLVANIA

1 Foglietta (D) —Dec. 3, 1928. Occupation: lawyer. Religion: Roman Catholic. Seniority: 73.

2 Blackwell (D) —Aug. 1, 1931. Occupation: labor official. Religion: Baptist. Seniority: 192.

3 Borski (D) —Oct. 20, 1948. Occupation: stockbroker. Religion: Roman Catholic. Seniority: 86.

4 Klink (D) —Sept. 23, 1951. Occupation: television journalist. Religion: United Church of Christ. Seniority: 195.

5 Clinger (R) —April 4, 1929. Occupation: lawyer. Religion: Presbyterian. Seniority: 21.

6 Holden (D) —March 5, 1957. Occupation: sheriff. Religion: Roman Catholic. Seniority: 195.

7 Weldon (R) —July 22, 1947. Occupation: teacher, consultant. Religion: Protestant. Seniority: 79.

8 Greenwood (R) —May 4, 1951. Occupation: state official. Religion: Presbyterian. Seniority: 128.

9 Shuster (R) —Jan. 23, 1932. Occupation: computer industry executive. Religion: United Church of Christ. Seniority: 10.

10 McDade (R) —Sept. 29, 1931. Occupation: lawyer. Religion: Roman Catholic. Seniority: 2.

11 Kanjorski (D) —April 2, 1937. Occupation: lawyer. Religion: Roman Catholic. Seniority: 118.

12 Murtha (D) —June 17, 1932. Occupation: car wash owner and operator. Religion: Roman Catholic. Seniority: 33.

13 Margolies-Mezvinsky (D) —June 21, 1942. Occupation: television journalist. Religion: Jewish. Seniority: 195.

14 Coyne (D) —Aug. 24, 1936. Occupation: accountant. Religion: Roman Catholic. Seniority: 73.

15 McHale (D) —July 26, 1950. Occupation: lawyer, adjunct professor. Religion: Roman Catholic. Seniority: 195.

16 Walker (R) —Dec. 23, 1942. Occupation: high school teacher, congressional aide. Religion: Presbyterian. Seniority: 17.

17 Gekas (R) —April 14, 1930. Occupation: lawyer. Religion: Greek Orthodox. Seniority: 48.

18 Santorum (R) —May 10, 1958. Occupation: lawyer, legislative aide. Religion: Roman Catholic. Seniority: 110.

19 Goodling (R) —Dec. 5, 1927. Occupation: public school superintendent. Religion: Methodist. Seniority: 15.

20 Murphy (D) —June 17, 1927. Occupation: lawyer. Religion: Roman Catholic. Seniority: 49.

21 Ridge (R) —Aug. 26, 1945. Occupation: lawyer. Religion: Roman Catholic. Seniority: 48.

RHODE ISLAND

1 Machtley (R) —July 13, 1948. Occupation: lawyer. Religion: Presbyterian. Seniority: 97.

2 Reed (D) —Nov. 12, 1949. Occupation: lawyer. Religion: Roman Catholic. Seniority: 171.

SOUTH CAROLINA

1 Ravenel (R) —March 29, 1927. Occupation: businessman. Religion: French Huguenot. Seniority: 79.

2 Spence (R) —April 9, 1928. Occupation: lawyer. Religion: Lutheran. Seniority: 7.

3 Derrick (D) —Sept. 30, 1936. Occupation: lawyer. Religion: Episcopalian. Seniority: 35.

4 Inglis (R) —Oct. 11, 1959. Occupation: lawyer. Religion: Presbyterian. Seniority: 128.

5 Spratt (D) —Nov. 1, 1942. Occupation: lawyer. Religion: Presbyterian. Seniority: 86.

6 Clyburn (D) —July 21, 1940. Occupation: state official. Religion: African Methodist Episcopal. Seniority: 195.

SOUTH DAKOTA

AL Johnson (D) —Dec. 28, 1946. Occupation: lawyer. Religion: Lutheran. Seniority: 124.

TENNESSEE

1 Quillen (R) —Jan. 11, 1916. Occupation: newspaper publisher, real estate and insurance broker, banker. Religion: Methodist. Seniority: 2.

2 Duncan (R) —July 21, 1947. Occupation: judge, lawyer. Religion: Presbyterian. Seniority: 96.

3 Lloyd (D) —Jan. 3, 1929. Occupation: radio station executive. Religion: Church of Christ. Seniority: 35.

4 Cooper (D) —June 19, 1954. Occupation: lawyer. Religion: Episcopalian. Seniority: 86.

5 Clement (D) —Sept. 23, 1943. Occupation: college president, marketing, management and real estate executive. Religion: Methodist. Seniority: 141.

6 Gordon (D) —Jan. 24, 1949. Occupation: lawyer. Religion: Methodist. Seniority: 118.

7 Sundquist (R) —March 15, 1936. Occupation: printing, advertising and marketing executive. Religion: Lutheran. Seniority: 48.

8 Tanner (D) —Sept. 22, 1944. Occupation: lawyer, businessman. Religion: Disciples of Christ. Seniority: 145.

9 Ford (D) —May 20, 1945. Occupation: funeral director. Religion: Baptist. Seniority: 35.

TEXAS

1 Chapman (D) —March 8, 1945. Occupation: lawyer. Religion: Methodist. Seniority: 123.

2 Wilson (D) —June 1, 1933. Occupation: lumberyard manager. Religion: Methodist. Seniority: 26.

3 Johnson (R) —Oct. 11, 1930. Occupation: home builder. Religion: Methodist. Seniority: 126.

4 Hall (D) —May 3, 1923. Occupation: lawyer, businessman. Religion: Methodist. Seniority: 73.

5 Bryant (D) —Feb. 22, 1947. Occupation: lawyer. Religion: Methodist. Seniority: 86.

6 Barton (R) —Sept. 15, 1949. Occupation: engineering consultant. Religion: Methodist. Seniority: 65.

7 Archer (R) —March 22, 1928. Occupation: lawyer, feed company executive. Religion: Roman Catholic. Seniority: 7.

8 Fields (R) —Feb. 3, 1952. Occupation: lawyer, cemetery executive. Religion: Baptist. Seniority: 32.

9 Brooks (D) —Dec. 18, 1922. Occupation: lawyer. Religion: Methodist. Seniority: 2.

10 Pickle (D) —Oct. 11, 1913. Occupation:

public relations and advertising executive. Religion: Methodist. Seniority: 10.

11 Edwards (D) —Nov. 24, 1951. Occupation: radio station executive. Religion: Methodist. Seniority: 171.

12 Geren (D) —Jan. 29, 1952. Occupation: lawyer. Religion: Baptist. Seniority: 162.

13 Sarpalius (D) —Jan. 10, 1948. Occupation: agriculture consultant, public school teacher. Religion: Methodist. Seniority: 145.

14 Laughlin (D) —Jan. 21, 1942. Occupation: lawyer. Religion: Methodist. Seniority: 145.

15 de la Garza (D) —Sept. 22, 1927. Occupation: lawyer. Religion: Roman Catholic. Seniority: 12.

16 Coleman (D) —Nov. 29, 1941. Occupation: lawyer. Religion: Presbyterian. Seniority: 86.

17 Stenholm (D) —Oct. 26, 1938. Occupation: cotton farmer. Religion: Lutheran. Seniority: 61.

18 Washington (D) —Oct. 12, 1941. Occupation: lawyer. Religion: Baptist. Seniority: 165.

19 Combest (R) —March 20, 1945. Occupation: farmer, congressional aide, electronics wholesaler. Religion: Methodist. Seniority: 65.

20 Gonzalez (D) —May 3, 1916. Occupation: teacher, public relations consultant, translator. Religion: Roman Catholic. Seniority: 7.

21 Smith (R) —Nov. 19, 1947. Occupation: lawyer, rancher. Religion: Christian Scientist. Seniority: 79.

22 DeLay (R) —April 8, 1947. Occupation: pest control executive. Religion: Baptist. Seniority: 65.

23 Bonilla (R) —Jan. 2, 1954. Occupation: television executive. Religion: Baptist. Seniority: 128.

24 Frost (D) —Jan. 1, 1942. Occupation: lawyer. Religion: Jewish. Seniority: 61.

25 Andrews (D) —Feb. 7, 1944. Occupation: lawyer. Religion: Episcopalian. Seniority: 86.

26 Armey (R) —July 7, 1940. Occupation: economist. Religion: Presbyterian. Seniority: 65.

27 Ortiz (D) —June 3, 1937. Occupation: law enforcement official. Religion: Methodist. Seniority: 86.

28 Tejeda (D) —Oct. 2, 1945. Occupation: lawyer. Religion: Roman Catholic. Seniority: 195.

29 Green (D) —Oct. 17, 1947. Occupation: lawyer. Religion: Methodist. Seniority: 195.

30 Johnson (D) —Dec. 3, 1935. Occupation: airport shop owner. Religion: Baptist. Seniority: 195.

UTAH

1 Hansen (R) —Aug. 14, 1932. Occupation: insurance executive, developer. Religion: Mormon. Seniority: 32.

2 Shepherd (D) —July 5, 1940. Occupation: university official. Religion: Protestant. Seniority: 195.

3 Orton (D) —Sept. 22, 1948. Occupation: lawyer. Religion: Mormon. Seniority: 171.

VERMONT

AL Sanders (I) —Sept. 8, 1941. Occupation: college lecturer, free-lance writer. Religion: Jewish.

VIRGINIA

1 Bateman (R) —Aug. 7, 1928. Occupation: lawyer. Religion: Protestant. Seniority: 48.

2 Pickett (D) —Aug. 31, 1930. Occupation: lawyer, accountant. Religion: Baptist. Seniority: 124.

3 Scott (D) —April 30, 1947. Occupation: lawyer. Religion: Episcopalian. Seniority: 195.

4 Sisisky (D) —June 9, 1927. Occupation: beer and soft drink distributor. Religion: Jewish. Seniority: 86.

5 Payne (D) —July 9, 1945. Occupation: real estate developer, businessman. Religion: Presbyterian. Seniority: 142.

6 Goodlatte (R) —Sept. 22, 1952. Occupation: lawyer, congressional aide. Religion: Christian Scientist. Seniority: 128.

7 Bliley (R) —Jan. 28, 1932. Occupation: funeral director. Religion: Roman Catholic. Seniority: 32.

8 Moran (D) —May 16, 1945. Occupation: investment banker. Religion: Roman Catholic. Seniority: 171.

9 Boucher (D) —Aug. 1, 1946. Occupation: lawyer. Religion: Methodist. Seniority: 86.

10 Wolf (R) —Jan. 30, 1939. Occupation: lawyer. Religion: Presbyterian. Seniority: 32.

11 Byrne (D) —Oct. 27, 1946. Occupation: human resources consultant. Religion: Roman Catholic. Seniority: 195.

WASHINGTON

1 Cantwell (D) —Oct. 13, 1958. Occupation: public relations consultant. Religion: Roman Catholic. Seniority: 195.

2 Swift (D) —Sept. 12, 1935. Occupation: broadcaster, congressional aide. Religion: Unitarian. Seniority: 61.

3 Unsoeld (D) —Dec. 3, 1931. Occupation: public official. Religion: Theist. Seniority: 145.

4 Inslee (D) —Feb. 9, 1951. Occupation: lawyer. Religion: Protestant. Seniority: 195.

5 Foley (D) —March 6, 1929. Occupation: lawyer. Religion: Roman Catholic. Seniority: 12.

6 Dicks (D) —Dec. 16, 1940. Occupation: congressional aide. Religion: Lutheran. Seniority: 49.

7 McDermott (D) —Dec. 28, 1936. Occupation: psychiatrist. Religion: Episcopalian. Seniority: 145.

8 Dunn (R) —July 29, 1941. Occupation: state party official. Religion: Episcopalian. Seniority: 128.

9 Kreidler (D) —Sept. 28, 1943. Occupation: optometrist. Religion: Church of Christ. Seniority: 195.

WEST VIRGINIA

1 Mollohan (D) —May 14, 1943. Occupation: lawyer. Religion: Baptist. Seniority: 86.

2 Wise (D) —Jan. 6, 1948. Occupation: lawyer. Religion: Episcopalian. Seniority: 86.

3 Rahall (D) —May 20, 1949. Occupation: broadcasting executive, travel agent. Religion: Presbyterian. Seniority: 49.

WISCONSIN

1 Barca (D) —Aug. 7, 1955. Occupation: educator, employment specialist. Religion: Roman Catholic. Seniority: 257.

2 Klug (R) —Jan. 16, 1953. Occupation: television journalist, business development and investment executive. Religion: Roman Catholic. Seniority: 110.

3 Gunderson (R) —May 10, 1951. Occupation: public official. Religion: Lutheran. Seniority: 32.

4 Kleczka (D) —Nov. 26, 1943. Occupation: accountant. Religion: Roman Catholic. Seniority: 117.

5 Barrett (D) —Dec. 8, 1953. Occupation: lawyer. Religion: Roman Catholic. Seniority: 195.

6 Petri (R) —May 28, 1940. Occupation: lawyer. Religion: Lutheran. Seniority: 30.

7 Obey (D) —Oct. 3, 1938. Occupation: real estate broker. Religion: Roman Catholic. Seniority: 21.

8 Roth (R) —Oct. 10, 1938. Occupation: real estate broker. Religion: Roman Catholic. Seniority: 21.

9 Sensenbrenner (R) —June 14, 1943. Occupation: lawyer. Religion: Episcopalian. Seniority: 21.

WYOMING

AL Thomas (R) —Feb. 17, 1933. Occupation: power company executive. Religion: Methodist. Seniority: 107.

Pronunciation Guide

The following is an informal pronunciation guide for some of the most often mispronounced names of members of Congress.

SENATORS

Alfonse M. D'Amato, R-N.Y. — da-MAH-toe
Dennis DeConcini, D-Ariz. — dee-con-SEE-nee
Pete V. Domenici, R-N.M. — da-MEN-ih-chee
Lauch Faircloth, R-N.C. — LOCK
Dianne Feinstein, D-Calif. — FINE-stine
Daniel K. Inouye, D-Hawaii — in-NO-ay

REPRESENTATIVES

Jim Bacchus, D-Fla. — BACK-us
Spencer Bachus, R-Ala. — BACK-us
Scotty Baesler, D-Ky. — BAA-zler
James A. Barcia, D-Mich. — BAR-sha
Xavier Becerra, D-Calif. — HAH-vee-air beh-SEH-ra
Anthony C. Beilenson, D-Calif. — BEE-lin-son
Doug Bereuter, R-Neb. — BEE-right-er
Michael Bilirakis, R-Fla. — bil-li-RACK-us
John A. Boehner, R-Ohio — BAY-ner
Henry Bonilla, R-Texas — bo-NEE-uh
David E. Bonior, D-Mich. — BON-yer
Rick Boucher, D-Va. — BOUGH-cher
Steve Buyer, R-Ind. — BOO-yer
Charles T. Canady, R-Fla. — CAN-uh-dee
Michael D. Crapo, R-Idaho — CRAY-poe
Peter A. DeFazio, D-Ore. — da-FAH-zee-o
Peter Deutsch, D-Fla. — DOYCH
Lincoln Diaz-Balart, R-Fla. — DEE-az BAA-lart
Eni F. H. Faleomavaega, D-Am. Samoa — EN-ee FOL-ee-oh-mav-ah-ENG-uh
Harris W. Fawell, R-Ill. — FAY-well
Vic Fazio, D-Calif. — FAY-zee-o
Thomas M. Foglietta, D-Pa. — fo-lee-ET-uh
Elton Gallegly, R-Calif. — GAL-uh-glee
Sam Gejdenson, D-Conn. — GAY-den-son
Robert W. Goodlatte, R-Va. — GOOD-lat
Luis V. Gutierrez, D-Ill. — loo-EES goo-tee-AIR-ez
George J. Hochbrueckner, D-N.Y. — HOCK-brewk-ner

Peter Hoekstra, R-Mich. — HOKE-struh
Amo Houghton, R-N.Y. — HO-tun
James M. Inhofe, R-Okla. — IN-hoff
John R. Kasich, R-Ohio — KAY-sick
Gerald D. Kleczka, D-Wis. — KLETCH-kuh
Scott L. Klug, R-Wis. — KLOOG
Jim Kolbe, R-Ariz. — COLE-bee
Mike Kopetski, D-Ore. — ka-PET-skee
Greg Laughlin, D-Texas — LAWF-lin
Rick A. Lazio, R-N.Y. — LAZZ-ee-o
Richard H. Lehman, D-Calif. — LEE-mun
Nita M. Lowey, D-N.Y. — LOW-e
Ronald K. Machtley, R-R.I. — MAKE-lee
Donald Manzullo, R-Ill. — man-ZOO-low
Marjorie Margolies-Mezvinsky, D-Pa. — mar-GO-lees mez-VIN-skee
Kweisi Mfume, D-Md. — kwy-EE-say mm-FU-may
David Minge, D-Minn. — MIN-gee
David R. Obey, D-Wis. — O-bee
Frank Pallone Jr., D-N.J. — pa-LOAN
Ed Pastor, D-Ariz.— pas-TORE
Nancy Pelosi, D-Calif. — pa-LOH-see
Tom Petri, R-Wis. — PEE-try
Glenn Poshard, D-Ill. — pa-SHARD
Arthur Ravenel Jr., R-S.C. — RAV-nel
Ralph Regula, R-Ohio — REG-you-luh
Dana Rohrabacher, R-Calif. — ROAR-ah-BAH-ker
Ileana Ros-Lehtinen, R-Fla. — il-ee-AH-na ross-LAY-tin-nen
Marge Roukema, R-N.J. — ROCK-ah-muh
Bill Sarpalius, D-Texas — sar-PAUL-us
José E. Serrano, D-N.Y. — ho-ZAY sa-RAH-no (rolled 'R')
Bart Stupak, D-Mich. — STEW-pack
W. J. "Billy" Tauzin, D-La. — TOE-zan
Frank Tejeda, D-Texas — tuh-HAY-duh
Robert G. Torricelli, D-N.J. — tor-uh-SELL-ee
Jolene Unsoeld, D-Wash. — UN-sold
Nydia M. Velázquez, D-N.Y. — NID-ee-uh veh-LASS-kez
Barbara F. Vucanovich, R-Nev. — voo-CAN-oh-vitch
Bill Zeliff, R-N.H. — ZELL-iff

Seniority in the Senate

Senate rank generally is determined according to the official date of the beginning of a member's service, except in the case of new members sworn in at times other than the beginning of a Congress. For those appointed or elected to fill unexpired terms, the date of the appointment, certification or swearing-in determines the senator's rank.

When members are sworn in on the same day, custom decrees that those with prior political experience take precedence. Counted as political experience, in order of importance, is senatorial, House and gubernatorial service. Information on prior experience is given where applicable to seniority ranking. The dates following senators' names refer to the beginning of their present service.

DEMOCRATS

1. Byrd—Jan. 7, 1959
2. Pell—Jan. 3, 1961
3. Kennedy—Nov. 7, 1962
4. Inouye—Jan. 9, 1963
5. Hollings—Nov. 9, 1966
6. Nunn—Nov. 8, 1972
7. Johnston—Nov. 14, 1972
8. Biden—Jan. 3, 1973
9. Glenn—Dec. 24, 1974
10. Ford—Dec. 28, 1974
11. Bumpers (ex-governor)—Jan. 14, 1975
12. Leahy—Jan. 14, 1975
13. Metzenbaum—Dec. 29, 1976
14. Riegle—Dec. 30, 1976
15. Sarbanes (ex-representative, three House terms)—Jan. 4, 1977
16. DeConcini—Jan. 4, 1977
    Moynihan—Jan. 4, 1977
    Sasser—Jan. 4, 1977
19. Baucus—Dec. 15, 1978
20. Pryor (ex-representative, three House terms)—Jan. 15, 1979
21. Boren (ex-governor)—Jan. 15, 1979
    Exon (ex-governor)—Jan. 15, 1979
23. Bradley—Jan. 15, 1979

Heflin—Jan. 15, 1979
Levin—Jan. 15, 1979
26. Mitchell—May 19, 1980
27. Dodd—Jan. 5, 1981
28. Lautenberg—Dec. 27, 1982
29. Bingaman—Jan. 3, 1983
30. Kerry—Jan. 2, 1985
31. Harkin (ex-representative, five House terms)—Jan. 3, 1985
    Simon (ex-representative, five House terms)—Jan. 3, 1985
33. Rockefeller—Jan. 15, 1985
34. Breaux (ex-representative, eight House terms)—Jan. 6, 1987
35. Mikulski (ex-representative, five House terms)—Jan. 6, 1987
36. Daschle (ex-representative, four House terms)—Jan. 6, 1987
    Shelby (ex-representative, four House terms)—Jan. 6, 1987
38. Reid (ex-representative, two House terms)—Jan. 6, 1987
39. Graham (ex-governor)—Jan. 6, 1987
40. Conrad—Jan. 6, 1987
41. Bryan (ex-governor)—Jan. 3, 1989
    Kerrey (ex-governor)—Jan. 3, 1989
    Robb (ex-governor)—Jan. 3, 1989
44. Kohl—Jan. 3, 1989
    Lieberman—Jan. 3, 1989
46. Akaka—May 16, 1990
47. Wellstone—Jan. 3, 1991
48. Wofford—May 9, 1991
49. Feinstein—Nov. 4, 1992
50. Dorgan—Dec. 15, 1992
51. Mathews—Jan. 2, 1993
52. Boxer (ex-representative, five House terms)—Jan. 5, 1993
53. Campbell (ex-representative, three House terms)—Jan. 5, 1993
54. Feingold—Jan. 5, 1993
    Moseley-Braun—Jan. 5, 1993
    Murray—Jan. 5, 1993

REPUBLICANS

1. Thurmond—Nov. 7, 1956 *
2. Hatfield—Jan. 10, 1967
3. Stevens—Dec. 24, 1968
4. Dole (ex-representative, four House terms)—Jan. 3, 1969
5. Packwood—Jan. 3, 1969
6. Roth—Jan. 1, 1971

7. Domenici—Jan. 3, 1973
   Helms—Jan. 3, 1973
9. Danforth—Dec. 27, 1976
10. Chafee—Dec. 29, 1976
11. Hatch—Jan. 4, 1977
    Lugar—Jan. 4, 1977
    Wallop—Jan. 4, 1977
14. Durenberger—Nov. 8, 1978
15. Kassebaum—Dec. 23, 1978
16. Cochran—Dec. 27, 1978
17. Simpson—Jan. 1, 1979
18. Warner—Jan. 2, 1979
19. Cohen (ex-representative, three House terms)—Jan. 15, 1979
20. Pressler (ex-representative, two House terms)—Jan. 15, 1979
21. Grassley (ex-representative, three House terms)—Jan. 5, 1981
22. D'Amato—Jan. 5, 1981
    Murkowski—Jan. 5, 1981
    Nickles—Jan. 5, 1981
    Specter—Jan. 5, 1981
26. Gramm (ex-representative, three House terms)—Jan. 3, 1985
27. McConnell—Jan. 3, 1985
28. McCain (ex-representative, two House terms)—Jan. 6, 1987
29. Bond (ex-governor)—Jan. 6, 1987
30. Gorton (ex-senator)—Jan. 3, 1989
31. Lott (ex-representative, eight House terms)—Jan. 3, 1989
32. Jeffords (ex-representative, seven House terms)—Jan. 3, 1989
33. Coats (ex-representative, four House terms)—Jan. 3, 1989
34. Mack (ex-representative, three House terms)—Jan. 3, 1989
35. Burns—Jan. 3, 1989
36. Smith—Dec. 7, 1990
37. Brown (ex-representative, five House terms)—Jan. 3, 1991
    Craig (ex-representative, five House terms)—Jan. 3, 1991
39. Gregg (ex-representative, four House terms)—Jan. 5, 1993
40. Bennett—Jan. 5, 1993
    Coverdell—Jan. 5, 1993
    Faircloth—Jan. 5, 1993
    Kempthorne—Jan. 5, 1993
44. Hutchison—June 14, 1993

Thurmond began his Senate service Nov. 7, 1956, as a Democrat. He became a Republican on Sept. 16, 1964. The Republican Conference allowed his seniority to count from his 1956 election to the Senate.

Seniority in the House

House rank generally is determined according to the official date of the beginning of a member's service, except in the case of members elected to fill vacancies, in which instance the date of election determines rank.

When members are sworn in on the same day, those with prior House experience take precedence, starting with those with the longest consecutive service. Experience as a senator or governor is disregarded. Prior experience is given where applicable to seniority ranking. The dates following members' names refer to the beginning of their present service.

Bernard Sanders of Vermont was the lone independent in the House during the first session of the 103rd Congress.

DEMOCRATS

1. Whitten (Miss.)—Nov. 4, 1941
2. Brooks (Texas)—Jan. 3, 1953
3. Natcher (Ky.)—Aug. 1, 1953
4. Dingell (Mich.)—Dec. 13, 1955
5. Rostenkowski (Ill.)—Jan. 7, 1959
   Smith (Iowa)—Jan. 7, 1959
7. Gonzalez (Texas)—Nov. 4, 1961
8. Edwards (Calif.)—Jan. 9, 1963
   Gibbons (Fla.)—Jan. 9, 1963
10. Pickle (Texas)—Dec. 21, 1963
11. Yates (Ill.) (seven terms previously)— Jan. 4, 1965
12. Conyers (Mich.)—Jan. 4, 1965
    de la Garza (Texas)—Jan. 4, 1965
    Foley (Wash.)—Jan. 4, 1965
    Ford (Mich.)—Jan. 4, 1965
    Hamilton (Ind.)—Jan. 4, 1965
17. Bevill (Ala.)—Jan. 10, 1967
    Montgomery (Miss.)—Jan. 10, 1967
19. Clay (Mo.)—Jan. 3, 1969
    Stokes (Ohio)—Jan. 3, 1969
21. Obey (Wis.)—April 1, 1969
22. Dellums (Calif.)—Jan. 21, 1971
    Mazzoli (Ky.)—Jan. 21, 1971
    Rangel (N.Y.)—Jan. 21, 1971
25. Brown (Calif.) (four terms previously)—Jan. 3, 1973
26. Moakley (Mass.)—Jan. 3, 1973
    Rose (N.C.)—Jan. 3, 1973
    Schroeder (Colo.)—Jan. 3, 1973
    Stark (Calif.)—Jan. 3, 1973
    Studds (Mass.)—Jan. 3, 1973
    Wilson (Texas)—Jan. 3, 1973
32. Collins (Ill.)—June 5, 1973
33. Murtha (Pa.)—Feb. 5, 1974
34. Jacobs (Ind.) (four terms previously)—Jan. 14, 1975
35. Derrick (S.C.)—Jan. 14, 1975
    English (Okla.)—Jan. 14, 1975
    Ford (Tenn.)—Jan. 14, 1975
    Hefner (N.C.)—Jan. 14, 1975
    Hughes (N.J.)—Jan. 14, 1975
    LaFalce (N.Y.)—Jan. 14, 1975

Lloyd (Tenn.)—Jan. 14, 1975
Miller (Calif.)—Jan. 14, 1975
Mineta (Calif.)—Jan. 14, 1975
Neal (N.C.)—Jan. 14, 1975
Oberstar (Minn.)—Jan. 14, 1975
Sharp (Ind.)—Jan. 14, 1975
Waxman (Calif.)—Jan. 14, 1975
48. Markey (Mass.)—Nov. 2, 1976
49. Applegate (Ohio)—Jan. 4, 1977
    Beilenson (Calif.)—Jan. 4, 1977
    Bonior (Mich.)—Jan. 4, 1977
    Dicks (Wash.)—Jan. 4, 1977
    Gephardt (Mo.)—Jan. 4, 1977
    Glickman (Kan.)—Jan. 4, 1977
    Kildee (Mich.)—Jan. 4, 1977
    Murphy (Pa.)—Jan. 4, 1977
    Rahall (W.Va.)—Jan. 4, 1977
    Skelton (Mo.)—Jan. 4, 1977
    Vento (Minn.)—Jan. 4, 1977
    Volkmer (Mo.)—Jan. 4, 1977
61. Dixon (Calif.)—Jan. 15, 1979
    Fazio (Calif.)—Jan. 15, 1979
    Frost (Texas)—Jan. 15, 1979
    Hall (Ohio)—Jan. 15, 1979
    Hutto (Fla.)—Jan. 15, 1979
    Matsui (Calif.)—Jan. 15, 1979
    Sabo (Minn.)—Jan. 15, 1979
    Stenholm (Texas)—Jan. 15, 1979
    Swift (Wash.)—Jan. 15, 1979
    Synar (Okla.)—Jan. 15, 1979
    Williams (Mont.)—Jan. 15, 1979
72. Tauzin (La.)—May 17, 1980
73. Coyne (Pa.)—Jan. 5, 1981
    Foglietta (Pa.)—Jan. 5, 1981
    Frank (Mass.)—Jan. 5, 1981
    Gejdenson (Conn.)—Jan. 5, 1981
    Hall (Texas)—Jan. 5, 1981
    Lantos (Calif.)—Jan. 5, 1981
    McCurdy (Okla.)—Jan. 5, 1981
    Schumer (N.Y.)—Jan. 5, 1981
    Wyden (Ore.)—Jan. 5, 1981
82. Hoyer (Md.)—May 19, 1981
83. Kennelly (Conn.)—Jan. 12, 1982
84. Martinez (Calif.)—July 13, 1982
85. Carr (Mich.) (three terms previously)—Jan. 3, 1983
86. Andrews (Texas)—Jan. 3, 1983
    Berman (Calif.)—Jan. 3, 1983
    Borski (Pa.)—Jan. 3, 1983
    Boucher (Va.)—Jan. 3, 1983
    Bryant (Texas)—Jan. 3, 1983
    Coleman (Texas)—Jan. 3, 1983
    Cooper (Tenn.)—Jan. 3, 1983
    Durbin (Ill.)—Jan. 3, 1983
    Evans (Ill.)—Jan. 3, 1983
    Kaptur (Ohio)—Jan. 3, 1983
    Lehman (Calif.)—Jan. 3, 1983
    Levin (Mich.)—Jan. 3, 1983
    Lipinski (Ill.)—Jan. 3, 1983
    McCloskey (Ind.)—Jan. 3, 1983
    Mollohan (W.Va.)—Jan. 3, 1983
    Ortiz (Texas)—Jan. 3, 1983
    Owens (N.Y.)—Jan. 3, 1983
    Penny (Minn.)—Jan. 3, 1983
    Richardson (N.M.)—Jan. 3, 1983
    Rowland (Ga.)—Jan. 3, 1983
    Sisisky (Va.)—Jan. 3, 1983
    Slattery (Kan.)—Jan. 3, 1983
    Spratt (S.C.)—Jan. 3, 1983

Torres (Calif.)—Jan. 3, 1983
Torricelli (N.J.)—Jan. 3, 1983
Towns (N.Y.)—Jan. 3, 1983
Valentine (N.C.)—Jan. 3, 1983
Wheat (Mo.)—Jan. 3, 1983
Wise (W.Va.)—Jan. 3, 1983
115. Ackerman (N.Y.)—March 1, 1983
116. Darden (Ga.)—Nov. 8, 1983
117. Kleczka (Wis.)—April 3, 1984
118. Gordon (Tenn.)—Jan. 3, 1985
    Kanjorski (Pa.)—Jan. 3, 1985
    Manton (N.Y.)—Jan. 3, 1985
    Traficant (Ohio)—Jan. 3, 1985
    Visclosky (Ind.)—Jan. 3, 1985
123. Chapman (Texas)—Aug. 3, 1985
124. Bilbray (Nev.)—Jan. 6, 1987
    Cardin (Md.)—Jan. 6, 1987
    DeFazio (Ore.)—Jan. 6, 1987
    Flake (N.Y.)—Jan. 6, 1987
    Hayes (La.)—Jan. 6, 1987
    Hochbrueckner (N.Y.)—Jan. 6, 1987
    Johnson (S.D.)—Jan. 6, 1987
    Kennedy (Mass.)—Jan. 6, 1987
    Lancaster (N.C.)—Jan. 6, 1987
    Lewis (Ga.)—Jan. 6, 1987
    Mfume (Md.)—Jan. 6, 1987
    Pickett (Va.)—Jan. 6, 1987
    Price (N.C.)—Jan. 6, 1987
    Sawyer (Ohio)—Jan. 6, 1987
    Skaggs (Colo.)—Jan. 6, 1987
    Slaughter (N.Y.)—Jan. 6, 1987
140. Pelosi (Calif.)—June 2, 1987
141. Clement (Tenn.)—Jan. 19, 1988
142. Payne (Va.)—June 14, 1988
143. Costello (Ill.)—Aug. 9, 1988
144. Pallone (N.J.)—Nov. 8, 1988
145. Engel (N.Y.)—Jan. 3, 1989
    Hoagland (Neb.)—Jan. 3, 1989
    Johnston (Fla.)—Jan. 3, 1989
    Laughlin (Texas)—Jan. 3, 1989
    Lowey (N.Y.)—Jan. 3, 1989
    McDermott (Wash.)—Jan. 3, 1989
    McNulty (N.Y.)—Jan. 3, 1989
    Neal (Mass.)—Jan. 3, 1989
    Parker (Miss.)—Jan. 3, 1989
    Payne (N.J.)—Jan. 3, 1989
    Poshard (Ill.)—Jan. 3, 1989
    Sangmeister (Ill.)—Jan. 3, 1989
    Sarpalius (Texas)—Jan. 3, 1989
    Tanner (Tenn.)—Jan. 3, 1989
    Unsoeld (Wash.)—Jan. 3, 1989
160. Long (Ind.)—March 28, 1989
161. Browder (Ala.)—April 4, 1989
162. Condit (Calif.)—Sept. 12, 1989
    Geren (Texas)—Sept. 12, 1989
164. Taylor (Miss.)—Oct. 17, 1989
165. Washington (Texas)—Dec. 9, 1989
166. Serrano (N.Y.)—March 20, 1990
167. Mink (Hawaii) (six terms previously)— Sept. 22, 1990
168. Andrews (N.J.)—Nov. 6, 1990
169. Thornton (Ark.) (three terms previously)—Jan. 3, 1991
170. Abercrombie (Hawaii) (one term previously)—Jan. 3, 1991
171. Andrews (Maine)—Jan. 3, 1991
    Bacchus (Fla.)—Jan. 3, 1991
    Brewster (Okla.)—Jan. 3, 1991
    Collins (Mich.)—Jan. 3, 1991

Cramer (Ala.)—Jan. 3, 1991
DeLauro (Conn.)—Jan. 3, 1991
Dooley (Calif.)—Jan. 3, 1991
Edwards (Texas)—Jan. 3, 1991
Jefferson (La.)—Jan. 3, 1991
Kopetski (Ore.)—Jan. 3, 1991
LaRocco (Idaho)—Jan. 3, 1991
Moran (Va.)—Jan. 3, 1991
Orton (Utah)—Jan. 3, 1991
Peterson (Minn.)—Jan. 3, 1991
Peterson (Fla.)—Jan. 3, 1991
Reed (R.I.)—Jan. 3, 1991
Roemer (Ind.)—Jan. 3, 1991
Swett (N.H.)—Jan. 3, 1991
Waters (Calif.)—Jan. 3, 1991
190. Olver (Mass.)—June 4, 1991
191. Pastor (Ariz.)—Sept. 24, 1991
192. Blackwell (Pa.)—Nov. 5, 1991
193. Clayton (N.C.)—Nov. 3, 1992
Nadler (N.Y.)—Nov. 3, 1992
195. Baesler (Ky.)—Jan. 5, 1993
Barcia (Mich.)—Jan. 5, 1993
Barlow (Ky.)—Jan. 5, 1993
Barrett (Wis.)—Jan. 5, 1993
Becerra (Calif.)—Jan. 5, 1993
Bishop (Ga.)—Jan. 5, 1993
Brown (Fla.)—Jan. 5, 1993
Brown (Ohio)—Jan. 5, 1993
Byrne (Va.)—Jan. 5, 1993
Cantwell (Wash.)—Jan. 5, 1993
Clyburn (S.C.)—Jan. 5, 1993
Coppersmith (Ariz.)—Jan. 5, 1993
Danner (Mo.)—Jan. 5, 1993
Deal (Ga.)—Jan. 5, 1993
Deutsch (Fla.)—Jan. 5, 1993
English (Ariz.)—Jan. 5, 1993
Eshoo (Calif.)—Jan. 5, 1993
Fields (La.)—Jan. 5, 1993
Filner (Calif.)—Jan. 5, 1993
Fingerhut (Ohio)—Jan. 5, 1993
Furse (Ore.)—Jan. 5, 1993
Green (Texas)—Jan. 5, 1993
Gutierrez (Ill.)—Jan. 5, 1993
Hamburg (Calif.)—Jan. 5, 1993
Harman (Calif.)—Jan. 5, 1993
Hastings (Fla.)—Jan. 5, 1993
Hilliard (Ala.)—Jan. 5, 1993
Hinchey (N.Y.)—Jan. 5, 1993
Holden (Pa.)—Jan. 5, 1993
Inslee (Wash.)—Jan. 5, 1993
Johnson (Ga.)—Jan. 5, 1993
Johnson (Texas)—Jan. 5, 1993
Klein (N.J.)—Jan. 5, 1993
Klink (Pa.)—Jan. 5, 1993
Kreidler (Wash.)—Jan. 5, 1993
Lambert (Ark.)—Jan. 5, 1993
Maloney (N.Y.)—Jan. 5, 1993
Mann (Ohio)—Jan. 5, 1993
Margolies-Mezvinsky (Pa.)—Jan. 5, 1993
McHale (Pa.)—Jan. 5, 1993
McKinney (Ga.)—Jan. 5, 1993
Meehan (Mass.)—Jan. 5, 1993
Meek (Fla.)—Jan. 5, 1993
Menendez (N.J.)—Jan. 5, 1993
Minge (Minn.)—Jan. 5, 1993
Pomeroy (N.D.)—Jan. 5, 1993
Reynolds (Ill.)—Jan. 5, 1993
Roybal-Allard (Calif.)—Jan. 5, 1993
Rush (Ill.)—Jan. 5, 1993
Schenk (Calif.)—Jan. 5, 1993
Scott (Va.)—Jan. 5, 1993
Shepherd (Utah)—Jan. 5, 1993

Strickland (Ohio)—Jan. 5, 1993
Stupak (Mich.)—Jan. 5, 1993
Tejeda (Texas)—Jan. 5, 1993
Thurman (Fla.)—Jan. 5, 1993
Tucker (Calif.)—Jan. 5, 1993
Velázquez (N.Y.)—Jan. 5, 1993
Watt (N.C.)—Jan. 5, 1993
Woolsey (Calif.)—Jan. 5, 1993
Wynn (Md.)—Jan. 5, 1993
256. Thompson (Miss.)—April 14, 1993
257. Barca (Wis.)—June 8, 1993
258. Farr (Calif.)—June 16, 1993

REPUBLICANS

1. Michel (Ill.)—Jan. 3, 1957
2. McDade (Pa.)—Jan. 9, 1963
Quillen (Tenn.)—Jan. 9, 1963
4. Myers (Ind.)—Jan. 10, 1967
5. Fish (N.Y.)—Jan. 3, 1969
6. Crane (Ill.)—Nov. 25, 1969
7. Archer (Texas)—Jan. 21, 1971
Spence (S.C.)—Jan. 21, 1971
Young (Fla.)—Jan. 21, 1971
10. Gilman (N.Y.)—Jan. 3, 1973
Moorhead (Calif.)—Jan. 3, 1973
Regula (Ohio)—Jan. 3, 1973
Shuster (Pa.)—Jan. 3, 1973
14. Young (Alaska)—March 6, 1973
15. Goodling (Pa.)—Jan. 14, 1975
Hyde (Ill.)—Jan. 14, 1975
17. Leach (Iowa)—Jan. 4, 1977
Stump (Ariz.)—Jan. 4, 1977
Walker (Pa.)—Jan. 4, 1977
20. Livingston (La.)—Aug. 27, 1977
21. Bereuter (Neb.)—Jan. 15, 1979
Clinger (Pa.)—Jan. 15, 1979
Gingrich (Ga.)—Jan. 15, 1979
Lewis (Calif.)—Jan. 15, 1979
Roth (Wis.)—Jan. 15, 1979
Sensenbrenner (Wis.)—Jan. 15, 1979
Snowe (Maine)—Jan. 15, 1979
Solomon (N.Y.)—Jan. 15, 1979
Thomas (Calif.)—Jan. 15, 1979
30. Petri (Wis.)—April 3, 1979
31. Porter (Ill.)—Jan. 22, 1980
32. Bliley (Va.)—Jan. 5, 1981
Dreier (Calif.)—Jan. 5, 1981
Emerson (Mo.)—Jan. 5, 1981
Fields (Texas)—Jan. 5, 1981
Gunderson (Wis.)—Jan. 5, 1981
Hansen (Utah)—Jan. 5, 1981
Hunter (Calif.)—Jan. 5, 1981
McCollum (Fla.)—Jan. 5, 1981
Roberts (Kan.)—Jan. 5, 1981
Rogers (Ky.)—Jan. 5, 1981
Roukema (N.J.)—Jan. 5, 1981
Shaw (Fla.)—Jan. 5, 1981
Skeen (N.M.)—Jan. 5, 1981
Smith (N.J.)—Jan. 5, 1981
Wolf (Va.)—Jan. 5, 1981
47. Oxley (Ohio)—June 25, 1981
48. Bateman (Va.)—Jan. 3, 1983
Bilirakis (Fla.)—Jan. 3, 1983
Boehlert (N.Y.)—Jan. 3, 1983
Burton (Ind.)—Jan. 3, 1983
Gekas (Pa.)—Jan. 3, 1983
Johnson (Conn.)—Jan. 3, 1983
Kasich (Ohio)—Jan. 3, 1983
Lewis (Fla.)—Jan. 3, 1983
McCandless (Calif.)—Jan. 3, 1983
Packard (Calif.)—Jan. 3, 1983

Ridge (Pa.)—Jan. 3, 1983
Smith (Ore.)—Jan. 3, 1983
Sundquist (Tenn.)—Jan. 3, 1983
Vucanovich (Nev.)—Jan. 3, 1983
62. Schaefer (Colo.)—March 29, 1983
63. Saxton (N.J.)—Nov. 6, 1984
64. Dornan (Calif.) (three terms previously)—Jan. 3, 1985
65. Armey (Texas)—Jan. 3, 1985
Barton (Texas)—Jan. 3, 1985
Bentley (Md.)—Jan. 3, 1985
Callahan (Ala.)—Jan. 3, 1985
Coble (N.C.)—Jan. 3, 1985
Combest (Texas)—Jan. 3, 1985
DeLay (Texas)—Jan. 3, 1985
Fawell (Ill.)—Jan. 3, 1985
Gallo (N.J.)—Jan. 3, 1985
Kolbe (Ariz.)—Jan. 3, 1985
Lightfoot (Iowa)—Jan. 3, 1985
McMillan (N.C.)—Jan. 3, 1985
Meyers (Kan.)—Jan. 3, 1985
78. Ballenger (N.C.)—Nov. 4, 1986
79. Baker (La.)—Jan. 6, 1987
Bunning (Ky.)—Jan. 6, 1987
Gallegly (Calif.)—Jan. 6, 1987
Grandy (Iowa)—Jan. 6, 1987
Hastert (Ill.)—Jan. 6, 1987
Hefley (Colo.)—Jan. 6, 1987
Herger (Calif.)—Jan. 6, 1987
Houghton (N.Y.)—Jan. 6, 1987
Inhofe (Okla.)—Jan. 6, 1987
Kyl (Ariz.)—Jan. 6, 1987
Morella (Md.)—Jan. 6, 1987
Ravenel (S.C.)—Jan. 6, 1987
Smith (Texas)—Jan. 6, 1987
Upton (Mich.)—Jan. 6, 1987
Weldon (Pa.)—Jan. 6, 1987
94. Shays (Conn.)—Aug. 18, 1987
95. McCrery (La.)—April 16, 1988
96. Duncan (Tenn.)—Nov. 8, 1988
97. Cox (Calif.)—Jan. 3, 1989
Gillmor (Ohio)—Jan. 3, 1989
Goss (Fla.)—Jan. 3, 1989
Hancock (Mo.)—Jan. 3, 1989
Machtley (R.I.)—Jan. 3, 1989
Paxon (N.Y.)—Jan. 3, 1989
Rohrabacher (Calif.)—Jan. 3, 1989
Schiff (N.M.)—Jan. 3, 1989
Stearns (Fla.)—Jan. 3, 1989
Walsh (N.Y.)—Jan. 3, 1989
107. Thomas (Wyo.)—April 25, 1989
108. Ros-Lehtinen (Fla.)—Aug. 29, 1989
109. Molinari (N.Y.)—March 20, 1990
110. Allard (Colo.)—Jan. 3, 1991
Barrett (Neb.)—Jan. 3, 1991
Boehner (Ohio)—Jan. 3, 1991
Camp (Mich.)—Jan. 3, 1991
Cunningham (Calif.)—Jan. 3, 1991
Doolittle (Calif.)—Jan. 3, 1991
Franks (Conn.)—Jan. 3, 1991
Gilchrest (Md.)—Jan. 3, 1991
Hobson (Ohio)—Jan. 3, 1991
Klug (Wis.)—Jan. 3, 1991
Nussle (Iowa)—Jan. 3, 1991
Ramstad (Minn.)—Jan. 3, 1991
Santorum (Pa.)—Jan. 3, 1991
Taylor (N.C.)—Jan. 3, 1991
Zeliff (N.H.)—Jan. 3, 1991
Zimmer (N.J.)—Jan. 3, 1991
126. Johnson (Texas)—May 18, 1991
127. Ewing (Ill.)—July 2, 1991
128. Bachus (Ala.)—Jan. 5, 1993
Baker (Calif.)—Jan. 5, 1993

Bartlett (Md.)—Jan. 5, 1993
Blute (Mass.)—Jan. 5, 1993
Bonilla (Texas)—Jan. 5, 1993
Buyer (Ind.)—Jan. 5, 1993
Calvert (Calif.)—Jan. 5, 1993
Canady (Fla.)—Jan. 5, 1993
Castle (Del.)—Jan. 5, 1993
Collins (Ga.)—Jan. 5, 1993
Crapo (Idaho)—Jan. 5, 1993
Diaz-Balart (Fla.)—Jan. 5, 1993
Dickey (Ark.)—Jan. 5, 1993
Dunn (Wash.)—Jan. 5, 1993
Everett (Ala.)—Jan. 5, 1993
Fowler (Fla.)—Jan. 5, 1993
Franks (N.J.)—Jan. 5, 1993
Goodlatte (Va.)—Jan. 5, 1993

Grams (Minn.)—Jan. 5, 1993
Greenwood (Pa.)—Jan. 5, 1993
Hoekstra (Mich.)—Jan. 5, 1993
Hoke (Ohio)—Jan. 5, 1993
Horn (Calif.)—Jan. 5, 1993
Huffington (Calif.)—Jan. 5, 1993
Hutchinson (Ark.)—Jan. 5, 1993
Inglis (S.C.)—Jan. 5, 1993
Istook (Okla.)—Jan. 5, 1993
Kim (Calif.)—Jan. 5, 1993
King (N.Y.)—Jan. 5, 1993
Kingston (Ga.)—Jan. 5, 1993
Knollenberg (Mich.)—Jan. 5, 1993
Lazio (N.Y.)—Jan. 5, 1993
Levy (N.Y.)—Jan. 5, 1993
Linder (Ga.)—Jan. 5, 1993

Manzullo (Ill.)—Jan. 5, 1993
McHugh (N.Y.)—Jan. 5, 1993
McInnis (Colo.)—Jan. 5, 1993
McKeon (Calif.)—Jan. 5, 1993
Mica (Fla.)—Jan. 5, 1993
Miller (Fla.)—Jan. 5, 1993
Pombo (Calif.)—Jan. 5, 1993
Pryce (Ohio)—Jan. 5, 1993
Quinn (N.Y.)—Jan. 5, 1993
Royce (Calif.)—Jan. 5, 1993
Smith (Mich.)—Jan. 5, 1993
Talent (Mo.)—Jan. 5, 1993
Torkildsen (Mass.)—Jan. 5, 1993
175. Portman (Ohio)—May 5, 1993

The Committees: Influence and Power

In the 103rd Congress, as in all those before it, the bulk of congressional work was done in committees, not on the floor of the House or Senate. Legislation was written by committees; hearings were held by committees; oversight investigations were conducted by committees.

Especially in the House, influence often was closely related to the committee or committees on which a member served. Assignment to a powerful committee virtually guaranteed large campaign contributions.

While many members sought a particular committee because they had an interest in issues within that panel's jurisdiction, others' preferences were based on political need. Members from large agricultural districts gravitated toward the Agriculture committees. Those from districts with major military installations often sought out the Armed Services panels.

Traditionally, the premier committee assignments sought by representatives to the House had been to Appropriations, Ways and Means, and Rules, although Rules had lost some of its attraction. In recent years, members also sought seats on Budget and on Energy and Commerce.

In the Senate, where the members served on more panels, the most popular committees traditionally had been Appropriations and Finance. The Armed Services committee was also in demand.

Some panels waxed and waned, but Finance, Appropriations, and Ways and Means were never eclipsed because they controlled the flow of money into and out of federal coffers. These committees had been thrust to the center of action by Congress' tendency to pile much of its legislative work onto a handful of fiscal measures.

Major vs. Minor

In both chambers, committees were ranked as major and minor. In the House, Energy and Commerce was a major committee, while Post Office and Civil Service was a minor committee. Agriculture, Nutrition and Forestry was a major Senate committee, while Small Business was minor.

In most cases the distinction was based on the traditional importance of the panel. But both the House and Senate Budget committees were classified as minor, even though they often had been in the limelight in previous years.

The House also had three "exclusive" committees — Appropriations, Rules, and Ways and Means — whose members generally could not serve on other committees. In addition to these three, the House had eight major and 10 minor committees.

In the Senate, there were 12 major and 10 minor committees. While representatives generally served on only two panels — and sometimes just one — senators often served on four. The feeling that senators were stretched too thin by serving on too many panels led Senate leaders to seek stricter enforcement in 1985 of the Senate rule that limited senators to two major committees and one minor panel. Usually, the chairman of a committee was the member of the majority party with the most committee seniority.

Senate

Senate Democrats were able to make the all-important majority assignments for the 103rd Congress and the three previous ones, having won back majority status in the 1986 elections.

The number of senators on each committee, as well as the ratio of Republicans to Democrats, was generally determined through negotiations between leaders of the parties. The majority party, however, clearly held the upper hand.

Senators were assigned to committee openings by their party caucuses, with assignments based on members' desires and seniority.

House

Democrats were assigned to House committees by the 35-member Democratic Steering and Policy Committee, chaired by Speaker of the House Thomas S. Foley, Wash. The committee consisted of 12 members elected by region, 10 appointed by Foley and 13 who held party leadership jobs.

A member seeking a particular committee had to be nominated by a member of Steering and Policy, so it helped to have a patron on the inside.

House Republicans got their assignments from the Republican Committee on Committees, chaired by Minority Leader Robert H. Michel, R-Ill. It had 23 members: Michel and the whip, representatives elected from the freshman and sophomore classes, and members elected according to the voting strength of their states. ∎

Key to Listings

Order of lists. Committee and subcommittee rosters list Democrats on the left in roman type and Republicans on the right in *italics*. (Bernard Sanders, a House independent, is listed below the Republicans on the right.)

The lists are arranged by seniority, as determined by each committee. New House Democratic rules also stipulate that their new members' seniority be determined by the order of appointment by the Steering Committee.

Members of party committees are listed alphabetically.

Office buildings, addresses. The following abbreviations are used for congressional office buildings:

- SD — Dirksen Senate Office Building
- SH — Hart Senate Office Building
- SR — Russell Senate Office Building
- CHOB — Cannon House Office Building
- LHOB — Longworth House Office Building
- RHOB — Rayburn House Office Building
- OHOB — O'Neill House Office Building
- FHOB — Ford House Office Building

A map of Capitol Hill appears on page 69-B. All mail should be addressed to the main committee rooms. The zip code for mail addressed to offices of the Senate is 20510; for the House, 20515.

Names and numbers. Phone and room numbers are listed for each committee and subcommittee, and for the key staff members. Following the committee rosters are a list of each member's committee assignments (p. 58-B) and a directory of phone and room numbers for each member (p. 64-B). To reach the U.S. Capitol switchboard, call (202) 224-3121.

Party Committees, 103rd Congress, 1st Session

(As of Dec. 31, 1993)

SENATE DEMOCRATS

President .... Al Gore, Tenn.
President Pro Tempore .... Robert C. Byrd, W.Va.
Majority Leader................... George J. Mitchell, Maine
Majority Whip .... Wendell H. Ford, Ky.
Conference Chairman .... George J. Mitchell, Maine
Conference Secretary .... David Pryor, Ark.
Assistant Floor Leader .... Barbara A. Mikulski, Md.
Chief Deputy Whip.................. John B. Breaux, La.
Deputy Whips (by region, each listed with an assistant deputy whip):

East................................ Patrick J. Leahy, Vt.
                                    John Kerry, Mass. (asst.)
South .... Bob Graham, Fla.
                                    Charles S. Robb, Va. (asst.)
Midwest .... Tom Harkin, Iowa
                                    Byron L. Dorgan, N.D. (asst.)
West .... Barbara Boxer, Calif.
                                    Patty Murray, Wash. (asst.)

Policy Committee

Phone: (202) 224-5551   **Room: S-118 Capitol**

An arm of the Democratic Caucus that advises on legislative priorities.

George J. Mitchell, Maine, chairman
Tom Daschle, S.D., co-chairman
Jeff Bingaman, N.M., vice chairman
John Glenn, Ohio, vice chairman
Charles S. Robb, Va., vice chairman
Paul S. Sarbanes, Md., vice chairman

Daniel K. Akaka, Hawaii	Carol Moseley-Braun, Ill.
Dale Bumpers, Ark.	Daniel Patrick Moynihan, N.Y.
Ben Nighthorse Campbell, Colo.	Claiborne Pell, R.I.
Byron L. Dorgan, N.D.	David Pryor, Ark. (ex officio)
Russell D. Feingold, Wis.	Donald W. Riegle Jr., Mich.
Wendell H. Ford, Ky. (ex officio)	John D. Rockefeller IV, W.Va.
Howell Heflin, Ala.	
Ernest F. Hollings, S.C.	
Frank R. Lautenberg, N.J.	

Steering Committee

Phone: (202) 224-3735   **Room: S-309 Capitol**

Makes Democratic committee assignments.

Daniel K. Inouye, Hawaii, chairman

Max Baucus, Mont.	Barbara Boxer, Calif.
Joseph R. Biden Jr., Del.	John B. Breaux, La.
David L. Boren, Okla.	Richard H. Bryan, Nev.

Robert C. Byrd, W.Va.	John Kerry, Mass.
Kent Conrad, N.D.	Herb Kohl, Wis.
Dennis DeConcini, Ariz.	Patrick J. Leahy, Vt.
Christopher J. Dodd, Conn.	Carl Levin, Mich.
Jim Exon, Neb.	Howard M. Metzenbaum, Ohio
Wendell H. Ford, Ky.	George J. Mitchell, Maine
Bob Graham, Fla.	Sam Nunn, Ga.
Tom Harkin, Iowa	David Pryor, Ark.
Edward M. Kennedy, Mass.	Jim Sasser, Tenn.

Democratic Senatorial Campaign Committee

Phone: (202) 224-2447   **Room: 430 S. Capitol St. S.E. 20003**

Campaign support committee for Democratic senatorial candidates.

Bob Graham, Fla., chairman

SENATE REPUBLICANS

Minority Leader .... Bob Dole, Kan.
Assistant Minority Leader .... Alan K. Simpson, Wyo.
Conference Chairman.................... Thad Cochran, Miss.
Conference Secretary..................... Trent Lott, Miss.
Deputy Whips:..................... Christopher S. Bond, Mo.
                                    Hank Brown, Colo.
                                    Thad Cochran, Miss.
                                    Paul Coverdell, Ga.
                                    Dave Durenberger, Minn.
                                    Charles E. Grassley, Iowa
                                    Judd Gregg, N.H.
                                    Nancy Landon Kassebaum, Kan.
                                    John McCain, Ariz.
                                    Frank H. Murkowski, Alaska
                                    Larry Pressler, S.D.
                                    Robert C. Smith, N.H.
                                    Arlen Specter, Pa.
                                    Malcolm Wallop, Wyo.
                                    John W. Warner, Va.

Policy Committee

Phone: (202) 224-2946   **Room: SR-347**

Advises on party action and policy.

Don Nickles, Okla., chairman

John H. Chafee, R.I.	*Trent Lott, Miss.*
Thad Cochran, Miss.	*Richard G. Lugar, Ind.*
Alfonse M. D'Amato, N.Y.	*Frank H. Murkowski, Alaska*
John C. Danforth, Mo.	*Bob Packwood, Ore.*
Bob Dole, Kan.	*Larry Pressler, S.D.*
Pete V. Domenici, N.M.	*William V. Roth Jr., Del.*
Phil Gramm, Texas	*Alan K. Simpson, Wyo.*
Orrin G. Hatch, Utah	*Ted Stevens, Alaska*
Mark O. Hatfield, Ore.	*Strom Thurmond, S.C.*
Jesse Helms, N.C.	*Malcolm Wallop, Wyo.*
Nancy Landon Kassebaum, Kan.	*John W. Warner, Va.*

Committee on Committees

Phone: (202) 224-2644   **Room: SD-183**

Makes Republican committee assignments.

Conrad Burns, Mont., chairman

Robert F. Bennett, Utah	*Judd Gregg, N.H.*
Paul Coverdell, Ga.	*Dirk Kempthorne, Idaho*
Lauch Faircloth, N.C.	*Frank H. Murkowski, Alaska*

National Republican Senatorial Committee

Phone: (202) 675-6000   **Room: 425 Second St. N.E. 20002**

Campaign support committee for Republican senatorial candidates.

Phil Gramm, Texas, chairman

Robert F. Bennett, Utah	*Dirk Kempthorne, Idaho*
Hank Brown, Colo.	*Richard G. Lugar, Ind.*
Conrad Burns, Mont.	*Connie Mack, Fla.*
Daniel R. Coats, Ind.	*John McCain, Ariz.*
Paul Coverdell, Ga.	*Bob Packwood, Ore.*
Alfonse M. D'Amato, N.Y.	*Ted Stevens, Alaska*
Lauch Faircloth, N.C.	*John W. Warner, Va.*
Slade Gorton, Wash.	

HOUSE DEMOCRATS

Speaker of the House	Thomas S. Foley, Wash.
Majority Leader	Richard A. Gephardt, Mo.
Majority Whip	David E. Bonior, Mich.
Caucus Chairman	Steny H. Hoyer, Md.
Caucus Vice Chairman	Vic Fazio, Calif.
Chief Deputy Whips	Butler Derrick, S.C.
	Barbara B. Kennelly, Conn.
	John Lewis, Ga.
	Bill Richardson, N.M.
Floor Whip	Martin Frost, Texas
Ex-Officio Whip	Joe Moakley, Mass.
Deputy Whips	Tom Bevill, Ala.
	W. G. "Bill" Hefner, N.C.
	Norman Y. Mineta, Calif.
	Charles B. Rangel, N.Y.
	Martin Olav Sabo, Minn.
	Patricia Schroeder, Colo.
	Charles W. Stenholm, Texas
	Esteban E. Torres, Calif.
	Jolene Unsoeld, Wash.
	Alan Wheat, Mo.
	Pat Williams, Mont.
Whip Task Force Chairmen	Bart Gordon, Tenn.
	David R. Obey, Wis.

At-Large Whips:

Thomas H. Andrews, Maine	Robert T. Matsui, Calif.
Xavier Becerra, Calif.	Frank McCloskey, Ind.
Howard L. Berman, Calif.	Dave McCurdy, Okla.
Robert A. Borski, Pa.	Robert Menendez, N.J.
Rick Boucher, Va.	George Miller, Calif.
Leslie L. Byrne, Va.	Alan B. Mollohan, W.Va.
Benjamin L. Cardin, Md.	Richard E. Neal, Mass.
Bob Carr, Mich.	James L. Oberstar, Minn.
Barbara-Rose Collins, Mich.	Timothy J. Penny, Minn.
George "Buddy" Darden, Ga.	David Price, N.C.
Rosa DeLauro, Conn.	Charlie Rose, N.C.
Norm Dicks, Wash.	Dan Rostenkowski, Ill.
Richard J. Durbin, Ill.	Bobby L. Rush, Ill.
Don Edwards, Calif.	Charles E. Schumer, N.Y.
Lane Evans, Ill.	Philip R. Sharp, Ind.
William D. Ford, Mich.	Norman Sisisky, Va.
Barney Frank, Mass.	David E. Skaggs, Colo.
Sam Gejdenson, Conn.	Louise M. Slaughter, N.Y.
Dan Glickman, Kan.	John M. Spratt Jr., S.C.
William J. Jefferson, La.	Mike Synar, Okla.
Eddie Bernice Johnson, Texas	W. J. "Billy" Tauzin, La.
Harry A. Johnston, Fla.	Robert G. Torricelli, N.J.
Paul E. Kanjorski, Pa.	Bruce F. Vento, Minn.
Dale E. Kildee, Mich.	Peter J. Visclosky, Ind.
H. Martin Lancaster, N.C.	Harold L. Volkmer, Mo.
Larry LaRocco, Idaho	Maxine Waters, Calif.
Richard H. Lehman, Calif.	Bob Wise, W.Va.
Nita M. Lowey, N.Y.	Ron Wyden, Ore.

Assistant Whips (by zone number):

1	Anna G. Eshoo, Calif.
	Matthew G. Martinez, Calif.
2	Jim McDermott, Wash.
3	Tim Johnson, S.D.
4	Sidney R. Yates, Ill.
5	Jim Slattery, Kan.
6	John Bryant, Texas
	Jim Chapman, Texas
7	Jack Reed, R.I.
8	Gary L. Ackerman, N.Y.
	Maurice D. Hinchey, N.Y.
9	Donald M. Payne, N.J.
10	Sander M. Levin, Mich.
	Tom Sawyer, Ohio
11	Romano L. Mazzoli, Ky.
12	James E. Clyburn, S.C.
13	Robert E. "Bud" Cramer, Ala.
14	Pete Peterson, Fla.

Steering and Policy Committee

Phone: (202) 225-8550   **Room: H-226 Capitol**

Scheduling of legislation and Democratic committee assignments.

Thomas S. Foley, Wash., chairman
Richard A. Gephardt, Mo., vice chairman
Steny H. Hoyer, Md., second vice chairman

David E. Bonior, Mich.	Butler Derrick, S.C.
Jack Brooks, Texas	John D. Dingell, Mich.
Maria Cantwell, Wash.	Julian C. Dixon, Calif.
Benjamin L. Cardin, Md.	Richard J. Durbin, Ill.
E. "Kika" de la Garza, Texas	Vic Fazio, Calif.

Sam Gejdenson, Conn.
Dan Glickman, Kan.
Barbara B. Kennelly, Conn.
Gerald D. Kleczka, Wis.
Ron Klink, Pa.
John Lewis, Ga.
Thomas J. Manton, N.Y.
Patsy T. Mink, Hawaii
Joe Moakley, Mass.
John P. Murtha, Pa.
William H. Natcher, Ky.

David R. Obey, Wis.
Ed Pastor, Ariz.
Bill Richardson, N.M.
Dan Rostenkowski, Ill.
J. Roy Rowland, Ga.
Al Swift, Wash.
Mike Synar, Okla.
W. J. "Billy" Tauzin, La.
Melvin Watt, N.C.
Alan Wheat, Mo.

Personnel Committee

Phone: (202) 225-4068   **Room: B-343-D RHOB**

Selects, appoints and supervises Democratic patronage positions.

Jack Brooks, Texas, chairman

Democratic Congressional Campaign Committee

Phone: (202) 863-1500   **Room: 430 S. Capitol St., S.E. 20003**

Campaign support committee for Democratic House candidates.

Vic Fazio, Calif., chairman
Dan Rostenkowski, Ill., vice chairman

Ex Officio Members:

Thomas S. Foley, Wash.
Richard A. Gephardt, Mo.
David E. Bonior, Mich.
Steny H. Hoyer, Md.
Butler Derrick, S.C.
Barbara B. Kennelly, Conn.
John Lewis, Ga.
Bill Richardson, N.M.

Co-Chairmen:

Benjamin L. Cardin, Md.
Robert E. "Bud" Cramer, Ala.
Barney Frank, Mass.
Bart Gordon, Tenn.
Greg Laughlin, Texas
Thomas J. Manton, N.Y.
John P. Murtha, Pa.
Nancy Pelosi, Calif.
Jim Slattery, Kan.

At-Large Members
  of Oversight Subcommittee:

Howard L. Berman, Calif.
John D. Dingell, Mich.
Martin Frost, Texas
H. Martin Lancaster, N.C.
Martin Olav Sabo, Minn.
Mike Synar, Okla.

Speaker's Appointments,
  Full Committee:

Rosa DeLauro, Conn.
Lee H. Hamilton, Ind.
David R. Obey, Wis.
Lynn Schenk, Calif.
Charles W. Stenholm, Texas
W. J. "Billy" Tauzin, La.
Maxine Waters, Calif.
Ron Wyden, Ore.

HOUSE REPUBLICANS

Minority Leader . . . . *Robert H. Michel, Ill.*
Minority Whip . . . . *Newt Gingrich, Ga.*
Conference Chairman . . . . *Dick Armey, Texas*
Conference Vice Chairman . . . . *Bill McCollum, Fla.*
Conference Secretary . . . . *Tom DeLay, Texas*
Chief Deputy Whip . . . . *Robert S. Walker, Pa.*

Deputy Whips . . . . *Joe L. Barton, Texas*
Tom DeLay, Texas
Dennis Hastert, Ill.
Nancy L. Johnson, Conn.
Jon Kyl, Ariz.
Gerald B. H. Solomon, N.Y.

Assistant Deputy Whips: . . . . *Thomas J. Bliley Jr., Va.*
John A. Boehner, Ohio
Dan Burton, Ind.
Robert L. Livingston, La.
Bill Paxon, N.Y.
Pat Roberts, Kan.
Olympia J. Snowe, Maine

Regional Whips:
East . . . . *Dean A. Gallo, N.J.*
Midwest and Plains . . . . *Jim Ross Lightfoot, Iowa*
South . . . . *Ileana Ros-Lehtinen, Fla.*
West . . . . *Barbara F. Vucanovich, Nev.*

Committee on Committees

Phone: (202) 225-0600   **Room: H-230 Capitol**

Makes Republican committee assignments.

Robert H. Michel, Ill., chairman

Wayne Allard, Colo.
Bill Archer, Texas
Bill Baker, Calif.
Cass Ballenger, N.C.
Thomas J. Bliley Jr., Va.
Jim Bunning, Ky.
Jennifer Dunn, Wash.
Dean A. Gallo, N.J.
Newt Gingrich, Ga.
Dennis Hastert, Ill.
James M. Inhofe, Okla.

Scott L. Klug, Wis.
John Linder, Ga.
Joseph M. McDade, Pa.
Ron Packard, Calif.
Ralph Regula, Ohio
Gerald B. H. Solomon, N.Y.
Floyd D. Spence, S.C.
Bob Stump, Ariz.
Fred Upton, Mich.
C. W. Bill Young, Fla.
Don Young, Alaska

Policy Committee

Phone: (202) 225-6168   **Room: 1616 LHOB**

Advises on party action and policy.

Henry J. Hyde, Ill., chairman

Bill Archer, Texas
Dick Armey, Texas
Doug Bereuter, Neb.
John A. Boehner, Ohio
Steve Buyer, Ind.
Michael D. Crapo, Idaho
Tom DeLay, Texas
Tillie Fowler, Fla.
Gary A. Franks, Conn.
Dean A. Gallo, N.J.
Newt Gingrich, Ga.
Bill Goodling, Pa.
Steve Gunderson, Wis.
Mel Hancock, Mo.
Dennis Hastert, Ill.
Peter Hoekstra, Mich.
Duncan Hunter, Calif.

Ernest Jim Istook Jr., Okla.
Nancy L. Johnson, Conn.
John R. Kasich, Ohio
Tom Lewis, Fla.
Bill McCollum, Fla.
Joseph M. McDade, Pa.
Jan Meyers, Kan.
Robert H. Michel, Ill.
Michael G. Oxley, Ohio
Bill Paxon, N.Y.
Ileana Ros-Lehtinen, Fla.
Ed Royce, Calif.
Lamar Smith, Texas
Gerald B. H. Solomon, N.Y.
Floyd D. Spence, S.C.
Craig Thomas, Wyo.
Barbara F. Vucanovich, Nev.

Research Committee

Phone: (202) 225-0871   **Room: 1622 LHOB**

Serves as an advisory body to Republican members of Congress. The committee and its task forces work to develop various policy options for the Republican Conference.

Duncan Hunter, Calif., chairman

Dick Armey, Texas	*Jim Ross Lightfoot, Iowa*
Doug Bereuter, Neb.	*Bill McCollum, Fla.*
John A. Boehner, Ohio	*Robert H. Michel, Ill.*
Dan Burton, Ind.	*Susan Molinari, N.Y.*
Charles T. Canady, Fla.	*Jack Quinn, N.Y.*
Michael D. Crapo, Idaho	*H. James Saxton, N.J.*
Tom DeLay, Texas	*Steven H. Schiff, N.M.*
Newt Gingrich, Ga.	*Olympia J. Snowe, Maine*
Mel Hancock, Mo.	*Cliff Stearns, Fla.*
Henry J. Hyde, Ill.	*Barbara F. Vucanovich, Nev.*

National Republican Congressional Committee

Phone: (202) 479-7000   **Room: 320 First St. S.E. 20003**

Campaign support committee for Republican House candidates.

Bill Paxon, N.Y., chairman
Susan Molinari, N.Y., chief vice chairman
Rick Santorum, Pa., chief vice chairman
H. James Saxton, N.J., chief vice chairman

Vice Chairmen:

John A. Boehner, Ohio
John T. Doolittle, Calif.
Nancy L. Johnson, Conn.
Robert L. Livingston, La.
Jim Nussle, Iowa
Deborah Pryce, Ohio

Ex Officio Members:

Robert H. Michel, Ill.
Newt Gingrich, Ga.
Dick Armey, Texas
Bill McCollum, Fla.
Tom DeLay, Texas
Henry J. Hyde, Ill.
Duncan Hunter, Calif.

Spencer Bachus, Ala.	*Pat Roberts, Kan.*
Helen Delich Bentley, Md.	*Ileana Ros-Lehtinen, Fla.*
Jim Bunning, Ky.	*Ed Royce, Calif.*
Dave Camp, Mich.	*Dan Schaefer, Colo.*
C. Christopher Cox, Calif.	*Steven H. Schiff, N.M.*
Jennifer Dunn, Wash.	*Olympia J. Snowe, Maine*
Bob Franks, N.J.	*Gerald B. H. Solomon, N.Y.*
Dennis Hastert, Ill.	*James M. Talent, Mo.*
Scott L. Klug, Wis.	*Barbara F. Vucanovich, Nev.*
Jon Kyl, Ariz.	*Robert S. Walker, Pa.*
John Linder, Ga.	

Senate Committees, 103rd Congress, 1st Session

(As of Dec. 31, 1993)

AGRICULTURE, NUTRITION AND FORESTRY

Phone: (202) 224-2035   **Room: SR-328A**

Majority Chief of Staff: Charles Riemenschneider, (202) 224-2035, SR-328A
Minority Staff Director: Chuck Conner, (202) 224-6901, SR-328A

Agriculture in general; animal industry and diseases; crop insurance and soil conservation; farm credit and farm security; food from fresh waters; food stamp programs; forestry in general; home economics; human nutrition; inspection of livestock, meat and agricultural products; pests and pesticides; plant industry, soils and agricultural engineering; rural development, rural electrification and watersheds; school nutrition programs. Chairman and ranking minority member are members ex officio of all subcommittees of which they are not regular members.

Party Ratio: **D 10 - R 8**

Patrick J. Leahy, Vt., chairman	Richard G. Lugar, Ind., ranking member
David Pryor, Ark.	Bob Dole, Kan.
David L. Boren, Okla.	Jesse Helms, N.C.
Howell Heflin, Ala.	Thad Cochran, Miss.
Tom Harkin, Iowa	Mitch McConnell, Ky.
Kent Conrad, N.D.	Larry E. Craig, Idaho
Tom Daschle, S.D.	Paul Coverdell, Ga.
Max Baucus, Mont.	Charles E. Grassley, Iowa
Bob Kerrey, Neb.	
Russell D. Feingold, Wis.	

SUBCOMMITTEES

Agricultural Credit

Phone: (202) 224-2035   **Room: SR-328A**

Conrad, chairman	Grassley
Daschle	Craig
Boren	Coverdell
Baucus	

Agricultural Production and Stabilization of Prices

Phone: (202) 224-2035   **Room: SR-328A**

Pryor, chairman	Helms
Baucus	Dole
Kerrey	Cochran
Feingold	McConnell
Boren	Craig
Heflin	Grassley
Harkin	

Agricultural Research, Conservation, Forestry and General Legislation

Phone: (202) 224-2035   **Room: SR-328A**

Daschle, chairman	Craig
Kerrey	Cochran
Harkin	

Domestic and Foreign Marketing and Product Promotion

Phone: (202) 224-2035   **Room: SR-328A**

Boren, chairman	Cochran
Pryor	Helms
Conrad	Coverdell
Baucus	McConnell
Feingold	Grassley
Heflin	

Nutrition and Investigations

Phone: (202) 224-2035   **Room: SR-328A**

Harkin, chairman	McConnell
Pryor	Dole
Kerrey	Helms
Feingold	

Rural Development and Rural Electrification

Phone: (202) 224-2035   **Room: SR-328A**

Heflin, chairman	Coverdell
Conrad	Dole
Daschle	

APPROPRIATIONS

Phone: (202) 224-3471   **Room: S-128 Capitol**

Majority Staff Director: Jim English, (202) 224-7200, S-128 Capitol
Minority Staff Director: J. Keith Kennedy, (202) 224-7335, SD-135

Appropriation of revenue; rescission of appropriations; new spending authority under the Budget Act. Chairman and ranking

minority member are members ex officio of all subcommittees.

Party Ratio: D 16 - R 13

Robert C. Byrd, W.Va., chairman	*Mark O. Hatfield, Ore., ranking member*
Daniel K. Inouye, Hawaii	*Ted Stevens, Alaska*
Ernest F. Hollings, S.C.	*Thad Cochran, Miss.*
J. Bennett Johnston, La.	*Alfonse M. D'Amato, N.Y.*
Patrick J. Leahy, Vt.	*Arlen Specter, Pa.*
Jim Sasser, Tenn.	*Pete V. Domenici, N.M.*
Dennis DeConcini, Ariz.	*Don Nickles, Okla.*
Dale Bumpers, Ark.	*Phil Gramm, Texas*
Frank R. Lautenberg, N.J.	*Christopher S. Bond, Mo.*
Tom Harkin, Iowa	*Slade Gorton, Wash.*
Barbara A. Mikulski, Md.	*Mitch McConnell, Ky.*
Harry Reid, Nev.	*Connie Mack, Fla.*
Bob Kerrey, Neb.	*Conrad Burns, Mont.*
Herb Kohl, Wis.	
Patty Murray, Wash.	
Dianne Feinstein, Calif.	

SUBCOMMITTEES

Agriculture, Rural Development and Related Agencies

Phone: (202) 224-7240   **Room: SD-140**

Bumpers, chairman	*Cochran*
Harkin	*Specter*
Kerrey	*Bond*
Johnston	*Gramm*
Kohl	*Gorton*
Feinstein	

Commerce, Justice, State and Judiciary

Phone: (202) 224-7277   **Room: S-146A Capitol**

Hollings, chairman	*Domenici*
Inouye	*Stevens*
Bumpers	*Hatfield*
Lautenberg	*Gramm*
Sasser	*McConnell*
Kerrey	

Defense

Phone: (202) 224-7255   **Room: SD-119**

Inouye, chairman	*Stevens*
Hollings	*D'Amato*
Johnston	*Cochran*
Byrd	*Specter*
Leahy	*Domenici*
Sasser	*Nickles*
DeConcini	*Gramm*
Bumpers	*Bond*
Lautenberg	
Harkin	

District of Columbia

Phone: (202) 224-2731   **Room: S-205 Capitol**

Kohl, chairman	*Burns*
Murray	*Mack*
Feinstein	

Energy and Water Development

Phone: (202) 224-7260   **Room: SD-132**

Johnston, chairman	*Hatfield*
Byrd	*Cochran*
Hollings	*Domenici*
Sasser	*Nickles*
DeConcini	*Gorton*
Reid	*McConnell*
Kerrey	

Foreign Operations

Phone: (202) 224-7209   **Room: SD-136**

Leahy, chairman	*McConnell*
Inouye	*D'Amato*
DeConcini	*Specter*
Lautenberg	*Nickles*
Harkin	*Mack*
Mikulski	*Gramm*
Feinstein	

Interior

Phone: (202) 224-7233   **Room: SD-127**

Byrd, chairman	*Nickles*
Johnston	*Stevens*
Leahy	*Cochran*
DeConcini	*Domenici*
Bumpers	*Gorton*
Hollings	*Hatfield*
Reid	*Burns*
Murray	

Labor, Health and Human Services and Education

Phone: (202) 224-7283   **Room: SD-186**

Harkin, chairman	*Specter*
Byrd	*Hatfield*
Hollings	*Stevens*
Inouye	*Cochran*
Bumpers	*Gorton*
Reid	*Mack*
Kohl	*Bond*
Murray	

Legislative Branch

Phone: (202) 224-7338   **Room: SD-132**

Reid, chairman	*Mack*
Mikulski	*Burns*
Murray	

Military Construction

Phone: (202) 224-7276   **Room: SD-131**

Sasser, chairman	*Gorton*
Inouye	*Stevens*
Reid	*McConnell*
Kohl	

Transportation

Phone: (202) 224-7281   **Room: SD-156**

Lautenberg, chairman	*D'Amato*
Byrd	*Domenici*
Harkin	*Hatfield*
Sasser	*Specter*
Mikulski	

Treasury, Postal Service and General Government

Phone: (202) 224-6280   **Room: SD-190**

DeConcini, chairman	*Bond*
Mikulski	*D'Amato*
Kerrey	

VA, HUD and Independent Agencies

Phone: (202) 224-7211   **Room: SD-142**

Mikulski, chairwoman	*Gramm*
Leahy	*D'Amato*
Johnston	*Nickles*
Lautenberg	*Bond*
Kerrey	*Burns*
Feinstein	

ARMED SERVICES

Phone: (202) 224-3871   **Room: SR-228**

Majority Staff Director: Arnold Punaro, (202) 224-3871, SR-228
Minority Staff Director: Richard L. Reynard, (202) 224-9348, SR-228

Defense and defense policy generally; aeronautical and space activities peculiar to or primarily associated with the development of weapons systems or military operations; maintenance and operation of the Panama Canal, including the Canal Zone; military research and development; national security aspects of nuclear energy; naval petroleum reserves (except Alaska); armed forces generally; Selective Service System; strategic and critical materials. Chairman and ranking minority member are non-voting members ex officio of all subcommittees of which they are not regular members.

Party Ratio: D 12 - R 10

Sam Nunn, Ga., chairman	*Strom Thurmond, S.C.,*
Jim Exon, Neb.	*ranking member*
Carl Levin, Mich.	*John W. Warner, Va.*
Edward M. Kennedy, Mass.	*William S. Cohen, Maine*
Jeff Bingaman, N.M.	*John McCain, Ariz.*

John Glenn, Ohio	*Trent Lott, Miss.*
Richard C. Shelby, Ala.	*Daniel R. Coats, Ind.*
Robert C. Byrd, W.Va.	*Robert C. Smith, N.H.*
Bob Graham, Fla.	*Dirk Kempthorne, Idaho*
Charles S. Robb, Va.	*Lauch Faircloth, N.C.*
Joseph I. Lieberman, Conn.	*Kay Bailey Hutchison, Texas*
Richard H. Bryan, Nev.	

SUBCOMMITTEES

Coalition Defense and Reinforcing Forces

Phone: (202) 224-3871   **Room: SR-228**

Levin, chairman	*Warner*
Exon	*Cohen*
Glenn	*Coats*
Shelby	*Smith*
Byrd	*Kempthorne*
Graham	*Hutchison*
Lieberman	

Defense Technology, Acquisition and Industrial Base

Phone: (202) 224-3871   **Room: SR-228**

Bingaman, chairman	*Smith*
Levin	*Cohen*
Kennedy	*Lott*
Byrd	*Coats*
Graham	*Kempthorne*
Robb	*Faircloth*
Lieberman	

Force Requirements and Personnel

Phone: (202) 224-3871   **Room: SR-228**

Shelby, chairman	*Coats*
Kennedy	*McCain*
Byrd	*Faircloth*
Bryan	

Military Readiness and Defense Infrastructure

Phone: (202) 224-3871   **Room: SR-228**

Glenn, chairman	*McCain*
Bingaman	*Smith*
Shelby	*Faircloth*
Robb	*Hutchison*
Bryan	

Nuclear Deterrence, Arms Control and Defense Intelligence

Phone: (202) 224-3871   **Room: SR-228**

Exon, chairman	*Lott*
Levin	*Warner*
Bingaman	*Kempthorne*
Glenn	*Hutchison*
Bryan	

Regional Defense and Contingency Forces

Phone: (202) 224-3871   **Room: SR-228**

Kennedy, chairman | *Cohen*
Exon | *Warner*
Graham | *McCain*
Robb | *Lott*
Lieberman |

BANKING, HOUSING AND URBAN AFFAIRS

Phone: (202) 224-7391   **Room: SD-534**

Majority Staff Director: Steven B. Harris, (202) 224-7391, SD-534
Minority Staff Director: Howard Menell, (202) 224-7391, SD-534

Banks, banking and financial institutions; price controls; deposit insurance; economic stabilization and growth; defense production; export and foreign trade promotion; export controls; federal monetary policy including Federal Reserve System; financial aid to commerce and industry; issuance and redemption of notes; money and credit including currency and coinage; nursing home construction; public and private housing including veterans' housing; renegotiation of government contracts; urban development and mass transit; international economic policy. Chairman and ranking minority member are members ex officio of all subcommittees of which they are not regular members.

Party Ratio: D 11 - R 8

Donald W. Riegle Jr., Mich., chairman | *Alfonse M. D'Amato, N.Y., ranking member*
Paul S. Sarbanes, Md. | *Phil Gramm, Texas*
Christopher J. Dodd, Conn. | *Christopher S. Bond, Mo.*
Jim Sasser, Tenn. | *Connie Mack, Fla.*
Richard C. Shelby, Ala. | *Lauch Faircloth, N.C.*
John Kerry, Mass. | *Robert F. Bennett, Utah*
Richard H. Bryan, Nev. | *William V. Roth Jr., Del.*
Barbara Boxer, Calif. | *Pete V. Domenici, N.M.*
Ben Nighthorse Campbell, Colo. |
Carol Moseley-Braun, Ill. |
Patty Murray, Wash. |

SUBCOMMITTEES

Economic Stabilization and Rural Development

Phone: (202) 224-7391   **Room: SD-534**

Shelby, chairman | *Faircloth*
Campbell | *Bennett*
Dodd | *Gramm*
Kerry | *Mack*
Bryan |

Housing and Urban Affairs

Phone: (202) 224-6348   **Room: SD-535**

Sarbanes, chairman | *Bond*
Kerry | *Domenici*
Bryan | *Mack*
Boxer | *Faircloth*
Moseley-Braun | *Roth*
Dodd |

International Finance and Monetary Policy

Phone: (202) 224-1564   **Room: SD-534**

Sasser, chairman | *Mack*
Murray | *Gramm*
Sarbanes | *Bennett*
Kerry | *Roth*
Boxer | *Bond*
Campbell |

Securities

Phone: (202) 224-9213   **Room: SD-534**

Dodd, chairman | *Gramm*
Sasser | *Roth*
Shelby | *Bond*
Bryan | *Faircloth*
Moseley-Braun | *Domenici*
Murray |

BUDGET

Phone: (202) 224-0642   **Room: SD-621**

Majority Staff Director: Larry Stein, (202) 224-0553, SD-621
Minority Staff Director: Bill Hoagland, (202) 224-0769, SD-634A

Federal budget generally; concurrent budget resolutions; Congressional Budget Office.

Party Ratio: D 12 - R 9

Jim Sasser, Tenn., chairman | *Pete V. Domenici, N.M., ranking member*
Ernest F. Hollings, S.C. |
J. Bennett Johnston, La. | *Charles E. Grassley, Iowa*
Donald W. Riegle Jr., Mich. | *Don Nickles, Okla.*
Jim Exon, Neb. | *Phil Gramm, Texas*
Frank R. Lautenberg, N.J. | *Christopher S. Bond, Mo.*
Paul Simon, Ill. | *Trent Lott, Miss.*
Kent Conrad, N.D. | *Hank Brown, Colo.*
Christopher J. Dodd, Conn. | *Slade Gorton, Wash.*
Paul S. Sarbanes, Md. | *Judd Gregg, N.H.*
Barbara Boxer, Calif. |
Patty Murray, Wash. |

COMMERCE, SCIENCE AND TRANSPORTATION

Phone: (202) 224-5115   **Room: SD-508**

Majority Chief Counsel & Staff Director: Kevin Curtin, (202) 224-0427, SR-254
Republican Staff Director: Jonathan Chambers, (202) 224-5183, SD-554

Interstate commerce and transportation generally; Coast Guard;

coastal zone management; communications; highway safety; inland waterways, except construction; marine fisheries; merchant marine and navigation; non-military aeronautical and space sciences; oceans, weather and atmospheric activities; interoceanic canals generally; regulation of consumer products and services; science, engineering and technology research, development and policy; sports; standards and measurement; transportation and commerce aspects of outer continental shelf lands. Chairman and ranking minority member are non-voting members ex officio of all subcommittees of which they are not regular members.

Party Ratio: **D 11 - R 9**

Ernest F. Hollings, S.C., chairman
Daniel K. Inouye, Hawaii
Wendell H. Ford, Ky.
Jim Exon, Neb.
John D. Rockefeller IV, W.Va.
John Kerry, Mass.
John B. Breaux, La.
Richard H. Bryan, Nev.
Charles S. Robb, Va.
Byron L. Dorgan, N.D.
Harlan Mathews, Tenn.

John C. Danforth, Mo., ranking member
Bob Packwood, Ore.
Larry Pressler, S.D.
Ted Stevens, Alaska
John McCain, Ariz.
Conrad Burns, Mont.
Slade Gorton, Wash.
Trent Lott, Miss.
Kay Bailey Hutchison, Texas

SUBCOMMITTEES

Aviation

Phone: (202) 224-9350   **Room: SH-428**

Ford, chairman
Exon
Inouye
Kerry
Bryan

Pressler
McCain
Stevens
Gorton

Communications

Phone: (202) 224-9340   **Room: SH-227**

Inouye, chairman
Hollings
Ford
Exon
Kerry
Breaux
Rockefeller
Robb

Packwood
Pressler
Stevens
McCain
Burns
Gorton

Consumer

Phone: (202) 224-0415   **Room: SH-227**

Bryan, chairman
Ford
Dorgan
Mathews

Gorton
McCain
Burns

Foreign Commerce and Tourism

Phone: (202) 224-9325   **Room: SH-428**

Kerry, chairman
Hollings
Rockefeller
Bryan
Dorgan
Mathews

McCain
Packwood
Pressler

Merchant Marine

Phone: (202) 224-4914   **Room: SH-425**

Breaux, chairman
Inouye
Mathews

Lott
Stevens

National Ocean Policy Study

Phone: (202) 224-4912   **Room: SH-425**

Hollings, chairman
Kerry, vice chairman
Inouye
Ford
Breaux
Robb
<Vacancy>

Stevens
Danforth
Packwood
Pressler
Gorton
Lott
Hutchison

Science, Technology and Space

Phone: (202) 224-9360   **Room: SH-427**

Rockefeller, chairman
Hollings
Kerry
Bryan
Robb

Burns
Pressler
Lott
Hutchison

Surface Transportation

Phone: (202) 224-9350   **Room: SH-428**

Exon, chairman
Rockefeller
Inouye
Breaux
Robb
Dorgan
Mathews

Hutchison
Packwood
Burns
Lott
McCain

ENERGY AND NATURAL RESOURCES

Phone: (202) 224-4971   **Room: SD-304**

Majority Staff Director: Benjamin Cooper, (202) 224-5360, SD-358
Minority Staff Director: G. Robert Wallace, (202) 224-1004, SD-312

Energy policy, regulation, conservation, research and development; coal; energy-related aspects of deep-water ports; hydroelec-

tric power, irrigation and reclamation; mines, mining and minerals generally; national parks, recreation areas, wilderness areas, wild and scenic rivers, historic sites, military parks and battlefields; naval petroleum reserves in Alaska; non-military development of nuclear energy; oil and gas production and distribution; public lands and forests; solar energy systems; territorial possessions of the United States. Chairman and ranking minority member are members ex officio of all subcommittees of which they are not regular members.

Party Ratio: D 11 - R 9

J. Bennett Johnston, La., chairman
Dale Bumpers, Ark.
Wendell H. Ford, Ky.
Bill Bradley, N.J.
Jeff Bingaman, N.M.
Daniel K. Akaka, Hawaii
Richard C. Shelby, Ala.
Paul Wellstone, Minn.
Ben Nighthorse Campbell, Colo.
Harlan Mathews, Tenn.
Byron L. Dorgan, N.D.

Malcolm Wallop, Wyo., ranking member
Mark O. Hatfield, Ore.
Pete V. Domenici, N.M.
Frank H. Murkowski, Alaska
Don Nickles, Okla.
Larry E. Craig, Idaho
Robert F. Bennett, Utah
Arlen Specter, Pa.
Trent Lott, Miss.

SUBCOMMITTEES

Energy Research and Development

Phone: (202) 224-7569   **Room: SH-312**

Ford, chairman
Shelby, vice chairman
Bumpers
Bingaman
Wellstone
Mathews
Dorgan

Domenici
Specter
Nickles
Craig
Lott

Mineral Resources Development and Production

Phone: (202) 224-7568   **Room: SD-362**

Akaka, chairman
Mathews, vice chairman
Bumpers
Ford
Campbell

Craig
Murkowski
Nickles
Bennett

Public Lands, National Parks and Forests

Phone: (202) 224-7934   **Room: SD-308**

Bumpers, chairman
Campbell, vice chairman
Bradley
Bingaman
Akaka
Shelby
Wellstone
Dorgan

Murkowski
Hatfield
Lott
Domenici
Bennett
Craig
Specter

Renewable Energy, Energy Efficiency and Competitiveness

Phone: (202) 224-4756   **Room: SH-212**

Bingaman, chairman
Wellstone, vice chairman
Bradley
Akaka
Shelby
Mathews

Nickles
Specter
Lott
Hatfield
Domenici

Water and Power

Phone: (202) 224-6836   **Room: SD-306**

Bradley, chairman
Ford
Campbell
Dorgan

Bennett
Hatfield
Murkowski

ENVIRONMENT AND PUBLIC WORKS

Phone: (202) 224-6176   **Room: SD-456**

Majority Staff Director: Peter L. Scher, (202) 224-7845, SD-458
Minority Staff Director & Chief Counsel: Steven J. Shimberg, (202) 224-7854, SD-410

Environmental policy, research and development; air, water and noise pollution; construction and maintenance of highways; environmental aspects of Outer Continental Shelf lands; environmental effects of toxic substances other than pesticides; fisheries and wildlife; flood control and improvements of rivers and harbors; non-military environmental regulation and control of nuclear energy; ocean dumping; public buildings and grounds; public works, bridges and dams; regional economic development; solid waste disposal and recycling; water resources.

Party Ratio: D 10 - R 7

Max Baucus, Mont., chairman
Daniel Patrick Moynihan, N.Y.
George J. Mitchell, Maine
Frank R. Lautenberg, N.J.
Harry Reid, Nev.
Bob Graham, Fla.
Joseph I. Lieberman, Conn.
Howard M. Metzenbaum, Ohio
Harris Wofford, Pa.
Barbara Boxer, Calif.

John H. Chafee, R.I., ranking member
Alan K. Simpson, Wyo.
Dave Durenberger, Minn.
John W. Warner, Va.
Robert C. Smith, N.H.
Lauch Faircloth, N.C.
Dirk Kempthorne, Idaho

SUBCOMMITTEES

Clean Air and Nuclear Regulation

Phone: (202) 224-3597   **Room: SH-505**

Lieberman, chairman
Moynihan
Graham
Metzenbaum

Simpson
Faircloth
Kempthorne

Clean Water, Fisheries and Wildlife

Phone: (202) 224-5031   **Room: SH-415**

Graham, chairman   *Chafee*
Mitchell   *Durenberger*
Lautenberg   *Faircloth*
Reid   *Kempthorne*
Lieberman
Wofford

Superfund, Recycling and Solid Waste Management

Phone: (202) 224-3597   **Room: SH-505**

Lautenberg, chairman   *Durenberger*
Moynihan   *Simpson*
Graham   *Smith*
Metzenbaum   *Warner*
Wofford
Boxer

Toxic Substances, Environmental Oversight, Research and Development

Phone: (202) 224-3597   **Room: SH-505**

Reid, chairman   *Smith*
Lautenberg   *Warner*
Lieberman   *Simpson*
Wofford   *Faircloth*
Boxer

Water Resources, Transportation, Public Buildings and Economic Development

Phone: (202) 224-3597   **Room: SH-505**

Moynihan, chairman   *Warner*
Mitchell   *Durenberger*
Reid   *Smith*
Metzenbaum   *Kempthorne*
Boxer

FINANCE

Phone: (202) 224-4515   **Room: SD-205**

Majority Staff Director: Lawrence O'Donnell Jr., (202) 224-4515, SD-205
Minority Chief of Staff: Edmund J. Mihalski, (202) 224-5315, SH-203

Revenue measures generally; taxes; tariffs and import quotas; reciprocal trade agreements; customs; revenue sharing; federal debt limit; Social Security; health programs financed by taxes or trust funds. Chairman and ranking minority member are members ex officio of all subcommittees of which they are not regular members.

Party Ratio: D 11 - R 9

Daniel Patrick Moynihan, N.Y.,   *Bob Packwood, Ore.,*
  chairman   *ranking member*
Max Baucus, Mont.   *Bob Dole, Kan.*

David L. Boren, Okla.   *William V. Roth Jr., Del.*
Bill Bradley, N.J.   *John C. Danforth, Mo.*
George J. Mitchell, Maine   *John H. Chafee, R.I.*
David Pryor, Ark.   *Dave Durenberger, Minn.*
Donald W. Riegle Jr., Mich.   *Charles E. Grassley, Iowa*
John D. Rockefeller IV, W.Va.   *Orrin G. Hatch, Utah*
Tom Daschle, S.D.   *Malcolm Wallop, Wyo.*
John B. Breaux, La.
Kent Conrad, N.D.

SUBCOMMITTEES

Deficits, Debt Management and Long-Term Economic Growth

Phone: (202) 224-4515   **Room: SD-205**

Bradley, chairman   *Wallop*
Riegle

Energy and Agricultural Taxation

Phone: (202) 224-4515   **Room: SD-205**

Daschle, chairman   *Hatch*
Boren   *Dole*
Breaux   *Wallop*

Health for Families and the Uninsured

Phone: (202) 224-4515   **Room: SD-205**

Riegle, chairman   *Chafee*
Bradley   *Roth*
Mitchell   *Durenberger*
Rockefeller   *Danforth*

International Trade

Phone: (202) 224-4515   **Room: SD-205**

Baucus, chairman   *Danforth*
Moynihan   *Packwood*
Boren   *Roth*
Bradley   *Chafee*
Mitchell   *Grassley*
Riegle   *Hatch*
Rockefeller   *Wallop*
Daschle
Breaux
Conrad

Medicare and Long-Term Care

Phone: (202) 224-4515   **Room: SD-205**

Rockefeller, chairman   *Durenberger*
Baucus   *Packwood*
Mitchell   *Dole*
Pryor   *Chafee*
Daschle   *Grassley*
Conrad   *Hatch*

Private Retirement Plans and Oversight of the Internal Revenue Service

Phone: (202) 224-4515　　**Room: SD-205**

Pryor, chairman　　　　　*Grassley*
Moynihan

Social Security and Family Policy

Phone: (202) 224-4515　　**Room: SD-205**

Breaux, chairman　　　　*Dole*
Moynihan　　　　　　　*Durenberger*

Taxation

Phone: (202) 224-4515　　**Room: SD-205**

Boren, chairman　　　　*Roth*
Baucus　　　　　　　*Packwood*
Pryor　　　　　　　*Danforth*
Conrad

FOREIGN RELATIONS

Phone: (202) 224-4651　　**Room: SD-446**

Majority Staff Director: Geryld B. Christianson, (202) 224-4651, SD-446
Minority Staff Director: James W. Nance, (202) 224-3941, SD-452

Relations of the United States with foreign nations generally; treaties; foreign economic, military, technical and humanitarian assistance; foreign loans; diplomatic service; International Red Cross; international aspects of nuclear energy; International Monetary Fund; intervention abroad and declarations of war; foreign trade; national security; oceans and international environmental and scientific affairs; protection of U.S. citizens abroad; United Nations; World Bank and other development assistance organizations. Chairman and ranking minority member are members ex officio of all subcommittees of which they are not regular members.

Party Ratio:　D 11 - R 9

Claiborne Pell, R.I., chairman
Joseph R. Biden Jr., Del.
Paul S. Sarbanes, Md.
Christopher J. Dodd, Conn.
John Kerry, Mass.
Paul Simon, Ill.
Daniel Patrick Moynihan, N.Y.
Charles S. Robb, Va.
Harris Wofford, Pa.
Russell D. Feingold, Wis.
Harlan Mathews, Tenn.

Jesse Helms, N.C.,
　ranking member
Richard G. Lugar, Ind.
Nancy Landon Kassebaum,
　Kan.
Larry Pressler, S.D.
Frank H. Murkowski, Alaska
Hank Brown, Colo.
James M. Jeffords, Vt.
Paul Coverdell, Ga.
Judd Gregg, N.H.

SUBCOMMITTEES

African Affairs

Phone: (202) 224-4651　　**Room: SD-446**

Simon, chairman　　　　*Jeffords*
Moynihan　　　　　　*Kassebaum*
Feingold

East Asian and Pacific Affairs

Phone: (202) 224-4651　　**Room: SD-446**

Robb, chairman　　　　*Murkowski*
Biden　　　　　　　*Lugar*
Kerry　　　　　　　*Pressler*
Mathews

European Affairs

Phone: (202) 224-4651　　**Room: SD-446**

Biden, chairman　　　　*Lugar*
Sarbanes　　　　　　*Kassebaum*
Simon　　　　　　　*Brown*
Feingold　　　　　　*Gregg*

International Economic Policy, Trade, Oceans and Environment

Phone: (202) 224-4651　　**Room: SD-446**

Sarbanes, chairman　　*Kassebaum*
Biden　　　　　　　*Helms*
Dodd　　　　　　　*Murkowski*
Kerry　　　　　　　*Brown*
Wofford　　　　　　*Jeffords*
Feingold

Near Eastern and South Asian Affairs

Phone: (202) 224-4651　　**Room: SD-446**

Moynihan, chairman　　*Brown*
Sarbanes　　　　　　*Pressler*
Robb　　　　　　　*Jeffords*
Wofford　　　　　　*Coverdell*
Mathews　　　　　　*Gregg*

Terrorism, Narcotics and International Operations

Phone: (202) 224-4651　　**Room: SD-446**

Kerry, chairman　　　*Pressler*
Pell　　　　　　　*Helms*
Dodd　　　　　　　*Murkowski*
Simon　　　　　　　*Coverdell*
Moynihan

Western Hemisphere and Peace Corps Affairs

Phone: (202) 224-4651　　**Room: SD-446**

Dodd, chairman　　　*Coverdell*
Robb　　　　　　　*Helms*
Wofford　　　　　　*Lugar*
Mathews

GOVERNMENTAL AFFAIRS

Phone: (202) 224-4751   Room: SD-340

Majority Staff Director: Leonard Weiss, (202) 224-4751, SD-340
Minority Staff Director: Franklin G. Polk, (202) 224-2627, SD-350

Archives of the United States; budget and accounting measures; census and statistics; federal civil service; congressional organization; intergovernmental relations; government information; District of Columbia; organization and management of nuclear export policy; executive branch organization and reorganization; Postal Service; efficiency, economy and effectiveness of government. Chairman and ranking minority member are non-voting members ex officio of all subcommittees of which they are not regular members.

Party Ratio: D 8 - R 5

John Glenn, Ohio, chairman	*William V. Roth Jr., Del.,*
Sam Nunn, Ga.	*ranking member*
Carl Levin, Mich.	*Ted Stevens, Alaska*
Jim Sasser, Tenn.	*William S. Cohen, Maine*
David Pryor, Ark.	*Thad Cochran, Miss.*
Joseph I. Lieberman, Conn.	*John McCain, Ariz.*
Daniel K. Akaka, Hawaii	
Byron L. Dorgan, N.D.	

SUBCOMMITTEES

Federal Services, Post Office and Civil Service

Phone: (202) 224-2254   Room: SH-601

Pryor, chairman	*Stevens*
Sasser	*Cochran*
Akaka	

General Services, Federalism and the District of Columbia

Phone: (202) 224-4718   Room: SH-432

Sasser, chairman	*McCain*
Lieberman	*Stevens*
Akaka	

Oversight of Government Management

Phone: (202) 224-3682   Room: SH-442

Levin, chairman	*Cohen*
Pryor	*Stevens*
Lieberman	*Cochran*
Akaka	*McCain*
Nunn	
Dorgan	

Permanent Investigations

Phone: (202) 224-3721   Room: SR-100

Nunn, chairman	*Roth*
Glenn, vice chairman	*Stevens*
Levin	*Cohen*
Sasser	*Cochran*
Pryor	*McCain*
Lieberman	
Dorgan	

Regulation and Government Information

Phone: (202) 224-9000   Room: SH-605

Lieberman, chairman	*Cochran*
Nunn	*Cohen*
Levin	*McCain*
Dorgan	

INDIAN AFFAIRS

Phone: (202) 224-2251   Room: SH-838

Majority Staff Director: Patricia Zell, (202) 224-2251, SH-838
Minority Staff Director: Daniel Lewis, (202) 224-2251, SH-838

Problems and opportunities of Indians, including Indian land management and trust responsibilities, education, health, special services, loan programs and claims against the United States.

Party Ratio: D 10 - R 8

Daniel K. Inouye, Hawaii,	*John McCain, Ariz.,*
chairman	*ranking member*
Dennis DeConcini, Ariz.	*Frank H. Murkowski, Alaska*
Tom Daschle, S.D.	*Thad Cochran, Miss.*
Kent Conrad, N.D.	*Slade Gorton, Wash.*
Harry Reid, Nev.	*Pete V. Domenici, N.M.*
Paul Simon, Ill.	*Nancy Landon Kassebaum,*
Daniel K. Akaka, Hawaii	*Kan.*
Paul Wellstone, Minn.	*Don Nickles, Okla.*
Byron L. Dorgan, N.D.	*Mark O. Hatfield, Ore.*
Ben Nighthorse Campbell,	
Colo.	

JUDICIARY

Phone: (202) 224-5225   Room: SD-224

Majority Chief Counsel: Cynthia Hogan, (202) 224-5225, SD-224
Minority Chief Counsel: Sharon Prost, (202) 224-7703, SD-147

Civil and criminal judicial proceedings in general; penitentiaries; bankruptcy, mutiny, espionage and counterfeiting; civil liberties; constitutional amendments; apportionment of representatives; government information; immigration and naturalization; interstate compacts in general; claims against the United States; patents, copyrights and trademarks; monopolies and unlawful restraints of trade; holidays and celebrations. Chairman and ranking minority member are members ex officio of all subcommittees of which they are not regular members.

Party Ratio: D 10 - R 8

Joseph R. Biden Jr., Del.,	*Orrin G. Hatch, Utah,*
chairman	*ranking member*
Edward M. Kennedy, Mass.	*Strom Thurmond, S.C.*
Howard M. Metzenbaum, Ohio	*Alan K. Simpson, Wyo.*
Dennis DeConcini, Ariz.	*Charles E. Grassley, Iowa*
Patrick J. Leahy, Vt.	*Arlen Specter, Pa.*
Howell Heflin, Ala.	*Hank Brown, Colo.*
Paul Simon, Ill.	*William S. Cohen, Maine*
Herb Kohl, Wis.	*Larry Pressler, S.D.*
Dianne Feinstein, Calif.	
Carol Moseley-Braun, Ill.	

SUBCOMMITTEES

Antitrust, Monopolies and Business Rights

Phone: (202) 224-5701   **Room: SH-308**

Metzenbaum, chairman   *Thurmond*
DeConcini   *Specter*
Heflin   *Hatch*
Simon

Constitution

Phone: (202) 224-5573   **Room: SD-524**

Simon, chairman   *Brown*
Metzenbaum   *Hatch*
DeConcini
Kennedy

Courts and Administrative Practice

Phone: (202) 224-4022   **Room: SH-223**

Heflin, chairman   *Grassley*
Metzenbaum   *Thurmond*
Kohl   *Cohen*
Moseley-Braun

Immigration and Refugee Affairs

Phone: (202) 224-7878   **Room: SD-520**

Kennedy, chairman   *Simpson*
Simon

Juvenile Justice

Phone: (202) 224-4933   **Room: SH-305**

Kohl, chairman   *Cohen*
Biden   *Pressler*
Moseley-Braun

Patents, Copyrights and Trademarks

Phone: (202) 224-8178   **Room: SH-327**

DeConcini, chairman   *Hatch*
Kennedy   *Simpson*
Leahy   *Grassley*
Heflin   *Brown*
Feinstein

Technology and the Law

Phone: (202) 224-3406   **Room: SH-815**

Leahy, chairman   *Specter*
Kohl   *Pressler*
Feinstein

LABOR AND HUMAN RESOURCES

Phone: (202) 224-5375   **Room: SD-428**

**Majority Staff Director & Chief Counsel: Nick Littlefield,
   (202) 224-5465, SD-428**
Minority Staff Director: Susan K. Hatten, (202) 224-6770, SH-835

Education, labor, health and public welfare in general; aging; arts and humanities; biomedical research and development; child labor; convict labor; domestic activities of the Red Cross; equal employment opportunity; handicapped and statistics; mediation and arbitration of labor disputes; occupational safety and health; private pensions; public health; railway labor and retirement; regulation of foreign laborers; student loans; wages and hours; agricultural colleges; Gallaudet University; Howard University; St. Elizabeths Hospital in Washington, D.C. Chairman and ranking minority member are members ex officio of all subcommittees of which they are not regular members.

Party Ratio: D 10 - R 7

Edward M. Kennedy, Mass.,   *Nancy Landon Kassebaum,*
  chairman   *Kan., ranking member*
Claiborne Pell, R.I.   *James M. Jeffords, Vt.*
Howard M. Metzenbaum, Ohio   *Daniel R. Coats, Ind.*
Christopher J. Dodd, Conn.   *Judd Gregg, N.H.*
Paul Simon, Ill.   *Strom Thurmond, S.C.*
Tom Harkin, Iowa   *Orrin G. Hatch, Utah*
Barbara A. Mikulski, Md.   *Dave Durenberger, Minn.*
Jeff Bingaman, N.M.
Paul Wellstone, Minn.
Harris Wofford, Pa.

SUBCOMMITTEES

Aging

Phone: (202) 224-3239   **Room: SH-615**

Mikulski, chairman   *Gregg*
Pell   *Coats*
Metzenbaum   *Durenberger*
Dodd
Wofford

Children, Families, Drugs and Alcoholism

Phone: (202) 224-5630   **Room: SH-639**

Dodd, chairman   *Coats*
Pell   *Kassebaum*
Mikulski   *Jeffords*
Bingaman   *Gregg*
Kennedy   *Thurmond*
Wellstone   *Durenberger*
Wofford

Disability Policy

Phone: (202) 224-6265   **Room: SH-113**

Harkin, chairman   *Durenberger*
Metzenbaum   *Jeffords*
Simon   *Hatch*
Bingaman

Education, Arts and Humanities

Phone: (202) 224-7666 **Room: SD-648**

Pell, chairman | *Jeffords*
Metzenbaum | *Kassebaum*
Dodd | *Coats*
Simon | *Gregg*
Mikulski | *Thurmond*
Bingaman | *Hatch*
Kennedy | *Durenberger*
Wellstone
Wofford
Harkin

Employment and Productivity

Phone: (202) 224-5575 **Room: SD-644**

Simon, chairman | *Thurmond*
Harkin | *Coats*
Mikulski | *Gregg*
Bingaman | *Hatch*
Wofford

Labor

Phone: (202) 224-5546 **Room: SH-608**

Metzenbaum, chairman | *Hatch*
Harkin | *Kassebaum*
Dodd | *Jeffords*
Kennedy | *Thurmond*
Wellstone

RULES AND ADMINISTRATION

Phone: (202) 224-6352 **Room: SR-305**

Majority Staff Director: James O. King, (202) 224-6352, SR-305
Minority Staff Director: Al McDermott, (202) 224-8923, SR-479

Senate administration in general; corrupt practices; qualifications of senators; contested elections; federal elections in general; Government Printing Office; Congressional Record; meetings of Congress and attendance of members; presidential succession; the Capitol, congressional office buildings, the Library of Congress, the Smithsonian Institution and the Botanic Garden.

Party Ratio: D 9 - R 7

Wendell H. Ford, Ky., chairman | *Ted Stevens, Alaska,*
Claiborne Pell, R.I. | *ranking member*
Robert C. Byrd, W.Va. | *Mark O. Hatfield, Ore.*
Daniel K. Inouye, Hawaii | *Jesse Helms, N.C.*
Dennis DeConcini, Ariz. | *John W. Warner, Va.*
Daniel Patrick Moynihan, N.Y. | *Bob Dole, Kan.*
Christopher J. Dodd, Conn. | *Mitch McConnell, Ky.*
Dianne Feinstein, Calif. | *Thad Cochran, Miss.*
Harlan Mathews, Tenn.

SELECT ETHICS

Phone: (202) 224-2981 **Room: SH-220**

Staff Director and Chief Counsel: Victor M. Baird, (202) 224-2981, SH-220

Studies and investigates standards and conduct of Senate members and employees and may recommend remedial action.

Party Ratio: D 3 - R 3

Richard H. Bryan, Nev., chairman | *Mitch McConnell, Ky., vice chairman*
Barbara A. Mikulski, Md. | *Robert C. Smith, N.H.*
Tom Daschle, S.D. | *Larry E. Craig, Idaho*

SELECT INTELLIGENCE

Phone: (202) 224-1700 **Room: SH-211**

Majority Staff Director: Norm Bradley, (202) 224-1700, SH-211
Minority Staff Director: David Addington, (202) 224-1700, SH-211

Legislative and budgetary authority over the Central Intelligence Agency, the Defense Intelligence Agency, the National Security Agency and intelligence activities of the Federal Bureau of Investigation and other components of the federal intelligence community. The majority leader and minority leader are members ex officio of the committee.

Party Ratio: D 9 - R 8

Dennis DeConcini, Ariz., chairman | *John W. Warner, Va., vice chairman*
Howard M. Metzenbaum, Ohio | *Alfonse M. D'Amato, N.Y.*
John Glenn, Ohio | *John C. Danforth, Mo.*
Bob Kerrey, Neb. | *Slade Gorton, Wash.*
Richard H. Bryan, Nev. | *John H. Chafee, R.I.*
Bob Graham, Fla. | *Ted Stevens, Alaska*
John Kerry, Mass. | *Richard G. Lugar, Ind.*
Max Baucus, Mont. | *Malcolm Wallop, Wyo.*
J. Bennett Johnston, La.

SMALL BUSINESS

Phone: (202) 224-5175 **Room: SR-428A**

Majority Staff Director: John W. Ball III, (202) 224-5175, SR-428A
Minority Staff Director: Thomas G. Hohenthaner, (202) 224-8485, SR-428A

Problems of small business; Small Business Administration.

Party Ratio: D 12 - R 10

Dale Bumpers, Ark., chairman | *Larry Pressler, S.D., ranking member*
Sam Nunn, Ga. | *Malcolm Wallop, Wyo.*
Carl Levin, Mich. | *Christopher S. Bond, Mo.*
Tom Harkin, Iowa | *Conrad Burns, Mont.*
John Kerry, Mass. | *Connie Mack, Fla.*
Joseph I. Lieberman, Conn. | *Paul Coverdell, Ga.*
Paul Wellstone, Minn. | *Dirk Kempthorne, Idaho*
Harris Wofford, Pa. | *Robert F. Bennett, Utah*
Howell Heflin, Ala. | *John H. Chafee, R.I.*
Frank R. Lautenberg, N.J. | *Kay Bailey Hutchison, Texas*
Herb Kohl, Wis.
Carol Moseley-Braun, Ill.

SUBCOMMITTEES

Competitiveness, Capital Formation and Economic Opportunity

Phone: (202) 224-5175   **Room: SR-428A**

Lieberman, chairman   *Mack*
Harkin   *Bond*
Lautenberg

Export Expansion and Agricultural Development

Phone: (202) 224-5175   **Room: SR-428A**

Wofford, chairman   *Coverdell*
Harkin   *Pressler*
Bumpers   *Bennett*
Lautenberg   *Chafee*
Moseley-Braun   *Hutchison*

Government Contracting and Paperwork Reduction

Phone: (202) 224-5175   **Room: SR-428A**

Nunn, chairman   *Bond*
Lieberman   *Wallop*
Harkin   *Hutchison*
Kohl

Innovation, Manufacturing and Technology

Phone: (202) 224-5175   **Room: SR-428A**

Levin, chairman   *Burns*
Kerry   *Kempthorne*
Bumpers   *Bennett*
Heflin

Rural Economy and Family Farming

Phone: (202) 224-5175   **Room: SR-428A**

Wellstone, chairman   *Pressler*
Nunn   *Wallop*
Levin   *Burns*
Bumpers   *Coverdell*
Heflin   *Kempthorne*
Kohl

Urban and Minority-Owned Business Development

Phone: (202) 224-5175   **Room: SR-428A**

Kerry, chairman   *Chafee*
Nunn   *Mack*
Wellstone   *Pressler*
Wofford
Moseley-Braun

SPECIAL AGING

Phone: (202) 224-5364   **Room: SD-G31**

Majority Staff Director: Portia Mittelman, (202) 224-5364, SD-G31
Minority Staff Director: Mary Gerwin, (202) 224-1467, SH-628

Problems and opportunities of older people including health, income, employment, housing, and care and assistance. Reports findings and makes recommendations to the Senate but cannot report legislation.

Party Ratio: D 11 - R 10

David Pryor, Ark., chairman   *William S. Cohen, Maine,*
John Glenn, Ohio   *ranking member*
Bill Bradley, N.J.   *Larry Pressler, S.D.*
J. Bennett Johnston, La.   *Charles E. Grassley, Iowa*
John B. Breaux, La.   *Alan K. Simpson, Wyo.*
Richard C. Shelby, Ala.   *James M. Jeffords, Vt.*
Harry Reid, Nev.   *John McCain, Ariz.*
Bob Graham, Fla.   *Dave Durenberger, Minn.*
Herb Kohl, Wis.   *Larry E. Craig, Idaho*
Russell D. Feingold, Wis.   *Conrad Burns, Mont.*
Donald W. Riegle Jr., Mich.   *Arlen Specter, Pa.*

VETERANS' AFFAIRS

Phone: (202) 224-9126   **Room: SR-414**

Majority Staff Director: Jim Gottleib, (202) 224-9126, SR-414
Minority Staff Director: John Moseman, (202) 224-2074, SH-202

Veterans' measures in general; compensation; life insurance issued by the government on account of service in the armed forces; national cemeteries; pensions; readjustment benefits; veterans' hospitals, medical care and treatment; vocational rehabilitation and education.

Party Ratio: D 7 - R 5

John D. Rockefeller IV, W.Va.,   *Frank H. Murkowski, Alaska,*
chairman   *ranking member*
Dennis DeConcini, Ariz.   *Strom Thurmond, S.C.*
George J. Mitchell, Maine   *Alan K. Simpson, Wyo.*
Bob Graham, Fla.   *Arlen Specter, Pa.*
Daniel K. Akaka, Hawaii   *James M. Jeffords, Vt.*
Tom Daschle, S.D.
Ben Nighthorse Campbell,
Colo.

House Committees, 103rd Congress, 1st Session

(As of Dec. 31, 1993)

AGRICULTURE

Phone: 225-2171   Room: 1301 LHOB

Majority Staff Director: Dianne Powell, 225-2171, 1301 LHOB
Minority Staff Director: Gary Mitchell, 225-0029, 1304 LHOB

Agriculture generally; production, marketing and stabilization of agricultural prices; animal industry and diseases of animals; crop insurance and soil conservation; dairy industry; farm credit and security; forestry in general; human nutrition and home economics; inspection of livestock and meat products; plant industry, soils and agricultural engineering; rural electrification; commodities exchanges; rural development. Chairman and ranking minority member are members ex officio of all subcommittees of which they are not regular members.

Party Ratio: D 29 - R 19

E. de la Garza, Texas, chairman
George E. Brown Jr., Calif.
Charlie Rose, N.C.
Glenn English, Okla.
Dan Glickman, Kan.
Charles W. Stenholm, Texas
Harold L. Volkmer, Mo.
Timothy J. Penny, Minn.
Tim Johnson, S.D.
Bill Sarpalius, Texas
Jill L. Long, Ind.
Gary A. Condit, Calif.
Collin C. Peterson, Minn.
Cal Dooley, Calif.
Eva Clayton, N.C.
David Minge, Minn.
Earl F. Hilliard, Ala.
Jay Inslee, Wash.
Tom Barlow, Ky.
Earl Pomeroy, N.D.
Tim Holden, Pa.
Cynthia A. McKinney, Ga.
Scotty Baesler, Ky.
Karen L. Thurman, Fla.
Sanford D. Bishop Jr., Ga.
Bennie Thompson, Miss.
Sam Farr, Calif.
Pat Williams, Mont.
Blanche Lambert, Ark.

Pat Roberts, Kan., ranking
member
Bill Emerson, Mo.
Steve Gunderson, Wis.
Tom Lewis, Fla.
Bob Smith, Ore.
Larry Combest, Texas
Wayne Allard, Colo.
Bill Barrett, Neb.
Jim Nussle, Iowa
John A. Boehner, Ohio
Thomas W. Ewing, Ill.
John T. Doolittle, Calif.
Jack Kingston, Ga.
Robert W. Goodlatte, Va.
Jay Dickey, Ark.
Richard W. Pombo, Calif.
Charles T. Canady, Fla.
Nick Smith, Mich.
Terry Everett, Ala.

SUBCOMMITTEES

Department Operations and Nutrition

Phone: 225-1496   Room: 1301A LHOB

Stenholm, chairman
Brown (Calif.)
Sarpalius
Dooley
Inslee
English (Okla.)
Glickman
McKinney
Bishop
Volkmer
Clayton
Holden
Rose
Farr
Johnson (S.D.)
Pomeroy
Lambert

Smith (Ore.)
Emerson
Gunderson
Allard
Barrett (Neb.)
Ewing
Kingston
Canady
Boehner

Environment, Credit and Rural Development

Phone: 225-0301   Room: 1430 LHOB

English (Okla.), chairman
Johnson (S.D.)
Long
Clayton
Minge
Barlow
Pomeroy
Holden
McKinney
Thurman
Penny
Sarpalius
Peterson (Minn.)
Hilliard
Inslee
Baesler
Thompson
Farr

Combest
Gunderson
Allard
Barrett (Neb.)
Nussle
Ewing
Dickey
Pombo
Smith (Mich.)

Foreign Agriculture and Hunger

Phone: 225-1867   Room: 1336 LHOB

Penny, chairman
Rose
Barlow
McKinney
Baesler
Thurman
Stenholm

Allard
Lewis (Fla.)
Doolittle
Canady
Everett

General Farm Commodities

Phone: 225-0301   **Room: 1430 LHOB**

Johnson (S.D.), chairman	*Emerson*
Glickman	*Smith (Ore.)*
Peterson (Minn.)	*Combest*
Volkmer	*Barrett (Neb.)*
Long	*Nussle*
Dooley	*Boehner*
Minge	*Ewing*
Pomeroy	*Doolittle*
Rose	*Dickey*
English (Okla.)	*Smith (Mich.)*
Stenholm	
Sarpalius	
Condit	
Barlow	
Bishop	
Thompson	
Williams	

Livestock

Phone: 225-1867   **Room: 1336 LHOB**

Volkmer, chairman	*Gunderson*
Condit	*Lewis (Fla.)*
Hilliard	*Smith (Ore.)*
Stenholm	*Boehner*
Holden	*Goodlatte*
Long	*Pombo*
Peterson (Minn.)	
Rose	
Dooley	
Thurman	
Sarpalius	

Specialty Crops and Natural Resources

Phone: 225-8906   **Room: 1336 LHOB**

Rose, chairman	*Lewis (Fla.)*
Baesler	*Emerson*
Bishop	*Doolittle*
Brown (Calif.)	*Kingston*
Condit	*Goodlatte*
Clayton	*Dickey*
Thurman	*Pombo*
Minge	*Everett*
Inslee	
Pomeroy	
English (Okla.)	
Stenholm	
Peterson (Minn.)	
Farr	
Volkmer	

APPROPRIATIONS

Phone: 225-2771   Room: H-218 Capitol

Majority Staff Director: Frederick G. Mohrman, 225-2771, H-218 Capitol

Minority Staff Director: Jim Kulikowski, 225-3481, 1016 LHOB

Appropriation of revenue for support of the federal government; rescissions of appropriations; transfers of unexpended balances; new spending authority under the Congressional Budget Act. Chairman and ranking minority member are members ex officio of all subcommittees of which they are not regular members.

Party Ratio: D 37 - R 23

William H. Natcher, Ky., chairman	*Joseph M. McDade, Pa., ranking member*
Jamie L. Whitten, Miss.	*John T. Myers, Ind.*
Neal Smith, Iowa	*C.W. Bill Young, Fla.*
Sidney R. Yates, Ill.	*Ralph Regula, Ohio*
David R. Obey, Wis.	*Robert L. Livingston, La.*
Louis Stokes, Ohio	*Jerry Lewis, Calif.*
Tom Bevill, Ala.	*John Edward Porter, Ill.*
John P. Murtha, Pa.	*Harold Rogers, Ky.*
Charles Wilson, Texas	*Joe Skeen, N.M.*
Norm Dicks, Wash.	*Frank R. Wolf, Va.*
Martin Olav Sabo, Minn.	*Tom DeLay, Texas*
Julian C. Dixon, Calif.	*Jim Kolbe, Ariz.*
Vic Fazio, Calif.	*Dean A. Gallo, N.J.*
W.G. Hefner, N.C.	*Barbara F. Vucanovich, Nev.*
Steny H. Hoyer, Md.	*Jim Ross Lightfoot, Iowa*
Bob Carr, Mich.	*Ron Packard, Calif.*
Richard J. Durbin, Ill.	*Sonny Callahan, Ala.*
Ronald D. Coleman, Texas	*Helen Delich Bentley, Md.*
Alan B. Mollohan, W.Va.	*James T. Walsh, N.Y.*
Jim Chapman, Texas	*Charles H. Taylor, N.C.*
Marcy Kaptur, Ohio	*David L. Hobson, Ohio*
David E. Skaggs, Colo.	*Ernest Jim Istook Jr., Okla.*
David Price, N.C.	*Henry Bonilla, Texas*
Nancy Pelosi, Calif.	
Peter J. Visclosky, Ind.	
Thomas M. Foglietta, Pa.	
Esteban E. Torres, Calif.	
George "Buddy" Darden, Ga.	
Nita M. Lowey, N.Y.	
Ray Thornton, Ark.	
Jose E. Serrano, N.Y.	
Rosa DeLauro, Conn.	
James P. Moran Jr., Va.	
Pete Peterson, Fla.	
John W. Olver, Mass.	
Ed Pastor, Ariz.	
Carrie P. Meek, Fla.	

SUBCOMMITTEES

Agriculture, Rural Development, FDA and Related Agencies

Phone: 225-2638   **Room: 2362 RHOB**

Durbin, chairman	*Skeen*
Whitten	*Myers*
Kaptur	*Vucanovich*
Thornton	*Walsh*
DeLauro	
Peterson (Fla.)	
Pastor	
Smith (Iowa)	

Commerce, Justice, State and Judiciary

Phone: 225-3351   **Room: H-309 Capitol**

Smith (Iowa), chairman   *Rogers*
Carr   *Kolbe*
Mollohan   *Taylor (N.C.)*
Moran
Skaggs
Price

Defense

Phone: 225-2847   **Room: H-144 Capitol**

Murtha, chairman   *McDade*
Dicks   *Young (Fla.)*
Wilson   *Livingston*
Hefner   *Lewis (Calif.)*
Sabo   *Skeen*
Dixon
Visclosky
Darden

District of Columbia

Phone: 225-5338   **Room: H-302 Capitol**

Dixon, chairman   *Walsh*
Stokes   *Istook*
Durbin   *Bonilla*
Kaptur
Skaggs
Pelosi

Energy and Water Development

Phone: 225-3421   **Room: 2362 RHOB**

Bevill, chairman   *Myers*
Fazio   *Gallo*
Chapman   *Rogers*
Peterson (Fla.)
Pastor
Meek

Foreign Operations, Export Financing and Related Programs

Phone: 225-2041   **Room: H-307 Capitol**

Obey, chairman   *Livingston*
Yates   *Porter*
Wilson   *Lightfoot*
Olver   *Callahan*
Pelosi
Torres
Lowey
Serrano

Interior

Phone: 225-3081   **Room: B-308 RHOB**

Yates, chairman   *Regula*
Murtha   *McDade*
Dicks   *Kolbe*
Bevill   *Packard*
Skaggs
Coleman

Labor, Health and Human Services, and Education

Phone: 225-3508   **Room: 2358 RHOB**

Natcher, chairman   *Porter*
Smith (Iowa)   *Young (Fla.)*
Obey   *Bentley*
Stokes   *Bonilla*
Hoyer
Pelosi
Lowey
Serrano
DeLauro

Legislative Branch

Phone: 225-5338   **Room: H-302 Capitol**

Fazio, chairman   *Young (Fla.)*
Moran   *Packard*
Obey   *Taylor (N.C.)*
Murtha
Carr
Chapman

Military Construction

Phone: 225-3047   **Room: B-300 RHOB**

Hefner, chairman   *Vucanovich*
Foglietta   *Callahan*
Meek   *Bentley*
Dicks   *Hobson*
Dixon
Fazio
Hoyer
Coleman

Transportation

Phone: 225-2141   **Room: 2358 RHOB**

Carr, chairman   *Wolf*
Durbin   *DeLay*
Sabo   *Regula*
Price
Coleman
Foglietta

Treasury, Postal Service and General Government

Phone: 225-5834   **Room: H-164 Capitol**

Hoyer, chairman	*Lightfoot*
Visclosky	*Wolf*
Darden	*Istook*
Olver	
Bevill	
Sabo	

Veterans Affairs, Housing and Urban Development, and Independent Agencies

Phone: 225-3241   **Room: H-143 Capitol**

Stokes, chairman	*Lewis (Calif.)*
Mollohan	*DeLay*
Chapman	*Gallo*
Kaptur	
Torres	
Thornton	

ARMED SERVICES

Phone: 225-4151   **Room: 2120 RHOB**

Staff Director: Marilyn A. Elrod, 225-4158, 2117 RHOB
Professional Staff Member: Andrew K. Ellis, 225-9647, 2340 RHOB

Jurisdiction pursuant to House Rule X--(1) Common defense generally (2) the Department of Defense generally, including the Departments of the Army, Navy, and Air Force generally (3) ammunition depots; forts; arsenals; Army, Navy, and Air Force reservations and establishments (4) conservation, development, and use of naval petroleum and oil shale reserves (5) pay, promotion, retirement, and other benefits and privileges of members of the armed forces (6) scientific research and development in support of the armed services (7) selective service (8) size and composition of the Army, Navy, and Air Force (9) soldiers' and sailors' homes (10) strategic and critical materials necessary for the common defense and (11) military applications of nuclear energy. In addition, the committee has the special oversight function provided for in clause 3(a) with respect to international arms control and disarmament, and military dependents' education.

Party Ratio: **D 34 * - R 22**

Ronald V. Dellums, Calif., chairman	*Floyd D. Spence, S.C., ranking member*
G.V. "Sonny" Montgomery, Miss.	*Bob Stump, Ariz.*
Patricia Schroeder, Colo.	*Duncan Hunter, Calif.*
Earl Hutto, Fla.	*John R. Kasich, Ohio*
Ike Skelton, Mo.	*Herbert H. Bateman, Va.*
Dave McCurdy, Okla.	*James V. Hansen, Utah*
Marilyn Lloyd, Tenn.	*Curt Weldon, Pa.*
Norman Sisisky, Va.	*Jon Kyl, Ariz.*

* Delegates and/or resident commissioner are not counted in official ratio.

John M. Spratt Jr., S.C.	*Arthur Ravenel Jr., S.C.*
Frank McCloskey, Ind.	*Robert K. Dornan, Calif.*
Solomon P. Ortiz, Texas	*Joel Hefley, Colo.*
George J. Hochbrueckner, N.Y.	*Ronald K. Machtley, R.I.*
Owen B. Pickett, Va.	*H. James Saxton, N.J.*
H. Martin Lancaster, N.C.	*Randy Cunningham, Calif.*
Lane Evans, Ill.	*James M. Inhofe, Okla.*
James Bilbray, Nev.	*Steve Buyer, Ind.*
John Tanner, Tenn.	*Peter G. Torkildsen, Mass.*
Glen Browder, Ala.	*Tillie Fowler, Fla.*
Gene Taylor, Miss.	*John M. McHugh, N.Y.*
Neil Abercrombie, Hawaii	*James M. Talent, Mo.*
Thomas H. Andrews, Maine	*Terry Everett, Ala.*
Chet Edwards, Texas	*Roscoe G. Bartlett, Md.*
Don Johnson, Ga.	
Frank Tejeda, Texas	
David Mann, Ohio	
Bart Stupak, Mich.	
Martin T. Meehan, Mass.	
Robert A. Underwood, Guam *	
Jane Harman, Calif.	
Paul McHale, Pa.	
Tim Holden, Pa.	
Pete Geren, Texas	
Elizabeth Furse, Ore.	
Sam Farr, Calif.	

SUBCOMMITTEES

Military Acquisition

Phone: 225-6999   **Room: 2343 RHOB**

Dellums, chairman	*Spence*
Lloyd	*Bateman*
Spratt	*Weldon*
McCloskey	*Ravenel*
Evans	*Dornan*
Tanner	*Hefley*
Taylor (Miss.)	*Machtley*
Abercrombie	*Saxton*
Andrews (Maine)	*Cunningham*
Mann	*Inhofe*
Stupak	
McHale	
Holden	
Geren	
Sisisky	

Military Forces and Personnel

Phone: 225-7560   **Room: 2343 RHOB**

Skelton, chairman	*Kyl*
Montgomery	*Ravenel*
Pickett	*Buyer*
Lancaster	*Fowler*
Bilbray	*Talent*
Stupak	*Bartlett*
Meehan	
Underwood	
Harman	
Farr	
<Vacancy>	

Military Installations and Facilities

Phone: 225-7120   **Room: 2120 RHOB**

McCurdy, chairman	*Hunter*
Montgomery	*Fowler*
McCloskey	*McHugh*
Ortiz	*Everett*
Hochbrueckner	*Stump*
Bilbray	*Machtley*
Browder	*Saxton*
Taylor (Miss.)	*Torkildsen*
Abercrombie	
Edwards (Texas)	
Johnson (Ga.)	
Tejeda	
Underwood	

Oversight and Investigations

Phone: 225-2086   **Room: 2340 RHOB**

Sisisky, chairman	*Hansen*
Spratt	*Kyl*
Tanner	*Hefley*
Browder	*McHugh*
Edwards (Texas)	*Everett*
Johnson (Ga.)	*Dornan*
Tejeda	
Mann	
Harman	
Holden	

Readiness

Phone: 225-9644   **Room: 2339 RHOB**

Hutto, chairman	*Kasich*
Ortiz	*Bateman*
Pickett	*Weldon*
Lancaster	*Dornan*
Evans	*Cunningham*
Browder	*Inhofe*
Meehan	
Underwood	
McHale	
McCurdy	

Research and Technology

Phone: 225-5627   **Room: 2120 RHOB**

Schroeder, chairman	*Stump*
Hochbrueckner	*Buyer*
Pickett	*Torkildsen*
Lancaster	*Talent*
Bilbray	*Bartlett*
Edwards (Texas)	*Hunter*
Johnson (Ga.)	*Kasich*
Tejeda	*Hansen*
Meehan	
Harman	
Furse	
Hutto	
McCurdy	

BANKING, FINANCE AND URBAN AFFAIRS

Phone: 225-4247   **Room: 2129 RHOB**

Majority Clerk and Staff Director: Kelsay Meek, 225-7057, 2129 RHOB

Minority Staff Director: Tony Cole, 225-7502, B-301C RHOB

Banks and banking including deposit insurance and federal monetary policy; money and credit; currency; issuance and redemption of notes; gold and silver; coinage; valuation and revaluation of the dollar; urban development; private and public housing; economic stabilization; defense production; renegotiation; price controls; international finance; financial aid to commerce and industry.

Party Ratio: D 30 - R 20 - I 1

Henry B. Gonzalez, Texas, chairman	*Jim Leach, Iowa, ranking member*
Stephen L. Neal, N.C.	*Bill McCollum, Fla.*
John J. LaFalce, N.Y.	*Marge Roukema, N.J.*
Bruce F. Vento, Minn.	*Doug Bereuter, Neb.*
Charles E. Schumer, N.Y.	*Tom Ridge, Pa.*
Barney Frank, Mass.	*Toby Roth, Wis.*
Paul E. Kanjorski, Pa.	*Al McCandless, Calif.*
Joseph P. Kennedy II, Mass.	*Richard H. Baker, La.*
Floyd H. Flake, N.Y.	*Jim Nussle, Iowa*
Kweisi Mfume, Md.	*Craig Thomas, Wyo.*
Maxine Waters, Calif.	*Sam Johnson, Texas*
Larry LaRocco, Idaho	*Deborah Pryce, Ohio*
Bill Orton, Utah	*John Linder, Ga.*
Jim Bacchus, Fla.	*Joe Knollenberg, Mich.*
Herb Klein, N.J.	*Rick A. Lazio, N.Y.*
Carolyn B. Maloney, N.Y.	*Rod Grams, Minn.*
Peter Deutsch, Fla.	*Spencer Bachus, Ala.*
Luis V. Gutierrez, Ill.	*Michael Huffington, Calif.*
Bobby L. Rush, Ill.	*Michael N. Castle, Del.*
Lucille Roybal-Allard, Calif.	*Peter T. King, N.Y.*
Thomas M. Barrett, Wis.	
Elizabeth Furse, Ore.	
Nydia M. Velázquez, N.Y.	
Albert R. Wynn, Md.	
Cleo Fields, La.	
Melvin Watt, N.C.	
Maurice D. Hinchey, N.Y.	
Cal Dooley, Calif.	
Ron Klink, Pa.	**Bernard Sanders, Vt.**
Eric D. Fingerhut, Ohio	

SUBCOMMITTEES

Consumer Credit and Insurance

Phone: 225-8872   **Room: 604 OHOB**

Kennedy, chairman   *McCandless*
Gonzalez   *Castle*
LaRocco   *King*
Gutierrez   *Pryce*
Rush   *Linder*
Roybal-Allard   *Knollenberg*
Barrett (Wis.)   *Bereuter*
Furse   *Thomas (Wyo.)*
Velázquez   *Lazio*
Wynn   *Grams*
Fields (La.)   *Bachus*
Watt   *Baker (La.)*
Hinchey
Kanjorski
Flake   **Sanders**
Waters
Maloney
Deutsch

Economic Growth and Credit Formation

Phone: 226-7315   **Room: 109 FHOB**

Kanjorski, chairman   *Ridge*
Neal (N.C.)   *McCollum*
LaFalce   *Roth*
Orton   *Nussle*
Klein   *Roukema*
Velázquez   *King*
Dooley
Klink
Fingerhut

Financial Institutions Supervision, Regulation and Deposit Insurance

Phone: 226-3280   **Room: 212 OHOB**

Neal (N.C.), chairman   *McCollum*
LaFalce   *Leach*
Vento   *Baker (La.)*
Schumer   *Nussle*
Frank   *Thomas (Wyo.)*
Kanjorski   *Johnson (Texas)*
Kennedy   *Pryce*
Flake   *Linder*
Mfume   *Lazio*
LaRocco   *Grams*
Orton   *Bachus*
Bacchus   *Huffington*
Waters
Klein
Maloney
Deutsch
Barrett (Wis.)
Hinchey

General Oversight, Investigations and the Resolution of Failed Financial Institutions

Phone: 225-2828   **Room: 139 FHOB**

Flake, chairman   *Roth*
Neal (N.C.)   *Ridge*
Velázquez
Hinchey

Housing and Community Development

Phone: 225-7054   **Room: B-303 RHOB**

Gonzalez, chairman   *Roukema*
Vento   *Bereuter*
Schumer   *Ridge*
Mfume   *Baker (La.)*
LaFalce   *Thomas (Wyo.)*
Waters   *Knollenberg*
Klein   *Lazio*
Maloney   *Grams*
Deutsch   *Bachus*
Gutierrez   *Castle*
Rush   *Pryce*
Roybal-Allard   *Roth*
Barrett (Wis.)
Furse
Velázquez   **Sanders**
Wynn
Fields (La.)
Watt

International Development, Finance, Trade and Monetary Policy

Phone: 226-7515   **Room: B-304 RHOB**

Frank, chairman   *Bereuter*
Neal (N.C.)   *McCandless*
LaFalce   *McCollum*
Kennedy   *Roukema*
Waters   *Johnson*
LaRocco   *Huffington*
Orton   *King*
Bacchus   *Baker (La.)*
Gonzalez   *Nussle*
Kanjorski   *Castle*
Rush
Fields (La.)
Watt   **Sanders**
Fingerhut
<Vacancy>

BUDGET

Phone: 226-7200   Room: 214 OHOB

Chief of Staff: Eileen Baumgartner, 226-7234, 222 OHOB
Minority Staff Director: Rick May, 226-7270, H2-278 FHOB

Federal budget generally; concurrent budget resolutions; Congressional Budget Office. Chairman and ranking minority member

are members ex officio of all task forces of which they are not regular members. The majority leader's designate and the minority leader's designate are ex officio members of all task forces.

Party Ratio: D 26 - R 17

Martin Olav Sabo, Minn., chairman
Richard A. Gephardt, Mo.
Dale E. Kildee, Mich.
Anthony C. Beilenson, Calif.
Howard L. Berman, Calif.
Bob Wise, W.Va.
John Bryant, Texas
Charles W. Stenholm, Texas
Barney Frank, Mass.
Jim Cooper, Tenn.
Louise M. Slaughter, N.Y.
Mike Parker, Miss.
William J. Coyne, Pa.
Barbara B. Kennelly, Conn.
Michael A. Andrews, Texas
Alan B. Mollohan, W.Va.
Bart Gordon, Tenn.
David Price, N.C.
Jerry F. Costello, Ill.
Harry A. Johnston, Fla.
Patsy T. Mink, Hawaii
Bill Orton, Utah
Lucien E. Blackwell, Pa.
Earl Pomeroy, N.D.
Glen Browder, Ala.
Lynn Woolsey, Calif.

John R. Kasich, Ohio, ranking member
Alex McMillan, N.C.
Jim Kolbe, Ariz.
Christopher Shays, Conn.
Olympia J. Snowe, Maine
Wally Herger, Calif.
Jim Bunning, Ky.
Lamar Smith, Texas
C. Christopher Cox, Calif.
Wayne Allard, Colo.
David L. Hobson, Ohio
Dan Miller, Fla.
Rick A. Lazio, N.Y.
Bob Franks, N.J.
Nick Smith, Mich.
Bob Inglis, S.C.
Martin R. Hoke, Ohio

DISTRICT OF COLUMBIA

Phone: 225-4457   **Room: 1310 LHOB**

Majority Staff Director: Broderick D. Johnson, 225-4457, 1310 LHOB
Minority Staff Director: Dennis G. Smith, 225-7158, 1307 LHOB

Municipal affairs of the District of Columbia.

Party Ratio: D 8 * - R 4

Pete Stark, Calif., chairman
Ronald V. Dellums, Calif.
Alan Wheat, Mo.
Jim McDermott, Wash.
Eleanor Holmes Norton, D.C. *
John Lewis, Ga.
William J. Jefferson, La.
<Vacancy>

Thomas J. Bliley Jr., Va., ranking member
Dana Rohrabacher, Calif.
H. James Saxton, N.J.
Cass Ballenger, N.C.

SUBCOMMITTEES

Fiscal Affairs and Health

Phone: 225-4457   **Room: 1310 LHOB**

McDermott, chairman
Dellums
Jefferson
Wheat
Norton

Ballenger
Saxton

Government Operations and Metropolitan Affairs

Phone: 225-4457   **Room: 1310 LHOB**

Wheat, chairman
Stark
Lewis (Ga.)
Jefferson

Saxton
Rohrabacher

Judiciary and Education

Phone: 225-4457   **Room: 1310 LHOB**

Norton, chairman
Lewis (Ga.)
Stark
Dellums
McDermott

Rohrabacher
Ballenger

EDUCATION AND LABOR

Phone: 225-4527   **Room: 2181 RHOB**

Majority Staff Director: Patricia Rissler, 225-4527, 2181 RHOB
Minority Staff Director: James Eagen III, 225-6910, 2174 RHOB

Education and labor generally; child labor; convict labor; labor standards and statistics; mediation and arbitration of labor disputes; regulation of foreign laborers; school food programs; vocational rehabilitation; wages and hours; welfare of miners; work incentive programs; Indian education; juvenile delinquency; human services programs; Howard University; Columbia Institution for the Deaf, Dumb and Blind; Freedmen's Hospital. Chairman and ranking minority member are members ex officio of all subcommittees of which they are not regular members.

Party Ratio: D 28 * - R 15

William D. Ford, Mich., chairman
William L. Clay, Mo.
George Miller, Calif.
Austin J. Murphy, Pa.
Dale E. Kildee, Mich.
Pat Williams, Mont.
Matthew G. Martinez, Calif.
Major R. Owens, N.Y.
Tom Sawyer, Ohio
Donald M. Payne, N.J.
Jolene Unsoeld, Wash.
Patsy T. Mink, Hawaii
Robert E. Andrews, N.J.
Jack Reed, R.I.
Tim Roemer, Ind.
Eliot L. Engel, N.Y.
Xavier Becerra, Calif.
Robert C. Scott, Va.
Gene Green, Texas
Lynn Woolsey, Calif.
Carlos Romero-Barceló, P.R. *
Ron Klink, Pa.
Karan English, Ariz.
Ted Strickland, Ohio
Ron de Lugo, Virgin Islands *
Eni F.H. Faleomavaega, Am. Samoa *
Scotty Baesler, Ky.
Robert Underwood, Guam *

Bill Goodling, Pa., ranking member
Tom Petri, Wis.
Marge Roukema, N.J.
Steve Gunderson, Wis.
Dick Armey, Texas
Harris W. Fawell, Ill.
Cass Ballenger, N.C.
Susan Molinari, N.Y.
Bill Barrett, Neb.
John A. Boehner, Ohio
Randy Cunningham, Calif.
Peter Hoekstra, Mich.
Howard P. "Buck" McKeon, Calif.
Dan Miller, Fla.
Michael N. Castle, Del.

* Delegates and/or resident commissioner are not counted in official ratio.

SUBCOMMITTEES

Elementary, Secondary and Vocational Education

Phone: 225-4368   **Room: B-346A RHOB**

Kildee, chairman
Miller (Calif.)
Sawyer
Owens
Unsoeld
Reed
Roemer
Mink
Engel
Becerra
Green
Woolsey
English (Ariz.)
Strickland
Payne (N.J.)
Romero-Barceló

Goodling
Gunderson
McKeon
Petri
Molinari
Cunningham
Miller (Fla.)
Roukema
Boehner

Human Resources

Phone: 225-1850   **Room: B-346C RHOB**

Martinez, chairman
Kildee
Andrews (N.J.)
Scott
Woolsey
Romero-Barceló
Owens
Baesler

Molinari
Barrett (Neb.)
Miller (Fla.)
Castle

Labor Standards, Occupational Health and Safety

Phone: 225-1927   **Room: B-345A RHOB**

Murphy, chairman
Clay
Andrews (N.J.)
Miller (Calif.)
Strickland
Faleomavaega
<Vacancy>

Fawell
Ballenger
Hoekstra

Labor-Management Relations

Phone: 225-5768   **Room: 320 CHOB**

Williams, chairman
Clay
Kildee
Miller (Calif.)
Owens
Martinez
Payne (N.J.)
Unsoeld
Mink
Klink
Murphy
Engel
Becerra
Green
Woolsey
Romero-Barceló

Roukema
Gunderson
Armey
Barrett (Neb.)
Boehner
Fawell
Ballenger
Hoekstra
McKeon

Postsecondary Education and Training

Phone: 226-3681   **Room: 2451 RHOB**

Ford (Mich.), chairman
Williams
Sawyer
Unsoeld
Mink
Andrews (N.J.)
Reed
Roemer
Kildee
Scott
Klink
English (Ariz.)
Strickland
Becerra
Green

Petri
Gunderson
Cunningham
Miller (Fla.)
Roukema
Hoekstra
McKeon
Armey
Castle

Select Education and Civil Rights

Phone: 226-7532   **Room: 518 OHOB**

Owens, chairman
Payne (N.J.)
Sawyer
Scott
<Vacancy>
<Vacancy>

Ballenger
Barrett (Neb.)
Fawell

ENERGY AND COMMERCE

Phone: 225-2927   **Room: 2125 RHOB**

Majority Staff Director & Chief Counsel: Alan Roth, 225-2927, 2125 RHOB
Minority Chief Counsel & Staff Director: Margaret Durbin, 225-3641, 2322 RHOB

Interstate and foreign commerce generally; national energy policy generally; exploration, production, storage, supply, marketing, pricing and regulation of energy resources; nuclear energy; solar

energy; energy conservation; generation and marketing of power; inland waterways; railroads and railway labor and retirement; communications generally; securities and exchanges; consumer affairs; travel and tourism; public health and quarantine; health-care facilities; biomedical research and development; Department of Energy; Federal Energy Regulatory Commission. Chairman and ranking minority member are members ex officio of all subcommittees of which they are not regular members.

Party Ratio: D 27 - R 17

John D. Dingell, Mich., chairman
Henry A. Waxman, Calif.
Philip R. Sharp, Ind.
Edward J. Markey, Mass.
Al Swift, Wash.
Cardiss Collins, Ill.
Mike Synar, Okla.
W. J. Tauzin, La.
Ron Wyden, Ore.
Ralph M. Hall, Texas
Bill Richardson, N.M.
Jim Slattery, Kan.
John Bryant, Texas
Rick Boucher, Va.
Jim Cooper, Tenn.
J. Roy Rowland, Ga.
Thomas J. Manton, N.Y.
Edolphus Towns, N.Y.
Gerry E. Studds, Mass.
Richard H. Lehman, Calif.
Frank Pallone Jr., N.J.
Craig Washington, Texas
Lynn Schenk, Calif.
Sherrod Brown, Ohio
Mike Kreidler, Wash.
Marjorie Margolies-Mezvinsky, Pa.
Blanche Lambert, Ark.

Carlos J. Moorhead, Calif., ranking member
Thomas J. Bliley Jr., Va.
Jack Fields, Texas
Michael G. Oxley, Ohio
Michael Bilirakis, Fla.
Dan Schaefer, Colo.
Joe L. Barton, Texas
Alex McMillan, N.C.
Dennis Hastert, Ill.
Fred Upton, Mich.
Cliff Stearns, Fla.
Bill Paxon, N.Y.
Paul E. Gillmor, Ohio
Scott L. Klug, Wis.
Gary A. Franks, Conn.
James C. Greenwood, Pa.
Michael D. Crapo, Idaho

SUBCOMMITTEES

Commerce, Consumer Protection and Competitiveness

Phone: 226-3160   **Room: 151 FHOB**

Collins (Ill.), chairman
Towns
Slattery
Rowland
Manton
Lehman
Pallone

Stearns
McMillan
Paxon
Greenwood

Energy and Power

Phone: 226-2500   **Room: 331 FHOB**

Sharp, chairman
Markey
Lehman
Washington
Kreidler
Lambert
Swift
Synar
Tauzin
Hall (Texas)
Boucher
Cooper

Bilirakis
Barton
Hastert
Stearns
Klug
Franks (Conn.)
Crapo

Health and the Environment

Phone: 225-4952   **Room: 2415 RHOB**

Waxman, chairman
Synar
Wyden
Hall (Texas)
Richardson
Bryant
Rowland
Towns
Studds
Slattery
Cooper
Pallone
Washington
Brown (Ohio)
Kreidler

Bliley
Bilirakis
McMillan
Hastert
Upton
Paxon
Klug
Franks (Conn.)
Greenwood

Oversight and Investigations

Phone: 225-4441   **Room: 2323 RHOB**

Dingell, chairman
Brown (Ohio)
Margolies-Mezvinsky
Waxman
Collins (Ill.)
Wyden
Bryant

Schaefer
Moorhead
Upton
Gillmor

Telecommunications and Finance

Phone: 226-2424   **Room: 316 FHOB**

Markey, chairman
Tauzin
Boucher
Manton
Lehman
Schenk
Margolies-Mezvinsky
Synar
Wyden
Hall (Texas)
Richardson
Slattery
Bryant
Cooper

Fields (Texas)
Bliley
Oxley
Schaefer
Barton
McMillan
Hastert
Gillmor

Transportation and Hazardous Materials

Phone: 225-9304   **Room: 324 FHOB**

Swift, chairman
Lambert
Tauzin
Boucher
Rowland
Manton
Studds
Pallone
Schenk
Sharp
Markey
Richardson

Oxley
Fields (Texas)
Schaefer
Upton
Paxon
Gillmor
Crapo

FOREIGN AFFAIRS

Phone: 225-5021   **Room: 2170 RHOB**

Majority Chief of Staff: Michael H. Van Dusen, 225-5021, 2170 RHOB
Minority Chief of Staff: Richard J. Garon Jr., 225-6735, B-360 RHOB

Relations of the United States with foreign nations generally; foreign loans; international conferences and congresses; intervention abroad and declarations of war; diplomatic service; foreign trade; neutrality; protection of Americans abroad; Red Cross; United Nations; international economic policy; export controls including non-proliferation of nuclear technology and hardware; international commodity agreements; trading with the enemy; international financial and monetary organizations; international education.

Party Ratio: D 27 * - R 18

Lee H. Hamilton, Ind., chairman
Sam Gejdenson, Conn.
Tom Lantos, Calif.
Robert G. Torricelli, N.J.
Howard L. Berman, Calif.
Gary L. Ackerman, N.Y.
Harry A. Johnston, Fla.
Eliot L. Engel, N.Y.
Eni F.H. Faleomavaega,
    Am. Samoa *
James L. Oberstar, Minn.
Charles E. Schumer, N.Y.
Matthew G. Martinez, Calif.
Robert A. Borski, Pa.
Donald M. Payne, N.J.
Robert E. Andrews, N.J.
Robert Menendez, N.J.
Sherrod Brown, Ohio
Cynthia A. McKinney, Ga.
Maria Cantwell, Wash.
Alcee L. Hastings, Fla.
Eric D. Fingerhut, Ohio
Peter Deutsch, Fla.
Albert R. Wynn, Md.
Don Edwards, Calif.
Frank McCloskey, Ind.
Tom Sawyer, Ohio
Luis V. Gutierrez, Ill.

Benjamin A. Gilman, N.Y.,
    ranking member
Bill Goodling, Pa.
Jim Leach, Iowa
Toby Roth, Wis.
Olympia J. Snowe, Maine
Henry J. Hyde, Ill.
Doug Bereuter, Neb.
Christopher H. Smith, N.J.
Dan Burton, Ind.
Jan Meyers, Kan.
Elton Gallegly, Calif.
Ileana Ros-Lehtinen, Fla.
Cass Ballenger, N.C.
Dana Rohrabacher, Calif.
David A. Levy, N.Y.
Donald Manzullo, Ill.
Lincoln Diaz-Balart, Fla.
Ed Royce, Calif.

* Delegates and/or resident commissioner are not counted in official ratio.

SUBCOMMITTEES

Africa

Phone: 226-7807   **Room: 709 OHOB**

Johnston, chairman
Payne (N.J.)
Hastings
Torricelli
Edwards (Calif.)
Engel

Burton
Diaz-Balart
Royce
<Vacancy>

Asia and the Pacific

Phone: 226-7801   **Room: 707 OHOB**

Ackerman, chairman
Faleomavaega
Martinez
Torricelli
Brown (Ohio)
Fingerhut
Gutierrez

Leach
Rohrabacher
Royce
Roth

Economic Policy, Trade and the Environment

Phone: 226-7820   **Room: 702 OHOB**

Gejdenson, chairman
Oberstar
McKinney
Cantwell
Fingerhut
Wynn
Johnston
Engel
Schumer

Roth
Manzullo
Bereuter
Meyers
Ballenger
Rohrabacher

Europe and the Middle East

Phone: 225-3345   **Room: B-359 RHOB**

Hamilton, chairman
Engel
Schumer
Borski
Andrews (N.J.)
Brown (Ohio)
Hastings
Deutsch
Lantos

Gilman
Goodling
Meyers
Gallegly
Levy
Leach

International Operations

Phone: 225-3424   **Room: 2103 RHOB**

Berman, chairman
Faleomavaega
Martinez
Andrews (N.J.)
Menendez
Lantos
Johnston
Edwards (Calif.)

Snowe
Hyde
Diaz-Balart
Levy
Manzullo

International Security, International Organizations and Human Rights

Phone: 226-7825   **Room: B-358 RHOB**

Lantos, chairman	*Bereuter*
Berman	*Snowe*
Ackerman	*Smith (N.J.)*
Martinez	*Burton*
McCloskey	
Sawyer	

Western Hemisphere Affairs

Phone: 226-7812   **Room: 705 OHOB**

Torricelli, chairman	*Smith (N.J.)*
Menendez	*Ros-Lehtinen*
Oberstar	*Ballenger*
McKinney	*Gallegly*
Deutsch	
Wynn	

GOVERNMENT OPERATIONS

Phone: 225-5051   **Room: 2157 RHOB**

Majority Staff Director: Julian Epstein, 225-5051, 2157 RHOB
Minority Staff Director: Matthew Fletcher, 225-5074, 2153 RHOB

Budget and accounting measures; overall economy and efficiency in government including federal procurement; executive branch reorganization; general revenue sharing; intergovernmental relations; National Archives; off-budget treatment of federal agencies or programs. Chairman and ranking minority member are members ex officio of all subcommittees of which they are not regular members.

Party Ratio: D 26 - R 16 - I 1

John Conyers Jr., Mich., chairman	*William F. Clinger, Pa., ranking member*
Cardiss Collins, Ill.	*Al McCandless, Calif.*
Glenn English, Okla.	*Dennis Hastert, Ill.*
Henry A. Waxman, Calif.	*Jon Kyl, Ariz.*
Mike Synar, Okla.	*Christopher Shays, Conn.*
Stephen L. Neal, N.C.	*Steven H. Schiff, N.M.*
Tom Lantos, Calif.	*C. Christopher Cox, Calif.*
Major R. Owens, N.Y.	*Craig Thomas, Wyo.*
Edolphus Towns, N.Y.	*Ileana Ros-Lehtinen, Fla.*
John M. Spratt Jr., S.C.	*Dick Zimmer, N.J.*
Gary A. Condit, Calif.	*Bill Zeliff, N.H.*
Collin C. Peterson, Minn.	*John M. McHugh, N.Y.*
Karen L. Thurman, Fla.	*Steve Horn, Calif.*
Bobby L. Rush, Ill.	*Deborah Pryce, Ohio*
Carolyn B. Maloney, N.Y.	*John L. Mica, Fla.*
Thomas M. Barrett, Wis.	*Rob Portman, Ohio*
Donald M. Payne, N.J.	
Floyd H. Flake, N.Y.	
Jimmy Hayes, La.	
Craig Washington, Texas	**Bernard Sanders, Vt.**
Barbara-Rose Collins, Mich.	
Corrine Brown, Fla.	
Marjorie Margolies-Mezvinsky, Pa.	
Lynn Woolsey, Calif.	
Gene Green, Texas	
Bart Stupak, Mich.	

SUBCOMMITTEES

Commerce, Consumer and Monetary Affairs

Phone: 225-4407   **Room: B-377 RHOB**

Spratt, chairman	*Cox*
Rush	*Shays*
Margolies-Mezvinsky	*Horn*
Collins (Mich.)	
Green	

Employment, Housing and Aviation

Phone: 225-6751   **Room: B-349A RHOB**

Peterson (Minn.), chairman	*Zeliff*
Lantos	*Shays*
Rush	*McHugh*
Flake	
Thurman	
Collins (Mich.)	

Environment, Energy and Natural Resources

Phone: 225-6427   **Room: B-371C RHOB**

Synar, chairman	*Hastert*
Thurman	*McHugh*
Maloney	*Pryce*
Hayes	*Mica*
Washington	
Towns	**Sanders**

Human Resources and Intergovernmental Relations

Phone: 225-2548   **Room: B-372 RHOB**

Towns, chairman	*Schiff*
Waxman	*Mica*
Barrett (Wis.)	*Portman*
Payne (N.J.)	
Washington	**Sanders**

Information, Justice, Transportation and Agriculture

Phone: 225-3741   **Room: B-349C RHOB**

Condit, chairman	*Thomas (Wyo.)*
Owens	*Ros-Lehtinen*
Thurman	*Horn*
Woolsey	
Stupak	

Legislation and National Security

Phone: 225-5147   **Room: B-373 RHOB**

Conyers, chairman
Collins (Ill.)
English (Okla.)
Neal (N.C.)
Maloney
Lantos
Brown (Fla.)

McCandless
Clinger
Kyl
Zimmer

HOUSE ADMINISTRATION

Phone: 225-2061   **Room: H-326 Capitol**

Majority Staff Director: Bob Shea, 225-2061, H-326 Capitol
**Minority Staff Director: Mary Sue Englund, 225-8281,
  H-330 Capitol**

House administration generally; contested elections; federal elections generally; corrupt practices; qualifications of members of the House; Congressional Record; the House wing of the Capitol; Library of Congress; Smithsonian Institution; Botanic Garden. Chairman and ranking minority member are non-voting members ex officio of all subcommittees of which they are not regular members.

Party Ratio: D 12 - R 7

Charlie Rose, N.C., chairman
Al Swift, Wash.
William L. Clay, Mo.
Sam Gejdenson, Conn.
Martin Frost, Texas
Thomas J. Manton, N.Y.
Steny H. Hoyer, Md.
Gerald D. Kleczka, Wis.
Dale E. Kildee, Mich.
Butler Derrick, S.C.
Barbara B. Kennelly, Conn.
Benjamin L. Cardin, Md.

*Bill Thomas, Calif.,
  ranking member*
Newt Gingrich, Ga.
Pat Roberts, Kan.
Robert L. Livingston, La.
Bill Barrett, Neb.
John A. Boehner, Ohio
Jennifer Dunn, Wash.

SUBCOMMITTEES

Accounts

Phone: 226-7540   **Room: 611 OHOB**

Frost, chairman
Swift
Gejdenson
Hoyer
Kildee
Kennelly
Cardin

Roberts
Gingrich
Boehner
Dunn

Administrative Oversight

Phone: 225-2061   **Room: H-326 Capitol**

Rose, chairman
Clay

Thomas (Calif.)
Barrett (Neb.)

Elections

Phone: 226-7616   **Room: 802 OHOB**

Swift, chairman
Frost
Hoyer
Kleczka
Cardin

Livingston
Roberts
Dunn

Libraries and Memorials

Phone: 226-2307   **Room: 612 OHOB**

Clay, chairman
Frost
Derrick
Kennelly

Barrett (Neb.)
Roberts

Office Systems

Phone: 225-1608   **Room: 720 OHOB**

Gejdenson, chairman
Frost
Kleczka
Kennelly

Boehner
Barrett (Neb.)

Personnel and Police

Phone: 226-7641   **Room: 722 OHOB**

Manton, chairman
Clay
Kleczka
Derrick

Dunn
Livingston

JUDICIARY

Phone: 225-3951   **Room: 2138 RHOB**

General Counsel: Jon Yarowsky, 225-3951, 2138 RHOB
**Minority Chief Counsel: Alan F. Coffey Jr., 225-6906,
  B-351C RHOB**

Civil and criminal judicial proceedings generally; federal courts and judges; bankruptcy, mutiny, espionage and counterfeiting; civil liberties; constitutional amendments; immigration and naturalization; interstate compacts; claims against the United States; apportionment of representatives; meetings of Congress and attendance of members; penitentiaries; patent office; patents, copyrights and trademarks; presidential succession; monopolies and unlawful restraints of trade; internal security; revision and codification of U.S. statutes; state and territorial boundary lines. Chairman and ranking

member are non-voting members ex officio of all subcommittees of which they are not regular members.

Party Ratio: D 21 - R 14

Jack Brooks, Texas, chairman	Hamilton Fish Jr., N.Y.,
Don Edwards, Calif.	*ranking member*
John Conyers Jr., Mich.	*Carlos J. Moorhead, Calif.*
Romano L. Mazzoli, Ky.	*Henry J. Hyde, Ill.*
William J. Hughes, N.J.	*F. James Sensenbrenner Jr.,*
Mike Synar, Okla.	*Wis.*
Patricia Schroeder, Colo.	*Bill McCollum, Fla.*
Dan Glickman, Kan.	*George W. Gekas, Pa.*
Barney Frank, Mass.	*Howard Coble, N.C.*
Charles E. Schumer, N.Y.	*Lamar Smith, Texas*
Howard L. Berman, Calif.	*Steven H. Schiff, N.M.*
Rick Boucher, Va.	*Jim Ramstad, Minn.*
John Bryant, Texas	*Elton Gallegly, Calif.*
George E. Sangmeister, Ill.	*Charles T. Canady, Fla.*
Craig Washington, Texas	*Bob Inglis, S.C.*
Jack Reed, R.I.	*Robert W. Goodlatte, Va.*
Jerrold Nadler, N.Y.	
Robert C. Scott, Va.	
David Mann, Ohio	
Melvin Watt, N.C.	
Xavier Becerra, Calif.	

SUBCOMMITTEES

Administrative Law and Governmental Relations

Phone: 225-5741   **Room: B-351A RHOB**

Bryant, chairman	*Gekas*
Glickman	*Ramstad*
Frank	*Inglis*
Berman	*Goodlatte*
Mann	
Watt	

Civil and Constitutional Rights

Phone: 226-7680   **Room: 806 OHOB**

Edwards (Calif.), chairman	*Hyde*
Schroeder	*Coble*
Frank	*Canady*
Washington	
Nadler	

Crime and Criminal Justice

Phone: 226-2406   **Room: 362 FHOB**

Schumer, chairman	*Sensenbrenner*
Edwards (Calif.)	*Smith (Texas)*
Conyers	*Schiff*
Mazzoli	*Ramstad*
Glickman	*Gekas*
Sangmeister	
Washington	
Mann	

Economic and Commercial Law

Phone: 225-2825   **Room: B-353 RHOB**

Brooks, chairman	*Fish*
Conyers	*Gallegly*
Synar	*Canady*
Schroeder	*Inglis*
Glickman	*Goodlatte*
Berman	*Moorhead*
Boucher	
Scott	
Mann	
Watt	

Intellectual Property and Judicial Administration

Phone: 225-3926   **Room: 207 CHOB**

Hughes, chairman	*Moorhead*
Edwards (Calif.)	*Coble*
Conyers	*Fish*
Mazzoli	*Sensenbrenner*
Synar	*McCollum*
Frank	*Schiff*
Berman	
Reed	
Becerra	

International Law, Immigration and Refugees

Phone: 225-5727   **Room: B-370B RHOB**

Mazzoli, chairman	*McCollum*
Schumer	*Smith (Texas)*
Bryant	*Gallegly*
Sangmeister	*Canady*
Nadler	
Becerra	

MERCHANT MARINE AND FISHERIES

Phone: 225-4047   Room: 1334 LHOB

Majority Staff Director: Jeffrey Pike, 225-4047, 1334 LHOB
Minority Staff Director: Harry Burroughs, 225-2650, 1337 LHOB

Merchant marine generally; oceanography and marine affairs including coastal zone management; Coast Guard; fisheries and wildlife; regulation of common carriers by water and inspection of merchant marine vessels, lights and signals, lifesaving equipment and fire protection; navigation; Panama Canal, Canal Zone and interoceanic canals generally; registration and licensing of vessels and small boats; rules and international arrangements to prevent collisions at sea; international fishing agreements; Coast Guard and Merchant Marine academies and state maritime academies. Chairman and ranking minority member are members ex officio of

all subcommittees of which they are not regular members.

Party Ratio: D 29 - R 19

Gerry E. Studds, Mass.,
  chairman
William J. Hughes, N.J.
Earl Hutto, Fla.
W.J. Tauzin, La.
William O. Lipinski, Ill.
Solomon P. Ortiz, Texas
Thomas J. Manton, N.Y.
Owen B. Pickett, Va.
George J. Hochbrueckner,
  N.Y.
Frank Pallone Jr., N.J.
Greg Laughlin, Texas
Jolene Unsoeld, Wash.
Gene Taylor, Miss.
Jack Reed, R.I.
H. Martin Lancaster, N.C.
Thomas H. Andrews, Maine
Elizabeth Furse, Ore.
Lynn Schenk, Calif.
Gene Green, Texas
Alcee L. Hastings, Fla.
Dan Hamburg, Calif.
Blanche Lambert, Ark.
Anna G. Eshoo, Calif.
Tom Barlow, Ky.
Bart Stupak, Mich.
Bennie Thompson, Miss.
Maria Cantwell, Wash.
Peter Deutsch, Fla.
Gary L. Ackerman, N.Y.

*Jack Fields, Texas,
  ranking member
Don Young, Alaska
Herbert H. Bateman, Va.
H. James Saxton, N.J.
Howard Coble, N.C.
Curt Weldon, Pa.
James M. Inhofe, Okla.
Arthur Ravenel Jr., S.C.
Wayne T. Gilchrest, Md.
Randy Cunningham, Calif.
Jack Kingston, Ga.
Tillie Fowler, Fla.
Michael N. Castle, Del.
Peter T. King, N.Y.
Lincoln Diaz-Balart, Fla.
Richard W. Pombo, Calif.
Helen Delich Bentley, Md.
Charles H. Taylor, N.C.
Peter G. Torkildsen, Mass.*

SUBCOMMITTEES

Coast Guard and Navigation

Phone: 226-3587   **Room: 541 FHOB**

Tauzin, chairman
Hughes
Hutto
Lancaster
Barlow
Stupak
Lipinski
Pickett
Hochbrueckner
Pallone
Laughlin
Schenk
Hastings
Lambert
Taylor (Miss.)

*Coble
Bateman
Gilchrest
Fowler
Castle
King
Diaz-Balart
Inhofe
Pombo*

Environment and Natural Resources

Phone: 226-3547   **Room: 545 FHOB**

Studds, chairman
Hochbrueckner
Pallone
Laughlin
Unsoeld
Reed
Furse
Hamburg
Lambert
Eshoo
Hutto
Tauzin
Ortiz
Thompson

*Saxton
Young (Alaska)
Weldon
Ravenel
Gilchrest
Cunningham
Castle
Taylor (N.C.)*

Fisheries Management

Phone: 226-3514   **Room: 534 FHOB**

Manton, chairman
Hughes
Unsoeld
Taylor (Miss.)
Lancaster
Hamburg
Cantwell
Hutto

*Young (Alaska)
Coble
Ravenel
Kingston
Torkildsen*

Merchant Marine

Phone: 226-3533   **Room: 543 FHOB**

Lipinski, chairman
Pickett
Taylor (Miss.)
Andrews (Maine)
Schenk
Green
Hastings
Reed
Furse
Stupak
Manton
Ackerman
Thompson

*Bateman
Inhofe
Cunningham
Kingston
Fowler
King
Diaz-Balart
Bentley*

Oceanography, Gulf of Mexico and the Outer Continental Shelf

Phone: 226-2460   **Room: 575 FHOB**

Ortiz, chairman
Green
Eshoo
Laughlin
Schenk

*Weldon
Saxton*

NATURAL RESOURCES

Phone: 225-2761   **Room: 1324 LHOB**

Majority Staff Director: John Lawrence, 225-2761, 1324 LHOB
Minority Staff Director: Dan Kish, 225-6065, 1329 LHOB

Public lands, parks and natural resources generally; Geological Survey; interstate water compacts; irrigation and reclamation; Indian affairs; minerals, mines and mining; petroleum conservation on public lands; regulation of domestic nuclear energy industry, including waste disposal; territorial affairs of the United States. Chairman and ranking minority member are non-voting members ex officio of all subcommittees of which they are not regular members.

Party Ratio: D 28 * - R 15

George Miller, Calif., chairman	*Don Young, Alaska,*
Philip R. Sharp, Ind.	*ranking member*
Edward J. Markey, Mass.	*James V. Hansen, Utah*
Austin J. Murphy, Pa.	*Barbara F. Vucanovich, Nev.*
Nick J. Rahall II, W.Va.	*Elton Gallegly, Calif.*
Bruce F. Vento, Minn.	*Bob Smith, Ore.*
Pat Williams, Mont.	*Craig Thomas, Wyo.*
Ron de Lugo, Virgin Islands *	*John J. "Jimmy" Duncan Jr.,*
Sam Gejdenson, Conn.	*Tenn.*
Richard H. Lehman, Calif.	*Joel Hefley, Colo.*
Bill Richardson, N.M.	*John T. Doolittle, Calif.*
Peter A. DeFazio, Ore.	*Wayne Allard, Colo.*
Eni F.H. Faleomavaega,	*Richard H. Baker, La.*
Am. Samoa *	*Ken Calvert, Calif.*
Tim Johnson, S.D.	*Scott McInnis, Colo.*
Larry LaRocco, Idaho	*Richard W. Pombo, Calif.*
Neil Abercrombie, Hawaii	*Jay Dickey, Ark.*
Cal Dooley, Calif.	
Carlos Romero-Barceló, P.R. *	
Karan English, Ariz.	
Karen Shepherd, Utah	
Nathan Deal, Ga.	
Maurice D. Hinchey, N.Y.	
Robert A. Underwood, Guam *	
Sam Farr, Calif.	
Lane Evans, Ill.	
Patsy T. Mink, Hawaii	
Tom Barlow, Ky.	
Thomas M. Barrett, Wis.	

SUBCOMMITTEES

Bonneville Power Administration

Phone: 225-6042   **Room: 1328 LHOB**

DeFazio, chairman	*Smith (Ore.)*
Sharp	*Vucanovich*
Williams	*Thomas (Wyo.)*
Lehman	*Doolittle*
LaRocco	
Shepherd	

Energy and Mineral Resources

Phone: 225-8331   **Room: 818 OHOB**

Lehman, chairman	*Vucanovich*
Sharp	*Thomas (Wyo.)*
Murphy	*Doolittle*
Markey	*Allard*
Rahall	*McInnis*
LaRocco	*Pombo*
Deal	
DeFazio	
Barlow	
Farr	

Insular and International Affairs

Phone: 225-9297   **Room: H2-107 FHOB**

de Lugo, chairman	*Gallegly*
Faleomavaega	*Vucanovich*
Romero-Barceló	
Underwood	
Murphy	
Miller (Calif.)	
<Vacancy>	

National Parks, Forests and Public Lands

Phone: 226-7736   **Room: 812 OHOB**

Vento, chairman	*Hansen*
Markey	*Smith (Ore.)*
Rahall	*Thomas (Wyo.)*
Williams	*Duncan*
DeFazio	*Hefley*
Johnson (S.D.)	*Doolittle*
LaRocco	*Baker (La.)*
Abercrombie	*Calvert*
Romero-Barceló	*Dickey*
English (Ariz.)	
Shepherd	
Hinchey	
Underwood	
Murphy	
Richardson	
Mink	

Native American Affairs

Phone: 226-7393   **Room: 1522 LHOB**

Richardson, chairman	*Thomas (Wyo.)*
Williams	*Young (Alaska)*
Gejdenson	*Baker (La.)*
Faleomavaega	*Calvert*
Johnson (S.D.)	
Abercrombie	
English (Ariz.)	

Delegates and/or resident commissioner are not counted in official ratio.

Oversight and Investigations

Phone: 225-6042   **Room: 1328 LHOB**

Miller (Calif.), chairman	*Smith (Ore.)*
Gejdenson	*Hansen*
Dooley	*Vucanovich*
Deal	*Duncan*
Sharp	*Doolittle*
Vento	*Allard*
Lehman	*Calvert*
DeFazio	*Pombo*
English (Ariz.)	*Dickey*
Shepherd	
Hinchey	
Abercrombie	
Evans	
Barrett (Wis.)	

POST OFFICE AND CIVIL SERVICE

Phone: 225-4054   **Room: 309 CHOB**

Majority Staff Director: Gail E. Weiss, 225-4054, 309 CHOB
Minority Staff Director: Joseph A. Fisher, 225-8036, 300 CHOB

Postal and federal civil service; census and the collection of statistics generally; Hatch Act; holidays and celebrations; commemorative bills and resolutions.

Party Ratio: **D 15 * - R 8**

William L. Clay, Mo., chairman	*John T. Myers, Ind., ranking member*
Patricia Schroeder, Colo.	*Benjamin A. Gilman, N.Y.*
Frank McCloskey, Ind.	*Don Young, Alaska*
Gary L. Ackerman, N.Y.	*Dan Burton, Ind.*
Tom Sawyer, Ohio	*Constance A. Morella, Md.*
Paul E. Kanjorski, Pa.	*Tom Ridge, Pa.*
Eleanor Holmes Norton, D.C. *	*Tom Petri, Wis.*
Barbara-Rose Collins, Mich.	*Sherwood Boehlert, N.Y.*
Leslie L. Byrne, Va.	
Melvin Watt, N.C.	
Albert R. Wynn, Md.	
Greg Laughlin, Texas	
Sanford D. Bishop Jr., Ga.	
Sherrod Brown, Ohio	
Alcee L. Hastings, Fla.	

SUBCOMMITTEES

Census, Statistics and Postal Personnel

Phone: 226-7523   **Room: 515 OHOB**

Sawyer, chairman	*Petri*
McCloskey	*Ridge*
Wynn	

Civil Service

Phone: 225-4025   **Room: 122 CHOB**

McCloskey, chairman	*Burton*
Schroeder	*Morella*
Kanjorski	

Compensation and Employee Benefits

Phone: 226-7546   **Room: 209 CHOB**

Norton, chairman	*Morella*
Ackerman	*Young (Alaska)*
Byrne	

Oversight and Investigations

Phone: 225-6295   **Room: 219 CHOB**

Clay, chairman	*Boehlert*
Hastings	*<Vacancy>*
Laughlin	

Postal Operations and Services

Phone: 225-9124   **Room: 406 CHOB**

Collins (Mich.), chairman	*Young (Alaska)*
Watt	*Gilman*
Bishop	

* Delegates and/or resident commissioner are not counted in official ratio.

PUBLIC WORKS AND TRANSPORTATION

Phone: 225-4472   **Room: 2165 RHOB**

Chief of Staff: Paul Schoellhamer, 225-4472, 2165 RHOB
Minority Chief Counsel & Staff Director: Jack Schenendorf,
225-9446, 2163 RHOB

Flood control and improvement of rivers and harbors; construction and maintenance of roads; oil and other pollution of navigable waters; public buildings and grounds; public works for the benefit of navigation including bridges and dams; water power; transportation, except railroads; Botanic Garden; Library of Congress; Smithsonian Institution. Chairman and ranking minority member are members ex officio of all subcommittees of which they are not regular members.

Party Ratio: D 40 * - R 24

Norman Y. Mineta, Calif.,
  chairman
James L. Oberstar, Minn.
Nick J. Rahall II, W.Va.
Douglas Applegate, Ohio
Ron de Lugo, Virgin Islands *
Robert A. Borski, Pa.
Tim Valentine, N.C.
William O. Lipinski, Ill.
Bob Wise, W.Va.
James A. Traficant Jr., Ohio
Peter A. DeFazio, Ore.
Jimmy Hayes, La.
Bob Clement, Tenn.
Jerry F. Costello, Ill.
Mike Parker, Miss.
Greg Laughlin, Texas
Pete Geren, Texas
George E. Sangmeister, Ill.
Glenn Poshard, Ill.
Dick Swett, N.H.
Robert E. "Bud" Cramer, Ala.
Barbara-Rose Collins, Mich.
Eleanor Holmes Norton, D.C.*
Lucien E. Blackwell, Pa.
Jerrold Nadler, N.Y.
Sam Coppersmith, Ariz.
Leslie L. Byrne, Va.
Maria Cantwell, Wash.
Pat Danner, Mo.
Karen Shepherd, Utah
Robert Menendez, N.J.
James E. Clyburn, S.C.
Corrine Brown, Fla.
Nathan Deal, Ga.
James A. Barcia, Mich.
Dan Hamburg, Calif.
Bob Filner, Calif.
Walter R. Tucker III, Calif.
Eddie Bernice Johnson, Texas
Peter W. Barca, Wis.

Bud Shuster, Pa.,
  ranking member
William F. Clinger, Pa.
Tom Petri, Wis.
Sherwood Boehlert, N.Y.
James M. Inhofe, Okla.
Bill Emerson, Mo.
John J. "Jimmy" Duncan Jr.,
  Tenn.
Susan Molinari, N.Y.
Bill Zeliff, N.H.
Thomas W. Ewing, Ill.
Wayne T. Gilchrest, Md.
Jennifer Dunn, Wash.
Tim Hutchinson, Ark.
Bill Baker, Calif.
Mac Collins, Ga.
Jay C. Kim, Calif.
David A. Levy, N.Y.
Steve Horn, Calif.
Bob Franks, N.J.
Peter I. Blute, Mass.
Howard P. "Buck" McKeon,
  Calif.
John L. Mica, Fla.
Peter Hoekstra, Mich.
Jack Quinn, N.Y.

SUBCOMMITTEES

Aviation

Phone: 225-9161   **Room: 2251 RHOB**

Oberstar, chairman
de Lugo, vice chairman
Lipinski
Geren
Sangmeister
Collins (Mich.)
Coppersmith
Borski
Valentine
DeFazio
Hayes
Clement
Costello
Parker
Laughlin
Swett
Cramer
Blackwell
Cantwell
Danner
Shepherd
Brown (Fla.)

Clinger
Boehlert
Inhofe
Duncan
Ewing
Gilchrest
Dunn
Collins (Ga.)
Kim
Levy
Horn
McKeon
Mica

Economic Development

Phone: 225-6151   **Room: B-376 RHOB**

Wise, chairman
Blackwell, vice chairman
Coppersmith
Clyburn
Deal
Barcia
Filner
Oberstar
Traficant
Clement
Costello
Parker
Swett
Nadler
Danner
Shepherd
Menendez
Brown (Fla.)
Hamburg
Norton
Johnson
Barca

Molinari
Boehlert
Ewing
Dunn
Hutchinson
Baker (Calif.)
Collins (Ga.)
Kim
Franks (N.J.)
Blute
Mica
Hoekstra
Quinn

* Delegates and/or resident commissioner are not counted in official ratio.

Investigations and Oversight

Phone: 225-3274   **Room: 586 FHOB**

Borski, chairman   *Inhofe*
Collins (Mich.), vice chairman   *Duncan*
Wise   *Molinari*
Blackwell   *Zeliff*
Byrne   *Gilchrest*
Barcia   *Baker (Calif.)*
Filner
Barca
Poshard

Public Buildings and Grounds

Phone: 225-9961   **Room: B-376 RHOB**

Traficant, chairman   *Duncan*
Norton, vice chairman   *Petri*
Johnson   *Emerson*
Applegate
Clyburn
Tucker

Surface Transportation

Phone: 225-9989   **Room: B-376 RHOB**

Rahall, chairman   *Petri*
Valentine, vice chairman   *Clinger*
Clement   *Emerson*
Costello   *Zeliff*
Laughlin   *Dunn*
Poshard   *Hutchinson*
Swett   *Baker (Calif.)*
Cramer   *Collins (Ga.)*
DeFazio   *Kim*
Nadler   *Levy*
Byrne   *Franks (N.J.)*
Cantwell   *Blute*
Danner   *McKeon*
Menendez
Clyburn
Tucker
Hamburg
Johnson
Applegate
de Lugo
Lipinski
Traficant
Barca

Water Resources and the Environment

Phone: 225-0060   **Room: B-370A RHOB**

Applegate, chairman   *Boehlert*
Hayes, vice chairman   *Clinger*
Parker   *Petri*
Shepherd   *Inhofe*
Brown (Fla.)   *Emerson*
Deal   *Molinari*
Barcia   *Zeliff*

Filner   *Boehlert*
Oberstar   *Clinger*
Rahall   *Petri*
Wise   *Inhofe*
Geren   *Emerson*
Sangmeister   *Molinari*
Poshard   *Zeliff*
Norton   *Ewing*
Nadler   *Gilchrest*
Byrne   *Hutchinson*
Menendez   *Horn*
Hamburg   *Hoekstra*
Tucker   *Quinn*
Borski
Valentine
Lipinski

RULES

Phone: 225-9486   **Room: H-312 Capitol**

Majority Staff Director: George C. Crawford, 225-9486, H-312 Capitol
Minority Chief of Staff: Don Wolfensberger, 225-9191, H-305 Capitol

Rules and joint rules, order of business of the House; recesses and final adjournments of Congress; authorized to sit and act whether or not the House is in session.

Party Ratio: D 9 - R 4

Joe Moakley, Mass., chairman   *Gerald B. H. Solomon, N.Y.,*
Butler Derrick, S.C.   *ranking member*
Anthony C. Beilenson, Calif.   *James H. Quillen, Tenn.*
Martin Frost, Texas   *David Dreier, Calif.*
David E. Bonior, Mich.   *Porter J. Goss, Fla.*
Tony P. Hall, Ohio
Alan Wheat, Mo.
Bart Gordon, Tenn.
Louise M. Slaughter, N.Y.

SUBCOMMITTEES

Legislative Process

Phone: 225-2430   **Room: 1629 LHOB**

Derrick, chairman   *Quillen*
Frost   *Goss*
Wheat
Gordon
Moakley

Rules of the House

Phone: 225-9588   **Room: 1628 LHOB**

Beilenson, chairman   *Dreier*
Bonior   *Solomon*
Hall (Ohio)
Slaughter
Moakley

SCIENCE, SPACE AND TECHNOLOGY

Phone: 225-6371   **Room: 2320 RHOB**

Chief of Staff: Dr. Radford Byerly Jr., 225-6375, 2320 RHOB
Minority Staff Director: Dave Clement, 225-8772, 2320 RHOB

Astronautical research and development, including resources, personnel, equipment and facilities; National Institute of Standards and Technology, standardization of weights and measures and the metric system; National Aeronautics and Space Administration; National Aeronautics and Space Council; National Science Foundation; outer space, including exploration and control; science scholarships; scientific research, development and demonstration; federally owned or operated non-military energy laboratories; civil aviation research and development; environmental research and development; energy research, development and demonstration; National Weather Service. Chairman and ranking minority member are members ex officio of all subcommittees of which they are not regular members.

Party Ratio: D 33 - R 22

George E. Brown Jr., Calif., chairman
Marilyn Lloyd, Tenn.
Dan Glickman, Kan.
Harold L. Volkmer, Mo.
Ralph M. Hall, Texas
Dave McCurdy, Okla.
Tim Valentine, N.C.
Robert G. Torricelli, N.J.
Rick Boucher, Va.
James A. Traficant Jr., Ohio
Jimmy Hayes, La.
John Tanner, Tenn.
Pete Geren, Texas
Jim Bacchus, Fla.
Tim Roemer, Ind.
Robert E. "Bud" Cramer, Ala.
Dick Swett, N.H.
James A. Barcia, Mich.
Herb Klein, N.J.
Eric D. Fingerhut, Ohio
Paul McHale, Pa.
Jane Harman, Calif.
Don Johnson, Ga.
Sam Coppersmith, Ariz.
Anna G. Eshoo, Calif.
Jay Inslee, Wash.
Eddie Bernice Johnson, Texas
David Minge, Minn.
Nathan Deal, Ga.
Robert C. Scott, Va.
Xavier Becerra, Calif.
Peter W. Barca, Wis.
<Vacancy>

Robert S. Walker, Pa., ranking member
F. James Sensenbrenner Jr., Wis.
Sherwood Boehlert, N.Y.
Tom Lewis, Fla.
Harris W. Fawell, Ill.
Constance A. Morella, Md.
Dana Rohrabacher, Calif.
Steven H. Schiff, N.M.
Joe L. Barton, Texas
Dick Zimmer, N.J.
Sam Johnson, Texas
Ken Calvert, Calif.
Martin R. Hoke, Ohio
Nick Smith, Mich.
Ed Royce, Calif.
Rod Grams, Minn.
John Linder, Ga.
Peter I. Blute, Mass.
Jennifer Dunn, Wash.
Bill Baker, Calif.
Roscoe G. Bartlett, Md.
<Vacancy>

SUBCOMMITTEES

Energy

Phone: 225-8056   **Room: H2-390 FHOB**

Lloyd, chairman
Scott
Cramer
Swett
Klein
McHale
Coppersmith
Inslee
Roemer
McCurdy

Fawell
Schiff
Baker (Calif.)
Grams
Bartlett

Investigations and Oversight

Phone: 225-4494   **Room: 822 OHOB**

Hayes, chairman
Tanner
Lloyd
Johnson (Ga.)
Coppersmith
<Vacancy>

Morella
Barton
<Vacancy>

Science

Phone: 225-8844   **Room: 2319 RHOB**

Boucher, chairman
Hall (Texas)
Valentine
Barcia
Johnson (Ga.)
Eshoo
Johnson (Texas)
Minge
Barca

Boehlert
Barton
Johnson (Texas)
Smith (Mich.)
Blute

Space

Phone: 225-7858   **Room: 2320 RHOB**

Hall (Texas), chairman
Volkmer
Torricelli
Traficant
Bacchus
Cramer
Barcia
Fingerhut
Hayes
Tanner
Geren
Roemer
Harman
Eshoo
McCurdy
<Vacancy>

Sensenbrenner
Rohrabacher
Zimmer
Johnson (Texas)
Hoke
Royce
Dunn
Schiff
Calvert

Technology, Environment and Aviation

Phone: 225-9662   **Room: B-374 RHOB**

Valentine, chairman
Glickman
Geren
Roemer
Swett
Klein
McHale
Harman
Johnson (Ga.)
Coppersmith
Eshoo
Inslee
Johnson (Texas)
Minge
Deal
Becerra
Torricelli
Bacchus
Barca

Lewis (Fla.)
Morella
Calvert
Smith (Mich.)
Grams
Linder
Blute
Bartlett
Rohrabacher
Zimmer
Hoke
Royce

SELECT INTELLIGENCE

Phone: 225-4121   **Room: H-405 Capitol**

Chief Counsel: Michael W. Sheehy, 225-4121, H-405 Capitol
Minority Counsel: Stephen D. Nelson, 225-8246, H-405 Capitol

Legislative and budgetary authority over the Central Intelligence Agency and the director of central intelligence, the Defense Intelligence Agency, the National Security Agency, intelligence activities of the Federal Bureau of Investigation and other components of the federal intelligence community. House majority leader and minority leader are non-voting members ex officio of the full committee.

Party Ratio: **D 12 - R 7**

Dan Glickman, Kan., chairman
Bill Richardson, N.M.
Norm Dicks, Wash.
Julian C. Dixon, Calif.
Robert G. Torricelli, N.J.
Ronald D. Coleman, Texas
David E. Skaggs, Colo.
James Bilbray, Nev.
Nancy Pelosi, Calif.
Greg Laughlin, Texas
Robert E. "Bud" Cramer, Ala.
Jack Reed, R.I.

Larry Combest, Texas,
  ranking member
Doug Bereuter, Neb.
Robert K. Dornan, Calif.
C.W. Bill Young, Fla.
George W. Gekas, Pa.
James V. Hansen, Utah
Jerry Lewis, Calif.

SUBCOMMITTEES

Legislation

Phone: 225-7311   **Room: H-405 Capitol**

Coleman, chairman
Dicks
Bilbray
Pelosi
Laughlin
Cramer

Gekas
Hansen
Lewis (Calif.)

Oversight and Evaluation

Phone: 225-5658   **Room: H-405 Capitol**

Dicks, chairman
Pelosi
Reed
Torricelli
Coleman
Skaggs

Young (Fla.)
Hansen
Bereuter

Program and Budget Authorization

Phone: 225-7690   **Room: H-405 Capitol**

Glickman, chairman
Richardson
Dixon
Torricelli
Skaggs
Bilbray
Laughlin
Cramer

Combest
Bereuter
Dornan
Lewis (Calif.)

SMALL BUSINESS

Phone: 225-5821   **Room: 2361 RHOB**

Majority Staff Director: Jeanne Roslanowick, 225-5821, 2361 RHOB
Minority Staff Director: Steve Lynch, 225-4038, B-343C RHOB

Assistance to and protection of small business including financial aid; participation of small business enterprises in federal procurement and government contracts. Chairman and ranking minority member are members ex officio of all subcommittees of which they are not regular members.

Party Ratio: **D 27 - R 18**

John J. LaFalce, N.Y., chairman
Neal Smith, Iowa
Ike Skelton, Mo.
Romano L. Mazzoli, Ky.
Ron Wyden, Ore.
Norman Sisisky, Va.
John Conyers Jr., Mich.
James Bilbray, Nev.
Kweisi Mfume, Md.
Floyd H. Flake, N.Y.
Bill Sarpalius, Texas
Glenn Poshard, Ill.
Eva Clayton, N.C.
Martin T. Meehan, Mass.
Pat Danner, Mo.
Ted Strickland, Ohio
Nydia M. Velázquez, N.Y.
Cleo Fields, La.
Marjorie Margolies-Mezvinsky, Pa.
Walter R. Tucker III, Calif.
Ron Klink, Pa.
Lucille Roybal-Allard, Calif.
Earl F. Hilliard, Ala.
H. Martin Lancaster, N.C.
Thomas H. Andrews, Maine
Maxine Waters, Calif.
Bennie Thompson, Miss.

Jan Meyers, Kan.,
  ranking member
Larry Combest, Texas
Richard H. Baker, La.
Joel Hefley, Colo.
Ronald K. Machtley, R.I.
Jim Ramstad, Minn.
Sam Johnson, Texas
Bill Zeliff, N.H.
Mac Collins, Ga.
Scott McInnis, Colo.
Michael Huffington, Calif.
James M. Talent, Mo.
Joe Knollenberg, Mich.
Jay Dickey, Ark.
Jay C. Kim, Calif.
Donald Manzullo, Ill.
Peter G. Torkildsen, Mass.
Rob Portman, Ohio

SUBCOMMITTEES

Minority Enterprise, Finance and Urban Development

Phone: 225-7673   **Room: H2-568A FHOB**

Mfume, chairman	*Machtley*
Conyers	*Talent*
Flake	*Knollenberg*
Velázquez	*Dickey*
Tucker	*Portman*
Fields (La.)	
Roybal-Allard	
Hilliard	

Procurement, Taxation and Tourism

Phone: 225-9368   **Room: B-363 RHOB**

Bilbray, chairman	*Baker (La.)*
Sisisky	*Knollenberg*
Hilliard	*Portman*
Mfume	*<Vacancy>*
Clayton	
Klink	

Regulation, Business Opportunities and Technology

Phone: 225-7797   **Room: B-363 RHOB**

Wyden, chairman	*Combest*
Skelton	*Johnson (Texas)*
Strickland	*Dickey*
Andrews (Maine)	*Kim*
Sisisky	*Torkildsen*
Bilbray	*Huffington*
Meehan	
Tucker	

Rural Enterprises, Exports and the Environment

Phone: 225-8944   **Room: 1F CHOB**

Sarpalius, chairman	*Hefley*
Clayton	*Ramstad*
Danner	*Manzullo*
Poshard	*Collins (Ga.)*
Strickland	
Hilliard	
Thompson	

SBA Legislation and the General Economy

Phone: 225-5821   **Room: 2361 RHOB**

LaFalce, chairman	*Meyers*
Smith (Iowa)	*Zeliff*
Mazzoli	*Collins (Ga.)*
Poshard	*Huffington*
Meehan	*Talent*
Fields (La.)	*Ramstad*
Margolies-Mezvinsky	
Klink	
Roybal-Allard	

STANDARDS OF OFFICIAL CONDUCT

Phone: 225-7103   **Room: HT-2 Capitol**

Chief Counsel: Bernard Raimo Jr., 225-7103, HT-2M Capitol

Measures relating to the Code of Official Conduct; conduct of House members and employees; and functions designated in the Ethics in Government Act and the U.S. Code.

Party Ratio: D 7 - R 7

Jim McDermott, Wash., chairman	*Fred Grandy, Iowa, ranking member*
George "Buddy" Darden, Ga.	*Nancy L. Johnson, Conn.*
Benjamin L. Cardin, Md.	*Jim Bunning, Ky.*
Nancy Pelosi, Calif.	*Jon Kyl, Ariz.*
Kweisi Mfume, Md.	*Porter J. Goss, Fla.*
Robert A. Borski, Pa.	*David L. Hobson, Ohio*
Tom Sawyer, Ohio	*Steven H. Schiff, N.M.*

VETERANS' AFFAIRS

Phone: 225-3527   **Room: 335 CHOB**

Majority Counsel & Staff Director: Mack G. Fleming, 225-3527, 335 CHOB
Minority Counsel & Staff Director: Carl Commenator, 225-9756, 333 CHOB

Veterans measures generally; compensation, vocational rehabilitation and education of veterans; armed forces life insurance; pensions; readjustment benefits; veterans hospitals, medical care and treatment. Chairman and ranking minority member are members ex officio of all subcommittees of which they are not regular members.

Party Ratio: D 21 - R 14

G.V. "Sonny" Montgomery, Miss., chairman	*Bob Stump, Ariz., ranking member*
Don Edwards, Calif.	*Christopher H. Smith, N.J.*
Douglas Applegate, Ohio	*Dan Burton, Ind.*
Lane Evans, Ill.	*Michael Bilirakis, Fla.*
Timothy J. Penny, Minn.	*Tom Ridge, Pa.*
J. Roy Rowland, Ga.	*Floyd D. Spence, S.C.*
Jim Slattery, Kan.	*Tim Hutchinson, Ark.*
Joseph P. Kennedy II, Mass.	*Terry Everett, Ala.*
George E. Sangmeister, Ill.	*Steve Buyer, Ind.*
Jill L. Long, Ind.	*Jack Quinn, N.Y.*
Chet Edwards, Texas	*Spencer Bachus, Ala.*
Maxine Waters, Calif.	*John Linder, Ga.*
Bob Clement, Tenn.	*Cliff Stearns, Fla.*
Bob Filner, Calif.	*Peter T. King, N.Y.*
Frank Tejeda, Texas	
Luis V. Gutierrez, Ill.	
Scotty Baesler, Ky.	
Sanford D. Bishop Jr., Ga.	
James E. Clyburn, S.C.	
Mike Kreidler, Wash.	
Corrine Brown, Fla.	

SUBCOMMITTEES

Compensation, Pension and Insurance

Phone: 225-3569   **Room:** 335 CHOB

Slattery, chairman	*Bilirakis*
Applegate	*Everett*
Evans	*Stearns*
Sangmeister	*King*
Edwards (Texas)	
Tejeda	

Education, Training and Employment

Phone: 225-9166   **Room:** 337-A CHOB

Montgomery, chairman	*Hutchinson*
Penny	*Stump*
Clyburn	*Ridge*
Rowland	*Quinn*
Slattery	
Clement	

Hospitals and Health Care

Phone: 225-9154   **Room:** 338 CHOB

Rowland, chairman	*Smith (N.J.)*
Applegate	*Stump*
Kennedy	*Burton*
Long	*Bilirakis*
Edwards (Texas)	*Hutchinson*
Clement	*Everett*
Filner	*Buyer*
Tejeda	*Linder*
Gutierrez	
Baesler	
Bishop	
Kreidler	
Brown (Fla.)	

Housing and Memorial Affairs

Phone: 225-9164   **Room:** 337 CHOB

Sangmeister, chairman	*Burton*
Bishop	*Spence*
Brown (Fla.)	*Buyer*
Kreidler	

Oversight and Investigations

Phone: 225-9044   **Room:** 335 CHOB

Evans, chairman	*Ridge*
Waters	*Bachus*
Filner	*Everett*
Gutierrez	*Quinn*
Clyburn	
Kreidler	
Long	

WAYS AND MEANS

Phone: 225-3625   **Room:** 1102 LHOB

Majority Chief Counsel: Janice A. Mays, 225-3625, 1102 LHOB
Minority Chief of Staff: Phillip D. Moseley, 225-4021, 1106 LHOB

Revenue measures generally; reciprocal trade agreements; customs, collection districts and ports of entry and delivery; bonded debt of the United States; deposit of public moneys; transportation of dutiable goods; tax exempt foundations and charitable trusts; Social Security. Chairman and ranking minority member are members ex officio of all subcommittees of which they are not regular members.

Party Ratio: **D 24 - R 14**

Dan Rostenkowski, Ill., chairman	*Bill Archer, Texas, ranking member*
Sam M. Gibbons, Fla.	*Philip M. Crane, Ill.*
J. J. Pickle, Texas	*Bill Thomas, Calif.*
Charles B. Rangel, N.Y.	*E. Clay Shaw Jr., Fla.*
Pete Stark, Calif.	*Don Sundquist, Tenn.*
Andrew Jacobs Jr., Ind.	*Nancy L. Johnson, Conn.*
Harold E. Ford, Tenn.	*Jim Bunning, Ky.*
Robert T. Matsui, Calif.	*Fred Grandy, Iowa*
Barbara B. Kennelly, Conn.	*Amo Houghton, N.Y.*
William J. Coyne, Pa.	*Wally Herger, Calif.*
Michael A. Andrews, Texas	*Jim McCrery, La.*
Sander M. Levin, Mich.	*Mel Hancock, Mo.*
Benjamin L. Cardin, Md.	*Rick Santorum, Pa.*
Jim McDermott, Wash.	*Dave Camp, Mich.*
Gerald D. Kleczka, Wis.	
John Lewis, Ga.	
Lewis F. Payne Jr., Va.	
Richard E. Neal, Mass.	
Peter Hoagland, Neb.	
Michael R. McNulty, N.Y.	
Mike Kopetski, Ore.	
William J. Jefferson, La.	
Bill Brewster, Okla.	
Mel Reynolds, Ill.	

SUBCOMMITTEES

Health

Phone: 225-7785   **Room:** 1114 LHOB

Stark, chairman	*Thomas (Calif.)*
Levin	*Johnson (Conn.)*
Cardin	*Grandy*
Andrews (Texas)	*McCrery*
McDermott	
Kleczka	
Lewis (Ga.)	

Human Resources

Phone: 225-1025   **Room: B-317 RHOB**

Ford (Tenn.), chairman   *Santorum*
Matsui   *Shaw*
McDermott   *Grandy*
Levin   *Camp*
Kopetski
Reynolds
Cardin

Oversight

Phone: 225-5522   **Room: 1135 LHOB**

Pickle, chairman   *Houghton*
Ford (Tenn.)   *Herger*
Rangel   *Hancock*
Jefferson   *Santorum*
Brewster
Kleczka
Lewis (Ga.)

Select Revenue Measures

Phone: 225-9710   **Room: 1105 LHOB**

Rangel, chairman   *Hancock*
Payne (Va.)   *Sundquist*
Neal (Mass.)   *McCrery*
Hoagland   *Camp*
McNulty
Kopetski
Jacobs

Social Security

Phone: 225-9263   **Room: B-316 RHOB**

Jacobs, chairman   *Bunning*
Pickle   *Crane*
Jefferson   *Houghton*
Brewster
Reynolds

Trade

Phone: 225-3943   **Room: 1136 LHOB**

Gibbons, chairman   *Crane*
Rostenkowski   *Thomas (Calif.)*
Matsui   *Shaw*
Kennelly   *Sundquist*
Coyne   *Johnson (Conn.)*
Payne (Va.)
Neal (Mass.)
Hoagland
McNulty

Joint Committees, 103rd Congress, 1st Session

(As of Dec. 31, 1993)

JOINT ECONOMIC

Executive Director: Steve Quick, 224-5171, SD-G01
Republican Staff Director: Larry Hunter, 224-0374, SH-805

PHONE: 224-5171   ROOM: SD-G01

Studies and investigates recommendations in the annual Economic Report of the President. Reports findings and recommendations to the House and Senate.

Senate:
Paul S. Sarbanes, Md.,
    vice chairman
Edward M. Kennedy, Mass.
Jeff Bingaman, N.M.
Charles S. Robb, Va.
Byron L. Dorgan, N.D.
Barbara Boxer, Calif.

Senate:
William V. Roth Jr., Del.,
    ranking member
Connie Mack, Fla.
Larry E. Craig, Idaho
Robert F. Bennett, Utah

House:
David R. Obey, D-Wis.,
    chairman
Lee H. Hamilton, Ind.
Pete Stark, Calif.
Kweisi Mfume, Md.
Ron Wyden, Ore.
Michael A. Andrews, Texas

House:
Dick Armey, Texas
H. James Saxton, N.J.
C. Christopher Cox, Calif.
Jim Ramstad, Minn.

JOINT LIBRARY

Staff Director: Hilary Lieber, 226-7633, 103 OHOB
Deputy Staff Director: William Cochrane, 224-6352, SR-305

PHONE: 226-7633   ROOM: 103 OHOB

Management and expansion of the Library of Congress; receipt of gifts for the benefit of the library; development and maintenance of the Botanic Garden; placement of statues and other works of art in the Capitol.

Senate:
Claiborne Pell, R.I.,
vice chairman
Dennis DeConcini, Ariz.
Daniel Patrick Moynihan, N.Y.

House:
Charlie Rose, N.C., chairman
Martin Frost, Texas
Thomas J. Manton, N.Y.

Senate:
Mark O. Hatfield, Ore.
Ted Stevens, Alaska

House:
Bill Barrett, Neb.
Pat Roberts, Kan.

JOINT ORGANIZATION OF CONGRESS

Staff Director: G. Kim Wincup, 226-0650, 175D FHOB

PHONE: 226-0650   **ROOM: 175D FHOB**

Congressional mandate: The Committee shall 1) make a full and complete study of the organization and operation of the Congress of the United States; and, 2) recommend improvements in such organization and operation with a view toward strengthening the effectiveness of the Congress, simplifying its operations, improving its relationships with and oversight of other branches of the United States government and improving the orderly consideration of legislation. The study shall include an examination of: 1) the organization and operation of each house of the Congress, and the structure of, and the relationships between, the various standing, special, and select committees of the Congress; 2) the relationship between the two Houses of Congress; 3) the relationship between the Congress and the executive branch of the government; 4) the resources and working tools available to the legislative branch as compared to those available to the executive branch; and 5) the responsibilities of the leadership, their ability to fulfill those responsibilities, and how that relates to the ability of the Senate and the House of Representatives to perform their legislative functions. The committee shall report to the Senate and the House of Representatives the result of its study, together with its recommendations, not later than Dec. 31, 1993. All reports and findings of the Committee shall, when received, be referred to the appropriate committees of the Senate and the appropriate committees of the House of Representatives.

Senate:
David L. Boren, Okla.,
co-chairman
Jim Sasser, Tenn.
Wendell H. Ford, Ky.
Harry Reid, Nev.
Paul S. Sarbanes, Md.
David Pryor, Ark.
George J. Mitchell, Maine,
ex officio

House:
Lee H. Hamilton, Ind.,
co-chairman
David R. Obey, Wis.
Al Swift, Wash.
Sam Gejdenson, Conn.
John M. Spratt Jr., S.C.
Eleanor Holmes Norton, D.C.
Richard A. Gephardt, Mo.,
exofficio

Senate:
Pete V. Domenici, N.M.,
co-vice chairman
Nancy Landon Kassebaum,
Kan.
Trent Lott, Miss.
Ted Stevens, Alaska
William S. Cohen, Maine
Richard G. Lugar, Ind.
Bob Dole, Kan., ex officio

House:
David Dreier, Calif.,
co-vice chairman
Robert S. Walker, Pa.
Gerald B.H. Solomon, N.Y.
Bill Emerson, Mo.
Wayne Allard, Colo.
Jennifer Dunn, Wash.
Robert H. Michel, Ill., ex officio

JOINT PRINTING

Staff Director: John Chambers, 224-5241, SH-818

PHONE: 224-5241   **ROOM: SH-818**

Probes inefficiency and waste in the printing, binding and distribution of federal government publications. Oversees arrangement and style of the Congressional Record.

Senate:
Wendell H. Ford, Ky., chairman
Dennis DeConcini, Ariz.
Harlan Mathews, Tenn.

House:
Charlie Rose, N.C., vice
chairman
Sam Gejdenson, Conn.
Gerald D. Kleczka, Wis.

Senate:
Ted Stevens, Alaska
Mark O. Hatfield, Ore.

House:
Pat Roberts, Kan., ranking
member
Newt Gingrich, Ga.

JOINT TAXATION

Chief of Staff: Harry Gutman, 225-3621, 1015 LHOB

PHONE: 225-3621   **ROOM: 1015 LHOB**

Operation, effects and administration of the federal system of Internal Revenue taxes; measures and methods for simplification of taxes.

Senate:
Daniel Patrick Moynihan, N.Y.,
vice chairman *
Max Baucus, Mont.
David L. Boren, Okla.

House:
Dan Rostenkowski, Ill.,
chairman *
Sam M. Gibbons, Fla.
J.J. Pickle, Texas

Senate:
Bob Packwood, Ore.
Bob Dole, Kan.

House:
Bill Archer, Texas
Philip M. Crane, Ill.

* Chairmanship was for the first session of 103rd Congress only. For the second session, beginning January 1994, chairmanship was to switch to Senate side.

Senators' Committee Assignments

Akaka: Energy & Natural Resources; Governmental Affairs; Indian Affairs; Veterans' Affairs

Baucus: Agriculture, Nutrition & Forestry; Environment & Public Works (chairman); Finance; Joint Taxation; Select Intelligence

Bennett: Banking, Housing & Urban Affairs; Energy & Natural Resources; Joint Economic; Small Business

Biden: Foreign Relations; Judiciary (chairman)

Bingaman: Armed Services; Energy & Natural Resources; Joint Economic; Labor & Human Resources

Bond: Appropriations; Banking, Housing & Urban Affairs; Budget; Small Business

Boren: Agriculture, Nutrition & Forestry; Finance; Joint Organization of Congress (co-chairman); Joint Taxation

Boxer: Banking, Housing & Urban Affairs; Budget; Environment & Public Works; Joint Economic

Bradley: Energy & Natural Resources; Finance; Special Aging

Breaux: Commerce, Science & Transportation; Finance; Special Aging

Brown: Budget; Foreign Relations; Judiciary

Bryan: Armed Services; Banking, Housing & Urban Affairs; Commerce, Science & Transportation; Select Ethics (chairman); Select Intelligence

Bumpers: Appropriations; Energy & Natural Resources; Small Business (chairman)

Burns: Appropriations; Commerce, Science & Transportation; Small Business; Special Aging

Byrd: Appropriations (chairman); Armed Services; Rules & Administration

Campbell: Banking, Housing & Urban Affairs; Energy & Natural Resources; Indian Affairs; Veterans' Affairs

Chafee: Environment & Public Works (ranking member); Finance; Select Intelligence; Small Business

Coats: Armed Services; Labor & Human Resources

Cochran: Agriculture, Nutrition & Forestry; Appropriations; Governmental Affairs; Indian Affairs; Rules & Administration

Cohen: Armed Services; Governmental Affairs; Joint Organization of Congress; Judiciary; Special Aging (ranking member)

Conrad: Agriculture, Nutrition & Forestry; Budget; Finance; Indian Affairs

Coverdell: Agriculture, Nutrition & Forestry; Foreign Relations; Small Business

Craig: Agriculture, Nutrition & Forestry; Energy & Natural Resources; Joint Economic; Select Ethics; Special Aging

D'Amato: Appropriations; Banking, Housing & Urban Affairs (ranking member); Select Intelligence

Danforth: Commerce, Science & Transportation (ranking member); Finance; Select Intelligence

Daschle: Agriculture, Nutrition & Forestry; Finance; Indian Affairs; Select Ethics; Veterans' Affairs

DeConcini: Appropriations; Indian Affairs; Joint Library; Joint Printing; Judiciary; Rules & Administration; Select Intelligence (chairman); Veterans' Affairs

Dodd: Banking, Housing & Urban Affairs; Budget; Foreign Relations; Labor & Human Resources; Rules & Administration

Dole: Agriculture, Nutrition & Forestry; Finance; Joint Organization of Congress; Joint Taxation; Rules & Administration

Domenici: Appropriations; Banking, Housing & Urban Affairs; Budget (ranking member); Energy & Natural Resources; Indian Affairs; Joint Organization of Congress (vice chairman)

Dorgan: Commerce, Science & Transportation; Energy & Natural Resources; Governmental Affairs; Indian Affairs; Joint Economic

Durenberger: Environment & Public Works; Finance; Labor & Human Resources; Special Aging

Exon: Armed Services; Budget; Commerce, Science & Transportation

Faircloth: Armed Services; Banking, Housing & Urban Affairs; Environment & Public Works

Feingold: Agriculture, Nutrition & Forestry; Foreign Relations; Special Aging

Feinstein: Appropriations; Judiciary; Rules & Administration

Ford: Commerce, Science & Transportation; Energy & Natural Resources; Joint Inaugural Ceremonies (chairman); Joint Organization of Congress; Joint Printing (chairman); Rules & Administration (chairman)

Glenn: Armed Services; Governmental Affairs (chairman); Select Intelligence; Special Aging

Gorton: Appropriations; Budget; Commerce, Science & Transportation; Indian Affairs; Select Intelligence

Graham: Armed Services; Environment & Public Works; Select Intelligence; Special Aging; Veterans' Affairs

Gramm: Appropriations; Banking, Housing & Urban Affairs; Budget

Grassley: Agriculture, Nutrition & Forestry; Budget; Finance; Judiciary; Special Aging

Gregg: Budget; Foreign Relations; Labor & Human Resources

Harkin: Agriculture, Nutrition & Forestry; Appropriations; Labor & Human Resources; Small Business

Hatch: Finance; Judiciary (ranking member); Labor & Human Resources

Hatfield: Appropriations (ranking member); Energy & Natural Resources; Indian Affairs; Joint Library; Joint Printing; Rules & Administration

Heflin: Agriculture, Nutrition & Forestry; Judiciary; Small Business

Helms: Agriculture, Nutrition & Forestry; Foreign Relations (ranking member); Rules & Administration

Hollings: Appropriations; Budget; Commerce, Science & Transportation (chairman)

Hutchison: Armed Services; Commerce, Science & Transportation; Small Business

Inouye: Appropriations; Commerce, Science & Transportation; Indian Affairs (chairman); Rules & Administration

Jeffords: Foreign Relations; Labor & Human Resources; Special Aging; Veterans' Affairs

Johnston: Appropriations; Budget; Energy & Natural Resources (chairman); Select Intelligence; Special Aging

Kassebaum: Foreign Relations; Indian Affairs; Joint Organization of Congress; Labor & Human Resources (ranking member)

Kempthorne: Armed Services; Environment & Public Works; Small Business

Kennedy: Armed Services; Joint Economic; Judiciary; Labor & Human Resources (chairman)

Kerrey: Agriculture, Nutrition & Forestry; Appropriations; Select Intelligence

Kerry: Banking, Housing & Urban Affairs; Commerce, Science & Transportation; Foreign Relations; Select Intelligence; Small Business

Kohl: Appropriations; Judiciary; Small Business; Special Aging

Lautenberg: Appropriations; Budget; Environment & Public Works; Small Business

Leahy: Agriculture, Nutrition & Forestry (chairman); Appropriations; Judiciary

Levin: Armed Services; Governmental Affairs; Small Business

Lieberman: Armed Services; Environment & Public Works; Governmental Affairs; Small Business

Lott: Armed Services; Budget; Commerce, Science & Transportation; Energy & Natural Resources; Joint Organization of Congress

Lugar: Agriculture, Nutrition & Forestry (ranking member); Foreign Relations; Joint Organization of Congress; Select Intelligence

Mack: Appropriations; Banking, Housing & Urban Affairs; Joint Economic; Small Business

Mathews: Commerce, Science & Transportation; Energy & Natural Resources; Foreign Relations; Joint Printing; Rules & Administration

McCain: Armed Services; Commerce, Science & Transportation; Governmental Affairs; Indian Affairs (ranking member); Special Aging

McConnell: Agriculture, Nutrition & Forestry; Appropriations; Rules & Administration; Select Ethics (vice chairman)

Metzenbaum: Environment & Public Works; Judiciary; Labor & Human Resources; Select Intelligence

Mikulski: Appropriations; Labor & Human Resources; Select Ethics

Mitchell: Environment & Public Works; Finance; Joint Inaugural Ceremonies; Joint Organization of Congress; Veterans' Affairs

Moseley-Braun: Banking, Housing & Urban Affairs; Judiciary; Small Business

Moynihan: Environment & Public Works; Finance (chairman); Foreign Relations; Joint Library; Joint Taxation (vice chairman); Rules & Administration

Murkowski: Energy & Natural Resources; Foreign Relations; Indian Affairs; Veterans' Affairs (ranking member)

Murray: Appropriations; Banking, Housing & Urban Affairs; Budget

Nickles: Appropriations; Budget; Energy & Natural Resources; Indian Affairs

Nunn: Armed Services (chairman); Governmental Affairs; Small Business

Packwood: Commerce, Science & Transportation; Finance (ranking member); Joint Taxation

Pell: Foreign Relations (chairman); Joint Library (vice chairman); Labor & Human Resources; Rules & Administration

Pressler: Commerce, Science & Transportation; Foreign Relations; Judiciary; Small Business (ranking member); Special Aging

Pryor: Agriculture, Nutrition & Forestry; Finance; Governmental Affairs; Joint Organization of Congress; Special Aging (chairman)

Reid: Appropriations; Environment & Public Works; Indian Affairs; Joint Organization of Congress; Special Aging

Riegle: Banking, Housing & Urban Affairs (chairman); Budget; Finance; Special Aging

Robb: Armed Services; Commerce, Science & Transportation; Foreign Relations; Joint Economic

Rockefeller: Commerce, Science & Transportation; Finance; Veterans' Affairs (chairman)

Roth: Banking, Housing & Urban Affairs; Finance; Governmental Affairs (ranking member); Joint Economic (ranking member)

Sarbanes: Banking, Housing & Urban Affairs; Budget; Foreign Relations; Joint Economic (vice chairman); Joint Organization of Congress

Sasser: Appropriations; Banking, Housing & Urban Affairs; Budget (chairman); Governmental Affairs; Joint Organization of Congress

Shelby: Armed Services; Banking, Housing & Urban Affairs; Energy & Natural Resources; Special Aging

Simon: Budget; Foreign Relations; Indian Affairs; Judiciary; Labor & Human Resources

Simpson: Environment & Public Works; Judiciary; Special Aging; Veterans' Affairs

Smith: Armed Services; Environment & Public Works; Select Ethics

Specter: Appropriations; Energy & Natural Resources; Judiciary; Special Aging; Veterans' Affairs

Stevens: Appropriations; Commerce, Science & Transportation; Governmental Affairs; Joint Inaugural Ceremonies; Joint Library; Joint Organization of Congress; Joint Printing ; Rules & Administration (ranking member); Select Intelligence

Thurmond: Armed Services (ranking member); Judiciary; Labor & Human Resources; Veterans' Affairs

Wallop: Energy & Natural Resources (ranking member); Finance; Select Intelligence; Small Business

Warner: Armed Services; Environment & Public Works; Rules & Administration; Select Intelligence (vice chairman)

Wellstone: Energy & Natural Resources; Indian Affairs; Labor & Human Resources; Small Business

Wofford: Environment & Public Works; Foreign Relations; Labor & Human Resources; Small Business

Representatives' Committee Assignments

Abercrombie: Armed Services; Natural Resources

Ackerman: Foreign Affairs; Merchant Marine & Fisheries; Post Office & Civil Service

Allard: Agriculture; Budget; Joint Organization of Congress; Natural Resources

Andrews (Maine): Armed Services; Merchant Marine & Fisheries; Small Business

Andrews (N.J.): Education & Labor; Foreign Affairs

Andrews (Texas): Budget; Joint Economic; Ways & Means

Applegate: Public Works & Transportation; Veterans' Affairs

Archer: Joint Taxation; Ways & Means (ranking member)

Armey: Education & Labor; Joint Economic

Bacchus: Banking, Finance & Urban Affairs; Science, Space & Technology

Bachus: Banking, Finance & Urban Affairs; Veterans' Affairs

Baesler: Agriculture; Education & Labor; Veterans' Affairs

Baker (Calif.): Public Works & Transportation; Science, Space & Technology

Baker (La.): Banking, Finance & Urban Affairs; Natural Resources; Small Business

Ballenger: District of Columbia; Education & Labor; Foreign Affairs

Barca: Public Works & Transportation; Science, Space & Technology

Barcia: Public Works & Transportation; Science, Space & Technology

Barlow: Agriculture; Merchant Marine & Fisheries; Natural Resources

Barrett (Neb.): Agriculture; Education & Labor; House Administration; Joint Library

Barrett (Wis.): Banking, Finance & Urban Affairs; Government Operations; Natural Resources

Bartlett: Armed Services; Science, Space & Technology

Barton: Energy & Commerce; Science, Space & Technology

Bateman: Armed Services; Merchant Marine & Fisheries

Becerra: Education & Labor; Judiciary; Science, Space & Technology

Beilenson: Budget; Rules

Bentley: Appropriations; Merchant Marine & Fisheries

Bereuter: Banking, Finance & Urban Affairs; Foreign Affairs; Select Intelligence

Berman: Budget; Foreign Affairs; Judiciary

Bevill: Appropriations

Bilbray: Armed Services; Select Intelligence; Small Business

Bilirakis: Energy & Commerce; Veterans' Affairs

Bishop: Agriculture; Post Office & Civil Service; Veterans' Affairs

Blackwell: Budget; Public Works & Transportation

Bliley: District of Columbia (ranking member); Energy & Commerce

Blute: Public Works & Transportation; Science, Space & Technology

Boehlert: Post Office & Civil Service; Public Works & Transportation; Science, Space & Technology

Boehner: Agriculture; Education & Labor; House Administration

Bonilla: Appropriations

Bonior: Rules

Borski: Foreign Affairs; Public Works & Transportation; Standards of Official Conduct

Boucher: Energy & Commerce; Judiciary; Science, Space & Technology

Brewster: Ways & Means

Brooks: Judiciary (chairman)

Browder: Armed Services; Budget

Brown (Fla.): Government Operations; Public Works & Transportation; Veterans' Affairs

Brown (Ohio): Energy & Commerce; Foreign Affairs; Post Office & Civil Service

Brown (Calif.): Agriculture; Science, Space & Technology (chairman)

Bryant: Budget; Energy & Commerce; Judiciary
Bunning: Budget; Standards of Official Conduct; Ways & Means
Burton: Foreign Affairs; Post Office & Civil Service; Veterans' Affairs
Buyer: Armed Services; Veterans' Affairs
Byrne: Post Office & Civil Service; Public Works & Transportation
Callahan: Appropriations
Calvert: Natural Resources; Science, Space & Technology
Camp: Ways & Means
Canady: Agriculture; Judiciary
Cantwell: Foreign Affairs; Merchant Marine & Fisheries; Public Works & Transportation
Cardin: House Administration; Standards of Official Conduct; Ways & Means
Carr: Appropriations
Castle: Banking, Finance & Urban Affairs; Education & Labor; Merchant Marine & Fisheries
Chapman: Appropriations
Clay: Education & Labor; House Administration; Post Office & Civil Service (chairman)
Clayton: Agriculture; Small Business
Clement: Public Works & Transportation; Veterans' Affairs
Clinger: Government Operations (ranking member); Public Works & Transportation
Clyburn: Public Works & Transportation; Veterans' Affairs
Coble: Judiciary; Merchant Marine & Fisheries
Coleman: Appropriations; Select Intelligence
Collins (Ga.): Public Works & Transportation; Small Business
Collins (Ill.): Energy & Commerce; Government Operations
Collins (Mich.): Government Operations; Post Office & Civil Service; Public Works & Transportation
Combest: Agriculture; Select Intelligence (ranking member); Small Business
Condit: Agriculture; Government Operations
Conyers: Government Operations (chairman); Judiciary; Small Business
Cooper: Budget; Energy & Commerce
Coppersmith: Public Works & Transportation; Science, Space & Technology
Costello: Budget; Public Works & Transportation
Cox: Budget; Government Operations; Joint Economic
Coyne: Budget; Ways & Means
Cramer: Public Works & Transportation; Science, Space & Technology; Select Intelligence
Crane: Joint Taxation; Ways & Means
Crapo: Energy & Commerce
Cunningham: Armed Services; Education & Labor; Merchant Marine & Fisheries
Danner: Public Works & Transportation; Small Business
Darden: Appropriations; Standards of Official Conduct
de la Garza: Agriculture (chairman)
de Lugo: Education & Labor; Natural Resources; Public Works & Transportation
Deal: Natural Resources; Public Works & Transportation; Science, Space & Technology
DeFazio: Natural Resources; Public Works & Transportation
DeLauro: Appropriations
DeLay: Appropriations
Dellums: Armed Services (chairman); District of Columbia
Derrick: House Administration; Rules
Deutsch: Banking, Finance & Urban Affairs; Foreign Affairs; Merchant Marine & Fisheries
Diaz-Balart: Foreign Affairs; Merchant Marine & Fisheries
Dickey: Agriculture; Natural Resources; Small Business
Dicks: Appropriations; Select Intelligence
Dingell: Energy & Commerce (chairman)
Dixon: Appropriations; Select Intelligence
Dooley: Agriculture; Banking, Finance & Urban Affairs; Natural Resources
Doolittle: Agriculture; Natural Resources
Dornan: Armed Services; Select Intelligence
Dreier: Joint Organization of Congress (vice chairman); Rules
Duncan: Natural Resources; Public Works & Transportation

Dunn: House Administration; Joint Organization of Congress; Public Works & Transportation; Science, Space & Technology
Durbin: Appropriations
Edwards (Calif.): Foreign Affairs; Judiciary; Veterans' Affairs
Edwards (Texas): Armed Services; Veterans' Affairs
Emerson: Agriculture; Joint Organization of Congress; Public Works & Transportation
Engel: Education & Labor; Foreign Affairs
English (Ariz.): Education & Labor; Natural Resources
English (Okla.): Agriculture; Government Operations
Eshoo: Merchant Marine & Fisheries; Science, Space & Technology
Evans: Armed Services; Natural Resources; Veterans' Affairs
Everett: Agriculture; Armed Services; Veterans' Affairs
Ewing: Agriculture; Public Works & Transportation
Faleomavaega: Education & Labor; Foreign Affairs; Natural Resources
Farr: Agriculture; Armed Services; Natural Resources
Fawell: Education & Labor; Science, Space & Technology
Fazio: Appropriations
Fields (La.): Banking, Finance & Urban Affairs; Small Business
Fields (Texas): Energy & Commerce; Merchant Marine & Fisheries (ranking member)
Filner: Public Works & Transportation; Veterans' Affairs
Fingerhut: Banking, Finance & Urban Affairs; Foreign Affairs; Science, Space & Technology
Fish: Judiciary (ranking member)
Flake: Banking, Finance & Urban Affairs; Government Operations; Small Business
Foglietta: Appropriations
Foley: Speaker of the House; Joint Inaugural Ceremonies
Ford (Mich.): Education & Labor (chairman)
Ford (Tenn.): Ways & Means
Fowler: Armed Services; Merchant Marine & Fisheries
Frank: Banking, Finance & Urban Affairs; Budget; Judiciary
Franks (Conn.): Energy & Commerce
Franks (N.J.): Budget; Public Works & Transportation
Frost: House Administration; Joint Library; Rules
Furse: Armed Services; Banking, Finance & Urban Affairs; Merchant Marine & Fisheries
Gallegly: Foreign Affairs; Judiciary; Natural Resources
Gallo: Appropriations
Gejdenson: Foreign Affairs; House Administration; Joint Organization of Congress; Joint Printing; Natural Resources
Gekas: Judiciary; Select Intelligence
Gephardt: Budget; Joint Inaugural Ceremonies; Joint Organization of Congress
Geren: Armed Services; Public Works & Transportation; Science, Space & Technology
Gibbons: Joint Taxation; Ways & Means
Gilchrest: Merchant Marine & Fisheries; Public Works & Transportation
Gillmor: Energy & Commerce
Gilman: Foreign Affairs (ranking member); Post Office & Civil Service
Gingrich: House Administration; Joint Printing
Glickman: Agriculture; Judiciary; Science, Space & Technology; Select Intelligence (chairman)
Gonzalez: Banking, Finance & Urban Affairs (chairman)
Goodlatte: Agriculture; Judiciary
Goodling: Education & Labor (ranking member); Foreign Affairs
Gordon: Budget; Rules
Goss: Rules; Standards of Official Conduct
Grams: Banking, Finance & Urban Affairs; Science, Space & Technology
Grandy: Standards of Official Conduct (ranking member); Ways & Means
Green: Education & Labor; Government Operations; Merchant Marine & Fisheries
Greenwood: Energy & Commerce
Gunderson: Agriculture; Education & Labor
Gutierrez: Banking, Finance & Urban Affairs; Veterans' Affairs
Hall (Ohio): Rules

Hall (Texas): Energy & Commerce; Science, Space & Technology

Hamburg: Merchant Marine & Fisheries; Public Works & Transportation

Hamilton: Foreign Affairs (chairman); Joint Economic; Joint Organization of Congress (co-chairman)

Hancock: Ways & Means

Hansen: Armed Services; Natural Resources; Select Intelligence

Harman: Armed Services; Science, Space & Technology

Hastert: Energy & Commerce; Government Operations

Hastings: Foreign Affairs; Merchant Marine & Fisheries; Post Office & Civil Service

Hayes: Government Operations; Public Works & Transportation; Science, Space & Technology

Hefley: Armed Services; Natural Resources; Small Business

Hefner: Appropriations

Herger: Budget; Ways & Means

Hilliard: Agriculture; Small Business

Hinchey: Banking, Finance & Urban Affairs; Natural Resources

Hoagland: Ways & Means

Hobson: Appropriations; Budget; Standards of Official Conduct

Hochbrueckner: Armed Services; Merchant Marine & Fisheries

Hoekstra: Education & Labor; Public Works & Transportation

Hoke: Budget; Science, Space & Technology

Holden: Agriculture; Armed Services

Horn: Government Operations; Public Works & Transportation

Houghton: Ways & Means

Hoyer: Appropriations; House Administration

Huffington: Banking, Finance & Urban Affairs; Small Business

Hughes: Judiciary; Merchant Marine & Fisheries

Hunter: Armed Services

Hutchinson: Public Works & Transportation; Veterans' Affairs

Hutto: Armed Services; Merchant Marine & Fisheries

Hyde: Foreign Affairs; Judiciary

Inglis: Budget; Judiciary

Inhofe: Armed Services; Merchant Marine & Fisheries; Public Works & Transportation

Inslee: Agriculture; Science, Space & Technology

Istook: Appropriations

Jacobs: Ways & Means

Jefferson: District of Columbia; Ways & Means

Johnson (Conn.): Standards of Official Conduct; Ways & Means

Johnson (Ga.): Armed Services; Science, Space & Technology

Johnson (S.D.): Agriculture; Natural Resources

Johnson, Eddie Bernice (Texas): Public Works & Transportation; Science, Space & Technology

Johnson, Sam (Texas): Banking, Finance & Urban Affairs; Science, Space & Technology; Small Business

Johnston: Budget; Foreign Affairs

Kanjorski: Banking, Finance & Urban Affairs; Post Office & Civil Service

Kaptur: Appropriations

Kasich: Armed Services; Budget (ranking member)

Kennedy: Banking, Finance & Urban Affairs; Veterans' Affairs

Kennelly: Budget; House Administration; Ways & Means

Kildee: Budget; Education & Labor; House Administration

Kim: Public Works & Transportation; Small Business

King: Banking, Finance & Urban Affairs; Merchant Marine & Fisheries; Veterans' Affairs

Kingston: Agriculture; Merchant Marine & Fisheries

Kleczka: House Administration; Joint Printing; Ways & Means

Klein: Banking, Finance & Urban Affairs; Science, Space & Technology

Klink: Banking, Finance & Urban Affairs; Education & Labor; Small Business

Klug: Energy & Commerce

Knollenberg: Banking, Finance & Urban Affairs; Small Business

Kolbe: Appropriations; Budget

Kopetski: Ways & Means

Kreidler: Energy & Commerce; Veterans' Affairs

Kyl: Armed Services; Government Operations; Standards of Official Conduct

LaFalce: Banking, Finance & Urban Affairs; Small Business (chairman)

Lambert: Agriculture; Energy & Commerce; Merchant Marine & Fisheries

Lancaster: Armed Services; Merchant Marine & Fisheries; Small Business

Lantos: Foreign Affairs; Government Operations

LaRocco: Banking, Finance & Urban Affairs; Natural Resources

Laughlin: Merchant Marine & Fisheries; Post Office & Civil Service; Public Works & Transportation; Select Intelligence

Lazio: Banking, Finance & Urban Affairs; Budget

Leach: Banking, Finance & Urban Affairs (ranking member); Foreign Affairs

Lehman: Energy & Commerce; Natural Resources

Levin: Ways & Means

Levy: Foreign Affairs; Public Works & Transportation

Lewis (Calif.): Appropriations; Select Intelligence

Lewis (Fla.): Agriculture; Science, Space & Technology

Lewis (Ga.): District of Columbia; Ways & Means

Lightfoot: Appropriations

Linder: Banking, Finance & Urban Affairs; Science, Space & Technology; Veterans' Affairs

Lipinski: Merchant Marine & Fisheries; Public Works & Transportation

Livingston: Appropriations; House Administration

Lloyd: Armed Services; Science, Space & Technology

Long: Agriculture; Veterans' Affairs

Lowey: Appropriations

Machtley: Armed Services; Small Business

Maloney: Banking, Finance & Urban Affairs; Government Operations

Mann: Armed Services; Judiciary

Manton: Energy & Commerce; House Administration; Joint Library; Merchant Marine & Fisheries

Manzullo: Foreign Affairs; Small Business

Margolies-Mezvinsky: Energy & Commerce; Government Operations; Small Business

Markey: Energy & Commerce; Natural Resources

Martinez: Education & Labor; Foreign Affairs

Matsui: Ways & Means

Mazzoli: Judiciary; Small Business

McCandless: Banking, Finance & Urban Affairs; Government Operations

McCloskey: Armed Services; Foreign Affairs; Post Office & Civil Service

McCollum: Banking, Finance & Urban Affairs; Judiciary

McCrery: Ways & Means

McCurdy: Armed Services; Science, Space & Technology

McDade: Appropriations (ranking member)

McDermott: District of Columbia; Standards of Official Conduct (chairman); Ways & Means

McHale: Armed Services; Science, Space & Technology

McHugh: Armed Services; Government Operations

McInnis: Natural Resources; Small Business

McKeon: Education & Labor; Public Works & Transportation

McKinney: Agriculture; Foreign Affairs

McMillan: Budget; Energy & Commerce

McNulty: Ways & Means

Meehan: Armed Services; Small Business

Meek: Appropriations

Menendez: Foreign Affairs; Public Works & Transportation

Meyers: Foreign Affairs; Small Business (ranking member)

Mfume: Banking, Finance & Urban Affairs; Joint Economic; Small Business; Standards of Official Conduct

Mica: Government Operations; Public Works & Transportation

Michel: Joint Inaugural Ceremonies; Joint Organization of Congress

Miller (Calif.): Education & Labor; Natural Resources (chairman)

Miller (Fla.): Budget; Education & Labor

Mineta: Public Works & Transportation (chairman)

Minge: Agriculture; Science, Space & Technology

Mink: Budget; Education & Labor; Natural Resources

Moakley: Rules (chairman)

Molinari: Education & Labor; Public Works & Transportation

Mollohan: Appropriations; Budget

Montgomery: Armed Services; Veterans' Affairs (chairman)

Moorhead: Energy & Commerce (ranking member); Judiciary

Moran: Appropriations

Morella: Post Office & Civil Service; Science, Space & Technology

Murphy: Education & Labor; Natural Resources

Murtha: Appropriations

Myers: Appropriations; Post Office & Civil Service (ranking member)

Nadler: Judiciary; Public Works & Transportation

Natcher: Appropriations (chairman)

Neal (Mass.): Ways & Means

Neal (N.C.): Banking, Finance & Urban Affairs; Government Operations

Norton: District of Columbia; Joint Organization of Congress; Post Office & Civil Service; Public Works & Transportation

Nussle: Agriculture; Banking, Finance & Urban Affairs

Oberstar: Foreign Affairs; Public Works & Transportation

Obey: Appropriations; Joint Economic (chairman); Joint Organization of Congress

Olver: Appropriations

Ortiz: Armed Services; Merchant Marine & Fisheries

Orton: Banking, Finance & Urban Affairs; Budget

Owens: Education & Labor; Government Operations

Oxley: Energy & Commerce

Packard: Appropriations

Pallone: Energy & Commerce; Merchant Marine & Fisheries

Parker: Budget; Public Works & Transportation

Pastor: Appropriations

Paxon: Energy & Commerce

Payne (N.J.): Education & Labor; Foreign Affairs; Government Operations

Payne (Va.): Ways & Means

Pelosi: Appropriations; Select Intelligence; Standards of Official Conduct

Penny: Agriculture; Veterans' Affairs

Peterson (Fla.): Appropriations

Peterson (Minn.): Agriculture; Government Operations

Petri: Education & Labor; Post Office & Civil Service; Public Works & Transportation

Pickett: Armed Services; Merchant Marine & Fisheries

Pickle: Joint Taxation; Ways & Means

Pombo: Agriculture; Merchant Marine & Fisheries; Natural Resources

Pomeroy: Agriculture; Budget

Porter: Appropriations

Portman: Government Operations; Small Business

Poshard: Public Works & Transportation; Small Business

Price: Appropriations; Budget

Pryce: Banking, Finance & Urban Affairs; Government Operations

Quillen: Rules

Quinn: Public Works & Transportation; Veterans' Affairs

Rahall: Natural Resources; Public Works & Transportation

Ramstad: Joint Economic; Judiciary; Small Business

Rangel: Ways & Means

Ravenel: Armed Services; Merchant Marine & Fisheries

Reed: Education & Labor; Judiciary; Merchant Marine & Fisheries; Select Intelligence

Regula: Appropriations

Reynolds: Ways & Means

Richardson: Energy & Commerce; Natural Resources; Select Intelligence

Ridge: Banking, Finance & Urban Affairs; Post Office & Civil Service; Veterans' Affairs

Roberts: Agriculture (ranking member); House Administration; Joint Library; Joint Printing (ranking member)

Roemer: Education & Labor; Science, Space & Technology

Rogers: Appropriations

Rohrabacher: District of Columbia; Foreign Affairs; Science, Space & Technology

Romero-Barcelo: Education & Labor; Natural Resources

Rose: Agriculture; House Administration (chairman); Joint Library (chairman); Joint Printing (vice chairman)

Ros-Lehtinen: Foreign Affairs; Government Operations

Rostenkowski: Joint Taxation (chairman); Ways & Means (chairman)

Roth: Banking, Finance & Urban Affairs; Foreign Affairs

Roukema: Banking, Finance & Urban Affairs; Education & Labor

Rowland: Energy & Commerce; Veterans' Affairs

Roybal-Allard: Banking, Finance & Urban Affairs; Small Business

Royce: Foreign Affairs; Science, Space & Technology

Rush: Banking, Finance & Urban Affairs; Government Operations

Sabo: Appropriations; Budget (chairman)

Sanders: Banking, Finance & Urban Affairs; Government Operations

Sangmeister: Judiciary; Public Works & Transportation; Veterans' Affairs

Santorum: Ways & Means

Sarpalius: Agriculture; Small Business

Sawyer: Education & Labor; Foreign Affairs; Post Office & Civil Service; Standards of Official Conduct

Saxton: Armed Services; District of Columbia; Joint Economic; Merchant Marine & Fisheries

Schaefer: Energy & Commerce

Schenk: Energy & Commerce; Merchant Marine & Fisheries

Schiff: Government Operations; Judiciary; Science, Space & Technology; Standards of Official Conduct

Schroeder: Armed Services; Judiciary; Post Office & Civil Service

Schumer: Banking, Finance & Urban Affairs; Foreign Affairs; Judiciary

Scott: Education & Labor; Judiciary; Science, Space & Technology

Sensenbrenner: Judiciary; Science, Space & Technology

Serrano: Appropriations

Sharp: Energy & Commerce; Natural Resources

Shaw: Ways & Means

Shays: Budget; Government Operations

Shepherd: Natural Resources; Public Works & Transportation

Shuster: Public Works & Transportation (ranking member)

Sisisky: Armed Services; Small Business

Skaggs: Appropriations; Select Intelligence

Skeen: Appropriations

Skelton: Armed Services; Small Business

Slattery: Energy & Commerce; Veterans' Affairs

Slaughter: Budget; Rules

Smith (Iowa): Appropriations; Small Business

Smith (Mich.): Agriculture; Budget; Science, Space & Technology

Smith (N.J.): Foreign Affairs; Veterans' Affairs

Smith (Ore.): Agriculture; Natural Resources

Smith (Texas): Budget; Judiciary

Snowe: Budget; Foreign Affairs

Solomon: Joint Organization of Congress; Rules (ranking member)

Spence: Armed Services (ranking member); Veterans' Affairs

Spratt: Armed Services; Government Operations; Joint Organization of Congress

Stark: District of Columbia (chairman); Joint Economic; Ways & Means

Stearns: Energy & Commerce; Veterans' Affairs

Stenholm: Agriculture; Budget

Stokes: Appropriations

Strickland: Education & Labor; Small Business

Studds: Energy & Commerce; Merchant Marine & Fisheries (chairman)

Stump: Armed Services; Veterans' Affairs (ranking member)

Stupak: Armed Services; Government Operations; Merchant Marine & Fisheries

Sundquist: Ways & Means

Swett: Public Works & Transportation; Science, Space & Technology

Swift: Energy & Commerce; House Administration; Joint Organization of Congress

Synar: Energy & Commerce; Government Operations; Judiciary

Talent: Armed Services; Small Business

Tanner: Armed Services; Science, Space & Technology

Tauzin: Energy & Commerce; Merchant Marine & Fisheries

Taylor (Miss.): Armed Services; Merchant Marine & Fisheries

Taylor (N.C.): Appropriations; Merchant Marine & Fisheries

Tejeda: Armed Services; Veterans' Affairs

Thomas (Calif.): House Administration (ranking member); Ways & Means

Thomas (Wyo.): Banking, Finance & Urban Affairs; Government Operations; Natural Resources

Thompson: Agriculture; Merchant Marine & Fisheries; Small Business

Thornton: Appropriations

Thurman: Agriculture; Government Operations

Torkildsen: Armed Services; Merchant Marine & Fisheries; Small Business

Torres: Appropriations

Torricelli: Foreign Affairs; Science, Space & Technology; Select Intelligence

Towns: Energy & Commerce; Government Operations

Traficant: Public Works & Transportation; Science, Space & Technology

Tucker: Public Works & Transportation; Small Business

Underwood: Armed Services; Education & Labor; Natural Resources

Unsoeld: Education & Labor; Merchant Marine & Fisheries

Upton: Energy & Commerce

Valentine: Public Works & Transportation; Science, Space & Technology

Velazquez: Banking, Finance & Urban Affairs; Small Business

Vento: Banking, Finance & Urban Affairs; Natural Resources

Visclosky: Appropriations

Volkmer: Agriculture; Science, Space & Technology

Vucanovich: Appropriations; Natural Resources

Walker: Joint Organization of Congress; Science, Space & Technology (ranking member)

Walsh: Appropriations

Washington: Energy & Commerce; Government Operations; Judiciary

Waters: Banking, Finance & Urban Affairs; Small Business; Veterans' Affairs

Watt: Banking, Finance & Urban Affairs; Judiciary; Post Office & Civil Service

Waxman: Energy & Commerce; Government Operations

Weldon: Armed Services; Merchant Marine & Fisheries

Wheat: District of Columbia; Rules

Whitten: Appropriations

Williams: Agriculture; Education & Labor; Natural Resources

Wilson: Appropriations

Wise: Budget; Public Works & Transportation

Wolf: Appropriations

Woolsey: Budget; Education & Labor; Government Operations

Wyden: Energy & Commerce; Joint Economic; Small Business

Wynn: Banking, Finance & Urban Affairs; Foreign Affairs; Post Office & Civil Service

Yates: Appropriations

Young (Alaska): Merchant Marine & Fisheries; Natural Resources (ranking member); Post Office & Civil Service

Young (Fla.): Appropriations; Select Intelligence

Zeliff: Government Operations; Public Works & Transportation; Small Business

Zimmer: Government Operations; Science, Space & Technology

Senators' Phone and Room Directory

(103rd Congress, 1st Session)

Capitol Switchboard: (202) 224-3121

Senate ZIP Code: 20510

SD — Dirksen Building   **SH** — Hart Building   **SR** — Russell Building

Name, Party, State	Phone	Room
Akaka, Daniel K., D-Hawaii	(202) 224-6361	SH-720
Baucus, Max, D-Mont.	224-2651	SH-511
Bennett, Robert F., R-Utah	224-5444	SD-241
Biden, Joseph R. Jr., D-Del.	224-5042	SR-221
Bingaman, Jeff, D-N.M.	224-5521	SH-110
Bond, Christopher S., R-Mo.	224-5721	SR-293
Boren, David L., D-Okla.	224-4721	SR-453
Boxer, Barbara, D-Calif.	224-3553	SH-112
Bradley, Bill, D-N.J.	224-3224	SH-731
Breaux, John B., D-La.	224-4623	SH-516
Brown, Hank, R-Colo.	224-5941	SH-716
Bryan, Richard H., D-Nev.	224-6244	SR-364
Bumpers, Dale, D-Ark.	224-4843	SD-229
Burns, Conrad, R-Mont.	224-2644	SD-183
Byrd, Robert C., D-W.Va.	224-3954	SH-311
Campbell, Ben Nighthorse, D-Colo.	224-5852	SR-380
Chafee, John H., R-R.I.	224-2921	SD-567
Coats, Daniel R., R-Ind.	224-5623	SR-404
Cochran, Thad, R-Miss.	224-5054	SR-326
Cohen, William S., R-Maine	224-2523	SH-322
Conrad, Kent, D-N.D.	224-2043	SH-724
Coverdell, Paul, R-Ga.	224-3643	SR-200
Craig, Larry E., R-Idaho	224-2752	SH-313
D'Amato, Alfonse M., R-N.Y.	224-6542	SH-520
Danforth, John C., R-Mo.	224-6154	SR-249
Daschle, Tom, D-S.D.	224-2321	SH-317
DeConcini, Dennis, D-Ariz.	224-4521	SH-328
Dodd, Christopher J., D-Conn.	224-2823	SR-444
Dole, Bob, R-Kan.	224-6521	SH-141
Domenici, Pete V., R-N.M.	224-6621	SD-427
Dorgan, Byron L., D-N.D.	224-2551	SH-713
Durenberger, Dave, R-Minn.	224-3244	SR-154
Exon, Jim, D-Neb.	224-4224	SH-528
Faircloth, Lauch, R-N.C.	224-3154	SH-702
Feingold, Russell D., D-Wis.	224-5323	SH-502
Feinstein, Dianne, D-Calif.	224-3841	SH-331
Ford, Wendell H., D-Ky.	224-4343	SR-173A
Glenn, John, D-Ohio	224-3353	SH-503
Gorton, Slade, R-Wash.	224-3441	SH-730
Graham, Bob, D-Fla.	224-3041	SH-524
Gramm, Phil, R-Texas	224-2934	SR-370
Grassley, Charles E., R-Iowa	224-3744	SH-135
Gregg, Judd, R-N.H.	224-3324	SR-393
Harkin, Tom, D-Iowa	224-3254	SH-531
Hatch, Orrin G., R-Utah	224-5251	SR-135
Hatfield, Mark O., R-Ore.	224-3753	SH-711
Heflin, Howell, D-Ala.	224-4124	SH-728
Helms, Jesse, R-N.C.	224-6342	SD-403
Hollings, Ernest F., D-S.C.	224-6121	SR-125
Hutchison, Kay Bailey, R-Texas	224-5922	SH-703
Inouye, Daniel K., D-Hawaii	(202) 224-3934	SH-722
Jeffords, James M., R-Vt.	224-5141	SH-513
Johnston, J. Bennett, D-La.	224-5824	SH-136
Kassebaum, Nancy Landon, R-Kan.	224-4774	SR-302
Kempthorne, Dirk, R-Idaho	224-6142	SD-367
Kennedy, Edward M., D-Mass.	224-4543	SR-315
Kerrey, Bob, D-Neb.	224-6551	SH-303
Kerry, John, D-Mass.	224-2742	SR-421
Kohl, Herb, D-Wis.	224-5653	SH-330
Lautenberg, Frank R., D-N.J.	224-4744	SH-506
Leahy, Patrick J., D-Vt.	224-4242	SR-433
Levin, Carl, D-Mich.	224-6221	SR-459
Lieberman, Joseph I., D-Conn.	224-4041	SH-316
Lott, Trent, R-Miss.	224-6253	SR-487
Lugar, Richard G., R-Ind.	224-4814	SH-306
Mack, Connie, R-Fla.	224-5274	SH-517
Mathews, Harlan, D-Tenn.	224-4944	SD-506
McCain, John, R-Ariz.	224-2235	SR-111
McConnell, Mitch, R-Ky.	224-2541	SR-120
Metzenbaum, Howard M., D-Ohio	224-2315	SR-140
Mikulski, Barbara A., D-Md.	224-4654	SH-709
Mitchell, George J., D-Maine	224-5344	SR-176
Moseley-Braun, Carol, D-Ill.	224-2854	SH-320
Moynihan, Daniel Patrick, D-N.Y.	224-4451	SR-464
Murkowski, Frank H., R-Alaska	224-6665	SH-706
Murray, Patty, D-Wash.	224-2621	SH-302
Nickles, Don, R-Okla.	224-5754	SH-133
Nunn, Sam, D-Ga.	224-3521	SD-303
Packwood, Bob, R-Ore.	224-5244	SR-259
Pell, Claiborne, D-R.I.	224-4642	SR-335
Pressler, Larry, R-S.D.	224-5842	SR-283
Pryor, David, D-Ark.	224-2353	SR-267
Reid, Harry, D-Nev.	224-3542	SH-324
Riegle, Donald W. Jr., D-Mich.	224-4822	SD-105
Robb, Charles S., D-Va.	224-4024	SR-493
Rockefeller, John D. IV, D-W.Va.	224-6472	SH-109
Roth, William V. Jr., R-Del.	224-2441	SH-104
Sarbanes, Paul S., D-Md.	224-4524	SH-309
Sasser, Jim, D-Tenn.	224-3344	SR-363
Shelby, Richard C., D-Ala.	224-5744	SH-509
Simon, Paul, D-Ill.	224-2152	SD-462
Simpson, Alan K., R-Wyo.	224-3424	SD-261
Smith, Robert C., R-N.H.	224-2841	SD-332
Specter, Arlen, R-Pa.	224-4254	SH-530
Stevens, Ted, R-Alaska	224-3004	SH-522
Thurmond, Strom, R-S.C.	224-5972	SR-217
Wallop, Malcolm, R-Wyo.	224-6441	SR-237
Warner, John W., R-Va.	224-2023	SR-225
Wellstone, Paul, D-Minn.	224-5641	SH-717
Wofford, Harris, D-Pa.	224-6324	SD-521

Representatives' Phone and Room Directory

(103rd Congress, 1st Session)

Capitol Switchboard: (202) 224-3121
House ZIP Code: 20515

Three-digit room numbers are in the Cannon Building; four-digit numbers begining with 1 are in the Longworth Building; four-digit numbers beginning with 2 are in the Rayburn Building.

Name, Party, State (District)	Phone	Room
Abercrombie, Neil, D-Hawaii (1) ... (202) 225-2726	.....	1440
Ackerman, Gary L., D-N.Y. (5)	225-2601	2445
Allard, Wayne, R-Colo. (4)	225-4676	422
Andrews, Michael A., D-Texas (25)	225-7508	303
Andrews, Robert E., D-N.J. (1)	225-6501	1005
Andrews, Thomas H., D-Maine (1)	225-6116	1530
Applegate, Douglas, D-Ohio (18)	225-6265	2183
Archer, Bill, R-Texas (7)	225-2571	1236
Armey, Dick, R-Texas (26)	225-7772	301
Bacchus, Jim, D-Fla. (15)	225-3671	432
Bachus, Spencer, R-Ala. (6)	225-4921	216
Baesler, Scotty, D-Ky. (6)	225-4706	508
Baker, Bill, R-Calif. (10)	225-1880	1724
Baker, Richard H., R-La. (6)	225-3901	434
Ballenger, Cass, R-N.C. (10)	225-2576	2238
Barca, Peter W., D-Wis. (1)	225-3031	1719
Barcia, James A., D-Mich. (5)	225-8171	1717
Barlow, Tom, D-Ky. (1)	225-3115	1533
Barrett, Bill, R-Neb. (3)	225-6435	1213
Barrett, Thomas M., D-Wis. (5)	225-3571	313
Bartlett, Roscoe G., R-Md. (6)	225-2721	312
Barton, Joe L., R-Texas (6)	225-2002	1514
Bateman, Herbert H., R-Va. (1)	225-4261	2350
Becerra, Xavier, D-Calif. (30)	225-6235	1710
Beilenson, Anthony C., D-Calif. (24)	225-5911	2465
Bentley, Helen Delich, R-Md. (2)	225-3061	1610
Bereuter, Doug, R-Neb. (1)	225-4806	2348
Berman, Howard L., D-Calif. (26)	225-4695	2201
Bevill, Tom, D-Ala. (4)	225-4876	2302
Bilbray, James, D-Nev. (1)	225-5965	2431
Bilirakis, Michael, R-Fla. (9)	225-5755	2240
Bishop, Sanford D. Jr., D-Ga. (2)	225-3631	1632
Blackwell, Lucien E., D-Pa. (2)	225-4001	410
Bliley, Thomas J. Jr., R-Va. (7)	225-2815	2241
Blute, Peter I., R-Mass. (3)	225-6101	1029
Boehlert, Sherwood, R-N.Y. (23)	225-3665	1127
Boehner, John A., R-Ohio (8)	225-6205	1020
Bonilla, Henry, R-Texas (23)	225-4511	1529
Bonior, David E., D-Mich. (10)	225-2106	2207
Borski, Robert A., D-Pa. (3)	225-8251	2161
Boucher, Rick, D-Va. (9)	225-3861	2245
Brewster, Bill, D-Okla. (3)	225-4565	1727
Brooks, Jack, D-Texas (9)	225-6565	2449
Browder, Glen, D-Ala. (3)	225-3261	1221
Brown, Corrine, D-Fla. (3)	225-0123	1037
Brown, George E. Jr., D-Calif. (42)	225-6161	2300
Brown, Sherrod, D-Ohio (13)	225-3401	1407
Bryant, John, D-Texas (5)	225-2231	205
Bunning, Jim, R-Ky. (4)	225-3465	2437
Burton, Dan, R-Ind. (6)	225-2276	2411

Name, Party, State (District)	Phone	Room
Buyer, Steve, R-Ind. (5) .... (202) 225-5037	.....	1419
Byrne, Leslie L., D-Va. (11)	225-1492	1609
Callahan, Sonny, R-Ala. (1)	225-4931	2418
Calvert, Ken, R-Calif. (43)	225-1986	1523
Camp, Dave, R-Mich. (4)	225-3561	137
Canady, Charles T., R-Fla. (12)	225-1252	1107
Cantwell, Maria, D-Wash. (1)	225-6311	1520
Cardin, Benjamin L., D-Md. (3)	225-4016	227
Carr, Bob, D-Mich. (8)	225-4872	2347
Castle, Michael N., R-Del. (AL)	225-4165	1205
Chapman, Jim, D-Texas (1)	225-3035	2417
Clay, William L., D-Mo. (1)	225-2406	2306
Clayton, Eva, D-N.C. (1)	225-3101	222
Clement, Bob, D-Tenn. (5)	225-4311	1230
Clinger, William F., R-Pa. (5)	225-5121	2160
Clyburn, James E., D-S.C. (6)	225-3315	319
Coble, Howard, R-N.C. (6)	225-3065	403
Coleman, Ronald D., D-Texas (16)	225-4831	440
Collins, Barbara-Rose, D-Mich. (15)	225-2261	1108
Collins, Cardiss, D-Ill. (7)	225-5006	2308
Collins, Mac, R-Ga. (3)	225-5901	1118
Combest, Larry, R-Texas (19)	225-4005	1511
Condit, Gary A., D-Calif. (18)	225-6131	1123
Conyers, John Jr., D-Mich. (14)	225-5126	2426
Cooper, Jim, D-Tenn. (4)	225-6831	125
Coppersmith, Sam, D-Ariz. (1)	225-2635	1607
Costello, Jerry F., D-Ill. (12)	225-5661	119
Cox, C. Christopher, R-Calif. (47)	225-5611	206
Coyne, William J., D-Pa. (14)	225-2301	2455
Cramer, Robert E. "Bud," D-Ala. (5)	225-4801	1318
Crane, Philip M., R-Ill. (8)	225-3711	233
Crapo, Michael D., R-Idaho (2)	225-5531	437
Cunningham, Randy "Duke," R-Calif. (51)	225-5452	117
Danner, Pat, D-Mo. (6)	225-7041	1217
Darden, George "Buddy," D-Ga. (7)	225-2931	2303
de la Garza, E. "Kika," D-Texas (15)	225-2531	1401
de Lugo, Ron, D-Virgin Islands (AL)	225-1790	2427
Deal, Nathan, D-Ga. (9)	225-5211	1406
DeFazio, Peter A., D-Ore. (4)	225-6416	1233
DeLauro, Rosa, D-Conn. (3)	225-3661	327
DeLay, Tom, R-Texas (22)	225-5951	407
Dellums, Ronald V., D-Calif. (9)	225-2661	2108
Derrick, Butler, D-S.C. (3)	225-5301	221
Deutsch, Peter, D-Fla. (20)	225-7931	425
Diaz-Balart, Lincoln, R-Fla. (21)	225-4211	509
Dickey, Jay, R-Ark. (4)	225-3772	1338
Dicks, Norm, D-Wash. (6)	225-5916	2467
Dingell, John D., D-Mich. (16)	225-4071	2328
Dixon, Julian C., D-Calif. (32)	225-7084	2400
Dooley, Cal, D-Calif. (20)	225-3341	1227

Name, Party, State (District)	Phone	Room
Doolittle, John T., R-Calif. (4)	(202) 225-2511	1524
Dornan, Robert K., R-Calif. (46)	225-2965	2402
Dreier, David, R-Calif. (28)	225-2305	411
Duncan, John J. "Jimmy" Jr., R-Tenn. (2)	225-5435	115
Dunn, Jennifer, R-Wash. (8)	225-7761	1641
Durbin, Richard J., D-Ill. (20)	225-5271	2463
Edwards, Chet, D-Texas (11)	225-6105	328
Edwards, Don, D-Calif. (16)	225-3072	2307
Emerson, Bill, R-Mo. (8)	225-4404	2454
Engel, Eliot L., D-N.Y. (17)	225-2464	1433
English, Glenn, D-Okla. (6)	225-5565	2206
English, Karan, D-Ariz. (6)	225-2190	1024
Eshoo, Anna G., D-Calif. (14)	225-8104	1505
Evans, Lane, D-Ill. (17)	225-5905	2335
Everett, Terry, R-Ala. (2)	225-2901	208
Ewing, Thomas W., R-Ill. (15)	225-2371	1317
Faleomavaega, Eni F. H., D-Am. Samoa (AL)	225-8577	109
Farr, Sam, D-Calif. (17)	225-2861	1216
Fawell, Harris W., R-Ill. (13)	225-3515	2342
Fazio, Vic, D-Calif. (3)	225-5716	2113
Fields, Cleo, D-La. (4)	225-8490	513
Fields, Jack, R-Texas (8)	225-4901	2228
Filner, Bob, D-Calif. (50)	225-8045	504
Fingerhut, Eric D., D-Ohio (19)	225-5731	431
Fish, Hamilton Jr., R-N.Y. (19)	225-5441	2354
Flake, Floyd H., D-N.Y. (6)	225-3461	1035
Foglietta, Thomas M., D-Pa. (1)	225-4731	341
Foley, Thomas S., D-Wash. (5)	225-2006	1201
Ford, Harold E., D-Tenn. (9)	225-3265	2211
Ford, William D., D-Mich. (13)	225-6261	2107
Fowler, Tillie, R-Fla. (4)	225-2501	413
Frank, Barney, D-Mass. (4)	225-5931	2404
Franks, Bob, R-N.J. (7)	225-5361	429
Franks, Gary A., R-Conn. (5)	225-3822	435
Frost, Martin, D-Texas (24)	225-3605	2459
Furse, Elizabeth, D-Ore. (1)	225-0855	316
Gallegly, Elton, R-Calif. (23)	225-5811	2441
Gallo, Dean A., R-N.J. (11)	225-5034	2447
Gejdenson, Sam, D-Conn. (2)	225-2076	2416
Gekas, George W., R-Pa. (17)	225-4315	2410
Gephardt, Richard A., D-Mo. (3)	225-2671	1432
Geren, Pete, D-Texas (12)	225-5071	1730
Gibbons, Sam M., D-Fla. (11)	225-3376	2204
Gilchrest, Wayne T., R-Md. (1)	225-5311	412
Gillmor, Paul E., R-Ohio (5)	225-6405	1203
Gilman, Benjamin A., R-N.Y. (20)	225-3776	2185
Gingrich, Newt, R-Ga. (6)	225-4501	2428
Glickman, Dan, D-Kan. (4)	225-6216	2371
Gonzalez, Henry B., D-Texas (20)	225-3236	2413
Goodlatte, Robert W., R-Va. (6)	225-5431	214
Goodling, Bill, R-Pa. (19)	225-5836	2263
Gordon, Bart, D-Tenn. (6)	225-4231	103
Goss, Porter J., R-Fla. (14)	225-2536	330
Grams, Rod, R-Minn. (6)	225-2271	1713
Grandy, Fred, R-Iowa (5)	225-5476	418
Green, Gene, D-Texas (29)	225-1688	1004
Greenwood, James C., R-Pa. (8)	225-4276	515
Gunderson, Steve, R-Wis. (3)	225-5506	2235
Gutierrez, Luis V., D-Ill. (4)	225-8203	1208
Hall, Ralph M., D-Texas (4)	225-6673	2236
Hall, Tony P., D-Ohio (3)	225-6465	2264
Hamburg, Dan, D-Calif. (1)	225-3311	114
Hamilton, Lee H., D-Ind. (9)	225-5315	2187
Hancock, Mel, R-Mo. (7)	225-6536	129

Name, Party, State (District)	Phone	Room
Hansen, James V., R-Utah (1)	(202) 225-0453	2466
Harman, Jane, D-Calif. (36)	225-8220	325
Hastert, Dennis, R-Ill. (14)	225-2976	2453
Hastings, Alcee L., D-Fla. (23)	225-1313	1039
Hayes, Jimmy, D-La. (7)	225-2031	2432
Hefley, Joel, R-Colo. (5)	225-4422	2442
Hefner, W. G. "Bill," D-N.C. (8)	225-3715	2470
Herger, Wally, R-Calif. (2)	225-3076	2433
Hilliard, Earl F., D-Ala. (7)	225-2665	1007
Hinchey, Maurice D., D-N.Y. (26)	225-6335	1313
Hoagland, Peter, D-Neb. (2)	225-4155	1113
Hobson, David L., R-Ohio (7)	225-4324	1507
Hochbrueckner, George J., D-N.Y. (1)	225-3826	229
Hoekstra, Peter, R-Mich. (2)	225-4401	1319
Hoke, Martin R., R-Ohio (10)	225-5871	212
Holden, Tim, D-Pa. (6)	225-5546	1421
Horn, Steve, R-Calif. (38)	225-6676	1023
Houghton, Amo, R-N.Y. (31)	225-3161	1110
Hoyer, Steny H., D-Md. (5)	225-4131	1705
Huffington, Michael, R-Calif. (22)	225-3601	113
Hughes, William J., D-N.J. (2)	225-6572	241
Hunter, Duncan, R-Calif. (52)	225-5672	133
Hutchinson, Tim, R-Ark. (3)	225-4301	1541
Hutto, Earl, D-Fla. (1)	225-4136	2435
Hyde, Henry J., R-Ill. (6)	225-4561	2110
Inglis, Bob, R-S.C. (4)	225-6030	1237
Inhofe, James M., R-Okla. (1)	225-2211	442
Inslee, Jay, D-Wash. (4)	225-5816	1431
Istook, Ernest Jim Jr., R-Okla. (5)	225-2132	1116
Jacobs, Andrew Jr., D-Ind. (10)	225-4011	2313
Jefferson, William J., D-La. (2)	225-6636	428
Johnson, Don, D-Ga. (10)	225-4101	226
Johnson, Eddie Bernice, D-Texas (30)	225-8885	1721
Johnson, Nancy L., R-Conn. (6)	225-4476	343
Johnson, Sam, R-Texas (3)	225-4201	1030
Johnson, Tim, D-S.D. (AL)	225-2801	2438
Johnston, Harry A., D-Fla. (19)	225-3001	204
Kanjorski, Paul E., D-Pa. (11)	225-6511	2429
Kaptur, Marcy, D-Ohio (9)	225-4146	2104
Kasich, John R., R-Ohio (12)	225-5355	1131
Kennedy, Joseph P. II, D-Mass. (8)	225-5111	1210
Kennelly, Barbara B., D-Conn. (1)	225-2265	201
Kildee, Dale E., D-Mich. (9)	225-3611	2239
Kim, Jay C., R-Calif. (41)	225-3201	502
King, Peter T., R-N.Y. (3)	225-7896	118
Kingston, Jack, R-Ga. (1)	225-5831	1229
Kleczka, Gerald D., D-Wis. (4)	225-4572	2301
Klein, Herb, D-N.J. (8)	225-5751	1728
Klink, Ron, D-Pa. (4)	225-2565	1130
Klug, Scott L., R-Wis. (2)	225-2906	1224
Knollenberg, Joe, R-Mich. (11)	225-5802	1218
Kolbe, Jim, R-Ariz. (5)	225-2542	405
Kopetski, Mike, D-Ore. (5)	225-5711	218
Kreidler, Mike, D-Wash. (9)	225-8901	1535
Kyl, Jon, R-Ariz. (4)	225-3361	2440
LaFalce, John J., D-N.Y. (29)	225-3231	2310
Lambert, Blanche, D-Ark. (1)	225-4076	1204
Lancaster, H. Martin, D-N.C. (3)	225-3415	2436
Lantos, Tom, D-Calif. (12)	225-3531	2182
LaRocco, Larry, D-Idaho (1)	225-6611	1117
Laughlin, Greg, D-Texas (14)	225-2831	236
Lazio, Rick A., R-N.Y. (2)	225-3335	314
Leach, Jim, R-Iowa (1)	225-6576	2186
Lehman, Richard H., D-Calif. (19)	225-4540	1226

Name, Party, State (District)	Phone	Room
Levin, Sander M., D-Mich. (12)	(202) 225-4961	106
Levy, David A., R-N.Y. (4)	225-5516	116
Lewis, Jerry, R-Calif. (40)	225-5861	2312
Lewis, John, D-Ga. (5)	225-3801	329
Lewis, Tom, R-Fla. (16)	225-5792	2351
Lightfoot, Jim Ross, R-Iowa (3)	225-3806	2444
Linder, John, R-Ga. (4)	225-4272	1605
Lipinski, William O., D-Ill. (3)	225-5701	1501
Livingston, Robert L., R-La. (1)	225-3015	2368
Lloyd, Marilyn, D-Tenn. (3)	225-3271	2406
Long, Jill L., D-Ind. (4)	225-4436	1513
Lowey, Nita M., D-N.Y. (18)	225-6506	1424
Machtley, Ronald K., R-R.I. (1)	225-4911	326
Maloney, Carolyn B., D-N.Y. (14)	225-7944	1504
Mann, David, D-Ohio (1)	225-2216	503
Manton, Thomas J., D-N.Y. (7)	225-3965	203
Manzullo, Donald, R-Ill. (16)	225-5676	506
Margolies-Mezvinsky, Marjorie, D-Pa. (13)	225-6111	1516
Markey, Edward J., D-Mass. (7)	225-2836	2133
Martinez, Matthew G., D-Calif. (31)	225-5464	2231
Matsui, Robert T., D-Calif. (5)	225-7163	2311
Mazzoli, Romano L., D-Ky. (3)	225-5401	2246
McCandless, Al, R-Calif. (44)	225-5330	2422
McCloskey, Frank, D-Ind. (8)	225-4636	306
McCollum, Bill, R-Fla. (8)	225-2176	2266
McCrery, Jim, R-La. (5)	225-2777	225
McCurdy, Dave, D-Okla. (4)	225-6165	2344
McDade, Joseph M., R-Pa. (10)	225-3731	2370
McDermott, Jim, D-Wash. (7)	225-3106	1707
McHale, Paul, D-Pa. (15)	225-6411	511
McHugh, John M., R-N.Y. (24)	225-4611	416
McInnis, Scott, R-Colo. (3)	225-4761	512
McKeon, Howard P. "Buck," R-Calif. (25)	225-1956	307
McKinney, Cynthia A., D-Ga. (11)	225-1605	124
McMillan, Alex, R-N.C. (9)	225-1976	401
McNulty, Michael R., D-N.Y. (21)	225-5076	217
Meehan, Martin T., D-Mass. (5)	225-3411	1223
Meek, Carrie P., D-Fla. (17)	225-4506	404
Menendez, Robert, D-N.J. (13)	225-7919	1531
Meyers, Jan, R-Kan. (3)	225-2865	2338
Mfume, Kweisi, D-Md. (7)	225-4741	2419
Mica, John L., R-Fla. (7)	225-4035	427
Michel, Robert H., R-Ill. (18)	225-6201	2112
Miller, Dan, R-Fla. (13)	225-5015	510
Miller, George, D-Calif. (7)	225-2095	2205
Mineta, Norman Y., D-Calif. (15)	225-2631	2221
Minge, David, D-Minn. (2)	225-2331	1508
Mink, Patsy T., D-Hawaii (2)	225-4906	2135
Moakley, Joe, D-Mass. (9)	225-8273	235
Molinari, Susan, R-N.Y. (13)	225-3371	123
Mollohan, Alan B., D-W.Va. (1)	225-4172	2242
Montgomery, G. V. "Sonny," D-Miss. (3)	225-5031	2184
Moorhead, Carlos J., R-Calif. (27)	225-4176	2346
Moran, James P. Jr., D-Va. (8)	225-4376	430
Morella, Constance A., R-Md. (8)	225-5341	223
Murphy, Austin J., D-Pa. (20)	225-4665	2210
Murtha, John P., D-Pa. (12)	225-2065	2423
Myers, John T., R-Ind. (7)	225-5805	2372
Nadler, Jerrold, D-N.Y. (8)	225-5635	424
Natcher, William H., D-Ky. (2)	225-3501	2333
Neal, Richard E., D-Mass. (2)	225-5601	131
Neal, Stephen L., D-N.C. (5)	225-2071	2469
Norton, Eleanor Holmes, D-D.C. (AL)	225-8050	1415
Nussle, Jim, R-Iowa (2)	225-2911	308

Name, Party, State (District)	Phone	Room
Oberstar, James L., D-Minn. (8)	(202) 225-6211	2366
Obey, David R., D-Wis. (7)	225-3365	2462
Olver, John W., D-Mass. (1)	225-5335	1323
Ortiz, Solomon P., D-Texas (27)	225-7742	2136
Orton, Bill, D-Utah (3)	225-7751	1122
Owens, Major R., D-N.Y. (11)	225-6231	2305
Oxley, Michael G., R-Ohio (4)	225-2676	2233
Packard, Ron, R-Calif. (48)	225-3906	2162
Pallone, Frank Jr., D-N.J. (6)	225-4671	420
Parker, Mike, D-Miss. (4)	225-5865	1410
Pastor, Ed, D-Ariz. (2)	225-4065	408
Paxon, Bill, R-N.Y. (27)	225-5265	1314
Payne, Donald M., D-N.J. (10)	225-3436	417
Payne, Lewis F. Jr., D-Va. (5)	225-4711	1119
Pelosi, Nancy, D-Calif. (8)	225-4965	240
Penny, Timothy J., D-Minn. (1)	225-2472	436
Peterson, Collin C., D-Minn. (7)	225-2165	1133
Peterson, Pete, D-Fla. (2)	225-5235	426
Petri, Tom, R-Wis. (6)	225-2476	2262
Pickett, Owen B., D-Va. (2)	225-4215	2430
Pickle, J. J., D-Texas (10)	225-4865	242
Pombo, Richard W., R-Calif. (11)	225-1947	1519
Pomeroy, Earl, D-N.D. (AL)	225-2611	318
Porter, John Edward, R-Ill. (10)	225-4835	1026
Portman, Rob, R-Ohio (2)	225-3164	238
Poshard, Glenn, D-Ill. (19)	225-5201	107
Price, David, D-N.C. (4)	225-1784	2458
Pryce, Deborah, R-Ohio (15)	225-2015	128
Quillen, James H., R-Tenn. (1)	225-6356	102
Quinn, Jack, R-N.Y. (30)	225-3306	331
Rahall, Nick J. II, D-W.Va. (3)	225-3452	2269
Ramstad, Jim, R-Minn. (3)	225-2871	322
Rangel, Charles B., D-N.Y. (15)	225-4365	2252
Ravenel, Arthur Jr., R-S.C. (1)	225-3176	231
Reed, Jack, D-R.I. (2)	225-2735	1510
Regula, Ralph, R-Ohio (16)	225-3876	2309
Reynolds, Mel, D-Ill. (2)	225-0773	514
Richardson, Bill, D-N.M. (3)	225-6190	2349
Ridge, Tom, R-Pa. (21)	225-5406	1714
Roberts, Pat, R-Kan. (1)	225-2715	1126
Roemer, Tim, D-Ind. (3)	225-3915	415
Rogers, Harold, R-Ky. (5)	225-4601	2468
Rohrabacher, Dana, R-Calif. (45)	225-2415	1027
Romero-Barceló, Carlos, D/NPP-P.R. (AL)	225-2615	1517
Ros-Lehtinen, Ileana, R-Fla. (18)	225-3931	127
Rose, Charlie, D-N.C. (7)	225-2731	2230
Rostenkowski, Dan, D-Ill. (5)	225-4061	2111
Roth, Toby, R-Wis. (8)	225-5665	2234
Roukema, Marge, R-N.J. (5)	225-4465	2244
Rowland, J. Roy, D-Ga. (8)	225-6531	2134
Roybal-Allard, Lucille, D-Calif. (33)	225-1766	324
Royce, Ed, R-Calif. (39)	225-4111	1404
Rush, Bobby L., D-Ill. (1)	225-4372	1725
Sabo, Martin Olav, D-Minn. (5)	225-4755	2336
Sanders, Bernard, I-Vt. (AL)	225-4115	213
Sangmeister, George E., D-Ill. (11)	225-3635	1032
Santorum, Rick, R-Pa. (18)	225-2135	1222
Sarpalius, Bill, D-Texas (13)	225-3706	126
Sawyer, Tom, D-Ohio (14)	225-5231	1414
Saxton, H. James, R-N.J. (3)	225-4765	438
Schaefer, Dan, R-Colo. (6)	225-7882	2448
Schenk, Lynn, D-Calif. (49)	225-2040	315
Schiff, Steven H., R-N.M. (1)	225-6316	1009
Schroeder, Patricia, D-Colo. (1)	225-4431	2208

Name, Party, State (District)	Phone	Room
Schumer, Charles E., D-N.Y. (9)	(202) 225-6616	2412
Scott, Robert C., D-Va. (3)	225-8351	501
Sensenbrenner, F. James Jr., R-Wis. (9)	225-5101	2332
Serrano, Jose E., D-N.Y. (16)	225-4361	336
Sharp, Philip R., D-Ind. (2)	225-3021	2217
Shaw, E. Clay Jr., R-Fla. (22)	225-3026	2267
Shays, Christopher, R-Conn. (4)	225-5541	1034
Shepherd, Karen, D-Utah (2)	225-3011	414
Shuster, Bud, R-Pa. (9)	225-2431	2188
Sisisky, Norman, D-Va. (4)	225-6365	2352
Skaggs, David E., D-Colo. (2)	225-2161	1124
Skeen, Joe, R-N.M. (2)	225-2365	2367
Skelton, Ike, D-Mo. (4)	225-2876	2227
Slattery, Jim, D-Kan. (2)	225-6601	2243
Slaughter, Louise M., D-N.Y. (28)	225-3615	2421
Smith, Bob, R-Ore. (2)	225-6730	108
Smith, Christopher H., R-N.J. (4)	225-3765	2353
Smith, Lamar, R-Texas (21)	225-4236	2443
Smith, Neal, D-Iowa (4)	225-4426	2373
Smith, Nick, R-Mich. (7)	225-6276	1708
Snowe, Olympia J., R-Maine (2)	225-6306	2268
Solomon, Gerald B. H., R-N.Y. (22)	225-5614	2265
Spence, Floyd D., R-S.C. (2)	225-2452	2405
Spratt, John M. Jr., D-S.C. (5)	225-5501	1536
Stark, Pete, D-Calif. (13)	225-5065	239
Stearns, Cliff, R-Fla. (6)	225-5744	332
Stenholm, Charles W., D-Texas (17)	225-6605	1211
Stokes, Louis, D-Ohio (11)	225-7032	2365
Strickland, Ted, D-Ohio (6)	225-5705	1429
Studds, Gerry E., D-Mass. (10)	225-3111	237
Stump, Bob, R-Ariz. (3)	225-4576	211
Stupak, Bart, D-Mich. (1)	225-4735	317
Sundquist, Don, R-Tenn. (7)	225-2811	339
Swett, Dick, D-N.H. (2)	225-5206	230
Swift, Al, D-Wash. (2)	225-2605	1502
Synar, Mike, D-Okla. (2)	225-2701	2329
Talent, James M., R-Mo. (2)	225-2561	1022
Tanner, John, D-Tenn. (8)	225-4714	1427
Tauzin, W. J. "Billy," D-La. (3)	225-4031	2330
Taylor, Charles H., R-N.C. (11)	225-6401	516
Taylor, Gene, D-Miss. (5)	225-5772	215
Tejeda, Frank, D-Texas (28)	225-1640	323

Name, Party, State (District)	Phone	Room
Thomas, Bill, R-Calif. (21)	(202) 225-2915	2209
Thomas, Craig, R-Wyo. (AL)	225-2311	1019
Thompson, Bennie, D-Miss. (2)	225-5876	1408
Thornton, Ray, D-Ark. (2)	225-2506	1214
Thurman, Karen L., D-Fla. (5)	225-1002	130
Torkildsen, Peter G., R-Mass. (6)	225-8020	120
Torres, Esteban E., D-Calif. (34)	225-5256	1740
Torricelli, Robert G., D-N.J. (9)	225-5061	2159
Towns, Edolphus, D-N.Y. (10)	225-5936	2232
Traficant, James A. Jr., D-Ohio (17)	225-5261	2446
Tucker, Walter R. III, D-Calif. (37)	225-7924	419
Underwood, Robert, D-Guam (AL)	225-1188	507
Unsoeld, Jolene, D-Wash. (3)	225-3536	1527
Upton, Fred, R-Mich. (6)	225-3761	2439
Valentine, Tim, D-N.C. (2)	225-4531	2229
Velázquez, Nydia M., D-N.Y. (12)	225-2361	132
Vento, Bruce F., D-Minn. (4)	225-6631	2304
Visclosky, Peter J., D-Ind. (1)	225-2461	2464
Volkmer, Harold L., D-Mo. (9)	225-2956	2409
Vucanovich, Barbara F., R-Nev. (2)	225-6155	2202
Walker, Robert S., R-Pa. (16)	225-2411	2369
Walsh, James T., R-N.Y. (25)	225-3701	1330
Washington, Craig, D-Texas (18)	225-3816	1711
Waters, Maxine, D-Calif. (35)	225-2201	1207
Watt, Melvin, D-N.C. (12)	225-1510	1232
Waxman, Henry A., D-Calif. (29)	225-3976	2408
Weldon, Curt, R-Pa. (7)	225-2011	2452
Wheat, Alan, D-Mo. (5)	225-4535	2334
Whitten, Jamie L., D-Miss. (1)	225-4306	2314
Williams, Pat, D-Mont. (AL)	225-3211	2457
Wilson, Charles, D-Texas (2)	225-2401	2256
Wise, Bob, D-W.Va. (2)	225-2711	2434
Wolf, Frank R., R-Va. (10)	225-5136	104
Woolsey, Lynn, D-Calif. (6)	225-5161	439
Wyden, Ron, D-Ore. (3)	225-4811	1111
Wynn, Albert R., D-Md. (4)	225-8699	423
Yates, Sidney R., D-Ill. (9)	225-2111	2109
Young, C. W. Bill, R-Fla. (10)	225-5961	2407
Young, Don, R-Alaska (AL)	225-5765	2331
Zeliff, Bill, R-N.H. (1)	225-5456	224
Zimmer, Dick, R-N.J. (12)	225-5801	228

CAPITOL HILL

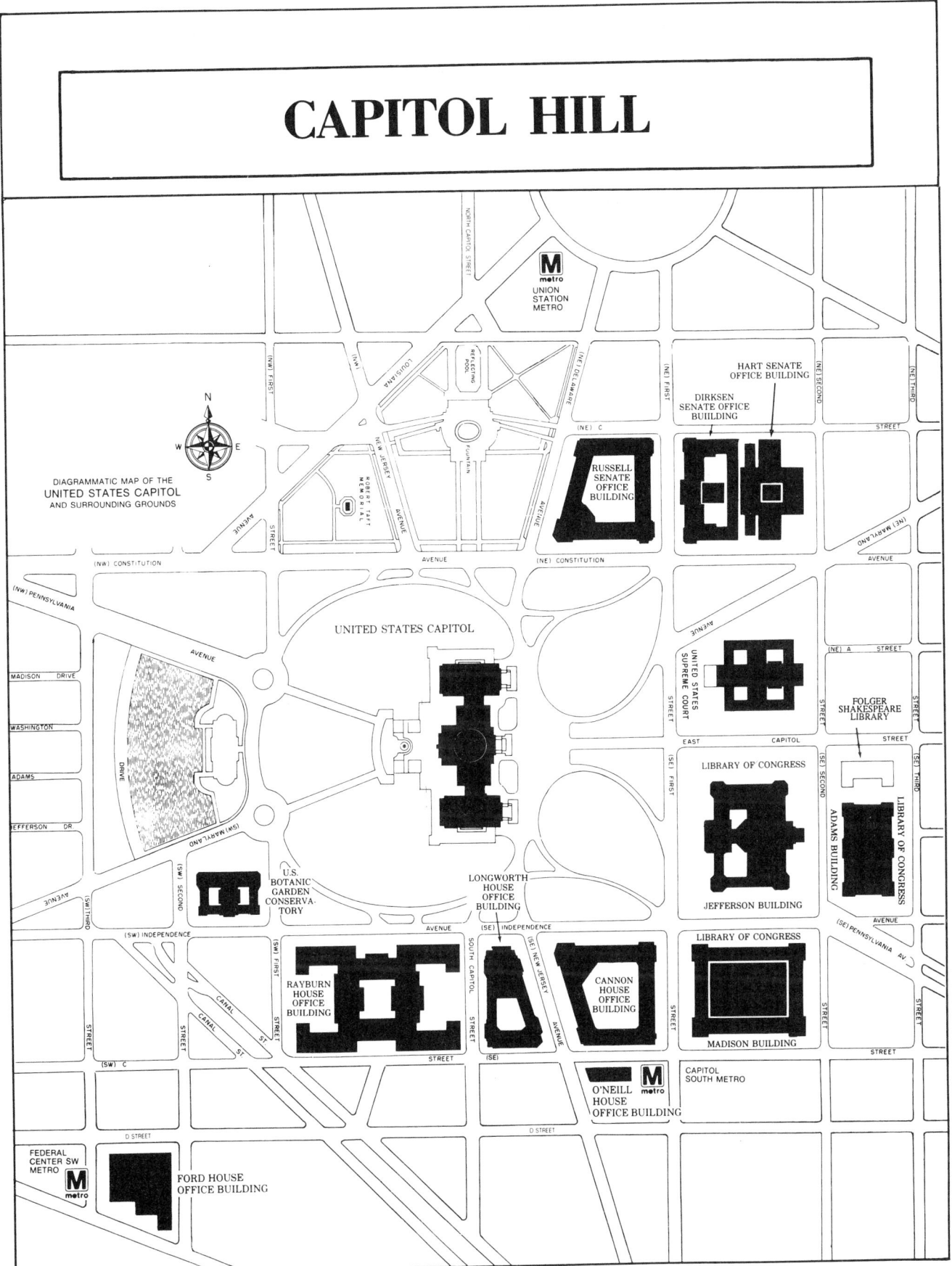

DIAGRAMMATIC MAP OF THE
UNITED STATES CAPITOL
AND SURROUNDING GROUNDS

UNION STATION METRO

HART SENATE OFFICE BUILDING

DIRKSEN SENATE OFFICE BUIILDING

RUSSELL SENATE OFFICE BUILDING

UNITED STATES SUPREME COURT

FOLGER SHAKESPEARE LIBRARY

LIBRARY OF CONGRESS

ADAMS BUILDING

LIBRARY OF CONGRESS

JEFFERSON BUILDING

UNITED STATES CAPITOL

U.S. BOTANIC GARDEN CONSERVATORY

LONGWORTH HOUSE OFFICE BUILDING

RAYBURN HOUSE OFFICE BUILDING

CANNON HOUSE OFFICE BUILDING

LIBRARY OF CONGRESS

MADISON BUILDING

O'NEILL HOUSE OFFICE BUILDING

CAPITOL SOUTH METRO

FEDERAL CENTER SW METRO

FORD HOUSE OFFICE BUILDING

ROBERT A TAFT MEMORIAL

REFLECTING POOL

FOUNTAIN

The Legislative Process in Brief

(Parliamentary terms used below are defined in the glossary, p. 73-B.)

Introduction of Bills

A House member (including the resident commissioner of Puerto Rico and non-voting delegates of the District of Columbia, Guam, the Virgin Islands and American Samoa) may introduce any one of several types of bills and resolutions by handing it to the clerk of the House or placing it in a box called the hopper.

A senator first gains recognition of the presiding officer to announce the introduction of a bill. If objection is offered by any senator, the introduction of the bill is postponed until the following day.

As the next step in either the House or Senate, the bill is numbered, referred to committee, labeled with the sponsor's name and sent to the Government Printing Office so that copies can be made for subsequent study and action. Senate bills may be jointly sponsored and carry several senators' names.

Until 1978, the House limited the number of members who could cosponsor any one bill; the ceiling was eliminated at the beginning of the 96th Congress.

A bill written in the executive branch and proposed as an administration measure usually is introduced by the chairman of the congressional committee that has jurisdiction over the subject.

Bills—Prefixed with HR in the House, S in the Senate, followed by a number. Used as the form for most legislation, whether general or special, public or private.

Joint Resolutions—Designated H J Res or S J Res. Subject to the same procedure as bills, with the exception of a joint resolution proposing an amendment to the Constitution. The latter must be approved by two-thirds of both houses and is thereupon sent directly to the administrator of general services for submission to the states for ratification instead of being presented to the president for his approval.

Concurrent Resolutions—Designated H Con Res or S Con Res. Used for matters affecting the operations of both houses. These resolutions do not become law.

Resolutions—Designated H Res or S Res. Used for a matter concerning the operation of either house alone and adopted only by the chamber in which it originates.

Committee Action

With few exceptions, bills are referred to the appropriate standing committees. The job of referral formally is the responsibility of the Speaker of the House and the presiding officer of the Senate, but this task usually is carried out on their behalf by the parliamentarians of the House and Senate.

Precedent, statute and the jurisdictional mandates of the committees as set forth in the rules of the House and Senate determine which committees receive what kinds of bills. An exception is the referral of private bills, which are sent to whatever committee is designated by their sponsors. Bills are technically considered "read for the first time" when referred to House committees.

When a bill reaches a committee, it is placed on the committee's calendar. At that time the bill comes under the sharpest congressional focus. Its chances for passage are quickly determined; the great majority of bills fall by the legislative roadside.

Failure of a committee to act on a bill is equivalent to killing it; the measure can be withdrawn from the committee's purview only by a discharge petition signed by a majority of the House membership on House bills or by adoption of a special resolution in the Senate. Discharge attempts rarely succeed.

The first committee action taken on a bill usually is a request for comment on it by interested government agencies. The committee chairman may assign the bill to a subcommittee for study and hearings, or it may be considered by the full committee. Hearings may be public, closed (executive session) or both. After considering a bill, a subcommittee reports to the full committee its recommendations for action and any proposed amendments.

The full committee then votes on its recommendation to the House or Senate. This procedure is called "ordering a bill reported."

Occasionally a committee may order a bill reported unfavorably; most of the time a report, submitted by the committee chairman to the House or Senate, calls for favorable action on the measure since the committee can effectively "kill" a bill by simply not taking any action.

After the bill is reported, the committee chairman instructs the staff to prepare a written report. The report describes the bill's purposes and scope, explains the committee revisions, notes proposed changes in existing law and, usually, includes the views of the executive branch agencies consulted. Often committee members opposing a bill include dissenting views in the report.

Usually, the committee "marks up" or proposes amendments to the bill. If they are substantial and the measure is complicated, the committee may order a "clean bill" introduced, which will embody the proposed amendments. The original bill then is put aside and the clean bill, with a new number, is reported to the floor.

The chamber must approve, alter or reject the committee amendments before the bill itself can be put to a vote.

Floor Action

After a bill is reported back to the house where it originated, it is placed on the calendar.

Debate. A bill is brought to debate by varying procedures. If it is a routine measure, it may await the call of the calendar. If it is urgent or important, it can be taken up in

the Senate either by unanimous consent or by a majority vote. The majority leader, in consultation with the minority leader and others, schedules the bills that will be taken up for debate.

In the House, precedence is granted if a special rule is obtained from the Rules Committee. A request for a special rule usually is made by the chairman of the committee that favorably reported the bill, supported by the bill's sponsor and other committee members. The request, considered by the Rules Committee in the same way that other committees consider legislative measures, is in the form of a resolution providing for immediate consideration of the bill.

The Rules Committee reports the resolution to the House, where it is debated and voted upon in the same fashion as regular bills. If the Rules Committee should fail to report a rule requested by a committee, there are several ways to bring the bill to the House floor — under suspension of the rules, on Calendar Wednesday or by a discharge motion.

The resolutions providing special rules are important because they specify how long the bill may be debated and whether it may be amended from the floor. If floor amendments are banned, the bill is considered under a "closed rule," which usually allows only changes proposed by the committee that first reported the measure to the House, subject to chamber acceptance.

When a bill is debated under an "open rule," amendments may be offered from the floor. Committee amendments always are taken up first but may be changed, like all amendments up to the second degree; that is, an amendment to an amendment to an amendment is not in order.

Duration of debate in the House depends on whether the bill is under discussion by the House proper or before the House when it is sitting as the Committee of the Whole House on the State of the Union.

In the House, the amount of time for debate either is determined by special rule or is allocated with an hour for each member if the measure is under consideration without a rule.

In the Committee of the Whole, the amount of time agreed on for general debate is equally divided between proponents and opponents. At the end of general discussion, the bill is read section by section for amendment. Debate on an amendment is limited to five minutes for each side; this is called the "five-minute rule." In practice, amendments regularly are debated more than 10 minutes, with members gaining the floor by offering pro forma amendments or obtaining unanimous consent to speak longer than five minutes.

Senate debate usually is unlimited. It can be halted only by unanimous consent or by "cloture," which requires a three-fifths majority of the entire Senate or, in the case of a proposed change in the Senate rules, a two-thirds vote.

The House considers almost all important bills within a parliamentary framework known as the Committee of the Whole. It is not a committee as the word usually is understood; it is the full House meeting under another name for the purpose of speeding action on legislation.

Technically, the House sits as the Committee of the Whole when it considers any tax measure or bill dealing with public appropriations. It also can resolve itself into the Committee of the Whole if a member moves to do so and the motion is carried. The Speaker appoints a member to serve as the chairman.

The rules of the House permit the Committee of the Whole to meet when a quorum of 100 members is present on the floor and to amend and act on bills, within certain time limitations. When the Committee of the Whole has acted, it "rises," the Speaker returns as the presiding officer of the House and the member appointed chairman of the Committee of the Whole reports the action of the committee and its recommendations.

The Committee of the Whole cannot pass a bill; it reports the measure to the full House with whatever changes it has approved. The full House then may pass or reject the bill — or, on occasion, recommit the bill to committee. Amendments adopted in the Committee of the Whole may be put to a second vote in the full House.

Beginning in the 103rd Congress, the delegates from the territories, the District of Columbia and the resident commissioner of Puerto Rico are allowed to vote in the Committee of the Whole. But any question decided by their votes must be re-voted by the House, without their participation.

Votes. Voting on bills may occur repeatedly before they are finally approved or rejected. The House votes on the rule for the bill and on various amendments to the bill. Voting on amendments often is a more illuminating test of a bill's support than is the final tally. Sometimes members approve final passage of bills after vigorously supporting amendments that, if adopted, would scuttle the legislation.

The Senate has three different methods of voting: an untabulated voice vote, a standing vote (called a division) and a recorded roll call to which members answer "yea" or "nay" when their names are called.

The House also employs voice and standing votes, but since January 1973 yeas and nays have been recorded by an electronic voting device, eliminating the need for time-consuming roll calls.

Since 1971, one-fifth of a quorum can demand that the votes of individual members be recorded, thereby forcing them to take a public position on amendments to key bills.

After amendments to a bill have been voted upon, a vote may be taken on a motion to recommit the bill to committee. If carried, this vote removes the bill from the chamber's calendar and is usually a death blow to the bill — unless the motion carries specific instructions on how to change the bill; in that case, the bill is usually re-reported immediately with the instructed changes. If the motion is unsuccessful, the bill then is "read for the third time." An actual reading usually is dispensed with. Until 1965, an opponent of a bill could delay this move by objecting and asking for a full reading of an engrossed (certified in final form) copy of the bill. After the "third reading," the vote on final passage is taken.

The final vote may be followed by a motion to reconsider, and this motion may be followed by a move to lay the motion on the table. Usually, those voting for the bill's passage vote for the tabling motion, thus safeguarding the final passage action. With that, the bill has been formally passed by the chamber. While a motion to reconsider a Senate vote is pending on a bill, the measure cannot be sent to the House.

Action in Second House

After a bill is passed, it is sent to the other chamber. This body may then take one of several steps. It may pass

the bill as is — accepting the other chamber's language. It may send the bill to committee for scrutiny or alteration, or reject the entire bill, advising the other house of its actions. Or it simply may ignore the bill submitted while it continues work on its own version of the proposed legislation. Frequently, one chamber may approve a version of a bill that is greatly at variance with the version passed by the other house, and then substitute its contents for the language of the other, retaining only the latter's bill number.

A provision of the Legislative Reorganization Act of 1970 permits a separate House vote on any non-germane amendment added by the Senate to a House-passed bill and requires a majority vote to retain the amendment. Previously, the House was forced to act on the bill as a whole; the only way to defeat the non-germane amendment was to reject the entire bill.

Often, the second chamber makes only minor changes. If these are readily agreed to by the other house, the bill then is sent to the president.

If the opposite chamber significantly alters the bill submitted to it, however, the measure usually is "sent to conference." The chamber that has possession of the "papers" (engrossed bill, engrossed amendments, messages of transmittal) requests a conference and the other chamber must agree to it. If the second house does not agree, the bill dies.

Conference, Final Action

Conference. A conference reconciles the differences between House and Senate versions of a legislative bill. The conferees usually are senior members appointed by the presiding officers of the two houses, from the committees that managed the bills. Under this arrangement the conferees of one house have the duty of trying to maintain their chamber's position in the face of amending actions by the conferees (also referred to as "managers") of the other house.

The number of conferees from each chamber varies, depending upon the length or complexity of the bill involved. A majority vote controls the action of each group; a large representation does not give one chamber a voting advantage over the other.

Theoretically, conferees are not allowed to write new legislation in reconciling the two versions before them, but this curb sometimes is bypassed. Many bills have been put into acceptable compromise form only after new language was provided by the conferees.

The 1970 Reorganization Act attempted to tighten restrictions on conferees by forbidding them to introduce any language on a topic that neither chamber sent to conference or to modify any topic beyond the scope of the differing versions of the bill.

Frequently, the ironing out of difficulties takes days or even weeks. As a conference proceeds, conferees reconcile differences between the versions. Generally, they grant concessions only insofar as they are sure that the chamber they represent will accept the compromises.

Occasionally, uncertainty over how either house will react, or the refusal of a chamber to back down on a disputed amendment, results in an impasse, and the bills die in conference even though each was approved by its sponsoring chamber.

Conferees may go back to their respective chambers for further instructions, when they report certain portions in disagreement. Then the chamber concerned can either "recede and concur" in the amendment of the other house or "insist on its amendment."

When the conferees have reached agreement, they prepare a conference report embodying their recommendations. The report, in document form, must be submitted to each house.

The conference report must be adopted by each house; adoption of the report is approval of the compromise bill. The chamber which asked for a conference yields to the other chamber the opportunity to vote first.

Final Steps. After a bill has been passed by both the House and Senate in identical form, all of the original papers are sent to the enrolling clerk of the chamber in which the bill originated. He then prepares an enrolled bill, which is printed on parchment paper.

When this bill has been certified as correct by the secretary of the Senate or the clerk of the House, depending on which chamber originated the bill, it is signed first (no matter whether it originated in the Senate or House) by the Speaker of the House and then by the presiding officer of the Senate. It is next sent to the White House to await action.

If the president approves the bill, he signs it, dates it and usually writes the word "approved" on the document. If he does not sign it within 10 days (Sundays excepted) and Congress is in session, the bill becomes law without his signature. Should Congress adjourn before the 10 days expire, and the president fails to sign the measure, it does not become law. This procedure is called the pocket veto.

A president vetoes a bill by refusing to sign it and, before the 10-day period expires, returning it to Congress with a message stating his reasons. The message is sent to the chamber that originated the bill. If no action is taken on the message, the bill dies.

Congress, however, can attempt to override the veto and enact the bill, "the objections of the president to the contrary notwithstanding." Overriding a veto requires a two-thirds vote of those present, who must number a quorum and vote by roll call.

Debate can precede this vote, with motions permitted to lay the message on the table, postpone action on it or refer it to committee. If the president's veto is overridden in both houses, the bill becomes law. Otherwise, it is dead.

When bills are passed finally and signed, or passed over a veto, they are given law numbers in numerical order as they become law. There are two series of numbers, one for public and one for private laws, starting at the number "1" for each two-year term of Congress. They are then identified by law number and by Congress — for example, Private Law 21, 97th Congress; Public Law 250, 97th Congress (or PL 97-250). ∎

Glossary of Congressional Terms

Act — The term for legislation once it has passed both houses of Congress and has been signed by the president or passed over his veto, thus becoming law. *(See also Pocket Veto, Veto.)*

Also used in parliamentary terminology for a bill that has been passed by one house and engrossed. *(See also Engrossed Bill.)*

Adjournment Sine Die — Adjournment without definitely fixing a day for reconvening; literally, "adjournment without a day." Usually used to connote the final adjournment of a session of Congress. A session can continue until noon, Jan. 3, of the following year, when, under the 20th Amendment to the Constitution, it automatically terminates. Both houses must agree to a concurrent resolution for either house to adjourn for more than three days.

Adjournment to a Day Certain — Adjournment under a motion or resolution that fixes the next time of meeting. Under the Constitution, neither house can adjourn for more than three days without the concurrence of the other. A session of Congress is not ended by adjournment to a day certain.

Amendment — A proposal of a member of Congress to alter the language, provisions or stipulations in a bill or in another amendment. An amendment usually is printed, debated and voted upon in the same manner as a bill.

Amendment in the Nature of a Substitute — Usually an amendment that seeks to replace the entire text of a bill. Passage of this type of amendment strikes out everything after the enacting clause and inserts a new version of the bill. An amendment in the nature of a substitute also can refer to an amendment that replaces a large portion of the text of a bill.

Appeal — A member's challenge of a ruling or decision made by the presiding officer of the chamber. In the Senate, the senator appeals to members of the chamber to override the decision. If carried by a majority vote, the appeal nullifies the chair's ruling. In the House, the decision of the Speaker traditionally has been final; seldom are there appeals to the members to reverse the Speaker's stand. To appeal a ruling is considered an attack on the Speaker.

Appropriations Bill — A bill that gives legal authority to spend or obligate money from the Treasury. The Constitution disallows money to be drawn from the Treasury "but in Consequence of Appropriations made by Law."

By congressional custom, an appropriations bill originates in the House, and it is not supposed to be considered by the full House or Senate until a related measure authorizing the funding is enacted. An appropriations bill grants the actual budget authority approved by authorization bills, but not necessarily the full amount permissible under the authorization. For decades, appropriations often have not been final until well after the fiscal year begins, requiring a succession of stopgap bills to continue the government's functions. About half of all budget authority, notably that for Social Security and interest on the federal debt, does not require annual appropriations; those programs exist under permanent appropriations. *(See also Authorization Bill, Backdoor Spending Authority, Budget Authority, Budget Process, Continuing Resolution, Entitlement Program, Supplemental Appropriations Bill.)*

Authorization Bill — Basic, substantive legislation that establishes or continues the legal operation of a federal program or agency, either indefinitely or for a specific period of time, or which sanctions a particular type of obligation or expenditure. An authorization normally is a prerequisite for an appropriation or other kind of budget authority. Under the rules of both chambers, the appropriation for a program or agency may not be considered until its authorization has been considered (although this requirement is often waived). An authorization sets the maximum amount of funds that can be given to a program or agency, but sometimes it merely authorizes "such sums as may be necessary." *(See also Backdoor Spending Authority.)*

Backdoor Spending Authority — Budget authority provided in legislation outside the normal appropriations process. The most common forms of backdoor spending are borrowing authority, contract authority, entitlements and loan guarantees that commit the government to payments of principal and interest on loans — such as guaranteed student loans — made by banks or other private lenders. Loan guarantees result in actual outlays only when there is a default by the borrower.

In some cases, such as interest on the public debt, a permanent appropriation is provided that becomes available without further action by Congress.

Bills — Most legislative proposals before Congress are in the form of bills and are designated by HR in the House of Representatives or S in the Senate, according to the house in which they originate, and by a number assigned in the order in which they are introduced during the two-year period of a congressional term. "Public bills" deal with general questions and become public laws if approved by Congress and signed by the president. "Private bills" deal with individual matters such as claims against the government, immigration and naturalization cases or land titles, and become private laws if approved and signed. *(See also Concurrent Resolution, Joint Resolution, Resolution.)*

Bills Introduced — In both the House and Senate, any number of members may join in introducing a single bill or resolution. The first member listed is the sponsor of the bill, and all subsequent members listed are the bill's cosponsors.

Many bills are committee bills and are introduced under the name of the chairman of the committee or subcommittee. All appropriations bills fall into this category. A committee frequently holds hearings on a number of related bills and may agree to one of them or to an entirely new bill. *(See also By Request, Clean Bill, Report.)*

Bills Referred — When introduced, a bill is referred to the committee or committees that have jurisdiction over the subject with which the bill is concerned. Under the standing rules of the House and Senate, bills are referred by the Speaker in the House and by the presiding officer in the Senate. In practice, the House and Senate parliamentarians act for these officials and refer the vast majority of bills.

Borrowing Authority — Statutory authority that permits a federal agency to incur obligations and make payments for specified purposes with borrowed money.

Budget — The document sent to Congress by the president early each year estimating government revenue and expenditures for the ensuing fiscal year.

Budget Act — The common name for the Congressional Budget and Impoundment Control Act of 1974, which established the current budget process and created the Congressional Budget Office. The act also put limits on presidential authority to spend appropriated money. It has undergone several major revisions since 1974. *(See also Budget Process, Impoundments.)*

Budget Authority — Authority for federal agencies to enter into obligations that will result in immediate or future outlays. The basic forms of budget authority are appropriations, contract authority and borrowing authority. Budget authority may be classified by (1) the period of availability (one-year, multiple-year or without a time limitation), (2) the timing of congressional action (current or permanent) or (3) the manner of determining the amount available (definite

or indefinite). *(See also Appropriations, Outlays)*

Budget Process — The annual budget process was created by the Congressional Budget and Impoundment Control Act of 1974, with a timetable that was modified in 1990. Under the law, the president must submit his proposed budget by the first Monday in February. Congress is supposed to complete an annual budget resolution by April 15, setting guidelines for congressional action on spending and tax measures.

The budget resolution sets a strict ceiling on discretionary budget authority, and it also may contain "reconciliation instructions" directing authorizing and tax-writing committees to meet specified deficit-reduction goals. The committees' proposals are then bundled into a reconciliation bill.

Budget rules enacted in the 1990 Budget Enforcement Act and extended in 1993 freeze discretionary outlays at the 1993 level or below through 1998. The caps can be adjusted annually to account for changes in the economy and other limited factors. In addition, pay-as-you-go rules require that any tax cuts, new entitlement programs or expansion of existing entitlement benefits be offset by an increase in taxes or a cut in entitlement spending. The rules hold Congress harmless for budget-deficit increases that lawmakers do not explicitly cause — for example, increases due to a recession or to an expansion in the number of beneficiaries qualifying for existing entitlement programs such as Medicare or food stamps.

If Congress exceeds the discretionary spending caps in its appropriations bills, the law requires an across-the-board cut — known as sequestration — in non-exempt discretionary spending accounts. If Congress violates the pay-as-you-go rules, entitlement programs are subject to a sequester. Supplemental appropriations are subject to similar controls, with the proviso that if both Congress and the president agree, spending designated as an emergency can exceed the caps. *(See also Budget Resolution, Reconciliation, Sequester Order.)*

Budget Resolution — A concurrent resolution that is passed by both chambers of Congress but does not require the president's signature. The measure sets a strict ceiling on the budget authority available for discretionary spending, along with nonbinding recommendations about how the spending should be allocated. It may also contain "reconciliation instructions" requiring authorizing and tax-writing committees to propose changes in existing law to meet deficit-reduction goals. The Budget Committees then bundles those proposals into a reconciliation bill. *(See also Budget process, Reconciliation.)*

By Request — A phrase used when a senator or representative introduces a bill at the request of an executive agency or private organization but does not necessarily endorse the legislation.

Calendar — An agenda or list of business awaiting possible action by each chamber. The House uses five legislative calendars. *(See also Consent, Discharge, House, Private and Union Calendar.)*

In the Senate, all legislative matters reported from committee go on one calendar. They are listed there in the order in which committees report them or the Senate places them on the calendar, but they may be called up out of order by the majority leader, either by obtaining unanimous consent of the Senate or by a motion to call up a bill. The Senate also uses one non-legislative calendar; this is used for treaties and nominations. *(See also Executive Calendar.)*

Calendar Wednesday — A procedure in the House, now rarely used, whereby committees, on Wednesdays, may be called in the order in which they appear in Rule X of the House, for the purpose of bringing up any of their bills from either the House or the Union Calendar, except bills that are privileged. General debate is limited to two hours. Bills called up from the Union Calendar are considered in the Committee of the Whole. Calendar Wednesday is not observed during the last two weeks of a session

and may be dispensed with at other times by a two-thirds vote. This procedure now routinely is dispensed with by unanimous consent.

Call of the Calendar — Senate bills that are not brought up for debate by a motion, unanimous consent or a unanimous consent agreement are brought before the Senate for action when the calendar listing them is "called." Bills must be called in the order listed. Measures considered by this method usually are noncontroversial, and debate on the bill and any proposed amendments is limited to a total of five minutes for each senator.

Chamber — The meeting place for the membership of either the House or the Senate; also the membership of the House or Senate meeting as such.

Clean Bill — Frequently after a committee has finished a major revision of a bill, one of the committee members, usually the chairman, will assemble the changes and what is left of the original bill into a new measure and introduce it as a "clean bill." The revised measure, which is given a new number, then is referred back to the committee, which reports it to the floor for consideration. This often is a timesaver, as committee-recommended changes in a clean bill do not have to be considered and voted on by the chamber. Reporting a clean bill also protects committee amendments that could be subject to points of order concerning germaneness.

Clerk of the House — An officer of the House of Representatives who supervises its records and legislative business. Many former administrative duties were transferred in 1992 to a new position, the director of non-legislative and financial services. *(See also Secretary of the Senate.)*

Cloture — The process by which a filibuster can be ended in the Senate other than by unanimous consent. A motion for cloture can apply to any measure before the Senate, including a proposal to change the chamber's rules. A cloture motion requires the signatures of 16 senators to be introduced. To end a filibuster, the cloture motion must obtain the votes of three-fifths of the entire Senate membership (60 if there are no vacancies), except when the filibuster is against a proposal to amend the standing rules of the Senate and a two-thirds vote of senators present and voting is required. The cloture request is put to a roll call vote one hour after the Senate meets on the second day following introduction of the motion. If approved, cloture limits each senator to one hour of debate. The bill or amendment in question comes to a final vote after 30 hours of consideration (including debate time and the time it takes to conduct roll calls, quorum calls and other procedural motions). *(See also Filibuster.)*

Committee — A division of the House or Senate that prepares legislation for action by the parent chamber or makes investigations as directed by the parent chamber.

There are several types of committees. Most standing committees are divided into subcommittees, which study legislation, hold hearings and report bills, with or without amendments, to the full committee. Only the full committee can report legislation for action by the House or Senate. *(See also Standing, Oversight Committees, Select or Special Committees.)*

Committee of the Whole — The working title of what is formally "The Committee of the Whole House [of Representatives] on the State of the Union." The membership is composed of all House members sitting as a committee. Any 100 members who are present on the floor of the chamber to consider legislation comprise a quorum of the committee. Any legislation, however, must first have passed through the regular legislative or Appropriations committee and have been placed on the calendar.

Technically, the Committee of the Whole considers only bills directly or indirectly appropriating money, authorizing appropriations or involving taxes or charges on the public. Because the Committee of the Whole need number only 100 representatives, a

quorum is more readily attained, and legislative business is expedited. Before 1971, members' positions were not individually recorded on votes taken in the Committee of the Whole. (See also Teller Vote.)

When the full House resolves itself into the Committee of the Whole, it replaces the Speaker with a "chairman." A measure is debated and amendments may be proposed, with votes on amendments as needed. (See also Five-Minute Rule.)

When the committee completes its work on the measure, it dissolves itself by "rising." The Speaker returns, and the chairman of the Committee of the Whole reports to the House that the committee's work has been completed. At this time, members may demand a roll call vote on any amendment adopted in the Committee of the Whole. The final vote is on passage of the legislation.

Beginning in 1993, the four delegates from the territories and the Resident Commissioner of Puerto Rico were allowed to vote on questions before the Committee of the Whole. If their votes are decisive in the outcome, however, the matter is automatically revoted, with the delegates and resident commissioner ineligible. They cannot vote on final passage of bills or on separate votes demanded after the Committee of the Whole rises.

Committee Veto — A requirement added to a few statutes directing that certain policy directives by an executive department or agency be reviewed by certain congressional committees before they are implemented. Under common practice, the government department or agency and the committees involved are expected to reach a consensus before the directives are carried out. (See also Legislative Veto.)

Concurrent Resolution — A concurrent resolution, designated H Con Res or S Con Res, must be adopted by both houses, but it is not sent to the president for approval and therefore does not have the force of law. A concurrent resolution, for example, is used to fix the time for adjournment of a Congress. It also is used to express the sense of Congress on a foreign policy or domestic issue. The annual budget resolution is a concurrent resolution. (See also Bills, Joint Resolution, Resolution.)

Conference — A meeting between representatives of the House and the Senate to reconcile differences between the two chambers on provisions of a bill. Members of the conference committee are appointed by the Speaker and the presiding officer of the Senate and are called "managers" for their respective chambers. In 1993, the Speaker was given the power to remove members from a conference committee and appoint new conferees.

A majority of the conferees for each house must reach agreement on the provisions of the bill (often a compromise between the versions of the two chambers) before it can be considered by either chamber in the form of a "conference report." When the conference report goes to the floor, it is difficult to amend, and, if it is not approved by both chambers, the bill may go back to conference under certain situations, or a new conference must be convened. Many rules and informal practices govern the conduct of conference committees.

Bills that are passed by both houses with only minor differences need not be sent to conference. Either chamber may "concur" in the other's amendments, completing action on the legislation. Sometimes leaders of the committees of jurisdiction work out an informal compromise instead of having a formal conference. (See also Custody of the Papers.)

Confirmations — (See Nominations.)

Congressional Record — The daily, printed account of proceedings in both the House and Senate chambers, showing substantially verbatim debate, statements and a record of floor action. Highlights of legislative and committee action are embodied in a Daily Digest section of the Record, and members are entitled to have their extraneous remarks printed in an appendix known as "Extension of Remarks." Members may edit and revise remarks made on the floor during debate, and quotations from debate reported by the press are not always found in the Record.

The Congressional Record provides a way to distinguish remarks spoken on the floor of the House and Senate from undelivered speeches. In the Senate, all speeches, articles and other matter that members insert in the Record without actually reading them on the floor are set off by large black dots, or bullets. However, a loophole allows a member to avoid the bulleting if he or she delivers any portion of the speech in person. In the House, undelivered speeches and other material are printed in a distinctive typeface. The record is also available in electronic form. (See also Journal.)

Congressional Terms of Office — Normally begin on Jan. 3 of the year following a general election and are two years for representatives and six years for senators. Representatives elected in special elections are sworn in for the remainder of a term. A person may be appointed to fill a Senate vacancy and serves until a successor is elected; the successor serves until the end of the term applying to the vacant seat.

Consent Calendar — Members of the House may place on this calendar most bills on the Union or House Calendar that are considered non-controversial. Bills on the Consent Calendar normally are called on the first and third Mondays of each month. On the first occasion that a bill is called in this manner, consideration may be blocked by the objection of any member. The second time, if there are three objections, the bill is stricken from the Consent Calendar. If fewer than three members object, the bill is given immediate consideration.

A bill on the Consent Calendar may be postponed in another way. A member may ask that the measure be passed over "without prejudice." In that case, no objection is recorded against the bill, and its status on the Consent Calendar remains unchanged. A bill stricken from the Consent Calendar remains on the Union or House Calendar. The consent calendar had seldom been used in recent years. (See also Calendar, House, Private and Union Calendar.)

Continuing Resolution — A joint resolution, cleared by Congress and signed by the president (when the new fiscal year is about to begin or has begun), to provide new budget authority for federal agencies and programs to continue in operation until the regular appropriations bills are enacted. The continuing resolution usually specifies a maximum rate at which an agency may incur obligations, based on the rate of the prior year, the president's budget request or an appropriations bill passed by either or both chambers of Congress but not yet enacted. Continuing resolutions also are called "CRs" or continuing appropriations.

Contract Authority — Budget authority contained in an authorization bill that permits the federal government to enter into contracts or other obligations for future payments from funds not yet appropriated by Congress. The assumption is that funds will be available for payment in a subsequent appropriation act.

Correcting Recorded Votes — Rules prohibit members from changing their votes after the result has been announced. But, occasionally, hours, days or months after a vote has been taken, a member may announce he or she was "incorrectly recorded." In the Senate, a request to change one's vote almost always receives unanimous consent, so long as it does not change the outcome. In the House, members are prohibited from changing their votes if tallied by the electronic voting system.

Cosponsor — (See Bills Introduced.)

Current Services Estimates — Estimated budget authority and outlays for federal programs and operations for the forthcoming fiscal year based on continuation of existing levels of service without policy changes but with adjustments for inflation and for demographic changes that affect programs. These estimates, accompanied by the underlying economic and policy assumptions upon which they are based, are transmitted by the president to Congress when the budget is submitted.

Custody of the Papers — To reconcile differences between the House and Senate versions of a bill, a conference may be arranged. The chamber with "custody of the papers" — the engrossed bill, engrossed amendments, messages of transmittal — is the only body empowered to request the conference. By custom, the chamber that asks for a conference is the last to act on the conference report once agreement has been reached on the bill by the conferees.

Custody of the papers sometimes is manipulated to ensure that a particular chamber acts either first or last on the conference report.

Deferral — Executive branch action to defer, or delay, the spending of appropriated money. The 1974 Congressional Budget and Impoundment Control Act requires a special message from the president to Congress reporting a proposed deferral of spending. Deferrals may not extend beyond the end of the fiscal year in which the message is transmitted. A federal district court in 1986 struck down the president's authority to defer spending for policy reasons; the ruling was upheld by a federal appeals court in 1987. Congress can prohibit proposed deferrals by enacting a law doing so; most often, cancellations of proposed deferrals are included in appropriations bills. *(See also Rescission.)*

Dilatory Motion — A motion made for the purpose of killing time and preventing action on a bill or amendment. House rules outlaw dilatory motions, but enforcement is largely within the discretion of the Speaker or chairman of the Committee of the Whole. The Senate does not have a rule banning dilatory motions, except under cloture.

Discharge a Committee — Occasionally, attempts are made to relieve a committee from jurisdiction over a measure before it. This is attempted more often in the House than in the Senate, and the procedure rarely is successful.

In the House, if a committee does not report a bill within 30 days after the measure is referred to it, any member may file a discharge motion. Once offered, the motion is treated as a petition needing the signatures of a majority of members (218 if there are no vacancies). After the required signatures have been obtained, there is a delay of seven days. Thereafter, on the second and fourth Mondays of each month, except during the last six days of a session, any member who has signed the petition must be recognized, if he or she so desires, to move that the committee be discharged. Debate on the motion to discharge is limited to 20 minutes, and, if the motion is carried, consideration of the bill becomes a matter of high privilege.

If a resolution to consider a bill is held up in the Rules Committee for more than seven legislative days, any member may enter a motion to discharge the committee. The motion is handled like any other discharge petition in the House. Occasionally, to expedite non-controversial legislative business, a committee is discharged by unanimous consent of the House, and a petition is not required. In 1993, the signatures on pending discharge petitions — previously kept secret — were made a matter of public record. *(For Senate procedure, see Discharge Resolution.)*

Discharge Calendar — The House calendar to which motions to discharge committees are referred when they have the required number of signatures (218) and are awaiting floor action.

Discharge Petition — *(See Discharge a Committee.)*

Discharge Resolution — In the Senate, a special motion that any senator may introduce to relieve a committee from consideration of a bill before it. The resolution can be called up for Senate approval or disapproval in the same manner as any other Senate business. *(For House procedure, see Discharge a Committee.)*

Division of a Question for Voting — A practice that is more common in the Senate but also used in the House whereby a member may demand a division of an amendment or a motion for purposes of voting. Where an amendment or motion can be divided, the individual parts are voted on separately when a member demands a division. This procedure occurs most often during the consideration of conference reports.

Division Vote — *(See Standing Vote.)*

Enacting Clause — Key phrase in bills beginning, "Be it enacted by the Senate and House of Representatives..." A successful motion to strike it from legislation kills the measure.

Engrossed Bill — The final copy of a bill as passed by one chamber, with the text as amended by floor action and certified by the clerk of the House or the secretary of the Senate.

Enrolled Bill — The final copy of a bill that has been passed in identical form by both chambers. It is certified by an officer of the house of origin (clerk of the House or secretary of the Senate) and then sent on for the signatures of the House Speaker, the Senate president pro tempore and the president of the United States. An enrolled bill is printed on parchment.

Entitlement Program — A federal program that guarantees a certain level of benefits to persons or other entities who meet requirements set by law, such as Social Security, farm price supports or unemployment benefits. It thus gives Congress no discretion over how much money to appropriate, and some entitlements carry permanent appropriations.

Executive Calendar — This is a non-legislative calendar in the Senate on which presidential documents such as treaties and nominations are listed. *(See also Calendar.)*

Executive Document — A document, usually a treaty, sent to the Senate by the president for consideration or approval. Executive documents are referred to committee in the same manner as other measures. Unlike legislative documents, however, treaties do not die at the end of a Congress but remain "live" proposals until acted on by the Senate or withdrawn by the president.

Executive Session — A meeting of a Senate or House committee (or occasionally of either chamber) that only its members may attend. Witnesses regularly appear at committee meetings in executive session — for example, Defense Department officials during presentations of classified defense information. Other members of Congress may be invited, but the public and news media are not allowed to attend.

Filibuster — A time-delaying tactic associated with the Senate and used by a minority in an effort to prevent a vote on a bill or amendment that probably would pass if voted upon directly. The most common method is to take advantage of the Senate's rules permitting unlimited debate, but other forms of parliamentary maneuvering may be used. The stricter rules of the House make filibusters more difficult, but delaying tactics are employed occasionally through various procedural devices allowed by House rules. *(For Senate filibusters, see Cloture.)*

Fiscal Year — Financial operations of the government are carried out in a 12-month fiscal year, beginning on Oct. 1 and ending on Sept. 30. The fiscal year carries the date of the calendar year in which it ends. (From fiscal year 1844 to fiscal year 1976, the fiscal year began July 1 and ended the following June 30.)

Five-Minute Rule — A debate-limiting rule of the House that is invoked when the House sits as the Committee of the Whole. Under the rule, a member offering an amendment is allowed to speak five minutes in its favor, and an opponent of the amendment is allowed to speak five minutes in opposition. Debate is then closed. In practice, amendments regularly are debated more than 10 minutes, with members gaining the floor by offering

pro forma amendments or obtaining unanimous consent to speak longer than five minutes. *(See also Committee of the Whole, Hour Rule, Strike Out the Last Word.)*

Floor Manager — A member who has the task of steering legislation through floor debate and the amendment process to a final vote in the House or the Senate. Floor managers usually are chairmen or ranking members of the committee that reported the bill. Managers are responsible for apportioning the debate time granted to supporters of the bill. The ranking minority member of the committee normally apportions time for the minority party's participation in the debate.

Frank — A member's facsimile signature, which is used on envelopes in lieu of stamps, for the member's official outgoing mail. The "franking privilege" is the right to send mail postage-free.

Germane — Pertaining to the subject matter of the measure at hand. All House amendments must be germane to the bill being considered. The Senate requires that amendments be germane when they are proposed to general appropriations bills or to bills being considered once cloture has been adopted or, frequently, when the Senate is proceeding under a unanimous consent agreement placing a time limit on consideration of a bill. The 1974 budget act also requires that amendments to concurrent budget resolutions be germane. In the House, floor debate must be germane, and the first three hours of debate each day in the Senate must be germane to the pending business.

Gramm-Rudman-Hollings Deficit Reduction Act — *(See Budget Process, Sequestration.)*

Grandfather Clause — A provision that exempts persons or other entities already engaged in an activity from rules or legislation affecting that activity.

Hearings — Committee sessions for taking testimony from witnesses. At hearings on legislation, witnesses usually include specialists, government officials and spokesmen for individuals or entities affected by the bill or bills under study. Hearings related to special investigations bring forth a variety of witnesses. Committees sometimes use their subpoena power to summon reluctant witnesses. The public and news media may attend open hearings but are barred from closed, or "executive," hearings. The vast majority of hearings are open to the public. *(See also Executive Session.)*

Hold-Harmless Clause — A provision added to legislation to ensure that recipients of federal funds do not receive less in a future year than they did in the current year if a new formula for allocating funds authorized in the legislation would result in a reduction to the recipients. This clause has been used most often to soften the impact of sudden reductions in federal grants.

Hopper — Box on House clerk's desk where members deposit bills and resolutions to introduce them. *(See also Bills Introduced.)*

Hour Rule — A provision in the rules of the House that permits one hour of debate time for each member on amendments debated in the House of Representatives sitting as the House. Therefore, the House normally amends bills while sitting as the Committee of the Whole, where the five-minute rule on amendments operates. *(See also Committee of the Whole, Five-Minute Rule.)*

House as in the Committee of the Whole — A procedure that can be used to expedite consideration of certain measures such as continuing resolutions and, when there is debate, private bills. The procedure only can be invoked with the unanimous consent of the House or a rule from the Rules Committee and has procedural elements of both the House sitting as the House of Representatives, such as the Speaker presiding and the previous question motion being in order, and the House sitting as the Committee of the Whole, with the five-minute rule being in order.

House Calendar — A listing for action by the House of public bills that do not directly or indirectly appropriate money or raise revenue. *(See also Calendar, Consent, Discharge, Private and Union Calendar.)*

Immunity — The constitutional privilege of members of Congress to make verbal statements on the floor and in committee for which they cannot be sued or arrested for slander or libel. Also, freedom from arrest while traveling to or from sessions of Congress or on official business. Members in this status may be arrested only for treason, felonies or a breach of the peace, as defined by congressional manuals.

Joint Committee — A committee composed of a specified number of members of both the House and Senate. A joint committee may be investigative or research-oriented, an example of the latter being the Joint Economic Committee. Others have housekeeping duties such as the joint committees on Printing and on the Library of Congress. In 1992, a Joint Committee on the Organziation of Congress was established to make recommendations for congressional reforms. *(See also Committee, Oversight, Select or Special Committee, Standing Committees.)*

Joint Resolution — A joint resolution, designated H J Res or S J Res, requires the approval of both houses and the signature of the president, just as a bill does, and has the force of law if approved. There is no practical difference between a bill and a joint resolution. A joint resolution generally is used to deal with a limited matter such as a single appropriation.

Joint resolutions also are used to propose amendments to the Constitution. They do not require a presidential signature but become a part of the Constitution when three-fourths of the states have ratified them. *(See also Concurrent Resolution, Resolution)*

Journal — The official record of the proceedings of the House and Senate. The Journal records the actions taken in each chamber, but, unlike the Congressional Record, it does not include the substantially verbatim report of speeches, debates, statements and the like. *(See also Congressional Record.)*

Law — An act of Congress that has been signed by the president or passed over his veto by Congress. Public bills, when signed, become public laws and are cited by the letters PL and a hyphenated number. The number before the hyphen corresponds to the Congress, and the one or more digits after the hyphen refer to the numerical sequence in which the president signed the bills during that Congress. Private bills, when signed, become private laws. *(See also Pocket Veto, Slip Laws, Statutes at Large, U.S. Code.)*

Legislative Day — The "day" extending from the time either house meets after an adjournment until the time it next adjourns. Because the House normally adjourns from day to day, legislative days and calendar days usually coincide. But in the Senate, a legislative day may, and frequently does, extend over several calendar days. *(See also Recess.)*

Legislative Veto — A procedure, held unconstitutional by the Supreme Court, permitting either the House or Senate, or both chambers, to review proposed executive branch regulations or actions and to block or modify those with which they disagreed.

The Supreme Court in 1983 struck down the legislative veto as an unconstitutional violation of the lawmaking procedure provided in the Constitution.

Loan Guarantees — Loans to third parties for which the federal government in the event of default guarantees, in whole or in part, the repayment of principal or interest to a lender or holder of a security.

Lobby — A group seeking to influence the passage or defeat of

legislation. Originally the term referred to persons frequenting the lobbies or corridors of legislative chambers to speak to lawmakers.

The definition of a lobby and the activity of lobbying is a matter of differing interpretation. By some definitions, lobbying is limited to direct attempts to influence lawmakers through personal interviews and persuasion. Under other definitions, lobbying includes attempts at indirect, or "grass-roots," influence, such as persuading members of a group to write or visit their district's representative and state's senators or attempting to create a climate of opinion favorable to a desired legislative goal.

The right to attempt to influence legislation is based on the First Amendment to the Constitution, which says Congress shall make no law abridging the right of the people "to petition the government for a redress of grievances."

Majority Leader — Floor leader for the majority party in each chamber. In the Senate, in consultation with the minority leader and his colleagues, the majority leader directs the legislative schedule for the chamber. He also is his party's spokesperson and chief strategist. In the House, the majority leader is second to the Speaker in the majority party's leadership and serves as his party's legislative strategist.

Majority Whip — In effect, the assistant majority leader, in either the House or Senate. His job is to help marshal majority forces in support of party strategy and legislation.

Manual — The official handbook in each house prescribing in detail its organization, procedures and operations.

Marking Up a Bill — Going through the contents of a piece of legislation in committee or subcommittee to, for example, consider its provisions, act on amendments to provisions and proposed revisions to the language, and insert new sections and phraseology. If the bill is extensively amended, the committee's version may be introduced as a separate bill, with a new number, before being considered by the full House or Senate. *(See also Clean Bill.)*

Minority Leader — Floor leader for the minority party in each chamber. *(See also Majority Leader.)*

Minority Whip — Performs duties of whip for the minority party. *(See also Majority Whip.)*

Morning Hour — The time set aside at the beginning of each legislative day for the consideration of regular, routine business. The "hour" is of indefinite duration in the House, where it is rarely used.

In the Senate, it is the first two hours of a session following an adjournment, as distinguished from a recess. The morning hour can be terminated earlier if the morning business has been completed. Business includes such matters as messages from the president, communications from the heads of departments, messages from the House, the presentation of petitions, reports of standing and select committees and the introduction of bills and resolutions. During the first hour of the morning hour in the Senate, no motion to proceed to the consideration of any bill on the calendar is in order except by unanimous consent. During the second hour, motions can be made but must be decided without debate. Senate committees may meet while the Senate conducts the morning hour.

Motion — In the House or Senate chamber, a request by a member to institute any one of a wide array of parliamentary actions. He or she "moves" for a certain procedure, such as the consideration of a measure. The precedence of motions, and whether they are debatable, is set forth in the House and Senate manuals.

Nominations — Presidential appointments to office subject to Senate confirmation. Although most nominations win quick Senate approval, some are controversial and become the topic of hearings and debate. Sometimes senators object to appointees for

patronage reasons — for example, when a nomination to a local federal job is made without consulting the senators of the state concerned. In some situations a senator may object that the nominee is "personally obnoxious" to him. Usually other senators join in blocking such appointments out of courtesy to their colleagues. *(See also Senatorial Courtesy.)*

One-Minute Speeches — Addresses by House members at the beginning of a legislative day. The speeches may cover any subject but are limited to one minute's duration.

Outlays — Actual spending that flows from the liquidation of budget authority. Appropriations bills provide budget authority — the authority to spend money. The outlays associated with appropriations bills are just estimates of future spending made by the Congressional Budget Office (CBO). The White House's Office of Management and Budget (OMB) also estimates outlays, but CBO's estimates govern bills for the purpose of congressional floor debate. OMB's numbers govern when it comes to determining whether legislation exceeds spending caps. While budget authority is analogous to putting money in a checking account, outlays are when the check actually is written. Outlays in a given fiscal year may result from budget authority provided in the current year or in previous years. *(See also Budget Authority, Budget Process)*

Override a Veto — If the president disapproves a bill and sends it back to Congress with his objections, Congress may try to override his veto and enact the bill into law. Neither house is required to attempt to override a veto. The override of a veto requires a recorded vote with a two-thirds majority of those present and voting in each chamber. The question put to each house is: "Shall the bill pass, the objections of the president to the contrary notwithstanding?" *(See also Pocket Veto, Veto.)*

Oversight Committee — A congressional committee, or designated subcommittee, that is charged with general oversight of one or more federal agencies' programs and activities. Usually, the oversight panel for a particular agency also is the authorizing committee for that agency's programs and operations.

Pair — A voluntary, informal arrangement that two lawmakers, usually on opposite sides of an issue, make on recorded votes. In many cases the result is to subtract a vote from each side, with no effect on the outcome. Pairs are not authorized in the rules of either house, are not counted in tabulating the final result and have no official standing. However, members pairing are identified in the Congressional Record, along with their positions on such votes, if known. A member who expects to be absent for a vote can pair with a member who plans to vote, with the latter agreeing to withhold his or her vote.

There are three types of pairs: 1) A live pair involves a member who is present for a vote and another who is absent. The member in attendance votes and then withdraws the vote, announcing that he or she has a live pair with colleague "X" and stating how the two members would have voted, one in favor, the other opposed. A live pair may affect the outcome of a closely contested vote, since it subtracts one "yea" or one "nay" from the final tally. A live pair may cover one or several specific issues. 2) A general pair, widely used in the House, does not entail any arrangement between two members and does not affect the vote. Members who expect to be absent notify the clerk that they wish to make a general pair. Each member then is paired with another desiring a pair, and their names are listed in the Congressional Record. The member may or may not be paired with another taking the opposite position, and no indication of how the members would have voted is given. 3) A specific pair is similar to a general pair, except that the opposing stands of the two members are identified and printed in the Record.

Petition — A request or plea sent to one or both chambers from an organization or private citizens' group asking support of particular legislation or favorable consideration of a matter not yet receiving congressional attention. Petitions are referred to appro-

priate committees. In the House, a petition signed by a majority of members (218) can discharge a bill from a committee. *(See also Discharge a Committee)*

Pocket Veto — The act of the president in withholding his approval of a bill after Congress has adjourned. When Congress is in session, a bill becomes law without the president's signature if he does not act upon it within 10 days, excluding Sundays, from the time he gets it. But if Congress adjourns sine die within that 10-day period, the bill will die even if the president does not formally veto it.

The Supreme Court in 1986 agreed to decide whether the president can pocket veto a bill during recesses and between sessions of the same Congress or only between Congresses. The justices in 1987 declared the case moot, however, because the bill in question was invalid once the case reached the court. *(See also Adjournment Sine Die, Veto.)*

Point of Order — An objection raised by a member that the chamber is departing from rules governing its conduct of business. The objector cites the rule violated, the chair sustaining his or her objection if correctly made. Order is restored by the chair's suspending proceedings of the chamber until it conforms to the prescribed "order of business."

President of the Senate — Under the Constitution, the vice president of the United States presides over the Senate. In his absence, the president pro tempore, or a senator designated by the president pro tempore, presides over the chamber.

President Pro Tempore — The chief officer of the Senate in the absence of the vice president; literally, but loosely, the president for a time. The president pro tempore is elected by his fellow senators, and the recent practice has been to elect the senator of the majority party with the longest period of continuous service.

Previous Question — A motion for the previous question, when carried, has the effect of cutting off all debate, preventing the offering of further amendments and forcing a vote on the pending matter. In the House, the previous question is not permitted in the Committee of the Whole, unless a rule governing debate provides otherwise. The motion for the previous question is a debate-limiting device and is not in order in the Senate.

Printed Amendment — A House rule guarantees five minutes of floor debate in support and five minutes in opposition, and no other debate time, on amendments printed in the Congressional Record at least one day prior to the amendment's consideration in the Committee of the Whole. In the Senate, while amendments may be submitted for printing, they have no parliamentary standing or status. An amendment submitted for printing in the Senate, however, may be called up by any senator.

Private Calendar — In the House, private bills dealing with individual matters such as claims against the government, immigration or land titles are put on this calendar. The Private Calendar must be called on the first Tuesday of each month, and the Speaker may call it on the third Tuesday of each month as well.

When a private bill is before the chamber, two members may block its consideration, which recommits the bill to committee. Backers of a recommitted private bill have recourse. The measure can be put into an "omnibus claims bill" — several private bills rolled into one. As with any bill, no part of an omnibus claims bill may be deleted without a vote. When the private bill goes back to the House floor in this form, it can be deleted from the omnibus bill only by majority vote. *(See also Calendar, Consent, Discharge, House and Union Calendar.)*

Privileged Questions — The order in which bills, motions and other legislative measures are considered on the floor of the Senate and House is governed by strict priorities. A motion to table, for instance, is more privileged than a motion to recommit. Thus, if a member moves to recommit a bill to committee for

further consideration, another member could supersede the first action by moving to table it, and a vote would occur first on the motion to table (or kill) the motion to recommit. A motion to adjourn is considered "of the highest privilege" and would have to be considered before virtually any other motion. *(See also Questions of Privilege.)*

Pro Forma Amendment — *(See Strike Out the Last Word.)*

Public Laws — *(See Law.)*

Questions of Privilege — These are matters affecting members of Congress individually or collectively. Matters affecting the rights, safety, dignity and integrity of proceedings of the House or Senate as a whole are questions of privilege in both chambers.

Questions involving individual members are called questions of "personal privilege." A member rising to ask a question of personal privilege is given precedence over almost all other proceedings. For instance, if a member feels that he or she has been improperly impugned in comments by another member, he or she can immediately demand to be heard on the floor on a question of personal privilege. An annotation in the House rules points out that the privilege rests primarily on the Constitution, which gives members a conditional immunity from arrest and an unconditional freedom to speak in the House.

In 1993, the House changed its rules to allow the Speaker to delay for two legislative days the floor consideration of a question of the privileges of the House unless it is offered by the majority leader or minority leader. *(See also Privileged Questions.)*

Quorum — The number of members whose presence is necessary for the transaction of business. In the Senate and House, it is a majority of the membership. A quorum is 100 in the Committee of the Whole House. If a point of order is made that a quorum is not present, the only business that is in order is either a motion to adjourn or a motion to direct the sergeant-at-arms to request the attendance of absentees. In practice, however, both chambers conduct much of their business without a quorum present.

Readings of Bills — Traditional parliamentary procedure required bills to be read three times before they were passed. This custom is of little modern significance. Normally a bill is considered to have its first reading when it is introduced and printed, by title, in the Congressional Record. In the House, its second reading comes when floor consideration begins. (This is the most likely point at which there is an actual reading of the bill, if there is any.) The second reading in the Senate is supposed to occur on the legislative day after the measure is introduced, but before it is referred to committee. The third reading (again, usually by title) takes place when floor action has been completed on amendments.

Recess — Distinguished from adjournment in that a recess does not end a legislative day and therefore does not interrupt unfinished business. The rules in each house set forth certain matters to be taken up and disposed of at the beginning of each legislative day. The House usually adjourns from day to day. The Senate often recesses, thus meeting on the same legislative day for several calendar days or even weeks at a time.

Recognition — The power of recognition of a member is lodged in the Speaker of the House and the presiding officer of the Senate. The presiding officer names the member to speak first when two or more members simultaneously request recognition. The order of recognition is governed by precedents and tradition for many situations. In the Senate, for instance, the majority leader has the right to be recognized first.

Recommit to Committee — A motion, made on the floor after a bill has been debated, to return it to the committee that reported it. If approved, recommittal usually is considered a death blow to the bill. In the House, a motion to recommit can be made only by a member opposed to the bill, and, in recognizing a member to make the motion, the Speaker gives preference to

members of the minority party over majority-party members.

A motion to recommit may include instructions to the committee to report the bill again with specific amendments or by a certain date. Or the instructions may direct that a particular study be made, with no definite deadline for further action. If the recommittal motion includes instructions to "report the bill back forthwith" and the motion is adopted, floor action on the bill continues with the changes directed by the instructions automatically incorporated into the bill; the committee does not actually reconsider the legislation.

Reconciliation — The 1974 budget act provided for a "reconciliation" procedure for bringing existing tax and spending laws into conformity with ceilings set in the congressional budget resolution. Under the procedure, the budget resolution sets specific deficit-reduction targets and instructs tax-writing and authorizing committees to propose changes in existing law to meet those targets. Those recommendations are consolidated without change by the Budget committees into an omnibus reconciliation bill, which then must be considered and approved by both chambers of Congress.

Special rules in the Senate limit debate on a reconciliation bill to 20 hours and bar extraneous or non-germane amendments. *(See also Budget Resolution, Sequestration.)*

Reconsider a Vote — A motion to reconsider the vote by which an action was taken has, until it is disposed of, the effect of putting the action in abeyance. In the Senate, the motion can be made only by a member who voted on the prevailing side of the original question or by a member who did not vote at all. In the House, it can be made only by a member on the prevailing side.

A common practice in the Senate after close votes on an issue is a motion to reconsider, followed by a motion to table the motion to reconsider. On this motion to table, senators vote as they voted on the original question, which allows the motion to table to prevail, assuming there are no switches. The matter then is finally closed, and further motions to reconsider are not entertained. In the House, as a routine precaution, a motion to reconsider usually is made every time a measure is passed. Such a motion almost always is tabled immediately, thus shutting off the possibility of future reconsideration, except by unanimous consent.

Motions to reconsider must be entered in the Senate within the next two days of actual session after the original vote has been taken. In the House, they must be entered either on the same day or on the next succeeding day the House is in session. Sometimes on a close vote, a member will switch his or her vote to be eligible to offer a motion to reconsider.

Recorded Vote — A vote upon which each member's stand is individually made known. In the Senate, this is accomplished through a roll call of the entire membership, to which each senator on the floor must answer "yea," "nay" or "present." Since January 1973, the House has used an electronic voting system for recorded votes, including yea-and-nay votes formerly taken by roll calls.

When not required by the Constitution, a recorded vote can be obtained on questions in the House on the demand of one-fifth (44 members) of a quorum or one-fourth (25) of a quorum in the Committee of the Whole. *(See also Yeas and Nays.)*

Report — Both a verb and a noun as a congressional term. A committee that has been examining a bill referred to it by the parent chamber "reports" its findings and recommendations to the chamber when it completes consideration and returns the measure. The process is called "reporting" a bill.

A "report" is the document setting forth the committee's explanation of its action. Senate and House reports are numbered separately and are designated S Rept or H Rept. When a committee report is not unanimous, the dissenting committee members may file a statement of their views, called minority or dissenting views and referred to as a minority report. Members in disagreement with some provisions of a bill may file additional or supplementary views. Sometimes a bill is reported without a committee recommendation.

Legislative committees occasionally submit adverse reports. However, when a committee is opposed to a bill, it usually fails to report the bill at all. Some laws require that committee reports — favorable or adverse — be made.

Rescission — What happens when Congress acts to rescind, or cancel, budget authority that was previously appropriated but has not yet been spent. Under the 1974 budget act, the president may recommend a rescission, but unless Congress approves the cut within 45 days of continuous session after receiving the proposal, the funds must be made available for obligation. *(See also Deferral.)*

Resolution — A "simple" resolution, designated H Res or S Res, deals with matters entirely within the prerogatives of one house or the other. It requires neither passage by the other chamber nor approval by the president, and it does not have the force of law. Most resolutions deal with the rules or procedures of one house. They also are used to express the sentiments of a single house such as condolences to the family of a deceased member or to comment on foreign policy or executive business. A simple resolution is the vehicle for a "rule" from the House Rules Committee. *(See also Concurrent and Joint Resolutions, Rules.)*

Rider — An amendment, usually not germane, that its sponsor hopes to get through more easily by including it in other legislation. A rider becomes law if the bill to which it is attached is enacted. Amendments providing legislative directives in appropriations bills are outstanding examples of riders, though technically legislation is banned from appropriations bills.

The House, unlike the Senate, has a strict germaneness rule; thus, riders usually are Senate devices to get legislation enacted quickly or to bypass lengthy House consideration and, possibly, opposition.

Rules — A rule is a standing order governing the conduct of House or Senate business and listed among the permanent rules of either chamber. The rules deal with issues such as duties of officers, the order of business, admission to the floor, parliamentary procedures on handling amendments and voting and jurisdictions of committees.

In the House, a rule also may be a resolution reported by its Rules Committee to govern the handling of a particular bill on the floor. The committee may report a rule, also called a special order, in the form of a simple resolution. If the House adopts the resolution, the temporary rule becomes as valid as any standing rule and lapses only after action has been completed on the measure to which it pertains. A rule sets the time limit on general debate. It also may waive points of order against provisions of the bill in question such as non-germane language or against certain amendments intended to be proposed to the bill from the floor. It may even forbid all amendments or all amendments except those proposed by the legislative committee that handled the bill. In this instance, it is known as a "closed" rule as opposed to an "open" rule, which puts no limitation on floor amendments, thus leaving the bill completely open to alteration by the adoption of germane amendments.

Secretary of the Senate — Chief administrative officer of the Senate, responsible for overseeing the duties of Senate employees, educating Senate pages, administering oaths, overseeing the registration of lobbyists and handling other tasks necessary for the continuing operation of the Senate. *(See also Clerk of the House.)*

Select or Special Committee — A committee set up for a special purpose and, usually, for a limited time by resolution of either the House or Senate. Most special committees are investigative and lack legislative authority: legislation is not referred to them, and they cannot report bills to their parent chamber. The House in 1993 terminated its four select committees. *(See also Committee, Joint, Oversight and Standing Committees.)*

Senatorial Courtesy — Sometimes referred to as "the cour-

tesy of the Senate," it is a general practice — with no written rule — applied to consideration of executive nominations. Generally, it means that nominations from a state are not to be confirmed unless they have been approved by the senators of the president's party of that state, with other senators following their colleagues' lead in the attitude they take toward consideration of such nominations. *(See also Nominations.)*

Sequester — An automatic, across-the-board spending cut. Under the 1985 Gramm-Rudman anti-deficit law, modified in 1987, a year-end, across-the-board spending cut known as a sequester would be triggered if the deficit exceeded a pre-set maximum. However, the Budget Enforcement Act of 1990, updated in 1993, effectively replaced that procedure through fiscal 1998.

Instead, if Congress exceeds an annual cap on discretionary spending, a sequester is triggered for all eligible discretionary spending to make up the difference. If Congress violates pay-as-you-go rules — which require that new or expanded mandatory spending (for entitlement programs such as Medicare and food stamps) and tax cuts be deficit-neutral — a sequester is triggered for all non-exempt entitlement programs. Similar procedures apply to supplemental appropriations bills. *(See also Budget Process.)*

Sine Die — *(See Adjournment Sine Die.)*

Speaker — The presiding officer of the House of Representatives, selected by the caucus of the party to which he belongs and formally elected by the whole House.

Special Session — A session of Congress after it has adjourned sine die, completing its regular session. Special sessions are convened by the president.

Spending Authority — The 1974 budget act defines spending authority as borrowing authority, contract authority and entitlement authority for which budget authority is not provided in advance by appropriation acts.

Sponsor — *(See Bills Introduced.)*

Standing Committees — Committees that are permanently established by House and Senate rules. The standing committees of the House were last reorganized by the committee reorganization of 1974. The last major realignment of Senate committees was in the committee system reorganization of 1977. The standing committees are legislative committees — legislation may be referred to them and they may report bills and resolutions to their parent chambers. *(See also Committee, Joint, Oversight and Select or Special Committees.)*

Standing Vote — A non-recorded vote used in both the House and Senate. (A standing vote also is called a division vote.) Members in favor of a proposal stand and are counted by the presiding officer. Then members opposed stand and are counted. There is no record of how individual members voted.

Statutes at Large — A chronological arrangement of the laws enacted in each session of Congress. Though indexed, the laws are not arranged by subject matter, and there is not an indication of how they changed previously enacted laws. *(See also Law, Slip Laws, U.S. Code.)*

Strike From the Record — Remarks made on the House floor may offend some member, who moves that the offending words be "taken down" for the Speaker's cognizance, and then expunged from the debate as published in the Congressional Record.

Strike Out the Last Word — A motion whereby a House member is entitled to speak for five minutes on an amendment then being debated by the chamber. A member gains recognition from the chair by moving to "strike out the last word" of the

amendment or section of the bill under consideration. The motion is pro forma, requires no vote and does not change the amendment being debated. *(See also Five-Minute Rule.)*

Substitute — A motion, amendment or entire bill introduced in place of the pending legislative business. Passage of a substitute measure kills the original measure by supplanting it. The substitute also may be amended. *(See also Amendment in the Nature of a Substitute.)*

Supplemental Appropriations Bill — Legislation appropriating funds after the regular annual appropriations bill for a federal department or agency has been enacted. A supplemental appropriation provides additional budget authority beyond original estimates for programs or activities, including new programs authorized after the enactment of the regular appropriation act, for which the need for funds is too urgent to be postponed until enactment of the next year's regular appropriation bill.

Suspend the Rules — Often a time-saving procedure for passing bills in the House. The wording of the motion, which may be made by any member recognized by the Speaker, is: "I move to suspend the rules and pass the bill . . ." A favorable vote by two-thirds of those present is required for passage. Debate is limited to 40 minutes and no amendments from the floor are permitted. If a two-thirds favorable vote is not attained, the bill may be considered later under regular procedures. The suspension procedure is in order every Monday and Tuesday and is intended to be reserved for non-controversial bills.

Table a Bill — Motions to table, or to "lay on the table," are used to block or kill amendments or other parliamentary questions. When approved, a tabling motion is considered the final disposition of that issue. One of the most widely used parliamentary procedures, the motion to table is not debatable, and adoption requires a simple majority vote.

In the Senate, however, different language sometimes is used. The motion may be worded to let a bill "lie on the table," perhaps for subsequent "picking up." This motion is more flexible, keeping the bill pending for later action, if desired. Tabling motions on amendments are effective debate-ending devices in the Senate.

Treaties — Executive proposals — in the form of resolutions of ratification — which must be submitted to the Senate for approval by two-thirds of the senators present. Treaties are normally sent to the Foreign Relations Committee for scrutiny before the Senate takes action. Foreign Relations has jurisdiction over all treaties, regardless of the subject matter. Treaties are read three times and debated on the floor in much the same manner as legislative proposals. After approval by the Senate, treaties are formally ratified by the president.

Trust Funds — Funds collected and used by the federal government for carrying out specific purposes and programs according to terms of a trust agreement or statute such as the Social Security and unemployment compensation trust funds. Such funds are administered by the government in a fiduciary capacity and are not available for the general purposes of the government.

Unanimous Consent — Proceedings of the House or Senate and action on legislation often take place upon the unanimous consent of the chamber, whether or not a rule of the chamber is being violated. Unanimous consent is used to expedite floor action and frequently is used in a routine fashion such as by a senator requesting the unanimous consent of the Senate to have specified members of his or her staff present on the floor during debate on a specific amendment. A single member's objection blocks a unanimous consent request.

Unanimous Consent Agreement — A device used in the Senate to expedite legislation. Much of the Senate's legislative business, dealing with both minor and controversial issues, is conducted through unanimous consent or unanimous consent agreements. On major legislation, such agreements usually are printed and

transmitted to all senators in advance of floor debate. Once agreed to, they are binding on all members unless the Senate, by unanimous consent, agrees to modify them. An agreement may list the order in which various bills are to be considered, specify the length of time bills and contested amendments are to be debated and when they are to be voted upon and, frequently, require that all amendments introduced be germane to the bill under consideration.

In this regard, unanimous consent agreements are similar to the "rules" issued by the House Rules Committee for bills pending in the House.

Union Calendar — Bills that directly or indirectly appropriate money or raise revenue are placed on this House calendar according to the date they are reported from committee. *(See also Calendar, Consent, Discharge, House and Private Calendar.)*

U.S. Code — A consolidation and codification of the general and permanent laws of the United States arranged by subject under 50 titles, the first six dealing with general or political subjects, and the other 44 alphabetically arranged from agriculture to war. The U.S. Code is updated annually, and a new set of bound volumes is published every six years. *(See also Law, Statutes at Large.)*

Veto — Disapproval by the president of a bill or joint resolution (other than one proposing an amendment to the Constitution). When Congress is in session, the president must veto a bill within 10 days, excluding Sundays, after he has received it; otherwise, it becomes law without his signature. When the president vetoes a bill, he returns it to the house of origin along with a message stating his objections. *(See also Pocket Veto, Override a Veto.)*

Voice Vote — In either the House or Senate, members answer "aye" or "no" in chorus, and the presiding officer decides the result. The term also is used loosely to indicate action by unanimous consent or without objection.

Whip — *(See Majority and Minority Whip.)*

Without Objection — Used in lieu of a vote on non-controversial motions, amendments or bills that may be passed in either the House or Senate if no member voices an objection.

Yeas and Nays — The Constitution requires that yea-and-nay votes be taken and recorded when requested by one-fifth of the members present. In the House, the Speaker determines whether one-fifth of the members present requested a vote. In the Senate, practice requires only 11 members. The Constitution requires the yeas and nays on a veto override attempt. *(See also Recorded Vote.)*

Yielding — When a member has been recognized to speak, no other member may speak unless he or she obtains permission from the member recognized. This permission is called yielding and usually is requested in the form, "Will the gentleman (or gentlelady) yield to me?" While this activity occasionally is seen in the Senate, the Senate has no rule or practice to parcel out time.

In the House, the floor manager of a bill usually apportions debate time by yielding specific amounts of time to members who have requested it. ∎

VOTE STUDIES

<u>PRESIDENTIAL SUPPORT</u>

When Congress Had To Choose, It Voted To Back Clinton

Only Eisenhower and LBJ topped Clinton's 86.4% success rate in a president's first year

When politicians and pundits — and ultimately historians — looked back at President Clinton's first year in office, they were likely to see a political roller coaster of ambitious goals and rapid retreats, skillful maneuvering and serious miscalculations, lucky breaks and unforeseen problems.

But when they looked specifically at the president's record in Congress, they were likely to conclude that he had a very good year.

In 1993, Clinton got his way with Congress on 86.4 percent of the 191 roll call votes on which he declared a position.

That was double President George Bush's success rate of 1992 and among the highest scores recorded in the 40 years that Congressional Quarterly had been measuring presidential support and presidential success in Congress.

And not only did Clinton win often, he won when it counted the most — on the August budget package vote and on the November showdown on the North American Free Trade Agreement (NAFTA).

Clinton's success record was strong in both chambers. In the House he prevailed 87.3 percent of the time, and in the Senate he earned an 85.4 percent rating.

He also scored well in every subject category, ranging from a high of 92.3 percent on economic issues to 83.8 percent on defense and foreign policy to 82.6 percent on domestic issues. *(Category breakdown, p. 8-C)*

Clinton's high success rate was due to several factors, but the most significant was that he was working with a Congress controlled by his own party.

In addition, Democrats in the House and Senate knew

Guide to Vote Studies

from the start that helping Clinton succeed was important to their own political futures.

That knowledge "is forcing them to sink or swim together," suggested Stephen Wayne, a Georgetown University government professor.

Indeed, most Democrats gave Clinton strong support. In 1992, House Republicans supported Bush an average of 71 percent of the time, while Senate Republicans backed him 73 percent of the time. In 1993, House Democrats supported Clinton an average of 77 percent of the time, while Senate Democrats contributed an average of 87 percent.

But it wasn't just Democratic loyalty that led to the victories. Clinton showed a willingness and considerable ability to work Congress, arguing, cajoling, trading and doing almost anything within reason to get his way. This was particularly apparent on the budget battle and the NAFTA debate.

Clinton has "worked the Congress very hard. You have to credit him," said Nicholas E. Calio, who was Bush's chief lobbyist in 1992.

"What he did on NAFTA was herculean," said House Minority Leader Robert H. Michel, R-Ill.

But there were also factors independent of Clinton that contributed to his extraordinarily high batting average. Clinton took over after 12 years of Republican administrations. During most of that time, Congress was controlled by Democrats who saw their agenda blocked or diluted by vetoes and veto threats. Once Clinton took office, some long-stalled legislation began to move (parental leave, the "motor voter" registration bill and the Hatch Act, to name a few), and the president gained points on his success rate simply by expressing his support for the bills.

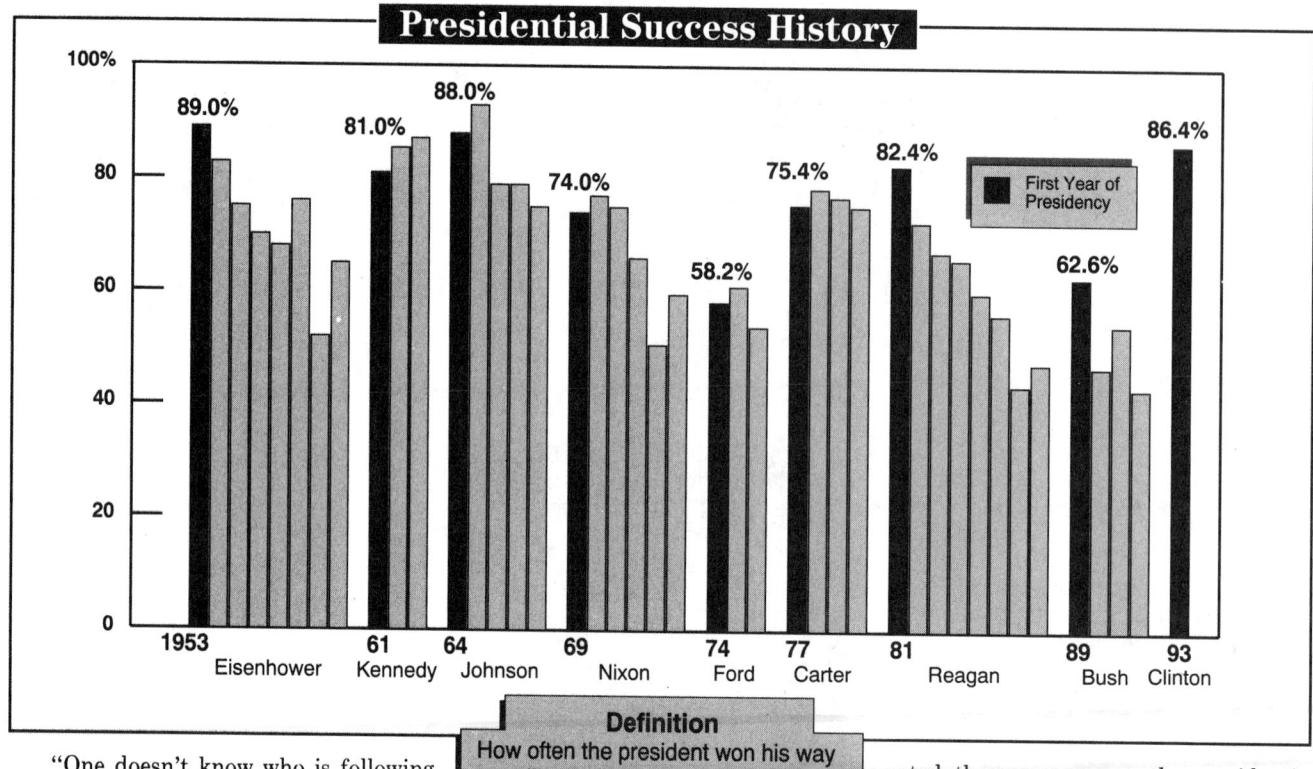

Presidential Success History

"One doesn't know who is following whom," said Wayne.

Clinton's tally ranked him near the top for presidents in their first year in office. In 1953, Republican Dwight D. Eisenhower had an 89 percent success rate, and in 1964, Democrat Lyndon B. Johnson's success rate was 88 percent. (A preliminary report in September on presidential success showed Clinton ahead of Johnson, but Clinton took several losses in the final weeks of the session on issues such as grazing fees on federal lands and termination of the superconducting super collider.) *(History, p. 5-C)*

Like Clinton, Eisenhower and Johnson worked with Congresses controlled by their own party. But that alone was not enough to ensure a top score. Democrat Jimmy Carter had a 75.4 percent success rate in 1977, his first year in office. John F. Kennedy had an 81 percent success rate his first year.

Ronald Reagan, who took office with a Democratic House and Republican Senate, scored 82.4 percent in 1981, his first year as president. But his success rate dropped steadily thereafter, bottoming out at 43.5 percent in 1987.

Some Caveats

In conducting their presidential support study, CQ reporters and editors examined each roll call vote to determine if Clinton took a position on it. Of the 597 recorded roll call votes in the House (other than quorum calls), CQ identified 102 on which the president took a position. Clinton won on 89. Of the 395 roll calls in the Senate, he took an unambiguous position on 89, and that position prevailed 76 times.

Those votes were the raw material for the two indicators used to measure presidential support:

● The first was presidential success. This measures how often Clinton won on votes on which he took a position.

● The second was members' support — how often a member

Definition

How often the president won his way on roll call votes on which he took a clear position.

1993 Data

Senate	76 victories
	13 defeats
House	89 victories
	13 defeats

Total Clinton success rate **86.4%**

Data, votes, pp. 8-C –13-C

voted the same way as the president's position. A 100 percent score for a House member, for instance, meant that member voted to back the president's position every time he or she voted on one of the 102 presidential position questions.

The CQ study, first conducted in 1953, had several limitations and should be regarded as only one of several tools for measuring a president's effectiveness.

One limitation was that the study did not include voice votes, even though some important issues were decided without a recorded vote, particularly in the Senate.

In addition, the study did not include presidential positions that never reached the floor. Thus, Clinton's setbacks on the nominations of Zoë Baird and Lani Guinier, for example, did not count against him in the study, although they clearly had an impact on his overall effectiveness in Congress.

The study also tended to conceal those instances in which the president settled for less than he sought. While Congress approved the National Service Act and an easing of the ban on gays in the military, for example, in both instances it gave Clinton far less than he had asked for. Yet, because Clinton supported the final versions of those measures, both still counted as victories in the presidential success study.

Although CQ did not measure how often this happened in 1993, Clinton's frequent willingness to compromise suggests that compromise could have had a significant impact.

Also, it is important to note that the CQ study gave equal standing to all floor votes, regardless of their significance. Clinton's pivotal victories on the budget-reconciliation bill and NAFTA counted the same in the CQ study as a comparatively insignificant vote, such as a 347-65 House vote to authorize maritime programs. Defeat of the reconciliation bill would have crippled Clinton, but a victory for the maritime bill did not alter his stature as a leader.

Clinton Bested Only by Ike, LBJ

President Clinton's high success score of 86.4 percent invites comparison with the only two presidents who had better scores for the first year in office, Dwight D. Eisenhower and Lyndon B. Johnson.

Since Congressional Quarterly started calculating presidential support scores in 1953, Eisenhower had held the first-year record (89 percent). In that year, Republicans narrowly controlled both chambers, and Eisenhower won big victories on statehood for Hawaii, confirmation of state title for tidelands and offshore oil and executive authority to reorganize portions of the government.

Other issues on which Eisenhower won in 1953 included the creation of the Department of Health, Education and Welfare (which became Health and Human Services), the issuing of 209,000 visas beyond immigration quotas and the capping of foreign aid. Eisenhower was rebuffed on measures creating 35,000 public housing units, increasing funds for international information and education and allowing surplus farm products to be sent abroad as foreign aid.

The year 1953 was the first in which CQ tried to determine which votes the president actually took a position on. Selection of these "Eisenhower issues," as they were called, was based on a standard of "sharply defined" presidential declarations. The decision apparently was made at the end of the year, rather than as the votes were taken (the recent practice). Changes had since been made in the number and types of votes selected, as well as in the methodology of calculating scores.

Capitalizing on the impetus of the assassination of President John F. Kennedy, Johnson achieved his high success rate in 1964 by pushing through several major legislative achievements, such as enactment of the 1964 Civil Rights Act, which outlawed discrimination in public accommodations and employment on the basis of

Eisenhower

Johnson

race and sex, and initial passage of Medicare (which did not make it through conference that year). Yet Johnson's 1964 score of 88 percent was only a prelude to his 93 percent score in 1965, a year widely regarded by political scientists as among the most productive in congressional history.

Johnson had only one major floor defeat on final passage of legislation in his first full year in the White House. He lost a fierce battle with Congress on legislation imposing mandatory quotas on the imports of meat. Members from livestock-producing states claimed meat imports were a prime cause for the depressed state of the industry.

The administration, the chief opponent of the legislation, felt that meat imports were not a major damaging factor to livestock producers. Under threat of a veto, Congress passed an acceptable compromise that scaled back the restrictions, and, in fact, made it possible that the quotas would never be imposed.

Civil rights, however, was the issue of 1964. In fact, so dominant was that legislation in the Senate that some votes were not used in computing Johnson's success score. In order to maintain consistency with previous studies, CQ editors selected just 10 key votes in the Senate on the issue for that year's vote studies, "lest the civil rights issue be overweighted."

Most of the disregarded votes were on amendments by Southern senators that attempted to restrict the reach of the Civil Rights Act of 1964. Johnson vigorously opposed these efforts and was successful on all but three. Had all these votes been included, Johnson's 1964 score would have been higher, probably even higher than Eisenhower's 1953 score. But other methodological changes, plus shifts in congressional voting procedures, also occurred in the ensuing decades, and their effect could not be measured in hindsight.

Some of the votes that show up in the CQ study as defeats for Clinton were only temporary setbacks; he lost preliminary votes on issues such as the Brady bill and the Hatch Act, but in the end he prevailed on those matters.

And some of Clinton's defeats were on topics that the White House chose not to lobby with much intensity. The administration nominally supported the superconducting super collider. But when deficit hawks in the House mobilized to terminate the $11 billion atom smasher in October, the administration kept a low profile.

Democratic Determination

Clinton's November 1992 election gave the Democrats control of both the executive and legislative branches for the first time in a dozen years. As Clinton took office, the Democratic leadership in Congress seemed intent on establishing an image of competence at governing. In the early weeks of the administration, Democrats locked arms and

gave overwhelming support to the Family and Medical Leave Act and to the fiscal 1994 budget resolution that represented the president's fiscal policy blueprint.

Democrats could point to these initiatives as evidence that the philosophy of the federal government had changed since the Reagan-Bush years. But the critical test of whether Democrats could put their stamp on government came on the budget-reconciliation bill in August. That measure, embodying a clear break from GOP fiscal policies, raised taxes on gasoline and other transportation fuels and on upper-income individuals, cut the defense budget and increased funds for some social and anti-poverty programs.

Republicans refused to have any part of the reconciliation bill; it did not get a single GOP vote in either chamber. With Democratic leaders watching whip counts intently and Clinton waging an intense and personal campaign to woo individual members, the president just barely managed to overcome defections from conservatives in his own

Leading Scorers: Clinton's Support, Opposition

Support indicates those who in 1993 voted most often for President Clinton's position; opposition shows how often members voted against the president's position. Scores are based on actual votes cast, and members are listed alphabetically when their scores are tied. Members not eligible for half the votes are not listed.

Support

Senate

Moseley-Braun

Chafee

Democrats		Republicans	
Moseley-Braun, Ill.	99%	Chafee, R.I.	57%
Dodd, Conn.	98	Jeffords, Vt.	57
Biden, Del.	97	Durenberger, Minn.	51
Glenn, Ohio	97	Kassebaum, Kan.	47
Kennedy, Mass.	97	Specter, Pa.	47
Murray, Wash.	96	Hatfield, Ore.	46
Sarbanes, Md.	96	Hutchison, Texas	46
Simon, Ill.	96	Packwood, Ore.	45
Inouye, Hawaii	95	Cohen, Maine	42
Lieberman, Conn.	95	Danforth, Mo.	42
Mikulski, Md.	95	Roth, Del.	40
Pell, R.I.	95	Domenici, N.M.	34
Robb, Va.	95	Lugar, Ind.	34
Rockefeller, W.Va.	95		

House

Bacchus

Boehlert

Democrats		Republicans	
Bacchus, Fla.	98%	Boehlert, N.Y.	74%
Dicks, Wash.	95	Morella, Md.	72
Pickle, Texas	95	Gilman, N.Y.	69
Rose, N.C.	95	Johnson, Conn.	67
Dixon, Calif.	94	Machtley, R.I.	67
Gibbons, Fla.	94	Horn, Calif.	64
Hoyer, Md.	94	Gallo, N.J.	63
Mineta, Calif.	94	Fish, N.Y.	62
Torricelli, N.J.	94	McDade, Pa.	62
Fazio, Calif.	93	Diaz-Balart, Fla.	61
Meek, Fla.	93	Torkildsen, Mass.	61
Smith, Iowa	93	Lazio, N.Y.	59

Opposition

Senate

Shelby

Smith

Democrats		Republicans	
Shelby, Ala.	54%	Smith, N.H.	89%
Hollings, S.C.	27	Faircloth, N.C.	88
Heflin, Ala.	25	Helms, N.C.	88
Exon, Neb.	22	Wallop, Wyo.	86
Nunn, Ga.	21	Craig, Idaho	85
Byrd, W.Va.	20	Kempthorne, Idaho	85
DeConcini, Ariz.	20	Nickles, Okla.	82
Bryan, Nev.	19	Lott, Miss.	80
Dorgan, N.D.	19	Brown, Colo.	79
Kerrey, Neb.	19	Gramm, Texas	78
Kohl, Wis.	19		

House

Tauzin

Nussle

Democrats		Republicans	
Tauzin, La.	52%	Nussle, Iowa	83%
Taylor, Miss.	52	Crane, Ill.	82
Condit, Calif.	50	Allard, Colo.	80
Hall, Texas	46	Herger, Calif.	80
Peterson, Minn.	44	Sensenbrenner, Wis.	80
Poshard, Ill.	43	Doolittle, Calif.	79
Deal, Ga.	41	Shuster, Pa.	78
Jacobs, Ind.	41	Archer, Texas	77
Murphy, Pa.	40	Hancock, Mo.	77
Penny, Minn.	40	Rohrabacher, Calif.	77
Stenholm, Texas	40	Royce, Calif.	77

	1	2	3
Alabama			
Heflin	71	24	75
Shelby	45	53	46
Alaska			
Murkowski	24	70	25
Stevens	31	65	33
Arizona			
DeConcini	76	19	80
McCain	27	70	28
Arkansas			
Bumpers	91	8	92
Pryor	87	8	92
California			
Boxer	91	9	91
Feinstein	89	8	92
Colorado			
Campbell	82	17	83
Brown	21	79	21
Connecticut			
Dodd	97	2	98
Lieberman	94	4	95
Delaware			
Biden	94	3	97
Roth	40	60	40
Florida			
Graham	90	10	90
Mack	25	75	25
Georgia			
Nunn	75	20	79
Coverdell	25	74	25
Hawaii			
Akaka	94	6	94
Inouye	85	4	95
Idaho			
Craig	15	85	15
Kempthorne	15	85	15
Illinois			
Moseley-Braun	99	1	99
Simon	96	4	96
Indiana			
Coats	29	70	30
Lugar	34	65	34

	1	2	3
Iowa			
Harkin	92	7	93
Grassley	25	75	25
Kansas			
Dole	28	72	28
Kassebaum	47	53	47
Kentucky			
Ford	92	8	92
McConnell	28	71	28
Louisiana			
Breaux	84	13	86
Johnston	85	13	86
Maine			
Mitchell	94	6	94
Cohen	42	58	42
Maryland			
Mikulski	93	4	95
Sarbanes	96	4	96
Massachusetts			
Kennedy	93	3	97
Kerry	93	7	93
Michigan			
Levin	93	7	93
Riegle	87	7	93
Minnesota			
Wellstone	91	8	92
Durenberger	48	46	51
Mississippi			
Cochran	26	74	26
Lott	19	79	20
Missouri			
Bond	31	65	33
Danforth	42	57	42
Montana			
Baucus	89	10	90
Burns	24	75	24
Nebraska			
Exon	76	21	78
Kerrey	80	19	81
Nevada			
Bryan	81	19	81
Reid	88	12	88

	1	2	3
New Hampshire			
Gregg	22	72	24
Smith	11	87	11
New Jersey			
Bradley	88	9	91
Lautenberg	85	15	85
New Mexico			
Bingaman	85	13	86
Domenici	34	66	34
New York			
Moynihan	93	7	93
D'Amato	28	69	29
North Carolina			
Faircloth	12	87	13
Helms	11	84	12
North Dakota			
Conrad	80	18	82
Dorgan	72	17	81
Ohio			
Glenn	97	3	97
Metzenbaum	91	8	92
Oklahoma			
Boren	87	10	90
Nickles	18	81	18
Oregon			
Hatfield	45	53	46
Packwood	45	54	45
Pennsylvania			
Wofford	87	10	90
Specter	42	47	47
Rhode Island			
Pell	93	4	95
Chafee	57	43	57
South Carolina			
Hollings	73	27	73
Thurmond	27	71	28
South Dakota			
Daschle	92	7	93
Pressler	25	74	25
Tennessee			
Mathews	90	9	91
Sasser	87	13	87

	1	2	3
Texas			
Gramm	21	76	22
Hutchison[1]†	45	53	46
Utah			
Bennett	31	66	32
Hatch	27	71	28
Vermont			
Leahy	92	7	93
Jeffords	56	42	57
Virginia			
Robb	94	4	95
Warner	28	71	28
Washington			
Murray	90	3	96
Gorton	30	67	31
West Virginia			
Byrd	80	20	80
Rockefeller	91	4	95
Wisconsin			
Feingold	85	15	85
Kohl	81	19	81
Wyoming			
Simpson	29	63	32
Wallop	13	83	14

Presidential Support and Opposition: Senate

1. Clinton Support Score, 1993. Percentage of 89 recorded votes in 1993 on which President Clinton took a position and on which a senator voted "yea" or "nay" *in agreement* with the president's position. Failures to vote lowered both support and opposition scores.

2. Clinton Opposition Score, 1993. Percentage of 89 recorded votes in 1993 on which President Clinton took a position and on which a senator voted "yea" or "nay" *in disagreement* with the president's position. Failures to vote lowered both support and opposition scores.

3. Clinton Support Score, 1993. Percentage of 89 recorded votes in 1993 on which President Clinton took a position and on which a senator was present and voted "yea" or "nay" *in agreement* with the president's position. In this version of the study, absences are not counted; therefore, failures to vote did not lower support or opposition scores. Opposition scores, not listed here, are the inverse of the support score; i.e., the opposition score is equal to 100 percent minus the individual's support score.

[1] *Kay Bailey Hutchison, R-Texas, was sworn in June 14, 1993, to succeed Bob Krueger, D. Krueger was appointed by Gov. Ann W. Richards, D, to fill the seat vacated by Lloyd Bentsen, D, who became Treasury secretary Jan. 20, 1993. Krueger was eligible for 42 presidential-support votes in 1993. His presidential-support score was 62 percent; opposition score 14 percent; support score, adjusted for absences, 81 percent. Bentsen was eligible for no presidential-support votes in 1993. Hutchison was eligible for 47 presidential-support votes in 1993.*

Presidential Support and Opposition: House

1. Clinton Support Score, 1993. Percentage of 102 recorded votes in 1993 on which President Clinton took a position and on which a representative voted "yea" or "nay" *in agreement* with the president's position. Failures to vote lowered both support and opposition scores.

2. Clinton Opposition Score, 1993. Percentage of 102 recorded votes in 1993 on which President Clinton took a position and on which a representative voted "yea" or "nay" *in disagreement* with the president's position. Failures to vote lowered both support and opposition scores.

3. Clinton Support Score, 1993. Percentage of 102 recorded votes in 1993 on which President Clinton took a position and on which a representative was present and voted "yea" or "nay" *in agreement* with the president's position. In this version of the study, absences were not counted; therefore, failures to vote did not lower support or opposition scores. Opposition scores, not listed here, are the inverse of the support score; i.e., the opposition score is equal to 100 percent minus the individual's support score.

NOTE: Delegates were eligible for 30 of the 102 presidential-support votes in 1993.

[1] *Rep. Sam Farr, D-Calif., was sworn in June 16, 1993, to succeed Leon E. Panetta, D, who became director of the Office of Management and Budget Jan. 21, 1993. Panetta was eligible for no presidential-support votes in 1993. Farr was eligible for 72 presidential-support votes in 1993.*

[2] *Rep. Vernon J. Ehlers, R-Mich., tentatively will be sworn in Jan. 25, 1994, to succeed Paul B. Henry, R, who died July 31, 1993. Henry was eligible for 45 presidential-support votes in 1993. His presidential-support score was 0 percent; opposition score, 0 percent; support score, adjusted for absences, 0 percent. Ehlers was eligible for no presidential-support votes in 1993.*

[3] *Rep. Bennie Thompson, D-Miss., was sworn in April 20, 1993, to succeed Mike Espy, D, who became Agriculture secretary Jan. 22, 1993. Espy was eligible for no presidential-support votes in 1993. Thompson was eligible for 83 presidential-support votes in 1993.*

[4] *Rep. Rob Portman, R-Ohio, was sworn in May 5, 1993, to succeed Bill Gradison, R, who resigned Jan. 31, 1993. Gradison was eligible for no presidential-support votes in 1993. Portman was eligible for 82 presidential-support votes in 1993.*

[5] *Rep. Thomas S. Foley, D-Wash., as Speaker of the House, voted at his discretion on 12 presidential-support votes in 1993.*

[6] *Rep. Peter W. Barca, D-Wis., was sworn in June 8, 1993, to succeed Les Aspin, D, who became Defense secretary Jan. 20, 1993. Aspin was eligible for no presidential-support votes in 1993. Barca was eligible for 73 presidential-support votes in 1993.*

KEY

† Not eligible for all recorded votes in 1993 or voted "present" to avoid possible conflict of interest.

Democrats *Republicans*
Independent

	1	2	3
Alabama			
1 *Callahan*	28	69	29
2 *Everett*	32	68	32
3 Browder	76	24	76
4 Bevill	82	16	84
5 Cramer	82	17	83
6 *Bachus*	33	67	33
7 Hilliard	75	21	78
Alaska			
AL *Young*	42	44	49
Arizona			
1 Coppersmith	84	15	85
2 Pastor	86	14	86
3 *Stump*	27	73	27
4 *Kyl*	30	67	31
5 *Kolbe*	44	56	44
6 English	77	23	77
Arkansas			
1 Lambert	72	27	72
2 Thornton	84	10	90
3 *Hutchinson*	31	69	31
4 Dickey	37	60	38
California			
1 Hamburg	75	25	75
2 *Herger*	20	77	20
3 Fazio	93	7	93
4 *Doolittle*	21	79	21
5 Matsui	88	8	92
6 Woolsey	78	20	80
7 Miller	74	23	77
8 Pelosi	77	19	81
9 Dellums	75	24	76
10 *Baker*	29	71	29
11 *Pombo*	25	73	26
12 Lantos	79	16	84
13 Stark	71	25	73
14 Eshoo	84	16	84
15 Mineta	94	6	94
16 Edwards	79	18	82
17 Farr[1]†	76	22	77
18 Condit	50	49	50
19 Lehman	69	26	72
20 Dooley	66	27	71
21 *Thomas*	52	47	52
22 *Huffington*	46	52	47
23 *Gallegly*	41	59	41
24 Beilenson	74	20	79
25 *McKeon*	30	67	31
26 Berman	78	10	89
27 *Moorhead*	33	67	33
28 *Dreier*	34	64	35
29 Waxman	82	18	82
30 Becerra	71	23	76
31 Martinez	77	20	80
32 Dixon	94	6	94
33 Roybal-Allard	80	18	82
34 Torres	87	11	89
35 Waters	77	22	78
36 Harman	85	10	90
37 Tucker	80	17	83
38 *Horn*	64	35	64
39 *Royce*	23	77	23
40 *Lewis*	42	56	43
41 *Kim*	35	65	35

	1	2	3
42 Brown	84	10	90
43 *Calvert*	37	61	38
44 *McCandless*	35	62	36
45 *Rohrabacher*	23	77	23
46 *Dornan*	30	66	32
47 *Cox*	32	63	34
48 *Packard*	30	61	33
49 Schenk	76	23	77
50 Filner	77	23	77
51 *Cunningham*	30	70	30
52 *Hunter*	25	71	26
Colorado			
1 Schroeder	72	26	73
2 Skaggs	82	18	82
3 *McInnis*	36	63	37
4 *Allard*	20	80	20
5 *Hefley*	28	72	28
6 *Schaefer*	33	67	33
Connecticut			
1 Kennelly	88	12	88
2 Gejdenson	83	17	83
3 DeLauro	84	16	84
4 *Shays*	55	45	55
5 *Franks*	49	51	49
6 *Johnson*	66	32	67
Delaware			
AL *Castle*	54	43	56
Florida			
1 Hutto	64	35	64
2 Peterson	91	9	91
3 Brown	86	9	91
4 Fowler	54	44	55
5 Thurman	74	26	74
6 *Stearns*	33	66	34
7 *Mica*	31	69	31
8 *McCollum*	40	58	41
9 *Bilirakis*	44	54	45
10 *Young*	34	63	35
11 Gibbons	93	6	94
12 *Canady*	31	69	31
13 *Miller*	39	61	39
14 *Goss*	41	59	41
15 *Bacchus*	97	2	98
16 *Lewis*	27	68	29
17 Meek	91	7	93
18 *Ros-Lehtinen*	57	42	57
19 Johnston	84	16	84
20 Deutsch	87	13	87
21 *Diaz-Balart*	60	38	61
22 *Shaw*	48	51	49
23 Hastings	89	11	89
Georgia			
1 *Kingston*	26	73	27
2 Bishop	88	12	88
3 *Collins*	29	71	29
4 *Linder*	32	68	32
5 Lewis	79	21	79
6 *Gingrich*	42	56	43
7 Darden	92	8	92
8 Rowland	71	29	71
9 Deal	58	40	59
10 Johnson	78	21	79
11 McKinney	76	23	77
Hawaii			
1 Abercrombie	69	23	75
2 Mink	73	26	73
Idaho			
1 LaRocco	80	20	80
2 *Crapo*	33	67	33
Illinois			
1 Rush	76	19	80
2 Reynolds	81	18	82
3 Lipinski	67	30	69
4 Gutierrez	72	24	75
5 Rostenkowski	75	19	80
6 *Hyde* †	38	58	40
7 Collins	77	22	78
8 *Crane*	18	82	18
9 Yates	75	17	82
10 *Porter*	45	50	47
11 Sangmeister	75	24	76
12 Costello	71	28	71
13 *Fawell*	43	56	44
14 *Hastert*	35	64	36
15 *Ewing*	31	69	31
16 *Manzullo*	29	71	29
17 Evans	69	27	71

ND Northern Democrats   SD Southern Democrats

The columns of numbers are headed **1**, **2**, **3** throughout.

District/Member	1	2	3
18 *Michel*	43	52	45
19 Poshard	57	43	57
20 Durbin	77	22	78
Indiana			
1 Visclosky	82	17	83
2 Sharp	76	20	80
3 Roemer	74	25	74
4 Long	70	30	70
5 *Buyer*	40	59	41
6 *Burton*	25	74	26
7 *Myers*	39	55	42
8 McCloskey	86	14	86
9 Hamilton	85	15	85
10 Jacobs	59	41	59
Iowa			
1 *Leach*	55	39	58
2 *Nussle*	17	83	17
3 *Lightfoot*	35	63	36
4 Smith	92	7	93
5 *Grandy*	40	59	41
Kansas			
1 *Roberts*	34	66	34
2 Slattery	75	23	77
3 *Meyers*	58	42	58
4 Glickman	86	14	86
Kentucky			
1 Barlow	76	23	77
2 Natcher	90	10	90
3 Mazzoli	78	22	78
4 *Bunning*	26	73	27
5 *Rogers*	47	53	47
6 Baesler	72	25	74
Louisiana			
1 *Livingston*	41	59	41
2 Jefferson	83	13	87
3 Tauzin	47	51	48
4 Fields	81	19	81
5 *McCrery*	44	56	44
6 *Baker*	36	62	37
7 Hayes	65	28	69
Maine			
1 Andrews	76	24	76
2 *Snowe*	41	59	41
Maryland			
1 *Gilchrest*	58	41	58
2 *Bentley*	47	50	48
3 Cardin	83	17	83
4 Wynn	80	20	80
5 Hoyer	93	6	94
6 *Bartlett*	35	65	35
7 Mfume	75	23	77
8 *Morella*	70	27	72
Massachusetts			
1 Olver	82	17	83
2 Neal	82	16	84
3 *Blute*	54	45	54
4 Frank	77	22	78
5 Meehan	77	22	78
6 *Torkildsen*	61	39	61
7 Markey	81	18	82
8 Kennedy	79	18	82
9 Moakley	74	16	82
10 Studds	79	20	80
Michigan			
1 Stupak	72	28	72
2 *Hoekstra*	38	62	38
3 Vacancy[2]	--	--	--
4 *Camp*	32	68	32
5 Barcia	61	37	62
6 *Upton*	51	49	51
7 *Smith*	32	62	34
8 Carr	73	25	74
9 Kildee	73	27	73
10 Bonior	80	16	84
11 *Knollenberg*	29	69	30
12 Levin	85	15	85
13 Ford	73	21	78
14 Conyers	63	17	79
15 Collins	76	23	77
16 Dingell	75	17	82
Minnesota			
1 Penny	60	40	60
2 Minge	66	33	66
3 *Ramstad*	45	55	45
4 Vento	80	20	80

District/Member	1	2	3
5 Sabo	81	18	82
6 *Grams*	33	65	34
7 Peterson	56	43	56
8 Oberstar	72	28	72
Mississippi			
1 *Whitten*	80	8	91
2 Thompson[3]†	71	22	77
3 Montgomery	75	25	75
4 Parker	67	33	67
5 Taylor	48	52	48
Missouri			
1 Clay	78	19	81
2 *Talent*	33	65	34
3 Gephardt	86	9	91
4 Skelton	73	25	74
5 Wheat	80	17	83
6 Danner	72	28	72
7 *Hancock*	23	75	23
8 *Emerson*	44	56	44
9 Volkmer	75	25	75
Montana			
AL Williams	63	28	69
Nebraska			
1 *Bereuter*	53	47	53
2 Hoagland	81	19	81
3 *Barrett*	40	60	40
Nevada			
1 Bilbray	79	21	79
2 *Vucanovich*	33	61	35
New Hampshire			
1 *Zeliff*	44	56	44
2 Swett	75	22	78
New Jersey			
1 Andrews	74	25	74
2 Hughes	76	24	76
3 *Saxton*	50	50	50
4 *Smith*	52	46	53
5 *Roukema*	45	49	48
6 Pallone	74	26	74
7 *Franks*	56	44	56
8 Klein	80	19	81
9 Torricelli	91	6	94
10 Payne	78	19	81
11 *Gallo*	63	37	63
12 *Zimmer*	37	61	38
13 Menendez	81	17	83
New Mexico			
1 *Schiff*	51	47	52
2 *Skeen*	45	51	47
3 Richardson	90	8	92
New York			
1 Hochbrueckner	86	11	89
2 *Lazio*	59	41	59
3 *King*	47	53	47
4 *Levy*	50	50	50
5 Ackerman	83	10	89
6 Flake	72	21	78
7 Manton	84	11	89
8 Nadler	75	24	76
9 Schumer	81	17	83
10 Towns	74	20	79
11 Owens	73	25	74
12 Velazquez	68	27	71
13 *Molinari*	52	47	52
14 Maloney	79	21	79
15 Rangel	76	22	78
16 Serrano	74	23	77
17 Engel	77	15	84
18 Lowey	84	16	84
19 Fish	62	37	62
20 *Gilman*	69	31	69
21 McNulty	79	21	79
22 *Solomon*	28	68	30
23 *Boehlert*	74	26	74
24 *McHugh*	38	58	40
25 *Walsh*	49	51	49
26 Hinchey	81	16	84
27 *Paxon*	29	70	30
28 Slaughter	74	25	75
29 LaFalce	72	25	74
30 *Quinn*	47	53	47
31 *Houghton*	56	41	58
North Carolina			
1 Clayton	76	23	77
2 Valentine	66	31	68

District/Member	1	2	3
3 Lancaster	81	19	81
4 Price	87	11	89
5 Neal	72	20	78
6 *Coble*	25	75	25
7 Rose	90	5	95
8 Hefner	79	19	81
9 *McMillan*	49	49	50
10 *Ballenger*	29	71	29
11 *Taylor*	27	71	28
12 Watt	79	21	79
North Dakota			
AL Pomeroy	76	24	76
Ohio			
1 Mann	81	19	81
2 *Portman*[4]†	35	65	35
3 Hall	61	24	72
4 *Oxley*	43	52	45
5 *Gillmor*	47	47	50
6 Strickland	75	24	76
7 *Hobson*	49	51	49
8 *Boehner*	34	66	34
9 Kaptur	69	27	71
10 *Hoke*	35	60	37
11 Stokes	82	12	88
12 *Kasich*	32	65	33
13 Brown	72	26	73
14 Sawyer	87	12	88
15 *Pryce*	46	54	46
16 *Regula*	58	42	58
17 Traficant	66	33	66
18 Applegate	66	33	66
19 Fingerhut	75	24	76
Oklahoma			
1 *Inhofe*	30	68	31
2 Synar	75	19	80
3 Brewster	68	30	69
4 McCurdy	84	10	90
5 *Istook*	30	69	31
6 English	61	38	61
Oregon			
1 Furse	80	19	81
2 *Smith*	30	64	32
3 Wyden	77	22	78
4 DeFazio	66	32	67
5 Kopetski	83	15	85
Pennsylvania			
1 Foglietta	78	18	82
2 Blackwell	78	20	80
3 Borski	85	11	89
4 Klink	65	33	66
5 *Clinger*	39	45	47
6 Holden	65	35	65
7 *Weldon*	47	51	48
8 *Greenwood*	43	56	44
9 *Shuster*	22	75	22
10 *McDade*	46	28	62
11 Kanjorski	73	27	73
12 Murtha	85	9	91
13 Margolies-Mezv.	77	23	77
14 Coyne	83	17	83
15 McHale	86	14	86
16 *Walker*	24	76	24
17 *Gekas*	31	68	32
18 Santorum	45	54	46
19 *Goodling*	41	57	42
20 Murphy	57	38	60
21 *Ridge*	46	44	51
Rhode Island			
1 *Machtley*	65	31	67
2 Reed	82	17	83
South Carolina			
1 *Ravenel*	38	62	38
2 *Spence*	41	59	41
3 Derrick	80	17	83
4 *Inglis*	25	75	25
5 Spratt	82	16	84
6 Clyburn	82	18	82
South Dakota			
AL Johnson	73	26	73
Tennessee			
1 *Quillen*	31	55	36
2 *Duncan*	25	75	25
3 Lloyd	83	14	86
4 Cooper	76	19	80
5 Clement	81	17	83

District/Member	1	2	3
6 Gordon	83	16	84
7 *Sundquist*	32	64	34
8 Tanner	71	29	71
9 Ford	54	16	77
Texas			
1 Chapman	78	17	82
2 Wilson	79	13	86
3 *Johnson, Sam*	27	73	27
4 Hall	54	46	54
5 Bryant	82	11	88
6 *Barton*	31	59	35
7 *Archer*	23	75	23
8 *Fields*	27	63	30
9 Brooks	86	10	90
10 Pickle	90	5	95
11 Edwards	82	17	83
12 Geren	72	27	72
13 Sarpalius	72	28	72
14 Laughlin	78	19	81
15 de la Garza	78	16	83
16 Coleman	90	9	91
17 Stenholm	60	39	60
18 Washington	63	22	74
19 *Combest*	30	70	30
20 Gonzalez	90	10	90
21 *Smith*	35	63	36
22 *DeLay*	25	75	25
23 *Bonilla*	33	67	33
24 Frost	87	9	91
25 Andrews	87	10	90
26 *Armey*	26	73	27
27 Ortiz	83	16	84
28 Tejeda	86	14	86
29 Green	77	19	81
30 Johnson, E. B.	90	10	90
Utah			
1 *Hansen*	32	67	33
2 Shepherd	79	21	79
3 Orton	62	38	62
Vermont			
AL *Sanders*	67	32	67
Virginia			
1 *Bateman*	50	46	52
2 Pickett	82	18	82
3 Scott	89	11	89
4 Sisisky	77	22	78
5 Payne	86	14	86
6 *Goodlatte*	42	58	42
7 *Bliley*	38	61	39
8 Moran	89	11	89
9 Boucher	82	15	85
10 *Wolf*	39	61	39
11 Byrne	76	24	76
Washington			
1 Cantwell	79	20	80
2 Swift	87	12	88
3 Unsoeld	75	23	77
4 Inslee	71	29	71
5 Foley[5]			
6 Dicks	91	5	95
7 McDermott	82	11	88
8 *Dunn*	47	52	48
9 Kreidler	80	20	80
West Virginia			
1 Mollohan	82	17	83
2 Wise	87	12	88
3 Rahall	64	34	65
Wisconsin			
1 Barca[6]†	67	33	67
2 *Klug*	50	49	50
3 *Gunderson*	51	49	51
4 Kleczka	80	19	81
5 Barrett	77	23	77
6 *Petri*	33	65	34
7 Obey	78	22	78
8 *Roth*	29	71	29
9 *Sensenbrenner*	20	80	20
Wyoming			
AL *Thomas*	32	67	33
Delegates			
de Lugo, V.I. †	57	37	61
Faleomavaega, Am.S. †	50	23	68
Norton, D.C. †	50	47	52
Romero-B., P.R. †	27	27	50
Underwood, Guam †	50	33	60

Southern states - Ala., Ark., Fla., Ga., Ky., La., Miss., N.C., Okla., S.C., Tenn., Texas, Va.
Omitted votes are quorum calls, which CQ does not include in its vote charts.

PARTY UNITY

With Democrat in White House, Partisanship Hit New High

Partisanship generally ruled the first session of the 103rd Congress, reaching levels in both the House and the Senate that had not been seen since Congressional Quarterly began measuring party divisions in 1954.

Democrats and Republicans in both chambers voted with the majority of their parties (and against the majority of the other party) more often in 1993 than in any year in the previous four decades.

The Senate prided itself on its traditional, proper comportment in contrast to the more raucously partisan wrangling associated with the House. But about two-thirds of the roll call votes in each chamber split along party lines in 1993, with a slightly higher percentage doing so in the Senate.

In the House, 65.5 percent of roll call votes were party-line votes (up from 64 percent in 1992). A slight rise in partisan votes had been predictable in the more fractious House due to post-election patterns and procedural squabbles.

But in the Senate, the partisanship measure jumped dramatically. Sixty-seven percent of roll call votes in the Senate followed party lines, an increase of 14 points from the 53 percent rate in 1992 (a year that featured many votes inspired and colored by the heated presidential election campaign).

The Senate reached this threshold of partisanship even without the frequent and acrimonious procedural votes that occurred in the House.

Individual members also showed unusually high levels of party loyalty in 1993. The average House Democrat voted with the majority of his party colleagues 89 percent of the time (excluding absences) on party-unity votes. Republicans were virtually as coherent: The average GOP member voted with his or her party majority 87 percent of the time. The pattern held in the Senate, where the average Democrat voted as a party person on 87 percent of the roll calls and the average Republican, on 86 percent.

Confluence of Factors

Several key factors were responsible for the intensity of partisanship and party unity. For the first time in 12 years, Democrats had a president in the White House who could rally and unite them. President Clinton, for his part, took

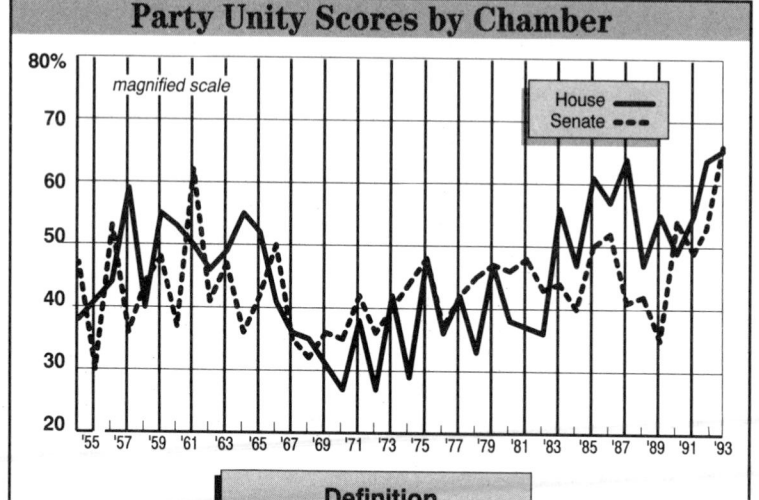

Party Unity Scores by Chamber

80%
70
60
50
40
30
20

magnified scale

House ——
Senate ---

'55 '57 '59 '61 '63 '65 '67 '69 '71 '73 '75 '77 '79 '81 '83 '85 '87 '89 '91 '93

Definition

The percentage of recorded floor votes in each chamber on which a majority of one party voted against a majority of the other party.

1993 Data

	Partisan Votes	Total Votes	Percent
Senate	265	395	67.1
House	391	597	65.5

Data, votes, pp. 17-C – 21-C

on controversial issues — from family leave and gays in the military to higher taxes and changes in campaign finance and election laws — that tended to divide members along strict party lines.

In the House, the burden of moving Clinton's program contributed to the Democratic leadership's decision to block many Republican floor amendments. This in turn spawned many GOP challenges, leading to procedural votes that, almost by definition, divided along party lines.

For Republicans, battling for political survival in the House, it was a policy decision to oppose Democrats at almost every turn, one they announced within a month of Clinton's election.

Accordingly, both parties often strove to cast issues and votes in clearly partisan terms.

"Parties have been jockeying to try to draw issues so that the lines are sharp," said Norman Ornstein, resident scholar at the American Enterprise Institute.

That impulse triumphed over any proclaimed interest in bipartisanship and cooperation. Even the 114 new members elected to the House in 1992 and 1993 promising change in the institution found themselves voting, by and large, as loyal soldiers for their parties.

In one crucial test of Clinton's presidency, the August vote on enacting Clinton's budget priorities into law, Democrats passed the package without a single Republican vote in either the House or Senate. It was the first time a majority party had passed legislation of that kind with absolutely no support from the opposition.

"That tells you something" about the political climate in the first session, Ornstein said.

Hail to the Chief

An overarching fact of life in the 103rd Congress was the Democrats' determination to prove wrong those who said they could not govern effectively even if they controlled both Congress and the White House.

"We have to demonstrate to the American people that we can govern," said John Lewis, D-Ga., a House chief deputy whip. "There is a conscious attempt on the part of

Leading Scorers: Party Unity

Support indicates those who in 1993 most consistently voted with their party's majority against the majority of the other party; opposition shows how often members voted against their party's majority. Scores are based on actual votes cast; members are ranked alphabetically when scores are tied. Members not eligible for half the votes are not listed.

Support

Senate

Mitchell   **Wallop**

Democrats		Republicans	
Mitchell, Maine	98%	Wallop, Wyo.	99%
Sarbanes, Md.	98	Gramm, Texas	98
Levin, Mich.	97	Craig, Idaho	97
Pell, R.I.	97	Faircloth, N.C.	97
Kennedy, Mass.	96	Helms, N.C.	97
Riegle, Mich.	96	Kempthorne, Idaho	97
Akaka, Hawaii.	95	Hatch, Utah	96
Boxer, Calif.	95	Lott, Miss.	96
Moseley-Braun, Ill.	95	Smith, N.H.	96
Moynihan, N.Y.	95	Dole, Kan.	95
Wellstone, Minn.	95	Mack, Fla.	95
		Nickles, Okla.	95

House

Becerra   **Bartlett**

Democrats		Republicans	
Becerra, Calif.	99%	Bartlett, Md.	99%
Coyne, Pa.	99	Hancock, Mo.	99
Dellums, Calif.	99	Stump, Ariz.	99
Frank, Mass.	99	Armey, Texas	98
Furse, Ore.	99	Boehner, Ohio	98
Markey, Mass.	99	Burton, Ind.	98
Payne, N.J.	99	Cunningham, Calif.	98
Rush, Ill.	99	Doolittle, Calif.	98
Serrano, N.Y.	99	Dornan, Calif.	98
Studds, Mass.	99	Fields, Texas	98
Wheat, Mo.	99	Hunter, Calif.	98
		Johnson, S., Texas	98
		Moorhead, Calif.	98
		Walker, Pa.	98

Opposition

Senate

Shelby   **Jeffords**

Democrats		Republicans	
Shelby, Ala.	63%	Jeffords, Vt.	54%
Heflin, Ala.	38	Chafee, R.I.	42
Exon, Neb.	29	Hatfield, Ore.	41
Nunn, Ga.	29	Durenberger, Minn.	39
Johnston, La.	22	Specter, Pa.	36
Hollings, S.C.	21	Cohen, Maine	31
Kerrey, Neb.	21	Packwood, Ore.	28
Bingaman, N.M.	20	Kassebaum, Kan.	23
Boren, Okla.	20	Roth, Del.	22
Breaux, La.	20	Warner, Va.	20
Campbell, Colo.	20		

House

Taylor   **Morella**

Democrats		Republicans	
Taylor, Miss.	63%	Morella, Md.	52%
Tauzin, La.	49	Gilman, N.Y.	47
Stenholm, Texas	48	Boehlert, N.Y.	40
Hall, Texas	46	Fish, N.Y.	38
Hutto, Fla.	46	Shays, Conn.	37
Jacobs, Ind.	46	Johnson, Conn.	33
Murphy, Pa.	41	Houghton, N.Y.	32
Orton, Utah	40	Snowe, Maine	32
Parker, Miss.	39	Gunderson, Wis.	31
Penny, Minn.	38	Leach, Iowa	31
		Machtley, R.I.	31
		Roukema, N.J.	31

the rank and file and the leadership to try to put gridlock behind us."

As for Republicans, being in the minority had gotten even tougher.

"The Democrats now have an administration in town, and not as many of them are crossing the line to vote with Republicans because they're being held in line," said Robert S. Walker, R-Pa., the House GOP's deputy whip.

Likewise, he said, his fellow Republicans were not inclined to work with Democrats either. Steven S. Smith, a political scientist and staff member at the Brookings Institution, agreed.

"For the first time in 12 years, the Democratic leadership had a president to back them up," Smith said.

And despite interparty squabbling that often threatened the president's success, he said, the White House remained the ultimate big gun: "The resources of the White House are considerable."

Those resources often were brought to bear on Democratic freshmen — most dramatically in August, when a last-minute Clinton call to Rep. Marjorie Margolies-Mezvinsky, D-Pa., secured the vote he needed to pass his budget package.

"You run and campaign on changing and bringing about dramatic changes in the way things take place, but when someone in the leadership talks about the need for party unity, that is a great incentive to stand with the party," Lewis said. "It's very hard to say no to the president."

That helped explain why House Democratic freshmen voted with their party an average of 92 percent of the time and Senate Democratic freshmen voted with their party 90 percent of the time on party-unity votes.

The Democrats' coherence, in turn, might help explain why the freshmen on the GOP side of both chambers were equally loyal to their party banner.

GOP House freshmen averaged a party-unity score of 89 percent, while GOP Senate freshmen averaged a party-unity score of 93 percent.

But Smith said more senior Democrats also felt pressure to toe the party line.

"Even moderate to conservative Democrats know that the public will hold the party accountable more fully when it has control of all the institutions," Smith said.

The Congressional Black Caucus, while jousting with Clinton and the Democratic leadership to secure some items in its own legislative agenda, remained loyal to the party in the process. Caucus Democrats voted with the party 97 percent of the time.

Change to Come?

Some experts predicted that partisanship would wane somewhat in 1994 as Clinton began the task of building coalitions across the parties on the issues of health care, crime and welfare.

"The president will start to move some of these programs toward the middle, because he can't win with a [strictly] partisan majority," Ornstein said.

In addition, all House members and a third of the Senate faced midterm elections. Party-line voting traditionally dipped in re-election years because, Ornstein said, it became "more important to show they voted *for* something."

"If we hadn't held tough, they would have rolled us and laughed while they did it."

—Sen. Alan K. Simpson, R-Wyo.

The extent to which Clinton might work with congressional Republicans was hard to discern. Thus far, on virtually every issue except the North American Free Trade Agreement, Republicans had had two choices: Fight Clinton or give in. In the first session, they usually chose to fight.

In a sense, the Democratic majority in the House had narrowed the GOP options with restrictive rules on floor debate and amendments.

The rules fights tended to intensify the partisanship, particularly in 1993, Ornstein said.

"The Democrats using the rules process in a way that has infuriated Republicans has contributed to that," Ornstein said. "When you have restrictive rules, you have take-it-or-leave-it alternatives."

Republicans retaliated by forcing procedural roll calls that did little but signal their displeasure and delay the proceedings.

"Even people who support the legislation will often vote against the rule, because they believe it is inherently unfair," Walker said. "Most Republicans don't have a problem voting against the [daily approval of the] Journal."

Lewis argued that rules that limited amendments were a matter of expediency.

"If you have open rules, you will never or seldom take care of the business of the American people, because you can bring almost anything to the floor," Lewis said.

Coherent Bloc in Senate

In the Senate as well, Republicans were greatly outnumbered. But the chamber's rules allowed a consistent minority to hold its own. With 41 votes sufficient to prolong debate ad infinitum, the GOP needed only that many of its 44 members to block most legislation other than the budget itself.

"They maintained a level of cohesiveness that was not expected," Brookings' Smith said.

In the Senate, the degree of partisanship evolved through the early weeks of the year, reaching a turning point in March when Democratic leaders used hardball procedural tactics to fight off amendments to Clinton's economic stimulus bill.

That helped Republican leader Bob Dole of Kansas forge a solid bloc that was not broken in any of the major votes on economic issues.

Even the most moderate of Senate Republicans, such as James M. Jeffords of Vermont, voted with their party more often in 1993 than they had in recent years. Jeffords, the Republican most likely to oppose his party in both 1992 and 1993, did so 54 percent of time in 1993, down from 61 percent in 1992.

"A united Republican Party in the Senate gives them the strength to obstruct legislation," Smith said. "That is one place where the Republicans can bring the Clinton steamroller to a halt."

Assistant Minority Leader Alan K. Simpson, R-Wyo., said the divisions in the Senate were not as acrimonious as in the House. But, he said, Republicans had little choice but to stick together.

"If we hadn't held tough, they would have rolled us and laughed while they did it," he said.   ■

Party-Unity Definitions

Party-unity votes. Recorded votes in the Senate or the House that split the parties, with a majority of voting Democrats opposing a majority of voting Republicans.

Party-unity support. Percentage of party-unity votes on which members voted "yea" or "nay" *in agreement* with a majority of their party. Failures to vote lowered scores for chambers and parties.

Opposition to party. Percentage of party-unity votes on which members voted "yea" or "nay" *in disagreement* with a majority of their party. Failures to vote lowered scores for chambers and parties.

Average Scores by Chamber

	1993		1992			1993		1992	
	Dem.	Rep.	Dem.	Rep.		Dem.	Rep.	Dem.	Rep.
Party Unity	85%	84%	79%	79%	**Opposition**	11%	13%	13%	16%
Senate	85	84	77	79	Senate	13	14	18	17
House	85	84	79	79	House	11	12	12	16

Sectional Support, Opposition

SENATE	Support	Opposition	HOUSE	Support	Opposition
Northern Democrats	88%	10%	Northern Democrats	87%	8%
Southern Democrats	76	21	Southern Democrats	80	16
Northern Republicans	81	16	Northern Republicans	83	14
Southern Republicans	91	6	Southern Republicans	88	9

1993 Victories, Defeats

	Senate	House	Total
Democrats won, Republicans lost	199	329	528
Republicans won, Democrats lost	66	62	128

Unanimous Voting by Parties

The number of times each party voted unanimously on 1993 party-unity votes. Scores for 1992 are in parentheses:

	Senate		House		Total	
Democrats voted unanimously	29	(12)	13	(18)	42	(30)
Republicans voted unanimously	57	(10)	65	(47)	122	(57)

Party-Unity Average Scores

Year	Democrats	Republicans	Year	Democrats	Republicans
1993	85%	84%	1976	65%	66%
1992	79	79	1975	69	70
1991	81	78	1974	63	62
1990	81	74	1973	68	68
1989	81	73	1972	57	64
1988	79	73	1971	62	66
1987	81	74	1970	57	59
1986	78	71	1969	62	62
1985	79	75	1968	57	63
1984	74	72	1967	66	71
1983	76	74	1966	61	67
1982	72	71	1965	69	70
1981	69	76	1964	67	69
1980	68	70	1963	71	72
1979	69	72	1962	69	68
1978	64	67	1961	71	72
1977	67	70			

Breakdown of Party-Unity Votes

Following are the votes, listed by roll call number, on which a majority of Democrats voted against a majority of Republicans.

House

(391 of 597 votes)

2	32	73	113	148	178	221	277	315	352	402	451	501	541	580
3	34	75	114	149	179	224	278	317	353	403	452	502	544	582
5	35	77	120	150	180	225	279	318	354	406	453	503	550	583
6	36	78	121	151	183	226	280	319	355	407	457	504	551	584
7	37	79	122	152	184	227	281	320	356	408	459	505	552	585
8	38	81	123	153	185	229	282	321	357	411	460	506	553	586
9	39	83	124	154	186	230	283	322	358	412	461	507	554	587
10	40	85	125	156	187	232	284	324	359	413	464	508	555	588
11	41	86	126	157	189	233	285	326	361	414	468	512	556	589
12	42	87	127	158	190	237	286	327	362	415	470	515	557	591
13	48	88	128	159	191	238	287	328	363	416	473	517	559	595
14	49	89	129	160	192	243	289	330	364	417	474	518	560	599
15	50	90	130	161	193	244	290	333	367	418	475	522	562	600
16	51	91	131	162	194	248	292	334	368	420	476	523	563	601
17	53	92	132	163	195	252	294	335	369	421	477	524	564	603
18	56	95	133	165	196	254	301	338	371	422	478	525	565	604
19	57	97	134	166	198	259	302	339	372	423	479	527	567	605
20	58	98	136	167	199	260	305	340	374	424	483	528	568	606
21	59	99	138	168	200	263	306	341	375	425	484	530	569	607
22	60	100	139	169	201	264	307	344	379	426	486	531	570	608
23	61	102	142	170	203	265	309	345	389	427	490	533	571	609
24	62	104	143	171	204	266	310	346	392	428	494	534	572	610
25	63	106	144	172	205	267	311	348	394	429	496	535	575	611
26	64	107	145	173	216	270	312	349	396	430	497	536	576	613
27	68	108	146	174	217	274	313	350	400	433	498	537	577	614
28	69	110	147	175	220	276	314	351	401	434	500	538	578	615
29														

Senate

(265 of 395 votes)

1	23	44	66	84	104	132	156	179	204	230	253	290	328	370
2	24	45	67	85	105	133	157	181	205	231	259	296	329	371
3	25	47	68	86	106	134	158	183	206	233	261	298	330	372
4	26	48	69	87	107	136	160	184	207	235	262	299	332	373
5	27	49	70	88	109	138	162	185	208	236	263	302	334	374
6	28	50	71	89	112	139	163	186	209	237	266	304	336	375
7	30	52	72	90	113	140	164	188	210	240	269	305	337	376
9	31	53	73	93	117	141	165	189	211	241	270	307	338	381
10	33	54	74	94	118	142	167	190	213	242	272	308	339	382
11	34	55	76	95	119	144	168	195	215	243	273	309	340	385
12	35	56	77	96	120	145	169	196	217	244	274	310	349	386
14	36	57	78	97	122	146	171	197	218	245	275	311	358	387
17	37	58	79	98	126	147	172	198	219	246	277	312	360	388
18	38	59	80	100	127	148	173	199	224	247	279	313	362	390
19	40	60	81	101	128	149	174	200	226	248	280	317	365	391
21	42	61	82	102	129	151	175	201	227	249	284	324	366	393
22	43	65	83	103	130	153	176	202	228	250	288	326	367	394
					131	154	177	203	229	251	289	327	369	395

Proportion of Partisan Roll Calls

How often a majority of Democrats voted against a majority of Republicans:

Year	House	Senate	Year	House	Senate	Year	House	Senate	Year	House	Senate
1954	38%	47%	1964	55%	36%	1974	29%	44%	1984	47%	40%
1955	41	30	1965	52	42	1975	48	48	1985	61	50
1956	44	53	1966	41	50	1976	36	37	1986	57	52
1957	59	36	1967	36	35	1977	42	42	1987	64	41
1958	40	44	1968	35	32	1978	33	45	1988	47	42
1959	55	48	1969	31	36	1979	47	47	1989	55	35
1960	53	37	1970	27	35	1980	38	46	1990	49	54
1961	50	62	1971	38	42	1981	37	48	1991	55	49
1962	46	41	1972	27	36	1982	36	43	1992	64	53
1963	49	47	1973	42	40	1983	56	44	1993	65	67

† Not eligible for all recorded votes in 1993 or voted "present" to avoid possible conflict of interest.

Democrats | Republicans

	1	2	3
Alabama			
Heflin	59	36	62
Shelby	36	61	37
Alaska			
Murkowski	82	7	92
Stevens	80	18	82
Arizona			
DeConcini	83	15	84
McCain	88	8	91
Arkansas			
Bumpers	89	10	90
Pryor	87	8	91
California			
Boxer	95	5	95
Feinstein	88	10	90
Colorado			
Campbell	77	19	80
Brown	91	9	91
Connecticut			
Dodd	91	8	92
Lieberman	83	17	83
Delaware			
Biden	91	8	92
Roth	77	22	78
Florida			
Graham	85	15	85
Mack	94	5	95
Georgia			
Nunn	66	27	71
Coverdell	91	6	94
Hawaii			
Akaka	95	5	95
Inouye	78	6	92
Idaho			
Craig	96	3	97
Kempthorne	97	3	97
Illinois			
Moseley-Braun	95	5	95
Simon	93	6	94
Indiana			
Coats	85	12	88
Lugar	88	12	88

	1	2	3
Iowa			
Harkin	92	6	93
Grassley	90	9	91
Kansas			
Dole	95	5	95
Kassebaum	76	23	77
Kentucky			
Ford	86	14	86
McConnell	92	6	94
Louisiana			
Breaux	78	20	80
Johnston	77	22	78
Maine			
Mitchell	98	2	98
Cohen	68	31	69
Maryland			
Mikulski	92	8	92
Sarbanes	97	2	98
Massachusetts			
Kennedy	95	4	96
Kerry	94	6	94
Michigan			
Levin	97	3	97
Riegle	93	4	96
Minnesota			
Wellstone	94	5	95
Durenberger	58	37	61
Mississippi			
Cochran	91	9	91
Lott	94	4	96
Missouri			
Bond	83	14	85
Danforth	80	18	82
Montana			
Baucus	80	15	85
Burns	92	8	92
Nebraska			
Exon	70	28	71
Kerrey	77	21	79
Nevada			
Bryan	83	17	83
Reid	86	14	86

	1	2	3
New Hampshire			
Gregg	87	10	90
Smith	94	4	96
New Jersey			
Bradley	88	8	92
Lautenberg	86	14	86
New Mexico			
Bingaman	79	20	80
Domenici	83	14	86
New York			
Moynihan	95	5	95
D'Amato	82	15	84
North Carolina			
Faircloth	96	3	97
Helms	89	3	97
North Dakota			
Conrad	81	18	82
Dorgan	76	16	83
Ohio			
Glenn	90	9	91
Metzenbaum	92	6	94
Oklahoma			
Boren	79	20	80
Nickles	94	5	95
Oregon			
Hatfield	56	39	59
Packwood	71	28	72
Pennsylvania			
Wofford	90	8	92
Specter	54	31	64
Rhode Island			
Pell	97	3	97
Chafee	57	41	58
South Carolina			
Hollings	76	20	79
Thurmond	91	6	93
South Dakota			
Daschle	89	9	90
Pressler	91	6	93
Tennessee			
Mathews	88	12	88
Sasser	86	13	87

	1	2	3
Texas			
Gramm	94	2	98
Hutchison[1]†	87	11	88
Utah			
Bennett	91	6	94
Hatch	94	4	96
Vermont			
Leahy	92	6	94
Jeffords	45	53	46
Virginia			
Robb	85	14	86
Warner	78	19	80
Washington			
Murray	85	6	94
Gorton	82	17	83
West Virginia			
Byrd	87	13	87
Rockefeller	91	6	94
Wisconsin			
Feingold	94	6	94
Kohl	84	16	84
Wyoming			
Simpson †	87	9	90
Wallop	95	1	99

Party Unity
and Party Opposition: Senate

1. Party Unity, 1993. Percentage of 265 party-unity recorded votes in 1993 on which a senator voted "yea" or "nay" *in agreement* with a majority of his or her party. (Party-unity roll calls are those on which a majority of voting Democrats opposed a majority of voting Republicans.) Failures to vote lowered both party-unity and party-opposition scores.

2. Party Opposition, 1993. Percentage of 265 party-unity recorded votes in 1993 on which a senator voted "yea" or "nay" *in disagreement* with a majority of his or her party. Failures to vote lowered both party-unity and party-opposition scores.

3. Party Unity, 1993. Percentage of 265 party-unity recorded votes in 1993 on which a senator was present and voted "yea" or "nay" *in agreement* with a majority of his or her party. In this version of the study, absences were not counted; therefore, failures to vote did not lower unity or opposition scores. Opposition scores, not listed here, are the inverse of the unity score; i.e., the opposition score is equal to 100 percent minus the individual's unity score.

[1] *Kay Bailey Hutchison, R-Texas, was sworn in June 14, 1993, to succeed Bob Krueger, D. Krueger was appointed by Gov. Ann W. Richards, D, to fill the seat vacated by Lloyd Bentsen, D, who became Treasury secretary Jan. 20, 1993. Krueger was eligible for 115 party-unity votes in 1993. His party-unity score was 58 percent; opposition score was 17 percent; unity score, adjusted for absences, was 78 percent. Bentsen was eligible for no party-unity votes in 1993. Hutchison was eligible for 150 party-unity votes in 1993.*

Party Unity and Party Opposition: House

1. Party Unity, 1993. Percentage of 391 party-unity recorded votes in 1993 on which a representative voted "yea" or "nay" *in agreement* with a majority of his or her party. (Party-unity roll calls are those on which a majority of voting Democrats opposed a majority of voting Republicans.) Failures to vote lowered both party-unity and party-opposition scores.

2. Party Opposition, 1993. Percentage of 391 party-unity recorded votes in 1993 on which a representative voted "yea" or "nay" *in disagreement* with a majority of his or her party. Failures to vote lowered both party-unity and party-opposition scores.

3. Party Unity, 1993. Percentage of 391 party-unity recorded votes in 1993 on which a representative was present and voted "yea" or "nay" *in agreement* with a majority of his or her party. In this version of the study, absences were not counted; therefore, failures to vote did not lower unity or opposition scores. Opposition scores, not listed here, are the inverse of the unity score; i.e., the opposition score is equal to 100 percent minus the individual's unity score.

NOTE: Delegates were eligible for 133 of the 391 party-unity votes in 1993.

[1] *Rep. Sam Farr, D-Calif., was sworn in June 16, 1993, to succeed Leon E. Panetta, D, who became director of the Office of Management and Budget on Jan. 21, 1993. Panetta was eligible for five party-unity votes in 1993. His party-unity score was 100 percent; opposition score was 0 percent; unity score, adjusted for absences, was 100 percent. Farr was eligible for 231 party-unity votes in 1993.*

[2] *Rep. Vernon J. Ehlers, R-Mich., tentatively will be sworn in Jan. 25, 1994, to succeed Paul B. Henry, R, who died July 31, 1993. Henry was eligible for 255 party-unity votes in 1993 and voted once. His party-unity score was 0 percent; opposition score was 0 percent; unity score, adjusted for absences, was 100 percent for one vote. Ehlers was eligible for no party-unity votes in 1993.*

[3] *Rep. Bennie Thompson, D-Miss., was sworn in April 20, 1993, to succeed Mike Espy, D, who became Agriculture secretary Jan. 22, 1993. Espy was eligible for five party-unity votes in 1993. His party-unity score was 100 percent; opposition score was 0 percent; unity score, adjusted for absences, was 100 percent. Thompson was eligible for 294 party-unity votes in 1993.*

[4] *Rep. Rob Portman, R-Ohio, was sworn in May 5, 1993, to succeed Bill Gradison, R, who resigned Jan. 31, 1993. Gradison was eligible for nine party-unity votes in 1993. His party-unity score was 89 percent; opposition score was 11 percent; unity score, adjusted for absences, was 89 percent. Portman was eligible for 282 party-unity votes in 1993.*

[5] *Rep. Bernard Sanders, I-Vt., voted as an independent. Had he voted as a Democrat, his party-unity score would have been 88 percent; opposition score would have been 5 percent; unity score, adjusted for absences, would have been 94 percent.*

[6] *Rep. Thomas S. Foley, D-Wash., as Speaker of the House, voted at his discretion on 31 of the 391 party-unity votes in 1993.*

[7] *Rep. Peter W. Barca, D-Wis., was sworn in June 8, 1993, to succeed Les Aspin, D, who became Defense secretary, Jan. 20, 1993. Aspin was eligible for one party-unity vote in 1993. His party-unity score was 0 percent; opposition score 0 percent; unity score, adjusted for absences, was 0 percent. Barca was eligible for 241 party-unity votes in 1993.*

KEY

† Not eligible for all recorded votes in 1993 or voted "present" to avoid possible conflict of interest.

Democrats *Republicans*
Independent

	1	2	3
Alabama			
1 Callahan	92	5	95
2 Everett	95	4	96
3 Browder	75	23	77
4 Bevill	77	18	81
5 Cramer	79	21	79
6 Bachus	96	3	97
7 Hilliard	90	6	94
Alaska			
AL Young	73	15	83
Arizona			
1 Coppersmith	90	8	92
2 Pastor	95	4	96
3 Stump	99	1	99
4 Kyl	95	3	97
5 Kolbe	83	15	85
6 English	94	5	95
Arkansas			
1 Lambert	86	13	87
2 Thornton	86	12	88
3 Hutchinson	91	8	92
4 Dickey	88	9	90
California			
1 Hamburg	93	3	97
2 Herger	94	4	96
3 Fazio	94	6	94
4 Doolittle	94	2	98
5 Matsui	92	4	96
6 Woolsey	96	2	98
7 Miller	90	2	98
8 Pelosi	93	2	98
9 Dellums	91	1	99
10 Baker	96	3	97
11 Pombo	86	13	87
12 Lantos	91	5	94
13 Stark	91	3	96
14 Eshoo	96	3	97
15 Mineta	94	5	95
16 Edwards	94	3	97
17 Farr[1]†	91	3	96
18 Condit	61	36	63
19 Lehman	79	12	87
20 Dooley	83	13	87
21 Thomas	86	11	89
22 Huffington	84	14	86
23 Gallegly	92	5	95
24 Beilenson	93	5	95
25 McKeon	94	4	96
26 Berman	86	3	97
27 Moorhead	98	2	98
28 Dreier	94	3	97
29 Waxman	90	2	98
30 Becerra	91	1	99
31 Martinez	86	8	92
32 Dixon	93	4	96
33 Roybal-Allard	95	3	97
34 Torres	86	3	97
35 Waters	92	4	96
36 Harman	88	7	92
37 Tucker	83	4	95
38 Horn	69	28	71
39 Royce	92	6	94
40 Lewis	83	15	84
41 Kim	92	8	92

	1	2	3
42 Brown	82	2	98
43 Calvert	89	8	92
44 McCandless	91	6	94
45 Rohrabacher	95	5	95
46 Dornan	92	2	98
47 Cox	89	4	96
48 Packard	82	5	95
49 Schenk	94	5	95
50 Filner	96	4	96
51 Cunningham	96	2	98
52 Hunter	91	2	98
Colorado			
1 Schroeder	77	21	79
2 Skaggs	93	6	94
3 McInnis	83	15	84
4 Allard	92	7	93
5 Hefley	94	6	94
6 Schaefer	94	5	95
Connecticut			
1 Kennelly	95	5	95
2 Gejdenson	97	2	98
3 DeLauro	95	4	96
4 Shays	63	37	63
5 Franks	85	14	86
6 Johnson	64	32	67
Delaware			
AL Castle	82	17	82
Florida			
1 Hutto	53	45	54
2 Peterson	90	10	90
3 Brown	92	5	95
4 Fowler	81	17	83
5 Thurman	88	11	89
6 Stearns	91	6	94
7 Mica	94	5	95
8 McCollum	90	8	91
9 Bilirakis	87	10	89
10 Young	82	11	88
11 Gibbons	86	8	91
12 Canady	94	6	94
13 Miller	84	15	85
14 Goss	94	6	94
15 Bacchus	87	11	89
16 Lewis	90	5	95
17 Meek	90	6	94
18 Ros-Lehtinen	75	24	76
19 Johnston	92	4	95
20 Deutsch	92	7	93
21 Diaz-Balart	75	23	76
22 Shaw	86	12	88
23 Hastings	90	3	97
Georgia			
1 Kingston	89	9	91
2 Bishop	89	7	92
3 Collins	94	6	94
4 Linder	97	3	97
5 Lewis	98	2	98
6 Gingrich	87	6	94
7 Darden	87	12	88
8 Rowland	73	26	74
9 Deal	68	31	69
10 Johnson	82	17	83
11 McKinney	93	2	98
Hawaii			
1 Abercrombie	90	5	95
2 Mink	95	3	97
Idaho			
1 LaRocco	85	13	87
2 Crapo	95	4	96
Illinois			
1 Rush	93	1	99
2 Reynolds	96	2	98
3 Lipinski	73	22	77
4 Gutierrez	90	4	96
5 Rostenkowski	88	6	94
6 Hyde †	82	14	85
7 Collins	94	2	98
8 Crane	93	3	97
9 Yates	91	2	98
10 Porter	71	24	75
11 Sangmeister	86	11	89
12 Costello	76	24	76
13 Fawell	86	14	86
14 Hastert	92	6	94
15 Ewing	93	5	95
16 Manzullo	95	4	96
17 Evans	94	3	97

ND Northern Democrats SD Southern Democrats

	1	2	3
18 Michel	89	7	93
19 Poshard	72	28	72
20 Durbin	93	6	94
Indiana			
1 Visclosky	90	9	91
2 Sharp	83	9	90
3 Roemer	81	18	82
4 Long	90	10	90
5 *Buyer*	95	5	95
6 *Burton*	97	2	98
7 *Myers*	74	22	77
8 McCloskey	93	5	95
9 Hamilton	83	17	83
10 Jacobs	54	46	54
Iowa			
1 *Leach*	63	28	69
2 *Nussle*	89	10	90
3 *Lightfoot*	87	10	89
4 Smith	85	11	88
5 *Grandy*	77	21	78
Kansas			
1 *Roberts*	91	6	94
2 Slattery	71	23	75
3 *Meyers*	76	22	77
4 Glickman	85	14	86
Kentucky			
1 Barlow	86	12	88
2 Natcher	92	8	92
3 Mazzoli	84	16	84
4 *Bunning*	94	4	96
5 *Rogers*	84	14	85
6 Baesler	84	14	85
Louisiana			
1 *Livingston*	87	10	90
2 Jefferson	91	4	96
3 Tauzin	48	46	51
4 Fields	94	4	96
5 *McCrery*	86	12	88
6 *Baker*	92	4	96
7 Hayes	65	30	68
Maine			
1 Andrews	97	2	98
2 *Snowe*	68	32	68
Maryland			
1 *Gilchrest*	71	27	73
2 *Bentley*	79	18	81
3 Cardin	92	5	95
4 Wynn	97	2	98
5 Hoyer	92	7	93
6 *Bartlett*	98	1	99
7 Mfume	90	5	95
8 *Morella*	47	51	48
Massachusetts			
1 Olver	96	2	98
2 Neal	94	4	96
3 *Blute*	73	21	78
4 Frank	96	1	99
5 Meehan	89	9	91
6 *Torkildsen*	75	24	76
7 Markey	96	1	99
8 Kennedy	93	3	97
9 Moakley	82	2	98
10 Studds	96	1	99
Michigan			
1 Stupak	85	13	87
2 *Hoekstra*	86	14	86
3 Vacancy[2]	--	--	--
4 *Camp*	92	8	92
5 Barcia	74	23	76
6 *Upton*	76	24	76
7 *Smith*	87	9	90
8 Carr	84	12	88
9 Kildee	92	8	92
10 Bonior	93	4	96
11 *Knollenberg*	94	4	96
12 Levin	96	4	96
13 Ford	91	3	97
14 Conyers	70	2	97
15 Collins	96	2	98
16 Dingell	87	7	92
Minnesota			
1 Penny	61	38	62
2 Minge	75	21	78
3 *Ramstad*	82	17	83
4 Vento	95	2	98
5 Sabo	96	2	98
6 *Grams*	95	4	96
7 Peterson	67	30	69
8 Oberstar	90	9	91
Mississippi			
1 Whitten	67	12	85
2 Thompson[3]†	87	3	96
3 Montgomery	72	28	72
4 Parker	59	38	61
5 Taylor	37	63	37
Missouri			
1 Clay	83	10	89
2 *Talent*	91	7	93
3 Gephardt	91	4	96
4 Skelton	70	27	72
5 Wheat †	95	1	99
6 Danner	87	13	87
7 *Hancock*	97	1	99
8 *Emerson*	88	10	89
9 Volkmer	78	21	78
Montana			
AL Williams	77	12	87
Nebraska			
1 *Bereuter*	80	19	81
2 Hoagland	83	15	84
3 *Barrett*	91	9	91
Nevada			
1 Bilbray	83	16	84
2 *Vucanovich*	86	9	91
New Hampshire			
1 *Zeliff*	89	8	92
2 Swett	85	10	90
New Jersey			
1 Andrews	81	14	85
2 Hughes	89	10	89
3 *Saxton*	82	16	84
4 *Smith*	69	28	71
5 *Roukema*	67	29	69
6 Pallone	90	10	90
7 *Franks*	77	22	78
8 Klein	94	5	95
9 Torricelli	83	9	90
10 Payne	95	1	99
11 *Gallo*	72	27	73
12 *Zimmer*	76	21	78
13 Menendez	90	8	91
New Mexico			
1 *Schiff*	81	17	82
2 *Skeen*	78	11	88
3 Richardson	89	7	92
New York			
1 Hochbrueckner	93	5	95
2 *Lazio*	74	26	74
3 *King*	92	8	92
4 *Levy*	90	10	90
5 Ackerman	90	3	97
6 Flake	91	3	96
7 Manton	82	10	89
8 Nadler	92	3	97
9 Schumer	93	3	97
10 Towns	86	2	98
11 Owens	92	2	98
12 Velazquez	95	2	98
13 *Molinari*	80	20	80
14 Maloney	91	4	95
15 Rangel	90	3	97
16 Serrano	94	1	99
17 Engel	86	2	98
18 Lowey	95	3	97
19 *Fish*	61	37	62
20 *Gilman*	52	47	53
21 McNulty	84	15	85
22 *Solomon*	93	4	96
23 *Boehlert*	59	40	60
24 *McHugh*	87	10	90
25 *Walsh*	78	20	79
26 Hinchey	92	3	97
27 *Paxon*	96	3	97
28 Slaughter	95	4	96
29 LaFalce	84	10	89
30 *Quinn*	84	15	85
31 *Houghton*	65	31	68
North Carolina			
1 Clayton	93	2	98
2 Valentine	72	23	76
3 Lancaster	79	19	81
4 Price	94	5	95
5 Neal	79	12	87
6 *Coble*	95	5	95
7 Rose	85	6	93
8 Hefner	88	8	92
9 *McMillan*	74	16	82
10 *Ballenger* †	93	6	94
11 *Taylor*	93	5	95
12 Watt	97	2	98
North Dakota			
AL Pomeroy	86	13	87
Ohio			
1 Mann	85	12	87
2 *Portman*[4]†	89	10	90
3 Hall	79	11	88
4 *Oxley*	87	11	89
5 *Gillmor*	72	26	74
6 Strickland	93	6	94
7 *Hobson*	83	17	83
8 *Boehner*	96	2	98
9 Kaptur	83	13	87
10 *Hoke*	79	14	85
11 Stokes	91	3	97
12 *Kasich*	80	17	82
13 Brown	91	5	94
14 Sawyer	96	3	97
15 *Pryce*	86	13	87
16 *Regula*	79	21	79
17 Traficant	85	15	85
18 Applegate	75	24	76
19 Fingerhut	86	13	87
Oklahoma			
1 *Inhofe*	94	3	97
2 Synar	86	7	93
3 Brewster	72	24	75
4 McCurdy	71	20	78
5 *Istook*	90	6	93
6 English	70	27	72
Oregon			
1 Furse	98	1	99
2 *Smith*	91	4	95
3 Wyden	95	4	96
4 DeFazio	84	10	89
5 Kopetski	93	4	96
Pennsylvania			
1 Foglietta	92	3	97
2 Blackwell	92	2	98
3 Borski	89	8	92
4 Klink	83	16	84
5 *Clinger*	67	21	76
6 Holden	80	19	81
7 *Weldon*	86	13	87
8 *Greenwood*	79	20	80
9 *Shuster*	90	6	93
10 *McDade*	59	18	77
11 Kanjorski	89	11	89
12 Murtha	83	13	86
13 Margolies-Mezv.	91	9	91
14 Coyne	98	1	99
15 McHale	88	11	89
16 *Walker*	98	2	98
17 *Gekas*	90	8	91
18 *Santorum*	77	16	83
19 *Goodling*	85	13	87
20 Murphy	55	38	59
21 *Ridge*	73	19	79
Rhode Island			
1 *Machtley*	66	30	69
2 Reed	96	4	96
South Carolina			
1 *Ravenel*	75	24	76
2 *Spence*	89	10	90
3 Derrick	86	11	88
4 *Inglis*	84	14	86
5 Spratt †	85	13	86
6 Clyburn	90	5	95
South Dakota			
AL Johnson	85	13	87
Tennessee			
1 *Quillen*	70	13	84
2 *Duncan*	88	11	89
3 Lloyd	73	21	78
4 Cooper	69	26	73
5 Clement	82	16	84
6 Gordon	87	11	89
7 *Sundquist*	86	8	91
8 Tanner	70	29	71
9 Ford	64	3	96
Texas			
1 Chapman	75	16	82
2 Wilson	70	15	83
3 *Johnson, Sam*	94	2	98
4 Hall	54	46	54
5 Bryant	92	5	95
6 *Barton*	80	5	94
7 *Archer*	83	14	86
8 *Fields*	82	1	98
9 Brooks	84	11	89
10 Pickle	78	13	86
11 Edwards	75	23	77
12 Geren	63	35	64
13 Sarpalius	69	29	70
14 Laughlin	70	25	74
15 de la Garza	76	19	80
16 Coleman	90	9	91
17 Stenholm	52	48	52
18 Washington	70	3	96
19 *Combest*	86	14	86
20 Gonzalez	95	5	95
21 *Smith*	94	4	96
22 *DeLay*	95	3	97
23 *Bonilla*	93	6	94
24 Frost	79	11	87
25 Andrews	72	24	75
26 *Armey*	95	2	98
27 Ortiz	77	20	80
28 Tejeda	82	18	82
29 Green	85	10	90
30 Johnson, E. B.	94	4	96
Utah			
1 *Hansen*	92	6	94
2 Shepherd	90	8	92
3 Orton	59	40	60
Vermont			
AL *Sanders*[5]	--	--	--
Virginia			
1 *Bateman*	70	25	73
2 Pickett	75	22	77
3 Scott	93	4	96
4 Sisisky	71	23	75
5 Payne	79	20	80
6 *Goodlatte*	92	8	92
7 *Bliley*	90	8	92
8 Moran	90	6	94
9 Boucher	88	7	93
10 *Wolf*	90	10	90
11 Byrne	91	7	93
Washington			
1 Cantwell	90	8	92
2 Swift	93	6	94
3 Unsoeld	92	3	97
4 Inslee	86	13	87
5 Foley[6]			
6 Dicks	88	7	92
7 McDermott	91	2	98
8 *Dunn*	90	9	90
9 Kreidler	97	2	98
West Virginia			
1 Mollohan	78	19	81
2 Wise	86	10	90
3 Rahall	76	20	79
Wisconsin			
1 Barca[7]†	85	15	85
2 *Klug*	74	24	76
3 *Gunderson*	69	31	69
4 Kleczka	88	7	92
5 Barrett	93	7	93
6 *Petri*	84	14	86
7 Obey	94	5	95
8 *Roth*	85	13	87
9 *Sensenbrenner*	90	10	90
Wyoming			
AL *Thomas*	90	7	93
Delegates			
de Lugo, V.I. †	91	2	98
Faleomavaega, Am.S. †	64	2	98
Norton, D.C. †	98	0	100
Romero-B., P.R. †	56	3	95
Underwood, Guam †	75	7	92

Southern states - Ala., Ark., Fla., Ga., Ky., La., Miss., N.C., Okla., S.C., Tenn., Texas, Va.
Omitted votes are quorum calls, which CQ does not include in its vote charts.

CONSERVATIVE COALITION

Clinton Keeps Southern Wing On His Team in 1993

The once-mighty "conservative coalition" of congressional Republicans and Southern Democrats had faded in recent years into a rather minor factor in the outcome of votes in the House and Senate. President Clinton's ability to keep it that way in 1993 was the key to success for much of his first-year economic program.

In lobbying for each of his fiscal 1994 budget measures, the new president from Arkansas focused much of his attention on Democratic lawmakers from his conservative-leaning home region. On each measure, he received one-sided support from his congressional counterparts, who eschewed alliances with Republicans that might have revived the conservative coalition and severely damaged the first Democratic president in 12 years.

Twelve years before, a group of self-styled "Boll Weevil" Democrats from the South allied with Republicans to give crucial victories to President Ronald Reagan on the tax and spending cuts that defined his first term in office.

In fact, on the relatively few votes in 1993 on which Southern Democrats and Republicans did join in a conservative coalition, they were more likely to support than oppose Clinton's position. On 14 House votes on which the conservative coalition developed and Clinton stated positions, the coalition and Clinton agreed 12 times. The coalition and the president were together on three of the five such votes in the Senate.

A 'Different Democrat'

"It does go to show there is something to Clinton being a different kind of Democrat, one of these Democratic Leadership Council Democrats," said David Rohde, a professor of political science at the University of Florida who followed the conservative coalition.

Rohde said that while Clinton did favor his party's large liberal constituency on most issues, he took positions far

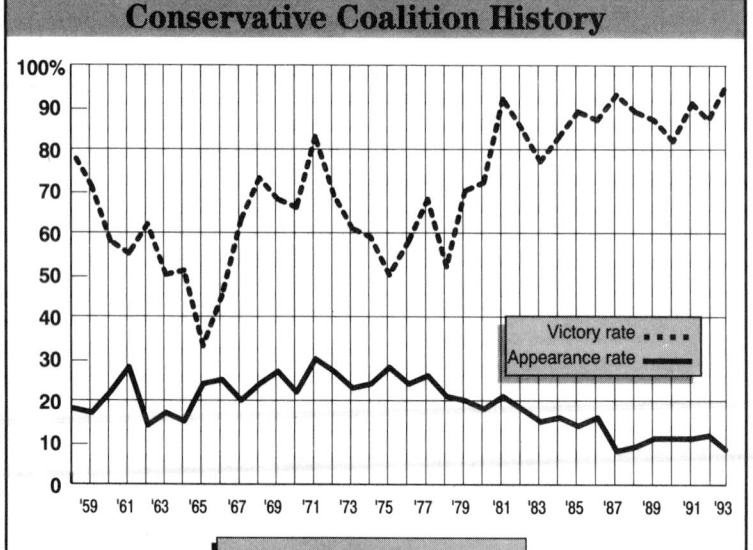

Conservative Coalition History

100%
90
80
70
60
50
40
30
20
10
0

'59 '61 '63 '65 '67 '69 '71 '73 '75 '77 '79 '81 '83 '85 '87 '89 '91 '93

Victory rate ....
Appearance rate ———

Definition

A voting block in the House and Senate consisting of a majority of Republicans and a majority of Southern Democrats, combined against a majority of Northern Democrats.

1993 Data

Senate   37 victories
         4 defeats
         41 appearances in 395 votes

House   43 victories
         1 defeat
         44 appearances in 597 votes

Total Congress appearance rate **8.6%**
Total Congress victory rate **94.1%**

Data, votes, pp. 26-C – 30-C

enough to the right on such issues as crime and defense spending to draw substantial support from conservative legislators.

But Thomas E. Mann, director of governmental studies at the Brookings Institution in Washington, said Clinton had to convince conservative constituents that the support he received from Southern members made him a "New Democrat."

"I'm sure he will try to and very much wants to," Mann said. "The reality is his poll standing in the South is lower than anywhere in the country."

The conservative coalition was defined as developing whenever majorities of Republicans and Southern Democrats voted contrary to a majority of Northern Democrats.

Altogether, the conservative coalition appeared in 1993 on 85 of 992 roll call votes in the House and Senate combined, or about 9 percent of the time. This was a near-record low, down from 12 percent in 1992 and second only to the 8 percent recorded in 1987.

The coalition turned up on 44 of 597 votes in the House, or 7 percent. It was slightly more prevalent in the Senate, where it was a factor on 41 of 395 votes, or 10 percent.

This was in sharp contrast to the pattern from the early 1950s, when Congressional Quarterly developed the conservative coalition study, through the 1970s. During those years, opposition to civil rights bills and conservative views on a wide range of fiscal and defense-related issues frequently galvanized "Solid South" Democrats to ally with Republicans against Northern members of their own party.

In those days, the conservative coalition appeared in 20 percent to 30 percent of all votes. Its frequency remained in the mid-teens through the early 1980s. But the coalition's cohesion and clout fell sharply toward the end of Reagan's presidency.

This ad hoc alliance rarely appeared in 1993 on macroeconomic policy issues. The biggest such issue on which the conservative coalition formed was the North American

Free Trade Agreement (NAFTA), with Republicans and Southern Democrats uniting to provide Clinton with a politically crucial victory.

The influence of a moderate-to-liberal segment of the Southern Democratic forces and the desire of most Democrats from the region to boost Clinton during his first year in office kept the coalition from developing on the major budget votes of 1993. On the other hand, the South's traditional social conservatism and its stalwart support for defense spending remained strong, and many moderate Southern Democrats joined with Republicans to re-create the coalition on a few dozen votes pertaining to such issues.

The dynamic that caused the coalition to appear infrequently, led at the same time to record levels of partisanship on votes in the House and Senate. But the new demographics of the South had caused the coalition to prevail most of the time in recent years, even as its appearances became fewer. In the House, the coalition was on the losing side on only one of the 44 votes in which it appeared, a success rate of 98 percent. In the Senate, the coalition won on 37 of 41 votes, or 90 percent. (Conservative coalition history and data, p. 22-C)

The combined success ratio for the conservative coalition, 94 percent, was an all-time record.

GOP Gains, Democrats Moderate

The changing composition of the South's congressional delegation had much to do with the declining prominence of the conservative coalition. In short, the number of hard-line white Democratic conservatives elected from the region had diminished.

Part of this had to do with Republican advances in the South over the past few decades. The GOP had become a force in the South, and its candidates had captured many districts traditionally held by Democrats who were key to formation of the conservative coalition.

In 1973, Republicans held 30 percent of 121 Southern House seats. In 1993, they held 38 percent — 52 of 137 seats. Republicans captured eight seats in 1992, a number equal to the region's gain from 1990 reapportionment.

The Senate showed even more parity, with Democrats holding a 14-12 edge over Republicans in Southern seats.

Southern Republicans in Congress showed up as a very conservative group. When participating in House votes, 39 of the 52 Southern Republicans joined with the conservative coalition on 90 percent or more of the votes on which it developed. Six of them had 100 percent conservative coalition support scores.

In the Senate, the lowest coalition support score among Southern Republicans was 88 percent; 10 of the 12 had scores of 90 percent or above.

Yet there was a paradox that undercut the viability of the conservative coalition. While Republicans had established a large foothold in the region, there were parts of the South — many of them represented by Democrats — that were far less conservative than they once had been.

The South had undergone important changes over the previous three decades. It was more urban and less agrarian. Much of the South — including Texas, Florida, North Carolina and Georgia — had enjoyed a Sun Belt economic boom that had greatly increased population; many of the

region's new residents migrated from the North. Freed by federal civil rights statutes from the restraints of racially discriminatory state laws, blacks had become politically and economically influential throughout the region.

Some districts and states still elected strongly conservative Democrats to Congress. However, 28 of the 68 white Southern Democrats in the House joined with the coalition 75 percent of the time or less; 11 scored under 50 percent. Mike Synar of Oklahoma set the low end of the spectrum at 13 percent support.

The range of coalition support scores was more narrow in the Senate, with most of the 14 Southern Democrats (all of them white) falling into the middle. Southern Democratic senators were led at 95 percent by Alabama's Richard C. Shelby, a frequent thorn in Clinton's side on budget issues; J. Bennett Johnston of Louisiana scored 90 percent. At the other end of the spectrum, in the mid-40s, were Charles S. Robb of Virginia and Dale Bumpers of Arkansas.

New Black Clout in the South

The rise of a large, mainly liberal-voting contingent of black House members from the South was another new political phenomenon that threatened the survival of the conservative coalition.

Black citizens had voted in great numbers in the South since passage of the federal Voting Rights Act in 1965. But until 1992, the region elected only a handful of black members to the House. There were only five during the 102nd Congress — 6 percent of all Southern Democratic members.

Redistricting, however, brought about a sea change in black political power. Driven by amendments to the Voting Rights Act in 1982, states across the South carefully crafted a dozen new districts with black-majority populations. All elected black members, giving Southern blacks a total of 17 seats — 20 percent of all Southern Democrats.

Among black Southern Democrats, Sanford D. Bishop Jr., Ga., had the highest conservative coalition support score — 59 percent — about average for his white colleagues.

The black contingent ended 1993 with voting records far more liberal than the norm for Southern Democrats. Sanford D. Bishop Jr., who came from a rural southwest Georgia district with an almost even black-white population split, had the highest conservative coalition support score, but even his 59 percent placed him in the middle ranks of his white Southern Democratic colleagues.

The liberal leanings of black Southern Democrats had a significant impact on whether the conservative coalition formed on some votes, particularly on social issues.

When the Brady bill (HR 1025) mandating a five-day waiting period prior to the purchase of a handgun passed the House on Nov. 10, Southern Democrats went 46-38 in favor of it. The black members' 15-2 vote in favor of the bill was crucial to keeping Southern Democrats from joining Republicans in a coalition against the bill; white Southern Democrats opposed the Brady bill by 31-36.

Black Southerners barely missed keeping an anti-abortion vote out of the conservative coalition column. All 17 black members voted June 30 against the Hyde amendment, which prohibited Medicaid from paying for abortions for poor women in most circumstances. White Southern Democrats supported the amendment, 44-24, giving it a 44-41 margin among the region's Democrats as a whole. The amendment passed, 255-178.

Leading Scorers: Conservative Coalition

High scorers in support are those who in 1993 voted most often with the conservative coalition. Opposition figures are for those who voted most often against the coalition. Scores are based on actual votes cast; names are listed alphabetically when scores are tied. Members who were not eligible for half the votes are not listed.

Support

Senate

| Shelby | Cochran | Exon |

Southern Democrats

Shelby, Ala.	95%	Ford, Ky.	80%
Johnston, La.	90	Mathews, Tenn.	68
Heflin, Ala.	89	Sasser, Tenn.	68
Nunn, Ga.	87	Boren, Okla.	63
Breaux, La.	83		

Republicans

Cochran, Miss.	100	Mack, Fla.	98
Gramm, Texas	100	McConnell, Ky.	98
Hutchison, Texas	100	Thurmond, S.C.	98
Lott, Miss.	100	Hatch, Utah	95
Coverdell, Ga.	98	Pressler, S.D.	95

Northern Democrats

Exon, Neb.	74	Kerrey, Neb.	60
Bryan, Nev.	61	Baucus, Mont.	58

House

| Hutto | Armey | Skelton |

Southern Democrats

Hutto, Fla.	100%	Bevill, Ala.	93%
Geren, Texas	95	Laughlin, Texas	93
Montgomery, Miss.	95	Lloyd, Tenn.	93
Parker, Miss.	95	Browder, Ala.	91
Sarpalius, Texas	95	Cramer, Ala.	91
		Stenholm, Texas	91%
		Tanner, Tenn.	91
		Taylor, Miss.	91

Republicans

Armey, Texas	100	Smith, Texas	100	Fields, Texas	98
Baker, Calif.	100	Boehner, Ohio	98	Johnson, Texas,	98
Bliley, Va.	100	Bonilla, Texas	98	Kim, Calif.	98
Callahan, Ala.	100	Buyer, Ind.	98	Michel, Ill.	98
Combest, Texas	100	Calvert, Calif.	98	Shaw, Fla.	98
Hansen, Utah	100	Cunningham,		Stump, Ariz.	98
Linder, Ga.	100	Calif.	98	Weldon, Pa.	98

Northern Democrats

Skelton, Mo.	86	Mollohan, W.Va.	79	McNulty, N.Y.	75
Orton, Utah	84	Murtha, Pa.	79	Volkmer, Mo.	75

Opposition

| Robb | Jeffords | Wellstone |

Southern Democrats

Robb, Va.	56%	Hollings, S.C.	41%
Bumpers, Ark.	55	Graham, Fla.	39
Pryor, Ark.	51	Boren, Okla.	37

Republicans

Jeffords, Vt.	73	Durenberger, Minn.	45
Hatfield, Ore.	55	Cohen, Maine	43
Chafee, R.I.	54		

Northern Democrats

Wellstone, Minn.	95	Pell, R.I.	88
Boxer, Calif.	90	Sarbanes, Md.	88
Bradley, N.J.	90	Harkin, Iowa	85
Feingold, Wis.	90	Moynihan, N.Y.	85
Kennedy, Mass.	90	Moseley-Braun, Ill.	83
Metzenbaum, Ohio	90	Simon, Ill.	83

| Washington | Shays | Conyers |

Southern Democrats

Washington, Texas	94%	Lewis, Ga.	91%
McKinney, Ga.	93	Synar, Okla.	88
Watt, N.C.	93	Clayton, N.C.	86
Ford, Tenn.	92	Thompson, Miss.	85

Republicans

Shays, Conn.	64	Nussle, Iowa	41
Leach, Iowa	54	Roukema, N.J.	40
Morella, Md.	53	Zimmer, N.J.	40
Johnson, Conn.	43		

Northern Democrats

Conyers, Mich.	100	Collins, Ill.	95
Furse, Ore.	98	Dellums, Calif.	95
Mink, Hawaii	98	Evans, Ill.	95
Owens, N.Y.	98	Hamburg, Calif.	95
Rush, Ill.	98	Payne, N.J.	95
Vento, Minn.	98	Rangel, N.Y.	95
Norton, D.C. *	97	Towns, N.Y.	95
Yates, Ill.	97	Wheat, Mo.	95
Andrews, Maine	95		

Delegate; eligible for 30 of 44 votes.

Coalition Counts Less on Budget

The changed nature of the Southern Democratic delegation was most evident on votes related to the federal budget. Despite near unity among Republicans in voting against Clinton's economic programs, Southern Democrats stood by their man in the White House in a big way, and the coalition rarely appeared on fiscal issues.

Not that all Democrats from the region bubbled with enthusiasm over a controversial administration plan that included substantial tax increases and some program cuts to reduce the federal deficit by $500 billion by 1999.

Led by such figures as Rep. Charles W. Stenholm of Texas, chairman of the Conservative Democratic Forum, Southern Democrats joined in a successful push to get Clinton to include more spending reductions in his budget and pledge to cut further in the future.

But when the votes were taken, Southern Democrats were strongly in Clinton's camp. In the House, the Southern delegation backed Clinton on the fiscal 1994 budget resolution (H Con Res 64) by 78-5, contributing to a 243-183 victory. Southern Democratic defections endangered the later budget-reconciliation bill (HR 2264), which put the tax increases and spending cuts into law. Yet the delegation stuck with Clinton, 62-23, and the bill passed on a 218-216 vote.

In the Senate, attention in June focused on three Southern Democrats — Shelby, Johnston and Sam Nunn of Georgia — whose votes against the reconciliation bill forced a 49-49 tie that had to be broken by Vice President Al Gore. Clinton managed, however, to hold on to 11 of the 14 Southern Democrats, and their votes were crucial to his razor-thin victory.

In November, Southern House Democrats, by 61-24, backed Clinton in his opposition to the unsuccessful proposal by Timothy J. Penny, D-Minn., and John R. Kasich, R-Ohio, to cut spending by $90 billion over five years.

The biggest economic vote on which the conservative coalition came together was NAFTA, the pact linking the United States, Mexico and Canada in a continental free-trade zone. Southern Democrats tended to be less allied than their Northern colleagues with labor unions, which spearheaded opposition to the agreement. Clinton also cajoled support from Southern members by giving assurances that certain of the region's agricultural and industrial products would receive special dispensations.

In the House, the 53-32 Southern Democratic vote for the bill to implement NAFTA (HR 3450) weighed heavily in the bill's passage by a 234-200 vote. Republicans joined in the conservative coalition by voting 132-43, while Northern Democrats broke against the pact, 49-124. In the Senate, where the victory margin was a more comfortable 61-38, Southern Democrats backed NAFTA by a 9-5 vote.

When the conservative coalition came together on fiscal issues, it was often to preserve rather than to cut spending for "big science" projects. In the House, the conservative coalition played a role in rescuing the space station, which a majority of Northern Democrats wanted to sacrifice to the cause of reducing the deficit.

Defense, Social Issues

The conservative coalition arose much more frequently and had more success in its traditional bailiwick of defense spending. On several occasions, the coalition rallied to Clinton's side: He moved to cut the defense budget but fought to stave off efforts by his party's liberal wing to make even deeper reductions.

In the House, the coalition helped preserve Clinton's spending levels for intelligence and such weapons programs as the Ballistic Missile Defense system and the Trident II and D-5 missiles. A conservative coalition appearance in the Senate helped Clinton win on the Trident II. The coalition also helped defeat a proposal by Reps. Barney Frank, D-Mass., and Christopher Shays, R-Conn. — opposed by Clinton — to cut $14.4 billion over five years by eliminating spending for the space station and several other science or defense-related projects.

The coalition suffered its only House defeat on a defense-related issue. During deliberations on the Veterans Administration-Housing and Urban Development appropriations bill (HR 2491), Southern Democrats voted 41-40 to join Republicans in a failed effort to preserve the Selective Service System. Ultimately, Congress voted to save the program.

And in both chambers, the coalition showed its greatest cohesion on social issues. Though the views of Southern Democrats resembled those of their Northern colleagues in some policy areas, the two groups parted ways on issues such as gay rights, abortion and immigration.

> Social issues "will be the last to go.... The cultural issues will have a longer half-life than economic ones."
>
> —Thomas E. Mann, Brookings Institution

"I think [these issues] will be the last to go," said Mann of the Brookings Institution. "The cultural issues will have a longer half-life than economic ones." Southern Democrats joined Republicans on several votes in breaking sharply against expanding homosexual rights. The conservative coalition formed in the House and Senate in opposition to lifting the ban on military service for homosexuals and in favor of codifying much tougher restrictions than those initially sought by Clinton.

The coalition also came together in the Senate on seven votes pertaining to crime, supporting provisions establishing federal penalties for "carjackings," gang activities and state gun crimes. But gun control, once a sure draw for the conservative coalition, was no longer so. The coalition formed in both chambers to support a phaseout after five years of the Brady bill's five-day waiting period. But Southern Democrats, by 9-5 in the Senate and 46-38 in the House, voted for the bill's passage.

Southern Democrats in the Senate joined in a reversal on one cultural issue of great social and regional import — a design patent for the insignia of the United Daughters of the Confederacy, which included a depiction of the Confederate flag. On July 22, Carol Moseley-Braun, D-Ill., the Senate's only black member, moved to table, and thus kill, an amendment by Jesse Helms, R-N.C., to extend the patent, Southern Democrats voted 4-10 against her motion; it was defeated, 48-52. But Moseley-Braun persisted and remonstrated the Senate over the pain that the Confederate symbol caused blacks, who associated it with slavery. A second motion to table the amendment was agreed to, 75-25, with Southern Democrats voting 13-1 in favor.

One issue that drew consistent conservative coalition opposition in the Senate was public financing of congressional campaigns. The coalition arose three times to help defeat public financing-related amendments to the campaign finance bill (S 3). It also came together to defeat a proposal to require broadcasters to provide candidates with free broadcast time. ∎

Conservative Coalition Definitions

Conservative coalition. As used in this study, "conservative coalition" means a voting alliance of Republicans and Southern Democrats against the Northern Democrats in Congress. This meaning, rather than any philosophic definition of the "conservative coalition" position, provides the basis for CQ's selection of coalition votes.

Conservative coalition support score. Percentage of conservative coalition votes on which a member voted "yea" or "nay" *in agreement* with the position of the conservative coalition. Failures to vote, even if a member announced a stand, lowered the score.

Conservative coalition vote. Any vote in the Senate or the House on which a majority of voting Southern Democrats and a majority of voting Republicans opposed the stand taken by a majority of voting Northern Democrats. Votes on which there was an even division within the ranks of voting Northern Democrats, Southern Democrats or Republicans are not included.

Conservative coalition opposition score. Percentage of conservative coalition votes on which a member voted "yea" or "nay" *in disagreement* with the position of the conservative coalition. Failures to vote, even if a member announced a stand, lowered the score.

Average Scores

Scores for 1992 are in parentheses:

Coalition Support	Southern Democrats		Republicans		Northern Democrats		Coalition Opposition	Southern Democrats		Republicans		Northern Democrats	
Senate	68%	(65)	82%	(76)	30%	(26)	Senate	29%	(30)	15%	(20)	67%	(69)
House	61	(62)	85	(82)	30	(29)	House	36	(30)	13	(13)	67	(64)

Regional Scores

Scores for 1992 are in parentheses:

Regional Support

Democrats	East		West		South		Midwest	
Senate	26%	(21)	38%	(32)	68%	(65)	29%	(28)
House	27	(25)	25	(28)	61	(62)	37	(32)

Republicans	East		West		South		Midwest	
Senate	63%	(56)	83%	(81)	93%	(87)	80%	(75)
House	80	(75)	88	(86)	91	(87)	82	(79)

Regional Opposition

Democrats	East		West		South		Midwest	
Senate	72%	(76)	59%	(62)	29%	(30)	68%	(65)
House	68	(66)	72	(64)	36	(30)	60	(62)

Republicans	East		West		South		Midwest	
Senate	34%	(40)	13%	(14)	4%	(8)	18%	(23)
House	18	(20)	9	(8)	8	(8)	16	(17)

*(CQ defines regions of the United States as follows: **East:** Conn., Del., Maine, Md., Mass., N.H., N.J., N.Y., Pa., R.I., Vt., W.Va. **West:** Alaska, Ariz., Calif., Colo., Hawaii, Idaho, Mont., Nev., N.M., Ore., Utah, Wash., Wyo. **South:** Ala., Ark., Fla., Ga., Ky., La., Miss., N.C., Okla., S.C., Tenn., Texas, Va. **Midwest:** Ill., Ind., Iowa, Kan., Mich., Minn., Mo., Neb., N.D., Ohio, S.D., Wis.)*

Conservative Coalition History

Following is the percentage of the recorded votes for both chambers of Congress on which the coalition appeared and its percentage of victories:

Year	Appearances	Victories	Year	Appearances	Victories
1993	9%	94%	1980	18%	72%
1992	12	87	1979	20	70
1991	11	91	1978	21	52
1990	11	82	1977	26	68
1989	11	87	1976	24	58
1988	9	89	1975	28	50
1987	8	93	1974	24	59
1986	16	87	1973	23	61
1985	14	89	1972	27	69
1984	16	83	1971	30	83
1983	15	77	1970	22	66
1982	18	85	1969	27	68
1981	21	92			

Conservative Coalition Vote Breakdown

Following is a list of votes, by roll call number, cast in 1993 on which a majority of Southern Democrats and a majority of Republicans voted against a majority of all other Democrats.

House	Senate
43 Victories	**37 Victories**

#	Vote Captions
68	National Institutes of Health - Project Aries *
171	National competitiveness
172	National competitiveness *
186	Supplemental funds - defense
249	National Endowment for Democracy
263	Space station
281	Space station
307	Abortion
309	Abortion *
313	District of Columbia domestic partners
315	District of Columbia domestic partners *
332	Steamtown park
338	National Endowment for the Arts *
341	Travel and Tourism Administration
342	Border Patrol *
352	National Service
374	National Service
393	Intelligence funds
396	Intelligence disclosure
412	Ballistic missiles
414	Technology Reinvestment Project
415	Trident II missiles
416	Trident II missiles
417	Burden-sharing
420	Troops in Europe
428	National Guard
460	Homosexuals in military
462	Homosexuals in military
471	Homosexuals in military *
477	Trident II missiles
478	Army School of the Americas
479	Rifle Practice Board
484	National Biological Survey
485	National Biological Survey
505	Jobless benefits
515	Selective Service System
544	Jobless benefits
559	Gun control
562	Gun control *
566	Trucking rates
575	NAFTA
595	D.C. statehood
610	Reinventing government - spending cuts

1 Defeat

#	
278	Selective Service System

#	Vote Captions
12	HIV immigration ban
13	HIV immigration ban
44	Budget - energy taxes
78	Budget - enhanced rescissions
130	Campaign finance
132	Campaign finance
133	Campaign finance
155	Campaign finance
163	Supplemental funds - welfare
182	Budget - immunization requirement
189	Budget - vaccine purchases
206	United Daughters of the Confederacy
217	District of Columbia domestic partners
218	District of Columbia displaced workers
227	Gun dealer fee
237	Supplemental funds - crop loss
250	Homosexuals in military
253	Defense funds
256	Nuclear testing
261	Anti-satellite program
262	Defense exports
273	Selective Service System
275	Advanced solid rocket motor
290	Abortion
296	Superconducting super collider
298	Advanced liquid metal reactor
309	Trident II missiles
312	Intelligence funds
325	Rifle Practice Board
354	Crime
358	Crime
360	Crime
361	Crime
362	Crime
376	Crime
386	Gun control
395	NAFTA

4 Defeats

#	
113	Wetlands determinations
269	National Endowment for the Arts
299	Gas reactor
330	Religious freedom bill

* Second vote on amendment adopted in the Committee of the Whole

Conservative Coalition Support and Opposition: House

1. Conservative Coalition Support, 1993. Percentage of 44 recorded votes in 1993 on which the conservative coalition appeared and on which a representative voted "yea" or "nay" *in agreement* with the position of the conservative coalition. Failures to vote lowered both support and opposition scores.

2. Conservative Coalition Opposition, 1993. Percentage of 44 recorded votes in 1993 on which the conservative coalition appeared and on which a representative voted "yea" or "nay" *in disagreement* with the position of the conservative coalition. Failures to vote lowered both support and opposition scores.

3. Conservative Coalition Support, 1993. Percentage of 44 recorded votes in 1993 on which the conservative coalition appeared and on which a representative was present and voted "yea" or "nay" *in agreement* with the position of the conservative coalition. In this version of the study, absences were not counted; therefore, failures to vote did not lower support or opposition scores. Opposition scores, not listed here, are the inverse of the support score; i.e., the opposition score is equal to 100 percent minus the individual's support score.

NOTE: Delegates were eligible for 30 of the 44 conservative coalition votes in 1993.

[1] *Rep. Sam Farr, D-Calif., was sworn in June 16, 1993, to succeed Leon E. Panetta, D, who became director of the Office of Management and Budget on Jan. 21, 1993. Panetta was eligible for no conservative coalition votes in 1993. Farr was eligible for 40 conservative coalition votes in 1993.*

[2] *Rep. Vernon J. Ehlers, R-Mich., tentatively will be sworn in Jan. 25, 1994, to succeed Paul B. Henry, R, who died July 31, 1993. Henry was eligible for 18 conservative coalition votes in 1993. His conservative coalition support score was 0 percent; opposition score, 0 percent; support score, adjusted for absences, 0 percent. Ehlers was eligible for no conservative coalition votes in 1993.*

[3] *Rep. Bennie Thompson, D-Miss., was sworn in April 20, 1993, to succeed Mike Espy, D, who became Agriculture secretary Jan. 22, 1993. Espy was eligible for no conservative coalition votes in 1993. Thompson was eligible for 43 conservative coalition votes in 1993.*

[4] *Rep. Rob Portman, R-Ohio, was sworn in May 5, 1993, to succeed Bill Gradison, R, who resigned Jan. 31, 1993. Gradison was eligible for no conservative coalition votes in 1993. Portman was eligible for 43 conservative coalition votes in 1993.*

[5] *Rep. Thomas S. Foley, D-Wash., as Speaker of the House, voted at his discretion on four of 44 conservative coalition votes in 1993.*

[6] *Rep. Peter W. Barca, D-Wis., was sworn in June 8, 1993, to succeed Les Aspin, D, who became Defense secretary Jan. 20, 1993. Aspin was eligible for no conservative coalition votes in 1993. Barca was eligible for 40 conservative coalition votes in 1993.*

KEY

† Not eligible for all recorded votes in 1993 or voted "present" to avoid possible conflict of interest.

Democrats *Republicans*
Independent

	1	2	3
Alabama			
1 *Callahan*	93	0	100
2 *Everett*	86	14	86
3 Browder	91	9	91
4 Bevill	89	7	93
5 Cramer	91	9	91
6 *Bachus*	93	5	95
7 Hilliard	30	68	30
Alaska			
AL *Young*	82	2	97
Arizona			
1 Coppersmith	23	73	24
2 Pastor	27	73	27
3 *Stump*	98	2	98
4 *Kyl*	93	5	95
5 *Kolbe*	80	16	83
6 English	16	84	16
Arkansas			
1 Lambert	50	50	50
2 Thornton	84	14	86
3 *Hutchinson*	91	9	91
4 *Dickey*	93	7	93
California			
1 Hamburg	5	86	5
2 *Herger*	91	7	93
3 Fazio	41	59	41
4 *Doolittle*	91	9	91
5 Matsui	34	66	34
6 Woolsey	9	91	9
7 Miller	7	91	7
8 Pelosi	7	93	7
9 Dellums	5	93	5
10 *Baker*	100	0	100
11 *Pombo*	89	11	89
12 Lantos	39	61	39
13 Stark	9	89	9
14 Eshoo	14	86	14
15 Mineta	34	64	35
16 Edwards	11	86	12
17 Farr[1]†	15	83	15
18 Condit	57	43	57
19 Lehman	48	43	52
20 Dooley	36	61	37
21 *Thomas*	91	7	93
22 *Huffington*	86	14	86
23 *Gallegly*	95	5	95
24 Beilenson	20	77	21
25 *McKeon*	93	5	95
26 Berman	20	73	22
27 *Moorhead*	93	7	93
28 *Dreier*	93	7	93
29 Waxman	18	75	20
30 Becerra	9	86	10
31 Martinez	43	55	44
32 Dixon	36	64	36
33 Roybal-Allard	20	80	20
34 Torres	16	77	17
35 Waters	14	86	14
36 Harman	41	57	42
37 Tucker	27	68	29
38 *Horn*	68	32	68
39 *Royce*	75	25	75
40 *Lewis*	89	11	89
41 *Kim*	98	2	98

	1	2	3
42 Brown	20	80	20
43 *Calvert*	98	2	98
44 *McCandless*	95	5	95
45 *Rohrabacher*	68	32	68
46 *Dornan*	93	5	95
47 *Cox*	91	9	91
48 *Packard*	75	2	97
49 Schenk	18	82	18
50 Filner	9	91	9
51 *Cunningham*	98	2	98
52 *Hunter*	86	5	95
Colorado			
1 Schroeder	20	80	20
2 Skaggs	27	73	27
3 *McInnis*	89	11	89
4 *Allard*	73	27	73
5 *Hefley*	95	5	95
6 *Schaefer*	89	11	89
Connecticut			
1 Kennelly	32	68	32
2 Gejdenson	18	82	18
3 DeLauro	20	80	20
4 *Shays*	36	64	36
5 *Franks*	93	7	93
6 *Johnson*	57	43	57
Delaware			
AL *Castle*	84	16	84
Florida			
1 Hutto	100	0	100
2 Peterson	73	27	73
3 Brown	39	52	43
4 *Fowler*	93	7	93
5 Thurman	57	43	57
6 *Stearns*	93	5	95
7 *Mica*	93	7	93
8 *McCollum*	95	5	95
9 *Bilirakis*	95	5	95
10 *Young*	91	9	91
11 Gibbons	45	50	48
12 *Canady*	93	7	93
13 *Miller*	80	20	80
14 *Goss*	95	5	95
15 Bacchus	48	50	49
16 *Lewis*	95	5	95
17 Meek	43	57	43
18 *Ros-Lehtinen*	77	23	77
19 Johnston	18	80	19
20 Deutsch	27	73	27
21 *Diaz-Balart*	75	23	77
22 *Shaw*	98	2	98
23 Hastings	18	73	20
Georgia			
1 *Kingston*	84	14	86
2 Bishop	59	41	59
3 *Collins*	91	9	91
4 *Linder*	100	0	100
5 Lewis	9	91	9
6 *Gingrich*	95	5	95
7 Darden	89	11	89
8 Rowland	89	11	89
9 Deal	80	20	80
10 Johnson	75	25	75
11 McKinney	7	91	7
Hawaii			
1 Abercrombie	14	86	14
2 Mink	2	98	2
Idaho			
1 LaRocco	52	45	53
2 *Crapo*	93	5	95
Illinois			
1 Rush	2	95	2
2 Reynolds	7	91	7
3 Lipinski	66	32	67
4 Gutierrez	11	82	12
5 Rostenkowski	25	75	25
6 *Hyde*	82	9	90
7 Collins	5	93	5
8 *Crane*	82	18	82
9 Yates	2	86	3
10 *Porter*	61	36	63
11 Sangmeister	48	48	50
12 Costello	66	32	67
13 *Fawell*	84	16	84
14 *Hastert*	93	7	93
15 *Ewing*	89	11	89
16 *Manzullo*	91	9	91
17 Evans	5	95	5

ND Northern Democrats   SD Southern Democrats

Member	1	2	3
18 *Michel*	93	2	98
19 Poshard	61	39	61
20 Durbin	34	66	34

Indiana

Member	1	2	3
1 Visclosky	45	55	45
2 Sharp	43	57	43
3 Roemer	50	50	50
4 Long	45	55	45
5 *Buyer*	98	2	98
6 *Burton*	91	9	91
7 *Myers*	93	5	95
8 McCloskey	27	70	28
9 Hamilton	68	32	68
10 Jacobs	39	59	40

Iowa

Member	1	2	3
1 *Leach*	43	50	46
2 *Nussle*	59	41	59
3 *Lightfoot*	95	5	95
4 Smith	59	39	60
5 *Grandy*	66	34	66

Kansas

Member	1	2	3
1 *Roberts*	95	5	95
2 Slattery	57	41	58
3 *Meyers*	75	23	77
4 Glickman	55	45	55

Kentucky

Member	1	2	3
1 Barlow	50	48	51
2 Natcher	64	36	64
3 Mazzoli	73	27	73
4 *Bunning*	84	14	86
5 *Rogers*	95	5	95
6 Baesler	64	34	65

Louisiana

Member	1	2	3
1 *Livingston*	95	5	95
2 Jefferson	23	73	24
3 Tauzin	82	11	88
4 Fields	20	80	20
5 *McCrery*	95	5	95
6 *Baker*	93	7	93
7 Hayes	82	14	86

Maine

Member	1	2	3
1 Andrews	5	95	5
2 *Snowe*	66	34	66

Maryland

Member	1	2	3
1 *Gilchrest*	61	39	61
2 *Bentley*	86	9	90
3 Cardin	20	80	20
4 Wynn	14	86	14
5 Hoyer	59	41	59
6 *Bartlett*	95	5	95
7 Mfume	7	91	7
8 *Morella*	45	52	47

Massachusetts

Member	1	2	3
1 Olver	14	86	14
2 Neal	16	82	16
3 *Blute*	73	23	76
4 Frank	9	91	9
5 Meehan	16	80	17
6 *Torkildsen*	80	20	80
7 Markey	9	89	9
8 Kennedy	14	86	14
9 Moakley	11	66	15
10 Studds	9	91	9

Michigan

Member	1	2	3
1 Stupak	41	59	41
2 *Hoekstra*	82	18	82
3 Vacancy[2]	--	--	--
4 *Camp*	84	16	84
5 Barcia	66	34	66
6 *Upton*	66	34	66
7 *Smith*	84	9	90
8 Carr	48	50	49
9 Kildee	23	77	23
10 Bonior	20	77	21
11 *Knollenberg*	89	11	89
12 Levin	23	77	23
13 Ford	14	82	14
14 Conyers	0	57	0
15 Collins	9	89	9
16 Dingell	39	55	41

Minnesota

Member	1	2	3
1 Penny	48	52	48
2 Minge	32	59	35
3 *Ramstad*	70	30	70
4 Vento	2	95	2
5 Sabo	11	84	12
6 *Grams*	95	5	95
7 Peterson	48	52	48
8 Oberstar	20	80	20

Mississippi

Member	1	2	3
1 Whitten	77	11	87
2 Thompson[3]†	14	81	15
3 Montgomery	95	5	95
4 Parker	93	5	95
5 Taylor	91	9	91

Missouri

Member	1	2	3
1 Clay	16	84	16
2 *Talent*	86	9	90
3 Gephardt	30	68	30
4 Skelton	86	14	86
5 Wheat	5	93	5
6 Danner	52	48	52
7 *Hancock*	95	5	95
8 *Emerson*	95	5	95
9 Volkmer	75	25	75

Montana

Member	1	2	3
AL Williams	25	68	27

Nebraska

Member	1	2	3
1 *Bereuter*	84	16	84
2 Hoagland	57	43	57
3 *Barrett*	91	9	91

Nevada

Member	1	2	3
1 Bilbray	68	30	70
2 *Vucanovich*	80	7	92

New Hampshire

Member	1	2	3
1 *Zeliff*	95	5	95
2 Swett	45	55	45

New Jersey

Member	1	2	3
1 Andrews	50	50	50
2 Hughes	55	45	55
3 *Saxton*	91	9	91
4 *Smith*	89	11	89
5 *Roukema*	59	39	60
6 Pallone	32	68	32
7 *Franks*	64	36	64
8 Klein	34	66	34
9 Torricelli	43	55	44
10 Payne	5	89	5
11 *Gallo*	93	7	93
12 *Zimmer*	59	39	60
13 Menendez	41	59	41

New Mexico

Member	1	2	3
1 *Schiff*	82	14	86
2 *Skeen*	80	5	95
3 Richardson	50	45	52

New York

Member	1	2	3
1 Hochbrueckner	52	48	52
2 *Lazio*	82	18	82
3 *King*	93	7	93
4 *Levy*	93	7	93
5 Ackerman	30	66	31
6 Flake	11	77	13
7 Manton	50	45	52
8 Nadler	7	86	7
9 Schumer	16	84	16
10 Towns	5	86	5
11 Owens	2	93	2
12 Velazquez	7	93	7
13 *Molinari*	84	16	84
14 Maloney	16	84	16
15 Rangel	5	91	5
16 Serrano	9	89	9
17 Engel	11	77	13
18 Lowey	18	82	18
19 *Fish*	91	9	91
20 Gilman	68	32	68
21 McNulty	75	25	75
22 *Solomon*	93	7	93
23 *Boehlert*	70	30	70
24 *McHugh*	84	14	86
25 *Walsh*	89	11	89
26 Hinchey	14	80	15
27 *Paxon*	95	5	95
28 Slaughter	20	80	20
29 LaFalce	39	61	39
30 *Quinn*	91	9	91
31 *Houghton*	86	11	88

North Carolina

Member	1	2	3
1 Clayton	14	86	14
2 Valentine	73	23	76
3 Lancaster	77	20	79
4 Price	45	52	47
5 Neal	57	23	71
6 *Coble*	73	27	73
7 Rose	52	41	56
8 Hefner	64	32	67
9 *McMillan*	80	7	92
10 *Ballenger*	86	14	86
11 *Taylor*	86	14	86
12 Watt	7	93	7

North Dakota

Member	1	2	3
AL Pomeroy	50	45	52

Ohio

Member	1	2	3
1 Mann	48	45	51
2 *Portman*[4]†	86	14	86
3 Hall	43	50	46
4 *Oxley*	93	5	95
5 *Gillmor*	93	5	95
6 Strickland	30	70	30
7 *Hobson*	82	18	82
8 *Boehner*	95	2	98
9 Kaptur	66	32	67
10 *Hoke*	75	14	85
11 Stokes	14	73	16
12 *Kasich*	86	14	86
13 Brown	23	77	23
14 Sawyer	30	66	31
15 *Pryce*	93	7	93
16 *Regula*	91	9	91
17 Traficant	64	36	64
18 Applegate	68	32	68
19 Fingerhut	41	57	42

Oklahoma

Member	1	2	3
1 *Inhofe*	93	7	93
2 Synar	11	80	13
3 Brewster	73	18	76
4 McCurdy	77	14	85
5 *Istook*	75	18	80
6 English	77	18	81

Oregon

Member	1	2	3
1 Furse	2	95	2
2 *Smith*	89	9	91
3 Wyden	11	89	11
4 DeFazio	25	75	25
5 Kopetski	27	70	28

Pennsylvania

Member	1	2	3
1 Foglietta	7	89	7
2 Blackwell	9	89	9
3 Borski	48	50	49
4 Klink	52	48	52
5 Clinger	84	11	88
6 Holden	57	43	57
7 Weldon	95	2	98
8 Greenwood	80	20	80
9 Shuster	82	11	88
10 McDade	68	11	86
11 Kanjorski	48	52	48
12 Murtha	77	20	79
13 Margolies-Mezv.	32	68	32
14 Coyne	7	93	7
15 McHale	55	45	55
16 *Walker*	91	9	91
17 *Gekas*	86	14	86
18 *Santorum*	77	23	77
19 *Goodling*	86	11	88
20 Murphy	45	48	49
21 *Ridge*	86	7	93

Rhode Island

Member	1	2	3
1 *Machtley*	82	16	84
2 Reed	23	75	23

South Carolina

Member	1	2	3
1 *Ravenel*	84	16	84
2 *Spence*	95	5	95
3 Derrick	61	32	66
4 *Inglis*	89	11	89
5 Spratt	82	18	82
6 Clyburn	45	55	45

South Dakota

Member	1	2	3
AL Johnson	50	45	52

Tennessee

Member	1	2	3
1 *Quillen*	95	5	95
2 *Duncan*	66	34	66
3 Lloyd	91	7	93
4 Cooper	86	11	88
5 Clement	64	34	65
6 Gordon	70	30	70
7 *Sundquist*	89	7	93
8 Tanner	91	9	91
9 Ford	7	80	8

Texas

Member	1	2	3
1 Chapman	86	9	90
2 Wilson	70	23	76
3 *Johnson, Sam*	98	2	98
4 Hall	86	14	86
5 Bryant	30	70	30
6 *Barton*	95	5	95
7 *Archer*	91	7	93
8 *Fields*	98	2	98
9 Brooks	77	20	79
10 Pickle	61	36	63
11 Edwards	84	14	86
12 Geren	95	5	95
13 Sarpalius	91	5	95
14 Laughlin	89	7	93
15 de la Garza	80	14	85
16 Coleman	57	39	60
17 Stenholm	91	9	91
18 Washington	5	75	6
19 *Combest*	100	0	100
20 Gonzalez	34	66	34
21 *Smith*	100	0	100
22 *DeLay*	95	5	95
23 *Bonilla*	98	2	98
24 Frost	68	18	79
25 Andrews	86	9	90
26 *Armey*	98	0	100
27 Ortiz	82	18	82
28 Tejeda	86	14	86
29 Green	39	57	40
30 Johnson, E. B.	34	66	34

Utah

Member	1	2	3
1 *Hansen*	100	0	100
2 Shepherd	34	64	35
3 Orton	82	16	84

Vermont

Member	1	2	3
AL *Sanders*	11	86	12

Virginia

Member	1	2	3
1 *Bateman*	93	7	93
2 Pickett	82	18	82
3 Scott	30	70	30
4 Sisisky	84	11	88
5 Payne	82	18	82
6 *Goodlatte*	84	16	84
7 *Bliley*	100	0	100
8 Moran	36	64	36
9 Boucher	50	45	52
10 *Wolf*	93	7	93
11 Byrne	34	66	34

Washington

Member	1	2	3
1 Cantwell	32	68	32
2 Swift	30	70	30
3 Unsoeld	11	84	12
4 Inslee	39	61	39
5 Foley[5]			
6 Dicks	48	52	48
7 McDermott	14	80	15
8 *Dunn*	91	9	91
9 Kreidler	14	86	14

West Virginia

Member	1	2	3
1 Mollohan	77	20	79
2 Wise	68	27	71
3 Rahall	66	34	66

Wisconsin

Member	1	2	3
1 Barca[6]†	45	55	45
2 *Klug*	64	36	64
3 *Gunderson*	70	30	70
4 Kleczka	48	50	49
5 Barrett	25	75	25
6 *Petri*	75	25	75
7 Obey	30	68	30
8 Roth	68	30	70
9 *Sensenbrenner*	61	39	61

Wyoming

Member	1	2	3
AL *Thomas*	86	14	86

Delegates

Member	1	2	3
de Lugo, V.I. †	10	80	11
Faleomavaega, Am.S. †	10	63	14
Norton, D.C. †	3	97	3
Romero-B., P.R. †	20	50	29
Underwood, Guam †	23	50	32

Southern states - Ala., Ark., Fla., Ga., Ky., La., Miss., N.C., Okla., S.C., Tenn., Texas, Va.
Omitted votes are quorum calls, which CQ does not include in its vote charts.

	1	2	3
Alabama			
Heflin	83	10	89
Shelby	93	5	95
Alaska			
Murkowski	80	5	94
Stevens	88	7	92
Arizona			
DeConcini	24	73	25
McCain	78	12	86
Arkansas			
Bumpers	44	54	45
Pryor	41	44	49
California			
Boxer	10	90	10
Feinstein	37	59	38
Colorado			
Campbell	46	51	48
Brown	83	17	83
Connecticut			
Dodd	29	68	30
Lieberman	56	44	56
Delaware			
Biden	32	66	33
Roth	78	22	78
Florida			
Graham	61	39	61
Mack	98	2	98
Georgia			
Nunn	80	12	87
Coverdell	95	2	98
Hawaii			
Akaka	29	71	29
Inouye	34	59	37
Idaho			
Craig	93	7	93
Kempthorne	90	10	90
Illinois			
Moseley-Braun	17	83	17
Simon	17	83	17
Indiana			
Coats	80	20	80
Lugar	88	10	90

	1	2	3
Iowa			
Harkin	15	83	15
Grassley	80	20	80
Kansas			
Dole	88	7	92
Kassebaum	85	12	88
Kentucky			
Ford	80	20	80
McConnell	98	2	98
Louisiana			
Breaux	80	17	83
Johnston	90	10	90
Maine			
Mitchell	20	80	20
Cohen	56	41	58
Maryland			
Mikulski	39	61	39
Sarbanes	12	88	12
Massachusetts			
Kennedy	10	90	10
Kerry	24	73	25
Michigan			
Levin	20	80	20
Riegle	22	73	23
Minnesota			
Wellstone	5	95	5
Durenberger	54	44	55
Mississippi			
Cochran	98	0	100
Lott	98	0	100
Missouri			
Bond	83	15	85
Danforth	71	27	73
Montana			
Baucus	54	39	58
Burns	85	15	85
Nebraska			
Exon	71	24	74
Kerrey	59	39	60
Nevada			
Bryan	61	39	61
Reid	49	49	50

	1	2	3
New Hampshire			
Gregg	71	27	73
Smith	90	10	90
New Jersey			
Bradley	10	85	10
Lautenberg	20	80	20
New Mexico			
Bingaman	49	49	50
Domenici	85	12	88
New York			
Moynihan	15	85	15
D'Amato	78	20	80
North Carolina			
Faircloth	93	7	93
Helms	83	5	94
North Dakota			
Conrad	51	49	51
Dorgan	32	56	36
Ohio			
Glenn	37	59	38
Metzenbaum	10	90	10
Oklahoma			
Boren	63	37	63
Nickles	85	12	88
Oregon			
Hatfield	44	54	45
Packwood	73	27	73
Pennsylvania			
Wofford	27	71	28
Specter	61	27	69
Rhode Island			
Pell	12	85	13
Chafee	46	54	46
South Carolina			
Hollings	59	41	59
Thurmond	98	2	98
South Dakota			
Daschle	51	44	54
Pressler	95	5	95
Tennessee			
Mathews	66	32	68
Sasser	68	32	68

KEY

† Not eligible for all recorded votes in 1993 or voted "present" to avoid possible conflict of interest.

Democrats   *Republicans*

	1	2	3
Texas			
Gramm	93	0	100
Hutchison[1]†	94	0	100
Utah			
Bennett	90	7	93
Hatch	95	5	95
Vermont			
Leahy	27	73	27
Jeffords	27	71	28
Virginia			
Robb	44	56	44
Warner	85	12	88
Washington			
Murray	22	71	24
Gorton	90	10	90
West Virginia			
Byrd	51	49	51
Rockefeller	37	54	41
Wisconsin			
Feingold	10	90	10
Kohl	24	76	24
Wyoming			
Simpson	88	7	92
Wallop	83	5	94

Conservative Coalition
Support and Opposition: Senate

1. Conservative Coalition Support, 1993. Percentage of 41 recorded votes in 1993 on which the conservative coalition appeared and on which a senator voted "yea" or "nay" *in agreement* with the position of the conservative coalition. Failures to vote lowered both support and opposition scores.

2. Conservative Coalition Opposition, 1993. Percentage of 41 recorded votes in 1993 on which the conservative coalition appeared and on which a senator voted "yea" or "nay" *in disagreement* with the position of the conservative coalition. Failures to vote lowered both support and opposition scores.

3. Conservative Coalition Support, 1993. Percentage of 41 recorded votes in 1993 on which the conservative coalition appeared and on which a senator was present and voted "yea" or "nay" *in agreement* with the position of the conservative coalition. In this version of the study, absences were not counted; therefore, failures to vote did not lower support or opposition scores. Opposition scores, not listed here, are the inverse of the support score; i.e., the opposition score is equal to 100 percent minus the individual's support score.

[1] *Kay Bailey Hutchison, R-Texas, was sworn in June 14, 1993, to succeed Bob Krueger, D. Krueger was appointed by Gov. Ann W. Richards, D, to fill the seat vacated by Lloyd Bentsen, D, who became Treasury secretary Jan. 20, 1993. Krueger was eligible for eight conservative coalition votes in 1993. His conservative coalition score was 63 percent; opposition score, 0 percent; support score, adjusted for absences, 100 percent. Bentsen was eligible for no conservative coalition votes in 1993. Hutchison was eligible for 33 conservative coalition votes in 1993.*

Freshmen Help Spur Congress To a Record Voting Rate

Missing a vote had become a relatively rare event in Congress. Despite an avalanche of votes, members voted 96.2 percent of the time in 1993. That was the highest level of voting participation for Congress since Congressional Quarterly began tracking recorded votes in 1953.

Thomas E. Mann, director of governmental studies at the Brookings Institution, said the fresh blood in Congress probably helped raise the scores.

"To the extent participation increased, it probably reflected that in the House there was high turnover — the last election got rid of members who had lost interest in their jobs," said Mann. "With large freshman classes, you have people who are more sensitive to charges of shirking responsibility."

"And finally," Mann said, "you have nervous Nellies on Capitol Hill and an angry public."

House members voted 96 percent of the time, and senators, 97.6 percent of the time. (The preponderance of House votes kept the overall percentage closer to the House total.)

In each chamber, participation increased by 3 percentage points over the previous year.

The overall score was nearly 3 percentage points higher than in 1992. The previous record of 95 percent occurred in 1989, 1990 and 1991.

Members managed to achieve these high scores in spite of large increases in the numbers of votes in both chambers.

In 1993, House members voted on 597 issues. (Including quorum calls — not counted in the study — the House took 615 votes, 127 more than the previous year and the most since 1980.) The Senate took 395 roll call votes, 125 more than in 1992.

The individual scores often served as a measure of a member's diligence in his or her job. However, members and observers of Congress alike cautioned against using the scores as an absolute gauge of a member's commitment, because members often were prevented from participating in floor votes by other significant duties, such as appointments with constituents and committee meetings to craft bills.

Voting participation scores were typically higher in non-election years, when members did not have to re-

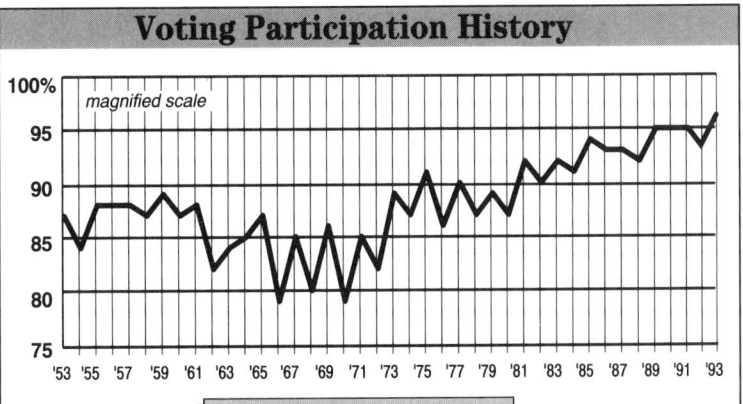

Voting Participation History

100%
95
90
85
80
75

magnified scale

'53 '55 '57 '59 '61 '63 '65 '67 '69 '71 '73 '75 '77 '79 '81 '83 '85 '87 '89 '91 '93

Definition

How often a member voted "yea" or "nay" on roll call votes on the floor of the House or Senate.

1993 Data

	Recorded Votes	Participation Rate
Senate	395	98%
House	597	96%
Total Congress	992	96%

Votes, pp. 33-C – 35-C

turn to their states and districts to campaign.

Since bottoming out at 79 percent in 1970, members' overall voting participation scores had risen steadily. "Members became sensitized to the issue back in the '70s, when the number of recorded votes went way up and voting participation percentages went way down," said Christopher J. Deering, a George Washington University political science professor. "A couple of members got burned on the issue during campaigns."

Deering said the days of vote-skipping were over: "[Members have] really cut that out because they know that it can be grist for an opponent."

Congressional leaders helped members keep up their voting participation scores by scheduling most roll calls between Tuesday and Thursday, allowing members to spend long weekends attending to business back home.

Rep. Bob Filner, D-Calif., a freshman who voted 100 percent of the time, argued that voting participation remained important to voters. "It resonates with them that you are doing your job. I am not sure there is any better record that you were on the job every day," he said.

Filner frequently found himself walking to the chamber to cast his ballot with the only other House freshman to achieve a perfect score, his neighbor in the Cannon House Office Building, California Republican Jay C. Kim. Filner said each would jokingly threaten to lock the other in a closet in order to prevent him from winning the top voting score.

Filner said he would try to extend his perfect attendance record for as long as possible. "I like to joke that Congressman [William H.] Natcher and I are the only Democrats with careers of perfect participation," Filner said.

Kentucky Democrat Natcher had participated in every floor vote since he took office in 1953. His string stretched to 14,125, excluding quorum votes.

Other members were skeptical about the importance of showing up for every vote. Craig Washington, D-Texas, missed 26 percent of the House votes. "It is just a question of priorities. I have to determine what the best use of my time is in serving my constituents," Washington said. Washington said that he regularly skipped procedural votes, such as the 44 votes to approve the House Journal,

Backlog, Revotes Raised Numbers

In 1993, the House took an extraordinary 597 roll call votes (excluding quorum calls), 26 percent more than in 1992, and the highest number of recorded votes since 1979. But did it necessarily cover more legislative ground as a result of the high number of votes? The answer seems to be both yes and no.

"There may have been more floor votes in both chambers, not so much because of the new administration, but because there were a backlog of things that members did not want to bring to the floor during the previous, Republican administration," said Christopher J. Deering, a political scientist at George Washington University.

Another reason the House took so many votes was that 69 of them were revotes, or separate votes on amendments that had been approved in the Committee of the Whole, a panel consisting of all House members that is used to expedite consideration of amendments.

Republicans forced the revotes because that excluded five votes — those of the resident commissioner of Puerto Rico and the delegates from American Samoa, Guam, the Virgin Islands and the District of Columbia. A new House rule gave them the power to vote on amendments in the Committee of the Whole — a rule bitterly opposed by Republicans, who said their voting power was diminished by the delegates, all of whom were Democrats.

The delegates could not vote on final passage, and House rules required an automatic revote if the delegates' votes made the difference between winning and losing. But that did not happen in 1993.

Instead, House Republicans demanded a separate vote at virtually every opportunity (though House rules prevented them from demanding separate votes on amendments that were rejected).

The outcome changed in four of the 69 instances where a second vote was taken.

Deering said that the practice of taking second votes on amendments raised an interesting question: Which one counted?

"Of course, it is the initial vote that counts," Deering said in response to his own question, "because it determines whether a second vote is taken."

Delegates Were Firm

Champions of voting rights for the delegates were unfazed by the Republican tactic.

Eleanor Holmes Norton, D-D.C., who initiated the rules change, insisted that the voting privilege increased the delegates' participation in the legislative process. Norton voted in 98 percent of the 189 roll call votes for which the delegates were eligible, the highest score of the delegates.

Norton

"It has made me more effective because of the many kinds of interaction I now have with my colleagues on the House floor," Norton said.

Virgin Islands Delegate Ron de Lugo also posted a high participation score, 95 percent. The other delegates had more trouble getting to votes — perhaps because of the travel difficulties presented by representing faraway places. Robert A. Underwood, of Guam, participated in 83 percent of the votes; Eni F. H. Faleomavaega of American Samoa voted in 62 percent; and Carlos Romero-Barceló of Puerto Rico voted in 58 percent.

but said he would not skip a vote that he thought would affect his district.

High Participation Scores for GOP

Overall, 18 House members and eight senators participated in 100 percent of the votes in their chambers. Thirty-seven senators and a whopping 117 House members cast votes 99 percent of the time. GOP members of Congress scored better than Democrats, 96.8 percent to 95.8 percent. In the House, Republicans voted more than a percentage point more frequently than their Democratic colleagues (96.7 percent to 95.5 percent). In the Senate, the Democrats posted a marginally higher score than the Republicans (97.8 percent to 97.3 percent).

The 114 first-term House members in the 103rd Congress logged higher participation scores than their veteran colleagues (97.5 percent to 95.9 percent). The 14 freshman senators, on the other hand, voted with slightly less frequency than non-freshmen (97.1 percent to 97.6 percent).

In the House, 21 representatives and three delegates voted less than 90 percent of the time. Republicans Joe L. Barton and Jack Fields of Texas both managed to vote 85 percent of the time, despite their unsuccessful campaigns for the Repub-

lican Senate nomination in the special election to fill the seat vacated by Treasury Secretary Lloyd Bentsen. Michigan Democrat John Conyers Jr. missed 29 percent of the votes because of his unsuccessful Detroit mayoral bid.

Serious health problems and illness in the family prevented some members from voting. James H. Quillen, R-Tenn., underwent heart bypass surgery. Massachusetts Democrat Joe Moakley was away from the chamber to attend to his wife, who was battling cancer.

Tennessee Democrat Harold E. Ford posted the lowest score of the representatives, 69 percent. Ford was on trial in Tennessee for five weeks in the early part of the year before he was acquitted in April of bank, mail and tax-fraud charges.

Only three senators voted less than 90 percent of the time. Republican Arlen Specter of Pennsylvania missed 14 percent of the votes after undergoing surgery to remove a brain tumor.

Some members took extra precautions to ensure that they did not miss votes, albeit with mixed results. Arkansas Republican Jay Dickey, who finished the year with 97 percent voting participation, took to the House floor Oct. 13 to offer a personal explanation for two missed roll calls: "Because of a malfunction of my beeper, I was unable to be here to record my vote," he said. ∎

State / Senator	1	2
Alabama		
Heflin	95	95
Shelby	98	98
Alaska		
Murkowski	89	89
Stevens	98	98
Arizona		
DeConcini	97	98
McCain	96	96
Arkansas		
Bumpers	98	98
Pryor	93	93
California		
Boxer	99	99
Feinstein	97	97
Colorado		
Campbell	96	96
Brown	100	100
Connecticut		
Dodd	99	99
Lieberman	99	99
Delaware		
Biden	97	97
Roth	99	99
Florida		
Graham	99	99
Mack	99	99
Georgia		
Nunn	94	94
Coverdell #	97	97
Hawaii		
Akaka	100	100
Inouye	88	87
Idaho		
Craig	99	99
Kempthorne	99	99
Illinois		
Moseley-Braun #	99	99
Simon	99	99
Indiana		
Coats	98	98
Lugar	99	99

State / Senator	1	2
Iowa		
Harkin	98	98
Grassley	99	99
Kansas		
Dole	98	98
Kassebaum	98	98
Kentucky		
Ford	100	100
McConnell #	98	98
Louisiana		
Breaux	98	98
Johnston	98	98
Maine		
Mitchell	100	100
Cohen #	99	99
Maryland		
Mikulski	99	99
Sarbanes	99	99
Massachusetts		
Kennedy	99	99
Kerry	99	99
Michigan		
Levin	99	99
Riegle	97	97
Minnesota		
Wellstone	99	99
Durenberger	96	96
Mississippi		
Cochran	99	99
Lott	99	99
Missouri		
Bond	97	97
Danforth	98	98
Montana		
Baucus #	96	96
Burns	99	99
Nebraska		
Exon	98	98
Kerrey	98	98
Nevada		
Bryan	99	99
Reid	99	99

State / Senator	1	2
New Hampshire		
Gregg	97	97
Smith #	98	98
New Jersey		
Bradley	96	96
Lautenberg	99	99
New Mexico		
Bingaman	98	98
Domenici	97	97
New York		
Moynihan	100	100
D'Amato	97	97
North Carolina		
Faircloth	98	98
Helms	92	92
North Dakota		
Conrad	99	99
Dorgan	92	92
Ohio		
Glenn	99	99
Metzenbaum	97	97
Oklahoma		
Boren	99	99
Nickles	99	99
Oregon		
Hatfield	95	95
Packwood	99	99
Pennsylvania		
Wofford	97	97
Specter #	86	86
Rhode Island		
Pell	99	99
Chafee #	98	98
South Carolina		
Hollings	96	96
Thurmond #	98	98
South Dakota		
Daschle	99	99
Pressler	98	98
Tennessee		
Mathews	98	98
Sasser	99	99

KEY

† Not eligible for all recorded votes in 1993 or voted "present" to avoid possible conflict of interest.

\# Member absent a day or more in 1993 due to illness or to a relative's death or illness.

Democrats	*Republicans*

State / Senator	1	2
Texas		
Gramm	93	94
Hutchison[1]†	99	99
Utah		
Bennett	96	96
Hatch	99	99
Vermont		
Leahy	98	98
Jeffords	97	97
Virginia		
Robb	99	99
Warner	96	96
Washington		
Murray #	92	92
Gorton	99	99
West Virginia		
Byrd	100	100
Rockefeller	96	96
Wisconsin		
Feingold	100	100
Kohl	100	100
Wyoming		
Simpson †#	96	96
Wallop	95	95

Voting Participation: Senate

1. Voting Participation, 1993. Percentage of 395 recorded votes in 1993 on which a senator voted "yea" or "nay."

2. Voting Participation, 1993. Percentage of 391 recorded votes in 1993 on which a senator voted "yea" or "nay." In this version of the study, votes to instruct the sergeant at arms to request the attendance of absent senators are not included.

NOTE: Scores are rounded to nearest percentage, except that no scores are rounded up to 100 percent. Members with 100 percent scores participated in all recorded votes for which they were eligible.

[1] *Kay Bailey Hutchison, R-Texas, was sworn in June 14, 1993, to succeed Bob Krueger, D. Krueger was appointed by Gov. Ann W. Richards, D, to fill the seat vacated by Lloyd Bentsen, D, who became Treasury secretary Jan. 20, 1993. Krueger was eligible for 146 votes in 1993, none of which included sergeant at arms votes. His voting participation score was 73 percent. Bentsen was not eligible to vote in 1993. Hutchison was eligible for 249 votes in 1993, 245 not including sergeant at arms votes.*

Voting Participation: House

1. Voting Participation, 1993. Percentage of 597 recorded votes in 1993 on which a representative voted "yea" or "nay."

2. Voting Participation, 1993. Percentage of 553 recorded votes in 1993 on which a representative voted "yea" or "nay." In this version of the study, votes of approval of the House Journal were not included.

NOTES: Scores are rounded to nearest percentage, except that no scores are rounded up to 100 percent. Members with a 100 percent score participated in all recorded votes for which they were eligible.

Delegates were eligible for 189 of the 597 votes in 1993 and for 189 of the 553 votes excluding the approval of the House Journal.

[1] *Rep. Sam Farr, D-Calif., was sworn in June 16, 1993, to succeed Leon E. Panetta, D, who became director of the Office of Management and Budget on Jan. 21, 1993. Panetta was eligible for five votes in 1993, none of which was a vote to approve the Journal. His voting participation score was 100 percent. Farr was eligible for 381 votes, 367 not including votes to approve the Journal.*

[2] *Rep. Vernon J. Ehlers, R-Mich., tentatively will be sworn in Jan. 25, 1994, to succeed Paul B. Henry, R, who died July 31, 1993. Henry was eligible for 375 votes in 1993, 341 not including votes to approve the Journal. His voting participation scores were 0 percent and 0 percent, respectively. Ehlers was not eligible to vote.*

[3] *Rep. Bennie Thompson, D-Miss., was sworn in April 20, 1993, to succeed Mike Espy, D, who became Agriculture secretary Jan. 22, 1993. Espy was eligible for five votes in 1993, none of which was a vote to approve the Journal. His voting participation score was 100 percent. Thompson was eligible for 466 votes, 442 not including votes to approve the Journal.*

[4] *Rep. Rob Portman, R-Ohio, was sworn in May 5, 1993, to succeed Bill Gradison, R, who resigned Jan. 31, 1993. Gradison was eligible for nine votes in 1993, seven not including votes to approve the Journal. His voting participation scores were 100 percent and 100 percent, respectively. Portman was eligible for 451 votes, 430 not including votes to approve the Journal.*

[5] *Rep. Thomas S. Foley, D-Wash., as Speaker of the House, voted at his discretion.*

[6] *Rep. Peter W. Barca, D-Wis., was sworn in June 8, 1993, to succeed Les Aspin, D, who became Defense secretary Jan. 20, 1993. Aspin was eligible for one vote in 1993, which did not include a vote to approve the Journal. His voting participation score was 0 percent. Barca was eligible for 405 votes in 1993, 387 not including votes to approve the Journal.*

KEY

† Not eligible for all recorded votes in 1993 or voted "present" to avoid possible conflict of interest.

Member absent a day or more in 1993 due to illness or to a relative's death or illness.

Democrats   *Republicans*
Independent

	1	2
Alabama		
1 Callahan #	96	97
2 *Everett* #	98	98
3 Browder	98	99
4 Bevill #	95	96
5 Cramer	99	99
6 *Bachus*	99	99
7 Hilliard #	95	95
Alaska		
AL *Young*	87	88
Arizona		
1 Coppersmith	98	98
2 Pastor	99	99
3 *Stump*	100	100
4 *Kyl*	98	98
5 *Kolbe*	97	97
6 English	99	99
Arkansas		
1 Lambert	99	99
2 Thornton	96	97
3 *Hutchinson*	99	99
4 *Dickey*	97	97
California		
1 Hamburg	97	97
2 *Herger*	98	99
3 Fazio	99	99
4 *Doolittle* #	97	97
5 Matsui	96	96
6 Woolsey	98	99
7 Miller	92	93
8 Pelosi	93	93
9 Dellums	92	93
10 *Baker*	99	99
11 *Pombo*	99	99
12 Lantos	97	98
13 Stark	94	95
14 Eshoo	99	99
15 Mineta	98	98
16 Edwards	97	97
17 Farr[1]†	96	96
18 Condit	96	96
19 Lehman	91	91
20 Dooley	94	95
21 *Thomas*	97	96
22 *Huffington*	97	98
23 *Gallegly*	97	97
24 Beilenson	97	97
25 *McKeon*	95	95
26 Berman #	88	88
27 *Moorhead*	99	99
28 *Dreier*	96	97
29 Waxman	93	93
30 Becerra #	93	93
31 Martinez	93	93
32 Dixon	98	99
33 Roybal-Allard	98	98
34 Torres	90	91
35 Waters	95	96
36 Harman	93	93
37 Tucker	89	91
38 *Horn*	98	98
39 *Royce*	98	99
40 *Lewis*	96	95
41 *Kim*	100	100

	1	2
42 Brown	86	91
43 *Calvert*	97	97
44 *McCandless*	98	98
45 *Rohrabacher*	99	100
46 *Dornan*	93	95
47 *Cox*	92	93
48 *Packard*	86	86
49 Schenk	98	99
50 Filner	100	100
51 *Cunningham* #	97	98
52 *Hunter*	92	93
Colorado		
1 Schroeder	98	98
2 Skaggs	99	99
3 *McInnis*	99	99
4 *Allard*	99	99
5 *Hefley*	99	99
6 *Schaefer*	98	98
Connecticut		
1 Kennelly	99	99
2 Gejdenson	99	99
3 DeLauro #	99	99
4 *Shays*	100	100
5 *Franks*	99	99
6 *Johnson*	97	97
Delaware		
AL *Castle*	99	99
Florida		
1 Hutto	97	97
2 Peterson	100	100
3 Brown	96	97
4 *Fowler*	97	97
5 Thurman	99	99
6 *Stearns*	98	98
7 *Mica*	99	99
8 *McCollum*	98	99
9 *Bilirakis*	96	97
10 *Young* #	94	94
11 Gibbons	94	95
12 *Canady*	99	99
13 *Miller*	98	99
14 *Goss*	100	100
15 Bacchus	97	97
16 *Lewis* #	94	94
17 Meek	94	93
18 *Ros-Lehtinen*	98	98
19 Johnston	95	95
20 Deutsch	99	99
21 *Diaz-Balart*	98	98
22 *Shaw*	96	96
23 Hastings	93	94
Georgia		
1 *Kingston*	98	98
2 Bishop	96	97
3 *Collins*	99	99
4 *Linder*	99	99
5 Lewis	99	99
6 *Gingrich*	91	92
7 Darden	99	99
8 Rowland	99	99
9 Deal	99	99
10 Johnson	98	99
11 McKinney	95	96
Hawaii		
1 Abercrombie	93	94
2 Mink	98	99
Idaho		
1 LaRocco	98	98
2 *Crapo*	99	99
Illinois		
1 Rush	93	94
2 Reynolds	98	98
3 Lipinski	94	94
4 Gutierrez	92	92
5 Rostenkowski	93	93
6 *Hyde* †	96	97
7 Collins	95	95
8 *Crane*	97	99
9 Yates #	94	94
10 *Porter* #	95	96
11 Sangmeister	96	96
12 Costello	99	99
13 *Fawell*	99	99
14 *Hastert* #	99	99
15 *Ewing*	98	99
16 *Manzullo*	99	99
17 Evans #	97	97

ND Northern Democrats   SD Southern Democrats

rights supporters and showed it to be wanting. It may also have foreshadowed the upcoming debate over Clinton's health plan (S 1757, HR 3600) and whether it would ensure access to abortions. If federal dollars were involved in a universal health plan — as they were in Medicaid — anti-abortion activists would try to keep the plan from including abortions.

The House made a bigger change in abortion law on the appropriations bill that paid for the Treasury, Postal Service and General Government spending (HR 2403 — PL 103-123). The bill lifted a decade-long ban on allowing women who were federal workers to receive abortions through their taxpayer-subsidized health-care plans. But anti-abortion lawmakers almost toppled the bill when the conference report was brought to the House floor Sept. 29. Working quietly, they lobbied members to vote against the measure. The measure barely prevailed, 207-206.

Abortion rights forces also found some success when the House and Senate passed a bill (HR 796 — H Rept 103-306) to make it a federal crime to intimidate by force or threat of force a woman seeking to obtain an abortion, or abortion clinic workers. But the clinic-access debate turned more on questions of terrorist activities vs. freedom of speech and assembly than it did on abortion rights. A number of abortion opponents supported the clinic access bill.

Over the course of the year, then, the debate over the Hyde amendment overshadowed any other gains that abortion rights supporters made in Congress. The vote demonstrated that, despite election-year gains of abortion rights supporters, there was still a large, bipartisan majority in the House that was wary of using taxpayer funds to pay for abortions. *(Senate vote 11, p. 55-C)*

6. Budget-Reconciliation

At the end of a long, torturous summer of negotiations over President Clinton's budget, the House was confronted with one final, climactic vote in which neither of the choices had much appeal for many lawmakers. It was the vote on the conference report for the budget-reconciliation bill (HR 2264) — the final version of Clinton's economic plan.

Wavering members were faced, on one hand, with the knowledge that rejecting the measure would cripple Clinton early in his presidency and throw the budget process into turmoil. But, hard as the bill was to swallow, most lawmakers found at least something to like in the budget deal — a tax and spending package that was estimated to reduce the deficit by almost $500 billion over the next five years.

A no vote would have killed the whole thing. But a yes vote evoked at least as many terrors. The final deal was the product of intense negotiations between the House and Senate, and many lawmakers found the terms inadequate — either the deal relied too heavily on taxes and not enough on spending cuts, or it was not generous enough in granting tax breaks for the poor and businesses.

Many members had come to Washington pledging to put an end to gridlock, but to vote yes on a controversial and possibly flawed measure merely to break a partisan stalemate struck many as foolish politics and bad policy.

No member felt the cross-pressures more intensely than freshman Democrat Marjorie Margolies-Mezvinsky of Pennsylvania. She had pledged during her campaign and even the day before the vote that she would vote against a

Margolies-Mezvinsky

bill that increased taxes. But Democratic leaders extracted a private promise from her to support the deficit-reduction package if her vote proved necessary to pass it.

In the end, Margolies-Mezvinsky's vote was necessary, and she voted yes. Her vote was among the last cast during the Aug. 5 roll call in the House, and it gave Clinton a razor-thin victory, 218-216: R 0-175; D 217-41 (ND 155-18, SD 62-23); I 1-0.

Twenty-four hours later, the Senate adopted the conference report, also with only one vote to spare, and that a tie-breaker supplied by Vice President Al Gore.

Again, not a single Republican voted with Clinton. It was the first time in postwar congressional history and possibly the first time ever that the majority party had passed major legislation with absolutely no support from the opposition.

The narrow House margin was something of a surprise. When the original version of the bill came before the House, it passed by the comparatively comfortable margin of 219-213. But it had returned in somewhat different form, owing to changes demanded in conference by the Senate. Conservative Democrats were particularly upset that the final bill was missing an "entitlement review" provision that would have set targets for spending on entitlement programs, such as Social Security and Medicare.

House leaders and the administration went into overdrive, cutting deals and making commitments to get the necessary votes. For example, Clinton issued an executive order setting up a complex process that would in effect bind the White House and the House to some action if entitlement spending exceeded projections.

Clinton went to Capitol Hill to lobby Democrats, and he and top White House officials were everywhere, working uncommitted or wavering members for votes right up until the roll call began.

When the vote was over and the conference report was adopted, Clinton claimed that he had succeeded in reorienting the nation's fiscal policy. Clinton asserted that his administration was setting the stage for lower long-term interest rates, economic growth and a healthier economy sometime in the future. The nervous Democrats who voted with him could only hope that he was right. *(Senate vote 4, p. 51-C)*

7. Thrift Bailout Financing

Rounding up the requisite votes to pass bills to salvage failed savings and loan institutions had never been an easy task for House leaders. In 1993, action on an unpopular bill (HR 1340) to finance the bailout's final round proved to be no exception. But unlike 1992, Congress ultimately met the challenge.

The key House vote to pass the bailout measure came in September, nearly a year and a half after Congress allowed the bulk of an earlier $25 billion appropriation for the Resolution Trust Corporation (RTC), the thrift salvage agency, to revert to the Treasury. The resulting delay left the cleanup essentially without money and cost taxpayers more than $1 billion as the RTC was forced to operate failed thrifts at a loss rather than move quickly to pay off depositors or transfer those deposits to other institutions.

The House had last faced the issue in April 1992, when a standoff between Democrats and Republicans scotched an effort to replenish the RTC's coffers. House Democratic leaders had agreed with the Bush administration that the RTC should be financed on a bipartisan basis — that majorities of both parties would be required to pass the financing bill. So when Republicans abandoned the 1992 effort, Democrats also jumped ship. The bailout languished without cash for 20 months, until the measure cleared on Nov. 23.

Members had always viewed voting for the bailout as politically risky, even though the taxpayer-provided money was used to make good on the federal government's deposit-insurance guarantee. Some saw a vote for the bailout as carrying the taint of the savings and loan debacle of the 1980s.

The RTC was also very unpopular with members, who criticized it for not always getting the best deal possible for taxpayers when selling the acquired assets of failed thrifts, for failing to give enough contracts to minority-owned businesses and law firms and for freezing out some smaller investors who wanted to purchase real estate and thrift franchises.

The election of Democrat Bill Clinton as president added a new twist: It put the responsibility for passing the financing bill squarely on Democrats, many of whom had never voted to replenish the bailout when it was being pushed by the Treasury Department

under Republican President George Bush. Moreover, the mood of the sizable freshman class on this issue was unknown.

Members ignored the administration's request for a "clean" $45 billion bill free of congressional mandates on agency operations. It likewise became obvious that the full financing request — $28 billion for the RTC and $17 billion to capitalize the thrift industry's new deposit insurance fund — would be pared significantly. As reported by the House Banking Committee in May, the bill included an $18.3 billion appropriation to be obtained by lifting the April 1, 1992, date on which the previous RTC appropriation reverted to the Treasury.

The bill was ready for floor action by early summer, and Democratic whip counts appeared favorable, but House leaders were skittish about bringing up the measure, having seen prior RTC bills rejected by wide margins.

Democratic leaders pressed top Banking Committee members to accommodate Republican concerns about provisions directing agency contracts to women- and minority-owned businesses and authorizing future appropriations for the new Savings Association Insurance Fund. Even so, those compromises barely picked up any GOP votes. The House on Sept. 14 narrowly passed HR 1340, 214-208: R 24-148; D 190-59 (ND 131-34, SD 59-25); I 0-1.

At one point during the roll call, the bill was behind by 20 votes, but Democratic vote counts proved accurate and the measure squeaked by. Once over that hurdle, the road to final action was less arduous, though it took until the last day of the session.

After passing HR 1340, the House took up a companion Senate bill (S 714), amended it to include the text of HR 1340 and passed it by voice vote. The Senate had passed S 714 on May 13 by a bipartisan 61-35 vote. The Senate adopted the conference report on S 714 by 54-45 on Nov. 20, and the House cleared the measure in the early hours of Nov. 23 by a healthier 235-191 margin.

8. Gays in the Military

Before passing the defense authorization bill (HR 2401), the House weighed in on the explosive issue of homosexuals in the military, a debate that had been centered primarily in the Senate for much of the year.

By the time the House took up the issue, President Clinton had abandoned his campaign pledge to lift the military's ban on homosexuals, settling for an easing of its application to gay service members who remained chaste and discreet about their orientation.

When the House Armed Services Committee drafted its version of the annual defense authorization bill late in July, it adopted without change language that had been written into the Senate version of the bill a few days earlier by Democrat Sam Nunn of Georgia, chairman of the Armed Services Committee.

That provision wrote into law the essentials of the military's previous regulations banning homosexual conduct by service members, a ban broad enough to cover a soldier's private disclosure to a friend of his or her homosexual orientation.

While many members of the House panel argued for an even more restrictive approach, Military Forces and Personal Subcommittee Chairman Ike Skelton, D-Mo., and a majority of others accepted the Senate language, partly in the hope of putting an end to the emotionally charged debate that had drowned out most other defense issues during the first several months of the Clinton presidency.

On the House floor, opponents of the gay ban offered an amendment to the defense authorization bill. Like an amendment by California Democrat Barbara Boxer that was defeated in the Senate, the amendment would have stripped from the defense bill the language reasserting the military ban and would have explicitly left the issue to the president.

In a key vote Sept. 28, the House rejected the amendment, by Martin T. Meehan, D-Mass., 169-264: R 11-163; D 157-101 (ND 131-43; SD 26-58); I 1-0.

Before that vote, the House also defeated, 144-291, a conservative amendment that would have toughened the ban by renewing the policy — which Clinton had ended — of questioning new recruits about their sexual orientation. And the House later adopted, 301-134, an amendment reaffirming the gay ban language in the bill.

The congressional language took a harder line than the position Clinton finally arrived at in July.

Clinton's stated policy asserted that "homosexual orientation is not a bar to military service" in the absence of conduct. But the Nunn-Skelton language rejected that view, declaring instead that the presence of openly homosexual members in a military unit "would create an unacceptable risk to the high standards of morale, good order and discipline and unit cohesion that are the essence of military capability."

The congressional provision left to the secretary of Defense the decision of whether to resume asking recruits about their sexual orientation, thus leaving intact the administration's decision in January to suspend that practice.

And it was silent on two other facets of administration

policy: Clinton's insistence that Pentagon investigators evenhandedly pursue any alleged violation of military law, which prohibited both homosexual and heterosexual sodomy; and his effort to curb dragnet-style hunts intended to discover service members who were secretly homosexual. *(Senate vote 7, p. 53-C)*

9. Endangered Species/Property Rights

For the previous 20 years, Congress had regularly embraced the environmental movement by passing laws to clean the air and water, to force polluters to clean up toxic waste sites and to preserve the nation's wilderness and endangered species.

But in 1993, landowners began to push the pendulum back in the other direction. A critical House vote helped spawn a political force that was likely to re-emerge during coming debates over the reauthorization of the 1973 Endangered Species Act (PL 93-205) and the overhaul of wetlands policy in the 1972 Federal Pollution Control Act (PL 92-500), known as the clean water law.

Landowners contended that enforcement of such environmental laws had driven down the market value of their private property and, in some cases, rendered their property useless for farming or development. A key test of that idea came Oct. 6, when the House considered a bill (HR 1845) to authorize a new survey of the nation's plants and animals, known as the National Biological Survey.

The National Biological Survey was the brainchild of Interior Secretary Bruce Babbitt, who billed it as a way to avoid legal conflicts arising from implementation of the endangered species law. Conservatives said the survey would lead to more regulations and to decisions over wetlands that would favor environmentalists instead of farmers.

To counter Babbitt's initiative, Charles H. Taylor, R-N.C., offered an amendment to the bill to require that the government obtain written permission from a landowner before entering private property to conduct the survey. It also required the government to disclose its findings to the landowner. Before passing the bill, House members overwhelmingly agreed to include Taylor's amendment, 309-115: R 171-3; D 138-111 (ND 72-95, SD 66-16); I 0-1.

Taylor

The House vote was particularly significant because it was usually the more conservative Senate that sided with landowners. In 1991, the Senate adopted by voice vote an amendment by then-Sen. Steve Symms, R-Idaho, that would have required the government to compensate landowners who could not use their property because of federal regulations.

The Fifth Amendment to the U.S. Constitution required the government to provide "just compensation" when it took away private property for public use — to build a highway, for example. The Supreme Court also had embraced the concept that regulations themselves can effectively cause the government to take away private property.

A driving force behind adoption of Taylor's amendment was conservative Democrats such as Reps. W. J. "Billy" Tauzin of Louisiana and Gary A. Condit of California, who represented a Central Valley farming district that was embroiled in a dispute over protecting the California smelt fish.

The vote on Taylor's amendment dampened the hopes of many environmentalists that Congress would be able to reauthorize the Endangered Species Act in the 103rd Congress. Tauzin was gathering support for a reauthorization bill (HR 1490) that he said would strike a balance between species conservation and financial impact on property owners. But environmentalists contended that Tauzin was trying to gut the law, which had helped bring species such as the bald eagle back from the brink of extinction.

"We won round one of a zillion rounds," said Charles S. Cushman, executive director of the Battleground, Wash.-based American Land Rights Association, an advocacy group for the rights of private property owners.

Environmental lobbyists were bracing for a long fight on similar issues. "We will see property rights amendments on everything," said Betsy Loyless, political director of the League of Conservation Voters. "The environmental community needs to focus on this."

10. Superconducting Super Collider

Like a group of big-game hunters searching for a prize trophy in the name of deficit reduction, House lawmakers emerged in 1993 with a big kill: The $11 billion superconducting super collider.

The coup de grâce for the giant atom smasher, an Energy Department project that sought to isolate the smallest atomic particles that are the building blocks of matter, followed a previous House vote to terminate the Energy Department project June 24 as part of the energy and water development spending bill (HR 2445) for fiscal 1994.

But that was essentially a reprise of House votes in previous years. On those occasions, the Senate would subsequently restore funding for the super collider, and the House, with members fearful of losing other pet projects in the energy-water bill, would ultimately cave in to the Senate position.

The key 1993 vote on the project's future was cast Oct. 19, when the energy-water bill came back from a House-Senate conference, and House members were forced to choose between killing the super collider or appeasing powerful appropriations conferees, who once again had restored the project to full funding.

But the actual vote was not so simple as "yea" or "nay."

The two main opponents of the project, Jim Slattery, D-Kan., and Sherwood Boehlert, R-N.Y., had to battle arcane House rules that favored appropriators and made the choice for House members difficult to follow, at best. Their task was to convince lawmakers that a complex parliamentary maneuver amounted to a vote to reaffirm the House's desire to kill the super collider.

Here is what occurred:

Before members voted on the final adoption of a conference report, House rules allowed the minority to offer one motion — and only one motion — to recommit the conference report to committee for further deliberation.

Slattery and Boehlert were not allowed to offer that motion, however. House rules and customs gave the nod to John T. Myers, R-Ind., the ranking minority leader of the subcommittee that wrote the bill.

Myers, a supporter of the super collider, offered a motion to recommit that had no instructions. If it prevailed, the final version of the spending bill would bounce back to the House with super collider funding intact. The only vote then would be up or down on the entire spending bill.

The only way for Slattery and Boehlert to pick the procedural lock was to call for a vote on the "previous question" — a step that asked the House to shut off debate on Myers' recommital motion and vote on it. In this case, Slattery and Boehlert wanted House members to defeat the previous question so they could amend Myers' motion with new instructions to terminate the super collider.

Slattery and Boehlert handed out pink slips naming those who voted against the super collider June 24 and urged them to vote "nay" on the previous question. Despite the pleas of appropriators and active support for the project from the Clinton administration, the "nays" prevailed, 159-264: R 61-111; D 98-152 (ND 47-121, SD 51-31); I 0-1.

Only 18 lawmakers switched their votes from June 24 to defend the project. And in a rare show of class solidarity, 81 of the 113 voting House freshmen stood with opponents of the super collider.

The House then voted on the motion to recommit as amended by Slattery to kill the super collider. At that point, super collider opponents pulled out green leaflets that told the same lawmakers to vote "yea." They prevailed again, by a vote of 282-143.

After the vote, Senate Energy and Water Appropriations Subcommittee Chairman J. Bennett Johnston, D-La., decided to give up the fight to save the super collider. He complained that House lawmakers had been carried away by an "emotional tide" for spending cuts that took as its victim one of the premier U.S. science projects.

In the end, the death of the super collider served only as a symbolic nod to fiscal austerity. The project still received $640 million in the fiscal 1994 energy and water appropriations bill (HR 2445). Lawmakers instead put those funds toward the costs of shutting down the project, already 20 percent complete in Waxahachie, Texas.

11. Somalia

Even after promising to withdraw U.S. forces from Somalia, the Clinton administration had trouble disengaging from the political skirmishing that persisted on Capitol Hill.

The administration escaped an embarrassing setback when the House endorsed the March 31 pullout date that President Clinton had previously accepted under strong Senate pressure. Yet the confusing, contradictory House actions of Nov. 9 underscored congressional opposition to an operation that, as of that date, had cost the lives of 35 U.S. troops.

Divided along party lines, lawmakers narrowly backed Clinton's timetable. The key vote came on an amendment to a non-binding resolution (H Con Res 170), which the House approved 226-201: R 2-170; D 224-130 (ND 150-21, SD 74-9); I 0-1.

Just an hour earlier, the House had voted 224-203 to call on the president to withdraw U.S. forces by Jan. 31. But under the "king of the hill" procedures that the Rules Committee set for debate, the vote was superseded by the adoption of the latter amendment.

The zigzagging votes had purely symbolic significance. The House had already signaled its support for a Senate-passed provision in the fiscal 1994 defense appropriations bill that put the force of law behind the March 31 date.

But a defeat would have reinforced the perception that the administration's foreign policy lacked public and congressional support. The timing was critical because the administration was about to face a tougher vote — with much higher stakes — on the North American Free Trade Agreement.

The administration strongly opposed the amendment backing the Jan. 31 pullout date that was offered by Benjamin A. Gilman, N.Y., the ranking Republican on the Foreign Affairs Committee. House Democratic leaders delayed the debate for several hours to allow the administration to lobby wavering members.

Despite those efforts, 55 Democrats bucked the administration in backing Gilman's amendment. All but three of the 171 Republicans voting backed the proposal.

It was clear that many of the Democrats — and even some Republicans — viewed Gilman's amendment as a low-cost opportunity to blast the administration's policy. The king-of-the-hill procedure afforded lawmakers the chance to reverse that vote by supporting the amendment by Lee H. Hamilton, D-Ind., chairman of the Foreign Affairs Committee, endorsing the March 31 deadline.

After losing in the initial skirmishing, Democrats hauled out the heavy artillery in support of Hamilton's amendment. House Speaker Thomas S. Foley, D-Wash., delivered an impassioned plea not to undercut the president's plan for an "orderly withdrawal" from Somalia.

"It would be a tragic moment for American resolve, American principle and the American position around the world," Foley said. "Do not do this to the president of the United States. We should not do this to any president, Republican or Democrat."

Republicans, who had complained for weeks that Democratic leaders had denied them a debate on Somalia, argued vehemently in favor of a quick withdrawal. "Helping the authors of our failed policy in Somalia save face is not worth the life of one American soldier," Gilman said.

While the GOP remained solid in opposing the superseding amendment, 24 Democrats who backed the Jan. 31 deadline turned around and supported Clinton's pullout date as well, providing the margin of victory. The group included such such senior lawmakers as Charles E. Schumer of New York and G. V. "Sonny" Montgomery of Mississippi.

But the debate highlighted position shifts by members of both parties. Gilman had forced quick action on the issue by invoking a provision of the 1973 War Powers Resolution, which most Republicans believed was unconstitutional. *(Senate vote 12, p. 55-C)*

12. Handgun Control

Few members of Congress embraced the so-called Brady bill as an anti-crime panacea, but advocates hoped the bill (HR 1025) to establish a five-day waiting period for handgun purchases would send a signal to constituents weary of crime that Congress was willing to take on gun violence and the lobbying clout of the powerful National Rifle Association (NRA).

And, in fact, House passage of the measure Nov. 10 opened the way for the first major federal gun control legislation since 1968. The bill was first introduced in 1987, six years after an assassination attempt on then-President Ronald Reagan permanently disabled his press secretary (and the

bill's namesake), James S. Brady. The House had passed a crime bill including Brady provisions in 1991, but that bill never became law. *(1991 Almanac, p. 271)*

But in 1993, a self-standing Brady bill passed on a 238-189 vote: R 54-119; D 184-69 (ND 138-31, SD 46-38).

The bill required would-be gun purchasers to wait five business days before purchasing a handgun, allowing local law enforcement officials to conduct a personal background check on them. The measure aimed to prevent the sale of handguns to convicted felons and other unqualified buyers, as well as to people making the purchase while they were angry. It also authorized $200 million per year toward creating an instant background checking system.

The bill had experienced almost annual setbacks in its battle for passage, despite a steady increase of gun violence nationwide, the support of the nation's law enforcement officers and a persistent personal campaign by Brady and his wife, Sarah. Detractors argued that the bill would fail to reduce crime while imposing unfair restrictions on people who wanted to buy guns legally. Criminals, they said, would purchase guns on the black market, while state and local authorities spent time and money trying to institute a gun purchase tracking system.

The biggest obstacle to passage was the NRA's enormous political clout. "It's a lobby that could put 15,000 letters in your district overnight," bill advocate William J. Hughes, D-N.J., once said.

Brady argued that he had endured far more than lawmakers were likely to suffer at the hands of the NRA, but politicians were reluctant to lend their support. It took four years from the bill's introduction before Reagan endorsed it. President George Bush had threatened to veto crime legislation that contained it.

President Clinton, however, backed Brady.

Lawmakers on both sides went into the House floor debate knowing there were almost certainly enough votes to pass some version of the bill — but which version was unclear. Neither side knew who would prevail on a series of Republican amendments that were endorsed by Judiciary Committee Chairman Jack Brooks, D-Texas, a Brady bill opponent.

One successful amendment, by George W. Gekas, R-Pa., mandated the end of the five-day waiting period five years after enactment. But Republican Bill McCollum of Florida was unsuccessful in offering an amendment that would have pre-empted state waiting periods once the instant-check system was in place. Clinton signed the bill Nov. 30, saying that "Americans are finally fed up with violence that cuts down another citizen with gunfire every 10 minutes." *(Senate vote 15, p. 58-C)*

13. NAFTA Implementation

When the House passed implementing legislation for the North American Free Trade Agreement (NAFTA) on Nov. 17, it brought to an end one of the most emotional, divisive and momentous national debates in many years. Despite overwhelming opposition from within his own party, President Clinton pushed hard to win congressional approval for the agreement and snatched a victory from near defeat. In the process, he charted a course for U.S. trade policy.

Never before had the United States been part of a trade agreement based on removing virtually all economic walls that guarded the nation from a country as poor and as different as Mexico. Bringing Mexico into a free-trade alliance along with Canada created a huge North American free trade zone with 358 million consumers and a $6.5 trillion market. Broadening that alliance to include other countries in Central and South America was widely viewed as the next step.

Even more important, the vote in favor of NAFTA reaffirmed the position of the United States as the world's leading champion of an open trading system, and it boosted continuing U.S. efforts to dismantle trade barriers worldwide.

But the debate and vote — especially in the House — also exposed deep anxiety about the pervasive job loss that had wracked the U.S. economy in preceding years. Organized labor and other NAFTA opponents charged that the agreement invited companies to relocate to Mexico and put U.S. workers out of their jobs. That charge struck a chord with many members, particularly Midwestern Democrats groping for a response to the upheaval in the industrial sector.

Opposition to the agreement scrambled conventional political alliances. Former independent presidential candidate Ross Perot joined with conservative Republican Pat Buchanan and liberal crusader Ralph Nader in opposing the agreement. Some environmental groups attacked the agreement, and some endorsed it. Farmers in the Midwest were avidly for it, but growers in Florida, California and elsewhere feared an increase in imports of Mexican fruits and vegetables.

NAFTA was one of the most explosive issues awaiting Clinton when he took office. He had endorsed the trade pact during the campaign but had finessed his position by insisting that "side agreements" with Mexico were needed to ensure enforcement of labor and environmental laws there. Clinton got the side deals, but they did nothing to mollify labor. Clinton could not remove the wedge that NAFTA drove through the Democratic Party.

Clinton proceeded to seek congressional approval for NAFTA anyway. Beginning his lobbying effort in early September, he turned to Republicans for the first time during his administration, asking them to provide the majority of the votes needed to pass the bill implementing NAFTA (HR 3450). After some initial reluctance to back a Democratic president, House Republicans responded to his appeal, urged on by their leadership.

In the dramatic House showdown, Republicans and Southern Democrats provided the victory margin. The measure passed 234-200: R 132-43; D 102-156 (ND 49-124, SD 53-32); I 0-1.

Passage in the Senate followed three days later, and was not in doubt, if no less important. *(Senate vote 16, p. 58-C)*

Though the victory demonstrated Clinton's ability to move beyond a traditional Democratic coalition on issues he considered important, it remained to be seen whether his success at putting together a centrist coalition would lead him to test similar bipartisan tactics in the future.

But Clinton's forceful defense of free trade, at the expense of alienating a major constituency within his own party, added credibility to his claim to be a new type of Democrat.

Even more important, the House vote symbolized a new era in U.S.-Mexico relations, which for years had been characterized by suspicion on both sides of the border, particularly in Mexico. Most economists predicted that reducing or eliminating trade and other barriers with Mexico would have only slight benefits for the massive U.S. economy over the following several years. But it could help raise the anemic Mexican standard of living, providing a huge future market for U.S. goods.

14. Mining Royalties

Members had tried since 1987 to revamp the 1872 Mining Law, one of the last remaining "homesteading" measures enacted to entice development of the West. But as with other natural resource and public lands issues, Western senators had long managed to outmuscle their House colleagues on mining disputes, so the 121-year-old law remained in a virtual stalemate.

The House in 1993 gave a big boost to supporters of an overhaul by passing a tough mining bill (HR 322) on Nov. 18. The lopsided vote was expected to give the House much leverage in negotiations with the Senate, which had passed a much leaner version by voice vote on May 25.

House passage came on a 316-108 vote: R 70-102; D 245-6 (ND 166-3, SD 79-3); I 1-0.

The 1872 Mining Law required no royalties to be collected from miners who extracted valuable ores from federal lands. It also allowed miners to buy, or "patent," claims on federal lands for as little as $2.50 an acre. The law required limited repair of abandoned hard-rock mines.

Under the House-passed bill, sponsored by Nick J. Rahall II, D-W.Va., miners would be required to pay an 8 percent royalty on hard-rock minerals but would be allowed to deduct the costs of transportation. The bill would eliminate patenting and require miners to pay an annual lease fee of $100 on existing claims and $200 a year for new claims.

The bill also would impose tough federal standards for the repair of federal land and require miners to be more environmentally sensitive.

The House passed HR 322 despite strong objections from Republicans that the measure would lead to a loss of jobs in states where the mining of gold, silver, copper and other hard-rock minerals was a dominant industry.

Rahall

Only six Democrats voted against the measure, while nine Republicans from Western, Rocky Mountain or Plains states voted for the measure, including New Mexico's Steven H. Schiff and Joe Skeen, who hailed from a state with large copper mines.

The Senate's alternative bill (S 775), crafted by Larry E. Craig, R-Idaho, imposed a 2 percent royalty but would have allowed most exploration, mining and development costs to be deducted. Patenting still would be allowed, although miners would be required to purchase federal land at fair market prices. The bill balked at establishing new federal reclamation standards, choosing instead to allow state laws to govern the repair of damaged public lands.

The House vote on mining was especially important because of the unusual "ticket to conference" strategy adopted by the Senate. At the behest of Energy and Natural Resources Committee Chairman J. Bennett Johnston, D-La., the Senate quickly moved Craig's bill through committee and the floor with no amendments and little debate. The Senate's leading mining reform advocate, Dale Bumpers, D-Ark., agreed to hold his fire until the House-Senate negotiations.

The Senate's Western coalition, usually in agreement on public lands issues, was expected to split on mining reform. And because the final bill was likely to be written in conference, the strength of the House vote gave House

negotiators added leverage against divided Senate conferees.

George Miller, D-Calif., chairman of the House Natural Resources Committee, Rahall and Energy and Mineral Resources Subcommittee Chairman Richard H. Lehman, D-Calif., crafted HR 322 so it would leave no doubt about the House's position on mining while still appeasing House Democrats from states containing most of the nation's hard-rock minerals.

"The House was not ambivalent on this issue," said Philip M. Hocker, president of the conservationist Mineral Policy Center. "The House does not want an ambivalent conference."

15. Campaign Finance

For most of 1993, House Democratic leaders resisted action on legislation to overhaul the campaign finance system. But in the waning days of the session, under pressure from the freshman class and editorial writers, they reversed course and used their clout to wrest a bill from defeat at the hands of an unusual bipartisan coalition.

Early in the year, House leaders delayed completion of a joint administration-congressional Democratic plan by demanding that the existing $5,000 limit on political action committee (PAC) contributions be maintained for House candidates. Then — after the plan was presented May 7 and the Senate passed its version June 17 — House leaders delayed further, saying they did not have the votes to pass a bill because of opposition to provisions calling for partial federal funding of campaigns.

For years, Democrats had struggled with the Supreme Court mandate that spending limits must be voluntary and accompanied by direct federal subsidies to candidates. Most Democrats supported restrictions on spending, but many resisted providing public benefits. With concern about the deficit high, the funding question became particularly salient.

Nearly all Republicans opposed any federal funding of congressional campaigns, and many objected to spending limits. Alone, they could do little to block a Democratic bill, but this time they were joined by an odd assortment of Democrats — some who resisted federal funding; some who said the spending and PAC limits were too high; and yet others who resisted change in the system that elected them. For months, Democratic leaders made little effort to unite their party on the issue.

By early fall, however, they were under pressure from first-term members who said voters would not tolerate inaction. Although October — once dubbed "reform month" — came and went without public action, Democratic leaders did begin serious private negotiations to reach a consensus within the House Democratic Caucus.

They cobbled together a funding mechanism that met with preliminary caucus approval. It relied heavily on voluntary taxpayer contributions and a new PAC registration fee. But when the Ways and Means Committee balked at waiving its right to review tax legislation, it was dropped from the plan, and an unfunded bill was readied for floor action.

In that way, the 1993 bill was identical to a plan Congress approved in 1992 that was vetoed by President George Bush. The two bills were also similar in that both included spending limits with up to one-third coming in federal money; both also capped PAC and large individual contributions at one-third of a candidate's total funds.

The 1993 spending limits, however, were potentially far higher than those in the 1992 bill. The new plan also permitted leadership PACs and allowed candidates to roll over substantial war chests from one election to the next, practices restricted in the earlier bill.

Once the bill was formally presented, the coalition that had stymied action began to lose steam. Naysayers were more adamant behind closed doors than in public; and many Democrats who had voted for or endorsed the 1992 bill when it was certain to be vetoed were reluctant to vote no now.

The loose coalition had one last card to play: the vote on the rule bringing the bill to the floor. From the Republican bloc to the scattered Democrats, all had amendments they wanted to support, but the rule forbade them.

To overcome their campaign to defeat the rule, Democratic leaders — even Speaker Thomas S. Foley, D-Wash. — worked the House floor for hours during an unusual Sunday session. The vote was delayed repeatedly as party whips counted and recounted their votes. Late in the day, Nov. 21, the House narrowly approved the rule, 220-207: R 3-168; D 216-39 (ND 156-15, SD 60-24); I 1-0.

Passage of the bill the next day was anticlimactic. Many members who were willing to vote against the rule were unwilling to vote against the package. *(Senate vote 3, p. 51-C)*

16. 'Reinventing Government'/Spending Cuts

When President Clinton eked out enough votes to pass his five-year deficit-reduction plan in August, the hard-fought victory came with a price: To win the votes of recalcitrant fiscal conservatives who thought the package of budget savings and tax increases did not cut enough, Clinton had to promise they would get another chance to glean more savings before the year's end.

Clinton kept that promise and gave lawmakers another vote on spending cuts, in the form of a package of rescissions from just-passed appropriations for fiscal 1994, plus selected cost-saving proposals from Vice President Al Gore's "reinventing government" initiative. But when that package (HR 3400) came to the floor Nov. 22, it opened the door for a bipartisan group of aggressive "deficit hawks" to offer their own deficit-reduction package, forcing the administration once again to scramble for votes to protect the president's five-year budget plan.

The showdown vote came on an amendment by Timothy J. Penny, D-Minn., and John R. Kasich, R-Ohio, who wanted to cut the budget by $90 billion over five years. It was Penny who had extracted the promise from Clinton and House Democratic leaders for a chance to offer a major deficit-cutting plan.

The original Clinton proposal was a relatively modest package of about $11.5 billion in savings. When the Congressional Budget Office later declared that the package would save only $305 million, the White House beefed up its plan by adding language already proposed by the administration to trim the federal work force by 252,000 employees over five years, bringing total savings to $37.1 billion in outlays.

By contrast, a large bulk of Penny-Kasich savings — $34.2 billion — would have come from cuts in the Medi-

care program, the health-care subsidy for the elderly and disabled.

Clinton was planning his own revisions to the Medicare system to help pay for his proposed overhaul of the health-care system, while the Penny-Kasich amendment would have steered Medicare savings only toward reducing the deficit.

The other feature of the Penny-Kasich bid that made the White House and Democratic leaders nervous was its mandate to lower ceilings on annual appropriations below levels ordered in the August deficit-reduction plan. Under that law, dis-cretionary spending was capped for five years at fiscal 1993 levels. The Penny-Kasich amendment would have reduced those limits by another $43 billion through fiscal 1998.

Penny   **Kasich**

"We have just begun to look for places to reduce the deficit," conceded Majority Leader Richard A. Gephardt, D-Mo., in a floor speech that paid homage to the spirit, if not the content, of the Penny-Kasich amendment. "But if we act on this amendment tonight, we act prematurely, because we not only cut, we take the caps down further."

Defense Appropriations Subcommittee Chairman John P. Murtha, D-Pa., helped lead the charge against the amendment on grounds that the lower spending limits would endanger defense spending, because budget rules no longer put up protective "fire walls" to insulate defense from spending cuts.

Other chairmen of Appropriations subcommittees launched their own lobbying assaults. One tactic criticized by lawmakers was a form letter by Energy and Water Appropriations Subcommittee Chairman Tom Bevill, D-Ala., and ranking Republican John T. Myers of Indiana threatening that specific water projects in members' districts might be at risk should the Penny-Kasich amendment pass.

Before the vote, Clinton called wavering lawmakers and recruited Cabinet secretaries and first lady Hillary Rodham Clinton to urge freshmen to vote against it.

Clinton prevailed again as the House rejected Penny-Kasich, 213-219: R 156-18; D 57-200 (ND 33-139, SD 24-61); I 0-1.

The vote was not only a late-session affirmation of Clinton's continued ability to thwart attempts by fiscal conservatives for more drastic deficit reduction; it also showed that he could still count on the votes of labor-oriented liberal Democrats just days after the fractious vote on the North American Free Trade Agreement (NAFTA).

In contrast to the NAFTA vote of Nov. 17, Clinton enjoyed help from labor groups, which considered the cuts too draconian: 125 Democrats came back to Clinton on the Penny-Kasich amendment after opposing him on the free trade agreement vote. Lobbyists for the AFL-CIO and other unions were lined up outside the House, calling on lawmakers to kill the amendment, though some continued to speak bitterly about Clinton's treatment of labor during the NAFTA debate.

Following are 1993 votes selected by Congressional Quarterly as key votes (House key votes and explanations of key votes, p. 36-C). Original vote number is provided in parentheses.

1. HR 1. Family and Medical Leave/Passage. Passage of the bill to require employers of more than 50 employees to provide 12 weeks of unpaid leave for an illness or to care for a new child or sick family member. Passed 265-163: R 40-134; D 224-29 (ND 162-8, SD 62-21); I 1-0, Feb. 3, 1993. (House vote 22.) A "yea" was a vote in support of the president's position.

2. H Con Res 64. Fiscal 1994 Budget Resolution/Adoption. Adoption of the concurrent resolution to set binding budget levels for the fiscal year ending Sept. 30, 1994: budget authority, $1.506 trillion; outlays, $1.495 trillion; revenues, $1.242 trillion; deficit, $253.5 billion. Adopted 243-183: R 0-172; D 242-11 (ND 164-6, SD 78-5); I 1-0, March 18, 1993. (House vote 85.) A "yea" was a vote in support of the president's position.

3. HR 1335. Fiscal 1993 Supplemental Appropriations/Rule. Adoption of the rule (H Res 132) to waive points of order against and provide for House floor consideration of the bill to provide $16.3 billion in new budget authority and approve $3.4 billion in trust fund spending to implement the administration's stimulus package to help the economy recover. The funds would be designated as emergency spending, making them exempt from discretionary spending caps. Adopted 240-185: R 0-172; D 239-13 (ND 165-4, SD 74-9); I 1-0, March 18, 1993. (House vote 86.) A "yea" was a vote in support of the president's position.

4. HR 2295. Fiscal 1994 Foreign Operations Appropriations/Aid to Russia. Callahan, R-Ala., amendment to cut the $1.6 billion fiscal 1993 supplemental appropriation for aid to Russia. Rejected in the Committee of the Whole 140-289: R 93-79; D 46-210 (ND 30-143, SD 16-67); I 1-0, June 17, 1993. (House vote 237.) A "nay" was a vote in support of the president's position.

5. HR 2518. Fiscal 1994 Labor, HHS, Education Appropriations/Abortion Prohibition. Hyde, R-Ill., amendment to prohibit funds in the bill from being spent for an abortion except when it is made known that it is a case of rape, incest or necessity to save the woman's life. Adopted in the Committee of the Whole 255-178: R 157-16; D 98-161 (ND 54-120, SD 44-41); I 0-1, June 30, 1993. (House vote 307.)

6. HR 2264. 1993 Budget-Reconciliation/Adoption. Adoption of the conference report to reduce the deficit by an estimated $496 billion over five years through almost $241 billion in additional taxes and $255 billion in spending cuts by closely tracking President Clinton's economic proposals. Of the cuts in the bill, $102 billion would come through a freeze of discretionary spending at fiscal 1993 levels through fiscal 1998. Adopted 218-216: R 0-175; D 217-41 (ND 155-18, SD 62-23); I 1-0, Aug. 5, 1933. (House vote 406.) A "yea" was a vote in support of the president's position.

7. HR 1340. Resolution Trust Corporation/Passage. Passage of the bill to provide $18.3 billion to resolve failed savings and loan institutions, authorize funds for the new Savings Association Insurance Fund for fiscal 1994-98, direct new management reforms, expand the Resolution Trust Corporation's affordable housing program and impose new requirements for contracting with businesses owned by minorities and women. Passed 214-208: R 24-148; D 190-59 (ND 131-34, SD 59-25); I 0-1, Sept. 14, 1993. (House vote 434.) A "yea" was a vote in support of the president's position.

8. HR 2401. Fiscal 1994 Defense Authorization/Gay Ban. Meehan, D-Mass., amendment to strike the provisions codifying a ban on homosexuals in the military and express the sense of Congress that the issue should be determined by the president and his advisers. Rejected in the Committee of the Whole 169-264: R 11-163; D 157-101 (ND 131-43, SD 26-58); I 1-0, Sept. 28, 1993. (House vote 460.)

KEY

Y	Voted for (yea).
#	Paired for.
+	Announced for.
N	Voted against (nay).
X	Paired against.
−	Announced against.
P	Voted "present."
C	Voted "present" to avoid possible conflict of interest.
?	Did not vote or otherwise make a position known.
D	Delegates ineligible to vote.

Democrats *Republicans*
Independent

Member	1	2	3	4	5	6	7	8
ALABAMA								
1 Callahan	N	N	N	Y	Y	N	N	N
2 Everett	N	N	N	Y	Y	N	N	N
3 Browder	N	Y	Y	N	Y	N	N	N
4 Bevill	Y	Y	Y	N	Y	N	N	N
5 Cramer	Y	Y	Y	N	Y	N	N	N
6 Bachus	N	N	N	Y	Y	N	N	N
7 Hilliard	Y	Y	Y	N	Y	N	Y	N
ALASKA								
AL Young	Y	N	N	?	Y	N	Y	N
ARIZONA								
1 Coppersmith	Y	Y	Y	N	N	N	Y	Y
2 Pastor	Y	Y	Y	N	N	Y	Y	Y
3 Stump	N	N	N	Y	N	N	N	N
4 Kyl	N	N	N	Y	N	N	N	N
5 Kolbe	N	N	N	Y	N	N	N	N
6 English	Y	Y	Y	N	Y	N	Y	Y
ARKANSAS								
1 Lambert	Y	Y	N	N	Y	N	Y	N
2 Thornton	Y	Y	Y	N	Y	N	Y	N
3 Hutchinson	N	N	N	Y	Y	N	N	N
4 Dickey	N	N	N	Y	Y	N	N	N
CALIFORNIA								
1 Hamburg	Y	Y	Y	N	N	Y	Y	Y
2 Herger	N	N	N	Y	N	N	N	N
3 Fazio	Y	Y	Y	N	Y	N	Y	Y
4 Doolittle	N	N	N	Y	N	N	N	N
5 Matsui	Y	Y	Y	N	Y	N	Y	Y
6 Woolsey	Y	Y	Y	N	N	Y	Y	Y
7 Miller	Y	Y	Y	N	Y	?	Y	Y
8 Pelosi	Y	Y	Y	−	N	Y	Y	Y
9 Dellums	Y	Y	Y	N	N	Y	Y	Y
10 Baker	N	N	N	Y	Y	N	N	N
11 Pombo	N	N	N	Y	N	N	N	N
12 Lantos	Y	Y	Y	N	Y	N	Y	Y
13 Stark	Y	Y	Y	N	N	Y	Y	Y
14 Eshoo	Y	Y	Y	N	Y	Y	Y	Y
15 Mineta	Y	Y	Y	N	Y	N	Y	Y
16 Edwards	Y	Y	Y	N	Y	Y	Y	Y
17 Farr			N	N	Y	Y	N	Y
18 Condit	Y	Y	Y	Y	Y	N	N	Y
19 Lehman	Y	Y	Y	N	N	Y	?	N
20 Dooley	Y	Y	Y	N	Y	N	Y	Y
21 Thomas	N	N	N	Y	N	N	N	N
22 Huffington	Y	N	N	Y	Y	N	?	Y
23 Gallegly	N	N	N	Y	Y	N	N	N
24 Beilenson	Y	Y	Y	N	N	Y	Y	Y
25 McKeon	N	N	N	Y	N	N	N	N
26 Berman	Y	Y	Y	N	Y	Y	Y	Y
27 Moorhead	N	N	N	Y	N	N	N	N
28 Dreier	N	N	N	Y	N	N	N	N
29 Waxman	Y	Y	Y	N	Y	Y	Y	Y
30 Becerra	Y	Y	Y	N	Y	N	Y	Y
31 Martinez	Y	Y	Y	N	N	Y	Y	Y
32 Dixon	Y	Y	Y	N	Y	Y	Y	Y
33 Roybal-Allard	Y	Y	Y	N	Y	N	Y	Y
34 Torres	Y	Y	Y	N	Y	N	Y	Y
35 Waters	Y	Y	Y	N	Y	Y	Y	Y
36 Harman	Y	Y	Y	N	Y	N	Y	Y
37 Tucker	Y	Y	Y	N	Y	N	Y	Y
38 Horn	Y	N	N	N	N	N	N	Y
39 Royce	N	N	N	Y	N	N	N	N
40 Lewis	N	N	N	Y	N	N	N	N
41 Kim	N	N	N	Y	N	N	N	N

Member	1	2	3	4	5	6	7	8
42 Brown	Y	Y	Y	N	N	Y	?	Y
43 Calvert	N	N	N	Y	N	N	N	N
44 McCandless	N	N	N	Y	N	N	N	N
45 Rohrabacher	N	N	N	Y	N	N	N	N
46 Dornan	N	N	N	Y	N	N	N	N
47 Cox	N	N	N	Y	N	N	N	N
48 Packard	N	N	N	Y	N	N	N	N
49 Schenk	Y	Y	Y	N	N	Y	Y	Y
50 Filner	Y	Y	Y	N	N	Y	N	Y
51 Cunningham	N	N	N	Y	N	N	N	N
52 Hunter	N	N	N	Y	Y	N	?	N
COLORADO								
1 Schroeder	Y	Y	Y	N	N	Y	N	Y
2 Skaggs	Y	Y	Y	N	N	Y	Y	Y
3 McInnis	N	N	N	Y	N	N	N	N
4 Allard	N	N	N	Y	N	N	N	N
5 Hefley	N	N	N	Y	N	N	N	N
6 Schaefer	N	N	N	Y	N	N	N	N
CONNECTICUT								
1 Kennelly	Y	Y	Y	N	N	Y	Y	Y
2 Gejdenson	Y	Y	Y	N	N	Y	Y	Y
3 DeLauro	Y	Y	Y	N	N	Y	Y	Y
4 Shays	Y	N	N	Y	N	Y	Y	Y
5 Franks	N	N	N	Y	N	N	Y	Y
6 Johnson	Y	N	N	N	N	N	Y	Y
DELAWARE								
AL Castle	Y	N	N	N	Y	N	N	N
FLORIDA								
1 Hutto	N	Y	Y	Y	Y	N	N	N
2 Peterson	Y	Y	Y	N	Y	N	Y	N
3 Brown	Y	Y	Y	N	Y	N	Y	N
4 Fowler	N	N	N	Y	Y	N	Y	N
5 Thurman	Y	Y	Y	N	Y	N	Y	N
6 Stearns	N	N	N	Y	Y	N	N	N
7 Mica	N	N	N	Y	Y	N	N	N
8 McCollum	N	N	N	Y	N	N	N	N
9 Bilirakis	N	N	N	Y	Y	N	N	N
10 Young	N	N	N	Y	N	N	N	N
11 Gibbons	Y	Y	Y	N	Y	Y	Y	Y
12 Canady	N	N	N	Y	Y	N	N	N
13 Miller	N	N	N	Y	Y	N	N	N
14 Goss	N	N	N	Y	Y	N	N	N
15 Bacchus	Y	Y	Y	N	N	Y	Y	Y
16 Lewis	N	N	N	Y	Y	N	N	N
17 Meek	Y	Y	Y	N	N	Y	Y	Y
18 Ros-Lehtinen	N	N	N	Y	Y	N	N	N
19 Johnston	Y	Y	Y	N	N	Y	Y	Y
20 Deutsch	Y	Y	Y	N	Y	Y	Y	Y
21 Diaz-Balart	N	N	N	Y	Y	N	N	N
22 Shaw	N	N	N	Y	Y	N	N	N
23 Hastings	Y	Y	Y	N	N	Y	Y	Y
GEORGIA								
1 Kingston	N	N	N	Y	Y	N	N	N
2 Bishop	Y	Y	Y	N	Y	N	Y	N
3 Collins	N	N	N	Y	Y	N	N	N
4 Linder	N	N	N	Y	N	N	N	N
5 Lewis	Y	Y	Y	N	N	Y	Y	Y
6 Gingrich	N	N	N	Y	N	N	N	N
7 Darden	Y	Y	Y	N	Y	N	Y	N
8 Rowland	N	Y	Y	N	Y	N	N	N
9 Deal	N	Y	Y	N	N	N	N	N
10 Johnson	N	Y	Y	N	Y	N	N	N
11 McKinney	Y	Y	Y	N	N	Y	Y	Y
HAWAII								
1 Abercrombie	Y	Y	Y	N	N	Y	Y	Y
2 Mink	Y	Y	Y	N	N	Y	Y	Y
IDAHO								
1 LaRocco	N	Y	Y	Y	N	Y	N	N
2 Crapo	N	N	N	Y	N	N	N	N
ILLINOIS								
1 Rush	Y	Y	Y	N	N	Y	Y	Y
2 Reynolds	Y	Y	Y	N	N	Y	Y	Y
3 Lipinski	Y	N	Y	N	Y	N	?	Y
4 Gutierrez	Y	Y	Y	N	N	Y	Y	Y
5 Rostenkowski	Y	Y	Y	N	Y	Y	Y	Y
6 Hyde	Y	N	N	N	Y	N	C	N
7 Collins	Y	Y	Y	N	N	Y	Y	Y
8 Crane	N	N	N	Y	N	N	N	N
9 Yates	Y	Y	Y	N	N	Y	Y	Y
10 Porter	N	N	N	Y	N	N	Y	N
11 Sangmeister	Y	Y	Y	N	N	Y	Y	Y
12 Costello	Y	Y	Y	N	N	Y	N	N
13 Fawell	N	N	N	Y	N	N	Y	N
14 Hastert	N	N	N	Y	N	N	N	N
15 Ewing	N	N	N	Y	Y	N	N	N
16 Manzullo	N	N	N	Y	N	N	N	N
17 Evans	Y	Y	Y	N	Y	N	Y	Y

ND Northern Democrats   SD Southern Democrats

	1	2	3	4	5	6	7	8
18 ***Michel***	N	N	N	N	Y	N	Y	N
19 Poshard	Y	Y	Y	Y	Y	Y	N	N
20 Durbin	Y	Y	Y	N	Y	Y	Y	Y
INDIANA								
1 Visclosky	Y	Y	Y	N	Y	Y	N	Y
2 Sharp	Y	Y	Y	N	Y	Y	N	Y
3 Roemer	Y	Y	Y	Y	Y	N	Y	N
4 Long	Y	N	Y	N	Y	N	N	N
5 ***Buyer***	N	N	N	Y	Y	N	N	N
6 ***Burton***	N	N	N	Y	Y	N	N	N
7 ***Myers***	N	?	?	N	Y	N	N	N
8 McCloskey	Y	Y	Y	N	Y	Y	Y	Y
9 Hamilton	N	Y	N	N	Y	Y	Y	N
10 Jacobs	Y	N	Y	Y	?	Y	Y	N
IOWA								
1 ***Leach***	Y	N	N	N	Y	N	Y	Y
2 ***Nussle***	N	N	N	Y	Y	N	N	N
3 ***Lightfoot***	N	N	N	N	Y	N	Y	N
4 Smith	Y	Y	Y	N	N	Y	Y	Y
5 ***Grandy***	N	N	N	N	Y	N	Y	Y
KANSAS								
1 ***Roberts***	N	N	N	N	Y	N	N	N
2 Slattery	N	Y	N	N	Y	Y	Y	N
3 ***Meyers***	N	N	N	N	N	N	N	N
4 Glickman	N	Y	Y	N	Y	Y	Y	N
KENTUCKY								
1 Barlow	Y	Y	Y	N	Y	Y	Y	N
2 Natcher	Y	Y	Y	N	Y	Y	Y	N
3 Mazzoli	Y	Y	Y	N	Y	Y	N	N
4 ***Bunning***	N	N	N	Y	Y	N	N	N
5 ***Rogers***	N	N	N	Y	Y	N	N	N
6 Baesler	Y	Y	N	N	Y	N	N	N
LOUISIANA								
1 ***Livingston***	N	N	N	N	Y	N	N	N
2 Jefferson	Y	Y	Y	N	N	Y	Y	Y
3 Tauzin	N	Y	N	Y	Y	N	N	N
4 Fields	Y	Y	Y	Y	N	Y	Y	Y
5 ***McCrery***	N	N	N	N	Y	N	N	N
6 ***Baker***	N	N	N	Y	Y	N	Y	N
7 Hayes	N	Y	Y	N	Y	N	Y	N
MAINE								
1 Andrews	Y	Y	Y	N	N	Y	Y	Y
2 ***Snowe***	Y	N	N	Y	N	N	N	N
MARYLAND								
1 ***Gilchrest***	N	N	N	N	Y	N	Y	N
2 ***Bentley***	N	N	N	N	Y	N	N	N
3 Cardin	Y	Y	Y	N	N	Y	Y	Y
4 Wynn	Y	Y	Y	N	N	Y	Y	Y
5 Hoyer	Y	Y	Y	N	N	Y	Y	Y
6 ***Bartlett***	N	N	N	Y	Y	N	N	N
7 Mfume	Y	Y	Y	Y	N	Y	Y	Y
8 ***Morella***	Y	N	N	N	N	N	Y	Y
MASSACHUSETTS								
1 Olver	Y	Y	Y	N	N	Y	Y	Y
2 Neal	Y	Y	Y	N	Y	Y	Y	Y
3 ***Blute***	Y	N	N	Y	Y	N	N	N
4 Frank	Y	Y	Y	N	N	Y	Y	Y
5 Meehan	Y	Y	Y	N	N	Y	Y	Y
6 ***Torkildsen***	N	N	N	N	Y	N	N	Y
7 Markey	Y	Y	Y	N	N	Y	Y	Y
8 Kennedy	Y	Y	Y	N	N	Y	Y	Y
9 Moakley	Y	Y	Y	N	?	Y	Y	Y
10 Studds	Y	Y	Y	N	N	Y	Y	Y
MICHIGAN								
1 Stupak	Y	Y	Y	N	Y	Y	Y	N
2 ***Hoekstra***	N	N	N	N	Y	N	N	N
3 Vacancy								
4 ***Camp***	N	N	N	Y	Y	N	N	N
5 Barcia	Y	Y	Y	Y	Y	Y	N	N
6 ***Upton***	N	N	N	N	Y	N	N	N
7 ***Smith***	N	N	N	N	Y	N	N	N
8 Carr	N	Y	Y	N	N	Y	N	Y
9 Kildee	Y	Y	Y	N	Y	Y	N	Y
10 Bonior	Y	Y	Y	N	Y	Y	Y	Y
11 ***Knollenberg***	N	N	N	N	Y	N	N	N
12 Levin	Y	Y	Y	N	N	Y	Y	Y
13 Ford	Y	Y	Y	N	N	Y	Y	Y
14 Conyers	Y	Y	Y	Y	N	Y	?	?
15 Collins	Y	Y	Y	Y	N	Y	Y	Y
16 Dingell	Y	Y	Y	N	N	Y	Y	N
MINNESOTA								
1 Penny	N	Y	Y	N	Y	Y	N	Y
2 Minge	Y	Y	Y	N	+	N	Y	Y
3 ***Ramstad***	Y	N	N	Y	Y	N	N	N
4 Vento	Y	Y	Y	N	N	Y	Y	Y

	1	2	3	4	5	6	7	8
5 Sabo	Y	Y	Y	N	N	Y	Y	Y
6 ***Grams***	N	N	N	Y	Y	N	N	N
7 Peterson	Y	Y	Y	N	Y	N	N	N
8 Oberstar	Y	Y	Y	N	Y	Y	Y	Y
MISSISSIPPI								
1 Whitten	Y	Y	Y	N	Y	Y	Y	N
2 Thompson				Y	N	Y	N	Y
3 Montgomery	N	Y	Y	N	Y	N	Y	N
4 Parker	N	Y	N	N	Y	N	Y	N
5 Taylor	Y	N	N	N	Y	N	N	N
MISSOURI								
1 Clay	Y	Y	Y	Y	N	Y	Y	Y
2 ***Talent***	N	N	N	N	Y	N	N	N
3 Gephardt	Y	Y	Y	N	Y	Y	Y	Y
4 Skelton	N	Y	Y	N	Y	Y	Y	N
5 Wheat	Y	Y	Y	N	N	Y	Y	Y
6 Danner	Y	Y	Y	Y	Y	N	Y	N
7 ***Hancock***	N	N	N	Y	Y	N	N	N
8 ***Emerson***	N	N	N	N	Y	N	N	N
9 Volkmer	Y	Y	Y	Y	Y	Y	Y	N
MONTANA								
AL Williams	Y	Y	?	N	N	Y	Y	N
NEBRASKA								
1 ***Bereuter***	N	N	N	N	Y	N	Y	N
2 Hoagland	Y	Y	Y	N	Y	Y	Y	Y
3 ***Barrett***	N	N	N	N	Y	N	Y	N
NEVADA								
1 Bilbray	Y	Y	Y	N	Y	Y	Y	N
2 ***Vucanovich***	N	N	N	Y	Y	N	N	N
NEW HAMPSHIRE								
1 ***Zeliff***	N	N	N	Y	Y	N	N	N
2 Swett	Y	Y	Y	?	Y	N	Y	Y
NEW JERSEY								
1 Andrews	Y	N	Y	Y	N	N	N	N
2 Hughes	Y	Y	N	N	Y	Y	N	N
3 ***Saxton***	Y	N	N	Y	Y	N	N	N
4 ***Smith***	Y	N	N	N	Y	N	N	N
5 ***Roukema***	Y	N	N	Y	N	N	Y	N
6 Pallone	Y	Y	Y	N	N	N	N	Y
7 ***Franks***	Y	N	N	N	N	N	N	N
8 Klein	Y	Y	Y	N	N	N	Y	N
9 Torricelli	Y	Y	Y	N	N	Y	N	Y
10 Payne	Y	Y	Y	N	N	Y	Y	Y
11 ***Gallo***	N	N	N	N	Y	N	N	N
12 ***Zimmer***	Y	N	N	Y	N	N	N	N
13 Menendez	Y	Y	Y	N	N	Y	N	Y
NEW MEXICO								
1 ***Schiff***	N	N	N	N	Y	N	N	N
2 ***Skeen***	N	N	N	N	+	N	N	N
3 Richardson	Y	Y	Y	N	N	Y	Y	Y
NEW YORK								
1 Hochbrueckner	Y	Y	Y	N	N	Y	Y	Y
2 ***Lazio***	Y	N	N	N	Y	N	Y	N
3 ***King***	N	N	N	N	Y	N	Y	N
4 ***Levy***	N	N	N	N	Y	N	Y	N
5 Ackerman	Y	Y	Y	N	N	Y	Y	Y
6 Flake	Y	Y	Y	Y	N	Y	Y	Y
7 Manton	Y	Y	Y	N	?	Y	Y	Y
8 Nadler	Y	Y	Y	N	N	Y	N	Y
9 Schumer	Y	Y	Y	N	N	Y	Y	Y
10 Towns	Y	Y	Y	Y	N	Y	?	Y
11 Owens	Y	Y	Y	N	N	Y	N	?
12 Velazquez	Y	Y	Y	Y	N	Y	Y	Y
13 ***Molinari***	Y	N	N	N	N	N	N	N
14 Maloney	Y	Y	Y	N	N	Y	Y	Y
15 Rangel	Y	Y	Y	Y	N	Y	Y	Y
16 Serrano	Y	Y	Y	N	N	Y	Y	Y
17 Engel	Y	Y	Y	N	N	Y	N	Y
18 Lowey	Y	Y	Y	N	N	Y	N	Y
19 ***Fish***	Y	N	N	N	Y	N	N	N
20 ***Gilman***	Y	N	N	N	N	N	N	Y
21 McNulty	Y	Y	Y	N	Y	Y	N	N
22 ***Solomon***	Y	N	N	Y	Y	N	N	N
23 ***Boehlert***	Y	N	N	N	N	N	Y	Y
24 ***McHugh***	Y	N	N	Y	N	N	N	N
25 ***Walsh***	Y	N	N	Y	Y	N	N	N
26 Hinchey	Y	Y	Y	N	N	Y	Y	Y
27 ***Paxon***	N	N	N	N	Y	N	N	N
28 Slaughter	Y	Y	Y	N	N	Y	N	Y
29 LaFalce	Y	Y	Y	N	Y	Y	Y	N
30 ***Quinn***	Y	N	N	Y	Y	N	N	N
31 ***Houghton***	N	N	N	N	Y	N	Y	N
NORTH CAROLINA								
1 Clayton	Y	Y	Y	N	N	Y	Y	Y
2 Valentine	N	Y	Y	Y	Y	Y	Y	N

	1	2	3	4	5	6	7	8
3 Lancaster	N	Y	N	Y	Y	Y	Y	N
4 Price	Y	Y	Y	N	N	Y	Y	N
5 Neal	Y	Y	Y	N	Y	Y	Y	N
6 ***Coble***	N	N	N	Y	Y	N	N	N
7 Rose	Y	Y	Y	N	N	Y	Y	?
8 Hefner	Y	Y	Y	N	Y	Y	N	N
9 ***McMillan***	N	N	N	N	?	N	Y	N
10 ***Ballenger***	N	N	N	N	Y	N	N	N
11 ***Taylor***	N	N	N	Y	Y	N	N	N
12 Watt	Y	Y	Y	N	N	Y	Y	Y
NORTH DAKOTA								
AL Pomeroy	Y	Y	Y	N	Y	Y	N	N
OHIO								
1 Mann	Y	Y	Y	N	Y	N	Y	N
2 ***Portman***				Y	Y	N	N	N
3 Hall	Y	Y	Y	N	Y	Y	Y	N
4 ***Oxley***	N	N	N	N	Y	N	N	N
5 ***Gillmor***	Y	N	N	N	Y	N	N	N
6 Strickland	Y	Y	Y	N	N	Y	Y	Y
7 ***Hobson***	N	N	N	N	Y	N	N	N
8 ***Boehner***	N	N	N	N	Y	N	N	N
9 Kaptur	Y	Y	Y	N	Y	Y	N	N
10 ***Hoke***	Y	N	N	Y	Y	N	N	N
11 Stokes	Y	Y	Y	N	N	Y	Y	Y
12 ***Kasich***	N	N	N	N	Y	N	N	N
13 Brown	Y	Y	Y	N	Y	Y	Y	Y
14 Sawyer	Y	Y	Y	N	N	Y	Y	Y
15 ***Pryce***	N	N	N	N	Y	N	N	N
16 ***Regula***	Y	N	N	Y	Y	N	N	N
17 Traficant	Y	N	Y	Y	N	N	N	N
18 Applegate	Y	Y	Y	Y	Y	Y	N	Y
19 Fingerhut	Y	Y	Y	N	N	Y	Y	Y
OKLAHOMA								
1 ***Inhofe***	N	N	N	Y	Y	N	N	N
2 Synar	Y	Y	Y	N	N	Y	N	Y
3 Brewster	N	Y	Y	Y	Y	N	N	N
4 McCurdy	Y	Y	Y	N	N	N	Y	N
5 ***Istook***	N	N	N	N	Y	N	N	N
6 English	Y	Y	Y	Y	Y	N	N	N
OREGON								
1 Furse	Y	Y	Y	N	N	Y	Y	Y
2 ***Smith***	N	N	N	N	Y	N	N	N
3 Wyden	Y	Y	Y	N	N	Y	Y	Y
4 DeFazio	Y	Y	Y	Y	N	Y	N	Y
5 Kopetski	Y	Y	Y	N	N	Y	Y	Y
PENNSYLVANIA								
1 Foglietta	Y	Y	Y	N	N	Y	Y	Y
2 Blackwell	Y	Y	Y	Y	N	Y	Y	Y
3 Borski	Y	Y	Y	N	Y	Y	?	N
4 Klink	Y	Y	Y	N	Y	Y	Y	N
5 ***Clinger***	N	N	N	N	Y	N	N	N
6 Holden	Y	Y	Y	N	Y	Y	N	N
7 ***Weldon***	Y	N	N	N	Y	N	N	N
8 ***Greenwood***	N	N	N	N	N	N	N	N
9 ***Shuster***	N	N	N	Y	Y	N	N	N
10 ***McDade***	Y	N	N	?	Y	N	Y	?
11 Kanjorski	Y	Y	Y	N	Y	Y	Y	N
12 Murtha	Y	Y	Y	N	Y	Y	Y	N
13 Margolies-Mezv.	Y	N	Y	N	N	Y	Y	Y
14 Coyne	Y	Y	Y	N	N	Y	Y	Y
15 McHale	Y	Y	Y	N	Y	Y	Y	N
16 ***Walker***	N	N	N	N	Y	N	N	N
17 ***Gekas***	N	N	N	Y	Y	N	N	N
18 ***Santorum***	N	N	N	Y	Y	N	N	N
19 ***Goodling***	N	N	N	N	Y	N	N	N
20 Murphy	Y	Y	N	Y	Y	Y	Y	N
21 ***Ridge***	N	N	N	N	Y	N	N	N
RHODE ISLAND								
1 ***Machtley***	Y	N	N	Y	N	N	N	N
2 Reed	Y	Y	Y	N	N	Y	Y	Y
SOUTH CAROLINA								
1 ***Ravenel***	Y	N	N	N	Y	N	N	N
2 ***Spence***	N	N	N	Y	Y	N	N	N
3 Derrick	Y	Y	Y	N	N	Y	Y	N
4 ***Inglis***	N	N	N	Y	Y	N	N	N
5 Spratt	Y	Y	Y	N	Y	Y	Y	N
6 Clyburn	Y	Y	Y	Y	N	Y	Y	Y
SOUTH DAKOTA								
AL Johnson	Y	Y	Y	N	Y	Y	Y	N
TENNESSEE								
1 ***Quillen***	N	?	?	Y	Y	N	N	N
2 ***Duncan***	N	N	N	Y	Y	N	N	N
3 Lloyd	Y	Y	Y	N	Y	N	N	N
4 Cooper	Y	Y	Y	N	Y	Y	N	N
5 Clement	Y	Y	Y	N	Y	N	N	N

	1	2	3	4	5	6	7	8
6 Gordon	Y	Y	Y	N	Y	Y	?	N
7 ***Sundquist***	N	N	N	Y	Y	N	N	N
8 Tanner	Y	Y	Y	N	Y	Y	N	N
9 Ford	?	?	?	Y	N	Y	Y	Y
TEXAS								
1 Chapman	Y	Y	Y	Y	Y	N	N	N
2 Wilson	Y	Y	Y	N	N	Y	Y	N
3 ***Johnson, Sam***	N	N	N	Y	Y	N	N	N
4 Hall	N	N	N	Y	Y	N	Y	N
5 Bryant	Y	Y	Y	N	N	Y	Y	Y
6 ***Barton***	N	N	N	N	Y	N	N	N
7 ***Archer***	N	N	N	Y	Y	N	N	N
8 ***Fields***	N	N	N	+	Y	N	N	N
9 Brooks	Y	Y	Y	N	N	Y	Y	N
10 Pickle	Y	Y	Y	?	N	Y	Y	Y
11 Edwards	Y	Y	Y	N	Y	N	Y	N
12 Geren	N	N	Y	N	Y	N	Y	N
13 Sarpalius	N	Y	Y	Y	Y	Y	Y	N
14 Laughlin	N	Y	Y	N	Y	N	Y	N
15 de la Garza	Y	Y	Y	?	Y	Y	Y	N
16 Coleman	Y	Y	Y	N	N	Y	Y	N
17 Stenholm	N	Y	N	N	Y	N	Y	N
18 Washington	Y	Y	Y	N	N	Y	Y	Y
19 ***Combest***	N	N	N	Y	Y	N	N	N
20 Gonzalez	Y	Y	Y	N	N	Y	Y	Y
21 ***Smith***	Y	N	N	Y	Y	N	N	N
22 ***DeLay***	N	N	N	Y	Y	N	N	N
23 ***Bonilla***	N	N	N	Y	Y	N	N	N
24 Frost	Y	Y	Y	N	N	Y	Y	N
25 Andrews	Y	Y	Y	N	N	Y	N	N
26 ***Armey***	N	N	N	N	Y	N	N	N
27 Ortiz	Y	Y	Y	N	Y	Y	Y	N
28 Tejeda	Y	Y	Y	N	Y	Y	Y	N
29 Green	Y	Y	Y	Y	N	Y	Y	Y
30 Johnson, E.B.	Y	Y	Y	N	N	Y	Y	Y
UTAH								
1 ***Hansen***	N	N	N	Y	Y	N	N	N
2 Shepherd	Y	Y	Y	N	N	Y	Y	Y
3 Orton	N	Y	Y	N	Y	N	Y	N
VERMONT								
AL *Sanders*	Y	Y	Y	Y	N	Y	N	Y
VIRGINIA								
1 ***Bateman***	N	N	N	N	Y	N	N	N
2 Pickett	N	N	Y	N	N	N	Y	N
3 Scott	Y	Y	Y	N	N	Y	Y	Y
4 Sisisky	N	N	Y	N	N	Y	Y	N
5 Payne	N	Y	Y	N	Y	Y	Y	N
6 ***Goodlatte***	N	N	N	N	Y	N	N	N
7 ***Bliley***	N	N	N	N	Y	N	N	N
8 Moran	Y	Y	Y	N	N	Y	Y	Y
9 Boucher	Y	Y	Y	N	N	Y	Y	N
10 ***Wolf***	N	N	N	N	Y	N	N	N
11 Byrne	Y	Y	Y	N	N	Y	Y	Y
WASHINGTON								
1 Cantwell	Y	Y	Y	N	N	Y	Y	Y
2 Swift	Y	Y	Y	N	N	Y	Y	Y
3 Unsoeld	Y	Y	Y	?	N	Y	Y	Y
4 Inslee	Y	Y	Y	Y	N	N	Y	Y
5 Foley					N	Y		
6 Dicks	Y	Y	Y	N	N	Y	Y	Y
7 McDermott	Y	Y	Y	N	N	Y	Y	Y
8 ***Dunn***	N	N	N	N	Y	N	N	N
9 Kreidler	Y	Y	Y	N	N	Y	Y	Y
WEST VIRGINIA								
1 Mollohan	Y	Y	Y	N	Y	Y	Y	N
2 Wise	Y	Y	Y	N	N	Y	Y	N
3 Rahall	Y	Y	Y	Y	Y	Y	N	N
WISCONSIN								
1 Barca				N	Y	Y	N	Y
2 ***Klug***	Y	N	N	N	Y	N	N	N
3 ***Gunderson***	N	N	N	N	Y	N	N	Y
4 Kleczka	Y	Y	Y	N	Y	Y	Y	Y
5 Barrett	Y	Y	Y	N	N	Y	Y	Y
6 ***Petri***	Y	N	N	Y	Y	N	Y	N
7 Obey	Y	Y	Y	N	Y	Y	Y	Y
8 ***Roth***	N	N	N	Y	Y	N	N	N
9 ***Sensenbrenner***	N	N	N	Y	Y	N	N	N
WYOMING								
AL ***Thomas***	Y	N	N	Y	Y	N	N	N
DELEGATES								
de Lugo, V.I.	D	D	D	N	N	D	D	Y
Faleomavaega, Am.S.	D	D	D	N	N	D	D	Y
Norton, D.C.	D	D	D	N	N	D	D	Y
Romero-B., P.R.	D	D	D	?	N	D	D	N
Underwood, Guam	D	D	D	N	Y	D	D	?

Southern states - Ala., Ark., Fla., Ga., Ky., La., Miss., N.C., Okla., S.C., Tenn., Texas, Va.
Omitted votes are quorum calls, which CQ does not include in its vote charts.

9. HR 1845. National Biological Survey/Non-Federal Property. Taylor, R-N.C., amendment to require the National Biological Survey to obtain written consent before going on non-federal lands and to require reports describing the survey's activities on non-federal lands. Adopted in the Committee of the Whole 309-115: R 171-3; D 138-111 (ND 72-95, SD 66-16); I 0-1, Oct. 6, 1993. (House vote 485.)

10. HR 2445. Fiscal 1994 Energy and Water Appropriations/Previous Question. Motion to order the previous question (thus ending debate and the possibility of amendment) on the Myers, R-Ind., motion to recommit to conference the conference report to provide $22,215,382,000 for energy and water development for fiscal 1994. Motion rejected 159-264: R 61-111; D 98-152 (ND 47-121, SD 51-31); I 0-1, Oct. 19, 1993. (House vote 510.) A "yea" was a vote in support of the president's position.

11. H Con Res 170. Somalia Troop Removal/March 31 Deadline. Hamilton, D-Ind., substitute amendment to change the deadline for the removal of U.S. troops from Somalia back to March 31, 1994, from the Jan. 31, 1994, date substituted by the Gilman, R-N.Y., amendment. Adopted 226-201: R 2-170; D 224-30 (ND 150-21, SD 74-9); I 0-1, Nov. 9, 1993. (House vote 556.) A "yea" was a vote in support of the president's position.

12. HR 1025. Brady Bill/Passage. Passage of the bill to require a five-business-day waiting period before an individual could purchase a handgun, to allow local officials to conduct a background check. Passed 238-189: R 54-119; D 184-69 (ND 138-31, SD 46-38); I 0-1, Nov. 10, 1993. (House vote 564.) A "yea" was a vote in support of the president's position.

13. HR 3450. NAFTA Implementation/Passage. Passage of the bill to approve the North American Free Trade Agreement and make the necessary changes to U.S. statutory law to implement it. Passed 234-200: R 132-43; D 102-156 (ND 49-124, SD 53-32); I 0-1, Nov. 17, 1993. (House vote 575.) A "yea" was a vote in support of the president's position.

14. HR 322. 1872 Mining Law Overhaul/Passage. Passage of the bill to require hard-rock mining companies to pay an 8 percent royalty on ores extracted from federal lands, with the money going toward cleanup of abandoned mines, and to require increased environmental regulation of such mining operations. Passed 316-108: R 70-102; D 245-6 (ND 166-3, SD 79-3); I 1-0, Nov. 18, 1993. (House vote 577.) A "yea" was a vote in support of the president's position.

15. HR 3. Campaign Finance/Rule. Adoption of the rule (H Res 319) to provide for House floor consideration of the bill to give House candidates up to $200,000 in federal benefits if they agree to voluntary spending limits of $600,000. The sums would be indexed for inflation from 1992 forward. Adopted 220-207: R 3-168; D 216-39 (ND 156-15, SD 60-24); I 1-0, Nov. 21, 1993. (House vote 599.) A "yea" was a vote in support of the president's position.

16. HR 3400. Fiscal 1994 Spending Cuts and Government Restructuring/Penny-Kasich Amendment. Penny, D-Minn., amendment to cut federal spending by $90 billion over five years through various proposals, including $34 billion in Medicare cuts, $52 billion in discretionary spending cuts and $4 billion in other entitlement cuts and user fee increases. Rejected in the Committee of the Whole 213-219: R 156-18; D 57-200 (ND 33-139, SD 24-61); I 0-1, Nov. 22, 1993. (House vote 609.) A "nay" was a vote in support of the president's position.

KEY

Y Voted for (yea).
\# Paired for.
+ Announced for.
N Voted against (nay).
X Paired against.
− Announced against.
P Voted "present."
C Voted "present" to avoid possible conflict of interest.
? Did not vote or otherwise make a position known.
D Delegates ineligible to vote.

Democrats **Republicans** *Independent*

Member	9	10	11	12	13	14	15	16
ALABAMA								
1 *Callahan*	Y	Y	N	N	Y	N	N	Y
2 *Everett*	Y	Y	N	N	N	N	N	Y
3 Browder	Y	Y	Y	N	Y	Y	Y	
4 Bevill	Y	Y	Y	N	N	Y	Y	N
5 Cramer	Y	Y	Y	N	Y	Y	Y	N
6 *Bachus*	Y	Y	N	N	Y	N	N	Y
7 Hilliard	Y	Y	Y	N	N	Y	Y	N
ALASKA								
AL *Young*	Y	Y	N	N	N	N	N	Y
ARIZONA								
1 Coppersmith	N	N	Y	Y	Y	Y	Y	Y
2 Pastor	N	Y	Y	Y	Y	Y	Y	N
3 *Stump*	Y	N	N	N	Y	N	N	Y
4 *Kyl*	Y	N	N	N	Y	N	?	Y
5 *Kolbe*	Y	Y	N	N	Y	N	N	Y
6 English	N	N	Y	Y	Y	Y	Y	N
ARKANSAS								
1 Lambert	Y	N	Y	N	Y	Y	Y	Y
2 Thornton	Y	Y	Y	N	Y	Y	Y	N
3 *Hutchinson*	N	N	N	N	N	N	N	Y
4 Dickey	Y	N	Y	N	Y	Y	Y	N
CALIFORNIA								
1 Hamburg	N	N	Y	Y	N	Y	Y	N
2 *Herger*	Y	N	N	N	Y	N	N	Y
3 Fazio	Y	Y	Y	Y	Y	Y	Y	N
4 *Doolittle*	Y	N	N	N	N	N	N	Y
5 Matsui	N	Y	Y	Y	Y	Y	Y	Y
6 Woolsey	N	N	Y	Y	N	Y	Y	N
7 Miller	N	N	Y	Y	N	Y	Y	N
8 Pelosi	N	N	Y	Y	Y	Y	Y	N
9 Dellums	N	N	Y	Y	N	Y	Y	N
10 *Baker*	Y	N	N	Y	Y	N	N	Y
11 *Pombo*	Y	N	N	N	N	N	N	Y
12 Lantos	Y	N	Y	Y	Y	Y	Y	N
13 Stark	N	N	Y	Y	N	Y	Y	N
14 Eshoo	N	N	Y	Y	Y	Y	Y	N
15 Mineta	N	Y	Y	Y	Y	Y	Y	N
16 Edwards	N	?	Y	Y	N	Y	Y	N
17 Farr	N	N	Y	Y	Y	Y	Y	N
18 Condit	Y	N	N	Y	N	Y	Y	Y
19 Lehman	Y	N	Y	Y	Y	Y	Y	N
20 Dooley	Y	Y	Y	Y	Y	Y	Y	N
21 *Thomas*	Y	Y	N	N	Y	N	N	Y
22 *Huffington*	Y	N	N	Y	Y	N	N	Y
23 *Gallegly*	Y	N	Y	N	Y	N	N	Y
24 Beilenson	N	N	Y	Y	Y	Y	Y	Y
25 *McKeon*	Y	N	N	N	Y	N	N	Y
26 Berman	N	N	Y	Y	Y	Y	Y	N
27 *Moorhead*	Y	Y	N	N	Y	N	N	Y
28 *Dreier*	Y	Y	N	N	Y	N	N	Y
29 Waxman	N	N	Y	Y	Y	Y	Y	N
30 Becerra	N	N	Y	Y	Y	Y	Y	N
31 Martinez	Y	N	Y	N	N	?	Y	N
32 Dixon	N	Y	Y	Y	Y	Y	Y	N
33 Roybal-Allard	N	N	Y	Y	Y	Y	Y	N
34 Torres	N	Y	Y	Y	Y	Y	Y	N
35 Waters	N	N	Y	Y	N	Y	Y	N
36 Harman	N	N	Y	Y	N	Y	Y	Y
37 Tucker	N	N	Y	Y	N	Y	Y	N
38 Horn	Y	Y	Y	Y	N	Y	Y	N
39 *Royce*	Y	N	N	N	N	N	N	Y
40 *Lewis*	Y	Y	N	N	Y	N	N	Y
41 *Kim*	Y	N	N	N	N	N	N	Y
42 Brown	N	Y	Y	Y	Y	Y	Y	N
43 *Calvert*	Y	N	N	N	Y	N	N	Y
44 *McCandless*	Y	Y	N	?	Y	N	N	Y
45 *Rohrabacher*	Y	N	N	N	Y	N	N	Y
46 *Dornan*	Y	Y	N	N	Y	N	N	Y
47 *Cox*	Y	Y	N	N	Y	N	N	Y
48 *Packard*	Y	Y	N	N	Y	N	N	Y
49 Schenk	Y	N	Y	N	Y	N	Y	Y
50 Filner	N	N	Y	N	Y	N	Y	N
51 *Cunningham*	Y	N	N	N	Y	N	N	Y
52 *Hunter*	Y	N	?	N	N	N	N	Y
COLORADO								
1 Schroeder	Y	N	?	Y	Y	Y	N	N
2 Skaggs	N	N	Y	Y	Y	Y	N	Y
3 *McInnis*	Y	N	N	N	Y	N	N	Y
4 *Allard*	Y	N	N	N	N	N	N	Y
5 *Hefley*	Y	N	N	N	N	N	N	Y
6 *Schaefer*	Y	N	N	N	Y	N	N	Y
CONNECTICUT								
1 Kennelly	N	N	Y	N	Y	Y	N	
2 Gejdenson	N	N	Y	Y	N	Y	Y	N
3 DeLauro	N	N	Y	Y	N	Y	Y	N
4 *Shays*	N	N	Y	Y	N	Y	Y	N
5 *Franks*	Y	Y	N	Y	Y	N	Y	Y
6 *Johnson*	Y	Y	N	Y	Y	Y	N	Y
DELAWARE								
AL *Castle*	Y	N	N	Y	Y	Y	N	Y
FLORIDA								
1 Hutto	Y	N	Y	N	Y	Y	N	
2 Peterson	Y	Y	Y	N	Y	Y	Y	N
3 Brown	Y	Y	Y	N	Y	Y	Y	N
4 *Fowler*	Y	N	N	Y	Y	Y	Y	Y
5 Thurman	Y	N	Y	N	Y	Y	Y	N
6 *Stearns*	Y	N	N	Y	N	N	N	Y
7 *Mica*	Y	Y	N	N	N	N	N	Y
8 *McCollum*	Y	Y	N	N	Y	N	N	Y
9 *Bilirakis*	Y	N	N	N	Y	N	N	Y
10 *Young*	Y	N	Y	N	Y	N	N	Y
11 Gibbons	N	Y	Y	Y	Y	Y	Y	N
12 *Canady*	Y	N	N	N	Y	N	N	Y
13 *Miller*	Y	N	N	N	Y	N	N	Y
14 *Goss*	Y	N	N	N	Y	N	N	Y
15 Bacchus	N	Y	Y	Y	Y	Y	Y	Y
16 *Lewis*	Y	N	?	N	Y	Y	N	Y
17 Meek	N	Y	Y	Y	Y	Y	Y	N
18 *Ros-Lehtinen*	Y	Y	N	Y	N	Y	N	Y
19 Johnson	N	N	Y	Y	N	Y	Y	N
20 Deutsch	N	N	Y	Y	N	Y	Y	N
21 *Diaz-Balart*	Y	Y	N	Y	N	Y	N	Y
22 *Shaw*	Y	Y	N	Y	N	Y	N	Y
23 Hastings	N	Y	Y	Y	Y	Y	Y	N
GEORGIA								
1 *Kingston*	Y	N	N	N	N	N	N	Y
2 Bishop	Y	Y	Y	N	Y	Y	Y	N
3 *Collins*	Y	N	N	Y	N	N	N	Y
4 *Linder*	Y	N	N	N	N	N	N	Y
5 Lewis	N	N	Y	Y	N	Y	Y	N
6 *Gingrich*	Y	Y	N	N	Y	N	N	Y
7 Darden	Y	Y	Y	Y	Y	Y	Y	N
8 Rowland	Y	Y	Y	N	Y	Y	Y	N
9 Deal	Y	N	—	Y	Y	N	Y	
10 Johnson	Y	N	Y	N	Y	Y	N	Y
11 McKinney	Y	N	Y	Y	N	Y	Y	N
HAWAII								
1 Abercrombie	N	N	Y	N	Y	N	Y	N
2 Mink	N	N	Y	N	Y	N	Y	N
IDAHO								
1 LaRocco	N	Y	Y	N	Y	N	Y	Y
2 *Crapo*	Y	Y	N	N	N	N	N	Y
ILLINOIS								
1 Rush	N	N	Y	N	Y	N	Y	N
2 Reynolds	N	Y	Y	Y	Y	Y	Y	N
3 Lipinski	Y	N	Y	N	N	Y	Y	N
4 Gutierrez	N	N	Y	N	Y	N	Y	N
5 Rostenkowski	N	N	Y	Y	N	Y	Y	N
6 *Hyde*	Y	N	N	Y	N	Y	N	Y
7 Collins	N	N	Y	N	Y	N	Y	N
8 *Crane*	Y	N	N	N	Y	N	N	Y
9 Yates	?	Y	Y	Y	Y	Y	Y	N
10 *Porter*	Y	N	N	Y	N	Y	N	Y
11 Sangmeister	Y	N	Y	Y	N	Y	Y	N
12 Costello	Y	N	N	N	N	N	Y	N
13 *Fawell*	Y	N	N	Y	N	Y	N	Y
14 *Hastert*	Y	N	N	N	Y	N	N	Y
15 *Ewing*	Y	N	N	N	Y	N	N	Y
16 *Manzullo*	Y	N	N	N	N	N	N	Y
17 Evans	N	N	N	Y	Y	Y	Y	N

ND Northern Democrats   SD Southern Democrats

	9	10	11	12	13	14	15	16
18 ***Michel***	Y	Y	N	N	Y	N	N	Y
19 Poshard	Y	N	N	N	N	Y	N	Y
20 Durbin	Y	N	Y	Y	Y	Y	Y	N
INDIANA								
1 Visclosky	N	N	Y	Y	N	Y	Y	N
2 Sharp	Y	N	Y	Y	N	Y	Y	Y
3 Roemer	Y	Y	Y	Y	N	Y	Y	Y
4 Long	Y	N	Y	Y	N	Y	Y	Y
5 ***Buyer***	Y	Y	N	N	Y	N	N	Y
6 ***Burton***	Y	?	N	N	N	N	N	Y
7 ***Myers***	Y	Y	N	N	N	N	N	N
8 McCloskey	?	Y	Y	Y	N	Y	Y	N
9 Hamilton	Y	N	Y	Y	Y	Y	Y	Y
10 Jacobs	Y	N	N	Y	N	Y	N	N
IOWA								
1 ***Leach***	Y	N	N	Y	Y	Y	N	Y
2 ***Nussle***	Y	N	N	N	Y	N	N	Y
3 ***Lightfoot***	Y	Y	N	N	Y	N	N	N
4 Smith	Y	Y	Y	N	Y	Y	Y	N
5 ***Grandy***	Y	N	N	N	Y	Y	N	Y
KANSAS								
1 ***Roberts***	Y	Y	N	N	Y	N	N	Y
2 Slattery	Y	N	Y	Y	N	Y	Y	Y
3 ***Meyers***	Y	N	N	Y	Y	Y	N	Y
4 Glickman	Y	N	Y	Y	Y	Y	Y	N
KENTUCKY								
1 Barlow	Y	Y	Y	N	N	Y	Y	Y
2 Natcher	Y	Y	Y	N	N	Y	Y	N
3 Mazzoli	Y	Y	N	Y	Y	Y	N	Y
4 ***Bunning***	Y	N	N	N	N	N	?	Y
5 ***Rogers***	Y	Y	N	N	N	N	N	N
6 Baesler	Y	N	Y	Y	Y	Y	N	Y
LOUISIANA								
1 ***Livingston***	Y	Y	N	N	Y	N	N	Y
2 Jefferson	N	Y	Y	Y	Y	Y	Y	N
3 Tauzin	Y	N	N	N	N	N	N	Y
4 Fields	N	Y	Y	Y	N	Y	Y	N
5 ***McCrery***	Y	Y	N	N	Y	N	N	Y
6 ***Baker***	Y	Y	N	N	Y	N	N	Y
7 Hayes	Y	Y	?	N	Y	N	N	Y
MAINE								
1 Andrews	N	N	Y	Y	N	Y	Y	N
2 ***Snowe***	Y	N	N	N	N	Y	N	Y
MARYLAND								
1 ***Gilchrest***	N	Y	N	Y	Y	?	N	Y
2 ***Bentley***	Y	Y	N	N	N	N	N	Y
3 Cardin	N	N	Y	Y	Y	Y	Y	N
4 Wynn	Y	N	Y	Y	N	Y	Y	N
5 Hoyer	Y	Y	Y	Y	Y	Y	Y	N
6 ***Bartlett***	Y	Y	N	N	N	N	N	Y
7 Mfume	N	N	Y	Y	N	Y	Y	N
8 ***Morella***	N	N	N	Y	Y	Y	Y	N
MASSACHUSETTS								
1 Olver	N	N	Y	Y	N	Y	Y	N
2 Neal	N	N	Y	Y	N	Y	Y	N
3 ***Blute***	Y	Y	N	Y	N	Y	N	Y
4 Frank	N	N	Y	Y	N	Y	Y	N
5 Meehan	N	N	N	Y	Y	Y	N	Y
6 ***Torkildsen***	Y	N	N	Y	Y	Y	N	Y
7 Markey	N	N	Y	Y	Y	Y	Y	N
8 Kennedy	N	N	Y	Y	Y	Y	Y	N
9 Moakley	N	?	?	#	N	Y	Y	N
10 Studds	N	N	Y	Y	Y	Y	Y	N
MICHIGAN								
1 Stupak	Y	N	N	N	N	Y	Y	N
2 ***Hoekstra***	Y	N	N	Y	Y	N	N	Y
3 Vacancy								
4 ***Camp***	Y	N	N	N	Y	N	N	Y
5 Barcia	Y	N	N	N	N	N	Y	N
6 ***Upton***	Y	N	N	Y	Y	N	Y	Y
7 ***Smith***	Y	?	N	Y	Y	N	N	Y
8 Carr	Y	N	Y	N	N	Y	N	N
9 Kildee	Y	N	N	Y	N	Y	Y	N
10 Bonior	N	Y	Y	Y	N	Y	Y	N
11 ***Knollenberg***	Y	N	N	N	Y	N	N	Y
12 Levin	N	N	Y	Y	N	Y	Y	N
13 Ford	N	N	Y	Y	N	Y	?	N
14 Conyers	?	N	Y	Y	N	Y	Y	N
15 Collins	Y	N	Y	Y	N	Y	Y	N
16 Dingell	N	N	Y	N	N	Y	Y	N
MINNESOTA								
1 Penny	Y	N	Y	N	Y	Y	Y	Y
2 Minge	Y	N	Y	Y	N	Y	Y	Y
3 ***Ramstad***	Y	N	N	Y	Y	Y	N	Y
4 Vento	N	N	Y	Y	N	Y	Y	N

	9	10	11	12	13	14	15	16
5 Sabo	N	N	Y	Y	N	Y	Y	N
6 ***Grams***	Y	Y	N	N	Y	N	N	Y
7 Peterson	Y	N	N	N	N	Y	Y	Y
8 Oberstar	Y	N	Y	N	N	Y	Y	N
MISSISSIPPI								
1 Whitten	Y	Y	Y	N	Y	Y	Y	N
2 Thompson	Y	Y	Y	Y	N	Y	Y	N
3 Montgomery	Y	Y	Y	N	Y	Y	Y	N
4 Parker	Y	N	Y	N	Y	Y	Y	N
5 Taylor	Y	N	N	N	N	Y	N	Y
MISSOURI								
1 Clay	N	Y	Y	Y	N	Y	Y	N
2 ***Talent***	Y	N	N	N	N	N	N	Y
3 Gephardt	N	Y	Y	Y	Y	Y	Y	N
4 Skelton	Y	Y	Y	N	Y	Y	N	N
5 Wheat	N	N	Y	Y	N	Y	Y	N
6 Danner	Y	N	Y	N	N	Y	Y	N
7 ***Hancock***	Y	N	N	N	Y	N	N	Y
8 ***Emerson***	Y	N	N	N	Y	N	N	Y
9 Volkmer	Y	Y	Y	N	N	Y	Y	N
MONTANA								
AL Williams	Y	N	Y	N	N	Y	Y	N
NEBRASKA								
1 ***Bereuter***	Y	N	N	N	Y	Y	N	Y
2 Hoagland	N	N	Y	Y	Y	Y	Y	Y
3 ***Barrett***	Y	N	N	N	Y	N	N	Y
NEVADA								
1 Bilbray	Y	N	Y	N	N	Y	Y	N
2 ***Vucanovich***	Y	Y	N	N	N	N	N	Y
NEW HAMPSHIRE								
1 ***Zeliff***	Y	N	N	N	Y	N	N	Y
2 Swett	Y	N	Y	Y	N	Y	Y	Y
NEW JERSEY								
1 Andrews	N	Y	N	Y	N	Y	N	Y
2 Hughes	Y	N	Y	Y	N	Y	Y	N
3 ***Saxton***	Y	N	N	Y	N	Y	N	Y
4 ***Smith***	Y	N	N	Y	N	Y	N	Y
5 ***Roukema***	Y	N	N	Y	Y	Y	N	Y
6 Pallone	N	N	Y	Y	N	Y	Y	N
7 ***Franks***	Y	Y	N	Y	Y	Y	N	Y
8 Klein	N	N	Y	Y	N	Y	Y	N
9 Torricelli	?	Y	Y	Y	N	Y	N	N
10 Payne	N	N	Y	Y	N	Y	Y	N
11 ***Gallo***	Y	Y	N	Y	Y	Y	N	Y
12 ***Zimmer***	Y	N	N	Y	Y	Y	N	Y
13 Menendez	Y	N	Y	Y	N	Y	Y	N
NEW MEXICO								
1 ***Schiff***	Y	?	N	N	Y	Y	N	Y
2 ***Skeen***	Y	Y	N	N	Y	Y	N	N
3 Richardson	N	Y	Y	N	Y	Y	Y	N
NEW YORK								
1 Hochbrueckner	Y	Y	Y	Y	N	Y	Y	N
2 ***Lazio***	Y	N	N	Y	Y	Y	N	N
3 ***King***	Y	N	N	N	Y	Y	N	N
4 ***Levy***	Y	N	N	N	Y	Y	N	N
5 Ackerman	?	Y	Y	Y	N	Y	Y	N
6 Flake	?	N	Y	Y	Y	Y	Y	N
7 Manton	N	Y	Y	Y	N	Y	Y	N
8 Nadler	N	Y	Y	Y	N	Y	Y	N
9 Schumer	N	N	Y	Y	N	Y	Y	N
10 Towns	N	N	Y	Y	N	Y	N	N
11 Owens	N	Y	Y	Y	N	Y	Y	N
12 Velazquez	N	N	Y	Y	N	Y	Y	N
13 ***Molinari***	Y	N	N	Y	Y	N	N	Y
14 Maloney	N	N	Y	Y	N	Y	Y	N
15 Rangel	N	N	Y	Y	N	Y	Y	N
16 Serrano	N	N	Y	Y	N	Y	Y	N
17 Engel	N	—	Y	Y	N	Y	Y	N
18 Lowey	N	Y	Y	Y	Y	Y	Y	N
19 ***Fish***	Y	N	N	Y	Y	Y	N	Y
20 ***Gilman***	Y	N	N	Y	N	Y	N	N
21 McNulty	Y	Y	N	Y	Y	Y	Y	N
22 ***Solomon***	Y	N	N	N	N	N	N	Y
23 ***Boehlert***	Y	N	N	Y	Y	Y	Y	N
24 ***McHugh***	Y	N	N	N	N	N	N	Y
25 ***Walsh***	Y	N	N	Y	N	N	N	Y
26 Hinchey	N	N	Y	Y	N	Y	Y	N
27 ***Paxon***	Y	N	N	N	Y	N	N	Y
28 Slaughter	Y	N	N	Y	N	Y	Y	N
29 LaFalce	N	N	Y	Y	N	Y	Y	N
30 ***Quinn***	Y	N	N	Y	N	N	N	Y
31 ***Houghton***	Y	N	Y	N	Y	N	N	Y
NORTH CAROLINA								
1 Clayton	N	N	Y	Y	N	Y	Y	N
2 Valentine	Y	N	Y	Y	Y	Y	N	N

	9	10	11	12	13	14	15	16
3 Lancaster	Y	N	Y	Y	N	Y	N	Y
4 Price	Y	N	Y	Y	Y	Y	Y	N
5 Neal	Y	N	Y	Y	Y	Y	Y	N
6 ***Coble***	Y	N	N	N	Y	N	N	Y
7 Rose	Y	Y	Y	Y	Y	?	Y	N
8 Hefner	Y	N	Y	Y	Y	Y	Y	N
9 ***McMillan***	Y	N	N	Y	Y	Y	N	Y
10 ***Ballenger***	Y	N	N	N	Y	N	N	Y
11 ***Taylor***	Y	Y	N	N	N	N	N	Y
12 Watt	N	N	Y	Y	N	Y	Y	N
NORTH DAKOTA								
AL Pomeroy	+	N	Y	N	N	Y	Y	Y
OHIO								
1 Mann	N	N	Y	Y	Y	Y	Y	Y
2 ***Portman***	Y	N	N	N	Y	Y	N	Y
3 Hall	Y	N	Y	Y	N	Y	?	?
4 ***Oxley***	?	Y	N	Y	Y	N	N	Y
5 ***Gillmor***	Y	N	N	N	Y	N	N	Y
6 Strickland	Y	N	Y	N	N	Y	Y	N
7 ***Hobson***	Y	N	N	N	Y	N	N	Y
8 ***Boehner***	Y	Y	N	N	Y	N	N	Y
9 Kaptur	Y	N	Y	Y	N	Y	N	Y
10 ***Hoke***	Y	N	N	N	N	N	N	Y
11 Stokes	N	Y	Y	Y	N	Y	Y	N
12 ***Kasich***	Y	N	N	N	Y	N	N	Y
13 Brown	Y	N	N	Y	N	Y	Y	N
14 Sawyer	Y	N	Y	Y	Y	Y	Y	N
15 ***Pryce***	Y	N	N	N	Y	N	N	Y
16 ***Regula***	Y	N	N	Y	N	Y	N	Y
17 Traficant	Y	Y	N	Y	N	Y	N	N
18 Applegate	Y	N	N	Y	N	Y	Y	N
19 Fingerhut	Y	N	N	Y	N	Y	Y	Y
OKLAHOMA								
1 ***Inhofe***	Y	N	N	N	N	N	N	Y
2 Synar	N	N	Y	Y	Y	Y	N	N
3 Brewster	Y	N	Y	N	Y	Y	N	N
4 McCurdy	?	?	Y	Y	Y	Y	N	Y
5 ***Istook***	Y	N	N	N	Y	N	N	Y
6 English	Y	N	Y	N	Y	Y	N	N
OREGON								
1 Furse	N	Y	Y	Y	N	Y	Y	N
2 ***Smith***	Y	N	N	N	Y	N	N	Y
3 Wyden	Y	N	N	Y	Y	Y	Y	N
4 DeFazio	Y	N	N	Y	N	Y	Y	N
5 Kopetski	Y	Y	Y	—	Y	Y	N	N
PENNSYLVANIA								
1 Foglietta	N	Y	Y	Y	N	Y	Y	N
2 Blackwell	N	Y	Y	Y	N	Y	Y	N
3 Borski	?	Y	Y	Y	N	Y	Y	N
4 Klink	Y	Y	Y	N	N	?	Y	Y
5 ***Clinger***	Y	N	N	N	Y	?	?	?
6 Holden	Y	N	Y	N	N	Y	Y	Y
7 ***Weldon***	Y	N	N	Y	N	Y	N	Y
8 ***Greenwood***	Y	N	N	Y	Y	Y	N	Y
9 ***Shuster***	Y	N	N	?	N	Y	N	Y
10 ***McDade***	Y	Y	N	Y	Y	Y	N	N
11 Kanjorski	Y	N	Y	N	N	Y	Y	N
12 Murtha	Y	Y	Y	N	N	Y	Y	N
13 Margolies-Mezv.	Y	N	Y	Y	N	Y	Y	Y
14 Coyne	N	Y	Y	Y	N	Y	Y	N
15 McHale	Y	Y	N	Y	N	Y	Y	Y
16 ***Walker***	Y	N	N	N	Y	N	N	Y
17 ***Gekas***	Y	N	N	N	Y	N	N	Y
18 ***Santorum***	Y	Y	N	N	N	N	N	Y
19 ***Goodling***	Y	N	N	Y	Y	N	N	Y
20 Murphy	N	?	Y	X	N	Y	N	Y
21 ***Ridge***	Y	N	N	N	Y	?	N	Y
RHODE ISLAND								
1 ***Machtley***	Y	N	N	Y	Y	Y	N	N
2 Reed	N	N	Y	Y	N	Y	Y	N
SOUTH CAROLINA								
1 ***Ravenel***	Y	N	N	N	N	Y	N	Y
2 ***Spence***	Y	Y	N	N	N	Y	N	Y
3 Derrick	?	Y	N	Y	N	Y	Y	N
4 ***Inglis***	Y	N	N	N	N	N	N	Y
5 Spratt	Y	N	Y	Y	Y	Y	Y	N
6 Clyburn	Y	Y	Y	Y	N	Y	Y	N
SOUTH DAKOTA								
AL Johnson	Y	N	N	Y	N	Y	Y	N
TENNESSEE								
1 ***Quillen***	Y	Y	N	N	Y	N	N	N
2 ***Duncan***	Y	N	N	N	N	Y	N	Y
3 Lloyd	Y	Y	Y	Y	Y	Y	N	N
4 Cooper	Y	Y	N	Y	Y	Y	Y	Y
5 Clement	Y	N	Y	Y	Y	Y	Y	N

	9	10	11	12	13	14	15	16
6 Gordon	Y	Y	Y	Y	Y	Y	Y	Y
7 ***Sundquist***	Y	N	N	N	Y	N	?	Y
8 Tanner	Y	N	Y	N	Y	Y	N	Y
9 Ford	N	?	Y	Y	Y	Y	Y	N
TEXAS								
1 Chapman	Y	Y	Y	Y	Y	?	N	N
2 Wilson	Y	Y	?	N	N	?	Y	N
3 ***Johnson, Sam***	Y	Y	N	N	N	N	N	Y
4 Hall	Y	Y	N	N	N	Y	Y	Y
5 Bryant	Y	?	Y	Y	Y	Y	Y	N
6 ***Barton***	Y	Y	N	N	Y	N	N	Y
7 ***Archer***	Y	N	N	N	Y	N	N	Y
8 ***Fields***	Y	Y	N	N	Y	N	N	Y
9 Brooks	Y	Y	Y	N	N	Y	Y	N
10 Pickle	Y	Y	Y	Y	Y	Y	Y	N
11 Edwards	Y	Y	Y	N	Y	Y	Y	Y
12 Geren	Y	Y	Y	N	Y	Y	N	Y
13 Sarpalius	Y	Y	Y	N	Y	Y	Y	N
14 Laughlin	Y	Y	Y	N	Y	Y	Y	Y
15 de la Garza	?	Y	Y	N	Y	Y	Y	N
16 Coleman	Y	Y	Y	N	Y	Y	Y	N
17 Stenholm	Y	Y	Y	N	Y	N	N	Y
18 Washington	N	N	Y	Y	N	Y	?	N
19 ***Combest***	Y	Y	N	N	Y	N	N	N
20 Gonzalez	N	Y	Y	Y	N	Y	Y	N
21 ***Smith***	Y	Y	N	N	Y	N	N	Y
22 ***DeLay***	Y	Y	N	N	Y	N	N	Y
23 ***Bonilla***	Y	Y	N	N	Y	N	N	Y
24 Frost	Y	Y	Y	Y	Y	Y	N	N
25 Andrews	Y	Y	Y	Y	Y	Y	N	Y
26 ***Armey***	Y	Y	N	N	Y	N	N	Y
27 Ortiz	Y	Y	Y	N	Y	Y	Y	N
28 Tejeda	Y	Y	Y	N	Y	Y	Y	N
29 Green	Y	Y	N	N	Y	Y	Y	N
30 Johnson, E.B.	Y	Y	Y	Y	Y	Y	Y	N
UTAH								
1 ***Hansen***	Y	Y	N	N	Y	N	N	Y
2 Shepherd	N	N	Y	Y	Y	Y	Y	N
3 Orton	Y	N	Y	N	N	N	Y	Y
VERMONT								
AL *Sanders*	N	N	N	N	N	Y	Y	N
VIRGINIA								
1 ***Bateman***	Y	Y	N	Y	Y	N	N	Y
2 Pickett	Y	Y	Y	N	Y	Y	N	N
3 Scott	Y	Y	Y	Y	N	Y	Y	N
4 Sisisky	Y	N	Y	N	N	Y	N	N
5 Payne	Y	Y	Y	N	Y	Y	Y	Y
6 ***Goodlatte***	Y	Y	N	N	Y	Y	N	Y
7 ***Bliley***	Y	Y	N	N	Y	N	N	Y
8 Moran	N	N	Y	Y	Y	Y	Y	N
9 Boucher	Y	Y	Y	N	N	Y	N	N
10 ***Wolf***	Y	N	N	Y	Y	Y	N	Y
11 Byrne	Y	N	N	Y	N	Y	Y	N
WASHINGTON								
1 Cantwell	Y	N	Y	Y	Y	Y	Y	Y
2 Swift	Y	Y	Y	Y	Y	Y	Y	N
3 Unsoeld	N	N	Y	N	N	Y	Y	N
4 Inslee	Y	N	Y	N	Y	Y	Y	Y
5 Foley			Y		Y		Y	N
6 Dicks	Y	Y	Y	Y	Y	?	Y	N
7 McDermott	N	Y	Y	Y	Y	Y	Y	N
8 ***Dunn***	Y	Y	N	N	Y	N	N	Y
9 Kreidler	N	N	Y	Y	Y	Y	Y	N
WEST VIRGINIA								
1 Mollohan	Y	Y	Y	N	N	Y	Y	N
2 Wise	Y	Y	Y	N	N	Y	Y	N
3 Rahall	N	Y	Y	N	N	Y	Y	N
WISCONSIN								
1 Barca	Y	N	Y	Y	N	Y	Y	Y
2 ***Klug***	Y	N	N	Y	Y	Y	N	Y
3 ***Gunderson***	Y	N	N	N	Y	Y	N	Y
4 Kleczka	Y	N	N	Y	N	Y	Y	N
5 Barrett	Y	N	Y	Y	N	Y	Y	Y
6 ***Petri***	Y	N	?	N	Y	Y	Y	Y
7 Obey	Y	N	Y	N	N	Y	Y	N
8 ***Roth***	Y	N	N	N	Y	Y	N	N
9 ***Sensenbrenner***	Y	N	N	Y	Y	Y	N	Y
WYOMING								
AL ***Thomas***	Y	N	N	N	Y	N	N	Y
DELEGATES								
de Lugo, V.I.	N	D	D	D	D	D	D	?
Faleomavaega, Am.S.	?	D	D	D	D	D	D	?
Norton, D.C.	N	D	D	D	D	D	D	?
Romero-B., P.R.	?	D	D	D	D	D	D	?
Underwood, Guam	N	D	D	D	D	D	D	?

Southern states - Ala., Ark., Fla., Ga., Ky., La., Miss., N.C., Okla., S.C., Tenn., Texas, Va.
Omitted votes are quorum calls, which CQ does not include in its vote charts.

KEY SENATE VOTES

1. Budget Resolution

The Senate vote on President Clinton's fiscal 1994 budget blueprint in March exemplified two themes that would reappear again and again in the battle over tax and spending issues in 1993.

First, Democrats evinced deep unease about voting for many of Clinton's economic proposals, particularly the tax increases that formed the core of his plan to reduce the deficit. Second, at crucial moments, Democrats put aside their fears and backed Clinton, saving his plan from imminent defeat.

The Senate version of the budget resolution (H Con Res 64) embodied a slightly modified version of Clinton's $1.5 trillion budget. Because the budget resolution set in motion the so-called reconciliation process, in which various committees drafted contributions to a bill putting tax increases and spending cuts into law, it provided the initial test of the Senate's willingness to follow the president's economic plan.

The budget resolution passed the Senate on March 25 on an almost strictly party-line vote of 54-45: R 0-43; D 54-2 (ND 41-0, SD 13-2).

The only two Democrats to vote against it were Bob Krueger of Texas, who was defeated in a special election May 1, and Richard C. Shelby of Alabama, who opposed Clinton's economic plan at every stage.

Throughout the six-day floor debate on the budget resolution, Democrats appeared sorely tempted to abandon key elements of Clinton's plan. Republicans crafted amendment after amendment to put them on the spot. But the Democrats stuck together and voted down amendments that, for example, would have stripped out a tax increase imposed on better-off Social Security beneficiaries, would have knocked out Clinton's proposed spending and tax increases and would have restored money that Clinton wanted to cut from defense.

The resolution did reflect an important shift in fiscal policy. It laid out a goal of cutting the deficit by more than $500 billion over five years, somewhat more than had been suggested by Clinton. It proposed net new taxes of $295 billion and net spending cuts of slightly more than $200 billion.

All of these figures would be adjusted as the budget moved through Congress, but the basic thrust of the plan would remain intact.

Keeping nervous Democrats in line required enormous lobbying pressure from Democratic leaders and from the president himself. Clinton and the leadership were able to succeed partly by appealing to lawmakers to give the president's program a chance. But many Democrats also knew that the specific tax and spending decisions would be made later in the year on the budget-reconciliation bill (HR 2264). *(House vote 2, p. 37-C)*

Thus, the vote on the budget resolution overstated the level of support among Democrats for the specifics of Clinton's program. Later in the summer, many of the same Democrats who voted for the budget gave the administration fits and forced revisions to key elements of the program. In particular, a proposed energy tax based on the heat content of fuels was dropped, and additional spending cuts were substituted for it.

Throughout the debate on the budget resolution, Re-publicans remained on the outside. Every GOP effort to make a substantive change in the blueprint was voted down. Not a single Republican voted for the Clinton plan, nor would any for the rest of the year.

2. Economic Stimulus

Senate Republicans in April killed President Clinton's first piece of fiscal legislation — an economic stimulus package — refusing to accept a multibillion-dollar increase in the deficit in exchange for several hundred thousand temporary jobs.

The bill's Democratic sponsors had the 50 votes needed to pass the bill but not the 60 needed to limit debate. The fourth and final attempt to end a GOP filibuster came April 21, after Clinton had agreed to cut 25 percent from the bill's spending in the hope of attracting a few Republican votes. The motion to invoke cloture failed, however, by a vote of 56-43: R 0-42; D 56-1 (ND 42-0, SD 14-1).

Billed as one of the three cornerstones of Clinton's economic program, the stimulus package took the form of a $16.3 billion supplemental appropriations bill for fiscal 1993 (HR 1335). It was a blend of diverse elements: public works projects to create jobs and spur economic development, summer jobs for youths and unskilled laborers, social programs for the poor and high-technology purchases for the federal government.

The White House had pushed the bill through the House without changes and tried to do the same in the Senate. The first hurdle it encountered was a trio of dissident Democrats — David L. Boren of Oklahoma, John B. Breaux of Louisiana and Richard H. Bryan of Nevada. Saying that the public wanted spending cuts, not increases, the trio wanted to postpone much of the spending in the bill until after Congress adopted a deficit-cutting budget-reconciliation bill.

When the stimulus package reached the Senate floor March 25, its manager, Senate Appropriations Committee Chairman Robert C. Byrd, D-W.Va., set up a parliamentary obstacle course to stop the dissident Democrats. He offered two slightly different versions of Clinton's entire stimulus package as substitute amendments, setting up an "amendment tree" that could wipe out any other amendments adopted by the Senate. The tactic

Byrd

bought time for Byrd, allowing the White House to negotiate a compromise with Boren, Breaux and Bryan. But it also provoked an angry response from Republicans, even after Byrd dismantled his amendment tree.

After failing in several attempts to cut the bill, Republicans released a letter March 31 announcing their willingness to filibuster unless changes were made in HR 1335. The Democrats clamped down further, taking control of the Senate floor and allowing no amendments to be offered. Senate Majority Leader George J. Mitchell, D-Maine, threatened to delay the two-week Senate recess that was scheduled to begin April 5 until the stimulus package passed. But Republicans held their ground, voting as a bloc against motions to limit debate on April 2, April 3 and April 5. With Democrat Richard C. Shelby of Alabama joining the Republicans, the bill's sponsors fell at least five votes short of cloture each time.

The Senate then recessed for two weeks, and Clinton

signaled his willingness to compromise. His proposed 25 percent cut, however, did not meet the basic Republican demand: any spending beyond the $4 billion for extended unemployment benefits had to be offset with cuts in other programs. Although a handful of Republican moderates said they were interested in compromising, none voted for cloture April 21.

Mitchell offered to trim the bill to $12.9 billion in appropriations and trust-fund spending, with $5 billion in offsetting cuts. Minority Leader Bob Dole, R-Kan., rejected that proposal, and Mitchell refused Dole's counteroffer of a $6.55 billion package with $2.55 billion in offsetting cuts.

By voice vote, the Senate then agreed to strip the bill down to one provision — a $4 billion emergency appropriation for extended unemployment benefits. The truncated measure quickly passed, and Clinton signed it into law April 23 (PL 103-24). *(House vote 3, p. 37-C)*

3. Campaign Finance

For three years in a row — from 1990 through 1992 — the Senate approved campaign finance legislation that would have provided substantial public funding to candidates who agreed to comply with spending limits.

But in 1993 Democrats could not break a Republican-led filibuster until they stripped out all public funding.

While concern over the deficit was a key factor, another was the occupant of the White House. Republicans had not tried to filibuster those previous bills because they knew that then-President George Bush would veto them. President Clinton, on the other hand, had promised to sign a bill.

Democrats had long argued that the way to reform the campaign finance system was to limit spending, which they said would keep incumbents from winning on the strength of their fundraising advantages. The only way limits could be imposed within the confines of the Supreme Court's 1976 decision in *Buckley v. Valeo* was to make them voluntary and encourage compliance by offering partial public financing.

Republicans, on the other hand, objected to spending caps, which they said would prevent challengers from being as visible as incumbents. They also objected to asking taxpayers to foot even part of the bill for congressional campaigns.

After two cloture votes failed on largely party lines to end the 1993 filibuster, Democrats agreed to a demand by five key Republicans that public funding be eliminated and replaced with a new 34 percent tax on contributions to candidates who rejected spending limits.

The tax amendment, offered by Sen. Dave Durenberger, R-Minn., passed on a 52-47 vote June 16, with 47 Democrats in support.

Though many said the tax would not pass constitutional muster — they argued that it was a tax on speech — the absence of public funding paved the way for a 62-37 vote to shut off debate hours later.

The bill as passed by the Senate set spending limits ranging from $8.25 million for a candidate in California to $2 million for those in small states. It banned political action committee contributions, prohibited groups that lobbied Congress from bundling individual contributions to a candidate and restricted the use of money raised outside federal guidelines in federal elections.

With the exception that it lacked public funding, the

bill essentially modeled a plan endorsed by Clinton on May 7. The Senate passed the bill on June 17 by a vote of 60-38: R 7-35; D 53-3 (ND 42-0; SD 11-3). *(House vote 15, p. 44-C)*

4. Budget-Reconciliation

It was the closest Senate vote in six years, and President Clinton came perilously close to seeing his entire economic plan go down to defeat at the hands of rebellious Democrats. But in the end, he won passage of the budget-reconciliation bill (HR 2264 — PL 103-66) that was designed to put a reworked version of his plan into law.

The bill passed only with the intervention of Vice President Al Gore, who cast the tie-breaking vote shortly after 3 a.m. June 25. The vote was 50-49: R 0-43; D 49-6 (ND 38-3, SD 11-3).

Clinton's heavy reliance on tax increases to reduce the deficit was initially the cause of the division among Senate Democrats. Conservative Democrats, many of them from energy producing states, balked at his proposal for an energy tax, based on the heat content of fuels. They wanted more emphasis on spending cuts, and when the bill came over from the House, some were determined to kill the energy tax, even if it meant bringing down the entire package. *(House vote 6, p. 39-C)*

The leading Democratic opponent was David L. Boren of Oklahoma, who had initially praised the Clinton plan but later became a vocal critic. In the weeks leading up to the Senate vote, Clinton had to rewrite key elements of his plan. But every attempt to produce a formula satisfactory to the conservatives caused problems with other party factions.

Deeper spending cuts drew protests from liberal senators, who wanted to defend programs for the poor and elderly. Pro-business moderates were upset that costly business tax breaks were to be scaled back to pay for a smaller energy tax.

Each group was able to exercise a sort of veto power over the deal because of Clinton's strategy to rely entirely on Democratic votes to pass his program. It was a strategy born partly of necessity, partly of choice. Republican leaders worked hard to keep their rank and file unified in opposition to Clinton's plan. The White House had almost no opportunity to seek a bipartisan coalition in support of its economic program.

At the same time, the White House and Senate Democratic leaders made little effort to attract moderate Republicans, some of whom said they would have supported tax increases if the administration had been willing to make a more serious attempt at cutting spending in entitlement programs, such as Social Security and Medicare.

The upshot was that Clinton's plan had to rise or fall with the Democrats alone.

Democrats escaped this quagmire with a laboriously crafted compromise that junked Clinton's energy tax and replaced it with an increase in federal excise taxes on gasoline and other transportation fuels. Liberals had to accept deeper cuts in Medicare, but they managed to limit the damage. And the moderates won a commitment from

Clinton to fight for business tax breaks when the final version of the bill was written in conference with the House.

When the bargaining was over, the broad outlines of Clinton's package looked roughly the same. But many key details had been changed.

Even then, when the bill went to the floor, there was plenty of doubt whether Democrats could energize their majority, put aside their worries about voting for tax increases and pass their president's plan.

When the roll was called, the Democrats lost six of their own, two of whom were up for re-election in 1994: Richard H. Bryan of Nevada and Frank R. Lautenberg of New Jersey. A third opponent, Dennis DeConcini of Arizona, later announced that he would not run for re-election the next year. Three Southern conservatives — J. Bennett Johnston of Louisiana, Sam Nunn of Georgia and Richard C. Shelby of Alabama — also voted no. Every Republican was opposed.

Two senators were absent: Patty Murray, D-Wash., and Arlen Specter, R-Pa. With 49 votes for the plan and 49 against, Gore had to break the tie.

Although the victory had Pyrrhic overtones, Clinton had accomplished something that had looked nearly impossible in the weeks before the vote. He had kept a recognizable version of his plan alive when it seemed headed for certain death in the Senate. And he set up a party-defining showdown for the Democrats later in the summer, when House and Senate leaders would sit down to write the final version of the bill. The conference agreement on HR 2264 ultimately was adopted by a 51-50 vote that reprised the June test, including Gore's tie-breaker.

5. National Service

President Clinton must never have believed it would be so difficult to enact his plan to create a National Service corps for young people to earn financial credit toward their postsecondary education in return for their contribution of community service. At stops across the country during the 1992 presidential campaign, he received more applause for mentioning National Service than for almost any other initiative.

But the feel-good program of the campaign turned into a gridlocked program in the Senate. It went through a series of revisions, compromises and delays before the Senate ultimately passed the National Service bill (HR 2010) on Aug. 3 by 58-41: R 7-37; D 51-4 (ND 38-3, SD 13-1).

Passage came only after a threatened Republican filibuster knocked the bill off the floor the week before, when Democrats scrambled — but failed — to come up with 60 votes to invoke cloture, stop Republican delaying tactics and bring the measure to a vote. Democrats had united in their attempts to stop the filibuster, but they failed by one vote July 29 to muster the necessary 60-vote majority. Four Democrats later voted against final passage: Robert C. Byrd of West Virginia, Ernest F. Hollings of South Carolina, and Jim Exon and Bob Kerrey of Nebraska.

Democratic sponsors broke the impasse by scaling back the measure to a three-year program with specified cost ceilings each year. That lured enough Republican support that a second cloture vote proved unnecessary. The cost ceilings of $300 million in fiscal 1994, $500 million in fiscal 1995 and $700 million in fiscal 1996 were projected to reduce the maximum number of service workers to about 100,000 from an earlier estimate of 150,000. Nonetheless,

Clinton proclaimed victory despite enactment of a bobtailed version of his campaign promise.

Once over the initial Senate hurdle, a conference compromise was quickly worked out that had no trouble winning adoption in the House or Senate, though final action in the Senate was delayed by the August congressional recess.

As enacted, the National Service program was designed to give awards of as much as $4,725 a year for no more than two years to individuals age 17 or older who performed community service before, during or after their postsecondary education. Local programs were to offer stipends to participants of as much as $7,400 a year, with the federal government providing 85 percent of the stipend. The federal government was to provide up to 85 percent of the cost of health-care and child-care benefits.

Nonprofit organizations, including institutions of higher education, local governments, school districts and state or federal agencies, were to run the individual programs. Young people would work in such positions as nurses' aides in hospitals or helpers in police departments, or in environmental jobs in national parks.

6. Supreme Court Nomination

The announced retirement of Supreme Court Justice Byron R. White in March gave the Democrats their first opportunity in 26 years to fill a Supreme Court vacancy. However, President Clinton's choice of U.S. Court of Appeals Judge Ruth Bader Ginsburg did not reflect a desire to begin reshaping a court that had been molded by Republican presidents. Instead, Clinton chose a non-controversial and well-respected centrist, acceptable to most parts of the political spectrum.

Concerned about the public perception that his presidency was drifting toward the left, Clinton made it clear from the outset that he was inclined to pick a centrist judge. He was still smarting from his recent withdrawal of Justice Department nominees Zoë Baird and Lani Guinier. Baird, nominated for attorney general, withdrew following disclosures that she had hired two illegal immigrants as domestic workers and failed to pay Social Security taxes on them. Guinier, nominated to head Justice's civil rights division, ran into ideological problems, particularly regarding writings on such issues as voting rights that suggested to many that she was too far to the left.

The president's choice of Ginsburg came only after he conducted a long and very public search, eventually passing over two touted finalists — Interior Secretary Bruce Babbitt and U.S. Appeals Court Judge Stephen G. Breyer.

Ginsburg, only the second woman to be nominated to the high court, seemed an ideal candidate. Considered a liberal on civil rights issues and somewhat conservative on criminal and business law, she was generally perceived as a political moderate. In addition, Ginsburg had impressive professional credentials and a solid reputation for personal integrity. A potential snag — her criticism of the landmark 1973 Supreme Court decision in *Roe v. Wade*, which legalized abortion nationwide — dissipated as a threat to her nomination after she publicly reiterated her support for abortion rights.

After four days of low-key testimony before the Senate Judiciary Committee in late July, the Senate confirmed Ginsburg on Aug. 3, 96-3: R 41-3; D 55-0 (ND 41-0, SD 14-0).

The Senate's overwhelming support for Clinton's choice reflected not only Ginsburg's qualities as a candidate but also the president's decision to consult with key senators

during the selection process. This was a break with the recent past, when Republican presidents and the Democratic-controlled Senate often squared off over high court nominations. Ginsburg's confirmation proceeded at a relatively fast pace, with the Senate vote coming a little more than seven weeks after her nomination — roughly half the time it took to confirm Clarence Thomas in 1991. Still, the process was not as speedy as it once was. White, for example, nominated by President John F. Kennedy in 1962, was confirmed within 12 days.

7. Gays in the Military

President Clinton's image and his relations with Congress during the first months of his administration were colored by a dispute over his campaign promise to eliminate the military's ban on homosexuals.

The first major party presidential nominee to openly seek gay support, Clinton had pledged months before he secured the Democratic nomination that he would lift the longstanding ban on gay and lesbian service members. Though Clinton repeated the promise several times during the campaign, it never became a focal point of the Democratic message, and George Bush's campaign did little to highlight it.

But the issue leapt into prominence almost immediately after the election, in part because it was one of the few controversial campaign pledges that Clinton did not either recant or turn over to a committee for study. The issue also rekindled the campaign debate over whether Clinton's avoidance of the draft during the Vietnam War demonstrated a fundamental antipathy toward the U.S. military.

The vast majority of senior military personnel, including Gen. Colin L. Powell Jr., chairman of the Joint Chiefs of Staff, vehemently opposed Clinton's pledge. Clinton's military critics, who maintained that abolition of the gay ban would undermine cohesion within combat units, were supported by many conservative members of Congress, particularly Senate Armed Services Committee Chairman Sam Nunn, D-Ga.

After an uproar that lasted for months and under the threat of being reversed by Congress, Clinton backed down and ordered only minor changes in the ban.

The new policy banned homosexual conduct, and its definition of "conduct" included a service member's private disclosure to a friend of his or her homosexual orientation.

However, under the new policy, recruits no longer would be asked if they were gay. Moreover, investigations of suspected homosexuals could be initiated only by a senior officer acting on the basis of credible information.

But the Senate Armed Services Committee declined to let the issue rest, adding language to the defense authorization bill that sealed the military's gay ban into law. In addition, the committee included in the bill strongly worded findings that homosexuality posed "an unacceptable risk" to morale, order and discipline in the armed forces. These findings were intended to buttress the new policy against anticipated court challenges.

In a key vote during debate on the fiscal 1994 defense authorization bill (S 1298), opponents of the gay ban attempted on Sept. 9 to remove from the bill all language on the issue and to explicitly cede the subject to the president. But that amendment, by Barbara Boxer, D-Calif., was rejected, 33-63: R 3-38; D 30-25 (ND 29-12; SD 1-13). *(House vote 8, p. 40-C)*

8. Strategic Defense

The Clinton administration renamed the Strategic Defense Initiative (SDI), endorsed a less ambitious focus for the anti-missile defense program and dramatically reduced its projected funding.

But the rechristened Ballistic Missile Defense program was not scaled back enough for the Senate. For the second year in a row, the Senate demonstrated its willingness to cut more money from the budget for anti-missile defenses than was requested by the Pentagon or recommended by the Senate Armed Services Committee.

The Senate's action in 1993 reduced funding for the Ballistic Missile Defense program to $2.8 billion, significantly less than the average annual budget of $3.6 billion that Defense Secretary Les Aspin had outlined for the Clinton administration's approach to anti-missile defense.

President Clinton had eliminated the budget increases that President George Bush had planned for the program, requesting $3.8 billion — including $121 million for procurement — instead of the $6.3 billion that Bush had projected for fiscal 1994.

Clinton also reshaped the anti-missile work along lines mandated by Congress in 1991, placing more emphasis on early deployment of ground-based defenses against attacks by a small number of intercontinental-range ballistic missiles or shorter-range "theater" missiles.

It was a far less ambitious approach than that of President Ronald Reagan, who founded SDI in 1983 with a vision of rendering nuclear missiles "impotent and obsolete." The program's original goal was to deploy a shield of anti-missile defenses that could make the United States impregnable to an all-out attack by the Soviet Union.

In drafting the fiscal 1994 defense authorization bill (HR 2401), the Armed Services Committee shifted part of the anti-missile defense request — $253 million sought for the Brilliant Eyes missile detection satellite — to another account, then approved $3.2 billion for the remaining projects.

In a key vote on the defense authorization bill, the Senate on Sept. 9 approved an amendment by Jim Sasser, D-Tenn., to cut the Ballistic Missile Defense program to $2.8 billion, not including the separate funding for Brilliant Eyes. The amendment was adopted 50-48: R 6-36; D 44-12 (ND 36-6; SD 8-6).

Advocates of the cut argued that the anti-missile program was still spending too much on "global" defenses that were relics of the Cold War nuclear competition with Moscow. Arguing the case on fiscal grounds, Sasser, chairman of the Budget Committee, said the biggest threat to U.S. national security was no longer ballistic missiles but a federal budget deficit that "threatens the very survival of our nation."

Opposing the cut, Howell Heflin, D-Ala., argued that even though the Soviet Union was gone, "we are still without any means of defending against attacks from hostile and possibly irrational Third World leaders."

Two staunch backers of the anti-missile program, Republicans Malcolm Wallop, Wyo., and Frank H. Murkowski, Alaska, did not vote.

The Senate's action essentially settled the funding issue because the version of the bill crafted by the House Armed

Services Committee and passed by the House authorized roughly the same amount.

In 1992, Senate Armed Services recommended $4.3 billion for the program for fiscal 1993. But the Senate on a procedural vote in effect endorsed an amendment by Sasser and Dale Bumpers, D-Ark., that would have cut the program by an additional $1 billion. Action on the defense bill was stalled for weeks of negotiations. Eventually, the Senate compromised on $3.8 billion for SDI in fiscal 1993, the level that Clinton requested for fiscal 1994. *(1992 Almanac, p. 498)*

9. Grazing Fees

Working against an unyielding phalanx of Western senators, the Clinton administration tried and failed in 1993 to initiate a plan to more than double grazing fees and impose tough environmental standards on publicly held rangeland. It was a major setback for President Clinton and his Interior secretary, Bruce Babbitt, who kicked off the year proposing to overhaul all public lands policies.

Members of Congress had tried since 1976 to force Western ranchers to pay market prices for leasing federal lands, most of which were in the West. The existing grazing fee rate, based on a formula established by a 1985 executive order by then-President Ronald Reagan, was $1.86 per "animal unit month" — enough forage to feed one cow and calf, five sheep or one horse for a month. That was about one-fifth the amount charged on private lands, although ranchers contended that it did not account for the costs of fences, stock ponds and other amenities that those who used commercial rangeland did not have to pay.

Another concern was the damage done by grazing. On many public lands, lush rangeland had turned to stubble and once-verdant areas near streams were nearly gone.

Nevertheless, Western senators fiercely opposed Clinton's proposals on grazing. At stake were the livelihoods of 27,000 ranchers — a fraction of the nation's ranchers but a politically potent force on an issue that had all the makings of a broader showdown on Western land policies for timber, mining and agriculture.

Malcolm Wallop of Wyoming, the ranking Republican on the Energy and Natural Resources Committee, set the tone early by pushing an amendment to Clinton's budget that would have cut out nearly all the proposed increases. While the amendment was killed, 59-40, on March 23 on a tabling motion by Budget Committee Chairman Jim Sasser, D-Tenn., Western opponents to overhauling public land policy made it clear that they would fight any attempt to impose new burdens on ranchers, miners and farmers.

A week later, Environment and Public Works Committee Chairman Max Baucus, D-Mont., led a small band of Western senators to lobby Clinton to reverse his budget proposals. To their surprise and to the chagrin of environmentalists, Clinton decided to back off on all the fee increases.

For the most part, the move left the proponents of overhauling public land policy looking to Congress to update such laws as the 1872 Mining Law. Still, on grazing, Babbitt had the administrative authority to increase fees without congressional approval.

Babbitt took a step in that direction Aug. 9, saying he would gradually raise grazing fees over three years to $4.28 per animal unit month. But Babbitt angered Western lawmakers and the cattle industry by also proposing an overhaul of rangeland management policies by tying the duration of a grazing permit to a rancher's environmental stewardship record.

On Sept. 14, during Senate debate on the fiscal 1994 appropriations bill for the Interior Department (HR 2520), Western senators argued that Babbitt's proposals were too sweeping to be implemented by executive order. Led by Pete V. Domenici, R-N.M., and Harry Reid, D-Nev., the Western senators pushed through an amendment to prohibit Babbitt from implementing the grazing package during fiscal 1994.

All but three senators from Western, Rocky Mountain or Plains states voted in favor of the one-year moratorium. Even some Easterners who supported grazing fee increases voted with Domenici and Reid, who prevailed 59-40: R 38-5; D 21-35 (ND 14-28, SD 7-7).

The vote demonstrated the unique balance of power in the Senate and the unusual voting allegiances it created. A contentious battle over the entire Interior spending bill ensued. Reid immediately began working on a compromise

Reid

and crafted an amendment that would only increase grazing fees moderately while codifying some of Babbitt's land management proposals.

House negotiators easily approved Reid's amendment in conference committee, while Senate conferees split on a party-line vote. The full House on Oct. 20 affirmed the compromise, 317-106, but it got no further. Using the Senate's unlimited debate rules, 40 Republicans and five Democrats from Western, Rocky Mountain and Plains states kept the Interior bill in a procedural stranglehold for three weeks.

During that time, Democratic sponsors of the grazing fee increase failed three times to cut off the filibuster, so Reid finally agreed on Nov. 9 to withdraw his compromise. In exchange, Domenici dropped the one-year moratorium, ended the filibuster and cleared the way for final passage of the fiscal 1994 Interior spending bill.

Both sides claimed victory. Babbitt retained the power to impose grazing fee increases but acknowledged that, as a result of the Senate's intransigence, he would proceed with extra deliberation and consultation with Western interests before doing so.

10. Ex-Soviet Aid

Patrick J. Leahy, D-Vt., said it was "a real roll of the dice" to bring the fiscal 1994 foreign operations appropriations bill to the Senate floor while Russia was teetering on the brink of political collapse.

The Senate began consideration of the measure (HR 2295) — which included $2.5 billion in aid

for Russia and its neighbors — on Sept. 22, just one day after Russian President Boris N. Yeltsin had thrown his nation into turmoil by disbanding Parliament.

With Yeltsin locked in a test of wills with his hard-line political rivals, Leahy feared that senators would be reluctant to vote for the massive aid package.

But the gamble paid off. The Senate overwhelmingly backed the legislation, handing President Clinton a foreign policy triumph. Clinton had urged the Senate to send a signal of support to the Russian leader.

In a key vote Sept. 23, the Senate approved the foreign operations bill, 88-10: R 36-7; D 52-3; (ND 40-2, SD 12-1).

Leahy, who chaired the Appropriations Subcommittee on Foreign Operations, really had no choice but to press for quick Senate action. The bill's unusual funding formula had created a tight timetable. Of the $2.5 billion in aid for the former Soviet Union, $1.6 billion was in the form of a supplemental appropriation for fiscal 1993.

That money — drawn from unexpended balances of defense and foreign aid funds — would have become unavailable on Sept. 30, the last day of the fiscal year.

Lawmakers ended up acting in time to fully fund the administration's request. Congress cleared the foreign operations bill Sept. 30, and Clinton signed it into law the same day.

Surprisingly, Russia's political chaos was barely mentioned during the Senate debate. The Senate adopted a host of conditions that reflected concerns over various policies being pursued by Moscow, but none were regarded as "killer" amendments that would have prevented disbursement of the aid.

Senators seemed generally content to follow Clinton's lead in backing Yeltsin. After the vote, Leahy told reporters that the Senate's virtual silence on the issue should be read as support for the administration's policy. After all, he said, any senator could have held up the bill.

No one was more pleased by the outcome than Strobe Talbott, the ambassador-at-large for the former Soviet Union. Talbott had been criticized by Leahy and other senators for not adequately consulting with Congress on the massive aid program for the former Soviet republics.

"It's a big victory for American foreign policy," Talbott said after the vote. "It would have been the worst possible signal to in any way pull back."

The administration and Congress remained committed to Yeltsin as a crisis in Moscow reached a bloody climax less than a week later. The standoff ended Oct. 4 as troops loyal to the Russian president launched a military assault on the Russian Parliament building, which had been occupied for two weeks by Yeltsin's opponents. *(House vote 4, p. 37-C)*

11. Abortion

From the beginning, Sen. Barbara A. Mikulski, D-Md., had insisted that she had the votes to lift the long-running ban on using federal dollars to pay for most abortions for poor women.

The House had been unable to kill the Hyde amendment, named after sponsor Henry J. Hyde, R-Ill. Instead, the House voted to relax slightly the restrictions on Medicaid, the federal-state health insurance program for the poor, allowing it to pay for abortions only in cases of rape and incest, as well as when the woman's life was in danger, a longstanding exception.

When the revised Hyde language came to the Senate as part of a spending bill (HR 2518) for the departments of Labor, Health and Human Services, and Education, Mikulski persuaded the Senate Appropriations Committee to strike it.

The committee's action would have allowed poor women to receive abortions under most circumstances — paid for by Medicaid.

Mikulski and the four other female Democratic senators — all abortion rights supporters — believed they could maintain that position on the floor. The Senate had always been more liberal than the House when it came to abortions paid for by Medicaid. For the previous decade, the House had usually voted to restrict Medicaid from paying for abortions except when the life of the woman was in danger. In the Senate, members had usually voted to allow Medicaid to pay for abortions in cases of rape and incest as well. But in conference, the House had always prevailed.

Mikulski

In 1993, female lawmakers in the Senate wanted to move beyond their usual position and drop all restrictions without any compromise. They worried that if they offered a compromise and lost, it would hurt attempts to insure abortion in President Clinton's universal health-care plan.

But Mikulski's calculation proved way off the mark. On Sept. 28, when abortion opponents forced a vote on the Appropriations Committee proposal to strike the Hyde language from the House-passed bill, the Senate voted it down, 40-59: R 6-38; D 34-21 (ND 31-11, SD 3-10).

In the end, 21 Democrats sided with 38 Republicans to defeat the amendment. While some of those Democrats supported a woman's right to an abortion, they would not go so far as to allow taxpayers' funds to be used to pay for the procedure.

The vote meant that the House language would stay in the bill, prohibiting Medicaid from paying for abortions except in cases of rape and incest and when the life of the woman was in danger. The vote also was a key test of clout for the five Democratic female senators, working together as a bloc. The large majority against federal funding suggested that future proposals — particularly on a health insurance reform bill affecting all women — would run into similar obstacles in the Senate.

Abortion rights supporters fared better on another abortion-related bill to make it a federal crime to intimidate by force or threat of force a woman seeking to obtain an abortion, or abortion clinic workers. The Senate passed that bill (S 636 — S Rept 103-117) on Nov. 16 by 69-30. But just as in the House, the clinic access debate turned more on the issue of free speech vs. fear of terrorism, rather than on the fundamental question of abortion.

At bottom, both House and Senate were willing to go only so far to protect and ensure access to abortion services. *(House vote 5, p. 38-C)*

12. Somalia/Peacekeeping

Amid a growing controversy over the U.S. role in international peacekeeping missions, the Senate voted Oct. 15 to effectively cut off funding for participation by U.S. forces in the United Nations' Somalia operation after March 31, 1994.

President Clinton already had agreed to that deadline, but only in the face of a growing threat that Congress might insist on an even earlier U.S. pullout.

In February, when the mission still retained broad congressional support, the Senate by voice vote adopted S J

Res 45, authorizing the initial phase of the humanitarian mission that had been launched in December 1992 by President George Bush. *(1992 Almanac, p. 535)*

But most of the 20,000 U.S. troops initially deployed were withdrawn from Somalia by May 4, when the military mission was handed over to a multilateral U.N. force.

Congressional approval for the U.S. commitment began to wane as troops loyal to Somali warlord Gen. Mohammed Farah Aidid began a relatively low-level but deadly cam-

paign of harassment against U.S. and other U.N. forces in the Somali capital of Mogadishu.

On Sept. 9, the Senate adopted 90-7 a non-binding amendment by Appropriations Committee Chairman Robert C. Byrd, D-W.Va. — attached to the defense authorization bill (HR 2401, formerly S 1298) — urging Clinton to report to Congress by Oct. 15 on the objectives of the Somalia operation and to seek congressional approval if he wanted to continue the deployment beyond Nov. 15.

The issue boiled over after 18 U.S. soldiers were killed Oct. 3 in a bloody battle with Aidid's forces as they tried to arrest several leaders of Aidid's clan. When the Appropriations panel marked up the defense appropriations bill (HR 3116) the following day, Byrd announced that he would force a Senate vote on an amendment to the bill intended to force an end to U.S. participation in the Somalia operation early in 1994.

Majority Leader George J. Mitchell, D-Maine, Armed Services Committee Chairman Sam Nunn, D-Ga., and other Senate leaders negotiated with Byrd and with the White House to work out a compromise Somalia amendment, which the Senate added to the defense appropriations bill Oct. 15.

The compromise measure endorsed Clinton's March 31 pullout date but cut off most U.S. funds after that. In a key vote Oct. 15, the Senate approved the compromise amendment, offered by Byrd, 76-23: R 24-20; D 52-3 (ND 38-3; SD 14-0).

Aside from writing into law Clinton's acquiescence in congressional demands for a firm end point to the Somalia deployment, the Byrd amendment also was significant on several other levels. It highlighted the opposition of many Republicans to such multinational peacekeeping ventures, and it marked the first time since the Vietnam War that either chamber had voted to cut off funds for an ongoing overseas military operation.

Before the Byrd amendment was adopted, the Senate first quashed an effort to mandate an earlier withdrawal date, voting 61-38 to table (kill) an amendment by John McCain, R-Ariz., to require a "prompt" withdrawal of U.S. forces.

A week after the Somalia showdown, Clinton survived another confrontation with GOP critics, as the Senate defeated, 33-65, an amendment that would have required congressional approval before the president placed U.S. forces under foreign command.

But deep dissatisfaction with Clinton's peacekeeping policies was underscored by passage of non-binding resolutions urging the administration to come to Congress before dispatching troops on such missions, including to Haiti and Bosnia. *(House vote 11, p. 42-C)*

13. Ethics Enforcement

The Constitution gave each chamber of Congress the power to "punish its members for disorderly behavior." After more than 200 years, however, the House and Senate could not shake the public perception that misbehavior was rampant on Capitol Hill, but punishment was not.

When ABC News asked a sample of Americans in August about allegations that Ways and Means Committee Chairman Dan Rostenkowski, D-Ill., had embezzled cash from the House Post Office, 68 percent said that sort of activity represented "business as usual in Congress."

It was in this atmosphere of public distrust that the Senate confronted sexual harassment allegations against Bob Packwood, R-Ore., first revealed in The Washington Post in November 1992.

Reconstituted with all new members in 1993, the Senate Ethics Committee toughened its image under its most prosecutorial-minded chairman in years, Richard H. Bryan, D-Nev. Within two weeks of being named, the panel barred questions about the Packwood accusers' sexual histories after hints that he might raise them in his defense, and it expanded its inquiry to include allegations that he tried to intimidate his accusers. Though accusers feared that the committee would limit its probe to the 11 women named by the Post, it mailed letters to every woman who had ever worked for Packwood.

After interviewing 150 witnesses, the committee in October prepared to wrap up the first phase of its inquiry so it could decide whether to hold public hearings. Its final task involved taking a deposition from Packwood.

But during his testimony, Packwood referred to his personal diaries. Despite concerns about the personal nature of such documents, the committee demanded to see

Rostenkowski   **Packwood**   **Bryan**

them. It was the clearest signal yet of a tough new era. Packwood initially allowed the panel to review them and copy relevant passages. But he balked when committee aides requested passages raising questions about whether he traded official favors for job offers to his estranged wife when he was in divorce court trying to minimize his alimony.

So the committee subpoenaed the diaries and asked the Senate to go to court to enforce the demand. Embodied in a resolution (S Res 153), the request sparked a wrenching fight unlike any the Senate had seen in years.

Packwood accused the committee of prying into the sexual lives of other lawmakers. Bryan accused Packwood of possible criminal acts. Members begged the two sides to compromise to avoid what one called "a floor debacle" — to no avail.

For 15 hours on Nov. 1-2, with a majority of senators present most of the time, the Senate debated fine legal points and big constitutional issues. Beneath the surface

were memories of the Anita Hill-Clarence Thomas imbroglio. *(1991 Almanac, p. 274)*

Bryan coolly stated the case against Packwood, who responded with insulted anger. Ethics members from both parties accused Packwood and his lawyers of bad faith. Freshman Democratic women insisted that the Senate take a hard line against sexual harassment by backing the committee.

Packwood's few public defenders — Republicans Alan K. Simpson, Wyo., Arlen Specter, Pa., and John C. Danforth, Mo. — protested that his privacy rights were being trampled. The precedent, they said, would haunt all senators forever.

For all the debate's complex facets, however, the mindset of the Senate was best framed by Ethics Committee Vice Chairman Mitch McConnell, R-Ky. "A lot of people — in the media, in the public — think that we can't handle the job of disciplining our fellow members and guarding the integrity of this institution," he said. "The question before us today is really whether we are up to the job."

It was clear from the start that Packwood's only hope was to limit the scope of the subpoena. On the second day, he offered to turn over all entries related to the sexual charges and to the job offers; an independent examiner would make sure he turned over everything required.

The committee refused the offer. Bryan said it would have required the examiner to ignore any other misdeeds that might be in the diaries. Nor would the examiner know for sure what was relevant. He insisted that the precedent set by the sweeping subpoena was limited because Packwood had introduced the diaries into the proceeding, and then let the committee peruse them and find other possible misdeeds that required further study.

On Nov. 2, Simpson offered the pivotal amendment — to limit the subpoena to "relevant" entries. He argued that the discovery process in civil proceedings was limited to relevant evidence. The Ethics Committee countered that its proceeding was more akin to that of a grand jury, which had broad subpoena powers.

In the end, the Senate decided that it could not risk the appearance that it treated its own more leniently than the government treated other citizens. The vote against Simpson's amendment, and the rebuke of Packwood, was overwhelming — 23-77: R 22-22; D 1-55 (ND 1-41, SD 0-14).

The Senate then approved the resolution to enforce the subpoena by 94-6.

14. Crime Bill/Assault Weapons

The annual Senate showdown over crime took an unusual turn in 1993 when key Republicans and Democrats struck a deal: Instead of fighting over whose approach to crime-fighting was more worthy, they stitched together a bill in early November that included enough money to make both sides happy. The result was a $22.3 billion measure (HR 3355) that included Republican prison proposals and Democratic rehabilitation efforts, as well as funds that both parties wanted for 100,000 new police officers.

Excess baggage was tossed overboard. The two sides agreed that they could not agree on how to limit death penalty appeals, so they dealt with that Republican issue separately, quietly killing it for the year and probably for the 103rd Congress. They also dealt separately with the Democrats' so-called Brady bill (HR 1025 — PL 103-159),

a five-day waiting period for handguns, which made it to the president's desk.

Only one thing stood in the way of the crime bill's final passage: the insistence of gun-control advocates, most of them Democrats, on a semiautomatic assault weapons ban. Though a narrow Senate majority had favored such a move since 1990, gun-control opponents might have been willing to filibuster the crime bill to death had it included a ban.

Gun-control advocates decided to risk it. Backed by the Clinton administration, Dianne Feinstein, D-Calif., crafted a compromise that was stricter than one successfully offered by Dennis DeConcini, D-Ariz., in 1990 and less strict than one advocated by the chamber's biggest anti-gun exponent, Howard M. Metzenbaum, D-Ohio. Feinstein's proposal banned the manufacture, sale and possession of 19 specific weapons, as well as so-called "copycats" and most 10-bullet-plus feeders. It explicitly exempted 650 named sporting and hunting guns and existing semiautomatic assault weapons.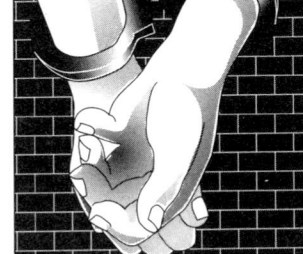

"It really comes down to a question of blood or guts — the blood of innocent people or the Senate of the United States having the guts to do what we should do when we take that oath to protect the welfare of our citizens," Feinstein said, as she and other advocates recounted the horror of recent random attacks with assault weapons.

Opponents reiterated their arguments — that toughening and enforcing existing criminal laws was the better solution; that relatively few crimes involved assault weapons; that knives and blunt objects killed more people than rifles; and that gun bans gave criminals an edge over law-abiding citizens seeking to protect themselves.

But their most compelling argument did not involve the amendment's merits. "This particular amendment could cause us to lose this bill," said Orrin G. Hatch, R-Utah. Added Phil Gramm, R-Texas, "The fragile alliance we put together could be torn apart."

The threats proved empty after the Senate rejected a motion to kill the amendment on Nov. 9 by a 49-51 vote (with Ben Nighthorse Campbell, D-Colo., switching his 1991 House position to vote for the amendment at the last minute). It became clear that a filibuster would not materialize the next day, when the two parties late on Nov. 10 struck a deal to allow the amendment and the bill to come to a final vote.

In the end, five Republicans who had voted to table Feinstein's amendment switched sides to vote for it, and the amendment carried on Nov. 17 by a comfortable margin, 56-43: R 10-34; D 46-9 (ND 38-3, SD 8-6).

Whether the gun ban would survive into law was very much in doubt. The House, by 247-177, had voted against a ban in 1991. DeConcini said he would not be surprised if the same thing happened again. He had good reason to say so: The National Rifle Association (NRA) was quite influential in the House. And the Senate bill contained many get-tough provisions that liberals abhorred; faced with a chance to scrap them, the Democrats might just be willing to dump the assault weapons ban.

Then again, the Senate vote — cast in the throes of a tenuous compromise on the rest of the crime bill — demon-

strated anew the mood in that chamber for gun control. Combined with the Brady bill vote to impose a waiting period on handgun purchases, the Senate once again put the NRA forces on the defensive.

15. Handgun Control

It took seven years of debate and a harrowing final week of political maneuvering, but the so-called Brady bill (HR 1025 — PL 103-159) finally became law as Congress adjourned for the year. Public pressure for the well-known handgun waiting-period measure was instrumental in breaking an eleventh-hour legislative logjam and passing the first major gun control legislation since 1968.

The bottleneck was in the Senate. The House had passed its version of the bill Nov. 10. But Senate Republicans led a filibuster against the bill, which imposed a five-day waiting period for handgun purchases and led to a nationwide system

of instant checks of criminal records to make sure guns were not sold to felons or other unqualified buyers. The bill was named after former White House press secretary James S. Brady, who was wounded during the 1981 assassination attempt on President Ronald Reagan.

Advocates said the measure would save lives by keeping guns away from some potential killers. But critics complained that it would simply inconvenience law-abiding gun owners while doing little or nothing to fight crime, and many on both sides described the bill as a modest measure that at best would make only a small dent in crime.

Throughout the week of Nov. 15, Senate Minority Leader Bob Dole, R-Kan., had negotiated with Majority Leader George J. Mitchell, D-Maine, and Senate Judiciary Committee Chairman Joseph R. Biden Jr., D-Del., over how to proceed. They eventually settled on a compromise version of the bill, to be voted on if supporters could muster the 60 votes for cloture needed to limit debate.

When they failed on two cloture votes on Nov. 19, many observers declared the bill dead for the year. But the legislation had a huge following. Brady's wife, Sarah, expressed frustration at the prospect of letting the bill die for the year, as did President Clinton. So did the public. And that unsettled some Republicans who had voted against cloture but did not want to be blamed for killing the bill.

Their concerns sent Dole back into negotiations. He emerged with a version that was only superficially different from the legislation Republicans had filibustered the night before. Instead of ending the waiting period after five years, the new compromise called for a four-year sunset and gave the attorney general the authority to extend it into a fifth year.

That version carried the Senate on Nov. 20, when more Republicans agreed to abandon the filibuster. The bill passed by 63-36: R 16-28; D 47-8 (ND 38-3, SD 9-5).

Republicans who voted against cloture but for final passage were Christopher S. Bond, Mo.; Daniel R. Coats, Ind.; William S. Cohen, Maine; Kay Bailey Hutchison, Texas; Richard G. Lugar, Ind.; Bob Packwood, Ore.; and Strom Thurmond, S.C. Meanwhile, Democrat Patrick J. Leahy of Vermont voted for cloture then voted against the bill.

More intrigue followed. During a raucous House-Senate negotiating session Nov. 22, Biden showed little interest in fighting for many aspects of the Senate version. Conferees essentially took the House bill intact. But while the House readily agreed to the conference version shortly after midnight, Dole balked in the Senate, accusing Democrats of abandoning the Senate's position.

A tense period ensued, with Mitchell threatening to reconvene the Senate after Thanksgiving to consider cloture votes. But Republicans did not want to be blamed for bucking public opinion by thwarting the bill. Opponents agreed to let the bill go through the Senate by voice vote Nov. 24 on the condition that Congress consider revising the law in 1994. *(House vote 12, p. 42-C)*

16. NAFTA Implementation

When the Senate on Nov. 20 passed the bill (HR 3450) implementing the North American Free Trade Agreement (NAFTA), the controversial trade deal had cleared its last hurdle and a wrenching national debate about trade policy had come to an end.

The outcome in the Senate was never in doubt, and the debate never reached the intensity it did in the House. That was because Republicans, who overwhelmingly supported the agreement, were proportionately more numerous in the Senate. Also, the body as a whole was less

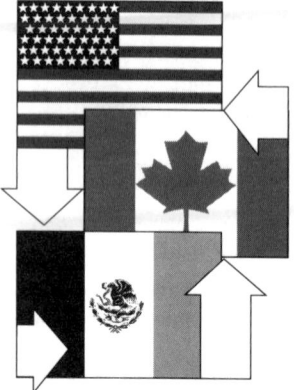

susceptible to the localized pressures for protection against foreign competition that nearly sank the trade deal in the House. *(House vote 13, p. 43-C)*

But the Senate vote was significant, nonetheless. It suggested that Clinton's victory on NAFTA in the House, achieved as it was through furious deal-cutting and bare-knuckles lobbying, was not an isolated event, owed exclusively to the persuasive powers of the president. The White House expended virtually no effort or time rounding up votes in the Senate. Yet NAFTA passed in that chamber by a comfortable margin, 61-38: R 34-10; D 27-28 (ND 18-23, SD 9-5).

The Senate vote exhibited the same divisions that made NAFTA such a tough sell in the House. Clinton once again owed his victory more to opposition Republicans than to members of his own party; Southern Democrats, as in the House, were key, however.

Senate NAFTA opponents included an unusual mix of liberals and conservatives. Many were from states that had suffered severe manufacturing job losses or had industries that expected fiercer competition as trade barriers with Mexico were removed. Conservatives opposed the agreement because they said it would create a multinational bureaucracy that would undermine U.S. sovereignty.

More representative of the sentiment in the Senate was that expressed by Democrats Edward M. Kennedy of Massachusetts and Tom Harkin of Iowa. Both had close ties to organized labor but voted for the agreement because, they said, Mexico offered their states expanded export opportunities. ∎

KEY

Y	Voted for (yea).
#	Paired for.
+	Announced for.
N	Voted against (nay).
X	Paired against.
−	Announced against.
P	Voted "present."
C	Voted "present" to avoid possible conflict of interest.
?	Did not vote or otherwise make a position known.

Democrats   *Republicans*

State / Senator	1	2	3	4	5	6	7	8
ALABAMA								
Heflin	Y	Y	N	Y	Y	Y	N	N
Shelby	N	N	N	N	Y	Y	N	N
ALASKA								
Murkowski	N	N	N	N	N	Y	−	?
Stevens	N	N	N	N	Y	Y	N	N
ARIZONA								
DeConcini	Y	Y	N	Y	N	Y	Y	Y
McCain	N	N	Y	N	N	Y	N	N
ARKANSAS								
Bumpers	Y	Y	Y	Y	Y	Y	N	Y
Pryor	Y	Y	Y	Y	Y	Y	N	Y
CALIFORNIA								
Boxer	Y	Y	Y	Y	Y	Y	Y	Y
Feinstein	Y	Y	Y	Y	Y	Y	Y	Y
COLORADO								
Campbell	Y	Y	Y	Y	Y	Y	Y	Y
Brown	N	N	N	N	N	Y	N	N
CONNECTICUT								
Dodd	Y	Y	Y	Y	Y	Y	Y	N
Lieberman	Y	Y	Y	Y	Y	Y	Y	N
DELAWARE								
Biden	Y	Y	Y	Y	Y	Y	Y	Y
Roth	N	N	N	N	N	Y	N	N
FLORIDA								
Graham	Y	Y	Y	Y	Y	Y	N	N
Mack	N	N	N	N	N	Y	N	N
GEORGIA								
Nunn	Y	Y	N	Y	N	Y	N	N
Coverdell	N	N	N	N	N	Y	N	N
HAWAII								
Akaka	Y	Y	Y	Y	Y	Y	Y	Y
Inouye	?	Y	Y	Y	Y	Y	Y	N
IDAHO								
Craig	N	N	N	N	N	Y	N	N
Kempthorne	N	N	N	N	N	Y	N	N
ILLINOIS								
Moseley-Braun	Y	Y	Y	Y	Y	Y	Y	Y
Simon	Y	Y	Y	Y	Y	Y	Y	Y
INDIANA								
Coats	N	N	N	N	N	Y	N	N
Lugar	N	N	N	N	N	Y	N	N

State / Senator	1	2	3	4	5	6	7	8
IOWA								
Harkin	Y	Y	Y	Y	Y	Y	Y	Y
Grassley	N	N	N	N	N	Y	N	Y
KANSAS								
Dole	N	N	N	N	N	Y	N	N
Kassebaum	N	N	Y	N	N	Y	N	Y
KENTUCKY								
Ford	Y	Y	Y	Y	Y	Y	N	Y
McConnell	N	N	N	N	N	Y	N	N
LOUISIANA								
Breaux	Y	Y	Y	N	Y	Y	N	Y
Johnston	Y	Y	Y	N	Y	Y	N	Y
MAINE								
Mitchell	Y	Y	Y	Y	Y	Y	N	Y
Cohen	N	N	Y	N	N	Y	N	Y
MARYLAND								
Mikulski	Y	Y	Y	Y	Y	Y	Y	Y
Sarbanes	Y	Y	Y	Y	Y	Y	Y	Y
MASSACHUSETTS								
Kennedy	Y	Y	Y	Y	Y	Y	Y	Y
Kerry	Y	Y	Y	Y	Y	Y	Y	Y
MICHIGAN								
Levin	Y	Y	Y	Y	Y	Y	Y	Y
Riegle	Y	Y	Y	+	+	Y	Y	Y
MINNESOTA								
Wellstone	Y	Y	Y	Y	Y	Y	Y	Y
Durenberger	N	N	Y	N	Y	Y	N	Y
MISSISSIPPI								
Cochran	N	N	N	N	N	Y	N	N
Lott	N	N	N	N	N	Y	N	N
MISSOURI								
Bond	N	N	N	N	N	Y	N	N
Danforth	N	N	N	N	N	Y	N	N
MONTANA								
Baucus	Y	Y	Y	Y	Y	Y	N	Y
Burns	N	N	N	N	N	Y	N	N
NEBRASKA								
Exon	Y	Y	Y	Y	N	Y	N	N
Kerrey	Y	Y	Y	N	Y	N	Y	Y
NEVADA								
Bryan	Y	Y	Y	N	Y	Y	N	N
Reid	Y	Y	Y	Y	Y	Y	N	Y

State / Senator	1	2	3	4	5	6	7	8
NEW HAMPSHIRE								
Gregg	N	N	N	N	N	Y	N	N
Smith	N	N	N	N	N	N	N	N
NEW JERSEY								
Bradley	Y	Y	Y	Y	Y	Y	Y	Y
Lautenberg	Y	Y	Y	N	Y	Y	Y	Y
NEW MEXICO								
Bingaman	Y	Y	Y	Y	Y	Y	Y	N
Domenici	N	N	N	N	N	Y	N	N
NEW YORK								
Moynihan	Y	Y	Y	Y	Y	Y	Y	Y
D'Amato	N	N	N	N	N	Y	Y	N
NORTH CAROLINA								
Faircloth	N	N	N	N	N	Y	N	N
Helms	N	N	N	N	N	N	N	N
NORTH DAKOTA								
Conrad	Y	Y	Y	Y	Y	Y	N	Y
Dorgan	Y	Y	Y	Y	Y	Y	N	Y
OHIO								
Glenn	Y	Y	Y	Y	Y	Y	?	Y
Metzenbaum	Y	Y	Y	Y	Y	Y	Y	Y
OKLAHOMA								
Boren	Y	Y	Y	Y	Y	Y	N	N
Nickles	N	N	N	N	N	N	N	N
OREGON								
Hatfield	N	N	N	N	N	Y	N	N
Packwood	N	N	N	N	N	Y	N	N
PENNSYLVANIA								
Wofford	Y	Y	Y	Y	Y	Y	Y	Y
Specter	N	N	?	?	Y	Y	N	N
RHODE ISLAND								
Pell	Y	Y	Y	Y	Y	Y	Y	Y
Chafee	N	N	Y	Y	Y	Y	Y	Y
SOUTH CAROLINA								
Hollings	Y	Y	N	Y	N	Y	N	Y
Thurmond	N	N	N	N	N	Y	N	N
SOUTH DAKOTA								
Daschle	Y	Y	Y	Y	Y	Y	N	Y
Pressler	N	N	Y	N	N	Y	N	N
TENNESSEE								
Mathews	Y	Y	Y	Y	Y	Y	N	Y
Sasser	Y	Y	Y	Y	Y	Y	N	Y

State / Senator	1	2	3	4	5	6	7	8
TEXAS								
Gramm	N	N	N	N	N	Y	N	N
Hutchison				N	N	Y	−	N
UTAH								
Bennett	N	N	N	N	N	Y	N	N
Hatch	N	N	N	N	N	Y	N	N
VERMONT								
Leahy	Y	Y	Y	Y	Y	Y	Y	Y
Jeffords	N	N	Y	N	Y	Y	Y	Y
VIRGINIA								
Robb	Y	Y	Y	Y	Y	Y	N	Y
Warner	N	N	N	N	N	Y	N	N
WASHINGTON								
Murray	Y	Y	Y	+	Y	Y	Y	Y
Gorton	N	N	N	N	N	Y	N	N
WEST VIRGINIA								
Byrd	Y	Y	Y	Y	N	Y	N	Y
Rockefeller	Y	Y	Y	Y	Y	Y	N	Y
WISCONSIN								
Feingold	Y	Y	Y	Y	Y	Y	Y	Y
Kohl	Y	Y	Y	Y	Y	Y	N	Y
WYOMING								
Simpson	N	−	−	N	N	Y	N	N
Wallop	N	N	N	N	N	Y	−	−

ND   Northern Democrats   SD   Southern Democrats

Southern states - Ala., Ark., Fla., Ga., Ky., La., Miss., N.C., Okla., S.C., Tenn., Texas, Va.

Following are 1993 votes selected by Congressional Quarterly as key votes (Senate key votes, p. 50-C; explanations of key votes, p. 36-C). Original vote number is provided in parentheses.

1. H Con Res 64. Fiscal 1994 Budget Resolution/Adoption. Adoption of the concurrent resolution to set binding budget levels for the fiscal year ending Sept. 30, 1994: budget authority, $1.505 trillion; outlays, $1.498 trillion; revenues, $1.251 trillion; deficit, $247.5 billion. Adopted 54-45: R 0-43; D 54-2 (ND 41-0, SD 13-2), March 25, 1993. (Senate vote 83.) A "yea" was a vote in support of the president's position.

2. HR 1335. Fiscal 1993 Supplemental Appropriations/Cloture. Motion to invoke cloture (thus limiting debate) on the bill to provide $12.2 billion in new budget authority and $3.1 billion in trust fund spending to implement the administration's compromise stimulus package to help in the economic recovery. The funds would be designated as emergency spending, making them exempt from discretionary spending caps. Motion rejected 56-43: R 0-42; D 56-1 (ND 42-0, SD 14-1), April 21, 1993. (Senate vote 105.) Three-fifths of the total Senate (60) is required to invoke cloture. A "yea" was a vote in support of the president's position.

3. S 3. Campaign Finance/Passage. Passage of the bill to encourage federal candidates to abide by voluntary spending limits by providing benefits such as reduced broadcast and mailing rates. Candidates who reject spending limits would be subject to a new federal tax on campaigns equal to the highest corporate rate, now 34 percent. Passed 60-38: R 7-35; D 53-3 (ND 42-0, SD 11-3), June 17, 1993. (Senate vote 158.) A "yea" was a vote in support of the president's position.

4. HR 2264. Fiscal 1994 Budget-Reconciliation/Passage. Passage of the bill to raise taxes by $243 billion, cut spending by $256 billion and reduce the deficit by $499 billion over five years by tracking President Clinton's economic proposals. Passed 50-49: R 0-43; D 49-6 (ND 38-3, SD 11-3), with Vice President Al Gore casting a "yea" vote, June 25, 1993. (In the session that began and the Congressional Record dated June 24.) (Senate vote 190.) A "yea" was a vote in support of the president's position.

5. HR 2010. National Service/Passage. Passage of the bill to authorize $300 million in fiscal 1994, $500 million in fiscal 1995 and $700 million in fiscal 1996 for the National Service program, which would provide people age 17 or older with $4,725 a year for up to two years in education awards in return for work in community service programs. Passed 58-41: R 7-37; D 51-4 (ND 38-3, SD 13-1), Aug. 3, 1993. (Senate vote 231.) A "yea" was a vote in support of the president's position.

6. Ginsburg Confirmation. Confirmation of Ruth Bader Ginsburg as an associate justice of the Supreme Court of the United States, replacing retired Associate Justice Byron R. White. Confirmed 96-3: R 41-3; D 55-0 (ND 41-0, SD 14-0), Aug. 3, 1993. (Senate vote 232.) A "yea" was a vote in support of the president's position.

7. S 1298. Fiscal 1994 Defense Authorization/Gay Ban. Boxer, D-Calif., amendment to strike language in the bill regarding homosexuals in the military and to express the sense of Congress that the policy regarding the subject should be determined by the president. Rejected 33-63: R 3-38; D 30-25 (ND 29-12, SD 1-13), Sept. 9, 1993. (Senate vote 250.)

8. S 1298. Fiscal 1994 Defense Authorization/Strategic Weapons. Sasser, D-Tenn., amendment to cut the Ballistic Missile Defense program from $3.4 billion to $3 billion. Adopted 50-48: R 6-36; D 44-12 (ND 36-6, SD 8-6), Sept. 9, 1993. (Senate vote 251.) A "nay" was a vote in support of the president's position.

SENATE KEY VOTES 9, 10, 11, 12, 13, 14, 15, 16

	9	10	11	12	13	14	15	16
ALABAMA								
Heflin	Y	Y	N	Y	N	N	N	N
Shelby	Y	Y	N	Y	N	N	N	N
ALASKA								
Murkowski	Y	Y	N	N	Y	N	N	Y
Stevens	Y	Y	Y	Y	N	N	N	N
ARIZONA								
DeConcini	Y	Y	N	Y	N	Y	Y	Y
McCain	Y	Y	N	N	N	N	N	Y
ARKANSAS								
Bumpers	N	Y	Y	Y	N	Y	Y	Y
Pryor	N	Y	?	Y	N	Y	Y	Y
CALIFORNIA								
Boxer	N	Y	Y	Y	N	Y	Y	N
Feinstein	Y	Y	Y	+	N	Y	Y	N
COLORADO								
Campbell	Y	Y	Y	Y	N	Y	N	N
Brown	Y	Y	N	N	Y	Y	N	Y
CONNECTICUT								
Dodd	Y	Y	Y	Y	N	Y	N	Y
Lieberman	N	Y	Y	Y	N	Y	Y	Y
DELAWARE								
Biden	N	Y	N	Y	N	Y	Y	Y
Roth	N	N	N	N	N	Y	Y	Y
FLORIDA								
Graham	N	Y	N	Y	N	Y	Y	Y
Mack	Y	Y	N	N	N	N	N	Y
GEORGIA								
Nunn	N	Y	N	Y	N	Y	Y	Y
Coverdell	Y	Y	N	Y	N	Y	N	N
HAWAII								
Akaka	N	Y	Y	Y	N	Y	Y	N
Inouye	Y	Y	Y	Y	N	Y	Y	N
IDAHO								
Craig	Y	N	N	N	Y	N	N	N
Kempthorne	Y	N	N	N	Y	N	N	N
ILLINOIS								
Moseley-Braun	N	Y	Y	Y	N	Y	Y	Y
Simon	N	Y	Y	Y	N	Y	Y	Y
INDIANA								
Coats	Y	Y	N	N	N	Y	Y	Y
Lugar	Y	Y	N	Y	N	Y	Y	Y

	9	10	11	12	13	14	15	16
IOWA								
Harkin	N	Y	Y	Y	N	Y	Y	Y
Grassley	N	Y	N	N	N	N	N	Y
KANSAS								
Dole	Y	Y	N	Y	Y	N	N	Y
Kassebaum	Y	Y	N	Y	N	Y	Y	Y
KENTUCKY								
Ford	Y	Y	N	Y	N	Y	Y	N
McConnell	Y	Y	N	Y	N	N	N	Y
LOUISIANA								
Breaux	Y	?	N	Y	N	N	N	Y
Johnston	N	Y	N	Y	N	N	N	Y
MAINE								
Mitchell	N	Y	Y	Y	N	Y	Y	Y
Cohen	N	Y	Y	Y	N	N	Y	N
MARYLAND								
Mikulski	N	Y	Y	Y	N	Y	Y	N
Sarbanes	N	Y	Y	Y	N	Y	Y	N
MASSACHUSETTS								
Kennedy	N	Y	Y	Y	N	Y	Y	Y
Kerry	N	Y	Y	Y	N	Y	Y	Y
MICHIGAN								
Levin	N	Y	Y	Y	N	Y	Y	N
Riegle	N	Y	Y	Y	N	Y	Y	N
MINNESOTA								
Wellstone	N	Y	Y	Y	N	Y	Y	Y
Durenberger	Y	Y	N	Y	Y	N	Y	Y
MISSISSIPPI								
Cochran	Y	Y	N	Y	N	N	N	Y
Lott	Y	Y	N	N	Y	N	N	Y
MISSOURI								
Bond	Y	Y	N	Y	N	Y	N	Y
Danforth	Y	Y	N	Y	Y	Y	Y	Y
MONTANA								
Baucus	Y	Y	Y	N	Y	N	Y	Y
Burns	Y	Y	N	Y	N	N	N	N
NEBRASKA								
Exon	N	Y	N	Y	N	Y	Y	N
Kerrey	Y	Y	Y	Y	N	Y	Y	Y
NEVADA								
Bryan	Y	Y	N	Y	N	N	N	N
Reid	Y	Y	N	Y	N	N	Y	N

	9	10	11	12	13	14	15	16
NEW HAMPSHIRE								
Gregg	Y	Y	N	N	N	N	N	Y
Smith	Y	N	N	N	N	N	N	N
NEW JERSEY								
Bradley	N	Y	Y	N	N	Y	Y	Y
Lautenberg	N	Y	Y	Y	N	Y	Y	N
NEW MEXICO								
Bingaman	Y	Y	N	Y	Y	Y	Y	Y
Domenici	Y	Y	N	Y	N	N	Y	Y
NEW YORK								
Moynihan	Y	Y	Y	Y	N	Y	Y	N
D'Amato	Y	Y	N	N	Y	N	N	N
NORTH CAROLINA								
Faircloth	Y	N	N	Y	N	N	N	N
Helms	Y	N	N	N	Y	N	N	N
NORTH DAKOTA								
Conrad	Y	Y	N	Y	N	Y	Y	N
Dorgan	Y	Y	N	Y	N	?	?	?
OHIO								
Glenn	N	Y	Y	Y	N	Y	Y	N
Metzenbaum	N	Y	Y	Y	N	Y	Y	N
OKLAHOMA								
Boren	Y	Y	N	Y	N	Y	Y	Y
Nickles	Y	Y	N	N	N	N	N	Y
OREGON								
Hatfield	Y	Y	N	Y	N	Y	Y	Y
Packwood	Y	Y	Y	Y	Y	Y	Y	Y
PENNSYLVANIA								
Wofford	N	Y	N	Y	N	Y	Y	N
Specter	N	Y	Y	Y	N	N	Y	N
RHODE ISLAND								
Pell	N	Y	Y	Y	N	Y	Y	Y
Chafee	Y	Y	Y	Y	N	Y	Y	Y
SOUTH CAROLINA								
Hollings	Y	N	Y	Y	N	N	N	N
Thurmond	Y	Y	N	Y	N	Y	N	Y
SOUTH DAKOTA								
Daschle	Y	Y	N	Y	N	Y	Y	Y
Pressler	Y	Y	N	N	Y	N	N	Y
TENNESSEE								
Mathews	Y	Y	N	Y	N	Y	Y	Y
Sasser	N	Y	N	Y	N	N	Y	N

	9	10	11	12	13	14	15	16
TEXAS								
Gramm	?	Y	N	Y	N	Y	N	Y
Hutchison	Y	Y	N	Y	N	N	Y	Y
UTAH								
Bennett	Y	Y	N	Y	N	N	N	Y
Hatch	Y	Y	N	Y	N	N	N	Y
VERMONT								
Leahy	N	Y	Y	Y	N	Y	N	Y
Jeffords	N	Y	Y	Y	N	Y	Y	Y
VIRGINIA								
Robb	N	Y	Y	Y	N	Y	Y	Y
Warner	Y	Y	N	Y	N	N	Y	Y
WASHINGTON								
Murray	N	Y	Y	Y	N	Y	Y	Y
Gorton	Y	Y	N	N	N	N	N	Y
WEST VIRGINIA								
Byrd	N	N	N	Y	N	Y	Y	N
Rockefeller	N	Y	Y	Y	N	Y	Y	N
WISCONSIN								
Feingold	N	Y	Y	N	N	Y	Y	N
Kohl	N	N	Y	N	N	Y	Y	N
WYOMING								
Simpson	Y	+	N	Y	Y	N	N	Y
Wallop	Y	N	N	N	Y	N	N	Y

ND Northern Democrats   SD Southern Democrats   Southern states - Ala., Ark., Fla., Ga., Ky., La., Miss., N.C., Okla., S.C., Tenn., Texas, Va.

9. HR 2520. Fiscal 1994 Interior Appropriations/Grazing Fees. Domenici, R-N.M., amendment to prohibit the administration for one year from using funds in the bill to implement higher grazing fees and other public land-management reforms. Adopted 59-40: R 38-5; D 21-35 (ND 14-28, SD 7-7), Sept. 14, 1993. (Senate vote 266.) A "nay" was a vote in support of the president's position.

10. HR 2295. Fiscal 1994 Foreign Aid Appropriations/Passage. Passage of the bill to provide $12,526,854,047 in new budget authority for foreign assistance and related programs in fiscal 1994. The bill includes the $2.5 billion requested by the administration for the former Soviet Union. The administration requested $14,425,993,066. Passed 88-10: R 36-7; D 52-3 (ND 40-2, SD 12-1), Sept. 23, 1993. (Senate vote 287.) A "yea" was a vote in support of the president's position.

11. HR 2518. Fiscal 1994 Labor, HHS, Education Appropriations/Abortion. Committee amendment to strike the Hyde amendment provisions included in the House bill that prohibit federal funds from covering abortions except in cases of rape, incest or when the life of the woman is endangered. Rejected 40-59: R 6-38; D 34-21 (ND 31-11, SD 3-10), Sept. 28, 1993. (Senate vote 290.) A "yea" was a vote in support of the president's position.

12. HR 3116. Fiscal 1994 Defense Appropriations/Somalia Policy. Byrd, D-W.Va., amendment to prohibit funding of U.S. military operations in Somalia after March 31, 1994, unless the president requests and Congress authorizes an extension. The amendment would also limit the U.S. mission to protecting U.S. personnel and bases, sustaining relief supplies and giving logistical and security aid to U.N. forces, and would require that U.S. forces in Somalia be under the command and control of U.S. command-

ers. Adopted 76-23: R 24-20; D 52-3 (ND 38-3, SD 14-0), Oct. 15, 1993 (In the session that began and the Congressional Record dated Oct. 14.) (Senate vote 314.)

13. S Res 153. Packwood Diaries/Relevancy Requirement. Simpson, R-Wyo., amendment to add that all materials requested in the Ethics Committee subpoena of the diaries of Sen. Bob Packwood, R-Ore., be relevant. Rejected 23-77: R 22-22; D 1-55 (ND 1-41, SD 0-14), Nov. 2, 1993. (Senate vote 347.)

14. S 1607. Omnibus Crime/Assault Weapons Ban. Feinstein, D-Calif., amendment to ban the manufacture, sale and future possession of 19 semiautomatic assault weapons and copycat guns. Adopted 56-43: R 10-34; D 46-9 (ND 38-3, SD 8-6), Nov. 17, 1993. (Senate vote 375.) A "yea" was a vote in support of the president's position.

15. HR 1025. Brady Bill/Passage. Passage of the bill to require a five-business-day waiting period before an individual could purchase a handgun, to allow local officials to conduct a background check. A compromise provided that the waiting period would expire four years after enactment unless the attorney general extended the waiting period for a fifth year. Passed 63-36: R 16-28; D 47-8 (ND 38-3, SD 9-5), Nov. 20, 1993. (Senate vote 394.) A "yea" was a vote in support of the president's position.

16. HR 3450. NAFTA Implementation/Passage. Passage of the bill to approve the North American Free Trade Agreement and make the necessary changes to U.S. statutory law to implement the trade agreement. Passed 61-38: R 34-10; D 27-28 (ND 18-23, SD 9-5), Nov. 20, 1993. (Senate vote 395.) A "yea" was a vote in support of the president's position.

Freshmen Toed Party Lines But Helped Cut Spending

First-term House Democrats proved liberal on social issues; Republicans strengthened conservative forces

An analysis of the floor votes of the 114 House freshmen 1993 votes showed them as a subtle but influential force in the House and within the parties — neither the outside agitators they initially promised to be nor the party sycophants they were later dubbed.

For a group elected on a broad theme of change, they proved remarkably reliable in their partisanship. On both sides of the aisle, first-term members were more likely to vote the party position than were those elected before 1992. Although they seldom joined hands across the aisle on any controversial matter, the newcomers did leave their imprint on both federal spending and social policy.

On fiscal matters, the freshmen were much more likely to vote against federal projects, notably big-science efforts, than were their veteran counterparts. On the Democratic side, the difference was conspicuous. The class helped kill two major federal projects and served notice that it stood ready to do so again.

On social policy, the newcomers proved so starkly partisan that they pushed their parties even further apart. Democratic newcomers far outpaced senior members on key votes in their support of abortion rights and gay rights — issues many senior members once hoped would recede from the agenda. On the Republican side, opposition to such rights among newcomers mirrored that of veterans. This solidified conservatives' hold on the House GOP leadership, because many freshmen succeeded moderates.

The Partisan Pattern

The idea that the freshman class would be rebellious came more from the mood of the electorate and the group's size than from any of their actions. In 1992, candidates from President Clinton on down found that voters responded to a generic message of change. The election of the largest class of House newcomers in more than 40 years signaled radical change to many.

But as their résumés indicated and their early votes bore out, the newcomers in both parties were political pros

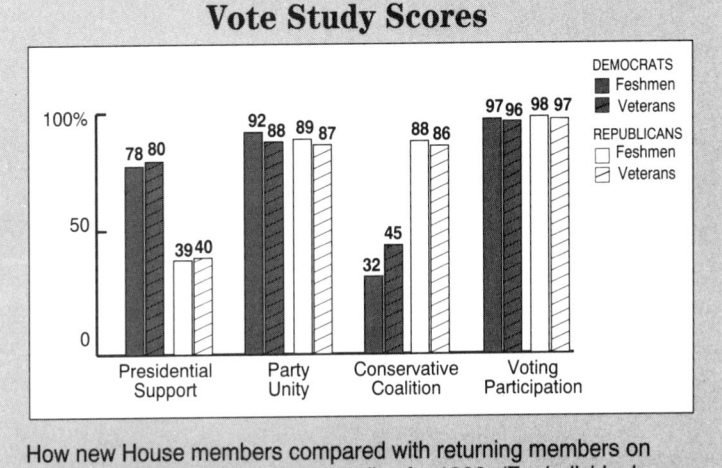

Vote Study Scores

DEMOCRATS
■ Freshmen
▨ Veterans

REPUBLICANS
□ Freshmen
▨ Veterans

Presidential Support: 78 80 39 40
Party Unity: 92 88 89 87
Conservative Coalition: 32 45 88 86
Voting Participation: 97 96 98 97

How new House members compared with returning members on Congressional Quarterly's vote studies for 1993. *(For individual definitions and studies, see list on p. 3-C)*

acculturated to the idea that institutional influence did not come from stepping on leadership toes and elbowing senior committee members. Moreover, they had been elected alongside Clinton, and most had pivoted off his campaign, aligning themselves either with him or against him. The first hard-fought vote of the year told the story. On the budget resolution that passed March 18, 98 percent of the first-term Democrats backed the president; 95 percent of the veteran Democrats did. All of the Republicans opposed him.

"The big fiscal issues are party-line votes," said James A. Thurber, a political scientist at American University. "There's no room for the freshmen to vote their consciences."

According to Congressional Quarterly's study of presidential support among House members, the freshmen were almost indistinguishable from veterans. On the Democratic side, newcomers backed Clinton on 78 percent of the votes on which he took a clear position, compared with 80 percent for senior members. Among Republicans, first-term members gave Clinton their votes 39 percent of the time, compared with 40 percent among veterans. *(Chart, above)*

The party-unity study — which measured votes on which a majority of Democrats opposed a majority of Republicans — showed freshmen even more loyal than veterans. Democratic newcomers voted with a majority of their party 92 percent of the time, compared with 88 percent for senior members. For Republicans, the difference narrowed to 89 percent for freshmen and 87 percent for veterans.

The Project Perspective

Freshman resistance to certain big-ticket programs emerged in June when the appropriations bills began coming to the floor.

Prior to that, it was rare for a majority of freshmen to vote in opposition to a majority of veterans in either party. It happened at least a dozen times in each party from June on, often on federal spending questions.

Key Spending Votes

On several controversial choices on whether to cut federal spending, first-term members voted differently than their more senior party colleagues:

Preserve Superconducting Super Collider. On Oct. 19, the House voted against ending debate on the conference report on the Energy and Water appropriations bill. As opponents of the $11 billion superconducting super collider made clear at the time, a "nay" vote was necessary to clear the way for an amendment to kill the collider. The opponents prevailed 159-264, with Democrats splitting 98-152 and Republicans splitting 61-111. Subsequently, the super collider was put on the path to extinction. *(Vote 510, p. 124-H)*

Freshman Democrats voting "nay"	**73%**	Freshman Republicans voting "nay"	**70%**
Veteran Democrats voting "nay"	**57%**	Veteran Republicans voting "nay"	**62%**

Preserve ASRM. On Oct. 6, the House voted against a rule to allow floor debate on the conference report on the VA-HUD appropriations bill. The key question was whether the bill should keep its $157.5 million for the Advanced Solid Rocket Motor (ASRM) project and its production site in Yellow Creek, Miss. Opponents of the project prevailed 123-305, with Democrats splitting 114-139 and Republicans dividing 9-165. About two weeks later, the House took up the bill again and deleted funds for the project. *(Vote 482, p. 118-H)*

Freshman Democrats voting "nay"	**80%**	Freshman Republicans voting "nay"	**98%**
Veteran Democrats voting "nay"	**47%**	Veteran Republicans voting "nay"	**94%**

Eliminate Space Station. On June 28, the House rejected by 196-220 an amendment to terminate the $2.1 billion space station as part of the VA-HUD appropriations bill. Democrats backed the amendment 140-108; Republicans opposed it 55-112. *(Vote 281, p. 68-H)*

Freshman Democrats voting "yea"	**61%**	Freshman Republicans voting "yea"	**38%**
Veteran Democrats voting "yea"	**55%**	Veteran Republicans voting "yea"	**31%**

Support Penny-Kasich Spending Cuts. On Nov. 22, the House rejected an amendment by Timothy J. Penny, D-Minn., and John R. Kasich, R-Ohio, to cut spending by $90 billion, largely through reductions in Medicare and future appropriations bills. Democrats voted overwhelmingly, 57-200, against the amendment; Republicans supported it 156-18. The House then passed a less ambitious package of cuts proposed by the Clinton administration. *(Vote 609, p. 148-H)*

Freshman Democrats voting "yea"	**32%**	Freshman Republicans voting "yea"	**90%**
Veteran Democrats voting "yea"	**19%**	Veteran Republicans voting "yea"	**90%**

By the fall, Democratic and Republican newcomers had provided the heft to pull the plug on the Advanced Solid Rocket Motor (ASRM) project and the superconducting super collider. They also helped opponents of the space station come within a whisker of axing it. *(Box, above)*

Among Democrats, the difference between first-term members' opposition to big-science projects and that of veteran Democrats was striking. While senior members were divided on the key votes, the freshman class was decisively and consistently opposed to federal funding of such projects.

The votes of freshmen occasionally made the difference between success and failure. On the ASRM, 80 percent of Democratic freshmen voted to kill the project, in direct opposition to 53 percent of veteran Democrats who voted for the project. In other instances, freshman votes set the tone for debate. On the super collider, newcomers' lopsided opposition was posted early on the tally board, helping

opponents of the project gain momentum.

But neither freshman Democrats nor Republicans were the front-line opponents of any of those programs. Instead, they joined coalitions that had been building strength over a period of years. With their votes, the newcomers put critics over the top.

Moreover, they succeeded in cutting programs only when an overwhelming majority of Democratic newcomers found common ground with Republican majorities. On the space station, a 61 percent majority of first-term Democrats voted to cut the project, along with a 55 percent majority of veterans. But strong majorities in both groups on the Republican side voted to retain the project, and it survived.

Similarly, though clear majorities of first-term Democrats supported cuts in the Pentagon and intelligence budgets, their efforts failed. A majority of freshman Democrats broke with the majority of veterans to support amendments to cut the Trident II missile, to reduce the Pentagon budget by $1.2 billion and to cut $500 million from the intelligence authorization. But with new and old Republicans leaning against the cuts, all the amendments were rejected.

Republican freshmen, meanwhile, supported many amendments to cut federal spending that Democrats rebuffed: to disallow extended jobless benefits in states with low unemployment rates, to cut $33 million in Amtrak funding and to cut $1 million from the Corporation for Public Broadcasting, to name just a few.

On most votes, the differences between first-term members and veterans were not substantial, but freshmen occasionally did set themselves apart on less public votes. A majority of the Republican freshmen stood alone in support of an amendment to end the office allowance for former presidents after five years.

And on a vote to cut $5 million from the Kissimmee River ecosystem restoration project in Florida, the majority of GOP freshmen supported the cut; the veteran Republicans opposed it. (A majority of freshman Democrats opposed the cut, in part due to appeals of classmate Rep. Carrie Meek, a popular Floridian and member of the Appropriations Committee.)

The GOP newcomers also parted company with party elders and showed a willingness to back some revenue measures when they voted against a prohibition on raising grazing fees on federal lands for one year. A majority of veteran Republicans backed the Senate-sponsored moratorium, which the administration strongly opposed. The Republican freshmen joined a Democratic majority, and the House voted to direct conferees to reject the Senate plan.

Macro Votes Went Party Line

When Rep. Marjorie Margolies-Mezvinsky, D-Pa., nervously cast the deciding vote in favor of the Clinton-backed budget-reconciliation bill on Aug. 5, her status as a freshman made the vote dramatic. But she was following in colleagues' footsteps.

Fully 88 percent of the first-term Democrats supported Clinton on the reconciliation vote, compared with 83 percent of the veterans. With Republicans unanimously in opposition, the bill would have gone down 215-219, had the first-term Democrats' votes paralleled those of senior members.

Months later, Reps. Timothy J. Penny, D-Minn., and John R. Kasich, R-Ohio, presented the House with an amendment to cut $90 billion in federal spending. The president and Democratic leaders opposed the Nov. 22 amendment, knowing that its defeat would be difficult.

The vote was perceived as particularly difficult for the freshmen, who by then touted their deficit-consciousness to constituents. In the end, the Democratic class did put some distance between itself and senior members, but not enough to change the outcome. Under considerable pressure to stand with the president, only 32 percent of first-term Democrats voted for the amendment, compared with 19 percent of the veteran members. Ninety percent of Republicans new and old supported it.

"The big budget questions involve a reordering of federal priorities. Of course, Democrats are going to vote like Democrats, and Republicans like Republicans," said Leslie L. Byrne, a first-term Democrat from Virginia.

Social Policy

The same might be said of social policy, and there the freshmen emerged as even more partisan.

On the Democratic side, the class was decisively more vigorous than were veterans in their opposition to abortion restrictions and the ban on gays in the military as well as in their support for family leave legislation:

● Among first-term Democrats, 73 percent supported an amendment that would have left the policy on gays in the military a matter of executive order rather than codifying it. Just 57 percent of senior Democrats voted for the amendment offered by first-term Rep. Martin T. Meehan, D-Mass.

● Seventy-seven percent of Democratic newcomers opposed an amendment to prohibit Medicaid funding of abortion except in cases of rape, incest and when the woman's life was in danger; 57 percent of senior Democrats opposed the amendment.

● Ninety-seven percent of the Democratic newcomers supported the family leave act to allow employees of large companies to take unpaid leave to care for a new child or sick relative; 86 percent of more senior Democrats did.

These differences might have been seen as minor matters of degree. But they appeared substantial when compared with the uniform posture of first-term Republicans and their veteran counterparts on key social policy votes:

● Six percent of GOP freshmen and GOP veterans supported the Meehan amendment to block the codification of military policy on gays.

● Ninety-two percent of first-term Republicans supported strict limits on abortion funding, compared with 90 percent of veterans.

● Twenty-one percent of the newcomers backed the family leave act, compared with 24 percent of senior Republicans.

One explanation offered for the differences among Democrats was the makeup of the class. Thirty-two percent of the Democratic freshmen were women, and 35 percent black or Hispanic. Of the veteran Democrats, 7 percent were women and 12 percent were minorities. ∎

Appendix D

TEXT

...His First Major Address to Congress

you sent me here — not to keep this seat warm, but to work for fundamental change, to make Washington work for all Americans, not just the special interests, and to chart a course that will enable us to compete and win in this new world.

Here's the challenge I will offer the Congress and the country on Wednesday. We'll invest in our future by nurturing our children and supporting their education, by rewarding work and family, by creating the jobs of the future and training our people to fill them. Our every effort will reflect what President Franklin Roosevelt called "bold, persistent experimentation," a willingness to stay with things that work and stop things that don't.

Change must begin at the top. That's why I cut the White House staff by 25 percent and ordered federal agencies to cut billions of dollars in administrative costs and to trim 100,000 federal positions by attrition. And in my budget there will be more than 150 specific cuts in government spending programs. Then I will ask the wealthiest Americans to pay their fair share.

That brings us to those of you who gave the most in the 1980s. I had hoped to invest in your future by creating jobs, expanding education, reforming health care and reducing the debt without asking more of you. And I've worked harder than I've ever worked in my life to meet that goal. But I can't — because the deficit has increased so much, beyond my earlier estimates and beyond even the worst official government estimates from last year. We just have to face the fact that to make the changes our country needs, more Americans must contribute today so that all Americans can do better tomorrow.

But I can assure you of this: You're not going alone any more, you're not going first, and you're no longer going to pay more and get less. Seventy percent of the new taxes I'll propose — 70 percent — will be paid by those who make more than $100,000 a year. And for the first time in more than a decade, we're all in this together. More important is the payoff. Our comprehensive plan for economic growth will create millions of long-term, good-paying jobs, including a program to jump-start our economy with another 500,000 jobs in 1993 and 1994. And as we make deep cuts in existing government programs, we'll make new investments where they'll do the most good, incentives to business to create new jobs, investments in education and training, special efforts for displaced defense workers, a fairer tax system to ensure that parents who work full time will no longer raise their children in poverty, welfare reform to move people from welfare to work, vaccinations and Head Start opportunities for all children who need them, and a system of affordable quality health care for all Americans.

Our national service plan will throw open the doors of college opportunity to the daughters and sons of the middle class, then we'll challenge them to give something back to our country — as teachers, police officers, community service workers — taking care of our own right here at home. And we'll do it all while reducing our debt.

Changing this fundamental will not be easy nor will it be quick. But at stake is the control of our economic destiny. Within minutes of the time I conclude my address to Congress Wednesday night, the special interests will be out in force. Those who've profited from the status quo will oppose the changes we seek — the budget cuts, the revenue increases, the new investment priorities. Every step of the way they'll oppose it. Many have already lined the corridors of power with high-priced lobbyists. They are the defenders of decline — and we must be the architects of the future.

I'm confident in our cause because I believe in America. And I know we have learned the hard lessons of the 1980s. This is your country. You demonstrated the power of the people in the last election. I urge you to stay informed and to stay involved. If you're vigilant and vocal, we can do what we have to do.

On this Presidents Day, we recall the many times in our history when past presidents have challenged this nation from this office in times of crisis. If you will join with me, we can create an economy in which all Americans work hard and prosper. This is nothing less than a call to arms to restore the vitality of the American dream.

When I was a boy we had a name for the belief that we should all pull together to build a better, stronger nation. We called it patriotism — and we still do.

Good night, and God bless America.

---

the revenue estimates, you and I know that both parties were given greater elbow room for irresponsibility. This is tightening the rein on the Democrats as well as the Republicans. Let's at least argue about the same set of numbers so the American people will think we're shooting straight with them.

As I said earlier, my recommendation makes more than 150 difficult reductions, to cut the federal spending by a total of $246 billion. We're eliminating programs that are no longer needed, such as nuclear power research and development.

We're slashing subsidies and canceling wasteful projects. But many of these programs were justified in their time and a lot of them were difficult for me to recommend reductions in — some really tough ones for me personally. I recommend that we reduce interest subsidies to the Rural [Electrification] Administration. That's a difficult thing for me to recommend, but I think that I cannot exempt the things that exist in my state or in my experience if I ask you to deal with things that are difficult for you to deal with. We're going to have to have no sacred cows except the fundamental, abiding interest of the American people.

I have to say that we all know our government has been just great at building programs. The time has come to show the American people that we can limit them, too, that we can not only start things, but we can actually stop things.

About the defense budget, I raise a hope and a caution. As we restructure our military forces to meet the new threats of the post-Cold War world, it is true that we can responsibly reduce our defense budget. And we may all doubt what that range of reductions is; but let me say that as long as I am president, I will do everything I can to make sure that the men and women who serve under the American flag will remain the best trained, the best prepared, the best equipped fighting force in the world, and every one of you should make that solemn pledge. We still have responsibilities around the world; we are the world's only superpower; this is still a dangerous and uncertain time, and we owe it to the people in uniform to make sure that we adequately provide for the national defense and for their interests and needs.

Backed by an effective national defense and a stronger economy, our nation will be prepared to lead a world challenged as it is everywhere by ethnic conflict, by the proliferation of weapons of mass destruction, by the global democratic revolution and by challenges to the health of our global environment.

I know this economic plan is ambitious, but I honestly believe it is necessary for the continued greatness of the United States. And I think it is paid for fairly, first by cutting government, then by asking the most of those who benefited the most in the past and by asking more Americans to contribute today so that all of us can prosper tomorrow.

Raising Taxes

For the wealthiest — those earning more than $180,000 per year — I ask you all who are listening tonight to support a raise in the top rate for federal income taxes from 31 to 36 percent. We recommend: a 10 percent surtax on incomes over

$250,000 a year. We recommend closing some loopholes that some people get away without paying any tax at all.

For businesses with taxable incomes in excess of $10 million, we recommend a raise in the corporate rate, also to 36 percent, as well as a cut in the deduction for business entertainment expenses.

Our plan seeks to attack tax subsides that actually reward companies more for shutting their operations down here and moving them overseas than for staying here and reinvesting in America.

I say that as someone who believes that American companies should be free to invest around the world and as a former governor who actively sought investment of foreign companies in my state. But the tax code should not express a preference to American companies for moving somewhere else, and it does in particular cases today.

We will seek to ensure that through effective tax enforcement, foreign corporations who do make money in America simply pay the same taxes that American companies make [sic] on the same income.

To middle-class Americans who have paid a great deal for the last 12 years and from whom I ask a contribution tonight, I will say again, as I did on Monday, you're not going it alone anymore — you're certainly not going first, and you're not going to pay more for less as you have too often in the past.

I want to emphasize the facts about this plan: 98.8 percent of America's families will have no increase in their income tax rates, only 1.2 percent at the top.

Let me be clear. There will also be no new cuts in benefits for Medicare.

As we move toward the fourth year with the explosion in health-care costs, as I said, projected to account for 50 percent of the growth of the deficit between now and the year 2000, there must be plan cuts in payments to providers — to doctors, to hospitals, to labs — as a way of controlling health-care costs, but I see these only as a stopgap until we can reform the entire health-care system. If you'll help me do that, we can be fair to the providers and to the consumers of health care.

Let me repeat this, because I know it matters to a lot of you on both sides of the aisle. This plan does not make a recommendation for new cuts in Medicare benefits for any beneficiary. Secondly, the only change we are making in Social Security is one that has already been publicized: The plan does ask older Americans with higher incomes who do not rely solely on Social Security to get by to contribute more. This plan will not affect the 80 percent of Social Security recipients who do not pay taxes on Social Security now. Those who do not pay tax on Social Security now will not be affected by this plan.

Our plan does include a broad-based tax on energy. And I want to tell you why I selected this and why I think it's a good idea. I recommend that we adopt a Btu tax on the heat content of energy as the best way to provide us with revenue to lower the deficit,

because it also combats pollution, promotes energy efficiency, promotes the independence economically of this country as well as helping to reduce the debt, and because it does not discriminate against any area. Unlike a carbon tax, it's not too hard on the coal states; unlike a gas tax, it's not too tough on people who drive a long way to work; unlike an ad valorem tax, it doesn't increase just when the price of an energy source goes up. And it is environmentally responsible; it will help us in the future as well as in the present with the deficit.

Taken together, these measures will cost an American family with an income of about $40,000 a year less than $17 a month. It will cost American families with incomes under $30,000 nothing because of other programs we propose, principally those raising the earned-income tax credit.

Because of our publicly stated determination to reduce the deficit, if we do these things, we will see the continuation of what's happened just since the election. Just since the election, since the secretary of the Treasury, the director of the Office of Management and Budget and others have begun to speak out publicly in favor of a tough deficit-reduction plan, interest rates have continued to fall, long-term. That means that for the middle class, who will pay something more each month, if they have any credit needs or demands, their increased energy costs will be more than offset by lower interest costs for mortgages, consumer loans, credit cards. This can be a wise investment for them and their country now.

I would also point out what the American people already know, and that is, because we're a big, vast country where we drive long distances, we have maintained far lower burdens on energy than any other advanced country. We will still have far lower burdens on energy than any other advanced country, and these will be spread fairly, with real attempts to make sure that no cost is imposed on families with incomes under $30,000, and that the costs are very modest until you get into the higher income groups where the income taxes trigger in.

Costs of Not Changing

Now I ask all of you to consider this. Whatever you think of the tax program, whatever you think of the spending cuts, consider the costs of not changing. Remember the numbers that you all know. If we just keep on doing what we're doing, by the end of the decade, we'll have a $650 billion-a-year deficit. If we just keep on doing what we're doing, by the end of the decade, 20 percent of our national income will go to health care every year, twice as much as any other country on the face of the globe. If we just keep on doing what we're doing, over 20 cents on the dollar will have to go to service the debt.

Unless we have the courage now to start building our future and stop borrowing from it, we're condemning ourselves to years of stagnation, interrupted by occasional recessions, to slow growth in jobs, to no more growth in incomes, to more debt, to more

disappointment. Unless we change, unless we increase investment and reduce the debt to raise productivity so that we can generate both jobs and incomes, we will be condemning our children and our children's children to a lesser life than we enjoyed.

Once Americans looked forward to doubling their living standards every 25 years. At present productivity rates, it'll take a hundred years to double living standards, until our grandchildren's grandchildren are born. I say that is too long to wait.

Tonight the American people know we have to change. But they're also likely to ask me tomorrow and all of you for the weeks and months ahead whether we have the fortitude to make the changes happen in the right way. They know that as soon as I leave this chamber and you go home, various interest groups will be out in force lobbying against this or that piece of this plan and that the forces of conventional wisdom will offer a thousand reasons why we well ought to do this but we just can't do it.

Our people will be watching and wondering — not to see whether you disagree with me on a particular issue but just to see whether this is going to [be] business as usual or a real new day — whether we're all going to conduct ourselves as if we know we're working for them. We must scale the walls of the people's skepticism, not with our words but with our deeds.

After so many years of gridlock and indecision, after so many hopeful beginnings and so few promising results, the American people are going to be harsh in their judgments of all of us if we fail to seize this moment. This economic plan can't please everybody. If the package is picked apart, there will be something that will anger each of us and won't please anybody. But if it taken as a whole, it will help all of us.

So I ask you all to begin by resisting the temptation to focus only on a particular spending cut you don't like or some particular investment that wasn't made — and nobody likes the tax increases — but let's just face facts. For 20 years, through administrations of both parties, incomes have stalled and debt has exploded and productivity has not grown as it should. We cannot deny the reality of our condition. We have got to play the hand we were dealt and play it as best we can.

My fellow Americans, the test of this plan cannot be what is in it for me; it has got to be what is in it for us.

If we work hard and if we work together, if we rededicate ourselves to creating jobs, to rewarding work, to strengthening our families, to reinvesting our government, we can lift our country's fortunes again. Today I ask everyone in this chamber and every American to look simply into your heart, to spark your own hopes, to fire your own imagination. There is so much good, so much possibility, so much excitement in this country now that if we act boldly and honestly, as leaders should, our legacy will be one of prosperity and progress. This must be America's new direction. Let us summon the courage to seize it.

Thank you. God bless America. ∎

Michel Urges Americans To Question Direction

House Minority Leader Robert H. Michel of Illinois delivered the Republican response to President Clinton's Feb. 17 address. Following is the Reuter transcript:

Good evening. Tonight you and I witnessed a colorful ritual — a new president of the United States addressing a joint session of Congress for the first time. The great chamber of the House rang out with cheers for the president. It was, as always, a thrilling spectacle. But now the last echo of the final cheer has faded away. The ceremony is over. It's time to put aside the pomp and circumstance. It's time to get to work for America.

That's what I'd like to briefly visit with you about: how your government can work better for you. Don't worry; I have no props, no flip-charts, no pointer, no electronic gimmicks. I don't even have a 1-800 number for you to call. I'd just like to talk with you as though we were having a cup of coffee back in my hometown of Peoria. It is a chance to ask some questions about where our nation is heading, the kinds of questions you might ask if you were here. We Americans are a questioning people; it is part of our national character. In fact, we may be the only nation whose national anthem begins and ends with a question. So, in questioning the direction of the administration, we are acting in a great American tradition.

All of us — Democrats, Republicans, Perot supporters, independents — want our new president to succeed. We want to help him do the right thing. But the only way we can help him is by candidly letting him know how we feel about his announced policies.

Our new president has an excellent chance to be successful. Because of the leadership of Presidents [Ronald] Reagan and [George] Bush, our nation does not face a nuclear threat. President Bush handed over to the president an economy that is growing, not shrinking, and a rate of worker productivity that is rising, not falling. As a matter of fact, the past 12 years of Republican leadership have built a strong foundation for progress.

We agree with the president that we have to put more people to work, but remember this: 80 to 85 percent of the new jobs in this country are created by small business. So the climate for starting and expanding businesses must be enhanced with tax incentives and deregulation, rather than imposing higher taxes and more governmental mandates.

The president speaks of the half million new jobs that will be created by his economic stimulus program. But, there are estimates that doing it his way will cost taxpayers some $55,000 per job. It should be noted that last year alone the private sector created a million-and-a-half new jobs on its own.

We have to make certain that government action helps, not hinders, the growing economy. After listening to the president tonight, I wonder if you know what the president's long-range economic strategy is. I don't — and I must say, I wonder if he does. All we are certain of is that the administration is engaged in a media blitz to sell his program. The president offers us what he calls a new direction but where he seems to be going is "back to the future," back to the failed big-government schemes of a generation ago, and that's not the direction we should be going.

The Clinton spin-doctors have even given us a new political vocabulary, if you will: "Investment" now means big government spending your tax dollars. "Change" now means reviving old, discredited big government tax-and-spend schemes. "Patriotism" now means agreeing with the Clinton program. The powerful, evocative word, "sacrifice" has been reduced to the level of a bumper sticker slogan. And, my favorite — "contribution" — is now the new word for "taxes." On April 15, just try telling the IRS you don't feel like contributing this year.

The administration is about to launch the biggest propaganda campaign in recent political history. The White House is even now becoming one big partisan political megaphone. But public relations campaigns are no substitute for sound public policy.

Tonight, the president mentioned a number of new programs that inevitably will cost considerable sums of money. As laudable as they might be, how do we pay for them? The president's answer is: more taxes on everyone. In 1992, candidate Clinton said: Tax only the super-rich. Then in 1993, President Clinton now says: If you earn more than $30,000, your taxes are going up. So much for not taxing the middle class.

The American people would do well to remember when you hear a Democrat call for taxes, do not ask for whom the tax rises — it will rise for you. There are those who say some taxes are a necessary evil. The difference is that Democrats stress the word "necessary," and we Republicans stress the word "evil."

The president was short on specifics again tonight — particularly as it relates to cutting spending. That's probably because he keeps juggling the figures. He offers no benchmarks, no coherent economic principles by which to judge what it is he is hoping to achieve. These fragmented, ad hoc proposals are the kind of thing that might be excused in the heat of a campaign. But, Mr. President, the campaign is over. You won. The time has come to park the bus and start the hard work of governing. And one of the hardest parts of that work is the vital question of health-care reform, which the president mentioned time and again. Will there be rationing of care? Will there be job-destroying mandates on employers?

Republicans believe in your right to select the doctor of your choice, and your right to immediate care without long waiting lines, and preserving the best of what our health-care system has to offer. Does the administration share these principles? As I said, these are some of the questions we have to ask, and then the answers we get will determine the kind of future we will have. And we Republicans are here to ask the tough questions, cut through the rhetoric and get the job done. But we do need your help.

My father, a French immigrant, used to tell me that it's better to listen 90 percent of the time — for that leaves you only 10 percent for talking. And throughout my life in public service, I've tried to take his advice. And I know my party is listening to your voice because we share your basic principles.

Our Republican governors, our state legislators, our elected officials, and of course, those of us in the U.S. House and Senate are all parts of the same team.

We owe it to you to make clear the ideas at the heart of our policies. And here are a few: We Republicans, and I think it's fair to say a great body of Perot supporters, insist on cutting spending as the best way to real deficit reduction. We'd like to support the president on an honest line-item veto that applies not only to pork barrel spending but to special interests' tax loopholes as well. And we will continue to press for a balanced-budget amendment. We want to help President Clinton in his efforts to spur savings and investments. We hope he will strive to maintain the current low rates of interest and inflation he inherited from George Bush. And let's not forget that we still live in a tough and often brutal world. Our national destiny is linked to our ability to compete in a global economy and to defend our interests and our values around the world. That's why we need to maintain a strong defense and stay on the cutting edge of high technology.

I'd like to address a few closing comments directly to the president himself. Mr. President, we wish you well. President Reagan and President Bush have given you a solid foundation of peace and a growing economy on which to build. You have a wonderful opportunity to succeed.

And when your domestic programs and policies are based on sound economic principles, common sense and traditional American values, we Republicans will be with you. And when your foreign policy is based on defending American interests and American values first and foremost, we'll be with you. But when those great values are missing from your proposals, we Republicans will be there to ask the tough questions and to provide effective answers. And to all of you, thanks for listening.

As the designated Republican questioner tonight, I know I speak for all elected Republicans among our governors, within the state legislatures, and in the House and Senate when I say, in the months ahead, we'll be visiting with you, whether the issue is health care, crime, education or the economy. We'll be listening and ready to react to your concerns. Do make your voice heard; you can make a difference. Thank you, and do have a good evening. ∎

Clinton Urges Participation In National Service

Following are excerpts from the text of President Clinton's address on voluntary service delivered at Rutgers University in New Brunswick, N.J., on March 1:

I came here to ask all of you to join me in a great national adventure. For, in the next few weeks, I will ask the United States Congress to join me in creating a new system of voluntary national service, something I believe in the next few years will change America forever and for the better.

My parents' generation won new dignity working their way out of the Great Depression through programs that provided them the opportunity to serve and to survive. Brave men and women in my own generation waged and won peaceful revolutions here at home for civil rights and human rights, and began service around the world in the Peace Corps and here at home in Vista.

Now Americans of every generation face profound challenges in meeting the needs that have been neglected for too long in this country — from city streets plagued by crime and drugs to classrooms where girls and boys must learn the skills they need for tomorrow, to hospital wards where patients need more care. All across America we have problems that demand our common attention.

For those who answer the call and meet these challenges, I propose that our country honor your service with new opportunities for education.

National service will be America at its best, building community, offering opportunity and rewarding responsibility. National service is a challenge for Americans from every background and walk of life, and it values something far more than money. National service is nothing less than the American way to change America.

It is rooted in the concept of community, the simple idea that none of us on our own will ever have as much to cherish about our own lives if we are out here all alone as we will if we work together, that somehow a society really is an organism in which the whole can be greater than the sum of its parts. And every one of us, no matter how many privileges with which we are born, can still be enriched by the contributions of the least of us, and that we will never fulfill our individual capacities until, as Americans, we can all be what God meant for us to be.

If that is so, if that is true, my fellow Americans, and if you believe it, it must therefore follow that each of us has an obligation to serve. For it is perfectly clear that all of us cannot be what we ought to be until those of us who can help others —

and that is nearly all of us — are doing something to help others live up to their potential.

The concept of community and the idea of service are as old as our history. They began the moment America was literally invented. Thomas Jefferson wrote in the Declaration of Independence: "With a firm reliance on the protection of divine providence, we mutually pledge to each other our lives, our fortune, and our sacred honor."

In the midst of the Civil War, President [Abraham] Lincoln signed into law two visionary programs that helped our people come together again and build America up. The Morrill Act helped states create new land grant colleges. This is a land grant university. The university in my home state was the first land grant college west of the Mississippi River.

In these places young people learned to make American agriculture and industry the best in the world. The legacy of the Morrill Act is not only our great colleges and universities like Rutgers, but the American tradition that merit and not money should give people a chance for higher education.

Mr. Lincoln also signed the Homestead Act that offered 100 acres of land for families who had the courage to settle the frontier and farm the wilderness. Its legacy is a nation that stretches from coast to coast.

Now we must create a new legacy that gives a new generation of Americans the right and the power to explore the frontiers of science and technology and space. The frontiers of the limitations of our knowledge must be pushed back so that we can do what we need to do.

And education is the way to do it, just as surely as it was more than a hundred years ago.

Seven decades after the Civil War, in the midst of the Great Depression, President [Franklin D.] Roosevelt created the Civilian Conservation Corps [CCC], which gave 2½ million young people the opportunity to support themselves while working in disaster relief and maintaining forests, beaches, rivers and parks. Its legacy is not only the restoration of our natural environment but the restoration of our national spirit.

Along with the Works Projects Administration — the WPA — the Civilian Conservation Corps symbolized government's efforts to provide a nation in depression with the opportunity to work, to build the American community through service. And all over America today you can see projects, even today in the 1990s, built by your par-

ents or your grandparents with a WPA plaque, the CCC plaque on it — the idea that people should be asked to serve and rewarded for doing it.

In the midst of World War II, President Roosevelt proposed a GI Bill of Rights, which offered returning veterans the opportunity for education in respect to their service to our country and the war.

Thanks to the GI Bill, which became a living reality in President [Harry S] Truman's time, more than 8 million veterans got advanced education, and half a century later the enduring legacy of the GI Bill is the strongest economy in the world and the broadest, biggest middle class that any nation has ever enjoyed.

For many in my own generation, the summons to citizenship and service came on this day, 32 years ago, when President John F. Kennedy created the Peace Corps. With [R.] Sargent Shriver and [Sen.] Harris Wofford [D-Pa.] and other dedicated Americans, he enabled thousands of young men and women to serve on the leading edge of the New Frontier, helping people all over the world to become what they ought to be, and bringing them the message by their very lives that America was a great country that stood for good values and human progress.

At its height the Peace Corps enrolled 16,000 young men and women. Its legacy is not simply good will and good works in countries all across the globe, but a profound and lasting change in the way Americans think about their own country and the world.

Shortly after the Peace Corps, Congress, under President [Lyndon B.] Johnson, created the Volunteers in Service to America.

Sen. [John D.] Jay Rockefeller [IV, D-W.Va.], whom I introduced a moment ago, and many thousands of other Americans went to the hills and hollows of poor places like West Virginia and Arkansas and Mississippi to lift up Americans through their service.

The lesson of our whole history is that honoring service and rewarding responsibility is the best investment America can make.

And I have seen it today across this great land: through the Los Angeles Conservation Corps, which took the children who lived in the neighborhoods where the riots occurred and gave them a chance to get out into nature and to clean up their own neighborhoods and to lift themselves and their friends in the effort; in Boston with the City Year program, with all these programs represented here in this room today — the spirit of service is sweeping this country and giving us a chance to put the quilt of America together in a way that makes strength out of diversity, that lifts us up out of our problems, and that keeps our people looking toward a better and brighter future.

National service recognizes a simple but powerful truth, that we make progress not by governmental action alone, but we

do best when the people and their government work at the grass roots in genuine partnership.

The idea of national service permeates many other aspects of the programs I have sought to bring to America. The economic plan I announced to Congress, for example, will offer every child the chance for a healthy start through immunization and basic health care and a head start.

But still it depends on parents doing the best they can as parents and children making the most of their opportunities.

The plan can help to rebuild our cities and our small communities through physical investments that will put people to work. But Americans still must work to restore the social fabric that has been torn in too many communities.

Unless people know we can work together in our schools, in our offices, in our factories — unless they believe we can walk the streets safely together, and unless we do that together, governmental action alone is doomed to fail.

The national service plan I propose will be built on the same principles as the old GI Bill: When people give something of invaluable merit to their country, they ought to be rewarded with the opportunity to further their education. National service will challenge our people to do the work that should and indeed must be done and cannot be done unless the American people voluntarily give themselves up to that work. It will invest in the future of every person who serves.

And as we rekindle the spirit of national service, I know it won't disappoint many of the students here to know that we also have to reform the whole system of student loans.

We should begin by making it easier for young people to pay back their student loans, in enabling them to hold jobs, enabling them to hold jobs that may accomplish much but pay little.

Today when students borrow money for an education, the repayment plan they make is based largely on how much they have to repay without regard to what the jobs they take themselves pay.

It is a powerful incentive, therefore, for young college graduates to do just the reverse of what we might want them to do: to take a job that pays more, even if it is less rewarding, because that is the job that will make the repayment of the loans possible.

It is also, unfortunately, a powerful incentive for some not to make the payments at all, which is unforgivable.

So what we seek to do is to enable the American students to borrow the money they need for college and pay it back as a small percentage of their own income over time. This is especially important after a decade in which the cost of a college education has gone up even more rapidly than the cost of health care, making a major contribution to one of the more disturbing statistics in America today, which is that the college dropout rate in this country is

now two-and-a-half times the high school dropout rate. We can do better than that through national service and adequate financing.

The present system is unacceptable not only for students but for the taxpayers as well. It's complicated, and it's expensive. It costs the taxpayers of our country about $4 billion every year to finance the student loan program because of loan defaults and the cost of administering the program, and I believe we can do better.

What we seek to do is to enable the American students to borrow the money they need for college and pay it back as a small percentage of their own income over time.

Beyond reforming this system for financing higher education, the national service program, more importantly, will create new opportunities for Americans to work off outstanding loans or to build up credits for future education and training opportunities.

We'll ask young people all across this country, and some who aren't so young, who want to further their college education, to serve in our schools as teachers or tutors in reading and mathematics.

We'll ask you to help our police forces across the nation, training members for a new police corps that will walk beats and work with neighborhoods and build the kind of community ties that will prevent crime from happening in the first place, so that our police officers won't have to spend all their time chasing criminals.

We'll ask young people to work to help control pollution and recycle waste, to paint darkened buildings and to clean up neighborhoods, to work with senior citizens and combat homelessness, and help children in trouble get out of it and build a better life.

And these are just a few of the things that you will be able to do, for most of the decisions about what you can do will be made by people like those in this room, people who run the programs represented by all of those wearing these different kinds of T-shirts. We don't see a national bureaucracy.

I have spoken often about how we need to reinvent the government to make it more efficient and less bureaucratic, to make it more responsive to people at the grass-roots level.

And I want national service to do just that. I want it to empower young people in their communities, not to empower yet another government bureaucracy in Washington. This is going to be your program, at your level, with your people.

And as you well know, that's what's

happening all across America today. People are already serving their neighbors and their neighborhoods. Just this morning I was inspired to see and to speak with students from Rutgers serving their community, from mentoring young people as big sisters to helping older people learn new skills.

I met a lady today who has 13 children and five great-grandchildren who dropped out of school the year before I was born, is about to become a high school graduate shortly, because of the efforts of this program.

She back there? Stand up.

I'm impressed by the spirit behind the Rutgers civic education and community service program. The understanding that community service enriches education, that students should not only take the lessons they learn in class out into the community, but bring the lessons they learn in the community back into the classroom.

In that spirit, during this academic year alone, more than 800 students from Rutgers are contributing more than 60,000 hours of community service, in New Brunswick and Camden and Newark, throughout this state.

This morning I also met with members of the New Jersey Youth Corps. Here they are. Stand up.

Young people who are looking for a second chance at school and who, when coming back to finish their high school degrees, also serve in their communities. Through this program, more than 6,500 young adults have contributed over 900,000 hours of service to the state of New Jersey.

They've done everything from paint senior citizens' homes to tutor and mentor children in after-school programs. For the future of our state and nation, we need more young people like those in the New Jersey Youth Corps who exemplify the spirit of service.

That spirit also moves people all across the nation. In my state, there's a young woman named Antoinette Jackson who's a senior in a small community called Gould, Ark. She's a member of the Delta Service Corps. The rural Mississippi Delta is still the poorest place in America, and in that area she works with the Lend a Hand program, which runs a thrift shop to provide hungry and homeless people with food and clothing. And in return, the Delta Corps is going to help her attend college so that she can make an even greater contribution.

The spirit of service also moves a young man I met about a year ago named Stephen Spalos who works with the City Year program in Boston. At age 23, he's had some hard times in his life, but as he puts it, City Year gave him a place and the tools to be able to start over. He works as a team leader, a mentor, a tutor, a project manager for a bunch of young people who restore senior citizens' homes.

Last year when I visited his project, he literally took his sweatshirt off his back and gave it to me so that I would never

forget the kids at City Year, and I still wear it when I go jogging, always remember what they're doing in Boston to help those kids.

The spirit of service moves Orah Fireman, a graduate of Wesleyan College. As a sophomore in high school, she worked with disadvantaged children in upstate New York.

That experience changed her life, and during her high school and college years she continued to work with children, and now that she's out of college, she has begun what will probably be a lifetime of service by working at a school for emotionally disturbed children in Boston.

She wants other people to have the opportunity to serve, and she wrote this: "Service work teaches responsibility and compassion. It fights alienation by proving to young people that they can make a difference. There's no lesson more important than that."

Well, there are stories like this in this room and all across America, and we're going to create thousands more of them through national service.

We'll work with groups with proven track records to serve their community, giving them the support they need. And if you have more good ideas, if you're entrepreneurs of national service, we'll let you compete for our form of venture capital — to develop new programs to serve your neighbors.

That's how we want the national service program to grow every year, rewarding results, building on success and bubbling up from the grass-roots energy and compassion and intellect of America.

I don't want service to wait while this potential is wasted. That's why I want to make this summer a summer of service, when young people can not only serve their communities but build a foundation for a new national effort.

I've asked Congress to invest in, and I'm asking young people to participate in, a special effort in national service and leadership training just this summer. We are going to recruit about 1,000 young people from every background, from high school dropouts to college graduates, to send to an intensive leadership training program for national service at the beginning of the summer.

Then we'll ask them to work on one of our country's most urgent problems — helping our children who are in danger of losing their God-given potential. Some of them will tutor; some will work on programs to immunize young children from preventable childhood diseases.

Some will help to develop and run recreational centers or reclaim urban parks from dealers and debris. Some will counsel people a few years younger than themselves to help keep them out of gangs and into good activities. And everyone will learn about serving our country and helping our communities.

At the end of this summer we'll bring all these people together for several days of debriefing and training, and then they'll all

join in a youth service summit. I will attend the meeting, and I expect to listen a lot more than I talk. I'll ask leaders from Congress, from business, labor, religious and community groups to attend the youth service summit, too.

We'll give those who serve the honor they deserve, and we'll learn a lot more about how to build this national service program. And from the thousand pioneers of this summer, I want the national service to grow 100-fold in the next four years.

I don't want service to wait while this potential is wasted. That's why I want to make this summer a summer of service, when young people can not only serve their communities but build a foundation for a new national effort.

But even when hundreds of thousands are serving, I want to maintain the pioneer spirit of this first few months because national service can make America new again. It can help solve our problems, educate our people and build our communities back together.

So if anybody here would like to be one of those 1,000, or if anybody who is listening to this speech by radio or television or reads about it would like to be one of those 1,000, drop me a card at the White House and just mark it "national service." We're going to pick them, and I can't promise you'll be selected, but I promise you'll be considered. I want to engage the energies of America in this effort.

I also want to say that you shouldn't wait for the summer or for a new program. We need to begin now. We are going to be looking for the kinds of ideas that we ought to be funding.

This is Monday. I ask you by Friday, every one of you, to think about what you think you can do and what we should do to be agents of renewal, to talk with your parents, your clergy, your friends, your teachers, to join the effort to renew our community and to rebuild our country, and to write to me about what you are doing.

It's time for millions of us to change our country block by block, neighborhood by neighborhood, time to return to our roots, and excitement, and idealism and an energy.

I have to tell you that there are some among us who do not believe that young Americans will answer a call to action, who believe that our people now measure their success merely in the accumulation of material things.

They believe this call to service will go unanswered. But I believe they are dead wrong.

And so, especially to the young Americans here, I ask you to prove that those who doubt you are wrong about your generation, and today I ask all of you who are young in spirit, whether you are a 10-year-old in a service program in our schools, who reads to still-younger children, or a 72-year-old who's become a foster grandparent. I ask you all to believe that you can contribute to your community and your country. And in so doing you will find the best in yourself. You will learn the lessons about your life that you might not ever learn any other way.

You will learn again that each of us has the spark of potential to accomplish something truly and enduringly unique.

You will experience the satisfaction of making a connection in a way with another person that you can do in no other way.

You will learn that the joy of mastering a new skill or discovering a new insight is exceeded only by the joy of helping someone else do the same thing.

You will know the satisfaction of being valued, not for what you own, or what you earn, or what position you hold, but just because of what you have given to someone else.

You will understand in personal ways the wisdom of the words spoken years ago by [the Rev.] Martin Luther King [Jr.] who said everybody can be great because everybody can serve.

I ask you all, my fellow Americans, to support our proposal for national service and to live a proposal for national service, to learn the meaning of America at its best and to re-create for others America at its best. We are not just another country. We have always been a special kind of community, linked by a web of rights and responsibilities, and bound together not by bloodlines but by beliefs.

At an age and time when people all across the world are being literally torn apart by racial hatreds, by ethnic hatreds, by religious divisions, we are a nation with all of our problems, where people can come together across racial and religious lines, and hold hands and work together, not just to endure our differences, but to celebrate them.

I ask you to make America celebrate that again.

I ask you, in closing, to commit yourselves to this season of service because America needs it. We need every one of you to live up to the fullest of your potential, and we need you to reach those who are not here, and who will never hear this talk, and who will never have the future they could otherwise have, if not for something that you could do.

The great challenge of your generation is to prove that every person here in this great land can live up to the fullest of their God-given capacity.

If we do it, the 21st century will be the American century. The American dream will be kept alive if you will today answer the call to service.

Thank you, and God bless you all. ■

PRESIDENTIAL ADDRESS

Clinton Announces Plan To Ease Business Credit

Program aims to reduce time spent on paperwork, bring banks and small businesses together

President Clinton on March 10 announced plans to ease banking regulations. Following are excerpts of the Reuter transcript of his remarks, which include references to charts prepared for Clinton's presentation.

. . . I am in debt to many people in this room and throughout this country who raised to me in many ways over the 16 months in which I was engaged in the campaign for the presidency the question of the credit crunch. From the beginnings of that campaign in New Hampshire across the country to Illinois and Michigan down to Florida across to California and in all points in between, I repeatedly ran into small-business men and [businesswomen]; I repeatedly met bankers themselves who said they wished that something could be done to open up credit again to creditworthy loans to generate jobs in the private sector.

Today we are taking a step to speed the economic recovery that will increase jobs by increasing access to credit for the main engine of our economy, small- and medium-size businesses. At the same time, by strengthening our banking system, our plan will move us beyond the banking problems of the last decade.

The initiative avoids the regulatory excess and duplication we've seen and focuses on real risks within our financial institutions, and on fair lending, equal opportunity and credit availability.

Every day small business is a big part of all of our lives. It's the coffee shop on the corner, the florist down the street, the stationery store that carries office supplies, the dry cleaner, the contractor who will remodel a kitchen. Many are businesses with fewer than a hundred employees, many more employ fewer than 20 people. But they keep communities and neighborhoods vibrant and vital.

They are the industry in a cottage, in a garage, in a spare bedroom. They're downtown in every town, and sometimes they grow into very large enterprises indeed.

Small business includes small farms, the agriculture community. Their contribution is evident every day on our table. But it is much more. They are the cultivators of an essential part of our history, our heritage, our culture.

Small business is also high-tech, the industries of tomorrow. From computer software to communications to biotechnology and environmental testing, all enterprises that create high-wage, high-skill jobs for Americans today, and they'll be there tomorrow.

Small business has been the route to a better life for immigrants who set up a family business, for men and women who save as they work for others until they can venture off on their own.

Often a small business is actually an outgrowth of the global economy. As larger firms downsize to remain competitive, they contract out to smaller firms. And many talented people who once worked for large companies are now going off on their own to seize opportunity in smaller enterprises, building businesses for themselves.

Owning one's own business is a cornerstone of the American dream, fortified by hard work, determination and creativity. My first experience in life with business was in my grandfather's little grocery store. He was the symbol of hope and opportunity to many people with whom he dealt in many ways, six days a week, at all hours of the day and night.

Today's small businesses are a barometer of the economic recovery, and as the strength of this recovery has been diluted by the inability to create jobs, it is clear that it's largely because small companies are still having a hard time. If you look at this chart here, you can see the number of small-business failures just since 1985 — 119,000 in '85-'86, 118,000 the next year, 111,000 in the next two-year period, but in '91-92 almost 185,000 small-business failures.

These businesses have been hit especially hard by the recession and by a problem not of their own making that can be summarized by two fearsome but now well-worn words: credit crunch. Small companies are simply unable in too many cases to get loans from banks.

And I want to show this. If you look here, the growth in commercial and industrial loans in '85-'86 in billions of dollars in the last two years, down to a negative — $36 billion.

Now, if these businesses can't begin or expand or try new ventures, that means stagnation for our economy — lost oppor-

tunity — and sometimes ruin for entrepreneurs. Indeed I've met business people in this country in the last year and a half who've never missed a payment on a loan and still have the loans canceled.

These problems are America's problems. When small businesses aren't prospering, they create fewer jobs and that means fewer jobs for America.

If you look at this last chart, you will see the real essence of why this has turned out to be, so far, a jobless recovery. In '85-'86, there was a positive change in small-business employment of 2.4 million; '87-'88, 2.8 million; '89-'90, 3.2 million; but down in '91-'92, 400,000.

Now, in every year of the 1980s, the Fortune 500 companies have reduced employment by several hundred thousand people a year in the United States. But all during the '80s, that reduction was more than offset by the creation of new jobs in the small-business sector, until the last couple of years.

If you had to put in a sentence why this has been a jobless recovery, it's because small-business job creation hasn't offset big-business job losses, and that is the central challenge we face as we take advantage of the incredible things going on now in the big- and small-business sector, with productivity increases, with the aggregate indications that we're in an economic recovery. We have to look for ways, all of us together, to try to help to spur small-business and medium-size business job growth so that we can put some jobs back into these [impressive] economic figures of the last quarter.

Nearly two-thirds of all of our workers are employed by small businesses, and as I said, millions of jobs in the last decade were created by them, even as larger employers were downsizing, contracting out or moving employment offshore.

We cannot afford not to try to resume this trend in the 1990s. We know that if we create a reliable and secure system of credit for America's small businesses, they'll create jobs for Americans and profits for themselves. That's why we have offered incentives, like investment tax credits for small employers, the new business capital gains tax, urban enterprise zones and a network of small-business community development banks.

In our country you can become successful if you have a better idea that you can turn into reality. But that reality can only occur if credit is available for most Americans. And we think we have a better idea for getting lenders and creditworthy borrowers together.

What we propose does not involve any changes in legislation. These steps can be taken quickly because they have been agreed to already by the four federal bank and thrift regulatory agencies — the Comptroller of the Currency, the Federal Reserve, the Federal Deposit Insurance Corporation and the Office of Thrift Supervision. Today I'll outline the basics of the plan, but the four bank and thrift regulators are issuing a joint interagency policy statement today that sets out more of the details. It will be available to all of you, and most of you will understand it.

I don't know if I left the implication that I didn't.

What we have done, first of all, is to re-examine our examination system, a system that bankers often felt has become too excessive in the wake of the banking and savings and loan failures of the '80s. With this plan, our examiners will be directed to do what they do best and not to spend endless hours on pointless paperwork. We'll strengthen our oversight by shifting our regulatory attention from unproductive and repetitive procedures, redirecting our resources to better use so that bank examiners will be able to seek out the real risks in today's environment. They'll go after bad loans and troubled banks. That means improved safety and soundness. But they will reduce the credit crunch because they will reduce attention to things that do not deserve them.

We will not, I will say again, we will not reduce attention to important regulation or to proper reserves for problem loans. The plan will not lower the capital requirements established in accordance with international standards. It will not cause a single bank to fail. And it will not cost the Deposit Insurance Funds one dollar.

Through a proper allocation of our regulatory resources, we will be able to focus more on examination procedures to further meaningful compliance with the Community Reinvestment Act and to promote fair opportunities for all of our people while reducing the hassles for all creditworthy loans.

Above all, borrowers can go to their banks expecting fair and equal treatment and a reasonable application process. Fairness is a goal for many good reasons, including the fact that women and other minorities have been very bullish for small business and for America. Female-owned companies now employ 11.5 million Americans.

A side effect of the savings and loan disaster was a reaction that forced many banks into a thinking mode that didn't distinguish between a good risk and a bad risk where small businesses were concerned. They were afraid to. This was a problem especially for community bankers, who frequently had to decide whether they could loan money to other members in their own community. Even if a banker could personally vouch that an applicant was a person of good character with an unblemished credit record and a good business track record, a loan might still be turned down because the banker felt his hands were tied by tight restrictions.

So while we ask bankers to give the small-businessmen and [businesswomen] credit, we'll give the bankers some credit too as they consider loans to small and medium-sized companies in their own communities and neighborhoods.

They'll be encouraged to use their judgment to determine whether a borrower is creditworthy. And we're telling bankers that as long as their institutions and their practices are sound, they shouldn't be afraid of the regulator.

If they disagree with a decision by a regulator, they'll now have a recourse, a workable and prompt appeals process. To bankers across the nation we say you are a pillar of our neighborhoods and communities. We know the demands of rebounding from the last decade have often been painful for many of you. Your comeback has been nothing short of amazing. But there is more work to do, and we need you to get it done.

And if it gets done there will be something to show for it, the kind of broad-based economic growth that benefits all of us. And we further say to bankers across the land that if you make sensible loans, the government should not come down on you. That's why we're taking this action today. We want bankers to get back into the business of lending money. And we're going to work with them to make it happen.

We're also making clear that taking collateral as part of a business loan should not be so burdensome or costly to discourage borrowers or lenders from making sound credit decisions. Often the only collateral the would-be borrower can offer is real estate. Of course we learned the hard way in the '80s that we'd have to be careful where loans involving commercial real estate are concerned. But care has been confused with regulatory excess. There has been too much of a burden for everyone.

The changes we propose will strike a balance so that we can have both safety and credit availability. These changes will also address the paper crunch in getting a small-business loan.

It simply shouldn't be as burdensome to get a $25,000 loan as it is to get a $25 million loan. It makes no sense for a small- or medium-sized business borrower or for an individual, for that matter, to be required in every case to produce a pile of paper like this one — pretty thick — when a loan can be made safely in many cases, particularly by banks who have demonstrated judgment in their business practices, with merely a promissory note and a financial statement and possibly a short credit application like this.

Under the current system, the paperwork — I expect every one of you to come back and show me your measured envelopes here.

We got to prove that the difference is what we're asserting it is today.

Under the current system, the paperwork is often daunting to the applicant and discourages banks from making smaller loans. Streamlining the process will make it easier to free up credit without compromising security. This is action that everyone — conscientious regulators, community-conscious banks and growing businesses can embrace.

With this approach, we want to marry the ingredients for a thriving business climate. Right now banks are healthier than they've been in years; 1990 was a record year for bank profitability. And these profits have been used to put banks in the strongest position they've been in in a quarter of a century.

At the same time, interest rates have gone down. Just three years ago the average interest rate on a small-business loan was 12 percent. So far this year the average is 8 percent. The climate for business ventures has been made even sunnier by economic growth that we've seen in the last quarter. That's a byproduct of the optimism for the growth that we are pressing for now with all the economic initiatives that are before the Congress and the country.

So both supply and demand for business loans are there. And would-be small-business owners are right to feel they have the wind at their backs. Now that we have banks in the strongest positions they've been in in a quarter-century, they ought to be able to give us the strongest economic boost we've had for small business in a quarter-century.

Until now the problem has been that everyone has had to face a 10-foot wall called the credit crunch. This action that this administration is taking today should take a big chunk out of that wall. The result should be a flow of billions of dollars of economic stimulus that doesn't cost the American taxpayers one red cent. The payoff will be in new jobs and in reversing the charts that I have shown you today.

At the same time, by encouraging new small-business ventures, we'll be laying the groundwork for a smarter work force that can compete more effectively in the global economy. Getting financing to these businesses is absolutely essential to the future growth of America. We'll see the benefits and so will our children.

This administration is firmly and unequivocally committed to the private sector as the engine of economic growth in America. We have no illusions, no abstractions, no preoccupations. We know that this is what works in this country.

In America, we put people first first by having a prosperous economy, founded on a thriving private sector. What's good for America is good for business, and we are determined to make the climate for business and for growth better and better and better, beginning today, where so many of you have told me for so long we ought to begin, with a real assault on the credit crunch. ■

NEWS CONFERENCE

Clinton Nominates Ginsburg To Supreme Court

Appeals court judge described as a centrist is chosen to replace Justice Byron White

President Clinton announced his nomination of Judge Ruth Bader Ginsburg to the Supreme Court at a Rose Garden news conference June 14. Following is the Reuter transcript of the session:

PRESIDENT CLINTON: Please be seated. I wish you all a good afternoon, and I thank the members of the Congress and other interested Americans who are here. In just a few days, when the Supreme Court concludes its term, Justice Byron [R.] White will begin a new chapter in his long and productive life. He has served the court as he has lived, with distinction, intelligence and honor, and he retires from public service with the deep gratitude of all the American people.

Article 2, Section 2 of the United States Constitution empowers the president to select a nominee to fill a vacancy on the Supreme Court of the United States. This responsibility is one of the most significant duties assigned to the president by the Constitution.

A Supreme Court justice has life tenure, unlike the president, and along with his or her colleagues decides the most significant questions of our time, and shapes the continuing contours of our liberty.

I care a lot about this responsibility, not only because I am a lawyer, but because I used to teach constitutional law, and I served my state as attorney general. I know well how the Supreme Court affects the lives of all Americans, personally and deeply.

I know clearly that a Supreme Court justice should have the heart and spirit, the talent and discipline, the knowledge, common sense and wisdom to translate the hopes of the American people as presented in the cases before it into an enduring body of constitutional law: a constitutional law that will preserve our most cherished values that are enshrined in that Constitution and at the same time enable the American people to move forward.

That is what I promised the American people, just as when I ran for president, and I believe it is a promise that I am delivering on today.

After careful reflection I am proud to nominate for associate justice of the Supreme Court Judge Ruth Bader Ginsburg of the United States Court of Appeals for the District of Columbia.

I will send her name to the Senate to fill the vacancy created by Justice White's retirement. As I told Judge Ginsburg last night when I called to ask her to accept the nomination, I decided on her for three reasons:

First, in her years on the bench she has genuinely distinguished herself as one of our nation's best judges: progressive in outlook, wise in judgment, balanced and fair in her opinions.

Second, over the course of a lifetime, in her pioneering work in behalf of the women of this country, she has compiled a truly historic record of achievement in the finest traditions of American law and citizenship.

And finally, I believe that in the years ahead, she will be able to be a force for consensus-building on the Supreme Court just as she has been on the Court of Appeals, so that our judges can become an instrument of our common unity in the expression of their fidelity to the Constitution.

Judge Ginsburg received her undergraduate degree from Cornell [University]. She attended both Harvard and Columbia [University] law schools and served on the law reviews of both institutions, the first woman to have earned this distinction. She was a law clerk to a federal judge, a law professor at Rutgers and Columbia [University] law schools; she argued six landmark cases in behalf of women before the United States Supreme Court and happily won five out of six.

For the past 13 years, she has served on the United States Court of Appeals for the District of Columbia, the second-highest court in our country, where her work has brought her national acclaim and on which she was able to amass a record that caused a national legal journal in 1991 to name her as one of the nation's leading centrist judges.

In the months and years ahead, the country will have the opportunity to get to know much more about Ruth Ginsburg's achievements, decency, humanity and fairness. People will find, as I have, that this nominee is a person of immense character. Quite simply, what's in her record speaks volumes about what is in her heart. Throughout her life, she has repeatedly stood for the individual, the person less well off, the outsider in society, and has given those people greater hope by telling them that they have a place in our legal system by giving them a sense that the Constitution and the laws protect all the American people, not simply the powerful.

Judge Ginsburg has also proven herself to be a healer, what attorneys call a moderate. Time and again, her moral imagination has cooled the fires of her colleagues' discord, ensuring that the right of jurists to dissent ennobles the law without entangling the court.

The announcement of this vacancy brought forth a unique outpouring of support from distinguished Americans on Judge Ginsburg's behalf. What caused that outpouring is the essential quality of the judge herself, her deep respect for others and her willingness to subvert self-interest to the interest of our people and their institutions.

In one of her own writings about what it is like to be a justice, Judge Ginsburg quotes Justice Louis Brandeis, who once said the Supreme Court is not a place for solo performers. If this is a time for consensus-building on the court, and I believe it is, Judge Ginsburg will be an able and effective architect of that effort.

It is important to me that Judge Ginsburg came to her reviews and attitudes by doing, not merely by reading and studying. Despite her enormous ability and academic achievements, she could not get a job with a law firm in the early 1960s because she was a woman and the mother of a small child.

Having experienced discrimination, she devoted the next 20 years of her career to fighting it and making this country a better place for our wives, our mothers, our sisters and our daughters. She herself argued and won many of the women's rights cases before the Supreme Court in the 1970s. Many admirers of her work say that she is to the women's movement what former Supreme Court Justice Thurgood Marshall was to the movement for the rights of African-Americans. I can think of no greater compliment to bestow on an American lawyer.

And she has done all of this and a lot of other things as well while raising a family with her husband, Marty, whom she married 39 years ago, as a very young woman.

Together they had two children, Jane and James, and they now have two grandchildren. Hers is a remarkable record of distinction and achievement, both professional and personal.

During the selection process, we reviewed the qualifications of more than 40 potential nominees. It was a long, exhaustive search, and during that time we identified several wonderful Americans whom I think could be outstanding nominees to the Supreme Court in the future.

Among the best were the secretary of the Interior, Bruce Babbitt, whose strong legal background as Arizona's attorney general and recent work balancing the competing interests of environmentalists and others in the very difficult issues affecting the American West made him a highly qualified candidate for the court.

And I had the unusual experience, something unique to me, of being flooded with calls all across America from Babbitt admirers who pleaded with me not to put him on the court and take him away from the Interior Department.

I also have carefully considered the chief judge of the 1st Circuit, Judge Stephen [G.] Breyer of Boston, a man whose character, confidence and legal scholarship impressed me very greatly.

I believe he has a very major role to play in public life. I believe he is superbly qualified to be on the court, and I think either one of these candidates, as well as the handful of others whom I closely considered, may well find themselves in that position some day in the future.

Let me say, in closing, that Ruth Bader Ginsburg cannot be called a liberal or a conservative. She has proved herself too thoughtful for such labels. As she herself put it in one of her articles, and I quote: The greatest figures of the American judiciary have been independent-thinking individuals with open but not empty minds, individuals willing to listen and to learn. They have exhibited a readiness to re-examine their own premises, liberal or conservative, as thoroughly as those of others.

That, I believe, describes Judge Ginsburg, and those, I too believe, are the qualities of a great justice. If, as I believe, the measure of a person's values can best be measured by examining the life the person lives, then Judge Ginsburg's values are the very ones that represent the very best in America.

I am proud to nominate this pathbreaking attorney, advocate and judge to be the 107th justice to the United States Supreme Court.

JUDGE GINSBURG: Mr. President, I am grateful beyond measure for the confidence you have placed in me, and I will strive, with all that I have, to live up to your expectations in making this appointment.

I appreciate, too, the special caring of Sen. Daniel Patrick Moynihan [D-N.Y.], the more so because I do not actually know the senator. I was born and brought up in New York, the state Sen. Moynihan represents, and he was the very first person to call with good wishes when President [Jimmy] Carter nominated me in 1980 to serve on the U.S. Court of Appeals for the District of Columbia Circuit. Sen. Moynihan has offered the same encouragement on this occasion.

May I introduce at this happy moment three people very special to me: my husband, Martin D. Ginsburg; my son-in-law, George T. Spera Jr.; and my son, James Steven Ginsburg. . . .

The announcement the president just made is significant, I believe, because it contributes to the end of the days when women, at least half the talent pool in our society, appear in high places only as one-at-a-time performers.

Recall that when President Carter took office in 1976 no woman ever served on the Supreme Court and only one woman, Shirley [M.] Hufstedler of California, then served at the next federal court level, the United States Courts of Appeals.

Today, Justice Sandra Day O'Connor graces the Supreme Court bench, and close to 25 women serve at the federal court of appeals level, too, as chief judges. I am confident that more will soon join them. That seems, to me, inevitable, given the change in law school enrollment.

My law school class, in the late 1950s, numbered over 500. That class included less than 10 women. As the president said, not a law firm in the entire city of New York bid for my employment as a lawyer when I earned my degree. Today, few law schools have female enrollment under 40 percent, and several have reached or passed the 50 percent mark.

And thanks to Title VII, no entry doors are barred. My daughter, Jane, reminded me a few hours ago, in a good luck call from Australia, of a sign of the change we have had the good fortune to experience. In her high school yearbook, on her graduation in 1973, the listing for Jane Ginsburg under ambition was to see her mother appointed to the Supreme Court.

The next line read: If necessary, Jane will appoint her.

Jane is so pleased, Mr. President, that you did it instead, and her brother, James, is, too.

I expect to be asked in some detail about my views of the work of a good judge on a high court bench. This afternoon is not the moment for extended remarks on that subject, but I might state a few prime guides.

Chief Justice [William H.] Rehnquist offered one I keep in the front of my mind. A judge is bound to decide each case fairly in accord with the relevant facts and the applicable law, even when the decision is not, as he put it, what the home crowd wants.

Next, I know no better summary than the one Justice O'Connor recently provided, drawn from a paper by New York University Law School Professor Burt Neuborne. The remarks concerned the enduring influence of Justice Oliver Wendell Holmes.

They read: When a modern constitutional judge is confronted with a hard case, Holmes is at her side with three gentle reminders. First, intellectual honesty about the available policy choices; second, disciplined self-restraint in respecting the majority's policy choice; and third, principled commitment to defense of individual autonomy even in the face of majority action.

To that I can only say Amen.

I am indebted to so many for this extraordinary chance and challenge, to a revived women's movement in the 1970s that opened doors for people like me, to the civil rights movement of the 1960s from which the women's movement drew inspiration, to my teaching colleagues at Rutgers and Columbia, and for 13 years, my D.C. Circuit colleagues, who shaped and heightened my appreciation of the value of collegiality.

Most closely, I have been aided by my life's partner, Martin D. Ginsburg, who has been since our teenage years my best friend and biggest booster; by my mother-in-law, Evelyn Ginsburg, the most supportive parent a person could have; and by a daughter and son with the taste to appreciate that Daddy cooks ever so much better than Mommy — and so phased me out of the kitchen at a relatively early age.

Finally, I know Hillary Rodham Clinton has encouraged and supported the president's decision to utilize the skills and talents of all the people of the United States. I did not until today know Mrs. Clinton, but I hasten to add that I am not the first member of my family to stand close to her. There is another I love dearly to whom the first lady is already an old friend. My wonderful granddaughter Clara — witness this super, unposed photograph taken last October when Mrs. Clinton visited the nursery school in New York and led the little ones in the toothbrush song. . . . This small person, right in front, is Clara.

I have a last thank-you. It is to my mother, Celia Amster Bader, the bravest and strongest person I have known, who was taken from me much too soon. I pray that I may be all that she would have been, had she lived in an age when women could aspire and achieve, and daughters are cherished as much as sons.

I look forward to stimulating weeks this summer; and, if I am confirmed, to working at a neighboring court, to the best of my ability, for the advancement of the law in the service of society.

Thank you.

Q: Mr. President, the result of the [Lani] Guinier nomination, sir, and your apparent focus on Judge Breyer, and your turn, late it seems, to Judge Ginsburg may have created an impression, perhaps unfair, of a certain zigzag quality in the decision-making process here. I wonder, sir, if you could kind of walk us through it and perhaps disabuse us of any notion we might have along those lines.

CLINTON: I have long since given up the thought that I could disabuse some of you of turning any substantive decision into anything but a political process. How you could ask a question like that after the statement she just made is beyond me. Good-bye. Thank you. ■

PRESIDENTIAL ADDRESS

Clinton Describes Retaliation Against Iraqi Complex

Following is the text of President Clinton's address to the nation June 26 on the U.S. attack on Baghdad.

CLINTON: My fellow Americans, this evening I want to speak with you about an attack by the government of Iraq against the United States and the actions we have just taken to respond.

This past April, the Kuwaiti government uncovered what they suspected was a car bombing plot to assassinate former President George Bush while he was visiting Kuwait City. The Kuwaiti authorities arrested 16 suspects, including two Iraqi nationals. Following those arrests, I ordered our own intelligence and law enforcement agencies to conduct a thorough and independent investigation. Over the past several weeks, officials from those agencies reviewed a range of intelligence information, traveled to Kuwait and elsewhere, extensively interviewed the suspects, and thoroughly examined the forensic evidence. This Thursday, Attorney General [Janet] Reno and Director of Central Intelligence [R. James] Woolsey gave me their findings.

Based on their investigation, there is compelling evidence that there was, in fact, a plot to assassinate former President Bush, and that this plot, which included the use of a powerful bomb made in Iraq, was directed and pursued by the Iraqi intelligence service.

We should not be surprised by such deeds, coming as they do from a regime like Saddam Hussein's, which has ruled by atrocity, slaughtered its own people, invaded two neighbors, attacked others, and engaged in chemical and environmental warfare. Saddam has repeatedly violated the will and conscience of the international community, but this attempt at revenge by a tyrant against the leader of the world coalition that defeated him in war is particularly loathsome and cowardly. We thank God it was unsuccessful.

The authorities who foiled it have the appreciation of all Americans. It is clear that this was no impulsive or random act. It was an elaborate plan devised by the Iraqi government, and directed against a former president of the United States because of actions he took as president. As such, the Iraqi attack against President Bush was an attack against our country, and against all Americans. We could not, and have not, let such action against our nation go unanswered.

From the first days of our Revolution, America's security has depended on the clarity of this message: Don't tread on us. A firm and commensurate response was essential to protect our sovereignty, to send a message to those who engage in state-sponsored terrorism, to deter further violence against our people, and to affirm the expectation of civilized behavior among nations.

Therefore, on Friday I ordered our forces to launch a cruise missile attack on the Iraqi intelligence service's principal command and control facility in Baghdad. Those missiles were launched this afternoon at 4:22 Eastern Daylight Time. They landed approximately an hour ago. I have discussed this action with the congressional leadership and with our allies and friends in the region, and I have called for an emergency meeting of the United Nations Security Council to expose Iraq's crime.

These actions were directed against the Iraqi government, which was responsible for the assassination plot. Saddam Hussein has demonstrated repeatedly that he will resort to terrorism or aggression if left unchecked. Our intent was to target Iraq's capacity to support violence against the United States and other nations, and to deter Saddam Hussein from supporting such outlaw behavior in the future.

Therefore, we directed our action against a facility associated with Iraq's support of terrorism, while making every effort to minimize the loss of innocent life.

There should be no mistake about the message we intend these actions to convey to Saddam Hussein, to the rest of the Iraqi leadership, and to any nation, group of persons who would harm our leaders or our citizens. We will combat terrorism. We will deter aggression. We will protect our people.

The world has repeatedly made clear what Iraq must do to return to the community of nations, and Iraq has repeatedly refused. If Saddam and his regime contemplate further illegal, provocative actions, they can be certain of our response.

Let me say to the men and women in our armed forces and our intelligence and law enforcement agencies who carried out the investigation and our military response: You have my gratitude, and the gratitude of all Americans. You have performed a difficult mission with courage and professionalism.

Finally, I want to say this to all the American people. While the Cold War has ended, the world is not free of danger, and I am determined to take the steps necessary to keep our nation secure. We will keep our forces ready to fight. We will work to head off emerging threats, and we will take action when action is required. That is precisely what we have done today.

Thank you, and God bless America.

Case Against Baghad:

At the U.N. Security Council on June 27, U.S. Representative Madeleine K. Albright presented the U.S. case against Iraq. Following is the Reuter transcript of her remarks:

ALBRIGHT: Mr. President, I come to the council today to brief you on a grave and urgent matter, an attempt to murder a president of the United States by the intelligence service of the government of Iraq, a member of the United Nations. Even by the standards of an Iraqi regime known for its brutality against its neighbors and its own people, this is an outrage. The attempt to murder President George Bush's life during his visit to Kuwait last April was an attack on the United States of America. I'm not asking the council for any action, but in our judgment, every member here today would regard an assassination attempt against its former head of state as an attack against itself and would react.

Let me begin by reviewing the events in question. On April 14, 1993, while President Bush was beginning a three-day visit to Kuwait City, Kuwaiti authorities thwarted a terrorist plot, seizing a powerful car bomb and other explosives, and arresting 16 suspects. The ringleaders of this plot were two Iraqi nationals.

Over the next two months, American law enforcement, forensic, and intelligence professionals conducted a meticulous and exhaustive investigation of this incident. They conducted detailed forensic examinations of the bombs and devices. Through the cooperation of the Kuwaiti government, they had independent access to all of the suspects in the case. They interviewed all involved several times. The process took time. There was no rush to judgment.

Based upon that investigation, the United States Department of Justice and the Central Intelligence Agency have concluded that Iraq planned, equipped and launched the terrorist operation that threatened the life of an American president. Further, it is the firm judgment of the United States intelligence community, based on all the sources of evidence available to it, that this assassination plot was directed and pursued by the Iraqi Intelligence Service, an arm of the government of Saddam Hussein.

The evidence that supports these conclusions includes forensic data, interviews with the suspects and other intelligence. The physical evidence is most impressive, and I will take some time to describe it to you.

A car bomb hidden in a Toyota Land Cruiser was smuggled across the Iraq-Kuwait border by the suspects during the night of

April 13, 1993. This bomb, and the other explosives that were seized by the Kuwaiti authorities, have been directly examined by FBI forensic experts. In their judgment, key components, including the remote-controlled firing device, the plastic explosives, the blasting cap, the integrated circuitry and the wiring were built by the same person or persons who built bombs previously recovered from the Iraqis. Certain aspects of these devices have been found only in devices linked to Iraq, and not in devices used by any other terrorist groups.

Similarly, the other explosives seized in the plot, including so-called cube bombs, contained components built by the same person or persons who built similar devices recovered in the past from the Iraqi Intelligence Service.

Let me show you some photographs that demonstrate the identical nature of the evidence seized in Kuwait with photos of Iraqi devices found elsewhere. The first photo is of the vehicle, of a Toyota Land Cruiser, that was turned into a car bomb by concealing approximately 80 kilograms of explosives in the vehicle's body panels.

The second photo shows the concealed wiring that was part of the bomb. This is a sophisticated device possessing devastating power. It was well hidden in the vehicle, and constructed to allow detonation by remote control, by a timer, or manually. The forensic experts have concluded that this bomb had a lethal radius of 400 yards. It would kill people occupying a four-square-block area. Hundreds of innocent people would have died.

The third set of photos shows that the front of the radio-controlled firing system found in Kuwait, and, above it, the front of another device recovered from an earlier terrorist bomb, known to be of Iraqi origin. Even an untrained eye can see that these are identical except for the serial numbers.

Next, we have a similar comparison of the insides of the two firing devices. The bottom photo is of the device found in Kuwait. As you can see, the selection of the components and the construction techniques in the two devices, including soldering, the use of connectors, and the wiring techniques, are also identical.

The fifth set of photos shows a comparison of the underside of the two firing devices. Again, you can see the obvious similarity of the circuit boards.

Finally, the last photograph shows the smaller cube bombs that were also seized by the Kuwaitis. The cube bombs contain the same type of integrated circuitry that was found in earlier known Iraqi terrorist devices.

In addition to this graphic evidence, we have the results of the interrogations of the suspects. The FBI conducted extensive interviews of all 16 suspects now on trial in Kuwait. The two main suspects are Iraqi nationals. They told the FBI that they had been recruited and received orders in Basra, Iraq, from individuals associated with the Iraqi Intelligence Service. They said the Iraqis provided them with the car bomb and other explosive devices on April 10, 1993.

One of the suspects said that he was recruited for the specific purpose of assassinating President Bush. The other main suspect told the FBI that he was instructed to guide the first suspect and the car bomb to Kuwait University, where President Bush and the emir of Kuwait were scheduled to appear, and to plant smaller explosives elsewhere in Kuwait.

During, and immediately after the Persian Gulf War, the Saddam Hussein government, through its controlled media, indicated that Iraq would hunt down and punish President Bush even after he left office. Since then, various classified intelligence sources support the conclusion of our investigation that the Iraqi government ordered this terrorist attack against President Bush.

From all the evidence available to our intelligence community, we are therefore highly confident that the Iraqi government, at its highest levels, directed its intelligence services to carry out an assassination attempt against President Bush.

As President Clinton indicated last night, this was a direct attack on the United States, an attack that required a direct United States response. Consequently, President Clinton yesterday instructed the United States armed forces to carry out a military operation against the headquarters of the Iraqi Intelligence Service in Baghdad. We responded directly, as we are entitled to do, under Article 51 of the United Nations Charter, which provides for the exercise of self-defense in such cases.

Our response has been proportional and aimed at a target directly linked to the operation against President Bush. It was designed to damage the terrorist infrastructure of the Iraqi regime, reduce its ability to promote terrorism, and deter further acts of aggression against the United States.

Let me say a word about the Iraqi intelligence apparatus. To survive in power, the Iraqi regime depends upon the fear created by its intelligence infrastructure. Renowned for its brutality, the Iraqi Intelligence Service, the largest part of this infrastructure, has responsibility for investigating and acting against any suspected disloyalty to Saddam Hussein. It is also responsible for conducting terrorism abroad, as it tried to do in this case, and for directing terror against Saddam's opponents at home.

We are all aware of the many acts of terror carried out by the Iraqi Intelligence Service against United Nations relief convoys in northern Iraq and on United Nations personnel and humanitarian aid workers in Iraq. This Iraqi Intelligence Service has also carried out assassinations of Iraqis seeking to escape Saddam's dictatorship, including a cold-blooded murder in Amman, Jordan, last year. The Iraqi Intelligence Service has been a major participant in the perpetration of Saddam's war crimes during the occupation of Kuwait, and the regime's crimes against humanity at home.

The Iraqi Intelligence Service headquarters building that was the target of last night's attack is the nerve center of the Iraqi Intelligence Service, the hub for all its activities.

Let me stress one point in particular. Our action is not directed against the Iraqi people. For far too long, they have suffered under the yoke of tyrannical repression of Saddam Hussein's regime. The United States looks forward to the day when that criminal regime is no longer able to oppress the Iraqi people, and the Iraqi nation can take its rightful place again among the family of nations.

Let me also say this: We regret the loss of civilian life. However, one should keep in mind that had the Iraqi attempt in Kuwait succeeded, hundreds of civilians could have died.

The specific incident was between Iraq and the United States directly, which is why we acted alone. Only the United States forces were involved. Our military action yesterday was aimed specifically at the instruments of terror that mounted the campaign against President Bush. Nevertheless, although we took action under Article 51 of the United Nations Charter, there is a broader context of which members of the Security Council are only too well aware.

Since its invasion of Kuwait, on Aug. 2, 1990, Iraq has repeatedly and consistently refused to comply with the resolutions of this council. Only a few days ago, the council found Iraq again to be in material breach of United Nations Security Council Resolution 687. The Iraqi regime today refuses to meet the requirements of the United Nations Special Commission on a range of matters relating to the destruction of weapons of mass destruction and ballistic missile programs.

The Iraqi regime refuses to accept United Nations Security Council Resolution 715, which mandates long-term monitoring of these weapons programs. The Iraqi regime rejects the delineation of the Kuwait-Iraq boundary. The Iraqi regime continues to repress its own people in violation of United Nations Security Council Resolution 688, instead choosing to impose a policy of economic deprivation, and even blockade, on some of its citizens. And the Iraqi regime refuses to accept United Nations Security Council Resolutions 706 and 712, which would allow Iraq to sell oil to meet the needs of its own citizens, a monumental act of abuse and disregard of the suffering of the Iraqi people.

My government's policy remains constant. We insist on full Iraqi compliance with all the United Nations resolutions. Through a policy of firmness and consistency, including readiness to use force if necessary, the international community must frustrate Iraq's efforts to ignore the will of the council.

The international community has spoken with one voice in insisting that Iraq abide by the principles of the United Nations Charter. We ignore crime of this magnitude at our collective peril, as members of an international society that seeks to uphold the rule of law. While the incident we are discussing today is an issue between Iraq and the United States, it should lead all nations represented here to redouble their resolve to ensure that the criminal regime in Baghdad is never again able to disturb the peace to which this institution is dedicated. ■

Clinton Announces Compromise On Gays in Military

President Clinton outlined his policy on gays in the military in a speech July 19 at the National Defense University at Fort McNair in Washington. Following is the Federal News Service transcript:

I have come here today to discuss a difficult challenge and one which has received an enormous amount of publicity and public and private debate over the last several months — our nation's policy toward homosexuals in the military.

I believe the policy I am announcing today represents a real step forward, but I know it will raise concerns in some of your minds, so I wanted you to hear my thinking and my decision directly and in person, because I respect you and because you are among the elite who will lead our armed forces into the next century, and because you will have to put this policy into effect, and I expect your help in doing it.

The policy I am announcing today is, in my judgment, the right thing to do and the best way to do it. It is right because it provides greater protection to those who happen to be homosexual and want to serve their country honorably in uniform, obeying all the military's rules against sexual misconduct. It is the best way to proceed because it provides a sensible balance between the rights of the individual and the needs of our military to remain the world's No. 1 fighting force.

As president of all the American people, I am pledged to protect and to promote individual rights. As commander in chief, I am pledged to protect and advance our security. In this policy I believe we have come close to meeting both objectives.

Let me start with this clear fact: Our military is one of our greatest accomplishments and our most valuable assets. It is the world's most effective and powerful fighting force, bar none. I have seen proof of this fact almost every day since I became president. I saw it last week when I visited Camp Casey along the DMZ [demilitarized zone] in Korea. I witnessed it at our military academies, at Annapolis and West Point, when I visited there. And I certainly relied on it three weeks ago when I ordered an attack on Iraq after that country's leadership attempted to assassinate President [George] Bush.

We owe a great deal to the men and women who protect us through their service, their sacrifice and their dedication; and we owe it to our own security to listen hard to them and act carefully as we consider any changes in the military. A force

ready to fight must maintain the highest priority under all circumstances.

Background

Let me review the events which bring us here today. Before I ran for president, this issue was already upon us. Some of the members of the military returning from the [Persian] Gulf War announced their homosexuality in order to protest the ban. The military's policy has been questioned in college ROTC programs. Legal challenges have been filed in court, including one that has since succeeded.

In 1991, the secretary of Defense, Dick Cheney, was asked about reports that the Defense Department spent an alleged $500 million to separate and replace about 17,000 homosexuals from the military service during the 1980s in spite of the findings of a government report saying there was no reason to believe that they could not serve effectively and with distinction.

Shortly thereafter, while giving a speech at the Kennedy School of Government at Harvard, I was asked by one of the students what I thought of this report and what I thought of lifting the ban. This question had never before been presented to me, and I had never had the opportunity to discuss it with anyone. I stated then what I still believe, that I thought there ought to be a presumption that people who wished to do so should be able to serve their country if they are willing to conform to the high standards of the military, and that the emphasis should be always on people's conduct, not their status.

For me — and this is very important — this issue has never been one of group rights but rather of individual ones, of the individual opportunity to serve and the individual responsibility to conform to the high standards of military conduct. For people who are willing to play by the rules, able to serve and make a contribution, I believed then and I believe now we should give them the chance to do so.

Existing Situation

The central facts of this issue are not much in dispute. First, notwithstanding the ban, there have been and are homosexuals in military service who serve with distinction. I have had the privilege of meeting some of these men and women, and I have been deeply impressed by their devotion to duty and to country. Second, there is no study showing them to be less capable or more prone to misconduct than heterosexual soldiers. Indeed, all the information we have indicates that they are not less capable or more prone to misbehavior.

Third, misconduct is already covered

by the laws and rules which also cover activities that are improper by heterosexual members of the military.

Fourth, the ban has been lifted in other nations and in police and fire departments in our country with no discernible negative impact on unit cohesion or capacity to do the job, though there is admittedly no absolute analogy to the situation we face and no study bearing on this specific issue.

Fifth, even if the ban were lifted entirely, the experience of other nations and police and fire departments in the United States indicates that most homosexuals would probably not declare their sexual orientation openly, thereby making an already hard life even more difficult in some circumstances.

But as the sociologist Charles Moskos noted after spending many years studying the American military, the issue might be tougher to resolve here in the United States than in Canada, Australia and in some other nations because of the presence in our country of both vocal gay rights groups and equally vocal anti-gay rights groups, including some religious groups who believe that lifting the ban amounts to endorsing a lifestyle they strongly disapprove of.

Clearly the American people are deeply divided on this issue, with most military people opposed to lifting the ban because of the feared impact on unit cohesion, rooted in disapproval of homosexual lifestyles, and a fear of invasion of privacy of heterosexual soldiers who must live and work in close quarters with homosexual military people.

However, those who have studied this issue extensively have discovered an interesting fact. People in this country who are aware of having known homosexuals are far more likely to support lifting the ban. In other words, they are likely to see this issue in terms of individual conduct and individual capacity, instead of the claims of a group with which they do not agree, and also to be able to imagine how this ban could be lifted without a destructive impact on group cohesion and morale.

Shortly after I took office and reaffirmed my position, the foes of lifting the ban in the Congress moved to enshrine the ban in law. I asked that congressional action be delayed for six months while the secretary of Defense worked with the Joint Chiefs [of Staff] to come up with a proposal for changing our current policy. I then met with the Joint Chiefs to hear their concerns and asked them to try to work through the issue with [Defense] Secretary [Les] Aspin.

I wanted to handle the matter in this way on grounds of both principle and practicality. As a matter of principle, it is my duty

as commander in chief to uphold the high standards of combat readiness and unit cohesion of the world's finest fighting force, while doing my duty as president to protect the rights of individual Americans and to put to use the abilities of all the American people. And I was determined to serve this principle as fully as possible through practical action, knowing this fact about our system of government: While the commander in chief and the secretary of Defense can change military personnel policies, Congress can reverse those changes by law in ways that are difficult, if not impossible, to veto.

For months now, the secretary of Defense and the service chiefs have worked through this issue in a highly charged, deeply emotional environment, struggling to come to terms with the competing consideration and pressures, and frankly, to work through their own ideas and deep feelings.

During this time, many dedicated Americans have come forward to state their own views on this issue. Most but not all of the military testimony has been against lifting the ban, but support for changing the policy has come from distinguished combat veterans, including Sens. Bob Kerrey, Chuck Robb, and John Kerry [of Neb., Va. and Mass., respectively] in the United States Congress. It has come from Lawrence J. Korb, who as an assistant secretary of Defense enforced the gay ban during the Reagan administration, and from former Sen. Barry Goldwater [Jr.], a distinguished veteran, former chairman of the Senate Armed Services Committee, founder of the Arizona National Guard and patron saint of the conservative wing of the Republican Party.

Sen. Goldwater's statement, published in The Washington Post recently, made it crystal clear that when this matter is viewed as an issue of individual opportunity and responsibility rather than one of alleged group rights, this is not a call for cultural license but, rather, a reaffirmation of the American value of extending opportunity to responsible individuals and of limiting the role of government over citizens' private lives. On the other hand, those who oppose lifting the ban are clearly focused not on the conduct of individual gay service members, but on how non-gay service members feel about gays in general and, in particular, those in the military service.

These past few days, I have been in contact with the secretary of Defense as he has worked through the final stages of this policy with the Joint Chiefs. We now have a policy that is a substantial advance over the one in place when I took office.

I have ordered Secretary Aspin to issue a directive consisting of these essential elements: One, service men and women will be judged based on their conduct, not their sexual orientation. Two, therefore, the practice, now six months old, of not asking about sexual orientation in the enlistment procedure will continue. Three, an open statement by a service member that he or she is a homosexual will recreate a rebuttable presumption that he or she intends to engage in prohibited conduct, but the service member will be given an opportunity to refute that presumption — in other words, to demonstrate that he or she intends to live by the rules of conduct that apply in the military service.

And four, all provisions of the Uniform Code of Military Justice will be enforced in an evenhanded manner as regards both heterosexuals and homosexuals. And, thanks to the policy provisions agreed [to] by the Joint Chiefs, there will be a decent regard to the legitimate privacy and associational rights of all service members. Just as is the case under current policy, unacceptable conduct, either heterosexual or homosexual, will be unacceptable 24 hours a day, seven days a week, from the time a recruit joins the service until the day he or she is discharged. Now, as in the past, every member of our military will be required to comply with the Uniform Code of Military Justice, which is federal law and military regulations, at all times and in all places.

'Honorable Compromise'

Let me say a few words now about this policy. It is not a perfect solution. It is not identical with some of my own goals. And it certainly will not please everyone, perhaps not anyone, and clearly not those who hold the most adamant opinions on either side of this issue. But those who wish to ignore the issue must understand that it is already tearing at the cohesion of the military, and it is today being considered by the federal courts in ways that may not be to the liking of those who oppose any change. And those who want the ban to be lifted completely on both status and conduct must understand that such action would have faced certain and decisive reversal by the Congress, and the cause for which many have fought for years would be delayed, probably for years.

Thus, on grounds of both principle and practicality, this is a major step forward. It is, in my judgment, consistent with my responsibilities as president and commander in chief to meet the need to change current policy. It is an honorable compromise that advances the cause of people who are called to serve our country by their patriotism, the cause of our national security, and our national interest in resolving an issue that has divided our military and our nation and diverted our attention from other matters for too long.

The time has come for us to move forward. As your commander in chief, I charge all of you to carry out this policy with fairness, with balance and with due regard for the privacy of individuals. We must and will protect unit cohesion and troop morale. We must and will continue to have the best fighting force in the world. But this is an end to witch hunts that spend millions of taxpayer dollars to ferret out individuals who have served their country well. Improper conduct on or off base should remain grounds for discharge, but we will proceed with an even hand against everyone regardless of sexual orientation.

Such controversies as this have divided us before, but our nation and our military have always risen to the challenge before. That was true of racial integration of the military and changes in the role of women in the military.

Each of these was an issue because it was an issue for society as well as for the military. And in each case, our military was a leader in figuring out how to respond most effectively.

In the early 1970s, when President [Richard M.] Nixon decided to transform our military into an all-volunteer force, many argued that it could not work. They said it would ruin our forces. But the leaders of our military not only made it work, they used the concept of an all-volunteer force to build the very finest fighting force our nation and the world have ever known.

Ultimately, the success of this policy will depend in large measure on the commitment it receives from the leaders of the military services. I very much respect and commend the Joint Chiefs for the good faith effort they have made through this whole endeavor. And I thank [Joint Chiefs Chairman] Gen. [Colin] Powell, the Joint Chiefs, and the commandant of the Coast Guard for joining me today and for their support of this policy.

I would also like to thank those who lobbied aggressively in behalf of changing the policy, including Congressman Barney Frank [D-Mass.], Congressman Gerry [E.] Studds [D-Mass.], the Campaign for Military Service, who worked with us and who clearly will not agree with every aspect of the policy announced today, but who should take some solace in knowing that their efforts have helped to produce a strong advance for the cause they seek to serve.

I must now look to Gen. Powell, to the Joint Chiefs, to all the other leaders in our military to carry out this policy through effective training and leadership. Every officer will be expected to exert the necessary effort to make this policy work. That has been the key every time the military has successfully addressed a new challenge, and it will be key in this effort, too.

Our military is a conservative institution, and I say that in the very best sense, for its purpose is to conserve the fighting spirit of our troops, to conserve the resources and the capacity of our troops, to conserve the military lessons acquired during our nation's existence, to conserve our very security and, yes, to conserve the liberties of the American people. Because it is a conservative institution, it is right for the military to be wary of sudden changes. Because it is an institution that embodies the best of America and must reflect the society in which it operates, it is also right for the military to make changes when the time for change is at hand.

I strongly believe that our military, like our society, needs the talents of every person who wants to make a contribution and who is ready to live by the rules. That is the heart of the policy that I have announced today. I hope in your heart you will find the will and the desire to support it and to lead our military in incorporating it into our nation's great asset and the world's best fighting force. ∎

Defense Guidelines on Conduct

Following are the Defense Dempartment's Department's official guidelines on homosexual conduct in the armed forces issued July 19, 1993:

Accession Policy:

Applicants for military service will no longer be asked or required to reveal if they are homosexual or bisexual, but applicants will be informed of the conduct that is proscribed for members of the armed forces, including homosexual conduct.

Discharge Policy:

Sexual orientation will not be a bar to service unless manifested by homosexual conduct. The military will discharge members who engage in homosexual conduct, which is defined as a homosexual act, a statement that the member is homosexual or bisexual, or a marriage or attempted marriage to someone of the same gender.

Investigations Policy:

No investigations or inquiries will be conducted solely to determine a service member's sexual orientation. Commanders will initiate inquiries or investigations when there is credible information that a basis for discharge or disciplinary action exists. Sexual orientation, absent credible information that a crime has been committed, will not be the subject of a criminal investigation. An allegation or statement by another that a service member is a homosexual, alone, is not grounds for either a criminal investigation or a commander's inquiry.

Activities:

Bodily contact between service members of the same sex that a reasonable person would understand to demonstrate a propensity or intent to engage in homosexual acts (e.g., handholding or kissing in most circumstances) will be sufficient to initiate separation.

Activities such as association with known homosexuals, presence at a gay bar, possessing or reading homosexual publications or marching in a gay rights rally in civilian clothes will not, in and of themselves, constitute credible information that would provide a basis for initiating an investigation or serve as the basis for an administrative discharge under this policy.

Speech within the context of priest-penitent, husband-wife or attorney-client communications remains privileged.

Off-Base Conduct:

No distinction will be made between off-base and on-base conduct.

From the time a member joins the service until discharge, the service member's duty and commitment to the unit is a 24-hour-a-day, seven-day-a-week obligation. Military members are required to comply with both the Uniform Code of Military Justice [UCMJ], which is federal law, and military regulations at all times and in all places. Unacceptable conduct, homosexual or heterosexual, is not excused because the service member is not "at work."

Investigations and Inquiries:

Neither investigations nor inquiries will be conducted solely to determine an individual's sexual orientation.

Commanders can initiate investigations into alleged homosexual conduct when there is credible information of homosexual acts, prohibited statements or homosexual marriage.

Commanders will exercise sound discretion regarding when credible information exists, and will evaluate the information's source and all attendant circumstances to assess whether the information supports a reasonable belief that a service member has engaged in proscribed homosexual conduct. Commanders, not investigators, determine when sufficient credible information exists to justify a detail of investigative resources to look into allegations.

Credible Information:

Credible information of homosexual conduct exists when the information, considered in light of its source and all attendant circumstances, supports a reasonable belief that a service member has engaged in such conduct. It requires a determination based on articulable facts, not just a belief of suspicion.

Security Clearances:

Questions pertaining to an individual's sexual orientation are not asked on personnel security questionnaires. An individual's sexual conduct, whether homosexual or heterosexual, is a legitimate security concern only if it could make an individual susceptible to exploitation or coercion, or indicate a lack of trustworthiness, reliability, or good judgment that is required of anyone with access to classified information.

The Threat of Extortion:

As long as service members continue to be separated from military service for engaging in homosexual conduct, credible information of such behavior can be a basis for extortion. Although the military cannot eliminate the potential for the victimization of homosexuals through blackmail, the policy reduces the risk to homosexuals by making certain categories of information largely immaterial to the military's initiation of investigations.

Only credible information that a service member engaged in homosexual conduct will form the basis for initiating an inquiry or investigation of a service member; suspicion of an individual's sexual orientation is not a basis, by itself, for official inquiry or action.

Extortion is a criminal offense, under both the UCMJ and U.S. Code, and offenders will be prosecuted. A service member convicted of extortion risks dishonorable discharge and up to three years confinement. Civilians found guilty of blackmail under the U.S. Code may be subject to a $2,000 fine and one-year imprisonment. The risk of blackmail will be addressed by educating all service members on the policy and by emphasizing the significant criminal sanctions facing convicted extortionists.

Outing:

A mere allegation or statement by another that a service member is a homosexual is not grounds for official action. Commanders will not take official action against members based on rumor, suspicion or capricious allegations.

However, if a third party provides credible information that a member has committed a crime or act that warrants discharge, e.g., engages in homosexual conduct, the commander may, based on the totality of the circumstances, conduct an investigation or inquiry, and take non-judicial or administrative action or recommend judicial action, as appropriate.

Commanders are responsible for initiating an investigation when credible information exists that a crime or basis for discharge has been committed. The commander examines the information and decides whether an investigation by the service investigative agency or a commander inquiry is warranted or if no action should be taken.

Harassment:

Commanders are responsible for maintaining good order and discipline.

All service members will be treated with dignity and respect. Hostile treatment or violence against a service member based on a perception of his or her sexual orientation will not be tolerated.

Former Postmaster Pleads Guilty; Documents Detail Alleged Scam

On July 19, former House Postmaster Robert V. Rota pleaded guilty to two counts of embezzlement and one count of conspiracy in connection with an alleged scheme to help members convert official expense money into cash for personal purposes, using the House Post Office.

In connection with the guilty pleas, J. Ramsey Johnson, U.S. attorney for the District of Columbia, filed a "factual proffer," in which the prosecutors laid out the facts they said they could have proved had the case gone to trial. The second document filed by Johnson, titled Information, contains the details of the indictment.

Following are the texts of the two documents:

Government's Factual Proffer

United States District Court for the District of Columbia

United States of America v. Robert V. Rota

In connection with the defendant's guilty plea in this matter, the United States proffers to the Court that had this case gone to trial on the charges to which the defendant is pleading guilty, the United States would have proved the following:

From July 1972 until March 1992, Defendant Robert V. Rota was Postmaster of the United States House of Representatives Post Office. As such, he was in charge of all postal operations associated with the United States House of Representatives. From at least 1978, Mr. Rota personally allowed the House Post Office to be used as a convenient and — until this investigation — largely untraceable source of illegal cash for selected Congressmen.

Mr. Rota provided cash to Members of Congress in three different ways: First, cash for official congressional vouchers, which falsely certified that the Congressmen had received postage stamps for the vouchers; second, cash for postage stamps, which the Congressmen had previously obtained with vouchers; and third, cash for checks drawn on congressional campaign and political action committee accounts. Mr. Rota's guilty plea focuses on the first two methods, each of which involved the embezzlement of United States funds by certain United States Congressmen.

Mr. Rota began giving cash from House Post Office funds to certain Congressmen shortly after he became Postmaster in 1972. On many occasions, he supplied cash by means of a two-step process, in which a Member of Congress would buy a large number of stamps through an official expense voucher, and then, shortly afterwards, would return the stamps to Mr. Rota and exchange them for cash. On other occasions, Mr. Rota gave cash to certain Members of Congress directly in exchange for official vouchers (each of which falsely certified that the Member had received postage stamps for the voucher). In either case, Mr. Rota obtained the cash from his Supervisor of Accounts, who was responsible for maintaining large amounts of cash and postage stamps in the House Post Office.

In 1979, a House Post Office employee reported a cash-for-vouchers exchange to law enforcement authorities, who began an investigation to determine whether Mr. Rota or others were giving cash to Members of Congress. On May 5, 1980, Justice Department attorneys interviewed Mr. Rota and his Supervisor of Accounts. Before the interview, Mr. Rota discussed with the Supervisor of Accounts the need to protect the Members of Congress and the need to be careful about what they said. During the interview itself, both Mr. Rota and the Supervisor of Accounts falsely denied that they had given cash to Congressmen.

After this successful cover-up, Mr. Rota did not end the practice of giving cash to selected Congressmen. To the contrary,

during the early and mid 1980s, he continued to provide cash in exchange for vouchers and stamps to several Members of Congress, including two who are designated in the Information as "Congressman A" and "Congressman B."

During a two-year period from May 1985 through May 1987, Mr. Rota personally handled stamp vouchers totaling $11,500 for Congressman A and $4,300 for Congressman B (as outlined in paragraph 24 of the Information). On some occasions, Mr. Rota provided large amounts of stamps to the Congressmen and later exchanged the stamps for cash, and on other occasions Mr. Rota gave cash directly in exchange for vouchers.

In approximately May of 1987, the long-time Supervisor of Accounts retired from the House Post Office and was replaced by an attorney whom Mr. Rota did not know. After that, when Congressman A and Congressman B asked Mr. Rota if he could still give them cash from the House Post Office, he explained that he could not trust the new employee to carry out the scheme. Mr. Rota discontinued the cash-for-vouchers practice, despite the requests from Congressman A and Congressman B, for the two-year period that this new employee occupied the position of Supervisor of Accounts.

In approximately May of 1989, the position of Supervisor of Accounts again became vacant. This time, with the personal intervention and insistence of Congressman A, Mr. Rota promoted a long-time House Post Office employee, who was a patronage employee of Congressman A, to be the new Supervisor of Accounts. Shortly after this person assumed his new position, Mr. Rota explained to him that they would give cash to Congressman A in exchange for postage vouchers, because Congressman A took care of them and they should take care of Congressman A in return. Later in 1989, Mr. Rota explained to his new Supervisor of Accounts that they would also give cash to Congressman B in exchange for postage vouchers, because Congressman B was a close friend of Mr. Rota.

During a 21-month period between late July 1989 and April 1991, Mr. Rota personally handled stamp vouchers totaling $9,800 for Congressman A and $5,000 for Congressman B (as outlined in paragraph 29 of the Information). On most of these occasions Mr. Rota gave cash to the Congressmen directly in exchange for postage vouchers. In addition to the incidents outlined in paragraph 29, during the summer of 1989 Mr. Rota twice delivered two other large sums of cash to Congressman A, having obtained the cash from his Supervisor of Accounts in exchange for stamps delivered by the Congressman.

Near the end of April 1991, a stamp clerk stole cash from the House Post Office, prompting an investigation by the United States Capitol Police. Shortly thereafter, the United States Attorney's Office and the United States Postal Inspection Service joined the investigation. In July 1991, Mr. Rota discussed with his Supervisor of Accounts the need to withhold information during interviews with the Postal Inspectors to protect the Congressmen.

In early 1992, the House of Representatives established a Task Force for the Investigation of the House Post Office. Mr. Rota resigned as House Postmaster on March 19, 1992. During a formal interview on April 7, 1992, Mr. Rota falsely stated to the House Task Force investigators that he was not aware of any occasion in which stamps were exchanged for cash.

Count One of the Information charges Mr. Rota with participating in a conspiracy, stretching from at least 1978 until April of 1992, comprising the range of events described above. Counts Two and Three are based on two of the particular incidents in which he provided cash to Congressmen.

The Government notes that Mr. Rota is not charged with converting any of this cash to his personal use, and that there is no

evidence that he did so. Rather, what Mr. Rota did was to place the services of his Office, and the United States funds under his control, at the disposal of certain United States Congressmen, knowing full well that he was aiding the embezzlement of money from those funds. What Mr. Rota got in return was to keep his job as an Officer of the United States House of Representatives.

Respectfully submitted,

J. RAMSEY JOHNSON
United States Attorney

Details of Indictment

INFORMATION

The United States Attorney informs the Court that:

COUNT ONE
(CONSPIRACY TO VIOLATE THE LAWS
OF THE UNITED STATES)

At all relevant times:

The House of Representatives Post Office

1. The Office of the Postmaster of the United States House of Representatives (the "House Post Office") was an arm of the United States House of Representatives, established to provide postal services to Members of the House of Representatives and others on Capitol Hill. These services included the delivery of United States mail, the sale of United States postage stamps, the sale of United States Postal money orders, and the provision of other special services relating to the transportation of the United States mail. In providing these services, the House Post Office functioned as a contract post office for the United States Postal Service.

2. Employees of the House Post Office were "patronage" employees of the House of Representatives. That is, an individual had to be "sponsored" by a Member of the House of Representatives in order to be employed at the House Post Office.

3. Defendant ROBERT V. ROTA was the Postmaster of the House Post Office, serving continuously as House Postmaster from 1972 until March of 1992. As House Postmaster, Defendant ROTA was a House Officer, elected by the Members of the House of Representatives. Defendant ROTA was responsible for managing and directing the operations of the House Post Office.

4. In carrying out the functions of the House Post Office, an employee known as the "Stamp Teller," and later known as the "Supervisor of Accounts," the "Director of Accountable Papers," or the "Assistant to the Postmaster, Accountable Papers," reported directly to defendant ROTA, and was responsible for the safekeeping and disbursement of all cash and postage stamps in the possession of the House Post Office. In this Information the term "Supervisor of Accounts" will be used to refer to the employee holding this position, regardless of its title at any particular time.

5. From at least 1978 until in or about May 1987, the position of Supervisor of Accounts was held by an individual who will be referred to in this Information as "Employee No. 1." From in or about May 1987 to in or about May 1989, the position was held by an individual who will be referred to as "Employee No. 2." From in or about May 1989 to in or about May 1992, the position was held by an individual who will be referred to as "Employee No. 3."

The Voucher System and the Use of Postage

6. The Committee on House Administration of the House of Representatives ("the Committee") was authorized by law to write rules and regulations governing the use of United States funds in support of the conduct of the official and representational duties of Members of the House of Representatives.

7. Under the rules and regulations prescribed by the Committee, each Member of the House of Representatives was entitled to an annual "Official Expenses Allowance," which could be used to cover ordinary and necessary business expenses incurred by the Member (and/or the Member's employees) within the United States in support of the conduct of the Member's official and representational duties. These allowances were drawn from funds of the United States administered by the House of Representatives. Members were prohibited from using these allowances to defray any personal, political, or campaign related expenses.

8. Under the rules and regulations prescribed by the Committee, Members of the House of Representatives were required to submit vouchers in order to use their Official Expenses Allowance to pay certain of these official expenses. Such vouchers had to be signed by the Member, certifying that he or she had paid for or received the item or service specified on the voucher.

9. Under the rules and regulations prescribed by the Committee, these vouchers were submitted to and processed by the Finance Office, which was part of the Office of the Clerk of the House of Representatives. Upon receipt of a Member's voucher, the Finance Office either reimbursed the Member for the expense certified on the voucher, or paid directly for the items or services described there. In either case, the Finance Office paid the expense out of United States funds, and then made a corresponding deduction from the Member's annual Official Expenses Allowance.

10. Under the rules and regulations prescribed by the Committee, Members of the House of Representatives were entitled to use vouchers to obtain postage stamps from the House Post Office, and then to use those stamps to send official mail instead of using the Congressional "frank" to do so, only in the following limited circumstances:

"[P]ostage or postage stamps are not to be used in lieu of the frank, but rather when the frank is insufficient, i.e., to pay the cost of certified, registered, insured, or express mail; to mail an item to a foreign country; or when the Member provides a stamped self-addressed envelope to recover documents or materials related to the conduct of official business."

In such circumstances, the Finance Office paid the United States Postal Service for the value of the stamps that were certified on the voucher as having been received by the Member.

11. Under the rules and regulations prescribed by the Committee, "[u]nused postage stamps shall be forwarded to the Clerk prior [to] the end of the Members service in the House."

The Conspiracy

12. From in or about 1978, and continuing through in or about April 1992, within the District of Columbia, defendant ROBERT V. ROTA willfully and knowingly combined, conspired, confederated, and agreed with other persons to commit offenses against the United States; that is, to convert to the use of particular Members of the House of Representatives, without authority, funds of the United States; that is, to cause cash from public funds to be given to particular Members of the House of Representatives (a) in exchange for vouchers which falsely stated that postage stamps had been given to the Members; and (b) in exchange for stamps that the Members had previously purchased by vouchers; in violation of Title 18, United States Code, Section 641 [Embezzlement of Government Property].

Goals of the Conspiracy

13. It was a goal of the conspiracy that defendant ROTA would enrich particular Members of the House of Representatives by giving them cash obtained from the House Post Office in exchange for House of Representatives vouchers and in exchange for postage stamps purchased with official House of Representatives funds.

14. It was a further goal of the conspiracy that defendant ROTA would maintain his position as one of the elected Officers of the House of Representatives, by earning the favor and support of particular Members of the House of Representatives by providing cash to them in exchange for vouchers and postage stamps.

The Manner and Means Used to Further
the Goals of the Conspiracy

The conspiracy was accomplished through the following manner and means, among others:

15. Defendant ROTA would and did arrange to obtain large sums of cash from the House Post Office, in exchange for official vouchers made out for postage stamps and signed by particular Members of the House of Representatives, and then would and did deliver the cash to the Members who had signed the vouchers, including two Members who will be referred to in this Information as "Congressman A" and "Congressman B."

16. Defendant ROTA would and did arrange to obtain large numbers of postage stamps from the House Post Office, in exchange for official vouchers signed by particular Members of the House of Representatives; shortly thereafter would and did return the stamps to the House Post Office, and direct employees to exchange the stamps for cash from the public funds maintained there; and then would and did deliver the cash to the Members who had signed the vouchers, including Congressman A and Congressman B.

17. Defendant ROTA would and did use employees of the House Post Office to facilitate the scheme to provide cash from public funds to particular Members of the House of Representatives, including:

(a) directing employees to prepare vouchers, from a voucher supply kept in the House Post Office (numbered in sequences beginning primarily with "262" and "263"), for the alleged purchase of stamps from the annual Official Expenses Allowances of particular Members of the House of Representatives;

(b) directing the Supervisor of Accounts to exchange the completed vouchers, after they were signed by the particular Members, for (1) cash, or (2) postage stamps to be later redeemed for cash.

18. At times during the course of the conspiracy, defendant ROTA would and did conceal and cover up the exchange of vouchers and postage stamps for cash, including the following:

(a) in or about May of 1980, discussing with Employee No. 1, who was the Supervisor of Accounts at the time, the fact that they had to protect the Members, and that they should be careful about what they said during their upcoming interview with Justice Department attorneys;

(b) in or about May of 1980, during the interview with Justice Department attorneys, falsely denying that Members of the House of Representatives had received cash from the House Post Office in exchange for vouchers or postage stamps;

(c) in or about July of 1991, discussing with Employee No. 3, who was then the Supervisor of Accounts, the fact that they needed to withhold information from the United States Postal Inspection Service during the course of a criminal investigation;

(d) in or about January or February of 1992, discussing with Employee No. 3 the fact that they needed to withhold information from Congressional investigators; and

(e) in or about April of 1992, falsely stating to Congressional investigators that he did not know whether or not Members of the House of Representatives had received cash from the House Post Office by returning postage stamps.

Overt Acts

In furtherance of the conspiracy and to accomplish its goals, defendant ROTA and other co-conspirators committed and caused to be committed the following overt acts, among others, within the District of Columbia and elsewhere:

19. On numerous occasions between 1978 and 1980, defendant ROTA gave cash from funds maintained at the House Post Office to each of several Members of the House of Representatives, including Congressman A, in exchange either for the Member's official voucher made out for postage, or for postage stamps that the Member had previously obtained by voucher from the House Post Office.

20. Between in or about April 1979 and in or about July 1979, defendant ROTA delivered $750.00 in cash to a Member of the House of Representatives, having obtained the cash from Employee No. 1 by giving her an official voucher made out for postage and signed by the Member, and directing her to exchange the voucher for cash.

21. Between in or about September 1979 and in or about early May 1980, defendant ROTA learned that the Justice Department was conducting an investigation of allegations that Members of the House of Representatives were receiving cash from the House Post Office in exchange for vouchers or postage stamps, which investigation was based in part on reports of the event described in the preceding paragraph.

22. On or about May 5, 1980, defendant ROTA discussed with Employee No. 1 the need to protect the Members, and to be careful about what they said in their upcoming interview with Justice Department attorneys.

23. On or about May 5, 1980, during the interview with Justice Department attorneys, defendant ROTA and Employee No. 1 falsely denied that Members of the House of Representatives had received cash from the House Post Office in exchange for postage stamps or vouchers.

24. On numerous occasions between May 1980 and May 1987, defendant ROTA gave cash from funds maintained at the House Post Office to each of several Members of the House of Representatives, including Congressman A and Congressman B, having obtained the cash from Employee No. 1 (who was the Supervisor of Accounts at the time) in exchange either for the Member's official voucher made out for postage, or for postage stamps that the Member had previously obtained by voucher from the House Post Office, including in the following instances:

Voucher Date	Voucher Number	Member	Amount	Description of Services Stated on Voucher
5/1/85	263851	Congressman A	$1,100	Postage Stamps
7/10/85	263853	Congressman A	$900	Postage Stamps
12/20/85	263856	Congressman A	$2,000	Postage Stamps
4/10/86	263854	Congressman A	$1,200	Postage Stamps
8/7/86	263847	Congressman A	$2,100	Postage Stamps
9/30/86	263848	Congressman B	$1,000	Postage Stamps
10/29/86	263849	Congressman B	$1,400	Postage Stamps
12/31/86	262751	Congressman B	$2,000	Postage Stamps
4/8/87	262793	Congressman A	$2,800	Postage Stamps
4/8/87	262799	Congressman B	$600	Postage Stamps
5/21/87	262809	Congressman B	$700	Postage Stamps

25. In or about the summer of 1987, defendant ROTA informed Congressman A and Congressman B, in response to their requests to ROTA to exchange vouchers for cash, that they could not make the exchange because Employee No. 2 had recently replaced Employee No. 1 as the new Supervisor of Accounts, and ROTA did not know whether they could trust Employee No. 2 to carry out the cash-for-vouchers scheme.

26. In or about May 1989, with the intervention and support of Congressman A, defendant ROTA promoted Employee No. 3, who was a patronage employee of Congressman A, to the position of Supervisor of Accounts, replacing Employee No. 2.

27. On or about July 26, 1989, defendant ROTA discussed with Employee No. 3, who was the new Supervisor of Accounts, that they would give cash to Congressman A in exchange for House of Representatives vouchers, because Congressman A took care of them, so they had to take care of Congressman A in return.

28. On or about December 29, 1989, defendant ROTA told Employee No. 3 that Congressman B wanted cash in exchange for House of Representatives vouchers, stating that Congressman B was a good friend of ROTA.

29. On numerous occasions between July 1989 and May 1991, defendant ROTA gave cash from funds maintained at the House Post Office to each of several Members of the House of Representatives, including Congressman A and Congressman B, having obtained the cash from Employee No. 3 (who was the Supervisor of Accounts at the time) in exchange either for the Member's official voucher made out for postage, or for postage stamps that the

Member had previously obtained by voucher from the House Post Office, including in the following instances:

Voucher Date	Voucher Number	Member	Amount	Description of Services Stated on Voucher
7/26/89	104790	Congressman A	$2,000	25 cent stamps
12/29/89	262862	Congressman B	$1,000	Postage stamps
12/29/89	516275	Congressman A	$1,500	25 cent stamps
4/25/90	249759	Congressman B	$2,000	Postage stamps
4/26/90	120734	Congressman A	$2,300	25 cent stamps
12/13/90	249781	Congressman B	$2,000	Postage stamps
12/ /90	[unknown]	Congressman A	$2,000	[unknown]
4/17/91	262806	Congressman A	$2,000	Postage stamps

30. In or about May or June 1991, defendant ROTA learned that a criminal investigation had begun of alleged irregularities at the House Post Office.

31. In or about July 1991, defendant ROTA discussed with Employee No. 3 the need to withhold information during interviews with United States Postal Inspectors.

32. Between in or about January 1992 and February 1992, defendant ROTA discussed with Employee No. 3 the need to withhold information about illegally giving cash to Members from a United States Congressional Committee investigating the House Post Office.

33. In or about April of 1992, defendant ROTA falsely stated to Congressional investigators that he did not know whether or not Members of the House of Representatives had received cash from the House Post Office by returning postage stamps.

(In violation of Title 18, United States Code, Section 371)

COUNT TWO
(EMBEZZLEMENT)

34. The United States Attorney restates paragraphs 1 through 11 of Count One.

35. On or about December 29, 1989, within the District of Columbia, defendant ROBERT V. ROTA aided and abetted Congressman B in willfully and knowingly embezzling and converting to Congressman B's own use, without authority, funds of the United States, which funds had come within the control of Congressman B as part of his annual Official Expenses Allowance.

(In violation of Title 18 U.S.C. Sections 641 and 2)

COUNT THREE
(EMBEZZLEMENT)

36. The United States Attorney restates paragraphs 1 through 11 of Count One.

37. On or about April 17, 1991, within the District of Columbia, defendant ROBERT V. ROTA aided and abetted Congressman A in willfully and knowingly embezzling and converting to Congressman A's own use, without authority, funds of the United States, which funds had come within the control of Congressman A as part of his annual Official Expenses Allowance.

(In violation of Title 18 U.S.C. Sections 641 and 2)

J. RAMSEY JOHNSON
United States Attorney in and for the District of Columbia

Ginsburg Adroit, Amiable But Avoids Specifics

Supreme Court nominee Judge Ruth Bader Ginsburg appeared before the Senate Judiciary Committee on July 20. Following are excerpts from the hearings, transcribed by the Federal News Service and beginning with Ginsburg's opening remarks:

JUDGE GINSBURG: . . . The president's confidence in my capacity to serve as a Supreme Court justice is responsible for the proceedings about to begin. There are no words to tell him what is in my heart. I can say simply this: If confirmed, I will try in every way to justify his faith in me.

I am, as you know, from my responses to your queries, a Brooklyn [N.Y.] native, born and bred. A first-generation American on my father's side, barely second-generation on my mother's. Neither of my parents had the means to attend college, but both taught me to love learning, to care about people and to work hard for whatever I wanted or believed in. Their parents had the foresight to leave the old country when Jewish ancestry and faith meant exposure to pogroms and denigration of one's human worth.

What has become of me could happen only in America. Like so many others, I owe so much to the entry this nation afforded to people yearning to breathe free. I have had the great good fortune to share life with a partner [Martin Ginsburg] truly extraordinary for his generation, a man who believed at age 18 when we met and who believes today that a woman's work, whether at home or on the job, is as important as a man's.

I became a lawyer in days when women were not wanted by most members of the legal profession. I became a lawyer because Marty and his parents supported that choice unreservedly. I have been deeply moved by the outpouring of good wishes received in recent weeks from family, neighbors, camp mates, classmates, students at Rutgers [University School of Law] and Columbia Law School, law teaching colleagues, lawyers with whom I have worked, judges across the country and many women and men who do not know me. That huge, spirit-lifting collection shows that for many of our people, an individual's sex is no longer remarkable or even unusual with regard to his or her qualifications to serve on the Supreme Court.

Indeed, in my lifetime, I expect to see three, four, perhaps even more women on the high court bench, women not shaped from the same mold, but of different complexions. Yes, there are miles in front; but what a distance we have traveled from the day President Thomas Jefferson told his secretary of State the appointment of women to public office is an innovation for which the public is not prepared. "Nor," Jefferson added, "am I."

The increasingly full use of the talent of all of this nation's people holds large promise for the future, but we could not have come to this point, and I surely would not be in this room today, without the determined efforts of men and women who kept dreams alive, dreams of equal citizenship in the days when few would listen. People like Susan B. Anthony, Elizabeth Cady Stanton [women's suffrage leaders] and Harriet Tubman [abolitionist] come to mind. I stand on the shoulders of those brave people.

Her View of Judging

Supreme Court justices are guardians of the great charter that has served as our nation's fundamental instrument of government for over 200 years. It is the oldest written Constitution still in force in the world. But the justices do not guard constitutional rights alone. Courts share that profound responsibility with Congress, the president, the states and the people. The constant realization of a more perfect union, the Constitution's aspiration, requires the widest, broadest, deepest participation on matters of government and government policy.

One of the world's greatest jurists, Judge Learned [B.] Hand, said, as Sen. [Carol] Moseley-Braun [D-Ill.] reminded us, that the spirit of liberty that imbues our Constitution must lie first and foremost in the hearts of the men and women who compose this great nation. Judge Hand defined that spirit in a way I fully embrace, as one which is not too sure it is right and so seeks to understand the minds of other men and women and to weigh the interests of others alongside its own without bias. The spirit Judge Learned Hand described strives for a community where the least shall be heard and considered side by side with the greatest. I will keep that wisdom in the front of my mind as long as I am capable of judicial service.

Some of you asked me during recent visits why I want to be on the Supreme Court. It is an opportunity beyond any other for one of my training to serve society. The controversies that come to the Supreme Court as the last judicial resort touch and concern the health and well-being of our nation and its people. They affect the preservation of liberty to ourselves and our posterity. Serving on this court is the highest honor, the most awesome trust that can be placed in a judge. It means working at my craft, working with and for the law as a way to keep our society both ordered and free.

Let me try to state in a nutshell how I view the work of judging. My approach, I believe, is neither liberal nor conservative. Rather, it is rooted in the place of the judiciary of judges in our democratic society. The Constitution's preamble speaks first of "we, the people" and then of their elected representatives. The judiciary is third in line, and it is placed apart from the political fray so that its members can judge fairly, impartially, in accordance with the law and without fear about the animosity of any appreciate group. In Alexander Hamilton's words, the mission of judges is to secure a steady, upright and impartial administration of the laws. I would add that the judge should carry out that function without fanfare but with due care. She should decide the case before her without reaching out to cover cases not yet seen. She should be ever mindful, as Judge and then [Supreme Court] Justice Benjamin [N.] Cardozo said, justice is not to be taken by storm. She is to be wooed by slow advances.

A Preview Would Be Wrong

We, this committee and I, are about to embark on many hours of hearings. You have arranged this hearing to aid you in the performance of a vital task — to prepare your Senate colleagues for consideration of my nomination. The record of the Constitutional Convention shows that the delegates had initially entrusted the power to appoint federal judges — most prominently, Supreme Court judges — not to the president, but to you and your colleagues, to the Senate acting alone. Only in the waning days of the convention did the framers settle on a nomination role for the president and an advice and consent role for the Senate. The text of the Constitution as finally formulated makes no distinction between the appointment process for Supreme Court justices and the process for other offices of the United States, for example, Cabinet officers. But, as history bears out, you and senators past have sensibly considered appointments in relation to the appointee's task.

Federal judges may long outlast the president who appoints them. They may serve as long as they can do the job. As the Constitution says, they may remain in office during good behavior. Supreme Court justices, most notably, participate in shaping a lasting body of constitutional decisions; they continuously confront matters on which the framers left things unsaid,

unsettled or uncertain.

For that reason, when the Senate considers a Supreme Court nomination, the senators are properly concerned about the nominee's capacity to serve the nation, not just for the here and now, but over the long term. You have been supplied, in the five weeks since the president supplied my nomination, with hundreds of pages about me and thousands of pages I have penned: my writings as a law teacher, mainly about procedure; 10 years of briefs filed when I was a courtroom advocate of the equal stature of men and women before the law; numerous speeches and articles on that same theme; 13 years of opinions, counting the unpublished together with the published opinions, well over 700 of them, all decisions I made as a member of the U.S. Court of Appeals for the District of Columbia Circuit, several comments on the roles of judges and lawyers in our legal system.

That body of material, I know, has been examined by the committee with care. It is the most tangible, reliable indicator of my attitude, outlook, approach and style. I hope you will judge my qualifications principally on that written record, a record spanning 34 years, and that you will find in that written record assurance that I am prepared to do the hard work and to exercise the informed, independent judgment that Supreme Court decision-making entails.

I think of these proceedings much as I do of the division between the written record and briefs on the one hand and oral argument on the other in appellate tribunals. The written record is by far the more important component in an appellate court's decision-making, but the oral argument often elicits helpful clarifications and concentrates the judges' minds on the character of the decision they are called upon to make.

There is, of course, this critical difference: You are well aware that I come to this proceeding to be judged as a judge, not as an advocate. Because I am and hope to continue to be a judge, it would be wrong for me to say or to preview in this legislative chamber how I would cast my vote on questions the Supreme Court may be called upon to decide. Were I to rehearse here what I would say and how I would reason on such questions, I would act injudiciously.

Judges in our system are bound to decide concrete cases, not abstract issues. Each case comes to court based on particular facts, and its decisions should turn on those facts and the governing law stated and explained in light of the particular arguments the parties or their representatives present. A judge sworn to decide impartially can offer no forecasts, no hints, for that would show not only disregard for the specifics of the particular case, it would display disdain for the entire judicial process.

Similarly, because you are considering my capacity for independent judging, my personal views on how I would vote on a publicly debated issue, were I in your shoes, were I a legislator, are not what you will be closely examining.

As [Supreme Court] Justice Oliver Wendell Holmes [Jr.] counseled, one of the most sacred duties of a judge is not to read her convictions into the Constitution. I have tried and I will continue to try to follow the model Justice Holmes set in holding that duty sacred. I see this hearing, as I know you do, as a grand opportunity once again to reaffirm that civility, courtesy and mutual respect [should] properly keynote our exchanges.

Judges, I am mindful, owe the elected branches, the Congress and the president respectful consideration of how court opinions affect their responsibilities, and I am heartened by legislative branch reciprocal sensitivity. As one of you said two months ago at a meeting of the Federal Judges' Association, we in Congress must be more thoughtful, more deliberate, in order to enable judges to do their job more effectively.

As for my own deportment or, in the Constitution's words, good behavior, I prize advice received on this nomination from a dear friend, Frank Griffin, a recently retired justice of the Supreme Court of Ireland. Justice Griffin wrote: "Courtesy to and consideration for one's colleagues, the legal profession and the public are among the greatest attributes a judge can have."

It is fitting, as I conclude this opening statement, to express my deep respect — my deep respect for and abiding appreciation to Justice Byron R. White for his 31 years and more of fine service on the Supreme Court. In acknowledging his colleagues' good wishes on the occasion of his retirement, Justice White wrote that he expects to sit on U.S. Courts of Appeals from time to time and so to be a consumer of, instead of a participant in, Supreme Court opinions. He expressed a hope shared by all lower court judges. He hoped the Supreme Court's mandates will be clear and crisp, leaving as little room as possible for disagreement about their meaning. If confirmed, I will take that counsel to heart and strive to write opinions that both get it right and keep it tight. Thank you for your patience.

The Meaning of the Constitution

SEN. JOSEPH R. BIDEN JR., D-DEL: ... I'd like to begin by asking you about how you will go about interpreting our Constitution, Judge. Judges, as you know better than I do, approach this job in many different ways. And these approaches often lead to very different results. You've made a great many statements about constitutional interpretation as a scholar and while as a judge in lectures that you've delivered, most recently in a talk you gave this year, which is referred to as the Madison lecture.

In that lecture, you said, and I'm quoting here, that, quote, our fundamental instrument of government is an evolving document. You also said you rejected the notion, "... that the great clauses of the Constitution must be confined to the interpretation which the framers would have placed on them." I could not agree more. If the meaning of the Constitution did not evolve over time we would not today have many of the individual rights all Americans now hold most dear, like the right to choose whomever we wish to marry. There's nothing in the Constitution, as you know, that gives someone a constitutional right to marry whom they want. It's not specifically enumerated, and were that not changed in *Loving v. Virginia*, there could still be laws on the books saying blacks can't marry whites and whites can't marry blacks. Or the right to get a job whoever you are, whether you're white or black, male or female.

But still there are hard questions about precisely how the Constitution evolves, about when the court should recognize a right not specifically mentioned in the Constitution or specifically contemplated by the authors of that document at that moment, whether it's an amendment or the core of the Constitution.

You spoke of these questions at some length in the Madison lecture. You said that the history of the United States Constitution is in large part a story of, and I quote, "the extension of the constitutional rights and protections, including to once excluded groups."

Judge, can you discuss with me for a moment what allows courts to recognize rights like the right to marry whomever you wish, like the right to be employed or not employed based on — without there being a distinction between males and females, like the right that was mentioned here earlier by several of my colleagues in the opening statement, for women to be included in — I thought the phrase that [Delegate] Eleanor Holmes Norton [D-D.C.] used was within the embrace of the 14th Amendment, or something to that effect, when in fact they were not contemplated to be part of that amendment when it was written.

What is it that allows the court to recognize such rights that the drafters of the Constitution or specific amendments did not specifically mention or even contemplate at the time the amendment, in the case of the 14th Amendment, or the Constitution and the Bill of Rights were drafted?

JUDGE GINSBURG: It's a large question, Mr. Chairman, and I'll do my best to respond. First, I think the credit goes to the Founders. When I visited Sen. [Strom] Thurmond [R-S.C.], he was kind enough to give me a pocket Constitution.... But this pocket Constitution contains another document, and it is our basic rights-declaring document. It is the Declaration of Independence. The declaration that created the United States. I think the framers are shortchanged if we view them as having a limited view of rights because they wrote — Thomas Jefferson wrote — "We hold these rights [sic] to be self-evident, that all men are created equal, that they are endowed by their creator with certain unalienable rights,

that among these" — "among these are life, liberty and the pursuit of happiness." And that government is formed to protect and secure those rights.

Now, when the Constitution was written, as you know, there was much concern over a bill of rights. There were some who thought a bill of rights dangerous because one couldn't enumerate all the rights of the people; one couldn't compose a complete catalog. The thing to do was to limit the powers of government, and that would keep government from trampling on people's rights.

But there was a sufficient call for a bill of rights, and so the framers put down what was in the front of their minds in the Bill of Rights, and if we look at the way they are stated in the Bill of Rights in contrast to the Declaration of Independence — let's take liberty as it appears in the Fifth Amendment — this statement in the Fifth Amendment — nor shall any person "be deprived of life, liberty or property without due process of law" — this is written as a restriction on the state. The right is already declared in the Declaration. It's an inalienable right, and the government is warned to keep off, both in the structure of the Constitution, by limiting the powers of government, and in the Bill of Rights.

And then as you also know, Mr. Chairman, the framers were fearful that this limited catalog might be understood, even though it's written as a restriction on government rather than a conferring of rights on people — that it might be understood as skimpy, as not stating everything that is. And so we do have the Ninth Amendment stating that the Constitution shall not be construed to deny or disparage other rights retained by the people.

So the Constitution is written — you might contrast it with the great French Declaration of the Rights of Man, which does confer a right — the state confers a right to speak freely. But in our Bill of Rights, it doesn't say the state gives one a right to speak. It says Congress shall make no law prohibiting the free exercise of religion or abridging the freedom of speech. So the whole thrust of it is people have rights and government must be kept from trampling on them, and the rights are stated with great breadth in the Declaration of Independence.

Now it is true, and it's a point I made in the Madison lecture, that the immediate implementation in the days of the Founding Fathers in many respects was limited. We the people was not then what it is today. The most eloquent speaker on that subject was [Supreme Court] Justice Thurgood Marshall when, during the series on the bicentennial, when songs of praise to the Constitution were sung, he reminded us that the Constitution's immediate implementation, even its text, had certain limitations, blind spots, blots on our record. But he said that the beauty of this Constitution is that through a combination of interpretation, constitutional amendment, laws passed by Congress, we the people has

grown ever larger. So now it includes people who were once held in bondage; it includes women, who were left out of the political community at the start. So I hope that begins to answer your question.

The view of the framers — their large view, I think was expansive. Their immediate view was tied to the circumstances in which they lived.

Racial Preferences

SEN. ORRIN G. HATCH, R-UTAH: Now, Judge Ginsburg, I'm concerned about a reverse discrimination case decided in the D.C. Circuit that you sought to overturn. Now, that's the case of *Hammon v. Starr*. That was in 1987 there, the court ruled the District of Columbia Fire Department's racial hiring quotas violated Title VII and the Equal Protection Clause. In that particular case, according to Judge [Kenneth W.] Starr's opinion, there was no evidence of any actual intentional discrimination in hiring by the D.C. Fire Department since the 1950s — in other words, no evidence of discrimination or intentional discrimination.

In fact, long before the quota hiring policy began, the majority of the new hires by the department had been black. In Judge [Abner V.] Mikva's opinion, dissenting from the court's denial of rehearing *en banc* in the case, an opinion which you joined, Judge Mikva wrote: "This case concerns one of the fundamental dilemmas our society faces — how to eliminate a manifest imbalance that reflected underrepresentation of women and minorities in the work force."

Now, because you joined in this opinion here, I take it that you agree with Judge Mikva that a, quote, manifest imbalance, end quote, in an employer's work force is sufficient justification under Title VII for either voluntary or court-ordered race- and sex-based quotas and preferences under Title VII, even if the imbalance is not traceable to any prior intentional discrimination.... Well, the problem with permitting a manifest imbalance, that is, a statistical disparity not traceable to any intentional discrimination, to justify quotas or other preferential euphemisms like numerical goals, is that statistical disparities can and do often occur for many reasons other than discrimination, and it's unfair to penalize innocent persons and deny them opportunities through quotas or other preferences simply because an employer's hiring statistics are not, quote, balanced, end quote, according to some notion of statistical proportionality.

It's an important issue. It's probably one of the most important issues in the future for our country. And I don't expect you to tell me how you would rule, but let me just pose a hypothetical situation to you: Suppose a small business in a major city that was majority-black had never hired a black person, even though that business in over a decade had hired more than 50 people. Further suppose that a disappointed black job applicant filed a

discrimination suit, but he or she was unable to provide provide any direct evidence of intentional discrimination [by the] employer.

Would such statistics, standing alone, in your view justify an inference of racial discrimination by the employer, and would that employer, in your view, to avoid an expensive and protracted lawsuit that could cost hundreds, even thousands, of dollars, be justified in using quotas or other forms of racial preferences to eliminate the quote, manifest imbalance, end quote, if that really is the law?

And just one other question: Would a federal court be justified in such a case in ordering that employer to resort to quotas or other forms of racial preferences to eliminate or reduce the quote, manifest imbalance, end quote? . . .

JUDGE GINSBURG: They come to us with a very large record of facts developed in the trial court, and then they come also with lengthy briefs on both sides. I study those records, intensely read the arguments, have my law clerks do additional research, come armed to the teeth to the oral argument so I can ask the testing questions. So I'm always suspicious when I'm given a kind of one, two, three hypothetical. . . .

But I can say this: I was thinking about a particular case, one that, in fact, went to the Supreme Court.

It was a Santa Clara [Calif.] Highway Department case —

SEN. HATCH: I'm aware of it —

JUDGE GINSBURG: — that involved one of these affirmative action programs.

SEN. HATCH: That was the *Johnson* case.

JUDGE GINSBURG: Right, Paul Johnson was the plaintiff, and he complained that Diane Joyce had gotten a job that he should have gotten, and it was a result of this affirmative action plan, and that was a case that was much discussed. I'll just tell you a non-legal reaction that I had to it. This was a department that had 238 positions. Not one before Diane Joyce was ever held by a woman.

There was an initial screening, and there were 12 people who qualified for the job. That was further reduced until there were seven considered well-qualified for the job. And then the final selection was made. And on the point score, Paul Johnson came out slightly higher than Diane Joyce. But part of the composite score was based on a subjective test — an interview — and they were scored on the basis of this interview. And I had to think back to the days when I was in law school and I did fine on the pen and paper tests and had good grades, and then I had interviews, and I didn't score as high as the men on the interviews. I was screened out on the basis of the interviews. So I wondered whether the kind of program that was involved in that case wasn't — was no kind of preference at all, but a safeguard, a check against unconscious bias, against the unconscious

bias that I think — it may even have been conscious way back in the '50s — but in a department that has 238 positions, none of them are women, whether the slight plus — I mean, one must always recognize that there's another interest at stake in this case, in this case, Paul Johnson's — whether the employer wasn't in fact engaged unconsciously in denying full and equal opportunity to the women.

These are very difficult cases, and each one has to be studied in its own particular context....

SEN. HATCH: ... Well, the reason I gave you the hypothetical example I did is because I have had a lot of experience with small-business people who are suffering the stings of these employment discrimination cases. The average cost of defending those cases before our 1991 civil rights bill that we enacted here, which I voted for — the average cost of defending it, defense alone, just paying their attorneys to defend them, is $80,000. That was before that statute, and I suspect that cost has gone up a little since then.

But in the 13 years — I give you that example I did because I have great faith in you. I have known you since 1980, and I have watched what you've done, I've admired you. I have no doubt that you're a person of total equality and a person who deserves to be on the Supreme Court.

But in response to the Judiciary Committee questionnaire, in the 13 years since you went on the bench in 1980, you've not had a single black law clerk to my knowledge, at least according to your secretary or intern, out of 57 such employees that you have hired. Now, I find no fault with that because I know that there was no desire to discriminate, even though your court sits in the middle of a majority-black city, Washington, D.C. Now, some, if they took the broad language of Abner Mikva in that case, might call that a quote, manifest imbalance, end quote.

Now, I would not suggest for a moment that that imbalance resulted from any intentional discrimination on your part. The crucial point to keep in mind, however, is that when the concept of, quote, discrimination, unquote, is divorced from intent and we rely on statistics alone, a small-business man or woman with your record of employing minorities might find himself or herself spending hundreds of thousands of dollars to fend off discrimination suits, and that in fact is what's happening around this country right now.

Such an employer might adopt quotas or other forms of preferences in order to avoid or avert such litigation under any number of federal civil rights laws. And I'm worried about it because it's not fair to the employer and it's not fair to the persons denied opportunities because of preferences. So naturally I'm concerned about preferences, and I know you are, and I know that you're a very good person. But I just want to point that out because that happens every day all over this country where there is no evidence of intent and in

fact was no evidence — no desire on the part of the employer to exclude anybody.

JUDGE GINSBURG: I appreciate that, Sen. Hatch, but I do want to say that I have tried —

SEN. HATCH: I know you did —

JUDGE GINSBURG: And I am going to try harder, and if you confirm me for this job, my attractiveness to black candidates is going to improve.

SEN. HATCH: Well, [laughter] that's wonderful. I like that. But let me just say, you can see my point. These things are tough cases; they are difficult; there should be some evidence of intent.

Abortion Rights

SEN. HOWARD M. METZENBAUM, D-OHIO: Judge Ginsburg, I've always believed it's important that the men and women who serve on the court have a good sense of the reality that litigants face in the practical implications of their decisions. I expect that your broad range of professional and personal experiences would give you an understanding of the world faced by the individuals who are before the court.

Having said that, I'm frank to say that I'm puzzled by your often repeated criticisms of the decision in *Roe v. Wade*, that the court went too far and too fast. You stated the decision need only have invalidated the Texas abortion law in question. You've also stated that *Roe* curtailed a trend towards liberalization of state abortion statutes.

I'm frank to say that some, including this senator, would question whether women really were making real progress towards obtaining reproductive freedom when *Roe* was decided in 1973. Would you be willing to explain your basis for making those statements about *Roe* and the state of abortion law at the time of the *Roe* decision?

JUDGE GINSBURG: Yes, Sen. Metzenbaum, I will — I will try.

The statement that you made about the law moving in a reform direction is taken directly from Justice [Harry A.] Blackmun's decision in *Roe* itself, where he said that until recently, the law had been almost solidly like the Texas law but that there had been a trend in the direction of reform to the extent that some one-third of the states in a span of a very few years had reformed their abortion laws from the point where only the life of the woman was protected to a few years later — some years later, one-third of the states moving from that position to a variety of positions, most of them following something on the order of the American Law Institute model, which [allowed abortion on] grounds of rape, incest and some other grounds, four states having by then moved to permit abortion on the woman's request as advised by her doctor.

So, I took that statement not from any source other than the very opinion, which I am hardly criticizing for making that point. I accept it just as it was made in *Roe v. Wade*.

SEN. METZENBAUM: Would you not have had some concern, or do you not have some concern that had the gradualism been the reality, that many more women would have been denied abortion or would have been forced into in an illegal abortion and possibly an unsafe abortion?

JUDGE GINSBURG: Senator, we — we can't see what the past might have been like. I wrote an article that was engaging in what-ifs. It — I expressed the view that if the court had simply done what courts usually do, stuck to the very case before it, gone no further, then there might have been a change — gradual changes. You know, we've seen it happen in this country so many times. We saw it with the law of marriage and divorce going in a span of some dozen years from adultery was the sole ground for divorce to no-fault divorce in every state in the union.

Once the states begin to change, then it takes a while, but eventually most of them move in the direction of change. There was — the one thing that one can say for sure, there was a massive attack on *Roe v. Wade*. It was a single target to hit at. I think two things happened. One is that a movement that had been very vigorous became relaxed, slightly relaxed, didn't [entirely relax], but it wasn't as vigorous as it had been or that it might have been were it not that the court seemed to have taken care of the problem.

So one thing is the — one side seemed to relax its energy while the other side had a single target around which to rally. But that was — that's my what-if — and I could be wrong about that. My view was that the people would have accepted — would have expressed themselves in an enduring way on this question. And as I said, this is a matter of speculation. This is my view of what-if. Other people can have a different view.

Ginsburg returned to the committee for another day of testimony on July 21.

Equal Rights

SEN. ARLEN SPECTER, R-PA.: Judge Ginsburg, [in a University of Washington Law Quarterly article you wrote on equal rights for women, you] went to the point about having the court extend what you categorized as a host of rights, and it really was more in line with a statement you made at the [2nd Circuit Judicial Conference] in 1976, where you put it this way: "The Supreme Court, by dynamic interpretation of the equal protection principle, could have done everything we asked today." And then as an advocate you had articulated a number of rights which you were looking for [that went beyond ratification of the Equal Rights Amendment].

JUDGE GINSBURG: ... The article contrasted having an equal rights amendment as distinguished from the equal protection clause as a guarantee of the equal citizenship of women before the law.

... This article is, as I said, an article in a symposium on the quest for equality.

There was one on race, there was one on equal employment opportunity, and there was one devoted to sexual equality under the 14th Amendment and the Equal Rights Amendment.

That article, like the 2nd Circuit Judicial Conference talk, focused on two things: the Equal Protection Clause as a guarantee of the equal citizenship of women vs. the Equal Rights Amendment. That was the entire context of the article, and what I said there, was it is part of our history.

It's a sad part of our history, Sen. Specter, but it is part of our history that at the time of the 14th Amendment, that great amendment that changed so much in this nation, it didn't change the status of women. And it is part of the history that the leading feminists of the day — Susan B. Anthony, Elizabeth Cady Stanton, Lucretia Mott — campaigned against the ratification of the 14th Amendment because it allowed a system to persist in the United States where women couldn't vote, they couldn't hold office.

If they married, they couldn't hold property in their own name, they couldn't contract for themselves. That's what life was like for women in the middle of the 19th century. Times change, and eventually, after nearly a century of struggle, women achieved the vote, and they became full citizens, and many people thought that when women became full citizens entitled to the vote, they had achieved equality that made them full and equal citizens with men entitled to the same equal protection before the laws.

The position was that yes, it took bold and dynamic interpretation from what the framers of the 14th Amendment intended. The framers of the 14th Amendment meant no change; they intended no change at all in the status of women before the law; but in 1920, when women achieved the vote, they became full citizens. And you have to read this document as a whole . . . changed, as Thurgood Marshall said, over the years by constitutional amendment and by judicial construction. And so it was certainly a bold change from the middle of the 19th century until the 1970s when women's equal citizenship was recognized before the law. I remain an advocate of the Equal Rights Amendment, I will tell you, for this reason: because I have a daughter and a granddaughter, and I would like the legislature of this country and of all the states to stand up and say we know what that history was in the 19th century and we want to make a clarion call that women and men are equal before the law just as every modern human rights document in the world does since 1970. I'd like to see that statement made just that way in the United States Constitution.

But that women are equal citizens and have been ever since the 19th Amendment was passed, I think that's the case, and that's what this Washington University Law Quarterly article is about; that's what the 2nd Circuit debate was about; and I do not think it should be applied out of context. This was a precisely focused article about women — women's entitlement to equal citizenship before the law.

Knowledge of the Law

SEN. HANK BROWN, R-COLO.: I suppose every first-year law student learns quickly that ignorance of the law is no excuse.... In thinking about the concept, though, that you are responsible whether you are aware of the law or not, or liable for violating it whether you are aware of the law or not, it appears that there are a variety of reasons for it. One is the philosophy that I think was reflected in our common law that, basically, laws reflect common sense or at least moral mandates, that if someone is well aware that — while they may not be aware of the statute number, they are aware that murder, robbery or other crimes are wrong; so that while people may not be aware of the exact law, they are aware of at least moral mandates that we have in our daily lives.

I suspect that another basis for it is simply that it's tough to function in society without that assumption. It would be tough to get convictions without it. But I noticed in the original case, the 1789 case, that at the time that was ruled, there were only 27 federal statutes. Clearly, that's different than our circumstance today. At the last count, I think there were some 26,000 pages of the U.S. Code, not counting any state laws; there were 128,900 and some pages of the Federal Code regulations, and my impression is that this year the Federal Register will print 70,000 pages of notices and regulations that are new....

I give you this background because I'd be interested in your thoughts as to whether or not it's fair to insist that ignorance of the law is no excuse when clearly what was once accomplishable by a conscientious citizen is beyond even remotely being possible now?

JUDGE GINSBURG: That question, Sen. Brown, I think is addressed first and foremost to people who sit in your seat and not in mine; that is, that you can, in all those statutes that you pass, you can put intent and knowledge requirements, and you often do, and sometimes courts have to interpret what is the intent, what is the knowledge that the individual has to have. Sometimes you do speak with a clear voice, and we love it when you do.

Other times we're not clear on exactly what the intent requirement was, and so we do our best to try to determine what you meant. But I think that lawmakers have to take that into account and when they expose individuals to a regulatory regime, to state what the intent or knowledge requirement should be, and there can be a difference based on the consequences.

It's one thing to say that you're going to send someone to prison for violating a law that that person didn't know existed; the other thing is to say that you're going to make that person subject to an order requiring compliance with the law; and then somewhere in between would be some kind of monetary exaction.

So what I would have to say in this area is that the courts take their instructions from the legislature, which deals with state of mind issues, whether absolute liability, liability without fault, knowledge, intent — all that is for the legislature to say. But I'm certain [that] every citizen has to be mindful that we are subject to so much more law than we once were.

Abortion Rights

SEN. BROWN: You have attracted some attention by observing with regard to *Roe v. Wade* that perhaps a different portion of the Constitution may well deserve attention with regard to that question, specifically, if I understand your articles correctly, the equal protection provisions of the Constitution rather than the right to privacy evolving from the due process right.

Would you share with us a description of how your writings — I don't mean your view necessarily, but how your writings — drawing a relationship between the right to choose and the Equal Protection Clause?

JUDGE GINSBURG: I'll be glad to try, senator. May I say first that it's never, in my mind, been an either/or, a rather one than the other; it's been both. And I'll try to explain how my own thinking developed on this issue, and it came out of a case involving a woman's choice for birth rather than the termination of her pregnancy. It's one of the briefs that you have; it's the case of *Captain Susan Struck v. Secretary of Defense*, and this was Capt. Susan Struck's story:

She became pregnant while she was serving in the Air Force in Vietnam. This was in the early '70s. She was offered a choice; she was told she could have an abortion at the base hospital — and let us remember that in the early '70s, before *Roe v. Wade*, abortion was available on service bases in this country to members of the service or, more often, dependents of members of the service. Capt. Susan Struck said, "I do not want an abortion; I want to bear this child. It's part of my religious faith that I do so. However, I will use only my accumulated leave time for the childbirth, I will surrender the child for adoption at birth, and I want to remain in the Air Force. That is my career."

She was told that that was not an option open to her if she wished to remain in the Air Force. In that case, we argued three things: One, that this regulation — if you're pregnant you're out unless you have an abortion — violated the equal protection principle because no man was ordered out of service because he had been a partner in a conception; no man was ordered out of service because he was about to become a father.

And then we said that the government is impeding, without cause, a woman's choice whether to bear or not to bear a child, and that was her personal choice and the interference with it was a violation of her liberty, her freedom to choose, guaran-

teed by the due process clause. And then finally we said that this is an unnecessary interference with her religious belief.

So all three strands were involved in Capt. Struck's case. The main emphasis was on her equality as a woman, vis-à-vis a man who was equally responsible for the conception, and then her personal choice, which the government said she could not have unless she gave up her career in the service.

In that case, all three strands were involved. Her equality right, her right to decide for herself whether she was going to bear the child, and her religious belief. So it was never an either/or or rather. It was always recognizing that the one thing that distinguishes women from men is that only women become pregnant. And if you were going to subject a woman to disadvantageous treatment on the basis of her pregnant status, which was what was happening here, you were going to deny her equal treatment under the law.

And that argument, that discrimination — disadvantageous treatment because of pregnancy — is sex discrimination — was something that the Supreme Court might have heard in the *Struck* case. But the Air Force decided that they were going to waive her discharge. And although they had won in the trial court and won in the court of appeals, the Supreme Court granted certiorari in that case, and at that point, perhaps with the advice of the solicitor general — I don't know — the Air Force decided that it would rather switch [than] fight, and Capt. Struck's discharge was waived, so she remained in the service, and the court never got that case.

In the case that they eventually got, they decided that discrimination on the basis of pregnancy was not discrimination on the basis of sex, and then this body, the Congress, in the pregnancy discrimination act, indicated that it thought otherwise.

But the *Struck* brief, which involved a woman's choice for birth, is the place where I first thought long and hard about this question, and never, ever thought of it as an either/or, one pocket or the other. But I did think about it first and foremost as differential treatment of the woman, based on her sex.

SEN. BROWN: I can see how the equal protection argument would apply to a policy that interfered with her plan to bear the child. Could that argument be applied for someone who wished to have the option of an abortion as well? Does it apply both to the decision to not have an abortion as well as to a decision to have an abortion, to terminate the pregnancy?

JUDGE GINSBURG: The argument was, it's her right to decide either way, her right to decide whether or not to bear a child....

But you asked me about my thinking about equal protection vs. individual autonomy, and my answer to you is it's both. This is something central to a woman's life, to her dignity. It's a decision that she must make for herself. And when government controls that decision for her, she's being

treated as less than a fully adult human responsible for her own choices.

SEN. BROWN: ... With regard to the equal protection argument, though, since this may well confer a right to choose on the woman, or could, would it also follow that the father would be entitled to a right to choose in this regard, or some rights in this regard?

JUDGE GINSBURG: That was an issue left open in *Roe v. Wade*, but if I recall correctly, it was closed [*Planned Parenthood of Southeastern Pennsylvania v. Casey*] in the court's most recent decision; there were a series of regulations that the court dealt with, and as I remember, it upheld most of them, but it struck down one of them, which was the notice to the husband. And it has something to do with a matter that the chairman raised earlier. I think there was an indication in that opinion that marriage and family life is not always all that we might wish it to be, and that there are women whose physical safety, even their lives, would be endangered, if the law required them to notify their partner.

So I believe that this case decision, which in other respects has been greeted in some quarters with great distress, in this respect answered a question that was left open in *Roe*, and said, and I believe it did strike down the notification to the husband.

SEN. BROWN: I was concerned that if the equal protection argument were relied on to ensure a right to choose, that looking for a sex-blind standard in this regard, that this same logic might also then convey rights on the father to this decision. Do you see that as following logically from the rights that might be conferred on the mother?

JUDGE GINSBURG: I will rest my answer on the *Casey* decision, which says in the end it's her body, her life, and men — to that extent — are not similarly situated. They don't bear the child.

SEN. BROWN: So the rights are not equal in this regard because the interests are not equal?

JUDGE GINSBURG: I said on the equality side of it, that it is essential to a woman's equality with man that her choice, that she be the decision-maker, that her choice be controlling, and that if you impose restraints and disadvantage her, you are disadvantaging her because of her sex.

Put that together with the general line of cases that have developed since — oh, a long string [of] cases about procreation, the centrality of that to an individual, starting from at least [*Skinner v. Oklahoma*, 1942] when the state law required sterilization for certain recidivists — that was a question of sterilizing a man — but the importance of procreation to an individual's autonomy. That applies to men as well as women.

The state controlling the woman is both denying her full autonomy and full equality with men, and that was the idea that I tried to express in this lecture. Never

as an either/or question, but just that there were these two strands, and that . . . I think that both of them are recognized in the cases since *Roe*.

Society's Problems

SEN. HERB KOHL, D-WIS.: What do you think are the major problems and challenges that face our society? I'll just throw out things like racism, sexism, guns, crime, drugs. Give us some indication as to what you think some of these major unresolved problems are that we're facing in our society today.

JUDGE GINSBURG: You listed a number of the ones that would be on the top of anyone's list. What the court doesn't get, though, as you get here is a problem of crime, a problem of violence. That's not what comes to the court. What comes to the court is a particular case raising an issue in a particular context, and we don't — unlike legislators, courts don't get big issues, abstract or general issues to decide, they get concrete cases.

That's in part the answer to that — and the court also has to decide questions of timing. Sometimes the court thinks it isn't — it will be able to judge better if it has more returns from the other federal courts. That is, maybe the first time an issue comes up, the court shouldn't take the case, that it will do better if it has the views of several judges on it. If all of the judges that have heard the case are in agreement, maybe the court will decide, well, it's not necessary for us to make a ruling. If there's a division, then there may be a greater need, but the idea of having what's called percolation, having an issue in the lower courts for a while, having commentators speak to it so that when the court ultimately judges the case, it will be better informed to make the decision, in some areas that's a wise thing to do. I think it was the case — one of the cases that I had that the Supreme Court reversed might have been an example of that, and it was a case involving the Fourth Amendment.

The Supreme Court had a decision that said the police — the police officers stop a car and open the trunk, and there's a suitcase in it, they can't open the suitcase without a warrant. Then a case came to a lower court about what about a cardboard box and what about a plastic bag? And there were these whole string of decisions in the lower courts about whether the luggage line was passed. And there was a kind of worthy container doctrine about when you needed a warrant. You needed it for a leather suitcase for sure; not so sure about lesser containers. Till my court got the case of a leather pouch and a paper bag, and the court originally decided — the three-judge panel decided the police needed a warrant before they could open the leather pouch, but they didn't need a warrant to open the paper bag — it had a tape — a piece of Scotch tape on it because that was a flimsy, unworthy container.

I wrote an opinion for the full court saying we have now seen this array going

from the leather suitcase to the lowly paper bag, and we can't ask police officers to make that kind of judgment. Either you can open a container or you can't without a warrant. Since the Supreme Court said you can't open the suitcase without a warrant, my court said you can't open any closed container without a warrant. The Supreme Court said, "You're right. You persuaded us about — that we don't want police officers on the spot to be drawing luggage lines, but you're wrong about where the end of it should be. Everything is open to the police. Once they have reasons to stop the car, they can open the trunk and inspect anything that's in it without a warrant."

But that was a case where the original notion that you could distinguish between containers on the basis of their character — it got — by the time that issue got to the Supreme Court, the court saw that the one thing that you could not do was establish a worthy container rule. They would not have seen that, I think, going in with the first case. It took a lot of cases in the lower courts, and really, there were cardboard boxes, there were plastic bag cases, all these kinds of cases. So that was an example where the Supreme Court was better informed, I think, in making the ultimate decision because that issue had been around in the circuits for a number of years, and there were all these cases that they could then look at when they made their final decision.

SEN. KOHL: I know how much you care for your grandchildren. It's perfectly obvious to all of us who have seen this confirmation hearing, and it's a great thing. As you know, what we are doing without their ability to represent themselves is imposing an enormous tax burden on them. We're building it up year by year, and they have no way to respond, to react, to protest, to vote us in or out. They just sit there and see it happen. And we all know that someday they're going to have to pay a price for that.

How can they be represented by the courts? Is there any way that your court can represent them? They are being — there's taxation without representation, an enormous burden of taxation without representation.

Does that in any way strike you as something that the courts might have a right to take a look at someday?

JUDGE GINSBURG: I think that you must represent them and their parents must represent them and we all must represent them. We all have to care about the next generation. In a democracy, the people and the legislators have to care about what's happening to the next generation.

SEN. KOHL: Justice [Louis] Brandeis once said that you can judge a person better by the books on their shelf than by the clients that they have in their office. So I am asking you, what's on your shelf? Could you tell us a little bit about your reading habits, the kinds of books you read, what books you've — what book you've most recently read?

JUDGE GINSBURG: Well, I can tell you the two books that I most recently read. I don't know that these are representative, but most recently I read "Wordstruck" by Robert MacNeil, and I read Marian Wright Edelman's book dedicated to her children, "The Measure of Our Success." I haven't been doing heavy reading these last five weeks except — [laughter] — except 700 of my opinions to try to remember what I said in them and refreshing my recollection of various areas of federal law.

I have a husband who was a voracious reader, and, in fact, is my — what shall I say? — he's my selector. He knows what my — what I would — what in — what I would enjoy. Every once in a while I go out and get something for myself like "The Bean Tree," which I read and enjoyed, but he — when he reads a book that he knows I would particularly like, he says, "Read this one," like "Love in the Time of Cholera," which I adored. So — well, I've told you the two books I've read most recently, and —

KOHL: Do you read a great deal of fiction or non-fiction, or is it equal?

JUDGE GINSBURG: I probably read more fiction, because there's so much non-fiction that I deal with every day....

KOHL: That's very good. Since your nomination, Judge Ginsburg, there have been reams and reams of information that have been printed and impressions that have been printed about you. Anything that you have read that has struck you particularly as being reflective of the kind of a person you are? Or don't you read these things? Don't they interest you? How would you describe the person that you would — just in general terms, a person that you would like us to know today on the eve of what may be your confirmation as a Supreme Court justice, recognizing that this is probably the last time that the American people will ever have a chance to glimpse you as a person and what you would like them to think most of all when they think of you?

JUDGE GINSBURG: As someone who cares about people and does the best she can with the talent she has to make a contribution to a better world.

Day Three

Ginsburg returned for a third day of testimony July 22.

SEN. HATCH: In 1975, while you were at the ACLU [American Civil Liberties Union], that organization adopted a policy statement favoring homosexual rights. According to what has been represented to me as minutes of a meeting on this matter, the following is noted:

Quote, In the second paragraph of the policy statement dealing with relations between adults and minors, Ruth Bader Ginsburg made a motion to eliminate the sentence reading — a quote within a quote — The state has a legitimate interest in controlling sexual behavior between adults and minors by criminal sanctions, unquote within a quote. She argued that this implied approval of statutory rape statutes, which are of questionable constitutionality, unquote. Now, I realize that these events took place over 18 years ago. So let me just ask you, do you have any doubt that the states have the constitutional authority to enact statutory rape laws to impose criminal sanctions on sexual conduct or contact between an adult and a minor, even where the minor allegedly consents?

JUDGE GINSBURG: Not at all, Sen. Hatch. What I did have a strong objection to was the sex classification.

SEN. HATCH: Sure.

JUDGE GINSBURG: I think child abuse is a deplorable thing, whether it's same sex, opposite sex, male, female. And the state has to draw lines based on age. What I do object to is the vision of the world that supposes that a woman is always the victim. So my only objection to that policy was the sex specificity.

SEN. HATCH: So as long as they treat males and females equally, that's your concern.

JUDGE GINSBURG: Yes. And I think that as much as we would not like these things to go on, children are abused, and it is among the most deplorable things, and it doesn't —

SEN. HATCH: And the state has power to correct it.

JUDGE GINSBURG: Yes, and has power to draw lines on the basis of age that are inevitably going to be arbitrary at the edge.

SEN. HATCH: Well, I'm relieved to hear that that was the basis for your objection, that the — it was a shock to me to learn that the — you know, that the Constitution — some people argue that the Constitution denies the state the right or the ability to protect young people and teenagers by forbidding sexual contact between them and an adult, even where the sexual contact is supposedly voluntary. And I'm concerned about that.

Death Penalty

SEN. HATCH: Let me just move on to the death penalty. Now, I have a question — one of the problems I had yesterday — you were very specific in talking about abortion, equal rights and a number of other issues. But you were not very specific on the death penalty. Now, there are people on this committee who are for and against the death penalty, as are people throughout the Congress. And my question about the constitutionality — is about the constitutionality of the death penalty. I'm not going to ask you your opinion about any specific statute or set of facts to which the death penalty might apply. Also, I recognize that your personal views regarding the morality or utility of capital punishment are not relevant, unless your personal views are so strong that you cannot be impartial or objective. Then that would be a relevant question and a relevant matter for us here today. Rather, I would just like to ask you

the following specific question.

Do you believe, as Justices [William] Brennan and [Thurgood] Marshall did, that the death penalty under all circumstances — even for whatever you would consider or many would consider to be the most heinous of crimes, but in this case what you would consider to be the most heinous of crimes — is incompatible with the Eighth Amendment's prohibition against cruel and unusual punishment?

JUDGE GINSBURG: ... At least since 1976 ... the Supreme Court by large majorities has rejected the position that the death penalty under any and all circumstances is unconstitutional. I recognize that there is no judge on the court that takes a position that the death penalty is unconstitutional under any and all circumstances. All of the justices on the court have rejected that view. There are many questions left unresolved. They are coming constantly before that court. I think at least two are before the court next year. I can tell you that I have — I do not have a closed mind on this subject. I don't want to commit my — I don't think it would be consistent with the line I have tried to hold to tell you that I would definitely accept or definitely reject any position. I can tell you that I am well aware of the precedent, and I have already expressed my views on the value of precedent.

SEN. HATCH: But do you agree with all the current sitting members that it is constitutional? It is within the Constitution?

JUDGE GINSBURG: I can tell you that I agree that that is the precedent. It has been clearly the precedent since 1976. I feel that I must draw the line at that point and hope that you will respect what I have tried to tell you, that I am very aware of the precedent; I am very aware of the principle of stare decisis.

SEN. HATCH: But, see, my question goes a little bit farther than that. I take it that you're not prepared to endorse the Brennan-Marshall approach that it's cruel and unusual punishment under the Eighth Amendment. But in response to my previous question, you stated that statutory rape laws are constitutional, yet you are unwilling to really answer the question or comment on the constitutionality — I'm not asking you to interpret that statute, just the Constitution — you're unwilling to comment on the constitutionality or unconstitutionality of the death penalty, and the thing I'm worried about is that it appears that your willingness to discuss the established principles of constitutional law may depend somewhat on whether your answer might solicit a favorable response from the committee....

JUDGE GINSBURG: Sen. Hatch, I have tried to be totally candid with this committee —

SEN. HATCH: And you have, you have.

JUDGE GINSBURG: — when you asked a question — I was asked a lot about abortion yesterday.

SEN. HATCH: Right. And you were very forthright talking about it.

JUDGE GINSBURG: I have written

about it; I have spoken about it as a teacher since the middle '70s.... Now, the death penalty is an area that I have never written about. I have —

SEN. HATCH: But you've taught constitutional law in major law schools in this country. It isn't a tough question. I mean I'm not really —

JUDGE GINSBURG: That — when you asked me what's in [the] Fifth Amendment —

SEN. HATCH: Right.

JUDGE GINSBURG: The Fifth Amendment uses the word capital. When you ask me what is the state of the precedent, but if you want me to take a pledge that there is —

SEN. HATCH: I don't want you to.

JUDGE GINSBURG: — that there is one position that I'm not going to take, I — that is what you must not ask a judge to do.

SEN. HATCH: But that's not what I asked you. I asked you, is it in the Constitution? Is it constitutional?

JUDGE GINSBURG: I can tell you that the Fifth Amendment reads, "No person shall be held to answer for a capital or otherwise infamous crime unless" — and the rest. But I'm not going to say to this committee that I will reject a position out of hand in a case — in a situation where I have never expressed an opinion. I have never had a death penalty case. I have never written about it. I have never spoken about it in the classroom. I can tell you that my — I have only —

SEN. HATCH: Have you ever discussed it?

JUDGE GINSBURG: — one passion, and it is to be a good judge and to judge fairly and not to tell in advance, not to give any hint, about how I am going to decide a question that I have never spoken about.

Discrimination

SEN. EDWARD M. KENNEDY, D-MASS.: During my round on Tuesday, Judge Ginsburg, we talked briefly about the very important role of the Supreme Court in construing civil rights laws, and I'd like to return to the topic this morning....

JUDGE GINSBURG: My view of the civil rights laws conform to my view concerning statutory interpretation generally: That is, it is the obligation of judges to construe statutes in the way that Congress meant them to be construed. Some statutes, not simply in the civil rights area but antitrust area, are meant to be broad charters: the Sherman Act. The Civil Rights Act states grand principles representing the highest aspirations of our nation to be a nation that is open and free where all people will have opportunity.

And that spirit imbues that law — just as free competition is the spirit in the antitrust laws, and the courts construe statutes in accord with the essential meaning that Congress had for passing them....

We live in a democracy that has through the years been opened to more and more people. Perhaps the most vital part of

the civil rights legislation in the middle '60s was the voting rights legislation.

SEN. KENNEDY: I agree.

JUDGE GINSBURG: That has been the history of our country, ever widening the participation in our democracy. And I think I expressed on the very first day of these hearings my discomfort with the notion that judges should pre-empt that process so that the people — the spirit of liberty is lost in the hearts of the men and women of this country. That's why I think the voting rights legislation, more than anything else, is so vital in our democracy.

SEN. KENNEDY: In another area, we've certainly made important progress, as you mentioned, in the areas of banning discrimination on the basis of race. We have on gender. We have on religious prejudice and more recently on disability with the passage of the Americans With Disabilities Act, banning discrimination against persons with disabilities. One form of discrimination still flourishes without any federal protection, and that is discrimination against gay men and lesbians. And I note that in a 1979 speech at a colloquium on legislation for women's rights, you stated that "I think discrimination based on sexual orientation should be deplored." By rank discrimination, I assume you meant intentional discrimination rather than discrimination on the basis of rank in the military. I share that view, and I think most Americans do. I'd like to ask you whether you still believe, as you did in 1979, that discrimination based on sexual orientation should be deplored.

JUDGE GINSBURG: I think rank discrimination against anyone is against the tradition of the United States and is to be deplored. Rank discrimination is not part of our nation's culture. Tolerance is. And a generous respect for differences based on — this country is great because of its accommodation of diversity. I mean, the first thing that I noticed when I came back to the United States from a prolonged stay in Sweden and after I was so accustomed to looking at people whose complexion was the same, and I took my first ride on a New York subway, and I thought, "What a wonderful country we live in — people who are so different in so many ways, and yet we, for the most part, get along with each other." The richness of the diversity of this country is a treasure, and it's a constant challenge, too, to remain tolerant and respectful of one another.

War Powers

SEN. SPECTER: Let me now move to a substantive area that I consider to be very important, and that is the role of the court on refereeing disputes between the president and the Congress on [the] War Powers act issue. And you wrote a concurring opinion in *Sanchez v.* — and *Espinoza v. President Reagan*. The issue on the gulf war was very [problematic] and President [George] Bush asserted very late in December of 1990 the intent to move into a conflict with Iraq over Kuwait without con-

gressional approval, and the leadership in the Congress stated their intention not to bring the matter to the floor. And it was in a very unusual procedural setting, where we had swearing-ins on Jan. 3, and [Democratic] Sen. [Tom] Harkin of Iowa brought the issue up in a way which I think forced the hand of the leadership, and the issue did come up, and we did have a vote on the resolution for the use of power.

Let me move to your concurring opinion, where — as the fastest way to get into the issue and into a dialogue — where you said that you would dismiss the War Powers claim for relief asserted by congressional plaintiffs as not ripe for judicial review. The judicial branch should not decide issues affecting the allocation of power between the president and Congress until the political leaders reach a constitutional impasse. Congress has formidable weapons at its disposal — the power of the purse and investigative resources far beyond those available in the third branch.

I would suggest to you, Judge Ginsburg, that the power of the purse is not very helpful, if the president goes into Kuwait without authorization from Congress, for the Congress to cut off his funding. It obviously can't be done when fighting men and women are at risk. And when you talk about the investigative resources far beyond those available in the third branch, I don't believe that our investigative resources, which are customarily very important, really bear on this issue. And if we are to have a resolution between the Congress and the president where we have a Korean War without a declaration of war, we have a Vietnam War without a declaration of war, and we have an issue about violation of the War Powers act in El Salvador, as the issue came before your court, how can this dispute of enormous constitutional proportion be decided unless the court will take jurisdiction and decide it?

JUDGE GINSBURG: Sen. Specter, my position in that case — I think you read that I said that the question was not ripe for our review.

SEN. SPECTER: I did.

JUDGE GINSBURG: It is a position that has been developed far more extensively than in that abbreviated statement that I made in the *Sanchez Espinoza* case by my colleague Carl McGowan, who has written on congressional standing as a matter of ripeness. It was the position adopted essentially by Justice [Lewis F.] Powell in the Supreme Court — I think it was in Goldwater against Carter — where the Supreme Court for various reasons held — was it the termination of the Taiwan Defense Treaty? Was that what was at issue, the executive's termination of that without —

SEN. SPECTER: It was Justice Powell, just had a single line: "Although I agree with the result reached by the court, I would not dismiss the complaint as ripe for judicial review." But I do not believe that either the Supreme Court or the circuit court — and the circuit had it in *Crockett v. Reagan* — has ever really dealt with the

issue, and I tried to with Justice [David H.] Souter, ask him if he thought the Korean War was a war. I answered the question in the question because I think the Korean War was a war, and he said he'd have to think about that. I said, "I'm going to ask you in the next round." Over the weekend, he came back, and I said, "Have you thought about it?" And he said, "Yes, I have." I said, "Well, was the Korean War a war?" He said, "I don't know."

And I think this is a matter that we really ought to explore with a nominee — standing, ripeness. You have written expansively, and I have admired your work on standing. I think that the court dismisses too many cases on the standing issue.

But isn't the Supreme Court there really to referee big, big issues? And it's harder to have a bigger issue than the constitutional authority of the Congress to declare war, or whether the president exceeds the War Powers act, if we don't come to you. And we can hardly come to you when the troops are in the field.

JUDGE GINSBURG: Sen. Specter, the question for me was: Who is the we? I have not ruled out the ultimate [justifiability] of a question of the kind you've raised. What I said was that I associate myself with the position taken by Justice Powell, taken in both decisions and law review articles by Carl McGowan, that the legislators must stand up and be counted in their own house.

And if Congress wants to put itself in conflict with the executive, by passing a resolution with a majority of both houses, saying, "We, the Congress, take the position that the executive is acting in opposition to our will," at that point I could not say there isn't a ripe controversy. But unless and until that occurs, I have taken the position, whether it's Republican senators, Democratic senators, that there is no ripe controversy between the legislature and the executive until the legislators who take the position in contrast to the executive win in their own branch. Until that point is reached, in my view there is no [justifiable] controversy between the two branches of government. The president is a unitary. The president takes a position. For Congress to take a position, Congress must act by majority vote. So I do not think that a group of senators can come to the court and say: Resolve a clash between the legislative and the executive branch.

That is my position with respect to ripeness. I know that there are disagreements. Some people say it belongs under some other head. I have said that position in an abbreviated way in *Sanchez* [*Espinoza*]. It is my position, there are people who can take — there are undoubtedly people who take other positions. On my court, there are people who have taken other positions. To the best of my judgment, the executive and the legislature, for them to have a controversy ripe for our court or any federal court to review, there must be a vote of the legislature. And if a

group of legislators does not prevail in Congress, does not prevail in Congress, they cannot come to the court and ask the court to resolve a clash that does not, in my mind, exist until it becomes the position of the Congress. That's about all I can say, Sen. Specter, on that subject.

Death Penalty

SEN. METZENBAUM: Just last month, a white man from Maryland, Kirk Bloodsworth, was set free after nine years in prison when it was conclusively proven that he did not commit the heinous rape and murder of a young girl. He had been sentenced to die.

Our committee held a hearing to understand the problems with the Supreme Court's decision in the case of *Herrera v. Collins*. In that case, Mr. Herrera was sentenced to die and later obtained evidence that allegedly proved his innocence. A Reagan-appointed federal judge, a district judge in Texas, wanted to conduct a timely hearing to review Herrera's new evidence of innocence. He was prepared to go forward with the hearing within two or three days. The state of Texas objected to the district court's decision to hold a hearing, and the case was sent to the Supreme Court for review. The Supreme Court rules that the Constitution does not require that a hearing be granted to a death row inmate who has newly discovered evidence which, if proven, could establish his innocence.

In the opinion for the court, Chief Justice [William H.] Rehnquist was unable to declare clearly and unequivocally that the Constitution forbids the execution of innocent people. The attorney who represented the state of Texas went even further than the chief justice. She bluntly asserted that if a death row inmate receives a fair trial, it does not violate the Constitution to execute that inmate even if everyone agrees that he is innocent.

Now, frankly, that's a shocking statement. It came from the prosecutor in that case. I'm extremely concerned with the court's opinion in *Herrera* and the argument made by the Texas prosecutor. Even though the Rehnquist opinion did not clearly hold that it was unconstitutional to execute an innocent person, it is possible to read that into his statements.

Do you believe the *Herrera* case stands for the principle that it is unconstitutional to execute an innocent person?

JUDGE GINSBURG: As I understand it, and the case is not fresh in my mind, what the court said was that the evidence in that case was insufficient to show innocence. It did not rule out a different ruling in a case with a stronger record. We heard yesterday from Sen. [Dianne] Feinstein [D-Calif.], who was expressing her anxiety with the number of cases that go on for years and years.

The colloquy that is occurring here is showing the tremendous tensions and difficulties in this area. . . . There must be a time when the curtain is drawn, and your anxiety is that no innocent person should

ever be put to death. Those tensions are coming before you, some of them, in the Powell commission report [on the reform of *habeas corpus* procedures] that you are going to have to address.

My understanding of *Herrera* is it's concerned with the situation that someone could say, 10 years after a conviction and multiple appeals, "I didn't do it," and then the process would start all over again. I can empathize —

SEN. METZENBAUM: No, I don't think —

JUDGE GINSBURG: — tremendously with the concern —

SEN. METZENBAUM: — I don't think anybody would argue that. I don't think anybody would argue that, Judge Ginsburg, that 10 years later he can say, "I didn't do it," because he's been saying for 10 years he didn't do it.

JUDGE GINSBURG: What the court said — and this is to the best of my recollection — that the evidence was too slim in *Herrera* to make out that claim, and it left the door open to a case where there was stronger evidence of innocence. That case is yet to come before the court in the future. So my understanding of this case is it, based on that particular record, said the evidence was too thin to show innocence, that the court was leaving open the question of whether you could have such a plea on a stronger showing than the one that was made in that case. And that's as far as the *Herrera* case went. It just left open a case where a stronger showing could be made.

SEN. METZENBAUM: Now, state courts, of course, should review any new claim of a death row inmate that he is innocent, but that review can be in an atmosphere of strong public [pressure] for execution, especially when the conviction is for a particularly heinous or vicious crime. Public pressure in these circumstances is most worrisome when the state trial and appellate judges are elected.

Historically, the federal courts have played a significant role in reviewing state dealt penalty verdicts. Federal judges have lifetime appointments and are more immune to the strong public sentiments that surround death penalty cases for heinous and violent crimes.

Now, the *Herrera* case raised significant new questions about the availability of the federal courts to hear the claim of a death row inmate that he has new evidence of his innocence. Would you care to explain your view on the general role federal courts should play in hearing the claims of death row inmates who have newly discovered evidence of their innocence?

JUDGE GINSBURG: Sen. Metzenbaum, that question of habeas review and its limits is before the Senate — before this committee, I believe —

SEN. METZENBAUM: But not before the court. Not before the court. So I think it's entirely proper for you to respond.

JUDGE GINSBURG: I can tell you

what the legislation that you have made is for the district in which I operate, and that is we do not have habeas review. You have given to the D.C. courts a fine post-conviction remedy; it is identical to the federal remedy. The Supreme Court said, sometime in the middle '70s, that is it. You go from the D.C. courts to the Supreme Court, the Supreme Court turns you down, there is no collateral review in the federal courts.

Important Cases

SEN. PATRICK J. LEAHY, D-VT.: Could you give me some of the cases you consider the most important Supreme Court cases? Take them from whatever era, time, recent or older or not, that the Supreme Court has decided? Just some of those that mean the most to you and why.

JUDGE GINSBURG: Starting from the beginning, *Marbury v. Madison*, establishing the principle of judicial review for constitutionality. Other great decisions of the Marshall court era, I'll just mention *Gibbons v. Ogden*. These are the — when I spoke of the Pledge of Allegiance before, I said "one nation indivisible," so I would put *Gibbons v. Ogden* in that camp of one nation. Then, going up to our times, I would put the great dissents of Holmes and Brandeis in *Abrams* and *Gitlow*, Brandeis' dissent in *Whitney v. California*.

These were — people think that free speech was always free in this country. It really wasn't; it is a development of our current century and those great cases that became — that are now, I think, just so well accepted. But they were originally stated as dissenting positions. *Brown v. Board of Education* has got to be there on any list. That gives you about half a dozen.

SEN. LEAHY: I take it you're — could I, in doing that, Judge — let me go to the dissents a moment because you and I talked about First Amendment rights and freedom of speech before.

How have you seen the evolution of our free speech rights in this country? Obviously, stated in the Bill of Rights, right from the beginning, but as you said, one that has been — one that has changed, evolved. We saw censorship during the Civil War and President Lincoln's time, everything from suspension of habeas corpus to suspension of freedom of speech; we've seen attacks on it that had been either direct government attacks or response in fear — the McCarthy era comes to mind where there were truly attacks on it. Do you see that right as still an evolving right in this country?

JUDGE GINSBURG: Free expression, I think, was an idea from the start, even before the limitations on it — the Alien and Sedition Act, which I think never was reversed by the Supreme Court but certainly has been reversed by the history of our country since that time. The idea was there from the beginning, though — I mentioned the Revolutionary War cartoon, "liberty of speech for those who speak the speech of liberty" — the idea was always there. The great opposition to the govern-

ment as censor was always there. But it is only in our time that that right has come to be recognized as fully as it is today with the line of cases ending in *Brandenburg v. Ohio* — truly recognizes that free speech means not freedom of thought and speech for those with whom we agree, but freedom of expression for the expression we hate. I think that there are always new contexts that will be presented. But that the dissenting positions of Holmes and Brandeis have become the law that everyone accepts, I think that is the case today.

SEN. LEAHY: Would you consider *Brandenburg* as one of the milestones in the court's history?

JUDGE GINSBURG: I certainly do, yes. That was in 1969. So the — the — I think it was 1969 — the McCarthy era was well over.

There were very many brave judges in the period of McCarthy who — including Learned Hand, who wrote one of the great early decisions in the *Dennis* case. There were some outstanding decisions of Justice [John M.] Harlan in that very difficult time for our country. But I think *Brandenburg* is not the least controversial now.....

SEN. LEAHY: How much weight do you put on the extent to which the holding has guided and been relied upon by the public? Is that something that must weigh heavily on you if there is a body of law that seems so settled that it has been well relied upon? Does — I'm thinking now the kind of thinking that must go through a Supreme Court justice's mind if they are going to overturn a past decision of the court. Are time and acceptance major factors to be considered?

JUDGE GINSBURG: Yes, they both are — how it has been working, what expectations, what reliance has built up around it. Those are major factors.

SEN. LEAHY: Change and — changed circumstances? Case that's settled in one era looking different in another?

JUDGE GINSBURG: Yeah, yeah....

SEN. LEAHY: Then lastly, Judge, what about, in your own moral belief, you, as an individual, it's your own moral belief that the earlier decision was wrong? ...

JUDGE GINSBURG: Well, that's why we have the law, and that's why we have a system of stare decisis, is just to keep judges from infusing their own moral beliefs, from making themselves king or queen. That's why I've answered the question that I've been asked a few times here, how do you feel about this or that, and I've said that's not relevant to the job for which you are considering me.

SEN. LEAHY: Would it be safe to say, however, Judge, that it can never totally disappear from your —

JUDGE GINSBURG: Yes, I think that is certainly true. I have to be aware of it. I have to be aware of it, and so I know that it's there, and that I must be sure that my own predilections — I don't confuse my own predilections with what is the law. ∎

NEWS CONFERENCE

Clinton Announces Policy On Illegal Immigration

At a White House news conference July 27, President Clinton outlined his new policy to prevent illegal immigration. Following is the text of the news conference, as provided by the Federal News Service:

PRESIDENT CLINTON: Several weeks ago I asked the vice president to work with our departments and agencies to examine what more might be done about the problems along our borders. I was especially concerned about the growing problems of alien smuggling and international terrorists hiding behind immigrant status, as well as the continuing flow of illegal immigrants across American borders. Following several weeks of intense efforts, including his personal involvement in resolving the recent alien smuggling incident with Mexico, the vice president presented me with a report spelling out what we might do.

I have reviewed that report and approved it. We have spoken to members of Congress, including those who are here today and others.

I want to particularly acknowledge Sen. [Edward M.] Kennedy [D-Mass.], Sen. [Alan K.] Simpson [R-Wyo.], Congressmen [Jack] Brooks [D-Texas] and [Romano L.] Mazzoli [D-Ky.] for all their work on this issue over many, many years.

We are also in debt to Sens. [Dianne] Feinstein and [Barbara] Boxer [Democrats of California] for their aggressive work in trying to deal with this growing problem, especially in the state of California, and I want to state publicly how much I appreciate the work the [Congressional] Hispanic Caucus has done to ensure that a balanced approach is adopted in dealing with this issue.

The simple fact is that we must not and we will not surrender our borders to those who wish to exploit our history of compassion and justice. We cannot tolerate those who traffic in human cargo, nor can we allow our people to be endangered by those who would enter our country to terrorize Americans. But the solution to the problem of illegal immigration is not simply to close our borders.

The solution is to welcome legal immigrants and legal, legitimate refugees and to turn away those who do not obey the laws. We must say no to illegal immigration so we can continue to say yes to legal immigration.

Today, we send a strong and clear message. We will make it tougher for illegal aliens to get into our country. We will treat organizing a crime syndicate to smuggle aliens as a serious crime. And we will increase the number of border patrol, equipping and training them to be first-class law enforcement officers.

These initiatives, for which I am asking the Congress for an additional $172.5 million in 1994, are an important step in regaining control over our borders and respect for our laws. When I made a commitment to combat this problem on June the 18th, I announced a plan of action. This is the next step in fulfilling that commitment.

Some will worry that our action today sends the wrong message, that this means we are against all immigration. That [it] is akin to America closing its doors. But nothing could be further from the truth. Let me be clear. Our nation has always been a safe haven for refugees and always been the world's greatest melting pot. What we announce today will not make it tougher for the immigrant who comes to this country legally, lives by our laws, gets a job and pursues the American dream.

This administration will promote family unification. We will reach out to those who have the skills we need to make our nation stronger. And we will welcome new citizens to our national family with honor and with dignity. But to treat terrorists and smugglers as immigrants dishonors the tradition of the immigrants who have made our nation great, and it unfairly taints the millions of immigrants who live here honorably and are a vital part of every segment of our society.

Today's initiatives are about stopping crime, toughening the penalties for the criminals and giving our law enforcement people the tools they need to do their job.

I'm also taking steps today to address the long-term challenges of reforming our immigration policy. I intend to appoint a new chair to the congressionally mandated Commission on Immigration Reform and to ask the Congress to expand the commission to include senior administration officials. I'm also asking our attorney general, Janet Reno, and the INS [Immigration and Naturalization Service] commissioner-designate, Doris [M.] Meissner, to make sure the INS is as professional and as effectively managed as it can be. Under their leadership, I have no doubt that it will be. With these efforts, I hope that we can begin a broad-based national discussion on this important issue and move towards significant resolution of the problems that plague all Americans.

Now, I'd like to ask the vice president to come forward, with my thanks for his outstanding work, to discuss the specifics of the initiatives.

VICE PRESIDENT GORE: The centerpiece of these initiatives is a legislative proposal carefully drawn to protect the rights of legal immigrants while allowing us to speed up the exclusion of illegal aliens at ports of entry. Right now, thousands of aliens arrive each year at airports and other entry points without proper documentation. What happens if, as they come off the airplane or off some smuggler's ship, they request political asylum? They're entitled to a range of administrative procedures that enable them to remain in the United States for many long months or even longer.

Of course, some deserve asylum. The facts show that most do not under our laws. Many never even show up for hearings and immediately become part of the large and growing illegal alien population. The legislation we announce today will help bring this abuse of our laws to an end. It enables us to promptly exclude those undocumented aliens who do not have credible claims for political asylum. At the same time, we provide protection for those who genuinely fear persecution if they are returned to their countries of origin, for the focus of our approach to immigration must not be on closing borders but on opening our hearts.

In addition to the expedited exclusion legislation, we are also proposing legislation aimed directly at the menace of alien smuggling by criminal syndicates. This measure will double prison sentences for convicted smugglers. It will make alien smuggling a predicate for the Racketeer Influenced and Corrupt Organizations Act, or RICO, prosecutions. It will authorize use of wiretaps in alien smuggling investigations. It will expand our authority to seize the assets of smugglers. These provisions will apply equally to organized criminal boat smugglers as well as to the large-scale organized gangs of so-called Coyotes who bring thousands of illegal aliens across our Southwest border every week.

Now, how do we prevent the illegal entry of undocumented aliens who have no reason to be in the United States? We will substantially increase funding for a range of administrative measures. It's time to make use of the full range of tools modern technology provides. For example, we will accelerate the automation of U.S. embassies and consulates as quickly as possible so they can better share information on people who should not receive visas — terrorists, drug smugglers and felons, for example.

We will also expand cooperative programs with foreign governments and airline carriers to make sure that improperly documented passengers are kept off airlines before they leave for the United States.

Finally, as a first step in slowing the flood of illegal immigrants who circumvent our understaffed and underequipped border patrol, we will significantly increase personnel, a kind of "more cops on the beat" approach. We will also give border agents the best possible equipment and technology. We're providing $45.1 million for training and equipment and up to 600 additional border patrol guards. That will improve their ability to interdict and return illegal aliens seeking to cross the border. We will also increase and improve border patrol training and review procedures to make sure that people they apprehend are treated in accordance with the law.

Now I'd like to ask Attorney General Janet Reno to talk a little bit about the enforcement provisions in this legislation.

ATTORNEY GENERAL RENO: This is an important step forward in dealing with what I believe will be one of the most critical issues that we face in this decade: how we maintain this nation's tradition of immigration while at the same time understanding and comprehending the burden that so many public services have felt as a result. I think we can do it, and I think this whole effort by the vice president is a first step in recognizing the Immigration and Naturalization Service as a true partner with the Department of State, with law enforcement agencies, with other national agencies to effectively deal with the problem in a comprehensive way, not in a piecemeal way.

With respect to the border patrol, Sen. Feinstein, Sen. [Bob] Graham [D-Fla.], Sen. Boxer have been saying, "When are you going to get more people?" And as I have said, we don't want to add people if we can't add them effectively. We've carefully reviewed this. We want to make sure that the equipment matches the people, that they are properly deployed, that they are used in the most effective manner possible.

With respect to the penalties, we want to increase the penalties for those who organize syndicates to smuggle people. We want to provide a full range of criminal investigative tools to do the job. And I think as a step towards addressing this critical problem, we have come a long way. We have much to do, and what it will require of all Americans is that we work together to address this critical problem.

If I were to have seen the Dade County [Florida] criminal justice system operate as the immigration and naturalization system has operated too often in the past in terms of review processes, I'm not sure it would have worked very well at all. We can do so much in terms of streamlining the effort, making it more effective, while at the same time ensuring due process for all people who are involved in the process. ■

PRESIDENTIAL ADDRESS

Clinton Hails Israel-PLO Pact As 'Historic Compromise'

President Clinton announced Sept. 10 that the United States was resuming a dialogue with the Palestine Liberation Organization. Following is the text of his remarks, transcribed by the Federal News Service:

Today marks a shining moment of hope for the people of the Middle East and, indeed, of the entire world. The Israelis and the Palestinians have now agreed upon a declaration of principles on interim self-government that opens the door to a comprehensive and lasting settlement. This declaration represents an historic and honorable compromise between two peoples who have been locked in a bloody struggle for almost a century. Too many have suffered for too long.

The agreement is a bold breakthrough. The Palestine Liberation Organization openly and unequivocally has renounced the use of violence and is pledged to live in peace with Israel. Israel in turn has announced its recognition of the PLO. I want to express my congratulations and praise for the courage and the vision displayed by the Israeli and Palestinian leadership and for the crucially helpful role played by Norway.

For too long the history of the Middle East has been defined in terms of violence and bloodshed. Today marks the dawning of a new era. Now there is an opportunity to define the future of the Middle East in terms of reconciliation and coexistence and the opportunities that children growing up there will have whether they are Israeli or Palestinian. I want to express the full support of the United States for this dramatic and promising step.

For more than a quarter of a century our nation has been directly engaged in efforts to resolve the Middle East conflict. We have done so because it reflects our finest values and our deepest interests: our interest in a stable Middle East, where Israelis and Arabs can live together in harmony and develop the potential of their region, which is tremendous. From Camp David to Madrid to the signing ceremony that will take place at the White House on Monday, administration after administration has facilitated this difficult but essential quest. From my first day in office, Secretary [of State Warren M.] Christopher and I have made this a priority. We are resolved to continue this process to achieve a comprehensive Arab-Israeli resolution.

In 1990, the United States suspended the U.S.-PLO dialogue begun two years earlier following an act of terrorism committed against Israel by a faction of the PLO. Yesterday, [PLO Chairman] Yasir Arafat wrote to Prime Minister [Yitzhak] Rabin, committing the PLO to accept Israel's right to exist in peace and security, to renounce terrorism, to take responsibility for the actions of its constituent groups, to discipline those elements who violate these new commitments, and to nullify key elements of the Palestinian covenant that denied Israel's right to exist.

These PLO commitments justify a resumption of our dialogue. As a result and in light of this week's events, I have decided to resume the dialogue and the contacts between the United States and the PLO.

The path ahead will not be easy. These new understandings, impressive though they are, will not erase the fears and suspicions of the past. But now the Israelis and the Palestinians have laid the foundations of hope. The United States will continue to be a full and an active partner in the negotiations that lie ahead to ensure that this promise of progress is fully realized.

All the peoples of the Middle East deserve the blessings of peace. I pledge to join them in our help and our support to achieve that objective. I look forward to joining with Russia, our co-sponsor in the Middle East peace process, and with the people of the world in witnessing the historic signing on Monday.

I also want to say I am very grateful for the overwhelming support this agreement has generated among members of both parties in the United States Congress. I especially thank leaders in the Congress from both parties who have foreign policy responsibilities who have come to meet with me this morning in the White House. . . .

This is a time for bipartisan support for this agreement and indeed a bipartisan effort to reassert and define America's role in a very new world. We were talking today in our meeting about how this period is not unlike the late 1940s, a time in which America was the first nation to recognize Israel, in which we formed the United Nations and other international institutions in an attempt to work toward the world which everyone hoped would follow from World War II.

Once again, we must develop a strong philosophy and a practical set of institutions that can permit us to follow our values and our interests and to work for a more peaceful, a more humane and a more democratic world. This is an enormous step toward that larger goal, and I think all Americans should be grateful for the opportunity that we have been presented to help make this historic peace work. ■

WHITE HOUSE CEREMONY

Leaders in 'Defining Drama' Express Hope for New Era

President Clinton pays tribute to efforts of the peacemakers as Israelis and Palestinians warily begin rapprochement

At a historic ceremony on the South Lawn of the White House on Sept. 13, Israel and the Palestine Liberation Organization signed an agreement promising self-government for Palestinians.

Participants at the ceremony hosted by President Clinton were Israeli Prime Minister Yitzhak Rabin, PLO Chairman Yasir Arafat, Israeli Foreign Minister Shimon Peres and PLO negotiator Mahmoud Abbas among others.

Following are transcripts by the Federal News Service of the remarks by the major speakers:

PRESIDENT CLINTON: Today we bear witness to an extraordinary act in one of history's defining dramas, a drama that began in a time of our ancestors when the word went forth from a sliver of land between the River Jordan and the Mediterranean Sea. That hallowed piece of earth, and land of life and revelation is the home to the memories and dreams of Jews, Muslims and Christians throughout the world.

As we all know, devotion to that land has also been the source of conflict and bloodshed for too long. Throughout this century, bitterness between the Palestinian and Jewish people has robbed the entire region of its resources, its potential and too many of its sons and daughters. The land has been so drenched in warfare and hatred, the conflicting claims of history etched so deeply in the souls of the combatants there, that many believe the past would always have the upper hand.

Then, 14 years ago, the past began to give way when at this place and upon this desk three men of great vision signed their names to the Camp David Accord. Today we honor the memories of [Israeli Prime Minister] Menachem Begin and [Egyptian President] Anwar Sadat, and we salute the wise leadership of President Jimmy Carter.

Then, as now, we heard from those who said that conflict would come again soon. But the peace between Egypt and Israel has endured. Just so, this bold, new venture today, this brave gamble that the future can be better than the past, must endure.

Two years ago in Madrid, another president took a major step on the road to peace by bringing Israel and all her neighbors together to launch direct negotiations, and today we also express our deep thanks

for the skillful leadership of President George Bush.

Ever since [President] Harry Truman first recognized Israel, every American president, Democrat and Republican, has worked for peace between Israel and her neighbors. Now the efforts of all who have labored before us bring us to this moment, a moment when we dare to pledge what for so [long] seemed difficult even to imagine: that the security of the Israeli people will be reconciled with the hopes of the Palestinian people, and there will be more security and more hope for all.

Today, the leadership of Israel and the Palestine Liberation Organization will sign a declaration of principles on interim Palestinian self-government. It charts a course toward reconciliation between two peoples who have both known the bitterness of exile. Now both pledge to put old sorrows and antagonisms behind them and to work for a shared future, shaped by the values of the Torah, the Koran and the Bible.

Let us salute also today the government of Norway for its remarkable role in nurturing this agreement.

But of all — above all, let us today pay tribute to the leaders who had the courage to lead their people toward peace, away from the scars of battle, the wounds and the losses of the past, toward a brighter tomorrow. The world today thanks Prime Minister Rabin, Foreign Minister Peres and Chairman Arafat. Their tenacity and vision has given us the promise of a new beginning.

What these leaders have done now must be done by others. Their achievement must be a catalyst for progress in all aspects of the peace process. And those of us who support them must be there to help in all aspects, for the peace must render the people who make it more secure.

A peace of the brave is within our reach. Throughout the Middle East, there is a great yearning for the quiet miracle of a normal life. We know a difficult road lies ahead. Every peace has its enemies, those who still prefer the easy habits of hatred to the hard labors of reconciliation.

But Prime Minister Rabin has reminded us that you do not have to make peace with your friends. And the Koran teaches that if the enemy inclines toward peace, do thou also incline toward peace.

Therefore, let us resolve that this new

mutual recognition will be a continuing process in which the parties transform the very way they see and understand each other. Let the skeptics of this peace recall what once existed among these people. There was a time when the traffic of ideas and commerce and pilgrims flowed uninterrupted among the cities of the fertile crescent. In Spain, in the Middle East, Muslims and Jews once worked together to write brilliant chapters in the history of literature and science. All this can come to pass again.

Mr. Prime Minister, Mr. Chairman, I pledge the active support of the United States of America to the difficult work that lies ahead. The United States is committed to ensuring that the people who are affected by this agreement will be made more secure by it, and to leading the world in marshaling the resources necessary to implement the difficult details that will make real the principles to which you commit yourselves today.

Together, let us imagine what can be accomplished if all the energy and ability the Israelis and the Palestinians have invested into your struggle can now be channeled into cultivating the land and freshening the waters, into ending the boycotts and creating new industry, into building a land as bountiful and peaceful as it is holy. Above all, let us dedicate ourselves today to your region's next generation. In this entire assembly, no one is more important than the group of Arab and Israeli children who are seated here with us today.

Mr. Prime Minister, Mr. Chairman, this day belongs to you.

And because of what you have done, tomorrow belongs to them. We must not leave them prey to the politics of extremism and despair, to those who would derail this process because they cannot overcome the fears and hatreds of the past. We must not betray their future. For too long, the young of the Middle East have been caught in a web of hatred not of their own making. For too long, they have been taught from the chronicles of war. Now, we can give them the chance to know the season of peace.

For them, we must realize the prophecy of Isaiah, that the cry of violence shall no more be heard in your land, nor rack nor ruin within your borders. The children of Abraham, the descendants of Isaac and

Ishmael, have embarked together on a bold journey. Together, today, with all our hearts and all our souls, we bid them Shalom, Salaam, Peace.

'It is a Revolution'

FOREIGN MINISTER PERES: . . . Mr. President, I would like to thank you and the great American people for peace and support. Indeed, I would like to thank all those who have made this day possible. What we are doing today is more than signing an agreement; it is a revolution. Yesterday a dream, today a commitment.

The Israeli and the Palestinian people, who fought each other for almost a century, have agreed to move decisively on the path of dialogue, understanding and cooperation. We live in an ancient land, and as our land is small, so must our reconciliation be great. As our wars have been long, so must our healing be swift. Deep gaps call for lofty bridges.

I want to tell the Palestinian delegation that we are sincere, that we mean business. We do not seek to shape your life or determine your destiny. Let all of us turn from bullets to ballots, from guns to shovels. We shall pray with you. We shall offer you our help in making Gaza prosper and Jericho blossom again.

As we have promised, we shall negotiate with you a permanent settlement, and with all our neighbors a comprehensive peace, peace for all.

We shall support the agreement with an economic structure. We shall convert the bitter triangle of Jordanians, Palestinians and the Israelis into a triangle of political triumph and economic prosperity. We shall lower our barriers and widen our roads so goods and guests will be able to move freely all about the places holy and other places.

This should be another genesis. We have to build a new commonwealth on our old soil: a Middle East of the people and a Middle East for their children. For their sake we must put an end to the waste of arms races and invest our resources in education.

Ladies and gentlemen, two parallel tragedies have unfolded. Let us become a civic community. Let us bid once and for all farewell to wars, to threats, to human misery. Let us bid farewell to enmity, and may there be no more victims on either side. Let us build a Middle East of hope where today's food is produced and tomorrow's prosperity is guaranteed, a region with a common market, a Near East with a long-range agenda.

We owe it to our own soldiers, to the memories of the victims of the Holocaust. Our hearts today grieve for the lost lives of young and innocent people yesterday in our own country. Let their memory be a foundation we are establishing today, a memory of peace on fresh and old tombs.

Suffering is first of all human. We also feel for the innocent loss of Palestinian lives. We begin a new day. The day may be long and the challenges enormous. Our cal-

endar must meet an intensive schedule.

Mr. President, historically you are presiding over a most promising day in the very long history of our region, of our people. I thank all of you, ladies and gentlemen, and let's pray together. Let's add hope to determination, as all of us since Abraham believe in freedom, in peace, in the blessing of our great land and great spirit.

[Speaking in Hebrew] From the eternal city of Jerusalem, from this green, promising lawn of the White House, let's say together in the language of our Bible: "Peace, peace to him that is far off and to him that is near," sayeth the Lord, "and I will hear."

Start of New Relationship

PLO NEGOTIATOR ABBAS: (Through interpreter) . . . In these historic moments, with feelings of joy that are mixed with a maximum sense of responsibility regarding events that are affecting our entire region, I greet you and I greet this distinguished gathering. I hope that this meeting in Washington will prove to be the onset of a positive and constructive change that will serve the interests of the Palestinian and the Israeli peoples.

We have come to this point because we believe that peaceful coexistence and cooperation are the only means for reaching understanding and for realizing the hopes of the Palestinians and the Israelis. The agreement we will sign reflects the decision we made in the Palestine Liberation Organization to turn a new page in our relationship with Israel.

We know quite well that this is merely the beginning of a journey that is surrounded by numerous dangers and difficulties.

And yet our mutual determination to overcome everything that stands in the way of the cause for peace, our common belief that peace is the only means to security and stability, and our mutual aspiration for a secure peace characterized by cooperation — all this will enable us to overcome all obstacles with the support of the international community. And here I would like to mention in particular the United States government, which will shoulder the responsibility of continuing to play an effective and distinct role in the next stage so that this great achievement may be completed.

In this regard, it is important to me to affirm that we are looking forward with a great deal of hope and optimism to a date that is two years from today when negotiations over the final status of our country are set to begin. We will then settle the remaining fundamental issues, especially those of Jerusalem, the refugees and the settlements. At that time, we will be laying the last brick in the edifice of peace whose foundation has been established today.

Economic development is the principal challenge facing the Palestinian people after years of struggle during which our national infrastructure and institutions were overburdened and drained.

We are looking to the world for its support and encouragement in our struggle for growth and development, which begins today.

I thank the government of the United States of America and the government of the Russian Federation for the part they played and for their efforts and their sponsorship of the peace process. I also appreciate the role played by the government of Norway in bringing about this agreement. And I look forward to seeing positive results soon on the remaining Arab-Israeli tracks so we can proceed together with our Arab brothers on this comprehensive quest for peace.

Accord Is Signed

Following the signing of the treaty by Peres and Abbas, Rabin and Arafat spoke:

PRIME MINISTER RABIN: . . . This signing of the Israeli-Palestinian declaration of principle here today, it's not so easy, neither for myself as a soldier in Israel's war, nor for the people of Israel, nor for the Jewish people in the Diaspora who are watching us now with great hope mixed with apprehension. It is certainly not easy for the families of the victims of the wars, violence, terror, whose pain will never heal; for the many thousands who defended our lives with their own and have even sacrificed their lives for our own. For them, this ceremony has come too late.

Today, on the eve of an opportunity, opportunity for peace, and perhaps end of violence and wars, we remember each and every one of them with everlasting love. We have come from Jerusalem, the ancient and eternal capital of the Jewish people. We have come from an anguished and grieving land. We have come from a people, a home, a family that has not known a single year, not a single month, in which mothers have not wept for their sons. We have come to try and put an end to the hostilities so that our children, our children's children, will no longer experience the painful cost of war: violence and terror. We have come to secure their lives and to ease the sorrow and the painful memories of the past, to hope and pray for peace.

Let me say to you, the Palestinians, we are destined to live together on the same soil in the same land. We, the soldiers who have returned from battles stained with blood; we who have seen our relatives and friends killed before our eyes; we who have attended their funerals and cannot look into the eyes of their parents; we who have come from a land where parents bury their children; we who have fought against you, the Palestinians, we say to you today in a loud and a clear voice: enough of blood and tears. Enough.

We have no desire for revenge, we have — we harbor no hatred towards you. We, like you, are people — people who want to build a home, to plant a tree, to love, live side by side with you in dignity, in affinity, as human beings, as free men. We are today giving peace a chance and saying to you

have joined together around the principle of providing universal comprehensive health care. It is a magic moment, and we must seize it.

I want to say to all of you, I have been deeply moved by the spirit of this debate, by the openness of all people to new ideas and argument and information. The American people would be proud to know that earlier this week, when a health-care university was held for members of Congress just to try to give everybody the same amount of information, over 320 Republicans and Democrats signed up and showed up for two days just to learn the basic facts of the complicated problem before us.

Both sides are willing to say we have listened to the people. We know the cost of going forward with this system is far greater than the cost of change. Both sides, I think, understand the literal ethical imperative of doing something about the system we have now. Rising above these difficulties and our past differences to solve this problem will go a long way toward defining who we are and who we intend to be as a people in this difficult and challenging era. I believe we all understand that.

And so tonight let me ask all of you, every member of the House, every member of the Senate, each Republican and each Democrat, let us keep this spirit and let us keep this commitment until this job is done. We owe it to the American people.

Health Security

Now if I might, I would like to review the six principles I mentioned earlier and describe how we think we can best fulfill those principles.

First and most important, security. This principle speaks to the human misery, to the cost, to the anxiety we hear about every day, all of us, when people talk about their problems with the present system. Security means that those who do not now have health-care coverage will have it, and for those who have it, it will never be taken away. We must achieve that security as soon as possible.

Under our plan, every American would receive a health-care security card that will guarantee a comprehensive package of benefits over the course of an entire lifetime, roughly comparable to the benefit package offered by most Fortune 500 companies.

This health-care security card will offer this package of benefits in a way that can never be taken away.

So let us agree on this: Whatever else we disagree on, before this Congress finishes its work next year, you will pass, and I will sign, legislation to guarantee this security to every citizen of this country.

With this card, if you lose your job or you switch jobs, you're covered. If you leave your job to start a small business, you're covered. If you're an early retiree, you're covered. If someone in your family has unfortunately had an illness that qualifies as a pre-existing condition, you're still covered.

If you get sick or a member of your family gets sick, even if it's a life-threatening illness, you're covered. And if the insurance company tries to drop you for any reason, you'll still be covered because that will be illegal.

This card will give comprehensive coverage. It will cover people for hospital care, doctor visits, emergency and lab services, diagnostic services like Pap smears and mammograms and cholesterol tests, substance abuse and mental health treatment. And equally important for both health-care and economic reasons, this program, for the first time, would provide a broad range of preventive services, including regular checkups and well-baby visits.

Now, it's just common sense. We know — any family doctor will tell you that people will stay healthier and long-term costs of the health system will be lower if we have comprehensive preventive services. You know how all of our mothers told us that an ounce of prevention was worth a pound of cure? Our mothers were right. And it's a lesson — like so many lessons from our mothers — that we have waited too long to live by. It is time to start doing it.

Health-care security must also apply to older Americans. This is something I imagine all of us in this room feel very deeply about. The first thing I want to say about that is that we must maintain the Medicare program. It works to provide that kind of security. But this time, and for the first time, I believe Medicare should provide coverage for the cost of prescription drugs.

Yes, it will cost some more in the beginning. But, again, any physician who deals with the elderly will tell you that there are thousands of elderly people in every state who are not poor enough to be on Medicaid, but just above that line and on Medicare, who desperately need medicine, who make decisions every week between medicine and food. Any doctor who deals with the elderly will tell you that there are many elderly people who don't get medicine who get sicker and sicker and eventually go to the doctor and wind up spending more money and draining more money from the health-care system than they would if they had regular treatment in the way that only adequate medicine can provide.

I also believe that over time we should phase in long-term care for the disabled and the elderly on a comprehensive basis.

As we proceed with this health-care reform, we cannot forget that the most rapidly growing percentage of Americans are those over 80. We cannot break faith with them. We have to do better by them.

Simplicity

The second principle is simplicity. Our health-care system must be simpler for the patients and simpler for those who actually deliver health care: our doctors, our nurses, our other medical professionals. Today we have more than 1,500 insurers with hundreds and hundreds of different forms. No other nation has a system like this. These forms are time-consuming for health-care providers, they're expensive for health-care consumers, they're exasperating for anyone who's ever tried to sit down around a table and wade through them and figure them out. The medical care industry is literally drowning in paperwork.

In recent years, the number of administrators in our hospitals has grown by four times the rate that the number of doctors has grown. A hospital ought to be a house of healing, not a monument to paperwork and bureaucracy.

Just a few days ago the vice president and I had the honor of visiting the Children's Hospital here in Washington, where they do wonderful, often miraculous things for very sick children. A nurse named Debbie Freiburg told us that — she's in the cancer and bone marrow unit — the other day a little boy asked her just to stay at his side during his chemotherapy, and she had to walk away from that child because she had been instructed to go to yet another class to learn how to fill out another form for something that didn't have a lick to do with the health care of the children she was helping. That is wrong, and we can stop it, and we ought to do it.

We met a very compelling doctor named Lillian Beard, a pediatrician, who said that she didn't get into her profession to spend hours and hours, some doctors up to 25 hours a week, just filling out forms. She told us she became a doctor to keep children well and to help save those who got sick.

We can relieve people like her of this burden. We learned, the vice president and I did, that in the Washington Children's Hospital alone, the administrators told us they spend $2 million a year in one hospital filling out forms that have nothing whatever to do with keeping up with the treatment of the patients. And the doctors there applauded when I was told, and I related to them, that they spend so much time filling out paperwork that if they only had to fill out those paperwork requirements necessary to monitor the health of the children, each doctor on that one hospital staff, 200 of them, could see another 500 children a year. That is 10,000 children a year.

I think we can save money in this business if we simplify it, and we can make the doctors and the nurses and the people that have given their lives to help us all be healthier a whole lot happier too on their jobs.

Under our proposal there would be one standard insurance form, not hundreds of them. We will simplify also, and we must, the government's rules and regulations because they are a big part of this problem.

This is one of those cases where the physician should heal thyself. We have to reinvent the way we relate to the health-care system, along with reinventing government. A doctor should not have to check with a bureaucrat in an office thousands of miles away before ordering a simple blood test. That's not right, and we can change it.

And doctors, nurses and consumers shouldn't have to worry about the fine print. If you have just one simple form, there won't be any fine print. People will know what it means.

The third principle is savings. Reform must produce savings in this health-care system. It has to. We are spending over 14 percent of our income on health care. Canada's is at 10. Nobody else is over nine. We're

competing with all these people for the future. And the other major countries, they cover everybody and they cover them with services as generous as the best company policies here in this country.

Rampant medical inflation is eating away at our wages, our savings, our investment capital, our ability to create new jobs in the private sector, and this public Treasury.

You know the budget we just adopted had steep cuts in defense, a five-year freeze on the discretionary spending, so critical to re-educating America and investing in jobs and helping us to convert from a defense to a domestic economy. But we passed a budget which has Medicaid increases of between 16 and 11 percent a year over the next five years, and Medicare increases of between 11 and 9 percent, in an environment where we assume inflation will be at 4 percent or less.

We cannot continue to do this. Our competitiveness, our whole economy, the integrity of the way the government works, and ultimately our living standards, depend upon our ability to achieve savings without harming the quality of health care. Unless we do this, our workers will lose $655 in income each year by the end of the decade. Small businesses will continue to face skyrocketing premiums, and a full third of small businesses now covering their employees say they will be forced to drop their insurance. Large corporations will bear bigger disadvantages in global competition, and health-care costs will devour more and more and more of our budget. Pretty soon all of you, and the people who succeed you, will be showing up here and writing out checks for health care and interest on the debt and worry about whether we've got enough defense — and that will be it, unless we have the courage to achieve the savings that are plainly there before us.

Every state and local government will continue to cut back on everything from education to law enforcement, to pay more and more for the same health care.

These rising costs are a special nightmare for our small businesses, the engine of our entrepreneurship and our job creation in America today. Health-care premiums for small businesses are 35 percent higher than those of large corporations today, and they will keep rising at double-digit rates unless we act.

So, how will we achieve these savings? Rather than looking at price controls, or looking away as the price spiral continues, rather than using the heavy hand of government to try to control what's happening, or continuing to ignore what's happening, we believe there is a third way to achieve these savings.

First, to give groups of consumers and small businesses the same market bargaining power that large corporations and large groups and public employees now have. We want to let market forces enable plans to compete. We want to force these plans to compete on the basis of price and quality, not simply to allow them to continue making money by turning people away who are sick or old, or performing mountains of unnecessary procedures. But we also believe we should

back this system up with limits on how much plans can raise their premiums year in and year out, forcing people again to continue to pay more for the same health care, without regard to inflation or the rising population needs.

We want to create what has been missing in this system for too long, and what every successful nation who has dealt with this problem has already had to do: to have a combination of private market forces and a sound public policy that will support that competition, but limit the rate at which prices can exceed the rate of inflation and population growth, if the competition doesn't work, especially in the early going.

The second thing I want to say is that unless everybody is covered — and this is a very important thing — unless everybody is covered, we will never be able to fully put the brakes on health-care inflation. Why is that? Because when people don't have any health insurance, they still get health care. But they get it when it's too late, when it's too expensive — often from the most expensive place of all, the emergency room. Usually by the time they show up, their illnesses are more severe, and their mortality rates are much higher in our hospitals than those who have insurance. So they cost us more.

And what else happens? Since they get the care but do not pay, who does pay? All the rest of us. We pay in higher hospital bills and higher insurance premiums. This cost shifting is a major problem.

Savings

The third thing we can do to save money is simply by simplifying the system, what we have already discussed. Freeing the health-care providers from these costly and unnecessary paperwork and administrative decisions will save tens of billions of dollars. We spend twice as much as any other major country does on paperwork. We spend at least a dime on the dollar more than any other major country. That is a stunning statistic. It is something that every Republican and every Democrat ought to be able to say we agree that we are going to squeeze this out. We cannot tolerate this. This has nothing to do with keeping people well or helping them when they are sick. We should invest the money in something else.

We also have to crack down on fraud and abuse in the system. That drains millions of dollars a year. It is a very large figure according to every health-care expert I've ever spoken with.

So I believe we can achieve large savings and that large savings can be used to cover the unemployed uninsured and will be used for people who realize those savings in the private sector to increase their ability to invest and grow, to hire new workers or to give their workers pay raises, many of them for the first time in years.

Now, nobody has to take my word for this. You can ask [former Surgeon General] Dr. [C. Everett] Koop. He's up here with us tonight, and I thank him for being here.

Since he left his distinguished tenure as our surgeon general, he has spent an enor-

mous amount of time studying our health-care system, how it operates, what's right and wrong with it. He said we could spend $200 billion ever year, more than 20 percent of the total budget, without sacrificing the high quality of American medicine.

Ask the public employees in California, who've held their own premiums down by adopting the same strategy that I want every American to be able to adopt, bargaining within the limits of a strict budget.

Ask Xerox, which saved an estimated $1,000 per worker on their health insurance premium. Ask the staff of the Mayo Clinic, that we all agree provides some of the finest health care in the world. They are holding their cost increases to less than half the national average.

Ask the people of Hawaii, the only state that covers virtually all of their citizens and has still been able to keep costs below the national average.

Now, people may disagree over the best way to fix this system. We may all disagree about how quickly we can do what, the thing that we have to do. But we cannot disagree that we can find tens of billions of dollars in savings in what is clearly the most costly and the most bureaucratic system in the entire world. And we have to do something about that, and we have to do it now.

Choice

The fourth principle is choice. Americans believe they ought to be able to choose their own health-care plan, keep their own doctors, and I think all of us agree. Under any plan we pass, they ought to have that right. But today under our broken health-care system, in spite of the rhetoric of choice, the fact is that that power is slipping away from more and more Americans.

Of course, it is usually the employer, not the employee, who makes the initial choice of what health-care plan the employee will be in, and if your employer offers only one plan, as nearly three-quarters of small and medium-size firms do today, you're stuck with that plan and the doctors that it covers.

We propose to give every American a choice among high-quality plans. You can stay with your current doctor, join a network of doctors and hospitals or join a health maintenance organization. If you don't like your plan, every year you'll have the chance to choose a new one. The choice will be left to the American citizen, the worker, not the boss and certainly not some government bureaucrat.

We also believe that doctors should have a choice as to what plans they practice in. Otherwise, citizens may have their own choices limited. We want to end the discrimination that is now growing against doctors and to permit them to practice in several different plans. Choice is important for doctors, and it is absolutely critical for our consumers. We've got to have it in whatever plan we pass.

Quality

The fifth principle is quality. If we reformed everything else in health care but failed to preserve and enhance the high quality of our medical care, we will have taken a

step backward, not forward.

Quality is something that we simply can't leave to chance. When you board an airplane, you feel better knowing that the plane had to meet standards designed to protect your safety. And we can't ask any less of our health-care system.

Our proposal will create report cards on health plans so that consumers can choose the highest quality health-care providers and reward them with their business. At the same time, our plan will track quality indicators so that doctors can make better and smarter choices of the kind of care they provide.

We have evidence that more efficient delivery of health care doesn't decrease quality. In fact, it may enhance it.

Let me just give you one example of one commonly performed procedure, the coronary bypass operation.

Pennsylvania discovered that patients who were charged $21,000 for this surgery received as good or better care as patients who were charged $84,000 for the same procedure in the same state. High prices simply don't always equal good quality.

Our plan will guarantee that high-quality information is available. In even the most remote areas of this country so that we can have high-quality service linking rural doctors, for example, with hospitals with high-tech urban medical centers. And our plan will ensure the quality of continuing progress on a whole range of issues, by speeding research on effective prevention and treatment measures, for cancer, for AIDS, for Alzheimer's [disease], for heart disease and for other chronic diseases.

We have to safeguard the finest medical research establishment in the entire world. And we will do that with this plan. Indeed, we will even make it better.

Responsibility

The sixth and final principle is responsibility. We need to restore a sense that we're all in this together and that we all have a responsibility to be a part of the solution.

Responsibility has to start with those who profit from the current system. Responsibility means insurance companies should no longer be allowed to cast people aside when they get sick. It should apply to laboratories that submit fraudulent bills, to lawyers who abuse malpractice claims, to doctors who order unnecessary procedures. It means drug companies should no longer charge three times more for prescription drugs made in America here in the United States than they charge for the same drugs overseas.

In short, responsibility should apply to anybody who abuses this system and drives up the cost for honest, hard-working citizens and undermines confidence in the honest, gifted health-care providers we have.

Responsibility also means changing some behaviors in this country that drive up our costs like crazy, and without changing them we'll never have the system we ought to have. We will never.

Let me just mention a few and start with the most important. The outrageous costs of violence in this country stem in large measure from the fact that this is the only country in the world where teenagers can roam the streets at random, with semiautomatic weapons and be better armed than the police.

Let's not kid ourselves, it's not that simple. We also have higher rates of AIDS, of smoking and excessive drinking, of teen pregnancy, of low-birthweight babies, and we have the third worst immunization rate of any nation in the Western Hemisphere. We have to change our ways if we ever really want to be healthy as a people and have an affordable health-care system. And no one can deny that.

But let me say this, and I hope every American will listen, because this is not an easy thing to hear. Responsibility in our health-care system isn't just about them. It's about you. It's about me. It's about each of us. Too many of us have not taken responsibility for our own health care and for our own relations to the health-care system. Many of us who've had fully paid health-care plans have used the system whether we needed it or not, without thinking what the costs were. Many people who use this system don't pay a penny for their care even though they can afford to.

I think those who don't have any health insurance should be responsible for paying a portion of their new coverage. There can't be any something for nothing, and we have to demonstrate that to people. This is not a free system. Even small contributions, as small as a $10 copayment when you visit a doctor, illustrates that this is something of value. There is a cost to it. It is not free.

And I want to tell you that I believe that all of us should have insurance. Why should the rest of us pick up the tab when a guy who doesn't think he needs insurance or says he can't afford it gets in an accident, winds up in an emergency room, gets good care and everybody else pays? Why should the small-businesspeople who are struggling to keep afloat and take care of their employees have to pay to maintain this wonderful health-care infrastructure for those who refuse to do anything?

Paying for It

If we're going to produce a better health-care system for every one of us, every one of us is going to have to do our part. There cannot be any such thing as a free ride. We have to pay for it. We have to pay for it. Tonight I want to say plainly how I think we should do that.

Most of the money would come, under my way of thinking, as it does today, from premiums paid by employers and individuals. That's the way it happens today. But under this health-care security plan, every employer and every individual will be asked to contribute something to health care. This concept was first conveyed to the Congress about 20 years ago by President [Richard M.] Nixon. And today a lot of people agree with the concept of shared responsibility between employers and employees and that the best thing to do is to ask every employer and every employee to share that.

The Chamber of Commerce has said that, and they're not in the business of hurting small business. The American Medical Association has said that. Some call it an employer mandate, but I think it's the fairest way to achieve responsibility in the health-care system. And it's the easiest for ordinary Americans to understand, because it builds on what we already have and what already works for so many Americans.

It is a reform that is not only easiest to understand but easiest to implement in a way that is fair to small business, because we can give a discount to help struggling small businesses meet the cost of covering their employees. We should require the least bureaucracy or disruption and create the cooperation we need to make the system cost-conscious even as we expand coverage. And we should do it in a way that does not cripple small businesses and low-wage workers.

Every employer should provide coverage, just as three-quarters do now. Those that pay are picking up the tab for those who don't today. I don't think that's right. To finance the rest of reform, we can achieve new savings, as I have outlined, in both the federal government and the private sector through better decision-making and increased competition. And we will impose new taxes on tobacco.

I don't think that should be the only source of revenues. I believe we should also ask for a modest contribution from big employers who opt out of the system to make up for what those who are in the system pay for medical research, for health education centers, for all the subsidies to small business, for all the things that everyone is contributing to. But between those two things, we believe we can pay for this package of benefits and universal coverage and a subsidy program that will help small business.

These sources can cover the cost of the proposal that I have described tonight. We subjected the numbers in our proposal to the scrutiny not only of all the major agencies in government. I know a lot of people don't trust them, but it'd be interesting for the American people to know that this was the first time that the financial experts on health care in all the different government agencies had ever been required to sit in a room together and agree on numbers. It had never happened before. But obviously that's not enough.

So then we gave these numbers to actuaries from major accounting firms and major Fortune 500 companies who have no stake in this other than to see that our efforts succeed. So I believe our numbers are good and achievable.

Now, what does this mean to an individual American citizen? Some will be asked to pay more. If you're an employer and you aren't insuring your workers at all, you'll have to pay more. But if you're a small business with fewer than 50 employees, you'll get a subsidy. If you're a firm that provides only very limited coverage, you may have to pay more. But some firms will pay the same or less for more coverage.

If you're a young single person in your 20s and you're already insured, your rates may go up somewhat because you're going to go into a big pool with middle-aged people and older people. And we want to enable people to keep their insurance even when

someone in their family gets sick. But I think that's fair, because when the young get older, they'll benefit from it, first. And secondly, even those who pay a little more today will benefit four, five, six, seven years from now by our bringing health-care costs closer to inflation.

Over the long run, we can all win. But some will have to pay more in the short run. Nevertheless, the vast majority of the Americans watching this tonight will pay the same or less for health-care coverage that will be the same or better than the coverage they have tonight. That is the central reality.

If you currently get your health insurance through your job, under our plan, you still will. And for the first time, everybody will get to choose from among at least three plans to belong to. If you're a small-business owner who wants to provide health insurance to your family and your employees but you can't afford to because the system is stacked against you, this plan will give you a discount that will finally make insurance affordable.

If you're already providing insurance, your rates may well drop because we'll help you as a small-businessperson join thousands of others to get the same benefits big corporations get at the same price they get those benefits. If you're self-employed, you'll pay less, and you'll get to deduct from your taxes 100 percent of your health-care premiums. If you're a large employer, your health-care costs won't go up as fast, so that you will have more money to put into higher wages and new jobs, and to put into the work of being competitive in this tough global economy.

Now, these, my fellow Americans, are the principles on which I think we should base our efforts: Security, simplicity, savings, choice, quality and responsibility. These are the guiding stars that we should follow on our journey toward health-care reform. Over the coming months, you'll be bombarded with information from all kinds of sources. There will be some who will stoutly disagree with what I have proposed, and with all other plans in the Congress, for that matter. And some of the arguments will be genuinely sincere and enlightening.

Others may simply be scare tactics by those who are motivated by the self-interest they have in the waste the system now generates, because that waste is providing jobs, incomes and money for some people. I ask you only to think of this: When you hear all of these arguments, ask yourself whether the cost of staying on this same course isn't greater than the cost of change. And ask yourself when you hear the arguments whether the arguments are in your interests or someone else's. This is something we have got to try to do together.

I want also to say to the representatives in Congress, you have a special duty to look beyond these arguments. I ask you instead to look into the eyes of a sick child who needs care; to think of the face of the woman who's been told not only that her condition is malignant but not covered by her insurance; to look at the bottom lines of the businesses driven to bankruptcy by health-care costs; to look at the for-sale signs in front of the homes of families who've lost everything because of their health-care costs.

I ask you to remember the kind of people I met for the last year and a half; the elderly couple in New Hampshire that broke down and cried because of their shame at having an empty refrigerator to pay for their drugs; the woman who lost a $50,000 job that she used to support her six children because her youngest child was so ill that she couldn't keep health insurance, and the only way to get care for the child was to get public assistance; a young couple that had a sick child and could only get insurance from one of the parent's employers that was a nonprofit corporation with 20 employees, and so they had to face the question of whether to let this poor person with a sick child go or raise the premiums of every employee in the firm by $200; and on and on and on.

I know we have differences of opinion, but we are here tonight in a spirit that is animated by the problems of those people and by the sure knowledge that if we can look into our hearts, we will not be able to say that the greatest nation in the history of the world is powerless to confront this crisis. Our history and our heritage tell us that we can meet this challenge. Everything about America's past tells us we will do it. So I say to you, let us write that new chapter in the American story. Let us guarantee every American comprehensive health benefits that can never be taken away.

In spite of all the work we've done together and all the progress we've made, there are still a lot of people who say it would be an outright miracle if we passed health-care reform. But my fellow Americans, in a time of change, you have to have miracles. And miracles do happen. I mean, just a few days ago we saw a simple handshake shatter decades of deadlock in the Middle East. We've seen the walls crumble in Berlin and South Africa. We see the ongoing brave struggle of the people of Russia to seize freedom and democracy. And now it is our turn to strike a blow for freedom in this country, the freedom of Americans to live without fear that their own nation's health-care system won't be there for them when they need it.

It's hard to believe that there was once a time in this century when that kind of fear gripped old age, when retirement was nearly synonymous with poverty and older Americans died in the street. That's unthinkable today because over half a century ago Americans had the courage to change, to create a Social Security system that ensures that no Americans will be forgotten in their later years.

Forty years from now, our grandchildren will also find it unthinkable that there was a time in this country when hard-working families lost their homes, their savings, their businesses, lost everything, simply because their children got sick or because they had to change jobs. Our grandchildren will find such things unthinkable tomorrow if we have the courage to change today.

This is our chance. This is our journey. And when our work is done, we will know that we have answered the call of history and met the challenge of our time. Thank you very much, and God bless America. ∎

REPUBLICAN RESPONSE

President Criticized On Plan's Details

The Republican response to President Clinton's address Sept. 22 was delivered by South Carolina Gov. Carroll A. Campbell Jr., Connecticut Rep. Nancy L. Johnson and Florida Sen. Connie Mack. Following is the transcript provided by the Federal News Service:

GOV. CAMPBELL: ... America is ready for health-care reform, and so are we. We're just sorry the president didn't spell out the details of his plan. There are many plans on the table for consideration. And the President and Mrs. [Hillary Rodham] Clinton deserve credit for bringing health care to the center stage of America.

As we begin the national debate, we hope you'll remember these words — choice, quality, jobs and cost. Those words are an important part of [Rep.] Nancy Johnson's comprehensive health-care proposal, which was one of the first to be introduced in the Congress.

REP. JOHNSON: Rarely is there an issue in Congress that so directly affects you and your family's health and well-being. Long before Bill Clinton became president, Republicans introduced solutions to America's health-care crisis. Tonight, we welcome the president's entry into this important dialogue. We support much of what he says. There are significant areas of agreement: for example, insurance reform to protect people from losing their health-care coverage when they change or lose their jobs; administrative reform to simplify paperwork; and malpractice reform to eliminate unnecessary costs. There are other areas of common ground, and in the months ahead, we are committed to work-

ing hard to reach agreement on a health-care plan that will serve all Americans.

But tonight, we must point out, in the brief time we have, some fundamental differences of approach you and your family need to think about. First, we are concerned about the president's Washington-mandated one-size-fits-all approach. Should government really force almost all Americans to change health plans and buy health insurance through state-run monopolies?

The president says he wants to reinvent government, because bureaucracy is so inefficient and unresponsive. I agree. And like many of you, I'm more than a little reluctant to create dozens of new bureaucracies with unprecedented power over my health care. We think we have a better way. Our proposals level the playing field for those who work for small businesses and others without insurance so they can afford coverage. We're also very troubled by the president's proposal to mandate the cost of health care on small business.

In my own state of Connecticut, many small employers are barely surviving. A new health-care tax would certainly force layoffs and discourage hiring. You know, America is different. We're the land of opportunity, because in America you can open your own business and expand it far easier than in any other country.

We need not sacrifice jobs or compromise economic opportunity to assure that all citizens have access to good health care. There are alternatives. For example, cutting the cost of insurance and expanding neighborhood health centers can create access to care without sacrificing jobs and opportunity. We believe that the American people want more choices, not more mandates.

Finally, we disagree with a key part of the president's approach to controlling health-care costs. We agree costs must be driven down and we are pleased he supports our proposals to do just that. But we oppose what amounts to national price fixing. We've had experience with that approach — all bad. Ask any veteran. Ask any welfare recipient. Ironically, this approach also penalizes those who are doing the most to cut costs by promoting wellness.

Companies that cut health-care costs by investing in fitness programs will pay the very same tax that companies that don't. The Republican health-care proposals are realistic. They expand access without mandates, preserve choice and flexibility, reduce costs and provide health-care security for you and your loved ones. Done right, health-care reform will provide increasingly better care and greater security for all Americans.

SEN. MACK: In this important national debate about health care, we must never lose sight of one simple truth: The health-care issue is not about numbers or percentages. It's about people. It's about families — yours and mine. I know this from personal experience. My wife, our daughter, my mother and I are all cancer survivors. My brother Michael died of cancer in 1979. Along with our doctors, we chose the treatment that was best for us during our illnesses. And we had a choice. And so

should you. But you may not under the president's plan — and it's frightening.

Read the Clinton administration's plan. It's loaded with more spending and more bureaucracy. It will devastate jobs in our economy. It will lead us to a system of government-controlled health care at a cost of $700 billion — that's billion with a capital "B." It would create literally dozens of new agencies. We would see an explosion in the size, scope and cost of government — a $700 billion explosion.

The president's plan will force too many Americans to change their health-care coverage. It will give a faceless government bureaucracy more control over your health care. It could even prevent your own doctor from treating you — and that's wrong. We want to reform the system to give you more control.

After all, the fundamental right of each American is the right to make choices for ourselves. You know more about your health-care needs than some bureaucrat. The emotional bond you have developed with your doctor could be lost when the government takes away your freedom to choose your own health care. I don't want bureaucracy to ration health care and decide when I'm sick and when I can't see my doctor. You and I know what's best for our families.

America has the highest quality of health care in the world, and people come from every corner of the globe — especially those living under government-controlled health-care systems. A woman in Florida told me that her father, who gets his care under Britain's government-controlled system, had to wait 18 months for a cataract operation. By then, his eyes were inoperable.

And just north of our border, Canadians wait seven months for cataract removal. We wouldn't tolerate that in America. My father had cataract surgery when he needed it. And I want to make certain that our senior citizens have the best care available when they need it.

We're amazingly close to some significant breakthroughs in medicine — maybe the kind of discoveries that could have saved my brother's life. The American spirit of innovation and ingenuity can only flourish with less government, not more government.

The debate tonight isn't about whether health care should be reformed, it's over how to do it. And we want it done right with less government and more freedom. The Clinton administration's plan will sacrifice health-care quality and lead to more spending, more government, fewer jobs and less freedom for all of us. Republicans believe maintaining health-care quality and ensuring individual choice is a better way.

GOV. CAMPBELL: There is common ground among the administration's plan, the bills introduced by Republicans in Congress and the principles endorsed by the nation's governors. For example, we all agree that we need to increase access to health care and reduce paperwork. We need to change malpractice laws to cut legal costs and duplication. And we need to focus on prevention to save lives and cut costs. We agree that you

shouldn't lose your health coverage just because you change jobs. And we want to make health insurance affordable for small businesses and individuals.

I know you believe, as I do, that America's health-care system has become nearly as cumbersome and bureaucratic as the federal government — and there's plenty of room for reform in both. But a one-size-fits-all federal health-care system will be bitter medicine for Americans to swallow. We need competition in the marketplace to bring quality and savings. And we need some answers about where we'll get the money to pay for this new system. More deficit spending is unacceptable. And we can't let the federal government shift more costs to state taxpayers and claim that they've made savings by capping Medicaid.

We have some tough questions that demand clear answers. Will you be allowed to choose your own doctor and the type of coverage you want? How many jobs will be lost if the federal government sets the price small businesses pay to provide employee coverage? Do you really want the federal government to control your health care? Should we rely on the government, with its track record, to manage one-seventh of our economy? Do we want to grow the government or grow the private sector?

We already have evidence that the federal bureaucracy can block real reform now going on in the states. Last week, Tennessee's Tenncare proposal, which expands coverage to more low-income Tennesseans for the same Medicaid dollars, was shot down by Washington.

In Arizona, [Republican] Gov. [Fife] Symington has saved as much as 40 percent of his state's Medicaid costs with a managed-care system. But he's having to go to Washington for a third time to ask for approval for reform that works. If we're serious about health-care reform, Tennessee should already have its waiver, and Arizona shouldn't have to ask if it's OK to save money for the taxpayers.

It's clear to me that we can't rely on heavy-handed government regulation and bureaucracies to lead the charge towards reform. The 238-page administration draft is a giant social experiment devised by theorists who have never met a payroll.

But I am encouraged that the president and Mrs. Clinton have signaled their willingness to talk and to compromise. Republicans have promised the same.

You know, my grandfather was a family doctor in rural South Carolina who believed that every individual deserved quality health care — and he delivered it. If a patient didn't have any money, my grandfather would accept farm products or sometimes he'd just tear the bill up. Those days are gone.

Do we need health-care reform? Yes, we do. But not at the expense of your right to make basic choices for your family. The cure must not be worse than the disease. Republicans will work with the administration to forge a health-care system that will work for you. We give you that commitment.

Thank you. God bless you, and good night. ∎

PRESIDENTIAL ADDRESS

Clinton Calls For Honest Look At U.N.'s Global Challenges

Following is the official White House text of President Clinton's address to the U.N. General Assembly in New York on Sept. 27:

Thank you very much. Mr. President, let me first congratulate you on your election as president of this General Assembly.

Mr. Secretary-General, distinguished delegates and guests, it is a great honor for me to address you and to stand in this great chamber which symbolizes so much of the 20th century — its darkest crises and its brightest aspirations.

I come before you as the first American president born after the founding of the United Nations. Like most of the people in the world today, I was not even alive during the convulsive World War that convinced humankind of the need for this organization, nor during the San Francisco Conference [on International Organization] that led to its birth. Yet I have followed the work of the United Nations throughout my life, with admiration for its accomplishments, with sadness for its failures, and conviction that through common effort our generation can take the bold steps needed to redeem the mission entrusted to the United Nations 48 years ago.

I pledge to you that my nation remains committed to helping make the United Nations' vision a reality. The start of this General Assembly offers us an opportunity to take stock of where we are, as common shareholders in the progress of humankind and in the preservation of our planet.

It is clear that we live at a turning point in human history. Immense and promising changes seem to wash over us every day. The Cold War is over. The world is no longer divided into two armed and angry camps. Dozens of new democracies have been born.

It is a moment of miracles. We see Nelson Mandela stand side by side with President [F. W.] De Klerk, proclaiming a date for South Africa's first non-racial election. We see Russia's first popularly elected president, Boris [N.] Yeltsin, leading his nation on its bold democratic journey. We have seen decades of deadlock shattered in the Middle East, as the prime minister of Israel [Yitzhak Rabin] and the chairman of the Palestine Liberation Organization [Yasir Arafat] reached past enmity and suspicion to shake each other's hands and exhilarate the entire world with the hope of peace.

We have begun to see the doomsday weapons of nuclear annihilation dismantled and destroyed. Thirty-two years ago, President [John F.] Kennedy warned this chamber that humanity lived under a nuclear sword of Damocles that hung by the slenderest of threads. Now the United States is working with Russia, Ukraine, Belarus and others to take that sword down, to lock it away in a secure vault where we hope and pray it will remain forever.

It is a new era in this hall as well. The superpower standoff that for so long stymied the United Nations' work almost from its first day has now yielded to a new promise of practical cooperation. Yet today we must all admit that there are two powerful tendencies working from opposite directions to challenge the authority of nation-states everywhere and to undermine the authority of nation-states to work together.

From beyond nations, economic and technological forces all over the globe are compelling the world toward integration. These forces are fueling a welcome explosion of entrepreneurship and political liberalization. But they also threaten to destroy the insularity and independence of national economies, quickening the pace of change and making many of our people feel more insecure.

At the same time, from within nations, the resurgent aspirations of ethnic and religious groups challenge governments on terms that traditional nation-states cannot easily accommodate.

These twin forces lie at the heart of the challenges not only to our national government, but also to all our international institutions. They require all of us in this room to find new ways to work together more effectively in pursuit of our national interests and to think anew about whether our institutions of international cooperation are adequate to this moment.

Thus, as we marvel at this era's promise of new peace, we must also recognize that serious threats remain. Bloody ethnic, religious and civil wars rage from Angola to the Caucasus to Kashmir. As weapons of mass destruction fall into more hands, even small conflicts can threaten to take on murderous proportions. Hunger and disease continue to take a tragic toll, especially among the world's children. The malignant neglect of our global environment threatens our children's health and their very security.

The repression of conscience continues in too many nations. And terrorism, which has taken so many innocent lives, assumes a horrifying immediacy for us here when militant fanatics bombed the World Trade Center and planned to attack even this very hall of peace.

Let me assure you, whether the fathers of those crimes, or the mass murderers who bombed Pan Am Flight 103, my government is determined to see that such terrorists are brought to justice.

As this moment of panoramic change, of vast opportunities and troubling threats, we must all ask ourselves what we can do and what we should do as a community of nations. We must once again dare to dream of what might be, for our dreams may be within our reach. For that to happen, we must all be willing to honestly confront the challenges of the broader world. That has never been easy.

When this organization was founded 48 years ago, the world's nations stood devastated by war or exhausted by its expense. There was little appetite for cooperative efforts among nations. Most people simply wanted to get on with their lives. But a far-sighted generation of leaders from the United States and elsewhere rallied the world. Their efforts built the institutions of postwar security and prosperity.

We are at a similar moment today. The momentum of the Cold War no longer propels us in our daily actions. And with daunting economic and political pressures upon almost every nation represented in this room, many of us are turning to focus greater attention and energy on our domestic needs and problems. And we must. But putting each of our economic houses in order cannot mean that we shut our windows to the world. The pursuit of self-renewal in many of the world's largest and most powerful economies — in Europe, in Japan, in North America — is absolutely crucial because unless the great industrial nations can recapture their robust economic growth, the global economy will languish.

Yet, the industrial nations also need growth elsewhere in order to lift their own. Indeed, prosperity in each of our nations and regions also depends upon active and responsible engagement in a host of shared concerns.

For example, a thriving and democratic Russia not only makes the world safer, it also can help to expand the world's economy. A strong GATT [General Agreement on Tariffs and Trade] agreement will create millions of jobs worldwide. Peace in the Middle East, buttressed as it should be by the repeal of outdated U.N. resolutions, can help to unleash that region's great economic potential and calm a perpetual source of tension in global affairs. And the growing economic power of China, coupled

with greater political openness, could bring enormous benefits to all of Asia and to the rest of the world.

We must help our publics to understand this distinction: Domestic renewal is an overdue tonic. But isolationism and protectionism are still poison. We must inspire our people to look beyond their immediate fears toward a broader horizon.

The Path of the United States

Let me start by being clear about where the United States stands. The United States occupies a unique position in world affairs today. We recognize that, and we welcome it. Yet, with the Cold War over, I know many people ask whether the United States plans to retreat or remain active in the world, and if active, to what end. Many people are asking that in our own country as well. Let me answer that question as clearly and plainly as I can.

The United States intends to remain engaged and to lead. We cannot solve every problem, but we must and will serve as a fulcrum for change and a pivot point for peace.

In a new era of peril and opportunity, our overriding purpose must be to expand and strengthen the world's community of market-based democracies. During the Cold War we sought to contain a threat to survival of free institutions. Now we seek to enlarge the circle of nations that live under those free institutions.

For our dream is of a day when the opinions and energies of every person in the world will be given full expression, in a world of thriving democracies that cooperate with each other and live in peace.

With this statement, I do not mean to announce some crusade to force our way of life and doing things on others, or to replicate our institutions, but we now know clearly that throughout the world, from Poland to Eritrea, from Guatemala to South Korea, there is an enormous yearning among people who wish to be the masters of their own economic and political lives. Where it matters most and where we can make the greatest difference, we will, therefore, patiently and firmly align ourselves with that yearning.

Today, there are still those who claim that democracy is simply not applicable to many cultures and that its recent expansion is an aberration, an accident, in history that will soon fade away. But I agree with President [Franklin D.] Roosevelt, who once said, "The democratic aspiration is no mere recent phase of human history. It is human history."

We will work to strengthen the free market democracies, by revitalizing our economy here at home, by opening world trade through the GATT, the North American Free Trade Agreement and other accords, and by updating our shared institutions, asking with you and answering the hard questions about whether they are adequate to the present challenges.

We will support the consolidation of market democracy where it is taking new root, as in the states of the former Soviet Union and all over Latin America. And we seek to foster the practices of good government that distribute the benefits of democracy and economic growth fairly to all people.

We will work to reduce the threat from regimes that are hostile to democracies and to support liberalization of non-democratic states when they are willing to live in peace with the rest of us.

As a country that has over 150 different racial, ethnic and religious groups within our borders, our policy is and must be rooted in a profound respect for all the world's religions and cultures. But we must oppose everywhere extremism that produces terrorism and hate.

And we must pursue our humanitarian goal of reducing suffering, fostering sustainable development, and improving the health and living conditions, particularly for our world's children.

On efforts from export control to trade agreements to peacekeeping, we will often work in partnership with others and through multilateral institutions, such as the United Nations. It is in our national interest to do so. But we must not hesitate to act unilaterally when there is a threat to our core interests or to those of our allies.

The United States believes that an expanded community of market democracies not only serves our own security interests, it also advances the goals enshrined in this body's charter and its Universal Declaration of Human Rights. For broadly based prosperity is clearly the strongest form of preventive diplomacy. And the habits of democracy are the habits of peace.

Democracy is rooted in compromise, not conquest. It rewards tolerance, not hatred. Democracies rarely wage war on one another. They make more reliable partners in trade, in diplomacy and in the stewardship of our global environment. And democracies with the rule of law and respect for political, religious and cultural minorities are more responsive to their own people and to the protection of human rights.

Non-Proliferation

But as we work toward this vision we must confront the storm clouds that may overwhelm our work and darken the march toward freedom. If we do not stem the proliferation of the world's deadliest weapons, no democracy can feel secure. If we do not strengthen the capacity to resolve conflict among and within nations, those conflicts will smother the birth of free institutions, threaten the development of entire regions and continue to take innocent lives.

If we do not nurture our people and our planet through sustainable development, we will deepen conflict and waste the very wonders that make our efforts worth doing.

Let me talk more about what I believe we must do in each of these three categories: non-proliferation, conflict resolution and sustainable development.

One of our most urgent priorities must be attacking the proliferation of weapons of mass destruction, whether they are nuclear, chemical or biological, and the ballistic missiles that can rain them down on populations hundreds of miles away.

We know this is not an idle problem. All of us are still haunted by the pictures of Kurdish women and children cut down by poison gas. We saw Scud missiles dropped during the gulf war that would have been far graver in their consequence if they had carried nuclear weapons. And we know that many nations still believe it is in their interest to develop weapons of mass destruction or to sell them or the necessary technologies to others for financial gain.

More than a score of nations likely possess such weapons, and their number threatens to grow. These weapons destabilize entire regions. They could turn a local conflict into a global human and environmental catastrophe. We simply have got to find ways to control these weapons and to reduce the number of states that possess them by supporting and strengthening the IAEA [International Atomic Energy Agency] and by taking other necessary measures.

I have made non-proliferation one of our nation's highest priorities. We intend to weave it more deeply into the fabric of all of our relationships with the world's nations and institutions. We seek to build a world of increasing pressures for non-proliferation but increasingly open trade and technology for those states that live by accepted international rules.

Today, let me describe several new policies that our government will pursue to stem proliferation. We will pursue new steps to control the materials for nuclear weapons. Growing global stockpiles of plutonium and highly enriched uranium are raising the danger of nuclear terrorism for all nations. We will press for an international agreement that would ban production of these materials for weapons forever.

As we reduce our nuclear stockpiles, the United States has also begun negotiations toward a comprehensive ban on nuclear testing. This summer I declared that to facilitate these negotiations, our nation would suspend our testing if all other nuclear states would do the same. Today, in the face of disturbing signs, I renew my call on the nuclear states to abide by that moratorium as we negotiate to stop nuclear testing for all time.

I am also proposing new efforts to fight the proliferation of biological and chemical weapons. Today, only a handful of nations has ratified the Chemical Weapons Convention. I call on all nations, including my own, to ratify this accord quickly so that it may enter into force by Jan. 13, 1995.

We will also seek to strengthen the Biological Weapons Convention by making every nation's biological activities and facilities open to more international students. I am proposing as well new steps to thwart the proliferation of ballistic missiles. Recently, working with Russia, Argentina, Hungary and South Africa, we have made significant progress toward that

goal. Now, we will seek to strengthen the principles of the Missile Technology Control Regime by transforming it from an agreement on technology transfer among just 23 nations to a set of rules that can command universal adherence.

We will also reform our own system of export controls in the United States to reflect the realities of the post-Cold War world, where we seek to enlist the support of our former adversaries in the battle against proliferation.

At the same time that we stop deadly technologies from falling into the wrong hands, we will work with our partners to remove outdated controls that unfairly burden legitimate commerce and unduly restrain growth and opportunity all over the world.

As we work to keep the world's most destructive weapons out of conflict, we must also strengthen the international community's ability to address those conflicts themselves. For as we all now know so painfully, the end of the Cold War did not bring us to the millennium of peace. And, indeed, it simply removed the lid from many cauldrons of ethnic, religious and territorial animosity.

U.N. Peacekeepers

The philosopher Isaiah Berlin has said that a wounded nationalism is like a bent twig forced down so severely that when released it lashes back with fury.

The world today is thick with both bent and recoiling twigs of wounded communal identities.

This scourge of bitter conflict has placed high demands on United Nations peacekeeping forces. Frequently the blue helmets have worked wonders. In Namibia, El Salvador, the Golan Heights and elsewhere, U.N. peacekeepers have helped to stop the fighting, restore civil authority and enable free elections.

In Bosnia, U.N. peacekeepers, against the danger and frustration of that continuing tragedy, [have] maintained a valiant humanitarian effort. And if the parties of that conflict take the hard steps needed to make a real peace, the international community including the United States must be ready to help in its effective implementation.

In Somalia, the United States and the United Nations have worked together to achieve a stunning humanitarian rescue, saving literally hundreds of thousands of lives and restoring the conditions of security for almost the entire country.

U.N. peacekeepers from over two dozen nations remain in Somalia today. And some, including brave Americans, have lost their lives to ensure that we complete our mission and to ensure that anarchy and starvation do not return just as quickly as they were abolished.

Many still criticize U.N. peacekeeping, but those who do should talk to the people of Cambodia, where the U.N.'s operations have helped to turn the killing fields into fertile soil through reconciliation. Last

May's elections in Cambodia marked a proud accomplishment for that war-weary nation and for the United Nations. And I am pleased to announce that the United States has recognized Cambodia's new government.

U.N. peacekeeping holds the promise to resolve many of this era's conflicts. The reason we have supported such missions is not, as some critics in the United States have charged, to subcontract American foreign policy, but to strengthen our security, protect our interests, and to share among nations the costs and effort of pursuing peace.

Peacekeeping cannot be a substitute for our own national defense efforts, but it can strongly supplement them.

Today, there is wide recognition that the U.N. peacekeeping ability has not kept pace with the rising responsibilities and challenges. Just six years ago, about 10,000 U.N. peacekeepers were stationed around the world. Today, the United Nations has some 80,000 deployed in 17 operations on four continents.

Yet, until recently, if a peacekeeping commander called in from across the globe when it was nighttime here in New York, there was no one in the peacekeeping office even to answer the call. When lives are on the line, you cannot let the reach of the United Nations exceed its grasp.

As the secretary-general and others have argued, if U.N. peacekeeping is to be a sound security investment for our nation and for other U.N. members, it must adapt to new times. Together we must prepare U.N. peacekeeping for the 21st century. We need to begin by bringing the rigors of military and political analysis to every U.N. peace mission.

In recent weeks in the Security Council, our nation has begun asking harder questions about proposals for new peacekeeping missions: Is there a real threat to international peace? Does the proposed mission have clear objectives? Can an end point be identified for those who will be asked to participate? How much will the mission cost?

From now on, the United Nations should address these and other hard questions for every proposed mission before we vote and before the mission begins.

The United Nations simply cannot become engaged in every one of the world's conflicts. If the American people are to say yes to U.N. peacekeeping, the United Nations must know when to say no. The United Nations must also have the technical means to run a modern world-class peacekeeping operation.

We support the creation of a genuine U.N. peacekeeping headquarters with a planning staff, with access to timely intelligence, with a logistics unit that can be deployed on a moment's notice, and a modern operations center with global communications.

And the United Nations' operations must not only be adequately funded, but also fairly funded. Within the next few

weeks, the United States will be current in our peacekeeping bills. I have worked hard with the Congress to get this done.

I believe the United States should lead the way in being timely in its payments, and I will work to continue to see that we pay our bills in full. But I am also committed to work with the United Nations to reduce our nation's assessment for these missions.

The assessment system has not been changed since 1973. And everyone in our country knows that our percentage of the world's economic pie is not as great as it was then. Therefore, I believe our rates should be reduced to reflect the rise of other nations that can now bear more of the financial burden. That will make it easier for me as president to make sure we pay in a timely and full fashion.

Changes in the United Nations' peacekeeping operations must be part of an even broader program of United Nations reform. I say that again not to criticize the United Nations, but to help to improve it. As our Ambassador Madeleine K. Albright has suggested, the United States has always played a twin role to the United Nations — first friend and first critic.

Reinventing Government

Today corporations all around the world are finding ways to move from the Industrial Age to the Information Age, improving service, reducing bureaucracy and cutting costs.

Here in the United States, our Vice President Al Gore and I have launched an effort to literally reinvent how our government operates. We see this going on in other governments around the world. Now the time has come to reinvent the way the United Nations operates as well.

I applaud the initial steps the secretary general [Boutros Boutros-Ghali] has taken to reduce and to reform the United Nations bureaucracy. Now, we must all do even more to root out waste.

Before this General Assembly is over, let us establish a strong mandate for an office of inspector general so that it can attain a reputation for toughness, for integrity, for effectiveness. Let us build new confidence among our people that the United Nations is changing with the needs of our times.

Ultimately, the key for reforming the United Nations, as in reforming our own government, is to remember why we are here and whom we serve.

It is wise to recall that the first words of the U.N. Charter are not "We, the governments," but, "We, the people of the United Nations." That means in every country the teachers, the workers, the farmers, the professionals, the fathers, the mothers, the children, from the most remote village in the world to the largest metropolis — they are why we gather in this great hall. It is their futures that are at risk when we act or fail to act. It is they who ultimately pay our bills.

As we dream new dreams in this age

when miracles now seem possible, let us focus on the lives of those people and especially on the children who will inherit this world.

Let us work with a new urgency and imagine what kind of world we could create for them in the coming generations.

Let us work with new energy to protect the world's people from torture and repression. As Secretary of State [Warren] Christopher stressed at the recent Vienna Conference, human rights are not something conditional, founded by culture, but rather something universal granted by God.

This General Assembly should create, at long last, a high commissioner for human rights. I hope you will do it soon and with vigor and energy and conviction.

Let us also work far more ambitiously to fulfill our obligations as custodians of this planet, not only to improve the quality of life for our citizens and the quality of our air and water and the Earth itself, but also because the roots of conflict are so often entangled with the roots of environmental neglect and the calamity of famine and disease.

During the course of our campaign in the United States last year, Vice President Gore and I promised the American people major changes in our nation's policy toward the global environment. Those were promises to keep, and today the United States is doing so.

Global Commitments

Today we are working with other nations to build on the promising work of the United Nations' Commission on Sustainable Development. We are working to make sure that all nations meet their commitments under the Global Climate Conven-

tion. We are seeking to complete negotiations on an accord to prevent the world's deserts from further expansion. And we seek to strengthen the World Health Organization's efforts to combat the plague of AIDS, which is not only killing millions, but also exhausting the resources of nations that can least afford it.

Let us make a new commitment to the world's children. It is tragic enough that 1.5 million children died as a result of wars over the past decade. But it is far more unforgivable that in that same period, 40 million children died from diseases completely preventable with simply vaccines or medicine. Every day — this day, as we meet here — over 30,000 of the world's children will die of malnutrition and disease.

Our UNICEF director, Jim Grant, has reminded me that each of those children had a name and a nationality, a family, a personality and a potential. We are compelled to do better by the world's children. Just as our own nation has launched new reforms to ensure that every child has adequate health care, we must do more to get basic vaccines and other treatment for curable diseases to children all over the world. It's the best investment we'll ever make.

We can find new ways to ensure that every child grows up with clean drinkable water, that most precious commodity of life itself. And the United Nations can work even harder to ensure that each child has at least a full primary education — and I mean that opportunity for girls as well as boys.

And to ensure a healthier and more abundant world, we simply must slow the world's explosive growth in population. We cannot afford to see the human waste doubled by the middle of the next century.

Our nation has, at last, renewed its

commitment to work with the United Nations to expand the availability of the world's family planning education and services. We must ensure that there is a place at the table for every one of our world's children. And we can do it.

At the birth of this organization 48 years ago, another time of both victory and danger, a generation of gifted leaders from many nations stepped forward to organize the world's efforts in behalf of security and prosperity.

One American leader during that period said this: "It is time we steered by the stars rather than by the light of each passing ship." His generation picked peace, human dignity and freedom. Those are good stars; they should remain the highest in our own firmament.

Now history has granted to us a moment of even greater opportunity, when old dangers and old walls are crumbling; future generations will judge us, every one of us, above all, by what we make of this magic moment.

Let us resolve that we will dream larger, that we will work harder so that they can conclude that we did not merely turn walls to rubble, but instead laid the foundation for great things to come.

Let us ensure that the tide of freedom and democracy is not pushed back by the fierce winds of ethnic hatred. Let us ensure that the world's most dangerous weapons are safely reduced and denied to dangerous hands. Let us ensure that the world we pass to our children is healthier, safer and more abundant than the one we inhabit today.

I believe — I know — that together we can extend this moment of miracles into an age of great work and new wonders. Thank you very much.   ■

Clinton: More Troops Needed For Safe Somalia Pullout

U.S. will complete military mission by March 31, 1994, but on 'our own terms,' president says

On Oct. 7, President Clinton delivered a televised address on the situation in Somalia. Following is the Federal News Service transcript of his comments:

My fellow Americans, today I want to talk with you about our nation's military involvement in Somalia.

A year ago we all watched with horror as Somali children and their families lay dying by the tens of thousands, dying the slow, agonizing death of starvation, a starvation brought on not only by drought but also by the anarchy that then prevailed in that country. This past weekend we all reacted with anger and horror as an armed Somali gang desecrated the bodies of our American soldiers and displayed a captured American pilot, all of them soldiers who were taking part in an international effort to end the starvation of the Somali people themselves.

These tragic events raise hard questions about our effort in Somalia. Why are we still there? What are we trying to accomplish? How did a humanitarian mission turn violent? And when will our people come home? These questions deserve straight answers. Let's start by remembering why our troops went into Somalia in the first place.

We went because only the United States could help stop one of the great human tragedies of this time. A third of a million people had died of starvation and disease. Twice that many more were at risk of dying. Meanwhile, tons of relief supplies piled up in the capital of Mogadishu because a small number of Somalis stopped food from reaching their own countrymen. Our consciences said, "Enough."

In our nation's best tradition, we took action with bipartisan support. President [George] Bush sent in 28,000 American troops as part of the United Nations humanitarian mission. Our troops created a secure environment so that food and medicine could get through. We saved close to 1 million lives. And throughout most of Somalia — everywhere but in Mogadishu — life began returning to normal. Crops are growing. Markets are reopening. So are schools and hospitals. Nearly a million Somalis still depend completely on relief supplies, but at least the starvation is gone. And none of this would have happened

without American leadership and America's troops.

Until June things went well with little violence. The United States reduced our troop presence from 28,000 down to less than 5,000, with other nations picking up where we left off.

But then, in June, the people who caused much of the problem in the beginning started attacking American, Pakistani and other troops who were there just to keep the peace. Rather than participate in building the peace with others, these people sought to fight and to disrupt, even if it means returning Somalia to anarchy and mass famine.

And make no mistake about it, if we were to leave Somalia tomorrow, other nations would leave, too. Chaos would resume, the relief effort would stop and starvation soon would return. That knowledge has led us to continue our mission. It is not our job to rebuild Somalia's society or even to create a political process that can allow Somalia's clans to live and work in peace. The Somalis must do that for themselves. The United Nations and many African states are more than willing to help. But we, we in the United States must decide whether we will give them enough time to have a reasonable chance to succeed.

We started this mission for the right reasons, and we're going to finish it in the right way. In a sense, we came to Somalia to rescue innocent people in a burning house. We've nearly put the fire out, but some smoldering embers remain. If we leave them now, those embers will reignite into flames and people will die again. If we stay a short while longer and do the right things, we've got a reasonable chance of cooling off the embers and getting other firefighters to take our place.

We also have to recognize that we cannot leave now and still have all our troops present and accounted for. And I want you to know that I am determined to work for the security of those Americans missing or held captive.

Anyone holding an American right now should understand above all else that we will hold them strictly responsible for our soldiers' well-being. We expect them to be well treated, and we expect them to be released.

So, now, we face a choice. Do we leave

when the job gets tough or when the job is well done? Do we invite the return of mass suffering, or do we leave in a way that gives the Somalis a decent chance to survive? Recently, [Joint Chiefs Chairman] Gen. Colin [L.] Powell [Jr.] said this about our choices in Somalia: "Because things get difficult, you don't cut and run. You work the problem and try to find a correct solution."

I want to bring our troops home from Somalia. Before the events of this week, as I've said, we had already reduced the number of our troops there from 28,000 to less than 5,000. We must complete that withdrawal soon, and I will. But we must also leave on our terms. We must do it right. And here is what I intend to do.

This past week's events make it clear that even as we prepare to withdraw from Somalia, we need more strength there. We need more armor, more airpower, to ensure that our people are safe and that we can do our job. Today, I have ordered 1,700 additional Army troops and 104 additional armored vehicles to Somalia to protect our troops and to complete our mission. I've also ordered an aircraft carrier and two amphibious groups with 3,600 combat Marines to be stationed offshore. These forces will be under American command. Their mission, what I am asking these young Americans to do, is the following:

First, they are there to protect our troops and our bases. We did not go to Somalia with a military purpose. We never wanted to kill anyone. But those who attack our soldiers must know they will pay a very heavy price.

Second, they are there to keep open and secure the roads, the port and the lines of communications that are essential for the United Nations and the relief workers to keep the flow of food and supplies and people moving freely throughout the country so that starvation and anarchy do not return.

Third, they are there to keep the pressure on those who cut off relief supplies and attack our people, not to personalize the conflict but to prevent a return to anarchy.

Fourth, through their pressure and their presence, our troops will help to make it possible for the Somali people, working with others, to reach agreement among themselves so that they can solve their

problems and survive when we leave.

That is our mission. I am proposing this plan because it will let us finish leaving Somalia on our own terms and without destroying all that two administrations have accomplished there, for if we were to leave today, we know what would happen. Within months, Somali children again would be dying in the streets. Our own credibility with friends and allies would be severely damaged. Our leadership in world affairs would be undermined at the very time when people are looking to America to help promote peace and freedom in the post-Cold War world. And all around the world, aggressors, thugs and terrorists will conclude that the best way to get us to change our policies is to kill our people. It would be open season on Americans.

That is why I am committed to getting this job done in Somalia not only quickly but also effectively. To do that, I am taking steps to ensure troops from other nations are ready to take the place of our own soldiers. We've already withdrawn some 20,000 troops, and more than that number have replaced them from over two dozen other nations. Now we will intensify efforts to have other countries deploy more troops to Somalia to assure that security will remain when we are gone. And we'll complete the replacement of U.S. military logistics personnel with civilian contractors who can provide the same support to the United Nations.

While we're taking military steps to protect our own people and to help the U.N. maintain a secure environment, we must pursue new diplomatic efforts to help the Somalis find a political solution to their problems. That is the only kind of outcome that can endure, for fundamentally the solution to Somalia's problems is not a military one, it is political.

Leaders of the neighboring African states, such as Ethiopia and Eritrea, have offered to take the lead in efforts to build a settlement among the Somali people that can preserve order and security.

I have directed my representatives to pursue such efforts vigorously, and I've asked Ambassador [Robert B.] Bob Oakley, who served effectively in two administrations as our representative in Somalia, to travel again to the region immediately to advance this process. Obviously, even then there is no guarantee that Somalia will rid itself of violence or suffering, but at least we will have given Somalia a reasonable chance.

This week some 15,000 Somalis took to the streets to express sympathy for our losses, to thank us for our effort. Most Somalis are not hostile to us, but grateful, and they want to use this opportunity to rebuild their country. It is my judgment and that of my military advisers that we may need up to six months to complete these steps and to conduct an orderly withdrawal.

We'll do what we can to complete the mission before then. All American troops will be out of Somalia no later than March 31, [1994,] except for a few hundred support personnel in non-combat roles.

If we take these steps, if we take the time to do the job right, I am convinced we will have lived up to the responsibilities of American leadership in the world, and we will have proved that we are committed to addressing the new problems of a new era. When our troops in Somalia came under fire this last weekend, we witnessed a dramatic example of the heroic ethic of our American military. When the first Blackhawk helicopter was down this weekend, the other American troops didn't retreat, although they could have. Some 90 of them formed a perimeter around the helicopter, and they held that ground under intensely heavy fire. They stayed with their comrades. That's the kind of soldiers they are; that's the kind of people we are.

So let us finish the work we set out to do. Let us demonstrate to the world, as generations of Americans have done before us, that when Americans take on a challenge, they do the job right.

Let me express my thanks, and my gratitude, and my profound sympathy to the families of the young Americans who were killed in Somalia. My message to you is your country is grateful, and so is the rest of the world, and so are the vast majority of the Somali people.

Our mission from this day forward is to increase our strength, do our job, bring our soldiers out and bring them home.

Thank you, and God bless America. ■

PRESIDENTIAL NEWS CONFERENCE

Clinton Says Haiti Must Put 'Democracy Back on Track'

Following is the official White House transcript of President Clinton's announcement Oct. 15 that he was ordering U.S. warships to enforce trade sanctions against Haiti.

PRESIDENT CLINTON: Ladies and gentlemen, during the past few days, we have witnessed a brutal attempt by Haiti's military and police authorities to thwart the expressed desire of the Haitian people for democracy.

On Monday, unruly elements, unrestrained by the Haitian military, violently prevented American and United Nations personnel from carrying out the steps toward that goal. Yesterday, gunmen assassinated prodemocracy Justice Minister [Guy] Malary.

There are important American interests at stake in Haiti and in what is going on there. First, there are about 1,000 American citizens living in Haiti or working there. Second, there are Americans there who are helping to operate our embassy. Third, we have an interest in promoting democracy in this hemisphere, especially in a place where such a large number of Haitians have clearly expressed their preference for president. And finally, we have a clear interest in working toward a government in Haiti that enables its citizens to live there in security so they do not have to flee in large numbers and at great risk to themselves to our shores and to other nations.

Two American administrations and the entire international community have consistently condemned the 1991 military coup that ousted President [Jean-Bertrand] Aristide. In response to United States, Latin American and United Nations sanctions and pressure, Haiti's military rulers agreed with civilian leaders on a plan to restore democracy. That plan was reached under the auspices of the Organization of the American States and the United Nations. It was concluded on July 3rd on Governors Island here in the United States.

Yesterday, the United Nations Security Council, upon the recommendations of its special negotiator for Haiti, Dante Caputo, voted to reimpose stiff sanctions against Haiti, including an embargo on oil imports, until order is restored and the Governors Island process is clearly resumed.

Those sanctions will go into effect on Monday night unless Haiti's security forces put democracy back on track between now and then. I will also be imposing additional unilateral sanctions, such as revoking visas and freezing the assets of those who are perpetrating the violence and their supporters.

The United States strongly supports the Governors Island process, the new civilian government of Prime Minister [Robert] Malval and the return to Haiti of President Aristide.

I have today ordered six destroyers to patrol the waters off Haiti so that they are in a position to enforce the sanctions fully when they come into effect Monday night. I have also offered and ordered an infantry company to be on standby at Guantánamo Naval Base in Cuba just a short distance from Haiti.

The purpose of these actions is this: to ensure the safety of the Americans in Haiti and to press for the restoration of democracy there through the strongest possible enforcement of the sanctions.

The military authorities in Haiti simply must understand that they cannot indefinitely defy the desires of their own people as well as the will of the world community. That path holds only suffering for their nation and international isolation for themselves. I call upon them again to restore order and security to their country, to protect their own citizens and ours and to comply with the Governors Island agreement.

Q: Mr. President, you warned yesterday about maintaining the safety of the provisional government in Haiti, and yet there was this assassination yesterday of the justice minister. You talk about the personal safety of Americans in Haiti — is there anything the United States can do to ensure the safety of President Aristide's cabinet? Are there any steps that you can take to help this fledgling democracy?

P: Well, we've had discussions with Prime Minister Malval. The vice president [Al Gore] talked to him yesterday, as well as to President Aristide. We have, as you probably know, a significant number of security forces there that we've been working to train, and there may be some things that we can do. But let me say this, we've made some — we've had discussions with him. We're in constant communications with him. And we are working with him. He has been very forthright in his asking us to reinforce the sanctions strongly and to do whatever we could to try to remind people that there is no other way out for Haiti but democracy. But what we do with regard to his safety, I think, in some ways is going to have to be decided as we go along and with his heavy involvement and support.

Q: Mr. President, are the naval ships going to stop merchant ships going in and out of Haiti and maybe board them to make sure that their embargo is being complied with?

P: That's what they're going to do. They're going to have a very wide berth to enforce the embargo, or the sanctions, very strongly. And we intend to use the six ships. There will be — one of them will be off the coast of Haiti within about an hour. They will be around Port-au-Prince by this evening. And they should all be in place by tomorrow.

Q: Mr. President, what if this embargo induces a new wave of immigrants who say they're political refugees? And what if these refugees come upon the U.S. destroyers, how will you handle that?

P: Our policy has not changed on that. We still believe that we should process the Haitians who are asking for asylum in Haiti, and that that is the safest thing for them. So we will continue to pursue the policy we have pursued for the last several months.

But the purpose of these destroyers is different. These destroyers are going there to enforce the sanctions and to do it very strongly.

Q: But if they come upon refugees, how will they handle them, though? Will they just let them go by? Will they turn them back?

P: We have no reason to believe that what we have been doing won't work there. And I want to emphasize that the purpose of — our policy has not changed, and we will continue to adhere to our policy with regard to refugees as we work with Haiti and the prime minister and the presidents are restored, the democratic government. But the purpose of the destroyers is to strongly enforce the sanctions.

Q: Mr. President, are you prepared to evacuate American citizens from Haiti if the security situation there does not improve?

P: As I said to you, we are moving an enhanced infantry company into Guantánamo so that we can be in a position to deal with whatever contingencies arise. I have taken the steps that I think are appropriate at this time. And at this time I have not made a decision to evacuate our personnel. But there are 1,000 Americans there. There are also 9,000 people who have a dual nationality. The 1,000 Americans, most of them are working. There are a handful of tourists there — not many. And there are 140 embassy personnel there.

Q: Mr. President, since you're dealing with people who agreed to the Governors Island accords in the face of sanctions and then reneged on their promise, what in your view will be sufficient indication of compliance and future compliance so that the embargo and other sanctions will be able to be lifted?

P: Well, I can tell you one thing that would clearly show a fundamental change, and that is if all the United Nations forces that were supposed to be there to try to help retrain the police and to retrain the army were permitted to do so in a clearly safe atmosphere where they could be also protected, that would be some evidence that we had fundamental change. Keep in mind, this is a different mission than Somalia, different from Bosnia, different from any of the existing U.N. missions.

The purpose of these people — the reason we could not even think about landing the United States forces that were there a couple of days ago is that primarily they were Seabees going there for the purpose of, in effect, helping the Haiti army to become like the Army Corps of Engineers in this country. They were helping them transform their whole mission — not to be fighters anymore, but to try to rebuild one of the most environmentally plundered and devastated lands in the entire world.

So if we were seriously proceeding, evidence of that would be all these French-speaking countries being able to bring their folks back in and retrain the police force to be a professional and ordinary, not a renegade, police force, and having the French-speaking Canadians and the United States in there showing the army how to build a country instead of tear up the fabric of the society.

Q: President Aristide is asking that the administration increase the Marine contingent at the U.S. Embassy in Port-au-Prince in order to protect the people in his government. Is that under consideration at this point? And if, let's say, members of his government should flee to the American embassy, would the embassy provide protection for them?

P: The answer to your first question is that is certainly something that I have not ruled out. I have not ruled out anything that I have spoken, just because I haven't spoken about it today. We had a good, long meeting this morning with [Acting Chairman of the Joint Chiefs of Staff] Admiral [David E.] Jeremiah and [incoming Joint Chiefs Chairman] General [John M.] Shalikashvili and others — Secretary of State [Warren M. Christopher], Secretary of Defense [Les Aspin]. And I am very concerned about the security and safety of the Americans there and the very brave prime minister and his government.

Again, I would say to you, whatever specific things we do with regard to the prime minister and his government, I would rather come out of statements they make, because I don't want anything I say to upset the balance of forces in Haiti now. But I wouldn't rule out a change in the deployment around the embassy.

Our first obligation, after all, is to protect the Americans there....

Q: I'm wondering, sir, if you have thought about and considered the possibility that you might need to have some kind of police force on the ground there in Haiti, much as has been necessary in Somalia in light of the fact that the place has been so violence-prone for so long?

P: One of the discussions that we had when the gang showed up on the dock [in Port-au-Prince] was the question of whether the protection for our Seabees, who... would have sidearms and access to rifles — was to whether that was adequate or not. That question will obviously have to be revisited depending upon the developments in the next few days. I wouldn't rule that out, but I think we ought to — let's see what happens over the next few days.

Q: Mr. President, how does this differ from the word blockade, which you the other day mentioned as a term of art associated with a declaration of war?

P: Well, in a literal sense, a blockade would physically stop all traffic going in and out of the country — in this case by water. The United Nations resolution and the sanctions attempt to stop virtually all commercial traffic that could be of some commercial benefit. It does not render illegal every single entering into or exit from Port-au-Prince, Cap Haitien or the country in general. So there is a legal difference in that sense.

But if you use the word in the common-sense parlance, we would block any prohibited materials and goods, and anything subject to the sanctions from going into the country. That is our goal.

Q: Mr. President, today was the day that Col. [Michel] François and Gen. [Raoul] Cedras were supposed to resign their posts.... Are there any conversations between the American Embassy people and Gen. Cedras and Col. François going on?

P: Well, as you know, [special envoy to Haiti] Mr. [Lawrence] Pezzullo went back yesterday. And our ambassador, Mr. [William L.] Swing, is down there now. And they are working hard to make sure that everyone in the country knows that the United States is determined to see the democratic process restored. I think they've made their position clear. ■

PRESIDENTIAL LETTER

Clinton Questions Bill Amendments

Following is the official text of a letter President Clinton sent Oct. 18 to Majority Leader George J. Mitchell, D-Maine, and Minority Leader Bob Dole, R-Kan., regarding amendments to the Defense Appropriations bill concerning Haiti, Bosnia and the use of U.S. armed forces in international operations:

I am writing to express grave concern about a number of amendments that may be offered to H.R. 3116, the Defense Appropriations bill for FY 94, regarding Haiti, Bosnia and the use of United States armed forces in international operations.

I am fundamentally opposed to amendments which improperly limit my ability to perform my constitutional duties as Commander-in-Chief, which may well have unconstitutional provisions, and which if adopted, could weaken the confidence of our allies in the United States. Such amendments would provide encouragement to aggressors and repressive rulers around the world who seek to operate without fear of reprisal.

America's adversaries and allies must know with certainty that the United States can respond decisively to protect the lives of Americans and to address crises that challenge American interests. Successive administrations have found it critical in world affairs to be able to state that no option has been ruled out.

I respect and acknowledge the importance of cooperation between the executive and legislative branches. There will inevitably be give and take between the executive branch and Congress as we work to redefine our role in the post Cold War world. But it is wrong and even dangerous to allow the questions of the moment to undercut the strength of our national security policies and to produce a fundamental shift in the proper relationship between our two branches of government.

The amendment regarding command and control of U.S. forces, which already has been introduced, would insert Congress into the detailed execution of military contingency planning in an unprecedented manner. The amendment would make it unreasonably difficult for me or any President to operate militarily with other nations when it is in our interest to do so — and as we have done effectively for half a century through NATO. It could lead to an all-or-nothing approach that causes the United States to shoulder the entire burden of a conflict even when a multinational approach would be most effective from the standpoint of military planning, burden sharing and other American national interests.

With regard to potential amendments on Haiti, let me caution against action that could aggravate that nation's violent conflict and undermine American interests. The situation on the ground in Haiti is highly unstable. Limiting my ability to act — or even creating the perception of such a limitation — could signal a green light to Haiti's military and police authorities in their brutal efforts to resist a return of democracy, could limit my ability to protect the more than 1,000 Americans currently in Haiti, and could trigger another mass exodus of Haitians, at great risk to their lives and great potential cost and disruption to our nation and others.

With regard to potential Bosnia amendments, our nation has worked with NATO to prepare to help implement a fair and enforceable peace settlement. This amendment thus could undermine our relationship with our NATO allies and frustrate the negotiation of an end to the aggression and ethnic cleansing in the former Yugoslavia. As you know, I have placed strict conditions on any U.S. involvement in Bosnia with which I believe most members of Congress would agree.

I am committed to full consultation with Congress on our foreign policy. As I have clearly stated for the record, I welcomed congressional authorization for U.S. operations in Somalia and would welcome similar action regarding U.S. efforts in Bosnia, should that become necessary. Further, as this Administration has done and is continuing to do, we will consult with and keep Congress fully informed on these and other issues that affect American national security.

I would welcome an opportunity to engage you and others in the bipartisan leadership in a full and constructive dialogue about the processes of executive-legislative relations regarding America's engagement in a changed world. But amendments such as these are not the right way for the American government to decide how we act in the world, and I urge the Senate to reject them. ■

PUBLIC LAWS

Public Laws

PL 103-1 (S J Res 2) Authorize the U.S. Secret Service to continue to furnish protection to the former vice president or his spouse. Introduced by MITCHELL, D-Maine, Jan. 5, 1993. Senate passed Jan. 5. House passed Jan. 5. President signed Jan. 15, 1993.

PL 103-2 (S J Res 1) Ensure that the compensation and other emoluments attached to the Office of the Secretary of the Treasury are those which were in effect Jan. 1, 1989. Introduced by GLENN, D-Ohio, Jan. 5, 1993. Senate passed Jan. 5. House passed Jan. 6. President signed Jan. 19, 1993.

PL 103-3 (HR 1) Grant family and temporary medical leave under certain circumstances. Introduced by FORD, D-Mich., Jan. 5, 1993. House Education and Labor reported, amended, Feb. 2 (H Rept 103-8, Part I). House Post Office and Civil Service reported, amended, Feb. 2 (H Rept 103-8, Part II). House passed, amended, Feb. 3. Senate passed, amended, Feb. 4. House agreed to Senate amendment pursuant to H Res 71 Feb. 4. President signed Feb. 5, 1993.

PL 103-4 (S 202) Designate the Federal Judiciary Building in Washington as the Thurgood Marshall Federal Judiciary Building. Introduced by MOYNIHAN, D-N.Y., Jan. 26, 1993. Senate passed Jan. 26. House passed Jan. 27. President signed Feb. 8, 1993.

PL 103-5 (H J Res 101) Designate Feb. 21 through Feb. 27, 1993, as National FFA [Future Farmers of America] Organization Awareness Week. Introduced by KOPETSKI, D-Ore., Feb. 4, 1993. House Post Office and Civil Service discharged. House passed Feb. 16. Senate passed Feb. 17. President signed Feb. 25, 1993.

PL 103-6 (HR 920) Extend the emergency unemployment compensation program. Introduced by ROSTENKOWSKI, D-Ill., Feb. 17, 1993. House Ways and Means reported, amended, Feb. 23 (H Rept 103-17). House passed, amended, Feb. 24. Senate passed, amended, March 3. House agreed to Senate amendments March 4. President signed March 4, 1993.

PL 103-7 (S 400) Amend the Employee Retirement Income Security Act of 1974 to provide for the treatment of settlement agreements reached with the Pension Benefit Guaranty Corporation. Introduced by JEFFORDS, R-Vt., Feb. 18, 1993. Senate Labor and Human Resources discharged. Senate passed, amended, March 11. House passed March 16. President signed March 17, 1993.

PL 103-8 (S J Res 22) Designate March 25, 1993, as Greek Independence Day: A National Day of Celebration of Greek and American Democracy. Introduced by SPECTER, R-Pa., Jan. 26, 1993. Senate Judiciary discharged. Senate passed March 11. House Post Office and Civil Service discharged. House passed March 16. President signed March 20, 1993.

PL 103-9 (S J Res 36) Proclaim March 20, 1993, as National Agriculture Day. Introduced by LEAHY, D-Vt., Jan. 28, 1993. Senate Judiciary discharged. Senate passed March 11. House Post Office and Civil Service discharged. House passed March 16. President signed March 20, 1993.

PL 103-10 (HR 750) Extend the Export Administration Act of 1979 and authorize appropriations under that act for fiscal 1993 and 1994. Introduced by GEJDENSON, D-Conn., Feb. 3, 1993. House passed, under suspension of the rules, Feb. 16. Senate passed March 11. President signed March 27, 1993.

PL 103-11 (S 284) Extend the suspended implementation of certain requirements of the food stamp program on Indian reservations. Introduced by PRESSLER, R-S.D., Feb. 3, 1993. Senate Agriculture, Nutrition and Forestry discharged. Senate passed, amended, March 29. House passed March 31. President signed April 1, 1993.

PL 103-12 (HR 1430) Provide for a temporary increase in the public debt limit. Introduced by ROSTENKOWSKI, D-Ill., March 23, 1993. House Ways and Means reported March 29 (H Rept 103-43). House passed April 2. Senate passed April 5. President signed April 6, 1993.

PL 103-13 (HR 904) Amend the Airport and Airway Safety, Capacity, Noise Improvement and Intermodal Transportation Act

of 1992 with respect to the establishment of the National Commission to Ensure a Strong Competitive Airline Industry. Introduced by OBERSTAR, D-Minn., Feb. 16, 1993. House Public Works and Transportation reported March 1 (H Rept 103-22). House passed, under suspension of the rules, March 2. Senate passed, amended, March 17. House agreed to Senate amendment, under suspension of the rules, March 23. President signed April 7, 1993.

PL 103-14 (H J Res 150) Designate April 2, 1993, as Education and Sharing Day, U.S.A. Introduced by GEPHARDT, D-Mo., March 15, 1993. House Post Office and Civil Service discharged. House passed March 25. Senate passed March 26. President signed April 12, 1993.

PL 103-15 (H J Res 156) Concerning the dedication of the United States Holocaust Memorial Museum. Introduced by YATES, D-Ill., March 17, 1993. House Administration discharged. House Natural Resources discharged. House passed April 1. Senate passed April 2. President signed April 12, 1993.

PL 103-16 (S 164) Authorize the adjustment of the boundaries of the South Dakota portion of the Sioux Ranger District of Custer National Forest. Introduced by DASCHLE, D-S.D., Jan. 21, 1993. Senate Energy and Natural Resources reported March 11 (S Rept 103-10). Senate passed March 17. House considered, under suspension of the rules, March 29. House passed, under suspension of the rules, March 30. President signed April 12, 1993.

PL 103-17 (S 252) Provide for certain land exchanges in the state of Idaho. Introduced by CRAIG, R-Idaho, Jan. 28, 1993. Senate Energy and Natural Resources reported March 11 (S Rept 103-12). Senate passed March 17. House considered, under suspension of the rules, March 29. House passed, under suspension of the rules, March 30. President signed April 12, 1993.

PL 103-18 (S 662) Amend Title 38, U.S. Code, and Title XIX of the Social Security Act to make technical corrections relating to the Veterans Health Care Act of 1992. Introduced by ROCKEFELLER, D-W.Va., March 26, 1993. Senate passed March 25. House considered, under suspension of the rules, March 29. House passed, under suspension of the rules, March 30. President signed April 12, 1993.

PL 103-19 (S J Res 27) Provide for the appointment of Hanna Holburn Gray as a citizen regent of the Board of Regents of the Smithsonian Institution. Introduced by MOYNIHAN, D-N.Y., Jan. 27, 1993. Senate Rules and Administration reported March 18 (S Rept 103-24). Senate passed March 22. House passed, amended, March 23. Senate agreed to House amendments March 29. President signed April 12, 1993.

PL 103-20 (S J Res 28) Provide for the appointment of Barber B. Conable Jr. as a citizen regent of the Board of Regents of the Smithsonian Institution. Introduced by MOYNIHAN, D-N.Y., Jan. 27, 1993. Senate Rules and Administration reported March 18 (S Rept 103-25). Senate passed March 22. House passed, amended, March 23. Senate agreed to House amendments March 29. President signed April 12, 1993.

PL 103-21 (S J Res 29) Provide for the appointment of Wesley Samuel Williams Jr. as a citizen regent of the Board of Regents of the Smithsonian Institution. Introduced by MOYNIHAN, D-N.Y., Jan. 27, 1993. Senate Rules and Administration reported March 18 (S Rept 103-26). Senate passed March 22. House passed, amended, March 23. Senate agreed to House amendments March 29. President signed April 12, 1993.

PL 103-22 (S J Res 53) Designate March 1993 and March 1994 both as Women's History Month. Introduced by HATCH, R-Utah, March 2, 1993. Senate Judiciary discharged. Senate passed March 29. House Post Office and Civil Service discharged. House passed March 30. President signed April 12, 1993.

PL 103-23 (HR 239) Amend the Stock Raising Homestead Act to resolve certain problems regarding subsurface estates. Introduced by LEHMAN, D-Calif., Jan. 5, 1993. House Natural Resources reported, amended, March 29 (H Rept 103-44). House considered, under suspension of the rules, March 29. House passed, under suspension of the rules, March 30. Senate passed

April 1. President signed April 16, 1993.

PL 103-24 (HR 1335) Making emergency supplemental appropriations for the fiscal year ending Sept. 30, 1993. Introduced by NATCHER, D-Ky., March 15, 1993. House Appropriations reported March 15 (H Rept 103-30). House considered March 17. House passed March 19. Senate Appropriations reported, amended, March 23. Senate considered March 25, 26, 29, 30, 31, April 1, 2, 3, 5, 19, 20. Senate passed, amended, April 21. House agreed to Senate amendment April 22. President signed April 23, 1993.

PL 103-25 (S 326) Revise the boundaries of the George Washington Birthplace National Monument. Introduced by WARNER, R-Va., Feb. 4, 1993. Senate Energy and Natural Resources reported, amended, March 11 (S Rept 103-14). Senate passed, amended, March 17. House Natural Resources reported April 19 (H Rept 103-55). House passed, under suspension of the rules, April 20. President signed May 3, 1993.

PL 103-26 (S 328) Provide for the rehabilitation of historic structures within the Sandy Hook Unit of Gateway National Recreation Area in the state of New Jersey. Introduced by BRADLEY, D-N.J., Feb. 4, 1993. Senate Energy and Natural Resources reported March 11 (S Rept 103-15). Senate passed March 17. House Natural Resources reported April 19 (H Rept 103-54). House passed, under suspension of the rules, April 20. President signed May 3, 1993.

PL 103-27 (S J Res 30) Designate the weeks of April 25 through May 2, 1993, and April 10 through April 17, 1994, as Jewish Heritage Week. Introduced by D'AMATO, R-N.Y., Jan. 28, 1993. Senate Judiciary reported March 25. Senate passed March 26. House Post Office and Civil Service discharged. House passed April 21. President signed May 3, 1993.

PL 103-28 (H J Res 127) Authorize the president to proclaim the last Friday of April 1993 as National Arbor Day. Introduced by KLEIN, D-N.J., March 2, 1993. House Post Office and Civil Service discharged. House passed April 21. Senate Judiciary discharged. Senate passed April 29. President signed May 6, 1993.

PL 103-29 (S J Res 62) Designate the week beginning April 25, 1993, as National Crime Victims' Right Week. Introduced by BIDEN, D-Del., March 10, 1993. Senate Judiciary discharged. Senate passed March 29. House Post Office and Civil Service discharged. House passed April 22. President signed May 6, 1993.

PL 103-30 (S J Res 66) Designate the weeks beginning April 18, 1993, and April 17, 1994, each as National Organ and Tissue Donor Awareness Week. Introduced by THURMOND, R-S.C., March 16, 1993. Senate Judiciary discharged. Senate passed April 7. House passed, amended, April 20. House proceedings vacated. House passed, amended, April 21. Senate agreed to House amendments April 22. President signed May 7, 1993.

PL 103-31 (HR 2) Establish national voter registration procedures for federal elections. Introduced by SWIFT, D-Wash., Jan. 5, 1993. House Education and Labor reported, amended, Feb. 2 (H Rept 103-8, Part I). House Post Office and Civil Service reported, amended, Feb. 2 (H Rept 103-8, Part II). House passed, amended, Feb. 3. Senate passed, amended, Feb. 4. House agreed to Senate amendment pursuant to H Res 71 on Feb. 4. President signed May 20, 1993.

PL 103-32 (S 214) Authorize the construction of a memorial on federal land in the District of Columbia or its environs to honor members of the armed forces who served in World War II and to commemorate United States participation in that conflict. Introduced by THURMOND, R-S.C., Jan. 26, 1993. Senate Energy and Natural Resources reported March 11 (S Rept 103-11). Senate passed March 17. House Administration discharged. House passed, amended, May 4. Senate agreed to House amendment May 12. President signed May 25, 1993.

PL 103-33 (S 801) Authorize the conduct and development of NAEP [National Assessment of Educational Progress] for fiscal 1994. Introduced by DORGAN, D-N.D., April 21, 1993. Senate passed April 21. House passed May 11. President signed May 25, 1993.

PL 103-34 (H J Res 80) Designate June 1, 1993, through June 7, 1993, as a Week for the National Observance of the Fiftieth Anniversary of World War II. Introduced by MYERS, R-Ind., Jan. 27, 1993. House Post Office and Civil Service discharged. House passed, amended, May 19. Senate passed May 24. President signed May 31, 1993.

PL 103-35 (HR 1378) Amend Title 10, U.S. Code, with respect to the applicability of qualification requirements for certain acquisition positions in the Department of Defense. Introduced by SISISKY, D-Va., March 17, 1993. House Armed Services reported, amended, May 6 (H Rept 103-83). House passed, amended, under suspension of the rules, May 11. Senate passed May 18. President signed May 31, 1993.

PL 103-36 (HR 1723) Authorize the establishment of a program under which employees of the Central Intelligence Agency may be offered separation pay to separate from service voluntarily to avoid or minimize the need for involuntary separations due to downsizing, reorganization, transfer of function or other similar action. Introduced by GLICKMAN, D-Kan., April 20, 1993. House Intelligence reported, amended, May 24 (H Rept 103-102). House passed, amended, under suspension of the rules May 24. Senate passed May 26. President signed June 8, 1993.

PL 103-37 (HR 2128) Amend the Immigration and Naturalization Act to authorize appropriations for refugee assistance for fiscal 1993 and 1994. Introduced by MAZZOLI, D-Ky., May 17, 1993. House Judiciary reported May 25 (H Rept 103-107). House passed, under suspension of the rules, May 25. Senate passed May 27. President signed June 8, 1993.

PL 103-38 (H J Res 78) Designate the weeks beginning May 23, 1993, and May 15, 1994, as Emergency Medical Services Week. Introduced by MANTON, D-N.Y., Jan. 27, 1993. House Post Office and Civil Service discharged. House passed May 25. Senate passed May 27. President signed June 8, 1993.

PL 103-39 (H J Res 135) Designate the months of May 1993 and May 1994 as National Trauma Awareness Month. Introduced by MINETA, D-Calif., March 4, 1993. House Post Office and Civil Service discharged. House passed May 25. Senate passed May 27. President signed June 8, 1993.

PL 103-40 (S 564) Establish in the Government Printing Office a means of enhancing electronic public access to a wide range of federal electronic information. Introduced by FORD, D-Ky., March 11, 1993. Senate Rules and Administration reported March 18 (S Rept 103-27). Senate passed March 22. House Administration reported May 25 (H Rept 103-108). House passed, under suspension of the rules, May 25. President signed June 8, 1993.

PL 103-41 (S J Res 43) Designate the weeks beginning June 6, 1993, and June 5, 1994, as Lyme Disease Awareness Week. Introduced by LIEBERMAN, D-Conn., Feb. 4, 1993. Senate Judiciary reported March 25. Senate passed March 26. House Post Office and Civil Service discharged. House passed May 25. President signed June 8, 1993.

PL 103-42 (HR 1313) Amend the National Cooperative Research Act of 1984 with respect to joint ventures entered into for the purpose of producing a product, process or service. Introduced by BROOKS, D-Texas, March 11, 1993. House Judiciary reported, amended, May 18 (H Rept 103-94). House passed, amended, under suspension of the rules, May 18. Senate Judiciary discharged. Senate passed May 28. President signed June 10, 1993.

PL 103-43 (S 1) Amend the Public Health Service Act to revise and extend the programs of the National Institutes of Health. Introduced by KENNEDY, D-Mass., Jan. 21, 1993. Senate Labor and Human Resources reported, amended, Jan. 27 (S Rept 103-2). Senate considered Feb. 16 and 17. Senate passed, amended, Feb. 18. House passed, amended, March 11. Conference report filed in the House on May 20 (H Rept 103-100). House agreed to conference report May 25. Senate agreed to conference report May 28. President signed June 10, 1993.

PL 103-44 (HR 890) Amend the Federal Deposit Insurance Act to provide for extended periods of time for claims on insured deposits. Introduced by FRANK, D-Mass., Feb. 16, 1993. House passed, amended, under suspension of the rules, March 2. Senate passed, amended, May 27. House agreed to Senate amendments June 9. President signed June 28, 1993.

PL 103-45 (HR 2343) Amend the Forest Resources Conservation and Shortage Relief Act of 1990 to permit states to adopt

timber export programs. Introduced by UNSOELD, D-Wash., June 8, 1993. House passed, amended, under suspension of the rules, June 14. Senate passed June 17. President signed July 1, 1993.

PL 103-46 (S 80) Increase the size of the Big Thicket National Preserve in the state of Texas by adding the Village Creek Corridor Unit, the Big Sandy Corridor Unit and the Canyonlands Unit. Introduced by GRAMM, R-Texas, Jan. 21, 1993. Senate Energy and Natural Resources reported March 11 (S Rept 103-9). Senate passed March 17. House Natural Resources reported June 21 (H Rept 103-142). House passed, under suspension of the rules, June 21. President signed July 1, 1993.

PL 103-47 (S J Res 88) Designate July 1, 1993, as National Youth Sports Program Day. Introduced by DeCONCINI, D-Ariz., May 6, 1993. Senate Judiciary reported May 27. Senate passed May 27. House Post Office and Civil Service discharged. House passed June 29. President signed July 1, 1993.

PL 103-48 (HR 765) Resolve the status of certain land relinquished to the United States under the act of June 4, 1897 (30 Stat. 11, 36). Introduced by DOOLEY, D-Calif., Feb. 3, 1993. House Natural Resources reported, amended, May 6 (H Rept 103-81, Part I). House passed, amended, under suspension of the rules, June 21. Senate Agriculture, Nutrition and Forestry discharged. Senate passed June 29. President signed July 2, 1993.

PL 103-49 (HR 1876) Provide authority for the president to enter into trade agreements to conclude the Uruguay Round of multilateral trade negotiations under the auspices of the General Agreement on Tariffs and Trade, to extend tariff proclamation authority to carry out such agreements and to apply congressional fast-track procedures to a bill implementing such agreements. Introduced by ROSTENKOWSKI, D-Ill., April 28, 1993. House Ways and Means reported June 14 (H Rept 103-128, Part I). House Rules reported June 16 (H Rept 103-128, Part II). House passed June 22. Senate passed June 30. President signed July 2, 1993.

PL 103-50 (HR 2118) Make supplemental appropriations for the fiscal year ending Sept. 30, 1993. Introduced by NATCHER, D-Ky., May 13, 1993. House Appropriations reported May 13 (H Rept 103-91). Supplemental report filed May 17 (H Rept 103-91, Part II). House passed, amended, May 26. Senate Appropriations reported, amended, June 8 (S Rept 103-54). Senate considered June 17. Senate passed, amended, June 22. Conference report filed in the House on June 30 (H Rept 103-165). House agreed to conference report July 1. Senate agreed to conference report July 1. President signed July 2, 1993.

PL 103-51 (HR 588) Designate the facility of the United States Postal Service located at 20 S. Main St., in Beaver, Utah, as the Abe Murdock United States Post Office Building. Introduced by HANSEN, R-Utah, Jan. 26, 1993. House passed, under suspension of the rules, May 24. Senate Governmental Affairs reported June 30. Senate passed July 1. President signed July 16, 1993.

PL 103-52 (H J Res 213) Designate July 2, 1993, and July 2, 1994, as National Literacy Day. Introduced by PAYNE, D-N.J., June 10, 1993. House Post Office and Civil Service discharged. House passed June 29. Senate Judiciary discharged. Senate passed July 1. President signed July 16, 1993.

PL 103-53 (H J Res 190) Designate July 17 through July 23, 1993, as National Veterans Golden Age Games Week. Introduced by QUILLEN, R-Tenn., May 4, 1993. House Post Office and Civil Service discharged. House passed July 13. Senate passed July 15. President signed July 22, 1993.

PL 103-54 (HR 2561) Authorize the transfer of naval vessels to certain foreign countries. Introduced by HAMILTON, D-Ind., June 30, 1993. House passed, amended, under suspension of the rules, July 13. Senate Armed Service reported July 21. Senate passed July 21. President signed July 28, 1993.

PL 103-55 (HR 1189) Entitle certain armored car crew members to lawfully carry a weapon in any state while protecting the security of valuable goods in interstate commerce in the service of an armored car company. Introduced by COLLINS, D-Ill., March 3, 1993. House Energy and Commerce reported April 22 (H Rept 103-62). House passed, under suspension of the rules, May 18. Senate Commerce, Science and Transportation discharged.

Senate passed, amended, June 30. House agreed to Senate amendment July 13. President signed July 28, 1993.

PL 103-56 (HR 843) Withdraw certain lands located in the Coronado National Forest from the mining and mineral leasing laws of the United States. Introduced by KOLBE, R-Ariz., Feb. 4, 1993. House Natural Resources reported, amended, May 11 (H Rept 103-85). House passed, amended, under suspension of the rules, May 11. Senate Energy and Natural Resources reported July 20 (S Rept 103-100). Senate passed July 26. President signed Aug. 2, 1993.

PL 103-57 (HR 847) Authorize the Board of Regents of the Smithsonian Institution to plan and design an extension of the National Air and Space Museum at Washington Dulles International Airport. Introduced by MINETA, D-Calif., Feb. 4, 1993. House passed, amended, under suspension of the rules, June 29. Senate passed July 22. President signed Aug. 2, 1993.

PL 103-58 (HR 1347) Modify the boundary of Hot Springs National Park. Introduced by DICKEY, R-Ark., March 16, 1993. House Natural Resources reported June 21 (H Rept 103-144). House passed, under suspension of the rules, June 21. Senate Energy and Natural Resources reported July 16 (S Rept 103-97). Senate passed July 21. President signed Aug. 2, 1993.

PL 103-59 (HR 2683) Extend the operation of the migrant student record transfer system. Introduced by FORD, D-Mich., July 21, 1993. House passed, under suspension of the rules, July 26. Senate Labor and Human Resources discharged. Senate passed July 28. President signed Aug. 2, 1993.

PL 103-60 (S J Res 54) Designate April 9, 1994, as National Former Prisoners of War Recognition Day. Introduced by MURKOWSKI, R-Alaska, March 2, 1993. Senate Judiciary reported March 25. Senate passed March 26. House Post Office and Civil Service discharged. House passed, amended, July 13. Senate agreed to House amendments July 21. President signed Aug. 2, 1993.

PL 103-61 (S J Res 111) Designate Aug. 1, 1993, as Helsinki Human Rights Day. Introduced by DeCONCINI, D-Ariz., July 13, 1993. Senate Judiciary reported July 22. Senate passed July 23. House passed July 26. President signed Aug. 2, 1993.

PL 103-62 (S 20) Provide for the establishment of strategic planning and performance measurement in the federal government. Introduced by ROTH, R-Del., Jan. 20, 1993. Senate Governmental Affairs reported, amended, June 16 (S Rept 103-58). Senate passed, amended, June 23. House passed July 15. President signed Aug. 3, 1993.

PL 103-63 (HR 63) Establish the Spring Mountains National Recreation Area in Nevada. Introduced by BILBRAY, D-Nev., Jan. 5, 1993. House Natural Resources reported, amended, April 20 (H Rept 103-59). House passed, amended, under suspension of the rules, April 20. Senate Energy and Natural Resources reported, amended, June 22 (S Rept 103-63). Senate passed, amended, June 29. House agreed to Senate amendments, under suspension of the rules, July 26. President signed Aug. 4, 1993.

PL 103-64 (HR 236) Establish the Snake River Birds of Prey National Conservation Area in the State of Idaho. Introduced by LaROCCO, D-Idaho, Jan. 5, 1993. House Natural Resources reported, amended, May 6 (H Rept 103-80, Part I). House passed, amended, under suspension of the rules, May 11. Senate Energy and Natural Resources reported July 23 (S Rept 103-108). Senate passed July 28. President signed Aug. 4, 1993.

PL 103-65 (HR 416) Extend the period during which Chapter 12 of Title 11 of the U.S. Code remains in effect. Introduced by SYNAR, D-Okla., Jan. 5, 1993. House Judiciary reported, amended, March 16 (H Rept 103-32). House passed, amended, under suspension of the rules, March 16. Senate passed Aug. 3. President signed Aug. 6, 1993.

PL 103-66 (HR 2264) Provide for the reconciliation pursuant to Section 7 of the concurrent resolution on the budget for fiscal 1994. Introduced by SABO, D-Minn., May 25, 1993. House Budget reported May 25 (H Rept 103-111). House passed May 27. Senate passed, amended, June 25. Conference report filed in the House Aug. 4. House agreed to the conference report Aug. 5. Senate agreed to conference report Aug. 6. President signed Aug. 10, 1993.

PL 103-67 (HR 490) Provide for the conveyance of certain lands and improvements in Washington, D.C., to the Columbia Hospital for Women to provide a site for the construction of a facility to house the National Women's Health Resource Center. Introduced by TRAFICANT, D-Ohio, Jan. 20, 1993. House Public Works and Transportation reported, amended, March 2 (H Rept 103-23, Part I). House passed, amended, under suspension of the rules, March 9. Senate Governmental Affairs reported Aug. 6 (S Rept 103-125). Senate passed Aug. 6. President signed Aug. 11, 1993.

PL 103-68 (HR 616) Amend the Securities and Exchange Act of 1934 to permit members of national securities exchanges to effect certain transactions with respect to accounts for which such members exercise investment discretion. Introduced by MARKEY, D-Mass., Jan. 26, 1993. House Energy and Commerce reported April 29 (H Rept 103-76). House passed, under suspension of the rules, May 4. Senate passed July 29. President signed Aug. 11, 1993.

PL 103-69 (HR 2348) Make appropriations for the legislative branch for the fiscal year ending Sept. 30, 1994. Introduced by FAZIO, D-Calif., June 8, 1993. House Appropriations reported June 8 (H Rept 103-117). House passed, amended, June 10. Senate Appropriations reported, amended, July 20 (S Rept 103-103). Senate passed, amended, July 23. Conference report filed in the House Aug. 2 (H Rept 103-210). House agreed to conference report Aug. 6. House receded and concurred in Senate amendments. Senate agreed to conference report Aug. 6. President signed Aug. 11, 1993.

PL 103-70 (H J Res 110) Authorize the administrator of the Federal Aviation Administration to conduct appropriate programs and activities to acknowledge the status of the county of Fond du Lac, Wis., as the World Capital of Aerobatics. Introduced by PETRI, R-Wis., Feb. 16, 1993. House passed, under suspension of the rules, July 26. Senate Commerce, Science and Transportation discharged. Senate passed Aug. 6. President signed Aug. 11, 1993.

PL 103-71 (H J Res 157) Designate Sept. 13, 1993, as Commodore John Barry Day. Introduced by GILMAN, R-N.Y., March 17, 1993. House Post Office and Civil Service discharged. House passed Aug. 5. Senate passed Aug 6. President signed Aug. 11, 1993.

PL 103-72 (S 1205) Amend the Fluid Milk Promotion Act of 1990 to define fluid milk processors to exclude de minimis processors. Introduced by LEAHY, D-Vt., July 1, 1993. Senate passed July 1. House Agriculture discharged. House passed Aug. 4. President signed Aug. 11, 1993.

PL 103-73 (S 1295) Amend the Rehabilitation Act of 1973 and the Education of the Deaf Act of 1986 to make technical and conforming amendments to the act. Introduced by HARKIN, D-Iowa, July 27, 1993. Senate passed July 27. House passed, under suspension of the rules, Aug. 2. President signed Aug. 11, 1993.

PL 103-74 (S J Res 99) Designate Sept. 9, 1993, and April 21, 1994, each as National D.A.R.E. [Drug Abuse Resistance Education] Day. Introduced by DeCONCINI, D-Ariz., June 8, 1993. Senate Judiciary reported July 22. Senate passed July 23. House Post Office and Civil Service discharged. House passed Aug. 5. President signed Aug. 11, 1993.

PL 103-75 (HR 2667) Make emergency supplemental appropriations for relief from the widespread flooding in the Midwest for the fiscal year ending Sept. 30, 1993. Introduced by NATCHER, D-Ky., July 20, 1993. House Appropriations reported July 20 (H Rept 103-184). House passed, amended, July 27. Senate Appropriations reported, amended, July 30. Senate considered Aug. 3. Senate passed, amended, Aug. 4. House agreed to Senate amendments Aug. 6. House agreed to Senate amendments with amendments Aug. 6. House disagreed to Senate amendments Aug. 6. Senate agreed to House amendments to Senate amendments Aug. 6. Senate receded from its amendments Aug. 6. President signed Aug. 12, 1993.

PL 103-76 (S 1273) Enhance the availability of credit in disaster areas by reducing the regulatory burden imposed upon insured depository institutions to the extent such action is consistent with the safety and soundness of the institutions. Introduced by BOND, R-Mo., July 21, 1993. Senate Banking, Housing and Urban Affairs discharged. Senate passed, amended, July 30. House

passed, amended, Aug. 3. Senate agreed to House amendments Aug. 5. President signed Aug. 12, 1993.

PL 103-77 (HR 631) Designate certain lands in the state of Colorado as components of the National Wilderness Preservation System. Introduced by SKAGGS, D-Colo., Jan. 26, 1993. House Natural Resources reported, amended, July 19 (H Rept 103-181). House passed, amended, under suspension of the rules, July 19. Senate Energy and Natural Resources reported Aug. 3 (S Rept 103-123). Senate passed Aug. 4. President signed Aug. 13, 1993.

PL 103-78 (HR 798) Amend Title 38, U.S. Code, to codify the rates of disability compensation for veterans with service-connected disabilities and the rates of dependency and indemnity compensation for survivors of such veterans as such rates took effect on Dec. 1, 1992. Introduced by SLATTERY, D-Kan., Feb. 3, 1993. House Veterans' Affairs reported, amended, April 22 (H Rept 103-63). House passed, amended, under suspension of the rules, April 27. Senate Veterans' Affairs discharged. Senate passed, amended, July 28. House agreed to Senate amendment Aug. 2. President signed Aug. 13, 1993.

PL 103-79 (HR 2034) Authorize major medical facility projects and leases for the Department of Veterans Affairs, to revise and extend the authority of the secretary of Veterans Affairs to enter into enhanced-use leases, and to revise certain authorities relating to Pershing Hall, France. Introduced by ROWLAND, D-Ga., May 6, 1993. House Veterans' Affairs reported May 13 (H Rept 103-92). House passed, amended, under suspension of the rules, May 18. Senate Veterans' Affairs discharged. Senate passed, amended, July 14. House agreed to Senate amendments with amendments Aug. 6. Senate agreed to House amendments to Senate amendments Aug. 6. President signed Aug. 13, 1993.

PL 103-80 (HR 2900) Clarify and revise the small-business exemption from the nutrition labeling requirements of the federal Food, Drug and Cosmetic Act. Introduced by DINGELL, D-Mich., Aug. 5, 1993. House Energy and Commerce discharged. House passed Aug. 6. Senate passed Aug. 6. President signed Aug. 13, 1993.

PL 103-81 (S 1274) Reduce the subsidy cost for the Guaranteed Business Loan Program of the Small Business Administration. Introduced by BUMPERS, D-Ark., July 21, 1993. Senate Small Business reported, amended, July 28. Senate passed, amended, July 30. House Small Business discharged. House passed, amended, Aug. 4. Senate agreed to House amendment Aug. 5. President signed Aug. 13, 1993.

PL 103-82 (HR 2010) Amend the National and Community Service Act of 1990 to establish a Corporation for National Service, enhance opportunities for national service and provide national service education awards to persons participating in such service. Introduced by MARTINEZ, D-Calif., May 6, 1993. House Education and Labor reported, amended, June 24 (H Rept 103-155). House considered July 13 and 21. House passed, amended, July 28. Senate passed, amended, Aug. 3. Conference report filed in the House on Aug. 5 (H Rept 103-219). House agreed to conference report Aug. 6. Senate agreed to conference report Sept. 8. President signed Sept. 21, 1993.

PL 103-83 (S J Res 50) Designate the weeks of Sept. 19, 1993, through Sept. 25, 1993, and of Sept. 18, 1994, through Sept. 24, 1994, as National Rehabilitation Week. Introduced by SPECTER, R-Pa., Feb. 24, 1993. Senate Judiciary discharged. Senate passed Sept. 10. House Post Office and Civil Service discharged. House passed Sept. 14. President signed Sept. 21, 1993.

PL 103-84 (S J Res 95) Designate October 1993 as National Breast Cancer Awareness Month. Introduced by PELL, D-R.I., May 19, 1993. Senate Judiciary reported July 22. Senate passed July 23. House Post Office and Civil Service discharged. House passed Sept. 14. President signed Sept. 21, 1993.

PL 103-85 (S J Res 126) Designate Sept. 10, 1993, as National POW/MIA Recognition Day and authorize the display of the National League of Families POW/MIA flag. Introduced by SMITH, R-N.H., Aug. 6, 1993. Senate passed Aug. 6. House Post Office and Civil Service discharged. House Veterans' Affairs discharged. House passed Sept. 9. President signed Sept. 21, 1993.

PL 103-86 (HR 3049) Extend the current interim exemption under the Marine Mammal Protection Act for commercial fisher-

ies until April 1, 1994. Introduced by STUDDS, D-Mass., Sept. 13, 1993. House passed, under suspension of the rules, Sept. 21. Senate passed Sept. 22. President signed Sept. 30, 1993.

PL 103-87 (HR 2295) Make appropriations for foreign operations, export financing and related programs for the fiscal year ending Sept. 30, 1994. Introduced by OBEY, D-Wis., May 27, 1993. House Appropriations reported, amended, June 10 (H Rept 103-125). House passed, amended, June 17. Senate Appropriations reported, amended, Sept. 14 (S Rept 103-142). Senate considered Sept. 22. Senate passed, amended, Sept. 23. Conference report filed in the House Sept. 28 (H Rept 103-267). House agreed to conference report Sept. 29. Senate agreed to conference report Sept. 30. President signed Sept. 30, 1993.

PL 103-88 (H J Res 267) Make continuing appropriations for fiscal 1994. Introduced by NATCHER, D-Ky., Sept. 27, 1993. House passed Sept. 29. Senate passed Sept. 29. President signed Sept. 30, 1993.

PL 103-89 (HR 3019) Amend Title 5, U.S. Code, to provide for a temporary extension and the orderly termination of the performance management and recognition system. Introduced by NORTON, D-D.C., Sept. 8, 1993. House Post Office and Civil Service reported Sept. 21 (H Rept 103-247). House passed, under suspension of the rules, Sept. 21. Senate passed Sept. 22. President signed Sept. 30, 1993.

PL 103-90 (HR 168) Designate the federal building to be constructed between Gay and Market streets and Cumberland and Church avenues in Knoxville, Tenn., as the Howard H. Baker Jr. U.S. Courthouse. Introduced by DUNCAN, R-Tenn., Jan. 5, 1993. House Public Works and Transportation reported, June 17 (H Rept 103-139). House passed, under suspension of the rules, June 29. Senate Environment and Public Works reported Sept. 14. Senate passed Sept. 15. President signed Oct. 1, 1993.

PL 103-91 (HR 873) Provide for the consolidation and protection of the Gallatin Range. Introduced by WILLIAMS, D-Mont., Feb. 4, 1993. House Natural Resources reported, amended, May 6 (H Rept 103-82, Part I). House Agriculture discharged. Failed passage under suspension of the rules May 11. House passed, amended, May 20. Senate Energy and Natural Resources reported, amended, Aug. 3 (S Rept 103-122). Senate passed, amended, Aug. 4. House agreed to Senate amendment, under suspension of the rules, Sept. 13. President signed Oct. 1, 1993.

PL 103-92 (H J Res 220) Designate the month of August as National Scleroderma Awareness Month. Introduced by ESHOO, D-Calif., June 29, 1993. House Post Office and Civil Service discharged. House passed Aug. 5. Senate Judiciary discharged. Senate passed Sept. 10. President signed Oct. 1, 1993.

PL 103-93 (S 184) Provide for the exchange of certain lands within the state of Utah. Introduced by HATCH, R-Utah, Jan. 26, 1993. Senate Energy and Natural Resources reported, amended, June 16 (S Rept 103-56). Senate passed, amended, June 25. House Natural Resources reported, amended, Aug. 2 (H Rept 103-207). House passed, amended, under suspension of the rules, Aug. 2. Senate agreed to House amendment with amendments Aug. 6. House agreed to Senate amendments to House amendment, under suspension of the rules, Sept. 13. President signed Oct. 1, 1993.

PL 103-94 (HR 20) Amend Title 5, U.S. Code, to restore to federal civilian employees their right to participate voluntarily, as private citizens, in the political processes of the nation, and to protect such employees from improper political solicitations. Introduced by CLAY, D-Mo., Jan. 5, 1993. House Post Office and Civil Service reported Feb. 22 (H Rept 103-16). House considered, under suspension of the rules, Feb. 23. Failed passage, under suspension of the rules, Feb. 24. House passed, amended, March 3. Senate Governmental Affairs discharged. Senate passed, amended, July 20. House agreed to Senate amendment Sept. 21. President signed Oct. 6, 1993.

PL 103-95 (HR 1513) Designate the U.S. Courthouse at 10th and Main streets in Richmond, Va., as the Lewis F. Powell Jr. U.S. Courthouse. Introduced by SCOTT, D-Va., March 29, 1993. House Public Works and Transportation reported April 29 (H Rept 103-74). House passed, under suspension of the rules, May 4. Senate Environment and Public Works discharged. Senate passed Sept. 20. President signed Oct. 6, 1993.

PL 103-96 (HR 2431) Designate the federal building in Jacksonville, Fla., as the Charles E. Bennett Federal Building. Introduced by BROWN, D-Fla., June 16, 1993. House Public Works and Transportation reported Sept. 9, 1993 (H Rept 103-227). House passed, under suspension of the rules, Sept. 13. Senate passed Sept. 15. President signed Oct. 6, 1993.

PL 103-97 (S 464) Redesignate the Pulaski Post Office at 111 W. College St. in Pulaski, Tenn., as the Ross Bass Post Office. Introduced by SASSER, D-Tenn., Feb. 25, 1993. Senate Governmental Affairs reported June 30. Senate passed July 1. House passed, under suspension of the rules, Sept. 21. President signed Oct. 6, 1993.

PL 103-98 (S 779) Continue the authorization of appropriations for the East Court of the National Museum of Natural History. Introduced by SASSER, D-Tenn., April 7, 1993. Senate Rules and Administration reported, May 24 (S Rept 103-48). Senate passed May 28. House Public Works and Transportation reported Sept. 9 (H Rept 103-232, Part I). House passed, under suspension of the rules, Sept. 21. President signed Oct. 6, 1993.

PL 103-99 (S J Res 61) Designate the week of Oct. 3, 1993, through Oct. 9, 1993, as Mental Illness Awareness Week. Introduced by SIMON, D-Ill., March 10, 1993. Senate Judiciary reported May 27. Senate passed May 27. House Post Office and Civil Service discharged. House passed Sept. 28. President signed Oct. 6, 1993.

PL 103-100 (S J Res 121) Designate Oct. 6, 1993, and Oct. 6, 1994, as German-American Day. Introduced by RIEGLE, D-Mich., Aug. 4, 1993. Senate passed Aug. 4. House Post Office and Civil Service discharged. House passed Sept. 28. President signed Oct. 6, 1993.

PL 103-101 (HR 2074) Authorize appropriations for the American Folklife Center for fiscal 1994 and 1995. Introduced by ROSE, D-N.C., May 11, 1993. House passed, amended, under suspension of the rules, Sept. 21. Senate passed Sept. 23. President signed Oct. 8, 1993.

PL 103-102 (HR 3051) Provide that certain property in the state of Oklahoma owned by an Indian housing authority for the purpose of providing low-income housing shall be treated as federal property under the act of Sept. 30, 1950 (PL 81-874). Introduced by BREWSTER, D-Okla., Sept. 13, 1993. House passed, under suspension of the rules, Sept. 21. Senate passed Sept. 23. President signed Oct. 8, 1993.

PL 103-103 (S 1130) Provide for continuing authorization of federal employee leave transfer and leave bank programs. Introduced by PRYOR, D-Ark., June 17, 1993. Senate Governmental Affairs reported June 30. Senate passed July 14. House Post Office and Civil Service reported, amended, Sept. 21 (H Rept 103-246). House passed, amended, under suspension of the rules, Sept. 21. Senate agreed to House amendment Sept. 23. President signed Oct. 8, 1993.

PL 103-104 (HR 38) Establish the Jemez National Recreation Area in New Mexico. Introduced by RICHARDSON, D-N.M., Jan. 5, 1993. House Natural Resources reported, amended, April 20 (H Rept 103-58). House considered, under suspension of the rules, April 20. House passed, amended, under suspension of the rules, April 21. Senate Energy and Natural Resources reported, amended, Sept. 14 (S Rept 103-139). Senate passed, amended, Sept. 22. House agreed to Senate amendments Sept. 29. President signed Oct. 12, 1993.

PL 103-105 (HR 2608) Provide for the reauthorization of the collection and publication of quarterly financial statistics by the secretary of Commerce through fiscal 1998. Introduced by SAWYER, D-Ohio, July 1, 1993. House Post Office and Civil Service reported Sept. 15 (H Rept 103-241). House passed, under suspension of the rules, Sept. 21. Senate passed, amended, Sept. 22. House agreed to Senate amendments Sept. 29. President signed Oct. 12, 1993.

PL 103-106 (S 1381) Improve administrative services and support provided to the National Forest Foundation. Introduced by DOMENICI, R-N.M., Aug. 5, 1993. Senate Agriculture, Nutrition and Forestry discharged. Senate passed Sept. 15. House passed Sept. 28. President signed Oct. 12, 1993.

PL 103-107 (S J Res 102) Designate the months of October

1993 and 1994 as Country Music Month. Introduced by SASSER, D-Tenn., June 15, 1993. Senate Judiciary reported July 22. Senate passed July 23. House Post Office and Civil Service discharged. House passed Oct. 5. President signed Oct. 12, 1993.

PL 103-108 (H J Res 218) Designate Oct. 16, 1993, and Oct. 16, 1994, each as World Food Day. GILMAN, R-N.Y., June 24, 1993. House Post Office and Civil Service discharged. House passed Oct 13. Senate passed Oct. 15. President signed Oct. 18, 1993.

PL 103-109 (H J Res 265) Designate Oct. 19, 1993, as National Mammography Day. Introduced by LLOYD, D-Tenn., Sept. 23, 1993. House Post Office and Civil Service discharged. House passed Oct. 13. Senate passed Oct. 15. President signed Oct. 18, 1993.

PL 103-110 (HR 2446) Make appropriations for military construction for the Department of Defense for the fiscal year ending Sept. 30, 1994. Introduced by HEFNER, D-N.C., June 17, 1993. House Appropriations reported June 17 (H Rept 103-136). House passed, amended, June 23. Senate Appropriations reported, amended, Sept. 23 (S Rept 103-148). Senate passed, amended, Sept. 30. Conference report filed in the House on Oct. 7 (H Rept 103-278). House agreed to conference report Oct. 13. House receded and concurred in Senate amendments Oct. 13. House receded and concurred with amendments in Senate amendments Oct. 13. Senate agreed to conference report Oct. 19. Senate agreed to House amendments to Senate amendments Oct. 19. President signed Oct. 21, 1993.

PL 103-111 (HR 2493) Make appropriations for Agriculture, rural development, Food and Drug Administration, and related agencies programs for the fiscal year ending Sept. 30, 1994. Introduced by DURBIN, D-Ill., June 23, 1993. House Appropriations reported June 23 (H Rept 103-153). House passed, amended, June 29. Senate Appropriations reported, amended, July 20 (S Rept 103-102). Senate considered July 26. Senate passed, amended, July 27. Conference report filed in the House Aug. 3 (H Rept 103-212). House agreed to conference report Aug. 6. House receded and concurred in Senate amendments Aug. 6. House receded and concurred with amendments in Senate amendments Aug. 6. Senate agreed to conference report Sept. 23. Senate agreed to House amendments to Senate amendments Sept. 23. Senate agreed with amendments to House amendments to Senate amendments Sept. 23. House agreed with amendment to Senate amendment to House amendment to Senate amendment Sept. 30. House agreed to Senate amendment to House amendment to Senate amendment Sept. 30. Senate agreed to House amendment to Senate amendment to House amendment to Senate amendment Oct 15. President signed Oct. 21, 1993.

PL 103-112 (HR 2518) Making appropriations for the Departments of Labor, Health and Human Services, and Education, and related agencies for the fiscal year ending Sept. 30, 1994. Introduced by NATCHER, D-Ky., June 24, 1993. House Appropriations reported June 24 (H Rept 103-156). House passed, amended, June 30. Senate Appropriations reported, amended, Sept. 15 (S Rept 103-143). Senate considered Sept. 23, 24, 27 and 28. Senate passed, amended, Sept. 29. Conference report filed in the House Oct. 5 (H Rept 103-275). House agreed to conference report Oct. 7. House receded and concurred in Senate amendments Oct. 7. House receded and concurred with amendments in Senate amendments Oct. 7. Senate agreed to conference report Oct. 18. Senate agreed to House amendments to Senate amendments Oct. 18. President signed Oct. 21, 1993.

PL 103-113 (H J Res 281) Make further continuing appropriations for fiscal 1994. Introduced by NATCHER, D-Ky., Oct. 20, 1993. House passed Oct. 21. Senate passed Oct. 21. President signed Oct. 21, 1993.

PL 103-114 (HR 2685) Amend Title 5, U.S. Code, to extend the Federal Physicians Comparability Allowance Act of 1978. Introduced by NORTON, D-D.C., July 21, 1993. House Post Office and Civil Service reported Sept. 15 (H Rept 103-242). House passed, under suspension of the rules, Sept. 21. Senate Governmental Affairs discharged. Senate passed Oct. 5. President signed Oct. 26, 1993.

PL 103-115 (S 1508) Amend the definition of a rural community for eligibility for economic recovery funds. Introduced by MURRAY, D-Wash., Sept. 30, 1993. Senate passed Sept. 30. House passed Oct. 6. President signed Oct. 26, 1993.

PL 103-116 (HR 2399) Provide for the settlement of land claims of the Catawba Tribe of Indians in the state of South Carolina and the restoration of the federal trust relationship with the tribe. Introduced by DERRICK, D-S.C., June 10, 1993. House Natural Resources reported, amended, Sept. 27 (H Rept 103-257, Part I). House passed, amended, under suspension of the rules, Sept. 27. Senate passed, amended, Oct. 5. House agreed to Senate amendments, under suspension of the rules, Oct. 12. President signed Oct. 27, 1993.

PL 103-117 (H J Res 111) Designate Oct. 21, 1993, as National Biomedical Research Day. Introduced by BONIOR, D-Mich., March 3, 1993. House Post Office and Civil Service discharged. House passed Sept. 28. Senate Judiciary discharged. Senate passed Oct. 15. President signed Oct. 27, 1993.

PL 103-118 (S J Res 21) Designate the week beginning Sept. 18, 1994, as National Historically Black Colleges and Universities Week. Introduced by THURMOND, R-S.C., Jan. 26, 1993. Senate Judiciary discharged. Senate passed Aug. 5. House Post Office and Civil Service discharged. House passed, amended, Oct. 13. Senate agreed to House amendments Oct. 15. President signed Oct. 27, 1993.

PL 103-119 (S J Res 92) Designate the month of October 1993 as National Down Syndrome Awareness Month. Introduced by MOYNIHAN, D-N.Y., May 11, 1993. Senate Judiciary reported July 22. Senate passed, amended, July 23. House Post Office and Civil Service discharged. House passed Oct. 13. President signed Oct. 27, 1993.

PL 103-120 (HR 2517) Enable the secretary of Housing and Urban Development to demonstrate innovative strategies for assisting homeless individuals, to develop the capacity of community development corporation and community housing development organizations to undertake community development and affordable housing projects and programs, to encourage pension fund investment in affordable housing. Introduced by GONZALEZ, D-Texas, June 24, 1993. House passed, amended, under suspension of the rules, June 29. Senate Banking, Housing and Urban Affairs discharged. Senate passed, amended, Sept. 23. House agreed to Senate amendments Oct. 6. President signed Oct. 27, 1993.

PL 103-121 (HR 2519) Make appropriations for the departments of Commerce, Justice and State, the judiciary and related agencies for the fiscal year ending Sept. 30, 1994. Introduced by SMITH, D-Iowa, June 24, 1993. House Appropriations reported June 24 (H Rept 103-157). House passed, amended, July 20. Senate Appropriations reported, amended, July 22 (S Rept 103-105). Senate considered July 27 and 28. Senate passed, amended, 29. Conference report filed in the House Oct. 14 (H Rept 103-293). House agreed to conference report Oct. 19. House receded and concurred in Senate amendments Oct. 19. House receded and concurred with amendments in Senate amendments Oct. 19. House receded and concurred in Senate amendment Oct. 20. House receded and concurred with amendments in Senate amendments Oct. 20. Senate agreed to conference report Oct. 21. Senate agreed to House amendments to Senate amendments Oct. 21. President signed Oct. 27, 1993.

PL 103-122 (HR 2750) Make appropriations for the Department of Transportation and related agencies for the fiscal year ending Sept. 30, 1994. Introduced by CARR, D-Mich., July 27, 1993. House Appropriations reported July 27 (H Rept 103-190). House considered Sept. 22. House passed, amended, Sept. 23. House passed, amended, June 23. Senate Appropriations reported, amended, Sept. 29 (S Rept 103-150). Senate considered Oct. 4 and 5. Senate passed, amended, Oct. 6. Conference reported filed in the House Oct. 18 (H Rept 103-300). House agreed to conference report Oct. 21. House receded and concurred in Senate amendments Oct. 21. House receded and concurred with amendments in Senate amendments Oct. 21. Senate agreed to conference report Oct. 21. Senate agreed to House amendments to Senate amendments Oct. 21. President signed Oct. 27, 1993.

PL 103-123 (HR 2403) Make appropriations for the Treasury Department, the U.S. Postal Service, the Executive Office of

the President and certain independent agencies, for the fiscal year ending Sept. 30, 1994. Introduced by HOYER, D-Md., June 14, 1993. House Appropriations reported June 14 (H Rept 103-127). House considered June 17 and 18. House passed, amended, June 22. Senate Appropriations reported, amended, July 22 (S Rept 103-106). Senate considered July 29 and 30. Senate passed, amended, Aug. 3. Conference report filed in the House on Sept. 24 (H Rept 103-256). House agreed to conference report Sept. 29. Senate agreed to conference report Oct. 26. President signed Oct. 28, 1993.

PL 103-124 (HR 2491) Make appropriations for the departments of Veterans Affairs and Housing and Urban Development, and for sundry independent agencies, boards, commissions, corporations and offices for the fiscal year ending Sept. 30, 1994. Introduced by STOKES, D-Ohio, June 22, 1993. House Appropriations reported June 22 (H Rept 103-150). House considered June 28. House passed, amended, June 29. Senate Appropriations reported, amended, Sept. 9 (S Rept 103-137). Senate considered Sept. 20 and 21. Senate passed, amended, Sept. 22. Conference report filed in the House on Oct. 4 (H Rept 103-273). House agreed to conference report Oct. 19. House receded and concurred in Senate amendments Oct. 19. House receded and concurred with amendments in Senate amendments Oct. 19. Senate agreed to conference report Oct. 21. Senate agreed to House amendments to Senate amendments Oct. 21. President signed Oct. 28, 1993.

PL 103-125 (S 1487) Middle East Peace Facilitation Act of 1993. Introduced by PELL, D-R.I., Sept. 23, 1993. Senate Foreign Relations reported, amended, Sept. 28. Senate passed Sept. 29. House Foreign Affairs reported, amended, Oct. 12 (H Rept 103-283, Part I). House passed, amended, under suspension of the rules, Oct. 12. Senate agreed to House amendment Oct. 15. President signed Oct. 28, 1993.

PL 103-126 (HR 2445) Make appropriations for energy and water development for the fiscal year ending Sept. 30, 1994. Introduced by BEVILL, D-Ala., June 17, 1993. House Appropriations reported June 17 (H Rept 103-135). House considered June 23. House passed, amended, June 24. Senate Appropriations reported, amended, Sept. 23 (S Rept 103-147). Senate considered Sept. 29. Senate passed, amended, Sept. 30. Conference report filed in the House Oct. 14 (H Rept 103-292). House recommitted conference report Oct. 19. Second conference report filed in the House on Oct. 22 (H Rept 103-305). House agreed to second conference report Oct. 26. House receded and concurred in Senate amendments Oct. 26. House receded and concurred with amendments in Senate amendments Oct. 26. Senate agreed to conference report Oct. 27. Senate agreed to House amendments to Senate amendments Oct. 27. President signed Oct. 28, 1993.

PL 103-127 (HR 2492) Make appropriations for the government of the District of Columbia and other activities chargeable in whole or in part against the revenues of said District for the fiscal year ending Sept. 30, 1994. Introduced by DIXON, D-Calif., June 23, 1993. House Appropriations reported June 23 (H Rept 103-152). House passed, amended, June 30. Senate Appropriations reported, amended, July 20 (S Rept 103-104). Senate passed, amended, July 27. Conference report filed in the House on Oct. 14 (H Rept 103-291). House rejected conference report Oct. 20. Second conference report filed in the House Oct. 20 (H Rept 103-303). House agreed to second conference report Oct. 27. House receded and concurred in Senate amendments Oct. 27. House receded and concurred with amendments in Senate amendments Oct. 27. Senate agreed to conference report Oct. 27. Senate agreed to House amendments to Senate amendments Oct. 27. President signed Oct. 29, 1993.

PL 103-128 (H J Res 283) Make further continuing appropriations for fiscal 1994. Introduced by NATCHER, D-Ky., Oct. 27, 1993. House passed Oct. 28. Senate passed Oct. 28. President signed Oct. 29, 1993.

PL 103-129 (HR 3123) Increase the interest rates electric and telephone borrowers pay under the lending programs administered by the Rural Electrification Administration and otherwise restructure the lending programs carried out by that administration. Introduced by DE LA GARZA, D-Texas, Sept. 22, 1993. House passed, amended, under suspension of the rules, Sept. 28. Senate passed Oct. 4. President signed Nov. 1, 1993.

PL 103-130 (S 1548) Amend the National Wool Act of 1954 to reduce the subsidies that wool and mohair producers receive for the 1994 and 1995 marketing years and to eliminate the wool and mohair programs for the 1996 and subsequent marketing years. Introduced by LEAHY, D-Vt., Oct. 14, 1993. Senate Agriculture, Nutrition and Forestry discharged. Senate passed Oct. 15. House passed Oct. 15. President signed Nov. 1, 1993.

PL 103-131 (S J Res 78) Designate the beach at 53°53' 51'' N, 166°34' 15'' W to 53°53' 48'' N, 166°34' 21'' W on Hog Island, which lies in the Northeast Bay of Unalaska, Alaska, as "Arkansas Beach" in commemoration of the 206th Regiment of the National Guard, which served during the Japanese attack on Dutch Harbor, Unalaska, on June 3 and 4, 1942. Introduced by MURKOWSKI, R-Alaska, March 31, 1993. Senate Energy and Natural Resources reported July 16 (S Rept 103-96). Senate passed July 21. House Natural Resources reported Oct. 15 (H Rept 103-294). House passed, under suspension of the rules, Oct. 18. President signed Nov. 1, 1993.

PL 103-132 (HR 328) Direct the secretary of Agriculture to convey certain lands to the town of Taos, N.M. Introduced by RICHARDSON, D-N.M., Jan. 5, 1993. House Natural Resources reported April 20 (H Rept 103-60). House considered, under suspension of the rules, April 20. House passed, amended, under suspension of the rules, April 21. Senate passed Oct. 20. President signed Nov. 2, 1993.

PL 103-133 (H J Res 228) Approve the extension of non-discriminatory treatment with respect to the products of Romania. Introduced by GEPHARDT, D-Mo., July 13, 1993. House Ways and Means reported Oct. 7 (H Rept 103-279). House passed, under suspension of the rules, Oct. 12. Senate Finance discharged. Senate passed Oct. 21. President signed Nov. 2, 1993.

PL 103-134 (HR 927) Designate the Pittsburgh Aviary in Pittsburgh, Pa., as the National Aviary in Pittsburgh. Introduced by COYNE, D-Pa., Feb. 17, 1993. House Merchant Marine and Fisheries reported July 13 (H Rept 103-169). House passed, under suspension of the rules, July 13. Senate Environment and Public Works reported Oct. 18. Senate passed Oct. 27. President signed Nov. 8, 1993.

PL 103-135 (HR 2824) Modify the project for flood control, James River Basin, Richmond, Va. Introduced by BLILEY, R-Va., Aug. 2, 1993. House Public Works and Transportation reported Sept. 9 (H Rept 103-235). House passed, under suspension of the rules, Sept. 13. Senate Environment and Public Works reported Oct. 21. Senate passed Oct. 27. President signed Nov. 8, 1993.

PL 103-136 (H J Res 205) Designate the week beginning Oct. 31, 1993, as "National Health Information Management Week." Introduced by DUNCAN, R-Tenn., May 27, 1993. House Post Office and Civil Service discharged. House passed Oct. 26. Senate passed Oct. 28. President signed Nov. 8, 1993.

PL 103-137 (S J Res 115) Designate Nov. 22, 1993, as National Military Families Recognition Day. Introduced by COCHRAN, R-Miss., July 22, 1993. Senate Judiciary reported Oct. 28. Senate passed Oct. 28. House Post Office and Civil Service discharged. House passed Nov. 2. President signed Nov. 8, 1993.

PL 103-138 (HR 2520) Make appropriations for the Department of the Interior and related agencies for the fiscal year ending Sept. 30, 1994. Introduced by YATES, D-Ill., June 24, 1993. House Appropriations reported June 24 (H Rept 103-158). House considered July 14. House passed, amended, July 15. Senate Appropriations reported, amended, July 28 (S Rept 103-114). Senate considered Sept. 14. Senate passed, amended, Sept. 15. Conference report filed in the House Oct. 15 (H Rept 103-299). House agreed to conference report Oct. 20. House receded and concurred in Senate amendments Oct. 20. House receded and concurred with amendments in Senate amendments Oct. 20. House insisted on its disagreement to a Senate amendment Oct. 20. Senate considered the conference report Oct. 21, 26, 28. Senate agreed to conference report Nov. 9. Senate agreed to House amendments to Senate amendments Nov. 9. Senate receded from its amendments Nov. 9. House receded from its amendment to Senate amendment Nov. 9. President signed Nov. 11, 1993.

PL 103-139 (HR 3116) Make appropriations for the Department of Defense for the fiscal year ending Sept. 30, 1994. Intro-

duced by MURTHA, D-Pa., Sept. 22, 1993. House Appropriations reported Sept. 22 (H Rept 103-254). House passed, amended, Sept 30. Senate Appropriations reported, amended, Oct. 4 (S Rept 103-153). Senate considered Oct. 13, 14, 15, 18, 19, 20. Senate passed, amended, Oct. 21. Conference report filed in the House Nov. 9 (H Rept 103-339). House agreed to conference report Nov. 10. Senate agreed to conference report Nov. 10. President signed Nov. 11, 1993.

PL 103-140 (S 616) Increase the rates of compensation for veterans with service-connected disabilities and the rates of dependency and indemnity compensation for the survivors of certain disabled veterans. Introduced by ROCKEFELLER, D-W.Va., March 18, 1993. Senate Veterans' Affairs reported, amended, June 15 (S Rept 103-55). Senate passed, amended, July 14. House Veterans' Affairs discharged. House passed, amended, Nov. 2. Senate agreed to House amendments Nov. 4. President signed Nov. 11, 1993.

PL 103-141 (HR 1308) Protect the free exercise of religion. Introduced by SCHUMER, D-N.Y., March 11, 1993. House Judiciary reported May 11 (H Rept 103-88). House passed, under suspension of the rules, May 11. Senate passed, amended, Oct. 27. House agreed to Senate amendment Nov. 3. President signed Nov. 16, 1993.

PL 103-142 (HR 175) Amend Title 18, U.S. Code, to authorize the Federal Bureau of Investigation to obtain certain telephone subscriber information. Introduced by EDWARDS, D-Calif., Jan. 5, 1993. House Judiciary reported March 29 (H Rept 103-46). House passed, under suspension of the rules, March 29. Senate Judiciary discharged. Senate passed Nov. 4. President signed Nov. 17, 1993.

PL 103-143 (HR 1345) Designate the federal building located at 280 S. First St. in San Jose, Calif., as the Robert F. Peckham United States Courthouse and Federal Building. Introduced by MINETA, D-Calif., March 16, 1993. House Public Works and Transportation reported April 29 (H Rept 103-71). House passed, under suspension of the rules, May 4. Senate Environment and Public Works reported Oct. 21 (S Rept 103-162). Senate passed Nov. 4. President signed Nov. 17, 1993.

PL 103-144 (S 836) Amend the National Trails System Act to provide for a study of El Camino Real de Tierra Adento. Introduced by BINGAMAN, D-N.M., April 28, 1993. Senate Energy and Natural Resources reported, amended, July 16 (S Rept 103-93). Senate passed, amended, July 21. House Natural Resources reported Nov. 4 (H Rept 103-326). House passed, under suspension of the rules, Nov. 8. President signed Nov. 17, 1993.

PL 103-145 (S 983) Amend the National Trails System Act to direct the secretary of the Interior to study the El Camino Real Para Los Texas for potential addition to the National Trails System. Introduced by JOHNSTON, D-La., May 19, 1993. Senate Energy and Natural Resources reported July 16 (S Rept 103-95). Senate passed July 21. House Natural Resources reported Nov. 4 (H Rept 103-327). House passed, under suspension of the rules, Nov. 8. President signed Nov. 17, 1993.

PL 103-146 (S J Res 131) Designate the week beginning Nov. 14, 1993, and the week beginning Nov. 13, 1994, each as Geography Awareness Week. Introduced by BRADLEY, D-N.J., Sept. 13, 1993. Senate Judiciary reported Oct. 28. Senate passed Oct. 28. House Post Office and Civil Service discharged. House passed Nov. 10. President signed Nov. 17, 1993.

PL 103-147 (S J Res 139) Designate the third Sunday in November of 1993 as National Children's Day. Introduced by GRAHAM, D-Fla., Oct. 4, 1993. Senate Judiciary reported Oct. 28. Senate passed Oct. 28. House Post Office and Civil Service discharged. House passed Nov. 8. President signed Nov. 17, 1993.

PL 103-148 (S J Res 142) Designate the week beginning Nov. 7, 1993, and the week beginning Nov. 6, 1994, each as National Women Veterans Recognition Week. Introduced by ROCKEFELLER, D-W.Va., Oct. 13, 1993. Senate Judiciary reported Oct. 28. Senate passed Oct. 28. House Post Office and Civil Service discharged. House passed, amended, Nov. 2. Senate agreed to House amendments Nov. 11. President signed Nov. 17, 1993.

PL 103-149 (HR 3225) Support the transition to non-racial democracy in South Africa. Introduced by JOHNSTON, D-Fla.,

Oct. 6, 1993. House Foreign Affairs reported, amended, Oct. 15 (H Rept 103-296, Part I). House Public Works and Transportation reported, amended, Nov. 8 (H Rept 103-296, Part II). House Banking, Finance and Urban Affairs reported, amended, Nov. 15 (H Rept 103-296, Part III). House Ways and Means reported Nov. 17. House passed, amended, Nov. 19. Senate passed Nov. 20. President signed Nov. 23, 1993.

PL 103-150 (S J Res 19) Acknowledge the 100th anniversary of the Jan. 17, 1893, overthrow of the Kingdom of Hawaii, and to offer an apology to Native Hawaiians on behalf of the United States for the overthrow of the Kingdom of Hawaii. Introduced by AKAKA, D-Hawaii Jan. 21, 1993. Senate Indian Affairs reported Aug. 6 (S Rept 103-126). Senate passed Oct. 27. House passed, under suspension of the rules, Nov. 15. President signed Nov. 23, 1993.

PL 103-151 (HR 2677) Authorize the Board of Regents of the Smithsonian Institution to plan, design, and construct the West Court of the National Museum of Natural History building. Introduced by MINETA, D-Calif., July 20, 1993. House Public Works and Transportation reported Sept. 9 (H Rept 103-231, Part I). House passed, under suspension of the rules, Sept. 13. Senate Rules and Administration reported Nov. 8 (S Rept 103-173). Senate passed Nov. 16. President signed Nov. 24, 1993.

PL 103-152 (HR 3167) Extend the emergency unemployment compensation program, and to establish a system of worker profiling. Introduced by ROSTENKOWSKI, D-Ill., Sept. 29, 1993. House Ways and Means reported, amended, Sept. 29 (H Rept 103-268). House passed, amended, Oct. 15. Senate considered Oct. 25, 26 and 27. Senate passed, amended, Oct. 28. Conference report filed in the House on Nov. 8 (H Rept 103-333). House recommitted conference report Nov. 9. Senate agreed to conference report Nov. 20. Second conference report filed in the House Nov. 21. (H Rept 103-404). House agreed to conference report Nov. 22. President signed Nov. 24, 1993.

PL 103-153 (H J Res 79) Authorize the president to issue a proclamation designating the weeks beginning Nov. 21, 1993, and Nov. 20, 1994, as National Family Week. Introduced by MYERS, R-Ind., Jan. 27, 1993. House Post Office and Civil Service discharged. House passed Nov. 8. Senate passed Nov. 11. President signed Nov. 24, 1993.

PL 103-154 (H J Res 159) Designate the month of November in 1993 and 1994 as National Hospice Month. Introduced by GEJDENSON, D-Conn., March 18, 1993. House Post Office and Civil Service discharged. House passed Nov. 18. Senate passed Nov. 20. President signed Nov. 24, 1993.

PL 103-155 (S 654) Amend the Indian Environmental General Assistance Program Act of 1992 to extend the authorization of appropriations. Introduced by McCAIN, R-Ariz., March 25, 1993. Senate Indian Affairs reported, amended, July 13 (S Rept 103-87). Senate passed, amended, July 20. House passed, amended, under suspension of the rules, Nov. 8. Senate agreed to House amendment Nov. 11. President signed Nov. 24, 1993.

PL 103-156 (S 1490) Amend PL 100-518 and the United States Grain Standards Act to extend through Sept. 30, 1998, the authority of the Federal Grain Inspection Service to collect fees to cover administrative and supervisory costs. Introduced by DASCHLE, D-S.D., Sept. 23, 1993. Senate passed, amended, Sept. 29. House passed, amended, Nov. 4. Senate agreed to House amendments Nov. 11. President signed Nov. 24, 1993.

PL 103-157 (S J Res 55) Designate the periods commencing on Nov. 28, 1993, and ending on Dec. 4, 1993, and commencing on Nov. 27, 1994, and ending on Dec. 3, 1994, as National Home Care Week. Introduced by HATCH, R-Utah, March 3, 1993. Senate Judiciary discharged. Senate passed Nov. 2. House Post Office and Civil Service discharged. House passed Nov. 18. President signed Nov. 24, 1993.

PL 103-158 (S J Res 129) Authorize the placement of a memorial cairn in Arlington National Cemetery, Arlington, Va., to honor the 270 victims of the terrorist bombing of Pan Am Flight 103. Introduced by KENNEDY, D-Mass., Sept. 7, 1993. Senate Veterans' Affairs reported Nov. 4. Senate passed Nov. 8. House passed Nov. 16. President signed Nov. 24, 1993.

PL 103-159 (HR 1025) Provide for a waiting period before

the purchase of a handgun, and for the establishment of a national instant criminal background check system to be contacted by firearms dealers before the transfer of any firearm. Introduced by SCHUMER, D-N.Y., Feb. 22, 1993. House Judiciary reported, amended, Nov. 10 (H Rept 103-344). House passed, amended, Nov. 10. Senate passed, amended, Nov. 20. Conference report filed in the House on Nov. 22 (H Rept 103-412). House agreed to the conference report Nov. 22. Senate agreed to the conference report Nov. 24. President signed Nov. 30, 1993.

PL 103-160 (HR 2401) Authorize appropriations for fiscal 1994 for military activities of the Department of Defense and to prescribe military personnel strengths for fiscal 1994. Introduced by DELLUMS, D-Calif., June 14, 1993. House Armed Services reported, amended, July 30 (H Rept 103-200). House considered Aug. 4 and Sept. 8, 9, 13 and 28. House passed, amended, Sept. 29. Senate passed, amended, Oct. 6. Conference report filed in the House Nov. 10 (H Rept 103-357). House agreed to conference report Nov. 15. Senate agreed to conference report Nov. 17. President signed Nov. 30, 1993.

PL 103-161 (HR 3341) Amend Title 38, U.S. Code, to increase the rate of special pension payable to people who have received the Medal of Honor. Introduced by SLATTERY, D-Kan., Oct. 21, 1993. House Veterans' Affairs reported Oct. 28 (H Rept 103-313). House passed, under suspension of the rules, Nov. 2. Senate Veterans' Affairs discharged. Senate passed Nov. 17. President signed Nov. 30, 1993. ∎

HOUSE
ROLL CALL
VOTES

* 2. Election of the Speaker. Nomination of Thomas S. Foley, D-Wash., Speaker since June 1989, and Robert H. Michel, R-Ill., the minority leader since 1981, for Speaker of the House of Representatives for the 103rd Congress. Foley elected 255-174: R 0-174; D 254-0 (ND 169-0, SD 85-0); I 1-0, Jan. 5, 1993. A "Y" on the chart represents a vote for Foley; an "N," a vote for Michel. All members-elect are eligible to vote on the election of the Speaker.

3. H Res 5. Rules of the House/Delegate Voting. Gephardt, D-Mo., motion to table (kill) the Solomon, R-N.Y., motion to refer the proposal to allow delegates and the resident commissioner to vote in the Committee of the Whole to a bipartisan committee to determine the constitutionality of the proposal. Approved 224-176: R 0-166; D 223-10 (ND 149-5, SD 74-5); I 1-0, Jan. 5, 1993.

* 5. H Res 5. Rules of the House/Order Previous Question. Slaughter, D-N.Y., motion to order the previous question (thus limiting debate and the possibility of amendment) on adoption of the resolution to adopt the rules of the 102nd Congress for the 103rd with changes approved by the Democratic Caucus, including amendments to allow delegates and the resident commissioner to vote in the Committee of the Whole, allow all committees to meet while the House is in session, provide for rolling quorums in committee, allow the Speaker to remove members from and add to conference and select committees, and allow privileged motions to be postponed for two days. Motion agreed to 249-176: R 0-173; D 248-3 (ND 165-3, SD 83-0); I 1-0, Jan. 5, 1993.

6. H Res 5. Rules of the House/Delegate Voting and Term Limits. Michel, R-Ill., motion to commit the resolution to adopt the rules and changes approved by the Democratic Caucus to a select committee made up of the majority and minority leader, with instructions to report the resolution back to the House after striking the amendment to allow delegates and the resident commissioner to vote in the Committee of the Whole, and adding a provision to place a six-year limit on members' chairing a committee or serving as a ranking member. Motion rejected 187-238: R 173-0; D 14-237 (ND 8-159, SD 6-78); I 0-1, Jan. 5, 1993.

7. H Res 5. Rules of the House/Adoption. Adoption of the resolution to adopt the rules of the 102nd Congress for the 103rd with changes approved by the Democratic Caucus, including amendments to allow delegates and the resident commissioner to vote in the Committee of the Whole, allow all committees to meet while the House is in session, provide for rolling quorums in committee, allow the Speaker to remove members from and add to conference and select committees, and allow privileged motions to be postponed for two days. Adopted 221-199: R 0-172; D 220-27 (ND 154-9, SD 66-18); I 1-0, Jan. 5, 1993.

8. Procedural Motion. Approval of the House Journal of Monday, Jan. 25. Approved 245-136: R 28-132; D 217-4 (ND 145-4, SD 72-0); I 0-0, Jan. 26, 1993.

9. H Res 20. Re-Establish the Select Committee on Narcotics/Previous Question. Moakley, D-Mass., motion to order the previous question (thus limiting debate and the possibility of amendment) on adoption of the resolution to re-establish the Select Committee on Narcotics Abuse and Control to carry out oversight and recommend to the appropriate committees legislation on the problems of narcotics, drug abuse or control. Motion agreed to 237-180: R 0-169; D 236-11 (ND 165-3, SD 71-8); I 1-0, Jan. 26, 1993.

10. H Res 20. Re-Establish the Select Committee on Narcotics/Adoption. Adoption of the resolution to re-establish for the duration of the 103rd Congress the Select Committee on Narcotics Abuse and Control for the purpose of oversight and recommending to the appropriate committees of the House legislation on the problems of narcotics, drug abuse or control. Rejected 180-237: R 15-154; D 164-83 (ND 117-51, SD 47-32); I 1-0, Jan. 26, 1993.

* Omitted votes are quorum calls, which CQ does not include in its vote charts.

**: Les Aspin, Cass Ballenger and Alan Wheat had not been sworn in as of Jan. 6.

KEY

Y	Voted for (yea).
#	Paired for.
+	Announced for.
N	Voted against (nay).
X	Paired against.
−	Announced against.
P	Voted "present."
C	Voted "present" to avoid possible conflict of interest.
?	Did not vote or otherwise make a position known.
D	Delegates ineligible to vote.

Democrats   *Republicans*
Independent

	2	3	5	6	7	8	9	10
ALABAMA								
1 *Callahan*	N	N	N	Y	N	N	N	N
2 *Everett*	N	N	N	Y	N	N	N	N
3 Browder	Y	Y	Y	N	Y	Y	N	N
4 Bevill	Y	Y	Y	N	Y	Y	Y	Y
5 Cramer	Y	Y	Y	N	N	Y	Y	N
6 *Bachus*	N	N	N	Y	N	N	N	N
7 Hilliard	Y	Y	Y	N	Y	Y	Y	Y
ALASKA								
AL *Young*	N	N	N	Y	N	N	N	?
ARIZONA								
1 Coppersmith	Y	Y	Y	N	Y	N	Y	N
2 Pastor	Y	Y	Y	N	Y	Y	Y	Y
3 *Stump*	N	N	N	Y	N	N	N	N
4 *Kyl*	N	N	N	Y	N	N	N	N
5 *Kolbe*	N	N	N	Y	N	N	N	N
6 English	Y	?	Y	N	Y	Y	Y	N
ARKANSAS								
1 Lambert	Y	Y	Y	N	Y	Y	Y	N
2 Thornton	Y	Y	Y	N	Y	Y	Y	Y
3 *Hutchinson*	N	N	N	Y	N	N	N	N
4 *Dickey*	N	N	N	Y	N	N	N	N
CALIFORNIA								
1 Hamburg	Y	Y	Y	N	Y	Y	Y	N
2 *Herger*	N	N	N	Y	N	N	N	Y
3 Fazio	Y	Y	Y	N	Y	Y	Y	Y
4 *Doolittle*	N	N	N	Y	N	N	N	N
5 Matsui	Y	?	Y	N	Y	Y	Y	Y
6 Woolsey	Y	Y	Y	N	Y	?	Y	Y
7 Miller	Y	Y	Y	N	Y	Y	Y	Y
8 Pelosi	Y	Y	Y	N	Y	Y	Y	Y
9 Dellums	Y	Y	Y	N	Y	Y	Y	Y
10 *Baker*	N	N	N	Y	N	N	N	N
11 *Pombo*	N	N	N	Y	N	N	N	N
12 Lantos	Y	Y	Y	N	Y	Y	Y	Y
13 Stark	Y	Y	Y	N	Y	Y	Y	Y
14 Eshoo	Y	Y	Y	N	Y	Y	Y	Y
15 Mineta	Y	Y	Y	N	Y	?	Y	Y
16 Edwards	Y	Y	Y	N	Y	Y	Y	Y
17 Panetta	Y	Y	Y	N				
18 Condit	Y	N	Y	N	Y	N	Y	N
19 Lehman	Y	Y	Y	N	Y	P	Y	Y
20 Dooley	Y	Y	Y	N	Y	N	Y	N
21 *Thomas*	N	N	N	Y	N	N	N	N
22 *Huffington*	N	N	N	Y	N	N	N	N
23 *Gallegly*	N	N	N	Y	N	N	N	N
24 Beilenson	Y	Y	Y	N	Y	Y	Y	N
25 *McKeon*	N	N	N	Y	N	N	N	N
26 Berman	Y	Y	Y	?	Y	Y	Y	Y
27 *Moorhead*	N	N	N	Y	N	N	N	N
28 *Dreier*	N	N	N	Y	N	N	N	N
29 Waxman	Y	?	Y	N	Y	Y	Y	Y
30 Becerra	Y	Y	Y	N	Y	Y	Y	Y
31 Martinez	Y	Y	Y	N	Y	Y	Y	Y
32 Dixon	Y	Y	Y	N	Y	Y	Y	Y
33 Roybal-Allard	Y	Y	Y	N	Y	Y	Y	Y
34 Torres	Y	+	Y	N	Y	Y	Y	Y
35 Waters	Y	Y	Y	N	Y	Y	Y	Y
36 Harman	Y	Y	Y	N	Y	Y	Y	N
37 Tucker	Y	?	Y	N	Y	Y	Y	Y
38 *Horn*	N	N	N	Y	N	N	N	N
39 *Royce*	N	N	N	Y	N	?	N	N
40 *Lewis*	N	N	N	Y	N	N	N	N
41 *Kim*	N	N	N	Y	N	N	N	N
42 Brown	Y	Y	Y	N	Y	?	Y	Y
43 *Calvert*	N	N	N	Y	N	N	N	N
44 *McCandless*	N	N	N	Y	N	N	N	N
45 *Rohrabacher*	N	N	N	Y	N	N	N	N
46 *Dornan*	N	N	N	Y	N	?	N	Y
47 *Cox*	N	N	N	Y	N	N	N	N
48 *Packard*	N	N	N	Y	N	N	N	N
49 Schenk	Y	Y	Y	N	Y	Y	Y	Y
50 Filner	Y	Y	Y	N	Y	Y	Y	Y
51 *Cunningham*	N	N	N	Y	N	P	N	N
52 *Hunter*	N	N	N	Y	N	N	N	N
COLORADO								
1 Schroeder	Y	Y	Y	N	Y	N	Y	Y
2 Skaggs	Y	Y	Y	N	N	Y	Y	N
3 *McInnis*	N	N	N	Y	N	N	N	N
4 *Allard*	N	N	N	Y	N	N	N	N
5 *Hefley*	N	N	N	Y	N	N	N	N
6 *Schaefer*	N	N	N	Y	N	N	N	N
CONNECTICUT								
1 Kennelly	Y	Y	Y	N	Y	Y	Y	Y
2 Gejdenson	Y	Y	Y	N	Y	?	Y	Y
3 DeLauro	Y	Y	Y	N	Y	Y	Y	Y
4 *Shays*	N	N	N	Y	N	N	N	N
5 *Franks*	N	N	N	Y	N	N	N	N
6 *Johnson*	N	N	N	Y	N	N	N	N
DELAWARE								
AL *Castle*	N	N	N	Y	N	N	N	N
FLORIDA								
1 Hutto	Y	N	Y	N	Y	N	N	N
2 Peterson	Y	Y	Y	N	Y	Y	Y	Y
3 Brown	Y	Y	Y	N	Y	Y	Y	Y
4 *Fowler*	N	N	N	Y	N	N	N	N
5 Thurman	Y	Y	Y	N	Y	Y	Y	Y
6 *Stearns*	N	N	N	Y	N	N	N	N
7 *Mica*	N	N	N	Y	N	N	N	N
8 *McCollum*	N	N	N	Y	N	N	N	N
9 *Bilirakis*	N	N	N	Y	N	N	N	N
10 *Young*	N	N	N	Y	N	N	N	N
11 Gibbons	Y	Y	Y	N	Y	?	?	?
12 *Canady*	N	N	N	Y	N	N	N	N
13 *Miller*	N	?	N	Y	N	N	N	N
14 *Goss*	N	N	N	Y	N	N	N	N
15 Bacchus	Y	Y	Y	N	Y	N	Y	N
16 *Lewis*	N	N	N	Y	N	N	N	N
17 Meek	Y	Y	?	N	Y	Y	Y	Y
18 *Ros-Lehtinen*	N	N	N	Y	N	N	N	N
19 Johnston	Y	Y	Y	N	Y	?	?	?
20 Deutsch	Y	Y	Y	N	Y	Y	Y	Y
21 *Diaz-Balart*	N	N	N	Y	N	N	N	Y
22 *Shaw*	N	N	N	Y	N	Y	N	Y
23 Hastings	Y	Y	Y	N	Y	?	?	?
GEORGIA								
1 *Kingston*	N	N	N	Y	N	N	N	N
2 Bishop	Y	Y	Y	N	Y	Y	Y	Y
3 *Collins*	N	N	N	Y	N	N	N	N
4 *Linder*	N	N	N	Y	N	N	N	N
5 Lewis	Y	Y	Y	N	Y	Y	Y	Y
6 *Gingrich*	N	N	N	Y	N	Y	N	N
7 Darden	Y	Y	Y	N	Y	Y	Y	Y
8 Rowland	Y	Y	Y	N	N	Y	Y	N
9 Deal	Y	Y	Y	N	N	Y	Y	N
10 Johnson	Y	?	Y	N	Y	Y	Y	N
11 McKinney	Y	Y	Y	N	Y	Y	Y	Y
HAWAII								
1 Abercrombie	Y	Y	Y	N	Y	Y	Y	Y
2 Mink	Y	Y	Y	N	Y	Y	Y	Y
IDAHO								
1 LaRocco	Y	Y	Y	N	Y	Y	Y	Y
2 *Crapo*	N	N	N	Y	N	N	N	N
ILLINOIS								
1 Rush	Y	Y	Y	N	Y	Y	Y	Y
2 Reynolds	Y	?	Y	N	Y	Y	Y	Y
3 Lipinski	Y	Y	N	Y	N	Y	Y	N
4 Gutierrez	Y	?	Y	N	Y	Y	Y	Y
5 Rostenkowski	Y	Y	Y	N	Y	Y	Y	Y
6 *Hyde*	N	N	N	Y	N	Y	N	N
7 Collins	Y	Y	Y	N	Y	Y	Y	Y
8 *Crane*	N	N	N	Y	N	?	N	N
9 Yates	Y	Y	Y	N	Y	Y	Y	Y
10 *Porter*	N	N	N	Y	N	N	Y	N
11 Sangmeister	Y	Y	Y	?	N	Y	Y	N
12 Costello	Y	Y	Y	N	Y	Y	Y	N
13 *Fawell*	N	N	N	Y	N	?	N	N
14 *Hastert*	N	N	N	Y	N	N	N	N
15 *Ewing*	N	N	N	Y	N	N	N	N
16 *Manzullo*	N	N	N	Y	N	N	N	N
17 Evans	Y	Y	Y	N	Y	Y	Y	Y

ND Northern Democrats   SD Southern Democrats

	2	3	5	6	7	8	9	10
18 ***Michel***	P	N	N	Y	N	N	?	N
19 Poshard	Y	N	N	Y	N	Y	Y	N
20 Durbin	Y	?	Y	N	Y	Y	Y	N
INDIANA								
1 Visclosky	Y	Y	Y	N	Y	Y	Y	N
2 Sharp	Y	Y	Y	N	Y	Y	Y	Y
3 Roemer	Y	Y	Y	Y	N	Y	Y	N
4 Long	Y	Y	Y	N	Y	Y	Y	Y
5 ***Buyer***	N	N	N	Y	N	Y	N	N
6 ***Burton***	N	N	N	Y	N	N	N	N
7 ***Myers***	N	N	N	Y	N	?	?	?
8 McCloskey	Y	Y	Y	N	Y	Y	Y	Y
9 Hamilton	Y	Y	Y	N	Y	Y	Y	Y
10 Jacobs	Y	Y	N	N	Y	N	N	N
IOWA								
1 ***Leach***	N	N	N	Y	N	N	N	N
2 ***Nussle***	N	N	N	Y	N	N	N	N
3 ***Lightfoot***	N	N	N	Y	N	N	N	N
4 Smith	Y	Y	Y	N	Y	?	?	?
5 ***Grandy***	N	N	N	Y	N	N	N	N
KANSAS								
1 ***Roberts***	N	N	N	Y	N	N	N	N
2 Slattery	Y	Y	Y	N	Y	?	Y	N
3 ***Meyers***	N	N	N	Y	N	N	N	N
4 Glickman	Y	Y	Y	N	Y	Y	Y	N
KENTUCKY								
1 Barlow	Y	Y	Y	N	Y	Y	Y	N
2 Natcher	Y	Y	Y	N	Y	Y	Y	Y
3 Mazzoli	Y	Y	Y	N	Y	Y	Y	Y
4 ***Bunning***	N	N	N	Y	N	N	N	N
5 ***Rogers***	N	N	N	Y	N	N	N	N
6 Baesler	Y	Y	Y	N	?	Y	Y	Y
LOUISIANA								
1 ***Livingston***	N	N	N	Y	N	N	N	N
2 Jefferson	Y	Y	Y	N	Y	Y	Y	Y
3 Tauzin	Y	Y	Y	N	Y	?	N	N
4 Fields	Y	Y	Y	N	Y	Y	Y	Y
5 ***McCrery***	N	N	N	Y	N	N	N	N
6 ***Baker***	N	N	N	Y	N	N	N	N
7 Hayes	Y	Y	Y	N	Y	Y	Y	N
MAINE								
1 Andrews	Y	Y	Y	N	Y	Y	Y	Y
2 ***Snowe***	N	N	N	Y	N	N	N	Y
MARYLAND								
1 ***Gilchrest***	N	?	N	Y	N	N	N	N
2 ***Bentley***	N	N	N	Y	N	N	N	N
3 Cardin	Y	Y	Y	N	Y	Y	Y	Y
4 Wynn	Y	Y	Y	N	Y	Y	Y	Y
5 Hoyer	Y	Y	Y	N	Y	Y	Y	Y
6 ***Bartlett***	N	N	N	Y	N	N	N	N
7 Mfume	Y	Y	Y	N	Y	Y	Y	Y
8 ***Morella***	N	N	N	Y	N	N	N	Y
MASSACHUSETTS								
1 Olver	Y	Y	Y	N	Y	Y	Y	Y
2 Neal	Y	Y	Y	N	Y	Y	Y	Y
3 ***Blute***	N	N	N	Y	N	N	N	N
4 Frank	Y	N	Y	N	Y	?	Y	Y
5 Meehan	Y	Y	Y	Y	Y	Y	Y	N
6 ***Torkildsen***	N	N	N	Y	N	N	N	N
7 Markey	Y	Y	Y	N	Y	?	Y	Y
8 Kennedy	Y	Y	Y	N	Y	Y	Y	Y
9 Moakley	Y	Y	Y	N	Y	Y	Y	Y
10 Studds	Y	Y	Y	N	Y	Y	Y	Y
MICHIGAN								
1 Stupak	Y	Y	Y	N	Y	Y	Y	N
2 ***Hoekstra***	N	N	N	Y	N	N	N	N
3 Henry	N	?	?	?	?	?	?	?
4 ***Camp***	N	N	N	Y	N	N	N	N
5 Barcia	Y	?	Y	N	Y	Y	Y	N
6 ***Upton***	N	N	N	Y	N	N	N	N
7 ***Smith***	N	N	N	Y	N	N	N	N
8 Carr	Y	?	Y	N	Y	?	Y	N
9 Kildee	Y	Y	Y	N	Y	Y	Y	N
10 Bonior	Y	Y	Y	N	Y	Y	Y	Y
11 ***Knollenberg***	N	N	N	Y	N	N	N	N
12 Levin	Y	Y	Y	N	Y	Y	Y	N
13 Ford	Y	Y	Y	N	Y	Y	Y	N
14 Conyers	Y	Y	Y	N	Y	?	Y	Y
15 Collins	Y	Y	Y	N	Y	Y	Y	Y
16 Dingell	Y	Y	Y	N	Y	Y	Y	N
MINNESOTA								
1 Penny	Y	Y	Y	N	Y	Y	Y	N
2 Minge	Y	Y	Y	Y	Y	Y	Y	N
3 ***Ramstad***	N	N	N	Y	N	N	N	N
4 Vento	Y	Y	Y	N	Y	Y	Y	Y

	2	3	5	6	7	8	9	10
5 Sabo	Y	Y	Y	N	Y	Y	Y	Y
6 ***Grams***	N	N	N	Y	N	N	N	N
7 Peterson	Y	Y	Y	N	Y	Y	Y	N
8 Oberstar	Y	Y	Y	N	Y	Y	Y	N
MISSISSIPPI								
1 Whitten	Y	Y	?	?	Y	?	Y	N
2 Espy	Y	Y	Y	N	Y			
3 Montgomery	Y	Y	Y	N	Y	Y	Y	N
4 Parker	Y	Y	Y	N	N	Y	Y	N
5 Taylor	Y	N	Y	Y	N	Y	N	N
MISSOURI								
1 Clay	Y	Y	?	N	Y	N	Y	Y
2 ***Talent***	N	N	N	Y	N	N	N	N
3 Gephardt	Y	Y	Y	N	Y	Y	Y	Y
4 Skelton	Y	Y	Y	N	Y	Y	Y	Y
5 Wheat **	?					Y	Y	Y
6 Danner	Y	Y	Y	N	Y	Y	Y	Y
7 ***Hancock***	N	N	N	Y	N	N	N	N
8 ***Emerson***	N	N	N	Y	N	N	N	Y
9 Volkmer	Y	Y	Y	N	Y	Y	Y	Y
MONTANA								
AL Williams	Y	N	Y	Y	Y	?	N	N
NEBRASKA								
1 ***Bereuter***	N	N	N	Y	N	N	N	N
2 Hoagland	Y	Y	Y	N	Y	Y	Y	N
3 ***Barrett***	N	N	N	Y	N	N	N	N
NEVADA								
1 Bilbray	Y	Y	Y	N	Y	Y	Y	N
2 ***Vucanovich***	N	N	N	Y	N	N	N	N
NEW HAMPSHIRE								
1 ***Zeliff***	N	N	N	Y	N	N	N	N
2 Swett	Y	Y	Y	N	Y	Y	Y	N
NEW JERSEY								
1 Andrews	Y	?	Y	N	Y	Y	Y	Y
2 Hughes	Y	Y	Y	N	?	Y	Y	Y
3 ***Saxton***	N	?	N	Y	N	N	N	N
4 ***Smith***	N	N	N	Y	N	Y	N	Y
5 ***Roukema***	N	N	N	Y	N	?	N	N
6 Pallone	Y	Y	Y	N	Y	Y	Y	Y
7 ***Franks***	N	?	N	Y	N	N	N	N
8 Klein	Y	Y	Y	N	?	Y	Y	Y
9 Torricelli	Y	?	Y	N	Y	Y	Y	N
10 Payne	Y	Y	Y	N	Y	Y	Y	Y
11 ***Gallo***	N	?	N	Y	N	N	N	N
12 ***Zimmer***	N	N	N	Y	N	N	N	N
13 Menendez	Y	?	Y	N	?	Y	Y	Y
NEW MEXICO								
1 ***Schiff***	N	N	N	Y	N	N	N	N
2 ***Skeen***	N	N	N	Y	N	Y	N	N
3 Richardson	Y	Y	Y	N	Y	Y	Y	Y
NEW YORK								
1 Hochbrueckner	Y	Y	Y	N	Y	Y	Y	Y
2 ***Lazio***	N	N	N	Y	N	N	N	N
3 ***King***	N	?	N	Y	N	N	N	N
4 ***Levy***	N	?	N	Y	N	Y	N	N
5 Ackerman	Y	Y	Y	N	Y	Y	Y	Y
6 Flake	Y	Y	Y	N	Y	Y	?	?
7 Manton	Y	Y	Y	N	Y	Y	Y	Y
8 Nadler	Y	Y	Y	N	Y	Y	Y	Y
9 Schumer	Y	Y	Y	N	Y	Y	Y	Y
10 Towns	Y	Y	Y	N	Y	Y	Y	Y
11 Owens	Y	Y	Y	N	Y	Y	Y	Y
12 Velazquez	Y	Y	Y	N	+	Y	Y	Y
13 ***Molinari***	N	N	N	Y	N	N	N	N
14 Maloney	Y	Y	Y	N	Y	?	Y	Y
15 Rangel	Y	Y	Y	N	Y	Y	Y	Y
16 Serrano	Y	Y	Y	N	Y	Y	Y	Y
17 Engel	Y	Y	Y	N	P	Y	Y	Y
18 Lowey	Y	Y	Y	N	Y	Y	Y	Y
19 ***Fish***	N	N	?	?	?	Y	N	N
20 ***Gilman***	N	N	N	Y	N	Y	N	Y
21 McNulty	Y	Y	Y	N	Y	Y	Y	Y
22 ***Solomon***	N	N	N	Y	N	N	N	N
23 ***Boehlert***	N	N	N	Y	N	N	N	N
24 ***McHugh***	N	N	N	Y	N	N	N	N
25 ***Walsh***	N	N	N	Y	N	?	N	N
26 Hinchey	Y	?	Y	N	Y	?	Y	Y
27 ***Paxon***	N	N	N	Y	N	N	N	N
28 Slaughter	Y	Y	Y	N	Y	?	Y	N
29 LaFalce	Y	Y	Y	N	Y	Y	Y	Y
30 ***Quinn***	N	N	N	Y	N	?	N	Y
31 ***Houghton***	N	N	N	Y	N	Y	N	N
NORTH CAROLINA								
1 Clayton	Y	?	Y	N	Y	?	Y	Y
2 Valentine	Y	Y	Y	N	N	Y	Y	Y

	2	3	5	6	7	8	9	10
3 Lancaster	Y	Y	Y	N	Y	?	Y	Y
4 Price	Y	Y	Y	N	Y	Y	N	Y
5 Neal	Y	Y	Y	N	Y	Y	Y	Y
6 ***Coble***	N	N	N	Y	N	N	N	N
7 Rose	Y	Y	Y	N	Y	Y	Y	Y
8 Hefner	Y	Y	Y	N	Y	?	Y	Y
9 ***McMillan***	N	N	N	Y	N	N	N	N
10 ***Ballenger*** **	?					N	N	N
11 ***Taylor***	N	N	N	Y	N	N	N	N
12 Watt	Y	Y	Y	N	Y	Y	Y	Y
NORTH DAKOTA								
AL Pomeroy	Y	Y	Y	N	Y	Y	Y	N
OHIO								
1 Mann	Y	Y	Y	N	?	Y	Y	N
2 ***Gradison***	N	N	N	Y	N	Y	N	N
3 Hall	Y	Y	Y	N	Y	Y	Y	Y
4 ***Oxley***	N	N	N	Y	N	N	N	Y
5 ***Gillmor***	N	N	N	Y	N	Y	N	Y
6 Strickland	Y	Y	?	?	?	Y	Y	Y
7 ***Hobson***	N	N	N	Y	N	N	N	N
8 ***Boehner***	N	N	N	Y	N	N	N	N
9 Kaptur	Y	Y	Y	N	Y	?	Y	N
10 ***Hoke***	N	?	N	Y	N	N	N	N
11 Stokes	Y	Y	Y	N	Y	Y	Y	Y
12 ***Kasich***	N	N	N	Y	N	Y	N	N
13 Brown	Y	Y	Y	N	Y	Y	Y	N
14 Sawyer	Y	Y	Y	N	Y	Y	Y	Y
15 ***Pryce***	N	N	N	Y	N	N	N	N
16 ***Regula***	N	N	N	Y	N	N	N	Y
17 Traficant	Y	Y	Y	N	Y	Y	Y	Y
18 Applegate	?	Y	Y	N	Y	Y	Y	Y
19 Fingerhut	Y	Y	Y	N	Y	Y	Y	N
OKLAHOMA								
1 ***Inhofe***	N	N	N	Y	N	N	N	Y
2 Synar	Y	Y	Y	N	Y	Y	N	Y
3 Brewster	Y	Y	Y	N	N	Y	Y	Y
4 McCurdy	Y	Y	Y	N	Y	Y	Y	N
5 ***Istook***	N	N	N	Y	N	N	N	N
6 English	Y	Y	Y	N	N	Y	Y	Y
OREGON								
1 Furse	Y	Y	Y	N	Y	Y	Y	Y
2 ***Smith***	N	N	N	Y	N	N	N	N
3 Wyden	Y	Y	Y	N	Y	Y	Y	Y
4 DeFazio	Y	Y	Y	N	Y	Y	Y	Y
5 Kopetski	Y	Y	Y	N	Y	Y	Y	N
PENNSYLVANIA								
1 Foglietta	Y	Y	Y	N	Y	?	Y	Y
2 Blackwell	Y	Y	Y	N	Y	Y	Y	Y
3 Borski	Y	Y	Y	N	Y	Y	Y	Y
4 Klink	Y	Y	Y	N	Y	P	Y	Y
5 ***Clinger***	N	N	N	Y	N	Y	?	?
6 Holden	Y	?	Y	N	Y	Y	Y	Y
7 ***Weldon***	N	N	N	Y	N	N	N	N
8 ***Greenwood***	N	N	N	Y	N	Y	N	N
9 ***Shuster***	N	N	N	Y	N	N	N	Y
10 ***McDade***	N	N	N	Y	N	?	?	?
11 Kanjorski	Y	Y	Y	N	Y	Y	Y	N
12 Murtha	Y	Y	Y	N	Y	Y	Y	Y
13 Margolies-Mezv.	Y	?	Y	N	N	Y	Y	N
14 Coyne	Y	Y	Y	N	Y	Y	Y	Y
15 McHale	Y	Y	Y	N	Y	Y	Y	Y
16 ***Walker***	N	N	N	Y	N	N	N	N
17 ***Gekas***	N	N	N	Y	N	N	N	N
18 ***Santorum***	N	N	N	Y	N	?	N	N
19 ***Goodling***	N	N	N	Y	N	N	N	N
20 Murphy	Y	Y	Y	N	Y	N	N	N
21 ***Ridge***	N	N	N	Y	N	N	N	N
RHODE ISLAND								
1 ***Machtley***	N	N	N	Y	N	?	N	N
2 Reed	Y	Y	Y	N	Y	Y	Y	Y
SOUTH CAROLINA								
1 ***Ravenel***	N	N	N	Y	N	Y	N	N
2 ***Spence***	N	N	N	Y	N	N	N	N
3 Derrick	Y	Y	Y	N	Y	Y	Y	N
4 ***Inglis***	N	N	N	Y	N	N	N	N
5 Spratt	Y	Y	Y	N	Y	Y	Y	N
6 Clyburn	Y	Y	Y	N	Y	Y	Y	Y
SOUTH DAKOTA								
AL Johnson	Y	N	Y	N	N	Y	Y	Y
TENNESSEE								
1 ***Quillen***	N	N	N	Y	N	Y	N	N
2 ***Duncan***	N	N	N	Y	N	N	N	N
3 Lloyd	Y	Y	Y	N	Y	Y	Y	Y
4 Cooper	Y	Y	Y	N	Y	Y	Y	N
5 Clement	Y	?	Y	N	Y	Y	Y	Y

	2	3	5	6	7	8	9	10
6 Gordon	Y	?	Y	N	Y	Y	Y	Y
7 ***Sundquist***	N	N	N	Y	N	N	N	N
8 Tanner	Y	Y	Y	N	Y	Y	Y	N
9 Ford	Y	Y	Y	N	Y	?	?	?
TEXAS								
1 Chapman	Y	?	Y	N	Y	Y	Y	N
2 Wilson	Y	Y	Y	N	Y	Y	N	Y
3 ***Johnson, Sam***	N	N	N	Y	N	N	N	N
4 Hall	Y	N	Y	Y	N	Y	Y	N
5 Bryant	Y	Y	Y	N	Y	Y	Y	N
6 ***Barton***	N	N	N	Y	N	?	?	?
7 ***Archer***	N	N	N	Y	N	Y	N	N
8 ***Fields***	N	N	N	Y	N	?	?	?
9 Brooks	Y	Y	Y	N	Y	Y	Y	Y
10 Pickle	Y	Y	Y	N	Y	Y	Y	N
11 Edwards	Y	Y	Y	N	Y	Y	Y	N
12 Geren	Y	N	Y	Y	N	Y	Y	N
13 Sarpalius	Y	Y	Y	N	Y	Y	Y	Y
14 Laughlin	Y	Y	Y	N	N	?	N	N
15 de la Garza	Y	Y	Y	N	Y	Y	Y	Y
16 Coleman	Y	Y	Y	N	Y	Y	Y	Y
17 Stenholm	Y	N	Y	Y	N	Y	Y	N
18 Washington	Y	Y	Y	N	Y	Y	Y	Y
19 ***Combest***	N	N	N	Y	N	Y	N	N
20 Gonzalez	Y	Y	Y	N	Y	Y	Y	Y
21 ***Smith***	N	N	N	Y	N	N	N	N
22 ***DeLay***	N	N	N	Y	N	N	N	N
23 ***Bonilla***	N	N	N	Y	N	N	N	N
24 Frost	Y	Y	Y	N	Y	?	?	?
25 Andrews	Y	Y	Y	N	Y	Y	N	N
26 ***Armey***	N	N	N	Y	N	N	N	N
27 Ortiz	Y	Y	Y	N	Y	Y	Y	Y
28 Tejeda	Y	Y	Y	N	Y	Y	Y	Y
29 Green	Y	Y	Y	N	Y	Y	Y	Y
30 Johnson, E. B.	Y	Y	Y	N	Y	Y	Y	Y
UTAH								
1 ***Hansen***	N	N	N	Y	N	Y	N	N
2 Shepherd	Y	Y	Y	N	Y	Y	Y	N
3 Orton	Y	Y	Y	Y	N	Y	Y	N
VERMONT								
AL *Sanders*	Y	Y	Y	N	Y	?	Y	Y
VIRGINIA								
1 ***Bateman***	N	N	N	Y	N	Y	N	N
2 Pickett	Y	?	Y	N	N	Y	Y	N
3 Scott	Y	Y	Y	N	Y	Y	Y	Y
4 Sisisky	Y	Y	Y	N	N	Y	Y	N
5 Payne	Y	Y	Y	N	N	Y	Y	N
6 ***Goodlatte***	N	N	N	Y	N	N	N	N
7 ***Bliley***	N	N	N	Y	N	N	N	N
8 Moran	Y	Y	Y	N	Y	Y	Y	Y
9 Boucher	Y	Y	Y	N	Y	?	Y	Y
10 ***Wolf***	N	N	N	Y	N	N	N	N
11 Byrne	Y	Y	Y	N	Y	Y	Y	Y
WASHINGTON								
1 Cantwell	Y	Y	Y	N	Y	Y	Y	Y
2 Swift	Y	Y	Y	N	Y	Y	Y	N
3 Unsoeld	Y	Y	Y	N	Y	Y	Y	N
4 Inslee	Y	Y	Y	N	Y	Y	Y	Y
5 Foley	P							
6 Dicks	Y	Y	Y	N	Y	Y	Y	Y
7 McDermott	Y	Y	Y	N	Y	Y	Y	Y
8 ***Dunn***	N	N	N	Y	—	N	N	N
9 Kreidler	Y	Y	Y	N	Y	?	Y	N
WEST VIRGINIA								
1 Mollohan	Y	Y	Y	N	Y	?	Y	Y
2 Wise	Y	Y	Y	N	Y	?	Y	Y
3 Rahall	Y	Y	Y	N	Y	Y	Y	Y
WISCONSIN								
1 Aspin **/Vacancy	?							
2 ***Klug***	N	N	N	Y	N	N	N	N
3 ***Gunderson***	N	N	N	Y	N	Y	N	N
4 Kleczka	Y	Y	Y	N	Y	Y	Y	Y
5 Barrett	Y	Y	Y	N	Y	Y	Y	Y
6 ***Petri***	N	N	N	Y	N	N	N	N
7 Obey	Y	Y	Y	N	Y	Y	Y	Y
8 ***Roth***	N	N	N	Y	N	?	N	N
9 ***Sensenbrenner***	N	N	N	Y	N	N	N	N
WYOMING								
AL ***Thomas***	N	N	N	Y	N	Y	N	N
DELEGATES								
de Lugo, V.I.	D	D	D	D	D	D	D	D
Faleomavaega, Am.S.	D	D	D	D	D	D	D	D
Norton, D.C.	D	D	D	D	D	D	D	D
Romero-B., P.R.	D	D	D	D	D	D	D	D
Underwood, Guam	D	D	D	D	D	D	D	D

Southern states - Ala., Ark., Fla., Ga., Ky., La., Miss., N.C., Okla., S.C., Tenn., Texas, Va.
Omitted votes are quorum calls, which CQ does not include in its vote charts.

11. Procedural Motion. Approval of the House Journal of Tuesday, Jan. 26. Approved 246-146: R 22-142; D 224-4 (ND 153-4, SD 71-0); I 0-0, Jan. 27, 1993.

12. HR 1. Family and Medical Leave/Previous Question. Gordon, D-Tenn., motion to order the previous question (thus limiting debate and the possibility of amendment) on adoption of the rule (H Res 58) to provide for House floor consideration of the bill to require employers of more than 50 employees to provide 12 weeks of unpaid leave for an illness or to care for a new child or sick family member. Motion agreed to 246-176: R 0-173; D 245-3 (ND 166-2, SD 79-1); I 1-0, Feb. 3, 1993.

13. HR 1. Family and Medical Leave/Rule. Adoption of the rule (H Res 58) to provide for House floor consideration of the bill to require employers of more than 50 employees to provide 12 weeks of unpaid leave for an illness or to care for a new child or sick family member. Adopted 259-164: R 16-158; D 242-6 (ND 162-5, SD 80-1); I 1-0, Feb. 3, 1993.

14. Constitutionality of Delegate Voting. Gephardt, D-Mo., motion to table (kill) the Solomon, R-N.Y., appeal of the ruling of the chair that the Solomon privileged resolution, to delay delegate voting until a constitutional determination is made, would constitute a change in House rules and therefore is not a privileged resolution and should be referred to the Rules Committee. Motion agreed to 251-174: R 0-174; D 250-0 (ND 169-0, SD 81-0); I 1-0, Feb. 3, 1993.

15. HR 1. Family and Medical Leave/Optional Benefits. Goodling, R-Pa., amendment to allow employers to satisfy the requirements of the bill by offering family and medical leave as an option under a "cafeteria" plan that employees may choose in place of other benefits usually offered by the employer. Rejected in the Committee of the Whole 187-244: R 157-16; D 30-227 (ND 9-166, SD 21-61); I 0-1, Feb. 3, 1993.

16. HR 1. Family and Medical Leave/Employer Discretion. Goodling, R-Pa., amendment to strike the provisions that allow employers to exempt the highest-paid 10 percent of employees from the bill and add provisions to allow employers to deny employees leave if the leave clearly would result in substantial and grievous economic injury to the employer or create a substantial health or safety risk. Rejected in the Committee of the Whole 185-238: R 156-15; D 29-222 (ND 9-162, SD 20-60); I 0-1, Feb. 3, 1993.

17. HR 1. Family and Medical Leave/Reduced Leave. Goodling, R-Pa., amendment to allow an employee to take reduced leave, working less than eight hours a day, only upon agreement with the employer. The bill would allow an employee to take reduced leave without the employer's consent when medically necessary. Adopted in the Committee of the Whole 223-209: R 174-0; D 49-208 (ND 15-160, SD 34-48); I 0-1, Feb. 3, 1993.

18. HR 1. Family and Medical Leave/Substitute. Adoption of the amendment in the nature of a substitute made in order as an original bill for the purpose of amendment under H Res 58, as amended during consideration in Committee of the Whole. Adopted in the Committee of the Whole 269-163: R 37-137; D 231-26 (ND 166-8, SD 65-18); I 1-0, Feb. 3, 1993.

KEY

Y Voted for (yea).
\# Paired for.
\+ Announced for.
N Voted against (nay).
X Paired against.
− Announced against.
P Voted "present."
C Voted "present" to avoid possible conflict of interest.
? Did not vote or otherwise make a position known.
D Delegates ineligible to vote.

Democrats *Republicans*
Independent

	11	12	13	14	15	16	17	18
ALABAMA								
1 *Callahan*	N	N	N	Y	Y	Y	Y	N
2 *Everett*	N	N	N	Y	Y	Y	Y	N
3 Browder	Y	Y	Y	N	Y	N	Y	N
4 Bevill	Y	Y	Y	N	N	N	Y	Y
5 Cramer	Y	Y	Y	N	N	Y	Y	Y
6 *Bachus*	N	N	N	Y	Y	Y	Y	N
7 Hilliard	?	Y	Y	Y	N	N	N	Y
ALASKA								
AL *Young*	N	N	Y	N	?	Y	Y	Y
ARIZONA								
1 Coppersmith	Y	Y	Y	Y	N	N	N	Y
2 Pastor	Y	Y	Y	Y	N	N	N	Y
3 *Stump*	N	N	N	N	Y	Y	Y	N
4 *Kyl*	N	N	N	N	Y	Y	Y	N
5 *Kolbe*	N	N	N	N	Y	Y	Y	N
6 English	Y	Y	Y	Y	N	N	N	Y
ARKANSAS								
1 Lambert	Y	Y	Y	N	N	N	Y	Y
2 Thornton	Y	Y	Y	N	N	N	Y	Y
3 *Hutchinson*	N	N	N	Y	Y	Y	Y	N
4 Dickey	N	N	N	N	Y	Y	Y	N
CALIFORNIA								
1 Hamburg	?	Y	?	Y	N	N	N	Y
2 *Herger*	N	N	N	N	Y	Y	Y	N
3 Fazio	Y	Y	Y	Y	N	N	N	Y
4 *Doolittle*	N	N	N	N	Y	Y	Y	N
5 Matsui	Y	Y	Y	N	N	N	N	Y
6 Woolsey	?	Y	Y	Y	N	N	N	Y
7 Miller	Y	Y	Y	N	N	N	N	Y
8 Pelosi	Y	Y	Y	N	N	N	N	Y
9 Dellums	Y	Y	Y	N	N	N	N	Y
10 *Baker*	N	N	N	N	Y	Y	Y	N
11 *Pombo*	N	N	N	N	Y	Y	Y	N
12 Lantos	Y	Y	Y	Y	N	N	N	Y
13 Stark	Y	Y	Y	N	N	N	N	Y
14 Eshoo	Y	Y	Y	Y	N	N	N	Y
15 Mineta	Y	Y	Y	Y	N	N	N	Y
16 Edwards	Y	Y	Y	Y	N	N	N	Y
17 Vacancy								
18 Condit	Y	Y	Y	Y	Y	N	Y	Y
19 Lehman	Y	Y	Y	Y	N	N	N	Y
20 Dooley	Y	Y	Y	Y	N	N	N	Y
21 *Thomas*	N	N	N	Y	Y	Y	Y	N
22 *Huffington*	N	N	N	Y	Y	Y	Y	Y
23 *Gallegly*	N	N	N	Y	Y	Y	Y	N
24 Beilenson	Y	Y	Y	N	N	N	N	Y
25 *McKeon*	N	N	N	N	Y	Y	Y	N
26 Berman	Y	Y	Y	N	N	N	N	Y
27 *Moorhead*	N	N	N	N	Y	Y	Y	N
28 *Dreier*	N	N	N	N	Y	Y	Y	N
29 Waxman	Y	Y	N	Y	N	N	N	Y
30 Becerra	Y	Y	Y	N	N	N	N	Y
31 Martinez	Y	Y	Y	Y	N	N	N	Y
32 Dixon	Y	Y	Y	Y	N	N	N	Y
33 Roybal-Allard	Y	Y	Y	Y	N	N	N	Y
34 Torres	Y	Y	Y	N	N	N	N	?
35 Waters	Y	Y	Y	N	?	N	Y	Y
36 Harman	Y	Y	Y	N	N	N	N	Y
37 Tucker	Y	Y	Y	N	N	N	N	Y
38 *Horn*	N	N	N	N	Y	Y	Y	Y
39 *Royce*	N	N	N	N	Y	Y	Y	N
40 *Lewis*	N	N	N	N	Y	Y	Y	N
41 *Kim*	N	N	N	N	Y	Y	Y	N

	11	12	13	14	15	16	17	18
42 Brown	?	Y	Y	Y	N	N	N	Y
43 *Calvert*	?	N	N	N	Y	Y	Y	N
44 *McCandless*	N	N	N	N	Y	Y	Y	N
45 *Rohrabacher*	?	N	N	N	Y	Y	Y	N
46 Dornan	N	N	N	N	Y	Y	Y	N
47 *Cox*	N	N	N	N	Y	Y	Y	N
48 *Packard*	Y	N	N	N	Y	Y	Y	N
49 Schenk	Y	Y	Y	Y	N	N	N	Y
50 Filner	Y	Y	Y	N	N	N	N	Y
51 *Cunningham*	N	N	N	N	Y	Y	Y	N
52 *Hunter*	N	N	N	N	Y	Y	Y	N
COLORADO								
1 Schroeder	N	Y	Y	Y	N	N	N	Y
2 Skaggs	Y	Y	Y	Y	N	N	Y	Y
3 *McInnis*	N	N	N	N	Y	Y	Y	N
4 *Allard*	N	N	N	N	Y	Y	Y	N
5 *Hefley*	N	N	N	N	Y	Y	Y	N
6 *Schaefer*	N	N	N	N	Y	Y	Y	N
CONNECTICUT								
1 Kennelly	Y	Y	Y	Y	N	N	N	Y
2 Gejdenson	Y	Y	Y	Y	N	N	N	Y
3 DeLauro	Y	Y	Y	Y	N	N	N	Y
4 *Shays*	N	N	Y	N	N	N	Y	Y
5 *Franks*	N	N	N	Y	Y	Y	Y	N
6 *Johnson*	N	N	N	N	Y	Y	Y	Y
DELAWARE								
AL *Castle*	N	N	N	N	Y	Y	Y	N
FLORIDA								
1 Hutto	Y	Y	Y	Y	N	N	N	N
2 Peterson	Y	Y	Y	Y	N	N	N	Y
3 Brown	Y	Y	Y	Y	N	N	N	Y
4 *Fowler*	N	N	N	N	Y	Y	Y	N
5 Thurman	P	Y	Y	Y	N	N	N	Y
6 *Stearns*	N	N	N	Y	Y	Y	Y	N
7 *Mica*	N	N	N	N	Y	Y	Y	N
8 *McCollum*	N	N	N	N	Y	Y	Y	N
9 *Bilirakis*	N	N	N	N	Y	Y	Y	N
10 *Young*	N	N	N	N	Y	Y	Y	Y
11 Gibbons	Y	Y	Y	Y	N	N	N	Y
12 *Canady*	N	N	N	N	Y	Y	Y	N
13 *Miller*	N	N	N	N	Y	Y	Y	N
14 *Goss*	N	N	N	N	Y	Y	Y	N
15 *Bacchus*	Y	Y	Y	Y	N	N	Y	Y
16 *Lewis*	N	N	N	N	Y	Y	Y	N
17 Meek	Y	Y	Y	Y	N	N	N	Y
18 *Ros-Lehtinen*	N	N	N	N	N	Y	Y	N
19 Johnston	?	Y	Y	Y	N	N	N	Y
20 Deutsch	Y	Y	Y	Y	N	N	N	Y
21 *Diaz-Balart*	N	N	Y	N	N	Y	Y	N
22 *Shaw*	Y	N	N	N	Y	Y	Y	N
23 Hastings	?	Y	Y	Y	N	?	N	Y
GEORGIA								
1 *Kingston*	Y	N	N	N	Y	Y	Y	N
2 Bishop	Y	Y	Y	Y	N	N	N	Y
3 *Collins*	N	N	N	N	Y	Y	Y	N
4 *Linder*	N	N	N	Y	Y	Y	Y	N
5 Lewis	Y	Y	Y	Y	N	N	N	Y
6 *Gingrich*	N	N	N	N	Y	Y	Y	N
7 *Darden*	Y	Y	Y	Y	N	N	N	Y
8 Rowland	Y	Y	Y	Y	Y	N	Y	Y
9 Deal	Y	Y	Y	Y	Y	Y	Y	N
10 Johnson	Y	Y	Y	Y	N	N	N	Y
11 McKinney	Y	Y	Y	Y	N	N	N	Y
HAWAII								
1 Abercrombie	?	Y	Y	Y	N	N	N	Y
2 Mink	Y	Y	Y	Y	N	N	N	Y
IDAHO								
1 LaRocco	Y	Y	Y	Y	N	N	N	Y
2 *Crapo*	N	N	N	N	Y	Y	Y	N
ILLINOIS								
1 Rush	Y	Y	Y	Y	N	N	N	Y
2 Reynolds	Y	Y	Y	Y	N	N	N	Y
3 Lipinski	Y	Y	Y	Y	N	N	N	Y
4 Gutierrez	?	Y	Y	Y	N	N	N	Y
5 Rostenkowski	Y	Y	Y	Y	N	N	N	Y
6 *Hyde*	Y	N	N	N	Y	Y	Y	Y
7 Collins	Y	Y	Y	Y	N	N	N	Y
8 *Crane*	?	N	N	N	Y	Y	Y	N
9 Yates	Y	Y	Y	Y	N	N	N	Y
10 *Porter*	?	N	N	N	Y	Y	Y	N
11 Sangmeister	Y	Y	Y	Y	N	N	N	Y
12 Costello	Y	Y	Y	Y	N	N	N	Y
13 *Fawell*	N	N	N	N	Y	Y	Y	N
14 *Hastert*	N	N	N	N	Y	Y	Y	N
15 *Ewing*	N	N	N	N	Y	Y	Y	N
16 *Manzullo*	N	N	N	N	Y	Y	Y	N
17 Evans	Y	Y	Y	Y	N	N	N	Y

ND Northern Democrats   SD Southern Democrats

	27	28	29	30	31	32	33	34
18 ***Michel***	N	N	N	Y	Y	?	Y	N
19 Poshard	Y	Y	Y	Y	Y	Y	Y	Y
20 Durbin	Y	Y	Y	Y	Y	Y	Y	Y
INDIANA								
1 Visclosky	Y	Y	Y	Y	Y	Y	Y	Y
2 Sharp	Y	Y	Y	Y	Y	Y	Y	Y
3 Roemer	Y	Y	Y	Y	Y	Y	Y	Y
4 Long	Y	Y	Y	Y	Y	Y	Y	Y
5 ***Buyer***	N	N	N	Y	Y	Y	Y	N
6 ***Burton***	N	N	N	Y	N	N	Y	N
7 ***Myers***	N	N	N	Y	Y	Y	Y	N
8 McCloskey	Y	Y	Y	+	+	Y	Y	Y
9 Hamilton	Y	N	N	Y	Y	Y	Y	Y
10 Jacobs	Y	N	Y	?	Y	N	Y	Y
IOWA								
1 ***Leach***	N	N	Y	Y	Y	N	Y	N
2 ***Nussle***	N	N	N	Y	N	N	Y	N
3 ***Lightfoot***	N	N	N	Y	Y	N	Y	N
4 Smith	Y	Y	Y	Y	Y	Y	Y	Y
5 ***Grandy***	N	N	N	Y	Y	N	Y	N
KANSAS								
1 ***Roberts***	N	N	N	Y	Y	N	Y	N
2 Slattery	?	Y	N	Y	Y	Y	Y	Y
3 ***Meyers***	N	N	N	Y	Y	N	Y	N
4 Glickman	Y	Y	N	Y	Y	Y	Y	Y
KENTUCKY								
1 Barlow	Y	Y	Y	Y	N	Y	Y	Y
2 Natcher	Y	Y	Y	Y	Y	Y	Y	Y
3 Mazzoli	Y	Y	Y	Y	Y	Y	Y	Y
4 ***Bunning***	N	N	N	Y	Y	N	Y	N
5 ***Rogers***	N	N	N	?	?	N	Y	N
6 Baesler	Y	Y	Y	Y	Y	Y	Y	Y
LOUISIANA								
1 ***Livingston***	N	N	N	Y	N	Y	Y	N
2 Jefferson	Y	Y	Y	Y	Y	Y	Y	Y
3 Tauzin	Y	N	N	Y	Y	Y	Y	Y
4 Fields	Y	Y	Y	Y	Y	Y	Y	Y
5 ***McCrery***	N	N	N	Y	Y	N	Y	N
6 ***Baker***	N	N	N	Y	Y	N	Y	N
7 Hayes	Y	Y	N	Y	Y	Y	Y	Y
MAINE								
1 Andrews	Y	Y	Y	Y	Y	Y	Y	Y
2 ***Snowe***	N	N	Y	Y	Y	Y	Y	N
MARYLAND								
1 ***Gilchrest***	N	N	N	Y	Y	N	Y	N
2 ***Bentley***	N	N	N	?	?	N	Y	N
3 Cardin	Y	Y	Y	Y	Y	Y	Y	Y
4 Wynn	Y	Y	Y	Y	Y	Y	Y	Y
5 Hoyer	Y	Y	Y	Y	Y	?	Y	Y
6 ***Bartlett***	N	N	N	Y	N	N	Y	N
7 Mfume	Y	Y	Y	Y	Y	Y	Y	Y
8 ***Morella***	Y	Y	Y	Y	Y	N	Y	Y
MASSACHUSETTS								
1 Olver	Y	Y	Y	Y	Y	Y	Y	Y
2 Neal	Y	Y	Y	Y	Y	Y	Y	Y
3 ***Blute***	N	N	Y	Y	N	N	Y	N
4 Frank	Y	Y	Y	Y	Y	Y	Y	Y
5 Meehan	Y	Y	Y	Y	Y	Y	Y	Y
6 ***Torkildsen***	N	N	N	Y	N	N	Y	N
7 Markey	Y	Y	Y	Y	Y	Y	Y	Y
8 Kennedy	Y	Y	Y	Y	Y	Y	Y	Y
9 Moakley	Y	Y	Y	Y	Y	Y	Y	Y
10 Studds	?	?	?	Y	Y	Y	Y	Y
MICHIGAN								
1 Stupak	Y	Y	Y	Y	Y	Y	Y	Y
2 ***Hoekstra***	N	N	N	Y	Y	N	Y	N
3 Henry	?	?	?	?	?	?	?	?
4 ***Camp***	N	N	N	Y	Y	N	Y	N
5 Barcia	Y	Y	Y	Y	Y	Y	Y	Y
6 ***Upton***	N	N	N	Y	Y	N	Y	N
7 ***Smith***	N	N	N	Y	N	N	Y	N
8 Carr	Y	Y	N	Y	Y	Y	Y	Y
9 Kildee	Y	Y	Y	Y	Y	Y	Y	Y
10 Bonior	Y	Y	Y	Y	Y	?	Y	Y
11 ***Knollenberg***	N	N	N	Y	N	N	Y	N
12 Levin	Y	Y	Y	Y	Y	Y	Y	Y
13 Ford	Y	Y	Y	?	?	Y	Y	Y
14 Conyers	Y	Y	Y	Y	Y	?	Y	Y
15 Collins	Y	Y	Y	Y	Y	Y	Y	Y
16 Dingell	Y	Y	Y	Y	Y	Y	Y	Y
MINNESOTA								
1 Penny	?	Y	N	Y	Y	Y	Y	Y
2 Minge	Y	Y	Y	Y	Y	Y	Y	Y
3 ***Ramstad***	N	N	Y	Y	Y	N	Y	N
4 Vento	Y	Y	Y	Y	Y	Y	Y	Y

	27	28	29	30	31	32	33	34
5 Sabo	Y	Y	Y	Y	Y	Y	Y	Y
6 ***Grams***	N	N	N	Y	N	N	Y	N
7 Peterson	Y	Y	Y	Y	Y	Y	Y	Y
8 Oberstar	Y	Y	Y	Y	Y	Y	Y	Y
MISSISSIPPI								
1 Whitten	?	?	?	?	?	?	?	?
2 Vacancy								
3 Montgomery	Y	N	N	Y	Y	Y	Y	Y
4 Parker	Y	N	N	?	?	Y	Y	Y
5 Taylor	Y	N	N	Y	Y	N	Y	Y
MISSOURI								
1 Clay	Y	Y	Y	Y	Y	N	Y	Y
2 ***Talent***	N	N	N	?	?	?	Y	N
3 Gephardt	Y	Y	Y	Y	Y	?	Y	Y
4 Skelton	Y	Y	N	?	?	?	?	?
5 Wheat	Y	Y	Y	Y	Y	Y	Y	Y
6 Danner	Y	Y	Y	Y	Y	Y	Y	Y
7 ***Hancock***	?	?	?	Y	N	N	Y	N
8 ***Emerson***	N	N	N	Y	Y	N	Y	N
9 Volkmer	Y	Y	Y	Y	Y	Y	Y	Y
MONTANA								
AL Williams	Y	Y	Y	Y	Y	Y	?	Y
NEBRASKA								
1 ***Bereuter***	N	N	N	Y	Y	N	Y	N
2 Hoagland	Y	Y	Y	Y	Y	Y	Y	Y
3 ***Barrett***	N	N	N	Y	Y	N	Y	N
NEVADA								
1 Bilbray	Y	Y	Y	Y	Y	Y	Y	Y
2 ***Vucanovich***	N	N	N	Y	Y	N	Y	N
NEW HAMPSHIRE								
1 ***Zeliff***	N	N	N	Y	Y	N	Y	N
2 Swett	Y	Y	Y	?	?	?	Y	Y
NEW JERSEY								
1 Andrews	Y	Y	Y	Y	Y	?	Y	Y
2 Hughes	Y	Y	Y	Y	Y	Y	Y	Y
3 ***Saxton***	N	N	Y	Y	Y	N	Y	N
4 ***Smith***	N	N	Y	Y	Y	Y	Y	N
5 ***Roukema***	Y	Y	Y	Y	Y	N	?	N
6 Pallone	Y	Y	Y	Y	Y	Y	Y	Y
7 ***Franks***	N	N	Y	Y	Y	N	Y	N
8 Klein	Y	Y	Y	Y	Y	Y	?	Y
9 Torricelli	Y	Y	Y	?	?	Y	Y	Y
10 Payne	Y	Y	Y	Y	Y	Y	Y	Y
11 ***Gallo***	N	N	N	Y	Y	N	Y	N
12 ***Zimmer***	N	N	Y	Y	Y	N	Y	N
13 Menendez	Y	Y	Y	Y	Y	Y	Y	Y
NEW MEXICO								
1 ***Schiff***	?	?	?	Y	Y	N	Y	N
2 ***Skeen***	N	N	N	Y	Y	N	Y	N
3 Richardson	Y	Y	Y	Y	Y	Y	Y	Y
NEW YORK								
1 Hochbrueckner	Y	Y	Y	Y	Y	Y	Y	Y
2 ***Lazio***	N	N	Y	Y	Y	N	Y	N
3 ***King***	N	N	N	Y	N	N	Y	N
4 ***Levy***	N	N	N	Y	Y	N	Y	N
5 Ackerman	Y	Y	Y	Y	Y	?	Y	Y
6 Flake	Y	Y	Y	?	?	Y	Y	Y
7 Manton	?	?	#	?	?	Y	Y	Y
8 Nadler	Y	Y	Y	Y	Y	Y	Y	Y
9 Schumer	Y	Y	Y	Y	Y	Y	Y	Y
10 Towns	Y	Y	Y	Y	Y	Y	Y	Y
11 Owens	Y	Y	Y	Y	Y	Y	Y	Y
12 Velazquez	Y	Y	Y	Y	Y	Y	Y	Y
13 ***Molinari***	N	N	Y	Y	Y	N	Y	N
14 Maloney	Y	Y	Y	Y	Y	Y	Y	Y
15 Rangel	Y	Y	Y	Y	Y	Y	Y	Y
16 Serrano	Y	Y	Y	Y	Y	?	Y	Y
17 Engel	Y	Y	Y	?	?	Y	Y	Y
18 Lowey	Y	Y	Y	Y	Y	Y	Y	Y
19 ***Fish***	N	N	Y	Y	Y	Y	Y	N
20 ***Gilman***	N	N	Y	Y	Y	Y	Y	N
21 McNulty	Y	Y	Y	Y	Y	Y	Y	Y
22 ***Solomon***	N	N	Y	Y	N	N	Y	N
23 ***Boehlert***	N	N	Y	Y	Y	Y	Y	N
24 ***McHugh***	N	N	Y	Y	Y	N	Y	N
25 ***Walsh***	N	N	Y	+	+	N	Y	N
26 Hinchey	Y	Y	Y	Y	Y	Y	Y	Y
27 ***Paxon***	N	N	N	Y	Y	N	Y	N
28 Slaughter	Y	Y	Y	Y	Y	Y	Y	Y
29 LaFalce	Y	Y	Y	Y	Y	Y	Y	Y
30 ***Quinn***	N	N	Y	Y	Y	N	Y	N
31 ***Houghton***	N	N	N	Y	Y	Y	Y	N
NORTH CAROLINA								
1 Clayton	Y	Y	Y	Y	Y	Y	Y	Y
2 Valentine	Y	N	N	Y	Y	?	Y	Y

	27	28	29	30	31	32	33	34
3 Lancaster	Y	Y	N	Y	Y	Y	Y	Y
4 Price	Y	Y	Y	Y	Y	Y	Y	Y
5 Neal	Y	Y	Y	Y	Y	Y	Y	Y
6 ***Coble***	N	N	N	Y	N	N	Y	N
7 Rose	?	?	?	Y	Y	Y	Y	Y
8 Hefner	Y	Y	Y	?	?	Y	Y	Y
9 ***McMillan***	N	N	N	Y	Y	Y	Y	N
10 ***Ballenger***	N	N	N	Y	Y	N	Y	N
11 ***Taylor***	?	?	?	Y	N	N	Y	N
12 Watt	Y	Y	Y	Y	Y	Y	Y	Y
NORTH DAKOTA								
AL Pomeroy	Y	Y	Y	Y	Y	Y	Y	Y
OHIO								
1 Mann	Y	Y	Y	Y	Y	Y	Y	Y
2 Vacancy								
3 Hall	Y	Y	Y	Y	Y	?	Y	Y
4 ***Oxley***	N	N	N	Y	Y	N	Y	N
5 ***Gillmor***	N	N	Y	Y	Y	Y	Y	N
6 Strickland	Y	Y	Y	Y	Y	Y	Y	Y
7 ***Hobson***	N	N	N	Y	Y	N	Y	N
8 ***Boehner***	N	N	N	Y	N	N	Y	N
9 Kaptur	Y	Y	Y	Y	Y	Y	Y	Y
10 ***Hoke***	N	N	Y	Y	Y	N	Y	N
11 Stokes	Y	Y	Y	Y	Y	Y	Y	Y
12 ***Kasich***	N	N	N	Y	N	Y	Y	N
13 Brown	Y	Y	Y	Y	Y	Y	Y	Y
14 Sawyer	Y	Y	Y	Y	Y	Y	Y	Y
15 ***Pryce***	N	N	N	Y	Y	?	Y	N
16 ***Regula***	N	N	Y	Y	Y	N	Y	N
17 Traficant	Y	Y	Y	Y	Y	Y	Y	Y
18 Applegate	Y	Y	Y	Y	Y	Y	?	Y
19 Fingerhut	Y	Y	Y	Y	Y	Y	Y	Y
OKLAHOMA								
1 ***Inhofe***	N	N	N	Y	Y	N	Y	N
2 Synar	Y	Y	Y	Y	Y	Y	Y	Y
3 Brewster	Y	N	N	?	?	Y	Y	Y
4 McCurdy	Y	Y	Y	Y	Y	Y	Y	Y
5 ***Istook***	N	N	N	Y	Y	N	Y	N
6 English	Y	N	Y	?	?	Y	Y	Y
OREGON								
1 Furse	Y	Y	Y	Y	Y	Y	Y	Y
2 ***Smith***	N	N	N	+	+	N	Y	N
3 Wyden	Y	Y	Y	Y	Y	Y	Y	Y
4 DeFazio	Y	Y	Y	Y	Y	Y	Y	Y
5 Kopetski	?	Y	Y	Y	Y	Y	Y	Y
PENNSYLVANIA								
1 Foglietta	Y	Y	Y	Y	Y	Y	Y	Y
2 Blackwell	?	Y	Y	Y	Y	Y	Y	Y
3 Borski	Y	Y	Y	Y	Y	Y	Y	Y
4 Klink	Y	Y	Y	Y	Y	Y	Y	Y
5 ***Clinger***	N	N	N	Y	Y	Y	Y	N
6 Holden	Y	N	Y	Y	Y	Y	Y	Y
7 ***Weldon***	N	N	Y	Y	Y	N	Y	N
8 ***Greenwood***	N	N	N	Y	Y	Y	Y	N
9 ***Shuster***	?	?	?	Y	N	N	Y	N
10 ***McDade***	N	N	Y	?	?	?	?	?
11 Kanjorski	Y	Y	Y	Y	Y	Y	Y	Y
12 Murtha	Y	Y	Y	Y	Y	Y	Y	Y
13 Margolies-Mezv.	Y	Y	Y	Y	Y	Y	Y	Y
14 Coyne	Y	Y	Y	Y	Y	Y	Y	Y
15 McHale	Y	Y	Y	Y	Y	Y	Y	Y
16 ***Walker***	N	N	N	Y	N	N	Y	N
17 ***Gekas***	N	N	N	+	−	N	Y	N
18 ***Santorum***	?	?	?	Y	Y	Y	Y	N
19 ***Goodling***	N	N	N	Y	Y	N	Y	N
20 Murphy	Y	Y	Y	Y	Y	N	Y	?
21 ***Ridge***	N	N	N	?	?	N	Y	N
RHODE ISLAND								
1 ***Machtley***	N	N	Y	Y	Y	N	Y	N
2 Reed	Y	Y	Y	?	?	Y	Y	Y
SOUTH CAROLINA								
1 ***Ravenel***	N	Y	Y	Y	Y	Y	Y	N
2 ***Spence***	N	N	N	Y	N	Y	Y	N
3 Derrick	Y	Y	Y	Y	Y	Y	Y	Y
4 ***Inglis***	N	N	N	Y	N	Y	Y	N
5 Spratt	Y	Y	Y	Y	Y	Y	Y	Y
6 Clyburn	Y	Y	Y	?	?	Y	Y	Y
SOUTH DAKOTA								
AL Johnson	Y	Y	Y	Y	Y	Y	Y	Y
TENNESSEE								
1 ***Quillen***	?	?	?	Y	Y	N	Y	N
2 ***Duncan***	N	N	N	Y	N	N	Y	N
3 Lloyd	Y	N	Y	?	?	?	?	?
4 Cooper	Y	Y	Y	Y	Y	Y	Y	Y
5 Clement	Y	Y	Y	Y	Y	Y	Y	Y

	27	28	29	30	31	32	33	34
6 Gordon	Y	Y	Y	Y	Y	Y	Y	Y
7 ***Sundquist***	N	N	N	Y	Y	N	Y	N
8 Tanner	Y	Y	Y	Y	Y	Y	Y	Y
9 Ford	?	?	?	Y	Y	Y	Y	Y
TEXAS								
1 Chapman	Y	Y	Y	?	?	Y	Y	Y
2 Wilson	Y	Y	Y	?	?	Y	Y	Y
3 ***Johnson, Sam***	N	N	N	Y	N	?	Y	N
4 Hall	Y	N	N	Y	Y	Y	Y	Y
5 Bryant	Y	Y	Y	Y	Y	Y	Y	Y
6 ***Barton***	?	?	?	?	?	?	?	?
7 ***Archer***	?	?	?	Y	N	Y	Y	N
8 ***Fields***	?	?	?	Y	N	?	?	?
9 Brooks	Y	Y	Y	Y	Y	Y	Y	Y
10 Pickle	?	?	?	Y	Y	Y	Y	Y
11 Edwards	Y	Y	Y	Y	Y	Y	Y	Y
12 Geren	Y	N	N	Y	Y	Y	Y	Y
13 Sarpalius	Y	N	N	Y	Y	Y	Y	Y
14 Laughlin	?	?	X	Y	Y	Y	Y	Y
15 de la Garza	Y	Y	Y	Y	Y	Y	Y	Y
16 Coleman	Y	Y	Y	Y	Y	Y	Y	Y
17 Stenholm	Y	N	N	Y	Y	Y	Y	Y
18 Washington	?	?	?	?	?	?	Y	?
19 ***Combest***	N	N	N	Y	Y	Y	Y	N
20 Gonzalez	Y	Y	Y	Y	Y	Y	Y	Y
21 ***Smith***	N	N	N	Y	Y	N	Y	N
22 ***DeLay***	N	N	N	Y	N	N	Y	N
23 ***Bonilla***	N	N	N	Y	Y	N	Y	N
24 Frost	Y	Y	Y	Y	Y	Y	Y	Y
25 Andrews	Y	Y	Y	Y	Y	Y	Y	Y
26 ***Armey***	N	N	N	Y	N	?	Y	N
27 Ortiz	Y	Y	Y	Y	Y	Y	Y	Y
28 Tejeda	Y	Y	Y	Y	Y	Y	Y	Y
29 Green	Y	Y	Y	Y	Y	Y	Y	Y
30 Johnson, E. B.	Y	Y	Y	Y	Y	Y	Y	Y
UTAH								
1 ***Hansen***	N	N	N	Y	Y	N	Y	N
2 Shepherd	Y	Y	Y	?	?	Y	Y	Y
3 Orton	Y	Y	N	Y	Y	Y	Y	Y
VERMONT								
AL *Sanders*	Y	Y	Y	Y	Y	Y	Y	Y
VIRGINIA								
1 ***Bateman***	N	N	N	Y	Y	Y	Y	N
2 Pickett	?	?	?	Y	Y	Y	Y	Y
3 Scott	Y	Y	Y	Y	Y	Y	Y	?
4 Sisisky	?	?	?	Y	Y	Y	Y	Y
5 Payne	Y	Y	N	Y	Y	Y	Y	Y
6 ***Goodlatte***	N	N	N	Y	Y	N	Y	N
7 ***Bliley***	N	N	N	Y	Y	N	Y	N
8 Moran	Y	Y	Y	Y	Y	Y	Y	Y
9 Boucher	Y	Y	Y	Y	Y	Y	Y	Y
10 ***Wolf***	N	N	N	Y	Y	N	Y	N
11 Byrne	Y	Y	Y	Y	Y	Y	Y	Y
WASHINGTON								
1 Cantwell	Y	Y	Y	Y	Y	Y	Y	Y
2 Swift	Y	Y	Y	Y	Y	Y	Y	Y
3 Unsoeld	Y	Y	Y	Y	Y	Y	Y	Y
4 Inslee	Y	Y	Y	Y	Y	Y	Y	Y
5 Foley								
6 Dicks	Y	Y	Y	Y	Y	Y	Y	Y
7 McDermott	Y	Y	Y	Y	Y	Y	Y	Y
8 ***Dunn***	N	N	N	Y	N	Y	Y	N
9 Kreidler	Y	Y	Y	Y	Y	Y	Y	Y
WEST VIRGINIA								
1 Mollohan	Y	Y	Y	Y	Y	Y	Y	Y
2 Wise	Y	Y	Y	Y	Y	Y	Y	Y
3 Rahall	Y	N	N	Y	Y	Y	Y	Y
WISCONSIN								
1 Vacancy								
2 ***Klug***	?	N	Y	Y	N	N	Y	N
3 ***Gunderson***	N	Y	N	Y	Y	Y	Y	N
4 Kleczka	Y	Y	Y	Y	Y	Y	Y	Y
5 Barrett	Y	Y	Y	Y	Y	Y	Y	Y
6 ***Petri***	N	N	Y	Y	Y	N	Y	N
7 Obey	Y	Y	Y	Y	Y	?	Y	Y
8 ***Roth***	N	N	N	Y	Y	N	Y	N
9 ***Sensenbrenner***	N	N	N	Y	N	N	Y	N
WYOMING								
AL ***Thomas***	?	N	N	Y	Y	N	Y	N
DELEGATES								
de Lugo, V.I.	D	D	D	D	D	D	D	D
Faleomavaega, Am.S.	D	D	D	D	D	D	D	D
Norton, D.C.	D	D	D	D	D	D	D	D
Romero-B., P.R.	D	D	D	D	D	D	D	D
Underwood, Guam	D	D	D	D	D	D	D	D

Southern states - Ala., Ark., Fla., Ga., Ky., La., Miss., N.C., Okla., S.C., Tenn., Texas, Va.
Omitted votes are quorum calls, which CQ does not include in its vote charts.

35. Procedural Motion. Approval of the House Journal of Wednesday, Feb. 17. Approved 242-144: R 23-140; D 218-4 (ND 153-3, SD 65-1); I 1-0, Feb. 18, 1993.

36. Procedural Motion. Approval of the House Journal of Monday, Feb. 22. Approved 231-147: R 15-142; D 216-5 (ND 142-4, SD 74-1); I 0-0, Feb. 23, 1993.

37. Procedural Motion. Walker, R-Pa., motion to adjourn. Motion rejected 143-254: R 143-25; D 0-228 (ND 0-152, SD 0-76); I 0-1, Feb. 23, 1993.

38. HR 920. Unemployment Benefits Extension/Previous Question. Bonior, D-Mich., motion to order the previous question (thus limiting debate and the possibility of amendment) on adoption of the rule (H Res 103) to waive points of order against and provide for House floor consideration of the bill to provide $5.7 billion to allow for the processing of claims from March 6 through Oct. 2 for federal extended emergency unemployment benefits. The funds would be designated as emergency spending and thus exempt from pay-as-you-go budget rules. Motion agreed to 243-172: R 0-172; D 242-0 (ND 162-0, SD 80-0); I 1-0, Feb. 24, 1993.

39. HR 920. Unemployment Benefits Extension/Rule. Adoption of the rule (H Res 103) to waive points of order against and provide for House floor consideration of the bill to provide $5.7 billion to allow for the processing of claims from March 6 through Oct. 2 for federal extended emergency unemployment benefits. The funds would be designated as emergency spending and thus exempt from the 1990 budget agreement's pay-as-you-go rules. Approved 237-178: R 0-171; D 236-7 (ND 162-1, SD 74-6); I 1-0, Feb. 24, 1993.

40. HR 920. Unemployment Benefits Extension/Recommit. Archer, R-Texas, motion to recommit to the House Ways and Means Committee the bill to extend unemployment benefits, with instructions to report it back with an amendment removing the emergency designation for the increased spending, thus requiring Ways and Means to find a funding mechanism for the bill in order to meet the pay-as-you-go rules of the 1990 budget agreement. Motion rejected 186-229: R 168-0; D 18-228 (ND 5-160, SD 13-68); I 0-1, Feb. 24, 1993. A "nay" was a vote in support of the president's position.

41. HR 920. Unemployment Benefits Extension/Passage. Passage of the bill to provide $5.7 billion to allow for the processing of claims from March 6 through Oct. 2 for federal extended emergency unemployment benefits. The funds would be designated as emergency spending and thus exempt from the 1990 budget agreement pay-as-you-go rules. Passed 254-161: R 27-141; D 226-20 (ND 160-5, SD 66-15); I 1-0, Feb. 24, 1993. A "yea" was a vote in support of the president's position.

42. HR 20. Hatch Act Revision/Passage. Clay, D-Mo., motion to suspend the rules and pass the bill to amend the 1939 Hatch Act, which bars federal employees from most political activities, to allow federal employees and postal workers to run for office, hold positions in political parties and volunteer for campaigns during non-working hours. Motion rejected 275-142: R 28-140; D 246-2 (ND 164-2, SD 82-0); I 1-0, Feb. 24, 1993. A two-thirds majority of those present and voting (278 in this case) is required for passage under suspension of the rules. A "yea" was a vote in support of the president's position.

	35	36	37	38	39	40	41	42
ALABAMA								
1 *Callahan*	N	N	Y	N	N	Y	N	N
2 *Everett*	N	N	Y	N	N	Y	Y	N
3 Browder	Y	Y	N	Y	Y	N	Y	Y
4 Bevill	Y	?	?	Y	Y	N	Y	Y
5 Cramer	Y	Y	N	Y	Y	N	Y	Y
6 *Bachus*	N	N	Y	N	N	Y	N	N
7 Hilliard	?	Y	?	Y	Y	N	Y	Y
ALASKA								
AL *Young*	N	N	Y	N	N	N	Y	Y
ARIZONA								
1 Coppersmith	Y	Y	N	Y	Y	N	Y	Y
2 Pastor	Y	Y	N	Y	Y	N	Y	Y
3 *Stump*	N	N	Y	N	N	Y	N	N
4 *Kyl*	N	N	Y	N	N	Y	N	N
5 *Kolbe*	N	N	Y	N	N	Y	N	N
6 English	Y	Y	N	Y	Y	N	Y	Y
ARKANSAS								
1 Lambert	Y	Y	N	Y	Y	N	Y	Y
2 Thornton	Y	Y	N	Y	Y	N	Y	Y
3 *Hutchinson*	N	N	Y	N	N	Y	N	N
4 Dickey	N	N	Y	N	N	Y	N	N
CALIFORNIA								
1 Hamburg	Y	?	N	Y	N	N	Y	Y
2 *Herger*	N	N	Y	N	N	Y	N	N
3 Fazio	Y	Y	N	Y	Y	N	Y	Y
4 *Doolittle*	N	N	Y	N	N	Y	N	N
5 Matsui	Y	Y	N	Y	Y	N	Y	Y
6 Woolsey	Y	Y	N	Y	Y	N	Y	Y
7 Miller	Y	Y	N	?	Y	N	Y	Y
8 Pelosi	Y	Y	N	Y	Y	N	Y	Y
9 Dellums	Y	?	N	Y	Y	N	Y	Y
10 *Baker*	?	N	Y	N	N	Y	N	N
11 *Pombo*	Y	Y	Y	N	N	Y	N	N
12 Lantos	Y	Y	N	Y	Y	?	?	#
13 Stark	?	Y	N	Y	Y	N	Y	Y
14 Eshoo	Y	Y	N	Y	Y	N	Y	Y
15 Mineta	Y	Y	N	Y	Y	N	Y	Y
16 Edwards	Y	Y	N	Y	Y	N	Y	Y
17 Vacancy								
18 Condit	Y	Y	N	Y	Y	Y	Y	Y
19 Lehman	Y	Y	N	Y	Y	N	Y	Y
20 Dooley	Y	?	N	Y	Y	N	Y	Y
21 *Thomas*	N	N	Y	N	N	Y	N	N
22 *Huffington*	N	N	Y	N	N	Y	N	N
23 *Gallegly*	?	N	Y	N	Y	N	N	N
24 Beilenson	Y	Y	N	Y	?	N	Y	N
25 *McKeon*	N	N	Y	N	N	Y	N	N
26 Berman	?	Y	N	Y	Y	N	Y	Y
27 *Moorhead*	N	N	Y	N	N	Y	N	N
28 *Dreier*	N	N	Y	N	N	Y	N	N
29 Waxman	Y	Y	N	Y	Y	N	Y	Y
30 Becerra	Y	Y	N	Y	Y	N	Y	Y
31 Martinez	Y	Y	N	Y	Y	N	Y	Y
32 Dixon	Y	Y	N	Y	Y	N	Y	Y
33 Roybal-Allard	Y	Y	N	Y	Y	N	Y	Y
34 Torres	Y	Y	N	Y	Y	N	Y	Y
35 Waters	?	Y	?	?	Y	N	Y	Y
36 Harman	Y	?	N	Y	Y	N	Y	Y
37 Tucker	?	?	N	Y	Y	N	Y	Y
38 *Horn*	?	N	N	N	N	Y	Y	N
39 *Royce*	N	N	Y	N	N	Y	N	N
40 *Lewis*	N	N	Y	N	N	Y	N	N
41 *Kim*	N	N	Y	N	N	Y	N	N

	35	36	37	38	39	40	41	42
42 Brown	Y	?	N	Y	Y	N	Y	Y
43 *Calvert*	N	?	Y	N	N	Y	N	N
44 *McCandless*	N	N	Y	N	N	Y	N	N
45 *Rohrabacher*	N	N	Y	N	N	Y	N	N
46 *Dornan*	N	Y	N	N	N	Y	N	N
47 *Cox*	N	?	Y	N	N	Y	N	N
48 *Packard*	N	N	Y	N	N	Y	N	N
49 Schenk	Y	Y	N	Y	Y	N	Y	Y
50 Filner	Y	Y	N	Y	Y	N	Y	Y
51 *Cunningham*	N	N	Y	N	N	Y	N	N
52 *Hunter*	N	N	Y	N	N	Y	N	N
COLORADO								
1 Schroeder	N	N	−	Y	Y	N	Y	Y
2 Skaggs	Y	Y	N	Y	Y	N	Y	Y
3 McInnis	Y	N	Y	N	N	Y	N	N
4 *Allard*	N	N	Y	N	N	Y	N	N
5 *Hefley*	N	N	Y	N	N	Y	N	N
6 *Schaefer*	N	?	Y	N	N	Y	N	N
CONNECTICUT								
1 Kennelly	Y	Y	N	Y	Y	N	Y	Y
2 Gejdenson	Y	Y	N	Y	Y	N	Y	Y
3 DeLauro	Y	Y	N	Y	Y	N	Y	Y
4 *Shays*	N	N	Y	N	Y	N	Y	Y
5 *Franks*	?	N	Y	N	N	Y	N	N
6 *Johnson*	N	N	Y	N	N	Y	N	N
DELAWARE								
AL *Castle*	N	N	Y	N	N	?	X	X
FLORIDA								
1 Hutto	Y	Y	N	Y	Y	Y	N	Y
2 Peterson	Y	Y	N	Y	Y	N	Y	Y
3 Brown	?	Y	N	Y	Y	N	Y	Y
4 *Fowler*	N	N	N	N	N	Y	N	N
5 Thurman	?	Y	N	Y	Y	N	Y	Y
6 *Stearns*	N	N	Y	N	N	Y	N	N
7 *Mica*	N	N	Y	N	N	Y	N	N
8 *McCollum*	N	N	Y	N	N	Y	N	N
9 *Bilirakis*	N	N	Y	N	N	Y	N	N
10 *Young*	?	?	Y	N	N	Y	N	N
11 Gibbons	?	?	N	Y	Y	N	Y	Y
12 *Canady*	N	N	Y	N	N	Y	N	N
13 *Miller*	N	N	Y	N	N	Y	N	N
14 *Goss*	N	N	Y	N	N	Y	N	N
15 *Bacchus*	Y	Y	N	Y	Y	N	Y	Y
16 *Lewis*	N	N	Y	N	N	Y	N	N
17 Meek	?	Y	N	Y	Y	N	Y	Y
18 *Ros-Lehtinen*	N	N	N	N	N	Y	N	N
19 Johnston	Y	Y	N	Y	Y	N	Y	Y
20 Deutsch	Y	+	N	Y	Y	N	Y	Y
21 *Diaz-Balart*	N	N	Y	N	N	Y	N	N
22 *Shaw*	N	?	Y	N	N	Y	N	N
23 Hastings	?	Y	N	Y	Y	N	Y	Y
GEORGIA								
1 *Kingston*	N	N	Y	N	N	Y	N	N
2 Bishop	?	Y	N	Y	Y	N	Y	Y
3 *Collins*	N	N	Y	N	N	Y	N	N
4 *Linder*	N	N	Y	N	N	Y	N	N
5 Lewis	Y	Y	N	Y	Y	N	Y	Y
6 *Gingrich*	N	N	Y	N	N	Y	N	N
7 Darden	Y	Y	N	Y	Y	N	Y	Y
8 Rowland	Y	Y	N	Y	Y	N	Y	Y
9 Deal	Y	Y	N	Y	Y	N	Y	Y
10 Johnson	?	Y	N	Y	Y	N	Y	Y
11 McKinney	Y	Y	N	Y	Y	N	Y	Y
HAWAII								
1 Abercrombie	Y	Y	N	?	?	?	?	#
2 Mink	Y	Y	N	Y	Y	N	Y	Y
IDAHO								
1 LaRocco	Y	Y	N	Y	Y	N	Y	Y
2 *Crapo*	N	N	Y	N	N	Y	N	N
ILLINOIS								
1 Rush	?	Y	N	Y	Y	N	Y	Y
2 Reynolds	Y	Y	?	Y	Y	N	Y	Y
3 Lipinski	Y	?	N	Y	Y	N	Y	Y
4 Gutierrez	Y	Y	N	Y	Y	N	Y	Y
5 Rostenkowski	Y	Y	N	Y	Y	N	Y	Y
6 *Hyde*	Y	Y	N	Y	N	Y	N	N
7 Collins	Y	Y	N	Y	Y	N	Y	Y
8 *Crane*	N	?	Y	N	N	Y	N	N
9 Yates	Y	?	?	?	?	?	#	#
10 *Porter*	Y	N	Y	N	N	Y	N	N
11 Sangmeister	Y	Y	N	Y	Y	N	Y	Y
12 Costello	Y	Y	N	Y	Y	N	Y	Y
13 *Fawell*	N	N	Y	N	N	Y	N	N
14 *Hastert*	N	N	Y	N	N	Y	N	N
15 *Ewing*	N	?	Y	N	N	Y	N	N
16 *Manzullo*	N	N	Y	N	N	Y	N	N
17 Evans	Y	?	?	?	?	?	#	#

ND   Northern Democrats   SD   Southern Democrats

	35	36	37	38	39	40	41	42
18 ***Michel***	N	N	Y	N	N	Y	N	N
19 Poshard	Y	Y	N	Y	Y	N	Y	Y
20 Durbin	Y	Y	N	Y	Y	N	Y	Y
INDIANA								
1 Visclosky	Y	Y	N	Y	Y	N	Y	Y
2 Sharp	Y	Y	N	Y	Y	N	Y	Y
3 Roemer	Y	Y	N	Y	Y	N	Y	Y
4 Long	Y	Y	?	Y	Y	N	Y	Y
5 ***Buyer***	N	N	Y	N	N	Y	N	N
6 ***Burton***	N	N	Y	N	N	Y	N	N
7 ***Myers***	Y	Y	N	N	N	Y	N	Y
8 McCloskey	Y	Y	N	Y	Y	N	Y	Y
9 Hamilton	Y	Y	N	Y	Y	N	Y	Y
10 Jacobs	N	N	N	Y	Y	N	Y	Y
IOWA								
1 ***Leach***	N	N	Y	N	N	Y	N	N
2 ***Nussle***	N	N	Y	N	?	Y	N	N
3 ***Lightfoot***	N	N	Y	N	N	Y	N	N
4 Smith	Y	Y	N	Y	Y	N	Y	Y
5 ***Grandy***	N	N	N	N	N	Y	N	N
KANSAS								
1 ***Roberts***	N	N	Y	N	N	Y	N	N
2 Slattery	?	Y	N	Y	Y	N	Y	Y
3 ***Meyers***	N	N	Y	N	N	Y	N	N
4 Glickman	Y	Y	N	Y	Y	N	Y	Y
KENTUCKY								
1 Barlow	Y	Y	N	Y	Y	N	Y	Y
2 Natcher	Y	Y	N	Y	Y	N	Y	Y
3 Mazzoli	Y	Y	N	Y	Y	N	Y	Y
4 ***Bunning***	N	?	Y	N	N	Y	N	N
5 ***Rogers***	N	N	Y	N	N	Y	Y	N
6 Baesler	Y	Y	N	Y	Y	N	Y	Y
LOUISIANA								
1 ***Livingston***	N	N	Y	N	N	Y	N	N
2 Jefferson	Y	?	?	Y	Y	N	Y	Y
3 Tauzin	Y	Y	N	Y	Y	Y	Y	Y
4 Fields	Y	Y	N	Y	Y	N	Y	Y
5 ***McCrery***	N	N	Y	N	N	Y	N	N
6 ***Baker***	N	N	Y	N	N	Y	N	N
7 Hayes	?	Y	N	Y	Y	Y	Y	Y
MAINE								
1 Andrews	Y	Y	N	Y	Y	N	Y	Y
2 ***Snowe***	Y	N	Y	N	N	Y	Y	N
MARYLAND								
1 ***Gilchrest***	N	N	Y	N	N	Y	Y	N
2 ***Bentley***	N	N	Y	N	N	Y	N	N
3 Cardin	Y	Y	N	Y	Y	N	Y	Y
4 Wynn	Y	Y	N	Y	Y	N	Y	Y
5 Hoyer	Y	Y	N	Y	Y	N	Y	Y
6 ***Bartlett***	N	N	Y	N	N	Y	N	N
7 Mfume	?	Y	N	Y	Y	N	Y	Y
8 ***Morella***	N	N	N	N	N	Y	Y	Y
MASSACHUSETTS								
1 Olver	Y	Y	?	Y	Y	N	Y	Y
2 Neal	Y	Y	N	Y	Y	N	Y	Y
3 ***Blute***	N	N	Y	N	N	Y	Y	N
4 Frank	Y	Y	N	Y	Y	N	Y	Y
5 Meehan	Y	Y	N	Y	Y	N	Y	Y
6 ***Torkildsen***	N	N	Y	N	N	Y	Y	N
7 Markey	Y	Y	N	Y	Y	N	Y	Y
8 Kennedy	Y	Y	N	Y	?	N	Y	Y
9 Moakley	Y	Y	N	Y	Y	N	Y	Y
10 Studds	Y	Y	N	Y	Y	N	Y	Y
MICHIGAN								
1 Stupak	Y	Y	N	Y	Y	N	Y	Y
2 ***Hoekstra***	N	N	N	N	N	Y	Y	N
3 Henry	?	?	?	?	?	?	?	?
4 ***Camp***	N	N	Y	N	N	Y	N	N
5 Barcia	Y	Y	N	Y	Y	N	Y	Y
6 ***Upton***	N	N	Y	N	N	Y	Y	Y
7 ***Smith***	Y	N	Y	N	N	Y	N	N
8 Carr	Y	Y	N	Y	Y	N	Y	Y
9 Kildee	Y	Y	N	Y	Y	N	Y	Y
10 Bonior	Y	Y	N	Y	Y	N	Y	Y
11 ***Knollenberg***	?	N	Y	N	N	Y	N	N
12 Levin	Y	Y	N	Y	Y	N	Y	Y
13 Ford	Y	Y	?	Y	Y	N	Y	Y
14 Conyers	Y	Y	N	Y	Y	N	Y	Y
15 Collins	Y	Y	N	Y	Y	N	Y	Y
16 Dingell	Y	Y	N	?	Y	N	Y	Y
MINNESOTA								
1 Penny	Y	Y	N	Y	Y	Y	N	Y
2 Minge	Y	Y	N	Y	N	Y	N	Y
3 ***Ramstad***	N	N	Y	N	N	Y	N	N
4 Vento	Y	Y	N	Y	Y	N	Y	Y
5 Sabo	Y	?	N	Y	Y	N	Y	Y
6 ***Grams***	N	N	N	N	N	Y	N	N
7 Peterson	Y	?	N	Y	Y	N	Y	Y
8 Oberstar	Y	Y	N	Y	Y	N	Y	Y
MISSISSIPPI								
1 Whitten	?	Y	?	Y	?	N	Y	Y
2 Vacancy								
3 Montgomery	Y	Y	N	Y	Y	N	N	Y
4 Parker	Y	Y	N	Y	N	Y	N	Y
5 Taylor	N	N	N	Y	N	Y	N	Y
MISSOURI								
1 Clay	?	N	N	Y	Y	N	Y	Y
2 ***Talent***	N	N	N	N	N	Y	N	N
3 Gephardt	Y	?	N	Y	Y	N	Y	Y
4 Skelton	Y	Y	N	Y	Y	N	Y	Y
5 Wheat	Y	Y	N	Y	Y	N	Y	Y
6 Danner	Y	Y	N	Y	Y	N	Y	Y
7 ***Hancock***	N	N	Y	N	N	Y	N	N
8 ***Emerson***	N	N	Y	N	N	Y	Y	Y
9 Volkmer	Y	Y	N	Y	Y	N	Y	Y
MONTANA								
AL Williams	Y	?	N	Y	Y	N	Y	Y
NEBRASKA								
1 ***Bereuter***	N	N	Y	N	N	Y	N	N
2 Hoagland	Y	Y	N	Y	Y	N	Y	Y
3 ***Barrett***	N	N	Y	N	N	Y	N	N
NEVADA								
1 Bilbray	Y	Y	N	Y	Y	N	Y	Y
2 ***Vucanovich***	N	N	Y	N	N	Y	N	N
NEW HAMPSHIRE								
1 ***Zeliff***	N	N	Y	N	N	Y	N	N
2 Swett	Y	Y	N	Y	Y	N	Y	Y
NEW JERSEY								
1 Andrews	Y	?	N	?	Y	N	Y	Y
2 Hughes	Y	Y	N	Y	Y	N	Y	Y
3 ***Saxton***	N	N	N	N	N	Y	N	Y
4 ***Smith***	Y	Y	Y	N	N	Y	Y	N
5 ***Roukema***	N	N	Y	N	N	Y	Y	N
6 Pallone	Y	Y	N	Y	Y	N	Y	Y
7 ***Franks***	N	N	Y	N	N	Y	N	N
8 Klein	Y	Y	N	Y	Y	N	Y	Y
9 Torricelli	Y	?	N	Y	Y	N	Y	Y
10 Payne	Y	Y	N	Y	Y	N	Y	Y
11 ***Gallo***	N	Y	N	N	N	Y	Y	Y
12 ***Zimmer***	N	N	Y	N	N	Y	N	N
13 Menendez	Y	Y	N	Y	Y	N	Y	Y
NEW MEXICO								
1 ***Schiff***	N	N	N	N	N	Y	N	N
2 ***Skeen***	Y	N	Y	N	N	Y	N	N
3 Richardson	Y	Y	?	Y	Y	N	Y	Y
NEW YORK								
1 Hochbrueckner	Y	Y	N	Y	Y	N	Y	Y
2 ***Lazio***	N	N	Y	N	N	Y	N	N
3 ***King***	N	N	Y	N	N	Y	N	N
4 ***Levy***	N	N	Y	N	N	Y	N	N
5 Ackerman	Y	?	?	?	?	?	#	?
6 Flake	?	Y	N	Y	Y	N	Y	Y
7 Manton	Y	Y	N	Y	Y	N	Y	Y
8 Nadler	Y	Y	N	Y	Y	N	Y	Y
9 Schumer	Y	Y	?	Y	Y	N	Y	Y
10 Towns	Y	?	?	Y	Y	N	Y	Y
11 Owens	?	?	?	Y	Y	N	Y	Y
12 Velazquez	Y	Y	?	Y	Y	N	Y	Y
13 ***Molinari***	N	N	N	N	N	Y	Y	N
14 Maloney	Y	Y	N	Y	Y	N	Y	Y
15 Rangel	?	Y	?	Y	Y	N	Y	Y
16 Serrano	Y	Y	N	Y	Y	N	Y	Y
17 Engel	Y	?	N	Y	Y	N	Y	Y
18 Lowey	Y	Y	N	Y	Y	N	Y	Y
19 ***Fish***	Y	Y	?	N	N	Y	Y	Y
20 ***Gilman***	Y	Y	N	N	N	Y	Y	Y
21 McNulty	Y	Y	N	Y	Y	N	Y	Y
22 ***Solomon***	N	?	?	?	?	?	?	?
23 ***Boehlert***	N	N	N	N	N	Y	Y	Y
24 ***McHugh***	N	N	Y	N	N	Y	Y	Y
25 ***Walsh***	N	N	Y	N	N	Y	Y	Y
26 Hinchey	Y	Y	N	Y	Y	N	Y	Y
27 ***Paxon***	N	N	Y	N	N	Y	N	N
28 Slaughter	Y	Y	N	Y	Y	N	Y	Y
29 LaFalce	Y	Y	?	Y	Y	N	Y	Y
30 ***Quinn***	N	?	Y	N	N	Y	Y	N
31 ***Houghton***	Y	Y	Y	N	N	Y	N	Y
NORTH CAROLINA								
1 Clayton	?	Y	N	?	Y	N	Y	Y
2 Valentine	Y	?	?	Y	Y	Y	N	Y
3 Lancaster	Y	Y	N	Y	Y	N	Y	Y
4 Price	Y	?	?	Y	Y	N	Y	Y
5 Neal	Y	Y	N	Y	Y	N	Y	Y
6 ***Coble***	N	N	Y	N	N	Y	N	N
7 Rose	Y	Y	N	Y	Y	N	Y	Y
8 Hefner	Y	Y	N	Y	Y	N	Y	Y
9 ***McMillan***	N	?	Y	N	N	Y	N	N
10 ***Ballenger***	N	N	Y	N	N	Y	N	N
11 ***Taylor***	N	N	Y	N	N	Y	N	N
12 Watt	Y	Y	N	Y	Y	N	Y	Y
NORTH DAKOTA								
AL Pomeroy	Y	Y	N	Y	Y	N	Y	Y
OHIO								
1 Mann	Y	Y	N	Y	Y	N	N	Y
2 Vacancy								
3 Hall	Y	Y	N	Y	Y	N	Y	Y
4 ***Oxley***	Y	?	Y	N	N	+	X	X
5 ***Gillmor***	Y	Y	Y	N	N	?	?	?
6 Strickland	Y	Y	N	Y	Y	N	Y	Y
7 ***Hobson***	N	N	Y	N	N	Y	N	N
8 ***Boehner***	N	N	Y	N	N	Y	N	N
9 Kaptur	Y	Y	N	Y	?	N	Y	Y
10 ***Hoke***	N	?	N	N	N	Y	N	N
11 Stokes	?	Y	N	Y	Y	N	Y	Y
12 ***Kasich***	Y	Y	Y	N	N	Y	N	N
13 Brown	Y	Y	N	Y	Y	N	Y	Y
14 Sawyer	Y	Y	N	Y	Y	N	Y	Y
15 ***Pryce***	N	N	Y	N	N	Y	N	N
16 ***Regula***	N	N	Y	N	N	Y	N	Y
17 Traficant	Y	Y	N	Y	Y	N	Y	Y
18 Applegate	Y	Y	N	Y	Y	N	Y	Y
19 Fingerhut	Y	Y	N	Y	Y	N	Y	Y
OKLAHOMA								
1 ***Inhofe***	N	N	Y	N	N	Y	N	N
2 Synar	Y	Y	N	Y	Y	N	Y	Y
3 Brewster	Y	Y	N	Y	Y	N	Y	Y
4 McCurdy	Y	Y	N	Y	N	Y	N	Y
5 ***Istook***	N	N	Y	N	N	Y	N	N
6 English	Y	Y	N	Y	N	Y	N	Y
OREGON								
1 Furse	Y	Y	N	Y	Y	N	Y	Y
2 ***Smith***	N	N	Y	N	N	Y	N	N
3 Wyden	Y	Y	N	Y	Y	N	Y	Y
4 DeFazio	Y	Y	N	Y	Y	N	Y	Y
5 Kopetski	Y	Y	N	Y	Y	N	Y	Y
PENNSYLVANIA								
1 Foglietta	Y	Y	N	Y	Y	N	Y	N
2 Blackwell	?	Y	N	Y	Y	N	Y	Y
3 Borski	Y	Y	N	Y	Y	N	Y	Y
4 Klink	Y	Y	N	Y	Y	N	Y	Y
5 ***Clinger***	Y	N	Y	N	N	Y	N	N
6 Holden	Y	Y	N	Y	Y	N	Y	Y
7 ***Weldon***	N	N	N	N	N	Y	N	Y
8 ***Greenwood***	N	N	Y	N	N	Y	N	N
9 ***Shuster***	N	N	Y	N	N	Y	N	N
10 ***McDade***	?	?	?	?	?	?	?	?
11 Kanjorski	Y	Y	N	Y	Y	N	Y	Y
12 Murtha	Y	Y	N	Y	Y	N	Y	Y
13 Margolies-Mezv.	Y	Y	N	Y	Y	N	Y	Y
14 Coyne	?	?	N	Y	Y	N	Y	Y
15 McHale	Y	Y	N	Y	Y	N	Y	Y
16 ***Walker***	N	N	Y	N	N	Y	N	N
17 ***Gekas***	N	N	Y	N	N	Y	N	N
18 ***Santorum***	N	N	N	N	N	Y	N	N
19 ***Goodling***	N	N	Y	N	N	Y	N	Y
20 Murphy	N	N	N	Y	Y	N	Y	Y
21 ***Ridge***	?	N	Y	N	N	Y	Y	Y
RHODE ISLAND								
1 ***Machtley***	N	N	Y	N	N	Y	Y	Y
2 Reed	Y	?	N	Y	Y	N	Y	Y
SOUTH CAROLINA								
1 ***Ravenel***	Y	Y	N	N	N	Y	N	Y
2 ***Spence***	N	N	Y	N	N	Y	N	N
3 Derrick	Y	Y	N	Y	Y	N	Y	Y
4 ***Inglis***	Y	Y	Y	N	N	Y	N	N
5 Spratt	Y	Y	N	Y	Y	N	Y	Y
6 Clyburn	Y	Y	?	Y	Y	N	Y	Y
SOUTH DAKOTA								
AL Johnson	Y	Y	N	Y	Y	Y	N	Y
TENNESSEE								
1 ***Quillen***	N	N	N	N	N	Y	N	Y
2 ***Duncan***	N	N	Y	N	N	Y	N	Y
3 Lloyd	?	Y	N	Y	Y	N	Y	Y
4 Cooper	Y	Y	N	?	?	?	?	?
5 Clement	Y	Y	N	Y	Y	N	N	Y
6 Gordon	Y	Y	N	Y	Y	N	Y	Y
7 ***Sundquist***	N	N	N	N	N	Y	N	Y
8 Tanner	Y	Y	N	Y	Y	N	Y	Y
9 Ford	?	?	?	?	?	?	?	?
TEXAS								
1 Chapman	?	Y	N	Y	?	N	Y	Y
2 Wilson	?	Y	N	?	Y	N	Y	Y
3 ***Johnson, Sam***	?	N	Y	N	N	Y	N	N
4 Hall	Y	Y	N	Y	Y	Y	N	Y
5 Bryant	Y	Y	N	Y	Y	N	Y	Y
6 ***Barton***	?	?	?	N	N	?	X	?
7 ***Archer***	Y	Y	Y	N	N	Y	N	N
8 ***Fields***	?	?	?	N	N	Y	N	N
9 Brooks	Y	Y	N	Y	Y	N	?	Y
10 Pickle	Y	Y	N	Y	Y	N	Y	Y
11 Edwards	Y	Y	N	Y	Y	N	N	Y
12 Geren	Y	Y	N	Y	Y	Y	Y	Y
13 Sarpalius	Y	Y	N	Y	Y	N	Y	Y
14 Laughlin	Y	Y	N	Y	Y	N	N	Y
15 de la Garza	Y	Y	N	Y	Y	N	Y	Y
16 Coleman	Y	Y	N	Y	Y	N	Y	Y
17 Stenholm	Y	Y	N	Y	N	Y	N	Y
18 Washington	?	?	N	Y	Y	?	Y	Y
19 ***Combest***	Y	Y	N	N	N	Y	N	N
20 Gonzalez	Y	Y	N	Y	Y	N	Y	Y
21 ***Smith***	N	N	Y	N	N	Y	N	N
22 ***DeLay***	N	N	Y	N	N	Y	N	N
23 ***Bonilla***	N	N	N	N	N	Y	N	N
24 Frost	?	Y	N	Y	Y	N	Y	Y
25 Andrews	Y	Y	N	Y	Y	N	Y	Y
26 ***Armey***	N	N	Y	N	N	Y	N	N
27 Ortiz	Y	Y	N	Y	Y	N	Y	Y
28 Tejeda	Y	Y	N	Y	Y	N	Y	Y
29 Green	Y	Y	N	Y	Y	N	Y	Y
30 Johnson, E. B.	?	Y	N	Y	Y	N	Y	Y
UTAH								
1 ***Hansen***	Y	N	Y	N	N	Y	N	N
2 Shepherd	Y	Y	N	Y	Y	N	Y	Y
3 Orton	Y	Y	N	Y	Y	Y	Y	Y
VERMONT								
AL *Sanders*	Y	?	N	Y	Y	N	Y	Y
VIRGINIA								
1 ***Bateman***	Y	Y	Y	N	N	Y	N	N
2 Pickett	Y	Y	N	Y	Y	N	N	Y
3 Scott	?	Y	N	Y	Y	N	Y	Y
4 Sisisky	Y	Y	N	Y	N	Y	Y	Y
5 Payne	Y	Y	N	Y	Y	N	Y	Y
6 ***Goodlatte***	N	N	Y	N	N	Y	N	N
7 ***Bliley***	N	N	Y	N	N	Y	N	N
8 Moran	Y	Y	N	Y	Y	N	Y	Y
9 Boucher	Y	Y	N	Y	Y	N	Y	Y
10 ***Wolf***	N	N	Y	N	N	Y	N	N
11 Byrne	Y	Y	N	Y	Y	N	Y	Y
WASHINGTON								
1 Cantwell	Y	Y	N	Y	Y	N	Y	Y
2 Swift	Y	Y	N	Y	Y	N	Y	Y
3 Unsoeld	Y	?	N	Y	Y	N	Y	Y
4 Inslee	Y	Y	N	Y	Y	N	N	Y
5 Foley								Y
6 Dicks	Y	Y	N	Y	Y	N	Y	Y
7 McDermott	Y	Y	N	Y	Y	N	Y	Y
8 ***Dunn***	N	N	Y	N	N	Y	N	N
9 Kreidler	Y	Y	N	Y	Y	N	Y	Y
WEST VIRGINIA								
1 Mollohan	Y	Y	N	Y	Y	N	Y	Y
2 Wise	Y	?	N	Y	Y	N	Y	Y
3 Rahall	Y	Y	?	Y	Y	N	Y	Y
WISCONSIN								
1 Vacancy								
2 ***Klug***	N	N	Y	N	N	Y	N	Y
3 ***Gunderson***	Y	N	N	N	N	Y	N	Y
4 Kleczka	Y	?	N	Y	Y	N	Y	Y
5 Barrett	Y	Y	N	Y	Y	N	Y	Y
6 ***Petri***	N	?	Y	N	N	Y	N	Y
7 Obey	Y	Y	N	Y	Y	N	Y	Y
8 ***Roth***	N	N	Y	N	N	Y	N	N
9 ***Sensenbrenner***	N	N	Y	N	N	Y	N	N
WYOMING								
AL ***Thomas***	N	N	Y	N	N	Y	N	Y
DELEGATES								
de Lugo, V.I.	D	D	D	D	D	D	D	D
Faleomavaega, Am.S.	D	D	D	D	D	D	D	D
Norton, D.C.	D	D	D	D	D	D	D	D
Romero-B., P.R.	D	D	D	D	D	D	D	D
Underwood, Guam	D	D	D	D	D	D	D	D

Southern states - Ala., Ark., Fla., Ga., Ky., La., Miss., N.C., Okla., S.C., Tenn., Texas, Va.
Omitted votes are quorum calls, which CQ does not include in its vote charts.

43. HR 890. Unclaimed Deposits/Passage. Neal, D-N.C., motion to suspend the rules and pass the bill to extend the time period given depositors to claim accounts insured by the Federal Deposit Insurance Corporation at failed institutions. Motion agreed to 409-1: R 166-0; D 242-1 (ND 164-0, SD 78-1); I 1-0, March 2, 1993. A two-thirds majority of those present and voting (274 in this case) is required for passage under suspension of the rules.

44. HR 904. Airline Competitiveness/Passage. Oberstar, D-Minn., motion to suspend the rules and pass the bill to increase the membership of the National Commission to Ensure a Strong Competitive Airline Industry to 22 members, allow the chairman to designate panels within the commission, and change the deadline for submission of the commission's report to 90 days after enactment. The commission was established in 1992 to analyze the financial condition of the airline industry. Motion agreed to 367-43: R 123-43; D 243-0 (ND 164-0, SD 79-0); I 1-0, March 2, 1993. A two-thirds majority of those present and voting (274 in this case) is required for passage under suspension of the rules. A "yea" was a vote in support of the president's position.

45. HR 868. Telemarketing Consumer Protection/Passage. Swift, D-Wash., motion to suspend the rules and pass the bill to require the Federal Trade Commission to issue rules to prohibit deceptive and abusive telemarketing activities; allow states to bring civil actions in federal courts to stop fraudulent telemarketing practices; and allow individuals who lost more than $50,000 through telemarketing schemes to sue in federal court. Motion agreed to 411-3: R 165-2; D 245-1 (ND 164-1, SD 81-0); I 1-0, March 2, 1993. A two-thirds majority of those present and voting (276 in this case) is required for passage under suspension of the rules.

46. HR 707. Emerging Telecommunications Technology/Passage. Markey, D-Mass., motion to suspend the rules and pass the bill to convert 200 megahertz of the electromagnetic radio spectrum to commercial entities. Motion agreed to 410-5: R 162-5; D 247-0 (ND 166-0, SD 81-0); I 1-0, March 2, 1993. A two-thirds majority of those present and voting (277 in this case) is required for passage under suspension of the rules.

47. HR 617. Limited Partnership Roll-Ups/Passage. Markey, D-Mass., motion to suspend the rules and pass the bill to grant small investors new rights when their limited partnerships are reorganized. Motion agreed to 408-6: R 161-6; D 246-0 (ND 165-0, SD 81-0); I 1-0, March 2, 1993. A two-thirds majority of those present and voting (276 in this case) is required for passage under suspension of the rules.

48. Procedural Motion. Approval of the House Journal of Monday, March 1. Approved 252-155: R 14-150; D 237-5 (ND 162-4, SD 75-1); I 1-0, March 2, 1993.

49. Procedural Motion. Approval of the House Journal of Tuesday, March 2. Approved 246-150: R 20-145; D 225-5 (ND 153-4, SD 72-1); I 1-0, March 3, 1993.

50. HR 20. Hatch Act Revision/Previous Question. Derrick, D-S.C., motion to order the previous question (thus limiting debate and the possibility of amendment) on adoption of the rule (H Res 106) to provide for House floor consideration of the bill to amend the 1939 Hatch Act barring federal employees from most political activities, to allow federal employees and postal workers to run for office, hold positions in political parties and volunteer for campaigns during non-working hours. Motion agreed to 248-166: R 3-165; D 244-1 (ND 166-1, SD 78-0); I 1-0, March 3, 1993.

KEY

Y   Voted for (yea).
\#   Paired for.
+   Announced for.
N   Voted against (nay).
X   Paired against.
—   Announced against.
P   Voted "present."
C   Voted "present" to avoid possible conflict of interest.
?   Did not vote or otherwise make a position known.
D   Delegates ineligible to vote.

Democrats   *Republicans*
Independent

	43	44	45	46	47	48	49	50
ALABAMA								
1 Callahan	?	?	?	?	?	?	N	N
2 Everett	Y	Y	Y	Y	Y	N	N	N
3 Browder	Y	Y	Y	Y	Y	Y	Y	Y
4 Bevill	Y	Y	Y	Y	Y	Y	Y	Y
5 Cramer	Y	Y	Y	Y	Y	Y	Y	Y
6 *Bachus*	Y	Y	Y	Y	N	N	N	N
7 Hilliard	Y	Y	Y	Y	Y	Y	Y	Y
ALASKA								
AL *Young*	?	?	?	?	?	?	?	?
ARIZONA								
1 Coppersmith	Y	Y	Y	Y	Y	Y	Y	Y
2 Pastor	Y	Y	Y	Y	Y	Y	Y	Y
3 *Stump*	Y	N	Y	Y	Y	N	N	N
4 *Kyl*	Y	Y	Y	Y	Y	N	N	N
5 *Kolbe*	Y	N	Y	Y	N	N	N	N
6 English	Y	Y	Y	Y	Y	Y	Y	Y
ARKANSAS								
1 Lambert	Y	Y	Y	Y	Y	Y	Y	Y
2 Thornton	Y	Y	Y	Y	Y	Y	Y	Y
3 *Hutchinson*	Y	Y	Y	Y	Y	N	Y	N
4 Dickey	Y	N	Y	Y	Y	N	N	N
CALIFORNIA								
1 Hamburg	Y	Y	Y	Y	Y	Y	?	Y
2 *Herger*	Y	N	Y	N	Y	N	N	N
3 Fazio	Y	Y	Y	Y	Y	Y	Y	Y
♦ *Doolittle*	Y	N	Y	Y	Y	N	N	N
5 Matsui	Y	Y	Y	Y	Y	Y	Y	Y
6 Woolsey	Y	Y	Y	Y	Y	Y	Y	Y
7 Miller	Y	Y	Y	Y	Y	Y	?	Y
8 Pelosi	Y	Y	Y	Y	Y	Y	Y	Y
9 Dellums	Y	Y	Y	Y	Y	Y	?	Y
10 *Baker*	Y	N	Y	Y	Y	N	N	N
11 *Pombo*	Y	N	Y	N	N	Y	Y	N
12 Lantos	Y	Y	Y	Y	Y	Y	Y	Y
13 Stark	Y	Y	Y	Y	Y	Y	Y	Y
14 Eshoo	Y	Y	Y	Y	Y	Y	Y	Y
15 Mineta	Y	Y	Y	Y	Y	Y	Y	Y
16 Edwards	Y	Y	Y	Y	Y	Y	Y	Y
17 Vacancy								
18 Condit	Y	Y	Y	Y	Y	Y	Y	Y
19 Lehman	Y	Y	Y	Y	Y	Y	Y	Y
20 Dooley	?	?	?	?	?	?	Y	Y
21 *Thomas*	Y	Y	Y	Y	Y	N	N	N
22 *Huffington*	Y	N	Y	Y	Y	N	N	N
23 *Gallegly*	Y	Y	Y	Y	Y	N	N	N
24 Beilenson	Y	Y	Y	Y	Y	Y	Y	Y
25 *McKeon*	Y	Y	Y	Y	Y	N	N	N
26 Berman	Y	Y	Y	Y	Y	?	?	Y
27 *Moorhead*	Y	N	Y	Y	N	N	N	N
28 *Dreier*	Y	N	Y	Y	N	N	N	N
29 Waxman	Y	Y	Y	Y	Y	Y	Y	Y
30 Becerra	?	?	Y	Y	Y	Y	Y	Y
31 Martinez	Y	Y	Y	Y	Y	Y	?	Y
32 Dixon	Y	Y	Y	Y	Y	Y	Y	Y
33 Roybal-Allard	Y	Y	Y	Y	Y	Y	Y	Y
34 Torres	Y	Y	Y	Y	Y	Y	Y	Y
35 Waters	Y	Y	Y	Y	Y	Y	Y	Y
36 Harman	Y	Y	Y	Y	Y	Y	Y	Y
37 Tucker	Y	Y	Y	Y	Y	Y	Y	Y
38 *Horn*	Y	Y	Y	Y	?	Y	N	N
39 *Royce*	Y	N	Y	N	N	N	N	N
40 *Lewis*	Y	Y	Y	Y	Y	N	N	N
41 *Kim*	Y	Y	Y	Y	Y	N	N	N

	43	44	45	46	47	48	49	50
42 *Brown*	Y	Y	Y	Y	Y	?	Y	Y
43 *Calvert*	Y	Y	Y	Y	N	N	N	N
44 *McCandless*	Y	Y	Y	Y	N	N	N	N
45 *Rohrabacher*	Y	N	Y	Y	N	N	N	N
46 *Dornan*	Y	N	Y	Y	N	N	N	N
47 *Cox*	?	?	?	?	?	?	?	?
48 *Packard*	Y	N	Y	Y	N	N	N	N
49 Schenk	Y	Y	Y	Y	Y	Y	?	Y
50 Filner	Y	Y	Y	Y	Y	Y	Y	Y
51 *Cunningham*	Y	N	Y	Y	N	N	N	N
52 *Hunter*	Y	N	Y	Y	N	N	N	N
COLORADO								
1 Schroeder	Y	Y	Y	Y	N	N	N	Y
2 Skaggs	Y	Y	Y	Y	Y	Y	Y	Y
3 *McInnis*	Y	Y	Y	Y	Y	N	Y	N
4 *Allard*	Y	N	Y	Y	N	N	N	N
5 *Hefley*	Y	Y	Y	Y	Y	N	N	N
6 *Schaefer*	Y	Y	Y	Y	Y	N	N	N
CONNECTICUT								
1 Kennelly	Y	Y	Y	Y	Y	Y	Y	Y
2 Gejdenson	Y	Y	Y	Y	Y	Y	Y	Y
3 DeLauro	Y	Y	Y	Y	Y	Y	Y	Y
4 *Shays*	Y	Y	Y	Y	Y	N	N	N
5 *Franks*	Y	Y	Y	Y	Y	N	N	N
6 *Johnson*	Y	Y	Y	Y	Y	N	N	N
DELAWARE								
AL *Castle*	?	N	Y	Y	Y	N	N	N
FLORIDA								
1 Hutto	Y	Y	Y	Y	Y	Y	Y	Y
2 Peterson	Y	Y	Y	Y	Y	Y	Y	Y
3 Brown	?	?	Y	Y	Y	Y	Y	Y
4 *Fowler*	Y	Y	Y	Y	Y	N	N	N
5 Thurman	Y	Y	Y	Y	Y	Y	?	Y
6 *Stearns*	Y	Y	Y	Y	Y	N	N	N
7 *Mica*	Y	Y	Y	Y	Y	N	N	N
8 *McCollum*	Y	Y	Y	Y	Y	N	N	N
9 *Bilirakis*	Y	Y	Y	Y	Y	N	N	N
10 *Young*	Y	Y	Y	Y	Y	N	N	?
11 Gibbons	Y	Y	Y	Y	Y	Y	Y	Y
12 *Canady*	Y	Y	Y	Y	Y	N	N	N
13 *Miller*	Y	Y	Y	Y	Y	N	N	N
14 *Goss*	Y	Y	Y	Y	Y	N	N	N
15 *Bacchus*	Y	Y	Y	Y	Y	Y	Y	Y
16 *Lewis*	Y	Y	Y	Y	Y	N	N	N
17 Meek	Y	Y	Y	Y	Y	Y	Y	Y
18 *Ros-Lehtinen*	Y	Y	Y	Y	N	N	N	N
19 Johnston	Y	Y	Y	Y	Y	Y	Y	Y
20 Deutsch	Y	Y	Y	Y	Y	?	Y	Y
21 *Diaz-Balart*	Y	Y	Y	Y	Y	N	N	N
22 *Shaw*	Y	Y	Y	Y	Y	N	N	N
23 Hastings	Y	Y	Y	Y	Y	Y	Y	Y
GEORGIA								
1 *Kingston*	Y	Y	Y	N	N	N	N	N
2 Bishop	Y	Y	Y	Y	Y	Y	Y	Y
3 *Collins*	Y	Y	Y	Y	N	N	N	N
4 *Linder*	Y	Y	Y	Y	N	N	N	N
5 Lewis	Y	Y	Y	Y	Y	Y	Y	Y
6 *Gingrich*	Y	Y	Y	Y	N	N	N	N
7 Darden	Y	Y	Y	Y	Y	Y	Y	Y
8 Rowland	Y	Y	Y	Y	Y	Y	Y	Y
9 Deal	Y	Y	Y	Y	Y	Y	Y	Y
10 Johnson	Y	Y	Y	Y	Y	Y	Y	Y
11 McKinney	Y	Y	Y	Y	Y	Y	Y	Y
HAWAII								
1 Abercrombie	Y	Y	Y	Y	Y	Y	Y	Y
2 Mink	Y	Y	Y	Y	Y	Y	Y	Y
IDAHO								
1 LaRocco	Y	Y	Y	Y	Y	Y	Y	Y
2 *Crapo*	Y	Y	Y	Y	Y	N	N	N
ILLINOIS								
1 Rush	Y	Y	Y	Y	Y	Y	Y	Y
2 Reynolds	Y	Y	Y	Y	Y	Y	Y	Y
3 Lipinski	Y	Y	Y	Y	Y	Y	Y	Y
4 Gutierrez	Y	Y	Y	Y	Y	Y	Y	Y
5 Rostenkowski	?	?	?	?	?	?	?	?
6 *Hyde*	Y	N	Y	Y	Y	Y	N	N
7 Collins	Y	Y	Y	Y	Y	Y	Y	Y
8 *Crane*	Y	N	Y	N	N	N	N	N
9 Yates	Y	Y	Y	Y	Y	Y	Y	Y
10 *Porter*	Y	Y	Y	Y	Y	N	N	N
11 Sangmeister	Y	Y	Y	Y	Y	Y	Y	Y
12 Costello	Y	Y	Y	Y	Y	Y	Y	Y
13 *Fawell*	Y	Y	Y	Y	Y	N	N	N
14 *Hastert*	Y	Y	Y	Y	Y	N	N	N
15 *Ewing*	Y	Y	Y	Y	Y	N	N	N
16 *Manzullo*	Y	N	Y	N	N	N	N	N
17 Evans	?	?	?	?	?	?	?	?

ND Northern Democrats   SD Southern Democrats

	43	44	45	46	47	48	49	50
18 **Michel**	Y	Y	Y	Y	Y	N	N	N
19 Poshard	Y	Y	Y	Y	Y	Y	Y	Y
20 Durbin	Y	Y	Y	Y	Y	Y	Y	Y
INDIANA								
1 Visclosky	Y	Y	Y	Y	Y	Y	Y	Y
2 Sharp	Y	Y	Y	Y	Y	Y	Y	Y
3 Roemer	Y	Y	Y	Y	Y	Y	+	+
4 Long	Y	Y	Y	Y	Y	Y	Y	Y
5 **Buyer**	Y	Y	Y	Y	Y	N	N	N
6 **Burton**	Y	N	Y	Y	Y	N	N	N
7 **Myers**	Y	Y	Y	Y	Y	Y	Y	N
8 McCloskey	Y	Y	Y	Y	Y	Y	Y	Y
9 Hamilton	Y	Y	Y	Y	Y	Y	Y	Y
10 Jacobs	Y	Y	Y	Y	Y	N	N	N
IOWA								
1 **Leach**	Y	Y	Y	Y	Y	N	N	N
2 **Nussle**	Y	N	Y	Y	Y	N	N	N
3 **Lightfoot**	Y	N	Y	N	Y	N	N	N
4 Smith	Y	Y	Y	Y	Y	Y	Y	Y
5 **Grandy**	Y	Y	Y	Y	Y	N	N	N
KANSAS								
1 **Roberts**	Y	Y	Y	Y	Y	N	N	N
2 Slattery	Y	Y	Y	Y	Y	Y	Y	Y
3 **Meyers**	Y	Y	Y	Y	Y	N	N	N
4 Glickman	Y	Y	Y	Y	Y	?	Y	Y
KENTUCKY								
1 Barlow	Y	Y	Y	Y	Y	Y	Y	Y
2 Natcher	Y	Y	Y	Y	Y	Y	Y	Y
3 Mazzoli	Y	Y	Y	Y	Y	Y	Y	Y
4 **Bunning**	Y	Y	Y	Y	Y	N	N	N
5 **Rogers**	Y	Y	Y	Y	Y	N	N	N
6 Baesler	Y	Y	Y	Y	Y	Y	Y	Y
LOUISIANA								
1 **Livingston**	Y	Y	Y	Y	Y	N	N	N
2 Jefferson	Y	?	Y	Y	Y	Y	?	Y
3 Tauzin	Y	Y	Y	Y	Y	Y	Y	?
4 Fields	Y	Y	Y	Y	Y	Y	Y	Y
5 **McCrery**	Y	Y	Y	Y	Y	N	N	N
6 **Baker**	Y	Y	Y	Y	Y	N	N	N
7 Hayes	Y	Y	Y	Y	Y	Y	Y	Y
MAINE								
1 Andrews	Y	Y	Y	Y	Y	Y	Y	Y
2 **Snowe**	Y	Y	Y	Y	Y	N	N	N
MARYLAND								
1 **Gilchrest**	Y	Y	Y	Y	Y	?	N	N
2 **Bentley**	Y	Y	Y	Y	Y	N	N	N
3 Cardin	Y	Y	Y	Y	Y	Y	Y	Y
4 Wynn	Y	Y	Y	Y	Y	Y	?	Y
5 Hoyer	Y	Y	Y	Y	Y	Y	Y	Y
6 **Bartlett**	Y	N	Y	Y	Y	N	N	N
7 Mfume	Y	Y	Y	Y	Y	N	Y	Y
8 **Morella**	Y	Y	Y	Y	Y	N	N	Y
MASSACHUSETTS								
1 Olver	Y	Y	Y	Y	Y	Y	Y	Y
2 Neal	Y	Y	Y	Y	Y	Y	Y	Y
3 **Blute**	Y	Y	Y	Y	Y	N	N	N
4 Frank	Y	Y	Y	Y	Y	Y	Y	Y
5 Meehan	Y	Y	Y	Y	Y	Y	Y	Y
6 **Torkildsen**	Y	Y	Y	Y	Y	N	N	N
7 Markey	Y	Y	Y	Y	Y	Y	Y	Y
8 Kennedy	Y	Y	Y	Y	Y	Y	Y	Y
9 Moakley	Y	Y	Y	Y	Y	Y	Y	Y
10 Studds	Y	Y	Y	Y	Y	Y	Y	Y
MICHIGAN								
1 Stupak	Y	Y	Y	Y	Y	Y	Y	Y
2 **Hoekstra**	Y	Y	Y	Y	Y	N	N	N
3 Henry	?	?	?	?	?	?	?	?
4 **Camp**	Y	Y	Y	Y	Y	N	N	N
5 Barcia	Y	Y	Y	Y	Y	Y	Y	Y
6 **Upton**	Y	Y	Y	Y	Y	N	N	N
7 **Smith**	Y	N	N	Y	Y	N	N	N
8 Carr	Y	Y	Y	Y	Y	Y	Y	Y
9 Kildee	Y	Y	Y	Y	Y	Y	Y	Y
10 Bonior	Y	Y	Y	Y	Y	Y	Y	Y
11 **Knollenberg**	Y	Y	Y	Y	Y	N	?	N
12 Levin	Y	Y	Y	Y	Y	Y	Y	Y
13 Ford	Y	Y	Y	Y	Y	Y	?	Y
14 Conyers	Y	Y	Y	Y	Y	Y	Y	Y
15 Collins	Y	Y	Y	Y	Y	Y	Y	Y
16 Dingell	Y	Y	Y	Y	Y	Y	Y	Y
MINNESOTA								
1 Penny	Y	Y	N	Y	Y	Y	Y	Y
2 Minge	Y	?	Y	Y	Y	Y	Y	Y
3 **Ramstad**	Y	Y	Y	Y	Y	N	N	N
4 Vento	Y	Y	Y	Y	Y	Y	Y	Y

	43	44	45	46	47	48	49	50
5 Sabo	Y	Y	Y	Y	Y	Y	Y	Y
6 **Grams**	Y	Y	Y	Y	Y	N	N	N
7 Peterson	Y	Y	Y	Y	Y	Y	Y	Y
8 Oberstar	Y	Y	Y	Y	Y	Y	Y	Y
MISSISSIPPI								
1 Whitten	Y	Y	Y	Y	Y	Y	?	Y
2 Vacancy								
3 Montgomery	Y	Y	Y	Y	Y	Y	Y	Y
4 Parker	Y	Y	Y	Y	Y	Y	Y	Y
5 Taylor	N	Y	Y	Y	Y	N	N	Y
MISSOURI								
1 Clay	Y	Y	Y	Y	Y	Y	N	Y
2 **Talent**	Y	Y	Y	Y	Y	N	N	N
3 Gephardt	Y	Y	Y	Y	Y	Y	Y	Y
4 Skelton	Y	Y	Y	Y	Y	Y	Y	Y
5 Wheat	Y	Y	Y	Y	Y	Y	Y	Y
6 Danner	Y	Y	Y	Y	Y	Y	Y	Y
7 **Hancock**	Y	?	N	Y	Y	N	N	N
8 **Emerson**	Y	Y	Y	Y	Y	N	N	N
9 Volkmer	Y	Y	Y	Y	Y	Y	Y	Y
MONTANA								
AL Williams	Y	Y	Y	Y	Y	Y	?	Y
NEBRASKA								
1 **Bereuter**	Y	Y	Y	Y	Y	N	N	N
2 Hoagland	Y	Y	Y	Y	Y	Y	Y	Y
3 **Barrett**	Y	Y	Y	Y	Y	N	N	N
NEVADA								
1 Bilbray	Y	Y	Y	Y	Y	Y	Y	Y
2 **Vucanovich**	Y	Y	Y	Y	Y	N	N	N
NEW HAMPSHIRE								
1 **Zeliff**	Y	Y	Y	N	Y	N	N	N
2 Swett	Y	Y	Y	Y	Y	Y	Y	Y
NEW JERSEY								
1 Andrews	Y	Y	Y	Y	Y	Y	Y	Y
2 Hughes	Y	Y	Y	Y	Y	Y	Y	Y
3 **Saxton**	Y	Y	Y	Y	Y	Y	?	N
4 **Smith**	Y	Y	Y	Y	Y	Y	Y	N
5 **Roukema**	?	?	?	?	?	?	?	X
6 Pallone	Y	Y	Y	Y	Y	Y	Y	Y
7 **Franks**	Y	Y	Y	Y	Y	N	N	N
8 Klein	Y	Y	Y	Y	Y	Y	Y	Y
9 Torricelli	Y	Y	Y	Y	?	Y	Y	Y
10 Payne	Y	Y	Y	Y	Y	Y	Y	Y
11 **Gallo**	Y	Y	Y	Y	Y	N	Y	N
12 **Zimmer**	Y	N	Y	Y	Y	N	N	N
13 Menendez	Y	Y	Y	Y	Y	Y	Y	Y
NEW MEXICO								
1 **Schiff**	Y	Y	Y	Y	Y	N	N	N
2 **Skeen**	Y	Y	Y	Y	Y	N	N	N
3 Richardson	Y	Y	Y	Y	Y	Y	Y	Y
NEW YORK								
1 Hochbrueckner	Y	Y	Y	Y	Y	Y	Y	Y
2 **Lazio**	Y	Y	Y	Y	Y	N	N	N
3 **King**	Y	Y	Y	Y	Y	N	N	N
4 **Levy**	Y	Y	Y	Y	Y	N	N	N
5 Ackerman	Y	Y	Y	Y	Y	Y	Y	Y
6 Flake	Y	Y	Y	Y	Y	Y	Y	Y
7 Manton	Y	Y	Y	Y	Y	Y	Y	Y
8 Nadler	Y	Y	Y	Y	Y	Y	Y	Y
9 Schumer	Y	Y	Y	Y	Y	Y	Y	Y
10 Towns	Y	Y	Y	Y	Y	Y	Y	Y
11 Owens	?	Y	Y	Y	Y	Y	Y	Y
12 Velazquez	Y	Y	Y	Y	Y	Y	Y	Y
13 **Molinari**	Y	Y	Y	Y	Y	N	N	N
14 Maloney	Y	Y	Y	Y	Y	Y	Y	Y
15 Rangel	Y	Y	Y	Y	Y	Y	Y	Y
16 Serrano	?	?	?	?	?	Y	Y	Y
17 Engel	Y	Y	Y	Y	Y	Y	Y	Y
18 Lowey	Y	Y	Y	Y	Y	Y	Y	Y
19 **Fish**	Y	Y	Y	Y	Y	Y	Y	N
20 **Gilman**	Y	Y	Y	Y	Y	N	Y	N
21 McNulty	Y	Y	Y	Y	Y	Y	Y	Y
22 **Solomon**	Y	Y	Y	Y	Y	N	N	N
23 **Boehlert**	Y	Y	Y	Y	Y	N	N	N
24 **McHugh**	Y	Y	Y	Y	Y	N	N	N
25 **Walsh**	Y	Y	Y	Y	Y	N	N	N
26 Hinchey	Y	Y	?	Y	Y	Y	Y	Y
27 **Paxon**	Y	N	Y	Y	Y	N	N	N
28 Slaughter	Y	Y	Y	Y	Y	Y	Y	Y
29 LaFalce	Y	Y	Y	Y	Y	Y	Y	Y
30 **Quinn**	Y	Y	Y	Y	Y	N	N	N
31 **Houghton**	Y	Y	Y	Y	Y	Y	Y	N
NORTH CAROLINA								
1 Clayton	Y	Y	Y	Y	Y	Y	?	#
2 Valentine	Y	Y	Y	Y	Y	Y	?	?

	43	44	45	46	47	48	49	50
3 Lancaster	Y	Y	Y	Y	Y	?	Y	Y
4 Price	Y	Y	Y	Y	Y	Y	Y	Y
5 Neal	Y	Y	Y	Y	Y	Y	Y	Y
6 **Coble**	Y	N	Y	Y	Y	N	N	N
7 Rose	Y	Y	Y	Y	Y	Y	Y	Y
8 Hefner	Y	Y	Y	Y	Y	Y	Y	Y
9 **McMillan**	Y	Y	Y	Y	Y	N	N	N
10 **Ballenger**	Y	N	Y	Y	Y	N	N	N
11 **Taylor**	Y	N	Y	Y	Y	N	N	N
12 Watt	Y	Y	Y	Y	Y	Y	Y	Y
NORTH DAKOTA								
AL Pomeroy	Y	Y	Y	Y	Y	Y	?	Y
OHIO								
1 Mann	Y	Y	Y	Y	Y	Y	Y	Y
2 Vacancy								
3 Hall	Y	Y	Y	Y	Y	Y	Y	Y
4 **Oxley**	Y	Y	Y	Y	Y	N	N	N
5 **Gillmor**	Y	Y	Y	Y	Y	Y	Y	N
6 Strickland	Y	Y	Y	Y	Y	Y	Y	Y
7 **Hobson**	Y	Y	Y	Y	Y	N	N	N
8 **Boehner**	Y	N	Y	Y	Y	N	N	N
9 Kaptur	Y	Y	Y	Y	Y	Y	Y	Y
10 **Hoke**	Y	Y	Y	N	Y	?	N	N
11 Stokes	Y	Y	Y	Y	Y	Y	Y	Y
12 **Kasich**	Y	Y	Y	Y	Y	N	N	N
13 Brown	Y	Y	Y	Y	Y	Y	Y	Y
14 Sawyer	Y	Y	Y	Y	Y	Y	Y	Y
15 **Pryce**	Y	Y	Y	Y	Y	N	N	N
16 **Regula**	Y	Y	Y	Y	Y	N	N	N
17 Traficant	Y	Y	Y	Y	Y	Y	Y	Y
18 Applegate	Y	Y	Y	Y	Y	Y	Y	Y
19 Fingerhut	Y	Y	Y	Y	Y	Y	Y	Y
OKLAHOMA								
1 **Inhofe**	Y	Y	Y	Y	Y	N	N	N
2 Synar	Y	Y	Y	Y	Y	Y	Y	Y
3 Brewster	Y	Y	Y	Y	Y	Y	Y	Y
4 McCurdy	Y	Y	Y	Y	Y	?	Y	Y
5 **Istook**	Y	Y	Y	Y	Y	N	N	N
6 English	Y	Y	Y	Y	Y	?	Y	Y
OREGON								
1 Furse	Y	Y	Y	Y	Y	Y	Y	Y
2 **Smith**	Y	Y	Y	Y	Y	N	N	N
3 Wyden	Y	Y	Y	Y	Y	Y	Y	Y
4 DeFazio	Y	Y	Y	Y	Y	Y	Y	Y
5 Kopetski	Y	Y	Y	Y	Y	Y	Y	Y
PENNSYLVANIA								
1 Foglietta	Y	Y	Y	Y	Y	Y	Y	Y
2 Blackwell	Y	Y	Y	Y	Y	Y	Y	Y
3 Borski	Y	Y	Y	Y	Y	Y	Y	Y
4 Klink	Y	Y	Y	Y	Y	Y	Y	Y
5 **Clinger**	Y	Y	Y	Y	Y	N	Y	N
6 Holden	Y	Y	Y	Y	Y	Y	Y	Y
7 **Weldon**	Y	Y	Y	Y	Y	N	N	N
8 **Greenwood**	Y	Y	Y	Y	Y	N	N	N
9 **Shuster**	Y	Y	Y	Y	Y	N	N	N
10 **McDade**	?	?	?	?	?	?	?	?
11 Kanjorski	Y	Y	Y	Y	Y	Y	Y	Y
12 Murtha	Y	Y	Y	Y	Y	Y	Y	Y
13 Margolies-Mezv.	Y	Y	Y	Y	Y	Y	Y	Y
14 Coyne	Y	Y	Y	Y	Y	Y	Y	Y
15 McHale	Y	Y	Y	Y	Y	Y	Y	Y
16 **Walker**	Y	N	Y	Y	N	N	N	N
17 **Gekas**	Y	N	Y	Y	Y	N	N	N
18 **Santorum**	Y	N	Y	Y	Y	N	Y	N
19 **Goodling**	Y	Y	Y	Y	Y	N	N	N
20 Murphy	Y	Y	Y	Y	Y	N	N	Y
21 **Ridge**	Y	Y	Y	Y	Y	N	N	N
RHODE ISLAND								
1 **Machtley**	Y	Y	Y	Y	Y	N	N	N
2 Reed	Y	Y	Y	Y	Y	Y	Y	Y
SOUTH CAROLINA								
1 **Ravenel**	Y	Y	Y	Y	Y	Y	Y	N
2 **Spence**	Y	Y	Y	Y	Y	N	N	N
3 Derrick	Y	Y	Y	Y	Y	Y	Y	Y
4 **Inglis**	Y	Y	Y	Y	Y	Y	Y	N
5 Spratt	Y	Y	Y	Y	Y	Y	Y	Y
6 Clyburn	Y	Y	Y	Y	Y	Y	Y	Y
SOUTH DAKOTA								
AL Johnson	Y	Y	Y	Y	Y	Y	Y	Y
TENNESSEE								
1 **Quillen**	Y	Y	Y	Y	Y	N	N	Y
2 **Duncan**	Y	N	Y	Y	Y	N	N	N
3 Lloyd	Y	Y	Y	Y	Y	Y	?	Y
4 Cooper	Y	Y	Y	Y	Y	Y	Y	Y
5 Clement	Y	Y	Y	Y	Y	Y	Y	Y

	43	44	45	46	47	48	49	50
6 Gordon	Y	Y	Y	Y	Y	Y	Y	Y
7 **Sundquist**	Y	N	Y	Y	N	N	N	Y
8 Tanner	Y	Y	Y	Y	Y	Y	Y	Y
9 Ford	?	?	?	?	?	?	?	?
TEXAS								
1 Chapman	Y	Y	Y	Y	Y	Y	Y	Y
2 Wilson	?	?	?	?	?	?	Y	Y
3 **Johnson, Sam**	Y	N	Y	Y	Y	N	N	N
4 Hall	Y	Y	Y	Y	Y	Y	Y	Y
5 Bryant	?	?	?	?	?	?	Y	?
6 **Barton**	?	?	?	?	?	?	N	N
7 **Archer**	Y	N	Y	Y	Y	Y	Y	N
8 **Fields**	?	?	?	?	?	?	?	?
9 Brooks	?	Y	Y	Y	Y	Y	Y	Y
10 Pickle	Y	Y	Y	Y	Y	Y	Y	Y
11 Edwards	Y	Y	Y	Y	Y	?	Y	Y
12 Geren	Y	Y	Y	Y	Y	Y	Y	Y
13 Sarpalius	Y	Y	Y	Y	Y	Y	Y	Y
14 Laughlin	Y	Y	Y	Y	Y	Y	Y	Y
15 de la Garza	Y	Y	Y	Y	Y	Y	Y	Y
16 Coleman	Y	Y	Y	Y	Y	Y	Y	Y
17 Stenholm	Y	Y	Y	Y	Y	Y	Y	Y
18 Washington	Y	Y	Y	Y	Y	Y	?	?
19 **Combest**	Y	Y	Y	Y	Y	Y	Y	N
20 Gonzalez	Y	Y	Y	Y	Y	Y	Y	Y
21 **Smith**	Y	Y	Y	Y	Y	N	N	N
22 **DeLay**	Y	N	Y	Y	N	N	?	N
23 **Bonilla**	Y	Y	Y	Y	Y	N	N	N
24 Frost	Y	Y	Y	Y	Y	Y	Y	Y
25 Andrews	Y	Y	Y	Y	Y	Y	Y	Y
26 **Armey**	Y	N	Y	Y	Y	N	N	N
27 Ortiz	Y	Y	Y	Y	Y	Y	Y	Y
28 Tejeda	Y	Y	Y	Y	Y	Y	Y	Y
29 Green	Y	Y	Y	Y	Y	Y	Y	Y
30 Johnson, E. B.	Y	Y	Y	Y	Y	Y	Y	Y
UTAH								
1 **Hansen**	Y	Y	Y	Y	Y	N	Y	N
2 Shepherd	Y	Y	Y	Y	Y	Y	Y	Y
3 Orton	Y	Y	Y	Y	Y	Y	Y	Y
VERMONT								
AL *Sanders*	Y	Y	Y	Y	Y	Y	Y	Y
VIRGINIA								
1 **Bateman**	Y	Y	Y	Y	Y	Y	Y	N
2 Pickett	Y	Y	Y	Y	Y	Y	Y	Y
3 Scott	Y	Y	Y	Y	Y	Y	Y	Y
4 Sisisky	Y	Y	Y	Y	Y	Y	?	Y
5 Payne	Y	Y	Y	Y	Y	Y	?	Y
6 **Goodlatte**	Y	Y	Y	Y	Y	N	N	N
7 **Bliley**	Y	Y	Y	Y	Y	N	N	N
8 Moran	Y	Y	Y	Y	Y	Y	Y	Y
9 Boucher	Y	Y	Y	Y	Y	Y	Y	Y
10 **Wolf**	Y	Y	Y	Y	Y	N	N	N
11 Byrne	Y	Y	Y	Y	Y	Y	?	Y
WASHINGTON								
1 Cantwell	Y	Y	Y	Y	Y	Y	Y	Y
2 Swift	Y	Y	Y	Y	Y	Y	Y	Y
3 Unsoeld	Y	Y	Y	Y	Y	Y	Y	Y
4 Inslee	Y	Y	Y	Y	Y	Y	Y	Y
5 Foley							Y	
6 Dicks	Y	Y	Y	Y	Y	Y	Y	Y
7 McDermott	Y	Y	Y	Y	Y	Y	Y	Y
8 **Dunn**	Y	Y	Y	Y	Y	N	N	N
9 Kreidler	Y	Y	Y	Y	Y	Y	Y	Y
WEST VIRGINIA								
1 Mollohan	Y	Y	Y	Y	Y	Y	Y	Y
2 Wise	Y	Y	Y	Y	Y	Y	Y	Y
3 Rahall	Y	Y	Y	Y	Y	Y	Y	Y
WISCONSIN								
1 Vacancy								
2 **Klug**	Y	N	Y	Y	Y	N	N	N
3 **Gunderson**	Y	Y	Y	Y	Y	Y	Y	N
4 Kleczka	Y	Y	Y	Y	Y	Y	Y	Y
5 Barrett	Y	Y	Y	Y	Y	Y	Y	Y
6 **Petri**	Y	Y	Y	Y	Y	N	N	N
7 Obey	Y	Y	Y	Y	Y	Y	Y	Y
8 **Roth**	Y	Y	Y	Y	Y	N	Y	N
9 **Sensenbrenner**	Y	N	Y	Y	Y	N	N	N
WYOMING								
AL **Thomas**	Y	Y	Y	Y	Y	N	N	N
DELEGATES								
de Lugo, V.I.	D	D	D	D	D	D	D	D
Faleomavaega, Am.S.	D	D	D	D	D	D	D	D
Norton, D.C.	D	D	D	D	D	D	D	D
Romero-B., P.R.	D	D	D	D	D	D	D	D
Underwood, Guam	D	D	D	D	D	D	D	D

Southern states - Ala., Ark., Fla., Ga., Ky., La., Miss., N.C., Okla., S.C., Tenn., Texas, Va.
Omitted votes are quorum calls, which CQ does not include in its vote charts.

KEY

Y   Voted for (yea).
Paired for.
+   Announced for.
N   Voted against (nay).
X   Paired against.
−   Announced against.
P   Voted "present."
C   Voted "present" to avoid possible conflict of interest.
?   Did not vote or otherwise make a position known.
D   Delegates ineligible to vote.

Democrats *Republicans*
Independent

51. HR 20. Hatch Act Revision/Rule. Adoption of the rule (H Res 106) to provide for House floor consideration of the bill to amend the 1939 Hatch Act barring federal employees from most political activities, to allow federal employees and postal workers to run for office, hold positions in political parties and volunteer for campaigns during non-working hours. Adopted 249-163: R 6-161; D 242-2 (ND 163-2, SD 79-0); I 1-0, March 3, 1993.

52. HR 20. Hatch Act Revision/Passage. Passage of the bill to amend the 1939 Hatch Act barring federal employees from most political activities, to allow federal employees and postal workers to run for office, hold positions in political parties and volunteer for campaigns during non-working hours. Passed 333-86: R 85-84; D 247-2 (ND 166-2, SD 81-0); I 1-0, March 3, 1993. A "yea" was a vote in support of the president's position.

53. HR 920. Unemployment Benefits Extension/Benefits Provisions. Motion to agree to Sections 1 through 6 of the Senate amendment to the bill to provide $5.7 billion to allow for the processing of claims from March 6 through Oct. 2 for federal extended emergency unemployment benefits and designate the funding as emergency spending and thus exempt from the pay-as-you-go budget rules. Motion agreed to 247-156: R 30-137; D 216-19 (ND 153-5, SD 63-14); I 1-0, March 4, 1993. A "yea" was a vote in support of the president's position.

54. HR 920. Unemployment Benefits Extension/COLA Provision. Motion to agree to Section 7 of the Senate amendment to the bill, which eliminates the cost of living adjustment for members of Congress in fiscal 1994. Motion agreed to (thus clearing the bill for the president) 403-0: R 164-0; D 238-0 (ND 162-0, SD 76-0); I 1-0, March 4, 1993.

55. HR 490. Columbia Hospital for Women Land Conveyance. Motion to suspend the rules and pass the bill to authorize the sale by the General Services Administration of 1.2 acres of land in the District of Columbia for $12.8 million to the Columbia Hospital for Women to enable the hospital to construct the National Women's Health Resource Center. Motion agreed to 339-69: R 99-69; D 240-0 (ND 162-0, SD 78-0); I 0-0, March 9, 1993. A two-thirds majority of those present and voting (272 in this case) is required for passage under suspension of the rules.

56. Procedural Motion. Approval of the House Journal of Monday, March 8. Approved 256-153: R 21-147; D 235-6 (ND 159-5, SD 76-1); I 0-0, March 9, 1993.

57. Procedural Motion. Approval of the House Journal of Tuesday, March 9. Approved 251-150: R 22-145; D 228-5 (ND 154-4, SD 74-1); I 1-0, March 10, 1993.

58. HR 4. National Institutes of Health Reauthorization/Previous Question. Slaughter, D-N.Y., motion to order the previous question (thus ending debate and the possibility of amendment) on adoption of the rule (H Res 119) to provide for House floor consideration of the bill to authorize $6.6 billion for the National Institutes of Health in fiscal 1994 and such sums as necessary in fiscal 1995-96. The bill codifies the Clinton executive order lifting the ban on fetal tissue research from induced abortions. Motion agreed to 247-170: R 2-169; D 244-1 (ND 165-1, SD 79-0); I 1-0, March 10, 1993.

	51	52	53	54	55	56	57	58
ALABAMA								
1 *Callahan*	N	N	N	+	N	N	N	N
2 *Everett*	N	Y	Y	+	Y	N	N	N
3 Browder	Y	Y	Y	Y	Y	Y	?	Y
4 Bevill	Y	Y	Y	Y	Y	Y	Y	Y
5 Cramer	Y	Y	Y	Y	Y	Y	Y	Y
6 *Bachus*	N	N	N	Y	Y	N	N	N
7 Hilliard	Y	Y	Y	Y	Y	?	Y	Y
ALASKA								
AL *Young*	?	#	?	?	?	N	N	N
ARIZONA								
1 Coppersmith	Y	Y	Y	Y	Y	Y	Y	Y
2 Pastor	Y	Y	Y	Y	Y	Y	Y	Y
3 *Stump*	N	N	N	Y	N	N	N	N
4 *Kyl*	N	N	N	Y	N	N	N	N
5 *Kolbe*	N	Y	N	Y	N	N	N	N
6 English	Y	Y	Y	Y	Y	Y	Y	Y
ARKANSAS								
1 Lambert	Y	Y	Y	Y	Y	Y	Y	Y
2 Thornton	Y	Y	Y	Y	Y	Y	Y	Y
3 *Hutchinson*	N	N	N	Y	Y	?	N	N
4 Dickey	N	Y	N	Y	+	N	N	N
CALIFORNIA								
1 Hamburg	Y	Y	Y	Y	Y	Y	Y	Y
2 *Herger*	N	N	N	Y	N	N	N	N
3 Fazio	Y	Y	Y	Y	Y	Y	Y	Y
4 *Doolittle*	N	N	N	Y	N	N	N	N
5 Matsui	Y	Y	Y	Y	Y	Y	Y	Y
6 Woolsey	Y	Y	Y	Y	Y	Y	Y	Y
7 Miller	Y	Y	?	Y	Y	Y	Y	Y
8 Pelosi	Y	Y	Y	Y	Y	Y	Y	Y
9 Dellums	Y	Y	Y	#	?	?	?	?
10 *Baker*	N	N	N	Y	N	N	N	N
11 *Pombo*	N	N	N	Y	Y	N	N	Y
12 Lantos	Y	Y	Y	Y	Y	Y	Y	Y
13 Stark	Y	Y	Y	Y	Y	Y	Y	Y
14 Eshoo	Y	Y	Y	Y	Y	Y	Y	Y
15 Mineta	Y	Y	Y	Y	Y	Y	Y	Y
16 Edwards	Y	Y	Y	Y	Y	Y	Y	Y
17 Vacancy								
18 Condit	Y	Y	Y	Y	?	?	Y	Y
19 Lehman	Y	Y	Y	Y	Y	Y	Y	Y
20 Dooley	Y	Y	Y	Y	Y	Y	Y	Y
21 *Thomas*	N	Y	N	Y	Y	N	N	N
22 *Huffington*	N	N	N	Y	Y	N	N	N
23 *Gallegly*	N	N	N	Y	N	N	N	N
24 Beilenson	N	N	Y	Y	Y	Y	Y	Y
25 *McKeon*	N	N	N	Y	Y	N	N	N
26 Berman	Y	Y	Y	Y	Y	Y	Y	Y
27 *Moorhead*	N	N	N	Y	N	N	N	N
28 *Dreier*	N	N	N	Y	N	N	N	N
29 Waxman	Y	Y	Y	Y	Y	Y	Y	Y
30 Becerra	Y	Y	Y	Y	Y	Y	Y	Y
31 Martinez	Y	Y	Y	Y	Y	Y	Y	Y
32 Dixon	Y	Y	Y	Y	Y	Y	Y	Y
33 Roybal-Allard	Y	Y	Y	Y	Y	Y	Y	Y
34 Torres	Y	Y	Y	Y	Y	Y	?	Y
35 Waters	Y	Y	Y	Y	Y	Y	Y	Y
36 Harman	Y	Y	Y	Y	Y	?	Y	Y
37 Tucker	Y	Y	?	?	Y	Y	Y	Y
38 *Horn*	N	Y	Y	Y	Y	N	N	N
39 *Royce*	N	N	N	Y	N	N	N	N
40 *Lewis*	N	N	N	Y	N	N	N	N
41 *Kim*	N	N	N	Y	N	N	N	N

	51	52	53	54	55	56	57	58
42 Brown	Y	Y	Y	Y	Y	Y	Y	Y
43 *Calvert*	N	N	N	Y	N	Y	N	N
44 *McCandless*	N	N	N	Y	N	N	N	N
45 *Rohrabacher*	N	N	N	Y	N	N	N	N
46 *Dornan*	N	N	N	Y	N	N	N	N
47 *Cox*	?	?	?	?	?	?	N	N
48 *Packard*	N	N	N	Y	N	N	N	N
49 Schenk	Y	Y	Y	Y	Y	Y	Y	Y
50 Filner	Y	Y	Y	Y	Y	Y	Y	Y
51 *Cunningham*	N	N	N	Y	X	?	?	N
52 *Hunter*	N	N	N	Y	N	N	N	N
COLORADO								
1 Schroeder	Y	Y	Y	Y	Y	N	N	Y
2 Skaggs	Y	Y	Y	Y	Y	Y	Y	Y
3 McInnis	N	N	N	Y	N	N	N	N
4 *Allard*	N	N	N	Y	N	N	N	N
5 *Hefley*	N	N	N	Y	N	N	N	N
6 *Schaefer*	N	Y	N	Y	N	N	N	N
CONNECTICUT								
1 Kennelly	Y	Y	Y	Y	Y	Y	Y	Y
2 Gejdenson	Y	Y	Y	Y	?	Y	Y	Y
3 DeLauro	Y	Y	Y	Y	Y	Y	Y	Y
4 *Shays*	Y	Y	N	Y	Y	N	N	Y
5 *Franks*	N	N	N	Y	N	Y	?	?
6 *Johnson*	N	Y	Y	Y	Y	N	N	N
DELAWARE								
AL *Castle*	N	Y	N	Y	Y	N	N	N
FLORIDA								
1 Hutto	Y	Y	N	Y	Y	Y	Y	Y
2 Peterson	Y	Y	Y	Y	Y	Y	Y	Y
3 Brown	Y	Y	Y	Y	Y	Y	Y	Y
4 *Fowler*	N	N	N	Y	N	N	N	N
5 Thurman	Y	Y	Y	Y	Y	Y	Y	Y
6 *Stearns*	N	N	N	Y	N	N	N	N
7 *Mica*	N	N	N	Y	N	N	N	N
8 *McCollum*	N	N	N	Y	N	Y	N	N
9 *Bilirakis*	N	Y	N	Y	N	N	N	N
10 *Young*	?	Y	N	Y	N	N	N	?
11 Gibbons	Y	Y	Y	Y	?	?	Y	?
12 *Canady*	N	N	N	Y	Y	N	N	N
13 *Miller*	N	Y	N	Y	N	N	N	N
14 *Goss*	N	Y	N	Y	N	N	N	N
15 Bacchus	Y	Y	Y	Y	Y	Y	Y	Y
16 *Lewis*	N	N	N	Y	N	N	N	N
17 Meek	Y	Y	Y	Y	Y	?	Y	?
18 *Ros-Lehtinen*	N	Y	N	Y	Y	N	N	N
19 Johnston	Y	Y	Y	Y	Y	Y	Y	Y
20 Deutsch	Y	Y	Y	Y	Y	Y	Y	Y
21 *Diaz-Balart*	N	Y	N	Y	Y	N	N	N
22 *Shaw*	N	Y	N	Y	Y	N	N	N
23 Hastings	Y	Y	Y	Y	?	?	?	?
GEORGIA								
1 *Kingston*	N	N	N	Y	N	N	Y	N
2 Bishop	Y	Y	Y	Y	Y	?	?	?
3 *Collins*	N	Y	Y	Y	N	N	?	N
4 *Linder*	N	N	N	Y	N	N	N	N
5 Lewis	Y	Y	Y	Y	Y	Y	Y	Y
6 *Gingrich*	N	N	N	Y	N	N	N	N
7 Darden	Y	Y	Y	Y	Y	Y	Y	Y
8 Rowland	Y	Y	Y	Y	Y	Y	Y	Y
9 Deal	Y	Y	Y	Y	Y	Y	Y	Y
10 Johnson	Y	Y	N	Y	Y	Y	Y	Y
11 McKinney	Y	Y	Y	Y	Y	Y	Y	Y
HAWAII								
1 Abercrombie	Y	Y	Y	Y	Y	Y	?	Y
2 Mink	Y	Y	Y	Y	Y	Y	Y	Y
IDAHO								
1 LaRocco	Y	Y	Y	Y	Y	Y	Y	Y
2 *Crapo*	N	N	N	Y	N	N	N	N
ILLINOIS								
1 Rush	Y	Y	+	Y	Y	Y	Y	Y
2 Reynolds	Y	Y	Y	Y	Y	Y	Y	Y
3 Lipinski	Y	Y	Y	Y	Y	Y	Y	Y
4 Gutierrez	Y	Y	?	Y	Y	Y	Y	Y
5 Rostenkowski	?	?	?	?	Y	Y	Y	Y
6 *Hyde*	N	Y	N	Y	Y	Y	N	N
7 Collins	Y	Y	Y	Y	Y	Y	Y	Y
8 *Crane*	N	N	N	Y	N	N	N	N
9 Yates	Y	Y	Y	Y	Y	Y	Y	Y
10 *Porter*	N	N	N	Y	Y	N	N	N
11 Sangmeister	Y	Y	Y	Y	Y	Y	Y	Y
12 Costello	Y	Y	Y	Y	Y	Y	Y	Y
13 *Fawell*	N	N	N	Y	N	N	N	N
14 *Hastert*	N	Y	N	Y	N	N	N	N
15 *Ewing*	N	N	N	Y	N	N	N	N
16 *Manzullo*	N	N	N	Y	N	N	N	N
17 Evans	?	Y	Y	Y	Y	Y	Y	Y

ND Northern Democrats   SD Southern Democrats

	51	52	53	54	55	56	57	58
18 ***Michel***	N	Y	N	Y	Y	N	N	N
19 Poshard	Y	Y	Y	Y	Y	Y	Y	Y
20 Durbin	Y	Y	Y	Y	Y	Y	Y	Y
INDIANA								
1 Visclosky	Y	Y	Y	Y	Y	Y	Y	Y
2 Sharp	?	Y	Y	Y	?	Y	Y	Y
3 Roemer	+	+	Y	Y	Y	Y	?	Y
4 Long	Y	Y	Y	Y	Y	Y	Y	Y
5 ***Buyer***	N	Y	N	Y	N	N	N	N
6 ***Burton***	N	Y	N	Y	N	N	N	N
7 ***Myers***	N	Y	N	Y	N	Y	N	N
8 McCloskey	Y	Y	Y	Y	Y	Y	Y	Y
9 Hamilton	Y	Y	Y	Y	Y	Y	Y	Y
10 Jacobs	Y	Y	Y	Y	Y	N	N	Y
IOWA								
1 ***Leach***	N	N	N	Y	Y	N	N	N
2 ***Nussle***	N	N	N	Y	Y	N	N	N
3 ***Lightfoot***	N	N	N	Y	Y	N	N	N
4 Smith	Y	Y	Y	P	Y	Y	Y	?
5 ***Grandy***	N	Y	N	Y	Y	N	N	N
KANSAS								
1 ***Roberts***	N	N	N	Y	Y	N	N	N
2 Slattery	Y	Y	Y	Y	Y	Y	Y	Y
3 ***Meyers***	N	Y	N	Y	N	N	N	N
4 Glickman	Y	Y	Y	Y	Y	Y	Y	Y
KENTUCKY								
1 Barlow	Y	Y	Y	Y	Y	Y	Y	Y
2 Natcher	Y	Y	Y	Y	Y	Y	Y	Y
3 Mazzoli	Y	Y	Y	Y	Y	Y	Y	Y
4 ***Bunning***	N	N	N	Y	Y	N	N	N
5 ***Rogers***	N	N	Y	Y	Y	N	N	N
6 Baesler	Y	Y	Y	Y	Y	Y	Y	Y
LOUISIANA								
1 ***Livingston***	N	Y	N	Y	N	N	N	N
2 Jefferson	Y	Y	?	?	Y	Y	Y	Y
3 Tauzin	Y	Y	Y	Y	Y	Y	?	Y
4 Fields	Y	Y	Y	Y	Y	Y	Y	Y
5 ***McCrery***	N	N	N	Y	Y	N	N	N
6 ***Baker***	N	N	N	Y	N	N	N	N
7 Hayes	Y	Y	Y	Y	Y	Y	Y	Y
MAINE								
1 Andrews	Y	Y	Y	Y	Y	Y	Y	Y
2 ***Snowe***	N	N	Y	Y	Y	Y	Y	N
MARYLAND								
1 ***Gilchrest***	N	Y	Y	Y	Y	N	N	N
2 ***Bentley***	N	Y	Y	N	N	N	N	N
3 Cardin	Y	Y	Y	Y	Y	Y	Y	Y
4 Wynn	Y	Y	Y	Y	Y	Y	Y	Y
5 Hoyer	Y	Y	Y	Y	Y	Y	Y	Y
6 ***Bartlett***	N	Y	N	Y	N	N	N	N
7 Mfume	Y	Y	Y	Y	Y	N	Y	Y
8 ***Morella***	Y	Y	Y	Y	Y	N	N	Y
MASSACHUSETTS								
1 Olver	Y	Y	Y	Y	Y	Y	Y	Y
2 Neal	Y	Y	Y	Y	Y	Y	Y	Y
3 ***Blute***	N	N	Y	Y	Y	N	N	N
4 Frank	Y	Y	Y	Y	Y	Y	Y	Y
5 Meehan	Y	Y	Y	Y	Y	Y	Y	Y
6 ***Torkildsen***	N	Y	Y	Y	Y	N	N	N
7 Markey	Y	Y	Y	Y	Y	Y	Y	Y
8 Kennedy	Y	Y	Y	Y	Y	Y	Y	Y
9 Moakley	Y	Y	Y	Y	Y	Y	Y	Y
10 Studds	Y	Y	Y	Y	Y	Y	Y	Y
MICHIGAN								
1 Stupak	Y	Y	Y	Y	Y	Y	Y	Y
2 ***Hoekstra***	N	N	Y	Y	Y	N	N	N
3 Henry	?	?	?	?	?	?	?	?
4 ***Camp***	N	N	N	Y	Y	N	N	N
5 Barcia	Y	Y	+	+	Y	Y	Y	Y
6 ***Upton***	N	N	Y	Y	N	N	N	N
7 ***Smith***	N	N	N	Y	Y	N	N	N
8 Carr	Y	Y	?	Y	Y	Y	Y	Y
9 Kildee	Y	Y	Y	Y	Y	Y	Y	Y
10 Bonior	Y	Y	?	?	Y	Y	Y	Y
11 ***Knollenberg***	N	N	N	Y	N	N	N	N
12 Levin	Y	Y	Y	Y	Y	Y	Y	Y
13 Ford	Y	Y	Y	Y	Y	Y	Y	Y
14 Conyers	?	Y	Y	Y	Y	Y	?	?
15 Collins	Y	Y	Y	Y	Y	Y	Y	Y
16 Dingell	Y	Y	?	+	Y	Y	Y	Y
MINNESOTA								
1 Penny	Y	Y	N	Y	Y	Y	Y	Y
2 Minge	Y	Y	N	Y	Y	Y	Y	Y
3 ***Ramstad***	N	Y	N	Y	Y	N	N	N
4 Vento	Y	Y	Y	Y	Y	Y	Y	Y

	51	52	53	54	55	56	57	58
5 Sabo	Y	Y	Y	Y	Y	Y	Y	Y
6 ***Grams***	N	N	N	Y	N	N	N	N
7 Peterson	Y	Y	Y	Y	Y	Y	Y	Y
8 Oberstar	Y	Y	Y	Y	Y	Y	Y	Y
MISSISSIPPI								
1 Whitten	Y	Y	Y	Y	Y	Y	?	Y
2 Vacancy								
3 Montgomery	Y	Y	N	Y	Y	Y	Y	Y
4 Parker	Y	Y	N	Y	Y	Y	Y	Y
5 Taylor	Y	Y	N	Y	Y	N	N	Y
MISSOURI								
1 Clay	Y	Y	Y	Y	Y	N	N	Y
2 ***Talent***	N	N	N	Y	Y	N	N	N
3 Gephardt	Y	Y	Y	Y	Y	Y	Y	Y
4 Skelton	Y	Y	Y	Y	Y	Y	Y	Y
5 Wheat	Y	Y	Y	Y	Y	Y	Y	Y
6 Danner	Y	Y	Y	Y	Y	Y	Y	Y
7 ***Hancock***	N	N	N	Y	N	N	N	N
8 ***Emerson***	N	Y	Y	Y	N	N	N	N
9 Volkmer	Y	Y	Y	Y	Y	Y	Y	Y
MONTANA								
AL Williams	Y	Y	Y	Y	Y	Y	Y	Y
NEBRASKA								
1 ***Bereuter***	N	Y	N	Y	Y	N	N	N
2 Hoagland	Y	Y	Y	Y	Y	Y	?	?
3 ***Barrett***	N	N	N	Y	Y	N	N	N
NEVADA								
1 Bilbray	Y	Y	Y	Y	Y	Y	Y	Y
2 ***Vucanovich***	N	Y	N	Y	N	N	N	N
NEW HAMPSHIRE								
1 ***Zeliff***	N	Y	N	Y	N	N	N	N
2 Swett	Y	Y	Y	Y	Y	Y	?	Y
NEW JERSEY								
1 Andrews	Y	Y	Y	Y	Y	Y	Y	Y
2 Hughes	Y	Y	Y	Y	Y	Y	Y	Y
3 ***Saxton***	N	Y	N	Y	Y	N	N	N
4 ***Smith***	N	Y	Y	Y	N	Y	Y	N
5 ***Roukema***	X	X	?	?	Y	N	N	N
6 Pallone	Y	Y	Y	Y	Y	Y	Y	Y
7 ***Franks***	N	Y	N	Y	Y	N	N	N
8 Klein	Y	Y	+	Y	Y	Y	Y	Y
9 Torricelli	Y	Y	Y	Y	Y	Y	Y	Y
10 Payne	Y	Y	Y	Y	Y	Y	Y	Y
11 ***Gallo***	N	Y	Y	Y	Y	N	N	N
12 ***Zimmer***	N	Y	N	Y	N	N	N	N
13 Menendez	Y	Y	Y	Y	Y	Y	Y	Y
NEW MEXICO								
1 ***Schiff***	N	N	N	Y	N	N	N	N
2 ***Skeen***	N	Y	N	Y	Y	N	N	N
3 Richardson	Y	Y	Y	Y	Y	Y	Y	Y
NEW YORK								
1 Hochbrueckner	Y	Y	Y	Y	Y	Y	Y	Y
2 ***Lazio***	N	Y	N	Y	Y	N	N	N
3 ***King***	N	Y	N	Y	N	N	N	N
4 ***Levy***	N	Y	N	Y	Y	N	N	N
5 Ackerman	Y	Y	Y	Y	Y	Y	Y	Y
6 Flake	Y	Y	Y	Y	Y	Y	?	Y
7 Manton	Y	Y	Y	Y	Y	Y	Y	Y
8 Nadler	Y	Y	Y	Y	Y	Y	Y	Y
9 Schumer	Y	Y	Y	Y	Y	Y	Y	Y
10 Towns	Y	Y	Y	Y	Y	Y	Y	Y
11 Owens	Y	Y	Y	Y	?	Y	Y	Y
12 Velazquez	Y	Y	Y	Y	Y	Y	Y	Y
13 ***Molinari***	N	Y	Y	Y	Y	N	N	N
14 Maloney	Y	Y	Y	?	#	+	Y	Y
15 Rangel	Y	Y	Y	Y	Y	Y	Y	Y
16 Serrano	Y	Y	Y	Y	Y	Y	Y	Y
17 Engel	Y	Y	Y	Y	Y	Y	Y	Y
18 Lowey	Y	Y	Y	Y	Y	Y	Y	Y
19 ***Fish***	N	Y	Y	Y	Y	Y	?	N
20 ***Gilman***	N	Y	Y	Y	Y	Y	Y	N
21 McNulty	Y	Y	Y	Y	Y	Y	Y	Y
22 ***Solomon***	N	Y	Y	Y	Y	N	N	N
23 ***Boehlert***	N	Y	Y	Y	Y	N	N	N
24 ***McHugh***	N	Y	Y	Y	Y	N	N	N
25 ***Walsh***	N	Y	Y	Y	Y	N	N	N
26 Hinchey	Y	Y	Y	Y	Y	Y	Y	Y
27 ***Paxon***	N	N	?	?	Y	N	N	N
28 Slaughter	Y	Y	Y	Y	Y	Y	Y	Y
29 LaFalce	Y	Y	Y	Y	Y	Y	?	Y
30 ***Quinn***	N	Y	Y	Y	Y	N	N	N
31 ***Houghton***	N	Y	N	Y	Y	Y	Y	N
NORTH CAROLINA								
1 Clayton	#	Y	+	+	Y	Y	?	Y
2 Valentine	?	?	?	?	Y	Y	Y	Y

	51	52	53	54	55	56	57	58
3 Lancaster	Y	Y	Y	Y	Y	Y	Y	Y
4 Price	Y	Y	Y	Y	Y	Y	Y	Y
5 Neal	Y	Y	Y	Y	Y	Y	?	Y
6 ***Coble***	N	N	N	Y	N	N	N	N
7 Rose	Y	Y	Y	Y	Y	Y	Y	Y
8 Hefner	Y	Y	Y	Y	Y	Y	Y	Y
9 ***McMillan***	N	Y	N	Y	N	N	N	N
10 ***Ballenger***	N	N	N	Y	N	N	N	N
11 ***Taylor***	–	N	N	Y	N	N	N	N
12 Watt	Y	Y	Y	Y	?	?	Y	Y
NORTH DAKOTA								
AL Pomeroy	Y	Y	Y	Y	Y	Y	Y	Y
OHIO								
1 Mann	Y	Y	N	Y	Y	Y	Y	Y
2 Vacancy								
3 Hall	Y	Y	Y	Y	Y	Y	?	Y
4 ***Oxley***	N	Y	N	Y	N	N	N	N
5 ***Gillmor***	N	Y	Y	Y	Y	Y	Y	N
6 Strickland	Y	Y	+	+	Y	Y	Y	Y
7 ***Hobson***	N	Y	N	Y	Y	N	N	N
8 ***Boehner***	N	N	N	P	Y	N	N	N
9 Kaptur	Y	Y	Y	Y	Y	Y	Y	Y
10 ***Hoke***	N	Y	N	Y	Y	N	N	N
11 Stokes	Y	Y	Y	Y	Y	Y	Y	Y
12 ***Kasich***	N	Y	N	Y	N	Y	Y	N
13 Brown	Y	Y	Y	Y	Y	Y	Y	Y
14 Sawyer	Y	Y	Y	Y	Y	Y	Y	Y
15 ***Pryce***	N	Y	N	Y	Y	N	N	N
16 ***Regula***	N	Y	Y	Y	Y	N	N	N
17 Traficant	Y	Y	Y	Y	Y	Y	Y	Y
18 Applegate	Y	Y	Y	Y	Y	Y	Y	Y
19 Fingerhut	Y	Y	Y	Y	Y	Y	Y	Y
OKLAHOMA								
1 ***Inhofe***	N	N	N	Y	N	N	N	N
2 Synar	Y	Y	Y	Y	Y	Y	Y	Y
3 Brewster	Y	Y	Y	Y	Y	Y	Y	Y
4 McCurdy	Y	Y	N	Y	Y	Y	Y	Y
5 ***Istook***	N	N	N	Y	N	N	N	N
6 English	Y	Y	N	Y	Y	Y	Y	Y
OREGON								
1 Furse	Y	Y	Y	Y	Y	Y	Y	Y
2 ***Smith***	N	Y	N	Y	N	N	N	N
3 Wyden	Y	Y	Y	Y	Y	Y	Y	Y
4 DeFazio	Y	Y	Y	Y	?	?	Y	Y
5 Kopetski	Y	Y	Y	Y	Y	Y	Y	Y
PENNSYLVANIA								
1 Foglietta	N	N	Y	Y	Y	Y	Y	Y
2 Blackwell	Y	Y	Y	Y	Y	Y	Y	Y
3 Borski	Y	Y	Y	Y	Y	Y	Y	Y
4 Klink	Y	Y	Y	Y	Y	Y	Y	Y
5 ***Clinger***	N	Y	N	Y	Y	Y	Y	N
6 Holden	Y	Y	Y	Y	Y	Y	Y	N
7 ***Weldon***	N	Y	N	Y	Y	N	N	N
8 ***Greenwood***	N	N	?	?	Y	N	N	N
9 ***Shuster***	N	N	N	Y	Y	N	N	N
10 ***McDade***	?	?	?	?	?	?	?	?
11 Kanjorski	Y	Y	Y	Y	Y	Y	Y	Y
12 Murtha	Y	Y	Y	Y	Y	Y	Y	Y
13 Margolies-Mezv.	Y	Y	Y	Y	+	Y	Y	Y
14 Coyne	Y	Y	Y	Y	Y	Y	Y	Y
15 McHale	Y	Y	Y	Y	Y	Y	Y	Y
16 ***Walker***	N	N	N	Y	N	N	N	N
17 ***Gekas***	N	N	N	Y	N	N	N	N
18 ***Santorum***	N	Y	N	Y	N	Y	N	N
19 ***Goodling***	N	Y	N	Y	N	N	N	N
20 Murphy	Y	Y	Y	Y	Y	N	N	Y
21 ***Ridge***	Y	Y	Y	Y	Y	N	?	N
RHODE ISLAND								
1 ***Machtley***	Y	Y	Y	Y	Y	N	?	N
2 Reed	Y	Y	Y	Y	Y	Y	Y	Y
SOUTH CAROLINA								
1 ***Ravenel***	N	Y	N	Y	Y	Y	Y	N
2 ***Spence***	N	Y	N	Y	N	Y	Y	N
3 Derrick	Y	Y	Y	Y	Y	Y	Y	Y
4 ***Inglis***	N	N	N	Y	Y	Y	Y	N
5 Spratt	Y	Y	Y	Y	Y	Y	Y	Y
6 Clyburn	Y	Y	Y	Y	Y	Y	Y	Y
SOUTH DAKOTA								
AL Johnson	Y	Y	N	Y	Y	Y	Y	Y
TENNESSEE								
1 ***Quillen***	Y	Y	N	Y	Y	N	N	N
2 ***Duncan***	N	Y	N	Y	Y	Y	Y	N
3 Lloyd	Y	Y	Y	Y	Y	Y	Y	Y
4 Cooper	Y	Y	Y	Y	Y	Y	Y	Y
5 Clement	Y	Y	N	Y	Y	Y	Y	Y

	51	52	53	54	55	56	57	58
6 Gordon	Y	Y	Y	Y	Y	Y	Y	Y
7 ***Sundquist***	Y	Y	N	Y	N	N	N	N
8 Tanner	Y	Y	Y	Y	Y	Y	Y	Y
9 Ford	?	?	?	?	?	?	?	?
TEXAS								
1 Chapman	Y	Y	Y	Y	Y	Y	Y	Y
2 Wilson	Y	Y	?	?	Y	Y	Y	Y
3 ***Johnson, Sam***	N	N	N	Y	N	N	N	N
4 Hall	Y	Y	N	Y	Y	Y	Y	Y
5 Bryant	?	?	?	?	Y	Y	Y	Y
6 ***Barton***	N	N	N	Y	?	?	Y	N
7 ***Archer***	N	N	N	Y	Y	Y	Y	N
8 ***Fields***	?	?	?	?	?	?	N	N
9 Brooks	Y	Y	Y	Y	Y	Y	Y	Y
10 Pickle	Y	Y	Y	Y	Y	Y	Y	Y
11 Edwards	?	Y	N	Y	+	Y	Y	Y
12 Geren	Y	Y	?	?	Y	Y	Y	Y
13 Sarpalius	Y	Y	Y	Y	Y	Y	Y	Y
14 Laughlin	Y	Y	N	Y	Y	Y	Y	Y
15 de la Garza	Y	Y	Y	Y	Y	Y	Y	Y
16 Coleman	Y	Y	Y	Y	Y	Y	Y	Y
17 Stenholm	Y	Y	N	Y	Y	Y	Y	Y
18 Washington	Y	Y	Y	P	Y	Y	Y	Y
19 ***Combest***	N	N	N	Y	N	Y	Y	N
20 Gonzalez	Y	Y	Y	Y	Y	Y	Y	Y
21 ***Smith***	N	N	N	Y	Y	N	N	N
22 ***DeLay***	N	N	N	Y	N	N	N	N
23 ***Bonilla***	N	N	N	Y	Y	N	N	N
24 Frost	Y	Y	Y	Y	Y	Y	Y	Y
25 Andrews	Y	Y	Y	Y	Y	Y	Y	Y
26 ***Armey***	N	N	N	Y	N	N	N	N
27 Ortiz	Y	Y	Y	Y	Y	Y	Y	Y
28 Tejeda	Y	Y	Y	Y	Y	Y	Y	Y
29 Green	Y	Y	Y	Y	Y	Y	Y	Y
30 Johnson, E. B.	Y	Y	Y	Y	Y	Y	Y	Y
UTAH								
1 ***Hansen***	N	Y	N	Y	N	N	N	N
2 Shepherd	Y	Y	Y	Y	Y	Y	Y	Y
3 Orton	Y	Y	Y	Y	Y	Y	Y	Y
VERMONT								
AL *Sanders*	Y	Y	Y	Y	?	?	Y	Y
VIRGINIA								
1 ***Bateman***	N	N	N	Y	N	Y	Y	N
2 Pickett	Y	Y	N	Y	Y	Y	Y	Y
3 Scott	Y	Y	Y	Y	?	?	Y	Y
4 Sisisky	Y	Y	Y	Y	Y	Y	Y	Y
5 Payne	Y	Y	Y	Y	Y	Y	Y	Y
6 ***Goodlatte***	N	Y	N	Y	Y	N	N	N
7 ***Bliley***	N	Y	N	Y	N	N	N	N
8 Moran	Y	Y	Y	Y	Y	Y	?	Y
9 Boucher	Y	Y	Y	Y	Y	Y	Y	Y
10 ***Wolf***	N	N	N	Y	Y	N	N	N
11 Byrne	Y	Y	Y	Y	Y	Y	Y	Y
WASHINGTON								
1 Cantwell	Y	Y	Y	Y	Y	Y	Y	Y
2 Swift	Y	Y	?	Y	Y	Y	Y	Y
3 Unsoeld	Y	Y	Y	Y	Y	Y	Y	Y
4 Inslee	Y	Y	N	Y	Y	Y	Y	Y
5 Foley								
6 Dicks	Y	Y	Y	Y	Y	Y	Y	Y
7 McDermott	Y	Y	Y	Y	Y	?	Y	Y
8 ***Dunn***	N	N	N	Y	Y	N	N	N
9 Kreidler	Y	Y	Y	Y	Y	Y	Y	Y
WEST VIRGINIA								
1 Mollohan	Y	Y	Y	Y	Y	Y	Y	Y
2 Wise	Y	Y	Y	Y	Y	Y	Y	Y
3 Rahall	Y	Y	Y	Y	Y	Y	Y	Y
WISCONSIN								
1 Vacancy								
2 ***Klug***	N	Y	N	Y	Y	N	N	N
3 ***Gunderson***	N	Y	N	Y	Y	Y	Y	Y
4 Kleczka	Y	Y	Y	Y	Y	Y	?	Y
5 Barrett	Y	Y	Y	Y	Y	Y	Y	Y
6 ***Petri***	N	Y	N	Y	N	N	N	N
7 Obey	Y	Y	Y	Y	Y	Y	Y	Y
8 ***Roth***	N	Y	N	Y	N	Y	Y	N
9 ***Sensenbrenner***	N	N	N	Y	N	N	N	N
WYOMING								
AL ***Thomas***	N	Y	N	Y	Y	N	N	N
DELEGATES								
de Lugo, V.I.	D	D	D	D	D	D	D	D
Faleomavaega, Am.S.	D	D	D	D	D	D	D	D
Norton, D.C.	D	D	D	D	D	D	D	D
Romero-B., P.R.	D	D	D	D	D	D	D	D
Underwood, Guam	D	D	D	D	D	D	D	D

Southern states - Ala., Ark., Fla., Ga., Ky., La., Miss., N.C., Okla., S.C., Tenn., Texas, Va.
Omitted votes are quorum calls, which CQ does not include in its vote charts.

59. HR 4. National Institutes of Health Reauthorization/Rule. Adoption of the rule (H Res 119) to provide for House floor consideration of the bill to authorize $6.6 billion for the National Institutes of Health in fiscal 1994 and such sums as necessary in fiscal 1995-96. The bill codifies the Clinton executive order lifting the ban on fetal tissue research from induced abortions. Adopted 248-170: R 6-165; D 241-5 (ND 163-2, SD 78-3); I 1-0, March 10, 1993.

60. HR 4. National Institutes of Health Reauthorization/Fetal Tissue Research. Waxman, D-Calif., substitute amendment to the Bliley, R-Va., amendment to add to the safeguards against women having abortions for the purpose of providing tissue for research by requiring that the abortion be performed in accordance with state law and requiring annual reports to Congress on the ethical safeguards for fetal tissue research. The Bliley amendment would add several other requirements, including that a woman provide consent for the abortion before the issue of tissue donation is raised, and be aware of any medical risks or interest in tissue research by the doctor. Adopted in the Committee of the Whole 253-173: R 37-135; D 215-38 (ND 147-25, SD 68-13); I 1-0, March 10, 1993. (Subsequently, the Bliley amendment as amended was adopted on vote 61.)

61. HR 4. National Institutes of Health Reauthorization/Fetal Tissue Research. Bliley, R-Va., amendment, as amended by the Waxman, D-Calif., amendment to add to the safeguards against women having abortions for the purpose of providing tissue for research by requiring that the abortions be performed in accordance with state law and requiring annual reports to Congress on the ethical safeguards for fetal tissue research. Adopted in the Committee of the Whole 261-162: R 45-127; D 215-35 (ND 148-21, SD 67-14); I 1-0, March 10, 1993.

62. HR 4. National Institutes of Health Reauthorization/Funding Freeze. Bereuter, R-Neb., amendment to freeze the authorizations in the bill at the fiscal 1993 appropriations levels. Rejected in the Committee of the Whole 193-234: R 157-16; D 36-217 (ND 16-157, SD 20-60); I 0-1, March 10, 1993.

63. Procedural Motion. Approval of the Journal of Wednesday, March 10. Approved 244-152: R 20-147; D 223-5 (ND 148-4, SD 75-1); I 1-0, March 11, 1993.

64. HR 4. National Institutes of Health Reauthorization/Fetal Tissue Research. Separate vote at the request of Solomon, R-N.Y., on the Bliley, R-Va., amendment adopted in the Committee of the Whole to add to the safeguards against women having abortions for the purpose of providing tissue for research. Previously the Bliley amendment was amended by a Waxman, D-Calif., amendment. Adopted 250-161: R 44-126; D 205-35 (ND 138-23, SD 67-12); I 1-0, March 11, 1993. (On separate votes, which may be demanded on an amendment adopted in the Committee of the Whole, the four delegates and the resident commissioner of Puerto Rico cannot vote. See vote 61).

65. HR 4. National Institutes of Health Reauthorization/Breast Cancer Research. Separate vote at the request of Solomon, R-N.Y., on the amendment adopted by voice vote in the Committee of the Whole offered by Waxman, D-Calif., to require a study of the environmental and other risks contributing to breast cancer on Long Island, N.Y., and to establish the Office of Alternative Medicine. Adopted 350-67: R 113-60; D 236-7 (ND 157-6, SD 79-1); I 1-0, March 11, 1993. (On separate votes, which may be demanded on an amendment adopted in the Committee of the Whole, the four delegates and the resident commissioner of Puerto Rico cannot vote.)

66. HR 4. National Institutes of Health Reauthorization/Back Injury Study. Separate vote at the request of Solomon, R-N.Y., on the amendment adopted by voice vote in the Committee of the Whole offered by Gilman, R-N.Y., to conduct a study of back injuries. Adopted 305-109: R 94-78; D 210-31 (ND 140-22, SD 70-9); I 1-0, March 11, 1993. (On separate votes, which may be demanded on an amendment adopted in the Committee of the Whole, the four delegates and the resident commissioner of Puerto Rico cannot vote.)

KEY

Y	Voted for (yea).
#	Paired for.
+	Announced for.
N	Voted against (nay).
X	Paired against.
−	Announced against.
P	Voted "present".
C	Voted "present" to avoid possible conflict of interest.
?	Did not vote or otherwise make a position known.
D	Delegates ineligible to vote.

Democrats   **Republicans**
Independent

	59	60	61	62	63	64	65	66
ALABAMA								
1 *Callahan*	N	N	N	Y	N	N	Y	N
2 *Everett*	N	N	N	Y	N	N	N	N
3 Browder	Y	Y	Y	N	Y	Y	Y	Y
4 Bevill	Y	Y	Y	N	Y	Y	Y	Y
5 Cramer	Y	Y	Y	N	Y	Y	Y	Y
6 *Bachus*	N	N	N	Y	N	N	N	N
7 Hilliard	Y	Y	Y	N	Y	Y	Y	Y
ALASKA								
AL *Young*	N	N	N	Y	N	N	Y	Y
ARIZONA								
1 Coppersmith	Y	Y	Y	N	Y	Y	Y	Y
2 Pastor	Y	Y	Y	N	Y	Y	Y	Y
3 *Stump*	N	N	N	Y	N	N	N	N
4 *Kyl*	N	N	N	Y	N	N	Y	N
5 *Kolbe*	N	Y	Y	N	Y	N	Y	N
6 English	Y	Y	Y	N	Y	Y	Y	Y
ARKANSAS								
1 Lambert	Y	Y	Y	N	Y	Y	Y	N
2 Thornton	Y	Y	Y	N	?	Y	Y	Y
3 *Hutchinson*	N	N	N	Y	N	N	N	N
4 *Dickey*	N	N	N	Y	N	N	N	N
CALIFORNIA								
1 Hamburg	Y	Y	Y	N	Y	Y	Y	Y
2 *Herger*	N	N	N	Y	N	N	N	N
3 Fazio	Y	Y	Y	N	Y	Y	Y	Y
4 *Doolittle*	N	N	N	Y	N	N	N	N
5 Matsui	Y	Y	Y	N	Y	Y	Y	Y
6 Woolsey	Y	Y	Y	N	Y	Y	Y	Y
7 Miller	Y	Y	Y	N	Y	Y	Y	Y
8 Pelosi	Y	Y	?	N	Y	Y	?	?
9 Dellums	?	Y	?	N	Y	Y	Y	Y
10 *Baker*	N	N	N	Y	N	N	N	N
11 *Pombo*	N	N	N	Y	N	N	N	N
12 Lantos	Y	Y	Y	N	Y	Y	Y	Y
13 Stark	Y	Y	Y	N	Y	Y	Y	Y
14 Eshoo	Y	Y	Y	N	Y	Y	Y	N
15 Mineta	Y	Y	Y	N	Y	?	?	?
16 Edwards	Y	Y	Y	N	Y	Y	Y	Y
17 Vacancy								
18 Condit	Y	Y	Y	Y	Y	Y	Y	Y
19 Lehman	Y	Y	Y	N	Y	Y	Y	Y
20 Dooley	Y	Y	Y	N	Y	Y	Y	N
21 *Thomas*	N	N	Y	Y	N	Y	N	N
22 *Huffington*	N	N	Y	N	N	N	Y	Y
23 *Gallegly*	N	N	N	Y	N	N	N	Y
24 Beilenson	Y	Y	Y	N	Y	Y	Y	Y
25 *McKeon*	N	N	N	Y	N	N	N	N
26 Berman	Y	Y	Y	N	?	Y	Y	Y
27 *Moorhead*	N	N	N	Y	N	N	N	Y
28 *Dreier*	N	N	N	Y	N	N	N	N
29 Waxman	Y	Y	Y	N	Y	Y	Y	Y
30 Becerra	Y	Y	Y	N	Y	Y	Y	Y
31 Martinez	Y	Y	Y	N	Y	Y	Y	Y
32 Dixon	Y	Y	Y	N	Y	Y	Y	Y
33 Roybal-Allard	Y	Y	Y	N	Y	Y	Y	Y
34 Torres	Y	Y	Y	N	Y	Y	Y	Y
35 Waters	Y	Y	Y	N	Y	Y	Y	?
36 Harman	Y	Y	Y	N	?	?	Y	Y
37 Tucker	Y	Y	Y	N	Y	Y	Y	Y
38 *Horn*	N	Y	Y	N	Y	N	Y	Y
39 *Royce*	N	N	N	Y	N	N	N	N
40 *Lewis*	N	N	N	Y	N	N	N	N
41 *Kim*	N	N	N	Y	N	N	N	Y

	59	60	61	62	63	64	65	66
42 Brown	Y	Y	Y	N	?	Y	Y	Y
43 *Calvert*	N	N	N	Y	N	N	N	N
44 *McCandless*	N	N	N	Y	N	N	N	Y
45 *Rohrabacher*	N	N	N	Y	N	N	N	Y
46 *Dornan*	N	N	N	Y	N	N	N	N
47 *Cox*	N	N	N	Y	?	N	Y	Y
48 *Packard*	N	N	N	Y	N	N	N	N
49 Schenk	Y	Y	Y	N	Y	Y	Y	Y
50 Filner	Y	Y	Y	N	Y	Y	Y	Y
51 *Cunningham*	N	N	N	Y	N	N	N	N
52 *Hunter*	?	N	N	Y	N	N	N	N
COLORADO								
1 Schroeder	Y	Y	Y	N	Y	Y	Y	Y
2 Skaggs	Y	Y	Y	N	Y	Y	Y	N
3 *McInnis*	N	Y	Y	Y	Y	Y	Y	Y
4 *Allard*	N	N	N	Y	N	N	N	N
5 *Hefley*	N	N	N	Y	N	N	N	N
6 *Schaefer*	N	N	N	Y	N	N	N	N
CONNECTICUT								
1 Kennelly	Y	Y	Y	N	Y	Y	Y	Y
2 Gejdenson	Y	Y	Y	N	Y	Y	Y	Y
3 DeLauro	Y	Y	Y	N	?	Y	Y	Y
4 *Shays*	Y	Y	Y	N	Y	Y	Y	Y
5 *Franks*	N	Y	Y	N	Y	N	Y	Y
6 Johnson	N	Y	Y	N	N	N	Y	Y
DELAWARE								
AL *Castle*	N	Y	Y	N	Y	N	Y	Y
FLORIDA								
1 Hutto	Y	N	N	Y	N	N	Y	Y
2 Peterson	Y	Y	Y	N	Y	Y	Y	Y
3 Brown	Y	Y	Y	N	Y	Y	Y	Y
4 *Fowler*	N	Y	Y	N	N	N	Y	N
5 Thurman	Y	Y	Y	N	Y	Y	Y	Y
6 *Stearns*	N	N	N	Y	N	N	N	N
7 *Mica*	N	N	N	Y	N	N	N	N
8 *McCollum*	N	N	N	Y	N	N	Y	N
9 *Bilirakis*	N	N	N	Y	N	N	N	Y
10 *Young*	N	N	N	Y	N	N	N	Y
11 Gibbons	Y	Y	Y	N	Y	Y	Y	Y
12 *Canady*	N	N	N	Y	N	N	N	N
13 *Miller*	N	Y	Y	N	N	N	Y	N
14 *Goss*	N	N	N	Y	N	N	N	Y
15 Bacchus	Y	Y	Y	N	Y	Y	Y	Y
16 *Lewis*	N	Y	Y	N	N	N	Y	Y
17 Meek	Y	Y	Y	N	Y	Y	Y	Y
18 *Ros-Lehtinen*	N	N	N	Y	N	N	N	Y
19 Johnston	Y	Y	Y	N	Y	Y	Y	Y
20 Deutsch	Y	Y	Y	N	Y	Y	Y	Y
21 *Diaz-Balart*	N	N	N	Y	N	N	N	Y
22 *Shaw*	N	N	Y	N	Y	N	Y	Y
23 Hastings	?	?	?	?	?	?	?	?
GEORGIA								
1 *Kingston*	N	N	N	N	N	N	N	N
2 Bishop	?	Y	?	N	Y	Y	Y	Y
3 *Collins*	N	N	N	Y	N	N	N	N
4 *Linder*	N	N	N	Y	N	N	N	N
5 Lewis	Y	Y	Y	N	Y	Y	Y	Y
6 *Gingrich*	N	N	N	Y	N	N	Y	Y
7 Darden	Y	Y	Y	N	Y	Y	Y	Y
8 Rowland	Y	Y	Y	N	Y	Y	Y	Y
9 Deal	Y	N	Y	N	Y	Y	Y	Y
10 Johnson	Y	Y	Y	N	Y	Y	Y	Y
11 McKinney	Y	Y	Y	N	Y	Y	Y	Y
HAWAII								
1 Abercrombie	Y	Y	Y	N	?	Y	Y	Y
2 Mink	Y	Y	Y	N	Y	Y	Y	Y
IDAHO								
1 LaRocco	Y	Y	Y	N	Y	Y	Y	Y
2 *Crapo*	N	N	N	Y	N	?	N	Y
ILLINOIS								
1 Rush	Y	Y	Y	N	Y	Y	Y	Y
2 Reynolds	Y	Y	Y	N	Y	Y	Y	Y
3 Lipinski	Y	N	Y	N	Y	Y	Y	Y
4 Gutierrez	Y	Y	Y	N	?	?	?	?
5 Rostenkowski	Y	Y	Y	N	Y	Y	Y	Y
6 *Hyde*	N	N	N	Y	N	N	Y	N
7 Collins	Y	Y	Y	N	?	?	?	?
8 *Crane*	N	N	N	Y	N	N	N	N
9 Yates	Y	Y	Y	N	Y	Y	Y	Y
10 *Porter*	N	Y	Y	N	Y	N	Y	Y
11 Sangmeister	Y	Y	?	N	Y	Y	Y	Y
12 Costello	Y	N	N	N	Y	N	Y	Y
13 *Fawell*	N	Y	Y	N	Y	N	Y	Y
14 *Hastert*	N	N	N	Y	N	N	N	N
15 *Ewing*	N	N	N	Y	N	N	N	N
16 *Manzullo*	N	N	N	Y	N	N	N	N
17 Evans	Y	Y	Y	N	Y	Y	Y	Y

ND   Northern Democrats   SD   Southern Democrats

	59	60	61	62	63	64	65	66
18 ***Michel***	N	N	N	Y	N	N	Y	Y
19 Poshard	Y	N	N	Y	Y	N	Y	Y
20 Durbin	Y	Y	Y	N	Y	Y	Y	N
INDIANA								
1 Visclosky	Y	Y	Y	N	Y	Y	Y	Y
2 Sharp	Y	Y	Y	N	Y	Y	Y	N
3 Roemer	Y	N	N	Y	Y	N	Y	N
4 Long	Y	Y	Y	Y	Y	Y	Y	Y
5 ***Buyer***	N	N	N	Y	N	N	Y	Y
6 ***Burton***	N	N	N	Y	N	N	N	N
7 ***Myers***	N	N	N	Y	Y	N	Y	Y
8 McCloskey	Y	Y	Y	N	Y	Y	Y	Y
9 Hamilton	Y	Y	Y	N	Y	Y	Y	Y
10 Jacobs	Y	Y	Y	N	N	Y	Y	Y
IOWA								
1 ***Leach***	N	?	Y	Y	N	Y	Y	Y
2 ***Nussle***	N	N	N	Y	N	N	Y	N
3 ***Lightfoot***	N	N	N	Y	N	N	Y	Y
4 Smith	?	Y	Y	N	Y	Y	Y	Y
5 ***Grandy***	N	N	N	Y	N	N	Y	Y
KANSAS								
1 ***Roberts***	N	N	N	Y	N	N	Y	N
2 Slattery	Y	Y	Y	N	Y	Y	Y	N
3 ***Meyers***	N	Y	Y	Y	N	Y	N	Y
4 Glickman	Y	Y	Y	N	Y	Y	Y	Y
KENTUCKY								
1 Barlow	Y	Y	Y	Y	Y	Y	Y	Y
2 Natcher	Y	Y	Y	N	Y	Y	Y	Y
3 Mazzoli	Y	N	N	N	Y	N	Y	Y
4 ***Bunning***	N	N	N	Y	N	N	Y	Y
5 ***Rogers***	N	N	N	Y	?	N	Y	Y
6 Baesler	Y	Y	Y	Y	Y	Y	Y	Y
LOUISIANA								
1 ***Livingston***	N	N	N	Y	?	N	Y	Y
2 Jefferson	Y	Y	Y	N	Y	Y	Y	Y
3 Tauzin	Y	N	N	N	Y	N	Y	Y
4 Fields	Y	Y	Y	N	Y	Y	Y	Y
5 ***McCrery***	N	N	N	Y	N	N	Y	Y
6 ***Baker***	N	N	N	Y	N	N	Y	Y
7 Hayes	Y	N	N	N	Y	N	Y	Y
MAINE								
1 Andrews	Y	Y	Y	N	Y	Y	Y	Y
2 ***Snowe***	Y	Y	Y	N	N	Y	Y	Y
MARYLAND								
1 ***Gilchrest***	N	Y	Y	Y	N	Y	Y	Y
2 ***Bentley***	N	Y	Y	Y	N	Y	Y	Y
3 Cardin	Y	Y	Y	N	?	?	Y	N
4 Wynn	Y	Y	Y	N	+	Y	Y	Y
5 Hoyer	Y	Y	Y	N	Y	Y	Y	Y
6 ***Bartlett***	N	N	N	Y	N	N	N	N
7 Mfume	Y	Y	Y	N	Y	Y	Y	Y
8 ***Morella***	Y	Y	Y	N	N	Y	Y	Y
MASSACHUSETTS								
1 Olver	Y	Y	Y	N	Y	Y	Y	Y
2 Neal	Y	Y	Y	N	Y	Y	Y	Y
3 ***Blute***	N	N	N	Y	N	N	Y	N
4 Frank	Y	Y	Y	N	Y	Y	Y	N
5 Meehan	Y	Y	Y	N	Y	Y	Y	Y
6 ***Torkildsen***	N	Y	Y	Y	N	Y	Y	N
7 Markey	Y	Y	Y	N	Y	?	?	?
8 Kennedy	Y	Y	Y	N	Y	Y	Y	Y
9 Moakley	Y	Y	Y	N	Y	Y	Y	Y
10 Studds	Y	Y	Y	N	Y	Y	Y	Y
MICHIGAN								
1 Stupak	Y	N	N	Y	Y	N	N	Y
2 ***Hoekstra***	N	N	N	Y	N	N	N	N
3 Henry	?	?	?	?	?	?	?	?
4 ***Camp***	N	N	N	Y	N	N	Y	Y
5 Barcia	Y	N	N	N	Y	N	Y	Y
6 ***Upton***	N	Y	Y	N	Y	N	Y	Y
7 ***Smith***	N	N	N	Y	N	?	N	N
8 Carr	Y	Y	Y	N	Y	Y	Y	Y
9 Kildee	Y	N	Y	N	Y	Y	Y	Y
10 Bonior	Y	Y	Y	N	Y	Y	Y	Y
11 ***Knollenberg***	N	N	N	Y	N	N	N	N
12 Levin	Y	Y	Y	N	Y	Y	Y	Y
13 Ford	Y	Y	?	N	Y	Y	Y	Y
14 Conyers	?	?	Y	N	Y	?	?	?
15 Collins	Y	Y	Y	N	Y	Y	Y	Y
16 Dingell	Y	Y	Y	N	Y	Y	Y	Y
MINNESOTA								
1 Penny	Y	N	N	N	Y	N	Y	N
2 Minge	Y	Y	N	Y	Y	Y	N	N
3 ***Ramstad***	N	Y	Y	Y	N	Y	Y	N
4 Vento	Y	Y	Y	N	Y	Y	Y	Y

	59	60	61	62	63	64	65	66
5 Sabo	Y	Y	Y	N	Y	Y	Y	Y
6 ***Grams***	N	N	N	Y	N	N	N	N
7 Peterson	N	N	N	Y	Y	N	N	Y
8 Oberstar	Y	N	N	N	Y	N	Y	Y
MISSISSIPPI								
1 Whitten	Y	Y	N	Y	Y	Y	Y	Y
2 Vacancy								
3 Montgomery	Y	Y	Y	Y	Y	Y	Y	Y
4 Parker	Y	N	N	Y	?	N	Y	Y
5 Taylor	N	N	N	Y	N	N	Y	N
MISSOURI								
1 Clay	Y	?	?	N	N	Y	Y	Y
2 ***Talent***	N	N	N	Y	N	N	Y	N
3 Gephardt	Y	Y	Y	N	Y	Y	Y	Y
4 Skelton	Y	N	N	Y	Y	N	N	N
5 Wheat	Y	Y	Y	N	Y	Y	Y	Y
6 Danner	Y	Y	Y	N	Y	Y	Y	Y
7 ***Hancock***	N	N	N	Y	N	N	N	N
8 ***Emerson***	N	N	N	Y	?	N	Y	N
9 Volkmer	N	N	N	Y	Y	N	Y	N
MONTANA								
AL Williams	Y	Y	Y	N	?	Y	Y	Y
NEBRASKA								
1 ***Bereuter***	Y	N	Y	Y	N	Y	Y	Y
2 Hoagland	?	?	?	?	Y	Y	Y	N
3 ***Barrett***	N	N	N	Y	N	N	Y	Y
NEVADA								
1 Bilbray	Y	Y	Y	N	Y	Y	Y	N
2 ***Vucanovich***	N	N	N	Y	N	N	Y	Y
NEW HAMPSHIRE								
1 ***Zeliff***	N	Y	Y	Y	N	Y	Y	Y
2 Swett	Y	Y	Y	N	Y	Y	Y	Y
NEW JERSEY								
1 Andrews	Y	Y	Y	N	Y	Y	Y	Y
2 Hughes	Y	Y	Y	N	Y	Y	Y	Y
3 ***Saxton***	N	N	N	Y	N	N	Y	Y
4 ***Smith***	N	N	N	Y	N	N	Y	Y
5 ***Roukema***	N	Y	Y	Y	N	Y	Y	N
6 Pallone	Y	Y	Y	N	Y	Y	Y	Y
7 ***Franks***	N	Y	Y	Y	N	Y	Y	Y
8 Klein	Y	Y	Y	N	Y	Y	Y	Y
9 Torricelli	Y	Y	Y	N	Y	Y	Y	Y
10 Payne	Y	Y	Y	N	Y	Y	Y	Y
11 ***Gallo***	N	Y	Y	N	N	Y	Y	Y
12 ***Zimmer***	N	Y	Y	Y	N	Y	N	N
13 Menendez	Y	Y	Y	N	Y	Y	Y	Y
NEW MEXICO								
1 ***Schiff***	N	N	N	Y	N	N	Y	Y
2 ***Skeen***	N	N	N	Y	N	N	Y	Y
3 Richardson	Y	Y	Y	N	Y	Y	Y	Y
NEW YORK								
1 Hochbrueckner	Y	Y	Y	N	Y	Y	Y	Y
2 ***Lazio***	N	N	Y	N	N	Y	Y	Y
3 ***King***	N	N	N	Y	N	N	Y	N
4 ***Levy***	N	N	N	Y	N	N	Y	Y
5 Ackerman	Y	Y	Y	N	Y	Y	Y	Y
6 Flake	Y	Y	Y	N	Y	Y	Y	Y
7 Manton	Y	N	N	N	Y	N	Y	Y
8 Nadler	Y	Y	Y	N	Y	Y	Y	Y
9 Schumer	Y	Y	Y	N	Y	Y	Y	Y
10 Towns	Y	Y	Y	N	Y	Y	Y	Y
11 Owens	Y	Y	Y	N	Y	Y	Y	Y
12 Velazquez	Y	Y	Y	N	Y	Y	Y	Y
13 ***Molinari***	N	Y	Y	N	N	Y	Y	Y
14 Maloney	?	Y	Y	N	Y	Y	Y	Y
15 Rangel	Y	Y	Y	N	Y	Y	Y	Y
16 Serrano	Y	Y	Y	N	Y	Y	Y	Y
17 Engel	Y	Y	Y	N	Y	Y	Y	Y
18 Lowey	Y	Y	Y	N	Y	Y	Y	Y
19 ***Fish***	N	N	N	Y	Y	N	N	Y
20 ***Gilman***	Y	Y	Y	N	Y	Y	Y	Y
21 McNulty	Y	N	N	N	Y	N	Y	Y
22 ***Solomon***	N	N	N	Y	N	N	Y	Y
23 ***Boehlert***	N	Y	Y	N	Y	Y	Y	Y
24 ***McHugh***	N	N	N	Y	N	N	Y	Y
25 ***Walsh***	N	N	N	Y	N	N	Y	Y
26 Hinchey	Y	Y	Y	N	Y	Y	Y	N
27 ***Paxon***	N	N	N	Y	N	N	N	N
28 Slaughter	Y	Y	Y	N	?	Y	Y	Y
29 LaFalce	Y	N	N	N	?	N	Y	Y
30 ***Quinn***	N	N	N	Y	N	N	Y	N
31 ***Houghton***	N	Y	Y	Y	Y	Y	Y	?
NORTH CAROLINA								
1 Clayton	Y	Y	Y	N	Y	Y	Y	Y
2 Valentine	Y	Y	Y	N	Y	Y	Y	Y

	59	60	61	62	63	64	65	66
3 Lancaster	Y	Y	Y	N	Y	Y	Y	Y
4 Price	Y	Y	Y	N	Y	Y	Y	Y
5 Neal	Y	Y	Y	Y	Y	Y	Y	Y
6 ***Coble***	N	N	N	Y	N	N	Y	N
7 Rose	Y	Y	Y	Y	Y	Y	Y	Y
8 Hefner	Y	Y	Y	N	Y	Y	Y	Y
9 ***McMillan***	Y	Y	Y	Y	N	Y	Y	Y
10 ***Ballenger***	N	N	N	Y	N	N	N	N
11 ***Taylor***	N	N	N	Y	N	N	N	Y
12 Watt	Y	Y	Y	N	Y	N	Y	N
NORTH DAKOTA								
AL Pomeroy	Y	Y	Y	N	Y	Y	Y	Y
OHIO								
1 Mann	Y	Y	Y	?	Y	Y	N	N
2 Vacancy								
3 Hall	Y	N	N	N	?	N	Y	Y
4 ***Oxley***	N	N	N	Y	N	N	Y	Y
5 ***Gillmor***	N	N	N	Y	Y	N	N	Y
6 Strickland	Y	Y	Y	N	Y	Y	Y	Y
7 ***Hobson***	N	N	Y	Y	N	Y	Y	Y
8 ***Boehner***	N	N	N	Y	N	N	N	N
9 Kaptur	Y	Y	Y	N	Y	Y	Y	Y
10 ***Hoke***	N	N	Y	Y	Y	N	Y	Y
11 Stokes	Y	Y	Y	N	Y	Y	Y	Y
12 ***Kasich***	N	N	N	Y	Y	N	Y	N
13 Brown	Y	Y	Y	N	Y	Y	Y	Y
14 Sawyer	Y	Y	Y	N	Y	Y	Y	Y
15 ***Pryce***	N	Y	Y	Y	N	Y	Y	N
16 ***Regula***	N	N	N	Y	N	N	Y	Y
17 Traficant	Y	Y	Y	N	Y	Y	Y	Y
18 Applegate	Y	N	N	N	Y	N	Y	Y
19 Fingerhut	Y	Y	Y	N	Y	Y	Y	Y
OKLAHOMA								
1 ***Inhofe***	N	N	N	Y	N	N	Y	N
2 Synar	Y	Y	Y	N	Y	Y	Y	Y
3 Brewster	Y	Y	Y	Y	Y	Y	Y	N
4 McCurdy	Y	Y	Y	N	Y	Y	Y	N
5 ***Istook***	N	N	N	Y	N	N	Y	N
6 English	Y	Y	Y	Y	Y	Y	Y	Y
OREGON								
1 Furse	Y	Y	Y	N	Y	Y	Y	Y
2 ***Smith***	N	N	N	Y	N	N	Y	Y
3 Wyden	Y	Y	Y	N	Y	Y	Y	Y
4 DeFazio	Y	Y	Y	N	Y	Y	Y	Y
5 Kopetski	Y	Y	Y	N	+	+	+	+
PENNSYLVANIA								
1 Foglietta	Y	Y	Y	N	?	?	Y	Y
2 Blackwell	Y	Y	Y	N	Y	Y	Y	Y
3 Borski	Y	Y	Y	N	Y	Y	Y	Y
4 Klink	Y	N	N	Y	Y	N	N	N
5 ***Clinger***	N	N	N	Y	Y	N	Y	Y
6 Holden	Y	N	Y	N	Y	N	Y	Y
7 ***Weldon***	N	N	N	Y	N	N	Y	Y
8 ***Greenwood***	N	Y	N	N	Y	Y	Y	Y
9 ***Shuster***	N	N	N	Y	N	N	N	Y
10 ***McDade***	?	?	?	?	?	?	?	?
11 Kanjorski	Y	N	Y	Y	Y	Y	N	N
12 Murtha	Y	N	Y	N	Y	N	Y	Y
13 Margolies-Mezv.	Y	Y	Y	N	Y	Y	Y	Y
14 Coyne	Y	Y	Y	N	Y	Y	Y	Y
15 McHale	Y	Y	Y	N	Y	Y	Y	Y
16 ***Walker***	N	N	N	Y	N	N	N	N
17 ***Gekas***	N	N	N	Y	N	N	N	N
18 ***Santorum***	N	N	?	Y	N	N	N	N
19 ***Goodling***	N	N	N	Y	N	N	N	Y
20 Murphy	Y	N	N	Y	N	N	Y	Y
21 ***Ridge***	N	Y	Y	Y	N	Y	Y	Y
RHODE ISLAND								
1 ***Machtley***	N	Y	Y	N	N	Y	Y	Y
2 Reed	Y	Y	Y	N	Y	Y	Y	Y
SOUTH CAROLINA								
1 ***Ravenel***	N	Y	Y	Y	Y	Y	Y	Y
2 ***Spence***	N	N	N	Y	Y	N	N	Y
3 Derrick	Y	Y	Y	N	Y	Y	Y	Y
4 ***Inglis***	N	N	N	Y	Y	N	N	N
5 Spratt	Y	Y	Y	N	Y	Y	Y	Y
6 Clyburn	Y	Y	Y	N	Y	Y	Y	Y
SOUTH DAKOTA								
AL Johnson	Y	Y	Y	N	?	Y	Y	Y
TENNESSEE								
1 ***Quillen***	N	N	N	Y	N	N	N	Y
2 ***Duncan***	N	N	N	Y	N	N	N	N
3 Lloyd	Y	Y	Y	N	Y	Y	Y	Y
4 Cooper	Y	Y	Y	N	Y	Y	Y	Y
5 Clement	Y	Y	Y	Y	Y	Y	Y	Y

	59	60	61	62	63	64	65	66
6 Gordon	Y	Y	Y	N	?	Y	Y	?
7 ***Sundquist***	N	N	N	Y	N	N	Y	Y
8 Tanner	Y	Y	Y	Y	Y	Y	Y	Y
9 Ford	?	?	?	?	?	?	?	?
TEXAS								
1 Chapman	Y	Y	Y	?	Y	Y	Y	Y
2 Wilson	Y	Y	Y	N	Y	?	?	?
3 ***Johnson, Sam***	N	N	N	Y	N	N	N	N
4 Hall	Y	N	N	N	Y	Y	Y	Y
5 Bryant	Y	Y	Y	N	Y	Y	Y	Y
6 ***Barton***	N	N	N	Y	?	?	Y	N
7 ***Archer***	N	N	N	Y	Y	N	N	N
8 ***Fields***	N	N	N	Y	?	N	Y	N
9 Brooks	Y	Y	Y	N	Y	Y	Y	Y
10 Pickle	Y	Y	Y	N	Y	Y	Y	Y
11 Edwards	Y	Y	Y	Y	Y	Y	Y	N
12 Geren	Y	Y	Y	Y	Y	Y	Y	Y
13 Sarpalius	Y	N	N	N	Y	Y	Y	N
14 Laughlin	Y	Y	Y	N	Y	Y	Y	Y
15 de la Garza	N	N	N	N	Y	N	N	Y
16 Coleman	Y	Y	Y	N	Y	Y	Y	Y
17 Stenholm	Y	N	N	Y	Y	N	Y	N
18 Washington	Y	Y	Y	N	?	Y	Y	Y
19 ***Combest***	N	N	N	Y	N	N	Y	Y
20 Gonzalez	Y	?	Y	N	Y	Y	Y	Y
21 ***Smith***	N	N	N	Y	N	N	Y	Y
22 ***DeLay***	N	N	N	Y	N	N	N	N
23 ***Bonilla***	N	N	N	Y	N	N	Y	N
24 Frost	Y	Y	Y	N	?	?	Y	Y
25 Andrews	Y	Y	Y	Y	Y	Y	Y	Y
26 ***Armey***	N	N	N	Y	N	N	N	N
27 Ortiz	N	N	N	Y	N	Y	Y	Y
28 Tejeda	Y	N	N	N	Y	N	Y	Y
29 Green	Y	Y	Y	N	Y	Y	Y	Y
30 Johnson, E. B.	Y	Y	Y	N	Y	Y	Y	Y
UTAH								
1 ***Hansen***	N	N	N	Y	N	N	Y	N
2 Shepherd	Y	Y	Y	N	Y	Y	Y	N
3 Orton	Y	N	N	Y	Y	N	Y	N
VERMONT								
AL *Sanders*	Y	Y	Y	N	Y	Y	Y	Y
VIRGINIA								
1 ***Bateman***	N	N	N	Y	Y	N	Y	Y
2 Pickett	Y	Y	Y	N	Y	Y	Y	Y
3 Scott	Y	Y	Y	N	Y	Y	Y	Y
4 Sisisky	Y	Y	Y	N	Y	Y	Y	Y
5 Payne	Y	Y	Y	Y	Y	Y	Y	Y
6 ***Goodlatte***	N	N	N	Y	N	N	Y	Y
7 ***Bliley***	N	N	N	Y	N	N	Y	Y
8 Moran	Y	Y	Y	?	Y	Y	Y	Y
9 Boucher	Y	Y	Y	N	?	?	?	?
10 ***Wolf***	N	N	N	Y	N	N	Y	Y
11 Byrne	Y	Y	Y	N	Y	Y	Y	Y
WASHINGTON								
1 Cantwell	Y	Y	Y	N	Y	Y	Y	Y
2 Swift	Y	Y	Y	N	Y	Y	Y	Y
3 Unsoeld	Y	Y	Y	N	Y	Y	Y	Y
4 Inslee	Y	Y	Y	Y	?	Y	Y	Y
5 Foley								
6 Dicks	Y	Y	Y	N	Y	Y	Y	Y
7 McDermott	Y	Y	Y	N	Y	Y	Y	Y
8 ***Dunn***	N	N	Y	Y	N	Y	N	N
9 Kreidler	Y	Y	Y	N	Y	Y	Y	Y
WEST VIRGINIA								
1 Mollohan	Y	N	N	N	Y	N	Y	Y
2 Wise	Y	Y	Y	N	?	Y	Y	Y
3 Rahall	Y	N	N	N	Y	N	Y	Y
WISCONSIN								
1 Vacancy								
2 ***Klug***	N	Y	Y	Y	N	Y	Y	N
3 ***Gunderson***	N	Y	Y	N	Y	Y	Y	Y
4 Kleczka	Y	Y	Y	N	Y	Y	Y	Y
5 Barrett	Y	Y	Y	N	Y	Y	Y	Y
6 ***Petri***	N	N	N	Y	N	N	N	N
7 Obey	Y	Y	?	N	Y	Y	Y	N
8 ***Roth***	N	N	N	Y	N	N	N	Y
9 ***Sensenbrenner***	N	N	N	Y	N	N	N	N
WYOMING								
AL ***Thomas***	?	N	N	Y	N	N	Y	Y
DELEGATES								
de Lugo, V.I.	D	Y	Y	N	D	D	D	D
Faleomavaega, Am.S.	D	Y	Y	N	D	D	D	D
Norton, D.C.	D	Y	Y	N	D	D	D	D
Romero-B., P.R.	D	Y	Y	N	D	D	D	D
Underwood, Guam	D	Y	Y	N	D	D	D	D

Southern states - Ala., Ark., Fla., Ga., Ky., La., Miss., N.C., Okla., S.C., Tenn., Texas, Va.
Omitted votes are quorum calls, which CQ does not include in its vote charts.

67. HR 4. National Institutes of Health Reauthorization/"Buy American." Separate vote at the request of Solomon, R-N.Y., on the amendment adopted by voice vote in the Committee of the Whole offered by Traficant, D-Ohio, to ensure that the goods and services purchased as a result of the bill are produced in the United States. Adopted 405-9: R 163-9; D 241-0 (ND 163-0, SD 78-0); I 1-0, March 11, 1993. (On separate votes, which may be demanded on an amendment adopted in the Committee of the Whole, the delegates cannot vote.)

68. HR 4. National Institutes of Health Reauthorization/Project Aries. Separate vote at the request of Solomon, R-N.Y., on the amendment adopted by voice vote in the Committee of the Whole offered by Sam Johnson, R-Texas, to prohibit further funding by NIH for Project Aries at the University of Washington at Seattle concerning the transmission of the HIV virus. Adopted 278-139: R 168-5; D 110-133 (ND 56-108, SD 54-25); I 0-1, March 11, 1993. (On separate votes, which may be demanded on an amendment adopted in the Committee of the Whole, the delegates cannot vote.)

69. HR 4. National Institutes of Health Reauthorization/Passage. Passage of a bill to authorize $6.6 billion for the National Institutes of Health in fiscal 1994 and such sums as necessary in fiscal 1995-96. The bill codifies the Clinton executive order lifting the ban on fetal tissue research from induced abortions. Passed 283-131: R 57-115; D 225-16 (ND 153-10, SD 72-6); I 1-0, March 11, 1993.

70. HR 4. National Institutes of Health Reauthorization/Instruct Conferees. Bliley, R-Va., motion to instruct the House conferees to agree to the Senate amendment to prevent the permanent immigration of persons infected with the HIV virus. Motion agreed to 356-58: R 171-0; D 185-57 (ND 118-44, SD 67-13); I 0-1, March 11, 1993.

71. HR 965. Child Safety Protection/Passage. Collins, D-Ill., motion to suspend the rules and pass the bill to require warning labels on toys that pose choking risks to small children and require the Consumer Product Safety Commission to develop federal bicycle helmet safety standards. Motion agreed to 362-38: R 126-35; D 235-3 (ND 158-2, SD 77-1); I 1-0, March 16, 1993. A two-thirds majority of those present and voting (267 in this case) is required for passage under suspension of the rules.

72. HR 1109. Merchant Seamen Re-Employment Rights. Studds, D-Mass., motion to suspend the rules and pass the bill to guarantee civilian merchant mariners job seniority and pension protection if they leave their jobs to serve on the Ready Reserve Force in a national emergency or war. The bill is retroactive to cover civilians who served in the Persian Gulf War. Motion agreed to 403-0: R 160-0; D 242-0 (ND 162-0, SD 80-0); I 1-0, March 16, 1993. A two-thirds majority of those present and voting (269 in this case) is required for passage under suspension of the rules. A "yea" was a vote in support of the president's position.

73. Procedural Motion. Motion to approve the House Journal of Tuesday, March 16. Approved 249-140: R 19-135; D 229-5 (ND 153-4, SD 76-1); I 1-0, March 17, 1993.

*75. Procedural Motion. Approval of the House Journal of Wednesday, March 17. Approved 253-155: R 17-152; D 235-3 (ND 159-2, SD 76-1); I 1-0, March 18, 1993.

Omitted votes are quorum calls, which CQ does not include in its vote charts.

KEY

- Y Voted for (yea).
- # Paired for.
- + Announced for.
- N Voted against (nay).
- X Paired against.
- − Announced against.
- P Voted "present."
- C Voted "present" to avoid possible conflict of interest.
- ? Did not vote or otherwise make a position known.
- D Delegates ineligible to vote.

Democrats **Republicans** *Independent*

	67	68	69	70	71	72	73	75
ALABAMA								
1 Callahan	Y	Y	N	Y	Y	Y	N	N
2 Everett	Y	Y	N	Y	Y	Y	N	N
3 Browder	Y	Y	?	Y	Y	Y	Y	Y
4 Bevill	Y	Y	Y	Y	Y	Y	?	Y
5 Cramer	Y	Y	Y	Y	Y	Y	Y	Y
6 Bachus	Y	Y	N	Y	N	Y	N	N
7 Hilliard	Y	N	N	Y	?	?	Y	Y
ALASKA								
AL Young	Y	Y	N	Y	Y	Y	N	N
ARIZONA								
1 Coppersmith	Y	N	Y	Y	Y	Y	Y	Y
2 Pastor	Y	N	Y	Y	Y	Y	Y	Y
3 Stump	N	Y	N	Y	N	Y	N	N
4 Kyl	Y	Y	N	Y	Y	Y	N	N
5 Kolbe	N	N	Y	Y	Y	Y	N	N
6 English	Y	N	Y	Y	Y	Y	Y	Y
ARKANSAS								
1 Lambert	Y	Y	Y	Y	Y	Y	Y	Y
2 Thornton	Y	Y	Y	Y	Y	Y	Y	Y
3 Hutchinson	Y	Y	N	Y	Y	Y	N	N
4 Dickey	Y	Y	N	Y	Y	Y	N	N
CALIFORNIA								
1 Hamburg	Y	N	Y	N	Y	Y	Y	Y
2 Herger	Y	Y	N	Y	N	Y	N	N
3 Fazio	Y	N	Y	Y	Y	Y	Y	Y
4 Doolittle	Y	Y	N	Y	N	Y	?	N
5 Matsui	Y	N	Y	N	Y	Y	Y	Y
6 Woolsey	Y	N	N	Y	Y	Y	Y	Y
7 Miller	Y	N	Y	Y	Y	Y	Y	Y
8 Pelosi	Y	N	Y	N	Y	Y	Y	Y
9 Dellums	Y	N	N	Y	Y	Y	?	Y
10 Baker	Y	Y	Y	Y	Y	Y	N	N
11 Pombo	Y	Y	N	Y	Y	Y	Y	Y
12 Lantos	Y	Y	Y	N	Y	Y	Y	Y
13 Stark	Y	N	Y	N	Y	Y	Y	Y
14 Eshoo	Y	N	Y	?	Y	Y	Y	Y
15 Mineta	?	?	?	?	Y	Y	Y	Y
16 Edwards	Y	N	Y	N	Y	Y	Y	Y
17 Vacancy								
18 Condit	Y	Y	Y	Y	Y	Y	Y	Y
19 Lehman	Y	Y	?	Y	?	?	Y	Y
20 Dooley	Y	Y	Y	Y	Y	N	Y	Y
21 Thomas	N	Y	Y	Y	Y	Y	N	N
22 Huffington	Y	Y	Y	Y	Y	Y	N	N
23 Gallegly	Y	Y	N	Y	Y	Y	N	N
24 Beilenson	Y	N	Y	Y	Y	Y	Y	Y
25 McKeon	Y	Y	N	Y	Y	Y	N	N
26 Berman	Y	N	Y	Y	Y	Y	Y	Y
27 Moorhead	Y	Y	N	Y	Y	Y	N	N
28 Dreier	N	Y	N	Y	Y	Y	N	N
29 Waxman	Y	N	Y	N	Y	Y	Y	Y
30 Becerra	Y	N	Y	N	Y	Y	?	Y
31 Martinez	Y	N	Y	Y	Y	Y	Y	Y
32 Dixon	Y	N	Y	N	Y	Y	Y	Y
33 Roybal-Allard	Y	N	Y	N	Y	Y	Y	Y
34 Torres	Y	Y	Y	Y	Y	Y	Y	?
35 Waters	Y	N	Y	N	?	Y	Y	Y
36 Harman	Y	N	Y	Y	Y	Y	Y	Y
37 Tucker	Y	Y	Y	Y	Y	Y	?	?
38 Horn	Y	Y	Y	Y	Y	Y	N	N
39 Royce	N	Y	N	Y	N	Y	N	N
40 Lewis	?	Y	Y	N	Y	Y	N	N
41 Kim	Y	Y	N	Y	Y	Y	N	N

	67	68	69	70	71	72	73	75
42 Brown	Y	N	Y	N	Y	Y	?	Y
43 Calvert	Y	Y	N	Y	Y	Y	N	N
44 McCandless	Y	Y	N	Y	Y	Y	N	N
45 Rohrabacher	Y	Y	N	Y	N	Y	N	N
46 Dornan	Y	Y	N	Y	?	?	?	?
47 Cox	Y	Y	N	Y	N	Y	N	N
48 Packard	Y	Y	N	Y	N	Y	N	N
49 Schenk	Y	N	Y	Y	Y	Y	Y	Y
50 Filner	Y	N	Y	Y	Y	Y	Y	Y
51 Cunningham	Y	Y	N	Y	N	Y	N	N
52 Hunter	Y	Y	N	Y	?	?	?	N
COLORADO								
1 Schroeder	Y	N	Y	Y	Y	Y	N	N
2 Skaggs	Y	N	Y	Y	Y	Y	Y	Y
3 McInnis	Y	Y	Y	Y	Y	Y	N	N
4 Allard	Y	Y	N	Y	N	Y	N	N
5 Hefley	Y	Y	N	Y	N	Y	N	N
6 Schaefer	Y	Y	N	Y	N	Y	N	N
CONNECTICUT								
1 Kennelly	Y	N	Y	Y	Y	Y	Y	Y
2 Gejdenson	Y	N	Y	N	Y	Y	Y	Y
3 DeLauro	Y	N	Y	Y	Y	Y	Y	Y
4 Shays	Y	Y	Y	Y	Y	Y	N	N
5 Franks	Y	Y	Y	Y	Y	Y	N	N
6 Johnson	Y	Y	Y	Y	Y	Y	N	N
DELAWARE								
AL Castle	Y	Y	Y	Y	Y	Y	N	N
FLORIDA								
1 Hutto	Y	Y	N	Y	Y	Y	Y	Y
2 Peterson	Y	Y	Y	Y	Y	Y	Y	Y
3 Brown	Y	Y	Y	N	+	+	Y	Y
4 Fowler	Y	Y	Y	Y	Y	Y	N	N
5 Thurman	Y	Y	Y	Y	Y	Y	Y	Y
6 Stearns	Y	Y	Y	Y	Y	Y	Y	N
7 Mica	Y	Y	N	Y	N	Y	N	N
8 McCollum	Y	Y	N	Y	Y	Y	N	N
9 Bilirakis	Y	Y	N	Y	?	?	N	N
10 Young	Y	Y	Y	Y	Y	Y	?	N
11 Gibbons	Y	N	Y	Y	Y	Y	Y	Y
12 Canady	Y	Y	N	Y	Y	Y	N	N
13 Miller	Y	Y	Y	Y	Y	Y	N	N
14 Goss	Y	N	Y	Y	Y	Y	N	N
15 Bacchus	Y	N	Y	Y	Y	Y	Y	Y
16 Lewis	Y	Y	Y	Y	Y	Y	N	N
17 Meek	Y	N	Y	Y	Y	Y	Y	Y
18 Ros-Lehtinen	Y	Y	N	Y	Y	Y	N	N
19 Johnston	Y	Y	Y	Y	Y	Y	Y	?
20 Deutsch	Y	Y	Y	Y	Y	Y	Y	Y
21 Diaz-Balart	Y	Y	Y	Y	Y	Y	N	N
22 Shaw	Y	Y	Y	Y	Y	Y	N	N
23 Hastings	?	?	?	?	Y	Y	Y	?
GEORGIA								
1 Kingston	Y	Y	N	Y	Y	Y	?	N
2 Bishop	Y	N	Y	N	Y	Y	Y	Y
3 Collins	Y	Y	N	Y	Y	Y	N	N
4 Linder	Y	Y	N	Y	N	Y	N	N
5 Lewis	Y	N	Y	N	Y	Y	Y	Y
6 Gingrich	Y	Y	N	Y	Y	Y	N	Y
7 Darden	Y	Y	Y	Y	Y	Y	Y	Y
8 Rowland	Y	Y	Y	Y	Y	Y	Y	Y
9 Deal	Y	Y	Y	Y	Y	Y	Y	Y
10 Johnson	Y	Y	Y	Y	Y	Y	Y	Y
11 McKinney	Y	N	Y	N	Y	Y	Y	Y
HAWAII								
1 Abercrombie	Y	N	Y	N	Y	Y	Y	Y
2 Mink	Y	N	Y	N	Y	Y	Y	Y
IDAHO								
1 LaRocco	Y	Y	Y	Y	Y	Y	Y	Y
2 Crapo	Y	Y	N	Y	N	Y	N	N
ILLINOIS								
1 Rush	Y	N	Y	N	Y	Y	Y	Y
2 Reynolds	Y	N	Y	N	Y	Y	Y	Y
3 Lipinski	Y	Y	Y	Y	Y	Y	Y	Y
4 Gutierrez	?	?	?	?	?	?	Y	Y
5 Rostenkowski	Y	N	Y	Y	Y	Y	Y	Y
6 Hyde	Y	Y	N	Y	N	Y	N	N
7 Collins	?	?	?	?	Y	Y	Y	Y
8 Crane	N	N	Y	N	Y	N	N	N
9 Yates	Y	N	Y	Y	Y	Y	Y	Y
10 Porter	Y	Y	Y	Y	Y	N	N	N
11 Sangmeister	Y	N	Y	Y	Y	Y	Y	Y
12 Costello	Y	N	N	Y	Y	Y	Y	Y
13 Fawell	Y	Y	Y	Y	Y	+	N	N
14 Hastert	Y	Y	N	Y	Y	Y	N	N
15 Ewing	Y	Y	N	Y	Y	Y	N	N
16 Manzullo	Y	Y	N	Y	N	Y	N	N
17 Evans	Y	N	Y	Y	Y	Y	Y	Y

ND Northern Democrats   SD Southern Democrats

	67	68	69	70	71	72	73	75
18 ***Michel***	Y	Y	N	Y	Y	Y	N	N
19 Poshard	Y	Y	N	Y	Y	Y	Y	Y
20 Durbin	Y	N	Y	Y	Y	Y	Y	Y
INDIANA								
1 Visclosky	Y	N	Y	Y	Y	Y	Y	Y
2 Sharp	Y	N	Y	Y	Y	Y	Y	Y
3 Roemer	Y	Y	N	Y	Y	Y	Y	Y
4 Long	Y	Y	Y	Y	Y	Y	Y	Y
5 ***Buyer***	Y	Y	N	Y	Y	Y	N	N
6 ***Burton***	Y	Y	N	Y	Y	Y	N	N
7 ***Myers***	Y	Y	N	Y	Y	Y	Y	Y
8 McCloskey	Y	N	Y	Y	Y	Y	?	Y
9 Hamilton	Y	Y	Y	Y	Y	Y	Y	Y
10 Jacobs	Y	Y	Y	Y	Y	Y	N	N
IOWA								
1 ***Leach***	Y	Y	Y	Y	Y	Y	N	N
2 ***Nussle***	Y	Y	N	Y	Y	Y	N	N
3 ***Lightfoot***	Y	Y	N	Y	?	?	N	N
4 Smith	Y	Y	Y	Y	Y	Y	Y	Y
5 ***Grandy***	Y	Y	N	Y	Y	Y	?	N
KANSAS								
1 ***Roberts***	Y	Y	N	Y	Y	Y	N	N
2 Slattery	Y	Y	Y	Y	Y	Y	?	Y
3 ***Meyers***	Y	Y	Y	Y	Y	Y	N	N
4 Glickman	Y	Y	Y	Y	Y	Y	Y	Y
KENTUCKY								
1 Barlow	Y	Y	Y	Y	Y	Y	Y	Y
2 Natcher	Y	Y	Y	Y	Y	Y	Y	Y
3 Mazzoli	Y	N	Y	Y	Y	Y	Y	Y
4 ***Bunning***	Y	Y	N	Y	Y	Y	N	N
5 ***Rogers***	Y	Y	N	Y	Y	Y	?	N
6 Baesler	Y	Y	Y	Y	Y	Y	Y	Y
LOUISIANA								
1 ***Livingston***	Y	Y	N	Y	N	Y	?	N
2 Jefferson	Y	N	Y	N	?	Y	Y	Y
3 Tauzin	Y	Y	N	Y	Y	Y	Y	Y
4 Fields	Y	N	Y	N	Y	Y	Y	Y
5 ***McCrery***	Y	Y	N	Y	Y	Y	?	N
6 ***Baker***	Y	Y	N	Y	Y	Y	N	N
7 Hayes	Y	Y	N	Y	Y	Y	Y	Y
MAINE								
1 Andrews	Y	N	Y	N	Y	Y	Y	Y
2 ***Snowe***	Y	Y	Y	Y	Y	Y	Y	Y
MARYLAND								
1 ***Gilchrest***	Y	Y	Y	Y	Y	Y	N	N
2 ***Bentley***	Y	Y	Y	Y	Y	Y	N	N
3 Cardin	Y	N	Y	Y	Y	Y	Y	Y
4 Wynn	Y	Y	Y	Y	Y	Y	Y	Y
5 Hoyer	Y	Y	Y	Y	Y	Y	Y	Y
6 ***Bartlett***	Y	Y	N	Y	Y	Y	N	N
7 Mfume	Y	N	Y	N	Y	Y	Y	Y
8 ***Morella***	Y	N	Y	Y	Y	Y	N	N
MASSACHUSETTS								
1 Olver	Y	N	Y	N	Y	Y	Y	Y
2 Neal	Y	N	Y	Y	Y	Y	Y	Y
3 ***Blute***	Y	Y	Y	Y	Y	Y	N	N
4 Frank	Y	N	Y	N	Y	Y	Y	Y
5 Meehan	Y	N	Y	Y	Y	Y	Y	Y
6 ***Torkildsen***	Y	Y	Y	Y	Y	Y	N	N
7 Markey	?	N	Y	N	Y	Y	Y	Y
8 Kennedy	Y	N	Y	Y	Y	Y	Y	Y
9 Moakley	Y	Y	Y	Y	Y	Y	Y	Y
10 Studds	Y	N	Y	N	Y	Y	Y	Y
MICHIGAN								
1 Stupak	Y	N	Y	Y	Y	Y	Y	Y
2 ***Hoekstra***	Y	Y	N	Y	Y	Y	N	N
3 Henry	?	?	?	?	?	?	?	?
4 ***Camp***	Y	Y	N	Y	Y	Y	N	N
5 Barcia	Y	Y	N	Y	Y	Y	?	Y
6 ***Upton***	Y	Y	Y	Y	Y	Y	N	N
7 ***Smith***	N	Y	N	Y	N	Y	N	N
8 Carr	Y	Y	Y	Y	Y	Y	Y	Y
9 Kildee	Y	Y	Y	Y	Y	Y	Y	Y
10 Bonior	Y	N	Y	N	Y	Y	Y	Y
11 ***Knollenberg***	Y	Y	N	Y	Y	Y	N	N
12 Levin	Y	N	Y	Y	Y	Y	Y	Y
13 Ford	Y	Y	Y	Y	Y	Y	?	Y
14 Conyers	?	?	?	?	Y	Y	Y	Y
15 Collins	Y	N	Y	N	Y	Y	Y	Y
16 Dingell	Y	Y	Y	Y	?	?	Y	Y
MINNESOTA								
1 Penny	Y	Y	Y	Y	N	Y	Y	Y
2 Minge	Y	N	Y	Y	Y	Y	Y	Y
3 ***Ramstad***	Y	Y	Y	Y	Y	Y	N	N
4 Vento	Y	N	Y	N	Y	Y	Y	Y

	67	68	69	70	71	72	73	75
5 Sabo	Y	N	Y	N	Y	Y	Y	Y
6 ***Grams***	Y	Y	–	Y	Y	Y	N	N
7 Peterson	Y	Y	N	Y	Y	Y	Y	?
8 Oberstar	Y	Y	Y	Y	Y	Y	Y	Y
MISSISSIPPI								
1 Whitten	Y	Y	Y	Y	Y	Y	?	Y
2 Vacancy								
3 Montgomery	Y	Y	Y	Y	Y	Y	Y	Y
4 Parker	Y	Y	N	Y	Y	Y	Y	Y
5 Taylor	Y	Y	N	Y	Y	Y	N	N
MISSOURI								
1 Clay	Y	N	Y	N	?	Y	N	?
2 ***Talent***	Y	Y	N	Y	N	Y	N	N
3 Gephardt	Y	N	Y	Y	Y	Y	Y	Y
4 Skelton	Y	Y	N	Y	Y	Y	Y	Y
5 Wheat	Y	N	Y	N	Y	Y	Y	Y
6 Danner	Y	Y	Y	Y	Y	Y	Y	Y
7 ***Hancock***	Y	Y	N	Y	N	Y	N	N
8 ***Emerson***	Y	Y	N	Y	Y	Y	N	N
9 Volkmer	Y	Y	N	Y	Y	Y	Y	Y
MONTANA								
AL Williams	Y	N	Y	Y	Y	Y	?	?
NEBRASKA								
1 ***Bereuter***	Y	Y	N	Y	Y	Y	?	N
2 Hoagland	Y	N	Y	Y	Y	Y	Y	Y
3 ***Barrett***	Y	Y	N	Y	Y	Y	N	N
NEVADA								
1 Bilbray	Y	Y	Y	Y	Y	Y	Y	Y
2 ***Vucanovich***	Y	Y	N	Y	Y	Y	?	N
NEW HAMPSHIRE								
1 ***Zeliff***	Y	Y	Y	Y	N	Y	N	N
2 Swett	Y	Y	Y	Y	Y	Y	Y	Y
NEW JERSEY								
1 Andrews	Y	N	Y	Y	Y	Y	Y	Y
2 Hughes	Y	Y	Y	Y	Y	Y	Y	Y
3 ***Saxton***	Y	Y	Y	Y	Y	Y	?	N
4 ***Smith***	Y	Y	N	Y	Y	Y	Y	Y
5 ***Roukema***	Y	Y	Y	Y	?	?	N	N
6 Pallone	Y	Y	Y	Y	Y	Y	Y	Y
7 ***Franks***	Y	Y	Y	Y	Y	Y	N	N
8 Klein	Y	Y	Y	Y	Y	Y	Y	Y
9 Torricelli	Y	Y	Y	Y	Y	Y	Y	Y
10 Payne	Y	N	Y	N	?	?	Y	Y
11 ***Gallo***	Y	Y	Y	Y	Y	Y	N	?
12 ***Zimmer***	Y	Y	Y	Y	N	Y	N	N
13 Menendez	Y	N	Y	Y	Y	Y	Y	Y
NEW MEXICO								
1 ***Schiff***	Y	N	Y	Y	Y	Y	N	N
2 ***Skeen***	Y	Y	N	Y	Y	Y	N	N
3 Richardson	Y	N	Y	Y	Y	Y	Y	Y
NEW YORK								
1 Hochbrueckner	Y	Y	Y	Y	Y	Y	Y	Y
2 ***Lazio***	Y	Y	Y	Y	Y	Y	N	N
3 ***King***	N	Y	N	Y	Y	Y	?	N
4 ***Levy***	Y	Y	Y	Y	Y	Y	N	N
5 Ackerman	Y	N	Y	Y	Y	Y	Y	Y
6 Flake	Y	N	Y	N	?	?	?	Y
7 Manton	Y	N	Y	Y	?	?	?	Y
8 Nadler	Y	N	Y	N	Y	Y	Y	Y
9 Schumer	Y	N	Y	Y	Y	Y	Y	Y
10 Towns	Y	N	Y	N	Y	Y	Y	Y
11 Owens	Y	N	Y	N	Y	Y	Y	Y
12 Velazquez	Y	N	Y	N	Y	Y	Y	Y
13 ***Molinari***	Y	Y	Y	Y	?	?	N	N
14 Maloney	Y	N	Y	Y	Y	Y	Y	Y
15 Rangel	Y	N	Y	N	Y	Y	Y	Y
16 Serrano	Y	N	Y	Y	Y	Y	Y	Y
17 Engel	Y	N	Y	N	?	?	Y	Y
18 Lowey	Y	N	Y	Y	Y	Y	Y	Y
19 ***Fish***	Y	Y	Y	Y	Y	Y	Y	Y
20 ***Gilman***	Y	Y	Y	Y	Y	Y	+	Y
21 McNulty	Y	Y	Y	Y	Y	Y	Y	Y
22 ***Solomon***	Y	Y	N	Y	Y	Y	N	N
23 ***Boehlert***	Y	Y	Y	Y	Y	Y	N	N
24 ***McHugh***	Y	Y	Y	Y	Y	Y	N	N
25 ***Walsh***	Y	Y	N	Y	Y	Y	N	N
26 Hinchey	Y	N	Y	Y	Y	Y	?	Y
27 ***Paxon***	Y	Y	N	Y	Y	Y	N	N
28 Slaughter	Y	N	Y	Y	+	+	Y	Y
29 LaFalce	Y	Y	Y	Y	Y	Y	Y	Y
30 ***Quinn***	Y	Y	N	Y	Y	Y	N	N
31 ***Houghton***	Y	Y	Y	Y	?	Y	Y	Y
NORTH CAROLINA								
1 Clayton	Y	N	Y	N	Y	Y	Y	Y
2 Valentine	Y	Y	Y	Y	Y	Y	Y	Y

	67	68	69	70	71	72	73	75
3 Lancaster	Y	Y	Y	Y	Y	Y	Y	Y
4 Price	Y	Y	Y	Y	Y	Y	Y	Y
5 Neal	Y	Y	Y	Y	Y	Y	Y	Y
6 ***Coble***	Y	Y	N	Y	N	Y	N	N
7 Rose	?	N	Y	Y	Y	Y	Y	Y
8 Hefner	Y	Y	Y	Y	Y	Y	Y	Y
9 ***McMillan***	Y	Y	Y	Y	Y	Y	N	N
10 ***Ballenger***	Y	Y	N	Y	N	Y	N	N
11 ***Taylor***	Y	Y	N	Y	–	+	N	N
12 Watt	Y	N	Y	N	Y	Y	Y	Y
NORTH DAKOTA								
AL Pomeroy	Y	N	Y	Y	Y	Y	Y	Y
OHIO								
1 Mann	Y	N	Y	Y	Y	Y	Y	Y
2 Vacancy								
3 Hall	Y	N	Y	Y	Y	Y	Y	Y
4 ***Oxley***	Y	Y	N	Y	Y	Y	Y	N
5 ***Gillmor***	Y	Y	N	Y	Y	Y	Y	Y
6 Strickland	Y	Y	Y	Y	Y	Y	Y	Y
7 ***Hobson***	Y	Y	Y	Y	Y	Y	N	N
8 ***Boehner***	Y	Y	N	Y	N	Y	N	N
9 Kaptur	Y	Y	Y	Y	Y	Y	Y	Y
10 ***Hoke***	Y	Y	N	Y	Y	Y	?	Y
11 Stokes	Y	N	Y	N	Y	Y	Y	Y
12 ***Kasich***	Y	Y	N	Y	?	?	Y	N
13 Brown	Y	N	Y	Y	Y	Y	Y	Y
14 Sawyer	Y	Y	Y	Y	Y	Y	Y	Y
15 ***Pryce***	Y	N	Y	Y	Y	Y	N	N
16 ***Regula***	Y	Y	N	Y	Y	Y	N	N
17 Traficant	Y	N	Y	Y	Y	Y	Y	Y
18 Applegate	Y	Y	Y	Y	Y	Y	Y	Y
19 Fingerhut	Y	Y	Y	Y	Y	Y	Y	Y
OKLAHOMA								
1 ***Inhofe***	Y	Y	N	Y	N	Y	?	N
2 Synar	Y	N	Y	N	Y	Y	Y	Y
3 Brewster	Y	?	Y	Y	Y	Y	Y	Y
4 McCurdy	Y	Y	Y	Y	Y	Y	Y	Y
5 ***Istook***	Y	Y	N	Y	N	Y	N	N
6 English	Y	Y	Y	Y	Y	Y	Y	Y
OREGON								
1 Furse	Y	N	Y	N	Y	Y	Y	Y
2 ***Smith***	Y	Y	N	Y	Y	Y	N	N
3 Wyden	Y	N	?	Y	Y	Y	Y	Y
4 DeFazio	Y	N	Y	Y	Y	Y	Y	?
5 Kopetski	+	–	+	–	Y	Y	Y	Y
PENNSYLVANIA								
1 Foglietta	Y	N	Y	N	Y	Y	Y	Y
2 Blackwell	Y	N	Y	N	Y	Y	Y	Y
3 Borski	Y	N	Y	Y	Y	Y	Y	Y
4 Klink	Y	Y	Y	?	Y	Y	Y	Y
5 ***Clinger***	Y	Y	N	Y	Y	Y	Y	N
6 Holden	Y	Y	Y	Y	Y	Y	Y	Y
7 ***Weldon***	Y	Y	N	Y	Y	Y	N	N
8 ***Greenwood***	Y	Y	Y	Y	Y	Y	N	N
9 ***Shuster***	Y	Y	N	Y	?	?	N	N
10 ***McDade***	?	?	?	?	Y	Y	N	N
11 Kanjorski	Y	Y	Y	Y	Y	Y	Y	Y
12 Murtha	Y	Y	Y	Y	Y	Y	Y	Y
13 Margolies-Mezv.	Y	N	Y	Y	Y	Y	Y	Y
14 Coyne	Y	N	Y	N	Y	Y	Y	Y
15 McHale	Y	N	Y	Y	Y	Y	Y	Y
16 ***Walker***	Y	Y	N	Y	N	Y	N	N
17 ***Gekas***	Y	Y	Y	Y	N	Y	N	N
18 ***Santorum***	Y	Y	N	Y	Y	Y	?	N
19 ***Goodling***	Y	Y	N	Y	Y	Y	N	N
20 Murphy	Y	Y	Y	Y	Y	Y	N	?
21 ***Ridge***	Y	Y	Y	Y	Y	Y	N	N
RHODE ISLAND								
1 ***Machtley***	Y	Y	Y	Y	Y	Y	?	N
2 Reed	Y	N	Y	Y	Y	Y	Y	Y
SOUTH CAROLINA								
1 ***Ravenel***	Y	Y	Y	Y	Y	Y	Y	Y
2 ***Spence***	Y	Y	Y	Y	Y	Y	Y	N
3 Derrick	Y	Y	?	Y	Y	Y	Y	Y
4 ***Inglis***	Y	Y	N	Y	N	Y	Y	Y
5 Spratt	Y	Y	Y	?	Y	Y	Y	?
6 Clyburn	Y	Y	Y	N	Y	Y	Y	Y
SOUTH DAKOTA								
AL Johnson	Y	Y	Y	Y	Y	Y	Y	Y
TENNESSEE								
1 ***Quillen***	Y	Y	N	?	?	?	?	?
2 ***Duncan***	Y	Y	N	Y	N	Y	N	N
3 Lloyd	Y	Y	Y	Y	?	?	?	Y
4 Cooper	Y	Y	Y	Y	Y	Y	Y	Y
5 Clement	Y	Y	Y	Y	Y	Y	Y	Y

	67	68	69	70	71	72	73	75
6 Gordon	?	Y	Y	Y	Y	Y	Y	Y
7 ***Sundquist***	Y	Y	N	Y	Y	Y	N	N
8 Tanner	Y	Y	Y	Y	Y	Y	Y	Y
9 Ford	?	?	?	?	?	?	?	?
TEXAS								
1 Chapman	Y	Y	Y	Y	Y	Y	Y	Y
2 Wilson	?	?	?	Y	Y	Y	?	?
3 ***Johnson, Sam***	Y	Y	N	Y	Y	Y	N	N
4 Hall	Y	Y	Y	Y	Y	Y	Y	Y
5 Bryant	Y	N	Y	Y	Y	Y	Y	Y
6 ***Barton***	Y	Y	N	?	?	?	N	N
7 ***Archer***	Y	Y	N	Y	N	Y	Y	Y
8 ***Fields***	Y	Y	N	Y	?	?	?	?
9 Brooks	Y	N	Y	Y	Y	Y	Y	Y
10 Pickle	Y	N	Y	Y	Y	Y	Y	Y
11 Edwards	Y	Y	Y	Y	Y	Y	Y	Y
12 Geren	Y	Y	Y	Y	Y	Y	Y	Y
13 Sarpalius	Y	Y	N	Y	Y	Y	Y	Y
14 Laughlin	Y	Y	Y	Y	?	Y	Y	?
15 de la Garza	Y	Y	Y	Y	Y	Y	?	Y
16 Coleman	Y	N	Y	Y	Y	Y	Y	Y
17 Stenholm	Y	Y	Y	Y	N	Y	Y	Y
18 Washington	Y	N	Y	N	Y	Y	?	?
19 ***Combest***	Y	Y	N	Y	Y	Y	Y	Y
20 Gonzalez	Y	N	Y	Y	Y	Y	Y	Y
21 ***Smith***	Y	Y	Y	Y	Y	Y	N	N
22 ***DeLay***	N	Y	N	Y	N	Y	N	N
23 ***Bonilla***	Y	Y	Y	Y	Y	Y	N	N
24 Frost	Y	Y	Y	Y	Y	Y	Y	Y
25 Andrews	Y	Y	Y	Y	Y	Y	Y	Y
26 ***Armey***	N	Y	N	Y	N	Y	N	N
27 Ortiz	Y	N	Y	Y	Y	Y	Y	Y
28 Tejeda	Y	Y	Y	Y	Y	Y	Y	Y
29 Green	Y	N	Y	Y	Y	Y	Y	Y
30 Johnson, E. B.	Y	N	Y	N	Y	Y	Y	Y
UTAH								
1 ***Hansen***	Y	Y	N	Y	N	Y	N	N
2 Shepherd	?	?	Y	Y	Y	Y	Y	Y
3 Orton	Y	Y	N	Y	Y	Y	Y	Y
VERMONT								
AL *Sanders*	Y	N	Y	N	Y	Y	Y	Y
VIRGINIA								
1 ***Bateman***	Y	Y	N	Y	Y	Y	Y	Y
2 Pickett	Y	Y	Y	Y	Y	Y	Y	Y
3 Scott	Y	N	Y	Y	Y	Y	Y	Y
4 Sisisky	Y	Y	Y	Y	Y	Y	Y	Y
5 Payne	Y	Y	Y	Y	Y	Y	Y	Y
6 ***Goodlatte***	Y	Y	N	Y	Y	Y	N	N
7 ***Bliley***	Y	Y	N	Y	Y	Y	N	N
8 Moran	Y	N	Y	Y	Y	Y	Y	Y
9 Boucher	?	?	?	?	Y	Y	Y	Y
10 ***Wolf***	Y	Y	N	Y	Y	Y	N	N
11 Byrne	Y	Y	Y	Y	Y	Y	Y	Y
WASHINGTON								
1 Cantwell	Y	N	Y	Y	Y	Y	Y	Y
2 Swift	Y	N	Y	Y	Y	Y	?	Y
3 Unsoeld	Y	N	Y	N	Y	Y	Y	?
4 Inslee	Y	N	Y	Y	Y	Y	Y	Y
5 Foley								
6 Dicks	Y	N	Y	?	Y	Y	Y	Y
7 McDermott	Y	N	Y	N	Y	Y	Y	Y
8 ***Dunn***	Y	Y	Y	Y	Y	Y	N	N
9 Kreidler	Y	N	Y	Y	Y	Y	Y	Y
WEST VIRGINIA								
1 Mollohan	Y	Y	N	Y	Y	Y	Y	Y
2 Wise	Y	Y	Y	Y	Y	Y	Y	Y
3 Rahall	Y	Y	N	Y	Y	Y	Y	Y
WISCONSIN								
1 Vacancy								
2 ***Klug***	Y	Y	Y	Y	Y	?	N	N
3 ***Gunderson***	Y	N	Y	Y	Y	Y	Y	N
4 Kleczka	Y	Y	Y	Y	Y	Y	Y	Y
5 Barrett	Y	N	Y	Y	Y	Y	Y	Y
6 ***Petri***	Y	Y	N	Y	Y	Y	N	N
7 Obey	Y	N	Y	Y	Y	Y	Y	Y
8 ***Roth***	Y	Y	N	Y	Y	Y	N	Y
9 ***Sensenbrenner***	Y	Y	N	Y	Y	Y	N	N
WYOMING								
AL ***Thomas***	Y	Y	Y	Y	Y	Y	N	N
DELEGATES								
de Lugo, V.I.	D	D	D	D	D	D	D	D
Faleomavaega, Am.S.	D	D	D	D	D	D	D	D
Norton, D.C.	D	D	D	D	D	D	D	D
Romero-B., P.R.	D	D	D	D	D	D	D	D
Underwood, Guam	D	D	D	D	D	D	D	D

Southern states - Ala., Ark., Fla., Ga., Ky., La., Miss., N.C., Okla., S.C., Tenn., Texas, Va.
Omitted votes are quorum calls, which CQ does not include in its vote charts.

76. Procedural Motion. Burton, R-Ind., motion to adjourn. Motion rejected 69-343: R 69-99; D 0-243 (ND 0-163, SD 0-80); I 0-1, March 18, 1993.

77. H Con Res 64. Fiscal 1994 Budget Resolution/Previous Question. Beilenson, D-Calif., motion to order the previous question (thus ending debate and the possibility of amendment) on adoption of the rule (H Res 133) to provide for House floor consideration of the concurrent resolution to set binding budget levels for the fiscal year ending Sept. 30, 1994: budget authority, $1.506 trillion; outlays, $1.495 trillion; revenues, $1.242 trillion; deficit, $253.5 billion. The resolution incorporates the guidelines of the administration's economic package plus an additional $63 billion in spending cuts. Motion agreed to 250-172: R 0-171; D 249-1 (ND 168-1, SD 81-0); I 1-0, March 18, 1993.

78. H Con Res 64. Fiscal 1994 Budget Resolution/Rule. Adoption of the rule (H Res 133) to provide for House floor consideration of the concurrent resolution to set binding budget levels for the fiscal year ending Sept. 30, 1994: budget authority, $1.506 trillion; outlays, $1.495 trillion; revenues, $1.242 trillion; deficit, $253.5 billion. The resolution incorporates the guidelines of the administration's economic package plus an additional $63 billion in spending cuts. Adopted 251-172: R 0-172; D 250-0 (ND 169-0, SD 81-0); I 1-0, March 18, 1993.

79. H Con Res 64. Fiscal 1994 Budget Resolution/Motion to Reconsider. Beilenson, D-Calif., motion to table (kill) the Moakley, D-Mass., motion to reconsider the adoption of the rule (H Res 133) to provide for House floor consideration of the concurrent resolution to set binding budget levels for the fiscal year ending Sept. 30, 1994: budget authority, $1.506 trillion; outlays, $1.495 trillion; revenues, $1.242 trillion; deficit, $253.5 billion. The resolution incorporates the guidelines of the administration's economic package plus an additional $63 billion in spending cuts. Motion agreed to 250-172: R 0-171; D 249-1 (ND 167-1, SD 82-0); I 1-0, March 18, 1993.

80. Procedural Motion. Burton, R-Ind., motion to adjourn. Motion rejected 60-360: R 60-113; D 0-246 (ND 0-166, SD 0-80); I 0-1, March 18, 1993.

81. H Con Res 64. Fiscal 1994 Budget Resolution/No-Tax Substitute. Kasich, R-Ohio, substitute amendment designed to achieve the same amount of deficit reduction as the Democratic resolution, approximately $500 billion over five years, without adding new taxes. Rejected in the Committee of the Whole 135-295: R 132-41; D 3-253 (ND 1-173, SD 2-80); I 0-1, March 18, 1993. A "nay" was a vote in support of the president's position.

82. H Con Res 64. Fiscal 1994 Budget Resolution/Spending Cut and Tax Substitute. Solomon, R-N.Y., substitute amendment to reduce the deficit by $682 billion over five years by cutting spending by $555 billion and adding $172 billion in new revenue. The substitute would eliminate most of the Democrats' tax increases, except for increased taxes on the wealthy. The substitute would also eliminate the superconducting super collider and the space station. Rejected in the Committee of the Whole 20-409: R 19-153; D 1-255 (ND 1-172, SD 0-83); I 0-1, March 18, 1993.

83. H Con Res 64. Fiscal 1994 Budget Resolution/Strike Resolving Clause. Burton, R-Ind., motion to strike the resolving clause, thus killing the measure. Motion rejected in the Committee of the Whole 122-302: R 120-50; D 2-251 (ND 2-169, SD 0-82); I 0-1, March 18, 1993.

	76	77	78	79	80	81	82	83
ALABAMA								
1 *Callahan*	Y	N	N	N	Y	Y	N	Y
2 *Everett*	Y	N	N	N	Y	Y	N	Y
3 Browder	N	Y	?	Y	N	N	N	N
4 Bevill	N	Y	Y	Y	N	N	N	N
5 Cramer	N	Y	Y	Y	N	N	N	N
6 *Bachus*	N	N	N	N	Y	N	N	Y
7 Hilliard	N	Y	Y	Y	N	N	N	N
ALASKA								
AL *Young*	Y	N	N	N	Y	N	N	Y
ARIZONA								
1 Coppersmith	N	Y	Y	Y	N	N	N	N
2 Pastor	N	Y	Y	Y	N	N	N	N
3 *Stump*	Y	N	N	N	Y	N	N	Y
4 *Kyl*	N	N	N	N	N	Y	N	Y
5 *Kolbe*	N	N	N	N	N	Y	N	Y
6 English	N	Y	Y	Y	N	N	N	N
ARKANSAS								
1 Lambert	N	Y	Y	Y	N	N	N	N
2 Thornton	N	Y	Y	Y	N	N	N	N
3 *Hutchinson*	N	N	N	N	N	N	N	Y
4 Dickey	N	N	N	N	Y	N	N	N
CALIFORNIA								
1 Hamburg	N	Y	Y	?	?	N	N	N
2 *Herger*	Y	?	N	N	Y	Y	N	Y
3 Fazio	N	Y	Y	Y	N	N	N	N
4 *Doolittle*	Y	N	N	N	Y	Y	N	Y
5 Matsui	N	Y	Y	Y	N	N	N	N
6 Woolsey	N	Y	Y	Y	N	N	N	N
7 Miller	?	Y	Y	Y	N	N	N	N
8 Pelosi	N	Y	Y	Y	N	N	N	N
9 Dellums	?	Y	Y	Y	N	N	N	N
10 *Baker*	Y	N	N	N	Y	Y	N	Y
11 *Pombo*	Y	N	N	N	Y	Y	N	Y
12 Lantos	N	Y	Y	Y	N	N	N	N
13 Stark	N	Y	Y	Y	N	N	N	N
14 Eshoo	N	Y	Y	Y	N	N	N	N
15 Mineta	N	Y	Y	Y	N	N	N	N
16 Edwards	N	Y	Y	Y	N	N	N	N
17 Vacancy								
18 Condit	N	Y	Y	Y	N	Y	N	N
19 Lehman	?	Y	Y	Y	N	N	N	N
20 Dooley	N	Y	Y	Y	N	N	N	N
21 *Thomas*	N	N	N	N	N	Y	N	N
22 *Huffington*	N	N	N	N	N	Y	N	Y
23 *Gallegly*	Y	N	N	N	Y	Y	N	Y
24 Beilenson	N	Y	Y	Y	N	N	N	N
25 *McKeon*	Y	N	N	N	Y	N	Y	Y
26 Berman	N	Y	Y	Y	?	N	N	N
27 *Moorhead*	N	N	N	N	N	Y	N	Y
28 *Dreier*	N	N	N	N	N	Y	N	Y
29 Waxman	N	Y	Y	Y	N	N	N	?
30 Becerra	N	Y	Y	Y	N	N	N	N
31 Martinez	N	Y	Y	Y	N	N	N	N
32 Dixon	N	Y	Y	Y	N	N	N	N
33 Roybal-Allard	N	Y	Y	Y	N	N	N	N
34 Torres	N	Y	Y	Y	N	N	N	N
35 Waters	N	Y	Y	Y	N	N	N	N
36 Harman	N	Y	Y	Y	N	N	N	N
37 Tucker	?	Y	Y	Y	N	N	N	N
38 *Horn*	Y	N	N	N	N	Y	N	N
39 *Royce*	N	N	N	N	N	Y	N	Y
40 *Lewis*	Y	N	N	N	Y	N	N	N
41 *Kim*	N	N	N	N	N	Y	N	Y

	76	77	78	79	80	81	82	83
42 Brown	N	Y	Y	Y	N	N	N	N
43 *Calvert*	N	N	N	N	Y	N	Y	N
44 *McCandless*	Y	N	N	N	Y	Y	N	Y
45 *Rohrabacher*	Y	N	N	N	Y	Y	N	Y
46 *Dornan*	?	N	N	N	Y	Y	N	Y
47 *Cox*	N	N	N	N	N	Y	N	Y
48 *Packard*	N	N	N	N	N	Y	N	Y
49 Schenk	N	Y	Y	Y	N	N	N	N
50 Filner	N	Y	Y	Y	N	N	N	N
51 *Cunningham*	N	N	N	N	N	Y	N	Y
52 *Hunter*	Y	N	N	N	Y	Y	N	Y
COLORADO								
1 Schroeder	N	Y	Y	Y	N	N	N	N
2 Skaggs	N	Y	Y	Y	N	N	N	N
3 *McInnis*	N	N	N	N	N	N	N	N
4 *Allard*	Y	N	N	N	Y	Y	N	Y
5 *Hefley*	Y	N	N	N	Y	N	N	Y
6 *Schaefer*	N	N	N	N	N	N	N	N
CONNECTICUT								
1 Kennelly	N	Y	Y	Y	N	N	N	N
2 Gejdenson	N	Y	Y	Y	N	N	N	N
3 DeLauro	N	Y	Y	Y	N	N	N	N
4 *Shays*	N	N	N	N	Y	Y	N	N
5 *Franks*	Y	N	N	N	Y	Y	N	Y
6 *Johnson*	Y	N	N	N	Y	Y	Y	Y
DELAWARE								
AL *Castle*	N	N	N	N	Y	N	Y	N
FLORIDA								
1 Hutto	N	Y	Y	Y	N	N	N	N
2 Peterson	N	Y	Y	Y	N	N	N	N
3 Brown	N	Y	Y	Y	N	N	N	N
4 *Fowler*	N	N	N	N	Y	N	N	N
5 Thurman	N	Y	Y	Y	N	N	N	N
6 *Stearns*	N	N	N	N	N	N	N	Y
7 *Mica*	Y	N	N	N	Y	Y	N	Y
8 *McCollum*	N	N	N	N	Y	Y	N	Y
9 *Bilirakis*	N	N	N	N	N	N	N	N
10 *Young*	N	N	N	N	N	Y	N	N
11 Gibbons	N	Y	Y	Y	N	N	N	N
12 *Canady*	N	N	N	N	Y	Y	N	Y
13 *Miller*	Y	N	N	N	Y	Y	N	Y
14 *Goss*	N	N	N	N	Y	Y	N	N
15 Bacchus	N	Y	Y	Y	N	N	N	N
16 *Lewis*	N	N	N	N	Y	N	N	N
17 Meek	N	Y	Y	Y	N	N	N	N
18 *Ros-Lehtinen*	N	N	N	N	N	N	N	N
19 Johnston	N	Y	Y	Y	?	N	N	N
20 Deutsch	N	Y	Y	Y	N	N	N	N
21 *Diaz-Balart*	N	N	N	N	N	N	N	N
22 *Shaw*	Y	N	N	N	Y	N	N	Y
23 Hastings	N	Y	Y	Y	N	N	N	N
GEORGIA								
1 *Kingston*	Y	N	N	N	Y	Y	N	Y
2 Bishop	N	Y	Y	Y	N	N	N	N
3 *Collins*	Y	N	N	N	Y	Y	N	Y
4 *Linder*	N	N	N	N	Y	Y	N	Y
5 Lewis	N	Y	Y	Y	N	N	N	N
6 *Gingrich*	?	N	N	N	Y	Y	N	Y
7 Darden	N	Y	Y	Y	N	N	N	N
8 Rowland	N	Y	Y	Y	N	N	N	N
9 Deal	N	Y	Y	Y	N	N	N	N
10 Johnson	N	Y	Y	Y	N	N	N	N
11 McKinney	N	Y	Y	Y	N	N	N	N
HAWAII								
1 Abercrombie	N	Y	Y	Y	N	N	N	N
2 Mink	N	Y	Y	Y	N	N	N	N
IDAHO								
1 LaRocco	N	Y	Y	Y	N	N	N	N
2 *Crapo*	Y	N	N	N	N	Y	N	Y
ILLINOIS								
1 Rush	N	Y	Y	Y	N	N	N	N
2 Reynolds	N	Y	Y	Y	N	N	N	N
3 Lipinski	N	Y	Y	Y	N	N	N	N
4 Gutierrez	N	Y	Y	Y	N	N	N	N
5 Rostenkowski	N	Y	Y	Y	N	N	N	N
6 *Hyde*	N	N	N	N	Y	Y	N	N
7 Collins	N	Y	Y	Y	N	N	N	N
8 *Crane*	Y	N	N	?	Y	Y	N	Y
9 Yates	N	Y	Y	Y	N	N	N	N
10 *Porter*	N	N	N	N	Y	N	N	N
11 Sangmeister	N	Y	Y	Y	N	N	N	N
12 Costello	N	Y	Y	Y	N	N	N	N
13 *Fawell*	Y	N	N	N	Y	Y	N	Y
14 *Hastert*	N	N	N	N	Y	Y	N	Y
15 *Ewing*	N	N	N	N	Y	Y	N	Y
16 *Manzullo*	N	N	N	N	N	Y	N	Y
17 Evans	N	Y	Y	Y	N	N	N	N

ND Northern Democrats   SD Southern Democrats

	76	77	78	79	80	81	82	83
18 ***Michel***	N	N	N	N	N	Y	N	Y
19 Poshard	N	Y	Y	Y	N	N	N	N
20 Durbin	N	Y	Y	Y	N	N	N	N
INDIANA								
1 Visclosky	N	Y	Y	Y	N	N	N	N
2 Sharp	N	Y	Y	Y	N	N	N	N
3 Roemer	N	Y	Y	Y	N	N	N	N
4 Long	N	Y	Y	Y	N	N	N	N
5 ***Buyer***	Y	N	N	N	Y	Y	N	Y
6 ***Burton***	Y	N	N	N	Y	N	N	Y
7 ***Myers***	Y	N	N	N	N	Y	?	?
8 McCloskey	N	Y	Y	Y	N	N	N	N
9 Hamilton	N	Y	Y	Y	N	N	N	N
10 Jacobs	N	N	Y	Y	N	N	N	Y
IOWA								
1 ***Leach***	N	N	N	N	N	N	N	Y
2 ***Nussle***	N	N	N	N	N	Y	N	Y
3 ***Lightfoot***	Y	N	N	N	N	N	N	Y
4 Smith	N	Y	Y	Y	N	N	N	N
5 ***Grandy***	N	N	N	N	N	Y	N	N
KANSAS								
1 ***Roberts***	Y	N	N	N	Y	Y	N	Y
2 Slattery	N	Y	Y	Y	N	N	N	N
3 ***Meyers***	N	N	N	N	N	Y	N	Y
4 Glickman	N	Y	Y	Y	N	N	N	N
KENTUCKY								
1 Barlow	N	Y	Y	Y	N	N	N	N
2 Natcher	N	Y	Y	Y	N	N	N	N
3 Mazzoli	N	Y	Y	Y	N	N	N	N
4 ***Bunning***	Y	N	N	N	Y	Y	N	N
5 ***Rogers***	N	N	N	N	N	N	N	Y
6 Baesler	N	Y	Y	Y	N	N	N	N
LOUISIANA								
1 ***Livingston***	Y	N	N	N	Y	Y	N	Y
2 Jefferson	N	Y	Y	Y	N	N	N	N
3 Tauzin	?	Y	Y	Y	N	N	N	N
4 Fields	N	Y	Y	Y	N	N	N	N
5 ***McCrery***	N	N	N	N	N	Y	Y	N
6 ***Baker***	Y	N	N	N	Y	Y	N	Y
7 Hayes	N	Y	Y	Y	N	N	N	N
MAINE								
1 Andrews	N	Y	Y	Y	N	N	N	N
2 ***Snowe***	N	N	N	N	N	Y	N	N
MARYLAND								
1 ***Gilchrest***	N	N	N	N	N	Y	Y	N
2 ***Bentley***	Y	N	N	N	Y	N	N	Y
3 Cardin	N	Y	Y	Y	N	N	N	N
4 Wynn	N	Y	Y	Y	N	N	N	N
5 Hoyer	N	Y	Y	Y	N	N	N	N
6 ***Bartlett***	Y	N	N	N	Y	Y	N	Y
7 Mfume	N	Y	Y	Y	N	N	N	N
8 ***Morella***	N	N	N	N	N	N	N	N
MASSACHUSETTS								
1 Olver	N	Y	Y	Y	N	N	N	N
2 Neal	N	Y	Y	Y	N	N	N	N
3 ***Blute***	Y	N	N	N	Y	N	N	Y
4 Frank	N	Y	Y	Y	N	N	N	N
5 Meehan	N	Y	Y	Y	N	N	N	N
6 ***Torkildsen***	Y	N	N	N	Y	Y	N	Y
7 Markey	N	Y	Y	Y	N	N	N	N
8 Kennedy	N	Y	Y	Y	N	N	N	N
9 Moakley	N	Y	Y	Y	N	N	N	N
10 Studds	N	Y	Y	Y	N	N	N	N
MICHIGAN								
1 Stupak	N	Y	Y	Y	N	N	N	N
2 ***Hoekstra***	Y	N	N	N	Y	Y	Y	Y
3 Henry	?	?	?	?	?	?	?	?
4 ***Camp***	N	N	N	N	N	Y	N	N
5 Barcia	N	Y	Y	Y	N	N	N	N
6 ***Upton***	N	N	N	N	N	Y	Y	Y
7 ***Smith***	N	N	N	N	N	Y	N	Y
8 Carr	N	Y	Y	Y	N	N	N	N
9 Kildee	N	Y	Y	Y	N	N	N	N
10 Bonior	N	Y	Y	Y	N	N	N	N
11 ***Knollenberg***	N	N	N	N	N	Y	N	Y
12 Levin	N	Y	Y	Y	N	N	N	N
13 Ford	N	?	?	Y	N	N	N	N
14 Conyers	N	Y	Y	Y	N	N	N	N
15 Collins	N	Y	Y	Y	N	N	N	N
16 Dingell	N	Y	Y	Y	N	N	N	N
MINNESOTA								
1 Penny	N	Y	Y	Y	N	N	N	N
2 Minge	N	Y	Y	Y	N	N	N	N
3 ***Ramstad***	N	N	N	N	N	Y	N	Y
4 Vento	N	Y	Y	Y	N	N	N	N

	76	77	78	79	80	81	82	83
5 Sabo	N	Y	Y	Y	N	N	N	N
6 ***Grams***	N	N	N	N	N	Y	N	Y
7 Peterson	N	Y	Y	Y	N	N	N	N
8 Oberstar	N	Y	Y	Y	N	N	N	N
MISSISSIPPI								
1 Whitten	N	Y	Y	Y	N	N	N	N
2 Vacancy								
3 Montgomery	N	Y	Y	Y	N	N	N	N
4 Parker	N	Y	Y	Y	N	N	N	N
5 Taylor	N	Y	Y	Y	N	Y	N	N
MISSOURI								
1 Clay	?	Y	Y	Y	N	N	N	N
2 ***Talent***	N	N	N	N	N	Y	N	Y
3 Gephardt	N	Y	Y	Y	N	N	N	N
4 Skelton	N	Y	Y	Y	N	N	N	N
5 Wheat	N	Y	Y	Y	N	N	N	N
6 Danner	N	Y	Y	Y	N	N	N	N
7 ***Hancock***	Y	N	N	N	Y	N	N	Y
8 ***Emerson***	N	N	N	N	N	Y	N	Y
9 Volkmer	N	Y	Y	Y	N	N	N	N
MONTANA								
AL Williams	?	Y	Y	Y	N	N	N	Y
NEBRASKA								
1 ***Bereuter***	N	N	N	N	N	N	N	N
2 Hoagland	N	Y	Y	Y	N	N	N	N
3 ***Barrett***	N	N	N	N	N	Y	N	Y
NEVADA								
1 Bilbray	N	Y	Y	Y	N	N	N	N
2 ***Vucanovich***	Y	N	N	N	Y	N	N	Y
NEW HAMPSHIRE								
1 ***Zeliff***	N	N	N	N	N	Y	N	Y
2 Swett	N	Y	Y	Y	N	N	N	N
NEW JERSEY								
1 Andrews	N	Y	Y	Y	N	N	N	N
2 Hughes	N	Y	Y	Y	N	N	N	N
3 ***Saxton***	N	N	N	N	N	Y	N	Y
4 ***Smith***	N	N	N	N	N	Y	N	Y
5 ***Roukema***	N	N	N	N	N	N	Y	N
6 Pallone	N	Y	Y	Y	N	N	N	N
7 ***Franks***	N	N	N	N	N	Y	N	Y
8 Klein	N	Y	Y	Y	N	N	N	N
9 Torricelli	N	Y	Y	Y	N	N	N	N
10 Payne	N	Y	Y	Y	N	N	N	N
11 ***Gallo***	?	N	N	N	N	Y	N	Y
12 ***Zimmer***	N	N	N	N	N	Y	N	Y
13 Menendez	N	Y	Y	Y	N	N	N	N
NEW MEXICO								
1 ***Schiff***	N	N	N	N	N	N	N	N
2 ***Skeen***	N	N	N	N	N	Y	N	N
3 Richardson	N	Y	Y	Y	N	N	N	N
NEW YORK								
1 Hochbrueckner	N	Y	Y	Y	N	N	N	N
2 ***Lazio***	Y	N	N	N	N	N	N	Y
3 ***King***	Y	N	N	N	N	Y	N	Y
4 ***Levy***	Y	N	N	N	N	Y	Y	Y
5 Ackerman	N	Y	Y	Y	N	N	N	N
6 Flake	N	Y	Y	Y	N	N	N	N
7 Manton	N	Y	Y	Y	N	N	N	N
8 Nadler	N	Y	Y	Y	N	N	N	N
9 Schumer	N	Y	Y	Y	N	N	N	N
10 Towns	N	Y	Y	Y	N	N	N	N
11 Owens	N	Y	Y	Y	N	N	N	N
12 Velazquez	N	Y	Y	Y	N	N	N	N
13 ***Molinari***	Y	N	N	N	Y	Y	N	N
14 Maloney	N	Y	Y	Y	N	N	N	—
15 Rangel	N	Y	Y	Y	N	N	N	N
16 Serrano	N	Y	Y	Y	N	N	N	N
17 Engel	N	Y	Y	Y	N	N	N	N
18 Lowey	N	Y	Y	Y	N	N	N	N
19 ***Fish***	N	N	N	N	N	Y	Y	N
20 ***Gilman***	N	N	N	N	N	Y	Y	N
21 McNulty	N	Y	Y	Y	N	N	N	N
22 ***Solomon***	Y	N	N	N	N	Y	Y	Y
23 ***Boehlert***	N	N	N	N	N	N	Y	Y
24 ***McHugh***	N	N	N	N	N	Y	Y	Y
25 ***Walsh***	Y	N	N	N	Y	Y	Y	N
26 Hinchey	N	Y	Y	?	?	N	N	N
27 ***Paxon***	Y	N	N	N	Y	Y	N	Y
28 Slaughter	N	Y	Y	Y	N	N	N	N
29 LaFalce	N	Y	Y	Y	N	N	N	N
30 ***Quinn***	N	N	N	N	N	Y	N	Y
31 ***Houghton***	Y	N	N	N	N	Y	Y	N
NORTH CAROLINA								
1 Clayton	N	Y	Y	Y	N	N	N	N
2 Valentine	N	Y	Y	Y	N	N	N	N

	76	77	78	79	80	81	82	83
3 Lancaster	N	Y	Y	Y	N	N	N	N
4 Price	N	Y	Y	Y	N	N	N	N
5 Neal	N	Y	Y	Y	N	N	N	N
6 ***Coble***	N	N	N	N	N	Y	N	Y
7 Rose	N	Y	Y	Y	N	N	N	N
8 Hefner	N	Y	Y	Y	N	N	N	N
9 ***McMillan***	N	N	N	N	N	Y	N	N
10 ***Ballenger***	Y	N	N	N	Y	Y	N	Y
11 ***Taylor***	P	N	N	N	Y	Y	N	?
12 Watt	N	Y	Y	Y	N	N	N	N
NORTH DAKOTA								
AL Pomeroy	N	Y	Y	Y	N	N	N	N
OHIO								
1 Mann	N	Y	Y	Y	N	N	N	N
2 Vacancy								
3 Hall	N	Y	Y	Y	N	N	N	N
4 ***Oxley***	N	N	N	N	N	Y	N	Y
5 ***Gillmor***	Y	N	N	N	N	Y	N	N
6 Strickland	N	Y	Y	Y	N	N	N	N
7 ***Hobson***	Y	N	N	N	Y	N	N	N
8 ***Boehner***	Y	N	N	N	Y	Y	N	Y
9 Kaptur	N	Y	Y	Y	?	N	N	N
10 ***Hoke***	N	N	N	N	Y	Y	N	N
11 Stokes	N	Y	Y	Y	N	N	N	N
12 ***Kasich***	N	N	N	N	N	Y	N	N
13 Brown	N	Y	Y	Y	N	N	N	N
14 Sawyer	N	Y	Y	Y	N	N	N	N
15 ***Pryce***	Y	N	N	N	N	Y	N	N
16 ***Regula***	N	N	N	N	N	N	Y	N
17 Traficant	N	Y	Y	Y	N	N	N	N
18 Applegate	N	Y	Y	Y	N	N	N	N
19 Fingerhut	N	Y	Y	Y	N	N	N	N
OKLAHOMA								
1 ***Inhofe***	N	N	N	N	N	Y	N	Y
2 Synar	N	Y	Y	Y	N	N	N	N
3 Brewster	N	?	Y	Y	N	N	N	N
4 McCurdy	N	Y	Y	Y	N	N	N	N
5 ***Istook***	N	N	N	N	N	Y	N	N
6 English	N	Y	Y	Y	N	N	N	N
OREGON								
1 Furse	N	Y	Y	Y	N	N	N	N
2 ***Smith***	Y	N	N	N	N	Y	N	N
3 Wyden	N	Y	Y	Y	N	N	N	N
4 DeFazio	N	Y	Y	Y	N	N	N	N
5 Kopetski	N	Y	Y	Y	N	N	N	N
PENNSYLVANIA								
1 Foglietta	?	Y	Y	Y	N	N	N	N
2 Blackwell	N	Y	Y	Y	N	N	N	N
3 Borski	N	Y	Y	Y	N	N	N	N
4 Klink	N	Y	Y	Y	N	N	N	N
5 ***Clinger***	N	N	N	N	N	Y	N	?
6 Holden	N	Y	Y	Y	N	N	N	N
7 ***Weldon***	N	N	N	N	N	Y	N	Y
8 ***Greenwood***	Y	N	N	N	Y	Y	N	Y
9 ***Shuster***	N	N	N	N	N	Y	N	N
10 ***McDade***	N	?	?	?	N	Y	N	N
11 Kanjorski	N	Y	Y	Y	N	N	N	N
12 Murtha	N	Y	Y	Y	N	N	N	N
13 Margolies-Mezv.	N	Y	Y	Y	N	N	N	N
14 Coyne	N	Y	Y	Y	N	N	N	N
15 McHale	N	Y	Y	Y	N	N	N	N
16 ***Walker***	N	N	N	N	N	Y	N	Y
17 ***Gekas***	Y	N	N	N	Y	Y	N	Y
18 ***Santorum***	N	N	N	N	N	Y	N	Y
19 ***Goodling***	Y	N	N	N	Y	Y	N	N
20 Murphy	N	Y	Y	Y	N	N	N	N
21 ***Ridge***	N	N	N	N	N	Y	N	N
RHODE ISLAND								
1 ***Machtley***	N	N	N	N	N	N	N	Y
2 Reed	N	Y	Y	Y	N	N	N	N
SOUTH CAROLINA								
1 ***Ravenel***	N	N	N	N	N	N	N	Y
2 ***Spence***	Y	N	N	N	Y	N	N	Y
3 Derrick	N	Y	Y	Y	N	N	N	N
4 ***Inglis***	N	N	N	N	N	Y	N	Y
5 Spratt	N	Y	Y	Y	N	N	N	N
6 Clyburn	N	Y	Y	Y	N	N	N	N
SOUTH DAKOTA								
AL Johnson	N	Y	Y	Y	N	N	N	N
TENNESSEE								
1 ***Quillen***	?	X	X	X	?	#	?	?
2 ***Duncan***	Y	N	N	N	Y	N	N	Y
3 Lloyd	N	Y	Y	Y	N	N	N	N
4 Cooper	N	Y	Y	Y	N	N	N	N
5 Clement	N	Y	Y	Y	N	N	N	N

	76	77	78	79	80	81	82	83
6 Gordon	N	Y	Y	Y	N	N	N	N
7 ***Sundquist***	Y	N	N	N	N	N	N	Y
8 Tanner	N	Y	Y	Y	N	N	N	N
9 Ford	?	?	?	?	?	?	?	?
TEXAS								
1 Chapman	N	Y	Y	Y	N	N	N	N
2 Wilson	?	Y	Y	Y	N	N	N	N
3 ***Johnson, Sam***	Y	N	N	N	Y	Y	N	Y
4 Hall	N	Y	Y	Y	N	N	N	N
5 Bryant	N	Y	Y	Y	N	N	N	N
6 ***Barton***	N	N	N	N	N	Y	N	N
7 ***Archer***	N	N	N	N	N	Y	N	Y
8 ***Fields***	?	N	N	N	Y	Y	N	Y
9 Brooks	N	Y	Y	Y	N	N	N	N
10 Pickle	N	Y	Y	Y	N	N	N	N
11 Edwards	N	Y	Y	Y	N	N	N	N
12 Geren	N	Y	Y	Y	N	Y	N	N
13 Sarpalius	N	Y	Y	Y	N	N	N	N
14 Laughlin	N	Y	Y	Y	N	N	N	N
15 de la Garza	N	Y	Y	Y	N	N	N	N
16 Coleman	N	Y	Y	Y	N	N	N	N
17 Stenholm	N	Y	Y	Y	N	N	N	N
18 Washington	?	#	#	#	?	X	N	?
19 ***Combest***	N	N	N	N	N	N	N	Y
20 Gonzalez	N	Y	Y	Y	N	N	N	N
21 ***Smith***	Y	N	N	N	N	Y	N	Y
22 ***DeLay***	Y	N	N	N	N	Y	N	Y
23 ***Bonilla***	Y	N	N	N	Y	Y	N	N
24 Frost	N	Y	Y	Y	N	N	N	N
25 Andrews	N	Y	Y	Y	N	N	N	N
26 ***Armey***	Y	N	N	N	Y	Y	N	Y
27 Ortiz	N	Y	Y	Y	N	N	N	N
28 Tejeda	N	Y	Y	Y	N	N	N	N
29 Green	N	Y	Y	Y	N	N	N	N
30 Johnson, E. B.	N	Y	Y	Y	N	N	N	N
UTAH								
1 ***Hansen***	N	N	N	N	Y	N	N	N
2 Shepherd	N	Y	Y	Y	N	N	N	N
3 Orton	N	Y	Y	Y	N	N	Y	N
VERMONT								
AL *Sanders*	N	Y	Y	Y	N	N	N	N
VIRGINIA								
1 ***Bateman***	N	N	N	N	N	N	N	Y
2 Pickett	N	Y	Y	Y	?	N	N	N
3 Scott	N	Y	Y	Y	N	N	N	N
4 Sisisky	N	Y	Y	Y	N	N	N	N
5 Payne	N	Y	Y	Y	N	N	N	N
6 ***Goodlatte***	N	N	N	N	N	N	N	Y
7 ***Bliley***	N	N	N	N	N	Y	N	N
8 Moran	N	Y	Y	Y	N	N	N	N
9 Boucher	N	Y	Y	Y	N	N	N	N
10 ***Wolf***	N	N	N	N	N	N	N	Y
11 Byrne	N	Y	Y	Y	N	N	N	N
WASHINGTON								
1 Cantwell	N	Y	Y	Y	N	N	N	N
2 Swift	N	Y	Y	Y	N	N	N	N
3 Unsoeld	N	Y	Y	Y	N	N	N	N
4 Inslee	N	Y	Y	Y	N	N	N	N
5 Foley								
6 Dicks	N	Y	Y	Y	N	N	N	N
7 McDermott	N	Y	Y	Y	N	N	N	N
8 ***Dunn***	Y	N	N	N	Y	Y	N	Y
9 Kreidler	N	Y	Y	Y	N	N	N	N
WEST VIRGINIA								
1 Mollohan	N	Y	Y	Y	N	N	N	N
2 Wise	N	Y	Y	Y	N	N	N	N
3 Rahall	N	Y	Y	Y	N	N	N	N
WISCONSIN								
1 Vacancy								
2 ***Klug***	N	N	N	N	N	Y	N	N
3 ***Gunderson***	N	N	N	N	N	Y	Y	N
4 Kleczka	N	Y	Y	Y	N	N	N	N
5 Barrett	N	Y	Y	Y	N	N	N	N
6 ***Petri***	N	N	N	N	N	N	N	Y
7 Obey	N	Y	Y	Y	N	N	N	N
8 ***Roth***	N	N	N	N	N	N	N	Y
9 ***Sensenbrenner***	N	N	N	N	N	Y	N	N
WYOMING								
AL ***Thomas***	Y	N	N	N	Y	Y	N	Y
DELEGATES								
de Lugo, V.I.	D	D	D	D	D	N	N	N
Faleomavaega, Am.S.	D	D	D	D	D	?	?	?
Norton, D.C.	D	D	D	D	D	N	N	N
Romero-B., P.R.	D	D	D	D	D	N	?	?
Underwood, Guam	D	D	D	D	D	N	N	N

Southern states - Ala., Ark., Fla., Ga., Ky., La., Miss., N.C., Okla., S.C., Tenn., Texas, Va.
Omitted votes are quorum calls, which CQ does not include in its vote charts.

84. H Con Res 64. Fiscal 1994 Budget Resolution/Black Caucus Substitute. Mfume, D-Md., amendment incorporating the Congressional Black Caucus budget substitute to provide for additional defense cuts and tax increases, with the resulting funds being used for education, job training, health and other domestic programs. Rejected in the Committee of the Whole 87-335: R 1-167; D 85-168 (ND 69-101, SD 16-67); I 1-0, March 18, 1993.

85. H Con Res 64. Fiscal 1994 Budget Resolution/ Adoption. Adoption of the concurrent resolution to set binding budget levels for the fiscal year ending Sept. 30, 1994: budget authority, $1.506 trillion; outlays, $1.495 trillion; revenues, $1.242 trillion; deficit, $253.5 billion. The resolution incorporates the guidelines of the administration's economic package plus an additional $63 billion in spending cuts. Adopted 243-183: R 0-172; D 242-11 (ND 164-6, SD 78-5); I 1-0, March 18, 1993. A "yea" was a vote in support of the president's position.

86. HR 1335. Fiscal 1993 Supplemental Appropriations/Rule. Adoption of the rule (H Res 132) to waive points of order against and provide for House floor consideration of the bill to provide $16.3 billion in new budget authority and approve $3.4 billion in trust fund spending to implement the administration's economic stimulus package. The funds would be designated as emergency spending and thus be exempt from the spending caps of the 1990 budget agreement. Adopted 240-185: R 0-172; D 239-13 (ND 165-4, SD 74-9); I 1-0, March 18, 1993. A "yea" was a vote in support of the president's position.

87. HR 1335. Fiscal 1993 Supplemental Appropriations/Motion to Recommit. McDade, R-Pa., motion to recommit the bill to the Appropriations Committee with instructions to report it back with an amendment to provide offsetting spending cuts for all spending in the bill except for $4 billion for unemployment benefits, thus making the bill comply with the discretionary spending caps of the 1990 budget agreement. Motion rejected 181-244: R 168-3; D 13-240 (ND 3-167, SD 10-73); I 0-1, March 19, 1993 (in the session that began and the Congressional Record dated March 18). A "nay" was a vote in support of the president's position.

88. HR 1335. Fiscal 1993 Supplemental Appropriations/Passage. Passage of the bill to provide $16.3 billion in new budget authority and approve $3.4 billion in trust fund spending to implement the administration's economic stimulus package. The funds would be designated as emergency spending and thus be exempt from the spending caps of the 1990 budget agreement. Passed 235-190: R 3-168; D 231-22 (ND 164-6, SD 67-16); I 1-0, March 19, 1993 (in the session that began and the Congressional Record dated March 18). A "yea" was a vote in support of the president's position.

89. Procedural Motion. Approval of the Journal of Tuesday, March 23. Approved 252-147: R 21-143; D 231-4 (ND 152-3, SD 79-1); I 0-0, March 24, 1993.

90. HR 670. Family Planning Amendments/Previous Question. Emerson, R-Mo., motion to order the previous question (thus ending debate and the possibility of amendment) on adoption of the rule (H Res 138) to provide for House floor consideration of the bill to authorize $238 million in fiscal 1994 and $270.5 million in fiscal 1995 for Title X family planning programs at clinics. The bill would codify the Clinton administration's lifting of the "gag rule," which prohibited staff at federally funded clinics from discussing abortion. Motion agreed to 252-164: R 4-163; D 247-1 (ND 165-1, SD 82-0); I 1-0, March 24, 1993.

91. HR 670. Family Planning Amendments/Rule. Adoption of the rule (H Res 138) to provide for House floor consideration of the bill to authorize $238 million in fiscal 1994 and $270.5 million in fiscal 1995 for Title X family planning programs at clinics. The bill would codify the Clinton administration's lifting of the "gag rule," which prohibited staff at federally funded clinics from discussing abortion. Adopted 247-169: R 10-158; D 236-11 (ND 160-6, SD 76-5); I 1-0, March 24, 1993.

KEY

Y	Voted for (yea).
#	Paired for.
+	Announced for.
N	Voted against (nay).
X	Paired against.
−	Announced against.
P	Voted "present."
C	Voted "present" to avoid possible conflict of interest.
?	Did not vote or otherwise make a position known.
D	Delegates ineligible to vote.

Democrats *Republicans*
Independent

	84	85	86	87	88	89	90	91
ALABAMA								
1 *Callahan*	N	N	N	Y	N	N	N	N
2 *Everett*	N	N	N	Y	N	N	N	N
3 Browder	N	Y	Y	N	Y	Y	Y	Y
4 Bevill	N	Y	Y	N	Y	Y	Y	Y
5 Cramer	N	Y	Y	N	Y	Y	Y	Y
6 *Bachus*	N	N	N	Y	N	N	N	N
7 Hilliard	Y	Y	Y	N	Y	Y	Y	Y
ALASKA								
AL *Young*	N	N	N	Y	N	N	N	N
ARIZONA								
1 *Coppersmith*	N	Y	Y	N	N	Y	Y	Y
2 Pastor	Y	Y	Y	N	Y	Y	Y	Y
3 *Stump*	N	N	N	Y	N	N	N	N
4 *Kyl*	N	N	N	Y	N	N	N	N
5 *Kolbe*	N	N	N	Y	N	N	N	N
6 English	N	Y	Y	N	Y	Y	Y	#
ARKANSAS								
1 Lambert	N	Y	N	N	Y	Y	Y	Y
2 Thornton	N	Y	Y	N	Y	Y	Y	Y
3 *Hutchinson*	N	N	N	Y	N	Y	N	N
4 Dickey	N	N	N	Y	N	N	N	N
CALIFORNIA								
1 Hamburg	Y	Y	Y	N	Y	Y	Y	Y
2 *Herger*	P	N	N	Y	N	N	N	N
3 Fazio	N	Y	Y	N	Y	Y	Y	Y
4 *Doolittle*	N	N	N	Y	N	?	?	X
5 Matsui	N	Y	Y	N	Y	Y	Y	Y
6 Woolsey	Y	Y	Y	N	Y	Y	Y	Y
7 Miller	Y	Y	Y	N	Y	Y	Y	Y
8 Pelosi	Y	Y	Y	N	Y	Y	Y	Y
9 Dellums	Y	Y	Y	N	Y	Y	Y	Y
10 *Baker*	N	N	N	Y	N	N	N	N
11 *Pombo*	N	N	N	Y	N	Y	N	N
12 Lantos	N	Y	Y	N	Y	Y	Y	Y
13 Stark	Y	Y	Y	N	Y	?	Y	Y
14 Eshoo	N	Y	Y	N	Y	Y	Y	Y
15 Mineta	Y	Y	Y	N	Y	Y	Y	Y
16 Edwards	?	Y	Y	N	Y	Y	Y	Y
17 Vacancy								
18 Condit	N	Y	Y	N	N	Y	Y	Y
19 Lehman	N	Y	Y	N	Y	Y	Y	Y
20 Dooley	N	Y	Y	N	Y	Y	Y	Y
21 *Thomas*	N	N	N	Y	N	N	N	N
22 *Huffington*	N	N	N	Y	N	N	N	N
23 *Gallegly*	N	N	N	Y	N	N	N	N
24 Beilenson	N	Y	Y	N	Y	Y	Y	Y
25 *McKeon*	N	N	N	Y	N	N	N	N
26 Berman	Y	Y	Y	N	Y	Y	Y	Y
27 *Moorhead*	N	N	N	Y	N	N	N	N
28 *Dreier*	N	N	N	Y	N	?	?	?
29 Waxman	Y	Y	Y	N	Y	Y	Y	Y
30 Becerra	Y	Y	Y	N	Y	Y	Y	Y
31 Martinez	N	Y	N	Y	Y	Y	Y	Y
32 Dixon	Y	Y	Y	N	Y	Y	Y	Y
33 Roybal-Allard	Y	Y	Y	N	Y	Y	Y	Y
34 Torres	Y	Y	Y	N	Y	Y	Y	#
35 Waters	Y	Y	Y	N	Y	Y	Y	Y
36 Harman	N	Y	Y	N	Y	Y	Y	Y
37 Tucker	Y	Y	Y	N	Y	?	Y	Y
38 *Horn*	N	N	N	Y	N	N	N	N
39 *Royce*	N	N	N	Y	N	N	N	N
40 *Lewis*	N	N	N	Y	N	N	N	N
41 *Kim*	N	N	N	Y	N	N	N	N
42 Brown	Y	Y	Y	N	Y	?	Y	Y
43 *Calvert*	N	N	N	Y	N	N	N	N
44 *McCandless*	N	N	N	Y	N	N	N	N
45 *Rohrabacher*	N	N	N	Y	N	N	N	N
46 *Dornan*	N	N	N	Y	N	N	N	N
47 *Cox*	N	N	N	Y	N	Y	N	N
48 *Packard*	N	N	N	Y	N	N	N	N
49 Schenk	N	Y	Y	N	Y	Y	Y	Y
50 Filner	Y	Y	Y	N	Y	Y	Y	Y
51 *Cunningham*	N	N	N	Y	N	N	N	N
52 *Hunter*	N	N	N	Y	N	N	N	N
COLORADO								
1 Schroeder	Y	Y	Y	N	Y	N	Y	Y
2 Skaggs	N	Y	Y	N	Y	Y	Y	Y
3 *McInnis*	N	N	N	Y	N	N	N	N
4 *Allard*	N	N	N	Y	N	N	N	N
5 *Hefley*	N	N	N	Y	N	N	N	N
6 *Schaefer*	N	N	N	Y	N	N	N	N
CONNECTICUT								
1 Kennelly	N	Y	Y	N	Y	Y	Y	Y
2 Gejdenson	N	Y	Y	N	Y	Y	Y	Y
3 DeLauro	N	Y	Y	N	Y	Y	Y	Y
4 *Shays*	N	N	N	Y	N	Y	N	N
5 *Franks*	N	N	N	Y	N	N	N	N
6 *Johnson*	N	N	N	Y	N	?	N	N
DELAWARE								
AL *Castle*	N	N	N	Y	N	N	N	N
FLORIDA								
1 Hutto	N	Y	Y	N	N	Y	Y	N
2 Peterson	N	Y	Y	N	Y	Y	Y	Y
3 Brown	Y	Y	Y	N	Y	Y	Y	Y
4 *Fowler*	N	N	N	Y	N	N	N	N
5 Thurman	N	Y	Y	N	Y	Y	Y	Y
6 *Stearns*	N	N	N	Y	N	N	N	N
7 *Mica*	N	N	N	Y	N	N	N	N
8 *McCollum*	N	N	N	Y	N	N	N	N
9 *Bilirakis*	N	N	N	Y	N	N	N	N
10 *Young*	N	N	N	Y	N	N	N	N
11 Gibbons	N	Y	Y	N	Y	Y	Y	Y
12 *Canady*	N	N	N	Y	N	N	N	N
13 *Miller*	N	N	N	Y	N	N	N	N
14 *Goss*	N	N	N	Y	N	N	N	N
15 Bacchus	N	Y	Y	N	Y	Y	Y	Y
16 *Lewis*	N	N	N	Y	N	?	?	X
17 Meek	Y	Y	Y	N	Y	Y	Y	Y
18 *Ros-Lehtinen*	N	N	N	Y	N	N	N	N
19 Johnston	N	Y	Y	N	Y	Y	Y	Y
20 Deutsch	N	Y	Y	N	Y	Y	Y	Y
21 *Diaz-Balart*	N	N	N	Y	N	N	N	N
22 *Shaw*	N	N	N	Y	N	?	?	?
23 Hastings	Y	Y	Y	N	Y	Y	Y	Y
GEORGIA								
1 *Kingston*	N	N	N	Y	N	N	N	N
2 Bishop	Y	Y	Y	N	Y	Y	Y	Y
3 *Collins*	N	N	N	Y	N	N	N	N
4 *Linder*	N	N	N	Y	N	N	N	N
5 Lewis	Y	Y	Y	N	Y	Y	Y	Y
6 *Gingrich*	P	N	N	Y	N	N	N	N
7 Darden	N	Y	Y	N	Y	Y	Y	Y
8 Rowland	N	Y	Y	N	Y	Y	Y	Y
9 Deal	N	Y	N	Y	Y	Y	Y	Y
10 Johnson	N	Y	Y	N	Y	Y	Y	Y
11 McKinney	Y	Y	Y	N	Y	Y	Y	Y
HAWAII								
1 Abercrombie	Y	Y	Y	N	Y	Y	Y	Y
2 Mink	Y	Y	Y	N	Y	Y	Y	Y
IDAHO								
1 LaRocco	N	Y	Y	N	Y	Y	Y	Y
2 *Crapo*	N	N	N	Y	N	N	N	N
ILLINOIS								
1 Rush	Y	Y	Y	N	Y	Y	Y	Y
2 Reynolds	Y	Y	Y	N	Y	Y	Y	Y
3 Lipinski	N	N	N	Y	N	Y	Y	Y
4 Gutierrez	Y	Y	Y	N	Y	Y	Y	Y
5 Rostenkowski	N	Y	Y	N	Y	Y	Y	Y
6 *Hyde*	N	N	N	Y	N	N	N	N
7 Collins	Y	Y	Y	N	Y	Y	Y	Y
8 *Crane*	N	N	N	Y	N	N	N	N
9 Yates	Y	Y	Y	N	Y	Y	Y	Y
10 *Porter*	N	N	N	Y	N	N	N	N
11 Sangmeister	N	Y	Y	N	Y	Y	Y	Y
12 Costello	N	Y	Y	N	Y	Y	Y	Y
13 *Fawell*	N	N	N	Y	N	N	N	N
14 *Hastert*	N	N	N	Y	N	N	N	N
15 *Ewing*	N	N	N	Y	N	N	N	N
16 *Manzullo*	N	N	N	Y	N	N	N	N
17 Evans	Y	Y	Y	N	Y	Y	Y	Y

	84	85	86	87	88	89	90	91
18 ***Michel***	N	N	N	Y	N	N	N	N
19 Poshard	N	Y	Y	N	Y	Y	Y	Y
20 Durbin	N	Y	Y	N	Y	Y	Y	Y
INDIANA								
1 Visclosky	N	Y	Y	N	Y	Y	Y	Y
2 Sharp	N	Y	Y	N	Y	?	?	?
3 Roemer	N	Y	Y	N	N	Y	Y	Y
4 Long	N	N	Y	N	Y	Y	Y	Y
5 ***Buyer***	N	N	N	Y	N	N	N	N
6 ***Burton***	N	N	N	Y	N	N	N	N
7 ***Myers***	?	?	?	?	?	Y	N	N
8 McCloskey	N	Y	Y	N	Y	Y	Y	Y
9 Hamilton	N	Y	N	N	Y	Y	Y	Y
10 Jacobs	Y	N	Y	N	Y	N	N	Y
IOWA								
1 ***Leach***	N	N	N	Y	N	N	N	N
2 ***Nussle***	N	N	N	Y	N	N	N	N
3 ***Lightfoot***	N	N	N	Y	N	N	N	N
4 Smith	N	Y	Y	N	Y	Y	Y	Y
5 ***Grandy***	Y	N	N	Y	N	?	N	N
KANSAS								
1 ***Roberts***	N	N	N	Y	N	N	N	N
2 Slattery	N	Y	N	N	Y	Y	Y	Y
3 ***Meyers***	N	N	N	Y	N	N	Y	Y
4 Glickman	N	Y	Y	N	Y	Y	Y	Y
KENTUCKY								
1 Barlow	N	Y	Y	N	Y	Y	Y	Y
2 Natcher	N	Y	Y	N	Y	Y	Y	Y
3 Mazzoli	N	Y	Y	N	Y	Y	Y	Y
4 ***Bunning***	N	N	N	Y	N	N	N	N
5 ***Rogers***	N	N	N	Y	Y	N	N	N
6 Baesler	N	Y	N	N	Y	Y	Y	Y
LOUISIANA								
1 ***Livingston***	N	N	N	Y	N	N	N	N
2 Jefferson	Y	Y	Y	N	Y	Y	Y	Y
3 Tauzin	N	Y	N	Y	N	?	Y	N
4 Fields	Y	Y	Y	N	Y	Y	Y	Y
5 ***McCrery***	N	N	N	Y	N	N	N	N
6 ***Baker***	N	N	N	Y	N	N	N	N
7 Hayes	N	Y	Y	N	N	Y	Y	Y
MAINE								
1 Andrews	Y	Y	Y	N	Y	Y	Y	Y
2 ***Snowe***	N	N	N	Y	N	Y	N	Y
MARYLAND								
1 ***Gilchrest***	N	N	N	Y	N	N	N	N
2 ***Bentley***	N	N	N	Y	N	N	N	N
3 Cardin	N	Y	Y	N	Y	Y	Y	Y
4 Wynn	Y	Y	Y	N	Y	Y	Y	Y
5 Hoyer	N	Y	Y	N	Y	?	Y	Y
6 ***Bartlett***	N	N	N	Y	N	N	N	N
7 Mfume	Y	Y	Y	N	Y	?	Y	Y
8 ***Morella***	N	N	N	Y	N	N	Y	Y
MASSACHUSETTS								
1 Olver	Y	Y	Y	N	Y	Y	Y	Y
2 Neal	N	Y	Y	N	Y	Y	Y	Y
3 ***Blute***	N	N	N	Y	N	N	N	N
4 Frank	Y	Y	Y	N	Y	Y	Y	Y
5 Meehan	N	Y	Y	N	Y	Y	Y	Y
6 ***Torkildsen***	N	N	N	Y	N	N	N	N
7 Markey	Y	Y	Y	N	Y	Y	Y	Y
8 Kennedy	Y	Y	Y	N	Y	Y	Y	Y
9 Moakley	Y	Y	Y	N	Y	Y	Y	Y
10 Studds	N	Y	Y	N	Y	Y	Y	Y
MICHIGAN								
1 Stupak	N	Y	Y	N	Y	Y	Y	Y
2 ***Hoekstra***	N	N	N	Y	N	N	N	N
3 Henry	?	?	?	?	?	?	?	?
4 ***Camp***	N	N	N	Y	N	N	N	N
5 Barcia	N	Y	Y	N	Y	?	Y	Y
6 ***Upton***	N	N	N	Y	N	N	N	N
7 ***Smith***	N	N	N	Y	N	N	N	N
8 Carr	N	Y	Y	N	Y	?	Y	Y
9 Kildee	N	Y	Y	N	Y	Y	Y	N
10 Bonior	Y	Y	Y	N	Y	Y	Y	Y
11 ***Knollenberg***	N	N	N	Y	N	N	N	N
12 Levin	N	Y	Y	N	Y	Y	Y	Y
13 Ford	N	Y	Y	N	Y	Y	Y	Y
14 Conyers	Y	Y	Y	N	Y	Y	Y	Y
15 Collins	Y	Y	Y	N	Y	Y	Y	Y
16 Dingell	?	Y	Y	N	Y	Y	Y	Y
MINNESOTA								
1 Penny	N	Y	Y	N	Y	Y	Y	Y
2 Minge	N	Y	Y	N	Y	Y	Y	Y
3 ***Ramstad***	N	N	N	Y	N	N	N	N
4 Vento	Y	Y	Y	N	Y	Y	Y	Y
5 Sabo	N	Y	Y	N	Y	Y	Y	Y
6 ***Grams***	N	N	N	Y	N	N	N	N
7 Peterson	N	Y	Y	N	Y	Y	Y	N
8 Oberstar	Y	Y	Y	N	Y	Y	Y	Y
MISSISSIPPI								
1 Whitten	N	Y	Y	N	Y	?	Y	Y
2 Vacancy								
3 Montgomery	N	Y	Y	N	N	Y	Y	Y
4 Parker	N	Y	N	Y	N	Y	Y	Y
5 Taylor	N	N	N	N	N	N	Y	N
MISSOURI								
1 Clay	Y	Y	Y	N	Y	?	Y	Y
2 ***Talent***	N	N	N	Y	N	N	N	N
3 Gephardt	N	Y	Y	N	Y	Y	Y	Y
4 Skelton	N	Y	Y	N	Y	Y	Y	Y
5 Wheat	Y	Y	Y	N	Y	Y	Y	Y
6 Danner	N	Y	Y	N	Y	Y	Y	Y
7 ***Hancock***	N	N	N	Y	N	N	N	N
8 ***Emerson***	N	N	N	Y	N	N	N	N
9 Volkmer	N	Y	Y	N	Y	Y	Y	N
MONTANA								
AL Williams	Y	Y	?	N	Y	Y	Y	Y
NEBRASKA								
1 ***Bereuter***	N	N	N	Y	N	N	N	N
2 Hoagland	N	Y	Y	N	Y	Y	Y	Y
3 ***Barrett***	N	N	N	Y	N	N	N	N
NEVADA								
1 Bilbray	N	Y	Y	N	Y	Y	Y	Y
2 ***Vucanovich***	N	N	N	Y	N	N	N	N
NEW HAMPSHIRE								
1 ***Zeliff***	N	N	N	Y	N	N	—	—
2 Swett	N	Y	Y	N	Y	?	?	?
NEW JERSEY								
1 Andrews	N	N	Y	N	Y	Y	Y	Y
2 Hughes	N	Y	N	N	Y	Y	Y	Y
3 ***Saxton***	N	N	N	Y	N	N	N	N
4 ***Smith***	N	N	N	Y	N	Y	N	N
5 ***Roukema***	N	N	N	Y	N	N	Y	Y
6 Pallone	N	Y	Y	N	Y	Y	Y	Y
7 ***Franks***	N	N	N	Y	N	N	N	N
8 Klein	N	Y	Y	N	Y	Y	Y	Y
9 Torricelli	N	Y	Y	N	Y	Y	Y	Y
10 Payne	Y	Y	Y	N	Y	Y	Y	Y
11 ***Gallo***	N	N	N	Y	N	N	N	Y
12 ***Zimmer***	N	N	N	Y	N	N	N	N
13 Menendez	P	Y	Y	N	Y	Y	Y	Y
NEW MEXICO								
1 ***Schiff***	N	N	N	Y	N	N	N	N
2 ***Skeen***	N	N	N	Y	N	N	N	N
3 Richardson	Y	Y	Y	N	Y	Y	Y	Y
NEW YORK								
1 Hochbrueckner	N	Y	Y	N	Y	Y	Y	Y
2 ***Lazio***	N	N	N	Y	N	N	N	Y
3 ***King***	N	N	N	Y	N	N	N	N
4 ***Levy***	N	N	N	Y	N	N	N	N
5 Ackerman	N	Y	Y	N	Y	Y	Y	Y
6 Flake	Y	Y	Y	N	Y	Y	Y	Y
7 Manton	N	Y	Y	N	Y	Y	Y	Y
8 Nadler	Y	Y	Y	N	Y	Y	Y	Y
9 Schumer	N	Y	Y	N	Y	Y	Y	Y
10 Towns	Y	Y	Y	N	Y	Y	Y	Y
11 Owens	Y	Y	Y	N	Y	?	Y	Y
12 Velazquez	Y	Y	Y	N	Y	Y	Y	Y
13 ***Molinari***	N	N	N	Y	N	N	N	N
14 Maloney	N	Y	Y	N	Y	Y	Y	Y
15 Rangel	Y	Y	Y	N	Y	?	Y	Y
16 Serrano	Y	Y	Y	N	Y	Y	Y	Y
17 Engel	Y	Y	Y	N	Y	Y	Y	Y
18 Lowey	N	Y	Y	N	Y	Y	Y	Y
19 ***Fish***	N	N	N	Y	N	Y	N	N
20 ***Gilman***	N	N	N	Y	N	Y	N	Y
21 McNulty	N	Y	Y	N	Y	Y	Y	Y
22 ***Solomon***	N	N	N	Y	N	N	N	N
23 ***Boehlert***	N	N	N	N	Y	N	N	Y
24 ***McHugh***	N	N	N	Y	N	N	N	N
25 ***Walsh***	N	N	N	N	Y	N	N	N
26 Hinchey	Y	Y	Y	N	Y	Y	Y	Y
27 ***Paxon***	N	N	N	Y	N	N	N	N
28 Slaughter	N	Y	Y	N	Y	Y	Y	Y
29 LaFalce	N	Y	Y	N	Y	Y	Y	Y
30 ***Quinn***	N	N	N	Y	N	N	N	N
31 ***Houghton***	N	N	N	Y	N	?	N	N
NORTH CAROLINA								
1 Clayton	Y	Y	Y	N	Y	Y	Y	Y
2 Valentine	N	Y	Y	Y	N	Y	Y	Y
3 Lancaster	N	Y	N	N	Y	Y	Y	Y
4 Price	N	Y	Y	N	Y	Y	Y	Y
5 Neal	N	Y	Y	N	N	Y	Y	Y
6 ***Coble***	N	N	N	Y	N	N	N	N
7 Rose	N	Y	Y	N	Y	Y	Y	Y
8 Hefner	N	Y	Y	N	Y	Y	Y	Y
9 ***McMillan***	N	N	N	Y	N	N	N	N
10 ***Ballenger***	N	N	N	Y	N	N	N	N
11 ***Taylor***	N	N	N	Y	N	N	N	N
12 Watt	Y	Y	Y	N	Y	Y	Y	Y
NORTH DAKOTA								
AL Pomeroy	N	Y	Y	N	Y	Y	Y	Y
OHIO								
1 Mann	N	Y	Y	N	N	Y	Y	Y
2 Vacancy								
3 Hall	N	Y	Y	N	Y	Y	Y	Y
4 ***Oxley***	N	N	N	Y	N	Y	N	N
5 ***Gillmor***	N	N	N	Y	N	Y	N	N
6 Strickland	N	Y	Y	N	Y	Y	Y	Y
7 ***Hobson***	N	N	N	Y	N	N	N	N
8 ***Boehner***	N	N	N	Y	N	N	N	N
9 Kaptur	N	Y	Y	N	Y	Y	Y	Y
10 ***Hoke***	N	N	N	Y	N	Y	N	N
11 Stokes	Y	Y	Y	N	Y	Y	Y	Y
12 ***Kasich***	N	N	N	Y	N	Y	N	N
13 Brown	N	Y	Y	N	Y	Y	Y	Y
14 Sawyer	N	Y	Y	N	Y	Y	Y	Y
15 ***Pryce***	N	N	N	Y	N	N	N	N
16 ***Regula***	N	N	N	Y	N	N	N	N
17 Traficant	N	N	Y	N	Y	Y	Y	Y
18 Applegate	N	Y	Y	N	Y	?	Y	Y
19 Fingerhut	N	Y	Y	N	Y	Y	Y	Y
OKLAHOMA								
1 ***Inhofe***	P	N	N	Y	N	N	N	N
2 Synar	N	Y	Y	N	Y	Y	Y	Y
3 Brewster	N	Y	Y	N	N	Y	Y	Y
4 McCurdy	N	Y	Y	N	Y	Y	Y	Y
5 ***Istook***	N	N	N	Y	N	N	N	N
6 English	N	Y	Y	Y	N	Y	Y	Y
OREGON								
1 Furse	Y	Y	Y	N	Y	Y	Y	Y
2 ***Smith***	N	N	N	Y	N	N	N	N
3 Wyden	Y	Y	Y	N	Y	Y	Y	Y
4 DeFazio	Y	Y	Y	N	Y	Y	Y	Y
5 Kopetski	Y	Y	Y	N	Y	Y	Y	Y
PENNSYLVANIA								
1 Foglietta	Y	Y	Y	N	Y	Y	Y	Y
2 Blackwell	Y	Y	Y	N	Y	Y	Y	Y
3 Borski	N	Y	Y	N	Y	Y	Y	Y
4 Klink	N	Y	Y	N	Y	Y	Y	Y
5 ***Clinger***	N	N	N	Y	N	N	N	N
6 Holden	N	Y	Y	N	Y	Y	Y	Y
7 ***Weldon***	N	N	N	Y	N	N	N	N
8 ***Greenwood***	N	N	N	Y	N	N	N	N
9 ***Shuster***	N	N	N	Y	N	N	N	N
10 ***McDade***	N	N	N	Y	N	N	N	N
11 Kanjorski	N	Y	Y	N	Y	Y	Y	Y
12 Murtha	N	Y	Y	N	Y	Y	Y	Y
13 Margolies-Mezv.	N	N	Y	N	N	Y	Y	Y
14 Coyne	Y	Y	Y	N	Y	Y	Y	Y
15 McHale	N	Y	Y	N	Y	Y	Y	Y
16 ***Walker***	N	N	N	Y	N	N	N	N
17 ***Gekas***	N	N	N	Y	N	N	N	N
18 ***Santorum***	N	N	N	Y	N	?	N	N
19 ***Goodling***	N	N	N	Y	N	N	N	N
20 Murphy	N	Y	N	Y	Y	N	Y	N
21 ***Ridge***	N	N	N	Y	N	N	N	N
RHODE ISLAND								
1 ***Machtley***	N	N	N	Y	N	N	N	Y
2 Reed	N	Y	Y	N	Y	Y	Y	Y
SOUTH CAROLINA								
1 ***Ravenel***	N	N	N	Y	N	Y	N	N
2 ***Spence***	N	N	N	Y	N	N	N	N
3 Derrick	N	Y	Y	N	Y	Y	Y	Y
4 ***Inglis***	N	N	N	Y	N	Y	N	N
5 Spratt	N	Y	Y	N	Y	Y	Y	Y
6 Clyburn	Y	Y	Y	N	Y	Y	Y	Y
SOUTH DAKOTA								
AL Johnson	N	Y	Y	N	Y	Y	Y	Y
TENNESSEE								
1 ***Quillen***	?	?	?	?	?	?	?	X
2 ***Duncan***	N	N	N	Y	N	N	N	N
3 Lloyd	N	Y	Y	N	Y	Y	Y	Y
4 Cooper	N	Y	Y	N	Y	Y	Y	Y
5 Clement	N	Y	Y	N	Y	Y	Y	Y
6 Gordon	N	Y	Y	N	Y	Y	Y	Y
7 ***Sundquist***	N	N	N	Y	N	N	N	N
8 Tanner	N	Y	Y	N	Y	Y	Y	Y
9 Ford	?	?	?	?	?	?	?	?
TEXAS								
1 Chapman	N	Y	Y	N	Y	Y	Y	Y
2 Wilson	N	Y	Y	N	Y	Y	Y	Y
3 ***Johnson, Sam***	N	N	N	Y	N	N	N	N
4 Hall	N	N	N	Y	N	Y	Y	N
5 Bryant	N	Y	Y	N	Y	Y	Y	Y
6 ***Barton***	N	N	N	?	?	N	N	N
7 ***Archer***	N	N	N	Y	N	Y	N	N
8 ***Fields***	N	N	N	Y	N	N	N	N
9 Brooks	N	Y	Y	N	Y	Y	Y	Y
10 Pickle	N	Y	Y	N	Y	?	?	#
11 Edwards	N	Y	Y	N	Y	Y	Y	Y
12 Geren	N	N	Y	Y	N	Y	Y	Y
13 Sarpalius	N	Y	Y	N	Y	Y	Y	Y
14 Laughlin	N	Y	Y	N	Y	Y	Y	Y
15 de la Garza	N	Y	Y	N	Y	Y	Y	Y
16 Coleman	N	Y	Y	N	Y	Y	Y	Y
17 Stenholm	N	Y	N	Y	N	Y	Y	N
18 Washington	Y	Y	Y	N	Y	Y	Y	Y
19 ***Combest***	N	N	N	Y	N	Y	N	N
20 Gonzalez	N	Y	Y	N	Y	Y	Y	Y
21 ***Smith***	N	N	N	Y	N	N	N	N
22 ***DeLay***	N	N	N	Y	N	N	N	N
23 ***Bonilla***	P	N	N	Y	N	N	N	N
24 Frost	N	Y	Y	N	Y	Y	Y	Y
25 Andrews	N	Y	Y	N	Y	Y	Y	Y
26 ***Armey***	N	N	N	Y	N	N	N	N
27 Ortiz	N	Y	Y	N	Y	Y	Y	Y
28 Tejeda	N	Y	Y	N	Y	Y	Y	Y
29 Green	Y	Y	Y	N	Y	Y	Y	Y
30 Johnson, E. B.	Y	Y	Y	N	Y	Y	Y	?
UTAH								
1 ***Hansen***	N	N	N	Y	N	N	?	N
2 Shepherd	N	Y	Y	N	Y	Y	Y	Y
3 Orton	N	Y	Y	Y	N	Y	Y	Y
VERMONT								
AL *Sanders*	Y	Y	Y	N	Y	?	Y	Y
VIRGINIA								
1 ***Bateman***	N	N	N	Y	N	Y	N	N
2 Pickett	N	N	Y	N	N	Y	Y	Y
3 Scott	Y	Y	Y	N	Y	Y	Y	Y
4 Sisisky	N	N	Y	Y	N	Y	Y	Y
5 Payne	N	Y	Y	N	Y	Y	Y	Y
6 ***Goodlatte***	N	N	N	Y	N	N	N	N
7 ***Bliley***	N	N	N	Y	N	N	N	N
8 Moran	N	Y	Y	N	Y	Y	Y	Y
9 Boucher	N	Y	Y	N	Y	Y	Y	Y
10 ***Wolf***	N	N	N	Y	N	N	N	N
11 Byrne	N	Y	Y	N	Y	Y	Y	Y
WASHINGTON								
1 Cantwell	N	Y	Y	N	Y	Y	Y	Y
2 Swift	N	Y	Y	N	Y	Y	Y	Y
3 Unsoeld	Y	Y	Y	N	Y	?	Y	Y
4 Inslee	N	Y	Y	N	Y	Y	Y	Y
5 Foley								
6 Dicks	N	Y	Y	N	Y	Y	Y	Y
7 McDermott	Y	Y	Y	N	Y	?	?	Y
8 ***Dunn***	N	N	N	Y	N	N	N	N
9 Kreidler	N	Y	Y	N	Y	Y	Y	Y
WEST VIRGINIA								
1 Mollohan	N	Y	Y	N	Y	Y	Y	N
2 Wise	N	Y	Y	N	Y	Y	Y	Y
3 Rahall	Y	Y	Y	N	Y	Y	Y	N
WISCONSIN								
1 Vacancy								
2 ***Klug***	N	N	N	Y	N	N	N	N
3 ***Gunderson***	N	N	N	N	N	Y	N	N
4 Kleczka	N	Y	Y	N	Y	Y	Y	Y
5 Barrett	N	Y	Y	N	Y	Y	Y	Y
6 ***Petri***	N	N	N	Y	N	N	N	N
7 Obey	N	Y	Y	N	Y	Y	Y	Y
8 ***Roth***	N	N	N	Y	N	Y	N	N
9 ***Sensenbrenner***	N	N	N	Y	N	N	N	N
WYOMING								
AL ***Thomas***	N	N	N	Y	N	N	N	N
DELEGATES								
de Lugo, V.I.	Y	D	D	D	D	D	D	D
Faleomavaega, Am.S.	?	D	D	D	D	D	D	D
Norton, D.C.	Y	D	D	D	D	D	D	D
Romero-B., P.R.	?	D	D	D	D	D	D	D
Underwood, Guam	Y	D	D	D	D	D	D	D

Southern states - Ala., Ark., Fla., Ga., Ky., La., Miss., N.C., Okla., S.C., Tenn., Texas, Va.
Omitted votes are quorum calls, which CQ does not include in its vote charts.

KEY

Y Voted for (yea).
\# Paired for.
\+ Announced for.
N Voted against (nay).
X Paired against.
\- Announced against.
P Voted "present."
C Voted "present" to avoid possible conflict of interest.
? Did not vote or otherwise make a position known.
D Delegates ineligible to vote.

Democrats *Republicans*
Independent

92. HR 670. Family Planning Amendments/Motion to Reconsider. Moakley, D-Mass., motion to table (kill) the Slaughter, D-N.Y., motion to reconsider the adoption of the rule (H Res 138) to provide for House floor consideration of the bill to authorize $238 million in fiscal 1994 and $270.5 million in fiscal 1995 for Title X family planning programs at clinics. The bill would codify the Clinton administration's lifting of the "gag rule," which prohibited staff at federally funded clinics from discussing abortion. Motion agreed to 252-165: R 9-160; D 242-5 (ND 165-0, SD 77-5); I 1-0, March 24, 1993.

93. Procedural Motion. Burton, R-Ind., motion to adjourn. Motion agreed to 32-374: R 32-135; D 0-238 (ND 0-159, SD 0-79); I 0-1, March 24, 1993.

* 95. HR 670. Family Planning Amendments/Patient Advisers. Waxman, D-Calif., amendment to the DeLay, R-Texas, amendment to add to the list of people allowed to advise patients at federally funded family planning facilities those who meet the criteria of the secretary of Health and Human Services and those allowed under state law. The DeLay amendment would require people giving advice to have a professional degree. Adopted in the Committee of the Whole 256-165: R 42-128; D 213-37 (ND 147-23, SD 66-14); I 1-0, March 24, 1993.

96. HR 670. Family Planning Amendments/Patient Advisers. DeLay, R-Texas, amendment, as amended by the Waxman, D-Calif., amendment, to require people advising patients at federally funded family planning facilities to have a professional degree, meet the criteria of the secretary of Health and Human Services or be allowed to offer such counseling under state law. Adopted in the Committee of the Whole 408-16: R 158-12; D 249-4 (ND 170-2, SD 79-2); I 1-0, March 24, 1993.

97. HR 670. Family Planning Amendments/Anti-Abortion Counselors. Waxman, D-Calif., amendment to clarify that an individual who provides counseling at a clinic but who objects to abortions would not be required to provide information but that the clinic would arrange for another person or clinic to give counseling. Adopted in the Committee of the Whole 260-163: R 50-120; D 209-43 (ND 144-27, SD 65-16); I 1-0, March 24, 1993.

98. HR 670. Family Planning Amendments/Motion to Rise. Waxman, D-Calif., motion that the Committee of the Whole rise and report the bill back to the House with no resolution. Motion agreed to in the Committee of the Whole 287-119: R 46-119; D 240-0 (ND 162-0, SD 78-0); I 1-0, March 24, 1993.

99. Procedural Motion. Taylor, D-Miss., motion to adjourn. Motion agreed to 265-134: R 34-130; D 230-4 (ND 154-2, SD 76-2); I 1-0, March 24, 1993.

100. Procedural Motion. Approval of the Journal of Wednesday, March 24. Approved 236-149: R 17-147; D 219-2 (ND 144-2, SD 75-0); I 0-0, March 25, 1993.

* Omitted votes are quorum calls, which CQ does not include in its vote charts.

	92	93	95	96	97	98	99	100
ALABAMA								
1 *Callahan*	N	N	N	Y	N	Y	N	N
2 *Everett*	N	N	N	Y	N	N	N	N
3 Browder	Y	N	Y	Y	Y	Y	Y	Y
4 Bevill	Y	N	Y	Y	Y	Y	Y	Y
5 Cramer	Y	N	Y	Y	Y	Y	Y	Y
6 *Bachus*	N	N	N	Y	N	N	N	N
7 Hilliard	Y	N	Y	Y	Y	Y	Y	Y
ALASKA								
AL *Young*	N	N	N	Y	N	N	N	N
ARIZONA								
1 Coppersmith	Y	N	Y	Y	Y	Y	Y	Y
2 Pastor	Y	N	Y	Y	Y	Y	Y	?
3 *Stump*	N	Y	N	Y	N	N	N	N
4 *Kyl*	N	N	N	Y	N	N	N	N
5 *Kolbe*	N	N	Y	Y	Y	N	N	N
6 English	Y	N	Y	Y	Y	Y	Y	Y
ARKANSAS								
1 Lambert	Y	N	Y	Y	Y	?	Y	Y
2 Thornton	Y	N	Y	Y	Y	Y	Y	Y
3 *Hutchinson*	N	N	N	Y	N	N	N	N
4 *Dickey*	N	N	N	Y	N	N	N	N
CALIFORNIA								
1 Hamburg	Y	N	Y	Y	Y	Y	Y	Y
2 *Herger*	N	N	N	Y	N	N	N	N
3 Fazio	Y	N	Y	Y	Y	Y	Y	Y
4 *Doolittle*	?	?	?	?	?	?	?	?
5 Matsui	Y	N	Y	Y	Y	Y	Y	Y
6 Woolsey	Y	N	Y	Y	Y	Y	Y	Y
7 Miller	Y	N	Y	Y	Y	?	?	?
8 Pelosi	Y	N	Y	Y	Y	Y	Y	?
9 Dellums	Y	?	Y	Y	Y	Y	Y	Y
10 *Baker*	N	Y	N	Y	N	N	N	N
11 *Pombo*	N	N	N	Y	N	N	N	Y
12 Lantos	Y	N	Y	Y	Y	Y	Y	Y
13 Stark	Y	N	Y	Y	Y	?	Y	Y
14 Eshoo	Y	N	Y	Y	Y	Y	Y	Y
15 Mineta	Y	N	Y	Y	Y	Y	Y	Y
16 Edwards	Y	?	Y	Y	Y	Y	Y	Y
17 Vacancy								
18 Condit	Y	N	Y	Y	Y	Y	Y	Y
19 Lehman	Y	N	Y	Y	Y	Y	Y	Y
20 Dooley	Y	N	Y	Y	Y	Y	Y	Y
21 *Thomas*	N	N	N	Y	Y	Y	N	N
22 *Huffington*	N	N	Y	Y	Y	Y	N	N
23 *Gallegly*	N	N	N	Y	N	N	N	N
24 Beilenson	Y	N	Y	Y	Y	Y	Y	Y
25 *McKeon*	N	Y	N	Y	N	N	N	N
26 Berman	Y	?	Y	Y	Y	?	?	Y
27 *Moorhead*	N	Y	N	Y	N	N	N	N
28 *Dreier*	?	?	?	?	?	?	?	?
29 Waxman	Y	N	Y	Y	Y	Y	Y	Y
30 Becerra	Y	N	Y	Y	Y	Y	Y	Y
31 Martinez	Y	?	Y	Y	Y	Y	Y	Y
32 Dixon	Y	N	Y	Y	Y	Y	Y	?
33 Roybal-Allard	Y	N	Y	Y	Y	Y	Y	Y
34 Torres	?	N	Y	Y	Y	Y	Y	Y
35 Waters	Y	N	Y	Y	Y	Y	Y	Y
36 Harman	Y	N	Y	Y	Y	Y	Y	Y
37 Tucker	Y	N	Y	Y	Y	?	?	?
38 *Horn*	N	N	Y	Y	Y	N	N	N
39 *Royce*	N	N	N	Y	N	N	N	N
40 *Lewis*	N	N	N	Y	N	N	N	N
41 *Kim*	N	N	N	Y	N	N	N	N

	92	93	95	96	97	98	99	100
42 Brown	Y	?	Y	Y	Y	Y	?	Y
43 *Calvert*	N	N	N	Y	Y	Y	N	N
44 *McCandless*	N	N	N	Y	N	N	N	N
45 *Rohrabacher*	N	Y	N	Y	N	N	N	N
46 *Dornan*	N	Y	N	Y	N	N	N	?
47 *Cox*	N	Y	N	Y	N	?	N	N
48 *Packard*	N	N	N	Y	N	N	N	N
49 Schenk	Y	N	Y	Y	Y	Y	Y	Y
50 Filner	Y	N	Y	Y	Y	Y	Y	Y
51 *Cunningham*	N	N	N	Y	N	N	N	N
52 *Hunter*	N	Y	N	Y	N	N	N	N
COLORADO								
1 Schroeder	Y	N	Y	Y	Y	Y	Y	Y
2 Skaggs	?	N	Y	Y	Y	Y	Y	Y
3 *McInnis*	N	Y	Y	Y	Y	Y	N	N
4 *Allard*	N	Y	N	Y	N	N	N	Y
5 *Hefley*	N	Y	N	Y	N	Y	N	N
6 *Schaefer*	N	Y	N	Y	N	N	N	N
CONNECTICUT								
1 Kennelly	Y	N	Y	Y	Y	Y	Y	Y
2 Gejdenson	Y	N	Y	Y	Y	Y	Y	Y
3 DeLauro	Y	N	Y	Y	Y	Y	Y	Y
4 *Shays*	Y	N	Y	Y	Y	Y	Y	N
5 *Franks*	N	Y	Y	Y	Y	N	N	N
6 *Johnson*	N	N	Y	Y	Y	Y	N	N
DELAWARE								
AL *Castle*	N	Y	Y	Y	Y	Y	Y	N
FLORIDA								
1 Hutto	N	N	N	Y	N	Y	?	Y
2 Peterson	Y	N	Y	Y	Y	Y	Y	Y
3 Brown	Y	N	Y	Y	Y	Y	Y	Y
4 *Fowler*	N	N	N	Y	N	N	N	N
5 Thurman	Y	N	Y	Y	Y	Y	Y	Y
6 *Stearns*	N	N	N	Y	N	N	N	N
7 *Mica*	N	Y	N	Y	N	Y	N	N
8 *McCollum*	N	N	N	Y	N	N	N	N
9 *Bilirakis*	N	N	N	Y	N	N	N	N
10 *Young*	N	N	N	Y	N	?	?	N
11 Gibbons	Y	N	Y	Y	Y	Y	Y	Y
12 *Canady*	N	N	N	Y	N	N	N	N
13 *Miller*	N	N	Y	Y	Y	N	N	N
14 *Goss*	N	N	N	Y	N	N	N	N
15 Bacchus	Y	N	Y	Y	Y	Y	Y	Y
16 *Lewis*	?	?	?	?	?	?	?	N
17 Meek	Y	N	?	Y	Y	Y	Y	Y
18 *Ros-Lehtinen*	N	N	N	Y	N	N	N	N
19 Johnston	Y	N	Y	Y	?	Y	Y	Y
20 Deutsch	Y	N	Y	Y	Y	Y	Y	Y
21 *Diaz-Balart*	N	N	N	Y	N	N	N	N
22 *Shaw*	N	N	N	Y	N	Y	N	N
23 Hastings	Y	N	Y	Y	Y	Y	Y	?
GEORGIA								
1 *Kingston*	N	Y	N	Y	N	N	N	N
2 Bishop	Y	N	Y	Y	Y	Y	Y	?
3 *Collins*	N	N	N	Y	N	N	N	N
4 *Linder*	N	N	N	Y	N	N	N	N
5 Lewis	Y	N	Y	Y	Y	Y	Y	Y
6 *Gingrich*	N	N	N	Y	N	N	N	N
7 Darden	Y	N	Y	Y	Y	Y	Y	Y
8 Rowland	Y	N	Y	Y	Y	Y	Y	Y
9 Deal	Y	N	Y	Y	Y	Y	Y	Y
10 Johnson	Y	N	Y	Y	Y	Y	Y	Y
11 McKinney	Y	N	Y	Y	Y	Y	Y	Y
HAWAII								
1 Abercrombie	Y	N	Y	Y	Y	Y	Y	Y
2 Mink	Y	N	Y	Y	Y	?	?	Y
IDAHO								
1 LaRocco	Y	N	Y	Y	Y	Y	Y	Y
2 *Crapo*	N	N	N	Y	N	N	N	N
ILLINOIS								
1 Rush	Y	N	Y	Y	Y	Y	Y	?
2 Reynolds	Y	N	Y	Y	Y	Y	Y	Y
3 Lipinski	Y	N	N	Y	N	Y	Y	Y
4 Gutierrez	Y	N	Y	Y	Y	Y	Y	Y
5 Rostenkowski	Y	N	Y	Y	Y	Y	Y	Y
6 *Hyde*	N	N	N	Y	N	Y	N	Y
7 Collins	Y	N	Y	Y	Y	Y	Y	Y
8 *Crane*	N	Y	N	Y	N	N	N	?
9 Yates	Y	N	Y	Y	Y	?	?	Y
10 *Porter*	N	N	Y	Y	Y	Y	N	Y
11 Sangmeister	Y	N	Y	Y	Y	Y	Y	Y
12 Costello	Y	N	N	N	N	Y	Y	Y
13 *Fawell*	N	N	Y	Y	Y	N	N	N
14 *Hastert*	N	N	N	Y	N	N	N	N
15 *Ewing*	N	N	N	Y	N	N	N	N
16 *Manzullo*	N	N	N	Y	N	N	N	N
17 Evans	Y	N	Y	Y	Y	Y	Y	Y

ND Northern Democrats   SD Southern Democrats

	92	93	95	96	97	98	99	100
18 ***Michel***	N	N	N	N	N	N	N	?
19 Poshard	Y	N	N	Y	N	Y	Y	Y
20 Durbin	Y	N	Y	Y	Y	Y	Y	Y
INDIANA								
1 Visclosky	Y	N	Y	Y	?	?	?	Y
2 Sharp	?	?	?	?	?	?	?	?
3 Roemer	Y	N	N	Y	N	Y	Y	Y
4 Long	Y	N	Y	Y	Y	Y	Y	Y
5 ***Buyer***	N	N	Y	Y	N	N	N	N
6 ***Burton***	N	Y	N	Y	N	N	N	N
7 ***Myers***	N	N	N	N	N	N	N	Y
8 McCloskey	Y	N	Y	Y	Y	Y	Y	Y
9 Hamilton	Y	N	Y	Y	Y	Y	Y	Y
10 Jacobs	Y	N	Y	Y	Y	Y	Y	N
IOWA								
1 ***Leach***	Y	N	Y	Y	Y	N	N	N
2 ***Nussle***	N	N	N	N	N	N	N	N
3 ***Lightfoot***	N	N	N	Y	N	N	N	N
4 Smith	Y	N	Y	Y	Y	Y	Y	Y
5 ***Grandy***	N	N	Y	Y	Y	N	Y	N
KANSAS								
1 ***Roberts***	N	N	N	N	N	N	Y	?
2 Slattery	Y	N	Y	Y	Y	Y	N	Y
3 ***Meyers***	Y	?	Y	Y	Y	N	N	N
4 Glickman	Y	N	Y	Y	Y	Y	Y	Y
KENTUCKY								
1 Barlow	Y	N	Y	Y	Y	Y	Y	Y
2 Natcher	Y	N	Y	Y	Y	Y	Y	Y
3 Mazzoli	Y	N	N	Y	N	Y	Y	Y
4 ***Bunning***	N	N	N	N	N	N	N	N
5 ***Rogers***	N	N	N	Y	N	Y	N	N
6 Baesler	Y	N	Y	Y	Y	Y	Y	Y
LOUISIANA								
1 ***Livingston***	N	Y	N	Y	N	N	N	N
2 Jefferson	Y	N	Y	Y	Y	Y	Y	?
3 Tauzin	N	N	N	Y	N	Y	Y	Y
4 Fields	Y	N	Y	Y	Y	Y	Y	Y
5 ***McCrery***	N	N	N	Y	N	N	N	N
6 ***Baker***	N	N	N	Y	N	N	N	N
7 Hayes	Y	N	N	Y	N	Y	Y	Y
MAINE								
1 Andrews	Y	N	Y	Y	Y	Y	Y	Y
2 ***Snowe***	Y	N	Y	Y	Y	N	N	N
MARYLAND								
1 ***Gilchrest***	N	N	Y	Y	Y	N	N	N
2 ***Bentley***	N	N	N	Y	N	Y	Y	N
3 Cardin	Y	N	Y	Y	Y	Y	Y	Y
4 Wynn	Y	N	Y	Y	Y	Y	Y	Y
5 Hoyer	Y	N	Y	Y	Y	Y	Y	Y
6 ***Bartlett***	N	Y	N	Y	N	N	N	N
7 Mfume	Y	N	Y	Y	Y	Y	Y	Y
8 ***Morella***	Y	N	Y	Y	Y	Y	N	N
MASSACHUSETTS								
1 Olver	Y	N	Y	Y	Y	Y	Y	?
2 Neal	Y	N	Y	Y	Y	Y	Y	Y
3 ***Blute***	N	N	N	Y	N	N	N	N
4 Frank	Y	N	Y	Y	Y	Y	Y	Y
5 Meehan	Y	N	Y	Y	Y	Y	Y	Y
6 ***Torkildsen***	N	N	Y	Y	Y	N	N	N
7 Markey	Y	N	Y	Y	Y	Y	Y	Y
8 Kennedy	Y	N	Y	Y	Y	Y	Y	Y
9 Moakley	Y	N	Y	Y	Y	Y	Y	Y
10 Studds	Y	N	Y	Y	Y	Y	Y	Y
MICHIGAN								
1 Stupak	Y	N	N	Y	N	Y	Y	Y
2 ***Hoekstra***	N	N	N	Y	N	N	Y	N
3 Henry	?	?	?	?	?	?	?	?
4 ***Camp***	N	N	N	Y	N	N	N	N
5 Barcia	Y	N	N	Y	N	Y	Y	Y
6 ***Upton***	N	N	Y	Y	Y	N	N	N
7 ***Smith***	N	N	N	Y	N	N	N	N
8 Carr	Y	N	?	Y	Y	Y	Y	?
9 Kildee	Y	N	N	Y	N	Y	Y	Y
10 Bonior	Y	N	Y	Y	Y	Y	N	Y
11 ***Knollenberg***	N	N	N	Y	N	N	N	N
12 Levin	Y	N	Y	Y	Y	Y	Y	Y
13 Ford	Y	N	Y	?	Y	Y	Y	Y
14 Conyers	Y	N	Y	Y	?	Y	Y	?
15 Collins	Y	N	Y	Y	Y	Y	Y	Y
16 Dingell	Y	?	Y	Y	Y	Y	Y	?
MINNESOTA								
1 Penny	Y	N	Y	Y	N	Y	Y	Y
2 Minge	Y	N	Y	Y	Y	Y	Y	?
3 ***Ramstad***	N	N	Y	Y	Y	N	N	N
4 Vento	Y	N	Y	Y	Y	Y	Y	Y
5 Sabo	Y	N	Y	Y	Y	Y	Y	Y
6 ***Grams***	N	N	N	Y	N	N	N	N
7 Peterson	Y	N	N	Y	N	Y	Y	Y
8 Oberstar	Y	N	N	Y	N	Y	Y	Y
MISSISSIPPI								
1 Whitten	Y	N	N	Y	N	?	?	?
2 Vacancy								
3 Montgomery	Y	N	N	Y	N	Y	Y	Y
4 Parker	Y	N	N	Y	N	Y	Y	Y
5 Taylor	N	N	N	Y	N	Y	Y	Y
MISSOURI								
1 Clay	Y	N	Y	Y	Y	Y	Y	?
2 ***Talent***	N	N	N	Y	N	Y	Y	N
3 Gephardt	Y	N	Y	Y	Y	Y	Y	Y
4 Skelton	Y	N	N	Y	N	Y	Y	Y
5 Wheat	Y	N	Y	Y	Y	Y	Y	Y
6 Danner	Y	N	Y	Y	Y	Y	Y	Y
7 ***Hancock***	N	Y	N	Y	N	N	N	N
8 ***Emerson***	N	Y	N	Y	N	N	N	N
9 Volkmer	Y	N	N	Y	N	Y	Y	?
MONTANA								
AL Williams	Y	?	Y	Y	Y	?	?	?
NEBRASKA								
1 ***Bereuter***	N	N	N	Y	N	N	N	N
2 Hoagland	Y	N	Y	Y	Y	Y	Y	Y
3 ***Barrett***	N	N	N	Y	N	N	N	N
NEVADA								
1 Bilbray	Y	N	Y	Y	Y	Y	Y	Y
2 ***Vucanovich***	N	N	N	N	N	N	N	N
NEW HAMPSHIRE								
1 ***Zeliff***	—	—	N	Y	Y	Y	N	N
2 Swett	?	?	?	Y	Y	Y	Y	Y
NEW JERSEY								
1 Andrews	Y	N	Y	Y	Y	Y	Y	?
2 Hughes	Y	N	Y	Y	Y	Y	Y	Y
3 ***Saxton***	N	N	N	Y	N	Y	Y	N
4 ***Smith***	N	Y	N	Y	N	N	Y	N
5 ***Roukema***	Y	N	N	Y	Y	N	N	N
6 Pallone	Y	N	Y	Y	Y	Y	Y	Y
7 ***Franks***	N	N	Y	Y	Y	Y	Y	N
8 Klein	Y	N	Y	Y	Y	Y	Y	Y
9 Torricelli	Y	N	Y	Y	Y	Y	Y	Y
10 Payne	Y	N	Y	Y	Y	Y	Y	Y
11 ***Gallo***	N	N	Y	Y	Y	N	N	N
12 ***Zimmer***	N	N	Y	Y	Y	N	N	N
13 Menendez	Y	N	Y	Y	Y	Y	Y	Y
NEW MEXICO								
1 ***Schiff***	N	N	Y	Y	Y	Y	N	N
2 ***Skeen***	N	N	N	Y	N	Y	N	N
3 Richardson	Y	N	Y	Y	Y	Y	Y	Y
NEW YORK								
1 Hochbrueckner	Y	N	Y	Y	Y	Y	Y	Y
2 ***Lazio***	N	N	Y	Y	Y	N	N	N
3 ***King***	N	N	N	Y	N	N	N	N
4 ***Levy***	N	N	N	Y	Y	N	N	N
5 Ackerman	Y	N	Y	Y	Y	Y	Y	Y
6 Flake	Y	N	Y	Y	Y	Y	Y	Y
7 Manton	Y	N	N	Y	N	?	?	?
8 Nadler	Y	N	Y	Y	Y	Y	Y	Y
9 Schumer	Y	N	Y	Y	Y	Y	Y	Y
10 Towns	Y	N	Y	Y	Y	Y	Y	Y
11 Owens	Y	N	Y	Y	Y	Y	Y	Y
12 Velazquez	Y	N	Y	Y	Y	Y	Y	Y
13 ***Molinari***	N	N	Y	Y	Y	N	N	N
14 Maloney	Y	N	Y	Y	Y	Y	?	?
15 Rangel	Y	?	Y	Y	Y	Y	Y	?
16 Serrano	Y	N	Y	Y	Y	Y	Y	?
17 Engel	Y	N	Y	Y	Y	Y	Y	Y
18 Lowey	Y	N	Y	Y	Y	Y	Y	Y
19 ***Fish***	N	N	N	Y	N	Y	N	Y
20 ***Gilman***	Y	N	Y	Y	Y	Y	N	Y
21 McNulty	Y	N	N	Y	N	Y	Y	Y
22 ***Solomon***	N	N	N	N	N	N	N	N
23 ***Boehlert***	Y	N	Y	Y	Y	Y	N	N
24 ***McHugh***	N	N	Y	Y	Y	N	N	N
25 ***Walsh***	N	N	N	Y	N	Y	N	N
26 Hinchey	Y	N	Y	Y	Y	Y	Y	Y
27 ***Paxon***	N	Y	N	Y	N	N	N	N
28 Slaughter	Y	N	Y	Y	Y	Y	Y	Y
29 LaFalce	Y	?	N	Y	N	Y	Y	Y
30 ***Quinn***	N	N	N	Y	N	N	N	N
31 ***Houghton***	N	N	Y	Y	Y	N	N	N
NORTH CAROLINA								
1 Clayton	Y	N	Y	Y	Y	Y	Y	Y
2 Valentine	Y	N	Y	Y	Y	Y	Y	Y
3 Lancaster	Y	N	Y	Y	Y	Y	Y	Y
4 Price	Y	N	Y	Y	Y	Y	Y	Y
5 Neal	Y	N	Y	Y	Y	Y	Y	Y
6 ***Coble***	N	N	N	Y	N	N	N	N
7 Rose	Y	N	Y	Y	Y	Y	Y	Y
8 Hefner	Y	N	Y	Y	Y	?	?	Y
9 ***McMillan***	N	N	Y	Y	Y	N	Y	N
10 ***Ballenger***	N	N	N	N	N	N	N	N
11 ***Taylor***	N	Y	N	Y	N	Y	?	N
12 Watt	Y	N	Y	N	Y	Y	Y	Y
NORTH DAKOTA								
AL Pomeroy	Y	N	Y	Y	Y	Y	Y	Y
OHIO								
1 Mann	Y	N	Y	Y	Y	Y	Y	Y
2 Vacancy								
3 Hall	Y	N	N	Y	N	Y	Y	Y
4 ***Oxley***	N	N	N	Y	N	Y	N	N
5 ***Gillmor***	N	N	N	Y	N	N	N	Y
6 Strickland	Y	N	Y	Y	Y	Y	Y	Y
7 ***Hobson***	N	N	Y	Y	Y	N	N	N
8 ***Boehner***	N	N	N	Y	N	N	N	N
9 Kaptur	Y	N	Y	Y	Y	Y	Y	Y
10 ***Hoke***	N	Y	Y	Y	Y	Y	Y	N
11 Stokes	Y	N	Y	Y	Y	Y	Y	Y
12 ***Kasich***	N	N	N	Y	N	?	Y	Y
13 Brown	Y	N	Y	Y	Y	Y	Y	Y
14 Sawyer	Y	N	Y	Y	Y	Y	Y	Y
15 ***Pryce***	N	N	Y	Y	Y	N	Y	N
16 ***Regula***	N	N	Y	Y	N	N	N	N
17 Traficant	Y	N	Y	Y	Y	Y	Y	Y
18 Applegate	Y	N	N	N	N	Y	?	Y
19 Fingerhut	Y	N	Y	Y	Y	Y	Y	Y
OKLAHOMA								
1 ***Inhofe***	N	N	N	Y	N	N	N	N
2 Synar	Y	N	Y	Y	Y	Y	Y	Y
3 Brewster	Y	N	Y	Y	Y	Y	Y	Y
4 McCurdy	Y	N	Y	Y	Y	Y	Y	?
5 ***Istook***	N	N	N	Y	N	Y	N	N
6 English	Y	N	N	Y	N	Y	Y	Y
OREGON								
1 Furse	Y	N	Y	Y	Y	Y	Y	Y
2 ***Smith***	N	N	N	N	N	N	Y	N
3 Wyden	Y	N	Y	Y	Y	Y	Y	Y
4 DeFazio	Y	N	Y	Y	Y	Y	?	Y
5 Kopetski	Y	N	Y	Y	Y	Y	Y	Y
PENNSYLVANIA								
1 Foglietta	Y	N	Y	Y	Y	Y	Y	Y
2 Blackwell	Y	N	Y	Y	Y	Y	Y	Y
3 Borski	Y	N	N	Y	N	Y	Y	Y
4 Klink	Y	N	N	Y	N	Y	Y	Y
5 ***Clinger***	N	N	N	Y	Y	Y	Y	Y
6 Holden	Y	N	N	Y	N	Y	Y	Y
7 ***Weldon***	N	N	N	Y	N	N	N	N
8 ***Greenwood***	N	N	Y	Y	Y	N	N	N
9 ***Shuster***	N	N	N	N	N	Y	Y	N
10 ***McDade***	N	N	N	Y	N	Y	?	?
11 Kanjorski	Y	N	N	Y	N	Y	Y	Y
12 Murtha	Y	N	Y	Y	N	Y	Y	Y
13 Margolies-Mezv.	Y	N	Y	Y	Y	Y	Y	Y
14 Coyne	Y	N	Y	Y	Y	Y	Y	?
15 McHale	Y	N	Y	Y	Y	Y	Y	Y
16 ***Walker***	N	N	N	Y	N	N	N	N
17 ***Gekas***	N	N	Y	Y	Y	N	N	N
18 ***Santorum***	N	Y	N	Y	N	N	N	N
19 ***Goodling***	N	N	N	Y	N	Y	Y	?
20 Murphy	Y	N	Y	Y	N	?	?	N
21 ***Ridge***	N	N	Y	Y	Y	Y	Y	N
RHODE ISLAND								
1 ***Machtley***	Y	N	Y	Y	Y	Y	Y	N
2 Reed	Y	N	Y	Y	Y	Y	Y	Y
SOUTH CAROLINA								
1 ***Ravenel***	N	N	N	Y	N	Y	Y	Y
2 ***Spence***	N	N	N	Y	N	N	Y	Y
3 Derrick	Y	N	Y	Y	Y	Y	Y	Y
4 ***Inglis***	N	N	N	Y	N	N	Y	Y
5 Spratt	Y	N	Y	Y	Y	Y	Y	Y
6 Clyburn	Y	N	Y	Y	Y	Y	Y	Y
SOUTH DAKOTA								
AL Johnson	Y	N	Y	Y	Y	Y	Y	Y
TENNESSEE								
1 ***Quillen***	?	?	?	?	?	?	?	?
2 ***Duncan***	N	Y	N	Y	N	N	N	N
3 Lloyd	Y	N	Y	Y	Y	Y	Y	Y
4 Cooper	Y	N	Y	Y	Y	Y	Y	Y
5 Clement	Y	N	Y	Y	Y	Y	Y	Y
6 Gordon	Y	N	Y	Y	Y	Y	Y	Y
7 ***Sundquist***	N	Y	N	Y	N	Y	N	N
8 Tanner	Y	N	Y	Y	N	Y	Y	Y
9 Ford	?	?	?	?	?	?	?	?
TEXAS								
1 Chapman	Y	N	Y	Y	Y	?	Y	?
2 Wilson	Y	N	Y	Y	Y	Y	Y	Y
3 ***Johnson, Sam***	N	?	N	Y	N	Y	N	N
4 Hall	N	N	N	Y	N	Y	Y	Y
5 Bryant	Y	N	Y	Y	Y	Y	Y	Y
6 ***Barton***	N	N	N	Y	N	Y	N	?
7 ***Archer***	N	N	N	Y	N	Y	Y	Y
8 ***Fields***	N	Y	N	Y	N	N	N	N
9 Brooks	Y	N	Y	Y	Y	Y	Y	Y
10 Pickle	?	?	?	?	?	?	?	?
11 Edwards	Y	N	Y	Y	Y	Y	Y	Y
12 Geren	Y	N	?	Y	Y	Y	Y	Y
13 Sarpalius	Y	N	N	Y	N	Y	Y	Y
14 Laughlin	Y	N	Y	Y	Y	Y	Y	Y
15 de la Garza	Y	?	Y	Y	N	Y	Y	Y
16 Coleman	Y	N	Y	Y	Y	Y	Y	Y
17 Stenholm	N	N	N	Y	N	Y	Y	Y
18 Washington	Y	?	Y	Y	Y	Y	Y	Y
19 ***Combest***	N	N	N	Y	N	?	?	Y
20 Gonzalez	Y	N	Y	Y	Y	Y	N	Y
21 ***Smith***	N	N	N	Y	N	N	N	N
22 ***DeLay***	N	Y	N	Y	N	N	N	N
23 ***Bonilla***	N	N	Y	Y	Y	N	N	N
24 Frost	Y	N	Y	Y	Y	Y	Y	Y
25 Andrews	Y	N	Y	Y	Y	Y	Y	Y
26 ***Armey***	N	Y	N	N	N	?	?	N
27 Ortiz	Y	N	N	Y	N	Y	N	Y
28 Tejeda	Y	—	N	N	N	Y	Y	Y
29 Green	Y	N	Y	Y	Y	Y	Y	Y
30 Johnson, E. B.	Y	N	Y	Y	Y	Y	Y	?
UTAH								
1 ***Hansen***	N	N	N	Y	N	Y	N	N
2 Shepherd	Y	N	Y	Y	Y	Y	Y	Y
3 Orton	Y	N	N	Y	N	Y	Y	Y
VERMONT								
AL *Sanders*	Y	N	Y	Y	Y	Y	Y	?
VIRGINIA								
1 ***Bateman***	N	N	N	Y	N	Y	?	Y
2 Pickett	Y	N	Y	Y	Y	Y	Y	Y
3 Scott	Y	N	Y	Y	Y	Y	Y	Y
4 Sisisky	Y	N	Y	Y	Y	Y	Y	Y
5 Payne	Y	N	Y	Y	Y	Y	Y	Y
6 ***Goodlatte***	N	N	N	Y	N	Y	Y	N
7 ***Bliley***	N	N	N	Y	N	N	Y	N
8 Moran	Y	N	Y	Y	Y	Y	Y	Y
9 Boucher	Y	N	Y	Y	Y	Y	Y	Y
10 ***Wolf***	N	N	N	Y	N	N	N	N
11 Byrne	Y	N	Y	Y	Y	Y	Y	Y
WASHINGTON								
1 Cantwell	Y	N	Y	Y	Y	Y	Y	Y
2 Swift	Y	N	Y	Y	Y	Y	Y	?
3 Unsoeld	Y	N	Y	Y	Y	Y	Y	Y
4 Inslee	Y	N	Y	Y	Y	Y	Y	?
5 Foley								
6 Dicks	Y	N	Y	Y	Y	Y	Y	Y
7 McDermott	Y	N	Y	Y	Y	Y	Y	Y
8 ***Dunn***	N	N	N	Y	Y	N	N	N
9 Kreidler	Y	N	Y	Y	Y	Y	Y	Y
WEST VIRGINIA								
1 Mollohan	Y	N	N	Y	N	Y	Y	Y
2 Wise	Y	N	Y	Y	Y	Y	Y	Y
3 Rahall	Y	N	N	Y	N	Y	Y	Y
WISCONSIN								
1 Vacancy								
2 ***Klug***	N	N	Y	Y	Y	N	N	N
3 ***Gunderson***	N	N	N	Y	Y	N	Y	Y
4 Kleczka	Y	N	Y	Y	Y	Y	Y	Y
5 Barrett	?	N	Y	Y	Y	Y	Y	Y
6 ***Petri***	N	N	N	Y	N	N	N	N
7 Obey	Y	N	Y	Y	Y	Y	Y	?
8 ***Roth***	N	N	N	Y	N	N	N	N
9 ***Sensenbrenner***	N	N	N	Y	N	N	N	N
WYOMING								
AL ***Thomas***	N	N	N	Y	N	N	N	N
DELEGATES								
de Lugo, V.I.	D	D	Y	Y	Y	Y	D	D
Faleomavaega, Am.S.	D	D	Y	Y	Y	?	D	D
Norton, D.C.	D	D	Y	Y	Y	Y	D	D
Romero-B., P.R.	D	D	?	?	?	?	D	D
Underwood, Guam	D	D	?	Y	Y	Y	D	D

Southern states - Ala., Ark., Fla., Ga., Ky., La., Miss., N.C., Okla., S.C., Tenn., Texas, Va.
Omitted votes are quorum calls, which CQ does not include in its vote charts.

101. Procedural Motion. Burton, R-Ind., motion to adjourn. Motion rejected 13-399: R 13-157; D 0-241 (ND 0-161, SD 0-80); I 0-1, March 25, 1993.

102. HR 670. Family Planning Amendments/State Control. DeLay, R-Texas, amendment to require that Title X funds go only to states. Rejected in the Committee of the Whole 142-277: R 115-52; D 27-224 (ND 15-154, SD 12-70); I 0-1, March 25, 1993.

103. HR 670. Family Planning Amendments/Patient Advisers. Separate vote at the request of Solomon, R-N.Y., on the DeLay, R-Texas, amendment adopted in the Committee of the Whole as amended by the Waxman, D-Calif., amendment, to require persons advising patients at federally funded family planning facilities to have a professional degree, meet the criteria of the secretary of Health and Human Services or be allowed to offer such counseling under state law. Adopted 418-0: R 170-0; D 247-0 (ND 166-0, SD 81-0); I 1-0, March 25, 1993. (On separate votes, which may be demanded on an amendment adopted in the Committee of the Whole, the four delegates and the resident commissioner of Puerto Rico cannot vote. See vote 96.)

104. HR 670. Family Planning Amendments/Conscience Exemption. Separate vote at the request of Solomon, R-N.Y., on the Waxman, D-Calif., amendment adopted in the Committee of the Whole to clarify that an individual who provides counseling at a clinic but who objects to abortions would not be required to provide information but that the clinic would arrange for another person or clinic to give counseling. Adopted 259-157: R 49-121; D 209-36 (ND 141-24, SD 68-12); I 1-0, March 25, 1993. (On separate votes, which may be demanded on an amendment adopted in the Committee of the Whole, the four delegates and the resident commissioner of Puerto Rico cannot vote. See vote 97.)

105. HR 670. Family Planning Amendments/Condom Standards. Separate vote at the request of Solomon, R-N.Y., on the Burton, R-Ind., amendment adopted in the Committee of the Whole and amended by Waxman, D-Calif., to require condoms distributed at Title X clinics to meet Food and Drug Administration standards for quality control and labeling and any subsequent standards. Adopted 417-0: R 170-0; D 246-0 (ND 164-0, SD 82-0); I 1-0, March 25, 1993. (On separate votes, which may be demanded on an amendment adopted in the Committee of the Whole, the four delegates and the resident commissioner of Puerto Rico cannot vote.)

106. HR 670. Family Planning Amendments/Motion to Recommit Parental Notice. Bliley, R-Va., motion to recommit to the House Energy and Commerce Committee the bill with instructions to report it back with an amendment to federally funded Title X clinics to give parents 48 hours' notice before performing an abortion on a minor. Motion rejected 179-243: R 138-34; D 41-208 (ND 26-141, SD 15-67); I 0-1, March 25, 1993. A "nay" was a vote in support of the president's position.

107. HR 670. Family Planning Amendments/Passage. Passage of the bill to authorize $238 million in fiscal 1994 and $270.5 million in fiscal 1995 for Title X family planning programs at clinics. The bill would codify the Clinton administration's lifting of the "gag rule" that prohibited staff at federally funded clinics from discussing abortion. Passed 273-149: R 51-121; D 221-28 (ND 150-17, SD 71-11); I 1-0, March 25, 1993. A "yea" was a vote in support of the president's position.

108. HR 670. Family Planning Amendments/Motion to Reconsider. Unsoeld, D-Wash., motion to table (kill) the Waxman, D-Calif., motion to reconsider the vote by which the House passed the bill to authorize $238 million in fiscal 1994 and $270.5 million in fiscal 1995 for Title X family planning programs. The bill would codify the Clinton administration's lifting of the "gag rule" that prohibited staff at federally funded clinics from discussing abortion. Motion agreed to 274-142: R 33-136; D 240-6 (ND 160-6, SD 80-0); I 1-0, March 25, 1993.

KEY

Y   Voted for (yea).
Paired for.
+   Announced for.
N   Voted against (nay).
X   Paired against.
—   Announced against.
P   Voted "present."
C   Voted "present" to avoid possible conflict of interest.
?   Did not vote or otherwise make a position known.
D   Delegates ineligible to vote.

Democrats   *Republicans*
Independent

	101	102	103	104	105	106	107	108
ALABAMA								
1 *Callahan*	N	Y	Y	N	Y	Y	N	N
2 *Everett*	N	Y	Y	N	Y	Y	N	?
3 Browder	N	N	Y	N	Y	N	Y	Y
4 Bevill	N	N	Y	Y	Y	N	Y	Y
5 Cramer	N	N	Y	Y	Y	N	Y	Y
6 *Bachus*	N	Y	Y	N	Y	N	N	N
7 Hilliard	N	N	Y	Y	Y	N	Y	Y
ALASKA								
AL *Young*	N	Y	Y	N	Y	N	Y	N
ARIZONA								
1 *Coppersmith*	N	N	Y	Y	Y	N	Y	Y
2 Pastor	N	N	Y	Y	Y	N	Y	Y
3 *Stump*	N	Y	Y	N	Y	N	N	N
4 *Kyl*	N	Y	Y	N	Y	N	N	N
5 *Kolbe*	N	N	Y	Y	Y	N	Y	Y
6 English	N	N	Y	Y	Y	N	Y	Y
ARKANSAS								
1 Lambert	N	N	?	Y	Y	N	Y	Y
2 Thornton	N	N	Y	Y	Y	N	Y	Y
3 *Hutchinson*	N	Y	Y	N	Y	Y	N	N
4 Dickey	N	Y	Y	N	Y	N	Y	N
CALIFORNIA								
1 Hamburg	N	N	Y	Y	Y	N	Y	Y
2 *Herger*	N	Y	Y	N	Y	N	N	N
3 Fazio	N	N	Y	Y	Y	N	Y	Y
4 *Doolittle*	Y	Y	N	Y	N	Y	N	N
5 Matsui	N	N	Y	Y	Y	N	Y	Y
6 Woolsey	N	N	Y	Y	Y	—	Y	Y
7 Miller	N	N	?	Y	Y	N	Y	Y
8 Pelosi	N	N	Y	Y	Y	N	Y	Y
9 Dellums	N	N	Y	Y	Y	N	Y	Y
10 *Baker*	Y	Y	N	Y	N	Y	N	N
11 *Pombo*	N	Y	Y	N	Y	N	N	N
12 Lantos	N	N	Y	Y	Y	N	Y	Y
13 Stark	N	N	Y	Y	Y	?	Y	Y
14 Eshoo	N	N	Y	Y	Y	N	Y	Y
15 Mineta	N	N	Y	Y	Y	N	Y	Y
16 Edwards	?	N	Y	Y	?	N	Y	Y
17 Vacancy								
18 Condit	N	N	Y	Y	Y	N	Y	Y
19 Lehman	N	N	Y	Y	N	?	Y	Y
20 Dooley	N	N	Y	Y	Y	N	Y	Y
21 *Thomas*	N	N	Y	N	N	N	N	N
22 *Huffington*	N	N	Y	N	Y	Y	N	Y
23 *Gallegly*	N	Y	Y	N	Y	Y	N	N
24 Beilenson	N	N	Y	Y	Y	N	Y	Y
25 *McKeon*	N	Y	Y	N	Y	N	N	N
26 Berman	N	N	Y	Y	Y	N	Y	?
27 *Moorhead*	N	Y	Y	N	Y	N	N	N
28 *Dreier*	?	?	?	?	?	?	?	?
29 Waxman	N	N	Y	Y	Y	N	Y	Y
30 Becerra	N	N	Y	Y	Y	N	Y	Y
31 Martinez	N	?	Y	Y	Y	N	Y	Y
32 Dixon	N	N	Y	Y	Y	N	Y	Y
33 Roybal-Allard	N	N	Y	Y	Y	N	Y	Y
34 Torres	N	N	Y	Y	Y	N	+	Y
35 Waters	N	N	Y	Y	Y	N	Y	Y
36 Harman	N	N	Y	Y	Y	N	Y	Y
37 Tucker	N	N	Y	Y	Y	N	Y	Y
38 *Horn*	N	N	Y	Y	Y	N	Y	Y
39 *Royce*	N	Y	Y	N	Y	N	Y	N
40 *Lewis*	N	N	Y	N	Y	N	Y	N
41 *Kim*	N	Y	Y	N	Y	Y	N	N

	101	102	103	104	105	106	107	108
42 Brown	N	N	Y	Y	N	Y	?	
43 *Calvert*	N	N	Y	N	Y	N	?	
44 *McCandless*	N	?	Y	N	Y	N	N	
45 *Rohrabacher*	N	Y	Y	N	Y	N	N	
46 *Dornan*	N	Y	Y	N	Y	N	N	
47 *Cox*	N	N	Y	N	Y	N	N	
48 *Packard*	N	Y	Y	N	Y	N	N	
49 Schenk	N	N	Y	Y	Y	N	Y	Y
50 Filner	N	N	Y	Y	Y	N	Y	Y
51 *Cunningham*	N	Y	Y	N	Y	N	N	N
52 *Hunter*	Y	Y	?	?	?	Y	N	N
COLORADO								
1 Schroeder	N	N	Y	Y	Y	N	Y	Y
2 Skaggs	N	N	Y	Y	Y	N	Y	Y
3 *McInnis*	N	N	Y	Y	Y	N	Y	Y
4 *Allard*	N	Y	Y	N	Y	Y	N	N
5 *Hefley*	N	N	Y	N	Y	N	N	N
6 *Schaefer*	N	Y	Y	N	Y	N	N	N
CONNECTICUT								
1 Kennelly	N	N	Y	Y	Y	N	Y	Y
2 Gejdenson	N	N	Y	Y	Y	N	Y	Y
3 DeLauro	N	N	Y	Y	Y	N	Y	Y
4 *Shays*	N	N	Y	Y	Y	N	Y	Y
5 *Franks*	Y	Y	N	Y	N	Y	N	N
6 *Johnson*	N	N	Y	Y	Y	N	Y	Y
DELAWARE								
AL *Castle*	N	N	Y	Y	Y	Y	Y	Y
FLORIDA								
1 Hutto	N	N	Y	N	Y	N	Y	Y
2 Peterson	N	N	Y	Y	Y	N	Y	Y
3 Brown	N	N	Y	Y	Y	N	Y	Y
4 *Fowler*	N	N	Y	Y	Y	N	Y	Y
5 Thurman	N	N	Y	Y	Y	N	Y	Y
6 *Stearns*	N	Y	Y	N	Y	N	N	N
7 *Mica*	N	Y	Y	N	Y	N	N	N
8 *McCollum*	N	Y	Y	N	Y	N	N	N
9 *Bilirakis*	N	Y	Y	N	Y	N	N	N
10 *Young*	N	Y	Y	N	Y	N	N	N
11 Gibbons	N	N	Y	Y	Y	N	Y	Y
12 *Canady*	N	Y	Y	N	Y	N	N	N
13 *Miller*	N	Y	Y	N	Y	N	N	N
14 *Goss*	N	Y	Y	N	Y	N	Y	N
15 Bacchus	N	N	Y	Y	Y	N	Y	Y
16 *Lewis*	N	N	Y	Y	Y	N	Y	Y
17 Meek	N	N	Y	Y	Y	N	Y	Y
18 *Ros-Lehtinen*	N	N	Y	Y	Y	N	N	N
19 Johnston	N	N	Y	Y	Y	N	Y	Y
20 Deutsch	N	N	Y	Y	Y	N	Y	Y
21 *Diaz-Balart*	N	Y	Y	N	Y	N	N	N
22 *Shaw*	N	Y	Y	N	Y	N	N	N
23 Hastings	N	N	Y	Y	Y	N	Y	Y
GEORGIA								
1 *Kingston*	N	Y	Y	N	Y	N	N	N
2 Bishop	N	N	Y	Y	Y	N	Y	Y
3 *Collins*	N	Y	Y	N	Y	N	N	N
4 *Linder*	N	Y	Y	N	Y	N	N	N
5 Lewis	N	N	Y	Y	Y	N	Y	Y
6 *Gingrich*	N	?	?	N	Y	N	N	N
7 Darden	N	N	Y	?	Y	N	Y	Y
8 Rowland	N	N	Y	Y	Y	N	Y	Y
9 Deal	N	N	Y	Y	Y	N	Y	Y
10 Johnson	N	N	Y	Y	Y	N	Y	Y
11 McKinney	N	N	Y	Y	Y	N	Y	Y
HAWAII								
1 Abercrombie	N	N	Y	Y	Y	N	Y	Y
2 Mink	N	N	Y	Y	Y	N	Y	Y
IDAHO								
1 LaRocco	N	N	Y	Y	?	N	Y	Y
2 *Crapo*	N	Y	Y	N	Y	Y	N	N
ILLINOIS								
1 Rush	N	N	Y	Y	Y	N	Y	Y
2 Reynolds	N	N	Y	Y	Y	N	Y	Y
3 Lipinski	N	Y	Y	N	Y	N	N	N
4 Gutierrez	N	N	Y	Y	Y	N	Y	Y
5 Rostenkowski	?	N	Y	Y	Y	N	Y	Y
6 *Hyde*	N	Y	Y	N	Y	N	N	N
7 Collins	N	N	Y	Y	Y	N	Y	Y
8 *Crane*	Y	Y	Y	N	Y	N	N	N
9 Yates	N	N	Y	Y	Y	N	Y	Y
10 *Porter*	N	N	Y	Y	Y	N	Y	Y
11 Sangmeister	N	N	Y	Y	Y	N	Y	Y
12 Costello	N	Y	Y	N	Y	N	Y	Y
13 *Fawell*	N	N	Y	Y	Y	N	Y	N
14 *Hastert*	N	Y	Y	N	Y	N	N	N
15 *Ewing*	N	Y	Y	N	Y	N	N	N
16 *Manzullo*	N	Y	Y	N	Y	N	N	N
17 Evans	N	N	Y	Y	Y	N	Y	Y

ND   Northern Democrats   SD   Southern Democrats

	101	102	103	104	105	106	107	108
18 ***Michel***	N	Y	Y	N	Y	Y	N	N
19 Poshard	N	Y	Y	N	Y	Y	N	N
20 Durbin	N	N	Y	Y	Y	N	Y	Y
INDIANA								
1 Visclosky	N	N	Y	Y	Y	N	Y	Y
2 Sharp	?	?	?	?	?	?	?	?
3 Roemer	N	Y	Y	N	Y	Y	Y	Y
4 Long	N	N	Y	Y	Y	N	Y	Y
5 ***Buyer***	N	Y	Y	N	Y	Y	N	N
6 ***Burton***	Y	Y	Y	N	Y	Y	N	N
7 ***Myers***	N	Y	Y	N	Y	Y	N	N
8 McCloskey	N	N	Y	Y	Y	N	Y	Y
9 Hamilton	N	N	Y	Y	Y	Y	Y	Y
10 Jacobs	N	N	Y	Y	Y	N	Y	Y
IOWA								
1 ***Leach***	N	N	Y	Y	Y	N	Y	Y
2 ***Nussle***	N	Y	Y	N	Y	Y	N	N
3 ***Lightfoot***	N	Y	Y	N	Y	Y	N	?
4 Smith	N	N	Y	Y	Y	N	Y	Y
5 ***Grandy***	N	N	Y	Y	Y	Y	N	N
KANSAS								
1 ***Roberts***	N	Y	Y	N	Y	Y	N	N
2 Slattery	N	N	Y	Y	Y	N	Y	Y
3 ***Meyers***	N	N	Y	Y	Y	N	Y	N
4 Glickman	N	N	Y	Y	Y	N	Y	Y
KENTUCKY								
1 Barlow	N	N	Y	Y	Y	N	Y	Y
2 Natcher	N	N	Y	Y	Y	N	Y	Y
3 Mazzoli	N	N	Y	N	Y	Y	Y	Y
4 ***Bunning***	N	Y	Y	N	Y	Y	N	N
5 ***Rogers***	N	Y	Y	N	Y	Y	N	N
6 Baesler	N	N	Y	Y	Y	N	Y	Y
LOUISIANA								
1 ***Livingston***	Y	Y	Y	N	Y	Y	N	N
2 Jefferson	N	N	Y	Y	Y	N	Y	Y
3 Tauzin	N	Y	Y	N	Y	Y	N	Y
4 Fields	N	N	Y	Y	Y	N	Y	Y
5 ***McCrery***	N	Y	Y	N	Y	Y	N	N
6 ***Baker***	N	Y	Y	N	Y	Y	N	N
7 Hayes	N	Y	Y	N	Y	Y	N	Y
MAINE								
1 Andrews	N	N	Y	Y	Y	N	Y	Y
2 ***Snowe***	N	N	Y	Y	Y	N	Y	Y
MARYLAND								
1 ***Gilchrest***	N	N	Y	Y	Y	Y	Y	N
2 ***Bentley***	N	N	Y	N	Y	Y	Y	Y
3 Cardin	N	N	Y	Y	Y	N	Y	Y
4 Wynn	N	N	Y	Y	Y	N	Y	Y
5 Hoyer	N	N	Y	Y	Y	N	Y	Y
6 ***Bartlett***	Y	Y	Y	N	Y	Y	N	N
7 Mfume	N	N	Y	Y	Y	N	Y	Y
8 ***Morella***	N	N	Y	Y	Y	N	Y	Y
MASSACHUSETTS								
1 Olver	N	N	Y	Y	Y	N	Y	Y
2 Neal	N	N	Y	Y	Y	N	Y	Y
3 ***Blute***	N	N	Y	N	Y	Y	N	N
4 Frank	N	N	Y	Y	Y	N	Y	Y
5 Meehan	N	N	Y	Y	Y	N	Y	Y
6 ***Torkildsen***	Y	N	Y	Y	Y	Y	Y	N
7 Markey	N	N	?	?	Y	N	Y	Y
8 Kennedy	N	N	Y	Y	Y	N	Y	Y
9 Moakley	N	N	Y	Y	Y	N	Y	Y
10 Studds	N	N	Y	Y	Y	N	Y	Y
MICHIGAN								
1 Stupak	N	Y	Y	N	Y	N	Y	Y
2 ***Hoekstra***	N	Y	Y	N	Y	Y	N	N
3 Henry	?	?	?	?	?	?	?	?
4 ***Camp***	N	Y	Y	N	Y	Y	N	N
5 Barcia	N	Y	Y	?	Y	Y	N	N
6 ***Upton***	N	N	Y	Y	Y	Y	N	N
7 ***Smith***	N	Y	Y	N	Y	Y	N	N
8 Carr	?	?	Y	Y	Y	N	Y	Y
9 Kildee	N	Y	Y	N	Y	Y	N	Y
10 Bonior	N	N	Y	Y	Y	N	Y	Y
11 ***Knollenberg***	N	Y	Y	N	Y	Y	N	N
12 Levin	N	N	Y	Y	Y	N	Y	Y
13 Ford	N	N	?	Y	Y	N	Y	Y
14 Conyers	N	N	Y	Y	Y	N	Y	Y
15 Collins	N	N	Y	Y	Y	N	Y	Y
16 Dingell	N	N	Y	Y	Y	N	Y	Y
MINNESOTA								
1 Penny	N	N	Y	N	Y	Y	Y	Y
2 Minge	N	N	Y	Y	Y	N	Y	Y
3 ***Ramstad***	N	N	Y	Y	Y	N	Y	Y
4 Vento	N	N	Y	Y	Y	N	Y	Y

	101	102	103	104	105	106	107	108
5 Sabo	N	N	Y	Y	Y	N	Y	Y
6 ***Grams***	N	N	Y	N	Y	Y	N	N
7 Peterson	N	Y	Y	N	Y	Y	N	Y
8 Oberstar	N	N	Y	N	Y	Y	N	Y
MISSISSIPPI								
1 Whitten	?	N	Y	Y	Y	N	Y	Y
2 Vacancy								
3 Montgomery	N	N	Y	Y	Y	Y	N	Y
4 Parker	N	Y	Y	Y	Y	Y	N	Y
5 Taylor	N	Y	Y	N	Y	Y	N	Y
MISSOURI								
1 Clay	N	N	Y	Y	Y	N	Y	Y
2 ***Talent***	?	Y	Y	?	?	Y	N	N
3 Gephardt	N	N	Y	Y	Y	N	Y	Y
4 Skelton	N	N	Y	N	Y	Y	N	Y
5 Wheat	N	N	Y	Y	Y	N	Y	Y
6 Danner	N	N	Y	Y	Y	N	Y	Y
7 ***Hancock***	N	Y	Y	N	Y	Y	N	N
8 ***Emerson***	N	Y	Y	N	Y	Y	N	N
9 Volkmer	N	Y	Y	N	Y	Y	N	Y
MONTANA								
AL Williams	?	N	Y	Y	Y	N	Y	Y
NEBRASKA								
1 ***Bereuter***	N	Y	Y	N	Y	Y	Y	Y
2 Hoagland	N	N	Y	Y	Y	N	Y	Y
3 ***Barrett***	N	Y	Y	N	Y	Y	N	N
NEVADA								
1 Bilbray	N	N	Y	Y	Y	N	Y	Y
2 ***Vucanovich***	N	Y	Y	N	Y	Y	N	N
NEW HAMPSHIRE								
1 ***Zeliff***	N	N	Y	Y	Y	N	Y	Y
2 Swett	N	N	Y	Y	Y	N	Y	Y
NEW JERSEY								
1 Andrews	N	N	Y	Y	Y	N	Y	Y
2 Hughes	N	N	Y	Y	Y	N	Y	Y
3 ***Saxton***	N	Y	Y	N	Y	Y	N	N
4 ***Smith***	N	Y	Y	N	Y	Y	N	N
5 ***Roukema***	N	N	Y	Y	Y	Y	Y	N
6 Pallone	N	N	Y	Y	Y	N	Y	Y
7 ***Franks***	N	N	Y	Y	Y	Y	Y	N
8 Klein	N	N	Y	Y	Y	N	Y	Y
9 Torricelli	?	N	Y	Y	Y	N	Y	Y
10 Payne	N	N	Y	Y	Y	N	Y	Y
11 ***Gallo***	N	N	Y	Y	Y	Y	Y	Y
12 ***Zimmer***	N	N	Y	Y	Y	Y	Y	N
13 Menendez	N	N	Y	Y	Y	N	Y	Y
NEW MEXICO								
1 ***Schiff***	N	N	Y	Y	Y	N	Y	Y
2 ***Skeen***	N	Y	Y	N	Y	N	Y	N
3 Richardson	N	N	Y	Y	Y	N	Y	Y
NEW YORK								
1 Hochbrueckner	N	N	Y	Y	Y	N	Y	Y
2 ***Lazio***	N	N	Y	Y	Y	Y	Y	Y
3 ***King***	N	Y	Y	N	Y	Y	N	N
4 ***Levy***	N	Y	Y	Y	Y	Y	N	N
5 Ackerman	N	N	Y	Y	Y	N	Y	Y
6 Flake	N	N	Y	Y	Y	Y	Y	Y
7 Manton	?	N	?	N	Y	Y	Y	Y
8 Nadler	N	N	Y	Y	Y	N	Y	Y
9 Schumer	N	N	Y	Y	Y	N	Y	Y
10 Towns	N	N	Y	Y	Y	N	Y	Y
11 Owens	N	N	Y	Y	Y	N	Y	Y
12 Velazquez	N	N	Y	Y	Y	N	Y	Y
13 ***Molinari***	N	N	Y	Y	Y	N	Y	Y
14 Maloney	N	N	Y	Y	Y	N	Y	Y
15 Rangel	N	N	Y	Y	Y	N	Y	Y
16 Serrano	N	N	Y	Y	Y	N	Y	Y
17 Engel	N	N	Y	Y	Y	N	Y	Y
18 Lowey	N	N	Y	Y	Y	N	Y	Y
19 ***Fish***	N	N	Y	N	Y	Y	Y	N
20 ***Gilman***	N	N	Y	Y	Y	N	Y	Y
21 McNulty	N	N	Y	N	Y	Y	Y	Y
22 ***Solomon***	N	Y	Y	N	Y	Y	N	N
23 ***Boehlert***	N	N	Y	Y	Y	N	Y	Y
24 ***McHugh***	N	N	Y	Y	Y	Y	Y	Y
25 ***Walsh***	N	Y	Y	N	Y	Y	N	N
26 Hinchey	N	N	Y	Y	Y	N	Y	Y
27 ***Paxon***	N	Y	Y	N	Y	Y	N	N
28 Slaughter	N	N	Y	Y	Y	N	Y	Y
29 LaFalce	?	Y	Y	N	Y	Y	N	Y
30 ***Quinn***	N	Y	Y	N	Y	Y	N	N
31 ***Houghton***	N	N	Y	Y	Y	Y	N	N
NORTH CAROLINA								
1 Clayton	N	N	Y	Y	Y	N	Y	Y
2 Valentine	N	N	Y	Y	Y	N	Y	Y

	101	102	103	104	105	106	107	108
3 Lancaster	N	N	Y	Y	Y	N	Y	Y
4 Price	N	N	Y	Y	Y	N	Y	Y
5 Neal	N	N	Y	Y	Y	N	Y	Y
6 ***Coble***	N	Y	Y	N	Y	Y	N	N
7 Rose	N	N	Y	Y	Y	N	Y	Y
8 Hefner	N	N	Y	Y	Y	N	Y	Y
9 ***McMillan***	N	N	Y	Y	Y	Y	Y	Y
10 ***Ballenger***	Y	Y	Y	N	Y	Y	N	N
11 ***Taylor***	N	Y	Y	N	Y	Y	N	N
12 Watt	N	N	Y	Y	Y	N	Y	Y
NORTH DAKOTA								
AL Pomeroy	N	N	Y	Y	Y	N	Y	Y
OHIO								
1 Mann	N	N	Y	Y	Y	N	Y	Y
2 Vacancy								
3 Hall	N	N	Y	N	?	Y	N	Y
4 ***Oxley***	N	Y	Y	N	Y	Y	N	N
5 ***Gillmor***	N	Y	Y	N	Y	Y	N	N
6 Strickland	N	N	Y	Y	Y	N	Y	Y
7 ***Hobson***	N	Y	Y	Y	Y	N	Y	N
8 ***Boehner***	N	Y	Y	N	Y	Y	N	N
9 Kaptur	N	N	Y	Y	?	N	Y	Y
10 ***Hoke***	Y	Y	Y	Y	Y	Y	N	N
11 Stokes	N	N	Y	Y	Y	N	Y	Y
12 ***Kasich***	N	Y	Y	N	Y	Y	N	N
13 Brown	N	N	Y	Y	Y	N	Y	Y
14 Sawyer	N	N	Y	Y	Y	N	Y	Y
15 ***Pryce***	N	N	Y	Y	Y	N	Y	N
16 ***Regula***	N	Y	Y	N	Y	N	Y	N
17 Traficant	N	N	Y	Y	Y	N	Y	Y
18 Applegate	N	N	Y	N	Y	Y	Y	Y
19 Fingerhut	N	N	Y	Y	Y	N	Y	Y
OKLAHOMA								
1 ***Inhofe***	N	Y	Y	N	Y	Y	N	N
2 Synar	N	N	Y	Y	Y	N	Y	Y
3 Brewster	N	N	Y	Y	Y	N	Y	Y
4 McCurdy	N	N	Y	Y	Y	N	Y	Y
5 ***Istook***	N	Y	Y	N	Y	Y	N	N
6 English	?	Y	Y	Y	Y	Y	Y	Y
OREGON								
1 Furse	N	?	Y	Y	Y	N	Y	Y
2 ***Smith***	N	Y	Y	N	Y	Y	N	N
3 Wyden	N	N	Y	Y	Y	N	Y	Y
4 DeFazio	N	N	Y	Y	Y	N	Y	Y
5 Kopetski	N	N	Y	Y	Y	N	Y	Y
PENNSYLVANIA								
1 Foglietta	N	N	Y	Y	Y	N	Y	Y
2 Blackwell	N	N	Y	Y	Y	N	Y	Y
3 Borski	N	N	Y	N	Y	N	Y	Y
4 Klink	N	Y	Y	N	Y	Y	N	N
5 ***Clinger***	N	N	Y	Y	Y	Y	N	N
6 Holden	N	Y	Y	?	Y	Y	N	N
7 ***Weldon***	N	N	Y	N	Y	Y	N	N
8 ***Greenwood***	N	N	Y	Y	Y	N	Y	Y
9 ***Shuster***	N	Y	Y	N	Y	Y	N	N
10 ***McDade***	?	?	Y	N	Y	Y	Y	Y
11 Kanjorski	N	N	Y	N	Y	Y	Y	Y
12 Murtha	N	N	Y	N	Y	N	Y	Y
13 Margolies-Mezv.	N	N	Y	Y	Y	N	Y	Y
14 Coyne	N	N	Y	Y	Y	N	Y	Y
15 McHale	N	N	Y	Y	Y	N	Y	Y
16 ***Walker***	N	Y	Y	N	Y	Y	N	N
17 ***Gekas***	N	N	Y	Y	Y	N	Y	Y
18 ***Santorum***	N	Y	Y	N	Y	Y	N	N
19 ***Goodling***	N	Y	Y	N	Y	Y	N	N
20 Murphy	N	N	Y	Y	Y	Y	N	?
21 ***Ridge***	N	N	Y	Y	Y	N	Y	Y
RHODE ISLAND								
1 ***Machtley***	N	N	Y	Y	Y	N	Y	Y
2 Reed	N	N	Y	Y	Y	N	Y	Y
SOUTH CAROLINA								
1 ***Ravenel***	N	N	Y	N	Y	N	Y	Y
2 ***Spence***	N	Y	Y	N	Y	Y	N	N
3 Derrick	N	N	Y	Y	Y	N	Y	Y
4 ***Inglis***	N	Y	Y	N	Y	Y	N	N
5 Spratt	N	N	Y	?	Y	Y	N	Y
6 Clyburn	N	N	Y	Y	Y	N	Y	?
SOUTH DAKOTA								
AL Johnson	N	N	Y	Y	Y	N	Y	Y
TENNESSEE								
1 ***Quillen***	?	#	?	?	?	#	X	?
2 ***Duncan***	N	Y	Y	N	Y	Y	N	N
3 Lloyd	N	N	Y	Y	Y	N	Y	Y
4 Cooper	N	N	Y	Y	Y	N	Y	Y
5 Clement	N	N	Y	Y	Y	N	Y	Y

	101	102	103	104	105	106	107	108
6 Gordon	N	N	Y	Y	Y	N	Y	Y
7 ***Sundquist***	N	Y	Y	N	Y	Y	N	N
8 Tanner	N	N	Y	Y	Y	N	Y	Y
9 Ford	?	?	?	?	?	?	?	?
TEXAS								
1 Chapman	N	N	Y	Y	Y	N	Y	Y
2 Wilson	N	N	Y	Y	Y	N	Y	Y
3 ***Johnson, Sam***	N	Y	Y	N	Y	Y	N	N
4 Hall	N	Y	Y	N	Y	Y	Y	Y
5 Bryant	N	N	Y	Y	Y	N	Y	Y
6 ***Barton***	N	?	Y	N	Y	Y	N	N
7 ***Archer***	N	?	Y	N	Y	Y	N	N
8 ***Fields***	N	Y	Y	N	Y	Y	N	N
9 Brooks	N	N	Y	Y	Y	N	Y	Y
10 Pickle	?	X	?	?	?	X	#	?
11 Edwards	N	N	Y	Y	Y	N	Y	Y
12 Geren	N	N	Y	Y	Y	Y	Y	Y
13 Sarpalius	N	Y	Y	N	Y	Y	N	Y
14 Laughlin	N	N	Y	Y	Y	N	Y	Y
15 de la Garza	N	Y	Y	N	Y	Y	N	Y
16 Coleman	N	N	Y	Y	Y	N	Y	Y
17 Stenholm	N	Y	Y	N	Y	Y	N	Y
18 Washington	N	N	Y	Y	Y	N	Y	?
19 ***Combest***	N	Y	Y	N	Y	Y	N	N
20 Gonzalez	N	N	Y	Y	Y	N	Y	Y
21 ***Smith***	N	Y	Y	N	Y	Y	Y	N
22 ***DeLay***	Y	Y	Y	N	Y	Y	N	N
23 ***Bonilla***	N	Y	Y	Y	Y	Y	N	N
24 Frost	N	N	Y	Y	Y	N	Y	Y
25 Andrews	N	N	Y	Y	Y	N	Y	Y
26 ***Armey***	N	Y	Y	N	Y	Y	N	N
27 Ortiz	N	Y	Y	N	Y	Y	N	Y
28 Tejeda	N	Y	Y	N	Y	Y	N	Y
29 Green	N	N	Y	Y	Y	N	Y	Y
30 Johnson, E. B.	N	N	Y	Y	Y	N	Y	Y
UTAH								
1 ***Hansen***	N	Y	Y	N	Y	Y	N	N
2 Shepherd	N	N	Y	Y	?	N	Y	Y
3 Orton	N	Y	Y	N	Y	Y	N	Y
VERMONT								
AL *Sanders*	N	N	Y	Y	Y	N	Y	Y
VIRGINIA								
1 ***Bateman***	N	Y	Y	N	Y	Y	N	Y
2 Pickett	N	N	Y	Y	Y	N	Y	Y
3 Scott	N	N	Y	Y	Y	N	Y	Y
4 Sisisky	N	N	Y	Y	Y	N	Y	Y
5 Payne	N	N	Y	Y	Y	N	Y	Y
6 ***Goodlatte***	N	Y	Y	N	Y	Y	N	N
7 ***Bliley***	N	Y	Y	N	Y	Y	N	N
8 Moran	N	N	Y	Y	Y	N	Y	Y
9 Boucher	N	N	Y	Y	Y	N	Y	Y
10 ***Wolf***	N	Y	Y	N	Y	Y	N	N
11 Byrne	N	N	Y	Y	Y	N	Y	Y
WASHINGTON								
1 Cantwell	N	N	Y	Y	Y	N	Y	Y
2 Swift	N	N	Y	Y	Y	N	Y	Y
3 Unsoeld	N	N	Y	Y	Y	N	Y	Y
4 Inslee	N	N	Y	Y	Y	N	Y	Y
5 Foley								
6 Dicks	?	N	Y	Y	Y	N	Y	Y
7 McDermott	N	N	Y	Y	Y	N	Y	Y
8 ***Dunn***	Y	Y	Y	Y	Y	Y	Y	Y
9 Kreidler	N	N	Y	Y	Y	N	Y	Y
WEST VIRGINIA								
1 Mollohan	N	Y	Y	N	Y	Y	N	Y
2 Wise	N	N	Y	Y	Y	N	Y	Y
3 Rahall	N	Y	Y	N	Y	Y	N	Y
WISCONSIN								
1 Vacancy								
2 ***Klug***	N	N	Y	Y	Y	N	Y	N
3 ***Gunderson***	N	N	Y	Y	Y	Y	Y	N
4 Kleczka	N	N	Y	Y	Y	N	Y	Y
5 Barrett	N	N	Y	Y	Y	N	Y	Y
6 ***Petri***	N	Y	Y	N	Y	Y	N	N
7 Obey	N	N	Y	Y	Y	N	Y	Y
8 ***Roth***	N	Y	Y	N	Y	Y	N	N
9 ***Sensenbrenner***	N	Y	Y	N	Y	Y	N	N
WYOMING								
AL ***Thomas***	N	Y	Y	N	Y	Y	N	N
DELEGATES								
de Lugo, V.I.	D	N	D	D	D	D	D	D
Faleomavaega, Am.S.	D	?	D	D	D	D	D	D
Norton, D.C.	D	N	D	D	D	D	D	D
Romero-B., P.R.	D	?	D	D	D	D	D	D
Underwood, Guam	D	N	D	D	D	D	D	D

Southern states - Ala., Ark., Fla., Ga., Ky., La., Miss., N.C., Okla., S.C., Tenn., Texas, Va.
Omitted votes are quorum calls, which CQ does not include in its vote charts.

109. H Con Res 64. Fiscal 1994 Budget Resolution/Instruct Conferees. Kasich, R-Ohio, motion to instruct the House conferees to insist on the highest possible deficit reduction and the lowest possible spending without increasing taxes on Social Security recipients. Motion agreed to 413-0: R 166-0; D 246-0 (ND 167-0, SD 79-0); I 1-0, March 25, 1993.

110. Procedural Motion/Passage. Approval of the Journal of Thursday, March 25. Approved 231-137: R 18-132; D 213-5 (ND 142-5, SD 71-0); I 0-0, March 29, 1993.

111. HR 175. FBI Access to Telephone Records/Passage. Brooks, D-Texas, motion to suspend the rules and pass the bill to give the Federal Bureau of Investigation limited access to unlisted phone numbers without a warrant in cases of suspected espionage or terrorism. Motion agreed to 367-6: R 151-0; D 216-6 (ND 149-2, SD 67-4); I 0-0, March 29, 1993. A two-thirds majority of those present and voting (249 in this case) is required for passage under suspension of the rules.

112. HR 829. DNA Identification/Passage. Brooks, D-Texas, motion to suspend the rules and pass the bill to authorize $10 million annually in fiscal years 1994-98 for grants to state and local governments to develop or improve criminal DNA identification and to authorize $4.5 million annually in fiscal years 1994-98 for the Federal Bureau of Investigation to establish a DNA data base of convicted offenders and to develop quality standards for use of DNA data. Motion agreed to 374-4: R 151-0; D 223-4 (ND 153-1, SD 70-3); I 0-0, March 29, 1993. A two-thirds majority of those present and voting (252 in this case) is required for passage under suspension of the rules.

113. Procedural Motion. Taylor, D-Miss., motion to adjourn. Motion rejected 155-221: R 1-152; D 154-69 (ND 97-52, SD 57-17); I 0-0, March 29, 1993.

114. Procedural Motion. Approval of the Journal of Monday, March 29. Approved 248-150: R 17-145; D 230-5 (ND 156-4, SD 74-1); I 1-0, March 30, 1993.

115. S 662. Veterans Health-Care Corrections/Passage. Montgomery, D-Miss., motion to suspend the rules and pass the bill to clarify language on how much the price of drugs for the Department of Veterans Affairs could increase and to restore the ceiling on the best-price rebate a drug manufacturer is required to pay in order to receive federal Medicaid matching funds. Motion agreed to 416-0: R 168-0; D 247-0 (ND 166-0, SD 81-0); I 1-0, March 30, 1993. A two-thirds majority of those present and voting (278 in this case) is required for passage under suspension of the rules.

116. S 252. Idaho Land Exchange/Passage. Vento, D-Minn., motion to suspend the rules and pass the bill to authorize the exchange of national forest lands in Idaho. Motion agreed to 417-0: R 168-0; D 248-0 (ND 167-0, SD 81-0); I 1-0, March 30, 1993. A two-thirds majority of those present and voting (278 in this case) is required for passage under suspension of the rules.

KEY

Y	Voted for (yea).
#	Paired for.
+	Announced for.
N	Voted against (nay).
X	Paired against.
−	Announced against.
P	Voted "present."
C	Voted "present" to avoid possible conflict of interest.
?	Did not vote or otherwise make a position known.
D	Delegates ineligible to vote.

Democrats *Republicans*
Independent

	109	110	111	112	113	114	115	116
ALABAMA								
1 *Callahan*	Y	N	Y	Y	N	N	Y	Y
2 *Everett*	Y	N	Y	Y	N	N	Y	Y
3 Browder	Y	Y	Y	Y	Y	Y	Y	Y
4 Bevill	Y	Y	Y	Y	Y	Y	Y	Y
5 Cramer	Y	Y	Y	Y	Y	?	Y	Y
6 *Bachus*	Y	N	Y	Y	N	N	Y	Y
7 Hilliard	Y	Y	N	N	N	Y	Y	Y
ALASKA								
AL *Young*	Y	N	Y	Y	N	N	Y	Y
ARIZONA								
1 Coppersmith	Y	Y	Y	Y	N	Y	Y	Y
2 Pastor	Y	Y	Y	Y	Y	Y	Y	Y
3 *Stump*	Y	N	Y	Y	N	N	Y	Y
4 *Kyl*	Y	N	Y	Y	N	N	Y	Y
5 *Kolbe*	Y	N	Y	Y	N	N	Y	Y
6 English	Y	Y	Y	Y	N	Y	Y	Y
ARKANSAS								
1 Lambert	Y	Y	Y	Y	Y	Y	Y	Y
2 Thornton	Y	Y	Y	Y	Y	Y	Y	Y
3 *Hutchinson*	Y	N	Y	Y	N	Y	Y	Y
4 *Dickey*	Y	N	Y	Y	N	N	Y	Y
CALIFORNIA								
1 Hamburg	Y	Y	N	N	Y	Y	Y	Y
2 *Herger*	Y	N	Y	N	N	N	Y	Y
3 Fazio	Y	Y	Y	N	Y	Y	Y	Y
4 *Doolittle*	Y	N	Y	N	N	N	Y	Y
5 Matsui	Y	Y	Y	N	Y	Y	Y	Y
6 Woolsey	Y	?	Y	Y	Y	Y	Y	Y
7 Miller	Y	Y	Y	Y	Y	Y	Y	Y
8 Pelosi	Y	Y	Y	Y	?	Y	Y	Y
9 Dellums	Y	Y	Y	Y	Y	?	?	?
10 *Baker*	Y	?	?	?	N	N	Y	Y
11 *Pombo*	Y	Y	Y	Y	N	N	Y	Y
12 Lantos	Y	Y	Y	N	Y	Y	Y	Y
13 Stark	?	Y	Y	Y	Y	Y	Y	Y
14 Eshoo	Y	Y	Y	N	Y	Y	Y	Y
15 Mineta	Y	Y	Y	N	Y	Y	Y	Y
16 Edwards	Y	Y	Y	N	Y	Y	Y	Y
17 Vacancy								
18 Condit	Y	Y	Y	Y	Y	Y	Y	Y
19 Lehman	Y	Y	Y	Y	Y	Y	Y	Y
20 Dooley	Y	Y	Y	Y	Y	Y	Y	Y
21 *Thomas*	Y	N	Y	Y	N	N	Y	Y
22 *Huffington*	Y	N	Y	N	N	N	Y	Y
23 *Gallegly*	Y	N	Y	Y	N	N	Y	Y
24 Beilenson	Y	Y	Y	Y	N	Y	Y	Y
25 *McKeon*	Y	N	Y	N	N	N	Y	Y
26 Berman	Y	Y	Y	N	Y	Y	Y	Y
27 *Moorhead*	Y	N	Y	N	N	N	Y	Y
28 *Dreier*	?	N	Y	N	N	N	Y	Y
29 Waxman	Y	Y	Y	Y	?	Y	Y	Y
30 Becerra	Y	Y	P	Y	Y	Y	Y	Y
31 Martinez	Y	Y	Y	Y	Y	Y	Y	Y
32 Dixon	Y	Y	Y	Y	N	Y	Y	Y
33 Roybal-Allard	Y	Y	Y	Y	Y	Y	Y	Y
34 Torres	Y	?	?	?	?	Y	Y	Y
35 Waters	Y	Y	N	Y	N	Y	Y	Y
36 Harman	Y	Y	Y	Y	Y	Y	Y	Y
37 Tucker	Y	?	Y	Y	Y	?	Y	Y
38 *Horn*	Y	N	Y	Y	N	N	Y	Y
39 *Royce*	Y	N	Y	N	N	N	Y	Y
40 *Lewis*	?	N	Y	N	N	N	Y	Y
41 *Kim*	Y	N	Y	N	N	N	Y	Y

	109	110	111	112	113	114	115	116
42 Brown	Y	Y	Y	Y	Y	Y	Y	Y
43 *Calvert*	Y	N	Y	N	N	N	Y	Y
44 *McCandless*	Y	N	Y	N	N	N	Y	Y
45 *Rohrabacher*	Y	N	Y	N	N	N	Y	Y
46 *Dornan*	Y	?	?	?	?	N	Y	Y
47 *Cox*	Y	?	?	?	N	N	Y	Y
48 *Packard*	Y	N	Y	N	N	N	Y	Y
49 *Schenk*	Y	?	Y	Y	Y	Y	Y	Y
50 Filner	Y	Y	Y	Y	Y	Y	Y	Y
51 *Cunningham*	Y	N	Y	N	N	N	Y	Y
52 *Hunter*	Y	?	?	?	?	N	Y	Y
COLORADO								
1 Schroeder	Y	N	Y	Y	Y	N	Y	Y
2 Skaggs	Y	?	?	?	?	Y	Y	Y
3 *McInnis*	Y	N	Y	Y	N	N	Y	Y
4 *Allard*	Y	N	Y	N	N	N	Y	Y
5 *Hefley*	Y	N	Y	Y	N	N	Y	Y
6 *Schaefer*	Y	N	Y	Y	N	N	Y	Y
CONNECTICUT								
1 Kennelly	Y	Y	Y	Y	N	Y	Y	Y
2 Gejdenson	Y	Y	Y	Y	Y	Y	Y	Y
3 DeLauro	Y	+	+	+	−	?	Y	Y
4 *Shays*	Y	N	Y	N	N	N	Y	Y
5 *Franks*	Y	N	Y	N	N	N	Y	Y
6 *Johnson*	Y	N	Y	N	N	N	Y	Y
DELAWARE								
AL *Castle*	Y	N	Y	N	N	N	Y	Y
FLORIDA								
1 Hutto	Y	?	?	?	?	Y	Y	Y
2 Peterson	Y	Y	Y	Y	Y	Y	Y	Y
3 Brown	Y	Y	Y	Y	N	Y	Y	Y
4 *Fowler*	Y	?	?	?	N	Y	Y	Y
5 Thurman	Y	Y	Y	Y	Y	Y	Y	Y
6 *Stearns*	Y	N	Y	N	N	N	Y	Y
7 Mica	Y	N	Y	N	Y	N	Y	Y
8 *McCollum*	Y	?	?	?	?	N	Y	Y
9 *Bilirakis*	Y	N	Y	N	N	N	Y	Y
10 *Young*	Y	N	Y	N	N	N	Y	Y
11 Gibbons	Y	Y	Y	Y	Y	Y	Y	Y
12 *Canady*	Y	N	Y	N	N	N	Y	Y
13 *Miller*	Y	?	?	?	N	N	Y	Y
14 *Goss*	Y	N	Y	N	N	N	Y	Y
15 Bacchus	Y	?	?	?	?	Y	Y	Y
16 *Lewis*	Y	N	Y	N	N	N	Y	Y
17 Meek	Y	Y	Y	Y	N	Y	Y	Y
18 *Ros-Lehtinen*	Y	N	Y	N	N	N	Y	Y
19 Johnston	Y	Y	Y	Y	Y	Y	Y	Y
20 Deutsch	Y	Y	Y	Y	Y	Y	Y	Y
21 *Diaz-Balart*	Y	N	Y	N	N	N	Y	Y
22 *Shaw*	Y	N	Y	N	N	N	Y	Y
23 Hastings	Y	?	?	?	?	Y	Y	Y
GEORGIA								
1 *Kingston*	Y	Y	Y	Y	N	N	Y	Y
2 Bishop	Y	Y	N	N	N	Y	Y	Y
3 *Collins*	Y	N	Y	N	N	N	Y	Y
4 *Linder*	Y	N	Y	N	N	N	Y	Y
5 Lewis	Y	Y	Y	Y	N	Y	Y	Y
6 *Gingrich*	?	N	Y	N	N	N	Y	Y
7 Darden	Y	Y	Y	Y	Y	Y	Y	Y
8 Rowland	Y	Y	Y	Y	Y	Y	Y	Y
9 Deal	Y	Y	Y	Y	Y	Y	Y	Y
10 Johnson	Y	Y	Y	Y	Y	Y	Y	Y
11 McKinney	Y	?	?	?	?	Y	Y	Y
HAWAII								
1 Abercrombie	Y	?	?	?	?	Y	Y	Y
2 Mink	Y	?	?	?	?	?	Y	Y
IDAHO								
1 LaRocco	Y	Y	Y	Y	N	Y	Y	Y
2 *Crapo*	Y	N	Y	Y	N	N	Y	Y
ILLINOIS								
1 Rush	Y	Y	Y	Y	Y	Y	Y	Y
2 Reynolds	Y	Y	Y	Y	N	Y	Y	Y
3 Lipinski	Y	Y	Y	Y	Y	Y	Y	Y
4 Gutierrez	Y	Y	Y	Y	Y	Y	Y	Y
5 Rostenkowski	Y	Y	Y	Y	Y	Y	Y	Y
6 *Hyde*	Y	Y	Y	N	Y	N	Y	Y
7 Collins	Y	Y	Y	Y	Y	Y	Y	Y
8 *Crane*	Y	N	Y	N	Y	?	Y	Y
9 Yates	Y	Y	Y	Y	?	Y	Y	Y
10 *Porter*	Y	N	Y	N	N	N	Y	Y
11 Sangmeister	Y	Y	Y	Y	Y	Y	Y	Y
12 Costello	Y	Y	Y	Y	Y	Y	Y	Y
13 *Fawell*	Y	N	Y	N	N	N	Y	Y
14 *Hastert*	Y	N	Y	N	N	N	Y	Y
15 *Ewing*	Y	N	Y	N	N	N	Y	Y
16 *Manzullo*	Y	N	Y	N	N	N	Y	Y
17 Evans	Y	Y	Y	Y	Y	Y	Y	Y

ND Northern Democrats   SD Southern Democrats

	109	110	111	112	113	114	115	116
18 ***Michel***	Y	N	Y	Y	N	N	Y	Y
19 Poshard	Y	Y	Y	Y	Y	Y	Y	Y
20 Durbin	Y	Y	Y	Y	Y	Y	Y	Y
INDIANA								
1 Visclosky	Y	Y	Y	Y	Y	Y	Y	Y
2 Sharp	?	?	Y	Y	N	Y	Y	Y
3 Roemer	Y	Y	Y	Y	N	Y	Y	Y
4 Long	Y	Y	Y	Y	Y	Y	Y	Y
5 ***Buyer***	Y	N	Y	Y	N	N	Y	Y
6 ***Burton***	Y	N	Y	Y	N	N	Y	Y
7 ***Myers***	Y	Y	Y	Y	N	Y	Y	Y
8 McCloskey	Y	Y	Y	Y	N	Y	Y	Y
9 Hamilton	Y	Y	Y	Y	N	Y	Y	Y
10 Jacobs	Y	N	Y	Y	Y	N	Y	Y
IOWA								
1 ***Leach***	Y	N	Y	Y	N	N	Y	Y
2 ***Nussle***	Y	N	Y	Y	N	N	Y	Y
3 ***Lightfoot***	Y	?	?	?	?	N	Y	Y
4 Smith	Y	Y	Y	Y	Y	Y	Y	Y
5 ***Grandy***	Y	N	Y	Y	N	N	Y	Y
KANSAS								
1 ***Roberts***	Y	N	Y	Y	N	N	Y	Y
2 Slattery	Y	Y	Y	Y	Y	Y	Y	Y
3 ***Meyers***	Y	N	Y	Y	N	N	Y	Y
4 Glickman	Y	Y	Y	Y	N	Y	Y	Y
KENTUCKY								
1 Barlow	Y	Y	?	Y	Y	Y	Y	Y
2 Natcher	Y	Y	Y	Y	Y	Y	Y	Y
3 Mazzoli	Y	Y	Y	Y	Y	Y	Y	Y
4 ***Bunning***	Y	N	Y	Y	N	N	Y	Y
5 ***Rogers***	Y	N	Y	Y	N	N	Y	Y
6 Baesler	Y	Y	Y	Y	Y	Y	Y	Y
LOUISIANA								
1 ***Livingston***	Y	N	Y	Y	N	?	Y	Y
2 Jefferson	Y	?	?	?	?	Y	Y	Y
3 Tauzin	Y	Y	Y	Y	Y	Y	Y	Y
4 Fields	Y	?	Y	Y	Y	Y	Y	Y
5 ***McCrery***	Y	N	Y	Y	N	N	Y	Y
6 ***Baker***	Y	?	?	?	?	N	Y	Y
7 Hayes	Y	Y	Y	Y	Y	Y	Y	Y
MAINE								
1 Andrews	Y	Y	Y	Y	N	Y	Y	Y
2 ***Snowe***	Y	Y	Y	Y	N	N	Y	Y
MARYLAND								
1 ***Gilchrest***	Y	N	Y	Y	N	N	Y	Y
2 ***Bentley***	Y	N	Y	Y	N	N	Y	Y
3 Cardin	Y	Y	Y	Y	?	Y	Y	Y
4 Wynn	Y	Y	Y	Y	Y	Y	Y	Y
5 Hoyer	Y	Y	Y	Y	N	Y	Y	Y
6 ***Bartlett***	Y	N	Y	Y	N	N	Y	Y
7 Mfume	Y	N	Y	Y	N	Y	Y	Y
8 ***Morella***	Y	N	Y	Y	N	N	Y	Y
MASSACHUSETTS								
1 Olver	Y	?	?	?	?	?	Y	Y
2 Neal	Y	Y	Y	Y	Y	Y	Y	Y
3 ***Blute***	Y	N	Y	Y	N	N	Y	Y
4 Frank	Y	Y	Y	Y	Y	Y	Y	Y
5 Meehan	Y	Y	Y	Y	N	Y	Y	Y
6 ***Torkildsen***	Y	N	Y	Y	N	N	Y	Y
7 Markey	Y	Y	Y	Y	Y	Y	Y	Y
8 Kennedy	Y	Y	Y	Y	N	Y	Y	Y
9 Moakley	Y	Y	Y	Y	Y	Y	Y	Y
10 Studds	Y	Y	Y	Y	Y	Y	Y	Y
MICHIGAN								
1 Stupak	Y	Y	Y	Y	Y	Y	Y	Y
2 ***Hoekstra***	Y	N	Y	Y	N	N	Y	Y
3 Henry	?	?	?	?	?	?	?	?
4 ***Camp***	Y	N	Y	Y	N	N	Y	Y
5 Barcia	Y	Y	Y	Y	Y	Y	Y	Y
6 ***Upton***	Y	N	Y	Y	N	N	Y	Y
7 ***Smith***	Y	Y	Y	Y	N	N	Y	Y
8 Carr	Y	Y	Y	Y	Y	Y	Y	Y
9 Kildee	Y	Y	Y	Y	N	Y	Y	Y
10 Bonior	Y	Y	Y	Y	N	Y	Y	Y
11 ***Knollenberg***	Y	N	Y	Y	N	N	Y	Y
12 Levin	Y	Y	Y	Y	N	Y	Y	Y
13 Ford	Y	Y	Y	Y	Y	Y	Y	Y
14 Conyers	Y	?	Y	Y	Y	?	?	?
15 Collins	Y	Y	Y	Y	Y	Y	Y	Y
16 Dingell	Y	Y	Y	Y	Y	Y	Y	Y
MINNESOTA								
1 Penny	Y	Y	Y	Y	Y	Y	Y	Y
2 Minge	Y	Y	Y	Y	Y	Y	Y	Y
3 ***Ramstad***	Y	N	Y	Y	N	N	Y	Y
4 Vento	Y	Y	Y	Y	N	Y	Y	Y
5 Sabo	Y	Y	Y	Y	N	Y	Y	Y
6 ***Grams***	Y	N	Y	Y	N	N	Y	Y
7 Peterson	Y	Y	Y	Y	Y	Y	Y	Y
8 Oberstar	Y	Y	Y	Y	N	Y	Y	Y
MISSISSIPPI								
1 Whitten	?	?	?	?	?	?	Y	Y
2 Vacancy								
3 Montgomery	Y	Y	Y	Y	Y	Y	Y	Y
4 Parker	Y	Y	Y	Y	Y	?	Y	Y
5 Taylor	Y	Y	Y	Y	Y	N	Y	Y
MISSOURI								
1 Clay	Y	N	Y	Y	Y	N	Y	Y
2 ***Talent***	Y	N	Y	Y	N	N	Y	Y
3 Gephardt	Y	Y	Y	Y	N	Y	Y	Y
4 Skelton	Y	Y	Y	Y	Y	Y	?	Y
5 Wheat	Y	Y	Y	Y	Y	Y	Y	Y
6 Danner	Y	Y	Y	Y	Y	Y	Y	Y
7 ***Hancock***	Y	N	Y	Y	N	N	Y	Y
8 ***Emerson***	Y	N	Y	Y	N	N	Y	Y
9 Volkmer	Y	Y	Y	Y	Y	Y	Y	Y
MONTANA								
AL Williams	Y	?	?	?	?	Y	Y	Y
NEBRASKA								
1 ***Bereuter***	Y	N	Y	Y	N	N	Y	Y
2 Hoagland	Y	Y	Y	Y	N	Y	Y	Y
3 ***Barrett***	Y	N	Y	Y	N	N	Y	Y
NEVADA								
1 Bilbray	Y	Y	Y	Y	Y	Y	Y	Y
2 ***Vucanovich***	Y	N	Y	Y	N	N	Y	Y
NEW HAMPSHIRE								
1 ***Zeliff***	Y	?	?	?	?	N	Y	Y
2 Swett	Y	Y	Y	Y	Y	Y	Y	Y
NEW JERSEY								
1 Andrews	Y	?	?	?	?	Y	Y	Y
2 Hughes	Y	Y	Y	Y	Y	Y	Y	Y
3 ***Saxton***	Y	N	Y	Y	N	N	Y	Y
4 ***Smith***	Y	N	Y	Y	N	N	Y	Y
5 ***Roukema***	Y	N	Y	Y	N	N	Y	Y
6 Pallone	Y	Y	Y	Y	Y	Y	Y	Y
7 ***Franks***	Y	N	Y	Y	N	N	Y	Y
8 Klein	Y	Y	Y	Y	N	Y	Y	Y
9 Torricelli	Y	?	?	?	?	Y	Y	Y
10 Payne	Y	Y	Y	Y	Y	Y	Y	Y
11 ***Gallo***	Y	N	Y	Y	N	N	Y	Y
12 ***Zimmer***	Y	N	Y	Y	N	N	Y	Y
13 Menendez	Y	Y	Y	Y	N	Y	Y	Y
NEW MEXICO								
1 ***Schiff***	Y	N	Y	Y	N	N	Y	Y
2 ***Skeen***	Y	N	Y	Y	N	N	Y	Y
3 Richardson	Y	Y	Y	Y	N	Y	Y	Y
NEW YORK								
1 Hochbrueckner	Y	Y	Y	Y	Y	Y	Y	Y
2 ***Lazio***	Y	N	Y	Y	N	N	Y	Y
3 ***King***	Y	N	Y	Y	N	?	?	?
4 ***Levy***	Y	N	Y	Y	N	N	Y	Y
5 Ackerman	Y	Y	Y	Y	Y	Y	Y	Y
6 Flake	Y	Y	Y	Y	Y	Y	Y	Y
7 Manton	Y	Y	Y	Y	Y	Y	Y	Y
8 Nadler	Y	Y	Y	Y	N	Y	Y	Y
9 Schumer	Y	Y	Y	Y	Y	Y	Y	Y
10 Towns	Y	?	?	?	?	Y	Y	Y
11 Owens	Y	?	?	?	?	Y	Y	Y
12 Velazquez	Y	Y	Y	Y	N	Y	Y	Y
13 ***Molinari***	Y	N	Y	Y	N	N	Y	Y
14 Maloney	Y	Y	?	Y	N	Y	Y	Y
15 Rangel	Y	?	?	Y	Y	Y	Y	Y
16 Serrano	Y	?	Y	Y	N	Y	Y	Y
17 Engel	Y	Y	Y	Y	Y	Y	Y	Y
18 Lowey	Y	Y	Y	Y	N	Y	Y	Y
19 ***Fish***	?	Y	Y	Y	N	Y	Y	Y
20 ***Gilman***	Y	Y	Y	Y	N	Y	Y	Y
21 McNulty	Y	Y	Y	Y	Y	Y	Y	Y
22 ***Solomon***	Y	N	Y	Y	N	N	Y	Y
23 ***Boehlert***	Y	N	Y	Y	N	N	Y	Y
24 ***McHugh***	Y	N	Y	Y	N	N	Y	Y
25 ***Walsh***	Y	N	Y	Y	N	N	Y	Y
26 Hinchey	Y	Y	Y	Y	Y	Y	Y	Y
27 ***Paxon***	Y	N	Y	Y	N	N	Y	Y
28 Slaughter	Y	Y	Y	Y	Y	Y	Y	Y
29 LaFalce	Y	Y	Y	Y	Y	Y	Y	Y
30 ***Quinn***	Y	N	Y	Y	N	N	Y	Y
31 ***Houghton***	Y	Y	Y	Y	N	?	Y	Y
NORTH CAROLINA								
1 Clayton	Y	Y	Y	Y	N	?	Y	Y
2 Valentine	Y	Y	Y	Y	Y	Y	Y	Y
3 Lancaster	Y	?	?	?	?	Y	Y	Y
4 Price	Y	Y	Y	Y	Y	Y	Y	Y
5 Neal	Y	Y	Y	Y	Y	Y	Y	Y
6 ***Coble***	Y	N	Y	Y	N	N	Y	Y
7 Rose	Y	Y	Y	Y	Y	Y	Y	Y
8 Hefner	Y	Y	Y	Y	Y	Y	Y	Y
9 ***McMillan***	Y	N	Y	Y	N	N	Y	Y
10 ***Ballenger***	Y	N	Y	Y	N	N	Y	Y
11 ***Taylor***	Y	N	Y	Y	N	N	Y	Y
12 Watt	Y	Y	Y	N	Y	Y	Y	Y
NORTH DAKOTA								
AL Pomeroy	Y	Y	Y	Y	N	Y	Y	Y
OHIO								
1 Mann	Y	Y	Y	Y	Y	Y	Y	Y
2 Vacancy								
3 Hall	Y	Y	Y	Y	Y	Y	Y	Y
4 ***Oxley***	Y	N	Y	Y	N	Y	Y	Y
5 ***Gillmor***	Y	Y	Y	Y	N	Y	Y	Y
6 Strickland	Y	Y	Y	Y	Y	Y	Y	Y
7 ***Hobson***	Y	N	Y	Y	N	N	Y	Y
8 ***Boehner***	Y	N	Y	Y	N	N	Y	Y
9 Kaptur	Y	Y	Y	Y	N	Y	Y	Y
10 ***Hoke***	Y	N	Y	Y	N	Y	Y	Y
11 Stokes	Y	Y	Y	Y	?	Y	Y	Y
12 ***Kasich***	Y	Y	Y	Y	N	Y	Y	Y
13 Brown	Y	?	?	?	?	Y	Y	Y
14 Sawyer	Y	Y	Y	Y	N	Y	Y	Y
15 ***Pryce***	Y	N	Y	Y	N	N	Y	Y
16 ***Regula***	Y	N	Y	Y	N	N	Y	Y
17 Traficant	Y	Y	Y	Y	N	Y	Y	Y
18 Applegate	Y	Y	Y	Y	Y	Y	Y	Y
19 Fingerhut	Y	Y	Y	Y	Y	Y	Y	Y
OKLAHOMA								
1 ***Inhofe***	Y	?	?	?	?	N	Y	Y
2 Synar	Y	Y	Y	Y	N	Y	Y	Y
3 Brewster	Y	Y	Y	Y	Y	?	Y	Y
4 McCurdy	Y	Y	Y	Y	Y	Y	?	?
5 ***Istook***	Y	?	?	?	?	N	Y	Y
6 English	Y	Y	Y	Y	Y	Y	Y	Y
OREGON								
1 Furse	Y	Y	Y	Y	N	Y	Y	Y
2 ***Smith***	?	?	?	?	?	?	Y	Y
3 Wyden	Y	Y	Y	Y	N	Y	Y	Y
4 DeFazio	?	?	?	?	Y	Y	Y	Y
5 Kopetski	Y	Y	Y	Y	Y	Y	Y	Y
PENNSYLVANIA								
1 Foglietta	Y	Y	Y	Y	Y	Y	Y	Y
2 Blackwell	Y	Y	Y	Y	Y	Y	Y	Y
3 Borski	Y	Y	Y	Y	Y	Y	Y	Y
4 Klink	Y	Y	Y	Y	Y	?	Y	Y
5 ***Clinger***	Y	Y	Y	Y	N	N	Y	Y
6 Holden	Y	Y	Y	Y	Y	Y	Y	Y
7 ***Weldon***	Y	N	Y	Y	N	N	Y	Y
8 ***Greenwood***	Y	N	Y	Y	N	N	Y	Y
9 ***Shuster***	Y	N	Y	Y	N	N	Y	Y
10 ***McDade***	Y	?	?	?	?	?	?	?
11 Kanjorski	Y	Y	Y	Y	Y	Y	Y	Y
12 Murtha	Y	Y	Y	Y	Y	Y	Y	Y
13 Margolies-Mezv.	Y	Y	Y	Y	N	Y	Y	Y
14 Coyne	Y	Y	Y	Y	Y	Y	Y	Y
15 McHale	Y	Y	Y	Y	N	Y	Y	Y
16 ***Walker***	Y	N	Y	Y	N	N	Y	Y
17 ***Gekas***	Y	N	Y	Y	N	N	Y	Y
18 ***Santorum***	Y	N	Y	Y	N	N	Y	Y
19 ***Goodling***	Y	N	Y	Y	N	N	Y	Y
20 Murphy	Y	N	Y	Y	Y	N	Y	Y
21 ***Ridge***	?	?	?	?	?	N	Y	Y
RHODE ISLAND								
1 ***Machtley***	Y	N	Y	Y	N	N	Y	Y
2 Reed	Y	Y	Y	Y	Y	Y	Y	Y
SOUTH CAROLINA								
1 ***Ravenel***	Y	Y	Y	Y	N	Y	Y	Y
2 ***Spence***	Y	Y	Y	Y	N	?	Y	Y
3 Derrick	Y	Y	Y	Y	Y	Y	Y	Y
4 ***Inglis***	Y	?	?	?	?	Y	Y	Y
5 Spratt	Y	Y	Y	Y	N	Y	Y	Y
6 Clyburn	Y	Y	Y	Y	N	Y	Y	Y
SOUTH DAKOTA								
AL Johnson	Y	Y	Y	Y	Y	Y	Y	Y
TENNESSEE								
1 ***Quillen***	?	?	?	?	?	?	?	?
2 ***Duncan***	Y	Y	Y	Y	N	N	Y	Y
3 Lloyd	Y	Y	Y	Y	Y	Y	Y	Y
4 Cooper	Y	?	?	?	?	Y	Y	Y
5 Clement	Y	?	?	Y	Y	Y	Y	Y
6 Gordon	Y	Y	Y	Y	Y	Y	Y	Y
7 ***Sundquist***	Y	?	Y	Y	N	N	Y	Y
8 Tanner	Y	Y	Y	Y	Y	Y	Y	Y
9 Ford	?	?	?	?	?	?	?	?
TEXAS								
1 Chapman	Y	Y	Y	Y	Y	Y	Y	Y
2 Wilson	Y	Y	Y	Y	Y	?	?	?
3 ***Johnson, Sam***	Y	?	?	?	?	?	Y	Y
4 Hall	Y	Y	Y	Y	Y	Y	Y	Y
5 Bryant	Y	Y	Y	Y	Y	Y	Y	Y
6 ***Barton***	?	?	?	?	?	?	?	?
7 ***Archer***	Y	Y	Y	Y	Y	Y	Y	Y
8 ***Fields***	Y	?	?	?	?	?	?	?
9 Brooks	?	Y	Y	Y	Y	Y	Y	Y
10 Pickle	?	?	?	?	N	Y	Y	Y
11 Edwards	Y	Y	Y	Y	Y	?	Y	Y
12 Geren	Y	Y	Y	Y	Y	?	Y	Y
13 Sarpalius	Y	Y	Y	Y	N	Y	Y	Y
14 Laughlin	Y	Y	Y	Y	Y	Y	Y	Y
15 de la Garza	Y	Y	Y	Y	Y	Y	Y	Y
16 Coleman	Y	Y	Y	Y	Y	Y	Y	Y
17 Stenholm	Y	Y	Y	Y	Y	Y	Y	Y
18 Washington	?	Y	N	Y	N	Y	Y	Y
19 ***Combest***	Y	Y	Y	Y	N	Y	Y	Y
20 Gonzalez	Y	Y	Y	Y	N	Y	Y	Y
21 ***Smith***	Y	?	?	?	?	N	Y	Y
22 ***DeLay***	Y	N	Y	Y	N	N	Y	Y
23 ***Bonilla***	Y	N	Y	Y	N	N	Y	Y
24 Frost	Y	Y	Y	Y	Y	Y	Y	Y
25 Andrews	Y	Y	Y	Y	Y	Y	Y	Y
26 ***Armey***	Y	?	?	?	?	N	Y	Y
27 Ortiz	Y	Y	Y	Y	N	Y	Y	Y
28 Tejeda	Y	Y	Y	Y	N	Y	Y	Y
29 Green	Y	Y	Y	Y	Y	Y	Y	Y
30 Johnson, E. B.	Y	Y	N	Y	Y	Y	Y	Y
UTAH								
1 ***Hansen***	Y	?	?	?	?	N	Y	Y
2 Shepherd	Y	Y	Y	Y	Y	Y	Y	Y
3 Orton	Y	Y	Y	Y	Y	Y	Y	Y
VERMONT								
AL *Sanders*	Y	?	?	?	?	Y	Y	Y
VIRGINIA								
1 ***Bateman***	Y	Y	Y	Y	N	?	+	+
2 Pickett	Y	Y	Y	Y	Y	Y	Y	Y
3 Scott	Y	Y	Y	Y	N	Y	Y	Y
4 Sisisky	Y	Y	Y	Y	Y	Y	Y	Y
5 Payne	Y	Y	Y	Y	Y	Y	Y	Y
6 ***Goodlatte***	Y	N	Y	Y	N	N	Y	Y
7 ***Bliley***	Y	N	Y	Y	N	N	Y	Y
8 Moran	Y	Y	Y	Y	N	Y	Y	Y
9 Boucher	Y	Y	Y	Y	Y	Y	Y	Y
10 ***Wolf***	Y	N	Y	Y	N	N	Y	Y
11 Byrne	Y	?	?	?	?	Y	Y	Y
WASHINGTON								
1 Cantwell	Y	Y	Y	Y	Y	Y	Y	Y
2 Swift	Y	Y	Y	Y	Y	Y	Y	Y
3 Unsoeld	Y	?	?	?	?	?	?	?
4 Inslee	Y	Y	Y	Y	N	Y	Y	Y
5 Foley								
6 Dicks	Y	?	?	?	?	?	Y	Y
7 McDermott	Y	Y	Y	Y	Y	Y	Y	Y
8 ***Dunn***	Y	N	Y	Y	N	N	Y	Y
9 Kreidler	Y	?	?	?	?	Y	Y	Y
WEST VIRGINIA								
1 Mollohan	Y	Y	Y	Y	Y	Y	Y	Y
2 Wise	Y	Y	Y	Y	Y	Y	Y	Y
3 Rahall	Y	Y	Y	Y	Y	?	Y	Y
WISCONSIN								
1 Vacancy								
2 ***Klug***	Y	N	Y	Y	N	N	Y	Y
3 ***Gunderson***	Y	N	Y	Y	N	Y	Y	Y
4 Kleczka	Y	Y	Y	Y	Y	Y	Y	Y
5 Barrett	Y	Y	Y	Y	Y	Y	Y	Y
6 ***Petri***	Y	N	Y	Y	N	N	Y	Y
7 Obey	Y	Y	Y	Y	Y	Y	Y	Y
8 ***Roth***	Y	N	Y	Y	N	N	Y	Y
9 ***Sensenbrenner***	Y	N	Y	Y	N	N	Y	Y
WYOMING								
AL ***Thomas***	Y	N	Y	Y	N	N	Y	Y
DELEGATES								
de Lugo, V.I.	D	D	D	D	D	D	D	D
Faleomavaega, Am.S.	D	D	D	D	D	D	D	D
Norton, D.C.	D	D	D	D	D	D	D	D
Romero-B., P.R.	D	D	D	D	D	D	D	D
Underwood, Guam	D	D	D	D	D	D	D	D

Southern states - Ala., Ark., Fla., Ga., Ky., La., Miss., N.C., Okla., S.C., Tenn., Texas, Va.
Omitted votes are quorum calls, which CQ does not include in its vote charts.

117. S 164. Custer National Forest Land Exchange/Passage. Vento, D-Minn., motion to suspend the rules and pass the bill to authorize the Forest Service to exchange land in order to establish a five-mile boundary for the South Dakota portion of the Sioux Ranger District of the Custer National Forest. 417-3: R 166-3; D 250-0 (ND 167-0, SD 83-0); I 1-0, March 30, 1993. A two-thirds majority of those present and voting (280 in this case) is required for passage under suspension of the rules.

118. HR 239. Stock-Raising Homestead Amendments/Passage. Lehman, D-Calif., motion to suspend the rules and pass the bill to establish procedures that prospectors would have to follow to gain access to stock-raising homestead lands to carry out mining claims. Motion agreed to 421-1: R 169-1; D 251-0 (ND 168-0, SD 83-0); I 1-0, March 30, 1993. A two-thirds majority of those present and voting (282 in this case) is required for passage under suspension of the rules.

119. H Res 118. Condemn Malta's Terrorist Release/Passage. Lantos, D-Calif., motion to suspend the rules and pass the bill to condemn Malta for releasing Mohammed Ali Rezaq, who was convicted of the 1985 hijacking of an Egyptian airliner to Malta that left 60 people dead. Motion agreed to 421-0: R 170-0; D 251-0 (ND 168-0, SD 83-0); I 0-0, March 30, 1993. A two-thirds majority of those present and voting (281 in this case) is required for passage under suspension of the rules.

120. H Res 107. 1993 Committee Funding Resolution/Recommit to Reduce Funding. Dunn, R-Wash., motion to recommit the resolution to the House Administration Committee with instructions to report it back with an amendment reducing the 1993 funding level of each committee to specified amounts averaging 25 percent less than in the prior year and requiring that at least one-third of the funds for each committee be available to the minority party. Motion rejected 171-246: R 168-1; D 3-244 (ND 2-162, SD 1-82); I 0-1, March 30, 1993.

121. H Res 107. 1993 Committee Funding Resolution/Adoption. Adoption of the resolution to authorize $52.3 million for 21 permanent committees of the House in 1993 and for three months' worth of funding for the four so-called select committees (Aging; Children, Youth and Families; Hunger; and Narcotics), plus $495,000 for the temporary Joint Committee on the Organization of Congress. The bill includes no funds for the four select committees after March 31, 1993, effectively killing them. Adopted 224-196: R 0-169; D 223-27 (ND 147-20, SD 76-7); I 1-0, March 30, 1993.

122. Procedural Motion. Taylor, D-Miss., motion to adjourn. Motion rejected 140-269: R 0-166; D 140-102 (ND 87-76, SD 53-26); I 0-1, March 30, 1993.

123. Procedural Motion. Approval of the Journal of Tuesday, March 30. Approved 255-159: R 18-154; D 237-5 (ND 159-4, SD 78-1); I 0-0, March 31, 1993.

124. H Con Res 64. Fiscal 1994 Budget Resolution/Same-Day Consideration. Adoption of the rule (H Res 142) to allow for House floor consideration of the fiscal 1994 budget resolution on the same day the rule providing for consideration of the resolution is reported without the two-thirds majority vote usually required for adoption of a rule reported the same day. Adopted 248-171: R 0-170; D 247-1 (ND 165-0, SD 82-1); I 1-0, March 31, 1993.

KEY

Y	Voted for (yea).
#	Paired for.
+	Announced for.
N	Voted against (nay).
X	Paired against.
−	Announced against.
P	Voted "present."
C	Voted "present" to avoid possible conflict of interest.
?	Did not vote or otherwise make a position known.
D	Delegates ineligible to vote.

Democrats *Republicans*
Independent

	117	118	119	120	121	122	123	124
ALABAMA								
1 *Callahan*	Y	Y	Y	N	Y	N	N	N
2 *Everett*	Y	Y	Y	N	Y	N	N	N
3 Browder	Y	Y	Y	N	Y	Y	Y	Y
4 Bevill	Y	Y	Y	N	Y	Y	Y	Y
5 Cramer	Y	Y	Y	N	Y	Y	Y	Y
6 *Bachus*	Y	Y	Y	N	N	N	N	N
7 Hilliard	Y	Y	Y	N	Y	Y	Y	Y
ALASKA								
AL *Young*	Y	Y	Y	N	N	N	N	N
ARIZONA								
1 Coppersmith	Y	Y	Y	N	Y	Y	Y	Y
2 Pastor	Y	Y	Y	N	Y	Y	Y	Y
3 *Stump*	N	Y	Y	N	N	N	N	N
4 *Kyl*	Y	Y	Y	N	N	N	N	N
5 *Kolbe*	Y	Y	Y	N	N	N	N	N
6 English	Y	Y	Y	N	Y	N	Y	Y
ARKANSAS								
1 Lambert	Y	Y	Y	N	Y	Y	Y	Y
2 Thornton	Y	Y	Y	N	Y	N	Y	Y
3 *Hutchinson*	Y	Y	Y	N	N	N	N	N
4 *Dickey*	Y	Y	Y	N	Y	N	N	N
CALIFORNIA								
1 Hamburg	Y	Y	Y	N	Y	Y	Y	Y
2 *Herger*	Y	Y	Y	N	N	N	N	N
3 Fazio	Y	Y	Y	N	Y	N	Y	Y
4 *Doolittle*	Y	Y	Y	N	N	N	N	N
5 Matsui	Y	Y	Y	N	Y	Y	Y	Y
6 Woolsey	Y	Y	Y	N	Y	Y	Y	Y
7 Miller	Y	Y	Y	N	Y	Y	Y	Y
8 Pelosi	Y	Y	Y	N	Y	Y	Y	Y
9 Dellums	Y	Y	Y	N	?	Y	Y	Y
10 *Baker*	Y	Y	Y	N	N	N	N	N
11 *Pombo*	Y	Y	Y	N	N	N	N	N
12 Lantos	Y	Y	Y	N	Y	N	Y	Y
13 Stark	Y	Y	Y	N	Y	Y	Y	Y
14 Eshoo	Y	Y	Y	N	Y	Y	Y	Y
15 Mineta	Y	Y	Y	N	Y	Y	Y	Y
16 Edwards	Y	Y	Y	N	Y	N	Y	Y
17 Vacancy								
18 Condit	Y	Y	Y	N	Y	Y	Y	Y
19 Lehman	Y	Y	Y	N	Y	Y	Y	Y
20 Dooley	Y	Y	Y	N	Y	N	Y	Y
21 *Thomas*	Y	Y	Y	Y	N	N	N	N
22 *Huffington*	Y	Y	Y	N	N	N	N	N
23 *Gallegly*	Y	Y	Y	N	?	N	N	N
24 Beilenson	Y	Y	Y	N	Y	N	Y	Y
25 *McKeon*	Y	Y	Y	N	N	N	N	N
26 Berman	Y	Y	Y	N	?	Y	Y	Y
27 *Moorhead*	Y	Y	Y	N	N	N	N	N
28 *Dreier*	Y	Y	Y	N	N	N	N	N
29 Waxman	Y	Y	Y	N	Y	N	Y	Y
30 Becerra	Y	Y	Y	N	Y	Y	Y	Y
31 Martinez	Y	Y	Y	N	Y	Y	Y	Y
32 Dixon	Y	Y	Y	N	Y	Y	Y	Y
33 Roybal-Allard	Y	Y	Y	N	Y	Y	Y	Y
34 Torres	Y	Y	Y	N	Y	Y	Y	Y
35 Waters	Y	Y	Y	N	Y	Y	Y	Y
36 Harman	Y	Y	Y	N	Y	Y	Y	Y
37 Tucker	Y	Y	Y	N	Y	Y	Y	Y
38 *Horn*	Y	Y	Y	N	N	N	N	N
39 *Royce*	Y	Y	Y	Y	N	N	N	N
40 *Lewis*	Y	Y	Y	N	?	?	N	N
41 *Kim*	Y	Y	Y	N	N	N	N	N
42 Brown	Y	Y	Y	N	Y	N	?	Y
43 *Calvert*	Y	Y	Y	N	N	N	N	N
44 *McCandless*	Y	Y	Y	N	N	N	N	N
45 *Rohrabacher*	Y	Y	Y	N	N	N	N	N
46 *Dornan*	Y	Y	Y	N	N	N	N	N
47 *Cox*	Y	Y	Y	N	N	N	N	N
48 *Packard*	Y	Y	Y	N	N	N	N	N
49 Schenk	Y	Y	Y	N	Y	N	Y	Y
50 Filner	Y	Y	Y	N	Y	Y	Y	Y
51 *Cunningham*	Y	Y	Y	N	N	N	N	N
52 *Hunter*	Y	Y	Y	N	N	N	N	N
COLORADO								
1 Schroeder	Y	Y	Y	N	Y	N	N	Y
2 Skaggs	Y	Y	Y	N	Y	N	Y	Y
3 *McInnis*	Y	Y	Y	N	N	N	N	N
4 *Allard*	Y	Y	Y	N	N	N	N	N
5 *Hefley*	Y	Y	Y	N	N	N	N	N
6 *Schaefer*	Y	Y	Y	N	N	N	N	N
CONNECTICUT								
1 Kennelly	Y	Y	Y	N	Y	N	Y	Y
2 Gejdenson	Y	Y	Y	N	Y	Y	Y	Y
3 DeLauro	Y	Y	Y	N	Y	Y	Y	Y
4 *Shays*	Y	Y	Y	N	N	N	N	N
5 *Franks*	Y	Y	Y	N	N	N	N	N
6 *Johnson*	Y	Y	Y	N	N	N	N	N
DELAWARE								
AL *Castle*	Y	Y	Y	N	N	N	N	N
FLORIDA								
1 Hutto	Y	Y	Y	N	Y	Y	Y	Y
2 Peterson	Y	Y	Y	N	Y	Y	Y	Y
3 Brown	Y	Y	Y	N	Y	Y	Y	Y
4 *Fowler*	Y	Y	Y	N	Y	Y	Y	Y
5 Thurman	Y	Y	Y	N	Y	Y	Y	Y
6 *Stearns*	Y	Y	Y	N	N	N	N	N
7 *Mica*	Y	Y	Y	N	N	N	N	N
8 *McCollum*	Y	Y	Y	N	N	N	N	N
9 *Bilirakis*	Y	Y	Y	N	N	N	N	N
10 *Young*	Y	Y	Y	N	N	N	N	N
11 Gibbons	Y	Y	Y	N	Y	?	Y	Y
12 *Canady*	Y	Y	Y	N	N	N	N	N
13 *Miller*	Y	Y	Y	N	N	N	N	N
14 *Goss*	Y	Y	Y	N	N	N	N	N
15 *Bacchus*	Y	Y	Y	N	Y	Y	Y	Y
16 *Lewis*	Y	Y	Y	N	Y	Y	Y	Y
17 Meek	Y	Y	Y	N	Y	Y	Y	Y
18 *Ros-Lehtinen*	Y	Y	Y	N	Y	Y	Y	Y
19 Johnston	Y	Y	Y	N	Y	Y	Y	Y
20 Deutsch	Y	Y	Y	N	Y	Y	Y	Y
21 *Diaz-Balart*	Y	Y	Y	N	Y	Y	Y	Y
22 *Shaw*	Y	Y	Y	N	N	Y	N	N
23 Hastings	Y	Y	Y	N	Y	N	Y	Y
GEORGIA								
1 *Kingston*	Y	Y	Y	N	N	N	N	N
2 Bishop	Y	Y	Y	N	Y	N	Y	Y
3 *Collins*	Y	Y	Y	N	N	N	N	N
4 *Linder*	Y	Y	Y	N	N	N	N	N
5 Lewis	Y	Y	Y	N	Y	Y	Y	Y
6 *Gingrich*	Y	Y	Y	N	N	N	N	N
7 Darden	Y	Y	Y	N	Y	Y	Y	Y
8 Rowland	Y	Y	Y	N	Y	Y	Y	Y
9 Deal	Y	Y	Y	N	Y	Y	Y	Y
10 Johnson	Y	Y	Y	N	Y	Y	Y	Y
11 McKinney	Y	Y	Y	N	Y	Y	Y	Y
HAWAII								
1 Abercrombie	Y	Y	Y	N	N	N	Y	Y
2 Mink	Y	Y	Y	N	Y	Y	Y	Y
IDAHO								
1 LaRocco	Y	Y	Y	N	Y	Y	Y	Y
2 *Crapo*	Y	Y	Y	N	N	N	N	N
ILLINOIS								
1 Rush	Y	Y	Y	N	Y	N	Y	Y
2 Reynolds	Y	Y	Y	N	Y	Y	Y	Y
3 Lipinski	Y	Y	Y	N	Y	Y	Y	Y
4 Gutierrez	Y	Y	Y	N	Y	Y	Y	Y
5 Rostenkowski	Y	Y	Y	N	Y	Y	Y	Y
6 *Hyde*	Y	Y	Y	N	N	N	N	N
7 Collins	Y	Y	Y	N	Y	Y	Y	Y
8 *Crane*	Y	Y	Y	N	N	N	N	N
9 Yates	Y	Y	Y	N	Y	Y	Y	Y
10 *Porter*	Y	Y	Y	N	N	N	N	N
11 Sangmeister	Y	Y	Y	N	Y	Y	Y	Y
12 Costello	Y	Y	Y	N	Y	Y	Y	Y
13 *Fawell*	Y	Y	Y	N	N	N	N	N
14 *Hastert*	Y	Y	Y	N	N	N	N	N
15 *Ewing*	Y	Y	Y	N	N	N	N	N
16 *Manzullo*	Y	Y	Y	N	N	N	N	N
17 Evans	Y	Y	Y	N	Y	Y	Y	Y

ND Northern Democrats   SD Southern Democrats

	117	118	119	120	121	122	123	124
18 ***Michel***	Y	Y	Y	Y	N	N	N	N
19 Poshard	Y	Y	Y	N	Y	N	Y	Y
20 Durbin	Y	Y	Y	N	Y	N	Y	Y
INDIANA								
1 Visclosky	Y	Y	Y	N	Y	N	Y	Y
2 Sharp	Y	Y	Y	?	?	?	Y	Y
3 Roemer	Y	Y	Y	N	N	N	Y	Y
4 Long	Y	Y	Y	N	Y	N	Y	Y
5 ***Buyer***	Y	Y	Y	Y	N	N	N	N
6 ***Burton***	Y	Y	Y	Y	N	N	N	N
7 ***Myers***	Y	Y	Y	Y	N	N	Y	N
8 McCloskey	Y	Y	Y	N	Y	N	Y	?
9 Hamilton	Y	Y	Y	N	Y	N	Y	Y
10 Jacobs	Y	Y	Y	Y	N	N	N	Y
IOWA								
1 ***Leach***	Y	Y	Y	Y	N	N	N	N
2 ***Nussle***	Y	Y	Y	+	N	N	N	N
3 ***Lightfoot***	Y	Y	Y	Y	N	N	N	N
4 Smith	Y	Y	Y	N	Y	Y	Y	Y
5 ***Grandy***	Y	Y	Y	Y	N	N	N	N
KANSAS								
1 ***Roberts***	Y	Y	Y	Y	N	N	N	N
2 Slattery	Y	Y	Y	N	Y	N	Y	Y
3 ***Meyers***	Y	Y	Y	Y	N	N	N	N
4 Glickman	Y	Y	Y	N	Y	N	Y	Y
KENTUCKY								
1 Barlow	Y	Y	Y	N	Y	Y	Y	Y
2 Natcher	Y	Y	Y	N	Y	Y	Y	Y
3 Mazzoli	Y	Y	Y	N	Y	N	Y	Y
4 ***Bunning***	Y	Y	Y	Y	N	N	N	N
5 ***Rogers***	Y	Y	Y	Y	N	N	N	N
6 Baesler	Y	Y	Y	N	Y	N	Y	Y
LOUISIANA								
1 ***Livingston***	Y	Y	Y	Y	N	N	N	N
2 Jefferson	Y	Y	Y	N	Y	Y	Y	Y
3 Tauzin	Y	Y	Y	N	Y	Y	Y	Y
4 Fields	Y	Y	Y	N	Y	N	Y	Y
5 ***McCrery***	Y	Y	Y	Y	N	N	N	N
6 ***Baker***	Y	Y	Y	Y	N	N	N	N
7 Hayes	Y	Y	Y	N	Y	Y	Y	Y
MAINE								
1 Andrews	Y	Y	Y	N	N	N	Y	Y
2 ***Snowe***	Y	Y	Y	Y	N	N	N	N
MARYLAND								
1 ***Gilchrest***	Y	Y	Y	Y	N	N	N	N
2 ***Bentley***	Y	Y	Y	Y	N	N	N	N
3 Cardin	Y	Y	Y	N	Y	N	Y	Y
4 Wynn	Y	Y	Y	N	Y	Y	Y	Y
5 Hoyer	Y	Y	Y	N	Y	N	Y	Y
6 ***Bartlett***	Y	Y	Y	Y	N	N	N	N
7 Mfume	Y	Y	Y	N	Y	N	Y	Y
8 ***Morella***	Y	Y	Y	Y	N	N	N	N
MASSACHUSETTS								
1 Olver	Y	Y	Y	N	Y	N	Y	Y
2 Neal	Y	Y	Y	N	Y	Y	Y	Y
3 ***Blute***	Y	Y	Y	Y	N	N	N	N
4 Frank	Y	Y	Y	N	Y	Y	Y	Y
5 Meehan	Y	Y	Y	Y	Y	N	Y	Y
6 ***Torkildsen***	Y	Y	Y	Y	N	N	N	N
7 Markey	Y	Y	Y	N	Y	Y	Y	Y
8 Kennedy	Y	Y	Y	N	Y	N	Y	Y
9 Moakley	Y	Y	Y	N	Y	N	Y	Y
10 Studds	Y	Y	Y	N	Y	N	Y	Y
MICHIGAN								
1 Stupak	Y	Y	Y	N	Y	Y	Y	Y
2 ***Hoekstra***	Y	Y	Y	Y	N	N	N	N
3 Henry	?	?	?	?	?	?	?	?
4 ***Camp***	Y	Y	Y	Y	N	N	N	N
5 Barcia	Y	Y	Y	N	Y	Y	Y	Y
6 ***Upton***	Y	Y	Y	Y	N	N	N	N
7 ***Smith***	Y	Y	Y	Y	N	N	N	N
8 Carr	Y	Y	Y	N	Y	Y	?	Y
9 Kildee	Y	Y	Y	N	Y	N	Y	Y
10 Bonior	Y	Y	Y	N	Y	N	Y	Y
11 ***Knollenberg***	Y	Y	Y	Y	N	N	N	N
12 Levin	Y	Y	Y	N	Y	N	Y	Y
13 Ford	Y	Y	Y	N	Y	Y	Y	Y
14 Conyers	?	?	?	X	#	?	Y	?
15 Collins	Y	Y	Y	N	Y	Y	Y	Y
16 Dingell	Y	Y	Y	N	Y	Y	Y	Y
MINNESOTA								
1 Penny	Y	Y	Y	N	Y	Y	Y	Y
2 Minge	Y	Y	Y	N	N	Y	Y	Y
3 ***Ramstad***	Y	Y	Y	Y	N	N	N	N
4 Vento	Y	Y	Y	N	Y	N	Y	Y

	117	118	119	120	121	122	123	124
5 Sabo	Y	Y	Y	N	Y	N	Y	Y
6 ***Grams***	Y	Y	Y	Y	N	N	N	N
7 Peterson	Y	Y	Y	N	N	Y	Y	Y
8 Oberstar	Y	Y	Y	N	Y	N	Y	Y
MISSISSIPPI								
1 Whitten	Y	Y	Y	N	Y	?	?	Y
2 Vacancy								
3 Montgomery	Y	Y	Y	N	Y	Y	Y	Y
4 Parker	Y	Y	Y	N	Y	Y	?	Y
5 Taylor	Y	Y	Y	N	Y	Y	N	Y
MISSOURI								
1 Clay	Y	Y	Y	N	Y	Y	N	Y
2 ***Talent***	Y	Y	Y	Y	N	N	N	N
3 Gephardt	Y	Y	Y	N	Y	N	Y	Y
4 Skelton	Y	Y	Y	N	Y	N	Y	Y
5 Wheat	Y	Y	Y	N	Y	N	Y	Y
6 Danner	Y	Y	Y	N	Y	N	Y	Y
7 ***Hancock***	N	Y	Y	Y	N	N	N	N
8 ***Emerson***	Y	Y	Y	Y	N	N	N	N
9 Volkmer	Y	Y	Y	N	N	Y	Y	Y
MONTANA								
AL Williams	Y	Y	Y	N	Y	N	Y	Y
NEBRASKA								
1 ***Bereuter***	Y	Y	Y	Y	N	N	N	N
2 Hoagland	Y	Y	Y	N	Y	N	Y	Y
3 ***Barrett***	Y	Y	Y	Y	N	N	N	N
NEVADA								
1 Bilbray	Y	Y	Y	N	Y	Y	Y	Y
2 ***Vucanovich***	Y	Y	Y	Y	N	N	N	N
NEW HAMPSHIRE								
1 ***Zeliff***	Y	Y	Y	Y	N	N	N	N
2 Swett	Y	Y	Y	N	Y	Y	Y	Y
NEW JERSEY								
1 Andrews	Y	Y	Y	N	Y	Y	Y	Y
2 Hughes	Y	Y	Y	N	N	Y	Y	Y
3 ***Saxton***	Y	Y	Y	Y	N	N	N	N
4 ***Smith***	Y	Y	Y	Y	N	N	N	N
5 ***Roukema***	Y	Y	Y	Y	N	N	N	N
6 Pallone	Y	Y	Y	N	Y	Y	Y	Y
7 ***Franks***	Y	Y	Y	Y	N	N	N	N
8 Klein	Y	Y	Y	N	Y	N	Y	Y
9 Torricelli	Y	Y	Y	N	Y	N	Y	Y
10 Payne	Y	Y	Y	N	Y	Y	Y	Y
11 ***Gallo***	Y	Y	Y	Y	N	N	N	N
12 ***Zimmer***	Y	Y	Y	Y	N	N	N	N
13 Menendez	Y	Y	Y	N	Y	N	Y	Y
NEW MEXICO								
1 ***Schiff***	Y	Y	Y	Y	N	N	N	N
2 ***Skeen***	Y	Y	Y	Y	N	N	N	N
3 Richardson	Y	Y	Y	N	Y	N	Y	Y
NEW YORK								
1 Hochbrueckner	Y	Y	Y	N	Y	Y	Y	Y
2 ***Lazio***	Y	Y	Y	Y	N	N	N	N
3 ***King***	Y	Y	Y	Y	N	N	N	N
4 ***Levy***	Y	Y	Y	Y	N	N	N	N
5 Ackerman	?	Y	Y	N	Y	Y	Y	Y
6 Flake	Y	Y	Y	N	Y	N	Y	Y
7 Manton	Y	Y	Y	N	Y	N	Y	Y
8 Nadler	Y	Y	Y	N	Y	N	?	#
9 Schumer	Y	Y	Y	N	Y	N	Y	Y
10 Towns	Y	Y	Y	N	Y	Y	Y	Y
11 Owens	Y	Y	Y	N	Y	N	Y	Y
12 Velazquez	Y	Y	Y	N	Y	N	Y	Y
13 ***Molinari***	Y	Y	Y	Y	N	N	N	N
14 Maloney	Y	Y	Y	?	N	N	+	Y
15 Rangel	Y	Y	Y	N	Y	Y	Y	Y
16 Serrano	Y	Y	Y	N	Y	N	Y	Y
17 Engel	Y	Y	Y	N	Y	Y	Y	Y
18 Lowey	Y	Y	Y	N	Y	N	Y	Y
19 ***Fish***	Y	Y	Y	Y	N	N	Y	N
20 ***Gilman***	Y	Y	Y	Y	N	N	Y	N
21 McNulty	Y	Y	Y	N	Y	N	Y	Y
22 ***Solomon***	Y	Y	Y	Y	N	N	N	N
23 ***Boehlert***	Y	Y	Y	Y	N	N	N	N
24 ***McHugh***	Y	Y	Y	Y	N	N	N	N
25 ***Walsh***	Y	Y	Y	Y	N	N	N	N
26 Hinchey	Y	Y	Y	N	Y	N	Y	Y
27 ***Paxon***	Y	Y	Y	Y	N	N	N	N
28 Slaughter	Y	Y	Y	N	N	N	Y	Y
29 LaFalce	Y	Y	Y	—	+	+	+	+
30 ***Quinn***	Y	Y	Y	Y	N	N	N	N
31 ***Houghton***	Y	Y	Y	Y	N	N	Y	N
NORTH CAROLINA								
1 Clayton	Y	Y	Y	N	Y	Y	?	Y
2 Valentine	Y	Y	Y	N	Y	Y	Y	Y

	117	118	119	120	121	122	123	124
3 Lancaster	Y	Y	Y	N	N	?	Y	Y
4 Price	Y	Y	Y	N	N	Y	Y	Y
5 Neal	Y	Y	Y	N	Y	Y	Y	Y
6 ***Coble***	Y	Y	Y	Y	N	N	N	N
7 Rose	Y	Y	Y	N	Y	Y	Y	Y
8 Hefner	Y	Y	Y	N	Y	Y	Y	Y
9 ***McMillan***	Y	Y	Y	Y	N	N	Y	N
10 ***Ballenger***	Y	Y	Y	Y	N	N	N	N
11 ***Taylor***	Y	Y	Y	Y	N	N	N	N
12 Watt	Y	Y	Y	N	Y	Y	Y	Y
NORTH DAKOTA								
AL Pomeroy	Y	Y	Y	N	Y	N	Y	Y
OHIO								
1 Mann	Y	Y	Y	N	Y	Y	Y	Y
2 Vacancy								
3 Hall	Y	Y	Y	N	N	Y	Y	?
4 ***Oxley***	Y	Y	Y	Y	N	?	Y	N
5 ***Gillmor***	Y	Y	Y	Y	N	N	Y	N
6 Strickland	Y	Y	Y	N	Y	Y	Y	Y
7 ***Hobson***	Y	Y	Y	Y	N	N	N	N
8 ***Boehner***	Y	Y	Y	Y	N	N	N	N
9 Kaptur	Y	Y	Y	N	Y	N	Y	Y
10 ***Hoke***	Y	Y	Y	Y	N	N	N	N
11 Stokes	Y	Y	Y	?	Y	Y	Y	Y
12 ***Kasich***	Y	Y	Y	Y	N	N	Y	?
13 Brown	Y	Y	Y	N	Y	N	Y	Y
14 Sawyer	Y	Y	Y	N	Y	Y	Y	Y
15 ***Pryce***	Y	Y	Y	Y	N	N	N	N
16 ***Regula***	Y	Y	Y	Y	N	N	N	N
17 Traficant	Y	Y	Y	N	Y	N	Y	Y
18 Applegate	Y	Y	Y	N	Y	Y	Y	Y
19 Fingerhut	Y	Y	Y	N	Y	Y	?	Y
OKLAHOMA								
1 ***Inhofe***	Y	Y	Y	Y	N	N	N	N
2 Synar	Y	Y	Y	N	Y	N	Y	Y
3 Brewster	Y	Y	Y	N	Y	Y	Y	Y
4 McCurdy	Y	Y	Y	N	N	Y	Y	Y
5 ***Istook***	Y	Y	Y	Y	N	N	N	N
6 English	Y	Y	Y	N	N	Y	Y	Y
OREGON								
1 Furse	Y	Y	Y	N	Y	Y	Y	Y
2 ***Smith***	Y	Y	Y	Y	N	N	N	N
3 Wyden	Y	Y	Y	N	Y	N	Y	Y
4 DeFazio	Y	Y	Y	N	N	Y	Y	Y
5 Kopetski	Y	Y	Y	N	Y	Y	Y	Y
PENNSYLVANIA								
1 Foglietta	Y	Y	Y	N	Y	Y	Y	Y
2 Blackwell	Y	Y	Y	N	Y	Y	Y	Y
3 Borski	Y	Y	Y	N	Y	Y	Y	Y
4 Klink	Y	Y	Y	N	Y	Y	Y	Y
5 ***Clinger***	Y	Y	Y	Y	N	N	Y	N
6 Holden	Y	Y	Y	N	N	Y	Y	Y
7 ***Weldon***	Y	Y	Y	Y	N	N	N	N
8 ***Greenwood***	Y	Y	Y	Y	N	N	N	N
9 ***Shuster***	Y	Y	Y	Y	N	N	N	?
10 ***McDade***	?	?	?	?	?	?	N	N
11 Kanjorski	Y	Y	Y	N	Y	Y	Y	Y
12 Murtha	Y	Y	Y	N	Y	Y	Y	Y
13 Margolies-Mezv.	Y	Y	Y	N	Y	N	Y	Y
14 Coyne	Y	Y	Y	N	Y	Y	Y	Y
15 McHale	Y	Y	Y	N	N	N	Y	Y
16 ***Walker***	Y	Y	Y	Y	N	N	N	N
17 ***Gekas***	Y	Y	Y	Y	N	N	N	N
18 ***Santorum***	Y	Y	Y	Y	N	N	N	N
19 ***Goodling***	Y	Y	Y	Y	N	N	N	N
20 Murphy	Y	Y	Y	N	Y	?	N	Y
21 ***Ridge***	Y	Y	Y	Y	N	N	N	N
RHODE ISLAND								
1 ***Machtley***	Y	Y	Y	Y	N	N	N	N
2 Reed	Y	Y	Y	N	Y	Y	Y	Y
SOUTH CAROLINA								
1 ***Ravenel***	Y	Y	Y	Y	N	?	Y	N
2 ***Spence***	Y	Y	Y	Y	N	N	N	N
3 Derrick	Y	Y	Y	N	Y	N	Y	Y
4 ***Inglis***	Y	Y	Y	Y	N	N	Y	N
5 Spratt	Y	Y	Y	N	Y	N	Y	Y
6 Clyburn	Y	Y	Y	N	Y	?	Y	Y
SOUTH DAKOTA								
AL Johnson	Y	Y	Y	N	Y	Y	Y	Y
TENNESSEE								
1 ***Quillen***	?	?	?	#	X	?	?	X
2 ***Duncan***	Y	Y	Y	Y	N	N	N	N
3 Lloyd	Y	Y	Y	N	Y	Y	Y	Y
4 Cooper	Y	Y	Y	N	Y	Y	Y	Y
5 Clement	Y	Y	Y	N	Y	Y	Y	Y

	117	118	119	120	121	122	123	124
6 Gordon	Y	Y	Y	N	Y	Y	Y	Y
7 ***Sundquist***	Y	Y	Y	Y	N	N	N	N
8 Tanner	Y	Y	Y	N	Y	Y	Y	Y
9 Ford	?	?	?	?	?	?	?	?
TEXAS								
1 Chapman	Y	Y	Y	N	Y	Y	Y	Y
2 Wilson	Y	Y	Y	N	Y	N	Y	Y
3 ***Johnson, Sam***	Y	Y	Y	Y	N	N	N	N
4 Hall	Y	Y	Y	N	N	N	Y	Y
5 Bryant	Y	Y	Y	N	Y	N	Y	Y
6 ***Barton***	?	?	?	?	X	?	?	?
7 ***Archer***	Y	Y	Y	Y	N	N	Y	N
8 ***Fields***	?	?	?	?	?	?	N	N
9 Brooks	Y	Y	Y	N	Y	Y	Y	Y
10 Pickle	Y	Y	Y	N	Y	N	Y	Y
11 Edwards	Y	Y	Y	N	Y	N	Y	Y
12 Geren	Y	Y	Y	N	Y	Y	Y	Y
13 Sarpalius	Y	Y	Y	N	Y	N	Y	Y
14 Laughlin	Y	Y	Y	N	Y	N	Y	Y
15 de la Garza	Y	Y	Y	N	Y	N	Y	Y
16 Coleman	Y	Y	Y	N	Y	Y	Y	Y
17 Stenholm	Y	Y	Y	N	Y	Y	Y	Y
18 Washington	Y	Y	Y	N	Y	N	Y	Y
19 ***Combest***	Y	Y	Y	Y	N	N	Y	N
20 Gonzalez	Y	Y	Y	N	Y	N	Y	Y
21 ***Smith***	Y	Y	Y	Y	N	N	N	N
22 ***DeLay***	Y	Y	Y	Y	N	N	N	N
23 ***Bonilla***	Y	Y	Y	Y	N	N	N	N
24 Frost	Y	Y	Y	N	Y	Y	Y	Y
25 Andrews	Y	Y	Y	N	Y	N	Y	Y
26 ***Armey***	Y	Y	Y	Y	N	N	N	N
27 Ortiz	Y	Y	Y	N	Y	N	Y	Y
28 Tejeda	Y	Y	Y	N	Y	N	Y	Y
29 Green	Y	Y	Y	N	Y	N	Y	Y
30 Johnson, E. B.	Y	Y	Y	N	Y	Y	Y	Y
UTAH								
1 ***Hansen***	Y	Y	Y	Y	N	N	N	N
2 Shepherd	Y	Y	Y	N	N	Y	?	Y
3 Orton	Y	Y	Y	N	Y	Y	Y	Y
VERMONT								
AL *Sanders*	Y	Y	?	N	Y	N	?	Y
VIRGINIA								
1 ***Bateman***	+	Y	Y	Y	N	N	Y	N
2 Pickett	Y	Y	Y	N	Y	Y	Y	Y
3 Scott	Y	Y	Y	N	Y	N	Y	Y
4 Sisisky	Y	Y	Y	N	Y	Y	Y	Y
5 Payne	Y	Y	Y	N	Y	Y	Y	Y
6 ***Goodlatte***	Y	Y	Y	Y	N	N	N	N
7 ***Bliley***	Y	Y	Y	Y	N	N	N	N
8 Moran	Y	Y	Y	N	Y	N	Y	Y
9 Boucher	Y	Y	Y	N	Y	Y	Y	Y
10 ***Wolf***	Y	Y	Y	Y	N	N	N	N
11 Byrne	Y	Y	Y	N	Y	Y	?	Y
WASHINGTON								
1 Cantwell	Y	Y	Y	N	Y	Y	Y	Y
2 Swift	Y	Y	Y	N	Y	N	Y	Y
3 Unsoeld	?	?	?	?	#	?	Y	Y
4 Inslee	Y	Y	Y	N	Y	N	Y	Y
5 Foley					Y	N		
6 Dicks	Y	Y	Y	N	Y	Y	Y	Y
7 McDermott	Y	Y	Y	N	Y	N	Y	Y
8 ***Dunn***	Y	Y	Y	Y	N	N	N	N
9 Kreidler	Y	Y	Y	N	Y	Y	Y	Y
WEST VIRGINIA								
1 Mollohan	Y	Y	Y	N	Y	N	Y	Y
2 Wise	Y	Y	Y	N	Y	Y	Y	Y
3 Rahall	Y	Y	Y	N	Y	Y	Y	Y
WISCONSIN								
1 Vacancy								
2 ***Klug***	Y	Y	Y	Y	N	N	N	N
3 ***Gunderson***	Y	Y	Y	Y	N	N	N	N
4 Kleczka	Y	Y	Y	N	Y	?	Y	Y
5 Barrett	Y	Y	Y	N	N	Y	Y	Y
6 ***Petri***	Y	Y	Y	Y	N	N	N	N
7 Obey	Y	Y	Y	N	Y	Y	Y	Y
8 ***Roth***	Y	Y	Y	Y	N	N	N	N
9 ***Sensenbrenner***	N	N	Y	Y	N	N	N	N
WYOMING								
AL ***Thomas***	Y	Y	Y	Y	N	N	N	N
DELEGATES								
de Lugo, V.I.	D	D	D	D	D	D	D	D
Faleomavaega, Am.S.	D	D	D	D	D	D	D	D
Norton, D.C.	D	D	D	D	D	D	D	D
Romero-B., P.R.	D	D	D	D	D	D	D	D
Underwood, Guam	D	D	D	D	D	D	D	D

Southern states - Ala., Ark., Fla., Ga., Ky., La., Miss., N.C., Okla., S.C., Tenn., Texas, Va.
Omitted votes are quorum calls, which CQ does not include in its vote charts.

125. H Con Res 64. Fiscal 1994 Budget Resolution/ Previous Question. Beilenson, D-Calif., motion to order the previous question (thus ending debate and the possibility of amendment) on adoption of the rule (H Res 145) to provide for House floor consideration of the concurrent resolution to set binding budget levels for the fiscal year ending Sept. 30, 1994. Motion agreed to 251-173: R 0-172; D 250-1 (ND 168-1, SD 82-0); I 1-0, March 31, 1993.

126. H Con Res 64. Fiscal 1994 Budget Resolution/Rule. Adoption of the rule (H Res 145) to provide for House floor consideration of the concurrent resolution to set binding budget levels for the fiscal year ending Sept. 30, 1994: budget authority, $1.507 trillion; outlays, $1.496 trillion; revenues, $1.242 trillion; deficit, $253.8 billion. The resolution incorporates the guidelines of the administration's economic package plus an additional $50 billion in spending cuts, ending up with $496 billion in deficit reduction over five years. The resolution would also provide for an increase in the federal debt limit through any one of three different options. Adopted 250-172: R 0-172; D 249-0 (ND 169-0, SD 80-0); I 1-0, March 31, 1993.

127. H Con Res 64. Fiscal 1994 Budget Resolution/Adoption. Adoption of the concurrent resolution to set binding budget levels for the fiscal year ending Sept. 30, 1994: budget authority, $1.507 trillion; outlays, $1.496 trillion; revenues, $1.242 trillion; deficit, $253.8 billion. The resolution incorporates the guidelines of the administration's economic package plus an additional $50 billion in spending cuts, ending up with $496 billion in deficit reduction over five years. The resolution would also provide for an increase in the federal debt limit through any one of three different options. Adopted 240-184: R 0-172; D 239-12 (ND 161-7, SD 78-5); I 1-0, March 31, 1993. A "yea" was a vote in support of the president's position.

128. Procedural Motion. Approval of the Journal of Wednesday, March 31. Approved 241-160: R 15-155; D 226-5 (ND 151-4, SD 75-1); I 0-0, April 1, 1993.

129. HR 2. National Voter Registration/Instruct Conferees. Thomas, R-Calif., motion to instruct the House conferees to accept the Senate provisions that allow states to register people to vote at public assistance or unemployment compensation agencies, rather than requiring it, as the House bill does. Motion rejected 192-222: R 170-0; D 22-221 (ND 8-156, SD 14-65); I 0-1, April 1, 1993.

130. HR 1430. Temporary Debt Limit Increase/Previous Question. Moakley, D-Mass., motion to order the previous question (thus ending debate and the possibility of amendment) on adoption of the rule (H Res 147) to provide for House floor consideration of the bill to temporarily increase the public debt limit by $225 billion from $4.145 trillion to $4.370 trillion through Sept. 30, 1993, to provide sufficient borrowing authority for the federal government to meet its obligations. Motion agreed to 244-168: R 0-167; D 243-1 (ND 162-1, SD 81-0); I 1-0, April 1, 1993.

131. HR 1430. Temporary Debt Limit Increase/Rule. Adoption of the rule (H Res 147) to provide for House floor consideration of the bill to temporarily increase the public debt limit by $225 billion from $4.145 trillion to $4.370 trillion through Sept. 30, 1993, to provide sufficient borrowing authority for the federal government to meet its obligations. Adopted 242-170: R 0-167; D 241-3 (ND 163-1, SD 78-2); I 1-0, April 1, 1993.

132. HR 1430. Temporary Debt Limit Increase/Recommit to Reduce Limit. Gingrich, R-Ga., motion to recommit the bill to the Ways and Means Committee with instructions to report it back with an amendment reducing the debt limit increase by $14 billion, an amount that would correspond to the Republican budget resolution proposed by Kasich, R-Ohio, on March 18 (See vote 81). Motion rejected 168-245: R 166-0; D 2-244 (ND 1-164, SD 1-80); I 0-1, April 2, 1993. A "nay" was a vote in support of the president's position.

KEY

Y	Voted for (yea).
#	Paired for.
+	Announced for.
N	Voted against (nay).
X	Paired against.
–	Announced against.
P	Voted "present."
C	Voted "present" to avoid possible conflict of interest.
?	Did not vote or otherwise make a position known.
D	Delegates ineligible to vote.

Democrats *Republicans*
Independent

	125	126	127	128	129	130	131	132
ALABAMA								
1 Callahan	N	N	N	N	Y	N	N	Y
2 Everett	N	N	N	N	Y	N	N	Y
3 Browder	Y	Y	Y	Y	Y	Y	Y	N
4 Bevill	Y	Y	Y	N	Y	Y	Y	N
5 Cramer	Y	Y	Y	N	Y	Y	Y	N
6 *Bachus*	N	N	N	N	Y	N	N	Y
7 Hilliard	Y	Y	Y	N	Y	Y	Y	N
ALASKA								
AL *Young*	N	N	N	N	Y	N	N	Y
ARIZONA								
1 Coppersmith	Y	Y	Y	N	Y	Y	Y	N
2 Pastor	Y	Y	Y	N	Y	Y	Y	N
3 *Stump*	N	N	N	N	Y	N	N	Y
4 *Kyl*	N	N	N	N	Y	N	N	Y
5 *Kolbe*	N	N	N	N	Y	N	N	Y
6 English	Y	Y	Y	N	Y	Y	Y	N
ARKANSAS								
1 Lambert	Y	Y	Y	N	Y	N	Y	N
2 Thornton	Y	Y	Y	?	Y	N	Y	N
3 *Hutchinson*	N	N	N	Y	Y	N	N	Y
4 *Dickey*	N	N	N	N	Y	N	N	Y
CALIFORNIA								
1 Hamburg	Y	Y	Y	N	Y	N	Y	N
2 *Herger*	N	N	N	N	Y	N	N	Y
3 Fazio	Y	Y	Y	N	Y	Y	Y	N
4 *Doolittle*	N	N	N	N	Y	N	N	Y
5 Matsui	Y	Y	Y	N	Y	Y	Y	N
6 Woolsey	Y	Y	Y	N	Y	Y	Y	N
7 Miller	Y	Y	Y	N	Y	Y	Y	N
8 Pelosi	Y	Y	Y	N	Y	Y	Y	N
9 Dellums	Y	Y	Y	?	N	Y	Y	N
10 *Baker*	N	N	N	N	Y	N	N	Y
11 *Pombo*	N	N	N	Y	Y	?	?	?
12 Lantos	Y	Y	Y	N	Y	?	?	?
13 Stark	Y	Y	Y	N	Y	?	Y	N
14 Eshoo	Y	Y	Y	N	Y	Y	Y	N
15 Mineta	Y	Y	Y	N	Y	Y	Y	N
16 Edwards	Y	Y	Y	N	Y	Y	Y	N
17 Vacancy								
18 Condit	Y	Y	Y	Y	Y	Y	Y	N
19 Lehman	Y	Y	Y	N	Y	Y	Y	N
20 Dooley	Y	Y	Y	N	Y	Y	Y	N
21 *Thomas*	N	N	N	N	Y	N	N	Y
22 *Huffington*	N	N	N	N	Y	N	N	Y
23 *Gallegly*	N	N	N	N	Y	N	N	Y
24 Beilenson	Y	Y	Y	Y	Y	Y	Y	N
25 *McKeon*	N	N	N	N	Y	N	N	Y
26 Berman	Y	Y	Y	?	N	Y	Y	N
27 *Moorhead*	N	N	N	N	Y	N	N	Y
28 *Dreier*	N	N	N	N	Y	N	N	Y
29 Waxman	Y	Y	Y	N	Y	Y	Y	N
30 Becerra	Y	Y	Y	N	Y	Y	Y	N
31 Martinez	Y	Y	Y	N	Y	Y	Y	N
32 Dixon	Y	Y	Y	?	Y	Y	Y	N
33 Roybal-Allard	Y	Y	Y	N	Y	Y	Y	N
34 Torres	Y	Y	Y	?	Y	Y	Y	N
35 Waters	Y	Y	Y	N	Y	Y	Y	N
36 Harman	Y	Y	Y	N	Y	Y	Y	N
37 Tucker	Y	Y	Y	N	Y	Y	Y	N
38 *Horn*	N	N	N	N	Y	N	N	Y
39 *Royce*	N	N	N	N	Y	N	N	Y
40 *Lewis*	N	N	N	N	Y	N	N	Y
41 *Kim*	N	N	N	N	Y	N	N	Y
42 Brown	Y	Y	Y	?	N	Y	Y	N
43 *Calvert*	N	N	N	N	Y	N	N	Y
44 *McCandless*	N	N	N	N	Y	N	N	Y
45 *Rohrabacher*	N	N	N	N	Y	N	N	Y
46 *Dornan*	N	N	N	N	Y	N	N	Y
47 *Cox*	N	N	N	N	Y	N	N	Y
48 *Packard*	N	N	N	N	Y	N	N	Y
49 Schenk	Y	Y	Y	Y	N	Y	Y	N
50 Filner	Y	Y	Y	Y	N	Y	Y	N
51 *Cunningham*	N	N	N	N	Y	N	N	Y
52 *Hunter*	N	N	N	N	Y	N	N	Y
COLORADO								
1 Schroeder	Y	Y	Y	N	N	Y	Y	N
2 Skaggs	Y	Y	Y	Y	Y	Y	Y	N
3 *McInnis*	N	N	N	N	Y	N	N	Y
4 *Allard*	N	N	N	N	Y	N	N	Y
5 *Hefley*	N	N	N	N	Y	N	N	Y
6 *Schaefer*	N	N	N	N	Y	N	N	Y
CONNECTICUT								
1 Kennelly	Y	Y	Y	N	Y	Y	Y	N
2 Gejdenson	Y	Y	Y	N	Y	Y	Y	N
3 DeLauro	Y	Y	Y	N	Y	Y	Y	N
4 *Shays*	N	N	N	N	Y	N	N	Y
5 *Franks*	N	N	N	N	Y	N	N	Y
6 *Johnson*	N	N	N	N	Y	N	N	Y
DELAWARE								
AL *Castle*	N	N	N	N	Y	N	N	Y
FLORIDA								
1 Hutto	Y	Y	Y	Y	Y	Y	Y	N
2 Peterson	Y	Y	Y	N	Y	Y	Y	N
3 Brown	Y	Y	Y	Y	–	Y	Y	N
4 Fowler	N	N	N	N	Y	?	?	?
5 Thurman	Y	Y	Y	N	Y	Y	Y	N
6 *Stearns*	N	N	N	N	Y	N	N	Y
7 *Mica*	N	N	N	N	Y	N	N	Y
8 *McCollum*	N	N	N	N	Y	N	N	Y
9 *Bilirakis*	N	N	N	N	Y	N	N	Y
10 *Young*	N	N	N	N	Y	N	N	Y
11 Gibbons	Y	Y	Y	N	Y	Y	Y	N
12 *Canady*	N	N	N	N	Y	N	N	Y
13 *Miller*	N	N	N	N	Y	N	N	Y
14 *Goss*	N	N	N	N	Y	N	N	Y
15 Bacchus	Y	Y	Y	N	Y	Y	Y	N
16 *Lewis*	N	N	N	N	Y	N	N	Y
17 Meek	Y	Y	Y	N	Y	Y	Y	N
18 *Ros-Lehtinen*	N	N	N	N	Y	N	N	Y
19 Johnston	Y	Y	Y	N	Y	Y	Y	N
20 Deutsch	Y	Y	Y	N	Y	Y	Y	N
21 *Diaz-Balart*	N	N	N	N	Y	N	N	Y
22 *Shaw*	N	N	N	N	Y	N	N	Y
23 Hastings	Y	Y	Y	N	Y	Y	Y	N
GEORGIA								
1 *Kingston*	N	N	N	N	Y	N	N	Y
2 Bishop	Y	Y	Y	N	Y	Y	Y	N
3 *Collins*	N	N	N	N	Y	N	N	Y
4 *Linder*	N	N	N	N	Y	N	N	Y
5 Lewis	Y	Y	Y	N	Y	Y	Y	N
6 *Gingrich*	N	N	N	?	Y	N	N	Y
7 Darden	Y	Y	Y	N	Y	Y	Y	N
8 Rowland	Y	Y	Y	N	Y	Y	Y	N
9 Deal	Y	Y	Y	N	Y	Y	Y	N
10 Johnson	Y	Y	Y	N	Y	Y	Y	N
11 McKinney	Y	Y	Y	N	Y	Y	Y	N
HAWAII								
1 Abercrombie	Y	Y	?	N	Y	N	Y	N
2 Mink	Y	Y	Y	N	Y	Y	Y	N
IDAHO								
1 LaRocco	Y	Y	Y	N	Y	Y	Y	N
2 *Crapo*	N	N	N	N	Y	N	N	Y
ILLINOIS								
1 Rush	Y	Y	Y	N	Y	Y	Y	N
2 Reynolds	Y	Y	Y	N	Y	Y	Y	N
3 Lipinski	Y	Y	N	Y	N	Y	Y	N
4 Gutierrez	Y	Y	Y	N	Y	Y	Y	N
5 Rostenkowski	Y	Y	Y	N	Y	Y	Y	N
6 *Hyde*	N	N	N	N	Y	N	N	Y
7 Collins	Y	Y	Y	N	Y	Y	Y	N
8 *Crane*	N	N	N	N	Y	N	N	Y
9 Yates	Y	Y	Y	N	Y	Y	Y	N
10 *Porter*	N	N	N	N	Y	N	N	Y
11 Sangmeister	Y	Y	Y	N	Y	Y	Y	N
12 Costello	Y	Y	Y	N	Y	Y	Y	N
13 *Fawell*	N	N	N	N	Y	N	N	Y
14 *Hastert*	N	N	N	N	Y	N	N	Y
15 *Ewing*	N	N	N	N	Y	N	N	Y
16 *Manzullo*	N	N	N	N	Y	N	N	Y
17 Evans	Y	Y	Y	N	Y	Y	Y	N

ND Northern Democrats   SD Southern Democrats

	125	126	127	128	129	130	131	132
18 ***Michel***	N	N	N	?	Y	N	N	?
19 Poshard	Y	Y	Y	Y	N	Y	Y	N
20 Durbin	Y	Y	Y	Y	N	Y	Y	N
INDIANA								
1 Visclosky	Y	Y	Y	Y	N	Y	Y	N
2 Sharp	Y	Y	Y	Y	N	Y	Y	N
3 Roemer	Y	Y	Y	Y	N	Y	Y	N
4 Long	Y	Y	N	Y	N	Y	Y	N
5 ***Buyer***	N	N	N	N	Y	N	N	Y
6 ***Burton***	N	N	N	N	Y	N	N	Y
7 ***Myers***	N	N	N	Y	Y	N	N	Y
8 McCloskey	Y	Y	Y	?	N	?	Y	N
9 Hamilton	Y	Y	Y	Y	N	Y	Y	N
10 Jacobs	N	Y	N	N	N	N	N	Y
IOWA								
1 ***Leach***	N	N	N	N	Y	N	N	Y
2 ***Nussle***	N	N	N	N	Y	N	N	Y
3 ***Lightfoot***	N	N	N	N	Y	N	N	Y
4 Smith	Y	Y	Y	Y	N	Y	Y	N
5 ***Grandy***	N	N	N	N	Y	N	N	Y
KANSAS								
1 ***Roberts***	N	N	N	N	Y	N	N	Y
2 Slattery	Y	Y	Y	Y	?	Y	Y	N
3 ***Meyers***	N	N	N	N	Y	N	N	Y
4 Glickman	Y	Y	Y	Y	N	Y	Y	N
KENTUCKY								
1 Barlow	Y	Y	Y	Y	N	Y	Y	N
2 Natcher	Y	Y	Y	Y	N	Y	Y	N
3 Mazzoli	Y	Y	Y	Y	N	Y	Y	N
4 ***Bunning***	N	N	N	N	Y	N	N	Y
5 ***Rogers***	N	N	N	N	Y	N	N	Y
6 Baesler	Y	Y	Y	Y	N	Y	Y	N
LOUISIANA								
1 ***Livingston***	N	N	N	N	Y	N	N	Y
2 Jefferson	Y	?	Y	Y	N	Y	Y	N
3 Tauzin	Y	Y	Y	Y	Y	Y	Y	N
4 Fields	Y	Y	Y	Y	N	Y	Y	N
5 ***McCrery***	N	N	N	N	?	N	N	Y
6 ***Baker***	N	N	N	N	Y	N	N	Y
7 Hayes	Y	Y	Y	Y	Y	Y	Y	N
MAINE								
1 Andrews	Y	Y	Y	Y	N	Y	Y	N
2 ***Snowe***	N	N	N	N	Y	N	N	Y
MARYLAND								
1 ***Gilchrest***	N	N	N	N	Y	N	N	Y
2 ***Bentley***	N	N	N	N	Y	N	N	Y
3 Cardin	Y	Y	Y	Y	N	Y	Y	N
4 Wynn	Y	Y	Y	Y	N	Y	Y	N
5 Hoyer	Y	Y	Y	Y	N	Y	Y	N
6 ***Bartlett***	N	N	N	N	Y	N	N	Y
7 Mfume	Y	Y	Y	?	N	Y	Y	N
8 ***Morella***	N	N	N	N	Y	N	N	Y
MASSACHUSETTS								
1 Olver	Y	Y	Y	Y	N	Y	Y	N
2 Neal	Y	Y	Y	Y	N	Y	Y	N
3 ***Blute***	N	N	N	N	Y	N	N	Y
4 Frank	Y	Y	Y	Y	N	Y	Y	N
5 Meehan	Y	Y	Y	Y	N	Y	Y	N
6 ***Torkildsen***	N	N	N	N	Y	N	N	Y
7 Markey	Y	Y	Y	Y	N	Y	Y	N
8 Kennedy	Y	Y	Y	Y	N	Y	Y	N
9 Moakley	Y	Y	Y	Y	N	Y	Y	N
10 Studds	Y	Y	Y	Y	N	Y	Y	N
MICHIGAN								
1 Stupak	Y	Y	Y	Y	N	Y	Y	N
2 ***Hoekstra***	N	N	N	N	Y	N	N	Y
3 Henry	?	?	?	?	?	?	?	?
4 ***Camp***	N	N	N	N	Y	N	N	Y
5 Barcia	Y	Y	Y	Y	N	Y	Y	N
6 ***Upton***	N	N	N	N	Y	N	N	Y
7 ***Smith***	N	N	N	N	Y	N	N	Y
8 Carr	Y	Y	Y	?	N	Y	Y	N
9 Kildee	Y	Y	Y	Y	N	Y	Y	N
10 Bonior	Y	Y	Y	?	N	Y	Y	N
11 ***Knollenberg***	N	N	N	N	Y	N	N	Y
12 Levin	Y	Y	Y	Y	N	Y	Y	N
13 Ford	Y	Y	Y	Y	N	Y	Y	N
14 Conyers	Y	Y	Y	Y	N	Y	Y	N
15 Collins	Y	Y	Y	Y	N	Y	Y	N
16 Dingell	Y	Y	Y	Y	N	Y	Y	N
MINNESOTA								
1 Penny	Y	Y	Y	Y	N	Y	Y	N
2 Minge	Y	Y	Y	Y	N	Y	Y	N
3 ***Ramstad***	N	N	N	N	Y	N	N	Y
4 Vento	Y	Y	Y	Y	N	Y	Y	N

	125	126	127	128	129	130	131	132
5 Sabo	Y	Y	Y	Y	N	Y	Y	N
6 ***Grams***	N	N	N	N	Y	N	N	Y
7 Peterson	Y	Y	Y	Y	N	Y	Y	N
8 Oberstar	Y	Y	Y	Y	N	Y	Y	N
MISSISSIPPI								
1 Whitten	Y	Y	Y	?	N	?	?	?
2 Vacancy								
3 Montgomery	Y	Y	Y	Y	Y	Y	Y	N
4 Parker	Y	Y	Y	Y	Y	Y	Y	Y
5 Taylor	Y	Y	N	N	Y	Y	Y	N
MISSOURI								
1 Clay	Y	Y	Y	?	N	Y	Y	N
2 ***Talent***	N	N	N	N	Y	N	N	Y
3 Gephardt	Y	Y	Y	?	N	Y	Y	N
4 Skelton	Y	Y	Y	Y	N	Y	Y	N
5 Wheat	Y	Y	Y	Y	N	Y	Y	N
6 Danner	Y	Y	Y	Y	N	Y	Y	N
7 ***Hancock***	N	N	N	N	Y	N	N	Y
8 ***Emerson***	N	N	N	N	Y	N	N	Y
9 Volkmer	Y	Y	Y	Y	Y	Y	Y	N
MONTANA								
AL Williams	Y	Y	Y	?	N	Y	Y	N
NEBRASKA								
1 ***Bereuter***	N	N	N	N	Y	N	N	Y
2 Hoagland	Y	Y	Y	Y	N	Y	Y	N
3 ***Barrett***	N	N	N	N	Y	N	N	Y
NEVADA								
1 Bilbray	Y	Y	Y	Y	N	Y	Y	N
2 ***Vucanovich***	N	N	N	N	Y	N	N	Y
NEW HAMPSHIRE								
1 ***Zeliff***	N	N	N	N	Y	N	N	Y
2 Swett	Y	Y	Y	Y	N	?	?	?
NEW JERSEY								
1 Andrews	Y	Y	N	Y	?	Y	Y	N
2 Hughes	Y	Y	Y	Y	N	Y	Y	N
3 ***Saxton***	N	N	N	N	Y	N	N	Y
4 ***Smith***	N	N	N	Y	Y	N	N	Y
5 ***Roukema***	N	N	N	N	Y	N	N	Y
6 Pallone	Y	Y	N	Y	N	Y	Y	N
7 ***Franks***	N	N	N	N	Y	N	N	Y
8 Klein	Y	Y	Y	Y	N	Y	Y	N
9 Torricelli	Y	Y	Y	Y	?	Y	Y	N
10 Payne	Y	Y	Y	Y	N	Y	Y	N
11 ***Gallo***	N	N	N	N	Y	N	N	Y
12 ***Zimmer***	N	N	N	N	Y	N	N	Y
13 Menendez	Y	Y	Y	Y	N	Y	Y	N
NEW MEXICO								
1 ***Schiff***	N	N	N	N	Y	N	N	Y
2 ***Skeen***	N	N	N	N	Y	N	N	Y
3 Richardson	Y	Y	Y	?	N	Y	Y	N
NEW YORK								
1 Hochbrueckner	Y	Y	Y	Y	N	Y	Y	N
2 ***Lazio***	N	N	N	N	Y	N	N	Y
3 ***King***	N	N	N	N	Y	N	N	Y
4 ***Levy***	N	N	N	N	Y	N	N	Y
5 Ackerman	Y	Y	Y	Y	N	Y	Y	N
6 Flake	Y	Y	Y	Y	N	Y	Y	N
7 Manton	Y	Y	Y	Y	N	Y	Y	N
8 Nadler	Y	Y	Y	Y	N	Y	Y	N
9 Schumer	Y	Y	Y	Y	N	Y	Y	N
10 Towns	Y	Y	Y	Y	N	Y	Y	N
11 Owens	Y	Y	Y	Y	N	Y	Y	N
12 Velazquez	Y	Y	Y	Y	N	Y	Y	N
13 ***Molinari***	N	N	N	N	Y	N	N	Y
14 Maloney	Y	Y	Y	Y	N	Y	Y	N
15 Rangel	Y	Y	Y	?	N	Y	Y	N
16 Serrano	Y	Y	Y	Y	N	Y	Y	N
17 Engel	Y	Y	Y	Y	N	Y	Y	N
18 Lowey	Y	Y	Y	Y	N	Y	Y	N
19 ***Fish***	N	N	N	Y	Y	N	N	Y
20 ***Gilman***	N	N	N	Y	Y	N	N	Y
21 McNulty	Y	Y	Y	Y	N	Y	Y	N
22 ***Solomon***	N	N	N	N	Y	N	N	Y
23 ***Boehlert***	N	N	N	N	Y	N	N	Y
24 ***McHugh***	N	N	N	N	Y	N	N	Y
25 ***Walsh***	N	N	N	N	Y	N	N	Y
26 Hinchey	Y	Y	Y	Y	N	Y	Y	N
27 ***Paxon***	N	N	N	N	Y	N	N	Y
28 Slaughter	Y	Y	Y	Y	N	Y	Y	N
29 LaFalce	+	+	+	Y	N	+	+	−
30 ***Quinn***	N	N	N	N	Y	N	N	Y
31 ***Houghton***	N	N	N	Y	Y	N	N	Y
NORTH CAROLINA								
1 Clayton	Y	Y	Y	Y	N	Y	Y	N
2 Valentine	Y	Y	Y	Y	Y	Y	Y	N

	125	126	127	128	129	130	131	132
3 Lancaster	Y	Y	Y	Y	Y	Y	Y	N
4 Price	Y	Y	Y	Y	N	Y	Y	N
5 Neal	Y	Y	Y	Y	N	Y	Y	N
6 ***Coble***	N	N	N	N	Y	N	N	Y
7 Rose	Y	Y	Y	Y	N	Y	Y	N
8 Hefner	Y	Y	Y	Y	N	Y	Y	N
9 ***McMillan***	N	N	N	N	Y	N	N	Y
10 ***Ballenger***	N	N	N	N	Y	N	N	Y
11 ***Taylor***	N	N	N	N	Y	N	N	Y
12 Watt	Y	Y	Y	?	X	Y	Y	N
NORTH DAKOTA								
AL Pomeroy	Y	Y	Y	Y	N	Y	Y	N
OHIO								
1 Mann	Y	Y	Y	Y	N	Y	Y	N
2 Vacancy								
3 Hall	Y	Y	Y	?	N	Y	Y	N
4 ***Oxley***	N	N	N	N	Y	N	N	Y
5 ***Gillmor***	N	N	N	Y	Y	N	N	Y
6 Strickland	Y	Y	Y	Y	N	Y	Y	N
7 ***Hobson***	N	N	N	N	Y	N	N	Y
8 ***Boehner***	N	N	N	N	Y	N	N	Y
9 Kaptur	Y	Y	Y	Y	N	Y	Y	N
10 ***Hoke***	N	N	N	N	Y	N	N	Y
11 Stokes	Y	Y	Y	Y	N	?	Y	N
12 ***Kasich***	N	N	N	Y	Y	N	N	Y
13 Brown	Y	Y	Y	Y	N	?	?	?
14 Sawyer	Y	Y	Y	Y	N	Y	Y	N
15 ***Pryce***	N	N	N	N	Y	N	N	Y
16 ***Regula***	N	N	N	N	Y	N	N	Y
17 Traficant	Y	Y	N	Y	N	Y	Y	N
18 Applegate	Y	Y	Y	Y	N	Y	Y	N
19 Fingerhut	Y	Y	Y	Y	N	Y	Y	N
OKLAHOMA								
1 ***Inhofe***	N	N	N	N	Y	N	N	Y
2 Synar	Y	Y	Y	Y	N	Y	Y	N
3 Brewster	Y	Y	Y	Y	N	Y	Y	N
4 McCurdy	Y	Y	Y	?	?	?	?	?
5 ***Istook***	N	N	N	N	Y	N	N	Y
6 English	Y	Y	Y	Y	Y	Y	Y	N
OREGON								
1 Furse	Y	Y	Y	Y	N	Y	Y	N
2 ***Smith***	N	N	N	N	Y	N	N	Y
3 Wyden	Y	Y	Y	Y	N	Y	Y	N
4 DeFazio	Y	Y	Y	Y	N	Y	Y	N
5 Kopetski	Y	Y	Y	Y	N	Y	Y	N
PENNSYLVANIA								
1 Foglietta	Y	Y	Y	Y	N	Y	Y	N
2 Blackwell	Y	Y	Y	Y	N	Y	Y	N
3 Borski	Y	Y	Y	Y	N	Y	Y	N
4 Klink	Y	Y	Y	Y	N	Y	Y	N
5 ***Clinger***	N	N	N	Y	Y	N	N	Y
6 Holden	Y	Y	Y	Y	N	Y	Y	N
7 ***Weldon***	N	N	N	N	Y	N	N	Y
8 ***Greenwood***	N	N	N	N	Y	N	N	Y
9 ***Shuster***	N	N	N	N	Y	N	N	Y
10 ***McDade***	N	N	N	N	Y	?	?	?
11 Kanjorski	Y	Y	Y	Y	N	Y	Y	N
12 Murtha	Y	Y	Y	Y	N	Y	Y	N
13 Margolies-Mezv.	Y	Y	N	Y	N	Y	Y	N
14 Coyne	Y	Y	Y	Y	N	Y	Y	N
15 McHale	Y	Y	Y	Y	N	Y	Y	N
16 ***Walker***	N	N	N	N	Y	N	N	Y
17 ***Gekas***	N	N	N	N	Y	N	N	Y
18 ***Santorum***	N	N	N	N	Y	?	?	?
19 ***Goodling***	N	N	N	N	Y	N	N	Y
20 Murphy	Y	Y	Y	N	N	Y	Y	N
21 ***Ridge***	N	N	N	N	Y	N	N	Y
RHODE ISLAND								
1 ***Machtley***	N	N	N	N	Y	N	N	Y
2 Reed	Y	Y	Y	Y	N	Y	Y	N
SOUTH CAROLINA								
1 ***Ravenel***	N	N	N	N	Y	N	N	Y
2 ***Spence***	N	N	N	N	Y	N	N	Y
3 Derrick	Y	Y	Y	Y	N	Y	Y	N
4 ***Inglis***	N	N	N	Y	Y	N	N	Y
5 Spratt	Y	Y	Y	Y	N	Y	Y	N
6 Clyburn	?	?	Y	?	?	Y	Y	N
SOUTH DAKOTA								
AL Johnson	Y	Y	Y	Y	N	Y	Y	N
TENNESSEE								
1 ***Quillen***	?	?	?	?	#	?	?	?
2 ***Duncan***	N	N	N	N	Y	N	N	Y
3 Lloyd	Y	Y	Y	?	Y	Y	Y	N
4 Cooper	Y	Y	Y	Y	N	Y	Y	N
5 Clement	Y	Y	Y	Y	N	Y	Y	N

	125	126	127	128	129	130	131	132
6 Gordon	Y	Y	Y	Y	N	Y	Y	N
7 ***Sundquist***	N	N	N	N	Y	N	N	Y
8 Tanner	Y	Y	Y	Y	Y	Y	N	N
9 Ford	?	?	?	?	?	?	?	?
TEXAS								
1 Chapman	Y	Y	Y	Y	N	Y	Y	N
2 Wilson	Y	Y	Y	Y	N	Y	Y	N
3 ***Johnson, Sam***	N	N	N	N	Y	N	N	Y
4 Hall	Y	Y	N	Y	N	Y	Y	N
5 Bryant	Y	Y	Y	Y	N	Y	Y	N
6 ***Barton***	?	?	?	N	Y	N	N	Y
7 ***Archer***	N	N	N	Y	Y	N	N	Y
8 ***Fields***	N	N	N	N	?	?	?	?
9 Brooks	Y	?	Y	Y	N	Y	Y	N
10 Pickle	Y	Y	Y	Y	N	Y	Y	N
11 Edwards	Y	Y	Y	Y	N	Y	Y	N
12 Geren	Y	Y	N	Y	N	Y	Y	N
13 Sarpalius	Y	Y	Y	Y	N	Y	Y	N
14 Laughlin	Y	Y	Y	Y	N	Y	Y	N
15 de la Garza	Y	Y	Y	Y	N	Y	Y	N
16 Coleman	Y	Y	Y	Y	N	Y	Y	N
17 Stenholm	Y	Y	Y	Y	Y	Y	Y	N
18 Washington	Y	Y	Y	?	N	Y	Y	N
19 ***Combest***	N	N	N	Y	Y	N	N	Y
20 Gonzalez	Y	Y	Y	Y	N	Y	Y	N
21 ***Smith***	N	N	N	N	Y	?	?	?
22 ***DeLay***	N	N	N	N	Y	N	N	Y
23 ***Bonilla***	N	N	N	N	Y	N	N	Y
24 Frost	Y	Y	Y	Y	N	Y	Y	N
25 Andrews	Y	Y	Y	Y	N	Y	Y	N
26 ***Armey***	N	N	N	N	Y	N	N	Y
27 Ortiz	Y	Y	Y	Y	N	Y	?	N
28 Tejeda	Y	Y	Y	Y	N	Y	Y	N
29 Green	Y	Y	Y	Y	N	Y	Y	N
30 Johnson, E. B.	Y	Y	Y	Y	N	Y	Y	N
UTAH								
1 ***Hansen***	N	N	N	N	Y	N	N	Y
2 Shepherd	Y	Y	Y	Y	N	Y	Y	N
3 Orton	Y	Y	Y	Y	Y	Y	Y	N
VERMONT								
AL *Sanders*	Y	Y	Y	?	N	Y	Y	N
VIRGINIA								
1 ***Bateman***	N	N	N	Y	Y	N	N	Y
2 Pickett	Y	Y	N	Y	N	Y	Y	N
3 Scott	Y	Y	Y	Y	N	Y	Y	N
4 Sisisky	Y	Y	N	Y	N	Y	Y	N
5 Payne	Y	Y	Y	Y	N	Y	Y	N
6 ***Goodlatte***	N	N	N	N	Y	N	N	Y
7 ***Bliley***	N	N	N	?	?	N	N	Y
8 Moran	Y	Y	Y	Y	N	Y	Y	N
9 Boucher	Y	Y	Y	Y	N	Y	Y	N
10 ***Wolf***	N	N	N	N	Y	N	N	Y
11 Byrne	Y	Y	Y	Y	N	Y	Y	N
WASHINGTON								
1 Cantwell	Y	Y	Y	Y	N	Y	Y	N
2 Swift	Y	Y	Y	Y	N	Y	Y	N
3 Unsoeld	Y	Y	Y	Y	N	Y	Y	N
4 Inslee	Y	Y	Y	Y	N	Y	Y	N
5 Foley								
6 Dicks	Y	Y	Y	Y	N	Y	Y	N
7 McDermott	Y	Y	Y	Y	N	Y	Y	N
8 ***Dunn***	N	N	N	N	Y	N	N	Y
9 Kreidler	Y	Y	Y	Y	N	Y	Y	N
WEST VIRGINIA								
1 Mollohan	Y	Y	Y	Y	N	Y	Y	N
2 Wise	Y	Y	Y	Y	?	Y	Y	N
3 Rahall	Y	Y	Y	?	?	?	?	?
WISCONSIN								
1 Vacancy								
2 ***Klug***	N	N	N	N	Y	N	N	Y
3 ***Gunderson***	N	N	N	Y	Y	N	N	Y
4 Kleczka	Y	Y	Y	Y	N	Y	Y	N
5 Barrett	Y	Y	Y	Y	N	Y	Y	N
6 ***Petri***	N	N	N	N	Y	N	N	Y
7 Obey	Y	Y	Y	Y	N	Y	Y	N
8 ***Roth***	N	N	N	N	Y	N	N	Y
9 ***Sensenbrenner***	N	N	N	N	Y	N	N	Y
WYOMING								
AL ***Thomas***	N	N	N	N	Y	N	N	Y
DELEGATES								
de Lugo, V.I.	D	D	D	D	D	D	D	D
Faleomavaega, Am.S.	D	D	D	D	D	D	D	D
Norton, D.C.	D	D	D	D	D	D	D	D
Romero-B., P.R.	D	D	D	D	D	D	D	D
Underwood, Guam	D	D	D	D	D	D	D	D

Southern states - Ala., Ark., Fla., Ga., Ky., La., Miss., N.C., Okla., S.C., Tenn., Texas, Va.
Omitted votes are quorum calls, which CQ does not include in its vote charts.

KEY

Y   Voted for (yea).
\#   Paired for.
\+   Announced for.
N   Voted against (nay).
X   Paired against.
\-   Announced against.
P   Voted "present."
C   Voted "present" to avoid possible conflict of interest.
?   Did not vote or otherwise make a position known.
D   Delegates ineligible to vote.

Democrats   *Republicans*
Independent

133. HR 1430. Temporary Debt Limit Increase/Passage. Passage of the bill to temporarily increase the public debt limit by $225 billion from $4.145 trillion to $4.370 trillion through Sept. 30, 1993, to provide sufficient borrowing authority for the federal government to meet its obligations. Passed 237-177: R 2-165; D 234-12 (ND 159-6, SD 75-6); I 1-0, April 2, 1993. A "yea" was a vote in support of the president's position.

134. Procedural Motion. Approval of the Journal of Thursday, April 1. Approved 237-155: R 11-149; D 226-6 (ND 152-5, SD 74-1); I 0-0, April 2, 1993.

* 136. Procedural Motion. Approval of the Journal of Monday, April 19. Approved 242-137: R 20-133; D 222-4 (ND 146-3, SD 76-1); I 0-0, April 20, 1993.

137. S 328. Gateway National Recreation Area Rehabilitation/Passage. Vento, D-Minn., motion to suspend the rules and pass the bill to authorize the use of federal lands within the Gateway National Recreation Area in Monmouth County, N.J., by the Marine Academy of Science and Technology. Motion agreed to (thus clearing the bill for the president) 410-0: R 166-0; D 243-0 (ND 163-0, SD 80-0); I 1-0, April 20, 1993. A two-thirds majority of those present and voting (274 in this case) is required for passage under suspension of the rules.

138. S 326. Washington Birthplace National Monument/Passage. Vento, D-Minn., motion to suspend the rules and pass the bill to expand the boundaries of the George Washington Birthplace National Monument in Westmoreland County, Va., and to provide for the administration of the monument. Motion agreed to 314-93: R 79-85; D 234-8 (ND 159-3, SD 75-5); I 1-0, April 20, 1993. A two-thirds majority of those present and voting (272 in this case) is required for passage under suspension of the rules.

139. Procedural Motion. Approval of the Journal of Tuesday, April 20. Approved 256-153: R 19-149; D 236-4 (ND 156-3, SD 80-1); I 1-0, April 21, 1993.

140. HR 328. Taos Land Conveyance/Passage. Vento, D-Minn., motion to suspend the rules and pass the bill to convey the Old Taos Ranger District Office and Warehouse in Taos, N.M., from the Forest Service to the town of Taos at fair market value. Motion agreed to 420-0: R 168-0; D 251-0 (ND 168-0, SD 83-0); I 1-0, April 21, 1993. A two-thirds majority of those present and voting (280 in this case) is required for passage under suspension of the rules.

141. HR 38. Jemez National Recreation Area/Passage. Vento, D-Minn., motion to suspend the rules and pass the bill to authorize such sums as necessary to establish the Jemez National Recreation Area within the Santa Fe National Forest in New Mexico. Motion agreed to 363-57: R 117-51; D 245-6 (ND 167-1, SD 78-5); I 1-0, April 21, 1993. A two-thirds majority of those present and voting (280 in this case) is required for passage under suspension of the rules.

* Omitted votes are quorum calls, which CQ does not include in its vote charts.

** Bennie Thompson, D-Miss., was sworn in April 20. The first vote for which he was eligible was vote 137.

	133	134	136	137	138	139	140	141
ALABAMA								
1 *Callahan*	N	N	N	Y	Y	N	Y	Y
2 *Everett*	N	N	N	Y	N	N	Y	N
3 Browder	Y	Y	Y	Y	Y	Y	Y	Y
4 Bevill	Y	Y	Y	Y	Y	Y	Y	Y
5 Cramer	Y	Y	Y	Y	Y	Y	Y	Y
6 *Bachus*	N	N	N	Y	N	N	Y	Y
7 Hilliard	Y	Y	Y	Y	Y	Y	Y	Y
ALASKA								
AL *Young*	N	?	N	Y	Y	N	Y	N
ARIZONA								
1 Coppersmith	Y	Y	Y	Y	Y	Y	Y	Y
2 Pastor	Y	Y	Y	Y	Y	Y	Y	Y
3 *Stump*	N	N	N	Y	N	N	Y	N
4 *Kyl*	N	N	N	Y	N	N	Y	N
5 *Kolbe*	N	N	N	Y	N	N	Y	Y
6 English	Y	Y	Y	Y	Y	Y	Y	Y
ARKANSAS								
1 Lambert	Y	Y	Y	Y	N	?	Y	Y
2 Thornton	Y	Y	Y	Y	Y	Y	Y	Y
3 *Hutchinson*	N	N	N	Y	Y	N	Y	N
4 *Dickey*	N	N	N	Y	Y	N	Y	Y
CALIFORNIA								
1 Hamburg	Y	Y	Y	Y	Y	Y	Y	Y
2 *Herger*	N	N	N	Y	N	N	Y	Y
3 Fazio	Y	Y	Y	Y	Y	Y	Y	Y
4 *Doolittle*	N	N	N	Y	N	N	Y	N
5 Matsui	Y	Y	Y	Y	Y	Y	Y	Y
6 Woolsey	Y	Y	Y	Y	Y	Y	Y	Y
7 Miller	Y	Y	Y	Y	Y	Y	Y	Y
8 Pelosi	Y	?	Y	Y	Y	Y	Y	Y
9 Dellums	Y	Y	Y	Y	Y	Y	Y	Y
10 *Baker*	N	N	N	Y	N	N	Y	N
11 *Pombo*	?	?	Y	Y	N	Y	Y	Y
12 Lantos	?	?	?	?	?	?	Y	Y
13 Stark	Y	Y	Y	Y	Y	Y	Y	Y
14 Eshoo	Y	Y	?	Y	Y	Y	Y	Y
15 Mineta	Y	Y	Y	Y	Y	Y	Y	Y
16 Edwards	Y	Y	?	Y	Y	?	Y	Y
17 Vacancy								
18 Condit	N	Y	Y	Y	Y	Y	Y	Y
19 Lehman	Y	Y	Y	Y	Y	Y	Y	Y
20 Dooley	Y	Y	Y	Y	Y	Y	Y	Y
21 *Thomas*	N	N	N	Y	N	N	Y	Y
22 *Huffington*	N	?	N	Y	N	N	Y	N
23 *Gallegly*	N	N	N	Y	N	N	Y	Y
24 Beilenson	Y	?	Y	Y	Y	Y	Y	Y
25 *McKeon*	N	N	N	Y	N	N	Y	N
26 Berman	Y	Y	Y	Y	Y	Y	Y	Y
27 *Moorhead*	N	N	N	Y	N	N	Y	N
28 *Dreier*	N	N	N	Y	N	N	Y	Y
29 Waxman	Y	Y	Y	Y	Y	?	Y	Y
30 Becerra	Y	Y	Y	Y	Y	Y	Y	Y
31 Martinez	Y	Y	Y	Y	Y	Y	Y	Y
32 Dixon	Y	Y	Y	Y	Y	Y	Y	Y
33 Roybal-Allard	Y	Y	Y	Y	Y	Y	Y	Y
34 Torres	Y	Y	?	?	Y	Y	Y	Y
35 Waters	Y	Y	?	Y	Y	Y	Y	Y
36 Harman	Y	Y	Y	Y	Y	Y	Y	Y
37 Tucker	Y	?	Y	Y	Y	Y	Y	Y
38 *Horn*	N	N	N	Y	N	N	Y	Y
39 *Royce*	N	N	N	Y	N	N	Y	N
40 *Lewis*	N	N	N	Y	N	N	Y	Y
41 *Kim*	N	N	N	Y	N	N	Y	Y

	133	134	136	137	138	139	140	141
42 Brown	Y	?	?	Y	Y	?	Y	Y
43 *Calvert*	N	N	N	Y	N	N	Y	Y
44 *McCandless*	N	N	N	Y	N	N	Y	Y
45 *Rohrabacher*	N	N	N	Y	N	N	Y	N
46 *Dornan*	N	N	?	Y	N	N	Y	N
47 *Cox*	N	N	N	Y	N	N	Y	Y
48 *Packard*	N	N	N	Y	N	N	Y	Y
49 *Schenk*	N	Y	Y	Y	Y	Y	Y	Y
50 Filner	Y	Y	Y	Y	Y	Y	Y	Y
51 *Cunningham*	N	N	N	Y	N	N	+	–
52 *Hunter*	N	N	?	Y	N	?	?	?
COLORADO								
1 Schroeder	Y	N	N	Y	N	Y	Y	Y
2 Skaggs	Y	Y	Y	Y	Y	Y	Y	Y
3 *McInnis*	N	N	Y	Y	Y	N	Y	Y
4 *Allard*	N	N	?	Y	Y	N	Y	N
5 *Hefley*	N	N	N	Y	N	N	Y	Y
6 *Schaefer*	N	N	N	Y	N	N	Y	N
CONNECTICUT								
1 Kennelly	Y	Y	Y	Y	Y	Y	Y	Y
2 Gejdenson	Y	Y	Y	Y	Y	Y	Y	Y
3 DeLauro	Y	Y	Y	Y	Y	Y	Y	Y
4 *Shays*	N	N	N	Y	N	N	Y	Y
5 *Franks*	N	N	N	Y	N	Y	Y	Y
6 *Johnson*	N	N	?	Y	N	N	Y	Y
DELAWARE								
AL *Castle*	N	N	N	Y	N	Y	Y	Y
FLORIDA								
1 Hutto	Y	Y	Y	Y	Y	Y	Y	Y
2 Peterson	Y	Y	Y	Y	Y	Y	Y	Y
3 Brown	Y	Y	Y	Y	Y	Y	Y	Y
4 *Fowler*	?	?	N	Y	N	N	Y	Y
5 Thurman	Y	Y	Y	Y	Y	Y	Y	Y
6 *Stearns*	N	N	Y	N	N	N	Y	N
7 *Mica*	N	N	N	Y	N	N	Y	Y
8 *McCollum*	N	N	N	Y	N	Y	Y	Y
9 *Bilirakis*	N	N	?	?	?	N	Y	Y
10 *Young*	N	?	N	Y	N	N	Y	Y
11 Gibbons	Y	Y	Y	Y	Y	Y	Y	Y
12 *Canady*	N	N	N	Y	?	N	Y	Y
13 *Miller*	N	N	N	Y	N	N	Y	N
14 *Goss*	N	N	N	Y	N	N	Y	Y
15 *Bacchus*	Y	Y	Y	Y	Y	Y	Y	Y
16 *Lewis*	N	N	N	Y	N	N	Y	N
17 Meek	Y	Y	Y	Y	Y	Y	Y	Y
18 *Ros-Lehtinen*	N	?	N	Y	N	Y	Y	Y
19 Johnston	Y	Y	Y	Y	Y	Y	Y	Y
20 Deutsch	Y	Y	+	Y	Y	Y	Y	Y
21 *Diaz-Balart*	N	N	N	Y	N	Y	Y	Y
22 *Shaw*	N	N	?	Y	Y	N	Y	Y
23 Hastings	Y	Y	Y	Y	Y	Y	Y	Y
GEORGIA								
1 *Kingston*	N	N	?	Y	N	N	Y	Y
2 Bishop	Y	Y	Y	Y	Y	Y	Y	Y
3 *Collins*	N	N	N	Y	N	N	Y	N
4 *Linder*	N	N	N	Y	N	N	Y	Y
5 Lewis	Y	Y	Y	Y	Y	Y	Y	Y
6 *Gingrich*	N	N	N	Y	N	Y	Y	Y
7 Darden	Y	Y	Y	Y	Y	Y	Y	Y
8 Rowland	Y	Y	Y	Y	Y	Y	Y	Y
9 Deal	Y	Y	Y	Y	Y	Y	Y	Y
10 Johnson	Y	Y	Y	Y	Y	Y	Y	Y
11 McKinney	Y	Y	Y	Y	Y	Y	Y	Y
HAWAII								
1 Abercrombie	Y	Y	Y	Y	Y	Y	Y	Y
2 Mink	Y	Y	Y	Y	Y	Y	Y	Y
IDAHO								
1 LaRocco	Y	Y	Y	Y	Y	Y	Y	Y
2 *Crapo*	N	N	N	Y	N	N	Y	N
ILLINOIS								
1 Rush	Y	Y	Y	Y	Y	Y	Y	Y
2 Reynolds	Y	Y	Y	Y	Y	Y	Y	Y
3 Lipinski	Y	Y	Y	Y	Y	Y	Y	Y
4 Gutierrez	Y	Y	Y	Y	Y	?	Y	Y
5 Rostenkowski	Y	Y	?	Y	Y	Y	Y	Y
6 *Hyde*	N	N	?	Y	N	N	Y	Y
7 Collins	Y	Y	Y	Y	Y	Y	Y	Y
8 *Crane*	N	N	N	Y	N	N	Y	N
9 Yates	Y	Y	?	Y	Y	Y	Y	Y
10 *Porter*	N	N	N	Y	N	N	Y	Y
11 Sangmeister	Y	Y	Y	Y	Y	Y	Y	Y
12 Costello	Y	Y	Y	Y	Y	Y	Y	Y
13 *Fawell*	N	N	N	Y	N	N	Y	Y
14 *Hastert*	N	N	N	Y	N	N	Y	N
15 *Ewing*	N	N	N	Y	N	N	Y	Y
16 *Manzullo*	N	N	N	Y	N	N	Y	N
17 Evans	Y	Y	Y	Y	Y	Y	Y	Y

ND Northern Democrats   SD Southern Democrats

	133	134	136	137	138	139	140	141
18 ***Michel***	?	N	N	Y	N	N	Y	N
19 Poshard	Y	Y	Y	Y	Y	Y	Y	Y
20 Durbin	Y	Y	Y	Y	Y	Y	Y	Y
INDIANA								
1 Visclosky	Y	Y	Y	Y	Y	Y	Y	Y
2 Sharp	Y	Y	Y	Y	Y	Y	Y	Y
3 Roemer	Y	Y	Y	Y	Y	Y	Y	Y
4 Long	Y	Y	Y	Y	Y	Y	Y	Y
5 ***Buyer***	N	N	N	Y	Y	N	Y	N
6 ***Burton***	N	N	N	Y	N	N	Y	N
7 ***Myers***	N	Y	Y	Y	N	Y	Y	N
8 McCloskey	Y	Y	Y	Y	Y	Y	Y	Y
9 Hamilton	Y	Y	Y	Y	Y	Y	Y	Y
10 Jacobs	N	N	N	Y	Y	N	Y	Y
IOWA								
1 ***Leach***	N	N	N	Y	Y	N	Y	Y
2 ***Nussle***	N	N	N	Y	N	N	Y	Y
3 ***Lightfoot***	N	N	N	Y	N	N	Y	N
4 Smith	Y	?	Y	Y	Y	Y	Y	Y
5 ***Grandy***	N	N	N	Y	Y	N	Y	Y
KANSAS								
1 ***Roberts***	N	N	N	Y	Y	N	Y	Y
2 Slattery	Y	Y	Y	Y	N	Y	Y	Y
3 ***Meyers***	N	N	N	Y	Y	N	Y	Y
4 Glickman	Y	Y	Y	Y	Y	Y	Y	Y
KENTUCKY								
1 Barlow	Y	Y	Y	Y	Y	Y	Y	Y
2 Natcher	Y	Y	Y	Y	Y	Y	Y	Y
3 Mazzoli	Y	Y	Y	Y	Y	Y	Y	Y
4 ***Bunning***	N	N	N	Y	Y	N	Y	Y
5 ***Rogers***	N	N	N	Y	Y	N	Y	Y
6 Baesler	Y	Y	Y	Y	Y	Y	Y	Y
LOUISIANA								
1 ***Livingston***	N	N	N	Y	Y	N	Y	Y
2 Jefferson	Y	Y	Y	Y	Y	Y	Y	Y
3 Tauzin	N	Y	Y	Y	Y	Y	Y	Y
4 Fields	Y	Y	Y	Y	Y	Y	Y	Y
5 ***McCrery***	N	N	Y	Y	Y	Y	Y	Y
6 ***Baker***	N	N	N	Y	N	N	Y	Y
7 Hayes	Y	Y	Y	Y	Y	Y	Y	Y
MAINE								
1 Andrews	Y	Y	Y	Y	Y	Y	Y	Y
2 ***Snowe***	N	N	N	Y	Y	Y	Y	Y
MARYLAND								
1 ***Gilchrest***	N	N	N	Y	Y	N	Y	Y
2 ***Bentley***	N	N	N	Y	N	N	Y	Y
3 Cardin	Y	Y	Y	Y	Y	Y	Y	Y
4 Wynn	Y	Y	Y	Y	Y	Y	Y	Y
5 Hoyer	Y	Y	Y	Y	Y	Y	Y	Y
6 ***Bartlett***	N	N	N	Y	N	N	Y	N
7 Mfume	Y	Y	Y	Y	Y	Y	Y	Y
8 ***Morella***	Y	?	?	Y	Y	N	Y	Y
MASSACHUSETTS								
1 Olver	Y	Y	Y	Y	Y	Y	Y	Y
2 Neal	Y	Y	Y	Y	Y	Y	Y	Y
3 ***Blute***	N	N	N	Y	Y	N	Y	Y
4 Frank	Y	Y	?	Y	Y	Y	Y	Y
5 Meehan	Y	Y	Y	Y	Y	Y	Y	Y
6 ***Torkildsen***	N	N	N	Y	Y	N	Y	Y
7 Markey	Y	Y	Y	Y	Y	Y	Y	Y
8 Kennedy	Y	Y	Y	Y	Y	Y	Y	Y
9 Moakley	Y	Y	Y	Y	Y	Y	Y	Y
10 Studds	Y	Y	Y	Y	Y	Y	Y	Y
MICHIGAN								
1 Stupak	Y	Y	Y	Y	Y	Y	Y	Y
2 ***Hoekstra***	N	N	N	Y	N	N	Y	N
3 Henry	?	?	?	?	?	?	?	?
4 ***Camp***	N	N	N	Y	Y	N	Y	Y
5 Barcia	Y	Y	Y	Y	Y	Y	Y	Y
6 ***Upton***	N	N	N	Y	Y	N	Y	Y
7 ***Smith***	N	N	N	Y	?	N	Y	N
8 Carr	Y	Y	?	Y	Y	Y	Y	Y
9 Kildee	Y	Y	Y	Y	Y	Y	Y	Y
10 Bonior	Y	Y	Y	Y	Y	Y	Y	Y
11 ***Knollenberg***	N	N	N	Y	N	N	Y	N
12 Levin	Y	Y	Y	Y	Y	Y	Y	Y
13 Ford	Y	?	?	Y	Y	Y	Y	Y
14 Conyers	Y	Y	?	?	?	Y	Y	Y
15 Collins	Y	Y	Y	Y	Y	Y	Y	Y
16 Dingell	Y	?	Y	Y	Y	Y	Y	Y
MINNESOTA								
1 Penny	Y	Y	Y	Y	N	Y	Y	N
2 Minge	N	Y	Y	Y	Y	Y	Y	Y
3 ***Ramstad***	N	N	N	Y	N	N	Y	N
4 Vento	Y	Y	Y	Y	Y	?	Y	Y
5 Sabo	Y	Y	Y	Y	Y	Y	Y	Y
6 ***Grams***	N	N	N	Y	Y	N	Y	Y
7 Peterson	Y	Y	Y	Y	Y	Y	Y	Y
8 Oberstar	Y	Y	Y	Y	Y	Y	Y	Y
MISSISSIPPI								
1 Whitten	?	?	Y	Y	Y	Y	Y	Y
2 Thompson **				Y	Y	Y	Y	Y
3 Montgomery	Y	Y	Y	Y	Y	Y	Y	Y
4 Parker	Y	Y	Y	Y	Y	Y	Y	Y
5 Taylor	N	N	N	Y	Y	N	Y	Y
MISSOURI								
1 Clay	Y	N	?	?	?	?	?	?
2 ***Talent***	N	N	N	Y	Y	N	Y	Y
3 Gephardt	Y	Y	?	Y	Y	Y	Y	Y
4 Skelton	Y	Y	Y	Y	Y	Y	Y	Y
5 Wheat	Y	Y	Y	Y	Y	Y	Y	Y
6 Danner	Y	Y	Y	Y	Y	Y	Y	Y
7 ***Hancock***	N	N	N	Y	N	N	Y	N
8 ***Emerson***	N	N	N	?	Y	N	Y	Y
9 Volkmer	Y	Y	Y	Y	Y	Y	Y	Y
MONTANA								
AL Williams	Y	Y	?	Y	Y	Y	Y	Y
NEBRASKA								
1 ***Bereuter***	N	N	N	Y	Y	N	Y	Y
2 Hoagland	Y	Y	Y	Y	Y	Y	Y	Y
3 ***Barrett***	N	N	N	Y	N	N	Y	Y
NEVADA								
1 Bilbray	Y	Y	Y	Y	Y	Y	Y	Y
2 ***Vucanovich***	N	N	N	Y	N	N	Y	N
NEW HAMPSHIRE								
1 ***Zeliff***	N	N	N	Y	N	N	Y	N
2 Swett	?	?	Y	Y	Y	Y	Y	Y
NEW JERSEY								
1 Andrews	Y	Y	?	Y	Y	Y	Y	Y
2 Hughes	Y	Y	Y	Y	Y	Y	Y	Y
3 ***Saxton***	N	N	N	Y	N	N	Y	Y
4 ***Smith***	N	?	N	Y	Y	N	Y	Y
5 ***Roukema***	Y	N	N	Y	Y	N	Y	Y
6 Pallone	Y	Y	Y	Y	Y	Y	Y	Y
7 ***Franks***	N	N	N	Y	Y	N	Y	Y
8 Klein	Y	Y	Y	Y	Y	Y	Y	Y
9 Torricelli	Y	Y	Y	Y	Y	Y	Y	Y
10 Payne	Y	Y	Y	Y	Y	Y	Y	Y
11 ***Gallo***	N	N	N	Y	Y	N	Y	Y
12 ***Zimmer***	N	N	N	Y	N	N	Y	Y
13 Menendez	Y	Y	Y	Y	Y	Y	Y	Y
NEW MEXICO								
1 ***Schiff***	N	N	N	Y	Y	N	Y	Y
2 ***Skeen***	N	N	N	Y	Y	N	Y	Y
3 Richardson	Y	Y	?	?	?	Y	Y	Y
NEW YORK								
1 Hochbrueckner	Y	Y	Y	Y	Y	Y	Y	Y
2 ***Lazio***	N	N	N	Y	N	N	Y	Y
3 ***King***	N	N	N	Y	N	N	Y	Y
4 ***Levy***	N	N	N	Y	N	N	Y	Y
5 Ackerman	Y	Y	Y	Y	Y	Y	Y	Y
6 Flake	Y	Y	Y	Y	Y	Y	Y	Y
7 Manton	Y	?	Y	Y	Y	Y	Y	Y
8 Nadler	Y	Y	Y	Y	Y	?	Y	Y
9 Schumer	Y	Y	Y	Y	Y	Y	Y	Y
10 Towns	Y	Y	?	Y	Y	Y	Y	Y
11 Owens	Y	Y	Y	Y	?	Y	?	?
12 Velazquez	Y	Y	Y	Y	Y	Y	Y	Y
13 ***Molinari***	N	N	N	Y	Y	N	Y	Y
14 Maloney	Y	Y	Y	Y	Y	Y	Y	Y
15 Rangel	Y	Y	Y	Y	Y	Y	Y	Y
16 Serrano	Y	Y	Y	Y	Y	Y	Y	Y
17 Engel	Y	Y	?	?	?	Y	Y	Y
18 Lowey	Y	Y	Y	Y	Y	?	Y	Y
19 ***Fish***	N	Y	Y	Y	Y	Y	Y	Y
20 ***Gilman***	N	Y	Y	Y	Y	Y	Y	Y
21 McNulty	Y	Y	Y	Y	Y	Y	Y	Y
22 ***Solomon***	N	N	N	Y	N	?	Y	Y
23 ***Boehlert***	N	N	N	Y	Y	N	Y	Y
24 ***McHugh***	N	N	N	Y	Y	N	Y	Y
25 ***Walsh***	N	N	N	Y	Y	N	?	?
26 Hinchey	Y	Y	Y	Y	Y	Y	Y	Y
27 ***Paxon***	N	N	N	Y	Y	N	Y	Y
28 Slaughter	Y	Y	Y	Y	Y	Y	Y	Y
29 LaFalce	+	+	Y	Y	Y	Y	Y	Y
30 ***Quinn***	N	N	?	Y	Y	N	Y	Y
31 ***Houghton***	N	Y	?	?	?	Y	Y	Y
NORTH CAROLINA								
1 Clayton	Y	Y	Y	Y	Y	Y	Y	Y
2 Valentine	Y	Y	Y	Y	Y	Y	Y	Y
3 Lancaster	Y	Y	Y	Y	Y	Y	Y	Y
4 Price	Y	Y	Y	Y	Y	Y	Y	Y
5 Neal	N	?	Y	Y	Y	Y	Y	Y
6 ***Coble***	N	N	N	Y	N	N	Y	N
7 Rose	Y	Y	Y	Y	Y	Y	Y	Y
8 Hefner	Y	Y	Y	Y	Y	?	?	?
9 ***McMillan***	N	N	N	Y	Y	N	Y	Y
10 ***Ballenger***	N	N	N	Y	N	N	Y	N
11 ***Taylor***	N	N	N	Y	N	N	Y	N
12 Watt	Y	Y	Y	Y	Y	Y	Y	Y
NORTH DAKOTA								
AL Pomeroy	Y	Y	Y	Y	Y	Y	Y	Y
OHIO								
1 Mann	Y	Y	Y	Y	Y	Y	Y	Y
2 Vacancy								
3 Hall	Y	Y	Y	Y	Y	?	Y	Y
4 ***Oxley***	N	N	N	Y	Y	N	Y	Y
5 ***Gillmor***	N	Y	Y	Y	Y	Y	Y	Y
6 Strickland	Y	Y	Y	Y	Y	Y	Y	Y
7 ***Hobson***	N	N	N	Y	Y	N	Y	Y
8 ***Boehner***	N	N	N	Y	Y	N	Y	Y
9 Kaptur	Y	Y	Y	Y	Y	Y	Y	Y
10 ***Hoke***	N	?	?	Y	?	N	Y	Y
11 Stokes	Y	N	Y	Y	Y	Y	Y	Y
12 ***Kasich***	N	Y	Y	Y	N	Y	Y	Y
13 Brown	?	Y	Y	Y	Y	Y	Y	Y
14 Sawyer	Y	Y	Y	Y	Y	Y	Y	Y
15 ***Pryce***	N	N	N	Y	Y	N	Y	Y
16 ***Regula***	N	N	N	Y	Y	N	Y	Y
17 Traficant	N	Y	Y	Y	Y	Y	Y	Y
18 Applegate	Y	Y	Y	Y	Y	Y	Y	Y
19 Fingerhut	Y	Y	Y	Y	Y	Y	Y	Y
OKLAHOMA								
1 ***Inhofe***	N	N	?	Y	N	N	Y	Y
2 Synar	Y	Y	Y	Y	Y	Y	Y	Y
3 Brewster	Y	Y	Y	Y	Y	?	Y	Y
4 McCurdy	?	?	Y	Y	Y	Y	Y	Y
5 ***Istook***	N	N	N	Y	Y	N	Y	N
6 English	N	Y	Y	Y	Y	Y	Y	Y
OREGON								
1 Furse	Y	Y	Y	Y	Y	Y	Y	Y
2 ***Smith***	N	N	N	Y	N	N	Y	Y
3 Wyden	Y	Y	Y	Y	Y	Y	Y	Y
4 DeFazio	N	?	Y	Y	Y	Y	Y	Y
5 Kopetski	Y	Y	Y	Y	Y	Y	Y	Y
PENNSYLVANIA								
1 Foglietta	Y	Y	?	Y	Y	Y	Y	Y
2 Blackwell	Y	Y	Y	Y	Y	Y	Y	Y
3 Borski	Y	Y	Y	Y	Y	Y	Y	Y
4 Klink	Y	Y	Y	Y	Y	Y	Y	Y
5 ***Clinger***	N	N	Y	Y	Y	Y	Y	Y
6 Holden	Y	Y	Y	Y	Y	Y	Y	Y
7 ***Weldon***	N	N	N	Y	N	N	Y	Y
8 ***Greenwood***	N	N	N	Y	Y	?	Y	Y
9 ***Shuster***	N	N	N	Y	N	N	Y	Y
10 ***McDade***	?	N	N	Y	Y	N	Y	Y
11 Kanjorski	Y	Y	Y	Y	Y	Y	Y	Y
12 Murtha	Y	Y	Y	Y	Y	Y	Y	Y
13 Margolies-Mezv.	Y	Y	Y	Y	Y	Y	Y	Y
14 Coyne	Y	Y	Y	Y	Y	Y	Y	Y
15 McHale	Y	Y	Y	Y	Y	Y	Y	Y
16 ***Walker***	N	N	N	Y	N	N	Y	N
17 ***Gekas***	N	N	?	Y	N	N	Y	N
18 ***Santorum***	N	N	Y	Y	N	Y	Y	Y
19 ***Goodling***	N	N	N	Y	N	N	Y	N
20 Murphy	Y	N	N	Y	Y	N	Y	Y
21 ***Ridge***	N	N	N	Y	Y	N	Y	Y
RHODE ISLAND								
1 ***Machtley***	N	N	?	Y	Y	Y	Y	Y
2 Reed	Y	Y	Y	Y	Y	Y	Y	Y
SOUTH CAROLINA								
1 ***Ravenel***	N	N	?	Y	Y	N	Y	Y
2 ***Spence***	N	N	Y	Y	Y	Y	Y	Y
3 Derrick	Y	Y	Y	Y	Y	Y	Y	Y
4 ***Inglis***	N	Y	Y	Y	N	Y	Y	Y
5 Spratt	Y	Y	Y	Y	Y	Y	Y	Y
6 Clyburn	Y	Y	Y	Y	Y	Y	Y	Y
SOUTH DAKOTA								
AL Johnson	Y	Y	Y	Y	Y	Y	Y	Y
TENNESSEE								
1 ***Quillen***	?	?	?	?	?	?	?	?
2 ***Duncan***	N	N	Y	Y	Y	N	Y	N
3 Lloyd	Y	?	Y	Y	Y	Y	Y	N
4 Cooper	Y	?	Y	Y	Y	Y	Y	Y
5 Clement	Y	Y	Y	Y	Y	Y	Y	N
6 Gordon	Y	Y	Y	Y	Y	Y	Y	Y
7 ***Sundquist***	N	?	?	?	?	N	Y	Y
8 Tanner	N	Y	Y	Y	N	Y	Y	N
9 Ford	?	?	Y	Y	Y	Y	Y	Y
TEXAS								
1 Chapman	Y	?	Y	Y	Y	Y	Y	Y
2 Wilson	Y	Y	Y	?	?	Y	Y	Y
3 ***Johnson, Sam***	N	?	N	Y	N	N	Y	N
4 Hall	N	Y	Y	Y	N	Y	Y	N
5 Bryant	Y	Y	?	Y	Y	Y	Y	Y
6 ***Barton***	N	N	?	?	?	?	?	?
7 ***Archer***	N	Y	Y	Y	N	Y	Y	Y
8 ***Fields***	?	?	?	?	?	?	?	?
9 Brooks	Y	?	?	Y	Y	Y	Y	Y
10 Pickle	Y	Y	Y	Y	Y	Y	Y	Y
11 Edwards	Y	Y	Y	Y	Y	Y	Y	Y
12 Geren	Y	Y	Y	Y	N	Y	Y	Y
13 Sarpalius	Y	Y	Y	Y	Y	Y	Y	Y
14 Laughlin	Y	Y	Y	Y	Y	Y	Y	Y
15 de la Garza	Y	Y	Y	Y	Y	Y	Y	Y
16 Coleman	Y	Y	Y	Y	Y	Y	Y	Y
17 Stenholm	Y	Y	Y	Y	N	Y	Y	N
18 Washington	Y	Y	Y	?	?	Y	Y	Y
19 ***Combest***	N	Y	Y	Y	Y	Y	Y	Y
20 Gonzalez	Y	Y	Y	Y	Y	Y	Y	Y
21 ***Smith***	?	?	N	Y	Y	N	Y	Y
22 ***DeLay***	N	Y	N	Y	N	N	Y	N
23 ***Bonilla***	N	N	N	Y	N	N	Y	Y
24 Frost	Y	?	?	Y	Y	Y	Y	Y
25 Andrews	Y	Y	Y	Y	Y	Y	Y	Y
26 ***Armey***	N	N	N	Y	N	N	Y	Y
27 Ortiz	Y	Y	Y	Y	Y	Y	Y	Y
28 Tejeda	Y	Y	Y	Y	Y	Y	Y	Y
29 Green	Y	Y	Y	+	+	Y	Y	Y
30 Johnson, E. B.	Y	Y	Y	Y	Y	Y	Y	Y
UTAH								
1 ***Hansen***	N	N	N	Y	Y	N	Y	Y
2 Shepherd	Y	Y	Y	Y	Y	Y	Y	Y
3 Orton	Y	Y	Y	Y	N	Y	Y	Y
VERMONT								
AL *Sanders*	Y	?	?	Y	Y	Y	Y	Y
VIRGINIA								
1 ***Bateman***	N	Y	?	Y	Y	Y	Y	Y
2 Pickett	Y	Y	?	Y	Y	Y	Y	Y
3 Scott	Y	Y	?	Y	Y	Y	Y	Y
4 Sisisky	Y	Y	?	Y	Y	?	?	?
5 Payne	Y	Y	Y	Y	Y	Y	Y	Y
6 ***Goodlatte***	N	N	N	Y	Y	N	Y	Y
7 ***Bliley***	N	N	N	Y	Y	N	Y	Y
8 Moran	Y	Y	Y	?	?	Y	Y	Y
9 Boucher	Y	Y	Y	Y	Y	Y	Y	Y
10 ***Wolf***	N	N	N	+	+	N	Y	Y
11 Byrne	Y	Y	Y	?	?	Y	Y	Y
WASHINGTON								
1 Cantwell	Y	Y	Y	Y	Y	Y	Y	Y
2 Swift	Y	Y	Y	Y	Y	Y	Y	Y
3 Unsoeld	Y	Y	?	?	?	Y	Y	Y
4 Inslee	Y	Y	Y	Y	Y	Y	Y	Y
5 Foley								
6 Dicks	Y	Y	Y	Y	Y	Y	Y	Y
7 McDermott	Y	Y	Y	Y	Y	?	Y	Y
8 ***Dunn***	N	N	N	Y	N	N	Y	N
9 Kreidler	Y	Y	Y	Y	Y	Y	Y	Y
WEST VIRGINIA								
1 Mollohan	Y	Y	Y	Y	Y	Y	Y	Y
2 Wise	Y	Y	Y	Y	Y	Y	Y	Y
3 Rahall	?	?	Y	Y	Y	Y	Y	Y
WISCONSIN								
1 Vacancy								
2 ***Klug***	N	N	N	Y	N	N	Y	Y
3 ***Gunderson***	N	N	Y	Y	Y	N	Y	Y
4 Kleczka	Y	Y	Y	Y	Y	Y	Y	Y
5 Barrett	Y	Y	Y	Y	Y	Y	Y	Y
6 ***Petri***	N	N	N	Y	Y	N	Y	Y
7 Obey	Y	Y	Y	Y	Y	Y	Y	Y
8 ***Roth***	N	N	Y	Y	N	N	Y	Y
9 ***Sensenbrenner***	N	N	N	Y	N	N	N	N
WYOMING								
AL ***Thomas***	N	N	N	Y	N	N	Y	Y
DELEGATES								
de Lugo, V.I.	D	D	D	D	D	D	D	D
Faleomavaega, Am.S.	D	D	D	D	D	D	D	D
Norton, D.C.	D	D	D	D	D	D	D	D
Romero-B., P.R.	D	D	D	D	D	D	D	D
Underwood, Guam	D	D	D	D	D	D	D	D

Southern states - Ala., Ark., Fla., Ga., Ky., La., Miss., N.C., Okla., S.C., Tenn., Texas, Va.
Omitted votes are quorum calls, which CQ does not include in its vote charts.

142. HR 1335. Fiscal 1993 Supplemental Appropriations/Concur in Senate Amendment. Natcher, D-Ky., motion to concur in the Senate amendment to eliminate all of the House provisions implementing the administration's economic stimulus package except for the $4 billion for extended unemployment benefits. The funds are designated as emergency spending and thus exempt from the spending caps of the 1990 budget agreement. Motion agreed to (thus clearing the bill for the president) 301-114: R 69-99; D 231-15 (ND 161-3, SD 70-12); I 1-0, April 22, 1993.

143. Procedural Motion. Approval of the Journal of Tuesday, April 27. Approved 253-149: R 18-144; D 234-5 (ND 157-5, SD 77-0); I 1-0, April 28, 1993.

144. HR 1578. Expedited Rescissions/Rule. Adoption of the rule (H Res 149) to provide for House floor consideration of the bill to allow the president to propose to rescind any part of an appropriations bill and require Congress to vote on that rescission proposal within a specified period. The bill would expire two years after enactment. Adopted 212-208: R 2-165; D 210-42 (ND 138-30, SD 72-12); I 0-1, April 28, 1993.

145. HR 1578. Expedited Rescission Authority/Tax Benefits. Michel, R-Ill., amendment to the Castle, R-Del., substitute amendment, to allow the president to veto targeted tax benefits in revenue bills. Adopted in the Committee of the Whole 257-157: R 170-0; D 87-156 (ND 56-104, SD 31-52); I 0-1, April 29, 1993. (Subsequently, the Castle substitute was rejected. See vote 146.)

146. HR 1578. Expedited Rescission Authority/Disapproval Procedures. Castle, R-Del., substitute amendment to require that a proposed presidential rescission take effect unless both chambers passed a motion of disapproval (which could be vetoed, ultimately forcing a two-thirds majority vote in both chambers in order to overturn a rescission). Rejected in the Committee of the Whole 198-219: R 165-4; D 33-214 (ND 21-143, SD 12-71); I 0-1, April 29, 1993.

147. HR 1578. Expedited Rescission Authority/Substitute Amendment. Adoption of the substitute amendment to allow the president to propose to rescind any part of an appropriations bill and require Congress to vote on that rescission proposal within a specified period of time. The bill would expire two years after enactment. Adopted in the Committee of the Whole 247-168: R 23-146; D 224-21 (ND 149-14, SD 75-7); I 0-1, April 29, 1993.

148. HR 1578. Expedited Rescission Authority/Substitute Amendment. Separate vote at the request of Walker, R-Pa., on the vote in the Committee of the Whole that adopted the substitute amendment to allow the president to propose to rescind any part of an appropriations bill and force Congress to vote on that rescission proposal within a specified period. The bill would expire two years after enactment. Adopted 248-163: R 24-145; D 224-17 (ND 144-15, SD 80-2); I 0-1, April 29, 1993. (On separate votes, which may be demanded on an amendment adopted in the Committee of the Whole, the four delegates and the resident commissioner of Puerto Rico cannot vote. See vote 147.)

149. HR 1578. Expedited Rescission Authority/Approval Procedures. Clinger, R-Pa., motion to recommit to the Rules Committee the bill to grant the president expedited rescission authority with instructions to report it back with an amendment to require that procedures could be changed only by statute or a three-fifths vote and to prohibit a rescission proposal from being considered under a special rule or suspension of the rules. Motion rejected 182-233: R 170-0; D 12-232 (ND 5-156, SD 7-76); I 0-1, April 29, 1993.

KEY

Y	Voted for (yea).
#	Paired for.
+	Announced for.
N	Voted against (nay).
X	Paired against.
−	Announced against.
P	Voted "present."
C	Voted "present" to avoid possible conflict of interest.
?	Did not vote or otherwise make a position known.
D	Delegates ineligible to vote.

Democrats   **Republicans**
Independent

Member	142	143	144	145	146	147	148	149
ALABAMA								
1 Callahan	N	N	N	Y	Y	N	N	Y
2 Everett	Y	N	N	Y	Y	N	N	Y
3 Browder	Y	Y	Y	N	N	Y	Y	N
4 Bevill	Y	Y	Y	N	N	Y	Y	N
5 Cramer	Y	Y	Y	N	N	Y	Y	N
6 Bachus	N	N	N	Y	Y	N	N	Y
7 Hilliard	Y	Y	N	N	N	Y	Y	N
ALASKA								
AL Young	Y	N	N	Y	Y	N	N	Y
ARIZONA								
1 Coppersmith	Y	Y	Y	Y	Y	Y	Y	Y
2 Pastor	Y	Y	Y	N	N	Y	Y	N
3 Stump	N	N	N	Y	Y	N	N	Y
4 Kyl	N	N	N	Y	Y	N	N	Y
5 Kolbe	Y	N	N	Y	N	N	N	Y
6 English	Y	Y	Y	N	N	Y	Y	N
ARKANSAS								
1 Lambert	Y	Y	Y	Y	N	Y	Y	N
2 Thornton	Y	Y	Y	N	N	Y	Y	N
3 Hutchinson	N	N	N	Y	Y	N	N	Y
4 Dickey	N	N	N	Y	Y	N	N	Y
CALIFORNIA								
1 Hamburg	Y	Y	N	N	N	Y	Y	N
2 Herger	N	N	N	Y	Y	N	N	Y
3 Fazio	Y	Y	Y	N	N	Y	Y	N
4 Doolittle	N	N	N	Y	Y	N	N	Y
5 Matsui	Y	Y	Y	N	N	Y	Y	N
6 Woolsey	Y	Y	Y	N	N	N	N	N
7 Miller	Y	Y	Y	N	N	Y	N	N
8 Pelosi	Y	Y	Y	?	N	Y	N	
9 Dellums	Y	Y	N	X	X	#	#	X
10 Baker	N	N	N	Y	Y	N	N	Y
11 Pombo	N	?	N	Y	Y	N	N	Y
12 Lantos	Y	Y	Y	Y	N	Y	Y	N
13 Stark	Y	Y	Y	?	N	Y	Y	N
14 Eshoo	Y	Y	Y	N	N	Y	Y	N
15 Mineta	Y	Y	Y	N	N	Y	Y	N
16 Edwards	Y	Y	Y	N	N	Y	Y	N
17 Vacancy								
18 Condit	Y	Y	Y	Y	Y	Y	Y	Y
19 Lehman	Y	Y	Y	Y	Y	Y	Y	Y
20 Dooley	Y	Y	Y	Y	Y	Y	Y	N
21 Thomas	N	N	N	Y	Y	?	N	Y
22 Huffington	Y	N	N	Y	Y	N	N	Y
23 Gallegly	Y	N	N	Y	N	N	N	Y
24 Beilenson	Y	Y	Y	Y	N	Y	Y	N
25 McKeon	N	N	N	Y	Y	Y	N	Y
26 Berman	Y	?	Y	?	?	?	?	?
27 Moorhead	N	N	N	Y	Y	N	N	Y
28 Dreier	N	N	N	Y	Y	N	N	Y
29 Waxman	Y	Y	Y	N	N	Y	?	N
30 Becerra	Y	Y	N	?	?	?	?	?
31 Martinez	Y	Y	N	N	N	N	N	N
32 Dixon	Y	Y	Y	N	N	Y	Y	N
33 Roybal-Allard	Y	Y	N	?	?	?	?	?
34 Torres	Y	?	?	?	?	?	?	?
35 Waters	Y	Y	N	N	N	Y	N	N
36 Harman	Y	Y	Y	Y	N	Y	Y	N
37 Tucker	Y	?	?	N	N	Y	N	N
38 Horn	Y	N	N	Y	Y	N	N	Y
39 Royce	N	N	N	Y	Y	N	N	Y
40 Lewis	N	N	N	Y	Y	N	N	Y
41 Kim	Y	N	N	Y	Y	N	N	Y
42 Brown	Y	?	Y	N	N	Y	Y	N
43 Calvert	Y	?	?	#	#	X	X	#
44 McCandless	N	N	N	Y	Y	N	N	Y
45 Rohrabacher	N	N	N	Y	Y	N	N	Y
46 Dornan	N	N	N	Y	Y	N	N	Y
47 Cox	N	?	?	Y	Y	N	N	Y
48 Packard	N	N	N	Y	Y	N	N	Y
49 Schenk	Y	?	#	Y	Y	Y	Y	N
50 Filner	Y	Y	N	N	N	N	N	N
51 Cunningham	N	N	N	Y	Y	N	N	Y
52 Hunter	N	?	?	Y	Y	N	N	Y
COLORADO								
1 Schroeder	Y	N	N	Y	N	Y	Y	N
2 Skaggs	Y	Y	Y	N	N	Y	Y	N
3 McInnis	N	Y	N	Y	Y	N	N	Y
4 Allard	N	N	N	Y	Y	N	N	Y
5 Hefley	N	N	N	Y	Y	N	N	Y
6 Schaefer	N	N	N	Y	Y	N	N	Y
CONNECTICUT								
1 Kennelly	Y	Y	Y	N	N	Y	Y	N
2 Gejdenson	?	Y	Y	N	N	Y	Y	N
3 DeLauro	Y	Y	Y	N	N	Y	Y	N
4 Shays	N	N	N	Y	Y	Y	Y	Y
5 Franks	N	N	N	Y	Y	N	N	Y
6 Johnson	Y	N	N	Y	Y	Y	Y	Y
DELAWARE								
AL Castle	N	N	N	Y	Y	N	N	Y
FLORIDA								
1 Hutto	N	Y	Y	Y	N	N	Y	N
2 Peterson	Y	Y	Y	N	N	Y	Y	N
3 Brown	Y	Y	N	N	N	N	Y	N
4 Fowler	N	N	N	Y	Y	N	N	Y
5 Thurman	Y	Y	Y	N	N	Y	Y	N
6 Stearns	N	N	Y	Y	N	N	N	Y
7 Mica	N	N	N	Y	Y	N	N	Y
8 McCollum	N	?	N	Y	Y	N	N	Y
9 Bilirakis	N	N	N	Y	Y	N	N	Y
10 Young	Y	N	N	Y	Y	N	N	Y
11 Gibbons	Y	Y	Y	N	Y	Y	Y	Y
12 Canady	N	N	Y	Y	Y	N	N	Y
13 Miller	N	N	N	Y	Y	N	N	Y
14 Goss	N	N	N	Y	Y	N	N	Y
15 Bacchus	Y	Y	Y	Y	Y	Y	Y	N
16 Lewis	N	N	N	Y	Y	N	N	Y
17 Meek	Y	Y	N	N	N	Y	Y	N
18 Ros-Lehtinen	Y	N	N	Y	Y	N	N	Y
19 Johnston	Y	Y	Y	N	Y	Y	Y	N
20 Deutsch	Y	Y	Y	Y	Y	Y	Y	N
21 Diaz-Balart	Y	N	N	Y	N	N	N	Y
22 Shaw	N	N	N	Y	Y	N	N	Y
23 Hastings	Y	Y	N	N	N	Y	Y	N
GEORGIA								
1 Kingston	N	N	N	Y	Y	N	N	Y
2 Bishop	Y	Y	Y	N	N	N	N	Y
3 Collins	N	N	Y	Y	Y	Y	Y	Y
4 Linder	N	N	N	Y	Y	N	N	Y
5 Lewis	Y	Y	Y	N	N	Y	Y	N
6 Gingrich	?	N	N	Y	Y	N	N	Y
7 Darden	Y	Y	Y	N	N	Y	Y	N
8 Rowland	Y	Y	Y	N	Y	Y	Y	N
9 Deal	N	Y	Y	Y	Y	Y	Y	N
10 Johnson	N	Y	Y	Y	Y	Y	Y	N
11 McKinney	Y	Y	N	N	N	N	Y	N
HAWAII								
1 Abercrombie	Y	Y	Y	N	N	Y	Y	N
2 Mink	Y	Y	Y	N	N	N	N	N
IDAHO								
1 LaRocco	Y	Y	Y	Y	N	Y	Y	N
2 Crapo	N	N	N	Y	Y	N	N	Y
ILLINOIS								
1 Rush	Y	Y	Y	N	N	Y	Y	N
2 Reynolds	Y	Y	Y	N	N	Y	Y	N
3 Lipinski	?	Y	Y	N	N	Y	Y	N
4 Gutierrez	Y	Y	Y	Y	Y	Y	Y	N
5 Rostenkowski	Y	Y	Y	N	N	Y	Y	N
6 Hyde	Y	N	N	Y	Y	N	N	Y
7 Collins	Y	Y	N	N	N	Y	Y	N
8 Crane	N	N	N	Y	Y	N	N	Y
9 Yates	Y	Y	N	Y	N	Y	Y	N
10 Porter	N	N	N	Y	Y	N	N	Y
11 Sangmeister	Y	Y	Y	N	N	Y	Y	N
12 Costello	Y	Y	Y	N	N	Y	Y	N
13 Fawell	Y	N	N	Y	Y	N	N	Y
14 Hastert	Y	N	N	Y	Y	N	N	Y
15 Ewing	Y	N	N	Y	Y	N	N	Y
16 Manzullo	N	N	N	Y	N	N	N	Y
17 Evans	Y	Y	N	N	N	N	N	N

ND Northern Democrats   SD Southern Democrats

	142	143	144	145	146	147	148	149
18 ***Michel***	Y	N	N	Y	Y	N	N	Y
19 Poshard	Y	Y	Y	Y	N	Y	Y	N
20 Durbin	Y	Y	Y	N	N	Y	Y	N
INDIANA								
1 Visclosky	Y	Y	Y	N	N	Y	Y	N
2 Sharp	Y	Y	Y	Y	N	Y	Y	N
3 Roemer	Y	Y	Y	Y	N	Y	Y	N
4 Long	Y	Y	Y	Y	N	Y	Y	N
5 ***Buyer***	N	N	N	Y	Y	N	N	Y
6 ***Burton***	N	N	N	Y	Y	N	N	Y
7 ***Myers***	Y	Y	N	Y	Y	N	N	Y
8 McCloskey	Y	Y	Y	Y	N	Y	Y	N
9 Hamilton	Y	Y	Y	Y	N	Y	Y	N
10 Jacobs	Y	N	Y	N	N	Y	Y	N
IOWA								
1 ***Leach***	Y	N	N	Y	Y	N	N	Y
2 ***Nussle***	N	N	N	Y	Y	N	N	Y
3 ***Lightfoot***	N	N	N	Y	Y	Y	Y	Y
4 Smith	Y	Y	N	Y	N	Y	Y	N
5 ***Grandy***	N	N	N	Y	Y	Y	Y	Y
KANSAS								
1 ***Roberts***	N	N	N	Y	Y	Y	Y	Y
2 Slattery	Y	Y	Y	Y	N	Y	Y	N
3 ***Meyers***	Y	N	N	Y	Y	Y	Y	Y
4 Glickman	Y	Y	Y	Y	N	Y	Y	N
KENTUCKY								
1 Barlow	Y	Y	Y	N	N	Y	Y	N
2 Natcher	Y	Y	Y	N	N	Y	Y	N
3 Mazzoli	Y	Y	Y	Y	N	Y	Y	N
4 ***Bunning***	N	N	N	Y	Y	N	N	Y
5 ***Rogers***	Y	N	N	Y	Y	N	N	Y
6 Baesler	Y	Y	Y	Y	Y	Y	Y	N
LOUISIANA								
1 ***Livingston***	N	N	N	Y	Y	Y	Y	Y
2 Jefferson	Y	?	Y	N	N	Y	Y	N
3 Tauzin	Y	Y	Y	Y	Y	Y	Y	Y
4 Fields	Y	?	Y	N	N	Y	Y	N
5 ***McCrery***	N	N	N	Y	Y	Y	Y	Y
6 ***Baker***	Y	N	N	Y	Y	N	N	Y
7 Hayes	Y	Y	Y	N	Y	Y	Y	Y
MAINE								
1 Andrews	Y	Y	Y	N	N	Y	Y	N
2 ***Snowe***	Y	N	N	Y	Y	Y	Y	Y
MARYLAND								
1 ***Gilchrest***	Y	N	N	Y	Y	N	N	Y
2 ***Bentley***	Y	N	N	Y	Y	N	N	Y
3 Cardin	Y	Y	Y	N	N	N	N	Y
4 Wynn	Y	Y	Y	N	N	Y	Y	N
5 Hoyer	Y	Y	Y	N	N	Y	Y	N
6 ***Bartlett***	N	N	N	Y	Y	N	N	Y
7 Mfume	Y	Y	N	N	N	Y	Y	N
8 ***Morella***	Y	N	N	Y	Y	N	N	Y
MASSACHUSETTS								
1 Olver	Y	Y	Y	N	N	Y	Y	N
2 Neal	Y	Y	Y	N	N	Y	Y	N
3 ***Blute***	Y	N	N	Y	Y	N	Y	Y
4 Frank	Y	Y	Y	Y	N	Y	Y	N
5 Meehan	Y	Y	Y	Y	Y	Y	Y	N
6 ***Torkildsen***	Y	N	N	Y	Y	Y	Y	Y
7 Markey	Y	Y	Y	N	N	Y	Y	N
8 Kennedy	Y	Y	Y	?	?	?	?	?
9 Moakley	Y	Y	Y	N	N	Y	Y	N
10 Studds	Y	Y	Y	N	N	Y	Y	N
MICHIGAN								
1 Stupak	Y	Y	Y	Y	N	Y	Y	N
2 ***Hoekstra***	Y	N	N	Y	Y	N	N	Y
3 Henry	?	?	?	?	?	?	?	?
4 ***Camp***	N	N	N	Y	Y	N	N	Y
5 Barcia	Y	Y	Y	Y	Y	Y	Y	N
6 ***Upton***	Y	N	N	Y	Y	N	N	Y
7 ***Smith***	N	Y	N	Y	Y	N	N	Y
8 Carr	Y	Y	N	Y	N	Y	Y	N
9 Kildee	Y	Y	Y	N	N	Y	Y	N
10 Bonior	Y	Y	Y	N	N	Y	Y	N
11 ***Knollenberg***	N	N	N	Y	Y	N	N	Y
12 Levin	Y	Y	Y	N	N	Y	Y	N
13 Ford	Y	Y	Y	N	N	Y	Y	N
14 Conyers	Y	Y	Y	N	N	Y	Y	N
15 Collins	Y	Y	N	N	N	?	Y	N
16 Dingell	Y	Y	Y	N	N	Y	Y	N
MINNESOTA								
1 Penny	N	Y	Y	Y	Y	Y	Y	N
2 Minge	Y	Y	Y	Y	Y	N	N	Y
3 ***Ramstad***	N	N	N	Y	Y	N	N	Y
4 Vento	Y	Y	Y	N	N	Y	?	N
5 Sabo	Y	Y	Y	Y	N	Y	Y	N
6 ***Grams***	N	N	N	Y	Y	N	N	Y
7 Peterson	Y	Y	Y	Y	Y	Y	Y	N
8 Oberstar	Y	Y	Y	N	N	Y	Y	N
MISSISSIPPI								
1 Whitten	Y	?	Y	N	N	Y	Y	N
2 Thompson	?	Y	N	N	N	Y	Y	N
3 Montgomery	Y	Y	Y	Y	N	Y	Y	N
4 Parker	N	Y	Y	Y	Y	Y	Y	Y
5 Taylor	N	Y	Y	Y	Y	Y	Y	N
MISSOURI								
1 Clay	?	N	N	N	N	Y	Y	N
2 ***Talent***	Y	N	N	Y	Y	N	N	Y
3 Gephardt	Y	Y	Y	N	N	Y	Y	N
4 Skelton	Y	Y	Y	Y	N	Y	Y	N
5 Wheat	Y	Y	N	?	?	?	?	?
6 Danner	Y	Y	Y	N	N	Y	Y	N
7 ***Hancock***	N	N	N	Y	Y	N	N	Y
8 ***Emerson***	Y	?	N	Y	Y	Y	Y	Y
9 Volkmer	Y	Y	Y	N	N	Y	Y	N
MONTANA								
AL Williams	Y	?	Y	Y	N	Y	Y	N
NEBRASKA								
1 ***Bereuter***	N	N	N	Y	Y	N	N	Y
2 Hoagland	Y	Y	Y	Y	N	Y	Y	N
3 ***Barrett***	N	N	N	Y	Y	N	N	Y
NEVADA								
1 Bilbray	Y	Y	Y	Y	Y	Y	Y	N
2 ***Vucanovich***	Y	N	N	Y	Y	Y	Y	Y
NEW HAMPSHIRE								
1 ***Zeliff***	N	N	N	Y	Y	N	N	Y
2 Swett	?	Y	Y	Y	Y	Y	Y	N
NEW JERSEY								
1 Andrews	Y	Y	Y	Y	Y	N	N	N
2 Hughes	Y	Y	Y	Y	N	Y	Y	N
3 ***Saxton***	N	N	N	Y	Y	N	N	Y
4 ***Smith***	Y	Y	N	Y	Y	N	N	Y
5 ***Roukema***	Y	N	N	Y	N	Y	Y	Y
6 Pallone	Y	Y	Y	Y	Y	N	N	N
7 ***Franks***	N	N	N	Y	Y	N	N	Y
8 Klein	Y	Y	Y	Y	N	N	N	N
9 Torricelli	Y	Y	Y	N	N	Y	N	N
10 Payne	Y	Y	N	N	N	Y	Y	N
11 ***Gallo***	Y	N	N	Y	Y	N	N	Y
12 ***Zimmer***	N	N	N	Y	Y	Y	Y	Y
13 Menendez	Y	Y	N	N	N	Y	Y	N
NEW MEXICO								
1 ***Schiff***	N	N	N	Y	Y	N	N	Y
2 ***Skeen***	Y	N	N	Y	Y	N	N	Y
3 Richardson	Y	Y	Y	Y	N	Y	Y	N
NEW YORK								
1 Hochbrueckner	Y	Y	Y	N	N	Y	Y	N
2 ***Lazio***	Y	?	N	Y	Y	N	N	Y
3 ***King***	Y	N	N	Y	Y	N	N	Y
4 ***Levy***	Y	N	N	Y	Y	N	N	Y
5 Ackerman	Y	Y	Y	N	N	Y	Y	N
6 Flake	Y	Y	Y	N	N	Y	Y	N
7 Manton	Y	Y	Y	N	N	Y	Y	N
8 Nadler	Y	?	Y	Y	N	Y	Y	N
9 Schumer	Y	Y	Y	Y	N	Y	Y	N
10 Towns	?	Y	N	?	?	?	?	?
11 Owens	Y	Y	N	N	N	Y	Y	N
12 Velazquez	Y	Y	N	N	N	Y	Y	N
13 ***Molinari***	Y	N	N	Y	Y	N	N	Y
14 Maloney	Y	Y	Y	N	N	Y	Y	N
15 Rangel	Y	Y	N	N	N	Y	Y	N
16 Serrano	Y	Y	N	?	?	?	?	?
17 Engel	Y	Y	Y	N	N	Y	Y	N
18 Lowey	Y	Y	Y	N	N	Y	Y	N
19 ***Fish***	Y	Y	N	Y	Y	N	N	Y
20 ***Gilman***	Y	Y	N	Y	Y	N	N	Y
21 McNulty	Y	Y	Y	N	N	Y	Y	N
22 ***Solomon***	Y	N	N	Y	Y	N	N	Y
23 ***Boehlert***	Y	N	N	Y	N	Y	Y	Y
24 ***McHugh***	Y	N	N	Y	Y	N	N	Y
25 ***Walsh***	Y	N	N	Y	Y	N	N	Y
26 Hinchey	Y	Y	Y	Y	N	Y	Y	N
27 ***Paxon***	N	N	N	Y	Y	N	N	Y
28 Slaughter	Y	Y	Y	N	N	Y	Y	N
29 LaFalce	Y	Y	Y	Y	N	Y	Y	N
30 ***Quinn***	Y	N	N	Y	Y	Y	Y	Y
31 ***Houghton***	Y	Y	N	Y	Y	N	N	Y
NORTH CAROLINA								
1 Clayton	Y	Y	Y	N	N	N	Y	N
2 Valentine	N	Y	Y	N	N	Y	Y	N
3 Lancaster	Y	Y	Y	N	N	Y	Y	N
4 Price	Y	Y	Y	N	N	Y	Y	N
5 Neal	Y	Y	Y	Y	N	Y	Y	N
6 ***Coble***	N	N	N	Y	Y	N	N	Y
7 Rose	Y	Y	Y	Y	N	Y	Y	N
8 Hefner	Y	Y	Y	N	N	Y	Y	N
9 ***McMillan***	N	?	N	Y	?	N	N	Y
10 ***Ballenger***	N	N	N	Y	Y	N	N	Y
11 ***Taylor***	N	N	N	Y	Y	N	N	Y
12 Watt	N	Y	N	N	N	Y	Y	N
NORTH DAKOTA								
AL Pomeroy	Y	Y	Y	Y	N	Y	Y	N
OHIO								
1 Mann	N	Y	Y	Y	Y	Y	Y	N
2 Vacancy								
3 Hall	Y	Y	Y	N	N	Y	Y	N
4 ***Oxley***	N	N	N	Y	Y	N	N	Y
5 ***Gillmor***	Y	Y	N	Y	Y	N	N	Y
6 Strickland	Y	Y	Y	N	N	Y	Y	N
7 ***Hobson***	N	N	N	Y	Y	Y	Y	Y
8 ***Boehner***	N	N	N	Y	Y	N	N	Y
9 Kaptur	Y	Y	Y	N	N	Y	Y	N
10 ***Hoke***	N	Y	?	Y	Y	N	N	Y
11 Stokes	Y	Y	N	N	N	Y	Y	N
12 ***Kasich***	Y	Y	N	Y	Y	N	N	Y
13 Brown	Y	Y	Y	N	N	Y	Y	N
14 Sawyer	Y	Y	Y	N	N	Y	Y	N
15 ***Pryce***	Y	N	N	Y	Y	N	N	Y
16 ***Regula***	Y	N	N	Y	Y	Y	Y	Y
17 Traficant	Y	Y	Y	N	N	N	N	N
18 Applegate	Y	Y	Y	N	N	N	N	N
19 Fingerhut	Y	Y	Y	Y	Y	Y	Y	N
OKLAHOMA								
1 ***Inhofe***	N	N	N	Y	Y	N	N	Y
2 Synar	Y	Y	N	N	N	N	N	N
3 Brewster	Y	Y	Y	N	N	Y	Y	N
4 McCurdy	Y	Y	Y	Y	N	Y	Y	N
5 ***Istook***	N	N	N	Y	Y	N	N	Y
6 English	Y	Y	Y	Y	N	Y	Y	N
OREGON								
1 Furse	Y	Y	Y	N	N	Y	Y	N
2 ***Smith***	Y	N	N	Y	Y	Y	Y	Y
3 Wyden	Y	Y	Y	N	N	Y	Y	N
4 DeFazio	Y	Y	Y	Y	N	Y	Y	N
5 Kopetski	Y	Y	Y	N	N	Y	Y	N
PENNSYLVANIA								
1 Foglietta	Y	N	N	?	?	?	?	?
2 Blackwell	Y	Y	N	N	N	Y	Y	N
3 Borski	Y	Y	Y	N	N	Y	Y	N
4 Klink	Y	Y	Y	N	N	Y	Y	N
5 ***Clinger***	Y	Y	N	Y	Y	N	N	Y
6 Holden	Y	Y	Y	N	Y	Y	Y	N
7 ***Weldon***	Y	N	N	Y	Y	N	N	Y
8 ***Greenwood***	N	N	N	Y	Y	N	N	Y
9 ***Shuster***	Y	N	N	Y	Y	N	N	Y
10 ***McDade***	Y	N	N	Y	Y	N	N	Y
11 Kanjorski	Y	Y	Y	N	N	Y	Y	N
12 Murtha	Y	Y	N	N	N	Y	Y	N
13 Margolies-Mezv.	Y	Y	Y	N	N	Y	Y	N
14 Coyne	Y	Y	Y	N	N	Y	Y	N
15 McHale	Y	Y	Y	N	Y	Y	Y	N
16 ***Walker***	N	N	N	Y	Y	N	N	Y
17 ***Gekas***	Y	N	N	Y	Y	N	N	Y
18 ***Santorum***	N	Y	N	Y	Y	N	N	Y
19 ***Goodling***	Y	N	N	Y	Y	N	N	Y
20 Murphy	Y	N	Y	Y	Y	Y	Y	N
21 ***Ridge***	Y	N	N	Y	Y	N	N	Y
RHODE ISLAND								
1 ***Machtley***	Y	N	N	Y	Y	N	N	Y
2 Reed	Y	Y	Y	N	N	N	N	N
SOUTH CAROLINA								
1 ***Ravenel***	N	N	N	Y	Y	N	N	Y
2 ***Spence***	N	N	N	Y	Y	N	N	Y
3 Derrick	Y	Y	Y	Y	N	Y	Y	N
4 ***Inglis***	N	Y	N	Y	Y	N	N	Y
5 Spratt	?	Y	Y	N	N	Y	Y	N
6 Clyburn	N	Y	Y	N	N	Y	Y	N
SOUTH DAKOTA								
AL Johnson	?	Y	Y	Y	N	Y	Y	N
TENNESSEE								
1 ***Quillen***	?	?	?	?	?	?	?	?
2 ***Duncan***	N	N	N	Y	Y	N	N	Y
3 Lloyd	Y	Y	Y	N	N	Y	Y	N
4 Cooper	Y	Y	Y	Y	Y	Y	Y	Y
5 Clement	Y	?	Y	Y	N	Y	Y	N
6 Gordon	Y	Y	Y	N	N	Y	Y	N
7 ***Sundquist***	Y	N	N	Y	Y	N	N	Y
8 Tanner	?	Y	Y	Y	N	Y	Y	N
9 Ford	Y	Y	Y	Y	N	Y	Y	N
TEXAS								
1 Chapman	Y	Y	N	Y	N	Y	Y	N
2 Wilson	Y	?	Y	N	Y	Y	Y	N
3 ***Johnson, Sam***	N	N	N	Y	Y	N	N	Y
4 Hall	N	Y	Y	Y	Y	Y	Y	Y
5 Bryant	Y	Y	Y	N	N	Y	Y	N
6 ***Barton***	?	?	?	?	?	?	?	?
7 ***Archer***	N	Y	N	Y	Y	N	N	Y
8 ***Fields***	?	?	?	?	?	?	?	?
9 Brooks	Y	?	Y	N	N	?	Y	N
10 Pickle	Y	Y	Y	N	N	Y	Y	N
11 Edwards	Y	Y	Y	Y	N	Y	Y	N
12 Geren	Y	Y	Y	Y	Y	Y	Y	Y
13 Sarpalius	Y	Y	Y	N	N	Y	Y	N
14 Laughlin	N	Y	Y	Y	N	Y	Y	N
15 de la Garza	Y	?	Y	N	N	Y	Y	N
16 Coleman	Y	Y	Y	N	N	Y	Y	N
17 Stenholm	N	Y	Y	N	N	Y	Y	N
18 Washington	Y	?	X	?	?	?	?	?
19 ***Combest***	N	Y	N	Y	Y	N	N	Y
20 Gonzalez	Y	Y	N	N	N	N	Y	N
21 ***Smith***	N	N	N	Y	Y	N	N	Y
22 ***DeLay***	N	N	N	Y	Y	Y	Y	Y
23 ***Bonilla***	N	N	N	Y	Y	N	N	Y
24 Frost	Y	Y	Y	N	N	Y	Y	N
25 Andrews	Y	Y	Y	N	N	Y	Y	N
26 ***Armey***	?	N	N	Y	Y	N	N	Y
27 Ortiz	Y	Y	N	?	?	?	?	?
28 Tejeda	Y	Y	N	N	N	N	N	N
29 Green	Y	Y	Y	N	N	Y	Y	N
30 Johnson, E. B.	Y	Y	Y	N	N	Y	Y	N
UTAH								
1 ***Hansen***	?	N	N	Y	Y	N	N	Y
2 Shepherd	Y	Y	Y	Y	N	Y	Y	N
3 Orton	Y	Y	Y	Y	N	Y	Y	N
VERMONT								
AL *Sanders*	Y	Y	N	N	N	N	N	N
VIRGINIA								
1 ***Bateman***	N	Y	N	Y	Y	N	N	Y
2 Pickett	N	Y	Y	N	N	Y	?	N
3 Scott	Y	Y	Y	N	N	Y	Y	N
4 Sisisky	Y	Y	Y	N	N	Y	Y	N
5 Payne	Y	Y	Y	N	N	Y	Y	N
6 ***Goodlatte***	N	N	N	Y	Y	N	N	Y
7 ***Bliley***	N	N	N	Y	Y	N	N	Y
8 Moran	Y	Y	Y	Y	N	Y	Y	N
9 Boucher	Y	Y	Y	N	N	Y	Y	N
10 ***Wolf***	Y	N	N	Y	Y	N	N	Y
11 Byrne	Y	Y	Y	Y	N	Y	Y	N
WASHINGTON								
1 Cantwell	Y	Y	Y	Y	Y	Y	Y	Y
2 Swift	Y	Y	Y	N	N	Y	Y	N
3 Unsoeld	Y	Y	Y	N	N	Y	Y	N
4 Inslee	N	Y	Y	N	N	Y	Y	N
5 Foley			Y		N	Y	Y	N
6 Dicks	Y	Y	Y	Y	N	Y	Y	N
7 McDermott	Y	Y	Y	—	N	Y	Y	N
8 ***Dunn***	Y	N	N	Y	Y	N	N	Y
9 Kreidler	Y	Y	Y	N	N	Y	Y	N
WEST VIRGINIA								
1 Mollohan	Y	Y	Y	N	N	Y	Y	N
2 Wise	Y	?	Y	N	N	Y	Y	N
3 Rahall	Y	Y	Y	N	N	Y	Y	N
WISCONSIN								
1 Vacancy								
2 ***Klug***	N	N	N	Y	Y	N	N	Y
3 ***Gunderson***	N	Y	N	Y	Y	N	N	Y
4 Kleczka	Y	Y	Y	N	N	Y	Y	N
5 Barrett	Y	Y	Y	Y	Y	Y	Y	N
6 ***Petri***	N	N	N	Y	Y	N	N	Y
7 Obey	Y	Y	Y	Y	N	Y	Y	N
8 ***Roth***	N	N	N	Y	Y	N	N	Y
9 ***Sensenbrenner***	N	N	N	Y	Y	N	N	Y
WYOMING								
AL ***Thomas***	N	?	N	Y	Y	N	?	Y
DELEGATES								
de Lugo, V.I.	D	D	D	?	?	?	D	D
Faleomavaega, Am.S.	D	D	D	?	?	?	D	D
Norton, D.C.	D	D	D	N	N	Y	D	D
Romero-B., P.R.	D	D	D	N	N	Y	D	D
Underwood, Guam	D	D	D	N	N	Y	D	D

Southern states - Ala., Ark., Fla., Ga., Ky., La., Miss., N.C., Okla., S.C., Tenn., Texas, Va.
Omitted votes are quorum calls, which CQ does not include in its vote charts.

150. HR 1578. Expedited Rescission Authority/Passage. Passage of the bill to allow the president to propose to rescind any part of an appropriations bill and force Congress to vote on that rescission proposal within a specified period. The bill would expire two years after enactment. Passed 258-157: R 84-86; D 174-70 (ND 111-50, SD 63-20); I 0-1, April 29, 1993. A "yea" was a vote in support of the president's position.

151. Procedural Motion. Approval of the House Journal of Tuesday, May 4. Approved 255-146: R 24-140; D 230-6 (ND 152-5, SD 78-1); I 1-0, May 5, 1993.

152. HR 2. National Motor-Voter Registration/ Rule. Adoption of the rule (H Res 163) to provide for House floor consideration of the conference report on the bill to require states to allow citizens to register to vote when applying for or renewing driver's licenses, at agencies providing public assistance and through the mail. The conference report includes language requiring that beneficiaries be notified that registering to vote is optional. Adopted 253-168: R 4-166; D 248-2 (ND 167-1, SD 81-1); I 1-0, May 5, 1993.

153. HR 2. National Motor-Voter Registration/ Proof of Citizenship. Livingston, R-La., motion to recommit to conference the report with instructions to report it back with an amendment to allow states to require proof of U.S. citizenship in order to register to vote. Motion rejected 170-253: R 167-3; D 3-249 (ND 3-164, SD 0-85); I 0-1, May 5, 1993.

154. HR 2. National Motor-Voter Registration/ Conference Report. Adoption of the conference report on the bill to require states to allow citizens to register to vote when applying for or renewing driver's licenses, at agencies providing public assistance and through the mail. The conference report includes language requiring that beneficiaries be notified that registering to vote is optional. Adopted (thus sent to the Senate) 259-164: R 20-150; D 238-14 (ND 163-4, SD 75-10); I 1-0, May 5, 1993. A "yea" was a vote in support of the president's position.

* 156. HR 820. National Competitiveness/Manufacturing Technology Centers. Rohrabacher, R-Calif., amendment to eliminate federal funding for manufacturing technology centers after six years. Rejected in the Committee of the Whole 201-221: R 169-1; D 32-219 (ND 20-149, SD 12-70); I 0-1, May 6, 1993.

157. HR 820. National Competitiveness/Manufacturing Programs. Bartlett, R-Md., amendment to eliminate the authorization for the National Science Foundation manufacturing programs. Rejected in the Committee of the Whole 170-248: R 165-5; D 5-242 (ND 5-161, SD 0-81); I 0-1, May 6, 1993.

158. HR 873. Gallatin Range Consolidation and Protection/Passage. Vento, D-Minn., motion to suspend the rules and pass the bill to direct the Forest Service to acquire private land in the Gallatin Range in Montana through purchases or exchanges to protect the greater Yellowstone ecosystem. Motion rejected 262-140: R 33-131; D 228-9 (ND 152-5, SD 76-4); I 1-0, May 11, 1993. A two-thirds majority of those present and voting (268 in this case) is required for passage under suspension of the rules.

Omitted votes are quorum calls, which CQ does not include in its vote charts.

** *Ron Portman, R-Ohio, was sworn in May 5. The first vote for which he was eligible was vote 152.*

KEY

Y   Voted for (yea).
Paired for.
+   Announced for.
N   Voted against (nay).
X   Paired against.
—   Announced against.
P   Voted "present."
C   Voted "present" to avoid possible conflict of interest.
?   Did not vote or otherwise make a position known.
D   Delegates ineligible to vote.

Democrats   *Republicans*
Independent

	150	151	152	153	154	156	157	158
ALABAMA								
1 Callahan	N	N	N	Y	N	Y	Y	N
2 Everett	N	N	N	Y	N	Y	Y	N
3 Browder	Y	Y	Y	N	N	N	N	Y
4 Bevill	Y	Y	Y	N	N	N	N	?
5 Cramer	Y	Y	Y	N	N	N	N	Y
6 Bachus	Y	Y	N	Y	N	Y	Y	N
7 Hilliard	N	Y	Y	N	Y	N	N	Y
ALASKA								
AL Young	N	N	N	Y	N	Y	Y	N
ARIZONA								
1 Coppersmith	Y	Y	Y	N	Y	N	N	Y
2 Pastor	N	Y	Y	N	Y	N	N	Y
3 Stump	N	N	N	Y	N	Y	Y	N
4 Kyl	N	N	N	Y	N	Y	Y	N
5 Kolbe	N	N	N	Y	N	Y	Y	N
6 English	Y	Y	Y	N	Y	Y	N	Y
ARKANSAS								
1 Lambert	Y	Y	Y	N	Y	N	N	Y
2 Thornton	Y	Y	Y	N	Y	N	N	Y
3 Hutchinson	Y	Y	N	Y	N	Y	Y	N
4 Dickey	Y	N	N	Y	N	Y	Y	N
CALIFORNIA								
1 Hamburg	N	Y	Y	N	Y	N	N	Y
2 Herger	N	N	N	Y	N	Y	Y	N
3 Fazio	Y	Y	Y	N	Y	N	N	Y
4 Doolittle	N	N	N	Y	N	Y	Y	N
5 Matsui	N	Y	Y	N	Y	N	N	Y
6 Woolsey	N	Y	Y	N	Y	N	N	Y
7 Miller	Y	Y	Y	N	Y	N	N	Y
8 Pelosi	N	?	Y	N	Y	N	N	Y
9 Dellums	X	Y	Y	N	Y	N	N	Y
10 Baker	N	N	N	Y	N	Y	Y	N
11 Pombo	Y	Y	N	Y	N	Y	Y	N
12 Lantos	Y	Y	Y	N	Y	N	N	Y
13 Stark	Y	Y	Y	N	Y	N	N	Y
14 Eshoo	Y	Y	Y	N	Y	N	N	Y
15 Mineta	Y	Y	Y	N	Y	N	N	Y
16 Edwards	N	Y	Y	N	Y	N	N	Y
17 Vacancy								
18 Condit	Y	Y	N	N	N	Y	N	N
19 Lehman	Y	Y	Y	Y	Y	Y	N	Y
20 Dooley	Y	?	Y	N	Y	Y	N	Y
21 Thomas	N	N	N	Y	N	Y	Y	N
22 Huffington	Y	N	N	Y	N	Y	N	N
23 Gallegly	N	N	N	Y	N	Y	Y	N
24 Beilenson	Y	Y	Y	N	N	N	N	Y
25 McKeon	Y	N	N	Y	N	Y	Y	N
26 Berman	?	Y	Y	N	Y	N	N	Y
27 Moorhead	N	N	N	Y	N	Y	Y	N
28 Dreier	N	N	N	Y	N	Y	Y	N
29 Waxman	N	Y	Y	N	Y	N	N	Y
30 Becerra	?	+	+	—	+	—	—	Y
31 Martinez	N	Y	Y	N	Y	N	N	Y
32 Dixon	N	Y	Y	N	Y	N	N	Y
33 Roybal-Allard	?	Y	Y	N	Y	N	N	Y
34 Torres	X	Y	Y	N	N	N	N	?
35 Waters	Y	Y	Y	N	Y	N	N	?
36 Harman	Y	Y	Y	N	N	N	N	Y
37 Tucker	N	?	Y	N	Y	?	?	Y
38 Horn	Y	N	N	Y	N	Y	N	Y
39 Royce	N	N	N	Y	N	Y	Y	N
40 Lewis	N	N	N	Y	N	Y	Y	N
41 Kim	Y	N	N	Y	N	Y	Y	N
42 Brown	Y	?	Y	N	Y	N	N	Y
43 Calvert	#	N	N	Y	N	Y	Y	N
44 McCandless	N	N	N	Y	N	?	N	N
45 Rohrabacher	N	N	N	Y	N	Y	Y	N
46 Dornan	N	N	N	Y	N	Y	Y	?
47 Cox	Y	N	N	Y	N	Y	Y	Y
48 Packard	N	N	N	Y	N	Y	Y	Y
49 Schenk	Y	Y	Y	N	Y	N	N	Y
50 Filner	N	Y	Y	N	N	N	N	Y
51 Cunningham	N	N	N	Y	N	Y	Y	N
52 Hunter	N	N	N	Y	N	Y	Y	N
COLORADO								
1 Schroeder	N	N	Y	N	Y	N	N	Y
2 Skaggs	Y	Y	Y	N	Y	N	N	Y
3 McInnis	Y	?	?	?	?	?	?	N
4 Allard	Y	N	N	Y	N	Y	Y	N
5 Hefley	Y	N	N	Y	N	Y	Y	Y
6 Schaefer	Y	N	N	Y	N	Y	Y	N
CONNECTICUT								
1 Kennelly	Y	Y	Y	N	Y	N	N	Y
2 Gejdenson	Y	Y	Y	N	Y	N	N	Y
3 DeLauro	Y	?	Y	N	Y	N	N	Y
4 Shays	Y	N	N	Y	Y	Y	Y	Y
5 Franks	N	N	N	Y	N	Y	Y	N
6 Johnson	Y	N	N	Y	Y	?	Y	N
DELAWARE								
AL Castle	Y	N	N	Y	N	Y	Y	N
FLORIDA								
1 Hutto	Y	Y	Y	N	N	Y	N	Y
2 Peterson	Y	Y	Y	N	N	N	N	Y
3 Brown	N	Y	Y	N	N	N	N	Y
4 Fowler	Y	N	N	Y	N	Y	Y	Y
5 Thurman	Y	Y	Y	N	Y	N	N	Y
6 Stearns	N	N	N	Y	N	Y	Y	N
7 Mica	Y	N	N	Y	N	Y	Y	N
8 McCollum	N	Y	Y	N	Y	Y	Y	N
9 Bilirakis	N	N	N	Y	Y	Y	Y	N
10 Young	N	N	?	?	?	Y	Y	N
11 Gibbons	Y	?	Y	N	Y	N	N	Y
12 Canady	Y	N	N	Y	N	Y	Y	N
13 Miller	Y	N	N	Y	N	Y	Y	N
14 Goss	Y	N	N	Y	N	Y	Y	N
15 Bacchus	Y	Y	Y	N	Y	N	N	Y
16 Lewis	N	N	N	Y	N	Y	Y	N
17 Meek	N	Y	Y	N	Y	N	?	Y
18 Ros-Lehtinen	N	N	N	Y	Y	Y	Y	?
19 Johnston	Y	Y	Y	N	Y	N	N	Y
20 Deutsch	Y	Y	Y	N	Y	N	N	Y
21 Diaz-Balart	N	N	N	Y	Y	Y	Y	N
22 Shaw	Y	N	N	Y	N	Y	Y	N
23 Hastings	N	Y	Y	N	N	N	N	Y
GEORGIA								
1 Kingston	Y	Y	N	Y	N	Y	Y	Y
2 Bishop	Y	Y	Y	N	N	N	N	Y
3 Collins	Y	N	N	Y	N	Y	Y	N
4 Linder	N	N	N	Y	N	Y	Y	N
5 Lewis	N	Y	Y	N	Y	N	N	Y
6 Gingrich	N	N	N	Y	N	Y	Y	?
7 Darden	Y	Y	Y	N	N	N	N	Y
8 Rowland	Y	Y	N	N	N	N	N	Y
9 Deal	Y	Y	Y	N	N	N	N	Y
10 Johnson	Y	Y	Y	N	N	N	N	Y
11 McKinney	N	?	Y	N	Y	N	N	Y
HAWAII								
1 Abercrombie	N	Y	Y	N	Y	N	N	Y
2 Mink	N	Y	Y	N	Y	N	N	Y
IDAHO								
1 LaRocco	Y	Y	Y	N	Y	Y	N	Y
2 Crapo	Y	N	N	Y	N	Y	Y	N
ILLINOIS								
1 Rush	N	Y	Y	N	Y	N	?	?
2 Reynolds	N	Y	Y	N	Y	N	?	Y
3 Lipinski	Y	Y	Y	N	N	N	N	Y
4 Gutierrez	Y	Y	Y	N	Y	?	?	Y
5 Rostenkowski	N	Y	Y	N	Y	N	N	Y
6 Hyde	N	?	N	Y	N	Y	Y	N
7 Collins	N	Y	Y	N	Y	?	?	?
8 Crane	N	N	N	Y	N	Y	Y	N
9 Yates	N	Y	Y	N	Y	N	N	Y
10 Porter	Y	?	N	Y	N	Y	Y	Y
11 Sangmeister	Y	Y	Y	N	Y	N	N	#
12 Costello	Y	Y	Y	N	Y	Y	N	Y
13 Fawell	Y	N	N	Y	N	Y	Y	N
14 Hastert	Y	N	N	Y	N	Y	Y	N
15 Ewing	Y	N	N	Y	N	Y	Y	N
16 Manzullo	Y	N	N	Y	N	Y	Y	N
17 Evans	N	Y	Y	N	Y	N	N	Y

ND Northern Democrats   SD Southern Democrats

	150	151	152	153	154	156	157	158
18 ***Michel***	N	N	N	Y	N	Y	Y	N
19 Poshard	Y	Y	Y	N	Y	Y	Y	Y
20 Durbin	Y	Y	Y	N	Y	N	N	Y
INDIANA								
1 Visclosky	Y	Y	Y	N	N	N	N	Y
2 Sharp	Y	Y	Y	N	Y	N	N	Y
3 Roemer	Y	Y	Y	N	Y	N	N	Y
4 Long	Y	Y	Y	N	Y	N	N	Y
5 ***Buyer***	Y	N	N	Y	N	Y	Y	N
6 ***Burton***	N	N	N	Y	N	Y	Y	N
7 ***Myers***	N	Y	N	Y	N	Y	Y	N
8 McCloskey	Y	Y	Y	N	Y	N	N	Y
9 Hamilton	Y	Y	Y	N	Y	N	N	Y
10 Jacobs	Y	N	Y	N	Y	Y	N	N
IOWA								
1 ***Leach***	Y	N	N	Y	Y	Y	Y	?
2 ***Nussle***	N	N	N	Y	N	Y	Y	N
3 ***Lightfoot***	N	?	N	Y	N	Y	Y	N
4 Smith	N	Y	Y	N	Y	N	N	Y
5 ***Grandy***	Y	N	N	Y	N	Y	Y	N
KANSAS								
1 ***Roberts***	Y	N	N	Y	N	Y	Y	N
2 Slattery	Y	Y	Y	N	Y	Y	N	N
3 ***Meyers***	Y	N	N	Y	Y	Y	Y	Y
4 Glickman	Y	Y	Y	N	Y	N	N	Y
KENTUCKY								
1 Barlow	Y	Y	Y	N	Y	N	N	Y
2 Natcher	Y	Y	Y	N	Y	N	N	Y
3 Mazzoli	Y	Y	Y	N	Y	N	N	Y
4 ***Bunning***	N	N	N	Y	N	Y	Y	N
5 ***Rogers***	N	N	N	Y	N	Y	Y	N
6 Baesler	Y	Y	Y	N	Y	Y	N	Y
LOUISIANA								
1 ***Livingston***	N	N	N	Y	N	Y	Y	N
2 Jefferson	N	Y	Y	N	Y	N	N	Y
3 Tauzin	Y	Y	Y	N	Y	Y	N	Y
4 Fields	N	Y	Y	N	Y	N	N	Y
5 ***McCrery***	Y	Y	N	Y	N	Y	N	N
6 ***Baker***	Y	N	N	Y	N	Y	Y	N
7 Hayes	Y	Y	Y	N	Y	N	N	Y
MAINE								
1 Andrews	Y	Y	Y	N	Y	N	N	Y
2 ***Snowe***	Y	N	N	Y	N	Y	Y	?
MARYLAND								
1 ***Gilchrest***	N	N	N	Y	Y	Y	Y	Y
2 ***Bentley***	N	N	N	Y	N	Y	Y	N
3 Cardin	Y	Y	Y	N	Y	N	N	Y
4 Wynn	Y	Y	Y	N	Y	N	N	Y
5 Hoyer	Y	Y	Y	N	Y	N	N	Y
6 ***Bartlett***	N	N	N	Y	N	Y	Y	N
7 Mfume	N	Y	Y	N	Y	N	N	?
8 ***Morella***	Y	N	N	Y	N	Y	Y	Y
MASSACHUSETTS								
1 Olver	Y	Y	Y	N	Y	N	N	Y
2 Neal	Y	Y	Y	N	Y	N	N	Y
3 ***Blute***	Y	N	N	Y	N	Y	Y	Y
4 Frank	Y	?	Y	N	Y	N	N	Y
5 Meehan	Y	Y	Y	N	Y	N	N	Y
6 ***Torkildsen***	Y	N	N	Y	N	Y	Y	Y
7 Markey	Y	N	Y	N	Y	N	N	Y
8 Kennedy	#	Y	Y	N	Y	N	N	Y
9 Moakley	Y	Y	Y	N	Y	N	N	Y
10 Studds	Y	Y	Y	N	Y	N	N	Y
MICHIGAN								
1 Stupak	Y	Y	Y	N	Y	Y	N	+
2 ***Hoekstra***	Y	N	N	Y	N	Y	Y	N
3 Henry	?	?	?	?	?	?	?	?
4 ***Camp***	N	N	N	Y	N	Y	Y	N
5 Barcia	Y	Y	Y	N	Y	N	N	Y
6 ***Upton***	Y	N	N	Y	Y	Y	Y	Y
7 ***Smith***	Y	N	N	Y	N	Y	Y	?
8 Carr	N	Y	Y	N	Y	N	N	?
9 Kildee	Y	Y	Y	N	Y	N	N	Y
10 Bonior	N	Y	Y	N	Y	N	N	Y
11 ***Knollenberg***	N	N	N	Y	N	Y	Y	N
12 Levin	Y	Y	Y	N	Y	N	N	Y
13 Ford	N	Y	Y	X	#	N	N	Y
14 Conyers	Y	?	Y	N	Y	N	N	Y
15 Collins	N	Y	Y	N	Y	N	N	Y
16 Dingell	Y	Y	Y	N	Y	N	N	Y
MINNESOTA								
1 Penny	Y	Y	Y	N	Y	Y	Y	N
2 Minge	Y	Y	Y	N	Y	Y	N	Y
3 ***Ramstad***	Y	N	N	Y	Y	Y	Y	Y
4 Vento	Y	Y	Y	N	Y	N	N	Y

	150	151	152	153	154	156	157	158
5 Sabo	N	Y	Y	N	Y	N	N	Y
6 ***Grams***	Y	N	N	Y	N	Y	Y	N
7 Peterson	Y	Y	Y	?	?	N	N	Y
8 Oberstar	N	Y	Y	N	Y	N	N	Y
MISSISSIPPI								
1 Whitten	N	?	?	N	Y	N	?	Y
2 Thompson	N	Y	?	N	Y	N	N	Y
3 Montgomery	Y	Y	Y	N	Y	N	N	Y
4 Parker	Y	Y	Y	N	Y	Y	N	Y
5 Taylor	Y	N	Y	N	Y	Y	N	Y
MISSOURI								
1 Clay	N	N	Y	N	Y	N	N	Y
2 ***Talent***	N	N	N	Y	N	Y	Y	N
3 Gephardt	Y	Y	Y	N	Y	N	N	Y
4 Skelton	Y	Y	Y	N	Y	N	N	Y
5 Wheat	?	Y	Y	N	Y	N	N	?
6 Danner	Y	Y	Y	N	Y	N	N	Y
7 ***Hancock***	N	N	N	Y	N	Y	Y	N
8 ***Emerson***	Y	N	N	Y	N	Y	Y	N
9 Volkmer	Y	Y	Y	N	Y	N	N	Y
MONTANA								
AL Williams	Y	Y	Y	N	Y	N	N	Y
NEBRASKA								
1 ***Bereuter***	Y	N	N	Y	N	Y	Y	N
2 Hoagland	Y	Y	Y	N	Y	Y	Y	Y
3 ***Barrett***	Y	N	N	Y	N	Y	Y	N
NEVADA								
1 Bilbray	Y	Y	Y	N	Y	N	N	Y
2 ***Vucanovich***	N	N	N	Y	N	Y	?	N
NEW HAMPSHIRE								
1 ***Zeliff***	Y	N	N	Y	N	Y	?	N
2 Swett	Y	Y	Y	N	Y	N	N	Y
NEW JERSEY								
1 Andrews	Y	Y	Y	N	Y	N	N	Y
2 Hughes	Y	Y	Y	N	Y	N	N	Y
3 ***Saxton***	Y	?	N	Y	N	Y	Y	N
4 ***Smith***	Y	?	?	?	?	Y	N	Y
5 ***Roukema***	Y	N	N	Y	N	?	Y	Y
6 Pallone	Y	Y	Y	N	Y	N	N	Y
7 ***Franks***	Y	N	N	Y	Y	Y	Y	N
8 Klein	Y	Y	Y	N	Y	N	N	Y
9 Torricelli	Y	Y	Y	N	Y	N	N	Y
10 Payne	N	Y	Y	N	Y	N	N	Y
11 ***Gallo***	Y	Y	N	Y	N	Y	Y	Y
12 ***Zimmer***	Y	?	?	?	?	Y	Y	Y
13 Menendez	N	Y	Y	N	Y	N	N	Y
NEW MEXICO								
1 ***Schiff***	N	N	N	Y	N	Y	Y	Y
2 ***Skeen***	N	N	N	Y	N	Y	Y	Y
3 Richardson	Y	Y	Y	N	Y	N	N	Y
NEW YORK								
1 Hochbrueckner	Y	Y	Y	N	Y	N	N	Y
2 ***Lazio***	Y	N	N	Y	N	Y	Y	N
3 ***King***	N	N	N	Y	N	Y	Y	N
4 ***Levy***	Y	N	N	Y	N	Y	Y	N
5 Ackerman	Y	Y	Y	N	Y	N	N	#
6 Flake	N	Y	Y	N	Y	N	N	Y
7 Manton	Y	Y	Y	N	Y	N	N	Y
8 Nadler	N	Y	Y	N	Y	N	N	Y
9 Schumer	Y	Y	Y	N	Y	N	N	Y
10 Towns	?	?	Y	N	Y	N	N	Y
11 Owens	N	Y	Y	N	Y	N	N	Y
12 Velazquez	N	Y	Y	N	Y	X	X	Y
13 ***Molinari***	N	N	N	Y	N	Y	Y	N
14 Maloney	Y	?	Y	N	Y	N	N	Y
15 Rangel	N	Y	Y	N	Y	N	N	Y
16 Serrano	?	Y	Y	N	Y	N	N	Y
17 Engel	N	Y	Y	N	Y	N	N	Y
18 Lowey	N	Y	Y	N	Y	N	N	Y
19 ***Fish***	Y	Y	N	Y	Y	Y	Y	Y
20 ***Gilman***	N	Y	N	Y	Y	Y	Y	Y
21 McNulty	Y	Y	Y	N	Y	N	N	Y
22 ***Solomon***	N	N	N	Y	N	Y	Y	N
23 ***Boehlert***	Y	N	N	Y	Y	Y	N	?
24 ***McHugh***	N	N	N	Y	N	Y	Y	?
25 ***Walsh***	N	N	N	Y	Y	Y	Y	Y
26 Hinchey	Y	Y	Y	N	Y	N	N	Y
27 ***Paxon***	N	N	N	Y	N	Y	Y	N
28 Slaughter	Y	P	Y	N	Y	N	N	Y
29 LaFalce	Y	Y	Y	N	Y	N	N	Y
30 ***Quinn***	Y	N	N	Y	N	Y	Y	N
31 ***Houghton***	Y	Y	N	Y	N	Y	Y	N
NORTH CAROLINA								
1 Clayton	N	Y	Y	N	Y	N	N	Y
2 Valentine	Y	?	Y	N	N	N	N	Y

	150	151	152	153	154	156	157	158
3 Lancaster	Y	Y	Y	N	Y	N	N	Y
4 Price	Y	Y	Y	N	Y	N	N	Y
5 Neal	Y	Y	Y	N	Y	N	N	Y
6 ***Coble***	N	N	N	Y	N	Y	Y	N
7 Rose	Y	Y	Y	N	Y	N	N	?
8 Hefner	Y	Y	Y	N	Y	N	N	Y
9 ***McMillan***	Y	?	N	Y	N	Y	Y	N
10 ***Ballenger***	N	N	N	Y	N	Y	Y	N
11 ***Taylor***	N	N	N	Y	N	Y	Y	N
12 Watt	N	Y	Y	N	Y	?	N	Y
NORTH DAKOTA								
AL Pomeroy	Y	Y	Y	N	Y	N	N	Y
OHIO								
1 Mann	Y	Y	Y	N	Y	N	N	Y
2 ***Portman*** **			N	Y	N	Y	Y	N
3 Hall	Y	Y	Y	N	Y	N	N	Y
4 ***Oxley***	N	Y	N	Y	N	Y	Y	N
5 ***Gillmor***	N	Y	N	Y	N	Y	Y	N
6 Strickland	Y	Y	Y	N	Y	N	N	Y
7 ***Hobson***	N	N	N	Y	N	Y	Y	N
8 ***Boehner***	N	N	N	Y	N	Y	Y	N
9 Kaptur	Y	Y	Y	N	Y	N	N	Y
10 ***Hoke***	Y	N	N	Y	Y	N	Y	N
11 Stokes	N	Y	Y	N	Y	N	N	?
12 ***Kasich***	N	Y	N	Y	N	Y	Y	N
13 Brown	Y	Y	Y	N	Y	N	N	Y
14 Sawyer	Y	Y	Y	N	Y	N	N	Y
15 ***Pryce***	N	N	N	Y	N	Y	Y	Y
16 ***Regula***	Y	N	N	Y	N	Y	Y	Y
17 Traficant	N	Y	Y	N	Y	N	N	Y
18 Applegate	N	Y	Y	Y	Y	N	Y	Y
19 Fingerhut	Y	Y	Y	N	Y	N	N	Y
OKLAHOMA								
1 ***Inhofe***	Y	?	X	#	X	#	#	N
2 Synar	N	Y	Y	N	Y	N	N	Y
3 Brewster	Y	Y	Y	N	N	N	N	N
4 McCurdy	Y	Y	Y	N	Y	N	N	?
5 ***Istook***	N	N	N	Y	N	Y	Y	N
6 English	Y	Y	Y	N	Y	Y	N	Y
OREGON								
1 Furse	Y	Y	Y	N	Y	N	N	Y
2 ***Smith***	Y	N	N	Y	N	Y	Y	N
3 Wyden	Y	Y	?	N	Y	N	N	Y
4 DeFazio	Y	?	Y	N	Y	Y	N	?
5 Kopetski	Y	Y	Y	N	Y	N	N	Y
PENNSYLVANIA								
1 Foglietta	?	Y	Y	N	Y	N	N	Y
2 Blackwell	N	Y	Y	N	Y	N	N	Y
3 Borski	N	Y	Y	N	Y	N	N	Y
4 Klink	Y	Y	Y	N	Y	N	N	Y
5 ***Clinger***	N	Y	Y	Y	N	Y	Y	N
6 Holden	Y	Y	Y	N	Y	N	N	Y
7 ***Weldon***	Y	N	N	Y	N	Y	Y	N
8 ***Greenwood***	Y	N	N	Y	N	Y	Y	Y
9 ***Shuster***	N	N	N	Y	N	Y	Y	N
10 ***McDade***	N	N	N	Y	N	Y	Y	N
11 Kanjorski	Y	Y	Y	N	Y	N	N	Y
12 Murtha	N	Y	Y	N	Y	N	N	Y
13 Margolies-Mezv.	Y	Y	Y	N	Y	N	N	Y
14 Coyne	N	Y	Y	N	Y	N	N	Y
15 McHale	Y	Y	Y	N	Y	N	N	Y
16 ***Walker***	N	N	N	Y	N	Y	Y	N
17 ***Gekas***	Y	N	N	Y	N	Y	Y	—
18 ***Santorum***	N	Y	N	Y	Y	Y	Y	N
19 ***Goodling***	Y	N	N	Y	N	Y	Y	N
20 Murphy	Y	N	Y	N	Y	Y	N	Y
21 ***Ridge***	N	?	N	Y	N	Y	Y	Y
RHODE ISLAND								
1 ***Machtley***	Y	N	N	Y	N	Y	Y	Y
2 Reed	N	Y	Y	N	Y	N	N	Y
SOUTH CAROLINA								
1 ***Ravenel***	N	N	N	Y	N	Y	Y	Y
2 ***Spence***	N	Y	N	Y	N	Y	Y	N
3 Derrick	Y	Y	Y	N	Y	N	N	Y
4 ***Inglis***	Y	Y	N	Y	N	Y	Y	N
5 Spratt	Y	Y	Y	N	Y	N	N	Y
6 Clyburn	N	Y	Y	N	Y	N	N	?
SOUTH DAKOTA								
AL Johnson	Y	Y	Y	N	Y	Y	N	Y
TENNESSEE								
1 ***Quillen***	?	Y	N	Y	N	Y	?	Y
2 ***Duncan***	Y	N	N	Y	N	Y	Y	N
3 Lloyd	Y	?	Y	N	Y	?	?	Y
4 Cooper	Y	Y	Y	N	Y	N	N	Y
5 Clement	Y	Y	Y	N	Y	N	N	Y

	150	151	152	153	154	156	157	158
6 Gordon	Y	Y	Y	N	Y	Y	N	Y
7 ***Sundquist***	Y	N	N	Y	N	Y	Y	N
8 Tanner	Y	Y	Y	N	Y	N	N	Y
9 Ford	N	Y	Y	N	Y	N	N	?
TEXAS								
1 Chapman	Y	Y	Y	N	Y	Y	N	Y
2 Wilson	Y	Y	Y	N	Y	?	N	Y
3 ***Johnson, Sam***	N	N	N	Y	N	Y	Y	N
4 Hall	Y	Y	N	N	Y	N	N	N
5 Bryant	Y	Y	Y	N	Y	N	N	Y
6 ***Barton***	?	N	N	Y	N	Y	Y	X
7 ***Archer***	N	Y	N	Y	N	Y	Y	N
8 ***Fields***	?	N	N	Y	N	Y	Y	N
9 Brooks	N	Y	Y	N	Y	N	N	Y
10 Pickle	Y	Y	Y	N	Y	N	N	Y
11 Edwards	Y	Y	Y	N	Y	Y	N	Y
12 Geren	Y	Y	Y	N	Y	N	N	Y
13 Sarpalius	N	Y	Y	N	Y	N	N	N
14 Laughlin	Y	Y	Y	N	Y	N	N	Y
15 de la Garza	Y	Y	Y	N	Y	N	N	Y
16 Coleman	N	Y	Y	N	Y	N	N	Y
17 Stenholm	Y	Y	Y	N	Y	N	N	N
18 Washington	?	?	Y	N	Y	N	N	Y
19 ***Combest***	N	Y	N	Y	N	Y	Y	N
20 Gonzalez	Y	Y	Y	N	Y	N	N	Y
21 ***Smith***	N	N	N	Y	N	Y	Y	N
22 ***DeLay***	N	N	N	Y	N	Y	Y	N
23 ***Bonilla***	Y	N	N	Y	N	Y	Y	N
24 Frost	Y	Y	Y	N	Y	N	N	Y
25 Andrews	Y	Y	Y	N	Y	N	N	Y
26 ***Armey***	N	N	N	Y	N	Y	Y	N
27 Ortiz	?	Y	Y	N	Y	N	N	Y
28 Tejeda	N	Y	Y	N	Y	N	N	Y
29 Green	Y	Y	Y	N	Y	N	N	Y
30 Johnson, E. B.	Y	Y	#	N	Y	N	N	Y
UTAH								
1 ***Hansen***	N	N	N	Y	N	Y	Y	Y
2 Shepherd	Y	Y	Y	N	Y	Y	N	Y
3 Orton	Y	Y	Y	N	Y	Y	Y	N
VERMONT								
AL *Sanders*	N	Y	Y	N	Y	N	N	Y
VIRGINIA								
1 ***Bateman***	Y	Y	N	Y	N	Y	Y	N
2 Pickett	Y	Y	Y	N	N	N	N	Y
3 Scott	N	Y	Y	N	Y	N	N	Y
4 Sisisky	Y	Y	Y	N	Y	N	N	Y
5 Payne	Y	Y	Y	N	Y	N	N	Y
6 ***Goodlatte***	Y	N	N	Y	N	Y	Y	N
7 ***Bliley***	N	N	N	Y	N	Y	Y	N
8 Moran	Y	Y	Y	N	Y	N	N	Y
9 Boucher	Y	Y	Y	N	Y	N	N	Y
10 ***Wolf***	N	N	N	Y	N	Y	Y	N
11 Byrne	Y	Y	Y	N	Y	N	?	Y
WASHINGTON								
1 Cantwell	Y	Y	Y	N	Y	N	N	Y
2 Swift	N	Y	Y	N	Y	N	N	Y
3 Unsoeld	N	Y	Y	N	Y	N	N	Y
4 Inslee	Y	Y	Y	N	Y	N	N	Y
5 Foley	Y							
6 Dicks	Y	Y	Y	N	Y	N	N	Y
7 McDermott	Y	Y	Y	N	Y	N	N	Y
8 ***Dunn***	Y	N	N	Y	N	Y	Y	N
9 Kreidler	Y	Y	Y	N	Y	N	N	Y
WEST VIRGINIA								
1 Mollohan	N	Y	Y	N	Y	N	N	?
2 Wise	Y	?	Y	N	Y	N	N	Y
3 Rahall	N	Y	Y	N	Y	N	N	Y
WISCONSIN								
1 Vacancy								
2 ***Klug***	Y	N	N	Y	Y	Y	Y	Y
3 ***Gunderson***	Y	Y	N	Y	Y	Y	Y	N
4 Kleczka	Y	Y	Y	N	Y	N	?	Y
5 Barrett	Y	Y	Y	N	Y	N	N	Y
6 ***Petri***	Y	N	N	Y	N	Y	Y	Y
7 Obey	Y	Y	Y	N	Y	N	N	Y
8 ***Roth***	Y	N	N	Y	N	Y	Y	N
9 ***Sensenbrenner***	Y	N	N	Y	N	Y	Y	N
WYOMING								
AL ***Thomas***	N	Y	N	Y	N	Y	Y	?
DELEGATES								
de Lugo, V.I.	D	D	D	D	D	N	N	D
Faleomavaega, Am.S.	D	D	D	D	D	N	N	D
Norton, D.C.	D	D	D	D	D	N	N	D
Romero-B., P.R.	D	D	D	D	D	N	N	D
Underwood, Guam	D	D	D	D	D	?	N	D

Southern states - Ala., Ark., Fla., Ga., Ky., La., Miss., N.C., Okla., S.C., Tenn., Texas, Va.
Omitted votes are quorum calls, which CQ does not include in its vote charts.

159. HR 820. National Competitiveness/Civilian Technology Program. Calvert, R-Calif., amendment to eliminate the authorization of $2 million in fiscal 1994 and $70 million in fiscal 1995 for civilian technology loan and civilian technology development programs. Rejected in Committee of the Whole 180-239: R 171-2; D 9-236 (ND 4-159, SD 5-77); I 0-1, May 12, 1993.

160. HR 820. National Competitiveness/Civilian Technology Program. Cox, R-Calif., en bloc amendment to eliminate the Department of Commerce's authority to buy preferred stock or guarantees or issue trust certificates in companies licensed under the Civilian Technology Development Program. Rejected in Committee of the Whole 180-237: R 172-1; D 8-235 (ND 5-157, SD 3-78); I 0-1, May 12, 1993.

161. HR 820. National Competitiveness/Civilian Technology Program. Meyers, R-Kan., en bloc amendment to reduce the authorization for the Civilian Technology Development Program to $1 million in fiscal 1994 and $10 million in fiscal 1995, shift the management of the program to the Small Business Administration and provide the government with a share of the profits. Rejected in Committee of the Whole 194-224: R 170-2; D 24-221 (ND 17-146, SD 7-75); I 0-1, May 12, 1993.

162. HR 820. National Competitiveness/Civilian Technology Loans. Walker, R-Pa., amendment to require that civilian technology loans be made available to Americans with incomes of $15,000 to $85,000. Rejected in Committee of the Whole 181-231: R 162-5; D 19-225 (ND 12-152, SD 7-73); I 0-1, May 13, 1993.

163. HR 820. National Competitiveness/Advanced Technology Program. Hoke, R-Ohio, amendment to eliminate the $100 million authorization in fiscal 1995 for the large-scale research and development consortia under the Advanced Technology Program. Rejected in Committee of the Whole 176-234: R 167-2; D 9-231 (ND 6-156, SD 3-75); I 0-1, May 13, 1993.

* 165. HR 820. National Competitiveness/Program Additions. Walker, R-Pa., substitute amendment to the Valentine, D-N.C., amendment to eliminate an $88 million authorization for six grant and loan programs the administration did not request. Rejected in Committee of the Whole 187-222: R 167-1; D 20-220 (ND 9-155, SD 11-65); I 0-1, May 19, 1993.

166. HR 820. National Competitiveness/Funding Freeze. Armey, R-Texas, substitute amendment to the Valentine, D-N.C., amendment to freeze the authorization for programs in the bill at the fiscal 1993 appropriation of $389 billion. Rejected in Committee of the Whole 199-217: R 168-3; D 31-213 (ND 13-154, SD 18-59); I 0-1, May 19, 1993. (The Valentine amendment to adjust FY 1995 authorization levels to reflect a budget resolution spending limit of $950 million subsequently was adopted by voice vote.)

167. HR 820. National Competitiveness/Funding Cut. Duncan, R-Tenn., amendment to cut $154.3 million over two years by reducing all program authorizations in the bill by 10 percent. Rejected in Committee of the Whole 208-213: R 172-1; D 36-211 (ND 19-149, SD 17-62); I 0-1, May 19, 1993.

* Omitted votes are quorum calls, which CQ does not include in its vote charts.

** Peter W. Barca, the apparent winner in Wisconsin's 1st District special election May 4, had not been sworn in pending a recount.

KEY

Y	Voted for (yea).
#	Paired for.
+	Announced for.
N	Voted against (nay).
X	Paired against.
−	Announced against.
P	Voted "present."
C	Voted "present" to avoid possible conflict of interest.
?	Did not vote or otherwise make a position known.
D	Delegates ineligible to vote.

Democrats **Republicans**
Independent

	159	160	161	162	163	165	166	167
ALABAMA								
1 Callahan	Y	Y	Y	Y	Y	Y	Y	Y
2 Everett	Y	Y	Y	Y	Y	Y	Y	Y
3 Browder	N	N	N	N	N	N	N	N
4 Bevill	?	N	N	N	N	N	N	N
5 Cramer	N	N	N	N	N	N	N	N
6 Bachus	Y	Y	Y	Y	Y	Y	Y	Y
7 Hilliard	N	N	N	N	N	N	N	N
ALASKA								
AL Young	Y	Y	Y	Y	Y	Y	?	Y
ARIZONA								
1 Coppersmith	N	N	N	N	N	N	N	N
2 Pastor	N	N	N	N	−	N	N	N
3 Stump	Y	Y	Y	Y	Y	Y	Y	Y
4 Kyl	Y	Y	Y	Y	Y	Y	Y	Y
5 Kolbe	Y	Y	Y	Y	Y	Y	Y	Y
6 English	N	N	N	N	N	N	N	N
ARKANSAS								
1 Lambert	N	N	Y	N	N	N	N	Y
2 Thornton	N	N	N	N	N	N	N	N
3 Hutchinson	Y	Y	Y	Y	Y	Y	Y	Y
4 Dickey	Y	Y	Y	Y	Y	Y	Y	Y
CALIFORNIA								
1 Hamburg	N	N	N	N	N	N	N	N
2 Herger	Y	Y	Y	Y	Y	Y	Y	Y
3 Fazio	N	N	N	N	N	N	N	N
4 Doolittle	Y	Y	Y	Y	Y	Y	Y	Y
5 Matsui	?	?	?	N	N	N	N	N
6 Woolsey	N	N	N	N	N	N	N	N
7 Miller	N	N	N	N	N	N	N	N
8 Pelosi	N	N	N	N	N	N	N	N
9 Dellums	X	?	?	?	?	N	N	N
10 Baker	Y	Y	Y	Y	Y	Y	Y	Y
11 Pombo	Y	Y	Y	Y	Y	Y	Y	Y
12 Lantos	N	N	N	N	N	N	N	N
13 Stark	N	N	N	N	N	N	N	N
14 Eshoo	N	N	N	N	N	N	N	N
15 Mineta	N	N	N	N	N	N	N	N
16 Edwards	N	N	N	N	N	N	N	N
17 Vacancy								
18 Condit	N	Y	Y	Y	Y	Y	Y	Y
19 Lehman	N	N	N	?	?	Y	Y	Y
20 Dooley	N	N	N	N	N	Y	N	Y
21 Thomas	Y	Y	Y	Y	N	Y	Y	Y
22 Huffington	Y	Y	Y	Y	Y	Y	Y	Y
23 Gallegly	Y	Y	Y	?	?	Y	Y	Y
24 Beilenson	N	N	N	N	N	N	N	N
25 McKeon	Y	Y	Y	Y	Y	Y	Y	Y
26 Berman	N	N	N	N	N	N	N	N
27 Moorhead	Y	Y	Y	Y	Y	Y	Y	Y
28 Dreier	Y	Y	Y	Y	Y	Y	Y	Y
29 Waxman	N	N	N	N	N	N	N	N
30 Becerra	N	N	N	N	N	N	N	N
31 Martinez	N	N	N	N	N	N	N	N
32 Dixon	N	N	N	N	N	N	N	N
33 Roybal-Allard	N	N	N	N	N	N	N	N
34 Torres	N	N	N	N	N	N	N	N
35 Waters	N	N	N	N	N	N	N	N
36 Harman	N	N	N	N	N	N	N	N
37 Tucker	N	N	N	?	?	N	N	N
38 Horn	Y	Y	Y	Y	Y	Y	Y	Y
39 Royce	Y	Y	Y	Y	Y	Y	Y	Y
40 Lewis	Y	Y	Y	Y	Y	Y	Y	Y
41 Kim	Y	Y	Y	Y	Y	Y	Y	Y

	159	160	161	162	163	165	166	167
42 Brown	N	N	N	N	N	N	N	N
43 Calvert	Y	Y	Y	Y	Y	Y	Y	Y
44 McCandless	Y	Y	Y	Y	Y	Y	Y	Y
45 Rohrabacher	Y	Y	Y	Y	Y	Y	Y	Y
46 Dornan	Y	Y	Y	Y	Y	Y	Y	Y
47 Cox	Y	Y	Y	Y	Y	Y	Y	Y
48 Packard	Y	Y	Y	Y	Y	?	#	?
49 Schenk	N	N	N	N	N	N	N	N
50 Filner	N	N	N	N	N	N	N	N
51 Cunningham	Y	Y	Y	Y	Y	Y	Y	Y
52 Hunter	Y	Y	Y	Y	Y	Y	Y	Y
COLORADO								
1 Schroeder	N	N	N	N	N	N	N	N
2 Skaggs	N	N	N	N	N	N	N	N
3 McInnis	Y	Y	Y	Y	Y	Y	Y	Y
4 Allard	Y	Y	Y	Y	Y	Y	Y	Y
5 Hefley	Y	Y	Y	Y	Y	Y	Y	Y
6 Schaefer	Y	Y	Y	Y	Y	Y	Y	Y
CONNECTICUT								
1 Kennelly	N	N	N	N	N	N	N	N
2 Gejdenson	N	N	N	N	N	N	N	N
3 DeLauro	N	N	N	N	N	N	N	N
4 Shays	Y	Y	Y	Y	Y	Y	Y	Y
5 Franks	Y	Y	Y	Y	Y	Y	Y	Y
6 Johnson	Y	Y	Y	Y	Y	Y	N	Y
DELAWARE								
AL Castle	Y	Y	Y	Y	Y	Y	Y	Y
FLORIDA								
1 Hutto	N	N	Y	Y	N	Y	Y	Y
2 Peterson	N	N	N	N	N	N	N	N
3 Brown	N	N	N	N	N	N	N	N
4 Fowler	Y	Y	Y	Y	Y	Y	Y	Y
5 Thurman	N	N	N	N	N	N	N	N
6 Stearns	Y	Y	Y	Y	Y	Y	Y	Y
7 Mica	Y	Y	Y	Y	Y	Y	Y	Y
8 McCollum	Y	Y	Y	Y	Y	Y	Y	Y
9 Bilirakis	Y	Y	Y	Y	Y	Y	Y	Y
10 Young	Y	Y	Y	Y	Y	Y	Y	Y
11 Gibbons	Y	N	N	N	N	N	N	N
12 Canady	Y	Y	Y	Y	Y	Y	Y	Y
13 Miller	Y	Y	Y	Y	Y	Y	Y	Y
14 Goss	Y	Y	Y	Y	Y	Y	Y	Y
15 Bacchus	N	N	N	N	N	N	N	N
16 Lewis	Y	Y	Y	Y	Y	Y	Y	Y
17 Meek	N	N	N	N	N	N	N	N
18 Ros-Lehtinen	Y	Y	Y	N	Y	Y	Y	Y
19 Johnston	N	N	N	N	N	N	N	N
20 Deutsch	N	N	N	N	N	N	N	N
21 Diaz-Balart	Y	Y	Y	Y	Y	Y	Y	Y
22 Shaw	Y	Y	Y	Y	Y	?	Y	Y
23 Hastings	N	N	N	N	N	N	N	N
GEORGIA								
1 Kingston	Y	Y	Y	Y	Y	Y	Y	Y
2 Bishop	N	N	N	N	N	N	N	N
3 Collins	Y	Y	Y	Y	Y	Y	Y	Y
4 Linder	Y	Y	Y	Y	Y	Y	Y	Y
5 Lewis	N	N	N	N	N	N	N	N
6 Gingrich	Y	Y	Y	Y	Y	Y	Y	Y
7 Darden	N	N	N	N	N	N	N	N
8 Rowland	N	N	N	Y	N	?	N	Y
9 Deal	N	N	N	N	N	N	N	N
10 Johnson	N	N	N	N	N	N	N	N
11 McKinney	N	N	N	N	N	N	N	N
HAWAII								
1 Abercrombie	?	?	N	N	N	N	N	N
2 Mink	N	N	N	N	N	N	N	N
IDAHO								
1 LaRocco	N	N	N	N	N	?	?	N
2 Crapo	Y	Y	Y	Y	Y	Y	Y	Y
ILLINOIS								
1 Rush	?	?	?	N	N	N	N	N
2 Reynolds	N	N	N	N	N	N	N	N
3 Lipinski	N	N	N	N	N	N	Y	N
4 Gutierrez	N	N	N	N	N	N	N	N
5 Rostenkowski	?	?	?	N	N	N	N	N
6 Hyde	Y	Y	Y	Y	Y	Y	Y	Y
7 Collins	N	N	N	N	N	N	N	N
8 Crane	Y	Y	Y	Y	Y	Y	Y	Y
9 Yates	N	N	N	N	N	N	?	N
10 Porter	#	#	Y	Y	Y	Y	#	Y
11 Sangmeister	N	N	N	N	N	X	X	N
12 Costello	N	N	Y	N	N	N	Y	N
13 Fawell	Y	Y	Y	Y	Y	Y	Y	Y
14 Hastert	Y	Y	Y	Y	Y	Y	Y	Y
15 Ewing	Y	Y	Y	Y	Y	Y	Y	Y
16 Manzullo	Y	Y	Y	?	?	Y	Y	Y
17 Evans	N	N	N	N	N	N	N	N

ND Northern Democrats   SD Southern Democrats

	159	160	161	162	163	165	166	167
18 ***Michel***	Y	Y	Y	Y	Y	Y	Y	Y
19 Poshard	N	N	Y	N	N	N	Y	Y
20 Durbin	N	N	N	N	N	N	N	Y
INDIANA								
1 Visclosky	N	N	N	N	N	N	N	N
2 Sharp	N	N	N	N	N	N	N	N
3 Roemer	N	N	N	N	N	N	N	Y
4 Long	N	N	N	N	N	N	N	N
5 ***Buyer***	Y	Y	Y	Y	Y	?	Y	Y
6 ***Burton***	Y	Y	Y	Y	Y	?	Y	Y
7 ***Myers***	Y	Y	Y	Y	Y	Y	Y	Y
8 McCloskey	N	N	N	N	N	N	N	N
9 Hamilton	N	N	N	N	N	N	N	Y
10 Jacobs	Y	Y	Y	Y	Y	Y	Y	Y
IOWA								
1 ***Leach***	?	?	?	?	?	?	?	?
2 ***Nussle***	Y	Y	Y	Y	Y	Y	Y	Y
3 ***Lightfoot***	Y	Y	Y	Y	Y	Y	Y	Y
4 Smith	N	N	Y	N	N	N	N	N
5 ***Grandy***	Y	Y	Y	Y	Y	Y	Y	Y
KANSAS								
1 ***Roberts***	Y	Y	Y	Y	Y	Y	Y	Y
2 Slattery	Y	Y	Y	N	?	?	Y	Y
3 ***Meyers***	Y	Y	Y	Y	Y	Y	Y	Y
4 Glickman	N	N	Y	N	N	N	?	?
KENTUCKY								
1 Barlow	N	N	N	N	N	N	N	N
2 Natcher	N	N	N	N	N	N	N	N
3 Mazzoli	N	N	Y	N	N	N	N	N
4 ***Bunning***	Y	Y	Y	Y	Y	Y	Y	Y
5 ***Rogers***	Y	Y	Y	Y	Y	Y	Y	Y
6 Baesler	Y	N	N	N	N	N	Y	Y
LOUISIANA								
1 ***Livingston***	Y	Y	Y	?	Y	Y	Y	Y
2 Jefferson	N	N	N	N	N	N	N	N
3 Tauzin	N	N	N	?	N	N	Y	Y
4 Fields	N	N	N	N	N	N	N	N
5 ***McCrery***	Y	Y	Y	Y	Y	?	Y	Y
6 ***Baker***	Y	Y	Y	Y	Y	Y	Y	Y
7 Hayes	N	N	N	N	N	N	N	N
MAINE								
1 Andrews	N	N	Y	N	N	N	N	N
2 ***Snowe***	Y	Y	Y	Y	Y	Y	Y	Y
MARYLAND								
1 ***Gilchrest***	Y	Y	Y	Y	Y	Y	Y	Y
2 ***Bentley***	N	N	N	Y	N	N	?	Y
3 Cardin	N	N	N	N	N	N	N	N
4 Wynn	N	N	N	N	N	N	N	N
5 Hoyer	N	N	N	N	?	N	N	N
6 ***Bartlett***	Y	Y	Y	Y	Y	Y	Y	Y
7 Mfume	N	N	Y	N	N	N	N	N
8 ***Morella***	Y	Y	Y	N	Y	Y	N	N
MASSACHUSETTS								
1 Olver	N	N	N	N	N	N	N	N
2 Neal	N	N	N	N	N	N	N	N
3 ***Blute***	Y	Y	Y	Y	Y	Y	Y	Y
4 Frank	N	N	N	N	N	N	?	N
5 Meehan	N	N	N	N	N	N	N	N
6 ***Torkildsen***	Y	Y	Y	?	Y	Y	Y	Y
7 Markey	N	N	N	N	N	N	N	N
8 Kennedy	N	N	N	N	N	N	N	N
9 Moakley	N	N	N	N	N	N	N	N
10 Studds	N	N	N	N	N	N	N	N
MICHIGAN								
1 Stupak	—	—	—	—	—	N	N	N
2 ***Hoekstra***	Y	Y	Y	Y	Y	Y	Y	Y
3 Henry	?	?	?	?	?	?	?	?
4 ***Camp***	Y	Y	Y	Y	Y	Y	Y	Y
5 Barcia	N	N	N	N	N	N	N	N
6 ***Upton***	Y	Y	Y	Y	Y	Y	Y	Y
7 ***Smith***	Y	Y	Y	Y	Y	Y	Y	Y
8 Carr	N	N	N	N	N	?	?	?
9 Kildee	N	N	N	N	N	N	N	N
10 Bonior	N	N	N	N	N	N	N	N
11 ***Knollenberg***	Y	Y	?	Y	Y	Y	Y	Y
12 Levin	N	N	N	N	N	N	N	N
13 Ford	N	N	N	N	N	N	N	N
14 Conyers	N	N	N	N	N	?	N	N
15 Collins	N	N	N	N	N	N	N	N
16 Dingell	N	N	?	N	N	N	N	N
MINNESOTA								
1 Penny	Y	Y	Y	Y	Y	Y	Y	Y
2 Minge	N	N	N	N	N	N	N	N
3 ***Ramstad***	Y	Y	Y	Y	Y	Y	Y	Y
4 Vento	N	N	N	N	N	N	N	N
5 Sabo	N	N	N	N	N	N	?	?
6 ***Grams***	Y	Y	Y	Y	Y	Y	Y	Y
7 Peterson	N	N	N	Y	Y	N	Y	Y
8 Oberstar	N	N	N	N	N	N	N	N
MISSISSIPPI								
1 Whitten	N	N	N	Y	N	?	?	?
2 Thompson	N	N	N	N	N	N	N	N
3 Montgomery	N	N	N	N	N	Y	Y	Y
4 Parker	N	N	N	Y	N	Y	Y	Y
5 Taylor	N	N	N	Y	N	N	Y	Y
MISSOURI								
1 Clay	N	N	N	N	?	N	N	N
2 ***Talent***	Y	Y	Y	Y	Y	Y	Y	Y
3 Gephardt	N	N	N	N	?	N	N	N
4 Skelton	N	N	Y	Y	N	N	N	N
5 Wheat	N	N	Y	N	N	N	N	N
6 Danner	N	N	N	N	N	N	N	N
7 ***Hancock***	Y	Y	Y	Y	Y	Y	Y	Y
8 ***Emerson***	Y	Y	Y	Y	Y	Y	Y	Y
9 Volkmer	N	N	N	N	N	N	N	N
MONTANA								
AL Williams	N	N	N	Y	N	N	N	N
NEBRASKA								
1 ***Bereuter***	N	Y	Y	Y	Y	Y	Y	Y
2 Hoagland	Y	Y	Y	N	Y	Y	Y	Y
3 ***Barrett***	Y	Y	Y	Y	Y	Y	Y	Y
NEVADA								
1 Bilbray	N	N	Y	Y	N	?	N	N
2 ***Vucanovich***	Y	Y	Y	Y	Y	Y	Y	Y
NEW HAMPSHIRE								
1 ***Zeliff***	Y	Y	Y	Y	?	Y	Y	Y
2 Swett	N	N	N	N	N	N	N	N
NEW JERSEY								
1 Andrews	N	N	N	N	N	N	N	N
2 Hughes	N	N	N	N	N	N	N	Y
3 ***Saxton***	Y	Y	Y	Y	Y	Y	Y	Y
4 ***Smith***	Y	Y	Y	Y	Y	Y	Y	Y
5 ***Roukema***	Y	Y	Y	Y	Y	Y	Y	Y
6 Pallone	N	N	N	N	N	N	Y	Y
7 ***Franks***	Y	Y	Y	Y	Y	Y	Y	Y
8 Klein	N	N	N	N	N	N	N	N
9 Torricelli	N	N	N	?	?	N	N	N
10 Payne	N	N	N	N	N	N	N	N
11 ***Gallo***	Y	Y	Y	Y	Y	Y	Y	Y
12 ***Zimmer***	Y	Y	Y	Y	Y	Y	Y	Y
13 Menendez	N	N	N	N	N	N	N	N
NEW MEXICO								
1 ***Schiff***	Y	Y	Y	Y	Y	Y	Y	Y
2 ***Skeen***	Y	Y	Y	Y	Y	Y	Y	Y
3 Richardson	N	N	N	N	N	N	N	Y
NEW YORK								
1 Hochbrueckner	N	N	N	N	N	N	N	N
2 ***Lazio***	Y	Y	Y	Y	Y	Y	Y	Y
3 ***King***	Y	Y	Y	Y	Y	Y	Y	Y
4 ***Levy***	Y	Y	Y	Y	Y	Y	Y	Y
5 Ackerman	N	N	N	N	N	N	N	N
6 Flake	?	?	X	N	N	N	N	N
7 Manton	N	N	N	N	N	?	?	?
8 Nadler	N	N	N	N	N	N	N	N
9 Schumer	?	X	?	N	N	N	N	N
10 Towns	N	N	N	N	?	N	N	N
11 Owens	N	N	N	N	N	N	N	N
12 Velazquez	N	N	N	N	N	N	N	N
13 ***Molinari***	Y	Y	Y	Y	Y	Y	Y	Y
14 Maloney	?	?	?	N	N	N	N	N
15 Rangel	N	N	?	N	N	N	N	N
16 Serrano	N	N	N	N	N	N	N	N
17 Engel	N	N	N	N	N	N	N	N
18 Lowey	N	N	N	N	N	N	N	N
19 ***Fish***	Y	Y	Y	Y	Y	Y	Y	Y
20 ***Gilman***	Y	Y	Y	Y	Y	Y	Y	Y
21 McNulty	N	N	N	N	N	N	N	N
22 ***Solomon***	Y	Y	Y	Y	Y	Y	Y	Y
23 ***Boehlert***	Y	Y	N	N	N	Y	N	Y
24 ***McHugh***	Y	Y	Y	Y	Y	Y	Y	Y
25 ***Walsh***	Y	Y	Y	Y	Y	Y	Y	Y
26 Hinchey	N	N	N	N	N	N	N	N
27 ***Paxon***	Y	Y	Y	Y	Y	Y	Y	Y
28 Slaughter	N	N	N	N	N	N	N	N
29 LaFalce	N	N	N	N	N	N	N	N
30 ***Quinn***	Y	Y	Y	Y	Y	Y	Y	Y
31 ***Houghton***	Y	Y	Y	Y	Y	Y	Y	Y
NORTH CAROLINA								
1 Clayton	N	N	N	N	N	N	N	N
2 Valentine	N	N	N	N	N	N	N	N
3 Lancaster	N	N	N	N	N	N	N	N
4 Price	N	N	N	N	N	N	N	N
5 Neal	N	N	N	?	?	N	N	?
6 ***Coble***	Y	Y	Y	Y	Y	Y	Y	Y
7 Rose	N	?	?	N	?	N	N	N
8 Hefner	N	N	N	N	N	?	?	?
9 ***McMillan***	Y	Y	Y	Y	Y	Y	Y	Y
10 ***Ballenger***	Y	Y	+	Y	Y	Y	Y	Y
11 ***Taylor***	Y	Y	Y	Y	Y	Y	Y	Y
12 Watt	N	N	N	N	N	N	N	N
NORTH DAKOTA								
AL Pomeroy	N	N	N	N	N	N	N	N
OHIO								
1 Mann	N	N	N	N	N	Y	N	N
2 ***Portman***	Y	Y	Y	Y	Y	Y	Y	Y
3 Hall	?	?	N	N	N	N	N	Y
4 ***Oxley***	Y	Y	Y	N	Y	Y	Y	Y
5 ***Gillmor***	Y	Y	Y	Y	Y	Y	Y	Y
6 Strickland	N	N	N	N	N	N	N	N
7 ***Hobson***	Y	Y	Y	Y	Y	Y	Y	Y
8 ***Boehner***	Y	Y	Y	Y	Y	Y	Y	Y
9 Kaptur	N	N	N	N	N	N	N	N
10 ***Hoke***	Y	Y	Y	Y	Y	Y	Y	Y
11 Stokes	N	N	N	Y	N	N	N	N
12 ***Kasich***	Y	Y	Y	Y	Y	Y	Y	Y
13 Brown	N	N	N	?	N	N	N	N
14 Sawyer	N	N	N	N	N	N	N	N
15 ***Pryce***	Y	Y	Y	Y	Y	Y	Y	Y
16 ***Regula***	Y	Y	Y	Y	Y	Y	Y	Y
17 Traficant	N	N	N	Y	N	N	N	N
18 Applegate	N	N	Y	Y	Y	N	N	Y
19 Fingerhut	N	N	N	N	N	N	N	N
OKLAHOMA								
1 ***Inhofe***	Y	Y	Y	Y	Y	Y	Y	Y
2 Synar	N	N	N	N	N	N	N	N
3 Brewster	N	N	N	N	N	?	?	?
4 McCurdy	?	?	?	N	N	N	?	?
5 ***Istook***	Y	Y	Y	Y	Y	Y	Y	Y
6 English	N	N	N	N	N	N	Y	N
OREGON								
1 Furse	N	N	N	N	N	N	N	N
2 ***Smith***	Y	Y	Y	Y	Y	Y	Y	Y
3 Wyden	N	N	N	N	N	N	N	N
4 DeFazio	N	N	N	N	N	N	Y	N
5 Kopetski	N	N	N	N	N	N	N	N
PENNSYLVANIA								
1 Foglietta	N	N	N	N	N	N	N	N
2 Blackwell	N	N	N	N	N	N	N	?
3 Borski	?	?	?	N	N	N	N	N
4 Klink	N	N	N	N	N	N	N	N
5 ***Clinger***	Y	Y	Y	Y	Y	Y	Y	Y
6 Holden	N	N	N	N	N	N	N	N
7 ***Weldon***	Y	Y	Y	Y	Y	Y	Y	Y
8 ***Greenwood***	Y	Y	Y	Y	Y	Y	Y	Y
9 ***Shuster***	Y	Y	Y	Y	Y	Y	Y	Y
10 ***McDade***	Y	Y	Y	?	Y	Y	Y	Y
11 Kanjorski	N	N	N	N	N	N	N	N
12 Murtha	N	N	N	N	N	N	N	N
13 Margolies-Mezv.	N	N	N	N	N	N	N	N
14 Coyne	N	N	N	N	N	N	N	N
15 McHale	N	N	N	N	N	N	N	N
16 ***Walker***	Y	Y	Y	Y	Y	Y	Y	Y
17 ***Gekas***	Y	Y	Y	Y	Y	Y	Y	Y
18 ***Santorum***	Y	Y	Y	Y	Y	Y	Y	Y
19 ***Goodling***	Y	Y	Y	Y	Y	Y	Y	Y
20 Murphy	N	N	Y	?	?	Y	N	?
21 ***Ridge***	Y	Y	Y	Y	Y	Y	Y	Y
RHODE ISLAND								
1 ***Machtley***	Y	Y	Y	Y	Y	Y	Y	Y
2 Reed	N	N	N	—	N	N	N	N
SOUTH CAROLINA								
1 ***Ravenel***	Y	Y	Y	Y	Y	Y	Y	Y
2 ***Spence***	Y	Y	Y	?	Y	Y	Y	Y
3 Derrick	N	N	N	N	N	Y	Y	Y
4 ***Inglis***	Y	Y	Y	Y	Y	Y	Y	Y
5 Spratt	N	N	N	N	N	N	N	Y
6 Clyburn	?	?	N	N	N	N	N	N
SOUTH DAKOTA								
AL Johnson	N	N	N	Y	N	N	N	N
TENNESSEE								
1 ***Quillen***	Y	Y	Y	Y	Y	Y	Y	Y
2 ***Duncan***	Y	Y	Y	Y	Y	Y	Y	Y
3 Lloyd	N	N	N	N	N	N	N	N
4 Cooper	N	N	N	N	N	N	N	Y
5 Clement	N	Y	Y	N	Y	Y	Y	Y
6 Gordon	N	N	N	N	N	N	N	N
7 ***Sundquist***	Y	Y	Y	Y	Y	Y	Y	Y
8 Tanner	N	N	N	?	?	N	N	N
9 Ford	N	N	N	N	N	?	N	N
TEXAS								
1 Chapman	N	N	N	N	N	?	?	?
2 Wilson	N	N	Y	N	?	N	Y	N
3 ***Johnson, Sam***	Y	Y	Y	Y	Y	Y	Y	Y
4 Hall	N	N	N	Y	N	Y	N	N
5 Bryant	N	N	N	N	?	?	?	N
6 ***Barton***	Y	Y	Y	?	Y	Y	Y	Y
7 ***Archer***	Y	Y	Y	Y	Y	Y	Y	Y
8 ***Fields***	Y	Y	Y	Y	Y	Y	Y	Y
9 Brooks	N	N	?	N	N	?	?	N
10 Pickle	N	N	N	N	N	N	N	N
11 Edwards	N	N	N	N	N	N	Y	Y
12 Geren	N	N	N	N	N	N	Y	N
13 Sarpalius	Y	N	Y	?	?	Y	Y	Y
14 Laughlin	N	N	N	N	N	Y	N	Y
15 de la Garza	N	N	N	?	?	N	N	N
16 Coleman	N	N	N	N	N	N	N	N
17 Stenholm	Y	Y	N	Y	Y	Y	Y	Y
18 Washington	N	N	N	N	N	?	?	N
19 ***Combest***	Y	Y	Y	Y	Y	Y	Y	Y
20 Gonzalez	N	N	N	N	N	N	N	N
21 ***Smith***	Y	Y	Y	Y	Y	Y	Y	Y
22 ***DeLay***	Y	Y	Y	Y	Y	Y	Y	Y
23 ***Bonilla***	Y	Y	Y	Y	Y	Y	Y	Y
24 Frost	N	N	N	N	N	N	N	N
25 Andrews	N	Y	N	N	N	Y	Y	Y
26 ***Armey***	Y	Y	Y	Y	Y	Y	Y	Y
27 Ortiz	N	N	N	N	N	N	N	N
28 Tejeda	N	N	N	N	N	N	N	N
29 Green	N	N	N	N	N	N	Y	N
30 Johnson, E. B.	N	N	N	N	N	N	N	N
UTAH								
1 ***Hansen***	Y	Y	Y	Y	Y	Y	Y	Y
2 Shepherd	N	N	N	N	N	N	N	N
3 Orton	N	N	N	N	N	N	N	Y
VERMONT								
AL *Sanders*	N	N	N	N	N	N	N	N
VIRGINIA								
1 ***Bateman***	Y	Y	Y	Y	?	Y	Y	Y
2 Pickett	N	N	N	N	N	N	N	N
3 Scott	N	N	N	N	N	N	N	N
4 Sisisky	Y	?	Y	N	N	Y	Y	N
5 Payne	N	N	N	N	N	N	Y	N
6 ***Goodlatte***	Y	Y	Y	Y	Y	Y	Y	Y
7 ***Bliley***	Y	Y	Y	Y	Y	Y	Y	Y
8 Moran	N	N	N	N	N	N	N	N
9 Boucher	N	N	N	N	N	N	N	N
10 ***Wolf***	Y	Y	Y	Y	Y	Y	Y	Y
11 Byrne	N	N	N	N	N	N	N	N
WASHINGTON								
1 Cantwell	N	N	N	N	N	N	N	N
2 Swift	N	N	N	N	N	N	N	N
3 Unsoeld	N	N	N	N	N	N	N	N
4 Inslee	N	N	N	N	N	N	N	N
5 Foley								
6 Dicks	N	N	N	N	N	N	N	N
7 McDermott	N	N	N	N	N	N	N	N
8 ***Dunn***	Y	Y	Y	Y	Y	Y	Y	Y
9 Kreidler	N	N	N	N	N	N	N	N
WEST VIRGINIA								
1 Mollohan	N	N	Y	N	N	N	N	N
2 Wise	N	N	N	?	N	N	N	N
3 Rahall	N	N	N	N	N	N	N	N
WISCONSIN								
1 Vacancy **								
2 ***Klug***	Y	Y	Y	Y	Y	Y	Y	Y
3 ***Gunderson***	Y	Y	Y	Y	Y	Y	Y	Y
4 Kleczka	N	N	N	N	N	Y	N	N
5 Barrett	N	N	N	N	N	N	N	N
6 ***Petri***	Y	Y	Y	Y	Y	Y	Y	Y
7 Obey	N	N	N	N	N	N	N	N
8 ***Roth***	Y	Y	Y	Y	Y	Y	Y	Y
9 ***Sensenbrenner***	Y	Y	Y	Y	Y	Y	Y	Y
WYOMING								
AL ***Thomas***	Y	Y	Y	Y	Y	Y	Y	Y
DELEGATES								
de Lugo, V.I.	N	N	N	N	N	N	N	N
Faleomavaega, Am.S.	N	?	N	?	?	?	N	N
Norton, D.C.	N	N	N	N	N	N	N	?
Romero-B., P.R.	?	?	?	?	?	?	N	N
Underwood, Guam	N	N	N	N	N	?	N	N

Southern states - Ala., Ark., Fla., Ga., Ky., La., Miss., N.C., Okla., S.C., Tenn., Texas, Va.
Omitted votes are quorum calls, which CQ does not include in its vote charts.

168. HR 820. National Competitiveness/Funding Cut. Stearns, R-Fla., amendment to cut $154.4 million over two years by reducing all program authorizations in the bill. Rejected in Committee of the Whole 203-225: R 172-1; D 31-223 (ND 14-159, SD 17-64); I 0-1, May 19, 1993.

169. HR 820. National Competitiveness/Budget Levels. Smith, R-Mich., amendment to require that any amount appropriated under the bill must be within the caps of the fiscal 1994 budget resolution. Rejected in Committee of the Whole 192-228: R 170-0; D 22-227 (ND 15-155, SD 7-72); I 0-1, May 19, 1993.

170. HR 820. National Competitiveness/American Workforce Quality Partnership Grants. DeLay, R-Texas, en bloc amendment to eliminate the $50 million in the bill for American Workforce Quality Partnership grants, providing funds to businesses for worker education and training. Rejected in Committee of the Whole 188-234: R 171-0; D 17-233 (ND 8-162, SD 9-71); I 0-1, May 19, 1993.

171. HR 820. National Competitiveness/Citizenship. Collins, R-Ga., amendment to require that funds go only to individuals who are U.S. citizens or nationals, aliens lawfully admitted for permanent residence, or aliens otherwise granted legal resident status. Adopted in Committee of the Whole 263-156: R 168-3; D 95-152 (ND 54-116, SD 41-36); I 0-1, May 19, 1993.

172. HR 820. National Competitiveness/Citizenship. Separate vote at the request of Kolbe, R-Ariz., on the amendment adopted in the Committee of the Whole offered by Collins, R-Ga., to require that all funds appropriated under the bill go to individuals who are U.S. citizens or nationals, aliens lawfully admitted for permanent residence, or aliens otherwise granted legal resident status. Adopted 288-127: R 167-3; D 121-123 (ND 74-92, SD 47-31); I 0-1, May 19, 1993. (On separate votes, which may be demanded on an amendment adopted in the Committee of the Whole, the four delegates and the resident commissioner of Puerto Rico cannot vote. See vote 171.)

173. HR 820. National Competitiveness/Passage. Passage of the bill to authorize $1.5 billion over two years for various grant, loan and technical aid programs for U.S. industry. Passed 243-167: R 12-158; D 230-9 (ND 153-8, SD 77-1); I 1-0, May 19, 1993. A "yea" was a vote in support of the president's position.

174. HR 873. Gallatin Range Consolidation/Land Purchases. DeLay, R-Texas, motion to recommit the bill to the Natural Resources Committee with instructions to report it back with an amendment to require that any lands acquired by the federal government under the bill be acquired through equal value land exchanges rather than purchases. Motion rejected 128-287: R 127-45; D 1-242 (ND 1-161, SD 0-81); I 0-0, May 20, 1993.

175. HR 873. Gallatin Range Consolidation/Passage. Passage of the bill to acquire 81,000 acres of land in the Gallatin National Forest in Montana for protection as part of the Greater Yellowstone Ecosystem. Passed 317-101: R 78-94; D 238-7 (ND 160-4, SD 78-3); I 1-0, May 20, 1993.

** Peter W. Barca, the apparent winner in Wisconsin's 1st District special election May 4, had not been sworn in pending a recount.

KEY

Y	Voted for (yea).
#	Paired for.
+	Announced for.
N	Voted against (nay).
X	Paired against.
−	Announced against.
P	Voted "present."
C	Voted "present" to avoid possible conflict of interest.
?	Did not vote or otherwise make a position known.
D	Delegates ineligible to vote.

Democrats **Republicans** *Independent*

	168	169	170	171	172	173	174	175
ALABAMA								
1 *Callahan*	Y	Y	Y	Y	Y	N	Y	N
2 *Everett*	Y	Y	Y	Y	Y	N	Y	N
3 Browder	N	N	N	Y	Y	Y	Y	N
4 Bevill	N	N	N	N	Y	Y	Y	N
5 Cramer	N	N	N	Y	Y	Y	Y	N
6 *Bachus*	Y	Y	Y	Y	Y	N	Y	N
7 Hilliard	N	N	N	N	N	Y	N	Y
ALASKA								
AL *Young*	Y	Y	Y	Y	Y	N	Y	Y
ARIZONA								
1 Coppersmith	N	N	N	N	N	Y	N	Y
2 Pastor	N	N	N	N	N	N	N	Y
3 *Stump*	Y	Y	Y	Y	Y	N	Y	N
4 *Kyl*	Y	Y	Y	Y	Y	N	Y	N
5 *Kolbe*	Y	Y	Y	Y	Y	N	N	Y
6 English	N	N	N	N	N	Y	N	Y
ARKANSAS								
1 Lambert	Y	N	N	Y	Y	Y	N	Y
2 Thornton	N	N	N	Y	Y	Y	N	Y
3 *Hutchinson*	Y	Y	Y	Y	Y	N	Y	N
4 Dickey	Y	Y	Y	Y	Y	N	N	N
CALIFORNIA								
1 Hamburg	N	N	N	N	Y	N	N	Y
2 *Herger*	Y	Y	Y	Y	Y	N	Y	N
3 Fazio	N	N	N	N	N	Y	N	Y
4 *Doolittle*	Y	Y	Y	Y	Y	N	Y	N
5 Matsui	N	N	N	N	N	Y	N	Y
6 Woolsey	N	N	N	N	N	Y	N	Y
7 Miller	N	N	N	N	N	Y	N	Y
8 Pelosi	N	N	?	N	N	Y	N	Y
9 Dellums	N	N	N	N	N	Y	N	Y
10 *Baker*	Y	Y	Y	Y	Y	N	Y	N
11 *Pombo*	Y	Y	Y	Y	Y	N	Y	N
12 Lantos	N	N	N	N	N	Y	N	Y
13 Stark	N	N	N	N	N	Y	N	Y
14 Eshoo	N	N	N	N	N	Y	N	Y
15 Mineta	N	N	N	N	N	Y	N	Y
16 Edwards	N	N	N	N	N	Y	N	Y
17 Vacancy								
18 Condit	Y	Y	Y	Y	Y	Y	N	N
19 Lehman	Y	Y	Y	Y	Y	Y	N	Y
20 Dooley	N	Y	Y	Y	Y	Y	N	Y
21 *Thomas*	Y	Y	Y	Y	Y	N	Y	N
22 *Huffington*	Y	Y	Y	Y	Y	N	Y	Y
23 *Gallegly*	Y	Y	Y	Y	Y	N	Y	N
24 Beilenson	N	N	N	N	N	Y	N	Y
25 *McKeon*	Y	Y	Y	Y	Y	N	Y	N
26 Berman	N	N	N	N	N	Y	N	Y
27 *Moorhead*	Y	Y	Y	Y	Y	N	Y	N
28 *Dreier*	Y	Y	Y	Y	Y	N	Y	Y
29 Waxman	N	?	N	?	N	Y	N	Y
30 Becerra	N	?	N	N	N	P	?	Y
31 Martinez	N	N	N	N	N	Y	N	Y
32 Dixon	N	N	N	N	N	Y	?	?
33 Roybal-Allard	N	N	N	N	N	P	N	Y
34 Torres	N	N	N	N	N	Y	N	Y
35 Waters	N	N	N	N	N	P	?	Y
36 Harman	N	N	N	N	N	Y	N	Y
37 Tucker	N	N	N	N	N	Y	N	Y
38 *Horn*	Y	Y	Y	Y	Y	N	Y	Y
39 *Royce*	Y	Y	Y	Y	Y	N	Y	N
40 *Lewis*	Y	Y	Y	Y	Y	N	Y	N
41 *Kim*	Y	Y	Y	Y	Y	N	Y	N

	168	169	170	171	172	173	174	175
42 Brown	N	N	N	N	N	Y	N	Y
43 *Calvert*	Y	Y	Y	Y	Y	N	Y	N
44 *McCandless*	Y	Y	Y	Y	Y	N	Y	N
45 *Rohrabacher*	Y	Y	Y	Y	Y	N	Y	N
46 *Dornan*	Y	Y	Y	Y	Y	N	Y	Y
47 *Cox*	Y	Y	Y	Y	Y	N	Y	Y
48 *Packard*	#	#	#	#	#	X	Y	N
49 Schenk	N	N	N	N	N	Y	N	Y
50 Filner	N	N	N	N	N	Y	N	Y
51 *Cunningham*	Y	Y	Y	Y	Y	N	Y	N
52 *Hunter*	Y	Y	Y	Y	?	N	N	Y
COLORADO								
1 Schroeder	N	N	N	Y	N	Y	N	Y
2 Skaggs	N	N	N	N	N	Y	N	Y
3 *McInnis*	Y	Y	Y	Y	Y	N	Y	N
4 *Allard*	Y	Y	Y	Y	Y	N	Y	N
5 *Hefley*	Y	Y	Y	Y	Y	Y	Y	Y
6 *Schaefer*	Y	Y	Y	Y	Y	N	Y	N
CONNECTICUT								
1 Kennelly	N	N	N	N	Y	Y	N	Y
2 Gejdenson	N	N	N	N	Y	Y	N	Y
3 DeLauro	N	N	N	N	Y	Y	N	Y
4 *Shays*	Y	Y	Y	Y	Y	N	Y	N
5 *Franks*	Y	Y	Y	Y	Y	N	N	Y
6 *Johnson*	Y	Y	Y	Y	Y	Y	N	Y
DELAWARE								
AL *Castle*	Y	Y	Y	Y	Y	N	Y	N
FLORIDA								
1 Hutto	Y	N	Y	Y	Y	Y	N	Y
2 Peterson	Y	N	N	N	N	Y	N	Y
3 Brown	N	N	N	N	N	P	N	Y
4 *Fowler*	Y	Y	Y	Y	Y	Y	Y	Y
5 Thurman	N	N	N	Y	Y	Y	N	Y
6 *Stearns*	Y	Y	Y	Y	Y	N	Y	N
7 *Mica*	Y	Y	Y	Y	Y	N	Y	N
8 *McCollum*	Y	Y	Y	Y	Y	N	Y	Y
9 *Bilirakis*	Y	Y	Y	Y	Y	N	Y	Y
10 *Young*	Y	Y	Y	Y	Y	N	Y	N
11 Gibbons	N	N	N	?	?	?	N	Y
12 *Canady*	Y	Y	Y	Y	Y	N	Y	N
13 *Miller*	Y	Y	Y	Y	Y	N	Y	N
14 *Goss*	Y	Y	Y	Y	Y	N	Y	Y
15 Bacchus	N	N	N	N	N	Y	N	Y
16 *Lewis*	Y	Y	Y	Y	Y	N	Y	N
17 Meek	N	N	N	N	N	Y	N	Y
18 *Ros-Lehtinen*	Y	Y	Y	N	N	Y	N	Y
19 Johnston	N	N	N	N	N	Y	N	Y
20 Deutsch	N	N	N	N	N	Y	N	Y
21 *Diaz-Balart*	Y	Y	Y	N	N	Y	N	Y
22 *Shaw*	Y	Y	Y	Y	Y	N	Y	Y
23 Hastings	N	N	N	N	N	Y	N	Y
GEORGIA								
1 *Kingston*	Y	Y	Y	Y	Y	N	Y	Y
2 Bishop	N	N	N	Y	Y	Y	N	Y
3 *Collins*	Y	Y	Y	Y	Y	N	Y	Y
4 *Linder*	Y	Y	Y	Y	Y	N	Y	Y
5 Lewis	N	N	N	N	N	Y	N	Y
6 *Gingrich*	Y	?	?	Y	Y	N	N	Y
7 Darden	N	N	N	Y	Y	Y	N	Y
8 Rowland	Y	N	N	Y	Y	Y	N	Y
9 Deal	N	N	N	Y	Y	Y	N	Y
10 Johnson	N	N	N	Y	Y	Y	N	Y
11 McKinney	N	N	N	N	N	Y	N	Y
HAWAII								
1 Abercrombie	N	N	N	N	N	Y	N	Y
2 Mink	N	N	N	N	N	Y	N	Y
IDAHO								
1 LaRocco	N	N	N	Y	Y	Y	N	Y
2 *Crapo*	Y	Y	Y	Y	Y	N	#	X
ILLINOIS								
1 Rush	N	−	N	N	N	Y	N	Y
2 Reynolds	N	N	N	?	N	Y	N	Y
3 Lipinski	N	N	N	Y	N	Y	N	Y
4 Gutierrez	N	N	N	N	N	N	?	?
5 Rostenkowski	N	N	N	N	N	Y	N	Y
6 *Hyde*	Y	Y	Y	Y	Y	N	Y	N
7 Collins	N	N	N	N	N	Y	N	Y
8 *Crane*	Y	Y	Y	Y	Y	N	Y	N
9 Yates	N	N	N	N	N	Y	N	Y
10 *Porter*	Y	Y	Y	Y	Y	N	Y	Y
11 Sangmeister	N	N	N	Y	Y	Y	N	Y
12 Costello	Y	N	Y	Y	Y	Y	N	Y
13 *Fawell*	Y	Y	Y	Y	Y	N	Y	N
14 *Hastert*	Y	Y	Y	Y	Y	N	Y	Y
15 *Ewing*	Y	Y	Y	Y	Y	N	Y	Y
16 *Manzullo*	Y	Y	Y	Y	Y	N	Y	N
17 Evans	N	N	N	N	N	Y	N	Y

ND Northern Democrats   SD Southern Democrats

	168	169	170	171	172	173	174	175
18 ***Michel***	Y	Y	Y	Y	Y	N	Y	N
19 Poshard	Y	Y	N	Y	Y	Y	N	Y
20 Durbin	N	N	N	Y	Y	Y	N	Y
INDIANA								
1 Visclosky	N	N	N	N	Y	Y	N	Y
2 Sharp	N	Y	N	Y	Y	Y	N	Y
3 Roemer	Y	N	N	Y	Y	Y	N	Y
4 Long	N	N	N	Y	Y	Y	N	Y
5 ***Buyer***	Y	Y	Y	Y	Y	N	Y	N
6 ***Burton***	Y	Y	Y	Y	Y	N	Y	N
7 ***Myers***	Y	Y	Y	Y	Y	N	N	Y
8 McCloskey	N	N	N	N	N	Y	N	Y
9 Hamilton	Y	N	N	N	N	Y	N	Y
10 Jacobs	Y	Y	Y	Y	Y	N	N	Y
IOWA								
1 ***Leach***	?	?	?	?	?	?	?	?
2 ***Nussle***	Y	Y	Y	Y	Y	N	Y	N
3 ***Lightfoot***	Y	Y	Y	Y	Y	N	Y	N
4 Smith	N	N	N	N	N	N	Y	Y
5 ***Grandy***	Y	Y	Y	N	N	N	N	Y
KANSAS								
1 ***Roberts***	Y	Y	Y	Y	Y	N	N	Y
2 Slattery	Y	N	N	Y	Y	N	N	N
3 ***Meyers***	Y	Y	Y	Y	Y	N	Y	Y
4 Glickman	N	Y	N	Y	Y	Y	N	Y
KENTUCKY								
1 Barlow	N	N	N	N	N	Y	N	Y
2 Natcher	N	N	N	N	N	Y	N	Y
3 Mazzoli	N	N	N	Y	Y	Y	N	Y
4 ***Bunning***	Y	Y	Y	Y	Y	N	Y	N
5 ***Rogers***	Y	Y	Y	Y	Y	N	Y	N
6 Baesler	Y	Y	Y	N	Y	N	N	Y
LOUISIANA								
1 ***Livingston***	Y	Y	Y	Y	Y	N	?	?
2 Jefferson	N	N	N	N	N	Y	N	Y
3 Tauzin	Y	Y	Y	Y	Y	Y	N	Y
4 Fields	N	N	N	N	N	Y	N	Y
5 ***McCrery***	Y	Y	Y	Y	Y	N	Y	Y
6 ***Baker***	Y	Y	Y	Y	Y	N	Y	N
7 Hayes	N	N	N	N	Y	Y	N	Y
MAINE								
1 Andrews	N	N	N	N	N	Y	N	Y
2 ***Snowe***	Y	Y	Y	Y	Y	N	N	Y
MARYLAND								
1 ***Gilchrest***	Y	Y	Y	Y	Y	Y	N	Y
2 ***Bentley***	Y	?	?	?	?	?	Y	N
3 Cardin	N	N	N	N	Y	Y	N	Y
4 Wynn	N	N	N	N	N	Y	N	Y
5 Hoyer	N	N	N	Y	Y	Y	N	Y
6 ***Bartlett***	Y	Y	Y	Y	Y	N	Y	N
7 Mfume	N	Y	N	N	N	Y	N	Y
8 ***Morella***	N	Y	Y	Y	Y	Y	N	Y
MASSACHUSETTS								
1 Olver	N	N	N	N	N	Y	N	Y
2 Neal	N	N	N	N	N	Y	N	Y
3 ***Blute***	Y	Y	Y	Y	Y	N	N	Y
4 Frank	N	N	N	N	Y	Y	N	Y
5 Meehan	N	Y	N	Y	Y	Y	N	Y
6 ***Torkildsen***	Y	Y	Y	Y	Y	N	N	Y
7 Markey	N	N	N	N	N	Y	N	Y
8 Kennedy	N	N	N	N	N	Y	N	Y
9 Moakley	N	N	N	N	N	Y	N	Y
10 Studds	N	N	N	N	N	Y	N	Y
MICHIGAN								
1 Stupak	N	N	N	N	N	Y	N	Y
2 ***Hoekstra***	Y	Y	Y	Y	Y	N	Y	N
3 Henry	?	?	?	?	?	?	?	?
4 ***Camp***	Y	Y	Y	Y	Y	N	Y	N
5 Barcia	N	N	N	Y	Y	Y	N	Y
6 ***Upton***	Y	Y	Y	Y	Y	N	Y	Y
7 ***Smith***	Y	Y	Y	Y	Y	N	Y	N
8 Carr	N	N	N	Y	Y	Y	N	Y
9 Kildee	N	N	N	N	Y	Y	N	Y
10 Bonior	N	N	N	N	N	Y	N	Y
11 ***Knollenberg***	Y	Y	Y	Y	Y	N	Y	N
12 Levin	N	N	N	N	N	Y	N	Y
13 Ford	N	N	N	N	N	Y	N	Y
14 Conyers	N	N	N	N	N	Y	N	Y
15 Collins	N	N	N	N	N	Y	N	Y
16 Dingell	N	N	N	N	N	Y	N	Y
MINNESOTA								
1 Penny	Y	Y	Y	Y	Y	N	N	N
2 Minge	N	N	N	Y	Y	Y	N	Y
3 ***Ramstad***	Y	Y	Y	Y	Y	N	N	Y
4 Vento	N	N	N	N	Y	Y	N	Y

	168	169	170	171	172	173	174	175
5 Sabo	N	N	N	?	?	Y	N	Y
6 ***Grams***	Y	Y	Y	Y	Y	N	Y	N
7 Peterson	Y	Y	Y	Y	Y	Y	N	Y
8 Oberstar	N	N	N	N	N	Y	N	Y
MISSISSIPPI								
1 Whitten	N	N	N	?	?	Y	N	Y
2 Thompson	N	N	N	N	N	Y	?	?
3 Montgomery	Y	N	N	Y	Y	Y	N	Y
4 Parker	Y	Y	Y	Y	Y	Y	N	Y
5 Taylor	Y	Y	Y	Y	Y	Y	N	Y
MISSOURI								
1 Clay	N	N	N	N	N	Y	N	Y
2 ***Talent***	Y	Y	Y	Y	Y	N	Y	Y
3 Gephardt	N	N	N	N	Y	Y	N	Y
4 Skelton	N	N	N	Y	Y	Y	N	Y
5 Wheat	N	N	N	N	N	Y	N	Y
6 Danner	N	N	N	N	Y	Y	N	Y
7 ***Hancock***	Y	Y	Y	Y	Y	N	Y	N
8 ***Emerson***	Y	Y	Y	Y	Y	N	N	Y
9 Volkmer	N	N	N	Y	Y	Y	N	Y
MONTANA								
AL Williams	N	N	N	Y	Y	Y	N	Y
NEBRASKA								
1 ***Bereuter***	Y	Y	Y	Y	Y	N	Y	Y
2 Hoagland	Y	Y	N	N	N	N	N	Y
3 ***Barrett***	Y	Y	Y	Y	Y	N	Y	N
NEVADA								
1 Bilbray	N	N	Y	Y	Y	Y	N	Y
2 ***Vucanovich***	Y	Y	Y	Y	Y	N	Y	N
NEW HAMPSHIRE								
1 ***Zeliff***	Y	Y	Y	Y	Y	N	Y	N
2 Swett	N	N	N	N	Y	Y	N	Y
NEW JERSEY								
1 Andrews	N	N	N	N	Y	Y	N	Y
2 Hughes	N	N	N	Y	Y	Y	N	Y
3 ***Saxton***	Y	Y	Y	Y	Y	N	Y	Y
4 ***Smith***	Y	Y	Y	Y	Y	?	N	Y
5 ***Roukema***	Y	Y	Y	Y	Y	N	N	Y
6 Pallone	Y	N	N	Y	Y	Y	N	Y
7 ***Franks***	Y	Y	Y	Y	Y	N	Y	N
8 Klein	N	N	N	Y	Y	Y	N	Y
9 Torricelli	N	N	N	Y	Y	Y	?	?
10 Payne	N	N	N	N	N	Y	N	Y
11 ***Gallo***	Y	Y	Y	Y	Y	N	N	Y
12 ***Zimmer***	Y	Y	Y	Y	Y	N	Y	Y
13 Menendez	N	N	N	Y	Y	Y	?	?
NEW MEXICO								
1 ***Schiff***	Y	Y	Y	?	?	N	N	Y
2 ***Skeen***	Y	Y	Y	Y	Y	N	N	Y
3 Richardson	N	N	N	N	N	Y	N	Y
NEW YORK								
1 Hochbrueckner	N	N	N	N	N	Y	N	Y
2 ***Lazio***	Y	Y	Y	Y	Y	N	Y	N
3 ***King***	Y	Y	Y	Y	Y	N	Y	N
4 ***Levy***	Y	Y	Y	Y	Y	N	Y	N
5 Ackerman	N	N	N	Y	Y	Y	N	Y
6 Flake	N	N	N	N	N	Y	N	Y
7 Manton	?	?	?	Y	Y	Y	N	Y
8 Nadler	N	N	?	?	?	?	N	Y
9 Schumer	N	N	N	N	N	Y	N	Y
10 Towns	N	N	N	N	N	Y	N	Y
11 Owens	N	N	N	N	N	Y	N	Y
12 Velazquez	N	N	N	N	N	P	N	Y
13 ***Molinari***	Y	Y	Y	Y	Y	N	N	Y
14 Maloney	N	N	N	Y	Y	Y	N	Y
15 Rangel	N	N	?	N	N	Y	X	#
16 Serrano	N	N	N	N	N	Y	N	Y
17 Engel	N	N	N	N	N	Y	N	Y
18 Lowey	N	N	N	N	N	Y	N	Y
19 ***Fish***	Y	Y	Y	Y	Y	Y	N	Y
20 ***Gilman***	Y	Y	Y	Y	Y	Y	N	Y
21 McNulty	N	N	N	N	Y	Y	N	Y
22 ***Solomon***	Y	Y	Y	Y	Y	N	Y	N
23 ***Boehlert***	Y	Y	Y	Y	Y	Y	N	Y
24 ***McHugh***	Y	Y	Y	Y	Y	N	Y	N
25 ***Walsh***	Y	Y	Y	Y	Y	N	N	Y
26 Hinchey	N	N	N	N	?	Y	N	Y
27 ***Paxon***	Y	Y	Y	Y	Y	N	Y	N
28 Slaughter	N	N	N	N	N	P	N	Y
29 LaFalce	N	N	N	N	N	Y	N	Y
30 ***Quinn***	Y	Y	Y	Y	Y	Y	Y	N
31 ***Houghton***	Y	?	Y	Y	Y	N	Y	N
NORTH CAROLINA								
1 Clayton	N	N	N	N	N	Y	N	Y
2 Valentine	N	N	N	N	N	Y	N	Y

	168	169	170	171	172	173	174	175
3 Lancaster	N	N	N	Y	Y	Y	N	Y
4 Price	N	N	N	N	N	Y	N	Y
5 Neal	N	N	N	Y	Y	Y	N	Y
6 ***Coble***	Y	Y	Y	Y	Y	N	Y	N
7 Rose	N	N	N	Y	Y	Y	N	Y
8 Hefner	?	?	?	?	?	?	N	Y
9 ***McMillan***	Y	Y	Y	Y	Y	N	Y	N
10 ***Ballenger***	Y	Y	Y	Y	Y	N	Y	N
11 ***Taylor***	Y	Y	Y	Y	Y	N	Y	N
12 Watt	N	N	N	N	N	Y	N	Y
NORTH DAKOTA								
AL Pomeroy	N	N	N	Y	Y	Y	N	Y
OHIO								
1 Mann	N	N	N	N	Y	Y	N	Y
2 ***Portman***	Y	Y	Y	Y	Y	N	N	Y
3 Hall	Y	N	N	Y	Y	Y	N	Y
4 ***Oxley***	Y	Y	Y	Y	Y	N	Y	N
5 ***Gillmor***	Y	Y	Y	Y	Y	N	N	Y
6 Strickland	N	N	N	Y	Y	Y	N	Y
7 ***Hobson***	Y	Y	Y	Y	Y	N	Y	Y
8 ***Boehner***	Y	Y	Y	Y	Y	N	Y	N
9 Kaptur	N	N	N	Y	Y	Y	N	Y
10 ***Hoke***	Y	Y	Y	Y	Y	N	Y	Y
11 Stokes	N	N	N	N	N	Y	N	Y
12 ***Kasich***	Y	Y	Y	Y	Y	N	Y	N
13 Brown	N	N	N	Y	Y	Y	N	Y
14 Sawyer	N	N	N	N	N	Y	N	Y
15 ***Pryce***	Y	Y	Y	Y	Y	N	Y	Y
16 ***Regula***	Y	Y	Y	Y	Y	Y	N	Y
17 Traficant	N	N	N	Y	Y	Y	N	Y
18 Applegate	Y	N	N	Y	Y	?	N	Y
19 Fingerhut	N	N	N	N	N	Y	N	Y
OKLAHOMA								
1 ***Inhofe***	Y	Y	Y	Y	Y	N	Y	N
2 Synar	X	X	X	X	X	#	?	?
3 Brewster	?	?	?	?	?	?	N	N
4 McCurdy	?	N	N	?	Y	Y	N	Y
5 ***Istook***	Y	Y	Y	Y	Y	N	Y	N
6 English	N	?	?	?	?	?	?	?
OREGON								
1 Furse	N	N	N	N	N	Y	?	?
2 ***Smith***	Y	Y	Y	Y	Y	N	Y	N
3 Wyden	N	N	N	N	N	Y	N	Y
4 DeFazio	N	N	N	Y	Y	Y	N	Y
5 Kopetski	N	N	N	N	N	Y	N	Y
PENNSYLVANIA								
1 Foglietta	N	N	N	N	N	Y	N	Y
2 Blackwell	?	N	N	N	N	Y	N	Y
3 Borski	N	N	N	Y	Y	Y	N	Y
4 Klink	N	N	N	N	Y	Y	N	Y
5 ***Clinger***	Y	Y	Y	Y	Y	N	N	Y
6 Holden	N	N	N	Y	Y	Y	N	Y
7 ***Weldon***	Y	Y	Y	Y	Y	N	N	Y
8 ***Greenwood***	Y	Y	Y	Y	Y	N	N	Y
9 ***Shuster***	Y	Y	Y	Y	Y	N	Y	Y
10 ***McDade***	Y	Y	Y	Y	Y	Y	N	Y
11 Kanjorski	N	N	N	N	N	Y	N	Y
12 Murtha	N	N	N	N	N	Y	N	Y
13 Margolies-Mezv.	N	N	N	Y	Y	Y	N	Y
14 Coyne	N	N	N	N	N	Y	N	Y
15 McHale	N	N	N	N	N	Y	N	Y
16 ***Walker***	Y	Y	Y	Y	Y	N	Y	N
17 ***Gekas***	Y	Y	Y	Y	Y	—	Y	Y
18 ***Santorum***	Y	Y	Y	Y	Y	Y	Y	Y
19 ***Goodling***	Y	Y	Y	Y	Y	N	Y	N
20 Murphy	N	N	Y	Y	Y	N	N	Y
21 ***Ridge***	Y	Y	Y	Y	Y	N	N	Y
RHODE ISLAND								
1 ***Machtley***	Y	Y	Y	Y	Y	Y	N	Y
2 Reed	N	N	N	N	N	Y	N	Y
SOUTH CAROLINA								
1 ***Ravenel***	Y	Y	Y	Y	Y	N	N	Y
2 ***Spence***	Y	Y	Y	Y	Y	N	Y	Y
3 Derrick	N	N	N	Y	Y	Y	N	Y
4 ***Inglis***	Y	Y	Y	Y	Y	N	Y	N
5 Spratt	N	N	N	Y	Y	Y	N	Y
6 Clyburn	N	N	N	N	N	Y	N	Y
SOUTH DAKOTA								
AL Johnson	N	Y	N	N	?	?	N	Y
TENNESSEE								
1 ***Quillen***	Y	Y	Y	Y	Y	N	Y	N
2 ***Duncan***	Y	Y	Y	Y	Y	N	Y	N
3 Lloyd	N	N	N	Y	Y	Y	N	Y
4 Cooper	Y	N	N	Y	Y	Y	N	Y
5 Clement	Y	Y	N	Y	Y	Y	N	Y

	168	169	170	171	172	173	174	175
6 Gordon	N	N	N	Y	Y	Y	N	Y
7 ***Sundquist***	Y	Y	Y	Y	Y	N	Y	N
8 Tanner	N	N	N	N	N	Y	N	Y
9 Ford	N	N	N	N	Y	Y	N	Y
TEXAS								
1 Chapman	Y	N	N	Y	Y	Y	N	Y
2 Wilson	N	?	N	Y	Y	Y	N	Y
3 ***Johnson, Sam***	Y	Y	Y	Y	Y	N	Y	N
4 Hall	N	N	N	Y	Y	Y	N	Y
5 Bryant	N	N	N	N	Y	Y	N	N
6 ***Barton***	Y	Y	Y	Y	Y	N	Y	N
7 ***Archer***	Y	Y	Y	Y	Y	N	Y	Y
8 ***Fields***	Y	Y	Y	Y	Y	N	Y	N
9 Brooks	N	N	N	Y	Y	Y	N	Y
10 Pickle	N	N	N	Y	Y	Y	N	Y
11 Edwards	Y	N	Y	Y	Y	Y	N	Y
12 Geren	N	N	N	Y	Y	Y	N	Y
13 Sarpalius	Y	N	N	Y	Y	Y	N	Y
14 Laughlin	Y	N	Y	Y	Y	Y	N	Y
15 de la Garza	N	N	?	?	?	?	?	?
16 Coleman	N	N	N	N	N	Y	N	Y
17 Stenholm	Y	N	N	Y	Y	Y	N	N
18 Washington	N	N	N	N	N	N	N	Y
19 ***Combest***	Y	Y	Y	Y	Y	N	Y	N
20 Gonzalez	N	N	N	N	N	Y	N	Y
21 ***Smith***	Y	Y	Y	Y	Y	N	Y	Y
22 ***DeLay***	Y	Y	Y	Y	Y	N	Y	N
23 ***Bonilla***	Y	Y	Y	Y	Y	N	Y	N
24 Frost	N	N	N	N	Y	Y	N	Y
25 Andrews	Y	Y	Y	Y	Y	Y	N	Y
26 ***Armey***	Y	Y	Y	Y	Y	N	Y	N
27 Ortiz	N	N	N	N	N	Y	N	Y
28 Tejeda	N	N	N	N	N	Y	N	Y
29 Green	N	N	N	Y	N	Y	N	Y
30 Johnson, E. B.	N	N	N	N	N	Y	N	Y
UTAH								
1 ***Hansen***	Y	Y	Y	Y	Y	N	N	Y
2 Shepherd	N	N	N	N	Y	Y	N	Y
3 Orton	N	Y	N	Y	Y	Y	Y	N
VERMONT								
AL *Sanders*	N	N	N	N	N	Y	?	Y
VIRGINIA								
1 ***Bateman***	Y	Y	Y	Y	Y	N	Y	Y
2 Pickett	N	N	N	N	Y	Y	N	Y
3 Scott	N	N	N	N	N	Y	N	Y
4 Sisisky	N	?	Y	Y	Y	Y	N	Y
5 Payne	N	Y	N	Y	Y	Y	N	Y
6 ***Goodlatte***	Y	Y	Y	Y	Y	N	Y	N
7 ***Bliley***	Y	Y	Y	Y	Y	N	Y	N
8 Moran	N	N	N	N	Y	Y	N	Y
9 Boucher	N	N	N	N	N	Y	N	Y
10 ***Wolf***	Y	Y	Y	Y	Y	N	Y	N
11 Byrne	N	N	N	Y	Y	Y	N	Y
WASHINGTON								
1 Cantwell	N	N	N	N	Y	Y	N	Y
2 Swift	N	N	?	N	N	Y	N	Y
3 Unsoeld	N	N	N	N	N	P	N	Y
4 Inslee	N	N	N	Y	Y	Y	N	Y
5 Foley								
6 Dicks	N	N	N	N	Y	Y	N	Y
7 McDermott	N	N	N	N	N	Y	N	Y
8 ***Dunn***	Y	Y	Y	Y	Y	N	Y	N
9 Kreidler	N	N	N	Y	Y	Y	N	Y
WEST VIRGINIA								
1 Mollohan	N	N	N	Y	Y	Y	N	Y
2 Wise	N	N	N	?	Y	Y	N	Y
3 Rahall	N	N	N	Y	Y	Y	N	Y
WISCONSIN								
1 Vacancy **								
2 ***Klug***	Y	Y	Y	Y	Y	N	N	Y
3 ***Gunderson***	Y	Y	Y	Y	Y	N	N	Y
4 Kleczka	N	N	N	N	Y	Y	N	Y
5 Barrett	N	N	N	Y	Y	Y	N	Y
6 ***Petri***	Y	Y	Y	Y	Y	N	N	Y
7 Obey	N	N	N	N	N	Y	N	Y
8 ***Roth***	Y	Y	Y	Y	Y	N	N	Y
9 ***Sensenbrenner***	Y	Y	Y	Y	Y	N	Y	N
WYOMING								
AL ***Thomas***	Y	Y	Y	Y	Y	N	Y	Y
DELEGATES								
de Lugo, V.I.	N	N	N	N	D	D	D	D
Faleomavaega, Am.S.	N	?	N	N	D	D	D	D
Norton, D.C.	N	N	N	N	D	D	D	D
Romero-B., P.R.	N	N	N	N	D	D	D	D
Underwood, Guam	N	N	N	N	D	D	D	D

Southern states - Ala., Ark., Fla., Ga., Ky., La., Miss., N.C., Okla., S.C., Tenn., Texas, Va.
Omitted votes are quorum calls, which CQ does not include in its vote charts.

176. HR 1159. Passenger Vessel Safety/Rule. Adoption of the rule (H Res 172) to provide for House floor consideration of the bill to prevent passenger vessels from circumventing Coast Guard safety standards by closing a loophole and requiring that bareboat chartered vessels carrying more than 12 passengers comply with U.S. passenger vessel safety laws. Adopted 308-0: R 128-0; D 180-0 (ND 123-0, SD 57-0); I 0-0, May 24, 1993.

177. HR 588. Abe Murdock Post Office Building/Passage. Collins, D-Mich., motion to suspend the rules and pass the bill to designate a postal facility in Beaver, Utah, as the "Abe Murdock United States Post Office Building." Abe Murdock was a former Democratic member of both the House and Senate. Motion agreed to 306-3: R 128-2; D 178-1 (ND 122-1, SD 56-0); I 0-0, May 24, 1993. A two-thirds majority of those present and voting (206 in this case) is required for passage under suspension of the rules.

178. S 1. National Institutes of Health Reauthorization/Conference Report. Adoption of the conference report to authorize $6.2 billion for the National Institutes of Health in fiscal 1994 and such sums as necessary in fiscal 1995-96. The conference report codifies the Clinton executive order lifting the ban on fetal tissue research from induced abortions and includes language allowing the government to prohibit immigration by those with the virus that causes AIDS. Adopted (thus clearing it for the Senate) 290-130: R 59-114; D 230-16 (ND 154-10, SD 76-6); I 1-0, May 25, 1993. A "yea" was a vote in support of the president's position.

179. S J Res 45. Somalia Troop Authorization/Authorization Period. Gilman, R-N.Y., substitute amendment to reduce from one year to six months the authorization of U.S. participation in Somalia and delete the section of the bill complying with the War Powers Resolution of 1973 (PL 93-148). Rejected in the Committee of the Whole 179-248: R 169-5; D 10-242 (ND 8-162, SD 2-80); I 0-1, May 25, 1993. A "nay" was a vote in support of the president's position.

180. S J Res 45. Somalia Troop Authorization/Authorization Period. Roth, R-Wis., amendment to end the U.S. troop authorization and financial aid in Somalia on June 30, 1993. Rejected in Committee of the Whole 127-299: R 124-48; D 3-250 (ND 2-168, SD 1-82); I 0-1, May 25, 1993. A "nay" was a vote in support of the president's position.

181. S J Res 45. Somalia Troop Authorization/Commendation. Solomon, R-N.Y., amendment to commend the U.S. armed forces for establishing a secure environment for humanitarian relief in Somalia. Adopted in Committee of the Whole 425-0: R 173-0; D 251-0 (ND 168-0, SD 83-0); I 1-0, May 25, 1993.

182. S J Res 45. Somalia Troop Authorization/Commendation. Separate vote at the request of Walker, R-Pa., on the amendment adopted in the Committee of the Whole offered by Solomon, R-N.Y., to commend the U.S. armed forces for establishing a secure environment for humanitarian relief in Somalia. Adopted 419-0: R 173-0; D 245-0 (ND 162-0, SD 83-0); I 1-0, May 25, 1993. (On separate votes, which may be demanded on an amendment adopted in the Committee of the Whole, the four delegates and the resident commissioner of Puerto Rico cannot vote. See vote 181).

183. S J Res 45. Somalia Troop Authorization/Passage. Passage of the bill to authorize under the War Powers Resolution the previous deployment of U.S. troops in Somalia under Operation Restore Hope and to authorize for one year after enactment the continued U.S. participation in a U.N.-led peacekeeping mission in Somalia. Passed 243-179: R 3-170; D 239-9 (ND 157-8, SD 82-1); I 1-0, May 25, 1993.

KEY

Y	Voted for (yea).
#	Paired for.
+	Announced for.
N	Voted against (nay).
X	Paired against.
−	Announced against.
P	Voted "present."
C	Voted "present" to avoid possible conflict of interest.
?	Did not vote or otherwise make a position known.
D	Delegates ineligible to vote.

Democrats *Republicans*
Independent

	176	177	178	179	180	181	182	183
ALABAMA								
1 Callahan	Y	Y	N	Y	Y	Y	Y	N
2 Everett	Y	Y	N	Y	Y	Y	Y	N
3 Browder	?	?	Y	N	N	Y	Y	Y
4 Bevill	Y	Y	N	N	Y	Y	Y	Y
5 Cramer	Y	Y	Y	N	N	Y	Y	Y
6 *Bachus*	Y	Y	N	Y	Y	Y	Y	N
7 Hilliard	?	?	?	?	?	?	?	?
ALASKA								
AL *Young*	?	?	Y	Y	Y	Y	Y	N
ARIZONA								
1 Coppersmith	+	+	Y	N	N	Y	Y	Y
2 Pastor	Y	Y	Y	N	N	Y	Y	Y
3 *Stump*	Y	Y	N	Y	Y	Y	Y	N
4 *Kyl*	Y	Y	N	Y	Y	Y	Y	N
5 *Kolbe*	Y	Y	Y	Y	Y	Y	Y	N
6 English	Y	Y	N	N	Y	Y	Y	Y
ARKANSAS								
1 Lambert	Y	Y	Y	N	N	Y	Y	Y
2 Thornton	Y	Y	N	N	Y	Y	Y	Y
3 *Hutchinson*	Y	Y	N	Y	N	Y	Y	N
4 Dickey	Y	Y	N	Y	N	Y	Y	N
CALIFORNIA								
1 Hamburg	Y	Y	Y	N	N	Y	Y	Y
2 *Herger*	Y	Y	N	Y	Y	Y	Y	N
3 Fazio	Y	Y	Y	N	N	Y	Y	Y
4 *Doolittle*	?	?	N	Y	Y	Y	Y	N
5 Matsui	?	?	Y	N	N	Y	Y	Y
6 Woolsey	?	?	Y	N	N	Y	Y	Y
7 Miller	Y	Y	Y	N	N	Y	Y	Y
8 Pelosi	Y	Y	Y	N	N	?	Y	Y
9 Dellums	Y	Y	N	N	N	Y	Y	Y
10 *Baker*	Y	Y	N	Y	Y	Y	Y	N
11 *Pombo*	Y	N	N	Y	Y	Y	Y	N
12 Lantos	Y	Y	N	N	Y	Y	Y	Y
13 Stark	Y	Y	Y	N	N	Y	Y	Y
14 Eshoo	Y	Y	Y	N	N	Y	Y	Y
15 Mineta	?	?	Y	N	N	Y	Y	Y
16 Edwards	Y	Y	Y	N	N	Y	Y	Y
17 Vacancy								
18 Condit	Y	Y	Y	N	N	Y	Y	Y
19 Lehman	?	?	Y	N	N	Y	Y	Y
20 Dooley	?	?	Y	N	N	Y	Y	Y
21 *Thomas*	?	?	Y	Y	Y	Y	Y	N
22 *Huffington*	Y	N	Y	Y	Y	Y	Y	N
23 *Gallegly*	?	?	Y	Y	Y	Y	Y	N
24 Beilenson	Y	Y	N	N	Y	Y	Y	Y
25 *McKeon*	?	?	N	Y	Y	Y	Y	N
26 Berman	?	?	?	N	N	Y	Y	Y
27 *Moorhead*	Y	Y	N	Y	Y	Y	Y	N
28 *Dreier*	Y	Y	N	Y	N	Y	Y	N
29 Waxman	Y	Y	N	N	N	Y	Y	Y
30 Becerra	Y	Y	N	N	N	Y	Y	Y
31 Martinez	Y	Y	Y	N	N	?	?	Y
32 Dixon	Y	Y	Y	N	N	Y	Y	Y
33 Roybal-Allard	Y	Y	N	N	N	Y	Y	Y
34 Torres	Y	Y	Y	N	N	Y	Y	Y
35 Waters	?	?	Y	N	N	Y	Y	Y
36 Harman	Y	Y	N	N	Y	Y	Y	Y
37 Tucker	Y	Y	Y	N	N	Y	Y	Y
38 *Horn*	Y	Y	Y	Y	Y	Y	Y	N
39 *Royce*	Y	Y	N	Y	Y	Y	Y	N
40 *Lewis*	Y	Y	?	Y	N	Y	Y	N
41 *Kim*	Y	Y	Y	Y	Y	Y	Y	N

	176	177	178	179	180	181	182	183
42 Brown	Y	Y	Y	N	N	Y	Y	Y
43 *Calvert*	?	?	N	Y	Y	Y	Y	N
44 *McCandless*	Y	Y	N	Y	Y	N	Y	N
45 *Rohrabacher*	Y	Y	N	Y	Y	Y	Y	N
46 *Dornan*	Y	Y	N	Y	Y	Y	Y	N
47 *Cox*	?	?	N	Y	Y	Y	Y	N
48 *Packard*	Y	Y	N	Y	Y	Y	Y	N
49 Schenk	Y	Y	Y	N	?	Y	Y	Y
50 Filner	Y	Y	Y	N	N	Y	Y	Y
51 *Cunningham*	Y	Y	N	Y	Y	Y	Y	N
52 *Hunter*	Y	Y	N	Y	Y	Y	Y	N
COLORADO								
1 Schroeder	?	?	Y	N	N	Y	Y	N
2 Skaggs	Y	Y	Y	N	N	Y	Y	Y
3 *McInnis*	Y	Y	Y	Y	N	Y	Y	N
4 *Allard*	Y	Y	N	Y	Y	Y	Y	N
5 *Hefley*	?	?	N	Y	Y	Y	Y	N
6 *Schaefer*	?	?	N	Y	Y	Y	Y	N
CONNECTICUT								
1 Kennelly	Y	Y	Y	N	N	Y	Y	Y
2 Gejdenson	?	?	Y	N	N	Y	Y	Y
3 DeLauro	Y	Y	Y	N	N	Y	Y	Y
4 *Shays*	Y	Y	Y	Y	Y	Y	Y	N
5 *Franks*	Y	Y	Y	Y	Y	Y	Y	N
6 *Johnson*	Y	Y	Y	Y	Y	Y	Y	N
DELAWARE								
AL *Castle*	Y	Y	N	Y	N	Y	Y	N
FLORIDA								
1 Hutto	?	?	N	N	N	Y	Y	Y
2 Peterson	Y	Y	N	N	N	Y	Y	Y
3 Brown	?	?	Y	N	N	Y	Y	Y
4 *Fowler*	?	?	N	Y	N	Y	Y	N
5 Thurman	Y	Y	N	N	N	Y	Y	Y
6 *Stearns*	Y	Y	N	Y	Y	Y	Y	N
7 Mica	Y	Y	N	N	Y	Y	Y	Y
8 *McCollum*	Y	Y	N	Y	Y	Y	Y	N
9 *Bilirakis*	Y	Y	N	Y	Y	Y	Y	N
10 *Young*	Y	Y	N	Y	N	Y	Y	N
11 Gibbons	Y	Y	Y	N	N	Y	Y	Y
12 *Canady*	Y	Y	N	Y	N	Y	Y	N
13 *Miller*	Y	Y	N	Y	Y	Y	Y	N
14 *Goss*	Y	Y	N	Y	N	Y	Y	N
15 *Bacchus*	Y	Y	N	N	N	Y	Y	Y
16 *Lewis*	Y	Y	N	Y	N	Y	Y	N
17 Meek	Y	Y	N	N	N	Y	Y	Y
18 *Ros-Lehtinen*	Y	Y	N	Y	N	Y	Y	N
19 Johnston	?	?	Y	N	N	Y	Y	Y
20 Deutsch	Y	Y	N	N	N	Y	Y	Y
21 *Diaz-Balart*	Y	Y	N	N	N	Y	Y	N
22 *Shaw*	?	?	Y	Y	Y	Y	Y	N
23 Hastings	?	?	Y	N	N	Y	Y	Y
GEORGIA								
1 *Kingston*	?	?	N	Y	Y	Y	Y	N
2 Bishop	+	+	Y	N	N	Y	Y	Y
3 *Collins*	Y	Y	N	Y	N	Y	Y	N
4 *Linder*	?	?	N	Y	Y	Y	Y	N
5 Lewis	Y	Y	N	N	N	Y	Y	Y
6 *Gingrich*	?	?	N	Y	N	Y	Y	N
7 *Darden*	Y	Y	Y	N	N	Y	Y	Y
8 Rowland	?	?	N	N	N	Y	Y	N
9 Deal	Y	Y	Y	N	N	Y	Y	Y
10 Johnson	Y	Y	N	N	N	Y	Y	Y
11 McKinney	?	?	Y	N	N	Y	Y	Y
HAWAII								
1 Abercrombie	?	?	Y	N	N	Y	Y	Y
2 Mink	Y	Y	Y	N	N	Y	Y	Y
IDAHO								
1 LaRocco	Y	Y	Y	N	N	Y	Y	Y
2 *Crapo*	?	?	N	Y	Y	Y	Y	N
ILLINOIS								
1 Rush	Y	Y	Y	N	N	Y	Y	Y
2 Reynolds	Y	Y	Y	N	N	Y	Y	Y
3 Lipinski	?	?	Y	N	N	Y	Y	Y
4 Gutierrez	?	?	Y	N	N	Y	Y	Y
5 Rostenkowski	?	?	Y	N	N	Y	Y	Y
6 *Hyde*	Y	Y	N	Y	N	Y	Y	N
7 Collins	Y	Y	Y	N	N	Y	Y	Y
8 *Crane*	?	?	N	Y	Y	N	Y	N
9 Yates	Y	Y	Y	N	N	Y	Y	Y
10 *Porter*	Y	Y	Y	N	N	Y	Y	N
11 Sangmeister	?	?	Y	N	N	Y	Y	Y
12 Costello	Y	Y	Y	N	N	Y	Y	Y
13 *Fawell*	Y	Y	N	Y	Y	Y	Y	N
14 *Hastert*	Y	N	N	Y	Y	Y	Y	N
15 *Ewing*	?	?	N	Y	Y	Y	Y	N
16 *Manzullo*	Y	Y	N	Y	Y	Y	Y	N
17 Evans	Y	Y	N	N	N	Y	Y	Y

ND Northern Democrats   SD Southern Democrats

	176	177	178	179	180	181	182	183
18 ***Michel***	Y	Y	N	Y	N	Y	Y	N
19 Poshard	Y	Y	N	N	N	Y	Y	Y
20 Durbin	Y	Y	Y	N	N	Y	Y	Y
INDIANA								
1 Visclosky	Y	Y	Y	N	N	Y	Y	Y
2 Sharp	Y	Y	Y	N	N	Y	Y	Y
3 Roemer	Y	Y	N	N	N	Y	Y	Y
4 Long	Y	Y	Y	N	N	Y	Y	Y
5 ***Buyer***	Y	Y	N	Y	N	Y	Y	N
6 ***Burton***	Y	Y	N	Y	Y	Y	Y	N
7 ***Myers***	Y	Y	N	Y	Y	Y	Y	N
8 McCloskey	Y	Y	Y	N	N	Y	Y	Y
9 Hamilton	Y	Y	Y	N	N	Y	Y	Y
10 Jacobs	Y	Y	Y	N	N	Y	Y	N
IOWA								
1 ***Leach***	?	?	?	?	?	?	?	?
2 ***Nussle***	Y	Y	N	Y	Y	Y	Y	N
3 ***Lightfoot***	Y	Y	N	Y	Y	Y	Y	N
4 Smith	Y	Y	Y	N	N	Y	Y	Y
5 ***Grandy***	?	?	Y	Y	Y	Y	Y	N
KANSAS								
1 ***Roberts***	Y	Y	N	Y	Y	Y	Y	N
2 Slattery	Y	Y	Y	N	N	Y	Y	Y
3 ***Meyers***	Y	Y	Y	Y	Y	Y	Y	N
4 Glickman	Y	Y	Y	N	N	Y	Y	Y
KENTUCKY								
1 Barlow	Y	Y	Y	N	N	Y	Y	Y
2 Natcher	Y	Y	Y	N	N	Y	Y	Y
3 Mazzoli	Y	Y	Y	N	N	Y	Y	N
4 ***Bunning***	Y	Y	N	Y	Y	Y	Y	N
5 ***Rogers***	Y	Y	N	Y	Y	Y	Y	N
6 Baesler	Y	Y	Y	N	N	Y	Y	Y
LOUISIANA								
1 ***Livingston***	?	Y	N	Y	Y	Y	Y	N
2 Jefferson	Y	Y	Y	N	N	Y	Y	Y
3 Tauzin	Y	Y	N	N	N	Y	Y	Y
4 Fields	Y	Y	Y	N	N	Y	Y	Y
5 ***McCrery***	Y	Y	N	Y	Y	Y	Y	N
6 ***Baker***	?	?	N	Y	Y	Y	Y	N
7 Hayes	?	?	N	N	N	Y	Y	Y
MAINE								
1 Andrews	Y	Y	Y	N	N	Y	Y	Y
2 ***Snowe***	Y	Y	Y	Y	Y	Y	Y	N
MARYLAND								
1 ***Gilchrest***	?	?	Y	Y	Y	Y	Y	N
2 ***Bentley***	Y	Y	Y	Y	Y	Y	Y	N
3 Cardin	?	?	Y	N	N	Y	Y	Y
4 Wynn	Y	Y	Y	N	N	Y	Y	Y
5 Hoyer	Y	?	Y	N	N	Y	Y	Y
6 ***Bartlett***	?	?	N	Y	Y	Y	Y	N
7 Mfume	Y	Y	Y	N	N	Y	Y	Y
8 ***Morella***	Y	Y	Y	Y	N	Y	Y	Y
MASSACHUSETTS								
1 Olver	Y	Y	Y	N	N	Y	Y	Y
2 Neal	?	?	Y	N	N	Y	Y	Y
3 ***Blute***	Y	Y	Y	Y	Y	Y	Y	N
4 Frank	Y	Y	Y	N	N	Y	Y	Y
5 Meehan	?	?	Y	N	N	Y	Y	Y
6 ***Torkildsen***	Y	Y	Y	Y	N	Y	Y	N
7 Markey	Y	Y	Y	N	N	Y	Y	Y
8 Kennedy	?	?	Y	N	N	Y	Y	Y
9 Moakley	Y	Y	Y	N	N	Y	Y	Y
10 Studds	Y	Y	Y	N	N	Y	Y	Y
MICHIGAN								
1 Stupak	?	?	Y	N	N	Y	Y	Y
2 ***Hoekstra***	Y	Y	N	Y	Y	Y	Y	N
3 Henry	?	?	?	?	?	?	?	?
4 ***Camp***	Y	Y	N	N	Y	Y	Y	N
5 Barcia	Y	Y	N	N	N	Y	Y	Y
6 ***Upton***	Y	Y	Y	Y	N	Y	Y	N
7 ***Smith***	+	+	N	Y	Y	Y	Y	N
8 Carr	?	?	Y	N	N	Y	Y	Y
9 Kildee	Y	Y	Y	N	N	Y	Y	Y
10 Bonior	Y	Y	+	—	—	+	+	+
11 ***Knollenberg***	?	?	N	Y	Y	Y	Y	N
12 Levin	Y	Y	Y	N	N	Y	Y	Y
13 Ford	Y	Y	Y	N	N	Y	?	Y
14 Conyers	?	?	?	?	?	?	?	?
15 Collins	Y	Y	Y	N	N	Y	Y	Y
16 Dingell	Y	Y	Y	N	N	Y	?	Y
MINNESOTA								
1 Penny	Y	N	Y	N	N	Y	Y	Y
2 Minge	?	Y	Y	N	N	Y	Y	Y
3 ***Ramstad***	Y	Y	Y	Y	Y	Y	Y	N
4 Vento	Y	Y	Y	N	N	Y	Y	Y

	176	177	178	179	180	181	182	183
5 Sabo	Y	Y	Y	N	N	Y	Y	Y
6 ***Grams***	Y	Y	N	Y	Y	Y	Y	N
7 Peterson	Y	Y	N	N	N	Y	Y	Y
8 Oberstar	Y	Y	Y	N	N	Y	Y	Y
MISSISSIPPI								
1 Whitten	Y	Y	?	N	N	Y	Y	Y
2 Thompson	?	?	?	?	?	?	?	Y
3 Montgomery	Y	Y	Y	N	N	Y	Y	Y
4 Parker	?	?	Y	Y	N	Y	Y	Y
5 Taylor	Y	Y	N	N	N	Y	Y	Y
MISSOURI								
1 Clay	Y	Y	Y	N	N	Y	Y	Y
2 ***Talent***	?	?	N	N	N	Y	Y	N
3 Gephardt	Y	Y	Y	N	N	Y	Y	Y
4 Skelton	?	?	N	N	N	Y	Y	Y
5 Wheat	Y	Y	Y	N	N	Y	Y	Y
6 Danner	Y	Y	Y	N	N	Y	Y	N
7 ***Hancock***	Y	Y	N	Y	Y	Y	Y	N
8 ***Emerson***	Y	Y	N	Y	N	Y	Y	N
9 Volkmer	Y	Y	N	N	N	Y	Y	Y
MONTANA								
AL Williams	?	?	?	?	?	?	?	?
NEBRASKA								
1 ***Bereuter***	Y	Y	N	Y	Y	Y	Y	N
2 Hoagland	Y	Y	Y	N	N	Y	Y	Y
3 ***Barrett***	Y	Y	N	Y	Y	Y	Y	N
NEVADA								
1 Bilbray	?	?	Y	N	N	Y	Y	Y
2 ***Vucanovich***	?	?	N	Y	Y	Y	Y	N
NEW HAMPSHIRE								
1 ***Zeliff***	?	?	Y	Y	Y	Y	Y	N
2 Swett	Y	Y	Y	N	N	Y	Y	Y
NEW JERSEY								
1 Andrews	Y	Y	Y	N	N	Y	Y	Y
2 Hughes	Y	Y	Y	N	N	?	?	Y
3 ***Saxton***	Y	Y	N	Y	Y	Y	Y	N
4 ***Smith***	Y	Y	N	Y	N	Y	Y	N
5 ***Roukema***	Y	Y	Y	Y	Y	Y	Y	N
6 Pallone	Y	Y	Y	N	N	Y	Y	Y
7 ***Franks***	Y	Y	Y	Y	Y	Y	Y	N
8 Klein	Y	Y	Y	N	N	Y	Y	Y
9 Torricelli	?	?	Y	N	N	Y	Y	Y
10 Payne	Y	Y	Y	N	N	Y	Y	Y
11 ***Gallo***	Y	Y	Y	Y	Y	Y	Y	N
12 ***Zimmer***	?	?	Y	Y	Y	Y	Y	N
13 Menendez	Y	Y	Y	N	N	Y	Y	Y
NEW MEXICO								
1 ***Schiff***	Y	Y	Y	Y	N	Y	Y	N
2 ***Skeen***	Y	Y	N	Y	N	Y	Y	N
3 Richardson	Y	Y	Y	N	N	Y	Y	Y
NEW YORK								
1 Hochbrueckner	?	?	Y	N	N	Y	Y	Y
2 ***Lazio***	Y	Y	Y	Y	N	Y	Y	Y
3 ***King***	Y	Y	N	Y	N	Y	Y	N
4 ***Levy***	Y	Y	Y	Y	Y	Y	Y	N
5 Ackerman	Y	Y	Y	N	N	Y	Y	Y
6 Flake	?	?	Y	N	N	Y	Y	Y
7 Manton	Y	Y	Y	N	N	Y	Y	Y
8 Nadler	Y	Y	Y	N	N	Y	Y	Y
9 Schumer	Y	Y	Y	N	N	Y	Y	Y
10 Towns	Y	Y	Y	N	N	Y	Y	Y
11 Owens	?	?	Y	N	N	Y	Y	Y
12 Velazquez	Y	Y	Y	N	N	Y	Y	Y
13 ***Molinari***	Y	Y	Y	Y	N	Y	Y	N
14 Maloney	?	?	Y	N	N	Y	Y	Y
15 Rangel	Y	Y	Y	N	N	Y	Y	Y
16 Serrano	Y	Y	Y	N	N	Y	Y	Y
17 Engel	?	?	+	?	N	Y	Y	Y
18 Lowey	Y	Y	Y	N	N	Y	Y	Y
19 ***Fish***	Y	Y	Y	Y	N	Y	Y	N
20 ***Gilman***	Y	Y	Y	Y	Y	Y	Y	N
21 McNulty	?	?	Y	N	N	Y	Y	Y
22 ***Solomon***	Y	Y	N	Y	Y	Y	Y	N
23 ***Boehlert***	Y	Y	Y	N	N	Y	Y	Y
24 ***McHugh***	Y	Y	Y	Y	Y	Y	Y	N
25 ***Walsh***	Y	Y	Y	Y	Y	Y	Y	N
26 Hinchey	Y	Y	Y	N	N	Y	Y	Y
27 ***Paxon***	Y	Y	N	Y	Y	Y	Y	N
28 Slaughter	Y	Y	Y	N	N	Y	Y	Y
29 LaFalce	Y	Y	Y	N	N	Y	Y	Y
30 ***Quinn***	Y	Y	N	Y	Y	Y	Y	N
31 ***Houghton***	Y	Y	Y	Y	?	?	?	X
NORTH CAROLINA								
1 Clayton	Y	Y	Y	N	N	Y	Y	Y
2 Valentine	Y	Y	Y	N	N	Y	Y	Y

	176	177	178	179	180	181	182	183
3 Lancaster	Y	Y	Y	N	N	Y	Y	Y
4 Price	Y	Y	Y	N	N	Y	Y	Y
5 Neal	?	?	Y	N	N	Y	Y	Y
6 ***Coble***	Y	Y	N	Y	Y	Y	Y	N
7 Rose	Y	Y	Y	N	N	Y	Y	Y
8 Hefner	?	?	Y	N	N	Y	Y	Y
9 ***McMillan***	Y	Y	Y	Y	Y	Y	Y	N
10 ***Ballenger***	+	+	N	Y	Y	Y	Y	N
11 ***Taylor***	?	?	N	Y	Y	Y	Y	N
12 Watt	Y	Y	Y	N	N	Y	Y	Y
NORTH DAKOTA								
AL Pomeroy	Y	Y	Y	N	N	Y	Y	Y
OHIO								
1 Mann	Y	Y	Y	N	N	Y	Y	Y
2 ***Portman***	Y	Y	N	Y	Y	Y	Y	N
3 Hall	Y	Y	N	N	N	Y	Y	Y
4 ***Oxley***	+	+	N	Y	Y	Y	Y	N
5 ***Gillmor***	Y	Y	Y	Y	N	Y	Y	N
6 Strickland	Y	Y	Y	N	N	Y	Y	Y
7 ***Hobson***	Y	Y	Y	Y	Y	Y	Y	N
8 ***Boehner***	?	?	N	Y	N	Y	Y	N
9 Kaptur	Y	Y	Y	N	?	?	?	#
10 ***Hoke***	?	?	N	Y	Y	Y	Y	N
11 Stokes	?	?	Y	N	N	Y	Y	Y
12 ***Kasich***	Y	Y	N	Y	N	Y	Y	N
13 Brown	Y	Y	Y	N	N	Y	Y	Y
14 Sawyer	Y	Y	Y	N	N	Y	Y	Y
15 ***Pryce***	Y	Y	Y	Y	N	Y	Y	N
16 ***Regula***	Y	Y	Y	Y	Y	Y	Y	N
17 Traficant	Y	Y	Y	N	N	Y	Y	Y
18 Applegate	?	?	Y	N	N	Y	Y	Y
19 Fingerhut	Y	Y	Y	N	N	Y	Y	Y
OKLAHOMA								
1 ***Inhofe***	?	?	N	Y	Y	Y	Y	N
2 Synar	Y	Y	Y	N	N	Y	Y	Y
3 Brewster	?	?	Y	N	N	Y	Y	Y
4 McCurdy	Y	?	Y	N	N	Y	Y	?
5 ***Istook***	Y	Y	N	Y	Y	Y	Y	N
6 English	Y	Y	Y	N	N	Y	Y	Y
OREGON								
1 Furse	Y	Y	Y	N	N	Y	Y	Y
2 ***Smith***	?	?	N	Y	Y	Y	Y	N
3 Wyden	Y	Y	Y	N	N	Y	Y	Y
4 DeFazio	?	?	Y	N	N	Y	Y	Y
5 Kopetski	Y	Y	Y	N	N	Y	Y	Y
PENNSYLVANIA								
1 Foglietta	?	?	Y	N	N	Y	Y	Y
2 Blackwell	Y	Y	?	N	N	Y	Y	Y
3 Borski	?	?	Y	N	N	Y	Y	Y
4 Klink	?	?	Y	N	Y	Y	Y	N
5 ***Clinger***	Y	Y	N	Y	Y	Y	Y	N
6 Holden	?	?	Y	N	N	Y	Y	Y
7 ***Weldon***	Y	Y	N	Y	Y	Y	Y	N
8 ***Greenwood***	Y	Y	Y	Y	N	Y	Y	N
9 ***Shuster***	Y	Y	Y	Y	Y	Y	Y	N
10 ***McDade***	Y	Y	N	Y	N	Y	Y	N
11 Kanjorski	Y	Y	Y	N	N	Y	Y	N
12 Murtha	Y	Y	Y	N	N	Y	Y	Y
13 Margolies-Mezv.	?	?	Y	N	N	Y	Y	Y
14 Coyne	?	?	Y	N	N	Y	Y	Y
15 McHale	Y	Y	Y	N	N	Y	Y	Y
16 ***Walker***	Y	Y	N	Y	Y	Y	Y	N
17 ***Gekas***	Y	Y	Y	Y	Y	Y	Y	N
18 ***Santorum***	?	?	N	Y	N	Y	Y	N
19 ***Goodling***	Y	Y	N	Y	Y	Y	Y	N
20 Murphy	?	?	N	Y	Y	Y	Y	Y
21 ***Ridge***	?	?	Y	Y	?	Y	Y	N
RHODE ISLAND								
1 ***Machtley***	Y	Y	Y	Y	Y	Y	Y	N
2 Reed	Y	Y	Y	N	N	Y	Y	Y
SOUTH CAROLINA								
1 ***Ravenel***	Y	Y	N	Y	Y	Y	Y	N
2 ***Spence***	Y	Y	Y	Y	Y	Y	Y	N
3 Derrick	Y	Y	Y	N	N	Y	Y	Y
4 ***Inglis***	?	?	N	Y	Y	Y	Y	N
5 Spratt	Y	Y	Y	N	N	Y	Y	Y
6 Clyburn	Y	Y	Y	N	N	Y	Y	Y
SOUTH DAKOTA								
AL Johnson	Y	Y	Y	Y	N	Y	Y	N
TENNESSEE								
1 ***Quillen***	?	?	N	Y	Y	Y	Y	N
2 ***Duncan***	Y	Y	N	Y	Y	Y	Y	N
3 Lloyd	Y	Y	Y	N	N	Y	Y	Y
4 Cooper	?	?	Y	N	N	Y	Y	Y
5 Clement	?	?	Y	N	N	Y	Y	Y

	176	177	178	179	180	181	182	183
6 Gordon	Y	Y	Y	N	N	Y	Y	Y
7 ***Sundquist***	?	?	N	Y	Y	Y	Y	N
8 Tanner	?	?	Y	N	N	Y	Y	Y
9 Ford	?	?	Y	N	N	Y	Y	Y
TEXAS								
1 Chapman	?	?	Y	N	N	Y	Y	Y
2 Wilson	Y	Y	Y	N	N	Y	Y	Y
3 ***Johnson, Sam***	?	?	N	N	Y	Y	Y	N
4 Hall	Y	Y	Y	N	N	Y	Y	Y
5 Bryant	Y	Y	Y	N	N	Y	Y	Y
6 ***Barton***	?	?	N	Y	Y	Y	Y	N
7 ***Archer***	Y	Y	N	Y	Y	Y	Y	N
8 ***Fields***	Y	Y	N	Y	Y	Y	Y	N
9 Brooks	Y	Y	Y	N	N	Y	Y	Y
10 Pickle	Y	Y	Y	N	N	Y	Y	Y
11 Edwards	?	?	Y	N	N	Y	Y	Y
12 Geren	?	?	Y	N	N	Y	Y	Y
13 Sarpalius	?	?	Y	N	N	Y	Y	Y
14 Laughlin	Y	Y	Y	N	N	Y	Y	Y
15 de la Garza	Y	Y	N	N	N	Y	Y	Y
16 Coleman	Y	Y	Y	N	N	Y	Y	Y
17 Stenholm	Y	Y	Y	?	N	Y	Y	Y
18 Washington	?	?	Y	N	N	Y	Y	Y
19 ***Combest***	Y	Y	N	Y	Y	Y	Y	N
20 Gonzalez	Y	Y	Y	N	N	Y	Y	Y
21 ***Smith***	Y	Y	Y	Y	Y	Y	Y	N
22 ***DeLay***	?	?	N	Y	Y	Y	Y	N
23 ***Bonilla***	Y	Y	Y	N	Y	Y	Y	N
24 Frost	?	?	Y	N	N	Y	Y	Y
25 Andrews	Y	Y	Y	N	N	Y	Y	Y
26 ***Armey***	?	?	N	Y	N	Y	Y	N
27 Ortiz	?	?	N	N	N	Y	Y	Y
28 Tejeda	Y	Y	Y	N	N	Y	Y	Y
29 Green	Y	Y	Y	N	Y	Y	Y	Y
30 Johnson, E. B.	Y	Y	Y	N	N	Y	Y	Y
UTAH								
1 ***Hansen***	Y	Y	N	Y	Y	Y	Y	N
2 Shepherd	Y	Y	Y	N	N	Y	Y	?
3 Orton	Y	Y	Y	N	N	Y	Y	Y
VERMONT								
AL *Sanders*	?	?	Y	N	N	Y	Y	Y
VIRGINIA								
1 ***Bateman***	Y	Y	N	Y	N	Y	Y	N
2 Pickett	Y	Y	Y	N	N	Y	Y	Y
3 Scott	Y	Y	Y	N	N	Y	Y	Y
4 Sisisky	Y	Y	Y	N	N	Y	Y	Y
5 Payne	?	?	Y	N	N	Y	Y	Y
6 ***Goodlatte***	Y	Y	N	Y	N	Y	Y	N
7 ***Bliley***	Y	Y	N	Y	N	Y	Y	N
8 Moran	Y	Y	Y	N	N	Y	Y	Y
9 Boucher	?	?	Y	N	N	Y	Y	Y
10 ***Wolf***	Y	Y	N	Y	N	Y	Y	N
11 Byrne	Y	Y	Y	N	N	Y	Y	Y
WASHINGTON								
1 Cantwell	Y	Y	Y	N	N	Y	Y	Y
2 Swift	?	?	Y	N	N	Y	Y	Y
3 Unsoeld	Y	Y	Y	N	N	Y	Y	Y
4 Inslee	Y	Y	Y	N	N	Y	Y	Y
5 Foley								
6 Dicks	?	?	Y	N	N	Y	Y	Y
7 McDermott	Y	Y	Y	N	N	Y	Y	Y
8 ***Dunn***	Y	Y	Y	Y	Y	Y	Y	N
9 Kreidler	Y	Y	Y	N	N	Y	Y	Y
WEST VIRGINIA								
1 Mollohan	Y	Y	N	N	N	Y	Y	Y
2 Wise	?	?	Y	N	N	Y	Y	Y
3 Rahall	?	?	N	N	N	Y	Y	Y
WISCONSIN								
1 Vacancy **								
2 ***Klug***	Y	Y	Y	Y	Y	Y	Y	N
3 ***Gunderson***	?	?	Y	Y	N	Y	Y	N
4 Kleczka	Y	Y	Y	N	N	Y	Y	Y
5 Barrett	Y	Y	Y	N	N	Y	Y	Y
6 ***Petri***	Y	Y	N	Y	Y	Y	Y	N
7 Obey	Y	Y	Y	N	N	Y	Y	Y
8 ***Roth***	Y	Y	N	Y	Y	Y	Y	N
9 ***Sensenbrenner***	Y	Y	N	Y	Y	Y	Y	N
WYOMING								
AL ***Thomas***	Y	Y	Y	Y	Y	Y	Y	N
DELEGATES								
de Lugo, V.I.	D	D	D	N	N	Y	D	D
Faleomavaega, Am.S.	D	D	D	N	N	Y	D	D
Norton, D.C.	D	D	D	N	N	Y	D	D
Romero-B., P.R.	D	D	D	?	N	Y	D	D
Underwood, Guam	D	D	D	N	N	Y	D	D

Southern states - Ala., Ark., Fla., Ga., Ky., La., Miss., N.C., Okla., S.C., Tenn., Texas, Va.
Omitted votes are quorum calls, which CQ does not include in its vote charts.

184. Procedural Motion. Approval of the Journal of Tuesday, May 25. Approved 255-153: R 17-147; D 238-6 (ND 159-5, SD 79-1); I 0-0, May 26, 1993.

185. HR 2118 & HR 2244. Fiscal 1993 Supplemental Appropriations Bills/Rules. Adoption of the rule (H Res 183) to waive points of order against and provide for House floor consideration of a bill (HR 2118) to provide $1.8 billion in new budget authority for underestimated or unanticipated needs in fiscal 1993 and a bill (HR 2244) to provide $931.5 million for summer jobs and other programs originally contained in President Clinton's failed $16.3 billion plan. Adoption of the rule also deleted all funding in HR 2118 for the Executive Office of the President. Adopted 251-174: R 1-171; D 249-3 (ND 166-2, SD 83-1); I 1-0, May 26, 1993.

186. HR 2118. Fiscal 1993 Supplemental Appropriations/Defense Spending. Andrews, D-Maine, amendment to cut the $1.2 billion in the bill for Defense Department activities, which would have forced the Defense Department to finance the activities by cutting existing programs. Rejected in Committee of the Whole 188-244: R 46-128; D 141-116 (ND 103-69, SD 38-47); I 1-0, May 26, 1993.

187. HR 2118. Fiscal 1993 Supplemental Appropriations/Funds Transfers. Wolf, R-Va., amendment to eliminate the provisions allowing the White House to transfer funds between White House accounts. Rejected in Committee of the Whole 165-267: R 165-9; D 0-257 (ND 0-173, SD 0-84); I 0-1, May 26, 1993.

188. HR 2118. Fiscal 1993 Supplemental Appropriations/Passage. Passage of the bill to provide $1.8 billion in new budget authority in fiscal 1993, including funds for Operation Restore Hope in Somalia, a cost of living adjustment for veterans, fees for federal jurors, the Civilian Health and Medical Program of the Uniformed Services, Small Business Administration loan subsidies, a shortfall in Pell grants and retirement expenses for former President George Bush. Passed 300-125: R 98-76; D 202-48 (ND 129-38, SD 73-10); I 0-1, May 26, 1993. A "yea" was a vote in support of the president's position.

189. HR 2244. Fiscal 1993 Supplemental Appropriations/Youth Stipends. Burton, R-Ind., en bloc amendment to eliminate the $80 million earmark for the Youth Fair Chance Program and strip language that would provide individuals ages 14 through 30 with stipends for transportation, food, grooming and other basic necessities to help with education and training while they participate in paid work experience and classroom programs. Rejected in Committee of the Whole 176-251: R 167-4; D 9-246 (ND 4-168, SD 5-78); I 0-1, May 26, 1993.

190. HR 2244. Fiscal 1993 Supplemental Appropriations/Wastewater Treatment. Burton, R-Ind., en bloc amendment to reduce by $90 million to $200 million the amount provided for the construction of wastewater treatment facilities and reinstate the 20 percent state matching requirement that the bill waives. Rejected in Committee of the Whole 175-246: R 155-16; D 20-229 (ND 10-156, SD 10-73); I 0-1, May 26, 1993.

191. HR 2244. Fiscal 1993 Supplemental Appropriations/Tree Planting. McInnis, R-Colo., amendment to strike the $14 million for the Natural Resources Development Tree Planting Program of the Small Business Administration. Rejected in Committee of the Whole 209-218: R 164-10; D 45-207 (ND 24-145, SD 21-62); I 0-1, May 26, 1993.

** Peter W. Barca, following a recount, has been ruled the winner in Wisconsin's 1st District special election May 4 and will be sworn in June 8.

KEY

Y Voted for (yea).
Paired for.
+ Announced for.
N Voted against (nay).
X Paired against.
− Announced against.
P Voted "present."
C Voted "present" to avoid possible conflict of interest.
? Did not vote or otherwise make a position known.
D Delegates ineligible to vote.

Democrats *Republicans*
Independent

	184	185	186	187	188	189	190	191
ALABAMA								
1 *Callahan*	N	N	N	Y	Y	Y	Y	Y
2 *Everett*	N	N	N	Y	Y	Y	Y	Y
3 Browder	Y	Y	N	N	Y	N	N	N
4 Bevill	Y	Y	N	N	Y	N	N	N
5 Cramer	Y	Y	N	N	Y	N	N	N
6 *Bachus*	N	N	N	Y	N	Y	Y	Y
7 Hilliard	Y	Y	Y	N	Y	N	N	N
ALASKA								
AL *Young*	N	N	N	Y	Y	Y	Y	Y
ARIZONA								
1 Coppersmith	Y	Y	Y	N	N	N	N	Y
2 Pastor	Y	Y	N	N	Y	N	N	N
3 *Stump*	N	N	N	Y	N	Y	Y	Y
4 *Kyl*	N	N	N	Y	N	Y	Y	Y
5 *Kolbe*	N	N	N	Y	Y	Y	Y	Y
6 English	Y	Y	Y	N	N	N	N	N
ARKANSAS								
1 Lambert	Y	Y	Y	N	N	N	N	Y
2 Thornton	Y	Y	N	N	Y	N	N	N
3 *Hutchinson*	N	N	N	Y	Y	Y	Y	Y
4 *Dickey*	P	N	N	N	N	Y	Y	Y
CALIFORNIA								
1 Hamburg	Y	Y	Y	N	N	N	N	N
2 *Herger*	N	N	N	Y	N	Y	Y	Y
3 Fazio	Y	Y	N	N	Y	N	N	N
4 *Doolittle*	N	N	N	Y	N	Y	Y	Y
5 Matsui	Y	Y	N	N	Y	N	N	N
6 Woolsey	Y	Y	Y	N	N	N	N	N
7 Miller	Y	Y	Y	N	Y	N	N	N
8 Pelosi	Y	Y	N	N	Y	N	N	N
9 Dellums	Y	Y	Y	N	N	N	N	N
10 *Baker*	N	N	N	Y	N	N	N	Y
11 *Pombo*	N	N	N	Y	Y	Y	Y	Y
12 Lantos	Y	Y	N	N	Y	N	N	N
13 Stark	Y	Y	Y	N	N	?	N	N
14 Eshoo	Y	Y	Y	N	N	N	N	N
15 Mineta	Y	Y	Y	N	N	N	N	N
16 Edwards	Y	Y	Y	N	N	N	N	N
17 Vacancy								
18 Condit	Y	Y	Y	N	N	N	N	Y
19 Lehman	Y	Y	N	N	Y	N	?	?
20 Dooley	Y	Y	Y	N	N	N	N	N
21 *Thomas*	N	N	N	Y	N	Y	Y	Y
22 *Huffington*	N	N	N	Y	N	Y	Y	Y
23 *Gallegly*	?	N	N	Y	Y	Y	Y	Y
24 Beilenson	Y	Y	N	N	N	N	N	N
25 *McKeon*	N	N	N	Y	N	Y	Y	Y
26 Berman	Y	Y	N	N	Y	N	N	N
27 *Moorhead*	N	N	N	Y	N	Y	Y	Y
28 *Dreier*	N	N	N	Y	N	Y	Y	Y
29 Waxman	Y	Y	Y	N	Y	N	N	N
30 Becerra	Y	Y	Y	N	N	N	N	N
31 Martinez	Y	Y	N	N	Y	N	?	N
32 Dixon	Y	Y	N	N	Y	N	N	N
33 Roybal-Allard	Y	Y	Y	N	N	N	N	N
34 Torres	Y	Y	N	N	Y	N	N	Y
35 Waters	Y	Y	N	N	Y	N	N	N
36 Harman	Y	Y	Y	N	Y	N	?	N
37 Tucker	?	Y	Y	N	N	N	N	?
38 *Horn*	N	N	N	Y	N	Y	Y	Y
39 *Royce*	N	N	N	Y	N	Y	Y	Y
40 *Lewis*	N	N	N	Y	N	?	Y	Y
41 *Kim*	N	N	N	Y	N	Y	Y	Y

	184	185	186	187	188	189	190	191
42 Brown	?	Y	N	N	Y	N	N	N
43 *Calvert*	N	N	N	Y	Y	Y	Y	Y
44 *McCandless*	N	N	N	Y	N	Y	Y	Y
45 *Rohrabacher*	N	N	N	Y	N	Y	Y	Y
46 *Dornan*	N	N	N	Y	N	Y	Y	Y
47 *Cox*	N	N	N	Y	N	Y	Y	Y
48 *Packard*	N	N	N	Y	Y	Y	Y	Y
49 Schenk	Y	Y	Y	N	Y	N	N	N
50 Filner	Y	Y	Y	N	Y	N	N	N
51 *Cunningham*	N	N	N	Y	Y	Y	Y	Y
52 *Hunter*	N	N	N	Y	Y	Y	Y	Y
COLORADO								
1 Schroeder	N	N	Y	N	N	N	N	N
2 Skaggs	Y	Y	N	N	N	N	N	N
3 *McInnis*	Y	N	Y	N	Y	Y	Y	Y
4 *Allard*	N	N	Y	N	Y	Y	Y	Y
5 *Hefley*	N	N	N	Y	Y	Y	Y	N
6 *Schaefer*	N	N	Y	Y	Y	Y	Y	Y
CONNECTICUT								
1 Kennelly	Y	Y	N	N	Y	N	N	N
2 Gejdenson	Y	Y	N	N	Y	N	N	N
3 DeLauro	Y	Y	N	N	Y	N	N	N
4 *Shays*	N	N	Y	Y	N	Y	N	Y
5 *Franks*	N	N	Y	Y	Y	Y	Y	Y
6 *Johnson*	N	N	N	Y	Y	Y	N	Y
DELAWARE								
AL *Castle*	N	N	Y	Y	N	Y	Y	Y
FLORIDA								
1 Hutto	Y	Y	N	N	Y	N	Y	N
2 Peterson	Y	Y	N	N	Y	N	N	N
3 Brown	Y	Y	N	N	Y	N	N	N
4 *Fowler*	N	N	N	Y	Y	Y	Y	Y
5 Thurman	Y	Y	N	N	N	N	N	N
6 *Stearns*	N	N	N	Y	Y	Y	Y	Y
7 *Mica*	N	N	N	Y	N	Y	Y	Y
8 *McCollum*	N	N	N	Y	N	Y	Y	Y
9 *Bilirakis*	?	X	N	Y	Y	Y	Y	Y
10 *Young*	N	N	N	Y	Y	Y	Y	Y
11 Gibbons	Y	Y	N	N	Y	?	N	N
12 *Canady*	N	N	N	Y	N	Y	Y	Y
13 *Miller*	?	N	N	Y	Y	Y	Y	Y
14 *Goss*	N	N	N	Y	N	Y	N	Y
15 Bacchus	Y	Y	N	N	Y	N	N	N
16 *Lewis*	N	N	N	Y	N	Y	Y	Y
17 Meek	Y	Y	N	N	Y	N	N	N
18 *Ros-Lehtinen*	N	N	N	Y	Y	Y	Y	N
19 Johnston	?	Y	Y	N	Y	N	N	N
20 Deutsch	Y	Y	N	N	Y	N	N	N
21 *Diaz-Balart*	N	N	N	Y	Y	Y	Y	N
22 *Shaw*	N	N	N	Y	Y	Y	Y	Y
23 Hastings	Y	Y	Y	N	Y	N	N	N
GEORGIA								
1 *Kingston*	N	N	N	Y	N	Y	Y	Y
2 Bishop	Y	Y	Y	N	Y	N	N	N
3 *Collins*	N	N	N	Y	N	Y	Y	Y
4 *Linder*	N	N	N	Y	Y	Y	Y	Y
5 Lewis	Y	Y	Y	N	Y	N	N	N
6 *Gingrich*	?	N	N	Y	Y	Y	?	Y
7 Darden	Y	Y	N	N	Y	N	N	N
8 Rowland	Y	Y	N	N	Y	N	N	Y
9 Deal	Y	Y	N	N	N	N	N	Y
10 Johnson	Y	Y	N	N	Y	N	Y	Y
11 McKinney	Y	Y	Y	N	Y	N	N	N
HAWAII								
1 Abercrombie	Y	Y	Y	N	N	N	N	N
2 Mink	Y	Y	N	N	Y	N	N	N
IDAHO								
1 LaRocco	Y	Y	Y	N	Y	N	N	N
2 *Crapo*	N	N	Y	Y	Y	Y	Y	Y
ILLINOIS								
1 Rush	Y	Y	Y	N	Y	N	N	N
2 Reynolds	Y	Y	Y	N	N	N	N	N
3 Lipinski	Y	Y	N	Y	N	Y	N	N
4 Gutierrez	Y	Y	Y	N	N	N	N	N
5 Rostenkowski	Y	Y	N	N	Y	N	?	?
6 *Hyde*	Y	N	N	Y	Y	Y	Y	Y
7 Collins	Y	Y	Y	N	N	N	N	N
8 *Crane*	N	N	N	Y	N	Y	N	Y
9 Yates	Y	Y	Y	N	N	N	N	N
10 *Porter*	N	N	Y	Y	N	Y	Y	Y
11 Sangmeister	Y	Y	N	N	Y	N	N	N
12 Costello	Y	Y	N	N	Y	N	N	N
13 *Fawell*	N	N	Y	Y	N	Y	Y	Y
14 *Hastert*	N	N	N	Y	Y	Y	Y	Y
15 *Ewing*	N	N	N	Y	Y	Y	Y	Y
16 *Manzullo*	N	N	N	Y	Y	Y	Y	Y
17 Evans	Y	Y	Y	N	Y	N	N	N

ND Northern Democrats   SD Southern Democrats

	184	185	186	187	188	189	190	191
18 **Michel**	N	N	N	Y	Y	Y	Y	Y
19 Poshard	Y	Y	Y	N	Y	N	N	N
20 Durbin	Y	Y	N	N	Y	N	N	N
INDIANA								
1 Visclosky	Y	Y	N	N	Y	N	N	N
2 Sharp	Y	Y	Y	N	N	N	N	N
3 Roemer	Y	Y	Y	N	Y	N	N	Y
4 Long	Y	Y	Y	N	N	N	N	N
5 **Buyer**	N	N	N	Y	Y	Y	Y	Y
6 **Burton**	N	N	N	Y	N	Y	Y	Y
7 **Myers**	Y	N	N	N	Y	Y	Y	N
8 McCloskey	Y	Y	N	N	Y	N	?	N
9 Hamilton	Y	Y	N	N	Y	N	N	Y
10 Jacobs	N	Y	Y	N	N	N	Y	N
IOWA								
1 **Leach**	?	?	?	?	?	?	?	?
2 **Nussle**	N	N	Y	N	N	Y	Y	Y
3 **Lightfoot**	N	N	N	Y	Y	Y	Y	N
4 Smith	Y	Y	N	N	Y	N	N	N
5 **Grandy**	N	N	Y	Y	Y	Y	Y	N
KANSAS								
1 **Roberts**	N	N	N	Y	N	Y	Y	Y
2 Slattery	Y	Y	Y	N	N	N	Y	Y
3 **Meyers**	N	N	Y	Y	Y	Y	Y	Y
4 Glickman	Y	Y	Y	N	N	N	Y	Y
KENTUCKY								
1 Barlow	Y	Y	Y	N	Y	N	N	N
2 Natcher	Y	Y	N	N	Y	N	N	N
3 Mazzoli	Y	Y	N	N	Y	N	N	N
4 **Bunning**	N	N	N	Y	N	Y	Y	Y
5 **Rogers**	N	N	N	Y	Y	Y	N	Y
6 Baesler	Y	Y	Y	N	N	N	N	Y
LOUISIANA								
1 **Livingston**	Y	N	N	Y	Y	Y	Y	Y
2 Jefferson	Y	Y	Y	N	Y	N	N	N
3 Tauzin	Y	Y	N	N	Y	Y	Y	Y
4 Fields	Y	Y	Y	N	Y	N	N	N
5 **McCrery**	N	N	N	Y	Y	Y	Y	Y
6 **Baker**	N	N	N	Y	N	Y	Y	Y
7 Hayes	Y	Y	N	N	Y	Y	N	N
MAINE								
1 Andrews	Y	Y	Y	N	N	N	N	N
2 **Snowe**	N	N	Y	Y	Y	Y	N	Y
MARYLAND								
1 **Gilchrest**	N	N	N	Y	Y	Y	N	N
2 **Bentley**	N	N	N	Y	Y	Y	Y	Y
3 Cardin	Y	Y	Y	N	N	N	N	Y
4 Wynn	Y	Y	Y	N	Y	N	N	N
5 Hoyer	Y	Y	N	N	Y	N	N	N
6 **Bartlett**	N	N	N	Y	Y	Y	Y	Y
7 Mfume	Y	Y	Y	N	Y	N	N	N
8 **Morella**	N	N	Y	Y	N	Y	Y	Y
MASSACHUSETTS								
1 Olver	Y	Y	N	N	Y	N	N	N
2 Neal	Y	Y	N	N	Y	N	N	N
3 **Blute**	N	N	Y	Y	Y	Y	N	Y
4 Frank	Y	Y	Y	N	Y	N	N	N
5 Meehan	Y	Y	Y	N	N	N	N	N
6 **Torkildsen**	N	N	Y	N	N	Y	N	Y
7 Markey	Y	Y	Y	N	Y	N	N	N
8 Kennedy	Y	Y	Y	N	Y	N	N	N
9 Moakley	Y	Y	N	N	Y	N	N	N
10 Studds	Y	Y	Y	N	Y	N	N	N
MICHIGAN								
1 Stupak	Y	Y	Y	N	Y	N	N	N
2 **Hoekstra**	N	N	N	Y	N	Y	Y	Y
3 Henry								
4 **Camp**	N	N	Y	Y	Y	Y	Y	Y
5 Barcia	Y	Y	Y	N	Y	N	?	N
6 **Upton**	N	N	N	Y	Y	Y	Y	Y
7 **Smith**	N	N	N	Y	N	Y	Y	Y
8 Carr	Y	N	N	N	Y	N	N	N
9 Kildee	Y	Y	Y	N	Y	N	N	N
10 Bonior	Y	Y	Y	N	Y	N	N	N
11 **Knollenberg**	N	N	N	Y	N	Y	Y	Y
12 Levin	Y	Y	Y	N	Y	N	N	N
13 Ford	Y	Y	N	N	Y	N	N	N
14 Conyers	?	#	?	N	?	N	N	N
15 Collins	Y	Y	Y	N	Y	N	N	N
16 Dingell	Y	Y	N	N	Y	N	N	N
MINNESOTA								
1 Penny	Y	Y	Y	N	N	N	Y	Y
2 Minge	Y	Y	Y	N	N	N	Y	N
3 **Ramstad**	N	N	Y	Y	N	Y	Y	Y
4 Vento	Y	Y	Y	N	Y	N	N	N

	184	185	186	187	188	189	190	191
5 Sabo	Y	Y	N	N	Y	N	N	N
6 **Grams**	N	N	Y	Y	N	Y	Y	Y
7 Peterson	Y	Y	Y	N	N	N	N	N
8 Oberstar	Y	Y	N	N	Y	N	N	N
MISSISSIPPI								
1 Whitten	?	Y	N	N	Y	N	N	N
2 Thompson	?	Y	Y	N	Y	?	N	N
3 Montgomery	Y	Y	N	N	Y	N	N	N
4 Parker	Y	Y	N	N	Y	N	N	Y
5 Taylor	N	Y	N	N	Y	N	Y	Y
MISSOURI								
1 Clay	N	Y	Y	N	Y	N	N	N
2 **Talent**	N	N	N	Y	Y	Y	Y	Y
3 Gephardt	Y	Y	N	N	Y	N	N	N
4 Skelton	Y	Y	N	N	Y	N	N	N
5 Wheat	Y	Y	Y	N	Y	N	N	N
6 Danner	Y	Y	Y	N	Y	N	N	Y
7 **Hancock**	N	N	Y	Y	N	Y	Y	Y
8 **Emerson**	N	N	N	Y	Y	Y	Y	Y
9 Volkmer	Y	Y	Y	N	Y	N	Y	N
MONTANA								
AL Williams	?	?	?	?	?	?	?	?
NEBRASKA								
1 **Bereuter**	N	N	Y	Y	N	Y	N	Y
2 Hoagland	Y	Y	Y	N	N	N	N	N
3 **Barrett**	N	N	Y	Y	Y	Y	Y	Y
NEVADA								
1 Bilbray	Y	Y	N	N	Y	N	N	Y
2 **Vucanovich**	N	N	N	Y	Y	Y	Y	Y
NEW HAMPSHIRE								
1 **Zeliff**	P	N	N	Y	Y	Y	Y	Y
2 Swett	Y	Y	N	N	Y	N	N	N
NEW JERSEY								
1 Andrews	Y	Y	N	N	Y	N	N	N
2 Hughes	Y	Y	Y	N	Y	N	N	N
3 **Saxton**	N	N	N	Y	Y	Y	Y	Y
4 **Smith**	Y	N	N	Y	Y	Y	Y	Y
5 **Roukema**	N	N	Y	Y	N	Y	Y	Y
6 Pallone	Y	Y	N	N	N	N	N	N
7 **Franks**	N	N	Y	Y	N	Y	Y	Y
8 Klein	Y	Y	Y	N	N	N	N	N
9 Torricelli	Y	Y	N	N	Y	N	N	N
10 Payne	Y	Y	Y	N	Y	N	N	N
11 **Gallo**	N	N	N	Y	Y	Y	Y	Y
12 **Zimmer**	N	N	Y	Y	N	Y	Y	Y
13 Menendez	Y	Y	Y	N	+	N	N	N
NEW MEXICO								
1 **Schiff**	N	N	N	N	Y	Y	Y	Y
2 **Skeen**	N	N	N	Y	Y	Y	Y	Y
3 Richardson	Y	Y	N	N	Y	N	N	N
NEW YORK								
1 Hochbrueckner	Y	Y	N	N	Y	N	N	N
2 **Lazio**	N	N	Y	Y	N	Y	Y	Y
3 **King**	N	N	N	Y	Y	Y	Y	Y
4 **Levy**	N	N	N	Y	Y	Y	Y	Y
5 Ackerman	Y	Y	Y	N	Y	N	N	N
6 Flake	Y	Y	Y	N	Y	N	N	N
7 Manton	Y	Y	N	N	Y	N	N	N
8 Nadler	Y	Y	Y	N	N	N	N	N
9 Schumer	Y	Y	Y	N	Y	N	N	N
10 Towns	Y	Y	Y	N	Y	N	N	N
11 Owens	Y	Y	Y	N	N	N	N	N
12 Velazquez	Y	Y	Y	N	N	N	N	N
13 **Molinari**	N	N	N	Y	Y	Y	N	Y
14 Maloney	Y	Y	Y	N	N	N	Y	Y
15 Rangel	Y	Y	Y	N	Y	N	?	N
16 Serrano	Y	Y	Y	N	Y	N	N	N
17 Engel	Y	Y	Y	N	Y	N	N	N
18 Lowey	Y	Y	N	N	Y	N	N	N
19 **Fish**	Y	N	N	Y	Y	N	Y	Y
20 **Gilman**	Y	N	N	Y	Y	Y	Y	Y
21 McNulty	Y	Y	N	N	Y	N	N	N
22 **Solomon**	N	N	N	Y	N	Y	Y	Y
23 **Boehlert**	N	N	N	Y	Y	Y	N	N
24 **McHugh**	N	N	N	Y	Y	Y	Y	Y
25 **Walsh**	N	N	N	Y	Y	Y	Y	Y
26 Hinchey	Y	Y	Y	N	Y	N	N	N
27 **Paxon**	N	N	N	Y	N	Y	Y	Y
28 Slaughter	Y	Y	N	N	Y	N	N	N
29 LaFalce	Y	Y	N	N	Y	N	Y	N
30 **Quinn**	N	N	N	Y	Y	Y	Y	Y
31 **Houghton**	?	N	N	Y	Y	Y	Y	Y
NORTH CAROLINA								
1 Clayton	Y	Y	Y	N	Y	N	N	N
2 Valentine	?	Y	Y	N	N	N	Y	Y

	184	185	186	187	188	189	190	191
3 Lancaster	Y	Y	N	N	Y	N	N	N
4 Price	Y	Y	N	N	Y	N	N	N
5 Neal	Y	Y	Y	N	Y	N	Y	Y
6 **Coble**	N	N	Y	Y	Y	Y	Y	Y
7 Rose	Y	Y	Y	N	?	N	N	N
8 Hefner	Y	Y	N	N	Y	N	N	N
9 **McMillan**	?	N	N	Y	Y	Y	Y	Y
10 **Ballenger**	N	N	N	Y	N	Y	Y	Y
11 **Taylor**	N	N	N	Y	Y	Y	Y	Y
12 Watt	Y	Y	Y	N	Y	N	N	N
NORTH DAKOTA								
AL Pomeroy	Y	Y	Y	N	Y	N	N	N
OHIO								
1 Mann	Y	Y	Y	N	N	N	N	N
2 **Portman**	N	N	Y	Y	N	Y	Y	Y
3 Hall	Y	Y	N	N	Y	N	N	N
4 **Oxley**	N	N	N	Y	N	Y	Y	Y
5 **Gillmor**	Y	N	Y	Y	Y	Y	Y	Y
6 Strickland	Y	Y	Y	N	Y	N	N	Y
7 **Hobson**	N	N	N	Y	Y	Y	Y	Y
8 **Boehner**	N	N	Y	Y	N	Y	Y	Y
9 Kaptur	Y	Y	N	N	Y	N	N	N
10 **Hoke**	Y	N	Y	Y	N	Y	?	Y
11 Stokes	Y	Y	N	N	Y	N	N	N
12 **Kasich**	Y	N	Y	Y	N	Y	Y	Y
13 Brown	Y	Y	Y	N	Y	N	N	N
14 Sawyer	Y	Y	N	N	Y	N	N	N
15 **Pryce**	N	N	Y	Y	Y	Y	Y	Y
16 **Regula**	N	N	N	Y	Y	Y	Y	N
17 Traficant	Y	Y	N	N	Y	N	N	Y
18 Applegate	Y	Y	N	N	Y	N	N	Y
19 Fingerhut	N	Y	Y	N	Y	N	N	N
OKLAHOMA								
1 **Inhofe**	N	?	N	Y	N	Y	Y	Y
2 Synar	Y	Y	Y	N	Y	N	N	N
3 Brewster	Y	Y	Y	N	Y	N	N	N
4 McCurdy	Y	Y	N	N	Y	N	Y	Y
5 **Istook**	?	N	Y	N	N	Y	Y	Y
6 English	Y	Y	N	N	N	N	Y	N
OREGON								
1 Furse	Y	Y	Y	N	N	N	N	N
2 **Smith**	N	N	N	Y	N	Y	Y	Y
3 Wyden	Y	Y	Y	N	Y	N	N	N
4 DeFazio	Y	Y	Y	N	N	N	N	?
5 Kopetski	?	Y	Y	N	Y	N	N	N
PENNSYLVANIA								
1 Foglietta	Y	Y	N	N	Y	N	N	N
2 Blackwell	Y	Y	Y	N	Y	N	N	N
3 Borski	Y	Y	N	N	Y	N	N	N
4 Klink	Y	Y	N	N	Y	N	N	Y
5 **Clinger**	Y	N	N	Y	Y	Y	Y	Y
6 Holden	Y	Y	N	N	Y	N	N	Y
7 **Weldon**	N	N	N	Y	Y	Y	Y	Y
8 **Greenwood**	N	N	Y	Y	N	Y	Y	Y
9 **Shuster**	N	N	N	Y	N	Y	Y	Y
10 **McDade**	N	N	N	Y	Y	Y	Y	Y
11 Kanjorski	Y	Y	N	N	Y	N	N	N
12 Murtha	Y	Y	N	N	Y	N	N	N
13 Margolies-Mezv.	Y	Y	N	N	Y	N	N	N
14 Coyne	Y	Y	N	N	Y	N	N	N
15 McHale	Y	Y	N	N	Y	N	N	Y
16 **Walker**	N	N	N	Y	N	Y	Y	Y
17 **Gekas**	N	N	N	Y	N	N	Y	Y
18 **Santorum**	N	Y	Y	N	N	Y	Y	Y
19 **Goodling**	N	N	N	Y	Y	Y	Y	Y
20 Murphy	N	Y	Y	N	Y	Y	N	Y
21 **Ridge**	N	N	Y	Y	N	?	?	Y
RHODE ISLAND								
1 **Machtley**	N	N	N	Y	Y	?	N	Y
2 Reed	Y	Y	N	N	Y	N	N	N
SOUTH CAROLINA								
1 **Ravenel**	Y	N	N	Y	Y	Y	Y	Y
2 **Spence**	N	N	N	Y	Y	Y	Y	Y
3 Derrick	Y	Y	N	N	Y	N	N	N
4 **Inglis**	Y	N	N	N	N	Y	Y	Y
5 Spratt	Y	Y	Y	N	Y	N	N	N
6 Clyburn	Y	Y	Y	N	Y	N	N	N
SOUTH DAKOTA								
AL Johnson	Y	Y	Y	N	Y	N	N	N
TENNESSEE								
1 **Quillen**	N	N	N	Y	Y	Y	N	Y
2 **Duncan**	N	N	Y	Y	N	Y	Y	Y
3 Lloyd	Y	Y	N	N	Y	N	N	Y
4 Cooper	Y	Y	N	N	Y	N	N	Y
5 Clement	Y	Y	Y	N	Y	N	N	N

	184	185	186	187	188	189	190	191
6 Gordon	Y	Y	Y	N	Y	N	N	Y
7 **Sundquist**	N	N	N	Y	Y	Y	N	Y
8 Tanner	Y	Y	N	N	Y	N	N	Y
9 Ford	?	Y	Y	N	Y	N	?	?
TEXAS								
1 Chapman	Y	Y	N	N	Y	N	N	N
2 Wilson	Y	?	N	N	Y	N	N	N
3 **Johnson, Sam**	N	N	N	Y	N	Y	Y	Y
4 Hall	Y	N	N	N	N	Y	N	Y
5 Bryant	Y	Y	Y	N	Y	N	N	N
6 **Barton**	N	N	Y	Y	N	Y	Y	Y
7 **Archer**	Y	N	N	Y	N	Y	Y	Y
8 **Fields**	N	N	N	Y	N	Y	Y	Y
9 Brooks	Y	Y	N	?	?	N	N	N
10 Pickle	Y	Y	N	N	Y	N	N	Y
11 Edwards	Y	Y	N	N	N	N	N	Y
12 Geren	Y	Y	N	N	Y	N	N	N
13 Sarpalius	Y	Y	N	N	Y	Y	N	Y
14 Laughlin	Y	Y	N	N	Y	N	N	N
15 de la Garza	Y	Y	N	N	Y	N	N	N
16 Coleman	Y	Y	N	N	Y	N	N	N
17 Stenholm	Y	Y	Y	N	N	N	N	Y
18 Washington	Y	Y	Y	N	Y	N	N	N
19 **Combest**	Y	N	N	Y	N	Y	Y	Y
20 Gonzalez	Y	Y	N	N	Y	N	N	N
21 **Smith**	N	N	N	Y	Y	Y	Y	Y
22 **DeLay**	N	N	N	Y	N	Y	Y	Y
23 **Bonilla**	N	N	N	Y	Y	Y	Y	Y
24 Frost	Y	Y	N	N	Y	N	N	N
25 Andrews	Y	Y	N	N	Y	N	Y	Y
26 **Armey**	N	N	N	Y	N	Y	Y	Y
27 Ortiz	Y	Y	N	N	Y	N	N	N
28 Tejeda	Y	Y	N	N	Y	N	N	N
29 Green	Y	Y	Y	N	N	N	N	N
30 Johnson, E. B.	Y	Y	Y	N	Y	N	N	N
UTAH								
1 **Hansen**	N	N	N	Y	Y	Y	Y	Y
2 Shepherd	Y	Y	Y	N	N	N	N	N
3 Orton	Y	Y	Y	N	N	N	Y	Y
VERMONT								
AL *Sanders*	?	Y	Y	N	N	N	N	N
VIRGINIA								
1 **Bateman**	Y	N	N	Y	Y	Y	Y	Y
2 Pickett	Y	Y	N	N	Y	N	N	N
3 Scott	Y	Y	N	N	Y	N	N	N
4 Sisisky	Y	Y	N	N	Y	N	N	N
5 Payne	Y	Y	Y	N	Y	N	N	N
6 **Goodlatte**	N	N	N	Y	Y	Y	N	Y
7 **Bliley**	N	N	N	Y	Y	Y	N	Y
8 Moran	Y	Y	Y	N	Y	N	Y	N
9 Boucher	Y	Y	N	N	Y	N	?	?
10 **Wolf**	N	N	N	Y	N	Y	Y	Y
11 Byrne	Y	Y	Y	N	Y	N	N	N
WASHINGTON								
1 Cantwell	Y	Y	Y	N	Y	N	N	N
2 Swift	Y	Y	N	N	Y	N	N	N
3 Unsoeld	Y	Y	Y	N	Y	N	N	N
4 Inslee	Y	Y	Y	N	Y	N	N	N
5 Foley								N
6 Dicks	Y	Y	N	N	Y	N	N	N
7 McDermott	Y	Y	Y	N	N	N	N	N
8 **Dunn**	N	N	N	Y	Y	Y	Y	Y
9 Kreidler	Y	Y	Y	N	Y	N	N	N
WEST VIRGINIA								
1 Mollohan	Y	Y	N	N	Y	N	N	N
2 Wise	?	Y	N	N	Y	N	N	N
3 Rahall	Y	Y	N	N	Y	N	N	N
WISCONSIN								
1 Vacancy **								
2 **Klug**	?	N	Y	Y	N	Y	Y	Y
3 **Gunderson**	Y	N	N	Y	Y	Y	Y	Y
4 Kleczka	Y	Y	Y	?	Y	Y	N	Y
5 Barrett	Y	Y	Y	N	N	N	N	N
6 **Petri**	N	N	N	Y	N	Y	Y	Y
7 Obey	Y	Y	N	N	Y	N	N	N
8 **Roth**	N	N	Y	Y	N	Y	Y	Y
9 **Sensenbrenner**	N	N	Y	Y	N	Y	Y	Y
WYOMING								
AL **Thomas**	N	N	N	Y	Y	Y	Y	Y
DELEGATES								
de Lugo, V.I.	D	D	?	N	D	N	N	N
Faleomavaega, Am.S.	D	D	N	N	D	N	N	N
Norton, D.C.	D	D	Y	N	D	N	N	N
Romero-B., P.R.	D	D	Y	N	D	?	?	?
Underwood, Guam	D	D	Y	N	D	N	N	?

Southern states - Ala., Ark., Fla., Ga., Ky., La., Miss., N.C., Okla., S.C., Tenn., Texas, Va.
Omitted votes are quorum calls, which CQ does not include in its vote charts.

192. HR 2244. Fiscal 1993 Supplemental Appropriations-/HOPE Housing Program. Kolbe, R-Ariz., amendment to restore $150 million of the $164.5 million that the bill cuts from the HOPE housing program. Rejected in Committee of the Whole 150-279: R 143-31; D 7-247 (ND 5-165, SD 2-82); I 0-1, May 26, 1993.

193. HR 2244. 1993 Supplemental Appropriations/ Passage. Passage of the bill to provide $931.5 million in new budget authority in fiscal 1993, including $320 million for summer youth employment programs, $290 million for EPA wastewater treatment facility grants, $200 million for local police programs and $51 million for Amtrak. Passed 287-140: R 38-136; D 248-4 (ND 167-1, SD 81-3); I 1-0, May 26, 1993. A "yea" was a vote in support of the president's position.

194. Procedural Motion. Approval of the House Journal of Wednesday, May 26. Approved 244-160: R 15-155; D 229-5 (ND 153-4, SD 76-1); I 0-0, May 27, 1993.

195. HR 2264. 1993 Budget Reconciliation/Previous Question. Derrick, D-S.C., motion to order the previous question (thus ending debate and the possibility of amendment) on adoption of the rule (H Res 186) to provide for consideration of the five-year budget reconciliation bill. Motion agreed to 252-178: R 0-175; D 251-3 (ND 167-2, SD 84-1); I 1-0, May 27, 1993.

196. HR 2264. 1993 Budget Reconciliation/Rule. Adoption of the rule (H Res 186) to provide for House floor consideration of the five-year, $337 billion bill to raise $250 billion in new revenues, mandate $87 billion in spending cuts in mandatory spending, and cut an additional $159 billion from the deficit, largely through discretionary spending cuts and interest savings, for a total of $496 billion in deficit reduction by closely following President Clinton's economic proposals. The rule incorporates into the bill provisions to freeze discretionary spending at or below fiscal 1993 levels through fiscal 1998, create an entitlement review process and establish a deficit-reduction trust fund. Adopted 236-194: R 0-175; D 235-19 (ND 161-9, SD 74-10); I 1-0, May 27, 1993.

***198. HR 2264. 1993 Budget Reconciliation.** Kasich, R-Ohio, substitute amendment to offer a Republican alternative that cut $355 billion from the deficit over five years through spending cuts without tax increases. Rejected in Committee of Whole 138-295: R 132-40; D 6-254 (ND 2-173, SD 4-81); I 0-1, May 27, 1993. A "nay" was a vote in support of the president's position.

199. HR 2264. 1993 Budget Reconciliation/Passage. Passage of the five-year, $337 billion bill that closely follows President Clinton's economic proposals. The bill would raise $250 billion in new revenues, mandate $87 billion in cuts in mandatory spending, and cut an additional $159 billion from the deficit, largely through discretionary spending cuts and interest savings, for a total of $496 billion in deficit reduction over five years. Proposals in the bill include: a new top income bracket of 36 percent with a 10 percent surtax on income of more than $250,000; a tax increase on the Social Security benefits of better-off recipients; an increase in the Medicare payroll tax; an energy (Btu) tax; an increase in the corporate income tax rate to 35 percent; an auction of the public radio spectrum; and an expansion of the earned-income tax credit. Also in the bill are provisions to freeze discretionary spending at or below fiscal 1993 levels through fiscal 1998 and create an entitlement review process and a deficit-reduction trust fund. Passed 219-213: R 0-175; D 218-38 (ND 150-21, SD 68-17); I 1-0, May 27, 1993. A "yea" was a vote in support of the president's position.

200. Procedural Motion. Approval of the House Journal of Thursday, May 27. Approved 240-144: R 20-138; D 219-6 (ND 143-5, SD 76-1); I 1-0, June 8, 1993.

Omitted votes are quorum calls, which CQ does not include in its vote charts.

** Peter W. Barca, following a recount, was ruled the winner in Wisconsin's 1st District special election May 4 and was sworn in June 8.

KEY

Y Voted for (yea).
Paired for.
+ Announced for.
N Voted against (nay).
X Paired against.
− Announced against.
P Voted "present."
C Voted "present" to avoid possible conflict of interest.
? Did not vote or otherwise make a position known.
D Delegates ineligible to vote.

Democrats **Republicans**
Independent

	192	193	194	195	196	198	199	200
ALABAMA								
1 Callahan	Y	Y	N	N	N	N	N	N
2 Everett	Y	N	N	N	N	Y	N	N
3 Browder	N	Y	Y	Y	Y	N	Y	?
4 Bevill	N	Y	Y	Y	Y	N	Y	Y
5 Cramer	N	Y	Y	Y	Y	N	Y	Y
6 Bachus	Y	N	N	N	N	Y	N	N
7 Hilliard	N	Y	Y	Y	Y	N	Y	Y
ALASKA								
AL Young	Y	Y	N	N	N	?	N	N
ARIZONA								
1 Coppersmith	N	Y	Y	Y	Y	N	N	Y
2 Pastor	N	Y	Y	Y	Y	N	Y	Y
3 Stump	Y	N	N	N	N	N	N	N
4 Kyl	Y	N	N	N	N	Y	N	N
5 Kolbe	Y	N	N	N	N	Y	N	N
6 English	N	Y	Y	Y	Y	N	Y	Y
ARKANSAS								
1 Lambert	N	Y	?	Y	N	N	Y	Y
2 Thornton	N	Y	Y	Y	Y	N	Y	Y
3 Hutchinson	N	Y	N	N	N	Y	N	N
4 Dickey	N	N	N	N	N	Y	N	N
CALIFORNIA								
1 Hamburg	N	Y	Y	Y	Y	N	Y	Y
2 Herger	N	N	N	N	N	Y	N	N
3 Fazio	N	Y	Y	Y	Y	N	Y	Y
4 Doolittle	N	N	N	N	N	Y	N	?
5 Matsui	N	Y	Y	Y	Y	N	Y	Y
6 Woolsey	N	Y	Y	Y	Y	N	Y	Y
7 Miller	N	Y	Y	Y	Y	N	Y	Y
8 Pelosi	N	Y	Y	Y	Y	N	Y	Y
9 Dellums	N	Y	?	Y	Y	N	Y	Y
10 Baker	N	N	N	N	N	Y	N	N
11 Pombo	N	N	N	N	N	Y	N	?
12 Lantos	N	Y	Y	Y	Y	N	Y	Y
13 Stark	N	Y	Y	Y	Y	N	Y	Y
14 Eshoo	N	Y	Y	Y	Y	N	Y	Y
15 Mineta	N	Y	Y	Y	Y	N	Y	Y
16 Edwards	N	Y	Y	Y	Y	N	Y	Y
17 Vacancy								
18 Condit	N	Y	Y	Y	Y	N	N	?
19 Lehman	N	Y	Y	Y	N	N	N	Y
20 Dooley	N	Y	Y	Y	Y	Y	Y	Y
21 Thomas	Y	N	N	N	N	Y	N	N
22 Huffington	N	N	N	N	N	N	N	?
23 Gallegly	Y	N	N	N	N	Y	N	N
24 Beilenson	N	Y	Y	Y	Y	N	Y	Y
25 McKeon	Y	N	N	N	N	Y	N	N
26 Berman	N	Y	Y	Y	Y	N	Y	Y
27 Moorhead	Y	N	N	N	N	Y	N	N
28 Dreier	Y	N	N	N	N	Y	N	N
29 Waxman	N	Y	Y	Y	Y	N	Y	Y
30 Becerra	N	Y	Y	Y	Y	N	Y	Y
31 Martinez	N	Y	?	Y	Y	N	Y	Y
32 Dixon	N	Y	Y	Y	Y	N	Y	Y
33 Roybal-Allard	N	Y	Y	Y	Y	N	Y	Y
34 Torres	N	Y	Y	Y	Y	N	Y	Y
35 Waters	N	Y	Y	Y	Y	N	Y	Y
36 Harman	N	Y	Y	Y	Y	N	Y	Y
37 Tucker	?	Y	Y	Y	Y	N	Y	?
38 Horn	Y	N	N	N	N	Y	N	N
39 Royce	N	N	N	N	N	Y	N	N
40 Lewis	N	N	N	N	N	Y	N	N
41 Kim	Y	N	N	N	N	Y	N	N
42 Brown	N	Y	?	?	Y	N	Y	?
43 Calvert	Y	N	N	N	N	Y	N	N
44 McCandless	N	N	N	N	N	Y	N	N
45 Rohrabacher	Y	N	N	N	N	Y	N	N
46 Dornan	Y	N	N	N	N	?	N	N
47 Cox	N	N	N	N	N	Y	N	N
48 Packard	Y	N	N	N	N	Y	N	N
49 Schenk	N	Y	Y	Y	Y	N	Y	Y
50 Filner	N	Y	Y	Y	Y	N	Y	Y
51 Cunningham	Y	N	N	N	N	Y	N	N
52 Hunter	Y	N	N	N	N	Y	N	N
COLORADO								
1 Schroeder	N	Y	N	Y	Y	N	Y	N
2 Skaggs	N	Y	Y	Y	Y	N	Y	Y
3 McInnis	N	N	N	N	N	N	N	Y
4 Allard	N	N	N	N	N	Y	N	N
5 Hefley	N	N	N	N	N	N	N	N
6 Schaefer	N	N	N	N	N	N	N	N
CONNECTICUT								
1 Kennelly	N	Y	Y	Y	Y	N	Y	Y
2 Gejdenson	N	Y	Y	Y	Y	N	Y	Y
3 DeLauro	N	Y	Y	Y	Y	N	Y	Y
4 Shays	Y	Y	N	N	N	Y	N	N
5 Franks	Y	N	N	N	N	Y	N	N
6 Johnson	Y	Y	N	N	N	Y	N	N
DELAWARE								
AL Castle	Y	N	Y	N	N	Y	N	N
FLORIDA								
1 Hutto	N	Y	Y	Y	Y	N	Y	Y
2 Peterson	N	Y	Y	Y	Y	N	Y	Y
3 Brown	N	Y	Y	Y	Y	N	Y	?
4 Fowler	Y	N	N	N	N	N	N	?
5 Thurman	N	Y	Y	Y	Y	N	Y	Y
6 Stearns	Y	N	N	N	N	N	N	−
7 Mica	Y	N	N	N	N	Y	N	N
8 McCollum	Y	N	Y	N	N	Y	N	?
9 Bilirakis	Y	N	N	N	N	Y	N	N
10 Young	Y	N	N	N	N	N	N	N
11 Gibbons	N	Y	Y	Y	Y	N	Y	Y
12 Canady	Y	N	N	N	N	N	N	N
13 Miller	Y	N	N	N	N	Y	N	N
14 Goss	Y	N	N	N	N	N	N	N
15 Bacchus	N	Y	Y	Y	Y	N	Y	Y
16 Lewis	Y	N	N	N	N	Y	N	N
17 Meek	N	Y	Y	Y	Y	N	Y	Y
18 Ros-Lehtinen	Y	Y	N	N	N	Y	N	N
19 Johnston	N	Y	Y	Y	Y	N	Y	Y
20 Deutsch	N	Y	Y	Y	Y	N	Y	Y
21 Diaz-Balart	Y	Y	N	N	N	Y	N	N
22 Shaw	Y	N	N	N	N	Y	N	N
23 Hastings	N	Y	Y	Y	Y	N	Y	Y
GEORGIA								
1 Kingston	Y	N	N	N	N	N	N	N
2 Bishop	N	Y	Y	Y	Y	N	Y	+
3 Collins	N	N	N	N	N	Y	N	N
4 Linder	Y	N	N	N	N	Y	N	N
5 Lewis	N	Y	Y	Y	Y	N	Y	Y
6 Gingrich	Y	N	N	N	N	Y	N	?
7 Darden	N	Y	Y	Y	Y	N	Y	Y
8 Rowland	N	Y	Y	Y	Y	N	N	?
9 Deal	N	Y	Y	Y	N	N	Y	Y
10 Johnson	N	Y	Y	Y	Y	N	Y	Y
11 McKinney	N	Y	Y	Y	Y	N	Y	Y
HAWAII								
1 Abercrombie	N	Y	Y	Y	Y	N	Y	Y
2 Mink	N	Y	Y	Y	Y	N	Y	Y
IDAHO								
1 LaRocco	N	Y	Y	Y	Y	N	Y	Y
2 Crapo	N	N	N	N	N	Y	N	N
ILLINOIS								
1 Rush	N	Y	Y	Y	Y	N	Y	Y
2 Reynolds	N	Y	Y	Y	Y	N	Y	Y
3 Lipinski	Y	Y	Y	Y	Y	N	N	Y
4 Gutierrez	N	Y	Y	Y	Y	N	Y	Y
5 Rostenkowski	N	Y	Y	Y	Y	N	Y	Y
6 Hyde	Y	N	N	N	N	Y	N	N
7 Collins	N	Y	Y	Y	Y	N	Y	Y
8 Crane	Y	N	?	N	N	N	N	N
9 Yates	N	Y	Y	Y	Y	N	Y	Y
10 Porter	Y	N	N	N	N	Y	N	N
11 Sangmeister	Y	Y	Y	Y	Y	N	Y	Y
12 Costello	N	Y	Y	Y	Y	N	Y	Y
13 Fawell	Y	N	N	N	N	Y	N	N
14 Hastert	Y	N	N	N	N	Y	N	N
15 Ewing	Y	N	P	N	N	Y	N	N
16 Manzullo	N	N	N	N	N	N	N	N
17 Evans	N	Y	Y	Y	Y	N	Y	Y

ND Northern Democrats   SD Southern Democrats

	192	193	194	195	196	198	199	200
18 ***Michel***	Y	N	N	N	N	Y	N	N
19 Poshard	N	Y	Y	Y	Y	N	Y	Y
20 Durbin	N	Y	Y	Y	Y	N	Y	Y
INDIANA								
1 Visclosky	N	Y	Y	Y	Y	N	Y	Y
2 Sharp	N	Y	Y	Y	Y	N	Y	Y
3 Roemer	N	Y	Y	Y	Y	N	N	Y
4 Long	N	Y	Y	Y	Y	N	N	Y
5 ***Buyer***	Y	N	?	N	N	Y	N	N
6 ***Burton***	Y	N	N	N	N	N	N	N
7 ***Myers***	N	Y	Y	N	N	Y	N	Y
8 McCloskey	N	Y	Y	Y	Y	N	Y	Y
9 Hamilton	N	Y	Y	N	N	N	Y	Y
10 Jacobs	N	Y	N	N	N	N	Y	N
IOWA								
1 ***Leach***	?	?	?	N	N	N	N	N
2 ***Nussle***	N	N	N	N	N	Y	N	N
3 ***Lightfoot***	Y	N	N	N	N	N	N	?
4 Smith	N	Y	Y	Y	Y	N	Y	Y
5 ***Grandy***	Y	N	N	N	N	N	N	N
KANSAS								
1 ***Roberts***	Y	N	N	N	N	N	N	N
2 Slattery	N	Y	Y	Y	Y	N	Y	Y
3 ***Meyers***	Y	Y	N	N	N	Y	N	N
4 Glickman	N	Y	Y	Y	Y	N	Y	Y
KENTUCKY								
1 Barlow	N	Y	Y	Y	Y	N	Y	Y
2 Natcher	N	Y	Y	Y	Y	N	Y	Y
3 Mazzoli	N	Y	Y	Y	Y	N	Y	Y
4 ***Bunning***	Y	N	N	N	N	Y	N	N
5 ***Rogers***	Y	Y	N	N	N	N	N	N
6 Baesler	N	Y	Y	Y	Y	N	N	Y
LOUISIANA								
1 ***Livingston***	Y	N	?	N	N	Y	N	N
2 Jefferson	N	Y	Y	Y	Y	N	Y	Y
3 Tauzin	N	Y	Y	Y	N	Y	Y	Y
4 Fields	N	Y	Y	Y	Y	N	Y	Y
5 ***McCrery***	N	Y	N	N	N	N	Y	Y
6 ***Baker***	Y	N	N	N	N	Y	N	N
7 Hayes	N	Y	Y	Y	?	N	N	Y
MAINE								
1 Andrews	N	Y	Y	Y	Y	N	Y	Y
2 ***Snowe***	N	N	N	N	N	Y	N	Y
MARYLAND								
1 ***Gilchrest***	Y	Y	N	N	N	Y	N	N
2 ***Bentley***	Y	Y	N	N	N	N	N	N
3 Cardin	N	Y	Y	Y	Y	N	Y	Y
4 Wynn	N	Y	Y	Y	Y	N	Y	Y
5 Hoyer	N	Y	Y	Y	Y	N	Y	Y
6 ***Bartlett***	Y	N	N	N	N	Y	N	?
7 Mfume	N	Y	Y	Y	Y	N	Y	Y
8 ***Morella***	N	Y	N	N	N	N	N	N
MASSACHUSETTS								
1 Olver	N	Y	Y	Y	Y	N	Y	Y
2 Neal	?	Y	Y	Y	Y	N	Y	Y
3 ***Blute***	Y	Y	N	N	N	Y	N	N
4 Frank	N	Y	Y	Y	Y	N	Y	Y
5 Meehan	N	Y	Y	Y	Y	N	Y	Y
6 ***Torkildsen***	N	Y	N	N	N	Y	N	N
7 Markey	N	Y	Y	Y	Y	N	Y	Y
8 Kennedy	N	Y	Y	Y	Y	N	Y	?
9 Moakley	N	Y	Y	Y	Y	N	Y	Y
10 Studds	N	Y	Y	Y	Y	N	Y	Y
MICHIGAN								
1 Stupak	N	Y	Y	Y	Y	N	Y	Y
2 ***Hoekstra***	N	Y	N	N	N	Y	N	N
3 Henry	?	?	?	?	?	?	?	?
4 ***Camp***	Y	N	N	N	N	Y	N	N
5 Barcia	N	Y	Y	Y	N	N	Y	Y
6 ***Upton***	Y	N	N	N	N	Y	N	N
7 ***Smith***	Y	N	N	N	N	Y	N	N
8 Carr	N	Y	Y	Y	Y	N	Y	Y
9 Kildee	N	Y	Y	Y	Y	N	Y	Y
10 Bonior	N	Y	Y	Y	Y	N	Y	Y
11 ***Knollenberg***	Y	N	N	N	N	Y	N	N
12 Levin	N	Y	Y	Y	Y	N	Y	Y
13 Ford	N	Y	Y	Y	Y	N	Y	Y
14 Conyers	N	Y	Y	Y	Y	N	Y	?
15 Collins	N	Y	Y	Y	Y	N	Y	Y
16 Dingell	N	Y	Y	Y	Y	N	Y	Y
MINNESOTA								
1 Penny	N	Y	Y	Y	Y	N	Y	+
2 Minge	N	Y	Y	Y	Y	N	N	Y
3 ***Ramstad***	N	N	N	N	N	Y	N	N
4 Vento	N	Y	Y	Y	Y	N	Y	Y

	192	193	194	195	196	198	199	200
5 Sabo	N	Y	?	Y	Y	N	Y	Y
6 ***Grams***	Y	N	N	N	N	Y	N	N
7 Peterson	N	N	N	Y	N	N	Y	?
8 Oberstar	N	Y	Y	Y	Y	N	Y	?
MISSISSIPPI								
1 Whitten	N	Y	?	Y	Y	N	Y	?
2 Thompson	N	Y	?	Y	Y	N	Y	Y
3 Montgomery	N	Y	Y	Y	Y	N	Y	Y
4 Parker	N	Y	Y	Y	N	N	N	Y
5 Taylor	N	Y	N	Y	Y	Y	N	N
MISSOURI								
1 Clay	N	Y	N	Y	Y	N	Y	N
2 ***Talent***	Y	N	N	N	N	Y	N	N
3 Gephardt	N	Y	Y	Y	Y	N	Y	Y
4 Skelton	N	Y	Y	Y	Y	N	N	Y
5 Wheat	N	Y	?	Y	Y	N	Y	Y
6 Danner	N	Y	Y	Y	Y	N	N	Y
7 ***Hancock***	Y	N	N	N	N	N	N	N
8 ***Emerson***	Y	N	N	N	N	N	N	N
9 Volkmer	N	Y	Y	Y	Y	N	Y	?
MONTANA								
AL Williams	?	?	?	Y	Y	N	Y	?
NEBRASKA								
1 ***Bereuter***	Y	N	N	N	N	N	N	N
2 Hoagland	N	Y	Y	Y	Y	Y	Y	Y
3 ***Barrett***	Y	N	N	N	N	N	N	N
NEVADA								
1 Bilbray	N	Y	Y	Y	Y	N	Y	Y
2 ***Vucanovich***	Y	Y	N	N	N	N	N	N
NEW HAMPSHIRE								
1 ***Zeliff***	Y	N	N	N	N	Y	N	?
2 Swett	N	Y	Y	Y	Y	N	N	Y
NEW JERSEY								
1 Andrews	Y	Y	Y	Y	Y	N	N	Y
2 Hughes	N	Y	Y	Y	N	N	Y	Y
3 ***Saxton***	Y	N	N	N	N	Y	N	N
4 ***Smith***	Y	Y	N	N	N	N	Y	Y
5 ***Roukema***	N	N	N	N	N	N	N	?
6 Pallone	Y	Y	Y	Y	Y	N	N	Y
7 ***Franks***	Y	Y	N	N	N	Y	N	N
8 Klein	N	Y	Y	Y	Y	N	N	Y
9 Torricelli	N	Y	Y	Y	Y	N	Y	Y
10 Payne	N	Y	Y	Y	Y	N	Y	Y
11 ***Gallo***	Y	N	N	N	N	N	Y	Y
12 ***Zimmer***	Y	N	N	N	N	Y	N	N
13 Menendez	N	Y	Y	Y	Y	N	Y	?
NEW MEXICO								
1 ***Schiff***	Y	Y	N	N	N	Y	N	N
2 ***Skeen***	Y	Y	N	N	N	Y	N	N
3 Richardson	N	Y	Y	Y	Y	N	Y	Y
NEW YORK								
1 Hochbrueckner	N	Y	Y	Y	Y	N	Y	Y
2 ***Lazio***	Y	Y	N	N	N	Y	N	Y
3 ***King***	Y	N	N	N	N	Y	N	N
4 ***Levy***	Y	Y	N	N	N	Y	N	N
5 Ackerman	N	Y	Y	Y	Y	N	Y	Y
6 Flake	N	Y	Y	Y	Y	N	Y	Y
7 Manton	N	Y	Y	Y	Y	N	Y	Y
8 Nadler	N	Y	Y	Y	Y	N	Y	Y
9 Schumer	N	Y	Y	Y	Y	N	Y	Y
10 Towns	N	Y	Y	Y	Y	N	Y	Y
11 Owens	N	Y	Y	Y	Y	N	Y	?
12 Velazquez	N	Y	Y	Y	Y	N	Y	Y
13 ***Molinari***	Y	N	N	N	N	Y	N	N
14 Maloney	N	Y	Y	Y	Y	N	N	Y
15 Rangel	N	Y	?	Y	Y	N	Y	?
16 Serrano	N	Y	Y	Y	Y	N	Y	Y
17 Engel	N	Y	?	Y	Y	N	Y	?
18 Lowey	N	Y	Y	Y	Y	N	Y	Y
19 ***Fish***	Y	Y	Y	N	N	N	Y	Y
20 ***Gilman***	Y	Y	Y	N	N	N	Y	Y
21 McNulty	N	Y	Y	Y	Y	N	Y	Y
22 ***Solomon***	Y	N	N	N	N	Y	N	N
23 ***Boehlert***	Y	Y	N	N	N	N	N	N
24 ***McHugh***	Y	Y	N	N	N	Y	N	N
25 ***Walsh***	Y	Y	N	N	N	Y	N	N
26 Hinchey	N	Y	Y	Y	Y	N	Y	Y
27 ***Paxon***	Y	N	N	N	N	Y	N	N
28 Slaughter	N	Y	Y	Y	Y	N	Y	Y
29 LaFalce	N	Y	Y	Y	Y	N	Y	?
30 ***Quinn***	Y	Y	N	N	N	Y	N	N
31 ***Houghton***	Y	N	Y	N	N	N	N	Y
NORTH CAROLINA								
1 Clayton	N	Y	?	Y	Y	N	Y	Y
2 Valentine	N	Y	Y	Y	Y	N	Y	Y

	192	193	194	195	196	198	199	200
3 Lancaster	N	Y	Y	Y	Y	N	Y	Y
4 Price	N	Y	Y	Y	Y	N	Y	?
5 Neal	N	Y	?	Y	Y	N	Y	Y
6 ***Coble***	Y	N	N	N	N	Y	N	N
7 Rose	N	Y	?	Y	Y	N	Y	Y
8 Hefner	N	Y	Y	Y	Y	N	Y	Y
9 ***McMillan***	Y	N	N	N	N	Y	N	N
10 ***Ballenger***	Y	N	N	N	N	Y	N	N
11 ***Taylor***	Y	N	N	N	N	N	N	N
12 Watt	N	Y	Y	Y	Y	N	Y	Y
NORTH DAKOTA								
AL Pomeroy	N	Y	Y	Y	Y	N	Y	Y
OHIO								
1 Mann	N	Y	Y	Y	Y	N	N	Y
2 ***Portman***	Y	N	N	N	N	Y	N	N
3 Hall	N	Y	?	Y	Y	N	Y	Y
4 ***Oxley***	Y	N	N	N	N	Y	N	N
5 ***Gillmor***	Y	Y	Y	N	N	N	N	Y
6 Strickland	N	Y	Y	Y	Y	N	Y	Y
7 ***Hobson***	Y	N	N	N	N	Y	N	N
8 ***Boehner***	Y	N	N	N	N	Y	N	N
9 Kaptur	N	Y	Y	Y	Y	N	Y	Y
10 ***Hoke***	Y	Y	N	N	N	N	Y	Y
11 Stokes	N	Y	Y	Y	Y	N	Y	Y
12 ***Kasich***	Y	N	Y	N	N	Y	N	Y
13 Brown	N	Y	Y	Y	Y	N	Y	Y
14 Sawyer	N	Y	Y	Y	Y	N	Y	Y
15 ***Pryce***	Y	N	N	N	N	Y	N	N
16 ***Regula***	Y	N	N	N	N	N	N	N
17 Traficant	N	Y	Y	Y	Y	N	N	Y
18 Applegate	N	Y	Y	Y	Y	N	Y	Y
19 Fingerhut	N	Y	?	Y	Y	N	Y	N
OKLAHOMA								
1 ***Inhofe***	Y	N	N	N	N	Y	N	?
2 Synar	N	Y	?	Y	Y	N	Y	Y
3 Brewster	N	N	Y	Y	Y	N	Y	Y
4 McCurdy	N	Y	Y	Y	N	N	Y	Y
5 ***Istook***	N	N	N	N	N	Y	N	N
6 English	N	Y	Y	Y	N	N	N	Y
OREGON								
1 Furse	N	Y	Y	Y	Y	N	Y	Y
2 ***Smith***	Y	N	N	N	N	N	N	N
3 Wyden	N	Y	Y	Y	Y	N	Y	Y
4 DeFazio	X	X	Y	Y	Y	N	Y	?
5 Kopetski	N	Y	?	Y	Y	N	Y	?
PENNSYLVANIA								
1 Foglietta	N	Y	Y	Y	Y	N	Y	?
2 Blackwell	N	Y	Y	Y	Y	N	Y	Y
3 Borski	N	Y	Y	Y	Y	N	Y	Y
4 Klink	N	Y	Y	Y	Y	N	Y	Y
5 ***Clinger***	Y	N	N	N	N	Y	N	?
6 Holden	N	Y	Y	Y	N	N	N	Y
7 ***Weldon***	Y	N	N	N	N	Y	N	N
8 ***Greenwood***	Y	N	N	N	N	Y	N	N
9 ***Shuster***	Y	N	N	N	N	Y	N	N
10 ***McDade***	Y	N	N	N	N	Y	N	N
11 Kanjorski	N	Y	Y	Y	Y	N	Y	Y
12 Murtha	N	Y	Y	Y	Y	N	Y	Y
13 Margolies-Mezv.	N	Y	Y	Y	Y	N	N	Y
14 Coyne	N	Y	Y	Y	Y	N	Y	Y
15 McHale	Y	Y	Y	Y	N	N	N	Y
16 ***Walker***	Y	N	N	N	N	Y	N	N
17 ***Gekas***	Y	N	N	N	N	Y	N	N
18 ***Santorum***	Y	Y	N	N	N	Y	N	N
19 ***Goodling***	N	N	N	N	N	Y	N	?
20 Murphy	N	Y	N	Y	Y	N	Y	N
21 ***Ridge***	Y	Y	N	N	N	Y	N	N
RHODE ISLAND								
1 ***Machtley***	Y	Y	N	N	N	N	N	N
2 Reed	N	Y	Y	Y	Y	N	Y	Y
SOUTH CAROLINA								
1 ***Ravenel***	Y	N	N	N	N	Y	N	N
2 ***Spence***	Y	N	N	N	N	N	N	?
3 Derrick	N	Y	Y	Y	Y	N	Y	Y
4 ***Inglis***	Y	N	Y	N	N	Y	N	?
5 Spratt	N	Y	Y	Y	Y	N	Y	Y
6 Clyburn	N	Y	?	Y	Y	N	Y	Y
SOUTH DAKOTA								
AL Johnson	N	Y	Y	Y	Y	N	N	Y
TENNESSEE								
1 ***Quillen***	Y	N	N	N	N	Y	N	N
2 ***Duncan***	N	N	N	N	N	N	N	N
3 Lloyd	N	Y	Y	Y	N	N	Y	Y
4 Cooper	N	Y	Y	Y	N	Y	Y	Y
5 Clement	N	Y	Y	Y	Y	N	N	Y

	192	193	194	195	196	198	199	200
6 Gordon	N	Y	Y	Y	Y	N	Y	Y
7 ***Sundquist***	Y	N	N	N	N	Y	N	N
8 Tanner	N	Y	Y	Y	Y	Y	Y	?
9 Ford	N	Y	Y	Y	Y	N	Y	?
TEXAS								
1 Chapman	N	Y	Y	Y	Y	N	N	Y
2 Wilson	N	Y	Y	Y	Y	N	N	Y
3 ***Johnson, Sam***	Y	N	N	N	N	Y	N	N
4 Hall	N	Y	Y	Y	N	N	N	Y
5 Bryant	N	Y	Y	Y	Y	N	Y	Y
6 ***Barton***	Y	N	N	N	N	Y	N	N
7 ***Archer***	Y	N	N	N	N	?	N	Y
8 ***Fields***	Y	N	N	N	N	Y	N	N
9 Brooks	N	Y	Y	Y	Y	N	Y	Y
10 Pickle	Y	Y	Y	Y	Y	N	Y	Y
11 Edwards	N	N	Y	Y	Y	N	N	Y
12 Geren	N	Y	Y	Y	Y	N	N	Y
13 Sarpalius	N	N	Y	N	N	N	N	Y
14 Laughlin	N	Y	Y	Y	Y	N	N	Y
15 de la Garza	N	Y	Y	Y	Y	N	Y	Y
16 Coleman	N	Y	Y	Y	Y	N	Y	Y
17 Stenholm	N	Y	Y	Y	Y	N	Y	Y
18 Washington	N	Y	Y	Y	Y	N	Y	Y
19 ***Combest***	Y	N	Y	N	N	N	N	Y
20 Gonzalez	N	Y	Y	Y	Y	N	Y	Y
21 ***Smith***	Y	N	N	N	N	Y	N	N
22 ***DeLay***	Y	N	N	N	N	Y	N	N
23 ***Bonilla***	Y	N	N	N	N	Y	N	N
24 Frost	N	Y	Y	Y	Y	N	Y	Y
25 Andrews	N	Y	Y	Y	Y	N	Y	Y
26 ***Armey***	Y	N	N	N	N	Y	N	N
27 Ortiz	N	Y	Y	Y	Y	N	Y	Y
28 Tejeda	N	Y	Y	Y	Y	N	Y	Y
29 Green	N	Y	Y	Y	Y	N	Y	Y
30 Johnson, E. B.	N	Y	Y	Y	Y	N	Y	Y
UTAH								
1 ***Hansen***	Y	N	N	N	N	Y	N	N
2 Shepherd	N	Y	?	Y	Y	N	Y	Y
3 Orton	N	Y	Y	Y	Y	N	N	Y
VERMONT								
AL *Sanders*	N	Y	?	Y	Y	N	Y	Y
VIRGINIA								
1 ***Bateman***	Y	Y	Y	N	N	N	N	Y
2 Pickett	N	Y	Y	Y	Y	N	N	Y
3 Scott	N	Y	Y	Y	Y	N	Y	Y
4 Sisisky	#	#	Y	Y	Y	N	Y	Y
5 Payne	Y	Y	Y	Y	Y	N	Y	Y
6 ***Goodlatte***	Y	N	N	N	N	N	N	N
7 ***Bliley***	Y	N	N	N	N	Y	N	N
8 Moran	N	Y	Y	Y	Y	N	Y	Y
9 Boucher	N	Y	Y	Y	Y	N	Y	Y
10 ***Wolf***	Y	N	N	N	N	Y	N	N
11 Byrne	N	Y	Y	Y	Y	N	Y	Y
WASHINGTON								
1 Cantwell	N	Y	Y	Y	N	N	Y	Y
2 Swift	N	Y	Y	Y	Y	N	Y	Y
3 Unsoeld	N	Y	Y	Y	Y	N	Y	Y
4 Inslee	N	Y	?	Y	Y	N	Y	Y
5 Foley						N	Y	
6 Dicks	N	Y	Y	Y	Y	N	Y	Y
7 McDermott	N	Y	Y	Y	Y	N	Y	Y
8 ***Dunn***	Y	N	N	N	N	Y	N	N
9 Kreidler	N	Y	Y	Y	Y	N	Y	Y
WEST VIRGINIA								
1 Mollohan	N	Y	Y	Y	Y	N	Y	?
2 Wise	N	Y	Y	Y	Y	N	Y	?
3 Rahall	N	Y	Y	Y	Y	N	Y	Y
WISCONSIN								
1 Vacancy **								
2 ***Klug***	Y	N	N	N	N	Y	N	N
3 ***Gunderson***	Y	Y	N	N	N	Y	N	N
4 Kleczka	N	Y	Y	Y	Y	N	Y	Y
5 Barrett	N	Y	Y	Y	Y	N	Y	Y
6 ***Petri***	N	N	N	N	N	N	N	N
7 Obey	N	Y	Y	Y	Y	N	Y	Y
8 ***Roth***	Y	N	Y	N	N	N	N	N
9 ***Sensenbrenner***	N	N	N	N	N	Y	N	N
WYOMING								
AL ***Thomas***	Y	N	N	N	N	Y	N	N
DELEGATES								
de Lugo, V.I.	N	D	D	D	D	N	D	D
Faleomavaega, Am.S.	N	D	D	D	D	N	D	D
Norton, D.C.	N	D	D	D	D	N	D	D
Romero-B., P.R.	?	D	D	D	D	N	D	D
Underwood, Guam	N	D	D	D	D	?	D	D

Southern states - Ala., Ark., Fla., Ga., Ky., La., Miss., N.C., Okla., S.C., Tenn., Texas, Va.
Omitted votes are quorum calls, which CQ does not include in its vote charts.

KEY

- Y Voted for (yea).
- # Paired for.
- + Announced for.
- N Voted against (nay).
- X Paired against.
- − Announced against.
- P Voted "present."
- C Voted "present" to avoid possible conflict of interest.
- ? Did not vote or otherwise make a position known.
- D Delegates ineligible to vote.

Democrats *Republicans*
Independent

201. Procedural Motion. Approval of the House Journal of Tuesday, June 8. Approved 256-144: R 23-139; D 232-5 (ND 154-4, SD 78-1); I 1-0, June 9, 1993.

202. HR 1159. Passenger Vessel Safety/Passage. Passage of the bill to prevent passenger vessels from circumventing Coast Guard safety standards by requiring that bareboat chartered vessels carrying 12 or more passengers comply with U.S. passenger vessel safety laws. Passed 409-4: R 165-3; D 243-1 (ND 165-1, SD 78-0); I 1-0, June 9, 1993.

203. Procedural Motion. Approval of the House Journal of Wednesday, June 9. Approved 240-146: R 18-139; D 221-7 (ND 151-5, SD 70-2); I 1-0, June 10, 1993.

204. HR 2348. Fiscal 1994 Legislative Branch Appropriations/Previous Question. Frost, D-Texas, motion to order the previous question (thus ending debate and the possibility of amendment) on adoption of the rule (H Res 192) to provide for House floor consideration of the bill to provide $1.785 billion in new budget authority for the operations of Congress and legislative branch agencies in fiscal 1994. The Senate will add funding for its expenses later. Motion agreed to 240-177: R 0-172; D 239-5 (ND 161-3, SD 78-2); I 1-0, June 10, 1993.

205. HR 2348. Fiscal 1994 Legislative Branch Appropriations/Rule. Adoption of the rule (H Res 192) to provide for House floor consideration of the bill to provide $1.785 billion in new budget authority for the operations of Congress and legislative branch agencies in fiscal 1994. The Senate will add funding for its expenses later. Adopted 226-185: R 0-168; D 225-17 (ND 156-8, SD 69-9); I 1-0, June 10, 1993.

206. Procedural Motion. Burton, R-Ind., motion to adjourn. Motion rejected 31-361: R 31-131; D 0-229 (ND 0-153, SD 0-76); I 0-1, June 10, 1993.

* 208. HR 2348. Fiscal 1994 Legislative Branch Appropriations/Rescissions. Stupak, D-Mich., amendment to rescind $1.6 million in unused funds from fiscal 1991 and 1992. Adopted in Committee of the Whole 415-2: R 166-0; D 248-2 (ND 168-2, SD 80-0); I 1-0, June 10, 1993.

209. HR 2348. Fiscal 1994 Legislative Branch Appropriations/Official Mail. Pomeroy, D-N.D., amendment to cut $5.8 million from the $45.8 million appropriation for House official mail costs. Adopted in Committee of the Whole 418-4: R 171-0; D 246-4 (ND 169-2, SD 77-2); I 1-0, June 10, 1993.

* Omitted votes are quorum calls, which CQ does not include in its vote charts.

** Peter W. Barca, D-Wis., was sworn in June 8. Vote 201 was the first vote for which he was eligible.

	201	202	203	204	205	206	208	209
ALABAMA								
1 Callahan	N	Y	N	N	?	N	Y	Y
2 Everett	N	Y	N	N	?	P	+	
3 Browder	Y	Y	Y	Y	?	Y	Y	Y
4 Bevill	Y	Y	Y	Y	Y	N	Y	Y
5 Cramer	Y	Y	Y	Y	Y	N	Y	Y
6 Bachus	N	Y	N	N	N	N	Y	Y
7 Hilliard	Y	Y	Y	Y	Y	N	Y	Y
ALASKA								
AL Young	N	Y	N	N	N	N	P	Y
ARIZONA								
1 Coppersmith	Y	Y	Y	Y	Y	N	Y	Y
2 Pastor	Y	Y	Y	Y	Y	N	Y	Y
3 Stump	N	N	N	N	N	N	Y	Y
4 Kyl	N	Y	N	N	N	N	Y	Y
5 Kolbe	N	Y	N	N	?	?	Y	Y
6 English	Y	Y	Y	Y	Y	N	Y	Y
ARKANSAS								
1 Lambert	Y	Y	Y	N	Y	N	Y	Y
2 Thornton	Y	Y	Y	Y	Y	N	Y	Y
3 Hutchinson	N	Y	N	N	N	N	Y	Y
4 Dickey	N	Y	N	N	N	Y	Y	Y
CALIFORNIA								
1 Hamburg	Y	Y	Y	Y	Y	?	Y	Y
2 Herger	N	Y	?	N	Y	Y	Y	Y
3 Fazio	Y	Y	Y	Y	Y	N	Y	Y
4 Doolittle	N	N	N	N	?	Y	Y	Y
5 Matsui	Y	Y	Y	Y	N	Y	?	Y
6 Woolsey	Y	Y	Y	Y	Y	N	Y	Y
7 Miller	Y	Y	Y	Y	Y	N	Y	Y
8 Pelosi	Y	Y	Y	Y	Y	?	Y	Y
9 Dellums	Y	Y	Y	Y	Y	N	Y	Y
10 Baker	N	Y	N	N	N	Y	Y	Y
11 Pombo	Y	Y	N	Y	N	Y	Y	Y
12 Lantos	Y	Y	Y	Y	Y	N	Y	Y
13 Stark	Y	Y	+	+	-		+	+
14 Eshoo	Y	Y	Y	Y	Y	?	Y	Y
15 Mineta	Y	Y	Y	Y	Y	N	Y	Y
16 Edwards	Y	Y	Y	Y	Y	N	Y	Y
17 Vacancy								
18 Condit	Y	Y	+	+	-		+	+
19 Lehman	Y	?	Y	Y	Y	N	Y	Y
20 Dooley	Y	Y	Y	Y	Y	N	Y	Y
21 Thomas	N	Y	N	N	N	P	Y	Y
22 Huffington	?	Y	N	N	N	Y	Y	Y
23 Gallegly	N	Y	N	N	N	N	Y	Y
24 Beilenson	Y	Y	Y	Y	Y	N	Y	Y
25 McKeon	N	Y	-	-	X	-	+	+
26 Berman	Y	Y	Y	Y	Y	N	Y	Y
27 Moorhead	N	Y	N	N	N	N	Y	Y
28 Dreier	N	Y	N	N	N	N	Y	Y
29 Waxman	Y	?	Y	Y	Y	N	Y	Y
30 Becerra	Y	Y	Y	Y	Y	?	Y	Y
31 Martinez	Y	Y	Y	Y	Y	N	Y	Y
32 Dixon	Y	Y	Y	Y	Y	N	Y	Y
33 Roybal-Allard	Y	Y	?	Y	Y	?	Y	Y
34 Torres	Y	Y	Y	Y	Y	?	Y	Y
35 Waters	Y	Y	Y	Y	Y	N	Y	Y
36 Harman	Y	Y	Y	Y	Y	?	Y	Y
37 Tucker	?	Y	Y	Y	Y	N	Y	Y
38 Horn	N	Y	N	N	N	N	Y	Y
39 Royce	N	Y	N	N	N	N	Y	Y
40 Lewis	N	Y	N	N	N	N	Y	Y
41 Kim	N	Y	N	N	N	Y	Y	Y

	201	202	203	204	205	206	208	209
42 Brown	?	Y	?	?	?	Y	?	Y
43 Calvert	N	Y	N	N	N	Y	Y	Y
44 McCandless	N	Y	N	N	N	Y	Y	Y
45 Rohrabacher	N	Y	N	N	N	Y	Y	Y
46 Dornan	N	?	?	N	N	N	Y	Y
47 Cox	N	Y	?	N	N	Y	Y	Y
48 Packard	N	Y	N	N	N	N	Y	Y
49 Schenk	Y	Y	Y	Y	Y	N	Y	Y
50 Filner	Y	Y	Y	Y	Y	N	Y	Y
51 Cunningham	?	Y	N	N	N	N	Y	Y
52 Hunter	?	Y	N	N	N	?	Y	Y
COLORADO								
1 Schroeder	N	Y	N	Y	Y	N	Y	Y
2 Skaggs	Y	Y	Y	Y	Y	N	Y	Y
3 McInnis	Y	Y	Y	N	N	N	Y	Y
4 Allard	N	N	N	N	N	N	Y	Y
5 Hefley	N	Y	N	N	?	Y	Y	Y
6 Schaefer	N	Y	N	N	N	N	Y	Y
CONNECTICUT								
1 Kennelly	Y	Y	Y	Y	Y	N	Y	Y
2 Gejdenson	Y	Y	Y	Y	Y	N	Y	Y
3 DeLauro	Y	Y	Y	Y	Y	N	Y	Y
4 Shays	N	Y	N	N	N	Y	Y	Y
5 Franks	N	Y	N	N	N	N	Y	Y
6 Johnson	−	Y	N	N	N	N	Y	Y
DELAWARE								
AL Castle	?	Y	N	N	N	N	Y	Y
FLORIDA								
1 Hutto	Y	Y	Y	Y	N	N	Y	Y
2 Peterson	Y	Y	Y	Y	N	Y	Y	Y
3 Brown	Y	Y	Y	Y	Y	N	Y	Y
4 Fowler	N	Y	N	N	N	N	Y	Y
5 Thurman	Y	Y	Y	Y	Y	N	Y	Y
6 Stearns	N	Y	N	N	N	N	Y	Y
7 Mica	N	Y	N	N	N	N	Y	Y
8 McCollum	N	Y	N	N	N	N	Y	Y
9 Bilirakis	N	Y	N	N	N	N	Y	Y
10 Young	N	Y	N	N	N	N	Y	Y
11 Gibbons	Y	Y	?	Y	?	?	Y	Y
12 Canady	N	Y	N	N	N	N	Y	Y
13 Miller	Y	Y	Y	Y	Y	N	Y	Y
14 Goss	N	Y	N	N	N	N	Y	Y
15 Bacchus	Y	Y	Y	Y	Y	N	Y	Y
16 Lewis	N	Y	N	N	N	N	Y	Y
17 Meek	Y	Y	Y	Y	Y	N	Y	Y
18 Ros-Lehtinen	N	Y	N	N	N	N	Y	Y
19 Johnston	Y	Y	Y	Y	Y	N	Y	Y
20 Deutsch	Y	Y	Y	Y	Y	N	Y	Y
21 Diaz-Balart	N	Y	N	N	N	N	Y	Y
22 Shaw	N	Y	N	N	N	N	Y	Y
23 Hastings	Y	Y	Y	Y	Y	N	Y	Y
GEORGIA								
1 Kingston	Y	Y	Y	N	N	Y	Y	Y
2 Bishop	+	+	?	Y	Y	Y	N	Y
3 Collins	?	?	N	N	N	N	Y	Y
4 Linder	N	Y	N	N	N	N	Y	Y
5 Lewis	Y	Y	Y	Y	Y	N	Y	Y
6 Gingrich	N	Y	N	N	?	P	Y	Y
7 Darden	Y	Y	Y	Y	Y	N	Y	Y
8 Rowland	?	?	Y	Y	Y	N	Y	Y
9 Deal	Y	Y	Y	Y	Y	N	Y	Y
10 Johnson	?	?	Y	Y	Y	N	Y	Y
11 McKinney	Y	Y	Y	Y	Y	N	Y	Y
HAWAII								
1 Abercrombie	Y	Y	Y	Y	Y	N	N	N
2 Mink	Y	Y	Y	Y	Y	N	Y	Y
IDAHO								
1 LaRocco	Y	Y	Y	Y	Y	N	Y	Y
2 Crapo	Y	Y	N	N	N	N	Y	Y
ILLINOIS								
1 Rush	Y	Y	Y	Y	Y	N	Y	Y
2 Reynolds	Y	Y	Y	Y	Y	N	Y	Y
3 Lipinski	Y	Y	Y	Y	Y	N	Y	Y
4 Gutierrez	Y	Y	Y	Y	Y	?	Y	Y
5 Rostenkowski	Y	Y	?	Y	Y	N	Y	Y
6 Hyde	N	Y	N	N	N	N	Y	Y
7 Collins	Y	Y	Y	Y	Y	N	Y	Y
8 Crane	N	Y	N	N	N	N	Y	Y
9 Yates	Y	Y	Y	Y	Y	N	Y	Y
10 Porter	N	Y	N	N	N	N	Y	Y
11 Sangmeister	Y	Y	Y	Y	Y	N	Y	Y
12 Costello	Y	Y	Y	Y	Y	N	Y	Y
13 Fawell	N	Y	N	N	N	N	Y	Y
14 Hastert	N	Y	N	N	N	N	Y	Y
15 Ewing	N	Y	N	N	N	N	Y	Y
16 Manzullo	N	Y	N	N	N	N	Y	Y
17 Evans	Y	Y	Y	Y	Y	N	Y	Y

ND Northern Democrats   SD Southern Democrats

	201	202	203	204	205	206	208	209
18 ***Michel***	N	Y	N	N	N	N	Y	Y
19 Poshard	Y	Y	Y	Y	Y	N	Y	Y
20 Durbin	Y	Y	Y	Y	Y	N	Y	Y
INDIANA								
1 Visclosky	Y	Y	Y	Y	Y	N	Y	Y
2 Sharp	Y	Y	Y	Y	N	N	Y	Y
3 Roemer	Y	Y	Y	Y	Y	N	Y	Y
4 Long	Y	Y	Y	Y	Y	N	Y	Y
5 ***Buyer***	N	Y	N	N	N	N	Y	Y
6 ***Burton***	N	Y	N	N	N	Y	Y	Y
7 ***Myers***	Y	Y	Y	N	N	Y	Y	Y
8 McCloskey	Y	Y	Y	Y	Y	N	Y	Y
9 Hamilton	Y	Y	Y	Y	Y	N	Y	Y
10 Jacobs	N	Y	N	N	N	N	Y	Y
IOWA								
1 ***Leach***	N	Y	N	N	N	N	Y	Y
2 ***Nussle***	N	Y	N	N	N	N	Y	Y
3 ***Lightfoot***	N	Y	N	N	N	N	Y	Y
4 Smith	?	Y	Y	Y	Y	N	Y	Y
5 ***Grandy***	N	Y	N	N	N	N	Y	Y
KANSAS								
1 ***Roberts***	N	Y	?	N	N	N	Y	Y
2 Slattery	Y	Y	Y	Y	Y	N	Y	Y
3 ***Meyers***	N	Y	N	N	N	N	Y	Y
4 Glickman	Y	Y	Y	Y	Y	N	Y	Y
KENTUCKY								
1 Barlow	Y	Y	Y	Y	Y	N	Y	Y
2 Natcher	Y	Y	Y	Y	Y	N	Y	Y
3 Mazzoli	Y	Y	Y	Y	Y	N	Y	Y
4 ***Bunning***	N	Y	N	N	N	N	Y	Y
5 ***Rogers***	N	Y	N	N	?	N	Y	Y
6 Baesler	Y	Y	Y	Y	Y	N	Y	Y
LOUISIANA								
1 ***Livingston***	?	?	N	N	N	N	Y	Y
2 Jefferson	Y	Y	Y	Y	Y	N	Y	Y
3 Tauzin	Y	Y	N	Y	Y	N	Y	Y
4 Fields	Y	Y	Y	Y	Y	N	Y	Y
5 ***McCrery***	Y	Y	Y	N	N	N	Y	Y
6 ***Baker***	N	Y	N	N	N	N	Y	Y
7 Hayes	Y	Y	Y	Y	Y	N	Y	Y
MAINE								
1 Andrews	Y	Y	Y	Y	Y	?	Y	Y
2 ***Snowe***	Y	Y	N	N	N	N	Y	Y
MARYLAND								
1 ***Gilchrest***	?	?	?	?	?	?	?	?
2 ***Bentley***	N	Y	N	N	N	Y	Y	Y
3 Cardin	Y	Y	Y	?	?	?	Y	Y
4 Wynn	Y	Y	Y	Y	Y	N	Y	Y
5 Hoyer	Y	Y	Y	Y	Y	N	Y	Y
6 ***Bartlett***	N	Y	N	N	N	Y	Y	Y
7 Mfume	Y	Y	Y	Y	Y	?	Y	Y
8 ***Morella***	N	Y	N	N	N	N	Y	Y
MASSACHUSETTS								
1 Olver	Y	Y	Y	?	Y	N	Y	Y
2 Neal	Y	Y	Y	Y	Y	N	Y	Y
3 ***Blute***	N	Y	N	N	N	N	Y	Y
4 Frank	Y	Y	Y	Y	Y	N	Y	Y
5 Meehan	Y	Y	Y	Y	Y	N	Y	Y
6 ***Torkildsen***	N	Y	N	N	N	Y	Y	Y
7 Markey	Y	Y	Y	Y	Y	N	Y	Y
8 Kennedy	Y	Y	Y	Y	Y	N	Y	Y
9 Moakley	Y	Y	Y	Y	Y	N	Y	Y
10 Studds	Y	Y	Y	Y	Y	N	Y	Y
MICHIGAN								
1 Stupak	Y	Y	Y	Y	Y	N	Y	Y
2 ***Hoekstra***	N	?	N	N	N	N	Y	Y
3 Henry	?	?	?	?	?	?	?	?
4 ***Camp***	N	Y	N	N	N	N	Y	Y
5 Barcia	Y	Y	Y	Y	Y	N	Y	Y
6 ***Upton***	N	Y	N	N	N	N	Y	Y
7 ***Smith***	N	Y	N	N	N	N	Y	Y
8 Carr	Y	Y	Y	Y	Y	N	Y	Y
9 Kildee	Y	Y	Y	Y	Y	N	Y	Y
10 Bonior	Y	Y	Y	Y	Y	N	Y	Y
11 ***Knollenberg***	N	Y	N	N	N	Y	Y	Y
12 Levin	Y	Y	Y	Y	Y	N	Y	Y
13 Ford	?	Y	Y	?	Y	N	Y	Y
14 Conyers	Y	Y	?	Y	Y	N	Y	Y
15 Collins	Y	Y	?	Y	Y	N	Y	Y
16 Dingell	Y	Y	Y	Y	Y	N	Y	Y
MINNESOTA								
1 Penny	Y	N	Y	N	N	N	Y	Y
2 Minge	?	Y	Y	Y	Y	N	Y	Y
3 ***Ramstad***	N	Y	N	N	N	N	Y	Y
4 Vento	Y	Y	Y	Y	Y	N	Y	Y

	201	202	203	204	205	206	208	209
5 Sabo	Y	Y	Y	Y	Y	N	Y	Y
6 ***Grams***	N	Y	N	N	N	N	Y	Y
7 Peterson	Y	Y	?	N	N	N	Y	Y
8 Oberstar	Y	Y	Y	Y	Y	N	Y	Y
MISSISSIPPI								
1 Whitten	Y	?	?	Y	Y	N	Y	Y
2 Thompson	?	Y	?	?	?	?	?	?
3 Montgomery	Y	Y	Y	Y	Y	N	Y	Y
4 Parker	Y	Y	Y	Y	N	N	Y	Y
5 Taylor	N	Y	N	Y	N	N	Y	Y
MISSOURI								
1 Clay	?	Y	N	Y	Y	N	Y	Y
2 ***Talent***	N	Y	N	N	N	N	Y	Y
3 Gephardt	Y	Y	Y	Y	Y	N	Y	Y
4 Skelton	Y	Y	Y	Y	Y	N	Y	Y
5 Wheat	Y	Y	?	Y	Y	N	Y	Y
6 Danner	Y	Y	Y	Y	Y	N	Y	Y
7 ***Hancock***	N	Y	N	N	N	?	Y	Y
8 ***Emerson***	N	Y	?	N	N	N	Y	Y
9 Volkmer	Y	Y	Y	Y	Y	N	Y	Y
MONTANA								
AL Williams	Y	Y	Y	Y	Y	N	Y	Y
NEBRASKA								
1 ***Bereuter***	N	Y	N	N	N	N	Y	Y
2 Hoagland	Y	Y	Y	Y	Y	N	Y	Y
3 ***Barrett***	N	Y	N	N	N	N	Y	Y
NEVADA								
1 Bilbray	Y	Y	Y	Y	Y	N	Y	Y
2 ***Vucanovich***	N	Y	N	N	N	N	Y	Y
NEW HAMPSHIRE								
1 ***Zeliff***	N	Y	N	N	N	N	Y	Y
2 Swett	?	Y	Y	Y	Y	N	Y	Y
NEW JERSEY								
1 Andrews	Y	Y	Y	Y	Y	N	Y	Y
2 Hughes	Y	Y	Y	Y	Y	N	Y	Y
3 ***Saxton***	N	Y	N	N	N	?	Y	Y
4 ***Smith***	Y	Y	Y	N	N	N	Y	Y
5 ***Roukema***	N	Y	N	N	N	N	Y	Y
6 Pallone	Y	Y	Y	Y	Y	N	Y	Y
7 ***Franks***	N	Y	N	N	N	N	Y	Y
8 Klein	Y	Y	Y	Y	Y	N	Y	Y
9 Torricelli	Y	Y	Y	Y	?	N	Y	Y
10 Payne	?	?	?	Y	Y	N	Y	Y
11 ***Gallo***	N	Y	N	N	N	N	Y	Y
12 ***Zimmer***	N	Y	N	N	N	N	Y	Y
13 Menendez	Y	Y	Y	Y	Y	N	Y	Y
NEW MEXICO								
1 ***Schiff***	N	Y	N	N	N	N	Y	Y
2 ***Skeen***	N	Y	N	N	N	N	Y	Y
3 Richardson	Y	Y	Y	Y	Y	N	Y	Y
NEW YORK								
1 Hochbrueckner	Y	Y	Y	Y	Y	N	Y	Y
2 ***Lazio***	N	Y	N	N	N	N	Y	Y
3 ***King***	N	Y	N	N	N	N	Y	Y
4 ***Levy***	N	Y	N	N	N	N	Y	Y
5 Ackerman	Y	Y	Y	Y	Y	N	Y	Y
6 Flake	Y	Y	Y	Y	Y	N	Y	Y
7 Manton	Y	Y	?	Y	Y	N	Y	Y
8 Nadler	Y	Y	Y	Y	Y	N	N	N
9 Schumer	Y	Y	Y	Y	Y	N	Y	Y
10 Towns	Y	Y	Y	Y	Y	N	Y	Y
11 Owens	Y	Y	Y	Y	Y	N	Y	Y
12 Velazquez	Y	?	Y	Y	Y	?	Y	Y
13 ***Molinari***	N	Y	N	N	N	Y	Y	Y
14 Maloney	Y	Y	Y	Y	Y	N	Y	Y
15 Rangel	?	Y	Y	Y	Y	?	Y	Y
16 Serrano	Y	Y	Y	Y	Y	?	Y	Y
17 Engel	Y	Y	?	?	#	?	?	?
18 Lowey	Y	Y	Y	Y	Y	N	Y	Y
19 ***Fish***	Y	Y	?	N	N	N	Y	Y
20 ***Gilman***	Y	Y	Y	N	N	N	Y	Y
21 McNulty	Y	Y	Y	Y	Y	N	Y	Y
22 ***Solomon***	N	Y	?	N	N	N	Y	Y
23 ***Boehlert***	N	Y	N	N	N	N	Y	Y
24 ***McHugh***	N	Y	?	N	N	N	Y	Y
25 ***Walsh***	N	Y	N	N	N	N	Y	Y
26 Hinchey	Y	Y	Y	Y	Y	N	Y	Y
27 ***Paxon***	N	Y	N	N	N	N	Y	Y
28 Slaughter	Y	Y	Y	Y	Y	N	Y	Y
29 LaFalce	Y	Y	Y	Y	Y	N	Y	Y
30 ***Quinn***	N	Y	N	N	N	N	Y	Y
31 ***Houghton***	Y	Y	Y	N	N	N	Y	Y
NORTH CAROLINA								
1 Clayton	Y	Y	Y	Y	Y	N	Y	Y
2 Valentine	Y	Y	Y	Y	N	N	Y	Y

	201	202	203	204	205	206	208	209
3 Lancaster	Y	Y	Y	Y	Y	N	Y	Y
4 Price	Y	Y	Y	Y	Y	N	Y	Y
5 Neal	Y	Y	?	Y	Y	N	Y	Y
6 ***Coble***	N	Y	N	N	N	N	Y	Y
7 Rose	Y	Y	?	Y	Y	N	Y	Y
8 Hefner	Y	Y	Y	Y	Y	N	Y	Y
9 ***McMillan***	N	Y	N	N	N	?	Y	Y
10 ***Ballenger***	N	Y	N	N	N	Y	Y	Y
11 ***Taylor***	N	Y	N	N	N	Y	Y	Y
12 Watt	Y	Y	Y	Y	Y	N	Y	Y
NORTH DAKOTA								
AL Pomeroy	Y	Y	Y	Y	Y	N	Y	Y
OHIO								
1 Mann	Y	Y	Y	Y	Y	N	Y	Y
2 ***Portman***	N	Y	N	N	N	N	Y	Y
3 Hall	Y	Y	?	Y	Y	N	Y	Y
4 ***Oxley***	N	Y	Y	N	N	N	Y	Y
5 ***Gillmor***	Y	Y	?	N	N	N	Y	Y
6 Strickland	Y	Y	Y	Y	Y	N	Y	Y
7 ***Hobson***	N	Y	N	N	N	N	Y	Y
8 ***Boehner***	N	Y	N	N	N	N	Y	Y
9 Kaptur	Y	Y	Y	Y	Y	N	Y	Y
10 ***Hoke***	N	Y	?	N	N	Y	Y	Y
11 Stokes	Y	Y	Y	Y	Y	N	Y	Y
12 ***Kasich***	Y	Y	Y	N	?	?	Y	Y
13 Brown	Y	Y	Y	Y	Y	N	Y	Y
14 Sawyer	Y	Y	Y	Y	Y	N	Y	Y
15 ***Pryce***	N	Y	N	N	N	Y	Y	Y
16 ***Regula***	N	Y	N	N	N	N	Y	Y
17 Traficant	Y	Y	Y	Y	Y	N	Y	Y
18 Applegate	Y	Y	Y	Y	Y	N	Y	Y
19 Fingerhut	N	Y	N	Y	N	N	Y	Y
OKLAHOMA								
1 ***Inhofe***	N	Y	N	N	N	N	Y	Y
2 Synar	Y	Y	Y	Y	Y	N	Y	N
3 Brewster	Y	Y	Y	Y	Y	N	Y	Y
4 McCurdy	Y	Y	Y	Y	Y	N	Y	?
5 ***Istook***	N	Y	?	N	N	N	Y	Y
6 English	Y	Y	Y	Y	Y	N	Y	Y
OREGON								
1 Furse	Y	Y	Y	Y	Y	N	Y	Y
2 ***Smith***	N	Y	N	N	N	N	Y	Y
3 Wyden	?	Y	Y	Y	Y	N	Y	Y
4 DeFazio	?	?	?	Y	Y	N	Y	Y
5 Kopetski	Y	Y	Y	Y	Y	N	Y	Y
PENNSYLVANIA								
1 Foglietta	Y	Y	Y	Y	Y	N	Y	Y
2 Blackwell	Y	Y	?	Y	Y	N	Y	Y
3 Borski	Y	Y	Y	Y	Y	N	Y	Y
4 Klink	Y	Y	Y	Y	Y	N	Y	Y
5 ***Clinger***	Y	Y	Y	N	N	N	Y	Y
6 Holden	Y	Y	Y	Y	Y	N	Y	Y
7 ***Weldon***	N	Y	N	N	N	N	Y	Y
8 ***Greenwood***	N	Y	N	N	N	N	Y	Y
9 ***Shuster***	N	Y	N	N	N	N	Y	Y
10 ***McDade***	N	Y	N	N	N	N	Y	Y
11 Kanjorski	Y	Y	Y	Y	Y	N	Y	Y
12 Murtha	Y	Y	Y	Y	Y	N	Y	Y
13 Margolies-Mezv.	Y	Y	Y	Y	Y	N	Y	Y
14 Coyne	Y	Y	Y	Y	Y	N	Y	Y
15 McHale	Y	Y	Y	Y	Y	N	Y	Y
16 ***Walker***	N	N	N	N	N	N	P	Y
17 ***Gekas***	N	Y	?	N	N	N	Y	Y
18 ***Santorum***	Y	Y	?	N	N	N	Y	Y
19 ***Goodling***	?	+	N	N	N	N	Y	Y
20 Murphy	N	Y	N	Y	Y	N	Y	Y
21 ***Ridge***	N	Y	N	N	N	N	Y	Y
RHODE ISLAND								
1 ***Machtley***	?	Y	N	N	N	N	Y	Y
2 Reed	Y	Y	Y	Y	Y	N	Y	Y
SOUTH CAROLINA								
1 ***Ravenel***	N	Y	N	N	N	N	Y	Y
2 ***Spence***	?	Y	Y	N	N	N	Y	Y
3 Derrick	Y	Y	Y	Y	Y	N	Y	Y
4 ***Inglis***	Y	Y	Y	N	N	N	Y	Y
5 Spratt	Y	Y	Y	Y	Y	N	Y	Y
6 Clyburn	Y	Y	?	?	?	?	?	?
SOUTH DAKOTA								
AL Johnson	Y	Y	Y	Y	Y	N	Y	Y
TENNESSEE								
1 ***Quillen***	N	Y	N	N	N	Y	Y	Y
2 ***Duncan***	N	Y	N	N	N	Y	Y	Y
3 Lloyd	Y	Y	Y	Y	Y	N	Y	Y
4 Cooper	Y	Y	Y	Y	N	N	Y	Y
5 Clement	Y	Y	Y	Y	Y	N	Y	Y

	201	202	203	204	205	206	208	209
6 Gordon	Y	Y	Y	Y	Y	N	Y	Y
7 ***Sundquist***	N	Y	N	N	N	Y	Y	Y
8 Tanner	Y	Y	Y	Y	Y	N	Y	Y
9 Ford	Y	Y	Y	Y	Y	N	Y	Y
TEXAS								
1 Chapman	Y	Y	Y	Y	Y	N	Y	Y
2 Wilson	Y	?	?	Y	Y	N	Y	Y
3 ***Johnson, Sam***	N	Y	N	N	N	N	Y	Y
4 Hall	Y	Y	Y	N	N	N	Y	Y
5 Bryant	Y	Y	Y	Y	Y	N	Y	Y
6 ***Barton***	Y	Y	?	N	N	N	Y	Y
7 ***Archer***	Y	Y	Y	N	N	N	Y	Y
8 ***Fields***	N	Y	?	N	N	N	Y	Y
9 Brooks	Y	?	Y	Y	Y	?	Y	Y
10 Pickle	Y	Y	Y	Y	Y	N	Y	Y
11 Edwards	?	Y	Y	Y	Y	N	Y	Y
12 Geren	Y	Y	Y	Y	Y	N	Y	Y
13 Sarpalius	Y	Y	Y	Y	Y	N	Y	Y
14 Laughlin	Y	Y	Y	Y	Y	N	Y	Y
15 de la Garza	Y	Y	?	Y	Y	?	Y	Y
16 Coleman	Y	Y	Y	Y	Y	N	Y	Y
17 Stenholm	Y	Y	Y	Y	N	N	Y	Y
18 Washington	?	?	?	Y	Y	N	Y	N
19 ***Combest***	Y	Y	Y	N	N	N	Y	Y
20 Gonzalez	Y	Y	Y	Y	Y	N	Y	Y
21 ***Smith***	N	Y	N	N	N	N	Y	Y
22 ***DeLay***	?	Y	N	N	N	Y	Y	Y
23 ***Bonilla***	N	Y	N	N	N	N	Y	Y
24 Frost	Y	Y	Y	Y	Y	N	Y	Y
25 Andrews	Y	Y	Y	Y	Y	N	Y	Y
26 ***Armey***	N	Y	N	N	N	Y	Y	Y
27 Ortiz	Y	Y	Y	Y	Y	N	Y	Y
28 Tejeda	Y	Y	Y	Y	Y	N	Y	Y
29 Green	Y	Y	Y	Y	Y	N	Y	Y
30 Johnson, E. B.	Y	Y	Y	Y	Y	N	Y	Y
UTAH								
1 ***Hansen***	N	Y	N	N	N	N	Y	Y
2 Shepherd	Y	Y	Y	Y	Y	N	Y	Y
3 Orton	Y	Y	Y	Y	N	N	Y	Y
VERMONT								
AL *Sanders*	Y	Y	Y	Y	Y	N	Y	Y
VIRGINIA								
1 ***Bateman***	Y	Y	+	–	–	–	+	+
2 Pickett	Y	Y	?	?	?	?	?	?
3 Scott	Y	Y	?	?	?	?	?	?
4 Sisisky	Y	Y	?	?	?	?	?	?
5 Payne	Y	Y	Y	Y	Y	N	Y	Y
6 ***Goodlatte***	N	?	N	N	N	N	Y	Y
7 ***Bliley***	N	Y	N	N	N	N	Y	Y
8 Moran	Y	Y	Y	Y	Y	N	Y	Y
9 Boucher	Y	Y	Y	Y	Y	?	Y	Y
10 ***Wolf***	N	Y	N	N	N	N	Y	Y
11 Byrne	Y	Y	Y	Y	Y	N	Y	Y
WASHINGTON								
1 Cantwell	Y	Y	Y	Y	Y	N	Y	Y
2 Swift	Y	Y	Y	Y	Y	N	Y	Y
3 Unsoeld	Y	Y	Y	Y	Y	N	Y	Y
4 Inslee	Y	Y	Y	Y	Y	N	Y	Y
5 Foley								
6 Dicks	Y	Y	Y	Y	Y	N	Y	Y
7 McDermott	?	Y	Y	Y	Y	N	Y	Y
8 ***Dunn***	N	Y	N	N	?	N	Y	Y
9 Kreidler	Y	Y	Y	Y	Y	N	Y	Y
WEST VIRGINIA								
1 Mollohan	Y	Y	Y	Y	Y	N	Y	Y
2 Wise	Y	Y	Y	Y	Y	N	Y	Y
3 Rahall	?	Y	Y	Y	Y	N	Y	Y
WISCONSIN								
1 Barca **	Y	Y	Y	Y	Y	N	Y	Y
2 ***Klug***	N	Y	N	N	N	Y	Y	Y
3 ***Gunderson***	Y	Y	Y	N	N	N	Y	Y
4 Kleczka	Y	Y	Y	Y	Y	N	Y	Y
5 Barrett	Y	Y	Y	Y	Y	N	Y	Y
6 ***Petri***	N	Y	N	N	N	N	Y	Y
7 Obey	Y	Y	Y	Y	Y	N	Y	Y
8 ***Roth***	Y	Y	N	N	N	Y	Y	Y
9 ***Sensenbrenner***	N	Y	N	N	N	N	Y	Y
WYOMING								
AL ***Thomas***	?	Y	N	N	N	Y	P	Y
DELEGATES								
de Lugo, V.I.	D	D	D	D	D	D	Y	Y
Faleomavaega, Am.S.	D	D	D	D	D	D	?	?
Norton, D.C.	D	D	D	D	D	D	Y	Y
Romero-B., P.R.	D	D	D	D	D	D	Y	Y
Underwood, Guam	D	D	D	D	D	D	Y	Y

Southern states - Ala., Ark., Fla., Ga., Ky., La., Miss., N.C., Okla., S.C., Tenn., Texas, Va.
Omitted votes are quorum calls, which CQ does not include in its vote charts.

210. HR 2348. Fiscal 1994 Legislative Branch Appropriations/Former Speakers. Shepherd, D-Utah, amendment to limit future spending for former Speakers to five years of staffing and office expenses after they leave the House and to cut off current spending for the three former Speakers' offices Oct. 1, 1998. Adopted in Committee of the Whole 383-36: R 170-1; D 212-35 (ND 145-24, SD 67-11); I 1-0, June 10, 1993.

211. HR 2348. Fiscal 1994 Legislative Branch Appropriations/Office Moves. Grams, R-Minn., amendment to prohibit funds in the bill from going to relocate members' House offices. Adopted in Committee of the Whole 340-76: R 159-12; D 180-64 (ND 123-43, SD 57-21); I 1-0, June 10, 1993.

212. HR 2348. Fiscal 1994 Legislative Branch Appropriations/Rescissions. Separate vote at the request of Walker, R-Pa., on the amendment offered by Stupak, D-Mich., and adopted in the Committee of the Whole to rescind $1.6 million in unused funds from fiscal 1991 and 1992. Adopted 398-3: R 166-0; D 231-3 (ND 156-2, SD 75-1); I 1-0, June 10, 1993. (On separate votes, which may be demanded on an amendment adopted in the Committee of the Whole, the four delegates and the resident commissioner of Puerto Rico cannot vote. See vote 208).

213. HR 2348. Fiscal 1994 Legislative Branch Appropriations/Official Mail. Separate vote at the request of Walker, R-Pa., on the amendment offered by Pomeroy, D-N.D., and adopted in the Committee of the Whole to cut $5.8 million from the $45.8 million appropriation for House official mail costs. Adopted 388-12: R 165-0; D 222-12 (ND 151-6, SD 71-6); I 1-0, June 10, 1993. (On separate votes, which may be demanded on an amendment adopted in the Committee of the Whole, the four delegates and the resident commissioner of Puerto Rico cannot vote. See vote 209).

214. HR 2348. Fiscal 1994 Legislative Branch Appropriations/Former Speakers. Separate vote at the request of Walker, R-Pa., on the amendment offered by Shepherd, D-Utah, and adopted in the Committee of the Whole to limit future spending for former Speakers to five years of staffing and office expenses after they leave the House and to cut off current spending for the three former Speakers' offices Oct. 1, 1998. Adopted 372-31: R 167-1; D 204-30 (ND 136-20, SD 68-10); I 1-0, June 10, 1993. (On separate votes, which may be demanded on an amendment adopted in the Committee of the Whole, the four delegates and the resident commissioner of Puerto Rico cannot vote. See vote 210).

215. HR 2348. Fiscal 1994 Legislative Branch Appropriations. Separate vote at the request of Walker, R-Pa., on the amendment offered by Grams, R-Minn., and adopted in the Committee of the Whole to prohibit funds in the bill from going to relocate members' House offices. Adopted 332-71: R 154-11; D 177-60 (ND 118-42, SD 59-18); I 1-0, June 10, 1993. (On separate votes, which may be demanded on an amendment adopted in the Committee of the Whole, the four delegates and the resident commissioner of Puerto Rico cannot vote. See vote 211).

216. HR 2348. Fiscal 1994 Legislative Branch Appropriations. Young, R-Fla., motion to recommit the bill to the House Appropriations Committee with instructions to report it back with an amendment reducing various accounts in the bill by 5 percent. Motion rejected 202-209: R 168-0; D 34-208 (ND 17-148, SD 17-60); I 0-1, June 10, 1993.

217. HR 2348. Fiscal 1994 Legislative Branch Appropriations/Passage. Passage of the bill to provide approximately $1.78 billion in new budget authority for the operations of Congress and legislative branch agencies in fiscal 1994. The Senate will add funding for its expenses later. Passed 224-187: R 6-163; D 217-24 (ND 149-14, SD 68-10); I 1-0, June 10, 1993.

KEY

Y	Voted for (yea).
#	Paired for.
+	Announced for.
N	Voted against (nay).
X	Paired against.
—	Announced against.
P	Voted "present."
C	Voted "present" to avoid possible conflict of interest.
?	Did not vote or otherwise make a position known.
D	Delegates ineligible to vote.

Democrats *Republicans*
Independent

	210	211	212	213	214	215	216	217
ALABAMA								
1 *Callahan*	Y	N	Y	Y	Y	N	Y	N
2 *Everett*	Y	Y	Y	Y	Y	Y	Y	N
3 Browder	Y	Y	Y	Y	Y	N	N	Y
4 Bevill	Y	Y	Y	Y	Y	N	N	Y
5 Cramer	Y	Y	Y	Y	Y	Y	Y	N
6 *Bachus*	Y	Y	Y	Y	Y	Y	Y	N
7 Hilliard	Y	Y	Y	Y	Y	Y	N	Y
ALASKA								
AL *Young*	Y	N	Y	Y	Y	N	Y	Y
ARIZONA								
1 *Coppersmith*	Y	Y	Y	Y	Y	Y	N	Y
2 Pastor	Y	N	Y	Y	Y	N	N	Y
3 *Stump*	Y	Y	Y	Y	Y	Y	Y	N
4 *Kyl*	Y	Y	Y	Y	Y	Y	Y	N
5 *Kolbe*	Y	Y	Y	Y	Y	Y	Y	N
6 English	Y	Y	Y	Y	Y	Y	N	Y
ARKANSAS								
1 Lambert	Y	Y	Y	Y	Y	Y	N	Y
2 Thornton	N	Y	Y	Y	N	Y	N	Y
3 *Hutchinson*	Y	Y	Y	Y	Y	Y	Y	N
4 *Dickey*	Y	Y	Y	Y	Y	Y	Y	N
CALIFORNIA								
1 Hamburg	Y	Y	Y	Y	Y	Y	N	Y
2 *Herger*	Y	Y	Y	Y	Y	Y	Y	N
3 Fazio	Y	Y	Y	Y	Y	Y	N	Y
4 *Doolittle*	Y	Y	Y	Y	Y	Y	Y	N
5 Matsui	Y	Y	Y	Y	Y	Y	N	Y
6 Woolsey	Y	Y	Y	Y	Y	Y	N	Y
7 Miller	Y	Y	Y	Y	Y	Y	N	Y
8 Pelosi	N	N	Y	N	N	N	N	Y
9 Dellums	N	N	Y	N	N	N	N	Y
10 *Baker*	Y	Y	Y	Y	Y	Y	Y	N
11 *Pombo*	Y	Y	Y	Y	Y	Y	Y	N
12 Lantos	Y	Y	Y	Y	Y	Y	N	Y
13 Stark	+	+	+	+	+	+	—	+
14 Eshoo	Y	Y	Y	Y	Y	Y	N	Y
15 Mineta	Y	Y	Y	Y	Y	Y	N	Y
16 Edwards	Y	Y	Y	Y	Y	Y	N	Y
17 Vacancy								
18 Condit	+	+	+	+	+	+	+	—
19 Lehman	Y	?	?	?	?	?	?	?
20 Dooley	Y	Y	Y	Y	Y	Y	N	Y
21 *Thomas*	Y	Y	Y	Y	Y	Y	Y	N
22 *Huffington*	Y	Y	Y	Y	Y	Y	Y	N
23 *Gallegly*	Y	Y	Y	Y	Y	Y	Y	N
24 Beilenson	Y	N	Y	Y	N	N	N	Y
25 *McKeon*	+	+	+	+	+	+	#	X
26 Berman	N	Y	Y	Y	?	Y	N	Y
27 *Moorhead*	Y	Y	Y	Y	Y	Y	Y	N
28 *Dreier*	Y	Y	Y	Y	Y	Y	Y	N
29 Waxman	Y	?	?	Y	Y	N	N	Y
30 Becerra	Y	N	Y	Y	Y	N	N	Y
31 Martinez	?	?	?	?	?	?	X	?
32 Dixon	Y	Y	Y	Y	Y	Y	N	Y
33 Roybal-Allard	Y	N	Y	Y	N	N	N	Y
34 Torres	Y	Y	Y	Y	N	N	N	Y
35 Waters	Y	Y	Y	Y	Y	N	N	Y
36 Harman	Y	N	Y	Y	?	N	Y	N
37 Tucker	Y	Y	Y	Y	Y	Y	N	Y
38 *Horn*	Y	Y	Y	Y	Y	Y	Y	N
39 *Royce*	Y	Y	Y	Y	Y	Y	Y	N
40 *Lewis*	Y	Y	?	?	?	?	#	X
41 *Kim*	Y	Y	Y	Y	Y	Y	Y	N

	210	211	212	213	214	215	216	217
42 Brown	?	?	?	?	?	?	?	?
43 *Calvert*	Y	Y	Y	Y	Y	Y	Y	N
44 *McCandless*	Y	Y	Y	Y	Y	Y	Y	N
45 *Rohrabacher*	Y	Y	Y	Y	Y	Y	Y	N
46 *Dornan*	Y	Y	?	?	Y	Y	Y	N
47 *Cox*	Y	Y	Y	Y	Y	Y	Y	N
48 *Packard*	Y	Y	Y	Y	Y	Y	Y	N
49 Schenk	Y	Y	Y	Y	Y	Y	Y	Y
50 Filner	Y	N	Y	Y	Y	N	N	Y
51 *Cunningham*	Y	Y	Y	Y	Y	Y	Y	N
52 *Hunter*	Y	Y	Y	Y	Y	Y	Y	N
COLORADO								
1 Schroeder	Y	Y	Y	Y	Y	N	N	Y
2 Skaggs	Y	Y	Y	Y	Y	Y	N	Y
3 *McInnis*	Y	Y	Y	Y	Y	Y	Y	N
4 *Allard*	Y	Y	Y	Y	Y	Y	Y	N
5 *Hefley*	Y	N	Y	Y	Y	N	Y	N
6 *Schaefer*	Y	Y	Y	Y	Y	Y	Y	N
CONNECTICUT								
1 Kennelly	Y	Y	Y	Y	Y	N	N	Y
2 Gejdenson	Y	Y	Y	Y	Y	Y	N	Y
3 DeLauro	Y	Y	Y	Y	Y	N	N	Y
4 *Shays*	Y	Y	Y	Y	Y	Y	N	Y
5 *Franks*	Y	Y	Y	Y	Y	Y	Y	N
6 *Johnson*	Y	Y	Y	Y	Y	Y	Y	N
DELAWARE								
AL *Castle*	Y	Y	Y	Y	Y	Y	Y	N
FLORIDA								
1 Hutto	Y	Y	Y	Y	Y	Y	Y	N
2 Peterson	Y	Y	Y	Y	Y	Y	N	Y
3 Brown	Y	N	Y	Y	Y	N	N	Y
4 *Fowler*	Y	Y	?	Y	Y	Y	Y	N
5 Thurman	Y	Y	Y	Y	Y	Y	Y	Y
6 *Stearns*	Y	N	Y	Y	Y	Y	Y	N
7 *Mica*	Y	Y	Y	Y	Y	Y	Y	N
8 *McCollum*	Y	Y	Y	Y	Y	Y	Y	N
9 *Bilirakis*	Y	Y	Y	Y	Y	Y	Y	N
10 *Young*	Y	Y	Y	Y	Y	Y	Y	N
11 Gibbons	Y	Y	Y	Y	Y	Y	N	Y
12 *Canady*	Y	Y	Y	Y	Y	Y	Y	N
13 *Miller*	Y	Y	Y	Y	Y	Y	Y	N
14 *Goss*	Y	Y	Y	Y	Y	Y	Y	N
15 *Bacchus*	Y	Y	Y	Y	Y	Y	Y	N
16 *Lewis*	Y	Y	?	Y	Y	Y	Y	—
17 Meek	?	?	?	?	N	N	N	Y
18 *Ros-Lehtinen*	Y	Y	Y	Y	Y	Y	Y	N
19 Johnston	Y	N	?	?	?	?	?	#
20 Deutsch	Y	Y	Y	Y	Y	Y	N	Y
21 *Diaz-Balart*	Y	Y	Y	Y	Y	Y	Y	N
22 *Shaw*	Y	N	Y	Y	Y	Y	Y	N
23 Hastings	N	N	Y	N	N	N	N	Y
GEORGIA								
1 *Kingston*	Y	Y	Y	Y	Y	Y	Y	N
2 Bishop	Y	Y	Y	Y	Y	Y	N	Y
3 *Collins*	Y	Y	Y	Y	Y	Y	Y	N
4 *Linder*	Y	Y	Y	Y	Y	Y	Y	N
5 Lewis	Y	Y	Y	Y	Y	Y	N	Y
6 *Gingrich*	Y	?	?	?	?	?	?	?
7 Darden	Y	N	Y	Y	Y	N	N	Y
8 Rowland	Y	Y	Y	Y	Y	Y	N	Y
9 Deal	Y	Y	Y	Y	Y	Y	N	Y
10 Johnson	Y	Y	Y	Y	Y	Y	N	Y
11 McKinney	Y	N	Y	N	Y	N	N	Y
HAWAII								
1 Abercrombie	N	N	N	N	N	N	N	Y
2 Mink	Y	Y	Y	Y	Y	Y	N	Y
IDAHO								
1 LaRocco	Y	N	Y	Y	Y	N	N	Y
2 *Crapo*	Y	Y	Y	Y	Y	Y	Y	N
ILLINOIS								
1 Rush	Y	Y	Y	Y	Y	Y	N	Y
2 Reynolds	Y	Y	Y	Y	Y	Y	N	Y
3 Lipinski	Y	N	Y	Y	Y	N	N	Y
4 Gutierrez	Y	Y	?	?	?	?	N	Y
5 Rostenkowski	Y	Y	Y	Y	Y	Y	N	Y
6 *Hyde*	Y	Y	Y	Y	Y	Y	Y	N
7 Collins	Y	Y	Y	Y	Y	Y	N	Y
8 *Crane*	Y	Y	Y	Y	Y	Y	Y	N
9 Yates	Y	N	Y	Y	?	N	N	Y
10 *Porter*	Y	Y	Y	Y	Y	Y	Y	N
11 Sangmeister	Y	Y	Y	Y	Y	Y	N	Y
12 Costello	Y	Y	Y	Y	Y	Y	N	Y
13 *Fawell*	Y	Y	Y	Y	Y	Y	Y	Y
14 *Hastert*	Y	Y	Y	Y	Y	Y	Y	N
15 *Ewing*	Y	Y	Y	Y	Y	Y	Y	N
16 *Manzullo*	Y	Y	Y	Y	Y	Y	Y	N
17 Evans	Y	N	Y	Y	Y	N	N	Y

ND Northern Democrats   SD Southern Democrats

	210	211	212	213	214	215	216	217
18 ***Michel***	Y	Y	Y	Y	Y	Y	Y	N
19 Poshard	Y	Y	Y	Y	Y	Y	Y	N
20 Durbin	Y	Y	Y	Y	Y	Y	N	Y
INDIANA								
1 Visclosky	Y	Y	Y	Y	Y	Y	N	Y
2 Sharp	Y	Y	Y	Y	Y	Y	Y	N
3 Roemer	Y	Y	Y	Y	Y	Y	Y	N
4 Long	Y	N	Y	Y	Y	N	N	Y
5 ***Buyer***	Y	Y	Y	Y	Y	Y	Y	N
6 ***Burton***	Y	Y	Y	Y	Y	Y	Y	N
7 ***Myers***	Y	Y	?	Y	Y	Y	Y	N
8 McCloskey	N	Y	Y	Y	N	Y	N	Y
9 Hamilton	Y	Y	Y	Y	Y	Y	N	Y
10 Jacobs	Y	Y	Y	Y	Y	Y	Y	N
IOWA								
1 ***Leach***	Y	Y	Y	Y	Y	Y	Y	N
2 ***Nussle***	Y	Y	Y	Y	Y	Y	Y	N
3 ***Lightfoot***	Y	Y	Y	Y	Y	Y	Y	N
4 Smith	N	Y	Y	Y	N	Y	N	Y
5 ***Grandy***	Y	Y	Y	Y	Y	Y	Y	N
KANSAS								
1 ***Roberts***	Y	N	Y	Y	Y	N	Y	N
2 Slattery	Y	Y	Y	Y	?	Y	N	N
3 ***Meyers***	+	Y	Y	Y	Y	Y	Y	N
4 Glickman	Y	Y	Y	Y	Y	Y	N	N
KENTUCKY								
1 Barlow	Y	Y	Y	Y	Y	Y	N	Y
2 Natcher	Y	Y	Y	Y	Y	Y	N	Y
3 Mazzoli	Y	Y	Y	Y	Y	Y	N	Y
4 ***Bunning***	Y	Y	Y	Y	Y	Y	Y	N
5 ***Rogers***	Y	Y	Y	Y	Y	Y	Y	N
6 Baesler	Y	Y	Y	Y	Y	Y	N	Y
LOUISIANA								
1 ***Livingston***	Y	Y	?	?	Y	?	Y	N
2 Jefferson	Y	Y	Y	Y	Y	?	N	Y
3 Tauzin	Y	Y	Y	Y	Y	Y	Y	Y
4 Fields	Y	Y	Y	Y	Y	Y	N	Y
5 ***McCrery***	Y	Y	Y	Y	Y	Y	Y	N
6 ***Baker***	Y	Y	Y	Y	Y	Y	Y	N
7 Hayes	Y	Y	Y	Y	Y	Y	Y	Y
MAINE								
1 Andrews	Y	?	Y	Y	Y	Y	Y	N
2 ***Snowe***	Y	Y	Y	Y	Y	Y	Y	N
MARYLAND								
1 ***Gilchrest***	?	?	?	?	?	?	?	?
2 ***Bentley***	Y	N	Y	Y	Y	N	Y	N
3 Cardin	Y	Y	Y	Y	Y	Y	N	Y
4 Wynn	Y	Y	Y	Y	Y	Y	N	Y
5 Hoyer	N	N	Y	?	?	N	N	Y
6 ***Bartlett***	Y	Y	Y	Y	Y	Y	Y	N
7 Mfume	Y	N	?	?	Y	N	N	Y
8 ***Morella***	Y	Y	Y	Y	Y	Y	Y	Y
MASSACHUSETTS								
1 Olver	Y	Y	Y	Y	Y	Y	N	Y
2 Neal	N	Y	Y	Y	N	Y	N	Y
3 ***Blute***	Y	Y	Y	Y	Y	Y	Y	N
4 Frank	Y	Y	?	Y	Y	Y	N	Y
5 Meehan	Y	Y	Y	Y	Y	Y	Y	N
6 ***Torkildsen***	Y	Y	Y	Y	Y	Y	Y	N
7 Markey	N	Y	Y	Y	N	Y	N	Y
8 Kennedy	Y	N	Y	Y	Y	N	N	Y
9 Moakley	N	Y	Y	Y	N	Y	N	Y
10 Studds	N	Y	Y	Y	Y	Y	N	Y
MICHIGAN								
1 Stupak	Y	Y	Y	Y	Y	Y	N	Y
2 ***Hoekstra***	Y	Y	Y	Y	Y	Y	Y	N
3 Henry	?	?	?	?	?	?	?	?
4 ***Camp***	Y	Y	Y	Y	Y	Y	Y	N
5 Barcia	Y	Y	Y	Y	Y	Y	N	Y
6 ***Upton***	Y	Y	Y	Y	Y	Y	Y	N
7 ***Smith***	Y	Y	Y	Y	Y	Y	Y	N
8 Carr	Y	Y	Y	Y	Y	Y	N	Y
9 Kildee	Y	Y	Y	Y	Y	Y	Y	Y
10 Bonior	N	Y	Y	Y	N	Y	N	Y
11 ***Knollenberg***	Y	Y	Y	Y	Y	Y	Y	N
12 Levin	Y	Y	Y	Y	Y	Y	N	Y
13 Ford	N	Y	Y	Y	Y	Y	N	Y
14 Conyers	N	N	Y	Y	N	N	N	Y
15 Collins	N	Y	Y	Y	N	Y	N	Y
16 Dingell	Y	N	Y	Y	Y	Y	N	Y
MINNESOTA								
1 Penny	Y	Y	Y	Y	Y	Y	Y	N
2 Minge	Y	Y	Y	Y	Y	Y	Y	N
3 ***Ramstad***	Y	Y	Y	Y	Y	Y	Y	N
4 Vento	Y	Y	Y	Y	Y	Y	N	Y

	210	211	212	213	214	215	216	217
5 Sabo	Y	Y	Y	Y	Y	Y	N	Y
6 ***Grams***	Y	Y	Y	Y	Y	Y	Y	N
7 Peterson	Y	Y	Y	Y	Y	Y	Y	N
8 Oberstar	Y	N	Y	Y	Y	N	N	Y
MISSISSIPPI								
1 Whitten	Y	N	Y	Y	Y	Y	N	Y
2 Thompson	?	?	?	?	?	?	?	?
3 Montgomery	Y	Y	Y	Y	Y	Y	N	Y
4 Parker	Y	Y	Y	Y	Y	Y	Y	N
5 Taylor	Y	Y	Y	Y	Y	Y	Y	Y
MISSOURI								
1 Clay	N	?	?	?	?	?	?	?
2 ***Talent***	Y	Y	Y	Y	Y	Y	Y	N
3 Gephardt	Y	Y	Y	Y	Y	Y	N	Y
4 Skelton	Y	Y	Y	Y	Y	Y	N	Y
5 Wheat	Y	Y	Y	Y	Y	Y	N	Y
6 Danner	Y	Y	Y	Y	Y	Y	N	Y
7 ***Hancock***	Y	Y	Y	Y	Y	Y	Y	N
8 ***Emerson***	Y	Y	Y	Y	Y	Y	Y	N
9 Volkmer	Y	Y	Y	Y	Y	Y	N	Y
MONTANA								
AL Williams	Y	N	Y	Y	Y	Y	N	Y
NEBRASKA								
1 ***Bereuter***	Y	Y	Y	Y	Y	Y	Y	N
2 Hoagland	Y	Y	Y	Y	Y	Y	N	Y
3 ***Barrett***	Y	Y	Y	Y	Y	Y	Y	N
NEVADA								
1 Bilbray	Y	Y	Y	Y	Y	Y	N	Y
2 ***Vucanovich***	Y	Y	Y	Y	Y	Y	Y	N
NEW HAMPSHIRE								
1 ***Zeliff***	Y	Y	Y	Y	Y	Y	Y	N
2 Swett	Y	Y	Y	Y	Y	Y	N	Y
NEW JERSEY								
1 Andrews	Y	Y	Y	Y	Y	Y	Y	Y
2 Hughes	Y	Y	Y	Y	Y	Y	N	Y
3 ***Saxton***	Y	Y	Y	Y	Y	Y	Y	N
4 ***Smith***	Y	Y	Y	Y	Y	Y	Y	N
5 ***Roukema***	Y	Y	Y	Y	Y	Y	Y	N
6 Pallone	Y	Y	Y	Y	Y	Y	N	Y
7 ***Franks***	Y	Y	Y	Y	Y	Y	Y	N
8 Klein	Y	Y	Y	Y	Y	Y	N	Y
9 Torricelli	Y	Y	Y	Y	Y	Y	N	Y
10 Payne	Y	Y	Y	Y	Y	Y	N	Y
11 ***Gallo***	Y	Y	Y	Y	Y	Y	Y	N
12 ***Zimmer***	Y	Y	Y	Y	Y	Y	Y	N
13 Menendez	Y	Y	Y	Y	Y	Y	N	Y
NEW MEXICO								
1 ***Schiff***	Y	Y	Y	Y	Y	Y	Y	N
2 ***Skeen***	Y	Y	Y	Y	Y	Y	Y	N
3 Richardson	Y	Y	Y	Y	Y	Y	N	Y
NEW YORK								
1 Hochbrueckner	Y	Y	Y	Y	Y	Y	N	Y
2 ***Lazio***	Y	Y	Y	Y	Y	Y	Y	N
3 ***King***	N	Y	Y	Y	N	Y	Y	N
4 ***Levy***	Y	Y	Y	Y	Y	Y	Y	N
5 Ackerman	N	N	Y	Y	N	N	N	Y
6 Flake	Y	N	Y	N	N	N	N	Y
7 Manton	Y	N	Y	?	Y	Y	N	Y
8 Nadler	Y	N	N	N	Y	N	N	Y
9 Schumer	Y	Y	Y	Y	Y	Y	N	?
10 Towns	N	N	Y	Y	N	N	N	Y
11 Owens	Y	Y	Y	Y	Y	?	N	Y
12 Velazquez	Y	N	?	?	?	?	N	Y
13 ***Molinari***	Y	Y	Y	Y	Y	Y	?	N
14 Maloney	Y	Y	Y	Y	Y	Y	N	Y
15 Rangel	N	N	Y	N	N	N	N	Y
16 Serrano	N	N	?	?	?	?	N	Y
17 Engel	?	?	?	?	?	?	?	?
18 Lowey	Y	Y	Y	Y	Y	Y	N	Y
19 ***Fish***	Y	Y	Y	Y	Y	Y	Y	N
20 ***Gilman***	Y	Y	Y	Y	Y	Y	Y	Y
21 McNulty	Y	Y	Y	Y	Y	Y	N	Y
22 ***Solomon***	Y	Y	Y	Y	Y	Y	Y	N
23 ***Boehlert***	Y	N	Y	Y	Y	N	Y	N
24 ***McHugh***	Y	Y	Y	Y	Y	Y	Y	N
25 ***Walsh***	Y	N	Y	Y	Y	N	Y	N
26 Hinchey	Y	Y	Y	Y	Y	Y	N	Y
27 ***Paxon***	Y	Y	Y	Y	Y	Y	Y	N
28 Slaughter	Y	Y	Y	Y	Y	Y	N	Y
29 LaFalce	Y	Y	Y	Y	Y	Y	N	Y
30 ***Quinn***	Y	Y	Y	Y	Y	Y	Y	N
31 ***Houghton***	Y	N	Y	Y	Y	N	Y	Y
NORTH CAROLINA								
1 Clayton	Y	?	?	?	?	?	X	?
2 Valentine	Y	Y	Y	Y	Y	Y	N	Y

	210	211	212	213	214	215	216	217
3 Lancaster	Y	Y	Y	Y	Y	Y	N	Y
4 Price	Y	Y	Y	Y	Y	Y	N	Y
5 Neal	Y	Y	Y	Y	Y	Y	N	Y
6 ***Coble***	Y	Y	Y	Y	Y	Y	Y	N
7 Rose	Y	Y	Y	Y	Y	Y	N	Y
8 Hefner	Y	Y	?	Y	Y	Y	N	Y
9 ***McMillan***	Y	Y	Y	Y	Y	Y	Y	N
10 ***Ballenger***	Y	Y	Y	Y	Y	Y	Y	N
11 ***Taylor***	Y	Y	Y	Y	Y	Y	Y	N
12 Watt	Y	N	Y	Y	Y	N	N	Y
NORTH DAKOTA								
AL Pomeroy	Y	Y	Y	Y	Y	Y	N	Y
OHIO								
1 Mann	Y	Y	Y	Y	Y	Y	Y	Y
2 ***Portman***	Y	Y	Y	?	Y	Y	Y	N
3 Hall	Y	N	Y	Y	Y	N	N	Y
4 ***Oxley***	Y	Y	Y	Y	Y	Y	Y	N
5 ***Gillmor***	Y	Y	Y	Y	Y	Y	Y	N
6 Strickland	Y	Y	Y	Y	Y	Y	N	Y
7 ***Hobson***	Y	Y	Y	Y	Y	Y	Y	N
8 ***Boehner***	Y	Y	Y	Y	Y	Y	Y	N
9 Kaptur	Y	Y	Y	Y	Y	Y	N	Y
10 ***Hoke***	Y	Y	Y	Y	Y	?	Y	N
11 Stokes	N	Y	Y	Y	N	N	N	Y
12 ***Kasich***	Y	Y	Y	Y	Y	Y	Y	N
13 Brown	Y	Y	Y	Y	Y	Y	N	Y
14 Sawyer	Y	Y	Y	Y	Y	Y	N	Y
15 ***Pryce***	Y	Y	Y	Y	Y	Y	Y	N
16 ***Regula***	Y	Y	Y	Y	Y	Y	Y	N
17 Traficant	Y	Y	Y	Y	Y	Y	N	Y
18 Applegate	Y	N	Y	Y	Y	N	N	Y
19 Fingerhut	Y	Y	Y	Y	Y	Y	Y	N
OKLAHOMA								
1 ***Inhofe***	Y	Y	Y	Y	Y	Y	Y	N
2 Synar	Y	N	Y	N	Y	N	N	Y
3 Brewster	Y	Y	Y	Y	Y	Y	N	Y
4 McCurdy	Y	Y	Y	Y	Y	Y	N	Y
5 ***Istook***	Y	Y	Y	?	?	?	Y	N
6 English	Y	Y	Y	Y	Y	Y	N	Y
OREGON								
1 Furse	Y	Y	Y	Y	Y	Y	N	Y
2 ***Smith***	Y	Y	Y	Y	Y	Y	Y	N
3 Wyden	Y	Y	Y	Y	Y	Y	N	Y
4 DeFazio	Y	N	Y	Y	Y	N	N	Y
5 Kopetski	Y	N	Y	Y	Y	N	N	Y
PENNSYLVANIA								
1 Foglietta	Y	Y	Y	Y	Y	Y	N	Y
2 Blackwell	Y	Y	Y	Y	Y	Y	N	Y
3 Borski	Y	Y	Y	Y	Y	Y	N	Y
4 Klink	Y	N	Y	Y	Y	N	N	Y
5 ***Clinger***	Y	Y	Y	Y	Y	Y	Y	N
6 Holden	Y	Y	Y	Y	Y	Y	N	Y
7 ***Weldon***	Y	Y	Y	Y	Y	Y	Y	N
8 ***Greenwood***	Y	Y	Y	Y	Y	Y	Y	N
9 ***Shuster***	Y	Y	Y	Y	Y	Y	Y	N
10 ***McDade***	Y	Y	Y	Y	Y	Y	Y	N
11 Kanjorski	Y	N	Y	Y	Y	N	N	Y
12 Murtha	Y	N	Y	Y	Y	N	N	Y
13 Margolies-Mezv.	Y	Y	Y	Y	Y	Y	N	Y
14 Coyne	N	N	Y	Y	N	N	N	Y
15 McHale	Y	Y	Y	Y	Y	Y	N	Y
16 ***Walker***	Y	Y	Y	Y	Y	Y	Y	N
17 ***Gekas***	Y	Y	Y	Y	Y	Y	Y	N
18 ***Santorum***	Y	Y	Y	Y	Y	Y	Y	N
19 ***Goodling***	Y	Y	Y	Y	Y	Y	Y	N
20 Murphy	Y	Y	Y	Y	Y	Y	N	Y
21 ***Ridge***	Y	Y	Y	Y	Y	Y	Y	N
RHODE ISLAND								
1 ***Machtley***	Y	Y	Y	Y	Y	Y	Y	N
2 Reed	Y	Y	Y	Y	Y	Y	N	Y
SOUTH CAROLINA								
1 ***Ravenel***	Y	Y	Y	Y	Y	Y	Y	N
2 ***Spence***	Y	Y	Y	Y	Y	?	Y	N
3 Derrick	Y	Y	Y	Y	Y	Y	N	Y
4 ***Inglis***	Y	Y	Y	Y	Y	Y	Y	N
5 Spratt	Y	Y	Y	Y	Y	Y	N	Y
6 Clyburn	?	?	?	?	?	?	?	?
SOUTH DAKOTA								
AL Johnson	Y	Y	Y	Y	Y	Y	N	Y
TENNESSEE								
1 ***Quillen***	Y	Y	Y	Y	Y	Y	Y	N
2 ***Duncan***	Y	Y	Y	Y	Y	Y	Y	N
3 Lloyd	Y	Y	Y	Y	Y	Y	Y	Y
4 Cooper	Y	Y	Y	Y	Y	Y	Y	N
5 Clement	Y	N	Y	Y	Y	Y	N	Y

	210	211	212	213	214	215	216	217
6 Gordon	Y	Y	Y	Y	Y	Y	N	Y
7 ***Sundquist***	Y	Y	Y	Y	Y	Y	Y	N
8 Tanner	Y	N	Y	Y	Y	N	Y	Y
9 Ford	Y	Y	Y	Y	Y	Y	?	Y
TEXAS								
1 Chapman	N	N	Y	Y	Y	N	N	Y
2 Wilson	N	Y	Y	Y	Y	Y	N	Y
3 ***Johnson, Sam***	Y	N	Y	Y	Y	N	Y	Y
4 Hall	Y	Y	Y	Y	Y	Y	Y	Y
5 Bryant	Y	Y	Y	Y	Y	Y	N	Y
6 ***Barton***	Y	N	Y	Y	Y	N	Y	N
7 ***Archer***	Y	Y	Y	Y	Y	Y	Y	N
8 ***Fields***	Y	Y	Y	Y	Y	Y	Y	N
9 Brooks	?	N	Y	Y	N	N	N	Y
10 Pickle	Y	Y	Y	Y	Y	Y	N	Y
11 Edwards	Y	Y	Y	Y	Y	Y	N	Y
12 Geren	Y	N	Y	Y	Y	N	N	Y
13 Sarpalius	N	N	Y	Y	Y	Y	N	Y
14 Laughlin	N	N	Y	Y	N	N	N	Y
15 de la Garza	Y	Y	Y	Y	Y	Y	N	Y
16 Coleman	N	N	Y	Y	N	N	N	Y
17 Stenholm	Y	Y	Y	Y	Y	Y	Y	N
18 Washington	N	N	N	N	N	N	N	Y
19 ***Combest***	Y	Y	Y	Y	Y	Y	Y	N
20 Gonzalez	N	N	Y	N	N	N	N	Y
21 ***Smith***	Y	Y	Y	Y	Y	Y	Y	N
22 ***DeLay***	Y	Y	Y	Y	Y	Y	Y	N
23 ***Bonilla***	Y	Y	Y	Y	Y	Y	Y	N
24 Frost	N	Y	Y	Y	N	Y	N	Y
25 Andrews	Y	Y	Y	Y	Y	Y	Y	Y
26 ***Armey***	Y	Y	Y	Y	Y	Y	Y	N
27 Ortiz	Y	Y	Y	Y	Y	Y	N	Y
28 Tejeda	Y	Y	Y	Y	Y	Y	N	Y
29 Green	Y	N	Y	Y	Y	N	N	Y
30 Johnson, E. B.	N	Y	Y	N	N	Y	N	Y
UTAH								
1 ***Hansen***	Y	Y	Y	Y	Y	Y	Y	N
2 Shepherd	Y	Y	Y	Y	Y	Y	N	Y
3 Orton	Y	Y	Y	Y	Y	Y	N	N
VERMONT								
AL *Sanders*	Y	Y	Y	Y	Y	Y	N	Y
VIRGINIA								
1 ***Bateman***	+	+	+	+	+	+	+	−
2 Pickett	?	?	?	?	?	?	?	#
3 Scott	?	?	?	?	?	?	?	?
4 Sisisky	?	?	?	?	?	?	?	?
5 Payne	Y	Y	Y	Y	Y	Y	N	Y
6 ***Goodlatte***	Y	Y	Y	Y	Y	Y	Y	N
7 ***Bliley***	Y	Y	Y	Y	Y	Y	Y	N
8 Moran	Y	N	Y	Y	Y	N	N	Y
9 Boucher	Y	Y	Y	Y	Y	Y	N	Y
10 ***Wolf***	Y	Y	Y	Y	Y	Y	Y	N
11 Byrne	Y	N	Y	Y	Y	N	N	Y
WASHINGTON								
1 Cantwell	Y	Y	Y	+	Y	Y	N	Y
2 Swift	N	N	Y	Y	N	N	N	Y
3 Unsoeld	N	N	Y	Y	N	N	N	Y
4 Inslee	Y	Y	Y	Y	Y	Y	Y	Y
5 Foley							N	
6 Dicks	Y	N	Y	Y	Y	N	N	Y
7 McDermott	Y	N	Y	Y	Y	N	N	Y
8 ***Dunn***	Y	Y	Y	Y	Y	Y	Y	N
9 Kreidler	Y	Y	Y	Y	Y	Y	N	Y
WEST VIRGINIA								
1 Mollohan	Y	N	Y	Y	Y	N	N	Y
2 Wise	Y	Y	Y	Y	Y	Y	N	Y
3 Rahall	Y	Y	Y	Y	Y	Y	N	Y
WISCONSIN								
1 Barca	Y	Y	Y	Y	Y	Y	N	Y
2 ***Klug***	Y	Y	Y	Y	Y	Y	Y	N
3 ***Gunderson***	Y	Y	Y	Y	Y	Y	Y	N
4 Kleczka	Y	Y	Y	Y	Y	Y	N	Y
5 Barrett	Y	Y	Y	Y	Y	Y	N	Y
6 ***Petri***	Y	Y	Y	Y	Y	Y	Y	N
7 Obey	Y	N	Y	Y	Y	N	N	Y
8 ***Roth***	Y	Y	Y	Y	Y	Y	Y	N
9 ***Sensenbrenner***	Y	Y	Y	Y	Y	Y	Y	N
WYOMING								
AL ***Thomas***	Y	Y	Y	Y	Y	Y	Y	N
DELEGATES								
de Lugo, V.I.	Y	N	D	D	D	D	D	D
Faleomavaega, Am.S.	?	?	D	D	D	D	D	D
Norton, D.C.	Y	Y	D	D	D	D	D	D
Romero-B., P.R.	Y	Y	D	D	D	D	D	D
Underwood, Guam	?	Y	D	D	D	D	D	D

Southern states - Ala., Ark., Fla., Ga., Ky., La., Miss., N.C., Okla., S.C., Tenn., Texas, Va.
Omitted votes are quorum calls, which CQ does not include in its vote charts.

218. HR 2201. Injury Prevention and Control/Passage. Kreidler, D-Wash., motion to suspend the rules and pass the bill to authorize $50 million in fiscal 1994 and such sums as necessary in fiscal 1995-98 for the Centers for Disease Control and Prevention to carry out programs to prevent and control injuries, including injuries from domestic violence and sexual assault. Motion agreed to 305-61: R 98-57; D 206-4 (ND 139-2, SD 67-2); I 1-0, June 14, 1993. A two-thirds majority of those present and voting (244 in this case) is required for passage under suspension of the rules.

219. HR 2202. Breast and Cervical Cancer Prevention/Passage. Waxman, D-Calif., motion to suspend the rules and pass the bill to authorize $135 million in fiscal 1994 and such sums as necessary in fiscal 1995-98 for grants to states to provide breast and cervical cancer screening for the poor. The bill also would authorize demonstration programs in three states for additional preventive health services for women. Motion agreed to 365-2: R 151-2; D 213-0 (ND 141-0, SD 72-0); I 1-0, June 14, 1993. A two-thirds majority of those present and voting (245 in this case) is required for passage under suspension of the rules.

220. Procedural Motion. Approval of the House Journal of Monday, June 14. Approved 237-151: R 19-145; D 217-6 (ND 150-5, SD 67-1); I 1-0, June 15, 1993.

221. HR 5. Striker Replacement/Rule. Adoption of the rule (H Res 195) to provide for House floor consideration of the bill to prohibit employers from hiring permanent replacements for striking union workers during economic strikes. Adopted 244-176: R 0-171; D 243-5 (ND 165-1, SD 78-4); I 1-0, June 15, 1993.

222. HR 5. Striker Replacement/Union Workplaces. Edwards, D-Texas, amendment to clarify that the bill does not apply to non-union workplaces and covers only union workplaces recognized or certified by the National Labor Relations Board. Rejected in the Committee of the Whole 94-339: R 41-132; D 53-206 (ND 11-163, SD 42-43); I 0-1, June 15, 1993.

223. HR 5. Striker Replacement/10-Week Moratorium. Ridge, R-Pa., substitute amendment to prohibit the permanent replacement of workers for the first 10 weeks of a strike after which the employer would be free to hire permanent replacements. Rejected in the Committee of the Whole 58-373: R 55-118; D 3-254 (ND 0-172, SD 3-82); I 0-1, June 15, 1993.

224. HR 5. Striker Replacement/Passage. Passage of the bill to prohibit employers from hiring permanent replacements for striking union workers during economic strikes. Passed 239-190: R 17-157; D 221-33 (ND 169-1, SD 52-32); I 1-0, June 15, 1993. A "yea" was a vote in support of the president's position.

225. Procedural Motion. Approval of the House Journal of Tuesday, June 15. Approved 246-149: R 19-143; D 226-6 (ND 156-5, SD 70-1); I 1-0, June 16, 1993.

KEY

Y	Voted for (yea).
#	Paired for.
+	Announced for.
N	Voted against (nay).
X	Paired against.
−	Announced against.
P	Voted "present."
C	Voted "present" to avoid possible conflict of interest.
?	Did not vote or otherwise make a position known.
D	Delegates ineligible to vote.

Democrats *Republicans*
Independent

	218	219	220	221	222	223	224	225
ALABAMA								
1 *Callahan*	N	Y	N	N	N	Y	N	N
2 *Everett*	+	+	?	N	N	N	N	N
3 Browder	Y	Y	Y	Y	Y	N	Y	Y
4 Bevill	Y	Y	Y	Y	Y	N	Y	Y
5 Cramer	Y	Y	Y	Y	N	N	Y	Y
6 *Bachus*	N	Y	N	N	N	Y	N	N
7 Hilliard	?	?	?	?	N	N	Y	Y
ALASKA								
AL *Young*	?	?	N	N	N	N	Y	?
ARIZONA								
1 Coppersmith	Y	Y	Y	Y	N	N	Y	Y
2 Pastor	Y	Y	Y	Y	N	N	Y	Y
3 *Stump*	N	N	N	N	N	N	N	N
4 *Kyl*	Y	Y	N	N	N	N	N	N
5 *Kolbe*	N	Y	N	N	Y	Y	N	N
6 English	Y	Y	Y	Y	N	N	Y	Y
ARKANSAS								
1 Lambert	Y	Y	Y	Y	Y	N	N	Y
2 Thornton	Y	Y	Y	Y	Y	Y	Y	Y
3 *Hutchinson*	N	Y	N	N	N	N	N	N
4 Dickey	Y	Y	N	N	Y	Y	N	N
CALIFORNIA								
1 Hamburg	Y	Y	Y	Y	N	N	Y	Y
2 *Herger*	N	Y	N	N	Y	N	N	?
3 Fazio	Y	Y	?	Y	N	N	Y	Y
4 *Doolittle*	N	Y	N	N	N	N	N	N
5 Matsui	Y	Y	Y	Y	N	N	Y	Y
6 Woolsey	Y	Y	?	Y	N	N	Y	Y
7 Miller	Y	Y	?	Y	N	Y	Y	Y
8 Pelosi	Y	Y	Y	Y	N	N	Y	Y
9 Dellums	?	?	Y	Y	N	Y	Y	Y
10 *Baker*	N	Y	N	N	N	N	N	N
11 *Pombo*	N	Y	N	N	N	N	N	N
12 Lantos	Y	Y	Y	Y	N	N	Y	Y
13 Stark	Y	Y	Y	Y	N	N	Y	Y
14 Eshoo	Y	Y	Y	Y	N	N	Y	Y
15 Mineta	Y	Y	Y	Y	N	N	Y	Y
16 Edwards	Y	Y	Y	Y	N	N	Y	Y
17 Vacancy								
18 Condit	Y	Y	Y	Y	Y	N	Y	Y
19 Lehman	Y	Y	Y	Y	N	N	Y	Y
20 Dooley	N	Y	Y	Y	Y	N	N	Y
21 *Thomas*	?	?	N	N	N	N	N	N
22 *Huffington*	?	?	?	N	Y	N	N	N
23 *Gallegly*	Y	Y	N	N	N	N	N	N
24 Beilenson	Y	Y	Y	Y	N	N	Y	Y
25 *McKeon*	+	+	N	N	N	N	N	N
26 Berman	Y	Y	Y	Y	N	N	Y	Y
27 *Moorhead*	Y	Y	N	N	N	N	N	N
28 *Dreier*	N	Y	N	N	N	N	N	N
29 Waxman	Y	Y	Y	Y	N	N	Y	Y
30 Becerra	Y	Y	Y	Y	N	N	Y	Y
31 Martinez	Y	Y	Y	Y	N	N	Y	Y
32 Dixon	Y	Y	Y	Y	N	N	Y	?
33 Roybal-Allard	Y	Y	Y	Y	N	N	Y	Y
34 Torres	Y	Y	Y	Y	N	N	Y	Y
35 Waters	?	?	Y	Y	N	N	Y	Y
36 Harman	?	?	Y	Y	N	N	Y	Y
37 Tucker	Y	Y	Y	Y	N	N	Y	Y
38 *Horn*	Y	Y	N	N	Y	N	Y	N
39 *Royce*	N	Y	N	N	N	N	N	N
40 *Lewis*	?	?	Y	Y	N	N	Y	Y
41 *Kim*	Y	Y	N	N	N	N	N	N

	218	219	220	221	222	223	224	225
42 Brown	Y	Y	?	Y	N	N	Y	?
43 *Calvert*	?	?	N	N	N	N	N	N
44 *McCandless*	Y	Y	N	N	N	N	N	N
45 *Rohrabacher*	N	Y	N	N	Y	Y	N	N
46 *Dornan*	Y	Y	N	N	N	N	N	N
47 *Cox*	Y	Y	N	N	N	N	N	Y
48 *Packard*	N	Y	N	N	N	N	N	N
49 Schenk	Y	Y	Y	Y	N	N	Y	Y
50 Filner	Y	Y	Y	Y	N	N	Y	Y
51 *Cunningham*	N	Y	N	N	N	N	N	N
52 *Hunter*	N	Y	N	N	Y	?	N	N
COLORADO								
1 Schroeder	Y	Y	N	Y	N	Y	N	Y
2 Skaggs	Y	Y	Y	Y	Y	N	Y	Y
3 *McInnis*	Y	Y	N	N	N	N	N	N
4 *Allard*	N	Y	N	N	N	Y	N	N
5 *Hefley*	N	Y	N	N	N	N	N	N
6 *Schaefer*	Y	Y	N	N	N	Y	N	N
CONNECTICUT								
1 Kennelly	Y	Y	Y	Y	N	N	Y	Y
2 Gejdenson	Y	Y	Y	Y	N	N	Y	Y
3 DeLauro	Y	Y	Y	Y	N	N	Y	Y
4 *Shays*	Y	Y	N	N	Y	N	N	N
5 *Franks*	Y	Y	N	N	N	N	N	N
6 *Johnson*	Y	Y	N	N	Y	Y	N	N
DELAWARE								
AL *Castle*	Y	Y	N	N	N	N	N	N
FLORIDA								
1 Hutto	Y	Y	Y	Y	Y	N	N	Y
2 Peterson	Y	Y	Y	Y	N	N	Y	Y
3 Brown	?	Y	Y	Y	N	N	Y	Y
4 *Fowler*	Y	Y	N	N	N	N	N	N
5 Thurman	Y	Y	Y	Y	N	Y	Y	Y
6 *Stearns*	Y	Y	N	N	N	N	N	N
7 *Mica*	N	Y	N	N	N	N	N	N
8 *McCollum*	Y	Y	N	N	Y	N	N	?
9 *Bilirakis*	?	?	?	X	Y	Y	N	N
10 *Young*	N	Y	N	N	Y	N	N	N
11 Gibbons	Y	Y	Y	Y	N	N	Y	Y
12 *Canady*	Y	Y	N	N	N	N	N	N
13 *Miller*	N	Y	N	N	N	N	N	N
14 *Goss*	N	Y	N	N	Y	N	N	N
15 *Bacchus*	Y	Y	Y	Y	N	Y	N	?
16 *Lewis*	?	?	N	N	Y	N	N	N
17 Meek	Y	Y	Y	Y	N	N	Y	Y
18 *Ros-Lehtinen*	Y	Y	N	N	N	N	N	N
19 Johnston	?	?	Y	Y	N	N	Y	Y
20 Deutsch	Y	Y	Y	Y	N	N	Y	Y
21 *Diaz-Balart*	Y	Y	N	N	N	N	N	N
22 *Shaw*	Y	Y	N	N	N	N	N	N
23 Hastings	Y	Y	?	Y	N	N	Y	Y
GEORGIA								
1 *Kingston*	Y	Y	N	N	N	N	N	N
2 Bishop	Y	Y	Y	Y	N	N	Y	Y
3 *Collins*	N	N	N	N	N	N	N	N
4 *Linder*	Y	Y	N	N	N	N	N	N
5 Lewis	Y	Y	?	Y	N	N	Y	Y
6 *Gingrich*	?	?	N	N	N	N	N	?
7 Darden	Y	Y	Y	Y	Y	N	Y	Y
8 Rowland	Y	Y	Y	Y	N	N	Y	Y
9 Deal	Y	Y	Y	Y	Y	N	Y	Y
10 Johnson	Y	Y	Y	Y	Y	N	Y	Y
11 McKinney	Y	Y	Y	Y	N	N	Y	Y
HAWAII								
1 Abercrombie	Y	Y	Y	Y	N	N	Y	Y
2 Mink	Y	Y	Y	Y	N	N	Y	Y
IDAHO								
1 LaRocco	Y	Y	Y	Y	N	N	Y	Y
2 *Crapo*	N	Y	N	N	N	N	N	N
ILLINOIS								
1 Rush	Y	Y	?	Y	N	N	Y	Y
2 Reynolds	Y	Y	Y	Y	N	N	Y	Y
3 Lipinski	?	?	?	Y	N	N	Y	Y
4 Gutierrez	?	?	Y	Y	N	N	Y	Y
5 Rostenkowski	?	?	?	?	N	N	Y	Y
6 *Hyde*	Y	Y	N	N	Y	N	N	?
7 Collins	Y	Y	Y	Y	N	N	Y	?
8 *Crane*	N	N	N	N	N	N	N	N
9 Yates	Y	Y	Y	Y	N	N	Y	Y
10 *Porter*	Y	Y	N	N	N	N	N	N
11 Sangmeister	?	?	Y	Y	N	N	Y	Y
12 Costello	?	?	Y	Y	N	N	Y	Y
13 *Fawell*	Y	Y	N	N	Y	N	N	N
14 *Hastert*	Y	Y	N	N	Y	Y	N	N
15 *Ewing*	Y	Y	N	N	N	N	N	Y
16 *Manzullo*	N	Y	N	N	N	N	N	N
17 Evans	Y	Y	Y	Y	N	N	Y	Y

ND Northern Democrats   SD Southern Democrats

	218	219	220	221	222	223	224	225
18 ***Michel***	Y	Y	N	N	N	N	N	N
19 Poshard	Y	Y	Y	Y	N	N	Y	Y
20 Durbin	Y	Y	Y	Y	N	N	Y	Y
INDIANA								
1 Visclosky	Y	Y	Y	Y	N	N	Y	Y
2 Sharp	Y	Y	?	Y	N	N	Y	Y
3 Roemer	Y	Y	Y	Y	N	N	Y	Y
4 Long	Y	Y	Y	Y	N	N	Y	Y
5 ***Buyer***	Y	Y	N	N	Y	Y	N	N
6 ***Burton***	N	Y	N	N	N	N	N	N
7 ***Myers***	Y	Y	?	N	N	N	N	Y
8 McCloskey	Y	Y	Y	Y	N	N	Y	Y
9 Hamilton	Y	Y	Y	Y	N	N	Y	Y
10 Jacobs	?	?	N	N	N	N	Y	N
IOWA								
1 ***Leach***	Y	Y	N	N	N	N	N	N
2 ***Nussle***	Y	Y	N	N	N	N	N	N
3 ***Lightfoot***	Y	Y	N	N	N	N	N	N
4 Smith	Y	Y	Y	?	N	N	Y	Y
5 ***Grandy***	Y	Y	N	N	N	Y	N	N
KANSAS								
1 ***Roberts***	N	Y	N	N	N	N	N	N
2 Slattery	Y	Y	Y	Y	Y	N	Y	Y
3 ***Meyers***	Y	Y	N	N	N	Y	N	N
4 Glickman	Y	Y	Y	Y	N	N	Y	Y
KENTUCKY								
1 Barlow	Y	Y	?	Y	N	N	Y	Y
2 Natcher	Y	Y	Y	Y	N	N	Y	Y
3 Mazzoli	Y	Y	Y	Y	N	Y	Y	Y
4 ***Bunning***	?	?	?	N	N	N	N	N
5 ***Rogers***	Y	Y	N	N	N	Y	N	N
6 Baesler	Y	Y	?	Y	Y	N	Y	Y
LOUISIANA								
1 ***Livingston***	?	?	N	N	Y	N	N	?
2 Jefferson	?	?	?	Y	N	N	Y	?
3 Tauzin	Y	Y	Y	N	Y	N	N	?
4 Fields	Y	Y	Y	Y	N	N	Y	Y
5 ***McCrery***	Y	Y	Y	N	N	N	N	N
6 ***Baker***	?	?	?	N	Y	Y	N	?
7 Hayes	Y	Y	Y	N	Y	Y	N	Y
MAINE								
1 Andrews	Y	Y	Y	Y	N	N	Y	Y
2 ***Snowe***	Y	Y	N	N	N	Y	N	N
MARYLAND								
1 ***Gilchrest***	Y	Y	N	N	N	Y	N	N
2 ***Bentley***	Y	Y	N	N	Y	Y	Y	N
3 Cardin	Y	Y	Y	Y	N	N	Y	Y
4 Wynn	Y	Y	Y	Y	N	N	Y	Y
5 Hoyer	Y	Y	Y	Y	N	N	Y	Y
6 ***Bartlett***	N	Y	N	N	N	N	N	N
7 Mfume	Y	Y	?	?	N	N	Y	Y
8 ***Morella***	Y	Y	N	N	N	N	N	?
MASSACHUSETTS								
1 Olver	Y	Y	Y	Y	N	N	Y	Y
2 Neal	Y	Y	Y	Y	N	N	Y	Y
3 ***Blute***	Y	Y	N	N	Y	Y	N	N
4 Frank	Y	Y	Y	?	N	N	Y	Y
5 Meehan	Y	Y	Y	Y	N	N	Y	Y
6 ***Torkildsen***	Y	Y	N	N	N	Y	N	N
7 Markey	?	?	Y	Y	N	N	Y	Y
8 Kennedy	?	?	Y	Y	N	N	Y	Y
9 Moakley	Y	Y	Y	Y	N	N	Y	Y
10 Studds	Y	Y	Y	Y	N	N	Y	Y
MICHIGAN								
1 Stupak	Y	Y	?	Y	N	N	Y	Y
2 ***Hoekstra***	Y	Y	N	N	N	N	N	N
3 Henry	?	?	?	?	?	?	?	?
4 ***Camp***	Y	Y	N	N	N	N	N	N
5 Barcia	Y	Y	Y	Y	N	N	Y	Y
6 ***Upton***	Y	Y	N	N	N	N	N	N
7 ***Smith***	N	Y	N	N	Y	Y	N	N
8 Carr	?	?	Y	Y	N	N	Y	Y
9 Kildee	Y	Y	Y	Y	N	N	Y	Y
10 Bonior	Y	Y	?	Y	N	N	Y	Y
11 ***Knollenberg***	Y	Y	N	N	N	N	N	N
12 Levin	Y	Y	Y	Y	N	N	Y	Y
13 Ford	Y	Y	Y	Y	N	N	Y	Y
14 Conyers	?	?	Y	Y	N	N	Y	Y
15 Collins	Y	Y	Y	Y	N	N	Y	Y
16 Dingell	?	?	Y	Y	N	N	Y	Y
MINNESOTA								
1 Penny	N	Y	Y	Y	Y	N	Y	Y
2 Minge	Y	Y	Y	Y	Y	N	Y	Y
3 ***Ramstad***	N	Y	N	N	N	N	N	N
4 Vento	Y	Y	Y	Y	N	N	Y	Y

	218	219	220	221	222	223	224	225
5 Sabo	Y	Y	Y	Y	N	N	Y	Y
6 ***Grams***	N	Y	N	N	N	N	N	N
7 Peterson	?	?	Y	Y	N	N	Y	Y
8 Oberstar	Y	Y	Y	Y	N	N	Y	Y
MISSISSIPPI								
1 Whitten	?	Y	?	Y	Y	N	N	?
2 Thompson	?	?	?	Y	N	N	Y	?
3 Montgomery	Y	Y	?	Y	Y	N	N	Y
4 Parker	Y	Y	Y	Y	Y	Y	N	Y
5 Taylor	N	Y	N	N	Y	N	N	N
MISSOURI								
1 Clay	Y	Y	N	Y	N	N	Y	N
2 ***Talent***	N	Y	N	N	N	N	N	N
3 Gephardt	Y	Y	Y	Y	N	N	Y	Y
4 Skelton	Y	Y	Y	Y	N	N	Y	Y
5 Wheat	Y	Y	Y	Y	N	?	Y	Y
6 Danner	Y	Y	Y	Y	N	N	Y	Y
7 ***Hancock***	N	Y	N	N	N	N	N	N
8 ***Emerson***	Y	Y	N	N	N	N	N	N
9 Volkmer	?	?	Y	Y	N	N	Y	Y
MONTANA								
AL Williams	Y	Y	Y	Y	N	N	Y	Y
NEBRASKA								
1 ***Bereuter***	Y	Y	N	N	N	Y	N	N
2 Hoagland	Y	Y	Y	Y	N	N	Y	Y
3 ***Barrett***	Y	Y	N	N	N	N	N	N
NEVADA								
1 Bilbray	Y	Y	Y	Y	Y	N	Y	Y
2 ***Vucanovich***	N	Y	N	N	N	N	N	N
NEW HAMPSHIRE								
1 ***Zeliff***	Y	Y	N	N	N	N	N	N
2 Swett	Y	Y	Y	Y	N	N	Y	Y
NEW JERSEY								
1 Andrews	Y	Y	Y	Y	N	N	Y	Y
2 Hughes	Y	Y	Y	Y	N	N	Y	Y
3 ***Saxton***	Y	Y	N	N	N	N	N	N
4 ***Smith***	Y	Y	Y	N	N	N	Y	Y
5 ***Roukema***	Y	Y	N	N	N	Y	N	N
6 Pallone	Y	Y	Y	Y	N	N	Y	Y
7 ***Franks***	Y	Y	N	N	Y	Y	Y	N
8 Klein	Y	Y	Y	Y	N	N	Y	Y
9 Torricelli	Y	Y	Y	Y	N	N	Y	?
10 Payne	?	?	Y	Y	N	N	Y	Y
11 ***Gallo***	Y	Y	N	N	N	N	N	N
12 ***Zimmer***	Y	Y	N	N	N	N	N	N
13 Menendez	Y	Y	Y	Y	N	N	Y	Y
NEW MEXICO								
1 ***Schiff***	Y	Y	N	N	N	Y	N	N
2 ***Skeen***	N	Y	N	N	N	N	N	?
3 Richardson	Y	Y	Y	Y	N	N	Y	Y
NEW YORK								
1 Hochbrueckner	Y	Y	?	Y	N	N	Y	Y
2 ***Lazio***	Y	Y	N	N	N	Y	Y	N
3 ***King***	Y	Y	N	N	N	N	Y	N
4 ***Levy***	Y	Y	N	N	N	N	Y	N
5 Ackerman	Y	Y	Y	Y	N	N	Y	Y
6 Flake	?	?	?	Y	N	N	Y	Y
7 Manton	Y	Y	Y	Y	N	N	Y	Y
8 Nadler	Y	Y	Y	Y	N	N	Y	Y
9 Schumer	Y	Y	Y	Y	N	N	Y	Y
10 Towns	Y	Y	Y	Y	N	N	Y	Y
11 Owens	?	?	Y	Y	N	N	Y	Y
12 Velazquez	?	?	Y	Y	N	N	Y	Y
13 ***Molinari***	Y	Y	N	N	N	N	N	N
14 Maloney	Y	Y	Y	Y	N	N	Y	Y
15 Rangel	?	?	Y	Y	?	?	?	?
16 Serrano	?	?	Y	Y	N	N	Y	Y
17 Engel	?	?	?	#	N	N	Y	?
18 Lowey	Y	Y	Y	Y	N	N	Y	?
19 ***Fish***	Y	Y	Y	N	N	N	Y	?
20 ***Gilman***	Y	Y	Y	N	N	N	Y	Y
21 McNulty	Y	Y	Y	Y	N	N	Y	Y
22 ***Solomon***	N	Y	?	?	?	?	?	?
23 ***Boehlert***	Y	Y	N	N	N	N	Y	N
24 ***McHugh***	?	?	?	N	N	N	Y	?
25 ***Walsh***	Y	Y	N	N	N	Y	N	N
26 Hinchey	Y	Y	Y	Y	N	N	Y	Y
27 ***Paxon***	Y	Y	N	N	N	N	N	N
28 Slaughter	Y	Y	Y	Y	N	N	Y	Y
29 LaFalce	Y	Y	Y	Y	N	N	Y	Y
30 ***Quinn***	Y	Y	N	N	N	N	Y	N
31 ***Houghton***	Y	?	Y	N	Y	Y	N	Y
NORTH CAROLINA								
1 Clayton	Y	Y	Y	Y	N	N	Y	P
2 Valentine	Y	Y	Y	Y	Y	N	N	Y

	218	219	220	221	222	223	224	225
3 Lancaster	?	?	Y	Y	N	N	N	Y
4 Price	Y	Y	Y	Y	Y	N	Y	Y
5 Neal	Y	Y	?	Y	Y	N	N	?
6 ***Coble***	Y	Y	N	N	N	N	N	N
7 Rose	Y	Y	Y	Y	Y	N	Y	Y
8 Hefner	Y	Y	?	Y	Y	N	Y	Y
9 ***McMillan***	Y	Y	N	N	N	N	N	N
10 ***Ballenger***	Y	Y	N	N	Y	N	N	N
11 ***Taylor***	+	+	N	N	N	Y	N	N
12 Watt	Y	Y	Y	Y	N	N	Y	Y
NORTH DAKOTA								
AL Pomeroy	Y	Y	Y	Y	N	N	Y	Y
OHIO								
1 Mann	Y	Y	Y	Y	N	N	Y	Y
2 ***Portman***	?	?	N	N	N	N	N	N
3 Hall	Y	Y	Y	Y	N	N	Y	?
4 ***Oxley***	N	?	Y	N	N	N	N	N
5 ***Gillmor***	Y	Y	Y	N	N	N	N	Y
6 Strickland	Y	Y	Y	Y	N	N	Y	Y
7 ***Hobson***	Y	Y	N	N	N	Y	N	N
8 ***Boehner***	N	Y	N	N	N	N	N	N
9 Kaptur	?	?	Y	Y	N	N	Y	Y
10 ***Hoke***	Y	Y	?	N	N	Y	N	N
11 Stokes	Y	Y	Y	Y	—	N	Y	Y
12 ***Kasich***	Y	Y	Y	N	N	N	N	Y
13 Brown	Y	Y	Y	Y	N	N	Y	Y
14 Sawyer	Y	Y	Y	Y	N	N	Y	Y
15 ***Pryce***	Y	Y	N	N	N	N	N	N
16 ***Regula***	Y	Y	N	N	Y	Y	Y	N
17 Traficant	Y	Y	Y	Y	N	N	Y	Y
18 Applegate	Y	Y	Y	Y	Y	N	Y	Y
19 Fingerhut	+	+	N	Y	N	N	Y	N
OKLAHOMA								
1 ***Inhofe***	N	Y	N	N	Y	N	N	N
2 Synar	Y	Y	Y	Y	N	N	Y	?
3 Brewster	Y	Y	Y	Y	Y	N	N	Y
4 McCurdy	?	?	Y	Y	Y	N	N	Y
5 ***Istook***	N	Y	N	N	Y	N	N	N
6 English	Y	Y	Y	Y	Y	N	N	?
OREGON								
1 Furse	Y	Y	Y	Y	N	N	Y	Y
2 ***Smith***	?	?	N	N	Y	Y	N	N
3 Wyden	Y	Y	Y	Y	N	N	Y	Y
4 DeFazio	Y	Y	Y	Y	N	?	Y	?
5 Kopetski	Y	Y	Y	Y	N	N	Y	Y
PENNSYLVANIA								
1 Foglietta	?	?	?	Y	N	N	Y	Y
2 Blackwell	Y	Y	Y	Y	N	N	Y	Y
3 Borski	?	?	Y	Y	N	N	Y	Y
4 Klink	?	?	Y	Y	N	N	Y	Y
5 ***Clinger***	+	+	Y	N	N	Y	N	N
6 Holden	Y	Y	Y	Y	N	N	Y	Y
7 ***Weldon***	Y	Y	N	N	N	Y	Y	N
8 ***Greenwood***	Y	Y	N	N	N	Y	N	N
9 ***Shuster***	N	Y	N	N	N	N	N	N
10 ***McDade***	Y	Y	N	N	N	Y	N	N
11 Kanjorski	Y	Y	Y	Y	N	N	Y	Y
12 Murtha	Y	Y	Y	Y	N	N	Y	Y
13 Margolies-Mezv.	Y	Y	Y	Y	N	N	Y	Y
14 Coyne	Y	Y	Y	Y	N	N	Y	Y
15 McHale	Y	Y	Y	Y	N	N	Y	Y
16 ***Walker***	N	Y	N	N	N	N	N	N
17 ***Gekas***	N	Y	N	N	N	Y	N	N
18 ***Santorum***	Y	Y	?	?	Y	Y	Y	Y
19 ***Goodling***	N	Y	N	N	N	Y	N	N
20 Murphy	?	?	N	Y	N	N	Y	N
21 ***Ridge***	?	?	N	N	N	Y	N	N
RHODE ISLAND								
1 ***Machtley***	Y	Y	N	N	N	Y	N	N
2 Reed	Y	Y	Y	Y	N	N	Y	Y
SOUTH CAROLINA								
1 ***Ravenel***	Y	Y	N	N	N	Y	N	N
2 ***Spence***	Y	Y	Y	N	Y	Y	N	Y
3 Derrick	Y	Y	Y	Y	Y	N	N	?
4 ***Inglis***	N	Y	N	Y	N	N	N	Y
5 Spratt	?	?	?	Y	Y	N	N	Y
6 Clyburn	?	?	Y	Y	N	N	Y	Y
SOUTH DAKOTA								
AL Johnson	Y	Y	Y	Y	Y	N	Y	Y
TENNESSEE								
1 ***Quillen***	N	Y	N	N	N	N	N	N
2 ***Duncan***	N	Y	N	N	Y	Y	N	N
3 Lloyd	Y	Y	?	?	N	N	Y	Y
4 Cooper	Y	Y	Y	Y	N	N	N	Y
5 Clement	Y	Y	Y	Y	Y	N	Y	Y

	218	219	220	221	222	223	224	225
6 Gordon	Y	Y	?	Y	N	N	Y	Y
7 ***Sundquist***	N	Y	N	N	N	N	N	N
8 Tanner	Y	Y	Y	Y	Y	N	Y	Y
9 Ford	?	?	?	Y	N	N	Y	?
TEXAS								
1 Chapman	Y	Y	Y	Y	N	N	Y	Y
2 Wilson	Y	Y	Y	Y	N	N	Y	Y
3 ***Johnson, Sam***	N	Y	N	N	N	N	N	N
4 Hall	Y	Y	Y	N	Y	N	N	Y
5 Bryant	?	?	Y	Y	N	N	Y	Y
6 ***Barton***	?	?	?	?	?	?	N	N
7 ***Archer***	N	Y	Y	N	N	N	N	Y
8 ***Fields***	Y	Y	N	N	N	N	N	N
9 Brooks	Y	Y	Y	Y	N	N	Y	Y
10 Pickle	Y	Y	Y	Y	Y	N	N	Y
11 Edwards	Y	Y	Y	Y	Y	N	Y	Y
12 Geren	Y	Y	Y	Y	Y	N	N	Y
13 Sarpalius	Y	Y	Y	Y	N	N	Y	Y
14 Laughlin	Y	Y	Y	Y	Y	N	Y	?
15 de la Garza	Y	Y	Y	Y	N	N	N	Y
16 Coleman	?	?	Y	Y	N	N	Y	Y
17 Stenholm	N	Y	Y	Y	Y	N	N	Y
18 Washington	?	Y	?	Y	N	N	Y	Y
19 ***Combest***	N	Y	Y	N	Y	N	N	Y
20 Gonzalez	Y	Y	Y	Y	N	N	Y	Y
21 ***Smith***	Y	Y	N	N	N	N	N	?
22 ***DeLay***	N	Y	N	N	Y	N	N	N
23 ***Bonilla***	Y	Y	N	N	Y	N	N	N
24 Frost	Y	Y	?	Y	N	N	Y	?
25 Andrews	Y	Y	Y	Y	N	N	Y	Y
26 ***Armey***	N	Y	N	N	N	N	N	N
27 Ortiz	Y	Y	Y	?	Y	N	N	?
28 Tejeda	Y	Y	Y	Y	Y	N	N	Y
29 Green	Y	Y	Y	Y	N	N	Y	Y
30 Johnson, E. B.	Y	Y	Y	Y	N	N	Y	Y
UTAH								
1 ***Hansen***	N	Y	N	N	N	Y	N	N
2 Shepherd	Y	Y	Y	Y	N	N	Y	Y
3 Orton	Y	Y	Y	Y	N	N	Y	Y
VERMONT								
AL *Sanders*	Y	Y	Y	Y	N	N	Y	Y
VIRGINIA								
1 ***Bateman***	Y	Y	Y	N	N	N	N	Y
2 Pickett	?	?	Y	Y	N	N	N	Y
3 Scott	?	?	Y	Y	N	N	Y	Y
4 Sisisky	Y	Y	Y	Y	Y	N	N	Y
5 Payne	Y	Y	Y	Y	Y	N	N	Y
6 ***Goodlatte***	Y	Y	N	N	N	N	N	N
7 ***Bliley***	Y	Y	N	N	N	N	N	N
8 Moran	Y	Y	Y	Y	N	N	Y	Y
9 Boucher	Y	Y	Y	Y	Y	N	?	Y
10 ***Wolf***	Y	Y	N	N	N	N	N	N
11 Byrne	Y	Y	Y	Y	N	N	Y	Y
WASHINGTON								
1 Cantwell	Y	Y	Y	Y	N	N	Y	Y
2 Swift	Y	Y	Y	Y	N	N	Y	Y
3 Unsoeld	Y	Y	Y	Y	N	N	Y	Y
4 Inslee	Y	Y	Y	Y	Y	N	Y	Y
5 Foley								
6 Dicks	Y	Y	Y	Y	N	?	Y	Y
7 McDermott	Y	Y	Y	Y	N	N	Y	Y
8 ***Dunn***	Y	Y	N	N	N	N	N	N
9 Kreidler	Y	Y	Y	Y	N	N	Y	Y
WEST VIRGINIA								
1 Mollohan	?	?	Y	Y	N	N	Y	Y
2 Wise	?	?	Y	Y	N	N	Y	Y
3 Rahall	Y	Y	Y	Y	N	N	Y	Y
WISCONSIN								
1 Barca	Y	Y	Y	Y	N	N	Y	Y
2 ***Klug***	Y	Y	N	N	N	Y	N	N
3 ***Gunderson***	Y	Y	Y	N	N	Y	N	Y
4 Kleczka	Y	Y	?	Y	N	N	Y	?
5 Barrett	Y	Y	Y	Y	N	N	Y	Y
6 ***Petri***	Y	Y	N	N	N	Y	N	N
7 Obey	Y	Y	Y	Y	N	N	Y	Y
8 ***Roth***	N	Y	Y	N	N	Y	N	N
9 ***Sensenbrenner***	N	Y	N	N	N	N	N	N
WYOMING								
AL ***Thomas***	N	Y	N	N	Y	N	N	Y
DELEGATES								
de Lugo, V.I.	D	D	D	D	N	N	D	D
Faleomavaega, Am.S.	D	D	D	D	N	N	D	D
Norton, D.C.	D	D	D	D	N	N	D	D
Romero-B., P.R.	D	D	D	D	N	N	D	D
Underwood, Guam	D	D	D	D	N	N	D	D

Southern states - Ala., Ark., Fla., Ga., Ky., La., Miss., N.C., Okla., S.C., Tenn., Texas, Va.
Omitted votes are quorum calls, which CQ does not include in its vote charts.

226. HR 2333, HR 2404. Fiscal 1994-95 State Department and Foreign Aid Authorizations/Rule. Adoption of the rule (H Res 197) to provide for House floor consideration of the bills to authorize $9.7 billion in fiscal 1994 for foreign aid and $7.3 billion in fiscal 1994, and $7.8 billion in fiscal 1995 for the operations of the State Department and related agencies. Adopted 294-129: R 73-98; D 220-31 (ND 142-26, SD 78-5); I 1-0, June 16, 1993.

227. HR 2404. Fiscal 1994-95 Foreign Aid Authorization/Agency for International Development. Hamilton, D-Ind., substitute amendment to the Gilman, R-N.Y., amendment to alter the administration of foreign assistance programs and terminate the development assistance authorities of the Agency for International Development (AID) at the end of fiscal 1995. Adopted in the Committee of the Whole 246-186: R 3-171; D 242-15 (ND 162-11, SD 80-4); I 1-0, June 16, 1993. (The Gilman amendment as amended by the Hamilton substitute amendment subsequently was adopted by roll call vote 228.)

228. HR 2404. Fiscal 1994-95 Foreign Aid Authorization/Agency for International Development. Gilman, R-N.Y., amendment, as amended by the Hamilton, D-Ind., substitute, to alter the administration of foreign assistance programs and terminate the existing development assistance authorities of the Agency for International Development at the end of fiscal 1995. Adopted in the Committee of the Whole 421-2: R 169-1; D 251-1 (ND 167-1, SD 84-0); I 1-0, June 16, 1993.

229. HR 2404. Fiscal 1994-95 Foreign Aid Authorization/Russian Aid. Kyl, R-Ariz., amendment to cut $704 million of the $904 million in the bill for aid to Russia and the other former Soviet republics. Rejected in the Committee of the Whole 118-317: R 91-83; D 27-233 (ND 18-157, SD 9-76); I 0-1, June 16, 1993. A "nay" was a vote in support of the president's position.

230. HR 2404. Fiscal 1994-95 Foreign Aid Authorization/India Human Rights. Burton, R-Ind., amendment to terminate the $41 million in aid to India unless the president certifies that India has repealed certain security laws that lead to human rights violations. Rejected in the Committee of the Whole 201-233: R 121-53; D 80-179 (ND 49-126, SD 31-53); I 0-1, June 16, 1993.

231. HR 2404. Fiscal 1994-95 Foreign Aid Authorization/Agency for International Development. Separate vote at the request of Kolbe, R-Ariz., on the amendment adopted in the Committee of the Whole offered by Gilman, R-N.Y., which was amended by a Hamilton, R-Ind., substitute to change the administration of foreign assistance programs and terminate the existing development assistance authorities of the Agency for International Development at the end of fiscal 1995. Adopted 426-0: R 175-0; D 250-0 (ND 167-0, SD 83-0); I 1-0, June 16, 1993. (On separate votes, which may be demanded on an amendment adopted in the Committee of the Whole, the four delegates and the resident commissioner of Puerto Rico cannot vote. See vote 228).

232. HR 2333. Fiscal 1994-95 State Department Authorization/U.N. Population Fund. Smith, R-N.J., amendment to prohibit funding of the U.N. Population Fund unless the president certifies that the population control program in China is not coercive or that the fund is no longer being used in China. Rejected in the Committee of the Whole 191-236: R 139-32; D 52-203 (ND 31-142, SD 21-61); I 0-1, June 16, 1993. A "nay" was a vote in support of the president's position.

233. HR 2295. Fiscal 1994 Foreign Operations Appropriations/Rule. Adoption of the rule (H Res 200) to provide for House floor consideration of the bill to provide $12,987,138,866 in new budget authority for foreign operations, export financing and related programs in fiscal 1994. The administration requested $14,421,987,300. Adopted 263-160: R 15-157; D 247-3 (ND 167-2, SD 80-1); I 1-0, June 17, 1993.

** Sam Farr, D-Calif., was sworn in June 16. Vote 226 was the first vote for which he was eligible.

KEY

Y	Voted for (yea).
#	Paired for.
+	Announced for.
N	Voted against (nay).
X	Paired against.
−	Announced against.
P	Voted "present."
C	Voted "present" to avoid possible conflict of interest.
?	Did not vote or otherwise make a position known.
D	Delegates ineligible to vote.

Democrats *Republicans*
Independent

	226	227	228	229	230	231	232	233
ALABAMA								
1 *Callahan*	N	N	Y	N	Y	Y	Y	Y
2 *Everett*	N	N	Y	Y	Y	Y	Y	N
3 Browder	Y	Y	Y	N	N	Y	Y	Y
4 Bevill	Y	Y	Y	N	N	Y	N	Y
5 Cramer	Y	Y	Y	N	N	Y	N	Y
6 *Bachus*	N	N	Y	N	Y	Y	Y	N
7 Hilliard	Y	Y	Y	N	N	Y	N	Y
ALASKA								
AL *Young*	Y	N	Y	N	Y	N	Y	?
ARIZONA								
1 Coppersmith	Y	Y	Y	N	N	Y	N	Y
2 Pastor	Y	Y	Y	N	N	Y	N	Y
3 *Stump*	N	N	Y	Y	Y	Y	Y	N
4 *Kyl*	Y	N	Y	Y	Y	Y	Y	N
5 *Kolbe*	Y	N	Y	Y	Y	N	N	N
6 English	Y	Y	Y	N	Y	Y	N	Y
ARKANSAS								
1 Lambert	Y	Y	Y	N	N	Y	N	Y
2 Thornton	Y	Y	Y	N	N	Y	?	Y
3 *Hutchinson*	N	N	Y	Y	Y	Y	Y	N
4 Dickey	Y	N	Y	Y	Y	Y	Y	N
CALIFORNIA								
1 Hamburg	N	Y	Y	N	N	Y	N	Y
2 *Herger*	Y	N	Y	Y	Y	Y	Y	N
3 Fazio	Y	Y	Y	N	Y	Y	N	Y
4 *Doolittle*	Y	N	Y	Y	Y	Y	Y	N
5 Matsui	?	Y	Y	N	N	Y	N	Y
6 Woolsey	Y	Y	Y	N	N	Y	N	Y
7 Miller	Y	Y	Y	N	Y	N	Y	Y
8 Pelosi	Y	Y	Y	N	Y	+	−	+
9 Dellums	?	Y	Y	N	N	Y	N	Y
10 *Baker*	N	N	Y	Y	Y	Y	Y	N
11 *Pombo*	N	N	Y	Y	Y	Y	Y	N
12 Lantos	N	Y	Y	N	N	Y	N	Y
13 Stark	Y	Y	Y	N	Y	N	Y	Y
14 Eshoo	Y	Y	Y	N	N	Y	N	Y
15 Mineta	Y	Y	Y	N	N	Y	N	Y
16 Edwards	Y	Y	N	N	N	Y	N	Y
17 Farr **	Y	+	+	N	Y	Y	N	Y
18 Condit	Y	N	Y	Y	Y	Y	N	Y
19 Lehman	Y	Y	Y	N	Y	Y	N	Y
20 Dooley	Y	Y	Y	N	Y	Y	N	Y
21 *Thomas*	Y	N	Y	N	Y	Y	N	N
22 *Huffington*	N	N	Y	Y	Y	Y	Y	N
23 *Gallegly*	Y	N	Y	Y	Y	Y	Y	N
24 Beilenson	Y	Y	Y	N	N	Y	N	Y
25 *McKeon*	Y	N	Y	Y	Y	Y	Y	N
26 Berman	Y	Y	N	N	Y	Y	N	Y
27 *Moorhead*	Y	N	Y	Y	Y	Y	Y	N
28 *Dreier*	N	N	Y	N	Y	Y	Y	N
29 Waxman	Y	Y	N	N	Y	N	Y	Y
30 Becerra	Y	Y	Y	N	Y	N	Y	Y
31 Martinez	Y	Y	Y	N	N	Y	N	Y
32 Dixon	Y	Y	Y	N	N	Y	N	Y
33 Roybal-Allard	Y	Y	Y	N	N	Y	N	Y
34 Torres	Y	Y	N	Y	N	Y	N	Y
35 Waters	Y	Y	Y	N	Y	N	Y	Y
36 Harman	Y	Y	Y	N	N	Y	N	Y
37 Tucker	Y	?	Y	N	N	N	N	Y
38 *Horn*	N	N	Y	N	Y	Y	Y	N
39 *Royce*	Y	N	Y	N	Y	Y	Y	N
40 *Lewis*	Y	N	Y	N	N	Y	N	Y
41 *Kim*	Y	N	Y	Y	Y	N	Y	N
42 Brown	Y	Y	Y	N	N	Y	N	Y
43 *Calvert*	N	N	Y	N	Y	Y	N	N
44 *McCandless*	N	N	Y	N	Y	Y	−	N
45 *Rohrabacher*	N	N	Y	Y	Y	Y	Y	N
46 *Dornan*	N	N	?	Y	Y	Y	Y	N
47 *Cox*	X	N	Y	Y	Y	Y	Y	N
48 *Packard*	N	N	Y	Y	Y	Y	Y	N
49 Schenk	Y	Y	Y	N	N	Y	N	Y
50 Filner	Y	Y	Y	N	N	Y	N	Y
51 *Cunningham*	N	N	Y	N	Y	Y	Y	N
52 *Hunter*	N	N	?	Y	Y	Y	Y	N
COLORADO								
1 Schroeder	Y	N	Y	N	N	Y	N	Y
2 Skaggs	Y	Y	N	N	N	Y	N	Y
3 *McInnis*	Y	N	Y	Y	Y	Y	N	Y
4 *Allard*	Y	N	Y	Y	Y	Y	Y	N
5 *Hefley*	N	N	Y	Y	Y	Y	Y	N
6 *Schaefer*	N	N	Y	Y	Y	Y	Y	N
CONNECTICUT								
1 Kennelly	Y	Y	Y	N	Y	Y	N	Y
2 Gejdenson	Y	Y	Y	N	Y	Y	N	Y
3 DeLauro	Y	Y	Y	N	Y	Y	N	Y
4 *Shays*	Y	N	Y	N	N	Y	N	Y
5 *Franks*	N	N	Y	Y	Y	Y	Y	N
6 *Johnson*	?	N	Y	N	N	Y	N	Y
DELAWARE								
AL *Castle*	N	N	Y	N	N	Y	N	N
FLORIDA								
1 Hutto	Y	Y	Y	N	N	Y	Y	Y
2 Peterson	Y	Y	Y	N	N	Y	N	Y
3 Brown	Y	Y	Y	N	N	Y	N	Y
4 *Fowler*	N	N	Y	N	N	Y	Y	N
5 Thurman	Y	Y	Y	Y	Y	Y	Y	Y
6 *Stearns*	N	N	Y	Y	Y	Y	Y	N
7 *Mica*	N	N	Y	Y	Y	Y	Y	N
8 *McCollum*	N	N	Y	N	N	Y	#	N
9 *Bilirakis*	N	N	Y	Y	Y	Y	Y	N
10 *Young*	N	N	Y	Y	Y	?	Y	N
11 Gibbons	Y	Y	N	N	Y	Y	N	Y
12 *Canady*	N	N	Y	Y	Y	Y	Y	N
13 *Miller*	Y	N	Y	Y	Y	Y	Y	N
14 *Goss*	N	N	Y	Y	Y	Y	Y	N
15 *Bacchus*	Y	Y	Y	N	Y	N	N	Y
16 *Lewis*	N	N	Y	Y	Y	Y	N	Y
17 *Meek*	Y	Y	N	Y	?	Y	N	Y
18 *Ros-Lehtinen*	N	N	Y	Y	Y	Y	Y	N
19 Johnston	Y	Y	Y	N	N	Y	N	Y
20 Deutsch	Y	Y	N	N	N	Y	N	Y
21 *Diaz-Balart*	N	N	Y	Y	Y	Y	Y	N
22 *Shaw*	N	N	Y	N	N	Y	N	N
23 Hastings	Y	Y	Y	N	N	Y	N	Y
GEORGIA								
1 *Kingston*	Y	N	Y	N	Y	Y	Y	N
2 Bishop	Y	Y	Y	N	N	Y	N	Y
3 *Collins*	N	N	Y	Y	Y	Y	Y	N
4 *Linder*	N	N	Y	N	N	Y	Y	N
5 Lewis	Y	Y	Y	N	N	Y	N	Y
6 *Gingrich*	Y	N	Y	N	N	Y	Y	N
7 Darden	Y	Y	Y	N	N	Y	N	Y
8 Rowland	Y	Y	Y	N	N	Y	N	Y
9 Deal	Y	Y	Y	N	Y	Y	Y	N
10 Johnson	Y	Y	Y	N	N	Y	N	Y
11 McKinney	Y	Y	Y	N	N	Y	N	Y
HAWAII								
1 Abercrombie	Y	Y	Y	N	N	Y	N	Y
2 Mink	Y	Y	Y	N	N	Y	N	Y
IDAHO								
1 LaRocco	Y	Y	Y	Y	Y	Y	N	Y
2 *Crapo*	N	N	Y	Y	Y	Y	Y	N
ILLINOIS								
1 Rush	Y	Y	Y	N	N	Y	N	Y
2 Reynolds	Y	Y	Y	N	N	Y	N	Y
3 Lipinski	N	Y	Y	N	Y	Y	Y	Y
4 Gutierrez	Y	Y	?	N	N	Y	N	Y
5 Rostenkowski	Y	Y	Y	N	N	Y	N	Y
6 *Hyde*	?	?	?	N	Y	Y	Y	N
7 Collins	#	?	?	N	N	N	N	Y
8 *Crane*	N	N	Y	Y	N	N	Y	N
9 Yates	N	Y	Y	N	N	Y	N	Y
10 *Porter*	Y	N	Y	N	N	Y	N	Y
11 Sangmeister	Y	Y	Y	N	Y	Y	N	Y
12 Costello	Y	Y	?	N	Y	Y	Y	Y
13 *Fawell*	N	N	Y	N	N	Y	Y	N
14 *Hastert*	Y	N	Y	N	Y	Y	Y	N
15 *Ewing*	Y	N	Y	Y	Y	Y	Y	N
16 *Manzullo*	N	N	Y	Y	Y	Y	Y	N
17 Evans	N	Y	Y	N	N	Y	N	Y

ND Northern Democrats   **SD** Southern Democrats

	226	227	228	229	230	231	232	233
18 ***Michel***	Y	N	Y	N	Y	Y	Y	Y
19 Poshard	Y	Y	Y	Y	Y	Y	Y	Y
20 Durbin	Y	Y	?	?	N	Y	N	Y
INDIANA								
1 Visclosky	Y	Y	Y	N	N	Y	N	Y
2 Sharp	Y	Y	Y	N	N	Y	N	Y
3 Roemer	Y	Y	Y	Y	N	Y	Y	Y
4 Long	Y	Y	Y	N	N	Y	N	Y
5 ***Buyer***	Y	N	Y	Y	N	Y	Y	N
6 ***Burton***	N	N	Y	Y	Y	Y	Y	N
7 ***Myers***	N	N	Y	N	N	Y	Y	N
8 McCloskey	Y	Y	?	N	N	Y	N	Y
9 Hamilton	Y	Y	Y	N	N	Y	N	Y
10 Jacobs	N	Y	Y	Y	Y	Y	Y	N
IOWA								
1 ***Leach***	Y	N	Y	N	N	Y	N	N
2 ***Nussle***	Y	N	Y	Y	Y	Y	Y	N
3 ***Lightfoot***	N	N	Y	N	Y	Y	Y	Y
4 Smith	Y	Y	Y	N	N	Y	N	Y
5 ***Grandy***	Y	N	Y	Y	Y	Y	Y	N
KANSAS								
1 ***Roberts***	Y	N	Y	N	Y	Y	Y	N
2 Slattery	Y	N	Y	N	Y	Y	Y	Y
3 ***Meyers***	Y	N	Y	N	N	Y	N	N
4 Glickman	Y	Y	Y	N	Y	Y	N	Y
KENTUCKY								
1 Barlow	Y	Y	Y	N	Y	Y	Y	Y
2 Natcher	Y	Y	Y	N	N	Y	N	Y
3 Mazzoli	Y	Y	Y	N	N	Y	Y	Y
4 ***Bunning***	N	N	Y	Y	Y	Y	Y	N
5 ***Rogers***	N	N	Y	Y	Y	Y	Y	N
6 Baesler	Y	Y	Y	N	N	Y	N	Y
LOUISIANA								
1 ***Livingston***	N	N	Y	N	Y	Y	Y	Y
2 Jefferson	Y	Y	Y	N	N	Y	N	Y
3 Tauzin	N	N	Y	Y	Y	Y	Y	Y
4 Fields	N	Y	Y	Y	Y	Y	N	Y
5 ***McCrery***	Y	N	Y	N	N	Y	Y	Y
6 ***Baker***	N	N	Y	Y	Y	Y	Y	N
7 Hayes	N	Y	Y	N	N	Y	Y	Y
MAINE								
1 Andrews	Y	Y	Y	N	N	Y	N	Y
2 ***Snowe***	N	N	Y	Y	Y	Y	N	N
MARYLAND								
1 ***Gilchrest***	N	N	Y	N	N	Y	N	N
2 ***Bentley***	N	N	Y	Y	?	Y	Y	N
3 Cardin	Y	Y	Y	N	N	Y	N	Y
4 Wynn	Y	Y	Y	N	N	Y	N	?
5 Hoyer	Y	Y	Y	N	N	Y	N	Y
6 ***Bartlett***	Y	N	Y	Y	N	Y	Y	N
7 Mfume	N	Y	Y	Y	Y	Y	N	Y
8 ***Morella***	Y	N	Y	N	N	Y	N	N
MASSACHUSETTS								
1 Olver	N	Y	Y	N	N	Y	N	Y
2 Neal	Y	Y	Y	N	N	Y	N	Y
3 ***Blute***	Y	N	Y	Y	N	Y	Y	N
4 Frank	Y	Y	Y	N	N	Y	N	Y
5 Meehan	Y	Y	Y	N	N	Y	N	Y
6 ***Torkildsen***	N	N	Y	N	N	Y	N	N
7 Markey	Y	Y	Y	N	N	Y	N	Y
8 Kennedy	N	Y	Y	N	N	Y	N	Y
9 Moakley	Y	Y	Y	N	N	Y	?	Y
10 Studds	N	Y	Y	N	N	Y	N	Y
MICHIGAN								
1 Stupak	N	Y	Y	N	Y	Y	Y	Y
2 ***Hoekstra***	Y	N	Y	N	Y	Y	Y	N
3 Henry	?	?	?	?	?	?	?	?
4 ***Camp***	Y	N	Y	Y	Y	Y	Y	N
5 Barcia	Y	Y	Y	Y	N	?	Y	?
6 ***Upton***	N	N	Y	N	Y	Y	N	N
7 ***Smith***	N	N	Y	N	N	Y	Y	N
8 Carr	Y	Y	Y	N	N	?	N	Y
9 Kildee	Y	Y	Y	N	N	Y	Y	Y
10 Bonior	Y	Y	Y	N	Y	Y	Y	Y
11 ***Knollenberg***	Y	N	Y	N	N	Y	Y	N
12 Levin	Y	Y	Y	N	N	Y	N	Y
13 Ford	Y	Y	Y	N	N	Y	N	Y
14 Conyers	Y	Y	Y	N	N	Y	N	Y
15 Collins	Y	Y	Y	Y	N	Y	N	Y
16 Dingell	N	Y	Y	N	N	Y	N	Y
MINNESOTA								
1 Penny	Y	Y	Y	N	N	Y	N	Y
2 Minge	Y	Y	Y	N	Y	Y	N	Y
3 ***Ramstad***	Y	N	Y	Y	Y	Y	N	N
4 Vento	Y	Y	Y	N	N	Y	N	Y
5 Sabo	Y	Y	Y	N	N	Y	N	Y
6 ***Grams***	Y	N	Y	Y	Y	Y	Y	N
7 Peterson	Y	Y	Y	N	Y	Y	Y	Y
8 Oberstar	Y	Y	Y	N	N	Y	Y	Y
MISSISSIPPI								
1 Whitten	Y	Y	Y	N	N	?	Y	Y
2 Thompson	Y	Y	Y	N	N	Y	N	Y
3 Montgomery	Y	Y	Y	N	Y	Y	Y	Y
4 Parker	Y	Y	Y	N	Y	Y	Y	Y
5 Taylor	N	N	Y	N	Y	Y	Y	N
MISSOURI								
1 Clay	Y	Y	Y	N	N	Y	N	Y
2 ***Talent***	N	N	Y	N	N	Y	Y	N
3 Gephardt	Y	Y	Y	N	N	Y	N	Y
4 Skelton	Y	Y	Y	N	Y	Y	Y	Y
5 Wheat	?	Y	Y	N	N	Y	N	Y
6 Danner	Y	Y	Y	Y	Y	Y	Y	Y
7 ***Hancock***	Y	N	Y	Y	Y	Y	Y	N
8 ***Emerson***	Y	N	Y	N	Y	Y	Y	N
9 Volkmer	N	Y	Y	N	Y	Y	Y	Y
MONTANA								
AL Williams	Y	N	N	N	Y	Y	N	Y
NEBRASKA								
1 ***Bereuter***	Y	Y	Y	N	N	Y	N	Y
2 Hoagland	Y	Y	Y	N	N	Y	N	Y
3 ***Barrett***	Y	N	Y	N	Y	Y	Y	N
NEVADA								
1 Bilbray	Y	Y	Y	N	N	Y	Y	Y
2 ***Vucanovich***	N	N	Y	Y	Y	Y	Y	N
NEW HAMPSHIRE								
1 ***Zeliff***	N	N	Y	N	Y	Y	N	N
2 Swett	N	Y	Y	N	N	Y	N	Y
NEW JERSEY								
1 Andrews	Y	Y	Y	Y	N	Y	N	Y
2 Hughes	N	N	Y	N	N	Y	N	Y
3 ***Saxton***	N	N	Y	Y	Y	Y	Y	N
4 ***Smith***	N	N	Y	N	Y	Y	Y	N
5 ***Roukema***	N	Y	Y	Y	Y	Y	N	N
6 Pallone	Y	Y	Y	N	N	Y	N	Y
7 ***Franks***	N	N	Y	N	N	Y	Y	N
8 Klein	Y	Y	Y	N	N	Y	N	Y
9 Torricelli	N	Y	Y	N	Y	Y	N	Y
10 Payne	Y	Y	Y	N	N	Y	N	Y
11 ***Gallo***	N	N	Y	N	Y	Y	N	N
12 ***Zimmer***	N	N	Y	Y	Y	Y	N	N
13 Menendez	Y	Y	Y	N	N	Y	N	Y
NEW MEXICO								
1 ***Schiff***	Y	N	Y	N	Y	Y	Y	N
2 ***Skeen***	Y	N	Y	N	Y	Y	Y	N
3 Richardson	Y	Y	Y	N	N	Y	N	Y
NEW YORK								
1 Hochbrueckner	Y	Y	Y	N	N	Y	N	Y
2 ***Lazio***	Y	N	Y	Y	N	Y	N	N
3 ***King***	N	N	Y	N	Y	Y	Y	N
4 ***Levy***	N	N	Y	N	N	Y	Y	N
5 Ackerman	Y	Y	Y	N	N	Y	N	Y
6 Flake	N	Y	Y	N	Y	Y	N	Y
7 Manton	Y	Y	Y	N	N	Y	Y	Y
8 Nadler	Y	Y	Y	N	N	Y	N	Y
9 Schumer	Y	Y	Y	N	?	?	X	Y
10 Towns	Y	Y	Y	N	N	Y	N	Y
11 Owens	Y	Y	Y	N	N	Y	N	Y
12 Velazquez	Y	Y	Y	N	Y	Y	N	Y
13 ***Molinari***	Y	N	?	N	N	Y	Y	N
14 Maloney	Y	Y	Y	N	N	Y	N	Y
15 Rangel	N	Y	Y	Y	N	Y	N	Y
16 Serrano	Y	Y	Y	N	N	Y	N	Y
17 Engel	Y	Y	Y	N	N	Y	N	Y
18 Lowey	Y	Y	Y	N	N	Y	N	Y
19 ***Fish***	Y	N	Y	N	Y	Y	?	Y
20 ***Gilman***	N	N	Y	N	N	Y	N	Y
21 McNulty	Y	Y	Y	N	N	Y	N	Y
22 ***Solomon***	N	N	Y	Y	Y	Y	Y	N
23 ***Boehlert***	Y	N	Y	N	N	Y	N	N
24 ***McHugh***	N	N	?	?	Y	Y	Y	N
25 ***Walsh***	N	N	Y	Y	N	Y	Y	N
26 Hinchey	Y	Y	?	N	Y	Y	N	Y
27 ***Paxon***	N	N	Y	N	Y	Y	Y	N
28 Slaughter	Y	N	?	N	Y	Y	N	Y
29 LaFalce	Y	Y	Y	N	Y	Y	Y	Y
30 ***Quinn***	N	N	Y	Y	Y	Y	Y	N
31 ***Houghton***	N	N	Y	N	N	Y	N	N
NORTH CAROLINA								
1 Clayton	Y	Y	Y	N	N	Y	N	Y
2 Valentine	Y	Y	Y	Y	Y	Y	Y	Y
3 Lancaster	Y	Y	Y	N	N	Y	N	Y
4 Price	Y	Y	Y	N	N	Y	N	Y
5 Neal	Y	Y	Y	N	N	Y	N	?
6 ***Coble***	N	N	Y	Y	Y	Y	Y	N
7 Rose	Y	?	?	N	Y	Y	N	Y
8 Hefner	Y	Y	Y	N	Y	Y	N	Y
9 ***McMillan***	N	N	Y	N	N	Y	Y	Y
10 ***Ballenger***	N	N	Y	N	Y	Y	Y	N
11 ***Taylor***	N	N	Y	Y	Y	Y	Y	N
12 Watt	Y	Y	Y	N	Y	Y	N	Y
NORTH DAKOTA								
AL Pomeroy	Y	Y	Y	N	N	Y	N	Y
OHIO								
1 Mann	Y	Y	Y	N	N	Y	N	Y
2 ***Portman***	N	N	Y	Y	N	Y	Y	N
3 Hall	Y	Y	Y	N	N	Y	Y	Y
4 ***Oxley***	Y	N	Y	N	N	Y	Y	N
5 ***Gillmor***	N	N	Y	N	Y	Y	Y	Y
6 Strickland	Y	Y	Y	N	Y	Y	N	Y
7 ***Hobson***	Y	N	Y	N	Y	Y	Y	N
8 ***Boehner***	Y	N	Y	N	Y	Y	Y	N
9 Kaptur	Y	Y	Y	N	N	Y	N	Y
10 ***Hoke***	N	N	Y	Y	Y	Y	Y	N
11 Stokes	Y	Y	Y	N	N	Y	N	Y
12 ***Kasich***	Y	N	Y	Y	Y	Y	Y	N
13 Brown	Y	Y	Y	N	N	Y	N	Y
14 Sawyer	Y	Y	Y	N	N	Y	N	Y
15 ***Pryce***	Y	N	Y	Y	Y	Y	Y	N
16 ***Regula***	N	N	Y	N	Y	Y	Y	N
17 Traficant	Y	N	Y	Y	Y	Y	N	Y
18 Applegate	Y	N	Y	Y	Y	Y	Y	Y
19 Fingerhut	Y	Y	Y	N	N	Y	N	Y
OKLAHOMA								
1 ***Inhofe***	N	N	Y	Y	Y	Y	Y	N
2 Synar	Y	Y	Y	N	N	Y	N	Y
3 Brewster	Y	Y	Y	N	Y	Y	N	Y
4 McCurdy	Y	Y	Y	N	N	Y	N	Y
5 ***Istook***	N	N	Y	N	Y	Y	Y	N
6 English	Y	Y	Y	N	Y	Y	N	Y
OREGON								
1 Furse	Y	Y	Y	N	Y	Y	N	Y
2 ***Smith***	Y	N	Y	N	Y	Y	Y	N
3 Wyden	Y	Y	Y	N	Y	Y	N	Y
4 DeFazio	Y	Y	Y	Y	Y	Y	N	Y
5 Kopetski	Y	Y	Y	N	N	Y	N	Y
PENNSYLVANIA								
1 Foglietta	Y	Y	Y	N	N	Y	Y	Y
2 Blackwell	Y	Y	Y	N	N	Y	N	Y
3 Borski	N	Y	Y	N	N	Y	Y	Y
4 Klink	N	N	Y	N	N	Y	Y	Y
5 ***Clinger***	?	N	Y	N	N	Y	Y	N
6 Holden	Y	Y	Y	N	N	Y	Y	Y
7 ***Weldon***	N	N	Y	N	Y	Y	Y	N
8 ***Greenwood***	Y	N	Y	N	Y	Y	N	N
9 ***Shuster***	N	N	Y	Y	Y	Y	Y	N
10 ***McDade***	N	N	Y	N	N	Y	Y	?
11 Kanjorski	Y	Y	Y	N	N	Y	Y	Y
12 Murtha	N	Y	Y	N	N	Y	N	Y
13 Margolies-Mezv.	Y	Y	Y	N	N	Y	N	Y
14 Coyne	N	Y	Y	N	N	Y	N	Y
15 McHale	Y	Y	Y	N	N	Y	N	Y
16 ***Walker***	Y	N	Y	Y	Y	Y	Y	N
17 ***Gekas***	N	N	N	Y	Y	Y	Y	N
18 ***Santorum***	N	N	Y	Y	N	Y	Y	N
19 ***Goodling***	Y	N	Y	N	N	Y	Y	N
20 Murphy	N	N	Y	Y	Y	Y	Y	Y
21 ***Ridge***	N	N	Y	N	N	Y	Y	N
RHODE ISLAND								
1 ***Machtley***	N	N	Y	N	Y	Y	N	N
2 Reed	Y	Y	Y	N	N	Y	N	Y
SOUTH CAROLINA								
1 ***Ravenel***	Y	N	Y	N	Y	Y	Y	N
2 ***Spence***	N	N	Y	N	Y	Y	Y	N
3 Derrick	Y	Y	Y	N	N	Y	N	Y
4 ***Inglis***	N	N	Y	Y	Y	Y	Y	N
5 Spratt	Y	Y	Y	N	N	Y	N	Y
6 Clyburn	Y	Y	Y	N	N	Y	N	Y
SOUTH DAKOTA								
AL Johnson	Y	Y	Y	N	N	Y	N	Y
TENNESSEE								
1 ***Quillen***	N	N	Y	Y	Y	Y	Y	N
2 ***Duncan***	N	N	Y	Y	Y	Y	Y	N
3 Lloyd	?	N	Y	N	Y	Y	N	Y
4 Cooper	Y	Y	Y	N	N	Y	N	Y
5 Clement	Y	Y	Y	N	N	Y	N	Y
6 Gordon	Y	Y	Y	N	Y	Y	N	Y
7 ***Sundquist***	N	N	Y	Y	Y	Y	Y	N
8 Tanner	Y	N	Y	Y	Y	Y	N	Y
9 Ford	Y	Y	Y	Y	N	Y	?	Y
TEXAS								
1 Chapman	Y	Y	Y	Y	Y	Y	N	Y
2 Wilson	Y	Y	Y	N	Y	Y	N	?
3 ***Johnson, Sam***	N	N	Y	Y	Y	Y	Y	N
4 Hall	Y	Y	Y	Y	Y	Y	Y	Y
5 Bryant	Y	Y	Y	N	N	Y	N	Y
6 ***Barton***	Y	N	Y	Y	Y	Y	Y	N
7 ***Archer***	Y	N	Y	Y	Y	Y	Y	N
8 ***Fields***	N	N	Y	Y	Y	Y	Y	—
9 Brooks	Y	Y	Y	N	Y	Y	N	Y
10 Pickle	Y	Y	Y	N	Y	Y	?	?
11 Edwards	Y	Y	Y	N	N	Y	N	Y
12 Geren	Y	Y	Y	N	Y	?	Y	Y
13 Sarpalius	Y	Y	Y	N	N	Y	Y	Y
14 Laughlin	Y	Y	Y	N	Y	Y	Y	Y
15 de la Garza	Y	Y	Y	N	N	Y	Y	?
16 Coleman	Y	Y	Y	N	N	Y	N	Y
17 Stenholm	Y	Y	Y	N	N	Y	Y	Y
18 Washington	?	Y	Y	N	N	Y	N	Y
19 ***Combest***	N	N	Y	Y	Y	Y	Y	N
20 Gonzalez	Y	Y	Y	N	N	Y	N	Y
21 ***Smith***	N	N	Y	Y	Y	Y	Y	N
22 ***DeLay***	N	N	Y	Y	Y	Y	Y	N
23 ***Bonilla***	Y	N	Y	Y	Y	Y	Y	N
24 Frost	Y	Y	Y	N	N	Y	N	Y
25 Andrews	Y	Y	Y	N	Y	Y	N	Y
26 ***Armey***	Y	N	Y	N	N	Y	Y	N
27 Ortiz	Y	Y	Y	N	N	Y	Y	Y
28 Tejeda	Y	Y	Y	N	N	Y	Y	Y
29 Green	Y	Y	Y	Y	N	Y	N	Y
30 Johnson, E. B.	Y	Y	Y	N	N	Y	N	Y
UTAH								
1 ***Hansen***	N	N	Y	Y	Y	Y	Y	N
2 Shepherd	Y	N	Y	N	Y	Y	N	Y
3 Orton	Y	Y	Y	N	Y	Y	Y	Y
VERMONT								
AL *Sanders*	Y	Y	Y	N	N	Y	N	Y
VIRGINIA								
1 ***Bateman***	N	N	Y	N	N	Y	Y	Y
2 Pickett	Y	Y	Y	N	N	Y	N	Y
3 Scott	Y	Y	Y	N	N	Y	N	Y
4 Sisisky	Y	Y	Y	N	N	Y	N	Y
5 Payne	Y	Y	Y	N	Y	Y	N	Y
6 ***Goodlatte***	Y	N	Y	N	Y	Y	Y	N
7 ***Bliley***	Y	N	Y	N	N	Y	Y	N
8 Moran	Y	Y	Y	N	Y	Y	N	Y
9 Boucher	Y	Y	Y	N	N	Y	N	Y
10 ***Wolf***	Y	N	Y	N	Y	Y	Y	N
11 Byrne	Y	Y	Y	N	Y	Y	N	Y
WASHINGTON								
1 Cantwell	Y	Y	Y	N	N	Y	N	Y
2 Swift	Y	Y	Y	N	N	Y	N	Y
3 Unsoeld	Y	Y	Y	N	N	Y	N	Y
4 Inslee	Y	Y	Y	Y	N	Y	N	Y
5 Foley								
6 Dicks	N	Y	Y	N	N	Y	N	Y
7 McDermott	Y	Y	Y	N	N	Y	N	Y
8 ***Dunn***	N	N	Y	N	Y	Y	Y	N
9 Kreidler	Y	Y	Y	N	N	Y	N	Y
WEST VIRGINIA								
1 Mollohan	N	Y	Y	N	N	Y	Y	Y
2 Wise	Y	Y	Y	N	N	Y	N	Y
3 Rahall	N	Y	Y	Y	N	Y	Y	N
WISCONSIN								
1 Barca	Y	Y	Y	N	N	Y	N	Y
2 ***Klug***	Y	N	Y	N	Y	Y	N	N
3 ***Gunderson***	Y	N	Y	N	N	Y	Y	Y
4 Kleczka	Y	Y	Y	N	N	?	Y	Y
5 Barrett	Y	Y	Y	N	N	Y	N	Y
6 ***Petri***	Y	N	Y	Y	N	Y	Y	N
7 Obey	Y	Y	Y	N	N	Y	N	Y
8 ***Roth***	N	N	Y	Y	Y	Y	Y	N
9 ***Sensenbrenner***	N	N	Y	Y	Y	Y	Y	N
WYOMING								
AL ***Thomas***	Y	N	Y	Y	Y	Y	Y	N
DELEGATES								
de Lugo, V.I.	D	Y	Y	N	N	D	N	D
Faleomavaega, Am.S.	D	Y	Y	N	N	D	N	D
Norton, D.C.	D	Y	Y	N	N	D	N	D
Romero-B., P.R.	D	?	?	?	?	D	?	D
Underwood, Guam	D	Y	Y	N	Y	D	Y	D

Southern states - Ala., Ark., Fla., Ga., Ky., La., Miss., N.C., Okla., S.C., Tenn., Texas, Va.
Omitted votes are quorum calls, which CQ does not include in its vote charts.

* 235. HR 2295. Fiscal 1994 Foreign Operations Appropriations/Funding Cut. Committee amendment to cut the administration's request of $14.4 billion by $1.4 billion, leaving approximately $13 billion, the amount recommended by the House Appropriations Committee. Adopted in Committee of the Whole 423-0: R 168-0; D 254-0 (ND 173-0, SD 81-0); I 1-0, June 17, 1993.

236. HR 2295. Fiscal 1994 Foreign Operations Appropriations/Aid to India. Obey, D-Wis., substitute amendment to the Burton, R-Ind., amendment, to cut development aid by $4.1 million. The Burton amendment would cut development aid by $41 million, which is the amount the administration requested for India. Adopted in Committee of the Whole 425-0: R 172-0; D 252-0 (ND 171-0, SD 81-0); I 1-0, June 17, 1993. (Subsequently, the Burton amendment as amended was adopted by voice vote.)

237. HR 2295. Fiscal 1994 Foreign Operations Appropriations/Aid to Russia. Callahan, R-Ala., amendment to cut the $1.6 billion fiscal 1993 supplemental appropriation for aid to Russia. Rejected in Committee of the Whole 140-289: R 93-79; D 46-210 (ND 30-143, SD 16-67); I 1-0, June 17, 1993. A "nay" was a vote in support of the president's position.

238. HR 2295. Fiscal 1994 Foreign Operations Appropriations/World Bank. Kasich, R-Ohio, amendment to cut the $55.8 million capital contribution to the World Bank. Rejected in Committee of the Whole 210-216: R 148-23; D 61-193 (ND 34-138, SD 27-55); I 1-0, June 17, 1993.

239. HR 2295. Fiscal 1994 Foreign Operations Appropriations/Committee Substitute. Separate vote at the request of Walker, R-Pa., on the committee substitute as amended that was adopted in the Committee of the Whole by voice vote to provide approximately $13 billion in new budget authority for foreign operations, export financing and related programs in fiscal 1994. Adopted 418-0: R 168-0; D 249-0 (ND 167-0, SD 82-0); I 1-0, June 17, 1993. (On separate votes, which may be demanded on an amendment adopted in the Committee of the Whole, the four delegates and the resident commissioner of Puerto Rico cannot vote.)

240. HR 2295. Fiscal 1994 Foreign Operations Appropriations/Passage. Passage of the bill to provide approximately $13 billion in new budget authority for foreign operations, export financing and related programs in fiscal 1994. The administration requested $14,421,987,300. Passed 309-111: R 107-63; D 202-47 (ND 138-29, SD 64-18); I 0-1, June 17, 1993. A "yea" was a vote in support of the president's position.

241. HR 2403. Fiscal 1994 Treasury-Postal Service Appropriations/Customs Service. Penny, D-Minn., amendment to cut the U.S. Customs Service appropriation by $4 million to the amount requested by the administration. Adopted in Committee of the Whole 298-104: R 119-45; D 179-59 (ND 119-42, SD 60-17); I 0-0, June 18, 1993.

242. HR 2403. Fiscal 1994 Treasury-Postal Service Appropriations/Bureau of Alcohol, Tobacco and Firearms. Deal, D-Ga., amendment to cut the Bureau of Alcohol, Tobacco and Firearms appropriation by $2 million to the amount requested by the administration. Adopted in Committee of the Whole 333-65: R 141-24; D 192-41 (ND 126-31, SD 66-10); I 0-0, June 18, 1993.

* Omitted votes are quorum calls, which CQ does not include in its vote charts.

KEY

Y	Voted for (yea).
#	Paired for.
+	Announced for.
N	Voted against (nay).
X	Paired against.
−	Announced against.
P	Voted "present."
C	Voted "present" to avoid possible conflict of interest.
?	Did not vote or otherwise make a position known.
D	Delegates ineligible to vote.

Democrats **Republicans**
Independent

	235	236	237	238	239	240	241	242
ALABAMA								
1 *Callahan*	Y	Y	Y	N	Y	N	N	Y
2 *Everett*	Y	Y	Y	Y	Y	N	Y	Y
3 Browder	Y	Y	N	?	Y	Y	Y	Y
4 Bevill	Y	Y	N	Y	Y	Y	Y	Y
5 Cramer	Y	Y	N	N	Y	Y	Y	Y
6 *Bachus*	?	Y	N	Y	Y	Y	Y	Y
7 Hilliard	Y	Y	Y	N	Y	+	?	?
ALASKA								
AL *Young*	?	?	?	?	?	?	?	?
ARIZONA								
1 *Coppersmith*	Y	Y	N	N	Y	Y	Y	Y
2 Pastor	Y	Y	N	N	Y	Y	N	Y
3 *Stump*	Y	Y	Y	Y	Y	N	N	Y
4 *Kyl*	Y	Y	Y	Y	Y	Y	Y	Y
5 *Kolbe*	Y	Y	N	Y	Y	Y	N	Y
6 English	Y	Y	N	N	Y	Y	N	Y
ARKANSAS								
1 Lambert	Y	Y	N	Y	Y	Y	Y	Y
2 Thornton	Y	Y	N	N	Y	Y	Y	Y
3 *Hutchinson*	Y	Y	Y	Y	Y	N	Y	Y
4 Dickey	Y	Y	N	Y	Y	Y	Y	Y
CALIFORNIA								
1 Hamburg	Y	Y	N	N	Y	Y	Y	Y
2 *Herger*	Y	Y	Y	Y	Y	N	Y	Y
3 Fazio	Y	Y	N	N	Y	Y	Y	Y
4 *Doolittle*	Y	Y	Y	Y	Y	N	N	Y
5 Matsui	Y	Y	N	N	Y	Y	Y	Y
6 Woolsey	Y	Y	N	N	Y	+	Y	Y
7 Miller	Y	Y	N	Y	Y	Y	?	?
8 Pelosi	+	+	−	−	+	#	X	X
9 Dellums	Y	Y	N	N	Y	Y	Y	Y
10 *Baker*	Y	Y	Y	Y	Y	N	Y	Y
11 *Pombo*	Y	Y	Y	Y	Y	N	Y	Y
12 Lantos	Y	Y	N	N	Y	Y	Y	Y
13 Stark	Y	Y	N	Y	Y	N	Y	N
14 Eshoo	Y	Y	N	N	Y	Y	Y	Y
15 Mineta	Y	Y	N	N	Y	Y	N	N
16 Edwards	Y	Y	N	N	Y	Y	Y	Y
17 Farr	Y	Y	N	N	Y	Y	Y	Y
18 Condit	Y	Y	Y	Y	Y	N	Y	Y
19 Lehman	Y	Y	N	N	Y	N	Y	Y
20 Dooley	Y	Y	N	N	Y	N	Y	Y
21 *Thomas*	Y	Y	N	Y	Y	N	Y	Y
22 *Huffington*	Y	Y	Y	Y	Y	N	Y	N
23 *Gallegly*	Y	Y	Y	Y	Y	N	Y	Y
24 Beilenson	Y	Y	N	N	Y	Y	Y	Y
25 *McKeon*	Y	Y	Y	Y	Y	N	Y	Y
26 Berman	Y	Y	N	N	Y	Y	N	Y
27 *Moorhead*	Y	Y	Y	Y	Y	N	Y	Y
28 *Dreier*	Y	Y	N	Y	Y	N	Y	Y
29 Waxman	Y	Y	N	N	Y	Y	N	N
30 Becerra	Y	Y	N	N	Y	N	N	Y
31 Martinez	Y	Y	N	Y	Y	Y	Y	Y
32 Dixon	Y	Y	N	N	Y	Y	N	Y
33 Roybal-Allard	Y	Y	N	N	Y	Y	N	Y
34 Torres	Y	Y	N	N	Y	Y	Y	Y
35 Waters	Y	Y	Y	N	Y	N	Y	N
36 Harman	Y	Y	N	N	Y	Y	?	?
37 Tucker	Y	?	Y	N	Y	N	Y	N
38 *Horn*	Y	Y	N	Y	Y	N	N	N
39 *Royce*	Y	Y	Y	Y	Y	N	Y	Y
40 *Lewis*	Y	Y	N	N	Y	N	N	N
41 *Kim*	Y	Y	Y	Y	Y	N	Y	Y

	235	236	237	238	239	240	241	242
42 Brown	Y	Y	N	N	Y	Y	Y	?
43 *Calvert*	Y	Y	N	Y	Y	N	Y	Y
44 *McCandless*	Y	Y	N	N	Y	N	Y	Y
45 *Rohrabacher*	Y	Y	Y	Y	Y	N	?	?
46 *Dornan*	Y	Y	Y	Y	Y	Y	?	?
47 *Cox*	?	Y	Y	Y	Y	+	Y	Y
48 *Packard*	Y	Y	Y	Y	Y	N	N	Y
49 Schenk	Y	Y	N	N	Y	Y	N	Y
50 Filner	Y	Y	N	N	Y	Y	Y	Y
51 *Cunningham*	Y	Y	Y	Y	Y	N	N	Y
52 *Hunter*	?	Y	Y	Y	?	Y	N	Y
COLORADO								
1 Schroeder	Y	Y	N	N	Y	Y	Y	Y
2 Skaggs	Y	Y	N	N	Y	Y	Y	Y
3 *McInnis*	Y	Y	Y	Y	Y	Y	Y	Y
4 *Allard*	Y	Y	Y	Y	Y	Y	Y	Y
5 *Hefley*	Y	Y	Y	N	Y	N	Y	N
6 *Schaefer*	Y	Y	Y	Y	Y	N	N	Y
CONNECTICUT								
1 Kennelly	Y	Y	N	N	Y	Y	Y	Y
2 Gejdenson	Y	Y	N	N	Y	Y	Y	Y
3 DeLauro	Y	Y	N	N	Y	Y	Y	Y
4 *Shays*	Y	Y	Y	Y	Y	Y	Y	Y
5 *Franks*	Y	Y	Y	Y	Y	Y	Y	Y
6 *Johnson*	Y	N	N	N	Y	Y	Y	Y
DELAWARE								
AL *Castle*	Y	Y	N	N	Y	Y	Y	Y
FLORIDA								
1 Hutto	Y	Y	Y	Y	Y	N	?	?
2 Peterson	Y	Y	N	N	Y	Y	Y	Y
3 Brown	Y	Y	N	N	Y	N	N	N
4 *Fowler*	Y	Y	Y	Y	Y	N	N	N
5 Thurman	Y	Y	N	N	Y	N	Y	Y
6 *Stearns*	Y	Y	Y	Y	Y	N	N	Y
7 *Mica*	Y	Y	Y	Y	Y	N	Y	Y
8 *McCollum*	Y	N	Y	Y	Y	N	Y	Y
9 *Bilirakis*	Y	Y	Y	N	Y	N	N	Y
10 *Young*	Y	Y	Y	Y	Y	N	N	Y
11 Gibbons	Y	N	N	N	Y	Y	Y	Y
12 *Canady*	Y	Y	Y	Y	Y	N	N	Y
13 *Miller*	Y	Y	Y	Y	Y	N	Y	Y
14 *Goss*	Y	Y	N	Y	Y	N	N	Y
15 Bacchus	Y	Y	N	N	Y	Y	Y	Y
16 *Lewis*	Y	Y	Y	Y	Y	Y	Y	Y
17 Meek	Y	Y	N	N	Y	Y	X	X
18 *Ros-Lehtinen*	Y	Y	Y	Y	Y	Y	N	N
19 Johnston	Y	Y	N	N	Y	Y	Y	Y
20 Deutsch	Y	Y	N	N	Y	Y	Y	Y
21 *Diaz-Balart*	Y	Y	Y	Y	Y	Y	N	N
22 *Shaw*	Y	Y	N	Y	Y	Y	Y	Y
23 Hastings	Y	Y	N	N	Y	Y	Y	N
GEORGIA								
1 *Kingston*	Y	Y	Y	Y	Y	Y	Y	Y
2 Bishop	Y	Y	N	N	Y	Y	+	+
3 *Collins*	Y	Y	Y	Y	Y	N	N	Y
4 *Linder*	Y	N	Y	Y	Y	Y	Y	Y
5 Lewis	Y	Y	N	N	Y	Y	Y	Y
6 *Gingrich*	Y	Y	N	Y	Y	?	?	?
7 Darden	Y	Y	N	N	Y	N	Y	Y
8 Rowland	Y	Y	N	N	Y	Y	Y	Y
9 Deal	Y	Y	N	N	Y	Y	Y	Y
10 Johnson	Y	Y	N	N	Y	Y	Y	Y
11 McKinney	Y	Y	N	N	Y	Y	Y	Y
HAWAII								
1 Abercrombie	Y	Y	N	N	Y	Y	Y	Y
2 Mink	Y	Y	N	N	Y	N	Y	Y
IDAHO								
1 LaRocco	Y	Y	N	Y	Y	N	Y	Y
2 *Crapo*	Y	Y	Y	Y	Y	N	Y	Y
ILLINOIS								
1 Rush	Y	Y	N	N	Y	Y	?	?
2 Reynolds	Y	Y	Y	Y	Y	Y	Y	Y
3 Lipinski	Y	Y	N	N	Y	Y	?	?
4 Gutierrez	Y	Y	N	N	Y	Y	N	N
5 Rostenkowski	Y	Y	N	N	Y	Y	Y	Y
6 *Hyde*	Y	Y	Y	N	Y	N	N	N
7 Collins	Y	Y	N	N	Y	N	N	N
8 *Crane*	Y	Y	Y	Y	Y	N	Y	Y
9 Yates	Y	Y	N	N	Y	Y	N	Y
10 *Porter*	Y	Y	N	N	Y	Y	Y	Y
11 Sangmeister	?	Y	N	Y	N	Y	Y	Y
12 Costello	Y	Y	N	Y	Y	Y	Y	Y
13 *Fawell*	Y	N	N	N	Y	Y	Y	Y
14 *Hastert*	Y	Y	Y	Y	Y	N	Y	Y
15 *Ewing*	Y	Y	Y	Y	Y	N	Y	Y
16 *Manzullo*	Y	Y	Y	Y	Y	Y	Y	Y
17 Evans	Y	Y	N	N	Y	N	Y	N

ND Northern Democrats   **SD** Southern Democrats

	235	236	237	238	239	240	241	242
18 ***Michel***	Y	Y	N	Y	Y	Y	N	Y
19 Poshard	Y	Y	Y	Y	Y	N	Y	Y
20 Durbin	Y	Y	N	Y	Y	Y	Y	Y
INDIANA								
1 Visclosky	Y	Y	N	N	Y	Y	N	N
2 Sharp	Y	Y	N	N	Y	Y	Y	Y
3 Roemer	Y	Y	Y	Y	Y	N	Y	Y
4 Long	Y	Y	N	N	Y	Y	Y	Y
5 ***Buyer***	Y	Y	Y	Y	Y	N	Y	Y
6 ***Burton***	Y	Y	Y	Y	Y	Y	Y	Y
7 ***Myers***	Y	Y	N	Y	Y	N	N	N
8 McCloskey	Y	Y	N	N	Y	Y	Y	Y
9 Hamilton	Y	Y	N	N	Y	Y	Y	Y
10 Jacobs	Y	Y	Y	Y	Y	N	Y	Y
IOWA								
1 ***Leach***	Y	Y	N	N	Y	Y	Y	Y
2 ***Nussle***	Y	Y	Y	Y	Y	N	Y	Y
3 ***Lightfoot***	Y	Y	N	N	Y	Y	Y	N
4 Smith	Y	Y	N	N	Y	Y	Y	Y
5 ***Grandy***	Y	Y	N	Y	Y	Y	Y	N
KANSAS								
1 ***Roberts***	Y	Y	N	Y	Y	Y	Y	Y
2 Slattery	Y	Y	N	Y	Y	N	Y	Y
3 ***Meyers***	Y	Y	N	Y	Y	Y	+	+
4 Glickman	Y	Y	N	Y	Y	Y	Y	N
KENTUCKY								
1 Barlow	Y	Y	N	Y	Y	Y	Y	Y
2 Natcher	Y	Y	N	N	Y	Y	Y	Y
3 Mazzoli	Y	Y	N	N	Y	Y	Y	N
4 ***Bunning***	Y	Y	Y	Y	Y	N	Y	N
5 ***Rogers***	Y	Y	Y	Y	Y	N	Y	Y
6 Baesler	Y	Y	N	Y	Y	Y	Y	N
LOUISIANA								
1 ***Livingston***	Y	Y	N	N	Y	Y	N	N
2 Jefferson	Y	Y	N	N	Y	Y	Y	Y
3 Tauzin	Y	Y	Y	Y	Y	N	Y	Y
4 Fields	Y	Y	Y	N	Y	N	Y	Y
5 ***McCrery***	Y	Y	N	Y	Y	Y	Y	Y
6 ***Baker***	Y	Y	Y	Y	Y	N	Y	Y
7 Hayes	Y	Y	N	Y	Y	N	Y	Y
MAINE								
1 Andrews	Y	Y	N	N	Y	Y	Y	Y
2 ***Snowe***	Y	Y	Y	Y	Y	Y	Y	Y
MARYLAND								
1 ***Gilchrest***	Y	Y	N	N	Y	Y	Y	Y
2 ***Bentley***	Y	Y	N	Y	Y	Y	Y	Y
3 Cardin	Y	Y	N	N	Y	Y	Y	Y
4 Wynn	Y	Y	N	N	Y	Y	Y	?
5 Hoyer	Y	Y	N	N	Y	Y	N	N
6 ***Bartlett***	Y	Y	Y	Y	Y	Y	Y	Y
7 Mfume	Y	Y	Y	N	Y	N	Y	Y
8 ***Morella***	Y	Y	N	N	Y	Y	Y	Y
MASSACHUSETTS								
1 Olver	Y	Y	N	N	Y	Y	N	Y
2 Neal	Y	Y	N	?	?	?	Y	Y
3 ***Blute***	Y	Y	Y	Y	Y	Y	Y	Y
4 Frank	Y	Y	N	N	Y	Y	Y	Y
5 Meehan	Y	Y	N	Y	Y	Y	Y	Y
6 ***Torkildsen***	Y	Y	N	Y	Y	Y	Y	Y
7 Markey	Y	Y	N	N	Y	Y	Y	Y
8 Kennedy	Y	Y	N	N	Y	Y	Y	Y
9 Moakley	Y	Y	N	N	Y	Y	?	?
10 Studds	Y	Y	N	N	Y	Y	Y	Y
MICHIGAN								
1 Stupak	Y	Y	N	N	Y	Y	Y	Y
2 ***Hoekstra***	Y	Y	N	Y	Y	Y	Y	Y
3 Henry	?	?	?	?	?	?	?	?
4 ***Camp***	Y	Y	Y	Y	Y	Y	Y	Y
5 Barcia	Y	Y	Y	Y	Y	Y	Y	Y
6 ***Upton***	Y	Y	N	Y	Y	Y	Y	N
7 ***Smith***	Y	Y	N	Y	Y	N	Y	Y
8 Carr	Y	Y	N	N	Y	Y	N	Y
9 Kildee	Y	Y	N	N	Y	Y	N	N
10 Bonior	Y	Y	N	N	Y	Y	N	Y
11 ***Knollenberg***	Y	Y	N	N	Y	Y	Y	Y
12 Levin	Y	Y	N	N	Y	Y	Y	Y
13 Ford	Y	Y	N	N	Y	Y	N	N
14 Conyers	Y	Y	Y	N	Y	N	N	Y
15 Collins	Y	Y	Y	N	Y	Y	N	N
16 Dingell	Y	Y	N	N	Y	Y	?	?
MINNESOTA								
1 Penny	Y	Y	N	N	Y	Y	Y	Y
2 Minge	Y	Y	N	Y	Y	N	Y	Y
3 ***Ramstad***	Y	Y	Y	Y	Y	Y	Y	Y
4 Vento	Y	Y	N	N	Y	Y	Y	Y

	235	236	237	238	239	240	241	242
5 Sabo	Y	Y	N	N	Y	Y	Y	Y
6 ***Grams***	Y	Y	Y	Y	Y	Y	Y	Y
7 Peterson	Y	Y	N	Y	Y	Y	Y	Y
8 Oberstar	Y	Y	N	Y	Y	Y	Y	Y
MISSISSIPPI								
1 Whitten	Y	Y	N	N	Y	N	Y	N
2 Thompson	Y	Y	Y	N	Y	Y	Y	?
3 Montgomery	Y	Y	N	Y	Y	N	Y	Y
4 Parker	Y	Y	N	Y	Y	Y	Y	Y
5 Taylor	Y	Y	N	Y	Y	N	Y	Y
MISSOURI								
1 Clay	Y	Y	Y	N	Y	Y	N	N
2 ***Talent***	Y	Y	N	Y	Y	Y	Y	Y
3 Gephardt	Y	Y	N	N	?	Y	Y	Y
4 Skelton	Y	Y	N	Y	Y	Y	Y	Y
5 Wheat	Y	Y	N	N	Y	+	Y	Y
6 Danner	Y	Y	Y	Y	Y	Y	Y	Y
7 ***Hancock***	Y	Y	Y	Y	Y	N	Y	?
8 ***Emerson***	Y	Y	N	Y	Y	Y	Y	Y
9 Volkmer	Y	Y	Y	Y	Y	N	Y	Y
MONTANA								
AL Williams	Y	?	N	N	Y	N	N	Y
NEBRASKA								
1 ***Bereuter***	Y	Y	N	N	Y	Y	Y	Y
2 Hoagland	Y	Y	N	N	Y	Y	Y	Y
3 ***Barrett***	Y	Y	N	Y	Y	N	Y	Y
NEVADA								
1 Bilbray	Y	Y	N	N	Y	Y	Y	Y
2 ***Vucanovich***	?	Y	Y	Y	Y	Y	Y	Y
NEW HAMPSHIRE								
1 ***Zeliff***	Y	Y	Y	Y	Y	Y	Y	Y
2 Swett	Y	Y	?	?	?	+	Y	Y
NEW JERSEY								
1 Andrews	Y	Y	Y	N	Y	Y	Y	Y
2 Hughes	Y	Y	N	Y	Y	N	Y	Y
3 ***Saxton***	Y	Y	Y	Y	Y	Y	Y	Y
4 ***Smith***	Y	Y	N	Y	Y	Y	Y	Y
5 ***Roukema***	Y	Y	Y	N	Y	Y	N	Y
6 Pallone	Y	Y	N	N	Y	Y	Y	Y
7 ***Franks***	Y	Y	N	Y	Y	Y	#	#
8 Klein	Y	Y	N	N	Y	Y	Y	Y
9 Torricelli	Y	Y	N	N	Y	Y	N	Y
10 Payne	Y	Y	N	N	Y	Y	?	?
11 ***Gallo***	Y	Y	N	N	Y	Y	?	?
12 ***Zimmer***	Y	Y	Y	Y	Y	Y	Y	Y
13 Menendez	Y	Y	N	N	Y	Y	N	Y
NEW MEXICO								
1 ***Schiff***	Y	Y	N	Y	Y	Y	Y	Y
2 ***Skeen***	Y	Y	N	Y	Y	Y	?	N
3 Richardson	Y	Y	N	N	Y	Y	Y	Y
NEW YORK								
1 Hochbrueckner	Y	Y	N	N	Y	Y	Y	Y
2 ***Lazio***	Y	Y	N	Y	Y	Y	N	N
3 ***King***	Y	Y	N	Y	Y	Y	N	Y
4 ***Levy***	Y	Y	N	Y	Y	Y	N	Y
5 Ackerman	Y	Y	N	N	Y	Y	N	N
6 Flake	Y	Y	Y	N	Y	N	?	X
7 Manton	Y	Y	N	N	Y	Y	Y	N
8 Nadler	Y	Y	N	N	Y	Y	N	N
9 Schumer	Y	Y	N	N	Y	Y	?	X
10 Towns	Y	Y	Y	N	Y	N	?	?
11 Owens	Y	Y	N	N	Y	Y	Y	Y
12 Velazquez	Y	Y	Y	N	Y	N	Y	Y
13 ***Molinari***	Y	Y	N	Y	Y	Y	N	Y
14 Maloney	Y	Y	N	N	Y	Y	Y	Y
15 Rangel	Y	Y	Y	N	Y	Y	N	N
16 Serrano	Y	Y	N	N	Y	Y	Y	N
17 Engel	Y	Y	N	N	Y	Y	Y	Y
18 Lowey	Y	Y	N	N	Y	Y	Y	Y
19 ***Fish***	Y	Y	N	Y	Y	Y	N	Y
20 ***Gilman***	Y	Y	N	N	Y	Y	N	Y
21 McNulty	Y	Y	N	N	Y	Y	N	Y
22 ***Solomon***	Y	Y	Y	Y	Y	N	Y	Y
23 ***Boehlert***	Y	Y	N	N	Y	Y	Y	Y
24 ***McHugh***	Y	Y	Y	Y	Y	Y	Y	Y
25 ***Walsh***	Y	Y	Y	N	Y	Y	Y	Y
26 Hinchey	Y	Y	N	N	Y	Y	Y	Y
27 ***Paxon***	Y	Y	N	Y	Y	Y	Y	Y
28 Slaughter	Y	+	N	N	Y	Y	Y	Y
29 LaFalce	Y	Y	N	N	Y	Y	N	Y
30 ***Quinn***	Y	Y	Y	Y	Y	Y	N	Y
31 ***Houghton***	Y	Y	N	N	Y	Y	Y	Y
NORTH CAROLINA								
1 Clayton	Y	Y	N	N	Y	Y	Y	Y
2 Valentine	Y	Y	Y	Y	Y	Y	Y	Y

	235	236	237	238	239	240	241	242
3 Lancaster	Y	Y	Y	Y	Y	Y	Y	Y
4 Price	Y	Y	N	N	Y	Y	Y	Y
5 Neal	?	?	N	N	Y	N	?	Y
6 ***Coble***	Y	Y	Y	Y	Y	Y	Y	Y
7 Rose	Y	Y	N	N	?	Y	N	Y
8 Hefner	Y	Y	N	N	Y	N	Y	Y
9 ***McMillan***	Y	Y	N	N	Y	Y	N	Y
10 ***Ballenger***	Y	Y	N	Y	Y	Y	Y	Y
11 ***Taylor***	Y	Y	Y	Y	Y	Y	Y	Y
12 Watt	Y	Y	N	N	Y	Y	Y	Y
NORTH DAKOTA								
AL Pomeroy	Y	Y	N	N	Y	Y	Y	Y
OHIO								
1 Mann	Y	Y	N	N	Y	Y	Y	Y
2 ***Portman***	Y	Y	Y	Y	Y	Y	Y	Y
3 Hall	Y	?	N	N	Y	Y	Y	Y
4 ***Oxley***	Y	Y	N	Y	Y	Y	Y	Y
5 ***Gillmor***	Y	Y	N	Y	Y	Y	Y	Y
6 Strickland	Y	Y	N	Y	Y	Y	Y	Y
7 ***Hobson***	Y	Y	N	Y	Y	Y	Y	Y
8 ***Boehner***	Y	Y	N	Y	Y	Y	Y	Y
9 Kaptur	Y	Y	N	N	Y	Y	?	?
10 ***Hoke***	Y	Y	Y	Y	Y	Y	Y	Y
11 Stokes	Y	Y	N	N	Y	Y	N	N
12 ***Kasich***	Y	Y	N	Y	Y	Y	Y	Y
13 Brown	Y	Y	N	N	Y	Y	?	?
14 Sawyer	Y	Y	N	N	Y	Y	Y	Y
15 ***Pryce***	Y	Y	N	Y	Y	Y	#	#
16 ***Regula***	Y	Y	Y	Y	Y	Y	Y	Y
17 Traficant	Y	Y	Y	Y	Y	N	Y	Y
18 Applegate	Y	Y	Y	Y	Y	N	Y	Y
19 Fingerhut	Y	Y	N	Y	Y	Y	+	+
OKLAHOMA								
1 ***Inhofe***	Y	Y	Y	Y	Y	Y	Y	Y
2 Synar	Y	Y	N	N	Y	Y	Y	Y
3 Brewster	Y	Y	Y	Y	Y	Y	Y	Y
4 McCurdy	Y	Y	N	N	Y	Y	Y	Y
5 ***Istook***	Y	Y	N	Y	Y	Y	Y	Y
6 English	Y	Y	Y	Y	Y	N	N	Y
OREGON								
1 Furse	Y	Y	N	N	Y	Y	Y	Y
2 ***Smith***	Y	Y	N	Y	Y	N	Y	Y
3 Wyden	Y	Y	N	N	Y	Y	Y	Y
4 DeFazio	Y	Y	Y	Y	Y	N	?	?
5 Kopetski	Y	Y	N	?	Y	Y	Y	Y
PENNSYLVANIA								
1 Foglietta	Y	Y	N	N	Y	Y	Y	N
2 Blackwell	Y	Y	Y	N	Y	Y	N	Y
3 Borski	Y	Y	N	N	Y	Y	Y	Y
4 Klink	Y	Y	N	Y	Y	N	Y	Y
5 ***Clinger***	Y	Y	N	N	Y	Y	Y	Y
6 Holden	Y	Y	N	N	Y	Y	Y	Y
7 ***Weldon***	Y	Y	N	+	Y	N	Y	Y
8 ***Greenwood***	Y	Y	N	Y	Y	Y	?	?
9 ***Shuster***	Y	Y	Y	Y	Y	N	Y	Y
10 ***McDade***	?	?	?	?	?	?	Y	N
11 Kanjorski	Y	Y	N	N	Y	Y	Y	Y
12 Murtha	Y	Y	N	N	Y	Y	Y	Y
13 Margolies-Mezv.	Y	Y	N	N	Y	Y	Y	Y
14 Coyne	Y	Y	N	N	Y	Y	Y	N
15 McHale	Y	Y	N	Y	Y	Y	Y	Y
16 ***Walker***	Y	Y	N	Y	Y	N	Y	Y
17 ***Gekas***	Y	Y	Y	Y	Y	N	Y	Y
18 ***Santorum***	Y	Y	Y	Y	Y	Y	Y	Y
19 ***Goodling***	Y	Y	N	Y	Y	N	N	N
20 Murphy	Y	Y	Y	Y	Y	N	Y	?
21 ***Ridge***	Y	Y	N	Y	Y	Y	?	Y
RHODE ISLAND								
1 ***Machtley***	Y	Y	Y	Y	Y	Y	Y	Y
2 Reed	Y	Y	N	N	Y	Y	Y	Y
SOUTH CAROLINA								
1 ***Ravenel***	Y	Y	N	Y	Y	Y	Y	Y
2 ***Spence***	Y	Y	Y	Y	Y	N	Y	Y
3 Derrick	Y	Y	N	N	Y	Y	Y	Y
4 ***Inglis***	Y	Y	Y	Y	?	N	Y	Y
5 Spratt	Y	Y	N	N	Y	Y	Y	Y
6 Clyburn	Y	Y	Y	N	Y	Y	Y	Y
SOUTH DAKOTA								
AL Johnson	Y	Y	N	N	Y	Y	Y	N
TENNESSEE								
1 ***Quillen***	Y	Y	Y	Y	Y	N	Y	N
2 ***Duncan***	Y	Y	Y	Y	Y	N	Y	Y
3 Lloyd	Y	Y	N	Y	Y	N	Y	Y
4 Cooper	Y	Y	N	N	Y	Y	Y	Y
5 Clement	Y	Y	N	Y	Y	Y	Y	Y

	235	236	237	238	239	240	241	242
6 Gordon	Y	Y	N	Y	Y	Y	Y	Y
7 ***Sundquist***	Y	Y	Y	Y	Y	Y	Y	Y
8 Tanner	Y	Y	N	Y	Y	N	Y	Y
9 Ford	Y	Y	Y	N	Y	Y	N	Y
TEXAS								
1 Chapman	Y	Y	Y	N	Y	N	Y	Y
2 Wilson	?	Y	N	N	Y	Y	Y	Y
3 ***Johnson, Sam***	Y	Y	Y	Y	Y	N	Y	Y
4 Hall	Y	Y	Y	Y	Y	N	N	Y
5 Bryant	Y	Y	N	N	Y	Y	N	N
6 ***Barton***	Y	Y	N	Y	Y	N	N	N
7 ***Archer***	Y	Y	Y	Y	Y	N	Y	Y
8 ***Fields***	+	+	+	+	+	–	N	Y
9 Brooks	Y	Y	N	N	Y	N	N	Y
10 Pickle	?	?	?	?	?	?	?	?
11 Edwards	Y	Y	N	Y	Y	Y	Y	Y
12 Geren	Y	Y	N	Y	Y	Y	Y	Y
13 Sarpalius	Y	Y	Y	N	Y	N	Y	Y
14 Laughlin	Y	Y	N	Y	Y	Y	N	Y
15 de la Garza	?	?	?	?	?	?	Y	Y
16 Coleman	Y	Y	N	N	Y	Y	N	N
17 Stenholm	Y	Y	N	Y	Y	Y	Y	Y
18 Washington	Y	?	N	Y	Y	Y	N	N
19 ***Combest***	Y	Y	Y	Y	Y	N	Y	N
20 Gonzalez	Y	Y	N	N	Y	Y	N	N
21 ***Smith***	Y	Y	Y	Y	Y	Y	N	N
22 ***DeLay***	Y	Y	Y	Y	Y	N	N	Y
23 ***Bonilla***	Y	Y	Y	Y	Y	N	N	Y
24 Frost	Y	Y	N	N	Y	Y	?	?
25 Andrews	Y	Y	N	N	Y	Y	Y	Y
26 ***Armey***	Y	Y	N	Y	Y	N	Y	Y
27 Ortiz	Y	Y	N	N	Y	Y	?	?
28 Tejeda	Y	Y	N	N	Y	Y	N	Y
29 Green	Y	Y	Y	Y	Y	Y	N	Y
30 Johnson, E. B.	Y	Y	N	N	Y	Y	N	N
UTAH								
1 ***Hansen***	Y	Y	Y	Y	Y	N	Y	Y
2 Shepherd	Y	Y	N	Y	Y	Y	Y	Y
3 Orton	Y	Y	N	N	Y	N	Y	Y
VERMONT								
AL *Sanders*	Y	Y	Y	Y	Y	N	?	?
VIRGINIA								
1 ***Bateman***	Y	Y	N	Y	Y	Y	N	Y
2 Pickett	Y	Y	N	N	Y	Y	N	Y
3 Scott	Y	Y	N	N	Y	Y	Y	Y
4 Sisisky	Y	Y	N	N	Y	Y	Y	Y
5 Payne	Y	Y	N	N	Y	Y	Y	Y
6 ***Goodlatte***	Y	Y	N	Y	?	Y	Y	Y
7 ***Bliley***	Y	Y	N	Y	Y	Y	Y	N
8 Moran	Y	Y	N	N	Y	Y	Y	Y
9 Boucher	Y	Y	N	N	Y	Y	Y	?
10 ***Wolf***	Y	Y	N	Y	Y	Y	N	N
11 Byrne	Y	Y	N	N	Y	Y	Y	Y
WASHINGTON								
1 Cantwell	Y	Y	N	N	Y	Y	Y	Y
2 Swift	Y	Y	N	N	Y	Y	N	Y
3 Unsoeld	Y	Y	?	N	Y	Y	Y	N
4 Inslee	Y	Y	Y	N	Y	N	Y	Y
5 Foley								
6 Dicks	Y	Y	N	N	Y	Y	Y	Y
7 McDermott	Y	Y	N	N	Y	Y	Y	N
8 ***Dunn***	Y	Y	N	Y	Y	Y	Y	Y
9 Kreidler	Y	Y	N	N	Y	Y	N	Y
WEST VIRGINIA								
1 Mollohan	Y	Y	N	Y	Y	N	Y	Y
2 Wise	Y	Y	N	Y	Y	Y	Y	Y
3 Rahall	Y	Y	Y	Y	Y	N	Y	N
WISCONSIN								
1 Barca	Y	Y	N	N	Y	Y	Y	Y
2 ***Klug***	Y	Y	N	Y	Y	Y	Y	Y
3 ***Gunderson***	Y	Y	N	Y	Y	Y	Y	Y
4 Kleczka	Y	Y	N	N	Y	Y	Y	Y
5 Barrett	Y	Y	N	N	Y	Y	Y	Y
6 ***Petri***	Y	Y	Y	Y	Y	N	Y	Y
7 Obey	Y	Y	N	N	Y	Y	Y	Y
8 ***Roth***	Y	Y	Y	Y	Y	N	Y	Y
9 ***Sensenbrenner***	Y	Y	Y	Y	Y	N	Y	Y
WYOMING								
AL ***Thomas***	Y	Y	Y	Y	+	X	+	+
DELEGATES								
de Lugo, V.I.	Y	Y	N	N	D	D	N	N
Faleomavaega, Am.S.	?	Y	N	N	D	D	N	?
Norton, D.C.	Y	Y	N	N	D	D	Y	Y
Romero-B., P.R.	?	?	?	?	D	D	?	?
Underwood, Guam	Y	Y	N	N	D	D	N	Y

Southern states - Ala., Ark., Fla., Ga., Ky., La., Miss., N.C., Okla., S.C., Tenn., Texas, Va.
Omitted votes are quorum calls, which CQ does not include in its vote charts.

243. HR 2403. Fiscal 1994 Treasury-Postal Service Appropriations/White House Payroll. Hefley, R-Colo., amendment to cut the appropriation for the White House office by $470,000. Rejected in Committee of the Whole 169-234: R 166-1; D 3-233 (ND 2-159, SD 1-74); I 0-0, June 18, 1993.

244. HR 2403. Fiscal 1994 Treasury-Postal Service Appropriations/White House Payroll. Lightfoot, R-Iowa, amendment to cut the appropriation for the White House office by $100,000. Rejected in Committee of the Whole 171-222: R 162-3; D 9-219 (ND 5-154, SD 4-65); I 0-0, June 18, 1993.

245. HR 2403. Fiscal 1994 Treasury-Postal Service Appropriations/U.S. Courthouse Funding. Pomeroy, D-N.D., en bloc amendment to cut funding for the construction of courthouses and joint federal buildings by 2 percent. Adopted in Committee of the Whole 339-50: R 154-10; D 185-40 (ND 127-31, SD 58-9); I 0-0, June 18, 1993.

246. HR 2403. Fiscal 1994 Treasury-Postal Service Appropriations/Former Presidents. Shepherd, D-Utah, amendment to limit office allowances for former presidents to five years of staffing and office expenses after they leave office and to cut off current spending for the five former presidents' offices Oct. 1, 1998, excluding Secret Service protection, pension benefits and presidential libraries. Adopted in Committee of the Whole 247-127: R 113-41; D 134-86 (ND 94-59, SD 40-27); I 0-0, June 18, 1993.

247. HR 1876. GATT Fast-Track Extension/Passage. Passage of the bill to extend through April 15, 1994, the administration's authority to negotiate an accord strengthening the General Agreement on Tariffs and Trade (GATT) and require Congress to consider the accord under expedited procedures that bar amendments. Passed 295-126: R 150-23; D 145-102 (ND 97-70, SD 48-32); I 0-1, June 22, 1993. A "yea" was a vote in support of the president's position.

248. HR 2333. State Department Authorization/Drug Testing. Solomon, R-N.Y., amendment to require the random drug testing of State Department employees. Rejected in Committee of the Whole 184-235: R 148-25; D 36-209 (ND 14-156, SD 22-53); I 0-1, June 22, 1993.

249. HR 2333. State Department Authorization/National Endowment for Democracy. Kanjorski, D-Pa., amendment to strike the $48 million authorization for the National Endowment for Democracy. Adopted in the Committee of the Whole 243-181: R 112-62; D 130-119 (ND 83-88, SD 47-31); I 1-0, June 22, 1993. A "nay" was a vote in support of the president's position.

250. HR 2333. State Department Authorization/Funding Cut. Separate vote at the request of Penny, D-Minn., on the amendment adopted in the Committee of the Whole offered by Roth, R-Wis., and amended by the Berman, D-Calif., substitute to reduce the authorizations for various accounts of the State Department by $200 million in fiscal 1994. Adopted 418-3: R 173-1; D 244-2 (ND 166-1, SD 78-1); I 1-0, June 22, 1993. (On separate votes, which may be demanded on an amendment adopted in the Committee of the Whole, the four delegates and the resident commissioner of Puerto Rico cannot vote.)

KEY

Y Voted for (yea).
\# Paired for.
\+ Announced for.
N Voted against (nay).
X Paired against.
− Announced against.
P Voted "present."
C Voted "present" to avoid possible conflict of interest.
? Did not vote or otherwise make a position known.
D Delegates ineligible to vote.

Democrats **Republicans**
Independent

	243	244	245	246	247	248	249	250
ALABAMA								
1 *Callahan*	Y	?	?	?	Y	Y	Y	Y
2 *Everett*	Y	Y	Y	Y	Y	Y	Y	Y
3 Browder	N	N	Y	N	N	Y	N	Y
4 Bevill	N	N	Y	N	N	Y	N	Y
5 Cramer	N	N	Y	Y	N	N	Y	Y
6 *Bachus*	Y	Y	Y	Y	Y	Y	N	Y
7 Hilliard	?	X	?	?	N	N	N	Y
ALASKA								
AL *Young*	?	?	?	?	N	Y	Y	Y
ARIZONA								
1 Coppersmith	N	N	Y	Y	Y	N	N	Y
2 Pastor	N	N	Y	N	Y	N	N	Y
3 *Stump*	Y	Y	Y	Y	Y	Y	Y	Y
4 *Kyl*	Y	Y	Y	Y	Y	Y	N	Y
5 *Kolbe*	Y	Y	Y	N	Y	N	N	Y
6 English	N	N	Y	N	Y	N	Y	Y
ARKANSAS								
1 Lambert	N	N	Y	N	N	N	N	Y
2 Thornton	N	N	Y	?	?	?	Y	?
3 *Hutchinson*	Y	N	Y	Y	Y	Y	N	Y
4 *Dickey*	N	N	Y	Y	Y	Y	Y	Y
CALIFORNIA								
1 Hamburg	N	N	Y	Y	N	N	Y	Y
2 *Herger*	Y	Y	Y	Y	Y	Y	Y	Y
3 Fazio	N	N	Y	Y	N	N	Y	Y
4 *Doolittle*	Y	Y	Y	Y	Y	Y	Y	Y
5 Matsui	N	N	N	Y	?	N	Y	Y
6 Woolsey	N	N	Y	N	N	N	N	Y
7 Miller	?	?	?	N	Y	N	Y	Y
8 Pelosi	−	X	+	X	Y	N	N	Y
9 Dellums	N	N	N	N	N	N	Y	Y
10 *Baker*	Y	Y	Y	Y	Y	Y	Y	Y
11 *Pombo*	Y	Y	Y	Y	Y	Y	N	Y
12 Lantos	N	N	Y	Y	Y	N	N	Y
13 Stark	N	N	N	N	N	N	Y	Y
14 Eshoo	N	N	Y	Y	Y	N	N	Y
15 Mineta	N	N	N	N	Y	N	N	Y
16 Edwards	N	N	Y	N	N	N	Y	Y
17 Farr	N	N	Y	N	N	N	N	Y
18 Condit	N	Y	Y	Y	Y	Y	Y	Y
19 Lehman	N	N	Y	N	N	Y	N	Y
20 Dooley	N	N	Y	N	Y	N	Y	Y
21 *Thomas*	Y	Y	Y	Y	Y	?	N	Y
22 *Huffington*	Y	Y	Y	Y	Y	Y	Y	Y
23 *Gallegly*	Y	Y	Y	Y	Y	Y	Y	Y
24 Beilenson	N	N	Y	N	Y	N	N	Y
25 *McKeon*	Y	Y	Y	Y	Y	Y	N	Y
26 Berman	N	N	Y	N	Y	N	N	Y
27 *Moorhead*	Y	Y	Y	Y	Y	Y	N	Y
28 *Dreier*	Y	Y	Y	Y	Y	Y	Y	Y
29 Waxman	N	N	Y	N	N	N	Y	Y
30 Becerra	N	N	?	N	N	Y	Y	Y
31 Martinez	N	N	Y	N	N	N	N	Y
32 Dixon	N	N	Y	Y	N	N	N	Y
33 Roybal-Allard	N	N	Y	N	N	Y	Y	Y
34 Torres	N	N	Y	N	N	N	N	Y
35 Waters	N	N	N	N	N	N	N	Y
36 Harman	?	?	?	?	?	?	?	?
37 Tucker	N	N	Y	N	Y	N	Y	Y
38 *Horn*	Y	Y	Y	N	Y	N	N	Y
39 *Royce*	Y	Y	Y	Y	Y	Y	N	Y
40 *Lewis*	?	Y	N	N	Y	N	Y	Y
41 *Kim*	Y	Y	Y	Y	Y	Y	Y	Y

	243	244	245	246	247	248	249	250
42 Brown	N	N	Y	Y	Y	N	N	Y
43 *Calvert*	Y	Y	Y	Y	Y	Y	N	Y
44 *McCandless*	Y	Y	Y	Y	Y	Y	Y	Y
45 *Rohrabacher*	Y	Y	Y	Y	Y	Y	N	Y
46 *Dornan*	Y	Y	Y	N	Y	N	N	Y
47 *Cox*	Y	Y	Y	N	Y	N	N	Y
48 *Packard*	Y	Y	Y	Y	Y	Y	N	Y
49 Schenk	N	N	Y	N	N	Y	N	Y
50 Filner	N	N	N	N	N	N	N	Y
51 *Cunningham*	Y	Y	Y	Y	Y	Y	Y	Y
52 *Hunter*	Y	Y	Y	N	N	Y	Y	Y
COLORADO								
1 Schroeder	N	N	Y	Y	N	N	Y	Y
2 Skaggs	N	N	Y	N	Y	N	N	Y
3 *McInnis*	Y	Y	Y	Y	Y	Y	Y	Y
4 *Allard*	Y	Y	Y	Y	Y	Y	Y	Y
5 *Hefley*	Y	Y	Y	Y	Y	Y	Y	Y
6 *Schaefer*	Y	Y	Y	Y	Y	Y	Y	Y
CONNECTICUT								
1 Kennelly	N	N	Y	Y	N	N	N	Y
2 Gejdenson	N	N	Y	N	N	N	N	Y
3 DeLauro	N	N	Y	Y	N	N	N	Y
4 *Shays*	Y	Y	Y	Y	Y	Y	Y	Y
5 *Franks*	Y	Y	Y	Y	Y	Y	Y	Y
6 *Johnson*	Y	Y	Y	Y	Y	Y	N	Y
DELAWARE								
AL *Castle*	Y	Y	Y	N	Y	Y	N	Y
FLORIDA								
1 Hutto	?	?	?	?	Y	Y	Y	Y
2 Peterson	N	N	Y	N	Y	N	N	Y
3 Brown	N	N	N	N	N	N	?	Y
4 *Fowler*	\#	\#	?	\#	Y	Y	Y	Y
5 Thurman	N	N	Y	N	N	Y	N	Y
6 *Stearns*	Y	Y	Y	N	Y	Y	N	Y
7 *Mica*	Y	Y	Y	Y	N	Y	N	Y
8 *McCollum*	Y	Y	N	Y	Y	Y	N	Y
9 *Bilirakis*	Y	Y	Y	Y	Y	Y	N	Y
10 *Young*	Y	Y	N	Y	N	Y	N	Y
11 Gibbons	N	N	N	N	Y	N	?	N
12 *Canady*	Y	Y	Y	N	Y	Y	Y	Y
13 *Miller*	Y	Y	Y	?	Y	Y	N	Y
14 *Goss*	Y	Y	Y	Y	Y	Y	N	Y
15 Bacchus	N	?	?	?	Y	Y	N	Y
16 *Lewis*	Y	Y	Y	N	N	Y	Y	Y
17 Meek	X	X	?	X	N	N	Y	?
18 *Ros-Lehtinen*	Y	Y	N	N	N	Y	N	Y
19 Johnston	N	N	?	X	N	N	N	Y
20 Deutsch	N	N	Y	Y	N	N	N	Y
21 *Diaz-Balart*	Y	Y	N	N	N	Y	N	Y
22 *Shaw*	Y	Y	Y	Y	Y	Y	N	Y
23 Hastings	N	N	N	N	N	N	N	Y
GEORGIA								
1 *Kingston*	Y	Y	Y	Y	N	Y	Y	Y
2 Bishop	−	−	+	+	N	N	N	Y
3 *Collins*	Y	Y	Y	Y	Y	Y	Y	Y
4 *Linder*	Y	Y	Y	Y	Y	Y	Y	Y
5 Lewis	N	N	N	N	N	N	N	Y
6 *Gingrich*	Y	Y	Y	Y	Y	Y	N	Y
7 Darden	N	N	Y	N	N	N	N	Y
8 Rowland	N	N	Y	N	N	Y	N	Y
9 Deal	N	N	Y	N	N	Y	N	Y
10 Johnson	N	N	Y	Y	Y	N	Y	Y
11 McKinney	N	N	N	N	N	N	Y	Y
HAWAII								
1 Abercrombie	N	N	Y	N	N	N	N	Y
2 Mink	N	N	Y	N	N	N	N	Y
IDAHO								
1 LaRocco	N	N	Y	Y	Y	N	Y	Y
2 *Crapo*	Y	Y	Y	Y	N	Y	Y	Y
ILLINOIS								
1 Rush	?	?	?	?	?	?	?	?
2 Reynolds	N	N	N	N	N	N	Y	Y
3 Lipinski	?	?	?	?	N	Y	Y	Y
4 Gutierrez	N	N	Y	N	N	N	N	Y
5 Rostenkowski	N	N	Y	?	Y	N	N	Y
6 *Hyde*	Y	Y	N	Y	Y	Y	N	Y
7 Collins	N	N	N	N	N	N	Y	Y
8 *Crane*	Y	Y	Y	Y	Y	Y	Y	Y
9 Yates	N	N	N	N	N	N	Y	Y
10 *Porter*	Y	Y	Y	Y	N	N	Y	Y
11 Sangmeister	N	N	Y	Y	Y	Y	N	Y
12 Costello	N	N	Y	N	N	Y	?	Y
13 *Fawell*	Y	Y	Y	Y	Y	Y	Y	Y
14 *Hastert*	Y	Y	Y	N	Y	Y	N	Y
15 *Ewing*	Y	Y	Y	Y	Y	Y	Y	Y
16 *Manzullo*	Y	Y	Y	Y	Y	Y	N	Y
17 Evans	N	N	N	Y	N	N	N	Y

ND Northern Democrats   SD Southern Democrats

	243	244	245	246	247	248	249	250
18 ***Michel***	Y	Y	Y	N	Y	Y	N	Y
19 Poshard	N	N	Y	Y	N	N	Y	Y
20 Durbin	N	N	Y	Y	N	N	Y	Y
INDIANA								
1 Visclosky	N	N	Y	N	Y	N	Y	Y
2 Sharp	N	N	Y	Y	Y	N	N	Y
3 Roemer	N	N	Y	Y	Y	N	N	Y
4 Long	N	N	Y	Y	N	N	Y	Y
5 ***Buyer***	Y	Y	N	Y	Y	Y	N	Y
6 ***Burton***	Y	Y	Y	Y	Y	Y	N	Y
7 ***Myers***	Y	Y	Y	Y	N	Y	N	Y
8 McCloskey	N	N	Y	Y	Y	N	N	Y
9 Hamilton	N	N	Y	Y	Y	N	N	Y
10 Jacobs	Y	N	Y	Y	N	N	Y	Y
IOWA								
1 ***Leach***	Y	Y	Y	Y	Y	N	N	N
2 ***Nussle***	Y	Y	Y	Y	Y	Y	Y	Y
3 ***Lightfoot***	Y	Y	Y	N	Y	N	Y	Y
4 Smith	N	N	Y	N	Y	N	N	Y
5 ***Grandy***	Y	Y	Y	Y	Y	N	Y	Y
KANSAS								
1 ***Roberts***	Y	Y	Y	Y	Y	Y	Y	Y
2 Slattery	N	N	Y	Y	Y	N	Y	Y
3 ***Meyers***	+	+	+	+	Y	Y	N	Y
4 Glickman	N	N	Y	Y	Y	N	Y	Y
KENTUCKY								
1 Barlow	N	N	Y	Y	Y	Y	Y	Y
2 Natcher	N	N	Y	N	Y	N	Y	Y
3 Mazzoli	N	N	N	Y	Y	Y	Y	Y
4 ***Bunning***	Y	Y	Y	N	Y	Y	N	Y
5 ***Rogers***	Y	Y	Y	N	N	Y	N	Y
6 Baesler	N	N	Y	N	Y	N	Y	Y
LOUISIANA								
1 ***Livingston***	Y	Y	Y	N	Y	N	N	Y
2 Jefferson	N	N	?	Y	N	N	N	Y
3 Tauzin	N	Y	Y	Y	Y	Y	Y	Y
4 Fields	N	N	Y	N	Y	N	N	Y
5 ***McCrery***	Y	Y	Y	Y	Y	Y	Y	Y
6 ***Baker***	Y	Y	Y	Y	Y	Y	Y	Y
7 Hayes	N	?	?	?	?	?	?	?
MAINE								
1 Andrews	N	N	Y	Y	N	N	Y	Y
2 ***Snowe***	Y	Y	Y	Y	N	N	Y	Y
MARYLAND								
1 ***Gilchrest***	Y	Y	Y	Y	Y	N	Y	Y
2 ***Bentley***	Y	N	Y	N	N	N	Y	Y
3 Cardin	N	N	Y	N	Y	N	N	Y
4 Wynn	N	N	Y	Y	N	N	N	Y
5 Hoyer	N	N	Y	N	Y	N	N	Y
6 ***Bartlett***	Y	Y	Y	Y	Y	Y	Y	Y
7 Mfume	N	N	Y	N	N	N	N	Y
8 ***Morella***	Y	Y	Y	Y	Y	N	N	Y
MASSACHUSETTS								
1 Olver	N	N	Y	N	Y	N	N	Y
2 Neal	N	N	Y	N	Y	N	N	Y
3 ***Blute***	Y	Y	Y	Y	Y	Y	Y	Y
4 Frank	N	N	Y	Y	Y	N	Y	Y
5 Meehan	N	N	Y	Y	Y	N	N	Y
6 ***Torkildsen***	Y	Y	Y	Y	Y	Y	Y	Y
7 Markey	N	N	Y	N	Y	N	N	Y
8 Kennedy	N	N	Y	N	Y	N	N	Y
9 Moakley	?	?	?	?	Y	N	N	Y
10 Studds	N	N	Y	N	Y	N	Y	Y
MICHIGAN								
1 Stupak	N	N	Y	Y	N	N	Y	Y
2 ***Hoekstra***	Y	Y	Y	Y	Y	Y	Y	Y
3 Henry	?	?	?	?	?	?	?	?
4 ***Camp***	Y	Y	Y	N	Y	Y	Y	Y
5 Barcia	N	N	Y	Y	N	N	Y	Y
6 ***Upton***	Y	Y	Y	Y	Y	Y	Y	Y
7 ***Smith***	Y	Y	Y	Y	Y	Y	Y	Y
8 Carr	N	N	N	Y	N	Y	Y	Y
9 Kildee	N	N	Y	Y	N	N	N	Y
10 Bonior	N	N	?	N	N	N	N	Y
11 ***Knollenberg***	Y	Y	Y	Y	+	Y	Y	Y
12 Levin	N	N	Y	Y	Y	N	N	Y
13 Ford	N	N	?	N	Y	N	N	Y
14 Conyers	N	?	?	?	?	?	?	?
15 Collins	N	N	N	N	N	N	N	Y
16 Dingell	N	?	N	N	Y	N	N	Y
MINNESOTA								
1 Penny	N	Y	Y	Y	Y	Y	Y	Y
2 Minge	N	Y	Y	Y	Y	N	Y	Y
3 ***Ramstad***	Y	Y	Y	Y	Y	Y	Y	Y
4 Vento	N	N	Y	?	Y	N	N	Y

	243	244	245	246	247	248	249	250
5 Sabo	?	?	?	?	Y	N	N	Y
6 ***Grams***	Y	Y	Y	Y	Y	Y	Y	Y
7 Peterson	N	N	Y	Y	N	N	Y	Y
8 Oberstar	N	N	Y	Y	N	N	N	Y
MISSISSIPPI								
1 Whitten	N	?	?	N	?	?	?	?
2 Thompson	?	?	?	?	?	?	N	Y
3 Montgomery	N	N	Y	N	Y	Y	Y	Y
4 Parker	N	Y	Y	Y	Y	Y	Y	Y
5 Taylor	N	Y	Y	Y	N	Y	Y	Y
MISSOURI								
1 Clay	N	N	N	N	N	N	Y	Y
2 ***Talent***	Y	Y	Y	Y	Y	Y	Y	Y
3 Gephardt	N	N	Y	Y	Y	N	N	Y
4 Skelton	N	N	?	?	Y	N	Y	Y
5 Wheat	N	N	Y	N	Y	N	N	Y
6 Danner	N	N	Y	Y	N	N	Y	Y
7 ***Hancock***	Y	Y	Y	Y	Y	Y	Y	Y
8 ***Emerson***	Y	Y	Y	Y	Y	Y	Y	Y
9 Volkmer	N	N	Y	Y	N	N	Y	Y
MONTANA								
AL Williams	N	N	N	N	N	N	N	Y
NEBRASKA								
1 ***Bereuter***	Y	Y	Y	Y	Y	Y	N	Y
2 Hoagland	N	N	Y	Y	Y	Y	Y	Y
3 ***Barrett***	Y	Y	?	?	Y	Y	Y	Y
NEVADA								
1 Bilbray	N	N	Y	Y	Y	Y	Y	Y
2 ***Vucanovich***	Y	Y	Y	N	Y	Y	N	Y
NEW HAMPSHIRE								
1 ***Zeliff***	Y	Y	Y	?	Y	Y	Y	Y
2 Swett	N	N	Y	Y	Y	N	Y	Y
NEW JERSEY								
1 Andrews	N	N	Y	Y	N	N	Y	Y
2 Hughes	N	N	Y	Y	Y	N	Y	Y
3 ***Saxton***	Y	Y	Y	Y	Y	Y	N	Y
4 ***Smith***	Y	Y	Y	Y	Y	Y	N	Y
5 ***Roukema***	Y	Y	Y	?	Y	Y	Y	Y
6 Pallone	N	N	Y	Y	N	N	N	Y
7 ***Franks***	#	#	?	#	Y	Y	N	Y
8 Klein	N	N	Y	Y	N	N	N	Y
9 Torricelli	N	N	N	?	Y	N	N	Y
10 Payne	N	N	Y	Y	N	N	N	Y
11 ***Gallo***	?	?	?	?	Y	N	N	Y
12 ***Zimmer***	Y	Y	Y	Y	Y	Y	Y	Y
13 Menendez	N	N	Y	Y	N	Y	N	Y
NEW MEXICO								
1 ***Schiff***	Y	Y	Y	Y	Y	N	N	Y
2 ***Skeen***	Y	Y	Y	N	Y	Y	N	Y
3 Richardson	N	N	Y	Y	Y	N	N	Y
NEW YORK								
1 Hochbrueckner	N	N	Y	N	Y	N	N	Y
2 ***Lazio***	Y	Y	N	N	Y	N	Y	Y
3 ***King***	Y	Y	N	N	Y	N	N	Y
4 ***Levy***	Y	Y	N	N	Y	N	N	Y
5 Ackerman	N	N	N	N	Y	N	N	Y
6 Flake	N	N	N	Y	?	?	?	?
7 Manton	N	N	Y	N	Y	N	N	Y
8 Nadler	N	N	N	N	N	N	Y	Y
9 Schumer	?	N	Y	Y	?	N	N	Y
10 Towns	?	?	?	?	N	N	N	Y
11 Owens	N	?	?	?	N	N	N	?
12 Velazquez	N	N	N	N	N	N	Y	Y
13 ***Molinari***	Y	Y	Y	N	Y	Y	N	Y
14 Maloney	N	N	Y	Y	N	N	N	Y
15 Rangel	N	N	N	N	N	N	N	Y
16 Serrano	N	N	Y	N	N	N	Y	Y
17 Engel	N	N	Y	N	N	N	N	Y
18 Lowey	N	N	Y	Y	Y	N	N	Y
19 ***Fish***	Y	Y	Y	N	N	Y	Y	Y
20 ***Gilman***	Y	Y	Y	N	Y	Y	N	Y
21 McNulty	N	N	Y	?	Y	Y	Y	Y
22 ***Solomon***	Y	Y	Y	?	N	Y	Y	Y
23 ***Boehlert***	Y	Y	Y	?	Y	N	N	Y
24 ***McHugh***	Y	Y	Y	N	Y	Y	Y	Y
25 ***Walsh***	Y	Y	Y	?	Y	Y	Y	Y
26 Hinchey	N	N	Y	Y	N	N	N	Y
27 ***Paxon***	Y	Y	Y	Y	Y	Y	Y	Y
28 Slaughter	N	N	Y	Y	Y	N	Y	Y
29 LaFalce	N	N	Y	?	Y	N	N	Y
30 ***Quinn***	Y	Y	Y	?	Y	Y	Y	Y
31 ***Houghton***	Y	Y	Y	?	Y	Y	N	Y
NORTH CAROLINA								
1 Clayton	N	N	Y	N	N	N	Y	Y
2 Valentine	N	N	Y	Y	N	Y	Y	Y

	243	244	245	246	247	248	249	250
3 Lancaster	N	N	Y	Y	N	Y	N	Y
4 Price	N	N	Y	Y	Y	N	N	Y
5 Neal	N	N	Y	Y	N	N	Y	Y
6 ***Coble***	Y	Y	Y	Y	N	Y	Y	Y
7 Rose	N	N	Y	Y	Y	?	N	Y
8 Hefner	N	N	Y	Y	Y	N	Y	Y
9 ***McMillan***	Y	?	?	?	Y	Y	Y	?
10 ***Ballenger***	Y	Y	Y	Y	Y	Y	N	Y
11 ***Taylor***	Y	Y	N	Y	Y	Y	N	Y
12 Watt	N	N	N	N	Y	N	N	Y
NORTH DAKOTA								
AL Pomeroy	N	N	Y	Y	N	N	N	Y
OHIO								
1 Mann	N	N	Y	Y	Y	N	Y	Y
2 ***Portman***	Y	Y	Y	N	Y	Y	Y	Y
3 Hall	N	N	Y	Y	Y	Y	Y	Y
4 ***Oxley***	Y	Y	Y	N	Y	Y	Y	Y
5 ***Gillmor***	Y	Y	Y	N	Y	N	Y	Y
6 Strickland	N	N	Y	Y	N	N	Y	Y
7 ***Hobson***	Y	Y	Y	N	Y	Y	N	Y
8 ***Boehner***	Y	Y	Y	?	Y	Y	Y	Y
9 Kaptur	?	?	?	?	N	N	Y	Y
10 ***Hoke***	Y	?	Y	N	Y	N	Y	Y
11 Stokes	N	N	N	N	Y	N	N	Y
12 ***Kasich***	Y	Y	Y	Y	Y	Y	Y	Y
13 Brown	?	?	?	?	N	N	Y	Y
14 Sawyer	N	N	Y	N	Y	N	N	Y
15 ***Pryce***	#	#	?	#	Y	Y	Y	Y
16 ***Regula***	Y	Y	Y	N	Y	Y	N	Y
17 Traficant	N	N	Y	N	N	Y	Y	Y
18 Applegate	Y	Y	Y	N	Y	Y	Y	Y
19 Fingerhut	—	—	Y	Y	N	N	Y	Y
OKLAHOMA								
1 ***Inhofe***	Y	Y	Y	Y	?	Y	N	Y
2 Synar	X	?	?	#	+	—	+	+
3 Brewster	N	N	Y	Y	Y	Y	Y	Y
4 McCurdy	N	N	Y	Y	Y	N	N	Y
5 ***Istook***	Y	Y	Y	Y	Y	Y	N	Y
6 English	N	N	Y	N	N	N	Y	Y
OREGON								
1 Furse	N	N	N	Y	N	N	Y	Y
2 ***Smith***	Y	Y	Y	Y	Y	Y	Y	Y
3 Wyden	N	N	N	Y	Y	N	Y	Y
4 DeFazio	?	?	?	?	N	N	Y	Y
5 Kopetski	N	N	N	Y	Y	N	N	Y
PENNSYLVANIA								
1 Foglietta	N	N	Y	N	Y	N	N	Y
2 Blackwell	N	N	N	P	Y	N	Y	Y
3 Borski	N	N	Y	Y	Y	N	N	Y
4 Klink	N	N	Y	Y	N	N	Y	Y
5 ***Clinger***	Y	Y	Y	N	Y	N	N	Y
6 Holden	N	N	Y	Y	N	Y	Y	Y
7 ***Weldon***	Y	Y	Y	Y	Y	Y	Y	Y
8 ***Greenwood***	Y	Y	Y	Y	Y	Y	Y	Y
9 ***Shuster***	Y	Y	Y	Y	N	Y	Y	Y
10 ***McDade***	Y	Y	Y	N	N	N	N	Y
11 Kanjorski	N	N	Y	Y	N	N	Y	Y
12 Murtha	N	N	Y	N	N	N	N	Y
13 Margolies-Mezv.	N	N	Y	Y	Y	N	Y	Y
14 Coyne	N	N	N	N	Y	N	N	Y
15 McHale	N	N	Y	Y	N	N	Y	Y
16 ***Walker***	Y	Y	Y	N	Y	Y	Y	Y
17 ***Gekas***	Y	Y	Y	N	Y	Y	Y	Y
18 ***Santorum***	Y	Y	Y	Y	Y	Y	Y	Y
19 ***Goodling***	Y	Y	Y	Y	Y	Y	N	Y
20 Murphy	?	?	?	?	N	Y	Y	Y
21 ***Ridge***	Y	Y	Y	Y	Y	N	?	Y
RHODE ISLAND								
1 ***Machtley***	Y	Y	Y	Y	Y	Y	Y	Y
2 Reed	N	N	Y	Y	Y	N	N	Y
SOUTH CAROLINA								
1 ***Ravenel***	Y	Y	Y	Y	N	Y	Y	Y
2 ***Spence***	Y	Y	?	?	N	Y	Y	Y
3 Derrick	N	N	Y	?	N	N	Y	Y
4 ***Inglis***	Y	Y	Y	Y	N	Y	Y	Y
5 Spratt	N	N	Y	Y	N	N	Y	Y
6 Clyburn	N	N	N	N	N	?	N	Y
SOUTH DAKOTA								
AL Johnson	N	N	Y	Y	Y	N	N	Y
TENNESSEE								
1 ***Quillen***	Y	Y	Y	X	N	Y	Y	Y
2 ***Duncan***	Y	Y	Y	Y	N	Y	Y	Y
3 Lloyd	N	N	?	?	N	Y	Y	Y
4 Cooper	N	N	Y	Y	Y	Y	N	Y
5 Clement	N	N	Y	Y	Y	N	N	Y

	243	244	245	246	247	248	249	250
6 Gordon	N	N	Y	Y	Y	N	Y	Y
7 ***Sundquist***	Y	Y	Y	N	Y	Y	Y	Y
8 Tanner	N	N	Y	Y	Y	N	Y	Y
9 Ford	N	?	?	?	N	N	N	Y
TEXAS								
1 Chapman	N	?	?	?	Y	N	Y	Y
2 Wilson	N	N	Y	Y	N	N	N	Y
3 ***Johnson, Sam***	Y	Y	Y	Y	Y	Y	Y	Y
4 Hall	N	N	Y	Y	Y	Y	Y	Y
5 Bryant	N	N	Y	N	Y	N	N	Y
6 ***Barton***	Y	Y	Y	Y	Y	Y	N	Y
7 ***Archer***	Y	Y	Y	Y	Y	Y	Y	Y
8 ***Fields***	Y	Y	Y	Y	Y	Y	Y	Y
9 Brooks	N	?	Y	N	Y	N	N	Y
10 Pickle	?	?	?	?	Y	N	N	Y
11 Edwards	N	N	Y	Y	Y	N	Y	Y
12 Geren	N	N	Y	Y	Y	Y	Y	Y
13 Sarpalius	N	N	Y	Y	Y	Y	Y	Y
14 Laughlin	N	N	Y	Y	Y	Y	Y	Y
15 de la Garza	N	N	Y	N	Y	N	Y	Y
16 Coleman	N	N	Y	N	Y	N	N	Y
17 Stenholm	N	Y	Y	Y	Y	Y	Y	Y
18 Washington	N	N	N	N	N	?	Y	N
19 ***Combest***	Y	Y	Y	Y	Y	Y	Y	Y
20 Gonzalez	N	N	Y	N	N	N	Y	Y
21 ***Smith***	Y	Y	Y	Y	Y	Y	Y	Y
22 ***DeLay***	Y	Y	Y	Y	Y	Y	Y	Y
23 ***Bonilla***	Y	Y	Y	Y	Y	Y	Y	Y
24 Frost	?	?	?	?	Y	N	P	Y
25 Andrews	Y	N	Y	Y	Y	?	?	?
26 ***Armey***	Y	Y	Y	Y	Y	Y	Y	Y
27 Ortiz	?	?	?	?	Y	N	N	Y
28 Tejeda	N	N	Y	Y	Y	N	Y	Y
29 Green	N	N	Y	Y	N	Y	N	Y
30 Johnson, E. B.	N	N	Y	N	N	N	N	Y
UTAH								
1 ***Hansen***	Y	Y	Y	Y	Y	Y	Y	Y
2 Shepherd	N	N	Y	Y	Y	Y	Y	Y
3 Orton	N	N	Y	Y	Y	Y	Y	Y
VERMONT								
AL *Sanders*	X	?	?	?	N	N	Y	Y
VIRGINIA								
1 ***Bateman***	Y	Y	Y	Y	Y	Y	Y	Y
2 Pickett	N	N	Y	N	Y	N	Y	Y
3 Scott	N	N	Y	N	Y	N	Y	Y
4 Sisisky	N	N	Y	N	Y	Y	Y	Y
5 Payne	N	N	Y	N	Y	Y	Y	Y
6 ***Goodlatte***	Y	Y	Y	Y	Y	Y	Y	Y
7 ***Bliley***	Y	Y	Y	Y	Y	Y	Y	Y
8 Moran	N	N	Y	Y	Y	N	N	Y
9 Boucher	?	?	?	?	Y	N	Y	Y
10 ***Wolf***	Y	Y	Y	N	Y	N	N	Y
11 Byrne	N	N	Y	Y	N	Y	Y	Y
WASHINGTON								
1 Cantwell	N	N	Y	Y	Y	N	Y	Y
2 Swift	N	N	N	N	Y	N	N	Y
3 Unsoeld	N	N	N	N	N	N	N	Y
4 Inslee	N	Y	Y	Y	Y	N	Y	Y
5 Foley								
6 Dicks	N	N	Y	Y	Y	N	N	Y
7 McDermott	N	N	Y	Y	Y	N	N	Y
8 ***Dunn***	Y	Y	Y	Y	Y	Y	N	Y
9 Kreidler	N	N	Y	Y	Y	N	Y	Y
WEST VIRGINIA								
1 Mollohan	N	N	Y	N	N	N	N	Y
2 Wise	N	N	Y	Y	Y	N	N	Y
3 Rahall	N	N	Y	N	N	N	Y	Y
WISCONSIN								
1 Barca	N	N	Y	Y	Y	N	Y	Y
2 ***Klug***	Y	Y	Y	Y	Y	Y	Y	Y
3 ***Gunderson***	Y	Y	Y	Y	Y	?	N	Y
4 Kleczka	N	N	Y	Y	Y	N	Y	Y
5 Barrett	N	N	Y	Y	Y	N	Y	Y
6 ***Petri***	Y	Y	Y	Y	Y	N	Y	Y
7 Obey	N	N	N	Y	N	N	N	Y
8 ***Roth***	Y	Y	Y	Y	Y	Y	Y	Y
9 ***Sensenbrenner***	Y	Y	Y	Y	Y	Y	Y	Y
WYOMING								
AL ***Thomas***	+	+	+	+	Y	Y	Y	Y
DELEGATES								
de Lugo, V.I.	N	N	Y	N	D	N	Y	D
Faleomavaega, Am.S.	?	?	?	?	D	?	?	D
Norton, D.C.	N	N	Y	N	D	N	Y	D
Romero-B., P.R.	?	?	?	?	D	?	Y	D
Underwood, Guam	N	N	N	N	D	N	Y	D

Southern states - Ala., Ark., Fla., Ga., Ky., La., Miss., N.C., Okla., S.C., Tenn., Texas, Va.
Omitted votes are quorum calls, which CQ does not include in its vote charts.

251. HR 2333. State Department Authorization/National Endowment for Democracy. Separate vote at the request of Solomon, R-N.Y., on the Kanjorski, D-Pa., amendment adopted in the Committee of the Whole to strike the $48 million authorization for the National Endowment for Democracy. Adopted 247-172: R 115-59; D 131-113 (ND 84-82, SD 47-31); I 1-0, June 22, 1993. (On separate votes, which may be demanded on an amendment adopted in the Committee of the Whole, the four delegates and the resident commissioner of Puerto Rico cannot vote. See vote 249.) A "nay" was a vote in support of the president's position.

252. HR 2333. State Department Authorization/Passage. Passage of the bill to authorize approximately $15 billion for the State Department, U.S. Information Agency and related agencies in fiscal 1994-95. Passed 273-144: R 41-129; D 231-15 (ND 159-9, SD 72-6); I 1-0, June 22, 1993.

253. HR 2403. Fiscal 1994 Treasury-Postal Appropriations/Former Presidents. Jacobs, D-Ind., amendment to cut $1.4 million from the bill by eliminating the staff and office allowance for all former presidents after they have been out of office for five years. Rejected in the Committee of the Whole 160-258: R 84-86; D 75-172 (ND 53-116, SD 22-56); I 1-0, June 22, 1993.

254. HR 2403. Fiscal 1994 Treasury-Postal Appropriations/Procedural Motion. Hoyer, D-Md., motion that the Committee of the Whole rise and report the bill back to the House, which would prevent additional amendments. Motion agreed to in the Committee of the Whole 241-171: R 0-169; D 240-2 (ND 163-1, SD 77-1); I 1-0, June 22, 1993.

255. HR 2403. Fiscal 1994 Treasury-Postal Appropriations/Bureau of Alcohol and Firearms. Separate vote at the request of Kolbe, R-Ariz., on the Deal, D-Ga., amendment adopted in the Committee of the Whole to cut the Bureau of Alcohol Tobacco and Firearms appropriation by $2.1 million to the amount requested by the administration. Adopted 353-62: R 154-18; D 198-44 (ND 128-35, SD 70-9); I 1-0, June 22, 1993. (On separate votes, which may be demanded on an amendment adopted in the Committee of the Whole, the four delegates and the resident commissioner of Puerto Rico cannot vote. See vote 242).

256. HR 2403. Fiscal 1994 Treasury-Postal Appropriations/Customs Service Cut. Separate vote at the request of Kolbe, R-Ariz., on the Penny, D-Minn., amendment adopted in the Committee of the Whole to cut the U.S. Customs Service appropriation by $4 million to the amount requested by the administration. Adopted 269-141: R 113-57; D 156-83 (ND 101-60, SD 55-23); I 0-1, June 22, 1993. (On separate votes, which may be demanded on an amendment adopted in the Committee of the Whole, the four delegates and the resident commissioner of Puerto Rico cannot vote. See vote 241.)

257. HR 2403. Fiscal 1994 Treasury-Postal Appropriations/Building Construction. Separate vote at the request of Kolbe, R-Ariz., on the Pomeroy, D-N.D., en bloc amendment adopted in the Committee of the Whole to cut funding for the construction of U.S. courthouses and joint federal buildings by 2 percent. Adopted 361-50: R 163-8; D 198-41 (ND 128-32, SD 70-9); I 0-1, June 22, 1993. (On separate votes, which may be demanded on an amendment adopted in the Committee of the Whole, the four delegates and the resident commissioner of Puerto Rico cannot vote. See vote 245).

258. HR 2403. Fiscal 1994 Treasury-Postal Appropriations/Former Presidents. Separate vote at the request of Kolbe, R-Ariz., on the Shepherd, D-Utah, amendment adopted in the Committee of the Whole to limit future spending for former Speakers to five years of staffing and office expenses after they leave office and to cut off current spending for the five former presidents' offices Oct. 1, 1998, excluding Secret Service protection, pension benefits and presidential libraries. Adopted 298-115: R 136-35; D 161-80 (ND 108-55, SD 53-25); I 1-0, June 22, 1993. (On separate votes, which may be demanded on an amendment adopted in the Committee of the Whole, the four delegates and the resident commissioner of Puerto Rico cannot vote. See vote 246.)

KEY

Y Voted for (yea).
\# Paired for.
\+ Announced for.
N Voted against (nay).
X Paired against.
− Announced against.
P Voted "present."
C Voted "present" to avoid possible conflict of interest.
? Did not vote or otherwise make a position known.
D Delegates ineligible to vote.

Democrats **Republicans**
Independent

ND Northern Democrats   SD Southern Democrats

	251	252	253	254	255	256	257	258
ALABAMA								
1 *Callahan*	Y	N	N	N	Y	N	Y	N
2 *Everett*	Y	N	Y	N	Y	Y	Y	Y
3 Browder	Y	Y	N	Y	Y	Y	Y	Y
4 Bevill	Y	Y	N	Y	Y	Y	Y	Y
5 Cramer	Y	Y	N	Y	Y	Y	Y	Y
6 *Bachus*	Y	N	Y	N	Y	N	Y	Y
7 Hilliard	N	Y	N	Y	Y	Y	Y	Y
ALASKA								
AL *Young*	Y	N	N	N	Y	N	Y	N
ARIZONA								
1 Coppersmith	N	Y	N	Y	Y	Y	Y	Y
2 Pastor	N	Y	N	Y	Y	Y	N	Y
3 *Stump*	Y	N	N	N	Y	N	Y	N
4 *Kyl*	N	N	Y	N	Y	Y	Y	Y
5 *Kolbe*	Y	Y	Y	N	Y	N	Y	Y
6 English	Y	Y	N	Y	N	Y	N	Y
ARKANSAS								
1 Lambert	N	Y	N	Y	Y	Y	Y	Y
2 Thornton	?	?	?	?	?	?	?	?
3 *Hutchinson*	Y	N	Y	N	Y	N	Y	Y
4 *Dickey*	Y	N	Y	N	Y	N	Y	Y
CALIFORNIA								
1 Hamburg	Y	Y	N	Y	Y	Y	Y	Y
2 *Herger*	Y	N	Y	N	Y	N	Y	Y
3 Fazio	N	Y	N	Y	N	Y	Y	Y
4 *Doolittle*	Y	N	N	N	Y	N	Y	N
5 Matsui	Y	Y	N	Y	N	Y	N	N
6 Woolsey	N	Y	N	Y	N	Y	N	Y
7 Miller	Y	Y	Y	Y	Y	Y	Y	Y
8 Pelosi	N	Y	N	Y	N	N	N	N
9 Dellums	Y	Y	N	Y	N	N	?	N
10 Baker	Y	N	Y	N	Y	N	Y	Y
11 *Pombo*	N	N	Y	N	Y	N	Y	Y
12 Lantos	N	Y	N	Y	Y	Y	Y	Y
13 Stark	Y	Y	Y	Y	N	N	Y	Y
14 Eshoo	N	Y	N	Y	N	Y	Y	Y
15 Mineta	N	Y	N	Y	N	N	N	N
16 Edwards	N	Y	N	Y	N	N	Y	N
17 Farr	N	Y	N	Y	Y	Y	Y	Y
18 Condit	Y	Y	Y	Y	Y	Y	Y	Y
19 Lehman	Y	Y	N	Y	Y	Y	Y	Y
20 Dooley	Y	Y	N	Y	Y	Y	Y	Y
21 *Thomas*	N	?	N	−	Y	Y	Y	Y
22 *Huffington*	Y	Y	N	N	Y	N	Y	Y
23 *Gallegly*	Y	N	Y	N	Y	N	Y	Y
24 Beilenson	N	Y	N	Y	N	N	Y	N
25 *McKeon*	Y	N	N	N	Y	N	Y	Y
26 Berman	N	Y	N	Y	N	Y	N	N
27 *Moorhead*	Y	N	N	N	Y	Y	Y	Y
28 *Dreier*	N	−	Y	N	Y	Y	Y	Y
29 Waxman	N	Y	N	?	N	N	Y	N
30 Becerra	Y	Y	Y	Y	Y	N	Y	Y
31 Martinez	Y	Y	N	Y	N	Y	Y	Y
32 Dixon	N	Y	N	Y	N	Y	Y	Y
33 Roybal-Allard	Y	Y	N	Y	N	Y	N	Y
34 Torres	N	Y	N	?	N	Y	Y	Y
35 Waters	N	Y	N	Y	N	Y	N	Y
36 Harman	?	?	?	?	?	?	?	?
37 Tucker	Y	Y	N	Y	Y	Y	Y	Y
38 *Horn*	N	Y	N	N	N	N	N	Y
39 *Royce*	N	N	Y	N	Y	Y	Y	Y
40 *Lewis*	N	N	N	N	Y	Y	Y	Y
41 *Kim*	Y	Y	Y	N	Y	Y	Y	Y

	251	252	253	254	255	256	257	258
42 Brown	?	Y	N	Y	Y	N	Y	N
43 *Calvert*	N	Y	N	N	Y	N	Y	Y
44 *McCandless*	Y	N	N	Y	Y	Y	Y	Y
45 *Rohrabacher*	N	N	Y	N	Y	Y	Y	Y
46 *Dornan*	Y	N	N	N	Y	Y	Y	Y
47 *Cox*	N	N	Y	N	Y	Y	Y	Y
48 *Packard*	N	N	Y	N	Y	N	Y	Y
49 Schenk	Y	Y	N	Y	Y	N	Y	Y
50 Filner	N	Y	N	Y	N	Y	Y	Y
51 *Cunningham*	Y	N	Y	N	Y	N	Y	Y
52 *Hunter*	Y	N	?	N	Y	N	Y	Y
COLORADO								
1 Schroeder	Y	Y	Y	Y	Y	N	Y	Y
2 Skaggs	N	Y	N	Y	Y	Y	Y	N
3 *McInnis*	Y	N	Y	N	Y	Y	Y	Y
4 *Allard*	N	N	Y	N	Y	Y	Y	Y
5 *Hefley*	Y	N	N	N	N	Y	Y	Y
6 *Schaefer*	Y	N	Y	N	Y	Y	Y	Y
CONNECTICUT								
1 Kennelly	N	Y	N	Y	Y	Y	Y	Y
2 Gejdenson	N	Y	N	Y	Y	Y	Y	N
3 DeLauro	N	Y	N	Y	Y	Y	Y	Y
4 *Shays*	Y	Y	N	Y	Y	Y	Y	Y
5 *Franks*	Y	N	Y	N	Y	Y	Y	Y
6 *Johnson*	N	Y	N	N	Y	Y	Y	Y
DELAWARE								
AL *Castle*	N	N	N	N	Y	Y	Y	N
FLORIDA								
1 Hutto	Y	Y	N	Y	Y	Y	Y	Y
2 Peterson	Y	Y	N	Y	Y	Y	Y	N
3 Brown	N	Y	N	Y	N	N	N	N
4 *Fowler*	Y	Y	N	N	N	N	N	Y
5 Thurman	Y	Y	N	Y	Y	Y	Y	Y
6 *Stearns*	Y	N	N	N	Y	N	Y	N
7 *Mica*	Y	N	Y	N	Y	N	Y	Y
8 *McCollum*	N	N	N	N	Y	N	N	Y
9 *Bilirakis*	Y	N	Y	N	Y	N	Y	Y
10 *Young*	Y	Y	Y	N	Y	Y	Y	Y
11 Gibbons	N	Y	N	Y	Y	Y	N	N
12 *Canady*	Y	N	Y	N	Y	N	Y	Y
13 *Miller*	N	N	Y	N	Y	N	Y	Y
14 *Goss*	N	N	N	N	Y	N	Y	Y
15 *Bacchus*	N	Y	N	Y	Y	Y	Y	Y
16 *Lewis*	Y	N	N	N	Y	Y	Y	Y
17 Meek	?	?	?	?	?	?	?	?
18 *Ros-Lehtinen*	N	N	Y	N	Y	N	Y	Y
19 Johnston	N	Y	N	Y	N	Y	N	Y
20 Deutsch	N	Y	N	Y	Y	Y	Y	Y
21 *Diaz-Balart*	N	N	N	N	N	N	N	N
22 *Shaw*	N	N	N	N	Y	N	Y	Y
23 Hastings	N	Y	N	Y	N	N	N	N
GEORGIA								
1 *Kingston*	Y	N	Y	N	Y	Y	Y	Y
2 Bishop	Y	Y	N	Y	Y	Y	Y	Y
3 *Collins*	Y	N	N	N	Y	Y	Y	Y
4 *Linder*	Y	N	N	Y	Y	Y	Y	Y
5 Lewis	N	Y	N	Y	N	N	N	N
6 *Gingrich*	N	N	N	Y	Y	N	Y	Y
7 Darden	N	Y	N	Y	Y	Y	Y	N
8 Rowland	Y	Y	N	Y	Y	Y	Y	Y
9 Deal	Y	Y	N	Y	Y	Y	Y	Y
10 Johnson	Y	Y	N	Y	Y	Y	Y	Y
11 McKinney	Y	Y	N	Y	Y	N	N	N
HAWAII								
1 Abercrombie	N	Y	N	Y	Y	N	N	N
2 Mink	Y	Y	N	Y	Y	N	Y	N
IDAHO								
1 LaRocco	Y	Y	Y	Y	Y	Y	Y	Y
2 *Crapo*	Y	N	Y	N	Y	?	Y	Y
ILLINOIS								
1 Rush	?	?	?	?	?	?	?	?
2 Reynolds	Y	Y	N	N	N	N	N	N
3 Lipinski	Y	Y	N	Y	N	Y	Y	N
4 Gutierrez	Y	Y	N	Y	Y	?	?	Y
5 Rostenkowski	Y	Y	N	Y	Y	Y	Y	Y
6 *Hyde*	N	N	N	N	N	Y	Y	Y
7 Collins	N	Y	N	N	N	N	N	N
8 *Crane*	Y	N	Y	N	Y	Y	Y	Y
9 Yates	Y	Y	Y	N	N	N	N	N
10 *Porter*	N	Y	N	Y	Y	Y	Y	Y
11 Sangmeister	Y	Y	N	Y	Y	Y	Y	Y
12 Costello	Y	Y	Y	Y	Y	Y	Y	Y
13 *Fawell*	Y	N	Y	N	Y	Y	Y	Y
14 *Hastert*	N	N	N	N	Y	Y	Y	Y
15 *Ewing*	Y	N	Y	N	Y	Y	Y	Y
16 *Manzullo*	Y	N	Y	N	Y	Y	Y	Y
17 Evans	Y	Y	Y	Y	N	N	N	Y

	251	252	253	254	255	256	257	258
18 ***Michel***	N	Y	N	N	Y	N	Y	N
19 Poshard	Y	Y	Y	Y	Y	Y	Y	Y
20 Durbin	Y	Y	Y	Y	Y	Y	Y	Y
INDIANA								
1 Visclosky	Y	Y	N	Y	N	N	Y	N
2 Sharp	N	Y	Y	Y	Y	Y	Y	Y
3 Roemer	N	Y	Y	Y	Y	Y	?	Y
4 Long	Y	Y	Y	Y	Y	Y	Y	Y
5 ***Buyer***	N	N	N	N	Y	N	N	Y
6 ***Burton***	N	N	Y	N	Y	Y	Y	Y
7 ***Myers***	N	Y	N	N	N	N	N	Y
8 McCloskey	N	Y	Y	Y	Y	Y	Y	Y
9 Hamilton	N	Y	Y	Y	Y	Y	Y	Y
10 Jacobs	Y	N	Y	N	Y	Y	Y	Y
IOWA								
1 ***Leach***	N	Y	Y	N	Y	Y	Y	Y
2 ***Nussle***	Y	N	Y	N	Y	Y	Y	Y
3 ***Lightfoot***	Y	Y	N	N	N	N	Y	N
4 Smith	N	Y	N	Y	Y	Y	Y	N
5 ***Grandy***	Y	Y	Y	N	N	Y	Y	Y
KANSAS								
1 ***Roberts***	Y	N	Y	N	?	?	?	?
2 Slattery	Y	Y	Y	Y	Y	Y	Y	Y
3 ***Meyers***	N	Y	Y	N	Y	Y	Y	Y
4 Glickman	Y	Y	Y	Y	Y	Y	Y	Y
KENTUCKY								
1 Barlow	Y	Y	Y	Y	Y	Y	Y	Y
2 Natcher	Y	Y	N	Y	Y	Y	Y	N
3 Mazzoli	Y	Y	N	Y	Y	Y	Y	Y
4 ***Bunning***	N	N	N	N	N	N	Y	N
5 ***Rogers***	N	N	N	N	Y	Y	Y	N
6 Baesler	Y	Y	N	Y	N	N	Y	Y
LOUISIANA								
1 ***Livingston***	N	Y	N	N	N	N	Y	N
2 Jefferson	N	Y	N	Y	N	Y	Y	Y
3 Tauzin	Y	N	Y	Y	Y	Y	Y	Y
4 Fields	N	Y	N	Y	Y	Y	Y	N
5 ***McCrery***	Y	N	Y	N	Y	Y	Y	Y
6 ***Baker***	Y	N	Y	N	Y	Y	Y	Y
7 Hayes	?	?	?	?	?	?	?	?
MAINE								
1 Andrews	Y	Y	?	Y	Y	Y	Y	Y
2 ***Snowe***	Y	Y	Y	N	Y	Y	Y	Y
MARYLAND								
1 ***Gilchrest***	Y	Y	N	N	Y	Y	Y	Y
2 ***Bentley***	Y	Y	N	N	Y	Y	Y	N
3 Cardin	N	Y	N	Y	Y	Y	Y	N
4 Wynn	N	Y	N	Y	Y	N	Y	Y
5 Hoyer	N	Y	N	Y	N	N	Y	N
6 ***Bartlett***	Y	?	N	N	Y	Y	Y	Y
7 Mfume	Y	N	Y	Y	Y	Y	Y	N
8 ***Morella***	N	Y	N	?	Y	Y	Y	Y
MASSACHUSETTS								
1 Olver	N	Y	N	Y	Y	N	Y	N
2 Neal	N	Y	N	Y	Y	Y	Y	N
3 ***Blute***	Y	N	N	N	Y	Y	Y	Y
4 Frank	Y	Y	Y	Y	Y	?	Y	Y
5 Meehan	N	Y	Y	Y	Y	Y	Y	Y
6 ***Torkildsen***	Y	N	N	N	Y	Y	Y	Y
7 Markey	N	Y	N	?	Y	Y	Y	Y
8 Kennedy	N	Y	N	Y	Y	Y	Y	N
9 Moakley	N	Y	N	Y	Y	N	N	N
10 Studds	Y	Y	N	Y	Y	Y	Y	N
MICHIGAN								
1 Stupak	Y	Y	N	Y	Y	Y	Y	Y
2 ***Hoekstra***	Y	N	Y	N	Y	Y	Y	Y
3 Henry	?	?	?	?	?	?	?	?
4 ***Camp***	Y	N	N	N	Y	Y	Y	N
5 Barcia	Y	Y	N	Y	Y	Y	?	Y
6 ***Upton***	Y	N	Y	N	N	Y	Y	Y
7 ***Smith***	Y	N	N	N	Y	Y	Y	Y
8 Carr	Y	Y	Y	Y	N	N	Y	N
9 Kildee	N	Y	N	Y	N	N	Y	Y
10 Bonior	N	Y	N	Y	Y	N	Y	N
11 ***Knollenberg***	Y	N	Y	N	Y	Y	Y	Y
12 Levin	N	Y	N	Y	Y	Y	Y	Y
13 Ford	N	Y	N	Y	Y	N	Y	N
14 Conyers	?	?	?	?	?	?	?	?
15 Collins	N	N	Y	N	Y	N	N	N
16 Dingell	N	N	N	Y	Y	N	N	?
MINNESOTA								
1 Penny	Y	Y	Y	Y	Y	Y	Y	Y
2 Minge	Y	N	Y	Y	Y	Y	Y	Y
3 ***Ramstad***	Y	N	Y	N	Y	Y	Y	Y
4 Vento	N	Y	Y	Y	Y	Y	Y	Y

	251	252	253	254	255	256	257	258
5 Sabo	N	Y	N	Y	N	N	Y	Y
6 ***Grams***	Y	N	Y	N	Y	Y	Y	Y
7 Peterson	N	N	Y	Y	Y	Y	Y	Y
8 Oberstar	N	Y	N	?	Y	Y	Y	Y
MISSISSIPPI								
1 Whitten	?	?	N	?	?	?	?	?
2 Thompson	N	Y	N	Y	Y	?	Y	N
3 Montgomery	Y	Y	N	Y	Y	Y	Y	Y
4 Parker	Y	Y	Y	Y	Y	Y	Y	Y
5 Taylor	Y	N	Y	N	Y	Y	Y	Y
MISSOURI								
1 Clay	Y	Y	N	Y	N	N	N	N
2 ***Talent***	Y	N	Y	N	Y	Y	Y	Y
3 Gephardt	N	Y	N	Y	?	?	Y	Y
4 Skelton	Y	Y	N	Y	Y	Y	Y	Y
5 Wheat	N	Y	N	Y	N	N	Y	N
6 Danner	Y	Y	Y	Y	Y	Y	Y	Y
7 ***Hancock***	Y	N	Y	N	Y	Y	Y	Y
8 ***Emerson***	Y	N	Y	N	Y	Y	Y	Y
9 Volkmer	Y	Y	Y	Y	Y	Y	Y	Y
MONTANA								
AL Williams	N	N	N	Y	Y	N	N	Y
NEBRASKA								
1 ***Bereuter***	N	Y	Y	N	Y	Y	Y	Y
2 Hoagland	Y	Y	Y	Y	Y	Y	Y	Y
3 ***Barrett***	Y	N	Y	N	Y	Y	Y	Y
NEVADA								
1 Bilbray	Y	Y	N	Y	Y	Y	Y	Y
2 ***Vucanovich***	N	N	N	N	Y	Y	Y	N
NEW HAMPSHIRE								
1 ***Zeliff***	Y	N	Y	N	Y	Y	Y	Y
2 Swett	Y	Y	Y	Y	Y	Y	Y	Y
NEW JERSEY								
1 Andrews	Y	Y	Y	Y	Y	Y	Y	Y
2 Hughes	Y	Y	N	Y	Y	Y	Y	Y
3 ***Saxton***	N	Y	N	N	Y	?	?	?
4 ***Smith***	N	N	N	N	Y	Y	Y	Y
5 ***Roukema***	Y	Y	N	N	Y	N	Y	Y
6 Pallone	N	Y	Y	Y	Y	Y	Y	Y
7 ***Franks***	N	N	Y	N	Y	Y	Y	Y
8 Klein	N	Y	N	Y	Y	Y	Y	Y
9 Torricelli	N	Y	N	?	?	?	?	?
10 Payne	N	Y	N	Y	N	N	Y	Y
11 ***Gallo***	N	Y	N	N	Y	Y	Y	Y
12 ***Zimmer***	Y	N	Y	N	Y	Y	Y	Y
13 Menendez	N	Y	N	Y	?	N	Y	Y
NEW MEXICO								
1 ***Schiff***	N	Y	N	N	Y	Y	Y	Y
2 ***Skeen***	N	Y	N	N	Y	N	Y	N
3 Richardson	N	Y	N	Y	Y	Y	Y	Y
NEW YORK								
1 Hochbrueckner	N	Y	N	Y	Y	Y	Y	N
2 ***Lazio***	Y	N	N	N	N	N	N	N
3 ***King***	N	Y	N	N	Y	N	N	N
4 ***Levy***	N	Y	N	N	Y	N	N	N
5 Ackerman	N	Y	N	Y	N	N	N	N
6 Flake	?	?	?	?	?	?	?	?
7 Manton	N	Y	N	?	Y	Y	N	N
8 Nadler	N	Y	N	Y	N	?	N	N
9 Schumer	N	Y	?	?	?	?	?	?
10 Towns	N	Y	N	Y	N	N	N	N
11 Owens	Y	Y	Y	Y	Y	Y	Y	Y
12 Velazquez	Y	Y	N	Y	N	Y	N	N
13 ***Molinari***	N	N	N	N	Y	N	Y	N
14 Maloney	N	Y	N	Y	Y	Y	Y	Y
15 Rangel	N	Y	?	Y	N	N	N	?
16 Serrano	Y	Y	N	Y	N	Y	Y	N
17 Engel	N	Y	N	Y	Y	Y	Y	N
18 Lowey	N	Y	N	Y	Y	Y	Y	Y
19 ***Fish***	Y	Y	Y	N	Y	N	Y	Y
20 ***Gilman***	N	Y	N	N	Y	N	Y	N
21 McNulty	Y	Y	N	Y	N	Y	Y	N
22 ***Solomon***	Y	N	Y	N	Y	Y	Y	Y
23 ***Boehlert***	N	?	N	N	Y	Y	Y	Y
24 ***McHugh***	Y	?	N	N	Y	Y	Y	N
25 ***Walsh***	Y	N	N	N	Y	Y	Y	Y
26 Hinchey	N	Y	N	Y	Y	Y	Y	Y
27 ***Paxon***	Y	N	N	N	Y	Y	Y	Y
28 Slaughter	Y	Y	N	Y	Y	Y	Y	Y
29 LaFalce	N	Y	N	Y	Y	Y	Y	N
30 ***Quinn***	Y	N	Y	N	Y	N	Y	Y
31 ***Houghton***	N	Y	N	N	Y	Y	Y	N
NORTH CAROLINA								
1 Clayton	Y	Y	N	Y	Y	Y	Y	N
2 Valentine	Y	Y	Y	Y	Y	Y	Y	Y

	251	252	253	254	255	256	257	258
3 Lancaster	N	Y	Y	Y	Y	Y	Y	Y
4 Price	N	Y	N	Y	Y	Y	Y	Y
5 Neal	Y	N	N	Y	Y	Y	Y	Y
6 ***Coble***	Y	N	Y	N	Y	Y	Y	Y
7 Rose	N	Y	N	Y	Y	N	Y	Y
8 Hefner	Y	Y	N	Y	Y	Y	Y	Y
9 ***McMillan***	?	Y	Y	N	Y	N	Y	Y
10 ***Ballenger***	N	N	N	N	Y	Y	Y	Y
11 ***Taylor***	Y	N	Y	N	Y	Y	Y	Y
12 Watt	N	Y	N	Y	Y	Y	N	N
NORTH DAKOTA								
AL Pomeroy	N	Y	N	Y	Y	Y	Y	Y
OHIO								
1 Mann	Y	Y	N	Y	Y	Y	Y	Y
2 ***Portman***	Y	N	N	N	Y	Y	Y	N
3 Hall	Y	Y	Y	Y	Y	Y	Y	Y
4 ***Oxley***	Y	N	N	N	Y	Y	Y	Y
5 ***Gillmor***	Y	N	N	?	Y	Y	Y	N
6 Strickland	Y	Y	Y	Y	Y	Y	Y	Y
7 ***Hobson***	N	N	N	N	Y	Y	Y	N
8 ***Boehner***	Y	N	N	N	Y	Y	Y	Y
9 Kaptur	Y	Y	Y	Y	Y	Y	Y	Y
10 ***Hoke***	Y	N	N	N	Y	Y	Y	N
11 Stokes	Y	Y	N	Y	N	N	N	N
12 ***Kasich***	Y	N	Y	N	Y	Y	Y	Y
13 Brown	Y	Y	Y	Y	Y	Y	Y	Y
14 Sawyer	N	Y	N	Y	Y	Y	Y	N
15 ***Pryce***	Y	N	N	N	Y	Y	Y	Y
16 ***Regula***	N	N	N	N	Y	Y	Y	N
17 Traficant	Y	N	N	Y	Y	Y	Y	N
18 Applegate	Y	N	Y	Y	Y	Y	Y	Y
19 Fingerhut	Y	Y	N	Y	Y	Y	Y	Y
OKLAHOMA								
1 ***Inhofe***	N	N	Y	N	Y	N	Y	Y
2 Synar	+	+	−	+	+	+	+	+
3 Brewster	Y	Y	N	Y	Y	Y	Y	Y
4 McCurdy	N	Y	?	Y	Y	Y	Y	Y
5 ***Istook***	N	N	?	N	Y	Y	Y	Y
6 English	Y	Y	Y	?	Y	N	Y	Y
OREGON								
1 Furse	Y	Y	N	Y	Y	N	N	Y
2 ***Smith***	Y	N	N	Y	Y	Y	Y	Y
3 Wyden	Y	Y	Y	Y	Y	Y	N	Y
4 DeFazio	Y	Y	Y	?	N	Y	Y	Y
5 Kopetski	?	Y	Y	Y	Y	Y	N	Y
PENNSYLVANIA								
1 Foglietta	N	Y	N	Y	N	Y	N	N
2 Blackwell	Y	Y	N	Y	N	N	N	N
3 Borski	N	Y	Y	Y	Y	Y	Y	Y
4 Klink	Y	Y	Y	Y	Y	Y	Y	Y
5 ***Clinger***	N	N	N	N	Y	Y	Y	N
6 Holden	Y	Y	Y	Y	Y	Y	Y	Y
7 ***Weldon***	Y	N	N	?	Y	Y	Y	Y
8 ***Greenwood***	Y	N	N	N	Y	Y	Y	Y
9 ***Shuster***	Y	N	Y	N	Y	Y	Y	Y
10 ***McDade***	N	Y	N	N	N	Y	Y	Y
11 Kanjorski	Y	Y	Y	Y	Y	Y	Y	Y
12 Murtha	Y	Y	N	Y	Y	Y	Y	N
13 Margolies-Mezv.	Y	Y	N	Y	Y	Y	Y	Y
14 Coyne	N	Y	N	Y	N	N	N	N
15 McHale	Y	Y	N	Y	Y	Y	Y	Y
16 ***Walker***	Y	N	N	N	Y	Y	Y	Y
17 ***Gekas***	Y	N	Y	N	Y	Y	Y	Y
18 ***Santorum***	Y	N	?	?	?	?	?	?
19 ***Goodling***	N	N	N	N	N	N	Y	Y
20 Murphy	Y	N	Y	Y	Y	Y	Y	Y
21 ***Ridge***	Y	Y	?	?	?	?	?	?
RHODE ISLAND								
1 ***Machtley***	Y	Y	N	N	Y	Y	Y	Y
2 Reed	N	Y	N	Y	Y	Y	Y	Y
SOUTH CAROLINA								
1 ***Ravenel***	Y	N	N	N	Y	Y	Y	Y
2 ***Spence***	Y	N	N	N	Y	N	Y	Y
3 Derrick	Y	Y	N	?	?	?	?	?
4 ***Inglis***	Y	N	Y	N	Y	Y	Y	Y
5 Spratt	Y	Y	Y	Y	Y	N	Y	Y
6 Clyburn	Y	Y	N	Y	Y	Y	Y	?
SOUTH DAKOTA								
AL Johnson	N	Y	Y	Y	N	Y	Y	Y
TENNESSEE								
1 ***Quillen***	Y	N	N	N	N	Y	Y	N
2 ***Duncan***	Y	N	Y	N	Y	Y	Y	Y
3 Lloyd	Y	N	Y	Y	Y	Y	Y	Y
4 Cooper	N	Y	N	Y	Y	Y	Y	Y
5 Clement	N	Y	Y	Y	Y	Y	Y	Y

	251	252	253	254	255	256	257	258
6 Gordon	Y	Y	N	Y	Y	Y	Y	Y
7 ***Sundquist***	Y	N	N	N	Y	Y	Y	N
8 Tanner	Y	N	Y	Y	Y	Y	Y	Y
9 Ford	N	Y	Y	Y	Y	N	Y	N
TEXAS								
1 Chapman	Y	?	N	Y	Y	N	Y	Y
2 Wilson	N	Y	?	Y	Y	Y	Y	Y
3 ***Johnson, Sam***	Y	N	Y	N	Y	Y	Y	Y
4 Hall	Y	Y	Y	Y	Y	N	Y	Y
5 Bryant	N	Y	N	Y	N	N	Y	N
6 ***Barton***	N	N	N	N	N	N	Y	N
7 ***Archer***	Y	N	N	N	Y	Y	Y	Y
8 ***Fields***	Y	N	N	N	Y	N	Y	Y
9 Brooks	N	Y	N	Y	Y	N	Y	N
10 Pickle	N	Y	N	Y	Y	N	Y	Y
11 Edwards	Y	Y	N	Y	Y	Y	Y	Y
12 Geren	Y	Y	Y	Y	Y	Y	Y	Y
13 Sarpalius	Y	N	Y	Y	Y	Y	Y	Y
14 Laughlin	Y	Y	Y	Y	Y	Y	Y	Y
15 de la Garza	N	Y	N	Y	Y	N	Y	N
16 Coleman	N	Y	N	Y	N	N	Y	N
17 Stenholm	Y	Y	Y	Y	Y	Y	Y	Y
18 Washington	Y	Y	?	Y	N	N	N	N
19 ***Combest***	Y	N	Y	N	N	Y	Y	Y
20 Gonzalez	Y	Y	N	Y	Y	Y	Y	N
21 ***Smith***	Y	N	N	N	N	N	Y	Y
22 ***DeLay***	Y	N	N	N	Y	N	Y	Y
23 ***Bonilla***	Y	N	Y	N	N	Y	Y	Y
24 Frost	P	Y	N	Y	Y	Y	Y	Y
25 Andrews	?	?	Y	Y	Y	Y	Y	Y
26 ***Armey***	Y	N	N	N	Y	Y	Y	Y
27 Ortiz	N	Y	Y	Y	Y	N	Y	Y
28 Tejeda	Y	Y	N	Y	Y	N	Y	Y
29 Green	N	Y	Y	Y	Y	N	Y	Y
30 Johnson, E. B.	N	Y	N	Y	N	N	N	N
UTAH								
1 ***Hansen***	Y	N	Y	N	Y	Y	Y	Y
2 Shepherd	Y	Y	N	Y	Y	Y	Y	Y
3 Orton	Y	Y	Y	Y	Y	Y	Y	Y
VERMONT								
AL *Sanders*	Y	Y	Y	Y	Y	N	N	Y
VIRGINIA								
1 ***Bateman***	Y	Y	N	N	Y	N	Y	Y
2 Pickett	Y	Y	N	Y	Y	N	Y	N
3 Scott	Y	Y	N	Y	Y	N	Y	N
4 Sisisky	Y	Y	N	Y	Y	Y	Y	Y
5 Payne	Y	Y	N	Y	Y	Y	Y	N
6 ***Goodlatte***	Y	N	Y	N	Y	Y	Y	Y
7 ***Bliley***	Y	Y	Y	N	Y	Y	Y	Y
8 Moran	N	Y	Y	Y	N	N	N	Y
9 Boucher	Y	Y	N	Y	Y	Y	Y	Y
10 ***Wolf***	N	N	N	N	N	N	Y	N
11 Byrne	Y	Y	Y	Y	Y	Y	Y	Y
WASHINGTON								
1 Cantwell	Y	Y	Y	Y	Y	Y	Y	Y
2 Swift	N	Y	N	Y	Y	N	N	N
3 Unsoeld	N	Y	N	Y	?	?	?	?
4 Inslee	Y	Y	Y	Y	Y	Y	Y	Y
5 Foley								
6 Dicks	N	Y	N	Y	Y	Y	Y	Y
7 McDermott	N	Y	N	Y	Y	N	N	N
8 ***Dunn***	N	N	N	Y	Y	Y	Y	Y
9 Kreidler	Y	Y	Y	Y	Y	N	Y	Y
WEST VIRGINIA								
1 Mollohan	N	Y	N	Y	Y	N	Y	N
2 Wise	N	Y	N	Y	Y	Y	Y	Y
3 Rahall	Y	N	N	Y	N	N	N	N
WISCONSIN								
1 Barca	Y	Y	N	Y	Y	Y	Y	Y
2 ***Klug***	Y	N	Y	N	Y	Y	Y	Y
3 ***Gunderson***	N	Y	Y	N	Y	Y	Y	Y
4 Kleczka	Y	Y	N	Y	Y	Y	Y	Y
5 Barrett	Y	Y	Y	Y	Y	Y	Y	Y
6 ***Petri***	Y	N	Y	N	Y	Y	Y	Y
7 Obey	N	Y	N	Y	Y	Y	Y	Y
8 ***Roth***	Y	Y	Y	N	Y	Y	Y	Y
9 ***Sensenbrenner***	Y	N	Y	N	Y	Y	Y	Y
WYOMING								
AL ***Thomas***	Y	N	?	N	Y	N	Y	Y
DELEGATES								
de Lugo, V.I.	D	D	N	Y	D	D	D	D
Faleomavaega, Am.S.	D	D	?	?	D	D	D	D
Norton, D.C.	D	D	N	Y	D	D	D	D
Romero-B., P.R.	D	D	N	Y	D	D	D	D
Underwood, Guam	D	D	N	Y	D	D	D	D

Southern states - Ala., Ark., Fla., Ga., Ky., La., Miss., N.C., Okla., S.C., Tenn., Texas, Va.
Omitted votes are quorum calls, which CQ does not include in its vote charts.

259. HR 2403. Fiscal 1994 Treasury-Postal Appropriations/Funding Cut. Myers, R-Ind., motion to recommit the bill to the House Appropriations Committee with instructions to report it back with an amendment to reduce appropriations in the bill by 2 percent with the exception of funding for the Customs Service, the Bureau of Alcohol, Tobacco and Firearms, and the Federal Buildings Fund. Motion rejected 180-235: R 167-3; D 13-231 (ND 9-156, SD 4-75); I 0-1, June 22, 1993.

260. HR 2403. Fiscal 1994 Treasury-Postal Appropriations/Passage. Passage of the bill to provide $22.7 billion in new budget authority for the Treasury Department, the Postal Service, the Executive Office of the President and certain independent agencies in fiscal 1994. The administration requested $22,006,136,000. Passed 263-153: R 35-135; D 227-18 (ND 155-11, SD 72-7); I 1-0, June 22, 1993.

261. HR 2446. Fiscal 1994 Military Construction Appropriations/Passage. Passage of the bill to provide $10,273,731,000 in new budget authority for military construction and family housing for the Department of Defense in fiscal 1994. The administration requested $10,794,341,000. Passed 347-67: R 123-49; D 223-18 (ND 146-15, SD 77-3); I 1-0, June 23, 1993.

262. HR 2200. NASA Authorization/Funding Cut. Hall, D-Texas, amendment to limit the fiscal 1994 NASA authorization to the rate of inflation, which would reduce authorizations by approximately $264 million. Adopted in Committee of the Whole 411-11: R 172-1; D 238-10 (ND 163-4, SD 75-6); I 1-0, June 23, 1993.

263. HR 2200. NASA Authorization/Space Station. Roemer, D-Ind., amendment to eliminate the seven-year $12.7 billion authorization for the space station, authorizing $825 million for costs associated with terminating the project. Rejected in Committee of the Whole 215-216: R 61-112; D 153-104 (ND 124-50, SD 29-54); I 1-0, June 23, 1993. A "nay" was a vote in support of the president's position.

264. HR 2445. Fiscal 1994 Energy and Water Appropriations/Kissimmee River Restoration. Duncan, R-Tenn., amendment to strike $5 million for the Kissimmee River ecosystem restoration project in Florida. Rejected in Committee of the Whole 100-324: R 90-81; D 10-242 (ND 9-160, SD 1-82); I 0-1, June 24, 1993.

265. HR 2445. Fiscal 1994 Energy and Water Appropriations/Water Projects. Burton, R-Ind., amendment to impose a 2.99567 percent across-the-board cut for water projects in the bill. Rejected in Committee of the Whole 96-329: R 87-86; D 9-242 (ND 8-161, SD 1-81); I 0-1, June 24, 1993.

266. HR 2445. Fiscal 1994 Energy and Water Appropriations/Interior Department Funding. Burton, R-Ind., amendment to impose a 7.20036 percent across-the-board cut in Interior Department funding in the bill. Rejected in Committee of the Whole 135-287: R 118-50; D 17-236 (ND 11-160, SD 6-76); I 0-1, June 24, 1993.

KEY

Y	Voted for (yea).
#	Paired for.
+	Announced for.
N	Voted against (nay).
X	Paired against.
−	Announced against.
P	Voted "present."
C	Voted "present" to avoid possible conflict of interest.
?	Did not vote or otherwise make a position known.
D	Delegates ineligible to vote.

Democrats **Republicans**
Independent

	259	260	261	262	263	264	265	266
ALABAMA								
1 *Callahan*	Y	N	Y	Y	N	Y	N	N
2 *Everett*	Y	N	Y	N	Y	N	Y	N
3 Browder	N	Y	Y	N	N	N	N	N
4 Bevill	N	Y	Y	N	N	N	N	N
5 Cramer	N	Y	Y	N	N	N	N	N
6 *Bachus*	Y	N	Y	N	N	N	N	N
7 Hilliard	N	Y	?	N	N	N	N	N
ALASKA								
AL *Young*	Y	N	Y	Y	N	Y	N	N
ARIZONA								
1 Coppersmith	N	Y	Y	Y	Y	N	N	N
2 Pastor	N	Y	Y	Y	Y	N	N	N
3 *Stump*	Y	N	Y	Y	N	Y	Y	Y
4 *Kyl*	Y	N	Y	N	Y	Y	Y	Y
5 *Kolbe*	Y	Y	Y	Y	Y	N	N	N
6 English	N	Y	+	+	Y	N	N	N
ARKANSAS								
1 Lambert	N	Y	Y	Y	Y	N	N	N
2 Thornton	?	?	Y	N	N	N	N	N
3 *Hutchinson*	Y	N	Y	N	N	Y	N	N
4 *Dickey*	Y	N	?	Y	Y	Y	N	N
CALIFORNIA								
1 Hamburg	N	Y	Y	Y	N	N	N	N
2 *Herger*	Y	N	N	Y	Y	Y	Y	N
3 Fazio	N	Y	Y	N	N	N	N	N
4 *Doolittle*	Y	N	N	Y	Y	Y	Y	Y
5 Matsui	N	Y	Y	N	N	N	N	N
6 Woolsey	N	Y	Y	Y	N	N	N	N
7 Miller	N	Y	Y	Y	N	N	N	N
8 Pelosi	N	Y	Y	Y	N	N	N	N
9 Dellums	N	Y	Y	Y	N	N	N	N
10 Baker	Y	N	Y	N	Y	N	Y	N
11 *Pombo*	Y	N	Y	N	N	N	N	N
12 Lantos	N	Y	Y	Y	N	N	N	N
13 Stark	N	Y	N	Y	N	N	N	N
14 Eshoo	N	Y	+	Y	N	N	N	Y
15 Mineta	N	Y	Y	Y	N	N	N	N
16 Edwards	N	Y	Y	Y	N	N	N	N
17 Farr	N	Y	Y	Y	N	N	N	N
18 Condit	Y	Y	N	Y	Y	N	N	Y
19 Lehman	N	Y	Y	Y	N	N	N	N
20 Dooley	N	Y	Y	Y	Y	N	N	N
21 *Thomas*	Y	N	Y	N	N	N	N	N
22 *Huffington*	Y	N	Y	N	N	N	N	N
23 *Gallegly*	Y	N	Y	Y	N	N	N	Y
24 Beilenson	N	Y	Y	Y	N	N	N	N
25 *McKeon*	Y	N	−	+	X	Y	Y	N
26 Berman	N	Y	Y	Y	N	N	N	N
27 *Moorhead*	Y	N	N	Y	N	Y	N	Y
28 *Dreier*	Y	N	N	Y	N	Y	Y	Y
29 Waxman	N	Y	Y	N	Y	N	N	N
30 Becerra	N	Y	Y	Y	N	N	N	N
31 Martinez	N	Y	Y	Y	N	N	N	N
32 Dixon	N	Y	Y	Y	N	N	N	N
33 Roybal-Allard	N	Y	Y	Y	N	N	N	N
34 Torres	N	Y	Y	Y	N	N	N	N
35 Waters	N	Y	Y	Y	N	N	N	N
36 Harman	?	?	Y	Y	N	N	N	N
37 Tucker	N	Y	Y	Y	N	?	?	?
38 *Horn*	Y	Y	Y	Y	N	N	N	N
39 *Royce*	Y	N	N	Y	N	Y	Y	Y
40 *Lewis*	Y	Y	Y	Y	N	N	N	N
41 *Kim*	Y	N	Y	Y	N	Y	Y	Y

	259	260	261	262	263	264	265	266
42 Brown	N	Y	Y	Y	N	N	N	N
43 *Calvert*	Y	N	Y	Y	N	N	N	N
44 *McCandless*	Y	N	Y	N	Y	N	N	Y
45 *Rohrabacher*	Y	N	N	N	Y	Y	Y	Y
46 *Dornan*	Y	N	N	Y	N	Y	N	N
47 *Cox*	Y	N	Y	N	Y	N	N	Y
48 *Packard*	Y	N	Y	Y	N	Y	N	N
49 Schenk	N	Y	Y	Y	Y	N	N	N
50 Filner	N	Y	Y	Y	N	N	N	N
51 *Cunningham*	Y	N	Y	N	Y	N	Y	Y
52 *Hunter*	Y	N	Y	N	Y	Y	Y	Y
COLORADO								
1 Schroeder	N	Y	Y	Y	Y	N	N	Y
2 Skaggs	N	Y	Y	Y	N	N	N	N
3 *McInnis*	Y	N	Y	N	Y	N	Y	N
4 *Allard*	Y	N	N	Y	Y	Y	Y	Y
5 *Hefley*	Y	N	Y	N	Y	N	Y	?
6 *Schaefer*	Y	N	N	Y	Y	Y	N	Y
CONNECTICUT								
1 Kennelly	N	Y	Y	Y	N	N	N	N
2 Gejdenson	N	Y	Y	Y	N	N	N	N
3 DeLauro	N	Y	Y	Y	N	N	N	N
4 *Shays*	Y	N	Y	Y	Y	N	Y	Y
5 *Franks*	Y	N	Y	Y	N	N	Y	Y
6 *Johnson*	Y	Y	Y	Y	N	Y	N	Y
DELAWARE								
AL *Castle*	Y	N	Y	Y	N	Y	N	Y
FLORIDA								
1 Hutto	N	N	Y	Y	N	N	N	Y
2 Peterson	N	Y	Y	Y	N	N	N	N
3 Brown	N	Y	Y	Y	N	N	N	N
4 *Fowler*	Y	Y	Y	Y	N	N	N	Y
5 Thurman	N	Y	N	Y	N	N	N	N
6 *Stearns*	Y	N	Y	N	Y	N	Y	Y
7 *Mica*	Y	Y	Y	Y	N	N	Y	?
8 *McCollum*	Y	N	Y	N	Y	N	Y	Y
9 *Bilirakis*	Y	N	Y	N	Y	N	N	N
10 *Young*	Y	N	Y	N	N	N	N	N
11 Gibbons	N	Y	Y	Y	N	N	N	N
12 *Canady*	Y	N	Y	N	N	N	N	Y
13 *Miller*	Y	N	N	Y	N	N	Y	Y
14 *Goss*	Y	N	N	Y	N	N	N	Y
15 Bacchus	N	Y	Y	N	N	N	N	N
16 *Lewis*	Y	N	Y	N	N	N	Y	Y
17 Meek	?	#	Y	?	N	N	N	N
18 *Ros-Lehtinen*	Y	N	Y	N	N	N	N	Y
19 Johnston	N	Y	Y	Y	N	N	N	N
20 Deutsch	N	Y	Y	N	N	N	N	N
21 *Diaz-Balart*	Y	N	Y	N	N	N	N	Y
22 *Shaw*	Y	Y	Y	N	N	N	N	Y
23 Hastings	N	Y	Y	Y	N	N	N	N
GEORGIA								
1 *Kingston*	Y	Y	Y	Y	Y	Y	Y	Y
2 Bishop	N	Y	Y	Y	N	N	N	N
3 *Collins*	Y	N	Y	Y	Y	Y	Y	Y
4 *Linder*	Y	N	N	Y	N	N	N	N
5 Lewis	N	Y	Y	Y	N	N	N	N
6 *Gingrich*	Y	N	Y	N	Y	?	Y	Y
7 Darden	N	Y	Y	Y	N	N	N	N
8 Rowland	N	Y	Y	Y	N	N	N	N
9 Deal	N	Y	N	Y	N	N	N	Y
10 Johnson	N	Y	Y	Y	N	N	N	Y
11 McKinney	N	Y	Y	Y	N	N	N	N
HAWAII								
1 Abercrombie	N	Y	Y	N	N	N	N	N
2 Mink	N	Y	Y	Y	Y	N	N	N
IDAHO								
1 LaRocco	N	Y	Y	Y	N	N	N	N
2 *Crapo*	Y	N	N	Y	N	N	Y	Y
ILLINOIS								
1 Rush	?	?	?	Y	Y	N	N	N
2 Reynolds	N	Y	Y	Y	N	N	N	N
3 Lipinski	N	Y	Y	Y	N	N	N	N
4 Gutierrez	N	Y	Y	Y	N	N	N	N
5 Rostenkowski	N	Y	Y	Y	N	N	N	N
6 *Hyde*	Y	N	Y	N	N	N	N	?
7 Collins	N	Y	Y	?	Y	N	N	N
8 *Crane*	Y	N	N	Y	N	Y	Y	Y
9 Yates	N	Y	Y	Y	N	N	N	N
10 *Porter*	Y	?	Y	Y	Y	Y	Y	Y
11 Sangmeister	N	Y	Y	Y	N	N	N	N
12 Costello	N	Y	Y	Y	N	N	N	N
13 *Fawell*	Y	N	N	Y	Y	Y	Y	Y
14 *Hastert*	Y	N	Y	Y	N	Y	Y	N
15 *Ewing*	Y	N	Y	Y	N	Y	N	Y
16 *Manzullo*	Y	N	Y	Y	Y	N	N	Y
17 Evans	N	Y	Y	Y	Y	N	N	N

ND Northern Democrats   SD Southern Democrats

	259	260	261	262	263	264	265	266
18 ***Michel***	Y	N	Y	Y	N	N	N	Y
19 Poshard	N	Y	Y	Y	Y	N	N	N
20 Durbin	N	Y	Y	Y	Y	N	N	N
INDIANA								
1 Visclosky	N	Y	Y	Y	Y	N	N	N
2 Sharp	Y	N	?	?	Y	N	N	N
3 Roemer	N	Y	Y	N	Y	N	N	N
4 Long	N	Y	Y	Y	Y	N	N	N
5 ***Buyer***	Y	N	Y	Y	N	Y	Y	Y
6 ***Burton***	Y	N	N	Y	N	Y	Y	Y
7 ***Myers***	Y	N	Y	Y	N	N	N	N
8 McCloskey	N	Y	Y	Y	Y	N	N	N
9 Hamilton	Y	Y	Y	Y	Y	N	N	N
10 Jacobs	Y	N	N	Y	Y	Y	Y	Y
IOWA								
1 ***Leach***	Y	N	Y	Y	Y	N	Y	Y
2 ***Nussle***	Y	N	N	Y	Y	Y	Y	Y
3 ***Lightfoot***	Y	Y	Y	Y	N	N	N	Y
4 Smith	N	Y	Y	Y	N	N	N	N
5 ***Grandy***	Y	Y	Y	Y	Y	Y	Y	Y
KANSAS								
1 ***Roberts***	#	X	Y	Y	N	N	Y	N
2 Slattery	N	Y	Y	Y	N	N	Y	Y
3 ***Meyers***	Y	N	Y	Y	N	N	N	Y
4 Glickman	N	Y	Y	Y	N	N	Y	Y
KENTUCKY								
1 Barlow	N	Y	Y	Y	Y	N	N	N
2 Natcher	N	Y	Y	Y	N	N	N	N
3 Mazzoli	N	Y	Y	Y	Y	N	N	N
4 ***Bunning***	Y	N	N	Y	Y	Y	N	Y
5 ***Rogers***	Y	Y	Y	Y	N	N	N	N
6 Baesler	N	Y	Y	Y	Y	N	N	N
LOUISIANA								
1 ***Livingston***	N	Y	Y	Y	N	N	N	N
2 Jefferson	N	Y	Y	Y	N	N	N	N
3 Tauzin	Y	Y	?	Y	Y	N	N	N
4 Fields	N	Y	Y	Y	Y	N	N	N
5 ***McCrery***	Y	N	Y	Y	N	Y	N	N
6 ***Baker***	Y	N	N	Y	N	Y	N	Y
7 Hayes	?	?	?	?	N	N	N	N
MAINE								
1 Andrews	N	Y	Y	Y	Y	N	?	N
2 ***Snowe***	Y	N	Y	Y	Y	N	Y	Y
MARYLAND								
1 ***Gilchrest***	Y	Y	Y	Y	N	N	N	Y
2 ***Bentley***	N	Y	Y	Y	N	N	N	Y
3 Cardin	N	Y	Y	Y	Y	N	N	N
4 Wynn	N	Y	Y	Y	Y	N	N	N
5 Hoyer	N	Y	Y	Y	N	N	N	N
6 ***Bartlett***	Y	N	Y	Y	N	Y	Y	Y
7 Mfume	N	Y	Y	Y	Y	?	N	N
8 ***Morella***	N	Y	Y	Y	N	N	N	N
MASSACHUSETTS								
1 Olver	N	Y	Y	Y	Y	N	N	N
2 Neal	N	Y	Y	Y	N	N	N	N
3 ***Blute***	Y	N	Y	Y	Y	Y	Y	Y
4 Frank	N	Y	?	Y	Y	N	N	N
5 Meehan	N	Y	Y	Y	Y	N	N	N
6 ***Torkildsen***	Y	N	N	Y	N	Y	Y	Y
7 Markey	N	Y	Y	Y	Y	N	N	N
8 Kennedy	N	Y	Y	Y	Y	N	N	N
9 Moakley	N	Y	Y	Y	Y	N	N	N
10 Studds	N	Y	Y	Y	Y	N	N	N
MICHIGAN								
1 Stupak	N	Y	Y	Y	Y	N	N	N
2 ***Hoekstra***	Y	N	N	Y	Y	Y	Y	Y
3 Henry	?	?	?	?	?	?	?	?
4 ***Camp***	Y	N	Y	Y	Y	Y	Y	Y
5 Barcia	N	Y	Y	Y	N	N	N	N
6 ***Upton***	Y	N	N	Y	Y	Y	Y	Y
7 ***Smith***	Y	N	Y	Y	Y	?	N	Y
8 Carr	N	Y	Y	Y	N	N	N	N
9 Kildee	N	Y	Y	Y	Y	N	N	N
10 Bonior	N	Y	?	Y	N	N	N	N
11 ***Knollenberg***	Y	N	N	Y	Y	Y	Y	Y
12 Levin	N	Y	Y	Y	Y	N	N	N
13 Ford	N	Y	Y	Y	Y	N	?	N
14 Conyers	?	?	Y	Y	Y	N	N	N
15 Collins	N	Y	Y	Y	Y	N	N	N
16 Dingell	N	Y	Y	Y	Y	N	N	N
MINNESOTA								
1 Penny	Y	Y	N	Y	Y	N	Y	Y
2 Minge	N	N	N	Y	Y	Y	N	Y
3 ***Ramstad***	Y	N	Y	Y	Y	Y	Y	Y
4 Vento	N	Y	N	Y	Y	N	N	N

	259	260	261	262	263	264	265	266
5 Sabo	N	Y	Y	Y	Y	N	N	N
6 ***Grams***	Y	N	N	Y	N	Y	N	N
7 Peterson	N	N	Y	Y	Y	N	N	Y
8 Oberstar	N	Y	Y	Y	Y	N	N	N
MISSISSIPPI								
1 Whitten	?	?	Y	Y	N	N	N	N
2 Thompson	N	Y	Y	Y	Y	?	?	?
3 Montgomery	N	Y	Y	Y	N	N	N	N
4 Parker	N	Y	Y	Y	N	N	N	N
5 Taylor	N	N	Y	Y	N	N	N	N
MISSOURI								
1 Clay	N	Y	Y	N	N	N	N	N
2 ***Talent***	Y	N	N	Y	N	N	N	Y
3 Gephardt	N	Y	Y	Y	N	N	N	N
4 Skelton	N	Y	Y	Y	Y	N	N	N
5 Wheat	N	Y	Y	Y	Y	N	N	N
6 Danner	N	Y	Y	Y	Y	Y	N	N
7 ***Hancock***	Y	N	N	Y	N	Y	Y	Y
8 ***Emerson***	Y	Y	Y	Y	N	N	N	N
9 Volkmer	Y	N	Y	Y	N	Y	N	N
MONTANA								
AL Williams	N	Y	Y	Y	Y	N	N	N
NEBRASKA								
1 ***Bereuter***	Y	N	Y	Y	Y	Y	Y	Y
2 Hoagland	N	Y	Y	Y	Y	N	Y	N
3 ***Barrett***	Y	N	Y	Y	N	N	N	N
NEVADA								
1 Bilbray	N	Y	Y	Y	Y	N	N	N
2 ***Vucanovich***	Y	N	Y	Y	Y	N	N	N
NEW HAMPSHIRE								
1 ***Zeliff***	Y	N	N	Y	N	Y	Y	Y
2 Swett	N	Y	Y	Y	Y	N	N	?
NEW JERSEY								
1 Andrews	N	Y	Y	Y	N	N	N	N
2 Hughes	N	N	Y	Y	Y	N	N	N
3 ***Saxton***	#	N	Y	Y	N	N	+	Y
4 ***Smith***	Y	N	Y	Y	N	N	N	N
5 ***Roukema***	Y	N	N	Y	Y	N	N	Y
6 Pallone	N	N	N	Y	Y	N	N	N
7 ***Franks***	Y	N	N	Y	Y	N	N	N
8 Klein	N	Y	N	Y	Y	N	N	N
9 Torricelli	?	?	Y	Y	N	N	N	N
10 Payne	N	Y	Y	Y	Y	N	N	N
11 ***Gallo***	Y	Y	Y	Y	N	N	N	N
12 ***Zimmer***	Y	N	Y	Y	Y	N	Y	Y
13 Menendez	N	Y	Y	Y	Y	N	N	N
NEW MEXICO								
1 ***Schiff***	Y	Y	Y	Y	N	N	N	N
2 ***Skeen***	Y	Y	+	+	X	—	—	—
3 Richardson	N	Y	Y	Y	Y	N	N	N
NEW YORK								
1 Hochbrueckner	N	Y	Y	Y	N	N	N	N
2 ***Lazio***	Y	N	N	Y	Y	N	N	Y
3 ***King***	Y	N	Y	Y	Y	Y	N	Y
4 ***Levy***	Y	N	Y	Y	Y	Y	N	Y
5 Ackerman	N	Y	Y	Y	Y	N	N	N
6 Flake	X	?	Y	Y	Y	N	N	N
7 Manton	N	Y	Y	Y	N	N	N	N
8 Nadler	N	Y	Y	Y	Y	N	N	N
9 Schumer	X	?	?	?	Y	?	?	N
10 Towns	N	Y	?	?	#	?	?	?
11 Owens	N	Y	Y	Y	Y	N	N	N
12 Velazquez	N	Y	Y	Y	Y	N	N	N
13 ***Molinari***	Y	N	Y	Y	Y	N	N	Y
14 Maloney	N	Y	Y	Y	Y	N	N	N
15 Rangel	N	Y	Y	Y	Y	N	N	N
16 Serrano	N	Y	Y	Y	Y	N	N	N
17 Engel	N	Y	Y	Y	N	?	—	—
18 Lowey	N	Y	Y	Y	Y	N	N	N
19 ***Fish***	Y	Y	Y	Y	Y	N	N	Y
20 ***Gilman***	Y	Y	Y	Y	N	N	N	Y
21 McNulty	N	Y	Y	Y	Y	N	Y	N
22 ***Solomon***	Y	Y	N	Y	Y	Y	Y	Y
23 ***Boehlert***	Y	Y	Y	Y	N	N	N	Y
24 ***McHugh***	Y	Y	Y	Y	Y	Y	Y	?
25 ***Walsh***	Y	Y	Y	Y	Y	N	N	N
26 Hinchey	N	Y	?	?	?	?	?	?
27 ***Paxon***	Y	N	N	Y	Y	Y	Y	?
28 Slaughter	N	Y	Y	Y	Y	N	N	N
29 LaFalce	N	Y	Y	Y	Y	N	N	N
30 ***Quinn***	Y	N	N	Y	N	Y	N	Y
31 ***Houghton***	Y	Y	Y	Y	N	N	Y	Y
NORTH CAROLINA								
1 Clayton	N	Y	Y	Y	Y	N	N	N
2 Valentine	N	Y	Y	Y	N	N	N	N

	259	260	261	262	263	264	265	266
3 Lancaster	N	Y	Y	Y	Y	N	N	N
4 Price	N	Y	Y	Y	Y	N	N	N
5 Neal	N	Y	Y	Y	Y	N	N	N
6 ***Coble***	Y	N	N	Y	Y	Y	Y	Y
7 Rose	N	Y	Y	Y	N	N	N	N
8 Hefner	N	Y	Y	Y	Y	N	N	N
9 ***McMillan***	Y	N	Y	Y	Y	N	N	Y
10 ***Ballenger***	Y	N	N	Y	Y	Y	Y	Y
11 ***Taylor***	Y	N	N	Y	N	Y	Y	Y
12 Watt	N	Y	Y	N	Y	N	N	N
NORTH DAKOTA								
AL Pomeroy	N	Y	N	Y	Y	N	N	N
OHIO								
1 Mann	N	Y	Y	Y	Y	N	N	N
2 ***Portman***	Y	N	N	Y	Y	N	Y	Y
3 Hall	N	Y	Y	Y	Y	Y	N	N
4 ***Oxley***	Y	N	Y	Y	N	N	Y	Y
5 ***Gillmor***	Y	N	Y	Y	N	N	N	N
6 Strickland	N	Y	Y	Y	Y	N	N	N
7 ***Hobson***	Y	Y	Y	Y	N	N	N	N
8 ***Boehner***	Y	N	N	Y	N	Y	Y	Y
9 Kaptur	N	Y	Y	Y	Y	N	N	N
10 ***Hoke***	Y	N	N	Y	N	Y	N	N
11 Stokes	N	Y	Y	Y	N	N	N	N
12 ***Kasich***	Y	N	Y	Y	Y	Y	N	N
13 Brown	N	Y	Y	Y	Y	N	N	N
14 Sawyer	N	Y	Y	Y	N	N	N	N
15 ***Pryce***	Y	N	Y	Y	N	Y	N	N
16 ***Regula***	Y	Y	Y	Y	N	N	N	N
17 Traficant	N	Y	Y	Y	N	N	N	N
18 Applegate	N	N	Y	Y	N	N	N	N
19 Fingerhut	Y	Y	N	Y	N	N	N	N
OKLAHOMA								
1 ***Inhofe***	Y	N	Y	Y	N	Y	Y	Y
2 Synar	—	+	+	+	+	—	—	—
3 Brewster	N	N	Y	Y	Y	N	N	N
4 McCurdy	N	Y	Y	Y	N	N	?	N
5 ***Istook***	Y	Y	N	Y	Y	Y	Y	Y
6 English	N	Y	Y	Y	Y	N	N	N
OREGON								
1 Furse	N	Y	Y	Y	Y	N	N	N
2 ***Smith***	Y	N	Y	Y	Y	Y	N	N
3 Wyden	N	Y	N	Y	Y	N	N	N
4 DeFazio	N	Y	N	Y	Y	N	N	N
5 Kopetski	N	Y	Y	Y	N	N	N	N
PENNSYLVANIA								
1 Foglietta	N	Y	Y	Y	Y	N	N	N
2 Blackwell	N	Y	Y	Y	Y	N	N	N
3 Borski	N	Y	Y	Y	N	?	N	N
4 Klink	N	Y	Y	Y	Y	N	N	N
5 ***Clinger***	Y	N	Y	Y	N	N	N	N
6 Holden	N	Y	Y	Y	Y	N	N	N
7 ***Weldon***	Y	N	Y	Y	N	Y	Y	Y
8 ***Greenwood***	Y	N	N	Y	N	N	Y	Y
9 ***Shuster***	Y	N	Y	Y	Y	N	N	N
10 ***McDade***	Y	Y	Y	Y	N	N	N	Y
11 Kanjorski	N	Y	Y	Y	Y	N	N	N
12 Murtha	N	Y	Y	Y	N	N	N	N
13 Margolies-Mezv.	N	Y	—	+	Y	N	N	N
14 Coyne	N	Y	Y	?	Y	N	N	N
15 McHale	N	Y	Y	Y	N	N	N	N
16 ***Walker***	Y	N	N	Y	N	Y	Y	Y
17 ***Gekas***	Y	N	Y	Y	Y	Y	Y	N
18 ***Santorum***	?	X	Y	Y	Y	Y	N	Y
19 ***Goodling***	?	?	Y	Y	Y	Y	Y	Y
20 Murphy	N	N	Y	Y	Y	Y	Y	Y
21 ***Ridge***	?	?	Y	Y	N	Y	Y	Y
RHODE ISLAND								
1 ***Machtley***	Y	N	Y	Y	Y	N	N	N
2 Reed	N	Y	Y	Y	Y	N	N	N
SOUTH CAROLINA								
1 ***Ravenel***	Y	Y	Y	Y	Y	N	N	N
2 ***Spence***	Y	N	Y	Y	N	N	Y	N
3 Derrick	?	#	?	?	#	N	N	N
4 ***Inglis***	Y	N	Y	Y	Y	Y	Y	Y
5 Spratt	N	Y	Y	Y	Y	N	N	N
6 Clyburn	N	Y	Y	Y	Y	N	N	N
SOUTH DAKOTA								
AL Johnson	N	Y	Y	Y	Y	N	N	N
TENNESSEE								
1 ***Quillen***	Y	Y	Y	Y	N	N	N	Y
2 ***Duncan***	Y	N	N	Y	Y	Y	Y	?
3 Lloyd	N	N	Y	Y	N	N	N	N
4 Cooper	Y	Y	Y	Y	N	N	Y	Y
5 Clement	N	Y	Y	Y	Y	N	N	N

	259	260	261	262	263	264	265	266
6 Gordon	N	Y	Y	Y	Y	N	N	N
7 ***Sundquist***	Y	N	Y	Y	Y	Y	Y	Y
8 Tanner	N	Y	Y	Y	N	Y	N	N
9 Ford	N	Y	Y	Y	Y	N	N	N
TEXAS								
1 Chapman	N	Y	Y	Y	N	N	N	N
2 Wilson	N	Y	Y	Y	N	N	N	N
3 ***Johnson, Sam***	Y	N	N	Y	N	N	Y	Y
4 Hall	Y	N	Y	Y	N	N	N	N
5 Bryant	N	Y	Y	Y	N	N	N	N
6 ***Barton***	Y	N	Y	Y	N	N	N	N
7 ***Archer***	Y	N	Y	Y	N	Y	Y	Y
8 ***Fields***	Y	N	Y	Y	N	N	N	Y
9 Brooks	N	Y	Y	Y	N	N	N	N
10 Pickle	N	Y	Y	Y	N	N	N	N
11 Edwards	N	N	Y	Y	N	N	N	N
12 Geren	N	Y	Y	Y	N	N	N	N
13 Sarpalius	N	N	Y	Y	N	N	N	N
14 Laughlin	N	Y	Y	Y	N	N	N	N
15 de la Garza	N	Y	Y	Y	N	N	N	N
16 Coleman	N	Y	Y	Y	N	N	N	N
17 Stenholm	Y	Y	Y	Y	N	N	N	Y
18 Washington	N	Y	N	N	Y	N	N	?
19 ***Combest***	Y	N	Y	Y	N	N	Y	Y
20 Gonzalez	N	Y	Y	Y	N	N	N	N
21 ***Smith***	Y	N	Y	Y	N	Y	Y	Y
22 ***DeLay***	Y	N	Y	Y	N	Y	N	Y
23 ***Bonilla***	Y	N	Y	Y	N	Y	Y	Y
24 Frost	N	Y	Y	Y	N	N	N	N
25 Andrews	N	Y	Y	Y	N	N	N	Y
26 ***Armey***	Y	N	Y	Y	N	N	Y	Y
27 Ortiz	N	Y	Y	Y	N	N	N	N
28 Tejeda	N	Y	Y	Y	N	N	N	N
29 Green	N	Y	Y	Y	N	N	N	N
30 Johnson, E. B.	N	Y	Y	Y	N	N	N	N
UTAH								
1 ***Hansen***	Y	N	Y	Y	N	?	Y	N
2 Shepherd	N	Y	N	Y	Y	N	N	N
3 Orton	N	Y	N	Y	Y	N	N	Y
VERMONT								
AL *Sanders*	N	Y	Y	Y	Y	N	N	N
VIRGINIA								
1 ***Bateman***	Y	Y	Y	Y	N	N	N	N
2 Pickett	N	Y	Y	Y	N	N	N	N
3 Scott	N	Y	Y	Y	N	N	N	N
4 Sisisky	N	Y	Y	Y	Y	N	N	N
5 Payne	N	Y	Y	Y	Y	N	N	Y
6 ***Goodlatte***	Y	N	Y	Y	Y	Y	N	Y
7 ***Bliley***	Y	Y	Y	Y	N	N	N	Y
8 Moran	N	Y	Y	Y	Y	N	N	N
9 Boucher	N	Y	Y	Y	N	N	N	N
10 ***Wolf***	Y	Y	Y	Y	N	Y	Y	Y
11 Byrne	N	Y	Y	Y	N	N	N	N
WASHINGTON								
1 Cantwell	Y	Y	Y	Y	Y	N	N	N
2 Swift	N	Y	Y	Y	N	N	N	N
3 Unsoeld	N	Y	Y	Y	Y	N	N	N
4 Inslee	Y	Y	Y	Y	Y	N	N	N
5 Foley								
6 Dicks	N	Y	Y	Y	N	N	N	N
7 McDermott	N	Y	+	+	N	N	N	N
8 ***Dunn***	Y	N	N	Y	N	Y	Y	Y
9 Kreidler	N	Y	Y	Y	Y	N	N	N
WEST VIRGINIA								
1 Mollohan	N	Y	Y	Y	N	N	N	N
2 Wise	N	Y	Y	Y	N	N	N	N
3 Rahall	N	N	N	Y	N	N	N	N
WISCONSIN								
1 Barca	N	N	Y	Y	Y	N	N	N
2 ***Klug***	Y	N	N	Y	N	N	Y	Y
3 ***Gunderson***	Y	N	Y	Y	Y	N	N	Y
4 Kleczka	?	Y	Y	Y	Y	N	N	N
5 Barrett	N	Y	Y	Y	Y	N	N	N
6 ***Petri***	Y	N	Y	Y	Y	Y	Y	Y
7 Obey	N	Y	Y	Y	Y	N	N	N
8 ***Roth***	Y	N	Y	Y	N	Y	Y	Y
9 ***Sensenbrenner***	Y	N	N	Y	N	Y	Y	Y
WYOMING								
AL ***Thomas***	Y	N	Y	Y	Y	Y	N	N
DELEGATES								
de Lugo, V.I.	D	D	D	Y	Y	N	N	N
Faleomavaega, Am.S.	D	D	D	?	?	?	?	?
Norton, D.C.	D	D	D	Y	Y	N	N	N
Romero-B., P.R.	D	D	D	Y	Y	N	N	N
Underwood, Guam	D	D	D	Y	Y	N	N	N

Southern states - Ala., Ark., Fla., Ga., Ky., La., Miss., N.C., Okla., S.C., Tenn., Texas, Va.
Omitted votes are quorum calls, which CQ does not include in its vote charts.

267. HR 2445. Fiscal 1994 Energy and Water Appropriations/Advanced Liquid Metal Reactor. Coppersmith, D-Ariz., amendment to strike $31.9 million to eliminate the Energy Department's advanced liquid metal reactor program. Adopted in Committee of the Whole 267-162: R 76-97; D 190-65 (ND 139-34, SD 51-31); I 1-0, June 24, 1993.

268. HR 2445. Fiscal 1994 Energy and Water Appropriations/Space Reactor. Markey, D-Mass., amendment to cut $25 million, leaving $5 million to terminate the Energy Department's SP-100 space reactor development program. Adopted in Committee of the Whole 333-98: R 112-62; D 220-36 (ND 161-12, SD 59-24); I 1-0, June 24, 1993.

269. HR 2445. Fiscal 1994 Energy and Water Appropriations/Superconducting Super Collider. Slattery, D-Kan., amendment to cut $400 million, leaving $220 million to terminate the superconducting super collider project. Adopted in Committee of the Whole 280-150: R 108-65; D 171-85 (ND 132-41, SD 39-44); I 1-0, June 24, 1993. A "nay" was a vote in support of the president's position.

270. HR 2445. Fiscal 1994 Energy and Water Appropriations/Advanced Liquid Metal Reactor. Separate vote at the request of Solomon, R-N.Y., on the amendment adopted in the Committee of the Whole offered by Coppersmith, D-Ariz., to strike $31.9 million to eliminate the Energy Department's advanced liquid metal reactor program. Adopted 272-146: R 76-93; D 195-53 (ND 138-27, SD 57-26); I 1-0, June 24, 1993. (On separate votes, which may be demanded on an amendment adopted in the Committee of the Whole, the four delegates and the resident commissioner of Puerto Rico cannot vote. See vote 267.)

271. HR 2445. Fiscal 1994 Energy and Water Appropriations/Space Reactor. Separate vote at the request of Solomon, R-N.Y., on the amendment adopted in the Committee of the Whole offered by Markey, D-Mass., to cut $25 million, leaving $5 million to terminate the Energy Department's SP-100 space reactor development program. Adopted 329-91: R 108-60; D 220-31 (ND 159-9, SD 61-22); I 1-0, June 24, 1993. (On separate votes, which may be demanded on an amendment adopted in the Committee of the Whole, the four delegates and the resident commissioner of Puerto Rico cannot vote. See vote 268.)

272. HR 2445. Fiscal 1994 Energy and Water Appropriations/Superconducting Super Collider. Separate vote at the request of Solomon, R-N.Y., on the amendment adopted in the Committee of the Whole offered by Slattery, D-Kan., to cut $400 million, leaving $220 million to terminate the superconducting super collider project. Adopted 280-141: R 107-62; D 172-79 (ND 132-36, SD 40-43); I 1-0, June 24, 1993. (On separate votes, which may be demanded on an amendment adopted in the Committee of the Whole, the four delegates and the resident commissioner of Puerto Rico cannot vote. See vote 269.) A "nay" was a vote in support of the president's position.

273. HR 2445. Fiscal 1994 Energy and Water Appropriations/Passage. Passage of the bill to provide $21.7 billion in new budget authority for energy and water development in fiscal 1994. The administration requested $22,238,648,000. Passed 350-73: R 101-69; D 248-4 (ND 166-3, SD 82-1); I 1-0, June 24, 1993.

274. HR 2491. Fiscal 1994 VA, HUD Appropriations/Rule. Adoption of the rule (H Res 208) to waive certain points of order against and provide for House floor consideration of the bill to provide $87,946,121,032 in new budget authority for the departments of Veterans Affairs and Housing and Urban Development and for other independent agencies, boards, commissions, corporations and offices in fiscal 1994. The administration requested $89,268,383,032. Adopted 206-132: R 23-123; D 183-9 (ND 123-2, SD 60-7); I 0-0, June 28, 1993.

KEY

Y	Voted for (yea).
#	Paired for.
+	Announced for.
N	Voted against (nay).
X	Paired against.
−	Announced against.
P	Voted "present."
C	Voted "present" to avoid possible conflict of interest.
?	Did not vote or otherwise make a position known.
D	Delegates ineligible to vote.

Democrats **Republicans**
Independent

	267	268	269	270	271	272	273	274
ALABAMA								
1 Callahan	N	N	N	N	N	N	Y	?
2 Everett	N	N	N	N	N	N	Y	?
3 Browder	N	N	N	N	N	N	Y	Y
4 Bevill	N	N	N	N	N	N	Y	Y
5 Cramer	N	N	N	N	N	N	Y	Y
6 Bachus	Y	N	N	N	N	N	Y	N
7 Hilliard	N	N	N	N	N	N	Y	Y
ALASKA								
AL Young	N	Y	N	N	Y	N	Y	Y
ARIZONA								
1 Coppersmith	Y	Y	Y	Y	Y	Y	Y	Y
2 Pastor	N	Y	N	N	Y	N	Y	N
3 Stump	N	N	N	N	N	N	N	N
4 Kyl	Y	N	Y	N	Y	Y	N	N
5 Kolbe	N	Y	N	N	Y	N	Y	N
6 English	Y	Y	Y	Y	Y	Y	Y	Y
ARKANSAS								
1 Lambert	Y	Y	Y	Y	Y	Y	Y	Y
2 Thornton	N	N	Y	N	Y	Y	Y	Y
3 Hutchinson	N	Y	N	Y	N	Y	N	N
4 Dickey	Y	Y	Y	Y	Y	Y	Y	N
CALIFORNIA								
1 Hamburg	Y	Y	Y	Y	Y	Y	Y	?
2 Herger	Y	Y	Y	Y	Y	Y	Y	N
3 Fazio	N	Y	N	N	Y	N	Y	Y
4 Doolittle	Y	Y	Y	Y	Y	Y	Y	N
5 Matsui	N	Y	N	N	Y	N	Y	Y
6 Woolsey	Y	Y	Y	Y	Y	Y	Y	Y
7 Miller	Y	Y	?	Y	Y	Y	Y	?
8 Pelosi	Y	Y	Y	Y	Y	Y	Y	?
9 Dellums	Y	Y	Y	Y	Y	Y	Y	?
10 Baker	N	N	Y	N	N	Y	N	N
11 Pombo	N	Y	N	Y	N	Y	N	N
12 Lantos	Y	Y	Y	Y	Y	Y	Y	?
13 Stark	Y	Y	Y	Y	Y	Y	Y	Y
14 Eshoo	Y	Y	Y	Y	Y	Y	Y	Y
15 Mineta	N	N	N	N	N	N	Y	Y
16 Edwards	Y	Y	Y	Y	N	Y	Y	Y
17 Farr	Y	Y	Y	Y	Y	Y	Y	?
18 Condit	Y	Y	Y	Y	Y	Y	Y	?
19 Lehman	Y	Y	Y	Y	Y	Y	Y	?
20 Dooley	Y	Y	Y	Y	Y	Y	Y	?
21 Thomas	N	N	N	N	N	N	N	N
22 Huffington	N	Y	Y	N	Y	N	N	N
23 Gallegly	N	Y	N	N	Y	N	Y	N
24 Beilenson	Y	Y	?	?	?	?	Y	Y
25 McKeon	N	N	Y	N	N	Y	N	N
26 Berman	Y	Y	Y	Y	Y	Y	Y	#
27 Moorhead	N	N	N	N	N	N	N	N
28 Dreier	N	N	N	N	N	N	N	N
29 Waxman	Y	Y	Y	Y	Y	Y	Y	?
30 Becerra	Y	Y	Y	Y	Y	Y	Y	?
31 Martinez	Y	Y	Y	Y	Y	Y	Y	Y
32 Dixon	Y	Y	N	Y	N	Y	Y	?
33 Roybal-Allard	Y	Y	Y	Y	Y	Y	Y	?
34 Torres	N	N	N	N	N	N	Y	?
35 Waters	Y	Y	Y	Y	Y	Y	Y	?
36 Harman	Y	Y	Y	Y	Y	Y	Y	?
~ 37 Tucker	?	#	#	?	#	#	?	?
38 Horn	N	N	N	N	N	N	Y	+
39 Royce	Y	Y	Y	Y	Y	Y	Y	N
40 Lewis	N	N	N	?	?	?	#	Y
41 Kim	Y	Y	Y	Y	Y	Y	Y	N

	267	268	269	270	271	272	273	274
42 Brown	Y	N	N	N	Y	N	Y	Y
43 Calvert	Y	Y	Y	Y	?	?	?	N
44 McCandless	Y	Y	Y	Y	Y	Y	Y	N
45 Rohrabacher	N	Y	N	Y	N	Y	N	N
46 Dornan	N	N	N	N	N	N	Y	?
47 Cox	Y	N	Y	?	?	N	Y	X
48 Packard	N	N	N	N	N	N	Y	N
49 Schenk	Y	N	N	N	Y	N	Y	?
50 Filner	Y	Y	Y	Y	Y	Y	Y	Y
51 Cunningham	Y	Y	N	?	?	N	N	N
52 Hunter	N	N	N	N	N	N	N	N
COLORADO								
1 Schroeder	Y	Y	Y	Y	Y	Y	Y	Y
2 Skaggs	Y	Y	Y	Y	Y	Y	Y	Y
3 McInnis	Y	Y	Y	Y	Y	Y	Y	N
4 Allard	Y	Y	Y	Y	Y	Y	Y	Y
5 Hefley	Y	Y	Y	Y	Y	Y	Y	N
6 Schaefer	N	Y	N	N	Y	N	Y	N
CONNECTICUT								
1 Kennelly	Y	Y	Y	Y	Y	Y	Y	Y
2 Gejdenson	Y	Y	Y	Y	Y	Y	Y	Y
3 DeLauro	Y	Y	Y	Y	Y	Y	Y	Y
4 Shays	Y	Y	Y	Y	Y	Y	Y	N
5 Franks	Y	Y	N	Y	N	N	N	N
6 Johnson	N	Y	N	N	Y	N	Y	Y
DELAWARE								
AL Castle	Y	Y	Y	Y	Y	Y	Y	N
FLORIDA								
1 Hutto	Y	Y	Y	Y	Y	Y	Y	Y
2 Peterson	N	Y	N	Y	N	Y	Y	Y
3 Brown	N	N	N	N	N	N	Y	?
4 Fowler	Y	N	Y	N	Y	Y	Y	Y
5 Thurman	Y	Y	Y	Y	Y	Y	Y	Y
6 Stearns	Y	N	Y	N	Y	N	X
7 Mica	N	N	N	N	N	N	N	—
8 McCollum	N	N	N	N	N	N	N	N
9 Bilirakis	N	N	Y	N	N	Y	N	N
10 Young	Y	N	Y	N	Y	Y	Y	N
11 Gibbons	N	Y	N	N	Y	N	Y	?
12 Canady	N	Y	N	Y	N	Y	N	N
13 Miller	Y	Y	Y	Y	Y	N	Y	N
14 Goss	N	Y	N	Y	N	Y	N	N
15 Bacchus	Y	N	N	Y	N	N	Y	Y
16 Lewis	N	N	Y	N	N	Y	N	N
17 Meek	N	N	N	N	N	N	Y	?
18 Ros-Lehtinen	N	Y	N	N	Y	N	Y	N
19 Johnston	Y	Y	Y	Y	Y	Y	Y	Y
20 Deutsch	Y	Y	Y	Y	Y	Y	Y	Y
21 Diaz-Balart	Y	N	N	Y	N	N	Y	N
22 Shaw	N	N	Y	N	N	Y	Y	N
23 Hastings	Y	N	N	Y	N	N	Y	Y
GEORGIA								
1 Kingston	N	Y	N	Y	N	Y	N	N
2 Bishop	Y	N	Y	N	Y	N	Y	N
3 Collins	Y	Y	Y	Y	Y	N	Y	X
4 Linder	Y	Y	Y	Y	N	Y	N	N
5 Lewis	Y	Y	Y	Y	Y	Y	Y	Y
6 Gingrich	N	N	N	N	N	N	N	?
7 Darden	Y	N	Y	N	Y	N	Y	Y
8 Rowland	Y	Y	Y	Y	Y	Y	Y	Y
9 Deal	Y	Y	Y	Y	Y	Y	Y	?
10 Johnson	Y	Y	Y	Y	Y	Y	Y	?
11 McKinney	Y	Y	Y	Y	Y	Y	Y	Y
HAWAII								
1 Abercrombie	N	N	Y	Y	Y	Y	Y	Y
2 Mink	Y	Y	Y	Y	Y	Y	Y	Y
IDAHO								
1 LaRocco	N	Y	N	N	Y	N	Y	?
2 Crapo	N	N	N	N	N	N	N	N
ILLINOIS								
1 Rush	Y	Y	N	Y	Y	N	Y	?
2 Reynolds	Y	Y	N	Y	Y	N	Y	Y
3 Lipinski	Y	Y	Y	Y	Y	Y	Y	Y
4 Gutierrez	Y	Y	Y	Y	Y	Y	Y	Y
5 Rostenkowski	N	Y	Y	N	Y	Y	Y	Y
6 Hyde	N	N	N	N	N	N	Y	N
7 Collins	Y	Y	Y	Y	Y	Y	Y	Y
8 Crane	N	Y	N	N	Y	N	Y	?
9 Yates	N	Y	N	N	Y	N	Y	Y
10 Porter	N	Y	N	N	Y	Y	Y	N
11 Sangmeister	N	Y	Y	N	Y	Y	Y	#
12 Costello	Y	Y	Y	Y	Y	Y	Y	Y
13 Fawell	N	Y	N	N	Y	N	N	N
14 Hastert	N	Y	N	N	Y	N	Y	N
15 Ewing	N	Y	N	Y	N	Y	N	N
16 Manzullo	N	Y	N	Y	N	Y	N	N
17 Evans	Y	Y	Y	Y	Y	Y	Y	Y

ND Northern Democrats   SD Southern Democrats

	267	268	269	270	271	272	273	274
18 ***Michel***	N	N	N	N	N	N	N	N
19 Poshard	Y	Y	Y	Y	Y	Y	Y	Y
20 Durbin	N	Y	Y	N	Y	Y	Y	Y
INDIANA								
1 Visclosky	N	Y	Y	N	Y	Y	Y	Y
2 Sharp	Y	Y	Y	Y	Y	Y	Y	Y
3 Roemer	Y	Y	N	Y	Y	N	Y	Y
4 Long	Y	Y	Y	Y	Y	Y	Y	Y
5 ***Buyer***	N	Y	N	N	Y	N	N	N
6 ***Burton***	N	Y	Y	N	Y	Y	N	N
7 ***Myers***	N	N	N	N	N	N	Y	N
8 McCloskey	Y	Y	N	Y	Y	N	Y	Y
9 Hamilton	Y	Y	Y	Y	Y	Y	Y	Y
10 Jacobs	Y	Y	Y	Y	Y	Y	N	Y
IOWA								
1 ***Leach***	N	Y	Y	N	Y	Y	Y	N
2 ***Nussle***	Y	Y	Y	Y	Y	Y	Y	Y
3 ***Lightfoot***	N	N	N	N	N	N	Y	N
4 Smith	N	N	N	N	N	N	Y	Y
5 ***Grandy***	Y	Y	Y	Y	Y	Y	Y	N
KANSAS								
1 ***Roberts***	N	Y	N	N	Y	N	N	N
2 Slattery	Y	Y	Y	Y	Y	Y	Y	Y
3 ***Meyers***	Y	Y	Y	Y	Y	Y	Y	N
4 Glickman	Y	Y	Y	Y	Y	Y	Y	Y
KENTUCKY								
1 Barlow	Y	Y	Y	Y	Y	Y	Y	Y
2 Natcher	N	N	N	N	N	N	Y	Y
3 Mazzoli	N	Y	Y	Y	Y	Y	Y	Y
4 ***Bunning***	Y	Y	Y	Y	Y	Y	Y	N
5 ***Rogers***	—	N	N	N	N	N	Y	N
6 Baesler	Y	Y	Y	Y	Y	Y	Y	+
LOUISIANA								
1 ***Livingston***	N	N	N	N	N	N	Y	N
2 Jefferson	Y	Y	Y	Y	Y	Y	Y	Y
3 Tauzin	Y	Y	Y	Y	Y	Y	Y	Y
4 Fields	Y	Y	N	Y	Y	N	Y	Y
5 ***McCrery***	N	Y	N	N	Y	N	Y	N
6 ***Baker***	N	Y	N	N	Y	N	N	N
7 Hayes	N	N	N	N	N	N	Y	Y
MAINE								
1 Andrews	Y	Y	Y	Y	Y	Y	Y	?
2 ***Snowe***	Y	Y	Y	Y	Y	Y	Y	N
MARYLAND								
1 ***Gilchrest***	Y	Y	N	Y	Y	N	Y	N
2 ***Bentley***	N	N	N	N	N	N	Y	N
3 Cardin	Y	Y	Y	Y	Y	Y	Y	?
4 Wynn	Y	Y	Y	Y	Y	Y	Y	Y
5 Hoyer	N	Y	N	N	Y	N	Y	Y
6 ***Bartlett***	N	N	N	N	N	N	N	N
7 Mfume	Y	Y	Y	Y	Y	Y	Y	?
8 ***Morella***	Y	Y	Y	Y	Y	Y	Y	N
MASSACHUSETTS								
1 Olver	Y	Y	Y	Y	Y	Y	Y	Y
2 Neal	Y	Y	Y	Y	Y	Y	Y	?
3 ***Blute***	Y	Y	N	Y	Y	N	Y	—
4 Frank	Y	Y	Y	Y	Y	Y	Y	Y
5 Meehan	Y	Y	Y	Y	Y	Y	Y	Y
6 ***Torkildsen***	Y	Y	Y	Y	Y	Y	N	?
7 Markey	Y	Y	Y	Y	Y	Y	Y	Y
8 Kennedy	Y	Y	Y	Y	Y	Y	Y	?
9 Moakley	Y	Y	Y	Y	Y	Y	Y	Y
10 Studds	Y	Y	Y	Y	Y	Y	Y	Y
MICHIGAN								
1 Stupak	Y	Y	Y	Y	Y	Y	Y	Y
2 ***Hoekstra***	Y	Y	Y	Y	Y	Y	Y	N
3 Henry	?	?	?	?	?	?	?	?
4 ***Camp***	N	Y	Y	N	Y	Y	Y	N
5 Barcia	Y	Y	Y	Y	Y	Y	Y	Y
6 ***Upton***	Y	Y	Y	Y	Y	Y	Y	N
7 ***Smith***	Y	N	Y	Y	Y	Y	N	N
8 Carr	N	Y	Y	N	Y	Y	Y	Y
9 Kildee	N	Y	Y	N	Y	Y	Y	Y
10 Bonior	N	Y	N	N	Y	N	Y	Y
11 ***Knollenberg***	N	Y	Y	N	Y	Y	N	N
12 Levin	Y	Y	Y	Y	Y	Y	Y	Y
13 Ford	Y	Y	Y	Y	Y	Y	Y	Y
14 Conyers	Y	Y	Y	Y	Y	Y	Y	?
15 Collins	Y	Y	Y	Y	Y	Y	Y	Y
16 Dingell	Y	Y	Y	?	Y	Y	Y	Y
MINNESOTA								
1 Penny	Y	Y	Y	Y	Y	Y	Y	Y
2 Minge	Y	Y	Y	Y	Y	Y	N	Y
3 ***Ramstad***	Y	Y	Y	Y	Y	Y	N	N
4 Vento	Y	Y	Y	Y	Y	Y	Y	?

	267	268	269	270	271	272	273	274
5 Sabo	Y	Y	Y	Y	Y	Y	Y	Y
6 ***Grams***	N	N	N	N	N	N	Y	N
7 Peterson	Y	Y	Y	Y	Y	Y	Y	Y
8 Oberstar	Y	Y	Y	Y	Y	Y	Y	Y
MISSISSIPPI								
1 Whitten	?	N	N	N	N	N	Y	Y
2 Thompson	?	?	?	?	?	?	X	Y
3 Montgomery	N	Y	Y	Y	Y	Y	Y	Y
4 Parker	Y	Y	Y	Y	Y	Y	Y	?
5 Taylor	Y	Y	Y	Y	Y	Y	Y	N
MISSOURI								
1 Clay	Y	Y	Y	Y	Y	Y	Y	Y
2 ***Talent***	Y	Y	Y	Y	Y	Y	Y	N
3 Gephardt	N	Y	N	N	Y	N	Y	Y
4 Skelton	N	Y	N	Y	Y	N	Y	Y
5 Wheat	Y	Y	Y	Y	Y	Y	Y	Y
6 Danner	Y	Y	Y	Y	Y	Y	Y	Y
7 ***Hancock***	N	Y	Y	N	Y	Y	N	N
8 ***Emerson***	N	Y	N	N	N	N	Y	N
9 Volkmer	N	Y	N	N	Y	N	Y	Y
MONTANA								
AL Williams	Y	Y	Y	Y	Y	Y	Y	?
NEBRASKA								
1 ***Bereuter***	N	N	Y	N	N	Y	Y	?
2 Hoagland	Y	Y	Y	Y	Y	Y	Y	Y
3 ***Barrett***	N	Y	Y	N	Y	Y	Y	N
NEVADA								
1 Bilbray	N	Y	Y	N	Y	Y	Y	N
2 ***Vucanovich***	N	Y	N	N	Y	Y	Y	N
NEW HAMPSHIRE								
1 ***Zeliff***	Y	Y	Y	Y	Y	Y	N	N
2 Swett	Y	Y	Y	Y	Y	Y	Y	?
NEW JERSEY								
1 Andrews	Y	Y	N	?	Y	N	Y	Y
2 Hughes	Y	Y	Y	Y	Y	Y	Y	Y
3 ***Saxton***	Y	Y	Y	Y	Y	Y	N	N
4 ***Smith***	Y	Y	Y	Y	Y	Y	Y	?
5 ***Roukema***	Y	Y	Y	Y	Y	Y	Y	N
6 Pallone	Y	Y	Y	Y	Y	Y	Y	Y
7 ***Franks***	N	N	N	N	N	N	Y	N
8 Klein	Y	Y	Y	Y	Y	Y	Y	Y
9 Torricelli	N	N	N	N	N	N	Y	?
10 Payne	Y	Y	Y	Y	Y	Y	Y	?
11 ***Gallo***	N	N	N	N	N	N	Y	Y
12 ***Zimmer***	Y	Y	Y	Y	Y	Y	Y	N
13 Menendez	Y	Y	Y	Y	Y	Y	Y	?
NEW MEXICO								
1 ***Schiff***	N	N	N	N	N	N	Y	?
2 ***Skeen***	—	X	—	—	X	—	+	X
3 Richardson	Y	Y	Y	Y	Y	Y	Y	#
NEW YORK								
1 Hochbrueckner	N	Y	N	N	Y	N	Y	Y
2 ***Lazio***	Y	Y	Y	Y	Y	Y	Y	N
3 ***King***	Y	N	Y	Y	N	Y	Y	N
4 ***Levy***	N	Y	Y	N	Y	Y	Y	N
5 Ackerman	Y	Y	N	Y	Y	N	Y	?
6 Flake	Y	Y	Y	Y	Y	Y	Y	?
7 Manton	Y	Y	X	?	#	X	#	#
8 Nadler	Y	Y	N	Y	Y	N	Y	Y
9 Schumer	Y	Y	Y	Y	Y	Y	Y	Y
10 Towns	Y	Y	N	Y	Y	N	Y	?
11 Owens	Y	Y	Y	Y	Y	Y	Y	?
12 Velazquez	Y	Y	Y	Y	Y	Y	Y	?
13 ***Molinari***	Y	Y	Y	Y	Y	Y	Y	N
14 Maloney	Y	Y	Y	Y	Y	Y	Y	Y
15 Rangel	Y	Y	Y	Y	Y	Y	Y	#
16 Serrano	Y	Y	Y	Y	Y	Y	Y	?
17 Engel	+	+	Y	Y	Y	Y	Y	+
18 Lowey	Y	Y	N	Y	Y	N	Y	Y
19 ***Fish***	Y	Y	Y	Y	Y	Y	Y	N
20 ***Gilman***	Y	Y	Y	Y	Y	Y	Y	—
21 McNulty	Y	Y	N	Y	Y	N	Y	Y
22 ***Solomon***	N	N	Y	N	N	Y	N	N
23 ***Boehlert***	Y	Y	Y	Y	Y	Y	Y	?
24 ***McHugh***	N	Y	Y	N	Y	?	Y	N
25 ***Walsh***	Y	Y	Y	Y	Y	Y	Y	N
26 Hinchey	?	?	?	?	?	?	?	Y
27 ***Paxon***	N	Y	Y	Y	Y	Y	N	N
28 Slaughter	Y	Y	Y	Y	Y	Y	Y	Y
29 LaFalce	Y	Y	Y	Y	Y	Y	Y	Y
30 ***Quinn***	N	Y	Y	N	Y	Y	Y	Y
31 ***Houghton***	N	Y	Y	N	N	Y	Y	N
NORTH CAROLINA								
1 Clayton	Y	Y	Y	Y	Y	Y	Y	Y
2 Valentine	N	Y	Y	Y	Y	Y	Y	Y

	267	268	269	270	271	272	273	274
3 Lancaster	Y	Y	Y	Y	Y	Y	Y	Y
4 Price	Y	Y	Y	Y	Y	Y	Y	Y
5 Neal	Y	Y	Y	Y	Y	Y	N	Y
6 ***Coble***	Y	Y	Y	Y	Y	Y	N	N
7 Rose	N	N	N	N	N	N	Y	Y
8 Hefner	Y	Y	Y	Y	Y	Y	Y	Y
9 ***McMillan***	N	Y	Y	N	Y	Y	N	?
10 ***Ballenger***	Y	Y	Y	Y	Y	Y	Y	—
11 ***Taylor***	N	Y	N	N	Y	N	N	N
12 Watt	Y	Y	Y	Y	Y	Y	Y	Y
NORTH DAKOTA								
AL Pomeroy	Y	Y	Y	Y	Y	Y	Y	Y
OHIO								
1 Mann	Y	Y	Y	Y	Y	Y	Y	?
2 ***Portman***	N	Y	Y	N	Y	Y	N	—
3 Hall	Y	Y	Y	Y	Y	Y	Y	Y
4 ***Oxley***	N	N	N	N	N	N	N	Y
5 ***Gillmor***	Y	Y	Y	Y	Y	Y	N	?
6 Strickland	N	Y	Y	N	Y	Y	Y	Y
7 ***Hobson***	Y	Y	Y	Y	Y	Y	Y	N
8 ***Boehner***	N	N	N	N	N	N	N	—
9 Kaptur	Y	Y	Y	Y	Y	Y	Y	Y
10 ***Hoke***	Y	Y	Y	Y	Y	Y	N	Y
11 Stokes	N	Y	Y	Y	Y	Y	Y	Y
12 ***Kasich***	Y	Y	?	?	?	?	?	N
13 Brown	Y	Y	Y	Y	Y	Y	Y	?
14 Sawyer	Y	Y	Y	Y	Y	Y	Y	?
15 ***Pryce***	Y	Y	Y	Y	Y	Y	Y	N
16 ***Regula***	Y	Y	Y	Y	Y	Y	Y	N
17 Traficant	N	N	N	N	N	N	Y	Y
18 Applegate	N	Y	Y	N	Y	Y	Y	?
19 Fingerhut	Y	Y	Y	Y	Y	Y	Y	Y
OKLAHOMA								
1 ***Inhofe***	N	Y	Y	Y	Y	Y	N	N
2 Synar	+	+	+	+	+	+	+	Y
3 Brewster	Y	Y	Y	Y	Y	Y	Y	Y
4 McCurdy	Y	Y	Y	Y	Y	Y	Y	?
5 ***Istook***	N	Y	Y	N	Y	Y	Y	—
6 English	Y	Y	Y	Y	Y	Y	Y	Y
OREGON								
1 Furse	Y	Y	N	Y	Y	N	Y	Y
2 ***Smith***	N	N	Y	N	N	Y	Y	Y
3 Wyden	Y	Y	Y	Y	Y	Y	Y	Y
4 DeFazio	Y	Y	Y	Y	Y	Y	Y	Y
5 Kopetski	Y	Y	N	Y	Y	N	Y	Y
PENNSYLVANIA								
1 Foglietta	N	Y	Y	Y	Y	Y	Y	?
2 Blackwell	N	Y	N	Y	Y	Y	Y	Y
3 Borski	Y	Y	N	Y	Y	N	Y	Y
4 Klink	Y	Y	Y	Y	Y	Y	Y	Y
5 ***Clinger***	N	Y	Y	N	Y	Y	Y	?
6 Holden	Y	Y	Y	Y	Y	Y	Y	Y
7 ***Weldon***	Y	N	Y	Y	N	Y	Y	?
8 ***Greenwood***	Y	Y	Y	Y	Y	Y	N	Y
9 ***Shuster***	N	N	Y	N	N	Y	Y	Y
10 ***McDade***	N	N	N	N	N	N	Y	N
11 Kanjorski	Y	Y	Y	Y	Y	Y	Y	Y
12 Murtha	N	N	N	N	N	N	Y	Y
13 Margolies-Mezv.	Y	Y	Y	Y	Y	Y	Y	Y
14 Coyne	Y	Y	N	Y	Y	N	Y	Y
15 McHale	Y	Y	N	Y	Y	N	Y	Y
16 ***Walker***	N	N	Y	N	N	Y	N	N
17 ***Gekas***	N	Y	Y	N	Y	Y	N	N
18 ***Santorum***	Y	Y	N	Y	Y	N	Y	N
19 ***Goodling***	N	Y	Y	Y	Y	Y	Y	N
20 Murphy	N	Y	Y	Y	Y	Y	N	Y
21 ***Ridge***	Y	Y	Y	Y	Y	Y	Y	?
RHODE ISLAND								
1 ***Machtley***	Y	Y	Y	Y	Y	Y	Y	N
2 Reed	Y	Y	Y	Y	Y	Y	Y	Y
SOUTH CAROLINA								
1 ***Ravenel***	Y	Y	Y	Y	Y	Y	Y	N
2 ***Spence***	N	N	N	N	N	N	Y	N
3 Derrick	Y	Y	N	Y	Y	N	Y	Y
4 ***Inglis***	Y	Y	Y	Y	Y	Y	N	N
5 Spratt	Y	Y	Y	Y	Y	Y	Y	Y
6 Clyburn	Y	Y	Y	Y	Y	Y	Y	Y
SOUTH DAKOTA								
AL Johnson	Y	Y	Y	Y	Y	Y	Y	?
TENNESSEE								
1 ***Quillen***	Y	Y	N	Y	Y	N	N	Y
2 ***Duncan***	Y	Y	Y	Y	Y	Y	N	N
3 Lloyd	N	Y	N	N	Y	N	Y	?
4 Cooper	Y	Y	Y	Y	Y	Y	Y	?
5 Clement	N	Y	Y	N	Y	Y	Y	Y

	267	268	269	270	271	272	273	274
6 Gordon	Y	Y	Y	Y	Y	Y	Y	Y
7 ***Sundquist***	Y	Y	Y	Y	Y	Y	N	?
8 Tanner	Y	Y	Y	Y	Y	Y	Y	Y
9 Ford	Y	Y	Y	Y	Y	Y	Y	?
TEXAS								
1 Chapman	N	N	N	N	N	N	Y	Y
2 Wilson	N	N	N	N	Y	N	Y	Y
3 ***Johnson, Sam***	N	Y	N	Y	Y	N	N	N
4 Hall	Y	N	N	Y	N	N	Y	Y
5 Bryant	Y	Y	N	Y	Y	N	Y	N
6 ***Barton***	N	N	N	N	N	N	N	N
7 ***Archer***	N	N	Y	N	N	Y	N	N
8 ***Fields***	N	N	N	N	N	N	N	N
9 Brooks	N	N	N	N	N	N	Y	Y
10 Pickle	N	Y	N	N	Y	N	Y	?
11 Edwards	Y	Y	N	Y	Y	N	Y	Y
12 Geren	Y	Y	N	Y	Y	Y	Y	?
13 Sarpalius	Y	Y	N	Y	Y	N	Y	Y
14 Laughlin	N	Y	N	Y	Y	N	Y	N
15 de la Garza	N	N	N	N	N	N	Y	Y
16 Coleman	N	N	N	N	N	N	Y	N
17 Stenholm	Y	Y	N	Y	Y	N	Y	Y
18 Washington	Y	Y	Y	Y	Y	Y	Y	?
19 ***Combest***	N	N	N	N	N	N	N	N
20 Gonzalez	N	N	N	N	N	N	Y	Y
21 ***Smith***	N	N	N	N	N	N	Y	N
22 ***DeLay***	N	N	N	N	N	N	N	Y
23 ***Bonilla***	N	N	N	N	N	N	N	N
24 Frost	N	N	N	N	N	N	Y	Y
25 Andrews	N	N	N	N	N	N	Y	Y
26 ***Armey***	N	N	N	?	X	?	X	X
27 Ortiz	N	Y	N	Y	Y	N	Y	N
28 Tejeda	N	Y	N	N	Y	N	Y	N
29 Green	N	N	N	N	Y	N	Y	N
30 Johnson, E. B.	N	N	N	N	N	N	Y	Y
UTAH								
1 ***Hansen***	N	N	N	N	N	N	Y	N
2 Shepherd	Y	Y	Y	Y	Y	Y	Y	Y
3 Orton	Y	Y	Y	Y	Y	Y	Y	Y
VERMONT								
AL *Sanders*	Y	Y	Y	Y	Y	Y	Y	?
VIRGINIA								
1 ***Bateman***	N	N	N	N	N	N	Y	Y
2 Pickett	N	N	N	N	N	N	Y	Y
3 Scott	Y	Y	N	Y	Y	N	Y	?
4 Sisisky	Y	Y	Y	Y	Y	Y	Y	Y
5 Payne	Y	Y	N	Y	Y	N	Y	?
6 ***Goodlatte***	Y	Y	N	Y	Y	Y	Y	N
7 ***Bliley***	N	N	Y	N	N	Y	Y	N
8 Moran	Y	Y	N	Y	Y	N	Y	Y
9 Boucher	Y	Y	N	Y	Y	N	Y	?
10 ***Wolf***	N	Y	Y	N	Y	Y	N	N
11 Byrne	Y	Y	Y	Y	Y	Y	Y	Y
WASHINGTON								
1 Cantwell	Y	Y	Y	Y	Y	Y	Y	Y
2 Swift	N	Y	Y	N	Y	Y	Y	Y
3 Unsoeld	Y	N	Y	Y	N	Y	Y	?
4 Inslee	N	N	Y	N	N	Y	Y	Y
5 Foley								
6 Dicks	Y	Y	N	Y	Y	Y	Y	Y
7 McDermott	Y	Y	Y	Y	Y	Y	Y	Y
8 ***Dunn***	Y	Y	N	Y	Y	N	N	N
9 Kreidler	Y	Y	Y	Y	Y	Y	Y	Y
WEST VIRGINIA								
1 Mollohan	N	N	N	N	N	N	Y	Y
2 Wise	Y	Y	Y	Y	Y	Y	Y	Y
3 Rahall	Y	Y	Y	Y	Y	Y	Y	Y
WISCONSIN								
1 Barca	Y	Y	Y	Y	Y	Y	Y	Y
2 ***Klug***	Y	Y	Y	Y	Y	Y	N	N
3 ***Gunderson***	N	Y	Y	N	Y	Y	Y	N
4 Kleczka	Y	Y	Y	Y	Y	Y	Y	Y
5 Barrett	Y	Y	Y	Y	Y	Y	Y	Y
6 ***Petri***	Y	Y	Y	Y	Y	Y	N	N
7 Obey	Y	Y	Y	Y	Y	Y	Y	Y
8 ***Roth***	Y	Y	Y	Y	Y	Y	N	N
9 ***Sensenbrenner***	Y	Y	Y	Y	Y	Y	N	N
WYOMING								
AL ***Thomas***	N	Y	Y	N	Y	Y	Y	Y
DELEGATES								
de Lugo, V.I.	Y	Y	N	D	D	D	D	D
Faleomavaega, Am.S.	?	?	?	D	D	D	D	D
Norton, D.C.	Y	Y	Y	D	D	D	D	D
Romero-B., P.R.	Y	Y	N	D	D	D	D	D
Underwood, Guam	Y	Y	N	D	D	D	D	D

Southern states - Ala., Ark., Fla., Ga., Ky., La., Miss., N.C., Okla., S.C., Tenn., Texas, Va.
Omitted votes are quorum calls, which CQ does not include in its vote charts.

KEY

Y   Voted for (yea).
Paired for.
+   Announced for.
N   Voted against (nay).
X   Paired against.
−   Announced against.
P   Voted "present."
C   Voted "present" to avoid possible conflict of interest.
?   Did not vote or otherwise make a position known.
D   Delegates ineligible to vote.

Democrats   *Republicans*
Independent

*276. HR 2491. Fiscal 1994 VA, HUD Appropriations/ CDBGs. Burton, R-Ind., amendment to cut $223.7 million from the appropriations for Community Development Block Grants (CDBGs). Rejected in Committee of the Whole 154-237: R 132-31; D 22-205 (ND 12-137, SD 10-68); I 0-1, June 28, 1993.

277. HR 2491. Fiscal 1994 VA, HUD Appropriations/ Disaster Assistance. Penny, D-Minn., amendment to cut $50 million in community development grants for disaster assistance to areas damaged by Hurricane Andrew, Hurricane Iniki and Typhoon Omar. Adopted in Committee of the Whole 202-194: R 146-17; D 56-176 (ND 26-126, SD 30-50); I 0-1, June 28, 1993.

278. HR 2491. Fiscal 1994 VA, HUD Appropriations/ Selective Service System. Solomon, R-N.Y., en bloc amendment to transfer $20 million from the HUD Policy Development and Research Account to prevent the termination of the Selective Service System. Rejected in Committee of the Whole 202-207: R 131-35; D 71-171 (ND 30-131, SD 41-40); I 0-1, June 28, 1993.

279. HR 2491. Fiscal 1994 VA, HUD Appropriations/ Development and Research Programs. Grams, R-Minn., amendment to cut $48 million from HUD Policy Development and Research programs. Adopted in Committee of the Whole 220-194: R 159-9; D 61-184 (ND 30-133, SD 31-51); I 0-1, June 28, 1993.

280. HR 2491. Fiscal 1994 VA, HUD Appropriations/ HOPE. Kolbe, R-Ariz., amendment to increase funding for Homeownership and Opportunities for People Everywhere (HOPE) grants by $10 million. HOPE assists low-income residents in buying government-owned housing units. Adopted in Committee of the Whole 214-199: R 161-5; D 53-193 (ND 24-139, SD 29-54); I 0-1, June 28, 1993.

281. HR 2491. Fiscal 1994 VA, HUD Appropriations/ Space Station. Roemer, D-Ind., amendment to cut $1.2 billion from NASA's research and development account and eliminate the $2.1 billion earmark for the space station, leaving $825 million for costs associated with terminating the project. Rejected in Committee of the Whole 196-220: R 55-112; D 140-108 (ND 113-51, SD 27-57); I 1-0, June 28, 1993. A "nay" was a vote in support of the president's position.

282. HR 2491. Fiscal 1994 VA, HUD Appropriations/ Office of Science and Technology Policy. Hefley, R-Colo., amendment to cut $970,000 for the Office of Science and Technology Policy in the Executive Office of the President. Adopted in Committee of the Whole 267-149: R 162-5; D 105-143 (ND 67-97, SD 38-46); I 0-1, June 28, 1993.

283. HR 2491. Fiscal 1994 VA, HUD Appropriations/ CIESIN. Hefley, R-Colo., amendment to cut $18 million for the Consortia for International Earth Science Information Network (CIESIN). Rejected in the Committee of the Whole 176-240: R 156-13; D 20-226 (ND 12-151, SD 8-75); I 0-1, June 28, 1993.

* Omitted votes are quorum calls, which CQ does not include in its vote charts.

	276	277	278	279	280	281	282	283
ALABAMA								
1 *Callahan*	?	?	?	?	?	N	Y	Y
2 *Everett*	Y	Y	Y	Y	Y	N	Y	Y
3 Browder	N	Y	Y	N	N	Y	N	N
4 Bevill	N	N	Y	N	N	N	N	N
5 Cramer	N	Y	Y	N	N	N	N	N
6 *Bachus*	Y	Y	Y	Y	Y	N	Y	Y
7 Hilliard	N	N	N	N	N	N	N	N
ALASKA								
AL *Young*	N	N	Y	Y	N	N	Y	Y
ARIZONA								
1 Coppersmith	−	−	−	−	+	+	+	−
2 Pastor	N	N	N	N	N	N	N	N
3 *Stump*	Y	Y	Y	Y	Y	N	Y	Y
4 *Kyl*	Y	Y	Y	Y	Y	N	Y	Y
5 *Kolbe*	Y	Y	Y	Y	Y	Y	Y	Y
6 English	N	N	N	N	Y	Y	N	N
ARKANSAS								
1 Lambert	N	N	N	N	Y	Y	N	N
2 Thornton	N	N	N	N	N	N	N	N
3 *Hutchinson*	Y	Y	Y	Y	Y	Y	Y	Y
4 *Dickey*	Y	Y	Y	Y	Y	Y	Y	Y
CALIFORNIA								
1 Hamburg	−	?	−	?	?	+	−	?
2 *Herger*	Y	Y	Y	Y	Y	Y	Y	Y
3 Fazio	N	N	N	N	N	N	N	N
4 *Doolittle*	Y	Y	Y	Y	Y	N	Y	Y
5 Matsui	N	N	N	N	N	N	N	N
6 Woolsey	N	N	N	N	Y	N	N	N
7 Miller	N	N	N	N	N	N	N	N
8 Pelosi	N	N	N	N	N	N	N	N
9 Dellums	N	N	N	N	Y	Y	N	N
10 *Baker*	Y	Y	Y	Y	Y	N	Y	Y
11 *Pombo*	Y	Y	Y	Y	Y	Y	Y	Y
12 Lantos	N	N	N	N	N	N	N	N
13 Stark	N	N	N	N	Y	?	?	
14 Eshoo	N	N	N	N	N	N	N	N
15 Mineta	N	N	N	N	N	N	N	N
16 Edwards	N	N	N	N	N	N	N	N
17 Farr	N	N	N	N	N	N	N	N
18 Condit	Y	Y	Y	Y	Y	Y	Y	Y
19 Lehman	?	?	?	N	N	Y	N	Y
20 Dooley	N	N	N	N	Y	Y	Y	N
21 *Thomas*	Y	Y	Y	Y	Y	Y	N	Y
22 *Huffington*	Y	N	Y	N	N	Y	N	Y
23 *Gallegly*	Y	Y	Y	Y	Y	N	Y	Y
24 Beilenson	N	N	N	N	N	Y	N	N
25 *McKeon*	Y	Y	N	Y	Y	N	Y	Y
26 Berman	?	X	?	?	?	X	?	?
27 *Moorhead*	Y	Y	Y	Y	Y	N	Y	Y
28 *Dreier*	Y	Y	Y	Y	Y	N	Y	Y
29 Waxman	?	?	N	N	N	Y	N	?
30 Becerra	?	?	?	?	?	?	?	?
31 Martinez	N	N	N	N	N	N	N	N
32 Dixon	N	N	N	N	N	N	N	N
33 Roybal-Allard	N	N	N	N	N	N	N	N
34 Torres	N	N	N	N	N	N	N	N
35 Waters	?	?	N	N	N	N	N	N
36 Harman	?	?	Y	Y	N	N	N	N
37 Tucker	N	N	N	N	N	N	N	N
38 *Horn*	Y	Y	N	Y	N	N	N	Y
39 *Royce*	Y	Y	Y	Y	Y	N	Y	Y
40 *Lewis*	N	N	N	Y	N	N	N	N
41 *Kim*	N	Y	Y	Y	Y	N	Y	Y

	276	277	278	279	280	281	282	283
42 Brown	N	N	N	N	N	N	N	N
43 *Calvert*	N	Y	Y	Y	Y	N	Y	Y
44 *McCandless*	Y	Y	Y	Y	Y	N	Y	Y
45 *Rohrabacher*	Y	Y	N	Y	Y	N	Y	Y
46 *Dornan*	Y	Y	Y	Y	Y	N	Y	Y
47 *Cox*	Y	Y	N	Y	Y	N	Y	Y
48 *Packard*	Y	Y	Y	Y	Y	N	Y	Y
49 Schenk	N	N	N	Y	Y	N	Y	N
50 Filner	N	N	N	N	N	N	N	N
51 *Cunningham*	N	N	N	N	N	N	N	N
52 *Hunter*	?	?	Y	Y	Y	?	Y	Y
COLORADO								
1 Schroeder	N	N	N	N	Y	Y	N	Y
2 Skaggs	N	N	N	Y	N	Y	N	N
3 *McInnis*	Y	Y	N	Y	Y	N	Y	Y
4 *Allard*	Y	Y	N	Y	Y	Y	Y	Y
5 *Hefley*	Y	Y	Y	Y	Y	N	Y	Y
6 *Schaefer*	Y	N	Y	Y	N	Y	N	Y
CONNECTICUT								
1 Kennelly	N	N	N	N	N	N	Y	N
2 Gejdenson	N	N	N	N	N	N	N	N
3 DeLauro	N	N	N	N	N	N	N	N
4 *Shays*	N	Y	N	Y	Y	Y	Y	N
5 *Franks*	Y	Y	Y	Y	Y	N	Y	Y
6 *Johnson*	N	Y	N	N	N	N	Y	N
DELAWARE								
AL *Castle*	Y	Y	Y	Y	Y	N	Y	Y
FLORIDA								
1 Hutto	N	Y	Y	Y	N	N	Y	Y
2 Peterson	N	N	N	N	N	N	Y	N
3 Brown	N	N	N	N	N	N	N	N
4 *Fowler*	Y	Y	Y	Y	Y	Y	Y	Y
5 Thurman	N	Y	N	N	N	N	N	N
6 *Stearns*	#	#	#	Y	Y	N	Y	Y
7 Mica	Y	N	Y	Y	N	Y	Y	Y
8 *McCollum*	Y	Y	Y	Y	Y	N	Y	Y
9 *Bilirakis*	Y	Y	Y	Y	Y	N	Y	Y
10 *Young*	Y	Y	Y	?	N	Y	N	Y
11 Gibbons	N	N	N	N	N	N	N	N
12 *Canady*	Y	Y	Y	Y	Y	N	Y	Y
13 *Miller*	Y	Y	N	Y	N	Y	N	Y
14 *Goss*	Y	Y	Y	Y	Y	N	Y	Y
15 Bacchus	N	N	N	N	N	N	N	N
16 *Lewis*	Y	Y	N	Y	N	Y	N	Y
17 Meek	N	N	N	N	N	N	N	N
18 *Ros-Lehtinen*	N	N	Y	Y	N	N	Y	Y
19 Johnston	N	N	N	N	N	Y	N	N
20 Deutsch	N	N	N	N	N	N	N	N
21 *Diaz-Balart*	N	N	Y	?	?	X	?	?
22 *Shaw*	Y	N	Y	Y	Y	N	Y	Y
23 Hastings	N	N	N	N	N	N	N	N
GEORGIA								
1 *Kingston*	Y	Y	Y	Y	Y	Y	Y	Y
2 Bishop	N	N	Y	N	N	N	N	N
3 *Collins*	Y	Y	Y	Y	Y	Y	Y	Y
4 *Linder*	Y	Y	Y	Y	Y	N	Y	Y
5 Lewis	N	N	N	N	N	N	N	N
6 *Gingrich*	Y	N	Y	Y	?	N	Y	Y
7 Darden	N	Y	Y	Y	N	N	N	N
8 Rowland	N	Y	Y	N	N	N	N	N
9 Deal	Y	Y	Y	Y	N	N	N	N
10 Johnson	Y	Y	Y	Y	N	Y	N	N
11 McKinney	?	N	N	N	Y	Y	N	N
HAWAII								
1 Abercrombie	N	N	N	N	Y	N	N	N
2 Mink	N	N	N	N	Y	N	N	N
IDAHO								
1 LaRocco	?	?	?	?	?	Y	Y	N
2 *Crapo*	Y	Y	Y	Y	Y	N	Y	Y
ILLINOIS								
1 Rush	N	N	N	N	N	Y	Y	N
2 Reynolds	N	N	N	N	N	Y	N	N
3 Lipinski	N	N	Y	Y	Y	N	Y	N
4 Gutierrez	N	N.	N	N	N	Y	N	N
5 Rostenkowski	N	N	N	N	N	Y	N	N
6 *Hyde*	Y	Y	Y	Y	Y	N	Y	Y
7 Collins	N	N	N	N	N	N	N	N
8 *Crane*	Y	Y	Y	Y	Y	N	Y	Y
9 Yates	N	N	N	N	N	Y	N	N
10 *Porter*	Y	Y	Y	Y	Y	Y	Y	Y
11 Sangmeister	?	#	?	?	X	#	Y	N
12 Costello	N	N	Y	N	Y	Y	Y	N
13 *Fawell*	Y	Y	Y	Y	Y	Y	Y	Y
14 *Hastert*	Y	Y	Y	Y	Y	Y	Y	Y
15 *Ewing*	Y	Y	Y	Y	Y	N	Y	Y
16 *Manzullo*	Y	Y	Y	Y	Y	Y	Y	Y
17 Evans	N	N	N	N	N	Y	N	N

ND   Northern Democrats   SD   Southern Democrats

	276	277	278	279	280	281	282	283
18 ***Michel***	Y	Y	Y	Y	Y	N	Y	Y
19 Poshard	N	N	Y	Y	N	Y	Y	Y
20 Durbin	N	N	N	N	N	Y	Y	N
INDIANA								
1 Visclosky	N	N	N	N	N	Y	N	N
2 Sharp	N	N	N	N	N	Y	Y	Y
3 Roemer	N	Y	Y	N	N	Y	Y	N
4 Long	N	N	N	N	N	Y	Y	Y
5 ***Buyer***	Y	Y	Y	Y	Y	N	Y	Y
6 ***Burton***	Y	Y	Y	Y	Y	N	Y	Y
7 ***Myers***	Y	Y	Y	Y	N	N	Y	Y
8 McCloskey	N	N	N	N	N	Y	Y	N
9 Hamilton	N	N	N	N	N	Y	Y	Y
10 Jacobs	Y	Y	N	Y	N	Y	Y	Y
IOWA								
1 ***Leach***	Y	Y	N	Y	Y	Y	Y	Y
2 ***Nussle***	Y	Y	N	Y	Y	Y	Y	Y
3 ***Lightfoot***	N	N	Y	N	Y	N	Y	Y
4 Smith	N	N	Y	N	N	?	N	N
5 ***Grandy***	Y	Y	Y	Y	Y	Y	Y	Y
KANSAS								
1 ***Roberts***	Y	Y	Y	Y	Y	N	Y	Y
2 Slattery	Y	Y	N	Y	N	N	Y	N
3 ***Meyers***	Y	Y	Y	Y	Y	N	Y	Y
4 Glickman	Y	Y	N	Y	N	N	Y	N
KENTUCKY								
1 Barlow	N	Y	N	N	Y	Y	Y	N
2 Natcher	N	N	N	N	N	N	N	N
3 Mazzoli	N	N	Y	N	N	Y	N	N
4 ***Bunning***	Y	Y	Y	Y	Y	Y	Y	Y
5 ***Rogers***	N	N	Y	Y	Y	N	Y	Y
6 Baesler	—	—	Y	N	Y	Y	Y	N
LOUISIANA								
1 ***Livingston***	Y	N	Y	Y	Y	N	Y	Y
2 Jefferson	N	N	Y	N	Y	N	N	N
3 Tauzin	Y	N	Y	Y	Y	Y	Y	Y
4 Fields	N	N	Y	N	Y	N	N	N
5 ***McCrery***	Y	Y	Y	Y	Y	N	Y	Y
6 ***Baker***	Y	Y	Y	Y	Y	N	Y	Y
7 Hayes	N	N	Y	Y	Y	N	Y	N
MAINE								
1 Andrews	N	?	N	N	N	Y	N	N
2 ***Snowe***	N	Y	Y	Y	Y	Y	Y	Y
MARYLAND								
1 ***Gilchrest***	Y	Y	N	N	Y	N	Y	N
2 ***Bentley***	Y	?	Y	Y	Y	N	Y	Y
3 Cardin	N	N	N	N	N	Y	N	N
4 Wynn	N	N	N	N	N	Y	N	N
5 Hoyer	N	N	Y	N	N	Y	N	N
6 ***Bartlett***	Y	Y	Y	Y	Y	N	Y	Y
7 Mfume	?	N	N	N	#	Y	N	N
8 ***Morella***	Y	Y	Y	Y	Y	N	Y	Y
MASSACHUSETTS								
1 Olver	N	N	N	N	N	Y	N	N
2 Neal	?	?	N	N	N	N	Y	N
3 ***Blute***	+	+	+	+	+	+	+	+
4 Frank	N	N	N	N	N	Y	N	N
5 Meehan	N	N	X	?	?	#	?	?
6 ***Torkildsen***	Y	Y	Y	Y	Y	N	Y	Y
7 Markey	N	N	N	N	N	Y	N	N
8 Kennedy	?	X	N	N	N	Y	N	N
9 Moakley	N	N	N	N	N	Y	N	N
10 Studds	N	N	N	N	N	Y	N	N
MICHIGAN								
1 Stupak	N	N	Y	N	N	Y	N	N
2 ***Hoekstra***	N	Y	N	Y	Y	Y	Y	N
3 Henry	?	?	?	?	?	?	?	?
4 ***Camp***	Y	Y	N	Y	Y	Y	Y	N
5 Barcia	N	N	Y	N	N	N	N	N
6 ***Upton***	N	Y	N	Y	Y	Y	Y	N
7 ***Smith***	Y	Y	Y	Y	Y	Y	Y	N
8 Carr	N	N	N	N	N	N	N	N
9 Kildee	N	N	N	N	N	Y	N	N
10 Bonior	N	N	N	N	N	N	N	N
11 ***Knollenberg***	Y	Y	N	Y	Y	Y	Y	N
12 Levin	N	Y	N	N	N	Y	Y	N
13 Ford	?	N	N	N	N	Y	N	N
14 Conyers	?	?	?	?	N	Y	N	N
15 Collins	N	N	N	N	N	Y	N	N
16 Dingell	N	N	N	N	N	Y	N	N
MINNESOTA								
1 Penny	Y	Y	N	Y	Y	Y	Y	Y
2 Minge	Y	Y	N	Y	Y	Y	Y	N
3 ***Ramstad***	Y	Y	Y	Y	Y	Y	Y	Y
4 Vento	?	X	?	?	X	Y	Y	N

	276	277	278	279	280	281	282	283
5 Sabo	N	N	N	N	N	Y	N	N
6 ***Grams***	Y	Y	Y	Y	Y	N	Y	Y
7 Peterson	Y	Y	N	N	N	Y	Y	N
8 Oberstar	N	N	N	N	N	Y	N	N
MISSISSIPPI								
1 Whitten	N	N	Y	N	N	N	N	N
2 Thompson	N	N	N	N	N	N	N	N
3 Montgomery	N	Y	Y	Y	N	N	Y	N
4 Parker	?	?	?	Y	N	N	Y	N
5 Taylor	Y	Y	Y	Y	Y	N	Y	Y
MISSOURI								
1 Clay	N	N	N	N	N	N	N	N
2 ***Talent***	Y	Y	Y	Y	Y	N	Y	Y
3 Gephardt	N	N	N	N	N	N	N	N
4 Skelton	N	N	Y	Y	N	Y	Y	N
5 Wheat	N	N	N	N	N	Y	N	?
6 Danner	N	Y	N	N	N	Y	Y	N
7 ***Hancock***	Y	Y	Y	Y	Y	N	Y	Y
8 ***Emerson***	Y	Y	Y	Y	Y	N	Y	Y
9 Volkmer	N	Y	Y	Y	N	N	N	N
MONTANA								
AL Williams	N	Y	N	Y	N	Y	Y	N
NEBRASKA								
1 ***Bereuter***	N	Y	Y	N	Y	Y	Y	Y
2 Hoagland	Y	Y	N	Y	N	Y	Y	Y
3 ***Barrett***	N	Y	N	Y	Y	N	Y	Y
NEVADA								
1 Bilbray	N	N	Y	Y	Y	Y	Y	N
2 ***Vucanovich***	N	N	Y	N	Y	N	Y	Y
NEW HAMPSHIRE								
1 ***Zeliff***	Y	Y	N	Y	Y	N	Y	Y
2 Swett	N	N	N	Y	N	Y	Y	N
NEW JERSEY								
1 Andrews	N	N	Y	N	Y	N	Y	N
2 Hughes	N	N	Y	N	N	Y	N	N
3 ***Saxton***	N	Y	Y	Y	Y	N	Y	N
4 ***Smith***	?	Y	Y	Y	Y	N	Y	Y
5 ***Roukema***	N	Y	Y	Y	N	Y	Y	Y
6 Pallone	N	N	Y	N	Y	Y	Y	N
7 ***Franks***	Y	Y	Y	Y	Y	Y	Y	Y
8 Klein	N	N	N	N	N	Y	N	N
9 Torricelli	?	?	N	N	N	N	?	N
10 Payne	?	?	?	?	?	?	?	?
11 ***Gallo***	N	N	Y	N	Y	N	Y	N
12 ***Zimmer***	Y	Y	N	Y	Y	Y	Y	Y
13 Menendez	N	N	Y	N	Y	Y	Y	N
NEW MEXICO								
1 ***Schiff***	N	Y	Y	Y	Y	N	Y	Y
2 ***Skeen***	—	—	X	+	#	X	+	+
3 Richardson	?	?	?	?	?	X	?	?
NEW YORK								
1 Hochbrueckner	N	N	Y	N	N	N	N	N
2 ***Lazio***	Y	Y	Y	Y	Y	Y	Y	Y
3 ***King***	Y	Y	Y	Y	Y	Y	Y	Y
4 ***Levy***	Y	Y	Y	Y	Y	Y	Y	Y
5 Ackerman	N	N	N	N	N	Y	N	N
6 Flake	N	N	N	N	N	Y	N	N
7 Manton	?	?	?	?	N	N	Y	N
8 Nadler	N	N	N	N	N	Y	N	N
9 Schumer	N	N	N	N	N	Y	Y	N
10 Towns	N	N	N	N	N	N	N	N
11 Owens	N	N	N	N	N	Y	N	N
12 Velazquez	N	N	N	N	N	Y	N	N
13 ***Molinari***	Y	Y	Y	Y	Y	Y	Y	Y
14 Maloney	N	N	N	N	N	Y	Y	N
15 Rangel	X	N	N	N	N	Y	N	N
16 Serrano	?	?	N	N	N	Y	N	N
17 Engel	—	—	N	N	N	N	N	N
18 Lowey	N	N	N	N	N	Y	Y	N
19 ***Fish***	N	N	Y	Y	Y	Y	Y	Y
20 ***Gilman***	N	Y	Y	Y	Y	N	Y	Y
21 McNulty	N	N	Y	N	N	Y	N	N
22 ***Solomon***	Y	Y	Y	Y	Y	Y	Y	Y
23 ***Boehlert***	N	N	Y	Y	Y	N	N	Y
24 ***McHugh***	Y	Y	Y	Y	Y	Y	Y	Y
25 ***Walsh***	N	Y	Y	Y	Y	Y	Y	Y
26 Hinchey	N	N	N	N	Y	N	Y	N
27 ***Paxon***	Y	Y	Y	Y	Y	Y	Y	Y
28 Slaughter	N	N	N	N	N	Y	Y	N
29 LaFalce	N	N	N	N	N	Y	N	N
30 ***Quinn***	N	Y	Y	Y	Y	N	Y	Y
31 ***Houghton***	Y	Y	Y	Y	Y	N	N	Y
NORTH CAROLINA								
1 Clayton	?	N	N	N	N	Y	N	N
2 Valentine	N	Y	N	Y	N	N	N	N

	276	277	278	279	280	281	282	283
3 Lancaster	N	Y	Y	Y	Y	Y	Y	Y
4 Price	N	N	N	N	N	Y	N	N
5 Neal	N	N	N	Y	N	Y	Y	N
6 ***Coble***	Y	Y	Y	Y	Y	Y	Y	Y
7 Rose	N	N	N	N	N	Y	N	N
8 Hefner	N	N	N	N	N	Y	N	N
9 ***McMillan***	?	?	?	?	?	?	?	?
10 ***Ballenger***	Y	Y	Y	Y	Y	Y	Y	Y
11 ***Taylor***	Y	Y	N	Y	Y	N	Y	Y
12 Watt	N	N	N	N	N	Y	N	N
NORTH DAKOTA								
AL Pomeroy	N	N	N	N	N	Y	Y	N
OHIO								
1 Mann	?	?	?	N	N	Y	N	N
2 ***Portman***	+	+	Y	Y	Y	Y	?	Y
3 Hall	N	N	N	N	Y	Y	Y	N
4 ***Oxley***	Y	Y	Y	Y	Y	N	Y	Y
5 ***Gillmor***	Y	Y	Y	Y	Y	N	Y	Y
6 Strickland	N	N	N	N	N	Y	N	N
7 ***Hobson***	Y	Y	N	Y	Y	N	Y	Y
8 ***Boehner***	+	+	+	Y	Y	N	Y	Y
9 Kaptur	N	N	N	N	N	Y	Y	N
10 ***Hoke***	Y	Y	N	Y	Y	N	Y	Y
11 Stokes	N	N	N	N	N	N	N	N
12 ***Kasich***	Y	Y	N	Y	Y	Y	Y	Y
13 Brown	?	?	N	N	N	Y	Y	N
14 Sawyer	N	N	N	N	N	N	N	N
15 ***Pryce***	Y	Y	Y	Y	Y	N	Y	Y
16 ***Regula***	Y	Y	Y	Y	Y	N	Y	Y
17 Traficant	N	N	N	N	N	N	N	N
18 Applegate	?	N	N	Y	N	N	Y	N
19 Fingerhut	N	Y	Y	Y	N	N	N	N
OKLAHOMA								
1 ***Inhofe***	Y	Y	Y	Y	Y	N	Y	Y
2 Synar	N	N	N	N	N	Y	N	Y
3 Brewster	Y	Y	N	Y	N	Y	N	N
4 McCurdy	N	Y	Y	Y	Y	N	Y	Y
5 ***Istook***	+	+	—	+	+	#	+	?
6 English	N	Y	Y	Y	Y	Y	Y	N
OREGON								
1 Furse	N	N	N	N	N	Y	N	N
2 ***Smith***	Y	Y	Y	Y	Y	Y	Y	Y
3 Wyden	N	Y	N	N	N	Y	Y	N
4 DeFazio	N	N	N	Y	Y	Y	Y	N
5 Kopetski	N	Y	N	N	N	N	N	N
PENNSYLVANIA								
1 Foglietta	N	N	N	N	Y	Y	N	N
2 Blackwell	N	N	N	N	Y	Y	N	N
3 Borski	N	N	N	N	Y	N	Y	N
4 Klink	N	N	Y	N	N	Y	Y	N
5 ***Clinger***	N	Y	N	Y	Y	N	Y	Y
6 Holden	N	N	N	Y	N	Y	Y	N
7 ***Weldon***	Y	Y	Y	Y	Y	?	Y	Y
8 ***Greenwood***	Y	Y	Y	Y	Y	N	Y	Y
9 ***Shuster***	Y	Y	Y	Y	Y	Y	Y	Y
10 ***McDade***	N	N	N	N	Y	N	Y	Y
11 Kanjorski	N	N	N	N	N	Y	N	N
12 Murtha	N	N	Y	N	N	N	N	N
13 Margolies-Mezv.	Y	Y	N	Y	N	Y	Y	N
14 Coyne	N	N	N	N	N	Y	N	N
15 McHale	N	Y	Y	N	Y	N	Y	N
16 ***Walker***	Y	Y	N	Y	Y	N	N	Y
17 ***Gekas***	N	Y	Y	Y	Y	Y	Y	Y
18 ***Santorum***	Y	Y	N	Y	Y	Y	Y	Y
19 ***Goodling***	N	Y	Y	Y	Y	Y	Y	Y
20 Murphy	Y	Y	N	Y	N	?	?	?
21 ***Ridge***	N	Y	Y	Y	Y	N	?	Y
RHODE ISLAND								
1 ***Machtley***	Y	Y	Y	Y	Y	Y	Y	Y
2 Reed	N	N	Y	N	N	Y	N	N
SOUTH CAROLINA								
1 ***Ravenel***	Y	Y	Y	Y	Y	Y	Y	Y
2 ***Spence***	Y	Y	Y	Y	Y	N	Y	Y
3 Derrick	N	Y	N	N	N	Y	Y	N
4 ***Inglis***	Y	Y	Y	Y	Y	Y	Y	Y
5 Spratt	N	Y	Y	Y	N	Y	Y	N
6 Clyburn	N	N	N	N	N	Y	N	N
SOUTH DAKOTA								
AL Johnson	N	N	Y	Y	N	Y	N	Y
TENNESSEE								
1 ***Quillen***	N	N	Y	N	N	N	Y	N
2 ***Duncan***	Y	Y	Y	Y	Y	Y	Y	Y
3 Lloyd	N	N	Y	Y	N	N	N	N
4 Cooper	?	?	Y	Y	N	N	Y	N
5 Clement	N	Y	N	Y	Y	N	Y	N

	276	277	278	279	280	281	282	283
6 Gordon	N	Y	Y	N	N	Y	Y	N
7 ***Sundquist***	?	?	?	?	?	?	?	?
8 Tanner	N	Y	Y	Y	Y	N	Y	N
9 Ford	?	?	?	?	?	?	?	?
TEXAS								
1 Chapman	N	N	N	?	?	N	N	N
2 Wilson	N	Y	Y	N	N	N	Y	?
3 ***Johnson, Sam***	Y	Y	Y	Y	Y	N	Y	Y
4 Hall	Y	Y	Y	Y	Y	N	N	N
5 Bryant	N	N	Y	N	N	N	N	N
6 ***Barton***	Y	Y	Y	Y	Y	N	Y	N
7 ***Archer***	Y	Y	N	Y	Y	N	Y	Y
8 ***Fields***	Y	Y	Y	Y	Y	N	Y	Y
9 Brooks	N	N	Y	N	N	N	N	N
10 Pickle	N	Y	Y	N	Y	N	N	N
11 Edwards	Y	Y	N	Y	Y	N	N	N
12 Geren	N	Y	Y	Y	Y	N	Y	N
13 Sarpalius	Y	Y	N	N	N	N	N	N
14 Laughlin	N	Y	Y	Y	Y	N	N	N
15 de la Garza	N	N	N	N	Y	N	Y	N
16 Coleman	N	N	N	N	N	N	N	N
17 Stenholm	Y	Y	Y	Y	Y	N	Y	Y
18 Washington	?	?	?	N	Y	Y	N	N
19 ***Combest***	Y	Y	Y	Y	Y	N	Y	Y
20 Gonzalez	N	N	N	N	N	N	N	N
21 ***Smith***	Y	Y	Y	Y	Y	N	Y	Y
22 ***DeLay***	Y	Y	N	Y	Y	N	Y	Y
23 ***Bonilla***	Y	Y	Y	Y	Y	N	Y	Y
24 Frost	N	N	N	Y	N	N	Y	N
25 Andrews	Y	Y	Y	Y	Y	N	Y	N
26 ***Armey***	?	#	#	Y	Y	N	Y	Y
27 Ortiz	N	N	N	N	Y	N	Y	N
28 Tejeda	N	N	Y	N	N	N	N	N
29 Green	N	N	N	N	N	N	N	N
30 Johnson, E. B.	N	N	N	N	N	N	N	N
UTAH								
1 ***Hansen***	Y	Y	Y	Y	Y	N	Y	Y
2 Shepherd	N	Y	Y	N	N	Y	Y	N
3 Orton	N	Y	Y	Y	Y	Y	Y	Y
VERMONT								
AL *Sanders*	N	N	N	N	N	Y	N	N
VIRGINIA								
1 ***Bateman***	Y	Y	Y	Y	Y	N	Y	N
2 Pickett	N	N	Y	N	N	N	N	N
3 Scott	N	N	N	N	Y	N	N	N
4 Sisisky	N	Y	?	Y	Y	Y	Y	N
5 Payne	N	Y	Y	Y	Y	Y	N	N
6 ***Goodlatte***	Y	Y	Y	Y	Y	Y	Y	Y
7 ***Bliley***	Y	Y	Y	Y	Y	N	Y	Y
8 Moran	N	N	Y	?	Y	N	N	N
9 Boucher	N	N	N	N	N	N	Y	N
10 ***Wolf***	Y	Y	Y	Y	Y	N	Y	Y
11 Byrne	N	N	N	N	Y	N	N	N
WASHINGTON								
1 Cantwell	Y	Y	N	Y	N	Y	Y	N
2 Swift	N	N	N	N	N	N	Y	N
3 Unsoeld	?	?	?	?	?	#	?	?
4 Inslee	Y	Y	N	Y	N	Y	N	N
5 Foley								
6 Dicks	N	Y	N	Y	N	N	Y	N
7 McDermott	N	N	N	N	N	N	N	N
8 ***Dunn***	Y	Y	Y	Y	Y	N	Y	Y
9 Kreidler	N	N	N	N	N	Y	Y	N
WEST VIRGINIA								
1 Mollohan	N	N	N	N	N	N	N	N
2 Wise	N	N	Y	Y	N	N	N	N
3 Rahall	N	N	N	N	N	N	Y	N
WISCONSIN								
1 Barca	N	Y	Y	Y	N	Y	Y	N
2 ***Klug***	Y	Y	N	Y	Y	N	Y	Y
3 ***Gunderson***	Y	Y	Y	Y	Y	Y	Y	Y
4 Kleczka	N	N	N	N	N	Y	Y	N
5 Barrett	N	Y	N	N	N	Y	Y	N
6 ***Petri***	Y	Y	Y	Y	Y	Y	Y	Y
7 Obey	N	N	N	N	N	Y	N	N
8 ***Roth***	Y	Y	Y	Y	Y	N	Y	Y
9 ***Sensenbrenner***	Y	Y	N	Y	Y	N	Y	Y
WYOMING								
AL ***Thomas***	Y	Y	N	Y	Y	Y	Y	Y
DELEGATES								
de Lugo, V.I.	N	N	N	N	Y	Y	N	N
Faleomavaega, Am.S.	?	?	?	?	?	?	?	?
Norton, D.C.	N	N	N	N	N	Y	N	N
Romero-B., P.R.	N	N	Y	N	?	?	?	?
Underwood, Guam	N	N	N	N	N	Y	N	N

Southern states - Ala., Ark., Fla., Ga., Ky., La., Miss., N.C., Okla., S.C., Tenn., Texas, Va.
Omitted votes are quorum calls, which CQ does not include in its vote charts.

284. HR 2491. Fiscal 1994 VA, HUD Appropriations/Disaster Assistance. Separate vote at the request of Stokes, D-Ohio, on the Penny, D-Minn., amendment adopted in the Committee of the Whole to cut $50 million in community development block grants for disaster assistance to areas damaged by Hurricane Andrew, Hurricane Iniki and Typhoon Omar. Rejected 170-244: R 140-29; D 30-214 (ND 19-144, SD 11-70); I 0-1, June 29, 1993. (On separate votes, which may be demanded on an amendment adopted in the Committee of the Whole, delegates cannot vote. See vote 284.)

285. HR 2491. Fiscal 1994 VA, HUD Appropriations/Development and Research Programs. Separate vote at the request of Stokes, D-Ohio, on the Grams, R-Minn., amendment adopted in the Committee of the Whole to cut $48 million from HUD's policy development and research programs. Rejected 198-214: R 162-6; D 36-207 (ND 20-143, SD 16-64); I 0-1, June 29, 1993. (On separate votes, which may be demanded on an amendment adopted in the Committee of the Whole, delegates cannot vote. See vote 279.)

286. HR 2491. Fiscal 1994 VA, HUD Appropriations/HOPE. Separate vote at the request of Stokes, D-Ohio, on the Kolbe, R-Ariz., amendment adopted in the Committee of the Whole to increase funding for Homeownership and Opportunities for People Everywhere (HOPE) grants by $10 million. Adopted 216-204: R 165-4; D 51-199 (ND 17-149, SD 34-50); I 0-1, June 29, 1993. (On separate votes, which may be demanded on an amendment adopted in the Committee of the Whole, delegates cannot vote. See vote 280.)

287. HR 2491. Fiscal 1994 VA, HUD Appropriations/Office of Science and Technology Policy. Separate vote at the request of Solomon, R-N.Y., on the Hefley, R-Colo., amendment adopted in the Committee of the Whole to cut $970,000 for the Office of Science and Technology Policy. Adopted 251-171: R 164-4; D 87-166 (ND 58-111, SD 29-55); I 0-1, June 29, 1993. (On separate votes, which may be demanded on an amendment adopted in the Committee of the Whole, delegates cannot vote. See vote 282.)

288. HR 2491. Fiscal 1994 VA, HUD Appropriations/Advanced Solid Rocket Motor. Separate vote at the request of Solomon, R-N.Y., on the Klug, R-Wis., amendment adopted by voice vote in the Committee of the Whole to cut by $4.5 million the $104.5 million for the costs associated with the termination of the Advanced Solid Rocket Motor program and cut the $32.6 million for the completion of a solid rocket construction facility in Yellow Creek, Miss. Adopted 379-43: R 162-7; D 216-36 (ND 155-14, SD 61-22); I 1-0, June 29, 1993. (On separate votes, which may be demanded on an amendment adopted in the Committee of the Whole, delegates cannot vote.)

289. HR 2491. Fiscal 1994 VA, HUD Appropriations/Funding Cut. Myers, R-Ind., motion to recommit the bill to the House Appropriations Committee with instructions to cut funding across the board 6 percent except for the Department of Veterans Affairs and an increase of $20 million for the Selective Service System. Motion rejected 178-244: R 158-13; D 20-230 (ND 9-158, SD 11-72); I 0-1, June 29, 1993.

290. HR 2491. Fiscal 1994 VA, HUD Appropriations/Passage. Passage of the bill to provide $88 billion in new budget authority for the departments of Veterans Affairs and Housing and Urban Development and for other agencies. The administration requested $89,268,383,032. Passed 313-110: R 76-94; D 236-16 (ND 155-13, SD 81-3); I 1-0, June 29, 1993.

291. HR 2493. Fiscal 1994 Agriculture Appropriations/Cooperative State Research Service. Fawell, R-Ill., en bloc amendment to cut $87.8 million for the Cooperative State Research Service's special research grants and earmarks for building and facilities. Rejected in the Committee of the Whole 88-343: R 74-98; D 14-244 (ND 13-161, SD 1-83); I 0-1, June 29, 1993.

KEY

- **Y** Voted for (yea).
- **#** Paired for.
- **+** Announced for.
- **N** Voted against (nay).
- **X** Paired against.
- **−** Announced against.
- **P** Voted "present."
- **C** Voted "present" to avoid possible conflict of interest.
- **?** Did not vote or otherwise make a position known.
- **D** Delegates ineligible to vote.

Democrats *Republicans*
Independent

Member	284	285	286	287	288	289	290	291
ALABAMA								
1 Callahan	Y	Y	Y	Y	N	Y	N	Y
2 Everett	Y	Y	Y	Y	N	Y	N	N
3 Browder	N	N	N	Y	N	N	Y	N
4 Bevill	N	N	N	N	N	N	Y	N
5 Cramer	N	N	N	N	N	N	Y	N
6 Bachus	Y	Y	Y	Y	N	N	N	N
7 Hilliard	N	N	N	N	Y	N	Y	N
ALASKA								
AL Young	N	Y	N	Y	Y	Y	Y	N
ARIZONA								
1 Coppersmith	N	N	Y	Y	Y	N	Y	N
2 Pastor	N	N	N	N	Y	N	Y	N
3 Stump	Y	Y	Y	Y	Y	Y	Y	N
4 Kyl	Y	Y	Y	Y	Y	Y	Y	Y
5 Kolbe	Y	Y	Y	Y	Y	Y	Y	N
6 English	N	N	N	Y	N	Y	N	N
ARKANSAS								
1 Lambert	N	N	N	N	Y	N	Y	N
2 Thornton	N	N	N	N	Y	N	Y	N
3 Hutchinson	Y	Y	Y	Y	Y	Y	Y	N
4 Dickey	Y	Y	Y	Y	Y	Y	Y	N
CALIFORNIA								
1 Hamburg	N	N	N	Y	Y	N	Y	N
2 Herger	Y	Y	Y	Y	Y	Y	Y	Y
3 Fazio	N	N	N	N	N	N	Y	N
4 Doolittle	Y	Y	Y	Y	Y	Y	N	Y
5 Matsui	N	N	N	N	N	N	Y	N
6 Woolsey	N	N	N	N	N	N	Y	N
7 Miller	?	N	N	N	Y	N	Y	N
8 Pelosi	N	N	N	N	Y	?	+	N
9 Dellums	N	N	N	N	Y	N	Y	N
10 Baker	Y	Y	Y	Y	Y	Y	Y	Y
11 Pombo	Y	Y	Y	Y	Y	Y	N	N
12 Lantos	N	N	N	Y	Y	N	Y	N
13 Stark	N	N	Y	N	Y	N	N	N
14 Eshoo	N	N	N	N	Y	N	Y	N
15 Mineta	N	N	N	N	N	N	Y	N
16 Edwards	N	N	N	Y	N	Y	?	N
17 Farr	N	N	N	N	Y	N	Y	N
18 Condit	N	Y	Y	Y	Y	Y	N	N
19 Lehman	Y	N	N	Y	N	Y	N	N
20 Dooley	N	N	Y	Y	N	Y	N	N
21 Thomas	Y	Y	Y	Y	Y	Y	N	N
22 Huffington	Y	Y	Y	Y	Y	Y	N	N
23 Gallegly	Y	Y	Y	Y	Y	Y	Y	Y
24 Beilenson	N	N	N	N	Y	N	N	N
25 McKeon	Y	Y	Y	Y	Y	Y	N	Y
26 Berman	N	N	N	N	Y	N	Y	N
27 Moorhead	Y	Y	Y	Y	Y	Y	N	Y
28 Dreier	Y	Y	Y	Y	Y	Y	N	Y
29 Waxman	N	N	N	N	Y	N	Y	?
30 Becerra	N	N	N	N	Y	?	Y	N
31 Martinez	N	N	N	Y	N	N	Y	N
32 Dixon	N	N	N	N	Y	N	Y	N
33 Roybal-Allard	N	N	N	N	Y	N	Y	N
34 Torres	N	N	N	Y	N	Y	N	N
35 Waters	N	N	N	N	Y	N	Y	N
36 Harman	N	Y	Y	N	Y	N	Y	Y
37 Tucker	?	?	?	?	?	N	Y	N
38 Horn	Y	Y	Y	N	Y	Y	N	N
39 Royce	Y	Y	Y	Y	Y	Y	N	Y
40 Lewis	N	N	Y	N	N	N	Y	N
41 Kim	Y	Y	Y	Y	Y	Y	Y	N

Member	284	285	286	287	288	289	290	291
42 Brown	N	N	N	N	N	Y	N	N
43 Calvert	Y	Y	Y	Y	Y	Y	Y	N
44 McCandless	Y	Y	Y	Y	Y	Y	Y	N
45 Rohrabacher	Y	Y	Y	Y	Y	Y	Y	Y
46 Dornan	Y	Y	Y	Y	Y	Y	N	Y
47 Cox	?	?	?	?	?	Y	N	Y
48 Packard	Y	Y	Y	Y	Y	Y	Y	N
49 Schenk	N	N	N	N	Y	N	Y	Y
50 Filner	N	N	N	N	Y	N	Y	N
51 Cunningham	Y	Y	Y	Y	Y	Y	N	Y
52 Hunter	Y	?	Y	Y	Y	Y	N	Y
COLORADO								
1 Schroeder	N	Y	N	N	Y	N	Y	N
2 Skaggs	N	Y	N	N	Y	N	Y	N
3 McInnis	Y	Y	Y	Y	Y	Y	Y	N
4 Allard	Y	Y	Y	Y	Y	Y	Y	N
5 Hefley	Y	Y	Y	Y	Y	Y	Y	N
6 Schaefer	Y	Y	Y	Y	Y	Y	N	Y
CONNECTICUT								
1 Kennelly	N	N	N	Y	Y	Y	N	N
2 Gejdenson	N	N	N	N	Y	N	Y	N
3 DeLauro	N	N	N	N	Y	N	Y	N
4 Shays	Y	Y	Y	Y	Y	N	Y	N
5 Franks	Y	Y	Y	Y	Y	Y	Y	N
6 Johnson	Y	N	Y	Y	Y	Y	Y	N
DELAWARE								
AL Castle	Y	Y	Y	Y	Y	Y	N	Y
FLORIDA								
1 Hutto	N	Y	N	Y	Y	Y	Y	N
2 Peterson	N	N	N	Y	Y	N	Y	N
3 Brown	N	N	N	N	Y	N	Y	N
4 Fowler	N	Y	N	Y	Y	Y	Y	N
5 Thurman	N	N	N	Y	Y	N	Y	N
6 Stearns	N	Y	Y	Y	Y	Y	Y	Y
7 Mica	N	Y	Y	Y	Y	Y	Y	N
8 McCollum	N	Y	Y	Y	Y	Y	Y	Y
9 Bilirakis	N	Y	Y	Y	Y	Y	Y	N
10 Young	?	?	?	?	?	?	?	?
11 Gibbons	N	N	N	N	N	Y	N	N
12 Canady	N	Y	Y	Y	Y	Y	Y	N
13 Miller	N	Y	Y	Y	Y	Y	N	Y
14 Goss	N	Y	Y	Y	Y	Y	N	Y
15 Bacchus	N	N	N	N	N	N	Y	N
16 Lewis	N	Y	Y	Y	Y	Y	N	N
17 Meek	N	?	N	N	N	Y	N	N
18 Ros-Lehtinen	N	Y	Y	Y	Y	N	Y	N
19 Johnston	?	?	N	Y	N	N	N	N
20 Deutsch	N	N	Y	N	Y	N	Y	N
21 Diaz-Balart	N	Y	Y	Y	N	Y	N	N
22 Shaw	N	Y	Y	Y	Y	Y	N	Y
23 Hastings	N	N	N	N	N	N	Y	N
GEORGIA								
1 Kingston	Y	Y	Y	Y	Y	Y	N	N
2 Bishop	N	N	N	N	Y	N	Y	N
3 Collins	Y	Y	Y	Y	Y	Y	N	N
4 Linder	Y	Y	Y	Y	Y	Y	N	Y
5 Lewis	N	N	N	N	Y	N	Y	N
6 Gingrich	N	Y	N	N	Y	N	N	N
7 Darden	N	N	N	N	Y	N	Y	N
8 Rowland	N	N	Y	Y	N	Y	N	N
9 Deal	Y	N	N	Y	N	Y	N	N
10 Johnson	Y	N	N	Y	N	Y	N	N
11 McKinney	N	N	Y	N	Y	N	Y	N
HAWAII								
1 Abercrombie	N	N	Y	N	Y	N	Y	N
2 Mink	N	N	N	N	Y	N	Y	N
IDAHO								
1 LaRocco	N	N	N	Y	Y	N	Y	N
2 Crapo	Y	Y	Y	Y	Y	Y	N	N
ILLINOIS								
1 Rush	N	N	N	N	Y	N	Y	N
2 Reynolds	N	N	N	N	Y	N	Y	?
3 Lipinski	N	N	Y	N	Y	N	Y	N
4 Gutierrez	N	N	Y	Y	?	N	Y	N
5 Rostenkowski	N	N	N	N	Y	N	Y	N
6 Hyde	Y	Y	Y	Y	Y	Y	Y	Y
7 Collins	N	N	N	N	Y	N	Y	N
8 Crane	Y	Y	Y	Y	Y	Y	N	N
9 Yates	N	N	N	N	Y	N	Y	N
10 Porter	Y	Y	Y	Y	Y	Y	Y	Y
11 Sangmeister	Y	N	N	Y	N	Y	N	N
12 Costello	N	Y	N	N	Y	N	Y	N
13 Fawell	Y	Y	Y	Y	Y	Y	N	Y
14 Hastert	Y	Y	Y	Y	Y	Y	N	N
15 Ewing	Y	Y	Y	Y	Y	Y	N	Y
16 Manzullo	Y	Y	Y	Y	Y	Y	N	Y
17 Evans	N	N	N	N	Y	N	Y	N

ND Northern Democrats SD Southern Democrats

	284	285	286	287	288	289	290	291
18 ***Michel***	Y	Y	Y	Y	Y	Y	N	N
19 Poshard	N	Y	N	Y	Y	N	Y	N
20 Durbin	N	N	N	N	Y	N	Y	N
INDIANA								
1 Visclosky	N	N	N	N	Y	N	Y	N
2 Sharp	N	N	N	N	Y	N	Y	N
3 Roemer	Y	N	N	Y	Y	N	N	N
4 Long	N	N	N	Y	Y	N	N	N
5 ***Buyer***	Y	Y	Y	Y	Y	Y	Y	N
6 ***Burton***	Y	Y	Y	Y	Y	Y	N	Y
7 ***Myers***	Y	Y	N	Y	Y	Y	N	N
8 McCloskey	N	N	N	Y	N	N	Y	N
9 Hamilton	N	N	N	Y	Y	Y	Y	N
10 Jacobs	Y	Y	N	Y	Y	Y	N	Y
IOWA								
1 ***Leach***	Y	Y	Y	Y	Y	Y	N	N
2 ***Nussle***	Y	Y	Y	Y	Y	Y	N	Y
3 ***Lightfoot***	N	N	Y	Y	N	Y	Y	N
4 Smith	N	N	N	N	Y	N	Y	N
5 ***Grandy***	Y	Y	Y	Y	Y	Y	N	N
KANSAS								
1 ***Roberts***	Y	Y	Y	Y	Y	Y	N	N
2 Slattery	Y	Y	N	Y	Y	N	Y	N
3 ***Meyers***	Y	Y	Y	Y	Y	Y	Y	N
4 Glickman	Y	Y	N	Y	Y	N	Y	N
KENTUCKY								
1 Barlow	N	?	Y	N	Y	N	Y	N
2 Natcher	N	N	N	N	N	N	Y	N
3 Mazzoli	N	N	N	N	Y	N	Y	N
4 ***Bunning***	Y	Y	Y	Y	Y	Y	N	N
5 ***Rogers***	N	Y	Y	Y	Y	Y	Y	N
6 Baesler	N	N	Y	N	Y	N	Y	N
LOUISIANA								
1 ***Livingston***	N	Y	Y	Y	N	Y	Y	N
2 Jefferson	N	N	Y	N	N	N	Y	N
3 Tauzin	N	Y	Y	Y	Y	Y	N	N
4 Fields	N	N	Y	N	N	N	Y	N
5 ***McCrery***	Y	Y	Y	Y	Y	Y	Y	N
6 ***Baker***	Y	Y	Y	Y	Y	Y	N	N
7 Hayes	N	N	Y	N	Y	N	Y	N
MAINE								
1 Andrews	N	N	N	N	Y	N	Y	Y
2 ***Snowe***	Y	Y	Y	Y	Y	Y	Y	N
MARYLAND								
1 ***Gilchrest***	Y	Y	Y	Y	Y	Y	Y	N
2 ***Bentley***	N	Y	Y	Y	Y	Y	Y	N
3 Cardin	N	N	N	N	Y	N	Y	N
4 Wynn	N	N	N	N	Y	N	Y	N
5 Hoyer	N	N	N	N	Y	N	Y	N
6 ***Bartlett***	Y	Y	Y	Y	Y	Y	N	N
7 Mfume	N	N	N	N	Y	N	Y	N
8 ***Morella***	Y	Y	Y	Y	Y	N	Y	N
MASSACHUSETTS								
1 Olver	N	N	N	N	Y	N	Y	N
2 Neal	N	N	N	Y	Y	N	Y	N
3 ***Blute***	+	+	+	+	+	+	−	+
4 Frank	N	N	N	N	Y	N	Y	Y
5 Meehan	?	?	N	Y	Y	N	Y	N
6 ***Torkildsen***	Y	Y	Y	Y	Y	Y	N	N
7 Markey	N	N	N	N	Y	N	Y	N
8 Kennedy	N	N	N	N	Y	N	Y	N
9 Moakley	N	N	N	N	Y	N	Y	N
10 Studds	N	N	N	N	Y	N	Y	N
MICHIGAN								
1 Stupak	N	N	N	N	Y	N	Y	N
2 ***Hoekstra***	Y	Y	Y	Y	Y	Y	N	Y
3 Henry	?	?	?	?	?	?	?	?
4 ***Camp***	Y	Y	Y	Y	Y	Y	Y	N
5 Barcia	N	N	N	N	Y	N	Y	N
6 ***Upton***	Y	Y	Y	Y	Y	Y	Y	N
7 ***Smith***	Y	Y	Y	Y	Y	Y	N	N
8 Carr	N	?	?	N	Y	N	Y	N
9 Kildee	N	N	N	N	Y	N	Y	N
10 Bonior	N	N	N	N	Y	N	Y	N
11 ***Knollenberg***	Y	Y	Y	Y	Y	Y	N	Y
12 Levin	Y	N	N	Y	Y	N	Y	N
13 Ford	N	N	N	N	Y	N	Y	N
14 Conyers	?	?	N	N	Y	N	Y	N
15 Collins	?	?	?	N	Y	N	Y	N
16 Dingell	N	N	N	N	Y	N	Y	N
MINNESOTA								
1 Penny	Y	Y	Y	Y	Y	Y	N	Y
2 Minge	Y	Y	Y	Y	Y	N	N	N
3 ***Ramstad***	Y	Y	Y	Y	Y	Y	N	Y
4 Vento	N	N	N	Y	Y	N	Y	N
5 Sabo	N	N	N	N	Y	N	Y	N
6 ***Grams***	Y	Y	Y	Y	Y	Y	N	Y
7 Peterson	N	N	N	Y	Y	N	Y	N
8 Oberstar	N	N	N	N	Y	N	Y	N
MISSISSIPPI								
1 Whitten	N	N	N	N	N	N	Y	N
2 Thompson	N	N	N	N	Y	N	Y	N
3 Montgomery	N	N	Y	Y	N	N	Y	N
4 Parker	N	Y	Y	Y	N	Y	N	N
5 Taylor	N	Y	Y	Y	N	Y	Y	Y
MISSOURI								
1 Clay	N	N	N	N	Y	N	Y	N
2 ***Talent***	Y	Y	Y	Y	Y	Y	Y	Y
3 Gephardt	N	N	N	N	N	N	Y	N
4 Skelton	N	N	N	Y	Y	N	Y	N
5 Wheat	N	N	N	N	Y	?	Y	N
6 Danner	N	N	N	Y	Y	N	Y	N
7 ***Hancock***	Y	Y	Y	Y	Y	Y	N	Y
8 ***Emerson***	Y	Y	Y	Y	Y	Y	Y	N
9 Volkmer	N	N	N	N	Y	N	Y	N
MONTANA								
AL Williams	N	Y	N	N	Y	N	Y	N
NEBRASKA								
1 ***Bereuter***	Y	N	Y	Y	Y	Y	Y	N
2 Hoagland	Y	Y	N	Y	Y	N	Y	N
3 ***Barrett***	Y	Y	Y	Y	Y	Y	Y	N
NEVADA								
1 Bilbray	Y	N	Y	Y	N	Y	Y	N
2 ***Vucanovich***	N	Y	Y	Y	N	Y	Y	N
NEW HAMPSHIRE								
1 ***Zeliff***	Y	Y	Y	Y	Y	Y	N	Y
2 Swett	N	N	N	Y	Y	Y	N	N
NEW JERSEY								
1 Andrews	N	N	Y	Y	Y	N	Y	Y
2 Hughes	N	N	N	N	Y	N	N	N
3 ***Saxton***	Y	Y	Y	Y	Y	Y	N	N
4 ***Smith***	Y	Y	Y	Y	Y	Y	Y	N
5 ***Roukema***	N	Y	N	Y	Y	Y	N	N
6 Pallone	N	N	Y	Y	Y	N	Y	N
7 ***Franks***	Y	Y	Y	Y	Y	Y	N	N
8 Klein	N	N	N	N	Y	N	Y	N
9 Torricelli	N	N	?	N	Y	N	Y	N
10 Payne	N	N	N	N	Y	N	Y	N
11 ***Gallo***	N	N	Y	Y	Y	N	Y	N
12 ***Zimmer***	Y	Y	Y	Y	Y	Y	N	Y
13 Menendez	N	N	N	Y	Y	N	Y	N
NEW MEXICO								
1 ***Schiff***	Y	Y	Y	Y	Y	Y	Y	N
2 ***Skeen***	−	+	+	+	+	−	+	−
3 Richardson	N	N	N	N	Y	N	Y	N
NEW YORK								
1 Hochbrueckner	N	N	N	N	N	N	Y	N
2 ***Lazio***	Y	Y	Y	Y	Y	Y	Y	Y
3 ***King***	Y	Y	Y	Y	Y	Y	Y	Y
4 ***Levy***	Y	Y	Y	Y	Y	Y	Y	Y
5 Ackerman	N	N	N	N	Y	N	Y	N
6 Flake	N	N	N	N	Y	N	Y	N
7 Manton	N	N	Y	Y	Y	N	Y	N
8 Nadler	N	N	N	N	Y	N	Y	N
9 Schumer	N	N	N	Y	Y	N	Y	N
10 Towns	N	N	N	N	Y	N	Y	N
11 Owens	?	N	N	N	Y	N	Y	N
12 Velazquez	N	N	N	N	Y	?	Y	N
13 ***Molinari***	Y	Y	Y	Y	Y	Y	Y	Y
14 Maloney	N	N	N	Y	Y	N	Y	Y
15 Rangel	N	N	N	N	Y	N	Y	N
16 Serrano	N	N	N	N	Y	N	?	N
17 Engel	−	−	−	−	+	N	Y	N
18 Lowey	?	?	?	?	?	N	Y	N
19 ***Fish***	N	Y	Y	Y	Y	Y	Y	N
20 ***Gilman***	Y	Y	Y	Y	Y	Y	Y	N
21 McNulty	N	N	N	N	N	N	Y	N
22 ***Solomon***	Y	Y	Y	Y	Y	Y	N	Y
23 ***Boehlert***	N	Y	Y	N	Y	N	Y	N
24 ***McHugh***	Y	Y	Y	Y	Y	Y	Y	N
25 ***Walsh***	N	Y	Y	Y	Y	N	Y	N
26 Hinchey	N	N	N	N	Y	N	Y	N
27 ***Paxon***	Y	Y	Y	Y	Y	Y	N	N
28 Slaughter	N	N	N	N	Y	N	Y	N
29 LaFalce	N	N	N	N	Y	N	Y	N
30 ***Quinn***	Y	Y	Y	Y	Y	N	Y	Y
31 ***Houghton***	Y	Y	Y	N	Y	Y	Y	N
NORTH CAROLINA								
1 Clayton	N	N	N	N	Y	N	Y	N
2 Valentine	?	N	N	N	Y	N	Y	N
3 Lancaster	N	N	Y	Y	Y	N	Y	N
4 Price	N	N	N	N	Y	N	Y	N
5 Neal	N	N	N	Y	Y	N	Y	N
6 ***Coble***	Y	Y	Y	Y	Y	Y	N	Y
7 Rose	N	N	Y	N	Y	N	Y	N
8 Hefner	N	N	N	N	Y	N	Y	N
9 ***McMillan***	?	?	?	?	?	?	?	?
10 ***Ballenger***	Y	Y	Y	Y	Y	Y	N	Y
11 ***Taylor***	Y	Y	Y	Y	Y	Y	N	N
12 Watt	N	N	N	N	Y	N	Y	N
NORTH DAKOTA								
AL Pomeroy	N	N	N	Y	Y	N	Y	N
OHIO								
1 Mann	N	N	N	N	Y	N	Y	Y
2 ***Portman***	Y	Y	Y	Y	Y	Y	N	N
3 Hall	N	N	Y	Y	Y	N	Y	N
4 ***Oxley***	Y	Y	Y	Y	Y	Y	N	N
5 ***Gillmor***	Y	Y	Y	Y	Y	Y	N	N
6 Strickland	N	N	N	N	Y	N	Y	N
7 ***Hobson***	Y	Y	Y	Y	Y	Y	Y	N
8 ***Boehner***	Y	Y	Y	Y	Y	Y	N	N
9 Kaptur	N	N	N	N	Y	N	Y	N
10 ***Hoke***	Y	Y	Y	Y	Y	N	Y	Y
11 Stokes	N	N	N	N	N	N	Y	N
12 ***Kasich***	Y	Y	Y	Y	Y	Y	N	Y
13 Brown	N	N	N	Y	Y	N	Y	N
14 Sawyer	N	N	N	N	Y	N	Y	N
15 ***Pryce***	Y	Y	Y	Y	Y	Y	N	N
16 ***Regula***	Y	Y	Y	Y	Y	Y	Y	N
17 Traficant	N	N	N	N	N	N	Y	N
18 Applegate	N	N	N	Y	Y	N	Y	Y
19 Fingerhut	N	Y	N	N	Y	Y	Y	Y
OKLAHOMA								
1 ***Inhofe***	Y	Y	Y	Y	Y	Y	N	Y
2 Synar	N	Y	N	N	Y	N	Y	N
3 Brewster	Y	N	N	N	Y	N	Y	N
4 McCurdy	Y	N	Y	Y	Y	N	Y	N
5 ***Istook***	Y	Y	Y	Y	Y	Y	N	N
6 English	Y	N	Y	Y	Y	N	Y	N
OREGON								
1 Furse	N	N	N	N	Y	N	Y	N
2 ***Smith***	Y	Y	Y	Y	Y	Y	N	N
3 Wyden	Y	N	N	Y	Y	N	Y	N
4 DeFazio	N	N	N	Y	Y	N	N	N
5 Kopetski	N	N	N	N	N	N	Y	N
PENNSYLVANIA								
1 Foglietta	N	N	N	N	Y	N	Y	N
2 Blackwell	N	N	Y	N	Y	N	Y	N
3 Borski	?	?	Y	Y	Y	N	Y	N
4 Klink	N	N	N	Y	Y	N	Y	N
5 ***Clinger***	Y	Y	Y	Y	Y	Y	Y	N
6 Holden	N	N	N	Y	Y	N	Y	N
7 ***Weldon***	Y	Y	Y	Y	Y	Y	N	Y
8 ***Greenwood***	Y	Y	Y	Y	Y	Y	Y	N
9 ***Shuster***	Y	Y	Y	Y	Y	Y	N	Y
10 ***McDade***	N	Y	Y	Y	Y	Y	Y	N
11 Kanjorski	N	N	N	N	Y	N	Y	N
12 Murtha	N	N	N	N	N	N	Y	N
13 Margolies-Mezv.	Y	N	N	Y	Y	N	Y	Y
14 Coyne	N	N	N	N	Y	N	Y	N
15 McHale	Y	?	Y	Y	Y	N	Y	N
16 ***Walker***	Y	Y	Y	Y	Y	Y	N	Y
17 ***Gekas***	Y	Y	Y	Y	Y	Y	N	N
18 ***Santorum***	Y	Y	Y	Y	Y	Y	N	Y
19 ***Goodling***	Y	Y	Y	Y	Y	Y	Y	Y
20 Murphy	Y	N	N	Y	Y	N	Y	Y
21 ***Ridge***	?	?	?	?	?	N	Y	N
RHODE ISLAND								
1 ***Machtley***	Y	Y	Y	Y	Y	Y	Y	N
2 Reed	N	N	N	N	Y	N	Y	N
SOUTH CAROLINA								
1 ***Ravenel***	Y	Y	Y	Y	Y	Y	Y	N
2 ***Spence***	Y	Y	Y	Y	Y	Y	Y	N
3 Derrick	N	N	N	Y	N	N	Y	N
4 ***Inglis***	Y	Y	Y	Y	Y	Y	N	Y
5 Spratt	Y	Y	N	Y	Y	N	Y	N
6 Clyburn	N	N	N	N	Y	N	Y	N
SOUTH DAKOTA								
AL Johnson	N	N	N	N	Y	Y	Y	N
TENNESSEE								
1 ***Quillen***	N	N	N	Y	Y	N	Y	N
2 ***Duncan***	Y	Y	Y	Y	Y	Y	N	N
3 Lloyd	N	N	N	N	Y	N	Y	N
4 Cooper	Y	Y	N	N	N	Y	Y	N
5 Clement	N	N	Y	Y	Y	N	Y	N
6 Gordon	N	N	N	Y	Y	N	Y	N
7 ***Sundquist***	N	Y	Y	Y	Y	Y	Y	N
8 Tanner	N	Y	Y	Y	N	Y	Y	N
9 Ford	?	?	Y	N	Y	N	Y	N
TEXAS								
1 Chapman	N	N	N	N	N	N	Y	N
2 Wilson	?	?	?	?	?	?	?	?
3 ***Johnson, Sam***	Y	Y	Y	Y	Y	Y	N	Y
4 Hall	N	Y	Y	N	N	Y	Y	N
5 Bryant	N	N	N	N	Y	N	Y	N
6 ***Barton***	Y	Y	Y	Y	Y	Y	N	N
7 ***Archer***	Y	Y	Y	Y	Y	Y	N	N
8 ***Fields***	Y	Y	Y	Y	Y	Y	N	N
9 Brooks	N	N	N	N	N	N	Y	N
10 Pickle	N	N	Y	N	Y	N	Y	N
11 Edwards	N	N	Y	Y	Y	N	Y	N
12 Geren	Y	Y	Y	Y	N	Y	Y	N
13 Sarpalius	N	Y	Y	N	Y	N	Y	N
14 Laughlin	N	Y	Y	N	Y	Y	Y	N
15 de la Garza	N	N	Y	N	Y	N	Y	N
16 Coleman	N	N	N	N	Y	N	Y	N
17 Stenholm	Y	Y	Y	Y	Y	Y	Y	N
18 Washington	N	N	Y	N	Y	N	Y	N
19 ***Combest***	Y	Y	Y	Y	Y	Y	N	N
20 Gonzalez	N	N	N	N	N	N	Y	N
21 ***Smith***	Y	Y	Y	Y	Y	Y	Y	N
22 ***DeLay***	N	Y	Y	Y	Y	Y	Y	Y
23 ***Bonilla***	Y	Y	Y	?	Y	Y	Y	N
24 Frost	N	N	N	Y	Y	N	Y	N
25 Andrews	Y	Y	Y	Y	Y	N	Y	N
26 ***Armey***	Y	Y	Y	Y	Y	Y	N	Y
27 Ortiz	N	N	Y	Y	Y	N	Y	N
28 Tejeda	N	N	N	N	Y	N	Y	N
29 Green	N	N	N	N	Y	−	Y	N
30 Johnson, E. B.	N	N	N	N	?	N	Y	N
UTAH								
1 ***Hansen***	Y	Y	Y	Y	Y	Y	N	N
2 Shepherd	Y	N	N	N	Y	N	Y	N
3 Orton	Y	N	N	Y	Y	Y	N	N
VERMONT								
AL *Sanders*	N	N	N	N	Y	N	Y	N
VIRGINIA								
1 ***Bateman***	Y	Y	Y	Y	Y	N	Y	N
2 Pickett	N	N	N	N	N	N	Y	N
3 Scott	N	N	Y	N	Y	N	Y	N
4 Sisisky	N	Y	Y	Y	Y	Y	Y	N
5 Payne	N	N	Y	N	Y	N	Y	N
6 ***Goodlatte***	Y	Y	Y	Y	Y	Y	N	N
7 ***Bliley***	Y	Y	Y	Y	Y	Y	Y	Y
8 Moran	Y	N	Y	N	Y	N	Y	N
9 Boucher	N	N	N	N	N	N	Y	N
10 ***Wolf***	Y	Y	Y	Y	Y	Y	N	N
11 Byrne	N	N	Y	N	Y	N	Y	N
WASHINGTON								
1 Cantwell	N	Y	N	Y	Y	N	Y	N
2 Swift	N	N	N	N	Y	N	Y	N
3 Unsoeld	N	N	N	N	Y	N	Y	N
4 Inslee	Y	Y	N	N	Y	N	Y	N
5 Foley								
6 Dicks	N	Y	N	Y	Y	N	?	N
7 McDermott	N	N	N	N	Y	N	Y	N
8 ***Dunn***	Y	Y	Y	Y	Y	Y	Y	Y
9 Kreidler	N	N	N	N	Y	N	Y	N
WEST VIRGINIA								
1 Mollohan	N	N	N	N	N	N	Y	N
2 Wise	N	Y	N	N	Y	N	Y	N
3 Rahall	N	N	N	Y	Y	N	Y	N
WISCONSIN								
1 Barca	N	Y	N	Y	Y	N	N	N
2 ***Klug***	Y	Y	Y	Y	Y	Y	N	Y
3 ***Gunderson***	Y	Y	Y	Y	Y	Y	Y	N
4 Kleczka	N	N	N	Y	Y	N	Y	N
5 Barrett	Y	N	N	Y	Y	N	Y	N
6 ***Petri***	Y	Y	Y	Y	Y	Y	N	Y
7 Obey	N	N	N	N	Y	N	Y	N
8 ***Roth***	Y	Y	Y	Y	Y	Y	N	N
9 ***Sensenbrenner***	Y	Y	Y	Y	Y	Y	N	Y
WYOMING								
AL ***Thomas***	Y	Y	Y	Y	Y	Y	N	N
DELEGATES								
de Lugo, V.I.	D	D	D	D	D	D	D	N
Faleomavaega, Am.S.	D	D	D	D	D	D	D	N
Norton, D.C.	D	D	D	D	D	D	D	N
Romero-B., P.R.	D	D	D	D	D	D	D	N
Underwood, Guam	D	D	D	D	D	D	D	?

Southern states - Ala., Ark., Fla., Ga., Ky., La., Miss., N.C., Okla., S.C., Tenn., Texas, Va.
Omitted votes are quorum calls, which CQ does not include in its vote charts.

292. HR 2493. Fiscal 1994 Agriculture Appropriations/ Rural Development Grants. Burton, R-Ind., amendment to cut rural development grants by $14.25 million. Rejected in the Committee of the Whole 145-288: R 133-39; D 12-248 (ND 10-165, SD 2-83); I 0-1, June 29, 1993.

293. HR 2493. Fiscal 1994 Agriculture Appropriations/ Rural Electrification Administration. Zimmer, R-N.J., amendment to cut $200 million from the Rural Electrification Administration's hardship loans to electric and telephone utilities. Rejected in the Committee of the Whole 117-314: R 85-86; D 32-227 (ND 30-146, SD 2-81); I 0-1, June 29, 1993.

294. HR 2493. Fiscal 1994 Agriculture Appropriations/ Socially Disadvantaged Farmers. Burton, R-Ind., amendment to cut the $3 million for outreach programs for farmers and ranchers who encountered economic hardship because of racial or ethnic prejudice. Rejected in the Committee of the Whole 178-251: R 150-21; D 28-229 (ND 15-159, SD 13-70); I 0-1, June 29, 1993.

295. HR 2493. Fiscal 1994 Agriculture Appropriations/ Whole Milk in School Lunch Programs. Volkmer, D-Mo., amendment to strike the provision of the bill that bars enforcement of a federal law requiring schools that receive school lunch funding to make whole milk available to students. Adopted in the Committee of the Whole 292-137: R 139-31; D 152-106 (ND 92-81, SD 60-25); I 1-0, June 29, 1993.

296. HR 2493. Fiscal 1994 Agriculture Appropriations/ Market Promotion Program. Durbin, D-Ill., amendment to the Schumer, D-N.Y., substitute amendment to the Armey, R-Texas, amendment, to cut $20 million from the Market Promotion Program. Schumer would have cut $57.7 million, and Armey would have eliminated the program by cutting all but $1 of the program's $147.7 million. Adopted in the Committee of the Whole 330-101: R 120-51; D 209-50 (ND 131-44, SD 78-6); I 1-0, June 29, 1993.

297. HR 2493. Fiscal 1994 Agriculture Appropriations/ Market Promotion Program. Schumer, D-N.Y., substitute amendment, as amended, to the Armey, R-Texas, amendment, to cut $20 million from the Market Promotion Program. Before being amended by a Durbin, D-Ill., amendment, the Schumer amendment would have cut $57.7 million, and Armey would have eliminated the program by cutting all but $1 of the program's $147.7 million. Adopted in the Committee of the Whole 337-90: R 120-51; D 216-39 (ND 138-33, SD 78-6); I 1-0, June 29, 1993.

298. HR 2493. Fiscal 1994 Agriculture Appropriations/ Market Promotion Program. Armey, R-Texas, amendment, as amended, to cut $20 million from the Market Promotion Program. Before being amended by a Schumer, D-N.Y., amendment, the Armey amendment would have eliminated the program by cutting all but $1 of the program's $147.7 million. Adopted in the Committee of the Whole 406-25: R 157-14; D 248-11 (ND 169-6, SD 79-5); I 1-0, June 29, 1993.

299. HR 2493. Fiscal 1994 Agriculture Appropriations/ Whole Milk in School Lunch Programs. Separate vote at the request of Solomon, R-N.Y., on the Volkmer, D-Mo., amendment adopted in the Committee of the Whole to strike the provision of the bill that bars enforcement of a federal law requiring schools that receive school lunch funding to make whole milk available to students. Adopted 299-127: R 146-25; D 152-102 (ND 89-81, SD 63-21); I 1-0, June 29, 1993. (On separate votes, which may be demanded on an amendment adopted in the Committee of the Whole, the four delegates and the resident commissioner of Puerto Rico cannot vote. See vote 295.)

KEY

Y Voted for (yea).
Paired for.
+ Announced for.
N Voted against (nay).
X Paired against.
− Announced against.
P Voted "present."
C Voted "present" to avoid possible conflict of interest.
? Did not vote or otherwise make a position known.
D Delegates ineligible to vote.

Democrats **Republicans** *Independent*

	292	293	294	295	296	297	298	299
ALABAMA								
1 *Callahan*	Y	N	Y	Y	Y	Y	Y	Y
2 *Everett*	N	N	Y	Y	Y	Y	Y	Y
3 Browder	N	N	N	Y	Y	Y	Y	N
4 Bevill	N	N	N	Y	Y	Y	Y	Y
5 Cramer	N	N	N	Y	Y	Y	Y	Y
6 *Bachus*	Y	N	Y	N	Y	Y	Y	Y
7 Hilliard	N	N	N	Y	Y	Y	Y	Y
ALASKA								
AL *Young*	N	N	Y	Y	N	N	Y	N
ARIZONA								
1 Coppersmith	N	Y	N	N	N	N	Y	N
2 Pastor	N	N	N	Y	Y	Y	Y	N
3 *Stump*	Y	Y	Y	N	N	N	Y	Y
4 *Kyl*	Y	N	Y	Y	N	N	Y	Y
5 *Kolbe*	Y	N	Y	Y	N	N	Y	Y
6 English	N	N	N	Y	Y	Y	Y	Y
ARKANSAS								
1 Lambert	N	N	N	N	Y	Y	Y	Y
2 Thornton	N	N	N	Y	Y	Y	Y	Y
3 *Hutchinson*	N	Y	Y	Y	Y	Y	Y	Y
4 *Dickey*	N	N	Y	Y	Y	Y	Y	Y
CALIFORNIA								
1 Hamburg	N	N	N	Y	Y	Y	Y	Y
2 *Herger*	Y	Y	Y	Y	Y	Y	Y	Y
3 Fazio	N	N	N	Y	Y	Y	N	Y
4 *Doolittle*	Y	Y	Y	N	Y	Y	Y	N
5 Matsui	?	N	N	N	Y	Y	Y	Y
6 Woolsey	N	N	N	Y	Y	Y	Y	Y
7 Miller	N	N	N	N	N	Y	N	N
8 Pelosi	N	N	N	Y	Y	Y	Y	N
9 Dellums	N	N	N	Y	Y	Y	Y	Y
10 *Baker*	Y	Y	Y	N	Y	Y	Y	Y
11 *Pombo*	Y	N	Y	Y	Y	Y	Y	Y
12 Lantos	N	N	N	Y	Y	Y	Y	N
13 Stark	N	Y	N	N	N	Y	N	N
14 Eshoo	N	Y	N	N	Y	Y	Y	N
15 Mineta	N	N	N	Y	Y	Y	Y	N
16 Edwards	N	N	N	Y	Y	Y	Y	N
17 Farr	N	N	N	Y	Y	Y	Y	N
18 Condit	Y	Y	Y	N	Y	Y	Y	N
19 Lehman	N	N	N	Y	Y	Y	Y	Y
20 Dooley	N	N	N	Y	Y	Y	Y	Y
21 *Thomas*	N	N	Y	Y	Y	Y	N	Y
22 *Huffington*	Y	Y	Y	Y	Y	Y	Y	Y
23 *Gallegly*	Y	Y	Y	Y	Y	Y	Y	Y
24 Beilenson	N	Y	N	N	N	N	Y	N
25 *McKeon*	Y	Y	Y	Y	Y	Y	Y	Y
26 Berman	N	N	N	Y	Y	Y	Y	N
27 *Moorhead*	Y	Y	Y	Y	Y	Y	Y	Y
28 *Dreier*	Y	Y	Y	Y	Y	Y	Y	Y
29 Waxman	N	N	N	N	N	N	Y	N
30 Becerra	N	N	N	N	Y	Y	Y	N
31 Martinez	N	N	?	?	?	?	?	?
32 Dixon	N	N	N	Y	Y	Y	Y	Y
33 Roybal-Allard	N	N	N	Y	Y	Y	Y	Y
34 Torres	N	N	N	+	Y	Y	Y	Y
35 Waters	N	Y	N	N	N	Y	N	Y
36 Harman	N	Y	N	N	Y	N	Y	N
37 Tucker	N	N	N	Y	Y	Y	Y	Y
38 *Horn*	Y	Y	Y	Y	Y	Y	N	Y
39 *Royce*	Y	Y	Y	Y	N	Y	Y	Y
40 *Lewis*	N	Y	N	Y	Y	Y	Y	Y
41 *Kim*	Y	Y	Y	Y	Y	Y	Y	Y

	292	293	294	295	296	297	298	299
42 Brown	N	N	N	?	Y	Y	Y	Y
43 *Calvert*	Y	N	Y	Y	Y	Y	Y	Y
44 *McCandless*	Y	N	Y	Y	Y	Y	Y	Y
45 *Rohrabacher*	Y	Y	Y	Y	N	N	Y	Y
46 *Dornan*	Y	Y	Y	Y	Y	N	Y	Y
47 *Cox*	Y	Y	Y	Y	Y	Y	Y	Y
48 *Packard*	Y	Y	Y	Y	Y	N	Y	Y
49 Schenk	N	Y	N	Y	Y	Y	Y	N
50 Filner	N	N	N	Y	Y	Y	Y	Y
51 *Cunningham*	Y	Y	Y	Y	Y	Y	Y	Y
52 *Hunter*	Y	Y	Y	Y	Y	Y	Y	Y
COLORADO								
1 Schroeder	Y	Y	N	N	N	N	Y	N
2 Skaggs	N	N	N	N	N	N	Y	N
3 *McInnis*	Y	N	Y	Y	N	Y	Y	Y
4 *Allard*	Y	N	Y	Y	Y	Y	Y	Y
5 *Hefley*	Y	Y	N	N	Y	N	Y	Y
6 *Schaefer*	Y	N	Y	Y	Y	Y	Y	Y
CONNECTICUT								
1 Kennelly	N	Y	N	N	Y	Y	Y	N
2 Gejdenson	N	N	N	N	Y	Y	Y	N
3 DeLauro	N	N	N	N	Y	Y	Y	N
4 *Shays*	Y	Y	N	N	N	N	Y	N
5 *Franks*	Y	Y	Y	N	Y	Y	Y	Y
6 *Johnson*	N	Y	Y	Y	Y	N	Y	Y
DELAWARE								
AL *Castle*	Y	N	Y	N	Y	Y	Y	N
FLORIDA								
1 Hutto	N	N	Y	Y	Y	Y	Y	Y
2 Peterson	N	N	N	Y	Y	Y	Y	Y
3 Brown	N	N	N	Y	Y	Y	Y	N
4 *Fowler*	Y	Y	Y	Y	Y	Y	Y	Y
5 Thurman	N	N	N	Y	Y	Y	Y	Y
6 *Stearns*	Y	N	Y	Y	Y	Y	Y	Y
7 *Mica*	Y	Y	Y	Y	Y	Y	Y	Y
8 *McCollum*	Y	Y	Y	N	N	N	Y	Y
9 *Bilirakis*	Y	Y	Y	Y	Y	Y	Y	Y
10 *Young*	Y	Y	Y	?	Y	Y	Y	Y
11 Gibbons	N	Y	N	N	Y	N	Y	N
12 *Canady*	Y	N	Y	Y	Y	Y	N	Y
13 *Miller*	Y	Y	Y	Y	Y	Y	Y	Y
14 *Goss*	Y	Y	Y	Y	Y	Y	Y	Y
15 Bacchus	N	N	N	Y	Y	Y	Y	Y
16 *Lewis*	Y	Y	Y	Y	Y	Y	Y	Y
17 Meek	N	N	N	Y	Y	Y	Y	N
18 *Ros-Lehtinen*	Y	Y	N	Y	Y	Y	Y	Y
19 Johnston	N	N	N	Y	Y	Y	Y	Y
20 Deutsch	N	N	N	Y	Y	Y	Y	Y
21 *Diaz-Balart*	Y	N	Y	Y	Y	Y	Y	Y
22 *Shaw*	Y	Y	Y	Y	N	N	Y	Y
23 Hastings	N	N	N	Y	Y	Y	Y	Y
GEORGIA								
1 *Kingston*	N	N	Y	Y	Y	Y	Y	Y
2 Bishop	N	−	N	Y	Y	Y	Y	Y
3 *Collins*	Y	Y	Y	Y	Y	Y	Y	Y
4 *Linder*	Y	Y	Y	N	N	N	Y	Y
5 Lewis	N	N	N	Y	Y	Y	Y	N
6 *Gingrich*	Y	Y	Y	Y	Y	Y	Y	Y
7 *Darden*	N	N	N	N	Y	Y	Y	N
8 Rowland	N	N	Y	N	Y	Y	Y	N
9 Deal	N	N	N	Y	N	Y	Y	Y
10 Johnson	N	N	N	Y	Y	Y	Y	Y
11 McKinney	N	N	N	Y	Y	Y	Y	Y
HAWAII								
1 Abercrombie	N	N	N	N	Y	Y	Y	N
2 Mink	N	N	N	Y	Y	Y	Y	Y
IDAHO								
1 LaRocco	N	N	N	Y	Y	Y	Y	Y
2 *Crapo*	N	N	Y	N	Y	Y	N	N
ILLINOIS								
1 Rush	N	N	N	Y	Y	Y	Y	Y
2 Reynolds	N	N	N	Y	Y	Y	Y	Y
3 Lipinski	N	N	Y	N	Y	N	Y	N
4 Gutierrez	N	N	N	Y	?	Y	N	Y
5 Rostenkowski	?	N	N	Y	Y	Y	Y	Y
6 *Hyde*	Y	Y	Y	N	N	N	Y	Y
7 Collins	N	N	N	Y	Y	Y	Y	Y
8 *Crane*	Y	Y	Y	N	N	Y	Y	Y
9 Yates	N	N	N	N	Y	Y	Y	N
10 *Porter*	Y	Y	Y	N	N	N	Y	N
11 Sangmeister	N	N	Y	Y	Y	Y	Y	Y
12 Costello	N	N	N	N	Y	Y	Y	N
13 *Fawell*	Y	Y	Y	N	N	Y	Y	N
14 *Hastert*	Y	N	Y	Y	N	N	Y	Y
15 *Ewing*	Y	N	N	Y	Y	Y	N	Y
16 *Manzullo*	Y	N	Y	Y	Y	Y	Y	Y
17 Evans	N	N	N	N	N	N	Y	N

ND Northern Democrats   SD Southern Democrats

	292	293	294	295	296	297	298	299
18 ***Michel***	Y	N	Y	N	Y	Y	Y	N
19 Poshard	N	N	N	N	Y	Y	Y	N
20 Durbin	N	N	N	N	Y	Y	Y	N
INDIANA								
1 Visclosky	N	Y	N	N	N	N	Y	N
2 Sharp	N	N	N	N	Y	Y	Y	N
3 Roemer	N	N	N	Y	N	Y	Y	Y
4 Long	N	N	N	Y	Y	Y	Y	Y
5 ***Buyer***	Y	N	Y	Y	Y	Y	Y	Y
6 ***Burton***	Y	Y	Y	Y	N	N	Y	Y
7 ***Myers***	Y	N	Y	N	Y	Y	Y	N
8 McCloskey	N	N	N	Y	Y	Y	Y	Y
9 Hamilton	N	N	N	Y	Y	Y	Y	Y
10 Jacobs	Y	Y	N	N	Y	N	Y	N
IOWA								
1 ***Leach***	N	N	Y	Y	Y	Y	Y	Y
2 ***Nussle***	Y	Y	Y	Y	Y	Y	Y	Y
3 ***Lightfoot***	N	N	Y	Y	Y	Y	Y	Y
4 Smith	N	N	N	N	Y	Y	Y	N
5 ***Grandy***	N	N	Y	Y	Y	Y	N	Y
KANSAS								
1 ***Roberts***	N	N	Y	Y	Y	Y	Y	Y
2 Slattery	Y	N	Y	N	Y	Y	Y	N
3 ***Meyers***	Y	Y	Y	Y	Y	Y	Y	Y
4 Glickman	N	N	Y	N	Y	Y	Y	N
KENTUCKY								
1 Barlow	N	N	N	N	Y	Y	Y	N
2 Natcher	N	N	N	N	Y	Y	Y	N
3 Mazzoli	N	N	N	Y	Y	Y	Y	Y
4 ***Bunning***	Y	N	Y	Y	Y	Y	Y	Y
5 ***Rogers***	N	N	Y	Y	Y	Y	Y	Y
6 Baesler	N	N	N	Y	Y	Y	Y	Y
LOUISIANA								
1 ***Livingston***	Y	N	N	Y	Y	Y	Y	Y
2 Jefferson	N	N	N	Y	Y	Y	Y	Y
3 Tauzin	N	N	N	Y	Y	Y	Y	Y
4 Fields	N	N	N	Y	N	N	N	Y
5 ***McCrery***	N	N	Y	Y	Y	Y	Y	Y
6 ***Baker***	N	N	Y	Y	N	N	N	Y
7 Hayes	N	N	N	Y	Y	Y	Y	Y
MAINE								
1 Andrews	N	N	N	N	N	N	Y	N
2 ***Snowe***	N	N	Y	Y	Y	Y	Y	Y
MARYLAND								
1 ***Gilchrest***	Y	N	Y	N	Y	Y	N	Y
2 ***Bentley***	Y	N	Y	Y	N	Y	Y	Y
3 Cardin	N	Y	Y	N	N	N	Y	N
4 Wynn	N	N	N	Y	Y	Y	Y	Y
5 Hoyer	N	N	N	N	Y	Y	Y	N
6 ***Bartlett***	Y	Y	Y	Y	Y	Y	Y	Y
7 Mfume	N	N	N	Y	Y	Y	Y	Y
8 ***Morella***	Y	Y	N	N	N	N	Y	N
MASSACHUSETTS								
1 Olver	N	N	N	Y	Y	Y	Y	?
2 Neal	N	Y	N	N	Y	Y	Y	N
3 ***Blute***	+	+	+	+	+	+	+	+
4 Frank	N	Y	N	N	N	N	Y	N
5 Meehan	Y	Y	Y	N	N	N	Y	N
6 ***Torkildsen***	Y	Y	Y	Y	N	N	Y	Y
7 Markey	N	N	N	N	N	N	Y	N
8 Kennedy	N	Y	N	N	N	Y	Y	N
9 Moakley	N	N	N	N	Y	Y	Y	N
10 Studds	N	N	N	N	N	N	Y	N
MICHIGAN								
1 Stupak	N	N	N	Y	Y	Y	Y	Y
2 ***Hoekstra***	Y	Y	Y	Y	Y	N	Y	Y
3 Henry	?	?	?	?	?	?	?	?
4 ***Camp***	Y	N	Y	Y	Y	Y	Y	Y
5 Barcia	N	N	N	Y	Y	Y	Y	Y
6 ***Upton***	Y	N	Y	Y	Y	Y	Y	Y
7 ***Smith***	Y	N	Y	Y	Y	Y	N	Y
8 Carr	N	N	N	N	Y	?	Y	N
9 Kildee	N	N	N	Y	Y	Y	Y	Y
10 Bonior	N	N	N	Y	Y	Y	N	Y
11 ***Knollenberg***	Y	Y	Y	Y	N	N	Y	Y
12 Levin	N	N	N	N	N	Y	Y	N
13 Ford	N	N	N	Y	Y	Y	Y	Y
14 Conyers	N	N	N	?	Y	Y	N	N
15 Collins	N	N	N	Y	N	Y	N	Y
16 Dingell	N	N	N	Y	Y	Y	Y	Y
MINNESOTA								
1 Penny	Y	N	Y	N	Y	Y	Y	N
2 Minge	N	N	N	N	Y	Y	Y	N
3 ***Ramstad***	Y	Y	Y	N	Y	N	Y	N
4 Vento	N	N	N	N	N	N	Y	N

	292	293	294	295	296	297	298	299
5 Sabo	N	N	N	N	Y	Y	Y	N
6 ***Grams***	Y	N	Y	N	N	Y	Y	N
7 Peterson	N	N	N	Y	Y	Y	Y	Y
8 Oberstar	N	N	N	Y	Y	?	Y	Y
MISSISSIPPI								
1 Whitten	N	N	N	N	Y	Y	Y	Y
2 Thompson	N	N	N	Y	Y	Y	Y	Y
3 Montgomery	N	?	Y	Y	Y	Y	Y	Y
4 Parker	N	N	N	Y	Y	Y	Y	Y
5 Taylor	N	N	Y	Y	Y	Y	Y	Y
MISSOURI								
1 Clay	N	N	N	Y	Y	Y	Y	Y
2 ***Talent***	Y	Y	Y	Y	Y	Y	Y	Y
3 Gephardt	N	N	N	N	Y	Y	Y	N
4 Skelton	N	?	N	Y	Y	Y	Y	Y
5 Wheat	N	N	N	Y	Y	Y	Y	Y
6 Danner	N	N	N	Y	Y	Y	Y	Y
7 ***Hancock***	Y	Y	Y	Y	Y	Y	Y	Y
8 ***Emerson***	N	N	Y	Y	Y	Y	Y	Y
9 Volkmer	N	N	N	Y	Y	Y	Y	Y
MONTANA								
AL Williams	N	N	N	Y	Y	Y	Y	Y
NEBRASKA								
1 ***Bereuter***	N	N	N	Y	Y	Y	Y	Y
2 Hoagland	N	N	Y	N	Y	Y	Y	N
3 ***Barrett***	N	N	Y	Y	Y	Y	Y	Y
NEVADA								
1 Bilbray	N	Y	Y	Y	N	Y	Y	Y
2 ***Vucanovich***	N	N	N	Y	Y	Y	Y	Y
NEW HAMPSHIRE								
1 ***Zeliff***	Y	Y	Y	Y	N	N	Y	Y
2 Swett	N	N	N	Y	N	N	Y	Y
NEW JERSEY								
1 Andrews	N	Y	N	Y	N	N	Y	Y
2 Hughes	N	Y	N	N	Y	Y	Y	Y
3 ***Saxton***	Y	Y	Y	Y	Y	Y	Y	Y
4 ***Smith***	Y	Y	Y	Y	Y	Y	Y	Y
5 ***Roukema***	Y	Y	Y	Y	Y	Y	Y	Y
6 Pallone	Y	Y	Y	Y	Y	Y	Y	Y
7 ***Franks***	Y	Y	Y	N	Y	N	Y	N
8 Klein	N	Y	N	N	Y	N	Y	N
9 Torricelli	N	N	N	N	Y	Y	Y	N
10 Payne	N	N	N	Y	Y	Y	Y	Y
11 ***Gallo***	N	Y	Y	N	Y	Y	Y	N
12 ***Zimmer***	Y	Y	Y	N	N	N	Y	N
13 Menendez	N	N	N	Y	Y	Y	Y	Y
NEW MEXICO								
1 ***Schiff***	Y	N	Y	Y	N	N	Y	Y
2 ***Skeen***	–	–	–	–	+	+	+	–
3 Richardson	N	N	N	Y	Y	Y	Y	Y
NEW YORK								
1 Hochbrueckner	N	N	N	Y	N	N	Y	Y
2 ***Lazio***	Y	Y	N	N	N	N	Y	N
3 ***King***	Y	Y	Y	N	N	N	Y	N
4 ***Levy***	Y	Y	Y	Y	N	N	Y	Y
5 Ackerman	N	N	N	Y	N	N	Y	Y
6 Flake	N	N	N	Y	Y	Y	Y	Y
7 Manton	N	N	N	Y	N	N	Y	Y
8 Nadler	N	N	N	Y	N	N	Y	N
9 Schumer	N	N	N	N	N	N	Y	N
10 Towns	N	N	N	Y	Y	?	Y	Y
11 Owens	N	N	N	N	N	Y	Y	N
12 Velazquez	N	N	N	Y	Y	Y	Y	Y
13 ***Molinari***	Y	Y	Y	Y	N	N	Y	Y
14 Maloney	N	N	N	N	Y	Y	Y	N
15 Rangel	N	N	N	Y	N	Y	Y	N
16 Serrano	N	N	N	Y	Y	Y	Y	Y
17 Engel	N	N	N	N	N	Y	Y	N
18 Lowey	N	N	N	N	Y	Y	Y	Y
19 ***Fish***	Y	Y	N	Y	Y	Y	Y	Y
20 ***Gilman***	Y	N	N	Y	Y	Y	Y	Y
21 McNulty	N	N	N	Y	Y	Y	Y	Y
22 ***Solomon***	Y	Y	Y	Y	N	N	Y	Y
23 ***Boehlert***	N	N	N	Y	Y	Y	Y	Y
24 ***McHugh***	N	N	Y	Y	Y	Y	Y	Y
25 ***Walsh***	N	N	N	Y	Y	Y	Y	Y
26 Hinchey	N	N	N	Y	Y	Y	Y	Y
27 ***Paxon***	Y	Y	Y	Y	Y	Y	Y	Y
28 Slaughter	N	Y	N	Y	Y	Y	Y	Y
29 LaFalce	N	Y	N	N	Y	Y	Y	N
30 ***Quinn***	Y	Y	Y	Y	Y	N	Y	Y
31 ***Houghton***	Y	N	Y	Y	Y	Y	N	Y
NORTH CAROLINA								
1 Clayton	N	N	N	Y	Y	Y	N	Y
2 Valentine	N	N	Y	Y	Y	N	Y	Y

	292	293	294	295	296	297	298	299
3 Lancaster	N	N	N	Y	Y	Y	N	Y
4 Price	N	N	N	Y	Y	Y	Y	Y
5 Neal	N	N	N	Y	Y	Y	Y	Y
6 ***Coble***	Y	N	Y	Y	N	Y	Y	Y
7 Rose	N	N	N	Y	Y	Y	N	Y
8 Hefner	N	N	N	Y	Y	Y	Y	Y
9 ***McMillan***	?	?	?	?	?	?	?	?
10 ***Ballenger***	Y	N	Y	Y	N	N	Y	Y
11 ***Taylor***	Y	N	N	Y	Y	N	Y	Y
12 Watt	N	N	N	Y	Y	Y	N	Y
NORTH DAKOTA								
AL Pomeroy	N	N	N	Y	Y	Y	Y	Y
OHIO								
1 Mann	Y	Y	Y	N	N	N	Y	N
2 ***Portman***	Y	Y	Y	Y	Y	Y	Y	Y
3 Hall	N	N	N	Y	Y	Y	Y	Y
4 ***Oxley***	Y	N	Y	Y	Y	Y	Y	Y
5 ***Gillmor***	N	N	N	N	N	Y	Y	Y
6 Strickland	N	N	N	Y	Y	Y	Y	Y
7 ***Hobson***	Y	N	Y	Y	Y	Y	Y	Y
8 ***Boehner***	N	Y	Y	Y	Y	Y	N	Y
9 Kaptur	N	N	N	N	Y	Y	Y	N
10 ***Hoke***	Y	Y	Y	Y	Y	Y	Y	Y
11 Stokes	N	N	N	N	N	Y	Y	Y
12 ***Kasich***	Y	Y	Y	Y	Y	Y	Y	Y
13 Brown	N	N	N	Y	Y	Y	Y	Y
14 Sawyer	N	N	N	Y	Y	Y	Y	Y
15 ***Pryce***	Y	N	Y	Y	Y	Y	Y	Y
16 ***Regula***	Y	N	Y	Y	Y	Y	Y	Y
17 Traficant	N	N	N	Y	Y	Y	Y	Y
18 Applegate	N	N	N	Y	Y	Y	N	Y
19 Fingerhut	N	N	N	N	N	N	Y	N
OKLAHOMA								
1 ***Inhofe***	Y	N	Y	Y	N	N	Y	Y
2 Synar	N	N	N	N	N	N	Y	N
3 Brewster	N	N	N	Y	N	Y	Y	Y
4 McCurdy	N	N	Y	N	Y	Y	Y	N
5 ***Istook***	Y	N	Y	Y	N	N	Y	Y
6 English	N	N	N	Y	Y	Y	Y	Y
OREGON								
1 Furse	N	N	N	N	Y	Y	Y	N
2 ***Smith***	Y	N	Y	Y	Y	Y	N	Y
3 Wyden	N	N	N	N	Y	Y	Y	N
4 DeFazio	N	N	N	?	Y	Y	Y	Y
5 Kopetski	N	N	N	Y	Y	Y	N	Y
PENNSYLVANIA								
1 Foglietta	N	N	N	N	N	Y	Y	Y
2 Blackwell	N	N	N	Y	Y	Y	Y	Y
3 Borski	N	N	N	Y	N	Y	Y	Y
4 Klink	N	N	N	Y	Y	N	Y	Y
5 ***Clinger***	N	N	Y	Y	Y	Y	Y	Y
6 Holden	N	N	N	Y	Y	Y	Y	Y
7 ***Weldon***	Y	Y	Y	Y	Y	Y	Y	Y
8 ***Greenwood***	Y	Y	Y	Y	Y	Y	Y	Y
9 ***Shuster***	N	N	Y	Y	N	N	Y	Y
10 ***McDade***	N	N	N	Y	Y	Y	Y	Y
11 Kanjorski	N	N	N	Y	N	N	Y	Y
12 Murtha	N	N	N	Y	Y	Y	Y	Y
13 Margolies-Mezv.	N	Y	N	N	Y	Y	Y	N
14 Coyne	N	N	N	N	Y	Y	Y	N
15 McHale	N	Y	N	Y	Y	Y	Y	Y
16 ***Walker***	Y	Y	Y	Y	N	N	Y	Y
17 ***Gekas***	Y	N	N	Y	N	N	Y	Y
18 ***Santorum***	Y	?	?	?	?	?	?	?
19 ***Goodling***	N	N	N	Y	Y	Y	Y	Y
20 Murphy	N	N	Y	Y	Y	Y	Y	Y
21 ***Ridge***	N	N	Y	Y	Y	N	Y	Y
RHODE ISLAND								
1 ***Machtley***	Y	Y	Y	Y	N	N	Y	Y
2 Reed	N	Y	N	N	N	N	Y	N
SOUTH CAROLINA								
1 ***Ravenel***	N	N	Y	Y	Y	Y	Y	Y
2 ***Spence***	Y	N	Y	Y	Y	Y	Y	Y
3 Derrick	N	N	Y	N	Y	Y	Y	N
4 ***Inglis***	Y	Y	Y	N	Y	Y	Y	N
5 Spratt	N	N	Y	N	Y	Y	Y	N
6 Clyburn	N	N	N	Y	Y	Y	Y	Y
SOUTH DAKOTA								
AL Johnson	N	N	N	Y	Y	Y	Y	Y
TENNESSEE								
1 ***Quillen***	N	N	Y	Y	N	Y	N	Y
2 ***Duncan***	Y	Y	Y	Y	Y	N	Y	Y
3 Lloyd	N	N	N	Y	N	N	Y	Y
4 Cooper	N	N	N	Y	Y	Y	Y	Y
5 Clement	N	N	N	N	N	Y	Y	N

	292	293	294	295	296	297	298	299
6 Gordon	N	N	N	Y	Y	Y	Y	Y
7 ***Sundquist***	N	N	Y	Y	N	Y	N	Y
8 Tanner	N	N	N	Y	Y	Y	Y	Y
9 Ford	N	N	N	N	Y	Y	Y	Y
TEXAS								
1 Chapman	N	N	N	Y	Y	Y	Y	Y
2 Wilson	N	N	N	Y	?	?	?	?
3 ***Johnson, Sam***	Y	Y	Y	N	N	N	Y	Y
4 Hall	N	N	Y	Y	Y	Y	Y	Y
5 Bryant	N	N	N	Y	Y	Y	Y	Y
6 ***Barton***	Y	Y	Y	Y	N	N	Y	Y
7 ***Archer***	Y	Y	Y	N	N	N	Y	Y
8 ***Fields***	Y	N	Y	Y	N	N	Y	Y
9 Brooks	N	N	N	Y	Y	Y	Y	Y
10 Pickle	N	N	N	Y	Y	Y	Y	Y
11 Edwards	N	N	N	Y	Y	Y	Y	Y
12 Geren	Y	Y	N	Y	Y	Y	Y	Y
13 Sarpalius	N	N	N	Y	Y	Y	Y	Y
14 Laughlin	N	N	N	N	Y	Y	Y	Y
15 de la Garza	N	N	N	Y	Y	Y	Y	Y
16 Coleman	N	N	N	N	Y	Y	Y	N
17 Stenholm	N	N	Y	Y	Y	Y	Y	Y
18 Washington	N	N	N	Y	Y	Y	Y	Y
19 ***Combest***	Y	N	Y	Y	Y	Y	Y	Y
20 Gonzalez	N	N	N	Y	Y	Y	Y	Y
21 ***Smith***	N	N	N	Y	Y	N	Y	Y
22 ***DeLay***	Y	Y	Y	N	N	N	Y	N
23 ***Bonilla***	Y	N	Y	Y	N	Y	Y	Y
24 Frost	N	N	N	Y	Y	Y	Y	Y
25 Andrews	Y	N	?	Y	Y	Y	Y	Y
26 ***Armey***	Y	Y	Y	N	N	N	Y	N
27 Ortiz	N	N	N	Y	Y	Y	Y	Y
28 Tejeda	N	N	N	Y	Y	Y	Y	Y
29 Green	N	N	Y	Y	N	N	Y	Y
30 Johnson, E. B.	N	N	N	Y	Y	Y	Y	Y
UTAH								
1 ***Hansen***	N	N	Y	Y	Y	Y	Y	Y
2 Shepherd	Y	Y	N	Y	N	Y	Y	N
3 Orton	N	N	Y	N	N	Y	Y	N
VERMONT								
AL *Sanders*	N	N	N	Y	Y	Y	Y	Y
VIRGINIA								
1 ***Bateman***	N	N	Y	Y	Y	Y	Y	Y
2 Pickett	N	N	N	Y	Y	Y	Y	Y
3 Scott	N	N	N	N	Y	Y	Y	N
4 Sisisky	N	N	Y	Y	Y	Y	Y	Y
5 Payne	N	N	Y	Y	Y	Y	Y	Y
6 ***Goodlatte***	Y	N	Y	Y	Y	Y	Y	Y
7 ***Bliley***	Y	N	Y	Y	Y	Y	Y	Y
8 Moran	N	N	?	N	Y	Y	Y	N
9 Boucher	N	N	N	N	Y	Y	Y	N
10 ***Wolf***	Y	N	Y	Y	Y	Y	Y	Y
11 Byrne	N	N	N	N	Y	Y	Y	N
WASHINGTON								
1 Cantwell	N	N	N	Y	Y	Y	Y	Y
2 Swift	N	N	N	Y	Y	Y	Y	Y
3 Unsoeld	N	N	N	N	Y	Y	Y	Y
4 Inslee	N	N	N	Y	Y	Y	Y	Y
5 Foley								
6 Dicks	N	N	N	N	Y	Y	Y	N
7 McDermott	N	N	N	N	Y	Y	Y	N
8 ***Dunn***	Y	Y	Y	Y	Y	Y	Y	Y
9 Kreidler	N	N	N	N	Y	Y	Y	N
WEST VIRGINIA								
1 Mollohan	N	N	N	Y	Y	Y	Y	Y
2 Wise	N	N	N	Y	Y	Y	Y	Y
3 Rahall	N	N	N	Y	Y	Y	Y	Y
WISCONSIN								
1 Barca	N	N	–	Y	Y	Y	Y	Y
2 ***Klug***	Y	N	Y	Y	Y	Y	Y	Y
3 ***Gunderson***	N	N	N	Y	Y	Y	Y	Y
4 Kleczka	N	N	?	Y	N	N	Y	Y
5 Barrett	N	Y	N	Y	N	N	Y	Y
6 ***Petri***	Y	N	Y	Y	N	N	Y	Y
7 Obey	N	N	N	Y	Y	Y	Y	Y
8 ***Roth***	Y	N	Y	Y	Y	Y	Y	Y
9 ***Sensenbrenner***	Y	Y	Y	Y	N	N	Y	Y
WYOMING								
AL ***Thomas***	Y	N	Y	Y	Y	Y	Y	Y
DELEGATES								
de Lugo, V.I.	N	N	N	Y	Y	Y	Y	D
Faleomavaega, Am.S.	N	N	N	Y	Y	Y	Y	D
Norton, D.C.	N	N	N	Y	Y	Y	Y	D
Romero-B., P.R.	N	N	N	Y	?	?	?	D
Underwood, Guam	N	N	N	N	Y	Y	Y	D

Southern states - Ala., Ark., Fla., Ga., Ky., La., Miss., N.C., Okla., S.C., Tenn., Texas, Va.
Omitted votes are quorum calls, which CQ does not include in its vote charts.

300. HR 2493. Fiscal 1994 Agriculture Appropriations/ Market Promotion Program. Separate vote at the request of Solomon, R-N.Y., on the Armey, R-Texas, amendment, as amended and adopted in the Committee of the Whole to cut $20 million from the Market Promotion Program. Before being amended, the Armey amendment would have eliminated the program by cutting all but $1 of the program's $147.7 million. Adopted 403-24: R 159-12; D 243-12 (ND 164-7, SD 79-5); I 1-0, June 29, 1993. (On separate votes, which may be demanded on an amendment adopted in the Committee of the Whole, delegates cannot vote. See vote 298.)

301. HR 2493. Fiscal 1994 Agriculture Appropriations/ Funding Cuts. Myers, R-Ind., amendment to recommit the bill to the House Appropriations Committee with instructions to report it back with an amendment to cut the Commodity Credit Corporation by $4.4 billion and all other programs by 5 percent. Motion rejected 172-255: R 152-19; D 20-235 (ND 10-161, SD 10-74); I 0-1, June 29, 1993.

302. HR 2493. Fiscal 1994 Agriculture Appropriations/ Passage. Passage of the bill to provide $70.8 billion in new budget authority for Agriculture, Rural Development, the Food and Drug Administration and related agencies in fiscal 1994. The administration requested $76,581,667,000. Passed 304-119: R 64-106; D 239-13 (ND 159-10, SD 80-3); I 1-0, June 29, 1993.

*304. HR 2518. Fiscal 1994 Labor, HHS, Education Appropriations/Corporation for Public Broadcasting. Crane, R-Ill., amendment to cut $292 million of the $292.64 million in the bill for the Corporation for Public Broadcasting. Rejected in the Committee of the Whole 56-373: R 55-117; D 1-255 (ND 1-171, SD 0-84); I 0-1, June 30, 1993.

305. HR 2518. Fiscal 1994 Labor, HHS, Education Appropriations/Corporation for Public Broadcasting. Hefley, R-Colo., amendment to cut $1 million from the Corporation for Public Broadcasting. Rejected in the Committee of the Whole 195-230: R 163-9; D 32-220 (ND 14-155, SD 18-65); I 0-1, June 30, 1993.

306. HR 2518. Fiscal 1994 Labor, HHS, Education Appropriations/Procedural Motion. Natcher, D-Ky., motion to rise and report the bill back to the full House, thus prohibiting additional amendments placing limits on the use of funds. Motion rejected in the Committee of the Whole 190-244: R 13-160; D 176-84 (ND 128-47, SD 48-37); I 1-0, June 30, 1993.

307. HR 2518. Fiscal 1994 Labor, HHS, Education Appropriations/Abortion Prohibition. Hyde, R-Ill., amendment to prohibit funds in the bill from being spent for an abortion except when it is made known that it is a case of rape, incest or necessity to save the life of the mother. Adopted in Committee of the Whole 255-178: R 157-16; D 98-161 (ND 54-120, SD 44-41); I 0-1, June 30, 1993.

308. HR 2518. Fiscal 1994 Labor, HHS, Education Appropriations/Direct Student Loans. Separate vote at the request of Armey, R-Texas, on the Gordon, D-Tenn., amendment adopted in the Committee of the Whole to provide that only direct student loan demonstration programs authorized by the 1992 Higher Education Act be eligible for funding. Adopted 397-28: R 171-0; D 226-27 (ND 146-22, SD 80-5); I 0-1, June 30, 1993. (On separate votes, which may be demanded on an amendment adopted in the Committee of the Whole, delegates cannot vote.)

Omitted votes are quorum calls, which CQ does not include in its vote charts.

KEY

Y	Voted for (yea).
#	Paired for.
+	Announced for.
N	Voted against (nay).
X	Paired against.
−	Announced against.
P	Voted "present."
C	Voted "present" to avoid possible conflict of interest.
?	Did not vote or otherwise make a position known.
D	Delegates ineligible to vote.

Democrats   **Republicans**
Independent

	300	301	302	304	305	306	307	308
ALABAMA								
1 Callahan	Y	Y	N	Y	Y	N	Y	Y
2 Everett	Y	Y	Y	Y	Y	N	Y	Y
3 Browder	Y	N	Y	N	N	N	Y	Y
4 Bevill	Y	N	Y	N	N	N	Y	Y
5 Cramer	Y	N	Y	N	N	N	Y	Y
6 *Bachus*	Y	Y	N	Y	Y	N	Y	Y
7 Hilliard	N	N	Y	N	N	N	Y	N
ALASKA								
AL *Young*	Y	Y	Y	Y	N	N	Y	Y
ARIZONA								
1 Coppersmith	Y	N	Y	N	N	Y	N	Y
2 Pastor	Y	N	Y	N	N	Y	N	Y
3 *Stump*	Y	Y	N	Y	Y	N	Y	Y
4 *Kyl*	Y	Y	N	Y	Y	N	Y	Y
5 *Kolbe*	Y	Y	N	N	N	N	Y	Y
6 English	Y	N	Y	N	N	Y	N	Y
ARKANSAS								
1 Lambert	Y	N	Y	N	N	Y	N	Y
2 Thornton	Y	N	Y	N	N	N	Y	Y
3 *Hutchinson*	Y	Y	Y	N	Y	N	Y	Y
4 Dickey	Y	Y	Y	N	Y	N	Y	Y
CALIFORNIA								
1 Hamburg	Y	N	Y	N	N	Y	N	Y
2 *Herger*	Y	Y	N	Y	Y	N	Y	Y
3 Fazio	N	N	Y	N	N	Y	N	Y
4 *Doolittle*	Y	Y	N	Y	Y	N	Y	Y
5 Matsui	Y	N	Y	N	N	N	Y	Y
6 Woolsey	Y	N	Y	N	N	Y	N	Y
7 Miller	Y	N	Y	N	?	N	Y	Y
8 Pelosi	Y	N	Y	N	N	N	N	N
9 Dellums	Y	N	Y	N	N	Y	N	Y
10 *Baker*	Y	Y	N	Y	Y	N	Y	P
11 *Pombo*	Y	Y	N	Y	Y	N	Y	Y
12 Lantos	Y	N	Y	N	N	Y	N	Y
13 Stark	Y	N	Y	N	N	N	N	N
14 Eshoo	Y	N	Y	N	N	N	N	Y
15 Mineta	Y	N	Y	N	N	Y	N	Y
16 Edwards	Y	N	Y	N	N	N	N	Y
17 Farr	Y	N	Y	N	N	N	N	Y
18 Condit	Y	Y	Y	Y	Y	Y	Y	Y
19 Lehman	N	N	Y	N	N	N	N	Y
20 Dooley	N	N	Y	N	N	?	N	Y
21 *Thomas*	N	N	Y	N	Y	N	Y	Y
22 *Huffington*	Y	Y	N	Y	Y	N	Y	Y
23 *Gallegly*	Y	Y	N	Y	Y	N	Y	Y
24 Beilenson	Y	N	N	N	N	N	N	Y
25 *McKeon*	Y	Y	N	Y	Y	N	Y	Y
26 Berman	Y	N	Y	N	N	N	N	N
27 *Moorhead*	Y	Y	N	Y	Y	Y	Y	Y
28 *Dreier*	Y	Y	N	Y	Y	N	Y	Y
29 Waxman	Y	N	Y	N	N	N	Y	Y
30 Becerra	Y	N	Y	N	N	Y	N	Y
31 Martinez	?	?	?	N	N	Y	N	Y
32 Dixon	Y	N	Y	N	N	N	Y	Y
33 Roybal-Allard	Y	N	Y	N	N	N	N	Y
34 Torres	Y	N	Y	N	N	Y	N	Y
35 Waters	Y	N	Y	N	N	N	N	N
36 Harman	Y	N	Y	N	N	N	N	Y
37 Tucker	Y	N	Y	N	N	N	N	Y
38 *Horn*	Y	Y	N	N	N	N	Y	Y
39 *Royce*	Y	Y	N	Y	Y	N	Y	Y
40 *Lewis*	Y	Y	Y	N	Y	N	Y	Y
41 *Kim*	Y	Y	Y	Y	Y	N	Y	Y

	300	301	302	304	305	306	307	308
42 Brown	Y	N	Y	N	?	Y	N	Y
43 *Calvert*	Y	Y	N	N	Y	N	Y	Y
44 *McCandless*	Y	Y	N	Y	Y	N	Y	Y
45 *Rohrabacher*	Y	Y	N	Y	Y	N	Y	Y
46 *Dornan*	Y	Y	N	Y	N	N	Y	Y
47 *Cox*	Y	Y	N	Y	Y	N	Y	Y
48 *Packard*	N	Y	N	Y	N	N	Y	Y
49 Schenk	Y	N	Y	N	N	N	Y	Y
50 Filner	Y	N	Y	N	N	Y	N	Y
51 *Cunningham*	Y	Y	N	Y	N	N	Y	Y
52 *Hunter*	Y	Y	N	Y	Y	N	Y	Y
COLORADO								
1 Schroeder	Y	N	N	N	N	Y	N	Y
2 Skaggs	Y	N	Y	N	N	Y	N	Y
3 *McInnis*	Y	Y	N	N	N	Y	N	Y
4 *Allard*	Y	Y	Y	Y	Y	N	Y	Y
5 *Hefley*	Y	Y	N	Y	Y	N	Y	Y
6 *Schaefer*	Y	Y	N	N	Y	N	Y	?
CONNECTICUT								
1 Kennelly	Y	N	Y	N	N	N	Y	Y
2 Gejdenson	Y	N	Y	N	N	N	N	N
3 DeLauro	Y	N	Y	N	N	N	Y	Y
4 *Shays*	Y	Y	N	N	N	Y	N	Y
5 Franks	Y	Y	N	Y	N	N	Y	Y
6 *Johnson*	Y	Y	N	N	N	Y	N	Y
DELAWARE								
AL *Castle*	Y	Y	N	N	N	Y	N	Y
FLORIDA								
1 Hutto	Y	Y	N	N	N	N	Y	Y
2 Peterson	Y	N	Y	N	N	N	Y	Y
3 Brown	Y	N	Y	N	N	N	Y	Y
4 *Fowler*	Y	Y	Y	N	Y	N	Y	Y
5 Thurman	Y	N	Y	N	N	N	Y	Y
6 *Stearns*	Y	N	N	N	N	N	Y	Y
7 *Mica*	Y	Y	N	Y	N	Y	N	Y
8 *McCollum*	Y	Y	N	N	N	N	Y	Y
9 *Bilirakis*	Y	Y	Y	N	Y	N	Y	Y
10 *Young*	Y	Y	Y	N	N	N	Y	Y
11 Gibbons	Y	Y	Y	?	?	Y	Y	Y
12 *Canady*	Y	N	Y	N	Y	N	Y	Y
13 *Miller*	Y	Y	N	Y	N	Y	N	Y
14 *Goss*	Y	Y	N	N	Y	N	Y	Y
15 Bacchus	Y	N	Y	N	N	N	Y	Y
16 *Lewis*	Y	Y	Y	N	Y	N	Y	Y
17 Meek	Y	N	Y	N	N	N	Y	Y
18 *Ros-Lehtinen*	Y	N	Y	N	Y	N	Y	Y
19 Johnston	Y	N	Y	N	N	Y	N	Y
20 Deutsch	Y	N	Y	N	N	N	Y	Y
21 *Diaz-Balart*	Y	N	Y	N	Y	N	Y	Y
22 *Shaw*	Y	Y	N	Y	Y	N	Y	Y
23 Hastings	Y	N	Y	N	N	N	N	N
GEORGIA								
1 *Kingston*	Y	Y	Y	Y	Y	N	Y	Y
2 Bishop	Y	N	Y	N	N	N	Y	Y
3 *Collins*	Y	N	Y	N	Y	N	Y	Y
4 *Linder*	Y	N	Y	N	Y	N	Y	Y
5 Lewis	Y	N	Y	N	N	N	Y	Y
6 *Gingrich*	Y	Y	N	N	Y	N	Y	Y
7 Darden	Y	N	Y	N	N	Y	Y	Y
8 Rowland	Y	N	Y	N	N	Y	Y	Y
9 Deal	Y	N	Y	N	N	N	Y	Y
10 Johnson	Y	N	Y	N	N	N	Y	Y
11 McKinney	Y	N	Y	N	N	Y	N	Y
HAWAII								
1 Abercrombie	Y	N	Y	N	N	Y	N	Y
2 Mink	Y	N	Y	N	N	Y	N	Y
IDAHO								
1 LaRocco	Y	N	Y	N	N	Y	N	Y
2 *Crapo*	N	Y	Y	N	Y	N	Y	Y
ILLINOIS								
1 Rush	Y	N	Y	N	N	N	N	N
2 Reynolds	Y	N	Y	N	N	N	Y	Y
3 Lipinski	Y	Y	Y	N	Y	N	Y	Y
4 Gutierrez	Y	N	Y	N	N	N	Y	Y
5 Rostenkowski	Y	N	Y	N	N	N	Y	Y
6 *Hyde*	Y	Y	Y	N	Y	N	Y	Y
7 Collins	Y	N	Y	N	N	N	Y	Y
8 *Crane*	Y	Y	N	Y	Y	N	Y	N
9 Yates	Y	N	Y	N	N	Y	N	N
10 *Porter*	Y	Y	N	N	N	Y	N	Y
11 Sangmeister	Y	N	Y	N	N	N	Y	Y
12 Costello	Y	N	Y	N	N	N	Y	Y
13 *Fawell*	Y	Y	N	N	N	N	Y	Y
14 *Hastert*	Y	Y	Y	N	Y	N	Y	Y
15 *Ewing*	Y	N	Y	N	N	N	Y	Y
16 *Manzullo*	Y	Y	N	Y	Y	N	Y	Y
17 Evans	Y	N	Y	N	N	N	Y	Y

ND   Northern Democrats   SD   Southern Democrats

	300	301	302	304	305	306	307	308
18 **Michel**	Y	Y	N	N	Y	N	Y	Y
19 Poshard	Y	N	Y	N	N	N	Y	Y
20 Durbin	Y	N	Y	N	N	N	Y	N
INDIANA								
1 Visclosky	Y	N	Y	N	N	N	Y	Y
2 Sharp	Y	N	Y	N	N	Y	Y	Y
3 Roemer	Y	Y	Y	N	Y	N	Y	Y
4 Long	Y	N	Y	N	Y	Y	Y	Y
5 **Buyer**	Y	Y	Y	Y	Y	N	Y	Y
6 **Burton**	Y	Y	N	Y	Y	N	Y	Y
7 **Myers**	Y	Y	N	Y	Y	N	Y	Y
8 McCloskey	Y	N	Y	N	N	N	Y	Y
9 Hamilton	Y	Y	Y	N	Y	N	Y	Y
10 Jacobs	Y	Y	N	N	Y	N	?	Y
IOWA								
1 **Leach**	Y	N	Y	N	Y	N	Y	Y
2 **Nussle**	Y	Y	N	N	Y	N	Y	Y
3 **Lightfoot**	Y	N	Y	N	Y	N	Y	Y
4 Smith	Y	N	Y	N	N	Y	N	Y
5 **Grandy**	N	N	Y	N	Y	N	Y	Y
KANSAS								
1 **Roberts**	Y	N	Y	N	Y	N	Y	Y
2 Slattery	Y	N	Y	N	N	N	Y	Y
3 **Meyers**	Y	Y	N	N	Y	N	N	Y
4 Glickman	Y	N	Y	N	N	N	Y	Y
KENTUCKY								
1 Barlow	Y	N	Y	N	N	N	Y	Y
2 Natcher	Y	N	Y	N	N	N	Y	Y
3 Mazzoli	Y	N	Y	N	N	N	Y	Y
4 **Bunning**	Y	Y	N	Y	Y	N	Y	Y
5 **Rogers**	Y	N	Y	N	Y	N	Y	Y
6 Baesler	Y	N	Y	N	N	N	Y	Y
LOUISIANA								
1 **Livingston**	Y	Y	Y	Y	Y	N	Y	Y
2 Jefferson	Y	N	Y	N	?	Y	N	Y
3 Tauzin	Y	Y	Y	N	Y	N	Y	Y
4 Fields	N	N	Y	N	N	Y	N	Y
5 **McCrery**	Y	Y	Y	N	Y	N	Y	Y
6 **Baker**	N	Y	Y	N	Y	N	Y	Y
7 Hayes	Y	Y	Y	N	N	N	Y	Y
MAINE								
1 Andrews	Y	N	Y	N	N	Y	N	Y
2 **Snowe**	Y	Y	Y	N	Y	Y	N	Y
MARYLAND								
1 **Gilchrest**	N	Y	Y	Y	Y	N	Y	Y
2 **Bentley**	Y	Y	Y	N	Y	N	Y	Y
3 Cardin	Y	N	Y	N	N	Y	N	Y
4 Wynn	Y	N	Y	N	N	Y	N	Y
5 Hoyer	Y	N	Y	N	N	Y	N	Y
6 **Bartlett**	Y	Y	?	Y	Y	N	Y	Y
7 Mfume	Y	N	Y	N	N	Y	N	Y
8 **Morella**	Y	N	Y	N	Y	Y	N	Y
MASSACHUSETTS								
1 Olver	Y	N	Y	N	N	Y	N	Y
2 Neal	Y	N	Y	N	N	N	Y	Y
3 **Blute**	+	+	–	N	N	N	Y	Y
4 Frank	Y	N	Y	N	N	Y	N	N
5 Meehan	Y	N	Y	N	N	Y	N	Y
6 **Torkildsen**	Y	N	Y	N	Y	N	Y	Y
7 Markey	Y	N	Y	N	N	Y	N	Y
8 Kennedy	Y	N	Y	N	N	Y	N	Y
9 Moakley	Y	N	Y	?	?	?	?	?
10 Studds	Y	N	Y	N	N	Y	N	N
MICHIGAN								
1 Stupak	Y	N	Y	N	N	N	Y	Y
2 **Hoekstra**	Y	Y	Y	N	Y	N	Y	Y
3 Henry	?	?	?	?	?	?	?	?
4 **Camp**	Y	Y	Y	N	Y	N	Y	Y
5 Barcia	Y	N	Y	N	N	N	Y	Y
6 **Upton**	Y	Y	Y	N	Y	N	Y	Y
7 **Smith**	N	Y	N	N	Y	N	Y	Y
8 Carr	Y	N	Y	N	N	Y	N	N
9 Kildee	Y	N	Y	N	N	N	Y	Y
10 Bonior	N	N	Y	N	N	Y	Y	Y
11 **Knollenberg**	Y	Y	N	P	P	N	Y	Y
12 Levin	Y	N	Y	N	N	Y	N	Y
13 Ford	Y	N	Y	N	N	Y	N	Y
14 Conyers	N	N	Y	N	N	Y	N	N
15 Collins	N	N	Y	N	N	Y	N	N
16 Dingell	Y	N	?	N	?	Y	N	?
MINNESOTA								
1 Penny	Y	Y	Y	N	Y	N	Y	Y
2 Minge	Y	N	Y	–	?	?	+	+
3 **Ramstad**	Y	Y	N	N	Y	N	Y	Y
4 Vento	Y	N	Y	N	N	Y	N	Y

	300	301	302	304	305	306	307	308
5 Sabo	Y	N	Y	N	N	Y	N	Y
6 **Grams**	Y	Y	N	Y	Y	N	Y	Y
7 Peterson	Y	N	Y	N	N	N	Y	Y
8 Oberstar	Y	N	Y	N	N	N	Y	Y
MISSISSIPPI								
1 Whitten	Y	N	Y	N	N	Y	Y	Y
2 Thompson	Y	N	Y	N	N	Y	N	Y
3 Montgomery	Y	N	Y	N	Y	N	Y	Y
4 Parker	Y	N	Y	N	Y	N	Y	Y
5 Taylor	Y	Y	N	N	Y	N	Y	Y
MISSOURI								
1 Clay	Y	N	Y	N	N	Y	N	Y
2 **Talent**	Y	Y	N	N	Y	N	Y	Y
3 Gephardt	Y	N	Y	N	N	Y	Y	Y
4 Skelton	Y	N	Y	N	Y	N	Y	Y
5 Wheat	Y	N	Y	N	N	Y	N	Y
6 Danner	Y	N	Y	N	N	N	Y	Y
7 **Hancock**	Y	Y	N	Y	Y	N	Y	Y
8 **Emerson**	Y	N	Y	Y	Y	N	Y	Y
9 Volkmer	Y	N	Y	N	Y	N	Y	Y
MONTANA								
AL Williams	Y	N	Y	N	N	Y	N	Y
NEBRASKA								
1 **Bereuter**	Y	N	Y	N	Y	N	Y	Y
2 Hoagland	Y	N	Y	N	N	N	Y	Y
3 **Barrett**	Y	Y	Y	N	Y	N	Y	Y
NEVADA								
1 Bilbray	Y	N	Y	N	N	N	Y	Y
2 **Vucanovich**	Y	Y	Y	N	Y	N	Y	Y
NEW HAMPSHIRE								
1 **Zeliff**	Y	Y	N	N	Y	N	Y	Y
2 Swett	Y	Y	Y	N	N	N	Y	Y
NEW JERSEY								
1 Andrews	Y	N	N	N	N	Y	N	Y
2 Hughes	Y	N	N	N	N	Y	Y	Y
3 **Saxton**	Y	Y	N	N	Y	N	Y	Y
4 **Smith**	Y	Y	Y	N	Y	N	Y	Y
5 **Roukema**	Y	Y	N	N	Y	Y	N	Y
6 Pallone	Y	N	N	N	N	Y	N	Y
7 **Franks**	Y	Y	N	Y	Y	Y	N	Y
8 Klein	Y	N	Y	N	N	Y	N	Y
9 Torricelli	Y	N	Y	?	?	Y	N	Y
10 Payne	Y	N	Y	N	N	Y	N	Y
11 **Gallo**	Y	Y	N	N	Y	N	Y	Y
12 **Zimmer**	Y	Y	N	Y	Y	Y	N	Y
13 Menendez	Y	N	Y	N	N	Y	N	Y
NEW MEXICO								
1 **Schiff**	Y	Y	N	N	N	N	Y	Y
2 **Skeen**	+	–	+	–	+	–	+	+
3 Richardson	Y	N	Y	N	N	Y	N	Y
NEW YORK								
1 Hochbrueckner	Y	N	Y	N	N	Y	N	Y
2 **Lazio**	Y	Y	N	N	N	N	Y	Y
3 **King**	Y	Y	N	N	Y	N	Y	Y
4 **Levy**	Y	Y	N	N	Y	N	Y	Y
5 Ackerman	Y	N	Y	N	N	Y	N	Y
6 Flake	Y	N	Y	N	N	Y	N	Y
7 Manton	Y	N	Y	N	N	N	?	Y
8 Nadler	Y	N	Y	N	N	Y	N	N
9 Schumer	Y	N	Y	N	N	Y	N	N
10 Towns	Y	N	Y	N	N	Y	N	Y
11 Owens	Y	N	Y	N	N	Y	N	Y
12 Velazquez	Y	N	Y	N	N	Y	N	Y
13 **Molinari**	Y	Y	N	N	N	N	Y	Y
14 Maloney	Y	N	Y	N	N	Y	N	Y
15 Rangel	Y	N	Y	N	N	Y	N	Y
16 Serrano	Y	N	Y	N	N	Y	N	N
17 Engel	Y	N	Y	N	N	Y	N	Y
18 Lowey	Y	N	Y	N	N	Y	N	Y
19 **Fish**	Y	Y	Y	N	Y	N	Y	Y
20 **Gilman**	Y	Y	Y	N	Y	N	Y	Y
21 McNulty	Y	N	Y	N	N	N	Y	Y
22 **Solomon**	Y	Y	N	Y	Y	N	Y	Y
23 **Boehlert**	Y	Y	Y	N	N	Y	N	Y
24 **McHugh**	Y	Y	N	N	Y	N	N	Y
25 **Walsh**	Y	Y	Y	N	N	N	Y	Y
26 Hinchey	Y	N	Y	N	N	Y	N	Y
27 **Paxon**	Y	Y	N	Y	Y	N	Y	Y
28 Slaughter	Y	N	Y	N	N	Y	N	Y
29 LaFalce	Y	N	?	N	N	N	Y	Y
30 **Quinn**	Y	Y	N	N	Y	N	Y	Y
31 **Houghton**	N	Y	Y	N	Y	N	Y	Y
NORTH CAROLINA								
1 Clayton	N	N	Y	N	N	Y	N	Y
2 Valentine	Y	Y	Y	N	N	Y	Y	Y

	300	301	302	304	305	306	307	308
3 Lancaster	N	N	Y	N	N	N	Y	Y
4 Price	Y	N	Y	N	N	Y	N	Y
5 Neal	Y	N	Y	N	N	Y	Y	Y
6 **Coble**	Y	Y	N	Y	Y	N	Y	Y
7 Rose	Y	N	?	N	N	Y	N	Y
8 Hefner	Y	N	Y	N	N	N	Y	Y
9 **McMillan**	?	?	?	?	?	?	?	?
10 **Ballenger**	Y	Y	N	N	Y	N	Y	Y
11 **Taylor**	Y	Y	N	N	Y	N	Y	Y
12 Watt	N	N	Y	N	N	Y	N	N
NORTH DAKOTA								
AL Pomeroy	Y	N	Y	N	N	Y	Y	Y
OHIO								
1 Mann	Y	N	Y	N	N	N	Y	Y
2 **Portman**	Y	Y	N	N	Y	N	Y	Y
3 Hall	Y	N	Y	N	N	N	Y	Y
4 **Oxley**	Y	N	Y	N	Y	N	Y	Y
5 **Gillmor**	Y	Y	Y	N	Y	N	Y	Y
6 Strickland	Y	N	Y	N	N	Y	N	Y
7 **Hobson**	Y	Y	Y	N	Y	N	Y	Y
8 **Boehner**	N	Y	Y	N	Y	N	Y	Y
9 Kaptur	Y	N	Y	N	N	N	Y	?
10 **Hoke**	Y	Y	N	N	Y	N	Y	Y
11 Stokes	Y	N	Y	N	N	Y	N	Y
12 **Kasich**	Y	Y	N	N	Y	N	Y	Y
13 Brown	Y	N	Y	N	Y	N	Y	Y
14 Sawyer	Y	N	Y	N	N	Y	N	Y
15 **Pryce**	Y	Y	Y	N	Y	N	Y	Y
16 **Regula**	Y	Y	Y	N	Y	N	Y	Y
17 Traficant	Y	N	Y	N	N	Y	N	Y
18 Applegate	Y	N	Y	N	N	N	Y	Y
19 Fingerhut	Y	Y	N	–	Y	Y	N	Y
OKLAHOMA								
1 **Inhofe**	Y	Y	N	Y	Y	N	Y	Y
2 Synar	Y	N	Y	N	N	Y	N	N
3 Brewster	Y	N	Y	N	Y	N	Y	Y
4 McCurdy	Y	N	Y	N	Y	Y	N	Y
5 **Istook**	Y	Y	N	Y	Y	N	Y	Y
6 English	Y	N	Y	N	Y	N	Y	Y
OREGON								
1 Furse	Y	N	Y	N	N	Y	N	Y
2 **Smith**	N	Y	N	N	Y	N	Y	Y
3 Wyden	Y	N	Y	N	N	Y	N	N
4 DeFazio	Y	Y	Y	N	N	Y	N	N
5 Kopetski	N	N	Y	N	N	Y	N	Y
PENNSYLVANIA								
1 Foglietta	Y	N	Y	N	?	Y	N	N
2 Blackwell	Y	N	Y	N	N	Y	N	Y
3 Borski	Y	N	Y	N	N	N	Y	Y
4 Klink	Y	N	Y	N	N	N	Y	Y
5 **Clinger**	Y	Y	Y	N	Y	N	Y	Y
6 Holden	Y	N	Y	N	N	N	Y	Y
7 **Weldon**	Y	Y	N	N	Y	N	Y	Y
8 **Greenwood**	Y	Y	Y	N	Y	N	N	Y
9 **Shuster**	Y	Y	N	Y	Y	N	Y	Y
10 **McDade**	Y	Y	N	N	Y	N	Y	Y
11 Kanjorski	Y	N	Y	N	N	N	Y	Y
12 Murtha	Y	N	Y	N	N	N	Y	Y
13 Margolies-Mezv.	Y	N	Y	N	N	Y	N	Y
14 Coyne	Y	N	Y	N	N	Y	N	N
15 McHale	Y	N	Y	N	N	N	Y	Y
16 **Walker**	Y	Y	N	Y	Y	N	Y	Y
17 **Gekas**	Y	Y	N	N	Y	N	Y	Y
18 **Santorum**	?	?	?	Y	Y	N	Y	Y
19 **Goodling**	Y	N	Y	N	Y	N	Y	Y
20 Murphy	Y	N	N	Y	Y	N	Y	Y
21 **Ridge**	Y	Y	Y	N	Y	N	Y	Y
RHODE ISLAND								
1 **Machtley**	Y	Y	Y	N	Y	Y	N	Y
2 Reed	Y	N	Y	N	N	Y	N	Y
SOUTH CAROLINA								
1 **Ravenel**	Y	Y	Y	N	Y	N	Y	Y
2 **Spence**	Y	Y	Y	N	Y	N	Y	Y
3 Derrick	Y	N	Y	N	Y	Y	N	Y
4 **Inglis**	Y	Y	N	N	Y	N	Y	Y
5 Spratt	Y	N	Y	N	N	N	Y	Y
6 Clyburn	Y	N	Y	N	N	Y	N	Y
SOUTH DAKOTA								
AL Johnson	Y	N	Y	N	N	N	Y	Y
TENNESSEE								
1 **Quillen**	N	N	Y	N	Y	N	Y	Y
2 **Duncan**	Y	Y	N	Y	Y	N	Y	Y
3 Lloyd	Y	Y	Y	N	N	N	Y	Y
4 Cooper	Y	Y	Y	N	Y	N	Y	Y
5 Clement	Y	N	Y	N	N	N	Y	Y

	300	301	302	304	305	306	307	308
6 Gordon	Y	N	Y	N	Y	Y	Y	Y
7 **Sundquist**	N	N	Y	N	Y	N	Y	Y
8 Tanner	Y	N	Y	N	Y	N	Y	Y
9 Ford	Y	N	Y	N	N	Y	N	Y
TEXAS								
1 Chapman	Y	N	Y	N	N	Y	Y	Y
2 Wilson	?	?	?	N	N	Y	N	Y
3 **Johnson, Sam**	Y	Y	N	Y	Y	N	Y	Y
4 Hall	Y	Y	Y	N	N	N	Y	Y
5 Bryant	Y	N	Y	N	N	Y	N	Y
6 **Barton**	Y	Y	N	Y	Y	N	Y	Y
7 **Archer**	Y	Y	N	Y	Y	N	Y	Y
8 **Fields**	Y	Y	N	Y	Y	N	Y	Y
9 Brooks	Y	N	Y	N	N	Y	N	Y
10 Pickle	Y	N	Y	N	N	Y	N	Y
11 Edwards	Y	N	Y	N	Y	N	Y	Y
12 Geren	Y	Y	Y	N	N	N	Y	Y
13 Sarpalius	Y	N	Y	N	Y	N	Y	Y
14 Laughlin	Y	N	Y	N	Y	N	Y	Y
15 de la Garza	Y	N	Y	N	N	N	Y	Y
16 Coleman	Y	N	Y	N	N	Y	N	Y
17 Stenholm	Y	N	Y	N	N	Y	Y	Y
18 Washington	Y	N	Y	N	N	Y	N	N
19 **Combest**	Y	Y	Y	N	Y	N	Y	Y
20 Gonzalez	Y	N	Y	N	N	Y	N	Y
21 **Smith**	Y	Y	Y	N	Y	N	Y	Y
22 **DeLay**	Y	Y	N	Y	Y	N	Y	Y
23 **Bonilla**	Y	Y	Y	N	Y	N	Y	Y
24 Frost	Y	N	Y	N	N	Y	N	Y
25 Andrews	Y	N	Y	N	Y	Y	N	Y
26 **Armey**	Y	Y	N	Y	Y	N	Y	Y
27 Ortiz	Y	N	Y	N	N	N	Y	Y
28 Tejeda	Y	N	Y	N	N	N	Y	Y
29 Green	Y	N	N	N	N	Y	N	Y
30 Johnson, E. B.	Y	N	Y	N	N	Y	N	Y
UTAH								
1 **Hansen**	Y	Y	N	N	Y	N	Y	Y
2 Shepherd	Y	N	Y	N	N	Y	N	Y
3 Orton	Y	Y	N	N	N	N	Y	Y
VERMONT								
AL *Sanders*	Y	N	Y	N	N	Y	N	N
VIRGINIA								
1 **Bateman**	Y	Y	Y	N	Y	N	Y	Y
2 Pickett	Y	N	Y	N	N	Y	N	Y
3 Scott	Y	N	Y	N	N	Y	N	Y
4 Sisisky	Y	N	Y	N	N	Y	N	Y
5 Payne	Y	N	Y	N	N	N	Y	Y
6 **Goodlatte**	Y	Y	N	N	Y	N	Y	Y
7 **Bliley**	Y	Y	N	N	Y	N	Y	Y
8 Moran	Y	N	Y	N	N	Y	N	Y
9 Boucher	Y	N	Y	N	N	Y	N	Y
10 **Wolf**	Y	Y	N	N	Y	N	Y	Y
11 Byrne	Y	N	Y	N	N	Y	N	Y
WASHINGTON								
1 Cantwell	Y	N	Y	N	N	Y	N	Y
2 Swift	Y	N	Y	N	N	Y	N	Y
3 Unsoeld	Y	N	Y	N	N	Y	N	Y
4 Inslee	Y	N	Y	N	Y	Y	N	Y
5 Foley						Y	N	
6 Dicks	Y	N	Y	N	N	Y	N	Y
7 McDermott	Y	N	Y	N	N	Y	N	Y
8 **Dunn**	Y	Y	N	N	Y	N	Y	Y
9 Kreidler	Y	N	Y	N	N	Y	N	Y
WEST VIRGINIA								
1 Mollohan	Y	N	Y	N	N	N	Y	Y
2 Wise	Y	N	Y	N	N	Y	N	Y
3 Rahall	Y	N	Y	N	N	N	Y	Y
WISCONSIN								
1 Barca	Y	N	N	N	N	Y	Y	Y
2 **Klug**	Y	Y	N	N	Y	N	Y	Y
3 **Gunderson**	Y	N	N	N	Y	N	Y	Y
4 Kleczka	Y	N	Y	N	N	N	Y	Y
5 Barrett	Y	N	Y	N	N	Y	N	Y
6 **Petri**	Y	Y	N	Y	Y	N	Y	Y
7 Obey	Y	N	Y	N	N	Y	Y	N
8 **Roth**	Y	Y	N	Y	Y	N	Y	Y
9 **Sensenbrenner**	Y	Y	N	Y	Y	N	Y	Y
WYOMING								
AL **Thomas**	Y	Y	N	N	Y	N	Y	Y
DELEGATES								
de Lugo, V.I.	D	D	D	N	N	Y	N	D
Faleomavaega, Am.S.	D	D	D	N	N	Y	N	D
Norton, D.C.	D	D	D	N	N	Y	N	D
Romero-B., P.R.	D	D	D	?	?	Y	N	D
Underwood, Guam	D	D	D	N	N	N	Y	D

Southern states - Ala., Ark., Fla., Ga., Ky., La., Miss., N.C., Okla., S.C., Tenn., Texas, Va.
Omitted votes are quorum calls, which CQ does not include in its vote charts.

309. HR 2518. Fiscal 1994 Labor, HHS, Education Appropriations/Abortion Prohibition. Separate vote at the request of Armey, R-Texas, on the Hyde, R-Ill., amendment adopted in the Committee of the Whole to prohibit funds in the bill from being spent for an abortion except when it is made known that it is a case of rape, incest or necessity to save the life of the mother. Adopted 256-171: R 157-16; D 99-154 (ND 55-113, SD 44-41); I 0-1, June 30, 1993. (On separate votes, which may be demanded on an amendment adopted in the Committee of the Whole, delegates cannot vote. See vote 307.)

310. HR 2518. Fiscal 1994 Labor, HHS, Education Appropriations/Spending Freeze. Livingston, R-La., motion to recommit the bill to the House Appropriations Committee with instructions to cut $4.8 billion by freezing spending at fiscal 1993 levels. Motion rejected 158-267: R 139-34; D 19-232 (ND 6-161, SD 13-71); I 0-1, June 30, 1993.

311. HR 2518. Fiscal 1994 Labor, HHS, Education Appropriations/Passage. Passage of the bill to provide $259.8 billion for the departments of Labor, Health and Human Services, and Education and related agencies of which $215.7 billion is for fiscal 1994. The administration requested $260.3 billion. Passed 305-124: R 67-106; D 237-18 (ND 157-13, SD 80-5); I 1-0, June 30, 1993.

312. HR 2492. Fiscal 1994 D.C. Appropriations/Crime and Youth Initiative. Walsh, R-N.Y., amendment to cut the $17.3 million for the District of Columbia Crime and Youth Initiative. The bill is $17 million over the formula that provides federal funds based on the D.C. tax base. Rejected in the Committee of the Whole 200-227: R 168-5; D 32-221 (ND 11-159, SD 21-62); I 0-1, June 30, 1993.

313. HR 2492. Fiscal 1994 D.C. Appropriations/Domestic Partners. Istook, R-Okla., amendment to prohibit the District from using funds to enforce its domestic partners ordinance, which allows unmarried couples or partners to register with the D.C. government. Under the law, partners of city employees can be eligible for the group health insurance offered to D.C. employees if the employee pays the higher premiums. Adopted in the Committee of the Whole 251-177: R 157-14; D 94-162 (ND 42-131, SD 52-31); I 0-1, June 30, 1993.

314. HR 2492. Fiscal 1994 D.C. Appropriations/Firefighters. Norton, D-D.C., amendment to eliminate the provision in the bill that requires the District to maintain current levels of firefighters and emergency medical personnel. Adopted in the Committee of the Whole 270-158: R 86-87; D 183-71 (ND 125-45, SD 58-26); I 1-0, June 30, 1993.

315. HR 2492. Fiscal 1994 D.C. Appropriations/Domestic Partners. Separate vote at the request of Solomon, R-N.Y., on the Istook, R-Okla., amendment adopted in the Committee of the Whole to prohibit funds from enforcing the District's domestic partners ordinance, which allows unmarried couples or partners to register with the D.C. government. Under the law, partners of city employees can be eligible for the group health insurance offered to D.C. employees if the employee pays the higher premiums. Adopted 253-167: R 158-14; D 95-152 (ND 42-124, SD 53-28); I 0-1, June 30, 1993. (On separate votes, which may be demanded on an amendment adopted in the Committee of the Whole, the four delegates and the resident commissioner of Puerto Rico cannot vote. See vote 313.)

316. HR 2492. Fiscal 1994 D.C. Appropriations/Firefighters. Separate vote at the request of Solomon, R-N.Y., on the Norton, D-D.C., amendment adopted in the Committee of the Whole to eliminate the provision in the bill that requires the District of Columbia to maintain existing levels of firefighters and emergency medical personnel. Adopted 266-154: R 88-84; D 177-70 (ND 119-45, SD 58-25); I 1-0, June 30, 1993. (On separate votes, which may be demanded on an amendment adopted in the Committee of the Whole, the four delegates and the resident commissioner of Puerto Rico cannot vote. See vote 314.)

KEY

Y	Voted for (yea).
#	Paired for.
+	Announced for.
N	Voted against (nay).
X	Paired against.
−	Announced against.
P	Voted "present."
C	Voted "present" to avoid possible conflict of interest.
?	Did not vote or otherwise make a position known.
D	Delegates ineligible to vote.

Democrats **Republicans**
Independent

	309	310	311	312	313	314	315	316
ALABAMA								
1 Callahan	Y	N	Y	Y	Y	N	Y	N
2 Everett	Y	N	N	Y	Y	N	Y	N
3 Browder	Y	N	Y	Y	Y	Y	Y	Y
4 Bevill	Y	N	Y	Y	Y	N	Y	N
5 Cramer	Y	N	Y	Y	Y	N	Y	N
6 Bachus	Y	Y	N	Y	?	N	Y	N
7 Hilliard	N	N	Y	N	N	Y	N	Y
ALASKA								
AL Young	Y	N	Y	Y	Y	N	Y	N
ARIZONA								
1 Coppersmith	N	N	Y	N	N	N	N	N
2 Pastor	N	?	Y	N	Y	N	Y	N
3 Stump	Y	Y	N	Y	Y	N	Y	N
4 Kyl	Y	Y	Y	Y	Y	Y	Y	Y
5 Kolbe	Y	Y	Y	N	Y	N	Y	Y
6 English	N	N	Y	N	N	N	N	N
ARKANSAS								
1 Lambert	N	N	Y	N	Y	Y	Y	Y
2 Thornton	Y	N	Y	N	Y	Y	Y	Y
3 Hutchinson	Y	Y	N	Y	Y	Y	Y	Y
4 Dickey	Y	Y	N	Y	Y	Y	Y	Y
CALIFORNIA								
1 Hamburg	N	N	N	N	N	Y	N	Y
2 Herger	Y	Y	N	Y	Y	N	Y	N
3 Fazio	N	N	Y	N	N	N	N	Y
4 Doolittle	Y	Y	N	Y	Y	Y	Y	Y
5 Matsui	N	N	Y	N	N	N	N	Y
6 Woolsey	N	N	Y	N	N	Y	N	Y
7 Miller	N	N	Y	N	N	Y	N	?
8 Pelosi	N	N	Y	N	N	N	N	N
9 Dellums	N	N	N	N	N	Y	N	Y
10 Baker	Y	Y	N	Y	Y	N	Y	N
11 Pombo	Y	Y	N	Y	Y	N	Y	N
12 Lantos	N	N	Y	N	N	N	N	N
13 Stark	N	N	Y	N	Y	Y	N	Y
14 Eshoo	N	N	Y	N	N	N	N	N
15 Mineta	N	N	N	N	N	Y	N	Y
16 Edwards	N	N	N	N	N	Y	N	Y
17 Farr	N	N	Y	N	N	N	N	N
18 Condit	Y	Y	Y	N	Y	Y	N	Y
19 Lehman	N	N	Y	N	N	Y	N	Y
20 Dooley	N	N	Y	N	N	?	N	Y
21 Thomas	Y	Y	N	Y	Y	Y	Y	Y
22 Huffington	Y	Y	N	Y	Y	N	Y	N
23 Gallegly	Y	Y	N	Y	Y	N	Y	N
24 Beilenson	N	N	Y	N	N	Y	N	Y
25 McKeon	Y	Y	N	Y	Y	N	Y	N
26 Berman	N	N	Y	N	Y	N	Y	N
27 Moorhead	Y	Y	N	Y	Y	N	Y	N
28 Dreier	Y	Y	N	Y	Y	N	Y	N
29 Waxman	N	N	Y	N	N	?	?	?
30 Becerra	N	N	Y	?	N	Y	N	Y
31 Martinez	N	N	Y	?	N	Y	N	Y
32 Dixon	N	N	Y	N	N	Y	N	Y
33 Roybal-Allard	N	N	Y	N	N	Y	N	Y
34 Torres	N	?	Y	N	N	Y	N	Y
35 Waters	N	N	Y	N	N	Y	N	Y
36 Harman	N	N	N	N	N	Y	N	Y
37 Tucker	N	N	Y	N	Y	Y	N	Y
38 Horn	N	N	Y	N	Y	Y	N	Y
39 Royce	Y	Y	N	Y	Y	Y	Y	Y
40 Lewis	Y	Y	N	Y	Y	Y	Y	Y
41 Kim	Y	Y	Y	Y	Y	Y	Y	Y

	309	310	311	312	313	314	315	316
42 Brown	N	N	Y	N	N	Y	N	Y
43 Calvert	Y	Y	N	Y	Y	N	Y	N
44 McCandless	Y	Y	N	Y	Y	Y	Y	Y
45 Rohrabacher	Y	Y	N	Y	N	Y	N	Y
46 Dornan	Y	Y	N	Y	Y	N	Y	N
47 Cox	Y	Y	N	Y	N	Y	N	Y
48 Packard	Y	Y	N	Y	N	Y	N	Y
49 Schenk	N	N	Y	N	N	Y	N	N
50 Filner	N	N	N	N	N	N	N	N
51 Cunningham	Y	Y	N	Y	N	Y	N	Y
52 Hunter	Y	Y	N	Y	N	Y	N	Y
COLORADO								
1 Schroeder	N	N	N	N	N	Y	N	Y
2 Skaggs	N	N	Y	N	N	Y	N	Y
3 McInnis	Y	Y	N	Y	Y	N	Y	N
4 Allard	Y	Y	N	Y	N	Y	N	N
5 Hefley	Y	Y	N	Y	Y	Y	Y	Y
6 Schaefer	Y	Y	N	Y	N	Y	N	Y
CONNECTICUT								
1 Kennelly	N	N	Y	N	N	Y	N	Y
2 Gejdenson	N	N	Y	N	N	Y	N	Y
3 DeLauro	N	N	N	N	N	N	N	N
4 Shays	N	N	Y	N	N	Y	N	Y
5 Franks	N	Y	Y	Y	Y	Y	Y	Y
6 Johnson	N	N	Y	N	N	Y	N	Y
DELAWARE								
AL Castle	Y	Y	N	Y	Y	Y	Y	Y
FLORIDA								
1 Hutto	Y	Y	Y	Y	Y	N	Y	N
2 Peterson	Y	N	Y	N	Y	Y	Y	Y
3 Brown	N	N	Y	N	N	N	N	Y
4 Fowler	Y	N	Y	Y	Y	N	Y	N
5 Thurman	Y	N	Y	N	Y	N	Y	N
6 Stearns	Y	Y	Y	Y	Y	N	Y	N
7 Mica	Y	Y	N	Y	Y	N	Y	N
8 McCollum	Y	Y	N	Y	Y	N	Y	N
9 Bilirakis	Y	Y	Y	Y	Y	Y	Y	Y
10 Young	Y	N	Y	Y	Y	Y	Y	Y
11 Gibbons	Y	N	Y	N	N	Y	Y	Y
12 Canady	Y	Y	N	Y	Y	Y	Y	Y
13 Miller	Y	Y	N	Y	Y	Y	Y	Y
14 Goss	Y	Y	N	Y	Y	Y	Y	Y
15 Bacchus	Y	N	Y	N	N	?	N	Y
16 Lewis	Y	Y	N	Y	Y	Y	Y	Y
17 Meek	N	N	Y	N	N	Y	N	Y
18 Ros-Lehtinen	Y	N	Y	Y	Y	N	Y	N
19 Johnston	N	N	Y	N	N	Y	N	Y
20 Deutsch	N	Y	N	N	N	N	N	N
21 Diaz-Balart	Y	N	Y	Y	Y	N	Y	N
22 Shaw	Y	Y	Y	Y	Y	Y	Y	Y
23 Hastings	N	N	Y	N	N	Y	N	Y
GEORGIA								
1 Kingston	Y	Y	N	Y	Y	Y	Y	Y
2 Bishop	N	N	Y	N	N	Y	N	Y
3 Collins	Y	Y	N	Y	Y	N	Y	N
4 Linder	Y	Y	N	Y	Y	Y	Y	Y
5 Lewis	N	N	Y	N	N	Y	N	Y
6 Gingrich	Y	Y	N	Y	Y	Y	Y	Y
7 Darden	Y	N	Y	N	N	Y	N	Y
8 Rowland	Y	N	Y	Y	Y	N	Y	N
9 Deal	Y	Y	Y	Y	Y	Y	Y	Y
10 Johnson	N	N	Y	N	Y	Y	N	Y
11 McKinney	N	N	N	N	N	Y	N	Y
HAWAII								
1 Abercrombie	N	N	Y	N	N	N	N	N
2 Mink	N	N	Y	N	N	Y	N	Y
IDAHO								
1 LaRocco	N	N	N	Y	N	Y	N	Y
2 Crapo	Y	Y	N	Y	?	Y	Y	Y
ILLINOIS								
1 Rush	N	?	Y	N	N	Y	N	Y
2 Reynolds	N	N	Y	N	N	Y	N	Y
3 Lipinski	Y	N	Y	N	Y	Y	Y	Y
4 Gutierrez	N	N	Y	N	N	N	N	Y
5 Rostenkowski	Y	N	Y	N	N	N	N	N
6 Hyde	Y	N	Y	Y	Y	Y	Y	Y
7 Collins	N	N	N	N	N	Y	N	Y
8 Crane	Y	Y	N	Y	Y	N	Y	N
9 Yates	N	N	Y	N	N	Y	N	Y
10 Porter	Y	N	Y	Y	Y	Y	Y	Y
11 Sangmeister	Y	N	Y	N	Y	N	Y	N
12 Costello	Y	N	Y	N	Y	Y	Y	Y
13 Fawell	Y	Y	N	Y	Y	N	Y	N
14 Hastert	Y	Y	N	Y	Y	N	Y	N
15 Ewing	Y	Y	N	Y	Y	Y	Y	Y
16 Manzullo	Y	Y	N	Y	Y	Y	Y	Y
17 Evans	N	N	Y	N	N	Y	N	Y

ND Northern Democrats   SD Southern Democrats

	309	310	311	312	313	314	315	316
18 ***Michel***	Y	Y	N	Y	Y	Y	Y	Y
19 Poshard	Y	N	Y	N	Y	Y	Y	Y
20 Durbin	Y	N	Y	N	N	Y	N	Y
INDIANA								
1 Visclosky	Y	N	Y	N	N	Y	N	Y
2 Sharp	Y	N	Y	N	N	Y	N	Y
3 Roemer	Y	N	Y	N	Y	Y	Y	Y
4 Long	Y	N	Y	N	N	Y	N	Y
5 ***Buyer***	Y	Y	N	Y	Y	N	Y	N
6 ***Burton***	Y	Y	N	Y	Y	N	Y	N
7 ***Myers***	Y	N	Y	Y	Y	N	Y	N
8 McCloskey	Y	N	Y	N	N	Y	N	Y
9 Hamilton	Y	N	Y	N	Y	Y	Y	Y
10 Jacobs	Y	Y	Y	N	N	Y	N	Y
IOWA								
1 ***Leach***	Y	Y	Y	Y	N	N	N	N
2 ***Nussle***	Y	Y	N	Y	Y	Y	Y	Y
3 ***Lightfoot***	Y	Y	N	Y	Y	N	Y	N
4 Smith	N	N	Y	N	N	Y	N	Y
5 ***Grandy***	Y	Y	Y	Y	Y	N	Y	N
KANSAS								
1 ***Roberts***	Y	Y	N	Y	Y	Y	Y	Y
2 Slattery	Y	N	Y	N	Y	Y	Y	Y
3 ***Meyers***	N	Y	N	Y	Y	Y	Y	Y
4 Glickman	Y	N	Y	N	N	Y	N	Y
KENTUCKY								
1 Barlow	Y	N	Y	N	N	N	Y	N
2 Natcher	Y	N	Y	N	N	Y	N	Y
3 Mazzoli	Y	N	Y	N	Y	N	Y	N
4 ***Bunning***	Y	Y	N	Y	Y	Y	Y	Y
5 ***Rogers***	Y	N	Y	Y	Y	Y	Y	Y
6 Baesler	Y	N	Y	N	Y	Y	Y	Y
LOUISIANA								
1 ***Livingston***	Y	Y	N	Y	Y	N	Y	N
2 Jefferson	N	N	Y	N	N	Y	N	Y
3 Tauzin	Y	Y	Y	Y	Y	N	Y	N
4 Fields	N	N	Y	N	N	Y	N	Y
5 ***McCrery***	Y	Y	Y	Y	Y	Y	Y	Y
6 ***Baker***	Y	Y	N	Y	Y	Y	Y	Y
7 Hayes	Y	N	Y	N	Y	Y	Y	Y
MAINE								
1 Andrews	N	N	Y	N	N	Y	N	Y
2 ***Snowe***	N	Y	Y	Y	Y	Y	Y	Y
MARYLAND								
1 ***Gilchrest***	Y	Y	Y	Y	N	Y	N	Y
2 ***Bentley***	Y	N	Y	Y	Y	N	Y	N
3 Cardin	N	N	Y	N	N	N	N	N
4 Wynn	N	N	Y	N	N	N	N	N
5 Hoyer	N	N	Y	N	N	N	N	N
6 ***Bartlett***	Y	Y	N	Y	Y	N	Y	N
7 Mfume	N	N	Y	N	N	Y	N	Y
8 ***Morella***	N	N	Y	N	N	N	N	N
MASSACHUSETTS								
1 Olver	N	N	Y	N	N	N	N	N
2 Neal	Y	N	Y	N	N	Y	N	Y
3 ***Blute***	Y	Y	Y	Y	N	Y	N	Y
4 Frank	N	N	Y	N	N	Y	N	Y
5 Meehan	N	N	Y	N	N	Y	N	Y
6 ***Torkildsen***	Y	N	Y	Y	N	Y	N	Y
7 Markey	N	N	Y	N	N	Y	N	Y
8 Kennedy	N	N	Y	N	N	Y	N	Y
9 Moakley	?	?	?	?	?	?	?	?
10 Studds	N	N	Y	N	N	Y	N	Y
MICHIGAN								
1 Stupak	Y	N	Y	N	Y	Y	Y	Y
2 ***Hoekstra***	Y	Y	Y	Y	Y	Y	Y	Y
3 Henry	?	?	?	?	?	?	?	?
4 ***Camp***	Y	Y	N	Y	Y	Y	Y	Y
5 Barcia	Y	N	Y	N	Y	Y	Y	Y
6 ***Upton***	Y	Y	Y	Y	Y	Y	Y	Y
7 ***Smith***	Y	Y	N	Y	Y	Y	Y	Y
8 Carr	N	N	Y	N	N	Y	N	Y
9 Kildee	Y	N	Y	N	N	Y	N	Y
10 Bonior	Y	N	Y	N	N	?	N	?
11 ***Knollenberg***	Y	Y	N	Y	Y	N	Y	N
12 Levin	N	N	Y	N	N	Y	N	Y
13 Ford	N	N	Y	N	N	N	N	N
14 Conyers	N	N	N	N	N	Y	?	?
15 Collins	N	N	N	N	N	Y	N	Y
16 Dingell	?	N	Y	?	Y	Y	?	Y
MINNESOTA								
1 Penny	Y	Y	Y	Y	Y	Y	Y	Y
2 Minge	+	?	?	?	+	+	+	+
3 ***Ramstad***	Y	Y	N	Y	Y	Y	Y	Y
4 Vento	N	N	Y	N	N	Y	N	Y
5 Sabo	N	N	Y	N	N	Y	N	Y
6 ***Grams***	Y	Y	N	Y	Y	Y	Y	Y
7 Peterson	Y	N	Y	Y	Y	Y	Y	Y
8 Oberstar	Y	N	Y	N	N	Y	N	Y
MISSISSIPPI								
1 Whitten	Y	N	Y	?	?	Y	Y	Y
2 Thompson	N	N	Y	N	N	Y	N	Y
3 Montgomery	Y	N	Y	Y	Y	N	Y	N
4 Parker	Y	N	Y	Y	Y	N	Y	N
5 Taylor	Y	Y	N	Y	Y	N	Y	N
MISSOURI								
1 Clay	N	N	Y	N	N	Y	N	Y
2 ***Talent***	Y	Y	N	Y	Y	N	Y	N
3 Gephardt	Y	N	Y	N	N	Y	N	Y
4 Skelton	Y	N	Y	N	Y	Y	Y	Y
5 Wheat	N	N	Y	N	N	Y	N	Y
6 Danner	Y	N	Y	N	Y	Y	Y	Y
7 ***Hancock***	Y	Y	N	Y	Y	N	Y	N
8 ***Emerson***	Y	Y	Y	N	Y	N	Y	N
9 Volkmer	Y	N	Y	N	Y	Y	Y	Y
MONTANA								
AL Williams	N	N	Y	Y	?	?	?	?
NEBRASKA								
1 ***Bereuter***	Y	Y	N	Y	Y	N	Y	N
2 Hoagland	Y	N	Y	N	N	N	N	N
3 ***Barrett***	Y	Y	Y	Y	Y	N	Y	N
NEVADA								
1 Bilbray	Y	N	Y	N	Y	N	Y	N
2 ***Vucanovich***	Y	N	Y	Y	Y	Y	Y	Y
NEW HAMPSHIRE								
1 ***Zeliff***	Y	Y	N	Y	Y	Y	Y	Y
2 Swett	Y	N	Y	N	Y	N	Y	N
NEW JERSEY								
1 Andrews	N	N	Y	N	N	N	N	N
2 Hughes	Y	N	Y	N	N	N	N	N
3 ***Saxton***	Y	Y	N	Y	Y	Y	Y	Y
4 ***Smith***	Y	Y	Y	Y	Y	N	Y	N
5 ***Roukema***	N	N	Y	Y	Y	N	Y	N
6 Pallone	N	N	N	N	N	N	N	N
7 ***Franks***	N	Y	N	Y	Y	N	Y	N
8 Klein	N	N	Y	N	N	N	N	N
9 Torricelli	N	N	Y	Y	N	N	N	N
10 Payne	N	N	Y	N	N	Y	N	Y
11 ***Gallo***	Y	N	Y	Y	Y	N	Y	N
12 ***Zimmer***	N	Y	N	Y	Y	Y	Y	Y
13 Menendez	N	N	Y	N	N	Y	N	Y
NEW MEXICO								
1 ***Schiff***	Y	Y	Y	Y	N	N	N	N
2 ***Skeen***	+	+	+	+	+	−	+	−
3 Richardson	N	N	Y	N	N	N	N	Y
NEW YORK								
1 Hochbrueckner	N	N	Y	N	N	N	N	N
2 ***Lazio***	Y	Y	Y	Y	N	Y	N	Y
3 ***King***	Y	Y	N	Y	Y	Y	Y	Y
4 ***Levy***	Y	Y	N	Y	Y	Y	Y	Y
5 Ackerman	N	N	Y	N	N	N	N	N
6 Flake	?	N	Y	N	N	Y	N	Y
7 Manton	Y	N	Y	N	Y	N	Y	N
8 Nadler	N	N	Y	N	N	Y	N	Y
9 Schumer	N	N	Y	N	N	N	N	N
10 Towns	N	N	Y	N	N	Y	N	Y
11 Owens	N	N	Y	N	N	Y	N	Y
12 Velazquez	N	N	Y	N	N	Y	N	Y
13 ***Molinari***	N	N	Y	Y	Y	N	Y	N
14 Maloney	N	N	Y	N	N	Y	N	Y
15 Rangel	N	N	Y	N	N	Y	N	Y
16 Serrano	N	N	Y	N	N	Y	N	Y
17 Engel	N	N	Y	N	N	N	N	N
18 Lowey	N	N	Y	N	N	N	N	N
19 ***Fish***	Y	Y	Y	Y	Y	Y	Y	Y
20 ***Gilman***	N	N	Y	Y	Y	N	Y	N
21 McNulty	Y	N	Y	N	Y	N	Y	N
22 ***Solomon***	Y	Y	N	Y	Y	Y	Y	Y
23 ***Boehlert***	N	N	Y	Y	N	N	N	N
24 ***McHugh***	N	Y	N	Y	Y	Y	Y	Y
25 ***Walsh***	Y	Y	Y	Y	Y	N	Y	N
26 Hinchey	N	N	Y	N	N	Y	N	?
27 ***Paxon***	Y	Y	N	Y	Y	Y	Y	Y
28 Slaughter	N	N	Y	N	N	N	N	N
29 LaFalce	Y	N	Y	N	Y	Y	Y	Y
30 ***Quinn***	Y	Y	N	Y	Y	N	Y	N
31 ***Houghton***	Y	Y	Y	Y	N	Y	N	Y
NORTH CAROLINA								
1 Clayton	N	N	N	N	N	Y	N	Y
2 Valentine	Y	N	Y	Y	Y	Y	Y	Y
3 Lancaster	Y	N	Y	N	Y	Y	Y	Y
4 Price	N	N	Y	N	N	Y	N	Y
5 Neal	Y	N	Y	N	Y	Y	Y	Y
6 ***Coble***	Y	Y	N	Y	Y	N	Y	N
7 Rose	N	N	Y	N	Y	Y	Y	Y
8 Hefner	Y	N	Y	N	Y	N	Y	N
9 ***McMillan***	?	?	?	?	?	?	?	?
10 ***Ballenger***	Y	Y	N	Y	Y	Y	Y	Y
11 ***Taylor***	Y	Y	N	Y	Y	N	Y	N
12 Watt	N	N	Y	N	N	Y	N	Y
NORTH DAKOTA								
AL Pomeroy	Y	N	Y	N	Y	N	Y	N
OHIO								
1 Mann	Y	N	Y	N	Y	N	Y	N
2 ***Portman***	Y	Y	N	Y	Y	Y	Y	Y
3 Hall	Y	N	Y	N	Y	N	Y	N
4 ***Oxley***	Y	Y	N	Y	Y	N	Y	N
5 ***Gillmor***	Y	N	N	Y	Y	Y	Y	Y
6 Strickland	N	N	Y	N	N	Y	N	Y
7 ***Hobson***	Y	Y	Y	Y	Y	N	Y	N
8 ***Boehner***	Y	Y	N	Y	Y	N	Y	Y
9 Kaptur	Y	N	Y	N	Y	N	Y	N
10 ***Hoke***	Y	Y	N	Y	Y	N	Y	N
11 Stokes	N	N	Y	N	N	Y	N	Y
12 ***Kasich***	Y	Y	Y	Y	Y	Y	Y	Y
13 Brown	Y	N	Y	N	N	Y	Y	Y
14 Sawyer	?	N	Y	N	N	Y	N	Y
15 ***Pryce***	Y	Y	Y	Y	Y	Y	Y	Y
16 ***Regula***	Y	Y	Y	Y	Y	Y	Y	Y
17 Traficant	N	N	Y	N	Y	Y	Y	Y
18 Applegate	Y	N	Y	N	N	N	N	N
19 Fingerhut	N	N	Y	N	N	Y	N	Y
OKLAHOMA								
1 ***Inhofe***	Y	Y	N	Y	Y	Y	Y	Y
2 Synar	N	N	Y	N	N	Y	N	Y
3 Brewster	Y	N	Y	N	Y	Y	Y	Y
4 McCurdy	N	N	Y	N	Y	Y	Y	Y
5 ***Istook***	Y	Y	N	Y	Y	Y	Y	Y
6 English	Y	Y	Y	N	Y	Y	Y	Y
OREGON								
1 Furse	N	N	Y	N	N	Y	N	Y
2 ***Smith***	Y	Y	N	Y	Y	Y	Y	Y
3 Wyden	N	N	Y	N	N	Y	N	Y
4 DeFazio	N	N	N	Y	N	Y	N	Y
5 Kopetski	N	N	Y	N	N	Y	N	Y
PENNSYLVANIA								
1 Foglietta	N	N	Y	N	N	Y	N	Y
2 Blackwell	N	N	Y	N	N	Y	N	Y
3 Borski	Y	N	Y	N	N	Y	N	Y
4 Klink	Y	N	Y	Y	Y	Y	Y	N
5 ***Clinger***	Y	Y	Y	Y	Y	N	Y	N
6 Holden	Y	N	Y	N	Y	Y	Y	Y
7 ***Weldon***	Y	Y	Y	N	Y	N	Y	N
8 ***Greenwood***	N	Y	Y	Y	Y	Y	Y	Y
9 ***Shuster***	Y	Y	N	Y	Y	N	Y	N
10 ***McDade***	Y	Y	Y	Y	Y	N	Y	N
11 Kanjorski	Y	N	Y	N	Y	N	Y	N
12 Murtha	Y	N	Y	N	Y	Y	Y	Y
13 Margolies-Mezv.	N	N	Y	N	N	Y	N	Y
14 Coyne	N	N	Y	N	N	Y	N	Y
15 McHale	Y	N	Y	N	Y	Y	Y	Y
16 ***Walker***	Y	Y	N	Y	Y	N	Y	N
17 ***Gekas***	Y	Y	N	N	Y	N	Y	N
18 ***Santorum***	Y	Y	Y	Y	Y	N	Y	N
19 ***Goodling***	Y	N	Y	Y	Y	N	Y	N
20 Murphy	Y	Y	Y	Y	Y	N	Y	N
21 ***Ridge***	Y	Y	Y	Y	Y	N	Y	N
RHODE ISLAND								
1 ***Machtley***	N	N	Y	Y	Y	Y	Y	Y
2 Reed	N	N	Y	N	N	N	N	N
SOUTH CAROLINA								
1 ***Ravenel***	Y	Y	Y	Y	Y	N	Y	N
2 ***Spence***	Y	Y	N	Y	Y	N	Y	N
3 Derrick	N	N	Y	Y	Y	Y	Y	Y
4 ***Inglis***	Y	Y	N	Y	Y	Y	Y	Y
5 Spratt	Y	N	Y	N	Y	Y	Y	Y
6 Clyburn	N	N	Y	N	N	Y	N	Y
SOUTH DAKOTA								
AL Johnson	Y	N	Y	Y	Y	Y	Y	Y
TENNESSEE								
1 ***Quillen***	Y	N	Y	Y	Y	N	Y	N
2 ***Duncan***	Y	Y	Y	Y	Y	Y	Y	Y
3 Lloyd	Y	N	Y	N	Y	N	Y	N
4 Cooper	Y	Y	Y	Y	Y	Y	Y	Y
5 Clement	Y	N	Y	N	Y	Y	Y	Y
6 Gordon	Y	N	Y	N	Y	N	Y	N
7 ***Sundquist***	Y	N	Y	Y	Y	N	Y	N
8 Tanner	Y	Y	Y	N	Y	Y	Y	Y
9 Ford	N	N	Y	N	N	Y	N	Y
TEXAS								
1 Chapman	Y	N	Y	N	Y	Y	Y	Y
2 Wilson	N	N	Y	Y	N	N	Y	N
3 ***Johnson, Sam***	Y	Y	N	Y	Y	N	Y	N
4 Hall	Y	Y	Y	Y	Y	Y	Y	Y
5 Bryant	N	N	Y	N	N	Y	N	Y
6 ***Barton***	Y	Y	N	Y	Y	Y	Y	Y
7 ***Archer***	Y	Y	N	Y	Y	Y	Y	Y
8 ***Fields***	Y	Y	N	Y	Y	Y	Y	Y
9 Brooks	N	N	Y	Y	Y	N	Y	N
10 Pickle	N	N	Y	N	Y	Y	?	Y
11 Edwards	Y	N	Y	N	Y	Y	Y	Y
12 Geren	Y	Y	Y	Y	Y	N	Y	N
13 Sarpalius	Y	N	Y	N	Y	Y	Y	Y
14 Laughlin	Y	Y	Y	?	?	?	?	?
15 de la Garza	Y	N	Y	N	Y	Y	Y	Y
16 Coleman	N	?	Y	N	N	N	N	Y
17 Stenholm	Y	Y	Y	Y	Y	N	Y	N
18 Washington	N	N	N	N	N	Y	N	Y
19 ***Combest***	Y	Y	N	Y	Y	N	Y	N
20 Gonzalez	N	N	Y	N	N	Y	N	Y
21 ***Smith***	Y	Y	N	Y	Y	N	Y	N
22 ***DeLay***	Y	Y	N	Y	Y	N	Y	N
23 ***Bonilla***	Y	N	Y	Y	Y	N	Y	N
24 Frost	N	N	Y	N	Y	Y	Y	Y
25 Andrews	N	Y	Y	Y	Y	Y	Y	Y
26 ***Armey***	Y	Y	N	Y	Y	N	Y	N
27 Ortiz	Y	N	Y	N	Y	N	Y	N
28 Tejeda	Y	N	Y	N	Y	N	Y	N
29 Green	N	N	Y	N	Y	N	Y	N
30 Johnson, E. B.	N	N	Y	N	N	Y	N	Y
UTAH								
1 ***Hansen***	Y	Y	N	Y	Y	Y	Y	Y
2 Shepherd	N	N	Y	N	Y	N	Y	N
3 Orton	Y	Y	N	Y	Y	Y	Y	Y
VERMONT								
AL *Sanders*	N	N	Y	N	N	Y	N	Y
VIRGINIA								
1 ***Bateman***	Y	N	Y	Y	Y	Y	Y	Y
2 Pickett	N	N	Y	Y	Y	Y	Y	Y
3 Scott	N	N	Y	N	N	Y	N	Y
4 Sisisky	N	N	Y	N	Y	Y	?	?
5 Payne	Y	N	Y	Y	Y	Y	Y	Y
6 ***Goodlatte***	Y	Y	N	Y	Y	Y	Y	Y
7 ***Bliley***	Y	Y	Y	Y	Y	Y	Y	Y
8 Moran	N	N	Y	N	N	N	N	N
9 Boucher	N	N	Y	N	Y	Y	Y	Y
10 ***Wolf***	Y	Y	Y	Y	Y	N	Y	N
11 Byrne	N	N	N	N	N	N	N	N
WASHINGTON								
1 Cantwell	N	N	Y	N	N	Y	N	Y
2 Swift	N	N	Y	N	N	Y	N	Y
3 Unsoeld	N	N	Y	N	N	Y	N	Y
4 Inslee	N	Y	Y	N	Y	Y	Y	Y
5 Foley	N							
6 Dicks	N	N	Y	Y	N	N	N	N
7 McDermott	N	N	Y	N	N	Y	N	Y
8 ***Dunn***	Y	N	N	Y	Y	Y	Y	Y
9 Kreidler	N	N	Y	N	N	Y	N	Y
WEST VIRGINIA								
1 Mollohan	Y	N	Y	N	Y	Y	Y	Y
2 Wise	N	N	Y	?	Y	Y	Y	Y
3 Rahall	Y	N	Y	N	Y	Y	Y	Y
WISCONSIN								
1 Barca	Y	N	Y	N	Y	N	Y	N
2 ***Klug***	Y	N	Y	Y	Y	Y	Y	Y
3 ***Gunderson***	Y	N	Y	Y	N	Y	N	Y
4 Kleczka	Y	N	Y	N	Y	Y	Y	N
5 Barrett	N	N	Y	N	Y	Y	Y	Y
6 ***Petri***	Y	Y	N	Y	Y	N	Y	N
7 Obey	Y	N	Y	N	N	Y	N	Y
8 ***Roth***	Y	Y	N	Y	Y	N	?	?
9 ***Sensenbrenner***	Y	Y	N	Y	Y	Y	Y	Y
WYOMING								
AL ***Thomas***	Y	Y	N	Y	Y	Y	Y	Y
DELEGATES								
de Lugo, V.I.	D	D	D	N	N	Y	D	D
Faleomavaega, Am.S.	D	D	D	N	N	?	D	D
Norton, D.C.	D	D	D	N	N	Y	D	D
Romero-B., P.R.	D	D	D	?	?	Y	D	D
Underwood, Guam	D	D	D	N	N	Y	D	D

Southern states - Ala., Ark., Fla., Ga., Ky., La., Miss., N.C., Okla., S.C., Tenn., Texas, Va.
Omitted votes are quorum calls, which CQ does not include in its vote charts.

HOUSE VOTES 317, 318, 319, 320, 321, 322, 323, 324

317. HR 2492. Fiscal 1994 D.C. Appropriations/Passage. Passage of the bill to provide $700 million in federal funds for the District of Columbia in fiscal 1994 and to approve the spending of $3,753,705,000 in funds raised from local taxes. The administration requested $705,101,000 in federal funds and $3,777,351,000 in local taxes. Passed 213-211: R 12-161; D 200-50 (ND 143-24, SD 57-26); I 1-0, June 30, 1993.

318. HR 2519. Fiscal 1994 Commerce, Justice, State Appropriations/Border Patrol. Hunter, R-Calif., amendment to provide an additional $60 million to the Immigration and Naturalization Service for increased border patrols. Adopted in the Committee of the Whole 265-164: R 153-17; D 111-147 (ND 70-104, SD 41-43); I 1-0, July 1, 1993.

319. HR 2118. Fiscal 1993 Supplemental Appropriations/Previous Question. Frost, D-Texas, motion to order the previous question (thus ending debate and the possibility of amendment) on adoption of the rule (H Res 216) to waive points of order against and provide for House floor consideration of the conference report on the bill to provide $1,003,413,538 in new budget authority by providing $3.5 billion in new spending and rescinding $2.5 billion in previously approved spending for fiscal 1993. The bill includes funding for U.S. military operations in Somalia and Iraq, rural water and waste disposal grants and loans, Small Business Administration loans, student loans, a summer jobs program and local law enforcement. Motion agreed to 250-172: R 0-170; D 249-2 (ND 165-2, SD 84-0); I 1-0, July 1, 1993.

320. HR 2118. Fiscal 1993 Supplemental Appropriations/Rule. Adoption of the rule (H Res 216) to waive points of order against and provide for House floor consideration of the conference report on the bill to provide $1,003,413,538 in new budget authority by providing $3.5 billion in new spending and rescinding $2.5 billion in previously approved spending for fiscal 1993. The bill includes funding for U.S. military operations in Somalia and Iraq, rural water and waste disposal grants and loans, Small Business Administration loans, student loans, a summer jobs program and local law enforcement. Adopted 243-170: R 0-166; D 242-4 (ND 160-2, SD 82-2); I 1-0, July 1, 1993.

321. HR 2118. Fiscal 1993 Supplemental Appropriations/Conference Report. Approval of the conference report on the bill to provide $1,003,413,538 in new budget authority by providing $3.5 billion in new spending and rescinding $2.5 billion in previously approved spending for fiscal 1993. The bill includes funding for U.S. military operations in Somalia and Iraq, rural water and waste disposal grants and loans, Small Business Administration loans, student loans, a summer jobs program and local law enforcement. Approved (thus sent to the Senate) 280-138: R 38-132; D 241-6 (ND 157-6, SD 84-0); I 1-0, July 1, 1993.

322. HR 2010. National Service/Rule. Adoption of the rule (H Res 215) to provide for House floor consideration of the bill to authorize $389 million in fiscal 1994 for a National Service program that will provide individuals with $5,000 a year for up to two years in education awards in return for work in community service programs. The bill also would authorize $5 million for the Points of Light Foundation. Adopted 239-159: R 3-159; D 235-0 (ND 158-0, SD 77-0); I 1-0, July 13, 1993.

323. HR 2520. Fiscal 1994 Interior Appropriations/Forest Service Roads. Porter, R-Ill., amendment to cut funding for the Forest Service by $11.9 million to limit the development of roads for logging on federal lands. Rejected in Committee of the Whole 164-262: R 75-95; D 89-166 (ND 71-102, SD 18-64); I 0-1, July 14, 1993.

324. HR 2520. Fiscal 1994 Interior Appropriations/National Trust for Historic Preservation. DeLay, R-Texas, amendment to cut $7 million of the $40 million for the Historic Preservation Fund to eliminate funding for the National Trust for Historic Preservation. Rejected in Committee of the Whole 116-315: R 98-75; D 18-239 (ND 12-161, SD 6-78); I 0-1, July 14, 1993.

KEY

Y	Voted for (yea).
#	Paired for.
+	Announced for.
N	Voted against (nay).
X	Paired against.
−	Announced against.
P	Voted "present."
C	Voted "present" to avoid possible conflict of interest.
?	Did not vote or otherwise make a position known.
D	Delegates ineligible to vote.

Democrats *Republicans* *Independent*

	317	318	319	320	321	322	323	324
ALABAMA								
1 *Callahan*	N	Y	N	N	Y	N	N	Y
2 *Everett*	N	Y	N	N	N	N	N	Y
3 Browder	N	N	Y	Y	Y	N	N	N
4 Bevill	Y	N	Y	Y	Y	Y	N	N
5 Cramer	N	N	Y	Y	Y	?	N	N
6 *Bachus*	N	Y	N	N	N	N	N	Y
7 Hilliard	Y	N	Y	Y	Y	Y	N	N
ALASKA								
AL *Young*	N	Y	N	N	N	N	N	Y
ARIZONA								
1 Coppersmith	Y	Y	Y	Y	Y	Y	Y	N
2 Pastor	Y	Y	Y	Y	Y	Y	N	N
3 *Stump*	N	Y	N	N	N	N	N	Y
4 *Kyl*	N	Y	N	N	N	N	N	Y
5 *Kolbe*	N	Y	N	N	N	N	N	N
6 English	Y	Y	Y	Y	Y	Y	N	N
ARKANSAS								
1 Lambert	Y	N	Y	Y	Y	Y	Y	N
2 Thornton	Y	N	Y	Y	Y	?	N	N
3 *Hutchinson*	N	Y	N	N	N	N	N	Y
4 *Dickey*	N	Y	N	N	N	N	N	Y
CALIFORNIA								
1 Hamburg	Y	Y	Y	Y	Y	Y	N	N
2 *Herger*	N	Y	N	N	N	N	N	Y
3 Fazio	Y	Y	Y	Y	Y	Y	N	N
4 *Doolittle*	N	Y	N	N	N	N	N	Y
5 Matsui	Y	N	Y	Y	Y	Y	N	N
6 Woolsey	Y	Y	Y	Y	Y	Y	N	N
7 Miller	?	Y	Y	Y	?	Y	Y	N
8 Pelosi	Y	N	Y	Y	Y	Y	N	N
9 Dellums	Y	N	?	?	Y	?	N	N
10 *Baker*	N	Y	N	N	N	N	N	N
11 *Pombo*	N	Y	N	N	N	N	N	Y
12 Lantos	Y	Y	Y	Y	Y	Y	Y	N
13 Stark	Y	Y	Y	?	Y	Y	Y	N
14 Eshoo	Y	Y	Y	Y	Y	Y	N	N
15 Mineta	Y	Y	Y	Y	Y	Y	N	N
16 Edwards	Y	Y	Y	?	Y	?	Y	N
17 Farr	Y	Y	Y	?	Y	Y	Y	N
18 Condit	N	Y	Y	Y	N	?	N	Y
19 Lehman	Y	Y	Y	Y	Y	Y	N	N
20 Dooley	Y	N	?	Y	N	Y	N	N
21 *Thomas*	N	Y	N	N	N	N	N	Y
22 *Huffington*	N	Y	N	N	N	?	N	Y
23 *Gallegly*	N	Y	N	N	N	?	Y	Y
24 Beilenson	Y	Y	Y	Y	Y	Y	Y	N
25 *McKeon*	N	Y	N	N	N	?	Y	Y
26 Berman	Y	Y	Y	?	Y	Y	Y	N
27 *Moorhead*	N	Y	N	N	N	N	N	Y
28 *Dreier*	N	Y	N	N	N	N	N	Y
29 Waxman	?	Y	?	?	?	Y	Y	N
30 Becerra	Y	Y	Y	Y	Y	Y	N	N
31 Martinez	Y	Y	Y	Y	Y	Y	N	N
32 Dixon	Y	Y	Y	Y	Y	Y	N	N
33 Roybal-Allard	Y	Y	Y	Y	Y	Y	N	N
34 Torres	Y	Y	Y	Y	Y	Y	N	N
35 Waters	Y	Y	Y	?	Y	Y	Y	N
36 Harman	Y	Y	Y	Y	Y	Y	N	N
37 Tucker	Y	Y	Y	Y	Y	?	N	N
38 *Horn*	N	Y	N	N	N	N	Y	N
39 *Royce*	N	Y	N	N	N	N	N	Y
40 *Lewis*	N	Y	N	N	N	N	N	Y
41 *Kim*	N	Y	N	N	Y	N	Y	Y
42 Brown	Y	N	Y	Y	Y	Y	Y	N
43 *Calvert*	N	Y	N	N	N	N	Y	Y
44 *McCandless*	N	Y	N	N	N	N	Y	Y
45 *Rohrabacher*	N	Y	N	N	N	N	Y	Y
46 *Dornan*	N	Y	N	N	N	N	N	Y
47 *Cox*	N	Y	N	N	N	?	N	Y
48 *Packard*	N	Y	N	N	N	N	N	N
49 Schenk	Y	Y	Y	Y	Y	Y	Y	N
50 Filner	Y	Y	Y	Y	Y	Y	Y	N
51 *Cunningham*	N	Y	N	N	N	N	Y	Y
52 *Hunter*	N	Y	N	N	N	N	N	Y
COLORADO								
1 Schroeder	N	N	Y	Y	Y	Y	Y	N
2 Skaggs	Y	N	Y	Y	Y	Y	Y	N
3 *McInnis*	N	Y	N	N	N	N	N	Y
4 *Allard*	N	N	N	N	N	N	N	Y
5 *Hefley*	N	Y	N	N	N	N	Y	Y
6 *Schaefer*	N	N	N	N	N	N	Y	Y
CONNECTICUT								
1 Kennelly	Y	N	Y	Y	Y	Y	Y	N
2 Gejdenson	Y	N	Y	Y	Y	Y	Y	N
3 DeLauro	Y	N	Y	Y	Y	Y	Y	N
4 *Shays*	Y	N	N	N	N	Y	Y	Y
5 *Franks*	Y	Y	N	N	N	N	Y	Y
6 *Johnson*	Y	N	N	Y	N	Y	N	Y
DELAWARE								
AL *Castle*	N	Y	N	N	N	N	N	N
FLORIDA								
1 Hutto	N	Y	Y	Y	Y	Y	N	Y
2 Peterson	Y	N	Y	Y	Y	Y	N	N
3 Brown	Y	Y	Y	Y	Y	Y	N	N
4 *Fowler*	N	Y	N	N	Y	N	N	N
5 Thurman	N	N	Y	Y	Y	Y	N	N
6 *Stearns*	N	Y	N	N	N	N	N	N
7 *Mica*	N	Y	N	N	N	N	Y	N
8 *McCollum*	N	Y	N	N	N	N	N	Y
9 *Bilirakis*	N	Y	N	?	N	Y	Y	Y
10 *Young*	N	Y	N	N	?	Y	Y	Y
11 Gibbons	Y	N	Y	Y	Y	Y	Y	N
12 *Canady*	N	Y	N	N	N	N	N	Y
13 *Miller*	N	Y	N	N	N	N	Y	N
14 *Goss*	N	Y	N	N	N	N	N	N
15 Bacchus	Y	Y	Y	Y	Y	Y	N	N
16 *Lewis*	N	Y	N	N	?	Y	Y	N
17 Meek	Y	Y	Y	Y	Y	Y	N	N
18 *Ros-Lehtinen*	N	Y	N	N	N	Y	N	Y
19 Johnston	Y	Y	Y	Y	Y	Y	N	N
20 Deutsch	Y	Y	Y	Y	Y	Y	N	N
21 *Diaz-Balart*	N	Y	N	N	N	Y	N	Y
22 *Shaw*	N	Y	N	N	N	Y	N	Y
23 Hastings	Y	N	Y	Y	Y	Y	Y	N
GEORGIA								
1 *Kingston*	N	Y	N	N	N	N	N	N
2 Bishop	Y	Y	Y	Y	Y	Y	N	N
3 *Collins*	N	Y	N	N	N	N	N	Y
4 *Linder*	N	Y	N	N	N	N	N	Y
5 Lewis	Y	N	Y	Y	Y	Y	N	N
6 *Gingrich*	N	Y	N	N	N	N	N	Y
7 Darden	Y	Y	Y	Y	Y	Y	N	N
8 Rowland	N	Y	Y	Y	Y	Y	N	N
9 Deal	Y	Y	Y	Y	Y	Y	N	N
10 Johnson	Y	Y	Y	Y	Y	Y	N	N
11 McKinney	Y	Y	Y	Y	Y	Y	N	N
HAWAII								
1 Abercrombie	Y	N	Y	Y	Y	Y	N	N
2 Mink	Y	N	Y	Y	Y	Y	N	N
IDAHO								
1 LaRocco	N	Y	Y	Y	Y	Y	N	N
2 *Crapo*	N	Y	N	N	N	N	N	Y
ILLINOIS								
1 Rush	Y	N	Y	Y	Y	Y	N	N
2 Reynolds	Y	N	Y	Y	Y	Y	N	N
3 Lipinski	N	N	?	?	?	?	N	N
4 Gutierrez	Y	Y	Y	Y	Y	Y	N	N
5 Rostenkowski	Y	N	Y	Y	Y	Y	N	N
6 *Hyde*	N	Y	N	?	N	N	N	Y
7 Collins	Y	Y	Y	Y	Y	Y	N	N
8 *Crane*	N	N	N	N	N	N	N	Y
9 Yates	Y	N	Y	Y	Y	Y	N	N
10 *Porter*	N	N	N	N	N	N	N	Y
11 Sangmeister	N	Y	Y	Y	Y	Y	N	N
12 Costello	N	Y	Y	Y	Y	Y	N	N
13 *Fawell*	N	Y	N	N	N	N	N	Y
14 *Hastert*	N	Y	N	N	N	N	N	Y
15 *Ewing*	N	Y	N	N	N	?	N	Y
16 *Manzullo*	N	Y	N	N	N	N	N	Y
17 Evans	Y	Y	Y	Y	Y	Y	Y	N

ND Northern Democrats   SD Southern Democrats

	317	318	319	320	321	322	323	324
18 ***Michel***	N	Y	N	N	Y	N	N	Y
19 Poshard	N	N	Y	Y	Y	Y	Y	Y
20 Durbin	Y	N	Y	Y	Y	Y	N	N
INDIANA								
1 Visclosky	Y	N	Y	Y	Y	Y	N	N
2 Sharp	Y	N	Y	Y	Y	Y	N	N
3 Roemer	N	N	Y	Y	Y	Y	N	N
4 Long	Y	Y	Y	Y	Y	Y	N	N
5 ***Buyer***	N	Y	N	N	N	N	N	Y
6 ***Burton***	N	Y	N	N	N	N	N	Y
7 ***Myers***	N	N	N	N	N	N	N	Y
8 McCloskey	Y	N	Y	Y	Y	Y	N	N
9 Hamilton	Y	N	Y	Y	Y	Y	N	N
10 Jacobs	Y	N	N	N	Y	Y	Y	N
IOWA								
1 ***Leach***	N	Y	N	N	N	N	?	?
2 ***Nussle***	N	Y	N	N	N	N	Y	Y
3 ***Lightfoot***	N	Y	N	N	Y	N	?	?
4 Smith	Y	N	Y	Y	Y	Y	?	?
5 ***Grandy***	N	N	N	N	Y	N	N	Y
KANSAS								
1 ***Roberts***	N	Y	N	N	N	N	N	N
2 Slattery	N	N	Y	Y	Y	Y	Y	N
3 ***Meyers***	N	Y	N	N	Y	N	Y	N
4 Glickman	Y	N	Y	Y	Y	Y	Y	N
KENTUCKY								
1 Barlow	Y	Y	Y	Y	Y	Y	N	N
2 Natcher	Y	N	Y	Y	Y	Y	N	N
3 Mazzoli	Y	Y	Y	Y	Y	Y	N	N
4 ***Bunning***	N	Y	N	N	N	N	N	Y
5 ***Rogers***	N	Y	N	N	Y	N	N	N
6 Baesler	Y	N	Y	Y	Y	Y	N	N
LOUISIANA								
1 ***Livingston***	Y	Y	N	N	N	N	N	N
2 Jefferson	Y	Y	Y	Y	Y	Y	N	N
3 Tauzin	N	Y	Y	N	Y	Y	N	N
4 Fields	Y	Y	Y	Y	Y	Y	N	N
5 ***McCrery***	N	N	N	N	Y	N	N	N
6 ***Baker***	N	N	N	N	N	N	Y	Y
7 Hayes	N	N	Y	Y	Y	Y	N	N
MAINE								
1 Andrews	Y	N	Y	Y	Y	Y	Y	N
2 ***Snowe***	N	Y	N	N	N	N	N	N
MARYLAND								
1 ***Gilchrest***	Y	Y	N	N	Y	N	Y	N
2 ***Bentley***	N	Y	N	N	N	N	N	Y
3 Cardin	Y	N	Y	Y	Y	Y	Y	N
4 Wynn	Y	N	Y	Y	Y	Y	N	N
5 Hoyer	Y	N	Y	Y	Y	Y	N	N
6 ***Bartlett***	N	Y	N	N	N	N	Y	Y
7 Mfume	Y	Y	Y	Y	Y	?	N	?
8 ***Morella***	Y	N	N	?	Y	N	Y	N
MASSACHUSETTS								
1 Olver	Y	N	Y	Y	Y	Y	N	N
2 Neal	Y	N	Y	Y	?	Y	N	N
3 ***Blute***	N	+	—	—	+	N	Y	N
4 Frank	Y	N	Y	Y	Y	Y	Y	N
5 Meehan	Y	N	Y	Y	Y	Y	Y	N
6 ***Torkildsen***	N	Y	N	N	Y	N	Y	N
7 Markey	Y	N	Y	Y	Y	Y	Y	N
8 Kennedy	Y	Y	Y	Y	Y	Y	Y	N
9 Moakley	?	?	?	?	?	Y	N	N
10 Studds	Y	N	Y	?	?	Y	N	N
MICHIGAN								
1 Stupak	Y	N	Y	Y	Y	Y	N	N
2 ***Hoekstra***	N	Y	N	N	N	N	N	N
3 Henry	?	?	?	?	?	?	?	?
4 ***Camp***	N	Y	N	N	N	N	N	Y
5 Barcia	Y	N	Y	Y	Y	Y	N	N
6 ***Upton***	N	Y	N	N	N	N	Y	N
7 ***Smith***	N	Y	N	N	N	N	Y	Y
8 Carr	Y	N	Y	Y	Y	Y	N	N
9 Kildee	Y	Y	Y	Y	Y	Y	N	N
10 Bonior	Y	N	Y	Y	Y	Y	N	N
11 ***Knollenberg***	N	Y	N	N	N	N	Y	Y
12 Levin	Y	Y	Y	Y	Y	Y	N	N
13 Ford	Y	N	Y	Y	Y	Y	N	N
14 Conyers	Y	N	Y	Y	?	?	?	?
15 Collins	Y	N	Y	Y	Y	Y	N	N
16 Dingell	Y	Y	Y	Y	Y	Y	N	N
MINNESOTA								
1 Penny	N	N	Y	Y	N	Y	Y	Y
2 Minge	?	Y	Y	Y	Y	Y	Y	Y
3 ***Ramstad***	N	Y	N	N	N	N	Y	Y
4 Vento	Y	N	Y	Y	Y	Y	Y	N
5 Sabo	Y	N	Y	Y	Y	Y	N	N
6 ***Grams***	N	Y	N	N	N	N	N	Y
7 Peterson	N	N	Y	N	N	Y	N	N
8 Oberstar	Y	N	Y	Y	Y	Y	N	N
MISSISSIPPI								
1 Whitten	Y	?	Y	Y	Y	Y	?	N
2 Thompson	Y	N	Y	Y	Y	Y	?	N
3 Montgomery	N	N	Y	Y	Y	Y	N	Y
4 Parker	N	N	Y	Y	Y	?	N	N
5 Taylor	N	N	Y	N	Y	?	N	Y
MISSOURI								
1 Clay	Y	N	Y	Y	?	Y	N	N
2 ***Talent***	N	Y	N	N	N	N	N	N
3 Gephardt	Y	N	Y	Y	Y	?	N	N
4 Skelton	Y	Y	Y	Y	Y	Y	N	Y
5 Wheat	Y	N	Y	Y	Y	Y	N	N
6 Danner	Y	Y	Y	Y	N	Y	N	N
7 ***Hancock***	N	Y	N	N	N	N	N	Y
8 ***Emerson***	N	Y	N	N	Y	N	N	N
9 Volkmer	N	N	Y	Y	Y	Y	N	N
MONTANA								
AL Williams	?	N	Y	Y	Y	Y	N	N
NEBRASKA								
1 ***Bereuter***	N	Y	N	N	N	N	N	N
2 Hoagland	Y	N	Y	Y	Y	Y	Y	N
3 ***Barrett***	N	Y	N	N	N	N	N	N
NEVADA								
1 Bilbray	Y	Y	Y	Y	Y	Y	N	Y
2 ***Vucanovich***	N	Y	N	N	Y	N	N	N
NEW HAMPSHIRE								
1 ***Zeliff***	N	Y	N	N	N	N	N	Y
2 Swett	Y	Y	Y	Y	Y	Y	N	N
NEW JERSEY								
1 Andrews	Y	N	Y	Y	Y	Y	N	N
2 Hughes	Y	N	Y	Y	Y	Y	Y	N
3 ***Saxton***	N	Y	N	N	N	N	Y	Y
4 ***Smith***	N	Y	N	N	Y	N	Y	Y
5 ***Roukema***	N	Y	N	N	N	N	Y	N
6 Pallone	N	Y	Y	Y	Y	Y	Y	N
7 ***Franks***	N	Y	N	N	N	N	Y	N
8 Klein	Y	N	Y	Y	Y	Y	Y	N
9 Torricelli	N	Y	Y	Y	Y	Y	Y	N
10 Payne	Y	Y	Y	Y	Y	Y	Y	N
11 ***Gallo***	Y	Y	N	N	N	N	Y	N
12 ***Zimmer***	N	Y	N	N	N	N	Y	N
13 Menendez	Y	Y	Y	Y	Y	Y	N	N
NEW MEXICO								
1 ***Schiff***	N	Y	N	N	Y	N	?	N
2 ***Skeen***	—	+	—	—	—	N	N	N
3 Richardson	Y	Y	Y	Y	Y	Y	Y	N
NEW YORK								
1 Hochbrueckner	Y	Y	Y	Y	Y	Y	Y	N
2 ***Lazio***	N	Y	N	N	Y	Y	Y	N
3 ***King***	N	Y	N	N	N	N	Y	Y
4 ***Levy***	N	Y	N	N	N	N	Y	Y
5 Ackerman	Y	Y	Y	Y	Y	Y	N	N
6 Flake	Y	N	Y	Y	Y	Y	N	N
7 Manton	Y	Y	Y	Y	Y	Y	N	N
8 Nadler	Y	Y	Y	Y	Y	Y	Y	N
9 Schumer	Y	Y	Y	Y	Y	Y	Y	N
10 Towns	Y	N	Y	Y	Y	?	N	N
11 Owens	Y	N	Y	Y	Y	Y	N	N
12 Velazquez	Y	Y	Y	Y	Y	Y	N	N
13 ***Molinari***	N	Y	N	N	N	N	Y	N
14 Maloney	Y	N	Y	Y	Y	Y	Y	N
15 Rangel	Y	Y	Y	Y	Y	Y	N	Y
16 Serrano	Y	Y	Y	Y	Y	Y	N	N
17 Engel	Y	Y	Y	Y	Y	Y	N	N
18 Lowey	Y	N	Y	Y	Y	Y	Y	N
19 ***Fish***	N	Y	N	N	Y	N	Y	N
20 ***Gilman***	Y	Y	N	N	Y	N	Y	N
21 McNulty	Y	Y	Y	Y	Y	Y	N	N
22 ***Solomon***	N	Y	N	N	N	N	Y	Y
23 ***Boehlert***	N	Y	N	N	Y	?	?	N
24 ***McHugh***	N	Y	N	N	N	N	Y	Y
25 ***Walsh***	N	Y	N	N	Y	N	Y	N
26 Hinchey	Y	Y	Y	Y	Y	Y	Y	N
27 ***Paxon***	N	Y	N	N	N	N	Y	Y
28 Slaughter	Y	N	Y	Y	Y	Y	Y	N
29 LaFalce	N	N	Y	Y	Y	Y	Y	N
30 ***Quinn***	N	Y	N	N	Y	N	Y	N
31 ***Houghton***	Y	?	?	?	?	N	Y	N
NORTH CAROLINA								
1 Clayton	Y	Y	Y	Y	Y	Y	N	N
2 Valentine	N	N	Y	Y	Y	Y	Y	N
3 Lancaster	N	N	Y	Y	Y	Y	N	N
4 Price	Y	N	Y	Y	Y	Y	N	N
5 Neal	Y	Y	Y	Y	Y	Y	Y	N
6 ***Coble***	N	N	N	N	N	N	N	Y
7 Rose	Y	N	Y	Y	Y	Y	N	N
8 Hefner	Y	N	Y	Y	Y	Y	N	N
9 ***McMillan***	?	Y	N	N	N	N	N	N
10 ***Ballenger***	N	Y	N	N	N	N	N	Y
11 ***Taylor***	N	Y	N	N	Y	N	N	N
12 Watt	Y	N	Y	Y	Y	Y	N	N
NORTH DAKOTA								
AL Pomeroy	Y	N	Y	?	Y	Y	N	N
OHIO								
1 Mann	Y	N	Y	Y	Y	Y	N	N
2 ***Portman***	N	N	N	N	N	N	N	N
3 Hall	N	N	Y	Y	Y	Y	N	N
4 ***Oxley***	N	Y	N	N	N	N	N	N
5 ***Gillmor***	N	Y	N	N	N	N	Y	N
6 Strickland	Y	N	Y	Y	Y	Y	Y	N
7 ***Hobson***	N	Y	N	N	Y	N	N	N
8 ***Boehner***	N	Y	N	N	N	N	N	Y
9 Kaptur	N	Y	Y	Y	Y	?	N	N
10 ***Hoke***	N	Y	N	N	Y	N	Y	Y
11 Stokes	Y	N	Y	Y	Y	?	N	N
12 ***Kasich***	N	Y	N	N	N	?	N	Y
13 Brown	Y	N	Y	Y	Y	Y	Y	N
14 Sawyer	Y	N	Y	Y	Y	Y	N	N
15 ***Pryce***	N	Y	N	N	Y	N	N	N
16 ***Regula***	N	N	N	N	Y	N	N	N
17 Traficant	Y	Y	Y	Y	Y	Y	N	N
18 Applegate	N	Y	Y	Y	Y	Y	Y	N
19 Fingerhut	Y	Y	Y	Y	Y	Y	Y	N
OKLAHOMA								
1 ***Inhofe***	N	Y	N	N	N	N	N	Y
2 Synar	Y	N	Y	Y	Y	Y	Y	N
3 Brewster	N	N	Y	Y	Y	Y	N	N
4 McCurdy	N	Y	Y	Y	Y	Y	Y	N
5 ***Istook***	N	Y	N	N	N	N	Y	Y
6 English	N	N	Y	Y	Y	Y	N	N
OREGON								
1 Furse	Y	N	Y	Y	Y	Y	Y	N
2 ***Smith***	N	Y	N	N	N	?	N	Y
3 Wyden	N	N	Y	Y	Y	Y	N	N
4 DeFazio	N	N	Y	Y	Y	?	N	N
5 Kopetski	Y	N	Y	Y	Y	Y	N	N
PENNSYLVANIA								
1 Foglietta	Y	N	Y	Y	Y	Y	N	N
2 Blackwell	Y	Y	Y	Y	Y	?	N	N
3 Borski	Y	N	Y	Y	Y	Y	N	N
4 Klink	Y	N	Y	Y	Y	Y	N	N
5 ***Clinger***	Y	Y	N	?	N	?	N	N
6 Holden	Y	N	Y	Y	Y	Y	Y	Y
7 ***Weldon***	N	Y	N	N	N	N	Y	N
8 ***Greenwood***	N	Y	N	N	N	N	Y	N
9 ***Shuster***	N	Y	N	N	N	N	N	Y
10 ***McDade***	N	N	N	N	Y	N	N	N
11 Kanjorski	Y	N	Y	Y	Y	Y	Y	N
12 Murtha	Y	N	Y	Y	Y	Y	N	N
13 Margolies-Mezv.	Y	Y	Y	Y	Y	Y	Y	N
14 Coyne	Y	N	Y	Y	Y	Y	N	N
15 McHale	Y	N	Y	Y	Y	Y	Y	N
16 ***Walker***	N	Y	N	N	N	N	Y	N
17 ***Gekas***	N	Y	N	N	N	N	Y	N
18 ***Santorum***	N	Y	N	N	N	N	N	Y
19 ***Goodling***	N	N	N	N	N	N	Y	Y
20 Murphy	N	N	N	Y	N	Y	N	Y
21 ***Ridge***	Y	Y	N	N	Y	N	N	N
RHODE ISLAND								
1 ***Machtley***	N	Y	N	N	N	N	Y	N
2 Reed	Y	N	Y	Y	Y	Y	Y	N
SOUTH CAROLINA								
1 ***Ravenel***	N	Y	N	N	Y	N	Y	N
2 ***Spence***	N	Y	N	N	N	N	?	N
3 Derrick	Y	N	Y	Y	Y	Y	N	N
4 ***Inglis***	N	Y	N	N	N	N	N	Y
5 Spratt	Y	N	?	?	Y	Y	N	N
6 Clyburn	Y	Y	Y	Y	Y	Y	N	N
SOUTH DAKOTA								
AL Johnson	Y	Y	Y	Y	Y	Y	Y	N
TENNESSEE								
1 ***Quillen***	N	Y	N	N	N	N	N	N
2 ***Duncan***	N	Y	N	N	N	?	Y	N
3 Lloyd	N	N	Y	Y	Y	Y	N	N
4 Cooper	Y	Y	Y	Y	Y	Y	Y	N
5 Clement	N	N	Y	Y	Y	Y	N	N
6 Gordon	Y	Y	Y	Y	Y	Y	N	N
7 ***Sundquist***	N	Y	N	N	N	N	N	N
8 Tanner	Y	Y	Y	Y	Y	Y	Y	N
9 Ford	Y	N	Y	Y	Y	Y	Y	N
TEXAS								
1 Chapman	N	N	Y	Y	Y	Y	N	N
2 Wilson	Y	Y	Y	Y	Y	?	?	?
3 ***Johnson, Sam***	N	Y	N	N	N	N	N	Y
4 Hall	N	Y	Y	Y	Y	Y	N	Y
5 Bryant	Y	Y	Y	Y	Y	?	Y	N
6 ***Barton***	N	Y	N	N	N	?	Y	Y
7 ***Archer***	N	Y	N	N	N	N	N	Y
8 ***Fields***	N	+	—	—	—	N	N	Y
9 Brooks	Y	Y	Y	Y	Y	Y	N	N
10 Pickle	Y	N	Y	Y	Y	Y	N	N
11 Edwards	N	N	Y	Y	Y	Y	N	Y
12 Geren	N	N	Y	Y	Y	Y	N	N
13 Sarpalius	N	Y	Y	Y	Y	Y	N	N
14 Laughlin	?	Y	Y	Y	Y	?	N	N
15 de la Garza	Y	Y	Y	Y	Y	Y	N	N
16 Coleman	Y	Y	Y	Y	Y	Y	N	N
17 Stenholm	N	N	Y	Y	?	Y	N	Y
18 Washington	Y	N	Y	Y	Y	Y	N	N
19 ***Combest***	N	Y	N	N	N	N	N	Y
20 Gonzalez	Y	N	Y	Y	Y	Y	N	N
21 ***Smith***	N	Y	N	N	N	N	Y	Y
22 ***DeLay***	N	Y	N	N	N	N	N	Y
23 ***Bonilla***	N	?	?	?	?	N	Y	Y
24 Frost	Y	Y	Y	Y	Y	Y	N	N
25 Andrews	N	Y	Y	Y	Y	Y	Y	N
26 ***Armey***	N	Y	N	N	N	N	N	Y
27 Ortiz	Y	Y	Y	Y	Y	Y	N	N
28 Tejeda	Y	Y	Y	Y	Y	Y	N	N
29 Green	Y	Y	Y	Y	Y	Y	Y	N
30 Johnson, E. B.	Y	N	Y	Y	Y	Y	N	N
UTAH								
1 ***Hansen***	N	Y	N	N	N	N	N	Y
2 Shepherd	Y	N	Y	Y	Y	Y	Y	N
3 Orton	N	N	Y	Y	Y	Y	N	Y
VERMONT								
AL *Sanders*	Y	Y	Y	Y	Y	Y	N	N
VIRGINIA								
1 ***Bateman***	N	Y	N	N	N	N	N	N
2 Pickett	N	Y	Y	Y	Y	Y	N	N
3 Scott	Y	Y	Y	Y	Y	Y	N	N
4 Sisisky	?	Y	Y	Y	Y	Y	Y	N
5 Payne	N	N	Y	Y	Y	Y	Y	N
6 ***Goodlatte***	N	Y	N	N	N	N	N	N
7 ***Bliley***	Y	Y	N	N	N	N	N	Y
8 Moran	Y	N	Y	Y	Y	?	Y	N
9 Boucher	Y	N	Y	Y	Y	Y	N	N
10 ***Wolf***	N	Y	N	N	N	N	N	N
11 Byrne	Y	Y	Y	Y	Y	Y	Y	N
WASHINGTON								
1 Cantwell	Y	N	Y	Y	Y	Y	N	N
2 Swift	Y	N	Y	Y	Y	Y	N	N
3 Unsoeld	Y	N	Y	Y	Y	Y	N	N
4 Inslee	Y	Y	Y	Y	Y	Y	N	N
5 Foley								
6 Dicks	Y	N	Y	Y	Y	Y	N	N
7 McDermott	Y	N	Y	Y	Y	Y	N	N
8 ***Dunn***	N	N	N	N	N	N	N	N
9 Kreidler	Y	N	Y	Y	Y	Y	N	N
WEST VIRGINIA								
1 Mollohan	N	N	Y	Y	Y	?	N	N
2 Wise	Y	N	Y	Y	Y	?	N	N
3 Rahall	N	N	Y	Y	Y	Y	Y	N
WISCONSIN								
1 Barca	Y	N	Y	Y	Y	Y	Y	Y
2 ***Klug***	N	Y	N	N	N	N	Y	N
3 ***Gunderson***	N	Y	N	N	Y	Y	N	N
4 Kleczka	Y	Y	Y	Y	Y	Y	N	N
5 Barrett	Y	N	Y	Y	Y	Y	Y	N
6 ***Petri***	N	Y	N	N	N	N	N	Y
7 Obey	Y	N	Y	Y	Y	Y	N	N
8 ***Roth***	N	Y	N	N	N	N	N	Y
9 ***Sensenbrenner***	N	N	N	N	N	N	Y	Y
WYOMING								
AL ***Thomas***	N	Y	N	N	N	N	N	Y
DELEGATES								
de Lugo, V.I.	D	Y	D	D	D	D	N	N
Faleomavaega, Am.S.	D	?	D	D	D	D	?	?
Norton, D.C.	D	N	D	D	D	D	N	N
Romero-B., P.R.	D	?	D	D	D	D	?	N
Underwood, Guam	D	N	D	D	D	D	N	N

Southern states - Ala., Ark., Fla., Ga., Ky., La., Miss., N.C., Okla., S.C., Tenn., Texas, Va.
Omitted votes are quorum calls, which CQ does not include in its vote charts.

KEY

Y Voted for (yea).
\# Paired for.
\+ Announced for.
N Voted against (nay).
X Paired against.
— Announced against.
P Voted "present."
C Voted "present" to avoid possible conflict of interest.
? Did not vote or otherwise make a position known.
D Delegates ineligible to vote.

Democrats **Republicans**
Independent

---

325. HR 2520. Fiscal 1994 Interior Appropriations/Oil Shale Research and Development. Sharp, D-Ind., amendment to cut $5 million of the $438 million for fossil energy research and development by the Energy Department to eliminate funding for oil shale research and development. Adopted in Committee of the Whole 395-37: R 149-24; D 245-13 (ND 167-7, SD 78-6); I 1-0, July 14, 1993.

326. HR 2520. Fiscal 1994 Interior Appropriations/National Endowment for the Arts. Crane, R-Ill., amendment to eliminate the $175 million in funding for the National Endowment for the Arts. Rejected in Committee of the Whole 105-322: R 90-83; D 15-238 (ND 5-163, SD 10-75); I 0-1, July 14, 1993.

327. HR 2264. 1993 Budget-Reconciliation/Previous Question. Kasich, R-Ohio, motion to order the previous question (thus ending debate and the possibility of amendment) on the Kasich motion to instruct the House conferees to accept the lower levels of new spending in the Senate bill and the Senate's higher threshold for taxing Social Security benefits. Motion rejected 184-238: R 171-0; D 13-237 (ND 4-161, SD 9-76); I 0-1, July 14, 1993.

328. HR 2264. 1993 Budget-Reconciliation/Substitute Motion to Instruct Conferees. Sabo, D-Minn., substitute amendment to the Kasich, R-Ohio, motion to instruct the House conferees to accept the Senate's higher threshold for taxing Social Security benefits. The Sabo amendment would omit the provisions of the Kasich motion to direct conferees to accept the lower levels of new spending in the Senate bill. Adopted 235-183: R 0-170; D 234-13 (ND 158-5, SD 76-8); I 1-0, July 14, 1993.

329. HR 2264. 1993 Budget-Reconciliation/Motion to Instruct Conferees. Kasich, R-Ohio, motion to instruct the House conferees, as amended by the Sabo, D-Minn., amendment, to accept the Senate's higher threshold for taxing Social Security benefits. Before being amended, the Kasich motion also would have directed the House conferees to accept the lower levels of new spending in the Senate bill. Adopted 415-0: R 169-0; D 245-0 (ND 163-0, SD 82-0); I 1-0, July 14, 1993.

330. HR 2520. Fiscal 1994 Interior Appropriations/National Endowment for the Arts. Stearns, R-Fla., amendment to cut the $174.6 million for the National Endowment for the Arts by 5 percent ($8.7 million). Adopted in the Committee of the Whole 240-184: R 162-10; D 78-173 (ND 39-130, SD 39-43); I 0-1, July 15, 1993.

331. HR 2520. Fiscal 1994 Interior Appropriations/Coal Research and Energy Conservation Programs. Walker, R-Pa., amendment to cut fossil energy research and development by approximately $50 million and increase energy conservation programs by approximately $25 million. Adopted in the Committee of the Whole 276-144: R 129-40; D 146-104 (ND 89-80, SD 57-24); I 1-0, July 15, 1993.

332. HR 2520. Fiscal 1994 Interior Appropriations/Steamtown. Andrews, D-Texas, amendment to cut the $3.1 million for operating expenses of Steamtown, USA, a national park in Scranton, Pa. Rejected in the Committee of the Whole 192-229: R 68-105; D 123-124 (ND 85-84, SD 38-40); I 1-0, July 15, 1993.

	325	326	327	328	329	330	331	332
ALABAMA								
1 *Callahan*	Y	Y	Y	N	Y	N	Y	N
2 *Everett*	Y	Y	Y	N	Y	Y	Y	Y
3 Browder	Y	N	N	Y	Y	Y	Y	Y
4 Bevill	Y	N	N	Y	Y	?	?	?
5 Cramer	Y	N	N	Y	Y	Y	Y	Y
6 *Bachus*	Y	Y	Y	N	Y	Y	Y	Y
7 Hilliard	Y	N	N	Y	Y	N	N	N
ALASKA								
AL *Young*	N	Y	Y	N	Y	Y	Y	N
ARIZONA								
1 Coppersmith	Y	N	N	Y	Y	N	Y	Y
2 Pastor	Y	N	N	Y	Y	N	N	N
3 *Stump*	N	Y	Y	N	Y	Y	Y	Y
4 *Kyl*	Y	Y	Y	N	Y	Y	Y	Y
5 *Kolbe*	N	N	Y	N	Y	#	#	?
6 English	Y	N	N	Y	N	Y	N	Y
ARKANSAS								
1 Lambert	Y	N	N	Y	Y	Y	Y	Y
2 Thornton	Y	N	N	Y	Y	Y	Y	N
3 *Hutchinson*	Y	Y	Y	N	Y	Y	Y	Y
4 *Dickey*	Y	Y	Y	N	Y	Y	Y	Y
CALIFORNIA								
1 Hamburg	Y	N	N	Y	Y	N	N	Y
2 *Herger*	Y	Y	Y	N	Y	Y	Y	N
3 Fazio	Y	N	N	Y	Y	N	N	Y
4 *Doolittle*	Y	Y	Y	N	Y	Y	Y	Y
5 Matsui	Y	N	N	Y	Y	N	N	N
6 Woolsey	Y	N	N	Y	Y	N	N	Y
7 Miller	Y	N	N	Y	Y	N	N	Y
8 Pelosi	Y	N	N	Y	Y	N	N	Y
9 Dellums	Y	N	N	Y	N	N	N	N
10 *Baker*	N	Y	Y	N	Y	Y	Y	N
11 *Pombo*	Y	Y	Y	N	Y	Y	Y	Y
12 Lantos	Y	N	N	Y	Y	N	Y	N
13 Stark	Y	N	N	Y	Y	N	Y	Y
14 Eshoo	Y	N	N	Y	Y	N	Y	Y
15 Mineta	Y	N	N	Y	Y	N	N	Y
16 Edwards	Y	N	N	Y	Y	N	N	N
17 Farr	Y	N	N	Y	Y	N	Y	Y
18 Condit	Y	Y	Y	N	Y	Y	Y	Y
19 Lehman	Y	N	N	Y	?	?	?	?
20 Dooley	Y	N	N	Y	Y	Y	Y	Y
21 *Thomas*	Y	N	?	?	?	Y	Y	N
22 *Huffington*	Y	N	Y	N	Y	Y	Y	Y
23 *Gallegly*	Y	Y	Y	N	Y	Y	Y	Y
24 Beilenson	Y	N	N	Y	Y	N	N	Y
25 *McKeon*	Y	Y	Y	N	Y	Y	Y	Y
26 Berman	Y	N	N	Y	N	N	N	N
27 *Moorhead*	Y	Y	Y	N	Y	Y	Y	Y
28 *Dreier*	Y	Y	Y	N	Y	Y	Y	N
29 Waxman	Y	N	N	Y	X	#	N	Y
30 Becerra	Y	N	N	Y	Y	N	N	N
31 Martinez	Y	N	N	Y	Y	N	N	N
32 Dixon	Y	N	N	Y	N	N	N	N
33 Roybal-Allard	Y	N	N	Y	N	Y	N	Y
34 Torres	Y	?	?	?	?	?	?	?
35 Waters	Y	N	?	Y	Y	N	N	N
36 Harman	Y	N	N	Y	Y	N	Y	Y
37 Tucker	Y	N	N	Y	N	N	N	N
38 *Horn*	Y	N	Y	N	Y	Y	Y	Y
39 *Royce*	Y	Y	Y	N	Y	Y	Y	Y
40 *Lewis*	N	N	Y	N	Y	N	Y	N
41 *Kim*	Y	N	Y	N	Y	Y	Y	N

	325	326	327	328	329	330	331	332
42 *Brown*	Y	N	N	Y	N	Y	N	Y
43 *Calvert*	Y	Y	Y	N	Y	Y	Y	N
44 *McCandless*	Y	Y	Y	N	Y	Y	Y	Y
45 *Rohrabacher*	Y	Y	Y	N	Y	Y	Y	Y
46 *Dornan*	Y	Y	Y	N	Y	Y	Y	Y
47 *Cox*	Y	Y	Y	N	Y	Y	?	Y
48 *Packard*	N	N	Y	N	Y	+	—	—
49 Schenk	Y	N	N	Y	Y	N	N	Y
50 Filner	Y	N	N	Y	N	N	N	Y
51 *Cunningham*	Y	Y	Y	N	Y	Y	Y	Y
52 *Hunter*	N	Y	Y	N	Y	Y	Y	N
COLORADO								
1 Schroeder	Y	N	N	Y	Y	N	Y	Y
2 Skaggs	Y	N	N	Y	Y	N	Y	Y
3 *McInnis*	Y	N	Y	N	Y	Y	Y	Y
4 *Allard*	Y	Y	Y	N	Y	Y	?	Y
5 *Hefley*	N	Y	N	Y	Y	N	Y	N
6 *Schaefer*	Y	N	Y	N	Y	Y	?	Y
CONNECTICUT								
1 Kennelly	Y	N	N	Y	Y	N	Y	N
2 Gejdenson	Y	N	N	Y	Y	N	Y	N
3 DeLauro	Y	N	N	Y	Y	N	Y	N
4 *Shays*	Y	N	Y	N	Y	Y	Y	Y
5 *Franks*	Y	N	Y	N	Y	Y	Y	Y
6 *Johnson*	N	N	Y	N	Y	Y	Y	Y
DELAWARE								
AL *Castle*	Y	N	Y	N	Y	N	Y	Y
FLORIDA								
1 Hutto	Y	Y	Y	Y	Y	Y	Y	N
2 Peterson	Y	N	N	Y	Y	N	Y	Y
3 Brown	Y	N	N	Y	Y	N	Y	N
4 *Fowler*	Y	N	Y	N	Y	Y	Y	Y
5 Thurman	Y	N	N	Y	Y	Y	Y	Y
6 *Stearns*	N	Y	Y	N	Y	Y	Y	N
7 *Mica*	Y	N	Y	N	Y	Y	N	Y
8 *McCollum*	Y	N	Y	N	Y	N	Y	Y
9 *Bilirakis*	Y	N	Y	N	Y	Y	Y	Y
10 *Young*	Y	N	Y	N	Y	?	Y	Y
11 Gibbons	Y	N	N	Y	Y	N	Y	N
12 *Canady*	Y	Y	Y	N	Y	Y	Y	Y
13 *Miller*	Y	N	Y	N	Y	Y	Y	Y
14 *Goss*	Y	N	Y	N	Y	Y	Y	N
15 Bacchus	Y	N	N	Y	Y	Y	Y	Y
16 *Lewis*	Y	Y	Y	N	Y	Y	N	N
17 Meek	Y	N	N	Y	Y	N	Y	N
18 *Ros-Lehtinen*	Y	N	Y	N	Y	Y	N	N
19 Johnston	Y	N	N	Y	Y	N	Y	?
20 Deutsch	Y	N	N	Y	Y	N	Y	Y
21 *Diaz-Balart*	Y	N	Y	N	Y	Y	Y	N
22 *Shaw*	Y	N	Y	N	Y	Y	Y	Y
23 Hastings	Y	N	N	Y	Y	N	?	?
GEORGIA								
1 *Kingston*	Y	Y	Y	N	Y	Y	Y	Y
2 Bishop	Y	N	N	Y	Y	Y	N	N
3 *Collins*	Y	Y	Y	N	Y	Y	N	N
4 *Linder*	Y	Y	Y	N	Y	Y	Y	N
5 Lewis	Y	N	N	Y	Y	N	N	N
6 *Gingrich*	Y	Y	Y	N	Y	Y	Y	N
7 Darden	Y	N	N	Y	Y	Y	Y	Y
8 Rowland	Y	N	N	Y	Y	Y	Y	N
9 Deal	Y	N	Y	N	Y	Y	Y	Y
10 Johnson	Y	N	N	Y	Y	Y	Y	Y
11 McKinney	Y	N	N	Y	Y	N	N	Y
HAWAII								
1 Abercrombie	Y	N	N	Y	Y	N	Y	N
2 Mink	Y	N	N	Y	Y	N	Y	Y
IDAHO								
1 LaRocco	Y	N	N	Y	Y	N	Y	Y
2 *Crapo*	Y	N	Y	N	Y	Y	Y	Y
ILLINOIS								
1 Rush	Y	N	?	Y	Y	N	X	N
2 Reynolds	Y	N	N	Y	Y	N	N	Y
3 Lipinski	Y	N	N	Y	Y	N	N	Y
4 Gutierrez	Y	N	N	Y	Y	N	N	Y
5 Rostenkowski	Y	N	N	Y	Y	N	N	Y
6 *Hyde*	Y	Y	Y	N	Y	Y	N	N
7 Collins	Y	N	N	Y	N	N	N	N
8 *Crane*	Y	Y	Y	N	Y	Y	Y	Y
9 Yates	N	N	N	Y	?	N	N	Y
10 *Porter*	Y	N	Y	N	Y	N	N	N
11 Sangmeister	Y	N	N	Y	Y	N	N	Y
12 Costello	Y	N	N	Y	Y	N	N	Y
13 *Fawell*	Y	Y	Y	N	Y	Y	N	Y
14 *Hastert*	Y	Y	Y	N	Y	Y	N	Y
15 *Ewing*	Y	Y	Y	N	Y	Y	Y	N
16 *Manzullo*	Y	Y	Y	N	Y	Y	Y	Y
17 Evans	Y	N	N	Y	Y	N	N	Y

ND Northern Democrats   SD Southern Democrats

	325	326	327	328	329	330	331	332
18 ***Michel***	N	Y	?	?	?	Y	N	N
19 Poshard	Y	N	N	Y	Y	Y	N	Y
20 Durbin	Y	N	N	Y	Y	N	N	N
INDIANA								
1 Visclosky	Y	N	N	N	Y	Y	N	N
2 Sharp	Y	N	?	Y	Y	N	Y	Y
3 Roemer	Y	N	N	Y	Y	Y	Y	Y
4 Long	Y	N	N	Y	Y	Y	N	Y
5 ***Buyer***	Y	Y	Y	N	Y	Y	Y	N
6 ***Burton***	Y	Y	Y	N	Y	Y	Y	Y
7 ***Myers***	N	Y	Y	N	Y	Y	N	N
8 McCloskey	Y	N	N	Y	Y	Y	N	N
9 Hamilton	Y	N	N	Y	Y	Y	N	Y
10 Jacobs	Y	N	N	Y	Y	Y	Y	Y
IOWA								
1 ***Leach***	?	?	?	?	?	N	Y	N
2 ***Nussle***	Y	N	Y	N	Y	Y	Y	Y
3 ***Lightfoot***	?	?	?	?	?	Y	N	N
4 Smith	?	?	?	?	?	N	N	N
5 ***Grandy***	Y	N	Y	N	Y	Y	Y	N
KANSAS								
1 ***Roberts***	Y	Y	Y	N	Y	Y	Y	Y
2 Slattery	Y	N	N	Y	Y	Y	Y	Y
3 ***Meyers***	Y	N	Y	N	Y	Y	Y	Y
4 Glickman	Y	N	N	Y	Y	N	Y	Y
KENTUCKY								
1 Barlow	Y	N	N	Y	Y	N	N	Y
2 Natcher	Y	N	N	Y	Y	N	N	N
3 Mazzoli	Y	N	N	Y	Y	N	N	N
4 ***Bunning***	Y	Y	Y	N	Y	Y	Y	Y
5 ***Rogers***	Y	N	Y	N	Y	Y	N	N
6 Baesler	Y	N	N	Y	Y	N	Y	N
LOUISIANA								
1 ***Livingston***	Y	Y	Y	N	Y	Y	Y	N
2 Jefferson	Y	N	N	Y	Y	N	N	N
3 Tauzin	Y	Y	Y	N	Y	?	Y	Y
4 Fields	Y	N	N	Y	Y	N	N	N
5 ***McCrery***	N	N	Y	N	Y	Y	Y	N
6 ***Baker***	Y	Y	Y	N	Y	Y	Y	Y
7 Hayes	N	Y	Y	N	Y	Y	Y	Y
MAINE								
1 Andrews	Y	N	N	Y	Y	N	Y	Y
2 ***Snowe***	Y	N	Y	N	Y	Y	Y	Y
MARYLAND								
1 ***Gilchrest***	Y	N	Y	N	Y	Y	Y	Y
2 ***Bentley***	Y	N	Y	N	Y	Y	N	N
3 Cardin	Y	N	N	Y	Y	N	Y	Y
4 Wynn	Y	N	N	Y	Y	Y	Y	N
5 Hoyer	Y	N	N	Y	Y	N	N	N
6 ***Bartlett***	Y	Y	Y	N	Y	Y	Y	Y
7 Mfume	Y	N	N	Y	Y	N	Y	Y
8 ***Morella***	Y	N	Y	N	Y	N	Y	N
MASSACHUSETTS								
1 Olver	Y	N	N	Y	Y	N	Y	N
2 Neal	Y	N	N	Y	Y	N	Y	Y
3 ***Blute***	Y	N	Y	N	Y	Y	Y	N
4 Frank	Y	?	N	Y	Y	N	Y	N
5 Meehan	Y	N	N	Y	Y	N	Y	Y
6 ***Torkildsen***	Y	N	Y	N	Y	Y	Y	N
7 Markey	Y	N	N	?	Y	N	Y	N
8 Kennedy	Y	N	N	?	?	N	Y	Y
9 Moakley	Y	N	N	Y	Y	N	N	N
10 Studds	Y	?	N	Y	Y	N	Y	Y
MICHIGAN								
1 Stupak	Y	N	N	Y	Y	N	Y	Y
2 ***Hoekstra***	Y	N	Y	N	Y	Y	Y	Y
3 Henry	?	?	?	?	?	?	?	?
4 ***Camp***	Y	N	Y	N	Y	Y	Y	N
5 Barcia	Y	Y	N	Y	Y	Y	Y	Y
6 ***Upton***	Y	N	Y	N	Y	Y	Y	Y
7 ***Smith***	Y	Y	Y	N	Y	Y	Y	Y
8 Carr	N	N	N	Y	Y	N	N	Y
9 Kildee	Y	N	N	Y	Y	N	Y	Y
10 Bonior	Y	N	N	Y	Y	N	N	N
11 ***Knollenberg***	Y	Y	Y	N	Y	Y	Y	N
12 Levin	Y	N	N	Y	Y	N	Y	Y
13 Ford	Y	N	N	Y	Y	N	N	N
14 Conyers	?	?	?	?	?	?	?	?
15 Collins	Y	N	N	Y	Y	N	N	N
16 Dingell	Y	?	N	Y	Y	N	N	N
MINNESOTA								
1 Penny	Y	N	Y	N	Y	Y	Y	Y
2 Minge	Y	N	N	Y	Y	Y	Y	Y
3 ***Ramstad***	Y	N	Y	N	Y	Y	Y	Y
4 Vento	Y	N	N	Y	Y	N	Y	Y

	325	326	327	328	329	330	331	332
5 Sabo	Y	N	N	Y	Y	N	N	N
6 ***Grams***	Y	Y	Y	N	Y	Y	Y	N
7 Peterson	Y	N	N	Y	Y	Y	Y	Y
8 Oberstar	Y	N	N	Y	Y	N	N	N
MISSISSIPPI								
1 Whitten	Y	N	N	Y	Y	N	N	N
2 Thompson	Y	N	N	Y	Y	N	?	?
3 Montgomery	Y	N	N	Y	Y	Y	Y	N
4 Parker	Y	N	Y	N	Y	Y	Y	N
5 Taylor	Y	Y	Y	N	Y	Y	Y	Y
MISSOURI								
1 Clay	Y	N	N	?	?	N	N	N
2 ***Talent***	Y	Y	Y	N	Y	Y	Y	Y
3 Gephardt	Y	N	N	Y	Y	N	N	Y
4 Skelton	Y	Y	N	Y	Y	Y	Y	Y
5 Wheat	Y	N	N	Y	Y	N	N	Y
6 Danner	Y	N	N	Y	Y	N	N	Y
7 ***Hancock***	Y	Y	Y	N	Y	Y	Y	Y
8 ***Emerson***	Y	Y	Y	N	Y	Y	N	Y
9 Volkmer	Y	N	N	Y	Y	Y	Y	Y
MONTANA								
AL Williams	N	N	N	Y	Y	N	N	Y
NEBRASKA								
1 ***Bereuter***	Y	N	Y	N	Y	Y	Y	N
2 Hoagland	Y	N	N	Y	Y	Y	Y	Y
3 ***Barrett***	Y	N	Y	N	Y	Y	Y	N
NEVADA								
1 Bilbray	Y	N	Y	Y	Y	N	Y	Y
2 ***Vucanovich***	N	Y	Y	N	Y	Y	Y	N
NEW HAMPSHIRE								
1 ***Zeliff***	Y	N	Y	N	Y	Y	Y	N
2 Swett	Y	N	N	?	Y	Y	Y	Y
NEW JERSEY								
1 Andrews	Y	N	N	Y	Y	N	Y	Y
2 Hughes	Y	N	N	Y	Y	N	Y	N
3 ***Saxton***	Y	N	Y	N	Y	Y	Y	N
4 ***Smith***	Y	N	Y	N	Y	Y	Y	N
5 ***Roukema***	Y	N	Y	N	Y	Y	N	Y
6 Pallone	Y	N	N	Y	Y	N	Y	N
7 ***Franks***	Y	N	Y	N	Y	Y	N	Y
8 Klein	Y	N	N	Y	Y	N	Y	N
9 Torricelli	N	N	N	Y	Y	N	N	Y
10 Payne	Y	N	N	Y	Y	N	N	N
11 ***Gallo***	Y	N	Y	N	Y	Y	Y	N
12 ***Zimmer***	Y	N	Y	N	Y	Y	Y	Y
13 Menendez	Y	N	N	Y	Y	N	Y	N
NEW MEXICO								
1 ***Schiff***	Y	N	Y	N	Y	Y	Y	N
2 ***Skeen***	Y	N	Y	N	Y	N	N	N
3 Richardson	Y	N	N	Y	Y	N	Y	Y
NEW YORK								
1 Hochbrueckner	Y	N	N	Y	Y	N	Y	N
2 ***Lazio***	Y	N	Y	N	Y	Y	Y	N
3 ***King***	Y	Y	Y	N	Y	Y	Y	N
4 ***Levy***	Y	Y	Y	N	Y	Y	Y	N
5 Ackerman	Y	N	N	Y	Y	X	Y	N
6 Flake	Y	N	N	Y	Y	N	Y	N
7 Manton	Y	N	N	Y	Y	N	N	N
8 Nadler	Y	N	N	Y	Y	N	Y	N
9 Schumer	Y	N	N	Y	Y	N	Y	Y
10 Towns	Y	?	?	?	?	?	X	?
11 Owens	Y	N	N	Y	Y	N	N	N
12 Velazquez	Y	N	N	Y	Y	N	Y	N
13 ***Molinari***	Y	N	Y	N	Y	Y	Y	N
14 Maloney	Y	N	N	Y	Y	N	Y	Y
15 Rangel	Y	?	N	Y	Y	N	Y	N
16 Serrano	Y	N	N	Y	Y	N	N	N
17 Engel	Y	N	N	Y	Y	N	N	N
18 Lowey	Y	N	N	Y	Y	N	N	N
19 ***Fish***	Y	N	N	Y	N	Y	Y	N
20 ***Gilman***	N	N	Y	N	Y	N	N	N
21 McNulty	Y	N	N	Y	Y	Y	Y	N
22 ***Solomon***	Y	Y	Y	N	Y	Y	Y	N
23 ***Boehlert***	Y	N	Y	N	Y	Y	Y	N
24 ***McHugh***	Y	Y	Y	N	Y	Y	Y	N
25 ***Walsh***	Y	N	Y	N	Y	Y	Y	N
26 Hinchey	Y	N	N	Y	Y	N	Y	N
27 ***Paxon***	Y	Y	Y	N	Y	Y	Y	N
28 Slaughter	Y	N	N	Y	Y	N	N	N
29 LaFalce	Y	N	N	Y	Y	N	Y	N
30 ***Quinn***	Y	Y	Y	N	Y	Y	Y	N
31 ***Houghton***	Y	N	Y	N	Y	N	N	N
NORTH CAROLINA								
1 Clayton	Y	N	N	Y	Y	N	Y	N
2 Valentine	Y	N	N	Y	Y	Y	Y	N

	325	326	327	328	329	330	331	332
3 Lancaster	Y	N	N	Y	Y	N	Y	Y
4 Price	Y	N	N	Y	Y	N	Y	Y
5 Neal	Y	N	N	Y	Y	Y	Y	Y
6 ***Coble***	Y	Y	Y	N	Y	Y	Y	Y
7 Rose	Y	N	N	Y	Y	N	Y	N
8 Hefner	Y	N	N	Y	Y	N	Y	N
9 ***McMillan***	Y	N	Y	N	?	Y	N	N
10 ***Ballenger***	Y	N	Y	N	Y	Y	Y	Y
11 ***Taylor***	Y	Y	Y	N	Y	Y	N	N
12 Watt	Y	N	N	Y	Y	N	Y	N
NORTH DAKOTA								
AL Pomeroy	Y	N	N	Y	Y	?	N	Y
OHIO								
1 Mann	Y	N	N	Y	Y	N	Y	Y
2 ***Portman***	Y	N	Y	N	Y	Y	Y	N
3 Hall	Y	N	N	Y	Y	N	N	N
4 ***Oxley***	Y	N	Y	N	Y	Y	N	N
5 ***Gillmor***	Y	N	Y	N	Y	Y	N	N
6 Strickland	Y	N	N	Y	Y	N	N	Y
7 ***Hobson***	Y	N	Y	N	Y	Y	N	N
8 ***Boehner***	Y	Y	Y	N	Y	Y	N	N
9 Kaptur	Y	N	N	Y	?	Y	N	Y
10 ***Hoke***	Y	N	Y	N	Y	Y	N	Y
11 Stokes	Y	N	N	Y	Y	N	N	Y
12 ***Kasich***	Y	N	Y	N	Y	Y	N	Y
13 Brown	Y	N	N	Y	Y	Y	N	Y
14 Sawyer	Y	N	N	Y	Y	N	N	Y
15 ***Pryce***	Y	N	Y	N	Y	Y	N	N
16 ***Regula***	N	N	Y	N	Y	Y	N	N
17 Traficant	N	N	N	Y	Y	Y	N	N
18 Applegate	Y	N	N	Y	?	Y	N	N
19 Fingerhut	Y	N	Y	N	Y	Y	Y	Y
OKLAHOMA								
1 ***Inhofe***	Y	Y	Y	N	Y	Y	Y	Y
2 Synar	Y	N	N	Y	Y	N	Y	Y
3 Brewster	Y	N	N	Y	Y	Y	Y	Y
4 McCurdy	Y	N	N	Y	Y	Y	Y	Y
5 ***Istook***	Y	Y	Y	N	Y	Y	Y	Y
6 English	Y	N	N	Y	Y	Y	Y	Y
OREGON								
1 Furse	Y	N	N	Y	Y	N	Y	Y
2 ***Smith***	N	Y	Y	?	?	Y	Y	N
3 Wyden	Y	N	N	Y	Y	N	Y	Y
4 DeFazio	Y	N	N	Y	Y	Y	Y	Y
5 Kopetski	Y	N	N	Y	Y	N	N	N
PENNSYLVANIA								
1 Foglietta	Y	N	N	Y	Y	N	N	N
2 Blackwell	Y	N	N	Y	Y	N	N	N
3 Borski	Y	N	N	Y	Y	N	N	N
4 Klink	Y	N	N	Y	Y	N	N	N
5 ***Clinger***	N	N	Y	N	Y	N	Y	N
6 Holden	Y	Y	N	Y	Y	Y	Y	Y
7 ***Weldon***	Y	N	Y	N	Y	Y	Y	N
8 ***Greenwood***	Y	Y	Y	N	Y	Y	Y	N
9 ***Shuster***	Y	Y	Y	N	Y	Y	Y	N
10 ***McDade***	N	N	Y	N	Y	Y	N	N
11 Kanjorski	Y	N	N	Y	Y	Y	N	N
12 Murtha	N	N	N	Y	Y	N	N	N
13 Margolies-Mezv.	Y	N	N	Y	Y	Y	N	N
14 Coyne	Y	N	N	Y	Y	N	N	N
15 McHale	Y	N	N	Y	Y	Y	N	Y
16 ***Walker***	Y	Y	Y	N	Y	Y	Y	Y
17 ***Gekas***	Y	Y	Y	N	Y	Y	Y	Y
18 ***Santorum***	Y	N	Y	N	Y	Y	N	N
19 ***Goodling***	Y	Y	Y	N	Y	Y	Y	N
20 Murphy	Y	N	N	Y	Y	Y	N	?
21 ***Ridge***	N	N	N	Y	Y	Y	?	N
RHODE ISLAND								
1 ***Machtley***	Y	N	Y	N	Y	N	Y	N
2 Reed	Y	N	N	Y	Y	N	Y	Y
SOUTH CAROLINA								
1 ***Ravenel***	Y	N	Y	N	Y	Y	Y	Y
2 ***Spence***	Y	N	Y	N	Y	Y	N	N
3 Derrick	Y	N	N	Y	Y	Y	N	Y
4 ***Inglis***	Y	Y	Y	N	Y	Y	Y	Y
5 Spratt	Y	N	N	Y	Y	Y	Y	Y
6 Clyburn	Y	N	N	Y	Y	N	N	N
SOUTH DAKOTA								
AL Johnson	Y	N	N	Y	Y	N	Y	Y
TENNESSEE								
1 ***Quillen***	N	Y	Y	N	Y	Y	N	N
2 ***Duncan***	Y	Y	Y	N	Y	Y	Y	Y
3 Lloyd	Y	N	Y	Y	Y	Y	Y	N
4 Cooper	Y	N	N	Y	Y	Y	N	Y
5 Clement	Y	N	N	Y	Y	N	N	Y

	325	326	327	328	329	330	331	332
6 Gordon	Y	N	N	Y	Y	Y	Y	Y
7 ***Sundquist***	N	Y	Y	N	Y	Y	N	Y
8 Tanner	Y	Y	N	Y	Y	Y	Y	Y
9 Ford	Y	N	N	Y	Y	N	Y	?
TEXAS								
1 Chapman	N	N	N	Y	Y	Y	N	N
2 Wilson	?	N	N	?	?	N	Y	N
3 ***Johnson, Sam***	Y	Y	Y	N	Y	Y	Y	Y
4 Hall	N	Y	Y	N	Y	Y	Y	Y
5 Bryant	Y	N	N	Y	Y	N	Y	Y
6 ***Barton***	Y	Y	Y	N	Y	Y	Y	N
7 ***Archer***	Y	Y	Y	N	Y	Y	Y	Y
8 ***Fields***	Y	Y	Y	N	Y	Y	Y	Y
9 Brooks	N	N	N	Y	Y	N	N	N
10 Pickle	Y	N	N	Y	Y	N	Y	N
11 Edwards	Y	N	N	Y	Y	Y	Y	Y
12 Geren	Y	Y	Y	N	Y	Y	Y	Y
13 Sarpalius	Y	Y	N	Y	Y	?	?	?
14 Laughlin	Y	Y	N	Y	Y	Y	Y	Y
15 de la Garza	Y	N	N	Y	?	Y	Y	N
16 Coleman	Y	N	N	Y	Y	N	N	?
17 Stenholm	Y	Y	N	Y	Y	Y	Y	Y
18 Washington	Y	N	N	Y	Y	N	N	N
19 ***Combest***	Y	Y	Y	N	Y	Y	Y	N
20 Gonzalez	N	N	N	Y	Y	N	N	N
21 ***Smith***	Y	Y	Y	N	Y	Y	Y	N
22 ***DeLay***	Y	Y	Y	N	Y	Y	Y	N
23 ***Bonilla***	Y	Y	Y	N	Y	Y	Y	N
24 Frost	Y	N	N	Y	Y	Y	Y	N
25 Andrews	Y	N	N	Y	Y	Y	Y	Y
26 ***Armey***	Y	Y	Y	N	Y	Y	Y	N
27 Ortiz	Y	N	N	Y	Y	Y	Y	N
28 Tejeda	Y	N	N	Y	Y	N	Y	N
29 Green	Y	N	N	Y	Y	N	Y	Y
30 Johnson, E. B.	Y	N	N	Y	Y	N	Y	N
UTAH								
1 ***Hansen***	N	N	Y	N	Y	Y	N	N
2 Shepherd	Y	N	N	Y	Y	N	Y	Y
3 Orton	N	Y	N	Y	Y	Y	Y	N
VERMONT								
AL *Sanders*	Y	N	N	Y	Y	N	Y	Y
VIRGINIA								
1 ***Bateman***	Y	N	Y	N	Y	Y	N	N
2 Pickett	N	N	N	N	?	Y	N	N
3 Scott	Y	N	N	Y	Y	N	N	N
4 Sisisky	Y	N	N	Y	Y	Y	N	N
5 Payne	Y	N	N	Y	Y	Y	N	Y
6 ***Goodlatte***	Y	Y	Y	N	Y	Y	N	Y
7 ***Bliley***	Y	Y	Y	N	Y	Y	N	N
8 Moran	Y	N	N	Y	Y	N	Y	N
9 Boucher	Y	N	N	Y	Y	N	N	N
10 ***Wolf***	Y	N	Y	N	Y	Y	Y	N
11 Byrne	Y	N	N	Y	Y	N	Y	N
WASHINGTON								
1 Cantwell	Y	N	N	Y	Y	Y	Y	Y
2 Swift	Y	N	N	Y	Y	N	N	N
3 Unsoeld	Y	N	N	Y	Y	N	Y	N
4 Inslee	Y	N	N	N	Y	Y	Y	Y
5 Foley								
6 Dicks	Y	N	N	?	Y	N	Y	N
7 McDermott	Y	N	N	Y	Y	N	Y	Y
8 ***Dunn***	Y	N	Y	N	Y	Y	Y	N
9 Kreidler	Y	N	N	Y	Y	N	Y	Y
WEST VIRGINIA								
1 Mollohan	Y	N	N	Y	Y	N	N	N
2 Wise	Y	N	N	Y	Y	Y	N	N
3 Rahall	Y	N	N	Y	Y	Y	N	N
WISCONSIN								
1 Barca	Y	N	N	Y	Y	N	Y	Y
2 ***Klug***	Y	N	Y	N	Y	Y	Y	Y
3 ***Gunderson***	Y	N	Y	N	Y	Y	Y	N
4 Kleczka	Y	N	N	Y	Y	N	N	Y
5 Barrett	Y	N	N	Y	Y	N	Y	Y
6 ***Petri***	Y	Y	Y	N	Y	Y	Y	N
7 Obey	Y	N	N	Y	Y	N	N	?
8 ***Roth***	Y	Y	Y	N	Y	Y	Y	Y
9 ***Sensenbrenner***	Y	Y	Y	N	Y	Y	Y	Y
WYOMING								
AL ***Thomas***	N	N	Y	N	Y	Y	N	N
DELEGATES								
de Lugo, V.I.	Y	N	D	D	D	N	N	N
Faleomavaega, Am.S.	?	?	D	D	D	?	?	?
Norton, D.C.	Y	N	D	D	D	N	Y	Y
Romero-B., P.R.	Y	N	D	D	D	N	?	?
Underwood, Guam	Y	N	D	D	D	N	N	N

Southern states - Ala., Ark., Fla., Ga., Ky., La., Miss., N.C., Okla., S.C., Tenn., Texas, Va.
Omitted votes are quorum calls, which CQ does not include in its vote charts.

333. HR 2520. Fiscal 1994 Interior Appropriations/Presidio. Duncan, R-Tenn., amendment to cut $14 million from the appropriation for the operation of the National Park Service in order to freeze funding for operating expenses at the former Presidio Army base in San Francisco at fiscal 1993 levels. Rejected in the Committee of the Whole 193-230: R 161-11; D 32-218 (ND 15-156, SD 17-62); I 0-1, July 15, 1993.

334. HR 2520. Fiscal 1994 Interior Appropriations/Land and Water Conservation Fund. Pombo, R-Calif., amendment to cut $1 million from the Land and Water Conservation Fund, thus eliminating funding for the creation of the Stone Lakes Wildlife Refuge wetlands project in California. Rejected in the Committee of the Whole 174-246: R 158-14; D 16-231 (ND 8-160, SD 8-71); I 0-1, July 15, 1993.

335. HR 2520. Fiscal 1994 Interior Appropriations/Motion to Rise. Yates, D-Ill., motion to rise and report the bill back to the House as amended in the Committee of the Whole, thereby prohibiting further amendments. Motion agreed to in the Committee of the Whole 243-177: R 1-170; D 241-7 (ND 166-3, SD 75-4); I 1-0, July 15, 1993.

336. HR 2520. Fiscal 1994 Interior Appropriations/Oil Shale Research and Development. Separate vote at the request of Solomon, R-N.Y., on the Sharp, D-Ind., amendment adopted in the Committee of the Whole to cut by $5 million the $438 million for the fossil energy research and development by the Energy Department to eliminate the earmark for oil shale research and development. Adopted 380-37: R 149-22; D 230-15 (ND 158-8, SD 72-7); I 1-0, July 15, 1993. (On separate votes, which may be demanded on an amendment adopted in the Committee of the Whole, the four delegates and the resident commissioner of Puerto Rico cannot vote. See vote 325.)

337. HR 2520. Fiscal 1994 Interior Appropriations/Coal Research and Energy Conservation. Separate vote at the request of Solomon, R-N.Y., on the Walker, R-Pa., amendment adopted in the Committee of the Whole to cut fossil energy research and development by about $50 million and increase energy conservation programs by about $25 million. Adopted 278-137: R 134-37; D 143-100 (ND 88-75, SD 55-25); I 1-0, July 15, 1993. (On separate votes, which may be demanded on an amendment adopted in the Committee of the Whole, the four delegates and the resident commissioner of Puerto Rico cannot vote. See vote 331.)

338. HR 2520. Fiscal 1994 Interior Appropriations/National Endowment for the Arts. Separate vote at the request of Solomon, R-N.Y., on the Stearns, R-Fla., amendment adopted in the Committee of the Whole to cut the $174.6 million for the National Endowment for the Arts by 5 percent ($8.7 million). Adopted 244-174: R 163-9; D 81-164 (ND 40-125, SD 41-39); I 0-1, July 15, 1993. (On separate votes, which may be demanded on an amendment adopted in the Committee of the Whole, the four delegates and the resident commissioner of Puerto Rico cannot vote. See vote 330.)

339. HR 2520. Fiscal 1994 Interior Appropriations/Passage. Passage of the bill to provide approximately $12.7 billion in new budget authority for the Department of Interior and related agencies for fiscal 1994. The administration requested $13,617,688,000. Passed 278-138: R 50-121; D 227-17 (ND 155-9, SD 72-8); I 1-0, July 15, 1993.

340. HR 2519. Fiscal 1994 Commerce, Justice, State Appropriations/Economic Development Administration. Hefley, R-Colo., amendment to cut the $26 million in salary and expenses for the Economic Development Administration. Rejected in the Committee of the Whole 122-300: R 116-55; D 6-244 (ND 3-165, SD 3-79); I 0-1, July 20, 1993.

KEY

Y   Voted for (yea).
Paired for.
+   Announced for.
N   Voted against (nay).
X   Paired against.
–   Announced against.
P   Voted ''present.''
C   Voted ''present'' to avoid possible conflict of interest.
?   Did not vote or otherwise make a position known.
D   Delegates ineligible to vote.

Democrats   **Republicans**
Independent

	333	334	335	336	337	338	339	340
ALABAMA								
1 *Callahan*	Y	Y	N	Y	N	Y	N	Y
2 *Everett*	Y	Y	N	Y	Y	Y	N	Y
3 Browder	N	N	Y	Y	Y	Y	Y	N
4 Bevill	?	?	?	?	?	?	?	?
5 Cramer	Y	N	Y	Y	N	Y	Y	N
6 *Bachus*	Y	Y	N	Y	Y	Y	N	Y
7 Hilliard	N	N	Y	Y	N	N	Y	N
ALASKA								
AL *Young*	Y	Y	N	N	N	Y	Y	Y
ARIZONA								
1 Coppersmith	N	N	Y	Y	Y	N	Y	N
2 Pastor	N	N	Y	Y	N	N	Y	N
3 *Stump*	Y	Y	N	N	N	Y	N	Y
4 *Kyl*	Y	Y	N	Y	Y	Y	N	Y
5 *Kolbe*	–	#	–	X	+	#	+	Y
6 English	N	N	Y	Y	N	N	Y	N
ARKANSAS								
1 Lambert	N	N	Y	Y	Y	Y	Y	N
2 Thornton	N	N	Y	Y	Y	Y	Y	N
3 *Hutchinson*	Y	Y	N	Y	Y	Y	Y	N
4 Dickey	Y	Y	N	Y	Y	Y	N	Y
CALIFORNIA								
1 Hamburg	N	N	Y	Y	Y	N	Y	?
2 *Herger*	Y	Y	N	Y	Y	Y	N	Y
3 Fazio	N	N	Y	Y	N	N	Y	N
4 *Doolittle*	Y	Y	N	Y	Y	Y	N	Y
5 Matsui	N	N	Y	Y	N	N	Y	N
6 Woolsey	N	N	Y	Y	N	N	Y	N
7 Miller	N	N	Y	Y	N	?	Y	N
8 Pelosi	N	N	Y	Y	N	N	Y	N
9 Dellums	N	N	Y	Y	N	N	Y	N
10 *Baker*	N	Y	N	N	Y	Y	N	Y
11 *Pombo*	Y	Y	N	Y	Y	Y	N	Y
12 Lantos	N	N	Y	Y	N	N	Y	N
13 Stark	N	N	Y	Y	N	N	Y	N
14 Eshoo	N	N	Y	Y	N	N	Y	N
15 Mineta	N	N	Y	Y	N	N	Y	N
16 Edwards	N	N	Y	Y	N	N	Y	N
17 Farr	N	N	Y	Y	N	N	Y	N
18 Condit	N	Y	Y	Y	Y	Y	N	N
19 Lehman	?	?	?	?	?	?	?	N
20 Dooley	N	N	Y	Y	Y	Y	Y	N
21 *Thomas*	Y	Y	N	Y	Y	Y	N	N
22 *Huffington*	N	Y	N	Y	Y	Y	N	Y
23 *Gallegly*	Y	Y	N	Y	Y	Y	N	Y
24 Beilenson	N	N	Y	Y	Y	N	Y	N
25 *McKeon*	Y	Y	N	Y	Y	Y	N	Y
26 Berman	N	N	Y	Y	N	Y	Y	N
27 *Moorhead*	Y	Y	N	Y	Y	Y	N	Y
28 *Dreier*	Y	Y	N	Y	Y	Y	N	Y
29 Waxman	N	N	?	#	?	?	?	N
30 Becerra	N	N	Y	Y	N	N	Y	N
31 Martinez	N	N	Y	Y	N	Y	Y	N
32 Dixon	N	N	Y	Y	N	N	Y	N
33 Roybal-Allard	N	N	Y	Y	N	N	Y	N
34 Torres	?	?	?	?	?	?	?	N
35 Waters	N	N	Y	Y	N	Y	Y	N
36 Harman	N	N	Y	Y	Y	N	Y	N
37 Tucker	N	N	Y	Y	N	Y	Y	X
38 *Horn*	N	Y	N	Y	Y	N	Y	–
39 *Royce*	Y	Y	N	Y	Y	Y	N	Y
40 *Lewis*	N	Y	N	N	Y	Y	N	N
41 *Kim*	Y	Y	N	Y	Y	Y	N	Y

	333	334	335	336	337	338	339	340
42 Brown	N	N	Y	Y	Y	N	Y	N
43 *Calvert*	Y	Y	N	Y	Y	Y	N	Y
44 *McCandless*	Y	Y	N	Y	Y	Y	N	Y
45 *Rohrabacher*	Y	Y	N	Y	Y	Y	N	Y
46 *Dornan*	Y	Y	N	Y	Y	Y	N	#
47 *Cox*	Y	Y	N	Y	Y	Y	N	Y
48 *Packard*	+	–	–	–	–	+	+	+
49 Schenk	N	N	Y	Y	N	N	Y	N
50 Filner	N	N	Y	Y	N	N	Y	N
51 *Cunningham*	Y	Y	N	Y	Y	Y	N	Y
52 *Hunter*	Y	Y	N	N	?	?	N	Y
COLORADO								
1 Schroeder	N	N	Y	Y	Y	N	Y	N
2 Skaggs	N	N	Y	Y	N	N	Y	N
3 *McInnis*	Y	Y	N	Y	?	Y	N	Y
4 *Allard*	Y	Y	N	Y	Y	Y	Y	Y
5 *Hefley*	Y	Y	N	N	Y	N	N	Y
6 *Schaefer*	Y	Y	N	Y	Y	Y	N	Y
CONNECTICUT								
1 Kennelly	N	N	Y	Y	N	Y	N	Y
2 Gejdenson	N	N	Y	Y	N	N	Y	N
3 DeLauro	N	N	Y	Y	N	N	Y	N
4 *Shays*	Y	N	Y	Y	Y	N	Y	N
5 *Franks*	Y	Y	N	Y	Y	Y	N	N
6 *Johnson*	Y	Y	N	N	Y	Y	N	Y
DELAWARE								
AL *Castle*	Y	Y	N	Y	N	Y	N	Y
FLORIDA								
1 Hutto	Y	N	N	Y	Y	Y	N	N
2 Peterson	N	N	Y	Y	N	Y	Y	N
3 Brown	N	N	Y	Y	N	N	Y	N
4 *Fowler*	Y	Y	N	Y	Y	Y	Y	Y
5 Thurman	N	N	Y	Y	Y	Y	Y	N
6 *Stearns*	Y	Y	N	N	Y	Y	N	N
7 *Mica*	Y	Y	N	Y	N	Y	N	N
8 *McCollum*	Y	Y	N	Y	Y	Y	N	Y
9 *Bilirakis*	Y	Y	N	Y	Y	Y	Y	Y
10 *Young*	Y	Y	N	Y	Y	Y	N	N
11 Gibbons	N	N	Y	Y	N	N	Y	N
12 *Canady*	Y	Y	N	Y	Y	Y	N	N
13 *Miller*	Y	Y	N	Y	Y	Y	N	Y
14 *Goss*	Y	Y	N	Y	Y	Y	N	Y
15 Bacchus	N	N	Y	Y	Y	Y	Y	N
16 *Lewis*	Y	Y	N	Y	Y	Y	Y	Y
17 Meek	N	N	Y	Y	N	N	Y	N
18 *Ros-Lehtinen*	Y	Y	N	Y	Y	Y	Y	N
19 Johnston	N	N	Y	Y	Y	Y	Y	N
20 Deutsch	N	N	Y	Y	N	Y	Y	N
21 *Diaz-Balart*	Y	Y	N	Y	Y	Y	Y	N
22 *Shaw*	Y	Y	N	Y	Y	Y	N	N
23 Hastings	?	?	?	?	?	?	?	N
GEORGIA								
1 *Kingston*	Y	Y	N	Y	Y	Y	N	N
2 Bishop	N	N	Y	Y	N	N	Y	N
3 *Collins*	Y	Y	N	Y	Y	Y	N	Y
4 *Linder*	Y	Y	N	Y	Y	Y	N	Y
5 Lewis	N	N	Y	Y	N	N	Y	N
6 *Gingrich*	Y	Y	?	Y	Y	Y	N	Y
7 *Darden*	N	N	Y	Y	N	Y	N	N
8 Rowland	N	N	Y	Y	Y	Y	Y	N
9 Deal	N	Y	Y	Y	Y	Y	Y	N
10 *Johnson*	N	Y	N	Y	Y	Y	N	N
11 McKinney	N	X	?	?	?	X	?	N
HAWAII								
1 Abercrombie	N	N	Y	Y	Y	N	Y	N
2 Mink	N	N	Y	Y	Y	N	Y	N
IDAHO								
1 LaRocco	N	N	Y	Y	Y	N	Y	N
2 *Crapo*	Y	Y	N	Y	Y	Y	N	Y
ILLINOIS								
1 Rush	?	N	Y	Y	Y	N	Y	N
2 Reynolds	N	N	Y	Y	N	N	Y	N
3 Lipinski	Y	N	Y	Y	N	Y	N	N
4 Gutierrez	N	N	Y	Y	N	N	Y	N
5 Rostenkowski	N	N	Y	Y	N	Y	Y	?
6 *Hyde*	Y	Y	N	Y	N	Y	N	Y
7 Collins	N	N	Y	Y	N	N	Y	N
8 *Crane*	Y	Y	N	Y	Y	Y	N	Y
9 Yates	N	N	Y	N	N	N	Y	N
10 *Porter*	Y	Y	N	Y	N	Y	Y	Y
11 Sangmeister	N	N	Y	Y	N	N	Y	N
12 Costello	Y	N	Y	Y	N	N	Y	N
13 *Fawell*	Y	Y	N	Y	N	Y	N	N
14 *Hastert*	Y	Y	N	Y	N	Y	N	Y
15 *Ewing*	Y	N	N	Y	N	Y	N	N
16 *Manzullo*	Y	Y	N	Y	Y	Y	N	Y
17 Evans	N	N	Y	Y	N	N	Y	N

ND   Northern Democrats   SD   Southern Democrats

	333	334	335	336	337	338	339	340
18 ***Michel***	Y	Y	N	N	N	Y	N	N
19 Poshard	Y	N	Y	Y	N	Y	Y	N
20 Durbin	N	N	Y	Y	N	N	Y	N
INDIANA								
1 Visclosky	N	N	Y	Y	N	Y	Y	N
2 Sharp	N	N	Y	Y	Y	N	Y	N
3 Roemer	N	N	N	Y	Y	Y	Y	N
4 Long	N	N	Y	Y	N	Y	Y	N
5 ***Buyer***	Y	Y	N	?	Y	Y	N	N
6 ***Burton***	Y	Y	N	Y	Y	Y	N	Y
7 ***Myers***	Y	Y	N	N	N	Y	N	Y
8 McCloskey	N	N	Y	Y	N	Y	Y	N
9 Hamilton	N	N	N	Y	N	Y	Y	N
10 Jacobs	N	Y	Y	Y	Y	Y	N	N
IOWA								
1 ***Leach***	N	Y	N	Y	Y	N	Y	Y
2 ***Nussle***	Y	Y	N	Y	Y	Y	N	Y
3 ***Lightfoot***	Y	Y	N	N	N	Y	Y	N
4 Smith	N	N	Y	N	N	N	Y	N
5 ***Grandy***	Y	Y	N	Y	Y	Y	N	N
KANSAS								
1 ***Roberts***	Y	Y	N	Y	Y	Y	N	Y
2 Slattery	N	Y	Y	Y	Y	Y	Y	Y
3 ***Meyers***	Y	N	N	Y	Y	Y	Y	Y
4 Glickman	N	N	Y	Y	Y	N	Y	N
KENTUCKY								
1 Barlow	N	N	Y	Y	N	Y	Y	N
2 Natcher	N	N	Y	Y	N	N	Y	N
3 Mazzoli	N	N	Y	Y	N	N	Y	N
4 ***Bunning***	Y	Y	N	Y	Y	Y	N	Y
5 ***Rogers***	Y	Y	N	Y	N	Y	Y	N
6 Baesler	N	N	Y	Y	Y	N	Y	N
LOUISIANA								
1 ***Livingston***	Y	Y	N	Y	Y	Y	Y	Y
2 Jefferson	N	N	Y	Y	N	N	Y	N
3 Tauzin	Y	Y	N	Y	Y	Y	N	N
4 Fields	N	N	Y	Y	N	N	Y	N
5 ***McCrery***	Y	Y	N	N	Y	Y	N	N
6 ***Baker***	Y	Y	N	Y	Y	Y	N	?
7 Hayes	Y	N	Y	N	Y	Y	N	N
MAINE								
1 Andrews	N	N	Y	Y	Y	N	Y	N
2 ***Snowe***	Y	Y	N	Y	Y	Y	N	N
MARYLAND								
1 ***Gilchrest***	Y	N	N	Y	Y	Y	Y	N
2 ***Bentley***	Y	Y	N	Y	N	Y	Y	N
3 Cardin	N	N	Y	Y	Y	N	Y	N
4 Wynn	N	N	Y	Y	Y	Y	Y	N
5 Hoyer	N	?	Y	Y	N	N	Y	N
6 ***Bartlett***	Y	Y	N	Y	N	Y	N	Y
7 Mfume	N	N	Y	Y	Y	N	Y	N
8 ***Morella***	N	N	N	Y	Y	N	Y	N
MASSACHUSETTS								
1 Olver	N	N	Y	Y	Y	N	Y	N
2 Neal	N	N	Y	Y	Y	N	Y	N
3 ***Blute***	Y	Y	N	Y	Y	Y	Y	N
4 Frank	N	N	Y	Y	Y	N	Y	N
5 Meehan	N	N	Y	Y	Y	N	Y	N
6 ***Torkildsen***	Y	N	N	Y	Y	Y	Y	N
7 Markey	N	N	Y	Y	Y	N	Y	N
8 Kennedy	N	N	Y	Y	Y	N	Y	N
9 Moakley	N	N	Y	Y	N	N	Y	?
10 Studds	N	N	Y	Y	Y	N	Y	N
MICHIGAN								
1 Stupak	N	N	Y	Y	Y	N	Y	N
2 ***Hoekstra***	Y	N	N	Y	Y	Y	N	N
3 Henry	?	?	?	?	?	?	?	?
4 ***Camp***	Y	N	N	Y	Y	Y	N	N
5 Barcia	N	N	Y	Y	Y	Y	N	N
6 ***Upton***	Y	N	N	Y	Y	Y	N	N
7 ***Smith***	Y	Y	N	Y	Y	Y	N	Y
8 Carr	N	N	Y	N	?	N	Y	N
9 Kildee	N	N	Y	Y	Y	N	Y	N
10 Bonior	N	?	Y	Y	N	N	Y	N
11 ***Knollenberg***	Y	Y	N	Y	Y	Y	N	Y
12 Levin	N	N	Y	Y	Y	N	Y	N
13 Ford	N	N	Y	Y	N	N	Y	N
14 Conyers	?	?	?	?	?	?	?	?
15 Collins	N	N	Y	Y	N	N	Y	N
16 Dingell	N	N	Y	Y	N	N	Y	N
MINNESOTA								
1 Penny	Y	Y	Y	Y	Y	Y	N	Y
2 Minge	N	Y	Y	Y	Y	Y	N	N
3 ***Ramstad***	Y	Y	?	Y	Y	Y	N	Y
4 Vento	N	N	Y	Y	Y	N	Y	N

	333	334	335	336	337	338	339	340
5 Sabo	N	N	Y	Y	N	N	Y	N
6 ***Grams***	Y	Y	N	Y	Y	Y	N	Y
7 Peterson	Y	N	Y	Y	Y	Y	N	N
8 Oberstar	N	N	Y	Y	N	N	Y	N
MISSISSIPPI								
1 Whitten	N	N	Y	N	N	N	N	N
2 Thompson	N	N	Y	Y	N	N	Y	N
3 Montgomery	N	Y	Y	Y	Y	Y	Y	N
4 Parker	Y	N	Y	Y	Y	Y	Y	N
5 Taylor	Y	N	N	Y	Y	Y	N	Y
MISSOURI								
1 Clay	N	N	Y	Y	N	N	Y	N
2 ***Talent***	Y	Y	N	Y	Y	Y	N	Y
3 Gephardt	N	?	Y	Y	?	?	Y	N
4 Skelton	N	N	Y	Y	Y	Y	N	N
5 Wheat	N	N	Y	Y	N	N	Y	N
6 Danner	Y	N	Y	Y	N	N	Y	N
7 ***Hancock***	Y	Y	N	Y	Y	Y	N	Y
8 ***Emerson***	Y	Y	N	Y	N	Y	N	N
9 Volkmer	Y	N	Y	Y	Y	Y	Y	N
MONTANA								
AL Williams	N	N	Y	N	N	N	Y	N
NEBRASKA								
1 ***Bereuter***	N	Y	N	Y	Y	Y	Y	Y
2 Hoagland	N	N	Y	Y	Y	Y	Y	N
3 ***Barrett***	Y	Y	N	Y	Y	Y	N	Y
NEVADA								
1 Bilbray	N	N	Y	Y	Y	N	Y	N
2 ***Vucanovich***	Y	Y	N	N	Y	Y	Y	Y
NEW HAMPSHIRE								
1 ***Zeliff***	Y	Y	N	Y	Y	Y	N	Y
2 Swett	N	N	Y	Y	Y	Y	Y	N
NEW JERSEY								
1 Andrews	Y	N	?	Y	Y	N	N	N
2 Hughes	N	N	Y	Y	Y	N	Y	N
3 ***Saxton***	Y	Y	N	Y	Y	Y	N	N
4 ***Smith***	Y	Y	N	Y	Y	Y	Y	N
5 ***Roukema***	Y	N	N	Y	N	Y	—	Y
6 Pallone	Y	N	Y	Y	Y	N	Y	N
7 ***Franks***	Y	Y	N	Y	Y	Y	N	N
8 Klein	N	N	Y	Y	Y	N	Y	N
9 Torricelli	N	N	Y	N	N	N	Y	N
10 Payne	N	N	Y	Y	N	N	Y	N
11 ***Gallo***	Y	Y	N	Y	Y	Y	Y	N
12 ***Zimmer***	Y	N	N	Y	Y	Y	N	Y
13 Menendez	Y	N	Y	Y	Y	N	Y	N
NEW MEXICO								
1 ***Schiff***	Y	Y	N	Y	Y	Y	Y	N
2 ***Skeen***	Y	Y	N	Y	N	N	Y	Y
3 Richardson	N	N	Y	Y	Y	N	Y	N
NEW YORK								
1 Hochbrueckner	N	?	Y	Y	Y	N	Y	N
2 ***Lazio***	Y	Y	N	Y	Y	Y	Y	Y
3 ***King***	Y	Y	N	Y	Y	Y	N	Y
4 ***Levy***	Y	Y	N	Y	Y	Y	N	Y
5 Ackerman	N	N	Y	Y	Y	N	Y	N
6 Flake	N	N	Y	Y	Y	N	Y	N
7 Manton	N	N	Y	Y	N	N	Y	N
8 Nadler	N	N	?	#	?	?	?	N
9 Schumer	N	N	Y	Y	Y	N	Y	N
10 Towns	?	?	?	?	?	?	?	N
11 Owens	N	N	Y	Y	N	N	Y	N
12 Velazquez	N	N	Y	Y	Y	N	Y	N
13 ***Molinari***	Y	Y	N	Y	Y	Y	Y	N
14 Maloney	N	N	Y	Y	Y	N	Y	N
15 Rangel	N	N	Y	Y	N	N	Y	N
16 Serrano	N	N	Y	Y	N	N	Y	N
17 Engel	N	N	Y	Y	N	N	Y	N
18 Lowey	N	N	Y	Y	N	N	Y	N
19 ***Fish***	?	Y	N	Y	Y	Y	Y	N
20 ***Gilman***	N	Y	N	N	N	N	Y	N
21 McNulty	N	N	Y	Y	Y	Y	Y	N
22 ***Solomon***	Y	Y	N	Y	Y	Y	N	Y
23 ***Boehlert***	Y	Y	N	Y	Y	Y	N	N
24 ***McHugh***	Y	Y	N	Y	Y	Y	N	Y
25 ***Walsh***	Y	Y	N	Y	Y	Y	Y	N
26 Hinchey	N	N	Y	Y	Y	N	Y	?
27 ***Paxon***	Y	Y	N	Y	Y	Y	N	Y
28 Slaughter	N	N	Y	Y	N	N	Y	N
29 LaFalce	N	N	Y	Y	Y	N	Y	N
30 ***Quinn***	Y	Y	N	Y	Y	Y	N	N
31 ***Houghton***	Y	Y	N	Y	Y	N	Y	N
NORTH CAROLINA								
1 Clayton	N	N	Y	Y	Y	N	Y	N
2 Valentine	Y	Y	Y	Y	Y	Y	Y	?

	333	334	335	336	337	338	339	340
3 Lancaster	N	N	Y	Y	Y	N	Y	N
4 Price	N	N	Y	Y	Y	N	Y	N
5 Neal	Y	N	Y	Y	Y	Y	Y	N
6 ***Coble***	Y	Y	N	Y	Y	Y	N	Y
7 Rose	N	N	Y	Y	Y	N	Y	N
8 Hefner	N	N	Y	Y	Y	N	Y	N
9 ***McMillan***	N	Y	N	Y	N	Y	Y	Y
10 ***Ballenger***	Y	Y	N	Y	Y	Y	N	Y
11 ***Taylor***	Y	Y	N	Y	N	Y	Y	Y
12 Watt	N	N	Y	Y	Y	N	Y	N
NORTH DAKOTA								
AL Pomeroy	N	N	Y	Y	?	N	Y	N
OHIO								
1 Mann	Y	N	Y	Y	Y	N	Y	?
2 ***Portman***	Y	Y	N	Y	Y	Y	N	Y
3 Hall	N	N	Y	Y	N	N	Y	N
4 ***Oxley***	Y	Y	N	Y	N	Y	N	Y
5 ***Gillmor***	Y	Y	N	Y	N	Y	?	Y
6 Strickland	N	N	Y	Y	N	N	Y	N
7 ***Hobson***	Y	Y	N	Y	N	Y	Y	Y
8 ***Boehner***	Y	Y	N	Y	N	Y	N	Y
9 Kaptur	N	Y	Y	Y	N	Y	Y	N
10 ***Hoke***	Y	Y	N	Y	Y	Y	N	Y
11 Stokes	N	N	Y	Y	N	N	Y	N
12 ***Kasich***	Y	Y	N	Y	N	Y	N	Y
13 Brown	N	N	Y	Y	N	Y	Y	N
14 Sawyer	N	N	Y	Y	N	N	Y	N
15 ***Pryce***	Y	Y	N	Y	N	Y	N	Y
16 ***Regula***	Y	Y	N	N	N	Y	Y	Y
17 Traficant	N	N	Y	N	N	Y	Y	N
18 Applegate	Y	N	Y	Y	N	Y	Y	N
19 Fingerhut	N	N	Y	Y	Y	Y	Y	N
OKLAHOMA								
1 ***Inhofe***	Y	Y	N	Y	Y	Y	N	Y
2 Synar	N	N	Y	Y	Y	N	Y	N
3 Brewster	Y	N	Y	Y	Y	Y	Y	N
4 McCurdy	N	N	Y	Y	Y	Y	Y	N
5 ***Istook***	Y	Y	N	Y	Y	Y	N	Y
6 English	Y	N	Y	Y	Y	Y	Y	N
OREGON								
1 Furse	N	N	Y	Y	Y	N	Y	N
2 ***Smith***	Y	Y	N	N	Y	Y	N	Y
3 Wyden	N	N	Y	Y	Y	N	Y	N
4 DeFazio	N	N	Y	Y	Y	Y	Y	N
5 Kopetski	N	N	Y	Y	N	N	Y	N
PENNSYLVANIA								
1 Foglietta	N	N	Y	Y	N	N	Y	N
2 Blackwell	N	N	Y	Y	N	N	Y	N
3 Borski	N	N	Y	Y	N	N	Y	N
4 Klink	N	N	Y	Y	N	N	Y	N
5 ***Clinger***	Y	Y	N	?	Y	N	Y	N
6 Holden	Y	N	Y	Y	N	Y	Y	N
7 ***Weldon***	Y	Y	N	Y	Y	Y	N	Y
8 ***Greenwood***	Y	Y	N	Y	Y	Y	N	Y
9 ***Shuster***	Y	Y	N	Y	Y	Y	N	N
10 ***McDade***	N	N	N	N	N	Y	Y	N
11 Kanjorski	N	Y	Y	Y	N	Y	Y	N
12 Murtha	N	N	Y	Y	N	N	Y	N
13 Margolies-Mezv.	N	N	Y	Y	N	Y	Y	N
14 Coyne	N	N	Y	Y	N	N	Y	N
15 McHale	N	N	Y	Y	N	Y	Y	N
16 ***Walker***	Y	Y	N	Y	Y	Y	N	Y
17 ***Gekas***	Y	Y	N	Y	Y	Y	N	Y
18 ***Santorum***	Y	Y	N	Y	N	Y	N	Y
19 ***Goodling***	Y	Y	N	Y	Y	Y	N	N
20 Murphy	Y	N	Y	Y	N	Y	?	N
21 ***Ridge***	Y	Y	N	N	N	Y	N	N
RHODE ISLAND								
1 ***Machtley***	Y	Y	N	Y	Y	Y	Y	N
2 Reed	N	N	Y	Y	Y	N	Y	N
SOUTH CAROLINA								
1 ***Ravenel***	Y	N	N	Y	Y	Y	Y	N
2 ***Spence***	Y	Y	N	Y	Y	Y	N	N
3 Derrick	N	N	Y	Y	N	Y	Y	N
4 ***Inglis***	Y	Y	N	Y	Y	Y	N	N
5 Spratt	N	N	Y	Y	Y	Y	Y	N
6 Clyburn	N	N	Y	Y	N	N	Y	N
SOUTH DAKOTA								
AL Johnson	N	N	Y	Y	Y	N	Y	N
TENNESSEE								
1 ***Quillen***	Y	Y	N	N	N	Y	Y	N
2 ***Duncan***	Y	Y	N	Y	Y	Y	N	Y
3 Lloyd	N	N	Y	Y	Y	Y	Y	N
4 Cooper	Y	N	Y	Y	N	Y	Y	N
5 Clement	Y	N	Y	Y	N	N	Y	N

	333	334	335	336	337	338	339	340
6 Gordon	N	N	Y	Y	Y	Y	Y	N
7 ***Sundquist***	Y	Y	Y	N	N	Y	N	N
8 Tanner	Y	N	Y	Y	Y	Y	Y	N
9 Ford	?	N	Y	Y	Y	N	Y	N
TEXAS								
1 Chapman	N	N	Y	N	N	Y	Y	N
2 Wilson	N	N	Y	Y	N	N	Y	N
3 ***Johnson, Sam***	Y	Y	N	Y	Y	Y	N	Y
4 Hall	Y	Y	N	N	Y	Y	Y	Y
5 Bryant	N	N	Y	Y	Y	N	Y	N
6 ***Barton***	Y	Y	N	Y	Y	Y	N	Y
7 ***Archer***	Y	Y	N	Y	Y	Y	N	Y
8 ***Fields***	Y	Y	N	Y	Y	Y	N	Y
9 Brooks	N	N	Y	N	N	N	Y	N
10 Pickle	?	N	Y	Y	Y	N	Y	N
11 Edwards	N	N	Y	Y	Y	Y	Y	N
12 Geren	Y	Y	Y	Y	Y	Y	N	N
13 Sarpalius	?	?	?	?	?	?	?	N
14 Laughlin	Y	Y	Y	Y	Y	Y	Y	N
15 de la Garza	N	N	Y	Y	Y	Y	Y	N
16 Coleman	?	?	?	?	?	?	?	N
17 Stenholm	Y	Y	Y	Y	Y	Y	N	Y
18 Washington	N	?	?	?	N	N	Y	N
19 ***Combest***	Y	Y	N	Y	Y	Y	N	Y
20 Gonzalez	N	N	Y	N	N	N	Y	N
21 ***Smith***	Y	Y	N	Y	Y	Y	N	Y
22 ***DeLay***	Y	Y	N	Y	Y	Y	N	Y
23 ***Bonilla***	Y	Y	N	Y	Y	Y	N	Y
24 Frost	N	N	Y	Y	Y	Y	Y	?
25 Andrews	N	N	Y	Y	Y	Y	Y	N
26 ***Armey***	Y	?	N	Y	Y	Y	N	Y
27 Ortiz	N	N	Y	Y	Y	Y	Y	N
28 Tejeda	N	N	Y	Y	Y	N	Y	N
29 Green	N	N	Y	Y	Y	N	Y	N
30 Johnson, E. B.	N	N	Y	Y	Y	N	Y	N
UTAH								
1 ***Hansen***	Y	Y	N	N	N	Y	Y	Y
2 Shepherd	N	N	Y	Y	Y	N	Y	N
3 Orton	Y	Y	Y	N	Y	Y	Y	Y
VERMONT								
AL *Sanders*	N	N	Y	Y	Y	N	Y	N
VIRGINIA								
1 ***Bateman***	N	N	N	Y	N	Y	Y	Y
2 Pickett	N	N	Y	N	N	Y	N	N
3 Scott	N	N	Y	Y	N	N	Y	N
4 Sisisky	N	N	Y	Y	N	Y	Y	N
5 Payne	N	N	Y	Y	N	Y	Y	N
6 ***Goodlatte***	Y	Y	N	Y	N	Y	N	Y
7 ***Bliley***	Y	Y	N	Y	N	Y	Y	Y
8 Moran	N	N	Y	Y	Y	N	Y	N
9 Boucher	N	N	Y	Y	N	N	Y	N
10 ***Wolf***	Y	Y	N	Y	Y	Y	N	N
11 Byrne	N	N	Y	Y	Y	N	Y	N
WASHINGTON								
1 Cantwell	N	N	Y	Y	Y	Y	Y	N
2 Swift	N	N	Y	Y	N	N	Y	N
3 Unsoeld	N	N	Y	Y	Y	N	Y	N
4 Inslee	N	N	Y	Y	Y	Y	Y	N
5 Foley								
6 Dicks	N	N	Y	Y	Y	N	Y	N
7 McDermott	N	N	Y	Y	Y	N	Y	N
8 ***Dunn***	Y	Y	N	Y	Y	Y	N	Y
9 Kreidler	N	N	Y	Y	Y	N	Y	N
WEST VIRGINIA								
1 Mollohan	N	N	Y	N	N	N	Y	N
2 Wise	N	N	Y	Y	N	Y	Y	N
3 Rahall	N	N	Y	Y	N	Y	Y	N
WISCONSIN								
1 Barca	N	N	Y	Y	Y	N	N	N
2 ***Klug***	Y	Y	N	Y	Y	Y	N	Y
3 ***Gunderson***	Y	Y	N	Y	Y	Y	Y	Y
4 Kleczka	N	N	N	Y	N	N	Y	N
5 Barrett	N	N	Y	Y	Y	N	Y	N
6 ***Petri***	Y	Y	N	Y	Y	Y	N	Y
7 Obey	N	N	Y	Y	N	N	Y	N
8 ***Roth***	Y	Y	N	Y	Y	Y	N	N
9 ***Sensenbrenner***	Y	Y	N	Y	Y	Y	N	Y
WYOMING								
AL ***Thomas***	Y	Y	N	N	N	Y	Y	Y
DELEGATES								
de Lugo, V.I.	N	N	Y	D	D	D	D	N
Faleomavaega, Am.S.	?	?	?	D	D	D	D	?
Norton, D.C.	N	N	Y	D	D	D	D	N
Romero-B., P.R.	N	N	Y	D	D	D	D	N
Underwood, Guam	N	N	Y	D	D	D	D	?

Southern states - Ala., Ark., Fla., Ga., Ky., La., Miss., N.C., Okla., S.C., Tenn., Texas, Va.
Omitted votes are quorum calls, which CQ does not include in its vote charts.

341. HR 2519. Fiscal 1994 Commerce, Justice, State Appropriations/Travel and Tourism Administration. Oberstar, D-Minn., amendment to restore the $22 million for the U.S. Travel and Tourism Administration that a point of order previously struck from the bill for being legislation on an appropriations bill. Rejected in the Committee of the Whole 158-263: R 25-148; D 132-115 (ND 95-70, SD 37-45); I 1-0, July 20, 1993.

342. HR 2519. Fiscal 1994 Commerce, Justice, State Appropriations/INS. Separate vote at the request of Walker, R-Pa., on the Hunter, R-Calif., amendment adopted in the Committee of the Whole to provide an additional $60 million to the Immigration and Naturalization Service for increased border patrols. Adopted 298-129: R 162-12; D 135-117 (ND 83-85, SD 52-32); I 1-0, July 20, 1993. (On separate votes, which may be demanded on an amendment adopted in the Committee of the Whole, the four delegates and the Resident Commissioner of Puerto Rico cannot vote. See vote 318.)

343. HR 2519. Fiscal 1994 Commerce, Justice, State Appropriations/NOAA. Separate vote at the request of Smith, D-Iowa, on the Walker, R-Pa., amendment adopted in the Committee of the Whole by voice vote July 1 to cut $9.6 million for the National Oceanic and Atmospheric Administration (NOAA). Rejected 70-356: R 59-114; D 11-241 (ND 6-162, SD 5-79); I 0-1, July 20, 1993. (On separate votes, which may be demanded on an amendment adopted in the Committee of the Whole, the four delegates and the Resident Commissioner of Puerto Rico cannot vote.)

344. HR 2519. Fiscal 1994 Commerce, Justice, State Appropriations/Small Business Administration. Separate vote at the request of Smith, D-Iowa, on the Penny, D-Minn., amendment adopted by voice vote July 1 in the Committee of the Whole to cut $22 million from the Small Business Administration. Rejected 183-242: R 143-29; D 40-212 (ND 24-144, SD 16-68); I 0-1, July 20, 1993. (On separate votes, which may be demanded on an amendment adopted in the Committee of the Whole, the four delegates and the Resident Commissioner of Puerto Rico cannot vote.)

345. HR 2519. Fiscal 1994 Commerce, Justice, State Appropriations/Motion to Recommit. Kolbe, R-Ariz., motion to recommit the bill to the House Appropriations Committee with instructions to report it back with an amendment to increase funding by $81.1 million to the levels requested by the administration for the Drug Enforcement Administration, the FBI and the detention of prisoners. Motion rejected 112-315: R 107-67; D 5-247 (ND 4-164, SD 1-83); I 0-1, July 20, 1993.

346. HR 2519. Fiscal 1994 Commerce, Justice, State Appropriations/Passage. Passage of the bill to provide approximately $20 billion in new budget authority for the departments of Commerce, Justice and State, the federal judiciary and related agencies in fiscal 1994. The administration requested $24,743,077,000. Passed 327-98: R 82-92; D 244-6 (ND 161-6, SD 83-0); I 1-0, July 20, 1993.

347. H J Res 208. China MFN Disapproval/Passage. Passage of the joint resolution to disapprove President Clinton's waiver of the Jackson-Vanik amendment to the 1974 Trade Act with respect to China for the period beginning July 3, 1993, through July 2, 1994. Jackson-Vanik bars most-favored-nation trade status to communist countries that do not allow free emigration. Rejected 105-318: R 63-108; D 41-210 (ND 25-143, SD 16-67); I 1-0, July 21, 1993. A "nay" was a vote supporting the president's position.

348. HR 2010. National Service/Rule. Adoption of the rule (H Res 217) to provide for further House floor consideration of the bill to authorize $389 million in fiscal 1994 for the National Service program, which would provide people 17 or older with $5,000 a year for up to two years in education awards in return for work in community service programs. The bill also would authorize $5 million for the Points of Light Foundation. Previously, on July 13 the House adopted a rule (H Res 215) providing for general debate of the bill. Adopted 261-164: R 11-161; D 249-3 (ND 169-1, SD 80-2); I 1-0, July 21, 1993.

KEY

Y Voted for (yea).
Paired for.
+ Announced for.
N Voted against (nay).
X Paired against.
− Announced against.
P Voted "present."
C Voted "present" to avoid possible conflict of interest.
? Did not vote or otherwise make a position known.
D Delegates ineligible to vote.

Democrats *Republicans*
Independent

	341	342	343	344	345	346	347	348
ALABAMA								
1 *Callahan*	N	Y	N	Y	N	N	N	N
2 *Everett*	N	Y	N	Y	N	N	Y	N
3 Browder	Y	N	N	N	N	Y	Y	Y
4 Bevill	N	N	N	N	N	Y	N	Y
5 Cramer	Y	N	N	N	Y	Y	Y	Y
6 *Bachus*	N	Y	N	Y	N	N	N	N
7 Hilliard	Y	Y	N	N	N	Y	N	Y
ALASKA								
AL *Young*	N	Y	N	N	N	Y	N	N
ARIZONA								
1 Coppersmith	Y	Y	Y	Y	N	Y	N	Y
2 Pastor	N	Y	N	N	N	Y	N	Y
3 *Stump*	N	Y	Y	Y	N	N	N	N
4 *Kyl*	N	Y	Y	Y	Y	Y	Y	N
5 *Kolbe*	N	Y	Y	Y	N	N	N	N
6 English	N	Y	N	N	N	Y	N	Y
ARKANSAS								
1 Lambert	Y	N	N	N	N	Y	N	Y
2 Thornton	N	N	N	N	N	Y	N	Y
3 *Hutchinson*	N	Y	Y	Y	N	Y	N	N
4 *Dickey*	N	Y	N	+	N	Y	N	N
CALIFORNIA								
1 Hamburg	?	Y	N	N	N	Y	N	Y
2 *Herger*	N	Y	Y	Y	N	N	N	N
3 Fazio	N	Y	N	N	N	Y	N	Y
4 *Doolittle*	N	Y	Y	Y	N	N	Y	N
5 Matsui	N	Y	N	N	Y	Y	N	Y
6 Woolsey	Y	Y	N	N	Y	Y	N	Y
7 Miller	N	N	N	N	N	Y	N	Y
8 Pelosi	Y	N	N	N	N	Y	N	Y
9 Dellums	Y	N	N	N	Y	Y	N	Y
10 *Baker*	N	Y	N	Y	Y	Y	Y	N
11 *Pombo*	N	Y	Y	Y	N	N	N	N
12 Lantos	N	Y	N	N	Y	Y	Y	Y
13 Stark	N	Y	N	N	N	Y	N	Y
14 Eshoo	Y	Y	N	N	N	Y	N	Y
15 Mineta	Y	Y	N	N	N	Y	N	Y
16 Edwards	?	Y	N	N	N	Y	N	Y
17 Farr	Y	Y	N	N	N	Y	N	Y
18 Condit	N	Y	Y	Y	N	Y	N	Y
19 Lehman	Y	Y	N	Y	N	N	N	Y
20 Dooley	N	N	Y	N	Y	N	N	Y
21 *Thomas*	N	Y	Y	Y	N	N	N	N
22 *Huffington*	N	Y	N	N	N	N	Y	N
23 *Gallegly*	N	Y	N	Y	N	N	N	N
24 Beilenson	N	N	N	N	N	Y	N	Y
25 *McKeon*	N	Y	Y	Y	N	N	N	N
26 Berman	N	Y	N	N	N	Y	N	Y
27 *Moorhead*	Y	Y	Y	Y	Y	N	N	N
28 *Dreier*	N	Y	Y	Y	N	N	N	N
29 Waxman	N	Y	N	N	N	Y	N	Y
30 Becerra	Y	Y	N	N	N	Y	N	Y
31 Martinez	Y	Y	N	N	N	Y	N	Y
32 Dixon	Y	Y	N	N	N	Y	N	Y
33 Roybal-Allard	Y	Y	N	N	N	Y	N	Y
34 Torres	Y	Y	N	N	N	Y	N	Y
35 Waters	Y	Y	N	N	N	Y	N	Y
36 Harman	N	Y	Y	Y	N	Y	N	Y
37 Tucker	?	?	?	?	?	?	N	Y
38 *Horn*	N	Y	N	Y	Y	Y	Y	N
39 *Royce*	N	Y	Y	Y	N	N	N	N
40 *Lewis*	Y	Y	N	Y	N	Y	N	N
41 *Kim*	N	Y	Y	Y	Y	N	N	N

ND Northern Democrats   SD Southern Democrats

	341	342	343	344	345	346	347	348
42 Brown	N	N	N	N	N	Y	N	Y
43 *Calvert*	N	Y	N	Y	N	Y	N	N
44 *McCandless*	N	Y	Y	Y	N	N	N	N
45 *Rohrabacher*	N	Y	Y	Y	N	N	N	N
46 *Dornan*	?	Y	Y	Y	N	#	X
47 *Cox*	N	Y	Y	Y	N	N	N	N
48 *Packard*	−	+	+	+	+	+	−	−
49 Schenk	Y	Y	N	N	Y	Y	N	Y
50 Filner	Y	Y	N	N	N	Y	N	Y
51 *Cunningham*	N	Y	Y	Y	N	N	N	N
52 *Hunter*	N	Y	Y	Y	Y	Y	Y	N
COLORADO								
1 Schroeder	N	Y	N	N	N	N	N	Y
2 Skaggs	N	N	N	N	N	Y	N	Y
3 *McInnis*	N	Y	Y	N	N	N	N	N
4 *Allard*	N	N	Y	Y	N	N	N	N
5 *Hefley*	N	Y	N	N	N	N	N	N
6 *Schaefer*	N	Y	Y	N	N	N	N	N
CONNECTICUT								
1 Kennelly	N	N	N	N	N	Y	N	Y
2 Gejdenson	Y	N	N	N	N	Y	Y	Y
3 DeLauro	N	N	N	N	N	Y	N	Y
4 *Shays*	N	Y	N	Y	Y	N	N	Y
5 *Franks*	N	Y	Y	Y	Y	Y	Y	N
6 *Johnson*	N	Y	N	Y	Y	Y	N	N
DELAWARE								
AL *Castle*	N	Y	N	Y	N	Y	N	N
FLORIDA								
1 Hutto	N	Y	N	N	N	Y	N	Y
2 Peterson	N	N	N	N	N	Y	N	Y
3 Brown	?	N	N	N	N	Y	N	Y
4 *Fowler*	N	Y	N	Y	Y	Y	N	N
5 Thurman	N	N	Y	N	N	Y	N	Y
6 *Stearns*	Y	Y	Y	Y	Y	N	Y	N
7 *Mica*	N	Y	N	Y	Y	N	N	N
8 *McCollum*	Y	Y	N	Y	Y	Y	Y	N
9 *Bilirakis*	N	Y	N	Y	Y	Y	N	N
10 *Young*	N	Y	Y	Y	Y	Y	N	N
11 Gibbons	N	N	N	N	N	Y	N	Y
12 *Canady*	N	Y	N	Y	N	N	N	N
13 *Miller*	N	Y	N	Y	Y	N	N	N
14 *Goss*	N	Y	N	Y	N	N	N	N
15 Bacchus	Y	Y	N	N	N	Y	N	Y
16 *Lewis*	N	Y	N	Y	Y	N	Y	N
17 Meek	Y	Y	N	N	N	Y	N	Y
18 *Ros-Lehtinen*	N	Y	N	N	Y	Y	Y	N
19 Johnston	Y	Y	N	N	N	Y	N	Y
20 Deutsch	Y	Y	N	N	N	Y	N	Y
21 *Diaz-Balart*	N	Y	N	Y	Y	Y	Y	N
22 *Shaw*	N	Y	N	N	N	Y	N	N
23 Hastings	Y	N	N	N	N	Y	N	Y
GEORGIA								
1 *Kingston*	N	Y	N	Y	N	N	Y	N
2 Bishop	Y	Y	N	N	N	Y	N	Y
3 *Collins*	N	Y	N	Y	N	N	Y	N
4 *Linder*	N	Y	Y	Y	Y	Y	Y	N
5 Lewis	Y	Y	N	N	N	Y	N	Y
6 *Gingrich*	N	Y	Y	Y	Y	N	N	N
7 Darden	N	Y	N	N	N	Y	N	Y
8 Rowland	N	Y	N	N	N	Y	N	Y
9 Deal	Y	Y	N	N	N	Y	Y	Y
10 Johnson	N	Y	N	N	N	Y	N	Y
11 McKinney	Y	Y	N	N	N	Y	N	Y
HAWAII								
1 Abercrombie	Y	Y	N	N	N	Y	?	#
2 Mink	Y	N	N	N	N	Y	N	Y
IDAHO								
1 LaRocco	Y	Y	N	Y	N	Y	N	Y
2 *Crapo*	N	Y	Y	Y	N	N	N	N
ILLINOIS								
1 Rush	Y	N	N	N	N	Y	N	Y
2 Reynolds	Y	N	N	N	N	Y	N	Y
3 Lipinski	Y	N	N	N	N	Y	N	Y
4 Gutierrez	?	Y	N	N	N	Y	Y	Y
5 Rostenkowski	N	N	N	N	N	Y	N	Y
6 *Hyde*	N	Y	N	Y	Y	Y	Y	N
7 Collins	Y	Y	N	N	N	Y	N	Y
8 *Crane*	N	N	N	N	N	N	N	N
9 Yates	?	N	N	N	N	Y	N	Y
10 *Porter*	N	N	N	N	N	Y	Y	N
11 Sangmeister	Y	Y	N	N	N	Y	N	Y
12 Costello	Y	N	N	N	N	Y	N	Y
13 *Fawell*	N	Y	N	Y	Y	N	N	N
14 *Hastert*	N	Y	N	Y	Y	N	N	N
15 *Ewing*	N	Y	N	Y	Y	N	N	N
16 *Manzullo*	N	Y	Y	Y	N	N	N	N
17 Evans	Y	Y	N	N	N	Y	N	Y

	341	342	343	344	345	346	347	348
18 ***Michel***	N	Y	N	Y	Y	Y	N	N
19 Poshard	N	N	N	N	N	Y	N	Y
20 Durbin	N	N	N	N	N	Y	N	Y
INDIANA								
1 Visclosky	N	N	N	N	N	Y	N	Y
2 Sharp	N	N	N	Y	N	Y	N	Y
3 Roemer	N	N	N	Y	N	Y	N	Y
4 Long	N	Y	N	N	N	Y	Y	Y
5 ***Buyer***	N	Y	N	Y	Y	N	N	N
6 ***Burton***	N	Y	Y	Y	N	N	Y	N
7 ***Myers***	N	Y	Y	Y	N	Y	N	N
8 McCloskey	Y	N	N	N	N	Y	N	Y
9 Hamilton	N	N	N	Y	N	Y	N	Y
10 Jacobs	N	N	N	N	N	N	N	Y
IOWA								
1 ***Leach***	N	Y	N	N	N	Y	N	N
2 ***Nussle***	N	Y	Y	N	N	Y	N	N
3 ***Lightfoot***	N	Y	N	N	Y	Y	N	N
4 Smith	N	N	N	N	N	Y	N	Y
5 ***Grandy***	N	Y	Y	N	Y	Y	N	N
KANSAS								
1 ***Roberts***	N	Y	Y	Y	N	N	N	N
2 Slattery	N	N	N	Y	N	N	N	Y
3 ***Meyers***	Y	Y	Y	N	N	Y	N	Y
4 Glickman	N	N	Y	N	N	Y	N	Y
KENTUCKY								
1 Barlow	N	Y	N	N	N	Y	Y	Y
2 Natcher	N	N	N	N	N	Y	N	Y
3 Mazzoli	N	Y	N	N	N	Y	N	Y
4 ***Bunning***	N	Y	Y	Y	Y	Y	Y	N
5 ***Rogers***	N	Y	N	N	Y	Y	Y	N
6 Baesler	N	N	N	Y	N	Y	N	Y
LOUISIANA								
1 ***Livingston***	Y	Y	N	Y	Y	Y	N	N
2 Jefferson	Y	Y	N	N	N	Y	N	Y
3 Tauzin	?	Y	N	N	N	Y	Y	Y
4 Fields	Y	Y	N	N	N	Y	N	Y
5 ***McCrery***	Y	N	Y	N	Y	N	N	N
6 ***Baker***	Y	N	N	Y	N	N	N	N
7 Hayes	Y	N	N	N	N	Y	N	Y
MAINE								
1 Andrews	N	N	N	N	N	Y	Y	Y
2 ***Snowe***	Y	Y	N	Y	Y	Y	Y	N
MARYLAND								
1 ***Gilchrest***	N	Y	N	N	Y	Y	Y	N
2 ***Bentley***	N	Y	N	N	N	Y	Y	N
3 Cardin	N	N	N	Y	N	Y	N	Y
4 Wynn	Y	N	N	N	N	Y	N	Y
5 Hoyer	N	N	N	N	N	Y	X	Y
6 ***Bartlett***	N	Y	N	Y	Y	N	N	N
7 Mfume	N	Y	N	N	N	Y	N	Y
8 ***Morella***	N	Y	N	N	N	Y	Y	Y
MASSACHUSETTS								
1 Olver	Y	N	N	N	N	Y	N	Y
2 Neal	Y	N	N	N	N	Y	N	Y
3 ***Blute***	Y	Y	N	Y	N	Y	N	Y
4 Frank	Y	N	N	N	N	Y	Y	Y
5 Meehan	Y	N	N	N	N	Y	N	Y
6 ***Torkildsen***	Y	Y	N	Y	N	Y	N	Y
7 Markey	Y	N	N	N	N	Y	Y	Y
8 Kennedy	Y	Y	N	N	N	Y	N	Y
9 Moakley	?	?	?	?	?	?	?	#
10 Studds	Y	N	N	N	N	Y	N	Y
MICHIGAN								
1 Stupak	Y	Y	N	N	N	Y	N	Y
2 ***Hoekstra***	N	Y	N	Y	Y	Y	N	N
3 Henry	?	?	?	?	?	?	?	?
4 ***Camp***	N	Y	N	Y	Y	N	N	N
5 Barcia	Y	N	N	N	N	N	N	Y
6 ***Upton***	Y	Y	N	Y	Y	N	Y	N
7 ***Smith***	N	Y	N	N	N	N	N	N
8 Carr	N	N	N	N	N	Y	N	Y
9 Kildee	Y	Y	N	N	N	Y	N	Y
10 Bonior	?	N	N	N	N	Y	N	Y
11 ***Knollenberg***	N	Y	N	Y	Y	N	N	N
12 Levin	N	Y	N	N	N	Y	N	Y
13 Ford	Y	Y	N	N	N	Y	N	Y
14 Conyers	?	?	?	?	?	?	Y	Y
15 Collins	Y	Y	N	N	N	Y	N	Y
16 Dingell	Y	Y	N	N	N	Y	N	Y
MINNESOTA								
1 Penny	N	N	Y	Y	N	Y	N	Y
2 Minge	N	N	Y	Y	N	Y	N	Y
3 ***Ramstad***	N	Y	N	Y	Y	N	N	N
4 Vento	Y	N	N	N	N	Y	N	Y

	341	342	343	344	345	346	347	348
5 Sabo	Y	N	N	N	N	Y	N	Y
6 ***Grams***	N	Y	Y	Y	Y	N	N	N
7 Peterson	Y	N	N	Y	N	Y	N	Y
8 Oberstar	Y	N	N	N	N	Y	N	Y
MISSISSIPPI								
1 Whitten	N	Y	N	N	N	Y	N	Y
2 Thompson	Y	Y	N	N	N	Y	N	Y
3 Montgomery	N	N	Y	Y	N	Y	N	Y
4 Parker	N	N	Y	Y	N	Y	N	Y
5 Taylor	N	N	Y	N	Y	Y	Y	N
MISSOURI								
1 Clay	N	Y	N	N	N	Y	N	Y
2 ***Talent***	N	Y	N	Y	Y	N	N	N
3 Gephardt	N	N	N	N	N	Y	N	Y
4 Skelton	Y	Y	N	N	N	Y	N	Y
5 Wheat	Y	Y	N	N	N	Y	Y	Y
6 Danner	Y	Y	N	N	N	Y	N	Y
7 ***Hancock***	N	Y	Y	Y	Y	N	?	N
8 ***Emerson***	N	Y	N	Y	Y	Y	N	N
9 Volkmer	N	N	N	N	N	Y	N	Y
MONTANA								
AL Williams	Y	N	N	N	N	Y	N	Y
NEBRASKA								
1 ***Bereuter***	N	Y	Y	N	N	Y	N	N
2 Hoagland	N	N	N	N	N	Y	N	Y
3 ***Barrett***	N	Y	Y	Y	N	Y	N	N
NEVADA								
1 Bilbray	Y	Y	N	N	N	Y	Y	Y
2 ***Vucanovich***	Y	Y	N	N	Y	Y	N	N
NEW HAMPSHIRE								
1 ***Zeliff***	Y	Y	N	Y	Y	N	N	N
2 Swett	Y	Y	N	N	N	Y	N	Y
NEW JERSEY								
1 Andrews	N	N	N	Y	N	Y	N	Y
2 Hughes	N	N	N	N	N	Y	N	Y
3 ***Saxton***	N	Y	N	Y	N	Y	Y	N
4 ***Smith***	N	Y	N	Y	N	Y	Y	N
5 ***Roukema***	N	Y	N	Y	Y	Y	N	N
6 Pallone	Y	Y	N	N	N	Y	Y	Y
7 ***Franks***	N	Y	N	Y	N	N	N	N
8 Klein	N	N	N	N	N	Y	N	Y
9 Torricelli	N	Y	N	N	N	Y	N	Y
10 Payne	N	N	N	N	N	Y	N	Y
11 ***Gallo***	N	Y	N	Y	N	Y	N	N
12 ***Zimmer***	N	Y	N	Y	Y	N	N	N
13 Menendez	N	Y	N	N	N	Y	N	Y
NEW MEXICO								
1 ***Schiff***	N	Y	N	Y	Y	Y	N	N
2 ***Skeen***	N	Y	N	N	N	Y	Y	N
3 Richardson	Y	Y	N	N	N	Y	N	Y
NEW YORK								
1 Hochbrueckner	Y	Y	N	N	N	Y	Y	Y
2 ***Lazio***	N	Y	N	Y	Y	Y	N	Y
3 ***King***	N	Y	N	Y	Y	N	N	N
4 ***Levy***	N	Y	N	Y	Y	N	N	N
5 Ackerman	Y	Y	N	N	N	Y	N	Y
6 Flake	Y	Y	N	N	N	Y	N	Y
7 Manton	Y	Y	N	N	N	Y	N	Y
8 Nadler	Y	Y	N	N	N	Y	Y	Y
9 Schumer	Y	Y	N	N	N	Y	N	Y
10 Towns	Y	Y	N	N	N	Y	N	Y
11 Owens	Y	N	N	N	N	Y	N	Y
12 Velazquez	Y	Y	N	N	N	Y	N	Y
13 ***Molinari***	N	Y	N	Y	Y	N	Y	N
14 Maloney	Y	Y	N	N	N	Y	N	Y
15 Rangel	Y	Y	N	N	N	Y	N	Y
16 Serrano	Y	Y	N	N	N	Y	N	Y
17 Engel	Y	Y	N	N	N	Y	N	Y
18 Lowey	N	N	N	N	N	Y	N	Y
19 ***Fish***	N	Y	N	Y	Y	Y	Y	Y
20 ***Gilman***	Y	Y	N	Y	Y	Y	Y	Y
21 McNulty	Y	Y	N	N	N	Y	N	Y
22 ***Solomon***	N	Y	Y	Y	N	N	Y	N
23 ***Boehlert***	Y	Y	N	Y	Y	Y	Y	N
24 ***McHugh***	N	Y	N	Y	Y	N	N	N
25 ***Walsh***	N	Y	N	Y	Y	Y	Y	N
26 Hinchey	?	Y	N	N	N	Y	N	Y
27 ***Paxon***	N	Y	Y	Y	N	N	N	N
28 Slaughter	Y	Y	N	N	N	Y	N	Y
29 LaFalce	Y	Y	N	N	N	Y	?	Y
30 ***Quinn***	N	Y	N	Y	Y	Y	N	N
31 ***Houghton***	Y	Y	N	Y	Y	Y	N	N
NORTH CAROLINA								
1 Clayton	N	Y	N	N	N	Y	N	Y
2 Valentine	N	N	N	N	N	Y	Y	Y

	341	342	343	344	345	346	347	348
3 Lancaster	Y	Y	N	N	N	Y	N	Y
4 Price	N	N	N	N	N	Y	N	Y
5 Neal	N	Y	N	N	N	Y	Y	Y
6 ***Coble***	N	N	Y	N	N	N	Y	N
7 Rose	N	Y	N	N	N	Y	N	Y
8 Hefner	N	N	N	N	N	Y	Y	Y
9 ***McMillan***	N	Y	N	Y	N	Y	Y	N
10 ***Ballenger***	N	Y	Y	Y	Y	N	Y	N
11 ***Taylor***	N	Y	Y	N	Y	N	Y	N
12 Watt	N	Y	N	N	N	Y	N	Y
NORTH DAKOTA								
AL Pomeroy	N	N	N	N	N	+	N	Y
OHIO								
1 Mann	?	?	?	?	?	?	N	Y
2 ***Portman***	N	N	Y	Y	N	Y	N	N
3 Hall	Y	N	N	N	N	Y	Y	Y
4 ***Oxley***	N	Y	N	Y	Y	Y	N	N
5 ***Gillmor***	N	Y	N	N	Y	Y	N	N
6 Strickland	Y	N	N	N	N	Y	N	Y
7 ***Hobson***	N	Y	N	Y	Y	Y	N	N
8 ***Boehner***	N	Y	N	Y	Y	N	N	N
9 Kaptur	N	Y	N	N	N	Y	Y	N
10 ***Hoke***	N	Y	N	Y	Y	Y	N	N
11 Stokes	N	Y	N	N	N	Y	N	Y
12 ***Kasich***	N	Y	N	Y	Y	Y	Y	N
13 Brown	Y	N	N	Y	N	Y	Y	Y
14 Sawyer	Y	Y	N	N	N	Y	N	Y
15 ***Pryce***	N	Y	N	Y	Y	Y	N	N
16 ***Regula***	N	N	N	N	Y	Y	N	N
17 Traficant	Y	Y	N	N	N	Y	Y	Y
18 Applegate	Y	Y	N	N	N	N	Y	Y
19 Fingerhut	Y	Y	N	Y	N	Y	N	Y
OKLAHOMA								
1 ***Inhofe***	N	Y	Y	Y	Y	N	N	N
2 Synar	Y	N	N	Y	N	Y	N	Y
3 Brewster	Y	Y	N	N	N	Y	N	Y
4 McCurdy	N	Y	N	Y	N	Y	N	Y
5 ***Istook***	N	Y	?	Y	Y	N	N	N
6 English	Y	N	N	Y	N	Y	N	Y
OREGON								
1 Furse	Y	N	N	N	N	Y	N	Y
2 ***Smith***	N	Y	N	Y	Y	N	N	N
3 Wyden	N	N	N	N	N	Y	N	Y
4 DeFazio	N	N	N	Y	N	Y	Y	Y
5 Kopetski	Y	Y	N	N	N	Y	N	Y
PENNSYLVANIA								
1 Foglietta	Y	N	N	N	N	Y	N	Y
2 Blackwell	Y	Y	N	N	N	Y	N	Y
3 Borski	Y	N	N	N	N	Y	N	Y
4 Klink	Y	N	N	N	N	Y	Y	Y
5 ***Clinger***	Y	Y	N	Y	Y	Y	N	N
6 Holden	N	N	N	N	N	Y	Y	Y
7 ***Weldon***	N	Y	N	Y	Y	N	Y	N
8 ***Greenwood***	N	Y	N	Y	Y	N	Y	N
9 ***Shuster***	Y	Y	N	Y	Y	N	N	N
10 ***McDade***	N	N	N	N	Y	Y	N	N
11 Kanjorski	N	N	N	N	N	Y	N	Y
12 Murtha	N	N	N	N	N	Y	N	Y
13 Margolies-Mezv.	Y	Y	N	N	N	Y	N	Y
14 Coyne	Y	N	N	N	N	Y	N	Y
15 McHale	N	N	N	N	N	Y	N	Y
16 ***Walker***	N	Y	Y	Y	Y	N	Y	N
17 ***Gekas***	Y	Y	N	Y	Y	N	N	N
18 ***Santorum***	N	Y	N	Y	Y	N	N	N
19 ***Goodling***	N	N	N	Y	N	Y	Y	N
20 Murphy	Y	N	N	Y	N	N	N	Y
21 ***Ridge***	N	Y	N	Y	Y	Y	?	N
RHODE ISLAND								
1 ***Machtley***	N	Y	N	Y	N	Y	N	Y
2 Reed	N	N	N	Y	N	Y	N	Y
SOUTH CAROLINA								
1 ***Ravenel***	Y	Y	N	Y	N	Y	Y	N
2 ***Spence***	Y	Y	N	Y	Y	N	Y	N
3 Derrick	N	Y	N	Y	N	Y	Y	Y
4 ***Inglis***	N	Y	N	Y	Y	N	Y	N
5 Spratt	Y	N	N	N	N	Y	Y	Y
6 Clyburn	Y	Y	N	N	N	Y	N	Y
SOUTH DAKOTA								
AL Johnson	Y	Y	N	N	N	Y	N	Y
TENNESSEE								
1 ***Quillen***	N	Y	N	N	N	Y	Y	N
2 ***Duncan***	N	Y	Y	Y	N	N	Y	N
3 Lloyd	Y	N	N	N	N	Y	Y	Y
4 Cooper	Y	Y	N	N	N	Y	Y	Y
5 Clement	Y	Y	N	N	N	Y	N	Y

	341	342	343	344	345	346	347	348
6 Gordon	N	Y	N	N	N	Y	N	Y
7 ***Sundquist***	N	Y	Y	N	N	Y	N	N
8 Tanner	N	Y	N	Y	N	Y	N	Y
9 Ford	Y	N	N	N	N	Y	N	Y
TEXAS								
1 Chapman	N	Y	N	N	N	Y	N	Y
2 Wilson	N	Y	N	N	N	Y	N	?
3 ***Johnson, Sam***	N	Y	Y	Y	N	N	N	N
4 Hall	Y	Y	Y	Y	N	Y	N	N
5 Bryant	Y	Y	N	N	N	Y	N	Y
6 ***Barton***	N	Y	Y	Y	N	N	Y	N
7 ***Archer***	N	Y	Y	Y	Y	N	N	N
8 ***Fields***	N	Y	N	Y	Y	N	N	N
9 Brooks	N	Y	N	N	N	Y	N	Y
10 Pickle	N	N	N	Y	N	Y	N	Y
11 Edwards	Y	N	N	N	N	Y	N	Y
12 Geren	N	N	N	N	N	Y	N	Y
13 Sarpalius	N	Y	N	N	N	Y	N	Y
14 Laughlin	N	Y	N	Y	N	Y	N	Y
15 de la Garza	Y	Y	N	N	N	Y	?	Y
16 Coleman	N	Y	N	N	N	Y	N	Y
17 Stenholm	N	N	N	Y	N	Y	N	Y
18 Washington	Y	N	N	N	N	?	Y	?
19 ***Combest***	N	Y	Y	N	N	N	N	N
20 Gonzalez	N	Y	N	N	N	Y	N	Y
21 ***Smith***	N	Y	N	Y	Y	Y	Y	N
22 ***DeLay***	N	Y	Y	Y	Y	N	N	X
23 ***Bonilla***	N	Y	Y	Y	Y	N	N	N
24 Frost	?	?	?	?	?	?	?	?
25 Andrews	N	Y	N	Y	N	Y	N	Y
26 ***Armey***	N	Y	Y	Y	Y	N	N	N
27 Ortiz	N	Y	N	N	N	Y	N	Y
28 Tejeda	N	Y	N	N	N	Y	N	Y
29 Green	Y	Y	N	N	N	Y	N	Y
30 Johnson, E. B.	Y	Y	N	N	N	Y	N	Y
UTAH								
1 ***Hansen***	N	Y	N	Y	N	N	N	N
2 Shepherd	Y	Y	N	Y	N	Y	N	Y
3 Orton	N	N	N	Y	N	Y	N	Y
VERMONT								
AL *Sanders*	Y	Y	N	N	N	Y	Y	Y
VIRGINIA								
1 ***Bateman***	Y	Y	N	Y	Y	Y	N	N
2 Pickett	N	Y	N	N	N	Y	N	Y
3 Scott	Y	Y	N	N	N	Y	N	Y
4 Sisisky	N	Y	N	N	N	Y	N	Y
5 Payne	N	N	N	N	N	Y	N	Y
6 ***Goodlatte***	N	Y	Y	Y	N	Y	N	N
7 ***Bliley***	N	Y	N	Y	Y	Y	Y	N
8 Moran	N	N	N	N	N	Y	Y	Y
9 Boucher	Y	N	N	N	N	Y	N	Y
10 ***Wolf***	N	Y	N	Y	Y	Y	Y	N
11 Byrne	N	Y	N	Y	N	Y	Y	Y
WASHINGTON								
1 Cantwell	N	N	N	N	N	Y	N	Y
2 Swift	Y	N	N	N	N	Y	N	Y
3 Unsoeld	N	N	N	N	N	Y	N	Y
4 Inslee	N	Y	N	Y	N	Y	N	Y
5 Foley								
6 Dicks	N	N	N	N	N	Y	N	Y
7 McDermott	N	N	N	N	N	Y	N	Y
8 ***Dunn***	N	N	N	Y	Y	N	N	N
9 Kreidler	Y	N	N	N	N	Y	N	Y
WEST VIRGINIA								
1 Mollohan	N	N	N	N	Y	Y	N	Y
2 Wise	Y	N	N	N	Y	Y	N	Y
3 Rahall	Y	N	N	N	Y	Y	Y	Y
WISCONSIN								
1 Barca	N	N	N	N	N	Y	N	Y
2 ***Klug***	N	Y	N	Y	N	N	Y	N
3 ***Gunderson***	N	Y	N	Y	Y	N	Y	Y
4 Kleczka	N	Y	N	N	N	Y	N	Y
5 Barrett	N	N	N	Y	N	Y	N	Y
6 ***Petri***	N	Y	N	Y	N	N	N	N
7 Obey	N	N	N	N	N	Y	N	Y
8 ***Roth***	Y	Y	N	Y	N	N	N	N
9 ***Sensenbrenner***	N	N	Y	Y	N	N	Y	N
WYOMING								
AL ***Thomas***	Y	Y	Y	Y	N	N	N	N
DELEGATES								
de Lugo, V.I.	?	D	D	D	D	D	D	D
Faleomavaega, Am.S.	Y	D	D	D	D	D	D	D
Norton, D.C.	Y	D	D	D	D	D	D	D
Romero-B., P.R.	Y	D	D	D	D	D	D	D
Underwood, Guam	?	D	D	D	D	D	D	D

Southern states - Ala., Ark., Fla., Ga., Ky., La., Miss., N.C., Okla., S.C., Tenn., Texas, Va.
Omitted votes are quorum calls, which CQ does not include in its vote charts.

KEY

Y Voted for (yea).
\# Paired for.
+ Announced for.
N Voted against (nay).
X Paired against.
− Announced against.
P Voted ''present.''
C Voted ''present'' to avoid possible conflict of interest.
? Did not vote or otherwise make a position known.
D Delegates ineligible to vote.

Democrats *Republicans*
Independent

349. HR 2010. National Service/Education Awards. Goodling, R-Pa., amendment to limit the amount of education awards a participant could receive to an amount no greater than the amount one could receive under other federal student financial aid programs. Rejected in the Committee of the Whole 156-270: R 147-23; D 9-246 (ND 3-171, SD 6-75); I 0-1, July 21, 1993.

350. HR 2010. National Service/Labor Union Consultation. Ballenger, R-N.C., amendment to eliminate the requirement that National Service applicants consult with local unions for their concurrence before engaging in similar work performed by local unions. Rejected in Committee of the Whole 153-276: R 143-30; D 10-245 (ND 0-174, SD 10-71); I 0-1, July 21, 1993.

351. HR 2010. National Service/Funding for Other Education Programs. Molinari, R-N.Y., amendment to prohibit the funding of the National Service program until certain funding levels for other federal education programs are met. Rejected in the Committee of the Whole 184-247: R 164-10; D 20-236 (ND 11-164, SD 9-72); I 0-1, July 21, 1993.

352. HR 2010. National Service/Budgetary Accounting. Solomon, R-N.Y., amendment to require that the authorizations in the bill be counted under the Labor, Health and Human Services budget function by the Office of Management and Budget. Adopted in the Committee of the Whole 259-171: R 172-1; D 87-169 (ND 43-131, SD 44-38); I 0-1, July 21, 1993.

353. Procedural Motion. Approval of the House Journal of Wednesday, July 21. Approved 250-151: R 20-146; D 229-5 (ND 154-4, SD 75-1); I 1-0, July 22, 1993.

354. HR 2667. Fiscal 1993 Disaster Supplemental Appropriations/Previous Question. Wheat, D-Mo., motion to order the previous question (thus ending debate and the possibility of amendment) on adoption of the rule (H Res 220) to provide for House floor consideration of the bill to provide $2,742,855,000 in new budget authority in fiscal 1993 for emergency relief from widespread flooding in the Midwest and other natural disasters. Motion agreed to 245-178: R 0-173; D 244-5 (ND 162-5, SD 82-0); I 1-0, July 22, 1993.

355. HR 2667. Fiscal 1993 Disaster Supplemental Appropriations/Rule. Adoption of the rule (H Res 220) to provide for House floor consideration of the bill to provide $2,742,855,000 in new budget authority in fiscal 1993 for emergency relief from widespread flooding in the Midwest and other natural disasters. Rejected 205-216: R 0-171; D 204-45 (ND 151-16, SD 53-29); I 1-0, July 22, 1993.

356. H Res 223. House Post Office Investigation/Delay Release. Gephardt, D-Mo., resolution to express the sense of the House that the House shall consider the public release of transcripts of a 1992 House Administration Committee investigation into the House Post Office when the U.S. attorney of the District of Columbia states that he has no objection to the release of the transcripts. Adopted 244-183: R 1-172; D 242-11 (ND 169-2, SD 73-9); I 1-0, July 22, 1993.

	349	350	351	352	353	354	355	356
ALABAMA								
1 *Callahan*	Y	Y	N	Y	N	N	N	N
2 *Everett*	Y	Y	Y	Y	N	N	N	N
3 Browder	N	N	N	Y	Y	Y	N	Y
4 Bevill	N	N	Y	Y	Y	Y	Y	Y
5 Cramer	N	N	N	Y	Y	Y	N	Y
6 *Bachus*	Y	Y	Y	Y	N	N	N	N
7 Hilliard	N	N	N	Y	Y	Y	Y	?
ALASKA								
AL *Young*	Y	N	Y	Y	?	N	N	N
ARIZONA								
1 Coppersmith	N	N	N	N	Y	Y	N	Y
2 Pastor	N	N	N	N	Y	Y	Y	Y
3 *Stump*	Y	Y	Y	Y	N	N	N	N
4 *Kyl*	Y	Y	Y	Y	N	N	N	N
5 *Kolbe*	Y	Y	Y	Y	N	N	N	N
6 English	N	N	N	N	Y	Y	Y	Y
ARKANSAS								
1 Lambert	N	N	N	Y	Y	Y	Y	Y
2 Thornton	N	N	N	N	Y	Y	Y	Y
3 *Hutchinson*	Y	Y	Y	Y	N	N	N	N
4 *Dickey*	Y	Y	Y	Y	N	N	N	N
CALIFORNIA								
1 Hamburg	N	N	N	N	Y	Y	Y	Y
2 *Herger*	Y	Y	Y	Y	N	N	N	N
3 Fazio	N	N	N	Y	Y	Y	Y	Y
4 *Doolittle*	Y	Y	Y	Y	N	N	N	N
5 Matsui	N	N	N	N	Y	Y	Y	Y
6 Woolsey	N	N	N	N	Y	Y	Y	Y
7 Miller	N	N	N	N	Y	Y	Y	Y
8 Pelosi	N	N	N	N	Y	Y	Y	Y
9 Dellums	N	N	N	N	Y	Y	Y	Y
10 *Baker*	Y	Y	Y	Y	N	N	N	N
11 *Pombo*	Y	Y	Y	Y	N	N	N	N
12 Lantos	N	N	N	N	Y	Y	Y	Y
13 Stark	N	N	N	N	Y	Y	Y	Y
14 Eshoo	N	N	N	N	Y	Y	Y	Y
15 Mineta	N	N	N	N	Y	Y	Y	Y
16 Edwards	N	N	N	N	Y	Y	Y	Y
17 Farr	N	N	N	N	Y	Y	Y	Y
18 Condit	N	N	Y	Y	Y	Y	N	Y
19 Lehman	N	N	N	N	Y	Y	Y	Y
20 Dooley	N	N	Y	Y	Y	Y	Y	Y
21 *Thomas*	Y	Y	Y	Y	N	N	N	N
22 *Huffington*	Y	Y	Y	Y	N	N	N	N
23 *Gallegly*	Y	Y	Y	Y	N	N	N	N
24 Beilenson	N	N	N	?	Y	Y	Y	Y
25 *McKeon*	Y	Y	Y	Y	N	N	N	N
26 Berman	N	N	N	N	Y	Y	Y	Y
27 *Moorhead*	Y	Y	Y	Y	N	N	N	N
28 *Dreier*	Y	Y	Y	Y	N	N	N	N
29 Waxman	N	N	N	N	Y	Y	Y	Y
30 Becerra	N	N	N	N	Y	Y	Y	Y
31 Martinez	N	N	N	N	Y	Y	Y	Y
32 Dixon	N	N	N	?	Y	Y	Y	Y
33 Roybal-Allard	N	N	N	N	Y	Y	Y	Y
34 Torres	N	N	N	N	Y	Y	Y	Y
35 Waters	N	N	N	N	Y	Y	Y	Y
36 Harman	N	N	N	N	Y	Y	Y	Y
37 Tucker	N	N	N	N	?	?	?	Y
38 *Horn*	N	Y	Y	N	N	N	N	N
39 *Royce*	Y	Y	Y	Y	N	N	N	N
40 *Lewis*	Y	Y	Y	Y	N	N	N	N
41 *Kim*	Y	Y	Y	Y	N	N	N	N

	349	350	351	352	353	354	355	356
42 Brown	N	N	N	N	?	Y	Y	Y
43 *Calvert*	Y	Y	Y	Y	N	N	N	N
44 *McCandless*	Y	Y	Y	Y	N	N	N	N
45 *Rohrabacher*	Y	Y	Y	Y	N	N	N	N
46 *Dornan*	?	Y	Y	Y	N	X	X	N
47 *Cox*	Y	Y	Y	Y	N	N	N	N
48 *Packard*	+	+	+	+	+	−	−	−
49 Schenk	N	N	N	N	Y	Y	Y	Y
50 Filner	N	N	N	N	Y	Y	Y	Y
51 *Cunningham*	Y	Y	Y	Y	N	N	N	N
52 *Hunter*	?	Y	Y	Y	N	N	N	N
COLORADO								
1 Schroeder	N	N	Y	N	N	Y	Y	Y
2 Skaggs	N	N	Y	N	Y	Y	Y	Y
3 *McInnis*	Y	Y	Y	Y	Y	N	N	N
4 *Allard*	Y	Y	Y	Y	N	N	N	N
5 *Hefley*	Y	Y	Y	Y	N	N	N	N
6 *Schaefer*	Y	Y	Y	Y	N	N	N	N
CONNECTICUT								
1 Kennelly	N	N	N	N	Y	Y	Y	Y
2 Gejdenson	N	N	N	N	Y	Y	Y	Y
3 DeLauro	N	N	N	N	Y	Y	Y	Y
4 *Shays*	N	N	N	Y	N	N	N	N
5 *Franks*	Y	Y	Y	Y	N	N	N	N
6 *Johnson*	N	N	Y	Y	N	N	N	N
DELAWARE								
AL *Castle*	N	Y	Y	Y	N	N	N	N
FLORIDA								
1 Hutto	Y	Y	N	Y	Y	Y	N	N
2 Peterson	N	N	N	Y	Y	Y	Y	Y
3 Brown	N	N	N	N	Y	Y	Y	Y
4 *Fowler*	Y	Y	Y	Y	N	N	N	N
5 Thurman	N	N	N	N	Y	Y	Y	Y
6 *Stearns*	Y	Y	Y	Y	N	N	N	N
7 *Mica*	Y	Y	Y	Y	N	N	N	N
8 *McCollum*	Y	Y	Y	Y	N	N	N	N
9 *Bilirakis*	Y	Y	Y	Y	N	N	N	N
10 *Young*	Y	Y	Y	Y	N	N	N	N
11 Gibbons	Y	N	N	?	Y	Y	Y	Y
12 *Canady*	Y	Y	Y	Y	N	N	N	N
13 *Miller*	Y	Y	Y	Y	N	N	N	N
14 *Goss*	N	Y	Y	Y	N	N	N	N
15 Bacchus	N	N	N	Y	Y	Y	Y	Y
16 *Lewis*	Y	Y	Y	Y	N	N	N	N
17 Meek	N	N	N	Y	Y	Y	Y	Y
18 *Ros-Lehtinen*	Y	N	Y	N	N	N	N	N
19 Johnston	N	N	N	N	Y	Y	Y	Y
20 Deutsch	N	N	N	N	Y	Y	N	Y
21 *Diaz-Balart*	N	Y	N	N	N	N	N	N
22 *Shaw*	Y	Y	Y	N	N	N	N	N
23 Hastings	N	N	N	Y	Y	Y	Y	Y
GEORGIA								
1 *Kingston*	Y	Y	Y	Y	N	N	N	N
2 Bishop	N	N	N	Y	Y	Y	Y	Y
3 *Collins*	Y	Y	Y	Y	N	N	N	N
4 *Linder*	Y	Y	Y	Y	N	N	N	N
5 Lewis	N	N	N	Y	Y	Y	Y	Y
6 *Gingrich*	Y	Y	Y	Y	N	N	N	N
7 Darden	N	N	N	N	?	Y	Y	Y
8 Rowland	N	Y	N	Y	Y	Y	Y	Y
9 Deal	N	N	Y	Y	N	Y	Y	Y
10 Johnson	N	N	N	Y	Y	N	Y	N
11 McKinney	N	N	N	?	?	Y	Y	Y
HAWAII								
1 Abercrombie	N	N	N	N	Y	Y	Y	Y
2 Mink	N	N	Y	N	Y	Y	Y	Y
IDAHO								
1 LaRocco	N	N	N	Y	Y	Y	Y	Y
2 *Crapo*	Y	Y	Y	Y	N	N	N	N
ILLINOIS								
1 Rush	N	N	N	Y	Y	Y	Y	Y
2 Reynolds	N	N	N	N	Y	Y	Y	Y
3 Lipinski	N	N	N	Y	Y	Y	Y	Y
4 Gutierrez	N	N	N	N	Y	Y	Y	Y
5 Rostenkowski	N	N	N	N	Y	Y	Y	Y
6 *Hyde*	Y	Y	Y	Y	N	N	N	N
7 Collins	N	N	N	N	Y	Y	Y	Y
8 *Crane*	Y	Y	Y	Y	?	N	N	N
9 Yates	N	N	N	N	Y	Y	Y	Y
10 *Porter*	Y	Y	Y	N	?	N	N	N
11 Sangmeister	N	N	N	N	Y	Y	Y	Y
12 Costello	N	N	N	N	Y	Y	Y	Y
13 *Fawell*	Y	Y	Y	Y	N	N	N	N
14 *Hastert*	Y	Y	Y	Y	N	N	N	N
15 *Ewing*	Y	Y	Y	Y	N	N	N	N
16 *Manzullo*	Y	Y	Y	Y	N	N	N	N
17 Evans	N	N	N	N	Y	Y	Y	Y

ND Northern Democrats   SD Southern Democrats

	349	350	351	352	353	354	355	356
18 ***Michel***	Y	Y	Y	Y	N	N	?	N
19 Poshard	N	N	N	Y	Y	Y	Y	Y
20 Durbin	N	N	N	N	Y	Y	Y	Y
INDIANA								
1 Visclosky	N	N	N	N	Y	Y	Y	Y
2 Sharp	N	N	N	Y	Y	Y	Y	Y
3 Roemer	N	N	N	N	Y	Y	N	Y
4 Long	N	N	N	N	Y	Y	Y	Y
5 ***Buyer***	Y	Y	Y	Y	N	N	N	N
6 ***Burton***	?	Y	Y	Y	N	N	N	N
7 ***Myers***	Y	Y	Y	Y	Y	N	N	N
8 McCloskey	N	N	N	N	?	Y	Y	Y
9 Hamilton	N	N	N	N	Y	Y	Y	Y
10 Jacobs	N	N	N	Y	N	N	N	Y
IOWA								
1 ***Leach***	N	N	Y	Y	N	N	N	N
2 ***Nussle***	Y	Y	Y	Y	N	N	N	N
3 ***Lightfoot***	Y	Y	Y	Y	N	N	N	N
4 Smith	N	N	N	N	Y	Y	Y	Y
5 ***Grandy***	Y	Y	Y	Y	N	N	N	P
KANSAS								
1 ***Roberts***	Y	Y	Y	Y	N	N	N	N
2 Slattery	Y	N	N	Y	Y	Y	N	Y
3 ***Meyers***	Y	Y	Y	?	N	N	N	N
4 Glickman	N	N	N	Y	Y	Y	N	Y
KENTUCKY								
1 Barlow	N	N	N	N	Y	Y	Y	Y
2 Natcher	N	N	N	N	Y	Y	Y	Y
3 Mazzoli	N	N	N	N	Y	Y	Y	N
4 ***Bunning***	Y	Y	Y	Y	N	N	N	N
5 ***Rogers***	Y	Y	Y	Y	N	N	N	N
6 Baesler	N	N	N	N	Y	Y	N	Y
LOUISIANA								
1 ***Livingston***	Y	Y	Y	Y	N	N	N	N
2 Jefferson	N	N	N	N	Y	Y	Y	Y
3 Tauzin	N	Y	Y	Y	Y	Y	N	N
4 Fields	N	N	N	Y	Y	Y	Y	Y
5 ***McCrery***	Y	Y	Y	Y	N	N	N	N
6 ***Baker***	Y	Y	Y	Y	N	N	N	N
7 Hayes	N	N	N	Y	Y	Y	N	Y
MAINE								
1 Andrews	N	N	Y	N	Y	Y	Y	Y
2 ***Snowe***	N	N	N	Y	N	N	N	N
MARYLAND								
1 ***Gilchrest***	Y	Y	Y	Y	N	N	N	N
2 ***Bentley***	Y	Y	Y	Y	N	N	N	N
3 Cardin	N	N	N	N	Y	Y	Y	Y
4 Wynn	N	N	N	N	Y	Y	Y	Y
5 Hoyer	N	N	N	N	Y	Y	Y	Y
6 ***Bartlett***	Y	?	Y	Y	N	N	N	N
7 Mfume	N	N	N	Y	Y	Y	Y	Y
8 ***Morella***	N	N	N	Y	N	N	N	N
MASSACHUSETTS								
1 Olver	N	N	N	N	Y	Y	Y	Y
2 Neal	N	N	N	N	Y	Y	Y	Y
3 ***Blute***	N	N	Y	Y	N	N	N	N
4 Frank	N	N	N	N	Y	Y	Y	Y
5 Meehan	N	N	N	Y	Y	Y	N	Y
6 ***Torkildsen***	N	N	Y	Y	N	N	N	N
7 Markey	N	N	N	N	Y	Y	Y	Y
8 Kennedy	N	N	N	N	Y	Y	Y	Y
9 Moakley	?	?	?	?	?	?	#	?
10 Studds	N	N	N	N	Y	Y	Y	Y
MICHIGAN								
1 Stupak	N	N	N	N	Y	Y	Y	Y
2 ***Hoekstra***	N	Y	N	Y	N	N	N	N
3 Henry	?	?	?	?	?	?	?	?
4 ***Camp***	Y	Y	Y	Y	N	N	N	N
5 Barcia	N	N	N	N	Y	Y	?	Y
6 ***Upton***	N	Y	N	Y	N	N	N	N
7 ***Smith***	N	Y	N	Y	N	N	N	N
8 Carr	N	N	N	N	Y	Y	Y	Y
9 Kildee	N	N	N	N	Y	Y	Y	Y
10 Bonior	N	N	N	N	Y	Y	Y	Y
11 ***Knollenberg***	Y	Y	Y	Y	N	N	N	N
12 Levin	N	N	N	N	Y	Y	Y	Y
13 Ford	N	N	N	N	Y	Y	Y	Y
14 Conyers	N	N	N	?	?	?	?	?
15 Collins	N	N	N	N	Y	Y	Y	Y
16 Dingell	N	N	N	N	?	Y	Y	Y
MINNESOTA								
1 Penny	Y	N	N	Y	Y	N	N	Y
2 Minge	N	N	N	Y	Y	Y	N	Y
3 ***Ramstad***	Y	Y	Y	Y	N	N	N	N
4 Vento	N	N	N	N	?	Y	Y	Y
5 Sabo	N	N	N	N	Y	Y	Y	Y
6 ***Grams***	Y	Y	Y	Y	N	N	N	N
7 Peterson	N	N	N	Y	Y	Y	N	N
8 Oberstar	N	N	N	N	Y	Y	Y	Y
MISSISSIPPI								
1 Whitten	N	N	N	N	?	Y	Y	Y
2 Thompson	N	N	N	N	Y	Y	Y	Y
3 Montgomery	N	N	N	Y	Y	Y	Y	Y
4 Parker	N	Y	N	Y	?	Y	N	N
5 Taylor	N	Y	Y	Y	N	Y	N	N
MISSOURI								
1 Clay	N	N	N	N	N	Y	Y	Y
2 ***Talent***	Y	Y	Y	Y	?	N	N	N
3 Gephardt	N	N	N	N	Y	#	#	Y
4 Skelton	?	?	N	N	Y	Y	Y	Y
5 Wheat	N	N	N	N	Y	Y	Y	Y
6 Danner	N	N	N	N	Y	Y	Y	Y
7 ***Hancock***	Y	Y	Y	Y	N	N	N	N
8 ***Emerson***	Y	Y	Y	Y	N	N	N	N
9 Volkmer	N	N	N	Y	Y	Y	Y	Y
MONTANA								
AL Williams	N	N	Y	Y	Y	N	Y	Y
NEBRASKA								
1 ***Bereuter***	N	Y	Y	Y	N	N	N	N
2 Hoagland	N	N	N	Y	Y	Y	Y	Y
3 ***Barrett***	Y	Y	Y	Y	N	N	N	N
NEVADA								
1 Bilbray	N	N	N	N	Y	Y	Y	Y
2 ***Vucanovich***	Y	Y	Y	Y	N	N	N	N
NEW HAMPSHIRE								
1 ***Zeliff***	Y	Y	Y	Y	N	N	N	N
2 Swett	N	N	N	N	Y	Y	N	Y
NEW JERSEY								
1 Andrews	N	N	N	N	Y	Y	N	Y
2 Hughes	N	N	N	Y	Y	Y	Y	Y
3 ***Saxton***	Y	Y	Y	Y	N	N	N	N
4 ***Smith***	Y	N	Y	Y	Y	N	N	N
5 ***Roukema***	Y	N	Y	Y	N	N	N	N
6 Pallone	N	N	N	Y	Y	Y	Y	Y
7 ***Franks***	Y	N	Y	Y	N	N	X	N
8 Klein	N	N	N	N	P	Y	Y	Y
9 Torricelli	N	N	N	N	Y	Y	Y	Y
10 Payne	N	N	N	N	Y	Y	Y	Y
11 ***Gallo***	Y	Y	Y	Y	N	N	N	N
12 ***Zimmer***	Y	Y	Y	Y	N	N	N	N
13 Menendez	N	N	N	Y	Y	Y	Y	Y
NEW MEXICO								
1 ***Schiff***	Y	Y	Y	Y	N	N	N	N
2 ***Skeen***	Y	Y	Y	Y	N	N	N	N
3 Richardson	N	N	N	Y	Y	Y	Y	Y
NEW YORK								
1 Hochbrueckner	N	N	N	Y	Y	Y	Y	Y
2 ***Lazio***	N	N	Y	Y	?	N	N	N
3 ***King***	Y	N	Y	Y	N	N	N	N
4 ***Levy***	Y	N	Y	Y	N	N	N	N
5 Ackerman	N	N	N	N	Y	Y	Y	Y
6 Flake	N	N	N	N	Y	Y	Y	Y
7 Manton	N	N	N	N	Y	Y	Y	Y
8 Nadler	N	N	N	N	?	Y	Y	Y
9 Schumer	N	N	N	N	Y	Y	Y	Y
10 Towns	N	N	N	N	Y	Y	Y	Y
11 Owens	N	N	N	N	Y	Y	Y	Y
12 Velazquez	N	N	N	N	Y	Y	Y	Y
13 ***Molinari***	Y	Y	Y	Y	N	N	N	N
14 Maloney	N	N	N	N	Y	?	?	Y
15 Rangel	N	N	N	N	Y	Y	Y	Y
16 Serrano	N	N	N	Y	Y	Y	Y	Y
17 Engel	N	N	N	N	Y	Y	Y	Y
18 Lowey	N	N	N	N	Y	Y	Y	Y
19 ***Fish***	Y	N	Y	Y	Y	N	N	N
20 ***Gilman***	N	N	N	Y	Y	N	N	N
21 McNulty	N	N	N	N	Y	Y	Y	Y
22 ***Solomon***	Y	Y	Y	Y	N	N	N	N
23 ***Boehlert***	Y	N	N	Y	N	N	N	N
24 ***McHugh***	Y	N	Y	Y	N	N	N	N
25 ***Walsh***	N	N	Y	Y	N	N	N	N
26 Hinchey	N	N	N	N	?	Y	Y	Y
27 ***Paxon***	Y	Y	Y	Y	N	N	N	N
28 Slaughter	N	N	N	Y	Y	Y	Y	Y
29 LaFalce	N	N	N	N	?	Y	Y	Y
30 ***Quinn***	Y	N	Y	Y	N	N	N	N
31 ***Houghton***	N	N	N	Y	Y	N	N	Y
NORTH CAROLINA								
1 Clayton	N	N	?	N	P	Y	Y	Y
2 Valentine	?	?	?	?	Y	Y	N	Y
3 Lancaster	N	Y	N	N	Y	Y	N	Y
4 Price	N	N	N	N	Y	Y	Y	Y
5 Neal	N	N	N	N	Y	Y	Y	Y
6 ***Coble***	Y	Y	Y	Y	N	N	N	N
7 Rose	N	N	N	N	Y	Y	Y	Y
8 Hefner	N	N	N	Y	Y	Y	Y	Y
9 ***McMillan***	Y	Y	Y	Y	N	N	N	N
10 ***Ballenger***	Y	Y	Y	Y	N	N	N	N
11 ***Taylor***	Y	Y	Y	Y	N	N	N	N
12 Watt	N	N	N	N	Y	Y	Y	Y
NORTH DAKOTA								
AL Pomeroy	N	N	N	Y	Y	Y	Y	Y
OHIO								
1 Mann	N	N	N	N	Y	Y	N	Y
2 ***Portman***	Y	Y	Y	Y	N	N	N	N
3 Hall	N	N	N	Y	Y	Y	Y	Y
4 ***Oxley***	Y	Y	Y	Y	Y	N	N	N
5 ***Gillmor***	Y	Y	Y	Y	Y	N	N	N
6 Strickland	N	N	N	N	Y	Y	Y	Y
7 ***Hobson***	Y	Y	Y	Y	N	N	N	N
8 ***Boehner***	Y	Y	Y	Y	N	N	N	N
9 Kaptur	N	N	N	N	Y	Y	Y	Y
10 ***Hoke***	Y	Y	Y	Y	N	N	N	N
11 Stokes	N	N	N	N	Y	Y	Y	Y
12 ***Kasich***	Y	Y	Y	Y	Y	N	N	N
13 Brown	N	N	N	N	Y	Y	Y	Y
14 Sawyer	N	N	N	N	Y	Y	Y	Y
15 ***Pryce***	Y	Y	Y	Y	N	N	N	N
16 ***Regula***	Y	Y	Y	Y	N	N	N	N
17 Traficant	N	N	N	Y	Y	Y	Y	Y
18 Applegate	N	N	N	Y	Y	Y	Y	Y
19 Fingerhut	N	N	N	Y	Y	Y	N	Y
OKLAHOMA								
1 ***Inhofe***	Y	Y	Y	Y	N	N	N	N
2 Synar	N	N	Y	Y	Y	Y	Y	Y
3 Brewster	Y	N	N	Y	Y	Y	N	Y
4 McCurdy	X	?	?	?	Y	Y	N	Y
5 ***Istook***	Y	Y	Y	Y	N	N	N	N
6 English	Y	N	N	N	Y	Y	Y	Y
OREGON								
1 Furse	N	N	N	N	Y	Y	Y	Y
2 ***Smith***	Y	Y	Y	Y	N	N	N	N
3 Wyden	N	N	N	N	Y	Y	Y	Y
4 DeFazio	N	N	N	Y	Y	Y	Y	Y
5 Kopetski	N	N	N	N	Y	Y	Y	Y
PENNSYLVANIA								
1 Foglietta	N	N	N	N	Y	Y	Y	Y
2 Blackwell	N	N	N	N	Y	Y	Y	Y
3 Borski	N	N	N	Y	Y	Y	Y	Y
4 Klink	N	N	N	Y	Y	Y	Y	Y
5 ***Clinger***	Y	Y	Y	Y	Y	N	N	N
6 Holden	N	N	N	N	Y	Y	Y	Y
7 ***Weldon***	Y	N	Y	Y	N	N	N	N
8 ***Greenwood***	Y	Y	Y	Y	N	N	N	N
9 ***Shuster***	Y	Y	Y	Y	N	N	N	N
10 ***McDade***	Y	N	Y	Y	N	N	N	N
11 Kanjorski	N	N	N	N	Y	Y	Y	Y
12 Murtha	N	N	N	N	Y	Y	Y	Y
13 Margolies-Mezv.	N	N	N	N	Y	Y	Y	N
14 Coyne	N	N	N	N	Y	Y	Y	Y
15 McHale	N	N	N	N	Y	Y	Y	Y
16 ***Walker***	Y	Y	Y	Y	N	N	N	N
17 ***Gekas***	Y	Y	Y	Y	N	N	N	N
18 ***Santorum***	Y	N	Y	Y	N	N	N	N
19 ***Goodling***	Y	Y	Y	Y	N	N	N	N
20 Murphy	N	N	Y	N	N	N	Y	Y
21 ***Ridge***	Y	Y	Y	Y	N	N	N	N
RHODE ISLAND								
1 ***Machtley***	N	N	Y	Y	N	N	N	N
2 Reed	N	N	N	N	Y	Y	Y	Y
SOUTH CAROLINA								
1 ***Ravenel***	Y	Y	Y	Y	N	N	N	N
2 ***Spence***	Y	Y	Y	Y	?	N	N	N
3 Derrick	N	N	N	Y	Y	Y	Y	Y
4 ***Inglis***	Y	Y	Y	Y	Y	N	N	N
5 Spratt	N	N	N	Y	?	Y	Y	Y
6 Clyburn	N	N	N	Y	Y	Y	Y	Y
SOUTH DAKOTA								
AL Johnson	N	N	Y	N	Y	Y	Y	Y
TENNESSEE								
1 ***Quillen***	Y	Y	Y	Y	N	N	N	N
2 ***Duncan***	Y	Y	Y	Y	N	N	N	N
3 Lloyd	N	N	Y	N	Y	Y	N	Y
4 Cooper	N	N	Y	Y	Y	Y	N	N
5 Clement	N	N	N	Y	Y	Y	Y	Y
6 Gordon	N	N	N	N	Y	Y	Y	Y
7 ***Sundquist***	Y	Y	Y	Y	N	N	N	N
8 Tanner	N	N	N	Y	Y	Y	N	Y
9 Ford	N	N	N	N	Y	Y	Y	N
TEXAS								
1 Chapman	N	N	N	N	Y	Y	Y	Y
2 Wilson	N	N	N	N	Y	?	?	Y
3 ***Johnson, Sam***	Y	Y	Y	Y	?	N	N	N
4 Hall	N	Y	N	N	Y	Y	N	N
5 Bryant	N	N	N	Y	Y	Y	Y	Y
6 ***Barton***	Y	Y	Y	Y	N	N	N	N
7 ***Archer***	Y	Y	Y	Y	Y	N	N	N
8 ***Fields***	Y	Y	Y	Y	N	N	N	N
9 Brooks	N	N	N	N	Y	Y	Y	Y
10 Pickle	N	N	N	Y	Y	Y	Y	Y
11 Edwards	N	N	Y	Y	Y	Y	Y	Y
12 Geren	Y	Y	Y	Y	?	Y	N	Y
13 Sarpalius	N	N	N	Y	Y	Y	N	Y
14 Laughlin	N	N	N	Y	Y	Y	Y	Y
15 de la Garza	?	N	Y	Y	Y	Y	Y	Y
16 Coleman	N	N	N	N	Y	Y	Y	Y
17 Stenholm	Y	Y	Y	Y	Y	Y	N	Y
18 Washington	N	?	N	N	?	Y	Y	Y
19 ***Combest***	Y	Y	Y	Y	Y	N	N	N
20 Gonzalez	N	N	N	N	Y	Y	Y	Y
21 ***Smith***	Y	Y	Y	Y	N	N	N	N
22 ***DeLay***	#	Y	Y	Y	?	N	N	N
23 ***Bonilla***	Y	Y	Y	Y	N	N	N	N
24 Frost	?	?	?	?	?	?	?	?
25 Andrews	N	N	N	Y	Y	Y	Y	Y
26 ***Armey***	Y	Y	Y	Y	N	N	N	N
27 Ortiz	N	N	N	Y	Y	Y	Y	Y
28 Tejeda	N	N	N	Y	Y	Y	Y	Y
29 Green	N	N	N	N	Y	Y	Y	Y
30 Johnson, E. B.	N	N	N	N	Y	Y	Y	Y
UTAH								
1 ***Hansen***	Y	Y	Y	Y	N	N	N	N
2 Shepherd	N	N	N	N	P	Y	Y	Y
3 Orton	N	N	N	Y	Y	Y	N	Y
VERMONT								
AL *Sanders*	N	N	N	N	Y	Y	Y	Y
VIRGINIA								
1 ***Bateman***	Y	Y	Y	Y	Y	N	N	N
2 Pickett	N	N	N	Y	Y	Y	N	Y
3 Scott	N	N	N	N	Y	Y	Y	Y
4 Sisisky	N	N	N	Y	Y	Y	N	Y
5 Payne	N	Y	N	Y	Y	Y	N	Y
6 ***Goodlatte***	Y	Y	Y	Y	N	N	N	N
7 ***Bliley***	Y	Y	Y	Y	N	N	N	N
8 Moran	N	N	N	N	Y	?	?	Y
9 Boucher	N	N	N	N	Y	Y	Y	Y
10 ***Wolf***	Y	Y	Y	Y	N	N	N	N
11 Byrne	N	N	N	N	Y	Y	N	?
WASHINGTON								
1 Cantwell	N	N	Y	Y	Y	Y	Y	Y
2 Swift	N	N	N	N	Y	Y	Y	Y
3 Unsoeld	N	N	N	N	Y	Y	Y	Y
4 Inslee	Y	N	N	Y	Y	Y	Y	Y
5 Foley							Y	Y
6 Dicks	N	N	N	N	Y	Y	Y	Y
7 McDermott	N	N	N	N	Y	Y	Y	Y
8 ***Dunn***	Y	Y	Y	Y	N	N	N	N
9 Kreidler	N	N	N	N	Y	Y	Y	Y
WEST VIRGINIA								
1 Mollohan	N	N	N	N	Y	Y	Y	Y
2 Wise	N	N	N	N	Y	Y	Y	Y
3 Rahall	N	N	N	Y	Y	Y	Y	Y
WISCONSIN								
1 Barca	N	N	N	N	Y	Y	Y	Y
2 ***Klug***	Y	Y	Y	Y	N	N	N	N
3 ***Gunderson***	N	N	N	Y	Y	N	N	N
4 Kleczka	N	N	N	N	Y	Y	Y	Y
5 Barrett	N	N	N	Y	Y	Y	Y	Y
6 ***Petri***	Y	N	Y	Y	Y	N	N	N
7 Obey	N	N	Y	Y	Y	Y	Y	Y
8 ***Roth***	N	Y	Y	Y	Y	N	N	N
9 ***Sensenbrenner***	Y	Y	Y	Y	N	N	N	N
WYOMING								
AL ***Thomas***	Y	Y	Y	Y	N	N	N	N
DELEGATES								
de Lugo, V.I.	N	N	N	N	D	D	D	D
Faleomavaega, Am.S.	N	N	N	N	D	D	D	D
Norton, D.C.	N	N	N	N	D	D	D	D
Romero-B., P.R.	N	N	N	N	D	D	D	D
Underwood, Guam	?	?	?	?	D	D	D	D

Southern states - Ala., Ark., Fla., Ga., Ky., La., Miss., N.C., Okla., S.C., Tenn., Texas, Va.
Omitted votes are quorum calls, which CQ does not include in its vote charts.

KEY

Y	Voted for (yea).
#	Paired for.
+	Announced for.
N	Voted against (nay).
X	Paired against.
−	Announced against.
P	Voted ''present.''
C	Voted ''present'' to avoid possible conflict of interest.
?	Did not vote or otherwise make a position known.
D	Delegates ineligible to vote.

Democrats **Republicans**
Independent

357. H Res 222. House Post Office Investigation/Immediate Release. Gephardt, D-Mo., motion to table (kill) the Michel, R-Ill., resolution to provide for the immediate public release of the transcripts of a 1992 House Administration Committee investigation into the House Post Office. Motion agreed to 242-186: R 0-173; D 241-13 (ND 168-2, SD 73-11); I 1-0, July 22, 1993.

358. Procedural Motion. Gephardt, D-Mo., motion to adjourn. Motion agreed to 235-190: R 0-172; D 234-18 (ND 156-13, SD 78-5); I 1-0, July 22, 1993.

359. Procedural Motion. Approval of the House Journal of Thursday, July 22. Approved 232-156: R 13-153; D 219-3 (ND 146-3, SD 73-0); I 0-0, July 23, 1993.

360. HR 2200. NASA Authorization/Advanced Solid Rocket Motor. Sensenbrenner, R-Wis., en bloc amendment to cut the $35 million in the bill to transfer the remaining activities of the Advanced Solid Rocket Motor program from Utah to Yellow Creek, Miss. Adopted in the Committee of the Whole 276-139: R 148-21; D 127-118 (ND 101-66, SD 26-52); I 1-0, July 23, 1993.

361. HR 2200. NASA Authorization/CIESIN. Walker, R-Pa., amendment to cut the $18 million in the bill for the Consortium for International Earth Science Information Network (CIESIN). Rejected in the Committee of the Whole 189-226: R 157-10; D 32-215 (ND 20-149, SD 12-66); I 0-1, July 23, 1993.

362. HR 2200. NASA Authorization/CIESIN. Hefley, R-Colo., amendment to cut the funding in the bill for the Consortium for International Earth Science Information Network (CIESIN) by $8 million. Rejected in the Committee of the Whole 188-220: R 157-7; D 31-212 (ND 20-148, SD 11-64); I 0-1, July 23, 1993.

363. Procedural Motion. Synar, D-Okla., motion that when the House adjourns that it next meet at noon on Monday, July 26. Motion agreed to 215-169: R 4-148; D 210-21 (ND 141-15, SD 69-6); I 1-0, July 23, 1993.

364. Procedural Motion. Gephardt, D-Mo., motion to adjourn. Motion agreed to 200-173: R 0-144; D 199-29 (ND 133-20, SD 66-9); I 1-0, July 23, 1993.

	357	358	359	360	361	362	363	364
ALABAMA								
1 *Callahan*	N	N	N	N	Y	Y	N	N
2 *Everett*	N	N	N	Y	Y	Y	N	N
3 Browder	Y	Y	N	N	N	N	Y	Y
4 Bevill	Y	Y	?	?	?	?	?	?
5 Cramer	Y	Y	Y	N	N	N	Y	Y
6 *Bachus*	N	N	N	N	Y	Y	N	N
7 Hilliard	Y	Y	Y	N	N	N	Y	Y
ALASKA								
AL *Young*	N	N	?	Y	Y	Y	N	N
ARIZONA								
1 Coppersmith	Y	Y	Y	N	N	N	Y	Y
2 Pastor	Y	Y	Y	Y	N	Y	Y	Y
3 *Stump*	N	N	N	Y	Y	Y	N	N
4 *Kyl*	N	N	N	Y	Y	Y	N	N
5 *Kolbe*	N	N	N	Y	Y	Y	N	N
6 English	Y	Y	Y	Y	N	N	N	Y
ARKANSAS								
1 Lambert	Y	Y	Y	N	N	N	N	N
2 Thornton	Y	Y	Y	N	N	N	Y	Y
3 *Hutchinson*	N	N	N	Y	Y	Y	N	N
4 *Dickey*	N	N	N	Y	Y	Y	N	N
CALIFORNIA								
1 Hamburg	Y	Y	Y	N	N	N	Y	Y
2 *Herger*	N	N	N	Y	Y	Y	N	N
3 Fazio	Y	Y	Y	N	N	N	Y	Y
4 *Doolittle*	N	N	N	Y	Y	Y	N	N
5 Matsui	Y	Y	Y	N	N	N	Y	Y
6 Woolsey	Y	Y	Y	N	N	N	Y	Y
7 Miller	Y	Y	Y	N	N	N	Y	Y
8 Pelosi	Y	Y	Y	N	N	N	Y	Y
9 Dellums	Y	Y	Y	N	N	N	Y	Y
10 *Baker*	N	N	N	Y	Y	Y	N	N
11 *Pombo*	N	N	N	Y	Y	Y	N	N
12 Lantos	Y	Y	Y	N	N	N	Y	Y
13 Stark	Y	Y	Y	N	Y	Y	Y	Y
14 Eshoo	Y	Y	Y	N	N	N	Y	Y
15 Mineta	Y	Y	Y	N	N	N	Y	Y
16 Edwards	Y	Y	?	N	N	N	Y	Y
17 Farr	Y	Y	Y	N	N	N	Y	Y
18 Condit	Y	Y	Y	Y	Y	Y	N	N
19 Lehman	Y	Y	Y	N	N	N	Y	Y
20 Dooley	Y	Y	?	?	?	?	?	?
21 *Thomas*	N	N	N	Y	Y	Y	N	N
22 *Huffington*	N	N	N	Y	Y	Y	N	N
23 *Gallegly*	N	?	?	?	?	?	?	?
24 Beilenson	Y	Y	Y	N	Y	N	Y	Y
25 *McKeon*	N	N	N	Y	Y	Y	N	N
26 Berman	Y	Y	Y	N	N	?	?	?
27 *Moorhead*	N	N	N	Y	Y	Y	N	N
28 *Dreier*	N	N	N	Y	Y	Y	N	N
29 Waxman	Y	Y	Y	N	N	N	Y	Y
30 Becerra	Y	Y	Y	N	N	N	Y	Y
31 Martinez	Y	Y	Y	N	Y	N	Y	Y
32 Dixon	Y	Y	?	N	N	N	Y	Y
33 Roybal-Allard	Y	Y	Y	N	N	N	Y	Y
34 Torres	Y	Y	Y	N	N	N	Y	Y
35 Waters	Y	Y	Y	N	N	N	Y	Y
36 Harman	Y	Y	Y	Y	N	?	?	?
37 Tucker	Y	Y	?	Y	N	N	Y	Y
38 *Horn*	N	N	N	Y	Y	Y	N	N
39 *Royce*	N	N	N	Y	Y	Y	N	N
40 *Lewis*	N	N	N	N	N	Y	N	N
41 *Kim*	N	N	N	Y	Y	Y	N	N

	357	358	359	360	361	362	363	364
42 Brown	Y	Y	Y	N	N	N	?	?
43 *Calvert*	N	N	N	Y	Y	Y	N	N
44 *McCandless*	N	N	?	?	?	?	?	?
45 *Rohrabacher*	N	N	N	Y	Y	Y	N	N
46 *Dornan*	N	N	N	Y	Y	Y	N	N
47 *Cox*	N	N	N	Y	Y	Y	N	N
48 *Packard*	+	−	−	+	+	+	−	−
49 Schenk	Y	Y	Y	N	N	N	Y	Y
50 Filner	Y	Y	Y	N	N	N	Y	Y
51 *Cunningham*	N	N	N	Y	Y	Y	N	N
52 *Hunter*	N	N	N	Y	?	Y	N	N
COLORADO								
1 Schroeder	Y	Y	?	+	+	+	+	+
2 Skaggs	Y	Y	?	N	N	N	Y	Y
3 *McInnis*	N	N	N	Y	Y	Y	N	N
4 *Allard*	N	N	N	Y	Y	Y	N	N
5 *Hefley*	N	N	N	Y	Y	Y	N	N
6 *Schaefer*	N	N	N	Y	Y	Y	N	N
CONNECTICUT								
1 Kennelly	Y	Y	Y	Y	N	N	Y	Y
2 Gejdenson	Y	Y	Y	N	N	N	Y	?
3 DeLauro	Y	Y	Y	N	N	N	Y	Y
4 *Shays*	N	N	N	Y	N	Y	N	N
5 *Franks*	N	N	N	Y	Y	Y	N	N
6 *Johnson*	N	N	N	Y	Y	Y	N	N
DELAWARE								
AL *Castle*	N	N	N	Y	Y	Y	N	N
FLORIDA								
1 Hutto	N	Y	Y	N	Y	Y	Y	Y
2 Peterson	Y	Y	Y	N	N	N	Y	Y
3 Brown	Y	Y	Y	Y	N	N	Y	Y
4 *Fowler*	N	N	N	Y	Y	Y	N	N
5 Thurman	Y	Y	Y	N	N	N	Y	Y
6 *Stearns*	N	N	N	Y	Y	Y	N	N
7 *Mica*	N	N	N	Y	Y	?	?	?
8 *McCollum*	N	N	N	Y	Y	Y	N	N
9 *Bilirakis*	N	N	N	Y	#	?	?	?
10 *Young*	N	N	N	Y	Y	Y	N	N
11 Gibbons	Y	Y	Y	N	N	N	Y	Y
12 *Canady*	N	N	N	Y	Y	Y	N	N
13 *Miller*	N	N	N	Y	Y	Y	N	N
14 *Goss*	N	N	N	Y	Y	Y	N	N
15 Bacchus	N	Y	Y	N	N	N	Y	Y
16 *Lewis*	N	N	N	Y	Y	Y	N	N
17 Meek	Y	Y	Y	N	N	N	Y	Y
18 *Ros-Lehtinen*	N	N	N	Y	Y	?	?	?
19 Johnston	Y	Y	Y	N	N	Y	Y	Y
20 Deutsch	Y	Y	Y	N	N	N	Y	?
21 *Diaz-Balart*	N	N	N	Y	Y	?	?	?
22 *Shaw*	N	N	N	Y	Y	Y	N	N
23 Hastings	Y	Y	Y	N	N	N	Y	Y
GEORGIA								
1 *Kingston*	N	N	N	Y	Y	Y	N	N
2 Bishop	Y	Y	Y	N	N	N	Y	Y
3 *Collins*	N	N	N	Y	Y	Y	N	N
4 *Linder*	N	N	N	Y	Y	Y	N	N
5 Lewis	Y	Y	Y	N	N	N	Y	Y
6 *Gingrich*	N	N	N	Y	Y	Y	N	?
7 Darden	Y	Y	Y	N	N	N	Y	Y
8 Rowland	Y	Y	Y	N	N	N	Y	Y
9 Deal	Y	Y	Y	N	N	N	Y	Y
10 Johnson	Y	Y	Y	N	N	N	Y	Y
11 McKinney	Y	Y	?	X	X	X	?	?
HAWAII								
1 Abercrombie	Y	Y	Y	N	N	N	Y	Y
2 Mink	Y	Y	Y	N	N	N	Y	Y
IDAHO								
1 LaRocco	Y	Y	Y	N	N	N	Y	Y
2 *Crapo*	N	N	N	Y	Y	Y	N	N
ILLINOIS								
1 Rush	Y	Y	?	N	N	N	Y	Y
2 Reynolds	Y	Y	Y	N	N	N	Y	Y
3 Lipinski	Y	Y	Y	N	N	N	Y	Y
4 Gutierrez	Y	Y	Y	N	N	N	Y	Y
5 Rostenkowski	Y	Y	Y	N	N	N	Y	Y
6 *Hyde*	N	N	N	Y	Y	N	N	N
7 Collins	Y	Y	?	?	?	X	?	?
8 *Crane*	N	N	N	Y	Y	Y	N	N
9 Yates	Y	Y	Y	N	N	N	Y	Y
10 *Porter*	N	N	N	Y	Y	Y	N	N
11 Sangmeister	Y	Y	Y	N	N	N	Y	Y
12 Costello	Y	N	Y	N	N	N	Y	Y
13 *Fawell*	N	N	N	Y	Y	Y	N	N
14 *Hastert*	N	N	N	Y	Y	N	N	N
15 *Ewing*	N	N	N	Y	Y	Y	N	N
16 *Manzullo*	N	N	N	Y	Y	Y	N	N
17 Evans	Y	Y	Y	Y	N	N	N	N

ND Northern Democrats   SD Southern Democrats

	357	358	359	360	361	362	363	364
18 ***Michel***	N	N	N	Y	Y	Y	N	N
19 Poshard	Y	N	Y	Y	Y	Y	N	N
20 Durbin	Y	Y	Y	Y	N	N	N	N
INDIANA								
1 Visclosky	Y	Y	Y	Y	N	N	Y	Y
2 Sharp	Y	Y	Y	Y	Y	Y	Y	Y
3 Roemer	Y	Y	Y	N	Y	N	Y	N
4 Long	Y	Y	Y	N	Y	Y	Y	N
5 ***Buyer***	N	N	N	Y	Y	Y	N	N
6 ***Burton***	N	N	N	Y	Y	Y	?	?
7 ***Myers***	N	N	Y	Y	Y	?	?	?
8 McCloskey	Y	Y	Y	N	N	N	Y	Y
9 Hamilton	Y	Y	Y	Y	Y	Y	Y	Y
10 Jacobs	Y	Y	N	Y	Y	Y	Y	Y
IOWA								
1 ***Leach***	N	N	N	Y	Y	Y	N	N
2 ***Nussle***	N	N	N	Y	Y	Y	N	N
3 ***Lightfoot***	N	N	N	Y	Y	Y	N	N
4 Smith	Y	N	Y	N	N	N	N	N
5 ***Grandy***	P	N	N	Y	Y	Y	N	N
KANSAS								
1 ***Roberts***	N	N	N	Y	#	#	?	?
2 Slattery	Y	Y	?	Y	N	N	N	N
3 ***Meyers***	N	N	N	Y	Y	Y	N	N
4 Glickman	Y	Y	Y	Y	Y	N	Y	Y
KENTUCKY								
1 Barlow	Y	Y	Y	N	N	N	Y	N
2 Natcher	Y	Y	Y	N	N	N	Y	Y
3 Mazzoli	N	Y	Y	Y	N	N	Y	Y
4 ***Bunning***	N	N	N	Y	Y	Y	N	N
5 ***Rogers***	N	N	N	Y	Y	Y	N	N
6 Baesler	Y	Y	Y	Y	N	N	Y	Y
LOUISIANA								
1 ***Livingston***	N	N	N	N	Y	Y	N	N
2 Jefferson	Y	Y	?	N	N	?	?	?
3 Tauzin	N	Y	Y	N	Y	Y	Y	N
4 Fields	Y	Y	?	?	?	?	?	?
5 ***McCrery***	N	N	N	Y	Y	Y	N	N
6 ***Baker***	N	N	?	?	?	?	?	?
7 Hayes	N	Y	Y	N	N	N	Y	Y
MAINE								
1 Andrews	Y	Y	Y	N	N	N	Y	Y
2 ***Snowe***	N	N	N	Y	Y	Y	N	N
MARYLAND								
1 ***Gilchrest***	N	N	N	Y	Y	Y	N	N
2 ***Bentley***	N	N	N	N	Y	Y	N	N
3 Cardin	Y	Y	Y	Y	N	N	Y	Y
4 Wynn	Y	Y	Y	N	N	N	Y	Y
5 Hoyer	Y	Y	Y	N	N	N	Y	Y
6 ***Bartlett***	N	N	N	Y	Y	Y	N	N
7 Mfume	Y	Y	Y	Y	N	N	Y	Y
8 ***Morella***	N	N	N	N	N	N	N	N
MASSACHUSETTS								
1 Olver	Y	Y	Y	Y	N	N	Y	Y
2 Neal	Y	Y	Y	Y	N	Y	Y	Y
3 ***Blute***	N	N	N	Y	Y	Y	N	N
4 Frank	Y	Y	Y	Y	N	N	Y	Y
5 Meehan	Y	N	Y	Y	N	Y	N	N
6 ***Torkildsen***	N	N	N	Y	Y	Y	N	N
7 Markey	Y	Y	?	Y	N	N	Y	Y
8 Kennedy	Y	Y	Y	N	N	Y	Y	Y
9 Moakley	?	?	?	?	?	?	?	?
10 Studds	Y	Y	Y	Y	N	N	Y	?
MICHIGAN								
1 Stupak	Y	N	Y	Y	N	N	Y	Y
2 ***Hoekstra***	N	N	N	Y	N	N	N	N
3 Henry	?	?	?	?	?	?	?	?
4 ***Camp***	N	N	N	Y	N	N	N	N
5 Barcia	Y	Y	Y	Y	N	N	N	N
6 ***Upton***	N	N	N	Y	N	N	N	N
7 ***Smith***	N	N	N	Y	N	N	Y	N
8 Carr	Y	Y	Y	N	N	N	Y	Y
9 Kildee	Y	Y	Y	Y	N	N	Y	Y
10 Bonior	Y	Y	?	N	N	N	Y	Y
11 ***Knollenberg***	N	N	N	Y	N	N	N	N
12 Levin	Y	Y	Y	Y	N	N	Y	Y
13 Ford	Y	Y	?	Y	N	N	Y	Y
14 Conyers	?	?	?	?	?	X	?	?
15 Collins	Y	Y	Y	Y	N	N	Y	Y
16 Dingell	Y	Y	Y	N	N	N	Y	Y
MINNESOTA								
1 Penny	Y	N	Y	Y	Y	Y	N	N
2 Minge	Y	N	Y	Y	Y	Y	N	N
3 ***Ramstad***	N	N	N	Y	Y	Y	N	N
4 Vento	Y	Y	?	?	?	?	?	?

	357	358	359	360	361	362	363	364
5 Sabo	Y	Y	Y	Y	N	N	Y	Y
6 ***Grams***	N	N	N	Y	Y	Y	N	N
7 Peterson	N	N	Y	Y	Y	Y	N	N
8 Oberstar	Y	Y	Y	Y	N	N	Y	Y
MISSISSIPPI								
1 Whitten	Y	Y	?	N	N	N	Y	Y
2 Thompson	Y	Y	Y	N	N	N	Y	Y
3 Montgomery	Y	Y	Y	N	Y	Y	Y	Y
4 Parker	N	N	?	N	N	N	N	N
5 Taylor	N	Y	Y	N	N	N	Y	Y
MISSOURI								
1 Clay	Y	Y	N	N	N	N	?	?
2 ***Talent***	N	N	N	Y	Y	Y	N	N
3 Gephardt	Y	Y	Y	N	N	N	Y	Y
4 Skelton	Y	Y	Y	Y	Y	N	Y	Y
5 Wheat	Y	Y	Y	N	N	N	Y	Y
6 Danner	Y	Y	Y	Y	N	N	Y	N
7 ***Hancock***	N	N	N	Y	Y	Y	N	N
8 ***Emerson***	N	N	N	N	Y	Y	N	N
9 Volkmer	Y	Y	Y	N	N	N	Y	Y
MONTANA								
AL Williams	Y	N	Y	Y	N	Y	N	N
NEBRASKA								
1 ***Bereuter***	N	N	N	Y	Y	Y	N	N
2 Hoagland	Y	Y	Y	Y	N	N	N	N
3 ***Barrett***	N	N	N	Y	Y	Y	N	N
NEVADA								
1 Bilbray	Y	Y	Y	Y	N	N	Y	Y
2 ***Vucanovich***	N	N	N	N	Y	Y	N	N
NEW HAMPSHIRE								
1 ***Zeliff***	N	N	N	Y	Y	Y	N	N
2 Swett	Y	N	Y	Y	N	N	Y	Y
NEW JERSEY								
1 Andrews	Y	Y	Y	Y	N	N	Y	Y
2 Hughes	Y	Y	Y	N	N	N	Y	Y
3 ***Saxton***	N	N	N	Y	Y	Y	N	N
4 ***Smith***	N	N	Y	Y	Y	Y	N	N
5 ***Roukema***	N	N	N	Y	Y	Y	N	N
6 Pallone	Y	Y	Y	Y	N	N	Y	Y
7 ***Franks***	N	N	N	Y	Y	Y	N	N
8 Klein	Y	Y	Y	N	N	N	Y	Y
9 Torricelli	Y	Y	Y	N	N	N	Y	Y
10 Payne	Y	Y	Y	N	N	N	Y	Y
11 ***Gallo***	N	N	N	Y	Y	Y	N	N
12 ***Zimmer***	N	N	N	Y	Y	Y	N	N
13 Menendez	Y	N	Y	N	N	N	Y	Y
NEW MEXICO								
1 ***Schiff***	N	N	N	Y	Y	Y	N	N
2 ***Skeen***	N	N	N	Y	Y	Y	N	?
3 Richardson	Y	Y	Y	Y	N	N	Y	Y
NEW YORK								
1 Hochbrueckner	Y	Y	Y	N	N	N	Y	Y
2 ***Lazio***	N	N	N	Y	Y	Y	N	N
3 ***King***	N	N	N	Y	Y	Y	N	N
4 ***Levy***	N	N	N	Y	Y	Y	N	N
5 Ackerman	Y	Y	Y	N	N	N	?	?
6 Flake	Y	Y	Y	N	N	N	Y	Y
7 Manton	Y	Y	Y	N	N	N	Y	Y
8 Nadler	Y	?	?	N	N	N	Y	Y
9 Schumer	Y	Y	Y	Y	N	N	Y	Y
10 Towns	Y	Y	Y	N	N	N	Y	N
11 Owens	Y	Y	Y	Y	N	N	?	?
12 Velazquez	Y	Y	Y	Y	N	N	Y	Y
13 ***Molinari***	N	N	N	Y	Y	Y	N	N
14 Maloney	Y	Y	Y	Y	N	N	Y	Y
15 Rangel	Y	Y	?	N	N	N	Y	Y
16 Serrano	Y	Y	Y	N	N	N	Y	Y
17 Engel	Y	Y	Y	N	N	N	Y	Y
18 Lowey	Y	Y	Y	Y	N	N	Y	Y
19 ***Fish***	N	N	Y	Y	Y	Y	N	N
20 ***Gilman***	N	N	N	Y	Y	Y	N	N
21 McNulty	Y	Y	Y	Y	N	N	Y	?
22 ***Solomon***	N	N	N	Y	Y	Y	N	N
23 ***Boehlert***	N	N	N	Y	Y	Y	N	N
24 ***McHugh***	N	N	N	Y	Y	Y	N	N
25 ***Walsh***	N	N	?	Y	Y	Y	?	?
26 Hinchey	Y	Y	?	Y	N	N	Y	Y
27 ***Paxon***	N	N	N	Y	Y	Y	N	N
28 Slaughter	Y	Y	Y	N	N	N	Y	Y
29 LaFalce	Y	Y	Y	Y	Y	N	?	?
30 ***Quinn***	N	N	N	Y	Y	Y	N	N
31 ***Houghton***	N	N	Y	N	Y	Y	?	?
NORTH CAROLINA								
1 Clayton	Y	Y	Y	?	N	N	Y	Y
2 Valentine	Y	Y	Y	N	N	N	Y	Y

	357	358	359	360	361	362	363	364
3 Lancaster	Y	Y	Y	Y	N	N	Y	Y
4 Price	Y	Y	Y	Y	N	N	Y	Y
5 Neal	Y	Y	?	Y	N	N	Y	Y
6 ***Coble***	N	N	N	Y	Y	Y	N	N
7 Rose	Y	?	Y	N	N	N	Y	Y
8 Hefner	Y	Y	Y	Y	N	N	Y	Y
9 ***McMillan***	N	N	N	Y	Y	Y	N	N
10 ***Ballenger***	N	N	N	Y	Y	+	—	—
11 ***Taylor***	N	N	N	Y	Y	Y	?	?
12 Watt	Y	Y	Y	N	N	N	Y	Y
NORTH DAKOTA								
AL Pomeroy	Y	N	Y	N	N	N	Y	N
OHIO								
1 Mann	Y	Y	Y	Y	Y	N	Y	Y
2 ***Portman***	N	N	N	Y	Y	Y	N	N
3 Hall	Y	Y	Y	Y	N	N	Y	?
4 ***Oxley***	N	N	N	Y	Y	Y	N	N
5 ***Gillmor***	N	N	Y	Y	Y	Y	N	N
6 Strickland	Y	Y	Y	Y	N	N	Y	Y
7 ***Hobson***	N	N	N	Y	Y	Y	N	N
8 ***Boehner***	N	?	N	Y	Y	Y	N	N
9 Kaptur	Y	Y	?	N	N	N	Y	Y
10 ***Hoke***	N	N	N	Y	Y	Y	N	N
11 Stokes	Y	Y	?	N	N	N	Y	Y
12 ***Kasich***	N	N	Y	Y	Y	Y	N	N
13 Brown	Y	Y	Y	Y	N	N	Y	Y
14 Sawyer	Y	Y	Y	Y	N	N	Y	Y
15 ***Pryce***	N	N	N	Y	Y	Y	N	N
16 ***Regula***	N	N	N	Y	Y	Y	N	N
17 Traficant	Y	Y	Y	Y	N	N	N	Y
18 Applegate	Y	Y	Y	Y	N	N	Y	Y
19 Fingerhut	Y	Y	Y	Y	N	N	Y	Y
OKLAHOMA								
1 ***Inhofe***	N	N	N	Y	Y	Y	?	?
2 Synar	Y	Y	Y	Y	Y	Y	Y	Y
3 Brewster	Y	Y	Y	N	N	N	Y	Y
4 McCurdy	Y	N	Y	Y	Y	Y	Y	Y
5 ***Istook***	N	N	N	Y	Y	Y	N	N
6 English	Y	Y	Y	N	N	Y	Y	Y
OREGON								
1 Furse	Y	Y	Y	N	N	N	Y	Y
2 ***Smith***	N	N	N	Y	Y	Y	N	N
3 Wyden	Y	Y	Y	Y	Y	N	Y	Y
4 DeFazio	Y	Y	?	?	N	N	Y	Y
5 Kopetski	Y	Y	Y	?	N	N	Y	Y
PENNSYLVANIA								
1 Foglietta	Y	Y	Y	Y	N	N	Y	Y
2 Blackwell	Y	Y	Y	N	N	N	Y	Y
3 Borski	Y	Y	Y	N	N	N	Y	Y
4 Klink	Y	Y	Y	Y	N	N	Y	Y
5 ***Clinger***	N	N	N	Y	Y	Y	N	N
6 Holden	Y	Y	Y	Y	N	N	?	?
7 ***Weldon***	N	N	N	Y	Y	Y	N	N
8 ***Greenwood***	N	N	N	Y	Y	Y	N	N
9 ***Shuster***	N	N	N	Y	Y	Y	N	?
10 ***McDade***	N	N	N	N	Y	Y	N	N
11 Kanjorski	Y	Y	Y	Y	N	N	Y	Y
12 Murtha	Y	Y	Y	N	N	N	Y	Y
13 Margolies-Mezv.	Y	Y	Y	Y	Y	Y	Y	Y
14 Coyne	Y	Y	Y	Y	N	N	Y	Y
15 McHale	Y	Y	Y	Y	N	N	Y	Y
16 ***Walker***	N	N	N	N	Y	Y	N	N
17 ***Gekas***	N	N	N	Y	Y	Y	N	N
18 ***Santorum***	N	N	?	?	?	?	?	?
19 ***Goodling***	N	N	N	Y	Y	Y	N	—
20 Murphy	N	Y	N	Y	Y	Y	?	?
21 ***Ridge***	N	N	N	Y	Y	Y	N	N
RHODE ISLAND								
1 ***Machtley***	N	N	N	Y	Y	?	?	?
2 Reed	Y	Y	Y	Y	N	N	Y	Y
SOUTH CAROLINA								
1 ***Ravenel***	N	N	N	Y	Y	Y	N	N
2 ***Spence***	N	N	N	Y	Y	Y	N	N
3 Derrick	Y	Y	Y	N	N	N	Y	Y
4 ***Inglis***	N	N	Y	Y	Y	Y	?	?
5 Spratt	Y	Y	Y	Y	N	N	Y	Y
6 Clyburn	Y	Y	Y	Y	N	N	Y	Y
SOUTH DAKOTA								
AL Johnson	Y	N	Y	Y	Y	Y	N	N
TENNESSEE								
1 ***Quillen***	N	N	N	N	Y	Y	?	?
2 ***Duncan***	N	N	N	Y	Y	Y	N	N
3 Lloyd	Y	N	Y	N	N	?	?	?
4 Cooper	N	Y	?	?	?	?	?	?
5 Clement	Y	Y	Y	N	N	N	Y	Y

	357	358	359	360	361	362	363	364
6 Gordon	Y	Y	Y	Y	Y	Y	Y	Y
7 ***Sundquist***	N	N	N	N	Y	Y	N	N
8 Tanner	Y	N	Y	N	N	N	N	N
9 Ford	N	Y	Y	N	N	N	Y	Y
TEXAS								
1 Chapman	Y	Y	?	Y	N	N	Y	Y
2 Wilson	Y	Y	?	N	N	?	Y	Y
3 ***Johnson, Sam***	N	N	?	Y	Y	Y	?	?
4 Hall	N	Y	Y	N	N	N	Y	Y
5 Bryant	Y	Y	Y	Y	N	N	Y	Y
6 ***Barton***	N	N	N	N	Y	Y	N	N
7 ***Archer***	N	N	Y	Y	Y	Y	N	N
8 ***Fields***	N	N	?	Y	Y	Y	N	N
9 Brooks	Y	Y	Y	N	N	N	Y	Y
10 Pickle	Y	Y	Y	N	N	N	?	Y
11 Edwards	Y	Y	Y	Y	N	N	Y	Y
12 Geren	Y	Y	Y	N	N	N	Y	Y
13 Sarpalius	Y	Y	Y	N	N	N	Y	Y
14 Laughlin	Y	Y	Y	N	N	N	?	?
15 de la Garza	Y	Y	Y	Y	N	N	Y	Y
16 Coleman	Y	Y	Y	N	N	N	Y	N
17 Stenholm	Y	Y	Y	Y	Y	Y	Y	Y
18 Washington	Y	Y	?	?	?	?	?	?
19 ***Combest***	N	N	Y	Y	Y	Y	N	N
20 Gonzalez	Y	Y	Y	N	N	N	Y	Y
21 ***Smith***	N	N	N	Y	Y	Y	N	N
22 ***DeLay***	N	N	N	N	Y	Y	N	N
23 ***Bonilla***	N	N	N	Y	Y	Y	N	N
24 Frost	?	?	?	?	?	?	?	?
25 Andrews	Y	Y	Y	Y	Y	Y	Y	Y
26 ***Armey***	N	N	N	Y	Y	Y	N	N
27 Ortiz	Y	Y	Y	N	Y	N	Y	Y
28 Tejeda	Y	Y	Y	Y	N	N	Y	Y
29 Green	Y	N	Y	N	N	N	N	N
30 Johnson, E. B.	Y	Y	Y	N	N	N	Y	Y
UTAH								
1 ***Hansen***	N	N	N	Y	Y	Y	N	N
2 Shepherd	Y	Y	Y	Y	N	N	Y	Y
3 Orton	Y	Y	Y	Y	Y	Y	Y	Y
VERMONT								
AL *Sanders*	Y	Y	?	Y	N	N	Y	Y
VIRGINIA								
1 ***Bateman***	N	N	Y	Y	Y	Y	N	?
2 Pickett	Y	Y	Y	N	Y	Y	Y	Y
3 Scott	Y	Y	Y	N	N	N	Y	Y
4 Sisisky	Y	Y	Y	Y	Y	Y	Y	Y
5 Payne	Y	Y	Y	Y	N	N	Y	Y
6 ***Goodlatte***	N	N	N	Y	Y	Y	N	N
7 ***Bliley***	N	N	N	Y	Y	Y	N	N
8 Moran	Y	Y	Y	N	?	?	Y	Y
9 Boucher	Y	Y	Y	N	N	N	Y	Y
10 ***Wolf***	N	N	N	Y	Y	Y	N	N
11 Byrne	N	Y	Y	N	N	N	Y	Y
WASHINGTON								
1 Cantwell	Y	Y	Y	Y	N	N	Y	Y
2 Swift	Y	Y	Y	N	N	N	Y	Y
3 Unsoeld	Y	Y	Y	Y	N	N	Y	Y
4 Inslee	Y	Y	Y	Y	N	N	Y	Y
5 Foley								Y
6 Dicks	Y	Y	Y	N	N	N	Y	Y
7 McDermott	Y	Y	?	?	?	?	?	?
8 ***Dunn***	N	N	N	Y	Y	Y	N	N
9 Kreidler	Y	Y	Y	Y	N	N	Y	Y
WEST VIRGINIA								
1 Mollohan	Y	Y	?	N	N	N	Y	Y
2 Wise	Y	Y	Y	Y	N	N	Y	Y
3 Rahall	Y	Y	Y	Y	N	N	Y	Y
WISCONSIN								
1 Barca	Y	Y	Y	Y	N	N	Y	Y
2 ***Klug***	N	N	N	Y	Y	Y	?	?
3 ***Gunderson***	N	N	Y	Y	Y	Y	N	?
4 Kleczka	Y	Y	Y	Y	N	N	Y	Y
5 Barrett	Y	Y	Y	Y	N	N	Y	Y
6 ***Petri***	N	N	N	Y	Y	Y	N	N
7 Obey	Y	Y	Y	Y	N	N	Y	Y
8 ***Roth***	N	N	N	#	?	#	?	?
9 ***Sensenbrenner***	N	N	N	Y	Y	Y	N	N
WYOMING								
AL ***Thomas***	N	N	N	Y	Y	Y	N	N
DELEGATES								
de Lugo, V.I.	D	D	D	N	N	N	D	D
Faleomavaega, Am.S.	D	D	D	Y	N	N	D	D
Norton, D.C.	D	D	D	N	N	N	D	D
Romero-B., P.R.	D	D	D	Y	N	N	D	D
Underwood, Guam	D	D	D	?	?	?	D	D

Southern states - Ala., Ark., Fla., Ga., Ky., La., Miss., N.C., Okla., S.C., Tenn., Texas, Va.
Omitted votes are quorum calls, which CQ does not include in its vote charts.

365. HR 1757. National Information Infrastructure/Passage. Boucher, D-Va., motion to suspend the rules and pass the bill to authorize $1 billion over 1994-98 for a coordinated federal program to expedite the development of applications for high-performance computing and high-speed networking. Motion agreed to 326-61: R 98-60; D 227-1 (ND 151-1, SD 76-0); I 1-0, July 26, 1993. A two-thirds majority of those present and voting (258 in this case) is required for passage under suspension of the rules. A "yea" was a vote in support of the president's position.

366. H Res 188. China Olympics Opposition/Passage. Lantos, D-Calif., motion to suspend the rules and pass the resolution to express the sense of the House of Representatives that, as a response to human rights violations, the 2000 Olympics should not be in China. Motion agreed to 287-99: R 121-39; D 165-60 (ND 117-32, SD 48-28); I 1-0, July 26, 1993. A two-thirds majority of those present and voting (258 in this case) is required for passage under suspension of the rules.

367. Procedural Motion. Approval of the House Journal of Monday, July 26. Approved 262-153: R 20-148; D 241-5 (ND 161-4, SD 80-1); I 1-0, July 27, 1993.

368. HR 2667. Fiscal 1993 Disaster Supplemental Appropriations/Rule. Adoption of the rule (H Res 226) to provide for House floor consideration of the bill to provide $2,742,855,000 in new budgetary authority in fiscal 1993 for emergency relief from widespread flooding in the Midwest and other natural disasters. (The House rejected another rule (H Res 220) on July 22. See vote 355.) Adopted 224-205: R 0-173; D 223-32 (ND 158-13, SD 65-19); I 1-0, July 27, 1993.

369. HR 2667. Fiscal 1993 Disaster Supplemental Appropriations/Youth Fair Chance. Porter, R-Ill., motion to recommit the bill to the House Appropriations Committee with instructions to report it back with an amendment to strike language added to the bill in the rule (H Res 226) pertaining to the Youth Fair Chance Program, which provides individuals ages 14 through 30 with stipends for transportation, food, grooming and other needs while they participate in paid work experience and classroom programs. Motion rejected 201-226: R 172-0; D 29-225 (ND 10-160, SD 19-65); I 0-1, July 27, 1993.

370. HR 2667. Fiscal 1993 Disaster Supplemental Appropriations/Passage. Passage of the bill to provide $2,767,855,000 in new budgetary authority in fiscal 1993 for emergency relief from widespread flooding in the Midwest and other natural disasters. Passed 400-27: R 145-27; D 254-0 (ND 170-0, SD 84-0); I 1-0, July 27, 1993. A "yea" was a vote in support of the president's position.

371. Procedural Motion. Approval of the House Journal of Tuesday, July 27. Approved 257-158: R 20-152; D 236-6 (ND 157-5, SD 79-1); I 1-0, July 28, 1993.

372. HR 2010. National Service/Volunteer Liability Protection. Bryant, D-Texas, amendment to the Porter, R-Ill., amendment, to require rather than allow states to impose certain conditions before granting volunteers of an organization liability protection. The Porter amendment provides nonprofit and government volunteers personal financial liability protection from tort claims alleging damage or injury during official work performed in good faith without misconduct for certain organizations. Adopted in the Committee of the Whole 239-194: R 3-170; D 235-24 (ND 163-13, SD 72-11); I 1-0, July 28, 1993.

KEY

Y	Voted for (yea).
#	Paired for.
+	Announced for.
N	Voted against (nay).
X	Paired against.
—	Announced against.
P	Voted "present."
C	Voted "present" to avoid possible conflict of interest.
?	Did not vote or otherwise make a position known.
D	Delegates ineligible to vote.

Democrats *Republicans*
Independent

	365	366	367	368	369	370	371	372
ALABAMA								
1 Callahan	N	N	N	N	Y	Y	N	N
2 Everett	N	Y	N	N	Y	Y	N	N
3 Browder	Y	Y	Y	Y	N	Y	Y	Y
4 Bevill	Y	Y	Y	N	Y	Y	Y	Y
5 Cramer	?	?	Y	Y	N	Y	Y	Y
6 Bachus	N	Y	N	N	Y	Y	N	N
7 Hilliard	Y	N	Y	Y	N	Y	Y	Y
ALASKA								
AL Young	N	Y	N	N	Y	Y	Y	N
ARIZONA								
1 Coppersmith	Y	Y	Y	Y	N	Y	Y	Y
2 Pastor	Y	Y	Y	Y	N	Y	Y	Y
3 Stump	N	N	N	N	Y	N	N	N
4 Kyl	N	Y	N	N	Y	Y	N	N
5 Kolbe	N	N	N	N	Y	Y	N	N
6 English	Y	Y	Y	Y	N	Y	+	Y
ARKANSAS								
1 Lambert	Y	Y	Y	Y	Y	Y	Y	Y
2 Thornton	Y	Y	Y	Y	N	Y	Y	Y
3 Hutchinson	N	Y	N	N	Y	Y	N	N
4 Dickey	N	Y	N	N	Y	Y	N	N
CALIFORNIA								
1 Hamburg	Y	Y	Y	Y	N	Y	Y	Y
2 Herger	N	N	N	N	Y	N	N	N
3 Fazio	Y	Y	Y	Y	N	Y	Y	Y
4 Doolittle	N	Y	N	N	Y	N	N	N
5 Matsui	Y	Y	Y	Y	N	Y	Y	Y
6 Woolsey	Y	Y	Y	Y	N	Y	Y	Y
7 Miller	Y	Y	Y	Y	N	Y	Y	Y
8 Pelosi	?	?	Y	Y	N	Y	Y	Y
9 Dellums	Y	N	Y	N	N	Y	Y	Y
10 Baker	Y	Y	N	N	Y	Y	N	N
11 Pombo	N	Y	N	N	Y	Y	Y	N
12 Lantos	Y	Y	Y	Y	N	Y	?	N
13 Stark	Y	Y	Y	Y	N	Y	Y	Y
14 Eshoo	Y	Y	Y	Y	N	Y	Y	Y
15 Mineta	Y	Y	Y	Y	N	Y	Y	Y
16 Edwards	Y	Y	Y	Y	N	Y	Y	Y
17 Farr	Y	Y	Y	Y	N	Y	Y	Y
18 Condit	Y	Y	Y	N	N	Y	N	Y
19 Lehman	Y	Y	Y	Y	N	Y	Y	Y
20 Dooley	Y	N	Y	N	N	Y	N	N
21 Thomas	Y	Y	N	N	Y	Y	N	N
22 Huffington	Y	Y	N	N	Y	Y	N	N
23 Gallegly	Y	Y	N	N	Y	Y	Y	N
24 Beilenson	Y	Y	Y	Y	N	Y	Y	N
25 McKeon	N	Y	N	N	Y	Y	N	N
26 Berman	?	?	Y	Y	N	Y	Y	Y
27 Moorhead	N	N	N	N	Y	N	N	N
28 Dreier	N	N	N	N	Y	Y	N	N
29 Waxman	Y	Y	Y	Y	N	Y	Y	Y
30 Becerra	Y	P	Y	Y	N	Y	Y	Y
31 Martinez	Y	N	Y	Y	N	Y	Y	Y
32 Dixon	Y	Y	Y	Y	N	Y	Y	Y
33 Roybal-Allard	Y	Y	Y	Y	N	Y	Y	Y
34 Torres	Y	Y	Y	Y	N	Y	Y	Y
35 Waters	Y	Y	Y	Y	N	Y	Y	Y
36 Harman	Y	Y	Y	Y	N	Y	Y	Y
37 Tucker	Y	Y	Y	Y	N	Y	Y	Y
38 Horn	Y	Y	N	N	N	Y	Y	N
39 Royce	N	Y	N	Y	Y	N	N	N
40 Lewis	Y	N	N	N	Y	Y	N	N
41 Kim	Y	N	N	N	Y	Y	N	N

	365	366	367	368	369	370	371	372
42 Brown	Y	N	?	Y	N	Y	?	Y
43 Calvert	Y	Y	N	N	Y	Y	N	N
44 McCandless	?	?	N	N	Y	Y	N	N
45 Rohrabacher	Y	Y	N	N	Y	N	N	N
46 Dornan	N	Y	N	Y	N	N	N	N
47 Cox	N	Y	N	N	Y	Y	N	N
48 Packard	-	+	-	-	-	+	-	-
49 Schenk	Y	Y	Y	Y	N	Y	Y	Y
50 Filner	Y	Y	Y	Y	N	Y	Y	Y
51 Cunningham	Y	Y	N	N	Y	N	N	N
52 Hunter	Y	Y	N	N	Y	N	N	N
COLORADO								
1 Schroeder	Y	Y	N	Y	N	Y	N	N
2 Skaggs	Y	N	Y	Y	N	Y	Y	Y
3 McInnis	Y	Y	N	N	Y	Y	N	N
4 Allard	Y	Y	N	N	Y	Y	N	N
5 Hefley	N	Y	N	N	Y	Y	N	N
6 Schaefer	N	N	N	N	Y	N	N	N
CONNECTICUT								
1 Kennelly	Y	N	Y	Y	N	Y	Y	Y
2 Gejdenson	Y	Y	Y	Y	N	Y	Y	Y
3 DeLauro	Y	Y	Y	Y	N	Y	Y	Y
4 Shays	Y	Y	N	N	Y	Y	N	N
5 Franks	Y	Y	N	N	Y	Y	N	N
6 Johnson	?	Y	Y	N	Y	Y	N	N
DELAWARE								
AL Castle	Y	Y	N	N	Y	Y	N	N
FLORIDA								
1 Hutto	?	?	Y	N	Y	Y	Y	N
2 Peterson	Y	Y	Y	Y	N	Y	Y	Y
3 Brown	Y	Y	Y	Y	N	Y	Y	Y
4 Fowler	Y	Y	N	N	Y	Y	N	N
5 Thurman	Y	N	Y	Y	N	Y	Y	Y
6 Stearns	Y	Y	N	N	Y	Y	N	N
7 Mica	N	N	N	N	Y	Y	N	N
8 McCollum	?	?	?	N	Y	Y	N	N
9 Bilirakis	?	Y	N	N	Y	Y	N	N
10 Young	Y	Y	N	N	Y	Y	N	N
11 Gibbons	Y	N	Y	Y	N	Y	Y	Y
12 Canady	N	Y	N	N	Y	Y	N	N
13 Miller	N	N	Y	N	Y	Y	N	N
14 Goss	N	N	N	N	Y	N	N	N
15 Bacchus	Y	Y	Y	Y	N	Y	Y	Y
16 Lewis	+	+	N	N	Y	Y	N	N
17 Meek	Y	Y	Y	Y	N	Y	Y	Y
18 Ros-Lehtinen	Y	Y	N	N	Y	Y	N	N
19 Johnston	Y	N	Y	Y	N	Y	Y	Y
20 Deutsch	Y	Y	Y	N	N	Y	Y	Y
21 Diaz-Balart	Y	Y	N	N	Y	Y	N	N
22 Shaw	Y	N	N	N	Y	Y	N	N
23 Hastings	Y	Y	Y	N	N	Y	Y	Y
GEORGIA								
1 Kingston	N	Y	Y	N	Y	Y	N	N
2 Bishop	Y	Y	Y	Y	N	Y	Y	Y
3 Collins	N	N	N	N	Y	Y	N	N
4 Linder	N	N	N	N	Y	Y	N	N
5 Lewis	Y	Y	Y	Y	N	Y	Y	Y
6 Gingrich	Y	Y	N	N	Y	Y	N	N
7 Darden	Y	N	Y	N	Y	Y	Y	Y
8 Rowland	Y	Y	Y	Y	Y	Y	Y	Y
9 Deal	Y	N	Y	Y	Y	Y	Y	Y
10 Johnson	Y	N	N	N	Y	Y	Y	Y
11 McKinney	Y	N	Y	N	Y	Y	Y	Y
HAWAII								
1 Abercrombie	Y	Y	Y	Y	N	Y	Y	Y
2 Mink	Y	Y	Y	Y	N	Y	Y	Y
IDAHO								
1 LaRocco	Y	Y	Y	Y	N	Y	Y	Y
2 Crapo	Y	Y	N	N	Y	N	N	N
ILLINOIS								
1 Rush	Y	Y	Y	Y	N	Y	Y	Y
2 Reynolds	Y	Y	Y	Y	N	Y	Y	Y
3 Lipinski	Y	Y	N	Y	Y	Y	Y	N
4 Gutierrez	Y	Y	Y	Y	N	Y	Y	Y
5 Rostenkowski	?	?	Y	Y	N	Y	Y	Y
6 Hyde	Y	N	N	N	Y	Y	N	N
7 Collins	?	?	Y	Y	N	Y	Y	Y
8 Crane	N	N	N	N	Y	N	N	N
9 Yates	Y	N	Y	Y	N	Y	Y	Y
10 Porter	Y	Y	N	N	Y	N	N	N
11 Sangmeister	Y	Y	Y	Y	N	Y	Y	Y
12 Costello	Y	Y	Y	Y	N	Y	Y	Y
13 Fawell	Y	Y	N	N	Y	Y	N	N
14 Hastert	Y	N	N	N	Y	Y	N	N
15 Ewing	Y	Y	Y	N	Y	Y	N	N
16 Manzullo	N	Y	N	N	Y	Y	N	N
17 Evans	Y	Y	Y	Y	N	Y	Y	Y

ND Northern Democrats   SD Southern Democrats

	365	366	367	368	369	370	371	372
18 ***Michel***	N	Y	N	N	Y	Y	N	N
19 Poshard	Y	Y	Y	Y	N	Y	Y	Y
20 Durbin	Y	Y	Y	Y	N	Y	Y	Y
INDIANA								
1 Visclosky	?	?	Y	Y	N	Y	Y	N
2 Sharp	?	?	Y	Y	N	Y	Y	Y
3 Roemer	Y	N	Y	N	N	Y	Y	Y
4 Long	Y	Y	Y	Y	N	Y	Y	Y
5 ***Buyer***	?	?	N	N	Y	Y	N	N
6 ***Burton***	N	Y	N	N	Y	Y	N	N
7 ***Myers***	N	N	Y	N	Y	N	Y	N
8 McCloskey	Y	Y	Y	Y	N	Y	Y	Y
9 Hamilton	Y	Y	Y	Y	N	Y	Y	Y
10 Jacobs	Y	N	N	N	N	Y	N	Y
IOWA								
1 ***Leach***	Y	N	N	N	Y	Y	N	N
2 ***Nussle***	N	N	N	N	Y	Y	N	N
3 ***Lightfoot***	?	?	N	N	Y	Y	N	N
4 Smith	Y	N	Y	Y	N	Y	Y	Y
5 ***Grandy***	Y	Y	N	N	Y	Y	N	N
KANSAS								
1 ***Roberts***	Y	N	N	N	Y	Y	N	N
2 Slattery	Y	N	Y	N	N	Y	Y	Y
3 ***Meyers***	Y	Y	N	N	Y	Y	N	N
4 Glickman	Y	N	Y	Y	N	Y	Y	N
KENTUCKY								
1 Barlow	Y	N	Y	Y	N	Y	Y	Y
2 Natcher	Y	Y	Y	Y	N	Y	Y	Y
3 Mazzoli	Y	Y	Y	Y	N	Y	Y	N
4 ***Bunning***	N	Y	N	N	Y	Y	N	N
5 ***Rogers***	Y	Y	N	N	Y	Y	N	N
6 Baesler	Y	N	Y	Y	N	Y	Y	Y
LOUISIANA								
1 ***Livingston***	N	Y	N	N	Y	Y	N	N
2 Jefferson	?	?	Y	Y	N	Y	Y	Y
3 Tauzin	Y	Y	Y	N	Y	Y	Y	N
4 Fields	Y	Y	Y	Y	N	Y	Y	Y
5 ***McCrery***	Y	Y	N	N	Y	Y	N	N
6 ***Baker***	?	?	N	N	Y	Y	N	Y
7 Hayes	Y	Y	Y	Y	Y	Y	Y	Y
MAINE								
1 Andrews	Y	Y	Y	Y	N	Y	Y	Y
2 ***Snowe***	Y	Y	N	N	Y	Y	N	N
MARYLAND								
1 ***Gilchrest***	Y	Y	N	N	Y	Y	N	N
2 ***Bentley***	?	?	N	N	#	?	N	N
3 Cardin	Y	Y	Y	Y	N	Y	Y	N
4 Wynn	Y	Y	Y	Y	N	Y	Y	Y
5 Hoyer	Y	Y	Y	Y	N	Y	Y	Y
6 ***Bartlett***	Y	Y	N	N	Y	Y	N	N
7 Mfume	?	?	Y	Y	N	Y	Y	Y
8 ***Morella***	Y	Y	Y	N	Y	Y	N	N
MASSACHUSETTS								
1 Olver	Y	Y	Y	Y	N	Y	Y	Y
2 Neal	Y	Y	Y	Y	N	Y	Y	Y
3 ***Blute***	Y	Y	N	N	Y	Y	N	N
4 Frank	Y	Y	Y	Y	N	Y	Y	N
5 Meehan	Y	Y	Y	N	Y	Y	Y	N
6 ***Torkildsen***	Y	Y	N	N	Y	Y	N	N
7 Markey	Y	Y	Y	Y	N	Y	Y	Y
8 Kennedy	?	?	Y	Y	N	Y	Y	Y
9 Moakley	?	?	?	#	X	?	?	?
10 Studds	Y	Y	Y	Y	N	Y	Y	Y
MICHIGAN								
1 Stupak	Y	Y	Y	Y	N	Y	Y	Y
2 ***Hoekstra***	N	N	N	N	Y	Y	N	N
3 Henry	?	?	?	?	?	?	?	?
4 ***Camp***	Y	Y	N	N	Y	Y	N	N
5 Barcia	Y	Y	Y	Y	Y	Y	Y	N
6 ***Upton***	Y	Y	N	N	Y	Y	N	N
7 ***Smith***	Y	N	N	N	Y	N	N	N
8 Carr	Y	Y	Y	Y	N	Y	Y	Y
9 Kildee	Y	Y	Y	Y	N	Y	Y	Y
10 Bonior	Y	Y	Y	Y	N	Y	Y	Y
11 ***Knollenberg***	N	N	N	N	Y	Y	N	N
12 Levin	Y	Y	Y	Y	N	Y	Y	Y
13 Ford	?	?	Y	Y	N	Y	Y	Y
14 Conyers	?	?	Y	Y	N	Y	Y	Y
15 Collins	Y	N	Y	Y	N	Y	Y	Y
16 Dingell	?	?	Y	Y	N	Y	Y	Y
MINNESOTA								
1 Penny	Y	N	Y	N	N	Y	Y	N
2 Minge	Y	P	Y	Y	N	Y	Y	Y
3 ***Ramstad***	Y	Y	N	N	Y	Y	N	N
4 Vento	Y	Y	Y	Y	N	Y	Y	Y

	365	366	367	368	369	370	371	372
5 Sabo	Y	Y	Y	Y	N	Y	Y	Y
6 ***Grams***	Y	Y	N	N	Y	Y	N	N
7 Peterson	Y	N	Y	N	Y	Y	Y	Y
8 Oberstar	Y	Y	Y	Y	N	Y	Y	Y
MISSISSIPPI								
1 Whitten	Y	Y	Y	Y	N	Y	Y	Y
2 Thompson	Y	Y	Y	Y	N	Y	Y	Y
3 Montgomery	Y	N	Y	Y	N	Y	Y	Y
4 Parker	Y	N	?	N	Y	Y	Y	N
5 Taylor	Y	Y	N	N	Y	Y	N	N
MISSOURI								
1 Clay	Y	Y	?	Y	N	Y	N	Y
2 ***Talent***	Y	Y	N	N	Y	Y	N	N
3 Gephardt	Y	Y	Y	Y	N	Y	Y	Y
4 Skelton	Y	Y	Y	Y	N	Y	Y	Y
5 Wheat	Y	Y	Y	Y	N	Y	Y	Y
6 Danner	Y	Y	Y	Y	N	Y	Y	Y
7 ***Hancock***	N	Y	N	N	Y	N	N	N
8 ***Emerson***	Y	Y	N	N	Y	Y	N	Y
9 Volkmer	Y	N	Y	Y	N	Y	Y	Y
MONTANA								
AL Williams	Y	N	Y	Y	N	Y	Y	Y
NEBRASKA								
1 ***Bereuter***	Y	Y	N	N	Y	Y	N	N
2 Hoagland	Y	N	Y	Y	N	Y	Y	Y
3 ***Barrett***	N	Y	N	N	Y	Y	N	N
NEVADA								
1 Bilbray	Y	Y	Y	Y	Y	Y	Y	Y
2 ***Vucanovich***	Y	N	N	N	Y	Y	N	N
NEW HAMPSHIRE								
1 ***Zeliff***	N	Y	N	N	Y	Y	N	N
2 Swett	Y	Y	Y	Y	N	Y	Y	Y
NEW JERSEY								
1 Andrews	Y	Y	Y	Y	N	Y	Y	Y
2 Hughes	Y	N	Y	Y	Y	Y	Y	Y
3 ***Saxton***	Y	Y	N	N	Y	Y	N	N
4 ***Smith***	Y	Y	Y	N	Y	Y	Y	N
5 ***Roukema***	Y	N	N	N	Y	Y	N	N
6 Pallone	Y	Y	Y	Y	N	Y	Y	Y
7 ***Franks***	Y	N	N	N	Y	Y	N	N
8 Klein	Y	Y	Y	Y	N	Y	Y	Y
9 Torricelli	?	?	Y	Y	N	Y	Y	Y
10 Payne	Y	N	Y	Y	N	Y	Y	Y
11 ***Gallo***	Y	Y	Y	N	Y	Y	N	N
12 ***Zimmer***	Y	Y	N	N	Y	Y	N	N
13 Menendez	Y	Y	Y	Y	N	Y	Y	Y
NEW MEXICO								
1 ***Schiff***	Y	Y	N	N	Y	Y	N	N
2 ***Skeen***	Y	Y	N	N	Y	Y	N	N
3 Richardson	Y	Y	Y	Y	N	Y	Y	Y
NEW YORK								
1 Hochbrueckner	+	+	+	+	−	+	Y	Y
2 ***Lazio***	Y	Y	N	N	Y	Y	N	N
3 ***King***	Y	Y	N	N	Y	Y	N	N
4 ***Levy***	Y	Y	N	N	Y	Y	N	N
5 Ackerman	?	?	Y	Y	N	Y	Y	Y
6 Flake	Y	Y	Y	Y	N	Y	?	Y
7 Manton	?	?	Y	Y	N	Y	Y	Y
8 Nadler	Y	Y	Y	Y	N	Y	Y	Y
9 Schumer	Y	Y	Y	Y	N	Y	Y	Y
10 Towns	?	?	Y	Y	N	Y	?	Y
11 Owens	?	?	Y	Y	N	Y	Y	Y
12 Velazquez	Y	Y	Y	Y	N	Y	Y	Y
13 ***Molinari***	Y	Y	N	N	Y	Y	N	N
14 Maloney	Y	Y	Y	Y	N	Y	Y	Y
15 Rangel	Y	Y	Y	Y	N	Y	Y	Y
16 Serrano	Y	Y	Y	Y	N	Y	Y	Y
17 Engel	Y	Y	Y	Y	N	Y	Y	Y
18 Lowey	Y	Y	Y	Y	N	Y	Y	Y
19 ***Fish***	Y	Y	Y	N	Y	Y	Y	N
20 ***Gilman***	Y	Y	Y	N	Y	Y	Y	N
21 McNulty	N	Y	Y	Y	N	Y	Y	Y
22 ***Solomon***	N	Y	N	N	Y	N	N	N
23 ***Boehlert***	Y	Y	N	N	Y	Y	N	N
24 ***McHugh***	Y	Y	N	N	Y	Y	?	N
25 ***Walsh***	Y	Y	N	N	Y	Y	N	N
26 Hinchey	Y	Y	Y	Y	N	Y	Y	Y
27 ***Paxon***	Y	Y	N	N	Y	N	N	N
28 Slaughter	Y	Y	Y	Y	N	Y	Y	Y
29 LaFalce	Y	Y	Y	Y	N	Y	Y	Y
30 ***Quinn***	Y	Y	N	N	Y	Y	N	N
31 ***Houghton***	Y	Y	Y	N	Y	Y	N	N
NORTH CAROLINA								
1 Clayton	Y	Y	Y	Y	N	Y	Y	Y
2 Valentine	Y	Y	Y	N	N	Y	?	Y

	365	366	367	368	369	370	371	372
3 Lancaster	Y	Y	Y	N	N	Y	Y	Y
4 Price	Y	Y	Y	Y	N	Y	Y	Y
5 Neal	Y	Y	Y	Y	N	Y	Y	Y
6 ***Coble***	N	Y	N	N	Y	Y	N	N
7 Rose	Y	Y	Y	Y	N	Y	Y	?
8 Hefner	?	?	Y	Y	N	Y	Y	Y
9 ***McMillan***	Y	N	?	N	Y	Y	N	N
10 ***Ballenger***	Y	Y	N	N	Y	Y	N	N
11 ***Taylor***	?	?	N	N	Y	Y	N	N
12 Watt	Y	N	Y	Y	N	Y	Y	Y
NORTH DAKOTA								
AL Pomeroy	Y	N	Y	Y	N	Y	Y	Y
OHIO								
1 Mann	Y	Y	Y	N	N	Y	Y	Y
2 ***Portman***	Y	Y	N	N	Y	Y	N	N
3 Hall	Y	Y	Y	Y	N	Y	Y	Y
4 ***Oxley***	Y	N	N	N	Y	Y	Y	N
5 ***Gillmor***	?	?	Y	N	Y	Y	Y	Y
6 Strickland	Y	Y	Y	Y	N	Y	?	Y
7 ***Hobson***	Y	Y	N	N	Y	Y	N	N
8 ***Boehner***	N	N	N	N	Y	N	N	N
9 Kaptur	Y	?	Y	Y	N	Y	Y	Y
10 ***Hoke***	N	N	N	N	Y	Y	Y	N
11 Stokes	?	?	?	Y	N	Y	?	Y
12 ***Kasich***	N	Y	N	Y	Y	Y	Y	N
13 Brown	Y	Y	?	Y	N	Y	Y	Y
14 Sawyer	Y	Y	Y	Y	N	Y	Y	Y
15 ***Pryce***	Y	Y	N	N	Y	Y	N	N
16 ***Regula***	Y	Y	N	N	Y	Y	N	N
17 Traficant	Y	N	Y	Y	N	Y	Y	Y
18 Applegate	Y	Y	Y	Y	Y	Y	Y	Y
19 Fingerhut	+	+	Y	N	N	Y	Y	Y
OKLAHOMA								
1 ***Inhofe***	N	Y	N	N	Y	N	N	N
2 Synar	Y	Y	Y	Y	N	Y	Y	Y
3 Brewster	Y	N	Y	N	Y	Y	Y	Y
4 McCurdy	Y	N	Y	N	N	Y	Y	Y
5 ***Istook***	Y	N	N	N	Y	Y	N	N
6 English	Y	N	Y	Y	N	Y	Y	Y
OREGON								
1 Furse	Y	Y	Y	Y	N	Y	Y	Y
2 ***Smith***	N	N	N	N	Y	Y	N	N
3 Wyden	Y	Y	Y	Y	N	Y	Y	Y
4 DeFazio	Y	N	Y	Y	N	Y	Y	Y
5 Kopetski	Y	Y	Y	Y	N	Y	?	Y
PENNSYLVANIA								
1 Foglietta	Y	Y	Y	Y	N	Y	Y	Y
2 Blackwell	Y	Y	?	Y	N	Y	Y	Y
3 Borski	Y	Y	Y	Y	N	Y	Y	Y
4 Klink	Y	N	Y	Y	N	Y	Y	Y
5 ***Clinger***	Y	Y	Y	N	Y	Y	Y	N
6 Holden	Y	Y	Y	Y	N	Y	?	Y
7 ***Weldon***	Y	N	N	N	Y	Y	N	N
8 ***Greenwood***	N	Y	N	N	Y	Y	N	N
9 ***Shuster***	N	N	N	N	Y	N	N	N
10 ***McDade***	?	?	?	X	?	?	?	?
11 Kanjorski	Y	N	Y	Y	N	Y	Y	Y
12 Murtha	Y	Y	Y	Y	N	Y	Y	Y
13 Margolies-Mezv.	Y	Y	Y	Y	N	Y	Y	Y
14 Coyne	Y	Y	Y	Y	N	Y	Y	Y
15 McHale	Y	Y	Y	Y	N	Y	Y	Y
16 ***Walker***	Y	Y	N	N	Y	N	N	N
17 ***Gekas***	Y	N	N	N	Y	Y	N	N
18 ***Santorum***	Y	Y	Y	N	Y	N	N	N
19 ***Goodling***	Y	Y	N	N	Y	Y	N	N
20 Murphy	Y	N	N	N	Y	Y	N	Y
21 ***Ridge***	?	?	?	N	Y	Y	N	N
RHODE ISLAND								
1 ***Machtley***	Y	Y	N	N	Y	Y	N	N
2 Reed	Y	Y	Y	Y	N	Y	Y	Y
SOUTH CAROLINA								
1 ***Ravenel***	Y	Y	N	N	Y	Y	N	N
2 ***Spence***	N	N	N	N	Y	Y	N	N
3 Derrick	?	?	?	#	?	?	?	Y
4 ***Inglis***	N	Y	N	Y	Y	Y	Y	N
5 Spratt	Y	Y	Y	Y	N	Y	Y	Y
6 Clyburn	Y	Y	?	Y	N	Y	Y	Y
SOUTH DAKOTA								
AL Johnson	Y	N	Y	Y	N	Y	Y	Y
TENNESSEE								
1 ***Quillen***	?	?	N	N	Y	N	N	N
2 ***Duncan***	N	Y	N	N	Y	N	N	N
3 Lloyd	Y	Y	Y	N	Y	Y	Y	Y
4 Cooper	?	?	Y	Y	N	Y	Y	Y
5 Clement	Y	N	Y	Y	N	Y	Y	Y

	365	366	367	368	369	370	371	372
6 Gordon	Y	Y	Y	Y	N	Y	Y	Y
7 ***Sundquist***	?	?	N	N	Y	Y	N	N
8 Tanner	Y	N	Y	N	Y	Y	Y	N
9 Ford	?	?	Y	Y	N	Y	Y	Y
TEXAS								
1 Chapman	Y	N	Y	Y	Y	Y	?	Y
2 Wilson	Y	Y	Y	Y	N	Y	?	Y
3 ***Johnson, Sam***	N	Y	?	N	Y	Y	N	N
4 Hall	Y	Y	Y	N	Y	Y	Y	Y
5 Bryant	?	?	Y	Y	N	Y	Y	Y
6 ***Barton***	Y	Y	N	N	Y	Y	N	N
7 ***Archer***	N	N	Y	N	Y	N	Y	N
8 ***Fields***	Y	Y	N	N	Y	N	N	N
9 Brooks	?	?	Y	Y	N	Y	Y	Y
10 Pickle	Y	N	Y	Y	N	Y	Y	Y
11 Edwards	Y	Y	Y	Y	Y	Y	Y	N
12 Geren	Y	Y	Y	N	N	Y	Y	Y
13 Sarpalius	Y	Y	Y	Y	Y	Y	Y	Y
14 Laughlin	Y	N	Y	Y	N	Y	Y	Y
15 de la Garza	Y	Y	Y	Y	N	Y	Y	Y
16 Coleman	Y	Y	Y	Y	N	Y	Y	Y
17 Stenholm	Y	N	Y	N	N	Y	Y	N
18 Washington	Y	N	?	Y	N	Y	?	?
19 ***Combest***	N	Y	Y	N	Y	Y	Y	N
20 Gonzalez	Y	N	Y	Y	N	Y	Y	Y
21 ***Smith***	Y	Y	N	N	Y	Y	N	N
22 ***DeLay***	?	?	N	N	Y	N	N	N
23 ***Bonilla***	N	Y	N	N	Y	Y	N	N
24 Frost	Y	Y	Y	Y	N	Y	Y	Y
25 Andrews	Y	Y	Y	Y	Y	Y	Y	Y
26 ***Armey***	N	Y	N	N	Y	N	N	N
27 Ortiz	Y	N	Y	Y	N	Y	Y	Y
28 Tejeda	Y	Y	Y	Y	N	Y	Y	Y
29 Green	Y	N	Y	Y	N	Y	Y	Y
30 Johnson, E. B.	Y	Y	Y	Y	N	Y	Y	Y
UTAH								
1 ***Hansen***	N	N	N	N	Y	Y	N	N
2 Shepherd	Y	N	Y	Y	N	Y	Y	Y
3 Orton	Y	N	Y	N	Y	Y	Y	N
VERMONT								
AL *Sanders*	Y	Y	Y	Y	N	Y	Y	Y
VIRGINIA								
1 ***Bateman***	Y	N	Y	N	Y	Y	Y	N
2 Pickett	Y	N	Y	N	Y	Y	Y	Y
3 Scott	Y	Y	Y	Y	N	Y	Y	Y
4 Sisisky	Y	Y	Y	N	Y	Y	Y	Y
5 Payne	Y	Y	Y	N	Y	Y	Y	N
6 ***Goodlatte***	Y	Y	N	N	Y	Y	N	N
7 ***Bliley***	Y	Y	N	N	Y	Y	N	N
8 Moran	Y	Y	Y	Y	N	Y	Y	Y
9 Boucher	Y	Y	Y	Y	N	Y	Y	Y
10 ***Wolf***	Y	Y	N	N	Y	Y	N	N
11 Byrne	Y	Y	Y	Y	N	Y	Y	Y
WASHINGTON								
1 Cantwell	Y	Y	Y	Y	N	Y	Y	Y
2 Swift	Y	Y	Y	Y	N	Y	Y	Y
3 Unsoeld	Y	Y	Y	Y	N	Y	Y	Y
4 Inslee	Y	N	Y	N	N	Y	Y	Y
5 Foley				Y				
6 Dicks	Y	Y	Y	Y	N	Y	Y	Y
7 McDermott	Y	N	Y	Y	N	Y	Y	Y
8 ***Dunn***	Y	Y	N	N	Y	Y	N	N
9 Kreidler	Y	N	Y	Y	N	Y	Y	Y
WEST VIRGINIA								
1 Mollohan	Y	Y	Y	Y	N	Y	Y	Y
2 Wise	Y	Y	Y	Y	N	Y	Y	Y
3 Rahall	Y	Y	Y	Y	N	Y	Y	Y
WISCONSIN								
1 Barca	Y	Y	Y	Y	N	Y	Y	Y
2 ***Klug***	Y	Y	N	N	Y	Y	N	N
3 ***Gunderson***	Y	Y	N	N	Y	Y	Y	N
4 Kleczka	Y	Y	Y	Y	Y	Y	Y	Y
5 Barrett	Y	Y	Y	Y	N	Y	Y	Y
6 ***Petri***	N	Y	N	N	Y	Y	N	N
7 Obey	Y	Y	Y	Y	N	Y	Y	Y
8 ***Roth***	Y	N	N	N	Y	N	N	N
9 ***Sensenbrenner***	Y	Y	N	N	Y	N	N	N
WYOMING								
AL ***Thomas***	N	Y	N	N	Y	Y	N	N
DELEGATES								
de Lugo, V.I.	D	D	D	D	D	D	D	Y
Faleomavaega, Am.S.	D	D	D	D	D	D	D	Y
Norton, D.C.	D	D	D	D	D	D	D	Y
Romero-B., P.R.	D	D	D	D	D	D	D	Y
Underwood, Guam	D	D	D	D	D	D	D	Y

Southern states - Ala., Ark., Fla., Ga., Ky., La., Miss., N.C., Okla., S.C., Tenn., Texas, Va.
Omitted votes are quorum calls, which CQ does not include in its vote charts.

373. HR 2010. National Service/Volunteer Liability Protection. Porter, R-Ill., amendment, as amended, to provide non-profit and government volunteers personal financial liability protection from tort claims alleging damage or injury during official work performed in good faith without misconduct for certain organizations. Adopted in the Committee of the Whole 358-69: R 168-3; D 189-66 (ND 123-49, SD 66-17); I 1-0, July 28, 1993.

374. HR 2010. National Service/Religious Organizations. Cunningham, R-Calif., amendment to the Baker, R-Calif., amendment, to allow religious organizations to offer religious instruction and religious services to illegal aliens without losing their ability to participate in the National Service program as they would under the Baker amendment. The Baker amendment would require organizations to have a written policy stating that they do not provide services to illegal aliens in order to participate in the National Service program. Adopted in the Committee of the Whole 270-163: R 168-5; D 102-157 (ND 59-117, SD 43-40); I 0-1, July 28, 1993.

375. HR 2010. National Service/Illegal Aliens. Baker, R-Calif., amendment to require organizations to have written policies stating that they do not provide services to illegal aliens in order to participate in the National Service program. Rejected in the Committee of the Whole 180-253: R 152-21; D 28-231 (ND 10-166, SD 18-65); I 0-1, July 28, 1993.

376. HR 2010. National Service/Reduced Education Awards. Separate vote at the request of Walker, R-Pa., on the Stump, R-Ariz., amendment adopted by voice vote in the Committee of the Whole to reduce the bill's education awards from $5,000 to $4,725 a year. Adopted 419-6: R 173-0; D 246-5 (ND 163-5, SD 83-0); I 0-1, July 28, 1993. (On separate votes, which may be demanded on an amendment adopted in the Committee of the Whole, the four delegates and the resident commissioner of Puerto Rico cannot vote.)

377. HR 2010. National Service/Scorekeeping. Separate vote at the request of Walker, R-Pa., on the Solomon, R-N.Y., amendment adopted in the Committee of the Whole to require that the Office of Management and Budget count the authorizations in the bill under the Labor, Health and Human Services budget function. Adopted 385-38: R 170-1; D 215-36 (ND 140-28, SD 75-8); I 0-1, July 28, 1993. (On separate votes, which may be demanded on an amendment adopted in the Committee of the Whole, the four delegates and the resident commissioner of Puerto Rico cannot vote. See vote 352.)

378. HR 2010. National Service/Volunteer Liability Protection. Separate vote at the request of Walker, R-Pa., on the amendment adopted in the Committee of the Whole offered by Porter, R-Ill., to provide nonprofit and government volunteers personal financial liability protection from tort claims alleging damage or injury during official work performed in good faith without misconduct for certain organizations. Adopted 362-61: R 172-0; D 189-61 (ND 121-46, SD 68-15); I 1-0, July 28, 1993. (On separate votes, which may be demanded on an amendment adopted in the Committee of the Whole, the four delegates and the resident commissioner of Puerto Rico cannot vote. See vote 373.)

379. HR 2010. National Service/Passage. Passage of bill to authorize $389 million in fiscal 1994 for the National Service program, which would provide people age 17 or older with $4,725 a year for up to two years in education awards in return for work in community service programs. The bill also would authorize $5 million for the Points of Light Foundation. Passed 275-152: R 26-147; D 248-5 (ND 166-4, SD 82-1); I 1-0, July 28, 1993. A "yea" was a vote in support of the president's position.

380. HR 2200. NASA Authorization/Helium Purchases. Cox, R-Calif., amendment to let NASA buy helium from the private sector. Adopted in the Committee of the Whole 319-109: R 166-6; D 152-103 (ND 113-61, SD 39-42); I 1-0, July 29, 1993.

KEY

Y	Voted for (yea).
#	Paired for.
+	Announced for.
N	Voted against (nay).
X	Paired against.
−	Announced against.
P	Voted "present."
C	Voted "present" to avoid possible conflict of interest.
?	Did not vote or otherwise make a position known.
D	Delegates ineligible to vote.

Democrats   *Republicans*
Independent

	373	374	375	376	377	378	379	380
ALABAMA								
1 Callahan	Y	Y	Y	Y	Y	Y	N	Y
2 Everett	Y	Y	Y	Y	Y	Y	N	Y
3 Browder	Y	Y	N	Y	Y	Y	Y	N
4 Bevill	Y	Y	N	Y	Y	Y	Y	N
5 Cramer	Y	Y	N	Y	Y	Y	Y	N
6 Bachus	Y	Y	Y	Y	?	?	N	Y
7 Hilliard	Y	N	N	Y	Y	N	Y	N
ALASKA								
AL Young	Y	Y	Y	Y	Y	Y	N	Y
ARIZONA								
1 Coppersmith	Y	N	N	Y	N	Y	Y	Y
2 Pastor	Y	N	N	Y	Y	Y	Y	N
3 Stump	Y	Y	Y	Y	Y	Y	N	Y
4 Kyl	Y	Y	Y	Y	Y	Y	N	Y
5 Kolbe	Y	Y	N	Y	Y	Y	N	Y
6 English	Y	N	N	Y	Y	Y	Y	Y
ARKANSAS								
1 Lambert	Y	Y	N	Y	Y	Y	Y	Y
2 Thornton	Y	Y	N	Y	Y	Y	Y	Y
3 Hutchinson	Y	Y	Y	Y	Y	Y	N	Y
4 Dickey	Y	Y	Y	Y	Y	Y	Y	Y
CALIFORNIA								
1 Hamburg	N	N	N	Y	Y	N	Y	N
2 Herger	Y	Y	Y	Y	Y	Y	N	Y
3 Fazio	Y	N	N	Y	Y	Y	Y	N
4 Doolittle	Y	Y	Y	Y	Y	Y	N	Y
5 Matsui	Y	N	N	Y	Y	Y	Y	Y
6 Woolsey	Y	N	N	N	N	N	Y	Y
7 Miller	N	N	N	Y	Y	N	Y	N
8 Pelosi	N	N	N	Y	N	?	Y	N
9 Dellums	N	N	N	Y	N	N	Y	N
10 Baker	Y	Y	Y	Y	Y	Y	N	Y
11 Pombo	Y	Y	Y	Y	Y	Y	N	Y
12 Lantos	Y	N	N	Y	Y	Y	Y	Y
13 Stark	N	N	N	Y	Y	N	Y	N
14 Eshoo	Y	N	N	Y	Y	Y	Y	Y
15 Mineta	Y	N	N	Y	Y	Y	Y	N
16 Edwards	N	N	N	Y	Y	N	Y	N
17 Farr	Y	N	N	Y	Y	Y	Y	N
18 Condit	Y	Y	N	Y	Y	Y	Y	Y
19 Lehman	Y	N	N	Y	Y	Y	Y	N
20 Dooley	Y	N	N	Y	Y	Y	Y	Y
21 Thomas	Y	Y	Y	Y	Y	N	Y	Y
22 Huffington	Y	Y	Y	Y	Y	N	Y	Y
23 Gallegly	Y	Y	Y	Y	Y	Y	N	Y
24 Beilenson	Y	N	N	Y	N	Y	Y	N
25 McKeon	Y	Y	Y	Y	Y	Y	N	Y
26 Berman	Y	N	N	Y	Y	Y	Y	Y
27 Moorhead	Y	Y	Y	Y	Y	Y	N	Y
28 Dreier	Y	Y	Y	Y	Y	Y	N	Y
29 Waxman	Y	Y	N	Y	N	Y	Y	N
30 Becerra	N	N	N	Y	N	N	Y	N
31 Martinez	N	N	N	Y	Y	Y	Y	N
32 Dixon	N	N	N	Y	Y	Y	Y	N
33 Roybal-Allard	Y	N	N	Y	N	Y	Y	N
34 Torres	N	N	N	Y	Y	Y	Y	N
35 Waters	N	N	N	N	N	N	Y	N
36 Harman	Y	Y	N	?	Y	Y	Y	N
37 Tucker	Y	N	N	Y	Y	Y	Y	Y
38 Horn	Y	N	Y	Y	Y	Y	Y	Y
39 Royce	Y	Y	Y	Y	Y	Y	N	Y
40 Lewis	Y	Y	Y	Y	Y	Y	N	Y
41 Kim	Y	Y	Y	Y	Y	Y	N	Y

	373	374	375	376	377	378	379	380
42 Brown	Y	N	N	N	N	Y	N	Y
43 Calvert	Y	Y	Y	Y	Y	Y	N	Y
44 McCandless	Y	Y	Y	Y	Y	Y	N	Y
45 Rohrabacher	Y	Y	Y	Y	Y	Y	N	Y
46 Dornan	Y	Y	Y	Y	Y	Y	N	Y
47 Cox	Y	Y	Y	Y	Y	Y	N	Y
48 Packard	+	+	+	+	+	+	−	+
49 Schenk	Y	N	N	Y	Y	Y	Y	Y
50 Filner	Y	N	N	Y	Y	Y	Y	Y
51 Cunningham	Y	Y	Y	Y	Y	Y	N	Y
52 Hunter	Y	Y	Y	Y	Y	Y	N	Y
COLORADO								
1 Schroeder	N	Y	N	Y	Y	Y	Y	Y
2 Skaggs	N	Y	N	Y	Y	N	Y	Y
3 McInnis	N	Y	Y	Y	Y	Y	N	Y
4 Allard	Y	Y	Y	Y	Y	Y	N	Y
5 Hefley	Y	Y	Y	Y	Y	Y	N	Y
6 Schaefer	Y	Y	Y	Y	Y	Y	N	Y
CONNECTICUT								
1 Kennelly	?	N	N	Y	Y	Y	Y	Y
2 Gejdenson	Y	N	N	Y	Y	Y	Y	Y
3 DeLauro	Y	N	N	Y	Y	Y	Y	Y
4 Shays	Y	Y	N	Y	Y	Y	Y	Y
5 Franks	Y	Y	Y	Y	Y	Y	N	Y
6 Johnson	Y	Y	N	Y	Y	Y	Y	Y
DELAWARE								
AL Castle	Y	Y	Y	Y	Y	Y	N	Y
FLORIDA								
1 Hutto	Y	Y	Y	Y	Y	Y	Y	Y
2 Peterson	Y	N	N	Y	Y	Y	Y	Y
3 Brown	N	N	−	Y	Y	Y	Y	Y
4 Fowler	Y	Y	Y	Y	Y	Y	N	Y
5 Thurman	Y	N	N	Y	Y	Y	Y	Y
6 Stearns	Y	Y	Y	Y	Y	Y	N	Y
7 Mica	Y	Y	Y	Y	Y	Y	N	Y
8 McCollum	Y	Y	Y	Y	Y	Y	N	Y
9 Bilirakis	Y	Y	Y	Y	Y	Y	N	Y
10 Young	Y	Y	Y	Y	Y	Y	N	Y
11 Gibbons	Y	N	N	Y	N	Y	Y	Y
12 Canady	Y	Y	Y	Y	Y	Y	N	Y
13 Miller	Y	Y	Y	Y	Y	Y	N	Y
14 Goss	Y	Y	Y	Y	Y	Y	N	Y
15 Bacchus	Y	N	N	Y	Y	Y	Y	Y
16 Lewis	Y	Y	Y	Y	Y	Y	N	Y
17 Meek	N	N	N	Y	Y	Y	N	Y
18 Ros-Lehtinen	Y	N	N	Y	Y	Y	Y	Y
19 Johnston	Y	N	N	Y	Y	Y	Y	Y
20 Deutsch	N	N	N	Y	N	Y	N	Y
21 Diaz-Balart	Y	N	N	Y	Y	Y	Y	Y
22 Shaw	Y	Y	Y	Y	Y	Y	N	Y
23 Hastings	Y	N	N	Y	Y	Y	Y	Y
GEORGIA								
1 Kingston	Y	Y	Y	Y	Y	Y	N	Y
2 Bishop	N	N	N	Y	Y	N	Y	N
3 Collins	Y	Y	Y	Y	Y	Y	N	Y
4 Linder	Y	Y	Y	Y	Y	Y	N	Y
5 Lewis	N	N	N	Y	Y	Y	Y	N
6 Gingrich	Y	Y	Y	Y	Y	Y	N	Y
7 Darden	Y	N	Y	Y	Y	Y	Y	Y
8 Rowland	Y	Y	Y	Y	Y	Y	Y	Y
9 Deal	N	Y	Y	Y	Y	Y	Y	Y
10 Johnson	Y	N	Y	Y	Y	Y	Y	Y
11 McKinney	Y	N	N	Y	Y	Y	Y	N
HAWAII								
1 Abercrombie	N	N	N	N	Y	N	Y	N
2 Mink	N	N	N	N	Y	N	Y	N
IDAHO								
1 LaRocco	Y	N	Y	Y	Y	Y	Y	Y
2 Crapo	Y	Y	Y	Y	Y	Y	N	Y
ILLINOIS								
1 Rush	N	N	N	Y	N	N	Y	N
2 Reynolds	Y	N	N	Y	N	N	Y	N
3 Lipinski	Y	Y	Y	Y	Y	Y	Y	Y
4 Gutierrez	Y	N	N	Y	N	Y	Y	N
5 Rostenkowski	Y	Y	N	Y	Y	Y	N	Y
6 Hyde	Y	Y	Y	Y	Y	Y	N	Y
7 Collins	N	N	N	N	N	N	Y	N
8 Crane	Y	Y	Y	Y	Y	Y	N	Y
9 Yates	N	N	N	Y	N	N	Y	N
10 Porter	Y	Y	Y	Y	Y	Y	N	Y
11 Sangmeister	Y	Y	N	Y	Y	N	Y	N
12 Costello	N	Y	Y	Y	Y	N	Y	Y
13 Fawell	Y	Y	Y	Y	Y	Y	N	Y
14 Hastert	Y	Y	Y	Y	Y	Y	N	Y
15 Ewing	Y	Y	Y	Y	Y	Y	N	Y
16 Manzullo	Y	Y	Y	Y	Y	Y	N	Y
17 Evans	Y	N	N	Y	Y	Y	Y	Y

ND Northern Democrats   SD Southern Democrats

	373	374	375	376	377	378	379	380
18 ***Michel***	Y	Y	Y	Y	Y	Y	N	Y
19 Poshard	Y	Y	Y	Y	Y	Y	Y	Y
20 Durbin	Y	Y	N	Y	Y	Y	Y	Y
INDIANA								
1 Visclosky	Y	Y	N	Y	N	Y	Y	Y
2 Sharp	Y	Y	N	Y	Y	Y	Y	Y
3 Roemer	Y	N	N	Y	Y	Y	Y	Y
4 Long	Y	Y	N	Y	Y	Y	Y	Y
5 ***Buyer***	?	Y	Y	Y	Y	Y	N	Y
6 ***Burton***	Y	Y	Y	Y	Y	Y	N	Y
7 ***Myers***	Y	Y	Y	Y	Y	Y	N	Y
8 McCloskey	Y	Y	N	Y	Y	Y	Y	?
9 Hamilton	Y	Y	N	Y	Y	Y	Y	Y
10 Jacobs	Y	Y	Y	Y	Y	Y	Y	Y
IOWA								
1 ***Leach***	Y	Y	N	Y	Y	Y	Y	Y
2 ***Nussle***	Y	Y	Y	Y	Y	Y	N	Y
3 ***Lightfoot***	Y	Y	Y	Y	Y	Y	N	Y
4 Smith	Y	Y	N	Y	N	N	Y	N
5 ***Grandy***	Y	Y	N	Y	Y	Y	N	Y
KANSAS								
1 ***Roberts***	Y	Y	Y	Y	Y	Y	N	Y
2 Slattery	Y	Y	N	Y	Y	Y	Y	Y
3 ***Meyers***	Y	Y	Y	Y	Y	Y	N	Y
4 Glickman	Y	Y	N	Y	Y	Y	Y	Y
KENTUCKY								
1 Barlow	Y	N	N	Y	Y	Y	Y	Y
2 Natcher	Y	N	N	Y	N	Y	Y	Y
3 Mazzoli	Y	N	N	Y	Y	Y	Y	Y
4 ***Bunning***	Y	Y	Y	Y	Y	Y	N	Y
5 ***Rogers***	Y	Y	Y	Y	Y	Y	Y	Y
6 Baesler	Y	Y	N	Y	Y	Y	Y	Y
LOUISIANA								
1 ***Livingston***	Y	Y	Y	Y	Y	Y	N	Y
2 Jefferson	N	N	N	Y	N	Y	Y	N
3 Tauzin	Y	Y	Y	Y	Y	Y	Y	Y
4 Fields	N	N	N	Y	Y	Y	Y	N
5 ***McCrery***	Y	Y	Y	Y	Y	Y	N	Y
6 ***Baker***	?	Y	Y	Y	Y	Y	N	Y
7 Hayes	Y	Y	Y	Y	Y	Y	Y	N
MAINE								
1 Andrews	Y	N	N	Y	Y	Y	Y	Y
2 ***Snowe***	Y	Y	Y	Y	Y	Y	Y	Y
MARYLAND								
1 ***Gilchrest***	Y	Y	Y	Y	Y	Y	Y	Y
2 ***Bentley***	Y	Y	Y	Y	Y	Y	N	Y
3 Cardin	Y	Y	N	Y	Y	Y	Y	Y
4 Wynn	Y	N	N	Y	Y	N	Y	N
5 Hoyer	Y	N	N	Y	N	Y	Y	Y
6 ***Bartlett***	Y	Y	Y	Y	Y	Y	N	Y
7 Mfume	Y	N	N	?	Y	Y	Y	N
8 ***Morella***	Y	N	N	Y	Y	Y	Y	Y
MASSACHUSETTS								
1 Olver	N	N	N	Y	N	Y	Y	Y
2 Neal	Y	N	N	Y	Y	Y	Y	Y
3 ***Blute***	Y	Y	Y	Y	Y	Y	Y	Y
4 Frank	Y	N	N	Y	N	Y	Y	Y
5 Meehan	N	N	N	Y	Y	Y	Y	Y
6 ***Torkildsen***	Y	Y	Y	Y	Y	Y	Y	Y
7 Markey	Y	N	N	Y	Y	N	Y	Y
8 Kennedy	N	Y	N	Y	Y	N	Y	N
9 Moakley	?	?	?	?	?	?	?	?
10 Studds	Y	Y	N	Y	Y	Y	Y	Y
MICHIGAN								
1 Stupak	Y	N	N	Y	Y	Y	Y	Y
2 ***Hoekstra***	Y	Y	N	Y	Y	Y	Y	Y
3 Henry	?	?	?	?	?	?	?	?
4 ***Camp***	Y	Y	N	Y	Y	Y	N	Y
5 Barcia	Y	Y	N	Y	Y	Y	Y	Y
6 ***Upton***	Y	Y	N	Y	Y	Y	Y	Y
7 ***Smith***	Y	Y	Y	Y	Y	Y	N	N
8 Carr	Y	N	N	?	Y	Y	Y	Y
9 Kildee	Y	N	N	Y	Y	Y	Y	Y
10 Bonior	Y	N	N	Y	Y	N	Y	N
11 ***Knollenberg***	Y	Y	Y	Y	Y	Y	N	Y
12 Levin	Y	N	N	Y	Y	Y	Y	Y
13 Ford	N	N	N	Y	Y	N	Y	N
14 Conyers	?	N	N	Y	?	N	Y	Y
15 Collins	N	N	N	Y	Y	Y	Y	N
16 Dingell	N	N	N	Y	Y	N	?	N
MINNESOTA								
1 Penny	Y	Y	N	Y	Y	Y	Y	Y
2 Minge	Y	N	N	Y	Y	Y	Y	Y
3 ***Ramstad***	Y	Y	Y	Y	?	Y	N	Y
4 Vento	Y	N	N	Y	Y	Y	Y	Y
5 Sabo	Y	N	N	Y	?	?	Y	Y
6 ***Grams***	Y	Y	Y	Y	Y	Y	N	Y
7 Peterson	Y	N	N	Y	Y	Y	Y	Y
8 Oberstar	Y	N	N	Y	Y	Y	Y	Y
MISSISSIPPI								
1 Whitten	Y	Y	Y	Y	Y	Y	Y	Y
2 Thompson	Y	N	N	Y	Y	Y	Y	N
3 Montgomery	Y	N	N	Y	Y	Y	Y	Y
4 Parker	Y	Y	Y	Y	Y	Y	Y	Y
5 Taylor	Y	Y	N	Y	Y	Y	Y	Y
MISSOURI								
1 Clay	N	N	N	Y	N	N	Y	N
2 ***Talent***	Y	Y	Y	Y	Y	Y	N	Y
3 Gephardt	Y	N	N	Y	?	?	Y	N
4 Skelton	Y	Y	N	Y	Y	Y	Y	Y
5 Wheat	Y	N	N	Y	Y	Y	Y	N
6 Danner	N	Y	N	Y	Y	Y	Y	Y
7 ***Hancock***	Y	Y	Y	Y	Y	Y	N	Y
8 ***Emerson***	Y	Y	Y	Y	Y	Y	N	Y
9 Volkmer	Y	Y	N	Y	Y	Y	Y	N
MONTANA								
AL Williams	Y	Y	N	Y	Y	Y	Y	N
NEBRASKA								
1 ***Bereuter***	Y	Y	N	Y	Y	Y	Y	Y
2 Hoagland	N	Y	N	Y	Y	N	Y	Y
3 ***Barrett***	Y	Y	Y	Y	Y	Y	N	Y
NEVADA								
1 Bilbray	Y	Y	N	Y	Y	Y	Y	Y
2 ***Vucanovich***	Y	Y	Y	Y	Y	Y	N	Y
NEW HAMPSHIRE								
1 ***Zeliff***	Y	Y	Y	Y	Y	Y	N	Y
2 Swett	Y	N	N	Y	Y	Y	Y	Y
NEW JERSEY								
1 Andrews	Y	N	N	Y	Y	Y	Y	Y
2 Hughes	Y	Y	N	Y	Y	Y	Y	Y
3 ***Saxton***	Y	Y	Y	Y	Y	Y	N	Y
4 ***Smith***	Y	Y	Y	Y	Y	Y	N	Y
5 ***Roukema***	Y	Y	Y	Y	Y	Y	N	Y
6 Pallone	Y	Y	N	Y	Y	Y	Y	Y
7 ***Franks***	Y	Y	Y	Y	Y	Y	N	Y
8 Klein	Y	N	N	Y	Y	Y	Y	Y
9 Torricelli	Y	Y	N	Y	Y	Y	Y	Y
10 Payne	Y	N	N	Y	Y	N	Y	N
11 ***Gallo***	Y	Y	Y	Y	Y	Y	N	Y
12 ***Zimmer***	Y	Y	Y	Y	Y	Y	N	Y
13 Menendez	Y	N	N	Y	Y	Y	Y	N
NEW MEXICO								
1 ***Schiff***	Y	Y	Y	Y	Y	Y	N	Y
2 ***Skeen***	Y	Y	Y	Y	Y	Y	N	N
3 Richardson	Y	N	N	Y	Y	Y	Y	N
NEW YORK								
1 Hochbrueckner	Y	Y	N	Y	Y	Y	Y	N
2 ***Lazio***	Y	Y	Y	Y	Y	Y	Y	+
3 ***King***	Y	Y	Y	Y	Y	Y	N	Y
4 ***Levy***	Y	Y	Y	Y	Y	Y	N	Y
5 Ackerman	Y	N	N	Y	Y	Y	Y	Y
6 Flake	Y	N	N	Y	N	N	Y	Y
7 Manton	Y	N	N	Y	Y	Y	Y	N
8 Nadler	N	N	N	Y	Y	N	Y	N
9 Schumer	Y	Y	N	Y	Y	Y	Y	Y
10 Towns	Y	N	N	Y	Y	Y	Y	N
11 Owens	N	N	N	Y	Y	Y	Y	N
12 Velazquez	Y	N	N	Y	N	Y	Y	N
13 ***Molinari***	Y	Y	Y	Y	Y	Y	N	Y
14 Maloney	Y	N	N	Y	Y	Y	Y	Y
15 Rangel	?	N	N	Y	N	?	Y	?
16 Serrano	Y	N	N	Y	Y	Y	Y	N
17 Engel	N	N	N	Y	N	N	Y	N
18 Lowey	Y	N	N	Y	Y	Y	Y	Y
19 ***Fish***	Y	Y	N	Y	Y	Y	Y	Y
20 ***Gilman***	Y	N	N	Y	Y	Y	Y	N
21 McNulty	N	Y	N	Y	Y	N	Y	Y
22 ***Solomon***	Y	Y	Y	Y	Y	Y	N	Y
23 ***Boehlert***	Y	Y	N	Y	Y	Y	N	Y
24 ***McHugh***	Y	Y	Y	Y	Y	Y	N	Y
25 ***Walsh***	Y	Y	Y	Y	Y	Y	Y	Y
26 Hinchey	Y	N	N	Y	Y	Y	Y	Y
27 ***Paxon***	Y	Y	Y	Y	Y	Y	N	Y
28 Slaughter	N	N	N	Y	Y	Y	Y	Y
29 LaFalce	Y	Y	N	Y	Y	Y	Y	Y
30 ***Quinn***	Y	Y	Y	Y	Y	Y	Y	Y
31 ***Houghton***	Y	Y	N	Y	Y	Y	Y	Y
NORTH CAROLINA								
1 Clayton	N	N	N	Y	Y	N	Y	N
2 Valentine	Y	Y	Y	Y	Y	Y	Y	N
3 Lancaster	N	Y	N	Y	Y	N	Y	Y
4 Price	Y	Y	N	Y	N	Y	Y	Y
5 Neal	Y	?	Y	Y	Y	Y	Y	Y
6 ***Coble***	Y	Y	Y	Y	Y	Y	N	Y
7 Rose	?	N	N	Y	Y	Y	Y	N
8 Hefner	Y	Y	N	Y	N	Y	Y	Y
9 ***McMillan***	Y	Y	Y	Y	Y	Y	N	Y
10 ***Ballenger***	Y	Y	Y	Y	Y	Y	N	Y
11 ***Taylor***	N	Y	Y	Y	Y	Y	N	Y
12 Watt	N	N	N	Y	N	N	Y	N
NORTH DAKOTA								
AL Pomeroy	Y	Y	N	Y	Y	Y	Y	Y
OHIO								
1 Mann	N	N	N	Y	Y	N	Y	N
2 ***Portman***	Y	Y	Y	Y	Y	Y	N	Y
3 Hall	Y	N	N	Y	Y	Y	Y	Y
4 ***Oxley***	Y	Y	Y	Y	Y	Y	N	Y
5 ***Gillmor***	Y	Y	Y	Y	Y	Y	Y	Y
6 Strickland	Y	N	N	Y	Y	Y	Y	Y
7 ***Hobson***	Y	Y	Y	Y	Y	Y	N	Y
8 ***Boehner***	Y	Y	Y	Y	Y	Y	N	Y
9 Kaptur	Y	Y	N	Y	Y	Y	Y	Y
10 ***Hoke***	Y	Y	Y	Y	Y	Y	N	Y
11 Stokes	N	N	N	Y	N	N	Y	N
12 ***Kasich***	Y	Y	Y	Y	Y	Y	N	Y
13 Brown	Y	N	N	Y	Y	Y	Y	Y
14 Sawyer	Y	N	N	Y	Y	Y	Y	Y
15 ***Pryce***	Y	Y	Y	Y	Y	Y	N	Y
16 ***Regula***	Y	Y	Y	Y	Y	Y	N	Y
17 Traficant	N	Y	Y	Y	Y	N	Y	N
18 Applegate	N	Y	Y	Y	Y	N	Y	Y
19 Fingerhut	Y	N	N	Y	Y	Y	Y	Y
OKLAHOMA								
1 ***Inhofe***	Y	Y	Y	Y	Y	Y	N	Y
2 Synar	N	N	N	Y	Y	N	N	Y
3 Brewster	Y	N	N	Y	?	?	Y	Y
4 McCurdy	Y	Y	N	Y	Y	Y	Y	Y
5 ***Istook***	N	Y	Y	Y	Y	Y	N	Y
6 English	Y	Y	N	Y	Y	Y	Y	N
OREGON								
1 Furse	N	N	N	Y	N	N	Y	Y
2 ***Smith***	Y	Y	Y	Y	Y	Y	N	Y
3 Wyden	Y	N	N	Y	Y	Y	Y	Y
4 DeFazio	Y	N	N	Y	Y	Y	Y	N
5 Kopetski	N	N	N	Y	Y	N	Y	N
PENNSYLVANIA								
1 Foglietta	Y	N	N	Y	Y	N	Y	Y
2 Blackwell	Y	N	N	Y	Y	N	Y	Y
3 Borski	Y	N	N	Y	Y	Y	Y	Y
4 Klink	N	N	N	Y	Y	N	Y	Y
5 ***Clinger***	Y	Y	Y	Y	Y	Y	N	Y
6 Holden	N	Y	Y	Y	Y	Y	Y	Y
7 ***Weldon***	Y	Y	Y	Y	Y	Y	N	Y
8 ***Greenwood***	Y	Y	Y	Y	Y	Y	N	Y
9 ***Shuster***	Y	Y	Y	Y	Y	Y	N	Y
10 ***McDade***	?	?	?	?	?	?	?	?
11 Kanjorski	N	N	N	Y	Y	N	Y	Y
12 Murtha	Y	N	N	Y	Y	Y	Y	Y
13 Margolies-Mezv.	Y	N	N	Y	Y	Y	Y	Y
14 Coyne	N	N	N	Y	Y	N	Y	Y
15 McHale	Y	Y	N	N	Y	Y	Y	Y
16 ***Walker***	Y	Y	Y	Y	Y	Y	N	Y
17 ***Gekas***	Y	Y	Y	Y	Y	Y	N	Y
18 ***Santorum***	Y	Y	Y	Y	Y	Y	N	Y
19 ***Goodling***	Y	Y	N	Y	Y	Y	N	Y
20 Murphy	N	Y	Y	Y	Y	Y	Y	Y
21 ***Ridge***	Y	Y	Y	Y	Y	Y	N	Y
RHODE ISLAND								
1 ***Machtley***	Y	Y	Y	Y	Y	Y	Y	Y
2 Reed	Y	N	N	Y	Y	Y	Y	Y
SOUTH CAROLINA								
1 ***Ravenel***	Y	Y	Y	Y	Y	Y	N	Y
2 ***Spence***	Y	Y	Y	Y	Y	Y	N	Y
3 Derrick	Y	Y	N	Y	Y	Y	Y	?
4 ***Inglis***	Y	Y	Y	Y	Y	Y	N	Y
5 Spratt	Y	Y	N	Y	Y	Y	Y	Y
6 Clyburn	Y	N	N	Y	Y	Y	Y	N
SOUTH DAKOTA								
AL Johnson	Y	Y	N	Y	Y	Y	Y	Y
TENNESSEE								
1 ***Quillen***	Y	Y	Y	Y	Y	Y	N	Y
2 ***Duncan***	Y	Y	Y	Y	Y	Y	N	Y
3 Lloyd	Y	Y	Y	Y	Y	Y	Y	Y
4 Cooper	Y	Y	Y	Y	Y	Y	Y	Y
5 Clement	Y	Y	Y	Y	Y	Y	Y	Y
6 Gordon	Y	Y	N	Y	Y	Y	Y	Y
7 ***Sundquist***	Y	Y	Y	Y	Y	Y	N	Y
8 Tanner	Y	Y	N	Y	Y	Y	Y	N
9 Ford	N	N	N	Y	Y	Y	Y	Y
TEXAS								
1 Chapman	Y	Y	Y	Y	Y	Y	Y	N
2 Wilson	N	Y	N	Y	Y	Y	Y	?
3 ***Johnson, Sam***	Y	Y	Y	Y	Y	Y	N	Y
4 Hall	Y	Y	Y	Y	Y	Y	Y	N
5 Bryant	Y	N	N	Y	Y	Y	Y	?
6 ***Barton***	Y	Y	N	Y	Y	Y	N	N
7 ***Archer***	Y	Y	Y	Y	Y	Y	N	Y
8 ***Fields***	Y	Y	Y	Y	Y	Y	N	Y
9 Brooks	N	N	N	Y	Y	N	Y	N
10 Pickle	Y	Y	N	Y	Y	Y	Y	N
11 Edwards	Y	Y	N	Y	Y	Y	Y	N
12 Geren	Y	Y	Y	Y	Y	Y	Y	N
13 Sarpalius	Y	Y	N	Y	Y	Y	Y	N
14 Laughlin	Y	Y	Y	Y	Y	Y	Y	N
15 de la Garza	Y	N	N	?	Y	Y	?	N
16 Coleman	Y	N	N	Y	Y	Y	Y	N
17 Stenholm	Y	Y	Y	Y	Y	Y	Y	N
18 Washington	?	?	?	?	?	?	?	?
19 ***Combest***	Y	Y	Y	Y	Y	Y	N	N
20 Gonzalez	Y	N	N	Y	N	N	Y	N
21 ***Smith***	Y	Y	Y	Y	Y	Y	N	N
22 ***DeLay***	Y	Y	Y	Y	Y	Y	N	Y
23 ***Bonilla***	Y	Y	N	Y	Y	Y	N	Y
24 Frost	Y	Y	N	Y	Y	Y	Y	Y
25 Andrews	Y	Y	Y	Y	Y	Y	Y	N
26 ***Armey***	Y	Y	Y	Y	Y	Y	N	Y
27 Ortiz	Y	N	N	Y	Y	Y	Y	N
28 Tejeda	Y	N	N	Y	Y	Y	Y	N
29 Green	N	N	N	Y	Y	N	Y	N
30 Johnson, E. B.	Y	N	N	Y	Y	N	Y	N
UTAH								
1 ***Hansen***	Y	Y	Y	Y	Y	Y	N	Y
2 Shepherd	Y	N	N	Y	Y	Y	Y	Y
3 Orton	Y	Y	Y	Y	Y	Y	Y	Y
VERMONT								
AL *Sanders*	Y	N	N	N	N	Y	Y	Y
VIRGINIA								
1 ***Bateman***	Y	Y	Y	Y	Y	Y	N	Y
2 Pickett	Y	N	N	Y	Y	Y	Y	N
3 Scott	N	N	N	Y	Y	N	Y	N
4 Sisisky	Y	Y	N	Y	Y	Y	Y	Y
5 Payne	Y	Y	N	Y	Y	Y	Y	Y
6 ***Goodlatte***	Y	Y	Y	Y	Y	Y	N	Y
7 ***Bliley***	Y	Y	Y	Y	Y	Y	N	Y
8 Moran	Y	N	N	Y	N	N	Y	N
9 Boucher	Y	N	N	Y	Y	Y	Y	N
10 ***Wolf***	Y	Y	Y	Y	Y	Y	N	Y
11 Byrne	Y	Y	N	Y	Y	Y	Y	Y
WASHINGTON								
1 Cantwell	Y	Y	N	Y	Y	Y	N	Y
2 Swift	N	N	N	Y	N	N	Y	N
3 Unsoeld	N	N	N	Y	N	N	Y	Y
4 Inslee	N	Y	N	Y	Y	N	Y	Y
5 Foley								
6 Dicks	Y	N	N	Y	Y	Y	Y	Y
7 McDermott	Y	N	N	Y	N	N	Y	Y
8 ***Dunn***	Y	Y	Y	Y	Y	Y	N	Y
9 Kreidler	Y	N	N	Y	Y	Y	N	Y
WEST VIRGINIA								
1 Mollohan	N	Y	N	Y	N	N	N	N
2 Wise	Y	Y	N	Y	Y	Y	Y	Y
3 Rahall	Y	Y	N	Y	Y	Y	Y	N
WISCONSIN								
1 Barca	Y	Y	N	Y	Y	Y	Y	Y
2 ***Klug***	Y	Y	Y	Y	Y	Y	Y	Y
3 ***Gunderson***	Y	Y	N	Y	Y	Y	Y	Y
4 Kleczka	Y	Y	N	Y	Y	Y	Y	Y
5 Barrett	Y	Y	N	Y	Y	Y	Y	Y
6 ***Petri***	Y	Y	Y	Y	Y	Y	N	Y
7 Obey	Y	Y	N	Y	Y	Y	Y	Y
8 ***Roth***	Y	Y	Y	Y	Y	Y	N	Y
9 ***Sensenbrenner***	Y	Y	Y	Y	Y	Y	N	Y
WYOMING								
AL ***Thomas***	Y	Y	Y	Y	Y	Y	N	Y
DELEGATES								
de Lugo, V.I.	N	N	N	D	D	D	D	Y
Faleomavaega, Am.S.	N	N	N	D	D	D	D	N
Norton, D.C.	Y	N	N	D	D	D	D	Y
Romero-B., P.R.	Y	N	N	D	D	D	D	Y
Underwood, Guam	?	N	N	D	D	D	D	Y

Southern states - Ala., Ark., Fla., Ga., Ky., La., Miss., N.C., Okla., S.C., Tenn., Texas, Va.
Omitted votes are quorum calls, which CQ does not include in its vote charts.

381. HR 2200. NASA Authorization/Funding Cut. Separate vote at the request of Goss, R-Fla., on the Hall, D-Texas, amendment adopted in the Committee of the Whole to limit the fiscal 1994 NASA authorization to the rate of inflation, which would reduce authorizations by approximately $264 million. Adopted 416-6: R 170-0; D 245-6 (ND 168-1, SD 77-5); I 1-0, July 29, 1993. (On separate votes, which may be demanded on an amendment adopted in the Committee of the Whole, the four delegates and the Resident Commissioner of Puerto Rico cannot vote. See vote 262.)

382. HR 2200. NASA Authorization/Advanced Solid Rocket Motor. Separate vote at the request of Goss, R-Fla., on the Sensenbrenner, R-Wis., en bloc amendment adopted in the Committee of the Whole en bloc amendment to cut the $35 million in the bill to transfer the remaining activities of the Advanced Solid Rocket Motor program from Utah to Yellow Creek, Miss. Adopted 303-111: R 151-18; D 151-93 (ND 109-55, SD 42-38); I 1-0, July 29, 1993. (On separate votes, which may be demanded on an amendment adopted in the Committee of the Whole, the four delegates and the Resident Commissioner of Puerto Rico cannot vote. See vote 360.)

383. HR 2200. NASA Authorization/Helium Purchases. Separate vote at the request of Goss, R-Fla., on the Cox, R-Calif., amendment adopted in the Committee of the Whole to allow NASA to purchase helium from the private sector. Adopted 326-98: R 167-5; D 158-93 (ND 116-54, SD 42-39); I 1-0, July 29, 1993. (On separate votes, which may be demanded on an amendment adopted in the Committee of the Whole, the four delegates and the Resident Commissioner of Puerto Rico cannot vote. See vote 380.)

384. HR 1964. Maritime Administration Authorization/Moratorium and Waiver. Studds, D-Mass., en bloc amendment, as amended, to exempt certain private vessels from certain maritime laws in order to be documented for domestic maritime commerce; place a moratorium on the Department of Transportation from transferring vessels over 3,000 tons to a foreign registry; and make other technical corrections. Adopted in the Committee of the Whole 388-41: R 134-38; D 253-3 (ND 173-2, SD 80-1); I 1-0, July 29, 1993.

385. HR 1964. Maritime Administration Authorization/Waiver and Moratorium. Separate vote at the request of Solomon, R-N.Y., on the Studds, D-Mass., en bloc amendment adopted in the Committee of the Whole to exempt certain private vessels from certain maritime laws in order to be documented for domestic maritime commerce; place a moratorium on the Department of Transportation from transferring vessels over 3,000 tons to a foreign registry; and make other technical corrections. Adopted 382-40: R 136-36; D 245-4 (ND 167-2, SD 78-2); I 1-0, July 29, 1993. (On separate votes, which may be demanded on an amendment adopted in the Committee of the Whole, the four delegates and the Resident Commissioner of Puerto Rico cannot vote. See vote 384.)

386. HR 1964. Maritime Administration Authorization/Passage. Passage of the bill to authorize $621 million in fiscal 1994 for the Maritime Administration within the Department of Transportation. Passed 372-48: R 126-42; D 245-6 (ND 164-4, SD 81-2); I 1-0, July 29, 1993.

387. HR 2150. Coast Guard Authorization/Rule. Adoption of the rule (H Res 206) to provide for House floor consideration of the bill to authorize $3.6 billion in fiscal 1994 for the Coast Guard. Adopted 401-0: R 160-0; D 240-0 (ND 164-0, SD 76-0); I 1-0, July 30, 1993.

388. HR 2535. Persian Gulf Veterans Health Care/Passage. Montgomery, D-Miss., motion to suspend the rules and pass the bill to provide priority health care for veterans exposed to toxic substances or environmental hazards during the Persian Gulf War for conditions that become apparent before Oct. 1, 1996. Motion agreed to 411-0: R 170-0; D 240-0 (ND 163-0, SD 77-0); I 1-0, Aug. 2, 1993. A two-thirds majority of those present and voting (274 in this case) is required for passage under suspension of the rules.

** Rep. Paul B. Henry, R-Mich., died July 31, 1993. Vote 387 was the last vote for which he was eligible.

KEY

Y	Voted for (yea).
#	Paired for.
+	Announced for.
N	Voted against (nay).
X	Paired against.
−	Announced against.
P	Voted "present."
C	Voted "present" to avoid possible conflict of interest.
?	Did not vote or otherwise make a position known.
D	Delegates ineligible to vote.

Democrats **Republicans**
Independent

	381	382	383	384	385	386	387	388
ALABAMA								
1 Callahan	Y	N	Y	Y	Y	Y	Y	Y
2 Everett	Y	N	Y	Y	Y	Y	Y	Y
3 Browder	N	N	Y	Y	Y	Y	Y	Y
4 Bevill	Y	N	Y	Y	Y	Y	Y	Y
5 Cramer	N	N	N	Y	Y	Y	Y	Y
6 Bachus	Y	N	Y	Y	Y	Y	Y	Y
7 Hilliard	N	N	N	Y	Y	Y	Y	Y
ALASKA								
AL Young	Y	Y	Y	Y	Y	Y	Y	Y
ARIZONA								
1 Coppersmith	Y	N	Y	Y	Y	Y	Y	Y
2 Pastor	Y	Y	N	Y	Y	Y	Y	Y
3 Stump	Y	Y	Y	N	N	N	Y	Y
4 Kyl	Y	Y	Y	N	N	N	Y	Y
5 Kolbe	Y	Y	Y	N	N	Y	?	Y
6 English	Y	Y	Y	Y	Y	Y	Y	Y
ARKANSAS								
1 Lambert	Y	N	Y	Y	Y	Y	Y	?
2 Thornton	Y	N	Y	Y	Y	Y	Y	Y
3 Hutchinson	Y	Y	Y	Y	Y	Y	Y	Y
4 Dickey	Y	Y	Y	Y	Y	Y	Y	Y
CALIFORNIA								
1 Hamburg	Y	N	N	Y	Y	Y	Y	Y
2 Herger	Y	Y	Y	Y	Y	Y	Y	Y
3 Fazio	Y	N	N	Y	Y	Y	Y	Y
4 Doolittle	Y	Y	Y	N	N	N	Y	Y
5 Matsui	Y	Y	Y	Y	Y	Y	?	Y
6 Woolsey	Y	N	Y	Y	Y	Y	Y	Y
7 Miller	Y	Y	N	Y	Y	Y	Y	Y
8 Pelosi	Y	Y	N	Y	Y	Y	Y	Y
9 Dellums	Y	N	N	Y	Y	Y	Y	Y
10 Baker	Y	Y	Y	Y	Y	Y	Y	Y
11 Pombo	Y	Y	Y	Y	Y	Y	Y	Y
12 Lantos	Y	Y	Y	Y	Y	Y	Y	Y
13 Stark	Y	N	Y	Y	Y	Y	Y	Y
14 Eshoo	Y	Y	Y	Y	Y	Y	Y	Y
15 Mineta	Y	N	N	Y	Y	Y	Y	Y
16 Edwards	Y	N	N	Y	Y	Y	Y	Y
17 Farr	Y	N	N	Y	Y	Y	Y	Y
18 Condit	Y	Y	Y	Y	N	Y	Y	Y
19 Lehman	Y	Y	N	Y	Y	Y	Y	Y
20 Dooley	Y	Y	Y	Y	Y	Y	Y	Y
21 Thomas	Y	Y	Y	Y	Y	Y	Y	Y
22 Huffington	Y	Y	Y	N	N	Y	Y	Y
23 Gallegly	Y	Y	Y	Y	Y	Y	?	Y
24 Beilenson	Y	N	N	Y	Y	Y	Y	Y
25 McKeon	Y	Y	Y	Y	Y	Y	Y	Y
26 Berman	Y	N	Y	Y	Y	?	Y	Y
27 Moorhead	Y	Y	Y	Y	Y	N	Y	Y
28 Dreier	Y	Y	Y	N	N	N	Y	Y
29 Waxman	Y	N	N	Y	Y	Y	Y	Y
30 Becerra	Y	N	N	Y	Y	Y	Y	?
31 Martinez	?	?	Y	Y	Y	Y	Y	Y
32 Dixon	Y	N	N	Y	Y	Y	Y	Y
33 Roybal-Allard	Y	N	N	Y	Y	Y	Y	Y
34 Torres	Y	N	N	Y	Y	Y	Y	Y
35 Waters	Y	N	N	Y	Y	Y	Y	Y
36 Harman	Y	?	N	Y	Y	Y	Y	Y
37 Tucker	Y	Y	N	Y	Y	Y	Y	Y
38 Horn	Y	Y	Y	Y	Y	Y	Y	Y
39 Royce	Y	?	Y	N	N	N	Y	Y
40 Lewis	Y	N	Y	Y	Y	Y	Y	Y
41 Kim	Y	Y	Y	Y	Y	Y	Y	Y

	381	382	383	384	385	386	387	388
42 Brown	Y	N	N	Y	Y	Y	Y	Y
43 Calvert	Y	N	Y	Y	Y	Y	Y	Y
44 McCandless	Y	Y	Y	Y	Y	Y	Y	Y
45 Rohrabacher	Y	Y	Y	N	N	N	Y	Y
46 Dornan	Y	Y	Y	N	N	N	Y	Y
47 Cox	Y	Y	Y	Y	Y	Y	Y	Y
48 Packard	+	+	+	+	+	+	?	?
49 Schenk	Y	Y	Y	Y	Y	?	Y	Y
50 Filner	Y	N	Y	Y	Y	Y	Y	Y
51 Cunningham	Y	Y	Y	Y	Y	Y	Y	Y
52 Hunter	Y	Y	Y	Y	Y	N	Y	?
COLORADO								
1 Schroeder	Y	Y	Y	Y	Y	Y	Y	Y
2 Skaggs	Y	N	Y	Y	Y	Y	Y	Y
3 McInnis	Y	Y	Y	Y	Y	?	Y	Y
4 Allard	Y	Y	N	N	N	N	Y	Y
5 Hefley	Y	Y	Y	Y	Y	Y	Y	Y
6 Schaefer	Y	Y	Y	Y	Y	Y	Y	Y
CONNECTICUT								
1 Kennelly	Y	Y	Y	Y	Y	Y	Y	Y
2 Gejdenson	Y	Y	Y	Y	Y	Y	Y	Y
3 DeLauro	Y	Y	Y	Y	Y	Y	Y	Y
4 Shays	Y	Y	Y	Y	Y	Y	Y	Y
5 Franks	Y	Y	Y	Y	Y	Y	Y	Y
6 Johnson	Y	Y	Y	Y	Y	Y	Y	Y
DELAWARE								
AL Castle	Y	Y	Y	Y	Y	Y	Y	Y
FLORIDA								
1 Hutto	Y	Y	Y	Y	Y	Y	Y	Y
2 Peterson	Y	N	Y	Y	Y	Y	Y	Y
3 Brown	Y	Y	Y	Y	Y	Y	Y	Y
4 Fowler	Y	Y	Y	Y	Y	Y	?	Y
5 Thurman	Y	Y	Y	Y	Y	Y	Y	Y
6 Stearns	Y	Y	Y	Y	Y	Y	Y	Y
7 Mica	Y	N	Y	Y	Y	Y	Y	Y
8 McCollum	Y	Y	Y	Y	Y	Y	Y	Y
9 Bilirakis	Y	N	Y	Y	Y	Y	Y	Y
10 Young	Y	Y	Y	Y	Y	Y	Y	Y
11 Gibbons	Y	N	Y	Y	Y	Y	Y	Y
12 Canady	Y	Y	Y	Y	Y	Y	Y	Y
13 Miller	Y	Y	Y	Y	Y	Y	Y	Y
14 Goss	Y	Y	Y	Y	Y	Y	Y	Y
15 Bacchus	N	N	N	Y	Y	Y	Y	?
16 Lewis	Y	Y	Y	Y	Y	Y	Y	?
17 Meek	Y	N	N	Y	Y	Y	Y	Y
18 Ros-Lehtinen	Y	Y	Y	Y	Y	Y	?	Y
19 Johnston	Y	Y	Y	Y	Y	Y	Y	Y
20 Deutsch	Y	Y	N	Y	Y	Y	Y	Y
21 Diaz-Balart	Y	Y	Y	Y	Y	Y	Y	Y
22 Shaw	Y	Y	Y	Y	Y	Y	Y	Y
23 Hastings	Y	Y	N	Y	Y	Y	Y	Y
GEORGIA								
1 Kingston	Y	Y	Y	N	Y	Y	Y	Y
2 Bishop	Y	N	N	Y	Y	Y	Y	Y
3 Collins	Y	Y	N	Y	N	N	Y	Y
4 Linder	Y	Y	Y	Y	Y	Y	Y	Y
5 Lewis	Y	N	N	Y	Y	Y	Y	Y
6 Gingrich	Y	N	Y	N	N	Y	Y	Y
7 Darden	Y	N	Y	Y	Y	Y	Y	Y
8 Rowland	Y	Y	Y	Y	Y	Y	Y	Y
9 Deal	Y	Y	Y	Y	Y	Y	Y	?
10 Johnson	Y	N	Y	Y	Y	Y	Y	Y
11 McKinney	Y	N	N	Y	Y	Y	?	Y
HAWAII								
1 Abercrombie	Y	N	N	Y	Y	Y	Y	Y
2 Mink	Y	N	N	Y	Y	Y	Y	Y
IDAHO								
1 LaRocco	Y	Y	Y	Y	Y	Y	Y	Y
2 Crapo	Y	Y	Y	Y	Y	N	+	Y
ILLINOIS								
1 Rush	Y	N	N	Y	Y	Y	Y	?
2 Reynolds	Y	N	N	Y	Y	Y	Y	Y
3 Lipinski	Y	Y	Y	Y	Y	Y	?	Y
4 Gutierrez	Y	Y	Y	Y	Y	Y	Y	Y
5 Rostenkowski	N	N	N	Y	Y	Y	Y	Y
6 Hyde	Y	Y	Y	N	N	Y	Y	Y
7 Collins	Y	N	N	Y	Y	Y	Y	Y
8 Crane	Y	Y	Y	N	N	N	Y	Y
9 Yates	Y	Y	Y	N	Y	Y	Y	Y
10 Porter	Y	Y	Y	N	N	N	Y	+
11 Sangmeister	Y	Y	Y	Y	Y	Y	Y	Y
12 Costello	Y	Y	Y	Y	Y	Y	Y	Y
13 Fawell	Y	Y	Y	Y	Y	N	Y	Y
14 Hastert	Y	Y	Y	Y	Y	+	+	Y
15 Ewing	Y	Y	Y	Y	Y	Y	Y	Y
16 Manzullo	Y	Y	Y	N	N	N	Y	Y
17 Evans	Y	Y	Y	Y	Y	Y	Y	Y

ND Northern Democrats   SD Southern Democrats

	381	382	383	384	385	386	387	388
18 ***Michel***	Y	Y	Y	Y	Y	Y	Y	Y
19 Poshard	Y	Y	Y	Y	Y	Y	Y	Y
20 Durbin	Y	Y	Y	Y	Y	Y	Y	Y
INDIANA								
1 Visclosky	Y	Y	Y	Y	Y	Y	Y	Y
2 Sharp	Y	Y	Y	Y	Y	Y	Y	Y
3 Roemer	Y	N	Y	Y	Y	Y	Y	Y
4 Long	Y	N	Y	Y	Y	Y	Y	Y
5 ***Buyer***	Y	Y	Y	Y	Y	Y	Y	Y
6 ***Burton***	?	Y	Y	N	N	N	Y	Y
7 ***Myers***	Y	Y	Y	Y	Y	Y	Y	Y
8 McCloskey	?	N	Y	Y	Y	Y	Y	Y
9 Hamilton	Y	Y	Y	Y	Y	Y	Y	Y
10 Jacobs	Y	Y	Y	N	N	N	Y	Y
IOWA								
1 ***Leach***	Y	Y	Y	Y	Y	N	Y	Y
2 ***Nussle***	Y	Y	Y	Y	Y	N	Y	Y
3 ***Lightfoot***	Y	Y	Y	Y	Y	Y	Y	Y
4 Smith	Y	Y	Y	Y	Y	Y	Y	Y
5 ***Grandy***	Y	Y	Y	Y	Y	Y	Y	Y
KANSAS								
1 ***Roberts***	Y	Y	Y	N	N	N	Y	Y
2 Slattery	Y	Y	Y	Y	Y	Y	Y	Y
3 ***Meyers***	Y	Y	Y	Y	Y	Y	Y	Y
4 Glickman	Y	Y	Y	Y	Y	Y	Y	Y
KENTUCKY								
1 Barlow	Y	N	Y	Y	Y	Y	Y	Y
2 Natcher	Y	N	Y	Y	Y	Y	Y	Y
3 Mazzoli	Y	Y	Y	Y	Y	Y	Y	Y
4 ***Bunning***	Y	Y	Y	Y	Y	Y	Y	Y
5 ***Rogers***	Y	Y	Y	Y	Y	Y	Y	Y
6 Baesler	Y	Y	Y	Y	Y	Y	Y	Y
LOUISIANA								
1 ***Livingston***	Y	N	Y	Y	Y	Y	Y	Y
2 Jefferson	Y	?	Y	Y	Y	Y	?	Y
3 Tauzin	Y	Y	Y	Y	Y	Y	Y	Y
4 Fields	Y	N	N	Y	Y	Y	Y	?
5 ***McCrery***	Y	Y	Y	Y	Y	Y	Y	Y
6 ***Baker***	Y	Y	Y	Y	Y	Y	Y	Y
7 Hayes	Y	N	N	Y	Y	Y	Y	Y
MAINE								
1 Andrews	Y	Y	Y	Y	Y	Y	Y	Y
2 ***Snowe***	Y	Y	Y	Y	Y	Y	Y	Y
MARYLAND								
1 ***Gilchrest***	Y	Y	Y	Y	Y	Y	Y	Y
2 ***Bentley***	Y	Y	Y	Y	Y	Y	Y	Y
3 Cardin	Y	Y	Y	Y	Y	Y	Y	Y
4 Wynn	Y	N	N	Y	Y	Y	Y	Y
5 Hoyer	Y	N	Y	Y	Y	Y	Y	Y
6 ***Bartlett***	Y	Y	Y	Y	Y	Y	Y	Y
7 Mfume	Y	?	N	Y	Y	Y	Y	Y
8 ***Morella***	Y	Y	Y	Y	Y	?	Y	Y
MASSACHUSETTS								
1 Olver	Y	Y	Y	Y	Y	Y	Y	Y
2 Neal	Y	?	Y	Y	Y	Y	Y	Y
3 ***Blute***	Y	Y	Y	Y	Y	Y	Y	Y
4 Frank	Y	Y	Y	Y	Y	Y	Y	Y
5 Meehan	Y	Y	Y	Y	Y	Y	Y	Y
6 ***Torkildsen***	?	Y	Y	Y	Y	Y	Y	Y
7 Markey	Y	Y	Y	Y	Y	Y	Y	Y
8 Kennedy	Y	N	Y	Y	Y	?	Y	Y
9 Moakley	?	?	?	?	?	?	?	Y
10 Studds	Y	Y	Y	Y	Y	Y	Y	Y
MICHIGAN								
1 Stupak	Y	Y	Y	Y	Y	Y	Y	Y
2 ***Hoekstra***	Y	Y	Y	Y	Y	Y	Y	Y
3 Henry **	?	?	?	?	?	?	?	
4 ***Camp***	Y	Y	Y	Y	Y	Y	Y	Y
5 Barcia	Y	Y	Y	Y	Y	Y	Y	Y
6 ***Upton***	Y	Y	Y	Y	Y	Y	Y	Y
7 ***Smith***	Y	Y	N	Y	Y	Y	Y	Y
8 Carr	Y	N	Y	Y	Y	Y	Y	Y
9 Kildee	Y	Y	Y	Y	Y	Y	Y	Y
10 Bonior	Y	N	N	Y	Y	Y	Y	?
11 ***Knollenberg***	Y	Y	Y	Y	Y	N	Y	Y
12 Levin	Y	Y	Y	Y	Y	Y	Y	Y
13 Ford	Y	Y	Y	Y	Y	Y	Y	?
14 Conyers	Y	Y	Y	Y	Y	Y	Y	Y
15 Collins	N	Y	Y	Y	Y	Y	Y	Y
16 Dingell	Y	Y	N	Y	Y	Y	Y	Y
MINNESOTA								
1 Penny	Y	Y	Y	N	N	N	Y	Y
2 Minge	Y	Y	Y	Y	Y	N	Y	Y
3 ***Ramstad***	Y	Y	Y	N	N	N	Y	Y
4 Vento	Y	Y	Y	Y	Y	Y	Y	Y
5 Sabo	Y	Y	Y	Y	Y	Y	Y	?
6 ***Grams***	Y	Y	Y	Y	Y	Y	Y	Y
7 Peterson	Y	Y	Y	Y	Y	Y	Y	Y
8 Oberstar	Y	Y	N	Y	Y	Y	Y	Y
MISSISSIPPI								
1 Whitten	Y	N	N	?	Y	Y	Y	Y
2 Thompson	Y	N	N	Y	Y	Y	Y	Y
3 Montgomery	Y	N	Y	Y	Y	Y	Y	Y
4 Parker	Y	N	Y	Y	Y	Y	Y	Y
5 Taylor	Y	N	Y	Y	Y	Y	Y	Y
MISSOURI								
1 Clay	Y	N	N	Y	Y	Y	?	Y
2 ***Talent***	Y	Y	Y	Y	Y	Y	Y	Y
3 Gephardt	Y	N	N	?	Y	Y	Y	?
4 Skelton	Y	Y	Y	Y	Y	Y	Y	Y
5 Wheat	Y	Y	Y	Y	Y	Y	Y	Y
6 Danner	Y	Y	Y	Y	Y	Y	Y	Y
7 ***Hancock***	Y	Y	Y	N	N	N	Y	Y
8 ***Emerson***	Y	Y	Y	Y	Y	Y	Y	Y
9 Volkmer	Y	N	N	Y	Y	Y	Y	Y
MONTANA								
AL Williams	Y	Y	N	Y	?	Y	Y	Y
NEBRASKA								
1 ***Bereuter***	Y	Y	Y	N	N	N	Y	Y
2 Hoagland	Y	Y	Y	Y	Y	Y	Y	Y
3 ***Barrett***	Y	Y	Y	N	N	N	Y	Y
NEVADA								
1 Bilbray	Y	Y	Y	Y	Y	Y	Y	Y
2 ***Vucanovich***	Y	N	Y	Y	Y	Y	Y	Y
NEW HAMPSHIRE								
1 ***Zeliff***	Y	?	Y	Y	Y	Y	Y	Y
2 Swett	Y	Y	Y	Y	Y	Y	Y	Y
NEW JERSEY								
1 Andrews	Y	Y	Y	Y	Y	Y	Y	Y
2 Hughes	Y	N	Y	Y	Y	Y	Y	Y
3 ***Saxton***	Y	Y	Y	Y	Y	Y	Y	Y
4 ***Smith***	Y	Y	Y	Y	Y	Y	Y	Y
5 ***Roukema***	Y	Y	Y	Y	Y	Y	Y	Y
6 Pallone	Y	Y	Y	Y	Y	Y	Y	Y
7 ***Franks***	Y	Y	Y	Y	Y	Y	Y	Y
8 Klein	Y	N	Y	Y	Y	Y	Y	Y
9 Torricelli	Y	?	Y	Y	Y	Y	?	Y
10 Payne	Y	N	N	Y	Y	Y	Y	Y
11 ***Gallo***	Y	Y	Y	Y	Y	Y	Y	Y
12 ***Zimmer***	Y	Y	Y	N	N	N	Y	Y
13 Menendez	Y	N	Y	Y	Y	Y	Y	Y
NEW MEXICO								
1 ***Schiff***	Y	Y	Y	Y	Y	Y	Y	Y
2 ***Skeen***	Y	N	N	Y	Y	Y	Y	Y
3 Richardson	Y	Y	Y	Y	Y	Y	Y	Y
NEW YORK								
1 Hochbrueckner	Y	N	N	Y	Y	Y	Y	+
2 ***Lazio***	+	+	+	+	+	+	+	Y
3 ***King***	Y	Y	Y	Y	Y	Y	Y	Y
4 ***Levy***	Y	Y	Y	Y	Y	Y	Y	Y
5 Ackerman	Y	N	Y	Y	Y	Y	Y	Y
6 Flake	Y	N	Y	Y	Y	Y	?	Y
7 Manton	Y	N	N	Y	Y	Y	Y	Y
8 Nadler	Y	Y	N	Y	Y	Y	Y	Y
9 Schumer	Y	Y	Y	Y	Y	Y	Y	Y
10 Towns	Y	N	N	Y	Y	Y	Y	Y
11 Owens	Y	N	N	Y	Y	Y	Y	Y
12 Velazquez	Y	Y	N	Y	Y	Y	Y	Y
13 ***Molinari***	Y	Y	Y	Y	Y	Y	Y	Y
14 Maloney	Y	Y	Y	Y	Y	Y	Y	Y
15 Rangel	Y	N	?	Y	Y	Y	Y	Y
16 Serrano	Y	N	N	Y	Y	Y	Y	Y
17 Engel	Y	N	N	Y	Y	Y	Y	Y
18 Lowey	Y	Y	Y	Y	Y	Y	Y	Y
19 ***Fish***	Y	Y	Y	Y	Y	Y	Y	Y
20 ***Gilman***	Y	N	N	Y	Y	Y	Y	Y
21 McNulty	Y	Y	Y	Y	Y	Y	Y	Y
22 ***Solomon***	Y	Y	Y	Y	Y	Y	?	Y
23 ***Boehlert***	Y	Y	Y	Y	Y	Y	Y	Y
24 ***McHugh***	Y	Y	Y	Y	Y	Y	Y	Y
25 ***Walsh***	Y	Y	Y	Y	Y	Y	Y	Y
26 Hinchey	Y	Y	Y	Y	Y	?	Y	Y
27 ***Paxon***	Y	Y	Y	N	N	N	Y	Y
28 Slaughter	Y	Y	Y	Y	Y	Y	Y	Y
29 LaFalce	Y	Y	Y	Y	Y	Y	Y	Y
30 ***Quinn***	Y	Y	Y	Y	Y	Y	Y	Y
31 ***Houghton***	Y	Y	Y	Y	Y	Y	Y	Y
NORTH CAROLINA								
1 Clayton	Y	Y	Y	Y	Y	Y	Y	Y
2 Valentine	Y	Y	N	Y	Y	Y	Y	Y
3 Lancaster	Y	Y	Y	Y	Y	Y	?	Y
4 Price	Y	Y	Y	Y	Y	Y	Y	Y
5 Neal	Y	Y	Y	Y	Y	Y	?	Y
6 ***Coble***	Y	Y	Y	Y	Y	Y	Y	Y
7 Rose	Y	N	N	Y	Y	Y	Y	Y
8 Hefner	Y	Y	?	Y	Y	Y	Y	Y
9 ***McMillan***	Y	Y	Y	Y	Y	N	Y	Y
10 ***Ballenger***	Y	Y	Y	Y	Y	N	Y	Y
11 ***Taylor***	Y	Y	Y	Y	Y	Y	Y	Y
12 Watt	N	N	N	Y	Y	Y	Y	Y
NORTH DAKOTA								
AL Pomeroy	Y	N	Y	Y	Y	Y	Y	Y
OHIO								
1 Mann	Y	Y	N	Y	Y	Y	Y	Y
2 ***Portman***	Y	Y	Y	Y	Y	Y	Y	Y
3 Hall	Y	Y	Y	Y	Y	Y	Y	Y
4 ***Oxley***	Y	Y	Y	Y	Y	Y	Y	Y
5 ***Gillmor***	Y	Y	Y	Y	Y	Y	Y	Y
6 Strickland	Y	Y	Y	Y	Y	Y	Y	Y
7 ***Hobson***	Y	Y	Y	Y	Y	Y	Y	Y
8 ***Boehner***	Y	Y	Y	N	N	N	Y	Y
9 Kaptur	Y	Y	Y	Y	Y	Y	Y	Y
10 ***Hoke***	Y	?	Y	Y	Y	Y	Y	Y
11 Stokes	Y	N	N	Y	Y	Y	Y	Y
12 ***Kasich***	Y	Y	Y	Y	Y	Y	Y	Y
13 Brown	Y	Y	Y	Y	Y	Y	Y	Y
14 Sawyer	Y	Y	Y	Y	Y	Y	Y	Y
15 ***Pryce***	Y	Y	Y	Y	Y	Y	?	Y
16 ***Regula***	Y	Y	Y	Y	Y	Y	Y	Y
17 Traficant	Y	Y	N	Y	Y	Y	Y	Y
18 Applegate	Y	Y	Y	Y	Y	Y	Y	Y
19 Fingerhut	Y	Y	Y	Y	Y	Y	Y	Y
OKLAHOMA								
1 ***Inhofe***	Y	Y	Y	N	N	Y	?	Y
2 Synar	Y	Y	Y	Y	Y	Y	Y	Y
3 Brewster	Y	N	Y	Y	Y	Y	Y	Y
4 McCurdy	Y	Y	Y	Y	Y	Y	Y	Y
5 ***Istook***	Y	Y	Y	Y	Y	Y	Y	Y
6 English	Y	Y	Y	Y	Y	Y	Y	Y
OREGON								
1 Furse	Y	N	Y	Y	Y	Y	Y	Y
2 ***Smith***	Y	Y	Y	Y	Y	Y	Y	Y
3 Wyden	Y	Y	Y	Y	Y	Y	Y	Y
4 DeFazio	Y	Y	N	Y	Y	Y	Y	?
5 Kopetski	Y	N	N	Y	Y	Y	Y	Y
PENNSYLVANIA								
1 Foglietta	Y	Y	Y	Y	Y	Y	Y	Y
2 Blackwell	Y	N	Y	Y	Y	Y	Y	Y
3 Borski	Y	N	Y	Y	Y	Y	Y	Y
4 Klink	Y	Y	Y	Y	Y	Y	Y	Y
5 ***Clinger***	Y	Y	Y	Y	Y	Y	Y	+
6 Holden	Y	Y	Y	Y	Y	Y	Y	Y
7 ***Weldon***	Y	Y	Y	Y	Y	Y	Y	Y
8 ***Greenwood***	Y	Y	Y	Y	Y	Y	Y	Y
9 ***Shuster***	Y	Y	Y	Y	Y	?	Y	Y
10 ***McDade***	?	?	?	?	?	?	?	Y
11 Kanjorski	Y	Y	Y	Y	Y	Y	Y	Y
12 Murtha	Y	Y	Y	Y	Y	Y	Y	Y
13 Margolies-Mezv.	Y	Y	Y	Y	Y	Y	?	Y
14 Coyne	Y	Y	Y	Y	Y	Y	Y	Y
15 McHale	Y	Y	Y	Y	?	Y	Y	Y
16 ***Walker***	Y	N	Y	Y	Y	N	Y	Y
17 ***Gekas***	Y	N	Y	Y	Y	N	Y	Y
18 ***Santorum***	Y	Y	Y	Y	Y	Y	Y	Y
19 ***Goodling***	Y	Y	Y	Y	Y	Y	Y	Y
20 Murphy	Y	Y	Y	Y	Y	Y	Y	Y
21 ***Ridge***	Y	Y	Y	Y	Y	Y	?	Y
RHODE ISLAND								
1 ***Machtley***	Y	Y	Y	Y	Y	Y	Y	Y
2 Reed	Y	Y	Y	Y	Y	Y	Y	Y
SOUTH CAROLINA								
1 ***Ravenel***	Y	Y	Y	Y	Y	Y	Y	Y
2 ***Spence***	Y	Y	Y	Y	Y	Y	Y	Y
3 Derrick	?	?	?	?	?	?	Y	Y
4 ***Inglis***	Y	Y	Y	Y	Y	Y	Y	Y
5 Spratt	Y	Y	Y	Y	?	Y	Y	Y
6 Clyburn	Y	Y	N	Y	Y	Y	Y	Y
SOUTH DAKOTA								
AL Johnson	Y	Y	Y	Y	Y	Y	Y	Y
TENNESSEE								
1 ***Quillen***	Y	N	Y	Y	Y	Y	Y	Y
2 ***Duncan***	Y	Y	Y	Y	Y	N	Y	Y
3 Lloyd	Y	N	Y	Y	Y	Y	?	Y
4 Cooper	Y	N	Y	Y	Y	Y	Y	Y
5 Clement	Y	N	Y	Y	Y	Y	Y	Y
6 Gordon	Y	Y	Y	Y	Y	Y	Y	Y
7 ***Sundquist***	Y	N	Y	Y	Y	Y	Y	Y
8 Tanner	Y	N	N	Y	Y	Y	Y	Y
9 Ford	Y	Y	Y	?	?	Y	Y	?
TEXAS								
1 Chapman	Y	Y	Y	Y	Y	Y	?	?
2 Wilson	?	?	?	Y	Y	Y	Y	Y
3 ***Johnson, Sam***	Y	Y	Y	N	N	N	Y	Y
4 Hall	Y	N	N	N	N	N	Y	Y
5 Bryant	Y	Y	N	Y	Y	Y	Y	Y
6 ***Barton***	Y	N	N	N	N	N	Y	Y
7 ***Archer***	Y	Y	Y	N	N	N	Y	Y
8 ***Fields***	Y	Y	Y	Y	Y	Y	Y	Y
9 Brooks	Y	Y	N	Y	Y	Y	Y	Y
10 Pickle	Y	N	N	Y	Y	Y	Y	Y
11 Edwards	Y	Y	N	Y	Y	Y	Y	Y
12 Geren	Y	N	N	Y	Y	Y	Y	Y
13 Sarpalius	Y	Y	N	Y	Y	Y	Y	Y
14 Laughlin	Y	N	N	Y	Y	Y	Y	Y
15 de la Garza	Y	Y	Y	Y	Y	Y	Y	Y
16 Coleman	Y	Y	N	Y	Y	Y	?	?
17 Stenholm	Y	Y	N	Y	N	N	Y	Y
18 Washington	?	?	?	?	?	?	?	?
19 ***Combest***	Y	Y	N	N	N	Y	Y	Y
20 Gonzalez	Y	Y	N	Y	Y	Y	Y	Y
21 ***Smith***	Y	Y	Y	Y	Y	Y	Y	Y
22 ***DeLay***	Y	N	Y	N	N	N	Y	Y
23 ***Bonilla***	Y	Y	Y	N	N	N	Y	Y
24 Frost	Y	Y	Y	Y	Y	Y	?	Y
25 Andrews	Y	Y	N	Y	Y	Y	Y	Y
26 ***Armey***	Y	Y	Y	N	N	N	Y	Y
27 Ortiz	Y	?	N	Y	Y	Y	Y	Y
28 Tejeda	Y	Y	N	Y	Y	Y	Y	Y
29 Green	Y	Y	N	Y	Y	Y	Y	Y
30 Johnson, E. B.	Y	N	N	Y	Y	Y	Y	Y
UTAH								
1 ***Hansen***	Y	Y	Y	Y	Y	Y	?	Y
2 Shepherd	Y	Y	Y	Y	Y	Y	Y	Y
3 Orton	Y	Y	Y	Y	Y	Y	Y	Y
VERMONT								
AL *Sanders*	Y	Y	Y	Y	Y	Y	Y	Y
VIRGINIA								
1 ***Bateman***	Y	Y	Y	Y	Y	Y	?	Y
2 Pickett	Y	Y	N	Y	Y	Y	Y	Y
3 Scott	Y	N	N	Y	Y	Y	Y	Y
4 Sisisky	Y	Y	Y	Y	Y	Y	Y	Y
5 Payne	Y	Y	Y	Y	?	Y	Y	Y
6 ***Goodlatte***	Y	Y	Y	Y	Y	Y	Y	Y
7 ***Bliley***	Y	Y	Y	N	N	N	Y	Y
8 Moran	Y	Y	N	Y	Y	Y	Y	Y
9 Boucher	Y	N	N	Y	Y	Y	Y	Y
10 ***Wolf***	Y	Y	Y	Y	Y	Y	Y	Y
11 Byrne	Y	Y	Y	Y	Y	Y	Y	Y
WASHINGTON								
1 Cantwell	Y	?	Y	Y	Y	Y	Y	Y
2 Swift	Y	N	N	Y	Y	Y	Y	Y
3 Unsoeld	Y	Y	Y	Y	Y	Y	Y	Y
4 Inslee	Y	Y	Y	Y	Y	Y	Y	Y
5 Foley								
6 Dicks	Y	Y	Y	Y	Y	Y	Y	Y
7 McDermott	Y	N	Y	Y	Y	Y	Y	?
8 ***Dunn***	Y	Y	Y	Y	Y	Y	Y	Y
9 Kreidler	Y	Y	Y	Y	Y	Y	Y	Y
WEST VIRGINIA								
1 Mollohan	Y	?	N	Y	Y	Y	Y	Y
2 Wise	Y	Y	Y	Y	Y	Y	Y	Y
3 Rahall	Y	Y	N	Y	Y	Y	Y	Y
WISCONSIN								
1 Barca	Y	Y	Y	Y	Y	Y	Y	Y
2 ***Klug***	Y	Y	Y	N	N	N	Y	Y
3 ***Gunderson***	Y	Y	Y	N	Y	Y	Y	Y
4 Kleczka	Y	Y	Y	Y	Y	Y	Y	Y
5 Barrett	Y	Y	Y	Y	Y	Y	Y	Y
6 ***Petri***	Y	Y	Y	N	N	?	Y	Y
7 Obey	Y	Y	Y	Y	Y	Y	Y	Y
8 ***Roth***	Y	Y	Y	Y	Y	Y	Y	Y
9 ***Sensenbrenner***	Y	Y	Y	N	N	N	Y	Y
WYOMING								
AL ***Thomas***	Y	Y	Y	Y	Y	Y	Y	Y
DELEGATES								
de Lugo, V.I.	D	D	D	Y	D	D	D	D
Faleomavaega, Am.S.	D	D	D	Y	D	D	D	D
Norton, D.C.	D	D	D	Y	D	D	D	D
Romero-B., P.R.	D	D	D	Y	D	D	D	D
Underwood, Guam	D	D	D	Y	D	D	D	D

Southern states - Ala., Ark., Fla., Ga., Ky., La., Miss., N.C., Okla., S.C., Tenn., Texas, Va.
Omitted votes are quorum calls, which CQ does not include in its vote charts.

389. HR 2668. Community Investment Demonstration/ Passage. Gonzalez, D-Texas, motion to suspend the rules and pass the bill to encourage investment in low-income housing by pension funds by authorizing the Department of Housing and Urban Development to provide $100 million in rental assistance to low-income families living in housing built or rehabilitated with pension fund investment. Motion agreed to 309-106: R 66-104; D 242-2 (ND 166-0, SD 76-2); I 1-0, Aug. 2, 1993. A two-thirds majority of those present and voting (277 in this case) is required for passage under suspension of the rules. A "yea" was a vote in support of the president's position.

* 391. HR 2330. Intelligence Authorization/Funding Cut. Sanders, I-Vt., amendment to reduce the bill's authorization to 10 percent below the fiscal 1993 level. Rejected in Committee of the Whole 104-323: R 6-164; D 97-159 (ND 81-91, SD 16-68); I 1-0, Aug. 3, 1993. A "nay" was a vote in support of the president's position.

392. Procedural Motion. Approval, of the House Journal of Tuesday, Aug. 3. Approved 248-156: R 17-150; D 230-6 (ND 157-4, SD 73-2); I 1-0, Aug. 4, 1993.

393. HR 2330. Intelligence Authorization/Authorization Cut. Frank, D-Mass., amendment to cut the bill's authorization by $500 million. Rejected in Committee of the Whole 134-299: R 13-159; D 120-140 (ND 101-76, SD 19-64); I 1-0, Aug. 4, 1993. A "nay" was a vote in support of the president's position.

394. HR 2330. Intelligence Authorization/Willful Disclosure. Glickman, D-Kan., amendment to the Goss, R-Fla., amendment, to cover members of the Senate and executive branch by the Goss amendment. The Goss amendment requires House members to sign a statment that they will not willfully disclose classified information on penalty of censure or expulsion. Adopted in Committee of the Whole 262-171: R 4-168; D 257-3 (ND 174-1, SD 83-2); I 1-0, Aug. 4, 1993.

395. HR 2330. Intelligence Authorization/Willful Disclosure. Goss, R-Fla., amendment, as amended, to require members of the House, Senate and executive branch to sign a statement that they will not willfully disclose classified information on penalty of censure or expulsion. Before being amended by the Glickman, D-Kan., amendment, the Goss amendment would have applied only to members of the House. Adopted in Committee of the Whole 341-86: R 166-5; D 175-80 (ND 108-63, SD 67-17); I 0-1, Aug. 4, 1993.

396. HR 2330. Intelligence Authorization/Public Disclosure. Frank, D-Mass., amendment to require public disclosure of aggregate amounts associated with the bill. Rejected in Committee of the Whole 169-264: R 6-166; D 162-98 (ND 131-46, SD 31-52); I 1-0, Aug. 4, 1993.

397. HR 2330. Intelligence Authorization/Willful Disclosure. Separate vote at the request of Solomon, R-N.Y., on the Goss, R-Fla., amendment amended by Glickman, D-Kan., and adopted in the Committee of the Whole to require members of the House, Senate and executive branch to sign a statement that they will not willfully disclose classified information on penalty of censure or expulsion. Adopted 342-85: R 167-4; D 175-80 (ND 108-62, SD 67-18); I 0-1, Aug. 4, 1993. (On separate votes, which may be demanded on an amendment adopted in the Committee of the Whole, the four delegates and the Resident Commissioner of Puerto Rico cannot vote. See vote 395.)

* *Omitted votes are quorum calls, which CQ does not include in its vote charts.*

KEY

Y	Voted for (yea).
#	Paired for.
+	Announced for.
N	Voted against (nay).
X	Paired against.
—	Announced against.
P	Voted "present."
C	Voted "present" to avoid possible conflict of interest.
?	Did not vote or otherwise make a position known.
D	Delegates ineligible to vote.

Democrats **Republicans**
Independent

	389	391	392	393	394	395	396	397
ALABAMA								
1 Callahan	N	N	N	N	N	Y	N	Y
2 Everett	N	N	N	N	N	Y	N	Y
3 Browder	Y	N	Y	N	Y	?	N	Y
4 Bevill	Y	N	Y	N	Y	N	N	Y
5 Cramer	Y	N	Y	N	Y	Y	N	Y
6 Bachus	N	N	N	N	N	Y	N	Y
7 Hilliard	Y	Y	Y	Y	Y	N	N	N
ALASKA								
AL Young	Y	N	N	N	N	Y	N	Y
ARIZONA								
1 Coppersmith	Y	N	Y	N	Y	Y	Y	Y
2 Pastor	Y	Y	Y	Y	Y	Y	Y	Y
3 Stump	N	N	N	N	N	Y	N	Y
4 Kyl	N	N	N	N	N	Y	N	Y
5 Kolbe	N	N	N	N	N	Y	N	Y
6 English	Y	N	Y	Y	Y	Y	Y	Y
ARKANSAS								
1 Lambert	?	Y	Y	Y	Y	Y	N	Y
2 Thornton	Y	N	Y	N	Y	Y	N	Y
3 Hutchinson	N	N	N	N	N	Y	N	Y
4 Dickey	N	N	N	N	N	Y	N	Y
CALIFORNIA								
1 Hamburg	Y	Y	Y	Y	Y	N	Y	N
2 Herger	N	N	N	N	N	Y	N	Y
3 Fazio	Y	N	Y	N	Y	Y	N	Y
4 Doolittle	N	N	N	N	N	Y	N	Y
5 Matsui	Y	N	Y	N	?	N	N	N
6 Woolsey	Y	Y	Y	Y	Y	Y	Y	Y
7 Miller	Y	N	Y	N	Y	N	Y	Y
8 Pelosi	Y	N	Y	Y	Y	N	Y	Y
9 Dellums	Y	Y	Y	Y	Y	N	Y	Y
10 Baker	N	N	N	N	N	Y	N	Y
11 Pombo	N	N	Y	N	N	Y	N	Y
12 Lantos	Y	N	Y	N	Y	N	Y	Y
13 Stark	Y	Y	Y	Y	Y	N	Y	N
14 Eshoo	Y	Y	Y	Y	Y	Y	Y	Y
15 Mineta	Y	N	Y	N	Y	N	Y	N
16 Edwards	Y	Y	Y	Y	Y	N	Y	N
17 Farr	Y	Y	Y	Y	Y	Y	Y	Y
18 Condit	Y	Y	Y	Y	Y	Y	Y	Y
19 Lehman	Y	Y	Y	N	Y	Y	N	Y
20 Dooley	Y	Y	Y	Y	Y	Y	Y	Y
21 Thomas	N	N	N	N	N	Y	N	Y
22 Huffington	N	N	N	N	N	Y	N	Y
23 Gallegly	N	N	N	N	N	Y	N	Y
24 Beilenson	Y	N	Y	N	Y	N	Y	N
25 McKeon	N	N	N	N	N	Y	N	Y
26 Berman	Y	N	Y	N	Y	N	Y	Y
27 Moorhead	N	N	N	N	N	Y	N	Y
28 Dreier	N	N	N	N	N	Y	N	Y
29 Waxman	Y	N	?	N	Y	N	Y	Y
30 Becerra	?	Y	Y	Y	Y	Y	N	Y
31 Martinez	Y	N	Y	N	Y	Y	Y	Y
32 Dixon	Y	Y	Y	Y	Y	N	N	N
33 Roybal-Allard	Y	Y	Y	Y	Y	N	Y	N
34 Torres	Y	Y	?	Y	Y	?	Y	Y
35 Waters	Y	Y	Y	Y	Y	N	Y	N
36 Harman	Y	N	Y	N	Y	Y	Y	Y
37 Tucker	Y	Y	Y	Y	Y	Y	Y	Y
38 Horn	Y	N	N	N	N	Y	N	Y
39 Royce	N	N	N	N	N	Y	N	Y
40 Lewis	N	N	N	N	N	Y	N	Y
41 Kim	N	N	N	N	N	Y	N	Y

	389	391	392	393	394	395	396	397
42 Brown	Y	Y	?	Y	Y	Y	Y	Y
43 Calvert	N	N	N	N	N	Y	N	Y
44 McCandless	Y	N	N	N	N	Y	N	Y
45 Rohrabacher	N	N	N	N	N	Y	Y	Y
46 Dornan	N	N	N	N	N	Y	N	Y
47 Cox	N	N	?	N	N	Y	N	Y
48 Packard	?	?	?	?	?	?	?	?
49 Schenk	Y	N	Y	N	Y	Y	N	Y
50 Filner	Y	Y	Y	Y	Y	Y	N	Y
51 Cunningham	N	N	N	N	N	Y	N	Y
52 Hunter	N	N	N	N	N	Y	N	Y
COLORADO								
1 Schroeder	Y	Y	N	Y	Y	N	Y	N
2 Skaggs	Y	N	Y	N	Y	N	Y	N
3 McInnis	Y	N	N	N	N	Y	N	Y
4 Allard	N	N	N	N	N	N	N	N
5 Hefley	N	N	N	N	N	Y	N	Y
6 Schaefer	N	N	N	N	N	Y	N	Y
CONNECTICUT								
1 Kennelly	Y	N	Y	Y	Y	Y	N	Y
2 Gejdenson	Y	Y	Y	Y	Y	N	Y	N
3 DeLauro	Y	N	Y	Y	Y	Y	N	Y
4 Shays	Y	Y	N	Y	Y	Y	Y	Y
5 Franks	Y	N	N	N	N	Y	N	Y
6 Johnson	Y	N	N	N	N	Y	N	Y
DELAWARE								
AL Castle	Y	N	N	N	N	Y	N	Y
FLORIDA								
1 Hutto	Y	N	Y	N	Y	Y	N	Y
2 Peterson	Y	N	Y	N	Y	Y	N	Y
3 Brown	Y	N	Y	Y	Y	N	Y	N
4 Fowler	N	N	N	N	Y	Y	N	Y
5 Thurman	Y	Y	Y	Y	Y	Y	Y	Y
6 Stearns	N	N	N	N	N	N	N	N
7 Mica	N	N	N	N	N	Y	N	Y
8 McCollum	N	Y	N	N	N	Y	N	Y
9 Bilirakis	Y	N	N	N	N	Y	N	Y
10 Young	N	?	N	N	N	Y	N	Y
11 Gibbons	Y	N	Y	Y	Y	N	Y	N
12 Canady	N	N	N	N	N	Y	N	Y
13 Miller	N	N	N	N	N	Y	N	Y
14 Goss	N	N	N	N	N	Y	N	Y
15 Bacchus	#	N	Y	N	Y	Y	Y	Y
16 Lewis	?	N	N	N	N	Y	N	Y
17 Meek	Y	N	Y	N	Y	N	Y	N
18 Ros-Lehtinen	Y	N	N	N	N	Y	N	Y
19 Johnston	Y	N	Y	Y	Y	Y	N	Y
20 Deutsch	Y	N	Y	N	Y	N	Y	N
21 Diaz-Balart	Y	N	N	N	N	Y	N	Y
22 Shaw	N	N	N	N	N	Y	N	Y
23 Hastings	Y	N	Y	N	Y	N	Y	N
GEORGIA								
1 Kingston	N	N	Y	N	Y	N	Y	Y
2 Bishop	Y	Y	Y	N	Y	Y	N	Y
3 Collins	N	N	N	N	N	Y	N	Y
4 Linder	N	N	N	N	N	Y	N	Y
5 Lewis	Y	Y	Y	Y	Y	Y	Y	N
6 Gingrich	N	N	N	N	N	Y	N	Y
7 Darden	Y	N	Y	N	Y	Y	N	Y
8 Rowland	Y	N	Y	N	Y	Y	N	Y
9 Deal	?	N	Y	N	Y	N	Y	Y
10 Johnson	Y	N	Y	N	Y	N	Y	Y
11 McKinney	Y	Y	?	Y	Y	N	Y	N
HAWAII								
1 Abercrombie	Y	Y	Y	Y	Y	Y	Y	Y
2 Mink	Y	Y	Y	Y	Y	Y	Y	Y
IDAHO								
1 LaRocco	Y	N	Y	N	Y	Y	Y	Y
2 Crapo	N	N	N	N	N	Y	N	Y
ILLINOIS								
1 Rush	?	Y	Y	Y	Y	N	Y	N
2 Reynolds	Y	N	Y	N	Y	N	Y	N
3 Lipinski	Y	N	Y	Y	Y	Y	N	Y
4 Gutierrez	Y	Y	Y	Y	Y	N	Y	N
5 Rostenkowski	Y	Y	Y	Y	Y	?	Y	Y
6 Hyde	N	N	N	N	N	Y	N	Y
7 Collins	Y	Y	Y	Y	Y	N	Y	N
8 Crane	N	N	N	N	N	Y	N	Y
9 Yates	Y	Y	Y	Y	Y	N	Y	N
10 Porter	X	—	N	N	N	Y	N	Y
11 Sangmeister	Y	N	Y	N	Y	Y	Y	Y
12 Costello	Y	N	Y	N	Y	Y	N	Y
13 Fawell	N	N	N	N	N	Y	N	Y
14 Hastert	Y	N	N	N	N	Y	N	Y
15 Ewing	Y	N	N	N	N	Y	N	Y
16 Manzullo	N	N	N	Y	N	Y	N	Y
17 Evans	Y	Y	Y	Y	Y	Y	Y	Y

ND Northern Democrats   SD Southern Democrats

	389	391	392	393	394	395	396	397
18 ***Michel***	N	N	N	N	N	Y	N	Y
19 Poshard	Y	Y	Y	Y	Y	Y	N	Y
20 Durbin	Y	N	Y	Y	Y	Y	Y	Y
INDIANA								
1 Visclosky	Y	N	Y	N	Y	Y	N	Y
2 Sharp	Y	N	Y	N	Y	Y	Y	Y
3 Roemer	Y	Y	Y	Y	Y	Y	Y	Y
4 Long	Y	Y	Y	Y	Y	Y	Y	Y
5 ***Buyer***	N	N	N	N	N	Y	N	Y
6 ***Burton***	N	N	N	N	N	Y	N	Y
7 ***Myers***	N	N	Y	N	N	Y	N	Y
8 McCloskey	Y	N	Y	N	Y	N	Y	N
9 Hamilton	Y	N	Y	N	Y	Y	Y	Y
10 Jacobs	Y	Y	N	Y	Y	Y	Y	Y
IOWA								
1 ***Leach***	Y	N	N	N	N	Y	N	Y
2 ***Nussle***	Y	Y	N	Y	Y	Y	Y	Y
3 ***Lightfoot***	Y	N	N	N	N	Y	N	Y
4 Smith	Y	N	Y	N	Y	N	N	Y
5 ***Grandy***	Y	N	N	N	N	Y	N	Y
KANSAS								
1 ***Roberts***	N	N	N	N	N	Y	N	Y
2 Slattery	Y	N	Y	Y	Y	Y	Y	Y
3 ***Meyers***	N	N	N	N	N	Y	N	Y
4 Glickman	Y	N	Y	N	Y	N	Y	N
KENTUCKY								
1 Barlow	Y	N	?	N	Y	Y	N	Y
2 Natcher	Y	N	Y	N	Y	Y	N	Y
3 Mazzoli	Y	N	Y	N	Y	Y	Y	Y
4 ***Bunning***	N	N	N	N	N	Y	N	Y
5 ***Rogers***	N	N	N	N	N	Y	N	Y
6 Baesler	Y	N	Y	N	Y	Y	Y	Y
LOUISIANA								
1 ***Livingston***	N	N	N	N	N	Y	N	Y
2 Jefferson	Y	N	Y	?	Y	N	Y	N
3 Tauzin	Y	N	N	N	Y	Y	N	Y
4 Fields	Y	Y	Y	Y	Y	N	Y	N
5 ***McCrery***	N	N	N	N	N	Y	N	Y
6 ***Baker***	N	N	N	N	N	Y	N	Y
7 Hayes	Y	N	Y	N	Y	Y	N	Y
MAINE								
1 Andrews	Y	Y	Y	Y	Y	N	Y	N
2 ***Snowe***	Y	N	N	N	N	Y	N	Y
MARYLAND								
1 ***Gilchrest***	Y	N	?	N	N	?	N	Y
2 ***Bentley***	Y	N	N	N	N	Y	N	Y
3 Cardin	Y	N	Y	N	Y	Y	N	Y
4 Wynn	Y	Y	Y	Y	Y	N	Y	N
5 Hoyer	Y	N	Y	N	Y	Y	N	Y
6 ***Bartlett***	N	N	N	N	N	Y	N	Y
7 Mfume	Y	Y	Y	Y	Y	N	Y	N
8 ***Morella***	Y	N	N	N	N	Y	N	Y
MASSACHUSETTS								
1 Olver	Y	Y	Y	Y	Y	N	Y	N
2 Neal	Y	N	Y	Y	Y	Y	Y	Y
3 ***Blute***	Y	N	N	N	N	Y	N	Y
4 Frank	Y	Y	Y	Y	Y	N	Y	N
5 Meehan	Y	Y	Y	Y	Y	Y	Y	Y
6 ***Torkildsen***	Y	N	N	N	N	Y	N	Y
7 Markey	Y	Y	Y	Y	Y	N	Y	N
8 Kennedy	Y	Y	Y	Y	Y	Y	N	Y
9 Moakley	Y	N	Y	Y	Y	Y	Y	Y
10 Studds	Y	Y	Y	Y	Y	N	Y	N
MICHIGAN								
1 Stupak	Y	Y	Y	N	Y	Y	Y	Y
2 ***Hoekstra***	N	N	N	N	N	Y	N	Y
3 Vacancy								
4 ***Camp***	Y	N	N	N	N	Y	N	Y
5 Barcia	Y	N	Y	N	Y	?	N	Y
6 ***Upton***	Y	N	N	N	N	Y	N	Y
7 ***Smith***	N	N	N	N	N	Y	N	?
8 Carr	Y	N	Y	N	N	Y	N	Y
9 Kildee	Y	N	Y	N	Y	N	Y	N
10 Bonior	Y	Y	Y	Y	Y	Y	Y	Y
11 ***Knollenberg***	N	N	N	N	N	Y	N	Y
12 Levin	Y	N	Y	N	Y	Y	Y	Y
13 Ford	?	Y	Y	Y	Y	N	Y	N
14 Conyers	Y	?	Y	Y	Y	N	Y	N
15 Collins	Y	Y	Y	Y	Y	N	Y	N
16 Dingell	Y	N	Y	N	Y	N	N	N
MINNESOTA								
1 Penny	Y	Y	Y	Y	Y	Y	Y	Y
2 Minge	Y	Y	Y	Y	Y	Y	Y	Y
3 ***Ramstad***	N	N	N	N	N	Y	N	Y
4 Vento	Y	Y	Y	Y	Y	N	Y	N

	389	391	392	393	394	395	396	397
5 Sabo	Y	?	Y	Y	Y	?	Y	N
6 ***Grams***	N	N	N	N	N	Y	N	Y
7 Peterson	Y	Y	Y	Y	Y	Y	Y	Y
8 Oberstar	Y	Y	Y	Y	Y	N	Y	N
MISSISSIPPI								
1 Whitten	Y	N	?	N	Y	Y	N	Y
2 Thompson	Y	Y	Y	Y	Y	N	?	N
3 Montgomery	Y	N	Y	N	Y	Y	N	Y
4 Parker	Y	N	Y	N	Y	Y	N	Y
5 Taylor	N	N	N	N	Y	Y	N	Y
MISSOURI								
1 Clay	Y	Y	N	Y	Y	N	Y	N
2 ***Talent***	Y	?	?	?	?	?	?	?
3 Gephardt	Y	?	Y	N	Y	Y	Y	Y
4 Skelton	Y	N	Y	N	Y	Y	N	Y
5 Wheat	Y	N	?	N	Y	Y	Y	Y
6 Danner	Y	N	Y	N	Y	Y	Y	Y
7 ***Hancock***	N	N	N	N	N	Y	N	Y
8 ***Emerson***	Y	N	N	N	N	Y	N	Y
9 Volkmer	Y	N	Y	N	Y	Y	N	Y
MONTANA								
AL Williams	Y	Y	Y	Y	Y	N	Y	?
NEBRASKA								
1 ***Bereuter***	Y	N	N	N	N	Y	N	Y
2 Hoagland	Y	N	Y	N	Y	Y	N	Y
3 ***Barrett***	Y	N	N	N	N	Y	N	Y
NEVADA								
1 Bilbray	Y	N	Y	N	Y	Y	N	Y
2 ***Vucanovich***	N	N	N	N	N	Y	N	Y
NEW HAMPSHIRE								
1 ***Zeliff***	N	N	N	N	N	Y	N	Y
2 Swett	Y	N	?	Y	Y	Y	Y	Y
NEW JERSEY								
1 Andrews	Y	N	Y	N	Y	Y	N	Y
2 Hughes	Y	N	?	N	Y	Y	N	Y
3 ***Saxton***	Y	N	N	N	N	Y	N	Y
4 ***Smith***	Y	N	?	N	N	Y	N	Y
5 ***Roukema***	Y	N	N	Y	N	Y	N	Y
6 Pallone	Y	N	Y	N	Y	Y	N	Y
7 ***Franks***	Y	N	N	N	N	Y	N	Y
8 Klein	Y	N	Y	N	Y	Y	N	Y
9 Torricelli	Y	N	Y	N	Y	Y	Y	Y
10 Payne	Y	Y	Y	Y	Y	?	Y	N
11 ***Gallo***	Y	N	N	N	N	Y	N	Y
12 ***Zimmer***	Y	N	N	N	N	Y	Y	Y
13 Menendez	Y	N	Y	N	Y	Y	N	Y
NEW MEXICO								
1 ***Schiff***	Y	N	N	N	N	Y	N	Y
2 ***Skeen***	Y	N	N	N	N	Y	N	Y
3 Richardson	Y	N	Y	N	Y	Y	Y	Y
NEW YORK								
1 Hochbrueckner	+	N	Y	N	Y	Y	N	Y
2 ***Lazio***	Y	N	N	N	N	Y	N	Y
3 ***King***	Y	N	N	N	N	Y	N	Y
4 ***Levy***	Y	N	N	N	N	Y	N	Y
5 Ackerman	Y	N	Y	N	Y	Y	N	Y
6 Flake	Y	?	?	Y	Y	Y	Y	Y
7 Manton	Y	N	Y	N	Y	Y	N	Y
8 Nadler	Y	Y	Y	Y	Y	N	Y	N
9 Schumer	Y	N	Y	N	Y	N	Y	N
10 Towns	Y	Y	Y	Y	Y	Y	Y	N
11 Owens	Y	Y	?	Y	Y	Y	Y	Y
12 Velazquez	Y	Y	Y	Y	Y	Y	Y	N
13 ***Molinari***	Y	N	N	N	N	Y	N	Y
14 Maloney	Y	Y	Y	N	Y	Y	Y	Y
15 Rangel	Y	Y	Y	Y	Y	Y	Y	?
16 Serrano	Y	Y	Y	Y	Y	N	Y	N
17 Engel	Y	Y	Y	Y	Y	N	Y	N
18 Lowey	Y	N	Y	N	Y	Y	Y	Y
19 ***Fish***	Y	N	Y	N	N	N	N	N
20 ***Gilman***	Y	N	Y	N	N	Y	N	Y
21 McNulty	Y	N	Y	N	Y	Y	N	Y
22 ***Solomon***	N	N	N	N	N	Y	N	Y
23 ***Boehlert***	Y	N	N	N	N	Y	N	Y
24 ***McHugh***	Y	N	N	N	N	Y	N	Y
25 ***Walsh***	Y	N	N	N	N	Y	N	Y
26 Hinchey	Y	Y	Y	Y	Y	N	Y	N
27 ***Paxon***	N	N	N	N	N	Y	N	Y
28 Slaughter	Y	Y	Y	Y	Y	Y	N	Y
29 LaFalce	Y	N	Y	N	Y	N	N	N
30 ***Quinn***	Y	N	P	N	N	Y	N	Y
31 ***Houghton***	Y	?	Y	?	N	Y	N	Y
NORTH CAROLINA								
1 Clayton	Y	Y	Y	Y	Y	Y	Y	Y
2 Valentine	Y	Y	Y	Y	Y	Y	Y	Y

	389	391	392	393	394	395	396	397
3 Lancaster	Y	N	Y	N	Y	Y	N	Y
4 Price	Y	N	Y	N	Y	Y	Y	Y
5 Neal	Y	N	?	N	Y	Y	Y	Y
6 ***Coble***	N	Y	N	Y	N	Y	N	Y
7 Rose	Y	N	Y	N	Y	Y	Y	Y
8 Hefner	Y	N	Y	N	Y	Y	Y	Y
9 ***McMillan***	Y	N	N	N	N	Y	N	Y
10 ***Ballenger***	N	N	N	N	Y	Y	N	Y
11 ***Taylor***	N	N	N	N	N	Y	N	Y
12 Watt	Y	Y	Y	Y	Y	N	Y	N
NORTH DAKOTA								
AL Pomeroy	Y	N	Y	N	Y	Y	Y	Y
OHIO								
1 Mann	Y	N	Y	N	Y	Y	N	Y
2 ***Portman***	N	N	N	N	N	Y	N	Y
3 Hall	Y	N	?	Y	Y	Y	N	Y
4 ***Oxley***	Y	N	N	N	N	Y	N	Y
5 ***Gillmor***	Y	N	Y	N	N	N	N	Y
6 Strickland	Y	N	Y	Y	Y	Y	Y	Y
7 ***Hobson***	Y	N	N	N	N	Y	N	Y
8 ***Boehner***	N	N	N	N	N	Y	N	Y
9 Kaptur	Y	N	Y	N	Y	Y	N	Y
10 ***Hoke***	N	N	Y	N	N	Y	N	Y
11 Stokes	Y	Y	Y	Y	Y	N	Y	N
12 ***Kasich***	N	N	?	N	N	Y	N	Y
13 Brown	Y	Y	Y	Y	Y	Y	Y	Y
14 Sawyer	Y	N	Y	Y	Y	Y	Y	Y
15 ***Pryce***	N	N	N	N	N	Y	N	Y
16 ***Regula***	Y	N	N	N	N	Y	N	Y
17 Traficant	Y	N	Y	N	Y	Y	N	Y
18 Applegate	Y	N	Y	N	Y	Y	N	Y
19 Fingerhut	Y	N	Y	Y	Y	Y	Y	Y
OKLAHOMA								
1 ***Inhofe***	Y	N	N	N	N	Y	N	Y
2 Synar	Y	N	Y	Y	Y	N	Y	N
3 Brewster	Y	N	Y	N	Y	Y	N	Y
4 McCurdy	Y	N	?	N	Y	Y	N	Y
5 ***Istook***	N	N	N	N	N	Y	Y	Y
6 English	Y	N	Y	N	Y	Y	N	Y
OREGON								
1 Furse	Y	Y	Y	Y	Y	N	Y	Y
2 ***Smith***	N	N	N	N	N	Y	N	Y
3 Wyden	Y	Y	Y	Y	Y	Y	N	Y
4 DeFazio	#	Y	?	Y	Y	N	Y	N
5 Kopetski	Y	N	Y	Y	Y	Y	Y	Y
PENNSYLVANIA								
1 Foglietta	Y	N	Y	Y	Y	N	Y	N
2 Blackwell	Y	Y	Y	Y	Y	N	Y	N
3 Borski	Y	N	Y	N	Y	Y	N	Y
4 Klink	Y	Y	Y	Y	Y	Y	Y	Y
5 ***Clinger***	+	N	N	N	N	Y	N	Y
6 Holden	Y	N	Y	N	Y	Y	Y	Y
7 ***Weldon***	Y	N	N	N	N	Y	N	Y
8 ***Greenwood***	Y	N	N	N	N	Y	N	Y
9 ***Shuster***	N	N	N	N	N	Y	N	Y
10 ***McDade***	Y	N	N	N	N	N	N	Y
11 Kanjorski	Y	Y	Y	Y	Y	N	Y	Y
12 Murtha	Y	N	Y	N	Y	Y	N	Y
13 Margolies-Mezv.	Y	N	Y	N	Y	Y	Y	Y
14 Coyne	Y	Y	Y	Y	Y	N	Y	N
15 McHale	Y	N	Y	N	Y	Y	Y	Y
16 ***Walker***	N	N	N	N	N	Y	N	Y
17 ***Gekas***	N	N	N	N	N	Y	N	Y
18 ***Santorum***	Y	N	Y	N	N	Y	N	Y
19 ***Goodling***	Y	N	N	N	N	Y	N	Y
20 Murphy	Y	Y	?	Y	Y	Y	Y	Y
21 ***Ridge***	Y	N	N	N	N	Y	N	Y
RHODE ISLAND								
1 ***Machtley***	Y	N	N	N	N	Y	?	?
2 Reed	Y	N	Y	N	Y	N	Y	N
SOUTH CAROLINA								
1 ***Ravenel***	N	N	N	N	N	Y	N	Y
2 ***Spence***	N	N	N	N	N	Y	N	Y
3 Derrick	Y	Y	Y	N	Y	Y	Y	Y
4 ***Inglis***	N	N	N	N	N	Y	N	Y
5 Spratt	Y	N	?	N	Y	Y	Y	Y
6 Clyburn	Y	Y	Y	Y	Y	N	Y	N
SOUTH DAKOTA								
AL Johnson	Y	Y	Y	N	Y	Y	Y	Y
TENNESSEE								
1 ***Quillen***	N	Y	N	Y	N	N	N	N
2 ***Duncan***	N	Y	N	Y	N	Y	Y	Y
3 Lloyd	Y	N	Y	N	Y	Y	N	Y
4 Cooper	Y	N	Y	N	Y	Y	N	Y
5 Clement	Y	N	Y	N	Y	Y	Y	Y

	389	391	392	393	394	395	396	397
6 Gordon	Y	N	Y	N	Y	Y	N	Y
7 ***Sundquist***	N	N	N	Y	N	Y	N	Y
8 Tanner	Y	N	Y	N	Y	Y	N	Y
9 Ford	?	Y	Y	Y	Y	Y	Y	Y
TEXAS								
1 Chapman	?	N	?	N	Y	Y	?	Y
2 Wilson	Y	N	Y	N	Y	Y	N	Y
3 ***Johnson, Sam***	N	N	N	N	N	Y	N	Y
4 Hall	N	N	Y	N	Y	Y	N	Y
5 Bryant	Y	N	Y	Y	Y	Y	N	Y
6 ***Barton***	N	N	N	N	N	Y	N	Y
7 ***Archer***	N	N	Y	N	N	Y	N	Y
8 ***Fields***	N	N	?	N	N	Y	N	Y
9 Brooks	Y	N	Y	N	Y	Y	Y	Y
10 Pickle	Y	N	Y	N	N	Y	Y	Y
11 Edwards	Y	N	Y	?	Y	Y	N	Y
12 Geren	Y	N	Y	N	Y	Y	N	Y
13 Sarpalius	Y	N	Y	N	Y	Y	N	Y
14 Laughlin	Y	N	Y	N	Y	Y	N	Y
15 de la Garza	Y	?	?	N	Y	Y	N	Y
16 Coleman	?	N	Y	N	Y	N	N	N
17 Stenholm	Y	N	Y	N	Y	Y	N	Y
18 Washington	?	Y	?	Y	N	N	Y	N
19 ***Combest***	N	N	Y	N	N	Y	N	Y
20 Gonzalez	Y	Y	Y	Y	Y	N	Y	N
21 ***Smith***	N	N	N	N	N	Y	N	Y
22 ***DeLay***	N	N	N	N	N	Y	N	Y
23 ***Bonilla***	N	N	N	N	N	Y	N	Y
24 Frost	Y	N	Y	N	Y	Y	N	Y
25 Andrews	Y	N	Y	N	Y	Y	N	Y
26 ***Armey***	N	N	N	N	N	Y	N	Y
27 Ortiz	Y	N	Y	N	Y	Y	N	Y
28 Tejeda	Y	N	Y	N	Y	Y	N	Y
29 Green	Y	N	?	N	Y	Y	N	Y
30 Johnson, E. B.	Y	N	Y	N	Y	Y	N	N
UTAH								
1 ***Hansen***	N	N	N	N	N	Y	N	Y
2 Shepherd	Y	Y	N	Y	Y	Y	Y	Y
3 Orton	Y	N	Y	Y	Y	Y	N	Y
VERMONT								
AL *Sanders*	Y	Y	Y	Y	Y	N	Y	N
VIRGINIA								
1 ***Bateman***	Y	N	Y	N	N	Y	N	Y
2 Pickett	Y	N	Y	N	Y	Y	N	Y
3 Scott	Y	N	Y	N	Y	N	Y	N
4 Sisisky	Y	N	Y	N	Y	Y	N	Y
5 Payne	Y	N	Y	N	Y	Y	N	Y
6 ***Goodlatte***	N	N	N	N	N	Y	N	Y
7 ***Bliley***	?	N	N	N	N	Y	N	Y
8 Moran	Y	N	Y	N	Y	Y	Y	Y
9 Boucher	Y	N	Y	Y	Y	Y	N	Y
10 ***Wolf***	N	N	N	N	N	Y	N	Y
11 Byrne	Y	N	Y	N	Y	Y	Y	Y
WASHINGTON								
1 Cantwell	Y	Y	Y	Y	Y	Y	Y	Y
2 Swift	Y	N	Y	N	Y	Y	Y	Y
3 Unsoeld	Y	Y	Y	Y	Y	N	Y	N
4 Inslee	Y	Y	Y	Y	Y	Y	Y	Y
5 Foley								
6 Dicks	Y	N	Y	N	Y	Y	Y	Y
7 McDermott	?	Y	Y	Y	Y	N	Y	N
8 ***Dunn***	N	N	N	N	N	Y	N	Y
9 Kreidler	Y	N	Y	N	Y	Y	Y	Y
WEST VIRGINIA								
1 Mollohan	Y	N	Y	N	Y	N	N	N
2 Wise	Y	N	Y	N	Y	Y	N	Y
3 Rahall	Y	N	Y	N	Y	Y	N	Y
WISCONSIN								
1 Barca	Y	Y	Y	Y	Y	Y	N	Y
2 ***Klug***	N	N	N	N	N	Y	N	Y
3 ***Gunderson***	N	N	N	N	N	Y	N	Y
4 Kleczka	Y	N	Y	Y	Y	Y	N	Y
5 Barrett	Y	Y	Y	Y	Y	Y	Y	Y
6 ***Petri***	Y	Y	N	Y	N	Y	N	Y
7 Obey	Y	Y	Y	Y	Y	N	Y	N
8 ***Roth***	Y	N	N	Y	N	Y	N	Y
9 ***Sensenbrenner***	N	N	N	Y	N	Y	N	Y
WYOMING								
AL ***Thomas***	Y	N	N	N	?	?	N	Y
DELEGATES								
de Lugo, V.I.	D	N	D	N	Y	N	Y	D
Faleomavaega, Am.S.	D	N	D	N	Y	Y	Y	D
Norton, D.C.	D	Y	D	Y	Y	N	Y	D
Romero-B., P.R.	D	?	D	N	Y	Y	Y	D
Underwood, Guam	D	N	D	N	?	?	Y	D

Southern states - Ala., Ark., Fla., Ga., Ky., La., Miss., N.C., Okla., S.C., Tenn., Texas, Va.
Omitted votes are quorum calls, which CQ does not include in its vote charts.

398. HR 2330. Intelligence Authorization/Passage. Passage of the bill to authorize a classified amount for intelligence agencies and operations in fiscal 1994. Passed 400-28: R 166-6; D 234-21 (ND 154-17, SD 80-4); I 0-1, Aug. 4, 1993.

399. HR 2010. National Service/Motion to Instruct. Goodling, R-Pa., motion to instruct the House conferees to insist on the House provisions to require that the authorizations in the bill be counted under the Labor, Health and Human Services budget function by the Office of Management and Budget. Motion agreed to 422-7: R 173-0; D 248-7 (ND 166-5, SD 82-2); I 1-0, Aug. 4, 1993.

400. HR 2401. Fiscal 1994 Defense Authorization/Previous Question. Frost, D-Texas, motion to order the previous question (thus ending debate and the possibility of amendment) on adoption of the rule (H Res 233) to provide for House floor consideration of the bill to authorize $263 billion in fiscal 1994 for the Department of Defense. Motion agreed to 250-175: R 1-173; D 248-2 (ND 168-1, SD 80-1); I 1-0, Aug. 4, 1993.

401. HR 2401. Fiscal 1994 Defense Authorization/Rule. Adoption of the rule (H Res 233) to provide for House floor consideration of the bill to authorize $263 billion in fiscal 1994 for the Department of Defense. Adopted 248-173: R 1-172; D 246-1 (ND 167-0, SD 79-1); I 1-0, Aug. 4, 1993.

402. Procedural Motion. Approval of the House Journal of Wednesday, Aug. 4. Approved 255-155: R 17-150; D 237-5 (ND 160-4, SD 77-1); I 1-0, Aug. 5, 1993.

403. HR 2264. 1993 Budget Reconciliation/Rule. Adoption of the rule (H Res 240) to waive points of order against and provide for House floor consideration of the conference report to reduce the deficit by an estimated $496 billion over five years through almost $241 billion in additional taxes and $255 billion in spending cuts by closely tracking President Clinton's economic proposals. Adopted 253-179: R 0-174; D 252-5 (ND 169-3, SD 83-2); I 1-0, Aug. 5, 1993. (Adoption of the rule automatically incorporates into House rules provisions that can require the House to find offsetting spending cuts or revenue increases if certain targets for entitlement spending are exceeded and the president proposes a way to offset the overspending. The provisions are similar to those in President Clinton's executive order establishing an entitlement review process.)

*406. HR 2264. 1993 Budget Reconciliation/Adoption. Adoption of the conference report to reduce the deficit by an estimated $496 billion over five years through almost $241 billion in additional taxes and $255 billion in spending cuts by closely tracking President Clinton's economic proposals. Adopted 218-216: R 0-175; D 217-41 (ND 155-18, SD 62-23); I 1-0, Aug. 5, 1993. A "yea" was a vote in support of the president's position.

407. HR 2010. National Service/Rule. Adoption of the rule (H Res 241) to waive points of order against and provide for House floor consideration of the conference report on the bill to authorize $300 million in fiscal 1994, $500 million in fiscal 1995 and $700 million in fiscal 1996 for the National Service program, which would provide people age 17 or older with $4,725 a year for up to two years in education awards in return for work in community service programs. Local programs would offer stipends of up to $7,400 a year, with the federal government providing an 85 percent match for the stipend and 85 percent of health- and child-care costs. Adopted 256-166: R 8-162; D 247-4 (ND 165-3, SD 82-1); I 1-0, Aug. 6, 1993.

Omitted votes are quorum calls, which CQ does not include in its vote charts.

KEY

Y	Voted for (yea).
#	Paired for.
+	Announced for.
N	Voted against (nay).
X	Paired against.
—	Announced against.
P	Voted "present."
C	Voted "present" to avoid possible conflict of interest.
?	Did not vote or otherwise make a position known.
D	Delegates ineligible to vote.

Democrats **Republicans**
Independent

ND Northern Democrats   SD Southern Democrats

	398	399	400	401	402	403	406	407
ALABAMA								
1 Callahan	Y	Y	N	N	N	N	N	N
2 Everett	Y	Y	N	N	N	N	N	N
3 Browder	Y	Y	Y	Y	Y	Y	N	Y
4 Bevill	Y	Y	Y	Y	?	Y	Y	Y
5 Cramer	Y	Y	Y	Y	Y	Y	Y	Y
6 Bachus	Y	Y	N	N	N	N	N	N
7 Hilliard	N	Y	Y	Y	Y	Y	Y	Y
ALASKA								
AL Young	Y	Y	N	N	N	N	N	?
ARIZONA								
1 Coppersmith	Y	Y	Y	Y	Y	Y	N	Y
2 Pastor	Y	Y	Y	Y	Y	Y	Y	Y
3 Stump	Y	Y	N	N	N	N	N	N
4 Kyl	Y	Y	N	N	N	N	N	N
5 Kolbe	Y	Y	N	N	N	N	N	N
6 English	Y	Y	Y	Y	Y	Y	Y	Y
ARKANSAS								
1 Lambert	Y	Y	Y	Y	Y	Y	Y	N
2 Thornton	Y	Y	Y	Y	Y	Y	N	Y
3 Hutchinson	Y	Y	N	N	N	N	N	N
4 Dickey	Y	Y	N	N	N	N	N	?
CALIFORNIA								
1 Hamburg	N	Y	Y	Y	Y	Y	Y	Y
2 Herger	Y	Y	N	N	?	N	N	N
3 Fazio	Y	Y	Y	Y	Y	Y	Y	Y
4 Doolittle	Y	Y	N	N	N	N	N	N
5 Matsui	Y	Y	Y	Y	Y	Y	Y	Y
6 Woolsey	N	Y	Y	Y	Y	Y	Y	Y
7 Miller	Y	Y	?	?	Y	Y	Y	Y
8 Pelosi	Y	Y	Y	Y	Y	Y	Y	Y
9 Dellums	N	Y	Y	Y	Y	Y	Y	Y
10 Baker	Y	Y	N	N	?	N	N	N
11 Pombo	Y	Y	N	Y	N	N	N	N
12 Lantos	Y	Y	Y	Y	Y	Y	Y	Y
13 Stark	Y	Y	Y	Y	Y	Y	Y	Y
14 Eshoo	Y	Y	Y	Y	Y	Y	Y	Y
15 Mineta	Y	Y	Y	Y	Y	Y	Y	Y
16 Edwards	Y	Y	Y	Y	Y	Y	Y	Y
17 Farr	Y	Y	Y	Y	Y	Y	Y	Y
18 Condit	Y	Y	Y	Y	Y	Y	N	Y
19 Lehman	Y	Y	Y	Y	Y	Y	N	Y
20 Dooley	Y	Y	Y	Y	?	Y	N	Y
21 Thomas	Y	Y	N	N	N	N	N	N
22 Huffington	Y	Y	N	N	N	N	N	N
23 Gallegly	Y	Y	N	N	N	N	N	N
24 Beilenson	Y	Y	Y	Y	Y	Y	Y	Y
25 McKeon	Y	Y	N	N	N	N	N	N
26 Berman	Y	Y	Y	Y	Y	Y	Y	Y
27 Moorhead	Y	Y	N	N	N	N	N	N
28 Dreier	Y	Y	N	N	N	N	N	N
29 Waxman	Y	Y	Y	Y	Y	Y	Y	Y
30 Becerra	N	Y	Y	Y	Y	Y	Y	Y
31 Martinez	Y	Y	Y	Y	Y	Y	Y	Y
32 Dixon	Y	Y	Y	Y	?	Y	Y	Y
33 Roybal-Allard	Y	Y	Y	Y	Y	Y	Y	Y
34 Torres	Y	Y	Y	Y	Y	Y	Y	Y
35 Waters	Y	Y	Y	Y	Y	Y	Y	Y
36 Harman	Y	Y	Y	Y	Y	Y	Y	Y
37 Tucker	Y	Y	Y	Y	Y	Y	Y	Y
38 Horn	Y	Y	N	N	N	N	N	N
39 Royce	Y	Y	N	N	N	N	N	N
40 Lewis	Y	Y	N	N	N	N	N	N
41 Kim	Y	Y	N	N	N	N	N	N
42 Brown	Y	Y	Y	Y	?	Y	Y	Y
43 Calvert	Y	Y	N	N	N	N	N	N
44 McCandless	Y	Y	N	N	N	N	N	N
45 Rohrabacher	N	Y	N	N	N	N	N	N
46 Dornan	Y	Y	N	N	?	N	N	N
47 Cox	Y	Y	N	N	N	N	N	N
48 Packard	?	?	?	?	?	?	N	?
49 Schenk	Y	Y	Y	Y	Y	Y	Y	Y
50 Filner	Y	Y	Y	Y	Y	Y	Y	Y
51 Cunningham	Y	Y	N	N	N	N	N	N
52 Hunter	Y	Y	N	N	?	N	N	N
COLORADO								
1 Schroeder	N	Y	Y	Y	N	Y	Y	Y
2 Skaggs	Y	Y	Y	Y	Y	Y	Y	Y
3 McInnis	Y	Y	N	N	Y	N	N	N
4 Allard	Y	Y	N	N	N	N	N	N
5 Hefley	Y	Y	N	N	N	N	N	N
6 Schaefer	Y	Y	N	N	N	N	N	N
CONNECTICUT								
1 Kennelly	Y	Y	Y	Y	Y	Y	Y	Y
2 Gejdenson	Y	Y	Y	Y	Y	Y	Y	Y
3 DeLauro	Y	Y	Y	Y	Y	Y	Y	Y
4 Shays	N	Y	N	N	N	N	N	Y
5 Franks	Y	Y	N	N	N	N	N	N
6 Johnson	Y	Y	N	N	N	N	N	N
DELAWARE								
AL Castle	Y	Y	N	N	N	N	N	N
FLORIDA								
1 Hutto	Y	Y	Y	Y	Y	Y	N	Y
2 Peterson	Y	Y	Y	Y	Y	Y	Y	Y
3 Brown	Y	Y	Y	Y	Y	Y	Y	Y
4 Fowler	Y	Y	N	N	N	N	N	N
5 Thurman	Y	Y	Y	Y	Y	Y	Y	Y
6 Stearns	Y	Y	N	N	N	N	N	N
7 Mica	Y	Y	N	N	N	N	N	N
8 McCollum	Y	Y	N	N	N	N	N	N
9 Bilirakis	Y	Y	N	N	N	N	N	N
10 Young	Y	Y	N	?	N	N	?	
11 Gibbons	Y	Y	Y	Y	Y	Y	Y	Y
12 Canady	Y	Y	N	N	N	N	N	N
13 Miller	Y	Y	N	N	N	N	N	N
14 Goss	Y	Y	N	N	N	N	N	N
15 Bacchus	Y	Y	Y	Y	Y	Y	Y	Y
16 Lewis	Y	Y	N	N	N	N	N	N
17 Meek	Y	Y	Y	Y	Y	Y	Y	Y
18 Ros-Lehtinen	Y	Y	N	N	N	N	N	N
19 Johnston	Y	?	Y	Y	Y	Y	Y	?
20 Deutsch	Y	Y	Y	Y	Y	Y	Y	Y
21 Diaz-Balart	Y	Y	N	N	N	N	N	N
22 Shaw	Y	Y	N	N	N	N	N	N
23 Hastings	Y	Y	Y	Y	Y	Y	Y	Y
GEORGIA								
1 Kingston	Y	Y	N	N	Y	N	N	N
2 Bishop	Y	Y	Y	Y	Y	Y	Y	Y
3 Collins	Y	Y	N	N	N	N	N	N
4 Linder	Y	Y	N	N	N	N	N	N
5 Lewis	Y	Y	Y	Y	Y	Y	Y	Y
6 Gingrich	Y	Y	N	N	N	N	N	N
7 Darden	Y	Y	Y	Y	Y	Y	Y	Y
8 Rowland	Y	Y	Y	Y	Y	Y	N	Y
9 Deal	Y	Y	Y	Y	Y	Y	N	Y
10 Johnson	Y	Y	Y	Y	Y	Y	Y	Y
11 McKinney	N	Y	Y	Y	Y	Y	Y	Y
HAWAII								
1 Abercrombie	Y	Y	Y	Y	Y	Y	Y	Y
2 Mink	Y	Y	Y	Y	Y	Y	Y	Y
IDAHO								
1 LaRocco	Y	Y	Y	Y	Y	Y	Y	Y
2 Crapo	Y	Y	N	N	N	N	N	N
ILLINOIS								
1 Rush	Y	Y	Y	Y	Y	Y	Y	Y
2 Reynolds	Y	Y	Y	Y	Y	Y	Y	Y
3 Lipinski	Y	Y	Y	Y	Y	Y	N	Y
4 Gutierrez	Y	Y	Y	Y	Y	Y	Y	Y
5 Rostenkowski	Y	Y	Y	Y	Y	Y	Y	Y
6 Hyde	?	Y	N	N	N	N	N	N
7 Collins	Y	Y	Y	Y	Y	Y	Y	Y
8 Crane	Y	Y	N	N	N	N	N	N
9 Yates	Y	N	Y	Y	N	Y	Y	Y
10 Porter	Y	Y	N	N	N	N	N	N
11 Sangmeister	Y	Y	Y	Y	Y	Y	Y	Y
12 Costello	Y	Y	Y	Y	Y	Y	Y	Y
13 Fawell	Y	Y	N	N	N	N	N	N
14 Hastert	Y	Y	N	N	N	N	N	N
15 Ewing	Y	Y	N	N	N	N	N	N
16 Manzullo	Y	Y	N	N	N	N	N	N
17 Evans	Y	Y	Y	Y	Y	Y	Y	Y

	416	417	418	419	420	421	422	423
18 ***Michel***	N	N	N	Y	N	Y	N	Y
19 Poshard	Y	Y	Y	Y	Y	N	Y	Y
20 Durbin	Y	Y	Y	Y	Y	Y	Y	N
INDIANA								
1 Visclosky	N	N	N	Y	N	Y	Y	N
2 Sharp	Y	Y	Y	Y	Y	N	Y	N
3 Roemer	Y	N	Y	Y	Y	N	Y	N
4 Long	Y	Y	Y	Y	Y	N	Y	N
5 ***Buyer***	N	N	N	Y	N	Y	N	Y
6 ***Burton***	N	Y	Y	Y	N	Y	N	Y
7 ***Myers***	N	N	Y	Y	N	Y	N	Y
8 McCloskey	Y	N	Y	Y	Y	N	Y	N
9 Hamilton	N	N	N	Y	N	Y	Y	N
10 Jacobs	Y	Y	Y	Y	Y	N	Y	N
IOWA								
1 ***Leach***	Y	N	Y	Y	Y	Y	Y	Y
2 ***Nussle***	Y	Y	N	Y	Y	N	Y	Y
3 ***Lightfoot***	N	Y	Y	Y	Y	Y	N	Y
4 Smith	N	N	N	Y	N	N	?	?
5 ***Grandy***	Y	N	Y	Y	Y	N	Y	Y
KANSAS								
1 ***Roberts***	N	Y	Y	Y	N	Y	N	Y
2 Slattery	Y	Y	Y	Y	N	N	N	N
3 ***Meyers***	N	N	Y	Y	N	Y	N	Y
4 Glickman	Y	N	Y	Y	N	N	Y	N
KENTUCKY								
1 Barlow	Y	Y	Y	Y	Y	N	Y	N
2 Natcher	N	Y	Y	Y	N	N	N	N
3 Mazzoli	N	N	Y	Y	Y	N	Y	N
4 ***Bunning***	N	N	N	Y	N	Y	N	Y
5 ***Rogers***	N	N	Y	Y	N	Y	N	Y
6 Baesler	N	Y	Y	Y	N	Y	Y	N
LOUISIANA								
1 ***Livingston***	N	N	N	Y	N	Y	N	Y
2 Jefferson	Y	Y	Y	Y	Y	N	N	N
3 Tauzin	N	?	?	Y	Y	N	N	N
4 Fields	Y	Y	Y	Y	Y	N	Y	N
5 ***McCrery***	N	N	N	Y	N	Y	N	#
6 ***Baker***	N	N	N	Y	N	Y	N	Y
7 Hayes	N	Y	Y	Y	Y	N	?	?
MAINE								
1 Andrews	Y	Y	Y	Y	Y	N	Y	N
2 ***Snowe***	Y	N	Y	Y	Y	Y	N	N
MARYLAND								
1 ***Gilchrest***	Y	N	N	Y	N	Y	Y	N
2 ***Bentley***	N	N	Y	Y	N	Y	Y	N
3 Cardin	Y	Y	Y	Y	Y	N	Y	N
4 Wynn	Y	Y	Y	Y	Y	N	Y	N
5 Hoyer	N	N	Y	Y	N	N	Y	N
6 ***Bartlett***	N	N	N	Y	N	Y	N	Y
7 Mfume	Y	?	?	Y	Y	N	Y	N
8 ***Morella***	Y	N	Y	Y	Y	N	Y	N
MASSACHUSETTS								
1 Olver	N	N	Y	Y	Y	N	Y	N
2 Neal	Y	Y	Y	Y	Y	N	Y	N
3 ***Blute***	N	N	N	Y	Y	N	N	N
4 Frank	Y	Y	Y	Y	Y	N	Y	N
5 Meehan	Y	Y	Y	Y	Y	N	Y	N
6 ***Torkildsen***	N	N	N	Y	N	Y	N	N
7 Markey	Y	Y	Y	Y	Y	N	Y	N
8 Kennedy	Y	Y	Y	Y	Y	N	Y	N
9 Moakley	Y	Y	Y	Y	Y	N	Y	N
10 Studds	Y	Y	Y	Y	Y	N	Y	N
MICHIGAN								
1 Stupak	Y	Y	Y	Y	Y	Y	N	N
2 ***Hoekstra***	Y	N	N	Y	N	Y	Y	Y
3 Vacancy								
4 ***Camp***	N	Y	Y	Y	N	Y	N	Y
5 Barcia	Y	Y	N	Y	Y	N	Y	N
6 ***Upton***	Y	Y	Y	Y	Y	Y	Y	Y
7 ***Smith***	Y	N	N	Y	N	Y	N	Y
8 Carr	Y	Y	Y	Y	Y	N	Y	N
9 Kildee	Y	Y	Y	Y	Y	N	Y	N
10 Bonior	Y	Y	Y	Y	Y	N	Y	N
11 ***Knollenberg***	N	N	N	Y	N	Y	Y	Y
12 Levin	Y	N	Y	Y	N	N	Y	N
13 Ford	Y	Y	Y	Y	Y	N	Y	N
14 Conyers	?	?	?	?	?	?	?	X
15 Collins	Y	?	Y	Y	Y	?	Y	N
16 Dingell	Y	Y	Y	Y	Y	N	N	N
MINNESOTA								
1 Penny	Y	N	Y	Y	Y	N	Y	N
2 Minge	Y	Y	Y	Y	Y	N	Y	N
3 ***Ramstad***	Y	Y	N	Y	Y	Y	Y	Y
4 Vento	Y	Y	Y	Y	Y	N	Y	N
5 Sabo	Y	N	Y	Y	Y	N	Y	N
6 ***Grams***	N	N	N	Y	N	N	Y	Y
7 Peterson	Y	Y	Y	Y	Y	N	Y	N
8 Oberstar	Y	Y	Y	Y	Y	N	Y	N
MISSISSIPPI								
1 Whitten	N	N	?	?	?	N	N	N
2 Thompson	Y	Y	Y	Y	Y	N	Y	N
3 Montgomery	N	N	Y	Y	N	N	N	N
4 Parker	N	Y	Y	Y	N	N	N	N
5 Taylor	N	Y	Y	Y	N	N	N	N
MISSOURI								
1 Clay	Y	Y	Y	Y	Y	N	Y	N
2 ***Talent***	N	N	N	Y	N	Y	N	Y
3 Gephardt	Y	N	Y	Y	Y	N	Y	N
4 Skelton	N	N	Y	Y	N	N	?	N
5 Wheat	Y	Y	Y	Y	Y	N	Y	N
6 Danner	Y	Y	Y	Y	Y	N	Y	N
7 ***Hancock***	N	N	N	Y	N	Y	N	Y
8 ***Emerson***	N	N	Y	Y	N	Y	N	Y
9 Volkmer	N	N	Y	Y	Y	N	Y	N
MONTANA								
AL Williams	Y	N	Y	Y	Y	N	Y	N
NEBRASKA								
1 ***Bereuter***	N	N	N	Y	N	N	Y	Y
2 Hoagland	N	N	Y	Y	N	N	Y	N
3 ***Barrett***	N	N	N	Y	N	Y	Y	Y
NEVADA								
1 Bilbray	N	N	Y	Y	N	N	N	N
2 ***Vucanovich***	X	X	X	?	X	#	?	#
NEW HAMPSHIRE								
1 ***Zeliff***	N	N	N	Y	N	Y	N	Y
2 Swett	Y	Y	Y	Y	Y	N	Y	N
NEW JERSEY								
1 Andrews	N	Y	Y	Y	Y	Y	Y	N
2 Hughes	Y	N	Y	Y	Y	N	Y	N
3 ***Saxton***	N	N	N	Y	N	Y	Y	Y
4 ***Smith***	N	N	N	Y	N	Y	Y	Y
5 ***Roukema***	Y	N	Y	Y	Y	Y	Y	Y
6 Pallone	Y	Y	Y	Y	Y	N	Y	N
7 ***Franks***	N	Y	Y	Y	Y	N	Y	Y
8 Klein	N	Y	Y	Y	Y	N	Y	N
9 Torricelli	Y	Y	N	Y	Y	N	N	N
10 Payne	Y	Y	Y	Y	Y	N	Y	N
11 ***Gallo***	N	N	N	Y	N	Y	Y	N
12 ***Zimmer***	Y	Y	Y	Y	Y	Y	Y	Y
13 Menendez	N	Y	N	Y	Y	N	Y	N
NEW MEXICO								
1 ***Schiff***	N	Y	N	Y	N	Y	Y	N
2 ***Skeen***	N	N	N	Y	N	Y	N	Y
3 Richardson	N	N	Y	Y	N	N	Y	N
NEW YORK								
1 Hochbrueckner	N	Y	Y	Y	Y	N	Y	N
2 ***Lazio***	N	N	N	Y	N	N	Y	N
3 ***King***	N	N	N	Y	N	Y	N	Y
4 ***Levy***	N	N	N	Y	N	Y	N	Y
5 Ackerman	Y	N	Y	Y	N	X	#	X
6 Flake	Y	Y	Y	Y	N	N	Y	N
7 Manton	N	N	Y	Y	Y	N	Y	?
8 Nadler	Y	Y	Y	Y	Y	N	Y	N
9 Schumer	N	Y	Y	Y	Y	N	Y	N
10 Towns	Y	Y	Y	Y	Y	N	Y	N
11 Owens	Y	Y	Y	Y	Y	N	Y	N
12 Velazquez	Y	Y	Y	Y	Y	N	Y	N
13 ***Molinari***	N	N	N	Y	N	Y	N	Y
14 Maloney	Y	N	Y	Y	Y	N	Y	N
15 Rangel	?	Y	Y	Y	Y	N	Y	N
16 Serrano	Y	Y	Y	Y	Y	N	Y	N
17 Engel	?	Y	Y	Y	Y	N	Y	N
18 Lowey	Y	Y	Y	Y	Y	N	Y	N
19 ***Fish***	N	N	N	Y	N	N	Y	N
20 ***Gilman***	N	N	N	Y	N	N	Y	Y
21 McNulty	N	N	Y	Y	Y	?	N	N
22 ***Solomon***	N	N	N	Y	N	Y	N	Y
23 ***Boehlert***	N	N	Y	Y	Y	N	Y	N
24 ***McHugh***	N	N	Y	Y	N	Y	N	N
25 ***Walsh***	N	N	Y	Y	N	Y	N	N
26 Hinchey	Y	Y	Y	Y	Y	N	Y	N
27 ***Paxon***	N	N	N	Y	N	Y	N	Y
28 Slaughter	Y	Y	Y	Y	Y	N	Y	N
29 LaFalce	Y	Y	Y	Y	Y	N	Y	N
30 ***Quinn***	N	N	Y	Y	N	Y	N	N
31 ***Houghton***	N	N	Y	Y	N	Y	N	N
NORTH CAROLINA								
1 Clayton	Y	N	Y	Y	Y	N	Y	N
2 Valentine	N	N	Y	Y	N	N	N	N
3 Lancaster	N	N	N	Y	N	N	N	N
4 Price	N	N	Y	Y	N	N	Y	N
5 Neal	?	?	?	?	?	?	?	?
6 ***Coble***	Y	Y	N	Y	N	Y	N	Y
7 Rose	N	N	Y	Y	N	N	N	N
8 Hefner	N	Y	Y	Y	N	N	Y	N
9 ***McMillan***	N	N	N	Y	N	Y	Y	Y
10 ***Ballenger***	N	Y	N	Y	N	Y	Y	Y
11 ***Taylor***	N	Y	Y	Y	N	N	N	Y
12 Watt	Y	Y	Y	Y	Y	N	Y	N
NORTH DAKOTA								
AL Pomeroy	Y	Y	Y	Y	Y	Y	Y	N
OHIO								
1 Mann	N	N	N	Y	N	N	N	N
2 ***Portman***	N	N	Y	Y	N	Y	Y	Y
3 Hall	Y	N	Y	Y	Y	N	Y	N
4 ***Oxley***	N	N	N	Y	N	Y	N	Y
5 ***Gillmor***	N	Y	Y	Y	N	Y	N	Y
6 Strickland	Y	Y	Y	Y	Y	N	Y	N
7 ***Hobson***	Y	Y	Y	Y	N	Y	N	Y
8 ***Boehner***	N	N	N	Y	N	Y	N	Y
9 Kaptur	N	Y	Y	Y	Y	N	Y	N
10 ***Hoke***	?	?	?	?	?	?	Y	Y
11 Stokes	#	#	#	?	#	X	?	X
12 ***Kasich***	N	N	Y	Y	N	Y	Y	Y
13 Brown	Y	Y	Y	Y	Y	N	Y	N
14 Sawyer	Y	N	Y	Y	Y	N	Y	N
15 ***Pryce***	N	Y	N	Y	N	Y	Y	Y
16 ***Regula***	N	Y	Y	Y	N	Y	Y	Y
17 Traficant	Y	Y	Y	Y	Y	N	Y	N
18 Applegate	Y	Y	Y	Y	Y	N	Y	N
19 Fingerhut	Y	Y	Y	Y	Y	N	Y	N
OKLAHOMA								
1 ***Inhofe***	N	N	Y	Y	N	N	Y	Y
2 Synar	Y	N	Y	Y	Y	N	Y	N
3 Brewster	N	N	Y	Y	N	N	Y	Y
4 McCurdy	N	N	N	Y	N	N	Y	N
5 ***Istook***	N	N	Y	Y	Y	Y	Y	Y
6 English	N	Y	Y	Y	N	N	Y	N
OREGON								
1 Furse	Y	Y	Y	Y	Y	N	Y	N
2 ***Smith***	N	N	N	Y	N	Y	N	Y
3 Wyden	Y	Y	Y	Y	Y	N	Y	N
4 DeFazio	Y	Y	Y	Y	Y	N	Y	N
5 Kopetski	Y	Y	Y	Y	Y	—	Y	N
PENNSYLVANIA								
1 Foglietta	Y	Y	Y	Y	Y	N	Y	N
2 Blackwell	Y	Y	Y	Y	Y	N	Y	N
3 Borski	N	Y	Y	Y	Y	N	Y	N
4 Klink	Y	Y	Y	Y	Y	N	Y	N
5 ***Clinger***	N	N	Y	Y	N	Y	N	Y
6 Holden	Y	Y	Y	Y	Y	N	Y	N
7 ***Weldon***	N	N	N	Y	N	Y	N	Y
8 ***Greenwood***	Y	Y	Y	Y	Y	Y	Y	Y
9 ***Shuster***	N	N	N	Y	N	Y	N	Y
10 ***McDade***	N	N	N	Y	N	Y	N	Y
11 Kanjorski	Y	Y	Y	Y	Y	Y	Y	N
12 Murtha	N	N	N	Y	N	Y	N	N
13 Margolies-Mezv.	Y	N	Y	Y	Y	N	Y	N
14 Coyne	Y	Y	Y	Y	Y	N	Y	N
15 McHale	Y	Y	Y	Y	Y	N	Y	N
16 ***Walker***	N	N	N	Y	N	Y	N	Y
17 ***Gekas***	N	N	N	Y	N	Y	N	Y
18 ***Santorum***	Y	N	N	Y	N	N	N	N
19 ***Goodling***	N	N	N	Y	N	Y	N	Y
20 Murphy	Y	Y	Y	Y	Y	N	Y	?
21 ***Ridge***	N	N	Y	Y	N	Y	N	Y
RHODE ISLAND								
1 ***Machtley***	N	N	N	Y	N	Y	N	N
2 Reed	Y	N	Y	Y	Y	N	Y	N
SOUTH CAROLINA								
1 ***Ravenel***	N	Y	Y	Y	N	Y	Y	Y
2 ***Spence***	N	N	N	Y	N	Y	N	Y
3 Derrick	N	N	Y	Y	Y	Y	Y	N
4 ***Inglis***	N	N	N	Y	N	Y	N	Y
5 Spratt	N	N	Y	Y	N	Y	Y	N
6 Clyburn	N	N	Y	Y	Y	N	Y	N
SOUTH DAKOTA								
AL Johnson	N	Y	Y	Y	Y	N	Y	N
TENNESSEE								
1 ***Quillen***	N	N	N	Y	N	Y	N	Y
2 ***Duncan***	Y	Y	Y	Y	Y	Y	Y	Y
3 Lloyd	N	N	N	Y	N	N	Y	N
4 Cooper	N	N	Y	Y	Y	N	?	?
5 Clement	N	N	Y	Y	Y	N	Y	Y
6 Gordon	Y	N	Y	Y	N	N	Y	N
7 ***Sundquist***	N	N	Y	Y	N	Y	N	Y
8 Tanner	N	N	Y	Y	Y	N	Y	N
9 Ford	Y	?	?	Y	Y	N	?	?
TEXAS								
1 Chapman	N	Y	Y	Y	N	N	Y	N
2 Wilson	N	Y	Y	Y	N	N	N	N
3 ***Johnson, Sam***	N	N	N	Y	N	Y	N	Y
4 Hall	N	Y	Y	Y	Y	N	N	N
5 Bryant	Y	Y	Y	Y	Y	N	Y	?
6 ***Barton***	N	N	N	Y	N	Y	N	Y
7 ***Archer***	N	N	N	Y	N	Y	N	Y
8 ***Fields***	N	N	N	Y	N	Y	N	Y
9 Brooks	N	N	Y	Y	N	N	Y	N
10 Pickle	N	N	Y	Y	N	Y	N	?
11 Edwards	N	N	N	Y	N	N	N	N
12 Geren	N	N	N	Y	N	Y	N	N
13 Sarpalius	N	N	Y	Y	N	N	N	N
14 Laughlin	N	Y	N	Y	N	N	N	N
15 de la Garza	N	N	Y	Y	N	N	?	?
16 Coleman	N	N	Y	Y	Y	N	Y	N
17 Stenholm	N	N	Y	Y	N	N	N	N
18 Washington	Y	Y	Y	Y	Y	N	Y	N
19 ***Combest***	N	N	N	Y	N	Y	N	Y
20 Gonzalez	Y	N	N	Y	N	N	Y	N
21 ***Smith***	N	N	N	Y	N	Y	N	Y
22 ***DeLay***	N	N	N	Y	N	Y	N	Y
23 ***Bonilla***	N	N	N	Y	Y	Y	N	Y
24 Frost	N	Y	Y	Y	Y	Y	N	N
25 Andrews	N	Y	N	Y	N	N	N	Y
26 ***Armey***	N	N	N	Y	N	Y	N	Y
27 Ortiz	N	N	Y	Y	N	N	N	N
28 Tejeda	N	N	Y	Y	N	N	N	N
29 Green	N	Y	Y	Y	Y	N	Y	N
30 Johnson, E.B.	N	Y	Y	Y	Y	Y	N	N
UTAH								
1 ***Hansen***	N	N	Y	Y	N	Y	N	Y
2 Shepherd	N	Y	Y	Y	Y	N	Y	N
3 Orton	N	N	Y	Y	N	Y	Y	Y
VERMONT								
AL *Sanders*	Y	Y	Y	Y	Y	N	Y	N
VIRGINIA								
1 ***Bateman***	N	N	N	Y	N	Y	N	Y
2 Pickett	N	N	N	Y	N	Y	N	N
3 Scott	Y	Y	Y	Y	Y	N	N	N
4 Sisisky	N	N	N	Y	N	Y	N	N
5 Payne	N	N	Y	Y	N	N	N	N
6 ***Goodlatte***	Y	N	N	Y	N	N	N	Y
7 ***Bliley***	N	N	N	Y	N	Y	?	?
8 Moran	Y	N	Y	Y	Y	N	Y	N
9 Boucher	Y	Y	Y	Y	?	N	N	N
10 ***Wolf***	N	N	Y	Y	N	Y	Y	N
11 Byrne	Y	Y	Y	Y	Y	N	Y	N
WASHINGTON								
1 Cantwell	N	N	Y	Y	Y	N	Y	N
2 Swift	N	N	Y	Y	Y	N	Y	N
3 Unsoeld	Y	Y	Y	Y	Y	N	Y	N
4 Inslee	Y	Y	Y	Y	Y	N	Y	N
5 Foley								
6 Dicks	N	N	Y	Y	N	N	N	N
7 McDermott	Y	Y	?	?	?	?	?	?
8 ***Dunn***	N	N	N	Y	N	Y	Y	Y
9 Kreidler	Y	Y	Y	Y	Y	N	Y	N
WEST VIRGINIA								
1 Mollohan	N	N	N	Y	N	Y	Y	N
2 Wise	N	N	Y	Y	Y	N	Y	N
3 Rahall	Y	Y	Y	Y	Y	N	Y	N
WISCONSIN								
1 Barca	Y	Y	Y	Y	Y	N	Y	Y
2 ***Klug***	Y	N	Y	Y	N	Y	Y	Y
3 ***Gunderson***	N	N	Y	Y	N	Y	Y	Y
4 Kleczka	N	Y	Y	Y	N	N	Y	N
5 Barrett	Y	Y	Y	Y	Y	N	Y	N
6 ***Petri***	Y	Y	Y	Y	N	Y	N	Y
7 Obey	Y	Y	Y	Y	Y	N	Y	N
8 ***Roth***	Y	Y	Y	Y	Y	N	Y	Y
9 ***Sensenbrenner***	Y	Y	Y	Y	Y	N	Y	Y
WYOMING								
AL ***Thomas***	N	N	N	Y	N	Y	N	Y
DELEGATES								
de Lugo, V.I.	Y	Y	Y	Y	Y	N	Y	N
Faleomavaega, Am.S.	Y	Y	Y	Y	?	N	Y	N
Norton, D.C.	Y	Y	Y	Y	Y	N	Y	N
Romero-B., P.R.	Y	Y	?	Y	Y	N	Y	N
Underwood, Guam	Y	N	Y	Y	Y	N	Y	N

Southern states - Ala., Ark., Fla., Ga., Ky., La., Miss., N.C., Okla., S.C., Tenn., Texas, Va.
Omitted votes are quorum calls, which CQ does not include in its vote charts.

424. HR 2401. Fiscal 1994 Defense Authorization/Previous Question. Derrick, D-S.C., motion to order the previous question (thus limiting debate and the possibility of amendment) on adoption of the rule (H Res 248) providing for further consideration of 54 amendments to the fiscal 1994 defense authorization bill. Motion agreed to 237-169: R 0-167; D 236-2 (ND 159-1, SD 77-1); I 1-0, Sept. 13, 1993.

425. HR 2401. Fiscal 1994 Defense Authorization/Rule. Adoption of the rule (H Res 248) providing for further consideration of 54 amendments to the fiscal 1994 defense authorization bill. Adopted 234-169: R 0-167; D 233-2 (ND 158-1, SD 75-1); I 1-0, Sept. 13, 1993.

426. HR 2401. Fiscal 1994 Defense Authorization/Defense Response Fund. Sisisky, D-Va., amendment to create a defense response fund and authorize the secretary of Defense to use the funds to pay the incremental costs of carrying out peacekeeping or foreign disaster relief operations. Rejected in the Committee of the Whole 199-211: R 1-166; D 197-45 (ND 132-31, SD 65-14); I 1-0, Sept. 13, 1993.

427. HR 2401. Fiscal 1994 Defense Authorization/Post-Cold War Programs. Sisisky, D-Va., amendment to authorize $33 million for the secretary of Defense to train other countries in peacekeeping techniques, teach foreign militaries their appropriate role in a democracy, and for the establishment of a United Nations command, control and communications center of peacekeeping operations. Rejected in the Committee of the Whole 199-210: R 6-161; D 192-49 (ND 126-36, SD 66-13); I 1-0, Sept. 13, 1993.

428. HR 2401. Fiscal 1994 Defense Authorization/National Guard Civilian Technicians. Bonior, D-Mich., amendment to include the National Guard Civilian Technicians in the competitive service, providing them with the right to appeal disciplinary action by a state to the federal Merit System Protection Board. Rejected in the Committee of the Whole 156-256: R 22-146; D 133-110 (ND 113-50, SD 20-60); I 1-0, Sept. 13, 1993.

429. HR 2401. Fiscal 1994 Defense Authorization/Soviet Nuclear Dismantlement. Hunter, R-Calif., amendment to cut the Soviet nuclear dismantlement account from $400 million to $100 million and transfer the $300 million to the operations and maintenance accounts of the Army, Navy and Air Force. Rejected in the Committee of the Whole 149-263: R 132-36; D 17-226 (ND 9-154, SD 8-72); I 0-1, Sept. 13, 1993. A "nay" was a vote in support of the president's position.

430. HR 1340. Resolution Trust Corporation/Rule. Adoption of the rule (H Res 250) to provide for House floor consideration of the bill to provide $18.3 billion to resolve failed savings and loans institutions, authorize funds for the Savings Association Insurance Fund (SAIF) for fiscal 1994-98, direct new management reforms, expand the Resolution Trust Corporation's affordable housing program, and impose new requirements for contracting with minority- and women-owned businesses. Adopted 213-191: R 0-170; D 213-20 (ND 141-11, SD 72-9); I 0-1, Sept. 14, 1993.

431. HR 1340. Resolution Trust Corporation/Committee Amendments. Gonzalez, D-Texas, en bloc amendment to extend the authority of the Resolution Trust Corporation to accept failed thrifts for 18 months until April 1, 1995, reduce the authorization for the Savings Association Insurance Fund (SAIF) from $16 billion to $8 billion and make the affordable-housing and minority preference provisions in the bill budget-neutral. Adopted in the Committee of the Whole 411-15: R 160-13; D 250-2 (ND 169-1, SD 81-1); I 1-0, Sept. 14, 1993.

KEY

Y	Voted for (yea).
#	Paired for.
+	Announced for.
N	Voted against (nay).
X	Paired against.
−	Announced against.
P	Voted "present."
C	Voted "present" to avoid possible conflict of interest.
?	Did not vote or otherwise make a position known.
D	Delegates ineligible to vote.

Democrats *Republicans*
Independent

	424	425	426	427	428	429	430	431
ALABAMA								
1 *Callahan*	N	N	N	N	N	Y	N	Y
2 *Everett*	N	N	N	N	N	Y	N	Y
3 Browder	Y	Y	Y	Y	N	N	Y	Y
4 Bevill	Y	Y	Y	Y	Y	N	Y	Y
5 Cramer	Y	Y	Y	Y	N	Y	Y	Y
6 *Bachus*	N	N	N	N	Y	N	Y	N
7 Hilliard	Y	Y	Y	Y	N	Y	N	N
ALASKA								
AL *Young*	?	?	?	?	?	?	N	Y
ARIZONA								
1 Coppersmith	Y	Y	Y	Y	N	N	N	Y
2 Pastor	Y	Y	Y	Y	N	Y	Y	Y
3 *Stump*	N	N	N	N	N	Y	N	Y
4 *Kyl*	N	N	N	N	N	Y	N	Y
5 *Kolbe*	N	N	N	N	N	Y	N	Y
6 English	Y	Y	Y	N	Y	N	Y	Y
ARKANSAS								
1 Lambert	Y	Y	N	N	N	N	Y	Y
2 Thornton	Y	Y	Y	Y	N	N	Y	Y
3 *Hutchinson*	N	N	N	N	N	Y	N	Y
4 Dickey	N	N	N	N	N	Y	N	Y
CALIFORNIA								
1 Hamburg	Y	Y	Y	Y	Y	N	N	Y
2 *Herger*	N	N	N	N	N	Y	N	Y
3 Fazio	Y	Y	Y	Y	Y	N	Y	Y
4 *Doolittle*	N	N	N	N	N	Y	N	N
5 Matsui	Y	Y	Y	Y	Y	N	Y	Y
6 Woolsey	Y	Y	Y	Y	Y	N	Y	Y
7 Miller	?	?	?	?	?	?	?	?
8 Pelosi	Y	Y	Y	Y	Y	N	Y	Y
9 Dellums	Y	Y	Y	Y	N	Y	Y	Y
10 *Baker*	N	N	N	N	N	Y	N	Y
11 *Pombo*	N	N	N	N	N	Y	N	Y
12 Lantos	Y	Y	Y	Y	Y	N	Y	Y
13 Stark	Y	Y	Y	Y	Y	N	?	Y
14 Eshoo	Y	Y	N	N	Y	N	Y	Y
15 Mineta	Y	Y	Y	Y	N	N	#	Y
16 Edwards	Y	Y	Y	Y	N	Y	Y	Y
17 Farr	?	?	?	?	?	?	Y	Y
18 Condit	Y	Y	N	N	Y	N	N	Y
19 Lehman	?	?	?	?	?	?	?	?
20 Dooley	Y	Y	Y	Y	N	N	?	Y
21 *Thomas*	N	N	N	N	N	Y	N	Y
22 *Huffington*	N	N	N	N	N	Y	?	?
23 *Gallegly*	N	N	N	N	N	Y	N	Y
24 Beilenson	Y	Y	Y	Y	Y	N	Y	Y
25 *McKeon*	N	N	N	N	N	Y	N	Y
26 Berman	Y	Y	Y	Y	Y	N	Y	Y
27 *Moorhead*	N	N	N	N	N	Y	N	Y
28 *Dreier*	N	N	N	N	N	Y	N	Y
29 Waxman	Y	Y	Y	Y	Y	N	Y	Y
30 Becerra	Y	Y	Y	Y	Y	N	Y	Y
31 Martinez	?	?	Y	Y	N	Y	N	Y
32 Dixon	Y	Y	Y	Y	Y	N	Y	Y
33 Roybal-Allard	Y	Y	Y	Y	Y	N	Y	Y
34 Torres	Y	Y	Y	Y	N	Y	N	Y
35 Waters	Y	Y	Y	Y	Y	N	Y	Y
36 Harman	Y	Y	Y	Y	N	Y	Y	Y
37 Tucker	Y	Y	Y	N	Y	N	Y	?
38 *Horn*	N	N	N	N	Y	N	Y	Y
39 *Royce*	N	N	N	N	N	Y	N	Y
40 *Lewis*	N	N	N	N	N	Y	N	Y
41 *Kim*	N	N	N	N	N	Y	N	Y

	424	425	426	427	428	429	430	431
42 Brown	Y	Y	Y	Y	Y	N	Y	Y
43 *Calvert*	N	N	N	N	Y	N	Y	Y
44 *McCandless*	N	N	N	N	N	Y	N	Y
45 *Rohrabacher*	N	N	N	N	N	Y	N	Y
46 *Dornan*	N	N	N	N	N	Y	N	Y
47 *Cox*	?	N	N	N	N	N	N	Y
48 *Packard*	N	N	N	N	N	Y	N	Y
49 Schenk	Y	Y	Y	N	Y	N	Y	Y
50 Filner	Y	Y	N	Y	N	Y	N	Y
51 *Cunningham*	N	N	N	N	N	Y	N	Y
52 *Hunter*	N	N	N	N	N	Y	N	Y
COLORADO								
1 Schroeder	Y	Y	Y	Y	Y	N	Y	Y
2 Skaggs	Y	Y	Y	Y	N	N	Y	Y
3 *McInnis*	N	N	N	N	N	Y	N	Y
4 *Allard*	N	N	N	N	N	Y	N	N
5 *Hefley*	N	N	N	N	Y	Y	N	Y
6 *Schaefer*	N	N	N	N	N	Y	N	N
CONNECTICUT								
1 Kennelly	Y	Y	Y	Y	N	N	Y	Y
2 Gejdenson	Y	Y	Y	Y	Y	N	Y	Y
3 DeLauro	Y	Y	Y	Y	Y	N	Y	Y
4 *Shays*	N	N	N	N	N	N	N	Y
5 *Franks*	N	N	N	N	N	Y	N	Y
6 *Johnson*	N	N	N	N	N	N	N	Y
DELAWARE								
AL *Castle*	N	N	N	N	N	N	N	Y
FLORIDA								
1 Hutto	Y	Y	N	N	N	N	Y	Y
2 Peterson	Y	Y	N	N	N	Y	Y	Y
3 Brown	Y	Y	Y	Y	N	Y	Y	Y
4 *Fowler*	N	N	N	N	N	Y	N	Y
5 Thurman	Y	Y	Y	N	N	Y	Y	Y
6 *Stearns*	N	N	N	N	N	Y	N	Y
7 *Mica*	N	N	N	N	N	Y	N	Y
8 *McCollum*	N	N	N	N	N	Y	N	Y
9 *Bilirakis*	N	N	N	N	N	Y	N	Y
10 *Young*	N	N	N	N	N	Y	N	Y
11 Gibbons	Y	Y	Y	Y	N	Y	N	Y
12 *Canady*	N	N	N	N	N	Y	N	Y
13 *Miller*	N	N	N	N	N	Y	N	Y
14 *Goss*	N	N	N	N	N	Y	N	Y
15 Bacchus	Y	?	Y	Y	N	Y	Y	Y
16 *Lewis*	N	N	N	N	N	Y	N	Y
17 Meek	Y	Y	Y	Y	Y	N	Y	Y
18 *Ros-Lehtinen*	N	N	N	N	N	Y	N	Y
19 Johnston	Y	Y	Y	Y	Y	N	Y	Y
20 Deutsch	Y	Y	N	Y	N	Y	Y	Y
21 *Diaz-Balart*	N	N	N	Y	Y	N	N	Y
22 *Shaw*	N	N	N	N	N	Y	N	Y
23 Hastings	Y	Y	Y	Y	Y	N	Y	Y
GEORGIA								
1 *Kingston*	X	X	X	?	?	#	N	Y
2 Bishop	Y	Y	Y	Y	N	Y	Y	Y
3 *Collins*	N	N	N	N	N	Y	N	Y
4 *Linder*	N	N	N	N	N	Y	N	Y
5 Lewis	Y	Y	Y	Y	N	Y	Y	Y
6 *Gingrich*	N	N	N	N	N	Y	N	Y
7 Darden	Y	Y	Y	Y	N	Y	Y	Y
8 Rowland	Y	Y	Y	Y	Y	Y	Y	Y
9 Deal	Y	Y	N	N	N	Y	Y	Y
10 Johnson	Y	Y	Y	Y	Y	N	Y	Y
11 McKinney	Y	Y	Y	Y	N	Y	N	Y
HAWAII								
1 Abercrombie	Y	Y	Y	Y	Y	N	Y	Y
2 Mink	Y	Y	Y	Y	N	N	Y	Y
IDAHO								
1 LaRocco	Y	Y	Y	Y	N	N	Y	Y
2 *Crapo*	N	N	N	N	N	Y	N	Y
ILLINOIS								
1 Rush	Y	Y	Y	Y	N	Y	Y	Y
2 Reynolds	Y	Y	Y	Y	Y	N	Y	Y
3 Lipinski	?	?	?	?	?	?	?	?
4 Gutierrez	Y	?	?	?	?	?	Y	Y
5 Rostenkowski	Y	Y	Y	Y	N	Y	Y	Y
6 *Hyde*	N	N	N	N	N	Y	C	C
7 Collins	Y	Y	Y	Y	N	Y	Y	Y
8 *Crane*	N	N	N	N	N	Y	N	Y
9 Yates	Y	Y	Y	Y	N	Y	Y	Y
10 *Porter*	X	X	?	X	X	#	N	Y
11 Sangmeister	Y	Y	Y	Y	N	N	Y	Y
12 Costello	Y	Y	N	N	N	Y	Y	Y
13 *Fawell*	N	N	N	N	N	Y	N	Y
14 *Hastert*	N	N	N	N	N	Y	N	Y
15 *Ewing*	N	N	N	N	N	Y	N	Y
16 *Manzullo*	N	N	N	N	N	Y	N	Y
17 Evans	Y	Y	Y	Y	N	N	Y	Y

ND Northern Democrats   SD Southern Democrats

	424	425	426	427	428	429	430	431
18 ***Michel***	N	N	N	N	N	Y	N	Y
19 Poshard	Y	Y	N	N	N	N	Y	Y
20 Durbin	Y	Y	Y	Y	Y	N	Y	Y
INDIANA								
1 Visclosky	Y	Y	Y	N	N	N	Y	Y
2 Sharp	?	?	Y	Y	Y	N	N	Y
3 Roemer	Y	Y	Y	Y	N	N	Y	Y
4 Long	Y	Y	N	N	Y	N	Y	Y
5 ***Buyer***	N	N	N	N	N	Y	N	Y
6 ***Burton***	N	N	N	N	N	Y	N	Y
7 ***Myers***	N	N	N	N	N	N	N	Y
8 McCloskey	Y	Y	Y	Y	N	N	Y	Y
9 Hamilton	Y	Y	Y	Y	Y	N	Y	Y
10 Jacobs	N	Y	N	N	Y	Y	N	Y
IOWA								
1 ***Leach***	N	N	Y	Y	N	N	N	Y
2 ***Nussle***	N	N	N	N	N	Y	N	Y
3 ***Lightfoot***	N	N	N	N	N	Y	N	Y
4 Smith	Y	Y	Y	Y	N	N	Y	Y
5 ***Grandy***	N	N	N	Y	N	N	N	Y
KANSAS								
1 ***Roberts***	N	N	N	N	N	Y	N	Y
2 Slattery	Y	Y	N	N	Y	N	Y	Y
3 ***Meyers***	N	N	N	N	N	N	N	Y
4 Glickman	Y	Y	N	Y	Y	N	Y	Y
KENTUCKY								
1 Barlow	Y	Y	Y	Y	N	N	Y	Y
2 Natcher	Y	Y	Y	Y	N	N	Y	Y
3 Mazzoli	Y	Y	Y	Y	N	N	N	Y
4 ***Bunning***	N	N	N	N	N	N	N	Y
5 ***Rogers***	N	N	N	N	N	Y	N	Y
6 Baesler	Y	Y	Y	N	N	N	Y	Y
LOUISIANA								
1 ***Livingston***	N	N	N	N	N	N	N	Y
2 Jefferson	Y	Y	Y	Y	N	N	Y	Y
3 Tauzin	Y	Y	N	N	N	N	N	Y
4 Fields	Y	Y	Y	Y	N	N	Y	Y
5 ***McCrery***	N	N	N	N	N	N	N	Y
6 ***Baker***	N	N	N	N	N	Y	N	Y
7 Hayes	Y	Y	Y	N	N	N	Y	?
MAINE								
1 Andrews	Y	Y	Y	Y	Y	N	Y	Y
2 ***Snowe***	N	N	N	N	N	N	N	Y
MARYLAND								
1 ***Gilchrest***	N	N	N	N	N	Y	N	Y
2 ***Bentley***	N	N	N	N	N	N	N	N
3 Cardin	Y	Y	N	Y	N	N	Y	Y
4 Wynn	Y	Y	Y	Y	Y	N	Y	Y
5 Hoyer	Y	Y	Y	Y	Y	N	Y	Y
6 ***Bartlett***	N	N	N	N	N	Y	N	Y
7 Mfume	Y	Y	Y	Y	Y	N	?	Y
8 ***Morella***	N	N	N	N	N	N	N	Y
MASSACHUSETTS								
1 Olver	Y	Y	Y	Y	Y	N	Y	Y
2 Neal	Y	?	?	?	?	?	Y	Y
3 ***Blute***	N	N	N	N	N	Y	N	Y
4 Frank	Y	Y	Y	Y	Y	N	Y	Y
5 Meehan	Y	Y	Y	Y	N	N	Y	Y
6 ***Torkildsen***	N	N	N	N	N	Y	N	Y
7 Markey	Y	Y	Y	Y	N	N	Y	Y
8 Kennedy	Y	Y	Y	Y	N	N	Y	Y
9 Moakley	Y	Y	Y	Y	N	X	Y	Y
10 Studds	Y	Y	Y	Y	Y	N	Y	Y
MICHIGAN								
1 Stupak	Y	Y	Y	N	Y	N	Y	Y
2 ***Hoekstra***	N	N	N	N	N	Y	N	Y
3 Vacancy								
4 ***Camp***	N	N	N	N	N	Y	N	Y
5 Barcia	Y	Y	Y	N	Y	Y	N	Y
6 ***Upton***	N	N	N	Y	N	N	N	Y
7 ***Smith***	N	N	N	N	N	N	N	Y
8 Carr	Y	Y	Y	Y	?	N	Y	Y
9 Kildee	Y	Y	Y	Y	Y	N	Y	Y
10 Bonior	Y	Y	Y	Y	Y	N	Y	Y
11 ***Knollenberg***	N	N	N	N	N	Y	N	N
12 Levin	Y	Y	Y	Y	Y	N	Y	Y
13 Ford	Y	Y	Y	Y	Y	N	Y	Y
14 Conyers	#	#	?	?	?	?	?	?
15 Collins	Y	Y	Y	Y	Y	N	Y	Y
16 Dingell	Y	Y	Y	Y	Y	N	?	Y
MINNESOTA								
1 Penny	Y	Y	Y	Y	Y	N	?	Y
2 Minge	Y	Y	Y	Y	Y	N	Y	Y
3 ***Ramstad***	N	N	N	N	N	N	N	Y
4 Vento	Y	Y	Y	Y	Y	N	Y	Y

	424	425	426	427	428	429	430	431
5 Sabo	Y	Y	Y	Y	N	N	Y	Y
6 ***Grams***	N	N	N	N	N	Y	N	Y
7 Peterson	Y	Y	N	?	Y	N	Y	Y
8 Oberstar	Y	Y	Y	Y	Y	N	Y	Y
MISSISSIPPI								
1 Whitten	Y	Y	Y	Y	N	N	Y	Y
2 Thompson	Y	Y	Y	Y	N	N	Y	Y
3 Montgomery	Y	Y	Y	Y	N	N	Y	Y
4 Parker	Y	Y	Y	Y	N	N	Y	Y
5 Taylor	Y	Y	N	N	N	N	N	Y
MISSOURI								
1 Clay	Y	Y	Y	Y	Y	N	Y	Y
2 ***Talent***	N	N	N	N	Y	Y	N	Y
3 Gephardt	Y	Y	Y	Y	Y	N	Y	Y
4 Skelton	Y	Y	Y	Y	N	N	Y	Y
5 Wheat	Y	Y	Y	Y	Y	N	Y	Y
6 Danner	Y	Y	Y	N	N	N	Y	Y
7 ***Hancock***	N	N	N	N	N	Y	N	Y
8 ***Emerson***	N	N	N	N	Y	Y	N	Y
9 Volkmer	Y	Y	Y	N	Y	N	Y	Y
MONTANA								
AL Williams	Y	Y	N	N	Y	N	Y	Y
NEBRASKA								
1 ***Bereuter***	N	N	N	Y	N	N	N	Y
2 Hoagland	Y	Y	Y	Y	Y	N	Y	Y
3 ***Barrett***	N	N	N	N	N	N	N	Y
NEVADA								
1 Bilbray	Y	Y	Y	Y	Y	N	Y	Y
2 ***Vucanovich***	N	N	N	N	N	Y	N	Y
NEW HAMPSHIRE								
1 ***Zeliff***	N	?	N	N	N	N	N	Y
2 Swett	Y	Y	Y	Y	Y	N	Y	Y
NEW JERSEY								
1 Andrews	Y	Y	N	Y	N	Y	?	Y
2 Hughes	?	Y	N	N	N	N	Y	Y
3 ***Saxton***	N	N	N	N	N	Y	N	Y
4 ***Smith***	N	N	N	N	N	Y	N	Y
5 ***Roukema***	N	N	N	N	N	N	N	Y
6 Pallone	Y	Y	N	Y	N	N	Y	Y
7 ***Franks***	N	N	N	N	Y	Y	N	Y
8 Klein	Y	Y	Y	N	Y	N	Y	Y
9 Torricelli	Y	Y	Y	Y	Y	N	Y	Y
10 Payne	Y	Y	Y	Y	Y	N	Y	Y
11 ***Gallo***	N	N	N	N	N	Y	N	Y
12 ***Zimmer***	?	?	?	?	?	?	N	Y
13 Menendez	Y	Y	N	N	N	N	Y	Y
NEW MEXICO								
1 ***Schiff***	N	N	N	N	N	Y	N	Y
2 ***Skeen***	N	N	N	N	N	Y	N	Y
3 Richardson	Y	Y	Y	Y	N	N	Y	Y
NEW YORK								
1 Hochbrueckner	Y	Y	Y	Y	N	N	Y	Y
2 ***Lazio***	N	N	N	N	N	Y	N	Y
3 ***King***	N	N	N	N	N	Y	N	Y
4 ***Levy***	N	N	N	N	N	Y	N	Y
5 Ackerman	Y	Y	?	?	?	?	Y	Y
6 Flake	Y	Y	Y	Y	Y	N	Y	Y
7 Manton	Y	Y	Y	Y	N	N	Y	Y
8 Nadler	Y	Y	Y	Y	Y	N	Y	Y
9 Schumer	Y	Y	Y	Y	Y	N	Y	Y
10 Towns	Y	Y	?	?	?	?	?	?
11 Owens	?	?	?	?	?	?	N	Y
12 Velazquez	Y	Y	Y	Y	Y	N	Y	Y
13 ***Molinari***	N	N	N	N	N	N	N	Y
14 Maloney	Y	Y	N	Y	N	N	?	Y
15 Rangel	Y	Y	Y	Y	Y	N	Y	Y
16 Serrano	Y	Y	Y	Y	Y	N	Y	Y
17 Engel	Y	Y	Y	Y	Y	N	?	Y
18 Lowey	Y	Y	?	?	N	N	Y	Y
19 ***Fish***	N	N	N	N	Y	N	N	Y
20 ***Gilman***	N	N	N	N	N	N	N	Y
21 McNulty	Y	Y	Y	Y	N	N	Y	Y
22 ***Solomon***	N	N	N	N	N	Y	N	Y
23 ***Boehlert***	N	N	N	N	N	N	N	Y
24 ***McHugh***	N	N	N	N	Y	N	N	Y
25 ***Walsh***	N	N	N	N	Y	Y	N	Y
26 Hinchey	Y	Y	Y	Y	Y	N	Y	Y
27 ***Paxon***	N	N	N	N	N	Y	N	Y
28 Slaughter	Y	Y	Y	Y	N	N	Y	Y
29 LaFalce	Y	Y	Y	Y	Y	N	Y	Y
30 ***Quinn***	N	N	N	N	N	Y	N	Y
31 ***Houghton***	N	N	N	N	N	Y	N	Y
NORTH CAROLINA								
1 Clayton	Y	Y	Y	Y	Y	N	Y	Y
2 Valentine	Y	Y	N	N	N	Y	Y	Y

	424	425	426	427	428	429	430	431
3 Lancaster	Y	Y	Y	Y	N	N	N	Y
4 Price	Y	Y	Y	Y	N	N	Y	Y
5 Neal	Y	Y	N	Y	N	N	Y	Y
6 ***Coble***	N	N	N	N	N	Y	N	Y
7 Rose	?	?	?	?	?	?	Y	Y
8 Hefner	Y	Y	Y	Y	N	N	Y	Y
9 ***McMillan***	N	N	N	N	N	Y	N	Y
10 ***Ballenger***	N	N	N	N	N	N	N	Y
11 ***Taylor***	N	N	N	N	N	Y	N	N
12 Watt	Y	Y	Y	Y	Y	N	Y	Y
NORTH DAKOTA								
AL Pomeroy	Y	Y	N	N	N	N	Y	Y
OHIO								
1 Mann	Y	Y	Y	Y	N	N	Y	Y
2 ***Portman***	N	N	N	N	N	Y	N	Y
3 Hall	Y	Y	Y	N	N	N	?	Y
4 ***Oxley***	N	N	N	N	N	Y	N	Y
5 ***Gillmor***	N	N	N	N	N	Y	N	Y
6 Strickland	Y	Y	Y	N	Y	N	Y	Y
7 ***Hobson***	N	N	N	N	N	N	N	Y
8 ***Boehner***	N	N	N	N	N	Y	N	Y
9 Kaptur	Y	Y	Y	Y	N	N	N	Y
10 ***Hoke***	?	?	?	?	?	?	N	N
11 Stokes	Y	Y	Y	Y	Y	N	Y	Y
12 ***Kasich***	N	N	N	N	N	Y	?	Y
13 Brown	Y	Y	Y	N	Y	N	Y	Y
14 Sawyer	Y	Y	Y	Y	Y	N	Y	Y
15 ***Pryce***	N	N	N	N	N	Y	N	Y
16 ***Regula***	N	N	N	N	N	N	N	Y
17 Traficant	Y	Y	Y	Y	N	Y	Y	Y
18 Applegate	Y	Y	N	N	N	Y	Y	Y
19 Fingerhut	Y	Y	N	N	N	N	Y	Y
OKLAHOMA								
1 ***Inhofe***	N	N	N	N	N	Y	N	Y
2 Synar	Y	Y	Y	Y	N	N	N	Y
3 Brewster	Y	Y	Y	Y	N	N	Y	Y
4 McCurdy	Y	Y	Y	Y	N	N	Y	Y
5 ***Istook***	N	N	N	N	N	Y	N	Y
6 English	Y	Y	Y	N	N	N	Y	Y
OREGON								
1 Furse	Y	Y	N	Y	Y	N	Y	Y
2 ***Smith***	N	N	N	N	N	Y	N	Y
3 Wyden	Y	Y	Y	Y	Y	N	Y	Y
4 DeFazio	?	?	N	Y	Y	N	N	Y
5 Kopetski	Y	Y	Y	Y	Y	N	Y	Y
PENNSYLVANIA								
1 Foglietta	Y	Y	Y	Y	N	N	?	Y
2 Blackwell	Y	Y	Y	Y	Y	N	?	Y
3 Borski	Y	Y	Y	Y	N	N	?	?
4 Klink	Y	Y	Y	N	N	N	Y	Y
5 ***Clinger***	N	N	N	N	Y	Y	N	Y
6 Holden	Y	Y	Y	N	Y	N	Y	Y
7 ***Weldon***	N	N	N	N	N	Y	N	Y
8 ***Greenwood***	N	?	N	N	Y	N	Y	Y
9 ***Shuster***	?	?	?	?	?	?	N	Y
10 ***McDade***	N	N	N	N	N	N	N	Y
11 Kanjorski	Y	Y	N	N	N	N	Y	Y
12 Murtha	Y	Y	Y	N	N	N	Y	Y
13 Margolies-Mezv.	Y	Y	N	N	N	N	Y	Y
14 Coyne	Y	Y	Y	Y	Y	N	Y	Y
15 McHale	Y	Y	Y	Y	Y	N	Y	Y
16 ***Walker***	N	N	N	N	Y	Y	N	Y
17 ***Gekas***	N	N	N	N	Y	Y	N	Y
18 ***Santorum***	N	N	N	N	N	N	N	Y
19 ***Goodling***	N	N	N	N	N	N	N	Y
20 Murphy	Y	Y	N	N	Y	N	Y	Y
21 ***Ridge***	N	N	?	?	?	?	X	N
RHODE ISLAND								
1 ***Machtley***	N	N	N	N	Y	N	N	Y
2 Reed	Y	Y	Y	Y	Y	N	Y	Y
SOUTH CAROLINA								
1 ***Ravenel***	N	N	N	N	N	Y	N	Y
2 ***Spence***	N	N	N	N	N	Y	N	Y
3 Derrick	Y	Y	Y	N	N	N	Y	Y
4 ***Inglis***	N	N	N	N	N	N	N	Y
5 Spratt	Y	Y	Y	Y	N	N	Y	Y
6 Clyburn	Y	Y	Y	Y	N	N	Y	Y
SOUTH DAKOTA								
AL Johnson	?	?	N	N	Y	N	Y	Y
TENNESSEE								
1 ***Quillen***	N	N	N	N	Y	N	N	N
2 ***Duncan***	N	N	N	N	N	Y	N	Y
3 Lloyd	Y	Y	Y	Y	N	N	Y	Y
4 Cooper	N	N	N	Y	N	N	N	Y
5 Clement	Y	Y	N	N	N	N	Y	Y

	424	425	426	427	428	429	430	431
6 Gordon	Y	Y	N	N	N	N	Y	Y
7 ***Sundquist***	N	N	N	N	N	Y	?	Y
8 Tanner	Y	Y	Y	Y	N	N	Y	Y
9 Ford	Y	?	Y	Y	Y	N	Y	?
TEXAS								
1 Chapman	?	?	N	N	N	Y	Y	Y
2 Wilson	Y	Y	Y	Y	N	N	Y	Y
3 ***Johnson, Sam***	N	N	N	N	N	Y	N	N
4 Hall	Y	Y	Y	Y	N	Y	N	Y
5 Bryant	Y	Y	Y	Y	Y	N	Y	Y
6 ***Barton***	?	N	N	N	N	Y	N	Y
7 ***Archer***	N	N	N	N	N	Y	N	Y
8 ***Fields***	N	N	N	N	N	Y	N	Y
9 Brooks	?	?	Y	Y	N	N	Y	Y
10 Pickle	?	?	?	?	N	Y	Y	Y
11 Edwards	Y	Y	Y	Y	N	Y	Y	Y
12 Geren	Y	Y	Y	Y	N	N	Y	Y
13 Sarpalius	Y	Y	Y	Y	N	N	Y	Y
14 Laughlin	Y	Y	Y	Y	N	N	Y	Y
15 de la Garza	Y	Y	Y	Y	N	N	?	Y
16 Coleman	Y	Y	Y	Y	N	N	Y	Y
17 Stenholm	Y	Y	Y	Y	N	Y	Y	Y
18 Washington	?	?	?	?	?	?	Y	Y
19 ***Combest***	N	N	N	N	N	Y	N	N
20 Gonzalez	Y	Y	Y	Y	Y	N	Y	Y
21 ***Smith***	N	N	N	N	N	Y	N	Y
22 ***DeLay***	N	N	N	N	N	Y	N	Y
23 ***Bonilla***	N	N	N	N	N	Y	N	N
24 Frost	?	?	?	?	?	?	Y	?
25 Andrews	?	?	?	?	?	?	?	Y
26 ***Armey***	N	N	N	N	N	Y	N	Y
27 Ortiz	Y	Y	Y	Y	N	N	?	Y
28 Tejeda	Y	Y	Y	Y	N	N	Y	Y
29 Green	Y	Y	—	—	?	+	+	Y
30 Johnson, E.B.	Y	Y	Y	Y	N	N	Y	Y
UTAH								
1 ***Hansen***	N	N	N	N	N	Y	N	Y
2 Shepherd	Y	Y	N	N	Y	N	Y	Y
3 Orton	Y	Y	N	N	N	Y	Y	Y
VERMONT								
AL *Sanders*	Y	Y	Y	Y	Y	N	N	Y
VIRGINIA								
1 ***Bateman***	N	N	N	N	N	Y	N	Y
2 Pickett	Y	Y	Y	Y	N	N	Y	Y
3 Scott	Y	Y	Y	Y	Y	N	Y	Y
4 Sisisky	Y	Y	Y	Y	N	N	Y	Y
5 Payne	Y	Y	Y	Y	N	N	Y	Y
6 ***Goodlatte***	N	N	N	N	N	Y	N	Y
7 ***Bliley***	N	N	N	N	N	Y	N	Y
8 Moran	Y	Y	Y	Y	N	N	Y	Y
9 Boucher	Y	Y	Y	Y	N	N	Y	Y
10 ***Wolf***	N	N	N	N	N	Y	N	Y
11 Byrne	Y	Y	Y	Y	N	N	Y	Y
WASHINGTON								
1 Cantwell	Y	Y	N	Y	Y	N	N	Y
2 Swift	Y	Y	Y	Y	Y	N	Y	Y
3 Unsoeld	Y	Y	Y	Y	Y	N	Y	Y
4 Inslee	Y	Y	N	Y	Y	N	+	Y
5 Foley								
6 Dicks	Y	Y	Y	Y	Y	N	Y	Y
7 McDermott	Y	Y	Y	Y	N	N	Y	Y
8 ***Dunn***	N	N	N	N	Y	Y	N	Y
9 Kreidler	Y	Y	Y	Y	Y	N	Y	Y
WEST VIRGINIA								
1 Mollohan	Y	Y	Y	N	N	N	Y	Y
2 Wise	Y	Y	Y	Y	N	N	N	Y
3 Rahall	Y	N	N	N	N	N	N	N
WISCONSIN								
1 Barca	Y	Y	Y	Y	Y	N	Y	Y
2 ***Klug***	N	N	N	N	Y	N	N	Y
3 ***Gunderson***	N	N	N	N	N	N	N	Y
4 Kleczka	#	#	#	#	#	X	Y	Y
5 Barrett	Y	Y	N	Y	Y	N	Y	Y
6 ***Petri***	N	N	N	N	Y	Y	N	Y
7 Obey	Y	Y	Y	N	Y	N	?	Y
8 ***Roth***	N	N	N	N	N	Y	N	Y
9 ***Sensenbrenner***	N	N	N	N	Y	Y	N	Y
WYOMING								
AL ***Thomas***	N	N	?	?	N	Y	N	Y
DELEGATES								
de Lugo, V.I.	D	D	?	?	?	?	D	Y
Faleomavaega, Am.S.	D	D	Y	Y	Y	N	D	Y
Norton, D.C.	D	D	Y	Y	Y	N	D	Y
Romero-B., P.R.	D	D	?	?	?	?	D	Y
Underwood, Guam	D	D	Y	Y	N	N	D	Y

Southern states - Ala., Ark., Fla., Ga., Ky., La., Miss., N.C., Okla., S.C., Tenn., Texas, Va.
Omitted votes are quorum calls, which CQ does not include in its vote charts.

432. HR 1340. Resolution Trust Corporation/Committee Amendments. Separate vote at the request of Solomon, R-N.Y., on the en bloc amendment offered by Gonzalez, D-Texas, and adopted in the Committee of the Whole to extend the authority of the Resolution Trust Corporation to accept failed thrifts for 18 months until April 1, 1995, reduce the authorization for the Savings Association Insurance Fund (SAIF) from $16 billion to $8 billion and make the affordable housing and minority preference provisions in the bill budget-neutral. Adopted 406-15: R 160-13; D 245-2 (ND 162-1, SD 83-1); I 1-0, Sept. 14, 1993. (On a separate vote, which may be demanded on an amendment adopted in the Committee of the Whole, the four delegates and the resident commissioner of Puerto Rico cannot vote. See vote 431.)

433. HR 1340. Resolution Trust Corporation/Funding Elimination. McCollum R-Fla., motion to recommit the bill to the Banking Committee with instructions to report it back with an amendment striking the additional $18.3 billion in funding, eliminating the minority- and women-owned business preferences, deleting the extension of the statute of limitations, holding the RTC to current funding levels and maintaining the Resolution Trust Corporation's regional pay differentials to executive agency levels. Motion rejected 180-242: R 158-14; D 22-227 (ND 11-154, SD 11-73); I 0-1, Sept. 14, 1993. A "nay" was vote in support of the president's position.

434. HR 1340. Resolution Trust Corporation/Passage. Passage of the bill to provide $18.3 billion to resolve failed savings and loans institutions, authorize funds for the new Savings Association Insurance Fund (SAIF) for fiscal 1994-98, direct new management reforms, expand the Resolution Trust Corporation's affordable housing program, and impose new requirements for contracting with businesses owned by minorities and women. Passed 214-208: R 24-148; D 190-59 (ND 131-34, SD 59-25); I 0-1, Sept. 14, 1993. A "yea" was a vote in support of the president's position.

435. Procedural Motion. Burton, R-Ind., motion to adjourn. Motion rejected 11-376: R 10-152; D 1-224 (ND 1-149, SD 0-75); I 0-0, Sept. 21, 1993.

436. HR 808. Relief of James B. Stanley/Third Reading. Question of engrossment and third reading of the bill to pay James B. Stanley of Florida $400,577 for physical, psychological and economic injuries he sustained from LSD administered to him without his knowledge by the Army in 1958. Ordered engrossed and read a third time 390-1: R 163-1; D 227-0 (ND 153-0, SD 74-0); I 0-0, Sept. 21, 1993.

437. HR 20. Hatch Act Revision/Agree to Senate Amendments. Motion to agree to the Senate amendments to the bill to revise the 1939 Hatch Act to allow limited political involvement by federal workers. Motion agreed to (thus cleared for the president) 339-85: R 90-84; D 248-1 (ND 168-1, SD 80-0); I 1-0, Sept. 21, 1993. A "yea" was a vote in support of the president's position.

438. HR 808. Relief of James B. Stanley/Passage. Passage of the bill to pay James B. Stanley of Florida $400,577 for physical, psychological and economic injuries he sustained from LSD administered to him without his knowledge by the Army in 1958. Passed 425-0: R 173-0; D 251-0 (ND 169-0, SD 82-0); I 1-0, Sept. 21, 1993.

439. HR 3019. Performance Management and Recognition System Termination/Passage. Norton, D-D.C., motion to suspend the rules and pass the bill to provide for a one-month extension through Oct. 31, 1993, before terminating the Performance Management and Recognition System. Motion agreed to 426-1: R 174-0; D 251-1 (ND 168-1, SD 83-0); I 1-0, Sept. 21, 1993. A two-thirds majority of those present and voting (285 in this case) is required for passage under suspension of the rules.

KEY

Y Voted for (yea).
\# Paired for.
\+ Announced for.
N Voted against (nay).
X Paired against.
— Announced against.
P Voted "present."
C Voted "present" to avoid possible conflict of interest.
? Did not vote or otherwise make a position known.
D Delegates ineligible to vote.

Democrats *Republicans*
Independent

	432	433	434	435	436	437	438	439
ALABAMA								
1 *Callahan*	Y	Y	N	N	Y	N	Y	Y
2 *Everett*	Y	Y	N	?	?	Y	Y	Y
3 Browder	Y	N	N	N	Y	Y	Y	Y
4 Bevill	Y	N	N	N	Y	Y	Y	Y
5 Cramer	Y	N	N	N	Y	Y	Y	Y
6 *Bachus*	Y	Y	N	N	Y	N	Y	Y
7 Hilliard	N	Y	N	N	Y	Y	Y	Y
ALASKA								
AL *Young*	Y	N	Y	N	N	Y	Y	Y
ARIZONA								
1 Coppersmith	Y	N	Y	N	Y	Y	Y	Y
2 Pastor	Y	N	Y	N	Y	Y	Y	Y
3 *Stump*	Y	Y	N	Y	N	Y	N	Y
4 *Kyl*	Y	Y	N	N	Y	N	Y	Y
5 *Kolbe*	Y	N	N	N	Y	Y	Y	Y
6 English	Y	N	Y	N	Y	Y	Y	Y
ARKANSAS								
1 Lambert	Y	Y	N	N	Y	Y	Y	Y
2 Thornton	Y	N	Y	N	Y	Y	Y	Y
3 *Hutchinson*	Y	Y	N	N	Y	N	Y	Y
4 *Dickey*	Y	Y	N	N	Y	Y	Y	Y
CALIFORNIA								
1 Hamburg	Y	N	Y	N	Y	Y	Y	Y
2 *Herger*	Y	Y	N	N	Y	N	Y	Y
3 Fazio	Y	N	Y	N	Y	Y	Y	Y
4 *Doolittle*	N	Y	N	Y	Y	N	Y	Y
5 Matsui	Y	N	Y	?	Y	Y	Y	Y
6 Woolsey	Y	N	Y	N	Y	Y	Y	Y
7 Miller	?	?	?	N	Y	Y	Y	Y
8 Pelosi	Y	N	Y	N	Y	Y	Y	Y
9 Dellums	Y	N	Y	?	Y	Y	Y	Y
10 *Baker*	Y	Y	N	Y	Y	N	Y	Y
11 *Pombo*	Y	Y	N	N	Y	N	Y	Y
12 Lantos	Y	N	Y	N	Y	Y	Y	Y
13 Stark	Y	N	Y	?	Y	Y	Y	Y
14 Eshoo	Y	N	Y	N	Y	Y	Y	Y
15 Mineta	Y	Y	Y	?	Y	Y	Y	Y
16 Edwards	Y	N	Y	N	Y	Y	Y	Y
17 Farr	Y	N	Y	N	Y	Y	Y	Y
18 Condit	Y	Y	N	?	?	Y	Y	Y
19 Lehman	?	?	?	N	Y	Y	Y	Y
20 Dooley	Y	N	Y	N	Y	Y	Y	Y
21 *Thomas*	Y	Y	N	N	Y	Y	Y	Y
22 *Huffington*	?	?	?	N	Y	N	Y	Y
23 *Gallegly*	Y	Y	N	N	Y	Y	Y	Y
24 Beilenson	Y	N	Y	N	Y	N	Y	Y
25 *McKeon*	Y	Y	N	N	Y	N	Y	Y
26 Berman	Y	N	Y	?	?	Y	Y	Y
27 *Moorhead*	Y	Y	N	N	Y	N	Y	Y
28 *Dreier*	Y	Y	N	N	Y	Y	Y	Y
29 Waxman	Y	N	Y	N	Y	Y	Y	Y
30 Becerra	Y	N	Y	N	Y	Y	Y	Y
31 Martinez	Y	N	Y	N	Y	Y	Y	Y
32 Dixon	Y	N	Y	N	Y	Y	Y	Y
33 Roybal-Allard	Y	N	Y	N	Y	Y	Y	Y
34 Torres	Y	N	Y	?	?	Y	Y	Y
35 Waters	Y	N	Y	N	Y	Y	Y	Y
36 Harman	Y	N	Y	N	Y	Y	Y	Y
37 Tucker	?	N	Y	N	Y	Y	Y	Y
38 *Horn*	Y	Y	N	N	Y	Y	Y	Y
39 *Royce*	Y	Y	N	N	Y	N	Y	Y
40 *Lewis*	Y	Y	N	N	Y	N	Y	Y
41 *Kim*	Y	Y	N	N	Y	Y	Y	Y
42 Brown	?	?	?	Y	Y	Y	Y	Y
43 *Calvert*	Y	Y	N	N	Y	Y	Y	Y
44 *McCandless*	Y	Y	N	N	?	N	Y	Y
45 *Rohrabacher*	Y	Y	N	Y	Y	N	Y	Y
46 *Dornan*	Y	Y	N	?	?	N	Y	Y
47 *Cox*	Y	?	N	N	Y	N	Y	Y
48 *Packard*	Y	Y	N	N	Y	N	Y	Y
49 Schenk	Y	N	Y	N	Y	Y	Y	Y
50 Filner	Y	N	N	N	Y	Y	Y	Y
51 *Cunningham*	Y	Y	N	N	Y	N	Y	Y
52 *Hunter*	Y	Y	?	N	Y	N	Y	Y
COLORADO								
1 Schroeder	Y	N	N	N	Y	Y	Y	Y
2 Skaggs	Y	N	Y	N	Y	Y	Y	Y
3 *McInnis*	Y	Y	N	N	Y	Y	Y	Y
4 *Allard*	N	Y	N	Y	N	Y	Y	Y
5 *Hefley*	Y	Y	N	N	Y	N	Y	Y
6 *Schaefer*	N	Y	N	N	Y	Y	Y	Y
CONNECTICUT								
1 Kennelly	Y	N	Y	N	Y	Y	Y	Y
2 Gejdenson	Y	N	Y	?	Y	Y	Y	Y
3 DeLauro	Y	N	N	N	Y	Y	Y	Y
4 *Shays*	Y	N	Y	N	Y	Y	Y	Y
5 *Franks*	Y	Y	N	N	Y	Y	Y	Y
6 *Johnson*	Y	N	Y	N	Y	N	Y	Y
DELAWARE								
AL *Castle*	Y	Y	N	N	Y	Y	Y	Y
FLORIDA								
1 Hutto	Y	N	N	N	Y	Y	Y	Y
2 Peterson	Y	N	Y	N	Y	Y	Y	Y
3 Brown	Y	N	Y	—	Y	Y	Y	Y
4 *Fowler*	Y	Y	Y	N	Y	N	Y	Y
5 Thurman	Y	N	Y	N	Y	Y	Y	Y
6 *Stearns*	Y	Y	N	N	Y	N	Y	Y
7 *Mica*	Y	Y	N	N	Y	Y	Y	Y
8 *McCollum*	Y	Y	N	N	Y	N	Y	Y
9 *Bilirakis*	Y	Y	N	N	Y	Y	Y	Y
10 *Young*	Y	Y	N	N	Y	Y	Y	Y
11 Gibbons	Y	N	Y	N	Y	Y	Y	Y
12 *Canady*	Y	Y	N	N	Y	N	Y	Y
13 *Miller*	Y	Y	N	N	Y	Y	Y	Y
14 *Goss*	Y	Y	N	N	Y	Y	Y	Y
15 Bacchus	Y	N	Y	?	Y	Y	Y	Y
16 *Lewis*	Y	Y	N	N	Y	N	Y	Y
17 Meek	Y	N	Y	N	Y	Y	Y	Y
18 *Ros-Lehtinen*	Y	Y	N	?	?	Y	Y	Y
19 Johnston	Y	N	Y	N	Y	Y	Y	Y
20 Deutsch	Y	N	Y	?	?	Y	Y	Y
21 *Diaz-Balart*	Y	Y	N	N	Y	Y	Y	Y
22 *Shaw*	Y	Y	N	?	?	?	?	Y
23 Hastings	Y	N	Y	N	Y	Y	Y	Y
GEORGIA								
1 *Kingston*	Y	Y	N	?	?	N	Y	Y
2 Bishop	Y	N	Y	N	Y	Y	Y	Y
3 *Collins*	Y	Y	N	N	Y	Y	Y	Y
4 *Linder*	Y	Y	N	N	Y	N	Y	Y
5 Lewis	Y	N	N	N	Y	Y	Y	Y
6 *Gingrich*	Y	Y	N	N	Y	N	Y	Y
7 Darden	Y	Y	N	N	Y	Y	Y	Y
8 Rowland	Y	N	Y	N	Y	Y	Y	Y
9 Deal	Y	Y	N	N	Y	Y	Y	Y
10 Johnson	Y	N	N	N	Y	Y	Y	Y
11 McKinney	Y	N	Y	?	Y	Y	Y	Y
HAWAII								
1 Abercrombie	Y	N	Y	?	?	?	?	Y
2 Mink	Y	N	Y	N	Y	Y	Y	Y
IDAHO								
1 LaRocco	Y	N	Y	N	Y	Y	Y	Y
2 *Crapo*	Y	Y	N	N	Y	N	Y	Y
ILLINOIS								
1 Rush	Y	N	Y	N	Y	Y	Y	Y
2 Reynolds	Y	N	Y	N	Y	Y	Y	Y
3 Lipinski	?	?	?	N	Y	Y	Y	Y
4 Gutierrez	Y	N	Y	N	Y	Y	Y	Y
5 Rostenkowski	Y	N	Y	N	Y	Y	Y	Y
6 *Hyde*	?	C	C	N	Y	N	Y	Y
7 Collins	Y	N	Y	N	Y	Y	Y	Y
8 *Crane*	Y	Y	N	Y	N	Y	Y	Y
9 Yates	Y	N	Y	N	Y	Y	Y	Y
10 *Porter*	Y	Y	N	N	Y	N	Y	Y
11 Sangmeister	Y	N	Y	N	Y	Y	Y	Y
12 Costello	Y	N	N	N	Y	Y	Y	Y
13 *Fawell*	Y	Y	N	N	Y	N	Y	Y
14 *Hastert*	Y	Y	N	N	Y	N	Y	Y
15 *Ewing*	Y	Y	N	N	Y	N	Y	Y
16 *Manzullo*	Y	Y	N	N	Y	N	Y	Y
17 Evans	Y	N	N	N	Y	Y	Y	Y

ND Northern Democrats   SD Southern Democrats

	432	433	434	435	436	437	438	439
18 ***Michel***	Y	Y	Y	N	Y	Y	Y	Y
19 Poshard	Y	Y	N	N	Y	Y	Y	Y
20 Durbin	Y	N	Y	N	Y	Y	Y	Y
INDIANA								
1 Visclosky	Y	N	N	N	Y	Y	Y	Y
2 Sharp	Y	N	N	N	Y	Y	Y	Y
3 Roemer	Y	N	Y	N	Y	Y	Y	Y
4 Long	Y	N	N	N	Y	Y	Y	Y
5 ***Buyer***	Y	Y	N	N	Y	Y	Y	Y
6 ***Burton***	Y	Y	N	Y	Y	Y	Y	Y
7 ***Myers***	Y	Y	N	N	Y	Y	Y	Y
8 McCloskey	Y	N	Y	N	Y	Y	Y	Y
9 Hamilton	Y	N	Y	N	Y	Y	Y	Y
10 Jacobs	Y	N	Y	N	?	Y	Y	Y
IOWA								
1 ***Leach***	Y	N	Y	N	Y	N	Y	Y
2 ***Nussle***	Y	Y	N	N	Y	N	Y	Y
3 ***Lightfoot***	Y	Y	Y	N	Y	Y	Y	Y
4 Smith	Y	N	Y	N	Y	Y	Y	Y
5 ***Grandy***	Y	Y	Y	N	Y	Y	Y	Y
KANSAS								
1 ***Roberts***	Y	Y	N	N	Y	N	Y	Y
2 Slattery	Y	N	Y	N	Y	Y	Y	Y
3 ***Meyers***	Y	Y	N	N	Y	Y	Y	Y
4 Glickman	Y	N	Y	N	Y	Y	Y	Y
KENTUCKY								
1 Barlow	Y	N	Y	N	Y	Y	Y	Y
2 Natcher	Y	N	Y	N	Y	Y	Y	Y
3 Mazzoli	Y	N	N	N	Y	Y	Y	Y
4 ***Bunning***	Y	Y	N	N	Y	N	Y	Y
5 ***Rogers***	Y	Y	N	N	Y	N	Y	Y
6 Baesler	Y	Y	N	?	?	?	Y	Y
LOUISIANA								
1 ***Livingston***	Y	Y	N	N	Y	N	Y	Y
2 Jefferson	?	N	Y	N	Y	Y	Y	Y
3 Tauzin	Y	Y	N	N	Y	Y	Y	Y
4 Fields	Y	N	Y	N	Y	Y	Y	Y
5 ***McCrery***	Y	Y	N	N	Y	N	Y	Y
6 ***Baker***	Y	N	Y	?	Y	N	Y	Y
7 Hayes	Y	N	Y	N	Y	Y	Y	Y
MAINE								
1 Andrews	Y	N	Y	N	Y	Y	Y	Y
2 ***Snowe***	Y	Y	N	N	Y	N	Y	Y
MARYLAND								
1 ***Gilchrest***	Y	Y	Y	N	Y	Y	Y	Y
2 ***Bentley***	N	Y	N	?	?	Y	Y	Y
3 Cardin	Y	N	Y	N	Y	Y	Y	Y
4 Wynn	Y	N	Y	N	Y	Y	Y	Y
5 Hoyer	Y	N	Y	N	Y	Y	Y	Y
6 ***Bartlett***	Y	Y	N	N	Y	Y	Y	Y
7 Mfume	Y	N	Y	?	?	Y	Y	Y
8 ***Morella***	Y	N	Y	N	Y	Y	Y	Y
MASSACHUSETTS								
1 Olver	Y	N	Y	N	Y	Y	Y	Y
2 Neal	Y	N	Y	N	Y	Y	Y	Y
3 ***Blute***	Y	Y	N	N	Y	Y	Y	Y
4 Frank	Y	N	Y	N	Y	Y	Y	Y
5 Meehan	Y	N	Y	N	Y	Y	Y	Y
6 ***Torkildsen***	Y	Y	N	N	?	Y	Y	Y
7 Markey	Y	N	Y	N	Y	Y	Y	Y
8 Kennedy	Y	N	Y	N	Y	Y	Y	Y
9 Moakley	Y	N	Y	N	Y	Y	Y	Y
10 Studds	Y	N	Y	N	Y	Y	Y	Y
MICHIGAN								
1 Stupak	Y	N	Y	N	Y	Y	Y	Y
2 ***Hoekstra***	Y	Y	N	N	Y	N	Y	Y
3 Vacancy								
4 ***Camp***	Y	Y	N	N	Y	N	Y	Y
5 Barcia	Y	N	N	N	Y	Y	Y	Y
6 ***Upton***	Y	Y	N	N	Y	Y	Y	Y
7 ***Smith***	Y	Y	N	N	Y	N	Y	Y
8 Carr	Y	Y	N	N	?	Y	Y	Y
9 Kildee	Y	N	N	N	Y	Y	Y	Y
10 Bonior	Y	N	Y	N	?	Y	Y	Y
11 ***Knollenberg***	N	Y	N	N	Y	N	Y	Y
12 Levin	Y	N	Y	N	Y	Y	Y	Y
13 Ford	Y	N	Y	?	?	Y	Y	Y
14 Conyers	?	?	?	N	Y	Y	Y	Y
15 Collins	Y	N	Y	N	Y	Y	Y	Y
16 Dingell	Y	N	Y	N	Y	Y	Y	Y
MINNESOTA								
1 Penny	Y	Y	N	N	Y	Y	Y	N
2 Minge	Y	N	Y	N	Y	Y	Y	Y
3 ***Ramstad***	Y	Y	N	N	Y	Y	Y	Y
4 Vento	Y	N	Y	N	Y	Y	Y	Y
5 Sabo	Y	N	Y	N	Y	Y	Y	Y
6 ***Grams***	Y	Y	N	N	Y	N	Y	Y
7 Peterson	Y	Y	N	N	Y	Y	Y	Y
8 Oberstar	Y	N	Y	N	Y	Y	Y	Y
MISSISSIPPI								
1 Whitten	Y	N	Y	N	Y	Y	Y	Y
2 Thompson	Y	N	N	N	Y	Y	Y	Y
3 Montgomery	Y	N	Y	N	Y	Y	Y	Y
4 Parker	Y	N	Y	N	Y	Y	Y	Y
5 Taylor	Y	Y	N	N	Y	Y	Y	Y
MISSOURI								
1 Clay	Y	N	Y	N	Y	Y	Y	Y
2 ***Talent***	Y	Y	N	N	Y	N	Y	Y
3 Gephardt	Y	N	Y	N	?	Y	Y	Y
4 Skelton	Y	N	Y	N	Y	Y	Y	Y
5 Wheat	Y	N	Y	N	Y	Y	Y	Y
6 Danner	Y	N	Y	N	Y	Y	Y	Y
7 ***Hancock***	Y	Y	N	Y	Y	N	Y	Y
8 ***Emerson***	Y	Y	N	N	Y	Y	Y	Y
9 Volkmer	Y	N	Y	N	Y	Y	Y	Y
MONTANA								
AL Williams	Y	Y	Y	N	Y	+	+	+
NEBRASKA								
1 ***Bereuter***	Y	Y	Y	N	Y	Y	Y	Y
2 Hoagland	Y	N	Y	N	Y	Y	Y	Y
3 ***Barrett***	Y	Y	Y	N	Y	N	Y	Y
NEVADA								
1 Bilbray	Y	N	Y	N	Y	Y	Y	Y
2 ***Vucanovich***	Y	Y	N	N	Y	Y	Y	Y
NEW HAMPSHIRE								
1 ***Zeliff***	Y	Y	N	?	Y	Y	Y	Y
2 Swett	Y	N	Y	N	?	Y	Y	Y
NEW JERSEY								
1 Andrews	Y	N	N	N	Y	Y	Y	Y
2 Hughes	Y	N	N	N	Y	Y	Y	Y
3 ***Saxton***	Y	Y	N	N	Y	Y	Y	Y
4 ***Smith***	Y	Y	N	N	Y	Y	Y	Y
5 ***Roukema***	Y	N	Y	N	Y	Y	Y	Y
6 Pallone	Y	N	N	N	Y	Y	Y	Y
7 ***Franks***	Y	Y	N	N	Y	Y	Y	Y
8 Klein	Y	N	Y	?	?	Y	Y	Y
9 Torricelli	Y	N	N	N	Y	Y	Y	Y
10 Payne	Y	N	Y	?	?	Y	Y	Y
11 ***Gallo***	Y	Y	N	N	Y	Y	Y	Y
12 ***Zimmer***	Y	Y	N	N	Y	Y	Y	Y
13 Menendez	Y	N	N	N	Y	Y	Y	Y
NEW MEXICO								
1 ***Schiff***	Y	Y	N	N	Y	Y	Y	Y
2 ***Skeen***	Y	Y	N	N	Y	Y	Y	Y
3 Richardson	Y	N	Y	N	Y	Y	Y	Y
NEW YORK								
1 Hochbrueckner	Y	N	Y	N	Y	Y	Y	Y
2 ***Lazio***	Y	N	Y	N	Y	Y	Y	Y
3 ***King***	Y	N	Y	N	Y	Y	Y	Y
4 ***Levy***	Y	Y	Y	N	Y	Y	Y	Y
5 Ackerman	Y	N	Y	N	Y	Y	Y	Y
6 Flake	Y	N	Y	N	Y	Y	Y	Y
7 Manton	Y	N	Y	N	Y	Y	Y	Y
8 Nadler	Y	N	N	N	Y	Y	Y	Y
9 Schumer	Y	N	Y	N	Y	Y	Y	Y
10 Towns	?	?	?	N	?	Y	Y	Y
11 Owens	Y	N	N	?	Y	Y	Y	Y
12 Velazquez	Y	N	Y	N	Y	Y	Y	Y
13 ***Molinari***	Y	Y	N	?	Y	Y	Y	Y
14 Maloney	Y	N	Y	N	Y	Y	Y	Y
15 Rangel	Y	N	Y	?	Y	Y	Y	Y
16 Serrano	Y	N	Y	N	Y	Y	Y	Y
17 Engel	Y	N	N	?	Y	Y	Y	Y
18 Lowey	Y	N	N	N	Y	Y	Y	Y
19 ***Fish***	Y	Y	N	N	Y	Y	Y	Y
20 ***Gilman***	Y	Y	N	N	Y	Y	Y	Y
21 McNulty	Y	N	N	N	Y	Y	Y	Y
22 ***Solomon***	Y	Y	N	N	Y	Y	Y	Y
23 ***Boehlert***	Y	N	Y	N	Y	Y	Y	Y
24 ***McHugh***	Y	Y	N	N	Y	Y	Y	Y
25 ***Walsh***	Y	Y	N	N	Y	Y	Y	Y
26 Hinchey	?	N	Y	?	?	Y	Y	Y
27 ***Paxon***	Y	Y	N	N	Y	N	Y	Y
28 Slaughter	Y	N	N	N	Y	Y	Y	Y
29 LaFalce	Y	N	Y	N	Y	Y	Y	Y
30 ***Quinn***	Y	Y	N	N	Y	Y	Y	Y
31 ***Houghton***	Y	N	Y	N	Y	Y	Y	Y
NORTH CAROLINA								
1 Clayton	Y	N	Y	N	Y	Y	Y	Y
2 Valentine	Y	N	Y	N	?	Y	Y	Y
3 Lancaster	Y	Y	Y	N	Y	Y	Y	Y
4 Price	Y	N	Y	N	Y	Y	Y	Y
5 Neal	Y	N	Y	?	?	Y	Y	Y
6 ***Coble***	Y	Y	N	N	Y	N	Y	Y
7 Rose	Y	N	Y	N	Y	?	?	?
8 Hefner	Y	N	N	?	?	Y	Y	Y
9 ***McMillan***	Y	Y	Y	N	Y	Y	Y	Y
10 ***Ballenger***	Y	Y	N	N	Y	N	Y	Y
11 ***Taylor***	N	Y	N	Y	Y	N	Y	Y
12 Watt	Y	N	Y	N	Y	Y	Y	Y
NORTH DAKOTA								
AL Pomeroy	Y	N	N	N	Y	Y	Y	Y
OHIO								
1 Mann	Y	N	Y	N	Y	Y	Y	Y
2 ***Portman***	Y	Y	N	N	Y	N	Y	Y
3 Hall	Y	N	Y	N	Y	Y	Y	Y
4 ***Oxley***	Y	Y	N	N	Y	N	Y	Y
5 ***Gillmor***	Y	Y	N	N	Y	N	Y	Y
6 Strickland	Y	N	Y	N	Y	Y	Y	Y
7 ***Hobson***	Y	Y	N	N	Y	Y	Y	Y
8 ***Boehner***	Y	Y	N	N	Y	N	Y	Y
9 Kaptur	Y	Y	N	?	?	Y	Y	Y
10 ***Hoke***	N	Y	N	N	Y	Y	Y	Y
11 Stokes	Y	N	Y	N	Y	Y	Y	Y
12 ***Kasich***	Y	Y	N	N	Y	Y	Y	Y
13 Brown	Y	N	Y	N	Y	Y	Y	Y
14 Sawyer	Y	N	Y	N	Y	Y	Y	Y
15 ***Pryce***	Y	Y	N	N	Y	Y	Y	Y
16 ***Regula***	Y	Y	N	N	Y	Y	Y	Y
17 Traficant	Y	N	N	?	?	?	?	?
18 Applegate	Y	Y	N	N	Y	Y	Y	Y
19 Fingerhut	Y	N	Y	N	Y	Y	Y	Y
OKLAHOMA								
1 ***Inhofe***	Y	Y	N	N	Y	N	Y	Y
2 Synar	Y	N	N	N	Y	Y	Y	Y
3 Brewster	Y	N	N	N	Y	Y	Y	Y
4 McCurdy	Y	N	Y	N	Y	Y	Y	Y
5 ***Istook***	Y	Y	N	N	?	N	P	Y
6 English	Y	N	N	N	Y	Y	Y	Y
OREGON								
1 Furse	Y	N	Y	N	Y	Y	Y	Y
2 ***Smith***	Y	Y	N	N	Y	Y	Y	Y
3 Wyden	Y	N	Y	N	Y	Y	Y	Y
4 DeFazio	Y	N	N	?	Y	Y	Y	Y
5 Kopetski	Y	N	Y	N	Y	Y	Y	Y
PENNSYLVANIA								
1 Foglietta	Y	N	Y	?	Y	Y	Y	Y
2 Blackwell	Y	N	Y	?	?	Y	Y	Y
3 Borski	?	?	?	N	Y	Y	Y	Y
4 Klink	Y	N	Y	N	Y	Y	Y	Y
5 ***Clinger***	Y	Y	N	N	Y	Y	Y	Y
6 Holden	Y	N	N	N	Y	Y	Y	Y
7 ***Weldon***	Y	Y	N	N	Y	Y	Y	Y
8 ***Greenwood***	Y	Y	N	?	?	N	Y	Y
9 ***Shuster***	Y	Y	N	N	Y	N	Y	Y
10 ***McDade***	Y	Y	Y	?	?	Y	Y	Y
11 Kanjorski	Y	N	Y	N	Y	Y	Y	Y
12 Murtha	Y	N	Y	N	Y	Y	Y	Y
13 Margolies-Mezv.	Y	N	Y	N	Y	Y	Y	Y
14 Coyne	Y	N	Y	N	Y	Y	Y	Y
15 McHale	Y	N	Y	N	Y	Y	Y	Y
16 ***Walker***	Y	Y	N	N	Y	N	Y	Y
17 ***Gekas***	Y	Y	N	N	Y	Y	Y	Y
18 ***Santorum***	Y	Y	N	N	Y	Y	Y	Y
19 ***Goodling***	Y	Y	N	?	Y	Y	Y	Y
20 Murphy	Y	N	Y	N	Y	Y	Y	Y
21 ***Ridge***	N	Y	N	?	Y	Y	Y	Y
RHODE ISLAND								
1 ***Machtley***	Y	N	N	N	Y	Y	Y	Y
2 Reed	Y	N	Y	N	Y	Y	Y	Y
SOUTH CAROLINA								
1 ***Ravenel***	Y	Y	N	N	Y	Y	Y	Y
2 ***Spence***	Y	Y	N	N	Y	Y	Y	Y
3 Derrick	Y	N	Y	N	?	Y	Y	Y
4 ***Inglis***	Y	Y	N	N	Y	N	Y	Y
5 Spratt	Y	N	Y	N	Y	?	Y	Y
6 Clyburn	Y	N	Y	N	Y	Y	Y	Y
SOUTH DAKOTA								
AL Johnson	Y	N	Y	N	Y	Y	Y	Y
TENNESSEE								
1 ***Quillen***	N	Y	N	N	Y	Y	Y	Y
2 ***Duncan***	Y	Y	N	N	Y	Y	Y	Y
3 Lloyd	Y	N	N	N	Y	Y	Y	Y
4 Cooper	Y	N	N	?	?	Y	Y	Y
5 Clement	Y	Y	N	N	Y	Y	Y	Y
6 Gordon	Y	N	?	N	Y	Y	Y	Y
7 ***Sundquist***	Y	Y	N	N	Y	Y	Y	Y
8 Tanner	Y	N	N	N	Y	Y	Y	Y
9 Ford	Y	N	Y	N	Y	?	?	Y
TEXAS								
1 Chapman	Y	Y	N	N	Y	Y	Y	Y
2 Wilson	Y	?	Y	?	?	?	?	?
3 ***Johnson, Sam***	N	Y	N	N	Y	N	Y	Y
4 Hall	Y	N	Y	N	Y	Y	Y	Y
5 Bryant	Y	N	Y	N	Y	Y	Y	Y
6 ***Barton***	Y	Y	N	N	Y	N	Y	Y
7 ***Archer***	Y	Y	N	N	Y	N	Y	Y
8 ***Fields***	Y	Y	N	N	Y	N	Y	Y
9 Brooks	Y	N	Y	N	Y	Y	Y	Y
10 Pickle	Y	N	Y	N	Y	Y	Y	Y
11 Edwards	Y	N	Y	N	Y	Y	Y	Y
12 Geren	Y	N	Y	N	Y	Y	Y	Y
13 Sarpalius	Y	N	Y	N	Y	Y	Y	Y
14 Laughlin	Y	N	Y	N	Y	Y	Y	Y
15 de la Garza	Y	N	Y	N	?	Y	Y	Y
16 Coleman	Y	N	Y	N	Y	Y	Y	Y
17 Stenholm	Y	N	Y	N	Y	Y	Y	Y
18 Washington	Y	N	Y	?	Y	Y	Y	Y
19 ***Combest***	N	Y	N	N	Y	N	Y	Y
20 Gonzalez	Y	N	Y	N	Y	Y	Y	Y
21 ***Smith***	Y	Y	N	N	Y	N	Y	Y
22 ***DeLay***	Y	Y	N	Y	Y	N	Y	Y
23 ***Bonilla***	N	Y	N	N	Y	N	Y	Y
24 Frost	Y	N	Y	N	Y	Y	Y	Y
25 Andrews	Y	Y	N	N	Y	Y	Y	Y
26 ***Armey***	N	Y	N	N	Y	N	Y	Y
27 Ortiz	Y	N	Y	N	?	Y	Y	Y
28 Tejeda	Y	N	Y	N	Y	Y	Y	Y
29 Green	Y	N	Y	N	Y	Y	Y	Y
30 Johnson, E.B.	Y	N	Y	N	Y	Y	Y	Y
UTAH								
1 ***Hansen***	Y	Y	N	N	Y	Y	Y	Y
2 Shepherd	Y	N	Y	N	Y	Y	Y	Y
3 Orton	Y	N	Y	N	Y	Y	Y	Y
VERMONT								
AL *Sanders*	Y	N	N	?	?	Y	Y	Y
VIRGINIA								
1 ***Bateman***	Y	Y	N	N	Y	N	Y	Y
2 Pickett	Y	N	Y	N	Y	Y	Y	Y
3 Scott	Y	N	Y	N	Y	Y	Y	Y
4 Sisisky	Y	N	Y	?	Y	Y	Y	Y
5 Payne	Y	N	Y	N	Y	Y	Y	Y
6 ***Goodlatte***	Y	Y	N	N	Y	N	Y	Y
7 ***Bliley***	Y	Y	N	N	Y	Y	Y	Y
8 Moran	Y	N	Y	N	Y	Y	Y	Y
9 Boucher	Y	N	Y	N	Y	Y	Y	Y
10 ***Wolf***	Y	Y	N	N	Y	N	Y	Y
11 Byrne	Y	N	Y	N	Y	Y	Y	Y
WASHINGTON								
1 Cantwell	Y	N	Y	N	Y	Y	Y	Y
2 Swift	Y	N	Y	N	Y	Y	Y	Y
3 Unsoeld	Y	N	Y	N	Y	Y	Y	Y
4 Inslee	Y	N	Y	N	Y	Y	Y	Y
5 Foley								
6 Dicks	Y	N	Y	N	Y	Y	Y	Y
7 McDermott	Y	N	Y	N	Y	Y	Y	Y
8 ***Dunn***	Y	Y	N	N	Y	N	Y	Y
9 Kreidler	Y	N	Y	N	Y	Y	Y	Y
WEST VIRGINIA								
1 Mollohan	Y	N	Y	N	Y	Y	Y	Y
2 Wise	Y	N	Y	N	Y	Y	Y	Y
3 Rahall	N	Y	N	N	Y	Y	Y	Y
WISCONSIN								
1 Barca	Y	N	N	N	Y	Y	Y	Y
2 ***Klug***	Y	Y	N	N	Y	Y	Y	Y
3 ***Gunderson***	Y	Y	N	N	Y	Y	Y	Y
4 Kleczka	Y	N	Y	N	Y	Y	Y	Y
5 Barrett	Y	N	Y	N	Y	Y	Y	Y
6 ***Petri***	Y	N	Y	N	Y	Y	Y	Y
7 Obey	Y	N	Y	N	Y	Y	Y	Y
8 ***Roth***	Y	Y	N	N	Y	Y	Y	Y
9 ***Sensenbrenner***	Y	Y	N	N	Y	N	Y	Y
WYOMING								
AL ***Thomas***	Y	Y	N	N	Y	Y	Y	Y
DELEGATES								
de Lugo, V.I.	D	D	D	D	D	D	D	D
Faleomavaega, Am.S.	D	D	D	D	D	D	D	D
Norton, D.C.	D	D	D	D	D	D	D	D
Romero-B., P.R.	D	D	D	D	D	D	D	D
Underwood, Guam	D	D	D	D	D	D	D	D

Southern states - Ala., Ark., Fla., Ga., Ky., La., Miss., N.C., Okla., S.C., Tenn., Texas, Va.
Omitted votes are quorum calls, which CQ does not include in its vote charts.

440. S 464. Ross Bass Post Office/Passage. Collins, D-Mich., motion to suspend the rules and pass the bill to redesignate the Pulaski Post Office in Pulaski, Tenn., as the Ross Bass Post Office. Motion agreed to 420-3: R 170-3; D 249-0 (ND 168-0, SD 81-0); I 1-0, Sept. 21, 1993. A two-thirds majority of those present and voting (282 in this case) is required for passage under suspension of the rules.

441. HR 2056. Samuel E. Perry Postal Building/Passage. Collins, D-Mich., motion to suspend the rules and pass the bill to designate a federal building in Fredericksburg, Va., as the Samuel E. Perry Postal Building. Motion agreed to 423-2: R 171-2; D 251-0 (ND 168-0, SD 83-0); I 1-0, Sept. 21, 1993. A two-thirds majority of those present and voting (284 in this case) is required for passage under suspension of the rules.

442. HR 2294. Graham B. Pursell Jr. Post Office/Passage. Collins, D-Mich., motion to suspend the rules and pass the bill to designate the Main Post Office in Wichita Falls, Texas, as the Graham B. Pursell Jr. Post Office and Federal Building. Motion agreed to 422-4: R 170-4; D 251-0 (ND 168-0, SD 83-0); I 1-0, Sept. 21, 1993. A two-thirds majority of those present and voting (284 in this case) is required for passage under suspension of the rules.

443. HR 3051. Impact Aid Regarding Certain Indian Lands/Passage. Kildee, D-Mich., motion to suspend the rules and pass the bill to continue federal impact aid payments to certain school districts in Oklahoma that enroll American Indian children from low-income housing. Motion agreed to 358-69: R 114-60; D 243-9 (ND 164-5, SD 79-4); I 1-0, Sept. 21, 1993. A two-thirds majority of those present and voting (285 in this case) is required for passage under suspension of the rules.

444. HR 3049. Marine Mammals Fishing Exemption Extension/Passage. Studds, D-Mass., motion to suspend the rules and pass the bill to extend from Oct. 1, 1993, to April 1, 1994, the commercial fishing exemption from the ban on incidental takes of marine mammals while a new policy is developed. Motion agreed to 421-6: R 172-2; D 248-4 (ND 169-0, SD 79-4); I 1-0, Sept. 21, 1993. A two-thirds majority of those present and voting (285 in this case) is required for passage under suspension of the rules.

445. HR 2961. Walter B. Jones Center for the Sounds/ Passage. Studds, D-Mass., motion to suspend the rules and pass the bill to authorize the Walter B. Jones Center for the Sounds in the Pocosin Lakes National Wildlife Refuge in North Carolina in honor of the late chairman of the Merchant Marine and Fisheries Committee (House 1966-92). Motion agreed to 425-0: R 174-0; D 250-0 (ND 168-0, SD 82-0); I 1-0, Sept. 21, 1993. A two-thirds majority of those present and voting (284 in this case) is required for passage under suspension of the rules.

446. HR 2604. Brownsville, Texas, Wetlands Center/ Passage. Studds, D-Mass., motion to suspend the rules and pass the bill to authorize $5 million in fiscal 1994 and $4 million in each of fiscal 1995 and 1996 to establish the Brownsville Wetlands Policy Center at the Port of Brownsville, Texas. Motion agreed to 360-64: R 121-53; D 238-11 (ND 163-5, SD 75-6); I 1-0, Sept. 21, 1993. A two-thirds majority of those present and voting (283 in this case) is required for passage under suspension of the rules.

447. HR 2750. Fiscal 1994 Transportation Appropriations/Rule. Adoption of the rule (H Res 252) to provide for House floor consideration of the bill to provide $13,837,444,009 in new budget authority for the Department of Transportation and related agencies in fiscal 1994. Adoption of the rule automatically incorporated into the bill an amendment earmarking $28.2 million for the San Francisco Airport Bay Area Rapid Transit (BART) Extension Project and Tasman Corridor LRT Project. Adopted 257-163: R 95-77; D 161-86 (ND 119-47, SD 42-39); I 1-0, Sept. 22, 1993.

KEY

Y	Voted for (yea).
#	Paired for.
+	Announced for.
N	Voted against (nay).
X	Paired against.
−	Announced against.
P	Voted "present."
C	Voted "present" to avoid possible conflict of interest.
?	Did not vote or otherwise make a position known.
D	Delegates ineligible to vote.

Democrats *Republicans*
Independent

	440	441	442	443	444	445	446	447
ALABAMA								
1 *Callahan*	Y	Y	Y	N	Y	Y	Y	N
2 *Everett*	Y	Y	Y	N	Y	Y	N	N
3 Browder	Y	Y	Y	Y	Y	Y	Y	Y
4 Bevill	Y	Y	Y	Y	Y	Y	Y	N
5 Cramer	Y	Y	Y	Y	Y	Y	Y	Y
6 *Bachus*	Y	Y	Y	Y	Y	Y	Y	N
7 Hilliard	Y	Y	Y	Y	Y	Y	Y	?
ALASKA								
AL *Young*	Y	Y	Y	Y	Y	Y	Y	Y
ARIZONA								
1 Coppersmith	Y	Y	Y	Y	Y	Y	Y	Y
2 Pastor	Y	Y	Y	Y	Y	Y	Y	N
3 *Stump*	Y	Y	Y	N	Y	N	N	N
4 *Kyl*	Y	Y	Y	Y	Y	Y	Y	N
5 *Kolbe*	Y	Y	Y	Y	Y	Y	Y	N
6 English	Y	Y	Y	Y	Y	Y	Y	Y
ARKANSAS								
1 Lambert	Y	Y	Y	Y	Y	Y	Y	Y
2 Thornton	Y	Y	Y	Y	Y	Y	Y	Y
3 *Hutchinson*	Y	Y	Y	N	Y	N	N	Y
4 *Dickey*	Y	Y	Y	N	Y	Y	Y	Y
CALIFORNIA								
1 Hamburg	Y	Y	Y	Y	Y	Y	Y	Y
2 *Herger*	Y	Y	Y	N	Y	N	N	N
3 Fazio	Y	Y	Y	Y	Y	Y	Y	Y
4 *Doolittle*	Y	Y	Y	N	Y	Y	Y	Y
5 Matsui	Y	Y	Y	Y	Y	Y	Y	Y
6 Woolsey	Y	Y	Y	Y	Y	Y	Y	Y
7 Miller	Y	Y	Y	Y	Y	Y	Y	Y
8 Pelosi	Y	Y	Y	Y	Y	Y	Y	Y
9 Dellums	Y	Y	Y	Y	Y	Y	Y	Y
10 *Baker*	Y	Y	Y	N	Y	Y	Y	Y
11 *Pombo*	Y	Y	Y	N	Y	Y	Y	N
12 Lantos	Y	Y	Y	Y	Y	Y	Y	Y
13 Stark	Y	Y	Y	Y	Y	Y	Y	Y
14 Eshoo	Y	Y	Y	Y	Y	Y	Y	Y
15 Mineta	Y	Y	Y	Y	Y	Y	Y	Y
16 Edwards	Y	?	Y	Y	Y	Y	Y	Y
17 Farr	Y	Y	Y	Y	Y	Y	Y	Y
18 Condit	Y	Y	Y	N	Y	N	Y	N
19 Lehman	Y	Y	Y	Y	Y	Y	Y	N
20 Dooley	Y	Y	Y	Y	Y	Y	Y	Y
21 *Thomas*	Y	Y	Y	Y	Y	Y	Y	Y
22 *Huffington*	N	Y	N	N	N	Y	N	Y
23 *Gallegly*	Y	Y	Y	Y	Y	Y	Y	Y
24 Beilenson	Y	Y	Y	Y	Y	Y	Y	Y
25 *McKeon*	Y	Y	Y	Y	Y	Y	Y	?
26 Berman	Y	Y	Y	Y	Y	Y	Y	Y
27 *Moorhead*	Y	Y	Y	N	Y	Y	Y	Y
28 *Dreier*	Y	Y	Y	Y	Y	Y	Y	Y
29 Waxman	Y	Y	Y	Y	Y	Y	Y	Y
30 Becerra	Y	Y	Y	Y	Y	Y	Y	Y
31 Martinez	Y	Y	Y	Y	Y	Y	Y	Y
32 Dixon	Y	Y	Y	Y	Y	Y	Y	Y
33 Roybal-Allard	Y	Y	Y	Y	Y	Y	Y	Y
34 Torres	Y	Y	Y	Y	Y	Y	Y	Y
35 Waters	Y	Y	Y	Y	Y	Y	Y	Y
36 Harman	Y	Y	Y	Y	Y	Y	Y	Y
37 Tucker	Y	Y	Y	Y	Y	Y	Y	Y
38 Horn	Y	Y	Y	Y	Y	Y	Y	Y
39 *Royce*	Y	Y	N	N	Y	N	N	N
40 *Lewis*	Y	Y	Y	Y	Y	Y	N	N
41 *Kim*	Y	Y	Y	Y	Y	Y	Y	Y

	440	441	442	443	444	445	446	447
42 Brown	Y	Y	Y	Y	Y	Y	Y	Y
43 *Calvert*	Y	Y	Y	Y	Y	Y	Y	N
44 *McCandless*	Y	Y	Y	Y	Y	Y	Y	Y
45 *Rohrabacher*	Y	Y	Y	N	Y	N	N	N
46 *Dornan*	Y	Y	Y	Y	Y	Y	Y	N
47 *Cox*	Y	Y	Y	Y	Y	N	N	N
48 *Packard*	Y	Y	Y	Y	Y	N	N	N
49 Schenk	Y	Y	Y	Y	Y	Y	Y	Y
50 Filner	Y	Y	Y	Y	Y	Y	Y	Y
51 *Cunningham*	N	Y	N	N	Y	N	N	N
52 *Hunter*	Y	Y	Y	N	Y	Y	Y	N
COLORADO								
1 Schroeder	Y	Y	Y	Y	Y	Y	Y	N
2 Skaggs	Y	Y	Y	Y	Y	Y	Y	Y
3 *McInnis*	Y	Y	Y	Y	Y	Y	Y	Y
4 *Allard*	Y	Y	N	N	Y	N	N	N
5 *Hefley*	Y	Y	N	N	Y	N	N	Y
6 *Schaefer*	Y	Y	Y	N	Y	Y	Y	Y
CONNECTICUT								
1 Kennelly	Y	Y	Y	Y	Y	Y	Y	Y
2 Gejdenson	Y	Y	Y	Y	Y	Y	Y	Y
3 DeLauro	Y	Y	Y	Y	Y	Y	Y	N
4 *Shays*	Y	Y	Y	N	Y	Y	Y	Y
5 *Franks*	Y	Y	Y	Y	Y	Y	Y	N
6 *Johnson*	Y	Y	Y	Y	Y	Y	Y	Y
DELAWARE								
AL *Castle*	Y	Y	Y	Y	Y	Y	Y	N
FLORIDA								
1 Hutto	Y	Y	Y	N	Y	Y	Y	N
2 Peterson	Y	Y	Y	Y	Y	Y	Y	N
3 Brown	Y	Y	Y	Y	Y	Y	Y	Y
4 *Fowler*	Y	Y	Y	N	Y	N	N	N
5 Thurman	Y	Y	Y	Y	Y	N	N	N
6 *Stearns*	Y	Y	Y	N	Y	N	N	N
7 *Mica*	Y	Y	N	Y	Y	Y	Y	Y
8 *McCollum*	Y	Y	Y	Y	Y	Y	N	Y
9 *Bilirakis*	Y	Y	Y	Y	Y	Y	Y	N
10 *Young*	Y	Y	Y	Y	Y	Y	N	N
11 Gibbons	Y	Y	Y	Y	Y	Y	Y	Y
12 *Canady*	Y	Y	N	Y	Y	Y	Y	N
13 *Miller*	Y	Y	Y	N	Y	N	Y	N
14 Goss	Y	Y	Y	Y	Y	Y	N	Y
15 Bacchus	Y	Y	Y	Y	Y	Y	Y	Y
16 *Lewis*	Y	Y	Y	Y	Y	Y	N	N
17 Meek	Y	Y	Y	Y	Y	Y	?	N
18 *Ros-Lehtinen*	Y	Y	Y	Y	Y	Y	Y	N
19 Johnston	Y	Y	Y	Y	Y	Y	Y	Y
20 Deutsch	Y	Y	Y	Y	Y	Y	Y	Y
21 *Diaz-Balart*	Y	Y	Y	Y	Y	Y	Y	Y
22 *Shaw*	?	?	?	?	?	?	?	N
23 Hastings	Y	Y	Y	Y	Y	Y	Y	Y
GEORGIA								
1 *Kingston*	Y	Y	Y	N	Y	Y	N	N
2 Bishop	Y	Y	Y	Y	Y	Y	Y	Y
3 *Collins*	Y	Y	Y	N	Y	Y	N	Y
4 *Linder*	Y	Y	Y	Y	Y	Y	Y	?
5 Lewis	Y	Y	Y	Y	Y	Y	Y	Y
6 *Gingrich*	Y	Y	Y	Y	Y	Y	N	Y
7 Darden	Y	Y	Y	Y	Y	Y	Y	N
8 Rowland	Y	Y	Y	Y	Y	Y	Y	Y
9 Deal	Y	Y	Y	Y	Y	Y	Y	Y
10 Johnson	Y	Y	Y	Y	Y	Y	Y	Y
11 McKinney	Y	Y	Y	Y	Y	Y	N	Y
HAWAII								
1 Abercrombie	?	?	?	?	?	?	?	Y
2 Mink	Y	Y	Y	Y	Y	Y	Y	Y
IDAHO								
1 LaRocco	Y	Y	Y	Y	Y	Y	Y	Y
2 *Crapo*	Y	Y	Y	Y	Y	Y	Y	Y
ILLINOIS								
1 Rush	Y	Y	Y	Y	Y	Y	Y	Y
2 Reynolds	Y	Y	Y	Y	Y	Y	Y	Y
3 Lipinski	Y	Y	Y	Y	Y	Y	Y	Y
4 Gutierrez	Y	Y	Y	Y	Y	Y	Y	Y
5 Rostenkowski	Y	Y	Y	Y	Y	?	?	N
6 *Hyde*	Y	Y	Y	N	Y	N	N	N
7 Collins	Y	Y	Y	Y	Y	Y	Y	Y
8 *Crane*	Y	Y	N	N	Y	N	N	N
9 Yates	Y	Y	Y	Y	Y	Y	Y	Y
10 *Porter*	Y	Y	Y	Y	Y	Y	Y	Y
11 Sangmeister	Y	Y	Y	Y	Y	Y	Y	Y
12 Costello	Y	Y	Y	Y	Y	Y	Y	Y
13 *Fawell*	Y	Y	Y	Y	Y	Y	Y	Y
14 *Hastert*	Y	Y	N	Y	Y	Y	Y	N
15 *Ewing*	Y	?	Y	N	Y	N	N	Y
16 *Manzullo*	Y	Y	Y	N	Y	N	N	N
17 Evans	Y	Y	Y	Y	Y	Y	Y	Y

ND Northern Democrats   SD Southern Democrats

	440	441	442	443	444	445	446	447
18 ***Michel***	Y	Y	Y	Y	Y	Y	N	?
19 Poshard	Y	Y	Y	Y	Y	Y	Y	Y
20 Durbin	Y	Y	Y	Y	Y	Y	Y	N
INDIANA								
1 Visclosky	Y	Y	Y	Y	Y	Y	Y	N
2 Sharp	Y	Y	Y	Y	Y	Y	Y	N
3 Roemer	Y	Y	Y	Y	Y	Y	N	N
4 Long	Y	Y	Y	Y	Y	Y	Y	N
5 ***Buyer***	Y	Y	Y	Y	Y	Y	Y	N
6 ***Burton***	Y	Y	Y	N	Y	Y	Y	N
7 ***Myers***	Y	Y	Y	Y	Y	Y	Y	N
8 McCloskey	Y	Y	Y	Y	Y	Y	Y	N
9 Hamilton	Y	Y	Y	Y	Y	Y	Y	N
10 Jacobs	Y	Y	Y	Y	Y	Y	N	N
IOWA								
1 ***Leach***	Y	Y	Y	Y	Y	Y	Y	Y
2 ***Nussle***	Y	Y	Y	Y	Y	Y	Y	N
3 ***Lightfoot***	Y	Y	Y	Y	Y	Y	Y	N
4 Smith	Y	Y	Y	Y	Y	Y	Y	N
5 ***Grandy***	Y	Y	Y	Y	Y	Y	Y	Y
KANSAS								
1 ***Roberts***	Y	Y	Y	Y	Y	Y	Y	N
2 Slattery	Y	Y	Y	Y	Y	Y	Y	?
3 ***Meyers***	Y	Y	Y	Y	Y	Y	Y	Y
4 Glickman	Y	Y	Y	Y	Y	Y	Y	Y
KENTUCKY								
1 Barlow	Y	Y	Y	Y	Y	Y	Y	Y
2 Natcher	Y	Y	Y	Y	Y	Y	Y	N
3 Mazzoli	Y	Y	Y	Y	Y	Y	Y	N
4 ***Bunning***	Y	Y	Y	N	Y	Y	N	N
5 ***Rogers***	Y	Y	Y	Y	Y	Y	Y	N
6 Baesler	Y	Y	Y	Y	Y	Y	Y	Y
LOUISIANA								
1 ***Livingston***	Y	Y	Y	Y	Y	Y	Y	N
2 Jefferson	Y	Y	Y	Y	Y	Y	Y	Y
3 Tauzin	Y	Y	Y	Y	Y	Y	Y	Y
4 Fields	Y	Y	Y	Y	Y	Y	Y	Y
5 ***McCrery***	Y	Y	Y	Y	Y	Y	Y	N
6 ***Baker***	Y	Y	Y	Y	Y	Y	Y	Y
7 Hayes	Y	Y	Y	Y	Y	Y	Y	Y
MAINE								
1 Andrews	Y	Y	Y	Y	Y	Y	Y	Y
2 ***Snowe***	Y	Y	Y	Y	Y	Y	Y	Y
MARYLAND								
1 ***Gilchrest***	Y	Y	Y	Y	Y	Y	Y	Y
2 ***Bentley***	Y	Y	Y	Y	Y	Y	Y	N
3 Cardin	Y	Y	Y	Y	Y	Y	Y	Y
4 Wynn	Y	Y	Y	Y	Y	Y	Y	N
5 Hoyer	Y	Y	Y	Y	Y	Y	Y	N
6 ***Bartlett***	Y	Y	Y	N	Y	Y	N	Y
7 Mfume	Y	Y	Y	Y	Y	Y	Y	Y
8 ***Morella***	Y	Y	Y	Y	Y	Y	Y	Y
MASSACHUSETTS								
1 Olver	Y	Y	Y	Y	Y	Y	Y	N
2 Neal	Y	Y	Y	Y	Y	Y	Y	Y
3 ***Blute***	Y	Y	Y	Y	Y	Y	Y	Y
4 Frank	Y	Y	Y	Y	Y	Y	Y	Y
5 Meehan	Y	Y	Y	Y	Y	Y	Y	Y
6 ***Torkildsen***	Y	Y	Y	Y	Y	Y	Y	Y
7 Markey	Y	Y	Y	Y	Y	Y	Y	Y
8 Kennedy	Y	Y	Y	Y	Y	Y	Y	Y
9 Moakley	Y	Y	Y	Y	Y	Y	Y	Y
10 Studds	Y	Y	Y	Y	Y	Y	Y	Y
MICHIGAN								
1 Stupak	Y	Y	Y	Y	Y	Y	Y	N
2 ***Hoekstra***	Y	Y	Y	N	Y	Y	Y	Y
3 Vacancy								
4 ***Camp***	Y	Y	Y	Y	Y	Y	Y	N
5 Barcia	Y	Y	Y	Y	Y	Y	Y	N
6 ***Upton***	Y	Y	Y	N	Y	Y	Y	Y
7 ***Smith***	Y	Y	Y	Y	Y	Y	N	N
8 Carr	Y	Y	Y	Y	Y	Y	Y	N
9 Kildee	Y	Y	Y	Y	Y	Y	Y	N
10 Bonior	Y	Y	Y	Y	Y	Y	Y	Y
11 ***Knollenberg***	Y	Y	Y	N	Y	Y	Y	N
12 Levin	Y	Y	Y	Y	Y	Y	Y	N
13 Ford	Y	Y	Y	Y	Y	Y	Y	Y
14 Conyers	?	Y	Y	Y	Y	Y	Y	?
15 Collins	Y	Y	Y	Y	Y	Y	Y	?
16 Dingell	Y	Y	Y	Y	Y	Y	Y	Y
MINNESOTA								
1 Penny	Y	Y	Y	N	Y	Y	N	N
2 Minge	Y	Y	Y	Y	Y	Y	Y	Y
3 ***Ramstad***	Y	Y	Y	Y	Y	Y	N	N
4 Vento	Y	Y	Y	Y	Y	Y	Y	N

	440	441	442	443	444	445	446	447
5 Sabo	Y	Y	Y	Y	Y	Y	Y	N
6 ***Grams***	Y	Y	Y	Y	Y	Y	Y	N
7 Peterson	Y	Y	Y	Y	Y	Y	Y	N
8 Oberstar	Y	Y	Y	Y	Y	Y	Y	Y
MISSISSIPPI								
1 Whitten	Y	Y	Y	Y	Y	Y	Y	N
2 Thompson	Y	Y	Y	Y	Y	Y	Y	Y
3 Montgomery	Y	Y	Y	Y	Y	Y	Y	Y
4 Parker	Y	Y	Y	Y	Y	Y	Y	Y
5 Taylor	Y	Y	Y	N	Y	Y	N	Y
MISSOURI								
1 Clay	Y	Y	Y	Y	Y	Y	Y	Y
2 ***Talent***	Y	Y	Y	Y	Y	Y	N	Y
3 Gephardt	Y	Y	Y	Y	Y	Y	Y	Y
4 Skelton	Y	Y	Y	Y	Y	Y	Y	N
5 Wheat	Y	Y	Y	Y	Y	Y	Y	Y
6 Danner	Y	Y	Y	Y	Y	Y	Y	Y
7 ***Hancock***	Y	Y	Y	N	Y	Y	N	N
8 ***Emerson***	Y	Y	Y	Y	Y	Y	N	Y
9 Volkmer	Y	Y	Y	Y	Y	Y	Y	Y
MONTANA								
AL Williams	+	+	+	+	+	+	+	Y
NEBRASKA								
1 ***Bereuter***	Y	Y	Y	Y	Y	Y	Y	N
2 Hoagland	Y	Y	Y	Y	Y	Y	Y	N
3 ***Barrett***	Y	Y	Y	N	Y	Y	N	Y
NEVADA								
1 Bilbray	Y	Y	Y	Y	Y	Y	Y	Y
2 ***Vucanovich***	Y	Y	Y	Y	Y	Y	Y	N
NEW HAMPSHIRE								
1 ***Zeliff***	Y	Y	Y	N	Y	Y	N	Y
2 Swett	Y	Y	Y	Y	Y	Y	Y	Y
NEW JERSEY								
1 Andrews	Y	Y	Y	Y	Y	Y	Y	Y
2 Hughes	Y	Y	Y	Y	Y	Y	Y	Y
3 ***Saxton***	Y	Y	Y	Y	Y	Y	Y	Y
4 ***Smith***	Y	Y	Y	Y	Y	Y	Y	Y
5 ***Roukema***	Y	Y	Y	N	Y	Y	Y	Y
6 Pallone	Y	Y	Y	Y	Y	Y	Y	Y
7 ***Franks***	Y	Y	Y	Y	Y	Y	Y	Y
8 Klein	Y	Y	Y	Y	Y	Y	Y	Y
9 Torricelli	Y	Y	Y	Y	Y	Y	Y	Y
10 Payne	Y	Y	Y	Y	Y	Y	Y	Y
11 ***Gallo***	Y	Y	Y	Y	Y	Y	Y	N
12 ***Zimmer***	Y	Y	Y	N	Y	Y	N	Y
13 Menendez	Y	Y	Y	Y	Y	Y	Y	Y
NEW MEXICO								
1 ***Schiff***	Y	Y	Y	Y	Y	Y	Y	N
2 ***Skeen***	Y	Y	Y	Y	Y	Y	Y	N
3 Richardson	Y	Y	Y	Y	Y	Y	Y	Y
NEW YORK								
1 Hochbrueckner	Y	Y	Y	Y	Y	Y	Y	N
2 ***Lazio***	Y	Y	Y	Y	Y	Y	Y	Y
3 ***King***	Y	Y	Y	Y	Y	Y	Y	Y
4 ***Levy***	Y	Y	Y	Y	Y	Y	Y	Y
5 Ackerman	Y	Y	Y	Y	Y	Y	Y	Y
6 Flake	Y	Y	Y	Y	Y	Y	Y	Y
7 Manton	Y	Y	Y	Y	Y	Y	Y	Y
8 Nadler	Y	Y	Y	Y	Y	Y	Y	Y
9 Schumer	Y	Y	Y	Y	Y	Y	Y	Y
10 Towns	Y	Y	Y	Y	Y	Y	Y	?
11 Owens	Y	Y	Y	Y	Y	Y	Y	Y
12 Velazquez	Y	Y	Y	Y	Y	Y	Y	Y
13 ***Molinari***	Y	Y	Y	Y	Y	Y	Y	Y
14 Maloney	Y	Y	Y	Y	Y	Y	Y	Y
15 Rangel	Y	Y	Y	Y	Y	Y	Y	Y
16 Serrano	Y	Y	Y	Y	Y	Y	Y	Y
17 Engel	Y	Y	Y	Y	Y	Y	Y	?
18 Lowey	Y	Y	Y	Y	Y	Y	Y	N
19 ***Fish***	Y	Y	Y	Y	Y	Y	Y	Y
20 ***Gilman***	Y	Y	Y	Y	Y	Y	Y	Y
21 McNulty	Y	Y	Y	Y	Y	Y	Y	Y
22 ***Solomon***	Y	Y	Y	Y	Y	Y	Y	Y
23 ***Boehlert***	Y	Y	Y	Y	Y	Y	Y	Y
24 ***McHugh***	Y	Y	Y	Y	Y	Y	Y	Y
25 ***Walsh***	Y	Y	Y	Y	Y	Y	Y	Y
26 Hinchey	Y	Y	Y	Y	Y	Y	Y	Y
27 ***Paxon***	Y	Y	Y	N	Y	Y	N	N
28 Slaughter	Y	Y	Y	Y	Y	Y	Y	Y
29 LaFalce	Y	Y	Y	N	Y	Y	Y	Y
30 ***Quinn***	Y	Y	Y	Y	Y	Y	Y	Y
31 ***Houghton***	Y	Y	Y	Y	Y	Y	Y	Y
NORTH CAROLINA								
1 Clayton	Y	Y	Y	Y	Y	Y	Y	N
2 Valentine	Y	Y	Y	N	N	Y	N	Y

	440	441	442	443	444	445	446	447
3 Lancaster	Y	Y	Y	Y	Y	Y	Y	N
4 Price	Y	Y	Y	Y	Y	Y	Y	N
5 Neal	Y	Y	Y	Y	Y	Y	Y	?
6 ***Coble***	Y	Y	Y	N	Y	Y	N	N
7 Rose	?	?	?	?	?	?	?	Y
8 Hefner	Y	Y	Y	Y	Y	?	?	N
9 ***McMillan***	Y	Y	Y	N	Y	Y	Y	N
10 ***Ballenger***	Y	Y	Y	N	Y	Y	Y	Y
11 ***Taylor***	Y	Y	Y	Y	Y	Y	N	N
12 Watt	?	Y	Y	Y	N	Y	Y	N
NORTH DAKOTA								
AL Pomeroy	Y	Y	Y	Y	Y	Y	Y	Y
OHIO								
1 Mann	Y	Y	Y	Y	Y	Y	Y	Y
2 ***Portman***	Y	Y	Y	Y	Y	Y	Y	Y
3 Hall	Y	Y	Y	Y	Y	Y	Y	Y
4 ***Oxley***	Y	Y	Y	Y	Y	Y	Y	Y
5 ***Gillmor***	Y	Y	Y	Y	Y	Y	Y	Y
6 Strickland	Y	Y	Y	Y	Y	Y	Y	Y
7 ***Hobson***	Y	Y	Y	Y	Y	Y	Y	N
8 ***Boehner***	Y	Y	Y	Y	Y	Y	Y	N
9 Kaptur	Y	Y	Y	Y	Y	Y	Y	Y
10 ***Hoke***	?	Y	Y	Y	Y	Y	Y	N
11 Stokes	Y	Y	Y	Y	Y	Y	Y	?
12 ***Kasich***	Y	Y	Y	Y	Y	Y	Y	N
13 Brown	Y	Y	Y	Y	Y	Y	Y	Y
14 Sawyer	Y	Y	Y	Y	Y	Y	Y	Y
15 ***Pryce***	Y	Y	Y	Y	Y	Y	Y	Y
16 ***Regula***	Y	Y	Y	Y	Y	Y	Y	N
17 Traficant	?	?	?	?	?	?	?	?
18 Applegate	Y	Y	Y	Y	Y	Y	Y	Y
19 Fingerhut	Y	Y	Y	Y	Y	Y	Y	N
OKLAHOMA								
1 ***Inhofe***	Y	Y	Y	N	Y	Y	N	Y
2 Synar	Y	Y	Y	Y	Y	Y	Y	Y
3 Brewster	Y	Y	Y	Y	Y	Y	Y	N
4 McCurdy	Y	Y	Y	Y	N	Y	Y	N
5 ***Istook***	Y	Y	Y	Y	Y	Y	Y	N
6 English	Y	Y	Y	Y	Y	Y	Y	N
OREGON								
1 Furse	Y	Y	Y	Y	Y	Y	Y	N
2 ***Smith***	Y	Y	Y	Y	Y	Y	Y	N
3 Wyden	Y	Y	Y	Y	Y	Y	Y	N
4 DeFazio	Y	Y	Y	Y	Y	Y	Y	Y
5 Kopetski	Y	Y	Y	Y	Y	Y	Y	Y
PENNSYLVANIA								
1 Foglietta	Y	Y	Y	Y	Y	Y	Y	N
2 Blackwell	Y	Y	Y	Y	Y	Y	Y	Y
3 Borski	Y	Y	Y	Y	Y	Y	Y	Y
4 Klink	Y	Y	Y	N	Y	Y	Y	Y
5 ***Clinger***	Y	Y	Y	Y	Y	Y	Y	Y
6 Holden	Y	Y	Y	Y	Y	Y	Y	Y
7 ***Weldon***	Y	Y	Y	Y	Y	Y	Y	Y
8 ***Greenwood***	Y	Y	Y	Y	Y	Y	Y	N
9 ***Shuster***	Y	Y	Y	N	Y	Y	Y	Y
10 ***McDade***	Y	Y	Y	Y	Y	Y	Y	N
11 Kanjorski	Y	Y	Y	Y	Y	Y	Y	Y
12 Murtha	Y	Y	Y	Y	Y	Y	Y	N
13 Margolies-Mezv.	Y	Y	Y	Y	Y	Y	Y	Y
14 Coyne	Y	Y	Y	Y	Y	Y	Y	N
15 McHale	Y	Y	Y	Y	Y	Y	Y	Y
16 ***Walker***	Y	Y	Y	N	Y	Y	N	Y
17 ***Gekas***	Y	Y	Y	Y	Y	Y	Y	Y
18 ***Santorum***	Y	Y	Y	Y	Y	Y	Y	Y
19 ***Goodling***	Y	Y	Y	Y	Y	Y	Y	Y
20 Murphy	Y	Y	Y	Y	Y	Y	Y	N
21 ***Ridge***	Y	Y	Y	Y	Y	Y	Y	Y
RHODE ISLAND								
1 ***Machtley***	Y	Y	Y	Y	Y	Y	Y	Y
2 Reed	Y	Y	Y	Y	Y	Y	Y	Y
SOUTH CAROLINA								
1 ***Ravenel***	Y	Y	Y	Y	Y	Y	Y	N
2 ***Spence***	Y	Y	Y	Y	Y	Y	Y	Y
3 Derrick	Y	Y	Y	Y	Y	Y	Y	Y
4 ***Inglis***	Y	Y	Y	N	Y	Y	N	N
5 Spratt	Y	Y	Y	Y	Y	Y	Y	Y
6 Clyburn	Y	Y	Y	Y	Y	Y	Y	Y
SOUTH DAKOTA								
AL Johnson	Y	Y	Y	Y	Y	Y	Y	N
TENNESSEE								
1 ***Quillen***	Y	Y	Y	Y	Y	Y	Y	Y
2 ***Duncan***	Y	Y	Y	N	Y	Y	N	Y
3 Lloyd	Y	Y	Y	Y	Y	Y	Y	N
4 Cooper	Y	Y	Y	Y	Y	Y	N	N
5 Clement	Y	Y	Y	Y	Y	Y	Y	Y

	440	441	442	443	444	445	446	447
6 Gordon	Y	Y	Y	Y	Y	Y	Y	Y
7 ***Sundquist***	Y	Y	Y	Y	Y	Y	Y	Y
8 Tanner	Y	Y	Y	Y	Y	Y	N	N
9 Ford	Y	Y	Y	Y	Y	Y	Y	Y
TEXAS								
1 Chapman	Y	Y	Y	Y	Y	Y	Y	N
2 Wilson	?	?	?	?	?	?	?	?
3 ***Johnson, Sam***	Y	Y	Y	Y	Y	Y	Y	Y
4 Hall	Y	Y	Y	Y	Y	Y	Y	N
5 Bryant	?	Y	Y	Y	Y	Y	Y	N
6 ***Barton***	Y	Y	Y	N	Y	Y	N	Y
7 ***Archer***	Y	Y	Y	N	Y	Y	N	N
8 ***Fields***	Y	Y	Y	Y	Y	Y	Y	N
9 Brooks	Y	Y	Y	Y	Y	Y	Y	N
10 Pickle	Y	Y	Y	Y	Y	Y	Y	N
11 Edwards	Y	Y	Y	Y	Y	Y	Y	N
12 Geren	Y	Y	Y	Y	N	Y	Y	Y
13 Sarpalius	Y	Y	Y	Y	Y	Y	Y	N
14 Laughlin	Y	Y	Y	Y	Y	Y	Y	Y
15 de la Garza	Y	Y	Y	Y	Y	Y	Y	Y
16 Coleman	Y	Y	Y	Y	Y	Y	Y	N
17 Stenholm	Y	Y	Y	Y	Y	Y	Y	N
18 Washington	Y	Y	Y	Y	Y	Y	Y	?
19 ***Combest***	Y	Y	Y	Y	Y	Y	Y	N
20 Gonzalez	Y	Y	Y	Y	Y	Y	Y	Y
21 ***Smith***	Y	Y	Y	Y	Y	Y	Y	Y
22 ***DeLay***	Y	Y	Y	N	Y	Y	N	N
23 ***Bonilla***	Y	Y	Y	N	Y	Y	Y	N
24 Frost	Y	Y	Y	Y	Y	Y	Y	Y
25 Andrews	Y	Y	Y	N	Y	Y	Y	N
26 ***Armey***	Y	Y	Y	N	Y	Y	N	N
27 Ortiz	Y	Y	Y	Y	Y	Y	Y	N
28 Tejeda	Y	Y	Y	Y	Y	Y	Y	Y
29 Green	Y	Y	Y	Y	Y	Y	Y	N
30 Johnson, E.B.	Y	Y	Y	Y	Y	Y	Y	Y
UTAH								
1 ***Hansen***	Y	Y	Y	N	Y	Y	N	N
2 Shepherd	Y	Y	Y	Y	Y	Y	Y	N
3 Orton	Y	Y	Y	N	Y	Y	N	N
VERMONT								
AL *Sanders*	Y	Y	Y	Y	Y	Y	Y	Y
VIRGINIA								
1 ***Bateman***	Y	Y	Y	Y	Y	Y	Y	N
2 Pickett	Y	Y	Y	Y	Y	Y	Y	N
3 Scott	Y	Y	Y	Y	Y	Y	Y	Y
4 Sisisky	Y	Y	Y	Y	Y	Y	Y	N
5 Payne	Y	Y	Y	Y	Y	Y	Y	Y
6 ***Goodlatte***	Y	Y	Y	N	Y	Y	Y	Y
7 ***Bliley***	Y	Y	Y	N	Y	Y	Y	Y
8 Moran	Y	Y	Y	Y	Y	Y	Y	N
9 Boucher	Y	Y	Y	Y	Y	Y	Y	N
10 ***Wolf***	Y	Y	Y	Y	Y	Y	Y	N
11 Byrne	Y	Y	Y	Y	Y	Y	Y	Y
WASHINGTON								
1 Cantwell	Y	Y	Y	Y	Y	Y	Y	Y
2 Swift	Y	Y	Y	Y	Y	Y	Y	Y
3 Unsoeld	Y	Y	Y	Y	Y	Y	Y	Y
4 Inslee	Y	Y	Y	Y	Y	Y	Y	Y
5 Foley								Y
6 Dicks	Y	Y	Y	Y	Y	Y	Y	N
7 McDermott	Y	Y	Y	Y	Y	Y	Y	Y
8 ***Dunn***	Y	N	Y	Y	Y	Y	Y	Y
9 Kreidler	Y	Y	Y	Y	Y	Y	Y	Y
WEST VIRGINIA								
1 Mollohan	Y	Y	Y	Y	Y	Y	Y	N
2 Wise	Y	Y	?	Y	Y	Y	Y	Y
3 Rahall	Y	Y	Y	Y	Y	Y	Y	Y
WISCONSIN								
1 Barca	Y	Y	Y	Y	Y	Y	Y	Y
2 ***Klug***	Y	Y	Y	Y	Y	Y	Y	Y
3 ***Gunderson***	Y	Y	Y	Y	Y	Y	Y	Y
4 Kleczka	Y	Y	Y	Y	Y	Y	Y	Y
5 Barrett	Y	Y	Y	Y	Y	Y	Y	Y
6 ***Petri***	Y	Y	Y	N	Y	Y	Y	Y
7 Obey	Y	Y	Y	Y	Y	Y	Y	N
8 ***Roth***	Y	Y	Y	Y	Y	Y	N	Y
9 ***Sensenbrenner***	N	N	N	N	Y	Y	N	N
WYOMING								
AL ***Thomas***	Y	Y	Y	N	Y	Y	N	Y
DELEGATES								
de Lugo, V.I.	D	D	D	D	D	D	D	D
Faleomavaega, Am.S.	D	D	D	D	D	D	D	D
Norton, D.C.	D	D	D	D	D	D	D	D
Romero-B., P.R.	D	D	D	D	D	D	D	D
Underwood, Guam	D	D	D	D	D	D	D	D

Southern states - Ala., Ark., Fla., Ga., Ky., La., Miss., N.C., Okla., S.C., Tenn., Texas, Va.
Omitted votes are quorum calls, which CQ does not include in its vote charts.

448. HR 2750. Fiscal 1994 Transportation Appropriations/Letters of Intent. Clement, D-Tenn., amendment to eliminate the provisions that bar the Federal Aviation Administration from issuing new airport improvement grant letters of intent. Adopted in the Committee of the Whole 317-117: R 135-40; D 182-76 (ND 123-51, SD 59-25); I 0-1, Sept. 22, 1993.

449. HR 2750. Fiscal 1994 Transportation Appropriations/Restore Appropriations. Mineta, D-Calif., amendment to reappropriate $284 million, struck from the bill on points of order, for federal highway aid through the Highway Trust Fund. Adopted in the Committee of the Whole 281-154: R 101-73; D 179-81 (ND 130-45, SD 49-36); I 1-0, Sept. 22, 1993.

450. HR 2750. Fiscal 1994 Transportation Appropriations/Amtrak. Hefley, R-Colo., amendment to cut operating assistance for Amtrak by $331 million. Rejected in the Committee of the Whole 84-337: R 81-89; D 3-247 (ND 1-167, SD 2-80); I 0-1, Sept. 23, 1993

451. HR 2750. Fiscal 1994 Transportation Appropriations/Amtrak. Hefley, R-Colo., amendment to cut operating assistance for Amtrak by $33.1 million. Rejected in the Committee of the Whole 153-271: R 130-44; D 23-226 (ND 9-162, SD 14-64); I 0-1, Sept. 23, 1993.

452. HR 2750. Fiscal 1994 Transportation Appropriations/BART. Walker, R-Pa., amendment to strike language added by the rule earmarking $28.2 million for the San Francisco Airport Bay Area Rapid Transit (BART) Extension Project and Tasman Corridor LRT Project. Rejected in the Committee of the Whole 136-290: R 104-68; D 32-221 (ND 17-155, SD 15-66); I 0-1, Sept. 23, 1993.

453. HR 2750. Fiscal 1994 Transportation Appropriations/Interstate Commerce Commission. Hefley, R-Colo., amendment to eliminate the Interstate Commerce Commission (ICC), transferring its functions to the Transportation Department. The bill provides $44.9 million for the ICC and allows the ICC to spend $7.3 million in fees. Rejected in the Committee of the Whole 207-222: R 154-19; D 53-202 (ND 29-143, SD 24-59); I 0-1, Sept. 23, 1993.

454. HR 2750. Fiscal 1994 Transportation Appropriations/Letters of Intent. Separate vote at the request of Goss, R-Fla., on the amendment offered by Clement, D-Tenn., and adopted in the Committee of the Whole to eliminate the provisions that bar the Federal Aviation Administration from issuing new airport improvement grant letters of intent. Adopted 311-94: R 128-38; D 183-55 (ND 121-38, SD 62-17); I 0-1, Sept. 23, 1993. (On a separate vote, which may be demanded on an amendment adopted in the Committee of the Whole, the four delegates and the resident commissioner of Puerto Rico cannot vote. See vote 448.)

455. HR 2750. Fiscal 1994 Transportation Appropriations/Restore Appropriations. Separate vote at the request of Goss, R-Fla., on the amendment offered by Mineta, D-Calif., and adopted in the Committee of the Whole to reappropriate $284.7 million, struck from the bill on points of order, for federal highway aid through the Highway Trust Fund. Adopted 267-132: R 94-70; D 172-62 (ND 124-34, SD 48-28); I 1-0, Sept. 23, 1993. (On a separate vote, which may be demanded on an amendment adopted in the Committee of the Whole, the four delegates and the resident commissioner of Puerto Rico cannot vote. See vote 449.)

KEY

Y	Voted for (yea).
#	Paired for.
+	Announced for.
N	Voted against (nay).
X	Paired against.
−	Announced against.
P	Voted "present."
C	Voted "present" to avoid possible conflict of interest.
?	Did not vote or otherwise make a position known.
D	Delegates ineligible to vote.

Democrats **Republicans**
Independent

	448	449	450	451	452	453	454	455
ALABAMA								
1 *Callahan*	Y	Y	N	N	Y	Y	Y	Y
2 *Everett*	Y	Y	N	N	Y	Y	Y	Y
3 Browder	Y	Y	N	N	N	Y	Y	Y
4 Bevill	N	Y	N	N	N	N	Y	Y
5 Cramer	Y	Y	N	N	N	Y	Y	Y
6 *Bachus*	N	Y	N	N	Y	N	Y	N
7 Hilliard	Y	Y	N	N	N	N	Y	Y
ALASKA								
AL *Young*	Y	Y	Y	Y	N	Y	Y	Y
ARIZONA								
1 Coppersmith	Y	Y	N	N	N	N	Y	Y
2 Pastor	N	N	N	N	N	N	N	Y
3 *Stump*	Y	Y	Y	Y	Y	Y	Y	Y
4 *Kyl*	Y	Y	Y	Y	Y	Y	Y	Y
5 *Kolbe*	Y	Y	N	Y	Y	Y	Y	Y
6 English	Y	Y	N	N	N	N	Y	Y
ARKANSAS								
1 Lambert	Y	Y	N	N	N	Y	Y	Y
2 Thornton	Y	Y	N	N	N	Y	Y	Y
3 *Hutchinson*	Y	Y	?	Y	N	Y	Y	?
4 *Dickey*	Y	Y	N	Y	N	N	Y	Y
CALIFORNIA								
1 Hamburg	Y	Y	N	N	N	Y	Y	Y
2 *Herger*	Y	Y	?	Y	N	Y	Y	Y
3 Fazio	N	N	N	N	N	N	N	N
4 *Doolittle*	Y	Y	Y	Y	Y	Y	Y	Y
5 Matsui	N	N	N	N	N	N	Y	Y
6 Woolsey	Y	Y	N	N	N	Y	Y	Y
7 Miller	Y	Y	N	N	N	?	?	Y
8 Pelosi	N	Y	?	N	N	N	?	?
9 Dellums	Y	Y	N	N	N	N	Y	Y
10 *Baker*	Y	Y	Y	N	Y	Y	Y	Y
11 *Pombo*	N	Y	Y	N	Y	Y	Y	N
12 Lantos	Y	Y	N	N	N	Y	Y	Y
13 Stark	Y	Y	N	N	N	N	Y	Y
14 Eshoo	Y	Y	N	N	N	Y	Y	Y
15 Mineta	Y	Y	N	N	N	N	Y	Y
16 Edwards	Y	Y	?	N	X	?	Y	Y
17 Farr	Y	Y	N	N	N	N	?	?
18 Condit	N	Y	N	N	Y	N	Y	Y
19 Lehman	Y	N	N	N	Y	N	Y	Y
20 Dooley	Y	Y	N	N	Y	?	Y	Y
21 *Thomas*	Y	Y	N	N	Y	N	Y	Y
22 *Huffington*	N	Y	Y	Y	N	Y	N	Y
23 *Gallegly*	Y	Y	Y	Y	Y	Y	Y	Y
24 Beilenson	Y	Y	N	N	N	N	Y	Y
25 *McKeon*	Y	Y	Y	Y	N	N	?	?
26 Berman	Y	Y	N	N	N	N	?	?
27 *Moorhead*	Y	Y	Y	Y	Y	Y	Y	Y
28 *Dreier*	Y	N	Y	Y	Y	Y	Y	N
29 Waxman	Y	Y	N	N	N	N	Y	Y
30 Becerra	Y	Y	N	N	N	N	Y	Y
31 Martinez	Y	Y	N	N	N	N	?	?
32 Dixon	N	N	N	N	N	N	N	N
33 Roybal-Allard	Y	Y	N	N	N	N	Y	Y
34 Torres	N	Y	N	N	N	N	Y	N
35 Waters	Y	Y	N	N	N	N	Y	Y
36 Harman	Y	Y	N	N	N	N	Y	Y
37 Tucker	Y	Y	N	N	N	N	Y	Y
38 *Horn*	Y	Y	N	N	N	Y	Y	Y
39 *Royce*	Y	N	Y	Y	Y	Y	Y	N
40 *Lewis*	Y	N	N	N	N	Y	Y	Y
41 *Kim*	Y	Y	Y	Y	N	Y	Y	Y

	448	449	450	451	452	453	454	455
42 Brown	Y	Y	N	N	N	N	Y	Y
43 *Calvert*	Y	Y	N	N	Y	Y	Y	Y
44 *McCandless*	Y	Y	Y	Y	Y	Y	Y	Y
45 *Rohrabacher*	Y	Y	Y	Y	Y	Y	Y	N
46 *Dornan*	Y	N	Y	Y	Y	Y	Y	N
47 *Cox*	Y	N	Y	Y	Y	Y	Y	N
48 *Packard*	N	N	N	Y	N	Y	N	N
49 Schenk	Y	Y	N	N	N	N	Y	Y
50 Filner	N	Y	N	N	N	N	Y	Y
51 *Cunningham*	Y	Y	Y	Y	Y	Y	?	?
52 *Hunter*	Y	Y	Y	Y	?	Y	Y	Y
COLORADO								
1 Schroeder	Y	Y	N	Y	Y	Y	Y	Y
2 Skaggs	Y	N	N	N	N	N	Y	Y
3 *McInnis*	Y	N	Y	Y	Y	Y	Y	N
4 *Allard*	Y	N	Y	Y	Y	Y	Y	N
5 *Hefley*	N	Y	Y	Y	Y	Y	?	?
6 *Schaefer*	Y	N	Y	Y	Y	Y	Y	N
CONNECTICUT								
1 Kennelly	Y	Y	N	N	N	N	Y	Y
2 Gejdenson	Y	Y	N	N	N	N	Y	Y
3 DeLauro	N	Y	N	N	N	N	Y	Y
4 *Shays*	N	Y	Y	Y	Y	Y	N	Y
5 *Franks*	N	Y	N	N	Y	N	N	Y
6 *Johnson*	Y	Y	N	N	N	Y	Y	Y
DELAWARE								
AL *Castle*	Y	N	N	N	Y	Y	Y	N
FLORIDA								
1 Hutto	Y	Y	N	N	Y	Y	Y	N
2 Peterson	N	N	N	N	Y	N	N	N
3 Brown	Y	Y	N	N	N	Y	Y	Y
4 *Fowler*	Y	N	N	Y	Y	Y	Y	N
5 Thurman	Y	Y	N	N	Y	+	+	
6 *Stearns*	Y	N	Y	Y	Y	Y	Y	N
7 *Mica*	Y	N	N	N	N	Y	Y	N
8 *McCollum*	Y	N	N	Y	Y	Y	Y	N
9 *Bilirakis*	Y	N	Y	Y	N	Y	?	N
10 *Young*	Y	N	Y	N	Y	?	?	?
11 Gibbons	Y	N	N	N	N	N	?	?
12 *Canady*	N	N	Y	Y	Y	N	N	N
13 *Miller*	Y	N	Y	Y	Y	Y	Y	N
14 *Goss*	Y	N	Y	Y	N	Y	Y	N
15 *Bacchus*	Y	Y	N	N	Y	?	?	?
16 *Lewis*	Y	N	Y	N	Y	Y	Y	N
17 Meek	N	N	N	N	N	N	N	N
18 *Ros-Lehtinen*	Y	Y	Y	N	Y	Y	Y	Y
19 Johnston	Y	Y	N	N	N	N	Y	?
20 Deutsch	Y	Y	N	N	N	Y	Y	Y
21 *Diaz-Balart*	Y	Y	Y	N	Y	Y	Y	Y
22 *Shaw*	Y	?	Y	Y	N	Y	Y	Y
23 Hastings	Y	N	N	N	N	N	Y	N
GEORGIA								
1 *Kingston*	Y	Y	Y	Y	Y	Y	Y	Y
2 Bishop	Y	Y	N	N	?	N	Y	Y
3 *Collins*	Y	N	Y	N	Y	Y	Y	Y
4 *Linder*	Y	Y	Y	Y	Y	Y	Y	Y
5 Lewis	Y	Y	N	N	N	N	Y	Y
6 *Gingrich*	Y	Y	Y	Y	?	Y	?	?
7 Darden	N	N	N	N	N	N	N	N
8 Rowland	N	Y	N	N	N	Y	Y	Y
9 Deal	N	Y	N	N	N	N	N	N
10 Johnson	N	Y	N	N	N	N	N	Y
11 McKinney	Y	Y	?	N	N	N	Y	Y
HAWAII								
1 Abercrombie	Y	Y	N	N	N	N	Y	Y
2 Mink	Y	Y	N	N	N	N	Y	Y
IDAHO								
1 LaRocco	Y	Y	N	N	N	N	?	?
2 *Crapo*	Y	N	Y	Y	N	Y	Y	Y
ILLINOIS								
1 Rush	Y	Y	N	N	N	N	Y	Y
2 Reynolds	Y	Y	N	N	N	N	Y	Y
3 Lipinski	Y	Y	N	N	N	N	Y	Y
4 Gutierrez	Y	Y	N	N	N	N	Y	Y
5 Rostenkowski	N	Y	N	N	N	N	N	Y
6 *Hyde*	Y	Y	N	Y	Y	Y	Y	Y
7 Collins	Y	Y	N	N	N	N	Y	Y
8 *Crane*	Y	Y	Y	Y	Y	Y	Y	N
9 Yates	N	N	N	N	N	N	Y	Y
10 *Porter*	Y	N	Y	Y	N	N	Y	N
11 Sangmeister	Y	Y	N	N	N	N	Y	Y
12 Costello	Y	Y	N	N	N	N	Y	Y
13 *Fawell*	N	Y	Y	Y	Y	N	Y	N
14 *Hastert*	Y	N	Y	N	Y	N	Y	Y
15 *Ewing*	Y	Y	N	Y	N	Y	Y	Y
16 *Manzullo*	Y	N	Y	Y	Y	Y	Y	Y
17 Evans	Y	N	N	N	N	N	Y	N

ND Northern Democrats   **SD** Southern Democrats

	448	449	450	451	452	453	454	455
18 ***Michel***	Y	Y	N	N	Y	Y	Y	Y
19 Poshard	Y	Y	N	N	N	Y	Y	Y
20 Durbin	N	N	N	N	N	N	N	Y
INDIANA								
1 Visclosky	N	N	N	N	N	N	N	N
2 Sharp	N	N	N	N	Y	Y	N	N
3 Roemer	Y	N	N	N	N	Y	Y	N
4 Long	N	N	N	N	N	Y	N	Y
5 ***Buyer***	Y	N	Y	Y	Y	Y	Y	Y
6 ***Burton***	N	N	N	Y	Y	Y	N	N
7 ***Myers***	N	N	N	N	Y	Y	Y	N
8 McCloskey	N	N	N	N	N	N	Y	N
9 Hamilton	Y	N	N	N	Y	N	Y	N
10 Jacobs	Y	N	N	N	Y	Y	Y	Y
IOWA								
1 ***Leach***	Y	N	N	Y	Y	Y	Y	N
2 ***Nussle***	N	N	N	Y	Y	Y	N	N
3 ***Lightfoot***	N	N	N	Y	N	Y	N	N
4 Smith	N	N	N	N	Y	N	?	?
5 ***Grandy***	N	Y	N	Y	N	Y	N	Y
KANSAS								
1 ***Roberts***	Y	Y	N	Y	Y	Y	Y	Y
2 Slattery	Y	Y	N	N	Y	N	Y	Y
3 ***Meyers***	Y	Y	N	Y	Y	Y	Y	Y
4 Glickman	Y	Y	N	N	N	Y	Y	Y
KENTUCKY								
1 Barlow	N	Y	N	Y	N	N	Y	Y
2 Natcher	N	N	N	N	Y	N	N	N
3 Mazzoli	N	N	N	N	N	N	N	Y
4 ***Bunning***	Y	Y	Y	Y	Y	Y	Y	Y
5 ***Rogers***	Y	N	N	Y	N	N	Y	N
6 Baesler	N	N	N	N	N	Y	N	N
LOUISIANA								
1 ***Livingston***	N	N	Y	Y	Y	Y	N	N
2 Jefferson	Y	Y	N	N	N	N	Y	Y
3 Tauzin	Y	Y	?	?	?	?	?	?
4 Fields	Y	Y	N	N	N	N	Y	Y
5 ***McCrery***	N	Y	Y	Y	Y	Y	N	Y
6 ***Baker***	N	Y	Y	Y	Y	Y	N	Y
7 Hayes	Y	Y	N	N	N	Y	Y	Y
MAINE								
1 Andrews	Y	Y	N	N	N	N	Y	Y
2 ***Snowe***	Y	Y	N	N	N	Y	Y	Y
MARYLAND								
1 ***Gilchrest***	Y	Y	N	N	N	N	Y	Y
2 ***Bentley***	N	N	N	N	Y	Y	N	N
3 Cardin	Y	N	N	N	N	Y	Y	N
4 Wynn	N	Y	N	N	N	Y	N	Y
5 Hoyer	N	N	N	N	N	N	N	N
6 ***Bartlett***	Y	Y	Y	Y	Y	Y	Y	Y
7 Mfume	Y	Y	N	N	N	Y	Y	Y
8 ***Morella***	Y	Y	N	N	N	Y	Y	Y
MASSACHUSETTS								
1 Olver	Y	Y	N	N	N	N	Y	Y
2 Neal	Y	Y	N	N	N	Y	Y	Y
3 ***Blute***	Y	Y	N	N	N	Y	Y	Y
4 Frank	N	Y	N	N	N	Y	N	Y
5 Meehan	N	Y	N	N	N	Y	N	Y
6 ***Torkildsen***	Y	Y	N	N	Y	Y	Y	Y
7 Markey	Y	Y	N	N	N	N	Y	Y
8 Kennedy	N	Y	N	N	N	Y	N	Y
9 Moakley	Y	Y	N	N	N	N	Y	Y
10 Studds	Y	Y	N	N	N	N	Y	Y
MICHIGAN								
1 Stupak	N	N	N	Y	N	N	N	N
2 ***Hoekstra***	Y	Y	Y	Y	Y	Y	Y	Y
3 Vacancy								
4 ***Camp***	N	N	N	Y	Y	Y	N	N
5 Barcia	N	N	N	Y	N	N	N	Y
6 ***Upton***	Y	N	N	N	Y	Y	Y	N
7 ***Smith***	Y	N	Y	Y	Y	?	Y	N
8 Carr	N	N	N	N	Y	N	N	N
9 Kildee	N	N	N	N	N	N	N	N
10 Bonior	N	N	N	N	N	N	N	N
11 ***Knollenberg***	N	N	Y	Y	Y	Y	N	N
12 Levin	N	N	N	N	N	N	N	N
13 Ford	N	Y	N	N	N	N	Y	Y
14 Conyers	?	?	N	N	N	N	Y	Y
15 Collins	?	?	N	N	N	N	Y	Y
16 Dingell	N	N	N	N	N	N	Y	N
MINNESOTA								
1 Penny	N	N	N	Y	Y	Y	N	N
2 Minge	N	Y	Y	Y	Y	Y	N	Y
3 ***Ramstad***	Y	N	Y	Y	Y	Y	Y	N
4 Vento	Y	N	N	N	N	N	Y	Y

	448	449	450	451	452	453	454	455
5 Sabo	N	N	N	N	N	N	N	N
6 ***Grams***	Y	N	Y	Y	Y	Y	Y	N
7 Peterson	N	N	N	N	Y	N	Y	N
8 Oberstar	Y	Y	N	N	N	N	Y	Y
MISSISSIPPI								
1 Whitten	N	N	?	?	N	N	N	N
2 Thompson	Y	Y	N	N	N	N	Y	Y
3 Montgomery	Y	Y	N	N	N	Y	Y	Y
4 Parker	Y	Y	N	N	N	Y	Y	Y
5 Taylor	N	Y	N	N	N	Y	Y	Y
MISSOURI								
1 Clay	Y	Y	N	N	N	N	Y	Y
2 ***Talent***	Y	Y	Y	Y	N	Y	Y	Y
3 Gephardt	Y	N	N	N	N	N	Y	?
4 Skelton	?	Y	N	N	N	N	Y	Y
5 Wheat	Y	Y	N	N	N	N	Y	Y
6 Danner	Y	Y	N	N	N	N	?	?
7 ***Hancock***	Y	Y	?	?	?	?	?	?
8 ***Emerson***	Y	Y	N	Y	N	N	Y	Y
9 Volkmer	Y	Y	N	N	N	N	Y	Y
MONTANA								
AL Williams	Y	Y	N	N	N	Y	Y	Y
NEBRASKA								
1 ***Bereuter***	N	N	N	Y	Y	Y	N	N
2 Hoagland	Y	Y	N	N	N	Y	Y	Y
3 ***Barrett***	Y	N	N	Y	N	Y	Y	N
NEVADA								
1 Bilbray	Y	Y	N	Y	N	N	Y	Y
2 ***Vucanovich***	Y	Y	Y	Y	Y	Y	Y	Y
NEW HAMPSHIRE								
1 ***Zeliff***	N	Y	N	Y	N	N	Y	Y
2 Swett	Y	Y	N	N	N	N	Y	Y
NEW JERSEY								
1 Andrews	N	Y	N	N	N	Y	N	Y
2 Hughes	Y	Y	N	N	N	N	Y	Y
3 ***Saxton***	N	N	N	Y	Y	Y	N	N
4 ***Smith***	Y	Y	N	N	Y	N	Y	Y
5 ***Roukema***	N	Y	N	N	N	Y	N	Y
6 Pallone	Y	Y	N	N	N	N	Y	Y
7 ***Franks***	Y	Y	N	N	N	N	Y	Y
8 Klein	N	Y	N	N	N	N	Y	Y
9 Torricelli	Y	Y	N	N	N	N	Y	Y
10 Payne	Y	Y	N	N	N	N	Y	Y
11 ***Gallo***	N	Y	N	N	N	Y	N	Y
12 ***Zimmer***	N	N	N	Y	Y	Y	N	N
13 Menendez	Y	Y	N	N	N	N	Y	Y
NEW MEXICO								
1 ***Schiff***	Y	Y	N	Y	Y	Y	Y	Y
2 ***Skeen***	Y	N	N	N	Y	Y	Y	N
3 Richardson	Y	Y	N	N	N	N	Y	Y
NEW YORK								
1 Hochbrueckner	N	N	N	N	N	N	N	N
2 ***Lazio***	Y	Y	N	N	N	Y	Y	Y
3 ***King***	Y	Y	N	N	Y	Y	Y	Y
4 ***Levy***	Y	Y	N	N	N	Y	Y	Y
5 Ackerman	Y	Y	N	N	N	N	?	?
6 Flake	Y	Y	N	N	N	N	Y	Y
7 Manton	Y	Y	N	N	N	N	Y	Y
8 Nadler	Y	Y	N	N	N	N	Y	Y
9 Schumer	Y	Y	N	N	N	N	Y	Y
10 Towns	Y	Y	N	N	N	N	Y	Y
11 Owens	Y	Y	N	N	N	N	Y	Y
12 Velazquez	Y	Y	?	?	?	?	?	?
13 ***Molinari***	Y	Y	Y	Y	N	Y	Y	Y
14 Maloney	Y	Y	N	N	N	Y	Y	Y
15 Rangel	Y	Y	N	N	N	N	Y	Y
16 Serrano	Y	Y	?	N	N	N	Y	Y
17 Engel	Y	Y	N	N	N	N	Y	Y
18 Lowey	N	Y	N	N	N	N	N	Y
19 ***Fish***	Y	Y	N	N	Y	Y	Y	Y
20 ***Gilman***	Y	Y	N	N	N	N	Y	Y
21 McNulty	Y	Y	N	N	N	N	Y	Y
22 ***Solomon***	Y	N	N	Y	Y	Y	Y	N
23 ***Boehlert***	Y	Y	N	N	N	N	Y	Y
24 ***McHugh***	Y	N	N	Y	Y	Y	Y	N
25 ***Walsh***	Y	N	N	Y	N	Y	N	N
26 Hinchey	Y	Y	N	N	N	N	Y	Y
27 ***Paxon***	Y	Y	Y	Y	Y	Y	Y	Y
28 Slaughter	Y	Y	N	N	N	N	Y	Y
29 LaFalce	Y	Y	?	?	N	N	Y	Y
30 ***Quinn***	Y	Y	N	N	N	Y	Y	Y
31 ***Houghton***	Y	N	N	N	Y	Y	Y	N
NORTH CAROLINA								
1 Clayton	Y	N	N	?	N	N	Y	Y
2 Valentine	Y	Y	N	?	N	N	Y	Y

	448	449	450	451	452	453	454	455
3 Lancaster	Y	N	Y	Y	Y	N	Y	N
4 Price	N	N	N	N	Y	N	N	N
5 Neal	N	N	N	Y	N	N	N	N
6 ***Coble***	Y	Y	Y	Y	Y	Y	Y	Y
7 Rose	Y	Y	N	N	N	N	Y	Y
8 Hefner	N	N	N	N	Y	N	N	N
9 ***McMillan***	Y	N	N	N	Y	Y	Y	N
10 ***Ballenger***	Y	Y	Y	Y	N	Y	Y	Y
11 ***Taylor***	N	N	N	Y	Y	Y	N	N
12 Watt	Y	N	N	N	N	N	Y	Y
NORTH DAKOTA								
AL Pomeroy	Y	Y	N	N	N	N	Y	Y
OHIO								
1 Mann	N	Y	N	N	N	Y	N	Y
2 ***Portman***	Y	Y	Y	Y	Y	Y	Y	Y
3 Hall	N	N	N	N	N	N	Y	Y
4 ***Oxley***	Y	Y	N	Y	Y	N	Y	Y
5 ***Gillmor***	Y	N	Y	Y	Y	Y	Y	N
6 Strickland	Y	Y	N	N	N	N	Y	Y
7 ***Hobson***	N	N	N	Y	N	Y	N	N
8 ***Boehner***	Y	Y	Y	Y	Y	Y	Y	Y
9 Kaptur	N	N	?	?	#	N	N	N
10 ***Hoke***	N	Y	Y	N	Y	Y	N	Y
11 Stokes	N	N	N	N	N	N	N	N
12 ***Kasich***	Y	N	Y	Y	Y	Y	Y	N
13 Brown	N	Y	N	N	N	N	N	Y
14 Sawyer	Y	N	?	N	N	N	Y	N
15 ***Pryce***	Y	N	N	Y	Y	Y	Y	N
16 ***Regula***	N	N	N	N	N	Y	N	N
17 Traficant	Y	Y	N	N	N	N	Y	Y
18 Applegate	Y	Y	N	N	N	N	Y	Y
19 Fingerhut	Y	Y	N	N	Y	Y	Y	Y
OKLAHOMA								
1 ***Inhofe***	Y	Y	Y	Y	N	Y	Y	Y
2 Synar	Y	Y	N	?	Y	N	Y	Y
3 Brewster	Y	Y	N	Y	Y	N	Y	Y
4 McCurdy	Y	Y	N	Y	Y	Y	Y	Y
5 ***Istook***	N	Y	Y	Y	Y	Y	N	Y
6 English	Y	Y	N	Y	N	N	Y	Y
OREGON								
1 Furse	Y	N	N	N	N	N	Y	N
2 ***Smith***	Y	Y	Y	Y	Y	Y	Y	Y
3 Wyden	Y	N	N	N	N	N	Y	N
4 DeFazio	Y	Y	N	N	N	N	?	#
5 Kopetski	Y	Y	N	N	N	N	Y	Y
PENNSYLVANIA								
1 Foglietta	N	N	N	N	Y	N	N	N
2 Blackwell	Y	Y	N	N	N	N	Y	Y
3 Borski	Y	Y	N	N	N	N	Y	Y
4 Klink	N	N	N	N	N	?	?	?
5 ***Clinger***	Y	Y	N	Y	N	N	Y	Y
6 Holden	Y	Y	N	N	N	Y	Y	Y
7 ***Weldon***	Y	N	N	Y	Y	Y	Y	N
8 ***Greenwood***	N	N	N	N	Y	Y	N	N
9 ***Shuster***	Y	Y	N	Y	N	N	Y	Y
10 ***McDade***	N	N	N	Y	N	Y	N	N
11 Kanjorski	Y	Y	N	Y	N	N	Y	Y
12 Murtha	N	N	N	N	N	N	N	N
13 Margolies-Mezv.	Y	Y	N	N	N	N	Y	Y
14 Coyne	N	N	N	N	N	N	N	N
15 McHale	Y	Y	N	N	N	Y	Y	Y
16 ***Walker***	Y	N	Y	Y	Y	Y	Y	N
17 ***Gekas***	Y	N	N	N	N	Y	Y	Y
18 ***Santorum***	Y	N	N	N	Y	Y	Y	N
19 ***Goodling***	Y	Y	Y	Y	Y	Y	Y	Y
20 Murphy	Y	Y	N	N	Y	N	Y	Y
21 ***Ridge***	Y	Y	N	N	N	N	Y	Y
RHODE ISLAND								
1 ***Machtley***	Y	Y	N	N	N	Y	Y	Y
2 Reed	Y	Y	N	N	N	N	Y	?
SOUTH CAROLINA								
1 ***Ravenel***	Y	Y	Y	Y	Y	Y	Y	Y
2 ***Spence***	Y	Y	N	Y	Y	Y	Y	Y
3 Derrick	Y	Y	N	N	N	N	Y	Y
4 ***Inglis***	Y	Y	Y	Y	Y	Y	Y	Y
5 Spratt	Y	Y	N	N	N	N	Y	Y
6 Clyburn	Y	Y	N	N	N	N	Y	Y
SOUTH DAKOTA								
AL Johnson	N	N	N	N	Y	N	N	N
TENNESSEE								
1 ***Quillen***	Y	Y	N	N	Y	Y	Y	Y
2 ***Duncan***	Y	Y	N	Y	N	Y	Y	Y
3 Lloyd	Y	Y	N	N	?	Y	Y	Y
4 Cooper	Y	N	N	Y	N	Y	Y	N
5 Clement	Y	Y	N	N	N	Y	Y	Y

	448	449	450	451	452	453	454	455
6 Gordon	Y	Y	N	Y	N	Y	Y	Y
7 ***Sundquist***	Y	Y	N	Y	Y	Y	Y	Y
8 Tanner	Y	Y	N	Y	Y	Y	Y	Y
9 Ford	?	Y	N	N	N	N	Y	Y
TEXAS								
1 Chapman	N	N	N	N	N	Y	Y	N
2 Wilson	N	N	N	N	Y	N	N	N
3 ***Johnson, Sam***	N	N	Y	Y	Y	Y	Y	N
4 Hall	Y	N	N	Y	N	N	Y	Y
5 Bryant	N	N	N	N	N	N	Y	N
6 ***Barton***	Y	N	Y	Y	Y	Y	Y	N
7 ***Archer***	N	N	?	Y	Y	Y	N	N
8 ***Fields***	N	N	Y	Y	Y	N	N	N
9 Brooks	Y	N	N	N	N	N	Y	N
10 Pickle	Y	Y	N	Y	Y	N	Y	?
11 Edwards	Y	N	N	Y	Y	Y	Y	N
12 Geren	Y	Y	N	N	N	Y	Y	?
13 Sarpalius	Y	N	N	N	N	Y	Y	N
14 Laughlin	Y	Y	N	?	N	N	Y	Y
15 de la Garza	Y	N	N	N	N	N	Y	N
16 Coleman	Y	N	N	N	Y	N	N	N
17 Stenholm	Y	N	N	N	N	Y	Y	N
18 Washington	N	N	N	?	?	N	?	?
19 ***Combest***	Y	N	Y	Y	Y	Y	Y	N
20 Gonzalez	N	N	N	N	N	N	Y	Y
21 ***Smith***	Y	N	Y	Y	Y	Y	Y	N
22 ***DeLay***	N	N	Y	Y	Y	Y	N	N
23 ***Bonilla***	N	N	Y	Y	Y	Y	N	N
24 Frost	Y	N	N	N	N	N	Y	N
25 Andrews	N	N	Y	Y	Y	Y	N	N
26 ***Armey***	N	N	Y	Y	Y	Y	Y	N
27 Ortiz	Y	N	N	N	N	N	Y	N
28 Tejeda	Y	Y	N	N	N	N	Y	Y
29 Green	N	N	N	N	N	—	—	+
30 Johnson, E.B.	Y	Y	N	N	N	N	Y	Y
UTAH								
1 ***Hansen***	Y	Y	Y	Y	Y	Y	?	?
2 Shepherd	Y	N	N	N	N	N	Y	Y
3 Orton	Y	N	N	Y	Y	Y	Y	N
VERMONT								
AL *Sanders*	N	Y	N	N	N	N	N	Y
VIRGINIA								
1 ***Bateman***	Y	Y	N	Y	N	N	Y	Y
2 Pickett	Y	N	N	N	N	N	Y	N
3 Scott	Y	Y	N	N	N	N	Y	Y
4 Sisisky	Y	N	N	N	N	Y	Y	N
5 Payne	Y	Y	N	N	N	Y	Y	Y
6 ***Goodlatte***	Y	N	N	N	Y	Y	Y	N
7 ***Bliley***	Y	N	N	N	N	Y	Y	N
8 Moran	N	N	N	N	N	N	N	N
9 Boucher	N	N	N	N	N	N	N	N
10 ***Wolf***	N	N	N	N	N	N	N	N
11 Byrne	Y	Y	N	N	N	N	Y	Y
WASHINGTON								
1 Cantwell	Y	Y	N	N	N	N	Y	Y
2 Swift	Y	Y	N	N	N	N	Y	Y
3 Unsoeld	Y	Y	N	N	N	N	Y	Y
4 Inslee	Y	Y	N	N	N	N	Y	Y
5 Foley								
6 Dicks	Y	Y	N	N	N	N	Y	Y
7 McDermott	Y	Y	N	N	N	N	Y	Y
8 ***Dunn***	Y	Y	Y	Y	N	Y	Y	Y
9 Kreidler	N	Y	N	N	N	N	N	Y
WEST VIRGINIA								
1 Mollohan	N	Y	N	N	N	N	N	Y
2 Wise	Y	Y	N	N	N	N	Y	Y
3 Rahall	Y	Y	N	N	N	N	Y	Y
WISCONSIN								
1 Barca	Y	Y	N	N	N	N	Y	Y
2 ***Klug***	Y	Y	N	Y	Y	Y	Y	Y
3 ***Gunderson***	Y	Y	N	Y	Y	Y	Y	Y
4 Kleczka	Y	Y	N	N	N	N	Y	Y
5 Barrett	Y	Y	N	N	N	Y	Y	Y
6 ***Petri***	Y	Y	?	Y	N	Y	Y	?
7 Obey	N	Y	N	N	Y	N	Y	Y
8 ***Roth***	N	Y	N	Y	Y	Y	N	N
9 ***Sensenbrenner***	Y	Y	Y	Y	Y	Y	Y	N
WYOMING								
AL ***Thomas***	Y	Y	Y	Y	Y	Y	Y	Y
DELEGATES								
de Lugo, V.I.	Y	Y	N	N	N	N	D	D
Faleomavaega, Am.S.	Y	Y	?	?	?	?	D	D
Norton, D.C.	Y	Y	N	N	N	N	D	D
Romero-B., P.R.	Y	N	?	?	?	?	D	D
Underwood, Guam	Y	Y	N	N	N	N	D	D

Southern states - Ala., Ark., Fla., Ga., Ky., La., Miss., N.C., Okla., S.C., Tenn., Texas, Va.
Omitted votes are quorum calls, which CQ does not include in its vote charts.

KEY

Y Voted for (yea).
\# Paired for.
\+ Announced for.
N Voted against (nay).
X Paired against.
— Announced against.
P Voted "present."
C Voted "present" to avoid possible conflict of interest.
? Did not vote or otherwise make a position known.
D Delegates ineligible to vote.

Democrats **Republicans**
Independent

456. HR 2750. Fiscal 1994 Transportation Appropriations/Passage. Passage of the bill to provide approximately $13.4 billion in new budget authority for the Department of Transportation and related agencies for fiscal 1994. The administration requested $14,268,309,569. Passed 312-89: R 92-74; D 219-15 (ND 148-10, SD 71-5); I 1-0, Sept. 23, 1993.

457. Procedural Motion. Approval of the House Journal of Monday, Sept. 27. Approved 241-149: R 17-146; D 223-3 (ND 145-3, SD 78-0); I 1-0, Sept. 28, 1993.

458. H Res 134. Discharge Petition Disclosure/Adoption. Adoption of the resolution to make public the signatures of members on discharge petitions. Adopted 384-40: R 174-0; D 209-40 (ND 139-26, SD 70-14); I 1-0, Sept. 28, 1993.

459. HR 2401. Fiscal 1994 Defense Authorization/Rule. Adoption of the rule (H Res 254) to provide for further House floor consideration of amendments to the bill to authorize defense appropriations in fiscal 1994. Adopted 241-182: R 1-172; D 239-10 (ND 160-7, SD 79-3); I 1-0, Sept. 28, 1993.

460. HR 2401. Fiscal 1994 Defense Authorization/Gay Ban. Meehan, D-Mass., amendment to strike the provisions codifying a ban on homosexuals in the military and express the sense of Congress that the issue should be determined by the president and his advisers. Rejected in the Committee of the Whole 169-264: R 11-163; D 157-101 (ND 131-43, SD 26-58); I 1-0, Sept. 28, 1993.

461. HR 2401. Fiscal 1994 Defense Authorization/Gay Ban. Hunter, R-Calif., amendment to require military personnel to ask whether candidates for the military are homosexual or bisexual. Rejected in the Committee of the Whole 144-291: R 114-60; D 30-230 (ND 5-170, SD 25-60); I 0-1, Sept. 28, 1993. A "nay" was a vote in support of the president's position.

462. HR 2401. Fiscal 1994 Defense Authorization/Gay Ban. Skelton, D-Mo., amendment to reinstate the committee-reported language in the bill codifying policy regarding homosexuals in the military. Adopted in the Committee of the Whole 301-134: R 161-12; D 140-121 (ND 77-99, SD 63-22); I 0-1, Sept. 28, 1993.

463. HR 2401. Fiscal 1994 Defense Authorization/Somalia. Gephardt, D-Mo., amendment to require the president to report to Congress by Oct. 15, 1993, on the goals, objectives and duration of the U.S. deployment in Somalia and express the sense of Congress that the president should seek congressional authorization by Nov. 15, 1993, for continued deployment in Somalia. Adopted in the Committee of the Whole 406-26: R 158-16; D 247-10 (ND 172-4, SD 75-6); I 1-0, Sept. 28, 1993.

	456	457	458	459	460	461	462	463
ALABAMA								
1 Callahan	Y	N	Y	N	N	Y	Y	Y
2 Everett	Y	N	Y	N	N	Y	Y	Y
3 Browder	Y	Y	Y	Y	N	Y	Y	Y
4 Bevill	?	Y	Y	Y	N	Y	Y	Y
5 Cramer	Y	Y	Y	Y	N	Y	Y	Y
6 Bachus	N	N	Y	N	N	N	Y	N
7 Hilliard	Y	Y	N	Y	Y	N	N	Y
ALASKA								
AL Young	Y	N	Y	N	N	Y	Y	Y
ARIZONA								
1 Coppersmith	Y	Y	Y	Y	Y	N	N	Y
2 Pastor	Y	Y	Y	Y	Y	N	Y	Y
3 Stump	N	N	Y	N	N	Y	Y	N
4 Kyl	N	N	Y	N	N	N	Y	Y
5 Kolbe	Y	N	Y	N	N	N	N	Y
6 English	Y	?	Y	Y	Y	N	N	Y
ARKANSAS								
1 Lambert	Y	Y	Y	Y	N	N	Y	Y
2 Thornton	Y	Y	Y	Y	N	N	Y	Y
3 Hutchinson	Y	Y	Y	N	N	Y	Y	Y
4 Dickey	N	N	Y	N	N	Y	Y	Y
CALIFORNIA								
1 Hamburg	Y	Y	Y	Y	Y	N	N	Y
2 Herger	N	?	Y	N	N	Y	Y	Y
3 Fazio	Y	Y	N	Y	Y	N	N	Y
4 Doolittle	N	N	Y	N	N	Y	Y	Y
5 Matsui	Y	Y	Y	Y	Y	N	N	Y
6 Woolsey	Y	Y	Y	Y	Y	N	N	Y
7 Miller	?	?	Y	Y	Y	N	N	Y
8 Pelosi	?	?	N	Y	Y	N	N	Y
9 Dellums	Y	Y	Y	Y	Y	N	N	Y
10 Baker	Y	?	Y	N	N	Y	Y	Y
11 Pombo	N	Y	N	N	N	Y	Y	Y
12 Lantos	Y	Y	Y	Y	Y	N	N	Y
13 Stark	Y	?	N	Y	Y	N	N	Y
14 Eshoo	Y	Y	Y	Y	Y	N	N	Y
15 Mineta	Y	Y	Y	Y	Y	N	N	Y
16 Edwards	Y	N	Y	Y	Y	N	N	Y
17 Farr	?	?	Y	Y	Y	N	N	Y
18 Condit	N	Y	Y	?	Y	N	Y	Y
19 Lehman	Y	Y	Y	Y	N	N	Y	Y
20 Dooley	Y	Y	Y	Y	Y	N	N	Y
21 Thomas	Y	N	Y	N	N	N	Y	Y
22 Huffington	N	N	Y	N	N	N	N	Y
23 Gallegly	Y	N	Y	N	N	Y	Y	Y
24 Beilenson	Y	Y	Y	Y	Y	N	N	Y
25 McKeon	?	N	Y	N	N	Y	Y	Y
26 Berman	?	Y	Y	Y	Y	N	N	Y
27 Moorhead	N	N	Y	N	N	Y	Y	Y
28 Dreier	N	N	Y	N	N	N	Y	Y
29 Waxman	Y	Y	Y	Y	Y	N	N	Y
30 Becerra	Y	?	Y	Y	Y	N	N	Y
31 Martinez	#	Y	P	Y	Y	N	N	Y
32 Dixon	Y	Y	Y	Y	Y	N	N	Y
33 Roybal-Allard	Y	Y	N	Y	Y	N	N	Y
34 Torres	Y	?	N	Y	Y	N	N	Y
35 Waters	Y	Y	Y	Y	Y	N	N	Y
36 Harman	Y	Y	Y	Y	N	N	Y	Y
37 Tucker	Y	Y	Y	Y	Y	N	N	Y
38 Horn	Y	N	Y	N	N	N	N	Y
39 Royce	N	N	Y	N	N	Y	Y	Y
40 Lewis	Y	N	Y	N	N	N	Y	Y
41 Kim	Y	N	Y	N	N	N	Y	Y

	456	457	458	459	460	461	462	463
42 Brown	Y	?	?	Y	Y	N	N	Y
43 Calvert	Y	N	Y	N	N	N	Y	Y
44 McCandless	Y	N	Y	N	N	N	Y	Y
45 Rohrabacher	N	N	N	N	N	N	Y	Y
46 Dornan	Y	N	Y	N	N	Y	Y	N
47 Cox	N	N	Y	N	N	N	Y	Y
48 Packard	Y	N	Y	N	N	Y	Y	Y
49 Schenk	Y	Y	Y	Y	Y	N	N	Y
50 Filner	Y	Y	Y	Y	Y	N	N	Y
51 Cunningham	X	?	Y	N	N	Y	Y	Y
52 Hunter	N	N	Y	N	N	Y	Y	N
COLORADO								
1 Schroeder	Y	N	Y	Y	Y	N	N	Y
2 Skaggs	Y	Y	Y	Y	Y	N	N	Y
3 McInnis	N	Y	Y	N	N	Y	Y	Y
4 Allard	N	N	Y	N	N	Y	Y	Y
5 Hefley	?	N	Y	N	N	Y	Y	Y
6 Schaefer	N	N	Y	N	N	Y	Y	Y
CONNECTICUT								
1 Kennelly	Y	Y	Y	Y	Y	N	N	Y
2 Gejdenson	Y	Y	Y	Y	Y	N	N	Y
3 DeLauro	Y	Y	Y	Y	Y	N	N	Y
4 Shays	Y	N	Y	N	N	N	N	Y
5 Franks	Y	N	Y	N	N	Y	Y	Y
6 Johnson	Y	N	Y	N	N	N	N	Y
DELAWARE								
AL Castle	N	N	Y	N	N	N	Y	Y
FLORIDA								
1 Hutto	Y	Y	Y	Y	N	Y	Y	Y
2 Peterson	Y	Y	Y	Y	N	N	Y	Y
3 Brown	Y	?	N	Y	N	Y	Y	Y
4 Fowler	Y	N	Y	N	N	N	Y	Y
5 Thurman	+	Y	Y	Y	N	N	Y	Y
6 Stearns	N	N	Y	N	N	Y	Y	Y
7 Mica	Y	N	Y	N	N	Y	Y	Y
8 McCollum	Y	N	Y	N	N	Y	Y	Y
9 Bilirakis	X	N	Y	N	N	Y	Y	Y
10 Young	?	N	Y	N	Y	Y	Y	Y
11 Gibbons	?	?	Y	?	Y	Y	Y	Y
12 Canady	N	N	Y	N	N	Y	Y	Y
13 Miller	?	N	Y	N	N	Y	Y	Y
14 Goss	N	N	Y	N	N	Y	Y	Y
15 Bacchus	?	Y	Y	Y	Y	N	N	Y
16 Lewis	N	N	Y	N	N	Y	Y	Y
17 Meek	Y	Y	N	Y	Y	N	N	Y
18 Ros-Lehtinen	Y	N	Y	N	N	Y	Y	Y
19 Johnston	?	Y	Y	Y	Y	N	N	N
20 Deutsch	Y	Y	Y	Y	Y	N	N	Y
21 Diaz-Balart	Y	N	Y	N	N	Y	Y	Y
22 Shaw	Y	N	Y	N	N	Y	Y	Y
23 Hastings	Y	Y	Y	Y	Y	N	N	Y
GEORGIA								
1 Kingston	Y	N	Y	N	N	Y	Y	Y
2 Bishop	Y	Y	N	Y	N	N	Y	Y
3 Collins	Y	N	Y	N	N	Y	Y	Y
4 Linder	N	N	Y	N	N	Y	Y	Y
5 Lewis	Y	Y	N	Y	Y	N	N	Y
6 Gingrich	?	N	Y	N	N	N	Y	Y
7 Darden	Y	Y	N	?	N	N	Y	Y
8 Rowland	Y	Y	Y	Y	N	N	Y	Y
9 Deal	Y	Y	Y	Y	N	N	Y	Y
10 Johnson	Y	Y	Y	Y	N	N	Y	Y
11 McKinney	Y	Y	N	Y	Y	N	N	N
HAWAII								
1 Abercrombie	Y	Y	N	Y	Y	N	N	Y
2 Mink	Y	Y	Y	Y	Y	N	N	Y
IDAHO								
1 LaRocco	?	?	Y	Y	Y	N	N	Y
2 Crapo	N	N	Y	N	N	Y	Y	Y
ILLINOIS								
1 Rush	Y	Y	N	Y	Y	N	N	Y
2 Reynolds	Y	Y	Y	Y	Y	N	N	Y
3 Lipinski	Y	Y	Y	Y	N	N	N	Y
4 Gutierrez	Y	Y	Y	Y	Y	N	N	Y
5 Rostenkowski	Y	?	Y	Y	Y	N	N	Y
6 Hyde	Y	N	Y	N	N	Y	Y	Y
7 Collins	Y	?	N	Y	Y	N	N	Y
8 Crane	N	N	Y	N	N	Y	Y	Y
9 Yates	N	Y	N	Y	Y	N	N	Y
10 Porter	Y	?	Y	N	N	N	Y	Y
11 Sangmeister	Y	Y	Y	Y	N	N	Y	Y
12 Costello	Y	Y	Y	Y	N	N	Y	Y
13 Fawell	N	N	Y	N	N	Y	Y	Y
14 Hastert	Y	N	Y	N	N	Y	Y	Y
15 Ewing	Y	N	Y	N	N	Y	Y	Y
16 Manzullo	N	N	Y	N	N	Y	Y	Y
17 Evans	Y	Y	Y	Y	Y	N	N	Y

ND Northern Democrats   SD Southern Democrats

	456	457	458	459	460	461	462	463
18 ***Michel***	Y	N	Y	N	N	N	Y	Y
19 Poshard	Y	Y	Y	Y	N	N	Y	Y
20 Durbin	Y	Y	Y	Y	Y	N	Y	Y
INDIANA								
1 Visclosky	Y	Y	N	Y	Y	N	N	Y
2 Sharp	Y	Y	+	Y	Y	N	Y	Y
3 Roemer	Y	Y	Y	Y	N	N	Y	Y
4 Long	Y	Y	Y	Y	N	N	Y	Y
5 ***Buyer***	N	N	Y	N	N	Y	Y	Y
6 ***Burton***	N	N	Y	N	N	Y	Y	N
7 ***Myers***	Y	Y	Y	N	N	Y	Y	Y
8 McCloskey	Y	Y	Y	Y	Y	N	N	Y
9 Hamilton	Y	Y	Y	Y	N	N	Y	Y
10 Jacobs	?	N	Y	Y	N	N	Y	Y
IOWA								
1 ***Leach***	Y	N	Y	N	Y	N	N	Y
2 ***Nussle***	N	N	Y	N	N	N	Y	Y
3 ***Lightfoot***	Y	N	Y	N	N	Y	Y	Y
4 Smith	?	Y	N	Y	Y	N	N	Y
5 ***Grandy***	Y	N	Y	N	Y	N	Y	Y
KANSAS								
1 ***Roberts***	N	N	Y	N	N	Y	Y	N
2 Slattery	Y	Y	Y	Y	N	N	Y	Y
3 ***Meyers***	Y	?	Y	N	N	N	Y	Y
4 Glickman	Y	Y	Y	Y	N	N	Y	Y
KENTUCKY								
1 Barlow	Y	Y	Y	Y	N	Y	N	Y
2 Natcher	Y	Y	Y	Y	N	N	Y	Y
3 Mazzoli	Y	Y	N	Y	N	N	Y	Y
4 ***Bunning***	N	N	Y	N	N	Y	Y	Y
5 ***Rogers***	Y	N	Y	N	N	Y	Y	Y
6 Baesler	Y	Y	Y	Y	N	Y	Y	Y
LOUISIANA								
1 ***Livingston***	Y	N	Y	N	N	Y	Y	Y
2 Jefferson	Y	Y	Y	Y	Y	N	Y	?
3 Tauzin	?	Y	Y	Y	N	Y	Y	Y
4 Fields	Y	Y	Y	Y	Y	N	N	Y
5 ***McCrery***	Y	?	Y	N	N	N	Y	Y
6 ***Baker***	N	N	Y	N	N	Y	Y	Y
7 Hayes	Y	Y	Y	Y	N	N	Y	Y
MAINE								
1 Andrews	Y	Y	Y	Y	Y	N	N	Y
2 ***Snowe***	N	N	Y	N	N	Y	Y	Y
MARYLAND								
1 ***Gilchrest***	Y	N	Y	N	N	N	Y	Y
2 ***Bentley***	Y	N	Y	?	N	Y	Y	Y
3 Cardin	Y	Y	Y	Y	Y	N	N	Y
4 Wynn	Y	Y	Y	Y	Y	N	Y	Y
5 Hoyer	Y	Y	Y	Y	Y	N	Y	Y
6 ***Bartlett***	N	N	Y	N	N	Y	Y	Y
7 Mfume	Y	Y	Y	Y	Y	N	N	Y
8 ***Morella***	Y	N	Y	N	Y	N	N	Y
MASSACHUSETTS								
1 Olver	Y	Y	Y	Y	Y	?	N	Y
2 Neal	Y	Y	Y	Y	Y	N	N	Y
3 ***Blute***	Y	N	Y	N	N	N	Y	Y
4 Frank	Y	Y	Y	Y	Y	N	N	Y
5 Meehan	Y	Y	Y	Y	Y	N	N	Y
6 ***Torkildsen***	Y	N	Y	N	Y	N	N	Y
7 Markey	Y	Y	Y	Y	Y	N	N	Y
8 Kennedy	Y	Y	Y	Y	Y	N	N	Y
9 Moakley	Y	Y	N	Y	Y	N	N	Y
10 Studds	Y	Y	Y	Y	Y	N	N	Y
MICHIGAN								
1 Stupak	Y	Y	Y	Y	N	N	Y	Y
2 ***Hoekstra***	Y	N	Y	N	N	Y	Y	Y
3 Vacancy								
4 ***Camp***	Y	N	Y	N	N	Y	Y	Y
5 Barcia	Y	Y	Y	Y	N	Y	Y	Y
6 ***Upton***	Y	N	Y	N	N	N	Y	Y
7 ***Smith***	N	N	Y	N	N	N	Y	Y
8 Carr	Y	Y	Y	Y	Y	N	Y	Y
9 Kildee	Y	Y	Y	Y	Y	N	Y	Y
10 Bonior	Y	Y	Y	Y	Y	N	Y	Y
11 ***Knollenberg***	N	N	Y	N	N	Y	Y	Y
12 Levin	Y	Y	Y	Y	Y	N	Y	Y
13 Ford	Y	?	N	Y	Y	N	N	Y
14 Conyers	Y	?	—	?	?	N	N	N
15 Collins	Y	?	N	N	Y	N	N	Y
16 Dingell	Y	Y	N	Y	N	N	Y	Y
MINNESOTA								
1 Penny	N	Y	Y	Y	Y	N	Y	Y
2 Minge	N	Y	Y	Y	Y	N	Y	Y
3 ***Ramstad***	N	N	Y	N	N	N	Y	Y
4 Vento	Y	Y	Y	?	Y	N	N	Y

	456	457	458	459	460	461	462	463
5 Sabo	Y	Y	N	Y	Y	N	N	Y
6 ***Grams***	N	N	Y	N	N	Y	Y	Y
7 Peterson	N	Y	Y	Y	N	N	Y	Y
8 Oberstar	Y	Y	Y	Y	Y	N	N	Y
MISSISSIPPI								
1 Whitten	N	?	Y	Y	N	N	Y	?
2 Thompson	Y	Y	Y	Y	Y	N	N	Y
3 Montgomery	Y	Y	Y	Y	N	N	Y	Y
4 Parker	Y	Y	Y	Y	N	Y	Y	N
5 Taylor	N	Y	Y	Y	N	Y	Y	N
MISSOURI								
1 Clay	Y	N	N	Y	Y	N	N	Y
2 ***Talent***	Y	N	Y	N	N	Y	Y	Y
3 Gephardt	Y	Y	Y	Y	Y	N	Y	Y
4 Skelton	Y	Y	Y	Y	N	N	Y	Y
5 Wheat	Y	Y	Y	Y	Y	N	N	Y
6 Danner	?	Y	Y	Y	N	N	Y	Y
7 ***Hancock***	?	N	Y	N	N	Y	Y	N
8 ***Emerson***	Y	N	Y	N	N	Y	Y	Y
9 Volkmer	Y	Y	Y	Y	N	Y	Y	Y
MONTANA								
AL Williams	N	Y	Y	?	N	N	N	Y
NEBRASKA								
1 ***Bereuter***	N	N	Y	N	N	Y	Y	Y
2 Hoagland	Y	Y	Y	Y	Y	N	Y	Y
3 ***Barrett***	N	N	Y	N	N	Y	Y	Y
NEVADA								
1 Bilbray	Y	Y	Y	Y	N	N	Y	Y
2 ***Vucanovich***	Y	?	Y	N	N	Y	Y	Y
NEW HAMPSHIRE								
1 ***Zeliff***	N	N	Y	N	N	Y	Y	Y
2 Swett	Y	Y	Y	Y	Y	N	Y	Y
NEW JERSEY								
1 Andrews	N	Y	Y	Y	N	N	Y	Y
2 Hughes	Y	Y	Y	Y	N	N	Y	Y
3 ***Saxton***	Y	N	Y	N	N	N	Y	Y
4 ***Smith***	Y	Y	Y	Y	N	Y	Y	Y
5 ***Roukema***	Y	N	Y	N	N	N	Y	Y
6 Pallone	N	Y	Y	Y	Y	N	N	Y
7 ***Franks***	N	N	Y	N	N	N	Y	Y
8 Klein	Y	Y	Y	Y	N	N	Y	Y
9 Torricelli	Y	Y	Y	Y	Y	N	Y	Y
10 Payne	Y	Y	N	Y	Y	N	N	N
11 ***Gallo***	N	N	Y	N	N	N	Y	Y
12 ***Zimmer***	N	N	Y	N	N	Y	Y	Y
13 Menendez	Y	Y	Y	Y	Y	N	Y	Y
NEW MEXICO								
1 ***Schiff***	Y	N	Y	N	N	N	Y	Y
2 ***Skeen***	Y	N	Y	N	N	Y	Y	Y
3 Richardson	Y	Y	Y	Y	Y	N	Y	Y
NEW YORK								
1 Hochbrueckner	Y	Y	Y	Y	Y	N	Y	Y
2 ***Lazio***	N	N	Y	N	N	N	Y	Y
3 ***King***	N	N	Y	N	N	Y	Y	Y
4 ***Levy***	Y	N	Y	N	N	Y	Y	Y
5 Ackerman	?	Y	Y	Y	Y	N	N	Y
6 Flake	Y	Y	N	Y	Y	N	N	Y
7 Manton	Y	Y	Y	Y	Y	N	N	Y
8 Nadler	Y	?	Y	Y	Y	N	N	Y
9 Schumer	Y	Y	Y	Y	Y	N	N	Y
10 Towns	Y	?	?	Y	Y	N	N	N
11 Owens	Y	?	?	?	?	N	N	Y
12 Velazquez	?	Y	N	Y	Y	N	N	Y
13 ***Molinari***	Y	N	Y	N	N	N	Y	Y
14 Maloney	Y	?	Y	N	Y	N	N	Y
15 Rangel	Y	Y	N	Y	Y	N	N	Y
16 Serrano	Y	Y	Y	Y	Y	N	N	Y
17 Engel	Y	Y	Y	Y	Y	N	N	Y
18 Lowey	Y	Y	Y	Y	Y	N	N	Y
19 ***Fish***	Y	Y	Y	N	N	N	Y	Y
20 ***Gilman***	Y	Y	Y	N	Y	N	N	Y
21 McNulty	Y	Y	Y	Y	N	N	Y	Y
22 ***Solomon***	N	N	Y	N	N	Y	Y	Y
23 ***Boehlert***	Y	N	Y	N	Y	N	N	Y
24 ***McHugh***	N	N	Y	N	N	Y	Y	Y
25 ***Walsh***	Y	N	Y	N	N	N	Y	Y
26 Hinchey	Y	?	Y	Y	Y	N	N	Y
27 ***Paxon***	N	N	Y	N	N	Y	Y	Y
28 Slaughter	?	?	Y	Y	Y	N	N	Y
29 LaFalce	Y	Y	Y	Y	N	N	Y	Y
30 ***Quinn***	Y	?	Y	N	N	Y	Y	Y
31 ***Houghton***	Y	Y	Y	N	N	N	Y	Y
NORTH CAROLINA								
1 Clayton	Y	Y	N	Y	Y	N	Y	Y
2 Valentine	Y	Y	Y	Y	N	Y	Y	Y

	456	457	458	459	460	461	462	463
3 Lancaster	Y	Y	Y	Y	N	Y	Y	Y
4 Price	Y	Y	Y	Y	N	N	Y	Y
5 Neal	Y	Y	Y	Y	N	N	Y	Y
6 ***Coble***	Y	N	Y	N	N	Y	Y	N
7 Rose	Y	Y	Y	Y	?	N	Y	Y
8 Hefner	Y	Y	Y	Y	N	N	Y	Y
9 ***McMillan***	Y	N	Y	N	N	Y	Y	Y
10 ***Ballenger***	Y	N	Y	N	N	N	Y	Y
11 ***Taylor***	N	N	Y	N	N	Y	Y	Y
12 Watt	Y	Y	N	Y	Y	N	N	Y
NORTH DAKOTA								
AL Pomeroy	Y	Y	Y	Y	N	N	Y	Y
OHIO								
1 Mann	Y	Y	Y	Y	N	N	Y	Y
2 ***Portman***	N	N	Y	N	N	Y	Y	Y
3 Hall	Y	Y	Y	Y	N	Y	Y	Y
4 ***Oxley***	Y	N	Y	N	N	N	Y	Y
5 ***Gillmor***	Y	Y	Y	N	N	N	Y	Y
6 Strickland	Y	Y	Y	Y	Y	N	Y	Y
7 ***Hobson***	Y	N	Y	N	N	N	Y	Y
8 ***Boehner***	N	N	Y	N	N	Y	Y	Y
9 Kaptur	Y	Y	Y	Y	N	N	Y	Y
10 ***Hoke***	Y	N	Y	N	N	N	Y	Y
11 Stokes	Y	?	Y	Y	Y	N	N	Y
12 ***Kasich***	N	Y	Y	N	N	N	Y	Y
13 Brown	Y	Y	Y	Y	Y	N	N	Y
14 Sawyer	Y	Y	Y	Y	Y	N	Y	Y
15 ***Pryce***	Y	N	Y	N	N	N	Y	Y
16 ***Regula***	Y	N	Y	N	N	N	Y	Y
17 Traficant	Y	Y	Y	Y	N	N	Y	Y
18 Applegate	Y	Y	Y	Y	N	N	Y	Y
19 Fingerhut	Y	Y	Y	Y	Y	N	Y	Y
OKLAHOMA								
1 ***Inhofe***	Y	Y	Y	N	N	Y	Y	N
2 Synar	Y	Y	Y	Y	Y	N	N	Y
3 Brewster	Y	Y	Y	Y	N	Y	Y	Y
4 McCurdy	Y	Y	Y	Y	N	N	Y	Y
5 ***Istook***	N	N	Y	N	N	Y	+	Y
6 English	Y	Y	Y	Y	N	Y	Y	Y
OREGON								
1 Furse	Y	Y	Y	Y	Y	N	N	Y
2 ***Smith***	N	N	Y	N	N	Y	N	Y
3 Wyden	Y	Y	Y	Y	Y	N	N	Y
4 DeFazio	#	Y	Y	Y	Y	N	N	Y
5 Kopetski	Y	Y	Y	Y	Y	N	Y	Y
PENNSYLVANIA								
1 Foglietta	Y	?	?	Y	Y	N	N	Y
2 Blackwell	Y	Y	Y	Y	Y	N	N	Y
3 Borski	Y	Y	Y	Y	N	N	Y	Y
4 Klink	?	Y	N	N	N	N	Y	Y
5 ***Clinger***	Y	Y	Y	N	N	N	Y	Y
6 Holden	Y	Y	Y	Y	N	Y	Y	Y
7 ***Weldon***	Y	N	Y	N	N	N	Y	N
8 ***Greenwood***	Y	N	Y	N	N	N	Y	Y
9 ***Shuster***	Y	N	Y	N	N	N	Y	Y
10 ***McDade***	Y	?	?	?	?	?	?	?
11 Kanjorski	Y	Y	Y	Y	N	N	Y	Y
12 Murtha	Y	Y	N	Y	N	N	Y	Y
13 Margolies-Mezv.	Y	Y	Y	Y	Y	N	N	Y
14 Coyne	Y	Y	Y	Y	Y	N	N	Y
15 McHale	Y	Y	Y	N	N	N	Y	Y
16 ***Walker***	N	N	Y	N	N	Y	Y	N
17 ***Gekas***	N	N	Y	N	N	Y	Y	Y
18 ***Santorum***	Y	N	Y	N	N	N	Y	Y
19 ***Goodling***	Y	N	Y	N	N	N	Y	Y
20 Murphy	Y	Y	Y	N	N	N	Y	Y
21 ***Ridge***	Y	?	Y	N	N	N	Y	N
RHODE ISLAND								
1 ***Machtley***	Y	N	Y	N	N	N	Y	Y
2 Reed	Y	Y	Y	Y	Y	N	N	Y
SOUTH CAROLINA								
1 ***Ravenel***	Y	N	Y	N	N	Y	Y	Y
2 ***Spence***	Y	N	Y	N	N	N	Y	Y
3 Derrick	Y	Y	Y	Y	N	Y	Y	Y
4 ***Inglis***	N	Y	Y	N	N	Y	Y	Y
5 Spratt	Y	Y	Y	Y	N	N	Y	Y
6 Clyburn	Y	Y	Y	Y	Y	N	Y	Y
SOUTH DAKOTA								
AL Johnson	Y	Y	Y	Y	N	N	Y	Y
TENNESSEE								
1 ***Quillen***	Y	N	Y	N	N	Y	Y	Y
2 ***Duncan***	N	N	Y	N	N	Y	Y	Y
3 Lloyd	Y	Y	Y	Y	N	N	Y	Y
4 Cooper	Y	Y	Y	N	N	Y	Y	?
5 Clement	Y	Y	Y	Y	N	N	Y	Y

	456	457	458	459	460	461	462	463
6 Gordon	Y	Y	Y	Y	N	N	Y	Y
7 ***Sundquist***	Y	?	Y	N	N	Y	Y	Y
8 Tanner	Y	Y	Y	Y	N	Y	Y	Y
9 Ford	Y	?	Y	Y	Y	N	N	Y
TEXAS								
1 Chapman	Y	Y	Y	Y	N	N	Y	Y
2 Wilson	Y	?	Y	Y	N	Y	Y	Y
3 ***Johnson, Sam***	N	N	Y	N	N	Y	Y	Y
4 Hall	N	Y	Y	N	Y	Y	Y	Y
5 Bryant	Y	Y	Y	Y	Y	N	N	Y
6 ***Barton***	N	N	Y	N	N	Y	Y	N
7 ***Archer***	N	Y	Y	N	N	Y	Y	Y
8 ***Fields***	N	N	Y	N	N	Y	Y	N
9 Brooks	Y	Y	N	Y	N	N	Y	Y
10 Pickle	?	Y	N	Y	Y	N	N	Y
11 Edwards	Y	Y	Y	Y	N	N	Y	Y
12 Geren	?	Y	Y	Y	N	Y	Y	N
13 Sarpalius	Y	Y	Y	Y	N	Y	Y	Y
14 Laughlin	Y	Y	Y	Y	N	N	Y	Y
15 de la Garza	Y	Y	Y	Y	N	Y	Y	?
16 Coleman	Y	Y	Y	Y	N	N	Y	Y
17 Stenholm	N	Y	Y	Y	N	Y	Y	Y
18 Washington	Y	?	N	Y	Y	N	N	Y
19 ***Combest***	N	Y	Y	N	N	Y	Y	N
20 Gonzalez	Y	Y	N	Y	Y	N	N	N
21 ***Smith***	N	N	Y	N	N	Y	Y	Y
22 ***DeLay***	Y	N	Y	N	N	Y	Y	Y
23 ***Bonilla***	Y	N	Y	N	N	Y	Y	Y
24 Frost	Y	Y	Y	Y	N	N	Y	Y
25 Andrews	N	Y	Y	Y	N	Y	Y	Y
26 ***Armey***	N	N	Y	N	N	Y	Y	Y
27 Ortiz	Y	Y	Y	Y	N	Y	Y	Y
28 Tejeda	Y	Y	Y	Y	N	Y	Y	Y
29 Green	+	Y	Y	Y	Y	N	Y	Y
30 Johnson, E.B.	Y	Y	+	Y	Y	N	N	Y
UTAH								
1 ***Hansen***	?	N	Y	N	N	Y	Y	Y
2 Shepherd	Y	Y	Y	Y	Y	N	N	Y
3 Orton	N	Y	Y	Y	N	N	Y	Y
VERMONT								
AL *Sanders*	Y	Y	Y	Y	Y	N	N	Y
VIRGINIA								
1 ***Bateman***	Y	Y	Y	N	N	Y	Y	Y
2 Pickett	Y	Y	Y	Y	N	N	Y	Y
3 Scott	Y	Y	Y	Y	Y	N	N	Y
4 Sisisky	Y	Y	Y	Y	N	N	Y	Y
5 Payne	Y	Y	Y	Y	N	N	Y	Y
6 ***Goodlatte***	N	?	Y	N	N	Y	Y	Y
7 ***Bliley***	Y	N	Y	N	N	Y	Y	Y
8 Moran	Y	Y	Y	Y	Y	N	N	Y
9 Boucher	Y	Y	Y	N	N	N	Y	Y
10 ***Wolf***	Y	N	Y	N	N	Y	Y	Y
11 Byrne	Y	?	Y	?	Y	N	N	Y
WASHINGTON								
1 Cantwell	Y	Y	Y	Y	Y	N	N	Y
2 Swift	Y	?	Y	Y	Y	N	N	Y
3 Unsoeld	Y	Y	N	Y	Y	N	N	Y
4 Inslee	Y	Y	Y	Y	Y	N	Y	Y
5 Foley								
6 Dicks	Y	Y	Y	Y	Y	N	Y	Y
7 McDermott	Y	Y	Y	Y	Y	N	N	Y
8 ***Dunn***	Y	N	Y	N	N	N	Y	Y
9 Kreidler	Y	Y	Y	Y	Y	N	N	Y
WEST VIRGINIA								
1 Mollohan	Y	?	N	Y	N	N	Y	Y
2 Wise	Y	Y	Y	Y	N	N	Y	Y
3 Rahall	Y	Y	Y	N	N	Y	Y	Y
WISCONSIN								
1 Barca	N	Y	Y	Y	Y	N	Y	Y
2 ***Klug***	N	N	Y	N	N	N	Y	Y
3 ***Gunderson***	N	Y	Y	N	Y	N	N	Y
4 Kleczka	Y	Y	Y	Y	Y	N	Y	Y
5 Barrett	Y	Y	Y	N	Y	N	N	Y
6 ***Petri***	N	N	Y	N	N	Y	Y	Y
7 Obey	Y	Y	Y	Y	Y	N	Y	N
8 ***Roth***	N	N	Y	N	N	Y	Y	Y
9 ***Sensenbrenner***	N	N	Y	N	N	Y	Y	N
WYOMING								
AL ***Thomas***	N	N	Y	N	N	Y	Y	Y
DELEGATES								
de Lugo, V.I.	D	D	D	D	Y	N	N	Y
Faleomavaega, Am.S.	D	D	D	D	Y	N	Y	Y
Norton, D.C.	D	D	D	D	Y	N	N	Y
Romero-B., P.R.	D	D	D	D	N	N	Y	Y
Underwood, Guam	D	D	D	D	?	?	?	?

Southern states - Ala., Ark., Fla., Ga., Ky., La., Miss., N.C., Okla., S.C., Tenn., Texas, Va.
Omitted votes are quorum calls, which CQ does not include in its vote charts.

464. H J Res 267. Fiscal 1994 Continuing Appropriations/Passage. Passage of the joint resolution to provide continuing appropriations through Oct. 21 for the appropriations bills not yet signed into law. Passed 274-156: R 26-147; D 247-9 (ND 163-8, SD 84-1); I 1-0, Sept. 29, 1993.

465. HR 2520. Fiscal 1994 Interior Appropriations/Grazing Fees. Regula, R-Ohio, motion to instruct House conferees to reject the Senate amendment to prohibit the administration for one year from implementing higher grazing fees. Motion agreed to 314-109: R 86-85; D 227-24 (ND 154-14, SD 73-10); I 1-0, Sept. 29, 1993. A "yea" was a vote in support of the president's position.

466. HR 2519. Fiscal 1994 Commerce, Justice and State Appropriations/United Nations. Rogers, R-Ky., motion to instruct House conferees to accept the Senate amendment calling on the United Nations to create an independent office to oversee U.N. activities. Motion agreed to 420-0: R 173-0; D 246-0 (ND 166-0, SD 80-0); I 1-0, Sept. 29, 1993.

467. HR 2295. Fiscal 1994 Foreign Operations Appropriations/Conference Report. Adoption of the conference report to provide $12,982,665,866 in new budget authority for foreign assistance and related programs in fiscal 1994. The administration requested $14,425,993,066. Adopted (thus sent to the Senate) 321-108: R 107-66; D 214-41 (ND 146-24, SD 68-17); I 0-1, Sept. 29, 1993. A "yea" was a vote in support of the president's position.

468. HR 2401. Fiscal 1994 Defense Authorization/Overseas Base Closures. Separate vote at the request of Walker, R-Pa., on the amendment offered by Schroeder, D-Colo., and adopted in the Committee of the Whole to require the 1995 Base Closure Commission to include overseas military installations in its closure recommendations. Adopted 292-138: R 59-114; D 232-24 (ND 160-12, SD 72-12); I 1-0, Sept. 29, 1993. (On a separate vote, which may be demanded on an amendment adopted in the Committee of the Whole, the four delegates and the resident commissioner of Puerto Rico cannot vote. See vote 418.) A "nay" was a vote in support of the president's position.

469. HR 2401. Fiscal 1994 Defense Authorization/Overseas Base Spending Reduction. Separate vote at the request of Walker, R-Pa., on the amendment offered by Lloyd, D-Tenn., and adopted in the Committee of the Whole to reduce the amount spent on overseas bases by $580 million. Adopted 427-1: R 172-1; D 254-0 (ND 169-0, SD 85-0); I 1-0, Sept. 29, 1993. (On a separate vote, which may be demanded on an amendment adopted in the Committee of the Whole, the four delegates and the resident commissioner of Puerto Rico cannot vote. See vote 419.)

470. HR 2401. Fiscal 1994 Defense Authorization/Foreign Arms Sales. Separate vote at the request of Walker, R-Pa., on the amendment offered by Andrews, D-Maine, and adopted in the Committee of the Whole to prohibit the use of defense conversion funds to finance sales or transfers to a foreign country. Adopted 266-162: R 55-118; D 210-44 (ND 157-12, SD 53-32); I 1-0, Sept. 29, 1993. (On a separate vote, which may be demanded on an amendment adopted in the Committee of the Whole, the four delegates and the resident commissioner of Puerto Rico cannot vote. See vote 422.)

471. HR 2401. Fiscal 1994 Defense Authorization/Gays in the Military. Separate vote at the request of Walker, R-Pa., on the amendment offered by Skelton, D-Mo., and adopted in the Committee of the Whole to reinstate the committee-reported language in the bill codifying policy regarding homosexuals in the military. Adopted 295-133: R 161-12; D 134-120 (ND 74-97, SD 60-23); I 0-1, Sept. 29, 1993. (On a separate vote, which may be demanded on an amendment adopted in the Committee of the Whole, the four delegates and the resident commissioner of Puerto Rico cannot vote. See vote 462.)

KEY

Y Voted for (yea).
Paired for.
+ Announced for.
N Voted against (nay).
X Paired against.
− Announced against.
P Voted "present."
C Voted "present" to avoid possible conflict of interest.
? Did not vote or otherwise make a position known.
D Delegates ineligible to vote.

Democrats **Republicans** *Independent*

	464	465	466	467	468	469	470	471
ALABAMA								
1 *Callahan*	N	N	Y	N	Y	Y	N	Y
2 *Everett*	N	Y	Y	N	N	Y	N	Y
3 Browder	Y	Y	Y	Y	Y	Y	N	Y
4 Bevill	Y	Y	Y	Y	Y	Y	Y	Y
5 Cramer	Y	Y	Y	Y	Y	Y	N	Y
6 *Bachus*	N	Y	Y	N	N	Y	N	Y
7 Hilliard	Y	Y	Y	Y	Y	Y	Y	N
ALASKA								
AL *Young*	N	N	Y	N	Y	N	Y	N	Y
ARIZONA								
1 Coppersmith	Y	Y	Y	Y	N	Y	Y	N
2 Pastor	Y	Y	Y	Y	Y	Y	Y	N
3 *Stump*	N	N	Y	N	N	N	N	Y
4 *Kyl*	N	N	Y	N	N	Y	N	Y
5 *Kolbe*	Y	N	Y	N	Y	N	N	N
6 English	Y	N	Y	Y	Y	Y	Y	N
ARKANSAS								
1 Lambert	Y	Y	Y	Y	Y	Y	Y	Y
2 Thornton	Y	Y	Y	Y	Y	Y	Y	Y
3 *Hutchinson*	N	N	Y	N	N	Y	N	Y
4 *Dickey*	N	Y	Y	Y	N	Y	N	Y
CALIFORNIA								
1 Hamburg	Y	Y	Y	Y	Y	Y	Y	N
2 *Herger*	N	N	Y	N	N	Y	N	Y
3 Fazio	Y	N	Y	Y	Y	Y	Y	N
4 *Doolittle*	N	N	Y	N	N	N	N	Y
5 Matsui	Y	Y	Y	Y	Y	Y	Y	N
6 Woolsey	Y	Y	Y	Y	Y	Y	Y	N
7 Miller	Y	Y	?	Y	Y	Y	Y	N
8 Pelosi	Y	Y	Y	Y	Y	Y	Y	N
9 Dellums	Y	Y	Y	Y	Y	Y	Y	N
10 *Baker*	N	N	N	N	N	N	N	Y
11 *Pombo*	N	N	Y	N	N	N	N	Y
12 Lantos	Y	Y	Y	Y	Y	Y	Y	N
13 Stark	Y	Y	Y	N	Y	Y	Y	N
14 Eshoo	Y	Y	Y	Y	Y	Y	Y	N
15 Mineta	Y	Y	Y	Y	Y	Y	Y	N
16 Edwards	Y	Y	Y	Y	Y	Y	Y	N
17 Farr	Y	Y	Y	Y	Y	Y	Y	N
18 Condit	N	N	Y	N	Y	Y	Y	Y
19 Lehman	Y	N	Y	N	Y	Y	Y	N
20 Dooley	Y	N	Y	N	Y	Y	Y	Y
21 *Thomas*	N	N	Y	N	Y	Y	N	Y
22 *Huffington*	N	N	Y	N	Y	N	N	Y
23 *Gallegly*	N	N	Y	N	N	N	N	Y
24 Beilenson	Y	Y	Y	Y	Y	Y	Y	N
25 *McKeon*	N	N	Y	N	N	N	N	Y
26 Berman	Y	Y	Y	Y	N	Y	Y	N
27 *Moorhead*	N	N	Y	N	N	Y	N	Y
28 *Dreier*	N	N	Y	N	N	Y	N	Y
29 Waxman	Y	Y	Y	Y	Y	Y	Y	N
30 Becerra	Y	Y	?	Y	Y	Y	Y	N
31 Martinez	Y	Y	Y	Y	Y	Y	Y	N
32 Dixon	Y	Y	Y	Y	Y	Y	Y	N
33 Roybal-Allard	Y	Y	Y	Y	Y	Y	Y	N
34 Torres	Y	Y	Y	Y	Y	Y	Y	N
35 Waters	Y	Y	Y	Y	Y	Y	Y	N
36 Harman	Y	Y	Y	Y	Y	Y	Y	N
37 Tucker	Y	Y	Y	Y	Y	Y	Y	N
38 *Horn*	Y	Y	Y	Y	Y	Y	Y	N
39 *Royce*	N	Y	Y	Y	Y	Y	N	Y
40 *Lewis*	N	N	Y	N	Y	Y	N	Y
41 *Kim*	N	Y	Y	N	N	Y	Y	Y

ND Northern Democrats   SD Southern Democrats

	464	465	466	467	468	469	470	471
42 Brown	Y	Y	Y	Y	Y	Y	Y	N
43 *Calvert*	N	N	Y	Y	Y	Y	N	Y
44 *McCandless*	N	N	Y	N	N	Y	N	Y
45 *Rohrabacher*	N	Y	Y	N	N	Y	N	Y
46 *Dornan*	N	N	Y	N	N	Y	N	Y
47 *Cox*	N	N	Y	N	N	N	N	Y
48 *Packard*	N	N	Y	N	N	Y	N	Y
49 Schenk	Y	Y	Y	Y	Y	Y	Y	N
50 Filner	Y	Y	Y	Y	Y	Y	Y	N
51 *Cunningham*	N	N	Y	N	N	Y	N	Y
52 *Hunter*	N	N	Y	N	Y	N	Y	Y
COLORADO								
1 Schroeder	N	Y	Y	N	Y	Y	Y	N
2 Skaggs	Y	Y	Y	Y	Y	Y	Y	N
3 *McInnis*	N	N	Y	N	Y	Y	N	Y
4 *Allard*	N	N	Y	N	Y	Y	Y	Y
5 *Hefley*	N	N	Y	N	Y	N	Y	Y
6 *Schaefer*	N	N	Y	N	Y	N	Y	Y
CONNECTICUT								
1 Kennelly	Y	Y	Y	Y	Y	Y	Y	N
2 Gejdenson	Y	Y	Y	Y	Y	Y	Y	N
3 DeLauro	Y	Y	Y	Y	Y	Y	Y	N
4 *Shays*	N	Y	Y	N	Y	N	N	N
5 *Franks*	N	Y	Y	N	Y	N	N	Y
6 *Johnson*	Y	Y	Y	Y	Y	Y	N	N
DELAWARE								
AL *Castle*	N	Y	Y	Y	N	Y	N	Y
FLORIDA								
1 Hutto	Y	Y	Y	N	N	Y	N	Y
2 Peterson	Y	Y	Y	Y	Y	Y	Y	Y
3 Brown	Y	Y	Y	Y	Y	Y	Y	Y
4 *Fowler*	N	Y	Y	N	N	Y	Y	Y
5 Thurman	Y	Y	Y	N	Y	Y	Y	Y
6 *Stearns*	N	Y	Y	N	N	Y	N	Y
7 *Mica*	N	Y	Y	N	N	Y	N	Y
8 *McCollum*	N	N	Y	N	N	Y	N	Y
9 *Bilirakis*	N	Y	Y	Y	Y	Y	N	Y
10 *Young*	Y	Y	Y	N	Y	Y	N	Y
11 Gibbons	Y	Y	Y	N	Y	Y	Y	Y
12 *Canady*	N	N	Y	N	Y	Y	Y	Y
13 *Miller*	N	Y	Y	N	Y	Y	Y	Y
14 *Goss*	N	Y	Y	N	N	Y	N	Y
15 Bacchus	Y	Y	Y	N	Y	Y	N	N
16 *Lewis*	N	N	Y	N	Y	Y	N	N
17 Meek	Y	Y	Y	Y	Y	Y	Y	N
18 *Ros-Lehtinen*	N	Y	Y	N	N	Y	N	Y
19 Johnston	Y	Y	Y	Y	Y	Y	Y	N
20 Deutsch	Y	Y	Y	Y	Y	Y	Y	N
21 *Diaz-Balart*	N	Y	Y	N	N	Y	N	Y
22 *Shaw*	N	Y	Y	Y	N	Y	N	Y
23 Hastings	Y	Y	Y	Y	Y	Y	Y	N
GEORGIA								
1 *Kingston*	N	N	Y	N	N	Y	N	Y
2 Bishop	Y	Y	Y	Y	Y	Y	Y	Y
3 *Collins*	N	Y	Y	N	N	Y	N	Y
4 *Linder*	N	Y	Y	N	N	Y	N	Y
5 Lewis	Y	Y	Y	Y	Y	Y	Y	N
6 *Gingrich*	N	N	Y	N	N	Y	N	Y
7 Darden	Y	Y	Y	Y	Y	Y	N	Y
8 Rowland	Y	Y	Y	Y	Y	Y	N	Y
9 Deal	Y	Y	Y	Y	Y	Y	Y	Y
10 Johnson	Y	Y	Y	Y	Y	Y	N	Y
11 McKinney	Y	Y	Y	Y	Y	Y	Y	N
HAWAII								
1 Abercrombie	Y	Y	Y	Y	Y	Y	Y	N
2 Mink	Y	Y	Y	Y	Y	Y	Y	N
IDAHO								
1 LaRocco	Y	N	Y	Y	Y	Y	Y	Y
2 *Crapo*	N	N	Y	N	N	Y	N	Y
ILLINOIS								
1 Rush	Y	Y	Y	Y	Y	Y	Y	N
2 Reynolds	Y	Y	Y	Y	Y	Y	Y	N
3 Lipinski	Y	Y	Y	Y	Y	Y	Y	Y
4 Gutierrez	Y	Y	Y	Y	Y	Y	Y	N
5 Rostenkowski	Y	Y	Y	Y	Y	Y	Y	N
6 *Hyde*	Y	Y	Y	N	N	Y	N	Y
7 Collins	Y	Y	?	Y	Y	Y	Y	N
8 *Crane*	N	N	Y	N	N	Y	Y	Y
9 Yates	Y	Y	Y	Y	Y	Y	N	N
10 *Porter*	N	Y	Y	N	Y	N	N	Y
11 Sangmeister	Y	Y	Y	Y	Y	Y	Y	N
12 Costello	N	Y	Y	Y	Y	Y	Y	Y
13 *Fawell*	N	Y	Y	N	Y	Y	N	Y
14 *Hastert*	N	N	Y	N	N	Y	N	Y
15 *Ewing*	N	N	Y	N	N	Y	N	Y
16 *Manzullo*	N	N	Y	N	N	Y	N	Y
17 Evans	Y	Y	Y	Y	Y	Y	Y	N

	464	465	466	467	468	469	470	471
18 ***Michel***	Y	?	Y	Y	N	Y	N	Y
19 Poshard	N	Y	Y	N	Y	Y	Y	Y
20 Durbin	Y	Y	Y	Y	Y	Y	Y	Y
INDIANA								
1 Visclosky	Y	Y	Y	Y	N	Y	Y	N
2 Sharp	Y	Y	Y	Y	Y	Y	Y	Y
3 Roemer	Y	Y	Y	N	Y	Y	Y	Y
4 Long	Y	Y	Y	Y	Y	Y	Y	Y
5 ***Buyer***	N	N	Y	N	N	Y	N	Y
6 ***Burton***	N	N	Y	Y	Y	Y	N	Y
7 ***Myers***	Y	N	Y	N	Y	Y	N	Y
8 McCloskey	Y	Y	Y	Y	Y	Y	Y	N
9 Hamilton	Y	Y	Y	Y	N	Y	Y	Y
10 Jacobs	N	Y	Y	N	Y	Y	Y	Y
IOWA								
1 ***Leach***	N	Y	Y	Y	Y	Y	Y	N
2 ***Nussle***	N	N	Y	N	N	Y	Y	Y
3 ***Lightfoot***	Y	N	Y	Y	Y	Y	N	Y
4 Smith	Y	Y	Y	Y	N	Y	N	N
5 ***Grandy***	N	?	Y	Y	Y	Y	Y	Y
KANSAS								
1 ***Roberts***	N	N	Y	N	Y	Y	N	Y
2 Slattery	Y	Y	Y	Y	Y	Y	N	Y
3 ***Meyers***	N	Y	Y	Y	Y	Y	N	Y
4 Glickman	Y	Y	Y	Y	Y	Y	Y	Y
KENTUCKY								
1 Barlow	Y	Y	Y	Y	Y	Y	Y	N
2 Natcher	Y	Y	Y	Y	Y	Y	N	Y
3 Mazzoli	Y	Y	Y	Y	Y	Y	Y	Y
4 ***Bunning***	N	N	Y	N	N	Y	N	Y
5 ***Rogers***	Y	N	Y	N	Y	Y	N	Y
6 Baesler	Y	Y	Y	Y	Y	Y	Y	Y
LOUISIANA								
1 ***Livingston***	Y	N	Y	Y	N	Y	N	Y
2 Jefferson	Y	Y	Y	Y	Y	Y	Y	N
3 Tauzin	Y	N	Y	N	Y	Y	N	Y
4 Fields	Y	Y	Y	N	Y	Y	Y	N
5 ***McCrery***	N	N	Y	Y	N	Y	N	Y
6 ***Baker***	N	N	Y	Y	N	Y	N	Y
7 Hayes	Y	N	Y	N	Y	Y	N	Y
MAINE								
1 Andrews	Y	Y	Y	Y	Y	Y	Y	N
2 ***Snowe***	N	Y	Y	Y	Y	Y	N	Y
MARYLAND								
1 ***Gilchrest***	N	Y	Y	Y	N	Y	Y	Y
2 ***Bentley***	Y	N	Y	Y	Y	Y	Y	Y
3 Cardin	Y	Y	Y	Y	Y	Y	Y	N
4 Wynn	Y	Y	Y	Y	N	Y	Y	Y
5 Hoyer	Y	Y	Y	Y	Y	Y	Y	Y
6 ***Bartlett***	N	Y	Y	Y	N	Y	N	Y
7 Mfume	Y	Y	Y	Y	Y	Y	Y	N
8 ***Morella***	Y	Y	Y	Y	Y	Y	Y	N
MASSACHUSETTS								
1 Olver	Y	Y	Y	Y	Y	Y	Y	N
2 Neal	Y	Y	Y	Y	Y	Y	Y	N
3 ***Blute***	N	Y	Y	Y	N	Y	N	Y
4 Frank	Y	Y	Y	Y	Y	Y	Y	N
5 Meehan	Y	Y	Y	Y	Y	Y	Y	N
6 ***Torkildsen***	N	Y	Y	Y	N	Y	N	N
7 Markey	Y	Y	Y	Y	Y	Y	Y	N
8 Kennedy	Y	Y	Y	Y	Y	Y	Y	N
9 Moakley	Y	Y	Y	Y	Y	Y	Y	N
10 Studds	Y	Y	Y	Y	Y	Y	Y	N
MICHIGAN								
1 Stupak	Y	Y	Y	Y	Y	Y	N	Y
2 ***Hoekstra***	N	Y	Y	Y	N	Y	Y	Y
3 Vacancy								
4 ***Camp***	N	N	Y	Y	Y	Y	N	Y
5 Barcia	Y	N	Y	Y	Y	Y	Y	Y
6 ***Upton***	N	Y	Y	Y	Y	Y	Y	Y
7 ***Smith***	?	?	?	?	?	?	?	?
8 Carr	Y	Y	Y	Y	Y	Y	Y	Y
9 Kildee	Y	Y	Y	Y	Y	Y	Y	Y
10 Bonior	Y	Y	Y	Y	Y	Y	Y	Y
11 ***Knollenberg***	N	Y	Y	Y	N	Y	Y	Y
12 Levin	Y	Y	Y	Y	Y	Y	Y	Y
13 Ford	Y	Y	Y	?	Y	?	?	Y
14 Conyers	?	?	?	N	Y	Y	Y	N
15 Collins	Y	Y	Y	Y	Y	Y	Y	Y
16 Dingell	Y	?	?	Y	Y	Y	N	Y
MINNESOTA								
1 Penny	N	Y	Y	Y	Y	Y	Y	Y
2 Minge	N	Y	Y	N	Y	Y	Y	Y
3 ***Ramstad***	N	Y	Y	Y	Y	Y	Y	Y
4 Vento	Y	Y	Y	Y	Y	Y	Y	N

	464	465	466	467	468	469	470	471
5 Sabo	Y	Y	Y	Y	Y	Y	Y	N
6 ***Grams***	N	N	Y	Y	N	Y	Y	Y
7 Peterson	N	N	Y	Y	Y	Y	Y	Y
8 Oberstar	Y	Y	Y	Y	Y	Y	Y	N
MISSISSIPPI								
1 Whitten	Y	Y	Y	Y	?	Y	Y	Y
2 Thompson	Y	Y	Y	Y	Y	Y	Y	N
3 Montgomery	Y	N	Y	Y	Y	Y	Y	Y
4 Parker	Y	Y	Y	Y	Y	Y	Y	Y
5 Taylor	Y	Y	Y	N	Y	Y	N	Y
MISSOURI								
1 Clay	Y	Y	Y	?	Y	Y	Y	N
2 ***Talent***	Y	N	Y	Y	N	Y	N	Y
3 Gephardt	Y	Y	?	Y	Y	Y	Y	Y
4 Skelton	Y	Y	Y	Y	Y	Y	N	Y
5 Wheat	Y	Y	Y	Y	Y	Y	Y	N
6 Danner	Y	Y	Y	Y	Y	Y	Y	Y
7 ***Hancock***	N	N	Y	N	N	Y	N	Y
8 ***Emerson***	N	N	Y	Y	N	Y	N	Y
9 Volkmer	Y	Y	Y	N	Y	Y	Y	Y
MONTANA								
AL Williams	Y	N	Y	N	Y	?	?	N
NEBRASKA								
1 ***Bereuter***	N	Y	Y	Y	N	Y	Y	Y
2 Hoagland	Y	Y	Y	Y	Y	Y	Y	Y
3 ***Barrett***	N	N	Y	N	N	Y	Y	Y
NEVADA								
1 Bilbray	Y	N	Y	Y	Y	Y	N	Y
2 ***Vucanovich***	Y	N	Y	N	N	Y	N	Y
NEW HAMPSHIRE								
1 ***Zeliff***	N	Y	Y	Y	N	Y	N	Y
2 Swett	Y	Y	Y	Y	Y	Y	Y	Y
NEW JERSEY								
1 Andrews	Y	Y	Y	Y	Y	Y	Y	Y
2 Hughes	Y	Y	Y	N	Y	Y	Y	Y
3 ***Saxton***	N	Y	Y	Y	N	Y	Y	Y
4 ***Smith***	N	Y	Y	N	N	Y	Y	Y
5 ***Roukema***	N	Y	Y	Y	Y	Y	Y	Y
6 Pallone	Y	Y	Y	Y	Y	Y	Y	N
7 ***Franks***	N	Y	Y	Y	Y	Y	Y	Y
8 Klein	Y	Y	Y	Y	Y	Y	Y	Y
9 Torricelli	Y	Y	Y	Y	N	Y	N	Y
10 Payne	Y	Y	Y	Y	Y	Y	Y	N
11 ***Gallo***	Y	Y	Y	Y	N	Y	Y	Y
12 ***Zimmer***	N	Y	Y	Y	Y	Y	Y	Y
13 Menendez	Y	Y	Y	Y	N	Y	Y	Y
NEW MEXICO								
1 ***Schiff***	Y	N	Y	Y	N	Y	Y	Y
2 ***Skeen***	Y	N	Y	Y	N	Y	N	Y
3 Richardson	Y	Y	Y	Y	Y	Y	Y	Y
NEW YORK								
1 Hochbrueckner	Y	Y	Y	Y	Y	Y	Y	Y
2 ***Lazio***	N	Y	Y	Y	Y	Y	Y	Y
3 ***King***	N	Y	Y	Y	N	Y	N	Y
4 ***Levy***	N	Y	Y	Y	N	Y	N	Y
5 Ackerman	Y	Y	Y	Y	Y	Y	Y	N
6 Flake	Y	Y	Y	N	Y	Y	Y	Y
7 Manton	Y	Y	Y	Y	Y	Y	Y	Y
8 Nadler	Y	Y	Y	Y	Y	Y	Y	N
9 Schumer	Y	Y	Y	Y	Y	Y	Y	N
10 Towns	Y	Y	Y	Y	Y	Y	Y	N
11 Owens	Y	Y	Y	Y	Y	Y	Y	N
12 Velazquez	Y	Y	Y	N	Y	Y	Y	N
13 ***Molinari***	N	Y	Y	Y	N	Y	N	Y
14 Maloney	Y	Y	Y	Y	Y	Y	Y	N
15 Rangel	Y	Y	Y	Y	Y	Y	Y	N
16 Serrano	Y	?	Y	Y	Y	Y	Y	N
17 Engel	Y	Y	Y	Y	Y	Y	Y	N
18 Lowey	Y	Y	Y	Y	Y	Y	Y	Y
19 ***Fish***	Y	Y	Y	Y	N	Y	Y	Y
20 ***Gilman***	N	Y	Y	Y	N	Y	Y	N
21 McNulty	Y	Y	Y	Y	Y	Y	N	Y
22 ***Solomon***	N	Y	Y	N	N	Y	N	Y
23 ***Boehlert***	N	Y	Y	Y	Y	Y	Y	N
24 ***McHugh***	N	Y	Y	N	Y	Y	N	Y
25 ***Walsh***	N	N	Y	Y	Y	Y	N	Y
26 Hinchey	Y	Y	Y	Y	Y	Y	Y	N
27 ***Paxon***	N	Y	Y	Y	N	Y	Y	Y
28 Slaughter	Y	Y	Y	Y	Y	Y	Y	N
29 LaFalce	Y	Y	Y	Y	Y	Y	Y	Y
30 ***Quinn***	N	Y	Y	Y	Y	Y	Y	Y
31 ***Houghton***	Y	N	Y	Y	N	Y	N	Y
NORTH CAROLINA								
1 Clayton	Y	Y	Y	Y	Y	Y	Y	N
2 Valentine	Y	Y	Y	Y	Y	Y	Y	Y

	464	465	466	467	468	469	470	471
3 Lancaster	Y	Y	Y	Y	N	Y	N	Y
4 Price	Y	Y	Y	Y	Y	Y	Y	Y
5 Neal	Y	Y	Y	N	Y	Y	Y	Y
6 ***Coble***	N	Y	Y	Y	N	Y	N	Y
7 Rose	Y	Y	Y	Y	Y	Y	Y	Y
8 Hefner	Y	Y	Y	N	Y	Y	Y	Y
9 ***McMillan***	N	Y	Y	Y	N	Y	Y	Y
10 ***Ballenger***	N	N	Y	Y	N	Y	Y	Y
11 ***Taylor***	N	N	Y	Y	Y	Y	N	Y
12 Watt	Y	Y	Y	Y	Y	Y	Y	N
NORTH DAKOTA								
AL Pomeroy	Y	N	Y	Y	Y	Y	Y	Y
OHIO								
1 Mann	Y	Y	Y	Y	N	Y	N	Y
2 ***Portman***	N	Y	Y	Y	Y	Y	Y	Y
3 Hall	Y	Y	Y	Y	Y	Y	Y	Y
4 ***Oxley***	N	Y	Y	Y	N	Y	N	Y
5 ***Gillmor***	N	Y	Y	Y	Y	Y	N	Y
6 Strickland	Y	Y	Y	Y	Y	Y	Y	Y
7 ***Hobson***	Y	Y	Y	Y	Y	Y	N	Y
8 ***Boehner***	N	N	Y	Y	N	Y	N	Y
9 Kaptur	Y	Y	Y	Y	Y	Y	Y	Y
10 ***Hoke***	N	Y	Y	Y	Y	Y	Y	Y
11 Stokes	Y	Y	Y	Y	Y	Y	Y	N
12 ***Kasich***	N	Y	Y	Y	Y	Y	Y	Y
13 Brown	Y	Y	Y	Y	Y	Y	Y	N
14 Sawyer	Y	Y	Y	Y	Y	Y	Y	Y
15 ***Pryce***	N	Y	Y	Y	N	Y	Y	Y
16 ***Regula***	Y	Y	Y	Y	Y	Y	Y	Y
17 Traficant	Y	Y	Y	N	Y	Y	Y	Y
18 Applegate	Y	Y	Y	Y	Y	Y	Y	Y
19 Fingerhut	Y	Y	Y	Y	Y	Y	Y	Y
OKLAHOMA								
1 ***Inhofe***	N	N	Y	Y	N	Y	N	Y
2 Synar	Y	Y	Y	Y	Y	Y	Y	N
3 Brewster	Y	N	?	Y	Y	Y	Y	?
4 McCurdy	Y	Y	?	Y	N	Y	Y	Y
5 ***Istook***	N	Y	Y	Y	Y	Y	Y	Y
6 English	Y	Y	Y	N	Y	Y	Y	Y
OREGON								
1 Furse	Y	Y	Y	Y	Y	Y	Y	N
2 ***Smith***	N	N	Y	N	N	Y	N	N
3 Wyden	Y	Y	Y	Y	Y	Y	Y	N
4 DeFazio	Y	Y	Y	N	Y	Y	Y	N
5 Kopetski	Y	N	Y	Y	Y	Y	Y	Y
PENNSYLVANIA								
1 Foglietta	Y	Y	Y	Y	Y	Y	Y	N
2 Blackwell	Y	Y	Y	Y	Y	Y	Y	N
3 Borski	Y	Y	Y	Y	Y	Y	Y	Y
4 Klink	Y	?	Y	N	Y	Y	Y	Y
5 ***Clinger***	Y	Y	Y	Y	Y	Y	N	Y
6 Holden	Y	Y	Y	Y	Y	Y	Y	Y
7 ***Weldon***	N	Y	Y	N	N	Y	N	Y
8 ***Greenwood***	N	Y	Y	Y	Y	Y	Y	Y
9 ***Shuster***	N	Y	Y	N	N	Y	N	Y
10 ***McDade***	?	?	?	?	?	?	?	?
11 Kanjorski	Y	Y	Y	Y	Y	Y	Y	Y
12 Murtha	Y	Y	Y	Y	N	Y	N	Y
13 Margolies-Mezv.	Y	Y	Y	Y	Y	Y	Y	N
14 Coyne	Y	Y	Y	Y	Y	Y	Y	N
15 McHale	Y	Y	Y	Y	N	Y	Y	Y
16 ***Walker***	N	N	Y	N	N	Y	N	Y
17 ***Gekas***	N	N	Y	N	N	Y	N	Y
18 ***Santorum***	N	Y	Y	Y	N	Y	N	Y
19 ***Goodling***	Y	Y	Y	N	N	Y	N	Y
20 Murphy	Y	Y	Y	N	Y	Y	Y	Y
21 ***Ridge***	N	Y	Y	Y	Y	Y	N	Y
RHODE ISLAND								
1 ***Machtley***	N	Y	Y	Y	N	Y	N	Y
2 Reed	Y	Y	Y	Y	Y	Y	Y	N
SOUTH CAROLINA								
1 ***Ravenel***	N	Y	Y	Y	Y	Y	Y	Y
2 ***Spence***	N	Y	Y	N	N	Y	N	Y
3 Derrick	Y	Y	Y	Y	Y	Y	Y	Y
4 ***Inglis***	N	Y	Y	N	N	Y	N	Y
5 Spratt	Y	?	Y	Y	Y	Y	Y	Y
6 Clyburn	Y	Y	Y	Y	Y	Y	Y	Y
SOUTH DAKOTA								
AL Johnson	Y	N	Y	Y	Y	Y	Y	Y
TENNESSEE								
1 ***Quillen***	N	N	Y	N	Y	Y	N	Y
2 ***Duncan***	N	Y	Y	N	Y	Y	Y	Y
3 Lloyd	Y	?	Y	N	N	Y	Y	Y
4 Cooper	Y	Y	Y	Y	Y	Y	Y	Y
5 Clement	Y	Y	+	Y	Y	Y	Y	Y

	464	465	466	467	468	469	470	471
6 Gordon	Y	Y	Y	Y	Y	Y	Y	Y
7 ***Sundquist***	N	N	Y	Y	Y	Y	N	Y
8 Tanner	Y	Y	Y	N	Y	Y	Y	Y
9 Ford	Y	Y	Y	Y	Y	Y	Y	N
TEXAS								
1 Chapman	Y	Y	Y	Y	Y	Y	Y	Y
2 Wilson	Y	Y	?	Y	N	Y	N	Y
3 ***Johnson, Sam***	N	N	Y	N	N	Y	N	Y
4 Hall	Y	N	Y	N	Y	Y	N	Y
5 Bryant	Y	Y	Y	Y	Y	Y	Y	N
6 ***Barton***	N	N	Y	N	N	Y	N	Y
7 ***Archer***	N	Y	Y	N	N	Y	N	Y
8 ***Fields***	N	N	Y	N	N	Y	N	Y
9 Brooks	Y	Y	Y	N	Y	Y	Y	Y
10 Pickle	Y	Y	Y	Y	Y	Y	N	N
11 Edwards	Y	N	Y	N	Y	Y	N	Y
12 Geren	Y	N	Y	N	N	Y	N	Y
13 Sarpalius	Y	N	Y	N	Y	Y	N	Y
14 Laughlin	Y	Y	Y	N	N	Y	N	Y
15 de la Garza	Y	Y	Y	Y	Y	Y	N	Y
16 Coleman	Y	Y	Y	Y	Y	Y	Y	Y
17 Stenholm	Y	N	Y	Y	Y	Y	N	Y
18 Washington	Y	Y	Y	Y	Y	Y	Y	—
19 ***Combest***	N	N	Y	N	N	Y	N	Y
20 Gonzalez	Y	Y	Y	N	Y	Y	Y	N
21 ***Smith***	N	N	Y	Y	N	Y	N	Y
22 ***DeLay***	N	N	Y	N	N	Y	N	Y
23 ***Bonilla***	N	N	Y	N	N	Y	N	Y
24 Frost	Y	N	Y	Y	Y	Y	N	Y
25 Andrews	Y	Y	Y	Y	Y	Y	N	Y
26 ***Armey***	N	N	Y	N	N	Y	N	Y
27 Ortiz	Y	Y	Y	Y	Y	Y	N	Y
28 Tejeda	Y	Y	Y	Y	Y	Y	N	Y
29 Green	Y	Y	Y	Y	Y	Y	Y	Y
30 Johnson, E.B.	Y	Y	Y	Y	Y	Y	N	N
UTAH								
1 ***Hansen***	N	N	Y	N	Y	Y	N	Y
2 Shepherd	Y	Y	Y	Y	Y	Y	Y	N
3 Orton	Y	N	Y	N	Y	Y	Y	?
VERMONT								
AL *Sanders*	Y	Y	Y	N	Y	Y	Y	N
VIRGINIA								
1 ***Bateman***	Y	N	Y	Y	N	Y	N	Y
2 Pickett	N	Y	?	Y	N	Y	N	Y
3 Scott	Y	Y	Y	Y	Y	Y	Y	N
4 Sisisky	Y	Y	Y	Y	N	Y	N	Y
5 Payne	Y	Y	Y	Y	Y	Y	N	Y
6 ***Goodlatte***	N	Y	Y	Y	N	Y	N	Y
7 ***Bliley***	Y	N	Y	Y	N	Y	N	Y
8 Moran	Y	Y	Y	Y	Y	Y	Y	N
9 Boucher	Y	Y	Y	Y	Y	Y	N	Y
10 ***Wolf***	Y	N	Y	Y	Y	Y	Y	Y
11 Byrne	Y	Y	Y	Y	Y	Y	Y	N
WASHINGTON								
1 Cantwell	Y	Y	Y	Y	Y	Y	Y	N
2 Swift	Y	Y	Y	Y	Y	Y	Y	N
3 Unsoeld	Y	Y	Y	Y	Y	?	?	N
4 Inslee	Y	Y	Y	Y	Y	Y	Y	Y
5 Foley								
6 Dicks	Y	Y	Y	Y	Y	Y	N	Y
7 McDermott	Y	Y	Y	Y	Y	Y	Y	N
8 ***Dunn***	N	N	Y	Y	N	Y	Y	Y
9 Kreidler	Y	Y	Y	Y	Y	Y	Y	N
WEST VIRGINIA								
1 Mollohan	Y	Y	Y	N	N	Y	Y	Y
2 Wise	Y	Y	Y	Y	Y	Y	Y	Y
3 Rahall	Y	Y	Y	N	Y	Y	Y	Y
WISCONSIN								
1 Barca	Y	Y	Y	Y	Y	Y	Y	Y
2 ***Klug***	N	Y	Y	Y	Y	Y	Y	Y
3 ***Gunderson***	N	Y	Y	Y	Y	Y	Y	N
4 Kleczka	Y	Y	Y	Y	Y	Y	Y	Y
5 Barrett	Y	Y	Y	Y	Y	Y	Y	N
6 ***Petri***	N	Y	Y	N	Y	Y	Y	Y
7 Obey	Y	Y	Y	Y	Y	Y	Y	Y
8 ***Roth***	N	N	Y	N	Y	Y	Y	Y
9 ***Sensenbrenner***	N	Y	Y	N	Y	Y	Y	Y
WYOMING								
AL ***Thomas***	N	N	Y	N	N	Y	N	Y
DELEGATES								
de Lugo, V.I.	D	D	D	D	D	D	D	D
Faleomavaega, Am.S.	D	D	D	D	D	D	D	D
Norton, D.C.	D	D	D	D	D	D	D	D
Romero-B., P.R.	D	D	D	D	D	D	D	D
Underwood, Guam	D	D	D	D	D	D	D	D

Southern states - Ala., Ark., Fla., Ga., Ky., La., Miss., N.C., Okla., S.C., Tenn., Texas, Va.
Omitted votes are quorum calls, which CQ does not include in its vote charts.

KEY

Y	Voted for (yea).
#	Paired for.
+	Announced for.
N	Voted against (nay).
X	Paired against.
−	Announced against.
P	Voted ''present.''
C	Voted ''present'' to avoid possible conflict of interest.
?	Did not vote or otherwise make a position known.
D	Delegates ineligible to vote.

Democrats **Republicans** *Independent*

472. HR 2401. Fiscal 1994 Defense Authorization/Somalia. Separate vote at the request of Walker, R-Pa., on the amendment offered by Gephardt, D-Mo., and adopted in the Committee of the Whole to require the president to report to Congress by Oct. 15, 1993, on the U.S. deployment in Somalia and express the sense of Congress that the president should seek congressional authorization by Nov. 15, 1993, for continued deployment. Adopted 405-23: R 156-16; D 248-7 (ND 168-2, SD 80-5); I 1-0, Sept. 29, 1993. (On a separate vote, which may be demanded on an amendment adopted in the Committee of the Whole, the four delegates and the resident commissioner of Puerto Rico cannot vote. See vote 463.)

473. HR 2401. Fiscal 1994 Defense Authorization/U.S. Involvement with the United Nations. Spence, R-S.C., motion to recommit the bill to the House Armed Services Committee with instructions to report it back with an amendment to require the president to certify that it is vital and necessary to protect U.S. national interests before placing U.S. troops under the control of a foreign national on behalf of the United Nations. Motion rejected 192-238: R 172-1; D 20-236 (ND 13-158, SD 7-78); I 0-1, Sept. 29, 1993. A "nay" was a vote in support of the president's position.

474. HR 2401. Fiscal 1994 Defense Authorization/Passage. Passage of the bill to authorize about $263 billion in fiscal 1994 for the military activities of the Defense Department. Passed 268-162: R 38-136; D 230-25 (ND 146-24, SD 84-1); I 0-1, Sept. 29, 1993.

475. HR 3116. Fiscal 1994 Defense Appropriations/Rule. Adoption of the rule (H Res 263) to waive certain points of order against and provide for House floor consideration of the bill to provide about $240 billion in new budget authority for the military activities of the Defense Department in fiscal 1994. Adopted 254-176: R 0-174; D 253-2 (ND 169-1, SD 84-1); I 1-0, Sept. 29, 1993.

476. HR 2403. Fiscal 1994 Treasury-Postal Appropriations/Conference Report. Adoption of the conference report to provide $22,538,822,000 in new budget authority for the Treasury Department, the U.S. Postal Service, the Executive Office of the President and certain independent agencies in fiscal 1994. The administration requested $22,006,136,000. The bill lifts a prohibition on federal employees' health insurance coverage of abortions. Adopted (thus sent to the Senate) 207-206: R 11-158; D 195-48 (ND 133-28, SD 62-20); I 1-0, Sept. 29, 1993. A "yea" was a vote in support of the president's position.

477. HR 3116. Fiscal 1994 Defense Appropriations/D-5 Missile. Penny, D-Minn., amendment to eliminate the D-5 missile after fiscal 1993. Rejected in the Committee of the Whole 178-248: R 33-137; D 144-111 (ND 124-48, SD 20-63); I 1-0, Sept. 30, 1993. A "nay" was a vote in support of the president's position.

478. HR 3116. Fiscal 1994 Defense Appropriations/Army School of the Americas. Kennedy, D-Mass., amendment to cut the $2.9 million for the Army School of Americas. Rejected in the Committee of the Whole 174-256: R 24-150; D 149-106 (ND 130-45, SD 19-61); I 1-0, Sept. 30, 1993.

479. HR 3116. Fiscal 1994 Defense Appropriations/Rifle Practice Board. Maloney, D-N.Y., amendment to eliminate the $2.5 million for the Civilian Marksmanship Program. Rejected in the Committee of the Whole 190-242: R 37-137; D 153-104 (ND 121-53, SD 32-51); I 0-1, Sept. 30, 1993.

	472	473	474	475	476	477	478	479
ALABAMA								
1 *Callahan*	Y	Y	N	N	N	N	N	N
2 *Everett*	Y	Y	N	N	N	Y	N	N
3 Browder	Y	N	Y	Y	N	N	N	N
4 Bevill	Y	N	Y	Y	Y	N	N	N
5 Cramer	Y	N	Y	Y	N	N	N	N
6 *Bachus*	N	Y	N	N	N	N	N	N
7 Hilliard	Y	N	Y	Y	Y	Y	?	N
ALASKA								
AL *Young*	Y	Y	N	N	N	N	N	N
ARIZONA								
1 Coppersmith	Y	N	Y	Y	Y	Y	N	Y
2 Pastor	Y	N	Y	Y	Y	Y	N	Y
3 *Stump*	N	Y	N	N	N	N	N	N
4 *Kyl*	Y	Y	N	N	N	N	N	N
5 *Kolbe*	Y	Y	N	N	Y	N	N	N
6 English	Y	N	Y	Y	Y	Y	Y	Y
ARKANSAS								
1 Lambert	Y	N	Y	Y	Y	Y	Y	Y
2 Thornton	Y	N	Y	Y	Y	N	N	N
3 *Hutchinson*	Y	Y	N	N	N	N	Y	N
4 *Dickey*	Y	Y	N	N	N	N	Y	N
CALIFORNIA								
1 Hamburg	Y	N	N	Y	Y	Y	Y	Y
2 *Herger*	Y	Y	N	N	N	?	N	N
3 Fazio	Y	N	Y	Y	Y	N	N	N
4 *Doolittle*	Y	Y	N	N	N	N	N	N
5 Matsui	Y	N	Y	Y	Y	Y	Y	Y
6 Woolsey	Y	N	Y	Y	Y	Y	Y	Y
7 Miller	Y	N	N	Y	Y	Y	Y	Y
8 Pelosi	Y	N	Y	Y	Y	Y	Y	Y
9 Dellums	Y	N	Y	Y	Y	Y	Y	Y
10 *Baker*	Y	Y	N	N	N	N	N	N
11 *Pombo*	Y	Y	N	N	N	N	N	N
12 Lantos	Y	N	Y	Y	Y	N	N	Y
13 Stark	Y	N	Y	?	?	Y	Y	Y
14 Eshoo	Y	N	Y	Y	Y	Y	Y	Y
15 Mineta	Y	N	Y	Y	Y	N	Y	Y
16 Edwards	Y	N	N	?	Y	Y	Y	Y
17 Farr	Y	N	Y	Y	Y	Y	Y	Y
18 Condit	Y	Y	Y	Y	Y	N	Y	Y
19 Lehman	Y	N	Y	Y	Y	Y	Y	N
20 Dooley	Y	N	Y	Y	Y	Y	N	N
21 *Thomas*	Y	Y	N	N	N	N	N	N
22 *Huffington*	Y	Y	N	N	N	N	N	N
23 *Gallegly*	Y	Y	N	N	N	N	N	N
24 Beilenson	Y	N	Y	Y	Y	Y	N	Y
25 *McKeon*	Y	Y	N	N	N	N	N	N
26 Berman	Y	N	Y	Y	Y	Y	Y	Y
27 *Moorhead*	Y	Y	N	N	N	N	N	N
28 *Dreier*	Y	Y	N	N	N	N	N	Y
29 Waxman	Y	N	Y	Y	Y	Y	Y	Y
30 Becerra	Y	N	Y	Y	Y	Y	Y	Y
31 Martinez	Y	N	Y	?	N	Y	N	Y
32 Dixon	Y	N	Y	Y	N	Y	Y	Y
33 Roybal-Allard	Y	N	Y	Y	Y	Y	Y	Y
34 Torres	Y	N	Y	Y	Y	N	Y	Y
35 Waters	Y	N	Y	Y	Y	Y	Y	Y
36 Harman	Y	N	Y	Y	Y	N	Y	Y
37 Tucker	Y	N	Y	Y	Y	N	N	Y
38 *Horn*	Y	Y	Y	N	N	N	N	N
39 *Royce*	Y	Y	N	N	N	N	N	N
40 *Lewis*	Y	Y	N	N	N	N	N	N
41 *Kim*	Y	Y	N	N	N	N	N	N

	472	473	474	475	476	477	478	479
42 Brown	Y	N	Y	Y	Y	Y	Y	Y
43 *Calvert*	Y	Y	N	N	N	N	N	N
44 *McCandless*	Y	Y	N	N	N	N	N	N
45 *Rohrabacher*	Y	Y	N	N	N	N	N	N
46 *Dornan*	N	Y	N	N	N	N	N	N
47 *Cox*	Y	Y	N	N	N	N	N	N
48 *Packard*	Y	Y	N	N	N	N	N	N
49 Schenk	Y	N	Y	Y	Y	Y	Y	Y
50 Filner	Y	N	Y	Y	Y	Y	Y	Y
51 *Cunningham*	Y	Y	N	N	N	N	N	N
52 *Hunter*	N	Y	N	N	N	N	N	N
COLORADO								
1 Schroeder	Y	N	Y	Y	?	Y	Y	Y
2 Skaggs	Y	N	?	Y	Y	Y	N	N
3 *McInnis*	Y	Y	N	N	N	N	N	N
4 *Allard*	Y	Y	N	N	N	Y	N	N
5 *Hefley*	Y	Y	N	N	N	N	N	N
6 *Schaefer*	Y	Y	N	N	Y	N	N	N
CONNECTICUT								
1 Kennelly	Y	N	Y	Y	Y	Y	Y	Y
2 Gejdenson	Y	N	Y	Y	Y	Y	Y	Y
3 DeLauro	Y	N	Y	Y	Y	Y	Y	Y
4 *Shays*	Y	Y	N	N	Y	N	Y	Y
5 *Franks*	Y	Y	N	N	N	N	Y	N
6 *Johnson*	Y	Y	Y	N	Y	N	Y	N
DELAWARE								
AL *Castle*	Y	Y	Y	N	N	N	N	N
FLORIDA								
1 Hutto	Y	N	Y	Y	N	N	N	N
2 Peterson	Y	N	Y	Y	N	N	N	N
3 Brown	Y	N	Y	Y	Y	Y	N	Y
4 *Fowler*	Y	Y	N	N	N	N	N	N
5 Thurman	Y	N	Y	Y	Y	N	Y	N
6 *Stearns*	Y	Y	N	N	N	N	N	N
7 *Mica*	Y	N	N	N	N	N	N	N
8 *McCollum*	Y	Y	N	N	N	N	N	N
9 *Bilirakis*	Y	Y	N	N	N	N	N	N
10 *Young*	Y	Y	N	N	N	N	N	N
11 Gibbons	Y	N	Y	Y	Y	N	N	Y
12 *Canady*	Y	Y	N	N	N	N	N	N
13 *Miller*	Y	N	N	N	Y	N	Y	N
14 *Goss*	Y	Y	N	N	N	N	N	N
15 Bacchus	Y	N	Y	Y	Y	N	N	Y
16 *Lewis*	Y	Y	N	N	−	N	N	N
17 Meek	Y	N	Y	Y	Y	Y	N	Y
18 *Ros-Lehtinen*	Y	N	Y	Y	Y	N	N	Y
19 Johnston	N	N	N	Y	Y	Y	Y	Y
20 Deutsch	Y	N	Y	Y	Y	N	N	Y
21 *Diaz-Balart*	Y	Y	N	N	N	N	N	N
22 *Shaw*	Y	Y	N	N	N	N	N	N
23 Hastings	Y	N	Y	Y	Y	N	N	Y
GEORGIA								
1 *Kingston*	Y	Y	N	N	N	N	N	N
2 Bishop	Y	N	Y	Y	N	N	N	N
3 *Collins*	+	Y	N	N	N	N	N	N
4 *Linder*	Y	Y	N	N	N	N	N	N
5 Lewis	Y	N	Y	Y	Y	Y	Y	Y
6 *Gingrich*	Y	N	Y	Y	Y	N	N	N
7 Darden	Y	N	Y	Y	Y	N	N	N
8 Rowland	Y	N	Y	Y	Y	N	N	N
9 Deal	Y	N	Y	Y	N	N	N	N
10 Johnson	Y	N	Y	Y	Y	N	N	Y
11 McKinney	N	N	Y	Y	Y	Y	Y	Y
HAWAII								
1 Abercrombie	Y	N	Y	Y	Y	Y	Y	Y
2 Mink	Y	N	Y	Y	Y	Y	Y	Y
IDAHO								
1 LaRocco	Y	N	Y	Y	Y	Y	N	N
2 *Crapo*	Y	Y	N	N	N	N	N	N
ILLINOIS								
1 Rush	Y	N	N	Y	Y	Y	Y	Y
2 Reynolds	Y	N	Y	Y	Y	Y	Y	Y
3 Lipinski	Y	Y	Y	Y	N	N	N	Y
4 Gutierrez	Y	N	Y	Y	Y	Y	Y	Y
5 Rostenkowski	Y	N	Y	Y	N	N	N	Y
6 *Hyde*	Y	N	N	N	N	N	N	N
7 Collins	Y	N	N	Y	Y	Y	Y	Y
8 *Crane*	Y	N	N	N	N	N	N	N
9 Yates	Y	N	N	?	Y	Y	Y	Y
10 *Porter*	Y	Y	Y	N	+	Y	Y	Y
11 Sangmeister	Y	N	Y	Y	N	N	N	N
12 Costello	Y	N	Y	Y	N	N	Y	Y
13 *Fawell*	Y	Y	N	N	N	N	N	Y
14 *Hastert*	Y	Y	N	N	N	N	N	N
15 *Ewing*	Y	Y	N	N	N	N	N	N
16 *Manzullo*	Y	Y	Y	N	N	N	N	N
17 Evans	Y	N	Y	Y	Y	Y	Y	Y

ND Northern Democrats   **SD** Southern Democrats

	472	473	474	475	476	477	478	479
18 ***Michel***	Y	Y	N	N	N	N	N	N
19 Poshard	Y	Y	Y	Y	N	Y	Y	Y
20 Durbin	Y	N	Y	Y	Y	Y	Y	Y
INDIANA								
1 Visclosky	Y	N	Y	Y	Y	N	N	Y
2 Sharp	Y	N	Y	Y	Y	Y	N	N
3 Roemer	Y	N	Y	Y	N	Y	Y	Y
4 Long	Y	N	Y	Y	Y	Y	Y	Y
5 ***Buyer***	Y	Y	Y	N	N	N	N	N
6 ***Burton***	Y	Y	N	N	N	N	N	N
7 ***Myers***	Y	Y	N	N	N	N	N	N
8 McCloskey	Y	N	Y	Y	Y	Y	Y	N
9 Hamilton	Y	N	Y	Y	Y	N	N	N
10 Jacobs	Y	Y	Y	N	N	Y	Y	N
IOWA								
1 ***Leach***	Y	N	Y	N	Y	Y	N	Y
2 ***Nussle***	Y	Y	N	N	N	Y	Y	Y
3 ***Lightfoot***	Y	Y	N	N	Y	N	N	N
4 Smith	Y	N	Y	Y	Y	N	N	N
5 ***Grandy***	Y	Y	Y	N	N	Y	N	Y
KANSAS								
1 ***Roberts***	N	Y	N	N	N	N	N	N
2 Slattery	Y	Y	Y	Y	N	N	Y	Y
3 ***Meyers***	Y	Y	N	N	Y	N	Y	N
4 Glickman	Y	N	Y	Y	Y	N	Y	Y
KENTUCKY								
1 Barlow	Y	N	Y	Y	N	Y	Y	N
2 Natcher	Y	N	Y	Y	Y	N	N	N
3 Mazzoli	Y	Y	Y	Y	N	N	N	Y
4 ***Bunning***	Y	Y	N	N	N	N	N	Y
5 ***Rogers***	Y	Y	N	N	N	N	N	N
6 Baesler	Y	N	Y	Y	Y	N	Y	N
LOUISIANA								
1 ***Livingston***	Y	Y	N	N	N	N	N	N
2 Jefferson	Y	N	Y	Y	Y	Y	?	Y
3 Tauzin	Y	Y	Y	Y	N	N	N	N
4 Fields	Y	N	Y	Y	Y	Y	Y	Y
5 ***McCrery***	Y	Y	N	N	N	N	N	N
6 ***Baker***	Y	Y	N	N	N	N	N	N
7 Hayes	Y	N	Y	Y	N	N	N	N
MAINE								
1 Andrews	Y	N	Y	Y	Y	Y	Y	Y
2 ***Snowe***	Y	Y	Y	N	N	Y	N	N
MARYLAND								
1 ***Gilchrest***	Y	Y	Y	N	N	Y	Y	Y
2 ***Bentley***	Y	Y	N	N	N	N	N	N
3 Cardin	Y	N	Y	Y	Y	Y	Y	Y
4 Wynn	Y	N	Y	Y	Y	Y	Y	Y
5 Hoyer	Y	N	Y	Y	Y	N	N	N
6 ***Bartlett***	Y	Y	N	N	N	N	N	N
7 Mfume	Y	N	Y	Y	Y	Y	Y	Y
8 ***Morella***	Y	Y	Y	N	Y	Y	Y	Y
MASSACHUSETTS								
1 Olver	Y	N	Y	Y	Y	N	Y	Y
2 Neal	Y	N	Y	Y	Y	Y	Y	Y
3 ***Blute***	Y	Y	Y	N	N	N	Y	Y
4 Frank	Y	N	Y	Y	?	Y	Y	Y
5 Meehan	Y	N	Y	Y	Y	Y	Y	Y
6 ***Torkildsen***	Y	Y	Y	N	N	N	Y	Y
7 Markey	Y	N	Y	Y	Y	?	Y	Y
8 Kennedy	Y	N	Y	Y	Y	Y	Y	Y
9 Moakley	Y	N	Y	Y	Y	N	Y	Y
10 Studds	Y	N	N	Y	Y	Y	Y	Y
MICHIGAN								
1 Stupak	Y	N	Y	Y	N	Y	Y	N
2 ***Hoekstra***	Y	Y	N	N	N	Y	N	Y
3 Vacancy								
4 ***Camp***	Y	Y	Y	N	N	N	N	N
5 Barcia	Y	Y	Y	Y	N	Y	Y	N
6 ***Upton***	Y	Y	N	N	N	Y	Y	N
7 ***Smith***	?	Y	N	N	N	?	N	N
8 Carr	Y	N	Y	Y	Y	N	N	N
9 Kildee	Y	Y	Y	Y	N	Y	Y	Y
10 Bonior	Y	N	Y	Y	Y	Y	Y	Y
11 ***Knollenberg***	Y	Y	N	N	N	N	N	Y
12 Levin	Y	N	Y	Y	Y	Y	N	Y
13 Ford	Y	N	Y	Y	Y	?	?	Y
14 Conyers	Y	N	N	Y	Y	Y	Y	Y
15 Collins	Y	N	Y	Y	Y	Y	Y	N
16 Dingell	Y	N	Y	Y	Y	Y	N	N
MINNESOTA								
1 Penny	Y	N	Y	Y	N	Y	Y	Y
2 Minge	Y	N	N	Y	N	Y	Y	Y
3 ***Ramstad***	Y	Y	N	N	N	Y	Y	Y
4 Vento	Y	N	N	Y	Y	Y	Y	Y

	472	473	474	475	476	477	478	479
5 Sabo	Y	N	Y	Y	Y	Y	Y	Y
6 ***Grams***	Y	Y	N	N	—	N	N	Y
7 Peterson	Y	N	N	Y	N	Y	Y	N
8 Oberstar	Y	N	Y	Y	N	Y	Y	N
MISSISSIPPI								
1 Whitten	Y	N	Y	N	Y	N	N	N
2 Thompson	Y	N	Y	Y	Y	Y	N	Y
3 Montgomery	Y	N	Y	Y	N	N	N	N
4 Parker	N	Y	Y	Y	N	N	N	N
5 Taylor	N	Y	Y	Y	N	N	N	N
MISSOURI								
1 Clay	Y	N	Y	Y	?	Y	Y	Y
2 ***Talent***	Y	Y	Y	N	N	N	N	Y
3 Gephardt	Y	N	Y	Y	Y	Y	Y	N
4 Skelton	Y	N	Y	Y	N	N	N	N
5 Wheat	Y	N	Y	Y	Y	Y	Y	Y
6 Danner	Y	N	Y	Y	N	Y	Y	N
7 ***Hancock***	N	Y	N	N	N	N	N	N
8 ***Emerson***	Y	Y	N	N	N	N	N	N
9 Volkmer	Y	N	Y	Y	N	Y	Y	N
MONTANA								
AL Williams	Y	N	Y	Y	Y	Y	Y	N
NEBRASKA								
1 ***Bereuter***	Y	Y	N	N	N	N	N	N
2 Hoagland	Y	N	Y	Y	Y	N	N	Y
3 ***Barrett***	Y	Y	N	N	N	N	N	Y
NEVADA								
1 Bilbray	Y	N	Y	Y	Y	Y	N	N
2 ***Vucanovich***	Y	Y	Y	N	N	N	N	N
NEW HAMPSHIRE								
1 ***Zeliff***	Y	Y	N	N	N	N	N	N
2 Swett	Y	N	Y	Y	Y	Y	Y	Y
NEW JERSEY								
1 Andrews	Y	Y	Y	Y	Y	N	N	N
2 Hughes	Y	N	Y	Y	Y	Y	N	Y
3 ***Saxton***	Y	Y	Y	N	N	N	N	N
4 ***Smith***	Y	Y	Y	N	N	N	N	N
5 ***Roukema***	Y	Y	N	N	N	Y	Y	Y
6 Pallone	Y	N	Y	Y	N	Y	Y	Y
7 ***Franks***	Y	Y	N	N	N	N	Y	Y
8 Klein	Y	N	Y	Y	Y	N	N	Y
9 Torricelli	?	?	?	?	?	N	N	Y
10 Payne	N	N	Y	Y	Y	Y	Y	Y
11 ***Gallo***	Y	Y	N	N	Y	N	N	N
12 ***Zimmer***	Y	Y	N	N	N	Y	N	Y
13 Menendez	Y	N	Y	Y	Y	N	N	Y
NEW MEXICO								
1 ***Schiff***	Y	Y	N	N	N	N	Y	N
2 ***Skeen***	Y	Y	N	N	N	N	N	N
3 Richardson	Y	N	Y	Y	Y	N	N	N
NEW YORK								
1 Hochbrueckner	Y	N	Y	Y	Y	Y	Y	N
2 ***Lazio***	Y	Y	Y	N	N	N	N	N
3 ***King***	Y	Y	N	N	N	N	N	N
4 ***Levy***	Y	Y	N	N	N	N	N	N
5 Ackerman	Y	N	Y	Y	Y	N	Y	Y
6 Flake	Y	N	Y	Y	Y	Y	N	Y
7 Manton	Y	N	Y	Y	Y	N	N	Y
8 Nadler	Y	N	N	Y	Y	Y	Y	Y
9 Schumer	Y	N	Y	Y	Y	N	Y	Y
10 Towns	Y	N	Y	Y	Y	Y	Y	Y
11 Owens	Y	N	N	Y	Y	Y	Y	Y
12 Velazquez	Y	N	Y	Y	Y	Y	Y	Y
13 ***Molinari***	Y	Y	N	N	N	N	N	N
14 Maloney	Y	N	N	Y	Y	Y	Y	Y
15 Rangel	Y	N	N	Y	Y	?	Y	Y
16 Serrano	Y	N	Y	Y	Y	Y	Y	#
17 Engel	Y	N	Y	Y	Y	Y	Y	Y
18 Lowey	Y	N	Y	Y	Y	Y	N	Y
19 ***Fish***	Y	Y	N	N	N	N	N	N
20 ***Gilman***	Y	Y	N	N	Y	N	N	N
21 McNulty	Y	Y	Y	Y	Y	N	N	N
22 ***Solomon***	Y	Y	N	N	N	N	N	N
23 ***Boehlert***	Y	Y	N	N	N	N	N	N
24 ***McHugh***	Y	Y	N	N	N	N	N	N
25 ***Walsh***	Y	Y	N	N	N	N	N	N
26 Hinchey	Y	N	Y	Y	Y	Y	Y	N
27 ***Paxon***	N	Y	N	N	N	N	N	N
28 Slaughter	Y	N	Y	Y	Y	Y	Y	Y
29 LaFalce	Y	N	Y	?	N	Y	N	Y
30 ***Quinn***	Y	Y	Y	N	N	N	N	Y
31 ***Houghton***	Y	Y	N	N	Y	N	N	N
NORTH CAROLINA								
1 Clayton	Y	N	Y	Y	Y	Y	Y	Y
2 Valentine	Y	N	Y	Y	Y	N	N	Y

	472	473	474	475	476	477	478	479
3 Lancaster	Y	N	Y	Y	Y	N	N	N
4 Price	Y	N	Y	Y	Y	N	N	Y
5 Neal	Y	Y	Y	Y	Y	?	?	N
6 ***Coble***	N	Y	N	N	N	Y	N	Y
7 Rose	Y	N	Y	Y	Y	N	N	N
8 Hefner	Y	N	Y	Y	Y	N	N	Y
9 ***McMillan***	Y	Y	Y	N	N	N	N	N
10 ***Ballenger***	Y	Y	Y	N	N	N	N	N
11 ***Taylor***	Y	Y	N	N	N	Y	Y	N
12 Watt	Y	N	Y	Y	Y	Y	Y	Y
NORTH DAKOTA								
AL Pomeroy	Y	N	Y	Y	Y	Y	Y	N
OHIO								
1 Mann	Y	N	Y	Y	Y	N	Y	Y
2 ***Portman***	Y	Y	Y	N	N	N	N	Y
3 Hall	Y	N	Y	Y	?	Y	N	N
4 ***Oxley***	Y	Y	Y	N	—	N	N	N
5 ***Gillmor***	Y	Y	N	N	N	N	N	N
6 Strickland	Y	N	Y	Y	Y	Y	Y	N
7 ***Hobson***	Y	Y	N	N	N	Y	N	N
8 ***Boehner***	Y	Y	N	N	N	N	N	N
9 Kaptur	Y	Y	Y	Y	N	N	N	N
10 ***Hoke***	Y	Y	N	N	N	N	Y	N
11 Stokes	Y	N	Y	Y	Y	Y	Y	Y
12 ***Kasich***	Y	Y	Y	N	N	N	N	N
13 Brown	Y	N	Y	Y	Y	Y	Y	N
14 Sawyer	Y	N	Y	Y	Y	Y	Y	N
15 ***Pryce***	Y	Y	Y	N	N	N	N	N
16 ***Regula***	Y	Y	N	N	N	N	N	N
17 Traficant	Y	Y	Y	Y	Y	N	N	N
18 Applegate	Y	Y	N	Y	N	Y	Y	N
19 Fingerhut	Y	Y	Y	Y	Y	Y	N	Y
OKLAHOMA								
1 ***Inhofe***	N	Y	N	N	N	N	N	N
2 Synar	Y	N	Y	Y	Y	Y	Y	Y
3 Brewster	Y	N	Y	Y	?	N	N	N
4 McCurdy	Y	N	Y	Y	Y	N	N	Y
5 ***Istook***	Y	Y	Y	N	N	N	N	N
6 English	Y	N	Y	Y	Y	N	N	N
OREGON								
1 Furse	?	N	N	Y	Y	Y	Y	Y
2 ***Smith***	Y	Y	N	N	?	N	N	N
3 Wyden	Y	N	N	Y	Y	Y	Y	N
4 DeFazio	Y	N	N	Y	Y	Y	Y	N
5 Kopetski	Y	N	Y	Y	Y	Y	Y	N
PENNSYLVANIA								
1 Foglietta	Y	N	Y	Y	Y	Y	Y	Y
2 Blackwell	Y	N	Y	Y	Y	Y	Y	Y
3 Borski	Y	N	Y	Y	Y	N	Y	Y
4 Klink	Y	N	Y	Y	N	Y	Y	Y
5 ***Clinger***	Y	Y	Y	N	N	N	N	N
6 Holden	Y	N	Y	Y	N	Y	Y	N
7 ***Weldon***	N	Y	Y	N	N	N	N	N
8 ***Greenwood***	Y	Y	Y	N	N	N	Y	Y
9 ***Shuster***	Y	Y	N	N	N	N	N	N
10 ***McDade***	?	?	?	?	?	?	?	?
11 Kanjorski	Y	N	Y	Y	N	N	Y	N
12 Murtha	Y	N	Y	Y	?	N	N	N
13 Margolies-Mezv.	Y	N	N	Y	Y	Y	Y	Y
14 Coyne	Y	N	Y	Y	Y	Y	Y	Y
15 McHale	Y	N	Y	Y	Y	Y	Y	Y
16 ***Walker***	N	Y	N	N	N	N	N	N
17 ***Gekas***	Y	Y	N	N	N	N	N	N
18 ***Santorum***	Y	Y	N	N	N	Y	N	N
19 ***Goodling***	Y	Y	N	N	N	—	N	N
20 Murphy	Y	N	N	Y	N	N	Y	N
21 ***Ridge***	N	Y	N	N	N	?	N	Y
RHODE ISLAND								
1 ***Machtley***	Y	Y	Y	N	N	N	N	N
2 Reed	Y	N	Y	Y	Y	Y	N	Y
SOUTH CAROLINA								
1 ***Ravenel***	Y	Y	Y	N	N	N	N	N
2 ***Spence***	Y	Y	N	N	N	N	N	N
3 Derrick	Y	N	Y	Y	Y	N	Y	Y
4 ***Inglis***	Y	Y	N	N	N	N	N	N
5 Spratt	Y	N	Y	Y	Y	N	N	N
6 Clyburn	Y	N	Y	Y	Y	Y	N	N
SOUTH DAKOTA								
AL Johnson	Y	N	Y	Y	Y	N	N	Y
TENNESSEE								
1 ***Quillen***	Y	Y	N	N	N	N	N	N
2 ***Duncan***	Y	Y	N	N	N	Y	Y	Y
3 Lloyd	Y	N	Y	Y	N	N	N	N
4 Cooper	Y	N	Y	Y	Y	N	Y	N
5 Clement	Y	N	Y	Y	Y	N	N	Y

	472	473	474	475	476	477	478	479
6 Gordon	Y	N	Y	Y	Y	Y	Y	N
7 ***Sundquist***	Y	Y	Y	N	N	N	N	N
8 Tanner	Y	Y	Y	Y	Y	N	N	N
9 Ford	Y	N	Y	Y	Y	Y	Y	Y
TEXAS								
1 Chapman	Y	N	Y	Y	Y	N	N	N
2 Wilson	Y	N	Y	Y	Y	N	?	X
3 ***Johnson, Sam***	Y	Y	N	N	N	N	N	N
4 Hall	Y	Y	Y	Y	N	N	N	N
5 Bryant	Y	N	Y	Y	?	Y	Y	Y
6 ***Barton***	N	Y	N	N	N	N	N	N
7 ***Archer***	Y	Y	N	N	N	N	N	N
8 ***Fields***	N	Y	N	N	N	N	N	N
9 Brooks	Y	N	Y	Y	Y	N	N	N
10 Pickle	Y	N	Y	Y	Y	N	N	Y
11 Edwards	Y	N	Y	Y	N	N	N	N
12 Geren	N	N	Y	Y	N	N	N	N
13 Sarpalius	Y	N	Y	Y	N	N	N	N
14 Laughlin	Y	N	Y	Y	N	N	N	N
15 de la Garza	Y	N	Y	Y	N	N	N	N
16 Coleman	Y	N	Y	Y	Y	N	N	N
17 Stenholm	Y	N	Y	Y	N	N	N	N
18 Washington	Y	N	Y	Y	Y	?	?	?
19 ***Combest***	N	Y	N	N	N	N	N	N
20 Gonzalez	Y	N	Y	Y	Y	N	Y	Y
21 ***Smith***	Y	Y	N	N	N	N	N	N
22 ***DeLay***	Y	Y	N	N	N	N	N	N
23 ***Bonilla***	Y	Y	Y	N	N	N	N	N
24 Frost	Y	N	Y	Y	Y	N	N	N
25 Andrews	Y	N	Y	Y	Y	N	N	N
26 ***Armey***	Y	Y	N	N	N	N	N	N
27 Ortiz	Y	N	Y	Y	N	N	N	N
28 Tejeda	Y	N	Y	Y	N	N	N	N
29 Green	Y	N	Y	Y	Y	Y	N	N
30 Johnson, E.B.	Y	N	Y	Y	Y	N	N	N
UTAH								
1 ***Hansen***	Y	Y	N	N	N	N	N	N
2 Shepherd	Y	N	Y	Y	Y	N	Y	Y
3 Orton	Y	N	Y	Y	N	N	N	N
VERMONT								
AL *Sanders*	Y	N	N	Y	Y	Y	Y	N
VIRGINIA								
1 ***Bateman***	Y	?	Y	N	Y	N	N	N
2 Pickett	Y	N	Y	Y	Y	N	N	N
3 Scott	Y	N	Y	Y	Y	N	N	Y
4 Sisisky	Y	N	Y	Y	Y	N	N	N
5 Payne	Y	N	Y	Y	Y	N	N	N
6 ***Goodlatte***	Y	Y	N	N	N	Y	N	N
7 ***Bliley***	Y	Y	N	N	N	N	N	N
8 Moran	Y	N	Y	Y	Y	N	Y	Y
9 Boucher	Y	N	Y	Y	?	N	N	N
10 ***Wolf***	Y	Y	N	N	N	N	N	N
11 Byrne	Y	N	Y	Y	Y	Y	Y	Y
WASHINGTON								
1 Cantwell	Y	N	Y	Y	Y	N	Y	Y
2 Swift	Y	N	Y	Y	Y	N	Y	Y
3 Unsoeld	Y	N	Y	Y	Y	Y	Y	N
4 Inslee	Y	N	Y	Y	Y	Y	Y	Y
5 Foley								
6 Dicks	Y	N	Y	Y	?	N	N	N
7 McDermott	Y	N	Y	Y	Y	Y	Y	Y
8 ***Dunn***	Y	Y	N	N	N	N	N	Y
9 Kreidler	Y	N	Y	Y	Y	Y	Y	Y
WEST VIRGINIA								
1 Mollohan	Y	N	Y	Y	N	N	N	N
2 Wise	Y	N	Y	Y	Y	N	N	N
3 Rahall	Y	N	N	Y	N	Y	Y	N
WISCONSIN								
1 Barca	Y	N	Y	Y	Y	Y	Y	N
2 ***Klug***	Y	Y	N	N	N	Y	Y	Y
3 ***Gunderson***	Y	Y	N	N	N	Y	N	Y
4 Kleczka	Y	N	Y	Y	Y	N	Y	Y
5 Barrett	Y	N	Y	Y	Y	Y	Y	Y
6 ***Petri***	Y	Y	N	N	N	Y	N	Y
7 Obey	N	N	Y	Y	Y	Y	Y	N
8 ***Roth***	Y	Y	N	N	N	Y	N	N
9 ***Sensenbrenner***	N	Y	N	N	N	Y	Y	Y
WYOMING								
AL ***Thomas***	Y	Y	N	N	N	Y	N	N
DELEGATES								
de Lugo, V.I.	D	D	D	D	D	Y	Y	Y
Faleomavaega, Am.S.	D	D	D	D	D	Y	Y	Y
Norton, D.C.	D	D	D	D	D	Y	Y	Y
Romero-B., P.R.	D	D	D	D	D	Y	Y	?
Underwood, Guam	D	D	D	D	D	?	?	?

Southern states - Ala., Ark., Fla., Ga., Ky., La., Miss., N.C., Okla., S.C., Tenn., Texas, Va.
Omitted votes are quorum calls, which CQ does not include in its vote charts.

480. HR 3116. Fiscal 1994 Defense Appropriations/Passage. Passage of the bill to provide $239.6 billion in fiscal 1994 for the Defense Department. The Clinton administration requested $241,081,531,000. Passed 325-102: R 95-77; D 230-24 (ND 149-22, SD 81-2); I 0-1, Sept. 30, 1993.

481. HR 2493. Fiscal 1994 Agriculture Appropriations/Honey Subsidy. Durbin, D-Ill., motion to concur in the Senate amendment to the House amendment to the Senate amendment, to bar fiscal 1994 spending on the honey subsidy program. Motion agreed to 430-0: R 174-0; D 255-0 (ND 172-0, SD 83-0); I 1-0, Sept. 30, 1993. Previously, the House adopted by voice vote an amendment ending federal wool and mohair subsidies in the 1994 marketing year but allowing them for the remainder of the 1993 marketing year, returning the bill to the Senate.

482. HR 2491. Fiscal 1994 VA-HUD Appropriations/Conference Rule. Adoption of the rule (H Res 268) to provide for House floor consideration of the conference report to provide $87,690,272,032 in new budget authority for the departments of Veterans Affairs and Housing and Urban Development, and for related agencies. The administration requested $89,268,383,032. The conference report includes $124.9 million for the Advanced Solid Rocket Motor (ASRM) program, plus $32.6 million for construction of the ASRM production facility at Yellow Creek, Miss. Rejected 123-305: R 9-165; D 114-139 (ND 65-104, SD 49-35); I 0-1, Oct. 6, 1993.

483. HR 1845. National Biological Survey/Rule. Adoption of the rule (H Res 262) to provide for House floor consideration of the bill to authorize $180 million in fiscal 1994 and such sums as necessary in fiscal 1995-97 to establish a National Biological Survey to facilitate research and monitoring of America's biological and natural resources on an ecosystem basis. Adopted 238-188: R 11-164; D 226-24 (ND 161-6, SD 65-18); I 1-0, Oct. 6, 1993.

484. HR 1845. National Biological Survey/Volunteers. Tauzin, D-La., amendment to strike the provisions that allow the secretary of the Interior to accept the services of volunteers. Adopted in the Committee of the Whole 217-212: R 151-22; D 66-189 (ND 24-149, SD 42-40); I 0-1, Oct. 6, 1993.

485. HR 1845. National Biological Survey/Non-Federal Property. Taylor, R-N.C., amendment to require the National Biological Survey to obtain written consent before going on non-federal lands and to require reports describing the survey's activities on non-federal lands. Adopted in the Committee of the Whole 309-115: R 171-3; D 138-111 (ND 72-95, SD 66-16); I 0-1, Oct. 6, 1993.

486. HR 2518. Fiscal 1994 Labor, HHS, Education Appropriations/Conference Report. Adoption of the conference report to provide $256,328,263,000 in new budget authority, $216.8 billion in fiscal 1994, $39.2 billion in fiscal 1995 and $312 million in fiscal 1996 for the departments of Labor, Health and Human Services, and Education, and related agencies. The administration requested $260,471,113,000. Adopted (thus sent to the Senate) 311-115: R 71-103; D 239-12 (ND 160-9, SD 79-3); I 1-0, Oct. 7, 1993.

487. HR 2739. Airport Improvements/Child Restraints. Oberstar, D-Minn., substitute amendment to the Lightfoot, R-Iowa, amendment, to require airlines to provide child safety restraints upon request. The Lightfoot amendment would require the use of child safety restraints on airplanes. Adopted in the Committee of the Whole 270-155: R 105-68; D 165-86 (ND 101-68, SD 64-18); I 0-1, Oct. 7, 1993.

KEY

- **Y** Voted for (yea).
- **#** Paired for.
- **+** Announced for.
- **N** Voted against (nay).
- **X** Paired against.
- **−** Announced against.
- **P** Voted "present."
- **C** Voted "present" to avoid possible conflict of interest.
- **?** Did not vote or otherwise make a position known.
- **D** Delegates ineligible to vote.

Democrats   **Republicans**   *Independent*

	480	481	482	483	484	485	486	487
ALABAMA								
1 Callahan	N	Y	Y	N	Y	Y	Y	N
2 Everett	N	Y	N	N	Y	Y	N	N
3 Browder	Y	Y	Y	N	Y	Y	Y	Y
4 Bevill	Y	Y	Y	N	Y	Y	Y	Y
5 Cramer	Y	Y	Y	N	Y	Y	Y	Y
6 Bachus	Y	Y	N	N	Y	Y	N	Y
7 Hilliard	Y	Y	Y	Y	Y	Y	Y	Y
ALASKA								
AL Young	Y	Y	N	N	Y	Y	Y	Y
ARIZONA								
1 Coppersmith	Y	Y	N	Y	N	N	Y	Y
2 Pastor	Y	Y	Y	N	Y	N	N	Y
3 Stump	N	Y	N	N	N	Y	N	N
4 Kyl	N	Y	N	N	Y	Y	Y	Y
5 Kolbe	Y	Y	N	N	Y	N	N	Y
6 English	Y	Y	N	Y	N	N	Y	N
ARKANSAS								
1 Lambert	Y	Y	N	Y	Y	Y	Y	N
2 Thornton	Y	Y	Y	Y	Y	Y	Y	Y
3 Hutchinson	Y	Y	N	N	Y	Y	N	N
4 Dickey	Y	Y	N	Y	Y	Y	N	Y
CALIFORNIA								
1 Hamburg	N	Y	N	N	N	N	Y	Y
2 Herger	N	Y	N	N	Y	Y	N	N
3 Fazio	Y	Y	Y	Y	Y	Y	Y	Y
4 Doolittle	N	Y	N	N	Y	Y	N	Y
5 Matsui	Y	Y	Y	N	N	Y	N	Y
6 Woolsey	Y	Y	N	Y	N	N	Y	N
7 Miller	Y	Y	N	Y	N	N	Y	N
8 Pelosi	Y	Y	N	Y	N	N	Y	N
9 Dellums	Y	Y	N	N	Y	N	Y	?
10 Baker	N	Y	N	N	Y	Y	N	N
11 Pombo	N	Y	N	N	Y	Y	N	N
12 Lantos	Y	Y	N	Y	N	Y	Y	Y
13 Stark	N	Y	N	N	N	N	Y	N
14 Eshoo	Y	Y	N	N	N	N	Y	N
15 Mineta	Y	Y	Y	Y	N	N	Y	Y
16 Edwards	N	Y	Y	N	N	Y	N	Y
17 Farr	Y	Y	Y	Y	N	N	Y	Y
18 Condit	Y	Y	Y	Y	Y	Y	N	N
19 Lehman	Y	Y	N	N	Y	N	Y	N
20 Dooley	Y	Y	N	N	Y	Y	Y	N
21 Thomas	?	Y	N	N	Y	Y	N	N
22 Huffington	N	Y	N	N	Y	N	Y	Y
23 Gallegly	Y	Y	N	N	Y	Y	N	N
24 Beilenson	N	Y	Y	N	N	Y	Y	Y
25 McKeon	Y	Y	N	N	Y	Y	N	Y
26 Berman	Y	Y	Y	Y	N	N	Y	?
27 Moorhead	Y	Y	N	N	Y	Y	N	Y
28 Dreier	N	Y	N	N	Y	N	Y	N
29 Waxman	Y	Y	Y	N	Y	N	Y	Y
30 Becerra	Y	Y	N	Y	N	N	Y	N
31 Martinez	Y	Y	Y	Y	N	Y	N	Y
32 Dixon	Y	Y	Y	Y	N	N	Y	Y
33 Roybal-Allard	Y	Y	N	Y	N	N	N	Y
34 Torres	Y	Y	Y	Y	N	N	Y	Y
35 Waters	Y	N	N	Y	N	N	Y	N
36 Harman	Y	Y	N	N	Y	N	Y	Y
37 Tucker	Y	Y	N	Y	N	N	Y	Y
38 Horn	Y	Y	N	N	Y	Y	Y	Y
39 Royce	N	Y	N	N	Y	N	Y	Y
40 Lewis	Y	Y	N	N	Y	Y	N	?
41 Kim	N	Y	N	N	Y	Y	Y	Y
42 Brown	Y	Y	Y	N	N	Y	N	N
43 Calvert	N	Y	N	N	Y	Y	N	Y
44 McCandless	N	Y	N	N	Y	Y	N	Y
45 Rohrabacher	N	Y	N	N	Y	Y	N	Y
46 Dornan	N	Y	N	N	Y	Y	N	N
47 Cox	N	Y	N	N	Y	Y	N	N
48 Packard	Y	Y	N	N	Y	Y	N	Y
49 Schenk	Y	Y	N	Y	N	Y	N	Y
50 Filner	Y	Y	Y	N	N	N	N	N
51 Cunningham	Y	Y	N	N	Y	Y	N	Y
52 Hunter	N	Y	N	N	?	Y	N	N
COLORADO								
1 Schroeder	Y	Y	N	Y	N	Y	N	N
2 Skaggs	Y	Y	Y	Y	N	N	Y	Y
3 McInnis	N	Y	N	N	Y	Y	N	Y
4 Allard	N	Y	N	N	Y	Y	N	Y
5 Hefley	N	Y	N	N	Y	Y	N	N
6 Schaefer	N	Y	N	N	Y	Y	N	Y
CONNECTICUT								
1 Kennelly	Y	Y	Y	Y	N	N	Y	N
2 Gejdenson	Y	Y	Y	Y	N	N	Y	Y
3 DeLauro	Y	Y	Y	Y	N	N	Y	N
4 Shays	N	Y	N	Y	N	Y	Y	Y
5 Franks	Y	Y	N	Y	Y	Y	Y	Y
6 Johnson	Y	Y	N	Y	N	Y	N	Y
DELAWARE								
AL Castle	Y	Y	N	N	N	Y	N	Y
FLORIDA								
1 Hutto	Y	Y	N	Y	Y	Y	Y	Y
2 Peterson	Y	Y	Y	N	Y	Y	Y	Y
3 Brown	Y	Y	N	Y	N	Y	Y	Y
4 Fowler	Y	Y	N	N	Y	Y	Y	Y
5 Thurman	Y	Y	N	N	Y	Y	+	Y
6 Stearns	N	Y	N	N	Y	Y	N	Y
7 Mica	N	Y	N	N	Y	Y	N	Y
8 McCollum	N	Y	N	N	Y	Y	N	N
9 Bilirakis	Y	Y	N	N	Y	Y	N	Y
10 Young	Y	Y	N	N	Y	Y	Y	Y
11 Gibbons	Y	Y	Y	N	N	Y	Y	Y
12 Canady	N	Y	N	N	Y	Y	N	Y
13 Miller	N	Y	N	N	Y	Y	N	Y
14 Goss	N	Y	N	N	Y	Y	N	Y
15 Bacchus	Y	Y	Y	Y	N	Y	N	Y
16 Lewis	N	Y	N	N	Y	Y	N	Y
17 Meek	Y	Y	Y	N	Y	N	Y	Y
18 Ros-Lehtinen	N	Y	N	Y	N	Y	N	Y
19 Johnston	N	Y	Y	Y	N	N	Y	N
20 Deutsch	Y	Y	N	N	Y	N	Y	N
21 Diaz-Balart	N	Y	N	N	N	Y	N	Y
22 Shaw	Y	Y	N	N	Y	Y	N	Y
23 Hastings	Y	Y	?	?	?	N	Y	N
GEORGIA								
1 Kingston	Y	Y	N	N	Y	Y	Y	N
2 Bishop	Y	Y	Y	Y	Y	Y	Y	Y
3 Collins	Y	Y	N	N	Y	Y	N	N
4 Linder	N	Y	N	N	Y	Y	N	N
5 Lewis	Y	Y	Y	N	N	Y	N	N
6 Gingrich	Y	Y	N	N	Y	Y	?	N
7 Darden	Y	Y	Y	Y	N	Y	Y	N
8 Rowland	Y	Y	Y	Y	Y	Y	Y	Y
9 Deal	Y	Y	N	Y	N	Y	Y	N
10 Johnson	Y	Y	N	Y	N	Y	N	N
11 McKinney	Y	Y	N	Y	N	Y	Y	N
HAWAII								
1 Abercrombie	Y	Y	N	N	N	Y	N	N
2 Mink	Y	Y	N	Y	N	N	Y	N
IDAHO								
1 LaRocco	Y	Y	N	Y	N	N	Y	Y
2 Crapo	N	Y	N	N	Y	Y	N	N
ILLINOIS								
1 Rush	N	Y	N	N	N	N	Y	N
2 Reynolds	Y	Y	N	Y	N	N	Y	N
3 Lipinski	Y	Y	N	Y	Y	Y	Y	Y
4 Gutierrez	Y	Y	N	N	Y	N	Y	N
5 Rostenkowski	Y	Y	Y	N	N	Y	N	N
6 Hyde	N	Y	N	Y	N	Y	N	Y
7 Collins	N	Y	N	N	N	Y	N	Y
8 Crane	N	Y	N	N	Y	N	Y	N
9 Yates	N	Y	Y	Y	N	?	Y	Y
10 Porter	Y	Y	N	Y	N	Y	Y	N
11 Sangmeister	Y	Y	N	Y	N	Y	Y	Y
12 Costello	Y	Y	N	Y	Y	Y	Y	Y
13 Fawell	—	Y	N	N	Y	Y	N	Y
14 Hastert	N	Y	N	N	Y	Y	N	Y
15 Ewing	N	Y	N	N	Y	Y	N	N
16 Manzullo	Y	Y	N	N	Y	Y	N	Y
17 Evans	Y	Y	N	Y	N	N	Y	N

ND Northern Democrats   SD Southern Democrats

	480	481	482	483	484	485	486	487
18 ***Michel***	Y	Y	N	N	?	Y	Y	N
19 Poshard	Y	Y	N	Y	Y	Y	Y	Y
20 Durbin	Y	Y	Y	Y	N	Y	Y	Y
INDIANA								
1 Visclosky	Y	Y	Y	Y	N	N	Y	N
2 Sharp	Y	Y	N	Y	N	Y	Y	Y
3 Roemer	Y	Y	N	Y	N	Y	Y	N
4 Long	Y	Y	N	Y	N	Y	Y	N
5 ***Buyer***	Y	Y	N	N	Y	Y	N	Y
6 ***Burton***	N	Y	N	N	Y	Y	N	N
7 ***Myers***	Y	Y	Y	N	Y	Y	Y	N
8 McCloskey	Y	Y	Y	Y	N	?	Y	Y
9 Hamilton	Y	Y	N	Y	N	Y	Y	Y
10 Jacobs	Y	Y	N	N	N	Y	N	N
IOWA								
1 ***Leach***	N	Y	Y	N	N	Y	Y	N
2 ***Nussle***	N	Y	N	N	Y	Y	N	N
3 ***Lightfoot***	Y	Y	Y	N	Y	Y	N	N
4 Smith	Y	Y	Y	Y	Y	Y	Y	N
5 ***Grandy***	Y	Y	N	N	Y	Y	Y	N
KANSAS								
1 ***Roberts***	N	Y	N	N	Y	Y	N	Y
2 Slattery	Y	Y	N	Y	N	Y	Y	Y
3 ***Meyers***	Y	Y	N	N	N	Y	Y	Y
4 Glickman	Y	Y	N	Y	N	Y	Y	Y
KENTUCKY								
1 Barlow	Y	Y	N	Y	Y	Y	Y	Y
2 Natcher	Y	Y	Y	Y	N	Y	Y	Y
3 Mazzoli	Y	Y	Y	Y	Y	Y	Y	Y
4 ***Bunning***	Y	Y	N	N	Y	Y	N	Y
5 ***Rogers***	Y	Y	Y	N	Y	Y	Y	Y
6 Baesler	Y	Y	N	Y	N	Y	Y	Y
LOUISIANA								
1 ***Livingston***	Y	Y	N	N	Y	Y	Y	N
2 Jefferson	Y	Y	N	Y	Y	N	Y	N
3 Tauzin	Y	Y	N	N	Y	Y	N	Y
4 Fields	Y	Y	N	Y	Y	N	Y	N
5 ***McCrery***	Y	Y	N	N	Y	Y	Y	N
6 ***Baker***	Y	Y	N	N	Y	Y	N	N
7 Hayes	Y	Y	Y	N	Y	Y	?	N
MAINE								
1 Andrews	Y	Y	N	Y	N	N	Y	Y
2 ***Snowe***	Y	Y	N	N	N	Y	Y	Y
MARYLAND								
1 ***Gilchrest***	Y	Y	N	Y	N	N	Y	Y
2 ***Bentley***	N	Y	N	N	Y	Y	Y	Y
3 Cardin	Y	Y	N	Y	N	N	Y	N
4 Wynn	Y	Y	N	Y	N	Y	Y	Y
5 Hoyer	Y	Y	Y	Y	N	Y	Y	Y
6 ***Bartlett***	N	Y	N	N	Y	Y	N	N
7 Mfume	Y	Y	?	Y	N	N	Y	N
8 ***Morella***	Y	Y	N	Y	N	N	Y	N
MASSACHUSETTS								
1 Olver	Y	Y	N	Y	N	N	Y	N
2 Neal	Y	Y	N	Y	N	N	Y	Y
3 ***Blute***	Y	Y	N	N	Y	Y	Y	Y
4 Frank	Y	Y	Y	Y	N	N	Y	N
5 Meehan	Y	Y	N	Y	N	N	Y	Y
6 ***Torkildsen***	Y	Y	N	N	Y	Y	Y	Y
7 Markey	Y	Y	N	Y	N	N	Y	N
8 Kennedy	Y	Y	N	Y	N	N	Y	N
9 Moakley	Y	Y	Y	Y	N	N	Y	Y
10 Studds	Y	Y	N	Y	N	N	Y	Y
MICHIGAN								
1 Stupak	Y	Y	N	Y	N	Y	Y	Y
2 ***Hoekstra***	N	Y	N	N	Y	Y	N	N
3 Vacancy								
4 ***Camp***	Y	Y	N	N	Y	Y	N	Y
5 Barcia	Y	Y	N	Y	Y	Y	Y	Y
6 ***Upton***	Y	Y	N	N	Y	Y	Y	Y
7 ***Smith***	Y	Y	N	N	Y	Y	N	N
8 Carr	Y	Y	Y	Y	N	Y	Y	Y
9 Kildee	Y	Y	N	Y	N	Y	Y	Y
10 Bonior	Y	Y	Y	Y	N	N	Y	Y
11 ***Knollenberg***	N	Y	N	N	Y	Y	N	N
12 Levin	Y	Y	N	Y	N	N	Y	Y
13 Ford	Y	Y	N	Y	N	N	Y	Y
14 Conyers	N	Y	N	Y	N	?	Y	N
15 Collins	Y	Y	N	Y	N	Y	Y	Y
16 Dingell	Y	Y	Y	Y	N	N	Y	Y
MINNESOTA								
1 Penny	N	Y	N	N	Y	Y	N	Y
2 Minge	N	Y	N	Y	Y	Y	N	Y
3 ***Ramstad***	N	Y	N	N	N	Y	N	Y
4 Vento	N	Y	N	Y	N	N	Y	Y
5 Sabo	Y	Y	Y	Y	N	N	Y	Y
6 ***Grams***	N	Y	N	N	Y	Y	N	Y
7 Peterson	N	Y	N	Y	Y	Y	N	Y
8 Oberstar	Y	Y	N	Y	N	Y	Y	Y
MISSISSIPPI								
1 Whitten	Y	Y	Y	Y	Y	Y	Y	Y
2 Thompson	Y	Y	Y	Y	N	Y	Y	N
3 Montgomery	Y	Y	Y	Y	Y	Y	Y	Y
4 Parker	Y	Y	Y	N	Y	Y	Y	Y
5 Taylor	Y	Y	Y	N	Y	Y	N	Y
MISSOURI								
1 Clay	Y	Y	Y	Y	N	N	Y	Y
2 ***Talent***	Y	Y	N	N	Y	Y	N	N
3 Gephardt	Y	Y	Y	Y	N	N	Y	Y
4 Skelton	Y	Y	N	Y	Y	Y	Y	Y
5 Wheat	Y	Y	Y	Y	N	N	Y	Y
6 Danner	Y	Y	N	Y	Y	Y	Y	Y
7 ***Hancock***	N	Y	N	N	Y	Y	N	N
8 ***Emerson***	Y	Y	N	N	Y	Y	Y	Y
9 Volkmer	Y	Y	N	Y	Y	Y	Y	Y
MONTANA								
AL Williams	Y	Y	N	Y	N	Y	Y	Y
NEBRASKA								
1 ***Bereuter***	N	Y	N	N	Y	Y	N	Y
2 Hoagland	Y	Y	N	Y	N	N	Y	Y
3 ***Barrett***	Y	Y	N	N	Y	Y	Y	N
NEVADA								
1 Bilbray	Y	Y	N	Y	N	Y	Y	Y
2 ***Vucanovich***	Y	Y	N	N	Y	Y	Y	Y
NEW HAMPSHIRE								
1 ***Zeliff***	N	Y	N	N	Y	Y	N	N
2 Swett	Y	Y	N	Y	N	Y	Y	Y
NEW JERSEY								
1 Andrews	Y	Y	N	Y	N	N	Y	N
2 Hughes	Y	Y	N	Y	N	Y	N	Y
3 ***Saxton***	Y	Y	N	Y	Y	Y	N	Y
4 ***Smith***	Y	Y	N	N	N	Y	Y	Y
5 ***Roukema***	N	Y	N	N	Y	Y	Y	Y
6 Pallone	Y	Y	Y	Y	N	N	N	N
7 ***Franks***	Y	Y	N	N	Y	Y	Y	N
8 Klein	Y	Y	N	Y	N	N	Y	Y
9 Torricelli	Y	Y	Y	Y	N	?	Y	Y
10 Payne	Y	Y	N	Y	N	N	Y	N
11 ***Gallo***	Y	Y	N	N	Y	Y	Y	Y
12 ***Zimmer***	N	Y	N	Y	N	Y	N	Y
13 Menendez	Y	Y	Y	Y	N	Y	Y	Y
NEW MEXICO								
1 ***Schiff***	Y	Y	N	N	Y	Y	Y	Y
2 ***Skeen***	Y	Y	N	N	Y	Y	Y	Y
3 Richardson	Y	Y	Y	Y	N	N	Y	Y
NEW YORK								
1 Hochbrueckner	Y	Y	Y	Y	N	Y	Y	Y
2 ***Lazio***	Y	Y	N	N	Y	Y	Y	N
3 ***King***	N	Y	N	N	Y	Y	Y	N
4 ***Levy***	N	Y	N	N	Y	Y	Y	Y
5 Ackerman	Y	Y	Y	?	N	?	?	?
6 Flake	Y	Y	Y	Y	N	?	Y	?
7 Manton	Y	Y	N	Y	N	N	Y	Y
8 Nadler	N	Y	N	Y	N	N	Y	N
9 Schumer	Y	Y	Y	Y	N	N	Y	Y
10 Towns	Y	Y	N	Y	N	N	Y	Y
11 Owens	N	Y	Y	Y	N	N	Y	Y
12 Velazquez	Y	Y	N	Y	N	N	Y	N
13 ***Molinari***	N	Y	N	N	Y	Y	Y	Y
14 Maloney	N	Y	N	Y	N	N	Y	N
15 Rangel	Y	Y	Y	Y	N	N	Y	Y
16 Serrano	?	Y	Y	Y	N	N	Y	N
17 Engel	Y	Y	?	Y	N	N	Y	N
18 Lowey	Y	Y	Y	Y	N	N	Y	N
19 ***Fish***	Y	Y	N	N	Y	Y	Y	N
20 ***Gilman***	N	Y	N	N	N	Y	Y	Y
21 McNulty	Y	Y	Y	Y	N	Y	Y	?
22 ***Solomon***	N	Y	N	N	Y	Y	N	Y
23 ***Boehlert***	Y	Y	N	N	N	Y	Y	Y
24 ***McHugh***	N	Y	N	N	Y	Y	N	Y
25 ***Walsh***	Y	Y	N	N	Y	Y	N	N
26 Hinchey	Y	Y	N	Y	N	N	Y	N
27 ***Paxon***	Y	Y	N	N	Y	Y	N	Y
28 Slaughter	Y	Y	Y	Y	N	Y	Y	N
29 LaFalce	Y	Y	N	?	N	N	Y	Y
30 ***Quinn***	Y	Y	N	N	Y	Y	N	Y
31 ***Houghton***	Y	Y	Y	N	Y	Y	Y	Y
NORTH CAROLINA								
1 Clayton	Y	Y	N	Y	N	N	Y	N
2 Valentine	Y	Y	Y	Y	N	Y	Y	Y
3 Lancaster	Y	Y	N	Y	N	Y	Y	Y
4 Price	Y	Y	Y	Y	N	Y	Y	Y
5 Neal	Y	Y	N	Y	N	Y	Y	Y
6 ***Coble***	Y	Y	N	N	Y	Y	N	N
7 Rose	Y	Y	Y	Y	N	Y	Y	N
8 Hefner	Y	Y	Y	Y	N	Y	Y	Y
9 ***McMillan***	Y	Y	N	N	Y	Y	Y	N
10 ***Ballenger***	Y	Y	N	N	Y	Y	N	N
11 ***Taylor***	Y	Y	N	N	Y	Y	N	Y
12 Watt	N	Y	N	Y	N	N	Y	Y
NORTH DAKOTA								
AL Pomeroy	Y	Y	−	+	+	+	Y	Y
OHIO								
1 Mann	Y	Y	N	Y	N	N	Y	Y
2 ***Portman***	Y	Y	−	N	Y	Y	N	Y
3 Hall	Y	Y	Y	Y	N	Y	Y	Y
4 ***Oxley***	Y	Y	N	N	Y	?	N	Y
5 ***Gillmor***	Y	Y	N	Y	Y	Y	Y	Y
6 Strickland	Y	Y	N	Y	N	Y	Y	N
7 ***Hobson***	Y	Y	N	N	N	Y	Y	Y
8 ***Boehner***	N	Y	N	N	Y	Y	N	N
9 Kaptur	Y	Y	Y	Y	Y	Y	Y	Y
10 ***Hoke***	Y	Y	Y	N	Y	Y	N	Y
11 Stokes	Y	Y	Y	Y	N	N	Y	Y
12 ***Kasich***	Y	Y	N	N	Y	Y	Y	N
13 Brown	Y	Y	Y	Y	N	Y	Y	Y
14 Sawyer	Y	Y	Y	Y	N	Y	Y	Y
15 ***Pryce***	Y	Y	N	N	Y	Y	Y	Y
16 ***Regula***	Y	Y	N	N	Y	Y	Y	Y
17 Traficant	Y	Y	Y	Y	Y	Y	Y	Y
18 Applegate	N	Y	Y	Y	Y	Y	Y	Y
19 Fingerhut	Y	Y	N	Y	N	Y	Y	Y
OKLAHOMA								
1 ***Inhofe***	N	Y	N	N	Y	Y	N	Y
2 Synar	Y	Y	N	Y	N	N	Y	Y
3 Brewster	Y	Y	N	N	Y	Y	Y	Y
4 McCurdy	Y	Y	N	N	N	?	Y	Y
5 ***Istook***	Y	Y	N	N	Y	Y	N	Y
6 English	Y	Y	N	N	Y	Y	Y	Y
OREGON								
1 Furse	Y	Y	N	Y	N	N	Y	N
2 ***Smith***	N	Y	N	N	Y	Y	N	N
3 Wyden	N	Y	N	Y	N	Y	Y	N
4 DeFazio	N	Y	N	Y	N	Y	Y	N
5 Kopetski	Y	Y	Y	Y	N	Y	Y	N
PENNSYLVANIA								
1 Foglietta	Y	Y	Y	Y	N	N	Y	Y
2 Blackwell	Y	Y	N	Y	?	N	Y	Y
3 Borski	Y	Y	N	Y	N	?	Y	Y
4 Klink	Y	Y	N	N	Y	Y	Y	N
5 ***Clinger***	Y	Y	N	Y	Y	Y	Y	N
6 Holden	Y	Y	N	?	Y	Y	Y	N
7 ***Weldon***	Y	Y	N	Y	Y	Y	Y	Y
8 ***Greenwood***	Y	Y	N	N	N	Y	Y	N
9 ***Shuster***	Y	Y	N	N	Y	Y	N	Y
10 ***McDade***	?	?	N	N	Y	Y	Y	N
11 Kanjorski	Y	Y	Y	Y	N	Y	Y	Y
12 Murtha	Y	Y	Y	Y	Y	Y	?	N
13 Margolies-Mezv.	N	Y	N	Y	N	Y	Y	N
14 Coyne	Y	Y	Y	Y	N	N	Y	Y
15 McHale	Y	Y	N	Y	N	Y	Y	N
16 ***Walker***	N	Y	N	N	Y	Y	N	N
17 ***Gekas***	Y	Y	N	N	Y	Y	Y	Y
18 ***Santorum***	Y	Y	N	N	Y	Y	Y	Y
19 ***Goodling***	N	Y	N	N	Y	Y	Y	N
20 Murphy	Y	Y	N	Y	Y	N	Y	?
21 ***Ridge***	Y	Y	N	N	Y	Y	N	Y
RHODE ISLAND								
1 ***Machtley***	Y	Y	N	N	N	Y	Y	Y
2 Reed	Y	Y	N	Y	N	N	Y	Y
SOUTH CAROLINA								
1 ***Ravenel***	Y	Y	N	N	N	Y	Y	Y
2 ***Spence***	N	Y	N	N	Y	Y	N	Y
3 Derrick	Y	Y	Y	Y	?	?	Y	Y
4 ***Inglis***	N	Y	N	N	N	Y	N	N
5 Spratt	Y	Y	N	Y	N	Y	Y	Y
6 Clyburn	Y	Y	Y	Y	Y	Y	Y	Y
SOUTH DAKOTA								
AL Johnson	Y	Y	N	Y	N	Y	Y	Y
TENNESSEE								
1 ***Quillen***	Y	Y	Y	N	Y	Y	N	?
2 ***Duncan***	Y	Y	N	N	Y	Y	Y	Y
3 Lloyd	Y	Y	Y	N	Y	Y	Y	Y
4 Cooper	Y	Y	N	Y	Y	Y	Y	Y
5 Clement	Y	Y	N	Y	N	Y	Y	Y
6 Gordon	Y	Y	Y	Y	N	Y	Y	Y
7 ***Sundquist***	Y	Y	Y	N	Y	Y	N	Y
8 Tanner	Y	Y	Y	N	Y	Y	Y	Y
9 Ford	Y	Y	N	Y	N	N	Y	Y
TEXAS								
1 Chapman	Y	?	N	Y	Y	Y	Y	Y
2 Wilson	#	Y	Y	Y	Y	Y	Y	?
3 ***Johnson, Sam***	N	Y	N	N	Y	Y	N	Y
4 Hall	Y	Y	Y	?	Y	Y	Y	Y
5 Bryant	Y	Y	N	Y	Y	Y	Y	Y
6 ***Barton***	N	Y	N	N	Y	Y	N	Y
7 ***Archer***	N	Y	N	N	Y	Y	N	Y
8 ***Fields***	N	Y	N	N	Y	Y	N	Y
9 Brooks	Y	Y	Y	Y	Y	Y	Y	Y
10 Pickle	Y	Y	Y	Y	N	Y	Y	Y
11 Edwards	Y	Y	N	Y	Y	Y	Y	Y
12 Geren	Y	Y	Y	N	Y	Y	Y	Y
13 Sarpalius	Y	Y	Y	Y	Y	Y	Y	Y
14 Laughlin	Y	Y	Y	N	Y	Y	Y	Y
15 de la Garza	Y	Y	Y	Y	Y	?	?	?
16 Coleman	Y	Y	Y	Y	N	Y	Y	N
17 Stenholm	Y	Y	N	N	Y	Y	Y	Y
18 Washington	X	?	N	Y	N	N	Y	N
19 ***Combest***	N	Y	N	N	Y	Y	N	Y
20 Gonzalez	Y	Y	Y	Y	N	N	Y	Y
21 ***Smith***	N	Y	N	N	Y	Y	N	N
22 ***DeLay***	N	Y	N	N	Y	Y	N	Y
23 ***Bonilla***	Y	Y	N	N	Y	Y	Y	N
24 Frost	Y	Y	N	Y	?	Y	Y	Y
25 Andrews	Y	Y	N	N	Y	Y	Y	Y
26 ***Armey***	N	Y	N	N	Y	Y	N	Y
27 Ortiz	Y	Y	Y	Y	Y	Y	Y	Y
28 Tejeda	Y	Y	Y	Y	Y	Y	Y	Y
29 Green	Y	Y	Y	Y	N	Y	Y	?
30 Johnson, E.B.	Y	Y	Y	Y	N	Y	Y	Y
UTAH								
1 ***Hansen***	Y	Y	N	N	Y	Y	N	N
2 Shepherd	Y	Y	N	Y	N	N	Y	N
3 Orton	Y	Y	N	Y	Y	Y	N	N
VERMONT								
AL *Sanders*	N	Y	N	Y	N	N	Y	N
VIRGINIA								
1 ***Bateman***	Y	Y	N	N	Y	Y	Y	Y
2 Pickett	Y	Y	Y	Y	Y	Y	Y	Y
3 Scott	Y	Y	Y	Y	N	Y	Y	N
4 Sisisky	Y	Y	N	N	Y	Y	Y	Y
5 Payne	Y	Y	N	Y	N	Y	Y	Y
6 ***Goodlatte***	Y	Y	N	N	Y	Y	N	Y
7 ***Bliley***	Y	Y	N	N	Y	Y	Y	N
8 Moran	Y	Y	Y	Y	N	N	Y	Y
9 Boucher	Y	Y	Y	Y	N	Y	Y	Y
10 ***Wolf***	Y	Y	N	N	Y	Y	Y	N
11 Byrne	Y	Y	N	Y	N	Y	Y	N
WASHINGTON								
1 Cantwell	Y	Y	N	Y	N	Y	Y	Y
2 Swift	Y	Y	N	Y	N	Y	Y	N
3 Unsoeld	N	Y	Y	Y	N	N	Y	N
4 Inslee	Y	Y	N	Y	N	Y	Y	N
5 Foley								
6 Dicks	Y	Y	N	Y	N	Y	Y	Y
7 McDermott	N	Y	N	Y	N	N	Y	?
8 ***Dunn***	N	Y	N	N	Y	Y	N	N
9 Kreidler	Y	Y	N	Y	N	N	Y	N
WEST VIRGINIA								
1 Mollohan	Y	Y	Y	Y	Y	Y	Y	Y
2 Wise	Y	Y	N	Y	N	Y	Y	Y
3 Rahall	Y	Y	Y	?	N	N	?	Y
WISCONSIN								
1 Barca	Y	Y	N	Y	N	Y	Y	N
2 ***Klug***	N	Y	N	N	N	Y	Y	N
3 ***Gunderson***	Y	Y	N	N	Y	Y	Y	Y
4 Kleczka	Y	Y	N	Y	N	Y	Y	Y
5 Barrett	N	Y	N	Y	N	Y	Y	Y
6 ***Petri***	N	Y	N	N	Y	Y	N	Y
7 Obey	Y	Y	Y	Y	N	Y	Y	Y
8 ***Roth***	N	Y	N	N	Y	Y	N	N
9 ***Sensenbrenner***	N	Y	N	N	Y	Y	N	N
WYOMING								
AL ***Thomas***	Y	Y	N	N	Y	Y	N	N
DELEGATES								
de Lugo, V.I.	D	D	D	D	N	N	D	Y
Faleomavaega, Am.S.	D	D	D	D	?	?	D	?
Norton, D.C.	D	D	D	D	N	N	D	Y
Romero-B., P.R.	D	D	D	D	?	?	D	N
Underwood, Guam	D	D	D	D	N	N	D	N

Southern states - Ala., Ark., Fla., Ga., Ky., La., Miss., N.C., Okla., S.C., Tenn., Texas, Va.
Omitted votes are quorum calls, which CQ does not include in its vote charts.

488. HR 2739. Airport Improvements/Child Restraints. Lightfoot, R-Iowa, amendment, as amended, to require airlines to provide child safety restraints upon request. Before being amended the Lightfoot amendment would have required the use of child safety restraints on airplanes. Adopted in the Committee of the Whole 374-48: R 131-42; D 242-6 (ND 162-4, SD 80-2); I 1-0, Oct. 7, 1993.

489. HR 2739. Airport Improvements/National Airport. Moran, D-Va., amendment to exempt National Airport from a study of the limits placed by the federal government on airlines' access to National, O'Hare, J.F.K. and LaGuardia airports. Rejected in the Committee of the Whole 110-294: R 18-145; D 92-148 (ND 59-103, SD 33-45); I 0-1, Oct. 7, 1993.

490. HR 2739. Airport Improvements/Metro Washington Airports Authority. Wolf, R-Va., amendment to strike the provisions of the bill that would grant collective bargaining rights to certain employees of the Metropolitan Washington Airports Authority. Rejected in the Committee of the Whole 167-259: R 154-16; D 13-242 (ND 1-171, SD 12-71); I 0-1, Oct. 13, 1993.

491. HR 2739. Airport Improvements/Child Restraints. Separate vote at the request of Linder, R-Ga., on the Lightfoot, R-Iowa, amendment adopted in the Committee of the Whole, as amended, to require airlines to provide child safety restraints upon request. Adopted 375-49: R 132-41; D 242-8 (ND 162-5, SD 80-3); I 1-0, Oct. 13, 1993. (On a separate vote, which may be demanded on an amendment adopted in the Committee of the Whole, the four delegates and the resident commissioner of Puerto Rico cannot vote. See vote 488)

492. HR 2739. Airport Improvements/Passage. Passage of the bill to authorize $6.5 billion for construction at airports, $7.7 billion for upgrading the air traffic control system and $14.1 billion for the Federal Aviation Administration in fiscal 1994 through fiscal 1996. The bill also reauthorizes the Airport Improvement Program, which distributes ticket, cargo and fuel taxes to airports for runways, terminals and other facilities. Passed 384-42: R 133-41; D 250-1 (ND 168-1, SD 82-0); I 1-0, Oct. 13, 1993.

493. HR 1804. School Improvement/States' Rights. Goodling, R-Pa., amendment to state that nothing in the bill gives the federal government control over state and local activities regarding curriculum, instruction or the allocation of state and local resources. Adopted in the Committee of the Whole 420-0: R 173-0; D 246-0 (ND 165-0, SD 81-0); I 1-0, Oct. 13, 1993.

494. HR 1804. School Improvement/Substitute. Armey, R-Texas, substitute amendment to eliminate the commissions, standards and testing systems in the bill; authorize $400 million in fiscal 1994-98 for model schools, merit schools, school choice programs and decentralized management programs involving parents; allow local communities to define "school choice" to include private schools; require 25 percent of federal funds to be spent on school choice programs by school districts; and add provisions to strengthen parental control of education. Rejected in the Committee of the Whole 130-300: R 129-45; D 1-254 (ND 0-171, SD 1-83); I 0-1, Oct. 13, 1993. A "nay" was a vote in support of the president's position.

495. HR 1804. School Improvement/States' Rights. Separate vote at the request of Linder, R-Ga., on the Goodling, R-Pa., amendment adopted in the Committee of the Whole to state that nothing in the bill gives the federal government control over state and local activities regarding curriculum, instruction or the allocation of state and local resources. Adopted 424-0: R 173-0; D 250-0 (ND 167-0, SD 83-0); I 1-0, Oct. 13, 1993. (On a separate vote, which may be demanded on an amendment adopted in the Committee of the Whole, the four delegates and the resident commissioner of Puerto Rico cannot vote. See vote 493.)

KEY

Y Voted for (yea).
\# Paired for.
\+ Announced for.
N Voted against (nay).
X Paired against.
− Announced against.
P Voted "present."
C Voted "present" to avoid possible conflict of interest.
? Did not vote or otherwise make a position known.
D Delegates ineligible to vote.

Democrats **Republicans**
Independent

	488	489	490	491	492	493	494	495
ALABAMA								
1 *Callahan*	N	N	Y	N	Y	Y	Y	Y
2 *Everett*	Y	N	Y	Y	Y	Y	Y	Y
3 Browder	Y	N	N	Y	Y	Y	N	Y
4 Bevill	Y	Y	N	Y	Y	Y	N	Y
5 Cramer	Y	N	N	Y	Y	Y	N	Y
6 *Bachus*	Y	N	Y	Y	Y	Y	Y	Y
7 Hilliard	Y	N	N	Y	Y	Y	N	Y
ALASKA								
AL *Young*	Y	N	N	Y	Y	Y	N	Y
ARIZONA								
1 Coppersmith	Y	N	N	Y	Y	Y	N	Y
2 Pastor	Y	Y	N	Y	Y	Y	N	Y
3 *Stump*	N	N	Y	N	N	Y	Y	Y
4 *Kyl*	Y	N	Y	Y	Y	Y	Y	Y
5 *Kolbe*	Y	N	Y	Y	Y	Y	N	Y
6 English	Y	Y	N	Y	Y	Y	N	Y
ARKANSAS								
1 Lambert	Y	N	N	Y	Y	Y	N	Y
2 Thornton	Y	Y	N	Y	Y	Y	N	Y
3 *Hutchinson*	Y	N	Y	Y	Y	Y	Y	Y
4 *Dickey*	Y	N	?	?	Y	Y	Y	Y
CALIFORNIA								
1 Hamburg	Y	N	N	Y	Y	Y	N	Y
2 *Herger*	Y	N	Y	Y	Y	Y	Y	Y
3 Fazio	Y	N	N	Y	Y	Y	N	Y
4 *Doolittle*	N	N	Y	N	N	Y	Y	Y
5 Matsui	Y	N	N	?	Y	Y	N	Y
6 Woolsey	Y	Y	N	Y	Y	Y	N	Y
7 Miller	Y	?	N	Y	Y	Y	N	Y
8 Pelosi	Y	Y	N	Y	Y	Y	N	Y
9 Dellums	?	N	N	Y	Y	?	N	Y
10 *Baker*	Y	N	Y	Y	Y	Y	Y	Y
11 *Pombo*	N	N	Y	N	N	Y	Y	Y
12 Lantos	Y	Y	N	Y	Y	Y	N	Y
13 Stark	Y	N	N	Y	Y	Y	N	Y
14 Eshoo	Y	Y	?	Y	Y	Y	N	Y
15 Mineta	Y	N	N	Y	Y	Y	N	Y
16 Edwards	Y	N	N	Y	Y	Y	N	Y
17 Farr	Y	N	N	Y	Y	Y	N	Y
18 Condit	N	Y	N	Y	Y	N	N	Y
19 Lehman	Y	Y	N	Y	Y	Y	N	Y
20 Dooley	Y	Y	N	Y	Y	Y	N	Y
21 *Thomas*	Y	N	Y	Y	Y	Y	Y	Y
22 *Huffington*	Y	Y	N	Y	Y	Y	Y	Y
23 *Gallegly*	Y	N	Y	Y	Y	Y	Y	Y
24 Beilenson	Y	Y	N	Y	Y	Y	N	Y
25 *McKeon*	Y	N	?	Y	Y	Y	Y	Y
26 Berman	?	?	N	Y	Y	Y	N	Y
27 *Moorhead*	Y	N	Y	Y	Y	Y	Y	Y
28 *Dreier*	Y	N	Y	Y	Y	Y	Y	Y
29 Waxman	Y	Y	N	Y	Y	Y	N	Y
30 Becerra	Y	Y	N	Y	Y	Y	N	Y
31 Martinez	Y	N	N	Y	Y	Y	N	Y
32 Dixon	Y	?	N	Y	Y	Y	N	Y
33 Roybal-Allard	Y	Y	N	Y	Y	Y	N	Y
34 Torres	Y	N	?	?	Y	Y	N	Y
35 Waters	Y	?	N	Y	Y	?	N	Y
36 Harman	Y	Y	N	Y	Y	Y	N	Y
37 Tucker	Y	N	N	Y	Y	Y	N	Y
38 *Horn*	Y	Y	?	Y	Y	Y	N	Y
39 *Royce*	N	N	Y	N	N	Y	Y	Y
40 *Lewis*	?	?	Y	Y	Y	Y	Y	Y
41 *Kim*	Y	N	Y	Y	Y	Y	Y	Y

	488	489	490	491	492	493	494	495
42 Brown	?	N	N	Y	Y	?	N	Y
43 *Calvert*	Y	N	Y	Y	Y	Y	Y	Y
44 *McCandless*	Y	N	Y	Y	Y	Y	Y	Y
45 *Rohrabacher*	N	N	Y	N	Y	Y	Y	Y
46 *Dornan*	N	N	Y	N	N	Y	Y	Y
47 *Cox*	N	N	Y	N	Y	Y	Y	Y
48 *Packard*	Y	N	Y	Y	Y	Y	Y	Y
49 Schenk	Y	N	N	Y	Y	Y	N	Y
50 Filner	Y	N	N	Y	Y	Y	N	Y
51 *Cunningham*	Y	N	Y	Y	Y	Y	Y	Y
52 *Hunter*	N	?	Y	N	N	Y	Y	Y
COLORADO								
1 Schroeder	Y	N	N	Y	Y	Y	N	Y
2 Skaggs	Y	N	N	Y	Y	?	N	Y
3 *McInnis*	Y	N	Y	N	Y	Y	Y	Y
4 *Allard*	N	N	Y	N	N	Y	Y	Y
5 *Hefley*	N	Y	Y	N	N	Y	Y	Y
6 *Schaefer*	Y	?	Y	Y	N	Y	Y	Y
CONNECTICUT								
1 Kennelly	?	Y	N	Y	Y	Y	N	Y
2 Gejdenson	Y	N	N	Y	Y	Y	N	Y
3 DeLauro	Y	N	N	Y	Y	Y	N	Y
4 *Shays*	Y	N	N	Y	Y	Y	Y	Y
5 *Franks*	Y	N	Y	Y ·	Y	Y	Y	Y
6 *Johnson*	Y	Y	Y	Y	Y	Y	Y	Y
DELAWARE								
AL *Castle*	Y	N	Y	Y	Y	Y	N	Y
FLORIDA								
1 Hutto	Y	N	?	?	?	Y	N	Y
2 Peterson	Y	N	N	Y	Y	Y	N	Y
3 Brown	Y	N	N	Y	Y	Y	N	Y
4 *Fowler*	Y	Y	Y	Y	Y	Y	Y	Y
5 Thurman	Y	Y	N	Y	Y	Y	N	Y
6 *Stearns*	Y	N	Y	Y	Y	Y	Y	Y
7 *Mica*	N	N	Y	N	N	Y	Y	Y
8 *McCollum*	Y	N	Y	Y	Y	Y	Y	Y
9 *Bilirakis*	Y	N	Y	Y	Y	Y	Y	Y
10 *Young*	Y	N	Y	Y	Y	Y	Y	Y
11 Gibbons	Y	N	N	Y	Y	Y	N	Y
12 *Canady*	Y	N	Y	Y	Y	Y	Y	Y
13 *Miller*	Y	N	Y	Y	Y	Y	Y	Y
14 *Goss*	Y	N	Y	Y	Y	Y	Y	Y
15 Bacchus	Y	Y	N	Y	Y	Y	N	Y
16 *Lewis*	Y	N	Y	Y	Y	Y	Y	Y
17 Meek	Y	Y	N	Y	Y	?	N	Y
18 *Ros-Lehtinen*	Y	N	Y	Y	Y	Y	Y	Y
19 Johnston	Y	N	N	Y	Y	Y	N	Y
20 Deutsch	Y	N	N	Y	Y	Y	N	Y
21 *Diaz-Balart*	Y	N	Y	Y	Y	Y	Y	Y
22 *Shaw*	Y	N	Y	Y	Y	Y	Y	Y
23 Hastings	Y	Y	N	Y	Y	Y	N	Y
GEORGIA								
1 *Kingston*	N	N	Y	N	Y	Y	Y	Y
2 Bishop	Y	N	N	Y	Y	Y	N	Y
3 *Collins*	Y	N	Y	Y	Y	Y	Y	Y
4 *Linder*	N	N	Y	N	Y	Y	Y	Y
5 Lewis	Y	N	N	Y	?	Y	N	Y
6 *Gingrich*	Y	N	Y	Y	Y	Y	Y	Y
7 Darden	Y	N	N	Y	Y	Y	N	Y
8 Rowland	Y	N	Y	Y	Y	Y	N	Y
9 Deal	Y	N	Y	Y	Y	Y	N	Y
10 Johnson	Y	N	N	Y	Y	Y	N	Y
11 McKinney	Y	Y	N	Y	Y	?	N	Y
HAWAII								
1 Abercrombie	Y	Y	N	Y	Y	Y	N	Y
2 Mink	Y	Y	N	Y	Y	Y	N	Y
IDAHO								
1 LaRocco	Y	N	N	Y	Y	Y	N	Y
2 *Crapo*	N	N	Y	N	N	Y	Y	Y
ILLINOIS								
1 Rush	Y	Y	N	Y	Y	Y	N	Y
2 Reynolds	Y	Y	N	Y	Y	Y	N	?
3 Lipinski	Y	N	N	Y	Y	Y	N	Y
4 Gutierrez	Y	Y	N	Y	Y	Y	N	Y
5 Rostenkowski	Y	N	N	Y	Y	Y	N	Y
6 *Hyde*	Y	N	Y	Y	Y	Y	Y	Y
7 Collins	Y	Y	N	Y	Y	Y	N	Y
8 *Crane*	Y	N	Y	Y	Y	Y	Y	Y
9 Yates	Y	N	N	Y	Y	Y	N	Y
10 *Porter*	Y	?	Y	Y	N	Y	N	Y
11 Sangmeister	Y	N	N	Y	Y	Y	N	Y
12 Costello	Y	N	N	Y	Y	Y	N	Y
13 *Fawell*	Y	N	Y	Y	N	?	N	Y
14 *Hastert*	Y	N	Y	Y	Y	Y	Y	Y
15 *Ewing*	Y	N	Y	Y	Y	Y	N	Y
16 *Manzullo*	Y	N	Y	Y	Y	Y	Y	Y
17 Evans	Y	N	N	Y	Y	Y	N	Y

ND Northern Democrats   SD Southern Democrats

	488	489	490	491	492	493	494	495
18 ***Michel***	N	N	?	N	Y	Y	Y	Y
19 Poshard	Y	N	N	Y	Y	Y	N	Y
20 Durbin	Y	N	N	Y	Y	Y	N	Y
INDIANA								
1 Visclosky	Y	N	N	Y	Y	Y	N	Y
2 Sharp	Y	Y	N	Y	Y	Y	N	Y
3 Roemer	Y	N	N	Y	Y	Y	N	Y
4 Long	Y	N	N	Y	Y	Y	N	Y
5 ***Buyer***	Y	N	Y	Y	Y	Y	Y	Y
6 ***Burton***	N	N	Y	N	N	Y	Y	Y
7 ***Myers***	N	Y	Y	N	Y	Y	N	Y
8 McCloskey	Y	N	N	Y	Y	Y	N	Y
9 Hamilton	Y	N	N	Y	Y	Y	N	Y
10 Jacobs	Y	N	N	Y	Y	Y	N	Y
IOWA								
1 ***Leach***	Y	N	Y	Y	Y	Y	N	Y
2 ***Nussle***	N	N	Y	N	Y	Y	Y	Y
3 ***Lightfoot***	N	N	Y	N	Y	Y	Y	Y
4 Smith	Y	Y	N	Y	Y	Y	N	Y
5 ***Grandy***	Y	N	Y	Y	Y	Y	N	Y
KANSAS								
1 ***Roberts***	N	N	Y	N	N	Y	Y	Y
2 Slattery	Y	N	N	Y	Y	Y	N	Y
3 ***Meyers***	Y	Y	Y	Y	Y	Y	N	Y
4 Glickman	Y	N	N	Y	Y	Y	N	Y
KENTUCKY								
1 Barlow	Y	N	N	Y	Y	Y	N	Y
2 Natcher	Y	N	N	Y	Y	Y	N	Y
3 Mazzoli	Y	N	N	Y	Y	Y	N	Y
4 ***Bunning***	Y	N	Y	Y	Y	Y	Y	Y
5 ***Rogers***	Y	N	Y	Y	Y	Y	N	Y
6 Baesler	Y	Y	N	Y	Y	Y	N	Y
LOUISIANA								
1 ***Livingston***	Y	N	Y	Y	Y	Y	Y	Y
2 Jefferson	Y	Y	N	Y	Y	Y	N	Y
3 Tauzin	Y	N	Y	Y	Y	Y	N	Y
4 Fields	Y	Y	N	Y	Y	Y	N	Y
5 ***McCrery***	Y	N	Y	Y	Y	Y	N	Y
6 ***Baker***	N	N	Y	N	Y	Y	Y	Y
7 Hayes	Y	N	N	Y	Y	Y	N	Y
MAINE								
1 Andrews	Y	N	N	Y	Y	Y	N	Y
2 ***Snowe***	Y	N	Y	Y	Y	Y	N	Y
MARYLAND								
1 ***Gilchrest***	Y	Y	Y	Y	Y	Y	N	Y
2 ***Bentley***	Y	Y	Y	Y	N	Y	N	Y
3 Cardin	Y	Y	N	Y	Y	Y	N	Y
4 Wynn	Y	Y	N	Y	Y	Y	N	Y
5 Hoyer	Y	Y	N	Y	Y	Y	N	Y
6 ***Bartlett***	N	Y	Y	N	Y	Y	Y	Y
7 Mfume	Y	Y	N	Y	Y	+	N	Y
8 ***Morella***	Y	Y	N	Y	Y	Y	N	Y
MASSACHUSETTS								
1 Olver	Y	N	N	Y	Y	Y	N	Y
2 Neal	Y	N	N	Y	Y	Y	N	Y
3 ***Blute***	Y	N	Y	Y	Y	Y	N	Y
4 Frank	Y	Y	N	Y	Y	Y	N	Y
5 Meehan	Y	N	N	Y	Y	Y	N	Y
6 ***Torkildsen***	Y	N	Y	Y	Y	Y	N	Y
7 Markey	Y	?	N	Y	Y	Y	N	Y
8 Kennedy	Y	Y	N	Y	Y	Y	N	Y
9 Moakley	Y	N	N	Y	Y	Y	N	Y
10 Studds	Y	N	N	Y	Y	Y	N	Y
MICHIGAN								
1 Stupak	Y	Y	N	Y	Y	Y	N	Y
2 ***Hoekstra***	N	N	Y	N	Y	Y	Y	Y
3 Vacancy								
4 ***Camp***	Y	N	Y	Y	Y	Y	Y	Y
5 Barcia	Y	N	N	Y	Y	Y	N	Y
6 ***Upton***	N	N	Y	N	Y	Y	Y	Y
7 ***Smith***	N	N	Y	N	N	Y	Y	Y
8 Carr	Y	N	N	Y	N	Y	N	Y
9 Kildee	Y	N	N	Y	Y	Y	N	Y
10 Bonior	Y	N	N	Y	Y	Y	N	Y
11 ***Knollenberg***	N	N	Y	N	N	Y	Y	Y
12 Levin	Y	N	N	Y	Y	Y	N	Y
13 Ford	Y	N	N	Y	Y	Y	N	Y
14 Conyers	Y	N	N	Y	Y	?	N	Y
15 Collins	Y	Y	N	Y	Y	Y	N	Y
16 Dingell	Y	N	N	Y	Y	Y	N	Y
MINNESOTA								
1 Penny	N	N	N	N	Y	Y	N	Y
2 Minge	Y	N	N	Y	Y	Y	N	Y
3 ***Ramstad***	N	N	Y	N	Y	Y	N	Y
4 Vento	Y	N	N	Y	Y	Y	N	Y
5 Sabo	Y	N	N	Y	Y	Y	N	Y
6 ***Grams***	Y	N	Y	Y	N	Y	Y	Y
7 Peterson	Y	N	N	Y	Y	Y	N	Y
8 Oberstar	Y	N	N	Y	Y	Y	N	Y
MISSISSIPPI								
1 Whitten	Y	N	N	Y	Y	Y	N	Y
2 Thompson	Y	Y	N	Y	Y	Y	N	Y
3 Montgomery	Y	Y	Y	Y	Y	Y	N	Y
4 Parker	Y	Y	Y	N	Y	Y	N	Y
5 Taylor	Y	N	Y	Y	Y	Y	N	Y
MISSOURI								
1 Clay	Y	N	N	Y	Y	Y	N	Y
2 ***Talent***	Y	N	Y	Y	Y	Y	Y	Y
3 Gephardt	Y	Y	N	?	Y	Y	N	Y
4 Skelton	Y	N	N	Y	Y	Y	?	?
5 Wheat	Y	Y	N	Y	Y	Y	N	Y
6 Danner	Y	N	N	Y	Y	Y	N	Y
7 ***Hancock***	N	N	Y	N	N	Y	Y	Y
8 ***Emerson***	Y	N	Y	Y	Y	Y	Y	Y
9 Volkmer	Y	N	N	Y	Y	Y	N	Y
MONTANA								
AL Williams	Y	Y	N	Y	Y	Y	N	Y
NEBRASKA								
1 ***Bereuter***	Y	N	Y	Y	Y	Y	N	Y
2 Hoagland	Y	Y	N	Y	Y	Y	N	Y
3 ***Barrett***	Y	N	Y	Y	Y	Y	N	Y
NEVADA								
1 Bilbray	Y	N	N	Y	Y	Y	N	Y
2 ***Vucanovich***	Y	N	Y	Y	Y	Y	Y	Y
NEW HAMPSHIRE								
1 ***Zeliff***	Y	N	Y	Y	N	Y	Y	Y
2 Swett	Y	N	N	Y	Y	Y	N	Y
NEW JERSEY								
1 Andrews	Y	N	N	Y	Y	Y	N	Y
2 Hughes	Y	N	N	Y	Y	Y	N	Y
3 ***Saxton***	Y	N	Y	Y	Y	Y	N	Y
4 ***Smith***	Y	N	N	Y	Y	Y	N	Y
5 ***Roukema***	Y	N	Y	Y	Y	Y	N	Y
6 Pallone	Y	Y	N	Y	Y	Y	N	Y
7 ***Franks***	Y	N	N	Y	Y	Y	N	Y
8 Klein	Y	Y	N	Y	Y	Y	N	Y
9 Torricelli	Y	?	N	Y	Y	Y	N	Y
10 Payne	Y	Y	N	Y	Y	?	N	Y
11 ***Gallo***	Y	N	Y	Y	Y	Y	N	Y
12 ***Zimmer***	Y	N	Y	Y	N	Y	Y	Y
13 Menendez	Y	N	N	Y	Y	Y	N	Y
NEW MEXICO								
1 ***Schiff***	Y	N	Y	Y	Y	Y	Y	Y
2 ***Skeen***	Y	N	Y	Y	Y	Y	Y	Y
3 Richardson	Y	N	N	Y	Y	Y	N	Y
NEW YORK								
1 Hochbrueckner	Y	N	N	Y	Y	Y	N	Y
2 ***Lazio***	Y	N	Y	Y	Y	Y	Y	Y
3 ***King***	Y	N	Y	Y	Y	Y	Y	Y
4 ***Levy***	Y	N	Y	Y	Y	Y	Y	Y
5 Ackerman	?	?	?	?	?	?	?	?
6 Flake	?	?	N	Y	Y	Y	N	Y
7 Manton	Y	N	N	Y	Y	Y	N	Y
8 Nadler	Y	Y	N	Y	Y	Y	N	Y
9 Schumer	Y	N	N	Y	Y	Y	N	Y
10 Towns	Y	?	N	Y	Y	Y	N	Y
11 Owens	Y	Y	N	Y	Y	?	N	Y
12 Velazquez	Y	Y	N	Y	Y	Y	N	Y
13 ***Molinari***	Y	N	Y	Y	Y	Y	N	Y
14 Maloney	Y	N	N	Y	Y	Y	N	Y
15 Rangel	Y	Y	N	Y	?	?	N	Y
16 Serrano	Y	N	N	Y	Y	Y	N	Y
17 Engel	Y	Y	N	Y	Y	Y	N	Y
18 Lowey	Y	N	N	Y	Y	Y	N	Y
19 ***Fish***	Y	N	Y	Y	Y	Y	N	Y
20 ***Gilman***	Y	N	N	Y	Y	Y	N	Y
21 McNulty	?	?	N	Y	Y	Y	N	Y
22 ***Solomon***	Y	N	Y	Y	N	Y	Y	Y
23 ***Boehlert***	Y	N	N	Y	Y	Y	N	Y
24 ***McHugh***	Y	N	Y	Y	Y	Y	N	Y
25 ***Walsh***	Y	?	Y	Y	Y	Y	Y	Y
26 Hinchey	Y	Y	N	Y	Y	Y	N	Y
27 ***Paxon***	Y	N	Y	Y	N	Y	Y	Y
28 Slaughter	Y	N	N	Y	Y	Y	N	Y
29 LaFalce	Y	N	N	Y	Y	Y	N	Y
30 ***Quinn***	Y	N	N	Y	Y	Y	Y	Y
31 ***Houghton***	Y	?	Y	Y	Y	Y	N	Y
NORTH CAROLINA								
1 Clayton	Y	Y	N	Y	Y	Y	N	Y
2 Valentine	Y	N	Y	Y	Y	Y	N	Y
3 Lancaster	Y	Y	N	Y	Y	Y	N	Y
4 Price	Y	Y	N	Y	Y	Y	N	Y
5 Neal	Y	N	N	Y	Y	?	?	?
6 ***Coble***	N	N	Y	N	N	Y	Y	Y
7 Rose	Y	N	N	Y	Y	Y	N	Y
8 Hefner	Y	Y	N	Y	Y	Y	N	Y
9 ***McMillan***	Y	Y	Y	Y	Y	Y	Y	Y
10 ***Ballenger***	N	N	Y	N	N	Y	Y	Y
11 ***Taylor***	N	N	Y	N	Y	Y	Y	Y
12 Watt	Y	Y	N	Y	Y	Y	N	Y
NORTH DAKOTA								
AL Pomeroy	Y	N	N	Y	Y	Y	N	Y
OHIO								
1 Mann	Y	N	N	Y	Y	Y	N	Y
2 ***Portman***	Y	N	Y	Y	Y	Y	Y	Y
3 Hall	Y	Y	N	Y	Y	?	N	Y
4 ***Oxley***	Y	N	Y	Y	Y	Y	Y	Y
5 ***Gillmor***	Y	?	Y	Y	Y	Y	N	Y
6 Strickland	Y	N	N	Y	Y	Y	N	Y
7 ***Hobson***	Y	N	Y	Y	Y	Y	N	Y
8 ***Boehner***	N	N	Y	N	Y	Y	Y	Y
9 Kaptur	Y	N	N	Y	Y	Y	N	Y
10 ***Hoke***	N	N	Y	Y	Y	Y	Y	Y
11 Stokes	Y	Y	N	Y	Y	Y	N	Y
12 ***Kasich***	Y	N	Y	Y	Y	Y	Y	Y
13 Brown	Y	Y	N	Y	Y	Y	N	Y
14 Sawyer	Y	Y	N	Y	Y	Y	N	Y
15 ***Pryce***	Y	?	Y	Y	Y	Y	Y	Y
16 ***Regula***	Y	Y	Y	Y	Y	Y	N	Y
17 Traficant	Y	N	N	Y	Y	Y	N	Y
18 Applegate	Y	N	N	Y	Y	Y	N	Y
19 Fingerhut	Y	Y	N	Y	Y	Y	N	Y
OKLAHOMA								
1 ***Inhofe***	Y	N	Y	Y	Y	Y	Y	Y
2 Synar	Y	N	N	Y	Y	Y	N	Y
3 Brewster	Y	N	N	Y	Y	Y	N	Y
4 McCurdy	Y	N	N	Y	Y	Y	N	Y
5 ***Istook***	Y	N	Y	Y	Y	Y	Y	Y
6 English	Y	N	N	Y	Y	Y	N	Y
OREGON								
1 Furse	Y	N	N	Y	Y	Y	N	Y
2 ***Smith***	Y	N	Y	Y	N	Y	Y	Y
3 Wyden	Y	N	N	Y	Y	Y	N	Y
4 DeFazio	N	X	N	N	Y	Y	N	Y
5 Kopetski	Y	N	N	Y	Y	Y	N	Y
PENNSYLVANIA								
1 Foglietta	Y	Y	N	Y	Y	Y	N	Y
2 Blackwell	Y	Y	N	Y	Y	Y	N	Y
3 Borski	Y	N	N	Y	Y	Y	?	?
4 Klink	Y	N	N	Y	Y	Y	N	Y
5 ***Clinger***	Y	N	Y	Y	Y	Y	N	Y
6 Holden	Y	N	N	Y	Y	Y	N	Y
7 ***Weldon***	Y	N	N	Y	Y	Y	Y	?
8 ***Greenwood***	Y	?	Y	Y	Y	Y	Y	Y
9 ***Shuster***	Y	N	Y	Y	Y	Y	Y	Y
10 ***McDade***	Y	N	?	?	?	?	?	?
11 Kanjorski	N	Y	N	N	Y	Y	N	Y
12 Murtha	Y	N	?	?	?	?	?	?
13 Margolies-Mezv.	Y	N	N	Y	Y	Y	N	Y
14 Coyne	Y	N	N	Y	Y	Y	N	Y
15 McHale	Y	N	N	Y	Y	Y	N	Y
16 ***Walker***	N	N	Y	N	N	Y	Y	Y
17 ***Gekas***	Y	N	Y	Y	Y	Y	N	Y
18 ***Santorum***	Y	N	N	Y	Y	Y	N	Y
19 ***Goodling***	N	N	Y	N	N	Y	N	Y
20 Murphy	?	?	N	Y	Y	Y	N	Y
21 ***Ridge***	Y	?	Y	Y	Y	Y	Y	Y
RHODE ISLAND								
1 ***Machtley***	Y	?	Y	Y	Y	Y	N	Y
2 Reed	Y	Y	N	Y	Y	Y	N	Y
SOUTH CAROLINA								
1 ***Ravenel***	Y	N	N	Y	Y	Y	Y	Y
2 ***Spence***	Y	N	Y	Y	Y	Y	Y	Y
3 Derrick	Y	Y	N	Y	Y	Y	N	Y
4 ***Inglis***	N	N	Y	N	Y	Y	Y	Y
5 Spratt	Y	Y	N	Y	Y	Y	N	Y
6 Clyburn	Y	N	N	Y	Y	Y	N	Y
SOUTH DAKOTA								
AL Johnson	Y	N	N	Y	Y	Y	N	Y
TENNESSEE								
1 ***Quillen***	?	#	Y	Y	N	Y	Y	Y
2 ***Duncan***	Y	N	N	Y	N	Y	Y	Y
3 Lloyd	Y	N	N	Y	Y	Y	N	Y
4 Cooper	Y	Y	N	Y	Y	Y	N	Y
5 Clement	Y	N	N	Y	Y	Y	N	Y
6 Gordon	Y	N	N	Y	Y	Y	N	Y
7 ***Sundquist***	Y	N	Y	Y	N	Y	Y	Y
8 Tanner	Y	Y	Y	Y	Y	Y	N	Y
9 Ford	Y	N	N	Y	Y	Y	N	?
TEXAS								
1 Chapman	Y	?	N	Y	Y	Y	N	Y
2 Wilson	?	?	N	Y	Y	Y	N	Y
3 ***Johnson, Sam***	Y	N	Y	Y	N	Y	Y	Y
4 Hall	Y	N	Y	Y	Y	Y	Y	Y
5 Bryant	Y	?	N	Y	Y	Y	N	Y
6 ***Barton***	Y	N	Y	Y	Y	Y	Y	Y
7 ***Archer***	Y	N	Y	Y	Y	Y	Y	Y
8 ***Fields***	Y	N	Y	Y	Y	Y	Y	Y
9 Brooks	Y	N	N	Y	Y	Y	N	Y
10 Pickle	Y	N	N	Y	Y	Y	N	Y
11 Edwards	Y	Y	N	Y	Y	Y	N	Y
12 Geren	Y	N	N	Y	Y	Y	N	Y
13 Sarpalius	N	N	N	N	Y	Y	N	Y
14 Laughlin	Y	?	N	Y	Y	Y	N	Y
15 de la Garza	?	?	N	Y	Y	Y	N	Y
16 Coleman	Y	Y	N	Y	Y	Y	N	Y
17 Stenholm	N	N	Y	N	Y	Y	N	Y
18 Washington	Y	?	N	Y	Y	?	N	Y
19 ***Combest***	Y	N	Y	Y	N	Y	Y	Y
20 Gonzalez	Y	Y	N	Y	Y	Y	N	Y
21 ***Smith***	Y	N	Y	Y	Y	Y	Y	Y
22 ***DeLay***	N	N	Y	N	Y	Y	Y	Y
23 ***Bonilla***	N	Y	Y	N	N	Y	Y	Y
24 Frost	Y	N	N	Y	Y	Y	N	Y
25 Andrews	Y	N	N	Y	Y	Y	N	Y
26 ***Armey***	N	N	Y	N	Y	Y	Y	Y
27 Ortiz	Y	N	N	Y	Y	Y	N	Y
28 Tejeda	Y	N	N	Y	Y	Y	N	Y
29 Green	+	−	N	Y	Y	Y	N	Y
30 Johnson, E.B.	Y	Y	N	Y	Y	Y	N	Y
UTAH								
1 ***Hansen***	Y	N	Y	Y	Y	Y	Y	Y
2 Shepherd	Y	Y	N	Y	Y	Y	N	Y
3 Orton	Y	N	N	Y	Y	Y	N	Y
VERMONT								
AL *Sanders*	Y	N	N	Y	Y	Y	N	Y
VIRGINIA								
1 ***Bateman***	Y	Y	Y	Y	Y	Y	Y	Y
2 Pickett	Y	Y	Y	Y	Y	Y	N	Y
3 Scott	Y	Y	N	Y	Y	Y	N	Y
4 Sisisky	Y	Y	Y	Y	Y	Y	N	Y
5 Payne	Y	Y	N	Y	Y	Y	N	Y
6 ***Goodlatte***	Y	Y	Y	Y	N	Y	Y	Y
7 ***Bliley***	N	Y	Y	N	Y	Y	Y	Y
8 Moran	Y	Y	N	Y	Y	Y	N	Y
9 Boucher	Y	Y	?	?	?	Y	N	Y
10 ***Wolf***	Y	Y	Y	Y	N	Y	Y	Y
11 Byrne	Y	Y	N	Y	Y	Y	N	Y
WASHINGTON								
1 Cantwell	Y	N	N	Y	Y	Y	N	Y
2 Swift	Y	Y	N	Y	Y	Y	N	Y
3 Unsoeld	Y	Y	N	Y	Y	Y	N	Y
4 Inslee	Y	N	N	Y	Y	Y	N	Y
5 Foley								
6 Dicks	Y	N	N	Y	Y	Y	N	Y
7 McDermott	?	Y	N	Y	Y	Y	N	Y
8 ***Dunn***	N	N	Y	N	Y	Y	Y	Y
9 Kreidler	Y	N	N	N	Y	Y	N	Y
WEST VIRGINIA								
1 Mollohan	Y	N	N	Y	Y	Y	N	Y
2 Wise	Y	N	N	Y	Y	Y	N	Y
3 Rahall	Y	N	N	Y	Y	Y	N	Y
WISCONSIN								
1 Barca	Y	N	N	Y	Y	Y	N	Y
2 ***Klug***	Y	N	Y	Y	Y	Y	N	Y
3 ***Gunderson***	Y	N	Y	Y	Y	Y	N	Y
4 Kleczka	Y	N	N	Y	Y	Y	N	Y
5 Barrett	Y	N	N	Y	Y	Y	N	Y
6 ***Petri***	Y	N	Y	N	N	Y	N	Y
7 Obey	Y	N	N	Y	Y	Y	N	Y
8 ***Roth***	Y	N	Y	Y	N	Y	Y	Y
9 ***Sensenbrenner***	Y	N	Y	Y	N	Y	Y	Y
WYOMING								
AL ***Thomas***	Y	N	Y	Y	Y	Y	N	Y
DELEGATES								
de Lugo, V.I.	Y	N	N	D	D	Y	N	D
Faleomavaega, Am.S.	?	?	?	D	D	Y	N	D
Norton, D.C.	Y	Y	N	D	D	Y	N	D
Romero-B., P.R.	?	?	N	D	D	Y	?	D
Underwood, Guam	Y	Y	N	D	D	Y	?	D

Southern states - Ala., Ark., Fla., Ga., Ky., La., Miss., N.C., Okla., S.C., Tenn., Texas, Va.
Omitted votes are quorum calls, which CQ does not include in its vote charts.

496. HR 1804. School Improvement/Passage. Passage of the bill to authorize $427 million for fiscal 1994 for grants to states and local schools and for other costs associated with voluntary adoption of national education goals, standards and tests and improvements to public schools. Passed 307-118: R 57-116; D 249-2 (ND 165-2, SD 84-0); I 1-0, Oct. 13, 1993. A "yea" was a vote in support of the president's position.

497. HR 2351. National Endowments for the Arts and the Humanities/Previous Question. Beilenson, D-Calif., motion to order the previous question (thus ending debate and the possibility of amendment) on adoption of the rule (H Res 264) to provide for House floor consideration of the bill to authorize $174.6 million for the National Endowment for the Arts, $177.5 million for the National Endowment for the Humanities and $28.8 million for the Institute of Museum Services in fiscal 1994 and such sums as necessary in fiscal 1995. Motion agreed to 240-185: R 1-172; D 238-13 (ND 166-3, SD 72-10); I 1-0, Oct. 14, 1993.

498. HR 2351. National Endowments for the Arts and the Humanities/Rule. Adoption of the rule (H Res 264) to provide for House floor consideration of the bill to authorize $174.6 million for the National Endowment for the Arts, $177.5 million for the National Endowment for the Humanities and $28.8 million for the Institute of Museum Services in fiscal 1994 and such sums as necessary in fiscal 1995. Adopted 225-195: R 1-171; D 223-24 (ND 159-8, SD 64-16); I 1-0, Oct. 14, 1993.

*500. HR 2351. National Endowments for the Arts and the Humanities/NEA Authorization. Crane, R-Ill., amendment to eliminate the authorization for the National Endowment for the Arts (NEA). Rejected in the Committee of the Whole 103-326: R 89-85; D 14-240 (ND 6-165, SD 8-75); I 0-1, Oct. 14, 1993. A "nay" was a vote in support of the president's position.

501. HR 2351. National Endowments for the Arts and the Humanities/Spending Cut. Dornan, R-Calif., amendment to cut by 40 percent the bill's fiscal 1994 authorization levels for the National Endowment for the Arts, the National Endowment for the Humanities and the Institute of Museum Services. Rejected in the Committee of the Whole 151-281: R 126-48; D 25-232 (ND 8-166, SD 17-66); I 0-1, Oct. 14, 1993. A "nay" was a vote in support of the president's position.

502. HR 2351. National Endowments for the Arts and the Humanities/Illegal Aliens. Cunningham, R-Calif., motion to recommit the bill to the Education and Labor Committee with instructions to report the bill back with an amendment to prohibit the National Endowment for the Arts from providing assistance to illegal aliens. Rejected 210-214: R 163-10; D 47-203 (ND 20-148, SD 27-55); I 0-1, Oct. 14, 1993.

503. HR 2351. National Endowments for the Arts and the Humanities/Passage. Passage of the bill to authorize $174.6 million for the National Endowment for the Arts, $177.5 million for the National Endowment for the Humanities and $28.8 million for the Institute of Museum Services in fiscal 1994 and such sums as necessary in.fiscal 1995. Passed 304-119: R 68-106; D 235-13 (ND 162-5, SD 73-8); I 1-0, Oct. 14, 1993. A "yea" was a vote in support of the president's position.

504. HR 3167. Unemployment Benefits Extension/Previous Question. Bonior, D-Mich., motion to order the previous question (thus ending debate and the possibility of amendment) on adoption of the rule (H Res 273) to provide for House floor consideration of the bill to extend emergency benefits for the long-term unemployed. Motion agreed to 235-187: R 2-171; D 232-16 (ND 159-8, SD 73-8); I 1-0, Oct. 14, 1993.

Omitted votes are quorum calls, which CQ does not include in its vote charts.

KEY

Y	Voted for (yea).
#	Paired for.
+	Announced for.
N	Voted against (nay).
X	Paired against.
−	Announced against.
P	Voted "present."
C	Voted "present" to avoid possible conflict of interest.
?	Did not vote or otherwise make a position known.
D	Delegates ineligible to vote.

Democrats *Republicans*
Independent

	496	497	498	500	501	502	503	504
ALABAMA								
1 *Callahan*	N	N	N	Y	Y	Y	N	N
2 *Everett*	N	N	N	Y	Y	Y	N	N
3 Browder	Y	N	N	N	Y	Y	Y	Y
4 Bevill	Y	N	N	N	Y	Y	Y	Y
5 Cramer	Y	N	N	Y	Y	Y	Y	Y
6 *Bachus*	N	N	N	Y	Y	Y	N	N
7 Hilliard	Y	Y	Y	N	N	N	Y	Y
ALASKA								
AL *Young*	Y	N	N	Y	Y	Y	Y	N
ARIZONA								
1 Coppersmith	Y	Y	Y	N	N	N	Y	Y
2 Pastor	Y	Y	Y	N	N	N	Y	Y
3 *Stump*	N	N	N	Y	Y	Y	N	N
4 *Kyl*	N	N	N	Y	Y	Y	N	N
5 *Kolbe*	N	N	N	N	N	Y	N	N
6 English	Y	Y	Y	N	N	Y	Y	Y
ARKANSAS								
1 Lambert	Y	Y	Y	N	N	N	Y	Y
2 Thornton	Y	Y	Y	N	N	N	Y	Y
3 *Hutchinson*	N	N	N	Y	Y	Y	N	N
4 *Dickey*	N	N	N	Y	Y	Y	N	N
CALIFORNIA								
1 Hamburg	Y	Y	Y	N	N	N	Y	Y
2 *Herger*	N	N	N	Y	Y	Y	N	N
3 Fazio	Y	Y	Y	N	N	N	Y	Y
4 *Doolittle*	N	N	N	Y	Y	Y	N	N
5 Matsui	Y	Y	Y	N	N	?	Y	Y
6 Woolsey	Y	Y	Y	N	N	N	Y	Y
7 Miller	Y	Y	Y	N	N	N	Y	Y
8 Pelosi	Y	Y	Y	N	N	N	Y	Y
9 Dellums	Y	Y	Y	N	N	N	Y	Y
10 *Baker*	N	N	N	Y	Y	Y	N	N
11 *Pombo*	N	N	N	Y	Y	Y	N	N
12 Lantos	Y	Y	Y	N	N	N	Y	Y
13 Stark	Y	Y	Y	?	N	N	Y	N
14 Eshoo	Y	Y	Y	N	N	N	Y	Y
15 Mineta	Y	Y	Y	N	N	N	Y	Y
16 Edwards	Y	Y	Y	N	N	N	Y	Y
17 Farr	Y	Y	Y	N	N	N	Y	Y
18 Condit	Y	Y	N	Y	Y	Y	N	Y
19 Lehman	Y	Y	Y	N	N	Y	Y	Y
20 Dooley	Y	Y	Y	N	N	N	Y	Y
21 *Thomas*	Y	N	N	N	N	Y	N	N
22 *Huffington*	Y	N	N	Y	Y	Y	N	N
23 *Gallegly*	N	N	N	Y	Y	Y	N	N
24 Beilenson	Y	Y	Y	N	N	N	Y	Y
25 *McKeon*	Y	N	N	Y	Y	Y	N	N
26 Berman	Y	Y	Y	N	N	N	?	Y
27 *Moorhead*	N	N	N	Y	Y	Y	N	N
28 *Dreier*	N	N	N	Y	Y	Y	N	N
29 Waxman	Y	Y	Y	N	N	N	Y	Y
30 Becerra	Y	Y	Y	N	N	N	Y	Y
31 Martinez	Y	Y	Y	N	N	?	?	?
32 Dixon	Y	Y	Y	N	N	N	Y	Y
33 Roybal-Allard	Y	Y	?	N	N	N	Y	Y
34 Torres	Y	Y	Y	N	N	N	Y	Y
35 Waters	Y	Y	Y	N	N	?	Y	Y
36 Harman	Y	Y	Y	N	N	N	Y	Y
37 Tucker	Y	Y	Y	N	N	N	Y	Y
38 *Horn*	Y	N	N	N	N	N	Y	Y
39 *Royce*	N	N	N	Y	Y	Y	N	N
40 *Lewis*	N	N	N	N	N	Y	N	N
41 *Kim*	N	N	N	N	Y	Y	N	N

	496	497	498	500	501	502	503	504
42 Brown	Y	Y	Y	N	N	N	Y	Y
43 *Calvert*	N	N	N	Y	Y	Y	N	N
44 *McCandless*	N	N	N	Y	Y	Y	N	N
45 *Rohrabacher*	N	N	N	Y	Y	Y	N	N
46 *Dornan*	N	N	N	Y	Y	Y	N	N
47 *Cox*	N	N	N	Y	Y	Y	N	N
48 *Packard*	N	N	N	N	N	Y	N	N
49 Schenk	Y	Y	Y	N	N	N	Y	Y
50 Filner	Y	Y	Y	N	N	N	Y	Y
51 *Cunningham*	N	N	N	Y	Y	Y	N	N
52 *Hunter*	N	N	N	Y	Y	Y	N	N
COLORADO								
1 Schroeder	Y	Y	Y	N	N	N	Y	Y
2 Skaggs	Y	Y	Y	N	N	N	Y	Y
3 *McInnis*	N	N	N	N	Y	Y	N	N
4 *Allard*	N	N	N	Y	Y	Y	N	N
5 *Hefley*	N	N	N	Y	Y	Y	N	N
6 *Schaefer*	N	N	N	N	Y	Y	N	N
CONNECTICUT								
1 Kennelly	Y	Y	Y	N	N	N	Y	Y
2 Gejdenson	Y	Y	Y	N	N	N	Y	Y
3 DeLauro	Y	Y	Y	N	N	N	Y	Y
4 *Shays*	N	N	N	N	N	N	Y	N
5 *Franks*	Y	N	N	Y	Y	Y	N	N
6 *Johnson*	Y	N	N	N	N	Y	N	N
DELAWARE								
AL *Castle*	Y	N	N	N	N	Y	Y	N
FLORIDA								
1 Hutto	Y	N	N	Y	Y	Y	N	N
2 Peterson	Y	Y	Y	N	N	N	Y	Y
3 Brown	Y	Y	Y	N	N	N	Y	Y
4 *Fowler*	N	N	N	N	N	Y	N	N
5 Thurman	Y	Y	Y	N	N	N	Y	Y
6 *Stearns*	Y	N	N	Y	Y	Y	N	N
7 *Mica*	N	N	N	N	Y	Y	N	N
8 *McCollum*	N	N	N	N	Y	Y	N	N
9 *Bilirakis*	Y	N	N	N	Y	Y	N	N
10 *Young*	Y	N	N	Y	Y	Y	N	N
11 Gibbons	Y	Y	Y	N	N	N	Y	Y
12 *Canady*	N	N	N	Y	Y	Y	N	N
13 *Miller*	Y	N	N	Y	Y	Y	N	N
14 *Goss*	N	N	N	N	Y	Y	N	N
15 Bacchus	Y	Y	Y	N	N	N	Y	Y
16 *Lewis*	N	N	N	Y	Y	Y	N	N
17 Meek	Y	Y	Y	N	N	N	Y	Y
18 *Ros-Lehtinen*	N	N	N	Y	Y	Y	N	N
19 Johnston	Y	Y	Y	N	N	N	Y	Y
20 Deutsch	Y	Y	Y	N	N	N	Y	Y
21 *Diaz-Balart*	Y	N	N	N	N	Y	Y	Y
22 *Shaw*	N	N	N	Y	Y	Y	N	N
23 Hastings	Y	Y	Y	N	N	N	Y	Y
GEORGIA								
1 *Kingston*	N	N	N	Y	Y	Y	N	N
2 Bishop	Y	Y	Y	N	N	N	Y	Y
3 *Collins*	N	N	N	Y	Y	Y	N	N
4 *Linder*	N	N	N	Y	Y	Y	N	N
5 Lewis	Y	Y	Y	N	N	N	Y	Y
6 *Gingrich*	N	N	N	Y	Y	Y	N	N
7 Darden	Y	Y	Y	N	N	Y	Y	Y
8 Rowland	Y	Y	Y	N	N	N	Y	Y
9 Deal	Y	Y	N	N	Y	N	Y	Y
10 Johnson	Y	Y	Y	N	N	N	Y	Y
11 McKinney	Y	Y	Y	N	N	?	?	Y
HAWAII								
1 Abercrombie	Y	Y	Y	N	N	N	?	Y
2 Mink	Y	Y	Y	N	N	N	Y	Y
IDAHO								
1 LaRocco	Y	Y	Y	N	N	N	Y	Y
2 *Crapo*	N	N	N	Y	Y	Y	N	N
ILLINOIS								
1 Rush	Y	Y	Y	N	N	N	Y	Y
2 Reynolds	Y	Y	Y	N	N	N	Y	Y
3 Lipinski	Y	Y	Y	N	Y	Y	Y	Y
4 Gutierrez	Y	Y	Y	N	N	N	Y	Y
5 Rostenkowski	Y	Y	Y	N	N	N	Y	Y
6 *Hyde*	N	N	N	Y	Y	Y	N	N
7 Collins	Y	Y	Y	N	N	N	Y	Y
8 *Crane*	N	N	N	Y	Y	Y	N	N
9 Yates	Y	Y	Y	N	N	N	Y	Y
10 *Porter*	N	N	N	N	N	N	Y	N
11 Sangmeister	Y	Y	Y	N	N	N	Y	Y
12 Costello	Y	Y	Y	N	N	N	Y	Y
13 *Fawell*	N	N	N	N	N	Y	N	N
14 *Hastert*	N	N	N	Y	Y	Y	N	N
15 *Ewing*	N	N	N	Y	Y	Y	N	N
16 *Manzullo*	N	N	N	Y	Y	Y	N	N
17 Evans	Y	Y	Y	N	N	N	Y	Y

ND Northern Democrats   SD Southern Democrats

	496	497	498	500	501	502	503	504
18 ***Michel***	N	N	N	N	Y	Y	Y	N
19 Poshard	Y	Y	Y	N	Y	Y	Y	Y
20 Durbin	Y	Y	Y	N	N	Y	Y	Y
INDIANA								
1 Visclosky	Y	Y	Y	N	Y	N	Y	Y
2 Sharp	Y	Y	Y	N	N	Y	Y	Y
3 Roemer	Y	Y	Y	N	N	N	Y	Y
4 Long	Y	Y	Y	N	N	N	Y	Y
5 ***Buyer***	Y	N	N	Y	Y	Y	N	N
6 ***Burton***	N	N	N	Y	Y	Y	N	N
7 ***Myers***	Y	N	N	N	Y	Y	Y	N
8 McCloskey	Y	Y	Y	N	N	N	Y	Y
9 Hamilton	Y	N	Y	N	N	N	Y	Y
10 Jacobs	Y	N	N	N	N	Y	Y	N
IOWA								
1 ***Leach***	Y	N	N	N	N	Y	Y	N
2 ***Nussle***	Y	N	N	N	Y	Y	N	N
3 ***Lightfoot***	N	N	N	Y	Y	Y	N	N
4 Smith	Y	Y	Y	N	N	N	Y	Y
5 ***Grandy***	Y	N	N	N	N	N	Y	N
KANSAS								
1 ***Roberts***	N	N	N	Y	Y	Y	N	N
2 Slattery	Y	Y	Y	N	N	Y	Y	Y
3 ***Meyers***	Y	N	N	N	N	Y	Y	N
4 Glickman	Y	Y	Y	N	N	N	Y	Y
KENTUCKY								
1 Barlow	Y	Y	Y	N	N	N	Y	Y
2 Natcher	Y	Y	Y	N	N	N	Y	Y
3 Mazzoli	Y	Y	Y	N	N	N	Y	Y
4 ***Bunning***	N	N	N	Y	Y	Y	N	?
5 ***Rogers***	Y	N	N	N	N	Y	Y	N
6 Baesler	Y	Y	Y	N	N	N	Y	Y
LOUISIANA								
1 ***Livingston***	N	N	?	Y	Y	Y	N	N
2 Jefferson	Y	Y	Y	N	N	N	Y	Y
3 Tauzin	Y	Y	N	Y	Y	Y	N	Y
4 Fields	Y	Y	Y	N	N	N	Y	Y
5 ***McCrery***	N	N	N	Y	Y	Y	N	N
6 ***Baker***	N	N	N	Y	Y	Y	N	N
7 Hayes	Y	Y	?	N	Y	N	Y	Y
MAINE								
1 Andrews	Y	Y	Y	N	N	N	Y	Y
2 ***Snowe***	Y	N	N	N	Y	Y	Y	N
MARYLAND								
1 ***Gilchrest***	Y	N	N	N	Y	Y	Y	N
2 ***Bentley***	Y	N	N	N	N	Y	Y	N
3 Cardin	Y	Y	Y	N	N	N	Y	Y
4 Wynn	Y	Y	Y	N	N	N	Y	Y
5 Hoyer	Y	Y	Y	N	N	N	Y	Y
6 ***Bartlett***	N	N	N	Y	Y	Y	N	N
7 Mfume	Y	Y	Y	N	N	N	Y	Y
8 ***Morella***	Y	Y	Y	N	N	N	Y	N
MASSACHUSETTS								
1 Olver	Y	Y	Y	N	N	N	Y	Y
2 Neal	Y	Y	Y	N	N	N	Y	Y
3 ***Blute***	Y	N	N	N	N	Y	Y	N
4 Frank	Y	Y	Y	N	N	N	Y	Y
5 Meehan	Y	Y	Y	N	N	N	Y	Y
6 ***Torkildsen***	Y	N	N	N	N	Y	Y	N
7 Markey	Y	Y	Y	N	N	N	Y	Y
8 Kennedy	Y	Y	Y	N	N	N	Y	Y
9 Moakley	Y	Y	Y	N	N	N	Y	Y
10 Studds	Y	Y	Y	N	N	N	Y	Y
MICHIGAN								
1 Stupak	Y	Y	Y	N	N	Y	Y	Y
2 ***Hoekstra***	N	N	N	N	N	Y	Y	N
3 Vacancy								
4 ***Camp***	N	N	N	N	N	Y	Y	N
5 Barcia	Y	Y	N	Y	Y	Y	Y	Y
6 ***Upton***	Y	N	N	N	N	Y	Y	N
7 ***Smith***	Y	N	N	Y	Y	?	N	N
8 Carr	Y	Y	?	N	N	N	Y	Y
9 Kildee	Y	Y	Y	N	N	N	Y	Y
10 Bonior	Y	Y	Y	N	N	N	Y	Y
11 ***Knollenberg***	N	N	N	Y	Y	Y	N	N
12 Levin	Y	Y	Y	N	N	N	Y	Y
13 Ford	Y	Y	Y	N	N	N	Y	Y
14 Conyers	Y	Y	Y	?	N	N	Y	Y
15 Collins	Y	Y	Y	N	N	N	Y	Y
16 Dingell	Y	Y	Y	N	N	N	Y	Y
MINNESOTA								
1 Penny	N	Y	N	Y	N	Y	Y	N
2 Minge	Y	Y	N	N	N	N	Y	Y
3 ***Ramstad***	Y	N	N	N	N	Y	Y	N
4 Vento	Y	Y	Y	N	N	N	Y	Y

	496	497	498	500	501	502	503	504
5 Sabo	Y	Y	Y	N	N	N	Y	Y
6 ***Grams***	N	N	N	Y	Y	Y	N	N
7 Peterson	Y	Y	Y	N	N	N	Y	Y
8 Oberstar	Y	Y	Y	N	N	N	Y	Y
MISSISSIPPI								
1 Whitten	Y	Y	Y	N	N	N	?	Y
2 Thompson	Y	Y	Y	N	N	N	Y	Y
3 Montgomery	Y	Y	Y	N	N	Y	Y	Y
4 Parker	Y	Y	Y	N	N	Y	Y	Y
5 Taylor	Y	N	N	Y	Y	Y	N	N
MISSOURI								
1 Clay	Y	Y	Y	?	N	N	Y	Y
2 ***Talent***	N	N	N	Y	Y	Y	N	N
3 Gephardt	Y	?	?	?	?	N	Y	Y
4 Skelton	?	Y	N	Y	Y	Y	N	Y
5 Wheat	Y	Y	Y	N	N	N	Y	Y
6 Danner	Y	Y	N	N	N	Y	Y	Y
7 ***Hancock***	N	N	N	Y	Y	Y	N	N
8 ***Emerson***	N	N	N	Y	Y	Y	N	N
9 Volkmer	Y	Y	Y	N	N	Y	Y	Y
MONTANA								
AL Williams	Y	Y	Y	N	N	N	Y	Y
NEBRASKA								
1 ***Bereuter***	N	N	N	N	N	Y	Y	N
2 Hoagland	Y	Y	Y	N	N	N	Y	Y
3 ***Barrett***	N	N	N	N	Y	Y	Y	N
NEVADA								
1 Bilbray	Y	Y	Y	N	N	Y	Y	Y
2 ***Vucanovich***	N	N	N	Y	Y	Y	N	N
NEW HAMPSHIRE								
1 ***Zeliff***	N	N	N	N	N	Y	Y	N
2 Swett	Y	Y	Y	N	N	N	Y	N
NEW JERSEY								
1 Andrews	Y	Y	Y	N	N	N	Y	Y
2 Hughes	Y	Y	Y	N	N	N	Y	Y
3 ***Saxton***	Y	N	N	N	N	N	Y	N
4 ***Smith***	N	N	N	Y	Y	Y	N	N
5 ***Roukema***	N	N	N	N	N	Y	Y	N
6 Pallone	Y	Y	Y	N	N	N	Y	Y
7 ***Franks***	N	N	N	N	N	Y	Y	N
8 Klein	Y	Y	Y	N	N	N	Y	Y
9 Torricelli	Y	Y	Y	N	N	N	Y	Y
10 Payne	Y	Y	Y	N	N	N	Y	Y
11 ***Gallo***	Y	N	N	N	N	Y	Y	N
12 ***Zimmer***	N	N	N	N	Y	Y	Y	N
13 Menendez	Y	Y	Y	N	N	N	Y	Y
NEW MEXICO								
1 ***Schiff***	Y	N	N	N	N	Y	Y	N
2 ***Skeen***	N	N	N	N	N	Y	N	N
3 Richardson	Y	Y	Y	N	N	N	Y	Y
NEW YORK								
1 Hochbrueckner	Y	Y	Y	N	N	N	Y	Y
2 ***Lazio***	Y	N	N	N	N	Y	Y	N
3 ***King***	N	N	N	Y	Y	Y	N	N
4 ***Levy***	N	N	N	Y	Y	Y	N	N
5 Ackerman	?	Y	Y	N	N	N	Y	Y
6 Flake	Y	Y	Y	N	N	N	Y	Y
7 Manton	?	Y	Y	N	N	N	Y	Y
8 Nadler	Y	Y	Y	N	N	N	Y	Y
9 Schumer	Y	Y	Y	N	N	N	Y	Y
10 Towns	Y	Y	Y	N	N	N	Y	Y
11 Owens	Y	Y	Y	N	N	N	Y	Y
12 Velazquez	Y	Y	Y	N	N	N	Y	Y
13 ***Molinari***	Y	N	N	N	Y	Y	Y	N
14 Maloney	Y	Y	Y	N	N	N	Y	Y
15 Rangel	Y	Y	Y	N	N	N	Y	Y
16 Serrano	Y	Y	?	N	N	N	Y	Y
17 Engel	Y	?	Y	N	N	N	Y	?
18 Lowey	Y	Y	Y	N	N	N	Y	Y
19 ***Fish***	Y	N	N	N	N	Y	Y	N
20 ***Gilman***	Y	N	N	N	N	Y	Y	N
21 McNulty	Y	Y	Y	N	N	Y	Y	Y
22 ***Solomon***	N	N	N	Y	Y	Y	N	N
23 ***Boehlert***	Y	N	N	N	N	Y	Y	N
24 ***McHugh***	N	N	N	Y	Y	Y	N	N
25 ***Walsh***	Y	N	N	N	N	Y	Y	N
26 Hinchey	Y	Y	Y	N	N	N	Y	Y
27 ***Paxon***	N	N	N	Y	Y	Y	N	N
28 Slaughter	Y	Y	Y	N	N	N	Y	Y
29 LaFalce	Y	Y	Y	N	N	N	Y	Y
30 ***Quinn***	Y	N	N	Y	Y	Y	N	N
31 ***Houghton***	Y	N	N	N	N	N	Y	N
NORTH CAROLINA								
1 Clayton	Y	Y	Y	N	N	N	Y	Y
2 Valentine	Y	Y	N	N	N	Y	Y	Y

	496	497	498	500	501	502	503	504
3 Lancaster	Y	Y	Y	N	N	Y	Y	N
4 Price	Y	Y	Y	N	N	N	Y	Y
5 Neal	?	?	?	N	N	N	Y	Y
6 ***Coble***	N	N	N	Y	Y	Y	N	N
7 Rose	Y	Y	Y	N	N	N	Y	?
8 Hefner	Y	Y	Y	N	N	N	Y	Y
9 ***McMillan***	Y	N	N	N	N	N	Y	N
10 ***Ballenger***	N	N	N	N	Y	Y	Y	N
11 ***Taylor***	N	N	N	Y	Y	Y	N	N
12 Watt	Y	Y	Y	N	N	N	Y	Y
NORTH DAKOTA								
AL Pomeroy	Y	Y	Y	N	N	N	Y	Y
OHIO								
1 Mann	Y	Y	Y	N	N	N	Y	Y
2 ***Portman***	N	N	N	N	Y	Y	N	N
3 Hall	Y	Y	Y	N	N	N	Y	Y
4 ***Oxley***	N	N	N	N	Y	Y	N	N
5 ***Gillmor***	Y	N	N	N	Y	Y	Y	N
6 Strickland	Y	Y	Y	N	N	N	Y	Y
7 ***Hobson***	Y	N	N	N	Y	Y	Y	N
8 ***Boehner***	N	N	N	Y	Y	Y	N	N
9 Kaptur	Y	Y	Y	N	N	N	Y	Y
10 ***Hoke***	N	N	N	N	Y	Y	Y	N
11 Stokes	Y	Y	Y	N	N	N	Y	?
12 ***Kasich***	N	N	N	N	Y	Y	N	N
13 Brown	Y	Y	Y	N	Y	Y	Y	Y
14 Sawyer	Y	Y	Y	N	N	N	Y	Y
15 ***Pryce***	N	N	N	N	Y	Y	Y	N
16 ***Regula***	Y	N	N	N	N	Y	Y	N
17 Traficant	Y	Y	Y	N	N	N	Y	Y
18 Applegate	Y	Y	Y	N	N	Y	Y	N
19 Fingerhut	N	Y	Y	N	N	N	Y	Y
OKLAHOMA								
1 ***Inhofe***	N	N	N	Y	Y	Y	N	N
2 Synar	Y	Y	Y	N	N	N	Y	Y
3 Brewster	Y	Y	Y	N	N	N	Y	N
4 McCurdy	Y	Y	Y	N	N	N	Y	?
5 ***Istook***	N	N	N	Y	Y	Y	N	N
6 English	Y	N	N	N	N	N	Y	N
OREGON								
1 Furse	Y	Y	Y	N	N	N	Y	Y
2 ***Smith***	N	N	N	Y	Y	Y	N	N
3 Wyden	Y	Y	Y	N	N	N	Y	Y
4 DeFazio	Y	Y	Y	N	N	N	Y	Y
5 Kopetski	Y	Y	Y	N	N	N	Y	Y
PENNSYLVANIA								
1 Foglietta	Y	Y	Y	N	N	N	Y	Y
2 Blackwell	Y	Y	Y	N	N	N	Y	Y
3 Borski	?	Y	Y	N	N	N	Y	Y
4 Klink	Y	Y	Y	N	N	N	Y	Y
5 ***Clinger***	Y	N	N	N	N	Y	Y	N
6 Holden	Y	Y	Y	Y	Y	Y	N	N
7 ***Weldon***	?	N	N	N	Y	Y	Y	N
8 ***Greenwood***	N	N	N	Y	Y	Y	N	N
9 ***Shuster***	N	N	N	Y	Y	Y	N	N
10 ***McDade***	?	?	?	?	?	?	?	?
11 Kanjorski	Y	Y	Y	N	N	N	Y	Y
12 Murtha	?	?	?	?	?	?	?	?
13 Margolies-Mezv.	Y	Y	Y	N	N	N	Y	N
14 Coyne	Y	Y	Y	N	N	N	Y	Y
15 McHale	Y	Y	Y	N	N	N	Y	Y
16 ***Walker***	N	N	N	Y	Y	Y	N	N
17 ***Gekas***	N	N	N	Y	Y	Y	N	N
18 ***Santorum***	N	N	N	N	N	Y	Y	N
19 ***Goodling***	Y	N	N	N	Y	Y	N	N
20 Murphy	Y	N	N	N	N	?	Y	N
21 ***Ridge***	N	N	N	N	N	Y	Y	N
RHODE ISLAND								
1 ***Machtley***	Y	N	N	N	N	Y	Y	N
2 Reed	Y	Y	Y	N	N	N	Y	Y
SOUTH CAROLINA								
1 ***Ravenel***	Y	N	N	Y	Y	Y	N	N
2 ***Spence***	N	N	N	N	Y	Y	Y	N
3 Derrick	Y	Y	Y	N	N	N	Y	Y
4 ***Inglis***	N	N	N	Y	Y	Y	N	N
5 Spratt	Y	Y	Y	N	N	N	Y	Y
6 Clyburn	Y	Y	Y	N	N	N	Y	Y
SOUTH DAKOTA								
AL Johnson	Y	Y	Y	N	N	N	Y	Y
TENNESSEE								
1 ***Quillen***	Y	N	N	Y	Y	Y	N	N
2 ***Duncan***	Y	N	N	Y	Y	Y	N	N
3 Lloyd	Y	Y	Y	N	N	?	Y	Y
4 Cooper	Y	N	N	N	Y	Y	Y	Y
5 Clement	Y	Y	Y	N	N	N	Y	Y

	496	497	498	500	501	502	503	504
6 Gordon	Y	Y	Y	N	N	N	Y	Y
7 ***Sundquist***	Y	N	N	Y	Y	Y	N	N
8 Tanner	Y	Y	N	Y	Y	Y	N	Y
9 Ford	Y	Y	Y	N	N	N	Y	Y
TEXAS								
1 Chapman	Y	Y	Y	N	Y	Y	Y	Y
2 Wilson	Y	N	?	N	N	N	Y	Y
3 ***Johnson, Sam***	N	N	N	Y	Y	Y	N	N
4 Hall	Y	N	N	Y	Y	Y	N	Y
5 Bryant	Y	Y	Y	N	N	Y	Y	Y
6 ***Barton***	N	N	N	Y	Y	Y	N	N
7 ***Archer***	N	N	N	Y	Y	Y	N	N
8 ***Fields***	N	N	N	Y	Y	Y	N	N
9 Brooks	Y	Y	Y	N	N	Y	Y	Y
10 Pickle	Y	Y	Y	N	N	Y	Y	Y
11 Edwards	Y	Y	Y	N	N	N	Y	Y
12 Geren	Y	Y	Y	N	Y	Y	Y	Y
13 Sarpalius	Y	Y	N	Y	Y	Y	N	Y
14 Laughlin	Y	Y	N	Y	Y	Y	N	Y
15 de la Garza	Y	Y	Y	N	N	Y	Y	Y
16 Coleman	Y	Y	Y	N	N	N	Y	Y
17 Stenholm	Y	N	N	Y	Y	Y	N	N
18 Washington	Y	?	#	?	?	?	?	?
19 ***Combest***	N	N	N	Y	Y	Y	N	N
20 Gonzalez	Y	Y	Y	N	N	N	Y	Y
21 ***Smith***	N	N	N	Y	Y	Y	N	N
22 ***DeLay***	N	N	N	Y	Y	Y	N	N
23 ***Bonilla***	N	N	N	Y	Y	Y	N	N
24 Frost	Y	Y	Y	N	N	N	Y	Y
25 Andrews	Y	Y	Y	N	N	Y	Y	Y
26 ***Armey***	N	N	N	Y	Y	Y	N	N
27 Ortiz	Y	Y	Y	N	N	N	Y	Y
28 Tejeda	Y	Y	Y	N	N	N	Y	Y
29 Green	Y	?	?	?	?	?	?	?
30 Johnson, E.B.	Y	Y	Y	N	N	N	Y	Y
UTAH								
1 ***Hansen***	N	?	X	N	Y	Y	Y	N
2 Shepherd	Y	Y	Y	N	N	N	Y	Y
3 Orton	Y	Y	Y	Y	N	N	N	Y
VERMONT								
AL *Sanders*	Y	Y	Y	N	N	N	Y	Y
VIRGINIA								
1 ***Bateman***	Y	N	N	N	N	Y	Y	N
2 Pickett	Y	Y	Y	N	N	N	Y	Y
3 Scott	Y	Y	Y	N	N	N	Y	Y
4 Sisisky	Y	Y	Y	N	N	Y	Y	Y
5 Payne	Y	Y	Y	N	N	N	Y	Y
6 ***Goodlatte***	N	N	N	Y	Y	Y	N	N
7 ***Bliley***	N	N	N	Y	Y	Y	N	N
8 Moran	Y	Y	Y	N	N	N	Y	Y
9 Boucher	Y	Y	Y	N	N	N	Y	Y
10 ***Wolf***	N	N	N	N	Y	Y	Y	N
11 Byrne	Y	Y	Y	N	N	N	Y	N
WASHINGTON								
1 Cantwell	Y	Y	Y	N	N	N	Y	Y
2 Swift	Y	Y	Y	N	N	N	Y	Y
3 Unsoeld	Y	Y	Y	N	N	N	Y	Y
4 Inslee	Y	Y	Y	N	N	N	Y	Y
5 Foley								
6 Dicks	Y	Y	Y	N	N	N	Y	Y
7 McDermott	Y	Y	Y	N	N	N	Y	?
8 ***Dunn***	N	N	N	N	N	Y	Y	N
9 Kreidler	Y	Y	Y	N	N	N	Y	Y
WEST VIRGINIA								
1 Mollohan	Y	Y	Y	N	N	N	Y	Y
2 Wise	Y	Y	Y	N	N	N	Y	Y
3 Rahall	Y	Y	Y	N	N	N	Y	Y
WISCONSIN								
1 Barca	Y	Y	Y	N	N	N	N	Y
2 ***Klug***	Y	N	N	N	N	Y	Y	N
3 ***Gunderson***	Y	N	N	N	N	Y	Y	N
4 Kleczka	Y	Y	Y	N	N	N	Y	Y
5 Barrett	Y	Y	Y	N	N	N	Y	Y
6 ***Petri***	Y	N	N	Y	Y	Y	N	N
7 Obey	Y	Y	Y	N	N	N	Y	Y
8 ***Roth***	N	N	N	Y	Y	Y	N	N
9 ***Sensenbrenner***	N	N	N	Y	Y	Y	N	N
WYOMING								
AL ***Thomas***	N	N	N	N	Y	Y	N	N
DELEGATES								
de Lugo, V.I.	D	D	D	N	N	D	D	D
Faleomavaega, Am.S.	D	D	D	N	N	D	D	D
Norton, D.C.	D	D	D	N	N	D	D	D
Romero-B., P.R.	D	D	D	?	?	D	D	D
Underwood, Guam	D	D	D	N	N	D	D	D

Southern states - Ala., Ark., Fla., Ga., Ky., La., Miss., N.C., Okla., S.C., Tenn., Texas, Va.
Omitted votes are quorum calls, which CQ does not include in its vote charts.

505. HR 3167. Unemployment Benefits Extension/Rule. Adoption of the rule (H Res 273) to provide for House floor consideration of the bill to extend emergency benefits for the long-term unemployed. The rule included a self-executing amendment to the bill that would have shortened the emergency benefits program by one month from Feb. 5, 1994, to Jan. 1, 1994, and eliminated the financing provisions of the bill that limit the availability of certain welfare benefits to new immigrants. Rejected 149-274: R 2-171; D 146-103 (ND 111-57, SD 35-46); I 1-0, Oct. 14, 1993.

506. Procedural Motion. Approval of the House Journal of Thursday, Oct. 14. Approved 226-145: R 17-139; D 209-6 (ND 142-5, SD 67-1); I 0-0, Oct. 15, 1993.

507. HR 3167. Unemployment Benefits Extension/Rule. Adoption of the rule (H Res 265) to provide for House floor consideration of the bill to provide about $1 billion for extended unemployment benefits for workers who have exhausted their 26 weeks of state unemployment benefits for an additional seven or 13 weeks of compensation, depending on the unemployment rate in their state. The bill would require legal immigrants to wait five years to become eligible to receive Supplemental Security Income payments. Adopted 239-150: R 24-137; D 214-13 (ND 149-6, SD 65-7); I 1-0, Oct. 15, 1993.

508. HR 3167. Unemployment Benefits Extension/Low Unemployment States. Johnson, R-Conn., amendment to disallow extended benefits in states where the total unemployment rate is below 5 percent. Rejected in the Committee of the Whole 128-277: R 117-45; D 11-231 (ND 6-160, SD 5-71); I 0-1, Oct. 15, 1993.

509. HR 3167. Unemployment Benefits Extension/Passage. Passage of the bill to provide about $1 billion for extended unemployment benefits for workers who have exhausted their 26 weeks of state unemployment benefits for an additional seven or 13 weeks of compensation, depending on the unemployment rate in their state. The bill would require legal immigrants to wait five years to become eligible to receive Supplemental Security Income payments. Passed 302-95: R 80-80; D 221-15 (ND 158-3, SD 63-12); I 1-0, Oct. 15, 1993.

510. HR 2445. Fiscal 1994 Energy and Water Appropriations/Previous Question. Motion to order the previous question (thus ending debate and the possibility of amendment) on the Myers, R-Ind., motion to recommit to conference the conference report to provide $22,215,382,000 for energy and water development for fiscal 1994. Motion rejected 159-264: R 61-111; D 98-152 (ND 47-121, SD 51-31); I 0-1, Oct. 19, 1993. A "yea" was a vote in support of the president's position.

511. HR 2445. Fiscal 1994 Energy and Water Appropriations/Super Collider. Slattery, D-Kan., amendment to the Myers, R-Ind., motion to recommit to conference the conference report with instructions to terminate the superconducting super collider. Adopted 282-143: R 115-58; D 166-85 (ND 130-39, SD 36-46); I 1-0, Oct. 19, 1993. (Subsequently, the Myers motion to recommit as amended by the Slattery amendment was adopted by voice vote.) A "nay" was a vote in support of the president's position.

512. HR 2491. Fiscal 1994 VA-HUD Appropriations/Rule. Adoption of the rule (H Res 275) to waive points of order against and provide for House floor consideration of the conference report to provide $87,835,272,032 in new budget authority for the departments of Veterans Affairs and Housing and Urban Development and related agencies for fiscal 1994. The administration requested $89,268,383,032. Adopted 273-151: R 25-148; D 247-3 (ND 165-2, SD 82-1); I 1-0, Oct. 19, 1993.

KEY

Y   Voted for (yea).
Paired for.
+   Announced for.
N   Voted against (nay).
X   Paired against.
−   Announced against.
P   Voted "present."
C   Voted "present" to avoid possible conflict of interest.
?   Did not vote or otherwise make a position known.
D   Delegates ineligible to vote.

Democrats   **Republicans**
Independent

	505	506	507	508	509	510	511	512
ALABAMA								
1 *Callahan*	N	N	N	Y	N	Y	N	N
2 *Everett*	N	N	N	Y	Y	Y	N	N
3 Browder	N	Y	Y	N	Y	Y	N	Y
4 Bevill	N	?	Y	N	Y	N	Y	Y
5 Cramer	N	Y	Y	N	N	N	Y	Y
6 *Bachus*	N	?	N	Y	N	Y	N	N
7 Hilliard	Y	Y	Y	N	Y	N	Y	Y
ALASKA								
AL *Young*	N	?	?	?	?	Y	N	Y
ARIZONA								
1 Coppersmith	Y	Y	Y	N	N	N	Y	Y
2 Pastor	Y	Y	Y	N	Y	N	Y	N
3 *Stump*	N	N	N	Y	N	Y	N	N
4 *Kyl*	N	?	?	?	?	N	Y	N
5 *Kolbe*	N	?	X	#	X	Y	Y	N
6 English	Y	Y	Y	N	Y	N	Y	Y
ARKANSAS								
1 Lambert	N	Y	Y	N	Y	N	Y	Y
2 Thornton	Y	Y	Y	N	Y	Y	Y	Y
3 *Hutchinson*	N	N	N	Y	N	Y	N	N
4 *Dickey*	N	N	N	Y	N	Y	N	N
CALIFORNIA								
1 Hamburg	Y	Y	Y	N	Y	N	Y	Y
2 *Herger*	N	N	Y	Y	N	Y	N	N
3 Fazio	Y	Y	Y	N	Y	Y	N	Y
4 *Doolittle*	N	N	N	Y	N	Y	N	N
5 Matsui	Y	Y	Y	N	Y	N	Y	Y
6 Woolsey	Y	Y	N	N	Y	N	Y	Y
7 Miller	N	Y	Y	N	Y	N	Y	Y
8 Pelosi	Y	?	?	?	?	N	Y	Y
9 Dellums	Y	?	Y	N	Y	N	Y	Y
10 *Baker*	N	N	N	Y	Y	N	Y	N
11 *Pombo*	N	Y	N	Y	N	Y	N	N
12 Lantos	N	Y	Y	N	Y	N	Y	Y
13 Stark	N	Y	Y	N	Y	N	Y	Y
14 Eshoo	Y	Y	Y	N	Y	N	Y	Y
15 Mineta	Y	Y	N	N	Y	N	Y	N
16 Edwards	Y	Y	Y	N	Y	?	Y	Y
17 Farr	Y	Y	Y	N	Y	N	Y	Y
18 Condit	N	Y	Y	Y	N	Y	N	Y
19 Lehman	N	Y	Y	Y	Y	N	Y	Y
20 Dooley	N	Y	Y	Y	Y	Y	Y	Y
21 *Thomas*	N	N	Y	Y	Y	Y	N	N
22 *Huffington*	N	N	N	Y	N	Y	N	N
23 *Gallegly*	N	N	N	Y	Y	Y	N	N
24 Beilenson	N	Y	Y	N	Y	N	Y	Y
25 *McKeon*	N	N	N	Y	N	Y	N	N
26 Berman	Y	Y	Y	N	Y	N	Y	Y
27 *Moorhead*	N	N	N	Y	Y	N	N	N
28 *Dreier*	N	N	N	Y	N	Y	N	N
29 Waxman	Y	Y	Y	N	Y	N	Y	Y
30 Becerra	Y	Y	Y	N	Y	N	Y	Y
31 Martinez	?	?	?	?	?	N	Y	Y
32 Dixon	Y	Y	Y	N	Y	N	Y	Y
33 Roybal-Allard	Y	Y	Y	N	Y	N	Y	Y
34 Torres	Y	?	?	N	Y	Y	N	Y
35 Waters	Y	Y	Y	N	Y	N	Y	?
36 Harman	Y	Y	Y	Y	Y	N	Y	Y
37 Tucker	Y	Y	Y	N	Y	N	Y	Y
38 *Horn*	N	N	N	Y	N	Y	N	N
39 *Royce*	N	N	N	Y	N	N	N	N
40 *Lewis*	N	N	N	Y	Y	N	N	Y
41 *Kim*	N	N	N	Y	Y	N	Y	Y

	505	506	507	508	509	510	511	512
42 Brown	Y	?	?	N	Y	Y	N	Y
43 *Calvert*	N	N	N	Y	Y	N	Y	N
44 *McCandless*	N	N	N	Y	N	Y	N	N
45 *Rohrabacher*	N	N	N	Y	N	N	N	N
46 *Dornan*	N	N	N	Y	N	Y	N	N
47 *Cox*	N	N	N	Y	N	Y	N	N
48 *Packard*	N	N	N	Y	N	Y	N	N
49 Schenk	Y	Y	Y	N	Y	N	N	Y
50 Filner	Y	Y	Y	N	Y	N	Y	Y
51 *Cunningham*	N	N	N	Y	−	N	N	N
52 *Hunter*	N	?	?	Y	Y	N	Y	N
COLORADO								
1 Schroeder	Y	N	Y	N	Y	N	Y	Y
2 Skaggs	Y	Y	Y	N	Y	N	Y	Y
3 *McInnis*	N	Y	N	N	N	N	Y	N
4 *Allard*	N	N	N	Y	N	N	N	N
5 *Hefley*	N	N	N	N	N	N	N	N
6 *Schaefer*	N	N	N	?	?	N	Y	N
CONNECTICUT								
1 Kennelly	Y	Y	Y	N	Y	N	Y	Y
2 Gejdenson	Y	Y	Y	N	Y	N	Y	Y
3 DeLauro	Y	?	Y	N	Y	Y	Y	Y
4 *Shays*	N	N	N	Y	N	N	Y	Y
5 *Franks*	N	N	N	Y	Y	Y	N	N
6 *Johnson*	N	N	Y	Y	Y	Y	Y	Y
DELAWARE								
AL *Castle*	N	Y	N	N	Y	N	Y	N
FLORIDA								
1 Hutto	N	Y	N	Y	N	Y	N	Y
2 Peterson	N	Y	Y	N	Y	Y	N	Y
3 Brown	Y	Y	Y	N	Y	N	Y	Y
4 *Fowler*	N	N	N	#	X	N	Y	N
5 Thurman	N	Y	Y	N	Y	N	Y	Y
6 *Stearns*	N	N	N	Y	N	N	Y	N
7 *Mica*	N	N	N	Y	N	N	N	N
8 *McCollum*	N	N	N	?	N	Y	N	N
9 *Bilirakis*	N	N	N	Y	N	N	N	N
10 *Young*	N	N	N	Y	Y	N	Y	N
11 Gibbons	N	Y	Y	N	Y	Y	N	Y
12 *Canady*	N	N	N	Y	N	Y	N	N
13 *Miller*	N	Y	N	Y	N	N	N	N
14 *Goss*	N	N	N	N	N	N	Y	N
15 *Bacchus*	N	Y	Y	N	Y	N	Y	N
16 *Lewis*	N	N	N	Y	N	Y	N	N
17 Meek	Y	Y	Y	N	Y	N	Y	Y
18 *Ros-Lehtinen*	Y	N	N	N	Y	N	N	N
19 Johnston	Y	Y	Y	N	Y	N	Y	Y
20 Deutsch	Y	Y	Y	N	Y	N	Y	Y
21 *Diaz-Balart*	Y	N	N	N	Y	N	N	N
22 *Shaw*	N	N	N	Y	N	N	N	N
23 Hastings	Y	Y	Y	N	Y	N	Y	Y
GEORGIA								
1 *Kingston*	N	Y	N	Y	N	N	N	N
2 Bishop	Y	Y	Y	N	Y	N	Y	Y
3 *Collins*	N	N	N	Y	N	N	N	N
4 *Linder*	N	N	N	Y	N	N	N	N
5 Lewis	Y	Y	Y	N	Y	N	Y	Y
6 *Gingrich*	N	N	Y	Y	N	N	N	N
7 *Darden*	N	Y	Y	N	Y	Y	N	Y
8 Rowland	N	N	N	N	N	N	N	Y
9 Deal	N	Y	N	N	N	N	N	Y
10 Johnson	N	Y	N	N	N	N	N	Y
11 McKinney	Y	Y	Y	N	Y	N	Y	Y
HAWAII								
1 Abercrombie	Y	?	Y	N	Y	N	Y	Y
2 Mink	Y	Y	N	N	Y	N	Y	Y
IDAHO								
1 LaRocco	N	Y	Y	N	Y	Y	N	Y
2 *Crapo*	N	N	N	N	N	Y	N	N
ILLINOIS								
1 Rush	Y	Y	Y	N	Y	N	Y	Y
2 Reynolds	Y	Y	Y	N	Y	N	Y	Y
3 Lipinski	N	Y	Y	N	Y	N	Y	Y
4 Gutierrez	Y	Y	Y	N	Y	N	Y	Y
5 Rostenkowski	N	Y	Y	N	Y	N	Y	Y
6 *Hyde*	N	N	X	Y	Y	N	Y	N
7 Collins	Y	Y	Y	N	Y	N	Y	Y
8 *Crane*	N	N	N	Y	N	N	N	N
9 Yates	Y	Y	Y	N	Y	Y	Y	Y
10 *Porter*	N	N	N	Y	Y	N	Y	N
11 Sangmeister	N	Y	Y	N	Y	N	Y	Y
12 Costello	N	Y	N	Y	N	Y	N	Y
13 *Fawell*	N	N	−	Y	Y	Y	N	N
14 *Hastert*	N	N	Y	Y	N	N	Y	N
15 *Ewing*	N	N	N	Y	N	Y	Y	N
16 *Manzullo*	N	N	N	Y	N	N	Y	N
17 Evans	Y	Y	Y	N	Y	N	Y	Y

	505	506	507	508	509	510	511	512
18 ***Michel***	N	N	Y	Y	Y	Y	N	N
19 Poshard	N	Y	Y	N	Y	N	Y	Y
20 Durbin	N	Y	Y	N	Y	N	Y	Y
INDIANA								
1 Visclosky	Y	Y	Y	N	Y	N	Y	Y
2 Sharp	N	Y	Y	N	Y	N	Y	Y
3 Roemer	N	Y	Y	N	Y	Y	N	Y
4 Long	N	Y	Y	N	Y	N	Y	Y
5 ***Buyer***	N	N	N	N	N	Y	N	N
6 ***Burton***	N	N	N	N	N	?	Y	N
7 ***Myers***	N	Y	?	N	Y	Y	N	Y
8 McCloskey	N	Y	Y	N	Y	Y	N	?
9 Hamilton	N	Y	Y	N	Y	N	Y	Y
10 Jacobs	N	N	N	N	Y	N	Y	Y
IOWA								
1 ***Leach***	N	N	N	N	N	N	Y	N
2 ***Nussle***	N	N	N	Y	N	N	Y	N
3 ***Lightfoot***	N	N	N	N	N	Y	N	N
4 Smith	Y	Y	Y	N	Y	Y	N	Y
5 ***Grandy***	N	N	Y	Y	N	N	Y	Y
KANSAS								
1 ***Roberts***	N	N	N	N	N	Y	N	N
2 Slattery	N	?	?	?	?	N	Y	Y
3 ***Meyers***	N	N	N	N	Y	N	Y	N
4 Glickman	N	Y	Y	N	Y	N	Y	Y
KENTUCKY								
1 Barlow	N	Y	Y	N	Y	Y	N	Y
2 Natcher	Y	Y	Y	N	Y	N	Y	Y
3 Mazzoli	Y	Y	Y	N	Y	Y	Y	Y
4 ***Bunning***	?	?	?	?	#	N	Y	N
5 ***Rogers***	N	N	N	Y	Y	Y	N	Y
6 Baesler	N	Y	Y	N	Y	N	Y	Y
LOUISIANA								
1 ***Livingston***	N	?	N	Y	N	Y	N	N
2 Jefferson	Y	Y	Y	N	?	Y	N	Y
3 Tauzin	N	?	?	?	?	N	Y	Y
4 Fields	Y	Y	Y	N	Y	Y	N	Y
5 ***McCrery***	N	N	N	Y	N	Y	N	N
6 ***Baker***	N	?	X	#	X	Y	N	N
7 Hayes	N	Y	Y	N	Y	Y	N	Y
MAINE								
1 Andrews	Y	Y	Y	N	Y	N	Y	Y
2 ***Snowe***	N	N	Y	Y	Y	N	Y	N
MARYLAND								
1 ***Gilchrest***	N	N	N	Y	Y	Y	N	N
2 ***Bentley***	N	?	N	Y	Y	Y	N	N
3 Cardin	N	Y	Y	N	Y	N	Y	Y
4 Wynn	Y	Y	Y	N	Y	N	Y	Y
5 Hoyer	Y	?	Y	N	Y	Y	N	Y
6 ***Bartlett***	N	N	N	Y	N	Y	N	N
7 Mfume	Y	N	Y	N	Y	N	Y	Y
8 ***Morella***	N	?	Y	N	Y	N	Y	Y
MASSACHUSETTS								
1 Olver	Y	Y	Y	N	Y	N	Y	Y
2 Neal	Y	Y	Y	N	Y	N	Y	Y
3 ***Blute***	N	N	N	N	Y	Y	N	N
4 Frank	Y	Y	Y	N	Y	N	Y	Y
5 Meehan	Y	Y	Y	N	Y	N	Y	Y
6 ***Torkildsen***	N	N	N	N	Y	N	Y	N
7 Markey	Y	?	?	N	Y	N	Y	Y
8 Kennedy	Y	Y	Y	N	Y	N	Y	Y
9 Moakley	Y	Y	Y	N	Y	?	?	?
10 Studds	Y	Y	Y	N	Y	N	Y	Y
MICHIGAN								
1 Stupak	Y	Y	Y	N	Y	N	Y	Y
2 ***Hoekstra***	N	N	N	Y	Y	N	Y	N
3 Vacancy								
4 ***Camp***	N	N	Y	Y	Y	N	Y	N
5 Barcia	N	Y	Y	N	Y	N	Y	Y
6 ***Upton***	N	N	N	Y	Y	N	Y	N
7 ***Smith***	N	N	N	Y	N	?	?	?
8 Carr	N	Y	Y	N	Y	N	Y	Y
9 Kildee	Y	Y	Y	N	Y	N	Y	Y
10 Bonior	Y	Y	Y	N	Y	Y	N	Y
11 ***Knollenberg***	N	N	N	Y	N	N	Y	N
12 Levin	Y	Y	Y	N	Y	N	Y	Y
13 Ford	Y	Y	Y	N	Y	N	Y	Y
14 Conyers	Y	?	?	?	?	Y	N	N
15 Collins	Y	Y	Y	N	Y	N	Y	Y
16 Dingell	Y	?	#	X	#	N	Y	Y
MINNESOTA								
1 Penny	N	?	?	Y	N	N	Y	N
2 Minge	Y	Y	Y	N	Y	N	Y	Y
3 ***Ramstad***	N	N	N	N	N	N	Y	N
4 Vento	Y	Y	Y	N	Y	N	Y	Y

	505	506	507	508	509	510	511	512
5 Sabo	Y	Y	Y	N	Y	N	Y	Y
6 ***Grams***	N	N	N	N	N	Y	N	N
7 Peterson	N	Y	Y	N	Y	N	Y	Y
8 Oberstar	Y	?	?	?	#	N	Y	Y
MISSISSIPPI								
1 Whitten	Y	Y	Y	N	Y	Y	N	Y
2 Thompson	Y	Y	Y	N	Y	Y	N	Y
3 Montgomery	N	Y	Y	N	Y	Y	N	Y
4 Parker	N	?	?	N	Y	N	Y	Y
5 Taylor	N	N	N	Y	N	N	Y	Y
MISSOURI								
1 Clay	Y	N	Y	N	Y	Y	N	Y
2 ***Talent***	N	N	N	Y	Y	N	Y	N
3 Gephardt	Y	Y	Y	N	Y	Y	N	Y
4 Skelton	N	?	?	N	Y	Y	N	Y
5 Wheat	Y	Y	Y	N	?	N	Y	Y
6 Danner	N	Y	Y	N	Y	N	Y	Y
7 ***Hancock***	N	N	N	Y	N	N	Y	N
8 ***Emerson***	N	N	N	Y	Y	N	N	N
9 Volkmer	N	Y	Y	N	Y	Y	N	Y
MONTANA								
AL Williams	N	Y	Y	N	Y	N	Y	Y
NEBRASKA								
1 ***Bereuter***	N	N	N	?	?	N	Y	Y
2 Hoagland	N	Y	Y	Y	N	N	Y	Y
3 ***Barrett***	N	N	N	N	N	N	Y	N
NEVADA								
1 Bilbray	N	Y	Y	N	Y	N	Y	Y
2 ***Vucanovich***	N	N	N	Y	Y	Y	N	N
NEW HAMPSHIRE								
1 ***Zeliff***	N	N	N	Y	N	N	Y	N
2 Swett	N	Y	Y	N	Y	N	Y	Y
NEW JERSEY								
1 Andrews	Y	Y	Y	N	Y	Y	N	Y
2 Hughes	N	Y	Y	N	Y	N	Y	Y
3 ***Saxton***	N	N	N	Y	Y	N	Y	N
4 ***Smith***	N	Y	Y	N	Y	N	Y	N
5 ***Roukema***	N	N	Y	N	Y	N	Y	N
6 Pallone	Y	Y	Y	N	Y	N	Y	Y
7 ***Franks***	N	N	Y	Y	Y	Y	N	N
8 Klein	Y	Y	Y	N	Y	N	Y	Y
9 Torricelli	Y	Y	Y	N	Y	Y	N	Y
10 Payne	Y	Y	Y	N	Y	N	Y	Y
11 ***Gallo***	N	N	N	Y	Y	Y	N	Y
12 ***Zimmer***	N	N	N	Y	Y	N	Y	N
13 Menendez	Y	Y	N	N	Y	N	Y	Y
NEW MEXICO								
1 ***Schiff***	N	N	N	N	Y	?	?	N
2 ***Skeen***	N	N	N	?	?	Y	N	Y
3 Richardson	Y	Y	Y	N	Y	Y	N	Y
NEW YORK								
1 Hochbrueckner	N	Y	Y	N	Y	Y	N	Y
2 ***Lazio***	N	N	N	Y	Y	N	Y	N
3 ***King***	N	N	N	Y	Y	N	Y	N
4 ***Levy***	N	N	N	Y	Y	N	Y	N
5 Ackerman	N	?	?	?	?	Y	N	Y
6 Flake	Y	Y	Y	N	Y	N	Y	Y
7 Manton	Y	?	?	N	Y	Y	N	Y
8 Nadler	Y	?	N	N	Y	Y	N	Y
9 Schumer	Y	Y	Y	N	Y	N	Y	Y
10 Towns	Y	?	?	?	?	N	Y	Y
11 Owens	Y	Y	Y	N	Y	Y	Y	Y
12 Velazquez	Y	Y	Y	N	Y	N	Y	Y
13 ***Molinari***	N	N	N	Y	Y	N	Y	N
14 Maloney	Y	Y	Y	N	Y	N	Y	Y
15 Rangel	Y	Y	Y	N	Y	N	Y	Y
16 Serrano	Y	Y	Y	N	Y	N	Y	Y
17 Engel	?	?	?	N	Y	—	+	+
18 Lowey	Y	Y	Y	N	Y	Y	N	Y
19 ***Fish***	N	Y	Y	N	Y	N	Y	N
20 ***Gilman***	N	Y	Y	N	Y	N	Y	N
21 McNulty	N	Y	Y	N	Y	Y	N	Y
22 ***Solomon***	N	?	N	Y	Y	N	Y	N
23 ***Boehlert***	N	N	Y	N	Y	N	Y	Y
24 ***McHugh***	N	N	N	N	Y	N	Y	N
25 ***Walsh***	N	N	N	N	Y	N	Y	N
26 Hinchey	Y	?	Y	N	Y	N	Y	Y
27 ***Paxon***	N	N	N	Y	Y	N	Y	N
28 Slaughter	Y	Y	Y	N	Y	N	Y	Y
29 LaFalce	N	Y	Y	N	Y	N	Y	Y
30 ***Quinn***	N	N	N	N	Y	N	Y	N
31 ***Houghton***	N	Y	N	Y	Y	N	Y	Y
NORTH CAROLINA								
1 Clayton	Y	Y	Y	N	Y	N	Y	Y
2 Valentine	N	Y	Y	N	N	N	Y	Y

	505	506	507	508	509	510	511	512
3 Lancaster	N	Y	Y	N	N	N	Y	Y
4 Price	N	Y	Y	N	Y	N	Y	Y
5 Neal	N	?	?	N	Y	N	Y	Y
6 ***Coble***	N	N	N	N	N	N	Y	N
7 Rose	?	Y	Y	N	Y	Y	N	Y
8 Hefner	N	Y	Y	N	Y	N	Y	Y
9 ***McMillan***	N	N	N	N	N	N	Y	N
10 ***Ballenger***	N	N	N	N	N	N	Y	N
11 ***Taylor***	N	N	N	N	N	Y	N	N
12 Watt	Y	Y	Y	N	Y	N	Y	Y
NORTH DAKOTA								
AL Pomeroy	N	Y	Y	N	Y	N	Y	Y
OHIO								
1 Mann	Y	Y	Y	N	Y	N	Y	Y
2 ***Portman***	N	N	N	Y	N	N	Y	N
3 Hall	Y	?	Y	N	Y	N	Y	Y
4 ***Oxley***	N	N	N	N	N	Y	N	N
5 ***Gillmor***	N	Y	N	N	Y	N	Y	N
6 Strickland	N	Y	Y	N	Y	N	Y	Y
7 ***Hobson***	N	N	N	Y	Y	N	Y	N
8 ***Boehner***	N	N	N	Y	N	Y	N	N
9 Kaptur	Y	Y	Y	N	Y	N	Y	Y
10 ***Hoke***	N	N	N	Y	Y	N	Y	Y
11 Stokes	?	?	#	?	?	Y	N	Y
12 ***Kasich***	N	?	N	Y	Y	N	Y	N
13 Brown	Y	Y	Y	N	Y	N	Y	Y
14 Sawyer	Y	Y	Y	N	Y	N	Y	Y
15 ***Pryce***	N	N	N	Y	N	N	Y	N
16 ***Regula***	N	N	Y	Y	Y	N	Y	N
17 Traficant	N	Y	Y	N	Y	Y	N	Y
18 Applegate	N	Y	Y	N	Y	N	Y	Y
19 Fingerhut	N	Y	Y	N	Y	N	Y	Y
OKLAHOMA								
1 ***Inhofe***	N	N	N	N	N	N	Y	N
2 Synar	Y	?	X	X	?	N	Y	Y
3 Brewster	N	?	?	N	N	N	Y	Y
4 McCurdy	?	?	?	?	?	?	?	?
5 ***Istook***	N	N	N	N	N	N	Y	N
6 English	N	Y	Y	N	Y	N	Y	Y
OREGON								
1 Furse	Y	Y	Y	N	Y	Y	N	Y
2 ***Smith***	N	N	N	Y	N	N	Y	N
3 Wyden	Y	Y	Y	N	Y	N	Y	Y
4 DeFazio	N	Y	Y	N	Y	N	Y	Y
5 Kopetski	Y	Y	Y	N	Y	Y	N	Y
PENNSYLVANIA								
1 Foglietta	Y	Y	Y	N	Y	Y	Y	Y
2 Blackwell	Y	?	Y	N	Y	Y	Y	Y
3 Borski	N	Y	Y	N	Y	Y	N	Y
4 Klink	N	Y	Y	N	Y	Y	Y	Y
5 ***Clinger***	N	Y	N	Y	Y	N	Y	N
6 Holden	N	Y	Y	N	Y	N	Y	Y
7 ***Weldon***	N	N	Y	Y	Y	N	Y	N
8 ***Greenwood***	N	N	Y	Y	Y	N	Y	N
9 ***Shuster***	N	N	N	Y	Y	N	Y	N
10 ***McDade***	?	?	?	?	?	Y	N	N
11 Kanjorski	Y	Y	Y	N	Y	N	Y	Y
12 Murtha	?	Y	Y	N	Y	Y	N	Y
13 Margolies-Mezv.	N	Y	Y	N	Y	N	Y	Y
14 Coyne	N	Y	Y	N	Y	Y	N	Y
15 McHale	N	Y	Y	N	Y	N	Y	Y
16 ***Walker***	N	N	N	Y	N	N	Y	N
17 ***Gekas***	N	N	N	Y	Y	N	Y	N
18 ***Santorum***	N	Y	Y	Y	Y	Y	N	N
19 ***Goodling***	N	N	Y	Y	Y	N	Y	Y
20 Murphy	N	N	Y	N	Y	?	?	?
21 ***Ridge***	N	?	?	Y	Y	N	Y	Y
RHODE ISLAND								
1 ***Machtley***	N	N	Y	Y	Y	N	Y	N
2 Reed	Y	Y	Y	N	Y	N	Y	Y
SOUTH CAROLINA								
1 ***Ravenel***	N	N	N	Y	N	N	Y	N
2 ***Spence***	N	N	N	Y	Y	Y	N	N
3 Derrick	Y	Y	Y	N	Y	Y	N	Y
4 ***Inglis***	N	Y	N	N	N	N	Y	N
5 Spratt	N	Y	Y	N	Y	N	Y	Y
6 Clyburn	Y	Y	Y	N	Y	Y	Y	Y
SOUTH DAKOTA								
AL Johnson	N	Y	Y	N	Y	N	Y	Y
TENNESSEE								
1 ***Quillen***	N	N	N	Y	N	Y	Y	Y
2 ***Duncan***	N	N	N	Y	N	Y	N	N
3 Lloyd	N	Y	Y	?	?	Y	N	Y
4 Cooper	N	Y	Y	N	Y	Y	Y	Y
5 Clement	N	?	?	?	+	N	Y	Y

	505	506	507	508	509	510	511	512
6 Gordon	Y	Y	Y	N	Y	Y	Y	Y
7 ***Sundquist***	N	?	?	?	?	N	Y	Y
8 Tanner	N	Y	Y	N	Y	N	Y	Y
9 Ford	Y	Y	Y	N	Y	?	?	?
TEXAS								
1 Chapman	N	?	Y	N	Y	Y	N	Y
2 Wilson	Y	?	Y	N	Y	Y	N	Y
3 ***Johnson, Sam***	N	?	N	N	N	Y	N	N
4 Hall	N	Y	N	N	Y	Y	N	Y
5 Bryant	N	Y	Y	N	Y	?	?	Y
6 ***Barton***	N	N	N	Y	N	Y	N	Y
7 ***Archer***	N	Y	Y	Y	N	N	Y	N
8 ***Fields***	N	?	?	#	X	Y	N	N
9 Brooks	N	?	#	?	#	Y	N	Y
10 Pickle	N	Y	Y	N	N	Y	N	Y
11 Edwards	Y	?	Y	N	Y	Y	N	Y
12 Geren	N	Y	Y	N	Y	Y	N	Y
13 Sarpalius	N	Y	Y	N	Y	Y	N	Y
14 Laughlin	Y	?	?	N	Y	Y	N	Y
15 de la Garza	Y	Y	Y	N	Y	Y	N	Y
16 Coleman	Y	Y	Y	N	Y	Y	N	Y
17 Stenholm	N	Y	N	Y	N	Y	N	Y
18 Washington	?	?	?	X	?	N	Y	Y
19 ***Combest***	N	Y	N	Y	N	Y	N	N
20 Gonzalez	Y	Y	Y	N	Y	Y	N	Y
21 ***Smith***	N	N	N	Y	N	Y	N	N
22 ***DeLay***	N	N	Y	Y	N	Y	N	Y
23 ***Bonilla***	N	N	N	Y	Y	Y	N	N
24 Frost	Y	Y	Y	N	Y	Y	N	Y
25 Andrews	N	?	#	?	?	Y	N	Y
26 ***Armey***	N	N	N	Y	N	Y	N	N
27 Ortiz	Y	Y	Y	N	Y	Y	N	Y
28 Tejeda	Y	Y	Y	N	Y	Y	N	Y
29 Green	?	Y	Y	N	Y	Y	N	Y
30 Johnson, E.B.	Y	Y	Y	N	Y	Y	N	Y
UTAH								
1 ***Hansen***	N	N	N	N	N	Y	N	Y
2 Shepherd	N	Y	Y	N	Y	N	Y	Y
3 Orton	N	+	+	X	+	N	Y	Y
VERMONT								
AL *Sanders*	Y	?	Y	N	Y	N	Y	Y
VIRGINIA								
1 ***Bateman***	N	+	N	N	N	Y	N	—
2 Pickett	N	Y	Y	Y	Y	Y	N	Y
3 Scott	Y	Y	Y	N	Y	Y	N	Y
4 Sisisky	N	Y	Y	N	Y	N	Y	Y
5 Payne	N	Y	Y	N	N	Y	N	Y
6 ***Goodlatte***	N	N	N	Y	N	Y	N	N
7 ***Bliley***	N	N	N	Y	N	Y	Y	N
8 Moran	N	?	?	N	Y	N	Y	Y
9 Boucher	Y	?	?	?	?	Y	N	Y
10 ***Wolf***	N	N	N	N	Y	N	Y	N
11 Byrne	N	Y	Y	N	Y	N	Y	N
WASHINGTON								
1 Cantwell	Y	Y	Y	N	Y	N	Y	Y
2 Swift	Y	Y	Y	N	Y	Y	Y	Y
3 Unsoeld	Y	Y	Y	N	Y	N	Y	Y
4 Inslee	Y	Y	Y	N	Y	N	Y	Y
5 Foley								
6 Dicks	Y	Y	Y	N	Y	Y	N	Y
7 McDermott	Y	Y	Y	N	Y	Y	N	Y
8 ***Dunn***	N	N	N	Y	Y	Y	N	N
9 Kreidler	Y	Y	Y	N	Y	N	Y	Y
WEST VIRGINIA								
1 Mollohan	Y	Y	Y	N	Y	Y	N	Y
2 Wise	Y	Y	Y	N	Y	Y	Y	Y
3 Rahall	N	Y	Y	N	Y	Y	Y	Y
WISCONSIN								
1 Barca	Y	Y	Y	N	Y	N	Y	Y
2 ***Klug***	N	?	?	?	?	N	Y	Y
3 ***Gunderson***	N	N	N	N	Y	N	Y	Y
4 Kleczka	N	Y	Y	N	Y	N	Y	Y
5 Barrett	Y	Y	Y	N	Y	N	Y	Y
6 ***Petri***	N	N	N	N	N	N	Y	N
7 Obey	Y	Y	Y	N	Y	N	Y	Y
8 ***Roth***	N	N	N	N	N	N	Y	N
9 ***Sensenbrenner***	N	N	N	N	N	N	Y	N
WYOMING								
AL ***Thomas***	N	N	N	Y	N	N	Y	N
DELEGATES								
de Lugo, V.I.	D	D	D	N	D	D	D	D
Faleomavaega, Am.S.	D	D	D	N	D	D	D	D
Norton, D.C.	D	D	D	N	D	D	D	D
Romero-B., P.R.	D	D	D	?	D	D	D	D
Underwood, Guam	D	D	D	N	D	D	D	D

Southern states - Ala., Ark., Fla., Ga., Ky., La., Miss., N.C., Okla., S.C., Tenn., Texas, Va.
Omitted votes are quorum calls, which CQ does not include in its vote charts.

513. HR 2491. Fiscal 1994 VA-HUD Appropriations/ Conference Report. Adoption of the conference report to provide $87,835,272,032 in new budget authority for the departments of Veterans Affairs and Housing and Urban Development and related agencies for fiscal 1994. The administration requested $89,268,383,032. Adopted (thus sent to the Senate) 341-89: R 100-75; D 240-14 (ND 157-13, SD 83-1); I 1-0, Oct. 19, 1993.

514. HR 2491. Fiscal 1994 VA-HUD Appropriations/ ASRM. Stokes, D-Ohio, motion to recede and concur in the Senate amendment with an amendment to provide $100 million to terminate the Advanced Solid Rocket Motor (ASRM) program and redistribute $57.5 million to the National Aerospace Plane, National Science Foundation research activities, National Science Foundation grants to colleges and universities, and the Environmental Protection Agency's "superfund" program. Motion agreed to 401-30: R 166-9; D 234-21 (ND 165-6, SD 69-15); I 1-0, Oct. 19, 1993.

515. HR 2491. Fiscal 1994 VA-HUD Appropriations/ Selective Service. Solomon, R-N.Y., motion to recede and concur in the Senate amendment to provide $25 million for the Selective Service System to register 18-year-olds for a potential military draft. Motion agreed to 236-194: R 143-32; D 93-161 (ND 37-133, SD 56-28); I 0-1, Oct. 19, 1993.

516. HR 2401. Fiscal 1994 Defense Authorization/Close Conference. Dellums, D-Calif., motion to close classified portions of the conference on the defense authorization bill (HR 2401). Motion agreed to 422-2: R 171-0; D 250-2 (ND 168-1, SD 82-1); I 1-0, Oct. 19, 1993.

517. HR 2519. Fiscal 1994 Commerce, Justice and State Appropriations/Conference Report. Adoption of the conference report to provide $23,396,781,000 in new budget authority for the departments of Commerce, Justice and State, the judiciary and related agencies for fiscal 1994. The administration requested $24,928,085,000. Adopted (thus sent to the Senate) 303-100: R 73-92; D 229-8 (ND 150-8, SD 79-0); I 1-0, Oct. 19, 1993.

518. HR 2492. Fiscal 1994 D.C. Appropriations/Conference Report. Adoption of the conference report to provide $700,000,000 in federal funds for the District of Columbia in fiscal 1994 and approve the spending of $3,740,382,000 in funds raised from local taxes. The administration requested $705,101,000 in federal funds and $3,740,382,000 in local taxes. The conference report did not include restrictions on abortion that had been part of previous bills. Rejected 206-224: R 14-160; D 191-64 (ND 137-34, SD 54-30); I 1-0, Oct. 20, 1993.

519. HR 2519. Fiscal 1994 Commerce, Justice and State Appropriations/United Nations. Smith, D-Iowa, motion to recede and concur in the Senate amendment with an amendment to withhold 10 percent of U.S. dues to the United Nations until the United Nations establishes an inspector general's office; require activities to be mutually agreed upon by the U.S. and international organizations; and prohibit funding of interest costs on loans incurred after Oct. 1, 1984, through external borrowing by international organizations. Motion agreed to 422-2: R 168-2; D 253-0 (ND 168-0, SD 85-0); I 1-0, Oct. 20, 1993.

520. HR 2519. Fiscal 1994 Commerce, Justice and State Appropriations/U.N. Peacekeeping. Smith, D-Iowa, motion to recede and concur in the Senate amendment with an amendment to require the secretary of State to notify Congress 15 days before a mission change in U.N. peacekeeping operations. Motion agreed to 367-61: R 118-56; D 248-5 (ND 165-3, SD 83-2); I 1-0, Oct. 20, 1993.

KEY

Y	Voted for (yea).
#	Paired for.
+	Announced for.
N	Voted against (nay).
X	Paired against.
−	Announced against.
P	Voted "present."
C	Voted "present" to avoid possible conflict of interest.
?	Did not vote or otherwise make a position known.
D	Delegates ineligible to vote.

Democrats   **Republicans**
Independent

	513	514	515	516	517	518	519	520
ALABAMA								
1 Callahan	N	N	Y	Y	N	N	Y	Y
2 Everett	N	N	Y	Y	N	N	Y	Y
3 Browder	Y	N	Y	Y	Y	N	Y	Y
4 Bevill	Y	N	Y	Y	Y	Y	Y	Y
5 Cramer	Y	N	Y	Y	Y	N	Y	Y
6 Bachus	N	N	Y	Y	N	N	Y	N
7 Hilliard	Y	Y	Y	Y	Y	Y	Y	Y
ALASKA								
AL Young	Y	Y	Y	Y	Y	N	Y	N
ARIZONA								
1 Coppersmith	N	Y	N	Y	Y	Y	Y	Y
2 Pastor	Y	Y	N	Y	Y	Y	Y	Y
3 Stump	N	Y	Y	Y	N	N	N	N
4 Kyl	Y	Y	Y	Y	Y	N	Y	Y
5 Kolbe	N	Y	Y	Y	Y	Y	Y	Y
6 English	Y	Y	N	Y	Y	Y	+	Y
ARKANSAS								
1 Lambert	Y	Y	N	Y	Y	Y	Y	Y
2 Thornton	Y	Y	N	Y	Y	Y	Y	Y
3 Hutchinson	N	Y	Y	Y	Y	N	Y	Y
4 Dickey	N	Y	Y	Y	Y	N	Y	Y
CALIFORNIA								
1 Hamburg	Y	Y	N	Y	Y	Y	Y	Y
2 Herger	Y	Y	Y	Y	N	N	Y	N
3 Fazio	Y	Y	N	Y	Y	Y	Y	Y
4 Doolittle	N	Y	Y	Y	N	N	Y	N
5 Matsui	Y	Y	N	Y	Y	Y	Y	Y
6 Woolsey	Y	Y	N	Y	Y	Y	Y	Y
7 Miller	Y	Y	N	?	Y	Y	?	?
8 Pelosi	?	Y	N	Y	Y	Y	Y	Y
9 Dellums	Y	Y	N	Y	Y	Y	Y	Y
10 Baker	Y	Y	Y	Y	Y	N	Y	N
11 Pombo	N	Y	Y	N	N	N	N	N
12 Lantos	Y	Y	Y	Y	Y	Y	Y	Y
13 Stark	Y	Y	N	Y	Y	Y	Y	Y
14 Eshoo	Y	Y	N	?	Y	Y	Y	Y
15 Mineta	Y	N	N	Y	Y	Y	Y	Y
16 Edwards	Y	Y	N	?	Y	Y	Y	Y
17 Farr	Y	Y	N	Y	Y	Y	Y	Y
18 Condit	N	Y	Y	N	N	N	Y	Y
19 Lehman	Y	Y	N	Y	Y	Y	Y	Y
20 Dooley	Y	Y	N	?	Y	Y	Y	Y
21 Thomas	Y	Y	Y	Y	Y	N	Y	Y
22 Huffington	N	Y	N	Y	N	N	N	Y
23 Gallegly	Y	Y	Y	Y	N	N	Y	Y
24 Beilenson	N	Y	N	Y	Y	Y	Y	Y
25 McKeon	Y	Y	Y	Y	N	N	Y	Y
26 Berman	Y	Y	N	Y	Y	Y	Y	Y
27 Moorhead	N	Y	Y	Y	N	N	Y	Y
28 Dreier	N	Y	Y	Y	N	N	Y	Y
29 Waxman	Y	Y	N	Y	Y	Y	?	Y
30 Becerra	Y	Y	N	Y	Y	Y	Y	Y
31 Martinez	Y	Y	N	Y	Y	Y	Y	Y
32 Dixon	Y	Y	N	Y	Y	Y	Y	Y
33 Roybal-Allard	Y	Y	N	Y	Y	Y	Y	Y
34 Torres	Y	Y	N	Y	Y	Y	Y	Y
35 Waters	Y	Y	N	Y	Y	?	Y	Y
36 Harman	Y	Y	Y	Y	Y	Y	Y	Y
37 Tucker	Y	Y	N	Y	Y	Y	Y	Y
38 Horn	Y	Y	N	Y	Y	Y	Y	Y
39 Royce	N	Y	N	Y	N	N	Y	Y
40 Lewis	Y	Y	N	Y	N	N	Y	N
41 Kim	Y	Y	Y	Y	N	Y	N	N

	513	514	515	516	517	518	519	520
42 Brown	Y	Y	N	Y	Y	Y	Y	Y
43 Calvert	Y	Y	Y	Y	N	Y	N	Y
44 McCandless	Y	Y	Y	Y	N	N	Y	Y
45 Rohrabacher	N	Y	N	N	N	N	Y	Y
46 Dornan	N	Y	Y	N	N	N	N	Y
47 Cox	N	Y	N	Y	N	N	Y	Y
48 Packard	Y	Y	Y	Y	N	Y	N	Y
49 Schenk	Y	Y	N	Y	Y	Y	Y	Y
50 Filner	Y	Y	N	Y	Y	Y	Y	Y
51 Cunningham	Y	Y	Y	Y	N	Y	N	Y
52 Hunter	N	Y	Y	Y	N	Y	N	Y
COLORADO								
1 Schroeder	Y	Y	N	Y	N	Y	Y	Y
2 Skaggs	Y	Y	N	Y	Y	Y	Y	Y
3 McInnis	N	Y	Y	Y	N	N	Y	Y
4 Allard	N	Y	N	Y	N	N	Y	Y
5 Hefley	N	Y	Y	N	N	N	Y	Y
6 Schaefer	N	Y	Y	Y	N	N	Y	Y
CONNECTICUT								
1 Kennelly	Y	Y	N	Y	Y	Y	Y	Y
2 Gejdenson	Y	Y	N	Y	Y	Y	Y	Y
3 DeLauro	Y	Y	N	Y	Y	Y	Y	Y
4 Shays	Y	Y	N	Y	N	Y	Y	Y
5 Franks	Y	Y	Y	Y	Y	Y	Y	Y
6 Johnson	Y	Y	N	Y	?	Y	Y	Y
DELAWARE								
AL Castle	Y	Y	Y	Y	Y	N	Y	Y
FLORIDA								
1 Hutto	Y	Y	Y	Y	Y	N	Y	Y
2 Peterson	Y	Y	Y	Y	Y	Y	Y	Y
3 Brown	Y	Y	Y	Y	Y	Y	Y	Y
4 Fowler	Y	Y	Y	Y	N	Y	Y	Y
5 Thurman	Y	Y	Y	Y	Y	Y	Y	Y
6 Stearns	Y	Y	Y	Y	N	N	Y	Y
7 Mica	N	N	Y	N	N	N	Y	Y
8 McCollum	Y	Y	Y	Y	N	N	Y	Y
9 Bilirakis	Y	Y	Y	Y	Y	N	Y	N
10 Young	Y	Y	Y	Y	Y	N	Y	Y
11 Gibbons	Y	Y	N	Y	Y	N	Y	Y
12 Canady	Y	Y	Y	Y	Y	N	Y	Y
13 Miller	N	Y	N	Y	N	N	Y	Y
14 Goss	N	Y	Y	N	N	N	Y	Y
15 Bacchus	Y	N	N	Y	Y	Y	Y	Y
16 Lewis	N	Y	Y	N	N	N	Y	Y
17 Meek	Y	Y	Y	Y	Y	Y	Y	Y
18 Ros-Lehtinen	Y	Y	Y	Y	N	Y	Y	Y
19 Johnston	Y	Y	N	Y	Y	Y	Y	Y
20 Deutsch	Y	Y	N	Y	Y	Y	Y	Y
21 Diaz-Balart	Y	Y	Y	Y	N	Y	Y	Y
22 Shaw	Y	Y	Y	Y	Y	N	Y	Y
23 Hastings	Y	Y	N	Y	Y	Y	Y	Y
GEORGIA								
1 Kingston	Y	Y	Y	Y	N	N	Y	Y
2 Bishop	Y	Y	Y	Y	+	Y	Y	Y
3 Collins	N	Y	Y	Y	N	N	Y	N
4 Linder	Y	Y	Y	Y	N	N	Y	Y
5 Lewis	Y	Y	N	Y	Y	Y	Y	Y
6 Gingrich	Y	Y	Y	Y	N	N	Y	Y
7 Darden	Y	Y	Y	Y	Y	Y	Y	Y
8 Rowland	Y	Y	Y	Y	Y	Y	Y	Y
9 Deal	Y	Y	Y	Y	Y	Y	Y	Y
10 Johnson	Y	Y	Y	Y	Y	Y	Y	Y
11 McKinney	Y	Y	N	Y	Y	Y	Y	Y
HAWAII								
1 Abercrombie	Y	Y	Y	Y	Y	Y	Y	Y
2 Mink	Y	Y	N	Y	Y	Y	Y	Y
IDAHO								
1 LaRocco	Y	Y	N	Y	N	Y	N	Y
2 Crapo	N	Y	Y	Y	N	N	Y	Y
ILLINOIS								
1 Rush	Y	Y	N	Y	Y	Y	Y	Y
2 Reynolds	Y	Y	N	Y	Y	Y	Y	Y
3 Lipinski	Y	Y	Y	Y	Y	N	Y	Y
4 Gutierrez	Y	Y	N	Y	Y	Y	Y	Y
5 Rostenkowski	Y	Y	N	Y	?	Y	Y	Y
6 Hyde	Y	Y	Y	Y	Y	Y	Y	Y
7 Collins	Y	Y	N	Y	Y	Y	Y	Y
8 Crane	N	Y	N	N	N	N	Y	N
9 Yates	Y	Y	N	Y	Y	Y	Y	Y
10 Porter	Y	Y	Y	Y	Y	N	Y	Y
11 Sangmeister	Y	Y	N	Y	Y	Y	Y	Y
12 Costello	Y	Y	Y	Y	Y	N	Y	Y
13 Fawell	N	Y	Y	N	N	N	Y	Y
14 Hastert	Y	Y	Y	Y	?	N	Y	Y
15 Ewing	Y	Y	Y	Y	Y	N	Y	Y
16 Manzullo	N	Y	Y	Y	N	N	Y	Y
17 Evans	Y	Y	N	Y	Y	Y	Y	Y

ND   Northern Democrats   SD   Southern Democrats

	513	514	515	516	517	518	519	520
18 ***Michel***	Y	Y	Y	Y	?	N	?	Y
19 Poshard	Y	Y	Y	Y	Y	N	Y	Y
20 Durbin	Y	Y	N	Y	Y	Y	Y	Y
INDIANA								
1 Visclosky	Y	Y	N	Y	Y	Y	Y	Y
2 Sharp	Y	Y	N	Y	Y	Y	Y	Y
3 Roemer	N	Y	Y	Y	Y	N	Y	Y
4 Long	Y	Y	N	Y	Y	Y	Y	Y
5 ***Buyer***	Y	Y	Y	Y	N	N	Y	Y
6 ***Burton***	N	Y	Y	Y	N	N	N	N
7 ***Myers***	Y	Y	Y	Y	Y	N	Y	Y
8 McCloskey	Y	N	Y	Y	Y	Y	Y	Y
9 Hamilton	Y	Y	N	Y	Y	Y	Y	Y
10 Jacobs	N	Y	N	Y	N	Y	Y	N
IOWA								
1 ***Leach***	N	Y	N	Y	Y	N	Y	Y
2 ***Nussle***	N	Y	N	Y	Y	N	Y	Y
3 ***Lightfoot***	Y	N	Y	Y	N	N	Y	N
4 Smith	Y	Y	Y	Y	Y	Y	Y	Y
5 ***Grandy***	Y	Y	Y	Y	Y	N	?	Y
KANSAS								
1 ***Roberts***	N	Y	Y	Y	N	N	Y	Y
2 Slattery	Y	Y	N	Y	N	N	Y	Y
3 ***Meyers***	Y	Y	Y	Y	+	N	Y	Y
4 Glickman	Y	Y	N	Y	Y	Y	Y	Y
KENTUCKY								
1 Barlow	Y	Y	Y	Y	Y	N	Y	Y
2 Natcher	Y	Y	Y	Y	Y	Y	Y	Y
3 Mazzoli	Y	Y	Y	Y	Y	N	Y	Y
4 ***Bunning***	N	Y	Y	Y	N	N	Y	Y
5 ***Rogers***	Y	Y	Y	Y	Y	N	Y	Y
6 Baesler	Y	Y	Y	Y	Y	Y	Y	Y
LOUISIANA								
1 ***Livingston***	Y	N	Y	Y	Y	N	Y	Y
2 Jefferson	Y	Y	N	Y	Y	Y	Y	Y
3 Tauzin	Y	Y	?	Y	Y	N	Y	Y
4 Fields	Y	Y	Y	Y	Y	Y	Y	Y
5 ***McCrery***	Y	Y	Y	Y	Y	N	Y	Y
6 ***Baker***	N	Y	Y	Y	Y	N	Y	N
7 Hayes	Y	Y	Y	Y	?	N	Y	Y
MAINE								
1 Andrews	Y	Y	N	Y	Y	Y	Y	Y
2 ***Snowe***	Y	Y	Y	Y	Y	Y	Y	Y
MARYLAND								
1 ***Gilchrest***	Y	Y	N	Y	Y	Y	Y	Y
2 ***Bentley***	Y	Y	Y	Y	N	N	Y	Y
3 Cardin	Y	Y	N	Y	Y	Y	Y	Y
4 Wynn	Y	Y	N	Y	Y	Y	Y	Y
5 Hoyer	Y	Y	Y	Y	Y	Y	Y	Y
6 ***Bartlett***	N	Y	Y	Y	N	N	Y	N
7 Mfume	Y	Y	N	Y	Y	Y	Y	Y
8 ***Morella***	Y	Y	Y	Y	Y	Y	Y	Y
MASSACHUSETTS								
1 Olver	Y	Y	N	Y	Y	Y	Y	Y
2 Neal	Y	Y	N	Y	Y	N	Y	Y
3 ***Blute***	N	Y	Y	Y	Y	N	Y	Y
4 Frank	Y	Y	N	Y	Y	Y	Y	Y
5 Meehan	Y	Y	N	Y	Y	Y	Y	Y
6 ***Torkildsen***	N	Y	Y	Y	Y	N	Y	Y
7 Markey	Y	Y	N	Y	Y	Y	Y	Y
8 Kennedy	Y	Y	N	Y	Y	Y	Y	Y
9 Moakley	Y	Y	N	Y	Y	N	Y	Y
10 Studds	Y	Y	N	Y	Y	Y	Y	Y
MICHIGAN								
1 Stupak	Y	Y	Y	Y	Y	N	Y	Y
2 ***Hoekstra***	N	Y	Y	Y	Y	N	Y	N
3 Vacancy								
4 ***Camp***	Y	Y	N	Y	N	N	Y	Y
5 Barcia	Y	Y	Y	Y	Y	N	Y	N
6 ***Upton***	Y	Y	N	Y	N	N	Y	N
7 ***Smith***	N	Y	Y	Y	N	N	Y	N
8 Carr	Y	Y	N	Y	Y	Y	Y	Y
9 Kildee	Y	Y	N	Y	Y	N	Y	Y
10 Bonior	Y	Y	N	Y	Y	Y	Y	Y
11 ***Knollenberg***	N	Y	N	Y	N	N	Y	Y
12 Levin	Y	Y	N	Y	Y	Y	Y	Y
13 Ford	Y	Y	N	Y	?	Y	Y	Y
14 Conyers	Y	Y	N	Y	N	Y	Y	?
15 Collins	Y	Y	N	Y	Y	Y	Y	Y
16 Dingell	Y	Y	N	Y	?	Y	Y	Y
MINNESOTA								
1 Penny	N	Y	N	Y	N	N	Y	Y
2 Minge	N	Y	N	Y	Y	Y	Y	Y
3 ***Ramstad***	N	Y	Y	Y	N	N	Y	Y
4 Vento	Y	Y	N	Y	Y	Y	Y	Y

	513	514	515	516	517	518	519	520
5 Sabo	Y	Y	N	Y	Y	Y	Y	Y
6 ***Grams***	N	Y	Y	Y	N	N	Y	Y
7 Peterson	N	Y	N	Y	Y	N	Y	Y
8 Oberstar	Y	Y	N	Y	Y	N	Y	Y
MISSISSIPPI								
1 Whitten	Y	N	Y	Y	Y	Y	Y	Y
2 Thompson	Y	N	Y	Y	Y	Y	Y	Y
3 Montgomery	Y	N	Y	Y	Y	N	Y	Y
4 Parker	Y	N	Y	Y	Y	N	Y	Y
5 Taylor	Y	N	Y	Y	Y	N	Y	Y
MISSOURI								
1 Clay	Y	Y	N	Y	Y	Y	Y	Y
2 ***Talent***	Y	Y	Y	Y	N	N	Y	Y
3 Gephardt	Y	Y	N	Y	?	Y	Y	Y
4 Skelton	Y	Y	Y	Y	Y	N	Y	Y
5 Wheat	Y	Y	N	Y	Y	Y	Y	Y
6 Danner	Y	Y	N	Y	Y	N	Y	Y
7 ***Hancock***	N	Y	Y	Y	N	N	Y	N
8 ***Emerson***	Y	Y	Y	Y	Y	N	Y	N
9 Volkmer	Y	Y	Y	Y	Y	N	Y	Y
MONTANA								
AL Williams	Y	Y	N	Y	Y	Y	Y	Y
NEBRASKA								
1 ***Bereuter***	Y	Y	Y	Y	Y	N	Y	Y
2 Hoagland	N	Y	Y	Y	Y	Y	Y	Y
3 ***Barrett***	N	Y	N	Y	Y	N	Y	Y
NEVADA								
1 Bilbray	Y	Y	Y	Y	Y	Y	Y	Y
2 ***Vucanovich***	Y	Y	Y	Y	Y	N	Y	Y
NEW HAMPSHIRE								
1 ***Zeliff***	N	Y	Y	Y	N	N	Y	N
2 Swett	Y	Y	Y	Y	Y	Y	Y	Y
NEW JERSEY								
1 Andrews	Y	Y	Y	?	Y	Y	Y	Y
2 Hughes	Y	Y	Y	Y	Y	Y	Y	Y
3 ***Saxton***	Y	Y	Y	Y	N	N	Y	Y
4 ***Smith***	Y	Y	Y	Y	Y	N	Y	Y
5 ***Roukema***	N	Y	Y	Y	?	N	Y	Y
6 Pallone	N	Y	Y	Y	Y	Y	Y	Y
7 ***Franks***	N	Y	N	Y	N	N	Y	Y
8 Klein	Y	Y	N	Y	Y	Y	Y	Y
9 Torricelli	Y	N	N	Y	Y	Y	Y	Y
10 Payne	Y	Y	N	Y	Y	Y	Y	Y
11 ***Gallo***	Y	Y	Y	Y	Y	Y	Y	Y
12 ***Zimmer***	N	Y	N	Y	N	Y	Y	N
13 Menendez	Y	Y	Y	Y	Y	Y	Y	Y
NEW MEXICO								
1 ***Schiff***	Y	Y	Y	Y	Y	N	Y	Y
2 ***Skeen***	Y	Y	Y	Y	Y	N	Y	Y
3 Richardson	Y	Y	Y	Y	?	Y	Y	Y
NEW YORK								
1 Hochbrueckner	Y	N	Y	Y	+	Y	Y	Y
2 ***Lazio***	Y	Y	Y	Y	Y	N	Y	Y
3 ***King***	Y	Y	Y	Y	N	N	Y	Y
4 ***Levy***	Y	Y	Y	Y	N	N	Y	Y
5 Ackerman	Y	Y	N	Y	Y	Y	Y	Y
6 Flake	Y	Y	N	Y	Y	Y	Y	Y
7 Manton	Y	Y	N	Y	Y	N	Y	Y
8 Nadler	Y	Y	N	Y	Y	Y	Y	Y
9 Schumer	Y	Y	N	Y	Y	Y	Y	Y
10 Towns	Y	Y	N	Y	Y	Y	Y	Y
11 Owens	Y	Y	N	Y	Y	Y	Y	Y
12 Velazquez	Y	Y	N	Y	Y	Y	Y	Y
13 ***Molinari***	Y	Y	Y	Y	N	Y	Y	N
14 Maloney	Y	Y	N	Y	Y	Y	Y	Y
15 Rangel	Y	Y	N	Y	Y	Y	Y	Y
16 Serrano	Y	Y	N	Y	Y	Y	Y	Y
17 Engel	+	+	−	+	+	+	+	+
18 Lowey	Y	Y	N	Y	Y	Y	Y	Y
19 ***Fish***	Y	Y	Y	Y	Y	N	Y	Y
20 ***Gilman***	Y	Y	Y	Y	Y	Y	Y	Y
21 McNulty	Y	Y	Y	Y	Y	N	Y	Y
22 ***Solomon***	N	Y	Y	Y	N	N	Y	N
23 ***Boehlert***	Y	Y	Y	Y	Y	N	Y	Y
24 ***McHugh***	Y	Y	Y	Y	N	N	Y	N
25 ***Walsh***	Y	Y	Y	Y	Y	N	Y	N
26 Hinchey	Y	Y	N	Y	Y	Y	Y	?
27 ***Paxon***	N	Y	Y	Y	N	N	Y	Y
28 Slaughter	Y	Y	N	Y	Y	Y	Y	Y
29 LaFalce	Y	Y	N	Y	Y	N	Y	Y
30 ***Quinn***	Y	Y	Y	Y	Y	N	Y	N
31 ***Houghton***	Y	Y	Y	Y	Y	Y	Y	Y
NORTH CAROLINA								
1 Clayton	Y	Y	N	Y	Y	Y	Y	Y
2 Valentine	Y	Y	Y	Y	Y	N	Y	Y

	513	514	515	516	517	518	519	520
3 Lancaster	Y	Y	Y	Y	Y	Y	Y	Y
4 Price	Y	Y	N	Y	Y	Y	Y	Y
5 Neal	Y	Y	N	?	?	?	Y	Y
6 ***Coble***	N	Y	Y	Y	N	N	Y	N
7 Rose	Y	Y	N	Y	Y	Y	Y	Y
8 Hefner	Y	Y	N	Y	?	Y	Y	Y
9 ***McMillan***	Y	Y	Y	Y	?	N	?	?
10 ***Ballenger***	N	Y	Y	Y	N	N	Y	Y
11 ***Taylor***	Y	Y	Y	Y	N	N	Y	Y
12 Watt	Y	Y	N	Y	Y	Y	Y	Y
NORTH DAKOTA								
AL Pomeroy	Y	Y	N	Y	Y	Y	Y	Y
OHIO								
1 Mann	Y	Y	N	Y	Y	N	Y	Y
2 ***Portman***	N	Y	Y	Y	N	N	Y	Y
3 Hall	Y	Y	N	Y	Y	N	Y	Y
4 ***Oxley***	Y	Y	Y	Y	Y	N	Y	Y
5 ***Gillmor***	Y	Y	Y	Y	Y	N	?	Y
6 Strickland	Y	Y	N	Y	Y	Y	Y	Y
7 ***Hobson***	Y	Y	N	Y	Y	N	Y	Y
8 ***Boehner***	N	Y	Y	Y	N	N	Y	Y
9 Kaptur	Y	Y	N	Y	Y	N	Y	Y
10 ***Hoke***	Y	Y	N	Y	N	N	Y	Y
11 Stokes	Y	Y	N	Y	Y	Y	Y	Y
12 ***Kasich***	Y	Y	N	Y	Y	N	Y	Y
13 Brown	Y	Y	N	Y	Y	Y	Y	Y
14 Sawyer	Y	Y	N	Y	Y	Y	Y	Y
15 ***Pryce***	Y	Y	Y	Y	Y	N	Y	Y
16 ***Regula***	Y	Y	Y	Y	Y	N	Y	Y
17 Traficant	Y	N	N	Y	Y	Y	Y	N
18 Applegate	Y	Y	N	Y	Y	N	Y	Y
19 Fingerhut	Y	Y	Y	Y	Y	Y	Y	Y
OKLAHOMA								
1 ***Inhofe***	N	Y	Y	Y	N	N	Y	N
2 Synar	Y	Y	N	Y	Y	Y	Y	Y
3 Brewster	Y	Y	Y	Y	Y	N	Y	Y
4 McCurdy	Y	Y	Y	Y	Y	Y	Y	Y
5 ***Istook***	Y	Y	N	Y	N	N	Y	Y
6 English	Y	Y	Y	Y	Y	N	Y	Y
OREGON								
1 Furse	Y	Y	N	Y	Y	Y	Y	Y
2 ***Smith***	N	Y	Y	Y	N	N	Y	Y
3 Wyden	Y	Y	N	Y	Y	Y	Y	Y
4 DeFazio	Y	Y	N	N	Y	Y	Y	Y
5 Kopetski	Y	Y	N	Y	Y	Y	Y	Y
PENNSYLVANIA								
1 Foglietta	Y	Y	N	Y	Y	Y	Y	Y
2 Blackwell	Y	Y	N	Y	Y	Y	Y	Y
3 Borski	Y	Y	N	?	?	N	Y	Y
4 Klink	Y	Y	Y	Y	N	N	Y	Y
5 ***Clinger***	Y	Y	Y	Y	Y	Y	Y	Y
6 Holden	N	Y	Y	Y	Y	N	Y	Y
7 ***Weldon***	Y	Y	Y	Y	N	N	Y	Y
8 ***Greenwood***	Y	Y	Y	?	?	N	?	Y
9 ***Shuster***	N	Y	N	Y	N	N	Y	N
10 ***McDade***	Y	Y	Y	Y	?	N	Y	Y
11 Kanjorski	Y	Y	N	Y	Y	N	Y	Y
12 Murtha	Y	N	Y	Y	Y	Y	Y	Y
13 Margolies-Mezv.	N	Y	N	Y	Y	Y	Y	Y
14 Coyne	Y	Y	N	Y	Y	Y	Y	Y
15 McHale	Y	Y	Y	Y	Y	Y	Y	Y
16 ***Walker***	N	Y	N	Y	N	N	Y	N
17 ***Gekas***	N	N	Y	Y	N	N	Y	N
18 ***Santorum***	Y	Y	N	?	?	?	Y	Y
19 ***Goodling***	Y	Y	Y	Y	Y	N	Y	Y
20 Murphy	Y	Y	N	Y	?	N	Y	Y
21 ***Ridge***	Y	Y	Y	Y	N	N	Y	Y
RHODE ISLAND								
1 ***Machtley***	Y	Y	Y	Y	Y	N	Y	Y
2 Reed	Y	Y	Y	Y	Y	Y	Y	Y
SOUTH CAROLINA								
1 ***Ravenel***	Y	Y	Y	Y	Y	N	Y	N
2 ***Spence***	N	Y	Y	Y	N	N	Y	N
3 Derrick	Y	N	N	Y	Y	Y	Y	Y
4 ***Inglis***	N	Y	Y	Y	N	N	Y	Y
5 Spratt	Y	Y	Y	Y	C	Y	Y	Y
6 Clyburn	Y	Y	Y	Y	Y	Y	Y	Y
SOUTH DAKOTA								
AL Johnson	Y	Y	?	Y	Y	Y	Y	Y
TENNESSEE								
1 ***Quillen***	Y	N	Y	Y	Y	N	Y	Y
2 ***Duncan***	N	Y	Y	Y	N	N	Y	N
3 Lloyd	Y	Y	Y	Y	Y	N	Y	Y
4 Cooper	Y	Y	Y	Y	Y	Y	Y	Y
5 Clement	Y	Y	Y	Y	Y	N	Y	Y

	513	514	515	516	517	518	519	520
6 Gordon	Y	Y	Y	Y	Y	Y	Y	Y
7 ***Sundquist***	Y	N	Y	Y	N	N	Y	Y
8 Tanner	Y	N	Y	Y	Y	Y	Y	Y
9 Ford	?	?	N	Y	Y	Y	Y	Y
TEXAS								
1 Chapman	Y	Y	N	?	Y	Y	Y	Y
2 Wilson	Y	Y	Y	Y	Y	Y	Y	Y
3 ***Johnson, Sam***	N	Y	Y	Y	N	N	Y	Y
4 Hall	Y	N	Y	Y	Y	N	Y	N
5 Bryant	Y	Y	Y	Y	Y	Y	Y	Y
6 ***Barton***	N	Y	Y	Y	N	N	Y	N
7 ***Archer***	N	Y	N	Y	N	N	Y	N
8 ***Fields***	N	Y	Y	Y	N	N	Y	N
9 Brooks	Y	Y	Y	Y	Y	Y	Y	Y
10 Pickle	Y	N	Y	Y	Y	Y	Y	Y
11 Edwards	Y	Y	Y	Y	Y	N	Y	Y
12 Geren	Y	N	Y	Y	Y	N	Y	Y
13 Sarpalius	Y	Y	Y	Y	Y	N	Y	Y
14 Laughlin	Y	Y	Y	Y	Y	Y	Y	Y
15 de la Garza	Y	Y	N	Y	Y	N	Y	Y
16 Coleman	Y	Y	N	Y	Y	Y	Y	Y
17 Stenholm	Y	Y	Y	Y	Y	N	Y	Y
18 Washington	Y	Y	N	N	Y	Y	Y	Y
19 ***Combest***	N	Y	Y	Y	N	N	Y	N
20 Gonzalez	Y	Y	N	Y	Y	Y	Y	N
21 ***Smith***	Y	Y	Y	Y	Y	N	Y	Y
22 ***DeLay***	Y	Y	N	Y	N	N	Y	N
23 ***Bonilla***	Y	Y	Y	Y	Y	N	Y	N
24 Frost	Y	Y	Y	Y	Y	Y	Y	Y
25 Andrews	Y	Y	Y	Y	Y	Y	Y	Y
26 ***Armey***	N	Y	Y	Y	N	N	Y	Y
27 Ortiz	Y	Y	N	Y	Y	N	Y	Y
28 Tejeda	Y	Y	Y	Y	Y	N	Y	Y
29 Green	Y	Y	N	Y	Y	N	Y	Y
30 Johnson, E.B.	Y	Y	Y	Y	Y	Y	Y	Y
UTAH								
1 ***Hansen***	Y	Y	Y	?	?	N	Y	N
2 Shepherd	Y	Y	Y	Y	Y	Y	Y	Y
3 Orton	N	Y	Y	Y	N	N	Y	Y
VERMONT								
AL *Sanders*	Y	Y	N	Y	Y	Y	Y	Y
VIRGINIA								
1 ***Bateman***	Y	Y	Y	Y	Y	N	Y	Y
2 Pickett	Y	N	Y	Y	Y	N	Y	Y
3 Scott	Y	Y	N	Y	Y	Y	Y	Y
4 Sisisky	Y	Y	Y	Y	Y	Y	Y	Y
5 Payne	Y	Y	Y	Y	Y	N	Y	Y
6 ***Goodlatte***	N	Y	Y	Y	Y	N	Y	Y
7 ***Bliley***	Y	Y	Y	?	Y	N	Y	Y
8 Moran	Y	Y	Y	Y	?	Y	Y	Y
9 Boucher	Y	Y	N	Y	Y	Y	Y	Y
10 ***Wolf***	Y	Y	Y	Y	N	N	Y	Y
11 Byrne	N	Y	N	Y	Y	Y	Y	Y
WASHINGTON								
1 Cantwell	Y	Y	N	Y	Y	Y	Y	Y
2 Swift	Y	Y	N	Y	Y	Y	Y	Y
3 Unsoeld	Y	Y	N	Y	Y	Y	Y	Y
4 Inslee	Y	Y	N	Y	Y	Y	Y	Y
5 Foley								
6 Dicks	Y	Y	N	Y	Y	Y	Y	Y
7 McDermott	Y	Y	N	Y	Y	Y	Y	Y
8 ***Dunn***	Y	Y	Y	Y	N	N	Y	Y
9 Kreidler	Y	Y	N	Y	Y	Y	Y	Y
WEST VIRGINIA								
1 Mollohan	Y	Y	N	Y	Y	N	Y	Y
2 Wise	Y	Y	Y	Y	Y	Y	Y	Y
3 Rahall	Y	Y	Y	Y	Y	N	Y	Y
WISCONSIN								
1 Barca	Y	Y	Y	Y	Y	Y	Y	Y
2 ***Klug***	N	Y	N	Y	N	N	Y	N
3 ***Gunderson***	Y	Y	Y	Y	Y	N	Y	Y
4 Kleczka	Y	Y	N	Y	Y	Y	Y	Y
5 Barrett	Y	Y	N	Y	Y	Y	Y	Y
6 ***Petri***	N	Y	Y	Y	N	N	Y	N
7 Obey	Y	Y	N	Y	Y	Y	Y	Y
8 ***Roth***	N	Y	N	Y	N	N	Y	N
9 ***Sensenbrenner***	N	Y	N	Y	N	N	Y	N
WYOMING								
AL ***Thomas***	Y	Y	Y	Y	N	N	Y	Y
DELEGATES								
de Lugo, V.I.	D	D	D	D	D	D	D	D
Faleomavaega, Am.S.	D	D	D	D	D	D	D	D
Norton, D.C.	D	D	D	D	D	D	D	D
Romero-B., P.R.	D	D	D	D	D	D	D	D
Underwood, Guam	D	D	D	D	D	D	D	D

Southern states - Ala., Ark., Fla., Ga., Ky., La., Miss., N.C., Okla., S.C., Tenn., Texas, Va.
Omitted votes are quorum calls, which CQ does not include in its vote charts.

521. HR 2519. Fiscal 1994 Commerce, Justice and State Appropriations/National Endowment for Democracy. Smith, D-Iowa, motion to recede from the House position on funding for the National Endowment for Democracy. Motion agreed to 259-172: R 102-73; D 157-98 (ND 104-67, SD 53-31); I 0-1, Oct. 20, 1993.

522. HR 2520. Fiscal 1994 Interior Appropriations/Rule. Adoption of the rule (H Res 279) to provide for House floor consideration of the conference report to provide $13,388,038,000 in new budget authority for the Department of the Interior and related agencies in fiscal 1994. Adopted 253-174: R 34-138; D 218-36 (ND 153-17, SD 65-19); I 1-0, Oct. 20, 1993.

523. HR 2520. Fiscal 1994 Interior Appropriations/Bureau of Land Management. Yates, D-Ill., motion to recede and concur in the Senate amendment with an amendment to provide $599.9 million for the management of lands and resources instead of the $604 million proposed by the Senate; provide $15 million for mining law administration and $5 million for the administration of the mining claim fee program; and prohibit the destruction of healthy wild horses and burros. Motion agreed to 296-131: R 57-117; D 238-14 (ND 161-8, SD 77-6); I 1-0, Oct. 20, 1993.

524. HR 2520. Fiscal 1994 Interior Appropriations/Land Acquisition. Yates, D-Ill., motion to recede and concur in the Senate amendment with an amendment to provide $82.7 million for land acquisition by the U.S. Fish and Wildlife Administration instead of the $61.6 million proposed by the House and the $76.2 million proposed by the Senate. Motion agreed to 293-131: R 66-107; D 226-24 (ND 154-12, SD 72-12); I 1-0, Oct. 20, 1993.

525. HR 2520. Fiscal 1994 Interior Appropriations/Grazing Fees. Yates, D-Ill., motion to recede and concur in a Senate amendment with an amendment to increase grazing fees on public lands from the current level of $1.86 per animal unit to $3.45 by fiscal 1996 and implement new grazing and range management policies. Motion agreed to 317-106: R 85-86; D 231-20 (ND 158-12, SD 73-8); I 1-0, Oct. 20, 1993. A "yea" was a vote in support of the president's position. (Previously, the House adopted the conference report by voice vote, thus sending the bill to the Senate.)

526. HR 2445. Fiscal 1994 Energy and Water Appropriations/Conference Report. Adoption of the conference report to provide $22,215,382,000 for energy and water development in fiscal 1994. The administration requested $22,346,046,000. Adopted (thus sent to the Senate) 332-81: R 109-60; D 222-21 (ND 148-14, SD 74-7); I 1-0, Oct. 26, 1993.

527. HR 2445. Fiscal 1994 Energy and Water Appropriations/Super Collider. Bevill, D-Ala., motion to recede and concur in a Senate amendment with an amendment to terminate the superconducting super collider. Motion agreed to 227-190: R 59-112; D 168-77 (ND 113-50, SD 55-27); I 0-1, Oct. 26, 1993. A "nay" was a vote in support of the president's position.

528. HR 1845. National Biological Survey/Volunteers. Separate vote at the request of Vento, D-Minn., on the amendment offered by Tauzin, D-La., and adopted in the Committee of the Whole to strike the provisions that allow the Interior secretary to accept the services of volunteers. Adopted 227-194: R 151-20; D 76-173 (ND 35-131, SD 41-42); I 0-1, Oct. 26, 1993. (On a separate vote, which may be demanded on an amendment adopted in the Committee of the Whole, the four delegates and the resident commissioner of Puerto Rico cannot vote. See vote 484.)

KEY

Y Voted for (yea).
\# Paired for.
\+ Announced for.
N Voted against (nay).
X Paired against.
− Announced against.
P Voted "present."
C Voted "present" to avoid possible conflict of interest.
? Did not vote or otherwise make a position known.
D Delegates ineligible to vote.

Democrats *Republicans*
Independent

	521	522	523	524	525	526	527	528
ALABAMA								
1 *Callahan*	N	N	N	Y	N	Y	Y	Y
2 *Everett*	Y	N	N	N	Y	Y	Y	Y
3 Browder	N	Y	Y	Y	Y	Y	Y	Y
4 Bevill	N	Y	Y	Y	Y	Y	Y	Y
5 Cramer	N	Y	Y	Y	Y	Y	Y	Y
6 *Bachus*	Y	N	N	N	N	Y	Y	Y
7 Hilliard	N	Y	Y	Y	Y	Y	Y	N
ALASKA								
AL *Young*	N	N	N	Y	N	Y	N	Y
ARIZONA								
1 Coppersmith	Y	Y	Y	Y	Y	N	N	N
2 Pastor	Y	Y	Y	?	N	Y	Y	N
3 *Stump*	N	N	N	N	N	N	N	Y
4 *Kyl*	Y	N	Y	N	Y	N	N	Y
5 *Kolbe*	Y	N	Y	Y	Y	N	Y	Y
6 English	Y	N	Y	N	Y	N	Y	N
ARKANSAS								
1 Lambert	Y	N	Y	N	Y	Y	Y	Y
2 Thornton	Y	Y	Y	Y	Y	Y	Y	Y
3 *Hutchinson*	Y	N	N	N	N	Y	N	Y
4 *Dickey*	Y	N	N	N	Y	Y	N	Y
CALIFORNIA								
1 Hamburg	N	Y	Y	Y	Y	Y	Y	N
2 *Herger*	N	N	N	N	N	Y	N	Y
3 Fazio	Y	Y	Y	?	Y	Y	Y	N
4 *Doolittle*	Y	N	N	N	N	Y	N	Y
5 Matsui	Y	Y	Y	Y	Y	Y	Y	N
6 Woolsey	N	Y	Y	Y	Y	Y	Y	N
7 Miller	N	Y	Y	Y	Y	Y	Y	N
8 Pelosi	Y	Y	Y	Y	Y	Y	Y	N
9 Dellums	N	Y	Y	Y	Y	Y	Y	N
10 *Baker*	Y	N	N	N	N	Y	N	Y
11 *Pombo*	Y	N	N	N	N	N	N	Y
12 Lantos	Y	Y	Y	Y	Y	Y	Y	N
13 Stark	N	Y	Y	Y	Y	N	Y	N
14 Eshoo	Y	Y	Y	Y	Y	Y	Y	N
15 Mineta	Y	Y	Y	Y	Y	Y	Y	N
16 Edwards	Y	Y	Y	Y	Y	Y	Y	N
17 Farr	Y	Y	Y	Y	Y	Y	Y	N
18 Condit	N	N	N	N	Y	N	N	Y
19 Lehman	Y	N	Y	?	N	Y	Y	Y
20 Dooley	Y	N	Y	N	Y	Y	N	Y
21 *Thomas*	Y	N	N	N	Y	N	Y	Y
22 *Huffington*	Y	N	N	N	Y	Y	Y	Y
23 *Gallegly*	N	N	N	N	N	Y	N	Y
24 Beilenson	Y	Y	Y	Y	Y	Y	Y	N
25 *McKeon*	N	N	N	N	N	Y	Y	Y
26 Berman	Y	Y	Y	Y	Y	?	?	?
27 *Moorhead*	Y	N	N	N	N	N	N	Y
28 *Dreier*	Y	N	N	N	N	N	N	Y
29 Waxman	Y	Y	?	?	Y	Y	Y	N
30 Becerra	Y	Y	Y	Y	Y	Y	Y	N
31 Martinez	Y	N	Y	Y	Y	Y	Y	Y
32 Dixon	Y	Y	Y	Y	Y	Y	Y	N
33 Roybal-Allard	Y	Y	Y	Y	Y	Y	Y	N
34 Torres	Y	Y	Y	Y	Y	Y	Y	N
35 Waters	Y	Y	Y	Y	Y	Y	N	N
36 Harman	Y	Y	Y	Y	Y	Y	Y	N
37 Tucker	Y	Y	Y	Y	Y	Y	Y	N
38 *Horn*	Y	Y	N	Y	Y	?	?	?
39 *Royce*	Y	N	N	N	Y	N	N	Y
40 *Lewis*	Y	N	Y	Y	N	Y	N	Y
41 *Kim*	Y	N	N	N	Y	N	Y	Y

	521	522	523	524	525	526	527	528
42 Brown	Y	Y	Y	Y	Y	?	?	?
43 *Calvert*	Y	N	N	Y	N	Y	Y	Y
44 *McCandless*	N	N	Y	N	Y	Y	Y	Y
45 *Rohrabacher*	Y	N	N	N	N	N	N	Y
46 *Dornan*	Y	N	N	N	N	?	?	Y
47 *Cox*	Y	N	N	N	N	N	N	Y
48 *Packard*	Y	N	Y	N	Y	N	Y	Y
49 Schenk	N	Y	Y	Y	Y	Y	Y	N
50 Filner	N	Y	Y	Y	Y	Y	Y	N
51 *Cunningham*	Y	N	N	N	N	N	N	Y
52 *Hunter*	Y	N	N	?	N	N	Y	Y
COLORADO								
1 Schroeder	N	Y	Y	Y	Y	Y	N	Y
2 Skaggs	Y	Y	Y	Y	Y	Y	Y	N
3 *McInnis*	N	N	N	N	Y	Y	N	Y
4 *Allard*	N	N	N	N	N	N	N	Y
5 *Hefley*	N	N	N	N	N	N	N	Y
6 *Schaefer*	N	N	N	N	Y	N	N	Y
CONNECTICUT								
1 Kennelly	Y	Y	Y	Y	Y	Y	Y	N
2 Gejdenson	Y	Y	Y	Y	Y	Y	Y	N
3 DeLauro	Y	Y	Y	Y	Y	Y	Y	N
4 *Shays*	N	Y	N	Y	Y	N	Y	N
5 *Franks*	N	N	Y	N	Y	N	N	Y
6 *Johnson*	Y	Y	Y	Y	Y	Y	N	N
DELAWARE								
AL *Castle*	Y	N	N	N	Y	N	N	Y
FLORIDA								
1 Hutto	N	N	Y	N	N	Y	N	Y
2 Peterson	Y	Y	Y	Y	Y	Y	Y	N
3 Brown	Y	Y	Y	Y	Y	Y	Y	N
4 *Fowler*	N	N	Y	Y	Y	Y	N	Y
5 Thurman	N	Y	Y	Y	Y	Y	N	N
6 *Stearns*	N	N	N	N	Y	N	Y	N
7 *Mica*	N	N	N	N	N	N	N	N
8 *McCollum*	Y	N	Y	N	Y	N	N	Y
9 *Bilirakis*	Y	N	Y	Y	Y	N	Y	Y
10 *Young*	Y	Y	N	Y	N	Y	Y	Y
11 Gibbons	Y	Y	?	Y	Y	Y	Y	N
12 *Canady*	Y	N	Y	Y	Y	N	Y	Y
13 *Miller*	Y	N	Y	Y	Y	N	N	Y
14 *Goss*	Y	N	Y	Y	Y	N	N	Y
15 Bacchus	Y	Y	Y	Y	Y	Y	N	N
16 *Lewis*	N	N	N	Y	Y	N	N	Y
17 Meek	Y	?	Y	Y	Y	Y	Y	N
18 *Ros-Lehtinen*	Y	Y	Y	Y	Y	N	N	Y
19 Johnston	Y	Y	Y	Y	Y	Y	Y	N
20 Deutsch	Y	Y	Y	Y	Y	Y	Y	N
21 *Diaz-Balart*	Y	Y	Y	Y	Y	Y	N	Y
22 *Shaw*	Y	N	Y	N	Y	N	N	Y
23 Hastings	Y	Y	Y	Y	Y	Y	Y	Y
GEORGIA								
1 *Kingston*	Y	N	N	N	N	Y	Y	Y
2 Bishop	Y	Y	Y	Y	Y	Y	Y	N
3 *Collins*	N	N	N	N	N	N	N	Y
4 *Linder*	Y	N	N	N	Y	N	Y	Y
5 Lewis	Y	Y	Y	Y	Y	Y	Y	N
6 *Gingrich*	Y	N	Y	N	Y	Y	Y	Y
7 *Darden*	Y	Y	Y	Y	Y	Y	Y	N
8 Rowland	Y	N	Y	Y	Y	Y	Y	Y
9 Deal	Y	Y	Y	Y	Y	N	Y	N
10 Johnson	Y	Y	Y	Y	Y	Y	N	N
11 McKinney	N	Y	Y	Y	Y	Y	Y	N
HAWAII								
1 Abercrombie	Y	Y	?	Y	Y	?	?	Y
2 Mink	N	Y	Y	Y	Y	Y	Y	N
IDAHO								
1 LaRocco	N	N	Y	N	Y	N	N	N
2 *Crapo*	Y	N	N	N	Y	N	N	Y
ILLINOIS								
1 Rush	Y	Y	Y	Y	Y	Y	Y	N
2 Reynolds	Y	?	Y	Y	Y	Y	N	Y
3 Lipinski	N	N	Y	Y	Y	N	N	Y
4 Gutierrez	Y	Y	Y	Y	Y	Y	N	N
5 Rostenkowski	N	Y	Y	Y	Y	?	?	?
6 *Hyde*	Y	N	N	N	N	Y	Y	Y
7 Collins	Y	Y	Y	Y	Y	Y	Y	N
8 *Crane*	N	N	N	N	N	N	N	Y
9 Yates	N	Y	Y	Y	Y	Y	Y	N
10 *Porter*	Y	Y	Y	N	Y	+	+	−
11 Sangmeister	N	Y	Y	Y	Y	Y	N	N
12 Costello	N	Y	Y	Y	Y	N	N	Y
13 *Fawell*	N	N	N	N	Y	N	N	Y
14 Hastert	Y	−	−	−	+	Y	N	Y
15 *Ewing*	N	N	N	N	Y	N	N	Y
16 *Manzullo*	N	N	N	N	N	N	N	Y
17 Evans	N	Y	Y	Y	Y	Y	N	N

ND Northern Democrats   SD Southern Democrats

	521	522	523	524	525	526	527	528
18 ***Michel***	Y	?	N	Y	N	Y	Y	Y
19 Poshard	N	N	Y	Y	Y	Y	N	Y
20 Durbin	Y	Y	Y	Y	Y	Y	Y	N
INDIANA								
1 Visclosky	N	Y	Y	Y	Y	Y	Y	N
2 Sharp	Y	Y	Y	?	Y	N	N	N
3 Roemer	Y	Y	Y	Y	Y	Y	N	N
4 Long	N	Y	Y	Y	Y	Y	Y	N
5 ***Buyer***	Y	N	N	N	N	N	N	Y
6 ***Burton***	Y	N	N	N	N	N	N	Y
7 ***Myers***	N	Y	Y	Y	N	Y	Y	Y
8 McCloskey	Y	Y	Y	Y	Y	Y	Y	N
9 Hamilton	Y	Y	Y	Y	Y	Y	Y	N
10 Jacobs	N	Y	N	N	Y	N	N	N
IOWA								
1 ***Leach***	Y	N	Y	Y	Y	Y	N	N
2 ***Nussle***	N	N	N	N	Y	N	N	Y
3 ***Lightfoot***	N	N	N	N	N	Y	Y	Y
4 Smith	Y	Y	Y	Y	Y	?	Y	Y
5 ***Grandy***	N	N	Y	N	Y	Y	N	Y
KANSAS								
1 ***Roberts***	Y	N	N	N	N	N	N	Y
2 Slattery	N	Y	Y	N	Y	Y	Y	N
3 ***Meyers***	Y	Y	N	N	Y	Y	N	N
4 Glickman	Y	Y	Y	N	Y	Y	N	Y
KENTUCKY								
1 Barlow	Y	N	Y	Y	Y	Y	Y	Y
2 Natcher	Y	Y	Y	Y	Y	Y	Y	N
3 Mazzoli	N	Y	Y	Y	Y	Y	Y	Y
4 ***Bunning***	Y	N	N	N	N	Y	Y	Y
5 ***Rogers***	Y	N	Y	Y	N	Y	Y	Y
6 Baesler	N	N	Y	Y	Y	Y	Y	Y
LOUISIANA								
1 ***Livingston***	Y	Y	N	Y	N	Y	Y	Y
2 Jefferson	Y	Y	Y	Y	Y	Y	N	Y
3 Tauzin	N	N	Y	Y	N	Y	Y	Y
4 Fields	Y	Y	Y	Y	Y	Y	Y	Y
5 ***McCrery***	Y	N	Y	Y	Y	Y	Y	Y
6 ***Baker***	N	N	N	N	N	N	Y	Y
7 Hayes	N	N	Y	Y	N	Y	Y	Y
MAINE								
1 Andrews	N	Y	Y	Y	Y	Y	N	N
2 ***Snowe***	N	Y	Y	Y	Y	Y	Y	N
MARYLAND								
1 ***Gilchrest***	Y	Y	Y	Y	N	Y	N	N
2 ***Bentley***	N	N	Y	N	N	Y	Y	Y
3 Cardin	Y	Y	Y	Y	Y	Y	Y	N
4 Wynn	N	Y	Y	Y	Y	Y	Y	N
5 Hoyer	Y	Y	Y	Y	Y	Y	Y	N
6 ***Bartlett***	Y	N	N	N	N	N	N	Y
7 Mfume	N	Y	Y	Y	Y	Y	N	N
8 ***Morella***	Y	Y	Y	Y	Y	Y	Y	N
MASSACHUSETTS								
1 Olver	Y	Y	Y	Y	Y	Y	Y	N
2 Neal	Y	Y	Y	Y	Y	Y	Y	N
3 ***Blute***	N	Y	N	Y	Y	Y	N	Y
4 Frank	N	Y	Y	Y	Y	Y	Y	N
5 Meehan	N	Y	Y	Y	Y	Y	Y	N
6 ***Torkildsen***	N	Y	N	Y	Y	Y	N	Y
7 Markey	Y	Y	Y	Y	Y	Y	Y	N
8 Kennedy	Y	Y	Y	Y	Y	?	?	?
9 Moakley	Y	Y	Y	Y	Y	Y	Y	N
10 Studds	N	Y	Y	Y	Y	Y	Y	N
MICHIGAN								
1 Stupak	N	Y	Y	Y	Y	Y	N	N
2 ***Hoekstra***	N	N	Y	N	Y	Y	Y	?
3 Vacancy								
4 ***Camp***	N	N	Y	N	N	N	N	Y
5 Barcia	N	N	N	N	N	Y	N	Y
6 ***Upton***	N	N	Y	N	Y	N	N	Y
7 ***Smith***	N	N	N	N	N	N	N	Y
8 Carr	N	Y	Y	Y	Y	Y	Y	N
9 Kildee	Y	Y	Y	Y	Y	Y	Y	N
10 Bonior	Y	Y	Y	Y	Y	Y	Y	N
11 ***Knollenberg***	N	N	Y	N	Y	Y	N	Y
12 Levin	Y	Y	Y	Y	Y	Y	Y	N
13 Ford	N	Y	Y	Y	Y	Y	Y	N
14 Conyers	N	Y	Y	Y	Y	Y	N	N
15 Collins	Y	Y	Y	Y	Y	Y	Y	N
16 Dingell	Y	Y	Y	N	Y	Y	?	Y
MINNESOTA								
1 Penny	Y	Y	N	N	Y	N	N	Y
2 Minge	Y	Y	N	N	Y	N	N	Y
3 ***Ramstad***	N	Y	N	N	Y	N	N	N
4 Vento	Y	Y	Y	Y	Y	Y	Y	N

	521	522	523	524	525	526	527	528
5 Sabo	Y	Y	Y	?	Y	Y	Y	N
6 ***Grams***	N	N	N	N	N	N	Y	Y
7 Peterson	N	N	Y	N	N	N	N	Y
8 Oberstar	Y	Y	Y	Y	Y	Y	Y	N
MISSISSIPPI								
1 Whitten	N	Y	Y	Y	?	Y	Y	Y
2 Thompson	Y	Y	Y	Y	Y	Y	N	N
3 Montgomery	N	N	Y	Y	Y	Y	Y	Y
4 Parker	N	N	Y	Y	Y	Y	Y	Y
5 Taylor	N	N	N	Y	Y	Y	N	Y
MISSOURI								
1 Clay	N	Y	Y	Y	Y	Y	N	N
2 ***Talent***	N	N	N	N	N	N	N	Y
3 Gephardt	Y	Y	Y	Y	Y	?	?	?
4 Skelton	N	N	Y	Y	Y	Y	N	Y
5 Wheat	Y	Y	Y	Y	Y	Y	N	N
6 Danner	N	Y	Y	Y	Y	Y	N	Y
7 ***Hancock***	N	N	N	N	N	N	N	Y
8 ***Emerson***	N	N	N	N	N	Y	N	Y
9 Volkmer	N	N	Y	Y	Y	Y	Y	Y
MONTANA								
AL Williams	Y	N	Y	Y	N	Y	Y	N
NEBRASKA								
1 ***Bereuter***	Y	Y	Y	Y	Y	Y	N	Y
2 Hoagland	Y	Y	Y	Y	Y	Y	Y	N
3 ***Barrett***	N	N	N	N	N	Y	N	Y
NEVADA								
1 Bilbray	Y	Y	Y	Y	Y	Y	Y	N
2 ***Vucanovich***	Y	N	N	N	N	Y	Y	Y
NEW HAMPSHIRE								
1 ***Zeliff***	Y	N	N	N	N	N	N	Y
2 Swett	N	Y	Y	Y	Y	Y	N	N
NEW JERSEY								
1 Andrews	N	Y	Y	Y	Y	Y	Y	Y
2 Hughes	Y	Y	Y	Y	Y	Y	Y	N
3 ***Saxton***	Y	Y	Y	Y	Y	Y	N	Y
4 ***Smith***	Y	N	Y	Y	Y	Y	Y	N
5 ***Roukema***	N	Y	Y	Y	Y	Y	N	Y
6 Pallone	Y	Y	Y	Y	Y	Y	Y	N
7 ***Franks***	Y	N	N	N	Y	N	Y	Y
8 Klein	Y	Y	Y	Y	Y	Y	Y	N
9 Torricelli	Y	Y	Y	Y	Y	Y	N	N
10 Payne	Y	Y	Y	Y	Y	Y	N	N
11 ***Gallo***	Y	Y	Y	Y	Y	Y	Y	Y
12 ***Zimmer***	N	Y	Y	Y	Y	Y	Y	N
13 Menendez	Y	Y	Y	Y	Y	Y	N	N
NEW MEXICO								
1 ***Schiff***	Y	N	Y	Y	N	Y	Y	Y
2 ***Skeen***	Y	N	Y	Y	N	Y	Y	Y
3 Richardson	Y	Y	Y	Y	Y	Y	Y	N
NEW YORK								
1 Hochbrueckner	Y	Y	Y	Y	Y	Y	Y	N
2 ***Lazio***	N	N	Y	Y	Y	Y	Y	Y
3 ***King***	Y	N	N	N	Y	N	N	Y
4 ***Levy***	Y	N	Y	N	Y	Y	N	Y
5 Ackerman	Y	Y	Y	Y	Y	Y	Y	N
6 Flake	Y	Y	Y	Y	Y	Y	Y	Y
7 Manton	Y	Y	Y	Y	Y	Y	Y	N
8 Nadler	Y	Y	Y	Y	Y	N	Y	N
9 Schumer	Y	Y	Y	Y	Y	Y	Y	N
10 Towns	N	Y	Y	Y	Y	Y	N	N
11 Owens	N	Y	Y	Y	Y	Y	Y	N
12 Velazquez	N	Y	Y	Y	Y	Y	Y	N
13 ***Molinari***	Y	N	N	N	Y	Y	Y	Y
14 Maloney	Y	Y	Y	Y	Y	N	Y	N
15 Rangel	N	Y	Y	Y	Y	Y	N	N
16 Serrano	N	Y	Y	Y	Y	Y	Y	N
17 Engel	+	+	+	Y	Y	?	?	N
18 Lowey	Y	Y	Y	Y	Y	+	Y	N
19 ***Fish***	Y	Y	N	Y	Y	Y	Y	Y
20 ***Gilman***	Y	Y	N	Y	Y	Y	Y	N
21 McNulty	Y	Y	Y	Y	Y	Y	Y	N
22 ***Solomon***	N	N	N	N	Y	N	N	Y
23 ***Boehlert***	Y	N	N	Y	Y	Y	Y	N
24 ***McHugh***	N	N	N	N	Y	N	N	Y
25 ***Walsh***	N	N	N	Y	Y	Y	Y	Y
26 Hinchey	Y	Y	Y	Y	Y	Y	Y	N
27 ***Paxon***	Y	N	N	N	Y	N	N	Y
28 Slaughter	Y	Y	Y	Y	Y	Y	Y	N
29 LaFalce	Y	Y	Y	Y	Y	Y	Y	N
30 ***Quinn***	N	N	N	N	Y	Y	Y	Y
31 ***Houghton***	Y	N	Y	Y	N	Y	Y	Y
NORTH CAROLINA								
1 Clayton	Y	Y	Y	Y	Y	Y	Y	N
2 Valentine	N	N	Y	Y	Y	N	N	N

	521	522	523	524	525	526	527	528
3 Lancaster	Y	Y	Y	Y	Y	Y	Y	N
4 Price	Y	Y	Y	Y	Y	?	?	N
5 Neal	Y	Y	Y	Y	Y	Y	Y	N
6 ***Coble***	N	N	N	N	Y	N	N	Y
7 Rose	Y	Y	Y	Y	Y	?	?	?
8 Hefner	N	Y	Y	Y	Y	Y	Y	N
9 ***McMillan***	Y	N	Y	Y	Y	N	N	Y
10 ***Ballenger***	Y	N	N	N	N	Y	Y	Y
11 ***Taylor***	N	N	N	N	N	N	N	Y
12 Watt	Y	Y	Y	Y	Y	Y	Y	N
NORTH DAKOTA								
AL Pomeroy	Y	N	Y	Y	N	Y	N	Y
OHIO								
1 Mann	N	Y	N	Y	Y	Y	Y	N
2 ***Portman***	Y	Y	N	N	Y	Y	N	Y
3 Hall	N	Y	Y	?	Y	Y	N	N
4 ***Oxley***	Y	Y	N	N	?	N	N	Y
5 ***Gillmor***	Y	Y	Y	Y	Y	Y	N	Y
6 Strickland	N	Y	Y	Y	Y	Y	N	N
7 ***Hobson***	Y	Y	Y	Y	Y	Y	N	N
8 ***Boehner***	N	N	N	N	N	N	N	Y
9 Kaptur	N	Y	Y	Y	Y	Y	N	Y
10 ***Hoke***	Y	N	N	N	Y	N	N	Y
11 Stokes	N	Y	Y	Y	Y	Y	Y	N
12 ***Kasich***	Y	N	N	N	Y	Y	N	Y
13 Brown	Y	Y	Y	Y	Y	Y	Y	N
14 Sawyer	Y	Y	Y	Y	Y	Y	Y	N
15 ***Pryce***	N	Y	Y	N	Y	Y	N	Y
16 ***Regula***	Y	Y	Y	Y	Y	Y	N	Y
17 Traficant	N	Y	Y	Y	Y	Y	N	Y
18 Applegate	N	Y	Y	Y	Y	Y	Y	Y
19 Fingerhut	N	Y	Y	Y	Y	Y	Y	N
OKLAHOMA								
1 ***Inhofe***	Y	N	N	N	N	N	N	Y
2 Synar	Y	Y	Y	Y	Y	Y	Y	N
3 Brewster	N	N	Y	N	N	Y	Y	?
4 McCurdy	Y	N	Y	N	Y	Y	N	N
5 ***Istook***	Y	N	N	N	Y	Y	Y	Y
6 English	N	N	Y	N	Y	Y	Y	Y
OREGON								
1 Furse	Y	Y	Y	Y	Y	Y	Y	N
2 ***Smith***	Y	N	Y	N	N	N	Y	N
3 Wyden	N	Y	Y	Y	Y	Y	N	N
4 DeFazio	N	Y	Y	Y	Y	Y	N	N
5 Kopetski	Y	Y	Y	Y	N	Y	Y	N
PENNSYLVANIA								
1 Foglietta	N	Y	Y	Y	Y	Y	N	N
2 Blackwell	Y	Y	Y	Y	Y	?	?	?
3 Borski	Y	Y	Y	Y	Y	Y	Y	N
4 Klink	Y	N	Y	Y	Y	N	N	Y
5 ***Clinger***	Y	N	Y	Y	Y	Y	Y	Y
6 Holden	N	Y	Y	Y	Y	N	N	Y
7 ***Weldon***	N	N	Y	Y	Y	Y	N	Y
8 ***Greenwood***	N	N	N	N	Y	?	Y	N
9 ***Shuster***	N	N	N	N	Y	Y	Y	Y
10 ***McDade***	Y	Y	Y	Y	?	Y	Y	?
11 Kanjorski	N	Y	Y	Y	Y	Y	Y	N
12 Murtha	Y	Y	Y	Y	Y	Y	Y	Y
13 Margolies-Mezv.	N	Y	Y	Y	Y	N	Y	N
14 Coyne	N	Y	Y	Y	Y	Y	Y	N
15 McHale	N	Y	Y	Y	Y	Y	N	N
16 ***Walker***	Y	N	N	N	N	N	N	Y
17 ***Gekas***	N	?	N	N	Y	N	N	Y
18 ***Santorum***	N	N	N	N	Y	Y	N	Y
19 ***Goodling***	N	N	N	Y	N	Y	N	Y
20 Murphy	N	Y	Y	Y	?	Y	Y	Y
21 ***Ridge***	N	N	N	N	Y	?	?	Y
RHODE ISLAND								
1 ***Machtley***	N	Y	Y	Y	Y	Y	N	N
2 Reed	Y	Y	Y	Y	Y	Y	Y	N
SOUTH CAROLINA								
1 ***Ravenel***	N	Y	Y	Y	Y	Y	N	N
2 ***Spence***	Y	N	N	Y	Y	Y	N	Y
3 Derrick	N	Y	Y	Y	Y	Y	Y	N
4 ***Inglis***	N	N	N	N	N	N	N	Y
5 Spratt	Y	Y	Y	Y	Y	Y	Y	N
6 Clyburn	Y	Y	Y	Y	Y	Y	Y	N
SOUTH DAKOTA								
AL Johnson	Y	N	Y	Y	N	Y	Y	N
TENNESSEE								
1 ***Quillen***	N	Y	Y	Y	N	Y	N	Y
2 ***Duncan***	N	N	N	N	Y	N	N	Y
3 Lloyd	N	Y	Y	Y	Y	Y	Y	Y
4 Cooper	Y	Y	N	N	Y	Y	Y	Y
5 Clement	Y	Y	Y	Y	Y	Y	?	N

	521	522	523	524	525	526	527	528
6 Gordon	N	Y	Y	Y	Y	Y	Y	N
7 ***Sundquist***	N	N	N	N	N	N	N	Y
8 Tanner	N	N	Y	N	Y	Y	Y	Y
9 Ford	N	Y	Y	Y	?	Y	Y	N
TEXAS								
1 Chapman	?	Y	Y	Y	Y	Y	N	Y
2 Wilson	Y	Y	Y	Y	?	?	Y	Y
3 ***Johnson, Sam***	Y	N	N	N	N	N	Y	Y
4 Hall	Y	N	N	N	N	N	N	Y
5 Bryant	Y	Y	Y	Y	Y	Y	N	Y
6 ***Barton***	Y	N	N	N	N	N	Y	Y
7 ***Archer***	N	N	N	N	N	Y	Y	Y
8 ***Fields***	N	N	N	N	N	N	Y	Y
9 Brooks	Y	Y	Y	?	Y	?	Y	Y
10 Pickle	Y	Y	Y	Y	Y	Y	N	N
11 Edwards	Y	Y	Y	Y	N	Y	N	Y
12 Geren	Y	N	Y	N	N	N	N	Y
13 Sarpalius	N	Y	N	N	N	Y	Y	Y
14 Laughlin	Y	N	Y	Y	Y	Y	Y	Y
15 de la Garza	Y	Y	Y	Y	Y	Y	N	Y
16 Coleman	Y	Y	Y	Y	Y	Y	Y	N
17 Stenholm	N	N	N	N	N	N	N	Y
18 Washington	N	Y	?	Y	?	Y	N	N
19 ***Combest***	N	N	N	N	N	N	N	Y
20 Gonzalez	N	Y	Y	Y	Y	Y	Y	N
21 ***Smith***	Y	N	N	N	N	N	Y	Y
22 ***DeLay***	Y	N	N	N	N	?	Y	Y
23 ***Bonilla***	Y	N	N	N	N	N	Y	Y
24 Frost	Y	Y	Y	Y	Y	N	N	Y
25 Andrews	Y	Y	Y	Y	Y	Y	N	Y
26 ***Armey***	Y	N	N	N	N	N	Y	Y
27 Ortiz	Y	Y	Y	Y	Y	Y	Y	Y
28 Tejeda	Y	Y	Y	Y	Y	Y	N	Y
29 Green	Y	Y	Y	Y	Y	N	N	N
30 Johnson, E.B.	Y	Y	Y	Y	Y	N	Y	N
UTAH								
1 ***Hansen***	Y	N	N	N	N	Y	Y	Y
2 Shepherd	N	Y	Y	Y	Y	Y	Y	N
3 Orton	N	N	N	N	N	N	N	Y
VERMONT								
AL *Sanders*	N	Y	Y	Y	Y	Y	N	N
VIRGINIA								
1 ***Bateman***	Y	N	N	Y	+	Y	Y	Y
2 Pickett	N	N	N	N	Y	Y	N	Y
3 Scott	Y	Y	Y	Y	Y	Y	Y	N
4 Sisisky	N	Y	Y	Y	Y	Y	N	Y
5 Payne	Y	Y	Y	Y	Y	N	N	N
6 ***Goodlatte***	Y	N	N	N	Y	Y	N	Y
7 ***Bliley***	Y	N	Y	Y	Y	Y	Y	Y
8 Moran	Y	Y	Y	Y	Y	Y	Y	N
9 Boucher	Y	Y	Y	Y	Y	Y	Y	N
10 ***Wolf***	Y	N	N	Y	N	Y	Y	Y
11 Byrne	N	Y	Y	Y	Y	Y	Y	N
WASHINGTON								
1 Cantwell	N	Y	Y	Y	Y	Y	Y	N
2 Swift	Y	Y	Y	Y	Y	Y	Y	Y
3 Unsoeld	Y	Y	Y	Y	Y	Y	Y	N
4 Inslee	Y	Y	Y	Y	Y	Y	Y	N
5 Foley								
6 Dicks	Y	Y	Y	Y	Y	Y	Y	N
7 McDermott	Y	Y	Y	Y	Y	Y	Y	N
8 ***Dunn***	Y	N	N	N	N	N	N	Y
9 Kreidler	Y	Y	Y	Y	Y	Y	Y	N
WEST VIRGINIA								
1 Mollohan	Y	Y	Y	Y	Y	Y	Y	Y
2 Wise	Y	Y	Y	Y	Y	Y	Y	N
3 Rahall	Y	Y	Y	Y	Y	Y	Y	N
WISCONSIN								
1 Barca	N	Y	N	N	Y	Y	N	N
2 ***Klug***	N	Y	N	N	Y	N	N	N
3 ***Gunderson***	Y	N	Y	N	Y	Y	Y	Y
4 Kleczka	N	Y	Y	Y	Y	Y	N	Y
5 Barrett	N	Y	Y	N	Y	Y	N	N
6 ***Petri***	N	N	N	N	Y	N	N	Y
7 Obey	Y	Y	Y	Y	Y	Y	Y	N
8 ***Roth***	N	N	Y	N	Y	N	N	Y
9 ***Sensenbrenner***	N	N	N	N	Y	N	N	Y
WYOMING								
AL ***Thomas***	N	N	N	Y	N	Y	N	Y
DELEGATES								
de Lugo, V.I.	D	D	D	D	D	D	D	D
Faleomavaega, Am.S.	D	D	D	D	D	D	D	D
Norton, D.C.	D	D	D	D	D	D	D	D
Romero-B., P.R.	D	D	D	D	D	D	D	D
Underwood, Guam	D	D	D	D	D	D	D	D

Southern states - Ala., Ark., Fla., Ga., Ky., La., Miss., N.C., Okla., S.C., Tenn., Texas, Va.
Omitted votes are quorum calls, which CQ does not include in its vote charts.

KEY

Y	Voted for (yea).
#	Paired for.
+	Announced for.
N	Voted against (nay).
X	Paired against.
−	Announced against.
P	Voted "present."
C	Voted "present" to avoid possible conflict of interest.
?	Did not vote or otherwise make a position known.
D	Delegates ineligible to vote.

Democrats **Republicans**
Independent

529. HR 1845. National Biological Survey/Non-Federal Property. Separate vote at the request of Dreier, R-Calif., on the amendment offered by Taylor, R-N.C., and adopted in the Committee of the Whole to require the National Biological Survey to obtain written consent before going on non-federal lands and to require reports describing the survey's activities on non-federal lands. Adopted 325-94: R 167-3; D 158-90 (ND 89-75, SD 69-15); I 0-1, Oct. 26, 1993. (On a separate vote, which may be demanded on an amendment adopted in the Committee of the Whole, the four delegates and the resident commissioner of Puerto Rico cannot vote. See vote 485)

530. HR 1845. National Biological Survey/Passage. Passage of the bill to authorize $171.5 million in fiscal 1994 and such sums as necessary in fiscal 1995-97 to establish a National Biological Survey to monitor America's biological and natural resources. Passed 255-165: R 41-130; D 213-35 (ND 151-14, SD 62-21); I 1-0, Oct. 26, 1993.

531. Procedural Motion. Approval of the House Journal of Tuesday, Oct. 26. Approved 242-160: R 12-155; D 230-5 (ND 154-4, SD 76-1); I 0-0, Oct. 27, 1993.

532. HR 3116. Fiscal 1994 Defense Appropriations/Classified Information. Murtha, D-Pa., motion to close portions of the conference during discussion of classified information. Motion agreed to 409-3: R 169-0; D 239-3 (ND 161-1, SD 78-2); I 1-0, Oct. 27, 1993.

533. HR 2492. Fiscal 1994 D.C. Appropriations/Rule. Adoption of the rule (H Res 283) to waive points of order against and provide for House floor consideration of the conference report to provide $700,000,000 in federal funds for the District of Columbia in fiscal 1994 and approve the spending of $3,740,382,000 in funds raised from local taxes. The conference agreement would restrict the use of federal funds in most abortion cases but would allow the D.C. government to use locally raised revenue for abortion services. Adopted 239-187: R 21-152; D 217-35 (ND 148-21, SD 69-14); I 1-0, Oct. 27, 1993.

534. HR 2492. Fiscal 1994 D.C. Appropriations/Conference Report. Adoption of the conference report to provide $700,000,000 in federal funds for the District of Columbia in fiscal 1994 and approve the spending of $3,740,382,000 in funds raised from local taxes. The administration requested $705,101,000 in federal funds and $3,740,382,000 in local taxes. The conference agreement would restrict the use of federal funds in most abortion cases but would allow the D.C. government to use locally raised revenue for abortion services. Adopted (thus sent to the Senate) 225-201: R 22-150; D 202-51 (ND 143-26, SD 59-25); I 1-0, Oct. 27, 1993.

535. H J Res 283. Fiscal 1994 Continuing Appropriations/Rule. Adoption of the rule (H Res 287) to provide for House floor consideration of the joint resolution to provide continuing appropriations through Nov. 10 for the appropriations bills not yet signed into law. Passed 252-170: R 0-169; D 251-1 (ND 167-1, SD 84-0); I 1-0, Oct. 28, 1993.

536. H J Res 283. Fiscal 1994 Continuing Appropriations/Passage. Passage of the joint resolution to provide continuing appropriations through Nov. 10 for the appropriations bills not yet signed into law. Passed 256-157: R 13-151; D 242-6 (ND 160-5, SD 82-1); I 1-0, Oct. 28, 1993.

	529	530	531	532	533	534	535	536
ALABAMA								
1 Callahan	Y	N	N	Y	N	N	N	N
2 Everett	Y	N	N	Y	N	N	N	N
3 Browder	Y	N	Y	N	N	N	Y	Y
4 Bevill	Y	N	Y	N	N	N	Y	Y
5 Cramer	Y	N	Y	Y	Y	N	Y	Y
6 Bachus	Y	N	N	N	N	N	N	N
7 Hilliard	Y	Y	Y	Y	Y	Y	Y	Y
ALASKA								
AL Young	Y	N	N	?	N	N	?	?
ARIZONA								
1 Coppersmith	N	Y	Y	Y	Y	Y	Y	Y
2 Pastor	N	Y	Y	Y	Y	Y	Y	Y
3 Stump	Y	N	N	Y	N	N	N	N
4 Kyl	Y	N	N	Y	N	N	N	N
5 Kolbe	Y	N	N	Y	Y	N	Y	N
6 English	Y	Y	Y	Y	Y	Y	Y	Y
ARKANSAS								
1 Lambert	Y	N	Y	Y	Y	Y	Y	Y
2 Thornton	Y	Y	Y	Y	Y	N	Y	Y
3 Hutchinson	Y	N	N	Y	N	N	N	N
4 Dickey	?	N	N	Y	N	N	N	N
CALIFORNIA								
1 Hamburg	N	Y	Y	Y	Y	Y	Y	Y
2 Herger	Y	N	N	Y	N	N	N	N
3 Fazio	Y	Y	Y	Y	Y	Y	Y	Y
4 Doolittle	Y	N	N	Y	N	N	N	N
5 Matsui	N	Y	Y	Y	Y	Y	Y	Y
6 Woolsey	N	Y	Y	Y	Y	Y	Y	+
7 Miller	N	Y	Y	Y	Y	Y	Y	Y
8 Pelosi	N	Y	Y	Y	Y	Y	Y	Y
9 Dellums	N	Y	?	Y	Y	Y	Y	Y
10 Baker	Y	N	N	Y	N	N	N	N
11 Pombo	Y	N	Y	Y	N	N	N	N
12 Lantos	Y	Y	Y	Y	Y	Y	Y	Y
13 Stark	N	Y	Y	Y	Y	Y	Y	Y
14 Eshoo	N	Y	Y	Y	Y	Y	Y	Y
15 Mineta	N	Y	Y	Y	Y	Y	Y	Y
16 Edwards	N	Y	Y	Y	Y	Y	Y	Y
17 Farr	N	Y	Y	Y	Y	Y	Y	Y
18 Condit	Y	N	Y	Y	Y	N	Y	Y
19 Lehman	Y	?	Y	Y	Y	Y	Y	Y
20 Dooley	Y	Y	Y	Y	Y	Y	Y	Y
21 Thomas	Y	N	N	Y	N	N	Y	N
22 Huffington	Y	N	N	Y	N	N	N	N
23 Gallegly	Y	N	N	Y	N	N	N	N
24 Beilenson	N	Y	Y	Y	Y	Y	Y	Y
25 McKeon	Y	N	N	Y	N	N	N	N
26 Berman	?	?	?	?	?	?	#	#
27 Moorhead	Y	N	N	N	N	N	N	N
28 Dreier	Y	N	N	Y	N	N	N	N
29 Waxman	N	Y	Y	Y	Y	Y	Y	Y
30 Becerra	N	Y	Y	Y	Y	Y	Y	Y
31 Martinez	Y	Y	Y	Y	Y	Y	Y	Y
32 Dixon	N	Y	Y	Y	Y	Y	Y	Y
33 Roybal-Allard	N	Y	Y	Y	Y	Y	Y	Y
34 Torres	N	Y	?	?	Y	Y	Y	Y
35 Waters	N	Y	Y	Y	Y	Y	Y	Y
36 Harman	N	Y	Y	?	Y	Y	Y	Y
37 Tucker	?	Y	Y	Y	Y	Y	Y	Y
38 Horn	?	?	N	Y	Y	Y	N	?
39 Royce	Y	N	?	?	?	?	?	?
40 Lewis	Y	N	N	N	N	N	N	N
41 Kim	Y	N	N	Y	N	N	N	N
42 Brown	?	?	?	Y	Y	N	N	N
43 Calvert	Y	N	N	Y	N	N	N	N
44 McCandless	Y	N	N	Y	N	N	N	N
45 Rohrabacher	Y	N	N	N	N	N	N	N
46 Dornan	Y	N	?	Y	N	N	N	N
47 Cox	Y	N	N	Y	N	N	?	?
48 Packard	Y	N	N	Y	N	N	N	N
49 Schenk	Y	Y	Y	Y	Y	Y	Y	Y
50 Filner	N	Y	Y	Y	Y	Y	Y	Y
51 Cunningham	Y	N	N	Y	N	N	N	N
52 Hunter	Y	N	N	Y	N	N	N	N
COLORADO								
1 Schroeder	Y	Y	N	Y	Y	Y	Y	N
2 Skaggs	N	Y	Y	Y	Y	Y	Y	Y
3 McInnis	Y	N	N	Y	N	N	N	N
4 Allard	Y	N	N	Y	N	N	N	N
5 Hefley	Y	N	N	Y	N	N	N	N
6 Schaefer	Y	N	N	Y	N	N	N	N
CONNECTICUT								
1 Kennelly	Y	Y	Y	Y	Y	Y	Y	Y
2 Gejdenson	Y	Y	Y	Y	Y	Y	Y	Y
3 DeLauro	Y	Y	Y	Y	Y	Y	Y	Y
4 Shays	N	Y	N	Y	Y	N	N	N
5 Franks	Y	Y	N	Y	Y	N	N	N
6 Johnson	Y	Y	N	Y	Y	N	N	N
DELAWARE								
AL Castle	Y	Y	N	Y	N	N	N	N
FLORIDA								
1 Hutto	Y	N	Y	N	N	N	Y	Y
2 Peterson	Y	N	Y	Y	Y	Y	Y	Y
3 Brown	Y	Y	Y	Y	Y	Y	Y	Y
4 Fowler	Y	N	N	Y	N	N	N	N
5 Thurman	Y	Y	Y	Y	Y	Y	Y	Y
6 Stearns	Y	N	N	Y	N	N	N	N
7 Mica	Y	N	N	Y	N	N	N	N
8 McCollum	Y	N	N	Y	N	N	N	N
9 Bilirakis	Y	N	N	Y	N	N	N	N
10 Young	Y	N	N	Y	N	N	N	Y
11 Gibbons	N	Y	Y	Y	Y	Y	Y	Y
12 Canady	Y	N	N	Y	N	N	N	N
13 Miller	Y	N	N	Y	N	N	N	N
14 Goss	Y	N	N	Y	N	N	N	N
15 Bacchus	N	Y	Y	Y	Y	Y	Y	Y
16 Lewis	Y	N	N	Y	N	N	N	N
17 Meek	N	Y	Y	Y	Y	Y	Y	Y
18 Ros-Lehtinen	Y	Y	N	Y	N	N	N	N
19 Johnston	N	Y	Y	Y	Y	Y	Y	Y
20 Deutsch	N	Y	Y	Y	Y	Y	Y	Y
21 Diaz-Balart	Y	Y	N	Y	N	N	N	N
22 Shaw	Y	N	N	Y	N	N	N	N
23 Hastings	N	Y	Y	Y	Y	Y	Y	Y
GEORGIA								
1 Kingston	Y	N	N	Y	N	N	N	N
2 Bishop	Y	Y	Y	Y	Y	Y	Y	Y
3 Collins	Y	N	N	Y	N	N	N	N
4 Linder	Y	N	N	Y	N	N	N	N
5 Lewis	N	Y	Y	Y	Y	Y	Y	Y
6 Gingrich	Y	N	N	Y	N	N	N	N
7 Darden	Y	Y	Y	Y	Y	Y	Y	Y
8 Rowland	Y	N	Y	Y	Y	N	Y	Y
9 Deal	Y	Y	Y	Y	Y	Y	Y	Y
10 Johnson	Y	Y	Y	Y	Y	Y	Y	Y
11 McKinney	Y	Y	N	Y	Y	Y	Y	Y
HAWAII								
1 Abercrombie	N	Y	Y	Y	Y	Y	Y	Y
2 Mink	N	Y	Y	Y	Y	Y	Y	Y
IDAHO								
1 LaRocco	Y	Y	Y	Y	Y	Y	Y	Y
2 Crapo	Y	N	N	Y	N	N	N	N
ILLINOIS								
1 Rush	N	Y	Y	Y	Y	Y	Y	N
2 Reynolds	Y	Y	Y	Y	Y	Y	Y	Y
3 Lipinski	Y	Y	Y	Y	N	N	Y	Y
4 Gutierrez	N	Y	Y	Y	Y	Y	Y	Y
5 Rostenkowski	?	?	Y	Y	Y	Y	Y	Y
6 Hyde	Y	N	Y	N	N	N	N	N
7 Collins	N	Y	?	Y	Y	Y	Y	Y
8 Crane	Y	N	?	Y	N	N	N	N
9 Yates	N	Y	Y	Y	Y	Y	Y	Y
10 Porter	+	+	N	Y	N	N	N	N
11 Sangmeister	Y	Y	Y	Y	Y	Y	Y	Y
12 Costello	Y	N	Y	Y	Y	N	Y	Y
13 Fawell	Y	N	Y	N	Y	N	N	N
14 Hastert	Y	N	N	Y	N	N	N	N
15 Ewing	Y	N	N	Y	N	N	N	N
16 Manzullo	Y	N	N	Y	N	N	N	N
17 Evans	N	Y	Y	Y	Y	Y	Y	Y

ND Northern Democrats   SD Southern Democrats

	529	530	531	532	533	534	535	536
18 ***Michel***	Y	N	N	Y	N	N	N	N
19 Poshard	Y	N	Y	Y	N	N	Y	N
20 Durbin	Y	Y	Y	Y	Y	Y	Y	Y
INDIANA								
1 Visclosky	N	Y	Y	Y	Y	Y	Y	Y
2 Sharp	Y	Y	Y	?	?	Y	Y	Y
3 Roemer	Y	Y	Y	Y	Y	N	Y	Y
4 Long	Y	Y	Y	Y	Y	Y	Y	Y
5 ***Buyer***	Y	N	N	Y	N	N	N	N
6 ***Burton***	Y	N	N	Y	N	N	N	N
7 ***Myers***	Y	N	?	Y	N	?	N	Y
8 McCloskey	Y	Y	Y	Y	Y	Y	?	Y
9 Hamilton	Y	Y	Y	Y	Y	Y	Y	Y
10 Jacobs	Y	Y	N	Y	Y	Y	N	N
IOWA								
1 ***Leach***	Y	Y	N	Y	N	N	N	N
2 ***Nussle***	Y	N	N	Y	N	N	N	N
3 ***Lightfoot***	Y	N	N	Y	N	N	N	N
4 Smith	Y	Y	Y	Y	Y	Y	Y	Y
5 ***Grandy***	Y	Y	N	Y	N	N	N	N
KANSAS								
1 ***Roberts***	Y	N	N	Y	N	N	N	N
2 Slattery	Y	N	Y	Y	Y	Y	Y	Y
3 ***Meyers***	Y	Y	N	Y	Y	N	N	N
4 Glickman	Y	Y	Y	Y	Y	Y	Y	Y
KENTUCKY								
1 Barlow	Y	N	Y	Y	Y	Y	Y	Y
2 Natcher	Y	Y	Y	Y	Y	Y	Y	Y
3 Mazzoli	Y	Y	Y	Y	N	N	Y	Y
4 ***Bunning***	Y	N	N	Y	N	N	N	N
5 ***Rogers***	Y	N	N	?	N	N	N	Y
6 Baesler	Y	Y	Y	Y	Y	Y	Y	Y
LOUISIANA								
1 ***Livingston***	Y	N	?	Y	N	N	N	Y
2 Jefferson	N	Y	Y	Y	Y	Y	Y	Y
3 Tauzin	Y	Y	?	?	X	X	?	?
4 Fields	N	Y	Y	Y	Y	Y	Y	Y
5 ***McCrery***	Y	N	N	Y	N	N	N	N
6 ***Baker***	Y	N	N	Y	N	N	N	N
7 Hayes	Y	Y	P	Y	Y	N	Y	Y
MAINE								
1 Andrews	N	Y	Y	Y	Y	Y	Y	Y
2 ***Snowe***	Y	Y	Y	Y	Y	Y	N	N
MARYLAND								
1 ***Gilchrest***	N	Y	N	Y	N	N	N	N
2 ***Bentley***	Y	N	?	?	N	N	N	N
3 Cardin	N	Y	Y	Y	Y	Y	?	?
4 Wynn	Y	Y	Y	Y	Y	Y	Y	Y
5 Hoyer	Y	Y	?	Y	Y	Y	Y	Y
6 ***Bartlett***	Y	N	N	Y	N	N	N	N
7 Mfume	N	Y	Y	Y	Y	Y	Y	Y
8 ***Morella***	N	Y	N	Y	Y	Y	N	Y
MASSACHUSETTS								
1 Olver	N	Y	Y	Y	Y	Y	Y	Y
2 Neal	Y	Y	Y	Y	Y	Y	Y	Y
3 ***Blute***	Y	Y	N	Y	N	N	N	N
4 Frank	N	Y	Y	Y	Y	Y	Y	Y
5 Meehan	N	Y	Y	Y	Y	Y	Y	Y
6 ***Torkildsen***	Y	Y	N	Y	N	Y	N	N
7 Markey	N	Y	Y	Y	Y	Y	Y	Y
8 Kennedy	?	?	?	?	?	Y	Y	Y
9 Moakley	Y	Y	Y	Y	Y	Y	Y	Y
10 Studds	N	Y	Y	Y	Y	Y	Y	Y
MICHIGAN								
1 Stupak	Y	Y	Y	Y	N	N	Y	Y
2 ***Hoekstra***	?	?	N	Y	N	N	N	N
3 Vacancy								
4 ***Camp***	Y	N	N	Y	N	N	N	N
5 Barcia	Y	N	Y	?	N	N	Y	Y
6 ***Upton***	Y	N	N	Y	N	N	N	N
7 ***Smith***	Y	N	N	Y	N	N	N	N
8 Carr	Y	N	Y	Y	Y	Y	Y	Y
9 Kildee	Y	Y	Y	Y	N	N	Y	Y
10 Bonior	N	Y	?	Y	Y	Y	Y	Y
11 ***Knollenberg***	Y	N	N	Y	N	N	N	N
12 Levin	N	Y	Y	Y	Y	Y	Y	Y
13 Ford	N	Y	Y	Y	Y	Y	Y	Y
14 Conyers	N	Y	Y	?	Y	Y	Y	Y
15 Collins	N	Y	Y	Y	Y	Y	Y	Y
16 Dingell	Y	N	Y	Y	Y	Y	Y	Y
MINNESOTA								
1 Penny	Y	N	Y	Y	N	N	Y	Y
2 Minge	Y	Y	Y	Y	Y	Y	Y	Y
3 ***Ramstad***	Y	Y	N	Y	N	N	N	N
4 Vento	N	Y	Y	Y	Y	Y	Y	Y
5 Sabo	N	Y	Y	Y	Y	Y	Y	Y
6 ***Grams***	Y	N	N	Y	N	N	N	N
7 Peterson	Y	N	Y	Y	N	N	Y	?
8 Oberstar	Y	Y	Y	Y	N	N	Y	Y
MISSISSIPPI								
1 Whitten	Y	Y	?	?	?	Y	Y	Y
2 Thompson	Y	Y	Y	Y	Y	Y	Y	Y
3 Montgomery	Y	N	Y	Y	Y	N	Y	Y
4 Parker	Y	N	Y	Y	N	N	Y	Y
5 Taylor	Y	N	N	Y	N	N	Y	Y
MISSOURI								
1 Clay	N	Y	N	Y	Y	Y	Y	?
2 ***Talent***	Y	N	N	Y	N	N	N	Y
3 Gephardt	?	?	Y	Y	Y	Y	Y	Y
4 Skelton	Y	Y	?	Y	N	N	Y	Y
5 Wheat	N	Y	Y	Y	Y	Y	Y	Y
6 Danner	Y	Y	Y	Y	N	Y	Y	Y
7 ***Hancock***	Y	N	N	Y	N	N	N	N
8 ***Emerson***	Y	N	N	Y	N	N	N	N
9 Volkmer	Y	Y	Y	Y	N	N	Y	Y
MONTANA								
AL Williams	Y	Y	Y	Y	Y	Y	Y	Y
NEBRASKA								
1 ***Bereuter***	Y	Y	N	Y	N	N	N	N
2 Hoagland	N	Y	Y	Y	Y	Y	Y	Y
3 ***Barrett***	Y	N	N	Y	N	N	N	N
NEVADA								
1 Bilbray	Y	Y	?	Y	Y	Y	Y	Y
2 ***Vucanovich***	Y	N	N	Y	N	N	N	N
NEW HAMPSHIRE								
1 ***Zeliff***	Y	N	N	Y	Y	N	N	?
2 Swett	Y	Y	Y	Y	Y	Y	Y	Y
NEW JERSEY								
1 Andrews	Y	Y	Y	Y	Y	Y	Y	Y
2 Hughes	Y	Y	Y	Y	Y	Y	Y	Y
3 ***Saxton***	Y	Y	N	Y	N	N	N	N
4 ***Smith***	Y	Y	N	Y	N	N	N	Y
5 ***Roukema***	Y	Y	N	Y	Y	Y	N	N
6 Pallone	N	Y	Y	Y	Y	Y	Y	Y
7 ***Franks***	Y	Y	N	Y	N	N	N	N
8 Klein	N	Y	Y	Y	Y	Y	Y	Y
9 Torricelli	N	Y	Y	Y	Y	Y	Y	Y
10 Payne	N	Y	Y	Y	Y	Y	Y	Y
11 ***Gallo***	Y	Y	N	Y	Y	Y	N	N
12 ***Zimmer***	Y	Y	N	Y	Y	Y	N	N
13 Menendez	Y	Y	?	Y	Y	Y	Y	Y
NEW MEXICO								
1 ***Schiff***	Y	Y	N	Y	N	N	N	Y
2 ***Skeen***	Y	N	N	Y	N	N	N	Y
3 Richardson	N	Y	Y	Y	Y	Y	Y	Y
NEW YORK								
1 Hochbrueckner	Y	Y	Y	Y	Y	Y	Y	Y
2 ***Lazio***	Y	Y	N	Y	N	N	N	N
3 ***King***	Y	N	N	Y	N	N	N	N
4 ***Levy***	Y	N	N	Y	N	N	N	N
5 Ackerman	N	Y	Y	Y	Y	Y	Y	Y
6 Flake	Y	Y	Y	Y	Y	Y	Y	Y
7 Manton	Y	Y	Y	Y	Y	N	Y	Y
8 Nadler	N	Y	Y	Y	Y	Y	Y	Y
9 Schumer	N	Y	?	?	Y	Y	Y	Y
10 Towns	N	Y	Y	Y	Y	Y	?	?
11 Owens	N	Y	Y	Y	Y	Y	Y	Y
12 Velazquez	N	Y	Y	Y	Y	Y	Y	Y
13 ***Molinari***	Y	N	N	Y	Y	Y	N	N
14 Maloney	N	Y	Y	Y	Y	Y	Y	Y
15 Rangel	?	Y	?	Y	Y	Y	Y	Y
16 Serrano	N	Y	Y	Y	Y	Y	Y	Y
17 Engel	N	Y	Y	Y	Y	Y	Y	Y
18 Lowey	N	Y	Y	Y	Y	Y	Y	Y
19 ***Fish***	Y	Y	Y	Y	N	N	N	N
20 ***Gilman***	Y	Y	Y	Y	Y	Y	N	N
21 McNulty	Y	Y	?	Y	Y	N	Y	Y
22 ***Solomon***	Y	N	N	Y	N	N	N	N
23 ***Boehlert***	Y	Y	N	Y	Y	Y	N	N
24 ***McHugh***	Y	N	N	Y	N	N	N	N
25 ***Walsh***	Y	N	N	Y	N	N	N	N
26 Hinchey	N	Y	Y	Y	Y	Y	Y	Y
27 ***Paxon***	Y	N	N	Y	N	N	N	N
28 Slaughter	Y	Y	Y	Y	Y	Y	Y	Y
29 LaFalce	N	Y	Y	Y	N	N	Y	Y
30 ***Quinn***	Y	N	N	Y	N	N	N	N
31 ***Houghton***	Y	Y	Y	Y	Y	Y	N	+
NORTH CAROLINA								
1 Clayton	N	Y	Y	Y	Y	Y	Y	Y
2 Valentine	Y	Y	Y	Y	Y	Y	Y	Y
3 Lancaster	Y	Y	?	Y	Y	Y	Y	Y
4 Price	Y	Y	Y	Y	Y	Y	Y	Y
5 Neal	Y	Y	Y	Y	Y	Y	Y	Y
6 ***Coble***	Y	N	N	Y	N	N	N	N
7 Rose	?	?	Y	Y	Y	Y	Y	Y
8 Hefner	Y	Y	Y	Y	Y	Y	Y	Y
9 ***McMillan***	Y	Y	N	Y	N	N	N	N
10 ***Ballenger***	Y	N	N	Y	N	N	N	N
11 ***Taylor***	Y	Y	?	Y	N	N	N	N
12 Watt	N	Y	Y	Y	Y	Y	Y	Y
NORTH DAKOTA								
AL Pomeroy	Y	N	Y	Y	Y	Y	Y	Y
OHIO								
1 Mann	N	Y	Y	Y	N	N	Y	Y
2 ***Portman***	Y	N	N	Y	N	N	N	N
3 Hall	Y	Y	Y	Y	Y	N	Y	Y
4 ***Oxley***	Y	N	N	Y	N	N	N	?
5 ***Gillmor***	Y	Y	Y	Y	N	N	N	N
6 Strickland	Y	Y	Y	Y	Y	Y	Y	Y
7 ***Hobson***	Y	Y	N	Y	Y	N	N	N
8 ***Boehner***	Y	N	N	Y	N	N	N	N
9 Kaptur	Y	Y	Y	Y	Y	Y	Y	?
10 ***Hoke***	Y	N	N	Y	N	N	N	N
11 Stokes	N	Y	Y	?	#	#	Y	Y
12 ***Kasich***	Y	N	Y	Y	N	N	N	N
13 Brown	Y	Y	Y	Y	Y	Y	Y	Y
14 Sawyer	Y	Y	Y	Y	Y	Y	Y	Y
15 ***Pryce***	Y	N	N	Y	N	N	N	N
16 ***Regula***	Y	Y	N	Y	N	Y	N	Y
17 Traficant	Y	Y	Y	Y	Y	Y	Y	Y
18 Applegate	Y	N	Y	Y	N	N	Y	Y
19 Fingerhut	Y	Y	Y	Y	Y	Y	Y	Y
OKLAHOMA								
1 ***Inhofe***	Y	N	N	Y	N	N	N	N
2 Synar	N	Y	Y	Y	Y	Y	Y	Y
3 Brewster	Y	N	Y	Y	Y	N	Y	Y
4 McCurdy	Y	Y	Y	Y	Y	Y	Y	Y
5 ***Istook***	Y	N	N	Y	N	N	N	N
6 English	Y	N	Y	Y	N	N	Y	Y
OREGON								
1 Furse	N	Y	Y	Y	Y	Y	Y	Y
2 ***Smith***	Y	N	N	Y	N	N	X	X
3 Wyden	Y	Y	Y	Y	Y	Y	Y	Y
4 DeFazio	Y	Y	Y	N	Y	Y	Y	Y
5 Kopetski	Y	Y	Y	Y	Y	Y	Y	Y
PENNSYLVANIA								
1 Foglietta	N	Y	Y	Y	Y	Y	Y	Y
2 Blackwell	?	?	Y	Y	Y	Y	Y	Y
3 Borski	Y	Y	Y	Y	Y	Y	Y	Y
4 Klink	Y	N	Y	Y	N	N	Y	Y
5 ***Clinger***	Y	N	N	Y	N	N	—	—
6 Holden	Y	N	Y	Y	N	N	Y	Y
7 ***Weldon***	Y	Y	N	Y	N	N	N	N
8 ***Greenwood***	Y	Y	N	Y	Y	Y	N	N
9 ***Shuster***	Y	N	N	Y	N	N	N	N
10 ***McDade***	?	?	N	Y	N	N	N	Y
11 Kanjorski	Y	Y	Y	Y	N	Y	Y	Y
12 Murtha	Y	Y	Y	Y	Y	?	Y	Y
13 Margolies-Mezv.	Y	Y	Y	Y	Y	Y	Y	Y
14 Coyne	N	Y	Y	Y	Y	Y	Y	Y
15 McHale	Y	Y	Y	Y	Y	Y	Y	Y
16 ***Walker***	Y	N	N	Y	N	N	N	N
17 ***Gekas***	Y	N	N	Y	N	N	N	N
18 ***Santorum***	Y	Y	N	Y	N	N	N	N
19 ***Goodling***	Y	N	N	Y	N	N	N	N
20 Murphy	Y	N	N	Y	N	N	Y	Y
21 ***Ridge***	Y	N	N	Y	N	Y	N	N
RHODE ISLAND								
1 ***Machtley***	Y	Y	N	Y	Y	Y	N	?
2 Reed	N	Y	Y	Y	Y	Y	Y	Y
SOUTH CAROLINA								
1 ***Ravenel***	Y	Y	Y	Y	N	N	N	N
2 ***Spence***	Y	N	N	Y	N	N	N	N
3 Derrick	Y	Y	Y	Y	Y	Y	Y	Y
4 ***Inglis***	Y	N	Y	Y	N	N	N	N
5 Spratt	Y	Y	Y	Y	Y	Y	Y	Y
6 Clyburn	Y	Y	Y	Y	Y	Y	Y	Y
SOUTH DAKOTA								
AL Johnson	Y	Y	Y	Y	Y	Y	Y	Y
TENNESSEE								
1 ***Quillen***	Y	N	N	Y	N	N	N	N
2 ***Duncan***	Y	N	N	Y	N	N	N	N
3 Lloyd	Y	N	Y	Y	Y	Y	Y	Y
4 Cooper	Y	Y	Y	Y	Y	Y	Y	Y
5 Clement	Y	Y	Y	Y	N	N	Y	Y
6 Gordon	Y	Y	Y	Y	Y	Y	Y	Y
7 ***Sundquist***	Y	N	N	Y	N	N	N	N
8 Tanner	Y	Y	Y	Y	Y	Y	Y	Y
9 Ford	Y	?	Y	Y	Y	Y	Y	Y
TEXAS								
1 Chapman	Y	Y	?	?	Y	Y	Y	Y
2 Wilson	Y	Y	Y	?	Y	Y	Y	Y
3 ***Johnson, Sam***	Y	N	N	Y	N	N	N	N
4 Hall	Y	N	Y	Y	N	N	Y	Y
5 Bryant	Y	Y	Y	Y	Y	Y	Y	Y
6 ***Barton***	Y	N	N	Y	N	N	N	N
7 ***Archer***	Y	N	Y	Y	N	N	N	N
8 ***Fields***	Y	N	N	Y	N	N	N	N
9 Brooks	Y	Y	Y	Y	Y	Y	Y	Y
10 Pickle	Y	Y	Y	Y	Y	Y	Y	Y
11 Edwards	Y	N	?	Y	Y	N	Y	Y
12 Geren	Y	N	Y	?	Y	N	Y	Y
13 Sarpalius	Y	Y	Y	Y	N	N	Y	Y
14 Laughlin	Y	Y	Y	Y	Y	Y	Y	Y
15 de la Garza	Y	Y	Y	Y	N	N	Y	Y
16 Coleman	Y	Y	Y	Y	Y	Y	Y	Y
17 Stenholm	Y	N	Y	Y	N	N	Y	Y
18 Washington	N	Y	?	N	Y	Y	Y	Y
19 ***Combest***	Y	N	Y	Y	N	N	N	N
20 Gonzalez	N	Y	Y	Y	Y	Y	Y	Y
21 ***Smith***	Y	N	N	Y	N	N	N	N
22 ***DeLay***	Y	N	N	Y	N	N	N	N
23 ***Bonilla***	Y	N	N	Y	N	N	N	N
24 Frost	Y	Y	Y	Y	Y	Y	Y	Y
25 Andrews	Y	Y	Y	Y	Y	Y	Y	Y
26 ***Armey***	Y	N	N	Y	N	N	N	N
27 Ortiz	Y	Y	Y	Y	N	N	Y	Y
28 Tejeda	Y	Y	Y	Y	N	N	Y	Y
29 Green	Y	Y	Y	Y	Y	N	Y	Y
30 Johnson, E.B.	Y	Y	Y	Y	Y	Y	Y	Y
UTAH								
1 ***Hansen***	Y	N	N	Y	N	N	N	?
2 Shepherd	Y	Y	Y	Y	Y	Y	Y	Y
3 Orton	Y	Y	Y	Y	N	N	Y	Y
VERMONT								
AL *Sanders*	N	Y	?	Y	Y	Y	Y	Y
VIRGINIA								
1 ***Bateman***	Y	N	+	+	—	—	N	Y
2 Pickett	Y	N	?	Y	Y	N	Y	N
3 Scott	Y	Y	Y	Y	Y	Y	Y	Y
4 Sisisky	Y	N	Y	Y	Y	Y	Y	Y
5 Payne	Y	Y	Y	Y	Y	Y	Y	Y
6 ***Goodlatte***	Y	N	N	Y	N	N	N	N
7 ***Bliley***	Y	N	N	Y	N	Y	N	N
8 Moran	N	Y	Y	Y	Y	Y	Y	?
9 Boucher	Y	Y	Y	Y	Y	Y	Y	Y
10 ***Wolf***	Y	N	N	Y	N	N	N	Y
11 Byrne	Y	Y	Y	Y	Y	Y	Y	Y
WASHINGTON								
1 Cantwell	Y	Y	Y	Y	Y	Y	Y	Y
2 Swift	Y	Y	Y	?	Y	Y	Y	Y
3 Unsoeld	N	Y	Y	Y	Y	Y	Y	Y
4 Inslee	Y	Y	Y	Y	Y	Y	Y	Y
5 Foley								
6 Dicks	Y	Y	Y	Y	Y	Y	Y	Y
7 McDermott	N	Y	Y	Y	Y	Y	Y	Y
8 ***Dunn***	Y	N	N	Y	N	N	N	N
9 Kreidler	Y	Y	Y	Y	Y	Y	Y	Y
WEST VIRGINIA								
1 Mollohan	Y	Y	Y	Y	N	N	Y	Y
2 Wise	Y	Y	Y	Y	Y	Y	Y	Y
3 Rahall	N	Y	Y	Y	N	N	Y	Y
WISCONSIN								
1 Barca	Y	Y	Y	Y	Y	Y	Y	Y
2 ***Klug***	Y	Y	N	Y	Y	Y	N	N
3 ***Gunderson***	Y	Y	N	Y	N	N	N	N
4 Kleczka	Y	Y	Y	Y	Y	Y	Y	Y
5 Barrett	Y	Y	Y	Y	Y	Y	Y	Y
6 ***Petri***	Y	N	N	Y	N	N	N	N
7 Obey	Y	Y	Y	Y	Y	Y	Y	Y
8 ***Roth***	Y	N	N	Y	N	N	N	N
9 ***Sensenbrenner***	Y	N	N	Y	N	N	N	N
WYOMING								
AL ***Thomas***	Y	N	N	Y	N	N	?	N
DELEGATES								
de Lugo, V.I.	D	D	D	D	D	D	D	D
Faleomavaega, Am.S.	D	D	D	D	D	D	D	D
Norton, D.C.	D	D	D	D	D	D	D	D
Romero-B., P.R.	D	D	D	D	D	D	D	D
Underwood, Guam	D	D	D	D	D	D	D	D

Southern states - Ala., Ark., Fla., Ga., Ky., La., Miss., N.C., Okla., S.C., Tenn., Texas, Va.
Omitted votes are quorum calls, which CQ does not include in its vote charts.

537. HR 334. Lumbee Tribe Recognition/Substitute. Thomas, R-Wyo., substitute amendment to not extend federal recognition to the Lumbee Tribe as the bill does, but instead to set up a process for the tribe to apply through the Interior Department for recognition. Rejected in the Committee of the Whole 178-238: R 160-5; D 18-232 (ND 13-156, SD 5-76); I 0-1, Oct. 28, 1993.

538. HR 334. Lumbee Tribe Recognition/Passage. Passage of the bill to extend federal recognition to the Lumbee Tribe of Cheraw Indians of North Carolina, making the tribe eligible for federal benefits provided through the Bureau of Indian Affairs and Indian Health Services, contingent upon specific appropriations for the Lumbee Tribe. Passed 228-184: R 11-153; D 216-31 (ND 147-19, SD 69-12); I 1-0, Oct. 28, 1993.

539. HR 2684. Fish and Wildlife Foundation Authorization/Passage. Studds, D-Mass., motion to suspend the rules and pass the bill to authorize $25 million per year for fiscal 1994-98 for the National Fish and Wildlife Foundation; expand its board of directors; and authorize it to work with the National Oceanic and Atmospheric Administration on marine conservation projects. Motion agreed to 368-59: R 120-54; D 247-5 (ND 166-1, SD 81-4); I 1-0, Nov. 3, 1993. A two-thirds majority of those present and voting (285 in this case) is required for passage under suspension of the rules.

540. HR 3350. Federal Prison Substance Abuse Treatment/Passage. Brooks, D-Texas, motion to suspend the rules and pass the bill to require the Bureau of Prisons to accommodate all prisoners in substance abuse treatment programs by 1997. Motion agreed to 373-54: R 121-53; D 251-1 (ND 167-0, SD 84-1); I 1-0, Nov. 3, 1993. A two-thirds majority of those present and voting (285 in this case) is required for passage under suspension of the rules. A "yea" was a vote in support of the president's position.

541. HR 3351. Alternative Punishment For Young Offenders/Passage. Brooks, D-Texas, motion to suspend the rules and pass the bill to authorize $200 million per year for fiscal 1994-96 in grants to states to develop alternative methods of punishment — including boot camps, electronic monitoring, weekend incarceration, reimbursement of victims by offenders, community service — for youthful offenders. Motion rejected 235-192: R 9-165; D 225-27 (ND 158-9, SD 67-18); I 1-0, Nov. 3, 1993. A two-thirds majority of those present and voting (285 in this case) is required for passage under suspension of the rules. A "yea" was a vote in support of the president's position.

542. HR 3353. Anti-Juvenile Gangs and Drug Trafficking Grants/Passage. Brooks, D-Texas, motion to suspend the rules and pass the bill to authorize $100 million per year in fiscal 1994 and 1995 for state and local governments and organizations to develop programs to reduce gang activities and juvenile substance abuse. Motion agreed to 413-12: R 162-11; D 250-1 (ND 165-1, SD 85-0); I 1-0, Nov. 3, 1993. A two-thirds majority of those present and voting (284 in this case) is required for passage under suspension of the rules. A "yea" was a vote in support of the president's position.

543. HR 3354. State Prisoner Substance Abuse Treatment/Passage. Brooks, D-Texas, motion to suspend the rules and pass the bill to authorize $100 million per year for fiscal 1994-96 for grants to state governments to establish substance abuse treatment programs in state prisons. Motion agreed to 394-32: R 143-30; D 250-2 (ND 166-1, SD 84-1); I 1-0, Nov. 3, 1993. A two-thirds majority of those present and voting (284 in this case) is required for passage under suspension of the rules. A "yea" was a vote in support of the president's position.

544. HR 3167. Unemployment Benefits Extension/Employment Reduction. Archer, R-Texas, motion to instruct the House conferees to concur in the Senate amendment to reduce federal employment levels to those the vice president proposed in the National Performance Review. Motion agreed to 275-146: R 171-1; D 104-144 (ND 57-108, SD 47-36); I 0-1, Nov. 4, 1993.

KEY

Y Voted for (yea).
\# Paired for.
+ Announced for.
N Voted against (nay).
X Paired against.
− Announced against.
P Voted "present."
C Voted "present" to avoid possible conflict of interest.
? Did not vote or otherwise make a position known.
D Delegates ineligible to vote.

Democrats **Republicans**
Independent

	537	538	539	540	541	542	543	544
ALABAMA								
1 Callahan	Y	N	N	N	N	Y	N	Y
2 Everett	Y	N	Y	N	N	Y	Y	Y
3 Browder	N	Y	Y	Y	Y	Y	Y	Y
4 Bevill	N	Y	Y	Y	Y	Y	Y	Y
5 Cramer	N	Y	Y	Y	Y	Y	Y	Y
6 Bachus	Y	N	N	N	N	Y	N	Y
7 Hilliard	N	Y	Y	Y	Y	Y	Y	N
ALASKA								
AL Young	?	?	Y	Y	N	Y	Y	Y
ARIZONA								
1 Coppersmith	N	Y	Y	Y	Y	Y	Y	Y
2 Pastor	N	Y	Y	Y	Y	Y	Y	Y
3 Stump	Y	N	N	N	N	N	N	Y
4 Kyl	Y	N	Y	N	Y	Y	Y	Y
5 Kolbe	Y	N	Y	N	Y	Y	Y	Y
6 English	N	Y	Y	Y	Y	Y	Y	Y
ARKANSAS								
1 Lambert	N	Y	Y	Y	Y	Y	Y	Y
2 Thornton	N	Y	Y	Y	Y	Y	Y	N
3 Hutchinson	Y	N	Y	N	Y	Y	Y	Y
4 Dickey	Y	N	Y	N	Y	N	Y	Y
CALIFORNIA								
1 Hamburg	N	Y	Y	Y	Y	Y	Y	?
2 Herger	Y	N	N	N	N	Y	N	Y
3 Fazio	N	Y	Y	Y	Y	Y	Y	N
4 Doolittle	Y	N	N	N	N	Y	N	Y
5 Matsui	N	Y	Y	Y	Y	Y	Y	N
6 Woolsey	N	Y	Y	Y	Y	Y	Y	N
7 Miller	N	Y	Y	Y	Y	Y	Y	N
8 Pelosi	N	Y	Y	Y	Y	Y	Y	N
9 Dellums	N	Y	Y	Y	Y	Y	Y	N
10 Baker	Y	N	Y	N	Y	Y	Y	Y
11 Pombo	Y	N	N	N	N	Y	N	Y
12 Lantos	N	Y	Y	Y	Y	Y	Y	N
13 Stark	N	Y	Y	Y	Y	Y	Y	N
14 Eshoo	N	Y	Y	Y	Y	Y	Y	N
15 Mineta	N	Y	Y	Y	Y	Y	Y	N
16 Edwards	Y	Y	Y	Y	Y	Y	Y	N
17 Farr	N	Y	Y	Y	Y	Y	Y	N
18 Condit	N	N	Y	?	Y	Y	Y	Y
19 Lehman	Y	Y	Y	Y	Y	Y	Y	N
20 Dooley	N	Y	?	?	?	?	?	?
21 Thomas	Y	N	Y	N	Y	Y	Y	Y
22 Huffington	Y	N	Y	Y	Y	Y	Y	Y
23 Gallegly	Y	N	Y	N	Y	Y	Y	Y
24 Beilenson	N	Y	?	?	\#	?	?	?
25 McKeon	Y	N	Y	N	Y	Y	Y	Y
26 Berman	?	?	?	?	\#	?	?	?
27 Moorhead	Y	N	N	N	N	Y	Y	Y
28 Dreier	Y	N	N	N	N	Y	Y	N
29 Waxman	N	Y	Y	Y	Y	Y	Y	N
30 Becerra	N	Y	Y	Y	Y	Y	Y	N
31 Martinez	N	Y	Y	Y	Y	Y	Y	N
32 Dixon	N	Y	Y	Y	Y	Y	Y	N
33 Roybal-Allard	N	Y	Y	Y	Y	Y	Y	N
34 Torres	N	Y	Y	Y	Y	Y	Y	?
35 Waters	N	Y	Y	Y	Y	Y	Y	N
36 Harman	N	Y	Y	Y	Y	Y	Y	N
37 Tucker	N	Y	Y	Y	Y	Y	Y	N
38 Horn	Y	Y	Y	Y	N	Y	Y	Y
39 Royce	?	?	N	N	N	Y	N	Y
40 Lewis	Y	N	Y	N	Y	N	Y	Y
41 Kim	Y	N	Y	N	Y	Y	Y	Y

	537	538	539	540	541	542	543	544
42 Brown	N	Y	Y	Y	Y	Y	Y	Y
43 Calvert	Y	N	Y	N	Y	Y	Y	Y
44 McCandless	Y	N	Y	N	Y	N	Y	Y
45 Rohrabacher	Y	N	N	N	Y	N	Y	Y
46 Dornan	?	N	N	N	Y	Y	Y	Y
47 Cox	?	X	Y	N	Y	Y	Y	Y
48 Packard	Y	N	N	N	N	Y	N	Y
49 Schenk	N	Y	Y	Y	Y	Y	Y	N
50 Filner	N	Y	Y	Y	Y	Y	Y	N
51 Cunningham	Y	N	N	N	Y	Y	Y	Y
52 Hunter	Y	N	N	N	N	Y	Y	Y
COLORADO								
1 Schroeder	N	Y	Y	Y	Y	Y	Y	N
2 Skaggs	N	Y	Y	Y	Y	Y	Y	N
3 McInnis	Y	N	Y	N	Y	Y	Y	Y
4 Allard	Y	N	N	N	N	N	N	Y
5 Hefley	Y	N	N	N	N	Y	N	Y
6 Schaefer	Y	N	Y	N	Y	Y	Y	Y
CONNECTICUT								
1 Kennelly	Y	N	Y	Y	Y	Y	Y	N
2 Gejdenson	N	Y	Y	Y	Y	Y	Y	N
3 DeLauro	Y	N	Y	Y	Y	Y	Y	N
4 Shays	Y	N	Y	N	Y	Y	Y	Y
5 Franks	Y	N	Y	N	Y	Y	Y	Y
6 Johnson	Y	N	Y	N	Y	Y	Y	Y
DELAWARE								
AL Castle	Y	N	Y	N	Y	N	Y	Y
FLORIDA								
1 Hutto	N	N	Y	N	Y	Y	Y	Y
2 Peterson	N	Y	Y	Y	Y	Y	Y	N
3 Brown	N	Y	Y	Y	Y	Y	Y	Y
4 Fowler	Y	N	Y	N	Y	Y	Y	Y
5 Thurman	N	Y	Y	Y	Y	Y	Y	Y
6 Stearns	Y	N	N	N	N	Y	N	Y
7 Mica	Y	N	N	N	Y	Y	Y	Y
8 McCollum	Y	N	N	N	Y	Y	Y	Y
9 Bilirakis	Y	N	Y	N	Y	Y	Y	Y
10 Young	Y	N	N	N	N	Y	Y	Y
11 Gibbons	N	Y	Y	Y	Y	Y	Y	N
12 Canady	Y	N	Y	N	Y	Y	Y	Y
13 Miller	Y	N	Y	N	Y	Y	Y	Y
14 Goss	Y	N	N	N	Y	Y	Y	Y
15 Bacchus	N	Y	Y	Y	Y	Y	Y	Y
16 Lewis	Y	N	Y	N	Y	Y	Y	Y
17 Meek	N	Y	Y	Y	Y	Y	Y	N
18 Ros-Lehtinen	Y	?	Y	Y	Y	Y	Y	Y
19 Johnston	?	\#	Y	Y	Y	Y	Y	Y
20 Deutsch	N	Y	Y	Y	Y	Y	Y	Y
21 Diaz-Balart	Y	N	Y	N	Y	Y	Y	Y
22 Shaw	Y	N	N	N	Y	Y	Y	Y
23 Hastings	N	Y	Y	Y	Y	Y	Y	Y
GEORGIA								
1 Kingston	Y	N	Y	N	N	Y	Y	Y
2 Bishop	N	Y	Y	Y	Y	Y	Y	N
3 Collins	Y	N	N	N	N	Y	Y	Y
4 Linder	Y	N	N	N	Y	Y	Y	Y
5 Lewis	N	Y	Y	Y	Y	Y	Y	N
6 Gingrich	Y	N	Y	N	Y	Y	Y	Y
7 Darden	N	Y	Y	Y	Y	Y	Y	Y
8 Rowland	N	Y	Y	Y	Y	Y	Y	Y
9 Deal	N	Y	Y	Y	Y	Y	Y	Y
10 Johnson	N	Y	Y	Y	Y	Y	Y	Y
11 McKinney	N	Y	Y	Y	Y	Y	Y	N
HAWAII								
1 Abercrombie	N	Y	Y	Y	Y	?	Y	N
2 Mink	N	Y	Y	Y	Y	?	Y	N
IDAHO								
1 LaRocco	N	Y	Y	Y	Y	Y	Y	Y
2 Crapo	Y	N	Y	N	N	Y	Y	Y
ILLINOIS								
1 Rush	N	Y	Y	Y	Y	Y	Y	N
2 Reynolds	N	Y	Y	Y	Y	Y	Y	Y
3 Lipinski	N	Y	Y	Y	Y	Y	Y	Y
4 Gutierrez	N	Y	Y	Y	Y	Y	Y	Y
5 Rostenkowski	N	Y	Y	Y	Y	Y	Y	Y
6 Hyde	Y	N	Y	N	Y	Y	Y	Y
7 Collins	N	Y	Y	Y	Y	Y	Y	Y
8 Crane	Y	N	N	N	N	N	N	Y
9 Yates	N	Y	Y	Y	Y	Y	Y	N
10 Porter	Y	N	Y	N	Y	Y	Y	Y
11 Sangmeister	N	Y	Y	Y	Y	Y	Y	Y
12 Costello	N	Y	Y	Y	Y	Y	Y	Y
13 Fawell	Y	N	N	N	N	Y	N	Y
14 Hastert	Y	N	Y	N	Y	Y	Y	Y
15 Ewing	Y	N	Y	N	Y	Y	Y	Y
16 Manzullo	Y	N	Y	N	N	Y	N	Y
17 Evans	N	Y	Y	Y	Y	Y	Y	N

ND Northern Democrats   SD Southern Democrats

	537	538	539	540	541	542	543	544
18 ***Michel***	Y	N	N	N	N	Y	Y	Y
19 Poshard	N	Y	Y	Y	Y	Y	Y	Y
20 Durbin	N	Y	Y	Y	Y	Y	Y	Y
INDIANA								
1 Visclosky	N	Y	Y	Y	Y	Y	Y	N
2 Sharp	N	Y	Y	Y	Y	Y	Y	Y
3 Roemer	N	Y	Y	Y	Y	Y	Y	Y
4 Long	N	Y	Y	Y	Y	Y	Y	Y
5 ***Buyer***	Y	N	Y	Y	N	Y	Y	Y
6 ***Burton***	Y	N	N	N	N	N	N	Y
7 ***Myers***	Y	N	Y	Y	N	Y	Y	Y
8 McCloskey	N	Y	Y	Y	Y	Y	Y	N
9 Hamilton	N	Y	Y	Y	Y	Y	Y	Y
10 Jacobs	N	Y	Y	Y	Y	Y	Y	Y
IOWA								
1 ***Leach***	Y	Y	Y	Y	N	Y	Y	Y
2 ***Nussle***	Y	N	N	N	N	N	N	Y
3 ***Lightfoot***	Y	N	Y	N	N	Y	Y	Y
4 Smith	N	Y	Y	Y	Y	Y	Y	N
5 ***Grandy***	Y	N	Y	Y	N	Y	Y	Y
KANSAS								
1 ***Roberts***	Y	N	Y	Y	N	Y	Y	Y
2 Slattery	N	Y	Y	Y	Y	Y	Y	Y
3 ***Meyers***	Y	N	Y	N	N	Y	Y	Y
4 Glickman	N	Y	Y	Y	Y	Y	Y	Y
KENTUCKY								
1 Barlow	N	Y	Y	Y	Y	Y	Y	N
2 Natcher	N	Y	Y	Y	Y	Y	Y	N
3 Mazzoli	N	Y	Y	Y	Y	Y	Y	Y
4 ***Bunning***	Y	N	Y	Y	N	Y	Y	Y
5 ***Rogers***	Y	N	Y	Y	N	Y	Y	Y
6 Baesler	N	Y	Y	Y	Y	Y	Y	?
LOUISIANA								
1 ***Livingston***	Y	N	Y	Y	N	Y	Y	Y
2 Jefferson	N	Y	Y	Y	Y	Y	Y	N
3 Tauzin	?	?	Y	Y	N	Y	Y	Y
4 Fields	N	Y	Y	Y	Y	Y	Y	N
5 ***McCrery***	Y	N	Y	Y	N	Y	Y	Y
6 ***Baker***	Y	N	Y	N	N	Y	Y	Y
7 Hayes	N	N	Y	Y	N	Y	Y	Y
MAINE								
1 Andrews	N	Y	Y	Y	Y	Y	Y	N
2 ***Snowe***	N	Y	Y	N	N	Y	Y	Y
MARYLAND								
1 ***Gilchrest***	Y	N	Y	Y	N	Y	Y	Y
2 ***Bentley***	Y	N	Y	Y	N	Y	Y	N
3 Cardin	?	?	Y	Y	Y	Y	Y	N
4 Wynn	N	Y	Y	Y	Y	Y	Y	N
5 Hoyer	N	Y	Y	Y	Y	Y	Y	N
6 ***Bartlett***	Y	N	N	N	N	Y	N	Y
7 Mfume	N	Y	Y	Y	Y	Y	Y	N
8 ***Morella***	Y	N	Y	Y	N	Y	Y	—
MASSACHUSETTS								
1 Olver	N	Y	Y	Y	Y	Y	Y	N
2 Neal	N	Y	Y	Y	Y	Y	Y	Y
3 ***Blute***	Y	Y	Y	Y	N	Y	Y	Y
4 Frank	N	Y	Y	Y	Y	Y	Y	N
5 Meehan	N	Y	Y	Y	Y	Y	Y	Y
6 ***Torkildsen***	Y	Y	Y	Y	N	Y	Y	Y
7 Markey	N	?	Y	Y	Y	Y	Y	N
8 Kennedy	N	Y	Y	Y	Y	Y	Y	N
9 Moakley	N	Y	Y	Y	Y	Y	Y	N
10 Studds	N	Y	Y	Y	Y	Y	Y	N
MICHIGAN								
1 Stupak	N	Y	Y	Y	Y	Y	Y	Y
2 ***Hoekstra***	Y	N	Y	Y	N	Y	Y	Y
3 Vacancy								
4 ***Camp***	Y	N	Y	Y	N	Y	Y	Y
5 Barcia	N	Y	Y	Y	N	Y	?	Y
6 ***Upton***	Y	Y	Y	Y	N	Y	Y	Y
7 ***Smith***	Y	N	N	Y	N	Y	N	?
8 Carr	N	Y	?	?	Y	Y	Y	N
9 Kildee	N	Y	Y	Y	Y	Y	Y	N
10 Bonior	N	Y	Y	Y	Y	Y	Y	N
11 ***Knollenberg***	Y	N	Y	Y	N	Y	Y	Y
12 Levin	N	Y	Y	Y	Y	Y	Y	Y
13 Ford	N	Y	Y	Y	Y	Y	Y	N
14 Conyers	?	#	Y	Y	Y	Y	Y	N
15 Collins	N	Y	Y	Y	Y	Y	Y	N
16 Dingell	Y	N	Y	Y	Y	Y	Y	N
MINNESOTA								
1 Penny	?	N	N	Y	Y	N	N	Y
2 Minge	N	N	Y	Y	Y	Y	Y	Y
3 ***Ramstad***	Y	N	Y	Y	N	Y	Y	Y
4 Vento	N	Y	Y	Y	Y	Y	Y	N

	537	538	539	540	541	542	543	544
5 Sabo	N	Y	Y	Y	Y	Y	Y	N
6 ***Grams***	Y	N	N	N	N	Y	Y	Y
7 Peterson	N	Y	Y	Y	Y	Y	Y	Y
8 Oberstar	N	N	Y	Y	Y	Y	Y	N
MISSISSIPPI								
1 Whitten	N	Y	Y	Y	Y	Y	Y	N
2 Thompson	N	Y	Y	Y	Y	Y	Y	N
3 Montgomery	N	N	N	Y	N	Y	Y	Y
4 Parker	N	N	Y	Y	Y	Y	Y	Y
5 Taylor	?	N	N	Y	N	Y	Y	Y
MISSOURI								
1 Clay	N	Y	Y	Y	Y	Y	Y	N
2 ***Talent***	Y	N	Y	N	N	Y	N	Y
3 Gephardt	N	Y	Y	Y	Y	Y	Y	N
4 Skelton	N	Y	Y	Y	N	Y	Y	Y
5 Wheat	N	Y	Y	Y	Y	Y	Y	N
6 Danner	N	Y	Y	Y	Y	Y	Y	Y
7 ***Hancock***	Y	N	N	N	N	N	N	Y
8 ***Emerson***	Y	N	N	Y	N	Y	Y	Y
9 Volkmer	N	Y	Y	Y	N	Y	Y	N
MONTANA								
AL Williams	N	Y	Y	Y	Y	Y	Y	N
NEBRASKA								
1 ***Bereuter***	Y	N	Y	Y	Y	Y	Y	Y
2 Hoagland	N	N	Y	Y	Y	Y	Y	Y
3 ***Barrett***	Y	N	N	Y	N	Y	Y	Y
NEVADA								
1 Bilbray	N	Y	Y	Y	N	Y	Y	?
2 ***Vucanovich***	?	N	N	Y	N	Y	Y	Y
NEW HAMPSHIRE								
1 ***Zeliff***	Y	N	Y	Y	N	Y	Y	Y
2 Swett	N	Y	Y	Y	N	Y	Y	Y
NEW JERSEY								
1 Andrews	N	Y	Y	Y	Y	Y	Y	N
2 Hughes	N	N	Y	Y	Y	Y	Y	N
3 ***Saxton***	Y	N	Y	Y	N	Y	Y	Y
4 ***Smith***	Y	N	Y	Y	Y	Y	Y	Y
5 ***Roukema***	Y	N	Y	N	N	Y	Y	Y
6 Pallone	N	Y	Y	Y	Y	Y	Y	Y
7 ***Franks***	Y	N	Y	Y	Y	Y	Y	Y
8 Klein	N	Y	Y	Y	Y	Y	Y	N
9 Torricelli	Y	N	Y	Y	Y	Y	Y	Y
10 Payne	N	Y	Y	Y	Y	Y	Y	N
11 ***Gallo***	Y	N	Y	Y	N	Y	Y	Y
12 ***Zimmer***	Y	N	Y	Y	N	Y	Y	Y
13 Menendez	Y	N	Y	Y	Y	Y	Y	N
NEW MEXICO								
1 ***Schiff***	Y	N	Y	Y	N	Y	Y	Y
2 ***Skeen***	Y	N	Y	Y	N	Y	Y	Y
3 Richardson	N	Y	Y	Y	Y	Y	Y	N
NEW YORK								
1 Hochbrueckner	N	Y	Y	Y	Y	Y	Y	N
2 ***Lazio***	Y	N	Y	Y	N	Y	Y	Y
3 ***King***	Y	N	Y	Y	N	Y	Y	Y
4 ***Levy***	Y	N	Y	Y	N	Y	Y	Y
5 Ackerman	N	Y	Y	Y	Y	Y	Y	N
6 Flake	N	Y	Y	Y	Y	Y	Y	?
7 Manton	N	Y	Y	Y	Y	Y	Y	N
8 Nadler	N	Y	Y	Y	Y	Y	Y	N
9 Schumer	N	Y	Y	Y	Y	Y	Y	Y
10 Towns	?	?	Y	Y	Y	Y	Y	N
11 Owens	N	Y	Y	Y	Y	Y	Y	N
12 Velazquez	N	Y	?	?	?	?	?	N
13 ***Molinari***	Y	N	Y	Y	N	Y	Y	Y
14 Maloney	N	Y	Y	Y	Y	Y	Y	N
15 Rangel	X	Y	Y	Y	Y	Y	Y	N
16 Serrano	N	Y	Y	Y	Y	Y	Y	N
17 Engel	N	Y	Y	Y	Y	Y	Y	N
18 Lowey	N	Y	Y	Y	Y	Y	Y	N
19 ***Fish***	Y	N	Y	Y	N	Y	Y	Y
20 ***Gilman***	Y	Y	Y	Y	N	Y	Y	Y
21 McNulty	?	?	Y	Y	Y	Y	Y	Y
22 ***Solomon***	Y	N	Y	Y	N	Y	Y	Y
23 ***Boehlert***	Y	N	Y	Y	N	Y	Y	Y
24 ***McHugh***	Y	?	Y	Y	N	Y	Y	?
25 ***Walsh***	Y	?	Y	Y	N	Y	Y	Y
26 Hinchey	N	Y	Y	Y	Y	Y	Y	Y
27 ***Paxon***	Y	N	N	N	N	Y	Y	Y
28 Slaughter	N	Y	Y	Y	Y	Y	Y	N
29 LaFalce	Y	N	Y	Y	N	Y	Y	N
30 ***Quinn***	Y	N	Y	Y	N	Y	Y	Y
31 ***Houghton***	Y	N	Y	Y	N	Y	Y	Y
NORTH CAROLINA								
1 Clayton	N	Y	Y	Y	Y	Y	Y	N
2 Valentine	N	Y	Y	Y	N	Y	N	Y

	537	538	539	540	541	542	543	544
3 Lancaster	N	Y	Y	Y	Y	Y	Y	?
4 Price	N	Y	Y	Y	Y	Y	Y	N
5 Neal	N	Y	Y	Y	Y	Y	Y	Y
6 ***Coble***	N	Y	N	Y	N	Y	Y	Y
7 Rose	N	Y	Y	Y	Y	Y	Y	N
8 Hefner	N	Y	Y	Y	Y	Y	Y	N
9 ***McMillan***	N	Y	Y	Y	N	Y	Y	Y
10 ***Ballenger***	Y	N	Y	N	N	Y	N	Y
11 ***Taylor***	Y	N	Y	N	N	Y	N	Y
12 Watt	N	Y	Y	Y	Y	Y	Y	N
NORTH DAKOTA								
AL Pomeroy	Y	N	Y	Y	Y	Y	Y	Y
OHIO								
1 Mann	N	Y	Y	Y	Y	Y	Y	N
2 ***Portman***	Y	N	Y	Y	N	Y	Y	Y
3 Hall	N	Y	Y	Y	Y	Y	Y	N
4 ***Oxley***	Y	N	N	Y	N	Y	Y	Y
5 ***Gillmor***	Y	N	Y	Y	N	Y	Y	Y
6 Strickland	N	Y	Y	Y	Y	Y	Y	Y
7 ***Hobson***	Y	N	Y	Y	N	Y	Y	Y
8 ***Boehner***	Y	N	Y	Y	N	Y	Y	Y
9 Kaptur	N	Y	Y	Y	Y	Y	Y	Y
10 ***Hoke***	Y	N	Y	Y	N	Y	Y	Y
11 Stokes	N	Y	Y	Y	Y	Y	Y	N
12 ***Kasich***	?	N	N	Y	N	Y	Y	Y
13 Brown	N	Y	Y	Y	Y	Y	Y	Y
14 Sawyer	N	Y	Y	Y	Y	Y	Y	N
15 ***Pryce***	Y	N	Y	Y	N	Y	Y	Y
16 ***Regula***	Y	N	Y	Y	N	Y	Y	Y
17 Traficant	N	Y	Y	Y	Y	Y	Y	N
18 Applegate	N	Y	Y	Y	N	Y	Y	N
19 Fingerhut	N	Y	Y	Y	Y	Y	Y	Y
OKLAHOMA								
1 ***Inhofe***	Y	N	N	Y	N	Y	Y	Y
2 Synar	Y	N	Y	Y	Y	Y	Y	N
3 Brewster	Y	Y	Y	Y	Y	Y	Y	Y
4 McCurdy	Y	N	Y	Y	Y	Y	Y	Y
5 ***Istook***	Y	N	Y	Y	N	Y	Y	Y
6 English	Y	N	Y	Y	N	Y	Y	Y
OREGON								
1 Furse	N	Y	Y	Y	Y	Y	Y	N
2 ***Smith***	#	X	N	Y	N	Y	Y	Y
3 Wyden	N	Y	Y	Y	Y	Y	Y	N
4 DeFazio	N	Y	Y	Y	Y	Y	Y	N
5 Kopetski	N	Y	Y	Y	Y	Y	Y	N
PENNSYLVANIA								
1 Foglietta	N	Y	Y	Y	Y	Y	Y	N
2 Blackwell	N	Y	Y	Y	Y	Y	Y	N
3 Borski	N	Y	Y	Y	Y	Y	Y	N
4 Klink	N	Y	Y	Y	Y	Y	Y	N
5 ***Clinger***	+	—	Y	Y	N	Y	Y	Y
6 Holden	N	Y	Y	Y	Y	Y	Y	Y
7 ***Weldon***	Y	N	Y	Y	N	Y	Y	Y
8 ***Greenwood***	Y	N	Y	Y	N	Y	Y	Y
9 ***Shuster***	Y	N	N	N	N	Y	N	Y
10 ***McDade***	Y	?	Y	Y	N	Y	Y	Y
11 Kanjorski	N	Y	Y	Y	Y	Y	Y	N
12 Murtha	N	Y	Y	Y	Y	Y	Y	N
13 Margolies-Mezv.	N	Y	Y	Y	Y	Y	Y	Y
14 Coyne	N	Y	Y	Y	Y	Y	Y	N
15 McHale	N	Y	Y	Y	Y	Y	Y	Y
16 ***Walker***	Y	N	N	N	N	Y	N	Y
17 ***Gekas***	Y	N	N	N	N	Y	Y	Y
18 ***Santorum***	Y	N	N	Y	N	Y	Y	Y
19 ***Goodling***	Y	N	Y	Y	Y	Y	Y	Y
20 Murphy	N	Y	Y	Y	N	Y	Y	N
21 ***Ridge***	Y	Y	Y	Y	Y	Y	Y	Y
RHODE ISLAND								
1 ***Machtley***	Y	N	?	?	X	?	?	Y
2 Reed	N	N	Y	Y	Y	Y	Y	Y
SOUTH CAROLINA								
1 ***Ravenel***	N	Y	Y	Y	N	Y	Y	Y
2 ***Spence***	Y	N	Y	Y	N	Y	Y	Y
3 Derrick	N	Y	Y	Y	N	Y	Y	Y
4 ***Inglis***	?	?	N	Y	N	N	N	Y
5 Spratt	N	Y	Y	Y	N	Y	Y	Y
6 Clyburn	N	Y	Y	Y	Y	Y	Y	N
SOUTH DAKOTA								
AL Johnson	Y	N	Y	Y	Y	Y	Y	N
TENNESSEE								
1 ***Quillen***	N	?	Y	Y	N	Y	Y	Y
2 ***Duncan***	Y	N	N	N	N	Y	Y	Y
3 Lloyd	N	Y	Y	Y	Y	Y	Y	Y
4 Cooper	N	Y	Y	Y	Y	Y	Y	Y
5 Clement	N	Y	Y	Y	Y	Y	Y	N

	537	538	539	540	541	542	543	544
6 Gordon	N	Y	Y	Y	Y	Y	Y	Y
7 ***Sundquist***	Y	N	Y	Y	N	Y	Y	Y
8 Tanner	N	N	Y	N	Y	Y	Y	Y
9 Ford	N	Y	Y	Y	Y	Y	Y	N
TEXAS								
1 Chapman	N	Y	Y	Y	Y	Y	Y	Y
2 Wilson	N	Y	Y	Y	N	Y	Y	Y
3 ***Johnson, Sam***	Y	N	N	N	N	Y	N	Y
4 Hall	Y	N	N	Y	N	Y	Y	Y
5 Bryant	N	Y	Y	Y	Y	Y	Y	Y
6 ***Barton***	Y	N	N	Y	N	Y	Y	Y
7 ***Archer***	Y	N	N	N	N	Y	N	Y
8 ***Fields***	Y	N	Y	N	N	Y	N	Y
9 Brooks	N	?	Y	Y	Y	Y	Y	Y
10 Pickle	N	Y	Y	Y	Y	Y	Y	Y
11 Edwards	N	Y	Y	Y	Y	Y	Y	Y
12 Geren	N	Y	Y	Y	N	Y	Y	Y
13 Sarpalius	N	Y	Y	Y	N	Y	Y	Y
14 Laughlin	N	N	Y	Y	Y	Y	Y	Y
15 de la Garza	N	Y	Y	Y	Y	Y	Y	N
16 Coleman	N	Y	Y	Y	Y	Y	Y	N
17 Stenholm	N	N	N	Y	N	Y	Y	Y
18 Washington	N	Y	Y	Y	Y	Y	Y	Y
19 ***Combest***	Y	N	N	N	N	N	N	Y
20 Gonzalez	N	Y	Y	Y	Y	Y	Y	N
21 ***Smith***	Y	N	Y	Y	N	Y	Y	Y
22 ***DeLay***	Y	N	N	N	N	N	N	Y
23 ***Bonilla***	Y	N	N	Y	N	Y	Y	Y
24 Frost	N	Y	Y	Y	Y	Y	Y	Y
25 Andrews	N	Y	Y	Y	N	Y	Y	Y
26 ***Armey***	Y	N	N	N	N	N	N	Y
27 Ortiz	N	Y	Y	Y	N	Y	Y	Y
28 Tejeda	N	Y	Y	Y	Y	Y	Y	Y
29 Green	?	?	Y	Y	Y	Y	Y	N
30 Johnson, E.B.	N	Y	Y	Y	Y	Y	Y	N
UTAH								
1 ***Hansen***	Y	N	N	Y	N	Y	?	Y
2 Shepherd	N	Y	Y	Y	Y	Y	Y	Y
3 Orton	Y	N	Y	Y	N	Y	Y	Y
VERMONT								
AL *Sanders*	N	Y	Y	Y	Y	Y	Y	N
VIRGINIA								
1 ***Bateman***	?	N	Y	Y	N	?	Y	Y
2 Pickett	N	Y	Y	Y	Y	Y	Y	N
3 Scott	N	Y	Y	Y	Y	Y	Y	N
4 Sisisky	N	Y	Y	Y	Y	Y	Y	Y
5 Payne	N	Y	Y	Y	Y	Y	Y	Y
6 ***Goodlatte***	Y	N	Y	Y	N	Y	Y	Y
7 ***Bliley***	Y	N	N	Y	N	Y	Y	Y
8 Moran	N	Y	Y	Y	Y	Y	Y	N
9 Boucher	N	Y	Y	Y	Y	Y	Y	N
10 ***Wolf***	Y	N	Y	Y	N	Y	Y	Y
11 Byrne	N	Y	Y	Y	Y	Y	Y	N
WASHINGTON								
1 Cantwell	N	Y	Y	Y	Y	Y	Y	Y
2 Swift	Y	N	Y	Y	Y	Y	Y	N
3 Unsoeld	N	Y	Y	Y	Y	Y	Y	N
4 Inslee	Y	N	Y	Y	Y	Y	Y	Y
5 Foley								
6 Dicks	N	Y	Y	Y	Y	Y	Y	N
7 McDermott	N	Y	Y	Y	Y	Y	Y	N
8 ***Dunn***	Y	N	Y	Y	N	Y	Y	Y
9 Kreidler	N	N	Y	Y	Y	Y	Y	N
WEST VIRGINIA								
1 Mollohan	N	Y	Y	Y	Y	Y	Y	N
2 Wise	N	Y	Y	Y	Y	Y	Y	N
3 Rahall	N	Y	Y	Y	Y	Y	Y	N
WISCONSIN								
1 Barca	N	Y	Y	Y	Y	Y	Y	Y
2 ***Klug***	Y	N	N	Y	Y	Y	Y	Y
3 ***Gunderson***	Y	N	Y	Y	N	Y	Y	Y
4 Kleczka	N	Y	Y	Y	Y	Y	Y	Y
5 Barrett	N	Y	Y	Y	Y	Y	Y	Y
6 ***Petri***	Y	N	Y	Y	N	Y	Y	Y
7 Obey	N	Y	Y	Y	Y	Y	Y	N
8 ***Roth***	Y	N	Y	Y	N	Y	Y	Y
9 ***Sensenbrenner***	Y	N	N	N	N	N	N	Y
WYOMING								
AL ***Thomas***	Y	N	N	Y	N	Y	Y	Y
DELEGATES								
de Lugo, V.I.	N	D	D	D	D	D	D	D
Faleomavaega, Am.S.	N	D	D	D	D	D	D	D
Norton, D.C.	N	D	D	D	D	D	D	D
Romero-B., P.R.	?	D	D	D	D	D	D	D
Underwood, Guam	N	D	D	D	D	D	D	D

Southern states - Ala., Ark., Fla., Ga., Ky., La., Miss., N.C., Okla., S.C., Tenn., Texas, Va.
Omitted votes are quorum calls, which CQ does not include in its vote charts.

KEY

Y Voted for (yea).
\# Paired for.
\+ Announced for.
N Voted against (nay).
X Paired against.
− Announced against.
P Voted "present."
C Voted "present" to avoid possible conflict of interest.
? Did not vote or otherwise make a position known.
D Delegates ineligible to vote.

Democrats **Republicans**
Independent

545. HR 2151. Maritime Revitalization/Foreign-Built Ship Subsidies. Taylor, D-Miss., amendment to strike the provisions that allow U.S. shipping lines to receive subsidies for certain foreign-built ships. Rejected in the Committee of the Whole 64-362: R 12-160; D 52-201 (ND 31-139, SD 21-62); I 0-1, Nov. 4, 1993.

546. HR 2151. Maritime Revitalization/Cargo Preference Rate. Penny, D-Minn., amendment to limit the freight rate charged by U.S.-flag vessels for military and foreign-aid "preference" cargo to twice the relevant world freight rate. Rejected in the Committee of the Whole 109-309: R 73-96; D 36-212 (ND 26-143, SD 10-69); I 0-1, Nov. 4, 1993. A "nay" was a vote in support of the president's position.

547. HR 2151. Maritime Revitalization/Passage. Passage of the bill to authorize $1.2 billion over 10 years to subsidize oceangoing U.S.-flag cargo vessels. The bill also would authorize such sums as necessary to fund a new subsidy program for U.S. shipyards based on the production of multiple copies of the same ship design. Passed 347-65: R 116-54; D 230-11 (ND 153-8, SD 77-3); I 1-0, Nov. 4, 1993. A "yea" was a vote in support of the president's position.

548. H Con Res 170. Somalia Force Removal/Rule. Adoption of the rule (H Res 293) to provide for House floor consideration of the concurrent resolution to call on the president to remove U.S. troops from Somalia by Jan. 31, 1994. Adopted 390-8: R 160-5; D 229-3 (ND 151-2, SD 78-1); I 1-0, Nov. 8, 1993.

549. HR 2440. National Transportation Safety Board Authorization/Passage. Oberstar, D-Minn., motion to suspend the rules and pass the bill to authorize $38 million in fiscal 1994, $44 million in fiscal 1995 and $45 million in fiscal 1996 for the National Transportation Safety Board to investigate and determine the causes of transportation accidents. Motion agreed to 353-49: R 120-44; D 232-5 (ND 155-2, SD 77-3); I 1-0, Nov. 8, 1993. A two-thirds majority of those present and voting (268 in this case) is required for passage under suspension of the rules.

550. Procedural Motion. Approval of the House Journal of Monday, Nov. 8. Approved 256-154: R 19-149; D 236-5 (ND 160-4, SD 76-1); I 1-0, Nov. 9, 1993.

551. HR 3167. Unemployment Benefits Extension/Rule. Adoption of the rule (H Res 298) to waive points of order against and provide for House floor consideration of the conference report to provide $1.1 billion for extended unemployment benefits for workers who have exhausted their 26 weeks of state unemployment benefits for an additional seven or 13 weeks of compensation, depending on the unemployment rate in their state. Adopted 249-172: R 5-167; D 243-5 (ND 164-3, SD 79-2); I 1-0, Nov. 9, 1993.

552. HR 3167. Unemployment Benefits Extension/Employment Reduction. Crane, R-Ill., motion to recommit the bill to conference with instructions to report it back with provisions to reduce the number of federal employees to the level the vice president proposed in the National Performance Review. Motion agreed to 226-202: R 169-3; D 57-198 (ND 28-143, SD 29-55); I 0-1, Nov. 9, 1993.

	545	546	547	548	549	550	551	552
ALABAMA								
1 *Callahan*	N	N	Y	Y	N	?	N	Y
2 *Everett*	N	N	Y	Y	N	N	N	Y
3 Browder	Y	N	Y	Y	Y	Y	Y	Y
4 Bevill	Y	?	?	Y	Y	Y	Y	N
5 Cramer	N	N	Y	Y	Y	Y	Y	Y
6 *Bachus*	Y	Y	N	Y	N	N	N	Y
7 Hilliard	N	Y	Y	Y	Y	Y	Y	N
ALASKA								
AL *Young*	N	N	Y	Y	Y	N	N	N
ARIZONA								
1 Coppersmith	N	N	Y	Y	Y	Y	Y	Y
2 Pastor	N	N	Y	Y	Y	Y	Y	N
3 *Stump*	Y	Y	N	Y	N	N	N	Y
4 *Kyl*	N	Y	Y	Y	N	N	N	Y
5 *Kolbe*	N	Y	Y	Y	N	N	N	Y
6 English	N	N	Y	Y	Y	Y	Y	N
ARKANSAS								
1 Lambert	N	N	Y	Y	Y	Y	?	N
2 Thornton	N	?	?	Y	Y	Y	Y	N
3 *Hutchinson*	N	N	Y	Y	N	N	N	Y
4 Dickey	N	N	?	Y	Y	N	N	Y
CALIFORNIA								
1 Hamburg	N	N	Y	Y	Y	Y	Y	N
2 *Herger*	N	?	?	Y	N	N	N	Y
3 Fazio	N	N	Y	Y	Y	Y	Y	N
4 *Doolittle*	N	N	Y	Y	N	N	N	Y
5 Matsui	?	?	?	Y	Y	Y	Y	N
6 Woolsey	N	N	Y	Y	Y	Y	Y	N
7 Miller	N	N	Y	Y	Y	Y	Y	N
8 Pelosi	N	N	Y	Y	Y	Y	Y	N
9 Dellums	N	N	Y	N	Y	Y	?	N
10 *Baker*	N	N	Y	Y	Y	N	N	Y
11 *Pombo*	N	N	Y	Y	N	N	N	Y
12 Lantos	N	N	Y	Y	Y	Y	Y	N
13 Stark	N	N	Y	?	Y	Y	Y	N
14 Eshoo	N	N	Y	Y	Y	Y	Y	N
15 Mineta	N	N	Y	Y	Y	Y	Y	N
16 Edwards	N	N	Y	Y	Y	Y	Y	N
17 Farr	N	N	Y	Y	Y	Y	Y	N
18 Condit	Y	N	N	Y	N	Y	N	Y
19 Lehman	N	N	Y	Y	Y	Y	Y	N
20 Dooley	?	?	?	?	Y	Y	Y	Y
21 *Thomas*	N	Y	Y	Y	N	N	N	Y
22 *Huffington*	N	N	Y	N	Y	?	N	Y
23 *Gallegly*	N	N	Y	Y	N	N	N	Y
24 Beilenson	?	?	?	Y	Y	Y	?	N
25 *McKeon*	N	?	?	Y	N	N	N	Y
26 Berman	?	?	?	Y	Y	Y	Y	N
27 *Moorhead*	N	N	N	Y	N	N	N	Y
28 *Dreier*	N	N	N	N	N	N	Y	Y
29 Waxman	N	N	Y	Y	Y	Y	Y	N
30 Becerra	N	N	Y	?	Y	Y	Y	N
31 Martinez	Y	N	Y	Y	Y	Y	Y	N
32 Dixon	N	N	Y	Y	Y	Y	Y	N
33 Roybal-Allard	N	N	Y	Y	Y	Y	Y	N
34 Torres	N	N	Y	Y	Y	Y	Y	N
35 Waters	N	N	Y	Y	Y	Y	Y	N
36 Harman	N	N	?	?	?	Y	Y	Y
37 Tucker	N	N	Y	Y	Y	Y	Y	N
38 *Horn*	N	N	Y	Y	Y	N	N	Y
39 *Royce*	Y	Y	N	Y	N	N	N	Y
40 *Lewis*	N	N	Y	Y	?	N	N	Y
41 *Kim*	N	N	N	Y	N	N	N	Y
42 *Brown*	N	N	Y	Y	Y	?	Y	N
43 *Calvert*	N	N	Y	Y	N	N	N	Y
44 *McCandless*	N	Y	Y	Y	N	N	N	Y
45 *Rohrabacher*	N	Y	N	Y	N	N	N	Y
46 *Dornan*	N	N	N	Y	N	N	N	Y
47 *Cox*	N	Y	N	Y	N	N	N	Y
48 *Packard*	N	N	Y	Y	Y	N	N	Y
49 Schenk	N	N	Y	?	Y	Y	Y	Y
50 Filner	Y	N	Y	Y	Y	Y	Y	N
51 *Cunningham*	N	N	Y	Y	N	N	N	Y
52 *Hunter*	N	N	Y	N	N	N	N	Y
COLORADO								
1 Schroeder	N	N	Y	Y	Y	N	Y	N
2 Skaggs	N	N	Y	Y	Y	Y	Y	N
3 *McInnis*	N	N	Y	Y	Y	Y	Y	N
4 *Allard*	N	Y	N	Y	N	N	N	Y
5 *Hefley*	N	N	Y	Y	Y	N	N	Y
6 *Schaefer*	N	N	Y	Y	N	N	N	Y
CONNECTICUT								
1 Kennelly	N	N	Y	Y	Y	Y	Y	N
2 Gejdenson	N	N	Y	Y	Y	Y	Y	N
3 DeLauro	N	N	Y	Y	Y	Y	Y	N
4 *Shays*	N	N	Y	Y	Y	N	Y	N
5 *Franks*	N	N	Y	Y	N	N	Y	Y
6 *Johnson*	N	N	Y	Y	Y	Y	Y	N
DELAWARE								
AL *Castle*	N	Y	Y	Y	Y	N	N	Y
FLORIDA								
1 Hutto	N	N	Y	Y	Y	Y	Y	Y
2 Peterson	N	N	Y	Y	Y	Y	Y	N
3 Brown	N	N	Y	Y	Y	Y	Y	N
4 *Fowler*	N	N	Y	Y	N	N	N	Y
5 Thurman	N	N	Y	Y	Y	Y	Y	Y
6 *Stearns*	N	N	Y	Y	N	N	N	Y
7 *Mica*	N	N	Y	N	N	N	N	Y
8 *McCollum*	N	N	Y	Y	N	N	N	Y
9 *Bilirakis*	N	N	Y	Y	N	N	N	Y
10 *Young*	N	Y	Y	Y	N	N	N	Y
11 Gibbons	N	N	Y	?	?	Y	Y	N
12 *Canady*	N	N	Y	Y	N	N	N	Y
13 *Miller*	N	N	Y	Y	N	N	N	Y
14 *Goss*	N	N	Y	Y	N	N	N	Y
15 *Bacchus*	N	N	Y	Y	Y	Y	Y	N
16 *Lewis*	N	Y	Y	+	+	?	?	?
17 Meek	N	N	Y	?	?	Y	Y	N
18 *Ros-Lehtinen*	N	N	Y	Y	N	N	N	Y
19 Johnston	N	N	Y	Y	Y	Y	Y	N
20 Deutsch	N	N	Y	Y	Y	?	Y	N
21 *Diaz-Balart*	N	N	Y	Y	N	N	N	Y
22 *Shaw*	N	N	Y	Y	N	N	N	Y
23 Hastings	N	N	Y	Y	Y	Y	Y	N
GEORGIA								
1 *Kingston*	N	N	Y	N	Y	N	N	Y
2 Bishop	N	N	Y	Y	Y	Y	Y	N
3 *Collins*	N	Y	N	N	N	N	N	Y
4 *Linder*	N	Y	Y	Y	Y	N	N	Y
5 Lewis	N	N	Y	Y	Y	Y	Y	N
6 *Gingrich*	N	?	Y	Y	Y	N	N	Y
7 *Darden*	N	N	Y	Y	Y	Y	Y	N
8 Rowland	N	N	Y	Y	Y	Y	Y	N
9 Deal	Y	Y	Y	Y	Y	Y	Y	N
10 Johnson	N	N	Y	Y	Y	Y	Y	N
11 McKinney	Y	N	Y	N	Y	Y	Y	N
HAWAII								
1 Abercrombie	N	N	Y	Y	Y	Y	Y	N
2 Mink	N	N	Y	Y	Y	Y	Y	N
IDAHO								
1 LaRocco	N	Y	Y	Y	Y	Y	Y	N
2 *Crapo*	N	N	Y	Y	Y	N	N	Y
ILLINOIS								
1 Rush	N	N	Y	Y	Y	Y	Y	N
2 Reynolds	N	N	Y	Y	Y	Y	Y	N
3 Lipinski	N	N	Y	Y	Y	Y	Y	Y
4 Gutierrez	N	?	?	Y	Y	Y	Y	N
5 Rostenkowski	N	N	Y	Y	Y	Y	Y	N
6 *Hyde*	N	Y	Y	Y	N	N	N	Y
7 Collins	N	N	Y	Y	Y	Y	Y	N
8 *Crane*	Y	Y	N	N	N	N	N	Y
9 Yates	N	N	Y	Y	Y	Y	Y	N
10 *Porter*	N	Y	N	Y	Y	N	N	Y
11 Sangmeister	N	N	Y	?	?	Y	Y	N
12 Costello	Y	Y	Y	Y	Y	Y	Y	N
13 *Fawell*	N	N	Y	Y	N	N	N	Y
14 *Hastert*	N	Y	N	Y	N	N	N	Y
15 *Ewing*	N	Y	Y	?	?	N	N	Y
16 *Manzullo*	N	N	Y	Y	N	N	N	Y
17 Evans	N	N	Y	Y	Y	Y	Y	N

ND Northern Democrats   SD Southern Democrats

	545	546	547	548	549	550	551	552
18 ***Michel***	N	?	Y	Y	Y	N	N	Y
19 Poshard	Y	Y	Y	Y	Y	Y	Y	Y
20 Durbin	Y	Y	Y	Y	Y	Y	Y	N
INDIANA								
1 Visclosky	N	N	Y	Y	Y	Y	Y	N
2 Sharp	N	Y	N	Y	Y	Y	Y	N
3 Roemer	N	Y	Y	Y	Y	Y	Y	Y
4 Long	N	Y	Y	Y	Y	Y	Y	N
5 ***Buyer***	N	Y	Y	Y	Y	N	N	Y
6 ***Burton***	N	Y	N	Y	N	N	N	Y
7 ***Myers***	N	Y	Y	Y	Y	Y	N	Y
8 McCloskey	Y	Y	Y	Y	Y	Y	Y	N
9 Hamilton	N	Y	N	Y	Y	Y	Y	N
10 Jacobs	Y	Y	N	Y	Y	N	N	N
IOWA								
1 ***Leach***	Y	Y	N	Y	Y	Y	N	Y
2 ***Nussle***	Y	Y	N	Y	N	N	N	Y
3 ***Lightfoot***	Y	Y	N	Y	Y	N	N	Y
4 Smith	N	Y	N	Y	Y	Y	Y	N
5 ***Grandy***	Y	Y	N	Y	Y	N	N	Y
KANSAS								
1 ***Roberts***	N	Y	N	Y	N	N	N	Y
2 Slattery	N	Y	Y	?	?	?	Y	Y
3 ***Meyers***	N	Y	Y	Y	Y	N	N	Y
4 Glickman	Y	Y	Y	Y	Y	Y	Y	N
KENTUCKY								
1 Barlow	Y	N	Y	Y	Y	Y	?	N
2 Natcher	N	N	Y	Y	Y	Y	Y	N
3 Mazzoli	Y	N	Y	Y	Y	Y	Y	N
4 ***Bunning***	N	N	Y	Y	Y	N	N	Y
5 ***Rogers***	N	N	Y	Y	Y	N	N	Y
6 Baesler	?	?	?	Y	Y	Y	Y	N
LOUISIANA								
1 ***Livingston***	N	N	Y	Y	Y	N	N	Y
2 Jefferson	N	N	Y	Y	Y	Y	Y	N
3 Tauzin	N	N	Y	Y	Y	Y	Y	Y
4 Fields	Y	N	Y	Y	Y	Y	Y	N
5 ***McCrery***	N	N	Y	Y	N	N	N	Y
6 ***Baker***	N	N	Y	Y	Y	N	N	Y
7 Hayes	Y	N	Y	Y	Y	?	Y	Y
MAINE								
1 Andrews	N	N	Y	Y	Y	Y	Y	N
2 ***Snowe***	Y	N	Y	Y	Y	N	N	Y
MARYLAND								
1 ***Gilchrest***	N	N	Y	Y	Y	N	N	Y
2 ***Bentley***	N	N	Y	Y	Y	N	N	N
3 Cardin	N	N	Y	Y	Y	Y	Y	N
4 Wynn	N	N	Y	Y	Y	Y	Y	N
5 Hoyer	N	N	Y	Y	Y	Y	Y	N
6 ***Bartlett***	N	N	Y	Y	N	N	N	Y
7 Mfume	N	N	Y	Y	Y	Y	Y	N
8 ***Morella***	—	—	+	Y	Y	N	Y	N
MASSACHUSETTS								
1 Olver	N	N	Y	Y	Y	?	Y	N
2 Neal	N	N	Y	Y	Y	Y	Y	N
3 ***Blute***	N	N	Y	+	+	N	N	Y
4 Frank	N	N	Y	?	?	Y	Y	N
5 Meehan	N	N	Y	Y	Y	Y	Y	Y
6 ***Torkildsen***	N	N	Y	Y	Y	N	N	Y
7 Markey	N	N	Y	Y	Y	Y	Y	N
8 Kennedy	N	N	Y	Y	Y	Y	Y	N
9 Moakley	N	N	Y	?	?	?	?	?
10 Studds	N	N	Y	Y	Y	Y	Y	N
MICHIGAN								
1 Stupak	Y	N	Y	Y	Y	Y	Y	N
2 ***Hoekstra***	N	Y	N	Y	Y	N	N	Y
3 Vacancy								
4 ***Camp***	N	N	Y	?	?	N	N	Y
5 Barcia	N	N	Y	Y	Y	Y	Y	Y
6 ***Upton***	N	Y	N	Y	Y	N	N	Y
7 ***Smith***	N	Y	N	Y	Y	N	N	Y
8 Carr	N	Y	Y	Y	Y	Y	Y	N
9 Kildee	Y	N	Y	Y	Y	Y	Y	N
10 Bonior	?	N	Y	Y	Y	Y	Y	N
11 ***Knollenberg***	N	Y	N	Y	Y	N	N	Y
12 Levin	N	N	Y	Y	Y	Y	Y	N
13 Ford	Y	N	Y	Y	Y	Y	Y	N
14 Conyers	N	N	Y	Y	Y	Y	Y	N
15 Collins	N	N	Y	Y	Y	Y	Y	N
16 Dingell	Y	N	Y	Y	Y	Y	Y	N
MINNESOTA								
1 Penny	Y	Y	N	Y	N	Y	N	Y
2 Minge	N	Y	N	Y	Y	Y	Y	Y
3 ***Ramstad***	N	Y	N	Y	N	N	N	Y
4 Vento	N	N	Y	Y	Y	Y	Y	N

	545	546	547	548	549	550	551	552
5 Sabo	N	N	Y	Y	Y	Y	Y	N
6 ***Grams***	N	Y	N	Y	N	N	N	Y
7 Peterson	N	Y	Y	Y	Y	Y	Y	Y
8 Oberstar	N	N	Y	Y	Y	Y	Y	N
MISSISSIPPI								
1 Whitten	N	N	Y	Y	Y	?	Y	N
2 Thompson	N	N	Y	Y	Y	Y	Y	N
3 Montgomery	Y	Y	Y	Y	Y	Y	Y	N
4 Parker	Y	Y	Y	Y	Y	Y	Y	Y
5 Taylor	Y	N	N	Y	N	N	N	Y
MISSOURI								
1 Clay	N	N	Y	?	?	N	Y	N
2 ***Talent***	N	N	Y	Y	Y	N	N	Y
3 Gephardt	N	N	?	Y	Y	Y	?	N
4 Skelton	N	Y	Y	Y	Y	Y	Y	Y
5 Wheat	N	N	Y	Y	Y	Y	Y	N
6 Danner	N	Y	Y	Y	Y	Y	Y	N
7 ***Hancock***	N	Y	N	Y	N	N	N	Y
8 ***Emerson***	N	Y	Y	Y	Y	N	N	Y
9 Volkmer	N	N	Y	Y	Y	Y	Y	N
MONTANA								
AL Williams	Y	Y	Y	Y	Y	Y	Y	N
NEBRASKA								
1 ***Bereuter***	N	Y	N	Y	Y	N	N	Y
2 Hoagland	Y	Y	N	Y	Y	Y	Y	Y
3 ***Barrett***	N	Y	N	Y	Y	N	N	Y
NEVADA								
1 Bilbray	N	N	Y	Y	Y	Y	Y	Y
2 ***Vucanovich***	N	N	Y	Y	Y	N	N	Y
NEW HAMPSHIRE								
1 ***Zeliff***	N	Y	Y	Y	N	N	N	Y
2 Swett	N	N	Y	Y	Y	Y	Y	N
NEW JERSEY								
1 Andrews	Y	N	Y	Y	Y	Y	Y	N
2 Hughes	N	N	Y	Y	Y	Y	Y	N
3 ***Saxton***	N	N	Y	Y	Y	N	N	Y
4 ***Smith***	N	N	Y	Y	Y	Y	N	Y
5 ***Roukema***	N	N	Y	Y	Y	N	N	Y
6 Pallone	N	N	Y	Y	Y	Y	Y	N
7 ***Franks***	N	N	Y	Y	Y	N	N	Y
8 Klein	N	N	Y	Y	Y	Y	Y	N
9 Torricelli	N	N	Y	Y	Y	Y	Y	N
10 Payne	N	N	Y	Y	Y	Y	Y	N
11 ***Gallo***	N	N	Y	Y	Y	N	N	Y
12 ***Zimmer***	N	Y	N	N	Y	N	N	Y
13 Menendez	N	N	Y	Y	Y	Y	Y	N
NEW MEXICO								
1 ***Schiff***	N	N	Y	Y	Y	N	N	Y
2 ***Skeen***	N	Y	Y	Y	Y	N	N	Y
3 Richardson	N	N	Y	Y	Y	Y	Y	N
NEW YORK								
1 Hochbrueckner	N	N	Y	Y	Y	Y	Y	N
2 ***Lazio***	N	N	Y	Y	Y	N	N	Y
3 ***King***	N	N	Y	Y	N	N	N	Y
4 ***Levy***	N	N	Y	Y	Y	N	N	Y
5 Ackerman	N	N	Y	Y	Y	Y	Y	N
6 Flake	?	?	?	?	Y	Y	Y	N
7 Manton	N	N	Y	Y	Y	Y	Y	N
8 Nadler	N	N	Y	Y	Y	Y	Y	N
9 Schumer	N	N	Y	Y	Y	Y	Y	N
10 Towns	N	N	?	Y	Y	Y	Y	N
11 Owens	N	N	Y	N	Y	Y	Y	N
12 Velazquez	N	N	Y	Y	Y	Y	Y	N
13 ***Molinari***	N	N	Y	Y	Y	N	N	Y
14 Maloney	N	N	Y	Y	Y	Y	Y	N
15 Rangel	N	N	Y	Y	Y	?	Y	N
16 Serrano	N	N	Y	Y	Y	Y	Y	N
17 Engel	N	N	Y	Y	Y	?	Y	N
18 Lowey	N	N	Y	Y	Y	Y	Y	N
19 ***Fish***	N	N	Y	Y	Y	Y	Y	Y
20 ***Gilman***	N	N	Y	Y	Y	Y	Y	Y
21 McNulty	Y	N	Y	Y	Y	Y	Y	N
22 ***Solomon***	N	N	Y	Y	N	N	N	Y
23 ***Boehlert***	N	N	Y	Y	Y	N	N	Y
24 ***McHugh***	?	?	?	Y	N	N	N	Y
25 ***Walsh***	N	N	Y	Y	Y	N	N	Y
26 Hinchey	N	N	Y	?	Y	Y	Y	N
27 ***Paxon***	N	Y	N	Y	N	N	N	Y
28 Slaughter	Y	N	Y	Y	Y	Y	Y	N
29 LaFalce	N	N	Y	Y	Y	Y	Y	N
30 ***Quinn***	N	N	Y	Y	Y	N	N	Y
31 ***Houghton***	N	Y	Y	Y	Y	Y	Y	Y
NORTH CAROLINA								
1 Clayton	N	N	Y	Y	Y	Y	Y	N
2 Valentine	Y	N	Y	Y	Y	Y	Y	Y

	545	546	547	548	549	550	551	552
3 Lancaster	Y	N	Y	Y	Y	Y	Y	Y
4 Price	N	N	Y	Y	Y	Y	Y	N
5 Neal	N	N	Y	Y	Y	Y	Y	N
6 ***Coble***	N	N	Y	Y	N	N	N	Y
7 Rose	N	N	Y	Y	Y	?	?	?
8 Hefner	Y	N	Y	Y	Y	Y	Y	Y
9 ***McMillan***	N	N	Y	Y	Y	N	N	Y
10 ***Ballenger***	N	Y	Y	Y	N	N	N	Y
11 ***Taylor***	N	N	Y	Y	Y	N	N	Y
12 Watt	N	N	Y	Y	Y	Y	Y	N
NORTH DAKOTA								
AL Pomeroy	N	N	Y	Y	Y	Y	Y	Y
OHIO								
1 Mann	N	N	Y	Y	Y	Y	Y	N
2 ***Portman***	N	Y	Y	Y	Y	N	N	Y
3 Hall	N	N	Y	Y	Y	Y	Y	N
4 ***Oxley***	N	Y	N	Y	?	N	N	Y
5 ***Gillmor***	N	N	Y	Y	Y	Y	N	Y
6 Strickland	N	N	Y	Y	Y	Y	Y	Y
7 ***Hobson***	N	N	Y	Y	Y	N	N	Y
8 ***Boehner***	N	Y	Y	Y	N	N	N	Y
9 Kaptur	N	?	?	Y	Y	Y	?	Y
10 ***Hoke***	N	Y	N	Y	N	N	N	Y
11 Stokes	N	N	Y	?	?	Y	Y	N
12 ***Kasich***	Y	Y	Y	Y	N	Y	N	Y
13 Brown	N	N	Y	?	?	Y	Y	N
14 Sawyer	N	N	Y	Y	Y	Y	Y	N
15 ***Pryce***	N	N	Y	Y	Y	N	N	Y
16 ***Regula***	N	N	Y	Y	Y	N	N	Y
17 Traficant	Y	N	Y	Y	Y	Y	Y	N
18 Applegate	N	N	Y	Y	Y	Y	Y	N
19 Fingerhut	N	N	Y	Y	Y	Y	Y	Y
OKLAHOMA								
1 ***Inhofe***	N	N	Y	Y	Y	N	N	Y
2 Synar	N	N	Y	Y	Y	Y	Y	N
3 Brewster	N	N	Y	Y	Y	Y	Y	N
4 McCurdy	N	?	?	Y	Y	?	Y	N
5 ***Istook***	N	Y	Y	Y	Y	N	N	Y
6 English	N	Y	Y	Y	Y	Y	Y	N
OREGON								
1 Furse	N	N	Y	Y	Y	Y	Y	N
2 ***Smith***	N	Y	Y	?	?	N	N	Y
3 Wyden	N	N	?	Y	Y	Y	Y	N
4 DeFazio	Y	N	Y	?	?	Y	Y	N
5 Kopetski	?	N	Y	Y	Y	Y	Y	N
PENNSYLVANIA								
1 Foglietta	Y	N	Y	Y	Y	Y	Y	N
2 Blackwell	N	N	Y	Y	Y	?	Y	N
3 Borski	N	N	Y	Y	Y	Y	Y	N
4 Klink	N	N	Y	Y	Y	Y	Y	N
5 ***Clinger***	N	N	Y	Y	Y	Y	N	Y
6 Holden	Y	N	Y	Y	Y	Y	Y	N
7 ***Weldon***	N	N	Y	Y	Y	N	N	Y
8 ***Greenwood***	N	N	Y	Y	Y	Y	N	Y
9 ***Shuster***	N	Y	N	Y	Y	N	N	Y
10 ***McDade***	N	N	Y	Y	Y	N	N	Y
11 Kanjorski	Y	N	Y	Y	Y	Y	Y	N
12 Murtha	N	N	Y	?	?	Y	Y	N
13 Margolies-Mezv.	Y	N	Y	Y	Y	Y	Y	N
14 Coyne	N	N	Y	Y	Y	Y	Y	N
15 McHale	Y	Y	Y	Y	Y	Y	Y	N
16 ***Walker***	N	Y	N	Y	N	N	N	Y
17 ***Gekas***	N	N	Y	Y	Y	N	N	Y
18 ***Santorum***	N	N	Y	Y	Y	Y	N	Y
19 ***Goodling***	N	Y	N	N	Y	N	N	Y
20 Murphy	N	N	Y	Y	Y	N	Y	N
21 ***Ridge***	N	N	Y	Y	Y	N	N	Y
RHODE ISLAND								
1 ***Machtley***	?	N	Y	Y	Y	N	N	Y
2 Reed	Y	N	Y	Y	Y	Y	Y	N
SOUTH CAROLINA								
1 ***Ravenel***	N	N	Y	Y	Y	N	N	Y
2 ***Spence***	N	N	Y	Y	Y	N	N	Y
3 Derrick	N	N	Y	Y	Y	Y	Y	Y
4 ***Inglis***	N	N	Y	Y	N	Y	N	Y
5 Spratt	N	N	Y	?	?	Y	Y	Y
6 Clyburn	N	N	Y	Y	Y	?	Y	N
SOUTH DAKOTA								
AL Johnson	Y	Y	Y	?	?	Y	Y	N
TENNESSEE								
1 ***Quillen***	N	N	Y	Y	Y	N	N	Y
2 ***Duncan***	N	N	Y	Y	N	N	N	Y
3 Lloyd	N	N	Y	Y	Y	Y	Y	N
4 Cooper	N	Y	Y	Y	Y	Y	N	Y
5 Clement	N	N	Y	Y	Y	Y	Y	N

	545	546	547	548	549	550	551	552
6 Gordon	N	N	Y	Y	Y	Y	?	N
7 ***Sundquist***	N	N	Y	?	?	?	N	Y
8 Tanner	Y	N	Y	Y	Y	Y	Y	Y
9 Ford	?	N	Y	Y	Y	Y	Y	N
TEXAS								
1 Chapman	N	?	Y	?	Y	?	Y	Y
2 Wilson	N	N	Y	Y	Y	Y	Y	N
3 ***Johnson, Sam***	N	Y	N	Y	N	?	N	Y
4 Hall	Y	N	N	Y	N	Y	Y	Y
5 Bryant	N	N	Y	Y	Y	Y	Y	N
6 ***Barton***	N	Y	N	?	?	N	N	?
7 ***Archer***	N	Y	N	Y	N	Y	N	Y
8 ***Fields***	N	N	Y	Y	Y	N	?	Y
9 Brooks	N	N	Y	Y	Y	Y	Y	N
10 Pickle	N	N	Y	?	?	Y	Y	Y
11 Edwards	N	N	Y	Y	Y	Y	Y	Y
12 Geren	Y	N	Y	Y	Y	Y	Y	Y
13 Sarpalius	N	N	Y	Y	Y	Y	Y	Y
14 Laughlin	N	?	?	Y	Y	Y	Y	Y
15 de la Garza	N	Y	Y	Y	Y	Y	Y	N
16 Coleman	N	N	Y	Y	Y	Y	Y	N
17 Stenholm	Y	Y	N	Y	N	Y	Y	Y
18 Washington	N	N	Y	Y	Y	Y	Y	N
19 ***Combest***	N	Y	N	Y	Y	Y	N	Y
20 Gonzalez	N	N	Y	Y	Y	Y	Y	N
21 ***Smith***	N	Y	N	?	?	N	N	Y
22 ***DeLay***	N	Y	N	Y	N	N	N	Y
23 ***Bonilla***	N	Y	N	Y	Y	N	N	Y
24 Frost	N	N	Y	Y	Y	Y	Y	N
25 Andrews	N	N	Y	Y	Y	Y	Y	Y
26 ***Armey***	N	Y	N	Y	N	N	N	Y
27 Ortiz	N	N	Y	Y	Y	?	Y	N
28 Tejeda	N	N	Y	Y	Y	Y	Y	N
29 Green	N	N	Y	Y	Y	Y	Y	N
30 Johnson, E.B.	N	N	Y	Y	Y	Y	Y	N
UTAH								
1 ***Hansen***	N	Y	N	Y	Y	N	N	Y
2 Shepherd	Y	N	Y	Y	?	Y	Y	Y
3 Orton	Y	Y	Y	Y	Y	?	Y	Y
VERMONT								
AL *Sanders*	N	N	Y	Y	Y	Y	Y	N
VIRGINIA								
1 ***Bateman***	N	N	Y	Y	Y	Y	N	Y
2 Pickett	N	N	Y	?	?	Y	Y	N
3 Scott	N	N	Y	Y	Y	Y	Y	N
4 Sisisky	N	N	Y	Y	Y	Y	Y	Y
5 Payne	Y	Y	Y	Y	Y	Y	Y	Y
6 ***Goodlatte***	N	Y	N	Y	Y	N	N	Y
7 ***Bliley***	N	N	Y	Y	Y	N	N	Y
8 Moran	N	N	Y	Y	Y	Y	Y	N
9 Boucher	Y	Y	Y	Y	Y	Y	Y	N
10 ***Wolf***	N	N	Y	Y	Y	N	N	Y
11 Byrne	Y	N	Y	Y	Y	Y	Y	N
WASHINGTON								
1 Cantwell	N	N	Y	Y	Y	Y	Y	Y
2 Swift	N	N	Y	Y	Y	Y	Y	N
3 Unsoeld	N	N	Y	Y	Y	Y	Y	N
4 Inslee	N	N	Y	Y	Y	Y	Y	N
5 Foley								
6 Dicks	N	N	Y	Y	?	Y	Y	N
7 McDermott	N	N	Y	Y	Y	Y	Y	N
8 ***Dunn***	N	N	Y	Y	Y	N	N	Y
9 Kreidler	N	N	Y	Y	Y	Y	Y	N
WEST VIRGINIA								
1 Mollohan	N	N	Y	?	?	Y	Y	N
2 Wise	N	N	Y	?	?	Y	Y	N
3 Rahall	N	N	Y	Y	Y	Y	Y	N
WISCONSIN								
1 Barca	N	N	Y	Y	Y	Y	Y	Y
2 ***Klug***	N	Y	N	Y	N	N	N	Y
3 ***Gunderson***	N	Y	Y	Y	Y	N	N	Y
4 Kleczka	N	N	Y	Y	Y	Y	Y	N
5 Barrett	N	N	Y	Y	Y	Y	Y	Y
6 ***Petri***	N	Y	N	?	?	?	?	?
7 Obey	N	N	Y	Y	Y	Y	Y	N
8 ***Roth***	Y	Y	N	Y	Y	?	N	Y
9 ***Sensenbrenner***	Y	Y	N	Y	N	N	N	Y
WYOMING								
AL ***Thomas***	N	Y	N	Y	Y	N	N	Y
DELEGATES								
de Lugo, V.I.	N	N	D	D	D	D	D	D
Faleomavaega, Am.S.	N	?	D	D	D	D	D	D
Norton, D.C.	N	N	D	D	D	D	D	D
Romero-B., P.R.	Y	Y	D	D	D	D	D	D
Underwood, Guam	N	N	D	D	D	D	D	D

Southern states - Ala., Ark., Fla., Ga., Ky., La., Miss., N.C., Okla., S.C., Tenn., Texas, Va.
Omitted votes are quorum calls, which CQ does not include in its vote charts.

553. HR 1036. Employment Retirement Income Security Amendments/Training Programs. Goodling, R-Pa., amendment to maintain ERISA's pre-emption for state laws governing apprenticeships and training programs that are anti-competitive in nature. Rejected in the Committee of the Whole 174-255: R 154-19; D 20-235 (ND 0-173, SD 20-62); I 0-1, Nov. 9, 1993.

554. HR 1036. Employment Retirement Income Security Amendments/Passage. Passage of the bill to amend the Employment Retirement Income Security Act of 1974 (ERISA) to allow state laws to pre-empt ERISA in certain cases, including state statutes requiring employers to pay workers the prevailing wage when working on state contracts. Passed 276-150: R 37-134; D 238-16 (ND 170-0, SD 68-16); I 1-0, Nov. 9, 1993.

555. H Con Res 170. Somalia Troop Removal/Jan. 31 Deadline. Gilman, R-N.Y., amendment to change the deadline for the removal of U.S. troops in Somalia from March 31, 1994, to Jan. 31, 1994. Adopted 224-203: R 168-3; D 55-200 (ND 37-134, SD 18-66); I 1-0, Nov. 9, 1993. A "nay" was a vote in support of the president's position.

556. H Con Res 170. Somalia Troop Removal/March 31 Deadline. Hamilton, D-Ind., substitute amendment to change the deadline for the removal of U.S. troops in Somalia back to March 31, 1994, from the Jan. 31, 1994, date substituted by the Gilman, R-N.Y., amendment. Adopted 226-201: R 2-170; D 224-30 (ND 150-21, SD 74-9); I 0-1, Nov. 9, 1993. A "yea" was a vote in support of the president's position.

557. HR 1025. Brady Bill/Rule. Adoption of the rule (H Res 302) to provide for House floor consideration of the bill to require a five-business-day waiting period before an individual could purchase a handgun to allow local officials to conduct a background check. Adopted 238-182: R 13-156; D 224-26 (ND 149-17, SD 75-9); I 1-0, Nov. 10, 1993.

558. HR 1025. Brady Bill/Reason for Denial. Ramstad, R-Minn., amendment to require local officials to provide within 20 days the reasons for denying an individual a handgun. Adopted in the Committee of the Whole 431-2: R 174-0; D 256-2 (ND 172-1, SD 84-1); I 1-0, Nov. 10, 1993.

559. HR 1025. Brady Bill/Five-Year "Sunset." Gekas, R-Pa., amendment to sunset the five-day waiting period five years after enactment. Adopted in the Committee of the Whole 236-198: R 139-36; D 96-162 (ND 44-129, SD 52-33); I 1-0, Nov. 10, 1993.

560. HR 1025. Brady Bill/State Pre-emption. McCollum, R-Fla., amendment to pre-empt any state or local law requiring waiting periods for the purchase of handguns once a national instant check system is instituted. Rejected in the Committee of the Whole 175-257: R 110-65; D 65-191 (ND 29-142, SD 36-49); I 0-1, Nov. 10, 1993.

KEY

Y   Voted for (yea).
Paired for.
+   Announced for.
N   Voted against (nay).
X   Paired against.
—   Announced against.
P   Voted "present."
C   Voted "present" to avoid possible conflict of interest.
?   Did not vote or otherwise make a position known.
D   Delegates ineligible to vote.

Democrats *Republicans*
Independent

	553	554	555	556	557	558	559	560
ALABAMA								
1 *Callahan*	Y	N	Y	N	N	Y	Y	Y
2 *Everett*	Y	N	Y	N	N	Y	Y	Y
3 Browder	N	N	N	Y	Y	Y	Y	Y
4 Bevill	N	Y	N	Y	Y	Y	Y	Y
5 Cramer	Y	N	N	Y	Y	Y	Y	Y
6 *Bachus*	Y	N	Y	N	N	Y	Y	Y
7 Hilliard	N	Y	N	Y	N	Y	Y	Y
ALASKA								
AL *Young*	N	Y	Y	N	N	Y	Y	Y
ARIZONA								
1 Coppersmith	N	Y	N	Y	Y	Y	N	N
2 Pastor	N	Y	N	Y	Y	Y	N	N
3 *Stump*	Y	N	Y	N	N	Y	Y	Y
4 *Kyl*	Y	N	Y	N	N	Y	Y	Y
5 *Kolbe*	Y	N	Y	N	N	Y	Y	N
6 English	N	Y	N	Y	Y	Y	N	N
ARKANSAS								
1 Lambert	N	Y	Y	Y	Y	Y	Y	N
2 Thornton	N	Y	N	Y	Y	Y	Y	Y
3 *Hutchinson*	Y	N	Y	N	N	Y	Y	Y
4 *Dickey*	Y	N	N	Y	N	Y	Y	Y
CALIFORNIA								
1 Hamburg	N	Y	N	Y	Y	Y	N	N
2 *Herger*	Y	N	Y	N	N	Y	Y	Y
3 Fazio	N	Y	N	Y	Y	Y	N	N
4 *Doolittle*	Y	N	Y	N	N	Y	Y	Y
5 Matsui	N	Y	N	Y	Y	Y	N	N
6 Woolsey	N	Y	N	Y	Y	Y	N	N
7 Miller	N	Y	N	Y	Y	Y	N	N
8 Pelosi	N	Y	N	Y	Y	Y	N	N
9 Dellums	N	Y	N	Y	?	Y	?	N
10 *Baker*	Y	N	Y	N	N	Y	Y	Y
11 *Pombo*	Y	N	Y	N	N	Y	Y	Y
12 Lantos	N	Y	N	Y	Y	Y	N	N
13 Stark	N	Y	N	Y	Y	Y	N	N
14 Eshoo	N	Y	Y	Y	Y	Y	N	N
15 Mineta	N	Y	N	Y	Y	Y	N	N
16 Edwards	N	Y	N	Y	Y	Y	N	N
17 Farr	N	Y	N	Y	Y	Y	N	N
18 Condit	N	Y	Y	Y	N	Y	N	N
19 Lehman	N	Y	N	Y	Y	Y	N	N
20 Dooley	N	Y	N	Y	Y	Y	N	N
21 *Thomas*	Y	N	Y	N	N	Y	N	Y
22 *Huffington*	Y	N	Y	N	N	Y	Y	N
23 *Gallegly*	Y	N	Y	N	N	Y	Y	Y
24 Beilenson	N	Y	N	Y	Y	Y	N	N
25 *McKeon*	Y	N	Y	N	N	Y	N	Y
26 Berman	N	Y	N	Y	Y	Y	N	N
27 *Moorhead*	Y	N	Y	N	N	Y	Y	Y
28 *Dreier*	Y	N	Y	N	N	Y	Y	Y
29 Waxman	N	Y	N	Y	Y	Y	N	N
30 Becerra	N	Y	N	Y	Y	Y	N	N
31 Martinez	N	Y	N	Y	N	Y	Y	Y
32 Dixon	N	Y	N	Y	Y	Y	N	N
33 Roybal-Allard	N	Y	N	Y	Y	Y	N	N
34 Torres	N	Y	N	Y	Y	Y	N	N
35 Waters	N	Y	N	Y	Y	Y	N	—
36 Harman	N	Y	N	Y	Y	Y	N	N
37 Tucker	N	Y	N	Y	Y	Y	N	N
38 *Horn*	Y	Y	Y	N	N	Y	N	N
39 *Royce*	Y	N	Y	N	N	Y	Y	N
40 *Lewis*	Y	N	Y	N	N	Y	Y	Y
41 *Kim*	Y	N	Y	N	N	Y	Y	Y

	553	554	555	556	557	558	559	560
42 Brown	N	Y	N	Y	Y	?	N	N
43 *Calvert*	Y	N	Y	N	N	Y	Y	Y
44 *McCandless*	Y	N	Y	N	N	Y	Y	Y
45 *Rohrabacher*	Y	N	Y	N	N	Y	Y	N
46 *Dornan*	Y	N	Y	N	N	Y	Y	Y
47 *Cox*	Y	N	Y	N	N	Y	Y	Y
48 *Packard*	Y	N	Y	N	N	Y	Y	Y
49 Schenk	N	Y	N	Y	Y	Y	N	N
50 Filner	N	Y	Y	Y	Y	Y	N	N
51 *Cunningham*	Y	N	Y	N	N	Y	Y	Y
52 *Hunter*	Y	N	Y	?	?	Y	Y	Y
COLORADO								
1 Schroeder	N	Y	Y	?	Y	Y	N	N
2 Skaggs	N	Y	N	Y	Y	Y	N	N
3 *McInnis*	Y	N	Y	N	N	Y	Y	Y
4 *Allard*	Y	N	Y	N	N	Y	Y	Y
5 *Hefley*	Y	N	Y	N	N	Y	Y	N
6 *Schaefer*	Y	N	Y	N	N	Y	Y	Y
CONNECTICUT								
1 Kennelly	N	Y	N	Y	Y	Y	N	N
2 Gejdenson	N	Y	N	Y	Y	Y	N	N
3 DeLauro	N	Y	N	Y	Y	Y	N	N
4 *Shays*	N	Y	Y	N	Y	Y	N	N
5 *Franks*	Y	N	Y	N	N	Y	Y	Y
6 *Johnson*	Y	Y	Y	N	N	Y	N	N
DELAWARE								
AL *Castle*	Y	N	Y	N	N	Y	N	N
FLORIDA								
1 Hutto	Y	N	Y	Y	N	Y	Y	N
2 Peterson	N	Y	N	Y	Y	Y	N	N
3 Brown	N	Y	N	Y	Y	Y	N	N
4 *Fowler*	Y	N	Y	N	N	Y	Y	N
5 Thurman	Y	Y	N	Y	Y	Y	Y	Y
6 *Stearns*	Y	N	Y	N	N	Y	Y	Y
7 *Mica*	Y	N	Y	N	N	Y	Y	Y
8 *McCollum*	Y	N	Y	N	N	Y	Y	Y
9 *Bilirakis*	Y	N	Y	N	N	Y	Y	Y
10 *Young*	Y	N	Y	N	N	Y	N	N
11 Gibbons	N	Y	N	Y	Y	Y	N	N
12 *Canady*	Y	N	Y	N	N	Y	Y	Y
13 *Miller*	Y	N	Y	N	N	Y	Y	Y
14 *Goss*	Y	N	Y	N	N	Y	Y	N
15 Bacchus	N	Y	N	Y	Y	Y	N	N
16 *Lewis*	#	X	?	?	N	Y	Y	Y
17 Meek	N	Y	N	Y	Y	Y	N	N
18 *Ros-Lehtinen*	Y	Y	N	Y	N	N	N	N
19 Johnston	N	Y	N	Y	Y	Y	N	N
20 Deutsch	N	Y	N	Y	Y	Y	N	N
21 *Diaz-Balart*	Y	Y	N	N	N	N	N	N
22 *Shaw*	Y	N	Y	N	N	Y	Y	Y
23 Hastings	N	Y	N	Y	Y	Y	N	N
GEORGIA								
1 *Kingston*	Y	N	Y	N	N	Y	Y	Y
2 Bishop	N	Y	N	Y	Y	Y	Y	Y
3 *Collins*	Y	N	Y	N	N	Y	Y	Y
4 *Linder*	Y	N	Y	N	N	Y	Y	Y
5 Lewis	N	Y	N	Y	Y	Y	N	N
6 *Gingrich*	Y	N	Y	N	?	Y	Y	Y
7 Darden	N	Y	N	Y	Y	Y	Y	Y
8 Rowland	Y	Y	N	Y	Y	Y	Y	Y
9 Deal	Y	Y	Y	Y	Y	N	N	N
10 Johnson	Y	Y	N	Y	Y	Y	Y	Y
11 McKinney	N	Y	N	Y	Y	Y	N	N
HAWAII								
1 Abercrombie	N	Y	Y	Y	Y	Y	N	N
2 Mink	N	Y	Y	Y	Y	Y	N	N
IDAHO								
1 LaRocco	N	Y	N	Y	N	Y	Y	Y
2 *Crapo*	Y	N	Y	N	N	Y	Y	Y
ILLINOIS								
1 Rush	N	Y	N	Y	Y	Y	N	N
2 Reynolds	N	Y	N	Y	Y	Y	N	N
3 Lipinski	N	Y	N	Y	Y	Y	N	N
4 Gutierrez	N	Y	N	Y	Y	Y	N	N
5 Rostenkowski	N	Y	?	Y	Y	Y	N	N
6 *Hyde*	Y	N	Y	N	N	Y	Y	Y
7 Collins	N	Y	N	Y	Y	Y	N	N
8 *Crane*	Y	N	Y	N	N	Y	Y	Y
9 Yates	N	Y	N	Y	Y	Y	N	N
10 *Porter*	Y	N	Y	N	N	Y	Y	Y
11 Sangmeister	N	Y	N	Y	Y	Y	N	N
12 Costello	N	Y	N	Y	Y	Y	Y	Y
13 *Fawell*	Y	Y	Y	N	N	Y	Y	N
14 *Hastert*	Y	N	Y	N	N	Y	Y	Y
15 *Ewing*	Y	N	Y	N	N	Y	Y	Y
16 *Manzullo*	Y	N	Y	N	N	Y	Y	Y
17 Evans	N	Y	N	Y	Y	Y	N	N

ND   Northern Democrats   SD   Southern Democrats

	553	554	555	556	557	558	559	560
18 ***Michel***	Y	N	Y	N	?	Y	Y	Y
19 Poshard	N	Y	Y	N	Y	Y	Y	Y
20 Durbin	N	Y	N	Y	Y	Y	N	N
INDIANA								
1 Visclosky	N	Y	N	Y	Y	Y	N	N
2 Sharp	N	Y	N	Y	Y	Y	Y	N
3 Roemer	N	Y	N	Y	Y	Y	N	N
4 Long	N	Y	N	Y	Y	Y	Y	N
5 ***Buyer***	Y	N	Y	N	N	Y	Y	Y
6 ***Burton***	Y	N	Y	N	N	Y	Y	Y
7 ***Myers***	Y	N	Y	N	N	Y	Y	Y
8 McCloskey	N	Y	N	Y	?	Y	N	N
9 Hamilton	N	Y	N	Y	Y	Y	Y	N
10 Jacobs	N	Y	Y	N	Y	Y	N	N
IOWA								
1 ***Leach***	Y	Y	Y	N	N	Y	N	N
2 ***Nussle***	Y	N	Y	N	N	Y	Y	N
3 ***Lightfoot***	Y	N	Y	N	N	Y	Y	Y
4 Smith	N	Y	N	Y	N	Y	N	N
5 ***Grandy***	Y	N	Y	N	N	Y	N	N
KANSAS								
1 ***Roberts***	Y	N	Y	N	N	Y	Y	Y
2 Slattery	N	Y	N	Y	?	Y	N	N
3 ***Meyers***	Y	N	Y	N	Y	Y	N	N
4 Glickman	N	Y	N	Y	Y	Y	N	N
KENTUCKY								
1 Barlow	N	Y	N	Y	Y	Y	Y	Y
2 Natcher	N	Y	N	Y	Y	Y	Y	Y
3 Mazzoli	N	Y	N	Y	Y	Y	N	N
4 ***Bunning***	Y	N	Y	N	N	Y	Y	Y
5 ***Rogers***	Y	N	Y	N	N	Y	Y	Y
6 Baesler	N	Y	N	Y	Y	Y	N	N
LOUISIANA								
1 ***Livingston***	Y	N	Y	N	N	Y	Y	Y
2 Jefferson	N	Y	N	Y	Y	Y	N	N
3 Tauzin	?	N	Y	N	Y	Y	Y	Y
4 Fields	N	Y	N	Y	Y	Y	N	N
5 ***McCrery***	Y	N	Y	N	N	Y	Y	Y
6 ***Baker***	Y	N	Y	N	N	Y	Y	Y
7 Hayes	Y	Y	N	?	Y	Y	Y	Y
MAINE								
1 Andrews	N	Y	N	Y	Y	Y	N	N
2 ***Snowe***	Y	N	Y	N	N	Y	Y	Y
MARYLAND								
1 ***Gilchrest***	Y	N	Y	N	N	Y	N	N
2 ***Bentley***	Y	Y	Y	N	?	Y	N	N
3 Cardin	N	Y	N	Y	Y	Y	N	N
4 Wynn	N	Y	N	Y	Y	Y	N	N
5 Hoyer	N	Y	N	Y	Y	Y	N	N
6 ***Bartlett***	Y	N	Y	N	—	+	Y	Y
7 Mfume	N	Y	N	Y	Y	Y	N	N
8 ***Morella***	Y	Y	?	N	?	Y	N	N
MASSACHUSETTS								
1 Olver	N	Y	N	Y	Y	Y	N	N
2 Neal	N	Y	N	Y	Y	Y	N	N
3 ***Blute***	Y	Y	Y	N	N	Y	Y	N
4 Frank	N	Y	N	Y	Y	Y	N	N
5 Meehan	N	Y	Y	N	Y	Y	N	N
6 ***Torkildsen***	N	Y	Y	N	N	Y	Y	N
7 Markey	N	Y	N	Y	Y	Y	N	N
8 Kennedy	N	Y	N	Y	Y	Y	N	N
9 Moakley	X	#	X	?	?	?	?	?
10 Studds	N	Y	N	Y	Y	Y	N	N
MICHIGAN								
1 Stupak	N	Y	Y	N	N	Y	Y	Y
2 ***Hoekstra***	Y	N	Y	N	N	Y	Y	Y
3 Vacancy								
4 ***Camp***	Y	N	Y	N	N	Y	Y	Y
5 Barcia	N	Y	Y	N	Y	Y	Y	Y
6 ***Upton***	Y	N	Y	N	N	Y	N	N
7 ***Smith***	Y	X	Y	N	N	Y	N	N
8 Carr	N	Y	N	Y	Y	Y	Y	Y
9 Kildee	N	Y	Y	N	Y	Y	N	N
10 Bonior	N	Y	N	Y	Y	Y	N	N
11 ***Knollenberg***	Y	N	Y	N	N	Y	Y	Y
12 Levin	N	Y	N	Y	Y	Y	N	N
13 Ford	N	Y	N	Y	Y	Y	N	N
14 Conyers	N	Y	N	Y	Y	Y	N	N
15 Collins	N	Y	N	Y	Y	Y	N	N
16 Dingell	N	Y	N	Y	Y	Y	Y	Y
MINNESOTA								
1 Penny	N	Y	N	Y	Y	Y	N	N
2 Minge	N	Y	Y	Y	N	Y	Y	Y
3 ***Ramstad***	Y	N	Y	N	N	Y	Y	N
4 Vento	N	Y	N	Y	Y	Y	N	N
5 Sabo	N	Y	N	Y	Y	Y	N	N
6 ***Grams***	Y	N	#	N	N	Y	Y	Y
7 Peterson	N	Y	Y	N	N	Y	Y	Y
8 Oberstar	N	Y	N	Y	Y	Y	Y	Y
MISSISSIPPI								
1 Whitten	?	?	N	Y	Y	Y	Y	Y
2 Thompson	N	Y	N	Y	Y	Y	N	N
3 Montgomery	Y	N	Y	Y	Y	Y	Y	Y
4 Parker	Y	N	Y	Y	Y	Y	Y	Y
5 Taylor	Y	N	Y	N	N	Y	Y	Y
MISSOURI								
1 Clay	N	Y	N	Y	Y	Y	N	N
2 ***Talent***	Y	N	Y	N	N	Y	Y	Y
3 Gephardt	N	Y	N	Y	Y	Y	N	N
4 Skelton	N	Y	N	Y	N	Y	Y	Y
5 Wheat	N	Y	N	Y	Y	Y	N	N
6 Danner	N	Y	N	Y	N	Y	Y	Y
7 ***Hancock***	Y	N	Y	N	N	Y	Y	Y
8 ***Emerson***	Y	N	Y	N	N	Y	Y	Y
9 Volkmer	N	Y	N	Y	N	Y	Y	Y
MONTANA								
AL Williams	N	Y	N	Y	N	Y	N	Y
NEBRASKA								
1 ***Bereuter***	Y	N	Y	N	N	Y	N	N
2 Hoagland	N	Y	N	Y	Y	Y	N	N
3 ***Barrett***	Y	N	Y	N	N	Y	Y	Y
NEVADA								
1 Bilbray	N	Y	N	Y	Y	Y	Y	N
2 ***Vucanovich***	Y	N	Y	N	N	Y	Y	Y
NEW HAMPSHIRE								
1 ***Zeliff***	Y	?	Y	N	N	Y	Y	Y
2 Swett	N	Y	N	Y	Y	Y	Y	N
NEW JERSEY								
1 Andrews	N	Y	Y	N	Y	Y	N	N
2 Hughes	N	Y	N	Y	Y	Y	N	N
3 ***Saxton***	N	Y	Y	N	Y	Y	N	N
4 ***Smith***	N	Y	Y	N	Y	Y	N	N
5 ***Roukema***	Y	Y	Y	N	Y	Y	N	N
6 Pallone	N	Y	N	Y	Y	Y	N	N
7 ***Franks***	N	Y	Y	N	Y	Y	N	N
8 Klein	N	Y	N	Y	Y	Y	N	N
9 Torricelli	N	Y	N	Y	?	Y	N	N
10 Payne	N	Y	N	Y	Y	Y	N	N
11 ***Gallo***	N	Y	Y	N	Y	Y	N	N
12 ***Zimmer***	Y	Y	Y	N	N	Y	Y	N
13 Menendez	N	Y	N	Y	Y	Y	N	N
NEW MEXICO								
1 ***Schiff***	Y	N	Y	N	N	Y	Y	N
2 ***Skeen***	Y	N	Y	N	N	Y	Y	Y
3 Richardson	N	Y	N	Y	Y	Y	Y	Y
NEW YORK								
1 Hochbrueckner	N	Y	N	Y	Y	Y	N	N
2 ***Lazio***	N	Y	Y	N	N	Y	N	N
3 ***King***	N	Y	Y	N	N	Y	Y	N
4 ***Levy***	N	Y	Y	N	N	Y	Y	N
5 Ackerman	N	Y	N	Y	Y	Y	N	N
6 Flake	N	Y	N	Y	Y	Y	N	N
7 Manton	N	Y	Y	Y	Y	Y	N	N
8 Nadler	N	Y	Y	Y	Y	N	N	N
9 Schumer	N	Y	Y	Y	Y	Y	N	N
10 Towns	N	Y	N	Y	Y	Y	N	N
11 Owens	N	Y	N	Y	Y	Y	N	N
12 Velazquez	N	Y	N	Y	Y	Y	N	N
13 ***Molinari***	Y	Y	Y	N	N	Y	N	N
14 Maloney	N	Y	Y	Y	Y	Y	N	N
15 Rangel	N	Y	N	Y	?	Y	N	N
16 Serrano	N	Y	N	Y	Y	Y	N	N
17 Engel	N	Y	N	Y	Y	Y	N	N
18 Lowey	N	Y	N	Y	Y	Y	N	N
19 ***Fish***	N	Y	Y	N	Y	Y	Y	N
20 ***Gilman***	N	Y	Y	N	Y	Y	N	N
21 McNulty	N	Y	Y	N	Y	Y	Y	Y
22 ***Solomon***	N	Y	Y	N	N	Y	Y	Y
23 ***Boehlert***	N	Y	Y	N	N	Y	N	N
24 ***McHugh***	N	Y	Y	N	N	Y	Y	Y
25 ***Walsh***	Y	N	Y	N	N	Y	Y	N
26 Hinchey	N	Y	N	Y	Y	Y	N	N
27 ***Paxon***	Y	N	Y	N	N	Y	Y	Y
28 Slaughter	N	Y	N	Y	Y	Y	N	N
29 LaFalce	N	Y	N	Y	Y	Y	N	N
30 ***Quinn***	Y	Y	Y	N	N	Y	N	Y
31 ***Houghton***	Y	Y	N	Y	N	Y	Y	N
NORTH CAROLINA								
1 Clayton	N	Y	N	Y	Y	Y	N	N
2 Valentine	Y	N	N	Y	Y	Y	Y	N
3 Lancaster	N	Y	N	Y	Y	Y	Y	Y
4 Price	N	Y	N	Y	Y	Y	N	N
5 Neal	Y	Y	N	Y	Y	Y	Y	Y
6 ***Coble***	Y	N	Y	N	N	Y	Y	Y
7 Rose	?	Y	N	Y	Y	Y	N	N
8 Hefner	N	Y	N	Y	Y	Y	Y	Y
9 ***McMillan***	Y	N	Y	N	N	Y	N	N
10 ***Ballenger***	Y	N	Y	N	N	Y	Y	Y
11 ***Taylor***	Y	N	Y	N	N	Y	Y	N
12 Watt	N	Y	N	Y	Y	Y	N	N
NORTH DAKOTA								
AL Pomeroy	N	Y	N	Y	Y	Y	Y	N
OHIO								
1 Mann	N	#	N	Y	Y	Y	N	N
2 ***Portman***	Y	N	Y	N	N	Y	Y	N
3 Hall	N	Y	N	Y	Y	Y	N	N
4 ***Oxley***	Y	N	Y	N	Y	Y	N	N
5 ***Gillmor***	Y	N	Y	N	N	Y	Y	Y
6 Strickland	N	Y	N	Y	N	Y	Y	Y
7 ***Hobson***	Y	N	Y	N	N	Y	Y	Y
8 ***Boehner***	Y	N	Y	N	N	Y	Y	Y
9 Kaptur	N	Y	Y	Y	Y	Y	N	N
10 ***Hoke***	Y	N	Y	N	N	Y	Y	Y
11 Stokes	N	Y	N	Y	Y	Y	N	N
12 ***Kasich***	Y	N	Y	N	N	Y	Y	Y
13 Brown	N	Y	Y	N	Y	Y	N	N
14 Sawyer	N	Y	N	Y	Y	Y	N	N
15 ***Pryce***	Y	N	Y	N	N	Y	Y	Y
16 ***Regula***	Y	Y	Y	N	N	Y	Y	N
17 Traficant	N	Y	Y	N	Y	Y	Y	N
18 Applegate	N	Y	Y	N	Y	Y	Y	N
19 Fingerhut	N	Y	Y	N	Y	Y	N	N
OKLAHOMA								
1 ***Inhofe***	Y	N	Y	N	N	Y	Y	Y
2 Synar	N	Y	N	Y	Y	Y	N	N
3 Brewster	N	Y	Y	Y	Y	Y	Y	Y
4 McCurdy	N	Y	N	Y	Y	Y	Y	N
5 ***Istook***	Y	N	Y	N	N	Y	Y	Y
6 English	N	Y	Y	Y	Y	Y	Y	Y
OREGON								
1 Furse	N	Y	N	Y	Y	Y	N	N
2 ***Smith***	Y	N	Y	N	N	Y	Y	Y
3 Wyden	N	Y	Y	N	Y	Y	N	N
4 DeFazio	N	Y	Y	N	Y	Y	Y	N
5 Kopetski	N	Y	N	Y	Y	Y	Y	Y
PENNSYLVANIA								
1 Foglietta	N	Y	N	Y	Y	Y	N	N
2 Blackwell	N	Y	N	Y	Y	Y	N	N
3 Borski	N	Y	N	Y	Y	Y	N	N
4 Klink	N	Y	Y	Y	Y	Y	Y	N
5 ***Clinger***	Y	N	Y	N	N	Y	N	N
6 Holden	N	Y	N	Y	N	Y	Y	Y
7 ***Weldon***	N	Y	Y	N	N	Y	Y	Y
8 ***Greenwood***	Y	Y	Y	N	N	Y	Y	N
9 ***Shuster***	Y	N	Y	N	N	Y	Y	Y
10 ***McDade***	Y	Y	Y	N	N	Y	N	N
11 Kanjorski	N	Y	N	Y	Y	Y	Y	Y
12 Murtha	N	Y	N	Y	Y	Y	Y	Y
13 Margolies-Mezv.	N	Y	N	Y	Y	Y	N	N
14 Coyne	N	Y	N	Y	Y	Y	N	N
15 McHale	N	Y	Y	N	Y	Y	N	N
16 ***Walker***	Y	N	Y	N	N	Y	Y	Y
17 ***Gekas***	Y	N	Y	N	N	Y	Y	Y
18 ***Santorum***	N	Y	Y	N	N	Y	Y	Y
19 ***Goodling***	Y	N	Y	N	N	Y	Y	Y
20 Murphy	N	Y	Y	Y	Y	Y	Y	?
21 ***Ridge***	N	Y	Y	N	N	Y	Y	Y
RHODE ISLAND								
1 ***Machtley***	Y	Y	Y	N	N	Y	Y	N
2 Reed	N	Y	N	Y	Y	Y	N	N
SOUTH CAROLINA								
1 ***Ravenel***	Y	N	Y	N	N	Y	Y	Y
2 ***Spence***	Y	N	Y	N	N	Y	Y	Y
3 Derrick	Y	Y	Y	N	Y	Y	N	N
4 ***Inglis***	Y	N	Y	N	N	Y	Y	Y
5 Spratt	N	Y	N	Y	Y	Y	Y	N
6 Clyburn	N	Y	N	Y	Y	Y	Y	Y
SOUTH DAKOTA								
AL Johnson	N	Y	Y	N	Y	Y	Y	N
TENNESSEE								
1 ***Quillen***	Y	N	Y	N	N	Y	Y	Y
2 ***Duncan***	Y	N	Y	N	N	Y	Y	N
3 Lloyd	N	Y	N	Y	Y	Y	Y	N
4 Cooper	N	Y	N	Y	Y	Y	Y	N
5 Clement	N	Y	N	Y	Y	Y	N	N
6 Gordon	N	Y	N	Y	Y	Y	Y	N
7 ***Sundquist***	Y	N	Y	N	N	Y	Y	Y
8 Tanner	Y	N	N	Y	N	Y	Y	Y
9 Ford	N	Y	N	Y	Y	Y	N	N
TEXAS								
1 Chapman	N	Y	N	Y	Y	Y	Y	N
2 Wilson	N	Y	?	?	N	Y	Y	Y
3 ***Johnson, Sam***	Y	N	Y	N	N	Y	Y	Y
4 Hall	Y	N	Y	N	N	Y	Y	N
5 Bryant	N	Y	N	Y	Y	Y	N	N
6 ***Barton***	Y	N	N	N	N	Y	Y	Y
7 ***Archer***	Y	N	Y	N	N	Y	Y	Y
8 ***Fields***	Y	N	Y	N	N	Y	Y	Y
9 Brooks	N	Y	N	Y	Y	Y	Y	Y
10 Pickle	N	N	N	Y	Y	Y	N	N
11 Edwards	N	Y	N	Y	Y	Y	Y	N
12 Geren	Y	N	N	Y	N	Y	Y	Y
13 Sarpalius	Y	N	N	Y	Y	Y	Y	Y
14 Laughlin	Y	N	N	Y	Y	Y	Y	Y
15 de la Garza	N	Y	Y	Y	?	Y	Y	N
16 Coleman	N	Y	N	Y	Y	Y	Y	Y
17 Stenholm	Y	N	Y	Y	Y	Y	Y	Y
18 Washington	N	Y	N	Y	Y	Y	N	N
19 ***Combest***	Y	N	Y	N	N	Y	Y	Y
20 Gonzalez	N	Y	N	Y	Y	Y	N	N
21 ***Smith***	Y	N	Y	N	N	Y	Y	Y
22 ***DeLay***	Y	N	Y	N	N	Y	Y	Y
23 ***Bonilla***	Y	N	Y	N	N	Y	Y	Y
24 Frost	N	Y	N	Y	Y	Y	Y	Y
25 Andrews	N	Y	N	Y	Y	Y	Y	N
26 ***Armey***	Y	N	Y	N	N	Y	Y	Y
27 Ortiz	N	Y	Y	Y	Y	Y	Y	N
28 Tejeda	N	Y	N	Y	Y	Y	Y	Y
29 Green	N	Y	Y	N	Y	Y	Y	Y
30 Johnson, E.B.	N	Y	N	Y	Y	Y	N	N
UTAH								
1 ***Hansen***	Y	N	Y	N	N	Y	Y	Y
2 Shepherd	N	Y	Y	Y	Y	Y	N	N
3 Orton	N	Y	N	Y	N	Y	Y	Y
VERMONT								
AL *Sanders*	N	Y	Y	N	Y	Y	Y	N
VIRGINIA								
1 ***Bateman***	Y	N	Y	N	N	Y	N	N
2 Pickett	N	Y	N	Y	Y	Y	N	N
3 Scott	N	Y	N	Y	Y	Y	N	N
4 Sisisky	N	Y	N	Y	Y	Y	Y	Y
5 Payne	Y	N	N	Y	Y	Y	Y	Y
6 ***Goodlatte***	Y	N	Y	N	N	Y	Y	Y
7 ***Bliley***	Y	Y	Y	N	N	Y	Y	Y
8 Moran	N	Y	N	Y	Y	N	N	N
9 Boucher	N	Y	N	Y	Y	Y	Y	Y
10 ***Wolf***	Y	N	Y	N	N	Y	N	N
11 Byrne	N	Y	Y	N	Y	Y	N	N
WASHINGTON								
1 Cantwell	N	Y	N	Y	Y	Y	N	N
2 Swift	N	Y	N	Y	Y	Y	Y	Y
3 Unsoeld	N	Y	N	Y	Y	Y	Y	Y
4 Inslee	N	Y	N	Y	Y	Y	Y	Y
5 Foley			N	Y				
6 Dicks	N	Y	N	Y	Y	Y	N	N
7 McDermott	N	Y	N	Y	Y	Y	N	N
8 ***Dunn***	Y	N	Y	N	N	Y	Y	N
9 Kreidler	N	Y	N	Y	Y	Y	N	N
WEST VIRGINIA								
1 Mollohan	N	Y	N	Y	Y	Y	Y	Y
2 Wise	N	Y	N	Y	N	Y	Y	Y
3 Rahall	N	Y	N	Y	N	Y	Y	Y
WISCONSIN								
1 Barca	N	Y	N	Y	Y	Y	Y	N
2 ***Klug***	Y	N	Y	N	N	Y	N	N
3 ***Gunderson***	Y	Y	Y	N	N	Y	Y	Y
4 Kleczka	N	Y	N	Y	Y	Y	N	N
5 Barrett	N	Y	Y	Y	Y	Y	N	N
6 ***Petri***	?	?	?	?	N	Y	Y	N
7 Obey	N	Y	N	Y	N	Y	Y	N
8 ***Roth***	Y	N	Y	N	N	Y	Y	Y
9 ***Sensenbrenner***	Y	N	Y	N	Y	Y	N	N
WYOMING								
AL ***Thomas***	Y	N	Y	N	N	Y	Y	Y
DELEGATES								
de Lugo, V.I.	N	D	D	D	D	Y	N	N
Faleomavaega, Am.S.	N	D	D	D	D	Y	N	?
Norton, D.C.	?	D	D	D	D	Y	N	N
Romero-B., P.R.	?	D	D	D	D	?	?	?
Underwood, Guam	?	D	D	D	D	?	?	?

Southern states - Ala., Ark., Fla., Ga., Ky., La., Miss., N.C., Okla., S.C., Tenn., Texas, Va.
Omitted votes are quorum calls, which CQ does not include in its vote charts.

561. HR 1025. Brady Bill/Reason For Denial. Separate vote at the request of Solomon, R-N.Y., on the amendment offered by Ramstad, R-Minn., and adopted in the Committee of the Whole to require local officials to provide within 20 days the reasons for denying an individual a handgun. Adopted 425-4: R 175-0; D 249-4 (ND 166-3, SD 83-1); I 1-0, Nov. 10, 1993. (On a separate vote, which may be demanded on an amendment adopted in the Committee of the Whole, the four delegates and the resident commissioner of Puerto Rico cannot vote. See vote 558.)

562. HR 1025. Brady Bill/Five-Year "Sunset." Separate vote at the request of Solomon, R-N.Y., on the amendment offered by Gekas, R-Pa., and adopted in the Committee of the Whole to sunset the five-day waiting period five years after enactment. Adopted 238-192: R 138-36; D 99-156 (ND 45-125, SD 54-31); I 1-0, Nov. 10, 1993. (On a separate vote, which may be demanded on an amendment adopted in the Committee of the Whole, the four delegates and the resident commissioner of Puerto Rico cannot vote. See vote 559.)

563. HR 1025. Brady Bill/Funding Mandates. Schiff, R-N.M., motion to recommit the bill to the Judiciary Committee with instructions to report it back with an amendment to eliminate the unfunded mandates to the states in the bill by either authorizing additional funds for personal background checks or removing the mandate for personal background checks. Motion rejected 200-229: R 136-37; D 64-191 (ND 28-142, SD 36-49); I 0-1, Nov. 10, 1993.

564. HR 1025. Brady Bill/Passage. Passage of the bill to require a five-business-day waiting period before an individual could purchase a handgun to allow local officials to conduct a background check. Passed 238-189: R 54-119; D 184-69 (ND 138-31, SD 46-38); I 0-1, Nov. 10, 1993. A "yea" was a vote in support of the president's position.

565. HR 2401. Fiscal 1994 Defense Authorization/Conference Report. Adoption of the conference report to authorize $261 billion for defense programs in fiscal 1994. Adopted (thus sent to the Senate) 273-135: R 50-120; D 223-15 (ND 146-13, SD 77-2); I 0-0, Nov. 15, 1993.

566. HR 2121. Trucking Rates Settlements/Passage. Rahall, D-W.Va., motion to suspend the rules and pass the bill to establish a mechanism to settle the claims of bankrupt trucking companies and their creditors. Motion agreed to 292-116: R 168-2; D 124-114 (ND 68-91, SD 56-23); I 0-0, Nov. 15, 1993. A two-thirds majority of those present and voting (272 in this case) is required for passage under suspension of the rules. A "yea" was a vote in support of the president's position.

567. Procedural Motion. Approval of the House Journal of Monday, Nov. 15. Approved 250-157: R 18-152; D 232-5 (ND 154-4, SD 78-1); I 0-0, Nov. 16, 1993.

568. HR 322. Mining Law Overhaul/Small Miners. Williams, D-Mont., amendment to exempt miners with claims of fewer than 10 acres from administrative and environmental review costs. Rejected in the Committee of the Whole 183-250: R 136-37; D 47-212 (ND 29-147, SD 18-65); I 0-1, Nov. 16, 1993.

KEY

- Y Voted for (yea).
- # Paired for.
- + Announced for.
- N Voted against (nay).
- X Paired against.
- − Announced against.
- P Voted "present."
- C Voted "present" to avoid possible conflict of interest.
- ? Did not vote or otherwise make a position known.
- D Delegates ineligible to vote.

Democrats   **Republicans**   *Independent*

	561	562	563	564	565	566	567	568
ALABAMA								
1 *Callahan*	Y	Y	Y	N	?	?	N	Y
2 *Everett*	Y	Y	Y	N	N	N	N	Y
3 Browder	Y	Y	Y	N	Y	Y	Y	N
4 Bevill	Y	Y	Y	N	Y	Y	Y	N
5 Cramer	Y	Y	Y	N	Y	Y	Y	N
6 *Bachus*	Y	Y	Y	N	N	Y	N	Y
7 Hilliard	Y	Y	N	N	Y	N	?	N
ALASKA								
AL *Young*	Y	Y	Y	N	N	Y	N	Y
ARIZONA								
1 Coppersmith	Y	N	N	Y	Y	Y	N	Y
2 Pastor	Y	N	N	Y	Y	Y	Y	Y
3 *Stump*	Y	Y	Y	N	N	Y	N	Y
4 *Kyl*	Y	Y	Y	N	N	Y	N	Y
5 *Kolbe*	Y	Y	Y	N	N	Y	N	Y
6 English	Y	N	N	Y	Y	N	Y	Y
ARKANSAS								
1 Lambert	Y	Y	N	N	Y	Y	Y	N
2 Thornton	Y	Y	N	N	Y	Y	Y	N
3 *Hutchinson*	Y	Y	Y	N	N	Y	N	Y
4 Dickey	Y	Y	Y	N	N	Y	N	Y
CALIFORNIA								
1 Hamburg	Y	N	N	Y	N	N	Y	N
2 *Herger*	Y	Y	Y	N	N	Y	N	Y
3 Fazio	Y	N	N	Y	Y	Y	Y	N
4 *Doolittle*	Y	Y	Y	N	N	Y	N	Y
5 Matsui	Y	N	N	Y	Y	Y	Y	N
6 Woolsey	Y	N	N	Y	N	Y	Y	N
7 Miller	Y	N	N	Y	N	N	Y	N
8 Pelosi	Y	N	N	Y	Y	Y	Y	N
9 Dellums	Y	N	N	Y	N	Y	Y	N
10 *Baker*	Y	Y	Y	N	Y	N	Y	N
11 *Pombo*	Y	Y	Y	N	N	Y	Y	Y
12 Lantos	Y	N	N	Y	Y	Y	Y	N
13 Stark	Y	N	N	Y	N	Y	Y	N
14 Eshoo	Y	N	N	Y	Y	Y	Y	N
15 Mineta	Y	N	N	Y	Y	Y	Y	N
16 Edwards	Y	N	N	Y	N	N	Y	N
17 Farr	Y	N	N	Y	Y	Y	Y	N
18 Condit	Y	Y	Y	Y	Y	Y	Y	Y
19 Lehman	Y	Y	N	Y	Y	Y	Y	N
20 Dooley	Y	N	N	Y	Y	Y	Y	N
21 *Thomas*	Y	N	Y	Y	X	?	N	Y
22 *Huffington*	Y	Y	N	N	Y	N	N	N
23 *Gallegly*	Y	Y	Y	Y	Y	Y	N	Y
24 Beilenson	Y	N	N	Y	Y	Y	Y	N
25 *McKeon*	Y	Y	Y	N	N	Y	N	Y
26 Berman	Y	N	N	Y	Y	N	Y	N
27 *Moorhead*	Y	Y	Y	N	N	Y	N	Y
28 *Dreier*	Y	Y	Y	N	N	Y	N	Y
29 Waxman	Y	N	N	Y	Y	Y	Y	N
30 Becerra	Y	N	N	Y	Y	N	Y	N
31 Martinez	Y	Y	Y	N	Y	Y	Y	N
32 Dixon	Y	N	N	Y	Y	Y	Y	N
33 Roybal-Allard	Y	N	N	Y	Y	N	Y	N
34 Torres	Y	N	N	Y	Y	N	Y	N
35 Waters	Y	N	N	Y	N	N	Y	N
36 Harman	Y	N	N	Y	Y	Y	Y	N
37 Tucker	Y	Y	Y	Y	Y	Y	?	N
38 *Horn*	Y	Y	N	Y	N	Y	Y	N
39 *Royce*	Y	Y	Y	N	Y	N	Y	Y
40 *Lewis*	Y	Y	Y	N	Y	Y	N	Y
41 *Kim*	Y	Y	Y	N	N	Y	N	Y
42 Brown	Y	N	N	Y	Y	Y	?	N
43 *Calvert*	Y	Y	Y	N	N	Y	N	Y
44 *McCandless*	Y	Y	Y	?	?	N	Y	Y
45 *Rohrabacher*	Y	Y	Y	N	N	Y	N	Y
46 *Dornan*	Y	Y	Y	N	N	Y	N	Y
47 *Cox*	Y	Y	Y	N	N	Y	N	Y
48 *Packard*	Y	Y	Y	N	N	Y	N	Y
49 Schenk	N	N	N	Y	Y	Y	Y	N
50 Filner	Y	N	N	Y	N	Y	Y	N
51 *Cunningham*	Y	Y	Y	N	N	Y	N	Y
52 *Hunter*	Y	Y	Y	N	N	Y	N	Y
COLORADO								
1 Schroeder	Y	N	N	Y	Y	Y	Y	N
2 Skaggs	Y	N	N	Y	Y	Y	Y	N
3 *McInnis*	Y	Y	Y	N	Y	Y	Y	N
4 *Allard*	Y	Y	N	N	N	Y	N	Y
5 *Hefley*	Y	Y	Y	N	N	Y	N	Y
6 *Schaefer*	Y	Y	Y	N	N	Y	N	Y
CONNECTICUT								
1 Kennelly	N	N	N	Y	Y	Y	Y	N
2 Gejdenson	Y	N	N	Y	Y	N	Y	N
3 DeLauro	Y	N	N	Y	Y	N	Y	N
4 *Shays*	Y	N	N	Y	N	N	N	N
5 *Franks*	Y	Y	Y	N	N	N	N	N
6 Johnson	Y	N	N	Y	Y	Y	N	N
DELAWARE								
AL *Castle*	Y	N	N	Y	Y	Y	Y	Y
FLORIDA								
1 Hutto	Y	Y	Y	Y	Y	Y	Y	Y
2 Peterson	Y	N	N	N	Y	Y	Y	N
3 Brown	Y	N	N	Y	Y	N	Y	N
4 *Fowler*	Y	N	Y	N	Y	N	Y	N
5 Thurman	Y	N	N	Y	Y	Y	Y	N
6 *Stearns*	Y	Y	Y	N	Y	N	N	Y
7 *Mica*	Y	Y	N	N	N	Y	N	Y
8 *McCollum*	Y	Y	Y	N	N	Y	N	Y
9 *Bilirakis*	Y	Y	Y	N	N	Y	N	Y
10 *Young*	Y	N	N	Y	N	Y	N	?
11 Gibbons	Y	N	N	Y	Y	Y	Y	N
12 *Canady*	Y	Y	Y	N	N	Y	N	Y
13 *Miller*	Y	Y	N	N	Y	Y	N	Y
14 *Goss*	Y	Y	Y	N	Y	N	Y	N
15 Bacchus	Y	N	N	Y	Y	Y	Y	N
16 *Lewis*	Y	Y	Y	N	N	Y	N	N
17 Meek	Y	N	N	Y	Y	N	Y	N
18 *Ros-Lehtinen*	Y	N	N	Y	Y	N	Y	N
19 Johnston	Y	N	N	Y	N	N	Y	N
20 Deutsch	Y	N	N	Y	Y	N	Y	N
21 *Diaz-Balart*	Y	N	N	Y	Y	N	N	N
22 *Shaw*	Y	Y	Y	N	Y	N	Y	N
23 Hastings	Y	N	N	Y	Y	N	Y	N
GEORGIA								
1 *Kingston*	Y	Y	Y	N	N	Y	N	Y
2 Bishop	Y	Y	N	N	Y	N	Y	N
3 *Collins*	Y	Y	Y	N	Y	Y	N	Y
4 *Linder*	Y	Y	Y	N	N	Y	N	Y
5 Lewis	Y	N	N	Y	N	Y	Y	N
6 *Gingrich*	Y	Y	Y	N	N	Y	N	Y
7 Darden	Y	Y	Y	N	Y	Y	Y	N
8 Rowland	Y	Y	Y	Y	Y	Y	Y	N
9 Deal	Y	Y	Y	−	Y	Y	Y	N
10 Johnson	Y	N	N	Y	Y	N	Y	N
11 McKinney	Y	N	N	Y	N	Y	N	N
HAWAII								
1 Abercrombie	Y	N	N	Y	Y	N	?	N
2 Mink	Y	N	N	Y	N	Y	Y	N
IDAHO								
1 LaRocco	Y	Y	Y	N	Y	Y	Y	Y
2 *Crapo*	Y	Y	Y	N	N	Y	N	Y
ILLINOIS								
1 Rush	Y	N	N	Y	N	Y	N	N
2 Reynolds	Y	N	N	Y	N	Y	Y	N
3 Lipinski	Y	N	N	Y	Y	Y	Y	Y
4 Gutierrez	Y	N	N	Y	N	Y	Y	N
5 Rostenkowski	Y	N	N	Y	Y	N	Y	N
6 *Hyde*	Y	N	N	Y	N	Y	Y	N
7 Collins	Y	N	N	Y	N	N	Y	N
8 *Crane*	Y	Y	Y	N	N	Y	N	Y
9 Yates	Y	N	N	Y	N	Y	Y	N
10 *Porter*	Y	N	N	Y	N	Y	Y	N
11 Sangmeister	Y	Y	Y	Y	N	Y	Y	N
12 Costello	Y	Y	Y	N	Y	Y	Y	N
13 *Fawell*	Y	N	N	Y	N	Y	Y	N
14 *Hastert*	Y	Y	Y	N	N	Y	N	Y
15 *Ewing*	Y	Y	Y	N	N	Y	N	Y
16 *Manzullo*	Y	Y	N	Y	N	Y	N	Y
17 Evans	Y	N	N	Y	N	Y	Y	N

ND Northern Democrats   SD Southern Democrats

	561	562	563	564	565	566	567	568
18 ***Michel***	Y	Y	Y	N	N	Y	N	Y
19 Poshard	Y	Y	Y	N	Y	N	Y	N
20 Durbin	Y	N	N	Y	Y	N	Y	N
INDIANA								
1 Visclosky	Y	N	N	Y	Y	N	Y	N
2 Sharp	Y	Y	N	Y	Y	Y	Y	N
3 Roemer	Y	N	N	Y	Y	Y	Y	N
4 Long	Y	Y	N	Y	Y	Y	Y	N
5 ***Buyer***	Y	Y	N	N	Y	Y	N	Y
6 ***Burton***	Y	Y	Y	N	N	Y	N	Y
7 ***Myers***	Y	Y	Y	N	N	Y	Y	Y
8 McCloskey	Y	N	N	Y	Y	N	Y	N
9 Hamilton	Y	Y	N	Y	Y	Y	Y	Y
10 Jacobs	Y	N	N	Y	Y	Y	N	N
IOWA								
1 ***Leach***	Y	N	N	Y	N	Y	N	Y
2 ***Nussle***	Y	Y	Y	N	N	Y	N	Y
3 ***Lightfoot***	Y	Y	Y	N	N	Y	N	Y
4 Smith	Y	N	Y	N	Y	Y	Y	Y
5 ***Grandy***	Y	N	Y	N	Y	Y	N	Y
KANSAS								
1 ***Roberts***	Y	Y	Y	N	N	Y	N	Y
2 Slattery	Y	N	N	Y	?	?	?	N
3 ***Meyers***	Y	N	N	Y	N	Y	N	N
4 Glickman	Y	N	N	Y	#	N	Y	N
KENTUCKY								
1 Barlow	Y	Y	Y	N	?	?	Y	N
2 Natcher	Y	Y	Y	N	Y	Y	Y	N
3 Mazzoli	Y	N	N	Y	Y	Y	Y	N
4 ***Bunning***	Y	Y	Y	N	N	Y	N	Y
5 ***Rogers***	Y	Y	Y	N	N	Y	N	Y
6 Baesler	Y	N	N	Y	Y	Y	Y	N
LOUISIANA								
1 ***Livingston***	Y	Y	Y	N	N	Y	Y	Y
2 Jefferson	Y	N	N	Y	Y	N	Y	N
3 Tauzin	Y	Y	Y	N	Y	Y	Y	Y
4 Fields	Y	N	N	Y	Y	N	Y	N
5 ***McCrery***	Y	Y	Y	N	N	Y	N	Y
6 ***Baker***	Y	Y	Y	N	N	Y	N	Y
7 Hayes	Y	Y	Y	N	?	?	Y	Y
MAINE								
1 Andrews	Y	N	N	Y	Y	N	Y	N
2 ***Snowe***	Y	Y	Y	N	Y	Y	N	N
MARYLAND								
1 ***Gilchrest***	Y	N	N	Y	Y	Y	N	N
2 ***Bentley***	Y	N	N	N	N	Y	N	Y
3 Cardin	Y	N	N	Y	Y	N	Y	N
4 Wynn	Y	N	N	Y	Y	N	Y	N
5 Hoyer	Y	N	N	Y	Y	N	Y	N
6 ***Bartlett***	Y	Y	Y	N	N	Y	N	Y
7 Mfume	Y	N	N	Y	Y	N	Y	N
8 ***Morella***	Y	N	N	Y	N	Y	N	N
MASSACHUSETTS								
1 Olver	Y	N	N	Y	Y	N	Y	N
2 Neal	Y	N	N	Y	Y	N	Y	N
3 ***Blute***	Y	Y	Y	Y	Y	Y	N	N
4 Frank	Y	N	N	Y	Y	Y	Y	N
5 Meehan	Y	N	N	Y	Y	Y	Y	N
6 ***Torkildsen***	Y	Y	Y	Y	Y	Y	?	N
7 Markey	Y	N	N	Y	Y	Y	Y	N
8 Kennedy	Y	N	N	Y	Y	N	Y	N
9 Moakley	?	?	?	#	Y	N	Y	N
10 Studds	Y	N	N	Y	Y	Y	Y	N
MICHIGAN								
1 Stupak	Y	Y	N	N	Y	N	Y	Y
2 ***Hoekstra***	Y	Y	Y	Y	N	Y	N	N
3 Vacancy								
4 ***Camp***	Y	Y	Y	N	Y	Y	N	Y
5 Barcia	Y	Y	Y	N	Y	Y	?	N
6 ***Upton***	Y	N	Y	Y	Y	Y	N	N
7 ***Smith***	Y	Y	Y	Y	N	Y	Y	Y
8 Carr	Y	Y	Y	N	Y	N	Y	N
9 Kildee	Y	N	N	Y	Y	N	Y	N
10 Bonior	Y	N	N	Y	Y	N	Y	?
11 ***Knollenberg***	Y	Y	Y	N	N	Y	N	Y
12 Levin	Y	N	N	Y	Y	Y	Y	N
13 Ford	Y	N	N	Y	Y	N	Y	Y
14 Conyers	Y	N	N	Y	N	N	Y	N
15 Collins	Y	N	N	Y	Y	N	?	N
16 Dingell	Y	Y	N	N	Y	Y	Y	N
MINNESOTA								
1 Penny	Y	N	N	N	N	Y	Y	N
2 Minge	Y	Y	Y	Y	N	Y	Y	N
3 ***Ramstad***	Y	Y	N	Y	N	Y	N	N
4 Vento	Y	N	N	Y	Y	N	Y	N

	561	562	563	564	565	566	567	568
5 Sabo	Y	N	N	Y	Y	N	Y	N
6 ***Grams***	Y	Y	Y	N	N	Y	N	Y
7 Peterson	Y	Y	Y	N	Y	N	?	Y
8 Oberstar	Y	Y	N	N	N	N	Y	Y
MISSISSIPPI								
1 Whitten	Y	Y	N	N	Y	Y	?	N
2 Thompson	Y	N	N	Y	Y	N	Y	N
3 Montgomery	Y	Y	Y	N	Y	Y	Y	Y
4 Parker	Y	Y	Y	N	Y	Y	Y	Y
5 Taylor	Y	Y	Y	N	Y	Y	N	N
MISSOURI								
1 Clay	Y	N	N	Y	Y	N	N	N
2 ***Talent***	Y	Y	Y	N	Y	Y	N	Y
3 Gephardt	Y	N	N	Y	Y	N	Y	N
4 Skelton	Y	Y	Y	N	Y	Y	Y	Y
5 Wheat	Y	N	N	Y	#	?	Y	N
6 Danner	Y	Y	Y	N	Y	N	Y	N
7 ***Hancock***	Y	Y	Y	N	N	Y	N	Y
8 ***Emerson***	Y	Y	Y	N	Y	Y	N	Y
9 Volkmer	Y	Y	Y	N	Y	Y	Y	N
MONTANA								
AL Williams	Y	N	Y	N	Y	Y	Y	Y
NEBRASKA								
1 ***Bereuter***	Y	N	Y	N	N	Y	N	Y
2 Hoagland	Y	N	N	Y	Y	Y	Y	N
3 ***Barrett***	Y	Y	Y	N	N	Y	N	Y
NEVADA								
1 Bilbray	Y	Y	Y	N	Y	Y	Y	Y
2 ***Vucanovich***	Y	Y	Y	N	Y	Y	N	Y
NEW HAMPSHIRE								
1 ***Zeliff***	Y	Y	Y	N	N	Y	N	Y
2 Swett	Y	Y	N	Y	Y	N	Y	N
NEW JERSEY								
1 Andrews	Y	N	N	Y	Y	N	?	Y
2 Hughes	Y	N	N	Y	Y	N	Y	N
3 ***Saxton***	Y	N	N	Y	Y	Y	N	N
4 ***Smith***	Y	N	N	Y	Y	Y	Y	N
5 ***Roukema***	Y	N	N	Y	?	?	N	N
6 Pallone	Y	N	N	Y	Y	N	Y	N
7 ***Franks***	Y	N	N	Y	N	Y	N	N
8 Klein	Y	N	N	Y	Y	Y	Y	N
9 Torricelli	Y	N	N	Y	Y	Y	Y	N
10 Payne	?	N	N	Y	?	?	Y	N
11 ***Gallo***	Y	N	N	Y	N	Y	N	N
12 ***Zimmer***	Y	Y	N	Y	N	Y	N	N
13 Menendez	Y	N	N	Y	Y	N	Y	N
NEW MEXICO								
1 ***Schiff***	Y	Y	Y	N	N	Y	N	N
2 ***Skeen***	Y	Y	Y	N	N	Y	N	Y
3 Richardson	Y	Y	Y	N	Y	Y	Y	N
NEW YORK								
1 Hochbrueckner	Y	N	N	Y	Y	N	Y	N
2 ***Lazio***	Y	N	N	Y	Y	Y	N	N
3 ***King***	Y	Y	Y	N	N	Y	N	Y
4 ***Levy***	Y	Y	Y	N	N	Y	N	Y
5 Ackerman	Y	N	N	Y	Y	Y	Y	N
6 Flake	Y	N	N	Y	?	?	?	Y
7 Manton	Y	N	N	Y	Y	N	Y	Y
8 Nadler	N	N	N	Y	N	N	Y	N
9 Schumer	Y	N	N	Y	Y	N	Y	N
10 Towns	Y	N	N	Y	Y	N	Y	N
11 Owens	Y	N	N	Y	Y	N	Y	N
12 Velazquez	Y	N	N	Y	Y	N	Y	N
13 ***Molinari***	Y	N	N	Y	N	Y	N	Y
14 Maloney	Y	N	N	Y	Y	Y	Y	N
15 Rangel	Y	N	N	Y	Y	N	Y	N
16 Serrano	Y	N	N	Y	Y	N	Y	N
17 Engel	Y	N	N	Y	+	?	?	Y
18 Lowey	Y	N	N	Y	Y	N	Y	N
19 ***Fish***	Y	Y	Y	Y	N	Y	Y	Y
20 ***Gilman***	Y	N	N	Y	N	N	Y	N
21 McNulty	Y	Y	Y	Y	Y	N	Y	N
22 ***Solomon***	Y	Y	Y	N	N	Y	N	N
23 ***Boehlert***	Y	N	N	Y	N	Y	N	N
24 ***McHugh***	Y	Y	Y	N	N	Y	N	Y
25 ***Walsh***	Y	Y	N	Y	Y	Y	N	Y
26 Hinchey	Y	N	N	Y	Y	Y	Y	Y
27 ***Paxon***	Y	Y	Y	N	N	Y	N	Y
28 Slaughter	Y	N	N	Y	Y	Y	Y	N
29 LaFalce	Y	N	N	Y	Y	N	Y	N
30 ***Quinn***	Y	N	Y	Y	Y	Y	N	Y
31 ***Houghton***	Y	Y	Y	N	N	Y	Y	Y
NORTH CAROLINA								
1 Clayton	Y	N	N	Y	Y	N	Y	Y
2 Valentine	Y	Y	Y	Y	Y	Y	Y	N

	561	562	563	564	565	566	567	568
3 Lancaster	Y	Y	Y	Y	Y	Y	Y	N
4 Price	Y	N	N	Y	Y	Y	Y	N
5 Neal	Y	Y	Y	Y	Y	Y	Y	N
6 ***Coble***	Y	Y	Y	N	N	Y	N	Y
7 Rose	Y	Y	N	Y	Y	Y	Y	N
8 Hefner	Y	Y	N	Y	Y	Y	Y	Y
9 ***McMillan***	Y	N	Y	Y	Y	Y	N	Y
10 ***Ballenger***	Y	Y	Y	N	Y	Y	N	Y
11 ***Taylor***	Y	Y	Y	N	Y	Y	?	Y
12 Watt	Y	N	N	Y	Y	N	Y	N
NORTH DAKOTA								
AL Pomeroy	Y	Y	Y	N	Y	Y	Y	N
OHIO								
1 Mann	Y	N	N	Y	Y	N	Y	N
2 ***Portman***	Y	Y	Y	N	Y	Y	N	Y
3 Hall	Y	N	N	Y	Y	?	Y	N
4 ***Oxley***	Y	N	N	Y	Y	Y	N	Y
5 ***Gillmor***	Y	Y	Y	N	?	?	Y	Y
6 Strickland	Y	Y	N	N	Y	N	Y	N
7 ***Hobson***	Y	Y	Y	N	Y	Y	N	Y
8 ***Boehner***	Y	Y	Y	N	N	Y	N	Y
9 Kaptur	Y	Y	N	Y	Y	N	Y	N
10 ***Hoke***	Y	Y	Y	N	N	Y	N	N
11 Stokes	Y	N	N	Y	?	?	Y	N
12 ***Kasich***	Y	Y	Y	N	Y	Y	Y	Y
13 Brown	Y	N	N	Y	Y	N	Y	N
14 Sawyer	Y	N	N	Y	?	?	?	N
15 ***Pryce***	Y	Y	Y	N	Y	Y	N	Y
16 ***Regula***	Y	Y	Y	Y	N	Y	N	Y
17 Traficant	Y	Y	Y	Y	Y	Y	Y	N
18 Applegate	Y	Y	Y	Y	Y	Y	Y	Y
19 Fingerhut	Y	N	N	Y	+	+	Y	N
OKLAHOMA								
1 ***Inhofe***	Y	Y	Y	N	N	Y	N	Y
2 Synar	Y	N	N	Y	Y	Y	Y	N
3 Brewster	Y	Y	Y	N	Y	Y	Y	N
4 McCurdy	?	Y	Y	Y	Y	Y	Y	N
5 ***Istook***	Y	Y	Y	N	Y	Y	?	Y
6 English	Y	Y	Y	N	Y	Y	Y	N
OREGON								
1 Furse	Y	N	N	Y	X	+	Y	N
2 ***Smith***	Y	Y	Y	N	N	Y	N	Y
3 Wyden	Y	N	N	Y	Y	N	Y	N
4 DeFazio	Y	Y	N	Y	N	N	Y	Y
5 Kopetski	Y	Y	Y	—	Y	N	Y	N
PENNSYLVANIA								
1 Foglietta	Y	N	N	Y	#	?	Y	N
2 Blackwell	Y	N	N	Y	Y	N	?	Y
3 Borski	Y	N	N	Y	Y	Y	Y	N
4 Klink	Y	Y	Y	N	Y	Y	Y	Y
5 ***Clinger***	Y	Y	Y	N	Y	Y	N	?
6 Holden	Y	Y	Y	N	Y	N	Y	N
7 ***Weldon***	Y	Y	Y	Y	Y	Y	?	N
8 ***Greenwood***	Y	Y	N	Y	Y	Y	Y	N
9 ***Shuster***	Y	?	?	?	?	?	N	Y
10 ***McDade***	Y	N	Y	Y	Y	Y	N	Y
11 Kanjorski	Y	Y	N	N	Y	Y	Y	N
12 Murtha	Y	Y	N	N	Y	Y	Y	Y
13 Margolies-Mezv.	Y	N	N	Y	N	Y	Y	N
14 Coyne	Y	N	N	Y	Y	N	Y	N
15 McHale	Y	N	N	Y	Y	Y	Y	N
16 ***Walker***	Y	Y	Y	N	N	Y	N	Y
17 ***Gekas***	Y	Y	Y	N	Y	Y	N	Y
18 ***Santorum***	Y	Y	Y	N	N	Y	Y	Y
19 ***Goodling***	Y	Y	Y	Y	Y	Y	?	Y
20 Murphy	?	?	?	X	Y	Y	N	N
21 ***Ridge***	Y	Y	Y	N	Y	Y	N	Y
RHODE ISLAND								
1 ***Machtley***	Y	Y	N	Y	Y	Y	N	Y
2 Reed	Y	N	N	Y	Y	Y	Y	N
SOUTH CAROLINA								
1 ***Ravenel***	Y	Y	Y	N	Y	Y	N	N
2 ***Spence***	Y	Y	Y	N	N	Y	N	Y
3 Derrick	Y	N	N	Y	Y	Y	Y	N
4 ***Inglis***	Y	Y	Y	N	N	Y	Y	Y
5 Spratt	Y	Y	N	Y	Y	Y	Y	N
6 Clyburn	Y	Y	N	Y	Y	Y	Y	N
SOUTH DAKOTA								
AL Johnson	Y	Y	N	Y	Y	Y	Y	N
TENNESSEE								
1 ***Quillen***	Y	Y	Y	N	Y	Y	N	N
2 ***Duncan***	Y	Y	Y	N	N	Y	N	Y
3 Lloyd	Y	Y	Y	Y	Y	Y	?	Y
4 Cooper	Y	Y	N	Y	?	?	Y	Y
5 Clement	Y	N	Y	Y	?	+	?	N

	561	562	563	564	565	566	567	568
6 Gordon	Y	Y	N	Y	Y	Y	Y	N
7 ***Sundquist***	Y	Y	Y	N	Y	Y	N	Y
8 Tanner	Y	Y	Y	N	Y	Y	Y	N
9 Ford	Y	N	N	Y	Y	Y	Y	N
TEXAS								
1 Chapman	Y	Y	N	Y	?	?	?	?
2 Wilson	Y	Y	Y	N	Y	N	Y	N
3 ***Johnson, Sam***	Y	Y	Y	N	N	Y	N	Y
4 Hall	Y	Y	Y	N	Y	Y	Y	Y
5 Bryant	Y	N	N	Y	Y	N	Y	N
6 ***Barton***	Y	Y	Y	N	N	Y	N	Y
7 ***Archer***	Y	Y	Y	N	N	Y	Y	Y
8 ***Fields***	Y	Y	Y	N	N	Y	N	Y
9 Brooks	Y	Y	N	N	?	?	?	N
10 Pickle	Y	N	N	Y	Y	Y	Y	Y
11 Edwards	Y	Y	N	N	Y	Y	Y	N
12 Geren	Y	Y	Y	N	Y	Y	Y	Y
13 Sarpalius	Y	Y	Y	N	Y	Y	Y	N
14 Laughlin	Y	Y	Y	N	Y	Y	Y	Y
15 de la Garza	Y	Y	Y	N	Y	Y	Y	Y
16 Coleman	Y	Y	N	N	Y	N	Y	N
17 Stenholm	Y	Y	Y	N	Y	Y	Y	Y
18 Washington	Y	N	N	Y	N	N	Y	N
19 ***Combest***	Y	Y	Y	N	N	Y	Y	Y
20 Gonzalez	Y	N	N	Y	Y	Y	Y	N
21 ***Smith***	Y	Y	Y	N	N	Y	N	Y
22 ***DeLay***	Y	Y	Y	N	N	Y	N	Y
23 ***Bonilla***	Y	Y	Y	N	Y	Y	N	Y
24 Frost	Y	Y	Y	Y	Y	N	Y	N
25 Andrews	Y	Y	N	Y	Y	Y	Y	N
26 ***Armey***	Y	Y	Y	N	N	Y	N	Y
27 Ortiz	Y	Y	Y	N	Y	Y	Y	Y
28 Tejeda	Y	Y	Y	N	Y	Y	Y	Y
29 Green	Y	Y	N	N	Y	N	Y	N
30 Johnson, E.B.	Y	N	N	Y	Y	N	Y	N
UTAH								
1 ***Hansen***	Y	Y	Y	N	N	Y	N	Y
2 Shepherd	Y	N	N	Y	Y	Y	Y	N
3 Orton	Y	Y	Y	N	Y	Y	Y	Y
VERMONT								
AL *Sanders*	Y	Y	N	N	X	?	?	N
VIRGINIA								
1 ***Bateman***	Y	N	N	Y	Y	Y	Y	Y
2 Pickett	Y	N	Y	N	Y	Y	Y	N
3 Scott	Y	N	N	Y	Y	N	Y	N
4 Sisisky	Y	Y	Y	N	Y	Y	Y	?
5 Payne	Y	Y	Y	N	Y	Y	Y	N
6 ***Goodlatte***	Y	Y	Y	N	N	Y	N	Y
7 ***Bliley***	Y	Y	Y	N	N	Y	N	Y
8 Moran	N	N	N	Y	Y	Y	Y	N
9 Boucher	Y	Y	Y	N	Y	Y	Y	N
10 ***Wolf***	Y	N	N	Y	N	Y	N	Y
11 Byrne	Y	N	N	Y	Y	N	Y	N
WASHINGTON								
1 Cantwell	Y	N	N	Y	Y	Y	Y	N
2 Swift	Y	Y	N	Y	Y	N	Y	Y
3 Unsoeld	Y	Y	N	N	Y	N	Y	Y
4 Inslee	Y	Y	N	N	Y	N	Y	Y
5 Foley								
6 Dicks	Y	N	N	Y	Y	N	Y	N
7 McDermott	Y	N	N	Y	Y	Y	Y	N
8 ***Dunn***	Y	Y	Y	N	N	Y	N	Y
9 Kreidler	Y	N	N	Y	Y	Y	Y	N
WEST VIRGINIA								
1 Mollohan	Y	Y	Y	N	?	?	Y	Y
2 Wise	Y	Y	Y	N	?	?	?	N
3 Rahall	Y	Y	Y	N	N	Y	?	N
WISCONSIN								
1 Barca	Y	Y	Y	Y	Y	Y	Y	N
2 ***Klug***	Y	N	N	Y	N	Y	N	N
3 ***Gunderson***	Y	Y	Y	N	Y	Y	N	Y
4 Kleczka	Y	N	N	Y	Y	Y	Y	N
5 Barrett	Y	N	N	Y	Y	Y	Y	N
6 ***Petri***	Y	Y	N	N	N	Y	N	Y
7 Obey	Y	Y	N	N	N	Y	Y	N
8 ***Roth***	Y	Y	Y	N	Y	Y	N	N
9 ***Sensenbrenner***	Y	N	N	Y	N	Y	N	N
WYOMING								
AL ***Thomas***	Y	Y	Y	N	N	Y	N	Y
DELEGATES								
de Lugo, V.I.	D	D	D	D	D	D	D	N
Faleomavaega, Am.S.	D	D	D	D	D	D	D	N
Norton, D.C.	D	D	D	D	D	D	D	N
Romero-B., P.R.	D	D	D	D	D	D	D	N
Underwood, Guam	D	D	D	D	D	D	D	N

Southern states - Ala., Ark., Fla., Ga., Ky., La., Miss., N.C., Okla., S.C., Tenn., Texas, Va.
Omitted votes are quorum calls, which CQ does not include in its vote charts.

KEY

Y Voted for (yea).
\# Paired for.
\+ Announced for.
N Voted against (nay).
X Paired against.
− Announced against.
P Voted "present."
C Voted "present" to avoid possible conflict of interest.
? Did not vote or otherwise make a position known.
D Delegates ineligible to vote.

Democrats *Republicans*
Independent

569. HR 322. Mining Law Overhaul/Unsuitability Reviews. DeFazio, D-Ore., amendment to declare lands unsuitable for mining if mining activities would cause significant damage to an area's special characteristics, dropping the bill's requirement that the damage be permanent and irreparable as well as significant. The amendment also would expand the list of special characteristics to include Bureau of Land Management areas of critical environmental concern and Forest Service research natural areas. Rejected in the Committee of the Whole 199-232: R 38-135; D 160-97 (ND 118-56, SD 42-41); I 1-0, Nov. 16, 1993.

570. HR 322. Mining Law Overhaul/Land Restoration. Vucanovich, R-Nev., amendment to require miners to restore lands only to the maximum extent practicable. Rejected in the Committee of the Whole 149-278: R 134-38; D 15-239 (ND 5-168, SD 10-71); I 0-1, Nov. 16, 1993.

571. HR 322. Mining Law Overhaul/Defense Department Waiver. Hansen, R-Utah, amendment to allow the Defense secretary to waive the requirements of the bill to ensure adequate supplies of critical and strategic minerals needed for national security reasons. Rejected in the Committee of the Whole 193-238: R 161-13; D 32-224 (ND 7-167, SD 25-57); I 0-1, Nov. 16, 1993.

572. Procedural Motion. Approval of the House Journal of Tuesday, Nov. 16. Approved 230-143: R 16-138; D 214-5 (ND 141-4, SD 73-1); I 0-0, Nov. 17, 1993.

573. HR 3450. NAFTA Implementation/Rule. Adoption of the rule (H Res 311) to waive points of order against and provide for House floor consideration of the bill to approve the North American Free Trade Agreement and make the necessary changes to U.S. statutory law to implement it. Adopted 342-85: R 140-32; D 202-52 (ND 127-42, SD 75-10); I 0-1, Nov. 17, 1993.

*575. HR 3450. NAFTA Implementation/Passage. Passage of the bill to approve the North American Free Trade Agreement and make the necessary changes to U.S. statutory law to implement it. Passed 234-200: R 132-43; D 102-156 (ND 49-124, SD 53-32); I 0-1, Nov. 17, 1993. A "yea" was a vote in support of the president's position.

576. HR 322. Mining Law Overhaul/Job Loss. Crapo, R-Idaho, motion to recommit the bill to the Natural Resources Committee with instructions to report it back with provisions designed to prevent a net loss of jobs. Rejected 148-270: R 137-32; D 11-237 (ND 3-167, SD 8-70); I 0-1, Nov. 18, 1993.

577. HR 322. Mining Law Overhaul/Passage. Passage of the bill to require hard-rock mining companies to pay an 8 percent royalty on ores extracted from federal lands with the money to go to clean up abandoned mines, and increasing environmental regulation of such mining operations. Passed 316-108: R 70-102; D 245-6 (ND 166-3, SD 79-3); I 1-0, Nov. 18, 1993. A "yea" was a vote in support of the president's position.

* Omitted votes are quorum calls, which CQ does not include in its vote charts.

	569	570	571	572	573	575	576	577
ALABAMA								
1 *Callahan*	N	Y	Y	N	Y	Y	Y	N
2 *Everett*	N	Y	Y	N	N	Y	Y	N
3 Browder	N	N	N	Y	Y	N	N	Y
4 Bevill	N	N	N	Y	Y	N	N	Y
5 Cramer	N	N	N	Y	Y	N	N	Y
6 *Bachus*	N	Y	Y	N	Y	Y	Y	N
7 Hilliard	Y	N	N	Y	Y	N	N	Y
ALASKA								
AL *Young*	N	Y	Y	?	?	N	?	N
ARIZONA								
1 Coppersmith	Y	N	N	Y	Y	Y	N	Y
2 Pastor	N	N	N	Y	Y	Y	N	Y
3 *Stump*	N	Y	Y	N	Y	Y	Y	N
4 *Kyl*	N	Y	Y	N	Y	Y	Y	N
5 *Kolbe*	N	Y	Y	N	Y	Y	Y	N
6 English	N	N	N	Y	Y	Y	N	Y
ARKANSAS								
1 Lambert	Y	N	N	Y	Y	Y	N	Y
2 Thornton	N	N	N	Y	Y	Y	N	Y
3 *Hutchinson*	N	Y	Y	N	Y	Y	Y	N
4 *Dickey*	N	Y	Y	N	Y	Y	N	Y
CALIFORNIA								
1 Hamburg	Y	N	N	Y	N	N	N	Y
2 *Herger*	N	Y	Y	N	Y	Y	Y	N
3 Fazio	N	N	N	Y	Y	Y	N	Y
4 *Doolittle*	N	Y	Y	N	N	N	N	Y
5 Matsui	N	N	N	Y	Y	Y	N	Y
6 Woolsey	Y	N	N	Y	N	N	N	Y
7 Miller	N	N	N	Y	Y	N	N	Y
8 Pelosi	Y	N	N	Y	Y	Y	N	Y
9 Dellums	Y	N	N	Y	N	N	N	Y
10 *Baker*	N	Y	Y	N	Y	Y	Y	N
11 *Pombo*	N	Y	Y	N	N	N	N	N
12 Lantos	Y	N	N	Y	Y	Y	N	Y
13 Stark	N	N	N	Y	N	N	N	Y
14 Eshoo	Y	N	N	Y	Y	Y	N	Y
15 Mineta	N	N	N	Y	Y	Y	N	Y
16 Edwards	Y	N	N	Y	Y	N	N	Y
17 Farr	N	N	N	Y	Y	Y	N	Y
18 Condit	N	N	N	N	N	N	N	Y
19 Lehman	N	N	N	Y	Y	Y	N	Y
20 Dooley	N	N	N	Y	Y	Y	N	Y
21 *Thomas*	N	Y	Y	N	Y	Y	Y	N
22 *Huffington*	N	Y	Y	?	Y	Y	Y	Y
23 *Gallegly*	N	Y	Y	N	Y	N	Y	Y
24 Beilenson	Y	N	N	Y	Y	Y	N	Y
25 *McKeon*	N	Y	Y	N	Y	Y	Y	N
26 Berman	Y	N	N	Y	Y	Y	N	Y
27 *Moorhead*	N	Y	Y	N	Y	Y	Y	Y
28 *Dreier*	N	Y	Y	N	Y	Y	Y	N
29 Waxman	Y	N	N	Y	Y	N	N	Y
30 Becerra	Y	N	N	Y	N	N	Y	Y
31 Martinez	Y	N	N	Y	Y	N	N	?
32 Dixon	Y	N	N	?	Y	N	N	Y
33 Roybal-Allard	Y	N	N	Y	Y	Y	N	Y
34 Torres	Y	N	N	Y	Y	Y	N	Y
35 Waters	Y	N	N	?	N	N	N	Y
36 Harman	Y	N	N	Y	Y	Y	N	Y
37 Tucker	Y	N	N	Y	N	N	N	Y
38 *Horn*	N	N	N	Y	Y	Y	N	Y
39 *Royce*	N	Y	Y	N	Y	N	Y	N
40 *Lewis*	N	Y	Y	N	Y	Y	Y	N
41 *Kim*	N	Y	Y	N	Y	Y	Y	N
42 *Brown*	?	?	?	?	Y	Y	N	Y
43 *Calvert*	N	Y	Y	N	Y	Y	Y	N
44 *McCandless*	N	Y	Y	N	Y	Y	Y	N
45 *Rohrabacher*	N	Y	Y	N	Y	Y	Y	N
46 *Dornan*	N	Y	Y	?	N	Y	Y	N
47 *Cox*	N	Y	Y	N	Y	Y	Y	N
48 *Packard*	N	Y	Y	N	Y	Y	Y	N
49 Schenk	Y	N	N	Y	Y	N	N	Y
50 Filner	Y	N	N	N	N	N	N	Y
51 *Cunningham*	Y	N	Y	N	Y	Y	Y	Y
52 *Hunter*	N	Y	Y	N	N	N	Y	N
COLORADO								
1 Schroeder	Y	Y	N	N	Y	Y	N	Y
2 Skaggs	Y	Y	N	Y	Y	Y	N	Y
3 *McInnis*	N	Y	Y	Y	Y	Y	Y	N
4 *Allard*	N	Y	Y	N	Y	Y	Y	N
5 *Hefley*	N	Y	N	N	Y	Y	Y	N
6 *Schaefer*	N	Y	Y	N	Y	Y	Y	N
CONNECTICUT								
1 Kennelly	Y	N	N	Y	Y	N	N	Y
2 Gejdenson	Y	N	N	?	Y	N	N	Y
3 DeLauro	Y	N	N	Y	Y	N	N	Y
4 *Shays*	Y	N	N	N	Y	Y	N	Y
5 *Franks*	Y	N	Y	N	Y	Y	N	Y
6 *Johnson*	Y	Y	Y	N	Y	Y	N	Y
DELAWARE								
AL *Castle*	N	Y	Y	N	Y	Y	Y	Y
FLORIDA								
1 *Hutto*	N	Y	Y	?	Y	Y	Y	Y
2 Peterson	N	N	N	Y	Y	N	N	Y
3 Brown	Y	N	N	Y	Y	N	N	Y
4 *Fowler*	N	Y	Y	N	Y	Y	Y	Y
5 Thurman	N	N	N	Y	N	N	N	Y
6 *Stearns*	N	Y	Y	N	N	N	Y	N
7 *Mica*	N	Y	Y	N	N	Y	Y	N
8 *McCollum*	N	Y	Y	N	Y	Y	Y	N
9 *Bilirakis*	N	Y	Y	N	Y	N	Y	Y
10 *Young*	N	N	Y	N	Y	Y	N	Y
11 Gibbons	N	N	N	Y	Y	Y	N	Y
12 *Canady*	N	Y	Y	N	N	N	Y	Y
13 *Miller*	Y	Y	Y	N	Y	Y	Y	Y
14 *Goss*	Y	Y	Y	N	Y	Y	Y	Y
15 Bacchus	Y	N	N	Y	Y	Y	?	Y
16 *Lewis*	N	Y	?	N	Y	Y	Y	Y
17 Meek	Y	N	N	Y	N	N	N	Y
18 *Ros-Lehtinen*	Y	N	N	N	N	N	N	Y
19 Johnston	Y	N	N	Y	Y	N	N	Y
20 Deutsch	Y	N	N	Y	Y	N	N	Y
21 *Diaz-Balart*	N	N	Y	N	N	N	N	Y
22 *Shaw*	N	N	Y	N	Y	Y	Y	Y
23 Hastings	Y	N	N	Y	Y	Y	N	Y
GEORGIA								
1 *Kingston*	N	Y	Y	Y	Y	N	Y	N
2 Bishop	Y	N	N	Y	Y	N	N	Y
3 *Collins*	N	Y	Y	N	N	Y	Y	N
4 *Linder*	N	Y	Y	N	N	Y	Y	N
5 Lewis	Y	N	N	Y	N	N	N	Y
6 *Gingrich*	N	Y	Y	N	Y	Y	Y	Y
7 Darden	N	N	N	Y	Y	Y	N	Y
8 Rowland	N	N	Y	Y	Y	N	Y	N
9 Deal	Y	N	N	Y	Y	Y	N	Y
10 Johnson	Y	N	N	Y	Y	Y	N	Y
11 McKinney	+	N	N	?	Y	N	N	Y
HAWAII								
1 Abercrombie	N	N	N	Y	Y	N	N	Y
2 Mink	N	N	N	Y	Y	N	N	Y
IDAHO								
1 LaRocco	N	N	N	Y	Y	N	N	Y
2 *Crapo*	N	Y	Y	N	N	N	Y	N
ILLINOIS								
1 Rush	Y	N	N	Y	N	N	N	Y
2 Reynolds	Y	?	N	Y	Y	Y	N	Y
3 Lipinski	Y	N	N	Y	N	N	N	Y
4 Gutierrez	Y	N	N	Y	N	N	N	Y
5 Rostenkowski	N	N	N	Y	Y	Y	N	Y
6 *Hyde*	N	Y	Y	N	Y	Y	Y	Y
7 Collins	Y	N	N	Y	N	N	N	Y
8 *Crane*	N	Y	Y	?	Y	Y	Y	N
9 Yates	Y	N	?	Y	Y	N	N	Y
10 *Porter*	Y	N	Y	N	Y	Y	N	Y
11 Sangmeister	N	N	N	Y	Y	N	N	Y
12 Costello	Y	N	N	Y	Y	N	N	Y
13 *Fawell*	N	N	N	Y	Y	Y	N	Y
14 *Hastert*	N	Y	Y	N	Y	Y	Y	Y
15 *Ewing*	N	Y	Y	N	Y	Y	Y	N
16 *Manzullo*	N	Y	Y	N	Y	Y	Y	N
17 Evans	Y	N	N	Y	N	N	N	Y

ND Northern Democrats   SD Southern Democrats

	569	570	571	572	573	575	576	577
18 ***Michel***	N	Y	Y	N	Y	Y	Y	N
19 Poshard	N	N	N	Y	Y	N	N	Y
20 Durbin	N	N	N	Y	Y	Y	N	Y
INDIANA								
1 Visclosky	Y	N	N	?	Y	N	N	Y
2 Sharp	Y	N	N	Y	Y	N	N	Y
3 Roemer	Y	N	N	Y	N	N	N	Y
4 Long	N	N	N	Y	Y	N	N	Y
5 ***Buyer***	N	Y	Y	?	N	Y	Y	N
6 ***Burton***	N	Y	Y	N	N	N	Y	N
7 ***Myers***	N	Y	Y	Y	Y	N	Y	N
8 McCloskey	Y	N	N	Y	Y	N	N	Y
9 Hamilton	Y	N	Y	Y	Y	Y	N	Y
10 Jacobs	Y	N	N	N	Y	N	N	Y
IOWA								
1 ***Leach***	Y	N	Y	N	Y	Y	Y	Y
2 ***Nussle***	N	Y	Y	N	Y	Y	Y	N
3 ***Lightfoot***	N	Y	Y	N	Y	Y	Y	N
4 Smith	N	N	N	Y	Y	Y	N	Y
5 ***Grandy***	N	Y	Y	N	Y	Y	?	Y
KANSAS								
1 ***Roberts***	N	Y	Y	?	Y	Y	Y	N
2 Slattery	N	N	N	Y	Y	N	N	Y
3 ***Meyers***	Y	N	Y	?	Y	Y	Y	Y
4 Glickman	N	N	N	Y	Y	Y	N	Y
KENTUCKY								
1 Barlow	Y	N	N	Y	Y	N	N	Y
2 Natcher	N	N	N	Y	Y	N	N	Y
3 Mazzoli	N	N	N	Y	Y	Y	N	Y
4 ***Bunning***	N	Y	Y	N	N	N	Y	N
5 ***Rogers***	N	Y	Y	N	N	N	Y	N
6 Baesler	Y	N	N	Y	Y	Y	N	Y
LOUISIANA								
1 ***Livingston***	N	Y	Y	Y	Y	Y	Y	N
2 Jefferson	Y	N	N	?	Y	Y	N	Y
3 Tauzin	N	N	Y	Y	N	N	Y	N
4 Fields	Y	N	N	Y	Y	N	N	Y
5 ***McCrery***	N	Y	Y	N	Y	Y	?	N
6 ***Baker***	N	Y	Y	N	Y	Y	Y	N
7 Hayes	N	Y	Y	Y	Y	Y	Y	N
MAINE								
1 Andrews	Y	N	N	Y	Y	N	N	Y
2 ***Snowe***	Y	N	Y	N	N	N	N	Y
MARYLAND								
1 ***Gilchrest***	Y	Y	N	?	Y	Y	N	?
2 ***Bentley***	N	Y	Y	N	N	N	Y	N
3 Cardin	Y	N	N	?	Y	Y	N	Y
4 Wynn	Y	N	N	Y	Y	N	N	Y
5 Hoyer	Y	N	N	Y	Y	Y	N	Y
6 ***Bartlett***	N	Y	Y	N	N	N	Y	N
7 Mfume	Y	N	N	Y	N	N	N	Y
8 ***Morella***	Y	N	N	N	Y	Y	N	Y
MASSACHUSETTS								
1 Olver	Y	N	N	Y	Y	N	N	Y
2 Neal	N	N	N	Y	N	N	N	Y
3 ***Blute***	Y	N	Y	N	N	N	N	Y
4 Frank	Y	N	N	?	Y	N	N	Y
5 Meehan	Y	N	N	Y	Y	Y	N	Y
6 ***Torkildsen***	Y	N	Y	N	N	Y	N	Y
7 Markey	Y	N	N	Y	Y	Y	N	Y
8 Kennedy	Y	N	N	Y	Y	Y	N	Y
9 Moakley	Y	N	N	Y	Y	N	N	Y
10 Studds	Y	N	N	Y	Y	Y	N	Y
MICHIGAN								
1 Stupak	Y	N	N	Y	Y	N	N	Y
2 ***Hoekstra***	N	Y	Y	N	N	Y	Y	N
3 Vacancy								
4 ***Camp***	N	Y	Y	N	Y	Y	Y	N
5 Barcia	N	Y	N	Y	N	N	Y	N
6 ***Upton***	Y	N	N	N	N	Y	N	Y
7 ***Smith***	N	Y	Y	N	Y	Y	Y	N
8 Carr	N	N	N	Y	Y	N	N	Y
9 Kildee	Y	N	N	Y	N	N	N	Y
10 Bonior	Y	N	N	Y	Y	N	N	Y
11 ***Knollenberg***	N	Y	Y	N	Y	Y	Y	N
12 Levin	N	N	N	Y	Y	N	N	Y
13 Ford	N	N	N	?	Y	N	N	Y
14 Conyers	Y	N	N	?	Y	N	N	Y
15 Collins	Y	N	N	Y	N	N	N	Y
16 Dingell	N	Y	N	Y	Y	N	N	Y
MINNESOTA								
1 Penny	N	N	N	Y	Y	Y	N	Y
2 Minge	Y	N	N	Y	Y	N	N	Y
3 ***Ramstad***	N	N	Y	N	Y	Y	Y	Y
4 Vento	Y	N	N	Y	Y	N	N	Y

	569	570	571	572	573	575	576	577
5 Sabo	Y	N	N	Y	Y	N	N	Y
6 ***Grams***	N	Y	Y	N	Y	Y	Y	N
7 Peterson	N	N	N	Y	N	N	N	Y
8 Oberstar	Y	N	N	Y	N	N	N	Y
MISSISSIPPI								
1 Whitten	Y	N	N	Y	Y	Y	N	Y
2 Thompson	Y	N	N	?	Y	N	N	Y
3 Montgomery	N	Y	Y	Y	Y	Y	Y	Y
4 Parker	N	Y	Y	Y	Y	Y	Y	Y
5 Taylor	N	Y	Y	N	N	N	Y	Y
MISSOURI								
1 Clay	Y	N	N	N	Y	N	N	Y
2 ***Talent***	N	Y	Y	N	Y	N	Y	N
3 Gephardt	N	N	N	Y	Y	N	N	Y
4 Skelton	N	N	Y	?	Y	Y	Y	Y
5 Wheat	Y	N	N	Y	Y	N	N	Y
6 Danner	N	N	N	Y	N	N	N	Y
7 ***Hancock***	N	Y	Y	N	Y	Y	Y	N
8 ***Emerson***	N	Y	Y	?	Y	Y	Y	N
9 Volkmer	N	N	N	Y	N	N	N	Y
MONTANA								
AL Williams	N	N	N	Y	Y	N	N	Y
NEBRASKA								
1 ***Bereuter***	N	N	Y	?	Y	Y	Y	Y
2 Hoagland	Y	N	N	Y	Y	Y	N	Y
3 ***Barrett***	N	Y	Y	N	Y	Y	Y	N
NEVADA								
1 Bilbray	N	N	N	Y	Y	N	N	Y
2 ***Vucanovich***	N	Y	Y	?	Y	N	Y	N
NEW HAMPSHIRE								
1 ***Zeliff***	N	Y	Y	N	Y	Y	Y	N
2 Swett	N	N	N	Y	Y	N	N	Y
NEW JERSEY								
1 Andrews	Y	N	N	?	?	N	N	Y
2 Hughes	N	N	N	Y	Y	N	N	Y
3 ***Saxton***	Y	N	Y	N	N	N	N	Y
4 ***Smith***	Y	N	Y	?	Y	N	N	Y
5 ***Roukema***	?	?	Y	N	Y	Y	N	Y
6 Pallone	Y	N	N	Y	Y	N	N	Y
7 ***Franks***	Y	Y	Y	N	Y	Y	N	Y
8 Klein	N	N	N	Y	Y	N	N	Y
9 Torricelli	?	?	N	?	Y	N	N	Y
10 Payne	Y	N	N	Y	Y	N	N	Y
11 ***Gallo***	Y	Y	Y	N	Y	Y	N	Y
12 ***Zimmer***	Y	N	N	N	Y	Y	N	Y
13 Menendez	Y	N	N	Y	Y	N	N	Y
NEW MEXICO								
1 ***Schiff***	Y	Y	Y	N	Y	Y	Y	Y
2 ***Skeen***	N	Y	Y	N	Y	Y	Y	Y
3 Richardson	Y	N	N	Y	Y	Y	N	Y
NEW YORK								
1 Hochbrueckner	Y	N	N	Y	N	N	N	Y
2 ***Lazio***	Y	N	Y	N	Y	Y	Y	Y
3 ***King***	N	Y	Y	N	Y	Y	Y	Y
4 ***Levy***	N	Y	Y	N	Y	Y	Y	Y
5 Ackerman	Y	N	N	Y	Y	N	N	Y
6 Flake	N	N	N	?	Y	Y	N	Y
7 Manton	Y	N	N	?	Y	N	N	Y
8 Nadler	Y	N	N	Y	Y	N	N	Y
9 Schumer	Y	N	N	Y	Y	N	N	Y
10 Towns	Y	N	N	?	?	N	N	Y
11 Owens	Y	N	N	Y	Y	N	N	Y
12 Velazquez	Y	N	N	Y	N	N	N	Y
13 ***Molinari***	Y	N	Y	N	Y	Y	N	N
14 Maloney	Y	N	N	Y	Y	N	N	Y
15 Rangel	Y	N	N	?	Y	N	N	Y
16 Serrano	Y	N	N	?	Y	N	N	Y
17 Engel	Y	N	N	?	Y	N	N	Y
18 Lowey	Y	N	N	Y	Y	Y	N	Y
19 ***Fish***	Y	N	N	Y	Y	Y	N	Y
20 ***Gilman***	Y	N	N	Y	Y	N	N	Y
21 McNulty	N	N	Y	Y	N	N	N	Y
22 ***Solomon***	N	Y	Y	N	Y	N	Y	N
23 ***Boehlert***	Y	N	N	N	Y	Y	N	Y
24 ***McHugh***	N	Y	Y	N	N	N	Y	N
25 ***Walsh***	N	Y	Y	N	N	N	Y	N
26 Hinchey	Y	N	N	?	N	N	N	Y
27 ***Paxon***	N	Y	Y	N	Y	Y	Y	N
28 Slaughter	Y	N	N	Y	Y	N	N	Y
29 LaFalce	Y	N	N	Y	N	N	N	Y
30 ***Quinn***	N	Y	Y	N	Y	N	Y	N
31 ***Houghton***	N	Y	Y	Y	Y	Y	Y	N
NORTH CAROLINA								
1 Clayton	Y	N	N	Y	Y	N	N	Y
2 Valentine	Y	Y	?	Y	Y	Y	N	Y

	569	570	571	572	573	575	576	577
3 Lancaster	Y	N	Y	Y	Y	N	N	Y
4 Price	Y	N	N	Y	Y	Y	N	Y
5 Neal	Y	N	N	?	Y	Y	N	Y
6 ***Coble***	N	Y	Y	N	Y	Y	Y	N
7 Rose	N	N	N	?	Y	Y	?	?
8 Hefner	N	N	N	?	Y	Y	N	Y
9 ***McMillan***	N	Y	Y	N	Y	Y	Y	Y
10 ***Ballenger***	N	Y	Y	N	Y	Y	Y	N
11 ***Taylor***	N	Y	Y	N	N	N	Y	N
12 Watt	Y	N	N	Y	N	N	N	Y
NORTH DAKOTA								
AL Pomeroy	N	N	Y	Y	N	N	N	Y
OHIO								
1 Mann	Y	N	Y	Y	Y	Y	N	Y
2 ***Portman***	N	Y	Y	N	Y	Y	Y	Y
3 Hall	N	N	N	Y	Y	N	N	Y
4 ***Oxley***	N	Y	Y	N	Y	Y	Y	N
5 ***Gillmor***	Y	Y	Y	Y	Y	Y	Y	N
6 Strickland	N	N	N	Y	Y	N	N	Y
7 ***Hobson***	N	Y	Y	N	Y	Y	Y	Y
8 ***Boehner***	N	Y	Y	N	Y	Y	Y	N
9 Kaptur	Y	N	N	Y	N	N	N	Y
10 ***Hoke***	N	Y	Y	?	?	N	?	N
11 Stokes	Y	N	N	Y	Y	N	N	Y
12 ***Kasich***	N	Y	Y	?	Y	Y	Y	N
13 Brown	Y	N	N	Y	N	N	N	Y
14 Sawyer	N	N	N	Y	Y	Y	N	Y
15 ***Pryce***	Y	Y	Y	N	Y	Y	Y	Y
16 ***Regula***	N	N	N	N	Y	N	N	Y
17 Traficant	Y	N	N	Y	N	N	N	Y
18 Applegate	N	N	N	Y	Y	N	N	Y
19 Fingerhut	Y	N	N	Y	Y	N	N	Y
OKLAHOMA								
1 ***Inhofe***	N	Y	Y	N	Y	N	Y	N
2 Synar	Y	N	N	Y	Y	Y	N	Y
3 Brewster	N	N	N	Y	Y	Y	N	Y
4 McCurdy	N	N	Y	Y	Y	Y	N	Y
5 ***Istook***	N	Y	Y	?	N	Y	Y	N
6 English	N	?	N	?	Y	Y	N	Y
OREGON								
1 Furse	Y	N	N	Y	Y	N	N	Y
2 ***Smith***	N	Y	Y	N	Y	Y	Y	N
3 Wyden	Y	N	N	Y	Y	Y	N	Y
4 DeFazio	Y	N	N	Y	N	N	N	Y
5 Kopetski	Y	N	N	?	Y	Y	N	Y
PENNSYLVANIA								
1 Foglietta	Y	N	N	?	Y	N	N	Y
2 Blackwell	?	?	?	?	Y	N	N	Y
3 Borski	Y	N	N	Y	Y	N	N	Y
4 Klink	Y	N	N	Y	N	N	?	?
5 ***Clinger***	?	?	?	?	?	Y	?	?
6 Holden	Y	N	N	Y	N	N	N	Y
7 ***Weldon***	Y	N	Y	N	Y	N	N	Y
8 ***Greenwood***	Y	N	Y	Y	Y	Y	N	Y
9 ***Shuster***	N	Y	Y	N	Y	N	Y	Y
10 ***McDade***	Y	Y	Y	?	Y	Y	N	Y
11 Kanjorski	N	N	N	Y	Y	N	N	Y
12 Murtha	N	N	N	Y	Y	N	N	Y
13 Margolies-Mezv.	Y	N	N	?	Y	N	N	Y
14 Coyne	Y	N	N	Y	Y	N	N	Y
15 McHale	Y	N	N	Y	Y	N	N	Y
16 ***Walker***	N	Y	Y	N	Y	Y	Y	N
17 ***Gekas***	N	Y	Y	N	Y	Y	Y	N
18 ***Santorum***	N	N	Y	N	Y	N	Y	N
19 ***Goodling***	Y	Y	Y	N	Y	Y	Y	N
20 Murphy	Y	N	N	N	Y	N	N	Y
21 ***Ridge***	N	Y	N	N	Y	Y	?	?
RHODE ISLAND								
1 ***Machtley***	Y	N	Y	?	Y	Y	N	Y
2 Reed	Y	N	N	Y	N	N	N	Y
SOUTH CAROLINA								
1 ***Ravenel***	Y	N	N	N	Y	N	N	Y
2 ***Spence***	N	Y	Y	N	Y	N	Y	Y
3 Derrick	Y	N	N	Y	Y	N	N	Y
4 ***Inglis***	N	?	Y	Y	N	N	Y	N
5 Spratt	N	N	N	Y	Y	Y	N	Y
6 Clyburn	Y	N	N	Y	Y	N	N	Y
SOUTH DAKOTA								
AL Johnson	N	N	N	Y	Y	N	N	Y
TENNESSEE								
1 ***Quillen***	N	N	Y	N	Y	Y	Y	N
2 ***Duncan***	N	Y	Y	N	Y	Y	Y	Y
3 Lloyd	N	Y	Y	Y	Y	Y	N	Y
4 Cooper	Y	N	N	Y	Y	Y	N	Y
5 Clement	N	N	N	Y	Y	Y	N	Y

	569	570	571	572	573	575	576	577
6 Gordon	N	N	N	Y	Y	Y	N	Y
7 ***Sundquist***	N	Y	Y	N	Y	Y	Y	N
8 Tanner	N	N	Y	Y	Y	Y	N	Y
9 Ford	N	?	?	?	Y	Y	?	Y
TEXAS								
1 Chapman	?	N	Y	?	Y	Y	?	?
2 Wilson	N	?	?	?	Y	N	?	?
3 ***Johnson, Sam***	N	Y	Y	N	Y	Y	Y	N
4 Hall	N	Y	Y	Y	N	N	Y	Y
5 Bryant	Y	?	N	Y	Y	Y	N	Y
6 ***Barton***	N	Y	Y	?	Y	Y	Y	N
7 ***Archer***	N	Y	Y	Y	Y	Y	Y	N
8 ***Fields***	N	Y	Y	N	Y	Y	Y	N
9 Brooks	N	N	N	Y	Y	N	N	Y
10 Pickle	N	N	N	Y	Y	Y	N	Y
11 Edwards	N	N	Y	Y	Y	Y	N	Y
12 Geren	Y	N	Y	Y	Y	Y	N	Y
13 Sarpalius	N	N	N	Y	Y	Y	N	Y
14 Laughlin	Y	N	N	Y	Y	Y	N	Y
15 de la Garza	Y	Y	Y	Y	Y	Y	N	Y
16 Coleman	Y	N	Y	Y	Y	Y	N	Y
17 Stenholm	N	Y	Y	Y	Y	Y	Y	N
18 Washington	Y	N	N	Y	N	N	?	Y
19 ***Combest***	N	Y	Y	Y	Y	Y	Y	N
20 Gonzalez	Y	N	N	Y	N	N	N	Y
21 ***Smith***	N	Y	Y	N	Y	Y	Y	N
22 ***DeLay***	N	Y	Y	N	Y	Y	Y	N
23 ***Bonilla***	N	Y	Y	N	Y	Y	Y	N
24 Frost	N	N	Y	Y	Y	Y	N	Y
25 Andrews	Y	N	Y	Y	Y	Y	N	Y
26 ***Armey***	N	Y	Y	N	Y	Y	Y	N
27 Ortiz	N	N	N	Y	Y	Y	N	Y
28 Tejeda	Y	N	Y	Y	Y	Y	N	Y
29 Green	Y	N	N	Y	Y	N	N	Y
30 Johnson, E.B.	Y	N	Y	Y	Y	Y	N	Y
UTAH								
1 ***Hansen***	N	Y	Y	N	Y	Y	Y	N
2 Shepherd	Y	N	Y	?	Y	Y	N	Y
3 Orton	N	Y	Y	?	Y	N	Y	N
VERMONT								
AL *Sanders*	Y	N	N	?	N	N	N	Y
VIRGINIA								
1 ***Bateman***	N	Y	Y	Y	Y	Y	Y	N
2 Pickett	N	N	Y	Y	Y	Y	N	Y
3 Scott	Y	N	N	Y	N	N	N	Y
4 Sisisky	N	N	Y	Y	Y	N	?	Y
5 Payne	N	N	Y	Y	Y	Y	N	Y
6 ***Goodlatte***	N	Y	Y	N	Y	Y	Y	Y
7 ***Bliley***	N	Y	Y	N	Y	Y	Y	N
8 Moran	Y	N	N	Y	Y	Y	N	Y
9 Boucher	N	N	N	Y	Y	N	N	Y
10 ***Wolf***	N	Y	Y	N	Y	Y	Y	Y
11 Byrne	Y	N	N	Y	N	N	N	Y
WASHINGTON								
1 Cantwell	Y	N	N	Y	Y	Y	N	Y
2 Swift	N	N	N	Y	Y	Y	N	Y
3 Unsoeld	Y	N	N	Y	Y	N	N	Y
4 Inslee	N	N	N	Y	Y	Y	N	Y
5 Foley						Y		
6 Dicks	N	N	N	Y	Y	Y	?	?
7 McDermott	Y	N	N	Y	Y	Y	N	Y
8 ***Dunn***	N	Y	Y	N	Y	Y	Y	N
9 Kreidler	Y	N	N	Y	Y	Y	N	Y
WEST VIRGINIA								
1 Mollohan	N	N	N	?	?	N	N	Y
2 Wise	Y	N	N	Y	N	N	N	Y
3 Rahall	Y	N	N	Y	N	N	N	Y
WISCONSIN								
1 Barca	Y	N	N	Y	N	N	N	Y
2 ***Klug***	Y	N	Y	N	Y	Y	N	Y
3 ***Gunderson***	N	N	Y	N	Y	Y	N	Y
4 Kleczka	Y	N	N	?	N	N	N	Y
5 Barrett	Y	N	N	Y	Y	N	N	Y
6 ***Petri***	Y	N	N	N	Y	Y	Y	Y
7 Obey	Y	N	N	Y	N	N	N	Y
8 ***Roth***	N	Y	Y	?	Y	Y	Y	Y
9 ***Sensenbrenner***	Y	N	Y	N	Y	Y	Y	Y
WYOMING								
AL ***Thomas***	N	Y	Y	N	Y	Y	Y	N
DELEGATES								
de Lugo, V.I.	Y	N	N	D	D	D	D	D
Faleomavaega, Am.S.	N	N	N	D	D	D	D	D
Norton, D.C.	Y	N	N	D	D	D	D	D
Romero-B., P.R.	N	N	N	D	D	D	D	D
Underwood, Guam	N	N	N	D	D	D	D	D

Southern states - Ala., Ark., Fla., Ga., Ky., La., Miss., N.C., Okla., S.C., Tenn., Texas, Va.
Omitted votes are quorum calls, which CQ does not include in its vote charts.

578. HR 796. Freedom of Access to Abortion Clinics/Rule. Adoption of the rule (H Res 313) to provide for House floor consideration of the bill to establish federal criminal and civil penalties for persons who use force, the threat of force, or physical obstruction to block access to abortion clinics. Adopted 233-192: R 18-156; D 214-36 (ND 146-23, SD 68-13); I 1-0, Nov. 18, 1993.

579. HR 796. Freedom of Access to Abortion Clinics/Parental Exemption. DeLay, R-Texas, amendment to exempt parents or legal guardians from penalties resulting from the actions of a child. Adopted in the Committee of the Whole 350-82: R 169-4; D 181-77 (ND 117-56, SD 64-21); I 0-1, Nov. 18, 1993.

580. HR 796. Freedom of Access to Abortion Clinics/Substitute. Smith, R-N.J., substitute amendment to provide that physical obstruction must be accompanied by force or threats of force to be a crime; eliminate the punitive damages in the bill; establish standards for a court injunction; and prohibit state attorneys general from bringing suits under the bill. Rejected in the Committee of the Whole 177-255: R 133-40; D 44-214 (ND 26-147, SD 18-67); I 0-1, Nov. 18, 1993. A "nay" was a vote in support of the president's position.

581. HR 796. Freedom of Access to Abortion Clinics/Parental Exemption. Separate vote at the request of Walker, R-Pa., on the amendment adopted in the Committee of the Whole offered by DeLay, R-Texas, to exempt parents or legal guardians from penalties resulting from the actions of a child. Adopted 345-80: R 169-4; D 176-75 (ND 113-53, SD 63-22); I 0-1, Nov. 18, 1993. (On a separate vote, which may be demanded on an amendment adopted in the Committee of the Whole, the four delegates and the resident commissioner of Puerto Rico cannot vote. See vote 579.)

582. HR 796. Freedom of Access to Abortion Clinics/Civil Cause of Action. Sensenbrenner, R-Wis., motion to recommit the bill to the House Judiciary Committee with instructions to report it back with an amendment eliminating the bill's provisions providing a civil cause of action by individuals and state attorneys general. Motion rejected 182-246: R 138-34; D 44-211 (ND 25-145, SD 19-66); I 0-1, Nov. 18, 1993. (Subsequently, the House passed the bill by voice vote.)

583. Procedural Motion. Approval of the House Journal of Thursday, Nov. 18. Approved 238-150: R 18-144; D 219-6 (ND 144-4, SD 75-2); I 1-0, Nov. 19, 1993.

584. HR 3351. Youth Offenders Alternative Punishment/Rule. Adoption of the rule (H Res 314) to provide for House floor consideration of the bill to authorize $200 million per year for fiscal 1994-96 in grants to states to develop alternative punishments other than incarceration and probation for young offenders. Adopted 238-179: R 1-172; D 236-7 (ND 159-4, SD 77-3); I 1-0, Nov. 19, 1993.

585. HR 3351. Youth Offenders Alternative Punishment/Eligibility. McCollum, R-Fla., amendment to limit the programs in the bill to individuals under 18 who have not been convicted of a sexual assault, a firearm crime or a crime with a sentence over a year. Rejected in the Committee of the Whole 201-228: R 166-6; D 35-221 (ND 15-157, SD 20-64); I 0-1, Nov. 19, 1993.

KEY

Y Voted for (yea).
Paired for.
+ Announced for.
N Voted against (nay).
X Paired against.
− Announced against.
P Voted "present."
C Voted "present" to avoid possible conflict of interest.
? Did not vote or otherwise make a position known.
D Delegates ineligible to vote.

Democrats **Republicans**
Independent

	578	579	580	581	582	583	584	585
ALABAMA								
1 *Callahan*	N	Y	Y	Y	Y	N	N	Y
2 *Everett*	N	Y	Y	Y	Y	N	N	Y
3 Browder	Y	Y	Y	Y	Y	Y	Y	Y
4 Bevill	Y	Y	Y	Y	Y	Y	Y	Y
5 Cramer	Y	Y	N	Y	N	Y	Y	Y
6 *Bachus*	N	Y	Y	Y	Y	N	N	Y
7 Hilliard	Y	N	N	N	N	Y	Y	N
ALASKA								
AL *Young*	N	Y	Y	Y	Y	?	N	Y
ARIZONA								
1 Coppersmith	Y	N	N	N	N	Y	Y	N
2 Pastor	Y	Y	N	Y	N	Y	Y	N
3 *Stump*	N	Y	Y	Y	Y	N	N	Y
4 *Kyl*	N	Y	Y	Y	Y	N	N	Y
5 *Kolbe*	N	Y	N	Y	Y	N	N	Y
6 English	Y	Y	N	Y	N	Y	Y	N
ARKANSAS								
1 Lambert	Y	Y	N	Y	N	Y	Y	N
2 Thornton	Y	Y	N	Y	N	?	Y	N
3 *Hutchinson*	N	Y	Y	Y	Y	N	N	Y
4 *Dickey*	N	?	?	?	?	?	N	Y
CALIFORNIA								
1 Hamburg	Y	N	N	N	N	Y	N	N
2 *Herger*	N	Y	Y	Y	Y	N	N	?
3 Fazio	Y	Y	N	Y	N	Y	Y	N
4 *Doolittle*	N	Y	Y	Y	Y	N	N	Y
5 Matsui	Y	N	N	N	N	P	Y	N
6 Woolsey	Y	N	N	N	N	Y	Y	N
7 Miller	Y	Y	N	Y	N	Y	Y	N
8 Pelosi	Y	Y	N	Y	N	Y	Y	N
9 Dellums	Y	N	N	N	N	Y	Y	N
10 *Baker*	N	Y	Y	Y	Y	N	N	Y
11 *Pombo*	N	Y	Y	Y	Y	N	Y	Y
12 Lantos	Y	Y	N	Y	N	Y	Y	N
13 Stark	Y	N	N	N	N	Y	Y	N
14 Eshoo	Y	Y	N	Y	N	Y	Y	N
15 Mineta	Y	N	N	N	N	Y	Y	N
16 Edwards	Y	N	N	N	Y	Y	Y	N
17 Farr	Y	Y	N	Y	N	Y	Y	N
18 Condit	Y	Y	N	Y	N	Y	Y	Y
19 Lehman	Y	Y	N	Y	N	Y	Y	N
20 Dooley	Y	Y	N	Y	N	Y	Y	N
21 *Thomas*	N	Y	N	Y	Y	N	N	Y
22 *Huffington*	N	Y	Y	Y	Y	N	N	Y
23 *Gallegly*	N	Y	Y	Y	Y	N	N	Y
24 Beilenson	Y	Y	N	Y	?	Y	Y	N
25 *McKeon*	N	Y	Y	Y	Y	N	N	Y
26 Berman	Y	Y	N	Y	N	Y	Y	N
27 *Moorhead*	N	Y	Y	Y	Y	N	N	Y
28 *Dreier*	N	Y	Y	Y	Y	N	N	Y
29 Waxman	Y	N	N	N	N	Y	Y	N
30 Becerra	Y	N	N	N	N	Y	Y	N
31 Martinez	Y	N	Y	N	Y	Y	N	N
32 Dixon	Y	N	Y	N	N	Y	Y	N
33 Roybal-Allard	Y	Y	N	Y	N	Y	Y	N
34 Torres	Y	N	N	Y	N	Y	Y	N
35 Waters	Y	N	N	N	N	Y	Y	N
36 Harman	Y	Y	N	Y	N	Y	Y	N
37 Tucker	N	Y	Y	Y	N	?	Y	N
38 *Horn*	Y	N	N	N	N	N	N	Y
39 *Royce*	N	Y	Y	Y	Y	N	N	Y
40 *Lewis*	N	Y	Y	Y	N	Y	N	Y
41 *Kim*	N	Y	Y	Y	Y	N	N	Y

	578	579	580	581	582	583	584	585
42 Brown	?	N	N	N	N	?	?	N
43 *Calvert*	N	Y	Y	Y	Y	?	N	Y
44 *McCandless*	N	Y	N	Y	Y	N	N	Y
45 *Rohrabacher*	N	Y	Y	Y	Y	N	N	Y
46 *Dornan*	N	Y	Y	Y	Y	?	N	Y
47 *Cox*	N	Y	N	Y	Y	N	N	Y
48 *Packard*	N	Y	Y	Y	Y	N	N	Y
49 Schenk	Y	Y	N	Y	N	Y	Y	N
50 Filner	Y	N	N	N	N	Y	Y	N
51 *Cunningham*	N	Y	Y	Y	Y	N	N	Y
52 *Hunter*	N	Y	Y	Y	Y	?	N	Y
COLORADO								
1 Schroeder	Y	N	N	N	N	N	Y	N
2 Skaggs	Y	Y	N	Y	N	Y	Y	N
3 *McInnis*	N	Y	Y	Y	N	Y	N	Y
4 *Allard*	N	Y	Y	Y	Y	N	N	Y
5 *Hefley*	N	Y	Y	Y	Y	N	N	Y
6 *Schaefer*	N	Y	Y	Y	Y	N	N	Y
CONNECTICUT								
1 Kennelly	Y	Y	N	Y	N	Y	?	N
2 Gejdenson	Y	N	N	N	Y	Y	Y	N
3 DeLauro	Y	Y	N	Y	N	Y	Y	N
4 *Shays*	Y	Y	N	Y	N	N	N	Y
5 *Franks*	Y	Y	N	Y	N	N	N	Y
6 *Johnson*	Y	Y	N	Y	−	N	N	N
DELAWARE								
AL *Castle*	Y	Y	Y	Y	N	N	N	Y
FLORIDA								
1 Hutto	N	Y	Y	Y	Y	Y	Y	N
2 Peterson	Y	Y	N	Y	N	Y	Y	N
3 Brown	Y	N	N	N	N	Y	Y	N
4 *Fowler*	N	Y	N	N	N	N	N	Y
5 Thurman	N	N	N	N	N	Y	Y	N
6 *Stearns*	N	Y	Y	Y	Y	N	N	#
7 *Mica*	N	Y	Y	Y	Y	N	N	Y
8 *McCollum*	N	Y	Y	Y	Y	N	N	Y
9 *Bilirakis*	N	Y	Y	Y	Y	N	N	Y
10 *Young*	N	Y	Y	Y	N	N	N	Y
11 Gibbons	Y	Y	N	Y	N	Y	Y	N
12 *Canady*	N	Y	Y	Y	Y	N	N	Y
13 *Miller*	N	Y	Y	Y	Y	N	N	Y
14 *Goss*	N	Y	Y	Y	Y	N	N	Y
15 *Bacchus*	Y	N	N	N	N	Y	N	N
16 *Lewis*	N	Y	Y	N	N	Y	N	Y
17 Meek	Y	Y	N	N	N	Y	Y	N
18 *Ros-Lehtinen*	N	Y	Y	Y	N	N	N	Y
19 Johnston	Y	N	N	N	N	Y	Y	N
20 Deutsch	Y	N	N	N	N	Y	Y	Y
21 *Diaz-Balart*	N	Y	Y	N	N	Y	N	Y
22 *Shaw*	N	Y	Y	Y	Y	N	N	Y
23 Hastings	Y	N	N	N	N	Y	N	N
GEORGIA								
1 *Kingston*	N	Y	Y	Y	Y	N	N	Y
2 Bishop	Y	Y	N	Y	N	Y	N	N
3 *Collins*	N	Y	Y	Y	Y	Y	N	Y
4 *Linder*	N	Y	Y	Y	Y	N	N	Y
5 Lewis	Y	N	N	N	N	Y	Y	N
6 *Gingrich*	N	Y	Y	Y	Y	N	N	Y
7 *Darden*	Y	Y	N	Y	N	Y	Y	N
8 Rowland	Y	Y	N	Y	N	Y	Y	N
9 *Deal*	N	Y	Y	Y	Y	Y	Y	N
10 Johnson	Y	Y	N	Y	N	Y	Y	N
11 McKinney	Y	N	N	N	N	Y	N	N
HAWAII								
1 Abercrombie	Y	N	N	N	N	Y	Y	N
2 Mink	Y	N	N	N	N	?	Y	N
IDAHO								
1 LaRocco	Y	Y	N	Y	N	Y	Y	N
2 *Crapo*	N	Y	Y	Y	Y	N	N	Y
ILLINOIS								
1 Rush	Y	N	N	N	N	Y	Y	N
2 Reynolds	Y	Y	N	Y	N	Y	Y	N
3 Lipinski	N	Y	Y	Y	Y	Y	Y	Y
4 Gutierrez	Y	Y	N	?	N	Y	Y	N
5 Rostenkowski	Y	Y	N	Y	N	Y	Y	N
6 *Hyde*	N	Y	N	Y	N	Y	N	Y
7 Collins	Y	N	N	N	N	Y	Y	N
8 *Crane*	N	Y	Y	Y	Y	N	N	Y
9 Yates	Y	Y	N	N	N	Y	Y	N
10 *Porter*	Y	Y	N	Y	N	?	Y	N
11 Sangmeister	Y	Y	N	Y	N	Y	Y	N
12 Costello	N	Y	Y	Y	Y	Y	Y	Y
13 *Fawell*	N	Y	N	N	N	N	N	Y
14 *Hastert*	N	Y	Y	Y	N	N	N	Y
15 *Ewing*	Y	Y	Y	Y	Y	N	N	Y
16 *Manzullo*	N	Y	Y	Y	Y	N	N	Y
17 Evans	Y	N	N	N	N	Y	N	N

ND Northern Democrats   SD Southern Democrats

	578	579	580	581	582	583	584	585
18 ***Michel***	N	Y	Y	Y	Y	N	N	Y
19 Poshard	N	Y	Y	Y	Y	Y	Y	N
20 Durbin	Y	Y	N	Y	N	Y	Y	N
INDIANA								
1 Visclosky	Y	N	N	N	N	Y	Y	N
2 Sharp	Y	Y	N	Y	N	Y	Y	N
3 Roemer	Y	Y	N	Y	N	Y	Y	N
4 Long	Y	N	N	N	N	Y	Y	N
5 ***Buyer***	N	Y	Y	Y	Y	N	N	Y
6 ***Burton***	N	Y	Y	Y	Y	N	N	Y
7 ***Myers***	N	Y	Y	Y	Y	Y	N	Y
8 McCloskey	Y	Y	N	Y	N	?	Y	N
9 Hamilton	Y	Y	N	Y	Y	Y	Y	Y
10 Jacobs	Y	Y	N	Y	N	N	N	N
IOWA								
1 ***Leach***	N	Y	N	Y	N	N	N	Y
2 ***Nussle***	N	Y	Y	Y	Y	N	N	Y
3 ***Lightfoot***	N	Y	Y	Y	Y	N	N	Y
4 Smith	Y	Y	N	Y	N	Y	Y	N
5 ***Grandy***	N	Y	N	Y	Y	N	N	Y
KANSAS								
1 ***Roberts***	N	Y	Y	Y	Y	N	N	Y
2 Slattery	Y	Y	N	Y	N	Y	?	?
3 ***Meyers***	Y	Y	N	Y	N	N	N	Y
4 Glickman	Y	Y	N	Y	N	Y	Y	N
KENTUCKY								
1 Barlow	Y	Y	N	Y	Y	Y	Y	Y
2 Natcher	Y	N	N	N	N	Y	Y	N
3 Mazzoli	N	Y	Y	Y	Y	Y	Y	N
4 ***Bunning***	N	Y	Y	Y	Y	N	N	Y
5 ***Rogers***	N	Y	Y	Y	Y	?	N	Y
6 Baesler	Y	Y	N	Y	N	Y	Y	Y
LOUISIANA								
1 ***Livingston***	N	Y	Y	Y	Y	Y	N	Y
2 Jefferson	Y	N	N	N	N	?	Y	N
3 Tauzin	N	Y	Y	Y	Y	Y	Y	Y
4 Fields	Y	Y	N	Y	N	Y	Y	N
5 ***McCrery***	N	Y	Y	Y	Y	?	N	Y
6 ***Baker***	N	Y	Y	Y	Y	N	N	Y
7 Hayes	N	Y	Y	Y	Y	Y	Y	Y
MAINE								
1 Andrews	Y	N	N	N	N	Y	Y	N
2 ***Snowe***	Y	Y	N	Y	N	N	N	Y
MARYLAND								
1 ***Gilchrest***	N	Y	N	Y	Y	N	N	Y
2 ***Bentley***	N	Y	Y	Y	Y	N	N	N
3 Cardin	Y	Y	N	Y	N	Y	Y	N
4 Wynn	Y	N	N	N	N	?	Y	N
5 Hoyer	Y	Y	N	Y	N	?	Y	N
6 ***Bartlett***	N	Y	Y	Y	Y	N	N	Y
7 Mfume	Y	Y	N	Y	N	?	Y	N
8 ***Morella***	Y	N	N	N	N	N	N	N
MASSACHUSETTS								
1 Olver	Y	N	N	N	N	Y	Y	N
2 Neal	Y	Y	N	Y	N	Y	Y	N
3 ***Blute***	N	Y	Y	Y	Y	N	N	Y
4 Frank	Y	N	N	N	N	Y	Y	N
5 Meehan	Y	N	N	N	N	Y	Y	N
6 ***Torkildsen***	N	Y	N	Y	N	?	N	Y
7 Markey	Y	Y	N	Y	N	Y	Y	N
8 Kennedy	Y	Y	N	Y	N	Y	Y	N
9 Moakley	Y	Y	N	Y	N	Y	Y	N
10 Studds	Y	Y	N	Y	N	Y	Y	N
MICHIGAN								
1 Stupak	N	Y	Y	Y	Y	Y	Y	N
2 ***Hoekstra***	N	Y	Y	Y	Y	N	N	Y
3 Vacancy								
4 ***Camp***	N	Y	Y	Y	Y	N	N	Y
5 Barcia	N	Y	Y	Y	Y	Y	Y	N
6 ***Upton***	N	Y	N	Y	N	N	N	Y
7 ***Smith***	N	Y	Y	Y	Y	N	N	Y
8 Carr	Y	Y	N	Y	N	Y	Y	N
9 Kildee	N	Y	Y	Y	Y	Y	Y	N
10 Bonior	Y	Y	N	Y	N	Y	Y	N
11 ***Knollenberg***	N	Y	Y	Y	Y	N	N	Y
12 Levin	Y	Y	N	Y	N	Y	Y	N
13 Ford	Y	N	N	N	N	?	Y	N
14 Conyers	Y	N	?	N	N	Y	Y	N
15 Collins	Y	N	N	N	N	Y	Y	N
16 Dingell	Y	Y	N	Y	N	?	Y	N
MINNESOTA								
1 Penny	Y	Y	Y	Y	Y	Y	Y	N
2 Minge	Y	Y	N	Y	N	Y	Y	N
3 ***Ramstad***	N	Y	N	Y	N	N	N	N
4 Vento	Y	N	N	N	N	Y	Y	N

	578	579	580	581	582	583	584	585
5 Sabo	Y	N	N	N	N	Y	Y	N
6 ***Grams***	N	Y	Y	Y	Y	N	N	Y
7 Peterson	N	Y	Y	Y	Y	Y	N	Y
8 Oberstar	N	Y	Y	Y	N	Y	Y	N
MISSISSIPPI								
1 Whitten	?	Y	N	Y	N	?	Y	N
2 Thompson	Y	N	N	N	N	Y	Y	N
3 Montgomery	Y	Y	Y	Y	Y	Y	Y	N
4 Parker	Y	Y	Y	Y	Y	Y	Y	N
5 Taylor	N	Y	Y	Y	Y	N	N	Y
MISSOURI								
1 Clay	Y	N	N	N	N	N	Y	N
2 ***Talent***	N	Y	Y	Y	Y	N	N	Y
3 Gephardt	Y	Y	N	?	N	Y	Y	N
4 Skelton	N	Y	Y	Y	Y	Y	N	Y
5 Wheat	Y	Y	N	Y	N	Y	?	N
6 Danner	Y	Y	N	Y	N	Y	Y	N
7 ***Hancock***	N	Y	Y	Y	Y	N	N	Y
8 ***Emerson***	N	Y	Y	Y	Y	N	N	Y
9 Volkmer	N	Y	Y	Y	Y	Y	Y	N
MONTANA								
AL Williams	Y	Y	N	N	N	?	Y	Y
NEBRASKA								
1 ***Bereuter***	N	Y	N	Y	Y	N	N	Y
2 Hoagland	Y	Y	N	Y	N	Y	Y	N
3 ***Barrett***	N	Y	Y	Y	Y	N	N	Y
NEVADA								
1 Bilbray	Y	Y	N	Y	N	Y	Y	N
2 ***Vucanovich***	N	Y	Y	Y	Y	N	N	Y
NEW HAMPSHIRE								
1 ***Zeliff***	N	Y	N	Y	N	N	N	Y
2 Swett	Y	N	N	N	N	Y	Y	N
NEW JERSEY								
1 Andrews	Y	?	?	?	?	?	Y	N
2 Hughes	Y	Y	N	Y	N	Y	Y	N
3 ***Saxton***	N	Y	Y	Y	Y	N	N	Y
4 ***Smith***	N	Y	Y	Y	Y	Y	N	Y
5 ***Roukema***	Y	Y	N	Y	N	N	N	Y
6 Pallone	Y	Y	N	Y	N	Y	Y	N
7 ***Franks***	N	Y	N	Y	N	N	N	Y
8 Klein	Y	Y	N	Y	N	Y	Y	N
9 Torricelli	Y	N	N	N	N	Y	Y	Y
10 Payne	Y	N	N	N	N	Y	Y	N
11 ***Gallo***	Y	Y	N	Y	N	N	N	Y
12 ***Zimmer***	Y	Y	N	Y	N	N	N	Y
13 Menendez	Y	Y	N	Y	N	Y	Y	N
NEW MEXICO								
1 ***Schiff***	N	Y	N	Y	Y	N	N	Y
2 ***Skeen***	N	Y	Y	Y	Y	N	N	Y
3 Richardson	Y	Y	N	Y	N	Y	Y	Y
NEW YORK								
1 Hochbrueckner	Y	Y	N	Y	N	Y	Y	N
2 ***Lazio***	N	Y	N	Y	N	N	N	Y
3 ***King***	N	Y	Y	Y	Y	N	N	Y
4 ***Levy***	N	Y	Y	Y	Y	N	N	Y
5 Ackerman	Y	Y	N	Y	N	Y	Y	N
6 Flake	Y	Y	N	Y	N	Y	Y	N
7 Manton	N	Y	Y	Y	Y	?	Y	N
8 Nadler	Y	N	N	N	N	?	Y	N
9 Schumer	Y	Y	N	Y	N	Y	Y	N
10 Towns	Y	N	N	N	N	Y	Y	N
11 Owens	Y	N	N	N	N	Y	Y	N
12 Velazquez	Y	Y	N	Y	N	?	Y	N
13 ***Molinari***	Y	Y	N	Y	N	N	N	Y
14 Maloney	Y	N	N	N	N	Y	Y	N
15 Rangel	Y	N	N	N	N	?	Y	N
16 Serrano	Y	Y	N	Y	N	?	Y	N
17 Engel	Y	N	N	N	N	?	Y	N
18 Lowey	Y	Y	N	Y	N	Y	Y	N
19 ***Fish***	N	Y	Y	Y	Y	Y	N	Y
20 ***Gilman***	Y	N	N	N	N	N	Y	Y
21 McNulty	N	Y	Y	Y	Y	Y	Y	N
22 ***Solomon***	N	Y	Y	Y	Y	N	N	Y
23 ***Boehlert***	Y	N	N	N	N	N	N	Y
24 ***McHugh***	N	Y	Y	Y	Y	N	N	Y
25 ***Walsh***	N	Y	Y	Y	Y	N	N	Y
26 Hinchey	Y	N	N	N	N	Y	Y	N
27 ***Paxon***	N	Y	Y	Y	Y	N	N	Y
28 Slaughter	Y	Y	N	Y	N	Y	Y	N
29 LaFalce	N	Y	Y	Y	Y	Y	Y	Y
30 ***Quinn***	N	Y	Y	Y	Y	N	N	Y
31 ***Houghton***	N	Y	N	Y	N	Y	N	Y
NORTH CAROLINA								
1 Clayton	Y	Y	N	Y	N	Y	Y	N
2 Valentine	Y	Y	N	Y	Y	Y	Y	Y

	578	579	580	581	582	583	584	585
3 Lancaster	Y	Y	N	Y	N	Y	N	N
4 Price	Y	Y	N	Y	N	Y	Y	N
5 Neal	Y	Y	N	Y	N	Y	Y	N
6 ***Coble***	N	Y	Y	Y	Y	N	N	Y
7 Rose	?	N	N	N	N	Y	Y	N
8 Hefner	Y	Y	N	Y	N	Y	Y	N
9 ***McMillan***	N	Y	Y	Y	Y	N	N	Y
10 ***Ballenger***	N	Y	Y	Y	Y	N	N	Y
11 ***Taylor***	N	Y	Y	Y	Y	N	N	Y
12 Watt	Y	N	N	N	N	Y	Y	N
NORTH DAKOTA								
AL Pomeroy	Y	Y	N	Y	N	Y	Y	N
OHIO								
1 Mann	Y	Y	N	Y	N	Y	Y	N
2 ***Portman***	N	Y	Y	Y	Y	N	N	Y
3 Hall	Y	Y	Y	Y	Y	Y	Y	N
4 ***Oxley***	N	Y	Y	Y	Y	N	N	Y
5 ***Gillmor***	N	Y	Y	Y	Y	Y	N	Y
6 Strickland	Y	Y	N	Y	N	Y	Y	N
7 ***Hobson***	N	Y	N	Y	N	N	N	Y
8 ***Boehner***	N	Y	Y	Y	Y	N	X	Y
9 Kaptur	?	Y	N	?	N	Y	Y	N
10 ***Hoke***	N	Y	Y	Y	Y	N	N	Y
11 Stokes	Y	N	N	N	N	Y	#	N
12 ***Kasich***	N	Y	Y	Y	Y	?	N	Y
13 Brown	Y	Y	N	Y	N	Y	Y	N
14 Sawyer	Y	Y	N	Y	N	Y	Y	N
15 ***Pryce***	N	Y	N	Y	N	N	N	Y
16 ***Regula***	N	Y	Y	Y	N	N	N	Y
17 Traficant	Y	Y	N	Y	N	Y	Y	Y
18 Applegate	N	Y	Y	Y	Y	Y	Y	Y
19 Fingerhut	Y	Y	N	Y	N	Y	Y	N
OKLAHOMA								
1 ***Inhofe***	N	Y	Y	Y	Y	N	N	Y
2 Synar	Y	N	N	N	N	Y	Y	N
3 Brewster	N	Y	N	Y	N	Y	Y	Y
4 McCurdy	Y	Y	N	Y	N	Y	Y	N
5 ***Istook***	N	Y	Y	Y	Y	N	N	Y
6 English	Y	Y	N	Y	N	Y	Y	Y
OREGON								
1 Furse	Y	Y	N	Y	N	Y	Y	N
2 ***Smith***	N	Y	Y	Y	Y	N	N	Y
3 Wyden	Y	N	N	N	N	Y	Y	N
4 DeFazio	Y	Y	N	Y	N	Y	Y	N
5 Kopetski	Y	N	N	N	N	Y	Y	N
PENNSYLVANIA								
1 Foglietta	Y	Y	N	Y	N	Y	Y	N
2 Blackwell	Y	N	N	N	N	Y	Y	N
3 Borski	N	Y	Y	Y	Y	Y	Y	N
4 Klink	N	Y	Y	Y	Y	Y	Y	N
5 ***Clinger***	?	?	?	?	?	?	?	?
6 Holden	N	Y	Y	Y	Y	Y	Y	N
7 ***Weldon***	N	Y	Y	Y	Y	N	N	Y
8 ***Greenwood***	N	Y	N	Y	N	?	N	Y
9 ***Shuster***	N	Y	Y	Y	Y	N	N	Y
10 ***McDade***	N	Y	Y	Y	Y	N	N	Y
11 Kanjorski	Y	Y	Y	Y	Y	Y	Y	N
12 Murtha	Y	Y	Y	Y	Y	Y	Y	N
13 Margolies-Mezv.	Y	N	N	N	N	?	Y	N
14 Coyne	Y	N	N	N	N	Y	Y	N
15 McHale	Y	Y	N	Y	N	Y	Y	Y
16 ***Walker***	N	Y	Y	Y	Y	N	N	Y
17 ***Gekas***	N	Y	Y	Y	Y	N	N	Y
18 ***Santorum***	N	Y	Y	Y	Y	N	N	Y
19 ***Goodling***	N	Y	Y	Y	Y	N	N	Y
20 Murphy	N	Y	Y	Y	Y	Y	Y	N
21 ***Ridge***	Y	Y	N	Y	N	N	N	Y
RHODE ISLAND								
1 ***Machtley***	Y	Y	N	Y	N	N	N	Y
2 Reed	Y	Y	N	Y	N	Y	Y	N
SOUTH CAROLINA								
1 ***Ravenel***	N	Y	Y	Y	Y	N	N	Y
2 ***Spence***	N	Y	Y	Y	Y	Y	N	Y
3 Derrick	Y	Y	N	Y	N	Y	Y	N
4 ***Inglis***	N	Y	Y	Y	Y	Y	N	Y
5 Spratt	Y	Y	N	Y	N	Y	Y	N
6 Clyburn	Y	N	N	N	N	Y	Y	N
SOUTH DAKOTA								
AL Johnson	Y	Y	N	Y	N	Y	Y	N
TENNESSEE								
1 ***Quillen***	N	Y	Y	Y	Y	N	N	N
2 ***Duncan***	N	Y	Y	Y	Y	N	N	Y
3 Lloyd	Y	Y	N	Y	N	Y	Y	Y
4 Cooper	Y	Y	N	Y	N	?	?	Y
5 Clement	Y	Y	N	Y	N	Y	Y	N

	578	579	580	581	582	583	584	585
6 Gordon	Y	Y	N	Y	N	Y	Y	N
7 ***Sundquist***	N	Y	Y	Y	Y	N	N	Y
8 Tanner	Y	Y	Y	Y	Y	Y	Y	Y
9 Ford	Y	N	N	N	N	?	Y	N
TEXAS								
1 Chapman	Y	Y	N	Y	N	?	Y	N
2 Wilson	Y	Y	N	Y	N	Y	?	Y
3 ***Johnson, Sam***	N	Y	Y	Y	Y	N	N	Y
4 Hall	N	Y	Y	Y	Y	Y	Y	Y
5 Bryant	Y	Y	N	Y	N	Y	Y	N
6 ***Barton***	N	Y	Y	Y	Y	?	N	Y
7 ***Archer***	N	Y	Y	Y	Y	Y	N	Y
8 ***Fields***	N	Y	Y	Y	Y	N	N	Y
9 Brooks	Y	N	N	N	N	Y	Y	N
10 Pickle	Y	Y	N	Y	N	?	Y	N
11 Edwards	Y	Y	N	Y	N	Y	Y	N
12 Geren	?	Y	N	Y	N	Y	Y	Y
13 Sarpalius	Y	Y	Y	Y	Y	Y	Y	N
14 Laughlin	N	Y	N	Y	N	Y	Y	N
15 de la Garza	N	Y	Y	Y	Y	Y	Y	N
16 Coleman	Y	Y	N	Y	N	Y	Y	N
17 Stenholm	N	Y	Y	Y	Y	Y	N	Y
18 Washington	Y	N	N	N	N	?	?	?
19 ***Combest***	N	Y	Y	Y	Y	Y	N	Y
20 Gonzalez	Y	N	N	N	N	Y	Y	N
21 ***Smith***	N	Y	Y	Y	Y	N	N	Y
22 ***DeLay***	N	Y	Y	Y	Y	N	N	Y
23 ***Bonilla***	N	Y	Y	Y	Y	N	N	Y
24 Frost	Y	Y	N	Y	N	Y	Y	N
25 Andrews	Y	Y	N	Y	N	Y	?	N
26 ***Armey***	N	Y	Y	Y	Y	N	N	Y
27 Ortiz	N	Y	Y	Y	Y	Y	Y	N
28 Tejeda	N	Y	Y	Y	Y	Y	Y	N
29 Green	Y	Y	N	Y	N	Y	Y	N
30 Johnson, E.B.	Y	Y	N	Y	N	Y	Y	N
UTAH								
1 ***Hansen***	N	Y	Y	Y	Y	N	N	Y
2 Shepherd	Y	Y	N	?	N	Y	Y	N
3 Orton	N	Y	Y	Y	Y	Y	Y	Y
VERMONT								
AL *Sanders*	Y	N	N	N	N	Y	Y	N
VIRGINIA								
1 ***Bateman***	N	Y	Y	Y	Y	Y	N	Y
2 Pickett	Y	Y	N	Y	N	Y	Y	N
3 Scott	Y	N	N	N	N	Y	Y	N
4 Sisisky	?	Y	N	Y	N	Y	Y	N
5 Payne	Y	Y	N	Y	N	Y	Y	N
6 ***Goodlatte***	N	Y	Y	Y	Y	N	N	Y
7 ***Bliley***	N	Y	Y	Y	Y	N	N	Y
8 Moran	Y	Y	N	Y	N	Y	?	N
9 Boucher	Y	Y	N	Y	N	Y	Y	N
10 ***Wolf***	N	Y	Y	Y	Y	N	N	N
11 Byrne	Y	Y	N	Y	N	Y	Y	N
WASHINGTON								
1 Cantwell	Y	Y	N	Y	N	?	?	X
2 Swift	Y	Y	N	Y	N	Y	Y	N
3 Unsoeld	Y	N	N	N	N	Y	Y	N
4 Inslee	Y	Y	N	Y	N	Y	Y	N
5 Foley								
6 Dicks	?	?	?	?	?	?	?	?
7 McDermott	Y	N	N	N	N	?	?	?
8 ***Dunn***	N	Y	Y	Y	N	N	N	Y
9 Kreidler	Y	N	N	N	N	Y	Y	N
WEST VIRGINIA								
1 Mollohan	N	Y	Y	Y	Y	?	Y	N
2 Wise	Y	Y	N	Y	N	Y	Y	N
3 Rahall	N	Y	Y	Y	Y	Y	Y	N
WISCONSIN								
1 Barca	Y	Y	N	Y	N	Y	Y	N
2 ***Klug***	N	Y	N	Y	N	N	N	Y
3 ***Gunderson***	N	Y	N	Y	N	Y	N	Y
4 Kleczka	Y	Y	N	Y	N	Y	Y	N
5 Barrett	Y	Y	N	Y	N	Y	Y	N
6 ***Petri***	N	Y	Y	Y	Y	N	N	Y
7 Obey	N	Y	N	Y	N	Y	?	N
8 ***Roth***	N	Y	Y	Y	Y	N	N	Y
9 ***Sensenbrenner***	N	Y	Y	Y	Y	N	N	Y
WYOMING								
AL ***Thomas***	N	Y	Y	Y	Y	N	N	Y
DELEGATES								
de Lugo, V.I.	D	N	N	D	D	D	D	N
Faleomavaega, Am.S.	D	?	N	D	D	D	D	N
Norton, D.C.	D	N	N	D	D	D	D	N
Romero-B., P.R.	D	?	?	D	D	D	D	?
Underwood, Guam	D	Y	N	D	D	D	D	N

Southern states - Ala., Ark., Fla., Ga., Ky., La., Miss., N.C., Okla., S.C., Tenn., Texas, Va.
Omitted votes are quorum calls, which CQ does not include in its vote charts.

586. HR 3351. Youth Offenders Alternative Punishment/ Republican Substitute. Brooks, D-Texas, motion to table (kill) the McCollum, R-Fla., appeal of the chair's ruling sustaining the Brooks point of order against the McCollum motion to recommit the bill with instructions for not being germane by exceeding the scope of the bill. The McCollum instructions would strike the text of the bill and insert a comprehensive Republican crime proposal. Motion agreed to 251-172: R 0-172; D 250-0 (ND 167-0, SD 83-0); I 1-0, Nov. 19, 1993.

587. HR 3351. Youth Offenders Alternative Punishment/ Regional Prison Systems. Brooks, D-Texas, motion to table (kill) the McCollum, R-Fla., appeal of the chair's ruling sustaining the Brooks point of order against the McCollum motion to recommit the bill with instructions for not being germane. The McCollum instructions would establish a regional prison system in partnership with states to house violent prisoners. Motion agreed to 251-171: R 0-170; D 250-1 (ND 167-0, SD 83-1); I 1-0, Nov. 19, 1993.

588. HR 3351. Youth Offenders Alternative Punishment/ Terrorism Task Force. Brooks, D-Texas, motion to table (kill) the McCollum, R-Fla., appeal of the chair's ruling sustaining the Brooks point of order against the McCollum motion to recommit the bill with instructions for not being germane. The McCollum instructions would set up an interagency task force to prevent terrorism. Motion agreed to 246-171: R 0-170; D 245-1 (ND 165-0, SD 80-1); I 1-0, Nov. 19, 1993.

589. HR 3351. Youth Offenders Alternative Punishment/ Boot Camps. Sensenbrenner, R-Wis., motion to recommit the bill to the House Judiciary Committee with instructions to report it back with an amendment providing that 90 percent of the funds go to the boot camp prison programs. Motion rejected 177-243: R 163-6; D 14-236 (ND 6-160, SD 8-76); I 0-1, Nov. 19, 1993.

590. HR 3351. Youth Offenders Alternative Punishment/ Passage. Passage of the bill to authorize $200 million per year for fiscal 1994-96 in grants to states to develop alternative punishments other than incarceration and probation for young offenders. Passed 336-82: R 90-78; D 245-4 (ND 163-2, SD 82-2); I 1-0, Nov. 19, 1993. A "yea" was a vote in support of the president's position.

591. HR 51. D.C. Statehood/Rule. Adoption of the rule (H Res 316) to provide for House floor consideration of the bill to admit the District of Columbia into the union as the state of New Columbia. Adopted 252-172: R 38-135; D 213-37 (ND 148-19, SD 65-18); I 1-0, Nov. 20, 1993.

592. HR 3098. Youth Handgun Safety/Passage. Brooks, D-Texas, motion to suspend the rules and pass the bill to make it a federal crime to sell, deliver or transfer a handgun to individuals 18 or younger. Motion agreed to 422-0: R 172-0; D 249-0 (ND 167-0, SD 82-0); I 1-0, Nov. 20, 1993. A two-thirds majority of those present and voting (282 in this case) is required for passage under suspension of the rules. A "yea" was a vote in support of the president's position.

593. HR 1133. Violence Against Women/Passage. Brooks, D-Texas, motion to suspend the rules and pass the bill to authorize grants to states to reduce violent crimes against women. Motion agreed to 421-0: R 172-0; D 248-0 (ND 165-0, SD 83-0); I 1-0, Nov. 20, 1993. A two-thirds majority of those present and voting (281 in this case) is required for passage under suspension of the rules.

KEY

Y	Voted for (yea).
#	Paired for.
+	Announced for.
N	Voted against (nay).
X	Paired against.
−	Announced against.
P	Voted "present."
C	Voted "present" to avoid possible conflict of interest.
?	Did not vote or otherwise make a position known.
D	Delegates ineligible to vote.

Democrats   *Republicans*
Independent

	586	587	588	589	590	591	592	593
ALABAMA								
1 *Callahan*	N	N	N	Y	Y	N	Y	Y
2 *Everett*	N	N	N	Y	N	Y	N	Y
3 Browder	Y	Y	Y	N	Y	Y	Y	Y
4 Bevill	Y	Y	Y	N	Y	Y	Y	Y
5 Cramer	Y	Y	Y	N	Y	Y	Y	Y
6 *Bachus*	N	N	N	Y	N	N	Y	Y
7 Hilliard	Y	Y	Y	N	Y	Y	Y	Y
ALASKA								
AL *Young*	N	N	N	Y	N	Y	N	Y
ARIZONA								
1 Coppersmith	Y	Y	Y	N	Y	Y	Y	Y
2 Pastor	Y	Y	Y	N	Y	Y	Y	Y
3 *Stump*	N	N	N	Y	N	N	N	Y
4 *Kyl*	N	N	N	Y	N	N	N	Y
5 *Kolbe*	N	N	N	Y	N	N	Y	Y
6 English	Y	Y	Y	N	Y	Y	Y	Y
ARKANSAS								
1 Lambert	Y	Y	Y	N	Y	Y	Y	Y
2 Thornton	Y	Y	Y	N	Y	Y	Y	Y
3 *Hutchinson*	N	N	N	Y	N	N	Y	Y
4 *Dickey*	N	N	N	Y	N	N	Y	Y
CALIFORNIA								
1 Hamburg	Y	Y	Y	N	Y	Y	Y	Y
2 *Herger*	N	N	N	Y	N	N	N	Y
3 Fazio	Y	Y	Y	N	Y	Y	Y	Y
4 *Doolittle*	N	N	N	Y	N	N	Y	Y
5 Matsui	Y	Y	Y	N	Y	?	?	?
6 Woolsey	Y	Y	Y	N	Y	Y	Y	Y
7 Miller	Y	Y	Y	N	Y	Y	Y	Y
8 Pelosi	Y	Y	Y	N	Y	Y	Y	Y
9 Dellums	Y	Y	Y	N	Y	Y	Y	Y
10 *Baker*	N	N	N	Y	N	N	N	Y
11 *Pombo*	N	N	N	Y	N	N	N	Y
12 Lantos	Y	Y	Y	N	Y	Y	Y	Y
13 Stark	Y	Y	Y	N	Y	Y	Y	Y
14 Eshoo	Y	Y	Y	N	Y	Y	Y	Y
15 Mineta	Y	Y	?	N	Y	Y	Y	Y
16 Edwards	Y	Y	Y	N	Y	Y	Y	Y
17 Farr	Y	Y	Y	N	Y	Y	Y	Y
18 Condit	Y	Y	Y	Y	Y	Y	Y	Y
19 Lehman	Y	Y	Y	N	Y	Y	Y	Y
20 Dooley	Y	Y	Y	N	Y	Y	Y	Y
21 *Thomas*	N	N	?	Y	Y	N	Y	Y
22 *Huffington*	N	N	N	Y	N	Y	N	Y
23 *Gallegly*	N	N	N	Y	N	Y	N	Y
24 Beilenson	Y	Y	Y	N	Y	Y	Y	Y
25 *McKeon*	N	N	N	Y	N	Y	N	Y
26 Berman	Y	Y	Y	N	Y	Y	Y	Y
27 *Moorhead*	N	N	N	Y	N	Y	N	Y
28 *Dreier*	N	N	N	Y	N	N	Y	Y
29 Waxman	Y	Y	Y	N	Y	Y	Y	Y
30 Becerra	Y	Y	Y	N	Y	Y	Y	Y
31 Martinez	Y	Y	Y	N	Y	Y	Y	Y
32 Dixon	Y	Y	Y	N	Y	Y	Y	Y
33 Roybal-Allard	Y	Y	Y	N	Y	Y	Y	Y
34 Torres	Y	Y	Y	N	Y	Y	Y	Y
35 Waters	Y	Y	Y	N	Y	Y	Y	Y
36 Harman	Y	Y	Y	N	Y	Y	Y	Y
37 Tucker	Y	Y	Y	N	Y	Y	Y	Y
38 *Horn*	N	N	N	Y	N	Y	Y	Y
39 *Royce*	N	N	N	Y	N	N	N	Y
40 *Lewis*	N	N	N	Y	N	N	N	Y
41 *Kim*	N	N	N	Y	N	N	Y	Y
42 Brown	Y	Y	Y	N	Y	Y	Y	Y
43 *Calvert*	N	N	N	Y	N	Y	N	Y
44 *McCandless*	N	N	N	Y	N	Y	N	Y
45 *Rohrabacher*	N	N	N	Y	N	N	N	Y
46 *Dornan*	N	N	N	Y	N	N	N	Y
47 *Cox*	N	N	N	Y	N	N	N	Y
48 *Packard*	N	N	N	Y	N	N	N	Y
49 Schenk	Y	Y	Y	N	Y	Y	Y	Y
50 Filner	Y	Y	Y	N	Y	Y	Y	Y
51 *Cunningham*	N	N	N	Y	N	N	Y	Y
52 *Hunter*	N	N	N	Y	?	N	Y	Y
COLORADO								
1 Schroeder	Y	Y	Y	N	Y	Y	Y	Y
2 Skaggs	Y	Y	Y	N	Y	Y	Y	Y
3 *McInnis*	N	N	N	Y	N	N	Y	Y
4 *Allard*	N	N	N	Y	N	N	N	Y
5 *Hefley*	N	N	N	Y	N	N	N	Y
6 *Schaefer*	N	N	N	Y	N	Y	N	Y
CONNECTICUT								
1 Kennelly	Y	Y	Y	N	Y	Y	Y	Y
2 Gejdenson	Y	Y	Y	N	Y	Y	Y	Y
3 DeLauro	Y	Y	Y	N	Y	Y	Y	Y
4 *Shays*	N	N	N	Y	N	Y	Y	Y
5 *Franks*	N	N	N	Y	N	Y	N	Y
6 *Johnson*	N	N	N	Y	N	Y	Y	Y
DELAWARE								
AL *Castle*	N	N	N	Y	N	Y	N	Y
FLORIDA								
1 Hutto	Y	Y	Y	N	Y	N	Y	Y
2 Peterson	Y	Y	Y	N	Y	Y	Y	Y
3 Brown	Y	Y	Y	N	Y	Y	Y	Y
4 *Fowler*	N	N	N	Y	N	Y	N	Y
5 Thurman	Y	Y	Y	N	Y	Y	Y	Y
6 *Stearns*	?	?	?	?	X	N	Y	Y
7 *Mica*	N	N	N	Y	N	N	N	Y
8 *McCollum*	N	N	N	Y	N	N	N	Y
9 *Bilirakis*	N	N	N	Y	N	Y	N	Y
10 *Young*	N	N	N	Y	Y	Y	Y	Y
11 Gibbons	Y	Y	Y	N	Y	Y	Y	Y
12 *Canady*	N	N	N	Y	N	N	Y	Y
13 *Miller*	N	N	N	Y	N	N	N	Y
14 *Goss*	N	N	N	Y	N	N	N	Y
15 Bacchus	Y	Y	Y	N	Y	Y	Y	Y
16 *Lewis*	N	N	N	Y	N	Y	N	Y
17 Meek	Y	Y	Y	N	Y	Y	Y	Y
18 *Ros-Lehtinen*	N	N	N	?	?	Y	Y	Y
19 Johnston	Y	Y	Y	N	Y	Y	Y	Y
20 Deutsch	Y	Y	Y	N	Y	Y	Y	Y
21 *Diaz-Balart*	N	N	N	?	?	N	Y	Y
22 *Shaw*	N	N	N	Y	N	Y	N	Y
23 Hastings	Y	Y	Y	N	Y	Y	Y	Y
GEORGIA								
1 *Kingston*	N	N	N	Y	N	Y	N	Y
2 Bishop	Y	Y	Y	N	Y	Y	Y	Y
3 *Collins*	N	N	N	Y	N	N	N	Y
4 *Linder*	N	N	N	Y	N	N	N	Y
5 Lewis	Y	Y	Y	N	Y	Y	Y	Y
6 *Gingrich*	?	?	?	?	?	Y	Y	Y
7 Darden	Y	Y	Y	N	Y	Y	Y	Y
8 Rowland	Y	Y	Y	N	Y	Y	Y	Y
9 Deal	Y	Y	Y	N	Y	Y	Y	Y
10 Johnson	Y	Y	Y	N	Y	?	?	?
11 McKinney	Y	Y	Y	N	Y	Y	Y	Y
HAWAII								
1 Abercrombie	Y	Y	Y	N	Y	Y	Y	Y
2 Mink	Y	Y	Y	N	Y	Y	Y	Y
IDAHO								
1 LaRocco	Y	Y	Y	N	Y	Y	Y	Y
2 *Crapo*	N	N	N	Y	Y	N	Y	Y
ILLINOIS								
1 Rush	Y	Y	Y	N	Y	Y	Y	Y
2 Reynolds	Y	Y	Y	N	Y	?	?	?
3 Lipinski	Y	Y	Y	N	Y	Y	Y	Y
4 Gutierrez	Y	Y	Y	N	Y	Y	Y	Y
5 Rostenkowski	Y	Y	Y	N	Y	Y	Y	Y
6 *Hyde*	N	N	N	Y	N	N	Y	Y
7 Collins	Y	Y	Y	N	Y	Y	Y	Y
8 *Crane*	N	N	N	Y	N	N	N	Y
9 Yates	Y	Y	Y	N	Y	Y	Y	Y
10 *Porter*	N	N	N	Y	N	Y	N	Y
11 Sangmeister	Y	Y	Y	N	Y	Y	Y	Y
12 Costello	Y	Y	Y	N	Y	Y	Y	Y
13 *Fawell*	N	N	N	Y	N	N	N	Y
14 *Hastert*	N	N	N	Y	N	N	Y	Y
15 *Ewing*	N	N	N	Y	N	Y	N	Y
16 *Manzullo*	N	N	N	Y	Y	N	N	Y
17 Evans	Y	Y	Y	N	Y	Y	Y	Y

ND Northern Democrats   SD Southern Democrats

	586	587	588	589	590	591	592	593
18 ***Michel***	N	N	N	Y	N	N	Y	Y
19 Poshard	Y	Y	Y	N	Y	N	Y	Y
20 Durbin	Y	Y	Y	N	Y	Y	Y	Y
INDIANA								
1 Visclosky	Y	Y	Y	N	Y	Y	Y	Y
2 Sharp	Y	Y	Y	N	Y	Y	Y	Y
3 Roemer	Y	Y	Y	N	Y	Y	Y	Y
4 Long	Y	Y	Y	N	Y	Y	Y	Y
5 ***Buyer***	N	N	N	Y	Y	N	Y	Y
6 ***Burton***	N	N	N	Y	N	N	Y	Y
7 ***Myers***	N	N	N	Y	N	Y	Y	Y
8 McCloskey	Y	Y	Y	N	Y	Y	Y	Y
9 Hamilton	Y	Y	Y	N	Y	Y	Y	Y
10 Jacobs	Y	Y	Y	N	Y	Y	Y	Y
IOWA								
1 ***Leach***	N	N	N	Y	Y	N	Y	Y
2 ***Nussle***	N	N	N	Y	N	Y	Y	Y
3 ***Lightfoot***	N	N	N	Y	N	N	Y	Y
4 Smith	Y	Y	Y	N	Y	N	Y	Y
5 ***Grandy***	N	N	N	Y	N	Y	Y	Y
KANSAS								
1 ***Roberts***	N	N	N	Y	Y	N	Y	Y
2 Slattery	?	?	?	?	?	?	?	?
3 ***Meyers***	N	N	N	Y	N	N	Y	Y
4 Glickman	Y	Y	Y	N	Y	Y	Y	Y
KENTUCKY								
1 Barlow	Y	Y	Y	N	Y	N	Y	Y
2 Natcher	Y	Y	Y	N	Y	Y	Y	Y
3 Mazzoli	Y	Y	Y	N	Y	Y	Y	Y
4 ***Bunning***	N	N	N	Y	N	N	Y	Y
5 ***Rogers***	N	N	N	Y	Y	N	Y	Y
6 Baesler	Y	Y	Y	N	Y	Y	Y	Y
LOUISIANA								
1 ***Livingston***	N	N	N	Y	Y	Y	Y	Y
2 Jefferson	Y	Y	Y	N	Y	Y	Y	Y
3 Tauzin	Y	Y	Y	Y	Y	N	Y	Y
4 Fields	Y	Y	Y	N	Y	Y	Y	Y
5 ***McCrery***	N	N	N	Y	Y	N	Y	Y
6 ***Baker***	N	N	N	Y	Y	N	Y	Y
7 Hayes	Y	Y	Y	N	Y	Y	Y	Y
MAINE								
1 Andrews	Y	Y	Y	N	Y	Y	Y	Y
2 ***Snowe***	N	N	N	Y	Y	Y	Y	Y
MARYLAND								
1 ***Gilchrest***	N	N	N	Y	N	N	Y	Y
2 ***Bentley***	N	N	N	Y	Y	N	Y	Y
3 Cardin	Y	Y	Y	N	Y	Y	Y	Y
4 Wynn	Y	Y	Y	N	Y	Y	Y	Y
5 Hoyer	Y	Y	Y	N	Y	Y	Y	Y
6 ***Bartlett***	N	N	N	Y	N	N	Y	Y
7 Mfume	Y	Y	Y	N	Y	Y	Y	Y
8 ***Morella***	N	N	N	N	Y	Y	Y	Y
MASSACHUSETTS								
1 Olver	Y	Y	Y	N	Y	Y	Y	Y
2 Neal	Y	Y	Y	N	Y	Y	Y	Y
3 ***Blute***	N	N	N	Y	Y	N	Y	Y
4 Frank	Y	Y	Y	N	Y	Y	Y	Y
5 Meehan	Y	Y	Y	N	Y	Y	Y	Y
6 ***Torkildsen***	N	N	N	Y	Y	Y	Y	Y
7 Markey	Y	Y	Y	N	Y	Y	Y	Y
8 Kennedy	Y	Y	Y	N	Y	Y	Y	Y
9 Moakley	Y	Y	Y	N	Y	Y	Y	Y
10 Studds	Y	Y	Y	N	Y	Y	Y	Y
MICHIGAN								
1 Stupak	Y	Y	Y	N	Y	Y	Y	Y
2 ***Hoekstra***	N	N	N	Y	Y	N	Y	Y
3 Vacancy								
4 ***Camp***	N	N	N	Y	Y	N	Y	Y
5 Barcia	Y	Y	Y	N	Y	Y	Y	Y
6 ***Upton***	N	N	N	Y	Y	N	Y	Y
7 ***Smith***	N	N	N	N	Y	N	Y	Y
8 Carr	Y	Y	Y	N	Y	N	Y	Y
9 Kildee	Y	Y	Y	N	Y	Y	Y	Y
10 Bonior	Y	Y	Y	N	Y	Y	Y	Y
11 ***Knollenberg***	N	?	?	?	X	N	Y	Y
12 Levin	Y	Y	Y	N	Y	Y	Y	Y
13 Ford	Y	Y	Y	N	Y	N	Y	Y
14 Conyers	Y	Y	Y	N	Y	Y	Y	Y
15 Collins	Y	Y	Y	N	Y	Y	Y	Y
16 Dingell	Y	Y	Y	N	Y	N	Y	Y
MINNESOTA								
1 Penny	Y	Y	Y	N	Y	Y	Y	Y
2 Minge	Y	Y	Y	N	Y	Y	Y	Y
3 ***Ramstad***	N	N	N	Y	Y	N	Y	Y
4 Vento	Y	Y	Y	N	Y	Y	Y	Y

	586	587	588	589	590	591	592	593
5 Sabo	Y	Y	Y	N	Y	Y	Y	Y
6 ***Grams***	N	N	N	Y	Y	N	Y	Y
7 Peterson	Y	Y	Y	Y	Y	N	Y	Y
8 Oberstar	Y	Y	Y	N	Y	Y	Y	Y
MISSISSIPPI								
1 Whitten	Y	Y	Y	N	Y	Y	Y	Y
2 Thompson	Y	Y	Y	N	Y	Y	Y	Y
3 Montgomery	Y	Y	Y	N	Y	Y	Y	Y
4 Parker	Y	Y	Y	N	Y	Y	Y	Y
5 Taylor	Y	Y	Y	Y	N	N	Y	Y
MISSOURI								
1 Clay	Y	Y	Y	N	Y	Y	Y	Y
2 ***Talent***	N	N	N	Y	Y	N	Y	Y
3 Gephardt	Y	Y	Y	N	Y	Y	Y	Y
4 Skelton	Y	Y	Y	Y	N	N	Y	Y
5 Wheat	Y	Y	Y	N	Y	Y	Y	Y
6 Danner	Y	Y	Y	N	Y	N	Y	Y
7 ***Hancock***	N	N	N	Y	N	N	Y	Y
8 ***Emerson***	N	N	N	Y	N	N	Y	Y
9 Volkmer	Y	Y	Y	N	Y	N	Y	Y
MONTANA								
AL Williams	Y	Y	Y	N	N	Y	Y	Y
NEBRASKA								
1 ***Bereuter***	N	N	N	N	N	N	Y	Y
2 Hoagland	Y	Y	Y	N	Y	Y	Y	Y
3 ***Barrett***	N	N	N	Y	N	N	Y	Y
NEVADA								
1 Bilbray	Y	Y	Y	N	Y	Y	Y	Y
2 ***Vucanovich***	N	N	N	Y	N	Y	Y	Y
NEW HAMPSHIRE								
1 ***Zeliff***	N	N	N	Y	N	N	Y	Y
2 Swett	Y	Y	Y	N	Y	Y	Y	Y
NEW JERSEY								
1 Andrews	Y	Y	Y	N	Y	Y	Y	Y
2 Hughes	Y	Y	Y	N	Y	Y	Y	Y
3 ***Saxton***	N	N	N	Y	Y	Y	Y	Y
4 ***Smith***	N	N	N	Y	Y	N	Y	Y
5 ***Roukema***	N	N	N	Y	Y	?	?	?
6 Pallone	Y	Y	Y	N	Y	Y	Y	Y
7 ***Franks***	N	N	N	Y	Y	N	Y	Y
8 Klein	Y	Y	Y	N	Y	Y	Y	Y
9 Torricelli	Y	Y	Y	Y	Y	Y	Y	Y
10 Payne	Y	Y	Y	N	Y	Y	Y	Y
11 ***Gallo***	N	N	N	N	Y	Y	Y	Y
12 ***Zimmer***	N	N	N	Y	Y	N	Y	Y
13 Menendez	Y	Y	Y	?	?	Y	Y	Y
NEW MEXICO								
1 ***Schiff***	N	N	N	Y	N	N	Y	Y
2 ***Skeen***	N	N	N	Y	Y	Y	Y	Y
3 Richardson	Y	Y	Y	N	Y	Y	Y	Y
NEW YORK								
1 Hochbrueckner	Y	Y	Y	N	Y	Y	Y	Y
2 ***Lazio***	N	N	N	Y	Y	Y	Y	Y
3 ***King***	N	N	N	Y	N	Y	Y	Y
4 ***Levy***	N	N	N	Y	Y	Y	Y	Y
5 Ackerman	Y	Y	Y	N	Y	Y	Y	Y
6 Flake	Y	Y	Y	N	Y	Y	Y	Y
7 Manton	Y	Y	Y	N	Y	Y	Y	Y
8 Nadler	Y	Y	Y	N	Y	Y	Y	Y
9 Schumer	Y	Y	Y	N	Y	Y	Y	Y
10 Towns	Y	Y	Y	N	Y	Y	Y	Y
11 Owens	Y	Y	Y	N	Y	Y	Y	Y
12 Velazquez	Y	Y	Y	N	Y	Y	Y	Y
13 ***Molinari***	N	N	N	Y	N	N	Y	Y
14 Maloney	Y	Y	Y	N	Y	Y	Y	Y
15 Rangel	Y	Y	Y	N	Y	Y	Y	Y
16 Serrano	Y	Y	Y	N	?	Y	Y	Y
17 Engel	Y	Y	Y	N	Y	Y	Y	Y
18 Lowey	Y	Y	Y	N	Y	Y	Y	?
19 ***Fish***	N	N	N	Y	Y	Y	Y	Y
20 ***Gilman***	N	N	N	Y	Y	Y	Y	Y
21 McNulty	Y	Y	Y	N	Y	Y	Y	Y
22 ***Solomon***	N	N	N	Y	N	N	Y	Y
23 ***Boehlert***	N	N	N	Y	Y	Y	Y	Y
24 ***McHugh***	N	N	N	Y	N	N	Y	Y
25 ***Walsh***	N	N	N	Y	Y	Y	Y	Y
26 Hinchey	Y	Y	Y	N	Y	Y	Y	Y
27 ***Paxon***	N	N	N	Y	N	N	Y	Y
28 Slaughter	Y	Y	Y	N	Y	Y	Y	Y
29 LaFalce	Y	Y	Y	N	Y	Y	Y	Y
30 ***Quinn***	N	N	N	Y	Y	N	Y	Y
31 ***Houghton***	N	N	N	Y	Y	N	Y	Y
NORTH CAROLINA								
1 Clayton	Y	Y	Y	N	Y	Y	Y	Y
2 Valentine	Y	Y	?	N	Y	Y	Y	Y

	586	587	588	589	590	591	592	593
3 Lancaster	Y	Y	Y	N	Y	Y	Y	Y
4 Price	Y	Y	Y	N	Y	Y	Y	Y
5 Neal	Y	Y	Y	N	Y	Y	Y	Y
6 ***Coble***	N	N	N	Y	N	N	Y	Y
7 Rose	Y	Y	Y	N	Y	Y	Y	Y
8 Hefner	Y	Y	Y	N	Y	Y	Y	Y
9 ***McMillan***	N	N	N	Y	Y	N	Y	Y
10 ***Ballenger***	N	N	N	Y	N	N	Y	Y
11 ***Taylor***	N	N	N	Y	N	N	Y	Y
12 Watt	Y	Y	Y	N	Y	Y	Y	Y
NORTH DAKOTA								
AL Pomeroy	Y	Y	Y	N	Y	N	Y	Y
OHIO								
1 Mann	Y	Y	Y	N	Y	Y	Y	Y
2 ***Portman***	N	N	N	Y	Y	N	Y	Y
3 Hall	?	?	?	?	?	?	?	?
4 ***Oxley***	N	N	N	Y	Y	N	Y	Y
5 ***Gillmor***	N	N	N	Y	Y	N	Y	Y
6 Strickland	Y	Y	Y	N	Y	Y	Y	Y
7 ***Hobson***	N	N	N	Y	Y	N	Y	Y
8 ***Boehner***	N	N	N	Y	N	N	Y	Y
9 Kaptur	Y	Y	Y	N	Y	Y	Y	Y
10 ***Hoke***	N	N	N	Y	N	Y	Y	Y
11 Stokes	Y	Y	Y	N	Y	Y	Y	Y
12 ***Kasich***	N	N	N	Y	Y	N	Y	Y
13 Brown	Y	Y	Y	N	Y	Y	Y	Y
14 Sawyer	Y	Y	Y	N	Y	Y	Y	Y
15 ***Pryce***	N	N	N	Y	Y	N	Y	Y
16 ***Regula***	N	N	N	Y	Y	N	Y	Y
17 Traficant	Y	Y	Y	N	Y	Y	Y	Y
18 Applegate	Y	Y	Y	N	Y	Y	Y	Y
19 Fingerhut	Y	Y	Y	N	Y	Y	Y	Y
OKLAHOMA								
1 ***Inhofe***	N	N	N	Y	N	N	Y	Y
2 Synar	Y	Y	Y	N	Y	Y	Y	Y
3 Brewster	Y	Y	Y	N	Y	N	Y	Y
4 McCurdy	Y	Y	Y	Y	Y	Y	Y	Y
5 ***Istook***	N	N	N	Y	Y	N	Y	Y
6 English	Y	Y	Y	Y	Y	Y	Y	Y
OREGON								
1 Furse	Y	Y	Y	N	Y	Y	Y	Y
2 ***Smith***	N	N	N	Y	Y	N	Y	Y
3 Wyden	Y	Y	Y	N	Y	Y	Y	Y
4 DeFazio	Y	Y	?	N	Y	Y	Y	Y
5 Kopetski	Y	Y	Y	N	Y	Y	Y	Y
PENNSYLVANIA								
1 Foglietta	Y	Y	Y	N	Y	Y	Y	Y
2 Blackwell	Y	Y	Y	N	Y	Y	Y	Y
3 Borski	Y	Y	Y	N	Y	Y	Y	Y
4 Klink	Y	Y	Y	N	Y	N	Y	Y
5 ***Clinger***	?	?	?	?	?	?	?	?
6 Holden	Y	Y	Y	N	Y	N	Y	Y
7 ***Weldon***	N	?	N	Y	Y	N	Y	Y
8 ***Greenwood***	N	N	N	Y	Y	N	Y	Y
9 ***Shuster***	N	N	N	Y	N	N	Y	Y
10 ***McDade***	N	N	N	Y	Y	Y	Y	Y
11 Kanjorski	Y	Y	Y	N	Y	N	Y	Y
12 Murtha	Y	Y	Y	N	Y	Y	Y	Y
13 Margolies-Mezv.	Y	Y	Y	N	Y	Y	Y	?
14 Coyne	Y	Y	Y	N	Y	Y	Y	Y
15 McHale	Y	Y	Y	N	Y	Y	Y	Y
16 ***Walker***	N	N	N	Y	N	Y	Y	Y
17 ***Gekas***	N	N	N	Y	N	Y	Y	Y
18 ***Santorum***	N	N	N	Y	Y	N	Y	Y
19 ***Goodling***	N	N	N	Y	N	Y	Y	Y
20 Murphy	Y	Y	Y	N	Y	N	Y	Y
21 ***Ridge***	N	N	N	Y	Y	Y	?	?
RHODE ISLAND								
1 ***Machtley***	N	N	N	Y	Y	N	Y	Y
2 Reed	Y	Y	Y	N	Y	Y	Y	Y
SOUTH CAROLINA								
1 ***Ravenel***	N	N	N	Y	Y	N	Y	Y
2 ***Spence***	N	N	N	Y	Y	Y	Y	Y
3 Derrick	Y	Y	?	N	Y	Y	Y	Y
4 ***Inglis***	N	N	N	Y	N	N	Y	Y
5 Spratt	Y	Y	Y	N	Y	Y	Y	Y
6 Clyburn	Y	Y	Y	N	Y	Y	Y	Y
SOUTH DAKOTA								
AL Johnson	Y	Y	Y	N	Y	Y	Y	Y
TENNESSEE								
1 ***Quillen***	N	N	N	Y	N	N	Y	Y
2 ***Duncan***	N	N	N	Y	Y	N	Y	Y
3 Lloyd	Y	Y	Y	N	Y	Y	Y	Y
4 Cooper	Y	N	N	Y	Y	Y	Y	Y
5 Clement	Y	Y	Y	N	Y	Y	Y	Y

	586	587	588	589	590	591	592	593
6 Gordon	Y	Y	Y	N	Y	Y	Y	Y
7 ***Sundquist***	N	N	N	Y	Y	N	Y	Y
8 Tanner	Y	Y	Y	Y	Y	N	Y	Y
9 Ford	Y	Y	Y	N	Y	Y	Y	Y
TEXAS								
1 Chapman	Y	Y	Y	N	Y	N	?	Y
2 Wilson	Y	Y	Y	N	Y	N	Y	Y
3 ***Johnson, Sam***	N	N	N	Y	N	N	Y	Y
4 Hall	Y	Y	Y	N	Y	N	Y	Y
5 Bryant	Y	Y	Y	N	Y	N	Y	Y
6 ***Barton***	N	N	N	Y	N	N	Y	Y
7 ***Archer***	N	N	N	Y	N	N	Y	Y
8 ***Fields***	N	N	N	Y	N	N	Y	Y
9 Brooks	Y	Y	Y	N	Y	N	Y	Y
10 Pickle	?	Y	Y	N	Y	Y	Y	Y
11 Edwards	Y	Y	Y	N	Y	Y	Y	Y
12 Geren	Y	Y	Y	Y	Y	N	Y	Y
13 Sarpalius	Y	Y	Y	N	Y	Y	Y	Y
14 Laughlin	Y	Y	Y	N	Y	Y	Y	Y
15 de la Garza	Y	Y	Y	N	Y	N	Y	Y
16 Coleman	Y	Y	Y	N	Y	Y	Y	Y
17 Stenholm	Y	Y	Y	Y	Y	N	Y	Y
18 Washington	?	?	?	?	#	?	?	?
19 ***Combest***	N	N	N	Y	N	N	Y	Y
20 Gonzalez	Y	Y	Y	N	N	Y	Y	Y
21 ***Smith***	N	N	N	Y	N	N	Y	Y
22 ***DeLay***	N	N	N	Y	N	N	Y	Y
23 ***Bonilla***	N	N	N	Y	N	N	Y	Y
24 Frost	Y	Y	Y	N	Y	Y	Y	Y
25 Andrews	Y	Y	Y	N	Y	N	Y	Y
26 ***Armey***	N	N	N	Y	N	N	Y	Y
27 Ortiz	Y	Y	Y	N	Y	Y	Y	Y
28 Tejeda	Y	Y	Y	N	Y	Y	Y	Y
29 Green	Y	Y	Y	N	Y	N	Y	Y
30 Johnson, E.B.	Y	Y	+	N	Y	Y	Y	Y
UTAH								
1 ***Hansen***	N	N	N	Y	N	N	Y	Y
2 Shepherd	Y	Y	Y	N	Y	Y	Y	Y
3 Orton	Y	Y	Y	Y	Y	N	Y	Y
VERMONT								
AL *Sanders*	Y	Y	Y	N	Y	Y	Y	Y
VIRGINIA								
1 ***Bateman***	N	N	N	Y	Y	N	Y	Y
2 Pickett	Y	Y	Y	N	Y	Y	Y	Y
3 Scott	Y	Y	Y	N	Y	Y	Y	Y
4 Sisisky	Y	Y	Y	N	Y	Y	Y	Y
5 Payne	Y	Y	Y	N	Y	Y	Y	Y
6 ***Goodlatte***	N	N	N	Y	Y	N	Y	Y
7 ***Bliley***	N	N	N	Y	Y	Y	Y	Y
8 Moran	Y	Y	Y	N	Y	Y	Y	Y
9 Boucher	Y	Y	Y	N	Y	Y	Y	Y
10 ***Wolf***	N	N	N	Y	Y	N	Y	Y
11 Byrne	Y	Y	Y	N	Y	Y	Y	Y
WASHINGTON								
1 Cantwell	?	?	?	?	#	Y	Y	Y
2 Swift	Y	Y	Y	N	Y	Y	Y	Y
3 Unsoeld	Y	Y	Y	N	Y	Y	Y	Y
4 Inslee	Y	Y	Y	N	Y	Y	Y	Y
5 Foley								
6 Dicks	?	?	?	?	?	Y	Y	Y
7 McDermott	?	?	?	?	?	?	?	?
8 ***Dunn***	N	N	N	Y	N	Y	Y	Y
9 Kreidler	Y	Y	Y	N	Y	Y	Y	Y
WEST VIRGINIA								
1 Mollohan	Y	Y	Y	N	Y	Y	Y	Y
2 Wise	Y	Y	Y	N	Y	N	Y	Y
3 Rahall	Y	Y	Y	N	Y	N	Y	Y
WISCONSIN								
1 Barca	Y	Y	Y	N	Y	Y	Y	Y
2 ***Klug***	N	N	N	Y	Y	N	Y	Y
3 ***Gunderson***	N	N	N	Y	N	N	Y	Y
4 Kleczka	Y	Y	Y	N	Y	Y	Y	Y
5 Barrett	Y	Y	Y	N	Y	Y	Y	Y
6 ***Petri***	N	N	N	Y	Y	N	Y	Y
7 Obey	Y	Y	Y	N	Y	Y	Y	Y
8 ***Roth***	N	N	N	Y	Y	N	Y	Y
9 ***Sensenbrenner***	N	N	N	Y	N	N	Y	Y
WYOMING								
AL ***Thomas***	N	N	N	Y	Y	Y	Y	Y
DELEGATES								
de Lugo, V.I.	D	D	D	D	D	D	D	D
Faleomavaega, Am.S.	D	D	D	D	D	D	D	D
Norton, D.C.	D	D	D	D	D	D	D	D
Romero-B., P.R.	D	D	D	D	D	D	D	D
Underwood, Guam	D	D	D	D	D	D	D	D

Southern states - Ala., Ark., Fla., Ga., Ky., La., Miss., N.C., Okla., S.C., Tenn., Texas, Va.
Omitted votes are quorum calls, which CQ does not include in its vote charts.

KEY

Y Voted for (yea).
Paired for.
+ Announced for.
N Voted against (nay).
X Paired against.
− Announced against.
P Voted "present."
C Voted "present" to avoid possible conflict of interest.
? Did not vote or otherwise make a position known.
D Delegates ineligible to vote.

Democrats **Republicans**
Independent

594. HR 2457. Winter Run Chinook Salmon Captive Broodstock/Passage. Studds, D-Mass., motion to suspend the rules and pass the bill to direct the secretary of the Interior to conduct a salmon captive broodstock program. Motion agreed to 335-85: R 98-73; D 236-12 (ND 160-6, SD 76-6); I 1-0, Nov. 20, 1993. A two-thirds majority of those present and voting (280 in this case) is required for passage under suspension of the rules.

595. HR 51. D.C. Statehood/Passage. Passage of the bill to admit the District of Columbia into the union as the State of New Columbia. Rejected 153-277: R 1-172; D 151-105 (ND 123-49, SD 28-56); I 1-0, Nov. 21, 1993. A "yea" was a vote in support of the president's position.

596. HR 3548. Commemorative Coin Minting/Passage. Kennedy, D-Mass., motion to suspend the rules and pass the bill to authorize the minting of a Thomas Jefferson commemorative $1 coin, a Prisoner of War Commemorative Coin, a Vietnam Veterans Memorial Commemorative Coin and a Women in Military Service for America Memorial Coin. Motion agreed to 428-0: R 172-0; D 255-0 (ND 171-0, SD 84-0); I 1-0, Nov. 21, 1993. A two-thirds majority of those present and voting (286 in this case) is required for passage under suspension of the rules.

597. S Con Res 50. Opposition to Arab Boycott of Israel/Passage. Hamilton, D-Ind., motion to suspend the rules and pass the concurrent resolution to express the sense of Congress that the Arab boycott of Israel is detrimental to the Middle East peace process and should be dismantled. Motion agreed to 425-1: R 172-0; D 252-1 (ND 168-1, SD 84-0); I 1-0, Nov. 21, 1993. A two-thirds majority of those present and voting (284 in this case) is required for passage under suspension of the rules.

598. HR 2202. Preventive Health Amendments/Passage. Waxman, D-Calif., motion to suspend the rules and pass the bill to authorize funds for the early detection of women's reproductive and breast cancers. Motion agreed to 420-0: R 171-0; D 248-0 (ND 164-0, SD 84-0); I 1-0, Nov. 21, 1993. A two-thirds majority of those present and voting (280 in this case) is required for passage under suspension of the rules. A "yea" was a vote in support of the president's position.

599. HR 3. Campaign Finance/Rule. Adoption of the rule (H Res 319) to provide for House floor consideration of the bill to give House candidates up to $200,000 in federal benefits if they agree to voluntary spending limits of $600,000. The sums would be indexed for inflation from 1992 forward. Adopted 220-207: R 3-168; D 216-39 (ND 156-15, SD 60-24); I 1-0, Nov. 21, 1993. A "yea" was a vote in support of the president's position.

600. HR 3. Campaign Finance/Reconsider Rule Vote. Moakley, D-Mass., motion to table (kill) the Derrick, D-S.C., motion to reconsider the vote on adoption of the rule (H Res 319) to provide for House floor consideration of the bill to give House candidates up to $200,000 in federal benefits if they agree to voluntary spending limits of $600,000. The sums would be indexed for inflation from 1992 forward, and a separate funding mechanism would be required. Motion agreed to 250-161: R 2-161; D 247-0 (ND 165-0, SD 82-0); I 1-0, Nov. 21, 1993.

601. Procedural Motion. Approval of the House Journal of Sunday, Nov. 21. Approved 219-141: R 13-137; D 205-4 (ND 137-2, SD 68-2); I 1-0, Nov. 22, 1993.

	594	595	596	597	598	599	600	601
ALABAMA								
1 *Callahan*	N	N	Y	Y	Y	N	N	N
2 *Everett*	N	N	Y	Y	Y	N	N	N
3 Browder	Y	N	Y	Y	Y	Y	Y	Y
4 Bevill	Y	N	Y	Y	Y	Y	Y	Y
5 Cramer	Y	N	Y	Y	Y	Y	Y	Y
6 *Bachus*	N	N	Y	Y	Y	N	N	N
7 Hilliard	Y	Y	Y	Y	Y	Y	Y	Y
ALASKA								
AL *Young*	Y	N	Y	Y	Y	N	N	?
ARIZONA								
1 Coppersmith	Y	N	Y	Y	Y	Y	Y	Y
2 Pastor	Y	Y	Y	Y	Y	Y	Y	Y
3 *Stump*	N	N	Y	Y	Y	N	N	N
4 *Kyl*	N	?	?	?	?	?	?	N
5 *Kolbe*	Y	N	Y	Y	Y	N	N	N
6 English	Y	N	Y	Y	Y	Y	Y	?
ARKANSAS								
1 Lambert	Y	N	Y	Y	Y	Y	Y	Y
2 Thornton	Y	N	Y	Y	Y	Y	Y	Y
3 *Hutchinson*	N	N	Y	Y	Y	N	N	N
4 *Dickey*	N	N	Y	Y	Y	N	N	N
CALIFORNIA								
1 Hamburg	Y	Y	Y	Y	Y	Y	Y	Y
2 *Herger*	Y	N	Y	Y	Y	N	N	?
3 Fazio	Y	Y	Y	Y	Y	Y	Y	Y
4 *Doolittle*	Y	N	Y	Y	Y	N	N	?
5 Matsui	?	Y	Y	Y	Y	Y	Y	Y
6 Woolsey	Y	Y	Y	Y	Y	Y	Y	Y
7 Miller	Y	Y	Y	Y	Y	Y	Y	?
8 Pelosi	Y	Y	Y	Y	Y	Y	Y	Y
9 Dellums	Y	Y	Y	Y	Y	Y	Y	Y
10 *Baker*	Y	N	Y	Y	Y	N	N	?
11 *Pombo*	Y	N	Y	Y	Y	N	N	Y
12 Lantos	Y	Y	Y	Y	Y	Y	Y	Y
13 Stark	Y	Y	Y	Y	Y	Y	Y	Y
14 Eshoo	Y	Y	Y	Y	Y	Y	Y	Y
15 Mineta	Y	Y	Y	Y	Y	Y	Y	Y
16 Edwards	Y	Y	Y	Y	?	Y	Y	Y
17 Farr	Y	Y	Y	Y	Y	Y	Y	?
18 Condit	Y	N	Y	Y	Y	Y	Y	Y
19 Lehman	Y	N	Y	Y	Y	Y	Y	Y
20 Dooley	Y	N	Y	Y	Y	Y	Y	Y
21 *Thomas*	Y	N	Y	Y	Y	N	N	N
22 *Huffington*	Y	N	Y	Y	Y	N	N	N
23 *Gallegly*	Y	N	Y	Y	Y	N	N	N
24 Beilenson	Y	Y	Y	Y	Y	Y	Y	?
25 *McKeon*	Y	N	Y	Y	Y	N	N	N
26 Berman	Y	Y	Y	Y	Y	Y	?	Y
27 *Moorhead*	Y	N	Y	Y	Y	N	?	N
28 *Dreier*	N	N	Y	Y	Y	N	N	N
29 Waxman	Y	Y	Y	?	Y	Y	Y	?
30 Becerra	Y	Y	Y	Y	Y	Y	Y	?
31 Martinez	Y	Y	Y	Y	Y	Y	Y	?
32 Dixon	Y	Y	Y	Y	Y	Y	Y	?
33 Roybal-Allard	Y	Y	Y	Y	Y	Y	Y	Y
34 Torres	Y	Y	Y	Y	Y	Y	Y	Y
35 Waters	Y	Y	Y	Y	Y	Y	?	?
36 Harman	Y	Y	Y	Y	?	Y	Y	Y
37 Tucker	Y	Y	Y	Y	Y	Y	Y	Y
38 *Horn*	Y	N	Y	Y	Y	N	N	N
39 *Royce*	N	N	Y	Y	Y	N	N	N
40 *Lewis*	Y	N	Y	Y	Y	N	N	N
41 *Kim*	N	N	Y	Y	Y	N	N	N

	594	595	596	597	598	599	600	601
42 Brown	Y	Y	Y	?	?	Y	Y	Y
43 *Calvert*	Y	N	Y	Y	Y	N	N	N
44 *McCandless*	N	N	Y	Y	Y	N	N	N
45 *Rohrabacher*	N	N	Y	Y	Y	N	N	N
46 *Dornan*	N	N	Y	Y	Y	N	N	?
47 *Cox*	N	N	Y	Y	Y	N	N	N
48 *Packard*	Y	N	Y	Y	Y	N	N	N
49 Schenk	Y	Y	Y	Y	Y	Y	Y	Y
50 Filner	Y	Y	Y	Y	Y	Y	Y	Y
51 *Cunningham*	N	N	Y	Y	Y	N	N	N
52 *Hunter*	Y	N	Y	Y	Y	N	N	?
COLORADO								
1 Schroeder	Y	Y	Y	Y	Y	N	N	N
2 Skaggs	Y	N	Y	Y	Y	Y	Y	Y
3 *McInnis*	Y	N	Y	Y	Y	N	N	N
4 *Allard*	N	N	Y	Y	Y	N	N	N
5 *Hefley*	Y	N	Y	Y	Y	N	N	N
6 *Schaefer*	Y	N	Y	Y	Y	N	N	?
CONNECTICUT								
1 Kennelly	Y	Y	Y	Y	Y	Y	Y	Y
2 Gejdenson	Y	Y	Y	Y	Y	Y	Y	Y
3 DeLauro	Y	Y	Y	Y	Y	Y	Y	Y
4 *Shays*	Y	N	Y	Y	Y	N	N	N
5 *Franks*	Y	N	Y	Y	N	N	N	N
6 *Johnson*	Y	N	Y	Y	Y	N	?	N
DELAWARE								
AL *Castle*	Y	N	Y	Y	Y	N	N	N
FLORIDA								
1 Hutto	Y	N	Y	Y	Y	N	Y	Y
2 Peterson	Y	N	Y	Y	Y	Y	Y	Y
3 Brown	Y	Y	Y	Y	Y	Y	Y	Y
4 *Fowler*	N	N	Y	Y	Y	N	N	N
5 Thurman	Y	N	Y	Y	Y	Y	Y	Y
6 *Stearns*	N	N	Y	Y	Y	N	N	N
7 *Mica*	N	N	Y	Y	Y	N	N	N
8 *McCollum*	N	N	Y	Y	Y	N	N	N
9 *Bilirakis*	Y	N	Y	Y	Y	N	N	N
10 *Young*	Y	N	Y	Y	Y	N	N	N
11 Gibbons	Y	Y	Y	Y	Y	Y	Y	Y
12 *Canady*	N	N	Y	Y	Y	N	N	N
13 *Miller*	Y	N	Y	Y	Y	N	N	N
14 *Goss*	N	N	Y	Y	Y	N	N	N
15 Bacchus	N	Y	Y	Y	Y	Y	Y	Y
16 *Lewis*	Y	N	Y	Y	Y	N	N	N
17 Meek	Y	Y	Y	Y	Y	Y	Y	Y
18 *Ros-Lehtinen*	Y	N	Y	Y	Y	N	N	N
19 Johnston	Y	N	Y	Y	Y	Y	Y	Y
20 Deutsch	Y	Y	Y	Y	Y	Y	Y	Y
21 *Diaz-Balart*	Y	N	Y	Y	Y	N	N	N
22 *Shaw*	Y	N	Y	Y	Y	N	N	N
23 Hastings	Y	Y	Y	Y	Y	Y	Y	Y
GEORGIA								
1 *Kingston*	Y	N	Y	Y	Y	N	N	Y
2 Bishop	Y	Y	Y	Y	Y	Y	Y	Y
3 *Collins*	N	N	Y	Y	Y	N	N	N
4 *Linder*	N	N	Y	Y	Y	N	N	N
5 Lewis	Y	Y	Y	Y	Y	Y	Y	Y
6 *Gingrich*	Y	N	Y	Y	Y	N	N	N
7 Darden	Y	N	Y	?	Y	Y	Y	Y
8 Rowland	Y	N	Y	Y	N	Y	Y	Y
9 Deal	Y	N	Y	Y	Y	N	Y	Y
10 Johnson	?	N	Y	Y	Y	Y	Y	N
11 McKinney	Y	Y	Y	Y	Y	Y	Y	Y
HAWAII								
1 Abercrombie	Y	Y	Y	Y	Y	?	?	Y
2 Mink	Y	Y	Y	Y	Y	Y	Y	Y
IDAHO								
1 LaRocco	Y	N	Y	Y	Y	Y	Y	Y
2 *Crapo*	Y	N	Y	Y	Y	N	N	N
ILLINOIS								
1 Rush	Y	Y	Y	Y	Y	Y	Y	Y
2 Reynolds	?	Y	Y	Y	Y	Y	Y	Y
3 Lipinski	Y	N	Y	Y	Y	Y	Y	Y
4 Gutierrez	Y	Y	Y	Y	Y	Y	Y	Y
5 Rostenkowski	Y	Y	Y	Y	Y	N	Y	Y
6 *Hyde*	Y	N	Y	Y	N	N	Y	N
7 Collins	Y	Y	Y	Y	Y	Y	Y	Y
8 *Crane*	N	N	Y	Y	Y	N	N	?
9 Yates	Y	Y	Y	Y	Y	Y	Y	Y
10 *Porter*	Y	N	Y	Y	Y	N	N	?
11 Sangmeister	Y	N	Y	Y	Y	N	Y	?
12 Costello	Y	Y	Y	Y	Y	Y	Y	Y
13 *Fawell*	Y	N	Y	Y	Y	N	N	N
14 *Hastert*	Y	N	Y	Y	Y	N	N	N
15 *Ewing*	N	N	Y	Y	Y	N	N	N
16 *Manzullo*	N	N	Y	Y	Y	N	N	N
17 Evans	Y	Y	Y	Y	Y	Y	Y	Y

ND Northern Democrats   SD Southern Democrats

	594	595	596	597	598	599	600	601
18 ***Michel***	N	N	Y	Y	Y	N	N	N
19 Poshard	N	N	Y	Y	Y	N	Y	Y
20 Durbin	Y	Y	Y	Y	Y	Y	Y	Y
INDIANA								
1 Visclosky	Y	Y	Y	Y	Y	Y	Y	Y
2 Sharp	Y	Y	Y	Y	Y	Y	Y	Y
3 Roemer	Y	N	Y	Y	Y	Y	Y	Y
4 Long	Y	Y	Y	Y	Y	Y	Y	Y
5 ***Buyer***	N	N	Y	Y	Y	N	N	N
6 ***Burton***	N	N	Y	Y	Y	N	N	N
7 ***Myers***	Y	N	Y	Y	Y	N	N	Y
8 McCloskey	Y	Y	Y	Y	Y	Y	Y	Y
9 Hamilton	Y	N	Y	Y	Y	Y	Y	Y
10 Jacobs	Y	Y	Y	Y	Y	N	Y	N
IOWA								
1 ***Leach***	Y	N	Y	Y	Y	N	N	N
2 ***Nussle***	N	N	Y	Y	Y	N	N	N
3 ***Lightfoot***	N	N	Y	Y	Y	N	N	N
4 Smith	Y	N	Y	Y	Y	Y	Y	Y
5 ***Grandy***	N	N	Y	Y	Y	N	N	N
KANSAS								
1 ***Roberts***	N	N	Y	Y	Y	N	N	N
2 Slattery	?	Y	Y	Y	Y	Y	Y	?
3 ***Meyers***	Y	N	Y	Y	Y	N	N	?
4 Glickman	Y	Y	Y	Y	Y	Y	Y	Y
KENTUCKY								
1 Barlow	Y	N	Y	Y	Y	Y	Y	Y
2 Natcher	Y	Y	Y	Y	Y	Y	Y	Y
3 Mazzoli	Y	N	Y	Y	Y	N	Y	Y
4 ***Bunning***	N	N	Y	Y	Y	?	?	?
5 ***Rogers***	N	N	Y	Y	Y	N	N	N
6 Baesler	Y	N	Y	Y	Y	N	Y	Y
LOUISIANA								
1 ***Livingston***	Y	N	Y	Y	Y	N	N	N
2 Jefferson	Y	Y	Y	Y	Y	Y	Y	?
3 Tauzin	Y	N	Y	Y	Y	N	Y	Y
4 Fields	Y	Y	Y	Y	Y	Y	Y	Y
5 ***McCrery***	Y	N	Y	Y	Y	N	N	?
6 ***Baker***	Y	N	Y	Y	Y	N	N	N
7 Hayes	Y	N	Y	Y	Y	N	Y	Y
MAINE								
1 Andrews	Y	Y	Y	Y	Y	Y	Y	Y
2 ***Snowe***	Y	N	Y	Y	Y	N	N	N
MARYLAND								
1 ***Gilchrest***	Y	Y	Y	Y	Y	N	N	N
2 ***Bentley***	Y	N	Y	Y	Y	N	N	N
3 Cardin	Y	Y	Y	Y	Y	Y	Y	Y
4 Wynn	Y	Y	Y	Y	Y	Y	Y	Y
5 Hoyer	Y	N	Y	Y	Y	Y	Y	Y
6 ***Bartlett***	N	N	Y	Y	Y	N	N	N
7 Mfume	Y	Y	Y	Y	Y	Y	Y	Y
8 ***Morella***	Y	N	Y	Y	Y	Y	N	?
MASSACHUSETTS								
1 Olver	Y	Y	Y	Y	Y	Y	Y	Y
2 Neal	Y	Y	Y	Y	Y	Y	Y	Y
3 ***Blute***	Y	N	Y	Y	Y	N	N	N
4 Frank	Y	Y	Y	Y	Y	Y	Y	Y
5 Meehan	Y	Y	Y	Y	Y	N	Y	Y
6 ***Torkildsen***	Y	N	Y	Y	Y	N	N	N
7 Markey	Y	Y	Y	Y	Y	Y	Y	?
8 Kennedy	Y	Y	Y	Y	Y	Y	Y	Y
9 Moakley	Y	Y	Y	Y	Y	Y	Y	?
10 Studds	Y	Y	Y	Y	Y	Y	Y	Y
MICHIGAN								
1 Stupak	Y	N	Y	Y	Y	Y	Y	Y
2 ***Hoekstra***	Y	N	Y	Y	Y	N	N	N
3 Vacancy								
4 ***Camp***	Y	N	Y	Y	Y	N	N	N
5 Barcia	Y	N	Y	Y	Y	Y	Y	Y
6 ***Upton***	Y	N	Y	Y	Y	N	N	N
7 ***Smith***	N	N	Y	Y	Y	N	N	N
8 Carr	N	N	Y	Y	Y	N	Y	Y
9 Kildee	Y	Y	Y	Y	Y	Y	Y	Y
10 Bonior	Y	Y	Y	Y	Y	Y	Y	Y
11 ***Knollenberg***	Y	N	Y	Y	Y	N	N	N
12 Levin	Y	Y	Y	Y	Y	Y	Y	Y
13 Ford	Y	N	Y	Y	?	?	Y	?
14 Conyers	Y	Y	Y	Y	Y	Y	?	?
15 Collins	Y	Y	Y	Y	Y	Y	Y	Y
16 Dingell	Y	N	Y	?	?	Y	Y	Y
MINNESOTA								
1 Penny	N	Y	Y	Y	Y	Y	Y	Y
2 Minge	N	Y	Y	Y	Y	Y	Y	Y
3 ***Ramstad***	N	N	Y	Y	Y	N	N	N
4 Vento	Y	Y	Y	Y	Y	Y	Y	Y

	594	595	596	597	598	599	600	601
5 Sabo	Y	Y	Y	Y	Y	Y	Y	Y
6 ***Grams***	N	N	Y	Y	Y	N	N	N
7 Peterson	Y	N	Y	Y	Y	Y	Y	?
8 Oberstar	Y	Y	Y	Y	Y	Y	Y	Y
MISSISSIPPI								
1 Whitten	Y	N	Y	Y	Y	Y	Y	?
2 Thompson	Y	Y	Y	Y	Y	Y	Y	Y
3 Montgomery	Y	N	Y	Y	Y	Y	Y	Y
4 Parker	Y	N	Y	Y	Y	Y	Y	?
5 Taylor	N	N	Y	Y	Y	N	Y	N
MISSOURI								
1 Clay	Y	Y	Y	Y	Y	Y	Y	?
2 ***Talent***	Y	N	Y	Y	Y	N	N	N
3 Gephardt	Y	Y	Y	Y	Y	Y	Y	Y
4 Skelton	Y	N	Y	Y	Y	N	Y	Y
5 Wheat	Y	Y	Y	Y	Y	Y	Y	Y
6 Danner	Y	N	Y	Y	Y	Y	Y	Y
7 ***Hancock***	N	N	Y	Y	Y	N	N	N
8 ***Emerson***	N	N	Y	Y	Y	N	N	N
9 Volkmer	Y	N	Y	Y	Y	Y	Y	Y
MONTANA								
AL Williams	Y	N	Y	Y	Y	Y	Y	?
NEBRASKA								
1 ***Bereuter***	Y	N	Y	Y	Y	N	N	N
2 Hoagland	Y	N	Y	Y	Y	Y	Y	Y
3 ***Barrett***	N	N	Y	Y	Y	N	N	N
NEVADA								
1 Bilbray	Y	Y	Y	Y	Y	Y	Y	?
2 ***Vucanovich***	N	N	Y	Y	Y	N	N	N
NEW HAMPSHIRE								
1 ***Zeliff***	N	N	Y	Y	Y	N	N	N
2 Swett	Y	Y	Y	Y	Y	Y	Y	Y
NEW JERSEY								
1 Andrews	Y	Y	Y	Y	Y	N	Y	Y
2 Hughes	Y	N	Y	Y	Y	Y	Y	Y
3 ***Saxton***	Y	N	Y	Y	Y	N	N	N
4 ***Smith***	Y	N	Y	Y	Y	N	N	Y
5 ***Roukema***	?	N	Y	Y	Y	N	N	N
6 Pallone	Y	Y	Y	Y	Y	Y	Y	Y
7 ***Franks***	Y	N	Y	Y	Y	N	N	N
8 Klein	Y	Y	Y	Y	Y	Y	Y	Y
9 Torricelli	?	Y	Y	Y	Y	N	Y	Y
10 Payne	Y	Y	Y	Y	Y	Y	Y	Y
11 ***Gallo***	Y	N	Y	Y	Y	N	N	N
12 ***Zimmer***	Y	N	Y	Y	Y	N	N	N
13 Menendez	Y	Y	Y	Y	Y	Y	Y	Y
NEW MEXICO								
1 ***Schiff***	Y	N	Y	Y	Y	N	N	N
2 ***Skeen***	Y	N	Y	Y	Y	N	N	N
3 Richardson	Y	Y	Y	Y	?	Y	Y	Y
NEW YORK								
1 Hochbrueckner	Y	N	Y	Y	Y	Y	Y	Y
2 ***Lazio***	Y	N	Y	Y	Y	N	N	N
3 ***King***	N	N	Y	Y	Y	N	N	N
4 ***Levy***	N	N	Y	Y	Y	N	N	N
5 Ackerman	Y	N	Y	Y	Y	Y	Y	Y
6 Flake	Y	Y	Y	Y	Y	Y	Y	Y
7 Manton	Y	Y	Y	Y	Y	Y	Y	?
8 Nadler	Y	Y	Y	Y	Y	Y	Y	?
9 Schumer	Y	Y	Y	Y	Y	Y	Y	Y
10 Towns	Y	Y	Y	Y	Y	N	Y	Y
11 Owens	Y	Y	Y	Y	Y	Y	Y	Y
12 Velazquez	Y	Y	Y	Y	Y	Y	Y	Y
13 ***Molinari***	Y	N	Y	Y	Y	N	N	N
14 Maloney	Y	Y	Y	Y	Y	Y	Y	Y
15 Rangel	Y	Y	Y	Y	Y	Y	Y	?
16 Serrano	Y	Y	Y	?	Y	Y	Y	Y
17 Engel	Y	Y	Y	Y	Y	Y	Y	?
18 Lowey	Y	Y	Y	Y	Y	Y	Y	Y
19 ***Fish***	Y	N	Y	Y	Y	N	N	?
20 ***Gilman***	Y	N	Y	Y	Y	N	N	+
21 McNulty	Y	N	Y	Y	Y	Y	Y	Y
22 ***Solomon***	Y	N	Y	Y	Y	N	N	N
23 ***Boehlert***	Y	N	Y	Y	Y	Y	N	N
24 ***McHugh***	Y	N	Y	Y	Y	N	N	N
25 ***Walsh***	Y	N	Y	Y	Y	N	N	N
26 Hinchey	Y	Y	Y	Y	Y	Y	Y	?
27 ***Paxon***	N	N	Y	Y	Y	N	N	N
28 Slaughter	Y	Y	Y	Y	Y	Y	Y	?
29 LaFalce	Y	N	Y	Y	Y	Y	Y	?
30 ***Quinn***	Y	N	Y	Y	Y	N	N	N
31 ***Houghton***	Y	N	Y	Y	Y	N	N	Y
NORTH CAROLINA								
1 Clayton	Y	Y	Y	Y	Y	Y	Y	Y
2 Valentine	Y	N	Y	Y	Y	N	Y	?

	594	595	596	597	598	599	600	601
3 Lancaster	Y	N	Y	Y	Y	N	Y	Y
4 Price	Y	N	Y	Y	Y	Y	Y	Y
5 Neal	Y	N	Y	Y	Y	Y	Y	?
6 ***Coble***	N	N	Y	Y	Y	N	N	N
7 Rose	Y	Y	Y	Y	Y	Y	Y	Y
8 Hefner	Y	Y	Y	Y	Y	Y	Y	?
9 ***McMillan***	Y	N	Y	Y	Y	N	N	N
10 ***Ballenger***	N	N	Y	Y	Y	N	N	N
11 ***Taylor***	N	N	Y	Y	Y	N	N	N
12 Watt	Y	Y	Y	Y	Y	Y	Y	Y
NORTH DAKOTA								
AL Pomeroy	Y	N	Y	Y	Y	Y	Y	Y
OHIO								
1 Mann	Y	N	Y	Y	Y	Y	Y	Y
2 ***Portman***	Y	N	Y	Y	Y	N	N	N
3 Hall	?	?	?	?	?	?	?	?
4 ***Oxley***	N	N	Y	Y	Y	N	N	?
5 ***Gillmor***	Y	N	Y	Y	Y	N	N	Y
6 Strickland	Y	N	Y	Y	Y	Y	Y	Y
7 ***Hobson***	Y	N	Y	Y	Y	N	N	N
8 ***Boehner***	N	N	Y	Y	Y	N	N	N
9 Kaptur	Y	N	Y	Y	Y	N	Y	?
10 ***Hoke***	N	N	Y	Y	Y	N	P	N
11 Stokes	Y	Y	Y	Y	Y	Y	Y	Y
12 ***Kasich***	N	N	Y	Y	Y	N	?	Y
13 Brown	Y	Y	Y	Y	Y	Y	Y	Y
14 Sawyer	Y	Y	Y	Y	Y	Y	Y	Y
15 ***Pryce***	N	N	Y	Y	Y	N	N	N
16 ***Regula***	Y	N	Y	Y	Y	N	N	N
17 Traficant	Y	Y	Y	Y	Y	N	Y	Y
18 Applegate	Y	N	Y	Y	Y	Y	Y	Y
19 Fingerhut	Y	N	Y	Y	Y	Y	Y	Y
OKLAHOMA								
1 ***Inhofe***	N	N	Y	Y	Y	N	N	N
2 Synar	Y	Y	Y	Y	Y	N	Y	Y
3 Brewster	Y	N	Y	Y	Y	N	Y	?
4 McCurdy	Y	N	Y	Y	Y	N	Y	Y
5 ***Istook***	Y	N	Y	Y	Y	N	N	N
6 English	Y	N	Y	Y	Y	N	Y	?
OREGON								
1 Furse	Y	Y	Y	Y	Y	Y	Y	Y
2 ***Smith***	Y	N	Y	Y	Y	N	?	?
3 Wyden	Y	Y	Y	Y	Y	Y	Y	Y
4 DeFazio	Y	Y	Y	Y	Y	Y	Y	Y
5 Kopetski	Y	Y	Y	Y	Y	N	Y	Y
PENNSYLVANIA								
1 Foglietta	Y	Y	Y	Y	?	Y	Y	Y
2 Blackwell	Y	Y	Y	Y	Y	Y	Y	Y
3 Borski	Y	Y	Y	Y	Y	Y	Y	Y
4 Klink	Y	N	Y	Y	Y	Y	Y	Y
5 ***Clinger***	?	?	?	?	?	?	?	?
6 Holden	Y	N	Y	Y	Y	Y	Y	Y
7 ***Weldon***	Y	N	Y	Y	Y	N	N	N
8 ***Greenwood***	Y	N	Y	Y	Y	N	N	Y
9 ***Shuster***	Y	N	Y	Y	Y	N	?	N
10 ***McDade***	Y	N	Y	Y	Y	N	N	?
11 Kanjorski	Y	N	Y	Y	Y	Y	Y	Y
12 Murtha	Y	N	Y	Y	Y	Y	Y	P
13 Margolies-Mezv.	Y	Y	Y	Y	Y	Y	Y	Y
14 Coyne	Y	Y	Y	Y	Y	Y	Y	Y
15 McHale	Y	Y	Y	Y	Y	Y	Y	Y
16 ***Walker***	N	N	Y	Y	Y	N	N	N
17 ***Gekas***	?	N	Y	Y	Y	N	N	N
18 ***Santorum***	N	N	Y	Y	Y	N	N	N
19 ***Goodling***	Y	N	Y	Y	Y	N	N	N
20 Murphy	Y	N	Y	Y	Y	N	Y	?
21 ***Ridge***	?	N	Y	Y	Y	N	N	N
RHODE ISLAND								
1 ***Machtley***	N	N	Y	Y	Y	N	N	N
2 Reed	Y	N	Y	Y	Y	Y	Y	Y
SOUTH CAROLINA								
1 ***Ravenel***	Y	N	Y	Y	Y	N	N	N
2 ***Spence***	N	N	Y	Y	Y	N	N	N
3 Derrick	Y	N	Y	Y	Y	Y	Y	Y
4 ***Inglis***	N	N	Y	Y	Y	N	N	Y
5 Spratt	Y	N	Y	Y	Y	Y	Y	Y
6 Clyburn	Y	Y	Y	Y	Y	Y	Y	Y
SOUTH DAKOTA								
AL Johnson	Y	N	Y	Y	Y	Y	Y	Y
TENNESSEE								
1 ***Quillen***	Y	N	Y	Y	Y	N	N	N
2 ***Duncan***	N	N	Y	Y	Y	N	N	N
3 Lloyd	Y	N	Y	Y	Y	N	?	Y
4 Cooper	Y	N	Y	Y	Y	Y	Y	Y
5 Clement	Y	N	Y	Y	Y	Y	Y	Y

	594	595	596	597	598	599	600	601
6 Gordon	Y	N	Y	Y	Y	Y	Y	Y
7 ***Sundquist***	N	N	?	?	?	?	?	?
8 Tanner	Y	N	Y	Y	Y	N	Y	Y
9 Ford	Y	Y	Y	Y	Y	Y	Y	?
TEXAS								
1 Chapman	Y	N	Y	Y	Y	N	Y	?
2 Wilson	Y	N	Y	Y	Y	Y	Y	?
3 ***Johnson, Sam***	N	N	Y	Y	Y	N	N	N
4 Hall	N	N	Y	Y	Y	Y	Y	Y
5 Bryant	?	Y	Y	Y	Y	Y	Y	Y
6 ***Barton***	N	N	Y	Y	Y	N	N	?
7 ***Archer***	Y	N	Y	Y	Y	N	N	Y
8 ***Fields***	Y	N	Y	Y	Y	N	N	?
9 Brooks	Y	N	Y	Y	Y	Y	Y	Y
10 Pickle	Y	Y	Y	Y	Y	Y	Y	Y
11 Edwards	Y	N	Y	Y	Y	Y	Y	Y
12 Geren	Y	N	Y	Y	Y	N	Y	?
13 Sarpalius	N	N	Y	Y	Y	Y	Y	Y
14 Laughlin	Y	N	Y	Y	Y	Y	Y	Y
15 de la Garza	Y	N	Y	Y	Y	Y	Y	Y
16 Coleman	Y	N	Y	Y	Y	Y	Y	Y
17 Stenholm	N	N	Y	Y	Y	N	Y	Y
18 Washington	?	?	?	?	?	?	?	?
19 ***Combest***	N	N	Y	Y	Y	N	?	Y
20 Gonzalez	Y	Y	Y	Y	Y	Y	Y	Y
21 ***Smith***	Y	N	Y	Y	Y	N	N	N
22 ***DeLay***	N	N	Y	Y	Y	N	N	?
23 ***Bonilla***	N	N	Y	Y	Y	N	N	N
24 Frost	Y	N	Y	Y	Y	N	Y	Y
25 Andrews	Y	N	Y	Y	Y	N	Y	Y
26 ***Armey***	N	N	Y	Y	Y	N	N	N
27 Ortiz	Y	N	Y	Y	Y	Y	Y	Y
28 Tejeda	Y	Y	Y	Y	Y	Y	Y	Y
29 Green	Y	Y	Y	Y	Y	Y	Y	Y
30 Johnson, E.B.	Y	Y	Y	Y	Y	Y	Y	Y
UTAH								
1 ***Hansen***	Y	N	Y	Y	Y	N	N	N
2 Shepherd	Y	N	Y	Y	Y	Y	Y	Y
3 Orton	Y	N	Y	Y	Y	Y	Y	Y
VERMONT								
AL *Sanders*	Y	Y	Y	Y	Y	Y	Y	Y
VIRGINIA								
1 ***Bateman***	Y	N	Y	Y	?	N	N	?
2 Pickett	Y	N	Y	Y	Y	N	Y	Y
3 Scott	Y	Y	Y	Y	Y	Y	Y	?
4 Sisisky	Y	N	Y	Y	Y	N	?	Y
5 Payne	Y	N	Y	Y	Y	Y	Y	Y
6 ***Goodlatte***	N	N	Y	Y	Y	N	N	N
7 ***Bliley***	Y	N	Y	Y	Y	N	N	N
8 Moran	Y	N	Y	Y	Y	Y	Y	?
9 Boucher	Y	N	Y	Y	Y	N	Y	Y
10 ***Wolf***	Y	N	Y	Y	Y	N	N	?
11 Byrne	N	N	Y	Y	Y	Y	Y	Y
WASHINGTON								
1 Cantwell	Y	Y	Y	Y	Y	Y	Y	Y
2 Swift	Y	Y	Y	Y	Y	Y	Y	Y
3 Unsoeld	Y	Y	Y	Y	Y	Y	Y	Y
4 Inslee	Y	Y	Y	Y	Y	Y	Y	Y
5 Foley		Y		Y		Y		
6 Dicks	Y	Y	Y	Y	Y	Y	?	Y
7 McDermott	?	Y	Y	Y	Y	Y	Y	Y
8 ***Dunn***	Y	N	Y	Y	Y	N	N	N
9 Kreidler	Y	Y	Y	Y	Y	Y	Y	Y
WEST VIRGINIA								
1 Mollohan	Y	N	Y	Y	Y	Y	Y	?
2 Wise	Y	N	Y	Y	Y	Y	Y	Y
3 Rahall	Y	N	Y	N	Y	Y	Y	Y
WISCONSIN								
1 Barca	N	Y	Y	Y	Y	Y	Y	Y
2 ***Klug***	N	N	Y	Y	Y	N	N	N
3 ***Gunderson***	Y	N	Y	Y	Y	N	N	N
4 Kleczka	Y	Y	Y	Y	Y	Y	Y	?
5 Barrett	N	Y	Y	Y	Y	Y	Y	Y
6 ***Petri***	N	N	Y	Y	Y	Y	Y	N
7 Obey	Y	Y	Y	Y	Y	Y	Y	Y
8 ***Roth***	Y	N	Y	Y	Y	N	N	N
9 ***Sensenbrenner***	N	N	Y	Y	Y	N	N	N
WYOMING								
AL ***Thomas***	N	N	Y	Y	Y	N	?	N
DELEGATES								
de Lugo, V.I.	D	D	D	D	D	D	D	D
Faleomavaega, Am.S.	D	D	D	D	D	D	D	D
Norton, D.C.	D	D	D	D	D	D	D	D
Romero-B., P.R.	D	D	D	D	D	D	D	D
Underwood, Guam	D	D	D	D	D	D	D	D

Southern states - Ala., Ark., Fla., Ga., Ky., La., Miss., N.C., Okla., S.C., Tenn., Texas, Va.
Omitted votes are quorum calls, which CQ does not include in its vote charts.

*603. HR 3. Campaign Finance/Republican Substitute. Thomas, R-Calif., substitute amendment to eliminate political action committees; require candidates to collect a majority of their funds in their district; ban soft money and bundling; allow unlimited contributions from individuals in cases where an opponent spends more than $250,000 of personal money; and require public disclosure of all election activities and spending by corporations, unions and nonprofit groups. Rejected in the Committee of the Whole 173-263: R 162-12; D 11-250 (ND 4-172, SD 7-78); I 0-1, Nov. 22, 1993.

604. HR 3. Campaign Finance/Motion To Recommit. Fowler, R-Fla., motion to recommit to the House Administration Committee (thus killing) the bill to give House candidates up to $200,000 in federal benefits if they agree to voluntary spending limits of $600,000. The sums would be indexed for inflation from 1992 forward, and a separate funding mechanism would be required. Motion rejected 190-240: R 165-8; D 25-231 (ND 6-165, SD 19-66); I 0-1, Nov. 22, 1993.

605. HR 3. Campaign Finance/Passage. Passage of the bill to give House candidates up to $200,000 in federal benefits if they agree to voluntary spending limits of $600,000. The sums would be indexed for inflation from 1992 forward, and a separate funding mechanism would be required. Passed 255-175: R 22-151; D 232-24 (ND 165-6, SD 67-18); I 1-0, Nov. 22, 1993. A "yea" was a vote in support of the president's position.

606. HR 1025. Brady Bill/Conference With Senate. Adoption of the resolution (H Res 322) to agree to the request of the Senate for a conference on the bill to require a five-business-day waiting period before an individual could purchase a handgun to allow local officials to conduct a background check. Adopted 249-178: R 52-121; D 197-56 (ND 144-26, SD 53-30); I 0-1, Nov. 22, 1993.

607. HR 3400. Reinventing Government and Spending Cuts/Rule. Adoption of the rule (H Res 320) to provide for House floor consideration of the bill to cut federal spending by $37.1 billion through various proposals from the vice president's National Performance Review, including reducing the federal work force by 252,000 jobs. Adopted 247-183: R 28-145; D 218-38 (ND 143-28, SD 75-10); I 1-0, Nov. 22, 1993.

608. HR 3400. Reinventing Government and Spending Cuts/Administration-Backed Plan. Sabo, D-Minn., substitute amendment to cut federal spending by $37.1 billion in outlays over five years, $32.5 billion through 252,000 job reductions in the federal work force, $2 billion in fiscal 1994 rescissions and $2.6 billion through proposals from the vice president's National Performance Review to make government more efficient and effective. Adopted in the Committee of the Whole 272-163: R 21-152; D 250-11 (ND 165-11, SD 85-0); I 1-0, Nov. 22, 1993. A "yea" was a vote in support of the president's position.

609. HR 3400. Reinventing Government and Spending Cuts/Penny-Kasich Amendment. Penny, D-Minn., amendment to cut federal spending by $90 billion over five years through various proposals, including $34 billion in Medicare cuts, $52 billion in discretionary spending cuts and $4 billion in other entitlement cuts and user fee increases. Rejected in the Committee of the Whole 213-219: R 156-18; D 57-200 (ND 33-139, SD 24-61); I 0-1, Nov. 22, 1993. A "nay" was a vote in support of the president's position.

610. HR 3400. Reinventing Government and Spending Cuts/Frank-Shays Amendment. Frank, D-Mass., amendment to cut $14.4 billion over five years by canceling the space station, reducing funding for the Ballistic Missile Defense Program, terminating the advanced liquid metal reactor and increasing burden-sharing in Europe. Rejected in the Committee of the Whole 184-248: R 33-139; D 150-109 (ND 122-53, SD 28-56); I 1-0, Nov. 22, 1993. A "nay" was a vote in support of the president's position.

* Omitted votes are quorum calls, which CQ does not include in its vote charts.

KEY

Y	Voted for (yea).
#	Paired for.
+	Announced for.
N	Voted against (nay).
X	Paired against.
−	Announced against.
P	Voted "present."
C	Voted "present" to avoid possible conflict of interest.
?	Did not vote or otherwise make a position known.
D	Delegates ineligible to vote.

Democrats **Republicans**
Independent

	603	604	605	606	607	608	609	610
ALABAMA								
1 *Callahan*	Y	Y	N	N	N	N	Y	N
2 *Everett*	Y	Y	N	N	N	N	Y	N
3 Browder	N	N	Y	Y	Y	Y	Y	N
4 Bevill	N	N	Y	Y	Y	Y	N	N
5 Cramer	N	N	Y	Y	Y	Y	N	N
6 *Bachus*	Y	Y	N	N	N	N	Y	N
7 Hilliard	N	N	Y	N	Y	Y	N	N
ALASKA								
AL *Young*	Y	Y	N	N	N	N	Y	N
ARIZONA								
1 Coppersmith	N	N	Y	Y	Y	Y	Y	Y
2 Pastor	N	N	Y	Y	Y	Y	N	N
3 *Stump*	Y	Y	N	N	N	N	Y	N
4 *Kyl*	Y	Y	N	N	N	N	Y	N
5 *Kolbe*	Y	Y	N	N	N	N	Y	N
6 English	N	N	Y	Y	Y	Y	N	Y
ARKANSAS								
1 Lambert	N	Y	Y	Y	Y	Y	Y	Y
2 Thornton	N	N	Y	Y	Y	Y	N	N
3 *Hutchinson*	Y	Y	N	N	N	N	Y	N
4 *Dickey*	Y	Y	N	N	N	N	Y	N
CALIFORNIA								
1 Hamburg	N	N	Y	Y	Y	Y	N	Y
2 *Herger*	Y	Y	N	N	N	N	Y	N
3 Fazio	N	N	Y	Y	Y	Y	N	N
4 *Doolittle*	Y	Y	N	N	N	N	Y	N
5 Matsui	N	N	Y	Y	Y	Y	N	N
6 Woolsey	N	N	Y	Y	Y	Y	N	N
7 Miller	N	N	Y	Y	Y	Y	N	Y
8 Pelosi	N	N	Y	Y	Y	Y	N	N
9 Dellums	N	N	Y	Y	Y	Y	N	Y
10 *Baker*	Y	Y	N	N	N	N	Y	N
11 *Pombo*	Y	Y	N	N	N	N	Y	N
12 Lantos	N	N	Y	Y	Y	Y	N	Y
13 Stark	N	N	Y	Y	Y	Y	N	Y
14 Eshoo	N	N	Y	Y	Y	Y	N	N
15 Mineta	N	N	Y	Y	Y	Y	N	N
16 Edwards	N	N	Y	Y	Y	Y	N	Y
17 Farr	N	N	Y	Y	Y	Y	N	N
18 Condit	N	N	Y	Y	N	Y	N	Y
19 Lehman	N	N	Y	Y	Y	N	N	Y
20 Dooley	N	N	Y	?	Y	Y	Y	Y
21 *Thomas*	Y	Y	N	N	N	N	Y	N
22 *Huffington*	Y	Y	N	N	Y	N	Y	N
23 *Gallegly*	Y	Y	N	N	N	N	Y	N
24 Beilenson	N	N	Y	Y	Y	Y	Y	Y
25 *McKeon*	Y	Y	N	N	N	N	Y	N
26 Berman	N	N	Y	Y	Y	Y	N	N
27 *Moorhead*	Y	Y	N	N	N	N	Y	N
28 *Dreier*	Y	Y	N	N	N	N	Y	N
29 Waxman	N	N	Y	Y	Y	Y	N	Y
30 Becerra	N	N	Y	Y	Y	Y	N	Y
31 Martinez	N	N	Y	Y	Y	Y	N	N
32 Dixon	N	N	Y	Y	Y	Y	N	N
33 Roybal-Allard	N	N	Y	Y	Y	Y	N	Y
34 Torres	N	N	Y	Y	Y	Y	N	Y
35 Waters	N	N	Y	Y	Y	N	N	N
36 Harman	N	N	Y	Y	Y	Y	N	N
37 Tucker	N	N	Y	Y	Y	Y	N	N
38 *Horn*	Y	Y	N	N	N	N	N	N
39 *Royce*	Y	Y	N	N	N	N	Y	N
40 *Lewis*	Y	Y	N	N	N	N	Y	N
41 *Kim*	Y	Y	N	N	Y	N	Y	N

	603	604	605	606	607	608	609	610
42 Brown	N	N	Y	Y	Y	Y	N	N
43 *Calvert*	Y	Y	N	N	N	N	Y	N
44 *McCandless*	Y	Y	N	N	N	N	Y	N
45 *Rohrabacher*	Y	Y	N	N	N	N	Y	N
46 *Dornan*	Y	Y	N	N	N	N	Y	N
47 *Cox*	Y	Y	N	N	N	N	Y	N
48 *Packard*	Y	Y	N	N	N	N	Y	N
49 Schenk	N	N	Y	Y	Y	Y	Y	Y
50 Filner	N	N	Y	Y	Y	Y	N	N
51 *Cunningham*	Y	Y	N	N	N	N	Y	N
52 *Hunter*	Y	Y	N	N	N	N	Y	N
COLORADO								
1 Schroeder	N	N	Y	Y	Y	Y	N	Y
2 Skaggs	N	N	Y	Y	Y	Y	N	Y
3 *McInnis*	Y	Y	N	N	Y	N	Y	N
4 *Allard*	Y	?	N	N	N	N	Y	N
5 *Hefley*	N	N	N	N	N	N	Y	N
6 *Schaefer*	Y	Y	N	N	Y	N	Y	N
CONNECTICUT								
1 Kennelly	N	N	Y	Y	Y	Y	N	N
2 Gejdenson	N	N	Y	Y	Y	Y	N	N
3 DeLauro	N	N	Y	Y	Y	Y	N	N
4 *Shays*	Y	N	Y	Y	Y	Y	Y	Y
5 *Franks*	Y	Y	N	N	N	N	Y	N
6 *Johnson*	Y	Y	N	Y	N	Y	Y	N
DELAWARE								
AL *Castle*	Y	Y	N	Y	N	N	Y	N
FLORIDA								
1 Hutto	N	Y	N	Y	Y	Y	N	N
2 Peterson	N	N	Y	Y	Y	Y	N	N
3 Brown	N	N	Y	Y	Y	Y	N	N
4 *Fowler*	N	Y	N	Y	N	N	Y	N
5 Thurman	N	N	Y	N	Y	Y	N	N
6 *Stearns*	Y	Y	N	N	N	N	Y	N
7 *Mica*	Y	Y	N	N	N	N	Y	N
8 *McCollum*	Y	Y	N	N	N	N	Y	N
9 *Bilirakis*	Y	Y	N	Y	N	N	Y	N
10 *Young*	Y	Y	N	Y	N	Y	N	N
11 Gibbons	N	N	Y	Y	Y	Y	N	N
12 *Canady*	Y	Y	N	N	N	N	Y	N
13 *Miller*	Y	Y	N	Y	N	Y	Y	N
14 *Goss*	Y	Y	N	Y	N	Y	Y	N
15 Bacchus	N	N	Y	Y	Y	Y	N	N
16 *Lewis*	Y	Y	N	N	N	N	Y	N
17 Meek	N	N	Y	Y	Y	Y	N	N
18 *Ros-Lehtinen*	Y	Y	N	Y	N	N	Y	N
19 Johnston	N	N	Y	Y	Y	Y	N	Y
20 Deutsch	N	N	Y	Y	Y	Y	N	Y
21 *Diaz-Balart*	Y	Y	N	Y	N	N	Y	N
22 *Shaw*	Y	Y	N	N	N	N	Y	N
23 Hastings	N	N	Y	Y	Y	Y	N	N
GEORGIA								
1 *Kingston*	Y	Y	N	N	N	N	Y	Y
2 Bishop	N	N	Y	Y	Y	Y	N	Y
3 *Collins*	Y	Y	N	N	N	N	Y	N
4 *Linder*	Y	Y	N	N	N	N	Y	N
5 Lewis	N	N	Y	Y	Y	Y	N	N
6 *Gingrich*	Y	Y	N	N	N	N	Y	N
7 Darden	N	N	Y	Y	Y	Y	N	N
8 Rowland	N	N	Y	Y	Y	Y	Y	N
9 Deal	Y	N	Y	Y	Y	Y	Y	N
10 Johnson	N	N	Y	N	Y	Y	N	Y
11 McKinney	N	N	Y	Y	Y	Y	N	Y
HAWAII								
1 Abercrombie	N	N	Y	Y	N	N	N	Y
2 Mink	N	N	Y	Y	N	N	N	Y
IDAHO								
1 LaRocco	N	N	Y	Y	Y	Y	N	Y
2 *Crapo*	Y	Y	N	N	N	N	Y	N
ILLINOIS								
1 Rush	N	N	Y	Y	Y	Y	N	Y
2 Reynolds	N	N	Y	Y	Y	Y	N	Y
3 Lipinski	N	N	Y	Y	Y	Y	N	Y
4 Gutierrez	N	N	Y	Y	Y	Y	N	Y
5 Rostenkowski	N	Y	Y	Y	Y	Y	N	N
6 *Hyde*	Y	Y	N	Y	N	N	Y	N
7 Collins	N	N	Y	Y	Y	Y	N	N
8 *Crane*	Y	Y	N	N	N	N	Y	N
9 Yates	N	N	Y	Y	Y	Y	N	Y
10 *Porter*	Y	Y	N	Y	N	Y	Y	Y
11 Sangmeister	N	N	Y	Y	Y	Y	N	Y
12 Costello	Y	Y	N	Y	Y	Y	N	Y
13 *Fawell*	Y	Y	N	Y	N	Y	N	N
14 *Hastert*	Y	Y	N	N	N	N	Y	N
15 *Ewing*	Y	Y	N	Y	N	Y	Y	N
16 *Manzullo*	N	Y	N	N	N	N	Y	N
17 Evans	N	N	Y	Y	Y	Y	N	Y

ND Northern Democrats   SD Southern Democrats

	603	604	605	606	607	608	609	610
18 ***Michel***	Y	Y	N	Y	N	N	Y	?
19 Poshard	Y	Y	Y	N	Y	Y	Y	Y
20 Durbin	N	N	Y	Y	N	Y	N	Y
INDIANA								
1 Visclosky	N	N	Y	Y	Y	Y	N	Y
2 Sharp	N	N	Y	Y	Y	Y	Y	Y
3 Roemer	N	N	Y	Y	Y	Y	Y	Y
4 Long	N	N	Y	Y	Y	Y	Y	Y
5 ***Buyer***	N	Y	N	N	N	N	Y	N
6 ***Burton***	Y	Y	N	N	N	N	Y	N
7 ***Myers***	Y	Y	N	N	N	N	N	N
8 McCloskey	N	N	Y	Y	N	Y	N	Y
9 Hamilton	N	N	Y	Y	Y	Y	Y	N
10 Jacobs	N	Y	Y	Y	N	N	N	Y
IOWA								
1 ***Leach***	Y	Y	Y	Y	N	N	Y	Y
2 ***Nussle***	Y	Y	N	N	N	N	Y	Y
3 ***Lightfoot***	Y	Y	N	N	N	N	N	N
4 Smith	N	N	Y	N	Y	Y	N	N
5 ***Grandy***	Y	Y	N	N	Y	N	Y	Y
KANSAS								
1 ***Roberts***	Y	Y	N	N	N	N	Y	N
2 Slattery	N	N	Y	Y	Y	Y	Y	N
3 ***Meyers***	Y	Y	N	Y	N	Y	Y	N
4 Glickman	N	N	Y	Y	Y	Y	N	N
KENTUCKY								
1 Barlow	N	N	Y	N	Y	Y	Y	N
2 Natcher	N	N	Y	N	Y	Y	N	N
3 Mazzoli	N	N	Y	Y	Y	Y	Y	N
4 ***Bunning***	Y	Y	N	N	N	N	Y	N
5 ***Rogers***	Y	Y	N	N	N	Y	N	N
6 Baesler	N	N	Y	Y	Y	Y	Y	Y
LOUISIANA								
1 ***Livingston***	Y	Y	N	N	N	N	Y	N
2 Jefferson	N	N	Y	Y	Y	Y	N	N
3 Tauzin	Y	Y	N	N	Y	Y	Y	N
4 Fields	N	N	Y	Y	Y	Y	N	N
5 ***McCrery***	Y	Y	N	N	Y	N	Y	N
6 ***Baker***	N	Y	N	N	N	N	Y	N
7 Hayes	Y	Y	N	N	Y	Y	Y	N
MAINE								
1 Andrews	N	N	Y	Y	Y	Y	N	Y
2 ***Snowe***	N	Y	Y	N	N	N	Y	Y
MARYLAND								
1 ***Gilchrest***	Y	Y	N	Y	N	N	Y	Y
2 ***Bentley***	N	Y	N	Y	N	N	Y	N
3 Cardin	N	N	Y	Y	N	Y	N	Y
4 Wynn	N	N	Y	Y	Y	Y	N	Y
5 Hoyer	N	N	Y	Y	Y	Y	N	N
6 ***Bartlett***	Y	Y	N	N	N	N	Y	N
7 Mfume	N	N	Y	Y	N	Y	N	Y
8 ***Morella***	Y	N	Y	Y	N	Y	N	N
MASSACHUSETTS								
1 Olver	N	N	Y	Y	Y	Y	N	Y
2 Neal	N	N	Y	Y	Y	Y	N	N
3 ***Blute***	Y	Y	Y	Y	N	N	Y	Y
4 Frank	N	N	Y	Y	Y	Y	N	Y
5 Meehan	N	N	Y	Y	Y	Y	Y	Y
6 ***Torkildsen***	Y	Y	Y	Y	N	N	Y	N
7 Markey	N	N	Y	Y	Y	Y	N	Y
8 Kennedy	N	N	Y	Y	Y	Y	N	Y
9 Moakley	N	N	Y	Y	Y	Y	N	Y
10 Studds	N	N	Y	Y	Y	Y	N	Y
MICHIGAN								
1 Stupak	N	N	Y	N	Y	Y	N	Y
2 ***Hoekstra***	Y	Y	N	N	Y	N	Y	Y
3 Vacancy								
4 ***Camp***	Y	Y	N	N	N	N	Y	Y
5 Barcia	N	N	Y	N	Y	Y	N	Y
6 ***Upton***	Y	Y	N	Y	N	N	Y	Y
7 ***Smith***	Y	Y	N	Y	Y	Y	Y	N
8 Carr	N	N	N	Y	Y	Y	N	N
9 Kildee	N	N	Y	Y	Y	Y	N	Y
10 Bonior	N	N	Y	Y	Y	Y	N	N
11 ***Knollenberg***	Y	Y	N	N	N	N	Y	N
12 Levin	N	N	Y	Y	Y	Y	N	Y
13 Ford	N	N	Y	Y	N	Y	N	Y
14 Conyers	N	N	Y	Y	Y	N	N	Y
15 Collins	N	N	Y	Y	Y	Y	N	Y
16 Dingell	N	N	Y	N	Y	Y	N	N
MINNESOTA								
1 Penny	N	N	Y	N	Y	N	Y	Y
2 Minge	Y	N	Y	Y	Y	Y	Y	Y
3 ***Ramstad***	Y	Y	N	Y	Y	N	Y	Y
4 Vento	N	N	Y	Y	Y	Y	N	Y

	603	604	605	606	607	608	609	610
5 Sabo	N	N	Y	Y	Y	Y	N	N
6 ***Grams***	Y	Y	N	N	N	N	Y	N
7 Peterson	N	N	Y	N	Y	N	Y	Y
8 Oberstar	N	N	Y	N	Y	Y	N	Y
MISSISSIPPI								
1 Whitten	N	N	Y	Y	Y	Y	N	N
2 Thompson	N	N	Y	Y	Y	Y	N	Y
3 Montgomery	N	N	Y	N	Y	Y	N	N
4 Parker	N	N	Y	N	N	Y	N	N
5 Taylor	Y	Y	N	N	Y	Y	Y	N
MISSOURI								
1 Clay	N	N	Y	Y	Y	Y	N	N
2 ***Talent***	Y	Y	N	N	N	N	Y	N
3 Gephardt	N	N	Y	Y	Y	Y	N	N
4 Skelton	N	Y	N	N	Y	N	N	N
5 Wheat	N	N	Y	Y	Y	Y	N	Y
6 Danner	N	N	Y	N	Y	Y	N	Y
7 ***Hancock***	Y	Y	N	N	N	N	Y	N
8 ***Emerson***	N	Y	N	N	N	N	Y	N
9 Volkmer	N	N	Y	N	Y	Y	N	N
MONTANA								
AL Williams	N	N	Y	N	Y	Y	N	Y
NEBRASKA								
1 ***Bereuter***	Y	Y	N	Y	N	N	Y	Y
2 Hoagland	N	N	Y	Y	Y	Y	Y	Y
3 ***Barrett***	Y	Y	N	N	N	Y	Y	N
NEVADA								
1 Bilbray	N	N	Y	Y	Y	Y	N	Y
2 ***Vucanovich***	Y	Y	N	?	N	N	Y	N
NEW HAMPSHIRE								
1 ***Zeliff***	Y	Y	N	N	N	N	Y	N
2 Swett	N	N	Y	Y	Y	Y	Y	Y
NEW JERSEY								
1 Andrews	N	N	Y	Y	Y	N	Y	N
2 Hughes	N	N	Y	Y	Y	Y	N	Y
3 ***Saxton***	Y	Y	N	Y	Y	N	Y	N
4 ***Smith***	Y	Y	Y	Y	N	N	Y	N
5 ***Roukema***	Y	Y	N	Y	N	Y	Y	Y
6 Pallone	N	N	Y	Y	Y	Y	N	Y
7 ***Franks***	Y	Y	N	Y	N	N	Y	Y
8 Klein	N	N	Y	Y	Y	Y	N	Y
9 Torricelli	N	N	Y	Y	Y	Y	N	N
10 Payne	N	N	Y	Y	Y	Y	N	Y
11 ***Gallo***	Y	Y	N	Y	N	N	Y	N
12 ***Zimmer***	Y	N	Y	Y	N	N	Y	Y
13 Menendez	N	N	Y	Y	Y	Y	N	Y
NEW MEXICO								
1 ***Schiff***	Y	Y	N	N	N	N	Y	N
2 ***Skeen***	Y	Y	N	N	N	N	N	N
3 Richardson	N	N	Y	N	Y	Y	N	N
NEW YORK								
1 Hochbrueckner	N	N	Y	Y	Y	Y	N	N
2 ***Lazio***	Y	Y	N	Y	N	Y	N	N
3 ***King***	Y	Y	N	N	N	N	N	N
4 ***Levy***	Y	Y	N	N	N	N	N	N
5 Ackerman	N	N	Y	Y	Y	Y	N	Y
6 Flake	N	N	Y	Y	Y	Y	N	Y
7 Manton	N	N	Y	Y	Y	Y	N	N
8 Nadler	N	N	Y	Y	Y	Y	N	Y
9 Schumer	N	N	Y	Y	Y	Y	N	Y
10 Towns	N	N	N	Y	Y	Y	N	Y
11 Owens	N	N	Y	Y	N	Y	N	Y
12 Velazquez	N	N	Y	Y	Y	Y	N	Y
13 ***Molinari***	Y	Y	N	Y	N	N	Y	N
14 Maloney	N	N	Y	Y	Y	Y	N	Y
15 Rangel	N	N	Y	Y	N	Y	N	Y
16 Serrano	N	N	Y	Y	Y	Y	N	Y
17 Engel	N	N	Y	Y	Y	Y	N	N
18 Lowey	N	N	Y	Y	Y	Y	N	Y
19 ***Fish***	Y	Y	Y	Y	N	N	Y	N
20 ***Gilman***	Y	N	Y	Y	N	Y	N	N
21 McNulty	N	N	Y	Y	Y	Y	N	Y
22 ***Solomon***	Y	Y	N	N	N	N	Y	N
23 ***Boehlert***	N	N	Y	Y	Y	Y	N	N
24 ***McHugh***	Y	Y	N	N	N	N	Y	N
25 ***Walsh***	Y	Y	Y	Y	N	N	Y	Y
26 Hinchey	N	N	Y	Y	N	Y	N	Y
27 ***Paxon***	Y	Y	N	N	N	N	Y	N
28 Slaughter	N	N	Y	Y	Y	Y	N	Y
29 LaFalce	N	N	Y	Y	Y	Y	N	Y
30 ***Quinn***	Y	Y	Y	Y	N	N	Y	N
31 ***Houghton***	Y	Y	N	N	Y	N	Y	N
NORTH CAROLINA								
1 Clayton	N	N	Y	Y	Y	Y	N	Y
2 Valentine	N	N	Y	Y	Y	Y	N	Y

	603	604	605	606	607	608	609	610
3 Lancaster	N	N	N	Y	Y	Y	Y	N
4 Price	N	N	Y	Y	Y	Y	N	Y
5 Neal	N	N	Y	Y	Y	Y	N	Y
6 ***Coble***	Y	Y	N	N	N	N	Y	Y
7 Rose	N	N	Y	Y	Y	Y	N	N
8 Hefner	N	N	Y	Y	N	Y	N	Y
9 ***McMillan***	Y	Y	N	Y	Y	N	Y	N
10 ***Ballenger***	Y	Y	N	N	N	N	Y	N
11 ***Taylor***	Y	Y	N	N	N	N	Y	N
12 Watt	N	N	Y	Y	Y	Y	N	Y
NORTH DAKOTA								
AL Pomeroy	N	N	Y	N	N	Y	Y	Y
OHIO								
1 Mann	N	N	Y	Y	Y	Y	Y	Y
2 ***Portman***	Y	Y	N	N	N	N	Y	Y
3 Hall	?	?	?	?	?	?	?	?
4 ***Oxley***	Y	Y	N	N	Y	N	Y	N
5 ***Gillmor***	Y	Y	N	N	N	N	Y	N
6 Strickland	N	N	Y	N	Y	Y	N	Y
7 ***Hobson***	Y	Y	N	N	Y	N	Y	N
8 ***Boehner***	Y	Y	N	N	N	N	Y	N
9 Kaptur	N	N	N	Y	Y	Y	Y	Y
10 ***Hoke***	Y	Y	N	N	N	N	Y	N
11 Stokes	N	N	Y	Y	Y	Y	N	N
12 ***Kasich***	Y	Y	N	N	Y	N	Y	N
13 Brown	N	N	Y	Y	Y	Y	N	Y
14 Sawyer	N	N	Y	Y	Y	Y	N	Y
15 ***Pryce***	Y	Y	N	N	Y	N	Y	N
16 ***Regula***	Y	Y	N	Y	Y	N	Y	N
17 Traficant	N	N	N	Y	N	N	N	Y
18 Applegate	N	N	N	Y	Y	Y	N	N
19 Fingerhut	N	N	Y	Y	Y	Y	Y	N
OKLAHOMA								
1 ***Inhofe***	Y	Y	N	N	N	N	Y	N
2 Synar	N	Y	N	Y	Y	Y	N	Y
3 Brewster	N	N	N	N	Y	Y	N	Y
4 McCurdy	N	Y	Y	?	Y	Y	Y	N
5 ***Istook***	Y	Y	N	N	N	N	Y	Y
6 English	N	Y	N	Y	N	Y	N	Y
OREGON								
1 Furse	N	N	Y	Y	Y	Y	N	Y
2 ***Smith***	Y	Y	N	N	N	N	Y	?
3 Wyden	N	N	Y	Y	Y	Y	N	Y
4 DeFazio	N	N	Y	Y	Y	Y	N	Y
5 Kopetski	N	N	Y	N	Y	Y	N	N
PENNSYLVANIA								
1 Foglietta	N	N	Y	Y	Y	Y	N	Y
2 Blackwell	N	N	Y	Y	Y	Y	N	N
3 Borski	N	N	Y	Y	Y	Y	N	Y
4 Klink	N	N	Y	N	Y	Y	Y	Y
5 ***Clinger***	?	?	?	?	?	?	?	?
6 Holden	N	N	Y	N	Y	Y	Y	Y
7 ***Weldon***	Y	Y	Y	Y	N	N	Y	N
8 ***Greenwood***	Y	Y	N	Y	N	N	Y	N
9 ***Shuster***	Y	Y	N	N	N	N	Y	N
10 ***McDade***	Y	Y	N	Y	N	N	N	N
11 Kanjorski	N	N	Y	N	Y	Y	N	Y
12 Murtha	N	N	Y	Y	Y	Y	N	N
13 Margolies-Mezv.	Y	N	Y	Y	Y	Y	Y	Y
14 Coyne	N	N	Y	Y	Y	Y	N	Y
15 McHale	N	N	Y	Y	Y	Y	Y	N
16 ***Walker***	Y	Y	N	N	N	N	Y	N
17 ***Gekas***	Y	Y	N	N	N	N	Y	Y
18 ***Santorum***	Y	Y	N	N	N	N	Y	N
19 ***Goodling***	Y	Y	—	Y	N	N	Y	Y
20 Murphy	N	N	Y	N	Y	Y	Y	Y
21 ***Ridge***	Y	Y	Y	Y	N	?	Y	N
RHODE ISLAND								
1 ***Machtley***	Y	N	Y	Y	N	N	N	Y
2 Reed	N	N	Y	Y	Y	Y	N	Y
SOUTH CAROLINA								
1 ***Ravenel***	Y	Y	N	N	N	N	Y	N
2 ***Spence***	Y	Y	N	N	N	N	Y	N
3 Derrick	N	N	Y	Y	Y	Y	N	N
4 ***Inglis***	Y	Y	N	N	Y	N	Y	N
5 Spratt	N	N	Y	Y	N	Y	N	N
6 Clyburn	N	N	Y	Y	Y	Y	N	Y
SOUTH DAKOTA								
AL Johnson	N	N	Y	Y	Y	Y	N	Y
TENNESSEE								
1 ***Quillen***	Y	Y	N	N	N	N	N	N
2 ***Duncan***	Y	Y	Y	N	N	Y	Y	Y
3 Lloyd	N	Y	N	Y	Y	Y	N	N
4 Cooper	Y	N	Y	Y	Y	Y	Y	N
5 Clement	N	N	Y	Y	Y	Y	N	Y

	603	604	605	606	607	608	609	610
6 Gordon	N	N	Y	Y	Y	Y	Y	Y
7 ***Sundquist***	Y	Y	N	N	N	N	Y	N
8 Tanner	N	Y	N	N	Y	Y	Y	N
9 Ford	N	N	Y	Y	Y	Y	N	?
TEXAS								
1 Chapman	N	N	Y	?	Y	Y	N	N
2 Wilson	N	N	N	N	Y	Y	N	N
3 ***Johnson, Sam***	Y	Y	N	N	N	N	Y	N
4 Hall	Y	Y	Y	N	N	Y	Y	N
5 Bryant	N	N	Y	Y	N	Y	N	Y
6 ***Barton***	Y	Y	N	N	Y	N	Y	N
7 ***Archer***	Y	Y	N	N	N	N	Y	N
8 ***Fields***	Y	Y	N	N	N	N	Y	N
9 Brooks	N	N	Y	Y	Y	Y	N	N
10 Pickle	N	N	Y	Y	Y	Y	N	N
11 Edwards	N	N	Y	N	Y	Y	Y	N
12 Geren	N	Y	N	N	Y	Y	Y	N
13 Sarpalius	N	Y	N	N	N	Y	N	N
14 Laughlin	N	N	Y	N	Y	Y	Y	N
15 de la Garza	N	N	Y	N	Y	Y	N	N
16 Coleman	N	N	Y	N	N	Y	N	N
17 Stenholm	Y	Y	N	N	Y	Y	Y	Y
18 Washington	N	N	Y	Y	N	Y	N	Y
19 ***Combest***	Y	Y	N	N	N	N	N	N
20 Gonzalez	N	N	Y	Y	N	Y	N	N
21 ***Smith***	Y	Y	N	N	N	N	Y	N
22 ***DeLay***	Y	Y	N	N	Y	N	Y	N
23 ***Bonilla***	N	Y	N	N	N	N	Y	N
24 Frost	N	Y	N	Y	Y	Y	N	N
25 Andrews	N	Y	Y	Y	Y	Y	Y	N
26 ***Armey***	Y	Y	N	N	N	N	Y	N
27 Ortiz	N	N	Y	N	Y	Y	N	N
28 Tejeda	N	N	Y	N	Y	Y	N	N
29 Green	N	N	Y	N	Y	Y	N	N
30 Johnson, E.B.	N	N	Y	Y	Y	Y	N	N
UTAH								
1 ***Hansen***	Y	Y	N	N	N	N	Y	N
2 Shepherd	N	N	Y	Y	Y	Y	N	Y
3 Orton	N	Y	Y	N	Y	Y	Y	Y
VERMONT								
AL *Sanders*	N	N	Y	N	Y	Y	N	Y
VIRGINIA								
1 ***Bateman***	N	Y	N	Y	N	N	Y	N
2 Pickett	N	Y	N	N	Y	Y	N	N
3 Scott	N	N	Y	Y	Y	Y	N	N
4 Sisisky	N	Y	N	N	N	Y	N	N
5 Payne	N	N	Y	N	Y	Y	Y	Y
6 ***Goodlatte***	Y	Y	N	N	N	Y	Y	Y
7 ***Bliley***	Y	Y	N	N	?	N	Y	N
8 Moran	N	N	Y	Y	Y	Y	N	N
9 Boucher	N	N	Y	N	Y	Y	N	N
10 ***Wolf***	Y	Y	N	Y	N	N	Y	N
11 Byrne	N	N	Y	Y	Y	Y	N	Y
WASHINGTON								
1 Cantwell	N	N	Y	Y	Y	Y	Y	Y
2 Swift	N	N	Y	Y	Y	Y	N	N
3 Unsoeld	N	N	Y	Y	Y	Y	N	Y
4 Inslee	N	N	Y	N	Y	Y	Y	Y
5 Foley							N	
6 Dicks	N	N	Y	Y	Y	Y	N	N
7 McDermott	N	N	Y	Y	Y	Y	N	Y
8 ***Dunn***	Y	Y	N	Y	N	N	Y	N
9 Kreidler	N	N	Y	Y	Y	Y	N	Y
WEST VIRGINIA								
1 Mollohan	N	N	Y	N	N	Y	N	N
2 Wise	N	N	Y	N	Y	Y	N	N
3 Rahall	N	N	Y	N	N	Y	N	N
WISCONSIN								
1 Barca	N	N	Y	Y	N	Y	Y	Y
2 ***Klug***	N	N	Y	Y	Y	N	Y	Y
3 ***Gunderson***	Y	Y	N	N	N	N	Y	Y
4 Kleczka	N	N	Y	Y	Y	Y	N	Y
5 Barrett	N	N	Y	Y	Y	Y	N	Y
6 ***Petri***	Y	N	Y	N	N	N	Y	Y
7 Obey	N	N	Y	Y	Y	Y	N	Y
8 ***Roth***	Y	Y	Y	N	N	N	Y	Y
9 ***Sensenbrenner***	Y	Y	N	Y	N	N	Y	Y
WYOMING								
AL ***Thomas***	Y	Y	N	N	N	N	Y	Y
DELEGATES								
de Lugo, V.I.	N	D	D	D	D	Y	?	Y
Faleomavaega, Am.S.	N	D	D	D	D	Y	?	Y
Norton, D.C.	N	D	D	D	D	Y	?	Y
Romero-B., P.R.	N	D	D	D	D	Y	?	?
Underwood, Guam	N	D	D	D	D	N	?	N

Southern states - Ala., Ark., Fla., Ga., Ky., La., Miss., N.C., Okla., S.C., Tenn., Texas, Va.
Omitted votes are quorum calls, which CQ does not include in its vote charts.

1993 CQ ALMANAC — 149-H

611. HR 3400. Reinventing Government and Spending Cuts/Administration-Backed Plan. Separate vote at the request of Walker, R-Pa., on the substitute amendment offered by Sabo, D-Minn., and adopted in the Committee of the Whole to cut federal spending by $37.1 billion over five years, $32.5 billion through 252,000 job reductions in the federal work force, $2 billion in fiscal 1994 rescissions and $2.6 billion through proposals from the vice president's National Performance Review to make government more efficient and effective. Adopted 277-153: R 30-143; D 246-10 (ND 161-10, SD 85-0); I 1-0, Nov. 22, 1993. (On a separate vote, which may be demanded on an amendment adopted in the Committee of the Whole, the four delegates and the resident commissioner of Puerto Rico cannot vote. See vote 608.) A "yea" was a vote in support of the president's position.

612. HR 3400. Reinventing Government and Spending Cuts/Passage. Passage of the bill to cut federal spending by $37.1 billion over five years, $32.5 billion through 252,000 job reductions in the federal work force, $2 billion in fiscal 1994 rescissions and $2.6 billion through proposals from the vice president's National Performance Review to make government more efficient and effective. Passed 429-1: R 173-0; D 255-1 (ND 170-1, SD 85-0); I 1-0, Nov. 22, 1993. A "yea" was a vote in support of the president's position.

613. S 714. Resolution Trust Corporation Financing/Conference Report. Adoption of the conference report to provide $18.3 billion to finish the savings and loan cleanup sometime between Jan. 1 and June 30, 1995, terminate the Resolution Trust Corporation (RTC) on Dec. 31, 1995, and authorize $8.5 billion for the Saving Association Insurance Fund to be spent only if the savings and loan industry cannot pay for future failures itself through higher insurance premiums. The bill also would establish minorities preference for RTC contracts, incorporates management reforms, limits bonuses for RTC employees and extends the statute of limitations for five years in cases of fraud or intentional wrongdoing. Adopted (thus cleared for the president) 235-191: R 27-144; D 208-46 (ND 143-27, SD 65-19); I 0-1, Nov. 23, 1993 (in the session that began and the Congressional Record dated Nov. 22). A "yea" was a vote in support of the president's position.

614. HR 1025. Brady Bill/Conference Report. Adoption of the conference report to require a five-business-day waiting period before an individual could purchase a handgun to allow local officials to conduct a background check. Adopted (thus sent to the Senate) 238-187: R 56-116; D 182-70 (ND 137-33, SD 45-37); I 0-1, Nov. 23, 1993 (in the session that began and the Congressional Record dated Nov. 22). A "yea" was a vote in support of the president's position.

615. Unemployment Benefit Extension/Conference Report. Adoption of the conference report to provide about $1 billion for extended unemployment benefits for workers who have exhausted their 26 weeks of state unemployment benefits for an additional seven or 13 weeks of compensation, depending on the unemployment rate in their state. Adopted (thus cleared for the president) 320-105: R 81-91; D 238-14 (ND 167-2, SD 71-12); I 1-0, Nov. 23, 1993 (in the session that began and the Congressional Record dated Nov. 22).

KEY

Y	Voted for (yea).
#	Paired for.
+	Announced for.
N	Voted against (nay).
X	Paired against.
—	Announced against.
P	Voted "present."
C	Voted "present" to avoid possible conflict of interest.
?	Did not vote or otherwise make a position known.
D	Delegates ineligible to vote.

Democrats **Republicans**
Independent

	611	612	613	614	615
ALABAMA					
1 Callahan	N	Y	N	N	N
2 Everett	N	Y	N	N	N
3 Browder	Y	Y	N	N	Y
4 Bevill	Y	Y	N	N	Y
5 Cramer	Y	Y	N	N	N
6 Bachus	N	Y	N	N	N
7 Hilliard	Y	Y	Y	N	Y
ALASKA					
AL Young	N	Y	Y	N	N
ARIZONA					
1 Coppersmith	Y	Y	Y	Y	Y
2 Pastor	Y	Y	Y	Y	Y
3 Stump	N	Y	N	N	N
4 Kyl	N	Y	N	N	N
5 Kolbe	N	Y	Y	N	N
6 English	Y	Y	Y	Y	Y
ARKANSAS					
1 Lambert	Y	Y	Y	N	Y
2 Thornton	Y	Y	N	N	Y
3 Hutchinson	N	Y	N	N	N
4 Dickey	N	Y	N	N	N
CALIFORNIA					
1 Hamburg	Y	Y	Y	Y	Y
2 Herger	N	Y	N	N	Y
3 Fazio	Y	Y	Y	Y	Y
4 Doolittle	N	Y	N	N	Y
5 Matsui	Y	Y	Y	Y	Y
6 Woolsey	Y	Y	Y	Y	Y
7 Miller	Y	Y	N	Y	Y
8 Pelosi	Y	Y	Y	Y	Y
9 Dellums	Y	Y	Y	Y	Y
10 Baker	N	Y	N	Y	Y
11 Pombo	N	Y	N	N	Y
12 Lantos	Y	Y	Y	Y	Y
13 Stark	Y	Y	Y	Y	Y
14 Eshoo	Y	Y	Y	Y	Y
15 Mineta	Y	Y	Y	Y	Y
16 Edwards	Y	Y	Y	Y	Y
17 Farr	Y	Y	Y	Y	Y
18 Condit	N	Y	N	N	Y
19 Lehman	Y	Y	Y	Y	Y
20 Dooley	Y	Y	Y	Y	Y
21 Thomas	N	Y	N	Y	Y
22 Huffington	Y	Y	N	Y	Y
23 Gallegly	N	Y	N	Y	Y
24 Beilenson	Y	Y	Y	Y	Y
25 McKeon	N	Y	N	N	Y
26 Berman	Y	Y	Y	Y	Y
27 Moorhead	N	Y	N	N	N
28 Dreier	N	Y	Y	N	N
29 Waxman	Y	Y	Y	Y	Y
30 Becerra	Y	Y	Y	Y	Y
31 Martinez	Y	Y	Y	N	Y
32 Dixon	Y	Y	Y	Y	Y
33 Roybal-Allard	Y	Y	Y	Y	Y
34 Torres	Y	Y	Y	Y	?
35 Waters	N	Y	Y	Y	Y
36 Harman	Y	Y	Y	Y	Y
37 Tucker	Y	Y	Y	Y	Y
38 Horn	N	Y	N	Y	Y
39 Royce	N	Y	N	N	N
40 Lewis	N	Y	N	Y	N
41 Kim	N	Y	N	N	Y
42 Brown	Y	Y	Y	Y	Y
43 Calvert	N	Y	N	N	Y
44 McCandless	N	Y	N	N	N
45 Rohrabacher	N	Y	N	N	N
46 Dornan	N	Y	N	N	N
47 Cox	N	Y	N	N	N
48 Packard	N	Y	N	N	N
49 Schenk	Y	Y	Y	Y	Y
50 Filner	Y	Y	Y	Y	Y
51 Cunningham	N	Y	N	N	N
52 Hunter	N	Y	N	N	N
COLORADO					
1 Schroeder	Y	Y	N	Y	Y
2 Skaggs	Y	Y	Y	Y	Y
3 McInnis	N	Y	N	N	N
4 Allard	N	Y	N	N	N
5 Hefley	N	Y	N	N	N
6 Schaefer	N	Y	N	N	N
CONNECTICUT					
1 Kennelly	Y	Y	Y	Y	Y
2 Gejdenson	Y	Y	Y	Y	Y
3 DeLauro	Y	Y	N	Y	Y
4 Shays	Y	Y	Y	Y	Y
5 Franks	N	Y	Y	N	Y
6 Johnson	Y	Y	Y	Y	Y
DELAWARE					
AL Castle	N	Y	N	Y	Y
FLORIDA					
1 Hutto	Y	Y	N	Y	N
2 Peterson	Y	Y	Y	N	Y
3 Brown	Y	Y	Y	Y	Y
4 Fowler	N	Y	Y	N	Y
5 Thurman	Y	Y	Y	N	Y
6 Stearns	N	Y	N	Y	N
7 Mica	N	Y	N	N	N
8 McCollum	N	Y	N	N	N
9 Bilirakis	Y	Y	N	Y	N
10 Young	N	Y	N	Y	N
11 Gibbons	Y	Y	Y	Y	Y
12 Canady	N	Y	N	N	Y
13 Miller	N	Y	N	N	N
14 Goss	N	Y	N	Y	N
15 Bacchus	Y	Y	Y	Y	Y
16 Lewis	N	Y	N	N	N
17 Meek	Y	Y	Y	Y	Y
18 Ros-Lehtinen	Y	Y	N	Y	Y
19 Johnston	Y	Y	Y	Y	Y
20 Deutsch	Y	Y	Y	Y	Y
21 Diaz-Balart	Y	Y	N	Y	Y
22 Shaw	N	Y	N	Y	Y
23 Hastings	Y	Y	Y	Y	Y
GEORGIA					
1 Kingston	Y	Y	N	N	N
2 Bishop	Y	Y	Y	N	Y
3 Collins	Y	Y	N	N	N
4 Linder	N	Y	N	N	N
5 Lewis	Y	Y	Y	Y	Y
6 Gingrich	N	Y	N	N	N
7 Darden	Y	Y	Y	Y	Y
8 Rowland	Y	Y	Y	Y	Y
9 Deal	Y	Y	N	Y	Y
10 Johnson	Y	Y	Y	N	Y
11 McKinney	Y	Y	Y	Y	Y
HAWAII					
1 Abercrombie	N	Y	Y	Y	Y
2 Mink	N	Y	Y	Y	Y
IDAHO					
1 LaRocco	Y	Y	Y	N	Y
2 Crapo	N	Y	N	N	N
ILLINOIS					
1 Rush	Y	Y	Y	Y	Y
2 Reynolds	Y	Y	Y	Y	Y
3 Lipinski	Y	Y	Y	Y	Y
4 Gutierrez	Y	Y	Y	Y	Y
5 Rostenkowski	Y	Y	Y	Y	Y
6 Hyde	N	Y	C	Y	Y
7 Collins	Y	Y	Y	Y	Y
8 Crane	N	Y	N	N	N
9 Yates	Y	Y	Y	?	#
10 Porter	Y	Y	Y	Y	Y
11 Sangmeister	Y	Y	Y	Y	Y
12 Costello	Y	Y	N	N	Y
13 Fawell	N	Y	Y	Y	Y
14 Hastert	N	Y	N	N	Y
15 Ewing	N	Y	N	N	N
16 Manzullo	N	Y	N	N	N
17 Evans	Y	Y	N	Y	Y

ND Northern Democrats   SD Southern Democrats

Member	611	612	613	614	615
18 *Michel*	N	Y	N	Y	Y
19 Poshard	Y	Y	N	N	Y
20 Durbin	Y	Y	Y	Y	Y
INDIANA					
1 Visclosky	Y	Y	N	Y	Y
2 Sharp	Y	Y	?	Y	Y
3 Roemer	Y	Y	N	Y	Y
4 Long	Y	Y	N	Y	Y
5 *Buyer*	N	Y	N	N	N
6 *Burton*	N	Y	N	N	N
7 *Myers*	N	Y	?	N	Y
8 McCloskey	Y	Y	Y	Y	Y
9 Hamilton	Y	Y	Y	Y	Y
10 Jacobs	N	Y	Y	Y	Y
IOWA					
1 *Leach*	N	Y	Y	Y	Y
2 *Nussle*	N	Y	N	N	N
3 *Lightfoot*	N	Y	Y	N	N
4 Smith	Y	Y	Y	N	Y
5 *Grandy*	N	Y	Y	N	Y
KANSAS					
1 *Roberts*	N	Y	N	N	N
2 Slattery	Y	Y	Y	Y	Y
3 *Meyers*	Y	Y	N	Y	Y
4 Glickman	Y	Y	Y	Y	Y
KENTUCKY					
1 Barlow	Y	Y	Y	N	Y
2 Natcher	Y	Y	Y	N	Y
3 Mazzoli	Y	Y	Y	Y	Y
4 *Bunning*	N	Y	N	N	Y
5 *Rogers*	Y	Y	N	N	Y
6 Baesler	Y	Y	N	Y	Y
LOUISIANA					
1 *Livingston*	N	Y	N	N	N
2 Jefferson	Y	Y	Y	Y	Y
3 Tauzin	Y	Y	N	N	Y
4 Fields	Y	Y	Y	Y	Y
5 *McCrery*	N	Y	N	N	N
6 *Baker*	N	Y	Y	?	?
7 Hayes	Y	Y	?	?	?
MAINE					
1 Andrews	Y	Y	Y	Y	+
2 *Snowe*	Y	Y	N	N	Y
MARYLAND					
1 *Gilchrest*	N	Y	N	Y	Y
2 *Bentley*	N	Y	N	Y	Y
3 Cardin	Y	Y	Y	Y	Y
4 Wynn	Y	Y	Y	Y	Y
5 Hoyer	Y	Y	Y	Y	Y
6 *Bartlett*	N	Y	N	N	N
7 Mfume	Y	Y	Y	Y	Y
8 Morella	Y	Y	Y	Y	Y
MASSACHUSETTS					
1 Olver	Y	Y	Y	Y	Y
2 Neal	Y	Y	Y	Y	Y
3 *Blute*	N	Y	N	Y	Y
4 Frank	Y	Y	Y	Y	Y
5 Meehan	Y	Y	Y	Y	Y
6 *Torkildsen*	N	Y	N	Y	Y
7 Markey	Y	Y	Y	Y	Y
8 Kennedy	Y	Y	Y	Y	Y
9 Moakley	Y	Y	Y	Y	Y
10 Studds	Y	Y	Y	Y	Y
MICHIGAN					
1 Stupak	Y	Y	Y	N	Y
2 *Hoekstra*	N	Y	N	Y	Y
3 Vacancy					
4 *Camp*	N	Y	N	N	Y
5 Barcia	Y	Y	Y	N	Y
6 *Upton*	N	Y	N	Y	Y
7 *Smith*	Y	Y	N	Y	N
8 Carr	Y	Y	Y	N	Y
9 Kildee	Y	Y	Y	Y	Y
10 Bonior	Y	Y	Y	Y	Y
11 *Knollenberg*	N	Y	N	N	N
12 Levin	Y	Y	Y	Y	Y
13 Ford	Y	Y	Y	Y	Y
14 Conyers	Y	Y	Y	Y	Y
15 Collins	Y	Y	Y	Y	Y
16 Dingell	Y	Y	Y	N	Y
MINNESOTA					
1 Penny	N	Y	N	N	N
2 Minge	Y	Y	Y	Y	Y
3 *Ramstad*	N	Y	N	N	Y
4 Vento	Y	Y	Y	Y	Y
5 Sabo	Y	Y	Y	Y	Y
6 *Grams*	N	Y	N	N	N
7 Peterson	N	Y	N	N	Y
8 Oberstar	Y	Y	Y	N	Y
MISSISSIPPI					
1 Whitten	Y	Y	Y	?	Y
2 Thompson	Y	Y	N	Y	Y
3 Montgomery	Y	Y	Y	N	Y
4 Parker	Y	Y	Y	Y	Y
5 Taylor	Y	Y	N	N	N
MISSOURI					
1 Clay	Y	Y	Y	Y	Y
2 *Talent*	N	Y	N	N	N
3 Gephardt	Y	Y	Y	Y	Y
4 Skelton	Y	Y	Y	N	Y
5 Wheat	Y	Y	Y	Y	Y
6 Danner	Y	Y	Y	N	Y
7 *Hancock*	N	Y	N	N	N
8 *Emerson*	N	Y	N	N	N
9 Volkmer	Y	Y	Y	N	Y
MONTANA					
AL Williams	Y	?	Y	N	Y
NEBRASKA					
1 *Bereuter*	Y	Y	Y	N	N
2 Hoagland	Y	Y	Y	Y	N
3 *Barrett*	Y	Y	Y	N	N
NEVADA					
1 Bilbray	Y	Y	Y	N	Y
2 *Vucanovich*	N	Y	N	N	Y
NEW HAMPSHIRE					
1 *Zeliff*	N	Y	N	N	N
2 Swett	Y	Y	Y	Y	Y
NEW JERSEY					
1 Andrews	N	Y	N	Y	Y
2 Hughes	Y	Y	N	Y	Y
3 *Saxton*	N	Y	N	Y	Y
4 *Smith*	N	Y	N	Y	Y
5 *Roukema*	Y	Y	N	Y	Y
6 Pallone	Y	Y	Y	Y	Y
7 *Franks*	N	Y	N	Y	Y
8 Klein	Y	Y	Y	Y	Y
9 Torricelli	Y	Y	Y	Y	Y
10 Payne	Y	Y	Y	Y	Y
11 *Gallo*	N	Y	N	Y	Y
12 *Zimmer*	N	Y	N	Y	Y
13 Menendez	Y	Y	N	Y	Y
NEW MEXICO					
1 *Schiff*	N	Y	N	N	Y
2 *Skeen*	N	Y	N	N	N
3 Richardson	Y	Y	Y	N	Y
NEW YORK					
1 Hochbrueckner	Y	Y	Y	Y	Y
2 *Lazio*	Y	Y	Y	Y	Y
3 *King*	N	Y	Y	N	Y
4 *Levy*	Y	Y	Y	N	Y
5 Ackerman	Y	Y	Y	Y	Y
6 Flake	Y	Y	Y	Y	Y
7 Manton	Y	Y	Y	Y	Y
8 Nadler	Y	Y	Y	Y	Y
9 Schumer	Y	Y	Y	Y	Y
10 Towns	Y	Y	Y	Y	Y
11 Owens	N	Y	N	Y	Y
12 Velazquez	Y	Y	Y	Y	Y
13 *Molinari*	N	Y	N	Y	Y
14 Maloney	Y	Y	Y	Y	Y
15 Rangel	Y	Y	Y	Y	Y
16 Serrano	Y	Y	Y	Y	Y
17 Engel	Y	Y	Y	Y	Y
18 Lowey	Y	Y	Y	Y	Y
19 *Fish*	N	Y	Y	N	Y
20 Gilman	Y	Y	Y	N	Y
21 McNulty	Y	Y	Y	Y	Y
22 *Solomon*	N	Y	N	N	Y
23 *Boehlert*	Y	Y	Y	N	Y
24 *McHugh*	N	Y	N	N	Y
25 *Walsh*	N	Y	N	Y	Y
26 Hinchey	Y	Y	Y	Y	Y
27 *Paxon*	N	Y	N	N	Y
28 Slaughter	Y	Y	Y	Y	Y
29 LaFalce	Y	Y	Y	N	Y
30 *Quinn*	N	Y	N	Y	Y
31 *Houghton*	N	Y	Y	N	Y
NORTH CAROLINA					
1 Clayton	Y	Y	Y	Y	Y
2 Valentine	Y	Y	Y	Y	N
3 Lancaster	Y	Y	Y	Y	Y
4 Price	Y	Y	Y	Y	Y
5 Neal	Y	Y	Y	Y	Y
6 *Coble*	Y	Y	N	N	Y
7 Rose	Y	Y	Y	Y	Y
8 Hefner	Y	Y	N	Y	Y
9 *McMillan*	N	Y	Y	Y	N
10 *Ballenger*	N	Y	N	N	N
11 *Taylor*	N	Y	N	N	N
12 Watt	Y	Y	Y	Y	Y
NORTH DAKOTA					
AL Pomeroy	Y	Y	N	N	Y
OHIO					
1 Mann	Y	Y	Y	Y	Y
2 *Portman*	N	Y	N	N	N
3 Hall	?	?	?	?	?
4 *Oxley*	N	Y	N	N	N
5 *Gillmor*	N	Y	N	N	N
6 Strickland	Y	Y	Y	N	Y
7 *Hobson*	N	Y	N	N	N
8 *Boehner*	N	Y	N	N	N
9 Kaptur	Y	Y	N	Y	Y
10 *Hoke*	N	Y	N	N	N
11 Stokes	Y	Y	Y	Y	Y
12 *Kasich*	N	Y	N	N	N
13 Brown	Y	Y	Y	Y	Y
14 Sawyer	Y	Y	Y	Y	Y
15 *Pryce*	N	Y	N	N	N
16 *Regula*	N	Y	N	Y	Y
17 Traficant	N	N	N	Y	Y
18 Applegate	Y	Y	Y	Y	Y
19 Fingerhut	Y	Y	Y	Y	Y
OKLAHOMA					
1 *Inhofe*	N	Y	N	N	N
2 Synar	Y	Y	Y	Y	Y
3 Brewster	Y	Y	N	N	N
4 McCurdy	Y	Y	Y	Y	Y
5 *Istook*	N	Y	N	N	N
6 English	Y	Y	N	N	Y
OREGON					
1 Furse	Y	Y	Y	Y	Y
2 *Smith*	?	?	?	?	X
3 Wyden	Y	Y	Y	Y	Y
4 DeFazio	Y	Y	N	Y	Y
5 Kopetski	Y	Y	Y	N	Y
PENNSYLVANIA					
1 Foglietta	Y	Y	Y	Y	Y
2 Blackwell	Y	Y	Y	Y	Y
3 Borski	Y	Y	Y	Y	Y
4 Klink	Y	Y	Y	N	Y
5 *Clinger*	?	?	?	?	?
6 Holden	Y	Y	Y	N	Y
7 *Weldon*	Y	Y	N	Y	Y
8 *Greenwood*	N	Y	N	Y	Y
9 *Shuster*	N	Y	N	N	Y
10 *McDade*	Y	Y	N	Y	Y
11 Kanjorski	Y	Y	N	Y	Y
12 Murtha	Y	Y	Y	N	Y
13 Margolies-Mezv.	Y	Y	Y	Y	Y
14 Coyne	Y	Y	Y	Y	Y
15 McHale	Y	Y	Y	N	Y
16 *Walker*	N	Y	N	N	N
17 *Gekas*	N	Y	N	N	N
18 *Santorum*	N	Y	N	N	N
19 *Goodling*	N	Y	N	Y	Y
20 Murphy	Y	Y	Y	N	Y
21 *Ridge*	Y	Y	N	N	Y
RHODE ISLAND					
1 *Machtley*	Y	Y	Y	Y	Y
2 Reed	Y	Y	Y	Y	Y
SOUTH CAROLINA					
1 *Ravenel*	N	Y	N	N	N
2 *Spence*	N	Y	N	N	N
3 Derrick	Y	Y	Y	Y	Y
4 *Inglis*	N	Y	N	N	N
5 Spratt	Y	Y	Y	Y	Y
6 Clyburn	Y	Y	Y	Y	Y
SOUTH DAKOTA					
AL Johnson	Y	Y	Y	Y	Y
TENNESSEE					
1 *Quillen*	N	Y	N	N	N
2 *Duncan*	Y	Y	N	N	N
3 Lloyd	Y	Y	Y	N	Y
4 Cooper	Y	Y	N	Y	Y
5 Clement	Y	Y	N	Y	Y
6 Gordon	Y	Y	Y	Y	Y
7 *Sundquist*	Y	Y	N	N	N
8 Tanner	Y	Y	N	N	Y
9 Ford	Y	Y	Y	?	Y
TEXAS					
1 Chapman	Y	Y	N	Y	Y
2 Wilson	Y	Y	Y	N	?
3 *Johnson, Sam*	N	Y	N	N	N
4 Hall	Y	Y	N	Y	Y
5 Bryant	Y	Y	Y	Y	Y
6 *Barton*	N	Y	N	N	N
7 *Archer*	N	Y	N	N	N
8 *Fields*	N	Y	N	N	N
9 Brooks	Y	Y	Y	N	Y
10 Pickle	Y	Y	Y	Y	Y
11 Edwards	Y	Y	Y	Y	Y
12 Geren	Y	Y	Y	N	Y
13 Sarpalius	Y	Y	Y	Y	Y
14 Laughlin	Y	Y	Y	N	Y
15 de la Garza	Y	Y	Y	N	Y
16 Coleman	Y	Y	Y	Y	Y
17 Stenholm	Y	Y	Y	N	Y
18 Washington	Y	Y	Y	N	Y
19 *Combest*	N	Y	N	N	N
20 Gonzalez	Y	Y	Y	Y	Y
21 *Smith*	N	Y	N	N	N
22 *DeLay*	N	Y	N	N	N
23 *Bonilla*	N	Y	N	N	N
24 Frost	Y	Y	Y	Y	Y
25 Andrews	Y	Y	Y	Y	Y
26 *Armey*	N	Y	N	N	N
27 Ortiz	Y	Y	Y	N	Y
28 Tejeda	Y	Y	Y	N	Y
29 Green	Y	Y	Y	N	Y
30 Johnson, E.B.	Y	Y	Y	Y	Y
UTAH					
1 *Hansen*	N	Y	N	N	N
2 Shepherd	Y	Y	Y	Y	Y
3 Orton	Y	Y	Y	N	Y
VERMONT					
AL *Sanders*	Y	Y	N	N	Y
VIRGINIA					
1 *Bateman*	N	Y	Y	Y	Y
2 Pickett	Y	Y	Y	N	Y
3 Scott	Y	Y	Y	Y	Y
4 Sisisky	Y	Y	Y	N	Y
5 Payne	Y	Y	Y	N	N
6 *Goodlatte*	Y	Y	N	N	N
7 *Bliley*	N	Y	N	N	N
8 Moran	Y	Y	Y	N	Y
9 Boucher	Y	Y	Y	N	Y
10 *Wolf*	N	Y	N	N	Y
11 Byrne	Y	Y	N	Y	Y
WASHINGTON					
1 Cantwell	Y	Y	Y	Y	Y
2 Swift	Y	Y	Y	Y	Y
3 Unsoeld	Y	Y	Y	N	Y
4 Inslee	Y	Y	Y	N	Y
5 Foley	Y			Y	
6 Dicks	Y	Y	Y	Y	Y
7 McDermott	Y	Y	Y	Y	Y
8 *Dunn*	N	Y	N	N	Y
9 Kreidler	Y	Y	Y	Y	Y
WEST VIRGINIA					
1 Mollohan	Y	Y	Y	N	Y
2 Wise	Y	Y	Y	N	Y
3 Rahall	Y	Y	Y	N	Y
WISCONSIN					
1 Barca	Y	Y	Y	N	Y
2 *Klug*	N	Y	N	Y	Y
3 *Gunderson*	N	Y	N	Y	Y
4 Kleczka	Y	Y	Y	Y	Y
5 Barrett	Y	Y	Y	Y	Y
6 *Petri*	N	Y	N	N	N
7 Obey	Y	Y	Y	N	Y
8 *Roth*	Y	Y	N	N	N
9 *Sensenbrenner*	N	Y	N	Y	N
WYOMING					
AL *Thomas*	N	Y	N	N	N
DELEGATES					
de Lugo, V.I.	D	D	D	D	D
Faleomavaega, Am.S.	D	D	D	D	D
Norton, D.C.	D	D	D	D	D
Romero-B., P.R.	D	D	D	D	D
Underwood, Guam	D	D	D	D	D

Southern states - Ala., Ark., Fla., Ga., Ky., La., Miss., N.C., Okla., S.C., Tenn., Texas, Va.
Omitted votes are quorum calls, which CQ does not include in its vote charts.

SENATE
ROLL CALL
VOTES

KEY

Y Voted for (yea).
Paired for.
+ Announced for.
N Voted against (nay).
X Paired against.
− Announced against.
P Voted "present."
C Voted "present" to avoid possible conflict of interest.
? Did not vote or otherwise make a position known.

Democrats *Republicans*

	1	2	3	4	5	6	7	8
ALABAMA								
Heflin	Y	Y	Y	Y	Y	Y	N	N
Shelby	N	N	N	N	Y	N	N	N
ALASKA								
Murkowski	N	N	N	N	N	N	N	N
Stevens	N	N	N	N	N	N	N	N
ARIZONA								
DeConcini	Y	Y	Y	Y	Y	Y	Y	N
McCain	N	N	N	N	N	N	N	N
ARKANSAS								
Bumpers	Y	Y	N	Y	Y	Y	Y	N
Pryor	Y	Y	Y	Y	Y	Y	Y	N
CALIFORNIA								
Boxer	Y	Y	Y	Y	Y	Y	Y	N
Feinstein	Y	Y	Y	Y	Y	Y	Y	N
COLORADO								
Campbell	Y	Y	Y	N	Y	Y	Y	N
Brown	N	N	N	N	N	N	N	N
CONNECTICUT								
Dodd	Y	Y	Y	Y	Y	Y	Y	N
Lieberman	Y	Y	Y	Y	Y	Y	Y	N
DELAWARE								
Biden	Y	Y	Y	Y	Y	Y	Y	N
Roth	Y	Y	N	Y	N	N	Y	N
FLORIDA								
Graham	Y	Y	Y	Y	Y	Y	Y	N
Mack	N	N	N	N	N	N	N	N
GEORGIA								
Nunn	Y	N	Y	Y	Y	Y	Y	N
Coverdell	N	N	N	N	N	N	N	N
HAWAII								
Akaka	Y	Y	Y	Y	Y	Y	Y	N
Inouye	Y	Y	Y	Y	Y	Y	Y	N
IDAHO								
Craig	N	N	N	N	N	N	N	N
Kempthorne	N	N	N	N	N	N	N	N
ILLINOIS								
Moseley-Braun	Y	Y	Y	Y	Y	Y	Y	N
Simon	Y	Y	Y	Y	Y	Y	Y	N
INDIANA								
Coats	Y	N	N	Y	N	N	?	N
Lugar	N	N	N	N	N	N	N	N
IOWA								
Harkin	Y	Y	Y	Y	Y	Y	Y	N
Grassley	N	N	N	N	N	N	N	N
KANSAS								
Dole	N	N	N	N	N	N	N	N
Kassebaum	N	N	N	N	N	N	N	N
KENTUCKY								
Ford	Y	Y	Y	Y	Y	Y	Y	N
McConnell	N	N	N	N	N	N	N	N
LOUISIANA								
Breaux	Y	Y	Y	Y	Y	Y	Y	N
Johnston	Y	Y	Y	Y	Y	Y	Y	N
MAINE								
Mitchell	Y	Y	Y	Y	Y	Y	Y	N
Cohen	Y	N	N	Y	Y	N	Y	N
MARYLAND								
Mikulski	Y	Y	Y	Y	Y	Y	Y	N
Sarbanes	Y	Y	Y	Y	Y	Y	Y	N
MASSACHUSETTS								
Kennedy	Y	Y	Y	Y	Y	Y	Y	N
Kerry	Y	Y	Y	Y	Y	Y	Y	N
MICHIGAN								
Levin	Y	Y	Y	Y	Y	Y	Y	N
Riegle	Y	Y	Y	Y	Y	Y	Y	N
MINNESOTA								
Wellstone	Y	Y	Y	Y	Y	Y	Y	N
Durenberger	Y	N	N	?	Y	N	Y	N
MISSISSIPPI								
Cochran	N	N	N	N	N	N	N	N
Lott	N	N	N	N	N	N	N	N
MISSOURI								
Bond	Y	Y	Y	Y	Y	Y	Y	N
Danforth	Y	Y	N	Y	N	N	Y	N
MONTANA								
Baucus	Y	Y	Y	Y	Y	Y	Y	N
Burns	N	N	N	N	N	N	N	N
NEBRASKA								
Exon	Y	Y	Y	Y	Y	Y	Y	N
Kerrey	Y	Y	Y	Y	Y	Y	Y	N
NEVADA								
Bryan	Y	Y	Y	Y	Y	Y	Y	N
Reid	Y	Y	Y	Y	Y	Y	Y	N
NEW HAMPSHIRE								
Gregg	N	N	N	N	N	N	N	N
Smith	N	N	N	N	N	N	N	N
NEW JERSEY								
Bradley	Y	Y	Y	Y	Y	Y	Y	N
Lautenberg	Y	Y	Y	Y	Y	Y	Y	N
NEW MEXICO								
Bingaman	Y	Y	Y	Y	Y	Y	Y	N
Domenici	N	N	N	N	N	N	N	N
NEW YORK								
Moynihan	Y	Y	Y	Y	Y	N	Y	N
D'Amato	Y	N	N	N	N	N	Y	N
NORTH CAROLINA								
Faircloth	N	N	N	N	N	N	N	N
Helms	N	N	N	N	N	N	N	N
NORTH DAKOTA								
Conrad	Y	N	N	Y	Y	Y	Y	N
Dorgan	Y	Y	N	Y	Y	Y	Y	N
OHIO								
Glenn	Y	Y	Y	Y	Y	Y	Y	N
Metzenbaum	Y	Y	Y	Y	Y	Y	Y	N
OKLAHOMA								
Boren	Y	Y	Y	Y	Y	Y	Y	N
Nickles	N	N	N	N	N	N	N	N
OREGON								
Hatfield	N	N	N	N	N	N	N	N
Packwood	Y	Y	N	Y	Y	Y	Y	N
PENNSYLVANIA								
Wofford	Y	Y	Y	Y	Y	Y	Y	N
Specter	Y	N	N	N	N	N	Y	N
RHODE ISLAND								
Pell	Y	Y	Y	Y	Y	Y	Y	N
Chafee	Y	Y	N	Y	Y	N	Y	N
SOUTH CAROLINA								
Hollings	Y	Y	Y	Y	Y	Y	Y	N
Thurmond	N	N	N	N	?	?	?	?
SOUTH DAKOTA								
Daschle	Y	Y	Y	Y	Y	Y	Y	N
Pressler	N	N	N	N	N	N	N	N
TENNESSEE								
Mathews	Y	Y	Y	Y	Y	Y	Y	N
Sasser	Y	Y	N	Y	Y	Y	Y	N
TEXAS								
Krueger	Y	Y	N	Y	Y	N	Y	N
Gramm	N	N	N	N	N	?	N	N
UTAH								
Bennett	N	N	N	N	N	N	N	N
Hatch	N	N	N	N	N	N	N	N
VERMONT								
Leahy	Y	Y	Y	Y	Y	Y	Y	N
Jeffords	Y	Y	Y	Y	Y	Y	Y	N
VIRGINIA								
Robb	Y	Y	Y	Y	Y	Y	Y	N
Warner	N	N	N	N	N	N	N	N
WASHINGTON								
Murray	Y	Y	Y	Y	Y	Y	Y	N
Gorton	N	N	N	N	N	N	N	N
WEST VIRGINIA								
Byrd	Y	Y	Y	Y	Y	Y	Y	Y
Rockefeller	Y	Y	Y	Y	Y	Y	Y	N
WISCONSIN								
Feingold	Y	Y	Y	Y	Y	Y	Y	N
Kohl	Y	Y	Y	Y	Y	N	Y	N
WYOMING								
Simpson	N	N	N	N	N	N	N	N
Wallop	N	N	N	N	N	N	N	N

ND Northern Democrats   SD Southern Democrats   Southern states - Ala., Ark., Fla., Ga., Ky., La., Miss., N.C., Okla., S.C., Tenn., Texas, Va.

1. S 5. Family and Medical Leave/Tax Credits. Dodd, D-Conn., motion to table (kill) the Craig, R-Idaho, substitute amendment to provide employers with a 20 percent refundable tax credit for providing employees with 12 weeks of unpaid leave a year for illness or to care for a new child or sick family member; the cost would be offset by an increase in corporate estimated tax payments. Motion agreed to 67-33: R 11-32; D 56-1 (ND 42-0, SD 14-1), Feb. 3, 1993.

2. S 5. Family and Medical Leave/Written Notice. Dodd, D-Conn., motion to table (kill) the Gorton, R-Wash., amendment to require an employee to provide 30 days' written notice before taking unpaid family leave in foreseeable cases. Motion agreed to 60-40: R 6-37; D 54-3 (ND 41-1, SD 13-2), Feb. 3, 1993.

3. S 5. Family and Medical Leave/Binding Arbitration. Dodd, D-Conn., motion to table (kill) the Grassley, R-Iowa, amendment to replace the enforcement provisions of the bill with provisions establishing binding arbitration procedures. Motion agreed to 53-47: R 2-41; D 51-6 (ND 40-2, SD 11-4), Feb. 3, 1993.

4. S 5. Family and Medical Leave/Optional Benefits. Dodd, D-Conn., motion to table (kill) the Kassebaum, R-Kan., amendment to allow employers to satisfy the requirements of the bill by offering family and medical leave as an option under a "cafeteria" benefits plan. Motion agreed to 63-36: R 8-34; D 55-2 (ND 41-1, SD 14-1), Feb. 3, 1993.

5. S 5. Family and Medical Leave/Overtime Pay. Dodd, D-Conn., motion to table (kill) the Wallop, R-Wyo., amendment to amend the Fair Labor Standards Act to allow employees to take compensatory time in lieu of overtime pay. Motion agreed to 64-35: R 7-35; D 57-0 (ND 42-0, SD 15-0), Feb. 3, 1993.

6. S 5. Family and Medical Leave/Mediation. Dodd, D-Conn., motion to table (kill) the Danforth, R-Mo., amendment to provide for the voluntary settlements of complaints through the use of a mediator. Motion agreed to 56-42: R 3-38; D 53-4 (ND 40-2, SD 13-2), Feb. 3, 1993.

7. S 5. Family and Medical Leave/Additional Costs. Dodd, D-Conn., motion to table (kill) the Dole, R-Kan., amendment to exempt employers from being required to provide family and medical leave until the federal government certifies that compliance will not increase the expenses of the employer or the federal government provides assistance sufficient to offset the additional costs. Motion agreed to 67-31: R 11-30; D 56-1 (ND 42-0, SD 14-1), Feb. 4, 1993.

8. S 5. Family and Medical Leave/Homosexuals in Military. Dole, R-Kan., motion to table (kill) the Mitchell, D-Maine, amendment to the Dole amendment, to express the sense of Congress that the secretary of Defense shall report to Congress the results of a review of the current policy regarding homosexuals in the military and the anticipated effects of any change in that policy and that the Senate Armed Services Committee shall conduct hearings on the policy and conduct oversight hearings on the secretary's recommendations. Motion rejected 1-98: R 0-42; D 1-56 (ND 1-41, SD 0-15), Feb. 4, 1993. (The Mitchell amendment was subsequently adopted by voice vote.)

KEY

- Y Voted for (yea).
- \# Paired for.
- \+ Announced for.
- N Voted against (nay).
- X Paired against.
- — Announced against.
- P Voted "present."
- C Voted "present" to avoid possible conflict of interest.
- ? Did not vote or otherwise make a position known.

Democrats *Republicans*

	9	10	11	12	13	14	15	16
ALABAMA								
Heflin	N	Y	N	N	Y	N	Y	Y
Shelby	N	N	Y	N	Y	N	Y	Y
ALASKA								
Murkowski	N	N	Y	N	Y	Y	Y	+
Stevens	N	N	Y	N	Y	N	Y	Y
ARIZONA								
DeConcini	Y	Y	Y	N	Y	N	Y	Y
McCain	N	N	Y	N	Y	N	Y	Y
ARKANSAS								
Bumpers	Y	N	Y	Y	Y	N	Y	Y
Pryor	Y	N	Y	Y	Y	N	Y	Y
CALIFORNIA								
Boxer	Y	Y	Y	Y	N	N	Y	Y
Feinstein	Y	Y	Y	Y	N	N	Y	Y
COLORADO								
Campbell	Y	Y	Y	N	Y	N	Y	Y
Brown	N	N	N	N	Y	Y	Y	Y
CONNECTICUT								
Dodd	Y	Y	Y	Y	N	N	Y	Y
Lieberman	Y	Y	Y	Y	Y	N	Y	Y
DELAWARE								
Biden	Y	Y	Y	N	Y	N	Y	Y
Roth	N	N	Y	N	Y	Y	Y	Y
FLORIDA								
Graham	Y	Y	Y	N	Y	N	Y	Y
Mack	N	N	N	N	Y	Y	Y	Y
GEORGIA								
Nunn	Y	Y	Y	N	Y	N	Y	Y
Coverdell	N	N	N	N	Y	Y	Y	Y
HAWAII								
Akaka	Y	Y	Y	Y	N	N	Y	Y
Inouye	Y	Y	Y	Y	N	N	Y	Y
IDAHO								
Craig	N	N	N	N	Y	Y	Y	Y
Kempthorne	N	N	N	N	Y	Y	Y	Y
ILLINOIS								
Moseley-Braun	Y	Y	Y	Y	N	N	Y	Y
Simon	Y	Y	Y	Y	N	N	Y	+
INDIANA								
Coats	N	Y	Y	N	Y	Y	Y	Y
Lugar	N	N	N	N	Y	N	Y	Y
IOWA								
Harkin	Y	Y	Y	Y	Y	N	Y	Y
Grassley	N	N	N	N	Y	Y	Y	Y
KANSAS								
Dole	N	N	N	N	Y	N	Y	Y
Kassebaum	N	N	N	N	Y	N	Y	Y
KENTUCKY								
Ford	Y	Y	Y	N	Y	N	Y	Y
McConnell	N	N	N	N	Y	Y	Y	Y
LOUISIANA								
Breaux	Y	Y	Y	N	Y	N	Y	Y
Johnston	Y	Y	Y	N	Y	N	Y	Y
MAINE								
Mitchell	Y	Y	Y	Y	N	N	Y	Y
Cohen	N	Y	Y	N	Y	N	Y	Y
MARYLAND								
Mikulski	Y	Y	Y	Y	N	N	Y	Y
Sarbanes	Y	Y	Y	Y	N	N	Y	Y
MASSACHUSETTS								
Kennedy	Y	Y	Y	Y	N	N	Y	Y
Kerry	Y	Y	Y	Y	Y	N	Y	Y
MICHIGAN								
Levin	Y	Y	Y	Y	Y	N	Y	Y
Riegle	Y	Y	Y	?	?	?	?	Y
MINNESOTA								
Wellstone	Y	Y	Y	Y	N	N	Y	Y
Durenberger	Y	Y	Y	Y	Y	N	Y	Y
MISSISSIPPI								
Cochran	N	N	N	N	Y	Y	Y	Y
Lott	N	N	N	N	Y	Y	Y	Y
MISSOURI								
Bond	N	Y	Y	N	Y	?	?	Y
Danforth	N	Y	Y	N	Y	?	?	Y
MONTANA								
Baucus	Y	Y	Y	Y	N	N	Y	Y
Burns	N	N	Y	N	Y	Y	Y	Y
NEBRASKA								
Exon	Y	Y	Y	Y	N	N	Y	Y
Kerrey	Y	Y	Y	Y	Y	N	Y	Y
NEVADA								
Bryan	Y	Y	Y	N	Y	N	Y	Y
Reid	Y	Y	Y	N	Y	N	Y	Y
NEW HAMPSHIRE								
Gregg	N	N	N	N	Y	Y	Y	Y
Smith	N	N	N	N	Y	Y	N	Y
NEW JERSEY								
Bradley	Y	Y	Y	Y	N	N	Y	Y
Lautenberg	Y	Y	Y	Y	N	N	Y	Y
NEW MEXICO								
Bingaman	Y	N	Y	N	Y	N	Y	Y
Domenici	N	N	N	N	Y	N	Y	Y
NEW YORK								
Moynihan	Y	Y	Y	Y	N	N	Y	Y
D'Amato	Y	N	Y	N	Y	N	Y	Y
NORTH CAROLINA								
Faircloth	N	N	N	N	Y	Y	N	Y
Helms	N	N	N	N	Y	Y	N	Y
NORTH DAKOTA								
Conrad	Y	Y	Y	Y	N	Y	Y	Y
Dorgan	Y	Y	Y	Y	Y	N	Y	Y
OHIO								
Glenn	Y	Y	Y	Y	N	N	Y	Y
Metzenbaum	Y	Y	Y	Y	N	N	Y	Y
OKLAHOMA								
Boren	Y	N	Y	N	Y	N	Y	Y
Nickles	N	N	N	N	Y	Y	Y	Y
OREGON								
Hatfield	Y	N	Y	N	Y	N	Y	Y
Packwood	Y	Y	Y	Y	Y	N	Y	Y
PENNSYLVANIA								
Wofford	Y	Y	Y	Y	N	N	Y	Y
Specter	Y	N	Y	Y	Y	N	Y	Y
RHODE ISLAND								
Pell	Y	Y	Y	Y	N	Y	Y	Y
Chafee	Y	N	Y	Y	Y	N	Y	Y
SOUTH CAROLINA								
Hollings	Y	Y	N	Y	N	N	Y	Y
Thurmond	—	?	?	N	Y	N	Y	Y
SOUTH DAKOTA								
Daschle	Y	Y	Y	Y	N	N	Y	Y
Pressler	N	N	N	N	Y	Y	Y	Y
TENNESSEE								
Mathews	Y	Y	Y	N	Y	N	Y	Y
Sasser	Y	Y	Y	N	Y	N	Y	Y
TEXAS								
Krueger	Y	Y	Y	N	Y	N	Y	Y
Gramm	N	N	N	N	Y	Y	Y	Y
UTAH								
Bennett	N	N	N	N	Y	Y	Y	Y
Hatch	N	N	N	N	Y	Y	Y	Y
VERMONT								
Leahy	Y	Y	Y	Y	N	N	Y	Y
Jeffords	Y	Y	Y	Y	N	Y	Y	Y
VIRGINIA								
Robb	Y	Y	Y	Y	N	N	Y	Y
Warner	N	N	N	N	Y	N	Y	Y
WASHINGTON								
Murray	Y	Y	Y	Y	N	N	Y	Y
Gorton	N	N	N	N	Y	N	Y	Y
WEST VIRGINIA								
Byrd	Y	Y	Y	N	Y	N	Y	Y
Rockefeller	Y	Y	Y	?	Y	N	Y	Y
WISCONSIN								
Feingold	Y	Y	Y	Y	N	N	Y	Y
Kohl	Y	Y	Y	Y	N	N	Y	Y
WYOMING								
Simpson	N	N	N	N	Y	N	Y	Y
Wallop	N	?	—	N	Y	Y	N	Y

ND Northern Democrats   SD Southern Democrats   Southern states - Ala., Ark., Fla., Ga., Ky., La., Miss., N.C., Okla., S.C., Tenn., Texas, Va.

9. S 5. Family and Medical Leave/Homosexuals in Military. Mitchell, D-Maine, motion to table the Dole, R-Kan., amendment to the Dole amendment, as amended by the Mitchell amendment, to suspend all executive orders on homosexuals in the military since Jan. 1, 1993, until a thorough review of all executive orders on homosexuals in the military is conducted by July 15, 1993, and to require that all changes to the policy be approved by Congress. Motion agreed to 62-37: R 7-35; D 55-2 (ND 42-0, SD 13-2), Feb. 4, 1993. (Subsequently, the Dole amendment, as amended by the Mitchell amendment in vote 8, was adopted by voice vote.) A "yea" was a vote in support of the president's position.

10. S 5. Family and Medical Leave/Reduced Leave. Dodd, D-Conn., motion to table (kill) the Brown, R-Colo., amendment to allow an employee to take reduced leave, working less than eight hours a day, only upon agreement with the employer. The bill would allow an employee to take reduced leave without the employer's consent when medically necessary. Motion agreed to 59-39: R 7-34; D 52-5 (ND 41-1, SD 11-4), Feb. 4, 1993.

11. HR 1. Family and Medical Leave/Passage. Passage of the bill to require employers of more than 50 employees to provide 12 weeks of unpaid leave for an illness or to care for a new child or sick family member. Passed 71-27: R 16-25; D 55-2 (ND 42-0, SD 13-2), Feb. 4, 1993. (Before passage, the Senate struck all after the enacting clause and inserted the text of S 5, as amended.) A "yea" was a vote in support of the president's position.

12. S 1. NIH Reauthorization/Health Implications. Kennedy, D-Mass., amendment to provide a 90-day period for the study of the health significance of an administration proposal to lift the ban on the immigration of people infected with the AIDS virus. A competing Nickles, R-Okla., amendment would prohibit the permanent immigration of persons infected with HIV. Rejected 42-56: R 6-37; D 36-19 (ND 32-8, SD 4-11), Feb. 18, 1993.

13. S 1. NIH Reauthorization/Ban on HIV-Positive Immigrants. Nickles, R-Okla., amendment to prohibit the permanent immigration of persons infected with the AIDS virus. Adopted 76-23: R 42-1; D 34-22 (ND 20-21, SD 14-1), Feb. 18, 1993. A "nay" was a vote in support of the president's position.

14. S 1. NIH Reauthorization/Ethics Advisory Board. Helms, R-N.C., amendment to eliminate the requirement that the president appoint an ethics advisory board for reviewing research proposals at NIH. Rejected 23-74: R 23-18; D 0-56 (ND 0-41, SD 0-15), Feb. 18, 1993.

15. S 1. NIH Reauthorization/Passage. Passage of the bill to authorize $5.5 billion for the National Institutes of Health in fiscal 1994 and such sums as necessary in fiscal 1995-96, including $2.2 billion for the National Cancer Institute and $1.5 billion for the National Heart, Lung and Blood Institute. Passed 93-4: R 37-4; D 56-0 (ND 41-0, SD 15-0), Feb. 18, 1993.

16. S Res 71. Committee Funding Resolution/Pay Freeze for Senators. Mitchell, D-Maine, amendment to the Dole, R-Kan., amendment to express the sense of the Senate that senators' pay should be frozen for one year. Adopted 98-0: R 42-0; D 56-0 (ND 41-0, SD 15-0), Feb. 24, 1993.

KEY

- Y Voted for (yea).
- # Paired for.
- + Announced for.
- N Voted against (nay).
- X Paired against.
- − Announced against.
- P Voted "present."
- C Voted "present" to avoid possible conflict of interest.
- ? Did not vote or otherwise make a position known.

Democrats   *Republicans*

	17	18	19	20	21	22	23	24
ALABAMA								
Heflin	N	Y	N	Y	Y	N	Y	Y
Shelby	Y	Y	?	?	Y	Y	Y	Y
ALASKA								
Murkowski	−	−	−	?	N	Y	N	Y
Stevens	N	N	N	Y	N	Y	Y	Y
ARIZONA								
DeConcini	Y	Y	N	Y	Y	N	N	Y
McCain	Y	Y	N	Y	N	Y	N	N
ARKANSAS								
Bumpers	N	N	N	Y	Y	N	Y	Y
Pryor	N	N	N	Y	Y	N	Y	Y
CALIFORNIA								
Boxer	N	N	N	Y	Y	N	Y	Y
Feinstein	N	N	N	Y	Y	N	Y	Y
COLORADO								
Campbell	N	N	N	Y	Y	N	Y	Y
Brown	Y	Y	Y	Y	N	Y	N	N
CONNECTICUT								
Dodd	N	N	N	Y	Y	N	Y	Y
Lieberman	N	N	N	Y	Y	N	Y	Y
DELAWARE								
Biden	N	N	N	Y	Y	N	Y	Y
Roth	N	Y	N	Y	N	Y	N	N
FLORIDA								
Graham	N	N	N	Y	Y	N	Y	Y
Mack	Y	Y	Y	Y	N	Y	N	N
GEORGIA								
Nunn	N	Y	N	Y	Y	N	Y	Y
Coverdell	Y	Y	N	Y	N	Y	N	N
HAWAII								
Akaka	N	N	N	Y	Y	N	Y	Y
Inouye	N	N	N	Y	Y	N	Y	Y
IDAHO								
Craig	N	Y	Y	Y	N	Y	N	N
Kempthorne	N	Y	Y	Y	N	Y	N	N
ILLINOIS								
Moseley-Braun	N	N	N	Y	Y	N	Y	Y
Simon	N	N	N	Y	Y	N	Y	Y
INDIANA								
Coats	Y	Y	Y	Y	N	Y	N	N
Lugar	Y	Y	Y	Y	N	Y	N	N
IOWA								
Harkin	N	Y	N	Y	Y	N	Y	Y
Grassley	N	N	N	Y	N	Y	N	N
KANSAS								
Dole	Y	Y	Y	Y	N	Y	N	N
Kassebaum	N	Y	N	Y	N	Y	N	N
KENTUCKY								
Ford	N	N	N	Y	Y	N	Y	Y
McConnell	Y	Y	Y	Y	N	Y	N	N
LOUISIANA								
Breaux	N	N	N	Y	Y	N	Y	Y
Johnston	Y	Y	Y	Y	Y	N	Y	Y
MAINE								
Mitchell	N	N	N	Y	Y	N	Y	Y
Cohen	N	N	N	Y	N	Y	N	N
MARYLAND								
Mikulski	N	Y	N	Y	Y	N	Y	Y
Sarbanes	N	N	N	Y	Y	N	Y	Y
MASSACHUSETTS								
Kennedy	N	N	N	Y	Y	N	Y	Y
Kerry	N	N	N	Y	Y	N	Y	Y
MICHIGAN								
Levin	N	N	N	Y	Y	N	Y	Y
Riegle	N	N	N	Y	Y	N	Y	Y
MINNESOTA								
Wellstone	N	N	N	Y	Y	N	Y	Y
Durenberger	N	N	N	Y	N	Y	N	Y
MISSISSIPPI								
Cochran	Y	Y	N	Y	N	Y	N	N
Lott	Y	Y	Y	Y	N	Y	N	N
MISSOURI								
Bond	Y	Y	Y	Y	N	Y	N	N
Danforth	Y	Y	Y	Y	N	Y	N	N
MONTANA								
Baucus	?	N	N	Y	Y	N	Y	Y
Burns	N	N	Y	Y	N	Y	N	N
NEBRASKA								
Exon	N	N	N	Y	Y	N	Y	Y
Kerrey	N	N	Y	Y	Y	N	Y	Y
NEVADA								
Bryan	Y	Y	N	Y	Y	N	Y	Y
Reid	N	Y	N	Y	Y	N	Y	Y
NEW HAMPSHIRE								
Gregg	Y	Y	Y	Y	N	Y	N	Y
Smith	Y	Y	Y	N	N	Y	N	N
NEW JERSEY								
Bradley	N	Y	Y	Y	Y	N	Y	Y
Lautenberg	N	Y	Y	Y	Y	N	Y	Y
NEW MEXICO								
Bingaman	N	N	N	Y	Y	?	?	?
Domenici	N	N	N	?	N	Y	Y	Y
NEW YORK								
Moynihan	N	N	N	Y	Y	N	Y	Y
D'Amato	Y	Y	Y	N	Y	N	Y	Y
NORTH CAROLINA								
Faircloth	Y	Y	Y	Y	N	Y	N	N
Helms	Y	Y	Y	N	N	Y	N	N
NORTH DAKOTA								
Conrad	N	N	N	Y	Y	N	Y	Y
Dorgan	N	N	N	Y	Y	N	Y	Y
OHIO								
Glenn	N	N	N	Y	Y	N	Y	Y
Metzenbaum	N	N	N	Y	Y	N	Y	Y
OKLAHOMA								
Boren	N	N	N	Y	Y	N	Y	Y
Nickles	Y	Y	Y	Y	N	Y	N	N
OREGON								
Hatfield	N	N	N	Y	Y	N	Y	Y
Packwood	N	Y	N	Y	N	Y	N	N
PENNSYLVANIA								
Wofford	N	N	N	Y	Y	N	Y	Y
Specter	N	N	Y	N	Y	N	Y	Y
RHODE ISLAND								
Pell	N	N	N	Y	Y	N	Y	Y
Chafee	N	N	Y	N	Y	N	Y	Y
SOUTH CAROLINA								
Hollings	Y	Y	N	Y	Y	N	Y	Y
Thurmond	Y	Y	N	Y	N	Y	N	N
SOUTH DAKOTA								
Daschle	N	N	N	Y	Y	N	Y	Y
Pressler	N	N	Y	N	Y	N	N	N
TENNESSEE								
Mathews	N	N	N	Y	Y	N	Y	Y
Sasser	N	N	N	Y	Y	N	Y	Y
TEXAS								
Krueger	N	N	N	Y	Y	N	Y	Y
Gramm	Y	Y	Y	Y	N	Y	N	N
UTAH								
Bennett	Y	Y	N	Y	N	Y	N	N
Hatch	N	N	N	Y	N	Y	N	N
VERMONT								
Leahy	N	N	N	Y	Y	N	Y	Y
Jeffords	N	N	N	Y	N	Y	N	Y
VIRGINIA								
Robb	N	Y	N	Y	Y	N	Y	Y
Warner	Y	Y	N	?	N	Y	N	N
WASHINGTON								
Murray	N	N	N	Y	Y	N	Y	Y
Gorton	Y	Y	Y	Y	N	Y	N	Y
WEST VIRGINIA								
Byrd	N	N	N	Y	Y	N	Y	Y
Rockefeller	N	N	N	Y	Y	N	Y	Y
WISCONSIN								
Feingold	N	N	N	Y	Y	N	Y	Y
Kohl	N	N	N	Y	Y	N	Y	Y
WYOMING								
Simpson	Y	Y	Y	Y	N	Y	N	N
Wallop	Y	Y	Y	Y	N	Y	N	N

ND Northern Democrats   SD Southern Democrats   Southern states - Ala., Ark., Fla., Ga., Ky., La., Miss., N.C., Okla., S.C., Tenn., Texas, Va.

17. S Res 71. Committee Funding Resolution/Eliminate Special Aging Committee. Cochran, R-Miss., amendment to the Reid, D-Nev., amendment, to eliminate the Senate Special Committee on Aging by April 1, 1993. The Reid amendment would eliminate the committee by Jan. 1, 1994. Rejected 30-68: R 25-17; D 5-51 (ND 2-39, SD 3-12), Feb. 24, 1993.

18. S Res 71. Committee Funding Resolution/Eliminate Special Aging Committee. Reid, D-Nev., amendment to eliminate the Senate Special Committee on Aging by Jan. 1, 1994. Rejected 43-56: R 30-12; D 13-44 (ND 7-35, SD 6-9), Feb. 24, 1993.

19. S Res 71. Committee Funding Resolution/Funding Levels. Chafee, R-R.I., amendment to cut funds for all committees, except Appropriations, with funding levels higher than the Finance Committee to Finance's level. Committees with levels below Finance's would be reduced to 95 percent of their 1992 levels. Rejected 29-69: R 25-17; D 4-52 (ND 3-39, SD 1-13), Feb. 24, 1993.

20. S Res 71. Committee Funding Resolution/Adoption. Adoption of the resolution to authorize $55.3 million in 1993 and $56.4 million in 1994 for Senate committee operations. The authorization is 7.6 percent or $4.7 million below the 1992 authorization. Adopted 94-2: R 38-2; D 56-0 (ND 42-0, SD 14-0), Feb. 25, 1993.

21. S 382. Unemployment Benefits Extension/Offsetting Cuts. Moynihan, D-N.Y., motion to table (kill) the Packwood, R-Ore., amendment to cut federal overhead and administrative expenses to pay for the cost of extending unemployment benefits.

Motion agreed to 57-43: R 0-43; D 57-0 (ND 42-0, SD 15-0), March 3, 1993. A "yea" was a vote in support of the president's position.

22. S 382. Unemployment Benefits Extension/Budget Delay. Domenici, R-N.M., motion to waive the budget act with respect to the Sasser, D-Tenn., point of order against the Domenici amendment for violating the 1974 Congressional Budget Act. The Domenici amendment would express the sense of the Senate that the president should submit his budget before a concurrent budget resolution is considered. Motion rejected 44-55: R 43-0; D 1-55 (ND 0-41, SD 1-14), March 3, 1993. A three-fifths majority vote (60) of the total Senate is required to waive the budget act. (Subsequently, the chair upheld the Sasser point of order, and the Domenici amendment fell.)

23. S 382. Unemployment Benefits Extension/COLA for Federal Workers. Moynihan, D-N.Y., motion to table (kill) the Brown, R-Colo., amendment to eliminate the cost of living adjustment (COLA) for federal employees in fiscal 1994. Motion agreed to 58-41: R 2-41; D 56-0 (ND 41-0, SD 15-0), March 3, 1993.

24. HR 920. Unemployment Benefits Extension/Passage. Passage of the bill to provide $5.7 billion to extend federal emergency unemployment benefits from March 6 through Oct. 2. The funds would be designated as emergency spending and thus exempt from pay-as-you-go rules. Passed 66-33: R 10-33; D 56-0 (ND 41-0, SD 15-0), March 3, 1993. (Before passage, the Senate struck all after the enacting clause and inserted the text of S 382 as amended.) A "yea" was a vote in support of the president's position.

	25	26	27	28	29	30	31	32
ALABAMA								
Heflin	Y	Y	N	Y	Y	Y	Y	Y
Shelby	Y	Y	Y	Y	Y	?	?	Y
ALASKA								
Murkowski	N	N	Y	N	Y	N	N	Y
Stevens	N	N	N	N	Y	N	N	Y
ARIZONA								
DeConcini	Y	Y	N	Y	Y	Y	Y	Y
McCain	N	N	Y	N	Y	N	N	Y
ARKANSAS								
Bumpers	Y	Y	N	Y	Y	Y	Y	Y
Pryor	Y	Y	N	Y	Y	Y	Y	Y
CALIFORNIA								
Boxer	Y	Y	N	Y	Y	Y	Y	Y
Feinstein	·Y	Y	Y	Y	Y	Y	Y	Y
COLORADO								
Campbell	Y	Y	N	Y	Y	Y	?	Y
Brown	N	N	Y	N	Y	N	N	Y
CONNECTICUT								
Dodd	Y	Y	N	Y	Y	Y	Y	Y
Lieberman	Y	Y	N	Y	Y	Y	Y	Y
DELAWARE								
Biden	Y	Y	N	Y	Y	Y	Y	Y
Roth	N	N	Y	N	Y	N	N	Y
FLORIDA								
Graham	Y	Y	Y	Y	Y	Y	Y	Y
Mack	N	N	Y	N	Y	N	N	Y
GEORGIA								
Nunn	Y	Y	N	Y	Y	Y	N	Y
Coverdell	N	N	Y	N	Y	N	N	Y
HAWAII								
Akaka	Y	Y	N	Y	Y	Y	Y	Y
Inouye	Y	Y	?	?	Y	Y	Y	Y
IDAHO								
Craig	?	N	Y	N	Y	N	N	Y
Kempthorne	N	N	Y	N	Y	N	N	Y
ILLINOIS								
Moseley-Braun	Y	Y	N	Y	Y	Y	Y	Y
Simon	Y	Y	N	Y	Y	Y	Y	Y
INDIANA								
Coats	N	N	Y	N	Y	N	N	Y
Lugar	N	N	Y	N	Y	N	N	Y

	25	26	27	28	29	30	31	32
IOWA								
Harkin	Y	Y	N	Y	Y	Y	Y	Y
Grassley	N	N	Y	N	Y	N	N	Y
KANSAS								
Dole	N	N	Y	N	Y	N	N	Y
Kassebaum	N	N	Y	N	Y	N	N	Y
KENTUCKY								
Ford	Y	Y	N	Y	Y	Y	Y	Y
McConnell	N	N	Y	N	Y	N	N	Y
LOUISIANA								
Breaux	?	Y	N	Y	Y	Y	Y	Y
Johnston	?	Y	N	Y	Y	Y	Y	Y
MAINE								
Mitchell	Y	Y	N	Y	Y	Y	Y	Y
Cohen	N	N	Y	N	Y	N	N	Y
MARYLAND								
Mikulski	Y	Y	N	Y	Y	Y	Y	Y
Sarbanes	Y	Y	N	Y	Y	Y	Y	Y
MASSACHUSETTS								
Kennedy	Y	Y	N	Y	Y	Y	Y	Y
Kerry	Y	Y	N	Y	Y	Y	Y	Y
MICHIGAN								
Levin	Y	Y	N	Y	Y	Y	Y	Y
Riegle	Y	Y	N	Y	Y	Y	Y	Y
MINNESOTA								
Wellstone	Y	Y	–	Y	Y	Y	Y	Y
Durenberger	N	Y	Y	N	Y	Y	N	Y
MISSISSIPPI								
Cochran	N	N	N	N	Y	N	N	Y
Lott	N	N	Y	N	Y	N	N	Y
MISSOURI								
Bond	N	N	Y	N	Y	N	N	Y
Danforth	N	N	Y	N	Y	N	N	Y
MONTANA								
Baucus	Y	Y	N	Y	Y	Y	Y	Y
Burns	N	N	Y	N	Y	N	N	Y
NEBRASKA								
Exon	Y	Y	N	Y	Y	Y	Y	Y
Kerrey	Y	Y	N	Y	Y	Y	Y	Y
NEVADA								
Bryan	Y	Y	N	Y	Y	Y	Y	Y
Reid	Y	Y	N	Y	Y	Y	Y	Y

	25	26	27	28	29	30	31	32
NEW HAMPSHIRE								
Gregg	?	N	Y	N	Y	N	N	Y
Smith	N	N	Y	N	Y	N	N	Y
NEW JERSEY								
Bradley	Y	Y	N	Y	Y	Y	Y	Y
Lautenberg	Y	Y	N	Y	Y	Y	Y	Y
NEW MEXICO								
Bingaman	Y	Y	N	Y	Y	Y	Y	Y
Domenici	N	N	Y	N	Y	N	N	Y
NEW YORK								
Moynihan	Y	Y	N	Y	Y	Y	Y	Y
D'Amato	N	N	Y	N	Y	N	N	Y
NORTH CAROLINA								
Faircloth	N	N	Y	N	Y	N	N	Y
Helms	N	N	Y	N	Y	N	N	Y
NORTH DAKOTA								
Conrad	Y	Y	N	Y	Y	Y	Y	Y
Dorgan	Y	Y	N	Y	Y	Y	Y	Y
OHIO								
Glenn	Y	Y	N	Y	Y	Y	Y	Y
Metzenbaum	Y	Y	N	Y	Y	Y	Y	Y
OKLAHOMA								
Boren	Y	Y	Y	Y	Y	N	N	Y
Nickles	N	N	Y	N	Y	N	N	Y
OREGON								
Hatfield	Y	Y	N	?	?	?	?	?
Packwood	?	Y	Y	N	Y	N	N	Y
PENNSYLVANIA								
Wofford	Y	Y	N	Y	Y	Y	Y	Y
Specter	N	Y	Y	N	Y	N	N	Y
RHODE ISLAND								
Pell	Y	Y	N	Y	Y	Y	Y	Y
Chafee	N	N	Y	N	Y	N	N	Y
SOUTH CAROLINA								
Hollings	Y	Y	N	Y	Y	Y	Y	Y
Thurmond	–	N	Y	N	Y	N	N	Y
SOUTH DAKOTA								
Daschle	Y	Y	N	Y	Y	Y	Y	Y
Pressler	N	N	Y	N	Y	N	N	Y
TENNESSEE								
Mathews	Y	Y	N	Y	Y	Y	Y	Y
Sasser	?	Y	N	Y	Y	Y	Y	Y

KEY

Y	Voted for (yea).
#	Paired for.
+	Announced for.
N	Voted against (nay).
X	Paired against.
–	Announced against.
P	Voted "present."
C	Voted "present" to avoid possible conflict of interest.
?	Did not vote or otherwise make a position known.

Democrats   *Republicans*

	25	26	27	28	29	30	31	32
TEXAS								
Krueger								
Gramm	N	N	Y	N	Y	N	N	Y
UTAH								
Bennett	?	N	Y	N	Y	N	N	Y
Hatch	N	N	Y	N	Y	N	N	Y
VERMONT								
Leahy	?	Y	N	Y	Y	Y	Y	Y
Jeffords	N	Y	N	Y	Y	Y	N	Y
VIRGINIA								
Robb	Y	Y	Y	Y	Y	Y	Y	Y
Warner	N	N	Y	N	Y	N	N	Y
WASHINGTON								
Murray	Y	Y	N	Y	Y	Y	Y	Y
Gorton	N	N	Y	N	Y	N	N	Y
WEST VIRGINIA								
Byrd	Y	Y	N	Y	Y	Y	Y	Y
Rockefeller	?	Y	N	Y	Y	Y	Y	Y
WISCONSIN								
Feingold	Y	Y	N	Y	Y	Y	Y	Y
Kohl	Y	Y	Y	Y	Y	Y	Y	Y
WYOMING								
Simpson	N	N	Y	N	Y	N	N	Y
Wallop	–	N	Y	N	Y	N	N	Y

ND Northern Democrats   SD Southern Democrats   Southern states - Ala., Ark., Fla., Ga., Ky., La., Miss., N.C., Okla., S.C., Tenn., Texas, Va.

25. S 460. National "Motor Voter" Registration/Cloture. Motion to invoke cloture (limiting debate) on the motion to proceed to the bill to require states to allow citizens to register to vote while applying for or renewing driver's licenses or other public certificates. Motion rejected 52-36: R 1-36; D 51-0 (ND 40-0, SD 11-0), March 5, 1993. A three-fifths majority vote of the total Senate (60) is required to invoke cloture.

26. S 460. National "Motor Voter" Registration/Cloture. Motion to invoke cloture (thus limiting debate) on the motion to proceed to the bill to require states to allow citizens to register to vote while applying for or renewing driver's licenses or other public certificates. Motion agreed to 62-38: R 5-38; D 57-0 (ND 42-0, SD 15-0), March 9, 1993. A three-fifths majority vote of the total Senate (60) is required to invoke cloture.

27. S 460. National "Motor Voter" Registration/Line-Item Veto. McCain, R-Ariz., motion to waive the budget act with respect to the Ford, D-Ky., point of order against the McCain amendment. The McCain amendment would grant the president line-item veto authority. Motion rejected 45-52: R 39-4; D 6-48 (ND 2-38, SD 4-10), March 10, 1993. A three-fifths majority vote (60) of the total Senate is required to waive the budget act. (Subsequently, the chair upheld the Ford point of order, and the McCain amendment fell.)

28. S 460. National "Motor Voter" Registration/Exemptions. Ford, D-Ky., motion to table (kill) the Kempthorne, R-Idaho, amendment to exempt a state from coverage of the bill if a

state had more than 75 percent of the voting-age population registered to vote in the last election. Motion agreed to 56-41: R 1-41; D 55-0 (ND 41-0, SD 14-0), March 10, 1993.

29. Reno Nomination. Confirmation of President Clinton's nomination of Janet Reno of Florida to be attorney general. Confirmed 98-0: R 42-0; D 56-0 (ND 42-0, SD 14-0), March 11, 1993. A "yea" was a vote in support of the president's position.

30. S 460. National "Motor Voter" Registration/Beneficiary Exclusion. Wellstone, D-Minn., motion to table (kill) the McCain, R-Ariz., amendment to prohibit an agency from registering to vote any person who receives direct financial aid from the agency except for people with disabilities. Motion agreed to 55-42: R 2-40; D 53-2 (ND 42-0, SD 11-2), March 11, 1993.

31. S 460. National "Motor Voter" Registration/Delay Implementation. Ford, D-Ky., motion to table (kill) the Nickles, R-Okla., amendment to provide that the bill shall not take effect until one year after Congress provides for the costs of implementing it. Motion agreed to 53-43: R 0-42; D 53-1 (ND 41-0, SD 12-1), March 11, 1993.

32. S 460. National "Motor Voter" Registration/Modifications. Ford, D-Ky., amendment to incorporate several changes including those to exempt states that already permit polling-place registration on Election Day; require applications to state the penalties for a false application; assist those needing help with the application; and provide registration at military recruitment centers. Adopted 99-0: R 42-0; D 57-0 (ND 42-0, SD 15-0), March 16, 1993.

KEY

Y	Voted for (yea).
#	Paired for.
+	Announced for.
N	Voted against (nay).
X	Paired against.
−	Announced against.
P	Voted "present."
C	Voted "present" to avoid possible conflict of interest.
?	Did not vote or otherwise make a position known.

Democrats   *Republicans*

State / Senator	33	34	35	36	37	38	39	40
ALABAMA								
Heflin	Y	Y	Y	Y	Y	Y	Y	N
Shelby	Y	Y	Y	Y	N	Y	Y	Y
ALASKA								
Murkowski	N	N	N	N	N	N	Y	Y
Stevens	N	N	N	N	N	N	Y	Y
ARIZONA								
DeConcini	Y	Y	Y	Y	Y	Y	N	N
McCain	N	N	N	N	N	N	Y	Y
ARKANSAS								
Bumpers	Y	Y	Y	Y	Y	Y	Y	N
Pryor	Y	Y	Y	Y	Y	Y	Y	N
CALIFORNIA								
Boxer	Y	Y	Y	Y	Y	Y	Y	N
Feinstein	Y	Y	Y	Y	Y	Y	Y	N
COLORADO								
Campbell	Y	Y	Y	Y	Y	Y	Y	N
Brown	N	N	N	N	N	N	Y	Y
CONNECTICUT								
Dodd	Y	Y	Y	Y	Y	Y	Y	N
Lieberman	Y	Y	Y	Y	Y	Y	Y	N
DELAWARE								
Biden	Y	Y	Y	Y	Y	Y	Y	N
Roth	N	N	N	N	N	N	N	Y
FLORIDA								
Graham	Y	Y	Y	Y	Y	Y	N	N
Mack	N	N	N	N	N	N	Y	Y
GEORGIA								
Nunn	Y	Y	Y	Y	Y	Y	Y	N
Coverdell	N	N	N	N	N	N	Y	Y
HAWAII								
Akaka	Y	Y	Y	Y	Y	Y	Y	N
Inouye	Y	Y	Y	Y	?	Y	Y	N
IDAHO								
Craig	N	N	N	N	N	N	Y	Y
Kempthorne	N	N	N	N	N	N	Y	Y
ILLINOIS								
Moseley-Braun	Y	Y	Y	Y	Y	Y	Y	N
Simon	Y	Y	Y	Y	Y	Y	Y	N
INDIANA								
Coats	N	N	N	N	N	N	Y	Y
Lugar	N	N	N	N	N	N	Y	Y
IOWA								
Harkin	Y	Y	Y	Y	Y	Y	Y	N
Grassley	N	N	N	N	N	N	Y	Y
KANSAS								
Dole	N	N	N	N	N	N	Y	Y
Kassebaum	N	N	N	N	N	N	Y	Y
KENTUCKY								
Ford	Y	Y	Y	Y	Y	Y	Y	N
McConnell	N	N	N	N	N	N	Y	N
LOUISIANA								
Breaux	Y	Y	Y	Y	Y	Y	Y	N
Johnston	Y	Y	Y	Y	Y	Y	Y	N
MAINE								
Mitchell	Y	Y	Y	Y	Y	Y	Y	N
Cohen	N	N	N	N	N	N	Y	Y
MARYLAND								
Mikulski	Y	Y	Y	Y	Y	Y	Y	N
Sarbanes	Y	Y	Y	Y	Y	Y	Y	N
MASSACHUSETTS								
Kennedy	Y	Y	Y	Y	Y	Y	Y	N
Kerry	Y	Y	Y	Y	Y	Y	N	N
MICHIGAN								
Levin	Y	Y	Y	Y	Y	Y	Y	N
Riegle	Y	Y	Y	Y	Y	Y	Y	N
MINNESOTA								
Wellstone	Y	Y	Y	Y	Y	Y	Y	N
Durenberger	N	Y	Y	N	Y	Y	Y	N
MISSISSIPPI								
Cochran	N	N	N	N	N	N	Y	Y
Lott	N	N	N	N	N	N	Y	Y
MISSOURI								
Bond	N	N	N	N	N	N	Y	Y
Danforth	N	N	N	N	N	N	Y	Y
MONTANA								
Baucus	Y	Y	Y	Y	Y	Y	Y	N
Burns	N	N	N	N	N	N	Y	Y
NEBRASKA								
Exon	Y	Y	Y	Y	Y	Y	Y	N
Kerrey	Y	Y	Y	Y	Y	Y	Y	N
NEVADA								
Bryan	Y	Y	Y	Y	Y	Y	Y	N
Reid	Y	Y	Y	Y	Y	Y	N	N
NEW HAMPSHIRE								
Gregg	N	N	N	N	N	N	Y	Y
Smith	N	N	N	N	N	N	Y	Y
NEW JERSEY								
Bradley	Y	Y	Y	Y	Y	Y	Y	N
Lautenberg	Y	Y	Y	N	Y	Y	N	N
NEW MEXICO								
Bingaman	Y	Y	Y	Y	Y	Y	Y	N
Domenici	N	N	N	N	N	N	Y	Y
NEW YORK								
Moynihan	Y	Y	Y	Y	Y	Y	N	N
D'Amato	N	N	N	N	N	N	Y	Y
NORTH CAROLINA								
Faircloth	N	N	N	N	N	N	Y	Y
Helms	N	N	N	N	N	N	Y	Y
NORTH DAKOTA								
Conrad	Y	Y	Y	Y	Y	Y	Y	N
Dorgan	Y	Y	Y	Y	Y	Y	Y	N
OHIO								
Glenn	Y	Y	Y	Y	Y	Y	Y	N
Metzenbaum	Y	Y	?	Y	Y	Y	Y	N
OKLAHOMA								
Boren	Y	Y	Y	Y	Y	Y	Y	N
Nickles	N	N	N	N	N	N	Y	Y
OREGON								
Hatfield	Y	N	Y	Y	Y	Y	Y	N
Packwood	N	N	N	Y	Y	Y	Y	Y
PENNSYLVANIA								
Wofford	Y	Y	Y	Y	Y	Y	Y	N
Specter	N	N	N	N	N	N	Y	N
RHODE ISLAND								
Pell	Y	Y	Y	Y	Y	Y	Y	N
Chafee	N	?	N	N	N	N	N	Y
SOUTH CAROLINA								
Hollings	Y	Y	Y	Y	Y	Y	Y	N
Thurmond	N	N	N	N	N	N	Y	Y
SOUTH DAKOTA								
Daschle	Y	Y	Y	Y	Y	Y	Y	N
Pressler	N	?	?	?	?	?	Y	Y
TENNESSEE								
Mathews	Y	Y	Y	Y	Y	Y	Y	N
Sasser	Y	Y	Y	Y	Y	Y	Y	N
TEXAS								
Gramm	N	N	N	N	N	N	Y	Y
Hutchison								
UTAH								
Bennett	N	N	N	−	N	N	Y	Y
Hatch	N	N	N	N	N	N	Y	Y
VERMONT								
Leahy	Y	Y	Y	Y	Y	Y	Y	N
Jeffords	Y	N	N	N	Y	Y	Y	Y
VIRGINIA								
Robb	Y	Y	Y	Y	Y	Y	N	?
Warner	N	N	N	N	N	N	Y	Y
WASHINGTON								
Murray	Y	Y	Y	Y	Y	Y	Y	N
Gorton	N	N	N	N	N	N	Y	Y
WEST VIRGINIA								
Byrd	Y	Y	Y	Y	Y	Y	Y	N
Rockefeller	Y	Y	Y	Y	Y	Y	N	N
WISCONSIN								
Feingold	Y	Y	Y	Y	Y	Y	N	N
Kohl	Y	Y	Y	Y	Y	Y	Y	N
WYOMING								
Simpson	N	N	N	N	N	N	Y	Y
Wallop	N	N	N	N	N	N	Y	Y

ND Northern Democrats   SD Southern Democrats

Southern states - Ala., Ark., Fla., Ga., Ky., La., Miss., N.C., Okla., S.C., Tenn., Texas, Va.

33. S 460. National 'Motor Voter' Registration/Cloture. Motion to invoke cloture (thus limiting debate) on the bill to require states to allow citizens to register to vote while applying for or renewing driver's licenses. Motion rejected 59-41: R 2-41; D 57-0 (ND 42-0, SD 15-0), March 16, 1993. A three-fifths majority vote of the total Senate (60) is required to invoke cloture.

34. S 460. National 'Motor Voter' Registration/Penalties. Ford, D-Ky., motion to table (kill) the Simpson, R-Wyo., amendment to provide civil penalties for falsely claiming to be a U.S. citizen. Motion agreed to 58-40: R 1-40; D 57-0 (ND 42-0, SD 15-0), March 17, 1993.

35. S 460. National 'Motor Voter' Registration/Fraudulent Registrations. Ford, D-Ky., motion to table (kill) the Simpson, R-Wyo., amendment to terminate the mail registration and agency registration sections of the bill if a study finds that more than 3 percent of registered voters in federal elections are non-citizens or were fraudulently registered. Motion agreed to 58-40: R 2-40; D 56-0 (ND 41-0, SD 15-0), March 17, 1993.

36. S 460. National 'Motor Voter' Registration/Military Registration. Ford, D-Ky., motion to table (kill) the McCain, R-Ariz., amendment to require the registration of people in the military and people being inducted into the military at the time and place of induction. Motion agreed to 58-40: R 2-39; D 56-1 (ND 41-1, SD 15-0), March 17, 1993.

37. S 460. National 'Motor Voter' Registration/State Exemption. Ford, D-Ky., motion to table (kill) the Helms, R-N.C., amendment to exempt a state from the bill if the governor certifies that the state would have to raise taxes in order to comply. Motion agreed to 59-39: R 4-38; D 55-1 (ND 41-0, SD 14-1), March 17, 1993.

38. HR 2. National 'Motor Voter' Registration/Passage. Passage of the bill to require states to allow citizens to register to vote while applying for or renewing driver's licenses or through the mail. The bill would allow states the option of registering people at other public agencies. Passed 62-37: R 5-37; D 57-0 (ND 42-0, SD 15-0), March 17, 1993. (Before passage, the Senate struck all after the enacting clause and inserted the text of S 460 as amended.) A "yea" was a vote in support of the president's position.

39. S Con Res 18. Fiscal 1994 Budget Resolution/Barge Tax. Harkin, D-Iowa, amendment to express the sense of the Senate that nothing in the resolution assumes an increase in the tax on diesel fuel used by barges that transport goods along the inland waterways. Adopted 88-12: R 41-2; D 47-10 (ND 34-8, SD 13-2), March 18, 1993.

40. S Con Res 18. Fiscal 1994 Budget Resolution/Energy Tax. Nickles, R-Okla., amendment to cut $72.9 billion over five years from the revenue account in the resolution to reflect elimination of any new energy (Btu) tax and to cut an equal amount in spending in order to maintain the overall deficit reduction targets. Rejected 46-53: R 43-0; D 3-53 (ND 0-42, SD 3-11), March 18, 1993. A "nay" was a vote in support of the president's position.

	41	42	43	44	45	46	47	48
ALABAMA								
Heflin	Y	N	Y	N	Y	Y	Y	Y
Shelby	Y	N	N	N	Y	Y	Y	N
ALASKA								
Murkowski	Y	N	N	N	N	Y	Y	N
Stevens	?	?	N	N	N	Y	Y	N
ARIZONA								
DeConcini	Y	N	Y	Y	Y	N	Y	N
McCain	Y	N	N	N	N	Y	Y	N
ARKANSAS								
Bumpers	Y	Y	Y	Y	Y	Y	N	Y
Pryor	Y	Y	Y	Y	Y	Y	N	Y
CALIFORNIA								
Boxer	Y	Y	Y	Y	Y	N	N	Y
Feinstein	Y	Y	Y	Y	Y	Y	N	Y
COLORADO								
Campbell	Y	Y	Y	Y	Y	Y	Y	Y
Brown	Y	N	N	N	N	N	Y	N
CONNECTICUT								
Dodd	Y	Y	Y	Y	Y	Y	N	Y
Lieberman	Y	Y	Y	N	N	Y	Y	Y
DELAWARE								
Biden	Y	Y	Y	N	Y	N	N	Y
Roth	N	N	N	Y	Y	N	Y	Y
FLORIDA								
Graham	Y	Y	Y	Y	Y	Y	Y	Y
Mack	Y	N	N	N	N	N	N	Y
GEORGIA								
Nunn	Y	N	Y	N	Y	Y	Y	Y
Coverdell	Y	N	N	N	N	N	Y	N
HAWAII								
Akaka	Y	Y	Y	Y	Y	Y	Y	Y
Inouye	Y	Y	Y	Y	?	?	?	?
IDAHO								
Craig	Y	N	N	N	N	Y	Y	N
Kempthorne	Y	N	N	N	Y	N	Y	N
ILLINOIS								
Moseley-Braun	Y	Y	Y	Y	Y	N	N	Y
Simon	Y	Y	Y	Y	Y	N	N	Y
INDIANA								
Coats	Y	N	N	Y	N	Y	Y	N
Lugar	Y	N	N	Y	N	Y	Y	N
IOWA								
Harkin	Y	Y	Y	Y	Y	N	N	Y
Grassley	Y	N	N	Y	N	N	Y	N
KANSAS								
Dole	N	N	N	Y	N	Y	Y	N
Kassebaum	N	Y	N	N	N	Y	Y	N
KENTUCKY								
Ford	Y	Y	Y	Y	Y	Y	Y	N
McConnell	Y	N	N	N	N	Y	Y	N
LOUISIANA								
Breaux	Y	Y	Y	N	Y	Y	Y	N
Johnston	Y	Y	Y	N	Y	Y	Y	N
MAINE								
Mitchell	Y	Y	Y	Y	Y	Y	N	Y
Cohen	Y	N	N	N	N	Y	Y	Y
MARYLAND								
Mikulski	?	?	Y	Y	Y	Y	N	Y
Sarbanes	Y	Y	Y	Y	Y	Y	N	Y
MASSACHUSETTS								
Kennedy	Y	Y	Y	Y	Y	N	N	Y
Kerry	Y	Y	Y	N	Y	N	N	Y
MICHIGAN								
Levin	Y	Y	Y	Y	Y	Y	Y	N
Riegle	Y	Y	Y	Y	Y	Y	N	Y
MINNESOTA								
Wellstone	Y	Y	Y	Y	Y	N	N	Y
Durenberger	Y	N	N	Y	N	Y	Y	Y
MISSISSIPPI								
Cochran	Y	N	N	N	N	Y	Y	N
Lott	?	?	N	N	N	Y	Y	N
MISSOURI								
Bond	Y	N	N	N	N	Y	Y	N
Danforth	N	N	N	N	N	Y	Y	N
MONTANA								
Baucus	Y	Y	Y	Y	Y	Y	N	Y
Burns	Y	N	N	Y	N	Y	Y	N
NEBRASKA								
Exon	Y	Y	Y	Y	Y	Y	Y	Y
Kerrey	Y	Y	Y	Y	Y	Y	N	Y
NEVADA								
Bryan	Y	Y	Y	Y	Y	Y	Y	Y
Reid	Y	Y	Y	N	Y	Y	N	Y
NEW HAMPSHIRE								
Gregg	N	N	N	N	N	N	Y	N
Smith	N	N	N	N	N	Y	Y	N
NEW JERSEY								
Bradley	Y	Y	Y	N	Y	N	N	Y
Lautenberg	Y	Y	Y	N	N	N	N	Y
NEW MEXICO								
Bingaman	Y	Y	Y	N	Y	Y	Y	Y
Domenici	Y	N	N	N	N	Y	Y	N
NEW YORK								
Moynihan	Y	Y	Y	Y	Y	N	N	Y
D'Amato	Y	N	N	N	N	Y	Y	N
NORTH CAROLINA								
Faircloth	N	N	N	N	N	N	Y	N
Helms	N	N	N	N	N	Y	Y	N
NORTH DAKOTA								
Conrad	Y	Y	Y	Y	Y	Y	N	Y
Dorgan	Y	Y	Y	Y	Y	N	N	Y
OHIO								
Glenn	Y	Y	Y	Y	Y	N	N	Y
Metzenbaum	Y	Y	Y	N	N	N	N	Y
OKLAHOMA								
Boren	Y	Y	Y	N	Y	Y	Y	N
Nickles	N	N	N	N	N	Y	Y	N
OREGON								
Hatfield	Y	N	N	N	N	N	N	N
Packwood	N	N	N	N	N	N	Y	N
PENNSYLVANIA								
Wofford	Y	?	Y	N	Y	Y	N	Y
Specter	Y	Y	N	N	N	Y	Y	N
RHODE ISLAND								
Pell	Y	Y	Y	Y	Y	Y	N	Y
Chafee	Y	Y	N	N	N	Y	Y	Y
SOUTH CAROLINA								
Hollings	Y	Y	Y	Y	Y	N	N	Y
Thurmond	Y	N	N	N	N	Y	Y	N
SOUTH DAKOTA								
Daschle	Y	Y	Y	Y	Y	Y	N	Y
Pressler	Y	N	N	Y	N	Y	Y	N
TENNESSEE								
Mathews	Y	Y	Y	Y	Y	N	N	Y
Sasser	Y	Y	Y	Y	Y	Y	N	Y
TEXAS								
Krueger	Y	Y	Y	N	Y	Y	Y	Y
Gramm	Y	N	N	N	N	N	Y	N
UTAH								
Bennett	Y	N	N	N	N	Y	Y	N
Hatch	N	N	N	N	N	Y	Y	N
VERMONT								
Leahy	Y	Y	Y	N	Y	Y	N	Y
Jeffords	Y	Y	N	Y	Y	Y	Y	Y
VIRGINIA								
Robb	Y	Y	Y	N	Y	Y	Y	Y
Warner	Y	N	N	N	N	Y	Y·	N
WASHINGTON								
Murray	Y	Y	Y	Y	Y	N	N	Y
Gorton	Y	N	N	N	N	Y	Y	N
WEST VIRGINIA								
Byrd	Y	Y	Y	Y	Y	Y	N	Y
Rockefeller	?	Y	Y	Y	Y	Y	N	Y
WISCONSIN								
Feingold	Y	Y	Y	N	N	N	N	Y
Kohl	Y	N	Y	N	Y	N	N	Y
WYOMING								
Simpson	Y	N	N	N	N	Y	Y	N
Wallop	N	N	N	N	N	Y	Y	N

KEY

Y	Voted for (yea).
#	Paired for.
+	Announced for.
N	Voted against (nay).
X	Paired against.
−	Announced against.
P	Voted ''present.''
C	Voted ''present'' to avoid possible conflict of interest.
?	Did not vote or otherwise make a position known.

Democrats *Republicans*

ND Northern Democrats   SD Southern Democrats   Southern states - Ala., Ark., Fla., Ga., Ky., La., Miss., N.C., Okla., S.C., Tenn., Texas, Va.

41. S Con Res 18. Fiscal 1994 Budget Resolution/Head Start. Kennedy, D-Mass., amendment to ensure full funding for the Head Start program by fiscal 1998. Adopted 84-12: R 29-12; D 55-0 (ND 40-0, SD 15-0), March 19, 1993.

42. S Con Res 18. Fiscal 1994 Budget Resolution/Domestic Spending Freeze. Sasser, D-Tenn., motion to table (kill) the Grassley, R-Iowa, amendment to freeze domestic discretionary spending for five years. Motion agreed to 54-42: R 4-37; D 50-5 (ND 38-2, SD 12-3), March 19, 1993. A "yea" was a vote in support of the president's position.

43. S Con Res 18. Fiscal 1994 Budget Resolution/Community Policing. DeConcini, D-Ariz., amendment to ensure that the community policing program is funded at $1.7 billion in fiscal 1998, the full level requested by President Clinton in his investment program. Adopted 56-44: R 0-43; D 56-1 (ND 42-0, SD 14-1), March 23, 1993.

44. S Con Res 18. Fiscal 1994 Budget Resolution/Nonconventional Fuels. Wellstone, D-Minn., amendment to express the sense of the Senate that any energy (Btu) tax would not include a tax increase on non-conventional fuels, including solar, geothermal, wind, ethanol, methanol or biomass-derived fuels. Rejected 48-52: R 11-32; D 37-20 (ND 30-12, SD 7-8), March 23, 1993.

45. S Con Res 18. Fiscal 1994 Budget Resolution/Grazing Fees, Mining Royalties. Bingaman, D-N.M., amendment to express the sense of the Senate that assumptions of increased revenues from grazing fees and hard-rock mining royalties should be set at amounts to allow the mining and ranching industries to remain viable, rather than at some arbitrary revenue target. Adopted 54-45: R 2-41; D 52-4 (ND 37-4, SD 15-0), March 23, 1993.

46. S Con Res 18. Fiscal 1994 Budget Resolution/Defense Spending. Nunn, D-Ga., amendment to express the sense of the Senate that if the inflation estimates used in the president's budget are too low, then the national defense function and other appropriate budget functions should be increased accordingly, and if the federal pay freeze proposed by the president is not enacted, then pay increases for the Department of Defense should be allowed. Adopted 69-30: R 31-12; D 38-18 (ND 24-17, SD 14-1), March 23, 1993.

47. S Con Res 18. Fiscal 1994 Budget Resolution/Defense Spending. Nunn, D-Ga., amendment to express the sense of the Senate that if defense spending is reduced below the level requested by the president, the savings should be used only for deficit reduction. Adopted 56-43: R 42-1; D 14-42 (ND 8-33, SD 6-9), March 23, 1993.

48. S Con Res 18. Fiscal 1994 Budget Resolution/Revenues From Grazing, Mining, Recreation, Irrigation. Sasser, D-Tenn., motion to table (kill) the Wallop, R-Wyo., amendment to reduce the reconciliation instructions to the Energy and Natural Resources Committee by two-thirds, thereby eliminating the ability to enact the proposals to increase grazing fees, hard-rock mining royalties, recreation fees and irrigation surcharges. Motion agreed to 59-40: R 5-38; D 54-2 (ND 40-1, SD 14-1), March 23, 1993. A "yea" was a vote in support of the president's position.

KEY

- Y Voted for (yea).
- # Paired for.
- + Announced for.
- N Voted against (nay).
- X Paired against.
- — Announced against.
- P Voted "present."
- C Voted "present" to avoid possible conflict of interest.
- ? Did not vote or otherwise make a position known.

Democrats   *Republicans*

	49	50	51	52	53	54	55	56
ALABAMA								
Heflin	Y	N	Y	N	Y	N	N	Y
Shelby	Y	N	Y	N	N	N	Y	N
ALASKA								
Murkowski	N	N	Y	N	N	N	N	N
Stevens	N	N	Y	N	N	N	N	N
ARIZONA								
DeConcini	Y	Y	Y	Y	Y	Y	N	Y
McCain	N	N	Y	N	N	N	N	N
ARKANSAS								
Bumpers	Y	Y	Y	Y	Y	Y	Y	Y
Pryor	Y	Y	Y	Y	Y	Y	Y	Y
CALIFORNIA								
Boxer	Y	Y	Y	Y	Y	Y	Y	Y
Feinstein	Y	Y	Y	Y	Y	Y	Y	Y
COLORADO								
Campbell	N	Y	Y	Y	Y	Y	Y	Y
Brown	N	N	Y	N	N	N	N	N
CONNECTICUT								
Dodd	Y	Y	Y	Y	Y	Y	Y	Y
Lieberman	Y	N	Y	Y	Y	Y	Y	Y
DELAWARE								
Biden	Y	Y	Y	Y	Y	Y	Y	Y
Roth	N	Y	Y	Y	N	N	N	N
FLORIDA								
Graham	Y	Y	Y	Y	Y	Y	Y	Y
Mack	N	N	Y	N	N	N	N	N
GEORGIA								
Nunn	Y	N	Y	Y	Y	Y	Y	Y
Coverdell	N	N	Y	N	N	N	N	N
HAWAII								
Akaka	Y	Y	Y	Y	Y	Y	Y	Y
Inouye	?	?	?	?	?	?	?	?
IDAHO								
Craig	N	N	Y	N	N	N	N	N
Kempthorne	N	N	Y	N	N	N	N	N
ILLINOIS								
Moseley-Braun	Y	Y	Y	Y	Y	Y	Y	Y
Simon	Y	Y	?	Y	Y	Y	Y	Y
INDIANA								
Coats	N	N	Y	N	N	N	N	N
Lugar	N	N	Y	N	N	N	N	N

	49	50	51	52	53	54	55	56
IOWA								
Harkin	Y	Y	Y	Y	Y	Y	Y	Y
Grassley	N	Y	Y	N	N	N	N	N
KANSAS								
Dole	N	N	N	N	N	N	N	N
Kassebaum	N	N	N	N	N	Y	N	N
KENTUCKY								
Ford	Y	Y	Y	Y	Y	Y	Y	Y
McConnell	N	N	Y	N	N	N	N	N
LOUISIANA								
Breaux	Y	Y	Y	Y	Y	Y	Y	Y
Johnston	Y	Y	Y	Y	Y	Y	Y	Y
MAINE								
Mitchell	Y	Y	Y	Y	Y	Y	Y	Y
Cohen	N	N	Y	N	N	Y	N	N
MARYLAND								
Mikulski	Y	Y	Y	Y	Y	Y	Y	Y
Sarbanes	Y	Y	Y	Y	Y	Y	Y	Y
MASSACHUSETTS								
Kennedy	Y	Y	Y	Y	Y	Y	Y	Y
Kerry	Y	Y	Y	Y	Y	Y	Y	Y
MICHIGAN								
Levin	Y	Y	Y	Y	Y	Y	Y	Y
Riegle	Y	Y	Y	Y	Y	Y	Y	Y
MINNESOTA								
Wellstone	Y	Y	Y	Y	Y	Y	Y	Y
Durenberger	N	Y	Y	N	N	Y	N	N
MISSISSIPPI								
Cochran	N	N	Y	N	N	Y	N	N
Lott	N	N	N	N	N	N	N	N
MISSOURI								
Bond	N	N	Y	N	N	Y	N	N
Danforth	N	N	N	N	N	N	N	N
MONTANA								
Baucus	Y	Y	Y	Y	Y	Y	Y	Y
Burns	N	N	Y	N	N	Y	N	N
NEBRASKA								
Exon	Y	Y	Y	Y	Y	Y	Y	N
Kerrey	Y	Y	Y	Y	Y	Y	Y	Y
NEVADA								
Bryan	Y	Y	Y	Y	Y	Y	Y	Y
Reid	Y	Y	Y	Y	Y	Y	Y	Y

	49	50	51	52	53	54	55	56
NEW HAMPSHIRE								
Gregg	N	N	N	N	N	N	N	N
Smith	N	N	?	N	N	N	N	N
NEW JERSEY								
Bradley	Y	Y	Y	Y	Y	Y	Y	Y
Lautenberg	Y	Y	Y	Y	Y	Y	Y	Y
NEW MEXICO								
Bingaman	Y	Y	Y	Y	Y	Y	Y	Y
Domenici	N	N	N	N	N	Y	N	N
NEW YORK								
Moynihan	Y	Y	Y	Y	Y	Y	Y	Y
D'Amato	N	N	Y	N	N	Y	N	N
NORTH CAROLINA								
Faircloth	N	N	N	N	N	N	N	N
Helms	N	N	N	N	N	N	N	N
NORTH DAKOTA								
Conrad	N	Y	Y	Y	Y	Y	Y	Y
Dorgan	N	Y	Y	Y	Y	Y	Y	Y
OHIO								
Glenn	Y	Y	Y	Y	Y	Y	Y	Y
Metzenbaum	Y	Y	Y	Y	Y	Y	Y	Y
OKLAHOMA								
Boren	Y	Y	Y	Y	Y	Y	Y	Y
Nickles	N	N	N	N	N	N	N	N
OREGON								
Hatfield	N	Y	Y	N	N	Y	N	N
Packwood	N	Y	N	N	N	N	N	N
PENNSYLVANIA								
Wofford	Y	Y	Y	Y	Y	Y	Y	Y
Specter	N	N	Y	N	N	Y	N	Y
RHODE ISLAND								
Pell	Y	Y	Y	Y	Y	Y	Y	Y
Chafee	N	N	Y	N	N	Y	N	N
SOUTH CAROLINA								
Hollings	Y	Y	Y	Y	Y	Y	Y	Y
Thurmond	N	N	N	N	N	Y	N	N
SOUTH DAKOTA								
Daschle	Y	Y	Y	Y	Y	Y	Y	Y
Pressler	N	N	Y	N	N	Y	N	N
TENNESSEE								
Mathews	Y	Y	Y	Y	Y	Y	Y	Y
Sasser	Y	Y	Y	Y	Y	Y	Y	Y

	49	50	51	52	53	54	55	56
TEXAS								
Krueger	Y	Y	Y	N	Y	Y	N	Y
Gramm	N	N	N	N	N	N	N	N
UTAH								
Bennett	N	N	Y	N	N	N	N	N
Hatch	N	N	Y	N	N	N	N	N
VERMONT								
Leahy	Y	Y	Y	Y	Y	Y	Y	Y
Jeffords	N	Y	Y	Y	N	Y	N	N
VIRGINIA								
Robb	N	Y	Y	Y	Y	Y	Y	Y
Warner	N	N	Y	N	N	Y	N	N
WASHINGTON								
Murray	Y	Y	Y	Y	Y	Y	Y	Y
Gorton	N	N	Y	N	N	N	N	N
WEST VIRGINIA								
Byrd	Y	Y	Y	Y	Y	Y	Y	Y
Rockefeller	Y	Y	Y	Y	Y	Y	Y	Y
WISCONSIN								
Feingold	Y	Y	Y	Y	Y	Y	Y	Y
Kohl	N	Y	Y	Y	Y	Y	Y	Y
WYOMING								
Simpson	N	N	Y	N	N	N	N	N
Wallop	N	N	N	N	N	N	N	N

ND Northern Democrats   SD Southern Democrats   Southern states - Ala., Ark., Fla., Ga., Ky., La., Miss., N.C., Okla., S.C., Tenn., Texas, Va.

49. S Con Res 18. Fiscal 1994 Budget Resolution/Government Funding. Sasser, D-Tenn., motion to table (kill) the Brown, R-Colo., amendment to reduce government overhead by $16.6 billion over five years by freezing federal department and agency overhead expenses for two years and allowing only for an inflation increase for the three following years. Motion agreed to 51-48: R 0-43; D 51-5 (ND 37-4, SD 14-1), March 23, 1993.

50. S Con Res 18. Fiscal 1994 Budget Resolution/Defense Spending. Sasser, D-Tenn., motion to table (kill) the Domenici, R-N.M., amendment to increase defense spending over five years by $67.4 billion in budget authority and $57.1 billion in outlays and cut domestic spending accounts by the same amount, placing defense spending at a level consistent with $50 billion in cuts proposed by former President George Bush plus cuts of $60 billion proposed by President Clinton during the campaign. Motion agreed to 58-41: R 6-37; D 52-4 (ND 40-1, SD 12-3), March 23, 1993. A "yea" was a vote in support of the president's position.

51. S Con Res 18. Fiscal 1994 Budget Resolution/WIC. Leahy, D-Vt., amendment to ensure that the Women, Infants and Children (WIC) feeding program will be funded at the full level requested by the president in fiscal 1998. Adopted 82-15: R 27-15; D 55-0 (ND 40-0, SD 15-0), March 23, 1993.

52. S Con Res 18. Fiscal 1994 Budget Resolution/Barge Tax. Sasser, D-Tenn., motion to table (kill) the Gorton, R-Wash., amendment to reduce the amount the Finance Committee is directed to raise in taxes by $790 million and reduce the domestic discretionary spending account by the same amount; $790 million is the amount proposed to be raised from a tax on diesel fuel used by barges that transport goods along the inland waterways. Motion agreed to 55-44: R 2-41; D 53-3 (ND 41-0, SD 12-3), March 23, 1993.

53. S Con Res 18. Fiscal 1994 Budget Resolution/Airline Fuel Tax. Sasser, D-Tenn., motion to table (kill) the Murkowski, R-Alaska, amendment to reduce the revenues assumed to be raised by the energy (Btu) tax by $4.5 billion over five years and to exempt airline fuel from the tax and cut discretionary spending by the same amount. Motion agreed to 55-44: R 0-43; D 55-1 (ND 41-0, SD 14-1), March 23, 1993.

54. S Con Res 18. Fiscal 1994 Budget Resolution/Defense Conversion. Bingaman, D-N.M., amendment to ensure that defense conversion programs will be fully funded by fiscal 1998 at the levels requested by the president. Adopted 70-29: R 15-28; D 55-1 (ND 41-0, SD 14-1), March 23, 1993.

55. S Con Res 18. Fiscal 1994 Budget Resolution/Taxes on Small Businesses, Family Farms. Sasser, D-Tenn., motion to table (kill) the Pressler, R-S.D., amendment to express the sense of the Senate that tax increases on small businesses or family farms should not be above the highest corporate tax rate. Motion agreed to 52-47: R 0-43; D 52-4 (ND 40-1, SD 12-3), March 23, 1993.

56. S Con Res 18. Fiscal 1994 Budget Resolution/Education Spending. Simon, D-Ill., amendment to ensure full funding for education reforms at the level requested by the president for fiscal 1998. Adopted 56-43: R 1-42; D 55-1 (ND 40-1, SD 15-0), March 23, 1993.

	57	58	59	60	61	62	63	64
ALABAMA								
Heflin	N	Y	Y	N	N	Y	Y	Y
Shelby	N	Y	N	Y	N	Y	Y	Y
ALASKA								
Murkowski	N	N	N	Y	N	Y	Y	Y
Stevens	N	N	N	Y	Y	Y	Y	Y
ARIZONA								
DeConcini	N	Y	Y	N	Y	Y	Y	Y
McCain	N	N	N	Y	N	Y	Y	Y
ARKANSAS								
Bumpers	Y	Y	Y	N	Y	Y	Y	Y
Pryor	Y	Y	Y	N	Y	Y	Y	Y
CALIFORNIA								
Boxer	Y	Y	Y	N	Y	Y	Y	Y
Feinstein	Y	Y	Y	N	Y	Y	Y	Y
COLORADO								
Campbell	Y	Y	Y	N	Y	Y	Y	Y
Brown	N	Y	N	Y	N	Y	Y	Y
CONNECTICUT								
Dodd	Y	Y	Y	N	Y	Y	Y	Y
Lieberman	Y	Y	Y	N	Y	Y	Y	Y
DELAWARE								
Biden	Y	Y	Y	N	Y	Y	Y	Y
Roth	N	N	N	Y	Y	Y	Y	Y
FLORIDA								
Graham	Y	Y	Y	N	Y	Y	Y	Y
Mack	N	N	N	Y	N	Y	Y	Y
GEORGIA								
Nunn	Y	Y	Y	N	N	Y	Y	Y
Coverdell	N	N	N	Y	N	Y	Y	Y
HAWAII								
Akaka	Y	Y	Y	N	Y	Y	Y	Y
Inouye	?	?	?	?	?	?	?	?
IDAHO								
Craig	N	N	N	Y	N	Y	Y	Y
Kempthorne	N	N	N	Y	N	Y	Y	Y
ILLINOIS								
Moseley-Braun	Y	Y	Y	N	Y	Y	Y	Y
Simon	Y	Y	Y	N	Y	Y	Y	Y
INDIANA								
Coats	N	N	N	Y	N	Y	Y	Y
Lugar	N	Y	N	Y	N	Y	Y	Y

	57	58	59	60	61	62	63	64
IOWA								
Harkin	Y	Y	Y	N	Y	Y	Y	Y
Grassley	N	N	N	Y	N	Y	Y	Y
KANSAS								
Dole	N	N	N	Y	N	Y	Y	Y
Kassebaum	N	Y	N	Y	N	N	Y	Y
KENTUCKY								
Ford	Y	Y	Y	N	Y	Y	Y	Y
McConnell	N	N	N	Y	N	Y	Y	Y
LOUISIANA								
Breaux	Y	Y	Y	N	N	Y	Y	Y
Johnston	Y	Y	Y	N	Y	Y	Y	Y
MAINE								
Mitchell	Y	Y	Y	N	Y	Y	Y	Y
Cohen	N	Y	N	Y	Y	Y	Y	Y
MARYLAND								
Mikulski	Y	Y	Y	N	Y	Y	Y	Y
Sarbanes	Y	Y	Y	N	Y	Y	Y	Y
MASSACHUSETTS								
Kennedy	Y	Y	Y	N	Y	Y	Y	Y
Kerry	Y	Y	Y	N	Y	Y	Y	Y
MICHIGAN								
Levin	Y	Y	Y	N	Y	Y	Y	Y
Riegle	Y	Y	Y	N	Y	Y	Y	Y
MINNESOTA								
Wellstone	Y	Y	Y	N	Y	Y	Y	Y
Durenberger	N	N	N	Y	Y	Y	Y	Y
MISSISSIPPI								
Cochran	N	N	N	Y	N	Y	Y	Y
Lott	N	N	N	Y	N	Y	Y	Y
MISSOURI								
Bond	N	N	N	Y	Y	Y	Y	Y
Danforth	N	N	N	Y	N	N	N	N
MONTANA								
Baucus	Y	Y	Y	N	Y	Y	Y	Y
Burns	N	N	N	Y	Y	Y	Y	Y
NEBRASKA								
Exon	Y	Y	Y	N	Y	Y	Y	Y
Kerrey	Y	Y	Y	N	N	Y	Y	Y
NEVADA								
Bryan	Y	Y	Y	N	Y	Y	Y	Y
Reid	Y	Y	Y	N	Y	Y	Y	Y

	57	58	59	60	61	62	63	64
NEW HAMPSHIRE								
Gregg	N	Y	N	Y	Y	Y	N	Y
Smith	N	N	N	Y	Y	Y	N	Y
NEW JERSEY								
Bradley	Y	Y	Y	N	Y	Y	N	Y
Lautenberg	Y	Y	Y	N	Y	Y	N	Y
NEW MEXICO								
Bingaman	Y	Y	Y	N	Y	Y	Y	Y
Domenici	N	N	N	Y	N	Y	Y	Y
NEW YORK								
Moynihan	Y	Y	Y	N	Y	Y	Y	Y
D'Amato	N	N	N	Y	Y	Y	Y	Y
NORTH CAROLINA								
Faircloth	N	N	N	Y	N	Y	Y	N
Helms	N	N	N	Y	N	Y	Y	N
NORTH DAKOTA								
Conrad	Y	Y	Y	N	Y	Y	Y	Y
Dorgan	Y	Y	Y	N	Y	Y	Y	Y
OHIO								
Glenn	Y	Y	Y	N	N	Y	Y	Y
Metzenbaum	Y	Y	Y	N	Y	Y	Y	Y
OKLAHOMA								
Boren	Y	Y	Y	N	Y	Y	Y	Y
Nickles	N	N	N	Y	Y	Y	Y	Y
OREGON								
Hatfield	N	Y	N	Y	N	Y	Y	Y
Packwood	N	Y	N	Y	N	Y	Y	Y
PENNSYLVANIA								
Wofford	Y	Y	Y	N	Y	Y	Y	Y
Specter	N	Y	N	Y	Y	Y	Y	Y
RHODE ISLAND								
Pell	Y	Y	Y	N	Y	Y	Y	Y
Chafee	N	Y	N	Y	Y	Y	Y	Y
SOUTH CAROLINA								
Hollings	Y	Y	Y	N	Y	Y	Y	Y
Thurmond	N	N	N	Y	N	Y	Y	Y
SOUTH DAKOTA								
Daschle	Y	Y	Y	N	Y	Y	Y	Y
Pressler	N	Y	N	Y	Y	Y	Y	Y
TENNESSEE								
Mathews	Y	Y	Y	N	Y	Y	Y	Y
Sasser	Y	Y	Y	N	Y	Y	Y	Y

	57	58	59	60	61	62	63	64
TEXAS								
Krueger	N	Y	Y	N	N	Y	Y	Y
Gramm	N	N	N	Y	N	Y	Y	Y
UTAH								
Bennett	N	N	N	Y	N	Y	Y	Y
Hatch	N	N	N	Y	N	Y	Y	Y
VERMONT								
Leahy	Y	Y	Y	N	Y	Y	Y	Y
Jeffords	N	Y	N	N	Y	N	Y	Y
VIRGINIA								
Robb	Y	N	Y	N	N	Y	N	Y
Warner	N	Y	N	Y	N	Y	Y	Y
WASHINGTON								
Murray	Y	Y	Y	N	Y	Y	Y	Y
Gorton	N	N	N	Y	N	Y	Y	Y
WEST VIRGINIA								
Byrd	Y	Y	Y	N	Y	Y	Y	Y
Rockefeller	Y	Y	Y	N	Y	Y	Y	Y
WISCONSIN								
Feingold	Y	Y	Y	N	Y	Y	Y	Y
Kohl	Y	Y	Y	N	Y	Y	Y	Y
WYOMING								
Simpson	N	N	N	Y	N	Y	Y	Y
Wallop	N	N	N	Y	N	Y	Y	N

ND Northern Democrats   SD Southern Democrats

Southern states - Ala., Ark., Fla., Ga., Ky., La., Miss., N.C., Okla., S.C., Tenn., Texas, Va.

57. S Con Res 18. Fiscal 1994 Budget Resolution/Social Security Taxes. Sasser, D-Tenn., motion to table (kill) the Lott, R-Miss., amendment to eliminate the instructions to the Finance Committee for a $32 billion tax increase over five years on Social Security beneficiaries, to be derived by increasing the amount of benefits subject to tax. The amendment would have cut new spending by the same amount in order to meet the same deficit-reduction targets in the resolution. Motion agreed to 52-47: R 0-43; D 52-4 (ND 40-1, SD 12-3), March 24, 1993. A "yea" was a vote in support of the president's position.

58. S Con Res 18. Fiscal 1994 Budget Resolution/Social Security Taxes. Lautenberg, D-N.J., amendment to express the sense of the Senate that the Finance Committee should make every effort to find additional sources of revenue before imposing new taxes on Social Security recipients. Adopted 67-32: R 12-31; D 55-1 (ND 41-0, SD 14-1), March 24, 1993.

59. S Con Res 18. Fiscal 1994 Budget Resolution/Tax Increases. Sasser, D-Tenn., motion to table (kill) the Gramm, R-Texas, amendment to eliminate the individual income tax increase, the energy tax increase and the increased tax on Social Security recipients and cut an equivalent amount of new spending to achieve the same amount of deficit reduction as the resolution. Motion agreed to 55-44: R 0-43; D 55-1 (ND 41-0, SD 14-1), March 24, 1993. A "yea" was a vote in support of the president's position.

60. S Con Res 18. Fiscal 1994 Budget Resolution/Tax Increases, Spending Cuts. Dole, R-Kan., substitute amendment to eliminate all of the new taxes and spending proposed by the administration and reduce the deficit by $460 billion over five years through spending cuts and caps on entitlements. Rejected 42-57: R 41-2; D 1-55 (ND 0-41, SD 1-14), March 24, 1993. A "nay" was a vote in support of the president's position.

61. S Con Res 18. Fiscal 1994 Budget Resolution/Home Heating Oil Taxes. Kennedy, D-Mass., amendment to express the sense of the Senate that the energy (Btu) tax should not apply to fuel used for home heating. Adopted 62-37: R 15-28; D 47-9 (ND 39-2, SD 8-7), March 24, 1993.

62. S Con Res 18. Fiscal 1994 Budget Resolution/Savings From Reorganizing. Krueger, D-Texas, amendment to express the sense of the Senate that any savings from reorganizing and streamlining the federal government should go first to offset the costs of the stimulus package (HR 1335) and then for deficit reduction. Adopted 96-3: R 40-3; D 56-0 (ND 41-0, SD 15-0), March 24, 1993.

63. S Con Res 18. Fiscal 1994 Budget Resolution/Energy Taxes on Agriculture. Baucus, D-Mont., amendment to express the sense of the Senate that the agriculture industry should not absorb a disproportionate amount of the energy (Btu) tax. Adopted 93-6: R 40-3; D 53-3 (ND 39-2, SD 14-1), March 24, 1993.

64. S Con Res 18. Fiscal 1994 Budget Resolution/Health Costs. Sasser, D-Tenn., amendment to express the sense of the Senate that the reductions in health costs in this budget resolution should be augmented by future savings from a comprehensive health-care reform package that will be reflected in future budget resolutions. Adopted 95-4: R 39-4; D 56-0 (ND 41-0, SD 15-0), March 24, 1993.

KEY

Y Voted for (yea).
\# Paired for.
+ Announced for.
N Voted against (nay).
X Paired against.
− Announced against.
P Voted "present."
C Voted "present" to avoid possible conflict of interest.
? Did not vote or otherwise make a position known.

Democrats   *Republicans*

	65	66	67	68	69	70	71	72
ALABAMA								
Heflin	Y	N	Y	N	N	N	N	Y
Shelby	N	N	Y	N	N	N	N	N
ALASKA								
Murkowski	N	N	Y	N	N	N	N	N
Stevens	N	N	Y	N	N	N	N	N
ARIZONA								
DeConcini	Y	Y	Y	Y	Y	Y	Y	Y
McCain	N	N	N	N	N	N	N	N
ARKANSAS								
Bumpers	Y	Y	Y	Y	Y	Y	Y	Y
Pryor	Y	Y	Y	Y	Y	Y	Y	Y
CALIFORNIA								
Boxer	Y	Y	Y	Y	Y	Y	Y	Y
Feinstein	Y	Y	Y	Y	Y	Y	Y	Y
COLORADO								
Campbell	Y	Y	Y	Y	Y	Y	Y	Y
Brown	N	N	N	N	N	N	N	N
CONNECTICUT								
Dodd	Y	Y	Y	Y	Y	Y	Y	Y
Lieberman	Y	Y	Y	Y	Y	Y	N	Y
DELAWARE								
Biden	Y	Y	Y	Y	Y	Y	Y	Y
Roth	N	N	N	N	N	N	N	N
FLORIDA								
Graham	Y	Y	Y	Y	Y	Y	Y	Y
Mack	N	N	N	N	N	N	N	N
GEORGIA								
Nunn	N	Y	Y	Y	Y	Y	N	Y
Coverdell	N	N	N	N	N	N	N	N
HAWAII								
Akaka	Y	Y	Y	Y	Y	Y	Y	Y
Inouye	\#	?	?	?	?	?	?	?
IDAHO								
Craig	N	N	N	N	N	N	N	N
Kempthorne	N	N	N	N	N	N	N	N
ILLINOIS								
Moseley-Braun	Y	Y	Y	Y	Y	Y	Y	Y
Simon	Y	Y	Y	Y	Y	Y	Y	Y
INDIANA								
Coats	N	N	Y	N	N	N	N	N
Lugar	N	N	N	N	N	N	N	N
IOWA								
Harkin	Y	Y	Y	Y	Y	Y	Y	Y
Grassley	N	N	N	N	N	N	N	N
KANSAS								
Dole	N	N	N	N	N	N	N	N
Kassebaum	N	N	N	Y	N	N	N	N
KENTUCKY								
Ford	Y	Y	Y	Y	Y	Y	Y	Y
McConnell	N	N	N	N	N	N	N	N
LOUISIANA								
Breaux	Y	Y	Y	Y	Y	Y	Y	Y
Johnston	Y	Y	Y	Y	Y	Y	Y	Y
MAINE								
Mitchell	Y	Y	Y	Y	Y	Y	Y	Y
Cohen	N	N	N	N	N	N	N	N
MARYLAND								
Mikulski	Y	Y	Y	Y	Y	Y	Y	Y
Sarbanes	Y	Y	Y	Y	Y	Y	Y	Y
MASSACHUSETTS								
Kennedy	Y	Y	Y	Y	Y	Y	Y	Y
Kerry	Y	Y	Y	Y	Y	Y	Y	Y
MICHIGAN								
Levin	Y	Y	Y	Y	Y	Y	Y	Y
Riegle	Y	Y	Y	Y	Y	Y	Y	Y
MINNESOTA								
Wellstone	Y	Y	Y	N	Y	Y	Y	Y
Durenberger	N	N	Y	N	N	N	N	N
MISSISSIPPI								
Cochran	N	N	N	N	N	N	N	N
Lott	N	N	N	N	N	N	N	N
MISSOURI								
Bond	N	N	N	N	N	N	N	N
Danforth	N	N	Y	N	N	N	N	N
MONTANA								
Baucus	Y	Y	Y	Y	Y	Y	Y	Y
Burns	N	N	N	N	N	N	N	N
NEBRASKA								
Exon	Y	Y	Y	Y	Y	Y	Y	Y
Kerrey	N	Y	Y	Y	Y	Y	Y	Y
NEVADA								
Bryan	Y	Y	Y	Y	Y	Y	Y	Y
Reid	Y	Y	Y	Y	Y	Y	Y	Y
NEW HAMPSHIRE								
Gregg	N	N	N	N	N	N	N	N
Smith	N	N	N	N	N	N	N	N
NEW JERSEY								
Bradley	Y	Y	Y	Y	Y	Y	Y	Y
Lautenberg	Y	Y	Y	Y	Y	N	Y	N
NEW MEXICO								
Bingaman	N	Y	Y	Y	Y	Y	Y	Y
Domenici	N	N	Y	N	N	N	N	N
NEW YORK								
Moynihan	Y	Y	Y	Y	Y	Y	Y	Y
D'Amato	N	N	Y	N	N	N	N	N
NORTH CAROLINA								
Faircloth	N	N	N	N	N	N	N	N
Helms	N	?	?	?	?	?	?	?
NORTH DAKOTA								
Conrad	Y	Y	Y	Y	Y	Y	Y	Y
Dorgan	Y	Y	Y	Y	Y	Y	Y	Y
OHIO								
Glenn	Y	Y	Y	Y	Y	Y	Y	N
Metzenbaum	Y	Y	Y	Y	Y	Y	Y	Y
OKLAHOMA								
Boren	X	Y	Y	Y	Y	Y	Y	Y
Nickles	N	N	N	N	N	N	N	N
OREGON								
Hatfield	N	N	Y	N	N	N	N	N
Packwood	N	N	Y	N	N	N	N	N
PENNSYLVANIA								
Wofford	Y	Y	Y	Y	Y	Y	Y	Y
Specter	N	N	Y	N	N	N	N	N
RHODE ISLAND								
Pell	Y	Y	Y	Y	Y	Y	Y	Y
Chafee	N	N	Y	N	N	N	N	Y
SOUTH CAROLINA								
Hollings	Y	Y	Y	Y	Y	Y	Y	Y
Thurmond	N	N	N	N	N	N	N	N
SOUTH DAKOTA								
Daschle	Y	Y	Y	Y	Y	Y	Y	Y
Pressler	N	N	N	N	N	N	N	N
TENNESSEE								
Mathews	Y	Y	Y	Y	Y	Y	Y	Y
Sasser	Y	Y	Y	Y	Y	Y	Y	Y
TEXAS								
Krueger	Y	Y	Y	Y	Y	Y	N	N
Gramm	N	N	N	N	N	N	N	N
UTAH								
Bennett	N	N	N	N	N	N	N	N
Hatch	N	N	N	N	N	N	N	N
VERMONT								
Leahy	Y	Y	Y	Y	Y	Y	Y	Y
Jeffords	Y	N	Y	N	N	N	N	Y
VIRGINIA								
Robb	N	Y	Y	Y	Y	Y	N	Y
Warner	N	N	N	N	N	N	N	N
WASHINGTON								
Murray	Y	Y	Y	Y	Y	Y	Y	Y
Gorton	N	N	Y	N	N	N	N	N
WEST VIRGINIA								
Byrd	Y	Y	Y	Y	Y	Y	Y	Y
Rockefeller	Y	Y	Y	Y	Y	Y	Y	Y
WISCONSIN								
Feingold	Y	Y	Y	Y	Y	Y	Y	Y
Kohl	Y	Y	Y	Y	Y	Y	Y	Y
WYOMING								
Simpson	N	N	N	N	N	N	N	N
Wallop	N	N	N	N	N	N	N	N

ND Northern Democrats   SD Southern Democrats   Southern states - Ala., Ark., Fla., Ga., Ky., La., Miss., N.C., Okla., S.C., Tenn., Texas, Va.

65. S Con Res 18. Fiscal 1994 Budget Resolution/Entitlement Cap. Sasser, D-Tenn., motion to table (kill) the Nunn, D-Ga., amendment to adjust the numbers in the budget resolution to place a cap on non-Social Security entitlements that would allow for inflation, population growth and 1 percent additional growth in fiscal 1996 and 1997. Motion agreed to 51-47: R 1-42; D 50-5 (ND 39-2, SD 11-3), March 24, 1993. A "yea" was a vote in support of the president's position.

66. S Con Res 18. Fiscal 1994 Budget Resolution/Diesel Tax Exemption for Farming. Sasser, D-Tenn., motion to table (kill) the Burns, R-Mont., amendment to reduce the revenue levels in the resolution to allow for an exemption for off-road diesel fuel used for farming from the energy (Btu) tax and cut spending by the same amount to meet the same deficit-reduction targets. Motion agreed to 54-44: R 0-42; D 54-2 (ND 41-0, SD 13-2), March 24, 1993.

67. S Con Res 18. Fiscal 1994 Budget Resolution/Davis-Bacon Repeal. Sasser, D-Tenn., motion to table (kill) the Craig, R-Idaho, amendment to repeal the Davis-Bacon Act of 1931, which sets wage standards for federal contracts, cutting the deficit by $3.3 billion over five years. Motion agreed to 69-29: R 13-29; D 56-0 (ND 41-0, SD 15-0), March 24, 1993.

68. S Con Res 18. Fiscal 1994 Budget Resolution/Ethanol Tax Exemption. Sasser, D-Tenn., motion to table (kill) the Durenberger, R-Minn., amendment to reduce the revenue levels in the resolution to allow for an exemption from the energy (Btu) tax for ethanol and cut spending by the same amount to meet the same deficit-reduction targets. Motion agreed to 55-43: R 2-40; D

53-3 (ND 40-1, SD 13-2), March 24, 1993.

69. S Con Res 18. Fiscal 1994 Budget Resolution/Civil Service Survivors' Annuities. Sasser, D-Tenn., motion to table (kill) the Stevens, R-Alaska, amendment to eliminate the assumed reduction in federal civil service survivors' annuities. Motion agreed to 54-44: R 0-42; D 54-2 (ND 41-0, SD 13-2), March 24, 1993.

70. S Con Res 18. Fiscal 1994 Budget Resolution/Home Heating Oil. Sasser, D-Tenn., motion to table (kill) the Murkowski, R-Alaska, amendment to reduce the revenue levels in the resolution to allow for an exemption for home heating oil from the proposed energy (Btu) tax. Motion agreed to 52-46: R 0-42; D 52-4 (ND 39-2, SD 13-2), March 24, 1993.

71. S Con Res 18. Fiscal 1994 Budget Resolution/Defense Spending. Sasser, D-Tenn., motion to table (kill) the Warner, R-Va., amendment to express the sense of the Senate that Congress should promptly reconsider the defense budget in the event of war, a non-democratic government in Russia, the deployment of U.S. troops for humanitarian purposes or the establishment of a hostile country with nuclear capability. Motion agreed to 50-48: R 0-42; D 50-6 (ND 40-1, SD 10-5), March 24, 1993.

72. S Con Res 18. Fiscal 1994 Budget Resolution/Pay Freeze. Sasser, D-Tenn., motion to table (kill) the McCain, R-Ariz., amendment to eliminate the proposed freeze for military and federal civilian pay in fiscal 1994 and cut spending by the same amount to meet the same deficit-reduction targets. Motion agreed to 54-44: R 2-40; D 52-4 (ND 39-2, SD 13-2), March 24, 1993.

KEY

- Y Voted for (yea).
- # Paired for.
- + Announced for.
- N Voted against (nay).
- X Paired against.
- — Announced against.
- P Voted "present."
- C Voted "present" to avoid possible conflict of interest.
- ? Did not vote or otherwise make a position known.

Democrats *Republicans*

	73	74	75	76	77	78	79	80
ALABAMA								
Heflin	N	N	Y	N	Y	N	Y	N
Shelby	N	N	Y	Y	N	N	N	N
ALASKA								
Murkowski	N	N	Y	N	N	N	N	N
Stevens	N	N	Y	N	N	N	N	N
ARIZONA								
DeConcini	Y	Y	N	N	Y	Y	Y	Y
McCain	N	N	N	N	N	Y	N	N
ARKANSAS								
Bumpers	Y	Y	N	Y	N	Y	N	Y
Pryor	Y	Y	N	Y	N	Y	N	Y
CALIFORNIA								
Boxer	Y	Y	N	Y	Y	Y	Y	Y
Feinstein	Y	Y	Y	Y	Y	N	Y	Y
COLORADO								
Campbell	Y	Y	N	Y	Y	N	Y	Y
Brown	N	N	Y	N	N	N	N	N
CONNECTICUT								
Dodd	Y	Y	N	Y	Y	N	Y	Y
Lieberman	N	Y	Y	Y	Y	N	Y	Y
DELAWARE								
Biden	Y	Y	?	Y	Y	Y	Y	Y
Roth	N	N	Y	N	N	N	N	N
FLORIDA								
Graham	Y	Y	Y	Y	Y	Y	Y	Y
Mack	N	N	Y	Y	N	N	N	N
GEORGIA								
Nunn	Y	N	Y	Y	N	Y	N	Y
Coverdell	N	N	Y	N	N	N	N	N
HAWAII								
Akaka	Y	Y	Y	Y	Y	Y	Y	Y
Inouye	?	?	?	?	?	?	?	?
IDAHO								
Craig	N	N	Y	N	N	N	N	N
Kempthorne	N	N	Y	N	N	N	N	N
ILLINOIS								
Moseley-Braun	Y	Y	Y	Y	Y	Y	Y	Y
Simon	Y	Y	Y	N	Y	Y	Y	Y
INDIANA								
Coats	—	N	Y	N	N	N	N	N
Lugar	N	N	Y	N	N	N	N	N
IOWA								
Harkin	Y	Y	N	Y	Y	Y	Y	Y
Grassley	N	N	Y	N	N	N	N	N
KANSAS								
Dole	N	N	Y	N	N	N	N	N
Kassebaum	N	N	Y	N	N	N	N	N
KENTUCKY								
Ford	Y	Y	Y	Y	Y	Y	Y	Y
McConnell	N	N	Y	N	N	N	N	N
LOUISIANA								
Breaux	Y	Y	Y	Y	Y	N	Y	Y
Johnston	Y	Y	N	Y	Y	Y	Y	Y
MAINE								
Mitchell	Y	Y	N	Y	Y	Y	Y	Y
Cohen	N	N	Y	N	N	N	N	N
MARYLAND								
Mikulski	Y	Y	Y	Y	Y	Y	Y	Y
Sarbanes	Y	Y	N	Y	Y	Y	Y	Y
MASSACHUSETTS								
Kennedy	Y	Y	Y	Y	Y	Y	Y	Y
Kerry	Y	Y	Y	Y	Y	N	Y	Y
MICHIGAN								
Levin	Y	Y	N	Y	Y	Y	Y	Y
Riegle	Y	Y	Y	Y	Y	Y	Y	Y
MINNESOTA								
Wellstone	Y	Y	Y	Y	Y	Y	Y	Y
Durenberger	N	Y	Y	N	N	N	N	N
MISSISSIPPI								
Cochran	N	N	N	N	N	N	N	N
Lott	N	N	Y	N	N	N	N	N
MISSOURI								
Bond	N	N	Y	N	N	N	N	N
Danforth	N	N	Y	N	N	N	N	N
MONTANA								
Baucus	Y	Y	N	Y	Y	Y	Y	Y
Burns	N	N	Y	N	N	N	N	N
NEBRASKA								
Exon	Y	N	Y	N	Y	N	Y	Y
Kerrey	Y	N	Y	Y	Y	N	Y	Y
NEVADA								
Bryan	Y	Y	N	Y	N	Y	N	Y
Reid	Y	Y	N	Y	Y	Y	Y	Y
NEW HAMPSHIRE								
Gregg	N	N	Y	N	N	N	N	N
Smith	N	N	Y	N	N	N	N	N
NEW JERSEY								
Bradley	Y	Y	Y	Y	Y	Y	Y	Y
Lautenberg	Y	Y	Y	Y	Y	N	Y	Y
NEW MEXICO								
Bingaman	Y	Y	N	Y	Y	Y	Y	Y
Domenici	N	N	Y	N	N	N	N	N
NEW YORK								
Moynihan	Y	Y	Y	Y	Y	N	Y	Y
D'Amato	N	N	Y	N	N	N	N	N
NORTH CAROLINA								
Faircloth	N	N	+	N	N	N	N	N
Helms	?	?	Y	N	N	N	N	N
NORTH DAKOTA								
Conrad	Y	Y	N	Y	N	Y	N	Y
Dorgan	Y	Y	Y	Y	Y	Y	Y	Y
OHIO								
Glenn	Y	N	Y	Y	Y	N	Y	Y
Metzenbaum	Y	Y	N	Y	Y	Y	Y	Y
OKLAHOMA								
Boren	Y	Y	Y	Y	Y	N	Y	Y
Nickles	N	N	Y	N	N	N	N	N
OREGON								
Hatfield	Y	N	N	N	Y	N	Y	N
Packwood	N	N	Y	N	N	N	N	N
PENNSYLVANIA								
Wofford	Y	Y	Y	Y	Y	N	Y	Y
Specter	N	N	Y	N	N	N	N	N
RHODE ISLAND								
Pell	Y	Y	Y	Y	Y	Y	Y	Y
Chafee	Y	N	Y	N	N	N	N	N
SOUTH CAROLINA								
Hollings	Y	Y	Y	Y	Y	N	Y	Y
Thurmond	N	N	Y	N	N	N	N	N
SOUTH DAKOTA								
Daschle	Y	Y	Y	Y	Y	Y	Y	Y
Pressler	N	N	Y	N	N	N	N	N
TENNESSEE								
Mathews	Y	Y	Y	Y	Y	N	Y	Y
Sasser	Y	Y	Y	Y	Y	Y	Y	Y
TEXAS								
Krueger	Y	Y	Y	Y	N	N	N	Y
Gramm	N	N	Y	N	N	N	N	N
UTAH								
Bennett	N	N	Y	N	N	N	N	N
Hatch	N	N	Y	N	N	N	N	N
VERMONT								
Leahy	Y	Y	Y	Y	Y	N	Y	Y
Jeffords	N	N	N	N	Y	N	N	Y
VIRGINIA								
Robb	Y	Y	Y	Y	Y	N	Y	Y
Warner	N	N	Y	N	N	N	N	N
WASHINGTON								
Murray	Y	Y	N	Y	Y	Y	Y	Y
Gorton	N	N	Y	N	N	N	N	N
WEST VIRGINIA								
Byrd	Y	Y	Y	Y	Y	Y	Y	Y
Rockefeller	Y	Y	N	Y	Y	Y	Y	Y
WISCONSIN								
Feingold	Y	Y	N	Y	Y	Y	Y	Y
Kohl	Y	Y	Y	Y	Y	Y	Y	Y
WYOMING								
Simpson	N	N	Y	N	N	N	N	N
Wallop	N	N	Y	N	N	N	N	N

ND Northern Democrats   SD Southern Democrats   Southern states - Ala., Ark., Fla., Ga., Ky., La., Miss., N.C., Okla., S.C., Tenn., Texas, Va.

73. S Con Res 18. Fiscal 1994 Budget Resolution/Defense Spending. Sasser, D-Tenn., motion to table (kill) the Thurmond, R-S.C., amendment to increase defense spending over five years for pay raises and cut spending to meet deficit-reduction targets. Motion agreed to 55-42: R 2-39; D 53-3 (ND 40-1, SD 13-2), March 24, 1993.

74. S Con Res 18. Fiscal 1994 Budget Resolution/Student Loans. Sasser, D-Tenn., motion to table (kill) the Kassebaum, R-Kan., amendment to reduce the revenue instructions for the Senate Labor and Human Resources Committee to allow for the implementation of a direct federal student loan program and cut spending sufficiently to meet deficit-reduction targets. Motion agreed to 51-47: R 1-41; D 50-6 (ND 38-3, SD 12-3), March 25, 1993 (in the session that began and the Congressional Record dated March 24).

75. S Con Res 18. Fiscal 1994 Budget Resolution/Line-Item Veto. Bradley, D-N.J, amendment to express the sense of the Senate supporting for the 103rd Congress a presidential line-item veto for taxes and spending. Adopted 73-24: R 38-4; D 35-20 (ND 23-17, SD 12-3), March 25, 1993.

76. S Con Res 18. Fiscal 1994 Budget Resolution/Unemployment Insurance. Sasser, D-Tenn., motion to table (kill) the Brown, R-Colo., amendment to reduce the income security function to reflect the elimination of unemployment insurance for individuals with incomes above $120,000. Motion agreed to 53-46: R 1-42; D 52-4 (ND 38-3, SD 14-1), March 25, 1993.

77. S Con Res 18. Fiscal 1994 Budget Resolution/Legislative Operations. Sasser, D-Tenn., motion to table (kill) the Kempthorne, R-Idaho, amendment to adjust the figures in the budget resolution to reflect a cut of 25 percent from the legislative branch budget in fiscal 1994. Motion agreed to 56-43: R 2-41; D 54-2 (ND 41-0, SD 13-2), March 25, 1993.

78. S Con Res 18. Fiscal 1994 Budget Resolution/Enhanced Rescission. Sasser, D-Tenn., motion to table (kill) the Cohen, R-Maine, amendment to express the sense of the Senate supporting enhanced presidential rescission authority for appropriations, tax subsidies or mandatory spending. Motion rejected 34-65: R 2-41; D 32-24 (ND 28-13, SD 4-11), March 25, 1993. (Subsequently, the Cohen amendment was adopted by voice vote.)

79. S Con Res 18. Fiscal 1994 Budget Resolution/Taxes on Small Businesses, Farms. Sasser, D-Tenn., motion to table (kill) the Gramm, R-Texas, amendment to exempt Subchapter S corporations (small business and farms) from the proposed increase in the top marginal rate on income tax and cut spending by the same amount to meet deficit-reduction targets. Motion agreed to 54-45: R 0-43; D 54-2 (ND 41-0, SD 13-2), March 25, 1993.

80. S Con Res 18. Fiscal 1994 Budget Resolution/Line-Item Veto. Sasser, D-Tenn., motion to table (kill) the Bond, R-Mo., amendment to implement a presidential line-item veto and reduce outlays and budget authority figures in the resolution by an amount equivalent to what President Clinton claimed as a candidate would be saved if that were done. Motion agreed to 57-42: R 3-40; D 54-2 (ND 41-0, SD 13-2), March 25, 1993.

SENATE VOTES 81, 82, 83, 84, 85, 86, 87, 88

Senator	81	82	83	84	85	86	87	88
ALABAMA								
Heflin	Y	N	Y	?	Y	Y	Y	N
Shelby	N	N	N	N	N	N	Y	N
ALASKA								
Murkowski	N	N	N	N	N	N	N	N
Stevens	N	N	N	N	N	N	N	N
ARIZONA								
DeConcini	N	Y	Y	?	Y	Y	Y	Y
McCain	N	N	N	N	N	N	N	N
ARKANSAS								
Bumpers	Y	Y	Y	Y	Y	Y	Y	Y
Pryor	Y	Y	Y	Y	Y	Y	Y	Y
CALIFORNIA								
Boxer	Y	Y	Y	Y	Y	Y	Y	Y
Feinstein	Y	Y	Y	Y	Y	Y	?	Y
COLORADO								
Campbell	Y	Y	Y	?	Y	Y	Y	Y
Brown	N	N	N	N	N	N	N	N
CONNECTICUT								
Dodd	Y	Y	Y	Y	Y	Y	Y	Y
Lieberman	Y	Y	Y	Y	Y	Y	Y	Y
DELAWARE								
Biden	Y	Y	Y	?	Y	Y	Y	Y
Roth	N	?	N	N	N	N	N	N
FLORIDA								
Graham	Y	Y	Y	N	N	N	Y	Y
Mack	N	N	N	N	N	N	N	N
GEORGIA								
Nunn	Y	Y	Y	N	N	N	Y	Y
Coverdell	N	N	N	N	N	N	N	N
HAWAII								
Akaka	Y	Y	Y	Y	Y	Y	Y	Y
Inouye	?	?	?	?	Y	Y	Y	Y
IDAHO								
Craig	N	N	N	N	N	N	N	N
Kempthorne	N	N	N	N	N	N	N	N
ILLINOIS								
Moseley-Braun	Y	Y	Y	Y	Y	Y	Y	Y
Simon	Y	Y	Y	Y	Y	Y	Y	Y
INDIANA								
Coats	N	N	N	N	N	N	N	N
Lugar	N	N	N	N	N	N	N	N
IOWA								
Harkin	Y	Y	Y	Y	Y	Y	Y	Y
Grassley	N	N	N	N	N	N	N	N
KANSAS								
Dole	N	N	N	N	N	N	N	N
Kassebaum	Y	Y	N	N	N	N	N	Y
KENTUCKY								
Ford	Y	Y	Y	Y	Y	Y	Y	Y
McConnell	N	N	N	N	N	N	N	N
LOUISIANA								
Breaux	Y	Y	Y	Y	Y	Y	Y	Y
Johnston	Y	Y	Y	?	Y	Y	Y	Y
MAINE								
Mitchell	Y	Y	Y	Y	Y	Y	Y	Y
Cohen	Y	N	N	N	N	N	N	N
MARYLAND								
Mikulski	Y	Y	Y	Y	Y	Y	Y	Y
Sarbanes	Y	Y	Y	Y	Y	Y	Y	Y
MASSACHUSETTS								
Kennedy	Y	Y	Y	?	Y	Y	Y	Y
Kerry	Y	Y	Y	Y	Y	Y	Y	Y
MICHIGAN								
Levin	Y	Y	Y	Y	Y	Y	Y	Y
Riegle	Y	Y	Y	Y	Y	Y	Y	Y
MINNESOTA								
Wellstone	Y	Y	Y	Y	Y	Y	Y	Y
Durenberger	N	N	N	N	N	N	N	N
MISSISSIPPI								
Cochran	N	N	N	N	N	N	N	N
Lott	N	N	N	N	N	N	N	N
MISSOURI								
Bond	N	N	N	N	N	N	N	N
Danforth	N	N	N	N	N	N	N	N
MONTANA								
Baucus	Y	Y	Y	Y	Y	Y	Y	Y
Burns	N	N	N	N	N	N	N	N
NEBRASKA								
Exon	Y	Y	Y	N	N	N	Y	Y
Kerrey	Y	Y	Y	N	N	N	Y	Y
NEVADA								
Bryan	Y	Y	Y	Y	Y	Y	Y	Y
Reid	Y	Y	Y	Y	Y	Y	Y	Y
NEW HAMPSHIRE								
Gregg	N	N	N	N	N	N	N	N
Smith	N	N	N	N	N	N	N	N
NEW JERSEY								
Bradley	Y	Y	Y	Y	Y	Y	?	Y
Lautenberg	Y	Y	Y	Y	Y	Y	Y	Y
NEW MEXICO								
Bingaman	Y	Y	Y	Y	Y	Y	Y	Y
Domenici	N	N	N	N	N	N	N	N
NEW YORK								
Moynihan	Y	Y	Y	Y	Y	Y	Y	Y
D'Amato	N	N	N	N	N	N	N	N
NORTH CAROLINA								
Faircloth	N	N	N	N	N	N	N	N
Helms	N	N	N	N	N	N	N	N
NORTH DAKOTA								
Conrad	Y	Y	Y	Y	Y	Y	Y	Y
Dorgan	Y	Y	Y	Y	Y	Y	Y	Y
OHIO								
Glenn	Y	Y	Y	Y	Y	Y	Y	Y
Metzenbaum	Y	Y	Y	Y	Y	Y	Y	Y
OKLAHOMA								
Boren	Y	Y	Y	Y	Y	Y	Y	Y
Nickles	N	N	N	N	N	N	N	N
OREGON								
Hatfield	Y	N	N	N	N	N	N	N
Packwood	N	N	N	N	N	N	N	N
PENNSYLVANIA								
Wofford	Y	Y	Y	Y	Y	Y	Y	Y
Specter	Y	Y	N	N	N	N	N	N
RHODE ISLAND								
Pell	Y	Y	Y	Y	Y	Y	Y	Y
Chafee	Y	Y	N	N	N	N	N	N
SOUTH CAROLINA								
Hollings	Y	Y	Y	Y	Y	Y	Y	Y
Thurmond	N	N	N	N	N	N	N	N
SOUTH DAKOTA								
Daschle	Y	Y	Y	Y	Y	Y	Y	Y
Pressler	N	N	N	N	N	N	N	N
TENNESSEE								
Mathews	Y	Y	Y	Y	Y	Y	Y	Y
Sasser	Y	Y	Y	Y	Y	Y	Y	Y
TEXAS								
Krueger	Y	Y	N	Y	Y	Y	?	Y
Gramm	N	N	N	N	N	N	N	N
UTAH								
Bennett	N	N	N	N	N	N	N	N
Hatch	N	N	N	N	N	N	N	N
VERMONT								
Leahy	Y	Y	Y	Y	Y	Y	Y	Y
Jeffords	Y	N	N	N	N	N	N	N
VIRGINIA								
Robb	Y	Y	Y	Y	Y	Y	Y	Y
Warner	Y	Y	N	N	N	N	N	Y
WASHINGTON								
Murray	Y	N	Y	Y	Y	Y	Y	Y
Gorton	N	N	N	?	N	N	N	N
WEST VIRGINIA								
Byrd	Y	Y	Y	N	Y	Y	Y	Y
Rockefeller	Y	Y	Y	Y	Y	Y	Y	Y
WISCONSIN								
Feingold	Y	Y	Y	Y	Y	Y	Y	Y
Kohl	Y	Y	Y	Y	Y	Y	Y	Y
WYOMING								
Simpson	N	N	N	N	N	N	N	N
Wallop	N	N	N	N	N	N	N	N

ND Northern Democrats   SD Southern Democrats   Southern states - Ala., Ark., Fla., Ga., Ky., La., Miss., N.C., Okla., S.C., Tenn., Texas, Va.

81. S Con Res 18. Fiscal 1994 Budget Resolution/Mining Royalties. Sasser, D-Tenn., motion to table (kill) the Murkowski, R-Alaska, amendment to reduce the instructions to the Energy and Natural Resources Committee by the amount assumed to be raised through increased royalties from mining on federal lands. Motion agreed to 61-38: R 7-36; D 54-2 (ND 40-1, SD 14-1), March 25, 1993.

82. S Con Res 18. Fiscal 1994 Budget Resolution/Hydroelectric Power Taxes. Sasser, D-Tenn., motion to table (kill) the Craig, R-Idaho, amendment to reduce the revenue levels in the resolution to allow for an exemption for hydroelectric power from the energy (Btu) tax and cut spending by the same amount to meet deficit-reduction targets. Motion agreed to 57-41: R 4-38; D 53-3 (ND 40-1, SD 13-2), March 25, 1993.

83. H Con Res 64. Fiscal 1994 Budget Resolution/Adoption. Adoption of the concurrent resolution to set binding budget levels for the fiscal year ending Sept. 30, 1994: budget authority, $1.505 trillion; outlays, $1.498 trillion; revenues, $1.251 trillion; deficit, $247.5 billion. (Before adoption the Senate struck all after the resolving clause and inserted the text of S Con Res 18 as amended). Adopted 54-45: R 0-43; D 54-2 (ND 41-0, SD 13-2), March 25, 1993. A "yea" was a vote in support of the president's position.

84. HR 1335. Fiscal 1993 Supplemental Appropriations/CDBGs. Byrd, D-W.Va., motion to table (kill) the Brown, R-Colo., amendment to cut $103.5 million of the $2.5 billion for Community Development Block Grants. Motion rejected 44-48: R 0-42; D 44-6 (ND 34-3, SD 10-3), March 29, 1993. (A Byrd motion to reconsider the vote was postponed until March 30.) A "yea" was a vote in support of the president's position.

85. HR 1335. Fiscal 1993 Supplemental Appropriations/Reconsider CDBG Vote. Byrd, D-W.Va., motion to reconsider the vote by which the Senate failed to agree to a Byrd motion to table (kill) the Brown, R-Colo., Community Development Block Grants amendment. Motion agreed to 52-48: R 0-43; D 52-5 (ND 40-2, SD 12-3), March 30, 1993. A "yea" was a vote in support of the president's position.

86. HR 1335. Fiscal 1993 Supplemental Appropriations/CDBGs. Byrd, D-W.Va., motion to table (kill) the Brown, R-Colo., Community Development Block Grants amendment. Motion agreed to 52-48: R 0-43; D 52-5 (ND 40-2, SD 12-3), March 30, 1993. A "yea" was a vote in support of the president's position.

87. HR 1335. Fiscal 1993 Supplemental Appropriations/CDBGs. Byrd, D-W.Va., motion to table (kill) the Nickles, R-Okla., amendment to cut the $2.5 billion in the bill for Community Development Block Grants. Motion agreed to 54-43: R 0-43; D 54-0 (ND 40-0, SD 14-0), March 30, 1993. A "yea" was a vote in support of the president's position.

88. HR 1335. Fiscal 1993 Supplemental Appropriations/D.C. Funds. Byrd, D-W.Va., motion to table (kill) the Nickles, R-Okla., amendment to eliminate the $28.2 million in the bill for the District of Columbia. Motion agreed to 57-43: R 2-41; D 55-2 (ND 42-0, SD 13-2), March 31, 1993. A "yea" was a vote in support of the president's position.

KEY

Y	Voted for (yea).
#	Paired for.
+	Announced for.
N	Voted against (nay).
X	Paired against.
−	Announced against.
P	Voted "present."
C	Voted "present" to avoid possible conflict of interest.
?	Did not vote or otherwise make a position known.

Democrats *Republicans*

Senator	89	90	91	92	93	94	95	96
ALABAMA								
Heflin	Y	Y	Y	N	N	Y	?	Y
Shelby	N	Y	N	N	N	N	N	?
ALASKA								
Murkowski	N	Y	Y	Y	N	N	N	N
Stevens	N	Y	Y	Y	N	N	N	N
ARIZONA								
DeConcini	Y	Y	Y	N	Y	Y	Y	Y
McCain	N	Y	N	N	N	N	N	N
ARKANSAS								
Bumpers	Y	N	N	Y	Y	Y	Y	Y
Pryor	Y	N	Y	Y	Y	Y	Y	Y
CALIFORNIA								
Boxer	Y	N	N	N	Y	Y	Y	Y
Feinstein	Y	N	N	N	Y	Y	Y	Y
COLORADO								
Campbell	Y	N	Y	Y	Y	Y	Y	Y
Brown	N	Y	N	Y	N	N	N	N
CONNECTICUT								
Dodd	Y	N	Y	Y	Y	Y	Y	Y
Lieberman	Y	N	Y	Y	Y	Y	Y	Y
DELAWARE								
Biden	Y	N	Y	Y	Y	Y	Y	Y
Roth	N	Y	N	Y	Y	N	N	N
FLORIDA								
Graham	Y	N	N	N	Y	Y	Y	Y
Mack	N	Y	N	N	N	N	N	N
GEORGIA								
Nunn	Y	Y	N	N	Y	Y	Y	N
Coverdell	N	Y	N	N	N	N	N	N
HAWAII								
Akaka	Y	N	Y	Y	Y	Y	Y	Y
Inouye	Y	N	Y	Y	Y	Y	Y	Y
IDAHO								
Craig	N	Y	Y	Y	N	N	N	N
Kempthorne	N	Y	Y	Y	N	N	N	N
ILLINOIS								
Moseley-Braun	Y	N	Y	Y	Y	Y	Y	Y
Simon	Y	Y	Y	Y	Y	Y	Y	Y
INDIANA								
Coats	N	Y	Y	N	Y	N	N	N
Lugar	N	Y	Y	N	Y	N	N	N
IOWA								
Harkin	Y	N	Y	Y	Y	Y	Y	Y
Grassley	N	Y	N	Y	N	N	N	N
KANSAS								
Dole	N	Y	Y	Y	N	N	N	N
Kassebaum	N	Y	N	Y	N	N	N	N
KENTUCKY								
Ford	Y	N	Y	Y	Y	Y	Y	Y
McConnell	N	Y	Y	N	N	N	N	N
LOUISIANA								
Breaux	Y	N	Y	Y	Y	Y	Y	Y
Johnston	Y	N	Y	Y	Y	Y	Y	Y
MAINE								
Mitchell	Y	N	Y	Y	Y	Y	Y	Y
Cohen	N	Y	Y	Y	Y	N	N	N
MARYLAND								
Mikulski	Y	N	Y	Y	Y	Y	Y	Y
Sarbanes	Y	N	Y	Y	Y	Y	Y	Y
MASSACHUSETTS								
Kennedy	Y	N	Y	Y	Y	Y	Y	Y
Kerry	Y	N	Y	Y	Y	Y	Y	Y
MICHIGAN								
Levin	Y	N	N	N	Y	Y	Y	Y
Riegle	Y	N	Y	N	Y	Y	Y	Y
MINNESOTA								
Wellstone	Y	N	Y	Y	Y	Y	Y	Y
Durenberger	N	Y	Y	Y	N	N	N	N
MISSISSIPPI								
Cochran	N	Y	N	N	N	N	N	N
Lott	N	Y	N	N	N	N	N	N
MISSOURI								
Bond	N	Y	Y	N	?	N	N	N
Danforth	N	Y	Y	N	N	N	N	N
MONTANA								
Baucus	Y	N	Y	Y	Y	Y	Y	Y
Burns	N	Y	Y	Y	N	N	N	N
NEBRASKA								
Exon	Y	Y	Y	Y	Y	Y	Y	Y
Kerrey	Y	N	Y	Y	Y	Y	Y	Y
NEVADA								
Bryan	Y	N	N	Y	Y	Y	Y	Y
Reid	Y	N	Y	Y	Y	Y	Y	Y
NEW HAMPSHIRE								
Gregg	N	Y	Y	Y	N	N	N	N
Smith	N	Y	Y	Y	N	N	N	N
NEW JERSEY								
Bradley	Y	N	Y	Y	Y	Y	Y	Y
Lautenberg	Y	N	Y	Y	Y	Y	Y	Y
NEW MEXICO								
Bingaman	Y	N	N	Y	Y	Y	Y	Y
Domenici	N	Y	N	Y	N	N	N	N
NEW YORK								
Moynihan	Y	N	Y	Y	Y	Y	Y	Y
D'Amato	N	Y	Y	N	N	N	N	N
NORTH CAROLINA								
Faircloth	N	N	N	N	N	N	N	N
Helms	N	N	N	N	N	N	N	N
NORTH DAKOTA								
Conrad	Y	N	Y	Y	Y	Y	Y	Y
Dorgan	Y	N	Y	Y	Y	Y	Y	Y
OHIO								
Glenn	Y	N	Y	Y	Y	Y	Y	Y
Metzenbaum	Y	N	Y	Y	Y	Y	Y	Y
OKLAHOMA								
Boren	Y	N	N	N	Y	N	Y	N
Nickles	N	Y	N	N	N	N	N	N
OREGON								
Hatfield	N	N	N	N	N	N	N	N
Packwood	N	Y	Y	N	N	N	N	N
PENNSYLVANIA								
Wofford	Y	N	Y	Y	Y	Y	Y	Y
Specter	N	Y	Y	Y	N	N	N	N
RHODE ISLAND								
Pell	Y	N	Y	Y	Y	Y	Y	Y
Chafee	N	Y	Y	Y	N	N	N	N
SOUTH CAROLINA								
Hollings	Y	N	Y	Y	Y	Y	Y	Y
Thurmond	N	Y	Y	N	N	N	N	N
SOUTH DAKOTA								
Daschle	Y	N	Y	Y	Y	Y	Y	Y
Pressler	N	Y	Y	Y	N	N	N	N
TENNESSEE								
Mathews	Y	N	Y	Y	Y	Y	Y	Y
Sasser	Y	N	N	Y	Y	Y	Y	Y
TEXAS								
Krueger	Y	N	N	N	Y	N	Y	Y
Gramm	N	Y	N	N	N	N	N	N
UTAH								
Bennett	N	Y	N	Y	N	N	N	N
Hatch	N	Y	N	Y	N	N	N	N
VERMONT								
Leahy	Y	N	N	Y	Y	Y	Y	Y
Jeffords	N	Y	Y	Y	N	N	N	N
VIRGINIA								
Robb	Y	Y	Y	N	Y	Y	Y	Y
Warner	N	Y	Y	N	N	N	N	N
WASHINGTON								
Murray	Y	N	Y	Y	Y	Y	Y	Y
Gorton	N	Y	Y	Y	N	N	N	N
WEST VIRGINIA								
Byrd	Y	N	Y	Y	Y	Y	Y	Y
Rockefeller	Y	N	Y	Y	Y	Y	Y	Y
WISCONSIN								
Feingold	Y	Y	Y	N	Y	Y	Y	Y
Kohl	Y	Y	N	N	Y	Y	Y	Y
WYOMING								
Simpson	N	Y	Y	Y	N	N	N	N
Wallop	N	Y	Y	Y	N	N	N	N

ND Northern Democrats   SD Southern Democrats   Southern states - Ala., Ark., Fla., Ga., Ky., La., Miss., N.C., Okla., S.C., Tenn., Texas, Va.

89. HR 1335. Fiscal 1993 Supplemental Appropriations/ CDBGs, Highway Trust Fund. Byrd, D-W.Va., motion to table (kill) the Gramm, R-Texas, amendment to cut $195 million in Community Development Block Grant and Highway Trust Fund spending and prohibit funds for low-priority projects. Motion agreed to 56-44: R 0-43; D 56-1 (ND 42-0, SD 14-1), March 31, 1993. A "yea" was a vote in support of the president's position.

90. HR 1335. Fiscal 1993 Supplemental Appropriations/ Budget Requirements. Kohl, D-Wis., motion to waive the budget act with respect to the Byrd, D-W.Va., point of order against the Kohl amendment for violating the 1974 Congressional Budget Act and encroaching on Budget Committee jurisdiction. Motion rejected 52-48: R 43-0; D 9-48 (ND 5-37, SD 4-11), March 31, 1993. A three-fifths vote (60) of the total Senate is required to waive the budget act. (Subsequently, the chair upheld the Byrd point of order, and the Kohl amendment fell.) A "nay" was a vote in support of the president's position.

91. HR 1335. Fiscal 1993 Supplemental Appropriations/ Highway Trust Fund. Byrd, D-W.Va., motion to table (kill) the Graham, D-Fla., amendment to give states greater flexibility to distribute Highway Trust Fund money in the bill. Motion agreed to 70-30: R 26-17; D 44-13 (ND 35-7, SD 9-6), March 31, 1993.

92. HR 1335. Fiscal 1993 Supplemental Appropriations/ Highway Trust Fund. Byrd, D-W.Va., motion to table (kill) the Graham, D-Fla., amendment to change the way federal highway money is distributed to benefit states that contribute more than they receive from the Highway Trust Fund. Motion agreed to 68-32: R 25-18; D 43-14 (ND 35-7, SD 8-7), March 31, 1993.

93. HR 1335. Fiscal 1993 Supplemental Appropriations/ Amtrak. Byrd, D-W.Va., motion to table (kill) the Danforth, R-Mo., amendment to eliminate $188 million in the bill for Amtrak. Motion agreed to 61-38: R 7-35; D 54-3 (ND 42-0, SD 12-3), March 31, 1993. A "yea" was a vote in support of the president's position.

94. H Con Res 64. Fiscal 1994 Budget Resolution/Conference Report. Adoption of the conference report on the concurrent resolution to set binding budget levels for the fiscal year ending Sept. 30, 1994: budget authority, $1.507 trillion; outlays, $1.496 trillion; revenues, $1.242 trillion; deficit, $253.8 billion. The resolution also would provide for an increase in the federal debt limit. Adopted 55-45: R 0-43; D 55-2 (ND 42-0, SD 13-2), April 1, 1993. A "yea" was a vote in support of the president's position.

95. HR 1335. Fiscal 1993 Supplemental Appropriations/ EPA Programs. Byrd, D-W.Va., motion to table (kill) the Bond, R-Mo., amendment to eliminate $23.5 million for EPA programs. Motion agreed to 55-44: R 0-43; D 55-1 (ND 42-0, SD 13-1), April 1, 1993. A "yea" was a vote in support of the president's position.

96. HR 1335. Fiscal 1993 Supplemental Appropriations/ Budget Requirements. Byrd, D-W.Va., motion to table (kill) the Nickles, R-Okla., amendment to eliminate the emergency designation, thus requiring the bill to meet the pay-as-you-go requirements to the 1990 budget agreement. Motion agreed to 54-45: R 0-43; D 54-2 (ND 42-0, SD 12-2), April 1, 1993. A "yea" was a vote in support of the president's position.

KEY

- **Y** Voted for (yea).
- **#** Paired for.
- **+** Announced for.
- **N** Voted against (nay).
- **X** Paired against.
- **−** Announced against.
- **P** Voted "present."
- **C** Voted "present" to avoid possible conflict of interest.
- **?** Did not vote or otherwise make a position known.

Democrats   *Republicans*

	97	98	99	100	101	102	103	104
ALABAMA								
Heflin	Y	Y	Y	Y	?	Y	Y	Y
Shelby	Y	N	Y	N	?	N	N	N
ALASKA								
Murkowski	N	N	Y	N	?	N	N	N
Stevens	N	N	Y	N	N	N	N	N
ARIZONA								
DeConcini	Y	Y	Y	Y	Y	?	Y	Y
McCain	N	N	N	N	−	−	N	N
ARKANSAS								
Bumpers	Y	Y	Y	Y	Y	Y	Y	Y
Pryor	Y	Y	Y	Y	Y	Y	Y	Y
CALIFORNIA								
Boxer	Y	Y	Y	Y	Y	Y	Y	Y
Feinstein	Y	Y	Y	Y	Y	Y	Y	Y
COLORADO								
Campbell	Y	N	Y	Y	Y	Y	Y	Y
Brown	N	N	Y	N	N	N	N	N
CONNECTICUT								
Dodd	Y	Y	Y	Y	Y	Y	Y	Y
Lieberman	Y	Y	Y	Y	Y	Y	Y	Y
DELAWARE								
Biden	Y	Y	Y	Y	Y	Y	Y	Y
Roth	N	N	Y	N	N	N	N	N
FLORIDA								
Graham	Y	Y	Y	Y	Y	Y	Y	Y
Mack	N	N	Y	N	N	N	N	N
GEORGIA								
Nunn	Y	N	Y	Y	?	?	N	Y
Coverdell	N	N	Y	N	N	N	N	N
HAWAII								
Akaka	Y	Y	Y	Y	Y	Y	Y	Y
Inouye	Y	Y	Y	Y	Y	Y	Y	Y
IDAHO								
Craig	N	N	N	N	N	N	N	N
Kempthorne	N	N	N	N	N	N	N	N
ILLINOIS								
Moseley-Braun	Y	Y	Y	Y	Y	Y	Y	Y
Simon	Y	Y	Y	Y	Y	Y	Y	Y
INDIANA								
Coats	N	N	Y	N	N	?	N	N
Lugar	N	N	Y	N	N	N	N	N
IOWA								
Harkin	Y	Y	Y	Y	Y	?	Y	Y
Grassley	N	N	Y	N	N	N	N	N
KANSAS								
Dole	N	N	Y	N	N	N	N	N
Kassebaum	N	N	Y	N	N	N	N	N
KENTUCKY								
Ford	Y	Y	Y	Y	Y	Y	Y	Y
McConnell	N	N	Y	N	N	N	N	N
LOUISIANA								
Breaux	Y	Y	Y	Y	Y	Y	Y	Y
Johnston	Y	Y	Y	Y	Y	Y	Y	Y
MAINE								
Mitchell	Y	Y	Y	Y	Y	Y	Y	Y
Cohen	N	N	Y	N	N	N	N	N
MARYLAND								
Mikulski	Y	N	Y	Y	Y	Y	Y	Y
Sarbanes	Y	Y	Y	Y	Y	Y	Y	Y
MASSACHUSETTS								
Kennedy	Y	Y	Y	Y	Y	?	Y	Y
Kerry	Y	Y	Y	Y	Y	Y	Y	Y
MICHIGAN								
Levin	Y	Y	Y	Y	Y	Y	Y	Y
Riegle	Y	Y	Y	Y	Y	Y	Y	Y
MINNESOTA								
Wellstone	Y	Y	Y	Y	Y	Y	Y	Y
Durenberger	N	N	Y	N	N	?	−	−
MISSISSIPPI								
Cochran	N	N	Y	N	N	N	N	N
Lott	N	N	N	N	?	N	N	N
MISSOURI								
Bond	N	N	Y	N	N	?	N	N
Danforth	N	N	Y	N	N	N	N	N
MONTANA								
Baucus	Y	Y	Y	Y	Y	Y	Y	Y
Burns	N	N	Y	N	N	N	N	N
NEBRASKA								
Exon	Y	Y	Y	Y	Y	Y	N	N
Kerrey	Y	Y	Y	Y	Y	?	N	N
NEVADA								
Bryan	Y	Y	Y	Y	Y	Y	Y	Y
Reid	Y	Y	Y	Y	Y	Y	Y	Y
NEW HAMPSHIRE								
Gregg	N	N	?	?	?	?	N	N
Smith	N	N	N	N	N	?	N	N
NEW JERSEY								
Bradley	Y	Y	Y	Y	Y	Y	Y	Y
Lautenberg	Y	Y	Y	Y	Y	Y	Y	Y
NEW MEXICO								
Bingaman	Y	Y	Y	Y	Y	Y	Y	Y
Domenici	N	N	Y	N	N	N	N	N
NEW YORK								
Moynihan	Y	Y	Y	Y	Y	Y	Y	Y
D'Amato	N	N	Y	N	?	?	N	N
NORTH CAROLINA								
Faircloth	N	N	N	N	N	?	N	N
Helms	N	N	N	N	−	?	N	N
NORTH DAKOTA								
Conrad	Y	Y	Y	Y	?	?	Y	Y
Dorgan	Y	Y	Y	Y	Y	?	Y	Y
OHIO								
Glenn	Y	Y	Y	Y	Y	Y	Y	Y
Metzenbaum	Y	Y	Y	Y	Y	Y	Y	Y
OKLAHOMA								
Boren	Y	Y	Y	Y	Y	Y	Y	Y
Nickles	N	N	Y	N	N	?	N	N
OREGON								
Hatfield	N	N	Y	N	N	N	N	N
Packwood	N	N	Y	N	N	N	N	N
PENNSYLVANIA								
Wofford	Y	Y	Y	Y	Y	Y	Y	Y
Specter	N	N	Y	N	N	N	N	N
RHODE ISLAND								
Pell	Y	Y	Y	Y	Y	Y	Y	Y
Chafee	N	N	Y	N	N	N	N	N
SOUTH CAROLINA								
Hollings	Y	Y	Y	Y	Y	Y	Y	Y
Thurmond	N	N	Y	N	N	N	N	N
SOUTH DAKOTA								
Daschle	Y	Y	Y	Y	Y	Y	Y	Y
Pressler	N	N	Y	N	N	N	N	N
TENNESSEE								
Mathews	Y	Y	Y	Y	Y	Y	Y	Y
Sasser	Y	Y	Y	Y	Y	Y	Y	Y
TEXAS								
Krueger	Y	N	?	?	?	?	Y	Y
Gramm	N	N	Y	N	N	?	N	N
UTAH								
Bennett	N	N	Y	N	N	?	N	N
Hatch	N	N	Y	N	N	−	N	N
VERMONT								
Leahy	Y	Y	Y	Y	Y	Y	Y	Y
Jeffords	N	N	Y	N	N	?	N	N
VIRGINIA								
Robb	Y	N	Y	Y	Y	Y	Y	Y
Warner	N	N	Y	N	N	N	N	N
WASHINGTON								
Murray	Y	Y	Y	Y	Y	Y	Y	Y
Gorton	N	N	N	N	N	−	N	N
WEST VIRGINIA								
Byrd	Y	Y	Y	Y	Y	Y	Y	Y
Rockefeller	Y	Y	Y	Y	Y	Y	Y	Y
WISCONSIN								
Feingold	Y	Y	Y	Y	Y	Y	Y	N
Kohl	Y	Y	Y	Y	Y	Y	Y	N
WYOMING								
Simpson	N	N	Y	N	N	N	?	?
Wallop	N	N	N	N	N	N	N	N

ND Northern Democrats   SD Southern Democrats   Southern states - Ala., Ark., Fla., Ga., Ky., La., Miss., N.C., Okla., S.C., Tenn., Texas, Va.

97. HR 1335. Fiscal 1993 Supplemental Appropriations/ Veterans Programs. Byrd, D-W.Va., motion to table (kill) the Murkowski, R-Alaska, amendment to shift $25 million from non-recurring VA maintenance projects to other veterans programs. Motion agreed to 57-43: R 0-43; D 57-0 (ND 42-0, SD 15-0), April 1, 1993. A "yea" was a vote in support of the president's position.

98. HR 1335. Fiscal 1993 Supplemental Appropriations/ COLAs. Byrd, D-W.Va., motion to table (kill) the Domenici, R-N.M., amendment to cut discretionary spending in the bill by 18 percent to allow a federal employee COLA (excluding members of Congress) on Jan. 1, 1994. Motion agreed to 51-49: R 0-43; D 51-6 (ND 40-2, SD 11-4), April 1, 1993. A "yea" was a vote in support of the president's position.

99. Talbott Nomination. Confirmation of President Clinton's nomination of Strobe Talbott as ambassador at large and special adviser to the secretary of State to coordinate U.S. policy on the former Soviet republics. Confirmed 89-9: R 33-9; D 56-0 (ND 42-0, SD 14-0), April 2, 1993. A "yea" was a vote in support of the president's position.

100. HR 1335. Fiscal 1993 Supplemental Appropriations/ Cloture. Motion to invoke cloture (thus limiting debate) on the committee substitute to the bill to provide $16.1 billion in new budget authority and approve $3.2 billion in trust fund spending. Motion rejected 55-43: R 0-42; D 55-1 (ND 42-0, SD 13-1), April 2, 1993. A three-fifths majority vote of the total Senate (60) is required to invoke cloture. A "yea" was a vote in support of the president's position.

101. HR 1335. Fiscal 1993 Supplemental Appropriations/ Cloture. Motion to invoke cloture (thus limiting debate) on the committee substitute to the bill to provide $16.1 billion in new budget authority and approve $3.2 billion in trust fund spending. Motion rejected 52-37: R 0-37; D 52-0 (ND 41-0, SD 11-0), April 3, 1993. A three-fifths majority vote of the total Senate (60) is required to invoke cloture. A "yea" was a vote in support of the president's position.

102. HR 1335. Fiscal 1993 Supplemental Appropriations/ Cloture. Motion to invoke cloture (thus limiting debate) on the committee substitute to the bill to provide $16.2 billion in new budget authority and approve $3.2 billion in trust fund spending. Motion rejected 49-29: R 0-28; D 49-1 (ND 37-0, SD 12-1), April 5, 1993. A three-fifths majority vote of the total Senate (60) is required to invoke cloture. A "yea" was a vote in support of the president's position.

103. HR 1335. Fiscal 1993 Supplemental Appropriations/ Republican Substitute. Byrd, D-W.Va., motion to table (kill) the Hatfield, R-Ore., amendment to the committee substitute, to eliminate all new spending in the bill except for $6 billion for extended emergency unemployment benefits, along with other selected programs that would be offset by cutting administrative costs. Motion agreed to 53-45: R 0-41; D 53-4 (ND 40-2, SD 13-2), April 20, 1993. A "yea" was a vote in support of the president's position.

104. HR 1335. Fiscal 1993 Supplemental Appropriations/Clinton Reductions. Byrd, D-W.Va., amendment to the committee substitute amendment, to cut funding in the bill by 25 percent. The funds would be designated as emergency spending and thus would be exempt from the spending caps of the 1990 budget agreement. Adopted 52-46: R 0-41; D 52-5 (ND 38-4, SD 14-1), April 20, 1993. A "yea" was a vote in support of the president's position.

	105	106	107	108	109	110	111	112
ALABAMA								
Heflin	Y	Y	Y	Y	N	Y	Y	Y
Shelby	N	N	Y	Y	N	Y	Y	N
ALASKA								
Murkowski	N	N	N	N	N	Y	Y	N
Stevens	N	N	N	N	N	Y	Y	N
ARIZONA								
DeConcini	Y	Y	Y	N	Y	Y	Y	Y
McCain	N	N	N	N	N	Y	Y	Y
ARKANSAS								
Bumpers	Y	Y	Y	N	Y	Y	Y	Y
Pryor	Y	Y	Y	N	Y	Y	Y	Y
CALIFORNIA								
Boxer	Y	Y	Y	N	Y	Y	Y	Y
Feinstein	Y	Y	Y	Y	Y	Y	Y	Y
COLORADO								
Campbell	Y	Y	Y	N	N	Y	Y	?
Brown	N	N	N	N	N	Y	Y	N
CONNECTICUT								
Dodd	Y	Y	Y	N	Y	Y	Y	Y
Lieberman	Y	Y	Y	N	Y	Y	Y	Y
DELAWARE								
Biden	Y	Y	Y	N	N	Y	Y	Y
Roth	N	N	Y	N	N	Y	Y	Y
FLORIDA								
Graham	Y	Y	Y	Y	Y	Y	Y	Y
Mack	N	N	Y	N	N	Y	Y	N
GEORGIA								
Nunn	Y	Y	Y	N	N	Y	Y	Y
Coverdell	N	N	Y	N	N	Y	Y	N
HAWAII								
Akaka	Y	Y	Y	N	Y	Y	Y	Y
Inouye	Y	?	Y	N	Y	Y	Y	Y
IDAHO								
Craig	N	N	N	N	N	Y	Y	N
Kempthorne	N	N	N	N	N	Y	Y	N
ILLINOIS								
Moseley-Braun	Y	Y	Y	Y	Y	Y	Y	Y
Simon	Y	Y	Y	N	Y	Y	Y	Y
INDIANA								
Coats	N	N	N	N	N	Y	Y	N
Lugar	N	N	N	N	N	Y	Y	Y

	105	106	107	108	109	110	111	112
IOWA								
Harkin	Y	Y	Y	N	Y	Y	Y	Y
Grassley	N	N	N	N	N	Y	Y	Y
KANSAS								
Dole	N	N	N	N	N	Y	Y	N
Kassebaum	N	N	N	N	N	Y	Y	N
KENTUCKY								
Ford	Y	Y	Y	N	Y	Y	Y	Y
McConnell	N	N	N	N	N	Y	Y	N
LOUISIANA								
Breaux	Y	Y	Y	Y	Y	?	?	?
Johnston	Y	Y	Y	Y	Y	Y	Y	Y
MAINE								
Mitchell	Y	Y	Y	N	Y	Y	Y	Y
Cohen	N	N	N	N	N	Y	Y	Y
MARYLAND								
Mikulski	Y	Y	Y	N	Y	Y	Y	Y
Sarbanes	Y	Y	Y	N	Y	Y	Y	Y
MASSACHUSETTS								
Kennedy	Y	Y	Y	N	Y	Y	Y	Y
Kerry	Y	Y	Y	N	Y	Y	Y	Y
MICHIGAN								
Levin	Y	Y	Y	Y	Y	Y	Y	Y
Riegle	Y	Y	Y	N	Y	Y	Y	Y
MINNESOTA								
Wellstone	Y	Y	Y	N	Y	Y	Y	Y
Durenberger	N	N	Y	N	N	Y	Y	Y
MISSISSIPPI								
Cochran	N	N	Y	N	N	Y	Y	Y
Lott	N	N	Y	N	N	Y	Y	N
MISSOURI								
Bond	N	N	Y	N	N	Y	Y	N
Danforth	N	N	N	N	N	Y	Y	Y
MONTANA								
Baucus	Y	Y	Y	N	Y	Y	Y	Y
Burns	N	N	Y	N	N	Y	Y	Y
NEBRASKA								
Exon	Y	Y	Y	N	Y	Y	Y	Y
Kerrey	Y	Y	Y	N	Y	Y	Y	Y
NEVADA								
Bryan	Y	Y	Y	N	N	Y	N	Y
Reid	Y	Y	Y	N	N	Y	Y	Y

	105	106	107	108	109	110	111	112
NEW HAMPSHIRE								
Gregg	N	N	N	N	Y	Y	Y	?
Smith	N	N	N	N	N	Y	Y	N
NEW JERSEY								
Bradley	Y	?	?	?	Y	Y	Y	Y
Lautenberg	Y	Y	Y	Y	Y	Y	N	Y
NEW MEXICO								
Bingaman	Y	Y	Y	N	Y	Y	Y	Y
Domenici	N	N	Y	N	N	Y	Y	Y
NEW YORK								
Moynihan	Y	Y	Y	Y	Y	Y	Y	Y
D'Amato	N	N	N	N	N	Y	Y	Y
NORTH CAROLINA								
Faircloth	N	N	N	?	?	Y	Y	N
Helms	N	N	N	N	N	?	Y	N
NORTH DAKOTA								
Conrad	Y	Y	Y	N	Y	Y	Y	Y
Dorgan	Y	Y	Y	N	Y	Y	Y	Y
OHIO								
Glenn	Y	Y	Y	Y	Y	Y	Y	Y
Metzenbaum	Y	Y	Y	Y	Y	Y	Y	Y
OKLAHOMA								
Boren	Y	Y	Y	N	Y	Y	Y	Y
Nickles	N	N	N	N	N	Y	Y	N
OREGON								
Hatfield	N	N	N	N	N	Y	Y	Y
Packwood	N	N	N	N	N	Y	Y	N
PENNSYLVANIA								
Wofford	Y	Y	Y	N	Y	Y	Y	Y
Specter	N	N	N	N	N	Y	Y	Y
RHODE ISLAND								
Pell	Y	Y	Y	N	Y	Y	Y	Y
Chafee	N	N	Y	Y	Y	Y	N	Y
SOUTH CAROLINA								
Hollings	Y	Y	Y	?	Y	Y	Y	Y
Thurmond	N	N	N	N	N	Y	Y	N
SOUTH DAKOTA								
Daschle	Y	Y	Y	N	Y	Y	Y	Y
Pressler	N	N	N	N	N	Y	Y	N
TENNESSEE								
Mathews	Y	Y	Y	N	Y	Y	Y	Y
Sasser	Y	Y	Y	?	Y	Y	Y	Y

	105	106	107	108	109	110	111	112
TEXAS								
Krueger	Y	?	?	?	?	?	?	?
Gramm	N	N	N	N	N	Y	Y	N
UTAH								
Bennett	N	N	N	N	N	Y	Y	N
Hatch	N	N	N	N	N	Y	Y	N
VERMONT								
Leahy	Y	Y	Y	N	Y	Y	Y	Y
Jeffords	N	Y	N	N	Y	Y	Y	Y
VIRGINIA								
Robb	Y	Y	Y	Y	Y	Y	Y	Y
Warner	N	N	N	N	N	Y	Y	Y
WASHINGTON								
Murray	Y	Y	Y	N	Y	Y	Y	Y
Gorton	N	N	Y	N	N	Y	Y	Y
WEST VIRGINIA								
Byrd	Y	Y	Y	Y	Y	Y	Y	Y
Rockefeller	Y	Y	Y	Y	Y	Y	Y	Y
WISCONSIN								
Feingold	Y	Y	Y	N	Y	Y	Y	Y
Kohl	Y	Y	Y	N	Y	Y	Y	Y
WYOMING								
Simpson	—	—	N	N	N	Y	Y	N
Wallop	N	N	N	N	N	Y	Y	N

ND Northern Democrats   SD Southern Democrats   Southern states - Ala., Ark., Fla., Ga., Ky., La., Miss., N.C., Okla., S.C., Tenn., Texas, Va.

105. HR 1335. Fiscal 1993 Supplemental Appropriations/Cloture. Motion to invoke cloture (thus limiting debate) on the bill to provide $12.2 billion in new budget authority and $3.1 billion in trust fund spending to implement the administration's compromise stimulus package to help in the economic recovery. Motion rejected 56-43: R 0-42; D 56-1 (ND 42-0, SD 14-1), April 21, 1993. Three-fifths of the total Senate (60) is required to invoke cloture. A "yea" was a vote in support of the president's position.

106. S 171. Department of the Environment/Related Provisions. Glenn, D-Ohio, motion to table (kill) the Roth, R-Del., amendment to elevate the Environmental Protection Agency to Cabinet-level status and eliminate all other provisions in the bill. Motion agreed to 54-42: R 1-41; D 53-1 (ND 40-0, SD 13-1), April 27, 1993. A "yea" was a vote in support of the president's position.

107. S 171. Department of the Environment/Health Care. Roth, R-Del., motion to table (kill) the Specter, R-Pa., amendment to implement a comprehensive health-care reform package based on the concept of managed competition. Motion agreed to 65-33: R 10-33; D 55-0 (ND 41-0, SD 14-0), April 28, 1993.

108. S 171. Department of the Environment/Indian Lands Official. Glenn, D-Ohio, motion to table (kill) the McCain, R-Ariz., amendment to require the Department of the Environment to have an assistant secretary for Indian lands, responsible for policies affecting the environment of Indian lands and Native Americans. Motion rejected 16-79: R 1-41; D 15-38 (ND 9-32, SD 6-6), April 28, 1993. (Subsequently, the McCain amendment was adopted by voice vote.)

109. S 171. Department of the Environment/Economic and Employment Impact Statements. Glenn, D-Ohio, motion to table (kill) the Nickles, R-Okla., amendment to require an economic and employment impact statement to accompany each bill considered by Congress or each regulation proposed by the executive branch. Motion agreed to 50-48: R 2-40; D 48-8 (ND 38-4, SD 10-4), April 29, 1993.

110. S 171. Department of the Environment/Small-Business Ombudsman. Lieberman, D-Conn., amendment to establish within the Department of the Environment a small-business ombudsman office to provide assistance to small businesses and family farms in environmental compliance. Adopted 97-0: R 42-0; D 55-0 (ND 42-0, SD 13-0), April 29, 1993.

111. S 171. Department of the Environment/Cost-Benefit Analysis. Johnston, D-La., amendment to require the Department of the Environment to analyze the risks addressed by new regulatory proposals and the cost of implementing them, and certify that benefits to human health and the environment justify the regulations. Adopted: 95-3: R 42-1; D 53-2 (ND 40-2, SD 13-0), April 29, 1993.

112. S 171. Department of the Environment/Cost Offsets. Johnston, D-La., motion to table (kill) the Hatch, R-Utah, amendment to require that new regulations be accompanied by a cost-benefit analysis and to require that the costs of a new regulation be offset by revoking or revising existing regulations. Motion agreed to 70-26: R 17-25; D 53-1 (ND 41-0, SD 12-1), April 29, 1993.

KEY

- **Y** Voted for (yea).
- **#** Paired for.
- **+** Announced for.
- **N** Voted against (nay).
- **X** Paired against.
- **—** Announced against.
- **P** Voted "present."
- **C** Voted "present" to avoid possible conflict of interest.
- **?** Did not vote or otherwise make a position known.

Democrats *Republicans*

	113	114	115	116	117	118	119	120
ALABAMA								
Heflin	Y	Y	?	?	Y	Y	N	N
Shelby	Y	Y	Y	Y	Y	Y	Y	Y
ALASKA								
Murkowski	Y	N	Y	Y	N	N	N	Y
Stevens	?	?	Y	Y	N	N	N	Y
ARIZONA								
DeConcini	N	Y	Y	Y	Y	Y	Y	N
McCain	Y	Y	Y	N	N	N	Y	Y
ARKANSAS								
Bumpers	X	?	Y	Y	Y	Y	N	N
Pryor	N	Y	Y	?	Y	Y	N	N
CALIFORNIA								
Boxer	N	Y	Y	Y	Y	Y	Y	N
Feinstein	N	Y	Y	Y	Y	Y	Y	N
COLORADO								
Campbell	N	Y	Y	Y	Y	Y	?	N
Brown	Y	Y	Y	Y	N	N	N	Y
CONNECTICUT								
Dodd	N	Y	Y	Y	Y	Y	N	N
Lieberman	N	Y	Y	Y	Y	Y	Y	N
DELAWARE								
Biden	N	Y	Y	Y	Y	Y	Y	N
Roth	Y	Y	Y	Y	N	N	Y	Y
FLORIDA								
Graham	N	Y	Y	Y	Y	Y	Y	N
Mack	Y	Y	Y	N	N	N	N	Y
GEORGIA								
Nunn	?	?	Y	Y	Y	Y	Y	N
Coverdell	Y	Y	Y	Y	N	N	N	Y
HAWAII								
Akaka	N	Y	Y	Y	Y	Y	Y	N
Inouye	N	Y	Y	Y	Y	Y	Y	N
IDAHO								
Craig	Y	N	Y	Y	N	N	N	Y
Kempthorne	Y	N	Y	Y	N	N	N	Y
ILLINOIS								
Moseley-Braun	N	Y	Y	Y	Y	Y	Y	N
Simon	N	Y	Y	Y	Y	Y	Y	N
INDIANA								
Coats	Y	Y	Y	Y	N	N	N	Y
Lugar	?	?	Y	Y	N	N	N	Y

	113	114	115	116	117	118	119	120
IOWA								
Harkin	N	Y	Y	Y	Y	Y	Y	N
Grassley	Y	Y	Y	Y	N	N	Y	Y
KANSAS								
Dole	Y	Y	Y	Y	N	N	N	Y
Kassebaum	Y	Y	Y	Y	N	N	N	?
KENTUCKY								
Ford	N	Y	Y	Y	Y	Y	Y	N
McConnell	Y	Y	Y	Y	N	N	N	Y
LOUISIANA								
Breaux	N	Y	Y	Y	Y	Y	Y	N
Johnston	Y	Y	Y	Y	Y	Y	Y	N
MAINE								
Mitchell	N	Y	Y	Y	Y	Y	Y	N
Cohen	N	Y	Y	Y	Y	N	Y	Y
MARYLAND								
Mikulski	N	Y	Y	Y	Y	Y	Y	N
Sarbanes	N	Y	Y	Y	Y	Y	Y	N
MASSACHUSETTS								
Kennedy	N	Y	Y	Y	Y	Y	Y	N
Kerry	N	Y	Y	Y	Y	Y	Y	N
MICHIGAN								
Levin	N	Y	Y	Y	Y	Y	?	N
Riegle	N	Y	Y	Y	Y	Y	Y	N
MINNESOTA								
Wellstone	N	Y	Y	Y	Y	Y	Y	N
Durenberger	N	Y	Y	Y	Y	Y	N	Y
MISSISSIPPI								
Cochran	Y	Y	Y	Y	N	N	N	Y
Lott	Y	Y	Y	Y	N	N	N	Y
MISSOURI								
Bond	Y	Y	Y	Y	N	N	N	Y
Danforth	Y	N	Y	Y	N	N	N	Y
MONTANA								
Baucus	N	Y	Y	Y	Y	Y	Y	N
Burns	Y	Y	Y	Y	N	N	Y	Y
NEBRASKA								
Exon	N	Y	Y	Y	Y	Y	Y	N
Kerrey	N	N	Y	Y	Y	Y	Y	N
NEVADA								
Bryan	N	Y	Y	Y	Y	Y	Y	N
Reid	N	Y	Y	Y	Y	Y	Y	N

	113	114	115	116	117	118	119	120
NEW HAMPSHIRE								
Gregg	N	Y	Y	Y	N	N	Y	Y
Smith	N	N	Y	N	N	N	?	?
NEW JERSEY								
Bradley	N	Y	Y	Y	Y	Y	Y	N
Lautenberg	N	Y	Y	Y	Y	Y	Y	N
NEW MEXICO								
Bingaman	N	Y	Y	Y	Y	Y	Y	N
Domenici	Y	Y	Y	Y	Y	Y	N	Y
NEW YORK								
Moynihan	N	Y	Y	Y	Y	Y	Y	N
D'Amato	N	Y	Y	Y	N	N	N	Y
NORTH CAROLINA								
Faircloth	Y	Y	Y	N	N	N	Y	Y
Helms	Y	N	Y	N	N	N	N	Y
NORTH DAKOTA								
Conrad	Y	Y	Y	Y	Y	Y	Y	N
Dorgan	Y	Y	Y	Y	Y	Y	Y	N
OHIO								
Glenn	N	Y	Y	Y	Y	Y	Y	N
Metzenbaum	N	Y	Y	Y	Y	Y	Y	N
OKLAHOMA								
Boren	Y	Y	Y	Y	Y	Y	Y	N
Nickles	Y	N	Y	Y	N	N	N	Y
OREGON								
Hatfield	N	Y	Y	Y	Y	Y	Y	Y
Packwood	Y	Y	Y	Y	N	Y	N	Y
PENNSYLVANIA								
Wofford	N	Y	Y	Y	Y	Y	Y	N
Specter	N	Y	Y	Y	Y	Y	Y	Y
RHODE ISLAND								
Pell	?	+	Y	Y	Y	Y	Y	N
Chafee	N	Y	Y	Y	N	N	Y	Y
SOUTH CAROLINA								
Hollings	N	Y	Y	Y	Y	Y	Y	N
Thurmond	Y	N	Y	Y	N	N	N	Y
SOUTH DAKOTA								
Daschle	N	Y	Y	Y	Y	Y	Y	N
Pressler	Y	N	Y	Y	N	N	N	Y
TENNESSEE								
Mathews	Y	Y	Y	Y	Y	Y	Y	N
Sasser	Y	Y	Y	Y	Y	Y	Y	N

	113	114	115	116	117	118	119	120
TEXAS								
Krueger	Y	Y	Y	?	Y	Y	?	?
Gramm	Y	N	Y	Y	N	N	N	Y
UTAH								
Bennett	Y	N	Y	Y	N	N	N	Y
Hatch	Y	N	Y	Y	N	—	N	Y
VERMONT								
Leahy	N	Y	Y	Y	Y	Y	Y	N
Jeffords	N	Y	Y	Y	Y	Y	Y	Y
VIRGINIA								
Robb	N	Y	Y	Y	Y	Y	Y	N
Warner	#	?	Y	Y	N	N	N	Y
WASHINGTON								
Murray	N	Y	Y	Y	Y	Y	Y	N
Gorton	Y	Y	Y	Y	N	N	Y	Y
WEST VIRGINIA								
Byrd	N	Y	Y	Y	Y	Y	Y	N
Rockefeller	N	Y	Y	Y	?	?	?	?
WISCONSIN								
Feingold	N	Y	Y	Y	Y	Y	Y	N
Kohl	N	Y	Y	Y	Y	Y	Y	N
WYOMING								
Simpson	Y	N	Y	Y	N	N	Y	Y
Wallop	Y	N	N	N	N	N	N	Y

ND Northern Democrats   SD Southern Democrats   Southern states - Ala., Ark., Fla., Ga., Ky., La., Miss., N.C., Okla., S.C., Tenn., Texas, Va.

113. S 171. Department of the Environment/Wetlands Determinations. Bond, R-Mo., motion to table (kill) the Baucus, D-Mont., amendment to the Bond amendment, to provide that one federal agency be responsible for technical determinations about wetlands on agricultural lands. Motion rejected 40-54: R 31-9; D 9-45 (ND 2-39, SD 7-6), May 4, 1993. (Subsequently, the Bond amendment as amended by the Baucus amendment was adopted by voice vote.)

114. S 171. Department of the Environment/Passage. Passage of the bill to elevate the Environmental Protection Agency to Cabinet level. The bill would establish a Department of Environmental Protection, abolish the Council on Environmental Quality and create a Bureau of Environmental Statistics. Passed 79-15: R 26-14; D 53-1 (ND 40-1, SD 13-0), May 4, 1993. A "yea" was a vote in support of the president's position.

115. S 349. Lobbying Disclosure. Lautenberg, D-N.J., amendment to express the sense of the Senate that as soon as possible the Senate should adopt restrictions similar to those on the executive branch limiting the acceptance of gifts, meals and travel by members and staff. Adopted 98-1: R 42-1; D 56-0 (ND 42-0, SD 14-0), May 6, 1993.

116. S 349. Lobbying Disclosure/Passage. Passage of the bill to ensure that all professional lobbyists are registered and their clients identified. Passed 95-2: R 41-2; D 54-0 (ND 42-0, SD 12-0), May 6, 1993. A "yea" was a vote in support of the president's position.

117. HR 2. National "Motor-Voter" Registration/Cloture. Motion to invoke cloture (thus limiting debate) on the conference report to require states to allow citizens to register to vote when applying for or renewing a driver's license, at agencies providing public assistance and through the mail. Motion agreed to 63-37: R 6-37; D 57-0 (ND 42-0, SD 15-0), May 11, 1993. Three-fifths of the total Senate (60) is required to invoke cloture.

118. HR 2. National "Motor-Voter" Registration/Conference Report. Adoption of the conference report to require states to allow citizens to register to vote when applying for or renewing a driver's license, at agencies providing public assistance and through the mail. Adopted (thus cleared for the president) 62-36: R 6-36; D 56-0 (ND 41-0, SD 15-0), May 11, 1993. A "yea" was a vote in support of the president's position.

119. S 714. Resolution Trust Corporation Funding/Statute of Limitations. Metzenbaum, D-Ohio, amendment to extend the statute of limitations for tort actions brought by the Resolution Trust Corporation from three to five years. Adopted 63-32: R 16-26; D 47-6 (ND 37-2, SD 10-4), May 13, 1993.

120. S 714. Resolution Trust Corporation Funding/Binding Budget Totals. Gramm, R-Texas, motion to waive the budget act with respect to the Sasser, D-Tenn., point of order against the Gramm amendment. The Gramm amendment would make the five-year budget totals binding, with automatic cuts if the totals are exceeded. Motion rejected 43-53: R 41-0; D 2-53 (ND 0-41, SD 2-12), May 13, 1993. A three-fifths majority vote (60) of the total Senate is required to waive the budget act. (Subsequently, the chair upheld the Sasser point of order, and the Gramm amendment fell.)

KEY

Y	Voted for (yea).
#	Paired for.
+	Announced for.
N	Voted against (nay).
X	Paired against.
−	Announced against.
P	Voted "present."
C	Voted "present" to avoid possible conflict of interest.
?	Did not vote or otherwise make a position known.

Democrats   *Republicans*

State / Senator	121	122	123	124	125	126	127	128
ALABAMA								
Heflin	Y	?	?	?	?	?	?	?
Shelby	N	N	N	N	Y	Y	N	Y
ALASKA								
Murkowski	Y	N	N	Y	Y	Y	N	N
Stevens	Y	N	N	Y	Y	Y	N	N
ARIZONA								
DeConcini	N	+	Y	Y	Y	N	Y	N
McCain	N	?	Y	Y	Y	Y	N	N
ARKANSAS								
Bumpers	Y	Y	N	Y	Y	N	Y	Y
Pryor	Y	Y	N	Y	Y	N	N	Y
CALIFORNIA								
Boxer	Y	Y	N	Y	N	N	Y	Y
Feinstein	Y	Y	N	Y	N	N	Y	Y
COLORADO								
Campbell	Y	Y	N	Y	Y	N	Y	N
Brown	N	N	N	Y	Y	Y	N	N
CONNECTICUT								
Dodd	Y	Y	N	Y	Y	N	N	Y
Lieberman	Y	Y	N	Y	Y	Y	N	Y
DELAWARE								
Biden	Y	Y	N	Y	N	N	Y	?
Roth	Y	Y	N	Y	Y	Y	N	Y
FLORIDA								
Graham	N	Y	N	Y	N	N	N	Y
Mack	N	N	N	N	Y	Y	N	N
GEORGIA								
Nunn	N	Y	N	Y	Y	N	Y	Y
Coverdell	N	N	N	Y	Y	Y	N	N
HAWAII								
Akaka	N	Y	N	Y	Y	N	Y	Y
Inouye	Y	Y	N	Y	?	N	N	Y
IDAHO								
Craig	N	N	N	Y	Y	Y	N	N
Kempthorne	N	N	N	Y	Y	Y	N	N
ILLINOIS								
Moseley-Braun	Y	Y	N	Y	Y	N	Y	Y
Simon	Y	Y	Y	Y	Y	N	Y	Y
INDIANA								
Coats	N	N	N	Y	N	Y	N	N
Lugar	N	N	N	Y	Y	Y	N	Y
IOWA								
Harkin	N	Y	Y	Y	Y	N	N	Y
Grassley	Y	N	Y	Y	Y	Y	N	N
KANSAS								
Dole	Y	N	N	Y	Y	Y	N	N
Kassebaum	Y	Y	N	Y	Y	Y	N	N
KENTUCKY								
Ford	Y	Y	N	Y	N	Y	N	Y
McConnell	N	N	N	Y	Y	Y	N	N
LOUISIANA								
Breaux	Y	Y	N	Y	Y	N	N	Y
Johnston	Y	Y	N	Y	Y	N	N	Y
MAINE								
Mitchell	Y	Y	N	Y	Y	N	Y	Y
Cohen	Y	Y	Y	Y	Y	Y	Y	N
MARYLAND								
Mikulski	Y	Y	N	Y	N	N	N	Y
Sarbanes	Y	Y	N	Y	N	Y	N	Y
MASSACHUSETTS								
Kennedy	Y	+	N	Y	N	Y	N	Y
Kerry	Y	Y	N	Y	N	Y	N	Y
MICHIGAN								
Levin	Y	Y	N	Y	N	Y	N	Y
Riegle	Y	Y	N	Y	N	Y	N	Y
MINNESOTA								
Wellstone	N	Y	Y	Y	Y	N	Y	Y
Durenberger	Y	Y	N	Y	Y	Y	N	N
MISSISSIPPI								
Cochran	N	N	N	Y	Y	Y	N	N
Lott	N	N	N	Y	Y	Y	N	N
MISSOURI								
Bond	Y	Y	N	Y	Y	Y	N	N
Danforth	Y	?	N	N	N	Y	N	N
MONTANA								
Baucus	N	Y	N	Y	Y	N	Y	Y
Burns	−	N	N	Y	Y	Y	Y	N
NEBRASKA								
Exon	N	X	N	Y	Y	Y	Y	N
Kerrey	N	Y	N	Y	Y	N	Y	Y
NEVADA								
Bryan	Y	Y	N	Y	Y	N	Y	Y
Reid	Y	Y	N	Y	Y	N	N	Y
NEW HAMPSHIRE								
Gregg	Y	Y	N	Y	Y	Y	N	N
Smith	?	N	N	N	Y	Y	N	N
NEW JERSEY								
Bradley	N	?	Y	Y	Y	N	Y	Y
Lautenberg	N	Y	Y	Y	Y	Y	Y	Y
NEW MEXICO								
Bingaman	Y	Y	N	Y	N	Y	N	Y
Domenici	Y	Y	N	Y	Y	Y	N	N
NEW YORK								
Moynihan	Y	Y	N	Y	N	Y	N	Y
D'Amato	Y	Y	N	Y	Y	Y	N	N
NORTH CAROLINA								
Faircloth	N	N	N	Y	Y	Y	N	N
Helms	N	N	N	?	N	Y	N	?
NORTH DAKOTA								
Conrad	N	Y	Y	Y	N	N	N	Y
Dorgan	N	Y	N	Y	N	N	N	Y
OHIO								
Glenn	Y	Y	N	Y	N	Y	N	Y
Metzenbaum	Y	Y	Y	Y	Y	N	Y	Y
OKLAHOMA								
Boren	Y	?	N	Y	N	Y	N	Y
Nickles	N	N	N	Y	Y	Y	N	N
OREGON								
Hatfield	Y	Y	N	Y	Y	Y	N	N
Packwood	Y	Y	N	Y	Y	Y	N	N
PENNSYLVANIA								
Wofford	N	Y	Y	Y	N	Y	Y	Y
Specter	N	Y	N	Y	Y	Y	N	N
RHODE ISLAND								
Pell	Y	Y	N	Y	N	Y	N	Y
Chafee	Y	Y	N	Y	Y	Y	N	Y
SOUTH CAROLINA								
Hollings	N	N	N	Y	N	Y	N	N
Thurmond	Y	N	N	Y	Y	Y	N	N
SOUTH DAKOTA								
Daschle	Y	Y	N	Y	N	N	N	Y
Pressler	Y	N	N	Y	Y	Y	N	N
TENNESSEE								
Mathews	Y	N	N	Y	Y	N	Y	Y
Sasser	Y	N	N	Y	Y	N	Y	Y
TEXAS								
Krueger	?	#	?	?	?	?	?	?
Gramm	Y	N	N	N	Y	Y	N	N
UTAH								
Bennett	Y	Y	N	N	Y	Y	N	N
Hatch	Y	N	N	N	Y	Y	N	N
VERMONT								
Leahy	Y	Y	?	Y	Y	N	Y	Y
Jeffords	Y	?	N	N	Y	Y	N	Y
VIRGINIA								
Robb	Y	Y	N	Y	N	Y	N	Y
Warner	Y	N	N	Y	Y	Y	N	Y
WASHINGTON								
Murray	Y	Y	N	Y	N	N	N	Y
Gorton	Y	N	N	Y	Y	N	Y	N
WEST VIRGINIA								
Byrd	N	N	N	Y	N	N	Y	Y
Rockefeller	−	Y	N	Y	Y	N	Y	Y
WISCONSIN								
Feingold	N	Y	Y	Y	Y	N	Y	Y
Kohl	N	Y	N	Y	Y	N	Y	Y
WYOMING								
Simpson	Y	−	N	Y	Y	Y	N	N
Wallop	N	N	N	N	Y	Y	N	N

ND Northern Democrats   SD Southern Democrats   Southern states - Ala., Ark., Fla., Ga., Ky., La., Miss., N.C., Okla., S.C., Tenn., Texas, Va.

121. S 714. Resolution Trust Corporation Funding/Passage. Passage of the bill to provide $18.3 billion to the Resolution Trust Corporation to resolve failed savings and loans institutions. The bill would also authorize $16 billion to capitalize the new Savings Association Insurance Fund, $8.5 billion of it appropriated. Passed 61-35: R 25-16; D 36-19 (ND 26-15, SD 10-4), May 13, 1993. A "yea" was a vote in support of the president's position.

122. Achtenberg Nomination/Confirmation. Confirmation of President Clinton's nomination of Roberta Achtenberg to be an assistant secretary for Fair Housing and Equal Opportunity at the Department of Housing and Urban Development. Confirmed 58-31: R 13-26; D 45-5 (ND 37-1, SD 8-4), May 24, 1993. A "yea" was a vote supporting the president's position.

123. S 3. Campaign Finance/Contribution Limit. Wellstone, D-Minn., amendment to reduce the individual contribution limit to $100 per Senate election cycle from the existing $1,000 per election cycle, effective only if public financing included in the bill were increased. Rejected 13-84: R 3-40; D 10-44 (ND 10-31, SD 0-13), May 25, 1993.

124. S 3. Campaign Finance/Personal Contribution Limit. Wellstone, D-Minn., amendment to reduce the maximum amount an individual may contribute to his own campaign to $25,000 from $250,000 and still receive public financing. Adopted 88-9: R 34-8; D 54-1 (ND 42-0, SD 12-1), May 25, 1993.

125. S 3. Campaign Finance/PAC Contributions. Pressler, R-S.D., amendment to ban political action committees (PACs) in House and Senate campaigns. If the PAC ban were found unconstitutional, then PAC contributions would be limited to $1,000 in any federal election; an aggregate cap for PAC contributions would be set at 20 percent of the spending limit for both chambers. Adopted 85-12: R 40-3; D 45-9 (ND 33-8, SD 12-1), May 26, 1993.

126. S 3. Campaign Finance/Public Financing. McConnell, R-Ky., motion to table (kill) the Boren, D-Okla., amendment to the McConnell amendment, to allow the revenue generated from eliminating the tax deduction for lobbying expenses to fund the public financing of federal elections and reduce the deficit. The McConnell amendment would require that the revenue go exclusively to deficit reduction. Motion rejected 48-50: R 43-0; D 5-50 (ND 3-39, SD 2-11), May 26, 1993. (The Boren amendment and the McConnell amendment as amended by the Boren amendment were both subsequently adopted by voice vote).

127. S 3. Campaign Finance/Spending Limits. Kerry, D-Mass., amendment to state certain opinions of the Senate on the relationship between spending limits and confidence in public officials. Rejected 39-59: R 0-43; D 39-16 (ND 32-10, SD 7-6), May 26, 1993.

128. S 3. Campaign Finance/Term Limits. Boren, D-Okla., motion to table (kill) the Faircloth, R-N.C., amendment to impose term limits on candidates who receive public financing of six House terms and two Senate terms. Under the amendment, if an individual decided to run for an additional term, the individual would be required to repay all public financing previously received. Motion agreed to 57-39: R 6-36; D 51-3 (ND 38-3, SD 13-0), May 26, 1993.

KEY

Y Voted for (yea).
Paired for.
+ Announced for.
N Voted against (nay).
X Paired against.
− Announced against.
P Voted "present."
C Voted "present" to avoid possible conflict of interest.
? Did not vote or otherwise make a position known.

Democrats   *Republicans*

State / Senator	129	130	131	132	133	134	135	136
ALABAMA								
Heflin	?	?	?	?	?	N	N	Y
Shelby	Y	N	N	N	N	N	Y	N
ALASKA								
Murkowski	N	−	−	?	?	?	?	?
Stevens	N	N	N	N	N	N	N	N
ARIZONA								
DeConcini	Y	Y	N	Y	Y	Y	Y	Y
McCain	N	N	?	?	?	N	Y	N
ARKANSAS								
Bumpers	Y	Y	Y	N	Y	N	Y	N
Pryor	Y	Y	Y	N	Y	Y	Y	N
CALIFORNIA								
Boxer	N	Y	N	Y	N	Y	N	Y
Feinstein	Y	N	Y	Y	Y	Y	N	N
COLORADO								
Campbell	Y	N	Y	N	?	Y	N	Y
Brown	N	N	N	Y	N	Y	N	N
CONNECTICUT								
Dodd	Y	Y	Y	N	Y	N	N	Y
Lieberman	Y	N	Y	Y	Y	N	N	N
DELAWARE								
Biden	Y	Y	Y	Y	?	Y	N	Y
Roth	Y	N	N	N	N	N	N	N
FLORIDA								
Graham	Y	N	Y	Y	N	Y	Y	Y
Mack	N	N	N	N	N	N	N	N
GEORGIA								
Nunn	Y	N	Y	Y	N	?	?	?
Coverdell	N	N	N	N	N	?	?	?
HAWAII								
Akaka	Y	Y	Y	N	N	Y	N	Y
Inouye	Y	Y	N	N	?	Y	N	Y
IDAHO								
Craig	N	N	N	N	N	N	N	N
Kempthorne	N	N	N	N	N	N	N	N
ILLINOIS								
Moseley-Braun	Y	Y	Y	Y	Y	N	N	Y
Simon	Y	Y	Y	Y	Y	Y	Y	N
INDIANA								
Coats	N	N	N	N	N	N	N	N
Lugar	N	N	N	N	N	N	N	N
IOWA								
Harkin	Y	Y	Y	N	Y	Y	Y	Y
Grassley	N	N	N	N	N	N	N	N
KANSAS								
Dole	N	N	N	N	N	N	N	N
Kassebaum	Y	N	N	N	?	N	N	N
KENTUCKY								
Ford	Y	N	N	Y	N	Y	N	Y
McConnell	N	N	N	N	N	N	N	N
LOUISIANA								
Breaux	Y	N	Y	Y	N	Y	N	Y
Johnston	Y	N	Y	N	N	Y	N	Y
MAINE								
Mitchell	Y	Y	Y	N	Y	N	Y	N
Cohen	N	N	N	N	N	N	N	N
MARYLAND								
Mikulski	N	Y	Y	Y	N	N	N	Y
Sarbanes	Y	Y	Y	Y	N	Y	N	Y
MASSACHUSETTS								
Kennedy	Y	Y	Y	Y	Y	N	N	Y
Kerry	Y	Y	Y	Y	?	N	N	Y
MICHIGAN								
Levin	Y	N	Y	Y	N	N	N	Y
Riegle	Y	Y	Y	Y	N	N	N	Y
MINNESOTA								
Wellstone	Y	Y	Y	Y	Y	Y	Y	Y
Durenberger	N	N	N	Y	?	N	N	N
MISSISSIPPI								
Cochran	N	N	N	N	N	N	N	N
Lott	N	N	N	N	N	N	N	N
MISSOURI								
Bond	N	N	N	N	N	N	N	N
Danforth	N	N	N	N	?	?	?	?
MONTANA								
Baucus	+	+	+	−	−	−	−	+
Burns	N	N	N	N	N	N	N	N
NEBRASKA								
Exon	Y	N	?	?	?	N	N	N
Kerrey	N	N	N	N	N	N	N	Y
NEVADA								
Bryan	Y	N	Y	Y	Y	N	Y	Y
Reid	Y	Y	Y	Y	Y	N	N	Y
NEW HAMPSHIRE								
Gregg	N	N	N	?	N	N	N	
Smith	N	N	N	N	N	N	N	N
NEW JERSEY								
Bradley	Y	Y	Y	Y	N	N	Y	?
Lautenberg	Y	Y	Y	Y	N	N	Y	Y
NEW MEXICO								
Bingaman	Y	Y	Y	N	Y	Y	N	Y
Domenici	N	N	N	N	N	N	N	N
NEW YORK								
Moynihan	N	Y	Y	Y	N	Y	N	Y
D'Amato	Y	N	N	N	N	N	N	N
NORTH CAROLINA								
Faircloth	N	N	N	N	N	N	N	N
Helms	N	N	?	?	?	N	N	N
NORTH DAKOTA								
Conrad	Y	Y	Y	Y	Y	N	N	Y
Dorgan	Y	?	Y	Y	Y	N	N	Y
OHIO								
Glenn	Y	Y	Y	N	?	N	N	Y
Metzenbaum	Y	Y	Y	N	Y	N	N	Y
OKLAHOMA								
Boren	Y	Y	Y	N	N	Y	N	Y
Nickles	N	N	N	Y	?	N	N	N
OREGON								
Hatfield	Y	N	N	N	Y	−	−	−
Packwood	N	N	N	N	N	N	N	N
PENNSYLVANIA								
Wofford	Y	Y	Y	Y	?	N	N	Y
Specter	Y	N	?	?	N	N	N	N
RHODE ISLAND								
Pell	N	Y	Y	Y	Y	Y	Y	N
Chafee	N	N	N	N	N	N	N	N
SOUTH CAROLINA								
Hollings	Y	N	N	Y	?	?	?	?
Thurmond	?	N	N	N	N	N	N	N
SOUTH DAKOTA								
Daschle	Y	Y	Y	Y	?	Y	N	Y
Pressler	Y	N	N	N	N	N	N	N
TENNESSEE								
Mathews	Y	Y	Y	N	Y	N	Y	Y
Sasser	Y	Y	Y	N	Y	N	Y	N
TEXAS								
Krueger	?	?	?	?	?	Y	Y	?
Gramm	N	N	N	N	N	N	N	N
UTAH								
Bennett	N	N	N	N	N	?	?	?
Hatch	?	N	N	N	N	N	N	N
VERMONT								
Leahy	N	Y	Y	Y	Y	Y	Y	N
Jeffords	N	N	N	Y	?	N	N	N
VIRGINIA								
Robb	Y	N	Y	Y	N	Y	N	Y
Warner	N	N	N	Y	N	N	N	N
WASHINGTON								
Murray	Y	N	Y	Y	N	Y	N	Y
Gorton	N	N	N	Y	N	N	N	N
WEST VIRGINIA								
Byrd	Y	Y	Y	Y	Y	N	N	Y
Rockefeller	N	N	Y	Y	?	Y	Y	Y
WISCONSIN								
Feingold	Y	Y	Y	Y	Y	Y	N	Y
Kohl	N	N	Y	Y	N	N	Y	N
WYOMING								
Simpson	N	N	N	N	N	N	N	N
Wallop	N	N	N	N	?	N	N	N

ND Northern Democrats   SD Southern Democrats

Southern states - Ala., Ark., Fla., Ga., Ky., La., Miss., N.C., Okla., S.C., Tenn., Texas, Va.

129. S 3. Campaign Finance/Constitutional Amendment. Hollings, D-S.C., amendment to express the sense of the Senate that Congress should adopt a joint resolution proposing a constitutional amendment that would allow reasonable limits on campaign expenditures. Adopted 52-43: R 6-35; D 46-8 (ND 33-8, SD 13-0), May 27, 1993.

130. S 3. Campaign Finance/Public Financing. Kerry, D-Mass., amendment to set public financing of campaigns at 90 percent of the general election spending limits for candidates who raise 10 percent of the limits in contributions of less than $250. The amendment would pay for public financing through an elimination of tax deductions for lobbying expenses and limit public financing to an amount that taxpayers express by a $5 tax return checkoff. Rejected 35-60: R 0-42; D 35-18 (ND 30-10, SD 5-8), May 27, 1993.

131. S 3. Campaign Finance/Copies of Advertisements. Graham, D-Fla., amendment to require a candidate to file an exact copy of an advertisement or a public communication that refers directly or indirectly to an opponent with the Federal Election Commission and the secretary of state of the candidate's state. Adopted 47-45: R 0-39; D 47-6 (ND 37-3, SD 10-3), May 27, 1993.

132. S 3. Campaign Finance/Debate Requirement. Graham, D-Fla., amendment to require candidates to participate in at least one public debate in order to be eligible for public financing. Rejected 42-50: R 7-32; D 35-18 (ND 30-10, SD 5-8), May 27, 1993.

133. S 3. Campaign Finance/Spending Limits. DeConcini, D-Ariz., amendment to lower the voluntary spending limits for candidates receiving public financing. The amendment would set the primary spending limit at 50 percent of the general election limit rather than the 67 percent currently set by the bill; set the general election minimum spending limit at $900,000 rather than the $1.2 million in the bill; and change the spending limit formula to produce lower limits in other states. Rejected 26-53: R 2-32; D 24-21 (ND 22-10, SD 2-11), May 28, 1993.

134. S 3. Campaign Finance/Grants for Pamphlets. Graham, D-Fla., amendment to authorize grants to states to provide voters with information pamphlets on candidates for federal office who agree to abide by spending limits. Rejected 32-60: R 0-38; D 32-22 (ND 21-20, SD 11-2), June 8, 1993.

135. S 3. Campaign Finance/Broadcast Discounts. Graham, D-Fla., amendment to provide a 50 percent discount broadcast rate in states that have adopted voluntary spending limits for state and local candidates. Rejected 16-76: R 1-37; D 15-39 (ND 11-30, SD 4-9), June 8, 1993.

136. S 3. Campaign Finance/Indexing Spending Limits. Boren, D-Okla., motion to table (kill) the McConnell, R-Ky., amendment to remove the provisions in the bill indexing public funding for inflation. Motion agreed to 46-44: R 0-38; D 46-6 (ND 35-5, SD 11-1), June 8, 1993.

	137	138	139	140	141	142	143	144
ALABAMA								
Heflin	Y	N	Y	N	Y	Y	Y	N
Shelby	Y	Y	Y	N	N	N	Y	Y
ALASKA								
Murkowski	?	?	?	?	?	?	?	?
Stevens	Y	Y	N	N	N	N	Y	Y
ARIZONA								
DeConcini	Y	N	Y	Y	Y	Y	Y	N
McCain	Y	Y	N	N	N	N	Y	Y
ARKANSAS								
Bumpers	N	N	Y	Y	Y	Y	Y	N
Pryor	Y	N	Y	Y	Y	Y	Y	N
CALIFORNIA								
Boxer	Y	N	Y	Y	Y	Y	Y	N
Feinstein	N	N	Y	Y	Y	Y	Y	Y
COLORADO								
Campbell	Y	N	N	N	Y	Y	Y	Y
Brown	Y	Y	N	N	N	N	Y	Y
CONNECTICUT								
Dodd	Y	N	Y	Y	Y	Y	Y	N
Lieberman	Y	Y	Y	Y	Y	Y	Y	N
DELAWARE								
Biden	Y	?	Y	Y	Y	N	Y	N
Roth	Y	Y	Y	N	N	N	Y	Y
FLORIDA								
Graham	Y	N	?	Y	Y	Y	Y	N
Mack	N	Y	N	N	N	N	Y	Y
GEORGIA								
Nunn	?	?	?	?	?	?	Y	N
Coverdell	?	?	?	?	?	?	Y	Y
HAWAII								
Akaka	Y	N	Y	Y	Y	Y	Y	N
Inouye	Y	?	Y	Y	Y	Y	Y	N
IDAHO								
Craig	Y	Y	N	N	N	N	Y	Y
Kempthorne	Y	Y	N	N	N	N	Y	Y
ILLINOIS								
Moseley-Braun	Y	N	Y	Y	Y	Y	Y	N
Simon	Y	N	Y	Y	Y	Y	Y	N
INDIANA								
Coats	Y	Y	N	N	N	N	Y	Y
Lugar	N	Y	N	N	N	N	Y	Y
IOWA								
Harkin	Y	N	Y	N	Y	Y	Y	N
Grassley	Y	Y	N	N	N	N	Y	Y
KANSAS								
Dole	Y	N	N	N	N	N	Y	Y
Kassebaum	Y	Y	N	N	N	N	Y	Y
KENTUCKY								
Ford	Y	N	Y	Y	Y	Y	Y	N
McConnell	Y	Y	N	N	N	N	Y	Y
LOUISIANA								
Breaux	Y	N	Y	Y	Y	?	Y	Y
Johnston	N	N	Y	Y	Y	?	Y	N
MAINE								
Mitchell	Y	N	Y	Y	Y	Y	Y	N
Cohen	Y	Y	N	N	N	N	Y	Y
MARYLAND								
Mikulski	Y	N	Y	Y	Y	Y	Y	N
Sarbanes	Y	N	Y	Y	Y	Y	Y	N
MASSACHUSETTS								
Kennedy	Y	N	Y	Y	Y	Y	Y	N
Kerry	Y	N	Y	Y	Y	Y	Y	N
MICHIGAN								
Levin	Y	N	Y	Y	Y	Y	Y	N
Riegle	Y	N	Y	Y	Y	Y	Y	N
MINNESOTA								
Wellstone	Y	N	Y	Y	Y	Y	Y	N
Durenberger	Y	Y	N	N	N	N	Y	Y
MISSISSIPPI								
Cochran	Y	Y	N	N	N	N	Y	Y
Lott	Y	Y	N	N	N	N	Y	Y
MISSOURI								
Bond	Y	Y	N	N	N	N	Y	Y
Danforth	Y	Y	N	N	N	N	Y	N
MONTANA								
Baucus	+	–	+	+	+	+	Y	Y
Burns	Y	Y	N	N	N	N	Y	Y
NEBRASKA								
Exon	Y	Y	N	Y	Y	Y	Y	N
Kerrey	Y	N	N	Y	Y	Y	?	?
NEVADA								
Bryan	Y	N	Y	Y	Y	Y	Y	N
Reid	Y	N	Y	Y	Y	Y	Y	N
NEW HAMPSHIRE								
Gregg	Y	Y	N	N	N	N	Y	Y
Smith	Y	Y	N	N	N	N	Y	Y
NEW JERSEY								
Bradley	Y	N	Y	Y	Y	Y	Y	N
Lautenberg	Y	Y	Y	N	Y	N	Y	N
NEW MEXICO								
Bingaman	Y	N	Y	Y	Y	Y	Y	N
Domenici	Y	Y	?	?	?	?	?	?
NEW YORK								
Moynihan	Y	N	Y	Y	Y	Y	Y	N
D'Amato	Y	Y	N	N	N	N	Y	Y
NORTH CAROLINA								
Faircloth	Y	Y	N	N	N	N	Y	Y
Helms	Y	Y	N	N	N	N	Y	Y
NORTH DAKOTA								
Conrad	?	N	Y	Y	Y	Y	Y	N
Dorgan	Y	N	Y	Y	Y	N	Y	N
OHIO								
Glenn	Y	N	Y	Y	Y	Y	Y	N
Metzenbaum	Y	N	?	Y	Y	N	?	?
OKLAHOMA								
Boren	Y	N	Y	Y	Y	Y	Y	N
Nickles	Y	Y	N	N	N	N	Y	Y
OREGON								
Hatfield	+	+	–	–	–	–	+	+
Packwood	Y	Y	N	N	N	?	Y	Y
PENNSYLVANIA								
Wofford	Y	N	N	Y	Y	Y	?	N
Specter	Y	Y	N	N	N	N	Y	Y
RHODE ISLAND								
Pell	Y	N	Y	Y	Y	Y	Y	N
Chafee	Y	Y	N	N	N	?	Y	Y
SOUTH CAROLINA								
Hollings	?	?	?	?	?	Y	Y	Y
Thurmond	Y	Y	N	N	N	N	Y	Y
SOUTH DAKOTA								
Daschle	Y	N	Y	Y	Y	Y	Y	N
Pressler	Y	Y	N	N	N	N	Y	Y
TENNESSEE								
Mathews	Y	N	Y	Y	Y	Y	Y	N
Sasser	Y	N	Y	Y	Y	Y	Y	N
TEXAS								
Krueger	Y	?	?	?	Y	Y	Y	?
Gramm	Y	Y	N	N	N	N	Y	Y
UTAH								
Bennett	?	?	N	N	N	N	Y	Y
Hatch	Y	Y	N	N	N	N	Y	Y
VERMONT								
Leahy	Y	N	Y	Y	Y	Y	Y	N
Jeffords	Y	Y	N	N	N	N	Y	Y
VIRGINIA								
Robb	N	N	Y	Y	Y	Y	Y	N
Warner	Y	Y	N	N	N	N	?	?
WASHINGTON								
Murray	Y	N	Y	Y	Y	Y	Y	N
Gorton	Y	Y	N	N	N	N	Y	Y
WEST VIRGINIA								
Byrd	Y	N	Y	Y	Y	Y	Y	N
Rockefeller	N	N	Y	Y	Y	Y	Y	N
WISCONSIN								
Feingold	Y	N	Y	Y	Y	N	Y	N
Kohl	Y	N	Y	N	Y	Y	Y	N
WYOMING								
Simpson	Y	Y	N	N	N	N	Y	Y
Wallop	Y	Y	N	N	N	N	Y	Y

KEY

Y Voted for (yea).
\# Paired for.
\+ Announced for.
N Voted against (nay).
X Paired against.
– Announced against.
P Voted "present."
C Voted "present" to avoid possible conflict of interest.
? Did not vote or otherwise make a position known.

Democrats   *Republicans*

ND Northern Democrats   SD Southern Democrats

Southern states - Ala., Ark., Fla., Ga., Ky., La., Miss., N.C., Okla., S.C., Tenn., Texas, Va.

137. S 3. Campaign Finance/1994 Effective Date. McCain, R-Ariz., amendment to make the bill effective for the 1994 elections rather than the 1996 elections as provided in the bill. Adopted 85-7: R 37-2; D 48-5 (ND 38-2, SD 10-3), June 8, 1993.

138. S 3. Campaign Finance/Financing Sources. McConnell, R-Ky., motion to table (kill) the Boren, D-Okla., amendment to the Gregg, R-N.H., amendment, to provide that revenue generated from the elimination of the tax deduction for lobbying expenses be used for the public financing of public elections and to reduce the deficit. The Gregg amendment would require that if the elimination of the deduction is used by the 1993 budget reconciliation bill (HR 2264) for deficit reduction, then alternative financing for the bill must be found for it to become effective. Motion rejected 43-47: R 39-0; D 4-47 (ND 3-36, SD 1-11), June 8, 1993. (Subsequently, the Boren amendment and the Gregg amendment, as amended by the Boren amendment, were adopted by voice vote.)

139. S 3. Campaign Finance/Repeated Public Financing. Boren, D-Okla., motion to table (kill) the Bennett, R-Utah, amendment to prohibit candidates from receiving public financing if they have received public financing in the two previous general elections. Motion agreed to 47-43: R 0-39; D 47-4 (ND 36-4, SD 11-0), June 9, 1993.

140. S 3. Campaign Finance/Advertising Disclosure. Boren, D-Okla., motion to table (kill) the McConnell, R-Ky., amendment to require campaign commercials that are paid for with communication vouchers to include the sentence: "The preceding political advertisement was paid for with taxpayer funds." Motion agreed to 47-45: R 0-39; D 47-6 (ND 37-4, SD 10-2), June 9, 1993.

141. S 3. Campaign Finance/Funding for Challengers. Ford, D-Ky., motion to table (kill) the Bennett, R-Utah, amendment to limit public financing to challengers, thereby excluding incumbents. Motion agreed to 53-40: R 0-39; D 53-1 (ND 41-0, SD 12-1), June 9, 1993.

142. S 3. Campaign Finance/Compliance Expenditures. Boren, D-Okla., motion to table (kill) the McConnell, R-Ky., amendment to require that money spent on legal and accounting compliance be counted against general election expenditure limits. Currently, the bill provides an exclusion for such expenditures. Motion agreed to 47-44: R 0-37; D 47-7 (ND 35-6, SD 12-1), June 9, 1993.

143. S 3. Campaign Finance/Audits. Kempthorne, R-Idaho, amendment to require complete audits of campaigns by candidates who accept public financing. Prior to the amendment, the bill would have required that only 10 percent of a publicly financed campaign be audited. Adopted 92-0: R 39-0; D 53-0 (ND 39-0, SD 14-0), June 10, 1993.

144. S 3. Campaign Finance/Personal Loans. McCain, R-Ariz., amendment to limit the amount a wealthy candidate or candidate's family could lend his or her campaign and be repaid to 4 percent of a state's spending limit or $200,000, whichever is less. Rejected 44-49: R 38-1; D 6-48 (ND 3-37, SD 3-11), June 10, 1993.

KEY

- Y   Voted for (yea).
- #   Paired for.
- +   Announced for.
- N   Voted against (nay).
- X   Paired against.
- −   Announced against.
- P   Voted "present."
- C   Voted "present" to avoid possible conflict of interest.
- ?   Did not vote or otherwise make a position known.

Democrats   *Republicans*

	145	146	147	148	149	150	151	152
ALABAMA								
Heflin	Y	Y	Y	N	Y	Y	N	N
Shelby	N	N	N	N	N	N	N	N
ALASKA								
Murkowski	?	?	N	N	N	N	N	N
Stevens	N	N	N	N	N	Y	N	N
ARIZONA								
DeConcini	Y	Y	Y	Y	Y	Y	Y	Y
McCain	N	N	N	N	N	N	N	Y
ARKANSAS								
Bumpers	Y	Y	Y	Y	Y	Y	Y	N
Pryor	Y	Y	Y	Y	Y	?	Y	Y
CALIFORNIA								
Boxer	Y	Y	Y	Y	Y	Y	Y	N
Feinstein	Y	Y	Y	Y	Y	Y	Y	N
COLORADO								
Campbell	Y	Y	Y	Y	Y	Y	N	N
Brown	N	N	N	N	Y	N	Y	N
CONNECTICUT								
Dodd	Y	Y	Y	Y	Y	Y	Y	N
Lieberman	N	Y	Y	Y	Y	Y	N	N
DELAWARE								
Biden	Y	Y	Y	Y	Y	Y	Y	N
Roth	N	N	N	N	N	N	N	Y
FLORIDA								
Graham	Y	Y	Y	Y	Y	Y	Y	N
Mack	N	N	N	N	N	Y	N	N
GEORGIA								
Nunn	Y	Y	?	Y	N	Y	N	N
Coverdell	N	N	N	N	N	Y	N	N
HAWAII								
Akaka	Y	Y	Y	Y	Y	Y	Y	N
Inouye	Y	Y	Y	Y	Y	Y	Y	N
IDAHO								
Craig	N	N	N	N	N	Y	N	N
Kempthorne	N	N	N	N	N	Y	N	N
ILLINOIS								
Moseley-Braun	Y	Y	Y	Y	Y	Y	Y	Y
Simon	Y	Y	Y	Y	Y	Y	Y	Y
INDIANA								
Coats	N	N	N	N	N	Y	N	N
Lugar	N	N	N	N	N	N	N	N

	145	146	147	148	149	150	151	152
IOWA								
Harkin	Y	Y	Y	?	Y	Y	Y	Y
Grassley	N	N	N	N	N	Y	N	Y
KANSAS								
Dole	N	N	N	N	Y	N	N	N
Kassebaum	N	N	N	N	Y	Y	?	Y
KENTUCKY								
Ford	Y	Y	Y	Y	Y	Y	Y	N
McConnell	N	N	N	N	Y	N	N	N
LOUISIANA								
Breaux	Y	Y	Y	Y	Y	Y	Y	N
Johnston	Y	Y	Y	Y	Y	Y	Y	N
MAINE								
Mitchell	Y	Y	Y	Y	Y	Y	Y	N
Cohen	N	N	N	N	N	N	N	Y
MARYLAND								
Mikulski	Y	Y	Y	Y	Y	Y	Y	N
Sarbanes	Y	Y	Y	Y	Y	Y	Y	N
MASSACHUSETTS								
Kennedy	Y	Y	Y	Y	Y	Y	Y	N
Kerry	Y	Y	Y	Y	Y	Y	Y	N
MICHIGAN								
Levin	Y	Y	Y	Y	Y	Y	Y	N
Riegle	Y	Y	Y	Y	Y	Y	Y	N
MINNESOTA								
Wellstone	Y	Y	Y	Y	Y	Y	Y	Y
Durenberger	N	N	N	N	N	Y	N	Y
MISSISSIPPI								
Cochran	N	N	N	N	N	Y	N	N
Lott	N	N	N	N	N	Y	N	N
MISSOURI								
Bond	N	N	N	N	N	Y	N	N
Danforth	N	N	N	N	N	Y	N	N
MONTANA								
Baucus	Y	Y	Y	Y	Y	Y	Y	N
Burns	N	N	N	N	N	Y	N	N
NEBRASKA								
Exon	Y	N	N	Y	Y	Y	Y	N
Kerrey	?	?	Y	Y	Y	Y	Y	N
NEVADA								
Bryan	Y	Y	Y	Y	Y	Y	Y	Y
Reid	Y	Y	Y	Y	Y	Y	Y	Y

	145	146	147	148	149	150	151	152
NEW HAMPSHIRE								
Gregg	N	N	N	N	Y	N	N	N
Smith	N	N	N	N	Y	N	N	N
NEW JERSEY								
Bradley	?	Y	Y	Y	Y	Y	Y	N
Lautenberg	Y	Y	Y	Y	Y	Y	Y	Y
NEW MEXICO								
Bingaman	Y	Y	Y	Y	N	Y	Y	N
Domenici	?	?	N	N	N	Y	N	N
NEW YORK								
Moynihan	Y	Y	Y	Y	Y	Y	Y	N
D'Amato	N	N	N	N	N	Y	N	Y
NORTH CAROLINA								
Faircloth	N	N	N	N	N	N	N	N
Helms	N	N	N	Y	N	Y	N	N
NORTH DAKOTA								
Conrad	Y	Y	Y	Y	Y	Y	Y	Y
Dorgan	N	Y	Y	Y	Y	Y	Y	Y
OHIO								
Glenn	Y	Y	Y	Y	Y	Y	Y	N
Metzenbaum	?	?	Y	Y	Y	Y	Y	N
OKLAHOMA								
Boren	Y	Y	Y	Y	Y	Y	Y	N
Nickles	N	N	N	N	Y	N	N	N
OREGON								
Hatfield	−	−	N	N	Y	N	N	N
Packwood	N	N	N	N	N	Y	N	Y
PENNSYLVANIA								
Wofford	Y	Y	Y	Y	Y	N	Y	Y
Specter	N	N	?	?	?	?	?	?
RHODE ISLAND								
Pell	Y	Y	Y	Y	Y	Y	Y	Y
Chafee	N	N	N	N	N	Y	N	N
SOUTH CAROLINA								
Hollings	Y	Y	Y	N	Y	Y	Y	N
Thurmond	N	N	N	N	N	Y	N	N
SOUTH DAKOTA								
Daschle	Y	Y	Y	Y	Y	Y	Y	N
Pressler	N	N	N	N	N	Y	N	Y
TENNESSEE								
Mathews	Y	Y	?	Y	Y	Y	Y	N
Sasser	Y	Y	Y	Y	Y	Y	Y	N

	145	146	147	148	149	150	151	152
TEXAS								
Krueger	Y	Y						
Gramm	N	N	N	N	Y	N	N	N
Hutchison **			N	N	N	Y	N	Y
UTAH								
Bennett	N	N	N	N	N	Y	N	N
Hatch	N	N	N	N	N	Y	N	N
VERMONT								
Leahy	Y	Y	Y	Y	Y	Y	Y	N
Jeffords	Y	N	N	Y	N	Y	Y	N
VIRGINIA								
Robb	Y	Y	Y	Y	Y	Y	Y	N
Warner	?	?	N	?	?	Y	N	Y
WASHINGTON								
Murray	Y	Y	Y	Y	Y	Y	Y	N
Gorton	N	N	N	N	N	Y	N	N
WEST VIRGINIA								
Byrd	Y	Y	Y	Y	Y	Y	Y	Y
Rockefeller	Y	Y	Y	Y	Y	Y	Y	N
WISCONSIN								
Feingold	Y	Y	Y	Y	N	Y	Y	N
Kohl	N	Y	Y	Y	N	Y	Y	N
WYOMING								
Simpson	N	N	N	N	Y	N	N	N
Wallop	N	N	N	N	Y	N	N	N

ND Northern Democrats   SD Southern Democrats   Southern states - Ala., Ark., Fla., Ga., Ky., La., Miss., N.C., Okla., S.C., Tenn., Texas, Va.

---

145. S 3. Campaign Finance/Subsidy Cap. Boren, D-Okla., motion to table (kill) the Nickles, R-Okla., amendment to place a $1 million limit on the amount of subsidies that an eligible Senate candidate may receive. Motion agreed to 51-42: R 1-38; D 50-4 (ND 36-3, SD 14-1), June 10, 1993.

146. S 3. Campaign Finance/Cloture. Motion to invoke cloture (thus limiting debate) on the bill to provide public financing for candidates who abide by voluntary spending limits. Motion rejected 53-41: R 0-39; D 53-2 (ND 39-1, SD 14-1), June 10, 1993. Three-fifths of the total Senate (60) is required to invoke cloture.

147. S 3. Campaign Finance/Cloture. Motion to invoke cloture (thus limiting debate) on the bill to provide partial public financing for candidates who abide by voluntary spending limits. Motion rejected 52-45: R 0-43; D 52-2 (ND 41-1, SD 11-1), June 15, 1993. Three-fifths of the total Senate (60) is required to invoke cloture. A "yea" was a vote in support of the president's position.

148. S 3. Campaign Finance/Public Financing. Boren, D-Okla., motion to table (kill) the Shelby, D-Ala., amendment to eliminate the provisions in the bill that provide public financing of and spending limits for federal campaigns. Motion agreed to 53-44: R 1-41; D 52-3 (ND 41-0, SD 11-3), June 16, 1993.

149. S 3. Campaign Finance/Out-of-State Contributions. Boren, D-Okla., motion to table (kill) the Domenici, R-N.M., amendment to limit out-of-state contributions to 40 percent of the spending limit unless a candidate's opponent spends more than $25,000 of personal money. Motion agreed to 53-45: R 2-40; D 51-5 (ND 39-3, SD 12-2), June 16, 1993.

150. S 3. Campaign Finance/Free Broadcast Time. Boren, D-Okla., motion to table (kill) the Roth, R-Del., amendment to strike public financing from the bill and require television stations to provide free broadcast time to congressional candidates during the last 45 days of an election. Motion agreed to 91-7: R 38-5; D 53-2 (ND 41-1, SD 12-1), June 16, 1993.

151. S 3. Campaign Finance/Suspension for Deficits. Boren, D-Okla., motion to table (kill) the Gramm, R-Texas, amendment to prohibit public financing of congressional elections in years when there is a projected federal budget deficit or a year after there was a deficit. Motion agreed to 53-45: R 1-41; D 52-4 (ND 40-2, SD 12-2), June 16, 1993.

152. S 3. Campaign Finance/Individual Contribution Limit. Wellstone, D-Minn., amendment to limit individual contributions to $500 per election. Rejected 32-67: R 12-31; D 20-36 (ND 18-24, SD 2-12), June 16, 1993.

*** Kay Bailey Hutchison, R-Texas, defeated Democrat Bob Krueger in a special election and was sworn in June 14. Vote 147 was the first vote for which she was eligible.*

	153	154	155	156	157	158	159	160
ALABAMA								
Heflin	N	Y	N	Y	N	N	Y	N
Shelby	N	N	Y	Y	Y	N	Y	Y
ALASKA								
Murkowski	N	N	N	Y	N	N	Y	Y
Stevens	N	N	N	Y	N	N	Y	N
ARIZONA								
DeConcini	Y	Y	Y	N	N	Y	Y	Y
McCain	N	Y	Y	N	N	Y	Y	Y
ARKANSAS								
Bumpers	Y	Y	N	N	Y	Y	Y	N
Pryor	Y	Y	N	N	Y	Y	Y	N
CALIFORNIA								
Boxer	Y	Y	Y	N	Y	Y	Y	N
Feinstein	Y	Y	Y	N	Y	Y	Y	N
COLORADO								
Campbell	Y	Y	Y	N	Y	Y	Y	N
Brown	N	N	N	Y	N	N	Y	Y
CONNECTICUT								
Dodd	Y	Y	Y	N	Y	Y	Y	N
Lieberman	Y	Y	Y	N	Y	Y	Y	Y
DELAWARE								
Biden	Y	Y	Y	N	Y	Y	Y	N
Roth	N	N	Y	Y	?	N	Y	Y
FLORIDA								
Graham	Y	Y	N	N	Y	Y	Y	N
Mack	N	N	N	Y	N	N	Y	Y
GEORGIA								
Nunn	Y	Y	Y	N	Y	Y	Y	Y
Coverdell	N	N	N	Y	N	N	Y	Y
HAWAII								
Akaka	Y	Y	N	N	Y	Y	Y	N
Inouye	Y	Y	N	N	Y	Y	Y	N
IDAHO								
Craig	N	N	N	Y	N	N	Y	Y
Kempthorne	N	N	N	Y	N	N	Y	Y
ILLINOIS								
Moseley-Braun	Y	Y	Y	N	Y	Y	Y	N
Simon	Y	Y	Y	N	Y	Y	Y	N
INDIANA								
Coats	N	N	N	Y	N	N	Y	Y
Lugar	N	N	N	Y	N	N	?	Y
IOWA								
Harkin	N	Y	Y	N	Y	Y	Y	N
Grassley	N	N	N	Y	N	N	Y	Y
KANSAS								
Dole	N	N	N	Y	N	N	Y	Y
Kassebaum	Y	Y	N	N	Y	Y	Y	N
KENTUCKY								
Ford	Y	Y	N	N	Y	Y	Y	N
McConnell	N	N	N	Y	N	N	Y	Y
LOUISIANA								
Breaux	Y	Y	N	N	Y	Y	Y	N
Johnston	N	Y	Y	N	Y	Y	Y	N
MAINE								
Mitchell	Y	Y	Y	N	Y	Y	Y	N
Cohen	N	Y	Y	N	Y	Y	Y	Y
MARYLAND								
Mikulski	Y	Y	Y	N	Y	Y	Y	N
Sarbanes	Y	Y	N	N	Y	Y	Y	N
MASSACHUSETTS								
Kennedy	Y	Y	Y	N	Y	Y	Y	N
Kerry	Y	Y	Y	N	Y	Y	Y	N
MICHIGAN								
Levin	Y	Y	Y	N	Y	Y	Y	N
Riegle	Y	Y	Y	N	Y	Y	Y	N
MINNESOTA								
Wellstone	N	Y	Y	N	Y	Y	Y	N
Durenberger	Y	Y	N	N	Y	Y	Y	Y
MISSISSIPPI								
Cochran	N	N	N	Y	N	N	Y	N
Lott	N	N	N	Y	N	N	Y	Y
MISSOURI								
Bond	N	N	N	Y	N	N	Y	Y
Danforth	N	N	Y	Y	N	N	Y	Y
MONTANA								
Baucus	Y	Y	Y	N	Y	Y	Y	N
Burns	N	N	N	Y	N	N	Y	Y
NEBRASKA								
Exon	Y	Y	N	N	Y	Y	Y	N
Kerrey	Y	Y	N	N	Y	Y	Y	N
NEVADA								
Bryan	Y	Y	N	N	Y	Y	Y	N
Reid	Y	Y	N	N	Y	Y	Y	N
NEW HAMPSHIRE								
Gregg	N	N	N	Y	N	N	Y	Y
Smith	N	N	N	Y	N	N	?	Y
NEW JERSEY								
Bradley	Y	Y	Y	N	Y	Y	Y	N
Lautenberg	N	Y	Y	N	Y	Y	Y	N
NEW MEXICO								
Bingaman	Y	Y	Y	N	Y	Y	Y	N
Domenici	N	N	N	Y	N	N	Y	Y
NEW YORK								
Moynihan	Y	Y	Y	N	Y	Y	Y	N
D'Amato	N	N	N	Y	N	N	Y	Y
NORTH CAROLINA								
Faircloth	N	N	N	Y	N	N	Y	Y
Helms	N	N	N	Y	N	N	Y	Y
NORTH DAKOTA								
Conrad	Y	Y	N	N	Y	Y	Y	N
Dorgan	Y	Y	N	N	Y	Y	Y	N
OHIO								
Glenn	Y	Y	Y	N	Y	Y	Y	N
Metzenbaum	N	Y	Y	N	Y	Y	Y	N
OKLAHOMA								
Boren	Y	Y	N	N	Y	Y	Y	N
Nickles	N	N	N	Y	N	N	Y	Y
OREGON								
Hatfield	N	N	N	Y	N	N	Y	N
Packwood	N	N	N	Y	N	N	Y	N
PENNSYLVANIA								
Wofford	Y	Y	Y	N	Y	Y	Y	N
Specter	?	?	?	?	?	?	?	?
RHODE ISLAND								
Pell	Y	Y	Y	N	Y	Y	Y	N
Chafee	Y	Y	Y	N	Y	Y	Y	N
SOUTH CAROLINA								
Hollings	N	Y	Y	N	Y	N	Y	N
Thurmond	N	N	N	Y	N	N	Y	Y
SOUTH DAKOTA								
Daschle	Y	Y	N	N	Y	Y	Y	N
Pressler	Y	Y	Y	N	Y	Y	Y	Y
TENNESSEE								
Mathews	Y	Y	N	N	Y	Y	Y	N
Sasser	Y	Y	N	N	Y	Y	Y	N
TEXAS								
Gramm	N	N	N	Y	N	N	Y	Y
Hutchison	N	N	N	Y	N	N	Y	Y
UTAH								
Bennett	N	N	N	Y	N	N	Y	Y
Hatch	N	N	N	Y	N	N	Y	Y
VERMONT								
Leahy	Y	Y	Y	N	Y	Y	Y	N
Jeffords	Y	Y	N	N	Y	Y	Y	N
VIRGINIA								
Robb	Y	Y	N	N	Y	Y	Y	N
Warner	N	N	N	Y	N	N	Y	Y
WASHINGTON								
Murray	N	Y	N	N	Y	Y	Y	+
Gorton	N	N	N	Y	N	N	Y	N
WEST VIRGINIA								
Byrd	Y	Y	N	N	Y	Y	Y	N
Rockefeller	Y	Y	N	N	Y	Y	Y	N
WISCONSIN								
Feingold	Y	Y	N	N	Y	Y	Y	N
Kohl	Y	Y	N	N	Y	Y	Y	N
WYOMING								
Simpson	N	N	-	+	-	-	+	Y
Wallop	N	N	N	Y	N	N	+	Y

KEY

Y Voted for (yea).
\# Paired for.
\+ Announced for.
N Voted against (nay).
X Paired against.
— Announced against.
P Voted "present."
C Voted "present" to avoid possible conflict of interest.
? Did not vote or otherwise make a position known.

Democrats   *Republicans*

ND Northern Democrats   SD Southern Democrats   Southern states - Ala., Ark., Fla., Ga., Ky., La., Miss., N.C., Okla., S.C., Tenn., Texas, Va.

153. S 3. Campaign Finance/Tax on Non-Complying Campaigns. Durenberger, R-Minn., amendment to impose a tax equal to the highest corporate rate on campaigns that do not abide by voluntary spending limits and to strip most public funding from the bill except for candidates who face opponents who exceed spending limits or independent campaigns against them. Adopted 52-47: R 5-38; D 47-9 (ND 37-5, SD 10-4), June 16, 1993.

154. S 3. Campaign Finance/Cloture. Motion to invoke cloture (thus limiting debate) on the bill to tax campaigns that do not abide by voluntary spending limits, provide benefits for candidates who do comply and make numerous other changes in campaign finance law. Motion agreed to 62-37: R 7-36; D 55-1 (ND 42-0, SD 13-1), June 16, 1993. Three-fifths of the total Senate (60) is required to invoke cloture. A "yea" was a vote in support of the president's position.

155. S 3. Campaign Finance/Free Broadcast Time. Pell, D-R.I., amendment to require broadcasters to provide candidates who abide by voluntary spending limits with limited free broadcast time during the general election. Rejected 32-66: R 5-37; D 27-29 (ND 23-19, SD 4-10), June 17, 1993.

156. S 3. Campaign Finance/Constitutional Violations. McConnell, R-Ky., point of order against the bill for violating the Constitution by originating a revenue bill in the Senate and breaching the principles of the Supreme Court's decision in *Buckley v. Valeo*. Rejected 39-59: R 36-6; D 3-53 (ND 0-42, SD 3-11), June 17, 1993.

157. S 3. Campaign Finance/Discount Broadcast Elimina-

tion. Boren, D-Okla., motion to table (kill) the Nickles, R-Okla., amendment to eliminate the 50 percent reduced broadcast rate. Motion agreed to 53-44: R 5-36; D 48-8 (ND 36-6, SD 12-2), June 17, 1993.

158. S 3. Campaign Finance/Passage. Passage of the bill to provide benefits for candidates who comply with voluntary spending limits, to tax campaigns that do not abide by the limits and to make numerous other changes in campaign finance law. Passed 60-38: R 7-35; D 53-3 (ND 42-0, SD 11-3), June 17, 1993. A "yea" was a vote in support of the president's position.

159. HR 2118. Fiscal 1993 Supplemental Appropriations/Defense Rescission. Byrd, D-W.Va., amendment to rescind $1.2 billion in previously approved defense spending to offset new defense spending in the bill, including $750 million for Operation Restore Hope in Somalia. Adopted 95-0: R 39-0; D 56-0 (ND 42-0, SD 14-0), June 17, 1993.

160. HR 2118. Fiscal 1993 Supplemental Appropriations/Economic Growth Plan. Roth, R-Del., motion to waive the budget act with respect to the Byrd, D-W.Va., point of order against the Roth amendment for violating the budget act. The Roth amendment would provide $46 billion in tax cuts, including indexing of capital gains, a modification of passive-loss rules, IRA expansion, and repeal of luxury taxes, offset by $58 billion in spending cuts. Motion rejected 39-59: R 35-8; D 4-51 (ND 2-39, SD 2-12), June 22, 1993. A three-fifths majority vote (60) of the total Senate is required to waive the budget act. (Subsequently, the chair upheld the Byrd point of order, and the Roth amendment fell.)

KEY

Y Voted for (yea).
Paired for.
+ Announced for.
N Voted against (nay).
X Paired against.
− Announced against.
P Voted ''present.''
C Voted ''present'' to avoid possible conflict of interest.
? Did not vote or otherwise make a position known.

Democrats   *Republicans*

	161	162	163	164	165	166	167	168
ALABAMA								
Heflin	?	Y	N	Y	N	Y	Y	Y
Shelby	Y	Y	N	Y	Y	Y	N	N
ALASKA								
Murkowski	Y	Y	N	N	Y	Y	N	N
Stevens	Y	Y	N	N	Y	Y	N	N
ARIZONA								
DeConcini	Y	Y	Y	Y	N	Y	N	Y
McCain	Y	N	N	N	Y	Y	N	N
ARKANSAS								
Bumpers	Y	N	N	Y	N	Y	Y	Y
Pryor	Y	N	Y	Y	N	Y	Y	Y
CALIFORNIA								
Boxer	Y	Y	Y	Y	N	Y	Y	Y
Feinstein	Y	Y	N	Y	N	Y	Y	Y
COLORADO								
Campbell	N	N	Y	N	Y	Y	Y	Y
Brown	Y	N	Y	N	Y	Y	N	N
CONNECTICUT								
Dodd	Y	Y	Y	Y	N	Y	Y	Y
Lieberman	Y	Y	N	Y	N	Y	N	Y
DELAWARE								
Biden	Y	Y	N	Y	N	Y	Y	Y
Roth	Y	N	N	N	Y	Y	N	N
FLORIDA								
Graham	Y	Y	Y	Y	N	Y	Y	Y
Mack	N	N	N	N	Y	Y	N	N
GEORGIA								
Nunn	Y	Y	N	Y	N	Y	Y	Y
Coverdell	Y	N	N	N	Y	Y	N	N
HAWAII								
Akaka	Y	Y	Y	Y	N	Y	Y	Y
Inouye	Y	Y	Y	Y	N	Y	Y	Y
IDAHO								
Craig	N	N	N	N	Y	Y	N	N
Kempthorne	N	N	N	N	Y	Y	N	N
ILLINOIS								
Moseley-Braun	Y	N	Y	Y	N	Y	Y	Y
Simon	Y	N	Y	Y	N	Y	Y	Y
INDIANA								
Coats	Y	N	N	N	Y	Y	N	N
Lugar	Y	N	N	N	Y	Y	N	N
IOWA								
Harkin	N	N	Y	Y	N	Y	Y	Y
Grassley	N	N	N	N	Y	Y	N	N
KANSAS								
Dole	N	N	N	N	Y	Y	N	N
Kassebaum	Y	N	N	N	Y	Y	N	N
KENTUCKY								
Ford	Y	Y	N	Y	N	Y	Y	Y
McConnell	Y	N	N	N	Y	Y	N	N
LOUISIANA								
Breaux	Y	Y	Y	Y	N	Y	Y	Y
Johnston	Y	Y	N	Y	N	Y	Y	Y
MAINE								
Mitchell	Y	Y	Y	Y	N	Y	Y	Y
Cohen	Y	Y	N	N	Y	Y	N	N
MARYLAND								
Mikulski	Y	Y	N	Y	N	Y	Y	Y
Sarbanes	Y	Y	Y	Y	N	Y	Y	Y
MASSACHUSETTS								
Kennedy	Y	Y	Y	Y	N	Y	Y	Y
Kerry	Y	Y	Y	Y	N	Y	Y	Y
MICHIGAN								
Levin	Y	Y	Y	Y	N	Y	Y	Y
Riegle	Y	Y	Y	Y	N	Y	Y	Y
MINNESOTA								
Wellstone	N	N	Y	N	N	N	N	Y
Durenberger	N	N	N	N	Y	Y	N	N
MISSISSIPPI								
Cochran	Y	Y	N	N	Y	Y	N	N
Lott	Y	Y	N	N	Y	Y	N	N
MISSOURI								
Bond	N	N	N	N	Y	Y	N	N
Danforth	N	N	N	N	Y	Y	N	N
MONTANA								
Baucus	Y	N	N	Y	N	Y	Y	Y
Burns	N	N	N	N	Y	Y	N	N
NEBRASKA								
Exon	N	N	Y	Y	N	Y	Y	Y
Kerrey	N	N	Y	Y	N	Y	Y	Y
NEVADA								
Bryan	Y	Y	N	Y	N	Y	Y	Y
Reid	Y	Y	N	Y	N	Y	Y	Y
NEW HAMPSHIRE								
Gregg	Y	N	N	Y	Y	Y	N	N
Smith	Y	N	N	N	Y	Y	N	N
NEW JERSEY								
Bradley	Y	Y	Y	N	N	N	Y	Y
Lautenberg	Y	Y	N	Y	N	Y	N	Y
NEW MEXICO								
Bingaman	Y	N	N	Y	N	Y	Y	Y
Domenici	Y	N	N	N	Y	Y	N	N
NEW YORK								
Moynihan	N	Y	Y	Y	N	Y	Y	Y
D'Amato	N	N	N	N	Y	Y	N	N
NORTH CAROLINA								
Faircloth	N	N	N	N	Y	Y	N	N
Helms	Y	N	N	N	Y	Y	N	N
NORTH DAKOTA								
Conrad	N	N	N	Y	N	Y	Y	Y
Dorgan	N	N	N	Y	N	Y	Y	Y
OHIO								
Glenn	Y	N	Y	N	Y	Y	Y	Y
Metzenbaum	Y	Y	Y	N	N	Y	Y	Y
OKLAHOMA								
Boren	Y	N	Y	N	Y	Y	Y	Y
Nickles	Y	N	N	N	Y	Y	N	N
OREGON								
Hatfield	Y	Y	N	N	Y	Y	N	N
Packwood	Y	Y	N	N	Y	N	N	N
PENNSYLVANIA								
Wofford	Y	Y	N	Y	N	Y	Y	Y
Specter	?	?	?	?	?	?	?	?
RHODE ISLAND								
Pell	Y	Y	Y	Y	N	Y	Y	Y
Chafee	Y	N	N	N	Y	Y	N	N
SOUTH CAROLINA								
Hollings	Y	Y	Y	N	Y	Y	Y	Y
Thurmond	N	N	N	N	Y	Y	N	N
SOUTH DAKOTA								
Daschle	N	Y	Y	Y	N	Y	Y	Y
Pressler	N	N	N	N	Y	Y	N	?
TENNESSEE								
Mathews	Y	Y	N	Y	N	Y	Y	Y
Sasser	Y	Y	N	Y	N	Y	Y	Y

	161	162	163	164	165	166	167	168
TEXAS								
Gramm	Y	N	N	N	Y	Y	N	N
Hutchison	Y	N	N	N	Y	Y	N	N
UTAH								
Bennett	Y	N	N	N	Y	Y	N	N
Hatch	N	N	N	N	Y	Y	N	N
VERMONT								
Leahy	Y	Y	N	Y	N	Y	Y	Y
Jeffords	Y	N	Y	N	Y	Y	N	N
VIRGINIA								
Robb	Y	Y	Y	Y	N	Y	Y	Y
Warner	N	N	N	N	Y	Y	N	N
WASHINGTON								
Murray	+	+	+	+	−	+	+	+
Gorton	Y	Y	N	N	Y	Y	N	N
WEST VIRGINIA								
Byrd	Y	Y	Y	Y	N	Y	Y	Y
Rockefeller	Y	Y	Y	Y	N	Y	Y	Y
WISCONSIN								
Feingold	Y	Y	Y	N	N	N	Y	Y
Kohl	Y	N	N	Y	N	Y	N	Y
WYOMING								
Simpson	Y	N	N	N	Y	Y	N	N
Wallop	Y	N	N	N	Y	Y	N	N

ND Northern Democrats   SD Southern Democrats

Southern states - Ala., Ark., Fla., Ga., Ky., La., Miss., N.C., Okla., S.C., Tenn., Texas, Va.

161. HR 2118. Fiscal 1993 Supplemental Appropriations/ Corn Farmer Disaster Relief. Byrd, D-W.Va., motion to table (kill) the Pressler, R-S.D., amendment to allow corn farmers to plant soybeans without losing federal benefits. Motion agreed to 73-24: R 28-15; D 45-9 (ND 32-9, SD 13-0), June 22, 1993.

162. HR 2118. Fiscal 1993 Supplemental Appropriations/ Cargo Preference. Breaux, D-La., motion to table (kill) the Brown, R-Colo., amendment to express the sense of the Senate about overcharging for the transport of food aid to Russia. Motion rejected 47-51: R 8-35; D 39-16 (ND 28-13, SD 11-3), June 22, 1993. (Subsequently, the Brown amendment was adopted by voice vote.)

163. HR 2118. Fiscal 1993 Supplemental Appropriations/ Welfare Work Requirement. Moynihan, D-N.Y., motion to table (kill) the D'Amato, R-N.Y., amendment to cut federal welfare aid to states that do not abide by certain ''workfare'' requirements. Motion rejected 34-64: R 1-42; D 33-22 (ND 27-14, SD 6-8), June 22, 1993. (Subsequently, the D'Amato amendment was adopted by voice vote.)

164. S 1134. 1993 Budget Reconciliation/Small Business. Daschle, D-S.D., motion to waive the budget act with respect to the Domenici, R-N.M., point of order against the Mitchell, D-Maine, amendment for violating the 1974 budget act. The Mitchell amendment would provide a capital gains tax cut and increased expensing for small businesses. Motion rejected 54-44: R 3-40; D 51-4 (ND 37-4, SD 14-0), June 23, 1993. A three-fifths majority vote (60) of the total Senate is required to waive the budget act. (Subsequently, the chair upheld the Domenici point of order, and the Mitchell amendment fell.)

165. S 1134. 1993 Budget Reconciliation/Republican Substitute. Domenici, R-N.M., motion to waive the budget act with respect to the Sasser, D-Tenn., point of order against the Dole, R-Kan., amendment for violating the 1974 budget act. The Dole substitute would cut the deficit by $367 billion over five years through spending cuts alone. Motion rejected 43-55: R 42-1; D 1-54 (ND 0-41, SD 1-13), June 23, 1993. A three-fifths majority vote (60) of the total Senate is required to waive the budget act. (Subsequently, the chair upheld the Sasser point of order, and the Dole amendment fell.) A ''nay'' was a vote in support of the president's position.

166. S 1134. 1993 Budget Reconciliation/Expensing Allowance. Mitchell, D-Maine, amendment to raise to $20,500 the first-year small-business deduction for equipment and machinery. Adopted 93-5: R 42-1; D 51-4 (ND 37-4, SD 14-0), June 24, 1993.

167. S 1134. 1993 Budget Reconciliation/Gas Tax. Breaux, D-La., motion to table (kill) the Nickles, R-Okla., amendment to eliminate the 4.3-cent tax on transportation fuels. Motion agreed to 50-48: R 0-43; D 50-5 (ND 37-4, SD 13-1), June 24, 1993. A ''yea'' was a vote in support of the president's position.

168. S 1134. 1993 Budget Reconciliation/Entitlement Caps. Sasser, D-Tenn., motion to waive the budget act with respect to the Gramm, R-Texas, point of order against the Sasser amendment for violating the budget act. The Sasser amendment would cap entitlement spending. Motion rejected 54-43: R 0-42; D 54-1 (ND 41-0, SD 13-1), June 24, 1993. A three-fifths majority vote (60) of the total Senate is required to waive the budget act. (Subsequently, the chair upheld the Gramm point of order, and the Sasser amendment fell.)

	169	170	171	172	173	174	175	176
ALABAMA								
Heflin	N	N	Y	Y	N	N	Y	N
Shelby	N	N	Y	N	Y	N	Y	Y
ALASKA								
Murkowski	N	N	Y	N	Y	N	Y	Y
Stevens	N	N	Y	N	Y	N	Y	N
ARIZONA								
DeConcini	N	Y	Y	Y	Y	N	Y	N
McCain	N	N	Y	N	Y	N	Y	Y
ARKANSAS								
Bumpers	Y	Y	N	Y	N	Y	N	N
Pryor	Y	Y	N	N	Y	N	Y	N
CALIFORNIA								
Boxer	Y	N	N	Y	N	Y	N	N
Feinstein	Y	N	N	Y	N	Y	N	Y
COLORADO								
Campbell	Y	N	N	Y	N	N	Y	N
Brown	N	N	Y	N	Y	N	Y	Y
CONNECTICUT								
Dodd	Y	Y	Y	N	N	Y	N	N
Lieberman	Y	Y	Y	Y	Y	Y	Y	Y
DELAWARE								
Biden	Y	N	Y	Y	N	Y	N	Y
Roth	N	N	Y	N	Y	Y	Y	Y
FLORIDA								
Graham	Y	N	N	Y	N	Y	Y	Y
Mack	N	N	Y	N	Y	N	Y	Y
GEORGIA								
Nunn	Y	Y	Y	Y	N	Y	Y	Y
Coverdell	N	N	Y	N	Y	N	Y	Y
HAWAII								
Akaka	Y	N	N	Y	N	Y	N	N
Inouye	Y	N	N	X	N	Y	N	N
IDAHO								
Craig	N	N	Y	N	Y	N	Y	Y
Kempthorne	N	N	Y	N	Y	N	Y	Y
ILLINOIS								
Moseley-Braun	Y	N	N	Y	N	Y	N	N
Simon	Y	Y	N	Y	N	Y	N	Y
INDIANA								
Coats	N	N	Y	N	Y	Y	Y	Y
Lugar	N	N	Y	N	Y	Y	Y	Y

	169	170	171	172	173	174	175	176
IOWA								
Harkin	Y	N	N	Y	N	Y	N	N
Grassley	N	N	Y	N	Y	N	Y	Y
KANSAS								
Dole	N	N	Y	N	Y	N	Y	Y
Kassebaum	N	N	Y	Y	Y	N	Y	Y
KENTUCKY								
Ford	Y	Y	N	Y	N	N	N	N
McConnell	N	N	Y	N	Y	N	Y	Y
LOUISIANA								
Breaux	Y	N	N	N	N	N	N	N
Johnston	Y	N	N	Y	N	Y	N	N
MAINE								
Mitchell	Y	Y	N	Y	N	Y	N	N
Cohen	N	N	Y	N	Y	Y	Y	N
MARYLAND								
Mikulski	Y	N	N	Y	N	Y	N	N
Sarbanes	Y	N	N	Y	N	Y	N	N
MASSACHUSETTS								
Kennedy	Y	N	N	Y	N	Y	N	Y
Kerry	Y	N	Y	N	Y	N	Y	
MICHIGAN								
Levin	Y	N	N	Y	N	Y	N	N
Riegle	Y	N	N	Y	N	Y	N	N
MINNESOTA								
Wellstone	Y	N	N	Y	N	Y	N	N
Durenberger	N	N	Y	N	Y	N	Y	Y
MISSISSIPPI								
Cochran	N	N	Y	N	Y	N	Y	N
Lott	N	N	Y	N	Y	N	Y	Y
MISSOURI								
Bond	N	N	Y	N	Y	N	Y	Y
Danforth	Y	N	Y	Y	Y	Y	Y	Y
MONTANA								
Baucus	Y	N	N	N	N	N	N	N
Burns	N	N	Y	N	Y	N	Y	Y
NEBRASKA								
Exon	Y	Y	Y	Y	N	Y	N	N
Kerrey	Y	Y	Y	Y	N	?	N	N
NEVADA								
Bryan	N	N	N	Y	N	Y	Y	N
Reid	Y	Y	N	N	N	Y	N	N

	169	170	171	172	173	174	175	176
NEW HAMPSHIRE								
Gregg	N	Y	Y	N	Y	Y	Y	Y
Smith	N	N	Y	N	Y	Y	Y	Y
NEW JERSEY								
Bradley	Y	N	N	Y	N	Y	N	Y
Lautenberg	Y	N	N	Y	Y	Y	N	Y
NEW MEXICO								
Bingaman	N	Y	Y	N	N	N	Y	N
Domenici	N	N	Y	N	Y	N	Y	N
NEW YORK								
Moynihan	Y	N	N	N	N	Y	N	N
D'Amato	N	N	Y	N	Y	N	Y	Y
NORTH CAROLINA								
Faircloth	N	N	Y	N	Y	N	Y	Y
Helms	N	N	Y	N	Y	N	Y	Y
NORTH DAKOTA								
Conrad	Y	N	N	Y	N	N	N	N
Dorgan	Y	N	N	Y	N	N	N	N
OHIO								
Glenn	Y	N	N	Y	N	Y	N	N
Metzenbaum	Y	N	Y	N	Y	N	Y	N
OKLAHOMA								
Boren	Y	Y	N	Y	N	Y	Y	Y
Nickles	N	N	Y	N	Y	Y	Y	Y
OREGON								
Hatfield	N	N	Y	N	Y	N	N	N
Packwood	N	N	Y	N	Y	N	Y	Y
PENNSYLVANIA								
Wofford	Y	N	N	Y	N	Y	N	Y
Specter	?	?	?	?	?	?	?	?
RHODE ISLAND								
Pell	Y	N	N	Y	N	Y	N	N
Chafee	N	N	Y	N	Y	N	Y	Y
SOUTH CAROLINA								
Hollings	Y	Y	N	N	Y	N	Y	N
Thurmond	N	N	Y	N	Y	N	Y	Y
SOUTH DAKOTA								
Daschle	Y	Y	N	Y	N	Y	N	N
Pressler	N	N	Y	N	Y	N	Y	Y
TENNESSEE								
Mathews	Y	Y	Y	N	N	Y	N	N
Sasser	Y	Y	N	Y	N	Y	N	N

	169	170	171	172	173	174	175	176
TEXAS								
Gramm	N	N	Y	N	Y	N	Y	Y
Hutchison	N	N	Y	Y	Y	N	Y	Y
UTAH								
Bennett	?	N	Y	N	Y	N	Y	Y
Hatch	N	N	Y	N	Y	N	Y	Y
VERMONT								
Leahy	Y	N	N	Y	N	N	N	N
Jeffords	N	Y	Y	Y	Y	N	N	N
VIRGINIA								
Robb	Y	N	N	N	N	Y	Y	Y
Warner	N	N	Y	N	Y	Y	Y	Y
WASHINGTON								
Murray	+	–	–	\#	–	+	–	–
Gorton	N	N	Y	N	Y	Y	Y	Y
WEST VIRGINIA								
Byrd	Y	N	N	Y	N	Y	N	N
Rockefeller	Y	N	N	Y	N	Y	N	N
WISCONSIN								
Feingold	Y	N	N	Y	N	Y	N	N
Kohl	Y	N	Y	Y	Y	Y	N	Y
WYOMING								
Simpson	N	N	Y	N	Y	N	Y	Y
Wallop	N	N	Y	N	Y	N	Y	Y

ND   Northern Democrats   SD   Southern Democrats   Southern states - Ala., Ark., Fla., Ga., Ky., La., Miss., N.C., Okla., S.C., Tenn., Texas, Va.

169. S 1134. 1993 Budget Reconciliation/Social Security Tax. Moynihan, D-N.Y., motion to table (kill) the Lott, R-Miss., amendment to strike provisions of the bill that raise the percentage of Social Security benefits taxed for certain recipients. Motion agreed to 51-46: R 1-41; D 50-5 (ND 38-3, SD 12-2), June 24, 1993. A "yea" was a vote in support of the president's position.

170. S 1134. 1993 Budget Reconciliation/Health Care Trust Fund. Kerrey, D-Neb., amendment to create a National Health Care Trust Fund on a pay-as-you-go basis. Rejected 19-79: R 2-41; D 17-38 (ND 10-31, SD 7-7), June 24, 1993.

171. S 1134. 1993 Budget Reconciliation/Small Business Exemptions. Roth, R-Del., motion to waive the budget act with respect to the Sasser, D-Tenn., point of order against the Roth amendment to give tax relief to small business and family farms, offset by a cut in discretionary spending. Motion rejected 56-42: R 43-0; D 13-42 (ND 9-32, SD 4-10), June 24, 1993. A three-fifths majority vote (60) of the total Senate is required to waive the budget act. (Subsequently, the chair upheld the Sasser point of order, and the Roth amendment fell.)

172. S 1134. 1993 Budget Reconciliation/Social Security Threshold. DeConcini, D-Ariz., amendment to increase the income threshold for applying the tax increase on Social Security benefits. Rejected 46-51: R 3-40; D 43-11 (ND 34-6, SD 9-5), June 24, 1993.

173. S 1134. 1993 Budget Reconciliation/Sunset Taxes. Dole, R-Kan., motion to waive the budget act with respect to the Moynihan, D-N.Y., point of order against the Dole amendment to sunset the bill's new taxes after five years. Rejected 48-50: R 43-0; D 5-50 (ND 4-37, SD 1-13), June 24, 1993. A three-fifths majority vote (60) of the total Senate is required to waive the budget act. (Subsequently, the chair upheld Moynihan's point of order; Dole's amendment fell.)

174. S 1134. 1993 Budget Reconciliation/Wool and Mohair Price Supports. Bryan, D-Nev., motion to waive the budget act with respect to the Domenici, R-N.M., point of order against the Bryan amendment to eliminate wool and mohair price supports. Motion rejected 52-45: R 10-33; D 42-12 (ND 32-8, SD 10-4), June 24, 1993. A three-fifths majority vote (60) of the total Senate is required to waive the budget act. (Subsequently, the chair upheld the Domenici point of order, and the Bryan amendment fell.)

175. S 1134. 1993 Budget Reconciliation/Fire Walls. Domenici, R-N.M., motion to waive the budget act with respect to the Sasser, D-Tenn., point of order against the Domenici amendment to extend budget walls through fiscal 1995. Motion rejected 53-45: R 41-2; D 12-43 (ND 6-35, SD 6-8), June 24, 1993. A three-fifths majority vote (60) of the total Senate is required to waive the budget act. (Subsequently, the chair upheld Sasser's point of order; Domenici's amendment fell.)

176. S 1134. 1993 Budget Reconciliation/Line-Item Veto. Bradley, D-N.J., motion to waive the budget act with respect to the Sasser, D-Tenn., point of order against the Bradley amendment to create a two-year line-item veto for appropriations and taxes. Motion rejected 53-45: R 37-6; D 16-39 (ND 10-31, SD 6-8), June 24, 1993. A three-fifths majority vote (60) of the total Senate is required to waive the budget act. (Subsequently, the chair upheld the Sasser point of order; the Bradley amendment fell.)

	177	178	179	180	181	182	183	184
ALABAMA								
Heflin	Y	Y	Y	N	N	Y	Y	Y
Shelby	N	N	N	N	N	Y	Y	N
ALASKA								
Murkowski	N	N	N	N	Y	Y	N	N
Stevens	N	N	N	N	Y	Y	N	N
ARIZONA								
DeConcini	Y	Y	Y	Y	N	N	Y	Y
McCain	N	N	N	N	Y	Y	N	N
ARKANSAS								
Bumpers	Y	Y	Y	N	Y	Y	Y	Y
Pryor	Y	N	Y	N	Y	Y	Y	Y
CALIFORNIA								
Boxer	Y	N	Y	N	N	N	N	Y
Feinstein	Y	N	Y	N	N	Y	Y	Y
COLORADO								
Campbell	Y	N	Y	N	Y	N	Y	Y
Brown	N	N	N	N	Y	Y	N	N
CONNECTICUT								
Dodd	Y	N	Y	N	N	N	N	Y
Lieberman	Y	N	Y	N	N	Y	N	Y
DELAWARE								
Biden	Y	N	Y	N	Y	N	Y	Y
Roth	N	N	N	N	N	Y	N	N
FLORIDA								
Graham	Y	Y	Y	N	Y	N	Y	Y
Mack	N	N	N	N	Y	Y	N	N
GEORGIA								
Nunn	Y	N	N	N	Y	Y	Y	Y
Coverdell	N	N	N	N	Y	Y	N	N
HAWAII								
Akaka	Y	N	Y	N	N	N	Y	Y
Inouye	Y	N	Y	N	N	Y	Y	Y
IDAHO								
Craig	N	N	N	N	Y	Y	N	N
Kempthorne	N	N	N	N	Y	Y	N	N
ILLINOIS								
Moseley-Braun	Y	Y	Y	N	N	N	N	Y
Simon	Y	Y	Y	N	N	N	N	Y
INDIANA								
Coats	N	N	N	N	Y	Y	N	N
Lugar	N	N	N	N	Y	Y	N	N

	177	178	179	180	181	182	183	184
IOWA								
Harkin	Y	Y	N	N	Y	Y	Y	Y
Grassley	N	N	N	N	Y	Y	N	N
KANSAS								
Dole	N	N	N	N	Y	Y	N	N
Kassebaum	N	N	N	Y	Y	Y	N	N
KENTUCKY								
Ford	Y	N	Y	N	Y	N	Y	Y
McConnell	N	N	N	N	Y	Y	N	N
LOUISIANA								
Breaux	Y	N	N	N	N	N	N	Y
Johnston	Y	N	Y	N	N	Y	Y	Y
MAINE								
Mitchell	Y	N	Y	N	Y	N	Y	Y
Cohen	N	N	Y	N	Y	Y	N	N
MARYLAND								
Mikulski	Y	Y	Y	N	Y	Y	Y	Y
Sarbanes	Y	N	Y	N	Y	Y	Y	Y
MASSACHUSETTS								
Kennedy	Y	N	N	N	N	N	N	Y
Kerry	Y	N	N	N	N	N	N	Y
MICHIGAN								
Levin	Y	N	Y	Y	Y	Y	Y	Y
Riegle	Y	N	Y	N	Y	N	Y	Y
MINNESOTA								
Wellstone	Y	Y	Y	N	N	N	N	Y
Durenberger	N	N	N	N	N	Y	N	Y
MISSISSIPPI								
Cochran	N	N	N	N	Y	Y	N	N
Lott	N	N	N	Y	Y	Y	N	N
MISSOURI								
Bond	N	N	N	Y	Y	Y	N	N
Danforth	N	N	N	N	Y	N	N	N
MONTANA								
Baucus	Y	N	Y	N	Y	Y	Y	Y
Burns	N	N	N	N	Y	Y	N	N
NEBRASKA								
Exon	Y	N	N	Y	Y	Y	Y	Y
Kerrey	Y	N	N	Y	Y	Y	Y	Y
NEVADA								
Bryan	Y	N	Y	Y	Y	Y	Y	Y
Reid	Y	N	Y	Y	Y	Y	Y	Y

	177	178	179	180	181	182	183	184
NEW HAMPSHIRE								
Gregg	N	N	N	N	Y	Y	N	N
Smith	N	N	N	N	Y	Y	N	N
NEW JERSEY								
Bradley	Y	N	N	N	N	N	N	Y
Lautenberg	Y	Y	N	N	Y	Y	Y	Y
NEW MEXICO								
Bingaman	Y	N	Y	N	Y	Y	Y	Y
Domenici	N	N	N	N	Y	Y	N	N
NEW YORK								
Moynihan	Y	N	N	N	N	N	N	Y
D'Amato	N	N	N	N	Y	Y	N	N
NORTH CAROLINA								
Faircloth	N	N	N	Y	Y	Y	N	N
Helms	N	N	N	N	Y	Y	N	N
NORTH DAKOTA								
Conrad	Y	N	N	N	Y	Y	Y	Y
Dorgan	Y	N	N	Y	Y	N	Y	Y
OHIO								
Glenn	Y	N	Y	N	N	N	Y	Y
Metzenbaum	Y	Y	N	Y	N	N	Y	Y
OKLAHOMA								
Boren	Y	N	N	Y	Y	Y	Y	Y
Nickles	N	N	N	N	Y	Y	N	N
OREGON								
Hatfield	N	N	N	N	Y	N	N	N
Packwood	N	N	N	N	Y	N	N	N
PENNSYLVANIA								
Wofford	Y	N	Y	N	Y	N	Y	Y
Specter	?	?	?	?	?	?	?	?
RHODE ISLAND								
Pell	Y	Y	Y	N	N	N	N	Y
Chafee	N	N	N	N	N	N	N	Y
SOUTH CAROLINA								
Hollings	Y	N	Y	Y	Y	Y	Y	Y
Thurmond	N	N	N	N	Y	Y	N	N
SOUTH DAKOTA								
Daschle	Y	N	Y	Y	Y	Y	Y	Y
Pressler	N	N	N	N	Y	Y	N	N
TENNESSEE								
Mathews	Y	Y	Y	Y	N	Y	Y	Y
Sasser	Y	N	Y	Y	Y	N	Y	Y

	177	178	179	180	181	182	183	184
TEXAS								
Gramm	N	N	N	N	Y	Y	N	N
Hutchison	N	N	N	N	Y	Y	N	N
UTAH								
Bennett	N	N	N	N	Y	Y	N	N
Hatch	N	N	N	N	Y	Y	N	N
VERMONT								
Leahy	Y	N	Y	Y	N	Y	Y	Y
Jeffords	Y	Y	Y	N	Y	N	N	Y
VIRGINIA								
Robb	Y	N	Y	N	N	N	N	Y
Warner	N	N	N	N	Y	Y	N	N
WASHINGTON								
Murray	+	−	−	−	−	−	+	+
Gorton	N	N	N	N	Y	Y	N	N
WEST VIRGINIA								
Byrd	Y	N	N	N	Y	N	Y	Y
Rockefeller	Y	N	N	N	N	N	N	Y
WISCONSIN								
Feingold	Y	Y	Y	N	Y	N	Y	Y
Kohl	Y	N	Y	N	Y	Y	Y	Y
WYOMING								
Simpson	N	N	N	N	Y	Y	N	N
Wallop	N	N	N	N	Y	Y	N	N

ND Northern Democrats   SD Southern Democrats   Southern states - Ala., Ark., Fla., Ga., Ky., La., Miss., N.C., Okla., S.C., Tenn., Texas, Va.

177. S 1134. 1993 Budget Reconciliation/Presidential Tax Checkoff. Mitchell, D-Maine, motion to table (kill) the McConnell, R-Ky., amendment to strike an increase in the presidential election tax checkoff from $1 to $3. Motion agreed to 55-43: R 1-42; D 54-1 (ND 41-0, SD 13-1), June 24, 1993.

178. S 1134. 1993 Budget Reconciliation/Medicare. Graham, D-Fla., motion to waive the budget act with respect to the Rockefeller, D-W.Va., point of order against the Graham amendment to reduce Medicare cuts in the bill. Motion rejected 15-83: R 1-42; D 14-41 (ND 10-31, SD 4-10), June 24, 1993. A three-fifths majority vote (60) of the total Senate is required to waive the budget act. (Subsequently, the chair upheld the Rockefeller point of order, and the Graham amendment fell.)

179. S 1134. 1993 Budget Reconciliation/Bovine Growth Hormone. Kohl, D-Wis., motion to waive the budget act with respect to the Danforth, R-Mo., point of order against a provision to prohibit the sale of bovine growth hormone. Motion rejected 38-60: R 2-41; D 36-19 (ND 26-15, SD 10-4), June 24, 1993. A three-fifths majority vote (60) of the total Senate is required to waive the budget act. (Subsequently, the chair upheld the Danforth point of order, and the prohibition was stricken.)

180. S 1134. 1993 Budget Reconciliation/Medicare. Bryan, D-Nev., motion to waive the budget act with respect to the Moynihan, D-N.Y., point of order against the Bryan amendment to eliminate the Section 936 corporate tax break and recommend that the resulting revenue be spent on Medicare. Motion rejected 20-78: R 6-37; D 14-41 (ND 11-30, SD 3-11), June 24, 1993. A three-fifths majority vote (60) of the total Senate is required to waive the budget act. (Subsequently, the chair upheld the Moynihan point of order, and the Bryan amendment fell.)

181. S 1134. 1993 Budget Reconciliation/Transportation Trust Funds. Brown, R-Colo., amendment to require that the transportation fuels tax increase go to the Highway Trust Fund or the Airport and Airway Trust Fund. Adopted 66-32: R 40-3; D 26-29 (ND 20-21, SD 6-8), June 24, 1993.

182. S 1134. 1993 Budget Reconciliation/Immunization Requirements. Bumpers, D-Ark., motion to waive the budget act with respect to the Riegle, D-Mich., point of order against the Bumpers amendment to allow states to set child immunization requirements for welfare recipients. Motion agreed to 69-29: R 39-4; D 30-25 (ND 19-22, SD 11-3), June 25, 1993 (in the session that began and the Congressional Record dated June 24). A three-fifths majority vote (60) of the total Senate is required to waive the budget act. (Subsequently, the Bumpers amendment was adopted by voice vote.)

183. S 1134. 1993 Budget Reconciliation/Deficit Retirement Account. DeConcini, D-Ariz., motion to waive the budget act with respect to the Domenici, R-N.M., point of order against the DeConcini amendment to require that all new revenue from the bill go to retire the debt. Motion rejected 55-43: R 0-43; D 55-0 (ND 41-0, SD 14-0), June 25, 1993 (in the session that began and the Congressional Record dated June 24). A three-fifths majority vote (60) of the total Senate is required to waive the budget act. (Subsequently, the chair upheld the Domenici point of order, and the DeConcini amendment fell.)

184. S 1134. 1993 Budget Reconciliation/Hospital Trust Fund. Mitchell, D-Maine, motion to table (kill) the McCain, R-Ariz., amendment to require that the increases in Social Security taxes go to the Social Security Trust Fund instead of the Hospital Trust Fund. Motion agreed to 57-41: R 3-40; D 54-1 (ND 41-0, SD 13-1), June 25, 1993 (in the session that began and the Congressional Record dated June 24).

	185	186	187	188	189	190	191	192
ALABAMA								
Heflin	N	N	N	Y	Y	Y	Y	N
Shelby	Y	Y	N	Y	Y	N	Y	N
ALASKA								
Murkowski	Y	Y	N	Y	Y	N	?	?
Stevens	Y	Y	N	Y	Y	N	N	Y
ARIZONA								
DeConcini	N	N	N	Y	N	N	Y	Y
McCain	Y	Y	N	Y	Y	N	Y	Y
ARKANSAS								
Bumpers	N	N	N	N	Y	Y	Y	Y
Pryor	N	N	N	N	Y	Y	Y	?
CALIFORNIA								
Boxer	N	N	N	N	N	Y	Y	Y
Feinstein	N	N	N	N	N	Y	Y	N
COLORADO								
Campbell	N	N	N	Y	Y	Y	Y	N
Brown	Y	Y	N	Y	Y	N	N	Y
CONNECTICUT								
Dodd	N	N	N	N	N	Y	Y	Y
Lieberman	N	N	N	Y	N	Y	+	Y
DELAWARE								
Biden	N	N	N	N	N	Y	Y	Y
Roth	Y	Y	N	Y	N	N	Y	Y
FLORIDA								
Graham	N	N	N	Y	N	Y	Y	Y
Mack	Y	Y	N	Y	Y	N	N	Y
GEORGIA								
Nunn	N	Y	N	Y	Y	N	Y	Y
Coverdell	Y	Y	N	Y	Y	N	N	Y
HAWAII								
Akaka	N	N	N	N	Y	N	Y	N
Inouye	N	N	N	N	Y	Y	Y	Y
IDAHO								
Craig	Y	Y	N	Y	Y	N	N	Y
Kempthorne	Y	Y	N	Y	Y	N	N	Y
ILLINOIS								
Moseley-Braun	N	N	N	N	N	Y	Y	Y
Simon	N	N	N	N	Y	Y	Y	Y
INDIANA								
Coats	Y	Y	N	Y	Y	N	Y	Y
Lugar	Y	Y	N	Y	Y	N	Y	Y
IOWA								
Harkin	N	N	N	Y	Y	Y	Y	Y
Grassley	Y	Y	N	Y	Y	N	N	Y
KANSAS								
Dole	Y	Y	N	Y	Y	N	N	Y
Kassebaum	Y	Y	N	Y	Y	N	Y	Y
KENTUCKY								
Ford	N	N	N	Y	Y	Y	Y	Y
McConnell	Y	Y	N	Y	Y	N	N	Y
LOUISIANA								
Breaux	N	N	N	N	Y	?	?	Y
Johnston	N	N	N	N	Y	N	Y	Y
MAINE								
Mitchell	N	N	N	N	N	Y	Y	Y
Cohen	Y	Y	N	Y	Y	N	Y	Y
MARYLAND								
Mikulski	N	N	N	N	N	Y	Y	Y
Sarbanes	N	N	N	N	N	Y	Y	Y
MASSACHUSETTS								
Kennedy	N	N	N	N	N	Y	Y	Y
Kerry	N	N	N	N	N	Y	Y	Y
MICHIGAN								
Levin	N	N	N	N	N	Y	Y	Y
Riegle	N	N	N	N	N	Y	Y	Y
MINNESOTA								
Wellstone	N	N	N	N	N	Y	Y	-
Durenberger	Y	Y	N	Y	Y	N	Y	+
MISSISSIPPI								
Cochran	Y	Y	N	Y	Y	N	N	Y
Lott	Y	Y	N	Y	Y	N	N	Y
MISSOURI								
Bond	Y	Y	N	Y	Y	N	Y	Y
Danforth	Y	Y	N	Y	N	N	Y	Y
MONTANA								
Baucus	N	N	N	Y	Y	Y	Y	Y
Burns	Y	Y	N	Y	Y	N	N	Y
NEBRASKA								
Exon	N	N	N	Y	Y	Y	Y	Y
Kerrey	N	N	N	Y	Y	Y	Y	Y
NEVADA								
Bryan	N	N	N	Y	Y	N	Y	Y
Reid	N	N	N	N	Y	Y	Y	Y
NEW HAMPSHIRE								
Gregg	Y	Y	N	Y	Y	N	?	Y
Smith	Y	Y	N	Y	Y	N	N	Y
NEW JERSEY								
Bradley	N	N	N	N	N	Y	Y	Y
Lautenberg	N	N	N	N	N	Y	Y	Y
NEW MEXICO								
Bingaman	N	Y	N	Y	Y	Y	Y	Y
Domenici	Y	Y	N	Y	Y	N	Y	Y
NEW YORK								
Moynihan	N	N	N	N	N	Y	Y	Y
D'Amato	Y	Y	N	Y	Y	N	Y	Y
NORTH CAROLINA								
Faircloth	Y	Y	N	Y	Y	N	Y	N
Helms	Y	Y	N	Y	Y	N	N	N
NORTH DAKOTA								
Conrad	N	N	N	Y	N	Y	Y	N
Dorgan	N	N	N	Y	N	Y	Y	N
OHIO								
Glenn	N	N	N	N	N	Y	Y	Y
Metzenbaum	N	N	N	N	N	Y	Y	N
OKLAHOMA								
Boren	N	N	N	N	N	Y	Y	Y
Nickles	Y	Y	N	Y	Y	N	N	Y
OREGON								
Hatfield	N	Y	N	Y	Y	Y	Y	Y
Packwood	Y	Y	N	Y	Y	N	Y	Y
PENNSYLVANIA								
Wofford	N	N	N	N	N	Y	Y	N
Specter	?	?	?	?	?	?	?	?
RHODE ISLAND								
Pell	N	N	N	N	Y	Y	Y	+
Chafee	Y	Y	N	Y	Y	N	N	Y
SOUTH CAROLINA								
Hollings	N	N	N	N	Y	Y	Y	N
Thurmond	Y	Y	N	Y	Y	N	Y	N
SOUTH DAKOTA								
Daschle	N	N	N	N	Y	Y	Y	?
Pressler	Y	Y	N	Y	Y	N	N	Y
TENNESSEE								
Mathews	N	N	N	N	Y	Y	Y	Y
Sasser	N	N	N	N	Y	Y	Y	Y
TEXAS								
Gramm	Y	Y	N	Y	Y	N	N	Y
Hutchison	Y	Y	N	Y	Y	N	Y	Y
UTAH								
Bennett	Y	Y	N	Y	Y	N	Y	Y
Hatch	Y	Y	N	Y	Y	N	Y	Y
VERMONT								
Leahy	N	N	N	N	N	Y	Y	Y
Jeffords	Y	Y	N	Y	Y	N	N	Y
VIRGINIA								
Robb	N	N	N	Y	N	Y	Y	Y
Warner	Y	Y	N	Y	Y	N	Y	Y
WASHINGTON								
Murray	-	-	-	-	+	+	+	+
Gorton	Y	Y	N	Y	Y	N	Y	Y
WEST VIRGINIA								
Byrd	N	N	N	N	Y	Y	Y	N
Rockefeller	N	N	N	N	N	Y	Y	Y
WISCONSIN								
Feingold	N	N	N	N	Y	Y	Y	N
Kohl	N	N	N	Y	N	Y	Y	Y
WYOMING								
Simpson	Y	Y	N	Y	Y	N	Y	Y
Wallop	Y	Y	N	Y	Y	N	N	Y

ND Northern Democrats   SD Southern Democrats

Southern states - Ala., Ark., Fla., Ga., Ky., La., Miss., N.C., Okla., S.C., Tenn., Texas, Va.

185. S 1134. 1993 Budget Reconciliation/Sequester. Gramm, R-Texas, motion to waive the budget act with respect to the Sasser, D-Tenn., point of order against the Gramm amendment to impose a sequester if any of the six deficit targets are not met. Motion rejected 43-55: R 42-1; D 1-54 (ND 0-41, SD 1-13), June 25, 1993 (in the Congressional Record dated June 24). A three-fifths majority vote (60) of the total Senate is required to waive the budget act. (Subsequently, the chair upheld the point of order; the Gramm amendment fell.)

186. S 1134. 1993 Budget Reconciliation/Retroactive Taxes. Burns, R-Mont., motion to waive the budget act with respect to the Sasser, D-Tenn., point of order against the Burns amendment to bar retroactive tax increases in the bill. Motion rejected 46-52: R 43-0; D 3-52 (ND 1-40, SD 2-12), June 25, 1993 (in the Congressional Record dated June 24). A three-fifths majority vote (60) of the total Senate is required to waive the budget act. (Subsequently, the chair upheld the Sasser point of order; the Burns amendment fell.)

187. S 1134. 1993 Budget Reconciliation/Paperwork Reduction. Sasser, D-Tenn., motion to table (kill) the Pressler, R-S.D., amendment to strike provisions requiring small businesses to report transactions over $600 to the IRS. Motion rejected 0-98: R 0-43; D 0-55 (ND 0-41, SD 0-14), June 25, 1993 (in the Congressional Record dated June 24). (Subsequently, Pressler's amendment was adopted by voice vote.)

188. S 1134. 1993 Budget Reconciliation/Federal Overhead Reduction. Hutchison, R-Texas, motion to waive the budget act with respect to the Sasser, D-Tenn., point of order against the Hutchison amendment to cut federal overhead by 10 percent over two years. Motion rejected 58-40: R 43-0; D 15-40 (ND 11-30, SD 4-10), June 25, 1993 (in the Congressional Record dated June 24). A three-fifths majority vote (60) of the total Senate is required to waive the budget act. (Subsequently, the chair upheld the Sasser point of order; the Hutchison amendment fell.)

189. S 1134. 1993 Budget Reconciliation/Vaccine Bulk Purchase Plan. Bumpers, D-Ark., amendment to revise the way the Medicaid program pays for vaccines and reimburses vaccine manufacturers. Adopted 59-39: R 39-4; D 20-35 (ND 10-31, SD 10-4), June 25, 1993 (in the Congressional Record dated June 24).

190. HR 2264. 1993 Budget Reconciliation/Passage. Passage of the bill to raise taxes and cut mandatory spending to reduce the deficit by $516 billion over five years. Passed 50-49: R 0-43; D 49-6 (ND 38-3, SD 11-3), with Vice President Gore casting a "yea" vote, June 25, 1993 (in the Congressional Record dated June 24). (Before passage, the Senate struck all after the enacting clause and inserted the text of S 1134 as amended.) A "yea" was a vote in support of the president's position.

191. Carter Nomination/Confirmation. Confirmation of President Clinton's nomination of Ashton B. Carter to be an assistant secretary of Defense. Confirmed 76-18: R 23-18; D 53-0 (ND 40-0, SD 13-0), June 29, 1993. A "yea" was a vote in support of the president's position.

192. HR 1876. GATT Fast-Track Extension/Passage. Passage of the bill to extend through April 16, 1994, authority to negotiate a GATT accord to be considered under fast-track rules. Passed (thus cleared for the president) 76-16: R 37-4; D 39-12 (ND 29-9, SD 10-3), June 30, 1993. A "yea" was a vote in support of the president's position.

	193	194	195	196	197	198	199	200
ALABAMA								
Heflin	Y	Y	Y	Y	Y	N	Y	Y
Shelby	N	Y	Y	Y	Y	Y	Y	Y
ALASKA								
Murkowski	Y	Y	N	N	—	—	—	—
Stevens	Y	Y	N	N	N	N	N	Y
ARIZONA								
DeConcini	Y	Y	Y	Y	Y	Y	Y	Y
McCain	Y	Y	N	N	N	N	N	N
ARKANSAS								
Bumpers	Y	Y	Y	Y	Y	Y	Y	Y
Pryor	Y	Y	Y	Y	Y	Y	Y	Y
CALIFORNIA								
Boxer	Y	Y	Y	Y	Y	Y	Y	Y
Feinstein	Y	Y	Y	Y	Y	N	N	Y
COLORADO								
Campbell	N	Y	N	Y	Y	Y	Y	Y
Brown	Y	Y	N	N	N	N	N	N
CONNECTICUT								
Dodd	Y	Y	Y	Y	Y	Y	Y	Y
Lieberman	N	N	Y	Y	Y	Y	Y	Y
DELAWARE								
Biden	Y	Y	Y	Y	Y	Y	N	Y
Roth	Y	Y	N	N	N	N	N	N
FLORIDA								
Graham	Y	Y	Y	Y	Y	Y	Y	Y
Mack	Y	Y	N	N	N	N	N	N
GEORGIA								
Nunn	Y	Y	Y	Y	Y	Y	Y	Y
Coverdell	Y	Y	N	N	N	N	N	N
HAWAII								
Akaka	Y	Y	Y	Y	Y	Y	Y	Y
Inouye	Y	Y	Y	Y	Y	Y	Y	Y
IDAHO								
Craig	Y	Y	Y	N	N	N	N	N
Kempthorne	Y	Y	N	N	N	N	N	N
ILLINOIS								
Moseley-Braun	Y	N	Y	Y	Y	Y	Y	Y
Simon	N	N	Y	Y	Y	Y	Y	Y
INDIANA								
Coats	Y	Y	N	N	N	N	N	N
Lugar	Y	Y	N	N	N	N	N	N
IOWA								
Harkin	?	?	?	?	Y	Y	Y	Y
Grassley	?	?	?	?	N	N	N	N
KANSAS								
Dole	Y	Y	N	N	N	N	N	N
Kassebaum	Y	Y	N	N	N	N	N	N
KENTUCKY								
Ford	Y	Y	Y	Y	Y	Y	N	Y
McConnell	Y	Y	N	N	N	N	N	N
LOUISIANA								
Breaux	Y	Y	Y	Y	Y	Y	Y	Y
Johnston	Y	Y	Y	Y	Y	Y	Y	Y
MAINE								
Mitchell	Y	Y	Y	Y	Y	Y	Y	Y
Cohen	Y	Y	N	N	N	N	N	N
MARYLAND								
Mikulski	Y	Y	Y	Y	Y	Y	Y	Y
Sarbanes	Y	Y	Y	Y	Y	Y	Y	Y
MASSACHUSETTS								
Kennedy	Y	Y	Y	Y	Y	Y	Y	Y
Kerry	Y	Y	Y	Y	Y	N	N	Y
MICHIGAN								
Levin	Y	Y	Y	Y	Y	Y	Y	Y
Riegle	Y	Y	Y	Y	Y	Y	Y	Y
MINNESOTA								
Wellstone	N	Y	Y	Y	Y	Y	Y	Y
Durenberger	N	Y	Y	Y	N	Y	N	Y
MISSISSIPPI								
Cochran	Y	Y	N	Y	N	N	N	N
Lott	Y	Y	N	N	N	N	N	N
MISSOURI								
Bond	Y	Y	N	Y	N	N	N	N
Danforth	Y	Y	N	Y	N	N	N	N
MONTANA								
Baucus	Y	Y	Y	Y	Y	Y	Y	Y
Burns	Y	Y	N	N	N	N	N	N
NEBRASKA								
Exon	Y	Y	Y	Y	Y	Y	N	Y
Kerrey	Y	Y	Y	Y	Y	Y	N	Y
NEVADA								
Bryan	Y	Y	Y	Y	Y	Y	N	Y
Reid	Y	Y	Y	Y	Y	Y	N	Y
NEW HAMPSHIRE								
Gregg	Y	Y	N	N	N	N	N	N
Smith	Y	Y	N	N	N	N	N	N
NEW JERSEY								
Bradley	Y	Y	Y	Y	Y	Y	N	Y
Lautenberg	Y	Y	Y	Y	Y	Y	Y	Y
NEW MEXICO								
Bingaman	Y	Y	Y	Y	Y	Y	N	Y
Domenici	Y	Y	N	N	N	N	N	N
NEW YORK								
Moynihan	Y	Y	Y	Y	Y	Y	Y	Y
D'Amato	Y	Y	N	N	N	N	N	N
NORTH CAROLINA								
Faircloth	Y	Y	N	?	N	N	N	N
Helms	Y	Y	N	N	N	N	N	N
NORTH DAKOTA								
Conrad	Y	Y	Y	Y	Y	Y	Y	Y
Dorgan	Y	Y	Y	Y	Y	Y	Y	Y
OHIO								
Glenn	Y	Y	Y	Y	Y	Y	Y	Y
Metzenbaum	Y	N	Y	Y	Y	Y	Y	Y
OKLAHOMA								
Boren	Y	Y	N	Y	Y	Y	N	N
Nickles	Y	Y	N	Y	N	N	N	N
OREGON								
Hatfield	Y	Y	Y	N	Y	N	N	N
Packwood	Y	Y	N	N	N	N	N	N
PENNSYLVANIA								
Wofford	Y	Y	Y	Y	Y	Y	Y	Y
Specter	?	?	?	?	N	N	N	N
RHODE ISLAND								
Pell	Y	Y	Y	Y	Y	Y	Y	Y
Chafee	Y	Y	N	Y	N	N	N	N
SOUTH CAROLINA								
Hollings	Y	Y	Y	Y	Y	N	N	Y
Thurmond	Y	Y	N	N	N	N	N	N
SOUTH DAKOTA								
Daschle	Y	Y	Y	Y	Y	Y	Y	Y
Pressler	Y	Y	N	N	N	N	N	N
TENNESSEE								
Mathews	Y	Y	Y	Y	Y	Y	N	Y
Sasser	Y	Y	Y	Y	Y	Y	Y	Y
TEXAS								
Gramm	Y	Y	N	N	N	N	N	N
Hutchison	Y	Y	N	N	N	N	N	N
UTAH								
Bennett	Y	Y	N	N	N	N	N	N
Hatch	Y	Y	N	N	N	N	N	N
VERMONT								
Leahy	Y	Y	Y	Y	Y	Y	Y	Y
Jeffords	?	Y	Y	Y	N	N	N	Y
VIRGINIA								
Robb	Y	Y	Y	Y	Y	Y	N	Y
Warner	?	?	?	?	N	N	N	N
WASHINGTON								
Murray	Y	Y	Y	Y	Y	Y	Y	Y
Gorton	Y	Y	N	N	N	N	N	N
WEST VIRGINIA								
Byrd	Y	Y	Y	Y	Y	Y	Y	Y
Rockefeller	Y	Y	Y	Y	Y	Y	Y	Y
WISCONSIN								
Feingold	N	Y	Y	Y	Y	Y	Y	Y
Kohl	Y	Y	Y	Y	Y	Y	N	Y
WYOMING								
Simpson	Y	Y	N	N	N	N	N	N
Wallop	Y	Y	N	N	N	N	N	N

ND Northern Democrats   SD Southern Democrats   Southern states - Ala., Ark., Fla., Ga., Ky., La., Miss., N.C., Okla., S.C., Tenn., Texas, Va.

193. S 185. Hatch Act Revision/Merit System Protection Board. Roth, R-Del., amendment to retain provisions in existing law allowing a federal employee to be removed for the first violation of the Hatch Act unless the Merit Systems Protection Board votes unanimously to suspend the employee's pay for 30 days. Adopted 88-7: R 39-1; D 49-6 (ND 36-5, SD 13-1), July 14, 1993.

194. S 185. Hatch Act Revision/Federal Employee Limitations. Roth, R-Del., amendment to express the sense of the Senate that federal employees should not be authorized to solicit political contributions from the general public or to be candidates for local office, except as expressly provided under existing law. Adopted 92-4: R 41-0; D 51-4 (ND 37-4, SD 14-0), July 14, 1993.

195. S 185. Hatch Act Revision/Employee Referendum. Glenn, D-Ohio, motion to table (kill) the Roth, R-Del., amendment to provide for an employee referendum on whether the Hatch Act under existing law or as proposed under the bill should take effect. Motion agreed to 62-34: R 8-33; D 54-1 (ND 41-0, SD 13-1), July 14, 1993.

196. S 185. Hatch Act Revision/Military Personnel. Glenn, D-Ohio, motion to table (kill) the McCain, R-Ariz., amendment to include military personnel for coverage under the bill. Motion agreed to 62-33: R 8-32; D 54-1 (ND 40-1, SD 14-0), July 14, 1993.

197. S 185. Hatch Act Revision/Midsession Budget Review. Glenn, D-Ohio, motion to table (kill) the Domenici, R-N.M., amendment to express the sense of the Senate that the president should submit a midsession budget review to Congress by July 26. Motion agreed to 56-43: R 0-43; D 56-0 (ND 42-0, SD 14-0), July 20, 1993.

198. S 185. Hatch Act Revision/IRS Agents. Glenn, D-Ohio, motion to table (kill) the Roth, R-Del., amendment to prohibit tax auditors, tax examiners and revenue agents of the Internal Revenue Service from taking an active part in political management or political campaigns. Motion agreed to 51-48: R 2-41; D 49-7 (ND 38-4, SD 11-3), July 20, 1993.

199. S 185. Hatch Act Revision/Justice Department Employees. Glenn, D-Ohio, motion to table (kill) the Roth, R-Del., amendment to prohibit employees of the Criminal Division of the Justice Department from taking an active part in political management or political campaigns. Motion rejected 43-56: R 1-42; D 42-14 (ND 33-9, SD 9-5), July 20, 1993. (Subsequently, the Roth amendment was adopted by voice vote.)

200. S 185. Hatch Act Revision/Solicitations by Federal Employees. Glenn, D-Ohio, motion to table (kill) the Kassebaum, R-Kan., amendment to strike the section of the bill that allows federal employees to solicit political contributions. Motion agreed to 58-41: R 3-40; D 55-1 (ND 42-0, SD 13-1), July 20, 1993.

	201	202	203	204	205	206	207	208
ALABAMA								
Heflin	Y	N	Y	N	Y	N	Y	Y
Shelby	Y	N	Y	Y	Y	N	Y	Y
ALASKA								
Murkowski	−	Y	N	Y	N	N	Y	Y
Stevens	Y	Y	N	Y	N	N	N	N
ARIZONA								
DeConcini	Y	N	Y	Y	Y	Y	Y	Y
McCain	Y	Y	N	Y	N	N	N	N
ARKANSAS								
Bumpers	Y	N	Y	N	Y	Y	Y	Y
Pryor	Y	N	Y	N	Y	Y	Y	Y
CALIFORNIA								
Boxer	Y	N	Y	Y	Y	Y	Y	Y
Feinstein	Y	N	Y	Y	Y	Y	Y	Y
COLORADO								
Campbell	Y	N	?	N	N	Y	Y	Y
Brown	N	Y	N	Y	N	Y	Y	Y
CONNECTICUT								
Dodd	Y	−	Y	N	Y	Y	Y	Y
Lieberman	Y	N	Y	N	Y	Y	Y	Y
DELAWARE								
Biden	Y	N	Y	N	Y	Y	Y	Y
Roth	N	Y	N	Y	N	N	Y	Y
FLORIDA								
Graham	Y	N	Y	N	Y	Y	Y	Y
Mack	N	N	N	Y	N	N	N	N
GEORGIA								
Nunn	Y	N	Y	N	Y	N	Y	N
Coverdell	N	N	N	Y	N	N	N	N
HAWAII								
Akaka	Y	N	Y	N	Y	Y	Y	Y
Inouye	Y	N	Y	N	Y	Y	Y	Y
IDAHO								
Craig	Y	Y	N	Y	?	N	N	N
Kempthorne	N	Y	N	Y	N	N	N	N
ILLINOIS								
Moseley-Braun	Y	N	Y	N	Y	Y	Y	Y
Simon	Y	N	Y	N	Y	Y	Y	Y
INDIANA								
Coats	N	?	?	?	N	N	Y	Y
Lugar	N	Y	N	Y	N	N	Y	Y
IOWA								
Harkin	Y	N	Y	N	Y	Y	Y	Y
Grassley	N	Y	N	Y	N	N	N	N
KANSAS								
Dole	N	Y	N	Y	N	N	N	N
Kassebaum	Y	Y	N	Y	N	N	N	Y
KENTUCKY								
Ford	Y	N	Y	N	Y	N	Y	Y
McConnell	N	Y	N	Y	N	N	N	N
LOUISIANA								
Breaux	Y	N	Y	N	Y	N	Y	Y
Johnston	Y	N	Y	N	Y	N	Y	Y
MAINE								
Mitchell	Y	N	Y	N	Y	Y	Y	Y
Cohen	N	Y	N	Y	N	Y	Y	Y
MARYLAND								
Mikulski	Y	N	Y	N	Y	Y	Y	Y
Sarbanes	Y	N	Y	N	Y	Y	Y	Y
MASSACHUSETTS								
Kennedy	Y	N	Y	N	Y	Y	Y	Y
Kerry	Y	N	Y	N	Y	Y	Y	Y
MICHIGAN								
Levin	Y	N	Y	N	Y	Y	Y	Y
Riegle	Y	N	Y	N	Y	Y	Y	Y
MINNESOTA								
Wellstone	Y	N	Y	N	Y	Y	Y	Y
Durenberger	Y	N	Y	N	Y	N	Y	Y
MISSISSIPPI								
Cochran	N	Y	N	Y	N	N	N	N
Lott	N	Y	N	Y	N	N	N	N
MISSOURI								
Bond	N	Y	N	Y	N	N	N	N
Danforth	N	Y	N	Y	N	N	Y	Y
MONTANA								
Baucus	Y	N	Y	N	Y	Y	Y	Y
Burns	N	Y	N	Y	N	N	N	N
NEBRASKA								
Exon	Y	Y	Y	Y	N	Y	Y	Y
Kerrey	Y	N	Y	N	N	Y	Y	Y
NEVADA								
Bryan	Y	N	Y	N	Y	Y	Y	Y
Reid	Y	N	Y	N	Y	Y	Y	Y
NEW HAMPSHIRE								
Gregg	N	Y	N	Y	N	N	Y	Y
Smith	N	Y	N	Y	N	N	N	N
NEW JERSEY								
Bradley	Y	N	Y	Y	Y	Y	Y	Y
Lautenberg	Y	N	Y	N	Y	Y	Y	Y
NEW MEXICO								
Bingaman	Y	N	Y	N	Y	Y	Y	Y
Domenici	N	Y	N	Y	N	N	Y	Y
NEW YORK								
Moynihan	Y	N	Y	N	Y	Y	Y	Y
D'Amato	Y	Y	N	Y	N	N	Y	Y
NORTH CAROLINA								
Faircloth	N	Y	N	Y	N	N	N	N
Helms	N	?	N	Y	N	N	N	N
NORTH DAKOTA								
Conrad	Y	N	Y	N	Y	Y	Y	Y
Dorgan	Y	N	Y	N	Y	Y	Y	Y
OHIO								
Glenn	Y	N	Y	N	Y	Y	Y	Y
Metzenbaum	Y	N	Y	N	Y	Y	Y	Y
OKLAHOMA								
Boren	N	N	Y	N	Y	N	Y	Y
Nickles	N	Y	N	Y	N	N	N	N
OREGON								
Hatfield	Y	Y	N	Y	Y	N	N	N
Packwood	Y	Y	N	Y	N	N	N	N
PENNSYLVANIA								
Wofford	Y	N	Y	N	Y	Y	Y	Y
Specter	Y	Y	N	Y	N	Y	Y	Y
RHODE ISLAND								
Pell	Y	N	Y	N	Y	Y	Y	Y
Chafee	Y	N	Y	N	N	N	Y	Y
SOUTH CAROLINA								
Hollings	Y	N	Y	N	N	Y	Y	Y
Thurmond	N	Y	N	Y	N	N	N	N
SOUTH DAKOTA								
Daschle	Y	N	Y	N	Y	Y	Y	Y
Pressler	N	Y	N	Y	N	Y	Y	Y
TENNESSEE								
Mathews	Y	N	Y	N	Y	N	Y	Y
Sasser	Y	N	Y	N	Y	N	Y	Y
TEXAS								
Gramm	N	Y	N	Y	N	N	N	N
Hutchison	N	Y	N	Y	N	N	Y	Y
UTAH								
Bennett	N	Y	N	Y	N	N	Y	Y
Hatch	N	Y	N	Y	N	N	N	N
VERMONT								
Leahy	Y	N	Y	N	Y	Y	Y	Y
Jeffords	Y	N	Y	N	Y	Y	Y	Y
VIRGINIA								
Robb	Y	N	Y	N	Y	Y	Y	Y
Warner	Y	Y	N	Y	N	N	Y	Y
WASHINGTON								
Murray	Y	N	Y	N	Y	Y	Y	Y
Gorton	Y	Y	N	Y	N	N	Y	Y
WEST VIRGINIA								
Byrd	Y	N	Y	N	Y	N	N	N
Rockefeller	Y	N	Y	N	Y	Y	Y	Y
WISCONSIN								
Feingold	Y	N	Y	N	Y	Y	Y	Y
Kohl	Y	N	N	N	Y	Y	Y	Y
WYOMING								
Simpson	N	Y	N	Y	N	N	Y	Y
Wallop	N	Y	N	Y	N	N	N	N

KEY

Y Voted for (yea).
Paired for.
+ Announced for.
N Voted against (nay).
X Paired against.
− Announced against.
P Voted "present."
C Voted "present" to avoid possible conflict of interest.
? Did not vote or otherwise make a position known.

Democrats *Republicans*

ND Northern Democrats   SD Southern Democrats   Southern states - Ala., Ark., Fla., Ga., Ky., La., Miss., N.C., Okla., S.C., Tenn., Texas, Va.

201. HR 20. Hatch Act Revision/Passage. Passage of the bill to revise the 1939 Hatch Act to allow limited political involvement by federal workers. Passed 68-31: R 13-30; D 55-1 (ND 42-0, SD 13-1), July 20, 1993. (Before passage, the Senate struck all after the enacting clause and inserted the text of S 185 as amended.)

202. S 919. National Service/Substitute. Kassebaum, R-Kan., substitute amendment to authorize approximately $100 million in additional spending in fiscal 1994 rather than the $389 million currently in the bill; provide for a two-year transition for existing federal national service programs to be incorporated into a single federal entity; allow states and localities more autonomy to develop programs; allocate funds to states and localities on individual state plans rather than a single national plan; and provide a different set of stipends and benefits. Rejected 38-59: R 37-5; D 1-54 (ND 1-40, SD 0-14), July 21, 1993.

203. S 919. National Service/Military Personnel. Wofford, D-Pa., motion to table (kill) the McCain, R-Ariz., amendment to make veterans eligible for national service education awards. Motion agreed to 56-42: R 2-41; D 54-1 (ND 40-1, SD 14-0), July 21, 1993.

204. S 919. National Service/Emergency Spending Offsets. Coverdell, R-Ga., amendment to delay the National Service program until the deficit increase resulting from emergency spending in fiscal 1993 supplemental appropriations bills has been eliminated through rescissions and transfers. Rejected 46-53: R 41-2; D 5-51 (ND 4-38, SD 1-13), July 21, 1993.

205. S 919. National Service/Funding for Other Education Programs. Wofford, D-Pa., motion to table (kill) the Domenici, R-N.M., amendment to prohibit the funding of national service education awards until the funding levels for certain federal education programs are at least equal to fiscal 1993 levels. Motion agreed to 55-44: R 3-40; D 52-4 (ND 39-3, SD 13-1), July 22, 1993.

206. S 919. National Service/United Daughters of the Confederacy. Moseley-Braun, D-Ill., motion to table (kill) the Helms, R-N.C., amendment to extend for 14 years the design patent for the insignia of the United Daughters of the Confederacy. Motion rejected 48-52: R 4-40; D 44-12 (ND 40-2, SD 4-10), July 22, 1993.

207. S 919. National Service/United Daughters of the Confederacy. Bennett, R-Utah, motion to reconsider the vote on the Moseley-Braun, D-Ill., motion to table (kill) the Helms, R-N.C., amendment to extend for 14 years the design patent for the insignia of the United Daughters of the Confederacy. Motion agreed to 76-24: R 21-23; D 55-1 (ND 41-1, SD 14-0), July 22, 1993.

208. S 919. National Service/United Daughters of the Confederacy. Reconsideration of the Moseley-Braun, D-Ill., motion to table (kill) the Helms, R-N.C., amendment to extend for 14 years the design patent for the insignia of the United Daughters of the Confederacy. Motion agreed to 75-25: R 21-23; D 54-2 (ND 41-1, SD 13-1), July 22, 1993. (The Senate earlier failed to table the Helms amendment on Vote 206.)

KEY

Y	Voted for (yea).
#	Paired for.
+	Announced for.
N	Voted against (nay).
X	Paired against.
−	Announced against.
P	Voted "present."
C	Voted "present" to avoid possible conflict of interest.
?	Did not vote or otherwise make a position known.

Democrats   *Republicans*

	209	210	211	212	213	214	215	216
ALABAMA								
Heflin	N	N	Y	N	N	Y	N	Y
Shelby	Y	N	N	Y	Y	Y	N	Y
ALASKA								
Murkowski	N	Y	Y	Y	N	Y	N	Y
Stevens	N	Y	Y	Y	Y	Y	N	Y
ARIZONA								
DeConcini	Y	N	Y	N	Y	N	N	Y
McCain	N	Y	N	Y	N	N	N	Y
ARKANSAS								
Bumpers	Y	N	?	?	Y	Y	Y	Y
Pryor	Y	N	?	?	Y	Y	Y	Y
CALIFORNIA								
Boxer	Y	N	N	Y	Y	Y	Y	Y
Feinstein	Y	N	N	Y	N	Y	Y	Y
COLORADO								
Campbell	Y	N	Y	N	Y	N	Y	N
Brown	N	Y	N	N	N	N	N	Y
CONNECTICUT								
Dodd	Y	N	Y	N	Y	N	Y	Y
Lieberman	Y	N	Y	Y	N	N	Y	N
DELAWARE								
Biden	Y	N	N	Y	Y	Y	Y	Y
Roth	Y	Y	N	N	N	N	Y	N
FLORIDA								
Graham	Y	N	Y	N	Y	N	Y	Y
Mack	N	Y	N	Y	N	N	Y	Y
GEORGIA								
Nunn	Y	N	N	Y	N	Y	Y	Y
Coverdell	N	Y	N	Y	Y	N	Y	Y
HAWAII								
Akaka	Y	N	Y	Y	Y	Y	Y	Y
Inouye	Y	N	Y	N	Y	N	Y	Y
IDAHO								
Craig	N	Y	N	Y	N	Y	N	Y
Kempthorne	N	Y	N	Y	Y	Y	N	Y
ILLINOIS								
Moseley-Braun	Y	N	Y	N	Y	N	Y	Y
Simon	Y	N	Y	N	Y	N	Y	Y
INDIANA								
Coats	Y	Y	N	N	Y	N	Y	Y
Lugar	N	Y	N	Y	N	N	Y	Y

	209	210	211	212	213	214	215	216
IOWA								
Harkin	Y	N	Y	Y	N	Y	Y	Y
Grassley	N	Y	N	Y	N	Y	N	Y
KANSAS								
Dole	N	Y	Y	Y	Y	Y	N	Y
Kassebaum	N	Y	Y	Y	N	Y	N	Y
KENTUCKY								
Ford	Y	N	Y	N	Y	N	Y	Y
McConnell	N	Y	Y	Y	Y	Y	N	Y
LOUISIANA								
Breaux	Y	N	Y	Y	Y	Y	Y	Y
Johnston	Y	N	Y	Y	Y	Y	Y	Y
MAINE								
Mitchell	Y	N	Y	Y	N	N	Y	Y
Cohen	N	Y	N	Y	N	Y	Y	Y
MARYLAND								
Mikulski	Y	N	Y	Y	Y	N	Y	Y
Sarbanes	Y	N	Y	Y	Y	N	Y	Y
MASSACHUSETTS								
Kennedy	Y	N	Y	Y	Y	Y	Y	Y
Kerry	Y	N	N	Y	N	N	Y	Y
MICHIGAN								
Levin	Y	N	N	Y	N	Y	Y	Y
Riegle	Y	N	Y	Y	N	Y	Y	Y
MINNESOTA								
Wellstone	Y	N	Y	Y	Y	N	Y	N
Durenberger	Y	N	Y	Y	Y	Y	N	Y
MISSISSIPPI								
Cochran	N	Y	Y	Y	Y	Y	N	Y
Lott	N	Y	Y	Y	Y	Y	N	Y
MISSOURI								
Bond	Y	Y	Y	?	N	Y	Y	Y
Danforth	N	Y	N	Y	N	Y	N	Y
MONTANA								
Baucus	Y	N	Y	N	Y	N	Y	N
Burns	N	Y	N	Y	Y	Y	N	Y
NEBRASKA								
Exon	Y	Y	N	Y	N	Y	Y	Y
Kerrey	Y	N	N	?	N	Y	N	Y
NEVADA								
Bryan	Y	N	N	Y	N	N	Y	Y
Reid	Y	N	Y	N	Y	N	N	Y

	209	210	211	212	213	214	215	216
NEW HAMPSHIRE								
Gregg	N	Y	N	Y	N	N	Y	N
Smith	N	Y	N	N	N	N	Y	N
NEW JERSEY								
Bradley	Y	N	N	Y	N	N	Y	Y
Lautenberg	Y	N	N	Y	N	N	Y	Y
NEW MEXICO								
Bingaman	Y	N	N	Y	N	N	N	Y
Domenici	N	Y	Y	Y	Y	Y	N	Y
NEW YORK								
Moynihan	Y	N	Y	N	Y	N	Y	Y
D'Amato	N	Y	N	Y	N	N	Y	Y
NORTH CAROLINA								
Faircloth	N	Y	N	Y	N	N	N	Y
Helms	N	Y	N	N	N	Y	N	N
NORTH DAKOTA								
Conrad	Y	N	Y	N	Y	N	Y	N
Dorgan	Y	N	Y	Y	Y	Y	N	Y
OHIO								
Glenn	Y	N	N	Y	N	N	Y	Y
Metzenbaum	Y	N	N	Y	N	N	Y	N
OKLAHOMA								
Boren	Y	N	Y	N	Y	N	Y	Y
Nickles	N	Y	N	Y	N	N	Y	Y
OREGON								
Hatfield	N	Y	Y	Y	Y	Y	Y	Y
Packwood	Y	Y	N	Y	Y	Y	?	Y
PENNSYLVANIA								
Wofford	Y	N	Y	N	Y	N	Y	Y
Specter	Y	Y	Y	Y	Y	Y	Y	Y
RHODE ISLAND								
Pell	Y	N	Y	N	Y	N	Y	N
Chafee	Y	Y	N	Y	N	N	Y	Y
SOUTH CAROLINA								
Hollings	Y	N	?	?	Y	Y	Y	Y
Thurmond	N	Y	Y	Y	Y	Y	N	Y
SOUTH DAKOTA								
Daschle	Y	N	Y	N	Y	Y	Y	N
Pressler	N	Y	N	?	Y	Y	N	Y
TENNESSEE								
Mathews	Y	N	Y	N	Y	N	Y	Y
Sasser	Y	N	Y	Y	Y	Y	Y	Y

	209	210	211	212	213	214	215	216
TEXAS								
Gramm	?	?	?	?	Y	Y	N	Y
Hutchison	Y	Y	N	Y	Y	Y	N	Y
UTAH								
Bennett	N	Y	N	Y	Y	Y	N	Y
Hatch	N	Y	N	Y	Y	Y	N	Y
VERMONT								
Leahy	Y	N	?	?	N	Y	Y	Y
Jeffords	Y	N	Y	Y	Y	Y	Y	Y
VIRGINIA								
Robb	Y	N	N	Y	N	Y	Y	Y
Warner	N	Y	N	Y	N	Y	N	N
WASHINGTON								
Murray	Y	N	Y	Y	Y	Y	Y	Y
Gorton	N	Y	Y	Y	N	Y	Y	Y
WEST VIRGINIA								
Byrd	Y	N	Y	Y	Y	Y	Y	Y
Rockefeller	Y	N	Y	Y	Y	N	Y	Y
WISCONSIN								
Feingold	Y	N	N	Y	N	N	Y	Y
Kohl	Y	N	N	N	N	N	Y	Y
WYOMING								
Simpson	N	Y	N	Y	Y	Y	N	N
Wallop	N	Y	N	Y	N	Y	N	N

ND Northern Democrats   SD Southern Democrats   Southern states - Ala., Ark., Fla., Ga., Ky., La., Miss., N.C., Okla., S.C., Tenn., Texas, Va.

209. S 919. National Service/Family and Medical Leave. Dodd, D-Conn., motion to table (kill) the Craig, R-Idaho, amendment to strike the provisions of the bill that provide participants in the National Service program with family and medical leave during their participation in the program. Adopted 64-35: R 9-34; D 55-1 (ND 42-0, SD 13-1), July 22, 1993.

210. S 919. National Service/Substitute. Kassebaum, R-Kan., substitute amendment to authorize approximately $100 million in fiscal 1994 rather than the $389 million currently in the bill; create a single consolidated program of current federal programs over two years; provide states maximum flexibility; and provide fiscal constraints that limit the rate of expansion of the program. Rejected 42-57: R 41-2; D 1-55 (ND 1-41, SD 0-14), July 22, 1993.

211. HR 2348. Fiscal 1994 Legislative Branch Appropriations/Franking. Stevens, R-Alaska, motion to table (kill) the Mack, R-Fla., amendment to eliminate the use of funds for unsolicited mass mailings. Motion agreed to 48-47: R 16-27; D 32-20 (ND 25-16, SD 7-4), July 23, 1993.

212. HR 2348. Fiscal 1994 Legislative Branch Appropriations/Passage. Passage of the bill to provide approximately $2.3 billion in new budget authority for the operations of Congress and legislative branch agencies in fiscal 1994. The agencies covered by the bill requested $2,641,945,500. Passed 85-7: R 37-4; D 48-3 (ND 38-2, SD 10-1), July 23, 1993.

213. HR 2493. Fiscal 1994 Agriculture Appropriations/

Rural Development Administration. Bumpers, D-Ark., motion to table (kill) the Reid, D-Nev., amendment to prohibit funding of the seven regional offices of the Rural Development Administration after April 1, 1994. Motion rejected 43-57: R 23-21; D 20-36 (ND 13-29, SD 7-7), July 27, 1993. (Subsequently, the Reid amendment was adopted by voice vote.)

214. HR 2493. Fiscal 1994 Agriculture Appropriations/Market Promotion Program. Cochran, R-Miss., motion to table (kill) the Bryan, D-Nev., amendment to eliminate the $75 million for the Market Promotion Program, which provides money to corporations for advertising to promote U.S. agricultural exports. Motion agreed to 70-30: R 31-13; D 39-17 (ND 25-17, SD 14-0), July 27, 1993.

215. HR 2493. Fiscal 1994 Agriculture Appropriations/Wool and Mohair Subsidy. Bumpers, D-Ark., motion to table (kill) the Craig, R-Idaho, motion to recommit the bill to the Senate Appropriations Committee with instructions to report it back with an amendment to eliminate the provision barring federal subsidies in fiscal 1994 under the wool and mohair programs. Motion agreed to 63-36: R 17-26; D 46-10 (ND 34-8, SD 12-2), July 27, 1993.

216. HR 2493. Fiscal 1994 Agriculture Appropriations/Passage. Passage of the bill to provide approximately $71 billion in new budget authority for the Department of Agriculture, rural development and related agencies for fiscal 1994. The Clinton administration requested $76,581,667,000. Passed 90-10: R 37-7; D 53-3 (ND 39-3, SD 14-0), July 27, 1993.

KEY

Y Voted for (yea).
Paired for.
+ Announced for.
N Voted against (nay).
X Paired against.
− Announced against.
P Voted "present."
C Voted "present" to avoid possible conflict of interest.
? Did not vote or otherwise make a position known.

Democrats *Republicans*

	217	218	219	220	221	222	223	224
ALABAMA								
Heflin	N	N	N	Y	Y	Y	N	Y
Shelby	N	N	N	Y	Y	Y	N	Y
ALASKA								
Murkowski	N	N	Y	N	Y	Y	N	N
Stevens	N	N	Y	Y	Y	Y	N	N
ARIZONA								
DeConcini	N	Y	N	N	Y	N	N	Y
McCain	N	N	N	Y	Y	Y	N	N
ARKANSAS								
Bumpers	N	N	Y	Y	Y	N	Y	Y
Pryor	N	N	Y	Y	Y	Y	Y	Y
CALIFORNIA								
Boxer	Y	Y	Y	Y	Y	N	Y	Y
Feinstein	Y	Y	Y	Y	Y	N	Y	Y
COLORADO								
Campbell	Y	Y	Y	N	Y	N	Y	Y
Brown	N	N	N	Y	Y	Y	Y	N
CONNECTICUT								
Dodd	Y	Y	Y	Y	Y	Y	N	Y
Lieberman	N	N	Y	Y	Y	Y	N	Y
DELAWARE								
Biden	Y	Y	Y	Y	Y	N	?	Y
Roth	N	N	N	Y	Y	Y	N	N
FLORIDA								
Graham	Y	Y	Y	Y	Y	N	Y	Y
Mack	N	N	Y	Y	Y	Y	N	N
GEORGIA								
Nunn	N	N	Y	Y	Y	Y	N	Y
Coverdell	N	N	Y	Y	Y	Y	N	N
HAWAII								
Akaka	Y	Y	Y	Y	Y	N	Y	Y
Inouye	Y	Y	Y	Y	N	Y	N	Y
IDAHO								
Craig	N	N	N	Y	Y	Y	N	N
Kempthorne	N	N	N	Y	Y	Y	N	N
ILLINOIS								
Moseley-Braun	Y	Y	Y	Y	N	N	N	Y
Simon	Y	Y	Y	Y	N	N	N	Y
INDIANA								
Coats	N	N	N	Y	Y	Y	N	N
Lugar	N	N	N	Y	Y	N	N	N

	217	218	219	220	221	222	223	224
IOWA								
Harkin	?	Y	Y	Y	N	N	N	Y
Grassley	N	N	N	Y	Y	Y	Y	N
KANSAS								
Dole	N	N	N	Y	Y	Y	N	N
Kassebaum	N	N	Y	Y	Y	Y	N	N
KENTUCKY								
Ford	N	Y	Y	Y	Y	Y	Y	N
McConnell	N	N	N	Y	Y	Y	Y	N
LOUISIANA								
Breaux	Y	N	Y	Y	Y	Y	Y	Y
Johnston	N	N	Y	Y	Y	Y	N	Y
MAINE								
Mitchell	Y	Y	Y	Y	N	N	N	Y
Cohen	Y	N	Y	Y	N	Y	N	N
MARYLAND								
Mikulski	Y	Y	Y	Y	Y	N	N	Y
Sarbanes	Y	Y	Y	Y	N	N	N	Y
MASSACHUSETTS								
Kennedy	Y	Y	Y	Y	N	Y	N	Y
Kerry	Y	N	Y	Y	N	Y	N	Y
MICHIGAN								
Levin	Y	Y	Y	Y	N	N	N	Y
Riegle	Y	Y	Y	Y	Y	Y	N	Y
MINNESOTA								
Wellstone	Y	Y	Y	Y	N	N	N	Y
Durenberger	N	N	Y	N	N	N	N	Y
MISSISSIPPI								
Cochran	N	N	N	Y	Y	Y	N	N
Lott	N	N	N	Y	Y	Y	N	N
MISSOURI								
Bond	N	N	N	Y	Y	Y	N	N
Danforth	N	N	Y	N	Y	Y	N	N
MONTANA								
Baucus	N	Y	Y	Y	Y	Y	?	Y
Burns	N	N	Y	Y	Y	Y	N	N
NEBRASKA								
Exon	N	N	Y	Y	Y	Y	Y	Y
Kerrey	Y	N	Y	N	Y	Y	N	Y
NEVADA								
Bryan	N	N	Y	Y	Y	Y	Y	Y
Reid	Y	N	Y	Y	Y	Y	Y	Y

	217	218	219	220	221	222	223	224
NEW HAMPSHIRE								
Gregg	N	N	N	Y	Y	Y	Y	N
Smith	N	N	N	Y	Y	Y	N	N
NEW JERSEY								
Bradley	?	?	?	?	Y	Y	N	Y
Lautenberg	Y	Y	Y	Y	N	Y	N	Y
NEW MEXICO								
Bingaman	N	N	Y	Y	Y	N	Y	Y
Domenici	N	N	N	Y	Y	Y	N	N
NEW YORK								
Moynihan	Y	Y	Y	Y	Y	N	Y	Y
D'Amato	Y	N	N	Y	Y	Y	N	N
NORTH CAROLINA								
Faircloth	N	N	N	Y	Y	Y	Y	N
Helms	N	N	N	Y	Y	Y	?	N
NORTH DAKOTA								
Conrad	N	N	Y	Y	Y	Y	Y	Y
Dorgan	N	N	Y	Y	Y	Y	Y	Y
OHIO								
Glenn	Y	Y	Y	Y	N	Y	N	Y
Metzenbaum	Y	Y	Y	Y	N	N	N	Y
OKLAHOMA								
Boren	Y	Y	Y	Y	Y	N	N	Y
Nickles	N	N	N	Y	Y	Y	Y	N
OREGON								
Hatfield	Y	N	Y	Y	N	N	N	Y
Packwood	Y	N	Y	Y	Y	Y	N	N
PENNSYLVANIA								
Wofford	Y	Y	Y	Y	N	N	N	Y
Specter	Y	N	Y	Y	N	Y	N	N
RHODE ISLAND								
Pell	Y	Y	Y	Y	N	N	N	Y
Chafee	Y	N	Y	N	N	Y	N	Y
SOUTH CAROLINA								
Hollings	N	Y	Y	Y	Y	Y	N	Y
Thurmond	N	N	N	Y	Y	Y	N	N
SOUTH DAKOTA								
Daschle	Y	N	Y	Y	Y	Y	Y	Y
Pressler	N	N	N	Y	Y	Y	N	N
TENNESSEE								
Mathews	N	N	Y	Y	Y	Y	N	Y
Sasser	N	Y	Y	Y	Y	Y	Y	Y

	217	218	219	220	221	222	223	224
TEXAS								
Gramm	N	N	N	Y	Y	Y	N	N
Hutchison	N	N	N	Y	Y	Y	N	N
UTAH								
Bennett	N	N	Y	Y	Y	Y	N	N
Hatch	N	N	N	Y	Y	Y	N	N
VERMONT								
Leahy	Y	Y	Y	N	Y	N	Y	Y
Jeffords	Y	Y	Y	Y	N	Y	N	Y
VIRGINIA								
Robb	Y	Y	Y	N	Y	N	Y	Y
Warner	N	N	Y	Y	Y	Y	Y	N
WASHINGTON								
Murray	Y	Y	Y	Y	N	N	Y	Y
Gorton	Y	N	N	Y	Y	Y	N	N
WEST VIRGINIA								
Byrd	N	Y	Y	Y	Y	Y	N	Y
Rockefeller	Y	Y	Y	Y	Y	Y	N	Y
WISCONSIN								
Feingold	Y	Y	Y	Y	N	N	Y	Y
Kohl	Y	Y	Y	Y	N	Y	N	Y
WYOMING								
Simpson	N	N	N	Y	Y	Y	N	N
Wallop	N	N	N	Y	Y	Y	N	N

ND Northern Democrats   SD Southern Democrats   Southern states - Ala., Ark., Fla., Ga., Ky., La., Miss., N.C., Okla., S.C., Tenn., Texas, Va.

217. HR 2492. Fiscal 1994 District of Columbia Appropriations/Domestic Partners. Adoption of the committee amendment to allow the District of Columbia to implement a domestic partners ordinance. This amendment would delete from the bill the House provisions prohibiting the use of funds to enforce the ordinance. Rejected 43-55: R 8-36; D 35-19 (ND 31-9, SD 4-10), July 27, 1993.

218. HR 2492. Fiscal 1994 District of Columbia Appropriations/Displaced Workers. Kohl, D-Wis., motion to table (kill) the Gregg, R-N.H., amendment to strike the provisions of the bill that require outside contractors to hire displaced D.C. government employees. Motion rejected 38-61: R 1-43; D 37-18 (ND 31-10, SD 6-8), July 27, 1993. (Subsequently, the Gregg amendment was adopted by voice vote.)

219. HR 2492. Fiscal 1994 District of Columbia Appropriations/Passage. Passage of the bill to provide $698 million in federal funds for the District of Columbia in fiscal 1994 and approve the spending of $3,777,932,000 in funds raised from local taxes. The administration requested $705.1 million in federal funds and $3,725,932,000 in funds from local taxes. Passed 70-29: R 18-26; D 52-3 (ND 40-1, SD 12-2), July 27, 1993.

220. HR 2519. Fiscal 1994 Commerce, Justice, State Appropriations/Funding of Disaster Relief. Hollings, D-S.C., motion to table (kill) the Kerrey, D-Neb., amendment to express the sense of the Senate that fiscal 1993 disaster appropriations should be funded through a temporary gasoline tax. Motion agreed to 92-7: R 41-3; D 51-4 (ND 38-3, SD 13-1), July 27, 1993.

221. HR 2519. Fiscal 1994 Commerce, Justice, State Appropriations/Terrorist Death Penalty. Judgment of the Senate on the germaneness of the D'Amato, R-N.Y., amendment to establish a federal death penalty in cases where a murder occurs during a terrorist act. Ruled germane 75-25: R 37-7; D 38-18 (ND 24-18, SD 14-0), July 28, 1993. (Subsequently, the D'Amato amendment was adopted by voice vote.)

222. HR 2519. Fiscal 1994 Commerce, Justice, State Appropriations/Nicaragua Aid. Helms, R-N.C., amendment to withhold aid to the Nicaraguan government pending findings on Nicaragua's role in global terrorism. Adopted 77-23: R 41-3; D 36-20 (ND 24-18, SD 12-2), July 28, 1993.

223. HR 2519. Fiscal 1994 Commerce, Justice, State Appropriations/National Endowment for Democracy. Bumpers, D-Ark., motion to table (kill) the committee amendment to provide $35 million for the National Endowment for Democracy. Motion rejected 23-74: R 6-37; D 17-37 (ND 13-27, SD 4-10), July 28, 1993. (Subsequently, the committee amendment was adopted by voice vote.) A "nay" was a vote in support fo the president's position.

224. S 919. National Service/Cloture. Motion to invoke cloture (thus limiting debate) on the Kennedy, D-Mass., substitute amendment to authorize $300 million in fiscal 1994, $500 million in fiscal 1995 and $700 million in fiscal 1996 for a National Service program. Motion rejected 59-41: R 3-41; D 56-0 (ND 42-0, SD 14-0), July 29, 1993. Three-fifths of the total Senate (60) is required to invoke cloture.

KEY

Y Voted for (yea).
\# Paired for.
\+ Announced for.
N Voted against (nay).
X Paired against.
— Announced against.
P Voted "present."
C Voted "present" to avoid possible conflict of interest.
? Did not vote or otherwise make a position known.

Democrats   *Republicans*

	225	226	227	228	229	230	231	232
ALABAMA								
Heflin	N	Y	N	N	N	Y	Y	Y
Shelby	Y	Y	N	N	N	Y	Y	Y
ALASKA								
Murkowski	Y	N	N	Y	N	N	N	Y
Stevens	Y	N	N	Y	Y	N	N	Y
ARIZONA								
DeConcini	Y	Y	Y	N	Y	Y	Y	Y
McCain	Y	N	N	Y	?	?	N	Y
ARKANSAS								
Bumpers	Y	Y	N	Y	?	?	Y	Y
Pryor	Y	?	?	?	?	?	Y	Y
CALIFORNIA								
Boxer	Y	Y	Y	N	N	Y	Y	Y
Feinstein	Y	Y	Y	N	N	Y	Y	Y
COLORADO								
Campbell	Y	Y	N	N	?	?	Y	Y
Brown	N	Y	N	Y	Y	N	N	Y
CONNECTICUT								
Dodd	Y	Y	Y	N	N	Y	Y	Y
Lieberman	Y	Y	N	N	N	Y	Y	Y
DELAWARE								
Biden	Y	Y	Y	N	Y	Y	Y	Y
Roth	N	N	N	Y	N	Y	N	Y
FLORIDA								
Graham	Y	Y	Y	N	Y	Y	Y	Y
Mack	Y	Y	N	Y	Y	N	N	Y
GEORGIA								
Nunn	Y	Y	N	?	N	Y	Y	Y
Coverdell	Y	N	N	Y	Y	N	N	Y
HAWAII								
Akaka	Y	Y	Y	N	N	Y	Y	Y
Inouye	Y	Y	Y	N	N	Y	Y	Y
IDAHO								
Craig	N	N	N	Y	N	Y	N	Y
Kempthorne	N	N	N	Y	N	Y	N	Y
ILLINOIS								
Moseley-Braun	Y	Y	Y	N	N	Y	Y	Y
Simon	Y	Y	Y	N	?	?	Y	Y
INDIANA								
Coats	Y	Y	N	Y	?	?	N	Y
Lugar	Y	N	N	Y	N	N	N	Y

	225	226	227	228	229	230	231	232
IOWA								
Harkin	Y	Y	Y	N	N	Y	Y	Y
Grassley	Y	Y	N	Y	Y	N	N	Y
KANSAS								
Dole	Y	N	N	Y	Y	N	N	Y
Kassebaum	Y	N	N	Y	Y	N	N	Y
KENTUCKY								
Ford	Y	Y	N	N	N	Y	Y	Y
McConnell	Y	Y	N	Y	Y	N	N	Y
LOUISIANA								
Breaux	Y	Y	N	N	N	Y	Y	Y
Johnston	Y	Y	N	N	N	Y	Y	Y
MAINE								
Mitchell	Y	Y	Y	N	N	Y	Y	Y
Cohen	Y	N	?	?	?	?	N	Y
MARYLAND								
Mikulski	Y	Y	Y	N	N	Y	Y	Y
Sarbanes	Y	Y	Y	N	N	Y	Y	Y
MASSACHUSETTS								
Kennedy	Y	Y	Y	N	N	Y	Y	Y
Kerry	Y	Y	Y	N	N	Y	Y	Y
MICHIGAN								
Levin	Y	Y	Y	N	N	Y	Y	Y
Riegle	Y	Y	N	N	N	Y	+	+
MINNESOTA								
Wellstone	Y	Y	Y	N	N	Y	Y	Y
Durenberger	Y	N	N	N	Y	Y	Y	Y
MISSISSIPPI								
Cochran	Y	N	N	Y	Y	N	N	Y
Lott	N	N	N	Y	Y	N	N	Y
MISSOURI								
Bond	Y	Y	N	Y	Y	N	N	Y
Danforth	Y	Y	Y	Y	Y	N	N	Y
MONTANA								
Baucus	Y	Y	N	N	N	Y	Y	Y
Burns	Y	N	Y	Y	Y	N	N	Y
NEBRASKA								
Exon	Y	Y	N	Y	N	?	N	Y
Kerrey	Y	Y	N	N	N	Y	N	Y
NEVADA								
Bryan	Y	Y	N	N	N	Y	Y	Y
Reid	Y	Y	N	N	N	Y	Y	Y

	225	226	227	228	229	230	231	232
NEW HAMPSHIRE								
Gregg	N	N	N	Y	?	?	N	Y
Smith	N	N	N	Y	Y	N	N	N
NEW JERSEY								
Bradley	Y	Y	Y	N	N	Y	Y	Y
Lautenberg	Y	Y	Y	N	N	Y	Y	Y
NEW MEXICO								
Bingaman	Y	Y	Y	N	N	Y	Y	Y
Domenici	Y	N	N	Y	Y	N	N	Y
NEW YORK								
Moynihan	Y	Y	Y	N	N	Y	Y	Y
D'Amato	Y	N	N	Y	Y	N	N	Y
NORTH CAROLINA								
Faircloth	N	N	N	Y	Y	N	N	Y
Helms	N	N	N	Y	Y	N	N	N
NORTH DAKOTA								
Conrad	N	N	N	N	N	Y	Y	Y
Dorgan	Y	N	N	N	N	Y	Y	Y
OHIO								
Glenn	Y	Y	Y	N	N	Y	Y	Y
Metzenbaum	Y	Y	Y	N	N	Y	Y	Y
OKLAHOMA								
Boren	Y	N	N	N	Y	Y	Y	Y
Nickles	Y	N	N	Y	N	N	N	N
OREGON								
Hatfield	Y	Y	Y	Y	Y	Y	Y	Y
Packwood	Y	Y	N	Y	N	N	N	Y
PENNSYLVANIA								
Wofford	Y	Y	Y	N	N	Y	Y	Y
Specter	Y	Y	N	Y	N	Y	Y	Y
RHODE ISLAND								
Pell	Y	Y	Y	N	N	Y	Y	Y
Chafee	Y	Y	Y	Y	?	?	Y	Y
SOUTH CAROLINA								
Hollings	Y	Y	Y	?	?	?	N	Y
Thurmond	Y	N	N	Y	N	N	N	Y
SOUTH DAKOTA								
Daschle	Y	Y	N	N	N	?	Y	Y
Pressler	Y	N	N	Y	Y	N	N	Y
TENNESSEE								
Mathews	Y	Y	N	N	N	Y	Y	Y
Sasser	Y	Y	N	N	N	Y	Y	Y

	225	226	227	228	229	230	231	232
TEXAS								
Gramm	Y	N	N	?	?	?	N	Y
Hutchison	N	N	N	Y	Y	N	Y	Y
UTAH								
Bennett	Y	N	N	Y	Y	N	N	Y
Hatch	Y	N	N	Y	Y	Y	N	Y
VERMONT								
Leahy	Y	Y	N	N	N	Y	Y	Y
Jeffords	Y	N	N	?	Y	Y	Y	Y
VIRGINIA								
Robb	Y	Y	N	N	N	Y	Y	Y
Warner	Y	N	N	Y	N	?	N	Y
WASHINGTON								
Murray	Y	Y	Y	N	N	Y	Y	Y
Gorton	Y	Y	Y	N	N	Y	N	Y
WEST VIRGINIA								
Byrd	Y	Y	Y	N	N	Y	N	Y
Rockefeller	Y	Y	Y	N	N	Y	Y	Y
WISCONSIN								
Feingold	Y	Y	Y	N	N	Y	Y	Y
Kohl	Y	Y	Y	N	N	Y	Y	Y
WYOMING								
Simpson	Y	Y	N	Y	Y	N	N	Y
Wallop	N	N	N	+	+	N	N	Y

ND Northern Democrats   SD Southern Democrats   Southern states - Ala., Ark., Fla., Ga., Ky., La., Miss., N.C., Okla., S.C., Tenn., Texas, Va.

225. HR 2519. Fiscal 1994 Commerce, Justice, State Appropriations/Passage. Passage of the bill to provide $23.6 billion in new budget authority for the departments of Commerce, Justice and State, the judiciary, and related agencies for fiscal 1994. The administration requested $24,928,085,000. Passed 87-13: R 33-11; D 54-2 (ND 41-1, SD 13-1), July 29, 1993.

226. HR 2403. Fiscal 1994 Treasury-Postal Appropriations/Unauthorized Building. DeConcini, D-Ariz., motion to table (kill) the McCain, R-Ariz., amendment to the Metzenbaum, D-Ohio, amendment, to prohibit funding for unauthorized federal building projects in the bill. The Metzenbaum amendment would allow funding for only certain projects before Feb. 1, 1994. Motion agreed to 65-34: R 13-31; D 52-3 (ND 40-2, SD 12-1), July 29, 1993. (Subsequently, the Metzenbaum amendment was adopted by voice vote.)

227. HR 2403. Fiscal 1994 Treasury-Postal Appropriations/Gun Dealer Fee. Judgment of the Senate whether the Simon, D-Ill., amendment to raise the fee to register as a gun dealer to $375 a year from $10 was germane. Ruled non-germane 30-68: R 2-41; D 28-27 (ND 26-16, SD 2-11), July 30, 1993.

228. S 919. National Service/Review and Evaluation. Specter, R-Pa., amendment to require that the 1996 authorization be enacted by separate legislation after evaluation of the program. Rejected 41-52: R 39-1; D 2-51 (ND 1-41, SD 1-10), July 30, 1993.

229. S 919. National Service/Liability Protection. McConnell, R-Ky., motion to table (kill) the Biden, D-Del., amendment to the McConnell amendment to provide National Service volunteers protection under the Federal Tort Claims Act. The McConnell amendment would give volunteers working for certain nonprofit and government agencies protection from tort claims alleging damage or injury during official work performed in good faith without misconduct. Motion rejected 35-53: R 33-4; D 2-49 (ND 1-39, SD 1-10), July 30, 1993. (Subseqently, the McConnell amendment, as amended by the Biden amendment, was adopted by voice vote.)

230. S 919. National Service/Means Test. Kennedy, D-Mass., motion to table (kill) the Brown, R-Colo., amendment to apply the family contribution means test to education awards. Motion agreed to 55-31: R 6-31; D 49-0 (ND 38-0, SD 11-0), July 30, 1993.

231. HR 2010. National Service/Passage. Passage of the bill to authorize $300 million in fiscal 1994, $500 million in fiscal 1995 and $700 million in fiscal 1996 for the National Service program, which would provide people age 17 or older with $4,725 a year in education awards for up to two years in return for work in community service programs. Passed 58-41: R 7-37; D 51-4 (ND 38-3, SD 13-1), Aug. 3, 1993. A "yea" was a vote in support of the president's position. (Before passage, the Senate struck all after the enacting clause and inserted the text of S 919 as amended.)

232. Ginsburg Nomination/Confirmation. Confirmation of Ruth Bader Ginsburg as an associate justice of the Supreme Court of the United States, replacing retired Associate Justice Byron R. White. Confirmed 96-3: R 41-3; D 55-0 (ND 41-0, SD 14-0), Aug. 3, 1993. A "yea" was a vote in support of the president's position.

SENATE VOTES 233, 234, 235, 236, 237, 238, 239, 240

	233	234	235	236	237	238	239	240
ALABAMA								
Heflin	Y	Y	Y	N	N	Y	Y	Y
Shelby	Y	Y	N	Y	N	Y	Y	Y
ALASKA								
Murkowski	N	Y	Y	Y	N	N	Y	N
Stevens	Y	Y	N	Y	Y	N	Y	Y
ARIZONA								
DeConcini	Y	Y	Y	Y	Y	N	Y	Y
McCain	N	N	Y	N	Y	N	N	N
ARKANSAS								
Bumpers	Y	Y	N	Y	N	Y	N	Y
Pryor	Y	Y	N	Y	N	Y	Y	Y
CALIFORNIA								
Boxer	Y	Y	N	Y	N	Y	N	Y
Feinstein	Y	Y	N	Y	Y	N	Y	Y
COLORADO								
Campbell	Y	Y	N	Y	N	Y	N	Y
Brown	N	N	Y	N	Y	N	N	N
CONNECTICUT								
Dodd	Y	Y	N	Y	N	Y	N	Y
Lieberman	Y	N	N	Y	N	Y	N	Y
DELAWARE								
Biden	Y	Y	Y	Y	N	Y	Y	Y
Roth	Y	Y	Y	N	Y	N	Y	N
FLORIDA								
Graham	Y	Y	N	Y	N	Y	N	Y
Mack	N	N	Y	N	N	N	N	N
GEORGIA								
Nunn	Y	Y	Y	Y	N	Y	N	Y
Coverdell	N	N	Y	N	N	Y	Y	Y
HAWAII								
Akaka	Y	Y	N	Y	N	Y	Y	Y
Inouye	Y	Y	N	Y	N	Y	Y	Y
IDAHO								
Craig	N	N	Y	N	N	Y	N	N
Kempthorne	N	N	Y	N	N	Y	N	N
ILLINOIS								
Moseley-Braun	Y	Y	N	Y	N	Y	Y	Y
Simon	Y	Y	N	Y	N	Y	Y	Y
INDIANA								
Coats	N	Y	Y	Y	N	Y	N	N
Lugar	Y	Y	Y	Y	Y	N	Y	N

	233	234	235	236	237	238	239	240
IOWA								
Harkin	Y	Y	N	Y	N	Y	Y	Y
Grassley	N	N	Y	N	N	N	Y	Y
KANSAS								
Dole	N	Y	Y	N	N	Y	Y	Y
Kassebaum	Y	Y	Y	Y	N	Y	Y	Y
KENTUCKY								
Ford	Y	Y	Y	Y	N	Y	Y	Y
McConnell	N	N	Y	Y	N	Y	Y	Y
LOUISIANA								
Breaux	Y	Y	Y	Y	N	Y	Y	Y
Johnston	Y	Y	Y	Y	N	N	Y	Y
MAINE								
Mitchell	Y	Y	N	Y	Y	N	Y	N
Cohen	Y	Y	N	Y	Y	N	Y	N
MARYLAND								
Mikulski	Y	Y	N	Y	N	Y	N	Y
Sarbanes	Y	Y	N	Y	N	Y	N	Y
MASSACHUSETTS								
Kennedy	Y	Y	N	Y	N	Y	Y	Y
Kerry	Y	Y	N	Y	N	Y	Y	Y
MICHIGAN								
Levin	Y	Y	N	Y	N	Y	N	Y
Riegle	?	?	N	Y	Y	N	Y	Y
MINNESOTA								
Wellstone	Y	Y	N	Y	N	Y	Y	Y
Durenberger	Y	Y	Y	N	N	Y	Y	Y
MISSISSIPPI								
Cochran	N	Y	Y	N	N	Y	Y	N
Lott	N	N	Y	N	N	Y	N	N
MISSOURI								
Bond	N	N	Y	N	Y	Y	Y	Y
Danforth	Y	Y	Y	Y	N	Y	Y	Y
MONTANA								
Baucus	Y	Y	N	N	N	Y	N	Y
Burns	N	N	Y	N	Y	Y	Y	Y
NEBRASKA								
Exon	Y	Y	Y	Y	N	Y	Y	Y
Kerrey	Y	Y	N	Y	N	N	Y	Y
NEVADA								
Bryan	Y	Y	N	Y	N	Y	N	Y
Reid	Y	Y	Y	Y	N	Y	N	Y

	233	234	235	236	237	238	239	240
NEW HAMPSHIRE								
Gregg	N	Y	?	N	Y	N	Y	N
Smith	N	N	Y	N	Y	N	N	N
NEW JERSEY								
Bradley	Y	Y	N	Y	N	Y	N	Y
Lautenberg	Y	Y	N	Y	N	Y	N	Y
NEW MEXICO								
Bingaman	Y	Y	N	Y	N	Y	N	Y
Domenici	Y	N	Y	N	Y	N	N	N
NEW YORK								
Moynihan	Y	Y	N	Y	N	Y	N	Y
D'Amato	Y	N	Y	Y	N	Y	N	N
NORTH CAROLINA								
Faircloth	N	N	N	N	N	Y	N	N
Helms	N	N	Y	N	Y	N	Y	N
NORTH DAKOTA								
Conrad	Y	Y	Y	N	Y	N	Y	Y
Dorgan	Y	Y	Y	Y	N	Y	Y	Y
OHIO								
Glenn	Y	Y	N	Y	N	Y	N	Y
Metzenbaum	Y	Y	N	Y	N	Y	Y	Y
OKLAHOMA								
Boren	Y	Y	N	Y	N	Y	N	Y
Nickles	N	N	Y	N	N	N	N	N
OREGON								
Hatfield	Y	Y	Y	Y	N	Y	N	Y
Packwood	Y	Y	N	Y	N	Y	N	N
PENNSYLVANIA								
Wofford	Y	Y	Y	Y	N	Y	N	Y
Specter	Y	Y	N	Y	N	Y	N	N
RHODE ISLAND								
Pell	Y	Y	N	Y	N	Y	N	Y
Chafee	Y	Y	N	Y	N	Y	N	Y
SOUTH CAROLINA								
Hollings	Y	Y	N	Y	N	Y	N	Y
Thurmond	Y	Y	Y	N	N	Y	Y	Y
SOUTH DAKOTA								
Daschle	Y	Y	N	Y	N	Y	N	Y
Pressler	N	N	Y	N	N	Y	Y	Y
TENNESSEE								
Mathews	Y	Y	N	Y	N	Y	N	Y
Sasser	Y	Y	N	Y	N	Y	N	Y

	233	234	235	236	237	238	239	240
TEXAS								
Gramm	N	N	Y	N	N	Y	N	N
Hutchison	Y	Y	Y	Y	N	Y	N	N
UTAH								
Bennett	Y	Y	Y	N	N	Y	Y	Y
Hatch	N	Y	Y	N	N	Y	Y	Y
VERMONT								
Leahy	Y	Y	N	Y	N	Y	Y	Y
Jeffords	Y	Y	N	Y	N	Y	N	Y
VIRGINIA								
Robb	Y	Y	N	Y	N	Y	N	Y
Warner	N	N	Y	Y	Y	N	Y	Y
WASHINGTON								
Murray	Y	Y	N	Y	N	Y	N	Y
Gorton	N	N	Y	Y	Y	N	N	Y
WEST VIRGINIA								
Byrd	N	Y	N	Y	N	Y	N	Y
Rockefeller	Y	Y	N	Y	N	Y	Y	Y
WISCONSIN								
Feingold	Y	Y	N	Y	N	Y	Y	Y
Kohl	Y	Y	N	Y	N	Y	Y	Y
WYOMING								
Simpson	Y	Y	N	Y	N	Y	N	N
Wallop	N	N	Y	N	Y	N	Y	N

ND Northern Democrats   SD Southern Democrats   Southern states - Ala., Ark., Fla., Ga., Ky., La., Miss., N.C., Okla., S.C., Tenn., Texas, Va.

233. Payzant Nomination/Confirmation. Confirmation of Thomas W. Payzant of California to be assistant secretary for elementary and secondary education in the Department of Education. Confirmed 72-27: R 18-26; D 54-1 (ND 40-1, SD 14-0), Aug. 3, 1993. A "yea" was a vote in support of the president's position.

234. Hackney Nomination/Confirmation. Confirmation of Sheldon Hackney of Pennsylvania to be chairman of the National Endowment for the Humanities for a four-year term. Confirmed 76-23: R 22-22; D 54-1 (ND 40-1, SD 14-0), Aug. 3, 1993. A "yea" was a vote in support of the president's position.

235. HR 2403. Fiscal 1994 Treasury-Postal Appropriations/Abortion. Judgment of the Senate on the germaneness of the Nickles, R-Okla., amendment to the committee amendment to require women to pay special premiums in order to receive additional coverage for abortions under their federal health plans. The committee amendment would lift a 10-year ban on federal employees' health-care policies covering abortions. Ruled non-germane 48-51: R 36-7; D 12-44 (ND 7-35, SD 5-9), Aug. 3, 1993.

236. HR 2403. Fiscal 1994 Treasury-Postal Appropriations/Passage. Passage of the bill to provide $22 billion in new budget authority for the Treasury Department, the U.S. Postal Service, the Executive Office of the President and certain independent agencies for fiscal 1994. The administration requested $22,006,136,000. The bill lifts a 10-year ban on federal employees' health-care policies covering abortions. Passed 73-27: R 19-25; D 54-2 (ND 41-1, SD 13-1), Aug. 3, 1993.

237. HR 2667. Fiscal 1993 Disaster Supplemental Appropriations/Crop Loss. Byrd, D-W.Va., motion to table (kill) the question of germaneness before the Senate on the Harkin amendment to provide a possible additional $3.4 billion in emergency spending for Midwest flooding. Motion rejected 50-50: R 21-23; D 29-27 (ND 23-19, SD 6-8), Aug. 4, 1993.

238. HR 2667. Fiscal 1993 Disaster Supplemental Appropriations/Crop Loss. Judgment of the Senate on the germaneness of the Harkin, D-Iowa, amendment to provide a possible additional $3.4 billion in emergency spending for Midwest flooding. Ruled non-germane 46-54: R 21-23; D 25-31 (ND 18-24, SD 7-7), Aug. 4, 1993.

239. HR 2667. Fiscal 1993 Disaster Supplemental Appropriations/Additional Spending. Byrd, D-W.Va., amendment to comply with the administration's additional spending request of $133 million by increasing spending by $11.1 million for the Job Training Partnership Act, $2 million for the Commission on National and Community Service, $100 million for the Economic Development Administration and $20 million for the Small Business Administration. Adopted 86-14: R 30-14; D 56-0 (ND 42-0, SD 14-0), Aug. 4, 1993. A "yea" was a vote in support of the president's position.

240. HR 2667. Fiscal 1993 Disaster Supplemental Appropriations/Crop Loss. Harkin, D-Iowa, amendment to provide an additional $1 billion in emergency spending for Midwest flooding by doubling to 42 cents on the dollar the amount that farmers could collect for crop losses. Adopted 68-32: R 18-26; D 50-6 (ND 37-5, SD 13-1), Aug. 4, 1993. A "yea" was a vote in support of the president's position.

	241	242	243	244	245	246	247	248
ALABAMA								
Heflin	N	Y	Y	N	N	N	Y	Y
Shelby	Y	Y	N	Y	N	Y	N	Y
ALASKA								
Murkowski	N	N	Y	Y	Y	Y	N	—
Stevens	Y	Y	N	Y	Y	Y	N	N
ARIZONA								
DeConcini	Y	Y	Y	N	N	N	Y	Y
McCain	N	N	Y	Y	Y	Y	N	N
ARKANSAS								
Bumpers	Y	Y	N	N	N	N	Y	Y
Pryor	Y	Y	N	N	N	N	Y	Y
CALIFORNIA								
Boxer	Y	Y	N	N	N	Y	Y	Y
Feinstein	N	Y	N	N	N	Y	Y	Y
COLORADO								
Campbell	N	Y	N	N	N	N	Y	Y
Brown	N	Y	Y	Y	Y	Y	N	Y
CONNECTICUT								
Dodd	Y	Y	N	N	N	N	Y	Y
Lieberman	Y	Y	N	N	N	N	Y	Y
DELAWARE								
Biden	Y	Y	N	N	N	N	Y	Y
Roth	N	Y	N	Y	Y	Y	N	N
FLORIDA								
Graham	Y	Y	N	N	N	N	Y	Y
Mack	N	Y	Y	Y	Y	Y	N	N
GEORGIA								
Nunn	N	Y	Y	N	N	N	Y	Y
Coverdell	N	Y	N	Y	Y	Y	N	N
HAWAII								
Akaka	Y	Y	N	N	N	N	Y	Y
Inouye	Y	Y	N	N	N	N	Y	Y
IDAHO								
Craig	N	N	Y	Y	Y	Y	N	N
Kempthorne	N	N	Y	Y	Y	Y	N	N
ILLINOIS								
Moseley-Braun	Y	Y	N	N	N	N	Y	Y
Simon	Y	Y	N	N	N	N	Y	Y
INDIANA								
Coats	N	N	Y	Y	Y	Y	N	N
Lugar	N	Y	Y	Y	Y	Y	N	Y
IOWA								
Harkin	Y	N	N	N	N	N	Y	Y
Grassley	N	N	Y	Y	Y	Y	N	N
KANSAS								
Dole	N	N	Y	Y	Y	Y	N	N
Kassebaum	N	N	N	Y	Y	Y	N	Y
KENTUCKY								
Ford	Y	Y	N	N	N	N	Y	N
McConnell	Y	Y	N	Y	Y	Y	N	N
LOUISIANA								
Breaux	Y	Y	N	N	N	N	Y	N
Johnston	Y	Y	N	N	N	N	N	Y
MAINE								
Mitchell	Y	Y	N	N	N	N	Y	Y
Cohen	N	N	Y	Y	N	Y	N	Y
MARYLAND								
Mikulski	Y	Y	N	N	N	N	Y	Y
Sarbanes	Y	Y	N	N	N	N	Y	Y
MASSACHUSETTS								
Kennedy	Y	Y	N	N	N	N	Y	Y
Kerry	Y	Y	N	N	N	N	Y	Y
MICHIGAN								
Levin	Y	Y	N	N	N	N	Y	Y
Riegle	Y	Y	N	N	N	N	Y	Y
MINNESOTA								
Wellstone	Y	N	N	N	N	N	Y	Y
Durenberger	N	N	Y	Y	Y	Y	N	Y
MISSISSIPPI								
Cochran	Y	Y	N	Y	Y	Y	N	N
Lott	Y	N	N	Y	Y	Y	N	N
MISSOURI								
Bond	Y	N	N	Y	Y	Y	N	N
Danforth	Y	N	N	Y	N	Y	N	Y
MONTANA								
Baucus	Y	Y	N	N	N	N	Y	Y
Burns	N	N	N	Y	Y	N	N	N
NEBRASKA								
Exon	Y	N	N	N	N	N	Y	N
Kerrey	N	Y	N	N	N	N	Y	Y
NEVADA								
Bryan	N	Y	N	N	N	N	N	Y
Reid	Y	Y	N	N	N	N	Y	Y
NEW HAMPSHIRE								
Gregg	N	Y	Y	Y	Y	Y	N	N
Smith	N	Y	Y	Y	Y	Y	N	N
NEW JERSEY								
Bradley	?	?	?	?	N	N	Y	Y
Lautenberg	Y	Y	N	N	N	N	N	Y
NEW MEXICO								
Bingaman	N	Y	Y	N	N	N	Y	Y
Domenici	Y	Y	Y	Y	Y	Y	N	N
NEW YORK								
Moynihan	Y	Y	N	N	N	N	Y	Y
D'Amato	N	N	Y	Y	Y	Y	N	N
NORTH CAROLINA								
Faircloth	N	N	Y	Y	Y	Y	N	N
Helms	N	Y	N	Y	Y	Y	N	N
NORTH DAKOTA								
Conrad	Y	Y	N	N	N	N	Y	Y
Dorgan	Y	N	N	N	N	N	Y	Y
OHIO								
Glenn	Y	Y	N	N	N	N	Y	Y
Metzenbaum	N	Y	N	N	N	N	Y	Y
OKLAHOMA								
Boren	N	Y	N	N	N	N	Y	Y
Nickles	N	N	Y	Y	Y	Y	N	N
OREGON								
Hatfield	Y	Y	N	Y	Y	Y	N	Y
Packwood	N	Y	Y	N	Y	Y	N	Y
PENNSYLVANIA								
Wofford	Y	Y	N	N	N	N	Y	Y
Specter	N	N	N	Y	Y	Y	N	Y
RHODE ISLAND								
Pell	Y	Y	N	N	N	N	Y	Y
Chafee	N	Y	Y	Y	Y	Y	N	Y
SOUTH CAROLINA								
Hollings	Y	Y	N	N	N	N	Y	Y
Thurmond	N	N	Y	Y	Y	N	N	N
SOUTH DAKOTA								
Daschle	Y	N	N	N	N	N	Y	Y
Pressler	N	N	Y	Y	Y	Y	N	N
TENNESSEE								
Mathews	Y	Y	N	N	N	N	Y	Y
Sasser	Y	Y	N	N	N	N	Y	Y
TEXAS								
Gramm	N	N	Y	Y	Y	Y	N	N
Hutchison	N	N	Y	Y	Y	Y	N	N
UTAH								
Bennett	N	N	Y	Y	Y	Y	N	N
Hatch	N	N	Y	Y	Y	Y	N	N
VERMONT								
Leahy	Y	Y	N	N	N	N	Y	Y
Jeffords	N	Y	Y	Y	Y	Y	N	Y
VIRGINIA								
Robb	N	Y	Y	N	N	N	Y	Y
Warner	Y	Y	N	Y	N	N	N	N
WASHINGTON								
Murray	Y	Y	N	N	N	N	Y	Y
Gorton	N	N	Y	Y	Y	Y	N	Y
WEST VIRGINIA								
Byrd	Y	Y	N	N	N	N	Y	N
Rockefeller	Y	Y	N	N	N	N	Y	Y
WISCONSIN								
Feingold	Y	Y	N	N	N	N	Y	Y
Kohl	Y	Y	N	N	N	N	Y	Y
WYOMING								
Simpson	N	Y	Y	Y	Y	Y	N	Y
Wallop	N	N	Y	Y	Y	Y	N	N

KEY

Y Voted for (yea).
Paired for.
+ Announced for.
N Voted against (nay).
X Paired against.
— Announced against.
P Voted "present."
C Voted "present" to avoid possible conflict of interest.
? Did not vote or otherwise make a position known.

Democrats *Republicans*

ND Northern Democrats   SD Southern Democrats   Southern states - Ala., Ark., Fla., Ga., Ky., La., Miss., N.C., Okla., S.C., Tenn., Texas, Va.

241. HR 2667. Fiscal 1993 Disaster Supplemental Appropriations/Budget Offsets. Byrd, D-W.Va., motion to table (kill) the Durenberger, R-Minn., amendment to remove the bill's emergency designation and require the spending to be offset. Motion agreed to 54-45: R 9-35; D 45-10 (ND 35-6, SD 10-4), Aug. 4, 1993.

242. HR 2667. Fiscal 1993 Disaster Supplemental Appropriations/Crop Insurance. Byrd, D-W.Va., motion to table (kill) the question of germaneness on the Durenberger, R-Minn., amendment to reform the federal crop insurance program. Motion agreed to 68-31: R 18-26; D 50-5 (ND 36-5, SD 14-0), Aug. 4, 1993. (Subsequently, the chair ruled the amendment non-germane.)

243. HR 2667. Fiscal 1993 Disaster Supplemental Appropriations/Future Disasters. Durenberger, R-Minn., motion to waive the budget act with respect to the Byrd, D-W.Va., point of order against the Durenberger amendment to require the president, with congressional approval, to find offsets for future emergency appropriations for natural disasters. Motion rejected 35-64: R 30-14; D 5-50 (ND 2-39, SD 3-11), Aug. 4, 1993. A three-fifths majority vote (60) of the total Senate is required to waive the budget act. (Subsequently, the chair upheld the Byrd point of order, and the Durenberger amendment fell.)

244. HR 2264. 1993 Budget Reconciliation/Retroactive Taxes. McCain, R-Ariz., point of order that the retroactive taxes in the bill applicable before April 8, 1993, violate the Due Process Clause of the Fifth Amendment of the Constitution. Point of order rejected 44-56: R 43-1; D 1-55 (ND 0-42, SD 1-13), Aug. 6, 1993.

245. HR 2264. 1993 Budget Reconciliation/Immunization Purchases. Danforth, R-Mo., appeal of the chair's ruling rejecting the Danforth point of order against the provisions allowing states to purchase immunizations at the Centers for Disease Control price. Ruling of the chair upheld 43-57: R 43-1; D 0-56 (ND 0-42, SD 0-14), Aug. 6, 1993. (A three-fifths majority vote (60) of the total Senate is required to overturn a ruling of the chair that provisions of a reconciliation bill are extraneous.)

246. HR 2264. 1993 Budget-Reconciliation/Domestic Tobacco Content. Brown, R-Colo., appeal of the chair's ruling rejecting the Brown point of order against the provisions encouraging use of domestic tobacco in U.S.-manufactured tobacco products. Ruling of the chair upheld 43-57: R 38-6; D 5-51 (ND 3-39, SD 2-12), Aug. 6, 1993. (A three-fifths majority vote (60) of the total Senate is required to overturn a ruling of the chair that provisions of a reconciliation bill are extraneous.)

247. HR 2264. 1993 Budget Reconciliation/Adoption. Adoption of the conference report to reduce the deficit by an estimated $516 billion over five years through tax increases and spending cuts, closely tracking President Clinton's economic proposals. Adopted 51-50: R 0-44; D 50-6 (ND 40-2, SD 10-4), with Vice President Al Gore casting a "yea" vote, Aug. 6, 1993. A "yea" was a vote in support of the president's position.

248. Elders Nomination/Confirmation. Confirmation of Dr. Joycelyn Elders to be U.S. surgeon general. Confirmed 65-34: R 13-30; D 52-4 (ND 40-2, SD 12-2), Sept. 7, 1993. A "yea" was a vote in support of the president's position.

	249	250	251	252	253	254	255	256
ALABAMA								
Heflin	Y	N	N	Y	Y	N	Y	N
Shelby	Y	N	N	Y	Y	N	Y	N
ALASKA								
Murkowski	–	–	?	?	?	?	?	?
Stevens	Y	N	N	Y	Y	N	Y	N
ARIZONA								
DeConcini	Y	Y	Y	Y	N	N	N	Y
McCain	N	N	N	Y	Y	N	Y	?
ARKANSAS								
Bumpers	Y	N	Y	Y	N	N	N	Y
Pryor	Y	N	Y	Y	?	N	N	Y
CALIFORNIA								
Boxer	Y	Y	Y	Y	N	Y	N	Y
Feinstein	Y	Y	Y	Y	N	Y	Y	Y
COLORADO								
Campbell	Y	Y	Y	Y	Y	Y	Y	N
Brown	N	N	N	N	Y	N	Y	N
CONNECTICUT								
Dodd	Y	Y	N	Y	Y	N	Y	N
Lieberman	Y	Y	N	Y	Y	N	Y	N
DELAWARE								
Biden	Y	Y	Y	Y	N	N	Y	N
Roth	N	N	N	Y	Y	N	Y	N
FLORIDA								
Graham	Y	N	N	Y	Y	N	Y	N
Mack	N	N	N	N	Y	N	Y	N
GEORGIA								
Nunn	Y	N	N	Y	Y	N	Y	N
Coverdell	N	N	N	Y	Y	N	Y	N
HAWAII								
Akaka	Y	Y	Y	Y	Y	Y	Y	N
Inouye	Y	Y	N	Y	Y	Y	Y	N
IDAHO								
Craig	N	N	N	Y	Y	N	Y	N
Kempthorne	N	N	N	Y	Y	N	Y	N
ILLINOIS								
Moseley-Braun	Y	Y	Y	Y	N	Y	Y	Y
Simon	Y	Y	Y	Y	N	Y	N	Y
INDIANA								
Coats	N	N	N	Y	Y	N	Y	N
Lugar	N	N	N	Y	Y	N	Y	N
IOWA								
Harkin	Y	Y	Y	Y	N	N	N	Y
Grassley	N	N	Y	N	N	N	Y	Y
KANSAS								
Dole	N	N	N	Y	Y	N	Y	N
Kassebaum	N	N	Y	Y	Y	N	Y	N
KENTUCKY								
Ford	Y	N	Y	Y	Y	N	Y	N
McConnell	N	N	N	Y	Y	N	Y	N
LOUISIANA								
Breaux	Y	N	Y	Y	Y	N	Y	N
Johnston	Y	N	Y	Y	Y	Y	Y	N
MAINE								
Mitchell	Y	N	Y	Y	N	N	Y	N
Cohen	N	N	N	Y	Y	N	Y	N
MARYLAND								
Mikulski	Y	Y	Y	Y	Y	Y	Y	N
Sarbanes	Y	Y	Y	Y	N	N	N	Y
MASSACHUSETTS								
Kennedy	Y	Y	Y	Y	N	N	N	Y
Kerry	Y	Y	Y	Y	N	N	Y	Y
MICHIGAN								
Levin	Y	Y	Y	Y	Y	Y	N	N
Riegle	Y	Y	Y	Y	N	Y	N	Y
MINNESOTA								
Wellstone	Y	Y	Y	Y	N	N	N	Y
Durenberger	Y	N	Y	Y	Y	N	N	Y
MISSISSIPPI								
Cochran	N	N	N	Y	?	Y	Y	N
Lott	N	N	N	Y	Y	Y	Y	N
MISSOURI								
Bond	N	N	N	Y	Y	N	Y	N
Danforth	N	N	N	+	Y	N	Y	Y
MONTANA								
Baucus	Y	N	Y	N	N	N	N	N
Burns	N	N	N	Y	N	N	N	N
NEBRASKA								
Exon	N	N	N	Y	Y	N	Y	N
Kerrey	N	Y	Y	Y	Y	N	Y	N
NEVADA								
Bryan	Y	N	N	Y	Y	N	Y	N
Reid	Y	N	Y	Y	Y	N	N	N
NEW HAMPSHIRE								
Gregg	N	N	N	Y	Y	N	Y	N
Smith	N	N	N	Y	Y	Y	Y	N
NEW JERSEY								
Bradley	Y	Y	Y	Y	N	N	N	Y
Lautenberg	Y	Y	Y	Y	N	N	N	Y
NEW MEXICO								
Bingaman	Y	Y	N	Y	?	N	Y	N
Domenici	N	N	N	Y	Y	N	Y	?
NEW YORK								
Moynihan	Y	Y	Y	Y	N	N	N	N
D'Amato	N	Y	N	N	Y	N	Y	N
NORTH CAROLINA								
Faircloth	N	N	N	Y	Y	N	Y	N
Helms	N	N	N	Y	+	Y	?	?
NORTH DAKOTA								
Conrad	Y	N	Y	Y	N	N	Y	Y
Dorgan	Y	N	Y	Y	N	N	Y	Y
OHIO								
Glenn	Y	?	Y	Y	Y	N	Y	N
Metzenbaum	Y	Y	Y	Y	N	N	N	Y
OKLAHOMA								
Boren	Y	N	N	N	N	N	Y	N
Nickles	N	N	N	Y	Y	N	Y	N
OREGON								
Hatfield	Y	N	Y	Y	N	N	N	Y
Packwood	N	N	N	Y	Y	N	Y	N
PENNSYLVANIA								
Wofford	Y	N	Y	Y	N	N	N	Y
Specter	Y	N	N	Y	N	Y	Y	Y
RHODE ISLAND								
Pell	Y	Y	Y	Y	N	N	N	Y
Chafee	Y	Y	Y	Y	Y	N	Y	N
SOUTH CAROLINA								
Hollings	N	N	N	Y	Y	N	Y	N
Thurmond	N	N	N	Y	Y	N	Y	N
SOUTH DAKOTA								
Daschle	Y	N	Y	Y	?	N	N	Y
Pressler	N	N	N	Y	Y	Y	Y	N
TENNESSEE								
Mathews	Y	N	Y	Y	Y	N	Y	N
Sasser	Y	N	Y	Y	N	N	N	Y
TEXAS								
Gramm	N	N	N	Y	Y	N	?	?
Hutchison	?	–	N	Y	Y	N	Y	N
UTAH								
Bennett	N	N	N	Y	Y	N	Y	N
Hatch	N	N	N	Y	Y	N	Y	N
VERMONT								
Leahy	Y	Y	Y	Y	N	N	N	Y
Jeffords	Y	Y	Y	Y	N	N	N	Y
VIRGINIA								
Robb	Y	Y	N	Y	Y	N	Y	N
Warner	N	N	N	Y	Y	N	Y	N
WASHINGTON								
Murray	Y	Y	Y	Y	Y	N	Y	N
Gorton	N	N	N	N	Y	Y	Y	N
WEST VIRGINIA								
Byrd	N	N	Y	Y	Y	N	Y	N
Rockefeller	?	N	Y	Y	Y	N	Y	N
WISCONSIN								
Feingold	Y	Y	Y	N	N	N	N	Y
Kohl	Y	N	Y	Y	Y	N	N	Y
WYOMING								
Simpson	N	N	N	Y	Y	–	+	–
Wallop	N	–	–	?	?	?	?	?

ND   Northern Democrats   SD   Southern Democrats   Southern states - Ala., Ark., Fla., Ga., Ky., La., Miss., N.C., Okla., S.C., Tenn., Texas, Va.

249. HR 2010. National Service/Conference Report. Adoption of the conference report on the bill to authorize $300 million in fiscal 1994, $500 million in fiscal 1995 and $700 million in fiscal 1996 for the National Service program, which would provide people age 17 or older with $4,725 a year in education awards for up to two years in return for community service work. Adopted (thus cleared for the president) 57-40: R 6-36; D 51-4 (ND 38-3, SD 13-1), Sept. 8, 1993. A "yea" was a vote in support of the president's position.

250. S 1298. Fiscal 1994 Defense Authorization/Gay Ban. Boxer, D-Calif., amendment to strike language in the bill regarding homosexuals in the military and to express the sense of Congress that the policy regarding the subject should be determined by the president. Rejected 33-63: R 3-38; D 30-25 (ND 29-12, SD 1-13), Sept. 9, 1993.

251. S 1298. Fiscal 1994 Defense Authorization/Strategic Missile Defense Cut. Sasser, D-Tenn., amendment to cut the Ballistic Missile Defense program from $3.4 billion to $3 billion. Adopted 50-48: R 6-36; D 44-12 (ND 36-6, SD 8-6), Sept. 9, 1993. A "nay" was a vote in support of the president's position.

252. S 1298. Fiscal 1994 Defense Authorization/Somalia. Byrd, D-W.Va., amendment to the Byrd amendment, to express the sense of the Senate that the president should outline the goals, objectives and duration of deployment of U.S. troops to Somalia in a report to Congress by Oct. 15, 1993; the president should seek and receive congressional authorization for the continued deployment in Somalia by Nov. 15, 1993; and U.S. participation would end if Congress failed to specifically authorize continued involvement. Adopted 90-7: R

36-5; D 54-2 (ND 41-1, SD 13-1), Sept. 9, 1993.

253. S 1298. Fiscal 1994 Defense Authorization/Drug Treatment. Byrd, D-W.Va., motion to table (kill) the DeConcini, D-Ariz., amendment to transfer $50 million from the Defense Department's unobligated account to the Department of Health and Human Services for the drug treatment of women and children. Motion agreed to 61-32: R 35-5; D 26-27 (ND 16-24, SD 10-3), Sept. 9, 1993.

254. S 1298. Fiscal 1994 Defense Authorization/Base Closings. Feinstein, D-Calif., amendment to postpone the 1995 military base closing round until 1997. Rejected 18-79: R 7-34; D 11-45 (ND 10-32, SD 1-13), Sept. 10, 1993.

255. S 1298. Fiscal 1994 Defense Authorization/Ground-Wave Emergency Network. Exon, D-Neb., motion to table (kill) the Reid, D-Nev., amendment to terminate the Ground-Wave Emergency Network program of the Air Force. Motion agreed to 67-28: R 35-4; D 32-24 (ND 21-21, SD 11-3), Sept. 10, 1993.

256. S 1298. Fiscal 1994 Defense Authorization/Nuclear Testing. Harkin, D-Iowa, motion to table (kill) the Exon, D-Neb., amendment to reduce funding for nuclear testing by $53.4 million from $428.4 million to $375 million. The Harkin amendment would provide for a $206 million reduction. Motion rejected 31-62: R 6-31; D 25-31 (ND 22-20, SD 3-11), Sept. 10, 1993. (Subsequently, the Exon amendment and the Harkin amendment as amended by the Exon amendment were adopted by voice vote.)

KEY

Y	Voted for (yea).
#	Paired for.
+	Announced for.
N	Voted against (nay).
X	Paired against.
—	Announced against.
P	Voted "present."
C	Voted "present" to avoid possible conflict of interest.
?	Did not vote or otherwise make a position known.

Democrats   *Republicans*

	257	258	259	260	261	262	263	264
ALABAMA								
Heflin	Y	Y	Y	Y	N	Y	N	N
Shelby	Y	Y	Y	Y	N	Y	N	N
ALASKA								
Murkowski	?	Y	N	Y	N	N	Y	Y
Stevens	Y	Y	Y	Y	N	Y	N	Y
ARIZONA								
DeConcini	N	Y	N	Y	Y	N	Y	N
McCain	?	Y	Y	Y	N	Y	Y	Y
ARKANSAS								
Bumpers	Y	Y	N	N	Y	N	Y	N
Pryor	Y	Y	N	Y	Y	N	Y	N
CALIFORNIA								
Boxer	N	Y	N	Y	Y	N	N	N
Feinstein	Y	Y	Y	Y	N	Y	N	N
COLORADO								
Campbell	?	Y	Y	Y	N	N	Y	N
Brown	N	Y	N	Y	N	Y	Y	Y
CONNECTICUT								
Dodd	Y	Y	Y	Y	Y	Y	Y	Y
Lieberman	Y	Y	Y	Y	N	Y	Y	Y
DELAWARE								
Biden	Y	Y	Y	Y	Y	N	Y	N
Roth	Y	Y	N	Y	N	Y	Y	Y
FLORIDA								
Graham	Y	Y	Y	Y	N	Y	Y	Y
Mack	?	Y	N	Y	N	Y	N	N
GEORGIA								
Nunn	Y	Y	Y	Y	N	Y	N	Y
Coverdell	Y	Y	Y	Y	N	Y	Y	Y
HAWAII								
Akaka	Y	Y	N	N	Y	N	Y	Y
Inouye	Y	Y	Y	Y	N	Y	Y	Y
IDAHO								
Craig	Y	Y	Y	Y	N	Y	N	Y
Kempthorne	Y	Y	Y	Y	N	Y	N	Y
ILLINOIS								
Moseley-Braun	Y	Y	Y	Y	Y	N	Y	N
Simon	Y	Y	N	Y	Y	N	Y	N
INDIANA								
Coats	Y	Y	Y	Y	N	Y	Y	Y
Lugar	Y	Y	N	Y	N	Y	N	Y
IOWA								
Harkin	N	Y	N	Y	Y	N	Y	N
Grassley	Y	Y	N	Y	N	N	N	N
KANSAS								
Dole	Y	Y	N	Y	N	Y	N	Y
Kassebaum	Y	Y	N	Y	N	N	Y	Y
KENTUCKY								
Ford	Y	Y	Y	Y	N	Y	Y	Y
McConnell	Y	Y	N	Y	N	Y	N	N
LOUISIANA								
Breaux	Y	Y	Y	Y	N	Y	Y	Y
Johnston	Y	Y	Y	Y	N	Y	N	Y
MAINE								
Mitchell	Y	Y	Y	Y	Y	Y	Y	Y
Cohen	Y	Y	Y	Y	N	Y	Y	Y
MARYLAND								
Mikulski	N	Y	Y	N	Y	Y	Y	Y
Sarbanes	Y	Y	Y	Y	Y	N	N	Y
MASSACHUSETTS								
Kennedy	Y	Y	Y	Y	Y	Y	Y	N
Kerry	Y	Y	Y	Y	Y	Y	Y	Y
MICHIGAN								
Levin	Y	Y	Y	Y	Y	N	Y	Y
Riegle	N	Y	Y	Y	Y	N	Y	Y
MINNESOTA								
Wellstone	N	Y	Y	Y	Y	N	Y	N
Durenberger	Y	Y	Y	N	Y	Y	Y	Y
MISSISSIPPI								
Cochran	Y	Y	N	Y	N	Y	N	Y
Lott	Y	Y	N	Y	N	Y	N	Y
MISSOURI								
Bond	Y	Y	Y	Y	N	Y	N	N
Danforth	Y	Y	N	Y	N	Y	N	N
MONTANA								
Baucus	Y	Y	Y	Y	N	Y	Y	Y
Burns	Y	Y	N	Y	N	Y	N	Y
NEBRASKA								
Exon	Y	Y	Y	Y	N	N	Y	N
Kerrey	Y	Y	Y	Y	N	Y	Y	N
NEVADA								
Bryan	Y	Y	Y	Y	N	N	Y	Y
Reid	Y	Y	Y	Y	N	Y	N	Y
NEW HAMPSHIRE								
Gregg	Y	Y	N	Y	N	Y	Y	Y
Smith	Y	Y	Y	Y	N	Y	N	Y
NEW JERSEY								
Bradley	Y	Y	N	Y	Y	N	Y	Y
Lautenberg	N	Y	N	Y	Y	Y	Y	Y
NEW MEXICO								
Bingaman	Y	Y	Y	Y	Y	N	N	N
Domenici	?	Y	N	Y	N	Y	N	Y
NEW YORK								
Moynihan	Y	Y	Y	N	Y	N	Y	Y
D'Amato	Y	Y	N	Y	N	Y	N	N
NORTH CAROLINA								
Faircloth	?	Y	N	Y	N	Y	Y	Y
Helms	?	Y	N	Y	N	Y	N	Y
NORTH DAKOTA								
Conrad	N	Y	N	Y	N	Y	N	?
Dorgan	N	Y	Y	N	Y	N	Y	N
OHIO								
Glenn	Y	Y	Y	Y	N	N	N	Y
Metzenbaum	N	Y	N	Y	N	Y	N	N
OKLAHOMA								
Boren	Y	Y	Y	Y	N	Y	Y	?
Nickles	Y	Y	N	Y	N	Y	Y	Y
OREGON								
Hatfield	Y	Y	Y	N	Y	N	Y	Y
Packwood	Y	Y	N	Y	N	Y	N	Y
PENNSYLVANIA								
Wofford	Y	Y	Y	Y	N	Y	N	Y
Specter	Y	Y	Y	Y	N	Y	Y	Y
RHODE ISLAND								
Pell	Y	Y	Y	Y	Y	Y	Y	N
Chafee	Y	Y	Y	Y	Y	Y	N	Y
SOUTH CAROLINA								
Hollings	Y	Y	Y	Y	N	Y	Y	Y
Thurmond	Y	Y	Y	Y	N	Y	Y	Y
SOUTH DAKOTA								
Daschle	N	Y	N	Y	N	Y	N	Y
Pressler	N	Y	N	Y	N	Y	Y	N
TENNESSEE								
Mathews	Y	Y	N	Y	N	N	Y	N
Sasser	Y	Y	N	Y	N	Y	N	Y
TEXAS								
Gramm	?	Y	Y	Y	N	Y	?	?
Hutchison	Y	Y	Y	Y	N	Y	N	Y
UTAH								
Bennett	?	Y	N	Y	N	Y	N	N
Hatch	Y	Y	N	Y	N	Y	N	N
VERMONT								
Leahy	Y	Y	N	Y	Y	N	Y	Y
Jeffords	Y	Y	N	Y	Y	Y	Y	N
VIRGINIA								
Robb	Y	Y	Y	N	Y	N	Y	Y
Warner	Y	Y	Y	Y	N	Y	Y	Y
WASHINGTON								
Murray	Y	Y	N	Y	N	Y	N	Y
Gorton	Y	Y	Y	Y	N	Y	N	Y
WEST VIRGINIA								
Byrd	Y	Y	Y	N	Y	N	Y	Y
Rockefeller	Y	Y	Y	Y	Y	Y	Y	Y
WISCONSIN								
Feingold	N	Y	N	Y	N	Y	N	Y
Kohl	N	Y	N	N	Y	N	Y	N
WYOMING								
Simpson	+	Y	N	Y	N	Y	N	Y
Wallop	?	Y	Y	Y	N	Y	N	Y

ND Northern Democrats   SD Southern Democrats   Southern states - Ala., Ark., Fla., Ga., Ky., La., Miss., N.C., Okla., S.C., Tenn., Texas, Va.

257. S 1298. Fiscal 1994 Defense Authorization/Burden Sharing. Nunn, D-Ga., amendment to the Lautenberg, D-N.J., amendment, to express the sense of Congress on increased burden sharing by U.S. allies. The Lautenberg amendment would require host nations to pay at least 75 percent of the cost of basing troops in their country by 1996. Adopted 74-15: R 32-2; D 42-13 (ND 28-13, SD 14-0), Sept. 10, 1993. (Subsequently, the Lautenberg amendment as amended by the Nunn amendment was adopted by voice vote.)

258. S 1298. Fiscal 1994 Defense Authorization/Land Mines. Leahy, D-Vt., amendment to extend for three years the existing U.S. moratorium on the sale or transfer of land mines abroad. Adopted 100-0: R 44-0; D 56-0 (ND 42-0, SD 14-0), Sept. 14, 1993.

259. S 1298. Fiscal 1994 Defense Authorization/Defense Business Operations Fund. Glenn, D-Ohio, motion to table (kill) the Grassley, R-Iowa, amendment to terminate the Defense Business Operations Fund after 1994, unless it is determined that the fund complied with financial management standards in fiscal 1993. Motion agreed to 57-43: R 19-25; D 38-18 (ND 28-14, SD 10-4), Sept. 14, 1993.

260. S 1298. Fiscal 1994 Defense Authorization/Anti-Satellite Program. Shelby, D-Ala., substitute amendment to the Harkin, D-Iowa, amendment to ensure that no additional funds are spent to convert the Kinetic Energy Anti-Satellite program until the administration certifies that it is necessary to preserve an option to develop and deploy an ASAT program. The Harkin amendment would terminate the ASAT program. Adopted 90-10: R 42-2; D 48-8 (ND 35-7, SD 13-1), Sept. 14, 1993. (Subsequently, the Harkin amendment as amended by the Shelby amendment was rejected. See Vote 261.)

261. S 1298. Fiscal 1994 Defense Authorization/Anti-Satellite Program. Harkin, D-Iowa, amendment as amended by the Shelby, D-Ala., substitute amendment to ensure that no additional funds are spent to convert the Kinetic Energy Anti-Satellite program until the administration certifies that it is necessary to preserve an option to develop and deploy an ASAT program. Rejected 40-60: R 4-40; D 36-20 (ND 33-9, SD 3-11), Sept. 14, 1993.

262. S 1298. Fiscal 1994 Defense Authorization/Defense Exports. Nunn, D-Ga., motion to table (kill) the Bingaman, D-N.M., amendment to eliminate the $25 million authorization for the $1 billion loan guarantee program to export defense articles to NATO countries, Israel, Australia, South Korea and Japan. Motion agreed to 63-37: R 40-4; D 23-33 (ND 13-29, SD 10-4), Sept. 14, 1993.

263. S 1298. Fiscal 1994 Defense Authorization/Single-Stage-to-Orbit Rocket. Nunn, D-Ga., motion to table (kill) the Domenici, R-N.M., amendment to authorize $75 million for the next stage of work on the single-stage-to-orbit rocket program. Motion agreed to 66-33: R 18-25; D 48-8 (ND 37-5, SD 11-3), Sept. 14, 1993.

264. S 1298. Fiscal 1994 Defense Authorization/Levee Damage. Baucus, D-Mont., motion to table (kill) the Simon, D-Ill., amendment to authorize the Army to pay 100 percent of the cost to repair federal and non-federal levees damaged as a result of flooding in the Midwest. Motion agreed to 63-34: R 33-10; D 30-24 (ND 24-17, SD 6-7), Sept. 14, 1993.

KEY

- **Y** Voted for (yea).
- **#** Paired for.
- **+** Announced for.
- **N** Voted against (nay).
- **X** Paired against.
- **−** Announced against.
- **P** Voted "present."
- **C** Voted "present" to avoid possible conflict of interest.
- **?** Did not vote or otherwise make a position known.

Democrats *Republicans*

	265	266	267	268	269	270	271	272
ALABAMA								
Heflin	Y	Y	Y	N	N	Y	N	Y
Shelby	Y	Y	Y	Y	N	N	N	Y
ALASKA								
Murkowski	Y	Y	Y	N	Y	N	N	Y
Stevens	Y	Y	Y	N	?	?	N	Y
ARIZONA								
DeConcini	Y	Y	Y	N	Y	N	Y	N
McCain	Y	Y	Y	Y	N	N	N	Y
ARKANSAS								
Bumpers	Y	N	Y	N	N	Y	N	N
Pryor	Y	N	Y	N	N	Y	N	N
CALIFORNIA								
Boxer	N	N	N	N	Y	Y	Y	Y
Feinstein	Y	Y	Y	N	Y	Y	Y	Y
COLORADO								
Campbell	Y	Y	N	N	Y	Y	Y	Y
Brown	Y	Y	Y	Y	N	N	N	N
CONNECTICUT								
Dodd	Y	Y	Y	N	Y	N	Y	N
Lieberman	Y	N	N	N	Y	Y	N	Y
DELAWARE								
Biden	Y	N	N	N	Y	Y	N	Y
Roth	Y	N	Y	N	Y	N	N	Y
FLORIDA								
Graham	Y	N	Y	N	Y	Y	N	Y
Mack	Y	Y	Y	Y	N	N	N	Y
GEORGIA								
Nunn	Y	N	Y	Y	?	?	N	N
Coverdell	Y	Y	Y	Y	N	N	?	Y
HAWAII								
Akaka	Y	N	Y	N	Y	Y	N	N
Inouye	Y	Y	Y	N	Y	Y	Y	Y
IDAHO								
Craig	Y	Y	Y	N	N	N	N	Y
Kempthorne	Y	Y	Y	N	N	N	N	Y
ILLINOIS								
Moseley-Braun	Y	N	Y	N	Y	Y	N	Y
Simon	Y	N	Y	N	Y	Y	N	N
INDIANA								
Coats	Y	Y	Y	N	N	N	N	N
Lugar	Y	Y	Y	N	N	Y	N	Y
IOWA								
Harkin	Y	N	Y	N	Y	Y	N	Y
Grassley	Y	N	Y	N	N	N	N	Y
KANSAS								
Dole	Y	Y	Y	N	N	N	N	Y
Kassebaum	Y	Y	Y	N	N	Y	N	Y
KENTUCKY								
Ford	Y	Y	Y	N	N	Y	N	N
McConnell	Y	Y	Y	Y	N	N	N	Y
LOUISIANA								
Breaux	Y	Y	Y	N	?	?	N	Y
Johnston	Y	N	Y	N	Y	Y	N	Y
MAINE								
Mitchell	Y	N	Y	N	Y	Y	N	N
Cohen	Y	N	Y	N	Y	Y	N	N
MARYLAND								
Mikulski	Y	N	Y	N	Y	Y	N	N
Sarbanes	Y	N	Y	N	Y	Y	N	Y
MASSACHUSETTS								
Kennedy	Y	N	N	N	Y	Y	N	N
Kerry	Y	N	N	N	Y	Y	N	N
MICHIGAN								
Levin	Y	N	Y	N	Y	Y	Y	Y
Riegle	Y	N	Y	N	Y	Y	Y	Y
MINNESOTA								
Wellstone	N	N	N	N	Y	Y	N	N
Durenberger	Y	Y	Y	N	Y	Y	N	Y
MISSISSIPPI								
Cochran	Y	Y	Y	N	N	Y	N	Y
Lott	Y	Y	Y	N	N	N	N	Y
MISSOURI								
Bond	Y	Y	Y	N	Y	N	?	Y
Danforth	Y	Y	Y	N	Y	Y	N	Y
MONTANA								
Baucus	Y	Y	Y	N	Y	N	N	Y
Burns	Y	Y	Y	N	N	N	N	Y
NEBRASKA								
Exon	Y	N	Y	Y	N	N	?	N
Kerrey	Y	Y	Y	N	Y	Y	N	N
NEVADA								
Bryan	Y	Y	N	N	Y	Y	N	N
Reid	Y	Y	Y	N	Y	Y	N	N
NEW HAMPSHIRE								
Gregg	Y	Y	Y	N	N	N	N	Y
Smith	Y	Y	Y	Y	N	N	N	Y
NEW JERSEY								
Bradley	Y	N	N	N	Y	Y	N	N
Lautenberg	Y	N	N	N	Y	Y	N	N
NEW MEXICO								
Bingaman	Y	Y	N	N	Y	Y	N	Y
Domenici	Y	Y	Y	N	Y	?	N	Y
NEW YORK								
Moynihan	N	Y	Y	N	Y	Y	Y	N
D'Amato	Y	Y	Y	N	Y	Y	#	N
NORTH CAROLINA								
Faircloth	Y	Y	Y	Y	N	N	N	N
Helms	Y	Y	Y	Y	N	N	N	Y
NORTH DAKOTA								
Conrad	Y	Y	Y	N	Y	N	N	N
Dorgan	Y	Y	Y	N	Y	Y	N	N
OHIO								
Glenn	Y	N	Y	N	Y	Y	N	Y
Metzenbaum	N	N	?	?	Y	Y	N	N
OKLAHOMA								
Boren	Y	Y	N	N	Y	N	N	N
Nickles	Y	Y	Y	Y	N	N	N	Y
OREGON								
Hatfield	N	Y	Y	N	Y	N	Y	N
Packwood	Y	Y	Y	N	Y	Y	N	Y
PENNSYLVANIA								
Wofford	Y	N	Y	N	Y	Y	N	N
Specter	Y	N	Y	N	Y	Y	Y	N
RHODE ISLAND								
Pell	Y	N	Y	N	Y	Y	N	N
Chafee	Y	Y	Y	N	Y	Y	N	N
SOUTH CAROLINA								
Hollings	Y	Y	Y	N	N	Y	N	N
Thurmond	Y	Y	Y	N	N	N	Y	Y
SOUTH DAKOTA								
Daschle	Y	Y	Y	N	Y	N	Y	Y
Pressler	Y	Y	Y	N	Y	N	N	Y
TENNESSEE								
Mathews	Y	Y	Y	N	N	Y	N	N
Sasser	Y	N	Y	N	N	Y	N	N
TEXAS								
Gramm	?	?	?	?	?	?	N	Y
Hutchison	Y	Y	Y	N	N	N	N	Y
UTAH								
Bennett	Y	Y	Y	N	N	N	N	Y
Hatch	Y	Y	Y	N	N	N	Y	Y
VERMONT								
Leahy	Y	N	N	N	Y	Y	N	N
Jeffords	Y	N	N	N	Y	Y	Y	Y
VIRGINIA								
Robb	Y	N	Y	N	Y	Y	N	Y
Warner	Y	Y	Y	N	Y	N	N	N
WASHINGTON								
Murray	Y	N	N	N	Y	Y	N	Y
Gorton	Y	Y	Y	N	Y	N	Y	N
WEST VIRGINIA								
Byrd	Y	N	Y	N	N	N	N	Y
Rockefeller	Y	N	Y	N	Y	Y	N	?
WISCONSIN								
Feingold	N	N	N	N	Y	Y	N	N
Kohl	Y	N	N	N	Y	Y	N	N
WYOMING								
Simpson	Y	Y	Y	N	Y	N	Y	N
Wallop	N	Y	Y	N	N	N	X	Y

ND Northern Democrats   SD Southern Democrats

Southern states - Ala., Ark., Fla., Ga., Ky., La., Miss., N.C., Okla., S.C., Tenn., Texas, Va.

265. S 1298. Fiscal 1994 Defense Authorization/Passage. Passage of the bill to authorize about $261 billion for the military activities of the Defense Department in fiscal 1994. The bill would scrap plans for the Navy's A/F-X carrier-based bomber, cut funds requested for anti-missile defenses and codify provisions on homosexuals in the military. Passed 92-7: R 41-2; D 51-5 (ND 37-5, SD 14-0), Sept. 14, 1993.

266. HR 2520. Fiscal 1994 Interior Appropriations/Grazing Fees. Domenici, R-N.M., amendment to prohibit the administration for one year from using funds in the bill to implement higher grazing fees and other public land-management reforms. Adopted 59-40: R 38-5; D 21-35 (ND 14-28, SD 7-7), Sept. 14, 1993. A "nay" was a vote in support of the president's position.

267. HR 2520. Fiscal 1994 Interior Appropriations/Coal and Timber. Byrd, D-W.Va., motion to table (kill) the Bradley, D-N.J., amendment to reduce spending on the coal liquefaction program by $12 million to about $16 million and limit the amount of timber that may be cut in the Tongass National Forest to 350 million board feet. Motion agreed to 81-17: R 42-1; D 39-16 (ND 26-15, SD 13-1), Sept. 14, 1993.

268. HR 2520. Fiscal 1994 Interior Appropriations/National Endowment for the Arts. Helms, R-N.C., amendment to eliminate all funding, about $170 million, for the National Endowment for the Arts. Rejected 15-83: R 11-32; D 4-51 (ND 1-40, SD 3-11), Sept. 14, 1993.

269. HR 2520. Fiscal 1994 Interior Appropriations/National Endowment for the Arts. Jeffords, R-Vt., motion to table (kill) the Helms, R-N.C., amendment to require the National Endowment for the Arts to equitably distribute funds to states based on their population. Motion agreed to 57-39: R 14-28; D 43-11 (ND 39-3, SD 4-8), Sept. 15, 1993.

270. HR 2520. Fiscal 1994 Interior Appropriations/National Endowment for the Arts. Jeffords, R-Vt., motion to table (kill) the Helms, R-N.C., amendment to prohibit the National Endowment for the Arts from directly funding individuals. Motion agreed to 65-30: R 15-26; D 50-4 (ND 40-2, SD 10-2), Sept. 15, 1993.

271. S J Res 114. Base-Closure Disapproval/Adoption. Adoption of the joint resolution to disapprove the recommendations of the Defense Base Closure and Realignment Commission submitted by the president July 13, 1993. Rejected 12-83: R 4-36; D 8-47 (ND 7-34, SD 1-13), Sept. 20, 1993. A "nay" was a vote in support of the president's position.

272. HR 2491. Fiscal 1994 VA-HUD Appropriations/Space Station. Mikulski, D-Md., motion to table (kill) the Bumpers, D-Ark., amendment to terminate the space station program. Motion agreed to 59-40: R 36-8; D 23-32 (ND 17-24, SD 6-8), Sept. 21, 1993. A "yea" was a vote in support of the president's position.

	273	274	275	276	277	278	279	280
ALABAMA								
Heflin	Y	Y	Y	Y	Y	Y	N	Y
Shelby	Y	Y	Y	Y	Y	Y	N	Y
ALASKA								
Murkowski	Y	Y	Y	N	N	N	Y	N
Stevens	Y	Y	Y	N	N	N	Y	Y
ARIZONA								
DeConcini	N	N	N	N	Y	N	N	Y
McCain	Y	Y	Y	N	N	N	Y	Y
ARKANSAS								
Bumpers	Y	N	N	N	Y	N	N	Y
Pryor	Y	?	N	N	Y	N	N	Y
CALIFORNIA								
Boxer	N	Y	N	N	Y	N	N	Y
Feinstein	N	Y	Y	Y	Y	N	N	Y
COLORADO								
Campbell	N	Y	N	N	N	Y	N	Y
Brown	Y	Y	Y	Y	N	N	Y	N
CONNECTICUT								
Dodd	Y	Y	Y	Y	Y	N	N	Y
Lieberman	N	N	N	N	Y	Y	N	Y
DELAWARE								
Biden	N	Y	N	N	Y	N	N	Y
Roth	Y	Y	Y	N	N	N	Y	Y
FLORIDA								
Graham	Y	Y	Y	Y	N	Y	Y	Y
Mack	Y	Y	Y	N	N	N	Y	N
GEORGIA								
Nunn	Y	N	N	N	Y	Y	Y	Y
Coverdell	Y	Y	Y	N	N	N	Y	N
HAWAII								
Akaka	Y	Y	Y	Y	Y	N	N	Y
Inouye	Y	Y	Y	Y	Y	Y	N	Y
IDAHO								
Craig	Y	Y	N	N	N	Y	Y	N
Kempthorne	Y	?	N	N	N	N	Y	N
ILLINOIS								
Moseley-Braun	N	Y	Y	N	Y	N	N	Y
Simon	Y	N	N	N	Y	N	N	Y
INDIANA								
Coats	Y	N	Y	N	N	N	Y	Y
Lugar	Y	Y	Y	N	N	N	N	Y
IOWA								
Harkin	N	N	N	Y	Y	N	N	Y
Grassley	N	N	Y	N	N	N	Y	Y
KANSAS								
Dole	Y	N	Y	N	N	Y	Y	Y
Kassebaum	Y	N	Y	N	N	N	Y	N
KENTUCKY								
Ford	Y	N	Y	N	Y	N	N	Y
McConnell	Y	Y	Y	N	N	Y	Y	Y
LOUISIANA								
Breaux	Y	Y	Y	Y	Y	N	N	Y
Johnston	Y	?	Y	Y	Y	Y	N	Y
MAINE								
Mitchell	N	N	N	N	Y	N	N	Y
Cohen	N	N	N	N	N	N	Y	Y
MARYLAND								
Mikulski	Y	Y	Y	Y	Y	Y	N	Y
Sarbanes	N	?	N	N	Y	N	N	Y
MASSACHUSETTS								
Kennedy	N	Y	N	N	Y	N	N	Y
Kerry	N	N	N	N	Y	N	N	Y
MICHIGAN								
Levin	N	N	N	Y	Y	Y	N	Y
Riegle	Y	Y	Y	N	Y	N	N	Y
MINNESOTA								
Wellstone	N	N	N	N	Y	N	N	Y
Durenberger	Y	N	N	N	Y	N	Y	N
MISSISSIPPI								
Cochran	Y	Y	Y	N	N	N	Y	Y
Lott	Y	Y	Y	Y	N	N	Y	N
MISSOURI								
Bond	Y	?	N	Y	N	Y	N	Y
Danforth	Y	Y	Y	N	Y	N	Y	N
MONTANA								
Baucus	N	N	N	N	Y	N	Y	Y
Burns	N	N	N	N	N	Y	N	N
NEBRASKA								
Exon	N	N	Y	N	N	N	Y	Y
Kerrey	N	N	N	N	N	N	N	Y
NEVADA								
Bryan	Y	N	Y	N	Y	Y	Y	N
Reid	N	Y	Y	N	Y	N	N	Y
NEW HAMPSHIRE								
Gregg	N	Y	N	N	N	N	Y	N
Smith	Y	Y	Y	N	N	N	Y	N
NEW JERSEY								
Bradley	N	N	N	N	N	N	N	Y
Lautenberg	N	N	N	N	N	N	N	Y
NEW MEXICO								
Bingaman	Y	Y	N	N	Y	Y	Y	Y
Domenici	Y	Y	Y	N	N	Y	Y	Y
NEW YORK								
Moynihan	N	Y	N	Y	N	N	N	Y
D'Amato	Y	N	Y	N	N	N	N	N
NORTH CAROLINA								
Faircloth	Y	Y	Y	N	N	N	Y	N
Helms	Y	?	Y	N	N	N	Y	N
NORTH DAKOTA								
Conrad	Y	N	N	N	Y	N	Y	Y
Dorgan	Y	N	N	N	Y	N	Y	Y
OHIO								
Glenn	Y	Y	Y	Y	Y	N	N	Y
Metzenbaum	N	N	N	N	Y	?	N	Y
OKLAHOMA								
Boren	N	N	Y	N	Y	N	Y	Y
Nickles	N	Y	Y	N	N	Y	Y	Y
OREGON								
Hatfield	N	Y	Y	Y	N	Y	Y	Y
Packwood	N	Y	Y	N	N	Y	Y	Y
PENNSYLVANIA								
Wofford	N	Y	N	N	Y	N	N	Y
Specter	Y	N	N	N	N	N	?	Y
RHODE ISLAND								
Pell	N	N	N	Y	Y	N	N	Y
Chafee	N	N	N	N	N	N	N	N
SOUTH CAROLINA								
Hollings	Y	N	N	N	N	N	N	Y
Thurmond	Y	Y	Y	N	N	Y	Y	Y
SOUTH DAKOTA								
Daschle	Y	Y	N	Y	Y	N	N	Y
Pressler	Y	Y	Y	N	N	N	Y	N
TENNESSEE								
Mathews	N	N	Y	N	Y	N	Y	Y
Sasser	Y	N	Y	N	Y	N	N	Y
TEXAS								
Gramm	Y	Y	Y	Y	N	Y	Y	Y
Hutchison	Y	Y	Y	Y	N	Y	Y	N
UTAH								
Bennett	N	Y	N	N	N	N	Y	N
Hatch	Y	Y	N	N	N	N	Y	N
VERMONT								
Leahy	N	Y	N	N	Y	Y	N	Y
Jeffords	N	N	N	N	N	N	N	Y
VIRGINIA								
Robb	N	Y	N	Y	Y	Y	N	Y
Warner	Y	N	Y	N	N	Y	N	Y
WASHINGTON								
Murray	N	Y	N	N	Y	Y	N	Y
Gorton	Y	Y	Y	N	N	Y	Y	Y
WEST VIRGINIA								
Byrd	Y	N	N	N	Y	N	N	Y
Rockefeller	+	Y	N	Y	Y	Y	N	Y
WISCONSIN								
Feingold	N	N	N	N	Y	N	N	N
Kohl	N	N	N	N	N	Y	N	Y
WYOMING								
Simpson	Y	Y	Y	N	N	Y	Y	N
Wallop	Y	Y	Y	N	N	N	Y	N

KEY

Y Voted for (yea).
Paired for.
+ Announced for.
N Voted against (nay).
X Paired against.
− Announced against.
P Voted ''present.''
C Voted ''present'' to avoid possible conflict of interest.
? Did not vote or otherwise make a position known.

Democrats   *Republicans*

ND Northern Democrats   SD Southern Democrats

Southern states - Ala., Ark., Fla., Ga., Ky., La., Miss., N.C., Okla., S.C., Tenn., Texas, Va.

273. HR 2491. Fiscal 1994 VA-HUD Appropriations/Selective Service. Mikulski, D-Md., motion to table (kill) the Bradley, D-N.J., amendment to cut $20 million in the bill for the Selective Service System and leave $5 million for termination costs. Motion agreed to 58-41: R 34-10; D 24-31 (ND 13-28, SD 11-3), Sept. 21, 1993.

274. HR 2491. Fiscal 1994 VA-HUD Appropriations/Space Station. Mikulski, D-Md., motion to table (kill) the Warner, R-Va., amendment to require further congressional approval before NASA could spend the final $1 billion in the bill for the space station. Motion agreed to 55-39: R 30-11; D 25-28 (ND 20-21, SD 5-7), Sept. 21, 1993.

275. HR 2491. Fiscal 1994 VA-HUD Appropriations/Advanced Solid Rocket Motor. Mikulski, D-Md., motion to table (kill) the Bumpers, D-Ark., amendment to terminate the Advanced Solid Rocket Motor project. Motion agreed to 53-47: R 32-12; D 21-35 (ND 11-31, SD 10-4), Sept. 22, 1993.

276. HR 2491. Fiscal 1994 VA-HUD Appropriations/Search for Extraterrestrials. Mikulksi, D-Md., motion to table (kill) the Bryan, D-Nev., amendment to eliminate funding for the program to.search for extraterrestrial intelligence. Motion rejected 23-77: R 6-38; D 17-39 (ND 12-30, SD 5-9), Sept. 22, 1993. (Subsequently, the Bryan amendment was adopted by voice vote.)

277. HR 2491. Fiscal 1994 VA-HUD Appropriations/National Service Initiative. Mikulski, D-Md., motion to table (kill) the Nickles, R-Okla., amendment to reduce funding for the National Service Initiative from $321 million to $300 million. Motion rejected 45-55: R 1-43; D 44-12 (ND 32-10, SD 12-2), Sept. 22, 1993.

278. HR 2491. Fiscal 1994 VA-HUD Appropriations/School Asbestos. Mikulski, D-Md., motion to table (kill) the Simon, D-Ill., amendment to provide $30 million for school asbestos removal. Motion rejected 31-68: R 13-31; D 18-37 (ND 12-29, SD 6-8), Sept. 22, 1993. (Subsequently, the Simon amendment was adopted by voice vote.)

279. HR 2491. Fiscal 1994 VA-HUD Appropriations/Community Development Block Grants. Brown, R-Colo., amendment to cut the Community Development Block Grant program by $176.3 million to the level requested by the administration. Rejected 48-51: R 37-6; D 11-45 (ND 7-35, SD 4-10), Sept. 22, 1993.

280. HR 2491. Fiscal 1994 VA-HUD Appropriations/VA Facilities. Rockefeller, D-W.Va., motion to table (kill) the Murkowski, R-Alaska, amendment to reduce from $369 million to $272 million the amount for construction of new Department of Veterans Affairs inpatient facilities. Motion agreed to 73-27: R 19-25; D 54-2 (ND 40-2, SD 14-0), Sept. 22, 1993.

	281	282	283	284	285	286	287	288
ALABAMA								
Heflin	Y	Y	Y	Y	N	Y	Y	Y
Shelby	Y	Y	Y	Y	Y	Y	Y	Y
ALASKA								
Murkowski	Y	Y	Y	N	Y	Y	Y	Y
Stevens	Y	Y	Y	N	N	Y	Y	Y
ARIZONA								
DeConcini	Y	?	Y	Y	N	Y	Y	N
McCain	Y	Y	Y	N	N	Y	Y	?
ARKANSAS								
Bumpers	Y	Y	Y	N	Y	Y	Y	N
Pryor	Y	Y	Y	N	N	Y	Y	Y
CALIFORNIA								
Boxer	Y	Y	Y	N	Y	Y	Y	N
Feinstein	Y	Y	Y	Y	N	Y	Y	Y
COLORADO								
Campbell	Y	Y	Y	N	Y	Y	Y	Y
Brown	Y	Y	Y	N	N	Y	Y	Y
CONNECTICUT								
Dodd	Y	Y	Y	Y	Y	Y	Y	N
Lieberman	Y	Y	Y	Y	Y	Y	Y	N
DELAWARE								
Biden	Y	?	?	Y	Y	Y	Y	N
Roth	N	Y	Y	N	Y	Y	N	N
FLORIDA								
Graham	Y	Y	Y	N	Y	Y	Y	N
Mack	Y	Y	Y	Y	Y	Y	Y	N
GEORGIA								
Nunn	Y	Y	N	N	Y	Y	Y	N
Coverdell	Y	Y	Y	Y	Y	Y	Y	Y
HAWAII								
Akaka	Y	Y	Y	Y	Y	Y	Y	N
Inouye	Y	Y	Y	Y	Y	Y	Y	N
IDAHO								
Craig	Y	Y	Y	N	N	Y	N	Y
Kempthorne	Y	Y	Y	N	N	Y	N	Y
ILLINOIS								
Moseley-Braun	Y	Y	Y	Y	Y	Y	Y	N
Simon	Y	N	Y	Y	Y	Y	Y	N
INDIANA								
Coats	Y	Y	Y	N	Y	Y	Y	N
Lugar	Y	Y	Y	Y	Y	Y	Y	N

	281	282	283	284	285	286	287	288
IOWA								
Harkin	Y	Y	Y	Y	Y	Y	Y	N
Grassley	Y	Y	Y	N	N	Y	Y	Y
KANSAS								
Dole	Y	Y	Y	N	N	Y	Y	Y
Kassebaum	Y	Y	Y	Y	Y	Y	Y	Y
KENTUCKY								
Ford	Y	Y	Y	Y	N	Y	Y	N
McConnell	Y	Y	Y	Y	Y	Y	Y	Y
LOUISIANA								
Breaux	Y	Y	Y	Y	N	Y	?	Y
Johnston	Y	Y	Y	Y	Y	Y	Y	Y
MAINE								
Mitchell	Y	Y	Y	Y	Y	Y	Y	N
Cohen	Y	Y	Y	N	N	Y	Y	N
MARYLAND								
Mikulski	Y	Y	Y	Y	Y	Y	Y	N
Sarbanes	Y	Y	Y	Y	Y	Y	Y	N
MASSACHUSETTS								
Kennedy	Y	Y	Y	Y	Y	Y	Y	N
Kerry	Y	Y	Y	Y	Y	Y	Y	N
MICHIGAN								
Levin	Y	Y	Y	Y	Y	Y	Y	N
Riegle	Y	Y	Y	N	Y	Y	Y	N
MINNESOTA								
Wellstone	Y	N	Y	Y	Y	Y	Y	N
Durenberger	Y	Y	Y	N	Y	Y	Y	Y
MISSISSIPPI								
Cochran	Y	Y	Y	Y	Y	Y	Y	Y
Lott	Y	Y	Y	N	N	Y	Y	Y
MISSOURI								
Bond	Y	Y	Y	N	N	Y	Y	Y
Danforth	Y	Y	Y	Y	Y	Y	Y	X
MONTANA								
Baucus	Y	Y	Y	N	Y	Y	Y	Y
Burns	Y	Y	Y	N	Y	Y	Y	Y
NEBRASKA								
Exon	Y	Y	Y	Y	Y	Y	Y	N
Kerrey	Y	Y	Y	Y	Y	Y	Y	Y
NEVADA								
Bryan	Y	Y	Y	N	Y	Y	Y	N
Reid	Y	Y	Y	Y	Y	Y	Y	N

	281	282	283	284	285	286	287	288
NEW HAMPSHIRE								
Gregg	N	Y	Y	N	N	Y	Y	N
Smith	N	Y	Y	N	N	Y	N	N
NEW JERSEY								
Bradley	Y	Y	Y	Y	Y	Y	Y	N
Lautenberg	Y	Y	Y	Y	N	Y	Y	N
NEW MEXICO								
Bingaman	Y	N	Y	N	N	Y	Y	Y
Domenici	Y	Y	Y	N	Y	Y	Y	Y
NEW YORK								
Moynihan	Y	Y	Y	Y	Y	Y	Y	N
D'Amato	Y	Y	Y	N	Y	Y	Y	N
NORTH CAROLINA								
Faircloth	N	Y	Y	N	N	Y	N	Y
Helms	N	Y	Y	N	N	Y	N	Y
NORTH DAKOTA								
Conrad	Y	Y	Y	N	Y	Y	Y	Y
Dorgan	Y	Y	Y	N	Y	Y	Y	Y
OHIO								
Glenn	Y	Y	Y	Y	Y	Y	Y	N
Metzenbaum	Y	Y	Y	Y	Y	Y	Y	N
OKLAHOMA								
Boren	N	Y	Y	N	Y	Y	Y	N
Nickles	Y	Y	Y	N	N	Y	Y	N
OREGON								
Hatfield	Y	Y	Y	Y	Y	Y	Y	N
Packwood	Y	Y	Y	Y	Y	Y	Y	N
PENNSYLVANIA								
Wofford	Y	?	?	?	?	?	Y	Y
Specter	Y	Y	Y	Y	Y	Y	Y	N
RHODE ISLAND								
Pell	Y	Y	Y	Y	Y	Y	Y	N
Chafee	Y	?	Y	Y	Y	Y	Y	N
SOUTH CAROLINA								
Hollings	Y	Y	Y	N	Y	N	N	N
Thurmond	Y	Y	Y	N	N	Y	Y	Y
SOUTH DAKOTA								
Daschle	Y	Y	Y	Y	Y	Y	Y	Y
Pressler	Y	Y	Y	N	N	Y	Y	N
TENNESSEE								
Mathews	Y	Y	Y	Y	Y	Y	Y	N
Sasser	Y	Y	Y	Y	N	Y	Y	N

	281	282	283	284	285	286	287	288
TEXAS								
Gramm	Y	Y	Y	N	N	Y	Y	Y
Hutchison	Y	Y	Y	N	N	Y	Y	Y
UTAH								
Bennett	Y	Y	Y	Y	Y	Y	Y	Y
Hatch	Y	Y	Y	N	Y	Y	Y	Y
VERMONT								
Leahy	Y	Y	Y	Y	Y	Y	Y	N
Jeffords	Y	Y	Y	Y	Y	Y	Y	Y
VIRGINIA								
Robb	Y	Y	Y	Y	N	Y	Y	N
Warner	Y	Y	Y	N	N	Y	Y	N
WASHINGTON								
Murray	Y	Y	Y	Y	Y	Y	Y	N
Gorton	Y	Y	Y	N	Y	Y	Y	N
WEST VIRGINIA								
Byrd	Y	Y	Y	N	Y	Y	N	N
Rockefeller	Y	Y	Y	Y	Y	Y	Y	N
WISCONSIN								
Feingold	N	N	Y	Y	Y	Y	Y	N
Kohl	N	Y	Y	N	N	Y	N	N
WYOMING								
Simpson	Y	Y	Y	N	N	Y	+	#
Wallop	N	Y	Y	N	N	Y	N	Y

ND Northern Democrats   SD Southern Democrats   Southern states - Ala., Ark., Fla., Ga., Ky., La., Miss., N.C., Okla., S.C., Tenn., Texas, Va.

---

281. HR 2491. Fiscal 1994 VA-HUD Appropriations/ Passage. Passage of the bill to provide approximately $87.9 billion in new budget authority for the departments of Veterans Affairs and Housing and Urban Development, and for various independent entities and offices in fiscal 1994. Passed 91-9: R 38-6; D 53-3 (ND 40-2, SD 13-1), Sept. 22, 1993.

282. HR 2295. Fiscal 1994 Foreign Aid Appropriations/ Expropriated Property. Helms, R-N.C., amendment to prohibit countries that expropriate the property of U.S. citizens from receiving foreign aid. Adopted 92-4: R 43-0; D 49-4 (ND 35-4, SD 14-0), Sept. 23, 1993.

283. HR 2295. Fiscal 1994 Foreign Aid Appropriations/ Russian Troop Withdrawal. Byrd, D-W.Va., amendment to restrict Russian aid unless the president certifies that Russia has made "substantial progress" in establishing a timetable for troop withdrawal from Latvia and Estonia. Adopted 97-1: R 44-0; D 53-1 (ND 40-0, SD 13-1), Sept. 23, 1993.

284. HR 2295. Fiscal 1994 Foreign Aid Appropriations/ World Bank. McConnell, R-Ky., motion to table (kill) the Brown, R-Colo., amendment to eliminate the World Bank capital stock funding increases. Motion agreed to 55-44: R 12-32; D 43-12 (ND 33-8, SD 10-4), Sept. 23, 1993. A "yea" was a vote in support of the president's position.

285. HR 2295. Fiscal 1994 Foreign Aid Appropriations/ Defense Conversion. McConnell, R-Ky., motion to table (kill) the Smith, R-N.H., amendment to transfer $200 million from foreign aid to defense conversion technology reinvestment. Motion agreed to 64-35: R 22-22; D 42-13 (ND 34-7, SD 8-6), Sept. 23, 1993. A "yea" was a vote in support of the president's position.

286. HR 2295. Fiscal 1994 Foreign Aid Appropriations/ Vietnam. Kerrey, D-Neb., amendment to express the sense of Congress that the United States should support nonviolent democratic reform in Vietnam, reaffirm the importance of progress on the POW/MIA issue to diplomatic relations and support other measures to promote human rights in Vietnam. Adopted 99-0: R 44-0; D 55-0 (ND 41-0, SD 14-0), Sept. 23, 1993.

287. HR 2295. Fiscal 1994 Foreign Aid Appropriations/ Passage. Passage of the bill to provide $12,526,854,047 in new budget authority for foreign aid and related programs in fiscal 1994, including the $2.5 billion administration request for the former Soviet Union. The administration requested $14,425,993,066. Passed 88-10: R 36-7; D 52-3 (ND 40-2, SD 12-1), Sept. 23, 1993. A "yea" was a vote in support of the president's position.

288. HR 2493. Fiscal 1994 Agriculture Appropriations/ Wool and Mohair. Daschle, D-S.D., motion to table (kill) the Bryan, D-Nev., amendment to the House amendment to the Senate amendment to eliminate the wool and mohair subsidy program. Motion rejected 41-56: R 26-15; D 15-41 (ND 9-33, SD 6-8), Sept. 23, 1993. Subsequently, the Senate concurred with the Bryan amendment by voice vote and agreed to the conference report with two amendments.

	289	290	291	292	293	294	295	296
ALABAMA								
Heflin	Y	N	Y	N	Y	N	Y	N
Shelby	Y	N	Y	N	Y	Y	Y	Y
ALASKA								
Murkowski	N	N	Y	N	Y	Y	Y	Y
Stevens	Y	Y	Y	N	Y	Y	Y	Y
ARIZONA								
DeConcini	Y	N	Y	N	Y	Y	Y	N
McCain	N	N	Y	Y	Y	Y	N	Y
ARKANSAS								
Bumpers	Y	Y	Y	N	Y	Y	Y	N
Pryor	?	?	?	?	?	?	?	—
CALIFORNIA								
Boxer	Y	Y	Y	N	Y	Y	Y	N
Feinstein	Y	Y	Y	N	?	Y	Y	Y
COLORADO								
Campbell	Y	Y	Y	N	Y	Y	Y	Y
Brown	N	N	Y	Y	Y	Y	N	Y
CONNECTICUT								
Dodd	Y	Y	Y	N	Y	Y	Y	N
Lieberman	Y	Y	Y	N	Y	Y	Y	Y
DELAWARE								
Biden	Y	N	Y	N	Y	?	Y	Y
Roth	N	N	Y	N	Y	Y	N	N
FLORIDA								
Graham	Y	N	Y	N	Y	Y	Y	Y
Mack	N	N	Y	Y	Y	Y	Y	Y
GEORGIA								
Nunn	N	N	Y	N	Y	Y	Y	N
Coverdell	N	N	Y	Y	Y	Y	Y	Y
HAWAII								
Akaka	Y	Y	Y	N	Y	Y	Y	Y
Inouye	Y	Y	Y	N	Y	N	Y	N
IDAHO								
Craig	N	N	Y	N	Y	Y	N	Y
Kempthorne	N	N	Y	N	Y	Y	N	Y
ILLINOIS								
Moseley-Braun	Y	Y	Y	N	Y	Y	Y	Y
Simon	Y	Y	Y	N	Y	N	Y	Y
INDIANA								
Coats	N	N	Y	Y	Y	Y	Y	N
Lugar	N	N	+	?	Y	Y	Y	Y

	289	290	291	292	293	294	295	296
IOWA								
Harkin	Y	Y	Y	N	Y	Y	Y	N
Grassley	N	N	Y	N	Y	Y	Y	N
KANSAS								
Dole	N	N	Y	Y	Y	Y	Y	Y
Kassebaum	N	N	Y	?	Y	Y	Y	N
KENTUCKY								
Ford	Y	N	Y	N	Y	Y	Y	Y
McConnell	N	N	Y	Y	Y	Y	Y	Y
LOUISIANA								
Breaux	Y	N	Y	N	Y	Y	Y	Y
Johnston	Y	N	Y	N	Y	Y	Y	Y
MAINE								
Mitchell	Y	Y	Y	N	Y	Y	Y	N
Cohen	N	Y	Y	Y	Y	Y	Y	N
MARYLAND								
Mikulski	Y	Y	Y	N	Y	Y	Y	N
Sarbanes	Y	Y	Y	N	Y	Y	Y	N
MASSACHUSETTS								
Kennedy	Y	Y	Y	N	Y	Y	Y	N
Kerry	Y	Y	Y	N	Y	Y	Y	N
MICHIGAN								
Levin	Y	Y	Y	N	Y	Y	Y	N
Riegle	Y	Y	Y	N	Y	Y	Y	N
MINNESOTA								
Wellstone	Y	Y	Y	N	Y	N	Y	N
Durenberger	Y	N	Y	N	Y	Y	Y	N
MISSISSIPPI								
Cochran	N	N	Y	N	Y	Y	Y	Y
Lott	N	N	Y	Y	Y	Y	Y	Y
MISSOURI								
Bond	N	N	Y	Y	Y	Y	Y	N
Danforth	N	N	Y	Y	Y	Y	Y	Y
MONTANA								
Baucus	Y	Y	Y	N	Y	Y	Y	N
Burns	N	N	Y	N	Y	Y	Y	N
NEBRASKA								
Exon	Y	N	Y	N	Y	Y	Y	N
Kerrey	Y	Y	Y	N	Y	Y	Y	Y
NEVADA								
Bryan	Y	N	Y	N	Y	Y	Y	N
Reid	Y	N	Y	N	Y	Y	Y	Y

	289	290	291	292	293	294	295	296
NEW HAMPSHIRE								
Gregg	N	N	Y	Y	Y	Y	N	N
Smith	N	N	Y	Y	Y	Y	N	N
NEW JERSEY								
Bradley	Y	Y	Y	Y	Y	Y	Y	N
Lautenberg	Y	Y	Y	N	Y	Y	Y	N
NEW MEXICO								
Bingaman	Y	N	Y	N	Y	Y	Y	Y
Domenici	N	N	Y	N	Y	N	Y	Y
NEW YORK								
Moynihan	Y	Y	Y	N	Y	Y	Y	Y
D'Amato	Y	N	Y	N	Y	Y	Y	N
NORTH CAROLINA								
Faircloth	N	N	N	Y	Y	Y	N	N
Helms	N	N	N	Y	Y	Y	N	Y
NORTH DAKOTA								
Conrad	Y	N	Y	N	Y	Y	Y	Y
Dorgan	Y	N	Y	Y	Y	Y	Y	N
OHIO								
Glenn	Y	Y	Y	N	Y	Y	Y	Y
Metzenbaum	Y	Y	Y	N	Y	Y	Y	N
OKLAHOMA								
Boren	N	N	Y	N	Y	Y	Y	Y
Nickles	N	N	Y	Y	Y	Y	N	Y
OREGON								
Hatfield	Y	N	Y	N	Y	Y	Y	Y
Packwood	Y	Y	Y	N	Y	Y	Y	Y
PENNSYLVANIA								
Wofford	Y	N	Y	N	+	Y	Y	N
Specter	Y	Y	Y	N	Y	Y	Y	Y
RHODE ISLAND								
Pell	Y	Y	Y	N	Y	Y	Y	N
Chafee	N	Y	Y	N	Y	Y	Y	Y
SOUTH CAROLINA								
Hollings	Y	Y	Y	N	Y	Y	Y	N
Thurmond	N	N	Y	N	Y	Y	Y	Y
SOUTH DAKOTA								
Daschle	Y	N	Y	N	Y	Y	Y	Y
Pressler	N	N	Y	Y	Y	Y	Y	N
TENNESSEE								
Mathews	Y	N	Y	N	Y	Y	Y	Y
Sasser	Y	N	Y	N	Y	Y	Y	N

	289	290	291	292	293	294	295	296
TEXAS								
Gramm	N	N	Y	Y	Y	Y	N	Y
Hutchison	N	N	Y	Y	Y	Y	N	Y
UTAH								
Bennett	N	N	Y	N	Y	Y	Y	Y
Hatch	N	N	Y	Y	Y	Y	Y	N
VERMONT								
Leahy	Y	Y	Y	N	Y	Y	Y	N
Jeffords	N	Y	Y	N	Y	Y	Y	N
VIRGINIA								
Robb	Y	Y	Y	N	Y	Y	Y	N
Warner	N	N	Y	N	Y	Y	Y	N
WASHINGTON								
Murray	Y	Y	Y	N	Y	Y	Y	N
Gorton	Y	N	Y	N	Y	Y	Y	Y
WEST VIRGINIA								
Byrd	Y	N	Y	N	Y	Y	Y	Y
Rockefeller	Y	Y	Y	N	Y	Y	Y	Y
WISCONSIN								
Feingold	Y	Y	Y	Y	Y	Y	Y	N
Kohl	Y	Y	Y	Y	Y	Y	N	N
WYOMING								
Simpson	N	N	Y	N	Y	Y	Y	Y
Wallop	N	N	N	Y	Y	Y	Y	Y

ND   Northern Democrats   SD   Southern Democrats   Southern states - Ala., Ark., Fla., Ga., Ky., La., Miss., N.C., Okla., S.C., Tenn., Texas, Va.

289. HR 2518. Fiscal 1994 Labor, HHS, Education Appropriations/Davis-Bacon Act. Committee amendment to prohibit the Labor Department from implementing regulations that would allow the use of helpers on federal construction projects covered by the Davis-Bacon Act. Adopted 60-39: R 7-37; D 53-2 (ND 42-0, SD 11-2), Sept. 28, 1993.

290. HR 2518. Fiscal 1994 Labor, HHS, Education Appropriations/Abortion. Committee amendment to strike the Hyde amendment provisions included in the House bill that prohibit federal funds from covering abortions except in cases of rape, incest or when the life of the woman is endangered. Rejected 40-59: R 6-38; D 34-21 (ND 31-11, SD 3-10), Sept. 28, 1993. A ''yea'' was a vote in support of the president's position.

291. HR 2518. Fiscal 1994 Labor, HHS, Education Appropriations/Smoking. Lautenberg, D-N.J., amendment to require federally funded child-care facilities to establish policies to protect children from secondhand smoke. Adopted 95-3: R 40-3; D 55-0 (ND 42-0, SD 13-0), Sept. 28, 1993.

292. HR 2518. Fiscal 1994 Labor, HHS, Education Appropriations/Corporation for Public Broadcasting. McCain, R-Ariz., amendment to freeze funding for the Corporation for Public Broadcasting by cutting $27,359. Rejected 25-72: R 21-21; D 4-51 (ND 4-38, SD 0-13), Sept. 28, 1993.

293. HR 2518. Fiscal 1994 Labor, HHS, Education Ap-

propriations/Crown Heights Riots. D'Amato, R-N.Y., amendment to express the sense of the Senate that the Justice Department should undertake a civil rights investigation into the 1991 Crown Heights riots in New York City and the Aug. 19, 1991, murder of Yankel Rosenbaum. Adopted 97-0: R 44-0; D 53-0 (ND 40-0, SD 13-0), Sept. 29, 1993.

294. HR 2518. Fiscal 1994 Labor, HHS, Education Appropriations/Criminally Insane. Helms, R-N.C., amendment to prohibit the criminally insane from receiving Social Security benefits while in public institutions. Adopted 94-4: R 43-1; D 51-3 (ND 38-3, SD 13-0), Sept. 29, 1993.

295. HR 2518. Fiscal 1994 Labor, HHS, Education Appropriations/Passage. Passage of the bill to provide approximately $256.7 billion in new budget authority for the departments of Labor, Health and Human Services, and Education and related agencies for fiscal 1994. The administration requested $260,471,113,000. Passed 82-17: R 30-14; D 52-3 (ND 40-2, SD 12-1), Sept. 29, 1993.

296. HR 2445. Fiscal 1994 Energy and Water Appropriations/Super Collider. Johnston, D-La., motion to table (kill) the Bumpers, D-Ark., amendment to terminate the superconducting super collider. Motion agreed to 57-42: R 31-13; D 26-29 (ND 17-25, SD 9-4), Sept. 30, 1993. A ''yea'' was a vote in support of the president's position.

KEY

Y Voted for (yea).
\# Paired for.
\+ Announced for.
N Voted against (nay).
X Paired against.
− Announced against.
P Voted "present."
C Voted "present" to avoid possible conflict of interest.
? Did not vote or otherwise make a position known.

Democrats   *Republicans*

	297	298	299	300	301	302	303	304
ALABAMA								
Heflin	Y	Y	Y	Y	Y	?	?	Y
Shelby	Y	Y	Y	Y	Y	?	Y	Y
ALASKA								
Murkowski	Y	Y	Y	Y	Y	N	N	Y
Stevens	Y	Y	Y	Y	Y	N	N	Y
ARIZONA								
DeConcini	Y	N	N	N	Y	Y	Y	Y
McCain	Y	N	N	N	Y	N	Y	N
ARKANSAS								
Bumpers	Y	N	N	Y	Y	Y	N	N
Pryor	?	?	?	?	?	Y	N	N
CALIFORNIA								
Boxer	Y	N	Y	Y	Y	Y	N	Y
Feinstein	Y	N	Y	Y	Y	Y	N	Y
COLORADO								
Campbell	Y	Y	N	Y	Y	N	N	N
Brown	Y	Y	N	N	N	N	N	N
CONNECTICUT								
Dodd	Y	Y	N	Y	Y	Y	N	Y
Lieberman	Y	N	N	N	Y	Y	N	Y
DELAWARE								
Biden	Y	N	N	Y	Y	?	N	Y
Roth	N	N	N	N	N	N	N	N
FLORIDA								
Graham	Y	N	N	Y	Y	Y	Y	Y
Mack	Y	Y	Y	Y	Y	N	N	N
GEORGIA								
Nunn	Y	Y	Y	Y	Y	?	Y	N
Coverdell	Y	Y	N	N	Y	N	Y	N
HAWAII								
Akaka	Y	N	N	Y	Y	Y	N	Y
Inouye	Y	N	N	Y	Y	Y	N	Y
IDAHO								
Craig	N	Y	Y	Y	Y	N	N	N
Kempthorne	N	Y	Y	Y	Y	N	N	N
ILLINOIS								
Moseley-Braun	Y	Y	Y	Y	Y	Y	N	N
Simon	Y	Y	Y	Y	Y	Y	N	N
INDIANA								
Coats	Y	Y	N	N	Y	N	Y	N
Lugar	Y	Y	N	N	Y	Y	Y	N

	297	298	299	300	301	302	303	304
IOWA								
Harkin	Y	N	N	Y	Y	Y	N	N
Grassley	Y	Y	Y	Y	Y	N	N	N
KANSAS								
Dole	Y	Y	N	Y	Y	N	Y	N
Kassebaum	Y	Y	N	Y	Y	N	N	N
KENTUCKY								
Ford	Y	Y	Y	Y	Y	Y	Y	Y
McConnell	Y	Y	Y	Y	Y	?	?	?
LOUISIANA								
Breaux	Y	Y	Y	Y	Y	Y	N	Y
Johnston	Y	Y	Y	Y	Y	Y	N	Y
MAINE								
Mitchell	Y	N	N	Y	Y	Y	N	Y
Cohen	Y	Y	N	Y	Y	Y	N	Y
MARYLAND								
Mikulski	Y	Y	N	Y	Y	Y	N	Y
Sarbanes	Y	N	N	Y	Y	Y	N	Y
MASSACHUSETTS								
Kennedy	Y	N	N	Y	Y	Y	N	Y
Kerry	Y	N	N	Y	N	Y	N	Y
MICHIGAN								
Levin	Y	N	N	Y	Y	Y	Y	Y
Riegle	Y	N	N	Y	Y	Y	Y	Y
MINNESOTA								
Wellstone	Y	N	N	N	Y	N	N	N
Durenberger	Y	Y	N	Y	Y	?	Y	N
MISSISSIPPI								
Cochran	Y	Y	Y	Y	Y	N	N	Y
Lott	Y	Y	Y	Y	Y	N	N	Y
MISSOURI								
Bond	Y	?	Y	Y	Y	?	Y	N
Danforth	Y	Y	Y	Y	Y	N	Y	N
MONTANA								
Baucus	Y	N	N	Y	Y	Y	N	N
Burns	Y	Y	Y	Y	Y	N	N	N
NEBRASKA								
Exon	Y	N	N	Y	Y	Y	N	N
Kerrey	Y	N	N	Y	Y	Y	N	N
NEVADA								
Bryan	Y	N	N	Y	Y	Y	N	Y
Reid	Y	N	N	Y	Y	N	N	Y

	297	298	299	300	301	302	303	304
NEW HAMPSHIRE								
Gregg	N	N	N	N	N	N	N	N
Smith	N	Y	Y	N	N	N	N	N
NEW JERSEY								
Bradley	Y	N	N	Y	?	N	Y	
Lautenberg	Y	N	N	Y	Y	Y	N	Y
NEW MEXICO								
Bingaman	Y	N	Y	Y	Y	N	N	Y
Domenici	Y	Y	Y	Y	Y	N	N	N
NEW YORK								
Moynihan	Y	Y	N	Y	Y	Y	N	Y
D'Amato	Y	Y	N	Y	Y	N	N	Y
NORTH CAROLINA								
Faircloth	N	Y	N	N	N	N	N	N
Helms	N	Y	Y	N	N	N	N	N
NORTH DAKOTA								
Conrad	Y	N	N	Y	Y	Y	N	N
Dorgan	Y	N	N	Y	Y	Y	N	N
OHIO								
Glenn	Y	N	N	Y	Y	Y	Y	N
Metzenbaum	Y	N	N	N	Y	Y	Y	Y
OKLAHOMA								
Boren	Y	Y	Y	Y	Y	N	Y	N
Nickles	Y	Y	N	Y	Y	N	Y	N
OREGON								
Hatfield	Y	N	Y	Y	Y	Y	N	Y
Packwood	Y	Y	Y	Y	Y	Y	N	Y
PENNSYLVANIA								
Wofford	Y	N	N	Y	Y	?	N	Y
Specter	Y	Y	Y	Y	Y	Y	N	Y
RHODE ISLAND								
Pell	Y	N	N	Y	Y	Y	N	Y
Chafee	Y	N	N	Y	Y	N	N	Y
SOUTH CAROLINA								
Hollings	N	N	Y	Y	Y	Y	Y	Y
Thurmond	Y	Y	Y	Y	Y	N	Y	N
SOUTH DAKOTA								
Daschle	Y	Y	Y	Y	Y	Y	N	Y
Pressler	Y	Y	Y	Y	Y	N	N	N
TENNESSEE								
Mathews	Y	N	N	Y	Y	Y	Y	N
Sasser	Y	Y	Y	Y	Y	Y	Y	Y

	297	298	299	300	301	302	303	304
TEXAS								
Gramm	Y	Y	Y	Y	Y	N	Y	N
Hutchison	Y	Y	Y	Y	Y	N	Y	N
UTAH								
Bennett	Y	Y	Y	Y	Y	N	Y	N
Hatch	Y	Y	Y	Y	Y	N	Y	N
VERMONT								
Leahy	Y	N	N	Y	Y	Y	N	Y
Jeffords	Y	N	N	N	N	N	N	N
VIRGINIA								
Robb	Y	N	N	Y	Y	Y	Y	Y
Warner	Y	Y	N	Y	Y	N	Y	N
WASHINGTON								
Murray	Y	Y	N	Y	Y	Y	N	Y
Gorton	Y	Y	N	Y	Y	N	N	Y
WEST VIRGINIA								
Byrd	N	N	N	Y	Y	Y	N	Y
Rockefeller	Y	N	N	Y	Y	Y	N	Y
WISCONSIN								
Feingold	Y	N	N	N	N	N	N	Y
Kohl	N	N	N	N	N	Y	N	Y
WYOMING								
Simpson	Y	Y	N	N	Y	N	N	N
Wallop	N	Y	Y	N	Y	N	Y	Y

ND Northern Democrats   SD Southern Democrats

Southern states - Ala., Ark., Fla., Ga., Ky., La., Miss., N.C., Okla., S.C., Tenn., Texas, Va.

297. HR 2295. Fiscal 1994 Foreign Operations Appropriations/Conference Report. Adoption of the conference report to provide $12,982,665,866 in new budget authority for foreign aid and related programs in fiscal 1994, including the $2.5 billion administration request for the former Soviet Union. The administration requested $14,425,993,066. Adopted (thus cleared for the president) 88-11: R 36-8; D 52-3 (ND 40-2, SD 12-1), Sept. 30, 1993. A "yea was a vote in support of the president's position.

298. HR 2445. Fiscal 1994 Energy and Water Appropriations/Advanced Liquid Metal Reactor. Johnston, D-La., motion to table (kill) the Kerry, D-Mass, amendment to terminate the Advanced Liquid Metal Reactor/Integral Fast Reactor Program. Motion agreed to 53-45: R 37-6; D 16-39 (ND 8-34, SD 8-5), Sept. 30, 1993.

299. HR 2445. Fiscal 1994 Energy and Water Appropriations/Gas Reactor. Johnston, D-La., motion to table (kill) the Bradley, D-N.J., amendment, to terminate the $22 million Gas Turbine Modular Helium Reactor. Motion rejected 41-58: R 25-19; D 16-39 (ND 6-36, SD 10-3), Sept. 30, 1993. (Subsequently, the Bradley amendment was adopted by voice vote.)

300. HR 2445. Fiscal 1994 Energy and Water Appropriations/Army Corps of Engineers and Reclamation Bureau. Johnston, D-La., motion to table (kill) the Bradley, D-N.J., amendment to reduce funding for the Army Corps of Engineers and the Bureau of Reclamation. Motion agreed to 81-18: R 32-12; D 49-6 (ND 36-6, SD 13-0), Sept. 30, 1993.

301. HR 2445. Fiscal 1994 Energy and Water Appropriations/Passage. Passage of the bill to provide $22 billion in new budget authority for energy and water development in fiscal 1994. The administration requested $22,350,946,000. Passed 89-10: R 38-6; D 51-4 (ND 38-4, SD 13-0), Sept. 30, 1993.

302. HR 2750. Fiscal 1994 Transportation Appropriations/Interstate Commerce Commission. Exon, D-Neb., motion to table (kill) the Danforth, R-Mo., amendment to eliminate funding for the Interstate Commerce Commission. Motion agreed to 52-39: R 7-34; D 45-5 (ND 34-5, SD 11-0), Oct. 4, 1993.

303. HR 2750. Fiscal 1994 Transportation Appropriations/Minimum Allocations. Warner, R-Va., motion to waive the budget act with respect to the Lautenberg, D-N.J., point of order against the Warner amendment. The Warner amendment would strike a provision that slows the flow of highway money to minimum allocation states between Oct. 1, 1993, and Jan. 1, 1994. Motion rejected 35-63: R 19-24; D 16-39 (ND 7-35, SD 9-4), Oct. 5, 1993. A three-fifths majority vote (60) of the total Senate is required to waive the budget act. (Subsequently, the chair upheld the Lautenberg point of order, and the Warner amendment fell.)

304. HR2750. Fiscal 1994 Transportation Appropriations/Cargo Preference Limit. Lautenberg, D-N.J., motion to table (kill) the Brown, R-Colo., amendment to the Burns, R-Mont., amendment, to bar federal agencies from paying more than twice the average competitive world market shipping rate to transport goods. Motion agreed to 50-49: R 11-32; D 39-17 (ND 30-12, SD 9-5), Oct. 5, 1993.

	305	306	307	308	309	310	311	312
ALABAMA								
Heflin	Y	Y	Y	Y	Y	Y	Y	Y
Shelby	Y	Y	Y	Y	Y	Y	Y	Y
ALASKA								
Murkowski	Y	Y	?	N	Y	N	Y	Y
Stevens	Y	Y	N	N	Y	N	Y	Y
ARIZONA								
DeConcini	Y	Y	Y	Y	Y	N	N	N
McCain	Y	Y	N	N	Y	N	Y	Y
ARKANSAS								
Bumpers	Y	Y	Y	Y	N	N	N	N
Pryor	Y	Y	Y	Y	N	Y	N	N
CALIFORNIA								
Boxer	Y	Y	Y	Y	N	Y	N	N
Feinstein	Y	Y	Y	Y	+	?	−	?
COLORADO								
Campbell	Y	Y	Y	Y	Y	Y	N	N
Brown	N	Y	N	N	N	N	Y	N
CONNECTICUT								
Dodd	Y	Y	Y	Y	?	Y	Y	N
Lieberman	Y	Y	Y	Y	Y	Y	Y	Y
DELAWARE								
Biden	Y	Y	Y	Y	Y	Y	Y	Y
Roth	N	N	N	N	N	N	Y	Y
FLORIDA								
Graham	Y	Y	Y	Y	Y	N	Y	Y
Mack	Y	Y	?	Y	Y	N	Y	Y
GEORGIA								
Nunn	Y	Y	Y	Y	Y	Y	Y	Y
Coverdell	Y	?	N	N	Y	N	Y	Y
HAWAII								
Akaka	Y	Y	Y	Y	Y	Y	Y	Y
Inouye	Y	Y	Y	Y	Y	Y	Y	Y
IDAHO								
Craig	N	Y	N	N	Y	Y	Y	Y
Kempthorne	N	Y	N	N	Y	Y	Y	Y
ILLINOIS								
Moseley-Braun	Y	Y	Y	Y	Y	Y	N	N
Simon	Y	Y	Y	Y	Y	Y	N	N
INDIANA								
Coats	N	Y	N	N	Y	N	Y	Y
Lugar	N	Y	N	N	Y	N	Y	Y

	305	306	307	308	309	310	311	312
IOWA								
Harkin	Y	Y	Y	Y	N	Y	N	N
Grassley	N	Y	N	N	N	N	N	N
KANSAS								
Dole	N	Y	N	N	Y	N	Y	Y
Kassebaum	N	Y	N	Y	Y	N	Y	Y
KENTUCKY								
Ford	Y	Y	Y	Y	Y	Y	Y	N
McConnell	?	Y	N	N	Y	N	Y	Y
LOUISIANA								
Breaux	Y	Y	Y	Y	Y	Y	Y	N
Johnston	Y	Y	Y	Y	N	Y	N	Y
MAINE								
Mitchell	Y	Y	Y	Y	Y	N	N	N
Cohen	Y	Y	N	Y	Y	N	Y	Y
MARYLAND								
Mikulski	Y	Y	Y	Y	Y	N	Y	N
Sarbanes	Y	Y	Y	Y	N	Y	N	N
MASSACHUSETTS								
Kennedy	Y	Y	Y	Y	Y	Y	Y	Y
Kerry	Y	Y	Y	Y	N	Y	Y	Y
MICHIGAN								
Levin	Y	Y	Y	Y	N	Y	N	N
Riegle	Y	Y	Y	Y	N	Y	N	N
MINNESOTA								
Wellstone	N	Y	Y	Y	N	N	N	N
Durenberger	N	Y	N	Y	N	Y	N	Y
MISSISSIPPI								
Cochran	Y	Y	N	N	Y	Y	Y	Y
Lott	Y	Y	N	N	Y	Y	Y	Y
MISSOURI								
Bond	N	Y	N	N	Y	N	Y	Y
Danforth	N	Y	Y	Y	Y	Y	Y	Y
MONTANA								
Baucus	N	Y	Y	Y	N	Y	N	Y
Burns	N	N	N	N	Y	N	Y	Y
NEBRASKA								
Exon	Y	Y	Y	Y	Y	N	Y	N
Kerrey	Y	Y	Y	Y	N	Y	N	Y
NEVADA								
Bryan	Y	Y	Y	Y	N	Y	N	N
Reid	Y	Y	Y	Y	N	Y	N	Y

	305	306	307	308	309	310	311	312
NEW HAMPSHIRE								
Gregg	N	N	N	N	Y	N	Y	Y
Smith	N	N	N	N	Y	N	+	Y
NEW JERSEY								
Bradley	Y	Y	Y	Y	N	N	N	N
Lautenberg	Y	Y	Y	Y	N	N	N	N
NEW MEXICO								
Bingaman	Y	Y	Y	Y	Y	N	N	N
Domenici	Y	Y	N	N	Y	N	Y	N
NEW YORK								
Moynihan	Y	Y	Y	Y	Y	N	N	N
D'Amato	Y	Y	N	N	Y	N	Y	Y
NORTH CAROLINA								
Faircloth	N	N	N	N	Y	N	Y	Y
Helms	N	N	N	N	Y	N	Y	Y
NORTH DAKOTA								
Conrad	N	Y	Y	?	N	N	N	N
Dorgan	N	Y	Y	Y	N	N	N	N
OHIO								
Glenn	Y	Y	Y	Y	N	Y	N	N
Metzenbaum	Y	Y	Y	Y	N	N	N	N
OKLAHOMA								
Boren	Y	N	Y	N	Y	Y	Y	Y
Nickles	N	Y	N	N	Y	N	Y	Y
OREGON								
Hatfield	Y	Y	N	Y	−	N	N	N
Packwood	Y	Y	Y	Y	Y	Y	Y	Y
PENNSYLVANIA								
Wofford	Y	Y	Y	Y	N	N	N	N
Specter	Y	Y	N	Y	Y	N	N	Y
RHODE ISLAND								
Pell	Y	Y	Y	Y	N	Y	N	N
Chafee	Y	Y	N	Y	Y	Y	Y	Y
SOUTH CAROLINA								
Hollings	Y	Y	Y	Y	N	Y	N	N
Thurmond	N	Y	N	N	Y	Y	Y	Y
SOUTH DAKOTA								
Daschle	Y	Y	Y	Y	N	Y	N	N
Pressler	N	Y	N	N	Y	N	Y	Y
TENNESSEE								
Mathews	Y	Y	Y	Y	N	Y	N	N
Sasser	Y	Y	Y	Y	N	Y	N	N

	305	306	307	308	309	310	311	312
TEXAS								
Gramm	Y	Y	N	N	Y	N	Y	Y
Hutchison	Y	Y	N	N	Y	Y	Y	Y
UTAH								
Bennett	N	Y	N	N	Y	Y	Y	Y
Hatch	N	Y	N	N	Y	Y	Y	Y
VERMONT								
Leahy	Y	Y	Y	Y	N	N	N	Y
Jeffords	N	Y	Y	Y	N	Y	N	Y
VIRGINIA								
Robb	Y	Y	Y	Y	Y	N	Y	Y
Warner	Y	Y	N	N	Y	Y	Y	Y
WASHINGTON								
Murray	Y	Y	Y	Y	Y	N	N	N
Gorton	Y	Y	N	N	Y	N	+	Y
WEST VIRGINIA								
Byrd	Y	Y	Y	Y	N	Y	N	Y
Rockefeller	Y	Y	Y	Y	Y	Y	N	Y
WISCONSIN								
Feingold	Y	Y	Y	Y	N	N	N	N
Kohl	N	N	Y	N	N	N	N	N
WYOMING								
Simpson	N	Y	N	N	Y	N	Y	Y
Wallop	N	N	N	N	Y	N	?	Y

ND Northern Democrats   SD Southern Democrats

Southern states - Ala., Ark., Fla., Ga., Ky., La., Miss., N.C., Okla., S.C., Tenn., Texas, Va.

305. HR 2750. Fiscal 1994 Transportation Appropriations/Cargo Preference Exemption. Lautenberg, D-N.J., motion to table (kill) the Burns, R-Mont., amendment to exempt grain shipped to Russia from Pacific Northwest ports from cargo preference requirements, if the secretaries of Transportation and Agriculture determine that there is an insufficient number of U.S. ships available to carry the grain. Motion agreed to 69-30: R 18-25; D 51-5 (ND 37-5, SD 14-0), Oct. 5, 1993.

306. HR 2750. Fiscal 1994 Transportation Appropriations/Passage. Passage of the bill to provide approximately $14 billion in new budget authority for the Department of Transportation and related agencies in fiscal 1994. The administration requested $14,254,994,000. Passed 90-9: R 36-7; D 54-2 (ND 41-1, SD 13-1), Oct. 6, 1993.

307. Dellinger Confirmation. Motion to invoke cloture (thus limiting debate) on the nomination of Walter E. Dellinger III of North Carolina to be an assistant attorney general. Motion rejected 59-39: R 3-39; D 56-0 (ND 42-0, SD 14-0), Oct. 7, 1993. Three-fifths of the total Senate (60) is required to invoke cloture.

308. Dellinger Confirmation. Confirmation of Walter E. Dellinger III to be an assistant attorney general. Confirmed 65-34: R 10-34; D 55-0 (ND 41-0, SD 14-0), Oct. 13, 1993. A "yea" was a vote in support of the president's position.

309. HR 3116. Fiscal 1994 Defense Appropriations/Trident II Missiles. Inouye, D-Hawaii, amendment to the Bumpers, D-Ark., amendment, to allow the continued funding of Trident II submarine-launched missiles if the president certifies that it is in the national interest. The Bumpers amendment would prohibit funding for Trident II missiles unless the president certified that START treaty signatories had rejected a proposal to reduce the number of missiles carried by each submarine. Adopted 63-34: R 39-4; D 24-30 (ND 16-24, SD 8-6), Oct. 14, 1993. (Subsequently, the Bumpers amendment as amended was adopted by voice vote.) A "yea" was a vote in support of the president's position.

310. HR 3116. Fiscal 1994 Defense Appropriations/*Seawolf* Submarine. Inouye, D-Hawaii, motion to table (kill) the McCain, R-Ariz., amendment to prohibit funding of a third *Seawolf*-class submarine. Motion agreed to 52-47: R 13-31; D 39-16 (ND 27-14, SD 12-2), Oct. 14, 1993.

311. HR 3116. Fiscal 1994 Defense Appropriations/Theater Missile Defense Program. Inouye, D-Hawaii, motion to table (kill) the Sasser, D-Tenn., amendment to require U.S. allies and international organizations to pay 20 percent of the costs of the Theater Missile Defense Program unless the president certifies that such a requirement is against national security. Motion agreed to 54-42: R 37-4; D 17-38 (ND 10-31, SD 7-7), Oct. 14, 1993.

312. HR 3116. Fiscal 1994 Defense Appropriations/Intelligence Programs. Inouye, D-Hawaii, motion to table (kill) the Bumpers, D-Ark., amendment to cut intelligence-related programs by $400 million. Motion agreed to 64-35: R 39-5; D 25-30 (ND 17-24, SD 8-6), Oct. 14, 1993.

KEY

- Y Voted for (yea).
- # Paired for.
- + Announced for.
- N Voted against (nay).
- X Paired against.
- − Announced against.
- P Voted "present."
- C Voted "present" to avoid possible conflict of interest.
- ? Did not vote or otherwise make a position known.

Democrats *Republicans*

	313	314	315	316	317	318	319	320
ALABAMA								
Heflin	Y	Y	N	Y	N	Y	Y	Y
Shelby	Y	Y	Y	Y	N	Y	Y	Y
ALASKA								
Murkowski	N	N	Y	Y	Y	Y	Y	Y
Stevens	N	Y	Y	Y	Y	Y	Y	Y
ARIZONA								
DeConcini	Y	Y	Y	Y	?	?	Y	Y
McCain	N	N	Y	Y	N	Y	Y	Y
ARKANSAS								
Bumpers	Y	Y	Y	?	N	Y	N	Y
Pryor	Y	Y	?	Y	N	Y	Y	Y
CALIFORNIA								
Boxer	N	Y	Y	Y	N	Y	Y	Y
Feinstein	+	+	Y	Y	N	Y	Y	Y
COLORADO								
Campbell	N	Y	Y	Y	N	Y	Y	Y
Brown	N	N	N	N	Y	Y	Y	Y
CONNECTICUT								
Dodd	Y	Y	Y	Y	N	Y	Y	Y
Lieberman	Y	Y	Y	Y	N	Y	Y	Y
DELAWARE								
Biden	Y	Y	?	Y	N	Y	Y	Y
Roth	N	N	N	Y	Y	Y	Y	Y
FLORIDA								
Graham	Y	Y	Y	Y	N	Y	Y	Y
Mack	N	N	Y	Y	Y	Y	Y	Y
GEORGIA								
Nunn	Y	Y	Y	Y	N	Y	Y	Y
Coverdell	N	Y	Y	Y	Y	Y	Y	Y
HAWAII								
Akaka	Y	Y	Y	Y	N	Y	Y	Y
Inouye	Y	Y	Y	Y	N	Y	Y	Y
IDAHO								
Craig	N	N	N	Y	Y	Y	Y	Y
Kempthorne	N	N	N	Y	Y	Y	Y	Y
ILLINOIS								
Moseley-Braun	Y	Y	Y	Y	N	Y	N	Y
Simon	Y	Y	Y	Y	N	Y	N	Y
INDIANA								
Coats	N	N	Y	Y	Y	Y	Y	Y
Lugar	Y	Y	Y	Y	Y	Y	N	Y

	313	314	315	316	317	318	319	320
IOWA								
Harkin	Y	Y	Y	Y	N	Y	N	Y
Grassley	N	N	Y	Y	Y	N	Y	Y
KANSAS								
Dole	Y	Y	Y	Y	Y	Y	Y	Y
Kassebaum	Y	Y	Y	N	Y	N	Y	Y
KENTUCKY								
Ford	Y	Y	Y	Y	N	Y	Y	Y
McConnell	Y	Y	Y	Y	N	Y	Y	Y
LOUISIANA								
Breaux	Y	Y	Y	Y	N	Y	Y	Y
Johnston	N	Y	Y	Y	N	Y	Y	Y
MAINE								
Mitchell	Y	Y	Y	Y	N	Y	N	Y
Cohen	N	Y	Y	Y	Y	Y	Y	Y
MARYLAND								
Mikulski	Y	Y	Y	Y	N	Y	Y	Y
Sarbanes	Y	Y	Y	Y	N	Y	Y	Y
MASSACHUSETTS								
Kennedy	Y	Y	Y	Y	N	Y	Y	Y
Kerry	Y	Y	Y	Y	N	Y	Y	Y
MICHIGAN								
Levin	Y	Y	Y	Y	N	Y	N	Y
Riegle	Y	Y	Y	Y	N	Y	Y	Y
MINNESOTA								
Wellstone	Y	Y	Y	Y	N	Y	Y	Y
Durenberger	Y	Y	?	Y	N	Y	Y	Y
MISSISSIPPI								
Cochran	Y	Y	Y	Y	Y	Y	Y	Y
Lott	N	N	Y	Y	Y	Y	Y	Y
MISSOURI								
Bond	Y	Y	Y	Y	Y	Y	Y	Y
Danforth	Y	Y	Y	Y	N	Y	N	Y
MONTANA								
Baucus	Y	Y	Y	Y	N	Y	Y	Y
Burns	N	Y	Y	Y	Y	Y	Y	Y
NEBRASKA								
Exon	Y	Y	Y	Y	N	Y	Y	Y
Kerrey	Y	Y	Y	Y	N	Y	N	Y
NEVADA								
Bryan	Y	Y	Y	Y	N	Y	Y	Y
Reid	Y	Y	Y	Y	N	Y	Y	Y

	313	314	315	316	317	318	319	320
NEW HAMPSHIRE								
Gregg	N	N	N	N	Y	Y	N	Y
Smith	N	N	N	N	Y	Y	N	Y
NEW JERSEY								
Bradley	N	N	Y	Y	N	Y	N	Y
Lautenberg	N	Y	Y	Y	N	Y	N	Y
NEW MEXICO								
Bingaman	Y	Y	Y	Y	N	Y	Y	Y
Domenici	Y	Y	Y	Y	Y	Y	Y	Y
NEW YORK								
Moynihan	Y	Y	Y	Y	N	Y	Y	Y
D'Amato	N	N	Y	Y	Y	Y	Y	Y
NORTH CAROLINA								
Faircloth	N	Y	N	N	Y	Y	N	Y
Helms	N	N	N	Y	Y	Y	Y	Y
NORTH DAKOTA								
Conrad	N	Y	N	Y	N	Y	N	Y
Dorgan	N	Y	Y	Y	N	Y	Y	Y
OHIO								
Glenn	Y	Y	Y	Y	N	Y	Y	Y
Metzenbaum	Y	Y	Y	Y	N	Y	N	Y
OKLAHOMA								
Boren	Y	Y	Y	Y	N	Y	Y	Y
Nickles	N	N	Y	Y	Y	Y	N	Y
OREGON								
Hatfield	N	N	Y	Y	Y	Y	Y	N
Packwood	Y	Y	Y	Y	N	Y	Y	Y
PENNSYLVANIA								
Wofford	Y	Y	Y	Y	N	Y	Y	Y
Specter	Y	Y	Y	Y	?	?	Y	Y
RHODE ISLAND								
Pell	Y	Y	Y	Y	N	Y	Y	Y
Chafee	Y	Y	Y	Y	N	Y	Y	Y
SOUTH CAROLINA								
Hollings	N	Y	Y	Y	Y	Y	Y	Y
Thurmond	Y	Y	Y	Y	Y	Y	Y	Y
SOUTH DAKOTA								
Daschle	Y	Y	Y	Y	N	Y	Y	Y
Pressler	N	N	N	Y	Y	Y	Y	Y
TENNESSEE								
Mathews	Y	Y	Y	Y	N	Y	Y	Y
Sasser	Y	Y	+	Y	N	Y	Y	Y

	313	314	315	316	317	318	319	320
TEXAS								
Gramm	N	N	N	Y	N	Y	Y	Y
Hutchison	N	Y	N	Y	Y	Y	Y	Y
UTAH								
Bennett	N	Y	Y	Y	Y	Y	Y	Y
Hatch	N	Y	Y	Y	N	Y	Y	Y
VERMONT								
Leahy	Y	Y	Y	Y	N	Y	Y	Y
Jeffords	Y	Y	Y	Y	N	Y	Y	Y
VIRGINIA								
Robb	Y	Y	Y	Y	N	Y	N	Y
Warner	Y	N	Y	N	Y	Y	Y	Y
WASHINGTON								
Murray	Y	Y	Y	Y	N	Y	Y	Y
Gorton	N	N	Y	Y	Y	Y	Y	Y
WEST VIRGINIA								
Byrd	Y	Y	Y	Y	N	Y	Y	Y
Rockefeller	Y	Y	Y	Y	N	Y	Y	Y
WISCONSIN								
Feingold	N	N	Y	N	N	Y	N	Y
Kohl	N	N	N	Y	N	Y	N	Y
WYOMING								
Simpson	Y	Y	Y	Y	Y	Y	Y	Y
Wallop	N	N	?	Y	Y	N	Y	Y

ND Northern Democrats   SD Southern Democrats   Southern states - Ala., Ark., Fla., Ga., Ky., La., Miss., N.C., Okla., S.C., Tenn., Texas, Va.

313. HR 3116. Fiscal 1994 Defense Appropriations/Somalia Withdrawal. Thurmond, R-S.C., motion to table (kill) the McCain, R-Ariz., amendment to prohibit funding of U.S. military operations in Somalia except for the withdrawal of all U.S. troops. Motion agreed to 61-38: R 16-28; D 45-10 (ND 33-8, SD 12-2), Oct. 15, 1993 (in the session that began and the Congressional Record dated Oct. 14). A "yea" was a vote in support of the president's position.

314. HR 3116. Fiscal 1994 Defense Appropriations/Somalia Policy. Byrd, D-W.Va., amendment to prohibit funding of U.S. military operations in Somalia after March 31, 1994, except for limited purposes if the president requests and Congress authorizes an extension. U.S. forces would have to be under the command and control of U.S. commanders. Adopted 76-23: R 24-20; D 52-3 (ND 38-3, SD 14-0), Oct. 15, 1993 (in the session that began and the Congressional Record dated Oct. 14).

315. HR 2518. Fiscal 1994 Labor, HHS, Education Appropriations/Conference Report. Adoption of the conference report to provide $256,328,263,000 in new budget authority for the departments of Labor, Health and Human Services, and Education, and related agencies. Adopted (thus cleared for the president) 80-15: R 30-12; D 50-3 (ND 39-2, SD 11-1), Oct. 18, 1993.

316. HR 2446. Fiscal 1994 Military Construction Appropriations/Conference Report. Adoption of the conference report to provide $10,065,114,000 in new budget authority for military construction and family housing for the Department of Defense for fiscal 1994. Adopted (thus cleared for the president) 94-5: R 40-4; D 54-1 (ND 41-1, SD 13-0), Oct. 19, 1993.

317. HR 3116. Fiscal 1994 Defense Appropriations/Command of U.S. Troops. Nickles, R-Okla., amendment to prohibit funding for U.S. forces under the command of U.N. foreign offices unless the president submits a report and Congress authorizes it or the president determines that a waiver is necessary because of an emergency or national security. Rejected 33-65: R 32-11; D 1-54 (ND 0-41, SD 1-13), Oct. 19, 1993. A "nay" was a vote in support of the president's position.

318. HR 3116. Fiscal 1994 Defense Appropriations/Command of U.S. Troops. Nunn, D-Ga., amendment to express the sense of Congress that U.S. troops must be under the control of qualified commanders with a clear mission and that the president should consult with Congress before placing combat troops under foreign command. Adopted 96-2: R 41-2; D 55-0 (ND 41-0, SD 14-0), Oct. 19, 1993.

319. HR 3116. Fiscal 1994 Defense Appropriations/National Guard Aircraft. Inouye, D-Hawaii, motion to table (kill) the Bradley, D-N.J., amendment to cut the $150 million for National Guard tactical transport aircraft. Motion agreed to 80-20: R 38-6; D 42-14 (ND 30-12, SD 12-2), Oct. 20, 1993. (On vote 319, John Glenn, D-Ohio, received unanimous consent to change his vote from "nay" to "yea.")

320. HR 3116. Fiscal 1994 Defense Appropriations/Bosnia. Mitchell, D-Maine, amendment to express the sense of Congress that none of the funds in the bill should be used to deploy U.S. troops in Bosnia-Herzegovina unless authorized by Congress, except for humanitarian missions started before Oct. 20, 1993. Adopted 99-1: R 43-1; D 56-0 (ND 42-0, SD 14-0), Oct. 20, 1993.

KEY

- Y Voted for (yea).
- # Paired for.
- + Announced for.
- N Voted against (nay).
- X Paired against.
- − Announced against.
- P Voted "present."
- C Voted "present" to avoid possible conflict of interest.
- ? Did not vote or otherwise make a position known.

Democrats *Republicans*

	321	322	323	324	325	326	327	328
ALABAMA								
Heflin	N	Y	N	Y	Y	Y	Y	Y
Shelby	N	Y	Y	Y	Y	Y	Y	Y
ALASKA								
Murkowski	Y	Y	Y	Y	Y	N	Y	N
Stevens	Y	Y	Y	Y	Y	N	?	?
ARIZONA								
DeConcini	N	Y	Y	Y	Y	Y	N	Y
McCain	N	Y	Y	Y	Y	N	N	Y
ARKANSAS								
Bumpers	N	Y	Y	Y	N	Y	N	Y
Pryor	N	Y	Y	Y	N	Y	N	Y
CALIFORNIA								
Boxer	N	Y	Y	Y	N	Y	N	Y
Feinstein	N	Y	Y	Y	N	Y	N	Y
COLORADO								
Campbell	N	Y	Y	Y	Y	N	N	Y
Brown	Y	Y	N	N	Y	N	Y	N
CONNECTICUT								
Dodd	N	Y	Y	Y	N	Y	N	Y
Lieberman	N	Y	Y	Y	Y	Y	Y	Y
DELAWARE								
Biden	N	Y	Y	Y	Y	Y	N	Y
Roth	Y	Y	N	N	Y	N	Y	Y
FLORIDA								
Graham	N	Y	Y	Y	N	Y	N	Y
Mack	N	Y	Y	Y	Y	N	Y	N
GEORGIA								
Nunn	N	Y	Y	Y	Y	Y	N	Y
Coverdell	N	Y	Y	N	Y	N	Y	N
HAWAII								
Akaka	N	Y	Y	Y	Y	Y	N	Y
Inouye	N	Y	Y	Y	Y	Y	N	Y
IDAHO								
Craig	Y	Y	Y	N	Y	N	Y	N
Kempthorne	Y	Y	Y	N	Y	N	Y	N
ILLINOIS								
Moseley-Braun	N	Y	Y	Y	N	Y	N	Y
Simon	N	Y	Y	N	N	Y	N	Y
INDIANA								
Coats	N	Y	Y	N	Y	N	Y	N
Lugar	N	Y	N	Y	N	Y	N	Y
IOWA								
Harkin	N	Y	Y	Y	N	Y	N	Y
Grassley	Y	Y	Y	N	Y	N	Y	N
KANSAS								
Dole	Y	Y	Y	?	?	?	Y	N
Kassebaum	N	Y	N	Y	N	Y	N	Y
KENTUCKY								
Ford	N	Y	Y	Y	Y	Y	Y	N
McConnell	N	Y	N	Y	N	Y	N	Y
LOUISIANA								
Breaux	N	Y	Y	Y	Y	Y	Y	N
Johnston	N	Y	Y	Y	Y	Y	Y	N
MAINE								
Mitchell	N	Y	Y	Y	Y	Y	Y	N
Cohen	N	Y	Y	Y	Y	Y	Y	N
MARYLAND								
Mikulski	N	Y	Y	Y	N	Y	N	Y
Sarbanes	N	Y	Y	Y	N	Y	N	Y
MASSACHUSETTS								
Kennedy	N	Y	Y	Y	N	Y	N	Y
Kerry	N	Y	Y	Y	N	Y	N	Y
MICHIGAN								
Levin	N	Y	Y	Y	N	Y	N	Y
Riegle	N	Y	Y	Y	N	Y	?	+
MINNESOTA								
Wellstone	N	Y	Y	Y	N	Y	N	Y
Durenberger	N	Y	Y	N	Y	?	Y	N
MISSISSIPPI								
Cochran	N	Y	Y	Y	Y	N	Y	N
Lott	Y	Y	N	Y	Y	?	Y	N
MISSOURI								
Bond	N	Y	Y	Y	Y	N	Y	N
Danforth	N	Y	N	Y	N	Y	N	Y
MONTANA								
Baucus	N	Y	Y	Y	Y	N	N	Y
Burns	N	Y	Y	N	Y	N	Y	N
NEBRASKA								
Exon	N	Y	Y	Y	Y	Y	N	N
Kerrey	N	Y	Y	Y	Y	Y	Y	N
NEVADA								
Bryan	N	Y	Y	Y	N	Y	Y	Y
Reid	N	Y	Y	Y	N	Y	N	Y
NEW HAMPSHIRE								
Gregg	N	Y	N	N	Y	N	Y	N
Smith	Y	Y	N	N	Y	N	Y	N
NEW JERSEY								
Bradley	N	Y	Y	Y	N	Y	N	Y
Lautenberg	N	Y	Y	Y	N	Y	?	Y
NEW MEXICO								
Bingaman	N	Y	Y	Y	N	Y	N	Y
Domenici	Y	Y	Y	N	Y	N	Y	Y
NEW YORK								
Moynihan	N	Y	Y	Y	Y	Y	N	Y
D'Amato	Y	Y	Y	+	?	?	Y	Y
NORTH CAROLINA								
Faircloth	Y	Y	Y	N	Y	N	Y	N
Helms	Y	Y	N	?	?	?	Y	N
NORTH DAKOTA								
Conrad	N	Y	N	Y	N	Y	N	N
Dorgan	N	Y	N	Y	N	N	N	Y
OHIO								
Glenn	N	Y	Y	Y	N	Y	N	Y
Metzenbaum	N	Y	Y	N	N	Y	N	Y
OKLAHOMA								
Boren	N	Y	Y	Y	Y	Y	N	Y
Nickles	Y	Y	Y	N	Y	N	Y	N
OREGON								
Hatfield	Y	N	Y	Y	N	N	N	N
Packwood	N	Y	Y	Y	N	Y	Y	Y
PENNSYLVANIA								
Wofford	N	Y	Y	Y	Y	Y	N	Y
Specter	N	Y	Y	Y	Y	N	P	Y
RHODE ISLAND								
Pell	N	Y	Y	Y	N	Y	N	Y
Chafee	N	Y	Y	N	N	Y	Y	Y
SOUTH CAROLINA								
Hollings	N	Y	Y	Y	Y	Y	N	Y
Thurmond	Y	Y	Y	N	Y	N	Y	N
SOUTH DAKOTA								
Daschle	N	Y	Y	Y	Y	Y	N	N
Pressler	Y	Y	Y	N	Y	N	Y	N
TENNESSEE								
Mathews	N	Y	Y	Y	N	Y	Y	Y
Sasser	N	Y	Y	Y	Y	Y	Y	Y
TEXAS								
Gramm	N	Y	Y	N	Y	N	Y	N
Hutchison	N	Y	Y	Y	Y	N	Y	N
UTAH								
Bennett	N	Y	Y	N	Y	N	Y	N
Hatch	N	Y	Y	N	Y	N	Y	N
VERMONT								
Leahy	N	Y	Y	Y	Y	Y	?	?
Jeffords	N	Y	Y	N	Y	?	Y	Y
VIRGINIA								
Robb	N	Y	Y	Y	N	Y	N	Y
Warner	N	Y	Y	Y	Y	N	Y	Y
WASHINGTON								
Murray	N	Y	Y	Y	N	Y	N	Y
Gorton	N	Y	Y	Y	Y	N	Y	Y
WEST VIRGINIA								
Byrd	N	N	Y	N	Y	N	Y	Y
Rockefeller	N	Y	Y	Y	Y	Y	Y	N
WISCONSIN								
Feingold	N	Y	Y	Y	N	Y	N	Y
Kohl	N	Y	N	N	Y	N	Y	Y
WYOMING								
Simpson	N	Y	Y	N	Y	N	C	N
Wallop	Y	Y	N	N	Y	N	Y	N

ND Northern Democrats   SD Southern Democrats

Southern states - Ala., Ark., Fla., Ga., Ky., La., Miss., N.C., Okla., S.C., Tenn., Texas, Va.

321. HR 3116. Fiscal 1994 Defense Appropriations/Haiti. Helms, R-N.C., amendment to prohibit funding for U.S. military operations in Haiti unless Congress specifically authorizes the operations or the president certifies that U.S. citizens in Haiti are in imminent danger. Rejected 19-81: R 19-25; D 0-56 (ND 0-42, SD 0-14), Oct. 21, 1993.

322. HR 3116. Fiscal 1994 Defense Appropriations/Haiti. Mitchell, D-Maine, amendment to express the sense of Congress that Congress should authorize all U.S. military operations in Haiti unless U.S. citizens are in imminent need of protection and evacuation or the deployment is vital to national security interests. Adopted 98-2: R 43-1; D 55-1 (ND 41-1, SD 14-0), Oct. 21, 1993.

323. HR 2519. Fiscal 1994 Commerce, Justice and State Appropriations/Conference Report. Adoption of the conference report to provide $23,396,781,000 in new budget authority for the departments of Commerce, Justice and State, and the judiciary and related agencies for fiscal 1994. Adopted (thus cleared for the president) 90-10: R 37-7; D 53-3 (ND 40-2, SD 13-1), Oct. 21, 1993.

324. HR 3116. Fiscal 1994 Defense Appropriations/Merchant Marine Contractors. Inouye, D-Hawaii, motion to table (kill) the Grassley, R-Iowa, amendment to prohibit the Defense Department from entering into contracts with merchant marine contractors that pay their crews more than the military pays for comparable work. Motion agreed to 67-30: R 14-27; D 53-3 (ND 39-3, SD 14-0), Oct. 21, 1993.

325. HR 3116. Fiscal 1994 Defense Appropriations/ Rifle Practice Board. Inouye, D-Hawaii, motion to table (kill) the Lautenberg, D-N.J., amendment to eliminate $2.5 million in the bill for the Civilian Marksmanship Program. Motion agreed to 67-30: R 39-2; D 28-28 (ND 19-23, SD 9-5), Oct. 21, 1993.

326. HR 2520. Fiscal 1994 Interior Appropriations/Cloture. Motion to invoke cloture (thus limiting debate) on the conference report to provide $13,388,038,000 in new budget authority for the Department of the Interior and related agencies in fiscal 1994. Motion rejected 53-41: R 2-36; D 51-5 (ND 37-5, SD 14-0), Oct. 21, 1993. Three-fifths of the total Senate (60) is required to invoke cloture.

327. HR 3167. Unemployment Benefits Extension/Retroactive Taxes. Hutchison, R-Texas, motion to waive the budget act with respect to the Mitchell, D-Maine, point of order against the Hutchison amendment to repeal retroactive taxes in the 1993 Budget Reconciliation Act and cut agency administrative expenses by $9 billion over three years. Motion rejected 50-44: R 40-1; D 10-43 (ND 5-34, SD 5-9), Oct. 26, 1993. A three-fifths majority vote (60) of the total Senate is required to waive the budget act. (Subsequently, the chair upheld the Mitchell point of order, and the Hutchison amendment fell.)

328. HR 3167. Unemployment Benefits Extension/Budget Act Waiver. Moynihan, D-N.Y., motion to waive the budget act with respect to the Nickles, R-Okla., point of order against the bill to provide about $1 billion for extended unemployment benefits. Motion rejected 59-38: R 8-35; D 51-3 (ND 38-2, SD 13-1), Oct. 26, 1993. A three-fifths majority vote (60) of the total Senate is required to waive the budget act. (Subsequently, a motion to reconsider the vote was postponed until Oct. 27.)

	329	330	331	332	333	334	335	336
ALABAMA								
Heflin	Y	N	Y	Y	Y	Y	N	N
Shelby	Y	Y	Y	N	Y	Y	N	N
ALASKA								
Murkowski	N	Y	Y	Y	Y	N	N	Y
Stevens	?	Y	Y	Y	Y	N	N	Y
ARIZONA								
DeConcini	Y	N	Y	Y	Y	Y	Y	N
McCain	N	Y	Y	N	Y	N	N	Y
ARKANSAS								
Bumpers	Y	N	Y	Y	Y	Y	Y	N
Pryor	Y	N	Y	Y	Y	Y	Y	N
CALIFORNIA								
Boxer	Y	N	Y	Y	Y	Y	N	N
Feinstein	Y	Y	Y	Y	Y	Y	N	N
COLORADO								
Campbell	N	N	Y	Y	Y	Y	N	?
Brown	N	Y	Y	N	N	N	Y	N
CONNECTICUT								
Dodd	Y	N	Y	Y	Y	Y	N	N
Lieberman	Y	N	Y	Y	Y	Y	N	N
DELAWARE								
Biden	Y	N	Y	Y	Y	Y	N	N
Roth	Y	Y	Y	N	N	Y	Y	N
FLORIDA								
Graham	Y	Y	Y	Y	Y	Y	N	N
Mack	N	Y	Y	N	Y	N	N	Y
GEORGIA								
Nunn	Y	Y	Y	?	Y	Y	Y	N
Coverdell	N	Y	Y	N	Y	N	N	Y
HAWAII								
Akaka	Y	N	Y	Y	Y	Y	N	N
Inouye	Y	N	Y	Y	Y	Y	N	N
IDAHO								
Craig	N	N	Y	N	Y	N	N	Y
Kempthorne	N	N	Y	N	Y	N	N	Y
ILLINOIS								
Moseley-Braun	Y	N	Y	Y	Y	Y	N	N
Simon	Y	N	Y	Y	Y	Y	Y	Y
INDIANA								
Coats	N	N	Y	N	Y	N	N	Y
Lugar	N	N	Y	N	Y	N	N	Y

	329	330	331	332	333	334	335	336
IOWA								
Harkin	Y	N	Y	Y	Y	Y	N	N
Grassley	N	N	Y	N	Y	N	N	N
KANSAS								
Dole	N	N	Y	Y	Y	N	N	Y
Kassebaum	N	N	Y	Y	Y	N	?	Y
KENTUCKY								
Ford	Y	N	Y	Y	Y	Y	Y	N
McConnell	N	N	Y	N	Y	N	N	N
LOUISIANA								
Breaux	Y	Y	Y	Y	Y	Y	N	N
Johnston	Y	Y	Y	Y	Y	Y	N	N
MAINE								
Mitchell	Y	N	Y	Y	Y	Y	N	N
Cohen	Y	Y	Y	N	Y	N	Y	Y
MARYLAND								
Mikulski	Y	N	Y	Y	Y	Y	N	N
Sarbanes	Y	N	Y	Y	Y	Y	N	N
MASSACHUSETTS								
Kennedy	Y	N	Y	Y	Y	Y	N	N
Kerry	Y	N	Y	N	Y	Y	N	N
MICHIGAN								
Levin	Y	N	Y	Y	Y	Y	N	N
Riegle	+	N	Y	Y	Y	Y	N	N
MINNESOTA								
Wellstone	Y	N	Y	Y	Y	Y	N	N
Durenberger	N	N	Y	N	Y	N	N	?
MISSISSIPPI								
Cochran	N	Y	Y	N	Y	N	N	Y
Lott	N	Y	Y	N	Y	N	N	Y
MISSOURI								
Bond	N	Y	Y	N	Y	N	N	?
Danforth	N	N	Y	N	Y	N	N	Y
MONTANA								
Baucus	N	Y	Y	Y	Y	Y	N	N
Burns	N	Y	Y	Y	Y	N	N	Y
NEBRASKA								
Exon	Y	Y	Y	Y	Y	N	Y	Y
Kerrey	Y	Y	Y	Y	Y	N	Y	Y
NEVADA								
Bryan	Y	Y	Y	Y	Y	Y	Y	Y
Reid	Y	Y	Y	Y	Y	Y	Y	Y

	329	330	331	332	333	334	335	336
NEW HAMPSHIRE								
Gregg	N	N	Y	N	N	N	Y	Y
Smith	N	Y	Y	N	N	N	N	Y
NEW JERSEY								
Bradley	Y	N	Y	Y	Y	Y	Y	N
Lautenberg	Y	N	Y	Y	Y	Y	Y	N
NEW MEXICO								
Bingaman	N	N	Y	Y	Y	Y	N	Y
Domenici	N	N	Y	Y	Y	N	N	Y
NEW YORK								
Moynihan	Y	N	Y	Y	Y	Y	N	N
D'Amato	N	N	Y	N	Y	Y	+	+
NORTH CAROLINA								
Faircloth	N	Y	Y	N	N	N	N	Y
Helms	N	Y	N	N	N	N	N	Y
NORTH DAKOTA								
Conrad	N	Y	Y	Y	Y	Y	Y	Y
Dorgan	N	Y	Y	Y	Y	Y	Y	Y
OHIO								
Glenn	Y	N	Y	Y	Y	Y	N	N
Metzenbaum	?	N	Y	Y	Y	Y	N	Y
OKLAHOMA								
Boren	Y	N	Y	N	Y	N	Y	Y
Nickles	N	Y	N	N	N	N	N	Y
OREGON								
Hatfield	N	N	Y	Y	Y	N	N	Y
Packwood	N	N	Y	N	Y	Y	N	Y
PENNSYLVANIA								
Wofford	Y	N	Y	Y	Y	Y	Y	N
Specter	N	N	Y	Y	Y	Y	Y	Y
RHODE ISLAND								
Pell	Y	N	Y	Y	Y	Y	N	N
Chafee	Y	N	Y	Y	Y	N	Y	N
SOUTH CAROLINA								
Hollings	Y	Y	Y	Y	Y	Y	Y	N
Thurmond	N	Y	Y	N	Y	N	N	Y
SOUTH DAKOTA								
Daschle	Y	Y	Y	Y	Y	Y	N	N
Pressler	N	Y	Y	Y	Y	N	N	Y
TENNESSEE								
Mathews	Y	Y	N	Y	Y	Y	Y	N
Sasser	Y	Y	Y	N	Y	Y	Y	Y

	329	330	331	332	333	334	335	336
TEXAS								
Gramm	N	Y	Y	N	N	N	Y	Y
Hutchison	N	Y	Y	N	N	N	N	Y
UTAH								
Bennett	N	N	Y	N	N	N	N	Y
Hatch	N	N	Y	N	N	N	N	Y
VERMONT								
Leahy	?	N	Y	Y	Y	Y	Y	N
Jeffords	N	N	Y	N	Y	Y	N	?
VIRGINIA								
Robb	Y	N	Y	Y	Y	Y	N	N
Warner	N	N	Y	Y	Y	Y	Y	Y
WASHINGTON								
Murray	Y	N	Y	Y	Y	Y	N	N
Gorton	N	Y	Y	N	Y	Y	Y	Y
WEST VIRGINIA								
Byrd	Y	N	Y	Y	Y	Y	N	N
Rockefeller	Y	?	Y	Y	Y	Y	?	N
WISCONSIN								
Feingold	Y	N	Y	Y	Y	N	Y	N
Kohl	Y	N	Y	Y	Y	Y	Y	Y
WYOMING								
Simpson	N	Y	Y	N	Y	N	N	Y
Wallop	N	Y	Y	N	N	N	N	Y

ND Northern Democrats   SD Southern Democrats   Southern states - Ala., Ark., Fla., Ga., Ky., La., Miss., N.C., Okla., S.C., Tenn., Texas, Va.

---

329. HR 2520. Fiscal 1994 Interior Appropriations/Cloture. Motion to invoke cloture (thus limiting debate) on the conference report to provide $13,388,038,000 in new budget authority for the Department of the Interior and related agencies in fiscal 1994. Motion rejected 51-45: R 3-40; D 48-5 (ND 34-5, SD 14-0), Oct. 26, 1993. A three-fifths majority vote (60) of the total Senate is required to invoke cloture. A "yea" was a vote in support of the president's position.

330. HR 1308. Religious Freedom/Prisoners. Reid, D-Nev., amendment to exclude federal, state and local prisoners from the protections of the bill. Rejected 41-58: R 23-21; D 18-37 (ND 10-31, SD 8-6), Oct. 27, 1993.

331. HR 1308. Religious Freedom/Passage. Passage of the bill to reverse a 1990 Supreme Court decision that made it easier for states or the federal government to pass laws restricting individual religious rights. Passed 97-3: R 43-1; D 54-2 (ND 41-1, SD 13-1), Oct. 27, 1993. A "yea" was a vote in support of the president's position.

332. S J Res 19. U.S. Apology for Hawaii Overthrow/Passage. Passage of the joint resolution to offer an apology to Native Hawaiians on behalf of the United States for the overthrow of the Kingdom of Hawaii. Passed 65-34: R 12-32; D 53-2 (ND 42-0, SD 11-2), Oct. 27, 1993.

333. HR 2445. Fiscal 1994 Energy and Water Appropriations/Conference Report. Adoption of the conference report to provide $22,215,382,000 for energy and water development in fiscal 1994. Adopted (thus cleared for the president) 89-11: R 35-9; D 54-2 (ND 40-2, SD 14-0), Oct. 27, 1993.

334. HR 3167. Unemployment Benefits Extension/Budget Act Violation. Nickles, R-Okla., motion to reconsider the Moynihan, D-N.Y., motion to waive the budget act with respect to the Nickles point of order against the bill to provide extended unemployment benefits. Motion agreed to 61-39: R 8-36; D 53-3 (ND 40-2, SD 13-1), Oct. 27, 1993. A three-fifths majority vote (60) of the total Senate is required to waive the budget act. (The Senate previously rejected the Moynihan motion on Oct. 26. See vote 328.)

335. HR 3167. Unemployment Benefits Extension/Taxes and Space Station. Bumpers, D-Ark., motion to waive the budget act with respect to the Moynihan, D-N.Y., point of order against the Bumpers amendment to repeal retroactive taxes in the 1993 Budget Reconciliation Act and offset the lost revenue by terminating the space station. Motion rejected 36-61: R 10-32; D 26-29 (ND 18-23, SD 8-6), Oct. 27, 1993. A three-fifths majority vote (60) of the total Senate is required to waive the budget act. (Subsequently, the chair upheld the Moynihan point of order, and the Bumpers amendment fell.)

336. HR 3167. Unemployment Benefits Extension/High-Income Individuals. Brown, R-Colo., amendment to exclude individuals with taxable income for 1992 above $120,000 from receiving extended unemployment benefits. Adopted 52-43: R 39-1; D 13-42 (ND 11-30, SD 2-12), Oct. 27, 1993.

	337	338	339	340	341	342	343	344
ALABAMA								
Heflin	N	Y	N	Y	Y	Y	Y	Y
Shelby	Y	Y	Y	Y	Y	Y	Y	Y
ALASKA								
Murkowski	Y	Y	Y	N	Y	N	Y	Y
Stevens	N	Y	N	N	Y	Y	Y	Y
ARIZONA								
DeConcini	Y	Y	N	Y	Y	Y	?	?
McCain	Y	Y	Y	N	Y	N	?	?
ARKANSAS								
Bumpers	Y	N	N	Y	Y	Y	Y	Y
Pryor	N	N	N	Y	N	Y	Y	Y
CALIFORNIA								
Boxer	N	N	N	Y	?	?	?	Y
Feinstein	N	N	N	Y	?	+	Y	Y
COLORADO								
Campbell	?	?	N	N	Y	Y	Y	Y
Brown	Y	Y	Y	N	Y	N	Y	Y
CONNECTICUT								
Dodd	N	N	N	Y	Y	Y	Y	Y
Lieberman	N	Y	N	Y	Y	Y	Y	Y
DELAWARE								
Biden	N	N	N	Y	Y	Y	Y	?
Roth	Y	Y	Y	Y	Y	Y	Y	Y
FLORIDA								
Graham	Y	N	N	Y	Y	Y	Y	Y
Mack	Y	Y	Y	N	Y	N	Y	Y
GEORGIA								
Nunn	Y	N	N	Y	N	Y	Y	Y
Coverdell	Y	N	Y	N	Y	N	Y	Y
HAWAII								
Akaka	N	N	N	Y	N	Y	Y	Y
Inouye	N	N	N	Y	Y	Y	Y	Y
IDAHO								
Craig	Y	Y	Y	N	Y	N	Y	Y
Kempthorne	Y	Y	Y	N	Y	N	Y	Y
ILLINOIS								
Moseley-Braun	N	N	N	Y	Y	Y	?	?
Simon	N	N	N	Y	N	Y	Y	Y
INDIANA								
Coats	Y	Y	Y	N	Y	N	Y	Y
Lugar	Y	Y	Y	N	Y	N	Y	Y

	337	338	339	340	341	342	343	344
IOWA								
Harkin	N	Y	N	Y	Y	Y	Y	Y
Grassley	Y	Y	Y	N	Y	Y	Y	Y
KANSAS								
Dole	Y	Y	Y	N	Y	N	Y	Y
Kassebaum	Y	Y	Y	N	Y	Y	Y	Y
KENTUCKY								
Ford	N	N	N	Y	Y	Y	Y	Y
McConnell	Y	Y	?	?	?	?	Y	Y
LOUISIANA								
Breaux	N	N	N	Y	Y	Y	Y	Y
Johnston	N	N	N	Y	Y	Y	Y	Y
MAINE								
Mitchell	N	N	N	Y	Y	Y	Y	Y
Cohen	Y	Y	Y	Y	Y	Y	Y	Y
MARYLAND								
Mikulski	N	N	N	Y	N	Y	Y	Y
Sarbanes	N	N	N	Y	N	Y	?	?
MASSACHUSETTS								
Kennedy	N	N	N	Y	N	Y	?	?
Kerry	N	N	N	Y	N	Y	Y	Y
MICHIGAN								
Levin	N	N	N	Y	Y	Y	Y	Y
Riegle	N	N	N	Y	N	Y	Y	Y
MINNESOTA								
Wellstone	N	N	N	Y	N	Y	Y	Y
Durenberger	?	?	−	?	?	?	Y	Y
MISSISSIPPI								
Cochran	Y	Y	Y	N	Y	Y	Y	Y
Lott	Y	Y	Y	N	Y	Y	Y	Y
MISSOURI								
Bond	Y	Y	Y	N	Y	Y	Y	Y
Danforth	Y	Y	Y	N	N	Y	N	Y	Y
MONTANA								
Baucus	Y	N	N	Y	Y	Y	Y	Y
Burns	Y	Y	Y	N	Y	Y	Y	Y
NEBRASKA								
Exon	Y	N	N	Y	N	Y	N	Y
Kerrey	Y	N	N	Y	Y	N	Y	Y
NEVADA								
Bryan	N	Y	?	Y	Y	Y	Y	Y
Reid	N	Y	N	Y	Y	Y	Y	Y

	337	338	339	340	341	342	343	344
NEW HAMPSHIRE								
Gregg	Y	Y	Y	N	Y	N	Y	Y
Smith	Y	Y	Y	N	Y	N	Y	Y
NEW JERSEY								
Bradley	Y	N	N	Y	Y	Y	Y	Y
Lautenberg	Y	Y	N	Y	Y	Y	Y	Y
NEW MEXICO								
Bingaman	N	N	N	N	Y	Y	Y	Y
Domenici	Y	N	Y	N	N	Y	Y	Y
NEW YORK								
Moynihan	N	N	N	Y	Y	Y	Y	Y
D'Amato	+	+	Y	N	Y	Y	Y	Y
NORTH CAROLINA								
Faircloth	Y	Y	Y	N	Y	N	?	?
Helms	Y	Y	Y	N	Y	N	Y	Y
NORTH DAKOTA								
Conrad	Y	N	N	N	Y	Y	Y	Y
Dorgan	Y	N	N	N	Y	Y	Y	Y
OHIO								
Glenn	N	N	N	Y	N	Y	Y	Y
Metzenbaum	N	N	N	Y	N	Y	Y	Y
OKLAHOMA								
Boren	N	N	Y	Y	Y	Y	Y	Y
Nickles	Y	Y	Y	N	Y	N	Y	Y
OREGON								
Hatfield	N	N	N	Y	Y	Y	Y	Y
Packwood	Y	N	N	N	Y	Y	Y	Y
PENNSYLVANIA								
Wofford	Y	Y	N	Y	Y	Y	Y	Y
Specter	Y	Y	Y	N	Y	Y	Y	Y
RHODE ISLAND								
Pell	N	N	N	Y	N	Y	Y	Y
Chafee	Y	Y	Y	Y	Y	Y	?	Y
SOUTH CAROLINA								
Hollings	N	N	N	Y	N	Y	Y	Y
Thurmond	Y	Y	Y	N	Y	Y	Y	Y
SOUTH DAKOTA								
Daschle	N	N	N	Y	N	Y	Y	Y
Pressler	Y	Y	Y	N	Y	N	Y	Y
TENNESSEE								
Mathews	Y	N	N	Y	Y	Y	Y	Y
Sasser	Y	N	N	Y	Y	Y	Y	Y

	337	338	339	340	341	342	343	344
TEXAS								
Gramm	Y	Y	Y	N	Y	N	?	?
Hutchison	Y	Y	Y	N	Y	Y	Y	Y
UTAH								
Bennett	Y	Y	Y	N	Y	Y	Y	Y
Hatch	Y	Y	?	N	Y	Y	Y	Y
VERMONT								
Leahy	N	N	N	Y	Y	Y	Y	Y
Jeffords	Y	Y	Y	N	Y	Y	?	?
VIRGINIA								
Robb	Y	N	N	Y	Y	Y	Y	Y
Warner	Y	Y	Y	N	Y	Y	Y	Y
WASHINGTON								
Murray	N	N	N	Y	Y	Y	Y	Y
Gorton	Y	Y	Y	N	Y	Y	Y	Y
WEST VIRGINIA								
Byrd	N	N	N	Y	N	Y	Y	Y
Rockefeller	N	N	N	Y	Y	Y	Y	Y
WISCONSIN								
Feingold	Y	N	N	Y	Y	Y	Y	Y
Kohl	Y	N	N	Y	Y	Y	Y	Y
WYOMING								
Simpson	Y	N	Y	N	Y	Y	Y	Y
Wallop	Y	Y	Y	N	Y	N	Y	Y

ND Northern Democrats   SD Southern Democrats   Southern states - Ala., Ark., Fla., Ga., Ky., La., Miss., N.C., Okla., S.C., Tenn., Texas, Va.

337. HR 3167. Unemployment Benefits Extension/Super Collider. Gramm, R-Texas, motion to waive the budget act with respect to the Byrd, D-W.Va., point of order against the Gramm amendment for violating the budget act. The Gramm amendment would require that all savings from the termination of the superconducting super collider go to deficit reduction. Motion rejected 58-39: R 40-2; D 18-37 (ND 11-30, SD 7-7), Oct. 27, 1993. A three-fifths majority vote (60) of the total Senate is required to waive the budget act. (Subsequently, the chair upheld the Byrd point of order, and the Gramm amendment fell.)

338. HR 3167. Unemployment Benefits Extension/Social Security Earnings Test. McCain, R-Ariz., motion to waive the budget act with respect to the Moynihan, D-N.Y., point of order against the McCain amendment for violating the budget act. The McCain amendment would repeal the Social Security earnings tests. Motion rejected 46-51: R 37-5; D 9-46 (ND 7-34, SD 2-12), Oct. 27, 1993. A three-fifths majority vote (60) of the total Senate is required to waive the budget act. (Subsequently, the chair upheld the Moynihan point of order, and the McCain amendment fell.)

339. HR 3167. Unemployment Benefits Extension/Retroactive Taxes. Nickles, R-Okla., amendment to require a three-fifths majority roll call vote of all senators in order to consider proposals to raise taxes retroactively. Rejected 40-56: R 38-3; D 2-53 (ND 0-41, SD 2-12), Oct. 28, 1993.

340. HR 2520. Fiscal 1994 Interior Appropriations/Cloture. Motion to invoke cloture (thus limiting debate) on the conference report to provide $13,388,038,000 in new budget authority for the Department of the Interior and related agencies in fiscal 1994. The conference report includes changes to federal land-management policies. Motion rejected 54-44: R 3-39; D 51-5 (ND 37-5, SD 14-0), Oct. 28, 1993. A three-fifths majority vote (60) of the total Senate is required to invoke cloture. A "yea" was a vote in support of the president's postion.

341. HR 3167. Unemployment Benefits Extension/Employment Reduction. Gramm, R-Texas, amendment to reduce federal employment levels to those proposed by the vice president in the National Performance Review. Adopted 82-14: R 41-1; D 41-13 (ND 29-11, SD 12-2), Oct. 28, 1993.

342. HR 3167. Unemployment Benefits Extension/Passage. Passage of the bill to provide about $1 billion for extended unemployment benefits for workers who have exhausted their 26 weeks of state benefits for an additional seven or 13 weeks, depending on the unemployment rates in their states. Passed 76-20: R 24-18; D 52-2 (ND 38-2, SD 14-0), Oct. 28, 1993.

343. Procedural Motion. Mitchell, D-Maine, motion to instruct the sergeant at arms to request the attendance of absent senators. Motion agreed to 90-0: R 39-0; D 51-0 (ND 37-0, SD 14-0), Nov. 1, 1993.

344. Procedural Motion. Mitchell, D-Maine, motion to instruct the sergeant at arms to request the attendance of absent senators. Motion agreed to 93-0: R 40-0; D 53-0 (ND 39-0, SD 14-0), Nov. 1, 1993.

	345	346	347	348	349	350	351	352
ALABAMA								
Heflin	Y	Y	N	Y	Y	Y	Y	Y
Shelby	Y	Y	N	Y	Y	Y	Y	Y
ALASKA								
Murkowski	Y	Y	Y	Y	N	Y	Y	Y
Stevens	Y	Y	N	Y	N	Y	Y	Y
ARIZONA								
DeConcini	Y	Y	N	N	Y	Y	Y	Y
McCain	N	Y	N	Y	N	Y	Y	Y
ARKANSAS								
Bumpers	Y	Y	N	Y	Y	Y	Y	Y
Pryor	Y	Y	N	Y	Y	Y	Y	Y
CALIFORNIA								
Boxer	Y	Y	N	Y	Y	Y	Y	Y
Feinstein	Y	Y	N	Y	Y	Y	Y	Y
COLORADO								
Campbell	Y	Y	N	Y	Y	Y	Y	Y
Brown	Y	Y	Y	Y	Y	Y	Y	Y
CONNECTICUT								
Dodd	Y	Y	N	Y	Y	Y	Y	Y
Lieberman	Y	Y	N	Y	Y	Y	Y	Y
DELAWARE								
Biden	Y	Y	N	Y	Y	Y	Y	Y
Roth	Y	Y	N	Y	N	Y	Y	Y
FLORIDA								
Graham	Y	Y	N	Y	Y	Y	Y	Y
Mack	Y	Y	N	Y	N	Y	Y	Y
GEORGIA								
Nunn	Y	Y	N	Y	Y	Y	Y	Y
Coverdell	Y	Y	Y	Y	N	Y	Y	Y
HAWAII								
Akaka	Y	Y	N	Y	Y	Y	Y	Y
Inouye	Y	Y	N	Y	Y	Y	Y	Y
IDAHO								
Craig	Y	Y	Y	Y	N	Y	Y	Y
Kempthorne	Y	Y	Y	Y	N	Y	Y	Y
ILLINOIS								
Moseley-Braun	?	?	N	Y	Y	Y	Y	Y
Simon	Y	Y	N	Y	Y	Y	Y	N
INDIANA								
Coats	Y	Y	N	Y	N	Y	Y	Y
Lugar	Y	Y	N	Y	N	Y	Y	Y

	345	346	347	348	349	350	351	352
IOWA								
Harkin	Y	Y	N	Y	Y	Y	Y	Y
Grassley	Y	Y	N	Y	N	Y	Y	Y
KANSAS								
Dole	Y	Y	Y	Y	N	Y	Y	Y
Kassebaum	Y	Y	N	Y	N	Y	Y	Y
KENTUCKY								
Ford	Y	Y	N	Y	Y	Y	Y	Y
McConnell	Y	Y	N	Y	N	Y	Y	Y
LOUISIANA								
Breaux	Y	Y	N	Y	Y	Y	Y	Y
Johnston	Y	Y	N	Y	Y	Y	Y	Y
MAINE								
Mitchell	Y	Y	N	Y	Y	Y	Y	Y
Cohen	Y	Y	N	Y	N	Y	Y	Y
MARYLAND								
Mikulski	Y	Y	N	Y	Y	Y	Y	Y
Sarbanes	Y	Y	N	Y	Y	Y	Y	Y
MASSACHUSETTS								
Kennedy	Y	Y	N	Y	Y	Y	Y	Y
Kerry	Y	Y	N	Y	Y	Y	Y	Y
MICHIGAN								
Levin	Y	Y	N	Y	Y	Y	Y	Y
Riegle	Y	Y	N	Y	Y	Y	Y	Y
MINNESOTA								
Wellstone	Y	Y	N	Y	Y	Y	Y	Y
Durenberger	Y	Y	Y	Y	N	Y	Y	?
MISSISSIPPI								
Cochran	Y	Y	N	Y	N	Y	Y	Y
Lott	Y	Y	Y	Y	N	Y	Y	Y
MISSOURI								
Bond	Y	Y	Y	Y	N	Y	Y	Y
Danforth	Y	Y	Y	N	N	Y	Y	Y
MONTANA								
Baucus	Y	Y	N	Y	Y	Y	Y	Y
Burns	Y	Y	N	Y	N	Y	Y	Y
NEBRASKA								
Exon	Y	Y	N	Y	Y	Y	Y	Y
Kerrey	Y	Y	N	Y	Y	Y	Y	Y
NEVADA								
Bryan	Y	Y	N	Y	Y	Y	Y	Y
Reid	Y	Y	N	Y	Y	Y	Y	Y

	345	346	347	348	349	350	351	352
NEW HAMPSHIRE								
Gregg	Y	Y	N	Y	N	Y	Y	Y
Smith	Y	Y	N	Y	N	Y	Y	Y
NEW JERSEY								
Bradley	?	Y	N	Y	Y	Y	Y	Y
Lautenberg	Y	Y	N	Y	Y	Y	Y	Y
NEW MEXICO								
Bingaman	Y	Y	Y	Y	Y	Y	Y	Y
Domenici	Y	Y	Y	Y	N	Y	Y	Y
NEW YORK								
Moynihan	Y	Y	N	Y	Y	Y	Y	Y
D'Amato	Y	Y	Y	Y	N	Y	Y	Y
NORTH CAROLINA								
Faircloth	Y	Y	Y	Y	N	Y	N	Y
Helms	Y	Y	Y	N	N	Y	N	?
NORTH DAKOTA								
Conrad	Y	Y	N	Y	Y	Y	?	Y
Dorgan	Y	Y	N	Y	Y	Y	Y	Y
OHIO								
Glenn	Y	Y	N	Y	Y	Y	Y	Y
Metzenbaum	Y	Y	N	Y	Y	Y	Y	Y
OKLAHOMA								
Boren	Y	Y	N	Y	Y	Y	Y	Y
Nickles	Y	Y	N	Y	N	Y	Y	Y
OREGON								
Hatfield	Y	Y	Y	Y	N	Y	Y	N
Packwood	Y	Y	Y	N	N	Y	Y	Y
PENNSYLVANIA								
Wofford	Y	Y	N	Y	Y	Y	Y	Y
Specter	Y	Y	Y	N	N	Y	Y	Y
RHODE ISLAND								
Pell	Y	Y	N	Y	Y	Y	Y	N
Chafee	Y	Y	N	Y	N	Y	Y	Y
SOUTH CAROLINA								
Hollings	Y	Y	N	Y	Y	Y	Y	Y
Thurmond	Y	Y	Y	Y	N	Y	Y	Y
SOUTH DAKOTA								
Daschle	Y	Y	N	Y	Y	Y	Y	Y
Pressler	Y	Y	Y	Y	N	Y	Y	Y
TENNESSEE								
Mathews	Y	Y	N	Y	Y	Y	Y	N
Sasser	Y	Y	N	Y	Y	Y	Y	Y

KEY

Y	Voted for (yea).
#	Paired for.
+	Announced for.
N	Voted against (nay).
X	Paired against.
−	Announced against.
P	Voted "present."
C	Voted "present" to avoid possible conflict of interest.
?	Did not vote or otherwise make a position known.

Democrats   *Republicans*

	345	346	347	348	349	350	351	352
TEXAS								
Gramm	Y	Y	Y	Y	N	Y	Y	Y
Hutchison	Y	Y	N	Y	N	Y	Y	Y
UTAH								
Bennett	Y	Y	N	Y	N	Y	Y	Y
Hatch	Y	Y	N	Y	N	Y	Y	Y
VERMONT								
Leahy	Y	Y	N	Y	Y	Y	Y	Y
Jeffords	Y	Y	N	Y	Y	Y	Y	Y
VIRGINIA								
Robb	Y	Y	N	Y	Y	Y	Y	Y
Warner	Y	Y	N	Y	N	Y	Y	Y
WASHINGTON								
Murray	Y	Y	N	Y	Y	Y	Y	Y
Gorton	Y	Y	N	Y	N	Y	Y	Y
WEST VIRGINIA								
Byrd	Y	Y	N	Y	Y	Y	Y	Y
Rockefeller	Y	Y	N	Y	Y	Y	Y	Y
WISCONSIN								
Feingold	Y	Y	N	Y	Y	Y	N	Y
Kohl	Y	Y	N	Y	Y	Y	Y	Y
WYOMING								
Simpson	Y	Y	Y	N	N	Y	Y	Y
Wallop	Y	Y	Y	N	Y	N	Y	N

ND Northern Democrats   SD Southern Democrats   Southern states - Ala., Ark., Fla., Ga., Ky., La., Miss., N.C., Okla., S.C., Tenn., Texas, Va.

345. Procedural Motion. Mitchell, D-Maine, motion to instruct the sergeant at arms to request the attendance of absent senators. Motion agreed to 97-1: R 43-1; D 54-0 (ND 40-0, SD 14-0), Nov. 2, 1993.

346. Procedural Motion. Mitchell, D-Maine, motion to instruct the sergeant at arms to request the attendance of absent senators. Motion agreed to 99-0: R 44-0; D 55-0 (ND 41-0, SD 14-0), Nov. 2, 1993.

347. S Res 153. Packwood Diaries/Relevancy Requirement. Simpson, R-Wyo., amendment to add that all materials requested in the Ethics Committee subpoena of the diaries of Sen. Bob Packwood, R-Ore., be "relevant." Rejected 23-77: R 22-22; D 1-55 (ND 1-41, SD 0-14), Nov. 2, 1993.

348. S Res 153. Packwood Diaries/Adoption. Adoption of the resolution to authorize the Senate legal counsel to bring civil action to enforce the Ethics Committee's subpoena of the diaries of Sen. Bob Packwood, R-Ore. Adopted 94-6: R 39-5; D 55-1 (ND 41-1, SD 14-0), Nov. 2, 1993.

349. State Department Nominations/Cloture. Motion to invoke cloture (thus limiting debate) on the nominations of Alan John Blinken to be ambassador to Belgium; Tobi Trister Gati to be an assistant secretary of State; Swanee Grace Hunt to be ambassador to Austria; Thomas A. Loftus to be ambassador to Norway; and Daniel L. Spiegel to be the U.S. representative to the European Office of the United Nations. Motion rejected 58-42: R 2-42; D 56-0 (ND 42-0, SD 14-0), Nov. 3, 1993. A three-fifths majority vote (60) of the total Senate is required to invoke cloture. (The Senate subsequently approved the nominations by voice vote.)

350. S 1607. Omnibus Crime/Child Pornography. Grassley, R-Iowa, amendment to repudiate the Justice Department's brief in *Knox v. United States* and clarify congressional intent in a federal child pornography statute that child pornography is not limited only to instances in which children appear nude. Adopted 100-0: R 44-0; D 56-0 (ND 42-0, SD 14-0), Nov. 4, 1993.

351. S 1607. Omnibus Crime/Hate Crimes. Feinstein, D-Calif., amendment to allow enhanced penalties for hate crimes. Adopted 95-4: R 41-3; D 54-1 (ND 40-1, SD 14-0), Nov. 4, 1993.

352. S 1607. Omnibus Crime/Additional Funds. Byrd, D-W.Va., amendment to provide additional funds beyond those in the underlying bill, including $3.72 billion for 40,000 additional state and local law enforcement personnel for a total of 100,000 new officers; $3 billion for the construction and operation of regional prisons; $1 billion for the construction of jails, boot camps and other minimum-security facilities; $500 million for the construction of violent juvenile offender facilities; and $1.8 billion to combat violence against women. To fund the provisions, the amendment would create a Violent Crime Reduction Trust Fund of $22.3 billion over five years by fully implementing the reductions in federal employment proposed in the National Performance Review. Adopted 94-4: R 41-1; D 53-3 (ND 40-2, SD 13-1), Nov. 4, 1993.

ALABAMA	353	354	355	356	357	358	359	360
Heflin	N	Y	Y	N	Y	Y	Y	Y
Shelby	Y	Y	Y	Y	?	?	Y	Y
ALASKA								
Murkowski	Y	Y	?	?	Y	Y	Y	Y
Stevens	Y	Y	Y	Y	Y	Y	Y	Y
ARIZONA								
DeConcini	N	N	Y	Y	+	?	Y	N
McCain	Y	X	+	+	Y	Y	Y	Y
ARKANSAS								
Bumpers	Y	N	?	?	Y	N	Y	N
Pryor	Y	Y	Y	Y	Y	Y	Y	N
CALIFORNIA								
Boxer	Y	N	Y	N	Y	N	Y	N
Feinstein	Y	N	Y	Y	Y	Y	Y	Y
COLORADO								
Campbell	Y	Y	?	?	Y	N	Y	Y
Brown	Y	Y	Y	Y	Y	Y	N	Y
CONNECTICUT								
Dodd	N	N	Y	N	Y	N	Y	N
Lieberman	Y	N	Y	Y	Y	Y	Y	Y
DELAWARE								
Biden	N	N	Y	N	Y	N	Y	N
Roth	Y	Y	Y	Y	Y	Y	N	Y
FLORIDA								
Graham	Y	N	Y	Y	Y	Y	Y	Y
Mack	Y	N	Y	Y	Y	Y	Y	Y
GEORGIA								
Nunn	Y	Y	Y	Y	Y	Y	Y	Y
Coverdell	Y	Y	Y	Y	?	?	Y	Y
HAWAII								
Akaka	N	N	Y	Y	Y	N	N	Y
Inouye	Y	N	Y	N	Y	?	Y	N
IDAHO								
Craig	Y	Y	Y	Y	Y	Y	Y	Y
Kempthorne	Y	Y	Y	Y	Y	Y	Y	Y
ILLINOIS								
Moseley-Braun	Y	N	Y	Y	Y	N	Y	N
Simon	Y	N	Y	Y	Y	N	Y	N
INDIANA								
Coats	Y	Y	Y	Y	Y	N	Y	Y
Lugar	Y	Y	Y	Y	Y	Y	Y	Y

IOWA	353	354	355	356	357	358	359	360
Harkin	Y	N	Y	Y	Y	N	Y	N
Grassley	Y	Y	Y	Y	Y	Y	Y	Y
KANSAS								
Dole	Y	?	?	?	Y	Y	Y	Y
Kassebaum	Y	Y	Y	N	Y	Y	Y	Y
KENTUCKY								
Ford	N	Y	Y	N	Y	Y	Y	Y
McConnell	Y	Y	Y	Y	Y	Y	Y	Y
LOUISIANA								
Breaux	Y	Y	Y	Y	Y	Y	Y	Y
Johnston	?	Y	Y	Y	Y	Y	Y	Y
MAINE								
Mitchell	N	Y	Y	N	Y	N	N	Y
Cohen	Y	Y	Y	Y	Y	N	N	Y
MARYLAND								
Mikulski	Y	N	Y	Y	Y	N	Y	Y
Sarbanes	Y	N	Y	Y	Y	N	Y	N
MASSACHUSETTS								
Kennedy	N	N	Y	N	?	N	Y	N
Kerry	Y	Y	Y	Y	Y	N	Y	N
MICHIGAN								
Levin	N	Y	Y	N	Y	N	Y	N
Riegle	Y	Y	Y	Y	Y	Y	Y	Y
MINNESOTA								
Wellstone	N	N	Y	N	Y	N	Y	N
Durenberger	Y	Y	Y	N	Y	N	Y	N
MISSISSIPPI								
Cochran	Y	Y	Y	Y	Y	Y	Y	Y
Lott	Y	Y	Y	Y	Y	?	Y	Y
MISSOURI								
Bond	Y	Y	?	?	Y	Y	Y	Y
Danforth	Y	Y	Y	Y	Y	N	Y	?
MONTANA								
Baucus	Y	Y	Y	Y	Y	Y	Y	Y
Burns	Y	Y	Y	Y	Y	Y	Y	Y
NEBRASKA								
Exon	Y	Y	Y	N	Y	Y	Y	Y
Kerrey	Y	Y	Y	N	Y	Y	Y	+
NEVADA								
Bryan	Y	Y	Y	Y	Y	Y	Y	Y
Reid	Y	?	?	?	Y	Y	Y	Y

NEW HAMPSHIRE	353	354	355	356	357	358	359	360
Gregg	Y	Y	Y	Y	Y	N	N	Y
Smith	Y	Y	Y	Y	Y	Y	N	Y
NEW JERSEY								
Bradley	N	N	Y	Y	Y	N	Y	N
Lautenberg	Y	N	Y	Y	Y	N	Y	N
NEW MEXICO								
Bingaman	N	N	?	?	Y	N	Y	Y
Domenici	Y	Y	Y	Y	Y	Y	Y	Y
NEW YORK								
Moynihan	N	N	N	Y	Y	N	Y	N
D'Amato	Y	Y	Y	Y	Y	Y	Y	Y
NORTH CAROLINA								
Faircloth	Y	Y	Y	Y	Y	Y	N	Y
Helms	?	Y	Y	Y	Y	Y	N	Y
NORTH DAKOTA								
Conrad	Y	Y	Y	Y	Y	N	Y	Y
Dorgan	Y	Y	Y	Y	?	Y	N	Y
OHIO								
Glenn	Y	Y	Y	N	Y	N	Y	N
Metzenbaum	N	Y	Y	N	?	N	Y	N
OKLAHOMA								
Boren	Y	Y	Y	Y	Y	N	Y	N
Nickles	Y	Y	Y	Y	Y	Y	Y	Y
OREGON								
Hatfield	Y	N	Y	N	Y	N	Y	Y
Packwood	N	N	Y	N	N	Y	Y	N
PENNSYLVANIA								
Wofford	Y	Y	Y	Y	Y	N	Y	N
Specter	Y	Y	Y	N	Y	Y	Y	Y
RHODE ISLAND								
Pell	N	N	Y	Y	Y	N	Y	N
Chafee	Y	Y	Y	N	?	N	Y	N
SOUTH CAROLINA								
Hollings	Y	Y	Y	Y	?	N	Y	N
Thurmond	Y	Y	Y	Y	Y	Y	Y	Y
SOUTH DAKOTA								
Daschle	Y	Y	Y	Y	Y	Y	Y	N
Pressler	Y	Y	Y	Y	Y	Y	N	Y
TENNESSEE								
Mathews	+	?	+	?	Y	Y	Y	N
Sasser	Y	Y	Y	Y	Y	Y	Y	Y

TEXAS	353	354	355	356	357	358	359	360
Gramm	?	?	?	?	Y	Y	Y	Y
Hutchison	Y	Y	Y	Y	Y	?	N	Y
UTAH								
Bennett	+	+	+	+	Y	Y	Y	Y
Hatch	Y	Y	Y	Y	Y	Y	Y	Y
VERMONT								
Leahy	N	Y	Y	N	Y	N	Y	N
Jeffords	N	N	?	?	Y	N	Y	Y
VIRGINIA								
Robb	Y	N	Y	N	Y	N	Y	Y
Warner	Y	Y	Y	Y	Y	Y	Y	Y
WASHINGTON								
Murray	Y	N	Y	N	Y	N	Y	N
Gorton	Y	Y	Y	N	Y	Y	Y	Y
WEST VIRGINIA								
Byrd	Y	Y	Y	Y	Y	Y	Y	Y
Rockefeller	?	Y	Y	Y	Y	N	Y	N
WISCONSIN								
Feingold	N	N	Y	N	Y	N	Y	N
Kohl	Y	Y	Y	Y	Y	N	N	Y
WYOMING								
Simpson	Y	Y	Y	Y	Y	Y	Y	Y
Wallop	Y	#	+	+	Y	Y	Y	Y

ND   Northern Democrats   SD   Southern Democrats   Southern states - Ala., Ark., Fla., Ga., Ky., La., Miss., N.C., Okla., S.C., Tenn., Texas, Va.

353. S 1607. Omnibus Crime/Sex Crimes. Dole, R-Kan., amendment to establish clearer rules for the admission of evidence in similar sexual assault and child molestation cases. Adopted 75-19: R 39-2; D 36-17 (ND 26-15, SD 10-2), Nov. 5, 1993.

354. S 1607. Omnibus Crime/Illegal Aliens. Exon, D-Neb., motion to table (kill) the Graham, D-Fla., amendment to the Exon amendment, to require a report within two years on the impact of federal benefits to illegal aliens. The Exon amendment would prohibit the payment of federal benefits to illegal aliens. Motion agreed to 64-29: R 35-4; D 29-25 (ND 19-22, SD 10-3), Nov. 5, 1993.

355. S 1607. Omnibus Crime/Illegal Aliens. Exon, D-Neb., amendment to prohibit the payment of federal benefits to illegal aliens except in cases of medical emergencies. Adopted 85-2: R 35-1; D 50-1 (ND 38-1, SD 12-0), Nov. 5, 1993.

356. S 1607. Omnibus Crime/Armed Juveniles. Moseley-Braun, D-Ill., amendment to allow armed offenders 13 years or older to be prosecuted as adults for federal crimes. Adopted 64-23: R 30-6; D 34-17 (ND 24-15, SD 10-2), Nov. 5, 1993.

357. S 1607. Omnibus Crime/Repeat Felons. Lott, R-Miss., amendment to provide mandatory life imprisonment for individuals convicted of a third felony with a maximum penalty of more than five years. Adopted 91-1: R 40-1; D 51-0 (ND 39-0, SD 12-0), Nov. 8, 1993.

358. S 1607. Omnibus Crime/Juvenile Death Penalty. Hatch, R-Utah, motion to table (kill) the Simon, D-Ill., amendment to prohibit the death penalty for crimes committed when an individual is under the age of 18. Motion agreed to 52-41: R 33-8; D 19-33 (ND 10-29, SD 9-4), Nov. 8, 1993.

359. HR 2520. Fiscal 1994 Interior Appropriations/Conference Report. Adoption of the conference report to provide $13,388,038,000 in new budget authority for the Department of the Interior and related agencies in fiscal 1994. The administration requested $13,617,688,000. Before adoption, the Senate stripped out provisions to increase grazing fees and reform federal land-management policies. Adopted (thus sent back to the House for final action) 91-9: R 36-8; D 55-1 (ND 41-1, SD 14-0), Nov. 9, 1993.

360. S 1607. Omnibus Crime/Gang Activity. Dole, R-Kan., amendment to make criminal gang activity a federal offense with mandatory minimum penalties; authorize $100 million over five years to hire additional federal prosecutors to prosecute gang activity; and establish a $100 million grant program to work with juveniles and gang members under the Juvenile Justice and Delinquency Prevention Act. Adopted 60-38: R 38-5; D 22-33 (ND 13-28, SD 9-5), Nov. 9, 1993.

	361	362	363	364	365	366	367	368
ALABAMA								
Heflin	N	N	Y	Y	Y	N	Y	Y
Shelby	Y	Y	Y	Y	Y	Y	N	Y
ALASKA								
Murkowski	Y	Y	Y	Y	Y	N	Y	Y
Stevens	Y	Y	Y	Y	Y	Y	N	Y
ARIZONA								
DeConcini	Y	N	Y	Y	N	N	Y	Y
McCain	Y	Y	Y	Y	Y	Y	N	N
ARKANSAS								
Bumpers	Y	N	Y	Y	N	N	Y	Y
Pryor	Y	N	Y	Y	N	N	Y	?
CALIFORNIA								
Boxer	Y	N	Y	Y	N	N	Y	Y
Feinstein	Y	Y	Y	Y	N	N	Y	Y
COLORADO								
Campbell	Y	Y	Y	?	N	N	Y	Y
Brown	Y	Y	Y	Y	Y	Y	N	N
CONNECTICUT								
Dodd	Y	Y	Y	Y	N	Y	N	Y
Lieberman	Y	Y	Y	Y	N	Y	N	Y
DELAWARE								
Biden	Y	N	Y	Y	N	N	Y	Y
Roth	Y	Y	Y	Y	N	Y	N	N
FLORIDA								
Graham	Y	Y	Y	Y	N	N	Y	Y
Mack	Y	Y	Y	Y	Y	Y	N	Y
GEORGIA								
Nunn	?	Y	Y	Y	N	Y	N	Y
Coverdell	Y	Y	Y	Y	Y	Y	N	Y
HAWAII								
Akaka	N	N	Y	Y	N	N	Y	Y
Inouye	N	N	Y	Y	N	N	Y	Y
IDAHO								
Craig	Y	Y	Y	Y	Y	N	Y	Y
Kempthorne	Y	Y	Y	Y	Y	Y	N	Y
ILLINOIS								
Moseley-Braun	N	N	Y	N	N	N	Y	Y
Simon	N	N	Y	N	N	N	Y	Y
INDIANA								
Coats	N	N	Y	Y	Y	Y	N	Y
Lugar	Y	Y	Y	Y	Y	Y	N	Y

	361	362	363	364	365	366	367	368
IOWA								
Harkin	N	N	Y	Y	N	N	Y	Y
Grassley	Y	Y	Y	Y	Y	Y	N	Y
KANSAS								
Dole	Y	Y	Y	Y	Y	Y	N	Y
Kassebaum	Y	Y	Y	Y	N	Y	N	Y
KENTUCKY								
Ford	Y	Y	Y	Y	N	Y	Y	Y
McConnell	Y	Y	Y	Y	Y	Y	N	Y
LOUISIANA								
Breaux	Y	Y	Y	Y	Y	Y	N	Y
Johnston	Y	Y	Y	Y	Y	Y	Y	?
MAINE								
Mitchell	N	N	Y	Y	N	N	Y	Y
Cohen	N	N	Y	Y	Y	Y	N	Y
MARYLAND								
Mikulski	Y	Y	Y	Y	N	N	Y	Y
Sarbanes	Y	Y	Y	Y	N	N	Y	Y
MASSACHUSETTS								
Kennedy	N	N	Y	Y	N	N	Y	Y
Kerry	N	N	Y	Y	N	N	Y	Y
MICHIGAN								
Levin	N	N	Y	Y	N	N	Y	Y
Riegle	Y	Y	Y	Y	N	N	Y	Y
MINNESOTA								
Wellstone	N	N	Y	Y	N	N	Y	N
Durenberger	Y	N	Y	N	Y	N	N	Y
MISSISSIPPI								
Cochran	Y	Y	Y	Y	Y	Y	N	Y
Lott	Y	Y	Y	Y	Y	Y	N	Y
MISSOURI								
Bond	N	N	Y	Y	Y	Y	N	Y
Danforth	N	N	Y	N	Y	N	N	Y
MONTANA								
Baucus	Y	Y	Y	Y	N	N	Y	Y
Burns	Y	Y	Y	Y	Y	Y	N	Y
NEBRASKA								
Exon	Y	Y	Y	Y	N	Y	N	Y
Kerrey	N	Y	Y	Y	N	N	Y	Y
NEVADA								
Bryan	Y	Y	Y	Y	Y	N	Y	Y
Reid	Y	N	Y	Y	Y	Y	N	Y

	361	362	363	364	365	366	367	368
NEW HAMPSHIRE								
Gregg	N	N	Y	N	Y	Y	N	Y
Smith	Y	Y	Y	Y	Y	Y	N	N
NEW JERSEY								
Bradley	Y	N	Y	Y	N	N	Y	Y
Lautenberg	N	N	Y	Y	N	N	Y	Y
NEW MEXICO								
Bingaman	N	N	Y	Y	N	N	Y	Y
Domenici	N	Y	Y	Y	Y	Y	N	Y
NEW YORK								
Moynihan	N	N	Y	Y	N	N	Y	Y
D'Amato	Y	Y	Y	Y	Y	Y	N	Y
NORTH CAROLINA								
Faircloth	Y	Y	Y	Y	Y	Y	N	Y
Helms	Y	Y	Y	Y	Y	Y	N	N
NORTH DAKOTA								
Conrad	Y	Y	Y	Y	N	N	Y	Y
Dorgan	N	Y	Y	Y	Y	N	Y	Y
OHIO								
Glenn	N	N	Y	Y	N	N	Y	Y
Metzenbaum	N	N	Y	Y	N	N	Y	Y
OKLAHOMA								
Boren	Y	N	Y	Y	N	N	Y	Y
Nickles	N	Y	Y	Y	Y	Y	N	Y
OREGON								
Hatfield	N	N	Y	Y	N	N	Y	N
Packwood	N	N	Y	Y	Y	Y	N	Y
PENNSYLVANIA								
Wofford	Y	N	Y	Y	N	N	Y	Y
Specter	Y	Y	Y	Y	Y	N	Y	Y
RHODE ISLAND								
Pell	N	N	Y	Y	N	N	Y	Y
Chafee	Y	N	Y	Y	N	Y	N	Y
SOUTH CAROLINA								
Hollings	Y	N	Y	Y	N	Y	N	Y
Thurmond	Y	Y	Y	Y	Y	Y	N	Y
SOUTH DAKOTA								
Daschle	Y	Y	Y	Y	N	N	Y	Y
Pressler	Y	Y	Y	Y	Y	Y	N	?
TENNESSEE								
Mathews	Y	N	Y	Y	N	N	Y	Y
Sasser	Y	Y	Y	Y	Y	N	Y	Y

	361	362	363	364	365	366	367	368
TEXAS								
Gramm	Y	Y	Y	Y	Y	Y	N	Y
Hutchison	Y	Y	Y	Y	Y	Y	N	Y
UTAH								
Bennett	Y	Y	Y	Y	Y	Y	N	Y
Hatch	Y	Y	Y	Y	Y	Y	N	Y
VERMONT								
Leahy	N	N	Y	Y	N	N	Y	Y
Jeffords	N	N	Y	Y	Y	Y	N	Y
VIRGINIA								
Robb	Y	Y	Y	Y	N	N	Y	Y
Warner	Y	Y	Y	Y	Y	Y	N	Y
WASHINGTON								
Murray	N	N	Y	Y	N	N	Y	Y
Gorton	Y	Y	Y	Y	Y	Y	N	Y
WEST VIRGINIA								
Byrd	Y	Y	Y	Y	N	N	Y	Y
Rockefeller	Y	Y	Y	Y	N	N	Y	Y
WISCONSIN								
Feingold	N	N	Y	N	N	N	Y	N
Kohl	N	N	Y	Y	N	N	Y	Y
WYOMING								
Simpson	Y	Y	Y	Y	Y	Y	N	Y
Wallop	N	Y	Y	N	Y	N	N	N

ND Northern Democrats   SD Southern Democrats   Southern states - Ala., Ark., Fla., Ga., Ky., La., Miss., N.C., Okla., S.C., Tenn., Texas, Va.

361. S 1607. Omnibus Crime/Carjacking. Lieberman, D-Conn., amendment to make carjacking a federal offense regardless of whether the perpetrator used a gun and to authorize the death penalty if a carjacking results in death. Adopted 65-34: R 33-11; D 32-23 (ND 20-22, SD 12-1), Nov. 9, 1993.

362. S 1607. Omnibus Crime/Federal Jurisdiction of Firearm Offenses. D'Amato, R-N.Y., amendment to the Gramm, R-Texas, amendment to apply federal gun penalties to state offenses that involve a gun that had crossed state lines. The Gramm amendment would impose minimum federal penalties for gun-related crimes of violence or drug trafficking. Adopted 58-42: R 34-10; D 24-32 (ND 16-26, SD 8-6), Nov. 9, 1993. (Subsequently, the Gramm amendment, as modified by the D'Amato amendment, was approved by voice vote.)

363. S 1607. Omnibus Crime/Juvenile Handgun Control. Kohl, D-Wis., amendment to make it a federal crime to sell a handgun to a minor under 18 or for a minor to possess a handgun except with adult supervision in situations such as hunting or ranching. Adopted 100-0: R 44-0; D 56-0 (ND 42-0, SD 14-0), Nov. 9, 1993. A "yea" was a vote in support of the president's position.

364. S 1607. Omnibus Crime/Immigration Laws. Roth, R-Del., amendment to require state and local governments to cooperate with the Immigration and Naturalization Service regarding the enforcement of immigration laws. Adopted 93-6: R 41-3; D 52-3 (ND 38-3, SD 14-0), Nov. 9, 1993.

365. S 1607. Omnibus Crime/Assault Weapon Ban. Dole, R-Kan., motion to table (kill) the Levin, D-Mich., amendment to study improving the use of automated fingerprint systems. (The tabling motion was aimed at a second degree amendment by Feinstein, D-Calif., to ban the manufacture, sale and future possession of 19 semiautomatic assault weapons and "copycat" guns.) Motion rejected 49-51: R 39-5; D 10-46 (ND 4-38, SD 6-8), Nov. 9, 1993. A "nay" was a vote in support of the president's position.

366. S 1301. Fiscal 1994 Intelligence Authorization/Budget Disclosure. Warner, R-Va., motion to table (kill) the Metzenbaum, D-Ohio, amendment to express the sense of Congress that the aggregate amount requested and authorized for intelligence activities should be disclosed in an appropriate manner. Motion rejected 49-51: R 40-4; D 9-47 (ND 4-38, SD 5-9), Nov. 10, 1993.

367. S 1301. Fiscal 1994 Intelligence Authorization/Budget Disclosure. Metzenbaum, D-Ohio, amendment to express the sense of Congress that the total requested and authorized for intelligence be disclosed in an appropriate manner. Adopted 52-48: R 3-41; D 49-7 (ND 38-4, SD 11-3), Nov. 10, 1993.

368. HR 3116. Fiscal 1994 Defense Appropriations/Adoption. Adoption of the conference report to provide $240,534,878,000 for the Department of Defense in fiscal 1994. The administration requested $240,857,464,000. Adopted (thus cleared for the president) 88-9: R 36-7; D 52-2 (ND 40-2, SD 12-0), Nov. 10, 1993.

KEY

- Y Voted for (yea).
- # Paired for.
- + Announced for.
- N Voted against (nay).
- X Paired against.
- − Announced against.
- P Voted "present."
- C Voted "present" to avoid possible conflict of interest.
- ? Did not vote or otherwise make a position known.

Democrats   *Republicans*

	369	370	371	372	373	374	375	376
ALABAMA								
Heflin	N	Y	N	Y	N	Y	N	N
Shelby	Y	N	N	N	Y	Y	N	N
ALASKA								
Murkowski	N	Y	Y	Y	N	N	N	N
Stevens	Y	N	N	N	Y	N	N	N
ARIZONA								
DeConcini	Y	Y	N	N	Y	Y	Y	Y
McCain	N	Y	Y	Y	N	N	N	N
ARKANSAS								
Bumpers	Y	N	N	N	Y	Y	Y	N
Pryor	Y	N	N	N	Y	Y	Y	N
CALIFORNIA								
Boxer	Y	N	N	N	Y	Y	Y	Y
Feinstein	Y	N	N	N	Y	Y	Y	N
COLORADO								
Campbell	Y	N	N	N	Y	Y	Y	Y
Brown	N	Y	N	N	Y	N	Y	N
CONNECTICUT								
Dodd	Y	N	N	N	Y	Y	Y	Y
Lieberman	Y	N	N	N	Y	Y	Y	N
DELAWARE								
Biden	Y	N	N	N	Y	Y	Y	Y
Roth	N	Y	Y	Y	Y	Y	Y	Y
FLORIDA								
Graham	Y	N	N	N	Y	Y	Y	N
Mack	N	Y	Y	Y	N	Y	N	N
GEORGIA								
Nunn	Y	N	N	N	Y	Y	Y	N
Coverdell	N	Y	Y	Y	N	Y	N	N
HAWAII								
Akaka	Y	N	N	N	Y	Y	Y	Y
Inouye	Y	N	N	N	Y	Y	Y	Y
IDAHO								
Craig	N	Y	Y	Y	N	N	N	N
Kempthorne	N	Y	Y	Y	N	N	N	N
ILLINOIS								
Moseley-Braun	Y	N	N	N	Y	Y	Y	Y
Simon	Y	N	N	N	Y	Y	Y	Y
INDIANA								
Coats	N	Y	Y	Y	N	Y	Y	N
Lugar	N	Y	Y	Y	N	Y	N	N
IOWA								
Harkin	Y	N	N	N	Y	Y	Y	Y
Grassley	N	Y	Y	Y	N	Y	N	N
KANSAS								
Dole	Y	Y	Y	Y	Y	Y	N	N
Kassebaum	?	N	N	N	Y	N	Y	N
KENTUCKY								
Ford	N	Y	N	Y	Y	Y	Y	Y
McConnell	N	Y	Y	Y	Y	Y	Y	N
LOUISIANA								
Breaux	N	N	Y	Y	N	Y	N	N
Johnston	N	Y	Y	Y	N	Y	N	N
MAINE								
Mitchell	Y	N	N	N	Y	Y	Y	Y
Cohen	Y	N	N	N	Y	N	N	N
MARYLAND								
Mikulski	Y	N	N	N	Y	Y	Y	Y
Sarbanes	Y	N	N	N	Y	Y	Y	Y
MASSACHUSETTS								
Kennedy	Y	N	N	N	Y	Y	Y	Y
Kerry	Y	N	N	N	Y	Y	Y	Y
MICHIGAN								
Levin	Y	N	N	N	Y	Y	Y	Y
Riegle	Y	N	N	N	Y	Y	Y	Y
MINNESOTA								
Wellstone	Y	N	N	N	Y	Y	Y	Y
Durenberger	Y	N	N	N	Y	Y	N	Y
MISSISSIPPI								
Cochran	N	Y	Y	Y	N	N	N	N
Lott	N	Y	Y	Y	N	Y	N	N
MISSOURI								
Bond	N	Y	Y	Y	N	N	N	N
Danforth	N	Y	Y	Y	Y	N	Y	N
MONTANA								
Baucus	Y	N	N	N	Y	Y	Y	N
Burns	N	Y	Y	Y	N	N	N	N
NEBRASKA								
Exon	N	Y	Y	Y	N	Y	N	N
Kerrey	Y	N	N	N	Y	Y	Y	N
NEVADA								
Bryan	Y	N	N	N	Y	Y	N	N
Reid	Y	N	Y	N	Y	N	N	N
NEW HAMPSHIRE								
Gregg	N	Y	Y	Y	N	N	N	N
Smith	N	Y	Y	Y	N	N	N	N
NEW JERSEY								
Bradley	Y	N	N	N	Y	Y	Y	Y
Lautenberg	Y	N	N	N	Y	Y	Y	Y
NEW MEXICO								
Bingaman	Y	N	N	N	Y	Y	N	Y
Domenici	N	N	Y	N	Y	N	N	N
NEW YORK								
Moynihan	Y	N	N	N	Y	Y	Y	Y
D'Amato	N	Y	Y	N	Y	N	Y	N
NORTH CAROLINA								
Faircloth	N	Y	Y	Y	N	N	N	N
Helms	N	Y	Y	Y	N	N	N	N
NORTH DAKOTA								
Conrad	N	N	N	Y	Y	Y	Y	Y
Dorgan	?	?	?	?	?	?	?	?
OHIO								
Glenn	Y	N	N	N	Y	Y	Y	N
Metzenbaum	Y	N	N	N	Y	Y	Y	Y
OKLAHOMA								
Boren	?	N	N	N	Y	Y	Y	N
Nickles	N	Y	Y	N	N	N	N	N
OREGON								
Hatfield	N	Y	Y	Y	N	Y	Y	Y
Packwood	Y	N	N	N	Y	N	Y	N
PENNSYLVANIA								
Wofford	Y	N	N	N	Y	Y	Y	Y
Specter	Y	N	N	N	Y	N	N	N
RHODE ISLAND								
Pell	Y	N	N	N	Y	Y	Y	Y
Chafee	Y	N	N	N	Y	N	Y	N
SOUTH CAROLINA								
Hollings	Y	N	N	N	Y	Y	Y	N
Thurmond	N	Y	Y	Y	N	Y	N	N
SOUTH DAKOTA								
Daschle	Y	N	N	N	Y	Y	Y	Y
Pressler	N	Y	Y	Y	N	N	N	N
TENNESSEE								
Mathews	?	N	N	N	Y	Y	Y	N
Sasser	Y	N	N	N	Y	Y	N	N

	369	370	371	372	373	374	375	376
TEXAS								
Gramm	N	Y	Y	Y	N	N	N	N
Hutchison	N	N	N	Y	Y	N	N	N
UTAH								
Bennett	N	Y	Y	Y	N	Y	N	N
Hatch	N	Y	Y	Y	N	Y	N	N
VERMONT								
Leahy	Y	N	N	N	Y	Y	Y	Y
Jeffords	Y	N	N	N	Y	Y	Y	N
VIRGINIA								
Robb	Y	N	N	N	Y	Y	Y	Y
Warner	N	N	N	Y	N	N	N	N
WASHINGTON								
Murray	Y	N	N	N	Y	Y	Y	Y
Gorton	N	N	N	N	Y	N	N	N
WEST VIRGINIA								
Byrd	Y	N	N	N	Y	N	Y	N
Rockefeller	Y	N	N	N	Y	Y	Y	Y
WISCONSIN								
Feingold	Y	N	N	N	Y	Y	Y	Y
Kohl	Y	N	N	N	Y	Y	Y	Y
WYOMING								
Simpson	Y	N	N	N	Y	N	N	N
Wallop	N	Y	Y	Y	N	N	N	N

ND Northern Democrats   SD Southern Democrats

Southern states - Ala., Ark., Fla., Ga., Ky., La., Miss., N.C., Okla., S.C., Tenn., Texas, Va.

369. S 636. Freedom of Access to Abortion Clinics/ Penalties. Kennedy, D-Mass., compromise amendment to maintain the felony status but lessen the federal criminal and civil penalties for people who use force, the threat of force or physical obstruction to block access to abortion clinics. Adopted 56-40: R 9-34; D 47-6 (ND 39-2, SD 8-4), Nov. 16, 1993.

370. S 636. Freedom of Access to Abortion Clinics/Free Speech. Coats, R-Ind., motion to table (kill) the Kennedy, D-Mass., amendment to the Coats amendment, to provide that the bill not interfere with the First Amendment rights of free speech and peaceful assembly. The Coats amendment would provide a cause of action for anti-abortion protesters who are interfered with during a peaceful, lawful protest. Motion rejected 36-63: R 31-13; D 5-50 (ND 2-39, SD 3-11), Nov. 16, 1993. (Subsequently, the Kennedy amendment and the Coats amendment, as amended, were adopted by voice vote).

371. S 636. Freedom of Access to Abortion Clinics/State's Rights. Nickles, R-Okla., motion to table (kill) the Kennedy, D-Mass., amendment to the Hatch, R-Utah, amendment, to ensure that the bill does not affect a state's right to regulate abortions. The Hatch amendment would apply the bill's protections only to legal abortions. Motion rejected 35-64: R 31-13; D 4-51 (ND 2-39, SD 2-12), Nov. 16, 1993. (Subsequently, the Kennedy amendment and the Hatch amendment, as amended, were adopted by voice vote.)

372. S 636. Freedom of Access to Abortion Clinics/ Substitute. Hatch, R-Utah, substitute amendment to differenti-ate between peaceful and violent demonstrations, and to remove the bill's protections for illegal abortions. Rejected 38-61: R 32-12; D 6-49 (ND 2-39, SD 4-10), Nov. 16, 1993.

373. S 636. Freedom of Access to Abortion Clinics/ Passage. Passage of the bill to establish federal criminal and civil penalties for persons who use force, the threat of force or physical obstruction to block access to abortion clinics. Passed 69-30: R 18-26; D 51-4 (ND 40-1, SD 11-3), Nov. 16, 1993. A "yea" was a vote in support of the president's position.

374. S 1657. Habeas Corpus Revision/Table Bill. Biden, D-Del., motion to table (kill) the bill to limit federal habeas corpus appeals by individuals convicted in state court to a single petition filed within six months of final adjudication in state court. Motion agreed to 65-34: R 14-30; D 51-4 (ND 37-4, SD 14-0), Nov. 17, 1993.

375. S 1607. Omnibus Crime/Assault Weapon Ban. Feinstein, D-Calif., amendment to ban the manufacture, sale and future possession of 19 semiautomatic assault weapons and "copy-cat" guns. Adopted 56-43: R 10-34; D 46-9 (ND 38-3, SD 8-6), Nov. 17, 1993. A "yea" was a vote in support of the president's position.

376. S 1607. Omnibus Crime/Prison Caps. Biden, D-Del., motion to table (kill) the Helms, R-N.C., amendment to prohibit federal courts from placing a ceiling on the inmate population of a prison in the absense of a special court evaluation. Motion rejected 31-68: R 1-43; D 30-25 (ND 28-13, SD 2-12), Nov. 17, 1993. (Subsequently, the Helms amendment was adopted by voice vote).

KEY

- Y Voted for (yea).
- # Paired for.
- + Announced for.
- N Voted against (nay).
- X Paired against.
- − Announced against.
- P Voted "present."
- C Voted "present" to avoid possible conflict of interest.
- ? Did not vote or otherwise make a position known.

Democrats *Republicans*

	377	378	379	380	381	382	383	384
ALABAMA								
Heflin	Y	N	N	Y	Y	Y	Y	Y
Shelby	Y	N	N	Y	Y	N	N	Y
ALASKA								
Murkowski	Y	Y	N	Y	N	N	N	Y
Stevens	Y	Y	N	Y	Y	N	N	Y
ARIZONA								
DeConcini	Y	N	N	Y	Y	Y	Y	Y
McCain	Y	Y	Y	N	N	N	Y	Y
ARKANSAS								
Bumpers	Y	N	N	Y	Y	Y	Y	Y
Pryor	Y	N	N	Y	Y	Y	Y	Y
CALIFORNIA								
Boxer	Y	N	N	N	Y	Y	Y	Y
Feinstein	Y	N	N	Y	Y	Y	Y	Y
COLORADO								
Campbell	Y	N	N	Y	Y	N	Y	Y
Brown	Y	Y	N	N	N	Y	Y	Y
CONNECTICUT								
Dodd	Y	N	N	Y	Y	Y	Y	Y
Lieberman	Y	N	N	Y	Y	Y	Y	Y
DELAWARE								
Biden	N	N	N	Y	Y	Y	Y	Y
Roth	Y	N	N	N	N	Y	Y	Y
FLORIDA								
Graham	Y	N	N	Y	Y	Y	Y	Y
Mack	Y	Y	N	N	N	N	N	Y
GEORGIA								
Nunn	Y	N	N	Y	?	?	Y	Y
Coverdell	Y	N	N	N	N	N	Y	Y
HAWAII								
Akaka	N	N	Y	Y	Y	Y	Y	Y
Inouye	N	N	Y	Y	Y	Y	Y	Y
IDAHO								
Craig	Y	Y	N	Y	N	N	N	N
Kempthorne	Y	N	N	Y	N	N	N	N
ILLINOIS								
Moseley-Braun	N	N	Y	Y	Y	Y	Y	Y
Simon	N	N	Y	Y	Y	Y	Y	N
INDIANA								
Coats	Y	Y	N	Y	N	N	N	Y
Lugar	Y	Y	N	Y	N	N	N	Y
IOWA								
Harkin	N	N	Y	Y	Y	Y	Y	Y
Grassley	Y	Y	N	Y	N	Y	Y	Y
KANSAS								
Dole	Y	Y	N	N	N	N	N	Y
Kassebaum	Y	N	N	Y	N	Y	Y	Y
KENTUCKY								
Ford	Y	N	N	Y	Y	Y	Y	Y
McConnell	Y	Y	N	Y	N	N	N	Y
LOUISIANA								
Breaux	Y	N	N	Y	Y	Y	Y	Y
Johnston	Y	N	N	Y	Y	Y	Y	Y
MAINE								
Mitchell	N	N	Y	Y	Y	Y	Y	Y
Cohen	N	N	Y	Y	Y	Y	Y	Y
MARYLAND								
Mikulski	Y	N	N	Y	Y	Y	?	Y
Sarbanes	Y	N	Y	Y	Y	Y	Y	Y
MASSACHUSETTS								
Kennedy	N	N	Y	Y	Y	Y	Y	Y
Kerry	N	N	Y	Y	Y	Y	Y	Y
MICHIGAN								
Levin	N	N	Y	Y	Y	Y	Y	Y
Riegle	Y	N	N	Y	Y	Y	Y	Y
MINNESOTA								
Wellstone	N	N	Y	N	Y	Y	Y	Y
Durenberger	N	N	Y	Y	Y	Y	Y	N
MISSISSIPPI								
Cochran	Y	N	N	Y	Y	N	N	Y
Lott	Y	Y	N	Y	Y	N	N	Y
MISSOURI								
Bond	Y	N	N	Y	N	Y	N	Y
Danforth	N	N	Y	Y	N	Y	N	Y
MONTANA								
Baucus	Y	N	N	Y	Y	Y	Y	Y
Burns	Y	N	N	Y	N	Y	N	Y
NEBRASKA								
Exon	Y	Y	N	Y	Y	Y	Y	Y
Kerrey	Y	N	N	Y	Y	Y	Y	Y
NEVADA								
Bryan	Y	N	N	Y	Y	Y	N	Y
Reid	Y	N	N	Y	Y	N	N	Y
NEW HAMPSHIRE								
Gregg	Y	N	N	Y	Y	N	N	Y
Smith	Y	Y	N	Y	N	N	N	Y
NEW JERSEY								
Bradley	Y	N	N	Y	Y	Y	Y	Y
Lautenberg	N	N	Y	Y	Y	Y	Y	Y
NEW MEXICO								
Bingaman	Y	N	N	Y	Y	Y	Y	Y
Domenici	Y	Y	N	Y	N	Y	N	Y
NEW YORK								
Moynihan	N	N	Y	Y	Y	Y	Y	Y
D'Amato	Y	N	N	N	N	Y	Y	Y
NORTH CAROLINA								
Faircloth	Y	Y	N	Y	N	N	N	Y
Helms	Y	Y	N	N	N	N	N	Y
NORTH DAKOTA								
Conrad	Y	Y	N	Y	Y	Y	Y	Y
Dorgan	?	?	?	?	?	?	?	?
OHIO								
Glenn	N	N	Y	Y	Y	Y	Y	Y
Metzenbaum	N	N	Y	N	Y	Y	Y	Y
OKLAHOMA								
Boren	Y	N	N	Y	Y	Y	?	Y
Nickles	Y	N	N	N	N	N	N	Y
OREGON								
Hatfield	N	N	Y	N	Y	N	Y	N
Packwood	Y	N	N	N	Y	Y	Y	Y
PENNSYLVANIA								
Wofford	Y	N	N	Y	Y	Y	Y	Y
Specter	Y	N	N	N	Y	Y	Y	Y
RHODE ISLAND								
Pell	N	N	Y	Y	Y	Y	Y	Y
Chafee	N	N	Y	Y	Y	Y	Y	Y
SOUTH CAROLINA								
Hollings	Y	Y	N	Y	Y	Y	Y	Y
Thurmond	Y	N	N	Y	N	Y	Y	Y
SOUTH DAKOTA								
Daschle	Y	Y	N	Y	Y	Y	Y	Y
Pressler	Y	N	N	N	N	N	N	Y
TENNESSEE								
Mathews	Y	N	N	Y	Y	Y	Y	Y
Sasser	Y	Y	N	Y	Y	Y	Y	Y
TEXAS								
Gramm	Y	Y	N	N	N	?	N	Y
Hutchison	Y	Y	N	Y	N	Y	Y	Y
UTAH								
Bennett	Y	Y	N	Y	Y	Y	Y	Y
Hatch	Y	Y	N	N	N	Y	Y	Y
VERMONT								
Leahy	N	N	Y	Y	Y	Y	Y	Y
Jeffords	Y	N	N	Y	N	N	Y	Y
VIRGINIA								
Robb	Y	N	N	Y	Y	Y	Y	Y
Warner	Y	N	N	Y	Y	N	Y	Y
WASHINGTON								
Murray	N	N	Y	Y	Y	Y	Y	Y
Gorton	Y	N	N	N	N	Y	Y	Y
WEST VIRGINIA								
Byrd	Y	Y	N	Y	Y	Y	Y	Y
Rockefeller	Y	N	N	Y	Y	Y	Y	Y
WISCONSIN								
Feingold	N	N	Y	N	Y	Y	Y	N
Kohl	N	N	Y	Y	Y	Y	Y	Y
WYOMING								
Simpson	Y	N	N	Y	Y	Y	Y	Y
Wallop	Y	N	N	N	N	N	N	Y

ND Northern Democrats SD Southern Democrats

Southern states - Ala., Ark., Fla., Ga., Ky., La., Miss., N.C., Okla., S.C., Tenn., Texas, Va.

377. S 1607. Omnibus Crime/Drug Kingpin Death Penalty. D'Amato, R-N.Y., amendment to allow the death penalty for engaging in a continuing criminal drug enterprise. Adopted 74-25: R 39-5; D 35-20 (ND 21-20, SD 14-0), Nov. 17, 1993.

378. S 1607. Omnibus Crime/State Funding Contingency. Smith, R-N.H., amendment to withhold 50 percent of federal financial assistance provided under the bill from states that do not have truth-in-sentencing of at least 85 percent of a sentence for violent offenders, pretrial detention similar to the federal system, sentencing for violent offenders at least as long as federal law, and a suitable system for the recognition of victims' rights. Rejected 26-73: R 20-24; D 6-49 (ND 4-37, SD 2-12), Nov. 17, 1993.

379. S 1607. Omnibus Crime/Life Imprisonment. Levin, D-Mich., amendment to substitute life imprisonment without the possibility of parole where the bill would impose the death penalty. Rejected 26-73: R 6-38; D 20-35 (ND 20-21, SD 0-14), Nov. 17, 1993.

380. HR 2401. Fiscal 1994 Defense Authorization/Conference Report. Adoption of the conference report to authorize $261 billion for defense programs in fiscal 1994. Adopted (thus cleared for the president) 77-22: R 26-18; D 51-4 (ND 37-4, SD 14-0), Nov. 17, 1993.

381. S 24. Independent Counsel Reauthorization/Mandatory Coverage for Congress. Cohen, R-Maine, motion to table (kill) the McCain, R-Ariz., amendment to require the attorney general to use the independent counsel process for members of Congress, rather than making coverage discretionary. Motion agreed to 67-31: R 14-30; D 53-1 (ND 40-1, SD 13-0), Nov. 17, 1993.

382. S 24. Independent Counsel Reauthorization/Senate Approval of Independent Counsel. Cohen, R-Maine, motion to table (kill) the Cochran, R-Miss., amendment to subject the appointment of an independent counsel to the advice and consent of the Senate, if the attorney general determines that a potential conflict of interest exists for a high government official. Motion agreed to 68-29: R 17-26; D 51-3 (ND 39-2, SD 12-1), Nov. 17, 1993.

383. S 24. Independent Counsel Reauthorization/Passage. Passage of the bill to reauthorize the independent counsel law for five years after enactment, strengthen the fiscal and administrative controls of the process, clarify and strengthen the role of the attorney general, and make it clear that members of Congress are covered by the law. Passed 76-21: R 25-19; D 51-2 (ND 39-1, SD 12-1), Nov. 18, 1993. A "yea" was a vote in support of the president's position.

384. HR 3355. Omnibus Crime/Passage. Passage of the bill to authorize about $22 billion to combat crime through various programs, including the hiring of 100,000 new police officers, a ban on 19 semiautomatic assault weapons and the imposition of a federal death penalty for dozens of offenses. Passed 95-4: R 42-2; D 53-2 (ND 39-2, SD 14-0), Nov. 19, 1993. A "yea" was a vote in support of the president's position.

ALABAMA	385	386	387	388	389	390	391	392
Heflin	N	N	N	Y	N	N	N	Y
Shelby	N	N	N	Y	N	N	N	Y
ALASKA								
Murkowski	N	N	N	N	N	N	N	Y
Stevens	N	N	N	Y	N	N	N	Y
ARIZONA								
DeConcini	Y	N	Y	Y	Y	Y	N	Y
McCain	N	N	N	Y	Y	N	Y	Y
ARKANSAS								
Bumpers	Y	Y	Y	Y	Y	Y	N	Y
Pryor	Y	Y	Y	Y	Y	Y	N	Y
CALIFORNIA								
Boxer	Y	Y	Y	Y	Y	Y	N	Y
Feinstein	Y	Y	Y	Y	Y	Y	N	Y
COLORADO								
Campbell	N	N	N	Y	Y	N	N	Y
Brown	N	N	N	N	Y	N	Y	N
CONNECTICUT								
Dodd	Y	Y	Y	Y	Y	Y	N	Y
Lieberman	Y	Y	Y	Y	Y	Y	N	Y
DELAWARE								
Biden	Y	Y	Y	Y	N	Y	N	Y
Roth	N	N	Y	Y	Y	Y	Y	Y
FLORIDA								
Graham	Y	Y	Y	Y	Y	Y	N	Y
Mack	N	N	N	N	Y	N	Y	N
GEORGIA								
Nunn	Y	N	Y	Y	Y	Y	N	Y
Coverdell	N	N	N	N	Y	N	Y	N
HAWAII								
Akaka	Y	Y	Y	Y	Y	Y	N	Y
Inouye	Y	Y	Y	Y	N	Y	N	Y
IDAHO								
Craig	N	N	N	N	N	N	Y	N
Kempthorne	N	N	N	N	N	N	Y	N
ILLINOIS								
Moseley-Braun	Y	Y	Y	Y	Y	Y	N	Y
Simon	Y	Y	Y	Y	Y	Y	N	Y
INDIANA								
Coats	N	N	N	N	Y	N	Y	Y
Lugar	Y	N	N	Y	Y	N	Y	N

IOWA	385	386	387	388	389	390	391	392
Harkin	Y	Y	Y	Y	Y	Y	N	Y
Grassley	N	N	N	N	Y	N	Y	Y
KANSAS								
Dole	N	N	N	N	Y	N	Y	N
Kassebaum	Y	Y	Y	Y	Y	Y	N	Y
KENTUCKY								
Ford	N	N	Y	N	Y	Y	N	Y
McConnell	N	N	N	N	Y	N	Y	Y
LOUISIANA								
Breaux	N	N	N	Y	Y	N	N	Y
Johnston	N	N	N	Y	Y	N	N	Y
MAINE								
Mitchell	Y	Y	Y	Y	Y	Y	N	Y
Cohen	N	N	N	Y	N	N	N	Y
MARYLAND								
Mikulski	Y	Y	Y	Y	Y	Y	N	Y
Sarbanes	Y	Y	Y	Y	Y	Y	N	Y
MASSACHUSETTS								
Kennedy	Y	Y	Y	Y	Y	Y	N	Y
Kerry	Y	Y	Y	Y	Y	Y	N	Y
MICHIGAN								
Levin	Y	Y	Y	Y	N	Y	N	Y
Riegle	Y	Y	Y	Y	N	Y	N	Y
MINNESOTA								
Wellstone	Y	Y	Y	Y	N	Y	N	Y
Durenberger	Y	Y	Y	Y	Y	Y	Y	Y
MISSISSIPPI								
Cochran	N	N	N	N	Y	N	Y	N
Lott	N	N	N	N	N	N	Y	N
MISSOURI								
Bond	N	N	N	N	Y	N	Y	Y
Danforth	Y	Y	Y	N	Y	Y	N	N
MONTANA								
Baucus	N	N	Y	Y	Y	Y	N	Y
Burns	N	N	N	Y	N	N	Y	Y
NEBRASKA								
Exon	Y	N	Y	Y	N	Y	N	N
Kerrey	Y	Y	Y	Y	Y	Y	N	N
NEVADA								
Bryan	Y	N	N	Y	Y	N	N	Y
Reid	Y	Y	Y	Y	Y	Y	N	Y

NEW HAMPSHIRE	385	386	387	388	389	390	391	392
Gregg	N	N	N	N	Y	N	Y	N
Smith	N	N	N	N	N	N	Y	N
NEW JERSEY								
Bradley	Y	Y	Y	Y	Y	Y	N	Y
Lautenberg	Y	Y	Y	Y	Y	Y	N	Y
NEW MEXICO								
Bingaman	Y	N	Y	Y	Y	Y	N	Y
Domenici	N	N	N	Y	Y	N	N	Y
NEW YORK								
Moynihan	Y	Y	Y	Y	Y	Y	N	Y
D'Amato	N	N	N	Y	N	N	Y	Y
NORTH CAROLINA								
Faircloth	N	N	N	N	N	N	Y	N
Helms	N	N	N	N	N	?	Y	N
NORTH DAKOTA								
Conrad	N	N	Y	Y	Y	Y	N	Y
Dorgan	?	?	?	?	?	?	?	?
OHIO								
Glenn	Y	Y	Y	Y	N	Y	N	Y
Metzenbaum	Y	Y	Y	Y	N	Y	N	Y
OKLAHOMA								
Boren	Y	N	Y	Y	Y	Y	N	Y
Nickles	N	N	N	N	Y	N	Y	N
OREGON								
Hatfield	Y	Y	Y	Y	Y	Y	N	Y
Packwood	N	N	N	?	Y	N	Y	Y
PENNSYLVANIA								
Wofford	Y	N	Y	Y	Y	Y	N	Y
Specter	N	N	N	Y	N	N	N	Y
RHODE ISLAND								
Pell	Y	Y	Y	Y	Y	Y	N	Y
Chafee	Y	Y	Y	Y	Y	Y	N	Y
SOUTH CAROLINA								
Hollings	N	N	N	Y	N	N	N	Y
Thurmond	N	N	N	Y	Y	N	N	Y
SOUTH DAKOTA								
Daschle	Y	Y	Y	Y	Y	Y	N	Y
Pressler	N	N	N	N	N	N	Y	N
TENNESSEE								
Mathews	Y	Y	Y	Y	Y	Y	N	Y
Sasser	Y	N	Y	Y	Y	Y	N	Y

TEXAS	385	386	387	388	389	390	391	392
Gramm	N	N	N	N	Y	N	Y	N
Hutchison	N	N	N	N	Y	N	Y	Y
UTAH								
Bennett	N	N	N	N	Y	N	Y	Y
Hatch	N	N	N	N	Y	N	Y	Y
VERMONT								
Leahy	Y	N	Y	Y	Y	Y	N	Y
Jeffords	Y	Y	Y	Y	Y	Y	N	Y
VIRGINIA								
Robb	Y	Y	Y	Y	Y	Y	N	Y
Warner	Y	N	Y	Y	N	Y	Y	Y
WASHINGTON								
Murray	Y	Y	Y	Y	Y	Y	N	Y
Gorton	N	N	Y	N	Y	Y	Y	Y
WEST VIRGINIA								
Byrd	Y	Y	Y	Y	Y	Y	N	Y
Rockefeller	Y	Y	Y	Y	Y	Y	N	Y
WISCONSIN								
Feingold	Y	Y	Y	Y	N	Y	N	Y
Kohl	Y	Y	Y	Y	Y	Y	N	Y
WYOMING								
Simpson	N	N	N	N	Y	N	Y	Y
Wallop	N	N	N	N	Y	N	Y	N

ND Northern Democrats   SD Southern Democrats   Southern states - Ala., Ark., Fla., Ga., Ky., La., Miss., N.C., Okla., S.C., Tenn., Texas, Va.

385. S 414. Brady Bill/State Pre-emption. Mitchell, D-Maine, amendment to the Mitchell substitute amendment, to strike the provisions that pre-empt any state or local law requiring waiting periods for the purchase of handguns once a national instant check system is instituted. Adopted 54-45: R 8-36; D 46-9 (ND 38-3, SD 8-6), Nov. 19, 1993.

386. S 414. Brady Bill/Five-Year Sunset. Metzenbaum, D-Ohio, amendment to the Mitchell, D-Maine, substitute amendment, to strike the provisions that sunset the five-day waiting period five years after enactment. Rejected 43-56: R 6-38; D 37-18 (ND 32-9, SD 5-9), Nov. 19, 1993.

387. S 414. Brady Bill/Cloture. Motion to invoke cloture (thus limiting debate) on the bill to require a five-business-day waiting period before an individual could purchase a handgun, to allow local officials to conduct a background check. Motion rejected 57-42: R 9-35; D 48-7 (ND 39-2, SD 9-5), Nov. 19, 1993. A three-fifths majority (60) of the total Senate is required to invoke cloture.

388. Napolitano Confirmation/Cloture. Motion to invoke cloture (thus limiting debate) on the confirmation of Janet Ann Napolitano to be U.S. attorney for the District of Arizona. Motion agreed to 72-26: R 17-26; D 55-0 (ND 41-0, SD 14-0), Nov. 19, 1993. A three-fifths majority (60) of the total Senate is required to invoke cloture. (Subsequently, the nomination was confirmed by voice vote.) A "yea" was a vote in support of the president's position.

389. HR 3450. NAFTA Implementation/Side Agree-ments. Judgment of the Senate to affirm the ruling of the chair that the Stevens, R-Alaska, amendment, to strip from the bill the side agreements dealing with labor issues, environmental cleanup, border patrols and the establishment of the North American Development Bank, was prohibited from consideration by the Trade Act of 1974. Ruling of the chair upheld 73-26: R 30-14; D 43-12 (ND 32-9, SD 11-3), Nov. 19, 1993.

390. S 414. Brady Bill/Cloture. Motion to invoke cloture (thus limiting debate) on the bill to require a five-business-day waiting period before an individual could purchase a handgun. Motion rejected 57-41: R 9-34; D 48-7 (ND 39-2, SD 9-5), Nov. 19, 1993. A three-fifths majority (60) of the total Senate is required to invoke cloture. A "yea" was a vote in support of the president's position.

391. HR 3167. Unemployment Benefit Extension/Federal Employment Reduction. Gramm, R-Texas, motion to recommit the bill to conference with instructions that the Senate insist on the Senate amendment to reduce federal employment levels to those proposed in the National Performance Review. Motion rejected 36-63: R 36-8; D 0-55 (ND 0-41, SD 0-14), Nov. 20, 1993.

392. HR 3167. Unemployment Benefit Extension/Conference Report. Adoption of the conference report to provide about $1 billion for extended unemployment benefits for workers who have exhausted their 26 weeks of state unemployment benefits for an additional seven or 13 weeks of compensation, depending on the unemployment rates in their states. Adopted 79-20: R 26-18; D 53-2 (ND 39-2, SD 14-0), Nov. 20, 1993.

	393	394	395
ALABAMA			
Heflin	Y	N	N
Shelby	N	N	N
ALASKA			
Murkowski	Y	N	Y
Stevens	N	N	N
ARIZONA			
DeConcini	N	Y	Y
McCain	N	N	Y
ARKANSAS			
Bumpers	Y	Y	Y
Pryor	Y	Y	Y
CALIFORNIA			
Boxer	Y	Y	N
Feinstein	Y	Y	N
COLORADO			
Campbell	N	N	N
Brown	N	N	Y
CONNECTICUT			
Dodd	Y	Y	Y
Lieberman	Y	Y	Y
DELAWARE			
Biden	Y	Y	Y
Roth	Y	Y	Y
FLORIDA			
Graham	N	Y	Y
Mack	N	N	Y
GEORGIA			
Nunn	Y	Y	Y
Coverdell	N	N	Y
HAWAII			
Akaka	Y	Y	N
Inouye	Y	Y	N
IDAHO			
Craig	N	N	N
Kempthorne	N	N	N
ILLINOIS			
Moseley-Braun	Y	Y	Y
Simon	Y	Y	Y
INDIANA			
Coats	Y	Y	Y
Lugar	Y	Y	Y

	393	394	395
IOWA			
Harkin	N	Y	Y
Grassley	Y	N	Y
KANSAS			
Dole	Y	N	Y
Kassebaum	Y	Y	Y
KENTUCKY			
Ford	Y	Y	N
McConnell	N	N	Y
LOUISIANA			
Breaux	Y	N	Y
Johnston	Y	N	Y
MAINE			
Mitchell	Y	Y	Y
Cohen	Y	Y	N
MARYLAND			
Mikulski	Y	Y	N
Sarbanes	Y	Y	N
MASSACHUSETTS			
Kennedy	Y	Y	Y
Kerry	N	Y	Y
MICHIGAN			
Levin	Y	Y	N
Riegle	Y	Y	N
MINNESOTA			
Wellstone	N	Y	N
Durenberger	Y	Y	Y
MISSISSIPPI			
Cochran	N	N	Y
Lott	N	N	Y
MISSOURI			
Bond	Y	Y	Y
Danforth	Y	Y	Y
MONTANA			
Baucus	N	Y	Y
Burns	N	N	N
NEBRASKA			
Exon	N	Y	N
Kerrey	N	Y	Y
NEVADA			
Bryan	Y	N	N
Reid	Y	Y	N

	393	394	395
NEW HAMPSHIRE			
Gregg	Y	N	Y
Smith	N	N	N
NEW JERSEY			
Bradley	N	Y	Y
Lautenberg	N	Y	N
NEW MEXICO			
Bingaman	Y	Y	Y
Domenici	Y	N	Y
NEW YORK			
Moynihan	N	Y	N
D'Amato	Y	N	N
NORTH CAROLINA			
Faircloth	N	N	N
Helms	N	N	N
NORTH DAKOTA			
Conrad	N	Y	N
Dorgan	?	?	?
OHIO			
Glenn	Y	Y	N
Metzenbaum	N	Y	N
OKLAHOMA			
Boren	Y	Y	Y
Nickles	N	N	Y
OREGON			
Hatfield	Y	Y	Y
Packwood	Y	Y	Y
PENNSYLVANIA			
Wofford	N	Y	N
Specter	N	N	Y
RHODE ISLAND			
Pell	Y	Y	Y
Chafee	Y	Y	Y
SOUTH CAROLINA			
Hollings	N	N	N
Thurmond	N	Y	N
SOUTH DAKOTA			
Daschle	Y	Y	Y
Pressler	N	N	Y
TENNESSEE			
Mathews	Y	Y	Y
Sasser	Y	Y	N

	393	394	395
TEXAS			
Gramm	N	N	Y
Hutchison	N	Y	Y
UTAH			
Bennett	Y	N	Y
Hatch	N	N	Y
VERMONT			
Leahy	Y	N	Y
Jeffords	Y	Y	Y
VIRGINIA			
Robb	Y	Y	Y
Warner	N	Y	Y
WASHINGTON			
Murray	Y	Y	Y
Gorton	N	Y	Y
WEST VIRGINIA			
Byrd	N	Y	N
Rockefeller	N	Y	N
WISCONSIN			
Feingold	N	Y	N
Kohl	N	Y	N
WYOMING			
Simpson	Y	N	Y
Wallop	N	N	Y

ND   Northern Democrats   SD   Southern Democrats   Southern states - Ala., Ark., Fla., Ga., Ky., La., Miss., N.C., Okla., S.C., Tenn., Texas, Va.

393. S 714. Resolution Trust Corporation Financing/Conference Report. Adoption of the conference report to provide $18.3 billion to finish the savings and loan cleanup between Jan. 1 and June 30, 1995, terminate the Resolution Trust Corporation (RTC) on Dec. 31, 1995, and authorize $8.5 billion for the Saving Association Insurance Fund to be spent only if the savings and loan industry cannot pay for future failures itself through higher insurance premiums. The bill also establishes minorities preference for RTC contracts, incorporates management reforms, limits bonuses for RTC employees and extends the statute of limitations for five years in cases of fraud or intentional wrongdoing. Adopted (thus sent to the House) 54-45: R 20-24; D 34-21 (ND 23-18, SD 11-3), Nov. 20, 1993. A "yea" was a vote in support of the president's position.

394. HR 1025. Brady Bill/Passage. Passage of the bill to require a five-business-day waiting period before an individual could purchase a handgun, to allow local officials to conduct a background check. A compromise provided that the waiting period would expire four years after enactment unless the attorney general extended the waiting period for a fifth year. Passed 63-36: R 16-28; D 47-8 (ND 38-3, SD 9-5), Nov. 20, 1993. (Before passage the Senate struck everything after the enacting clause and inserted the text of S 414.) A "yea" was a vote in support of the president's position.

395. HR 3450. NAFTA Implementation/Passage. Passage of the bill to approve the North American Free Trade Agreement and make the necessary changes to U.S. statutory law to implement the trade agreement. Passed 61-38: R 34-10; D 27-28 (ND 18-23, SD 9-5), Nov. 20, 1993. A "yea" was a vote in support of the president's position.

INDEXES

Bill Number Index

Roll Call Vote Index

General Index